MOTOR IMPORTED CAR REPAIR MANUAL

9th Edition

First Printing

Michael J. Kromida, SAE
Editor

Dan Irizarry, SAE
Production Editor

Debra A. Luczak
Assistant Production Editor

Robert J. Ost
Production Assistant

Denver Steele
Manager, Electronic Data

Robert R. Savasta, SAE
Senior Associate Editor

Patrick Peyton, SAE
Associate Editor

John R. Lypen, SAE
Associate Editor

Daniel E. Doku
Associate Editor

Mark E. Flynn, SAE
Associate Editor

Warren Schildknecht, SAE
Special Projects Editor

James M. Garripoli
Assistant Editor

John E. DeGroat
Assistant Editor

Thomas G. Gaeta
Assistant Editor

Steve C. Anderson
Assistant Editor

Published by
MOTOR

**Hearst Books/Business Publishing Group,
A Division of The Hearst Corp.**

555 West 57th St., New York, N.Y. 10019

Printed in the U.S.A.

ISBN 0-87851-643-3

Frank A. Bennack, Jr.
President

Philip D. Shalala
*Group Vice President,
Hearst Books/Business
Publishing Group*

Kevin F. Carr
*Publisher
Motor Books*

Gordon L. Jones
*Vice President,
Hearst Books/Business
Publishing Group*

Dominic A. Mucchetti
*Vice President,
Group Publisher*

Louis C. Forier
*Editorial Director
Motor Books*

DIESEL ENGINE PERFORMANCE SPECIFICATIONS

FUEL, IGNITION & GENERAL MAINTENANCE

TROUBLESHOOTING

Table of Contents

TUNE UP SPECIFICATIONS

Table of Contents

The following specifications are published from the latest information available. This data should be used only in the absence of a decal affixed in the engine compartment.

When checking ignition timing, it may be necessary to disconnect certain hoses and/or electrical connectors. Refer to vehicle emission control label for specific instructions.

Before disconnecting spark plug wires from distributor cap, determine location of number 1 wire in cap, as distributor position may have been altered from that shown.

ACURA

Year	Model	Spark Plug Gap Inch	Ignition Timing			Curb Idle Speed		Fuel System Pressure Psi.
			Firing Order	Timing BTDC ①	Timing Mark	Man. Trans.	Auto. Trans.	
1986	Integra	.039	②	12°	③	800	800N	36
	Legend	.039	1-6-3-5-2-4	④	③	720	720N	36
1987	Integra	.039	②	12°	③	800	750N	36
	Legend	.039	1-6-3-5-2-4	④	③	720	720N	36

①—Before Top Dead Center.
②—No. 1 cylinder located at timing belt end of engine. Firing order: 1-3-4-2.
③—Located on crankshaft pulley.
④—Auto. Trans., 18°; manual trans., 23°

AUDI

Year	Model	Spark Plug Gap Inch	Ignition Timing			Curb Idle Speed		Fuel System Pressure Psi.
			Firing Order	Timing BTDC ①	Mark	Man. Trans.	Auto. Trans.	
1983	4000②	.028	④	⑦	—	850–1000	850–1000	68–78
	4000③	.028	⑤	⑦	—	775–925	850–1000	68–78
	5000③	.028	⑤	⑦	—	775–925	850–1000	68–78
	5000 Turbo	.028	⑤	21°⑥	—	790–910	790–910	68–78
	Coupe③	.028	⑤	⑦	—	775–925	850–1000	68–78
	Quattro Turbo③	.028	⑤	⑧	—	790–910	790–910	—
1984	4000②	.028	④	6°	—	850–1000	850–1000	75–82
	4000 Quattro③	.028	⑤	6°	—	750–850	750–850	75–81
	5000③	.028	⑤	6°	—	730–870	730–870	68–78
	5000 Turbo③	.028	⑤	6°	—	750–850	750–850	61–67
	Coupe GT③⑨	.028	⑤	⑦	—	775–925	850–1000	68–78
	Coupe GT③⑩	.028	⑤	6°	—	750–850	750–850	68–78
	Quattro Turbo③	.028	⑤	⑧	—	890–910	890–910	75–82
1985	4000S②	.031	④	6°	—	800–1000	800–1000	75–82
	4000S③	.032	⑤	8°	—	750–850	750–850	75–82
	Quattro Turbo③	.028	⑤	⑧	—	890–910	890–910	75–82
	5000S③	.028	⑤	6°	—	750–850	750–850	73–84
	5000S Turbo③	.028	⑤	TDC	—	750–850	750–850	84–91
	Coupe GT③	.032	⑤	6°	—	750–850	750–850	68–78
	Coupe GT③	.032	⑤	8°	—	750–850	750–850	75–82
1986	4000S②	.031	④	6°	—	800–900	800–900	68–78
	4000CS Quattro③	.032	⑤	8°	—	750–850	750–850	75–82
	5000S③	.028	⑤	6°	—	750–850	750-850	73-84
	5000CS③	.028	⑤	TDC	—	750–850	750–850	84–91
	Coupe GT③	.032	⑤	6°	—	750–850	750–850	75–82

①—Before Top Dead Center.
②—4 cylinder engine.
③—5 cylinder engine.
④—Timed at No. 1 cylinder, front of engine. Firing order 1-3-4-2.
⑤—Timed at No. 1 cylinder, front of engine. Firing order 1-2-4-5-3.
⑥—Before top dead center @ 3000 RPM, vacuum hoses disconnected.
⑦—Man. trans. 6° BTDC; auto. trans., 3° ATDC.
⑧—Distributor housing aligned with mark.
⑨—Exc. CIS-E Mode.
⑩—CIS-E Mode.

BMW

Year	Engine	Spark Plug Gap	Firing Order	Timing BTDC①	Ignition Timing: Timing Mark	Curb Idle Speed: Man. Trans.	Curb Idle Speed: Auto. Trans.	Fast Idle Speed: Man. Trans.	Fast Idle Speed: Auto. Trans.	Fuel Pump Pressure psi
1983–84	6-196/3210cc	.028	153624	6–14° ②	③	④	④	900–1000	900–1000	33–38
1983–85	4-107/1766cc	.031	1342	15° ⑤	⑥	⑦	⑦	900–1000	900–1000	40–47
1983–87	6-164/2693cc	.028	153624	4–12° ②	③	④	④	900–100	900–1000	33–38
1986–87	6-209/3400cc	.028	153624	13° ⑧	③	750–850	750–850	—	—	40–47
1987	4-140/2302	—	1342	1° ⑧	③	840–920	840–920	—	—	40–47
	6-153/2494cc	—	153624	—	③	680–760	680–760	—	—	40–47
	6-211/3453cc	—	153624	0° ⑧	③	750–850	750–850	—	—	40–47

①—BDTC: Before top dead center.
②—At 700 RPM.
③—Equipped with Motronic Control System.
④—With A/C on, 800–900 RPM; with A/C off, 650–750 RPM.
⑤—At 2000 RPM.
⑥—Timed at No. 1 cylinder front of engine. Disconnect vacuum hose at distributor & align ball on flywheel with pointer.
⑦—With A/C on, 800–900 RPM. With A/C off: 1983 models, 800–900 RPM; 1984–85 models, 700–800 RPM.
⑧—At specified curb idle speed.

DODGE/PLYMOUTH

Year	Engine	Spark Plug Gap Inch	Ignition Timing: Firing Order Fig.	Ignition Timing: Timing BTDC①	Ignition Timing: Mark Fig.	Curb Idle Speed: Man. Trans.	Curb Idle Speed: Auto. Trans. ②	Fast Idle Speed: Man. Trans.	Fast Idle Speed: Auto. Trans.	Fuel Pump Pressure psi
1983	1400	.041	C	5°	B	700	—	—	—	3.7–5.1
	1600	.041	C	5°	B	750	750	—	—	3.7–5.1
	2000	.041	A	5°	B	③	750	—	—	4.6–6
	2600	.041	A	5°	D	750	750	—	—	4.6–6
1984	1400	.041	C	5°	B	⑧	—	—	—	3.7–.1
	1600⑥	.041	C	5°	B	—	⑨	—	—	3.7–5.1
	1600⑦	.041	C	5°	B	700	—	—	—	—
	2000⑤	.041	A	5°	B	③	750	—	—	4.6–6
	2000④	.041	A	5°	B	750	750	—	—	4.6–6
	2600⑥	.041	A	7°	D	750	800	—	—	4.6–6
	2600⑦	.041	A	7°	D	850	850	—	—	—
1985	1500	⑩	E	⑮	F	700	750	—	—	—
	1600	⑩	C	8°	B	700	700	—	—	35.6
	2000⑪	⑩	A	⑯	B	700	700	—	—	—
	2000⑫	.041	A	5°	B	750	750	—	—	—
	2600⑥	.041	A	7°	D	750	800	—	—	—
	2600⑦	.041	A	10°	D	850	850	—	—	—
1986	1500	⑬	E	⑯	F	700	750	—	—	—
	1600	⑬	C	10°	B	700	700	—	—	35.6
	2000⑪	⑭	A	⑰	B	700	700	—	—	—
	2000⑫	.041	A	5°	B	750	750	—	—	—
	2600⑥	.041	A	7°	D	750	800	—	—	—
	2600⑦	.041	A	7°	D	850	850	—	—	—
1987	1500	㉑	E	⑯	F	700	750	2800	2700	2.7–3.7
	1600	㉑	C	⑱	B	700	700	—	—	35–38
	2000⑪	.041	A	5°	B	700	700	—	—	35–38
	2000⑫	.041	A	⑰	B	750	750	2450	2500	2.7–3.7
	2600⑥ ⑫	.041	A	⑲	D	750	800	2300	2350	2.8–4.2
	2600⑥ ⑳	.041	A	⑲	D	800	800	2300	2350	2.8–4.2
	2600⑦	.041	A	⑱	D	850	850	—	—	35–38

Continued

DODGE/PLYMOUTH–Continued

①—BDTC: Before top dead center.
②—In neutral unless otherwise specified.
③—5 speed manual trans., 700 RPM; 4 speed manual trans., 750 RPM.
④—Calif.
⑤—Exc. Calif.
⑥—Except turbocharged.
⑦—Turbocharged.
⑧—Less A/C, 650 RPM; with A/C, 700 RPM.
⑨—Less A/C, 700 RPM; with A/C, 750 RPM.
⑩—W22EPR-S11, W20EP-U-10 & W20EPR-U-10, .037 inch; all others, .041 inch.
⑪—Colt Vista.
⑫—Ram 50.
⑬—NGK, .037 inch; all others, .041 inch.
⑭—Nippondenso, .037 inch; all others, .041 inch.
⑮—Vehicles built prior to April, 1985: exc. high altitude, 3°; high altitude, 8°. Vehicles built in April, 1985, or later: exc. high altitude, 5°; high altitude, 10°.
⑯—Exc. high altitude, 5°; high altitude, 10°.
⑰—Exc. high altitude, 8°; high altitude, 13°.
⑱—Exc. high altitude, 10°; high altitude, 15°.
⑲—Exc. high altitude, 7°; high altitude, 12°
⑳—Ram Raider.
㉑—Exc. Nippondenso U-10 type, .039–.043 inch; Nippondenso U-10 type, .035–.039 inch.

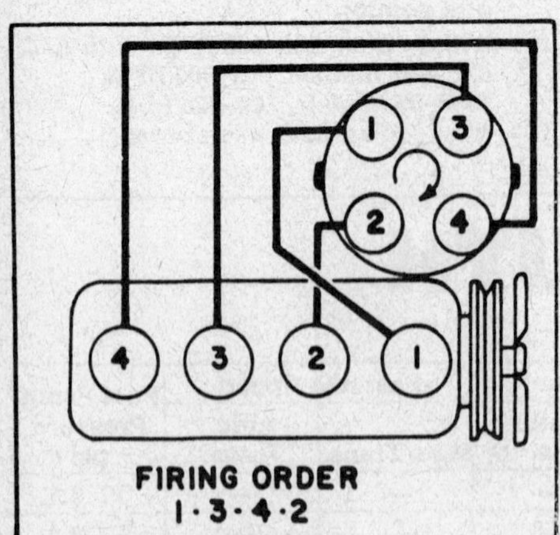

Fig. A

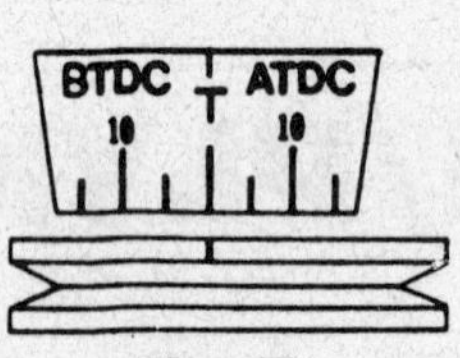

Fig. B

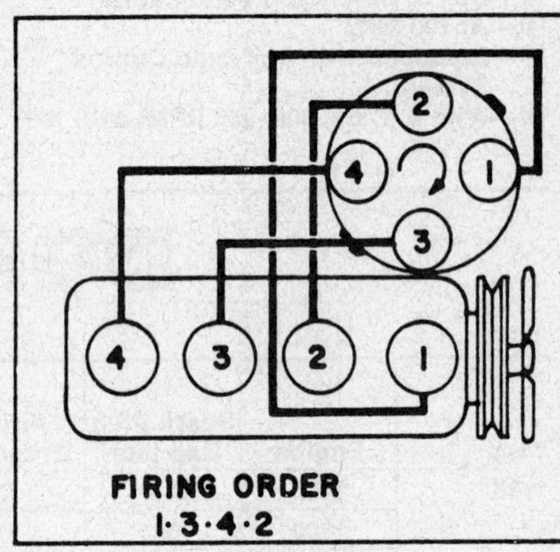

Fig. C

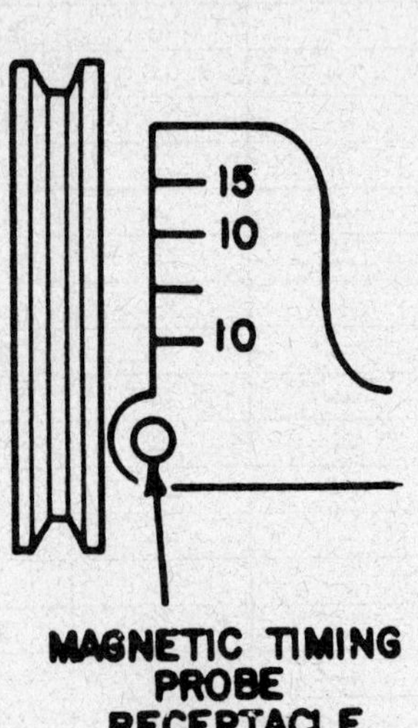

Fig. D

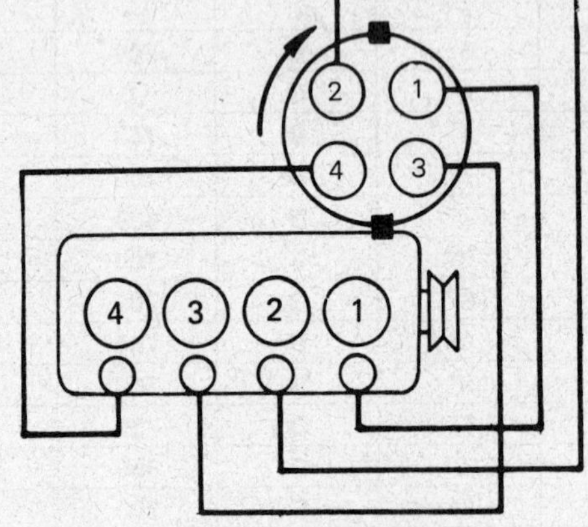

Fig. E

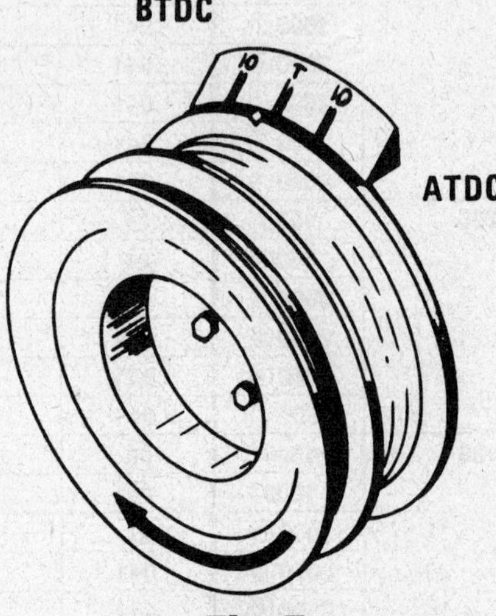

Fig. F

HONDA

Year	Model	Spark Plug Gap	Ignition Timing: Firing Order Fig.	Ignition Timing: Timing BTDC	Ignition Timing: Mark Fig.	Curb Idle Speed: Std. Trans.	Curb Idle Speed: Auto. Trans.	Fast Idle Speed: Std. Trans.	Fast Idle Speed: Auto. Trans.	Fuel Pump Pressure psi
1983	Civic 1300	.041	A	①	②	③	700D	3000	3000	2–3
	Civic 1500	.041	A	18°	⑱	700	700D	3000	3000	2–3
	Accord	.041	A	⑲	⑳	750	700D	2500	2500	2–3
	Prelude	.041	B	⑤	㉓	800	750D	2000	2000	2–3
1984	Accord	.041	㉖	㉗	㉘	750	700D	2500	2500	2.4–3.1
	Civic 1300	.041	㉖	㉙	F	㉚	—	3000	3000	2.7–3.8
	Civic 1500	.041	㉖	㉙	F	㉚	700D	3000	3000	2.7–3.8
	Prelude	.041	B	㉔	㉕	800	800D	1700	1800	2–3
1985	Accord ㉟	.041	㉖	㊲	㊳	㉝	㉒	2000–3000	2000–3000	2.4–3.1
	Accord ㊱	.041	㉖	18°	㉞	750	750	1000–1800	1000–1800	33–39
	Civic 1300	.041	㉖	㉙	F	㉑	—	2500–3500	—	2.4–3.3
	Civic 1500	.041	㉖	⑧	F	700	㉒	2500–3500	2500–3500	2.4–3.3
	CRX 1500 HF ㉟	.041	㉖	㉙	F	⑰	—	3000	—	2.4–3.3
	CRX 1500 Si ㊱	.041	㉖	㉙	F	750	—	1250–2250	—	3.3–3.9
	Prelude	.041	B	㉔	⑯	800	800	1750	1700	2.1–2.8
1986	Accord ㉟	.041	㉖	④	⑭	750	700	2000–3000	2000–3000	2.6–3.3
	Accord ㊱	.041	㉖	15°	⑭	750	750	1000–1800	1000–1800	33–39
	Civic 1300	.041	㉖	⑦	F	㉑	—	2500–3500	—	2.6–3.3
	Civic 1500 ㉟	.041	㉖	⑧	F	⑩	⑪	2500–3500	2500–3500	2.4–3.3
	Civic 1500 ㊱	.041	㉖	㉛	F	750	—	1250–2250	—	33–39
	CRX 1500 ㉟	.041	㉖	⑨	F	⑮	⑥	2500–3500	2500–3500	2.4–3.3
	CRX HF	.041	㉖	⑦	F	㉜	—	2500–3500	—	2.4–3.3
	CRX Si ㊱	.041	㉖	㉛	F	750	—	1250–2250	—	33–39
	Prelude ㉟	.041	B	㉔	⑭	800	800	1700	1800	2.1–2.8
	Prelude ㊱	.041	B	15°	⑭	750	750	1000–1800	1000–1800	36
1987	Accord ㉟	.041	㉖	④	⑭	750	700	2000–3000	2000–3000	2.6–3.3
	Accord ㊱	.041	㉖	15°	⑭	750	750	1000–1800	1000–1800	33–39
	Civic 1300	.041	㉖	⑦	F	㉑	—	2500–3500	—	2.4–3.3
	Civic 1500 ㉟	.041	㉖	⑧	F	⑩	⑪	2500–3500	2500–3500	2.4–3.3
	Civic 1500 ㊱	.041	㉖	㉛	F	750	—	1250–2250	—	33–39
	CRX 1500 ㉟	.041	㉖	⑧	F	⑮	⑥	2500–3500	2500–3500	2.4–3.3
	CRX HF	.041	㉖	⑫	F	⑬	—	2500–3500	—	2.4–3.3
	CRX Si ㊱	.041	㉖	㉛	F	750	—	1250–2250	—	33–39
	Prelude ㉟	.041	B	㉔	⑭	800	800	1250–1750	1200–1700	2.1–2.8
	Prelude ㊱	.041	B	15°	⑭	750	1000–1800	—	—	36

—Not Available.

①—1300 4 speed manual trans., 20° BTDC (redmark); 1300 5 speed manual trans., 18°BTDC (red mark).

②—4 speed manual trans., Fig. D; 5 speed manual trans., Fig. G.

③—4 speed manual trans., 700 RPM; 5 speed manual trans., 650 RPM.

④—Auto. trans., 15° BTDC. manual trans.: exc. Calif., 24° BTDC; Calif., 20° BTDC.

⑤—Manual trans. exc. Calif. & High altitude, 10°; all others, 12.°

⑥—Exc. Calif.: 650 RPM @ low altitude; 700 RPM @ high altitude. Calif., 700 RPM.

⑦—Exc. Calif., 21° BTDC; Calif., 16° BTDC.

⑧—Manual trans.: Exc. 4wd Wagon, 20° BTDC; 4wd Wagon, 15° BTDC. Auto. Trans.: less power steering, 15 BTDC; w/power steering, 17° BTDC.

⑨—Auto. trans., 15° BTDC; manual trans., 20° BTDC.

⑩—Exc. Calif.: 700 RPM @ low altitude; 750 RPM @ high altitude. Calif.: exc. 4wd Wagon, 700 RPM; 4wd Wagon, 750 RPM.

⑪—Exc. Calif.: 650 RPM @ low altitude; 700 RPM @ high altitude. Calif., 700 RPM.

⑫—Exc. Calif., 26° BTDC; Calif., 16° BTDC.

⑬—Exc Calif. & high altitude, 580 RPM; Calif., 750 RPM. High altitude: 700 RPM @ low altitude, 750 RPM @ high altitude.

⑭—Auto. Trans., Fig. C; manual trans., Fig. E.

⑮—All models, 700 RPM @ low altitude; models exc. Calif., 750 RPM @ h igh altitude.

⑯—Auto. Trans., Fig. R; manual trans., Fig. O.

⑰—Calif., 600 RPM; high altitude, 700 RPM; Exc. Calif. & high altitude, 580 RPM.

⑱—1500 auto. trans., Fig. H; 1500 Man.Trans., Fig. G.

⑲—Auto trans., 16° BTDC (red mark); manual trans., exc. Calif., 16° BTDC (white mark); manual trans., Calif., 12° BTDC (red mark).

⑳—Auto. trans., Fig. I; manual trans. exc. Calif., Fig. J; Calif., Fig. K.

㉑—Exc. high altitude, 650 RPM. High altitude: 750 RPM @ low altitude; 800 RPM @ high altitude.

㉒—Exc. high altitude, 700 RPM; high altitude, 650 RPM.

㉓—Calif. & high altitude, Fig. M; Calif. & auto. trans., Fig. L; manual trans. exc. high altitude manual trans., Fig. N.

㉔—Auto. trans., 12°; manual trans., 20°.

Continued

HONDA–Continued

㉕—Auto. trans., Fig. L; manual trans., Fig. O.
㉖—No. 1 cyl. located at front of engine (alternator end); cylinder numbering, 1-2-3-4; firing order, 1-3-4-2.
㉗—Manual trans. exc. Calif. & high altitude, 22°; Calif. & high altitude manual trans., 18°; auto. trans. all, 18°.
㉘—Exc. Federal w/manual trans., Q; manual trans. exc. Calif. & high altitude, Fig. P.
㉙—Red mark on crankshaft pulley.
㉚—4 speed manual trans., 650 RPM; 5 speed manual trans. exc. Calif., 600 RPM; Calif. 5 speed manual trans., 650 RPM.
㉛—Exc. Calif., 16°; Calif., 12°.
㉜—Exc. Calif. & high altitude, 580 RPM; Calif., 600 RPM. High altitude: 700 RPM @ low altitude. 750 RPM @ high altitude.
㉝—Exc. high altitude, 750 RPM; high altitude, 700 RPM.
㉞—Auto. Trans., Fig. R; manual trans., Fig. Q.
㉟—Carbureted engines.
㊱—Fuel injected engines.
㊲—Exc. Calif., manual trans., 22° (red mark); Calif., manual trans., 18° (red mark); Auto. Trans., 18° (red mark).
㊳—Auto. Trans., Fig. R; manual trans. exc. Calif., Fig. P; manual trans. Calif., Fig. Q.

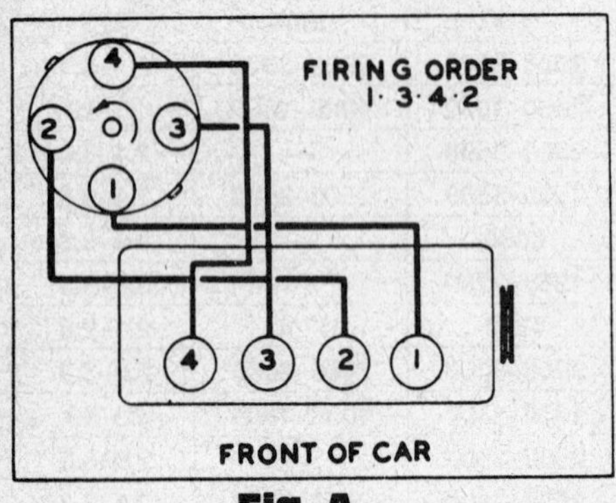

Fig. A

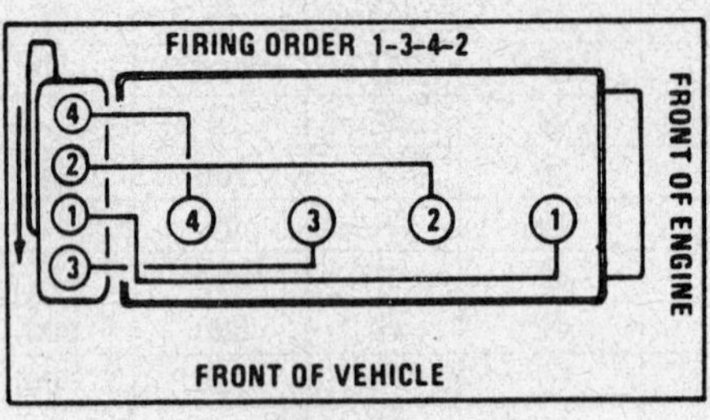

Fig. B

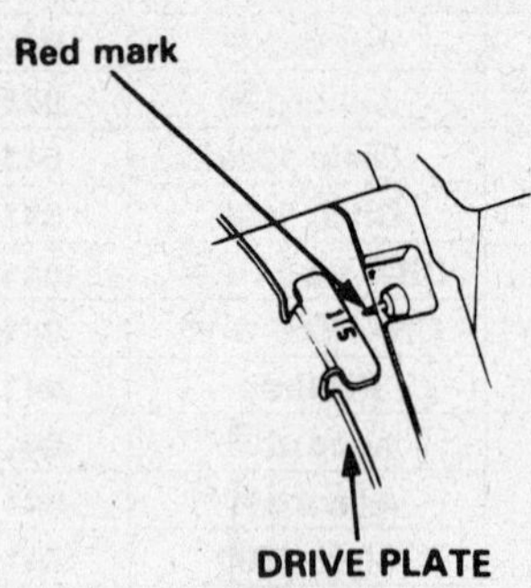

Fig. C

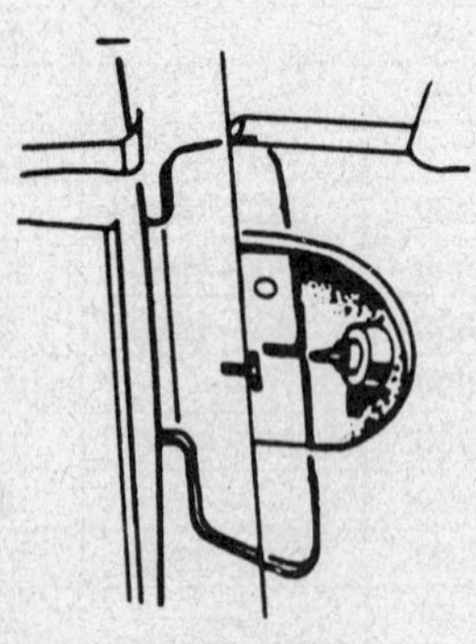
Fig. D

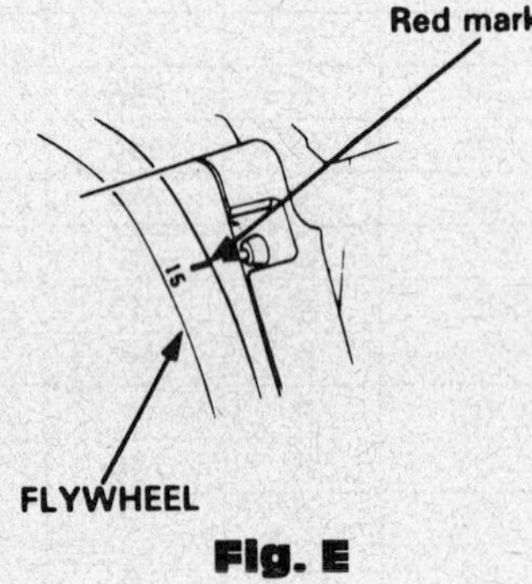

Fig. E

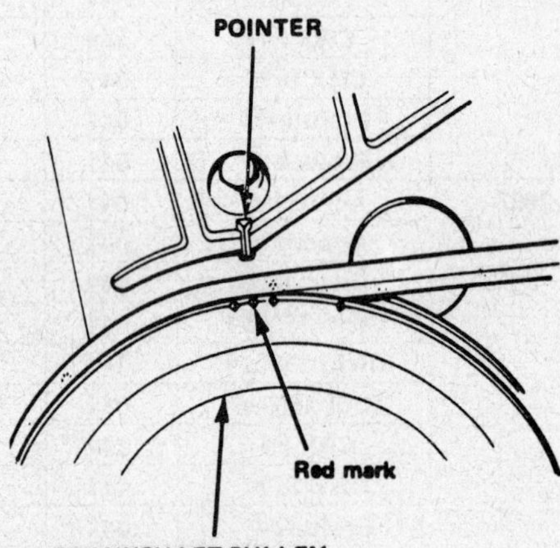

Fig. F

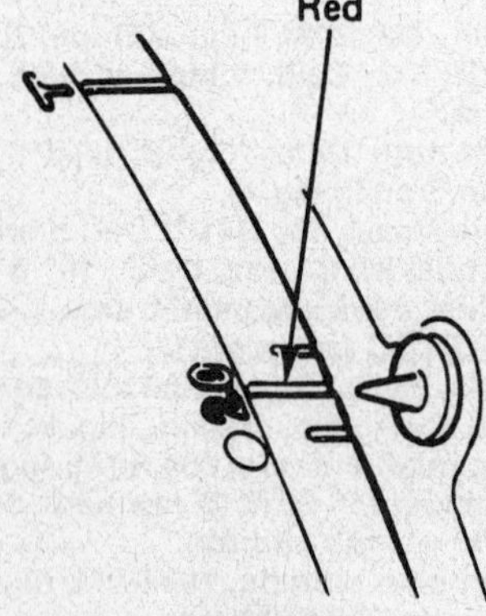

Fig. G

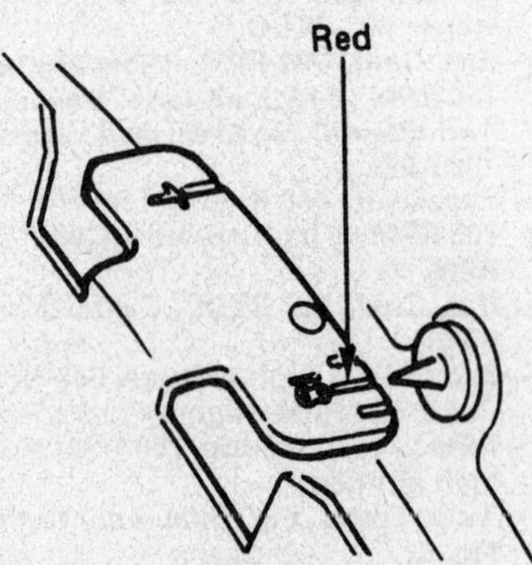

Fig. H

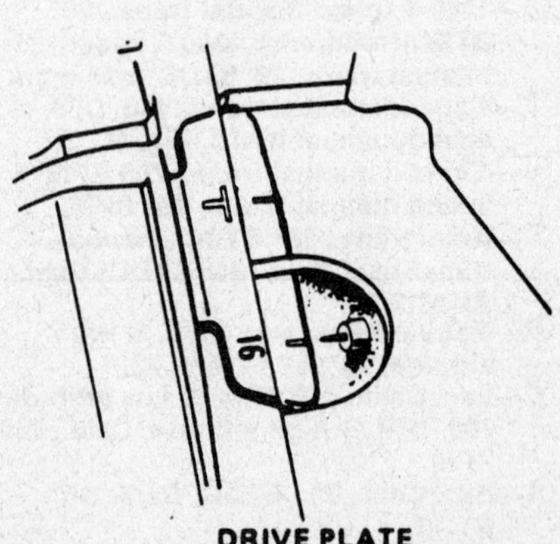

Fig. I

Continued

HONDA–Continued

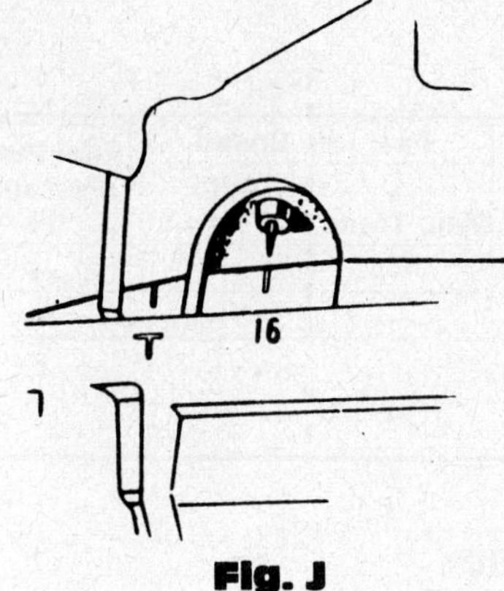

Fig. J

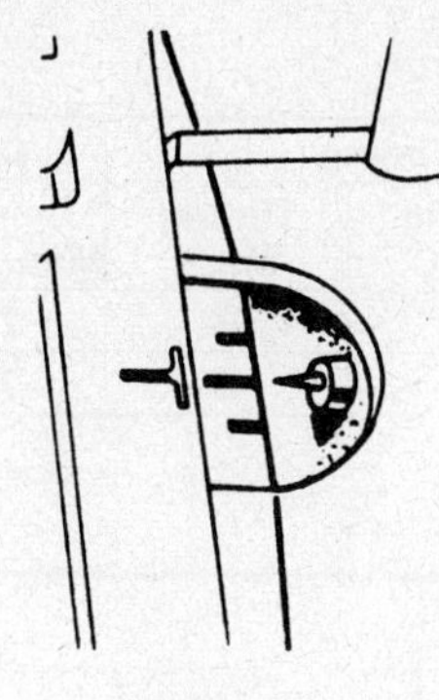
Fig. K

Fig. L

Fig. M

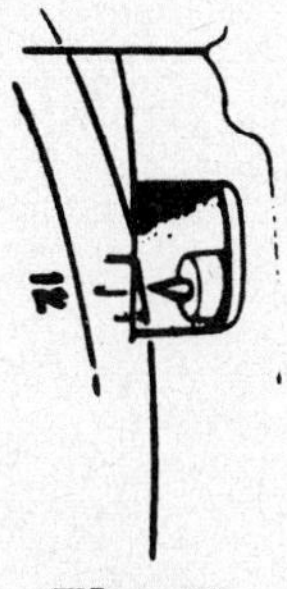

Fig. N

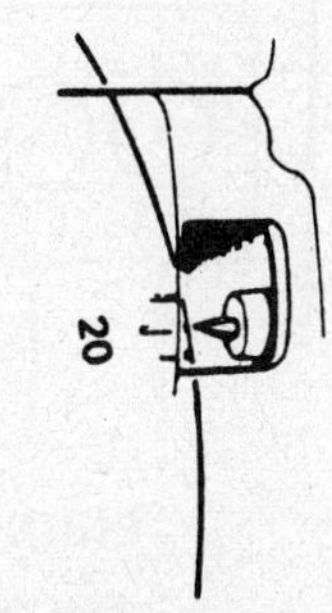

Fig. O

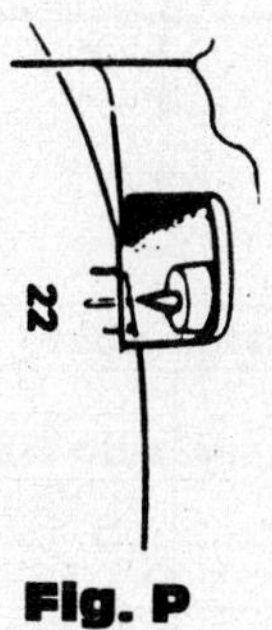

Fig. P

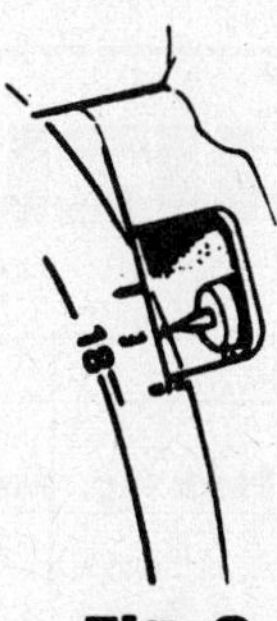

Fig. Q

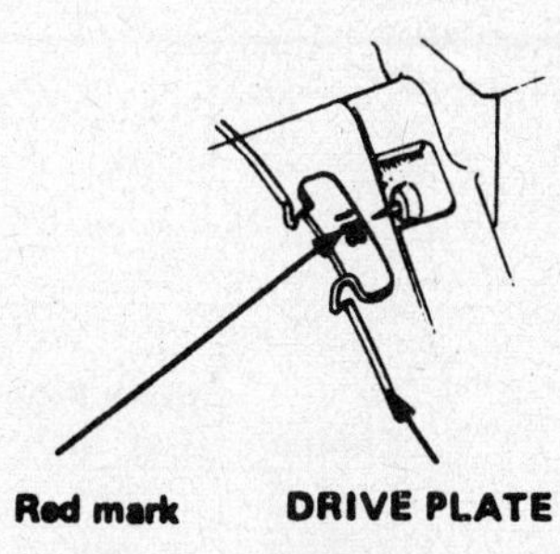

Fig. R

HYUNDAI

Year	Engine	Spark Plug Gap Inches	Ignition Timing			Curb Idle Speed		Fast Idle Speed		Fuel Pump Pressure lbs.
			Firing Order Fig.	Timing BTDC	Timing Mark	Man. Trans.	Auto. Trans.	Man. Trans.	Auto. Trans.	
1986–87	4-90/1.5L ①	.041	A	3°	B	700	750	—	—	—
	4-90/1.5L ②	.041	A	5°	B	700	750	—	—	—

①—Exc. California.
②—California.

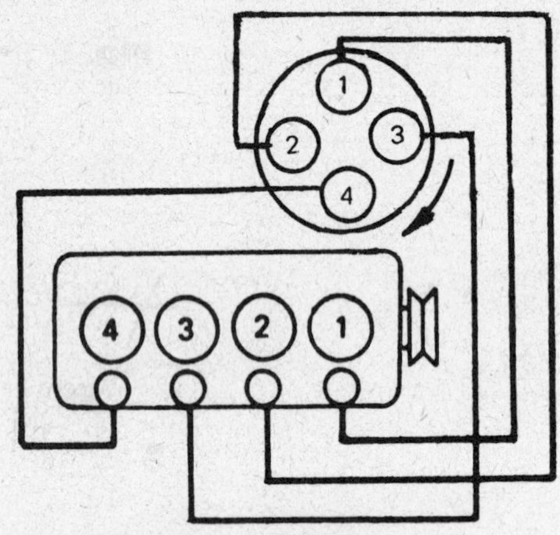

FIRING ORDER 1-3-4-2
FRONT OF VEHICLE

Fig. A

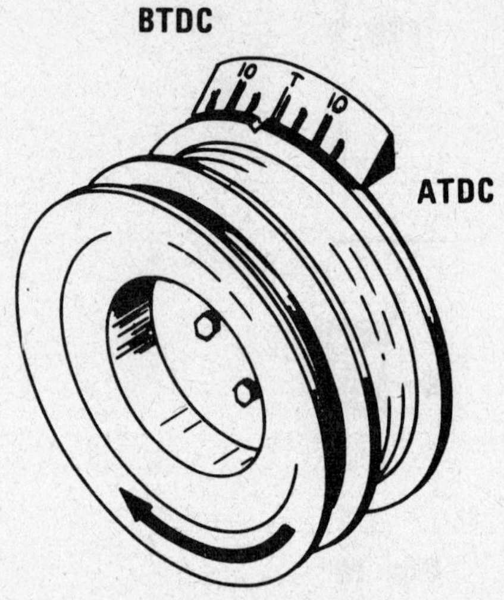

Fig. B

ISUZU

Year	Engine	Spark Plug Gap Inch	Ignition Timing			Curb Idle Speed		Fast Idle Speed		Fuel Pump Pressure psi
			Firing Order Fig.	Timing BTDC ①	Mark Fig.	Man. Trans.	Auto. Trans.	Man. Trans.	Auto Trans.	
1983–85	I Mark ②	.041	A	6°	B	750–850	850–950	③	③	—
1983–87	Pickup	.041	A	6°	B	④	850–950	③	③	—
1984–87	Impulse ⑤	.041	A	12°	B	850–950	850–959	③	③	—
	Trooper II	.041	A	6°	B	④	—	③	—	—
1985–87	I Mark ⑥ ⑦	.041	1-3-4-2	3°	—	750	1000	③	③	—
	Impulse ⑧	.041	1-3-4-2	12°	B	850–950	850–950	③	③	—

①—BTDC: Before top dead center, at or below specified curb idle speed.
②—Rear Wheel Drive.
③—On carbureted models, fast idle speed is adjusted by primary throttle valve opening angle. On fuel injected models, fast idle speed not adjustable.
④—Exc. Calif., 750–850 RPM; Calif., 850–950 RPM.
⑤—Exc. turbocharged engine.
⑥—Front wheel drive.
⑦—Carbureted engine.
⑧—Turbocharged engine.

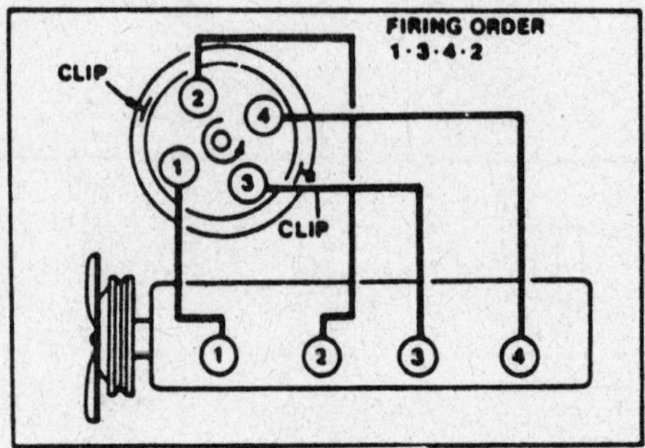

Fig. A

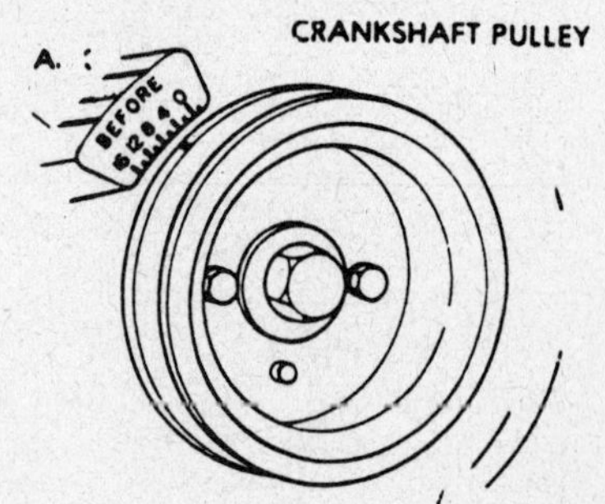

Fig. B

JAGUAR

Model	Engine	Spark Plug Gap	Firing Order	Ignition Timing: Timing BTDC ①	Ignition Timing: Mark Location	Curb Idle Speed	Fast Idle Speed	Fuel Pump Pressure PSI
XJ6	6-258/4235cc	.035	1-5-3-6-2-4	8②	Pulley	750	—	36
XJ-S.H.E.	V12-326/5343cc	.025	③	26④	Pulley	750	—	36

①—BTDC: Before top dead center.
②—Timed at No. 6 cyl. located front of engine.
③—Cylinders are numbered front to rear R = right bank, L = left bank, 1R-6L-5R-2L-3R-4L-6R-1L-2R-5L-4R-3L.
④—At 3000 RPM with vacuum advance hose disconnected & plugged.

MAZDA (PISTON ENGINE)

Year	Model	Spark Plug Gap Inch	Ignition Timing: Firing Order	Ignition Timing: Timing BTDC ①	Ignition Timing: Mark Fig.	Curb Idle Speed: Man. Trans.	Curb Idle Speed: Auto. Trans. ②	Fast Idle Speed: Man. Trans.	Fast Idle Speed: Auto Trans.	Fuel Pump Pressure psi
1983–84	GLC	.031	③	⑩	F	850	750D	3000–4000	3000–4000	⑧
	626	.031	④	6°	A	750	700D	3000–4000	3000–4000	⑨
	B2000	.031	④	8°	C	650	—	—	—	2.8–3.6
1985	GLC	.031	③	6°	F	850	750D	3000–4000	3000–4000	4.3–6.0
	626	.031	④	6°	A	750	700	3000–4000	3000–4000	2.8–4.3
1986	323	.041	③	⑥	F	850	1000	2000–2350⑪	⑪	⑤
	626	.031	③	6°	B	750	900	⑪	⑪	63.8–85.6
	B2000	.031	④	6°	E	825	—	3000–4000	—	4.0–4.4
1987	323	.041	③	⑥	F	800–900	950–1050	2000–2350⑪	2000–2350⑪	⑤
	626	.031	③	5–7°	B	800–850	900–950	⑪	⑪	64–85
	B2200	.031	④	5–7°	E	800–850	800–850	—	—	⑦
	B2600	.041	④	6–8	D	800–850	800–850	—	—	2.8–3.6

—Not available.
①—BTDC-Before top dead center.
②—D: Drive.
③—1-3-4-2. No. 1 cyl. located front of engine, passenger side of engine compartment.
④—1-3-4-2. No. 1 cyl., located at front of engine.
⑤—Carbureted engine, 4.0–5.0 psi; fuel injected engine, 64.0–85.3 psi.
⑥—All engines, 2° BTDC with vacuum hose disconnected; fuel injected engine, 7° BTDC with vacuum hose connected.
⑦—Auto. trans., 2.8–3.6 psi; manual trans., 3.7–4.7 psi.
⑧—1983, 2.8–3.8 psi; 1984, 4.3–6.0 psi.
⑨—1983, 2.8–3.8 psi; 1984, 2.8–4.3 psi.
⑩—Except 1983 sta. wag., 6° BTDC; 1983 sta. wag: 8° BTDC.
⑪—Fast idle speed not adjustable on fuel injected engines.

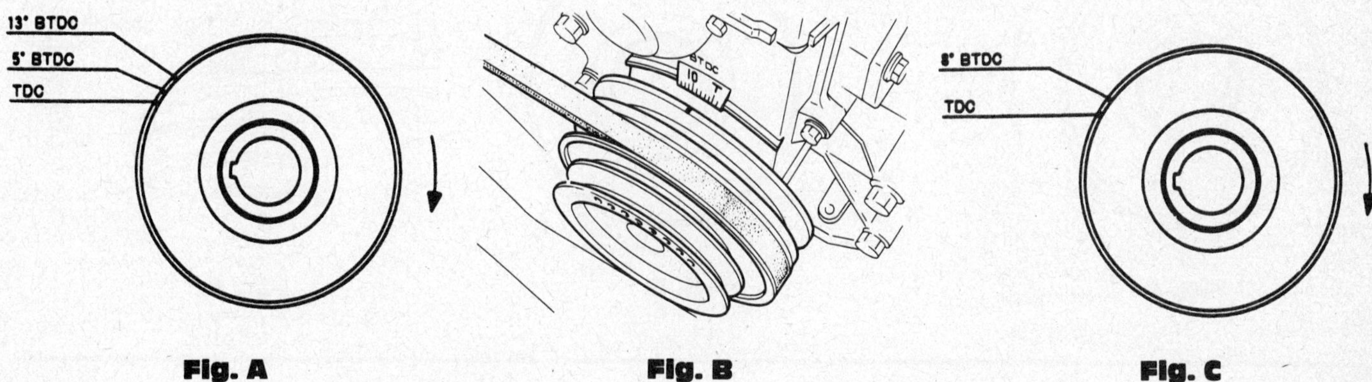

Fig. A Fig. B Fig. C

Continued

MAZDA (PISTON ENGINE)—Continued

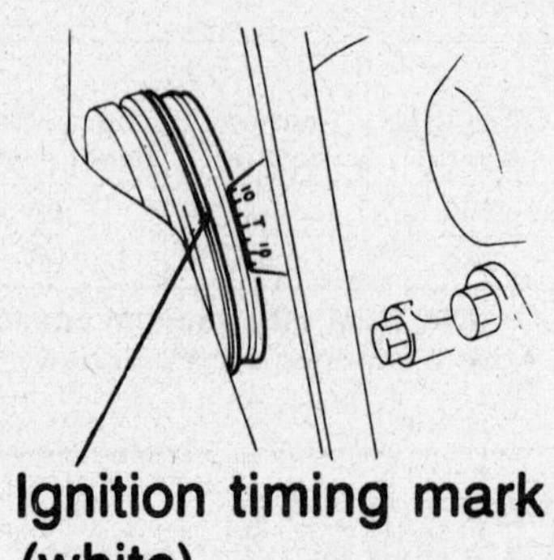

Fig. D

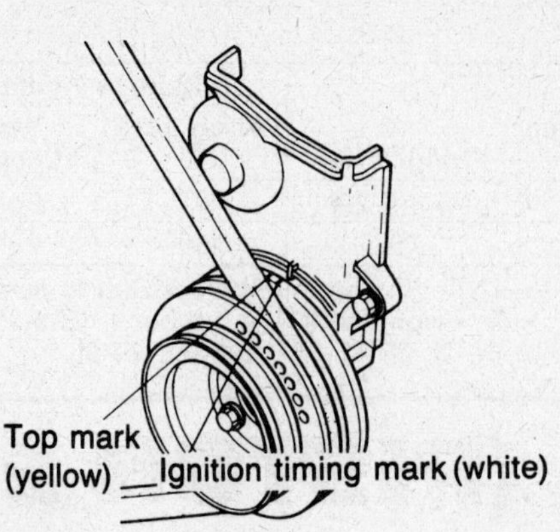

Fig. E

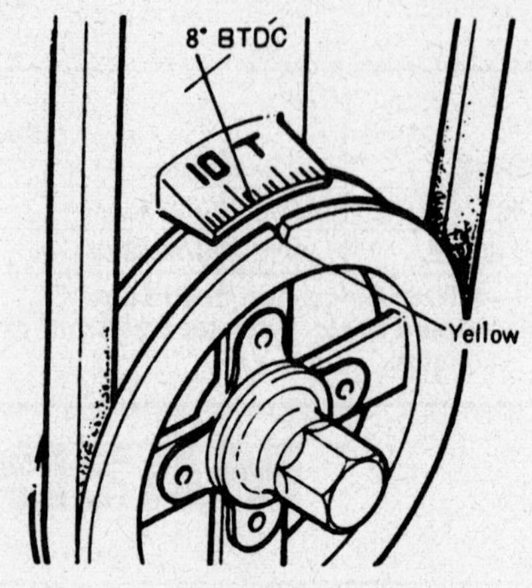

Fig. F

MAZDA (ROTARY ENGINE)

Year	Model	Spark Plug Gap	Ignition Timing: Timing ATDC ①: Firing Order	Ignition Timing: Timing ATDC ①: Leading Coil	Ignition Timing: Timing ATDC ①: Trailing Coil	Ignition Timing: Mark Fig.	Curb Idle Speed: Man. Trans.	Curb Idle Speed: Auto. Trans. ②	Fast Idle Speed: Man. Trans.	Fast Idle Speed: Auto. Trans.	Fuel Pump Pressure psi
1983–85	RX-7④	.055	1-2	TDC	20°	A	750	750D	③	③	2.8–3.6
1984–85	RX-7⑤	.055	1-2	5°	20°	B	800	—	—	—	50.8–72.5
1986	RX-7⑤	.080	1-2	5°	20°	C	750	750N	—	—	64–85
1987	RX-7⑤	.080	1-2	5°	20°	C	750	750	—	—	⑥

—Not Available.
①—A.T.D.C.-After top dead center.
②—D: Drive.
③—Manually controlled by dash-mounted control.
④—Exc. fuel injected engine.
⑤—Fuel injected engine.
⑥—Exc. turbocharged engine, 64–85 psi; turbocharged engine, 71–92 psi.

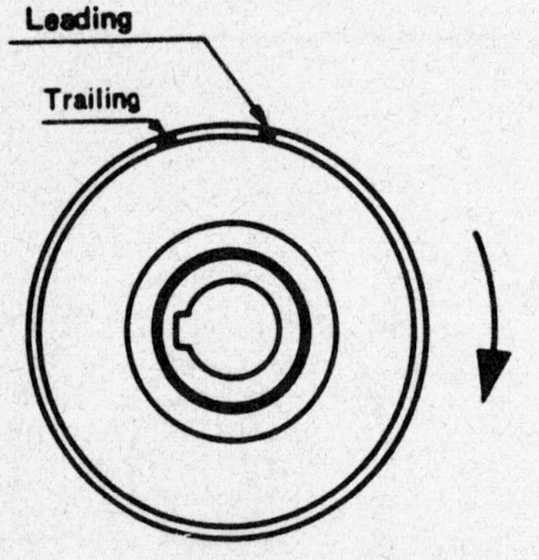

Fig. A

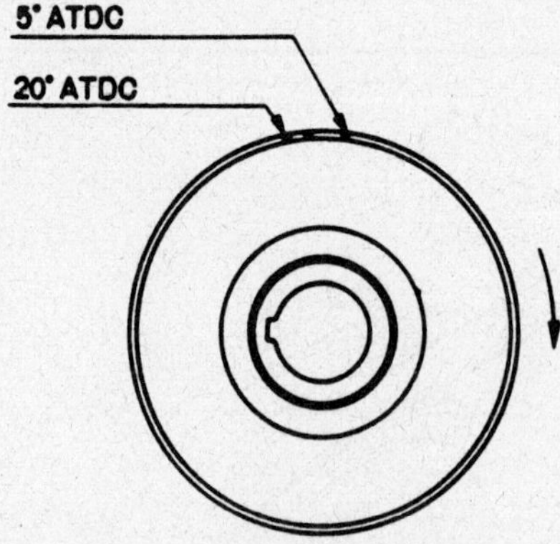

Fig. B

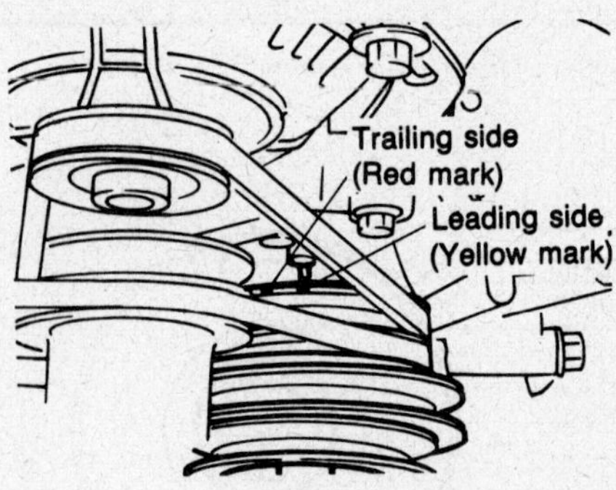

Fig. C

MERCEDES-BENZ

Year	Model	Spark Plug ① Gap Inch	Firing Order Fig.	IGNITION TIMING		Curb Idle Speed		Fast Idle Speed	
				Timing BTDC ①	Mark Fig.	Man. Trans.	Auto. Trans.	Man. Trans.	Auto. Trans.
1983	380SEC, SEL, SL	.032	A	10°	②	—	725	—	—
1984–86	190E 2.3	.032	③	5°	②	720N	720	—	—
	380SE, SL	.032	A	10°	②	—	725	—	—
	500SEC, SEL	.032	A	10°	②	—	675	—	—

①—BTDC: Before top dead center.
②—Mark located on damper or pulley.
③—No. 1 cylinder located at front of engine; firing order, 1-3-4-2.

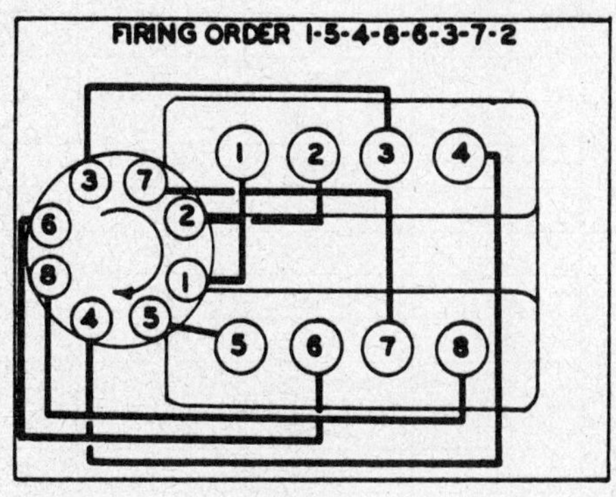

Fig. A

MERKUR

Year & Model	Engine	Spark Plug Gap Inch	Ignition Timing			Curb Idle Speed	Fuel Pump Pressure psi
			Firing Order	Timing BTDC ①	Mark Location		
1985–87 XR4Ti	4-140/2.3i	.034	1-3-4-2	②	Pulley	900	40

①—BTDC-Before top dead center.
②—Auto. trans., 10°; man. trans., 13°.

MITSUBISHI

Year	Engine	Spark Plug Gap Inches	Ignition Timing			Curb Idle Speed ①		Fast Idle Speed		Fuel Pump Pressure (psi)
			Firing Order	Timing BTDC	Mark Fig.	Man. Trans.	Auto. Trans.	Man. Trans.	Auto. Trans.	
1983	1800	⑤	1-3-4-2	5°	A	⑦	750/1300	—	—	—
	2000	.041	1-3-4-2	5°	A	⑧	750	—	—	3–4
	2600	.041	1-3-4-2	7°	B	750	800	—	—	3–4
	2600③	.041	1-3-4-2	10°	B	⑨	⑨	⑨	⑨	35.6
1984	1800③	⑤	1-3-4-2	7°	A	⑨	⑨	⑨	⑨	35.6
	2000	⑤	1-3-4-2	5°	A	700/750	750/850	—	—	—
	2600	.041	1-3-4-2	7°	B	750/925	750/925	⑦	⑦	—
	2600③	.041	1-3-4-2	10°	B	⑨	⑨	⑨	⑨	35.6

Continued

MITSUBISHI—Continued

Year	Engine	Spark Plug Gap Inches	Ignition Timing			Curb Idle Speed①		Fast Idle Speed		Fuel Pump Pressure (psi)
			Firing Order	Timing BTDC	Mark Fig.	Man. Trans.	Auto. Trans.	Man. Trans.	Auto. Trans.	
–	–	–	–	–	–	–	–	–	–	–
1985	1500	⑩	1-3-4-2	⑪		700	750	—	—	—
	1600③	⑩	1-3-4-2	8°	A	⑨	⑨	⑨	⑨	35.6
	1800③	⑩	1-3-4-2	10°	A	⑨	⑨	⑨	⑨	35.6
	2000	⑩	1-3-4-2	5°	A	700	700	—	—	—
	2400	⑤	1-3-4-2	5°	—	—	750	—	—	35.6
	2600	.041	1-3-4-2	7°	B	750	800	—	—	—
	2600③	.041	1-3-4-2	10°	B	⑨	⑨	⑨	⑨	35.6
1986	1500	⑩	1-3-4-2	⑫	C	700	750	—	—	—
	1600③	⑩	1-3-4-2	②	A	⑨	⑨	⑨	⑨	35.6
	1800③	⑩	1-3-4-2	10°	A	⑨	⑨	⑨	⑨	35.6
	2000	⑩	1-3-4-2	⑫	A	700	700	—	—	—
	2400	⑤	1-3-4-2	5°	—	—	⑨	—	⑨	35.6
	2600	.041	1-3-4-2	7°	B	750	800	—	—	—
	2600③	.041	1-3-4-2	10°	B	⑨	⑨	⑨	⑨	35.6
1987	1500	⑤	1-3-4-2	⑫	A	700/850	750/850	2800	2700	2.7–3.7
	1600③	⑤	1-3-4-2	②	A	700/850	700N/650D	⑨	⑨	35–38
	1800③	⑩	1-3-4-2	10°	A	⑨	⑨	⑨	⑨	35.6
	2000	⑤	1-3-4-2	6°	A	750/850	750/950	2500	2450	2.7–3.7
	2400	.041	1-3-4-2	5°	750/900	750N/700D	⑨	⑨	35–38	
	2600⑬	⑤	1-3-4-2	④	B	750/800	800/950	2350	2300	2.8–4.2
	2600⑭	.041	1-3-4-2	④	B	800/900	800/950	2350	2300	2.8–4.2
	2600③	.041	1-3-4-2	②	B	850/1000	850N/750D	⑨	⑨	35–38

①—Where two idle speeds are listed, the higher speed is with A/C on. On carbureted engines, make adjustments at throttle opener.
②—Exc. high altitude, 10°; high altitude, 15°.
③—Turbocharged engine.
④—Exc. high altitude, 7°; high altitude, 12°.
⑤—Nippondenso W20EPR-U10 or W22EPR-10, .037 inch other, .041 inch.
⑥—Exc. high altitude, 8°; high altitude, 13°.
⑦—4 speed, 700/1300 RPM; 5 speed, 650/1300 RPM.
⑧—Calif. models, 750; Exc. Calif. models w/4 speed, 750; Exc. Calif. models w/5 speed, 700.
⑨—Controlled by idle speed control servo.
⑩—NGK, .037 inch; others, .041 inch.
⑪—High alt., 8°; ext. high alt., 3°.
⑫—Exc. high altitude, 5°; high altitude, 10°
⑬—Pickup.
⑭—Montero.

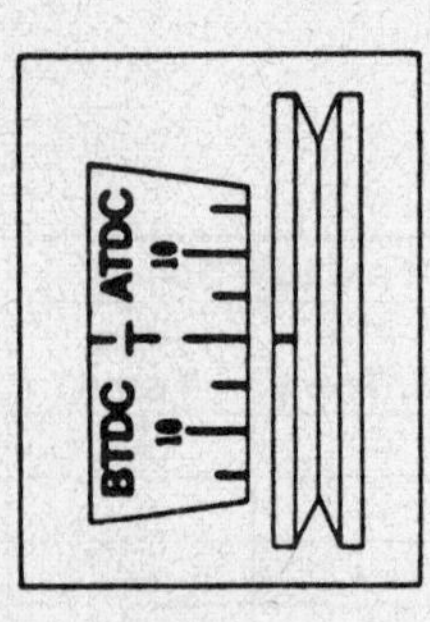

Fig. A

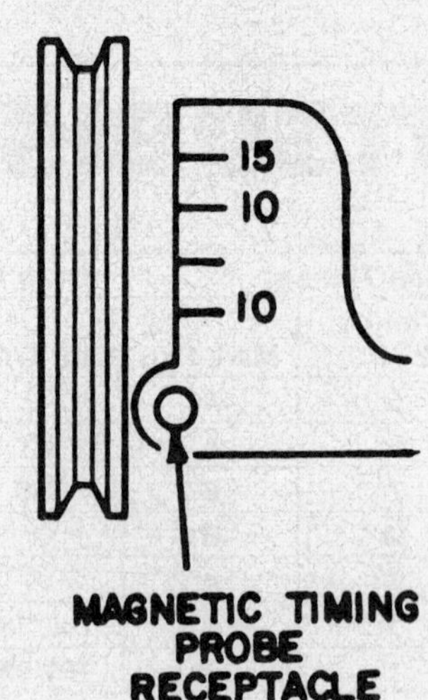

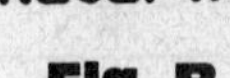

Fig. B

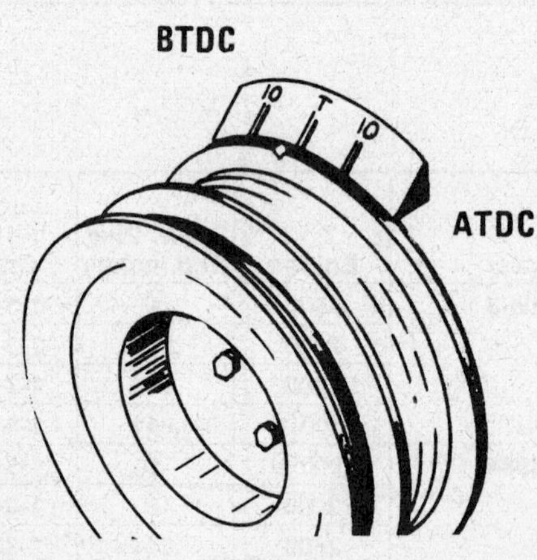

Fig. C

ISSAN/DATSU

Year	Engine	Spark Plug Gap Inch	Ignition Timing BTDC ①		Curb Idle Speed ②		Fast Idle Speed		Fuel Pump Pressure PSI
			Firing Order Fig.	Timing BTDC	Man. Trans.	Auto. Trans.	Man. Trans.	Auto. Trans.	
1983	CA20㊲	.041	A	0°	650	650	—	—	3.3
	E15③	.041	1-3-4-2	2°㉓	700	—	2400–3200	—	3.3
	E16③ ㊳	.041	1-3-4-2	5°㉓	750	650	㊱	㊵	3.3
	L24E㊴	.041	1-5-3-6-2-4	8°	700	650	—	—	36.3
	L28E㉒	.041	1-5-3-6-2-4	8°	700	700	—	—	36.3
	L28ET㉜	.041	1-5-3-6-2-4	24°	700	650	—	—	36.3
	Z22⑧	.033	1-3-4-2	3°	⑪	650	—	—	3.4
	Z22E㉙	.033	1-3-4-2	8°	750	700	—	—	36.3
1984	CA18ET㉙	.041	A	15°	⑥	⑦	—	—	36.3
	CA20E㉙ ㊲	.041	A	0°	750	700	—	—	36.3
	E16S③ ㊳	.041	1-3-4-2	⑫	㉞	650	2600–3400	2900–3700	3.8
	L24E㊴	.041	1-5-3-6-2-4	8°	㉟	㉟	—	—	36.3
	VG30E㉚	.041	B	20°	⑱	⑱	—	—	36.3
	VG30ET㉚	.041	B	20°	700	650	—	—	36.3
	Z20⑧	.033	1-3-4-2	5°	600	650	—	—	3.4
	Z24⑧	.033	1-3-4-2	3°	㉖	650	—	—	3.4
1985	CA18ET㉙	.041	A	15°	⑥	—	—	—	36.3
	CA20E㉙ ㊲	.041	A	⑲	750	700	—	—	36.3
	E16S③ ㊳	④	1-3-4-2	⑫	800	650	2600–3400⑤	2900–3700⑤	3.8
	VG30E㉚ ㊴	.041	B	20°	⑱	⑱	—	—	36.3
	VG30ET㉚	.041	B	20°	700	650	—	—	36.3
	Z20⑧	.033	1-3-4-2	5°	700	—	2600–3000	2600–3000	3.4
	Z24⑧	.033	1-3-4-2	3°	㉖	650	2200–2600	2600–3000	3.4
1986	CA18ET㉙	.041	1-3-4-2	15°	㉕	—	—	—	36.3
	CA20E⑬	.041	A	⑲	750	700	—	—	36.6
	CA20E⑨	.041	A	4°	750	700	—	—	36.6
	E16S③ ㊳	④	1-3-4-2	⑰	650	650	1800–2600	2600–3100	3.8
	VG30E㉚	.041	B	20°	⑱	⑱	—	—	36.3
	VG30ET㉚	.041	B	20°	700	650	—	—	36.3
	VG30i⑭	.041	—	12°	800/900	700D/900N	—	—	36.3
	Z20⑧	.033	1-3-4-2	5°	700	—	2600–3000	2600–3000	3.4
	Z24⑧	.033	1-3-4-2	3°	⑩	650	2200–2600	2600–3000	3.4
	Z24i⑧	.033	1-3-4-2	5°	900	—	—	—	14.2
1987	CA16DE㊳	㉔	—	15°	㉛	—	—	—	28–36
	CA20E㉙ ㊲	.041	A	15°	750	700D	—	—	36.3
	E16i③ ㊳	.041	1-3-4-2	7°	⑳	㉑	—	—	14
	E16S③	.033	1-3-4-2	⑯	㉗	㉘	—	—	2.8–3.8
	E16S③ ⑤	.033	1-3-4-2	⑯	800	700D	1800–2600	2100–2900	2.8–3.8
	VG30E㊴	.041	B	20°	㉟	⑱	—	—	36.3
	VG30E㉙	.041	B	20°	700	700	—	—	36.3
	VG30E㉚	.041	B	20°	⑱	⑱	—	—	61–71
	VG30ET㉚	.041	B	20°	700	650D	—	—	61–71
	VG30i⑭ ㉝	.041	—	12°	800/900	700D/900N	—	—	36.3
	Z24i⑭	.033	1-3-4-2	5°	900	650D/900N	—	—	36.3
	Z24i⑮	.033	1-3-4-2	10°	800/950	700D/950N	—	—	36.3

Continued

NISSAN/DATSUN—Continued

① —BTDC: Before Top Dead Center.
② —Where 2 idle speeds are listed, second speed is with A/C on.
③ —Sentra.
④ —Exc. Federal w/auto. trans., .041 inch; Federal w/auto. trans., .033 inch.
⑤ —California.
⑥ —Except high altitude, 750 RPM; high altitude, 680 RPM.
⑦ —Except high altitude, 700 RPM; high altitude, 630 RPM.
⑧ —Pickup.
⑨ —Stanza wagon.
⑩ —2 wheel drive cab and chassis, 700 RPM; others, 800 RPM.
⑪ —4 X 2, 650 RPM; 4 4, 800 RPM.
⑫ —Except Calif.; man. trans., 15° BTDC; auto. trans., 8° BTDC. Calif., 5° BTDC.
⑬ —Exc. Stanza Wagon.
⑭ —Pickup & Pathfinder.
⑮ —Van.
⑯ —Inspection, 7° BTDC w/all hoses connected. Adjust to 2° BTDC w/vacuum sensor hose disconnected and plugged.
⑰ —Exc. Calif., 10° BTDC; Calif., 5° ATDC.
⑱ —Exc. high altitude, 700 RPM; high altitude, 650 RPM.
⑲ —Auto. trans., 0°; man. trans., 4°.
⑳ —Inspection, 700–900 RPM with A/C off; 1000 RPM with A/C on. Adjust to 750 RPM w/throttle sensor harness disconnected and all accessories off.
㉑ —Inspection, 600–800D RPM with A/C off; 700D with A/C on. Adjust to 670D RPM w/throttle sensor harness disconnected and all accessories off.
㉒ —280Z, 280ZX models.
㉓ —ATDC: After top dead center.
㉔ —Specified spark plugs are preset. Do not check and/or adjust gap.
㉕ —Exc. high altitude, 750 RPM; high altitude, 680 RPM.
㉖ —2 wheel drive, 700 RPM; 4 wheel drive, 800 RPM.
㉗ —Inspection, 700–900 RPM. Adjust to 725 RPM with Vacuum Control Modulator (VCM) harness disconnected.
㉘ —Inspection, 600–800D RPM. Adjust to 625D RPM with Vacuum Control Modulator (VCM) harness disconnected.
㉙ —200SX models.
㉚ —300ZX models.
㉛ —Inspection, 750–850 RPM. Adjust to 750 RPM w/AAC valve harness disconnected.
㉜ —280ZX turbo models.
㉝ —1986½.
㉞ —Except Calif., 800 RPM; Calif., 750 RPM.
㉟ —Except high altitude, 700 RPM; high altitude, 650 RPM.
㊱ —Exc. Calif., 2400–3200 RPM; Calif., 2600–3400 RPM.
㊲ —Stanza.
㊳ —Pulsar.
㊴ —Maxima.
㊵ —Exc. Calif., 2700–3500 RPM; Calif., 2900–3700 RPM.

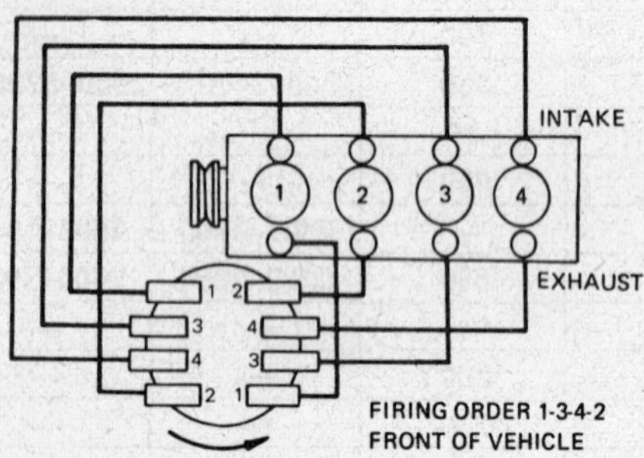

Fig. A

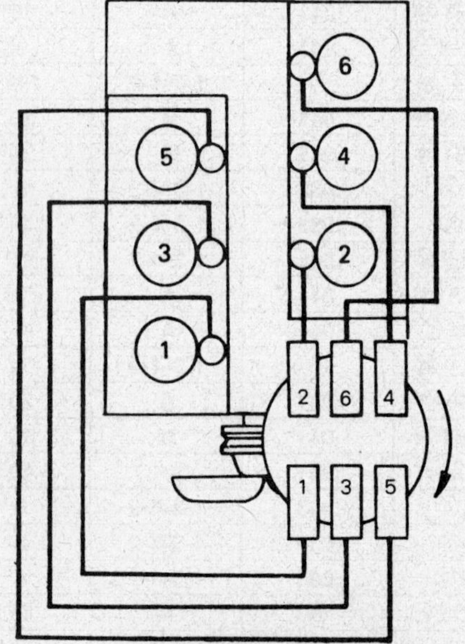

Fig. B

PEUGEOT

Year	Engine	Spark Plug		Ignition Timing		Curb Idle Speed		Fast Idle Speed	
		Gap Inch	Firing Order Fig.	Timing BTDC	Mark Fig.	Man. Trans.	Auto. Trans.	Man. Trans.	Auto. Trans.
1983–85	4-120	.024	A	8°	B	900–950	900–950	①	①
1985–86	4-134	.036	—	10°	—	900–950	900–950	—	—

①—Controlled by auxiliary air device.

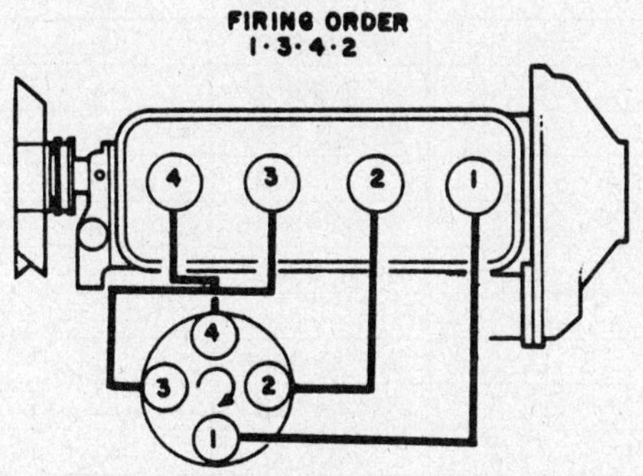

Fig. A

Fig. B

PORSCHE

Year	Model	Spark Plug Gap Inch	Firing Order Fig.	Timing BTDC ①	Ignition Timing		Curb Idle Speed	
					Mark Fig.	Man. Trans.	Auto. Trans.	Fuel System Pressure Psi
1983	944	.028	A	—	⑤	850–950	850–950	29④
	911SC	.028	B	5°	⑥	—	—	—
	928S	.028	D	20° @ 3000	C	600–700	600–700	33–39
1984	944	.028	A	5° @ 900	⑤	800–900	800–900	29④
	911 Carrera	.028	B	3° @ 800③	—	780–820	780–820	29④
	928S	.028	D	20° @ 3000	C	600–700	600–700	33–39
1985	944	.028	A	5° @ 900	⑤	820–860	820–860	29④
	911	.028	B	3°@ 800③	—	780–820	780–820	29④
	928S	.028	D	20° @ 3000	C	660–700	660–700	33–39
1986	944	.028	A	5° @ 900	⑤	820–860	820–860	29④
	944 Turbo	.028	—	②	—	800–880	800–880	33–39
	911 Carrera	.028	B	3° @ 800③	—	780–820	780–820	29④
	911 Turbo	.028	—	—	—	850–950	—	—
	928S	.028	D	20° @ 3000	C	660–700	660–700	33–39
1987	924S	.028	A	5° @ 900	⑤	820–860	820–860	29④
	944S	.028	—	②	—	800–880	800–880	33–39
	911 Carrera	.028	B	3° @ 800③	—	780–820	780–820	29④
	911 Turbo	.028	—	—	—	850–950	—	—
	928S	.028	D	20° @ 3000	C	660–700	660–700	33–39

①-Before Top Dead Center.
②—Ignition timing controlled by Digital Motor Electronic (Motronic) control system.
③—After top dead center.
④—At idle speed.
⑤—Mark located on flywheel.
⑥—Mark located on pulley.

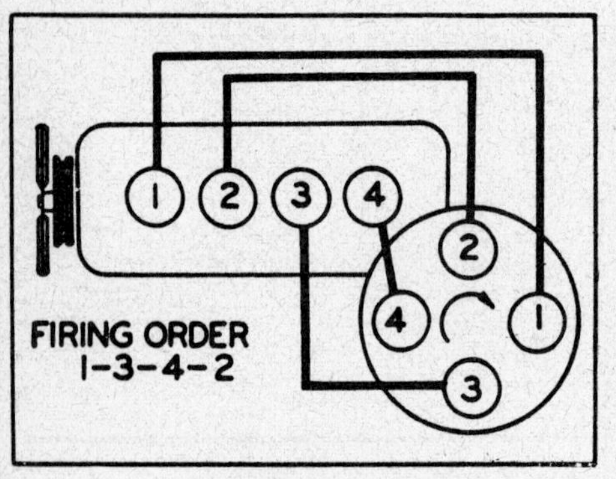

Fig. A

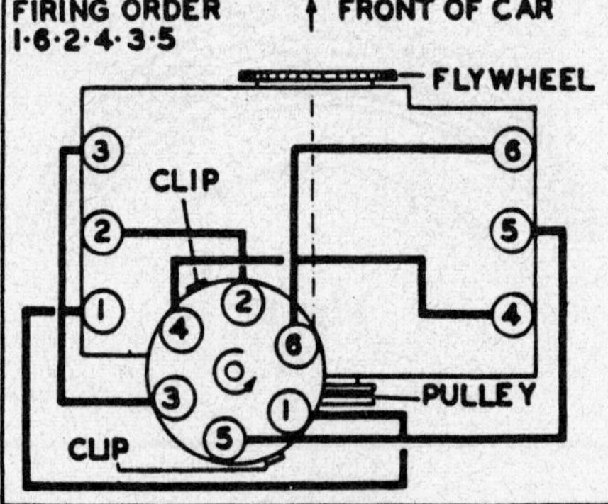

Fig. B

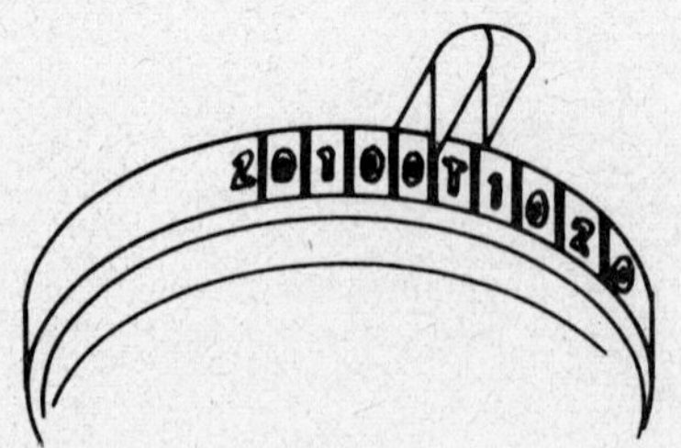

Fig. C

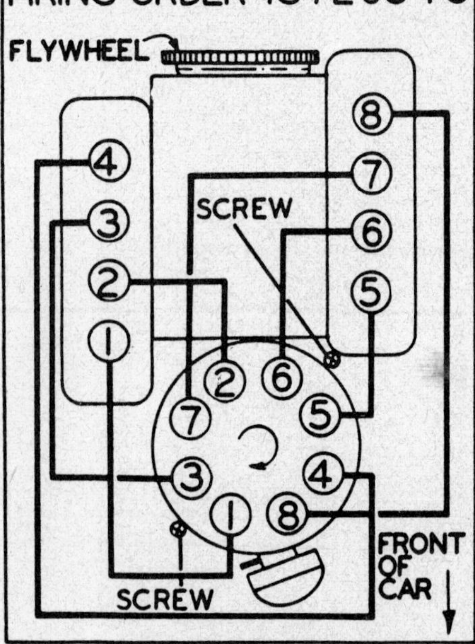

Fig. D

RENAULT

Year	Engine	Spark Plug Gap Inch	Ignition Timing			Curb Idle Speed		Fast Idle Speed		Fuel Pump Pressure PSI
			Firing Order	Timing BTDC ①	Mark Fig.	Man. Trans.	Auto. Trans.	Man. Trans.	Auto. Trans.	
1983	4-85/1397cc ④ ⑨	.024	⑫	8° ② ⑥	⑬	700	700	⑰	⑰	28
	4-85/1397cc ⑤ ⑨	.024	⑫	8° ② ⑥	⑬	⑩	⑩	⑩	⑩	14.5
	4-85/1397cc ⑮	.024	⑫	3°	⑬	800	—	⑪	—	2.5–4
	4-100/1647cc ⑧	.024	⑫	10°	⑬	—	—	⑰	⑰	—
	4-95/1565cc ⑭ ⑯	.024	⑫	10° ② ⑥	⑬	750	—	⑰	⑰	36 ⑦
	4-100/1647cc ⑭	.026	⑫	10° ②	⑬	800	650	⑰	⑰	36 ⑦
1984	4-85/1397cc ④ ⑨	.024	⑫	8° ② ⑥	⑬	700	700	⑰	⑰	28
	4-85/1397cc ⑤ ⑨	.024	⑫	8° ② ⑥	⑬	⑩	⑩	⑩	⑩	14.5
	4-95/1565cc ⑭ ⑯	.024	⑫	10° ② ⑥	⑬	750	—	⑰	⑰	36 ⑦
	4-132 ③ ⑭	.025	⑫	10° ② ⑥	⑬	800	700	⑰	⑰	36 ⑦
1985	4-85/1397cc ④ ⑨	.024	⑫	8° ② ⑥	⑬	700	700	⑰	⑰	28
	4-85/1397cc ⑤ ⑨	.024	⑫	8° ② ⑥	⑬	⑩	⑩	⑩	⑩	14.5
	4-105/1721cc ⑨	.032	⑫	⑥	⑬	⑩	⑩	⑩	⑩	17.3
1985–86	4-132 ③ ⑭	.025	⑫	10° ② ⑥	⑬	800	700	⑰	⑰	36 ⑦
1986–87	4-85/1397cc ④ ⑨	.032	⑫	8° ② ⑥	⑬	700	700	⑰	⑰	28
	4-85/1397cc ⑤ ⑨	.032	⑫	8° ② ⑥	⑬	⑩	⑩	⑩	⑩	14.5
	4-105/1721cc ⑨	.032	⑫	⑥	⑬	⑩	⑩	⑩	⑩	17.3
1987	4-120/1965cc ⑨	.032	⑫	⑥	⑬	⑩	⑩	⑩	⑩	17.3

① —BTDC: Before top dead center.
② —With vacuum sensor disconnected and plugged.
③ —Sportswagon.
④ —With multi-point fuel injection.
⑤ —With throttle body fuel injection.
⑥ —Not adjustable.
⑦ —With vacuum supply disconnected from pressure regulator.
⑧ —18i.
⑨ —Alliance or Encore.
⑩ —Controlled by idle control motor.
⑪ —Exc. Calif., 1900 RPM; Calif., 1500 RPM.
⑫ —Firing order, 1-3-4-2: No. 1 cyl. at flywheel or drive plate end of engine.
⑬ —Mark located on flywheel or converter, timed at No. 1 cyl.
⑭ —Fuego.
⑮ —Le Car.
⑯ —Turbo.
⑰ —Controlled by electronic control unit.

SAAB

Year	Model	Spark Plug Gap Inch	Firing Order Fig.	Ignition Timing: Timing BTDC ①	Ignition Timing: Mark Fig.	Curb Idle Speed: Man. Trans.	Curb Idle Speed: Auto. Trans.	Fast Idle Speed	Fuel Pump Pressure
1983–84	900	.024	C	20②	B	875	875	③	68.2–78.3
1985	900⑤	.024	A	20②	B	875	875	—	68.2–78.3
	900⑥	.024	A	16⑦	B	850	850	—	35
1986–87	900⑤	.024	A	20②	B	875	875	—	68.2–78.3
	900⑥	.024	A	④⑦	B	850	850	—	35
	9000	.024	—	④⑦	B	850	850	—	35

①—BTDC: Before Top Dead Center.
②—@ 2000 RPM.
③—Cold engine operation is controlled by the Idle Air Control (IAC) valve & fuel enrichment circuits; no adjustment required.
④—Exc. Turbo, 14° BTDC; Turbo, 16° BTDC.
⑤—8 valve engine.
⑥—16 valve engine.
⑦—@ 850 RPM.

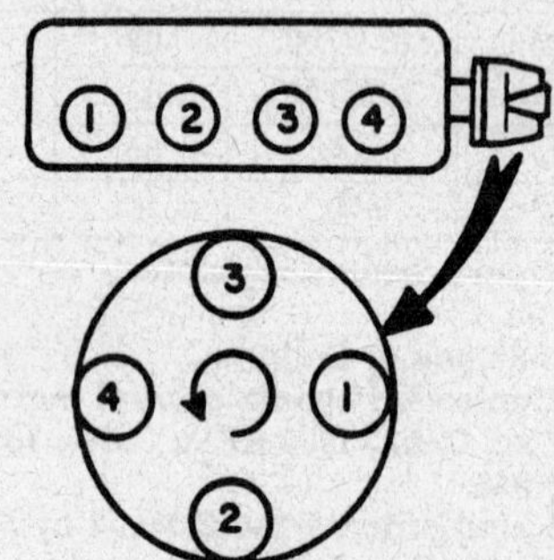

Fig. A

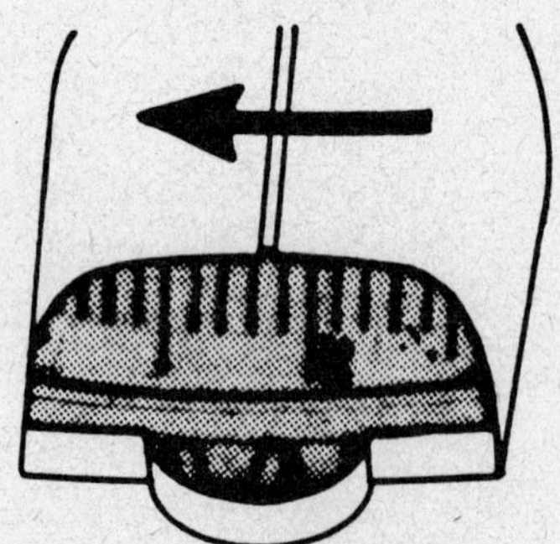

Fig. B

SPECTRUM

Year	Engine	Spark Plug Gap	Ignition Timing BTDC ①				Curb Idle Speed ②		Fast Idle Speed		Fuel Pump Pressure
			Firing Order	Man. Trans.	Auto. Trans.	Location	Man. Trans.	Auto. Trans.	Man. Trans.	Auto. Trans.	
1985–87	4-90L/1.5	.040	1-3-4-2	15°	10°	Damper	750/850	1000/980	—	—	—

①—BTDC-Before Top Dead Center.
②—Where 2 idle speeds are listed, second speed is with A/C on.

SPRINT

Year	Engine	Spark Plug Gap	Ignition Timing BTDC ①				Curb Idle Speed		Fast Idle Speed		Fuel Pump Pressure
			Firing Order Fig.	Man. Trans.	Auto. Trans.	Mark Location	Man. Trans.	Auto Tans.	Man. Trans.	Auto. Trans.	
1985	3-61/1.0L	.041	A	10° ④	6° ⑤	B	700–800	800–900	2100–2700	2100–2700	—
1986–87	3-61/1.0L ②	.041	A	10° ④	6° ⑤	B	700–800	800–900	2100–2700	2100–2700	4.2
	3-61/1.0L ③	.041	A	10° ⑥	—	B	650–750	—	2100–2700	—	4.2
1987	3-61/1.0L ⑦	.041	A	12° ⑥	—	B	700–800	—	—	—	⑧

①—BTDC-Before Top Dead Center.
②—Exc. ER models.
③—ER models.
④—At 750 RPM.
⑤—At 850 RPM.
⑥—At 700 RPM.
⑦—Turbocharged engine.
⑧—35–43 psi w/vacuum hose disconnected from regulator. 25–33 psi with engine idling & vacuum hose connected to regulator.

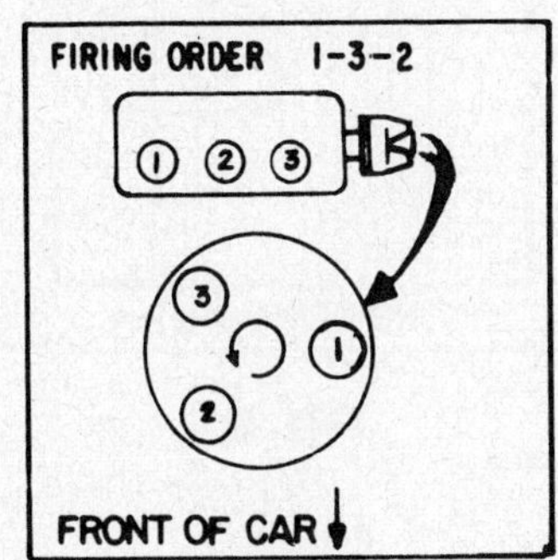

Fig. A

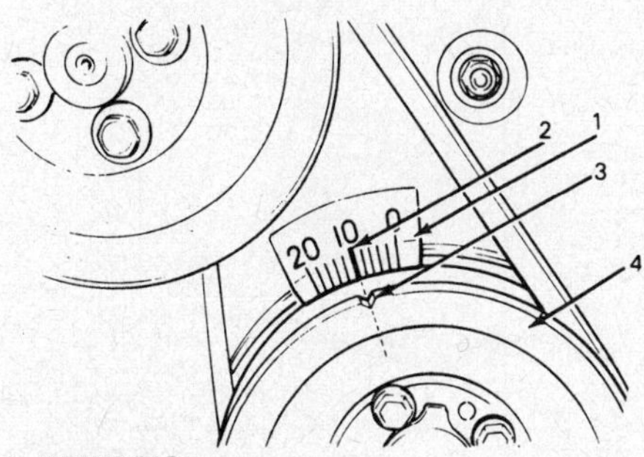

1. TIMING TAB
2. (MT) 10° (BTDC) (AT) 6° (BTDC)
3. TIMING NOTCH
4. CRANKSHAFT PULLEY

Fig. B

SUBARU

Year	Engine	Spark Plug Gap Inch	Ignition Timing			Curb Idle Speed		Fast Idle Speed		Fuel Pump Pressure psi
			Firing Order Fig.	Timing BTDC ①	Mark Fig.	Man. Trans.	Auto. Trans. ②	Man. Trans.	Auto. Trans.	
1983	1600	.041	A	8°	B	700	—	—	—	1.3–2.0
	1800	.041	A	8°	B	700	800N	—	—	1.3–2.0
1984	1600	.041	A	8°	B	650	—	—	—	1.35–2.06
	1800 Exc. Turbo	.041	A	8°	B	700	800N	—	—	1.35–2.06
	1800 Turbo	.041	A	15°	B	—	800N	—	—	61–71
1985	1800 2 Bbl.	.041	A	8°	B	700	800N	—	—	2.6–3.3
	1800 F.I.	.041	A	6°	B	700	800N	—	—	—
	1800 Turbo	.041	A	25°	B	700	800N	—	—	—
1986	1800 2 Bbl.	.041	A	8°	B	700	800N	—	—	2.6–3.3
	1800 F.I.④	.041	A	20°	B	—	700N	—	—	28–43
	1800 F.I.③	.041	A	6°	B	700	800N	—	—	61–71
	1800 Turbo	.041	A	25°	B	700	800N	—	—	61–71

①—B.T.D.C.-Before top dead center.
②—N: Neutral.
③—Multi-point injection.
④—Single point injection.

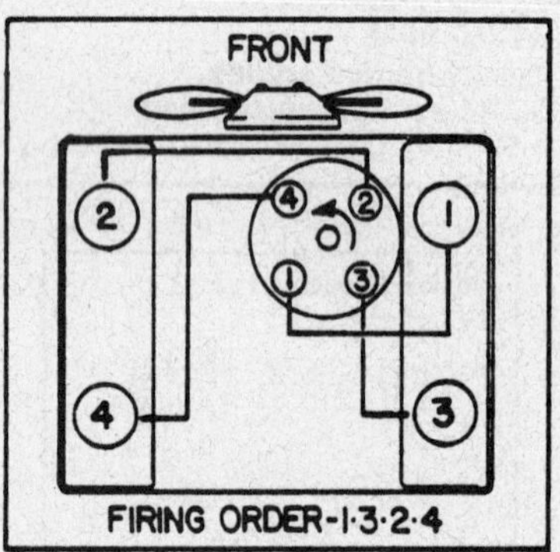

Fig. A

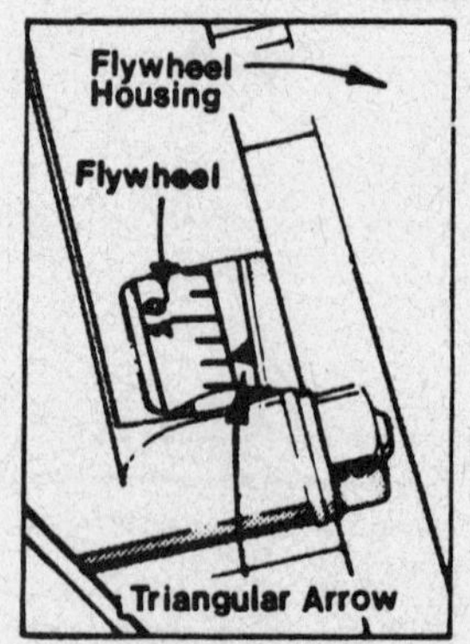

Fig. B

SUZUKI SAMURAI

Year	Engine	Spark Plug Gap	Ignition Timing			Curb Idle Speed②	Fast Idle Speed	Fuel Pump Pressure
			Firing Order Fig.	Timing BTDC ①	Mark Location			
1986–87	4-81/1.3L	.029	1-3-4-2	10°	A	800/900	—	—

①—BTDC: Before Top Dead Center.
②—If 2 speeds are listed, second speed is with idle-up actuator engaged (headlamps on, turning, etc.).

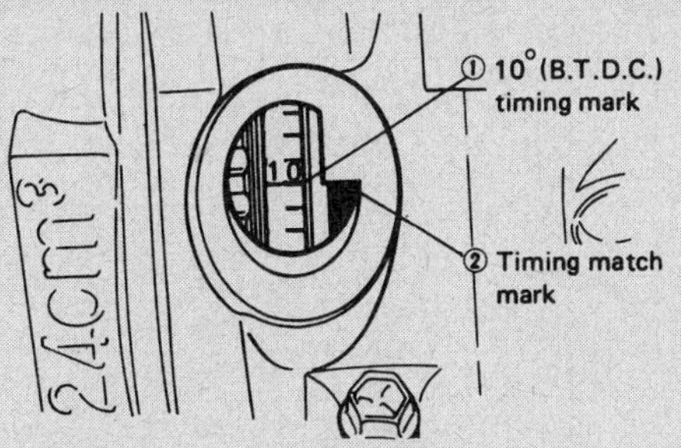

Fig. A

TOYOTA

Year	Engine	Spark Plug Gap Inch	Ignition Timing			Curb Idle Speed②		Fast Idle Speed		Fuel Pump Pressure Lbs.
			Firing Order	Timing BTDC①	Mark Fig.	Man. Trans.	Auto. Trans.	Man. Trans.	Auto. Trans.	
1983	4-1290cc	.043	M	5° ⑫	D	700	—	—	—	35–38
	4-1452cc	.043	N	5° ⑫	E	⑭	⑯	3000	3000	—
	4-1587cc	.043	N	5° ⑫	E	⑮	⑯	3000	3000	—
	4-1995cc	.043	O	5° ⑫	H	700	750	—	—	33–38
	4-2367cc	.031	K	5° ⑫	G	⑰	750	2600	2600	—
	6-2759cc	.043	L	10° ⑱	C	650	650	—	—	35–38
1984	4-1290cc	.043	M	5° ⑫	D	700	—	—	—	35–38
	4-1452cc	.043	N	5° ⑫	E	㉑	㉒	3000	3000	35–38
	4-1587cc ⑲	.043	N	5° ⑫	E	650	800	3000	3000	—
	4-1587cc ⑳	.043	N	5° ⑫	E	㉑	㉒	3000	3000	—
	4-1995cc	.043	O	5° ⑫	H	700	750	—	—	33–38
	4-1998cc	.043	㉘	8° ⑫	I	700	750	—	—	35–38
	4-2367cc	.031	K	5° ⑫	G	750	750	—	—	35–38
	6-2759cc	.043	L	10° ⑱	C	650	650	—	—	35–38
1985	4-1452cc	.043	N	5° ⑫	E	㉙	㉒	3000 ㉚	3000 ㉚	—
	4-1587cc ㉛	.043	N	5° ⑫	E	㉝	㉞	3000 ㉚	3000 ㉚	2.6–3.5
	4-1587cc ㉜	.043	N	10° ⑱	E	800	800	—	—	33–40
	4-1995cc	.043	O	5° ⑫	H	700	750	—	—	33–38
	4-1998cc	.043	㉘	8° ⑫	I	700	750	—	—	33–38
	4-2367cc ㉟	.031	K	5° ⑱	G	750	750	—	—	33–38
	4-2367cc ㊱	.031	K	0° ⑫	G	700	750	2600 ㉚	2600 ㉚	—
	6-2759cc	.043	L	10° ⑱	C	650	650	—	—	33–38
1986	4-1452cc ㉞	.043	N	5° ⑫	E	⑮	⑯	3000 ㉚	3000 ㉚	2.6–3.5
	4-1452cc ㊵	.043	N	5° ⑫	E	⑥	⑯	3000 ㉚	3000 ㉚	2.6–3.5
	4-1587cc ㉛	.043	N	5° ⑫	E	③	④	3000 ㉚	3000 ㉚	2.6–3.5
	4-1587cc ㉜	.043	N	10° ⑱	E	800	800	—	—	33–38
	4-1587cc ㊴	.043	N	5° ⑫	B	650	750	3000 ㉚	3000 ㉚	2.6–3.5
	4-1587cc ㉓	.043	N	10° ⑱	A	800	800	—	—	33–38
	4-1995cc	.043	O	10° ⑫	H	⑤	⑤	—	—	㊲
	4-1998cc	.043	㉘	10° ⑱	F	750	750	—	—	35–38
	4-2237cc	.043	㉘	12° ⑱	I	700	750	—	—	33–38
	4-2367cc ㉟	.031	K	5° ⑫	G	⑩	⑩	—	—	36–38
	4-2367cc ㊱	.031	K	0° ⑫	G	700	750	2600 ㉚	2600 ㉚	2.8–4.3
	6-2759cc	.043	L	10° ⑫	C	—	—	—	—	㊳

Continued

TOYOTA—Continued

Year	Engine	Spark Plug Gap Inch	Ignition Timing: Firing Order	Ignition Timing: Timing BTDC (1)	Ignition Timing: Mark Fig.	Curb Idle Speed (2): Man. Trans.	Curb Idle Speed (2): Auto. Trans.	Fast Idle Speed: Man. Trans.	Fast Idle Speed: Auto. Trans.	Fuel Pump Pressure Lbs.
1987	4-1452cc	.043	1-3-4-2	5° (12)	E	(15) (7)	(16) (7)	3000 (27)	3000 (27)	2.6–3.5
	4-1456cc	.043	1-3-4-2	3° (12)	J	700	900	3000 (27)	2800 (27)	3.0
	4-1587cc (31)	.043	1-3-4-2	5° (12)	E	(3) (7)	(4) (7)	3000 (27)	3000 (27)	2.5–3.5
	4-1587cc (39)	.043	1-3-4-2	5° (12)	B	650/800	750/900	3000 (27)	3000 (27)	2.5–3.5
	4-1587cc (32)	.043	1-3-4-2	10° (13)	E	800	800	—	—	33–39
	4-1587cc (11)	.043	1-3-4-2	10° (18)	E	800	800	—	—	33–38
	4-1587cc (23)	.043	1-3-4-2	10° (18)	A	800	800	—	—	33–38
	4-1998cc (24)	.043	(28)	10° (13)	F	700	700	—	—	38–44
	4-1998 (25)	.043	(28)	10° (13)	J	750	750	—	—	33–38
	4-2237cc	.043	1-3-4-2	12° (18)	I	700	750	—	—	33–38
	4-2367 (36)	.031	K	0°	G	700	750	2600 (27)	2600 (27)	—
	4-2367 (26)	.031	K	5°	G	750	750	—	—	33–38
	4-2367 (27)	.031	K	5°	G	800	800	—	—	33–38
	6-2759cc	.043	L	10° (18)	C	650	650	—	—	33–38
	6-2954cc (8)	.043	1-5-3-6-2-4	10° (13)	C	700	700	—	—	33–40
	6-2954cc (9)	.031	1-5-3-6-2-4	10° (13)	C	650	650	—	—	33–40

(1)—BTDC: Before Top Dead Center.
(2)—Where 2 speeds are listed, second speed is with throttle positioner activated.
(3)—Manual steering, 700 RPM; power steering, 750 RPM.
(4)—Manual steering, 800 RPM; power steering, 850 RPM.
(5)—Camry, 750 RPM; Celica, 700 RPM.
(6)—4 spd., 550 RPM; 5 & 6 spd. with manual steering, 800 RPM; 5 & 6 spd. with power steering, 650 RPM.
(7)—With throttle positioner activated, 1400 RPM.
(8)—7M-GE engine.
(9)—7M-GTE engine.
(10)—Turbocharged engine, 800 RPM; non-turbocharged engine, 750 RPM.
(11)—4A-GEC engine.
(12)—With distributor vacuum chamber hose(s) disconnected & plugged.
(13)—With check connector terminals T & E shorted.
(14)—Exc. power steering models, 4 spd., 550 RPM, 5 spd., 650 RPM; models with power steering, 800 RPM.
(15)—Manual steering, 650 RPM; power steering, 800 RPM.
(16)—Manual steering, 800 RPM; power steering, 900 RPM.
(17)—Exc. fuel injected engines, 700 RPM; fuel injected engines, 750 RPM.
(18)—With engine check connector terminals jumped, located near distributor.
(19)—Front wheel drive.
(20)—Rear wheel drive.
(21)—Manual steering, 700 RPM; power steering, 800 RPM.
(22)—Manual steering, 800 RPM; power steering, 900 RPM.
(23)—Model 4A-GELC engine.
(24)—3S-FE engine.
(25)—3S-GE engine.
(26)—22R-E engine.
(27)—22R-TE engine.
(28)—No. 1 cyl located at front of engine, cylinder numbering 1-2-3-4, firing order 1-3-4-2.
(29)—4 spd., 550 RPM; 5 spd. with manual steering, 650 RPM; 5 spd. with power steering, 800 RPM.
(30)—With cooling fan, choke opener and EGR system off.
(31)—Model 4A-C engine.
(32)—Model 4A-GE engine.
(33)—Front wheel drive models, 650 RPM. Rear wheel drive models: with manual steering, 700 RPM; with power steering, 800 RPM.
(34)—Front wheel drive models, 800 RPM. Rear wheel drive models: with manual steering, 800 RPM; with power steering, 900 RPM.
(35)—Exc. 22R engine.
(36)—22R engine.
(37)—Camry, 28–36 psi; Celica, 35–38 psi.
(38)—Cressida, 33–38 psi; Supra, 35–38 psi.
(39)—4A-LC engine.
(40)—3A-C engine.

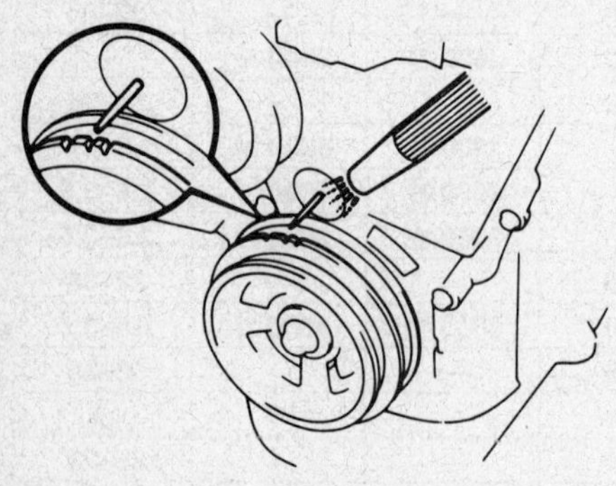

Fig. A

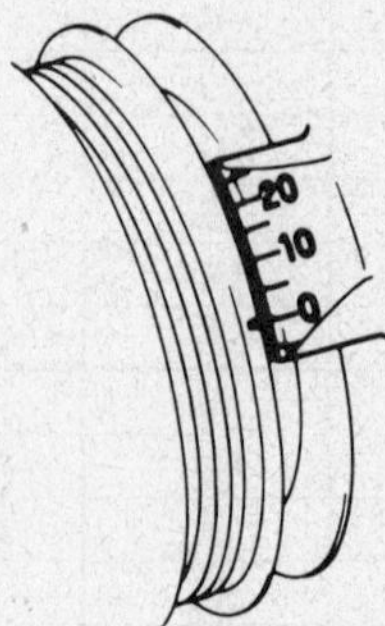

Fig. B

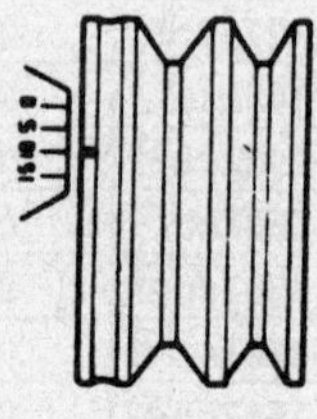

Fig. C

Continued

TOYOTA–Continued

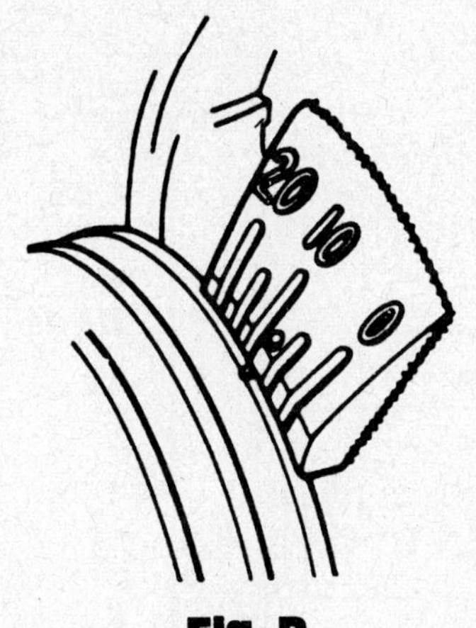

Fig. D

Fig. E

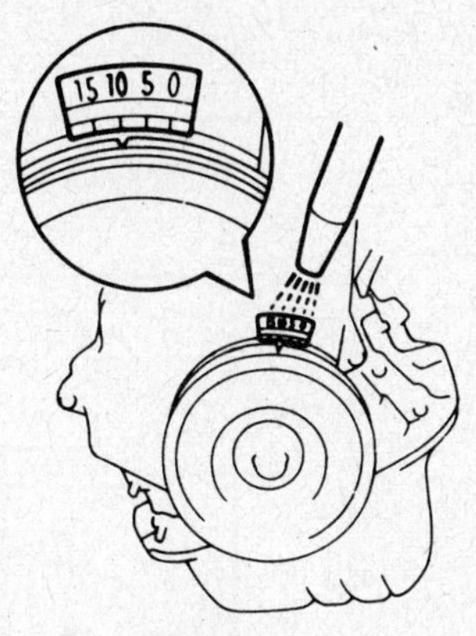

Fig. F

Fig. G

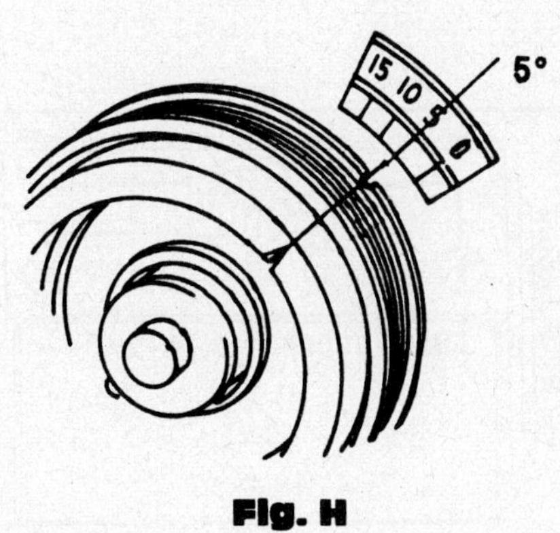

Fig. H

Fig. I

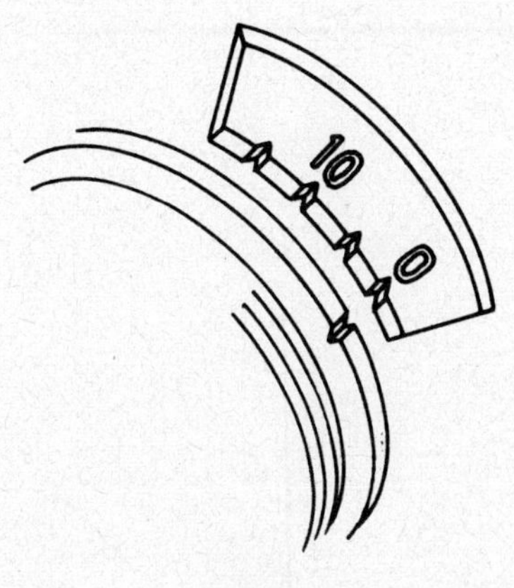

Fig. J

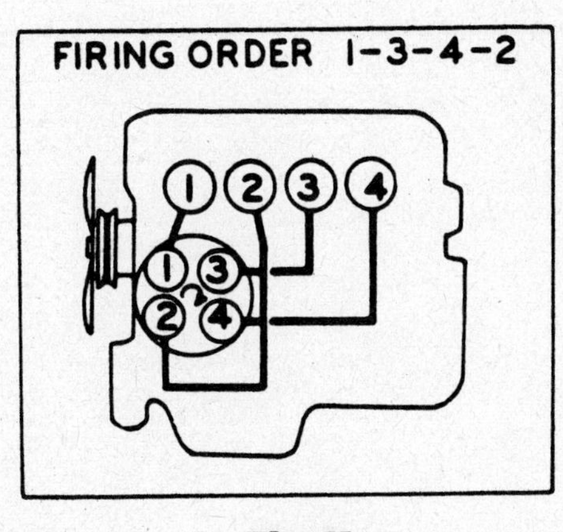

Fig. K

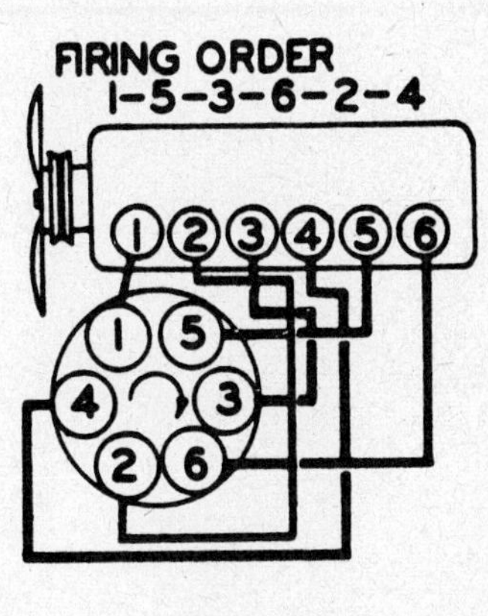

Fig. L

Continued

TOYOTA–Continued

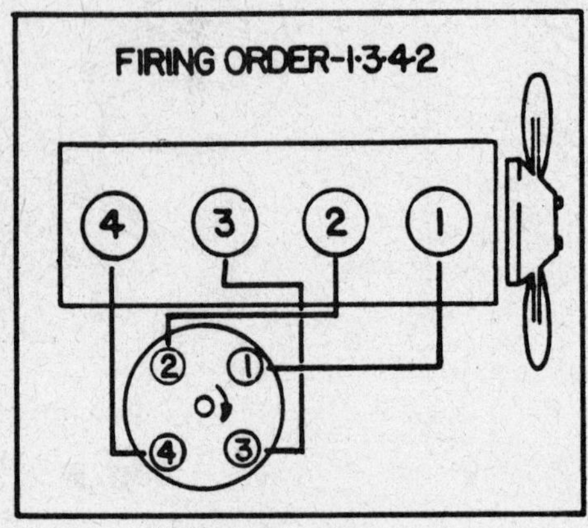

Fig. M

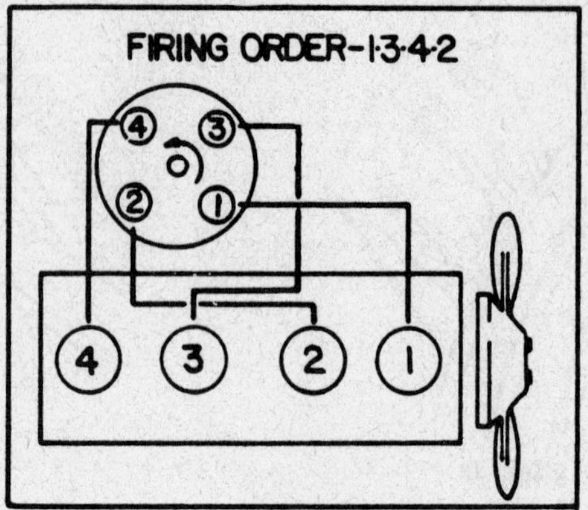

Fig. N

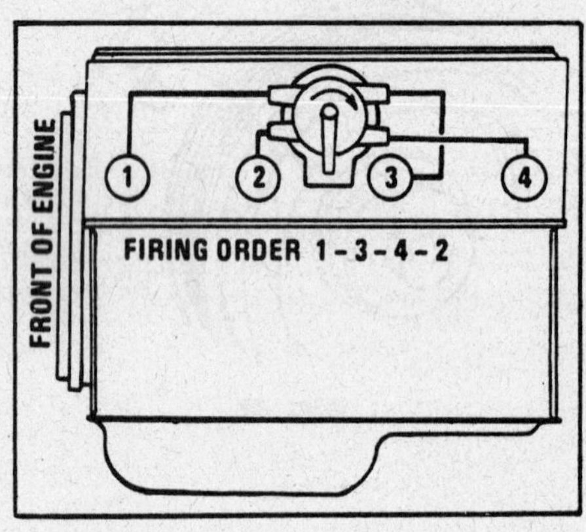

Fig. O

VOLKSWAGEN

Year	Model	Spark Plug Gap Inch	Ignition Timing: Firing Order Fig.	Ignition Timing: Timing	Ignition Timing: Mark Fig.	Curb Idle Speed: Man. Trans.	Curb Idle Speed: Auto. Trans.	Fast Idle Speed: Man. Trans.	Fast Idle Speed: Auto. Trans.	Fuel Pump Pressure
1983	Vanagon ② ④	.028	B	⑭	F	925	925	—	—	29-36
	Vanagon ② ⑤	.028	B	6	G	900	900	—	—	29-36
1983–84	Rabbit, Jetta, Scirocco	.028	A	⑧	—	⑥	⑥	⑮	⑮	⑦
	Pickup	.028	A	3° ①	C	925	925	—	—	64–74
	GTI	.028	A	6° ⑨	—	950	—	—	—	64–74
	Quantum ⑪	.028	—	⑩	⑬ 925	925	—	—	—	68-78
1983–86	Vanagon ③	.028	—	5° ①	—	850	850	—	—	—
1984	Quantum ⑫	.028	—	6° ⑨	E	750–850	750–850	—	—	68–78
1985–86	Cabriolet	.028	A	⑩	-	925	925	—	—	64–74
	Golf, Jetta ⑯	.028	A	6° ⑨	—	900	900	—	—	75–82
	Golf, Jetta ⑰	.028	A	6° ⑨	—	850	850	—	—	75–82
	Quantum ⑫	.028	—	6° ⑨	D	750–850	750–850	—	—	68–78
	Scirocco	.028	A	⑩	—	925	925	—	—	64–74

①—ATDC-After Top Dead Center, idle stabilizer bypassed, if equipped.
②—Air Cooled.
③—Water Cooled.
④—Exc. California.
⑤—California.
⑥—Exc. carbureted engine, 925 RPM; carbureted engine, 820–900 RPM.
⑦—Exc. carbureted engine, 64–74 psi; carbureted engine, 4.0–5.3 psi. @ 2000 RPM.
⑧—Auto. trans., 3° ATDC; man. trans. exc. with carburetor, 6° Before Top Dead Center (BTDC); man. trans. with carburetor, 7.5° BTDC.
⑨—Before Top Dead Center.
⑩—Auto. trans., 3° ATDC; man. trans., 6° BTDC.
⑪—4 cylinder engine.
⑫—5 cylinder engine.
⑬—Auto. trans., Fig. D; man. trans., Fig. E.
⑭—Point gap, .016 inch,; dwell, 44–50°; ignition timing, 7½° before top dead center.
⑮—Carbureted engine, 2600–3000 RPM.
⑯—Exc. GTI & GLI models.
⑰—GTI or GLI Models.

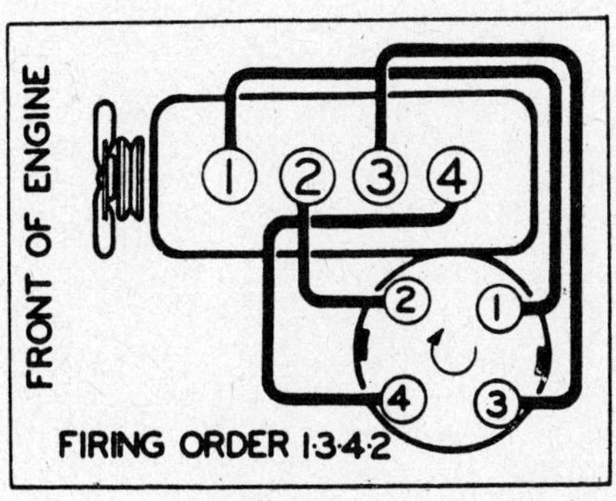

Fig. A

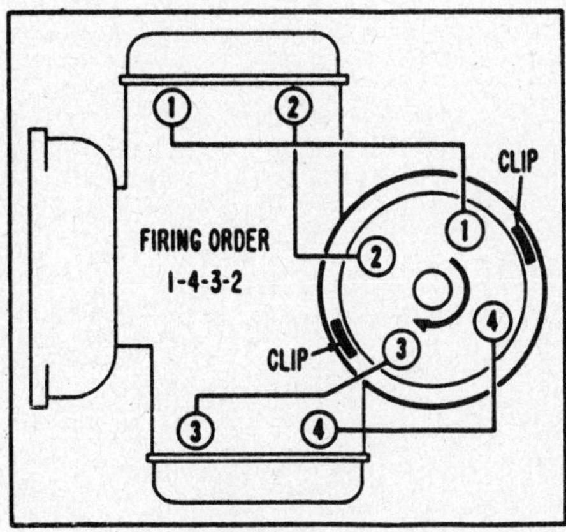

Fig. B

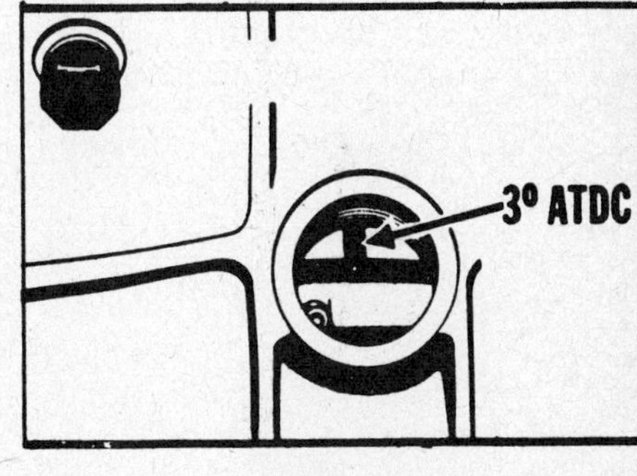

Fig. C

Continued

VOLKSWAGEN—Continued

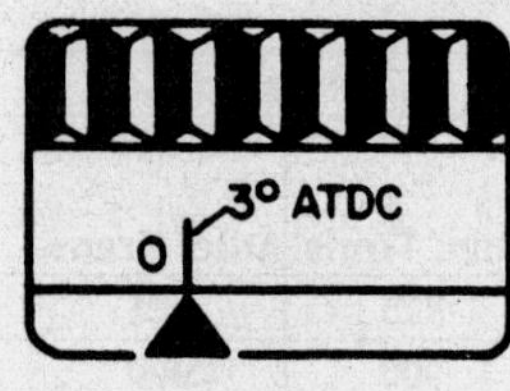

Fig. D

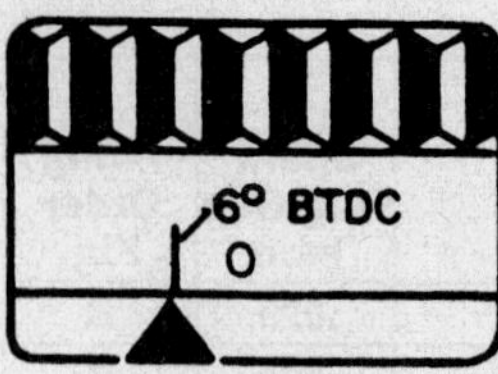

Fig. E

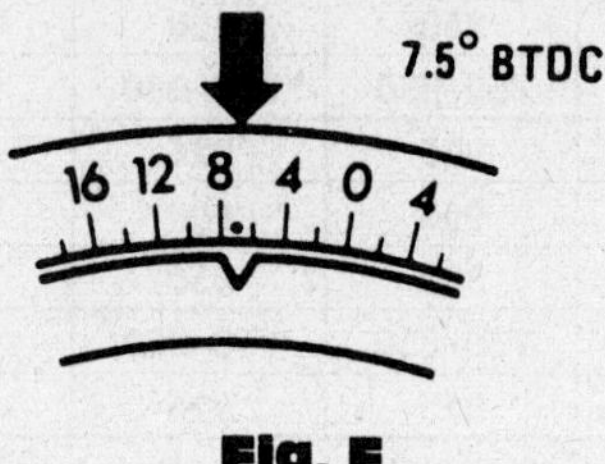

Fig. F

5°

AFTER

Fig. G

VOLVO

Year	Engine	Spark Plug Gap Inch	Ignition Timing			Curb Idle Speed②		Fuel Pump Pressure psi
			Firing Order Fig.	Timing BTDC ①	Mark Fig.	Std. Trans.	Auto. Trans.	
1983–84	B21F Turbo	.030	A	12°	C	900③	900③	—
	B23F	.030	A	12°	C	750/900③	750/900③	—
	B28F	.026	B	10°	D	750/900③	750/900③	—
1985	B21F Turbo	.030	A	12°	C	900③	900③	—
	B230F	.030	—	12°	—	750③	750③	36
	B28F	.026	B	—	D	—	—	—
1986	B230F	.030	—	12°	E	750③	750③	36
	B230F Turbo	.030	—	12°	E	—	—	—
	B28F	.026	B	—	D	—	—	—
1987	B230F	.030	—	12°	—	750③	750③	36
	B230FT	—	—	—	—	750/900③	750/900③	42
	B280F	.026	—	12.5°	F	③④	③④	35.5

—Not available.
①—BTDC: Before top dead center.
②—Where 2 speeds are listed, second speed is with A/C on.
③—Controlled by Constant Idle Speed (CIS) system.
④—750 RPM w/CIS system active; adjust to 700 RPM w/CIS system disconnected.

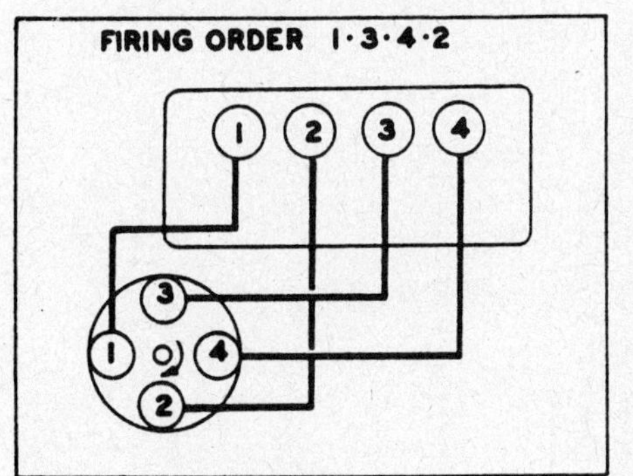

Fig. A

Fig. B

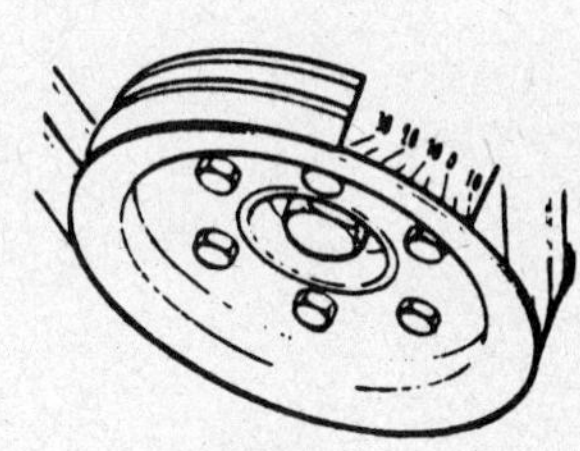
Fig. C

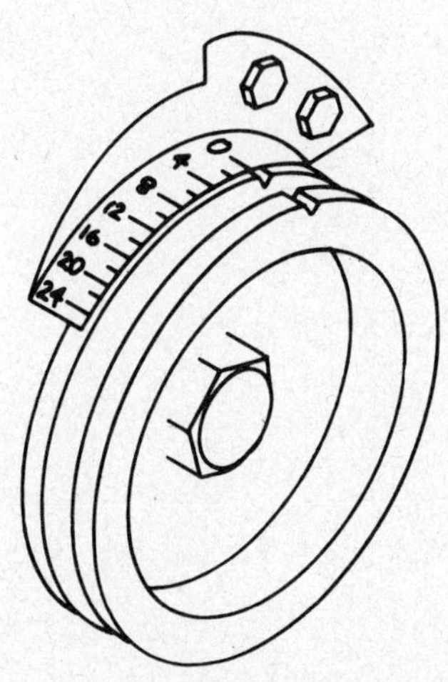
Fig. D

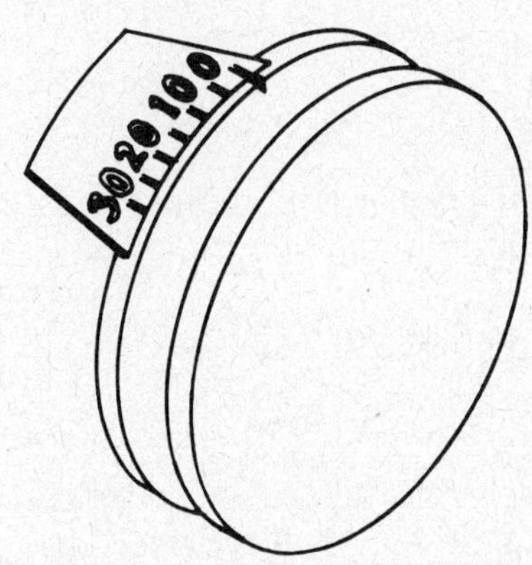
Fig. E

Fig. F

YUGO

Year	Engine	Spark Plug Gap Inches	Ignition Timing			Curb Idle Speed		Fast Idle Speed		Fuel Pump Pressure Lbs.
			Firing Order	Timing BTDC	Mark Fig.	Man. Trans.	Auto. Trans.	Man. Trans.	Auto. Trans.	
1986–87	4-68/1116cc	.030	1-3-4-2	10°	—	800	—	—	—	2.5

DIESEL ENGINE PERFORMANCE SPECIFICATIONS

The following specifications are published from the latest information available. This data should be used only in the absence of a decal affixed in the engine compartment.

When checking timing, it may be necessary to perform certain steps. Refer to vehicle emission control label for specific instructions.

Table of Contents

AUDI

Year	Model	Firing Order	Compression Pressure		Injection Timing BTDC ①	Injector Opening Test Pressure Psi.	Injector Leak Test Pressure Psi.	Idle RPM	Max. No Load RPM
			Normal Pressure Psi.	Max. Variation Between Cylinders Psi.					
1983	4000	1-3-4-2	406–493	72	②	1740–1885	1595	900–1000	5300–5400
	5000 Turbo	1-2-4-5-3	398–483	72	④	2030–2248	1595③	720–780	5050–5150

①—B.T.D.C.-Before top dead center.
②—Injection timing .036 inch (.905 mm) plunger stroke at TDC. With cold start knob pushed in, turn pump body to adjust.
③—Must hold pressure for 10 seconds.
④—Injection timing, .037 inch (.93 mm) plunger stroke at TDC. With cold start knob pushed in, turn pump body to adjust.

DODGE/PLYMOUTH

Year	Model	Firing Order	Injection Timing ATDC ①	Compression Pressure (psi)	Curb Idle Speed RPM	Injection Nozzle Pressure (psi)	
						New	Used
1983	2300	1-3-4-2	2°②	384③	750	1707–1849	1565
1984–85	2300	1-3-4-2	5°②	384③	750	1707–1849	1565

①—After top dead center.
②—At .039 inch plunger stroke.
③—At 250 RPM.

ISUZU

Year	Model	Firing Order	Injection Timing BTDC①	Cranking Compression Pressure (psi)	Injector Nozzle Pressure (psi)	Fuel Pump Delivery Pressure (psi)	Curb Idle Speed		Fast idle Speed	
							Man. Trans.	Auto. Tans.	Man. Trans.	Auto. Trans.
1983	4FB1②⑤	1-3-4-2	12°°	441	1706–1848	—	575–675	675–775	900–950	900–950
	C223③⑥	1-3-4-2	15°	441	1493–1636	—	700–800	—	900–950	—
1984–85	4FB1②⑤	1-3-4-2	12°	441	1706–1848	—	575–675	675–775	900–950	900–950
	C223③⑥	1-3-4-2	⑦	441	1493–1636	—	700–800	800–900	900–950	900–950
1986–87	C223③⑥	1-3-4-2	⑦	441	1493	—	750	850	—	—
	C223T⑧④	1-3-4-2	10°	441	1920	—	750	850	—	—

①—BTDC: Before top dead center.
②—I-Mark only.
③—Pickup only.
④—Pickup and Trooper II.
⑤—1817cc.
⑥—2238cc.
⑦—Exc Calif., 15°; Calif., 13°.
⑧—Turbocharged.

MAZDA

Year	Model	Firing Order	Injection Timing ATDC①	Cranking Compression Pressure (psi)	Injector Nozzle Pressure (psi)	Idle Speed
1983–84	B2200	1-3-4-2	2°	384–427	1958–2030	700
1985	626	1-3-4-2	TDC	384–427	1920	825

①—ATDC: After top dead center.

MERCEDES-BENZ

Year	Model	Firing Order	Injection Timing BTDC ①	Cranking Compression Pressure (psi)	Injector Nozzle Pressure (psi)		Fuel Pump Delivery Pressure② (psi)		Idle Speed	Max. Speed @ Zero Load or End of Control (RPM)
					New	Used	@ idle	@ 3000 (RPM)		
1983	240D	1-3-4-2	24°	319–348	1668–1784	1450③	8.7–11.6	11.6	700–800	4700–5200
	300CD, D, SD, TD Turbo	1-2-4-5-3	24°	348–435	1958–2074	1740③	8.7–11.6	11.6	650–850	4900–5200
1984–86	190D 2.2	1-3-4-2	24°	348–435	1668–1813	1450③	—	—	700–800	4900–5100
	300CD, D, SD, TD Turbo	1-2-4-5-3	24°	348–435	1958–2074	1740③	8.7–11.6	11.6	650–850	4900–5200
1987	300D, TD Turbo	1-5-3-6-2-4	④	—	1957–2102	1957③	—	—	610–650	5000–5300

①—BTDC: Before top dead center.
②—Measured between injection pump and main fuel filter.
③—Minimum.
④—Reference pulse nominal value, −15° ±1° ATDC.

MITSUBISHI

Year	Engine	Firing Order	Injection Timing ATDC ①	Cranking Compression Pressure (psi)	Injector Nozzle Pressure (psi)		Fuel Pump Delivery Pressure (psi)		Curb Idle Speed
					New	Used	@ Idle	@ 3000 (RPM)	
1983–84	2300	1-3-4-2	②	384	1707–1849	1565③	—	—	750
1985	2300	1-3-4-2	5°②	384	1707–1849	1565③	—	—	750

①—ATDC: After top dead center.
②—2° ATDC at .039 inch plunger stroke.
③—Minimum.

NISSAN/DATSUN

Year	Engine	Firing Order	Injection Timing B.T.D.C.①	Cylinder Compression Pressure @ 200 RPM	Injection Nozzle Opening Pressure Psi	Curb Idle Speed
1983	LD28	1-5-3-6-2-4	—	455	1778–1920	650
	SD22	1-3-4-2	20°	427	1422–1493	700
1983–86	CD17	1-3-4-2	—	455	1778–1920	750
1984–86	SD25	1-3-4-2	②	427	1422–1493	700

①—B.T.D.C.-Before top dead center.
②—1984, 18°; 1985–86, exc. Calif. 16°; Calif., 15°.

PEUGEOT

Model	Engine CID①/cc	Injection Order	Injection Timing	Fuel Injection Starting Pressure Psi	Curb Idle Speed	Fast Idle Speed
504	4-140/2304	1-3-4-2	②	1668	③	②
505	4-140/2304	1-3-4-2	②	1740	④	②
604	4-140/2304	1-3-4-2	②	—	830	—
505	4-152/2500	—	—	—	—	—

—Not Available.
①—Cubic inch displacement.
②—Refer to text.
③—Models with manual trans. less A/C, 750 RPM; models with manual trans. with A/C and models with auto. trans. less A/C 800 RPM; models with auto. trans. and A/C, 850 RPM.
④—Less A/C, 800 RPM; with A/C, 850 RPM.

TOYOTA

Year	Engine	Firing Order	Injection Timing	Cylinder Compression Pressure psi @ RPM	Injection Nozzle Opening Pressure		Curb Idle Speed	Maximum Speed
					New	Used		
1983	4-2188cc	1-3-4-2	TDC②	427 @ 250	1636–1778	1493–1778	700	4900
1984	4-1839cc	1-3-4-2	TDC①	427 @ 250	2062–2205	1920–2205	700	5100
	4-2446cc	1-3-4-2	TDC③	455 @ 250	2276–2389	1707–2389	700	5100
1985	4-1839cc	1-3-4-2	TDC①	427 @ 250	2062–2205	1920–2205	750	5100
	4-2446cc④	1-3-4-2	TDC①	427 @ 250	2062–2205	1920–2205	⑥	5100
	4-2446cc⑤	1-3-4-2	TDC⑦	455 @ 250	2276–2389	2062–2389	700	4900
1986	4-1974	1-3-4-2	TDC⑧	427 @ 250	2062–2205	1920–2205	750	5200

①—At .031 inch, (.80 mm) plunger lift.
②—At .039 inch, (1 mm) plunger lift.
③—Exc. Calif. models, at .0433–.0465 inch, (1.10–1.18 mm) plunger lift; California models, at .0382–.0406 inch, (.97–1.03 mm) plunger lift.
④—Corolla models.
⑤—Pickup models.
⑥—Auto. trans., 750 RPM; man. trans., 700 RPM.
⑦—2L-T engine, .039 inch (1 mm) plunger lift. 2L engine: exc. Calif., .045 inch (1.14 mm) plunger lift; Calif., .035 (.89 mm) plunger lift.
⑧—At .028 inch (.70 mm) plunger lift.

VOLKSWAGEN

Year	Model	Firing Order	Injection Pump Timing Plunger Lift (In.) At TDC	Compression Pressure		Injector Nozzles		Idle Speed	Max. Speed @ Zero Load RPM
				Cranking Pressure Psi	Maximum Variation Psi	Spray Test Psi①	Leak Test Psi		
1983–84	Rabbit, Jetta③	—	②	406–493	73	1740–1885	1595	800–950	5300--5400
1983–85	Vanagon	—	.0331–.0346	406–493	73	1740–1885	1595	800–850	4750–4850
1983–86	Quantum③	—	.0392–.0408	406–493	73	2248–2364	1505	900–1000	5050–5150
1985–86	Golf, Jetta④	—	.0372–.0388	493	72.5	1885–2001	1595	920–980	5300–5400
	Jetta③	—	.0372–.0388	493	72.5	2247–2363	1595	920–980	5050–5150

①—Used injectors.
②—Pump less paint dot, .0332–.0372 inch; pump with paint dot, .0440–.0480 inch.
③—Turbo diesel.
④—Exc. turbo.

VOLVO

Year	Engine	Injection Timing①	Fuel Injection Starting Pressure	Curb Idle Speed	Idle No Load RPM
1983–85	D24	.0323–.0354	1700–1845	750	5200
1983–86	D24T②	.0307–.0335③	2062–2318	750	5400

①—Pump plunger stroke, in inches, at Top Dead Center (TDC).
②—Turbodiesel.
③—For high altitude use, increase plunger stroke .0028 inch over standard setting for each 3300 ft. increase in altitude.

TROUBLESHOOTING

TABLE OF CONTENTS

Introduction

STARTING A STALLED ENGINE

When an engine fails to start the chances are that 90 per cent of the cases will involve the ignition system and seldom the fuel system or other miscellaneous reasons. If a systematic procedure is followed the trouble can almost always be found without the use of special equipment.

To begin with, turn on the ignition switch and if the ammeter shows a slight discharge (or if the telltale lamp lights) it indicates that current is flowing. A glance at the gas gauge will indicate whether or not there is fuel in the tank.

Operate the starter and if the engine turns over freely, both the battery and starter are functioning properly. On the other hand, if the starter action is sluggish it may be due to a discharged or defective battery, loose, corroded or dirty battery terminals, mechanical failure in the starter, starter switch or starter drive. If the starter circuit is okay, skip this phase of the discussion and proceed to ignition.

Starter Circuit Checkout

To determine which part of the starter circuit is at fault, turn on the light switch and again operate the starter. Should the lights go out or become dim, the trouble is either in the battery, its connections or cables. A hydrometer test of the battery should indicate better than 1.250 specific gravity, while a voltmeter, placed across the positive and negative posts, should indicate about 12 volts. If either of these tests prove okay, clean and tighten the battery connections and cable terminals or replace any cable which seems doubtful.

If the lights remain bright when the starter is operated, the trouble is between the battery and the starter, or the starter switch is at fault, since it is evident that there is no electrical connection between these points. If these connections are clean and tight, it is safe to assume that the starter or starter switch is defective.

Neutral Safety Switch

If the ammeter shows a slight discharge (or if the telltale lamp lights) when the ignition is turned on, but the system goes dead when the starting circuit is closed, the neutral safety switch may be at fault. To check, bypass the switch with a suitable jumper. If the engine now starts, adjust or replace the switch.

CAUTION: With the safety switch bypassed, the vehicle can be started in any gear. Be sure the transmission is in neutral or park and the parking brake is applied.

Secondary Ignition Checkout

First of all, remove the wire from one of the spark plugs, turn on the ignition and operate the starter. While the engine is cranking, hold the terminal of the spark plug wire about 1/4" away from the engine or spark plug base. If the spark is strong and jumps the gap, the trouble is confined to either the spark plugs or lack of fuel. Before going any further, wipe the outside of the plugs to remove any dirt or dampness which would create an easy path for the current to flow, then try to start the engine again. If it still fails to start, remove one of the spark plugs and if it is wet around the base, it indicates that the fuel system is okay, so it naturally follows that the spark plugs are at fault. Remove all the plugs, clean them and set the gaps. An emergency adjustment of spark plug gaps can be made by folding a piece of newspaper into 6 or 7 layers. When changing the gap, always bend the side (ground) electrode and never the center one as there is danger of breaking the insulation.

Fuel System Checkout

If the spark plug that was removed showed no indication of dampness on its base, check the fuel system. A quick check can be made by simply removing the carburetor air cleaner and looking down into the carburetor. Open and close the throttle manually and if fuel is present in the carburetor, the throttle will operate the accelerating pump, causing it to push gasoline through the pump jet. If it does, check the choke valve. If the engine is cold, the choke valve should be closed. If the choke won't close, the engine can be started by covering the carburetor throat while the engine is cranking, provided, of course, that fuel is reaching the carburetor.

Check the operation of the fuel pump by disconnecting the fuel lines from the pump to the carburetor. Crank the engine and if the pump is working, fuel will pulsate out of the line. If not, either the pump isn't working or the line from the tank to the pump is clogged. Before blaming the pump, however, disconnect the line at the inlet side of the pump which leads to the tank and, while a companion listens at the tank blow through the line. If a gurgling sound is heard back in the tank, the line is open and the trouble is in the pump. Remove the sediment bowl, if so equipped and clean the screen, then replace the bowl and screen, being sure that you have an airtight fit. If the pump still refuses to function, it should be removed and repaired.

The foregoing discussion will, in most cases, uncover the cause of why an engine won't start. However, if further diagnosis is necessary, the following list will undoubtedly provide the answer.

ENGINE NOISE TESTS

Loose Main Bearing

A loose main bearing is indicated by a powerful but dull thud or knock when the engine is pulling. If all main bearings are loose a noticeable clatter will be audible.

The thud occurs regularly every other revolution. The knock can be confirmed by shorting spark plugs on cylinders adjacent to the bearing. Knock will disappear or be less when plugs are shorted. This test should be made at a fast idle equivalent to 15 mph in high gear. If bearing is not quite loose enough to produce a knock by itself, the bearing may knock if oil is too thin or if there is no oil at the bearing.

Loose Flywheel

A loose flywheel is indicated by a thud or click which is usually irregular. To test, idle the engine at about 20 mph and shut off the ignition. If thud is heard, the flywheel may be loose.

Loose Rod Bearing

A loose rod bearing is indicated by a metallic knock which is usually loudest at about 30 mph with throttle closed. Knock can be reduced or even eliminated by shorting spark plug. If bearing is not loose enough to produce a knock by itself, the bearing may knock if oil is too thin or if there is no oil at the bearing.

Piston Pin

Piston pin, piston and connecting rod noises are difficult to tell apart.

A loose piston pin causes a sharp double knock which is usually heard when engine is idling. Severity of knock should increase when spark plug to this cylinder is short-circuited. However, on some engines the knock becomes more noticeable at 25 to 35 mph on the road.

Piston pin rubs against cylinder wall, caused by broken snap ring.

Hydraulic Lifters

The malfunctioning of a hydraulic valve lifter is almost always accompanied by a clicking or tapping noise. More or less hydraulic lifter noise may be expected when the engine is cold but if lifters are functioning properly the noise should disappear when the engine warms up.

If all or nearly all lifters are noisy, they may be stuck because of dirty or gummy oil.

If all lifters are noisy, oil pressure to them may be inadequate. Foaming oil may also cause this trouble. If oil foams there will be bubbles on the oil level dipstick. Foaming may be caused by water in the oil or by too high an oil level or by a very low oil level.

If the hydraulic plungers require an initial adjustment, they will be noisy if this adjustment is incorrect.

If one lifter is noisy the cause may be:

1. Plunger too tight in lifter body.
2. Weak or broken plunger spring.
3. Ball valve leaks.
4. Plunger worn.
5. Lock ring (if any) improperly installed or missing.
6. Lack of oil pressure to this plunger.

If ball valve leaks, clean plunger in special solvent such as acetone and reinstall. Too often, plungers are condemned as faulty when all they need is a thorough cleaning.

Gum and dirty oil are the most common causes of hydraulic valve lifter trouble. Engine oil must be free of dirt. Select a standard brand of engine oil and use no other. Mixing up one standard brand with another may cause gummy oil and sticking plungers. Do not use any special oils unless recommended by the truck manufacturer and change oil filter or element at recommended intervals.

Loose Engine Mountings

Occasional thud with vehicle in operation. Most likely to be noticed at the moment the throttle is opened or closed.

Excessive Crankshaft End Play

A rather sharp rap which occurs at idling speed but may be heard at higher speeds also. The noise should disappear when clutch is disengaged.

Fuel Pump Noise

Diagnosis of fuel pumps suspected as noisy requires that some form of sounding device be used. Judgment by ear alone is not sufficient, otherwise a fuel pump may be needlessly replaced in attempting to correct noise contributed by some other component. Use of a stethoscope, a long screwdriver, or a sounding rod is recommended to locate the area or component causing the noise. The sounding rod can easily be made from a length of copper tubing ¼ to ⅜ inch in diameter.

If the noise has been isolated to the fuel pump, remove the pump and run the engine with the fuel remaining in the carburetor bowl. If the noise level does not change, the source of the noise is elsewhere and the original fuel pump should be reinstalled. On models using a fuel pump push rod, check for excessive wear and/or galling of the push rod.

VAPOR LOCK

The term vapor lock means the flow of fuel to the mixing chamber in the carburetor has been stopped (locked) by the formation of vaporized fuel pockets or bubbles caused by overheating the fuel by a hot fuel pump, hot fuel lines or hot carburetor.

The more volatile the fuel the greater the tendency for it to vapor lock. Vapor lock is encouraged by high atmospheric temperature, hard driving, defective engine cooling and high altitude.

A mild case of vapor lock will cause missing and hard starting when engine is warm. Somewhat more severe vapor lock will stop the engine which cannot be started again until it has cooled off enough so that any vaporized fuel has condensed to a liquid.

PERCOLATION

Percolation means simply that gasoline in the carburetor bowl is boiling over into the intake manifold. This condition is most apt to occur immediately after a hot engine is shut off. Most carburetors have a provision for relieving the vapor pressure of overheated fuel in the carburetor bowl by means of ports. If, however, percolation should take place, the engine may be started by allowing it to cool slightly and then holding the throttle wide open while cranking to clear the intake manifold of excess fuel.

SPARK KNOCK, PING, DETONATION

All three expressions mean the same thing. It is a sharp metallic knock caused by vibration of the cylinder head and block. The vibration is due to split-second high-pressure waves resulting from almost instantaneous abnormal combustion instead of the slower normal combustion.

The ping may be mild or loud. A mild ping does no harm but a severe ping will reduce power. A very severe ping may shatter spark plugs, break valves or crack pistons.

Pinging is most likely to occur on open throttle at low or moderate engine speed. Pinging is encouraged by:

1. Overheated engine.
2. Low octane fuel.
3. Too high compression.
4. Spark advanced too far.
5. Hot mixture due to hot engine or hot weather.
6. Heavy carbon deposit which increases the compression pressure.
7. Clogged or restricted EGR passages.

Tendency to ping increases with mixture temperature including high atmospheric temperature; intake manifold heater valve "on" when engine is warm; hot cooling water; hot interior engine surfaces due to sluggish water circulation or water jackets clogged with rust or dirt especially around exhaust valves. Some of these troubles may be confined to one or two cylinders.

If an engine pings objectionably even when using the highest octane fuel available, retard the spark setting, but first be sure the EGR system is functioning, the cooling system is in good condition, the mixture is not too lean, and the combustion chambers are free of carbon deposits.

PRE-IGNITION

Pre-ignition means that the mixture is ignited before the spark occurs, being ignited by a red hot spot in the combustion chamber such as an incandescent particle of carbon; a thin piece of protruding metal; an overheated spark plug, or a bright red hot exhaust valve. The result is reduction of power and overheating accompanied by pinging. The bright red hot exhaust valve may be due to a leak, to lack of tappet clearance, to valve sticking, or to a weak or broken spring.

Pre-ignition may not be noticed if not severe. Severe pre-ignition results in severe pinging. The most common cause of pre-ignition is a badly overheated engine.

When the engine won't stop when the ignition is shut off, the cause is often due to red hot carbon particles resting on heavy carbon deposit in a very hot engine.

AFTER-BURNING

A subdued put-putting at the exhaust tail pipe may be due to leaky exhaust valves which permit the mixture to finish combustion in the muffler. If exhaust pipe or muffler is red hot, better let it cool, as there is some danger of setting the car on fire. Most likely to occur when mixture is lean.

ENGINE CONTINUES TO RUN AFTER IGNITION IS TURNED OFF

This condition, known as "dieseling," "run on," or "after running," is caused by improper idle speed and/or high temperature. Idle speed and engine temperature are affected by:

Carburetor Adjustment: High idle speed will increase the tendency to diesel because of the inertia of the engine crankshaft and flywheel. Too low an idle speed, particularly with a lean mixture, will result in an increase in engine temperature, especially if the engine is allowed to idle for long periods of time.

Ignition Timing: Because advanced ignition timing causes a corresponding increase in idle speed and retarded timing reduces idle speed, ignition timing influences the tendency to diesel in the same manner as Carburetor Adjustment.

Fuel Mixture: Enriching the idle fuel mixture decreases the tendency to diesel by causing the engine to run cooler.

Fuel Content: High octane fuels tend to reduce dieseling. Increased fuel content of lead alkyl increases the tendency to diesel. Phosphates and nickel fuel additives help prevent dieseling.

Spark Plugs: Plugs of too high a heat range for the engine in question can cause dieseling.

Throttle Plates: If the throttle plates are not properly aligned in the carburetor bore, a resulting leanness in fuel mixture occurs, contributing to dieseling.

Electrical System: Normally, during dieseling, ignition is self-supplied by a "hot spot," self-igniting fuel, etc. However, there is a possibility of the vehicle's electrical system supplying the necessary ignition. When the ignition switch is turned off, a small amount of current can flow from the alternator into the primary of the ignition coil through the alternator tell-tale light. This is particularly true when the warning light bulb has been changed for one of increased wattage.

NOTE: "Run on" is more prevalent in an engine when the ignition is turned off before the engine is allowed to return to idle. Therefore, it can be reduced by letting the engine return to idle before shutting off the ignition. "Run on" incidence can be reduced on automatic transmission units by turning off the engine when in gear.

A certain amount of "run on" can be expected from any gasoline engine regardless of make, size or configuration. (Diesel engines operate on this principle.) However, if the above suggestions are correctly employed, "Run on" will be reduced to an unnoticeable level.

GASOLINE ENGINE

Condition	Possible Cause	Correction
ENGINE WILL NOT START	1. Weak battery.	1. Test battery specific gravity. Recharge or replace as necessary.
	2. Corroded or loose battery connections.	2. Clean and tighten battery connections. Apply a coat of petroleum to terminals.
	3. Faulty starter.	3. Repair starter motor.
	4. Moisture on ignition wires and distributor cap.	4. Wipe wires and cap clean and dry.
	5. Faulty ignition cables.	5. Replace any cracked or shorted cables.
	6. Open or shorted primary ignition circuit.	6. Trace primary ignition circuit and repair as necessary.
	7. Malfunctioning ignition points or condensor (if equipped).	7. Replace ignition points & condensor as necessary (if equipped).
	8. Faulty coil.	8. Test and replace if necessary.
	9. Incorrect spark plug gap.	9. Set gap correctly.
	10. Incorrect ignition timing.	10. Reset timing.
	11. Dirt or water in fuel line or carburetor.	11. Clean lines and carburetor. Replace filter.
	12. Carburetor flooded.	12. Adjust float level—check seats.
	13. Incorrect carburetor float setting.	13. Adjust float level—check seats.
	14. Faulty fuel pump.	14. Install new fuel pump.
	15. Carburetor percolating. No fuel in the carburetor.	15. Measure float level. Adjust bowl vent. Inspect operation of manifold heat control valve.
ENGINE STALLS	1. Idle speed set too low.	1. Adjust carburetor.
	2. Incorrect choke adjustment.	2. Adjust choke.
	3. Idle mixture too lean or too rich.	3. Adjust carburetor.
	4. Incorrect carburetor float setting.	4. Adjust float setting.
	5. Leak in intake manifold.	5. Inspect intake manifold gasket and replace if necessary.
	6. Worn or burned distributor rotor.	6. Install new rotor.
	7. Incorrect ignition wiring.	7. Install correct wiring.
	8. Faulty coil.	8. Test and replace if necessary.
	9. Incorrect tappet lash.	9. Adjust to specifications.
ENGINE LOSS OF POWER	1. Incorrect ignition timing.	1. Reset timing.
	2. Worn or burned distributor rotor.	2. Install new rotor.
	3. Worn distributor shaft.	3. Remove and repair distributor.
	4. Dirty or incorrectly gapped spark plugs.	4. Clean plugs and set gap.
	5. Dirt or water in fuel line, carburetor or filter.	5. Clean lines, carburetor and replace filter.
	6. Incorrect carburetor float setting.	6. Adjust float level.
	7. Faulty fuel pump.	7. Install new pump.

GASOLINE ENGINE—Continued

Condition	Possible Cause	Correction
ENGINE LOSS OF POWER, Continued	8. Incorrect valve timing.	8. Check and correct valve timing.
	9. Blown cylinder head gasket.	9. Install new head gasket.
	10. Low compression.	10. Test compression of each cylinder.
	11. Burned, warped or pitted valves.	11. Install new valves.
	12. Plugged or restricted exhaust system.	12. Install new parts as necessary.
	13. Faulty ignition cables.	13. Replace any cracked or shorted cables.
	14. Faulty coil.	14. Test and replace as necessary.
ENGINE MISSES ON ACCELERATION	1. Dirty, or gap too wide in spark plugs.	1. Clean spark plugs and set gap.
	2. Incorrect ignition timing.	2. Reset timing.
	3. Dirt in carburetor.	3. Clean carburetor and replace filter.
	4. Acceleration pump in carburetor.	4. Install new pump.
	5. Burned, warped or pitted valves.	5. Install new valves.
	6. Faulty coil.	6. Test and replace if necessary.
ENGINE MISSES AT HIGH SPEED	1. Dirty or gap set too wide in spark plug.	1. Clean spark plugs and set gap.
	2. Worn distributor shaft.	2. Remove and repair distributor.
	3. Worn or burned distributor rotor.	3. Install new rotor.
	4. Faulty coil.	4. Test and replace if necessary.
	5. Incorrect ignition timing.	5. Reset timing.
	6. Dirty jets in carburetor.	6. Clean carburetor, replace filter.
	7. Dirt or water in fuel line, carburetor or filter.	7. Clean lines, carburetor and replace filter.
NOISY VALVES	1. High or low oil level in crankcase.	1. Check for correct oil level.
	2. Thin or diluted oil.	2. Change oil.
	3. Low oil pressure.	3. Check engine oil level.
	4. Dirt in valve lifters.	4. Clean lifters.
	5. Bent push rod.	5. Install new push rods.
	6. Worn rocker arms.	6. Inspect oil supply to rockers.
	7. Worn tappets.	7. Install new tappets.
	8. Worn valve guides.	8. Ream and install new valves with O/S stems.
	9. Excessive run-out of valve seats or valve faces.	9. Grind valve seats and valves.
	10. Incorrect tappet lash.	10. Adjust to specifications.
CONNECTING ROD NOISE	1. Insufficient oil supply.	1. Check engine oil level.
	2. Low oil pressure.	2. Check engine oil level. Inspect oil pump relief valve and spring.
	3. Thin or diluted oil.	3. Change oil to correct viscosity.
	4. Excessive bearing clearance.	4. Measure bearings for correct clearance.
	5. Connecting rod journals out-of-round.	5. Replace crankshaft or regrind journals.
	6. Misaligned (bent) connecting rods.	6. Replace bent connecting rods.
MAIN BEARING NOISE	1. Insufficient oil supply.	1. Check engine oil level.
	2. Low oil pressure.	2. Check engine oil level. Inspect oil pump relief valve and spring.
	3. Thin or diluted oil.	3. Change oil to correct viscosity.
	4. Excessive bearing clearance.	4. Measure bearings for correct clearances.
	5. Excessive end play.	5. Check thrust bearing for wear on flanges.
	6. Crankshaft journal worn out-of-round.	6. Replace crankshaft or regrind journals.
	7. Loose flywheel or torque converter.	7. Tighten to correct torque.
OIL PUMPING AT RINGS	1. Worn, scuffed, or broken rings.	1. Hone cylinder bores and install new rings.
	2. Carbon in oil ring slot.	2. Install new rings.
	3. Rings fitted too tight in grooves.	3. Remove the rings. Check grooves. If groove is not proper width, replace piston.

GASOLINE ENGINE—Continued

Condition	Possible Cause	Correction
OIL PRESSURE DROP	1. Low oil level.	1. Check engine oil level.
	2. Faulty oil pressure sending unit.	2. Install new sending unit.
	3. Clogged oil filter.	3. Install new oil filter.
	4. Worn parts in oil pump.	4. Replace worn parts or pump.
	5. Thin or diluted oil.	5. Change oil to correct viscosity.
	6. Excessive bearing clearance.	6. Measure bearings for correct clearance.
	7. Oil pump relief valve stuck.	7. Remove valve and inspect, clean, and reinstall.
	8. Oil pump suction tube loose, bent or cracked.	8. Remove oil pan and install new tube if necessary.
NO OIL PRESSURE	1. Low oil level.	1. Add oil to correct level.
	2. Oil pressure gauge or sending unit inaccurate.	2. Replace defective unit.
	3. Oil pump malfunction.	3. Repair oil pump.
	4. Oil pressure relief valve sticking.	4. Remove and inspect oil pressure relief valve assembly.
	5. Oil passages on pressure side of pump obstructed.	5. Inspect oil passages for obstructions.
	6. Oil pickup screen or tube obstructed.	6. Inspect oil pickup for obstructions.
LOW OIL PRESSURE	1. Low oil level.	1. Add oil to correct level.
	2. Oil excessively thin due to dilution, poor quality, or improper grade.	2. Drain and refill crankcase with recommended oil.
	3. Oil pressure relief spring weak or sticking.	3. Remove and inspect oil pressure relief valve assembly.
	4. Oil pickup tube and screen assembly has restriction or air leak.	4. Remove and inspect oil inlet tube and screen assembly. (Fill pickup with lacquer thinner to find leaks.)
	5. Excessive oil pump clearance.	5. Check clearances.
	6. Excessive main, rod, or camshaft bearing clearance.	6. Measure bearing clearances, repair as necessary.
HIGH OIL PRESSURE	1. Improper grade oil.	1. Drain and refill crankcase with correct grade oil.
	2. Oil pressure gauge or sending unit inaccurate.	2. Replace defective unit.
	3. Oil pressure relief valve sticking closed.	3. Remove and inspect oil pressure relief valve assembly.
EXTERNAL OIL LEAK	1. Fuel pump gasket broken or improperly seated.	1. Replace gasket.
	2. Cylinder head cover gasket broken or improperly seated.	2. Replace gasket; check cylinder head cover gasket flange and cylinder head gasket surface for distortion.
	3. Oil filter gasket broken or improperly seated.	3. Replace oil filter.
	4. Oil pan side gasket broken or improperly seated.	4. Replace gasket; check oil pan gasket flange for distortion.
	5. Oil pan front oil seal broken or improperly seated.	5. Replace seal; check timing chain cover and oil pan seal flange for distortion.
	6. Oil pan rear oil seal broken or improperly seated.	6. Replace seal; check oil pan rear oil seal flange; check rear main bearing cap for cracks, plugged oil return channels, or distortion in seal groove.
	7. Timing chain cover oil seal broken or improperly seated.	7. Replace seal.
	8. Oil pan drain plug loose or has stripped threads.	8. Repair as necessary and tighten.
	9. Rear oil gallery plug loose.	9. Use appropriate sealant on gallery plug and tighten.
	10. Rear camshaft plug loose or improperly seated.	10. Seat camshaft plug or replace and seal, as necessary.

GASOLINE ENGINE—Continued

Condition	Possible Cause	Correction
EXCESSIVE OIL CONSUMPTION	1. Oil level too high.	1. Lower oil level to specifications.
	2. Oil too thin.	2. Replace with specified oil.
	3. Valve stem oil seals are damaged, missing, or incorrect type.	3. Replace valve stem oil seals.
	4. Valve stems or valve guides worn.	4. Check stem-to-guide clearance and repair as necessary.
	5. Piston rings broken, missing.	5. Replace missing or broken rings.
	6. Piston rings incorrect size.	6. Check ring gap, repair as necessary.
	7. Piston rings sticking or excessively loose in grooves.	7. Check ring side clearance, repair as necessary.
	8. Compression rings installed upside down.	8. Repair as necessary.
	9. Cylinder walls worn, scored, or glazed.	9. Repair as necessary.
	10. Piston ring gaps not properly staggered.	10. Repair as necessary.
	11. Excessive main or connecting rod bearing clearance.	11. Check bearing clearance, repair as necessary.

OIL PRESSURE INDICATOR

Condition	Possible Cause	Correction
LIGHT NOT LIT, IGNITION ON AND ENGINE NOT RUNNING.	1. Bulb burned out.	1. Replace bulb.
	2. Open in light circuit.	2. Locate and correct open.
	3. Defective oil pressure switch.	3. Replace oil pressure switch.
LIGHT ON, ENGINE RUNNING ABOVE IDLE SPEED.	1. Grounded wiring between light and switch.	1. Locate and repair ground.
	2. Defective oil pressure switch.	2. Replace oil pressure switch.
	3. Low oil pressure.	3. Locate cause of low oil pressure and correct.

IGNITION, STARTER & FUEL

Condition	Possible Cause	Correction
NOTHING HAPPENS WHEN START ATTEMPT IS MADE	1. Undercharged or defective battery.	1. Check condition of battery and recharge or replace as required.
	2. Loose battery cables.	2. Clean and tighten cable connections.
	3. Burned fusible link in starting circuit.	3. Check for burned fusible link. Correct wiring problem.
	4. Incorrectly positioned or defective neutral start switch.	4. Check neutral start switch adjustment. If O.K., replace switch.
	5. Loose or defective wiring between neutral start switch and ignition switch.	5. Check for loose connections and opens between battery, horn relay, ignition switch, and solenoid "S" terminal. Check battery ground cable. Replace or repair defective item.
	6. Defective starter motor.	6. Repair or replace starter motor.
SOLENOID SWITCH CLICKS BUT STARTER DOES NOT CRANK	1. Undercharged or defective battery.	1. Test battery. Recharge or replace battery.
	2. Loose battery cables.	2. Check and tighten battery connections.
	3. Loose or defective wiring at starter.	3. Tighten connections or repair wiring as required.
	4. Defective solenoid.	4. Replace solenoid.
	5. "Hot stall" condition.	5. Check engine cooling system.
	6. Excessive engine rotational torque caused by mechanical problem within engine.	6. Check engine torque for excessive friction.
	7. Defective starter motor.	7. Repair or replace starter motor.

IGNITION, STARTER & FUEL—Continued

Condition	Possible Cause	Correction
SLOW CRANKING	1. Vehicle is overheating.	1. Check engine cooling system and repair as required.
	2. Undercharged or defective battery.	2. Recharge or replace battery.
	3. Loose or defective wiring between battery and engine block.	3. Repair or replace wiring.
	4. Loose or defective wiring between battery and solenoid "Bat" terminal.	4. Repair or replace wiring.
	5. Defective starter motor.	5. Repair or replace starter.
STARTER SPINS AND/OR MAKES LOUD GRINDING NOISE BUT DOES NOT TURN ENGINE	1. Defective starter motor.	1. Repair or replace starter motor.
	2. Defective ring gear.	2. Replace ring gear.
STARTER KEEPS RUNNING AFTER IGNITION SWITCH IS RELEASED—FROM "START" TO "RUN" POSITION	1. Defective ignition switch.	1. Replace ignition switch.
	2. Defective solenoid.	2. Replace solenoid.
STARTER ENGAGES ("Clunks") BUT ENGINE DOES NOT CRANK	1. Open circuit in solenoid armature or field coils.	1. Repair or replace solenoid or starter motor.
	2. Short or ground in field coil or armature.	2. Repair or replace starter motor.
HARD STARTING (Engine Cranks Normally)	1. Binding linkage, choke valve or choke piston.	1. Repair as necessary.
	2. Restricted choke vacuum and hot air passages.	2. Clean passages.
	3. Improper fuel level.	3. Adjust float level.
	4. Dirty, worn or faulty needle valve and seat.	4. Repair as necessary.
	5. Float sticking.	5. Repair as necessary.
	6. Exhaust manifold heat valve stuck.	6. Repair as necessary.
	7. Faulty fuel pump.	7. Replace fuel pump.
	8. Incorrect choke cover adjustment.	8. Adjust choke cover.
	9. Inadequate unloader adjustment.	9. Adjust unloader.
	10. Faulty ignition coil.	10. Test and replace as necessary.
	11. Improper spark plug gap.	11. Adjust gap.
	12. Incorrect initial timing.	12. Adjust timing.
	13. Incorrect valve timing.	13. Check valve timing; repair as necessary.
ROUGH IDLE OR STALLING	1. Incorrect curb or fast idle speed.	1. Adjust curb or fast idle speed.
	2. Incorrect initial timing.	2. Adjust timing to specifications.
	3. Improper idle mixture adjustment.	3. Adjust idle mixture.
	4. Damaged tip on idle mixture screw(s).	4. Replace mixture screw(s).
	5. Improper fast idle cam adjustment.	5. Adjust fast idle.
	6. Faulty PCV valve air flow.	6. Test PCV valve and replace as necessary.
	7. Exhaust manifold heat valve inoperative.	7. Lubricate or replace heat valve as necessary.
	8. Choke binding.	8. Locate and eliminate binding condition.
	9. Improper choke setting.	9. Adjust choke.
	10. Vacuum leak.	10. Check manifold vacuum and repair as necessary.
	11. Improper fuel level.	11. Adjust fuel level.
	12. Faulty distributor rotor or cap.	12. Replace rotor or cap.
	13. Leaking engine valves.	13. Check cylinder leakdown rate or compression and repair as necessary.
	14. Incorrect ignition wiring.	14. Check wiring and correct as necessary.
	15. Faulty coil.	15. Test coil and replace as necessary.
	16. Clogged air bleed or idle passages.	16. Clean passages.
	17. Restricted air cleaner.	17. Clean or replace air cleaner.
	18. Faulty EGR valve operation.	18. Test EGR system and repair as necessary.

IGNITION, STARTER & FUEL—Continued

Condition	Possible Cause	Correction
FAULTY LOW-SPEED OPERATION	1. Clogged idle transfer slots.	1. Clean transfer slots.
	2. Restricted idle air bleeds and passages.	2. Clean air bleeds and passages.
	3. Restricted air cleaner.	3. Clean or replace air cleaner.
	4. Improper fuel level.	4. Adjust fuel level.
	5. Faulty spark plugs.	5. Clean or replace spark plugs.
	6. Dirty, corroded, or loose secondary circuit connections.	6. Clean or tighten secondary circuit connections.
	7. Faulty ignition cable.	7. Replace ignition cable.
	8. Faulty distributor cap.	8. Replace cap.
FAULTY ACCELERATION	1. Improper pump stroke.	1. Adjust pump stroke.
	2. Incorrect ignition timing.	2. Adjust timing.
	3. Inoperative pump discharge check ball or needle.	3. Clean or replace as necessary.
	4. Worn or damaged pump diaphragm or piston.	4. Replace diaphragm or piston.
	5. Leaking main body cover gasket.	5. Replace gasket.
	6. Engine cold and choke too lean.	6. Adjust choke.
	7. Faulty spark plug(s).	7. Clean or replace spark plug(s).
	8. Leaking engine valves.	8. Check cylinder leakdown rate or compression, repair as necessary.
	9. Faulty coil.	9. Test coil and replace as necessary.
FAULTY HIGH-SPEED OPERATION	1. Incorrect ignition timing.	1. Adjust timing.
	2. Faulty distributor centrifugal advance.	2. Check centrifugal advance and repair as necessary.
	3. Faulty distributor vacuum advance.	3. Check vacuum advance and repair as necessary.
	4. Low fuel pump volume.	4. Replace fuel pump.
	5. Improper spark plug gap.	5. Adjust gap.
	6. Faulty choke operation.	6. Adjust choke.
	7. Partially restricted exhaust manifold, exhaust pipe, muffler, or tailpipe.	7. Eliminate restriction.
	8. Clogged vacuum passages.	8. Clean passages.
	9. Improper size or obstructed main jets.	9. Clean or replace as necessary.
	10. Restricted air cleaner.	10. Clean or replace as necessary.
	11. Faulty distributor rotor or cap.	11. Replace rotor or cap.
	12. Worn distributor shaft.	12. Replace shaft.
	13. Faulty coil.	13. Test coil and replace as necessary.
	14. Leaking engine valve(s).	14. Check cylinder leakdown or compression and repair as necessary.
	15. Faulty valve spring(s).	15. Inspect and test valve spring tension and replace as necessary.
	16. Incorrect valve timing.	16. Check valve timing and repair as necessary.
	17. Intake manifold restricted.	17. Pass chain through passages.
MISFIRE AT ALL SPEEDS	1. Faulty spark plug(s).	1. Clean or replace spark plug(s).
	2. Faulty spark plug cable(s).	2. Replace as necessary.
	3. Faulty distributor cap or rotor.	3. Replace cap or rotor.
	4. Faulty coil.	4. Test coil and replace as necessary.
	5. Primary circuit shorted or open intermittently.	5. Trace primary circuit and repair as necessary.
	6. Leaking engine valve(s).	6. Check cylinder leakdown rate or compression and repair as necessary.
	7. Faulty hydraulic tappet(s).	7. Clean or replace tappet(s).
	8. Faulty valve spring(s).	8. Inspect and test valve spring tension, repair as necessary.
	9. Worn lobes on camshaft.	9. Replace camshaft.
	10. Vacuum leak.	10. Check manifold vacuum and repair as necessary.
	11. Improper carburetor settings.	11. Adjust carburetor.
	12. Fuel pump volume or pressure low.	12. Replace fuel pump.
	13. Blown cylinder head gasket.	13. Replace gasket.
	14. Intake or exhaust manifold passage(s) restricted.	14. Pass chain through passages.

IGNITION, STARTER & FUEL—Continued

Condition	Possible Cause	Correction
POWER NOT UP TO NORMAL	1. Incorrect ignition timing.	1. Adjust timing.
	2. Faulty distributor rotor.	2. Replace rotor.
	3. Worn distributor shaft.	3. Replace shaft.
	4. Incorrect spark plug gap.	4. Adjust gap.
	5. Faulty fuel pump.	5. Replace fuel pump.
	6. Incorrect valve timing.	6. Check valve timing and repair as necessary.
	7. Faulty coil.	7. Test coil and replace as necessary.
	8. Faulty ignition cables.	8. Test cables and replace as necessary.
	9. Leaking engine valves.	9. Check cylinder leakdown rate or compression and repair as necessary.
	10. Blown cylinder head gasket.	10. Replace gasket.
	11. Leaking piston rings.	11. Check compression and repair as necessary.
INTAKE BACKFIRE	1. Improper ignition timing.	1. Adjust timing.
	2. Faulty accelerator pump discharge.	2. Repair as necessary.
	3. Improper choke operation.	3. Repair as necessary.
	4. Lean fuel mixture.	4. Check float level or manifold vacuum for vacuum leak.
EXHAUST BACKFIRE	1. Vacuum leak.	1. Check manifold vacuum and repair as necessary.
	2. Faulty A.I.R. diverter valve (if equipped).	2. Test diverter valve and replace as necessary (if equipped).
	3. Faulty choke operation.	3. Repair as necessary.
	4. Exhaust leak.	4. Locate and eliminate leak.
PING OR SPARK KNOCK	1. Incorrect ignition timing.	1. Adjust timing.
	2. Distributor centrifugal or vacuum advance malfunction.	2. Check advance and repair as necessary.
	3. Excessive combustion chamber deposits.	3. Use combustion chamber cleaner.
	4. Carburetor set too lean.	4. Adjust carburetor.
	5. Vacuum leak.	5. Check manifold vacuum and repair as necessary.
	6. Excessively high compression.	6. Check compression and repair as necessary.
	7. Fuel octane rating excessively low.	7. Try alternate fuel source.
	8. Heat riser stuck in heat on position.	8. Free-up or replace heat riser.
	9. Insufficient EGR flow.	9. Check EGR system operation.
SURGING (Cruising Speeds To Top Speeds)	1. Low fuel level.	1. Adjust fuel level.
	2. Low fuel pump pressure or volume.	2. Replace fuel pump.
	3. Improper PCV valve air flow.	3. Test PCV valve and replace as necessary.
	4. Vacuum leak.	4. Check manifold vacuum and repair as necessary.
	5. Dirt in carburetor.	5. Clean carburetor, replace filter.
	6. Undersize main jets.	6. Replace main jet(s).
	7. Clogged fuel filter screen.	7. Replace fuel filter.
	8. Restricted air cleaner.	8. Clean or replace air cleaner.
	9. Excessive EGR valve flow.	9. Check EGR system operation.

CHARGING SYSTEM

Condition	Possible Cause	Correction
ALTERNATOR FAILS TO CHARGE (No Output or Low Output)	1. Alternator drive belt loose.	1. Adjust drive belt to specifications.
	2. Regulator base improperly grounded.	2. Connect regulator to a good ground.
	3. Worn brushes and/or slip rings.	3. Install new brushes and/or slip rings.
	4. Sticking brushes.	4. Clean slip rings and brush holders. Install new brushes if necessary.
	5. Open field circuit.	5. Test all the field circuit connections, and correct as required.
	6. Open charging circuit.	6. Inspect all connections in charging circuit, and correct as required.

CHARGING SYSTEM—Continued

Condition	Possible Cause	Correction
ALTERNATOR FAILS TO CHARGE (No Output or Low Output), continued	7. Open circuit in stator windings.	7. Remove alternator and disassemble. Test stator windings. Install new stator if necessary.
	8. Open rectifiers.	8. Remove alternator and disassemble. Test the rectifiers. Install new rectifier assemblies if necessary.
LOW, UNSTEADY CHARGING RATE	1. High resistance in body to engine ground lead.	1. Tighten ground lead connections. Install new ground lead if necessary.
	2. Alternator drive belt loose.	2. Adjust alternator drive belt.
	3. High resistance at battery terminals.	3. Clean and tighten battery terminals.
	4. High resistance in charging circuit.	4. Test charging circuit resistance. Correct as required.
	5. Open stator winding.	5. Remove and disassemble alternator. Test stator windings. Install new stator if necessary.
LOW OUTPUT AND A LOW BATTERY	1. High resistance in charging circuit.	1. Test charging circuit resistance and correct as required.
	2. Shorted rectifier. Open rectifier.	2. Perform current output test. Test the rectifiers and install new rectifier heat sink assembly as required. Remove and disassemble the alternator.
	3. Grounded stator windings.	3. Remove and disassemble alternator. Test stator windings. Install new stator if necessary.
	4. Faulty voltage regulator.	4. Test voltage regulator. Replace as necessary.
EXCESSIVE CHARGING RATE TO A FULLY CHARGED BATTERY	1. Faulty ignition switch.	1. Install new ignition switch.
	2. Faulty voltage regulator.	2. Test voltage regulator. Replace as necessary.
NOISY ALTERNATOR	1. Alternator mounting loose.	1. Properly install and tighten alternator mounting.
	2. Worn of frayed drive belt.	2. Install a new drive belt and adjust to specifications.
	3. Worn bearings.	3. Remove and disassemble alternator. Install new bearings as required.
	4. Interference between rotor fan and stator leads.	4. Remove and disassemble alternator. Correct interference as required.
	5. Rotor or rotor fan damaged.	5. Remove and disassemble alternator. Install new rotor.
	6. Open or shorted rectifer.	6. Remove and disassemble alternator. Test rectifers. Install new rectifier heat sink assemble as required.
	7. Open or shorted winding in stator.	7. Remove and disassemble alternator. Test stator windings. Install new stator if necessary.
EXCESSIVE AMMETER FLUCTUATION	1. High resistance in the alternator and voltage regulator circuit.	1. Clean and tighten all connections as necessary.

CHARGING SYSTEM INDICATOR

Condition	Possible Cause	Correction
LIGHT ON, IGNITION OFF	1. Shorted positive diode.	1. Locate and replace shorted diode.
LIGHT NOT ON, IGNITION ON AND ENGINE NOT RUNNING	1. Bulb burned out.	1. Replace bulb.
	2. Open in light circuit.	2. Locate and correct open.
	3. Open in field.	3. Replace rotor.
LIGHT ON, ENGINE RUNNING ABOVE IDLE SPEED	1. No generator output.	1. Check and correct cause of no output.
	2. Shorted negative diode.	2. Locate and replace shorted diode.
	3. Loose or broken alternator belt.	3. Tighten or replace and tighten alternator belt.

COOLING SYSTEM

Condition	Possible Cause	Correction
HIGH TEMPERATURE INDICATION—OVERHEATING	1. Coolant level low.	1. Replenish coolant level.
	2. Fan belt loose.	2. Adjust fan belt.
	3. Radiator hose(s) collapsed.	3. Replace hose(s).
	4. Radiator blocked to airflow.	4. Remove restriction.
	5. Faulty radiator cap.	5. Replace cap.
	6. Vehicle overloaded.	6. Reduce load.
	7. Ignition timing incorrect.	7. Adjust ignition timing.
	8. Idle speed low.	8. Adjust idle speed.
	9. Air trapped in cooling system.	9. Purge air.
	10. Vehicle in heavy traffic.	10. Operate at fast idle intermittently to cool engine.
	11. Incorrect cooling system component(s) installed.	11. Install proper component(s).
	12. Faulty thermostat.	12. Replace thermostat.
	13. Water pump shaft broken or impeller loose.	13. Replace water pump.
	14. Radiator tubes clogged.	14. Flush radiator.
	15. Cooling system clogged.	15. Flush system.
	16. Casting flash in cooling passages.	16. Repair or replace as necessary. Flash may be visible by removing cooling system components or removing core plugs.
	17. Brakes dragging.	17. Repair brakes.
	18. Excessive engine friction.	18. Repair engine.
	19. Car working beyond cooling system capacity.	19. Install heavy-duty cooling fan and/or radiator.
	20. Antifreeze concentration over 68%.	20. Lower antifreeze content.
	21. Low anti-freeze concentration.	21. Add anti-freeze to provide a minimum 50% concentration.
LOW TEMPERATURE INDICATION—OVERCOOLING	1. Improper fan being used.	1. Install proper fan.
	2. Improper radiator.	2. Install proper radiator.
	3. Thermostat stuck open.	3. Replace thermostat.
	4. Improper fan pulley (too small).	4. Install proper pulley.
COOLANT LOSS—BOILOVER	Refer to Overheating Causes in addition to the following:	
NOTE: Immediately after shutdown, the engine enters a period known as heat soak. This is caused because the cooling system is inoperative but engine temperature is still high. If coolant temperature rises above boiling point, it may push some coolant out of the radiator overflow tube. If this does not occur frequently, it is considered normal.	1. Overfilled cooling system.	1. Reduce coolant level to proper specification.
	2. Quick shutdown after hard (hot) run.	2. Allow engine to run at fast idle prior to shutdown.
	3. Air in system resulting in occasional "burping" of coolant.	3. Purge system.
	4. Insufficient antifreeze allowing coolant boiling point to be too low.	4. Add antifreeze to raise boiling point.
	5. Antifreeze deteriorated because of age or contamination.	5. Replace coolant.
	6. Leaks due to loose hose clamps, loose nuts, bolts, drain plugs, faulty hoses, or defective radiator.	6. Pressure test system to locate leak then repair as necessary.
	7. Faulty head gasket.	7. Replace head gasket.
	8. Cracked head, manifold, or block.	8. Replace as necessary.
COOLANT ENTRY INTO CRANKCASE OR CYLINDER	1. Faulty head gasket.	1. Replace head gasket.
	2. Crack in head, manifold or block.	2. Replace as necessary.
COOLANT RECOVERY SYSTEM INOPERATIVE	1. Coolant level low.	1. Replenish coolant.
	2. Leak in system.	2. Pressure test to isolate leak and repair as necessary.
	3. Pressure cap not tight or gasket missing or leaking.	3. Repair as necessary.
	4. Pressure cap defective.	4. Replace cap.
	5. Overflow tube clogged or leaking.	5. Repair as necessary.
	6. Recovery bottle vent plugged.	6. Remove restriction.
NOISE	1. Fan contacting shroud.	1. Reposition shroud and check engine mounts.
	2. Loose water pump impeller.	2. Replace pump.
	3. Dry fan belt.	3. Apply belt dressing or replace belt.

COOLING SYSTEM—Continued

Condition	Possible Cause	Correction
NOISE, continued	4. Loose fan belt. 5. Rough surface on drive pulley. 6. Water pump bearing worn.	4. Adjust fan belt. 5. Replace pulley. 6. Remove belt to isolate. Replace pump.
NO COOLANT FLOW THROUGH HEATER CORE	1. Plugged return pipe in water pump. 2. Heater hose collapsed or plugged. 3. Plugged heater core. 4. Plugged outlet in thermostat housing. 5. Heater bypass hole in cylinder head plugged.	1. Remove obstruction. 2. Remove obstruction or replace hose. 3. Remove obstruction or replace core. 4. Remove flash or obstruction. 5. Remove obstruction.

COOLANT TEMPERATURE INDICATOR

Condition	Possible Cause	Correction
"HOT" INDICATOR; LIGHT NOT LIT WHEN CRANKING ENGINE	1. Bulb burned out. 2. Open in light circuit. 3. Defective ignition switch.	1. Replace bulb. 2. Locate and correct open. 3. Replace ignition switch.
LIGHT ON, ENGINE RUNNING	1. Wiring grounded between light and switch. 2. Defective temperature switch. 3. Defective ignition switch. 4. High coolant temperature.	1. Locate and correct grounded wiring. 2. Replace temperature switch. 3. Replace ignition switch. 4. Locate and correct cause of high coolant temperature.

EXHAUST SYSTEM

Condition	Possible Cause	Correction
LEAKING EXHAUST GASES	1. Leaks at pipe joints. 2. Damaged or improperly installed seals or packing. 3. Loose exhaust pipe heat tube extension connections. 4. Burned or rusted out exhaust pipe heat tube extensions.	1. Tighten U-bolt nuts at leaking joints. 2. Replace seals or packing as necessary. 3. Replace seals or packing as required. Tighten stud nuts or bolts. 4. Replace heat tube extensions as required.
EXHAUST NOISES	1. Leaks at manifold or pipe connections. 2. Burned or blown out muffler. 3. Burned or rusted out exhaust pipe. 4. Exhaust pipe leaking at manifold flange. 5. Exhaust manifold cracked or broken. 6. Leak between manifold and cylinder head.	1. Tighten clamps at leaking connections to specified torque. Replace gasket or packing as required. 2. Replace muffler assembly. 3. Replace exhaust pipe. 4. Tighten attaching bolt nuts. 5. Replace manifold. 6. Tighten manifold to cylinder head stud nuts or bolts.
LOSS OF ENGINE POWER AND/OR INTERNAL RATTLES IN MUFFLER	1. Dislodged tuning tubes and/or baffles in muffler.	1. Replace muffler.
LOSS OF ENGINE POWER	1. Imploding (inner wall collapse) of exhaust pipe.	1. Replace exhaust pipe.
ENGINE HARD TO WARM UP OR WILL NOT RETURN TO NORMAL IDLE	1. Heat control valve frozen in the open position.	1. Free up manifold heat control using a suitable manifold heat control solvent.
MANIFOLD HEAT CONTROL VALVE NOISE	1. Thermostat broken. 2. Broken, weak or missing anti-rattle spring.	1. Replace thermostat. 2. Replace spring.

CLUTCH & MANUAL TRANSMISSION

Condition	Possible Cause	Correction
CLUTCH CHATTER	1. Worn or damaged disc assembly.	1. Replace disc assembly.
	2. Grease or oil on disc facings.	2. Replace disc assembly and correct cause of contamination.
	3. Improperly adjusted cover assembly.	3. Replace cover assembly.
	4. Broken or loose engine mounts.	4. Replace or tighten mounts.
	5. Misaligned clutch housing.	5. Align clutch housing.
CLUTCH SLIPPING	1. Insufficient pedal free play.	1. Adjust release fork rod.
	2. Burned, worn, or oil soaked facings.	2. Replace disc assembly and correct cause of contamination.
	3. Weak or broken pressure springs.	3. Replace cover assembly.
DIFFICULT GEAR SHIFTING	1. Excessive pedal free play.	1. Adjust release fork rod.
	2. Excessive deflection in linkage or firewall.	2. Repair or replace linkage.
	3. Worn or damaged disc assembly.	3. Replace disc assembly.
	4. Improperly adjusted cover assembly.	4. Replace cover assembly.
	5. Clutch disc splines sticking.	5. Remove disc assembly and free up splines or replace disc.
	6. Worn or dry pilot bushing.	6. Lubricate or replace bushing.
	7. Clutch housing misaligned.	7. Align clutch housing.
CLUTCH NOISY	1. Dry clutch linkage.	1. Lubricate where necessary.
	2. Worn release bearing.	2. Replace release bearing.
	3. Worn disc assembly.	3. Replace disc assembly.
	4. Worn release levers.	4. Replace cover assembly.
	5. Worn or dry pilot bushing.	5. Lubricate or replace bushing.
	6. Dry contact-pressure plate lugs in cover.	6. Lubricate very lightly.
TRANSMISSION SHIFTS HARD	1. Incorrect clutch adjustment.	1. Adjust clutch pedal free-play.
	2. Clutch linkage binding.	2. Lubricate or repair linkage as required.
	3. Gearshift linkage incorrectly adjusted, bent, or binding.	3. Adjust linkage—correct any bind. Replace bent parts.
	4. Bind in steering column, or column is misaligned.	4. Disconnect shift rods at column. Check for bind/misalignment between tube and jacket by shifting lever into all positions. Correct as required.
	5. Incorrect lubricant.	5. Drain and refill transmission.
	6. Internal bind in transmissions—e.g. shift rails, interlocks, shift forks, synchronizer teeth.	6. Remove transmission and inspect shift mechanism. Repair as required.
	7. Clutch housing misalignment.	7. Check runout at rear face of clutch housing.
GEAR CLASH WHEN SHIFTING FROM ONE FORWARD GEAR TO ANOTHER	1. Incorrect clutch adjustment.	1. Adjust clutch.
	2. Clutch linkage binding.	2. Lubricate or repair linkage as required.
	3. Gear shift linkage incorrectly adjusted, bent, or binding.	3. Adjust linkage, correct binds, replace bent parts.
	4. Clutch housing misalignment.	4. Check runout at rear face of clutch housing.
	5. Damaged or worn transmission components: shift forks, synchronizers, shift rails and interlocks. Excessive end play due to worn thrust washers.	5. Inspect components. Repair or replace as required.
TRANSMISSION NOISY	1. Insufficient lubricant.	1. Check lubricant level and replenish as required.
	2. Incorrect lubricant.	2. Replace with proper lubricant.
	3. Clutch housing to engine or transmission to clutch housing bolts loose.	3. Check and correct bolt torque as required.
	4. Dirt, chips in lubricant.	4. Drain and flush transmission.
	5. Gearshift linkage incorrectly adjusted, bent or binding.	5. Adjust linkage, correct binds, replace bent parts.
	6. Clutch housing misalignment.	6. Check runout at rear face of clutch housing.

CLUTCH & MANUAL TRANSMISSION—Continued

Condition	Possible Cause	Correction
TRANSMISSION NOISY, continued	7. Worn transmission components: front-rear bearings, worn gear teeth, damaged gear teeth or synchronizer components.	7. Inspect components and repair as required.
JUMPS OUT OF GEAR	1. Gearshift linkage incorrectly adjusted.	1. Adjust linkage.
	2. Gearshift linkage bent or binding.	2. Correct bind, replace bent parts.
	3. Clutch housing misaligned.	3. Check runout at rear face of clutch housing.
	4. Worn pilot bushing.	4. Replace bushing.
	5. Worn or damaged clutch shaft roller bearings.	5. Replace bearings.
	6. Worn, tapered gear teeth; synchronizer parts worn.	6. Inspect and replace as required.
	7. Shifter forks, shift rails, or detent-interlock parts worn, missing, etc.	7. Inspect and replace as required.
	8. Excessive end play of output shaft gear train, countershaft gear or reverse idler gear.	8. Replace thrust washers, and snap rings (output shaft gear train).
WILL NOT SHIFT INTO ONE GEAR—ALL OTHERS OK	1. Gearshift linkage not adjusted correctly.	1. Adjust linkage.
	2. Bent shift rod at transmission.	2. Replace rod.
	3. Transmission shifter levers reversed.	3. Correctly position levers.
	4. Worn or damaged shift rails, shift forks, detent-interlock plugs, loose setscrew in shifter fork, worn synchronizer parts.	4. Inspect and repair or replace parts as required.
LOCKED IN ONE GEAR—CANNOT BE SHIFTED OUT OF THAT GEAR	1. Gearshift linkage binding or bent.	1. Correct bind, replace bent components.
	2. Transmission shifter lever attaching nuts loose or levers are worn at shifter fork shaft hole.	2. Tighten nuts, replace worn levers.
	3. Shift rails worn or broken, shifter fork bent, setscrew loose, detent-interlock plug missing or worn.	3. Inspect and replace worn or damaged parts.
	4. Broken gear teeth on countershaft gear, clutch shaft, or reverse idler gear.	4. Inspect and replace damaged part.

TRANSFER CASE

Condition	Possible Cause	Correction
TRANSFER CASE NOISY	1. Incorrect tire inflation pressures and/or tire and wheel size.	1. Check that all tire and wheel assemblies are the same size and inflation pressures are correct.
NOTE: If the vehicle has not been driven for a week or more, noise may occur during initial operation. This is a normal condition and the noise will usually stop after continued operation.	2. Incorrect lubricant level.	2. Check and fill lubricant as required.
	3. Worn or damaged bearings.	3. Inspect and replace as required.
	4. Worn or damaged drive chain.	4. Inspect and replace as required.
	5. Incorrectly aligned driveshafts or universal joints.	5. Inspect and align as required.
	6. Loose adapter bolts.	6. Check and correct bolt torque as required.
SHIFTER LEVER DIFFICULT TO MOVE	1. Dirty or contaminated linkage.	1. Clean and lubricate as required.
	2. Internal component damage.	2. Inspect and replace as required.
JUMPS OUT OF GEAR	1. Incorrectly adjusted or loose shift linkage.	1. Adjust and/or tighten linkage bolts.
	2. Loose mounting bolts.	2. Check and correct bolt torque as required
	3. Front and rear driveshaft slip yokes dry or loose.	3. Lubricate and repair slip yokes as required. Correct bolt torque as required.
	4. Internal case component damage.	4. Inspect and replace worn and/or damaged case components as required.

TRANSFER CASE—Continued

Condition	Possible Cause	Correction
FRONT AXLE SLIPS OUT OF ENGAGEMENT	1. Spring loose or broken. 2. Incorrect shift linkage or cable adjustment.	1. Inspect and replace as required. 2. Adjust linkage or cable as required.
TRANSFER CASE LEAKING	1. Excessive lubricant in case. 2. Worn and/or damaged seals or gaskets. 3. Loose mounting case bolts. 4. Scored yoke in seal contact area.	1. Correct lubricant level as required. 2. Inspect and replace as required. 3. Check and correct bolt torque as required 4. Repair or replace as required.

BRAKES

Condition	Possible Cause	Correction
LOW BRAKE PEDAL (Excessive pedal travel required to apply brake)	1. Excessive clearance between linings and drums. 2. Worn brake lining. 3. Bent, distorted brakeshoes. 4. Caliper pistons corroded. 5. Power unit push rod height incorrect.	1. Adjust brakes. 2. Inspect and replace lining if worn beyond minimum thickness specification. 3. Replace brakeshoes in axle sets. 4. Repair or replace calipers. 5. Check height with gauge (only). Replace power unit if push rod height is not within specifications.
LOW BRAKE PEDAL (Pedal may go to floor under steady pressure)	1. Leak in hydraulic system. 2. Air in hydraulic system. 3. Incorrect or non-recommended brake fluid (fluid boils away at below normal temp.).	1. Fill master cylinder to within ¼-inch of rim; have helper apply brakes and check calipers, wheel cylinders combination valve, tubes, hoses and fittings for leaks. Repair or replace parts as necessary. 2. Bleed air from system. 3. Flush hydraulic system with clean brake fluid. Refill with correct-type fluid.
LOW BRAKE PEDAL (Pedal goes to floor on first application—OK on subsequent applications)	1. Disc brakeshoe (pad) knock back; shoes push caliper piston back into bore. Caused by loose wheel bearings or excessive lateral runout of rotor (rotor wobble). 2. Calipers sticking on mounting surfaces of caliper and anchor. Caused by buildup of dirt, rust, or corrosion on abutment.	1. Adjust wheel bearings and check lateral runout of rotor(s). Refinish rotors if runout is over limits. Replace rotor if refinishing would cause rotor to fall below minimum thickness limit. 2. Clean mounting surfaces and lubricate surfaces with molydisulphide grease or equivalent.
FADING BRAKE PEDAL (Pedal falls away under steady pressure)	1. Leak in hydraulic system. 2. Master cylinder piston cups worn, or master cylinder bore is scored, worn or corroded.	1. Fill master cylinder reservoirs to within ¼-inch of rim; have helper apply brakes, check master cylinder, calipers, wheel cylinders combination valve, tubes, hoses, and fittings for leaks. Repair or replace parts as necessary. 2. Repair or replace master cylinder.

BRAKES—Continued

Condition	Possible Cause	Correction
DECREASING BRAKE PEDAL TRAVEL (Pedal travel required to apply brakes decreases, may be accompanied by hard pedal)	1. Caliper or wheel cylinder pistons sticking or seized.	1. Repair or replace calipers, or wheel cylinders.
	2. Master cylinder compensator ports blocked (preventing fluid return to reservoirs) or pistons sticking or seized in master cylinder bore.	2. Repair or replace master cylinder.
	3. Power brake unit binding internally.	3. Test unit as follows: a. Raise hood, shift transmission into neutral and start engine. b. Increase engine speed to 1500 RPM, close throttle and fully depress brake pedal. c. Slowly release brake pedal and stop engine. d. Remove vacuum check valve and hose from power unit. Observe for backward movement of brake pedal or power unit-to-brake pedal push rod. e. If pedal or push rod moves backward, power unit has internal bind—replace power brake unit.
	4. Incorrect power unit push rod height.	4. Adjust push rod height.
SPONGY BRAKE PEDAL (Pedal has abnormally soft, springy, spongy feel when depressed)	1. Air in hydraulic system.	1. Bleed brakes.
	2. Brakeshoes bent or distorted.	2. Replace brakeshoes.
	3. Brake lining not yet seated to drums and rotors.	3. Burnish brakes.
HARD BRAKE PEDAL (Excessive pedal pressure required to stop car. May be accompanied by brake fade)	1. Loose or leaking power brake unit vacuum hose.	1. Tighten connections or replace leaking hose.
	2. Brake lining contaminated by grease or brake fluid.	2. Determine cause of contaminations and correct. Replace contaminated brake lining in axle sets.
	3. Incorrect or poor quality brake lining.	3. Replace lining in axle sets.
	4. Bent, broken, distorted brakeshoes.	4. Replace brakeshoes and lining.
	5. Calipers binding or dragging on anchor. Rear brakeshoes dragging on support plate.	5. Sand or wire brush anchors and caliper mounting surfaces and lubricate surfaces lightly. Clean rust or burrs from rear brake support plate ledges and lubricate ledges. **NOTE:** If ledges are deeply grooved or scored, do not attempt to sand or grind them smooth—replace support plate.
	6. Rear brake drum(s) bell mouthed, flared or barrel shaped (distorted).	6. Replace rear drum(s).
	7. Caliper, wheel cylinder, or master cylinder pistons sticking or seized.	7. Repair or replace parts as necessary.
	8. Power brake unit vacuum check valve malfunction.	8. Test valve as follows: a. Start engine, increase engine speed to 1500 RPM, close throttle and immediately stop engine. b. Wait at least 90 seconds then try brake action. c. If brakes are not vacuum assisted for 2 or more applications, check valve is faulty.

BRAKES—Continued

Condition	Possible Cause	Correction
HARD BRAKE PEDAL, continued	9. Power brake unit has internal bind or incorrect push rod height (too long).	9. Test unit as follows: a. With engine stopped, apply brakes several times to exhaust all vacuum in system. b. Shift transmission into neutral, depress brake pedal and start engine. c. If pedal falls away under foot pressure and less pressure is required to hold pedal in applied position, power unit vacuum system is working. Test power unit as outlined in item (3) under Decreasing Brake Pedal Travel. If power unit exhibits bind condition, replace power unit. d. If power unit does not exhibit bind condition, disconnect master cylinder and check push rod height with appropriate gauge. If height is not within specifications, replace power unit.
	10. Master cylinder compensator ports (at bottom of reservoirs) blocked by dirt, scale, rust, or have small burrs (blocked ports prevent fluid return to reservoirs).	10. Repair or replace master cylinder. **CAUTION:** Do not attempt to clean blocked ports with wire, pencils, or similar implements.
	11. Brake hoses, tubes, fittings clogged or restricted.	11. Use compressed air to check or unclog parts. Replace any damaged parts.
	12. Brake fluid contaminated with improper fluids (motor oil, transmission fluid, or poor quality brake fluid) causing rubber components to swell and stick in bores.	12. Replace all rubber components and hoses. Flush entire brake system. Refill with recommended brake fluid.
GRABBING BRAKES (Severe reaction to brake pedal pressure)	1. Brake lining(s) contaminated by grease or brake fluid.	1. Determine and correct cause of contamination and replace brakeshoes and linings in axle sets.
	2. Parking brake cables incorrectly adjusted or seized.	2. Adjust cables. Free up or replace seized cables.
	3. Power brake unit binding internally or push rod height incorrect.	3. Test unit as outlined in item (3) under Decreasing Brake Pedal Travel. If o.k., check push rod height. If unit has internal bind or incorrect push rod height, replace unit.
	4. Incorrect brake lining or lining loose on brakeshoes.	4. Replace brakeshoes in axle sets.
	5. Brakeshoes bent, cracked, distorted.	5. Replace brakeshoes in axle sets.
	6. Caliper anchor plate bolts loose.	6. Tighten bolts.
	7. Rear brakeshoes binding on support plate ledges.	7. Clean and lubricate ledges. Replace support plate(s) if ledges are deeply grooved. Do not attempt to smooth ledges by grinding.
	8. Rear brake support plates loose.	8. Tighten mounting bolts.
	9. Caliper or wheel cylinder piston sticking or seized.	9. Repair or replace parts as necessary.
	10. Master cylinder pistons sticking or seized in bore.	10. Repair or replace master cylinder.
BRAKES GRAB, PULL, OR WON'T HOLD IN WET WEATHER	1. Brake lining water soaked.	1. Drive vehicle with brakes lightly applied to dry out lining. If problem persists after lining has dried, replace brakeshoe lining in axle sets.
	2. Rear brake support plate bent allowing excessive amount of water to enter drum.	2. Replace support plate.

BRAKES—Continued

Condition	Possible Cause	Correction
DRAGGING BRAKES (Slow or incomplete release of brakes)	1. Brake pedal binding at pivot.	1. Free up and lubricate.
	2. Power brake unit push rod height incorrect (too high) or unit has internal bind.	2. Replace unit if push rod height is incorrect. If height is o.k., check for internal bind as outlined in item (3) under Decreasing Brake Pedal Travel.
	3. Parking brake cables incorrectly adjusted or seized.	3. Adjust cables. Free up or replace seized cables.
	4. Brakeshoe return springs weak or broken.	4. Replace return springs. Replace brakeshoe if necessary in axle sets.
	5. Automatic adjusters malfunctioning.	5. Repair or replace adjuster parts as required.
	6. Caliper, wheel cylinder or master cylinder pistons sticking or seized.	6. Repair or replace parts as necessary.
	7. Master cylinder compensating ports blocked (fluid does not return to reservoirs).	7. Use compressed air to clear ports. Do not use wire, pencils, or similar objects to open blocked ports.
VEHICLE PULLS TO ONE SIDE WHEN BRAKES ARE APPLIED	1. Incorrect front tire pressure.	1. Inflate to recommended cold (reduced load) inflation pressures.
	2. Incorrect front wheel bearing adjustment or worn—damaged wheel bearings.	2. Adjust wheel bearings. Replace worn, damaged bearings.
	3. Brakeshoe lining on one side contaminated.	3. Determine and correct cause of contamination and replace brakeshoe lining in axle sets.
	4. Brakeshoes on one side bent, distorted, or lining loose on shoe.	4. Replace brakeshoes in axle sets.
	5. Support plate bent or loose on one side.	5. Tighten or replace support plate.
	6. Brake lining not yet seated to drums and rotors.	6. Burnish brakes.
	7. Caliper anchor plate loose on one side.	7. Tighten anchor plate bolts.
	8. Caliper or wheel cylinder piston sticking or seized.	8. Repair or replace caliper or wheel cylinder.
	9. Brakeshoe linings watersoaked.	9. Drive vehicle with brakes lightly applied to dry linings. Replace brakeshoes in axle sets if problem persists.
	10. Loose suspension component attaching or mounting bolts, incorrect front end alignment. Worn suspension parts.	10. Tighten suspension bolts. Replace worn suspension components. Check and correct alignment as necessary.
CHATTER OR SHUDDER WHEN BRAKES ARE APPLIED (Pedal pulsation and roughness may also occur)	1. Front wheel bearings loose.	1. Adjust wheel bearings.
	2. Brakeshoes distorted, bent, contaminated, or worn.	2. Replace brakeshoes in axle sets.
	3. Caliper anchor plate or support plate loose.	3. Tighten mounting bolts.
	4. Excessive thickness variation or lateral rim out of rotor.	4. Refinish or replace rotor.
	5. Rear drum(s) out of round, sharp spots.	5. Refinish or replace drum.
	6. Loose suspension component attaching or mounting bolts, incorrect front end alignment. Worn suspension parts.	6. Tighten suspension bolts. Replace worn suspension components. Check and correct alignment as necessary.
NOISY BRAKES (Squealing, clicking, scraping sound when brakes are applied)	1. Bent, broken, distorted brakeshoes.	1. Replace brakeshoes in axle sets.
	2. Brake lining worn out—shoes contacting drum or rotor.	2. Replace brakeshoes and lining in axle sets. Refinish or replace drums or rotors.
	3. Foreign material imbedded in brake lining.	3. Replace brake lining.
	4. Broken or loose hold-down or return springs.	4. Replace parts as necessary.
	5. Rough or dry drum brake support plate ledges.	5. Lubricate support plate ledges.
	6. Cracked, grooved, or scored rotor(s) or drum(s).	6. Replace rotor(s) or drum(s).

BRAKES—Continued

Condition	Possible Cause	Correction
PULSATING BRAKE PEDAL	1. Out of round drums or excessive thickness variation or lateral runout in disc brake rotor(s). 2. Bent rear axle shaft.	1. Refinish or replace drums or rotors. 2. Replace axle shaft.

STEERING

Condition	Possible Cause	Correction
EXCESSIVE PLAY OR LOOSENESS IN STEERING	1. Incorrectly adjusted front wheel bearings. 2. Worn steering shaft couplings. 3. Steering wheel loose on shaft, loose pitman arm, tie rods, steering arms or steering linkage ball studs. 4. Worn ball joints. 5. Worn intermediate rod or tie rod sockets.	1. Adjust bearings. 2. Inspect and replace as required. 3. Check and correct steering attachment torques as required. 4. Inspect and replace as required. 5. Inspect and replace as required.
HARD OR ERRATIC STEERING	1. Incorrect tire pressure. 2. Insufficient or incorrect lubrication. 3. Steering or linkage parts damaged or misaligned. 4. Incorrect front wheel alignment. 5. Incorrect steering gear adjustment.	1. Inflate tires to recommended pressure. 2. Lubricate as required. 3. Repair or replace parts as required. 4. Adjust wheel alignment angles. 5. Adjust steering gear.
POOR STEERING RETURNABILITY	1. Insufficient ball joint or linkage lubrication. 2. Steering gear adjusted too tightly. 3. Steering gear to column misaligned. 4. Incorrect front wheel alignment (caster).	1. Lubricate as required. 2. Adjust over center and thrust bearing preload. 3. Align steering column. 4. Check alignment and correct as required.
WHEEL SHIMMY OR TRAMP	1. Improper tire pressure. 2. Wheels, tires, or brake drums out-of-balance or out-of-round. 3. Inoperative, worn, or loose shock absorbers or mounting parts. 4. Loose or worn steering or suspension parts. 5. Loose or worn wheel bearings. 6. Incorrect steering gear adjustments. 7. Incorrect front wheel alignment.	1. Inflate tires to recommended pressures. 2. Inspect parts and replace unacceptable out-of-round parts. Rebalance parts. 3. Repair or replace shocks or mountings. 4. Tighten or replace as necessary. 5. Adjust or replace bearings. 6. Adjust steering gear. 7. Correct front wheel alignment.
TIRE WEAR	1. Improper tire pressure. 2. Failure to rotate tires. 3. Brakes grabbing. 4. Incorrect front wheel alignment. 5. Broken or damaged steering and suspension parts. 6. Wheel runout. 7. Excessive speed on turns.	1. Inflate tires to recommended pressures. 2. Rotate tires. 3. Adjust or repair brakes. 4. Align incorrect angles. 5. Repair or replace defective parts. 6. Replace faulty wheel. 7. Make driver aware of condition.
VEHICLE LEADS TO ONE SIDE	1. Improper tire pressures. 2. Front tires with uneven tread depth, wear pattern, or different cord design (i.e., one bias ply and one belted tire on front wheels). 3. Incorrect front wheel alignment. 4. Brakes dragging. 5. Faulty power steering gear valve assembly. 6. Pulling due to uneven tire construction.	1. Inflate tires to recommended pressures. 2. Install tires of same cord construction and reasonably even tread depth and wear pattern. 3. Align incorrect angles. 4. Adjust or repair brakes. 5. Replace valve assembly. 6. Replace faulty tire.

SUSPENSION

Condition	Possible Cause	Correction
FRONT BOTTOMING OR RIDING LOW	1. Incorrect tire pressure.	1. Inflate tires to recommended pressure.
	2. Incorrect tire and wheel usage.	2. Install correct tire and wheel assembly.
	3. Vehicle overloaded or unevenly loaded.	3. Correct as required.
	4. Broken or incorrectly installed front springs.	4. Repair or replace as required.
	5. Loose or broken shock absorbers.	5. Tighten or replace as required.
	6. Loose or broken shackles.	6. Tighten or replace as required.
	7. Incorrect springs.	7. Check springs and replace if necessary.
DOG TRACKING OF REAR WHEELS	1. Loose or damaged front and/or rear suspension parts.	1. Inspect, repair or replace as required.
	2. Loose rear spring U-bolts.	2. Check and correct bolt torque as required.
	3. Rear springs incorrectly installed on axle.	3. Repair as required.
	4. Incorrectly installed front springs.	4. Repair as required.
SWAY OR ROLL	1. Unequal load distribution (side to side).	1. Correct as required.
	2. Excessive load or body height.	2. Correct as required.
	3. Incorrect tire pressure.	3. Correct tire inflation pressure.
	4. Loose wheel lug nuts.	4. Torque lug nuts as required.
	5. Worn or loose stabilizer bar assembly.	5. Tighten or replace as required.
	6. Loose or defective shock absorbers.	6. Torque mounting bolts or replace as required.
	7. Broken or sagging spring.	7. Replace spring as required.
FRONT END NOISE	1. Insufficient ball joint or linkage lubricant.	1. Lubricate parts as required.
	2. Worn bushings or loose shock absorber.	2. Tighten bolts and/or replace bushings.
	3. Worn control arm bushings.	3. Replace bushings.
	4. Worn tie rod ends.	4. Replace tie rod ends.
	5. Worn or loose wheel bearings.	5. Adjust or replace wheel bearings.
	6. Loose stabilizer bar.	6. Torque all stabilizer bar attachments as required.
	7. Loose wheel lug nuts.	7. Torque lug nuts as required.
	8. Incorrectly positioned spring.	8. Correctly install spring.
	9. Loose suspension bolts.	9. Check and correct bolt torque as required.
FRONT AXLE NOISE	1. Incorrect lubricant level.	1. Check and fill lubricant as required.
	2. Excessive pinion end-play.	2. Check and adjust end play as required.
NOTE: A knocking noise heard at low speed or when coasting may be caused by loose differential side gears. If this is encountered, operate vehicle at speed where noise is loudest and apply brakes lightly. If loose gears are causing the problem, noise level should decrease as brakes are applied.	3. Incorrect pinion bearing preload.	3. Check and adjust pinion bearing preload.
	4. Worn and/or damaged pinion or differential bearings.	4. Inspect and replace worn and/or damaged bearings.
	5. Excessive differential bearing preload.	5. Check and adjust differential bearing preload.
	6. Damaged pinion gears.	6. Replace gears.

HEADLAMPS

Condition	Possible Cause	Correction
ONE HEADLAMP INOPERATIVE OR INTERMITTENT	1. Loose connection.	1. Secure connections to sealed beam including ground.
	2. Defective sealed beam.	2. Replace sealed beam.
ONE OR MORE HEADLIGHTS ARE DIM	1. Open ground connection at headlight.	1. Repair ground wire connection between sealed beam and body ground.
	2. Ground wire mislocated in headlight connector (type 2 sealed beam).	2. Relocate ground wire in connector.
ONE OR MORE HEADLIGHTS SHORT LIFE	1. Voltage regulator setting incorrect.	1. Readjust or replace regulator.
ALL HEADLIGHTS INOPERATIVE OR INTERMITTENT	1. Loose connection.	1. Check and secure connections at dimmer switch and light switch.
	2. Defective dimmer switch.	2. Check voltage at dimmer switch with test lamp. If test lamp bulb lights only at switch "Hot" wire terminal, replace dimmer switch.
	3. Open wiring—light switch to dimmer switch.	3. Check wiring with test lamp. If bulb lights at light switch wire terminal, but not at dimmer switch, repair open wire.
	4. Open wiring—light switch to battery.	4. Check "Hot" wire terminal at light switch with test lamp. If lamp does not light, repair open wire circuit to battery (possible open fusible link).
	5. Shorted ground circuit.	5. If, after a few minutes operation, headlights flicker "ON" and "OFF" and/or a thumping noise can be heard from the light switch (circuit breaker opening and closing), repair short to ground in circuit between light switch and headlights. After repairing short, check for headlight flickering after one minute operation. If flickering occurs, the circuit breaker has been damaged and light switch must be replaced.
	6. Defective light switch.	6. Check light switch. Replace light switch, if defective.
UPPER OR LOWER BEAM WILL NOT LIGHT OR INTERMITTENT	1.. Open connection or defective dimmer switch.	1. Check dimmer switch terminals with test lamp. If bulb lights at all wire terminals, repair open wiring between dimmer switch and headlights. If bulb will not light at one of these terminals, replace dimmer switch.
	2. Short circuit to ground.	2. Follow diagnosis above (all headlights inoperative or intermittent).

SIDE MARKER LAMPS

Condition	Possible Cause	Correction
ONE LAMP INOPERATIVE	1. Turn signal bulb burnt out (front lamp).	1. Switch turn signals on. If signal bulb does not light, replace bulb.
	2. Side marker bulb burnt out.	2. Replace bulb.
	3. Loose connection or open in wiring.	3. Using test lamp, check "Hot" wire terminal at bulb socket. If test lamp lights, repair open ground circuit. If lamp does not light, repair open "Hot" wire circuit.
FRONT OR REAR LAMPS INOPERATIVE	1. Loose connection or open ground connection.	1. If associated tail or park lamps do not operate, secure all connectors in "Hot" wire circuit. If park and turn lamps operate, repair open ground connections.
	2. Multiple bulbs burnt out.	2. Replace burnt out bulbs.

SIDE MARKER LAMPS—Continued

Condition	Possible Cause	Correction
ALL LAMPS INOPERATIVE	1. Blown fuse.	1. If park and tail lamps do not operate, replace blown fuse. If new fuse blows, check for short to ground between fuse panel and lamps.
	2. Loose connection.	2. Secure connector to light switch.
	3. Open in wiring.	3. Check tail light fuse with test lamp. If test lamp lights, repair open wiring between fuse and light switch. If not, repair open wiring between fuse and battery (possible open fusible link).
	4. Defective light switch.	4. Check light switch. Replace light switch, if defective.

TAIL, PARK AND LICENSE LAMPS

Condition	Possible Cause	Correction
ONE SIDE INOPERATIVE	1. Bulb burnt out.	1. Replace bulb.
	2. Open ground connection at bulb socket or ground wire terminal.	2. Jump bulb base socket connection to ground. If lamp lights, repair open ground circuit.
BOTH SIDES INOPERATIVE	1. Tail lamp fuse blown.	1. Replace fuse. If new fuse blows, repair short to ground in "Hot" wire circuit between fuse panel through light switch to lamps.
	2. Loose connection.	2. Secure connector at light switch.
	3. Open wiring.	3. Using test light, check circuit on both sides of fuse. If lamp does not light on either side, repair open circuit between fuse panel and battery (possible open fusible link). If test lamp lights at light switch terminal, repair open wiring between light switch and lamps.
	4. Multiple bulb burnout.	4. If test lamp lights at lamp socket "Hot" wire terminal, replace bulbs.
	5. Defective light switch.	5. Check light switch. Replace light switch, if defective.

TURN SIGNAL AND HAZARD WARNING LAMP

Condition	Possible Cause	Correction
TURN SIGNALS INOPERATIVE ONE SIDE	1. Bulb(s) burnt out (flasher cannot be heard).	1. Turn hazard warning system on. If one or more bulbs are inoperative replace necessary bulbs.
	2. Open wiring or ground connection.	2. Turn hazard warning system on. If one or more bulbs are inoperative, use test lamp and check circuit at lamp socket. If test lamp lights, repair open ground connection. If not, repair open wiring between bulb socket and turn signal switch.
	3. Improper bulb or defective turn signal switch.	3. Turn hazard warning system on. If all front and rear lamps operate, check for improper bulb. If bulbs are OK, replace defective turn signal switch.
	4. Short to ground (flasher can be heard, no bulbs operate).	4. Locate and repair short to ground by disconnecting front and rear circuits separately.

TURN SIGNAL AND HAZARD WARNING LAMP—Continued

Condition	Possible Cause	Correction
TURN SIGNALS INOPERATIVE	1. Blown turn signal fuse.	1. Turn hazard warning system on. If all lamps operate, replace blown fuse. If new fuse blows, repair short to ground between fuse and lamps.
	2. Defective flasher.	2. If turn signal fuse is OK and hazard warning system will operate lamps, replace defective turn signal flasher.
	3. Loose connection.	3. Secure steering column connector.
HAZARD WARNING LAMPS INOPERATIVE	1. Blown fuse.	1. Switch turn signals on. If lamps operate, replace fuse if blown. If new fuse blows, repair short to ground. (could be in stop light circuit).
	2. Defective hazard warning flasher.	2. If fuse is OK, switch turn signals on. If lamps operate, replace defective hazard flasher.
	3. Open in wiring or defective turn signal switch.	3. Using test lamp, check hazard switch feed wire in turn signal steering column connector. If lamp does not light on either side of connector, repair open circuit between flasher and connector. If lamp lights only on feed side of connector, clean connector contacts. If lamp lights on both sides of connector, replace defective turn signal switch assembly.

BACK-UP LAMP

Condition	Possible Cause	Correction
ONE LAMP INOPERATIVE OR INTERMITTENT	1. Loose or burnt out bulb.	1. Secure or replace bulb.
	2. Loose connection.	2. Tighten connectors.
	3. Open ground connections.	3. Repair bulb ground circuit.
BOTH LAMPS INOPERATIVE OR INTERMITTENT	1. Neutral start or back-up lamp switch maladjusted.	1. Readjust or replace bulb.
	2. Loose connection or open circuit.	2. Secure all connectors. If OK, check continuity of circuit from fuse to lamps with test lamp. If lamp does not light on either side of fuse, correct open circuit from battery to fuse.
	3. Blown fuse.	3. Replace fuse. If new fuse blows, repair short to ground in circuit from fuse through neutral start switch to back-up lamps.
	4. Defective neutral start or back-up lamp switch.	4. Check switch. Replace neutral start or back-up lamp switch, if defective.
	5. Defective ignition switch.	5. If test lamp lights at ignition switch battery terminal but not at output terminal, replace ignition switch.
LAMP WILL NOT TURN OFF	1. Neutral start or back-up switch maladjusted.	1. Readjust neutral start or back-up lamp switch.
	2. Defective neutral start or back-up lamp switch.	2. Check switch. Replace neutral start or back-up lamp switch, if defective.

STOP LIGHTS

Condition	Possible Cause	Correction
ONE BULB INOPERATIVE	1. Bulb burnt out.	1. Replace bulb.
ONE SIDE INOPERATIVE	1. Loose connection, open wiring or defective bulbs.	1. Turn on directional signal. If lamp does not operate, check bulbs. If bulbs are OK, secure all connections. If lamp still does not operate, use test lamp and check for open wiring.

STOP LIGHTS—Continued

Condition	Possible Cause	Correction
ONE SIDE INOPERATIVE, continued	2. Defective directional signal switch or canceling cam.	2. If lamp will operate by turning directional signal on, the switch is not centering properly during canceling operation. Replace defective cancelling cam or directional signal switch.
ALL INOPERATIVE	1. Blown fuse.	1. Replace fuse. If new fuse blows, repair short to ground in circuit between fuse and lamps.
	2. Stop-switch maladjusted or defective.	2. Check stop switch. Adjust or replace stop switch, if required.
WILL NOT TURN OFF	1. Stop switch maladjusted or defective.	1. Readjust switch. If switch still malfunctions, replace.

HORNS

Condition	Possible Cause	Correction
HORNS WILL NOT OPERATE	1. Loose connections in circuit.	1. Check and tighten connections. Be sure to check ground straps.
	2. Defective horn switch.	2. Replace defective parts.
	3. Defective horn relay.	3. Replace relay.
	4. Defects within horn.	4. Replace horn.
HORNS HAVE POOR TONE	1. Low available voltage at horn, or defects within horn.	1. Check battery and charging circuit. Although horn should blow at any voltage above 7.0 volts, a weak or poor tone may occur at operating voltage below 11.0 volts. If horn has weak or poor tone at operating voltage of 11.0 volts or higher, remove horn and replace.
HORNS OPERATE INTERMITTENTLY	1. Loose or intermittent connections in horn relay or horn switch.	1. Check and tighten connections.
	2. Defective horn switch.	2. Replace switch.
	3. Defective relay.	3. Replace relay.
	4. Defects within horn.	4. Replace horn.
HORNS BLOW CONSTANTLY	1. Sticking horn relay.	1. Replace relay.
	2. Horn relay energized by grounded or shorted wiring.	2. Check and adjust wiring.
	3. Horn button can be grounded by sticking closed.	3. Adjust or replace damaged parts.

SPEEDOMETER

Condition	Possible Cause	Correction
SPEEDOMETER NOT OPERATING PROPERLY	1. Noisy speedometer cable.	1. Loosen over-tightened casing nuts and snap-on at speedometer head. Replace housing and core. Replace broken cable.
	2. Pointer and odometer inoperative. Inaccurate reading.	2. Check tire size. Check for correct speedometer driven gear.
	3. Kinked cable.	3. Replace cable. Reroute casing so that bends have no less than 6″ radius.
	4. Defective speedometer head.	4. Replace speedometer.
	5. Casing connector loose on speedometer case.	5. Tighten connector.

Noise, Vibration & Harshness

ROAD TEST

A road test and customer interview can provide much of the information needed to identify the specific condition which must be dealt with.

1. Make notes during diagnosis routine. This will ensure diagnosis is complete and systematic. Take care not to overlook details.
2. Road test vehicle and study condition by reproducing it several times during test.
3. When condition is reproduced, perform road test checks immediately. Refer to "Road Test Quick Checks" to identify proper section of diagnostic procedure. Perform checks several times to ensure valid conclusions. While the quick checks may not locate the problem, they will indicate the areas where there are no problems.
4. Do not make changes or adjustments before a road test and inspection of vehicle are performed. Any changes made can hide problems or add additional problems. Check and note tire pressures, any leaks, loose nuts or bolts, shiny spots where components may be rubbing, and if any unusually heavy items are loaded onto truck.

ROAD TEST QUICK CHECKS

1. **25–50 mph**—Under light acceleration, a moaning noise can be heard possibly accompanied by a vibration in floor. Refer to "Tip-In Moan" diagnostic procedure.
2. **25–45 mph**—Under steady to heavy acceleration, a rumbling noise can be heard. Refer to "Incorrect Driveline Angle" diagnostic procedure.
3. **High Speed**—Under slow acceleration and deceleration, shaking is noticeable in steering column or wheel, seats, floor pan, trim panels, or front end sheet metal. Refer to "High Speed Shake" procedure.
4. **High Speed**—Vibration can be felt in floor pan or seats, with no visible shaking but with rumble, buzz, hum, or booming noise. Refer to "Driveline Vibration" procedure.
5. **High Speed**—Coast with clutch disengaged or with automatic transmission in neutral and engine idling. If vibration is present, refer to "Driveline Vibration" procedure. If vibration is no longer present, refer to "Engine and Accessory Vibration" or "High Speed Shake" procedures.
6. **0–High Speed**—Vibration can be felt when engine reaches particular RPM. Vibration can also be felt when vehicle is stationary. Refer to "Engine and Accessory Vibration."

TYPES OF CONDITIONS

High Speed Shake (35 mph)

This condition involves a visible shake and pumping feeling in steering column, seats, or floor pan. The vibration is of low frequency (about 9–15 cycles per second) and may be seen as front end sheet metal shake. The condition may or may not be intensified by lightly applying brakes.

Tip-In Moan (15–50 mph)

Acceleration between 15–50 mph is accompanied by vibration which causes moan or high frequency resonance in floor pan. This condition is usually worse at a particular engine speed and at a particular throttle opening during acceleration at that speed. A moaning sound may also be caused depending on which component is producing the noise.

Driveline Vibration (50 mph)

This condition does not involve a visible vibration, but is felt in floor pan as rumble, buzz, hum, drone, or boom. This condition is independent of engine speed and will occur at same speed in any gear, and is not sensitive to acceleration or deceleration and cannot be reduced by coasting in neutral. The condition can be duplicated by supporting vehicle on axle-type hoist and operating driveline in gear at appropriate speed.

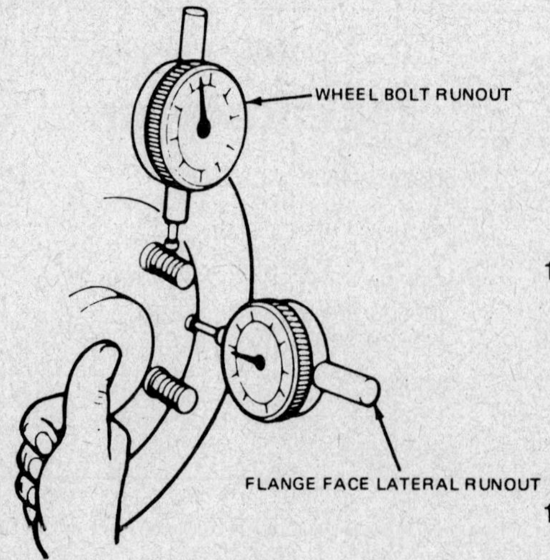

Fig. 1 Checking axle flange & wheel bolt run-out

Engine or Accessory Vibration (All Speeds)

This condition can occur at any vehicle speed but always at same engine RPM. Vibration will disappear during neutral coast and can be duplicated by operating engine at problem RPM with vehicle stationary. The condition can be caused by any component turning at engine speed when vehicle is stationary.

HIGH SPEED SHAKE

1. Apply brakes gently. If shake increases, proceed to step 2; if shake does not increase, proceed to step 10.
2. Lightly apply parking brake. If shake increases, proceed to step 3; if shake does not increase, proceed to step 6.
3. Check clearance between rear drum and brake shoe. Loosen cable tension if necessary. If clearance is correct, proceed to step 4; if clearance is not correct, proceed to step 7.
4. Using dial indicator, check axle flange run-out, Fig. 1. If run-out is acceptable, proceed to step 5. If run-out is unacceptable, proceed to step 8.
5. Check run-out of rear brake drum or disc. If run-out is acceptable, proceed to step 10. If run-out is unacceptable, proceed to step 9.
6. Check run-out of front brake disc. If run-out is acceptable, proceed to step 10. If run-out is unacceptable, proceed to step 9.
7. Adjust parking brake cable tension and road test vehicle. If shake is not eliminated, proceed to step 4.
8. Replace axle shaft and road test vehicle. If shake is not eliminated, proceed to step 5.
9. Replace or machine brake drums or discs and road test vehicle. If shake is not eliminated, proceed to step 10.
10. Raise and support vehicle. Turn wheels by hand and check for abnormal wear, damage, wheel bearing play or roughness. If abnormal wear or damage is found, proceed to step 12. If wheel bearing displays excessive play or roughness, proceed to step 13. If brakes drag, proceed to steps 5 and 6.
11. Road test vehicle, noting carefully which area of vehicle is shaking. If front end sheet metal is shaking heavily, proceed to step 14. If shaking is felt more in floor pan, seat and steering

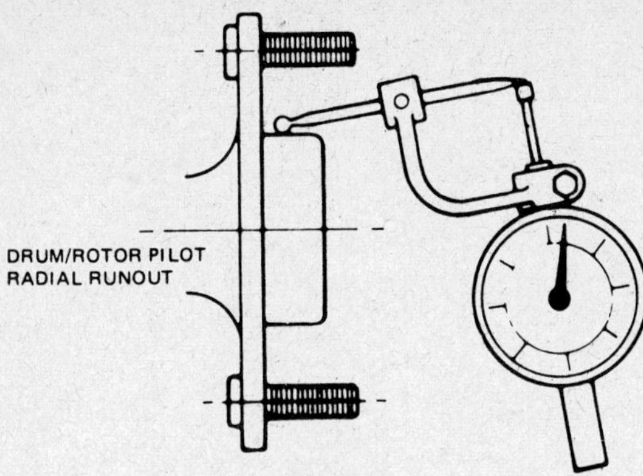

Fig. 2 Checking drum/rotor pilot radial run-out

column, proceed to step 15.

12. Replace worn or damaged tires and check for any other damaged components such as shock absorbers. Road test vehicle. If vehicle still shakes, proceed to step 15.
13. Check and adjust wheel bearings. Replace damaged wheel bearings and road test vehicle. If shake is not eliminated, proceed to step 15.
14. Check and tighten all major front end sheet metal attaching bolts and adjust hood rests. Road test vehicle. If shake is not eliminated, proceed to step 15.
15. Balance wheels on vehicle and check tires and rims for run-out. If wheel balancing is not necessary, proceed to step 16. If wheel and tire run-out are found, proceed to step 19.
16. Road test vehicle at speed at which condition was most apparent. If shake is not eliminated, proceed to step 17.
17. Install a known good set of wheels and tires on vehicle and road test. If shake is eliminated, proceed to step 18. If shake is not eliminated, proceed to step 23.
18. If one or more of the tires has a construction irregularity which causes tire to contact the road in an irregular manner, substitute known good tires until irregular tires are located.
19. Attempt to reduce run-out by mounting wheel in different position in relation to axle. If run-out is now acceptable, proceed to step 16. If run-out is still excessive, proceed to step 17. If repositioning indicates axle shaft run-out, proceed to step 22. If repositioning indicates tire and wheel run-out, proceed to step 20.
20. Attempt to correct run-out by repositioning tire on rim. If run-out is acceptable, proceed to step 15. If run-out is still excessive, proceed to step 21.
21. Replace component shown to be unserviceable and recheck run-out. If run-out is acceptable, proceed to step 15. If run-out is excessive, proceed to step 22.
22. Measure axle shaft run-out, Fig. 2. Replace shaft if run-out is excessive and check run-out of new shaft. Install wheel and check run-out again. If run-out is acceptable, proceed to step 15. If run-out is excessive, proceed to step 20.
23. Raise and support vehicle. Remove rear wheels and tires. Check all axle and brake rotor run-out measurements if not already checked. If axle and brake run-out are acceptable, proceed to step 24. If axle run-out is excessive, proceed to step 8. If brake disc run-out is excessive, proceed to step 9.
24. Check driveshaft run-out. If run-out is acceptable, proceed to step 25. If run-out is excessive, proceed to step 27.
25. Remove driveshaft and inspect universal joints. If joints are OK, proceed to step 26. If joints are defective, replace joints.
26. Install driveshaft and check for vibration. If vibration is unacceptable, proceed to step 27.
27. Measure ring gear run-out. If run-out is excessive, proceed to step 28.
28. Install new ring and pinion. Check run-out to ensure parts are within specifications. Recheck for vibration.

MOANING NOISE DURING LIGHT ACCELERATION

1. Inspect air cleaner for correct positioning of gasket, lid and gasket, element and duct. Correct if necessary and check condition. If noise is unacceptable, proceed to step 2.
2. On vehicles where a transmission extension housing damper is specified, ensure damper is installed. Recheck condition, if noise is unacceptable, proceed to step 3.
3. Loosen engine mounts, start engine, and shift from Neutral to Drive and back to normalize engine mounts. Tighten engine mounts and check condition; if noise is unacceptable, proceed to step 4.
4. With exhaust system hot, loosen hangers, and operate engine while shifting from Neutral to Drive and back to normalize exhaust system. Tighten hangers and recheck condition; if noise is unacceptable, proceed to step 5.
5. Inspect accessory drive belts for proper tension and accessory brackets for proper bolt torques. Adjust or tighten if necessary and check condition, if noise is unacceptable, proceed to step 6.
6. Loosen all bell housing bolts ¾ turn to test if noise is reduced. If noise is reduced, recheck step 2.

DRIVELINE VIBRATION

NOTE: Driveline vibration is a higher frequency, lower amplitude vibration than high speed shake, directly related to road speeds of 45 mph and higher. This type of vibration will be felt in the floor pan or heard as a rumble, hum, buzz or boom and will be present in all driving modes. The vibration may vary during acceleration, deceleration or coasting conditions. A driveline vibration can usually be duplicated with the axle supported, through light braking applications while accelerating and decelerating to simulate road load resistance.

1. Raise and support vehicle with drive wheels free. Operate driveline at problem speed. If vibration is present, proceed to step 3; if vibration is not present, proceed to step 2.
2. Retest vehicle to observe reported condition.
3. Evaluate noise and vibration by operating driveline at problem speed. If audible boom or rumble occurs above 45 mph, proceed to step 4. If buzzy feel occurs in floor pan above 45 mph, proceed to step 5. If a gravelly feel or grinding sound occurs at low speeds, proceed to step 4.
4. Install rear spring dampers if available for vehicle. If condition is still unacceptable or dampers are not available, proceed to step 5.
5. Scribe a line to index rear axle companion flange to driveshaft flange. Inspect drive shaft for dents, undercoating, proper seating of U-joint bearing caps, and tight U-joints. If driveshaft is in acceptable condition, proceed to step 6. Replace driveshaft if damaged. Replace U-joints if worn or improperly positioned.
6. Inspect wheel bearings. If bearings are OK, proceed to step 10; if wheel bearings are not in acceptable condition, proceed to step 7.
7. Replace wheel bearings and retest for vibration. If vibration is unacceptable proceed to step 10.
8. Repair or replace driveshaft. If vibration is unacceptable proceed to step 10.

9. Reposition U-joint bearing caps or replace U-joints. If vibration is unacceptable, proceed to step 10.
10. Disconnect driveshaft from rear axle companion flange and reconnect 180° from original position. Operate driveline at problem speed. If vibration is unacceptable, install rear axle pinion nose damper if available for vehicle. If pinion damper is not available or vibration is still unacceptable, proceed to step 11.
11. Disconnect driveshaft and return to original position. Refer to "Driveshaft Run-out," procedure and check run-out at front, center, and rear of driveshaft. If run-out is less than .035 inch at all positions, proceed to step 15 of "High Speed Shake" diagnosis. If run-out at front and/or center of driveshaft exceeds .035 inch while rear of shaft is acceptable, proceed to step 8. If run-out at rear of driveshaft exceeds .035 inch, proceed to "Driveshaft Run-out Check" procedure.
12. Balance driveshaft on vehicle and test vehicle at problem speed. If vibration is still unacceptable, proceed to step 17 of "High Speed Shake" diagnosis.

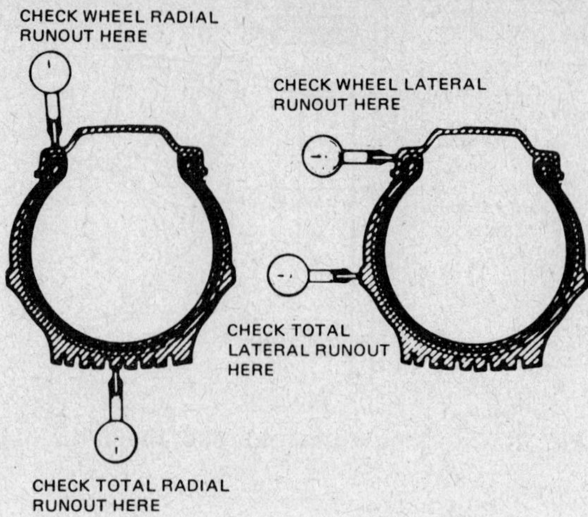

Fig. 3 Checking tire/wheel radial run-out

INCORRECT PINION ANGLE

1. Ensure U-joints are tight and all bearing caps are in plate. If U-joints are in good condition, proceed to step 3; if not, proceed to step 2.
2. Make an index mark on driveshaft and rear axle companion flange. Remove driveshaft and replace U-joints. Retest vehicle; if vibration is unacceptable, proceed to step 3.
3. Refer to "Driveline Pinion Angle Check" procedure to check pinion angle.
4. If pinion angle is correct, proceed to step 1 of "Driveline Vibration."

ENGINE OR ACCESSORY VIBRATION

1. With vehicle stationary, run engine at problem speed to check for condition. If vibration is present, proceed to step 2; if not, proceed to step 1 of "Driveline Vibration" diagnosis.
2. Inspect drive belts to check for wear or fraying. Ensure pulleys are not damaged or bent. Replace any damaged components and operate engine at problem speed. If vibration is present, proceed to step 3.
3. Check drive belt tension and adjust if necessary. Operate engine at problem speed. If vibration is still present, proceed to step 4.
4. Check torque of all accessory bracket bolts and retorque as necessary. Operate engine at problem speed; if vibration is still present, proceed to step 5.
5. Check pulley alignment and run-out visually at idle. Realign or replace pulleys if necessary. Operate engine at problem speed; if condition is still present, proceed to step 6.
6. Inspect belts for severe whipping at problem speed. If whip cannot be corrected by adjusting tension, replace belts. Operate engine at problem speed; if condition is still present, proceed to step 7.
7. Check engine accessories for noise while operating engine at problem speed. If vibration is still present, proceed to step 9. If vibration is not present, proceed to step 8.
8. Repair or replace noisy accessory. Connect and tension drive belt. Operate engine at problem speed; if vibration is still present, proceed to step 9.
9. Remove accessory from bracket. Inspect all hardware and bracket. Repair or replace as necessary.

CHECKS & ADJUSTMENTS

Tire/Wheel Run-out

1. After road test, promptly raise car on hoist to prevent flat spots in tires. Spin front wheels by hand to check for rough wheel bearings. Ensure bearings are not loose and adjust if necessary. If bearings are OK, proceed to step 2. If bearings have rough feel, proceed to step 2.
2. Check total radial and lateral run-out of tire and wheel assembly, Fig. 3. If both run-out measurements are less than .070 inch, balance tires. If lateral run-out exceeds .070 inch, proceed to step 3. If radial run-out exceeds .070 inch, proceed to step 4.
3. Check wheel rim lateral run-out. If run-out is less than .045 inch, replace tire and proceed to step 2. If run-out exceeds .045 inch, replace wheel and proceed to step 2.
4. Mark point of maximum run-out on tire thread. Check radial run-out of wheel. If radial run-out of wheel exceeds .045 inch, replace wheel and proceed to step 2. If radial run-out of wheel is less than .045 inch, proceed to step 5.
5. Mark point of least run-out on wheel. Remove tire from wheel and match point of maximum tire run-out with point of least run-out on wheel. Mount tire in this position and check total radial run-out of wheel and tire assembly. If total radial run-out is less than .070 inch, balance tires. If run-out exceeds .070 inch, replace tire and proceed to step 2.

Driveshaft Runout

1. Raise and support vehicle. Mark position of drive wheels or hub lugs for installation, then remove wheels.
2. On one piece driveshafts, proceed as follows:
   a. Using a suitable dial indicator, measure driveshaft run-out at front, center and rear of driveshaft. Rotate driveshaft by turning brake drum or brake rotor.
   b. If measured run-out exceeds .035 inch at front or center, replace driveshaft.
   c. If front and center run-out measurements are within specified amount and rear is not, mark rear run-out high point and proceed to step 4.
   d. If runout exceeds specified amount at all test points, proceed to "Driveshaft Balance."

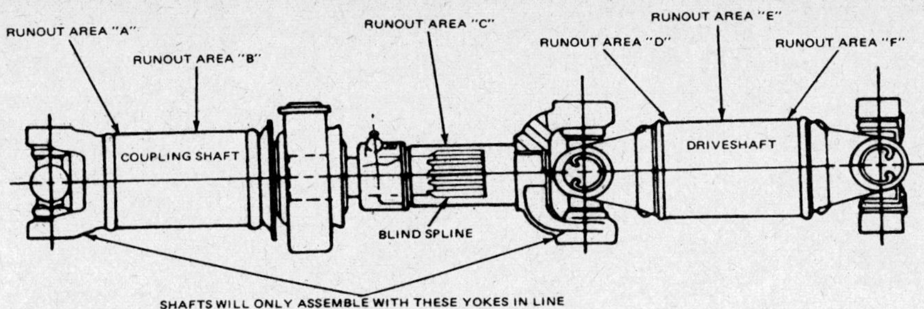

Fig. 4 Two piece driveshaft run-out check areas

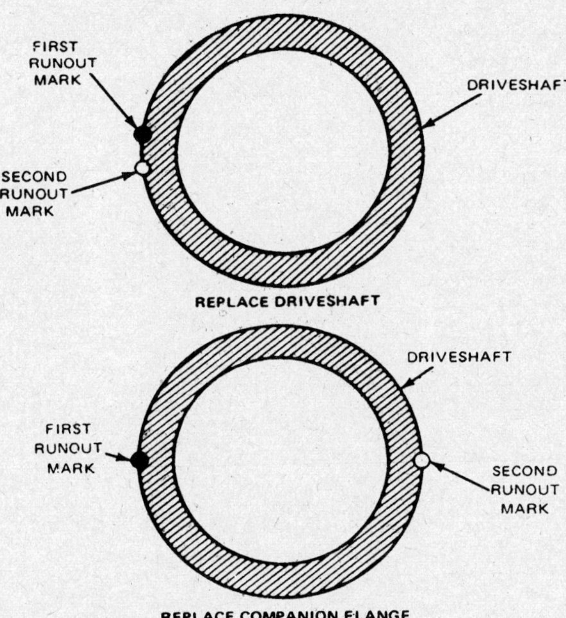

Fig. 5 Checking driveshaft run-out

3. On two piece driveshafts, proceed as follows:
   a. Using a suitable dial indicator, measure run-out at areas A through F as shown in Fig. 4. Rotate coupling shaft or driveshaft by turning rear wheel or drum.
   b. Mark run-out high points on coupling shaft and driveshaft.
   c. If run-out exceeds .035 inch at areas A, B or C, replace coupling shaft.
   d. If run-out exceeds .035 inch at areas D or E, replace driveshaft.
   e. If run-out at front, center or rear is less than .035 inch, proceed to "Driveshaft Balance."
   f. If run-out at area F exceeds .035 inch, mark run-out high point on shaft.
4. Note or mark indexing of driveshaft to rear axle pinion flange. Disconnect driveshaft, turn 180° and reconnect. Check run-out at rear of shaft. If run-out exceeds .035 inch, mark run-out high point and proceed to step 5. If run-out is within specified amount, check for vibration at road test speed. If vibration is still present proceed to "Driveshaft Balance."
5. Excessive driveshaft run-out may originate in the driveshaft, pinion yoke or flange. To determine which, compare the two run-out high points marked in steps 2, 3 and 4, Fig. 5. If the marks are within 1 inch of each other, replace driveshaft and recheck for vibration. If the marks are on opposite sides of the driveshaft, approximately 180° apart, the yoke or flange is worn and/or damaged.

NOTE: During replacement of a yoke type flange, driveshaft run-out should not exceed .035 inch when reconnected.

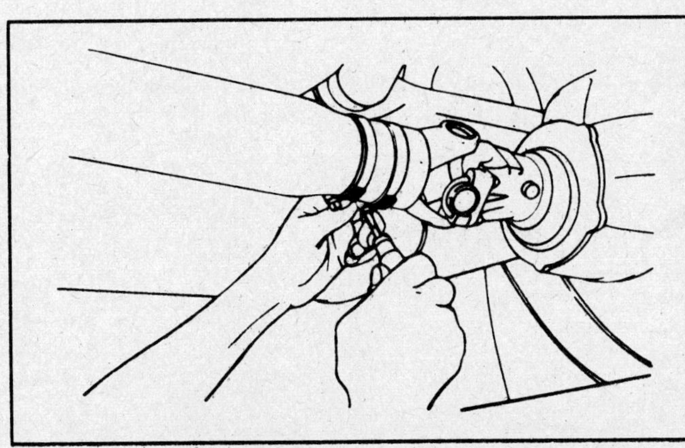

Fig. 6 Balancing driveshaft using hose clamps

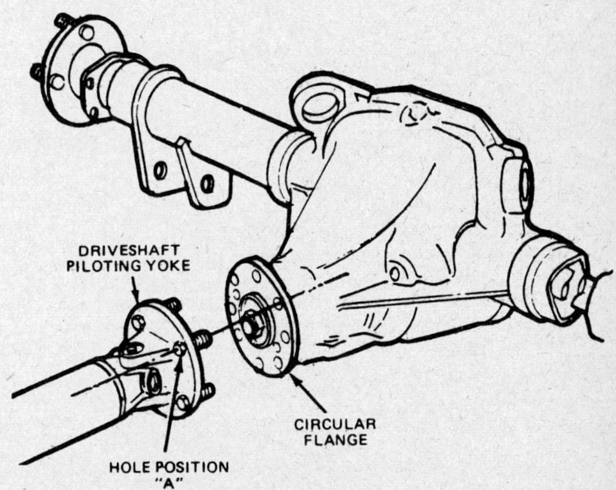

Fig. 7 Driveshaft indexing

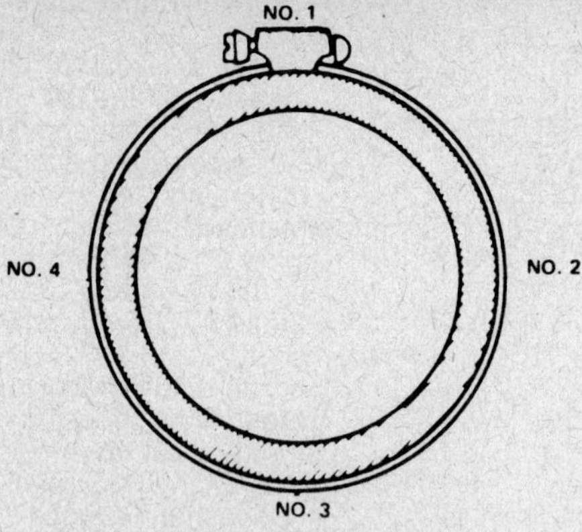

Fig. 8 Installing hose clamp

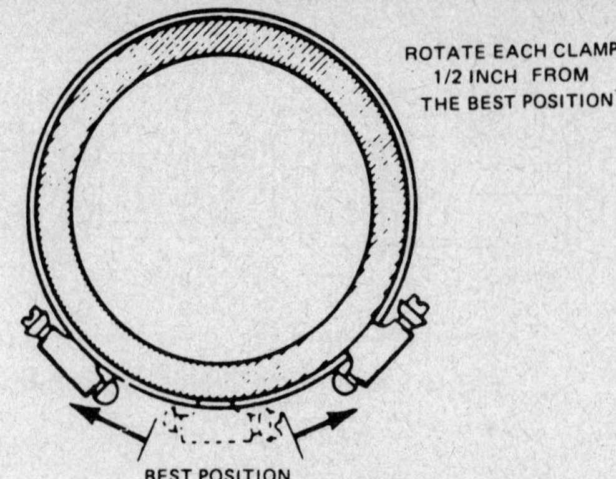

Fig. 9 Optimizing clamp location

When run-out is within specified amount, check for vibration at road speed and road test if vibration is not present or substantially reduced. if vibration persists, proceed to "Driveshaft Balance."

Driveshaft Balance

Two methods are possible depending on the method of connecting the driveshaft to the differential. Some vehicles are equipped with a drilled companion flange at the differential which allows re-indexing of the driveshaft in 45° increments. Driveshafts not equipped with this style flange can be balanced using worm-drive hose clamps, Fig. 6.

Re-indexing Method

1. Mark one hole of rear U-joint yoke flange with letter A. Number rear axle pinion flange holes 1 through 8 starting with hole opposite yoke flange hole A, Fig. 7. Position A-1 will be considered original index position.

NOTE: Check U-joints for binding while re-indexing.

---

2. Index driveshaft 180° to position A-5. Road test vehicle. If condition is still unsatisfactory, check condition in position A-3 and position A-7.
3. If further improvement is necessary, evaluate remaining positions that are located between best of previous positions A-3 and A-7.
4. Coat flange bolts with suitable thread locking compound and torque to 70–95 ft. lbs.

Hose Clamp Method

1. Make a mark to index rear axle companion flange to driveshaft. Disconnect driveshaft at flange, turn 180° and reconnect. If vibration increases, return driveshaft to original position. If vibration is reduced, proceed to step 2.
2. Mark rear of driveshaft with 4 equal sections numbered 1 through 4. Install a worm-drive hose clamp with screw at position 1 on driveshaft, Fig. 8. Operate driveline at problem speed. Check with clamp in each position. If vibration is worse in each position, proceed to step 5. If vibration is reduced in any one position, proceed to step 3. If vibration is reduced in any 2 positions, turn clamp between those positions and proceed to step 3.
3. Install additional clamp with screw in same position as first clamp in its best position. Operate driveline at problem speed. If vibration is same or increased, proceed to step 4.
4. Rotate each clamp screw ½ inch away in opposite directions, Fig. 9. If vibration is reduced, continue to move clamp screws apart until vibration is minimal. If vibration is still excessive, proceed to step 5.
5. Install wheels and road test vehicle to check if vibration might be acceptable on road. If vibration is unacceptable, proceed to step 17 of "High Speed Shake" diagnosis procedure.

Driveline Pinion Angle Checking

1. Raise vehicle on drive-on hoist, ensuring vehicle is at proper controlled height, Fig. 10.
2. Turn driveshaft so pinion U-joint bearing cap is facing down.
3. Place Vee magnet from pinion angle measuring tool T68P-4602-A or equivalent on driveshaft. Working from left side of vehicle, position pinion angle gauge on Vee magnet with adjusting screw towards front of vehicle. Adjust screw so bubble just contacts zero line, Fig. 11.
4. Move gauge to U-joint bearing cap with tool in same relative position as it was on Vee magnet, Fig. 12.
5. Read position on left edge of bubble on scale to determine driveshaft pinion angle. If pinion angle is not correct, adjust. Recheck and proceed to step 6.
6. Position Vee magnet on front of driveshaft and position gauge on magnet. Zero bubble and move gauge to downward facing U-joint bearing cap at rear of transmission. Read driveline angle and compare with specification.

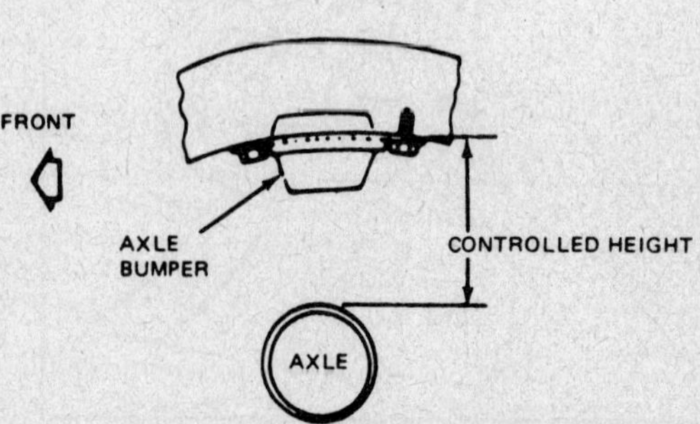

Fig. 10 Controlled height

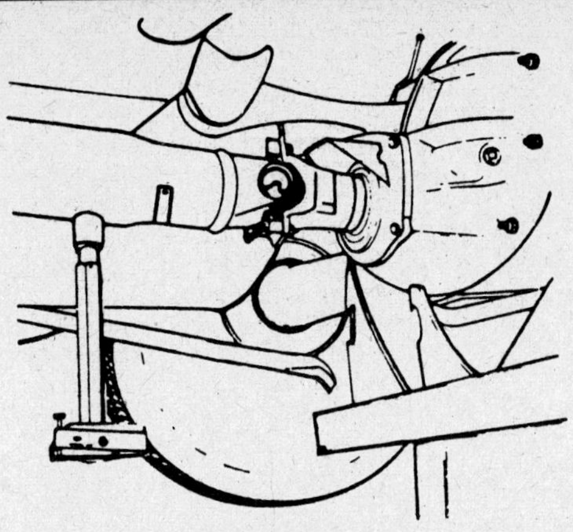

Fig. 11 Positioning driveline angle gauge on driveshaft

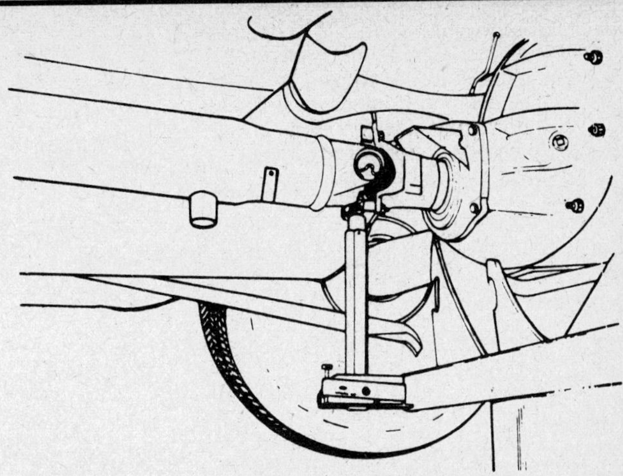

Fig. 12 Positioning driveline angle gauge on pinion U-joint cap

Electrical

CIRCUIT MALFUNCTIONS

There are three types of electrical malfunctions that cause an inoperative circuit. They are the open circuit, short circuit and grounded circuit.

Open Circuit

When there is a complete break in the normal current patch such as a broken wire, Fig. 1, it prevents the flow of electricity from the source of power to the electrical unit or from the electrical unit to the ground. In the automotive electrical circuit, the current usually flows through wires or cables, through switches and an electrical component. The component may be grounded through its mounting attachments or another wire to ground and back to the source. A break anywhere along this route results in an open circuit and a complete loss of power. A break in the circuit is an infinite high resistance. However, symptoms will appear different than the typical high resistance circuit. For example, there will be no heat created by this type of malfunction since there is no current flow. An ammeter will not produce a reading since there is no current flow. A voltmeter, depending on where it is placed in the circuit in relation to the "Open", may or may not register a reading.

A high resistance in a circuit reduces

Fig. 1 Open circuit

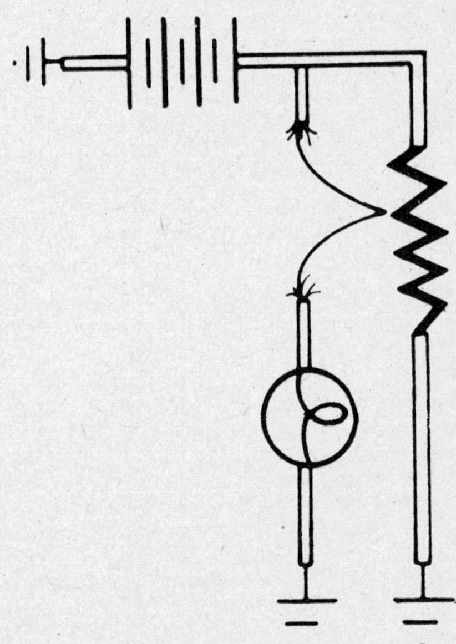

Fig. 2 Short circuit

current flow and causes the unit to operate intermittently or not at all. An open or high resistance circuit may be caused by a broken wire in the wiring harness, loose connections at terminals, broken leads or wiring within the units or poor ground connections between the unit and the ground.

Short Circuit

A short circuit, Fig. 2, is basically one that is completed the wrong way, such as two bare wires contacting each other so the current bypasses part of the circuit. When the current bypasses part of the circuit, it has found the path of least resistance and a higher current flow results. This causes blown fuses, wiring and component overheating, burned components and insulation, and inoperative components.

A short circuit causes more current flow through the conductor than the conductor can handle. This causes the conductor to overheat and, if the overload is severe or lasts long enough, will melt the wire and burn the insulation. If the wire melts through, there is no path for the current to flow and the circuit becomes an open circuit.

Grounded Circuit

A grounded circuit, Fig. 3, is similar to the short circuit since a grounded circuit also bypasses part of the normal circuit. However, the current flows directly to ground. A grounded circuit may be caused by a bare wire contacting the ground, or part of the circuit within a component contacting the frame or housing of the component. A grounded circuit may also be caused by deposits of dirt, oil or moisture around the connections or terminals since these deposits provide a path for the current to flow to ground. The current follows

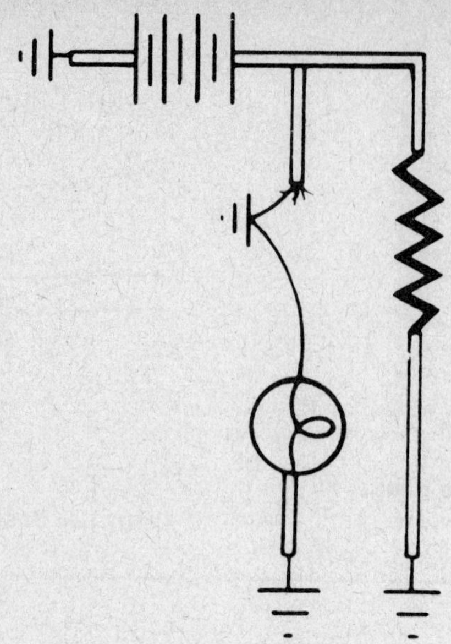

Fig. 3 Grounded circuit

the path of least resistance to complete the circuit back to ground.

CIRCUIT PROTECTION

Fuses

The most common circuit protector in the automotive electrical system is the fuse. The fuse consists of a thin wire or strip of metal enclosed in a glass tube. Some vehicles use a new type fuse where the wire is enclosed in plastic. The wire or metal strip melts when there is an overload caused by a short or grounded circuit. The fuse is designed to melt before the wiring or electrical components are damaged. The cause of the overload must be located and repaired before the new fuse is installed since the new fuse will also blow.

Fuses are rated in amperes. Since different circuits carry various amounts of current, depending upon load components and wire gauge, the properly rated fuse must be installed in the circuit. Never install a fuse with a higher amperage rating than the original.

Circuit Breakers

Circuit breakers incorporate a bimetallic strip which, when heated by an overloaded circuit, moves and opens the contacts to break the circuit. When the bimetallic strip cools, it returns to the original position, closing the contacts and completing the circuit. The circuit breaker will open and close the circuit until the overload is located and repaired or the circuit is opened with a switch.

Fusible Link

A fusible link is a short length of wire connected into a heavy feed circuit of the wiring system. The wire is generally four gauge sizes smaller than the circuit being protected and is used when the circuit is not protected by a fuse or circuit breaker. The fusible link is designed to melt in event of an overload before damage can occur to the circuit. Fusible links are marked on the insulation with the wire gauge size since the heavy insulation causes the link to appear heavier in wire size. Engine compartment wiring harnesses incorporate fusible links. When replacing a fusible link, the overload must be located and repaired and the same size fusible link installed in the circuit.

INDEX

Fuel System Service

DESCRIPTION

An automotive engine is basically a pump which produces motive force by drawing in air mixed with fuel, compressing and igniting this mixture to create a small explosion, then quickly expelling the by products of the combustion process. Acceptable engine performance, driveability and fuel economy, and proper control of exhaust emissions are dependant upon efficient combustion; with efficient combustion being primarily dependant upon the quality of air/fuel mixtures entering the engine.

To ensure efficient combustion, fuel must be thoroughly mixed with air entering the engine, the air/fuel mixture ratio must be maintained within a relatively narrow band, and the mixture must be free from contaminants such as dirt or water. The function of the fuel system is to deliver clean air and fuel to the engine, and to mix these elements in the proper proportions to ensure complete, efficient combustion under all operating conditions. In addition, the fuel system works in conjunction with emission control devices fitted to the vehicle in order to reduce emission of pollutants into the atmosphere.

Automotive fuel systems include a fuel storage tank, distributions lines and hoses, a pump to pressurize the system, air ducts and filters, carburetors or fuel injectors, and a system of collecting, storing and recycling fuel vapors so that they do not enter the atmosphere. In addition, some models are equipped with a turbocharger which uses energy from exhaust gasses to drive a turbine that forces air into the engine, increasing power output without increasing engine size.

The fuel tank, lines and pump serve as the fuel storage and distributions system, ensuring that a sufficient quantity of fuel is available to the engine under all operating conditions. Carburetors or fuel injectors are used to atomize liquid fuel to ensure thorough mixing, and to mix atomized fuel with air entering the engine. Air ducts, filters and housings (air cleaner), and the turbocharger, if equipped, are designed to provide an adequate supply of clean, temperature conditioned air to the engine intake tract.

Fuel systems on vehicles covered in this manual are calibrated to aid in controlling emission of pollutants to the atmosphere. Blow-by gasses from the crankcase and fuel vapors collected from the fuel tank are routed to the intake tract to be reburned by the Positive Crankcase Ventilation (PCV) and Evaporative Emission Control (EEC) systems respectively. Exhaust Gas Recirculation (EGR) is also used on most models to prevent formation of certain pollutants. Besides reducing emission levels, these systems allow fuel and ignition systems to be calibrated for increased engine performance and fuel economy, and therefore must be kept in proper operating condition.

INSPECTION & ADJUSTMENTS

AIR CLEANER

Periodic inspection and replacement of the engine air filter is an important step in maintaining fuel economy. A dirty, clogged air filter reduces the amount of air available to the engine, upsetting carburetor or fuel injection calibrations and causing excessive fuel consumption. The air filter should be checked frequently, and replaced if it is dirty. To remove and inspect air filter, proceed as follows:

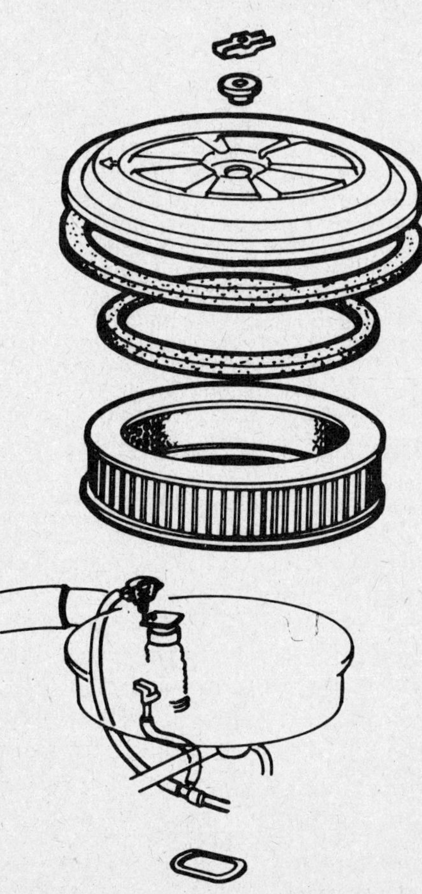

Fig. 1 Conventional carburetor mounted air cleaner exploded view

NOTE: When servicing air filter, also inspect condition air cleaner, air ducts and related vacuum hoses. Clean air cleaner assembly and repair or replace any hoses that are cracked, damaged or loose.

1. Remove nuts or release clips securing air cleaner cover using suitable tools, **Figs. 1, 2 and 3.**
2. Mark position of any hoses connected to cover and disconnect hoses, releasing clamps as needed.
3. Remove engine air filter from air cleaner housing.
4. Knock loose dirt from filter by tapping filter against a hard surface.
5. Hold filter up against light, **Fig. 4.** If light cannot be seen shining through air filter, or if it is damaged or oil soaked, filter must be replaced.
6. Remove PCV breather or air injection filters from housing, if equipped, **Figs. 5 and 6,** and replace as needed.
7. Clean loose dirt, leaves, etc. from air cleaner housing and inspect vacuum hoses, sensors and snorkel air door if equipped.
8. If housing is caked with dirt or oil soaked, remove and clean housing as follows:
   a. Disconnect air ducts and breather hoses from houisng, noting installation position.
   b. Remove fasteners securing housing to brackets, engine, etc., then carefully raise housing.
   c. Mark position of all vacuum hoses connected to housing, disconnect hoses and remove housing.
   d. Clean housing with suitable solvent, taking care not to soak sensors or air door vacuum diaphragm, then wipe housing dry.
   e. Reinstall housing ensuring that all hoses are properly connected and routed, and that housing gasket is properly positioned.

NOTE: Air cleaner mounting fasteners must be tightened securely, but not overtightened, as air cleaner housing or carburetor may be damaged.

9. Install replacement filters and air

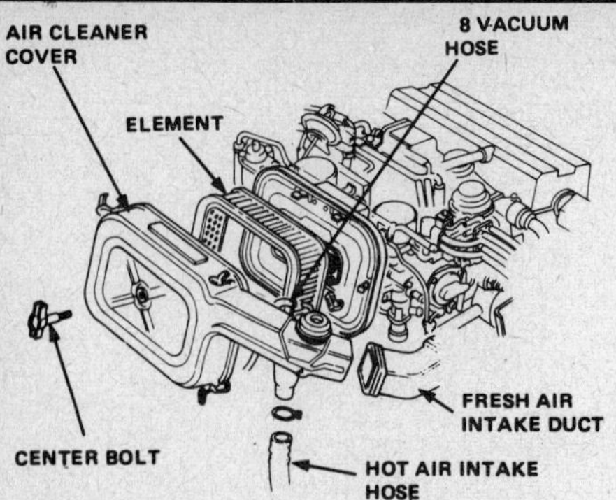

Fig. 2 Side draft carburetor air cleaner exploded view

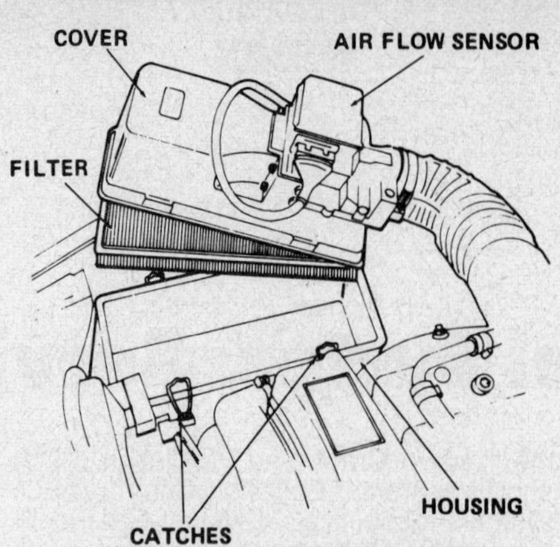

Fig. 3 Remote mounted air cleaner assembly. Typical of models w/fuel injection

Fig. 4 Air filter inspection

cleaner cover, ensuring that fasteners are secure and that hoses are properly routed.

10. Start engine, remove air duct from snorkel if equipped, and observe operation of air control door by looking through snorkel. With engine cold, door should be closed. As the engine warms up the door should gradually open.

NOTE: If air door fails to function as outlined, have system tested by a professional technician.

CARBURETORS

Carburetors consist of a group of different circuits, each of which operates at a specific engine speed to properly meter air and fuel for that mode of operation. A needle valve, operated by a float, controls entry of fuel into the carburetor, while the throttle plate controls the amount of air passing through the carburetor. Each of the different carburetor circuits use the speed of the air passing through the carburetor to draw liquid fuel from the float chamber, then vaporize and mix that fuel with air entering the engine.

The idle circuit provides air and fuel to the engine during no-load, closed throttle operation. Manifold vacuum draws air into the idle air bleed, past an opening to the float chamber and a regulating needle, and into the engine through a port located below the edge of the closed throttle plate, **Fig. 7.** Small amounts of fuel are drawn into the circuit by the vacuum created when air flows past the opening to the float chamber. This fuel is mixed with additional air drawn into the circuit from a transfer port which further atomizes the mixture. The basic air/fuel ratio is determined by the relative sizes of the air bleeds to the size of the opening into the float bowl, while the actual amount of mixture entering the engine is controlled by an adjustable needle valve. As the throttle plate is opened slightly, the transfer port becomes a fuel feed as it is exposed to manifold vacuum, providing additional fuel to compensate for increased air flow past the throttle plate.

The main metering circuit controls air/fuel metering during normal, part throttle operation. Air flowing through the carburetor passes through a narrowed section called a venturi creating a vacuum at the opening of the main feed tube, **Fig. 8.** The main feed tube is a passage that connects the venturi to the float chamber, allowing fuel to be drawn into the intake stream by the venturi vacuum. The amount of fuel drawn into the engine through the main feed tube is determined by the amount of air passing the main tube nozzle, and regulated by the size of the main jet, metering rods which open and close the jet, or by a mixture control solenoid on electronically controlled carburetors. Fuel is atomized or emulsified by the action of being drawn into the rushing air stream, and on some models, by small holes in the main tube which mix air with the fuel before it is discharged.

Additional circuits within the carburetor are used to compensate for rapid changes in throttle opening, and to provide additional enrichment for cold starting and wide open throttle operation. The two main compensation circuits are the accelerator pump circuit and the choke system. The accelerator pump is a diaphragm or plunger which is operated by the throttle linkage and injects fuel into the air stream when the throttle is opened. The choke system provides extra rich air/fuel mixtures to compensate for fuel puddling and other inefficiencies of cold engine operation.

The most common type choke is the external type flap, **Fig. 9,** which closes off the carburetor air inlet causing more fuel to be drawn into the engine through the carburetor main metering circuit. The choke enrichment device is activated manually by a cable or automatically by a temperature sensitive thermostat.

Since most of the carburetor's work is performed internally, and since calibration of the air/fuel metering is generally pre-set and sealed at the factory, relatively few adjustments are required. However, there are several important items that should be checked periodically, including cleaning and inspection of carburetor linkages, tightening of fasteners, and operational checks. At least twice a year, or whenever

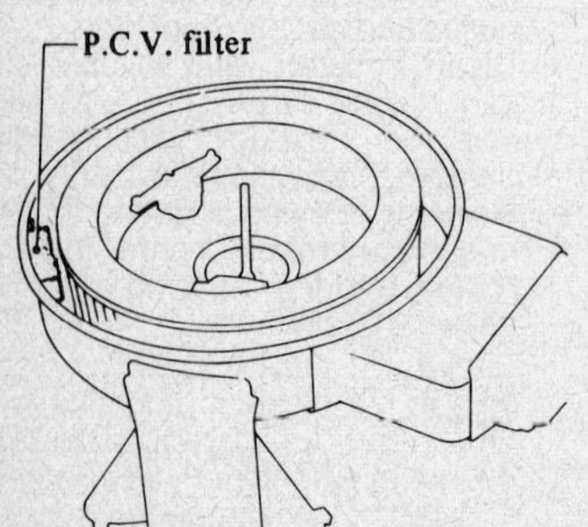

Fig. 5 Typical PCV breather filter

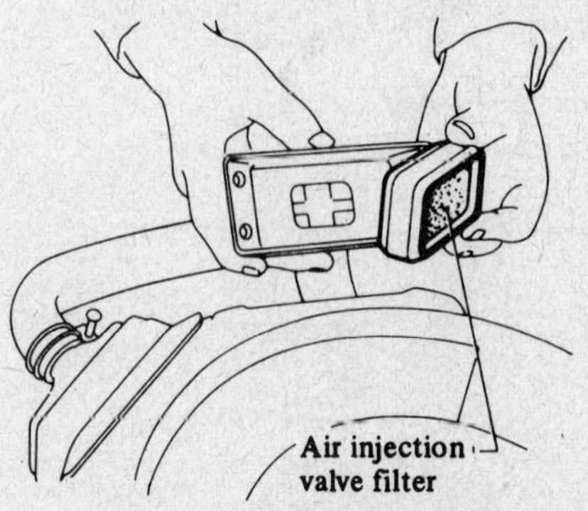

Fig. 6 Typical air cleaner mounted AIR filter

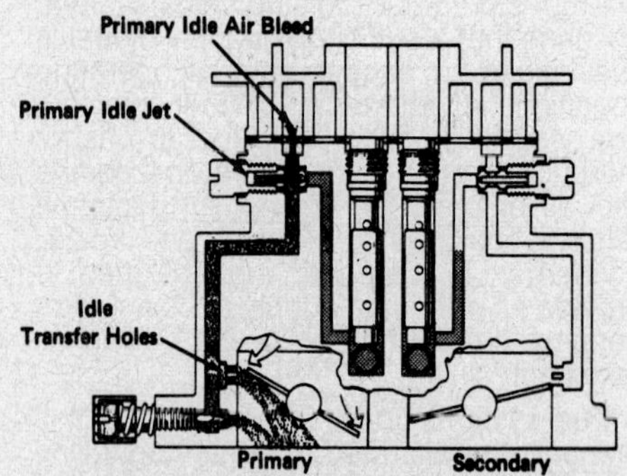

Fig. 7 Typical carburetor idle circuit operation

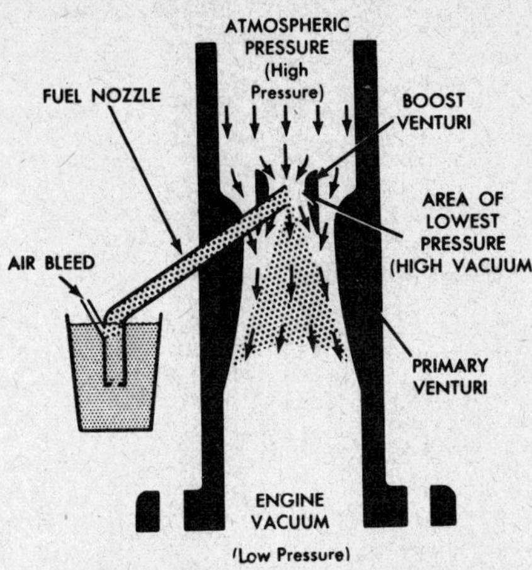

Fig. 8 Typical carburetor main metering circuit schematic

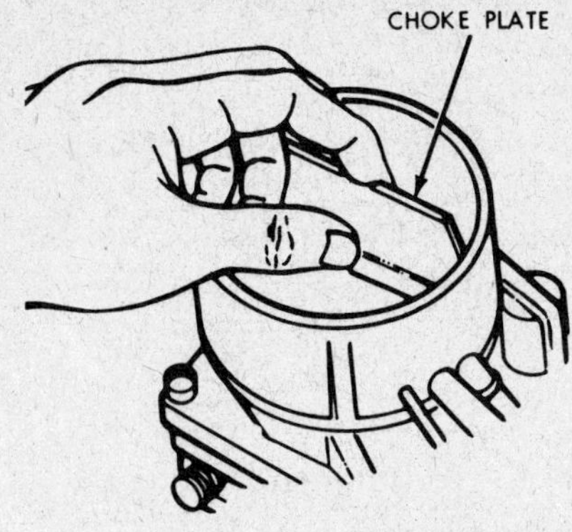

Fig. 9 Carburetor choke valve

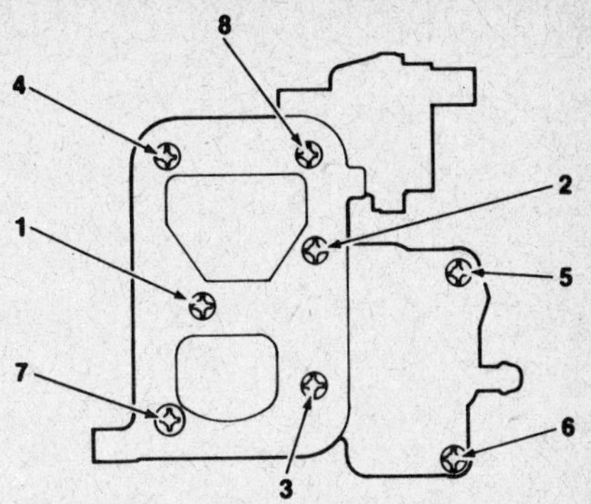

Fig. 10 Typical carburetor float bowl tightening sequence

driveability problems indicate a carburetor malfunction, perform the following inspection:

NOTE: Prior to suspecting a carburetor malfunction as the cause of driveability problems, ensure that ignition system components such as, cap, rotor, wires, spark plugs and distributor are satisfactory and properly adjusted. Also ensure that fuel and air filters, fuel distrubition system and emission control systems are satisfactory.

1. Begin with a cold engine, preferably before engine has been started after sitting overnight.
2. Remove air cleaner as needed to gain access to carburetor.
3. If possible, leave vacuum hoses connected to carburetor and engine; if this is not possible, plug open vacuum ports with short length of hose, stoppered with screws.

NOTE: Ensure that air cleaner is secured so that it does not interfere with carburetor linkages or fall into moving engine components.

4. Visually inspect carburetor body, throttle linkage, external choke linkages and fuel lines.
5. If components are loose, damaged, or if components appear to be missing, repair as needed.

NOTE: If you discover loose or missing components during inspection and are not sure as to how or where they should be installed, have carburetor inspected by a professional technician.

6. Ensure that float bowl cover retaining screws are secure, checking them with a suitable screw driver. Do not overtighten screws.
7. Ensure that carburetor mounting nuts are securely tightened, using a suitable wrench.
8. Check operation of automatic choke system as follows:
   a. Have an assistant fully depress then release accelerator pedal while you observe choke valve and linkages, **Figs. 9 and 11.**
   b. When pedal is released, choke valve should close fully and throttle should be held open slightly by fast idle linkage.
   c. Start engine while observing choke. If engine stalls, fully depress and release accelerator and restart engine.

   NOTE: If engine stalls continuously, carburetor should be checked by a professional technician.

   d. Engine should start and begin to run at fast idle. When engine starts, choke pull-off should open choke valve ⅛ to ½ inch.
   e. Allow engine to run for 1½-5 minutes then quickly depress and release accelerator.
   f. Choke valve should open further and engine should return to normal idle speed.
   g. Continue to observe choke as engine warms up. Choke should be fully open within 5-10 minutes of engine operation. Stop engine.
9. If choke mechanism fails to operate as outlined in previous step, check for binding or sticking choke plate and linkages, and repair as needed.

NOTE: If choke system malfunctions but no external problem is evident, have carburetor checked by professional technician.

10. Clean carburetor linkages and choke valve with suitable spray cleaner, taking care not to spray excessive cleaner into carburetor throat.
11. Lubricate linkages with multi-purpose grease, then restart engine.
12. Allow engine to warm fully, then if you have suitable test equipment, check idle speed as outlined on Emission Control Information label.
13. Road test vehicle, noting performance.
14. If engine stalls, hesitates, or surges at steady speed, and other engine systems are operating properly, have carburetor checked by a professional technician.

GASOLINE FUEL INJECTION

On models equipped with fuel injection, gasoline is forced under high pressure into the intake air stream in a fine mist, similar to the spray pattern of an aerosol can. The action of forcing liquid fuel through a very small opening creates this mist, sufficiently atomizing the fuel so that it readily mixes with the air. The orifice and plunger assembly that produces this mist is called a fuel injector.

Two basic types of fuel injectors are used, depending upon the placement of the injectors in the intake air stream. The most common type of fuel injection used is the multi-point system, which places simple plunger and orifice assemblies, **Fig. 12,** in position to spray fuel directly toward each intake valve. The second type of injection system used, called single point or throttle body injection, uses a plunger and orifice assembly mounted in a housing that includes a throttle plate and venturi, similar to a carburetor, **Fig. 13.** Like a carburetor, the throttle body injectors are centrally mounted on an intake manifold, and fuel is sprayed into the manifold and routed to the valves through manifold runners.

Fuel injector operation, and therefore the amount of fuel injected, is controlled either electronically or mechanically, with both type systems using an air flow sensor to determine the amount of fuel necessary for engine operating conditions. On electronically controlled systems, a small computer monitors air intake flow and other engine operating conditions, computes the proper amount of fuel necessary, then pulses the injectors accordingly. Injectors used on electronically controlled systems are operated by small, integral solenoids, that allow fuel to be injected whenever they receive a pulse from the computer. On most mechanically controlled systems, fuel is injected continuously, with the amount of fuel injected being controlled by fuel pressure within the system. Fuel pressure in mechanical systems is controlled by an air flow sensor, which increases fuel pressure as the amount of air entering the engine increases.

As testing and adjustment of fuel injection systems is a specialized operation, requiring use of special tools, most system

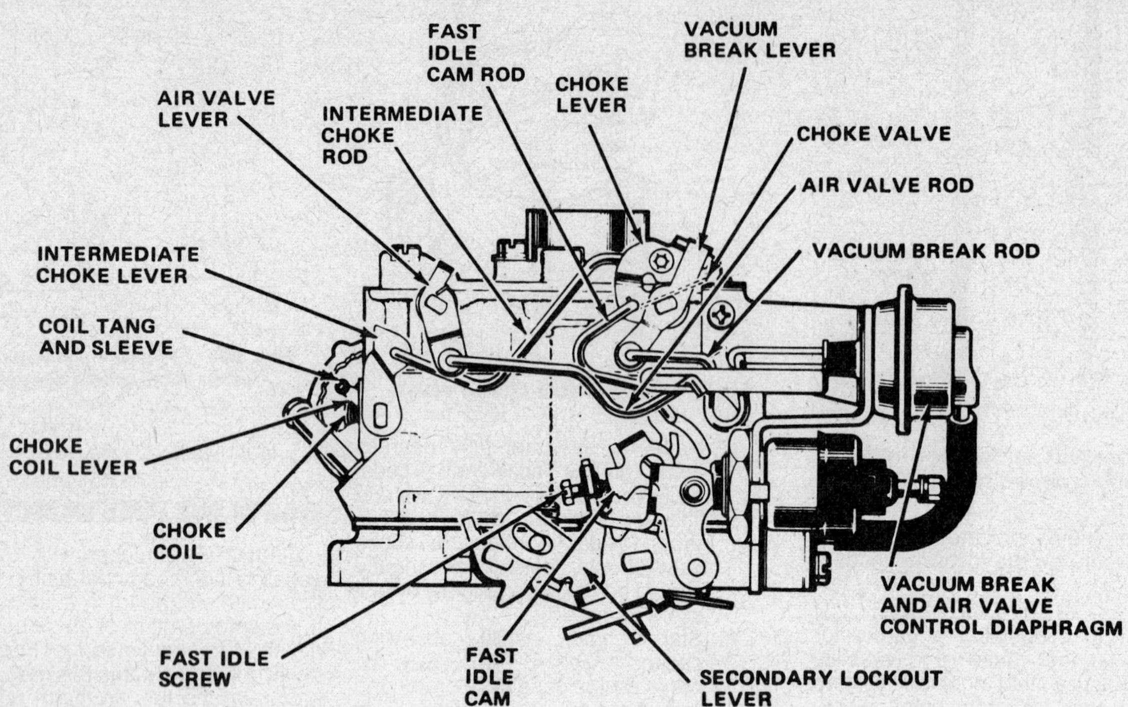

Fig. 11 Typical automatic choke linkages

checks should be performed by a professional technician that has been properly trained in system service. However, a periodic inspection of the system will aid in heading off potential trouble. Perform fuel injection inspection as follows:

CAUTION: The fuel delivery system is under extremely high pressure, and opening the fuel system without first relieving this pressure may cause personal injury, fire or damage to the vehicle.

1. Inspect fuel delivery lines and hoses, ensuring that pipe fittings are not leaking and that hoses are not cracked, chafed or oil soaked.
2. On electronically controlled systems, check wiring between system components. Ensure that wiring is properly routed and not chafed or broken, and that connections are secure and free from corrosion.
3. Check ducting and filter leading to flow sensor inlet. Ensure that filter is clean and that duct is free from obstructions.
4. Ensure that duct between flow sensor and manifold, if equipped, is not cut, broken or damaged. Damage to this duct will upset system calibration.

DIESEL FUEL INJECTION

On diesel engines, the fuel delivery system not only supplies fuel for combustion, but the timing of the fuel delivery is an essential factor in initiating and controlling the combustion process. Diesel fuel injectors spray fuel directly into the combustion chamber at the precise moment when engine compression has raised temperatures in the combustion chamber to a temperature that will ignite the fuel. Therefore, the injection of the fuel is what begins the combustion process in a diesel engine.

In order to precisely control fuel injection, diesel engines use a pump that is timed to the engine's mechanical rotation. This pump both pressurizes the fuel and times its injection to the mechanical rotation of the engine in order to control the combustion process. As each piston is nearing top dead center on it's compression stroke, a mechanically controlled plunger in the pump that controls the injector for that cylinder raises fuel pressure to a level that will open the injector. When the injector opens, fuel is sprayed into the cylinder, combustion occurs, and the injector closes due to the resulting pressure drop. This process occurs for each cylinder in turn, with the total amount of fuel delivered during each cycle being determined by an internal fuel pressure governor.

In order to precisely control fuel pressure and delivery, the injection pump is built to extremely close tolerances. In general, periodic maintenance of the system is limited to ensuring that fuel supplied to the pump is clean and free from moisture. If a system malfunction is suspected, the system should be checked by a professional technician, trained in diesel fuel system repair.

FUEL PUMP, FILTER, TANK & LINES

A commonly overlooked item in most fuel systems, and perhaps one of the most important maintenance items, is the fuel distribution system, **Fig. 14.** Because of precise calibration of carburetors and fuel injection systems, an adequate supply of clean fuel is essential. Even small traces of dirt or moisture can completely upset air/-fuel metering calibration, and in many instances, these contaminants can prevent an engine from running.

Performing a simple inspection of the fuel distribution system, on a regular basis, will often uncover impending failures, and can prevent malfunctions of the carburetor or fuel injection units.

1. Start at the rear of the vehicle by removing and inspecting the fuel tank filler cap. Ensure that gasket is satisfactory and cap is not damaged.
2. A small amount of air may be heard entering or leaving the tank, but if a long, loud rush of air is heard, cap or evaporative emission system may be malfunctioning.

NOTE: If tank is not being properly vented by the cap and/or evaporative emission system, have vehicle checked by a professional technician.

3. Inspect condition of fuel tank. If tank is damaged, or if there are signs of leakage, tank should be repaired.
4. Inspect rubber fuel hoses between tank and fuel lines or outboard electric pump, and between fuel lines and engine.
5. If hoses are cracked, leaking or deteriorated, they should be replaced.

CAUTION: On models with fuel injection, the fuel system is under high pressure. If system is opened without first relieving the pressure, personal injury or damage to vehicle may result.

6. Inspect metal fuel lines on chassis and engine. If fuel lines are crushed, badly

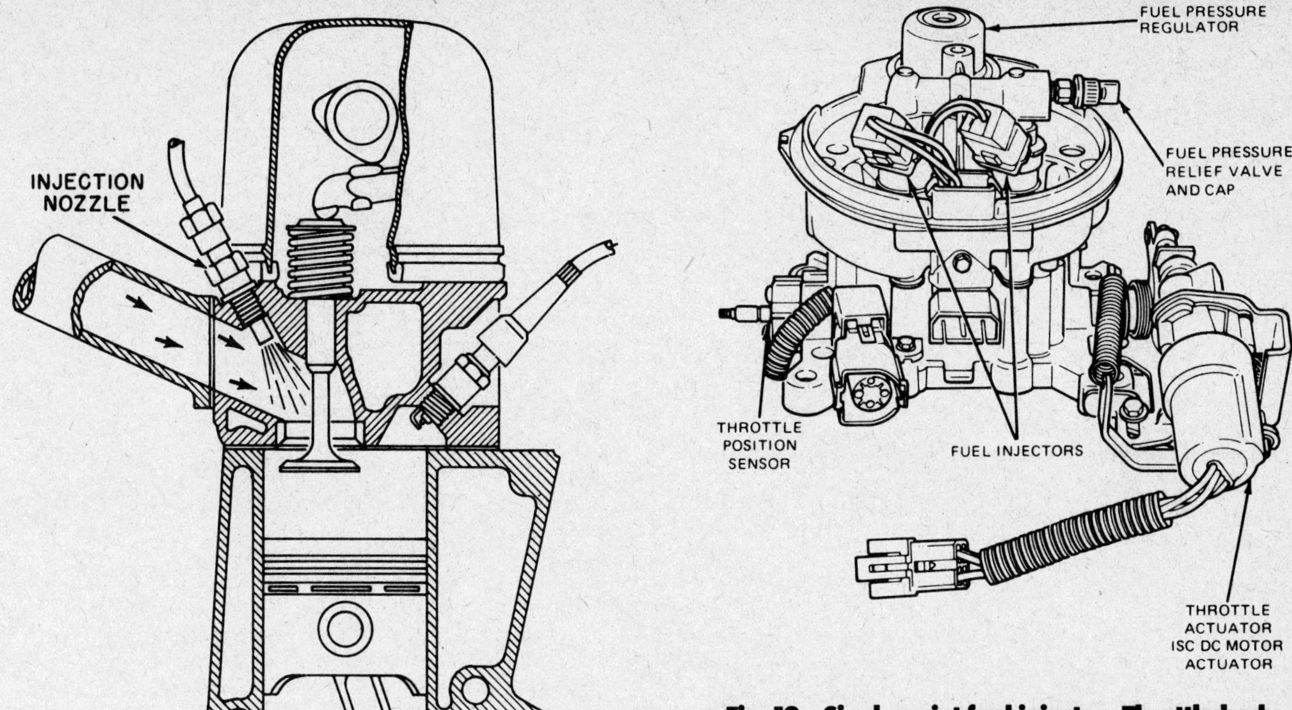

Fig. 13 Single point fuel injector. Throttle body type

Fig. 12 Multi-point fuel injector installation

rusted or leaking, they should be repaired or replaced.

7. Inspect fuel pump for leakage. Operate engine and listen for abnormal noises from pump. If a defect is suspected, have pump checked.
8. Remove fuel filter as outlined in "Fuel Filter, Replace," cut filter apart and check for contamination.
9. If filter shows signs of excessive contamination with sediment or rust, fuel system should be flushed by a professional technician.
10. On models with diesel engine, place drain pan under water separator in fuel filter and tank.
11. Open petcock or loosen drain plug and drain water from separator, just until fuel begins to run out, then tighten drain.

CAUTION: Draining fuel from system may present a fire hazzard. Make sure that no sources of sparks or open flame are in area where system is drained.

EVAPORATIVE EMISSION CONTROL (VAPOR STORAGE) SYSTEM

The evaporative emission system is de-

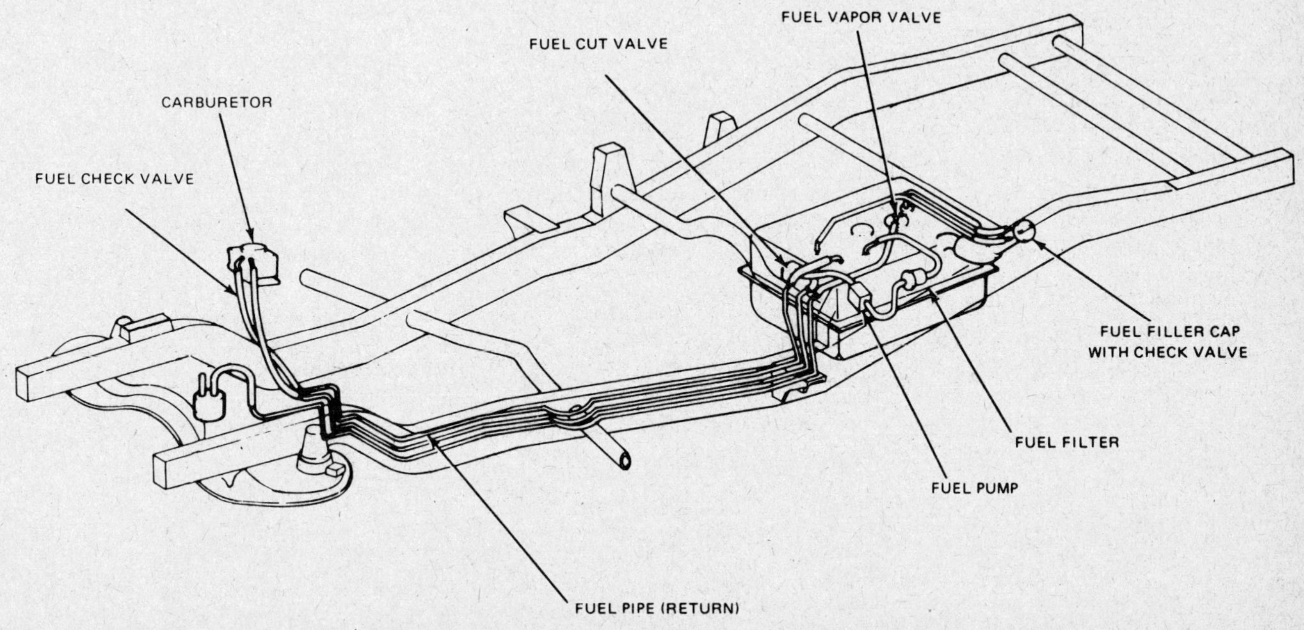

Fig. 14 Fuel distribution system schematic

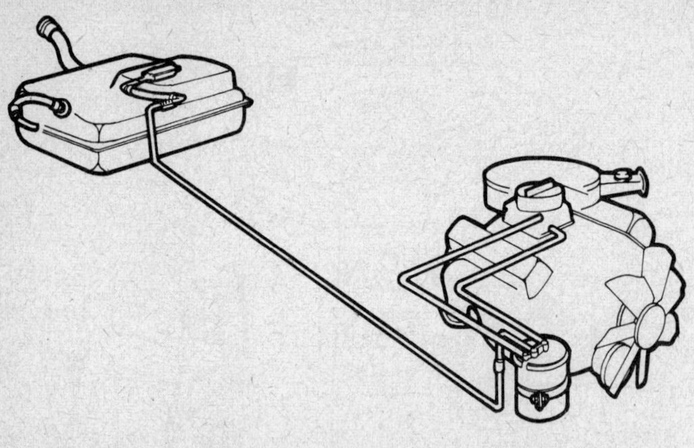

Fig. 15 Evaporative emission control system schematic

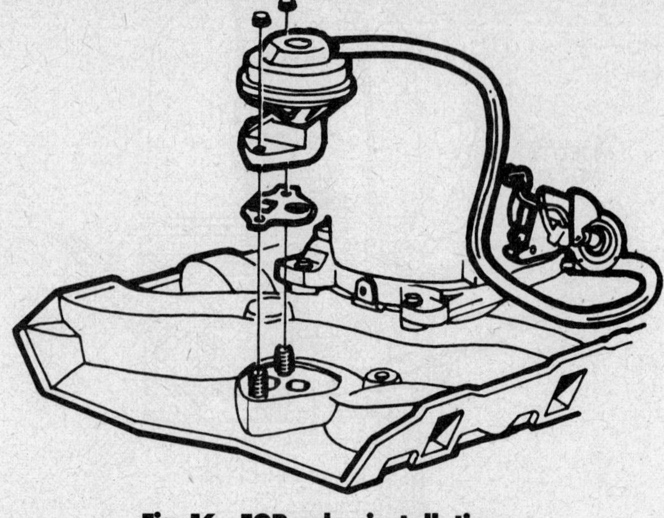

Fig. 16 EGR valve installation

signed to collect vapors formed in the fuel tank and carburetor float chamber, if equipped, store these vapors in an activated charcoal canister, and route the vapors into the engine to be burned. A series of hoses, valves, and a vapor separator are used to collect these vapors and route them to the storage canister and from the canister to the engine, **Fig 15.** Under certain operating conditions, such as during cold engine operation or full throttle operation, a purge valve opens allowing intake manifold vacuum to draw air through the storage canister. Vapors are drawn from the canister and burned, providing added mixture enrichment. This allows for added fuel economy as well as preventing emission of vapors to the atmosphere.

The evaporative emission system requires little service other than periodic inspection of hoses, and if equipped, replacement of the storage canister filter. However, if strong fuel odors are present in the engine or rear compartments, or if fuel tank venting is suspect, system operation should be checked.

EXHAUST GAS RECIRCULATION

Most models use Exhaust Gas Recirculation (EGR) to lower combustion temperatures and reduce formation of certain pollutants. Metered amounts of exhaust gas are allowed to enter the intake tract under certain operating conditions, reducing the amount of air/fuel mixture entering each cylinder while still allowing adequate cylinder filling. Reducing the amount of burnable mixture not only reduces combustion temperatures to prevent formation of NOx emissions, but actually increases fuel economy in two ways. Reducing the amount of air/fuel mixture in the cylinder reduces the overall amount of fuel used, and reducing the combustion temperature allows ignition timing to be calibrated for increased fuel economy and greater engine performance. Therefore, ensuring proper operation of the EGR system is essential to maintaining adequate engine performance and fuel economy.

Check operation of the exhaust gas recirculation system as follows:

1. Start engine and allow to warm up.
2. With engine at curb idle speed, disconnect vacuum hose from EGR valve and plug hose to prevent vacuum leak.
3. Attach hand vacuum pump to EGR valve fitting.
4. Operate pump to apply at least 4 inches of vacuum to valve.
5. Observe that engine begins to misfire and run roughly. If there is no change in engine performance, EGR valve is defective or gas passages are clogged with exhaust deposits.
6. Disconnect vacuum hose from valve.
7. Remove the two bolts holding valve to manifold or spacer, and remove valve, **Fig. 16.**
8. Clean old gasket off mating surface with scraper and wire brush.
9. Inspect and clean out gas passages in manifold or spacer with wire gun-bore brush or small round wire brush.
10. Exhaust deposits can be removed from EGR valve with wire brush or by tapping side of valve with soft mallet.
11. Ensure valve stem and diaphragm can move freely by pushing on diaphragm.
12. Check diaphragm for leakage by applying vacuum with hand vacuum pump.
13. Install new valve or reinstall old valve with new gasket and tighten bolts.
14. Reconnect vacuum hose and check operation. With engine warmed up, valve should be seen or felt to operate when throttle opening is increased beyond idle.
15. If valve fails to operate when engine is accelerated, check vacuum hose between valve and engine and repair as needed.
16. If hoses are satisfactory, have system tested by a professional technician.

CRANKCASE VENTILATION (PCV) SYSTEM

Crankcase ventilation is used to evacuate pressure build-up in the engine created by the reciprocating action of the pistons and to prevent blow-by gasses (small quantities of partially burned mixture that "blow" past the piston rings) from entering the atmosphere. Whenever the engine is running, crankcase gasses are drawn into the intake manifold or air cleaner through an oil separator assembly or spring loaded vent valve, **Figs. 17 and 18,** and reburned in the engine. A filter/breather element allows air to be drawn through the engine by intake manifold vacuum or the vacuum created in the air cleaner, preventing pressure or vacuum build-up in the crankcase.

Proper operation of the crankcase ventilation system is essential for preventing excessive oil consumption and leaks, rough engine idle and stalling. Check PCV system and valves as follows:

1. Inspect hoses between PCV valve and intake manifold or between oil separator and manifold or air cleaner.
2. Replace hoses that are damaged or deteriorated.
3. Inspect breather element in air cleaner or valve cover. Replace element or clean mesh strainer if clogged or dirty.
4. Check PCV valve as follows:
   a. Pull valve from grommet in valve cover or manifold, leaving hose connected, **Fig. 19.**
   b. Start engine and place thumb over end of valve. If no vacuum is present, check hose and manifold for restrictions.
   c. Stop engine and shake valve. Valve should rattle with a sharp metallic sound. If no rattle is heard or if sound is dull, replace valve.

FUEL FILTER

REPLACE

Several type fuel filters are used on imported vehicles. Checking and replacing the filter at regular intervals can ensure that proper vehicle performance is maintained. The fuel filter should always be inspected and replaced if signs of fuel starvation are noted such as loss of power on hills or at high speeds.

NOTE: Fuel systems on gasoline engines equipped with fuel injection are under high pressure which must be relieved prior to

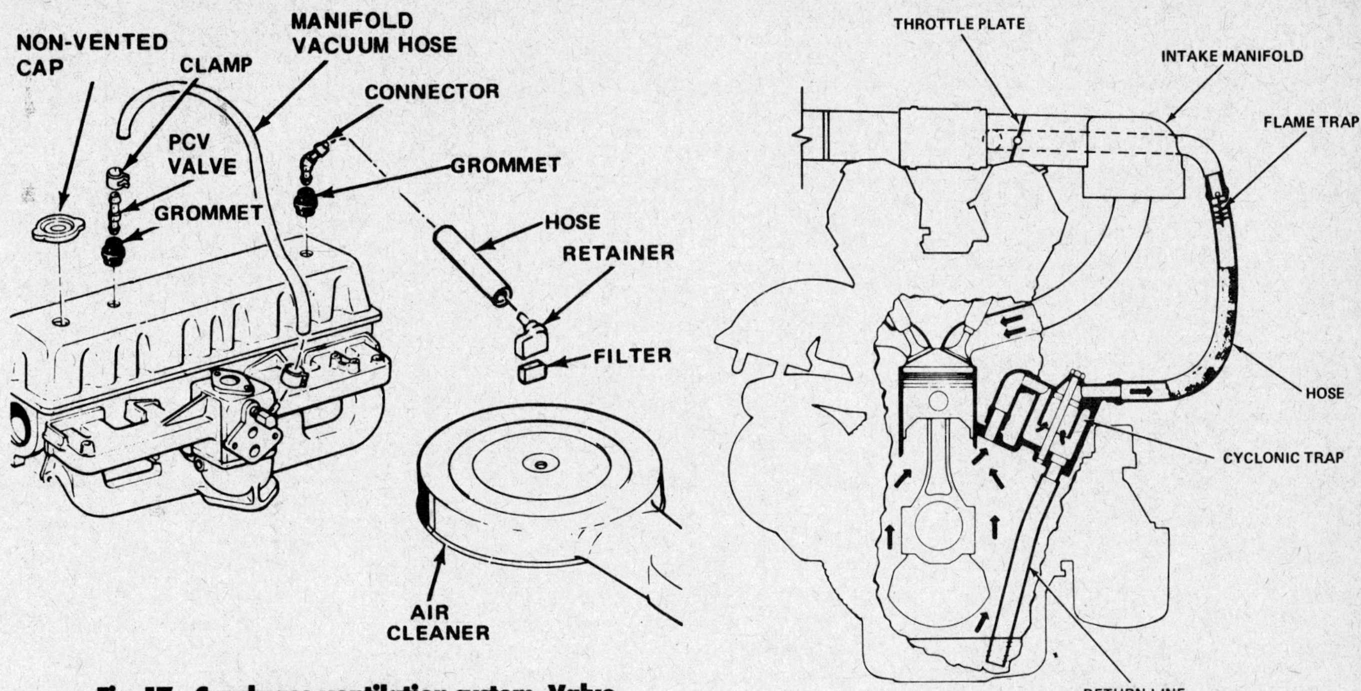

Fig. 17 Crankcase ventilation system. Valve controlled type

Fig. 18 Crankcase ventilation system. Oil separator type

opening the system. On most diesel engines, the fuel system must be bled after the fuel filter is replaced. Replacing fuel filters on either of these type vehicles requires specialized knowledge and is best left to the professional technician.

Refer to the owner's manual to identify and locate the fuel filter on your vehicle, then use following procedures as a guide for replacement.

CAUTION: Use extreme caution when opening and working with the fuel system. Work only in a well ventilated area and do not create any sparks. Always place a suitable drain pan under connections to be opened and wipe up spilled fuel immediately.

IN-LINE FILTER

1. Remove fuel tank cap.
2. If filter is located under vehicle, raise vehicle as needed and support with suitable stands.
3. Remove shrouds or other components, as needed, to gain access to filter, then place drain pan under filter.
4. Release filter from bracket, if equipped.
5. Loosen clamps securing hoses to filter and slide clamps away from filter, **Fig. 20.**

SERVICE NOTE: To prevent excessive fuel spillage when disconnecting filter, clamp hoses on either side of filter with suitable locking pliers. Tighten pliers just enough to close fuel hose or hose may be damaged.

6. Disconnect hoses from old filter and plug hoses to prevent fuel spillage.
7. Check condition of clamps and replace as needed.
8. Remove plugs and quickly install replacement filter, ensuring that filter is installed in proper direction and that hoses are fully seated on filter.
9. Slide clamps toward filter, ensure that clamps and hoses are properly positioned, **Fig. 21,** then tighten clamps securely.
10. Install filter in bracket, then remount other components removed.

CARBURETOR MOUNTED FILTERS

Externally Mounted

1. Loosen spring clip or clamp at fuel line end of hose and slide upward over flange of fuel line.
2. Unscrew filter from carburetor and remove filter with hose from vehicle.
3. Screw new filter into carburetor.

CAUTION: Screw new filter in only until snug. Filter usually will not fit flush against carburetor. Overtightening of filter will cause breakage with neck of filter becoming lodged in carburetor.

4. Install new hose, if provided, or original hose on filter and insert fuel line into other end of hose, securing with spring clips or clamps, **Fig. 21.**

Internally Mounted

1. Hold large nut with suitable wrench

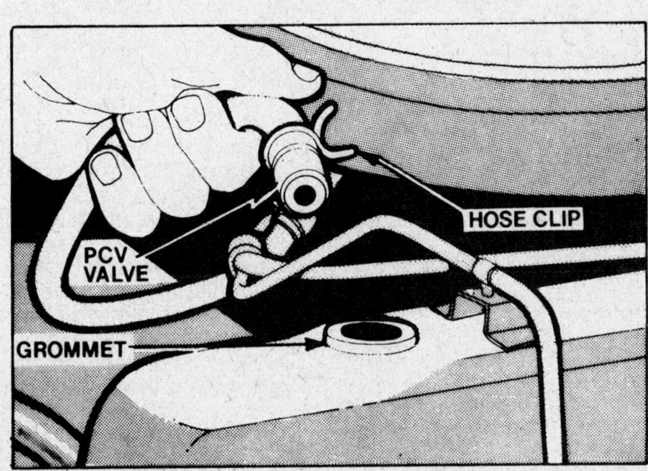

Fig. 19 PCV valve inspection

and loosen small nut, **Fig. 22.**

CAUTION: Use a flare nut wrench on small nut. Use of a conventional wrench will distort nut. Break nut loose by manually rapping wrench rather than pushing or pulling it.

2. Remove large nut together with gas filter, spring, and gaskets, noting installed direction of filter, **Fig. 23.**
3. Install paper gasket in large nut, then the replacement filter, ensuring that filter is installed in correct direction.
4. Insert spring into carburetor inlet, then the nut with filter. Ensure that gasket is properly positioned on nut.
5. Tighten nut until snug.
6. Hand start fuel line flare nut into large nut.
7. Hold large nut with suitable wrench, and tighten flare nut until snug.

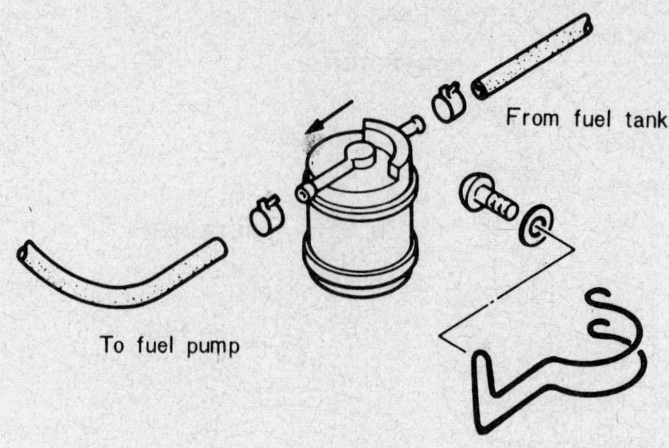

Fig. 20 In-line type fuel filter

CARBURETOR

REPLACE

The carburetor should only be replaced if a thorough engine diagnosis indicates the carburetor as the only possible cause for a driveability problem. It is usually wise to have the engine checked by a professional technician before condemning the carburetor as defective. And in many cases, even if the carburetor is malfunctioning, it can be repaired by a properly trained technician at a cost significantly less than the cost of a replacement unit.

Prior to replacing the carburetor on your vehicle, ensure that your have the proper replacement unit, tools and skills to complete the task. Read the replacement procedure for your vehicle and inspect the vehicle, keeping in mind that no procedure can take into account all of the possible variables of design, optional equipment, etc. During the replacement procedure, observe the following precautions:

1. Mark all components prior to removal and keep components in order once removed.
2. Mark the adjustment positions of all linkages to serve as a base adjustment once the new carburetor has been installed.
3. Take precautions not to allow nuts, washers or any other component to fall into the engine, as the engine may have to be disassembled to remove something that falls inside.
4. Do not allow dirt or any other foreign material to enter the engine, fuel or vacuum systems as they will impair engine operation.
5. Thoroughly clean all sealing surfaces prior to installing new parts.
6. Always replace gaskets, O-rings and seals.
7. Adjust carburetor to your engine using listed specifications and the underhood Emission Control Information Label as a guide.

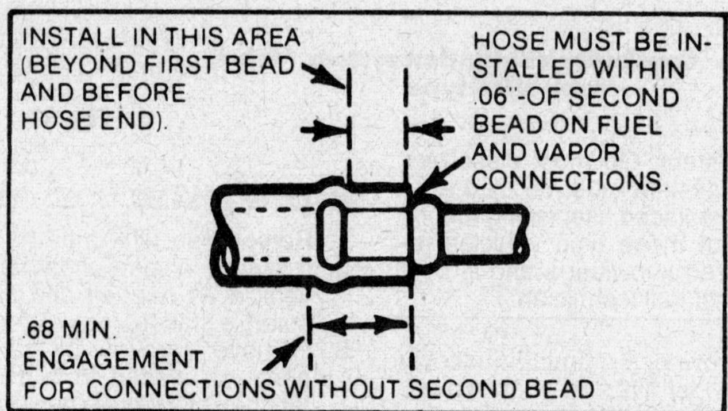

Fig. 21 Fuel hose and clamp installation

CAUTION: Gasoline is a dangerous substance. Use extreme caution when opening and working with the fuel system. Work only in a well ventilated area and do not create any sparks. Always place a suitable drain pan under connections and wipe up spilled fuel immediately.

DATSUN/NISSAN

1. Disconnect battery ground cable, then remove air cleaner assembly.
2. Mark position of vacuum hoses, then disconnect hoses from carburetor.
3. Release clamps and disconnect fuel lines from carburetor.
4. Disconnect throttle cable or torsion link from throttle lever.
5. Disconnect electrical connectors from choke, idle solenoids or fuel solenoids, as equipped, noting position for assembly.
6. Remove nuts securing carburetor to manifold, then lift carburetor from manifold.
7. Reverse procedure to install, using a new base gasket.

DODGE/PLYMOUTH & MITSUBISHI

1. Disconnect battery ground cable and remove air cleaner assembly.
2. Partially drain cooling system as outlined in "General Maintenance Section," then loosen clamp(s) and disconnect coolant hose(s) from choke cover.
3. Mark position of vacuum hoses between carburetor and engine, then disconnect hoses from carburetor.
4. Loosen clamp and disconnect fuel hose from carburetor.
5. Remove retaining pin from throttle control rod, or loosen throttle cable at mounting bracket, then disconnect throttle linkage from lever.
6. Remove mounting nuts, then lift carburetor from manifold.
7. Thoroughly clean mounting surface on manifold, then install new base gasket, ensuring that gasket is properly aligned with ports in manifold.
8. Reverse procedure to complete installation, tightening mounting nuts evenly to prevent vacuum leaks.

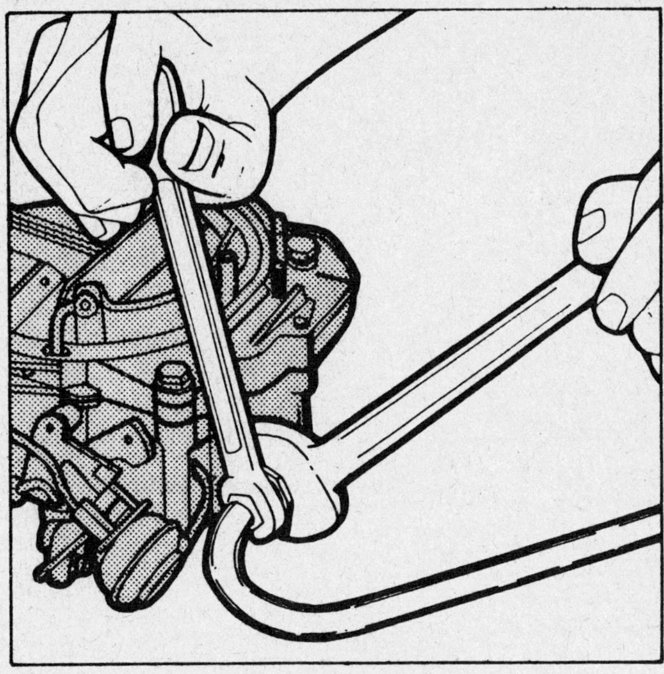

Fig. 22 Disconnecting fuel line from carburetor

HONDA

Exc. 1983-86 Prelude

1. Disconnect battery ground cable and remove air cleaner assembly.
2. Mark position of vacuum hoses between carburetor and engine, then disconnect hoses from carburetor.
3. Manually open throttle, disconnect throttle cable from lever, then, if necessary, loosen nuts and remove cable housing from bracket.
4. Disconnect electrical connectors from choke and, if equipped, fuel cut solenoids.
5. Release clamp and disconnect fuel hose from carburetor.
6. Remove mounting nuts, lock washers and spring washers, noting position for installation, then lift carburetor from manifold.
7. Mark position of vacuum hoses connected to carburetor insulator, then disconnect hoses and remove insulator assembly.
8. Replace insulator gasket and O-rings, then reverse procedure to install.

NOTE: It is adviseable to replace spring washers during installation.

1983 Prelude

1. Disconnect battery ground cable, partially drain cooling system as outlined in "General Maintenance Section" and remove air cleaner assembly.
2. Mark position of vacuum hoses between carburetor and engine, then disconnect vacuum hoses from carburetor.
3. Manually open throttle, disconnect throttle cable from lever, loosen cable retaining nuts and remove cable housing from bracket.
4. Disconnect vacuum hose from throttle opener, remove 3 screws (A), **Fig. 25,** then the steel vacuum lines.
5. Disconnect electrical connector to choke and coolant hoses from thermowax valve and right end of intake manifold.
6. Support carburetors, loosen insulator band clamps, then remove carburetors from insulators.
7. Reverse procedure to install, ensuring that carburetors are fully seated in insulators, **Fig. 26.**
8. Refill and bleed cooling system as outlined in "General Maintenance Section."

Fig. 23 Carburetor mounted fuel filter assembly. Internal type

1984-86 Prelude

1. Disconnect battery ground cable and partially drain cooling system as outlined in "General Maintenance Section."
2. Disconnect hoses and remove air cleaner cover, noting position of hoses for installation.
3. Disconnect breather hose from valve cover, vacuum hoses from air cleaner base and electrical connectors to solenoid, noting position for installation.
4. Remove 2 retaining bolts and 4 nuts, screen and flange assemblies and the air cleaner base.

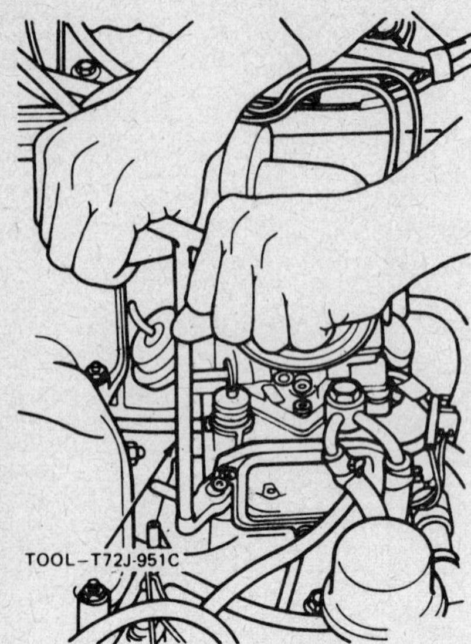

Fig. 24 Removing carburetor mounting nuts w/offset wrench

5. Mark position of vacuum hoses between carburetors and engine, then disconnect hoses from carburetors.
6. Manually open throttle, disconnect throttle cable from lever, loosen retaining nuts and remove cable housing from bracket.
7. Disconnect hoses from vacuum tube manifold, noting position for installation.
8. Disconnect 3 coolant hoses from thermowax valve.
9. Disconnect hoses from canister at air vent cut-off solenoid valve and vacuum tube manifold.
10. Disconnect electrical connectors from carburetor noting position for installation.
11. Remove fuel hose from vacuum tube manifold.
12. Support carburetors, loosen insulator band clamps and remove carburetors from insulators.
13. Reverse procedure to install, ensuring that carburetors are fully seated in insulators, **Fig. 26.**
14. Refill and bleed cooling system as outlined in "General Maintenance Section."

HYUNDAI

1. Disconnect battery ground cable.
2. Drain cooling system, then remove air cleaner assembly.
3. Disconnect throttle cable and vacuum hoses from carburetor.
4. Disconnect TPS and solenoid valve electrical connectors from carburetor.
5. Disconnect fuel lines from carburetor inlet nipples.
6. Remove carburetor attaching bolts and the carburetor.
7. Reverse procedure to install.

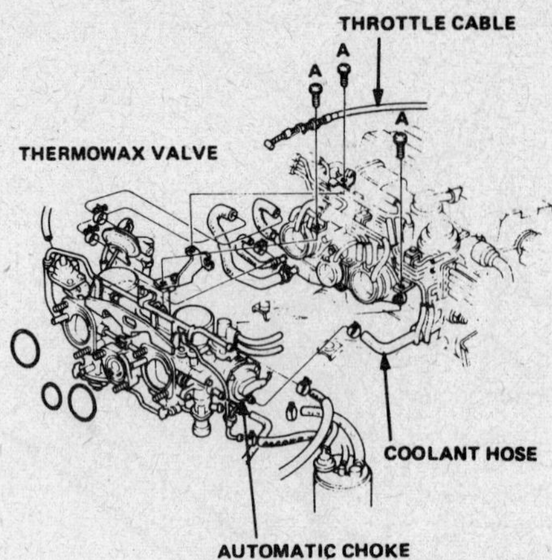

Fig. 25 Carburetor removal. 1983 Prelude

ISUZU

1. Disconnect battery ground cable.
2. Disconnect hoses from AIR pump and remove air cleaner assembly.
3. On models equipped with external throttle return spring, remove spring.
4. On all models, mark position of vacuum hoses between carburetor and engine, then disconnect hoses from carburetor.
5. Disconnect electrical connectors from choke and fuel solenoids, and remove clamp from water outlet pipe, as equipped.
6. Disconnect throttle cable, and if equipped, transmission detent cable, from throttle lever.
7. Release clamps and disconnect fuel supply and return hoses from carburetor.
8. Remove retaining nuts and washers, using a suitable offset wrench, **Fig. 24,** then lift carburetor from manifold.
9. Reverse procedure to install, using a new base gasket.

MAZDA

1. Disconnect battery ground cable and remove air cleaner assembly.
2. Disconnect electrical connectors to fuel and idle solenoids and electric choke, as equipped, noting position for installation.
3. Mark position of vacuum hoses between carburetor and engine, then disconnect hoses from carburetor.
4. Disconnect accelerator and cruise control cables from throttle lever, and on models with external throttle return spring, remove spring.
5. On models with manual choke, loosen retaining clamp and screw then disconnect cable.
6. On models with metering oil pump, remove connecting link and disconnect tubes and hoses from carburetor, noting position for installation.
7. Loosen clamps and disconnect fuel

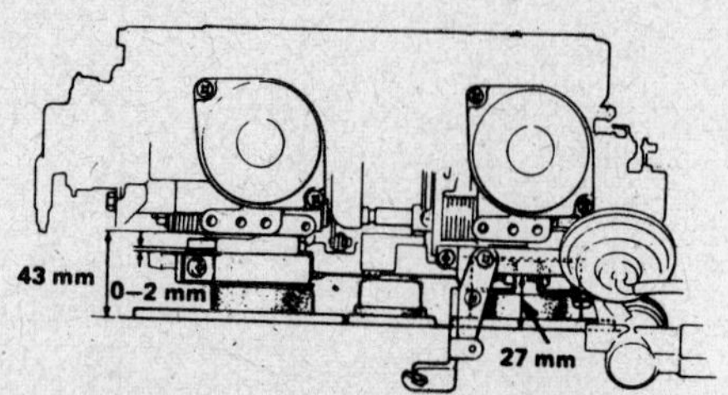

Fig. 26 Carburetor installation dimensions. 1983-86 Prelude

supply and return hoses, and if equipped, remove air vent solenoid coupler.
8. Remove mounting nuts, then lift carburetor from manifold.
9. Reverse procedure to install, using a new base gasket.

RENAULT LE CAR

1. Disconnect battery ground cable and remove air cleaner duct and adapter.
2. Mark position of vacuum hoses between carburetor and engine, then disconnect hoses from carburetor.
3. Loosen retaining clamp and screw, then disconnect choke cable from carburetor.
4. Disconnect control cables from throttle lever.
5. Loosen clamps and disconnect fuel supply and return lines.
6. Remove mounting nuts and washers, then lift carburetor from engine.
7. Reverse procedure to install, noting the following:
   a. Use a new base gasket during installation.
   b. Adjust choke cable so that choke valve closes fully.

SPECTRUM

1. Disconnect battery ground cable.
2. Drain cooling system, then remove air cleaner assembly.
3. Disconnect vacuum hoses, electrical connector, fuel line and throttle cable from carburetor.
4. Remove carburetor attaching bolts from bottom of intake manifold, then lift carburetor from engine.
5. Reverse procedure to install. Replace insulator holding EFE heater in between with new packings.

SPRINT

1. Disconnect battery ground cable.
2. Drain cooling system, then remove air cleaner assembly.
3. Disconnect vacuum hoses, electrical connectors, fuel line and throttle cable from carburetor.
4. Remove carburetor attaching nuts and

the carburetor.

5. Reverse procedure to install, using a new insulator between carburetor and intake manifold.

SUBARU

1. Disconnect battery ground cable and remove air cleaner assembly.
2. Drain cooling system as outlined in "General Maintenance Section."
3. Loosen clamps and disconnect fuel hoses.
4. Mark position of vacuum hoses between carburetor and engine, then disconnect hoses from carburetor.
5. Disconnect electrical connectors to carburetor, noting position for installation.
6. Disconnect throttle cable from lever.
7. Remove retaining nuts and washers, then lift carburetor from manifold.
8. Reverse procedure to install, using a new base gasket. Refill cooling system, then check for leaks.

TOYOTA

1. Disconnect battery ground cable and remove air cleaner assembly.
2. Inspect choke housing. On models with water heated choke (hoses running from engine to choke housing), partially drain cooling system as outlined in "General Maintenance Section," then disconnect hoses from choke housing.
3. Mark position of vacuum hoses between carburetor and engine, then disconnect hoses from carburetor.
4. Disconnect electrical connectors to carburetor, noting position for installation.
5. Remove clip and slip throttle rod from clevis on lever, or disconnect throttle cable from ball stud on lever, as equipped.
6. On automatic transmission models, disconnect kick-down linkage from throttle lever.
7. Release clamps and disconnect fuel supply and return hoses from carburetor.
8. Remove carburetor mounting nuts and washers, then lift carburetor from manifold.
9. Reverse procedure to install, using a new base gasket.
10. On models with water heated choke, refill cooling system as outlined in "General Maintenance Section."

VOLKSWAGEN RABBIT

1. Disconnect battery ground cable and remove air cleaner duct and adapter.
2. On all except 1983-84 models, drain cooling system as outlined in "General Maintenance Section," then disconnect hoses from choke housing.
3. On all models, disconnect electrical connectors to carburetor, noting position for installation.
4. Mark position of vacuum hoses between carburetor and engine, then disconnect hoses from carburetor.
5. Disconnect throttle cable from throttle lever, and if necessary, from retaining bracket.
6. Loosen clamps and disconnect fuel hoses.
7. Remove mounting nuts, washers and the carburetor.
8. Reverse procedure to install, using a new base gasket. On all except 1983-84 models, refill cooling system as outlined in "General Maintenance Section."

YUGO

1. Disconnect battery ground cable.
2. Drain cooling system, then remove air cleaner assembly.
3. Disconnect vacuum hoses, electrical connectors, fuel lines and throttle cable from carburetor.
4. Remove carburetor attaching nuts and the carburetor.
5. Reverse procedure to install, using new gaskets between carburetor and intake manifold.

General Maintenance

ADD 2 / ADD 1 SAFE

ADD SAFE

ADD SAFE MAX. OVERFILL

NOTE: LUBRICANT LEVEL SHOULD BE WITHIN THE SAFE RANGE.

Fig. 1 Typical engine oil level dipstick markings

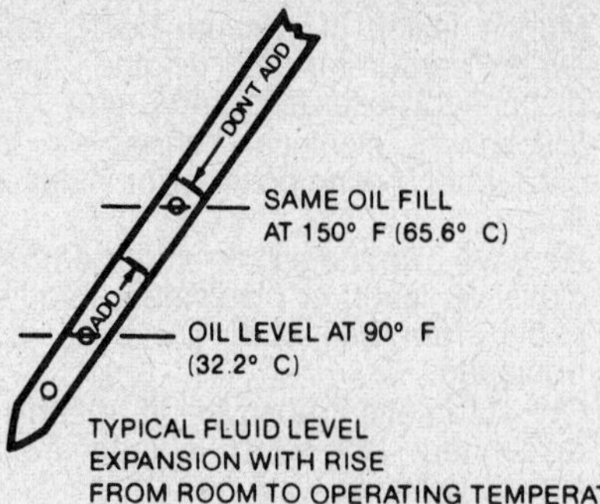

Fig. 2 Checking automatic transmission fluid level

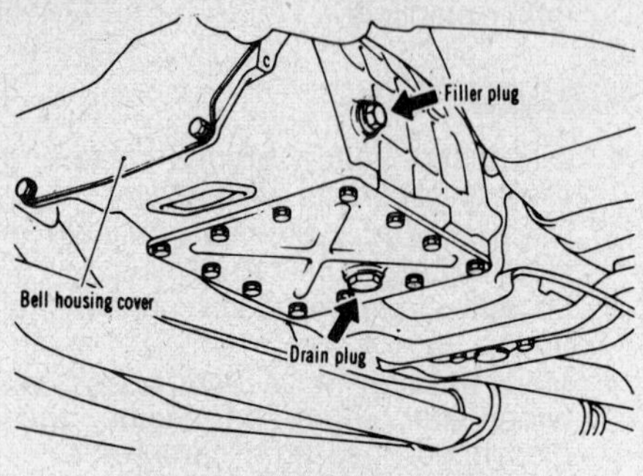

Fig. 3 Typical manual transmission filler plug

CHECKING & MAINTAINING FLUID LEVELS

NOTE: When checking fluid levels, ensure vehicle is on a level surface. If vehicle is not level, an accurate fluid level reading cannot be obtained.

ENGINE OIL LEVEL

1. Warm up engine, then turn ignition off and allow a few minutes for oil to return to crankcase.
2. Remove dipstick and wipe off.
3. Replace dipstick and ensure it is seated in tube.
4. Remove dipstick and inspect to see if oil level is between "Add" and "Full" marks, **Fig. 1.**

   NOTE: Add oil only if level is at or below "Add" mark.

5. If oil level is at "Add" mark, one quart of oil will bring level to "Full" mark, if oil level is below "Add" mark, add sufficient amount of oil to bring level between "Add" & "Full" marks.

   NOTE: Do not bring oil level above "Full" mark, as overfilling of crankcase could result in damage to engine gaskets and seals and cause leaks. Only add oil meeting the vehicle manufacturer's specifications.

6. Replace dipstick.

AUTOMATIC TRANSMISSION

1. Operate vehicle for 10-15 minutes to bring transmission fluid to normal operating temperature.
2. Stop vehicle and apply parking brake securely.
3. Operate shift selector through all ranges, then place selector lever in "Park" or "Neutral." Refer to owner's manual for specific checking position.
4. Thoroughly clean area around dipstick.
5. On all except Honda, ensure that engine is running at normal idle speed. On Honda, stop engine and check fluid level within one minute.
6. Remove dipstick from tube, wipe oil from dipstick with clean rag, then push dipstick all the way back into tube.
7. Pull dipstick from tube, hold stick level and read oil level from stick, **Fig. 2.**
8. If oil level is between "Add" and "Full" marks, oil level is correct. If level is below "A" mark, add sufficient amount of the specified fluid through dipstick tube to bring level to a point between "Add" and "Full" marks.

   NOTE: Do not over fill transmission, as damage may result. Generally, one pint of fluid is sufficient to raise fluid level from the "Add" to the "Full" mark.

9. Insert dipstick back into tube, ensuring that dipstick is fully seated.

MANUAL TRANSMISSION

NOTE: On some models, the manual transmission is equipped with a dipstick for checking fluid level. On models without a dipstick, use the following procedure to check and fill transmission.

1. Set parking brake and block wheels.
2. Clean area around filler plug on side of case, then remove plug using a suitable wrench, **Fig. 3.**
3. If fluid runs out of hole when plug is removed, or if fluid level is even with bottom of hole, level is correct.
4. Add specified type lubricant in order to bring level even with bottom of filler hole, then install plug.

   CAUTION: Do not overtighten filler plug as transmission case may be damaged.

DRIVE AXLE

NOTE: All automatic transaxle equipped vehicles except Audi, Fiat, Saab, Subaru, Toyota and Porsche 924, 928 and 944 with automatic transmission use a common fluid in the transmission and final drive. Refer to appropriate transmission checking section to check transaxle fluid level on all models not listed above.

1. Apply parking brake and block wheels.
2. Clean area surrounding differential or final drive housing filler plug, then remove plug using a suitable wrench or drive key, **Fig. 4.**

   NOTE: Many differential/final drive units are equipped with an internally broached filler plug. To prevent damaging the plug, only use a properly fitting tool for plug removal.

3. Add specified lubricant to bring the fluid level even with bottom of the filler hole, then reinstall filler plug.

COOLING SYSTEM

CAUTION: Do not remove radiator cap when engine is hot. If radiator cap must be removed, insulate cap with several layers of heavy cloth, then rotate cap counterclockwise until pressure begins to escape. Do not remove cap until system pressure is completely relieved.

Never add large quantities of coolant to an overheated engine until the engine has cooled. If coolant must be added, start engine and add coolant slowly to prevent engine damage. Use only permanent type anti-freeze that meets manufacturer's specifications, mixed in 50% solution with water, when coolant is needed.

Less Coolant Recovery Tank

1. With engine cold, remove radiator cap as follows:
   a. Rotate cap counterclockwise to first stop.
   b. Ensure that all cooling system pressure, if present, is relieved.
   c. Press down on cap, rotate counterclockwise to stop, then remove cap.
2. Inspect coolant level. Coolant level should be as shown in **Fig. 5.**
3. Add coolant as required to bring coolant to specified level.
4. Install cap, ensuring that cap is in fully locked position.

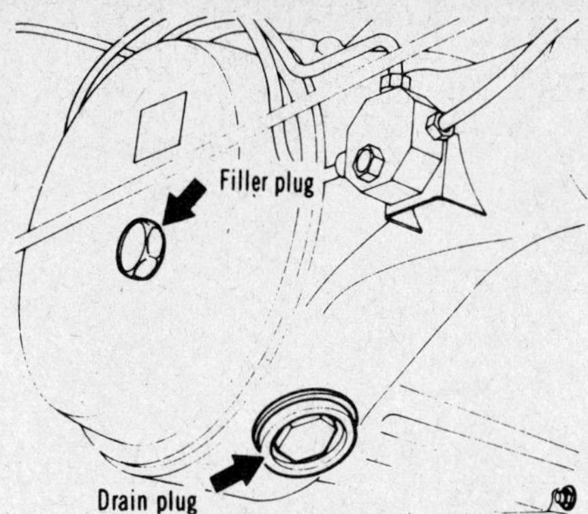

Fig. 4 Typical drive axle filler plug

With Coolant Recovery Tank

1. With engine cold, inspect coolant level in recovery tank.
2. If tank is dry, or if coolant does not cover outlet to radiator, check and correct cooling system leaks, then refer to "Cooling System Service" for refilling and bleeding procedures.
3. Start engine, run until it reaches normal operating temperature, then inspect coolant level in recovery tank.
4. If coolant is not at or near the "Full Hot" or upper mark on recovery tank, add coolant to tank to obtain proper level.

NOTE: If frequent addition of coolant is required, cooling system should be tested for leaks.

BRAKE/CLUTCH MASTER CYLINDER

CAUTION: Do not allow brake fluid to come into contact with skin, eyes or painted surfaces of vehicle. If fluid is accidently spilled or splashed, immediately flush affected area with clean cool water.

1. Thoroughly clean master cylinder cover(s) and surrounding area, then remove cover(s).
2. Fluid level should be up to the full mark on the reservoir, **Fig. 6,** or within ¼ inch of top of reservoir if no full mark is present.
3. Add sufficient brake fluid to bring fluid level to the specified level.

NOTE: Only add brake fluid which meets manufacturer's specifications and that has been stored in a tightly closed container. Do not allow petroleum based fluids, dirt or moisture to enter master cylinder, as system will be damaged.

4. Reinstall cover(s) and check system operation.

NOTE: Fluid level in reservoirs for disc brakes will decrease as linings wear. If levels are excessively low, inspect system for leakage and inspect linings for wear.

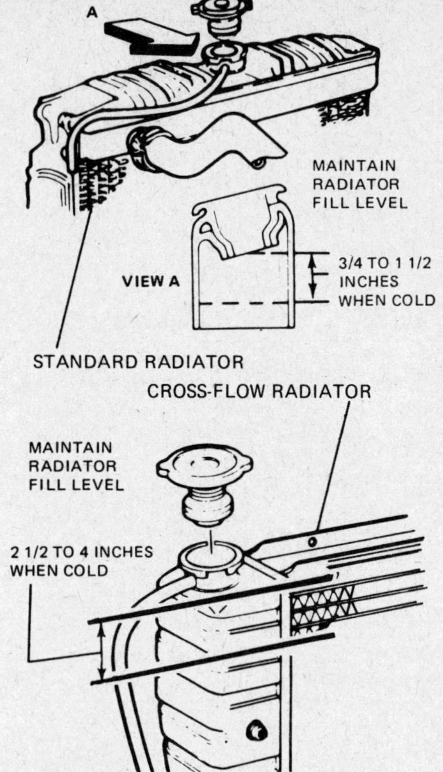

Fig. 5 Checking coolant level. Models less recovery tank

BATTERY

1. Remove filler cap and check fluid level in each cell.

NOTE: Keep flame and sparks away from top of battery as combustible gases present may explode. Do not allow battery electrolyte to contact skin, eyes, fabric or painted surfaces. Flush contacted area with water immediately and thoroughly and seek medical attention if necessary. Wear eye protection when working on or near battery, Do not wear rings or other metal jewelry when working on or near battery.

2. Add water as required to bring fluid level of each cell up to split ring located at bottom of filler well.

NOTE: In areas where water is known to be hard or have a high mineral or alkali content, distilled water must be used. If water is added during freezing temperatures, the vehicle should be driven several miles afterwards to mix the water and battery electrolyte.

3. Install fill caps.

POWER STEERING PUMP RESERVOIR

1. Start engine and allow to reach operating temperature, then turn ignition off.
2. Clean area around filler cap or dipstick, then remove filler cap or dipstick and inspect fluid level.

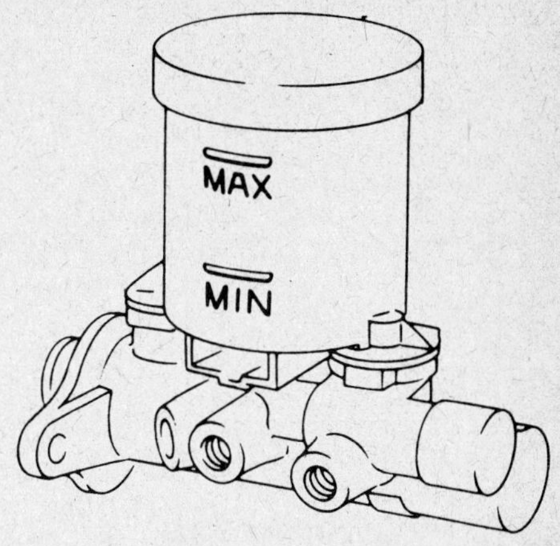

Fig. 6 Brake/clutch master cylinder markings

3. Fluid level should be between "Full" mark and end of dipstick, **Fig. 7.**

NOTE: On models without dipstick, fluid level should be half way up filler neck.

4. Add fluid as necessary, then install filler cap or dipstick.

NOTE: Only add fluid recommended by the vehicle manufacturer.

LUBRICATION & OIL CHANGE

ENGINE OIL & FILTER CHANGE

Under normal operating conditions, engine oil and filter should be changed at intervals recommended by vehicle manufacturer. Under severe operating conditions, such as extended stop and go driving or operation in dusty environments, intervals between oil changes should be reduced.

1. Operate engine until it reaches normal operating temperature, then stop engine and remove lower covers, as needed, to gain access to drain plug and filter.
2. Place suitable drain pan under engine, positioned so that pan will catch surge of oil when drain plug is removed, then loosen oil filler cap.
3. Remove drain plug from engine case or oil pan using a suitable wrench.

NOTE: On front wheel drive models, ensure that the plug is removed from engine oil pan, not the transaxle.

4. While oil is draining, clean and inspect drain plug. Replace drain pug and/or gasket if damaged or distorted.
5. When oil has drained completely, install and tighten drain plug.

NOTE: Do not overtighten drain plug, as this may strip threads from oil pan or engine case. If oil pan threads are stripped, several different drain hole repair kits are available. One type

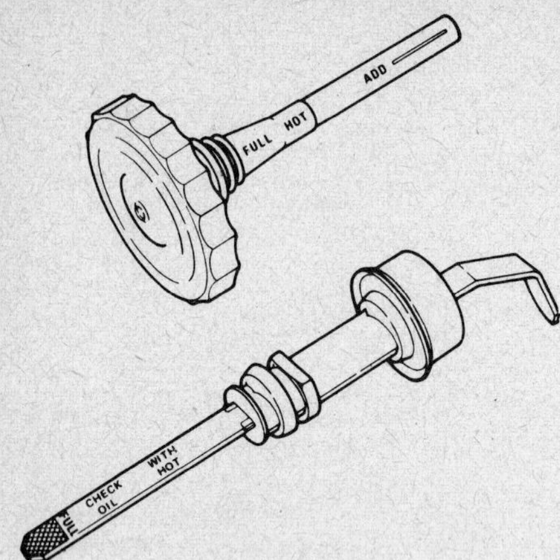

Fig. 7 Typical power steering reservoir dipsticks

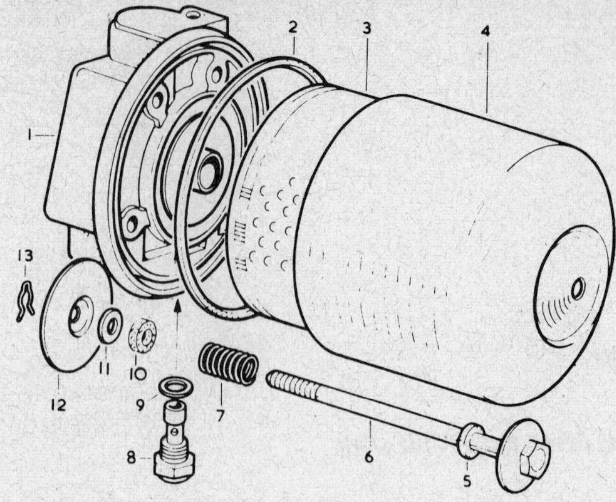

Fig. 8 Oil filter assembly exploded view. Replaceable element type

uses a self-tapping steel plug with a threaded brass plug in the center which becomes the new drain plug. Other kits use a rubber stopper which is removed and installed with a special tool. Select a repair kit that will best work with your vehicle after consulting a knowledgeable parts supplier.

6. Position drain pan under engine oil filter.
7. Replace cartridge element type filters as follows:
   a. Loosen center bolt securing filter housing and allow oil from filter to drain into pan.
   b. Unscrew center bolt, lower housing assembly and remove filter element from housing, **Fig. 8.**
   c. Clean filter housing and mounting adapter, ensuring that none of the old gasket remains on either component.
   d. Lubricate new gasket and position gasket on filter housing or mounting adapter, **Fig. 8.**
   e. Install new filter in housing, hold housing against mounting adapter and tighten center bolt hand tight.

   NOTE: Ensure that gasket remains in place while tightening center bolt.

   f. Tighten center bolt using a suitable wrench.
8. Replace spin-on type filter cartridge as follows:
   a. Turn filter counterclockwise with suitable wrench, **Figs. 9 and 10,** then remove filter.
   b. Clean oil and gasket residue from filter mounting surface.
   c. Coat gasket on new filter with a thin film of clean engine oil, then thread filter onto adapter.
   d. Hand tighten filter until gasket contacts mounting surface, then tighten filter one additional turn to ensure proper sealing.

   CAUTION: Do not over tighten filter as this may cause leaks and make subsequent filter removal difficult.

   e. Wipe filter and mounting adapter clean.
9. Clean oil strainer on Volkswagen air cooled engine as follows:
   a. Remove 5 nuts securing oil strainer plate and loosen the 6th nut several turns.
   b. Gently pry strainer plate from engine case, then remove retaining nut and strainer assembly.
   c. Thoroughly clean strainer mounting surface and strainer, new sealing washers and the retaining nuts.
   d. Torque retaining nuts to 7-9 ft. lbs.
10. Remove oil filler cap and add specified quantity of suitable oil to engine.

    NOTE: Use only the type and grade motor oil specified by the vehicle manufacturer for anticipated driving conditions.

11. Start engine and inspect drain plug and oil filter for leaks. If leakage is evident, stop engine and correct leaks as required.
12. Stop engine and check oil level on dipstick. Add oil as needed to bring oil level to a point just below "Full" mark on dipstick.

CHASSIS LUBRICATION

Although many of the steering and suspension components on modern imported cars and trucks are sealed—requiring no periodic lubrication—inspection and lubrication of sliding surfaces throughout the vehicle is still an important maintenance item. The first step in chassis maintenance is to identify and locate components that require lubrication. Refer to the vehicle owner's manual to identify these components and for recommended lubrication intervals, and to **Figs. 11 and 12,** which show common steering, suspension and driveline lubrication points.

In addition to luricating front end and driveline components, operating linkages such as throttle and parking brake cables and gear selector controls; and body components such as hood, door and trunk hinges require lubrication. Use the owner's manual as a guide to where and when these components require lubrication and to select the proper type lubricant for each component. As with any other maintenance service, lubrication intervals should be reduced when the vehicle is operated under severe conditions: wet or dusty climates, areas where salt is used to clear roads, etc.

NOTE: To prolong overall vehicle life and to make service easier, flush underbody and suspension with water prior to lubrication. This will remove dirt, mud and harmful salt deposits, and make components easier to identify and service.

Steering, Suspension & Driveline

1. Locate lubrication points at ball joints and suspension bushings, steering linkage points and universal joints as outlined above.
2. As you locate fittings, clean fitting with a rag to prevent injecting dirt along with the grease.
3. If plugs are installed in the joint, remove the plugs and install suitable grease fittings.

NOTE: If joints do not have provisions for grease fittings, clean and inspect joint and dust boots. If dust boots are intact and no abnormal play is evident, no further service is required. If dust boots are damaged or if joint shows excessive wear, replacement may be

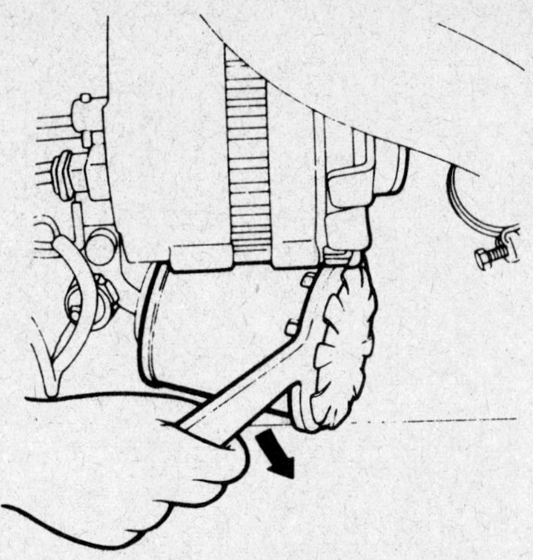

Fig. 9 Removing oil filter w/cup type wrench

necessary.

4. When lubrication points have been located and cleaned, fit nozzle of grease gun over each fitting. Nozzle tip should be a catch fit, requiring only slight straight on pressure to lock tip on fitting.
5. Pump grease gun handle slowly, just until grease begins to flow from bleed holes at base of dust boot or until boot can be seen to swell slightly.

CAUTION: Do not inject excess grease into joints, as pressure may damage dust boot.

6. If grease oozes out from sides of gun tip, do not keep pumping handle, as the fitting is not taking grease properly.
7. If fittings fail to take grease, remove nozzle, clean fitting and try once more to lubricate fitting while applying slight pressure on nozzle. If fitting still will not take grease, fitting should be replaced.

NOTE: While lubricating suspension and driveline components, inspect seals on transmission, drive axle, engine and steering gear, and inspect components for damage. Check fluid levels in any assembly found to be leaking, and plan to repair leaking, damaged or worn components.

Control Cables & Linkages

1. Locate pivot points on control linkages and dust boots on cables identified in the owner's manual as requiring lubrication.
2. Lubricate linkage pivots with suitable water resistant multi-purpose grease or motor oil. Apply lubricants sparingly to avoid making a mess.
3. With brake actuator released, pull back boot where prking brake cable enters passenger compartment and lubricate cable.
4. Fully apply parking brake, then pull back boots where cable enters each wheel and lubricate cables.
5. Lubricate throttle, heater and transmission control cables with suitable lubricant.

NOTE: Use lubricants recommended by vehicle manufacturer.

6. If control cables bind or stick, disconnect one end of cable and drip suitable penetrating oil down between inner cable and housing.
7. Check operation of all controls and adjust or repair as outlined in service sections.

Body Components

1. Lubricate door, hood and rear compartment hinges with oil or suitable multi-purpose grease. Apply lubricant sparingly to all sliding contact areas, **Fig. 13**.

NOTE: For long neglected hinges, flush contact areas with penetrating oil to free mechanism, wipe clean, then lubricate as outlined.

2. Lubricate exposed contact areas of door, hood and rear compartment latches with multi-purpose grease.
3. Apply suitable lock lubricant to door, ignition and rear compartment lock cylinders.
4. Insert and remove key several times and operate lock to work lubrication into cylinder.
5. Spray suitable silicone lubricant on all weather strips, keeping excess spray from contacting interior components and painted surfaces.
6. Apply a thin film of silicone grease to door, hood and rear compartment in-

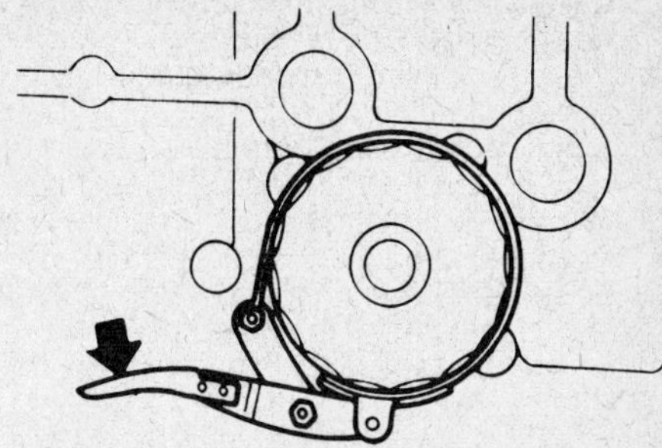

Fig. 10 Removing oil filter w/strap type wrench

sulators (rubber bumpers).

Wheel Bearings

NOTE: Permanently sealed and lubricated bearings, used on many models, cannot be repacked, and must be replaced if lubricant is lost. Refer to service sections for bearing identification, removal, installation and adjustment.

1. Remove hub assembly from spindle and bearings from hub, keeping all components in order for reassembly, **Fig. 14.**
2. Clean all old grease from hub and spindle.
3. Wash all old lubricant from bearings with suitable solvent and allow bearings to air dry. Do not dry bearings with compressed air.

NOTE: Do not use solvents, such as gasoline, that will leave deposits on bearings and prevent new grease from adhering to bearing surfaces.

4. Inspect bearing cones, rollers and races, and mounting surfaces of hub and spindle.
5. Replace bearings that are cracked, damaged, excessively worn, or that fail to operate smoothly.

NOTE: Bearings and races must be replaced as an assembly.

6. Replace spindle and/or hub if bearings have "spun" and damaged mounting surfaces.
7. Place a small amount of suitable wheel bearing grease in palm of hand and force grease into large end of roller cage, through bearing, until grease

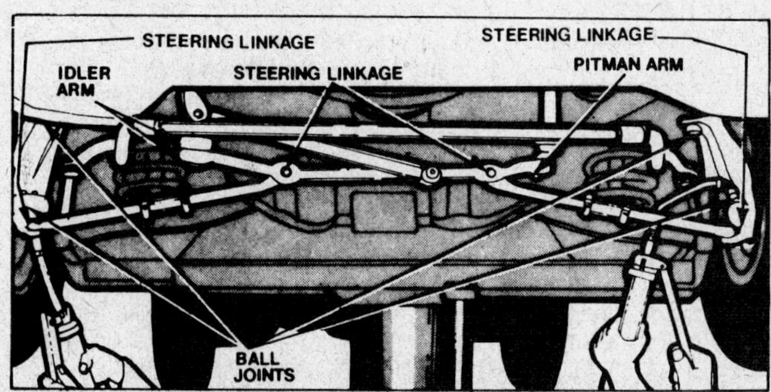

Fig. 11 Typical front suspension lubrication points

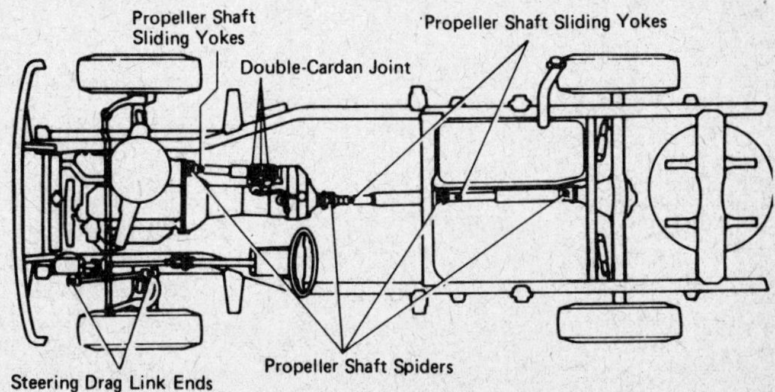

Fig. 12 Typical driveline lubrication points

oozes out from small end of cage, then coat outside of rollers.
8. Repeat packing procedure with each bearing.
9. Apply a thin film of grease to spindle and lip of oil seal, and pack approximately 1 tablespoon of grease into center of hub.
10. Assemble bearings into hub, install hub assembly, then adjust wheel bearings as outlined in service section.

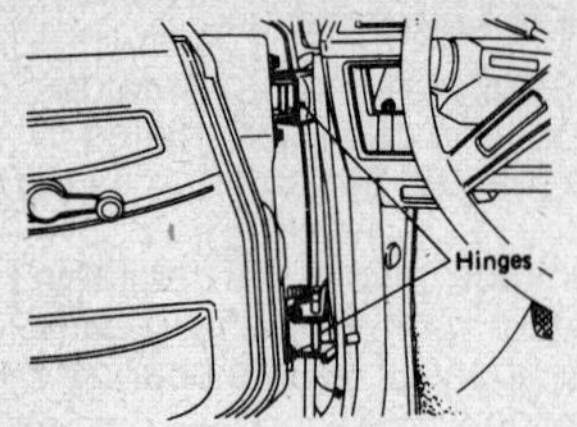

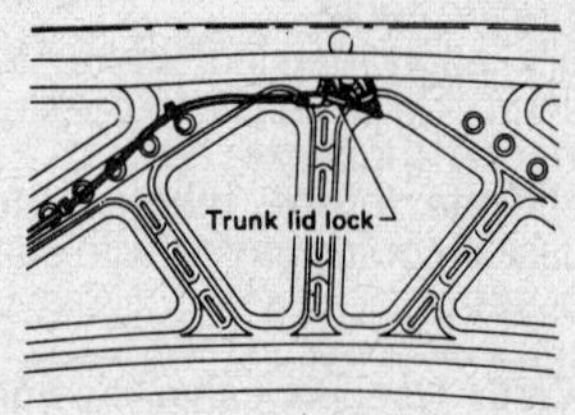

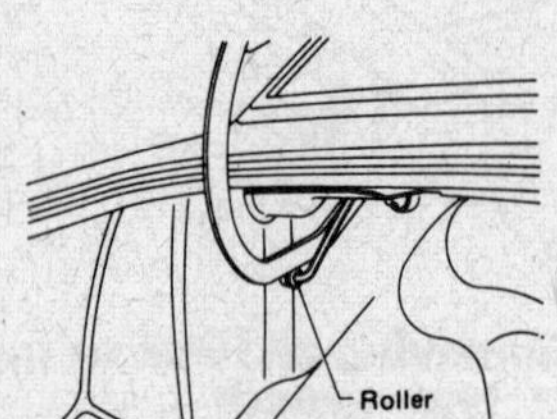

Fig. 13 Typical body lubrication points

COOLING SYSTEM SERVICE

CAUTION: Do not remove radiator cap when engine is hot. If radiator cap must be removed, insulate cap with several layers of heavy cloth, then rotate cap counterclockwise until pressure begins to escape. Do not remove cap until system pressure is completely relieved.

Never add large quantities of coolant to an overheated engine until engine has cooled. If coolant must be added, start engine and add coolant slowly to prevent engine damage.

When addition of coolant is necessry, use only permanent type anti-freeze that meets manufacturer's specifications, mixed in 50% solution with water.

INSPECTION

1. Inspect radiator for leaks around tank and neck seams, and at transmission oil cooler, if equipped, and repair or replace as needed.
2. Inspect radiator cooling fins for damage or blockage and clean or straighten core fins as needed.
3. Inspect coolant hoses (radiator, heater, by-pass etc.) for damage or deterioration, **Fig. 15,** and replace defective hoses and clamps.
4. Inspect water pump for leakage and worn bearings. If pump is leaking, noisy, or if shaft bearing has excessive play, pump should be replaced.
5. Ensure that fan blade is not damaged or loose, and that fan shroud, if equipped is properly aligned.
6. Inspect drive belts and adjust or replace as needed.
7. Check coolant level and internal condition of radiator. If coolant is contaminated, or radiator is clogged with deposits, flush system and replace coolant.

DRAINING THE SYSTEM

1. Remove lower engine cover, as needed, to provide access to radiator and engine drains or lower hose connection.
2. Place heater control in fully hot position and remove cap from coolant recovery tank, if equipped.
3. Place a suitable drain pan under radiator drain or lower hose connection.
4. On models with radiator drain, open petcock or remove drain plug taking care not to damage or distort radiator, **Fig. 16.**
5. On models without radiator drain, loosen clamp securing lower hose to radiator and disconnect hose, taking care not to damage radiator outlet.
6. Slowly loosen, then remove radiator cap and allow coolant to drain into pan.
7. When coolant stops flowing from radiator, place drain pan under block drain, if equipped, and open petcock or remove drain plug, **Fig. 17.**

FLUSHING THE SYSTEM

There are several flushing procedures that can be performed without using special tools. The method outlined below requires only the use of a garden hose and, if the block is to be flushed, removal of the thermostat. Additional methods include the use of a flushing "T" that is spliced into the heater hose or the use of chemical flushing agents. Flushing "T's" and chemical agents are commonly available from aftermarket suppliers and are furnished with instructions.

Reverse Flushing Radiator

1. Drain cooling system, then close petcocks or install drain plugs. If system was drained by disconnecting lower hose, leave hose disconnected.

CAUTION: Do not over tighten radiator drains, as radiator may be damaged.

2. Disconnect lower hose from radiator and upper hose from connection on engine.
3. Install radiator cap and secure upper radiator hose so that it points away from engine toward a suitable drain.
4. Insert garden hose into radiator lower hose outlet and seal connection by wrapping a rag around hose and outlet, **Fig. 18.**
5. Turn water on and allow water to flow up through radiator and out through upper hose until water runs clear.
6. Turn off water, reconnect hoses, then refill system.

Reverse Flushing Engine Block

1. Drain cooling system then close petcocks or install drain plugs. If system was drained by disconnecting lower hose from radiator, leave hose disconnected.
2. Disconnect upper and lower hoses from radiator.
3. Remove thermostat from lower hose or from housing on top of engine. If thermostat is installed in housing, reinstall housing using a new gasket.
4. Secure lower hose so that it points away from engine and insert garden hose into upper hose.
5. Turn water on and allow water to flow through engine until it runs clear.
6. Turn water off, reconnect hoses and install thermostat, then refill cooling system.

NOTE: Always use new gasket when installing thermostat.

Reverse Flushing Heater Core

NOTE: Care must be taken when flushing heater core not to allow water pressure to burst core.

1. Drain cooling system, then disconnect heater hoses from engine.
2. Connect core outlet hose (usually the smaller hose) to garden hose and secure core inlet hose so it points away from engine.
3. Turn on water, using just enough pressure to force water through core.
4. Allow water to flow through core until it runs clear, then turn water off, reconnect hoses and refill system.

REFILLING THE SYSTEM

NOTE: The cooling systems on many

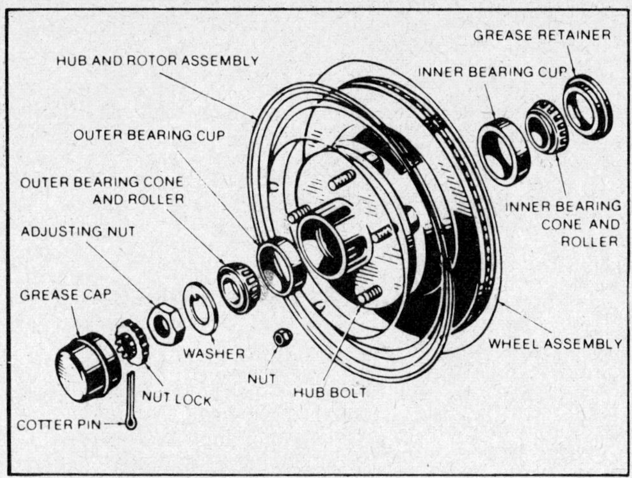

Fig. 14 Typical wheel bearing & hub assembly exploded view

ALWAYS CHECK hose for chafed or burned areas that may cause an untimely and costly failure.

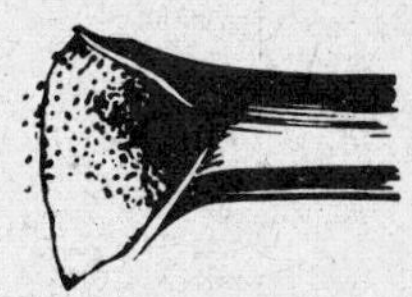

SOFT hose indicates inside deterioration. This deterioration can contaminate the cooling system and cause particles to clog the radiator.

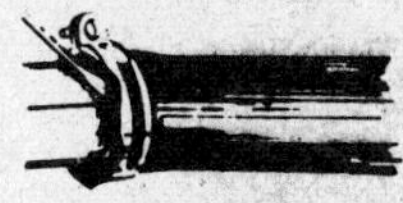

HARDENED hose can fail at any time. Tightening hose clamps will not seal the connection or stop leaks.

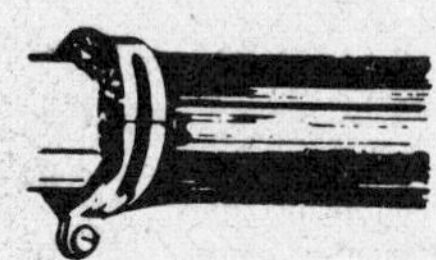

SWOLLEN hose or oil soaked ends indicate danger and possible failure from oil or grease contamination. Squeeze the hose to locate cracks and breaks that cause leaks.

Fig. 15 Coolant hose inspection

models are equipped with bleed screws to remove air trapped in the system and ensure complete filling. Filling procedures must be followed carefully on these models to prevent possible overheating and engine damage.

EXC. MODELS W/BLEED SCREW OR REMOTE FILLER

1. Ensure that drain plugs and petcocks are securely tightened and that all hoses are properly connected.
2. Remove cap from radiator and recovery tank, if equipped, and place heater control in "Hot" position.
3. Refer to specifications and add sufficient anti-freeze to radiator to ensure a 50% solution.
4. Continue filling radiator with water, pouring water in slowly so that trapped air can escape.
5. When no more water can be poured into radiator, start engine and run at fast idle until thermostat opens.

NOTE: Coolant level in radiator will drop suddenly when thermostat opens.

6. Top up radiator with water and on models with recovery tank, fill tank to "Full Hot" mark, then install radiator cap.
7. Stop engine and allow to cool, then ensure that coolant level is correct.

MODELS W/BLEED SCREW OR REMOTE FILLER

BMW

1. Follow steps 1-6 outlined for models without bleed screw.
2. With engine running at fast idle, loosen bleeder screw on pump housing and allow air to escape, maintaining coolant level in recovery tank.
3. When coolant flows from bleeder without bubbles, close screw.

Honda & Saab

Follow procedure outlined for models without bleed screw, noting the following: Open bleed screw prior to filling system with coolant. When coolant runs from bleeder without bubbles, tighten screw. Bleed screw is located on thermostat housing on all except 1984-86 Civic, and on the water outlet on 1984-86 Civic.

Jaguar XJ-12 w/Fuel Injection & XJ-S Exc. HE

1. Ensure that block and radiator drains are securely tightened, remove recovery tank cap and open bleed vent on radiator.
2. Refer to specifications and mix a sufficient quantity of anti-freeze with water in a suitable container to ensure a 50% solution.
3. Slowly pour coolant into recovery tank until no more can be added, wait 1-2 minutes and add more coolant as needed. Repeat process until no more coolant can be added.
4. Close radiator vent and install recovery tank cap.
5. Place heater control in warm position (approximately 80°), start engine and run at 1000 RPM for 3 minutes.
6. Open bleed valve. When air has been purged, remove recovery tank cap, add coolant until it runs from bleed valve, then close valve and install cap.

XJ-12 W/Carburetors

1. Ensure that block and radiator drains are securely tightened, remove caps from recovery tank and engine filler pipe and open radiator bleed valve.
2. Refer to specifications and mix sufficient anti-freeze with water in a suitable container to ensure a 50% solution.
3. Slowly pour coolant into engine fill pipe until recovery tank is full, then install recovery tank cap.
4. Continue to add coolant to engine pipe until coolant flows from bleed valve, then close valve and install cap on engine pipe.
5. Run engine until it reaches normal operating temperature, allow engine to cool and ensure that coolant is at proper level.

Jaguar XJ-S HE

Follow procedure outlined for models without remote filler noting the following: Add coolant through engine filler pipe until recovery tank is full, then install recovery tank cap. Continue filling system until no more coolant can be added, then install engine filler cap. Run engine until it reaches normal operating temperature, allow engine to cool, then ensure that coolant is at proper level.

Nissan Stanza

1. Ensure that engine and radiator drains are securely tightened, remove caps from radiator and recovery tank, and set heater control at "Hot."
2. Fully depress pin in 3-way valve using a .012 inch (3 mm) diameter rod, **Fig. 19.**

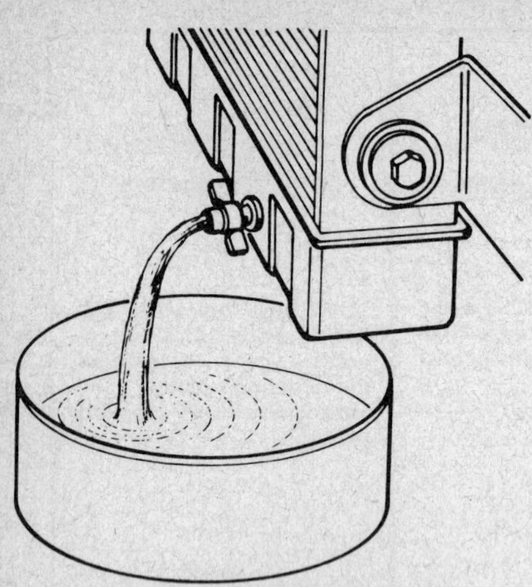

Fig. 16 Draining the radiator

CAUTION: Do not start engine with valve pin depressed.

3. Refer to specifications and mix sufficient anti-freeze with water in a suitable container to ensure a 50% solution.
4. Slowly pour coolant into radiator until coolant reaches top of neck.
5. Remove rod from 3-way valve and continue filling system as outlined for models without bleed valve.

Porsche 924 & 924 Turbo

1. Ensure that engine and radiator drains are securely tightened, remove recovery tank cap and place heater control in "Hot" position.
2. On non-turbo models, loosen clamp and remove plug from bleed valve on heater hose. On Turbo, loosen bleed screw on thermostat housing 1 turn.
3. Refer to specifications and mix sufficient anti-freeze with water, in a suitable container, to ensure a 50% solution.
4. Slowly pour coolant into recovery tank until level stabilizes at full mark on tank.
5. Start engine and run until it reaches normal operating temperature.
6. Close bleeder when no more air bubbles are visible, then fill system to full mark on recovery tank and install cap.

Porsche 944

1. Ensure that engine and radiator drains are securely tightened, remove recovery tank cap and place heater control in "Hot" position.
2. Fully loosen bleed valve screw on heater hose.
3. Refer to specifications and mix sufficient anti-freeze with water, in a suitable container, to ensure a 50% solution.
4. Slowly pour coolant into recovery tank until it begins to run out bleed valve.
5. Drain sufficient coolant from system to return recovery tank level to half full, then tighten bleed screw several turns.
6. Start engine and run at fast idle until it reaches normal operating temperature.
7. Close bleeder when no more air bubbles are visible, then fill system to full mark on recovery tank and install cap.

Renault Alliance & Encore

1. Ensure that engine and radiator drains are tightened securely, remove recovery tank and remote filler caps and place heater control at "Hot."
2. Tap plastic "T" fitting joining hoses from remote filler to ensure proper operation of check valve.

NOTE: To ensure proper filling, hose from coolant recovery tank (1) must be routed under radiator inlet hose (2), **Fig. 20.**

3. Refer to specifications and add sufficient anti-freeze to system to ensure a 50% solution. Pour anti-freeze in through remote filler, do not add to radiator.

NOTE: Maintain coolant level below purge hole in filler so that trapped air can escape from system.

4. Continue filling system with water until coolant level is just below overflow port in remote filler.
5. Fill recovery tank to full mark with anti-freeze/water solution.
6. Install recovery tank and remote filler caps, start engine and run for several minutes after themostat opens.
7. Allow engine to cool, then check and fill recovery tank as needed.

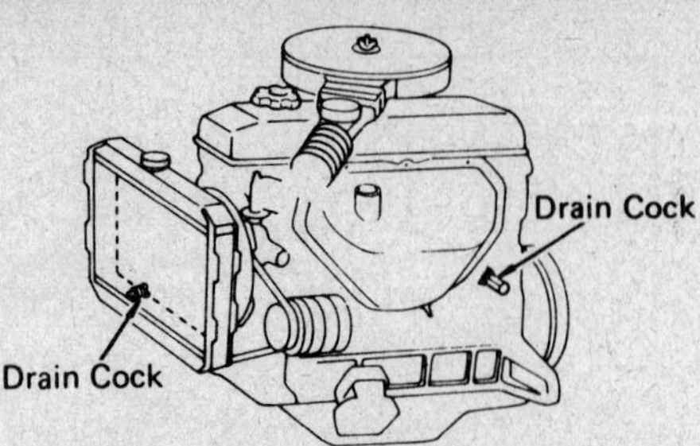

Fig. 17 Typical engine & radiator drains

NOTE: A second heat/cool cycle may be necessary to completely purge air from system.

Renault Fuego, Le Car & 18i

1. Ensure that engine and radiator drains are securely tightened, remove recovery tank and radiator caps, and place heater control in "Hot" position.
2. Refer to specifications and mix sufficient anti-freeze with water, in a suitable container, to ensure a 50% solution.
3. Remove recovery tank from bracket, leaving hose connected, and secure as high as possible.
4. On Fuego and 18i, open bleed screws on heater hose and upper radiator hose. On Le Car, open bleed screws on heater core bleed hose and hose between expansion tank and carburetor.
5. Slowly pour coolant into radiator until no more can be added, pour a small amount of coolant into recovery tank and install radiator cap.
6. Continue filling system through recovery tank until coolant runs from bleed valves, then close bleed valves.

NOTE: Coolant level in recovery tank should be approximately 1½ inches from bottom on Fuego and 18i or 2¾

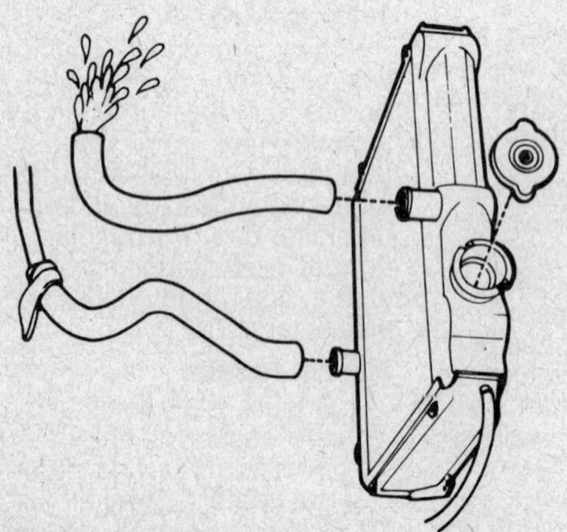

Fig. 18 Reverse flushing the radiator

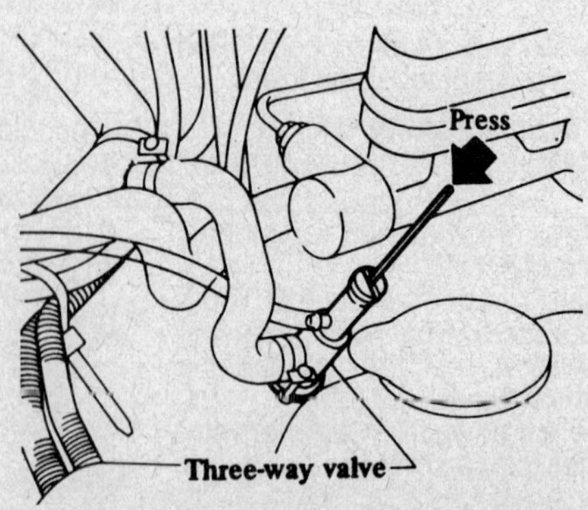

Fig. 19 Three-way cooling system bleed valve. Nissan Stanza

Fig. 20 Remote filler hose installation. Renault Alliance & Encore

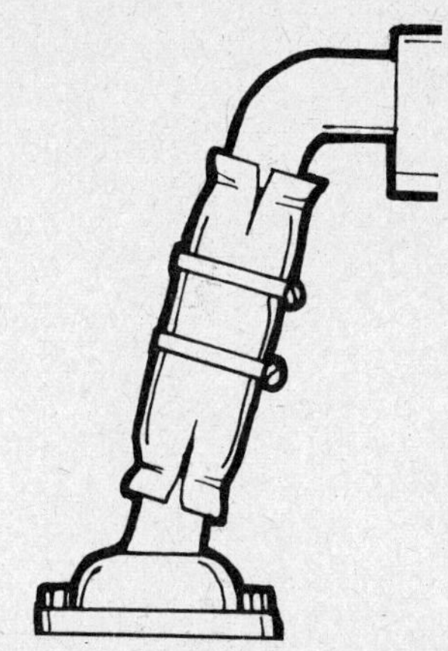

Fig. 21 Coolant hose removal

inches from bottom on Le Car.

7. Start engine and run until thermostat has opened, then re-open bleed screws.
8. Close bleed screws as soon as there is a continuous flow of coolant with no air bubbles.
9. Stop engine and return recovery tank to proper position.
10. Allow engine to cool and check coolant level.

Volkswagen Vanagon

1. Reconnect hoses to water pump and radiator, if removed, place heater control in "Hot" position and open bleed valve on radiator.
2. Refer to specifications and mix sufficient anti-freeze with water, in a suitable container, to ensure a 50% solution.
3. Slowly pour coolant into expansion tank until tank remains full.
4. Start engine and run at fast idle. When coolant flows from bleed valve with no bubbles, close valve.
5. Fill cooling system to "Full Hot" mark on expansion tank, install cap and stop engine.
6. Allow engine to cool and ensure that coolant level in expansion tank is within specifications.

HOSE REPLACEMENT

Hoses carrying engine coolant must be replaced whenever they are leaking, and should be replaced if periodic inspection, **Fig. 15,** shows them to be deteriorated. Use the following procedures as a guide to hose replacement on your vehicle.

1. Prior to beginning the actual replacement, obtain proper replacement hoses, new clamps and specified engine coolant, noting the following:
   a. Measure length of heater hoses and have the proper size replacement hoses cut slightly longer. Hoses can be trimmed to fit during installation, but they cannot be stretched.
   b. Match replacement molded hoses to the original to ensure proper fit.
   c. If a universal type hose can be bent to obtain an adequate fit without collapsing or placing excessive strain on radiator connections.
   d. Installing new hose clamps during hose replacement is cheap insurance against a future failure.
   e. When refilling cooling system, use only the type anti-freeze recommended by the vehicle manufacturer.
2. Drain cooling system as outlined. If coolant is to be re-used, use a clean container that is large enough to hold total system capacity, **Fig. 16.**

NOTE: If only upper engine hoses are being replaced, cooling system need only be drained partially.

3. Loosen clamps and slide them toward the middle of hose to be replaced. If clamps are siezed, pry them away from hose carefully to prevent damaging connections.

CAUTION: Radiator and heater core connections are extremely fragile, and can be bent or broken if excessive force is used.

4. Note proper installation position, then remove hoses as follows:
   a. Twist hose back and forth gently to break bond, then slide hose off connector.
   b. If bond cannot be broken by gentle twisting, attempt to pry hose from connector with a suitable lever, taking care not to damage connector.
   c. If hoses are really stuck, cut hose the length of the connector, **Fig. 21,** then peel hose from connector.

CAUTION: Do not cut hose too deeply, as sealing surface of connector may be damaged.

   d. Release hose from retaining straps or brackets, if equipped, then remove hose and clamps.
5. Remove all remnants of old hose from connectors using a suitable scraper or abrasive and ensure that connectors are not distorted.
6. Position clamps on replacement hose so that they can be easily tightened and so that they do not interfere with other components.
7. Coat inside of hose ends with soapy solution to aid installation, slide hose onto connectors and align in position noted in step 4.

NOTE: Ensure that hose is secured in retaining straps or brackets, if equipped.

8. Align clamps on hoses as shown in **Fig. 22,** then tighten clamps.
9. Refill cooling system and bleed as needed.
10. Check for leaks.

DRIVE BELTS

Proper belt tension is important not only to minimize noise and prolong belt life, but also to protect the accessories being driven.

Belts which are adjusted too tight may cause failure to the bearing of the accessory which it drives. Premature wear and breakage of the belt may also result. Belts which are too loose will slip on their pulleys and cause a screeching sound. Loose belts can also cause the battery to go dead, the engine to overheat, steering to become hard (if equipped with power steering) and air conditioner to malfunction.

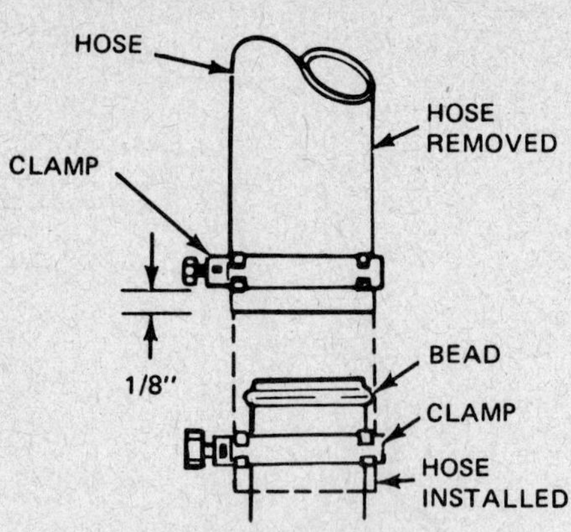

Fig. 22 Coolant hose installation

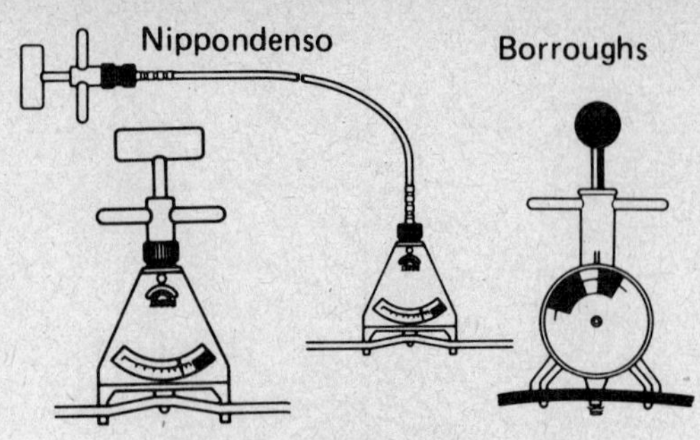

Fig. 23 Typical drive belt tension gauge

DRIVE BELT TENSION GAUGE

The use of a belt tension gauge will quickly indicate whether a belt is properly adjusted or not. Low cost tension gauges give spot readings while the more expensive ones give continuous readins as the belt tension is adjusted, **Fig. 23.**

DRIVE BELT INSPECTION

All belts should be inspected at regular intervals for uneven wear, fraying and glazing.

CAUTION: Do not inspect belts while engine is running.

Small cracks on the underside of the belt can be enlarged for inspection by flexing the belt. Cracks expose the interior to damage, leading to breakage without warning.

Grease rots ordinary rubber belts. It also causes the belts to slip.

Glazed belts, indicated with a shiny friction surface cause the belts to slip. This can cause overheating, a low charging rate, and hard steering in the case of vehicles with power steering.

Always make sure to inspect the underside of belts. Belts that appear sound from the top may be severely split on the sides and bottom, ready to fail.

PIVOT BOLT
PULLEYS
ADJUSTING BOLT
DRIVE BELT

Fig. 24 Drive belt adjuster. Pivot & adjusting bolt type

DRIVE BELT TENSION ADJUSTMENT

1. Run engine until it reaches normal operating temperature, then turn engine off.

CAUTION: Do not attempt to check or adjust any drive belt while engine is running. Turn engine off.

2. Using belt tension gauge following manufacturer's instructions, check tension of each belt, individually. Refer to individual vehicle chapter for belt tension specifications.
3. If adjustment is necessary, proceed as follows:
   a. Pivot Bolt and Adjusting Bolt, **Fig. 24:** using a suitable wrench, loosen adjusting bolt and pivot bolt, then using a pry bar, move accessory toward or away from engine until tension gauge reaches specified reading. Make sure to tighten bolts before relieving force applied to pry bar.

   CAUTION: Do not pry against power steering housing or air pump housing.

   b. Adjusting Bolt and Adjusting Bolt Slots, **Fig. 25:** loosen adjusting slot bolts, then loosen or tighten adjusting bolt until tension gauge reaches specified reading. Make sure to tighten adjusting slot bolts.
   c. Idler Pulley Pivot Bolt and Adjusting Bolt, **Fig. 26:** loosen idler pulley pivot bolt and adjusting bolt, then insert a ½ inch flex handle into pulley arm slot and apply force on handle until tension gauge reaches specified reading. Make sure to tighten pivot bolt and adjusting bolt before relieving force on handle.
4. To check tension on a belt without a belt tension gauge, proceed as follows:
   a. Place a straight edge along the belt from pulley to pulley, **Fig. 27.**
   b. Using a ruler, depress belt at midpoint between pulleys. Measure amount of deflection. For belt with a free span of less than 12 inches between pulleys, amount of deflection should be ¼ inch. For belts with a free span of more than 12 inches between pulleys, amount of deflection should be ½ inch.
   c. Adjust belt tension, if necessary, as described previously.
5. Recheck belt tension, and readjust if necessary.

DRIVE BELT REPLACEMENT

To replace a belt, loosen the adjusting bolt and pivot bolt. Move accessory as required to obtain maximum slack on belt. Remove belt by lifting off the pulleys and working it around the fan or other accessories, as necessary. Occasionally on multiple belt arrangements, it will be necessary to remove one or more additional belts in order to remove the defective belt. To install belt, reverse the removal procedure and adjust belt tension as described previously.

NOTE: On accessories which are driven by dual belts, it is advisable to replace both belts even if only one needs replacement.

TIMING BELT INSPECTION

The overhead camshaft, used on many imported models, is synchronized to and driven by the crankshaft through a toothed, reinforced rubber drive belt. As failure of this belt may result in costly engine repairs, the timing belt should be replaced if it exhibits any of the following conditions.

1. Hardened back surface, indicated by a

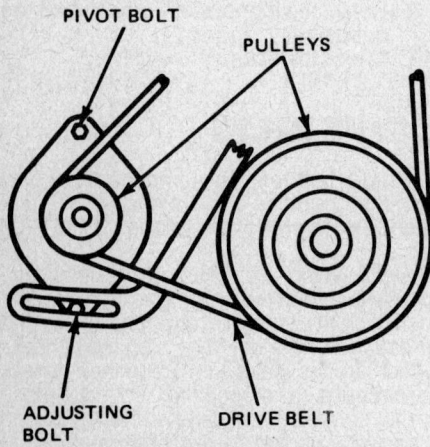

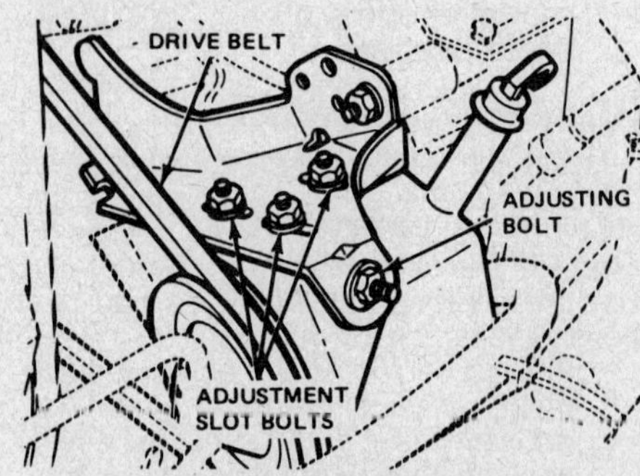

Fig. 25 Drive belt adjuster. Adjusting bolt & adjusting bolt slot type

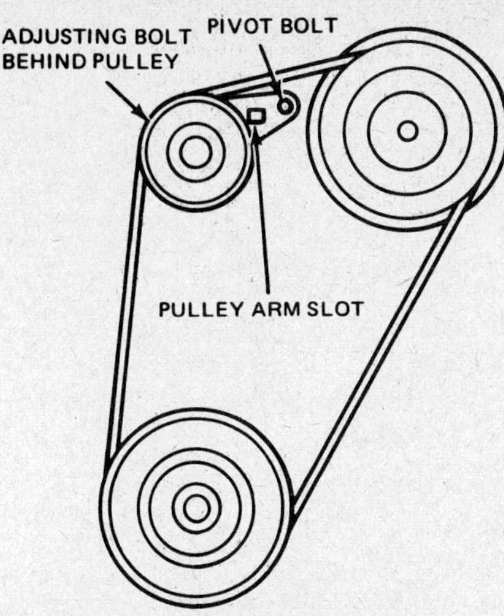

Fig. 26 Drive belt adjuster. Idler pulley type

glossy non-elastic surface, so hard that no mark is left when a fingernail is forced into the surface.

2. Cracked back surface.
3. Cracked or separated reinforcing fabric.
4. Badly worn teeth, indicated in first stage by worn fabric on drive side and in second stage by worn fabric on load side of tooth. Coating will be worn away, fabric will appear fluffy and whitened, and core of belt may be visible.
5. Cracked or missing teeth.
6. Sides of belt worn or cracked.

NOTE: Refer to individual service sections for timing belt replacement.

BATTERY SERVICE

CONSTRUCTION & OPERATION

To understand why batteries malfunction, some knowledge of batteries is important. Simply stated, the battery is constructed of two unlike materials, a positive plate and a negative plate with a porous separator between the two plates. This assembly placed in a suitable battery case and filled slightly above the top of the plates with electrolyte (sulphuric acid and distilled water) forms a cell. The 12 volt battery is composed of 6 cells interconnected by plate straps. Note that batteries have varying number of plates per cell, but each cell in any given battery has the same number of plates.

The battery performs the following four basic functions in a vehicle:

1. Supplies electrical energy to the starter motor to crank and start the engine and also to the ignition system while the engine is being started.
2. Supplies electrical energy for accessories such as radio, tape deck, heater, and lights when engine is not running and the ignition switch is in the "OFF" or the "Accessory" position.
3. Supplies additional electrical energy for accessories while the engine is running when the output alternator is exceeded by the various accessories.
4. Stabilizes voltage in the electrical system. Satisfactory operation of the ignition system and any other electrical device is impossible with a damaged, weak or even underpowered (low rating) battery.

Sealed Batteries

Sealed batteries, called "Maintenance Free" or "Freedom" batteries, are available on some vehicles, and can also be purchased from other sources.

The sealed batteries have unique chemistry and construction methods which provide advantages.

Water never needs to be added to the battery.

The battery is completely sealed except for two small vent holes on the side. The vent holes allow what small amount of gasses are produced in the battery to escape. The special chemical composition inside the battery reduces the production of gas to an extremely small amount at normal charging voltages.

The battery has a very strong ability to withstand damaging effects of overcharge, and the terminals are tightly sealed to minimize leakage. A charge indicator in the cover indicates state of charge.

Compared to a conventional battery in which performance decreases steadily with age, the sealed battery delivers more available power at any time during its life. The battery has a reduced tendency to self-discharge as compared to a conventional battery.

BATTERY RATING & CAPACITY

The two most commonly used ratings are the 20 hour rating of 80° F and the cold cranking load capacity of the battery at 0° F, specified in amps. Batteries are also rated by watts in the Peak Watt Rating (PWR) which is actually the cold cranking ability of the battery at 0° F.

Another battery rating method is the reserve capacity rating in minutes. The purpose of this rating is to determine the length of time a vehicle can be operated with a faulty charging system (malfunctioning alternator or regulator). Batteries are normally marketed by the Ampere-Hour rating which is based on the 20 hour rating. The Ampere-Hour rating is also normally stamped on the battery case or on a label attached to the battery. A battery capable of furnishing 4 amps for a period of 20 hours is classified as an 80 ampere hour battery (4 amps x 20 hours = 80).

The Ampere-Hour rating should not be confused with the cranking performance of a battery at 0° F. Batteries with the same Ampere-Hour ratings can have various 0° F cranking capacities. The higher quality battery will have a higher Ampere-Hour rating and a higher cranking capacity rating at 0° F. Note that battery capacity will increase with larger number of plates per cell, larger size of plates, and larger battery case size allowing for more electrolyte solution.

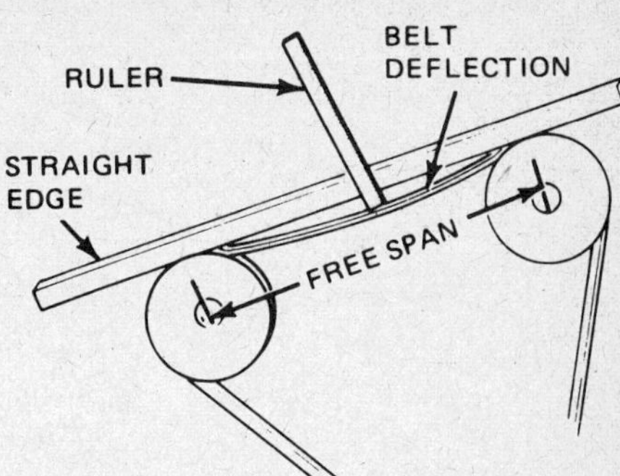

Fig. 27 Checking belt tension

SELECTING A REPLACEMENT BATTERY

Long and troublefree service can be better assured when the capacity or wattage rating of the replacement battery is at least equal to the wattage rating of the battery originally engineered for the application by the manufacturer.

The use of an undersized battery may result in poor performance and early failure. Sub-zero temperatures reduce capacity of a fully charged battery to 45% of its normal power and at the same time increase cranking load to 3½ times the normal warm weather load.

Hot weather can also place excessive electrical loads on the battery. Difficulty in starting may occur when cranking is attempted shortly after a hot engine has been turned off or stalls. High compression engines can be as difficult to start under such conditions as on the coldest day. Consequently, good performance can be obtained only if the battery has ample capacity to cope with these conditions.

A battery of greater capacity should be considered if the electrical load has been increased through the addition of accessories, or if driving conditions are such that the generator cannot keep the battery charged.

CAUSES OF DISCHARGED BATTERIES

There are numerous reasons that could cause a battery to discharge and appear to be defective, therefore the battery should not be targeted as the primary source of electrical and/or starting problems before it has been tested.

The following are some common conditions that could discharge a good battery:

1. Lights left "ON" or doors not closed properly, leaving dome light "ON."
2. Excessive use of accessories with the engine not running.
3. Improper installation of aftermarket accessories.
4. Alternator belt loose or damaged.
5. Dirty battery case causing a self-discharge condition.
6. Loose battery cable terminals.
7. Low alternator output.
8. High resistance in charging circuits caused by other loose electrical connections.

SAFETY PRECAUTIONS

CAUTION: Electrolyte solution in the battery is a strong and dangerous acid. It is extremely harmful to eyes, skin and clothing. If acid contact any part of the body, flush immediately with water for a period not less than 15 minutes. If acid is accidentally swallowed, drink large quantities of milk or water, followed by milk of magnesia, a beaten raw egg or vegetable oil. Call physician immediately.

When batteries are being charged, highly explosive hydrogen and oxygen gases form in each battery cell. Some of this gas escapes through the vent holes in the plugs on top of battery case and forms an explosive atmosphere surrounding the battery. This explosive gas will remain in and/or around the battery for several hours after the battery has been charged. Sparks or flames can ignite this gas and cause a dangerous battery explosion.

The following precautions must be observed to avoid battery explosion, personal harm and damage to the vehicle's electrical system.

1. Do not smoke near batteries being charged or those which have been recently charged. It is a good practice never to smoke near a battery even though the battery is in the vehicle.
2. Always shield your eyes when working with batteries.
3. Do not disconnect live (working) circuits (lights or accessories operating) at the terminals of batteries since sparking usually occurs at a point where such a circuit is disconnected.
4. Use extreme caution when connecting or disconnecting booster leads or cable clamps from battery chargers. Make sure live (working) circuits are disconnected before connecting or disconnecting the booster leads or cable clamps. Poor booster lead connections are a common cause of electrical arcing causing battery explosions.

TESTING BATTERY (SPECIFIC GRAVITY)

NOTE: The specific gravity of a sealed battery cannot be checked.

A hydrometer can be used to measure the specific gravity of the electrolyte in each cell. There are several types of hydrometers available, the least expensive consisting of a glass tube, a rubber bulb at the end of the tube and several balls within the tube. To use this type, the specific gravity of the battery must be interpreted by the number of balls which float to the surface of the electrolyte, according to the manufacturer's instructions.

The hydrometer indicates the concentration of the battery electrolyte, and electrolyte concentration relates directly to the battery's state of charge.

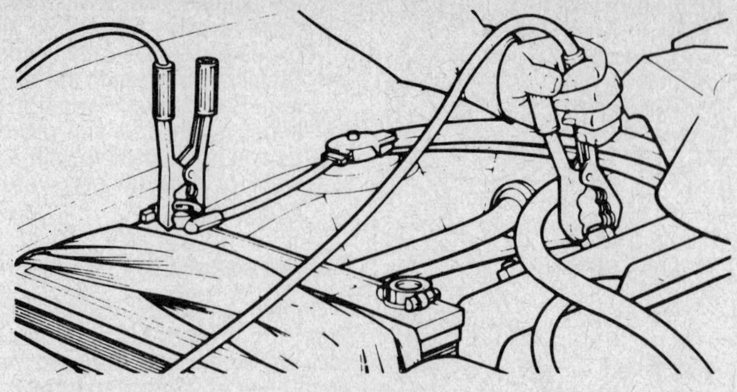

Fig. 28 Booster cable connections on vehicle w/dead battery

BOOST STARTING A VEHICLE WITH A DISCHARGED BATTERY

1. Be sure the ignition key is in the off position and all accessories and lights are off.
2. Shield eyes. Use goggles or similar eye protection.
3. Connect the booster cables from the positive (+) battery terminal of the discharged battery (vehicle to be started) to the positive (+) battery terminal of the vehicle used as the booster.
4. Connect one end of the other cable to negative (-) terminal of the good battery.
5. Connect one end of the other cable to engine bolthead or similar good contact spot on the vehicle being started, **Fig. 28.**

CAUTION: Never connect booster cable to negative terminal of dead battery.

6. Start engine of vehicle with boosting battery, wait several minutes to allow a charge to build up, then start engine of disabled vehicle.
7. Disconnect negative booster cable from each vehicle, then the positive cable.

NOTE: To prevent damage to other electrical components on the vehicle being started, make certain engine is at idle speed before disconnecting jumper cables.

CHARGING THE BATTERY

There are two separate methods of recharging batteries which differ basically in the rate of charge.

Slow Charging Method

Slow charging is the best and only method of completely recharging a battery. This method, when properly applied, may be used safely under all possible conditions providing the electrolyte is at proper level and the battery is capable of being fully charged. The normal charging rate is 5 amperes.

A fully charged battery is indicated when all cell specific gravities do not increase when checked at three one-hour intervals and all cells are gassing freely.

Charge periods of 24 hours or more may be required because of the low charging rate.

Quick Charging Method

In order to get a car back on the road in the least amount of time, it is sometimes necessary to quick charge a battery. The battery cannot be brought up to full charged condition by the quick charge method. It can, however, be substantially recharged or boosted but, in order to bring it to a fully charged condition, the charging cycle must be finished by charging at a low or normal rate. Some quick chargers have a provision for finishing the charging cycle at a low rate to bring the battery up to a fully charged condition.

CAUTION: Too high a current during quick charging will damage battery plates.

REPLACING BATTERY

Careless installation of a new battery can ruin the battery. In removing the old battery, note the location of the positive battery post so the new battery can be installed in the same position. Always remove the negative (ground) cable first.

Use an open-end wrench to loosen the clamp. If the nut is very tight, use one wrench on the head of the bolt and the other on the nut to avoid straining and possible cracking the battery cover. A pair of battery pliers can be used to loosen the nut, but a wrench should always be used on the head of the bolt.

If a cable terminal is corroded to the post, do not try to loosen it by hammering, or by resting a tool on the battery and prying — either method can break the battery container. Use a screw type terminal puller, or spread the cable terminals slightly with a screwdriver.

Clean any corrosion from the cables, battery case, or hold-downs, and inspect them. Paint any corroded steel parts with acid-proof paint. Make sure the cable is of the correct size and that its insulation and clamp terminal are in good condition.

Put the new battery in position, making sure it sits level, and tighten the hold-downs a little at a time, alternately, to avoid distorting and breaking the battery case.

The hold-downs should be snug enough to prevent bouncing, but not be too tight.

NOTE: Before connecting the cables, check the battery terminals to be sure the battery is not reversed.

Clean the battery post bright with sandpaper or a wire brush.

Don't hammer the terminals down on the posts, as the battery case may crack. Spread the terminals slightly if necessary. Connect the starter cable first and the negative (ground) cable last, tightening the terminal bolts after making sure the cables don't interfere with the vent plugs or rub against the hold-downs.

PERIODIC MAINTENANCE

The battery case, mounting and electrolyte level, cables and cable ends should be inspected whenever other underhood items such as engine oil, coolant and transmission fluid levels are checked.

Inspection

1. Check battery electrolyte level as outlined previously, and correct as needed.
2. Inspect battery case and mountings. Ensure that battery is securely mounted and that both battery and mount are free from dirt or heavy deposits of corrosion. Clean or repair as required.
3. Inspect cable ends for damage, looseness and corrosion, and clean or repair as needed.
4. Inspect cables. If cable insulation is worn or damaged, or if cable strands are broken, frayed or corroded, cable should be replaced.

Service

1. Disconnect clamp type cable ends from battery as follows:

NOTE: Always disconnect negative cable first.

a. Support clamp to prevent damaging battery and loosen nut with a suitable wrench or battery pliers. If through bolt begins to turn in clamp, hold bolt head with second wrench.

b. Spread clamp slightly using battery pliers or by twisting screwdriver in clamp opening, taking care not to damage post.

c. Remove clamp using a twisting motion.

CAUTION: If cable clamp is siezed on battery post, do not hammer or pry against clamp to loosen it as battery will be damaged. Remove clamp from battery post using a suitable puller.

2. Disconnect sensor wires from battery, if equipped, noting position for installation.
3. Loosen battery hold-down retainers using a suitable tool.

NOTE: It may be necessary to remove corrosion from battery retainers with a wire brush, then soak threads with penetrating oil to prevent breakage.

4. Lift battery from vehicle and place battery on a secure, insulated surface.
5. Clean heavy deposits from top of battery and battery mount with a wire brush, then mix a solution of baking soda and water to complete cleaning.
6. Plug battery vents to prevent solution from entering battery, then apply solution to battery and mount with a suitable brush.

CAUTION: Even a small amount of baking soda can damage battery, so be sure that battery vents are completely sealed and that solution does not enter battery.

7. Flush battery and mount with water, then wipe dry with suitable rags.
8. After cleaning battery mount and hold-down hardware, paint them with acid resistant paint to retard corrosion.
9. Clean battery posts and cable clamps with special battery cleaning tool, wire brush or sand paper, ensuring that all corrosion is removed. Replace any cable clamps or cables that are damaged.
10. Install battery in mount, ensuring that terminals are properly aligned.

NOTE: Take care not to spill electrolyte when installing battery. If electrolyte is accidentally spilled, flush area with water immediately.

11. Install battery hold-down and ensure that battery is secure in mount, then connect sensor wire, if equipped.
12. Reconnect positive cable to positive post and tighten cable clamp, then repeat with negative cable, ensuring that clamps are fully seated on post.

NOTE: It may be necessary to spread clamp slightly prior to installation. Do not force clamp onto post as battery will be damaged.

Ignition System Service

BASIC OPERATION

Combustion of air/fuel mixture in gasoline engines is initiated by spark ignition. Complete burning (combustion) of the air/fuel mixtures is essential for proper engine performance, acceptable driveability and fuel economy, and exhaust emission control. In order to ensure that the air/fuel mixtures burn completely, the spark that begins combustion must be of sufficient heat (voltage) and duration, and it must be applied at exactly the right moment during each cylinder's operating cycle.

The part of the vehicle electrical system that produces spark to ignite the air/fuel mixtures is the ignition system. Spark is created by producing an electric arc between electrodes of the spark plug, **Fig. 1,** which is installed in the combustion chamber of each cylinder. Depending upon engine design and operating conditions, 5000 to 30,000 volts of electricity are required to produce a spark of sufficient energy to ensure proper combustion of air/fuel mixtures.

The ignition system receives energy to produce spark from the vehicle battery and charging system. Since the nominal voltage of most automotive electrical systems is 12 volts, one of the main functions of the ignition system is to increase battery voltage to the voltage required to produce an arc across the spark plug of sufficient heat and duration. The other main function of ignition systems is to deliver these "stepped-up" voltages to the spark plug of each cylinder at exactly the right time to ensure that air/fuel mixtures burn completely and transfer the maximum amount of energy to produce power.

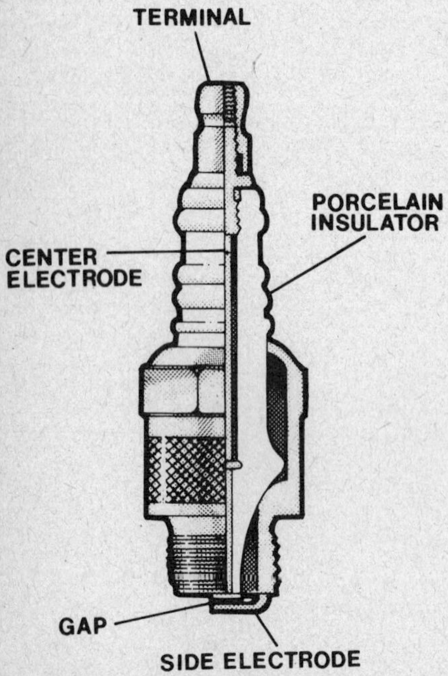

TERMINAL
PORCELAIN INSULATOR
CENTER ELECTRODE
GAP
SIDE ELECTRODE

Fig. 1 Typical spark plug cross-sectional view

Ignition systems are broken down into two main sub-systems which relate to the two main system functions. The primary (low voltage) side of the system performs the function of increasing battery voltage to the levels necessary to produce spark. The secondary side of the system delivers the high voltage to the spark plugs.

The ignition coil is the transformer that steps-up battery voltage to produce spark, and also the division point between primary and secondary ignition circuits. The coil consists of two coils of wire, insulated from each other, which are wound around an iron core, **Fig. 2.** The primary windings consist of a few turns of large diameter wire, while the secondary windings consist of many turns of fine wire. The coil creates high voltages necessary to produce spark through magnetic induction.

As battery voltage (current) flows through the coil primary windings, a magnetic field is produced. When current flow through the primary windings is momentarily interrupted, the magnetic field instantly collapses and high voltage is induced in the coil secondary windings. This induced voltage is discharged through the spark plug, creating spark to initiate combustion.

Secondary voltage strength is determined by the strength of the magnetic field created by current flow in the primary windings, the speed with which the magnetic field collapses and the difference between the number of turns or wire in the primary and secondary sides of the coil. The longer current flows in the primary windings (dwell period), the stronger the magnetic field created will be. The stronger the magnetic field is and the quicker it collapses, the higher the voltages in the secondary circuit will be. In addition, secondary voltages increase as the difference between the number of turns of wire in the primary and secondary windings increase.

The ignition distributor, **Fig. 3,** acts as both the switch that turns current flow on and off in the primary circuit, and as the mechanism that delivers secondary (high) voltages to each spark plug at the right time. The distributor is driven by the engine and synchronized to the engine's mechanical operation. When the distributor is properly installed and adjusted, it will momentarily stop current flow in the primary circuit and connect the coil secondary windings to the spark plug of each cylinder just as the piston in that cylinder is reaching top dead center on the compression stroke. This synchronization between ignition system electrical operation and engine mechanical operation is referred to as ignition timing.

Common practice is to relate the ignition firing point to the rotation of the crankshaft, and to express this relationship in degrees. The point of crankshaft rotation where the piston is at Top Dead Center (TDC) is expressed as zero degrees. Generally, the ignition system is adjusted so that the firing point will occur before TDC, which is referred to as ignition advance. If the firing point is set to occur after TDC, it is referred to as spark retard.

In order for air/fuel mixtures to transfer maximum energy to the engine, the mixture must reach the point of complete combustion just after each piston has reached TDC on its compression stroke. Because there is a slight lag between the time that the mixture begins to burn (ignition) and the time that complete combustion is achieved, ignition must occur before the piston has reached TDC and begun its downward travel. If the spark occurs too late, energy is lost because the piston is already moving downward when the mixture reaches its maximum explosive force. If spark occurs too early, the piston must fight against the explosive force in order to rise, which absorbs energy and ultimately causes damage to engine components. Therefore, correct timing of the ignition system is essential for efficient engine operation.

Basic ignition timing is determined by the installation position of the distributor. However, ideal ignition timing to ensure proper combustion varies constantly with changing engine operating conditions. Ignition systems have built in electronic, mechanical and/or vacuum operated devices which advance or retard ignition timing from the basic setting to compensate for changing loads, air/fuel mixtures and engine speeds.

CONVENTIONAL IGNITION SYSTEMS

Conventional ignition systems use a cam operated switch to interrupt current flow in the primary circuit. The contacts of this switch, called breaker points, are mounted in the distributor housing and op-

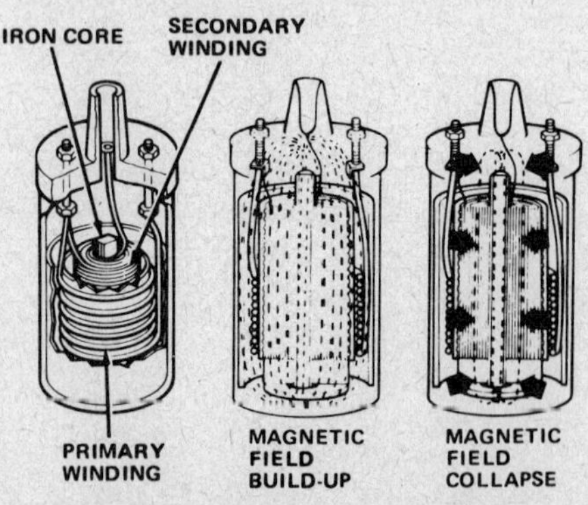

Fig. 2 Typical ignition coil construction & operation

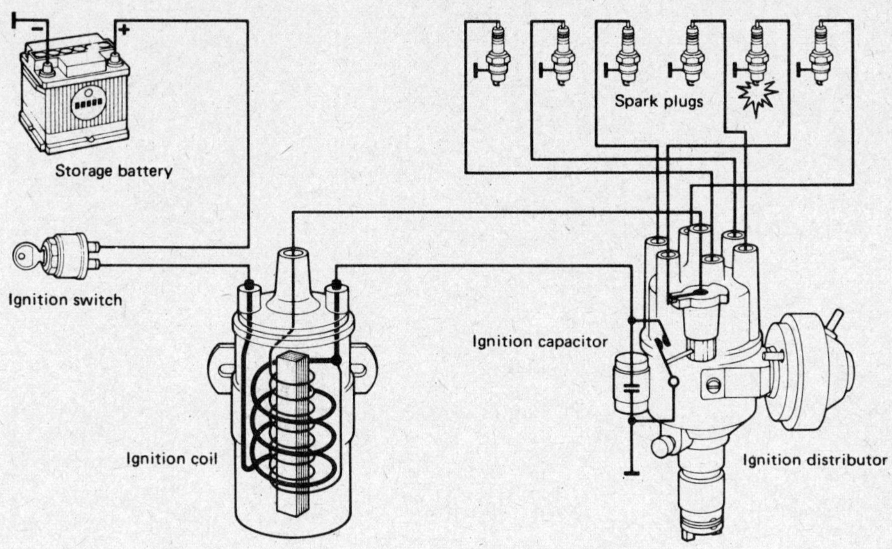

Fig. 3 Conventional ignition system schematic

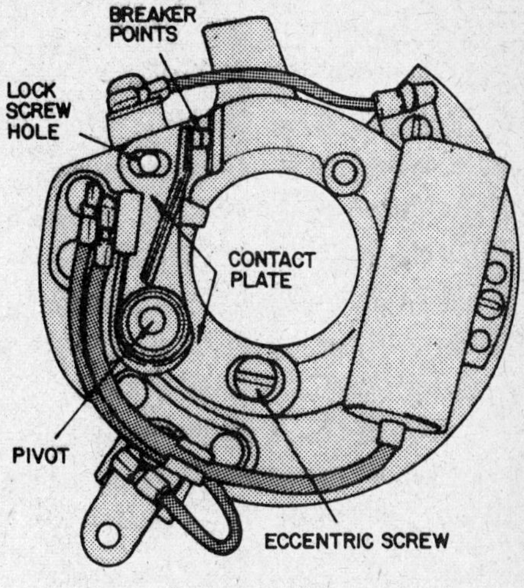

Fig. 4 Typical breaker point assembly installation

erated by a cam on the rotating distributor shaft, **Fig. 3,** which has the same number of lobes as the engine has cylinders. A rubbing block on the moveable contact of the breaker point assembly, **Fig. 4,** rides on the distributor shaft cam, and the contacts are opened each time a lobe rotates past the rubbing block.

Battery voltage is supplied to the ignition coil through the ignition switch, and the circuit is completed to ground through the breaker point contacts. A ballast resistor between the ignition switch and coil, or a resistor within the coil, limits voltage in the primary circuit in order to prolong breaker contact life. However, on most models the primary resistance is by-passed during starting in order to provide increased spark energy. The ignition capacitor, usually called a condenser, is connected in parallel with the breaker points, **Fig. 3,** and acts to reduce arcing across the contacts as they open, further increasing contact life.

Voltage from the ignition coil is supplied to the moveable contact of the breaker point assembly, usually through the contact arm spring. The moveable contact is insulated from the ground path by the rubbing block and insulators at the contact arm pivot and spring mount/terminal connection, **Fig. 4,** allowing current to flow through the primary ignition circuit only when contacts are closed. The amount of time that the contacts are closed and allowing current to flow through the primary circuit is referred to as the dwell period, and it is the dwell period which determines the magnetic field strength in the primary coil windings, and ultimately, secondary circuit voltage output. Dwell period is controlled by a number of factors, including dwell angle, engine speed and mechanical inefficiencies of the system.

Dwell angle is the number of degrees that the distributor shaft rotates from the time that the breaker point contacts close until they are opened again by the next cam. Dwell angle is determined by the number of degrees of distributor rotation per engine cycle (720°) divided by the number of lobes on the cam, cam lobe design, and the breaker point contact gap adjustment. The fewer number of cylinders the engine has, and/or the smaller the breaker contact gap, the larger the dwell angle will be. The dwell angle remains constant as long as the contact gap remains fixed and the contact arm spring keeps the rubbing block in contact with the distributor cam, and serves as the primary checking and adjustment parameter for the contact breaker system.

While the dwell angle remains fixed as long as the system is operating properly, the dwell period (coil saturation) varies constantly with engine RPM and is adversely affected if the system is not adjusted and operating properly. At low engine speeds, the actual amount of time that current flows through the coil primary windings is more than adequate to produce high secondary voltages, but if current flows through the breaker contacts for too long, they become overheated and damaged. As engine speed increases, the actual amount of time that current flows through the system decreases, and secondary voltage strength decreases proportionally. The decrease in secondary voltages at higher RPM is compounded by the mechanical instability of the contact arm as it is required to open and close the contacts at a faster rate. Therefore, distributor cam design and the specified contact gap are a compromise which must allow for adequate coil saturation at high RPM, while allowing for acceptable contact life during low speed operation. It is the mechanical limitations of this system, and the necessary compromises in performance required by these limitations, that have led to the increased use of electronically triggered ignition systems.

In a conventional ignition distributor, the breaker points and condenser of the primary circuit and a cap with terminals to distribute secondary voltage to the spark plug of each cylinder are mounted on the distributor housing, **Fig. 5.** An engine driven shaft rotates within this housing and cap assembly, on which is mounted the breaker point operating cam and a rotor contact. While distributor design varies from vehicle to vehicle, all conventional distributors operate in a similar manner.

A centrally located terminal inside the distributor cap receives secondary voltage pulses from the ignition coil each time the primary circuit is opened by the breaker points. These voltage pulses are distributed to the proper terminal for the cylinder to be fired by the shaft mounted rotor. These terminals are evenly spaced around the inner perimeter of the cap, and as the rotor spins it contacts each terminal, in turn, delivering secondary voltage.

The distributor shaft, along with the cam and distributor rotor are driven by and timed to the engine's mechanical operation. The cam is indexed so that the lobes that open the breaker point contacts each time a piston nears top dead center on its compression stroke. The rotor is indexed so that it completes the secondary voltage circuit to the proper terminal in the cap for each cylinder, just as the cam is opening the breaker points. Therefore, proper ignition timing is dependent upon the relative fixed installation position of the distributor housing in relation to the rotating distributor shaft.

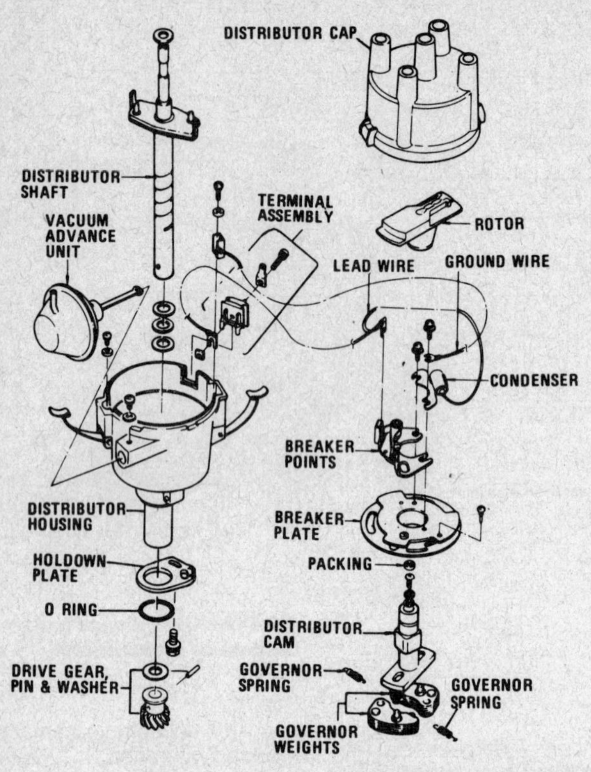

Fig. 5 Conventional ignition distributor exploded view

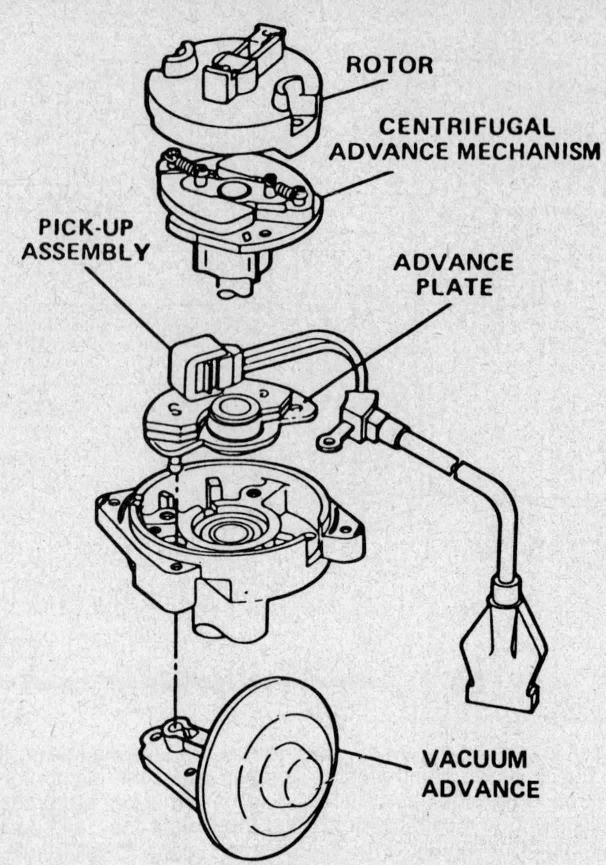

Fig. 6 Typical electronic ignition distributor exploded view. Single pole magnetic pick-up type

While an engine can operate fairly well with the ignition timing set at a fixed value, acceptable fuel economy and performance are dependant upon being able to tailor ignition timing to various vehicle operating conditions. Two systems, found on most ignition systems, are used to adjust ignition timing during engine operation to compensate for operating conditions. A mechanical advance system is used to alter the installation position of the breaker point operating cam on the distributor shaft, and a vacuum diaphragm capsule is used to alter the installation position of the breaker point contacts in relation to the operating cam.

On models with a centrifugal (mechanical) advance system, the distributor shaft is formed in two pieces, providing a separation between the part of the shaft that is driven by the engine and the part on which the breaker point cam is mounted, **Fig. 5**. An assembly of springs, levers, governor weights and pins holds the parts of the shaft in proper alignment while allowing them to rotate independent of one another slightly. As engine speed increases, weights are forced outward against spring tension, operating a lever which in turn advances the breaker point cam and distributor rotor in the direction of distributor shaft rotation. This action effectively causes the ignition spark to be created and delivered earlier in relation to piston position than the base timing setting allows. When engine speed decreases, the springs pull the weights in and the breaker cam and distributor rotor return to the base timing position.

On models with vacuum advance (or retard), the breaker points are mounted on a plate within the distributor housing. The plate is able to rotate concentrically around the distributor shaft, allowing the breaker point installation position to be altered in relation to the operating cam. A diaphragm capsule operated by engine vacuum is connected to the plate, and when vacuum is applied to the capsule the plate rotates. To advance the ignition timing, the plate is rotated in the opposite direction of shaft rotation; to retard the timing, the plate is rotated in the same direction as the distributor shaft rotates. A spring within the diaphragm capsule returns the breaker plate to the base timing position when the vacuum signal is removed.

ELECTRONIC IGNITION SYSTEMS

In order to properly ignite air/fuel mixtures required for exhaust emission control under all operating conditions, many vehicles covered in this manual use electronic ignition systems. On electronic systems, the breaker points, operating cam and condenser used on conventional systems to control primary circuit voltage have been replaced by a non-mechanical triggering mechanism and an electronic control unit (module). This allows the electronic systems to control current flow through the ignition primary circuit with more flexibility and precision, resulting in higher secondary voltages and more precise ignition timing. In addition, because there is no mechanical triggering mechanism to wear out, electronic systems require less maintenance.

Although electronic ignition components differ in design from manufacturer to manufacturer, or even within a single manufacturer's vehicle line, all current systems operate in a similar manner. Each system consists of a control module which controls current flow in the primary circuit, and on some systems ignition timing; a distributor which containes a trigger and sensor mechanism, and on some models the module, and mechanical and/or vacuum operated advance mechanisms; a coil which steps-up batter voltages to produce spark; a distributor cap with terminals for each cylinder and a rotor which directs secondary voltages to the proper cap terminal; specially insulated wires to carry secondary voltages from the distributor cap to each spark plug; primary (low voltage) wiring that links the control module, trigger sensor, ignition coil and the vehicle electrical system. Installation and mounting of these components varies from vehicle to vehicle.

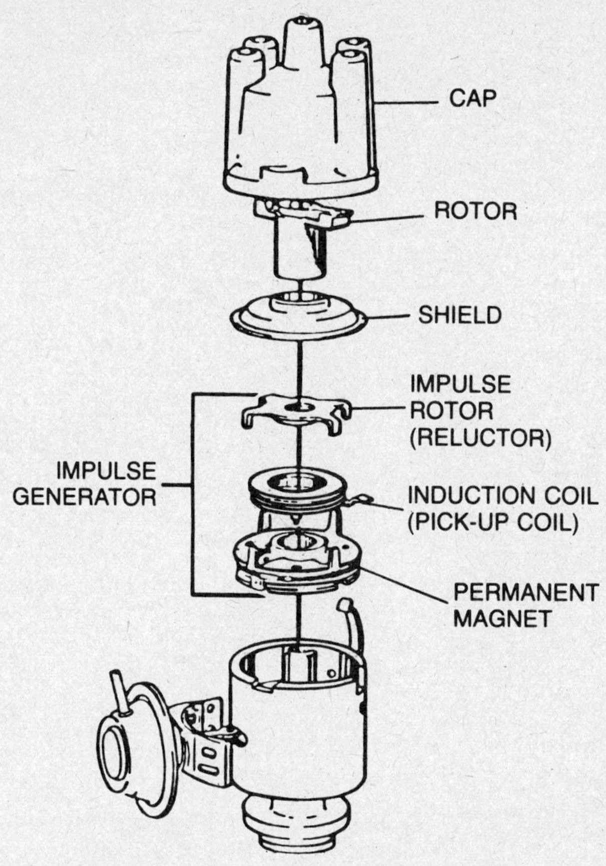

Fig. 7 Typical electronic ignition distributor exploded view. Multi-pole magnetic pick-up type

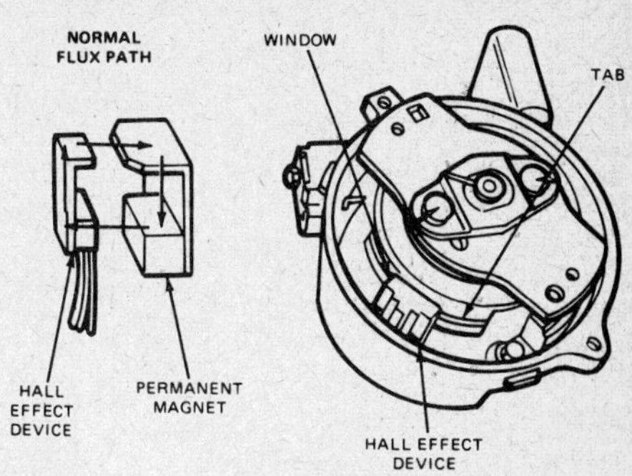

Fig. 8 Typical Hall effect generator

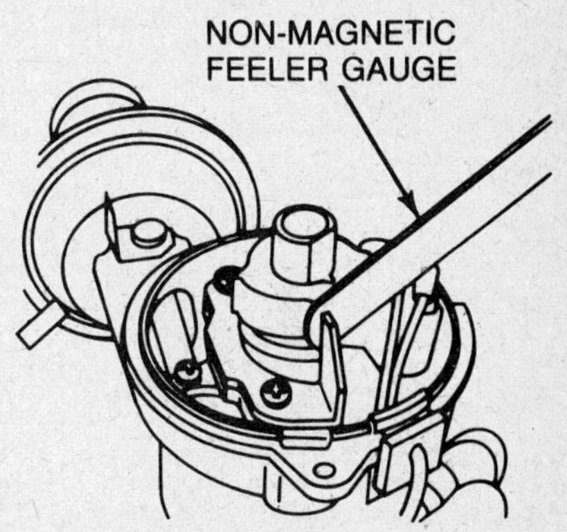

Fig. 9 Air gap check. Magnetic pulse type distributor

The electronic ignition coil consists of primary and secondary windings like coils used with breaker point systems. Current flow through the coil primary windings is switched on and off by the electronic control module, which on most systems, has the ability to vary the "on" time (dwell period) to match secondary voltages to engine operating conditions. Module operation is controlled by a magnetic "impulse" type mechanism which consists of a trigger wheel mounted on the distributor shaft and a sensor coil, or by a Hall type sensor.

The device most widely used to control electronic ignition module operation is an impulse generator known as a pick-up coil. In systems using this device, current switching in the primary ignition circuit is controlled by the module based on voltage pulses generated through magnetic induction. While construction of induction pick-up and trigger assemblies varies, **Figs. 6 and 7,** all of the systems operate on the same basic principle.

The pick-up, consisting of many turns of fine wire wrapped around a pole piece and permanent magnet with a number of internally protruding "teeth," is mounted on the distributor housing or breaker plate, replacing the breaker point assembly used in conventional systems. A trigger wheel with the same number of externally protruding "teeth" as the engine has cylinders is mounted on the distributor shaft, replacing the cam used in conventional systems. The trigger wheel, also called a stator, rotor or reluctor, rotates past or within the pick-up coil pole piece, with the teeth of the two assemblies separated by a narrow air gap. When the teeth of the two assemblies are aligned, the action of the trigger wheel teeth moving through the air gap creates a magnetic field which in turn induces voltage in the windings of the pick-up. The ignition control module uses these voltage pulses to control current switching in the primary circuit as outlined previously.

The other type device used to control ignition module operation is a semi-conductor pulse generator that uses the Hall effect principle to generate control signals. The Hall effect generator, **Fig. 8,** consists of a semi-conductor element and a permanent magnet which are separated by an air gap, a slotted umbrella type rotor (trigger) which passes through the air gap, and an integrated circuit. Whenever the semi-conductor element is exposed to the force field of the permanent magnet, a voltage is generated across the semi-conductor called the Hall effect, but when the magnetic field is blocked, no Hall effect voltage is generated.

In this type system, the semi-conductor, magnet and integrated circuit are mounted on the distributor housing or breaker plate replacing the breaker contacts used in conventional systems, and the slotted trigger rotor is mounted on the distributor shaft, **Fig. 8.** As the rotor passes through the air gap, Hall effect voltages are switched on and off by the action of the vanes and slots (windows) passing between the magnet and the semi-conductor. When a slot is in the air gap, voltage is generated across the semi-conductor, but when a rotor vane is in the gap, no voltage is generated. These alternating voltage pulses are conditioned by the integrated circuit and used by the ignition module to control current switching in the primary ignition circuit.

On some electronic ignition systems, all spark timing functions are controlled by the electronic module, allowing for more precise control of engine operation and exhaust emissions. However, most systems on vehicles covered in this manual use mechanical and/or vacuum controlled systems to alter spark timing to suit operating conditions. Operation of these spark control systems is similar to the operation of systems used on models with conventional breaker point ignition.

IGNITION SERVICE

IGNITION SYSTEM TUNE-UP

The following is an outline of the visual inspections and repair procedures neces-

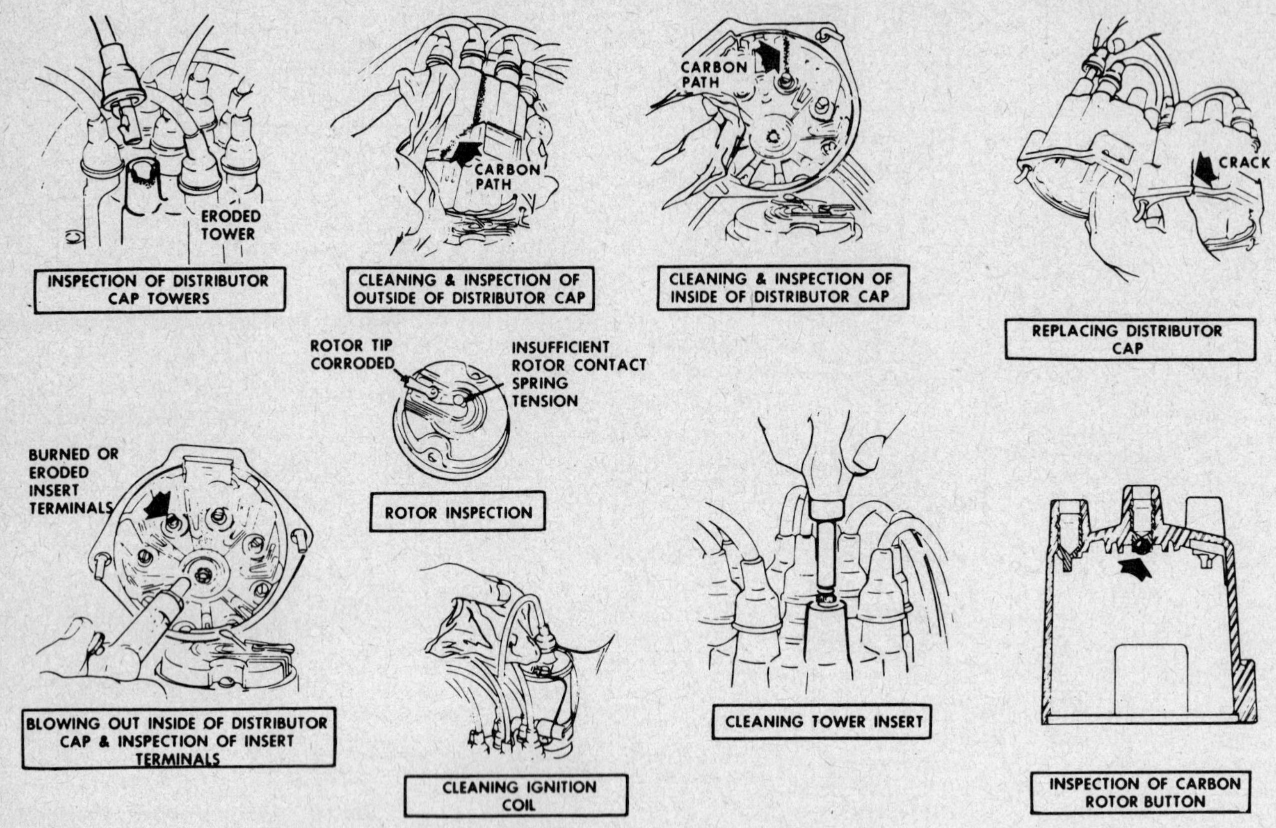

Fig. 10 Distributor cap & rotor inspection

sary to ensure proper operation of the ignition systems described previously. Refer to appropriate headings for actual repair, replacement and inspection procedures for each component or sub-assembly. Follow all listed precautions to ensure successful repairs.

1. Inspect battery, cables and connections.
2. Ensure that battery is fully charged, connections are tight and free from corrosion, and that cables are not frayed or damaged.

NOTE: Refer to "General Maintenance Section" for battery service procedures.

3. Inspect wiring and connections between the distributor and remotely mounted ignition coil, control module and fuel control computer, if equipped.
4. Ensure that all connections are tight and free from corrosion, and that wiring is properly routed and not pinched or damaged.

NOTE: An electrically conductive silicone grease is used in the wiring connectors of most electronic ignition systems. Do not remove this grease from the connectors.

5. Inspect spark plug wires. Ensure that wires are properly retained in the clamps provided to keep them away from other engine components.
6. Spark plug wires that are cracked, broken, burned or saturated with oil should be replaced.
7. Inspect distributor cap and rotor for cracks, burned terminals and insulation, and carbon tracking.
8. On conventional systems, check breaker points and condenser, and replace if necessary. On electronic systems, check distributor air gap using a non-magnetic feeler gauge, Fig. 9.

NOTE: Although the distributor air gap is not adjustable on many models, the correct air gap is essential for proper ignition system operation.

CAUTION: Using a ferrous metal (steel, iron, etc.) gauge to check the distributor air gap will damage ignition system components.

9. Inspect ignition coil, noting the following:
   a. Coil should be replaced if terminals are burned or damaged.
   b. Oil filled coils should be replaced if there are signs of leakage or cracks around the high tension tower or primary terminals.
   c. On open type coils, replace coil if windings are burned or terminals are loose.

NOTE: Slight play in the windings of open type coils is normal, and does not indicate a defective coil.

10. Remove and inspect spark plugs, and replace as needed.
11. Check basic ignition timing.
12. Check operation of centrifugal, vacuum and/or electronic ignition timing control mechanisms.

DISTRIBUTOR CAP & ROTOR, REPLACE

Observe the following precautions when replacing the cap and rotor:

1. Note installation position of the No. 1 spark plug wire on the distributor cap.
2. Mark each spark plug wire with the corresponding cylinder number, using tape, paint etc. If wiring positions become confused, refer to the "Tune Up Specifications" section in the individual chapters.
3. Note the installation position of the cap on the distributor housing, and ensure that the cap is properly seated during installation.
4. Note the rotor installation position on the distributor shaft, and ensure that the rotor is properly indexed and seated during installation.

CAUTION: If the cap and/or rotor are improperly installed, cranking the engine will damage distributor components. If the ignition wires are incorrectly installed, the engine may backfire, resulting in component damage and a possible engine compartment fire.

Removal

1. Disconnect battery ground cable to prevent short circuits or accidental cranking of engine.
2. Release spring clips securing cap to distributor, or loosen retaining screws using a suitable screwdriver.
3. Lift cap from distributor taking care not to damage rotor or carbon button in center of cap.
4. If plug wires are still connected, invert cap for inspection taking care not to stretch or dislodge wires.
5. Loosen screws securing rotor, if equipped, then remove rotor from distributor shaft.

NOTE: If rotor is seized on shaft, pry rotor from shaft using suitable levers taking care not to damage distributor components.

Inspection

1. Inspect cap as shown in Fig. 10. Cap should be replaced if it is cracked, carbon tracked, burnt, or if terminals are excessively worn or corroded.
2. Inspect rotor contacts and replace rotor if contacts are damaged or severely pitted.
3. Inspect rotor body and replace rotor if plastic is cracked or if there are signs of burning (indicated by gray-white spots).

Installation

1. Install rotor on distributor shaft, ensuring that all locating tabs and notches are aligned, and that rotor is fully seated. Tighten retaining screws evenly, if equipped.
2. If cap is to be replaced, transfer spark plug wires, one at a time, to proper terminals on replacement cap.
3. Position cap on distributor housing, ensuring that all locating tabs are engaged in their respective slots and that cap is fully seated.
4. Secure cap to distributor as follows:
   a. On caps retained with bale clips, press each clip into its slot by hand, while holding cap in position.
   b. On caps retained with screws, tighten screws securely and evenly, but do not over tighten screws as cap may be damaged.
5. Check installation position of cap and wires against firing order diagram shown in "Tune-Up Specifications" section before starting engine.

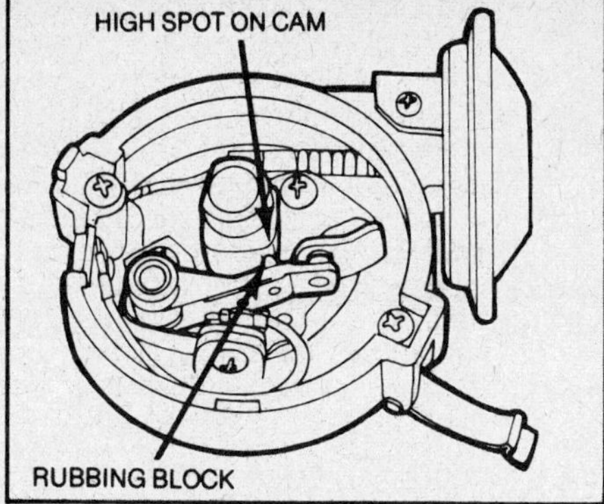

Fig. 11 Aligning high spot on breaker cam w/rubbing block

BREAKER POINTS & CONDENSER, REPLACE

1. Remove distributor cap and rotor as outlined previously.
2. Insepect contacts and rubbing block, and replace breaker point assembly if contacts are burned, pitted or contaminated with oil, or if rubbing block is worn.

NOTE: Condenser should be replaced whenever the breaker point assembly is replaced.

3. Disconnect electrical connectors from condenser and ignition coil as follows:
   a. On models with spade type terminals, separate connectors noting position of wires for assembly.
   b. On models with screw terminal connection on side of distributor housing, remove screw or nut and remove wires from insulator block.
   c. On models with screw connection on contact assembly, loosen screw or nut and disconnect wires from contacts.

CAUTION: Note installation position of all wires, insulators and retainers to ensure proper assembly. Improper installation may cause a short circuit and result in a no-start condition or component damage.

4. Loosen screw(s) securing contact assembly to breaker plate or distributor housing, then remove screws with a magnetized screw driver or probe.
5. Remove contact assembly, noting position of ground strap, if equipped.
6. Loosen screw securing condenser to breaker plate or distributor housing, then remove screw and condenser. If condenser is mounted inside distributor, use a suitable magnet to prevent dropping screw into distributor.

CAUTION: If screws are dropped into distributor, they must be removed before cranking engine. Screws left inside distributor may jam advance weights and/or shaft, damaging the distributor.

7. Clean breaker assembly mounting surface and operating cam with a clean rag, then inspect distributor.
8. If cam is rough or worn, or if distributor shaft has excessive side play, points will not remain adjusted properly and distributor should be replaced.
9. Coat breaker cam with suitable lubricant and lightly lubricate exposed advance weights, wiping away excess lubricants.

NOTE: Do not apply more than two match heads of lubricant to breaker cam.

10. Install replacement condenser and tighten screw securely. Do not over tighten retaining screw as threads are easily stripped.
11. Position replacement breaker point assembly in housing ensuring that pivot is properly seated and ground strap, if equipped, is installed on top of contact flange.
12. Install retaining screw(s) hand tight and align adjustment slot on contact assembly with slot in mounting plate for preliminary adjustment.
13. Reconnect condenser and coil wires in position noted during disassembly, then tighten retainer, if equipped.

NOTE: Ensure that wire terminals are not contacting grounded contact assembly flange or distributor housing, and that wiring is aligned so that it will not contact moving parts inside distributor.

14. Rotate engine until rubbing block contact arm is bearing against high spot on breaker cam, Fig. 11.
15. Adjust contact gap to specifications as follows:
    a. Move contact mounting flange using eccentric adjuster screw, Fig. 4, or slot, Fig. 12.
    b. Check gap using a clean dry feeler gauge the same size as the specified contact gap.
    c. If gap is too large, move base of contact assembly away from cam. If gap is too narrow, move contact base toward cam.
    d. When gap has been adjusted so that feeler gauge can be drawn between contacts with a very slight drag, tighten retaining screws.
    e. Recheck adjustment, and if it has changed after tightening screws, loosen screws slightly and repeat adjustment procedure.
16. Ensure that primary wiring is properly aligned, then install rotor and cap.
17. Connect suitable dwell meter to engine following manufacturer's instructions, start engine and check dwell.
18. If contact gap has been properly adjusted, dwell should be within 2° of specifications. If dwell is not as specified, readjust contact gap.

NOTE: Increasing contact gap decreases dwell angle, while decreasing contact gap increases dwell angle.

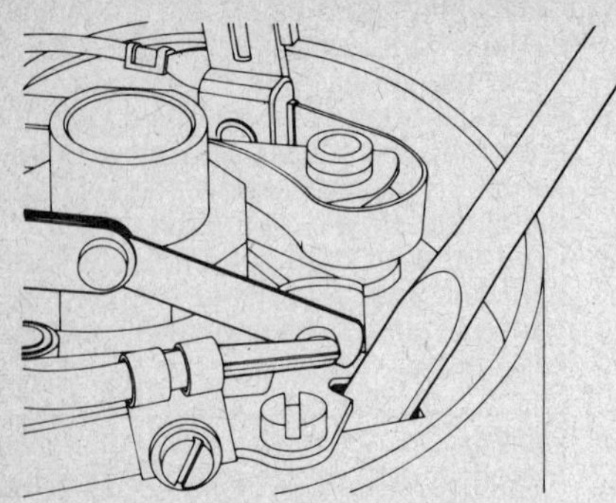

Fig. 12 Adjusting breaker contacts w/slotted type adjuster

19. When dwell is within specifications, check ignition timing following instructions on Emission Control Information Label.

NOTE: If engine will not start after replacing breaker points or condenser, recheck installation position of wiring, contacts and condenser. Ensure that wiring, moveable contact arm and spring are not grounded.

SPARK PLUGS, REPLACE

1. Mark each spark plug wire with the corresponding cylinder number, using tape, paint, etc. Refer to "Tune-Up Specifications" for cylinder numbering.
2. Disconnect wires from each spark plug as follows:
   a. Grasp wire boot firmly and twist boot back and forth approximately ½ turn to free boot from plug.
   b. Still holding boot, pull wire away from plug with a slight twisting motion.
   c. Pull wires off by the boot only. Pulling on the wires may cause internal breakage.
3. Blow out loose dirt adjacent to spark plugs before loosening each plug.

NOTE: If compressed air is not available, remove dirt by blowing through a straw or short length of hose.

4. Install a suitable spark plug socket over spark plug.
5. Connect ratchet to spark plug socket using extensions, if necessary, to allow ratchet handle to swing, then turn plug counterclockwise until loose (approximately 1 full turn).
6. Loosen each plug as outlined in steps 4 and 5, then briefly crank engine to "blow out" loosened carbon.
7. Remove spark plugs by hand, using plug socket and a suitable extension to reach plugs.
8. If a spark plug cannot be turned by hand after performing steps 4-6, proceed as follows:
   a. Apply penetrating oil to plug threads and retighten plug with ratchet.
   b. Wait 1-2 minutes, then attempt to remove plug as outlined previously.
   c. If plug is still too tight to be unscrewed by hand, alternately tighten and loosen plug (steps "a" and "b") until it becomes free.

CAUTION: If spark plug does not loosen after performing steps "a" and "b" a few times, plug may be incorrectly installed, seized, or damaged. Retighten plug and have plug removed by a professional technician.

9. Inspect plugs and replace as needed. Correct any problem causing abnormal spark plug condition.
10. Adjust gaps for each spark plug to be installed using a round, wire type feeler gauge, Fig. 13, and a suitable bending tool.

CAUTION: Always use a sutable tool to adjust spark plug gap. Tapping ground electrode against a hard surface or prying against the center electrode may damage spark plug. Never install a spark plug without first checking the electrode gap.

11. Install spark plugs, using the plug socket and extension to turn each plug clockwise, by hand, until plug is seated against cylinder head.

NOTE: If plugs cannot be installed by hand, ensure that threads in cylinder head are free from dirt and damage. If threads are damaged, have engine repaired by a competent technician.

12. Torque spark plugs to specifications found in individual chapters. If torque wrench is not available, turn each taper-seat type plug 1/16 turn clockwise from hand tight position; turn each gasket seat plug ¼ turn.
13. Lightly coat inside of each plug wire boot with a suitable silicone grease to prevent boots from seizing on plugs, then reconnect wires.
14. Check installation position of plug wires against engine firing order. Ensure that wires are properly connected before starting engine.

SPARK PLUG WIRES, REPLACE

1. Remove spark plug wires individually, even if the entire set is being replaced, to ensure that each wire is routed properly.
2. On systems where wires are held in a retainer, release clips securing retainer to cap, free wires from cap terminals by turning boot back and forth, and allow assembly to rest in position on distributor.
3. On all models, disconnect spark plug wire at distributor, noting installation position.
4. Release wire from all looms and clamps between distributor and spark plug, then disconnect wire from plug.
5. Select a replacement wire of the same length and type, and having the same type terminals (straight, angled, etc.) as the wire that was removed.

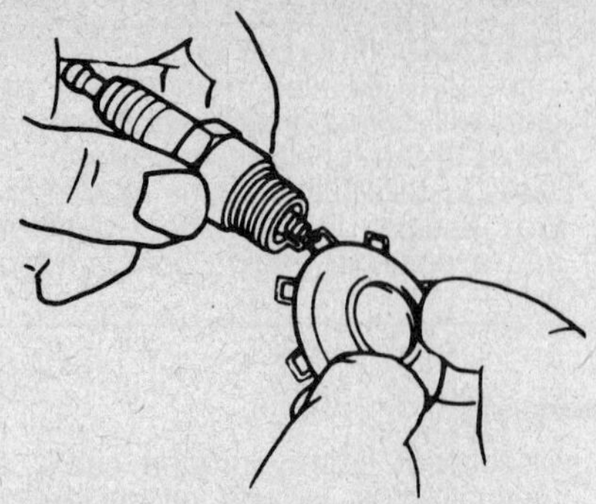

Fig. 13 Checking spark plug gap w/wire type gauge

6. Lightly coat inside of spark plug terminal boot with a suitable silicone grease to prevent wire from seizing on plug, then connect new wire to plug.

NOTE: Ensure that wire is fully seated on spark plug terminal end.

7. Route replacement wire through all looms and clamps installed to prevent wire from contacting hot or moving engine components.
8. Lightly lubricate inside of distributor terminal boot with suitable silicone grease, then connect wire to distributor cap terminal.
9. Repeat procedure with remaining wires that must be replaced.
10. Check installation position of all wires against engine firing order.
11. Ensure that wires are properly installed and fully seated before starting engine.

DISTRIBUTOR, REPLACE

The following is a general procedure which includes many of the precautions that must be observed whenever an ignition distributor is removed and installed on a gasoline engine. Steps 1 through 7 of the removal procedure can be used to check whether distributor installation position is correct, or to properly index the engine for distributor installation if the engine has been rotated with the distributor removed. However, because distributor installation position is critical to proper engine performance, and because there are many possible mistakes that can result in severe engine damage and even personal injury, removal and installation of the distributor should not be attempted by the beginner.

Read the procedure and included precautions carefully, noting each step that may (or may not) apply to your vehicle. If there is any doubt as to whether you possess the required mechanical skills or the proper tools to perform the steps as outlined, seek the assistance of a professional technician.

1. Disconnect wire from No. 1 spark plug, then remove plug as outlined.
2. Disconnect coil wire from center terminal on distributor cap, then ground coil wire to engine using a suitable jumper wire.
3. Crank engine in short bursts, holding thumb over spark plug opening, until compression pressure can be felt at opening.
4. When compression pressure can be felt at opening, disengage starter and observe timing marks.

NOTE: Refer to "Tune-Up Specifications" for timing mark locations.

5. Stationary and movable marks should be quite close to each other. Rotate engine by hand, as needed, to align timing marks at 0° (TDC) position.
6. Mark position of No. 1 spark plug wire terminal on distributor housing, then remove distributor cap.
7. If rotor contact is pointing at mark made in step 6, proceed to next step; if not, proceed as follows:
   a. If contact is pointing directly away from mark (180° out), rotate engine exactly 1 full revolution, until timing marks are aligned at TDC, then proceed to step 8.
   b. If rotor contact is not pointing at or directly away from housing reference mark with timing marks aligned at TDC, distributor is incorrectly installed or defective, or engine timing chain may be defective. Engine should be checked by a professional technician.
8. Disconnect battery ground cable, then mark position of rotor contact and housing reference mark on engine using chalk, paint, etc.
9. Disconnect electrical connectors to distributor, then remove hold-down bolt and clamp.

NOTE: Special hold down bolts are used on some models to prevent distributor position adjustment. Do not attempt to remove these bolts unless you have the proper tool.

10. Lift distributor straight out of engine while observing rotor. Rotor may move away from reference position due to design of distributor drive gear. Note position of rotor when distributor is fully withdrawn.

CAUTION: Do not rotate engine with distributor removed. If engine is rotated, it will be necessary to return engine to TDC on the compression stroke of the reference cylinder before the distributor can be reinstalled.

Installation

1. Ensure that engine position has not changed while distributor was removed.
2. If distributor is being replaced, temporarily install cap on replacement distributor and mark position of cap reference terminal on housing.
3. Rotate distributor shaft so that rotor contact is pointing at reference mark on distributor housing.

NOTE: If rotor position changed as distributor was removed from engine, position rotor as noted in step 10 of removal procedure.

4. Align mark on distributor housing with mark on engine, then insert distributor into engine.
5. Distributor should seat fully in engine, and rotor contact mark on engine and mark on distributor housing should be aligned.

NOTE: If so equipped, ensure that oil pump driveshaft is properly engaged with distributor shaft. It may be necessary to crank engine with starter after distributor drive gear is partially engaged in order to engage oil pump shaft and allow distributor to seat.

6. Install distributor hold down clamp and retaining bolts.

NOTE: If it was necessary to rotate engine to allow full engagement of distributor shaft, recheck that distributor housing reference mark and rotor contact are aligned with reference cylinder at TDC on the compression stroke.

7. Reconnect electrical connectors and reinstall distributor cap.
8. Check basic ignition timing and adjust as needed.

IGNITION TIMING ADJUSTMENTS

During normal service, engines sparked by electronic ignition systems do not require ignition timing adjustments. Because there are no mechanical control components in the ignition system to wear out, ignition timing cannot change unless it is altered by adjustment or there is a component failure. However, as an aid to vehicle performance diagnosis, basic ignition timing should be checked to ensure that the ignition system is operating within specifications.

Observe the following precautions when checking or adjusting ignition timing.

1. Always use a timing light recommended by the manufacturer as suitable for your systems.
2. Never pierce the spark plug wire insulation when connecting the timing light. Once the insulation has been broken, voltage will jump to ground and the spark plug will not fire properly.
3. Since timing must be checked with the engine running at normal operating temperature, keep test equipment leads, clothing and your hands away from hot or moving engine components.

NOTE: Suitable eye protection should be worn when working around a running engine.

4. Refer to "Tune-Up Specifications" in the individual chapters and the underhood Emission Control Information label when performing adjustments.
5. Clean movable and stationary timing marks with a suitable solvent, then "highlight" the fixed reference mark and the specified adjustment value with chalk, white or yellow paint, etc.
6. Always adjust ignition timing to manufacturer's specifications. If there is any doubt about the correct specifications, or if vehicle performance is unsatisfactory with timing adjusted to specifications, seek assistance of a professional technician.

Checking & Adjustment

1. Connect timing light sensor lead to No. 1 spark plug wire and power leads to battery following manufacturer's instructions.
2. Connect suitable tachometer to ignition coil following manufacturer's instructions.
3. Start engine and run until it reaches normal operating temperature, then ensure that idle speed is within specifications.
4. Prepare engine for adjustment following instructions on underhood Emission Control Information Label.
5. Aim timing light at timing marks. Strobe action of lamp will act to "stop" moving mark.

NOTE: Refer to "Tune Up Specifications" for timing mark locations.

6. If movable indicator does not appear to "stop" at number indicating specified timing value, adjust distributor position as follows:
   a. Loosen distributor hold down bolt just enough to allow distributor to be rotated.
   b. If movable indicator "Stops" after specified timing value (timing retarded), rotate distributor in the direction opposite rotor rotation.
   c. If movable indicator "stops" before specified timing value (timing advanced), rotate distributor in the direction of rotor rotation.

   NOTE: Move distributor in small amounts and recheck timing marks after each adjustment.

   d. When timing marks are aligned at specified value, tighten distributor hold down, then recheck timing to ensure that distributor has not moved.
7. If ignition timing cannot be adjusted to specifications within the normal adjustment range of distributor, recheck installation of test equipment.
8. If test equipment is properly connected, check for malfunction in the centrifugal or vacuum advance mechanisms.
9. If advance mechanisms are operating properly, but timing cannot be adjusted to specifications, have engine checked by a professional technician.

TROUBLESHOOTING

ENGINE CRANKS BUT WILL NOT START

1. Visually inspect engine electrical wiring and connectors for breaks, chafing, burns and damage, and repair wiring as needed.
2. Modify a spark plug by removing the side electrode, disconnect wire from one spark plug and insert modified plug into wire.
3. Hold modified plug against a suitable engine ground, then have an assistant crank engine.
4. If spark is evident, ignition system is satisfactory. If no spark is present, disconnect coil lead from center terminal of distributor cap.
5. Insert modified plug into coil wire and repeat step 3.
6. If spark is evident, check for defective cap and/or rotor, and replace as needed.
7. If no spark is evident in step 6, check voltage feed to ignition coil.
8. If sufficient voltage is available to ignition coil, inspect breaker contacts and rotor, if equipped, or have electronic ignition system tested by a professional technician.

ENGINE STARTS BUT RUNS ROUGH

1. Check for disconnected, broken or improperly routed vacuum hoses.
2. Check fuel delivery system, and ensure that a sufficient supply of fuel is available to engine.
3. Check ignition timing, and adjust to specifications.
4. Check for defective cap, rotor or ignition wires. With engine running, listen for "snapping" sound of secondary voltage jumping from wires to ground.
5. On conventional systems, inspect breaker points as outlined previously, and if points are pitted or burned, replace breaker points and condenser.
6. Remove and inspect spark plugs.
7. On models with electronic ignition, have system tested by a technician.

ACURA (Japan)

INDEX OF SERVICE OPERATIONS

General Engine Specifications

Year	Model	Engine CID ①/cc	Fuel System	Bore & Stroke Inches (mm)	Compression Ratio	Net Brake HP @ RPM	Net Torque Lbs. Ft. @ RPM	Normal Oil Pressure PSI
1986-87	Integra	4-97/1590	Fuel Inj.	2.95 x 3.54 (75 x 90)	9.3	113 @ 6250	99 @ 5500	60-78②
	Legend	V6-152/2494	Fuel Inj.	3.31 x 2.95 (84 x 75)	9.0	151 @ 5800	154 @ 4500	71-82②

①—Cubic inch displacement.
②—At 3000 RPM.

Valve Specifications

Year	Model	Valve Lash		Valve Angles		Valve Spring Pressure Lbs. @ In.	Stem Clearance		Stem Diameter	
		Int.	Exh.	Seat	Face		Intake	Exhaust	Intake	Exhaust
1986	Integra	.005	.006	45	45	—	.001-.002	.002-.003	.2591-.2594	.2579-.2583
	Legend	Zero①	Zero①	45	45	—	.001-.002	.002-.003	.2591-.2594	.2579-.2583
1987	Integra	.005	.006	45	45	—	.002-.004	.004-.006	.2591-.2594	.2579-.2583
	Legend	Zero①	Zero①	45	45	—	.001-.002	.002-.003	.2591-.2594	.2579-.2583

—Not available.
①—Hydraulic valve lifters.

Alternator & Regulator Specifications

Year	Model	Alternator			Regulated Voltage
		Rated Hot Output Amps	Hot Output Amps @ 5000 RPM	Hot Output Amps @ 6000 RPM	
1986-87	Integra	55	55	65	13.9-15.1
	Legend	75	70 ①	—	13.9-15.1

—Not available.
①—5500 RPM.

Starting Motor Specifications

Year	Model	Brush Spring Tension, Lbs.	Torque Test	
			Amperes	Volts
1986	Integra	①	350	8
	Legend	3.2-4.5	350	8
1987	Integra	①	350	8
	Legend	3.7-5.3	350	8

—Not available.
①—Mitsuba starter, 4.11-5.22 lbs.; ND starter, 3.22-4.53 lbs.

Pistons, Pins, Rings, Crankshaft & Bearings

Year	Model	Piston Clearance ①	Ring End Gap ①		Wristpin Diameter	Rod Bearings		Main Bearings			Shaft End Play
			Comp.	Oil		Shaft Diameter	Bearing Clearance	Shaft Diameter	Bearing Clearance	Thrust on Bear. No.	
1986–87	Integra	.0004	.015	.020	.7479	1.7707–1.7717	.0008–.0015	2.1644–2.1654	.0009–.0017	3	.004–.014
	Legend	.0002	.020	.020	.8660	2.0463–2.0472	.0010–.0020	2.5187–2.5197	.0009–.0019	3	.004–.014

①—Minimum.

Final Drive Gear Specifications

Year	Model	Carrier Type	Final Drive Gear Backlash		Differential Side Clearance ①		Pinion To Side Gear Backlash	
			Method	Clearance In.	Method	Clearance In.	Method	Clearance In.
1986–87	Integra	②	—	.0033–.0056	—	—	③	.002–.006
	Legend	②	—	.0060–.0080	—	—	③	.002–.006

—Not available.
①—Measured between snap ring and outer bearing race.
②—Integral with trans.
③—Thrust washers.

Engine Tightening Specifications

Year	Model	Spark Plugs Ft. Lbs.	Cylinder Head Bolts Ft. Lbs.	Intake Manifold Ft. Lbs.	Exhaust Manifold Ft. Lbs.	Camshaft Sprocket Ft. Lbs.	Connecting Rod Cap Bolts Ft. Lbs.	Main Bearing Cap Bolts Ft. Lbs.	Flywheel to Crankshaft Ft. Lbs.
1986	Integra	13	47	16	23	27	23	40	①
	Legend	13	49	16	22	23	36	30	②
1987	Integra	13	48	16	23	27	23	40	①
	Legend	13	56	16	22	23	33	28	②

①—Auto. trans., 54 ft. lbs.; man. trans., 76 ft. lbs.
②—Auto. trans., 54 ft. lbs., man. trans., 87 ft. lbs.

Brake Specifications

Year	Model	Nominal Thickness		Minimum Thickness		Thickness Variation (Parallelism)	Run Out (TIR)
		Front	Rear	Front	Rear		
1986–87	Integra	.750	.390	.670	.310	.0003	①
	Legend	.830	.390	.750	.310	.0006	.004

①—Front, .004 inch; rear, .006 inch.

Wheel Alignment Specifications

Year	Model	Caster Angle, Degrees		Camber Angle, Degrees				King Pin Inclination	Toe-In Inch	
		Limits	Desired	Limits		Desired			Front	Rear
				Front	Rear	Front	Rear			
1986	Integra	+1 1/6 to +3 1/6	+2 1/6	−1 1/2 to +1/2	−1 to −1/2	−1/2	−3/4	13°	.039	.079
	Legend	+2/3 to +2 2/3	+1 2/3	−1 to +1	−1 to +1	0	0	—	0	.08
1987	Integra	+1 1/6 to +3 1/6	+2 1/6	−1 1/2 to +1/2	−1 to −1/2	/−1/2	−3/4	13 1/3°	.039	.079
	Legend	+2/3 to +2 2/3	+1 2/3	−1 to +1	−1 to +1	0	0	—	0	.08

—Not available.

Cooling System & Capacity Data

Year	Model	Cooling Capacity Qts.	Radiator Cap Relief Pressure, Lbs.	Thermo Opening Temp.	Fuel Tank Gals.	Engine Oil Refill Qts. w/Filter	Transaxle Oil	
							5 Speed Pts.	Auto. Trans. Pts.
1986–87	Integra	6.0 ①	11—15	196	13.2	3.1	4.8	②
	Legend	4.6 ①	14–17	196	18.0	4.8	4.6	③

①—Includes reserve tank.
②—Refill capacity, 5 pts.; total capacity, 11.4 pts.
③—Refill capacity, 6.8 pts.; total capacity, 13.8 pts.

ELECTRICAL SECTION

INDEX

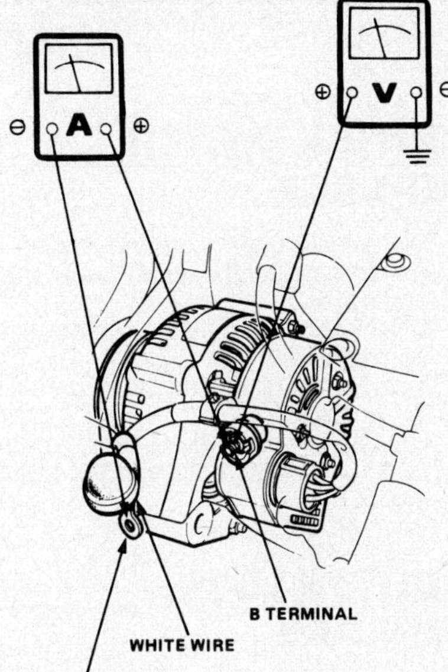

Fig. 1 Alternator test connections

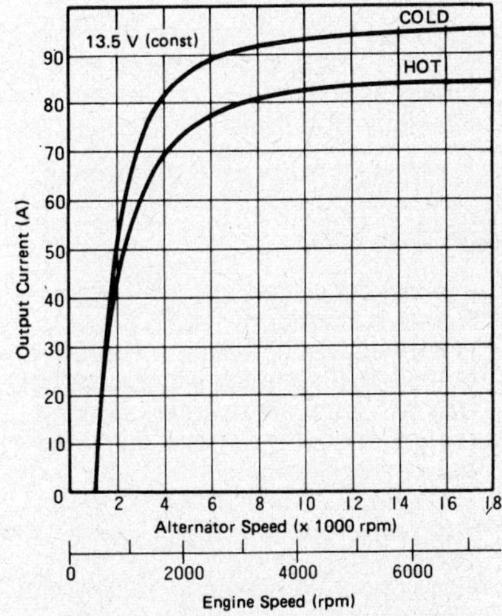

Fig. 3 Alternator test specifications. Legend

ALTERNATOR IN-VEHICLE TESTING

ALTERNATOR & REGULATOR TEST

1. Ensure battery is fully charged and that alternator belt, connections at alternator and main fuses are in satisfactory condition.
2. On Integra models, ensure fuse No. 4 in the dash fuse panel is in satisfactory condition.
3. On Legend models, ensure fuse No. 11 in the dash fuse panel and No. 36 in the underhood relay box are in satisfactory condition.
4. On all models, disconnect electrical connector from alternator.
5. Turn ignition switch on and ensure battery voltage exists between alternator connector black/yellow wire terminal and ground and, on Legend models, between yellow/blue wire terminal and ground.
6. If voltage is indicated as described in step 5, connect a voltmeter and ammeter to alternator as shown, **Fig. 1.**
7. Start engine, turn on headlamps and rear defroster and set blower fan on high speed.
8. Observe amperage and voltage output and compare to specifications, **Figs. 2 and 3. If voltage remains above 13.5 volts, apply a greater electrical load to lower voltage. If voltage remains above 16 volts, stop engine and replace voltage regulator.**
9. Turn off all electrical loads and check output voltage at 1500 RPM. If voltage indication is still 13.9-15.1 volts, the alternator and regulator are operating normally. If charge warning lamp remains lit, refer to "Charge Warning Lamp Test."
10. Insert a screwdriver into brush holder screw hole in alternator and cover, **Fig. 4.**
11. While contacting the brush screw, ground screwdriver against cover and note amperage reading at various speeds. **Ground screwdriver for as short a time as possible. Do not allow system voltage to exceed 16 volts, as electrical system components may be damaged.**

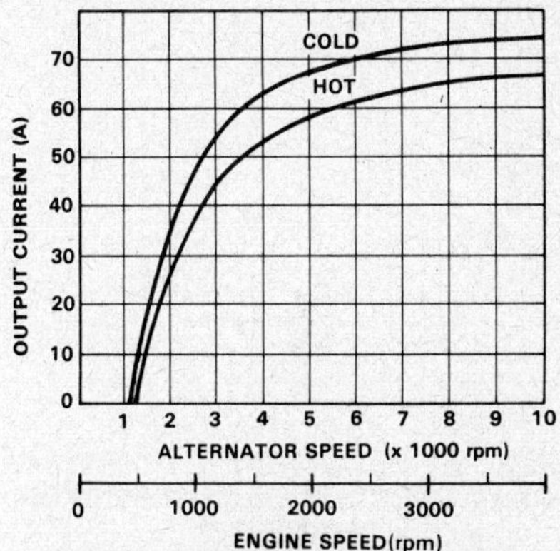

Fig. 2 Alternator test specifications. Integra

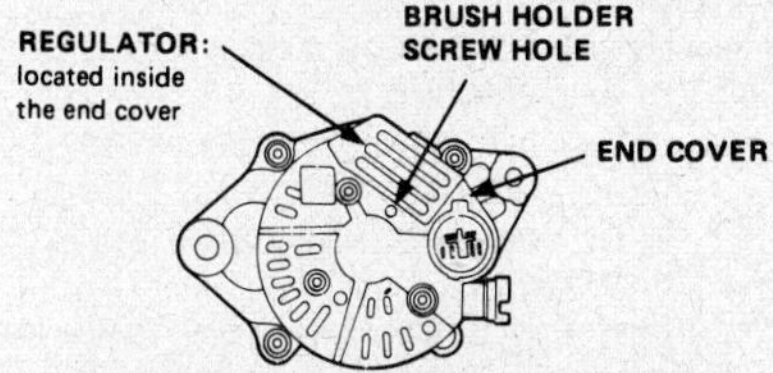

Fig. 4 Grounding brush holder screw to test alternator output

12. Compare current output with specifications, **Figs. 2 and 3,** noting the following:
    a. If output is not within specifications and, on Integra models, battery voltage is available at alternator black/yellow wire terminal, alternator is defective.
    b. If output is within specifications and, on Integra models, battery voltage is available at alternator black/yellow wire terminal, voltage regulator is defective.

CHARGE WARNING LAMP TEST

Integra

1. Ensure alternator belt is properly adjusted and that all electrical connections are secure and free from corrosion.
2. Observe warning lamp with ignition on and engine not running.
3. If warning lamp does not light, disconnect electrical connector from alternator and short the white/blue wire in

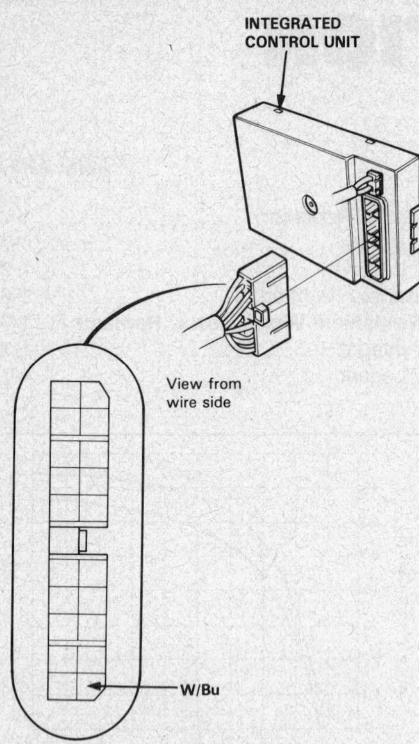

Fig. 5 Integrated control unit electrical connector. Legend

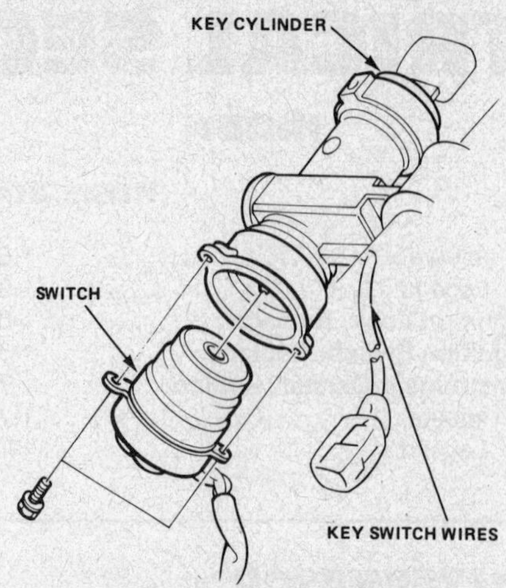

Fig. 6 Ignition switch replacement

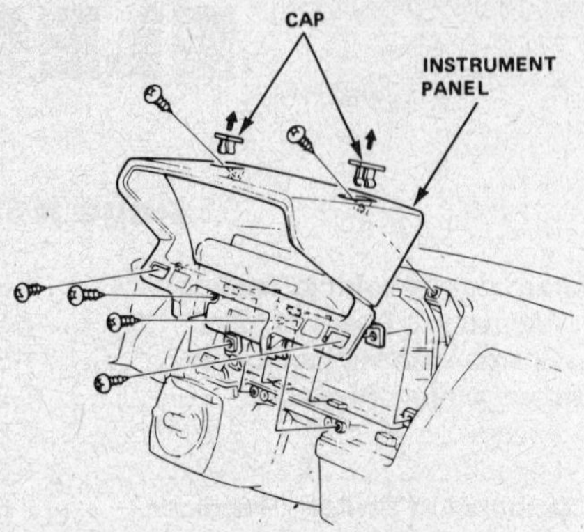

Fig. 7 Instrument panel removal. Integra

terminal to ground.

4. If lamp still does not light, check the following:
   a. Blown fuse No. 4 in dash fuse panel or defective bulb.
   b. Open in black/yellow wire between warning lamp and fuse panel or between fuse panel and ignition switch.
   c. Open in white/blue wire between warning lamp and voltage regulator.
5. If lamp lights in step 3, perform "Alternator & Regulator Test."
6. Run engine at idle and observe warning lamp.
7. If lamp stays lit, perform "Alternator & Regulator Test."
8. If system is charging normally, proceed as follows:
   a. Stop engine and disconnect 3-pin connector from alternator on 1986 models, or 4-pin connector on 1987 models.
   b. Turn ignition on and observe warning lamp.
   c. If lamp goes out, a defective voltage regulator is indicated.
   d. If lamp remains lit, disconnect retractable headlamp control unit and integrated control unit and observe warning lamp.
   e. If lamp remains lit, a short to ground in blue/white wire between warning lamp and one of the control units is indicated.

Legend

1. Ensure alternator belt is properly adjusted and that all electrical connections are secure and free from corrosion.
2. Observe warning lamp with ignition on and engine not running.
3. If warning lamp does not light, disconnect electrical connector from alternator and short the white/blue wire in terminal to ground.
4. If lamp still does not light, check the following:
   a. Blown fuse No. 11 in dash fuse panel or defective bulb.
   b. Open in black/yellow wire between warning lamp and fuse panel or between fuse panel and ignition switch.
   c. Open in white/blue wire between warning lamp and voltage regulator.
5. If lamp lights in step 3, perform "Alternator & Regulator Test."
6. Run engine at idle and observe warning lamp.
7. If lamp remains lit, check condition of fuse No. 36 in underhood relay box and white/green wire between relay box and alternator. If fuse and wire are satisfactory, perform "Alternator & Regulator Test."
8. If system is charging normally, proceed as follows:
   a. Remove lower dashboard panel, then disconnect 21-pin connector from integrated control unit behind the fuse panel, **Fig. 5**, and observe warning lamp.
   b. If lamp goes out, a short in the integrated control unit is indicated.
   c. If lamp remains lit, a short to ground in the white/blue wire between warning lamp and control unit is indicated.

STARTER
REPLACE

1. Disconnect battery ground cable.
2. Disconnect all electrical connectors from starter motor.
3. Remove starter motor attaching bolts and the starter motor.
4. Reverse procedure to install.

IGNITION SWITCH
REPLACE

1. Disconnect battery ground cable.
2. Remove steering column lower panel and cover.
3. Disconnect 6-pin electrical connector from switch.
4. Insert ignition key and move switch to "0" position.
5. Unfasten switch wires, then remove switch attaching bolts and the switch, **Fig. 6.**
6. Reverse procedure to install.

IGNITION LOCK
REPLACE

1. Remove ignition switch as previously described.
2. Insert ignition key and move switch to "I" position.
3. Depress pin and remove lock cylinder from body.
4. Turn ignition key to "lock" position and align lock cylinder with body.
5. Turn key almost to "I" position and insert lock cylinder until pin contacts body.
6. Turn key to "I" position, then depress pin and insert lock cylinder until pin clicks into place.
7. Install ignition switch.

COMBINATION SWITCH
REPLACE

1. Disconnect battery ground cable.
2. Remove steering wheel.
3. Remove steering wheel lower cover.
4. On models equipped with cruise control, remove cruise control slip ring.
5. On all models, remove turn signal cancelling sleeve.
6. Remove upper column holder, bending plate, bending plate base and bending plate guide.
7. Disconnect combination switch electrical connector.
8. Remove combination switch attaching screws and the switch.
9. Reverse procedure to install.

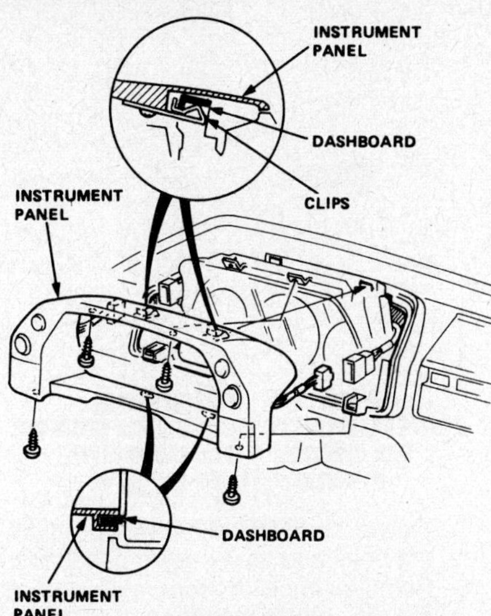

Fig. 8 Instrument panel removal. Legend

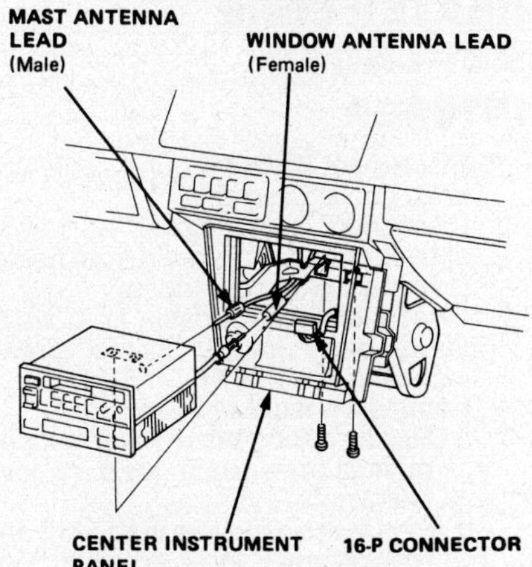

Fig. 11 Radio replacement. Legend

INSTRUMENT CLUSTER
REPLACE
INTEGRA

1. Disconnect battery ground cable.
2. Remove left side lower dash panel and switch by pushing it out, then disconnecting the electrical connectors.
3. Remove instrument panel caps and attaching screws, then the instrument panel, **Fig. 7.**
4. Remove instrument cluster attaching screws, then pull cluster away from dash.
5. Disconnect speedometer cable and electrical connector from instrument cluster, then remove the cluster from vehicle.
6. Reverse procedure to install.

LEGEND

1. Disconnect battery ground cable.
2. Remove instrument panel attaching screws and the instrument panel, **Fig. 8.**
3. Remove instrument cluster attaching screws, then pull cluster away from dash.
4. Disconnect speedometer cable and electrical connectors from instrument cluster, then remove the cluster from vehicle.
5. Reverse procedure to install.

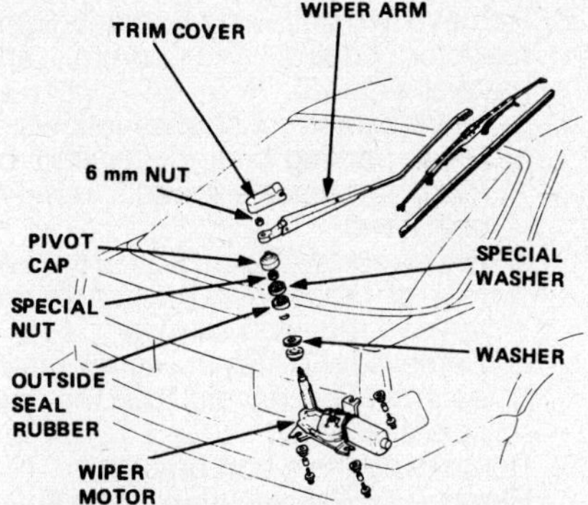

Fig. 9 Rear wiper motor replacement. Integra

WINDSHIELD WIPER MOTOR
REPLACE
INTEGRA
Front

1. Disconnect battery ground cable.
2. Remove cap nuts and wiper arm.
3. Pry off air scoop trim clip, then remove the air scoop.
4. Pry wiper linkage away from motor arm.
5. Remove wiper motor cover, then disconnect motor electrical connector.
6. Remove wiper motor attaching bolts and the motor.
7. Reverse procedure to install, noting the following:
   a. Apply suitable grease to joints and ensure linkages operate smoothly.
   b. Following installation, ensure tips of wiper arms rest .8-1.2 inch from the air scoop.

Rear

1. Disconnect battery ground cable.
2. Remove hatch trim panel, then the trim cover, wiper arm attaching nut, pivot cap, nut and outside seal rubber, **Fig. 9.**
3. Disconnect electrical connector from wiper motor, then remove motor attaching bolts and the motor.
4. Reverse procedure to install.

LEGEND

1. Position wiper arms in the winter (exposed) position.
2. Disconnect battery ground cable.
3. With wiper arm lifted away from windshield, pull lock pin tab out to release spring pressure.
4. Remove wiper arm cap nuts and the wiper arms.
5. Pry wiper linkage away from motor arm.
6. Unfasten wiper connectors from bracket, then disconnect electrical connectors from wiper motor.

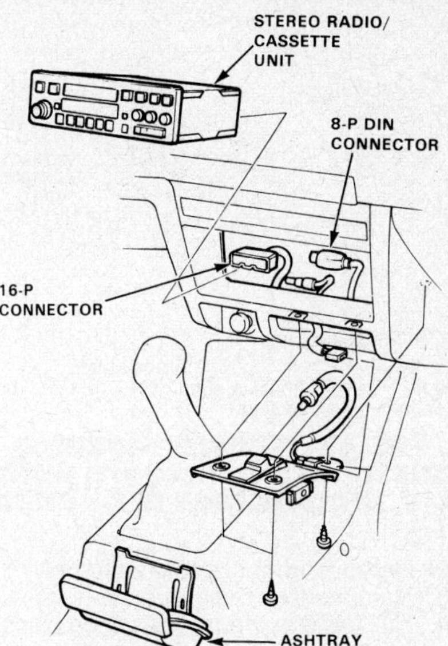

Fig. 10 Radio replacement. Integra

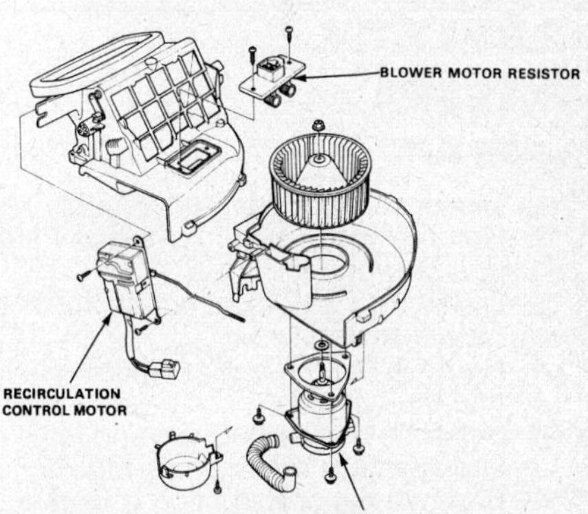

Fig. 12 Exploded view of blower housing assembly. Integra

7. Remove wiper motor attaching bolts and the motor.
8. Reverse procedure to install, noting the following:
   a. Apply suitable grease to joints and ensure linkages operate smoothly.
   b. Prior to installing wiper arms, turn ignition switch on and wiper switch off. Following installation, ensure tips of wiper arms rest .32-.39 inch from the air scoop.

RADIO
REPLACE
INTEGRA

1. Disconnect battery ground cable.
2. Remove ashtray and ashtray bracket.
3. Remove two lower radio attaching screws.
4. Push radio out from dash, then disconnect electrical connectors and antenna lead and remove radio, **Fig. 10.**
5. Reverse procedure to install.

LEGEND

1. Disconnect battery ground cable.

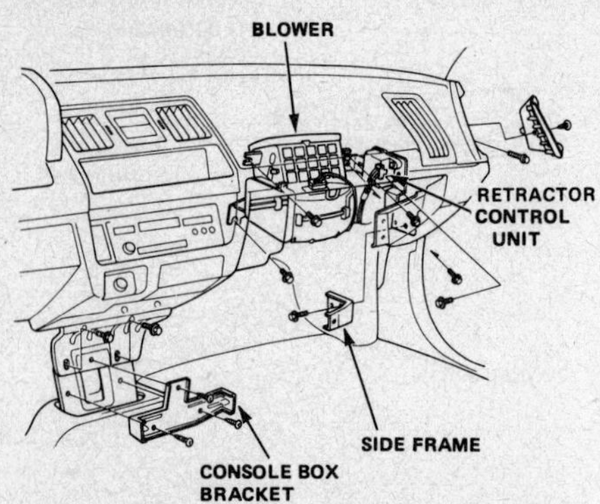

Fig. 13 Blower housing installation. Integra with A/C, models less A/C similar

2. Remove front console assembly.
3. Remove four radio attaching screws.
4. Pull radio out from dash, then disconnect electrical connector and antenna leads and remove radio, **Fig. 11.**
5. Reverse procedure to install.

BLOWER MOTOR

REPLACE

INTEGRA

Less A/C

1. Disconnect battery ground cable.
2. Remove glove box, glove box frame and blower duct.
3. Disconnect electrical connector from blower motor.
4. Remove three housing retaining bolts and the housing.
5. Separate blower housing and remove impeller from motor shaft, **Fig. 12.**
6. Remove motor mounting screws and the motor.
7. Reverse procedure to install.

With A/C

1. Disconnect battery ground cable.
2. Remove glove box and glove box frame.
3. Remove two bolts securing headlamp retractor control, the control and bracket, **Fig. 13.**
4. Remove center console as follows:
   a. Raise parking brake lever and, on manual transaxle models, remove shift knob.
   b. Pry up screw covers from front and rear of brake lever housing, then remove retaining screws.
   c. Remove two retaining screws from each side of console, then the console assembly.
5. Remove console box bracket.
6. Remove bolts securing instrument panel lower bracket to bracket B, **Fig. 14,** then pry instrument panel bracket forward approximately 1/2 inch to provide clearance.
7. Loosen sealing band on right side of housing and disconnect electrical connector from blower motor.
8. Remove three bolts securing blower housing and the housing, **Fig. 13.**
9. Separate blower housing and remove impeller from motor shaft, **Fig. 12.**
10. Remove motor mounting screws and the motor.
11. Reverse procedure to install.

LEGEND

1. Disconnect battery ground cable and discharge refrigerant.
2. Remove glove box lower cover, glove box, glove box frame and the side heater duct.
3. Remove evaporator assembly as follows:
   a. Disconnect harness connector from evaporator sensor.
   b. Remove four self-tapping screws and three mounting bolts, then the evaporator housing assembly.
   c. Pull evaporator sensor from core.
   d. Remove self-tapping screws and clips securing upper housing, then separate housing and remove evaporator cover and the evaporator.
4. Disconnect electrical connectors from blower housing, then remove attaching bolts and the housing assembly.
5. Remove impeller from motor shaft, **Fig. 15,** motor mounting screws and the motor.
6. Reverse procedure to install.

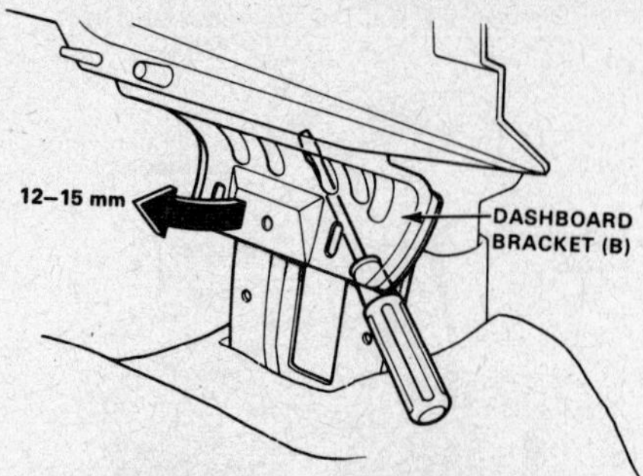

Fig. 14 Aligning instrument panel bracket to allow component removal. Integra

HEATER CORE

REPLACE

INTEGRA

1. Disconnect battery ground cable and drain cooling system.
2. Disconnect heater hoses at firewall and allow coolant to drain from heater core, then plug core tubes.
3. Disconnect control cable from water valve and remove heater lower mounting nut, **Fig. 16.**
4. Remove console as follows:
   a. Raise parking brake lever and, on manual transaxle models, remove shift knob.
   b. Pry up screw covers from front and rear of brake lever housing, then remove retaining screws.
   c. Remove two retaining screws from each side of console, then the console assembly.
   d. Remove console box bracket.
5. Disconnect air mix cable from heater

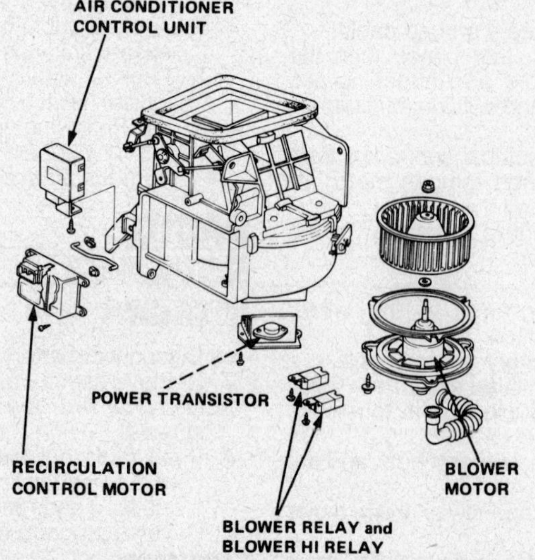

Fig. 15 Exploded view of blower housing assembly. Legend

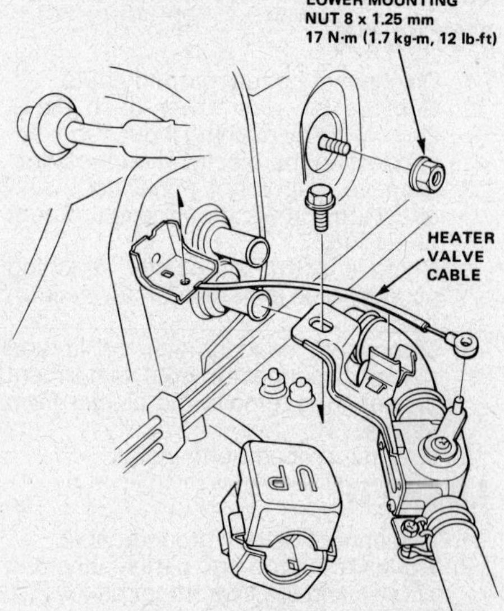

Fig. 16 Heater housing removal. Integra

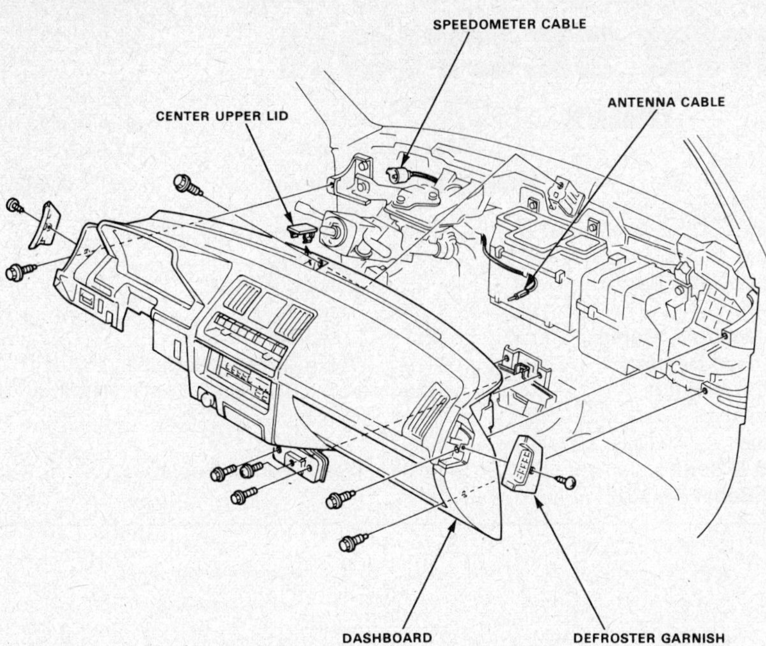

Fig. 17 Instrument panel installation. Integra

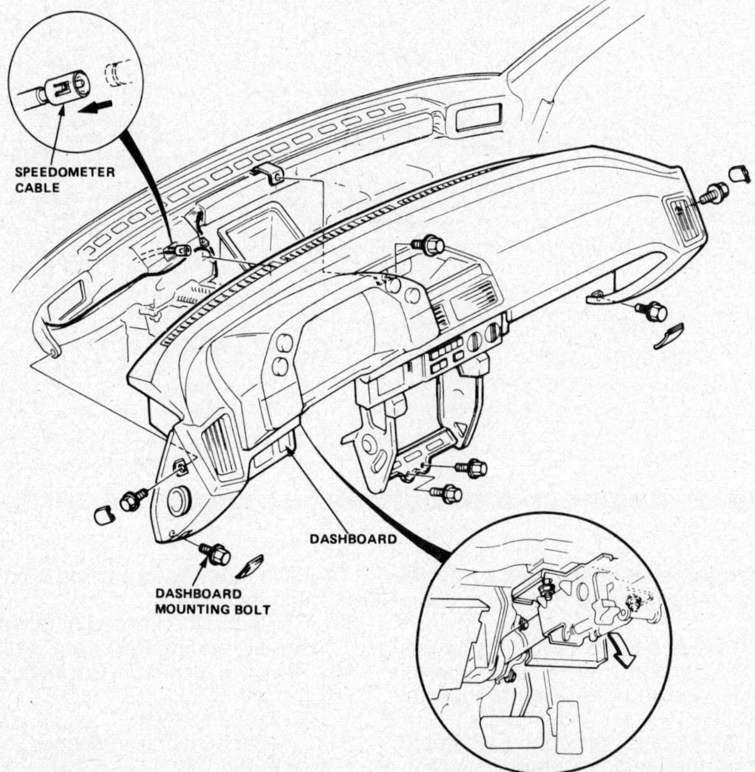

Fig. 18 Instrument panel installation. Legend

housing.

6. Remove instrument panel as follows:
   a. Remove steering wheel, fuse panel cover and lower dash trim panel.
   b. Disconnect instrument panel wiring harness from fuse panel.
   c. Disconnect antenna lead from radio and the heat control cable.
   d. Remove steering column bracket bolts and lower steering column.
   e. Remove bolt and disconnect ground strap from right side of steering column.
   f. Open glove box and remove instrument panel mounting bolt on right side.
   g. Remove two nuts securing hood release handle.
   h. Remove center upper lid from top of instrument panel and defroster garnishes from each end of instrument panel, **Fig. 17.**
   i. Remove six retaining bolts and one screw, pull instrument panel away from cowl and disconnect speedometer cable, then remove instrument panel assembly.
7. Disconnect electrical connectors from heater assembly.
8. Remove two heater housing mounting bolts, then the heater assembly.
9. Remove screws securing heater core retaining plate and the plate, then withdraw core from housing.
10. Reverse procedure to install, noting the following:
    a. Apply sealer to grommets when installing heater housing.
    b. Install and adjust control cables as necessary.
    c. When filling cooling system, loosen bleed bolt in water outlet. When coolant running from bleeder is free of bubbles, retighten bolt.

LEGEND

1. Disconnect battery ground cable and drain cooling system.
2. Disconnect heater hoses at firewall, allow coolant to drain from heater core, then plug core tubes.
3. Remove instrument panel as follows:
   a. Remove steering wheel, left and right lower dash panels and left air duct.
   b. Remove ashtray, six screws securing front console and front console section.
   c. Disconnect instrument panel harness at fuse panel and release harness from holder.
   d. Remove bolt securing instrument panel ground and disconnect ground strap from steering column.
   e. Remove screws securing radio panel, pull radio away from dash and disconnect electrical connectors, then remove radio assembly.
   f. Disconnect control cables from heater housing.
   g. Remove center dash pocket assembly.
   h. Remove instrument panel mounting bolts, **Fig. 18.** Pull assembly straight back and disconnect speedometer cable, then remove instrument panel assembly.
4. Disconnect electrical connectors and vacuum hoses from heater assembly, noting position for installation reference.
5. Remove lower mounting nuts and upper mounting bolts, then remove heater assembly.
6. Remove screws securing heater core retaining plate and the plate, then withdraw heater core from housing.
7. Reverse procedure to install, noting the following:
   a. Apply sealer to grommets when installing heater housing.
   b. Install and adjust control cables as necessary.
   c. Connect vacuum hoses, ensuring hoses are properly routed, and are not kinked or pinched.
   d. When filling cooling system, loosen bleed bolt in water outlet. When coolant running from bleeder is free of bubbles, retighten bolt.

ENGINE SECTION

INDEX

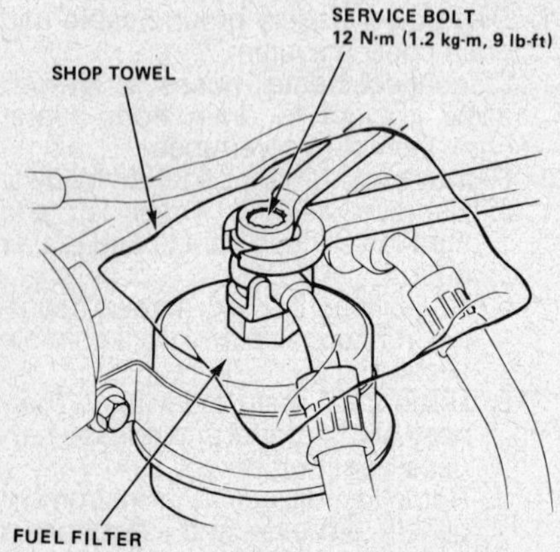

Fig. 1 Relieving fuel system pressure

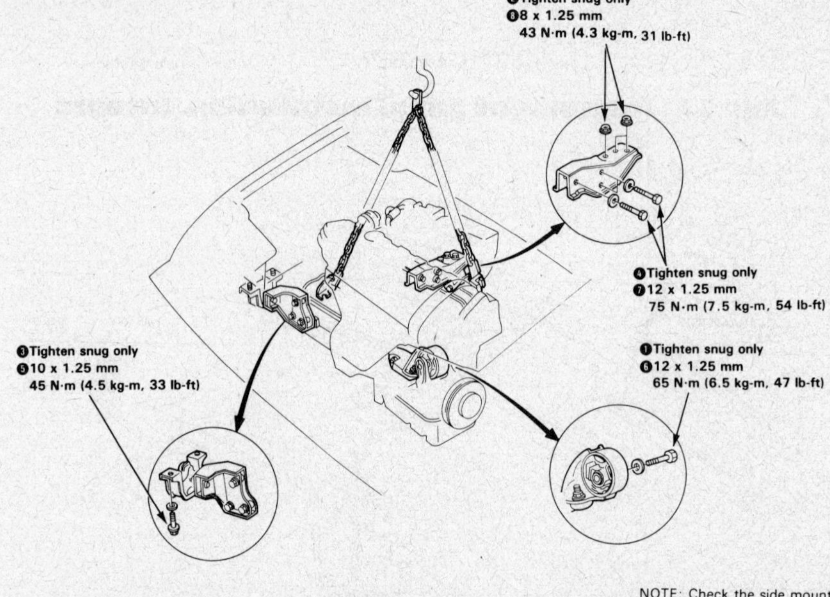

Fig. 2 Engine mount bolt torque sequence. Integra

ENGINE REPLACE

INTEGRA

1. Disconnect both battery cables.
2. Disconnect windshield washer tube, then scribe hood hinge locations and remove hood.
3. Drain engine oil, cooling system and transaxle fluid into suitable containers. **Install engine oil and transaxle drain plugs using new washers.**
4. Remove air intake duct and front air intake duct.
5. Relieve fuel system pressure by loosening the service bolt on top of fuel filter, **Fig. 1,** one complete revolution, then disconnect fuel lines from filter.
6. Loosen throttle cable locknut and adjusting nut, then slip cable end out of throttle bracket and accelerator linkage. **Use care to avoid bending cable when removing it.**
7. Remove power steering pump attaching bolts and drive belt, then unfasten pump and position aside, leaving hose connected.
8. Remove center console assembly.
9. Disconnect radiator hoses, heater hoses, transaxle oil cooler lines and speedometer cable. **Do not remove speedometer cable holder, as the gear may fall into transaxle housing.**
10. On models equipped with A/C, unfasten A/C compressor and position aside, leaving refrigerant lines attached.
11. On all models, disconnect alternator wiring, then remove alternator attaching bolt and the alternator.
12. Attach suitable hoist equipment to engine block brackets and raise hoist just enough to remove slack from chain.
13. Remove rear transaxle mount bracket and the front transaxle mount attaching bolts.
14. Remove engine side mount attaching bolt.
15. Disconnect any remaining vacuum lines, coolant hoses, fuel lines and electrical connectors from engine.
16. Raise engine approximately six inches and ensure all hoses and wires have been disconnected from engine and transaxle.
17. Carefully lift engine and transaxle assembly and remove from vehicle.
18. Reverse procedure to install, noting the following:
    a. Torque engine mount bolts to specifications, in sequence shown in **Fig. 2.**
    b. Install new spring clips on each end of driveshaft and ensure each clip snaps properly into place.
    c. Bleed air from cooling system at bleed bolt with heater valve open.

LEGEND

1. Remove battery and battery tray.
2. Scribe hood hinge locations and remove hood.
3. Remove air intake tube, air cleaner and resonator tube as an assembly.
4. Remove splash guard from under engine.
5. Drain engine oil, cooling system and

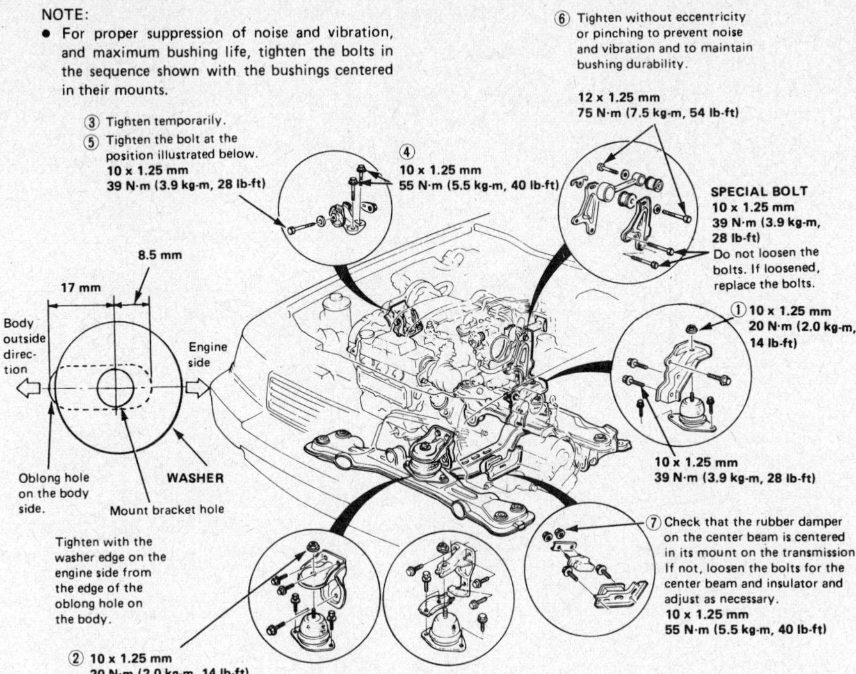

NOTE:
• For proper suppression of noise and vibration, and maximum bushing life, tighten the bolts in the sequence shown with the bushings centered in their mounts.
③ Tighten temporarily.
⑤ Tighten the bolt at the position illustrated below.
10 x 1.25 mm
39 N·m (3.9 kg-m, 28 lb-ft)
④
10 x 1.25 mm
55 N·m (5.5 kg-m, 40 lb-ft)
⑥ Tighten without eccentricity or pinching to prevent noise and vibration and to maintain bushing durability.
12 x 1.25 mm
75 N·m (7.5 kg-m, 54 lb-ft)
SPECIAL BOLT
10 x 1.25 mm
39 N·m (3.9 kg-m, 28 lb-ft)
Do not loosen the bolts. If loosened, replace the bolts.
① 10 x 1.25 mm
20 N·m (2.0 kg-m, 14 lb-ft)
8.5 mm
17 mm
Body outside direction
Engine side
Oblong hole on the body side.
WASHER
Mount bracket hole
10 x 1.25 mm
39 N·m (3.9 kg-m, 28 lb-ft)
⑦ Check that the rubber damper on the center beam is centered in its mount on the transmission. If not, loosen the bolts for the center beam and insulator and adjust as necessary.
10 x 1.25 mm
55 N·m (5.5 kg-m, 40 lb-ft)
Tighten with the washer edge on the engine side from the edge of the oblong hole on the body.
② 10 x 1.25 mm
20 N·m (2.0 kg-m, 14 lb-ft)
A/T
M/T

Fig. 3 Engine mount bolt torque sequence. Legend

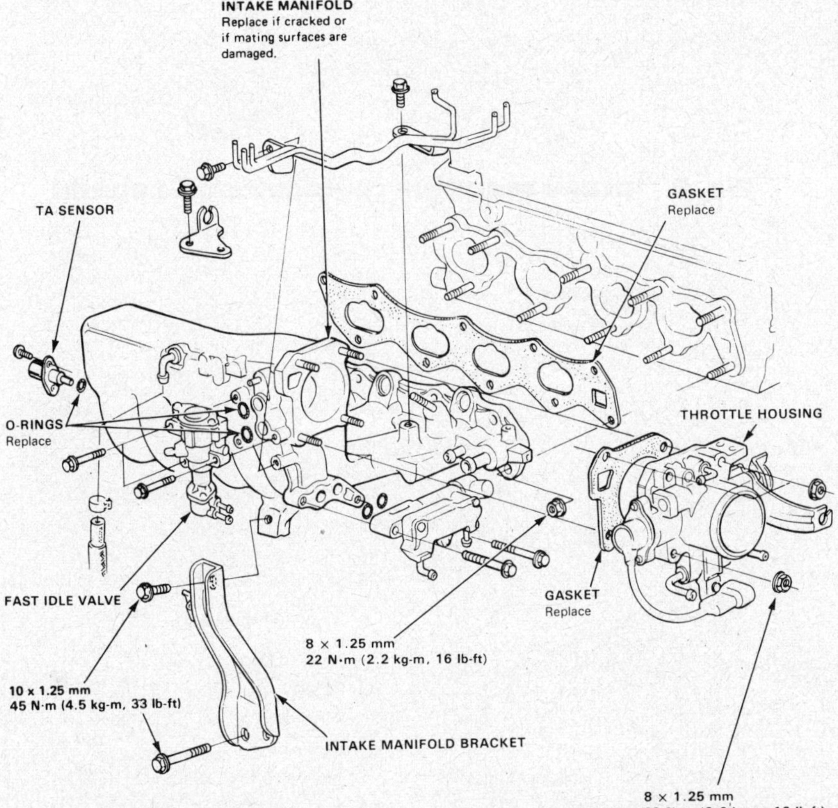

INTAKE MANIFOLD
Replace if cracked or if mating surfaces are damaged.
TA SENSOR
GASKET
Replace
O-RINGS
Replace
THROTTLE HOUSING
FAST IDLE VALVE
GASKET
Replace
8 x 1.25 mm
22 N·m (2.2 kg-m, 16 lb-ft)
10 x 1.25 mm
45 N·m (4.5 kg-m, 33 lb-ft)
INTAKE MANIFOLD BRACKET
8 x 1.25 mm
22 N·m (2.2 kg-m, 16 lb-ft)

Fig. 4 Intake manifold replacement. Integra

transaxle fluid into suitable containers. **Install engine oil and transaxle drain plugs using new washers.**

6. Disconnect pressure switch electrical connector from oil filter case.
7. Disconnect two water hoses from engine oil cooler.
8. Remove plug and drain oil from oil filter case, then remove the case from engine block.
9. Disconnect upper and lower radiator hoses from radiator.
10. On models equipped with automatic transaxle, disconnect transaxle cooler lines from radiator.
11. On all models, disconnect engine sub-harness connectors from body side.
12. Disconnect electrical connector and hoses from power steering pump.
13. Disconnect cruise control actuator hose.
14. Disconnect vacuum hose from power brake booster.
15. Relieve fuel system pressure by loosening the service bolt on top of fuel filter, **Fig. 1,** one complete revolution.
16. Disconnect fuel lines from fuel filter.
17. Disconnect throttle cable from throttle body, then the rubber tube from control box from connection stay.
18. Remove speed sensor, then unfasten A/C compressor and position aside, leaving refrigerant lines attached.
19. Remove exhaust pipe from front and rear manifolds.
20. On models equipped with automatic transaxle, remove center console assembly, then position shift lever in Reverse and disconnect control wire by removing lock pin.
21. On models equipped with manual transaxle, remove change rod and extension and the clutch release cylinder.
22. On all models, remove ball joint using a suitable tool, then disconnect driveshaft from transaxle.
23. Attach suitable hoist equipment to engine block brackets and raise hoist just enough to remove slack from chain.
24. Remove engine side mount bracket bolts, then the front and rear engine mount nuts and torque rod.
25. Ensure all hoses and wires have been disconnected from engine and transaxle, then carefully lift engine and remove front and rear engine brackets from mount bolts.
26. Tilt engine approximately 30°, then carefully lift and remove engine and transaxle assembly from vehicle.
27. Reverse procedure to install, noting the following:
    a. Torque engine mount bolts to specifications, in sequence shown in **Fig. 3.**
    b. Install new spring clips on each end of driveshaft and ensure each clip snaps properly into place.
    c. Bleed air from cooling system at bleed bolt with heater valve open.

INTAKE MANIFOLD REPLACE

Refer to **Figs. 4 and 5** when replacing intake manifold.

EXHAUST MANIFOLD REPLACE

Refer to **Figs. 6 and 7** when replacing exhaust manifold.

CYLINDER HEAD REPLACE

INTEGRA

1. Disconnect battery ground cable, then drain cooling system.
2. Disconnect air intake duct and vacuum hose, then remove air cleaner cover.
3. Relieve fuel system pressure by loosening the service bolt on top of fuel filter, **Fig. 1,** one complete revolution, then disconnect fuel lines from filter.
4. Remove engine secondary ground cable from valve cover.
5. Disconnect brake booster vacuum tube from intake manifold.
6. Loosen throttle cable locknut and adjusting nut, then slip cable end out of throttle bracket and accelerator linkage. **Use care to avoid bending cable when removing it.**
7. Disconnect ignition wires from spark plugs, then remove distributor assembly.
8. Disconnect vacuum lines from charcoal canister.
9. Disconnect No. 1 control box emission hoses from tubing manifold.
10. On models equipped with A/C, disconnect idle control solenoid hoses.
11. On all models, disconnect engine sub-harness connectors and couplers from cylinder head and intake manifold.
12. Disconnect oxygen sensor electrical connector.
13. Disconnect upper radiator hose, heater inlet hose and bypass inlet hose from cylinder head.
14. Remove coolant hose between thermostat housing and intake manifold.
15. Remove exhaust manifold and bracket attaching bolts, then the manifold.
16. Remove intake manifold and bracket attaching bolts.
17. Disconnect hose between intake manifold and breather chamber, then remove valve cover and upper timing belt cover.
18. Loosen timing belt tension bolt and remove the belt. **Do not bend or crimp timing belt more than 90° or to less than 1 inch in diameter.**
19. Remove timing belt lower cover attaching bolts from cylinder head.
20. Remove camshaft holder attaching bolts, then the camshaft holders, camshaft and rocker arms.
21. Remove cylinder head attaching bolts and the cylinder head. **Loosen cylinder head attaching bolts 1/3 turn at a time until all bolts are loose, to prevent warpage.**
22. Reverse procedure to install, noting the following:
    a. Clean cylinder head and engine block mating surfaces prior to installation.
    b. Ensure "UP" mark on timing belt pulley is positioned on top when installing cylinder head.
    c. Install cylinder head using a new gasket, ensuring dowel pins and oil control jet are properly aligned with cutouts in gasket.

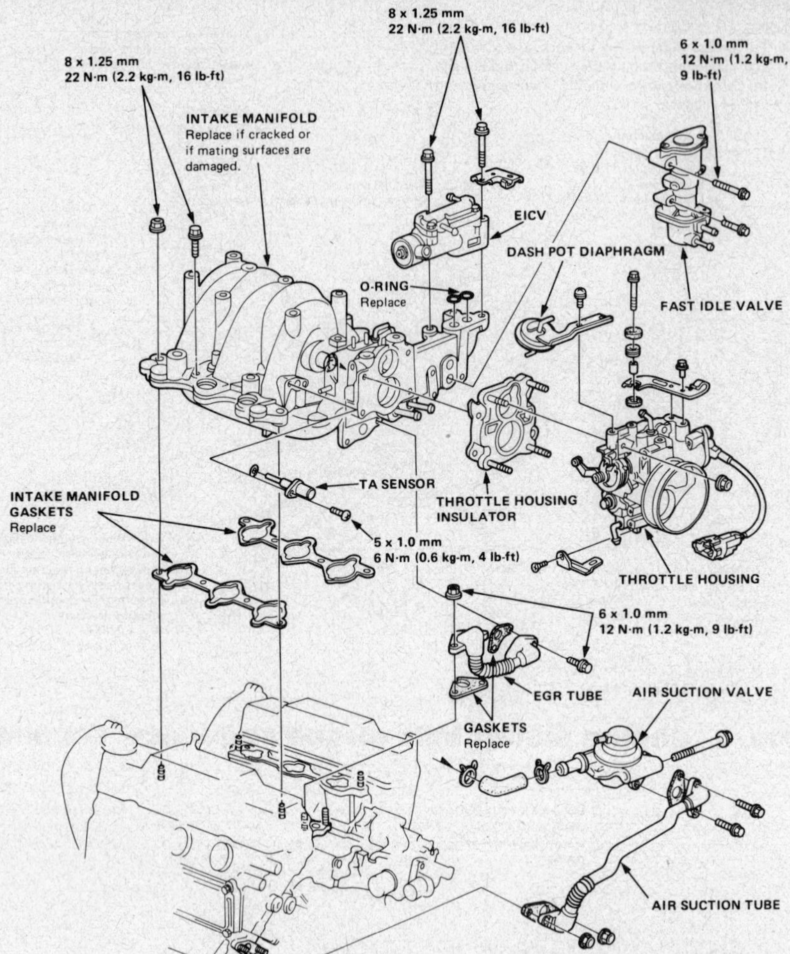

Fig. 5 Intake manifold replacement. Legend

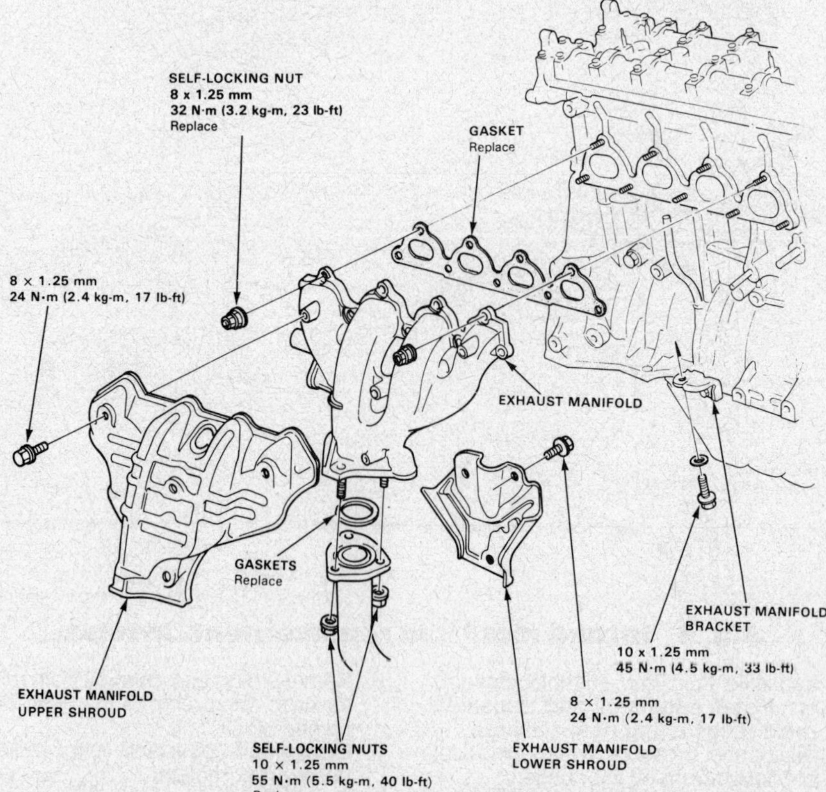

Fig. 6 Exhaust manifold replacement. Integra

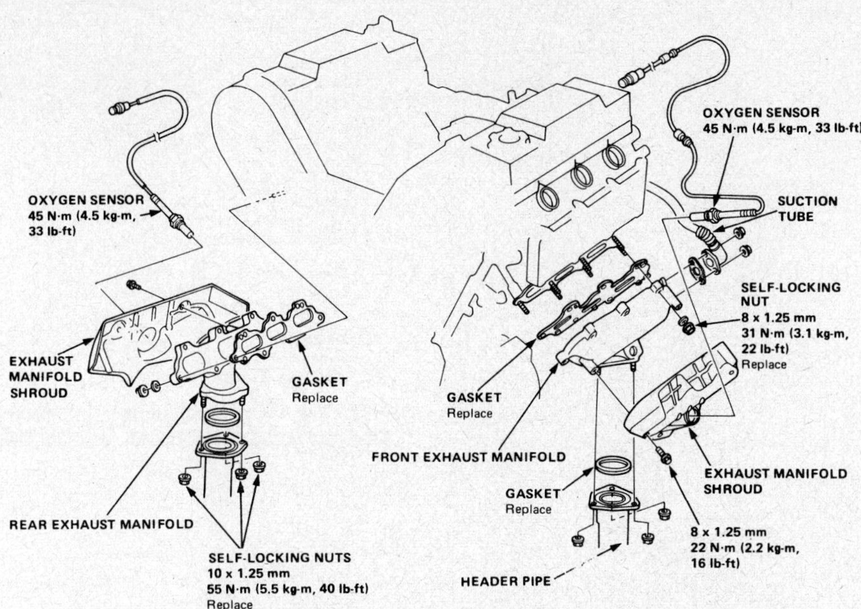

Fig. 7 Exhaust manifold replacement. Legend

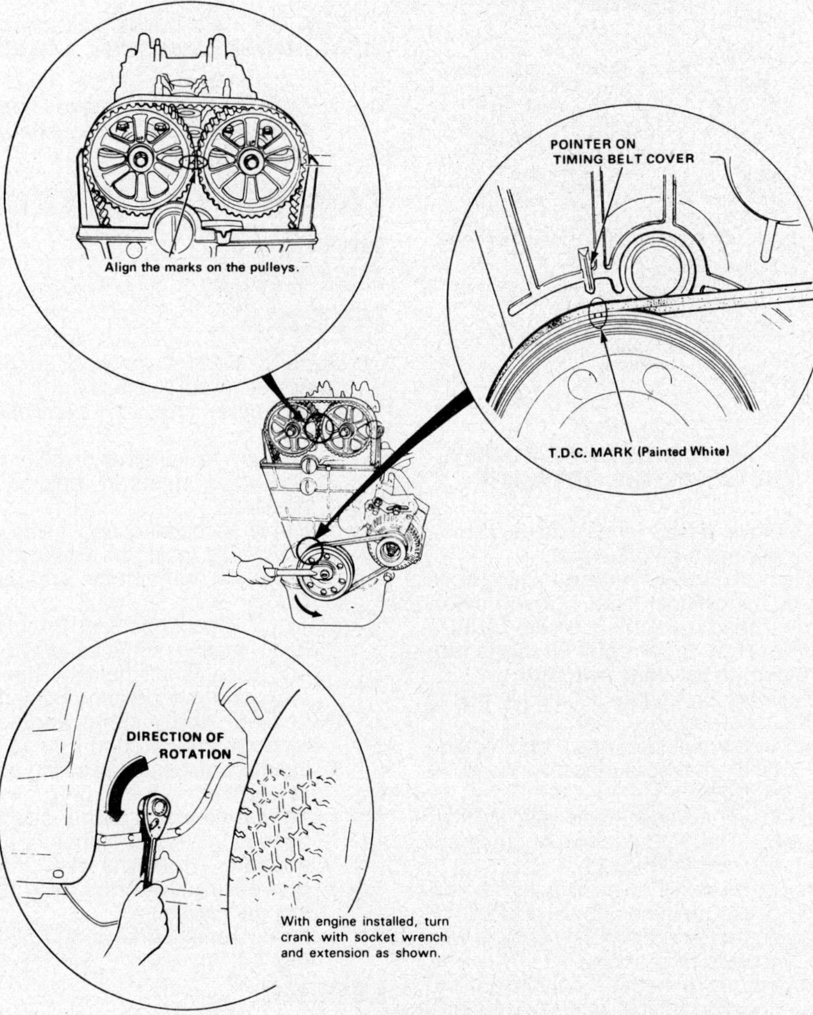

Fig. 8 Timing gear marks. Integra

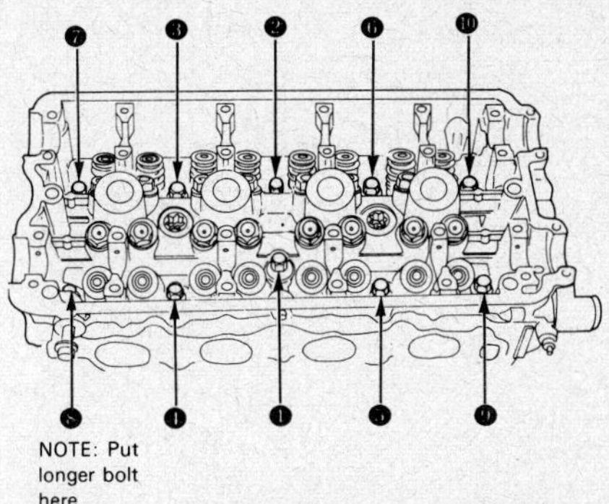

Fig. 9 Cylinder head bolt torque sequence. Integra

d. Apply clean engine oil to cylinder head attaching bolts and washers.
e. Torque cylinder head attaching bolts in two steps; first to 22 ft. lbs., then to 48 ft. lbs. in sequence, **Fig. 9.**
f. Install timing belt with cylinder No. 1 at TDC of compression stroke, **Fig. 8.**
g. Torque intake manifold nuts to specifications in crossing pattern in two or three steps.

LEGEND

1. Disconnect battery ground cable, then drain cooling system.
2. Disconnect brake booster vacuum tube from intake manifold.
3. Remove engine secondary ground cable from cylinder head and transaxle housing.
4. Disconnect radio condenser electrical connector, ignition coil wire and ignition primary connector.
5. Remove air cleaner cover.
6. Relieve fuel system pressure by loosening the service bolt on top of fuel filter, **Fig. 1,** one complete revolution, then disconnect fuel lines from filter.
7. Disconnect throttle cable from throttle body and the charcoal canister hose from throttle valve.
8. Disconnect engine sub-harness connectors and couplers from cylinder head and intake manifold.
9. Disconnect oxygen sensor electrical connector.
10. Disconnect upper radiator hose, heater inlet hose and bypass inlet hose from cylinder head.
11. Remove coolant hose between intake manifold and water passage.
12. Disconnect connecting pipe to valve body hose and bypass outlet hose.
13. Disconnect ignition wires from spark plugs, then remove distributor assembly.
14. Remove intake manifold cover, wire harness cover and alternator pulley cover.
15. Remove alternator and alternator drive belt.
16. Remove power steering pump and disconnect pump hoses.
17. On models equipped with A/C, disconnect idle control solenoid hoses.
18. On models equipped with cruise control, remove cruise control actuator.
19. On all models, remove exhaust pipe

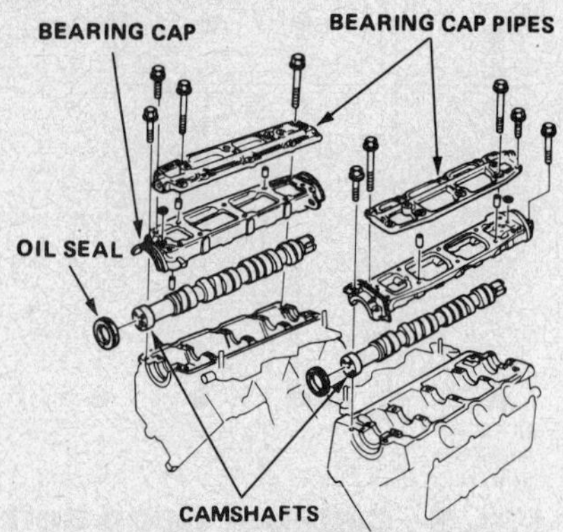

Fig. 10 Bearing cap & camshaft removal

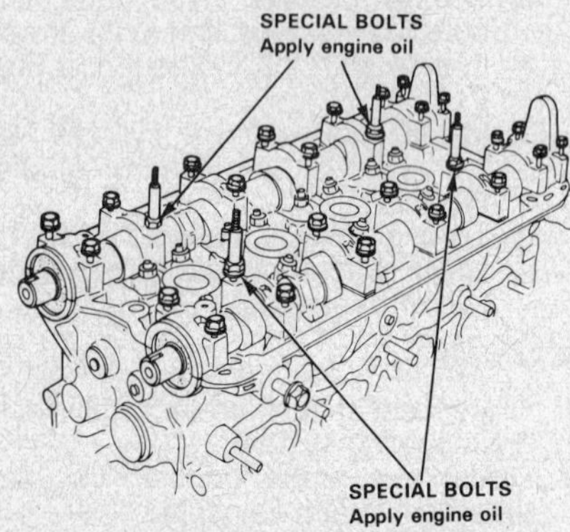

Fig. 13 Camshaft holder installation. Integra

header nuts, then disconnect header pipes from manifolds.

20. Remove air cleaner base attaching bolts, then disconnect hose between intake manifold and breather chamber.
21. Remove air cleaner base from intake manifold.
22. Remove EGR tube nuts from cylinder head, then the exhaust manifold cover nuts.
23. Remove air suction tube nuts from exhaust manifold and air suction valve.
24. Remove intake manifold from cylinder head.
25. Remove water passage assembly from front and rear cylinder heads.
26. Remove timing belt upper covers, then loosen tension bolt and remove timing belt. **Advance crankshaft approximately 15° prior to removing timing belt to prevent interference between valve and piston. Do not bend or crimp timing belt more than 90° or to less than 1 inch in diameter.**
27. Position cam so that no valve is fully open, then remove front and rear pulley attaching bolts and the pulleys. **On the rear pulley, remove top two bolts first, then the remaining bolt.**
28. Remove upper cover back plates, then the valve covers and head side covers.
29. Remove bearing cap pipes, bearing caps and camshafts, **Fig. 10.**

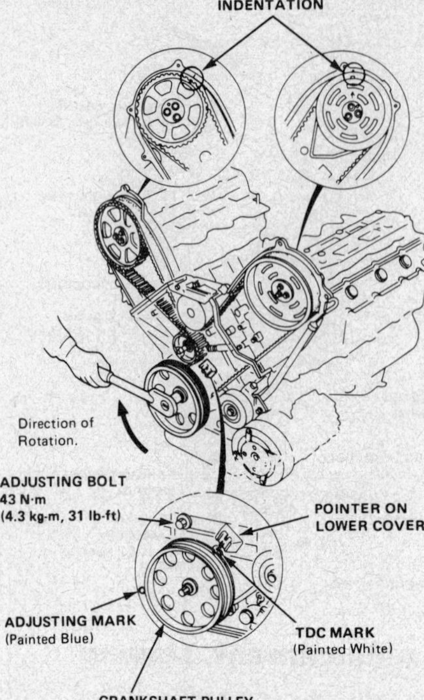

Fig. 11 Timing gear marks. Legend

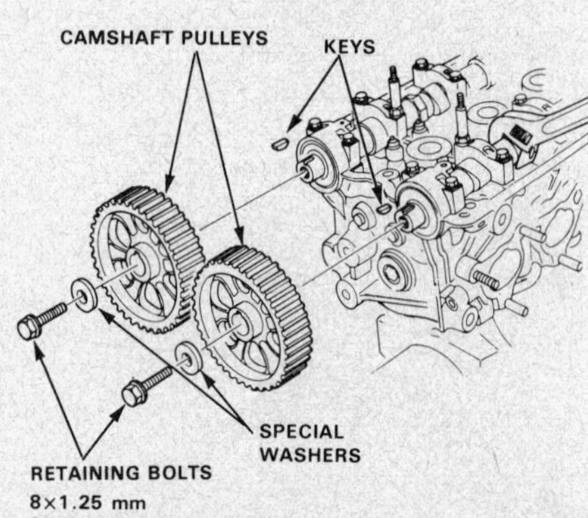

Fig. 14 Camshaft pulley installation. Integra

30. Remove intake and exhaust inside rocker arms and pushrods.
31. Remove cylinder head attaching bolts and the cylinder head. **Loosen cylinder head attaching bolts 1/3 turn one at a time until all bolts are loose, to prevent warpage.**
32. Reverse procedure to install, noting the following:
    a. Clean cylinder head and engine block mating surfaces prior to installation.
    b. Install cylinder head with cylinder No. 1 at TDC position of compression stroke, **Fig. 11.**
    c. Install cylinder head using a new gasket, ensuring dowel pins and oil control jet are properly aligned with cutouts in gaskets.
    d. Torque exhaust manifold nuts to specifications in a criss-cross pattern in two or three steps, beginning with the inner nuts.
    e. Torque cylinder head attaching

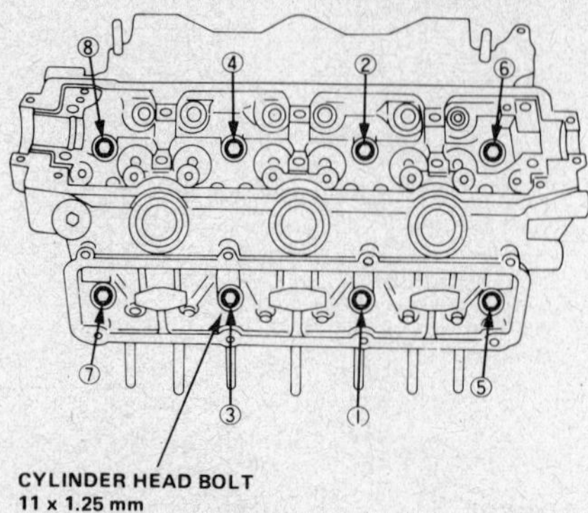

Fig. 12 Cylinder head bolt torque sequence. Legend

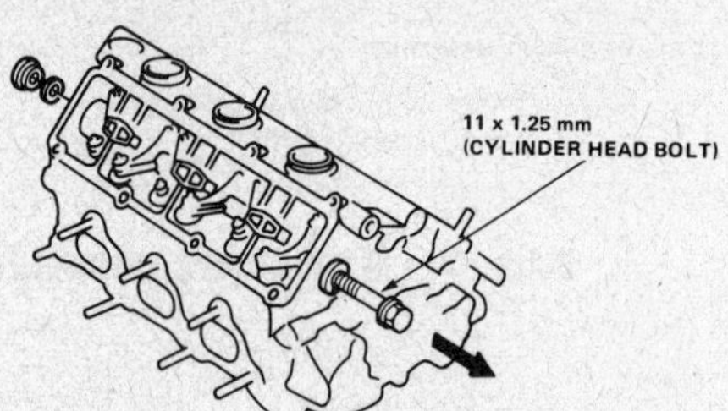

Fig. 15 Exhaust rocker arm shaft removal. Legend

bolts in two steps; first to 29 ft. lbs., then to 56 ft. lbs. in sequence, **Fig. 12.**

CAMSHAFTS & ROCKER ARMS

REPLACE

INTEGRA

1. Perform steps 1 through 20 under "Cylinder Head, Replace."
2. Install rocker arms and camshaft as follows:
    a. Position rocker arms on pivot bolts and valve stems in their original positions.
    b. Install camshafts and seals with open side facing in. **Ensure keyways on camshafts are facing up.**
    c. Apply suitable sealant to cylinder head mating surfaces of Nos. 1 and 6 camshaft holders, then install and temporarily tighten all holders. **Apply clean engine oil to bolts indicated in Fig. 13.**
    d. Install camshaft seals using a suitable driver.
    e. Torque camshaft holder attaching bolts to 9 ft. lbs. **Alternately tighten bolts two turns at a time to prevent rocker arms from binding on valves.**
    f. Install camshaft keys and pulleys, **Fig. 14.**

LEGEND

1. Perform steps 1 through 30 under "Cylinder Head, Replace."
2. Remove exhaust rocker arm assem-

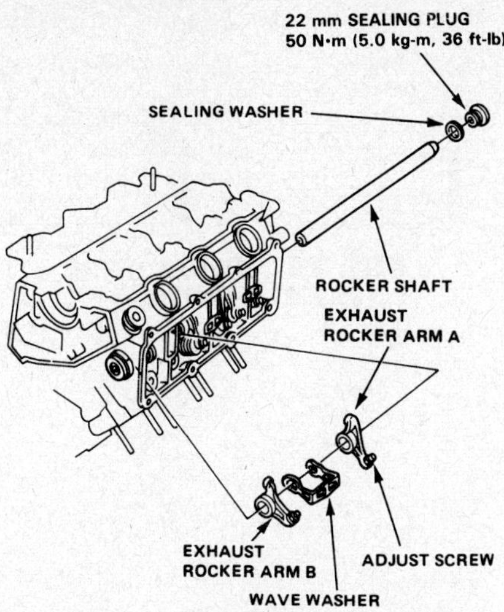

Fig. 16 Exhaust rocker arm installation. Legend

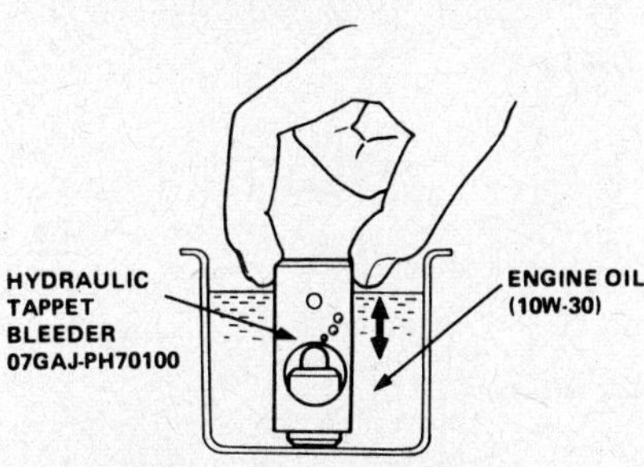

Fig. 19 Hydraulic valve lifter test. Legend

bly as follows:

a. Remove rocker shaft sealing bolt from transaxle side of cylinder head and install a long 111.25 mm bolt to the rocker shaft.
b. Remove rocker shaft, rocker arms and wave washers using installed bolt, **Fig. 15.**

3. Install exhaust rocker arm assembly as follows:
   a. Apply clean engine oil to rocker shaft mounting surfaces.
   b. Tap rocker arm shaft into position from transaxle side, then install rocker arms and wave washers, **Fig. 16. Ensure wave washers are fully seated in cylinder head groove.**
   c. Fully insert rocker shaft, then install sealing plug and torque to 36 ft. lbs.
4. Install pushrods, then the exhaust inside rocker arm and intake rocker arms, **Fig. 17.**
5. Install camshafts and camshaft oil seals, noting the following:
   a. Ensure camshaft in front position has a groove for driving the distributor.
   b. Ensure camshaft is positioned parallel with rocker arm slipper surface.
   c. To prevent interference between piston and valve, advance crankshaft by 15° from TDC of compression stroke on cylinder No. 1.
   d. Position camshaft in rear position on cylinder head so cam is not pushing the valve.
   e. Position oil seals with spring side facing inward.
   f. Do not lubricate cam holder side of oil seal.
6. Apply suitable sealant to oil seal mounting surface and on head contact surface, then install and temporarily tighten bearing caps.
7. Install camshaft oil seal until it contacts bearing cap, then torque attaching bolts to specifications in sequence, **Fig. 18.**
8. Install timing belt upper cover plate, then the camshaft pulleys.

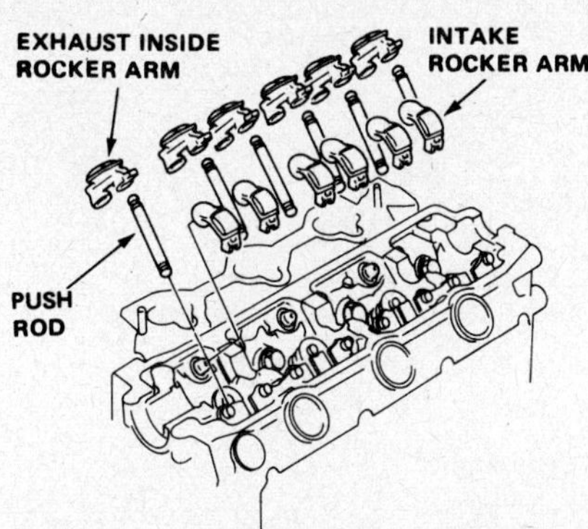

Fig. 17 Exhaust inside rocker arm & intake rocker arm installation. Legend

HYDRAULIC LIFTER SERVICE

LEGEND

The hydraulic valve lifters cannot be disassembled and must be serviced as an assembly.

1. Inspect lifters for excessive wear or damage or an obstructed oil passage.
2. Measure free length of each valve lifter as follows:
   a. Attach suitable tappet bleeder tool to tappet, then depress and release bleeder slowly with assembly submerged in clean engine oil, **Fig. 19.**
   b. Operate bleeder until there are no air bubbles from lifter.
   c. Remove lifter from oil and attempt to quickly compress it by hand.
   d. Measure compression stroke of lifter using a suitable dial indicator. Compression should measure 0-.003 inch.

VALVES

ADJUST

INTEGRA

Valves should be adjusted cold when cylinder head temperature is below 100°F.

1. Position cylinder No. 1 at TDC of compression stroke with "UP" marks on camshaft pulley on top and TDC grooves on back side of pulley aligning with cylinder head surface, **Fig. 20. Distributor rotor should also be pointing toward No. 1 plug wire.**
2. Loosen locknut and turn adjustment screw until feeler gauge slides back and forth with slight amount of drag, then torque intake and exhaust valve locknuts to 13 ft. lbs.
3. Rotate crankshaft 180° counterclockwise. The "UP" marks on pulley should be at exhaust side and distributor rotor should point toward No. 3 plug wire. Check clearance on cylinder No. 3 and adjust as in step 2.
4. Rotate crankshaft 180° counterclockwise. The "UP" marks on pulley should be at bottom and distributor rotor should point toward No. 4 plug wire. Check clearance on cylinder No. 4 and adjust as in step 2.
5. Rotate crankshaft 180° counterclockwise. The "UP" marks on pulley should be at intake side and distributor rotor should point toward No. 2 plug wire. Check clearance of cylinder No. 2 and adjust as in step 2.

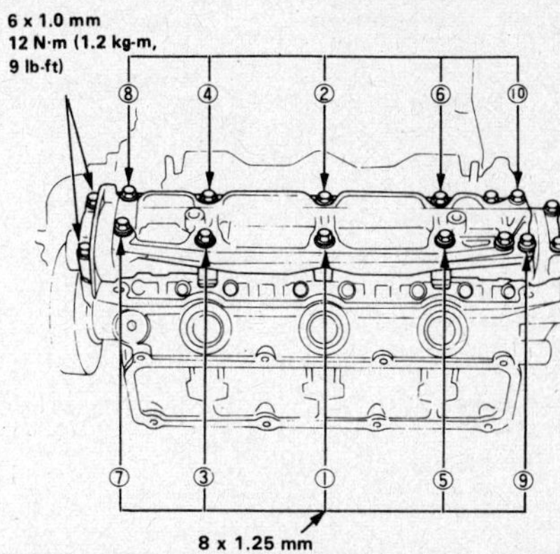

Fig. 18 Camshaft bearing cap bolt torque sequence. Legend

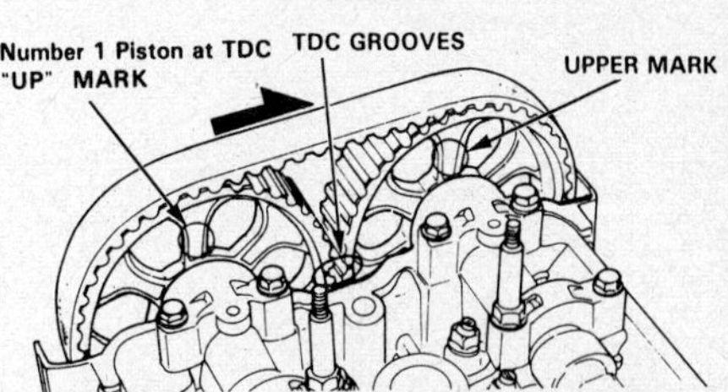

Fig. 20 Camshaft pulley timing marks. Integra

LEGEND

The V6-152/2494cc engine used on Legend models uses hydraulic valve lifters which do not normally require adjustment. However, if cylinder head or valve requires service, they should be adjusted as follows:

1. Position front and rear camshafts at TDC of compression stroke of cylinder No. 1, **Fig. 11.**
2. Tighten cylinder No. 1 adjusting screw until screw contacts valve, then tighten an additional 1½ turns and torque locknut to 16 ft. lbs., **Fig. 21.**
3. Repeat adjustment sequence for Nos. 2 and 4 cylinders.

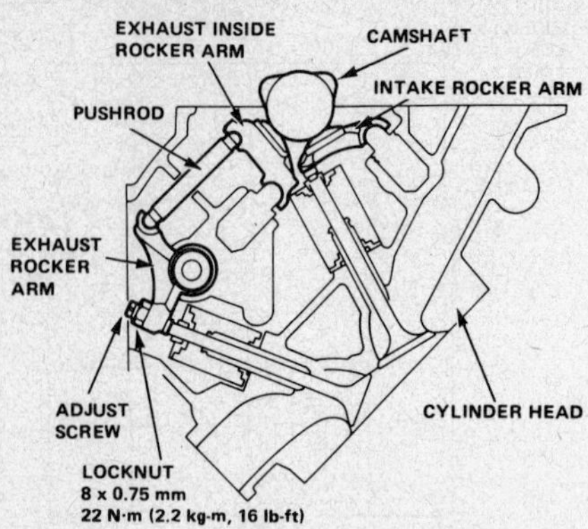

Fig. 21 Valve adjustment. Legend

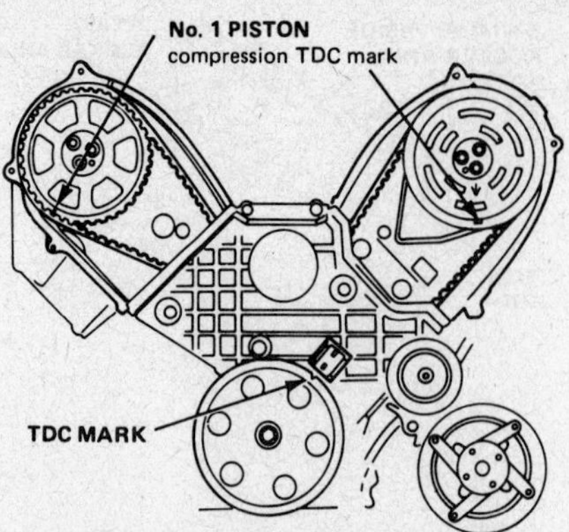

Fig. 22 Valve adjustment timing mark reference. Legend

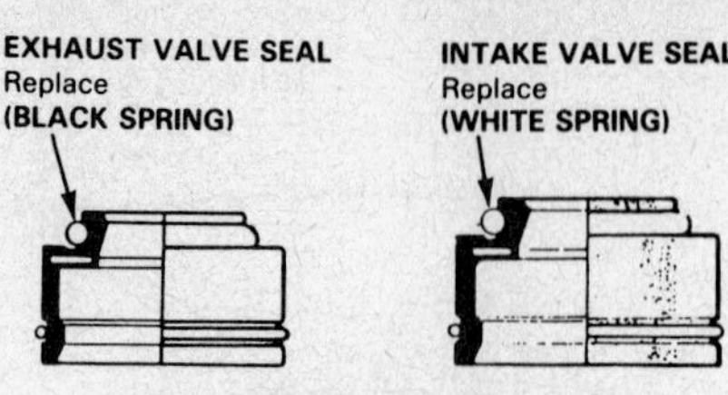

Fig. 23 Valve seal identification

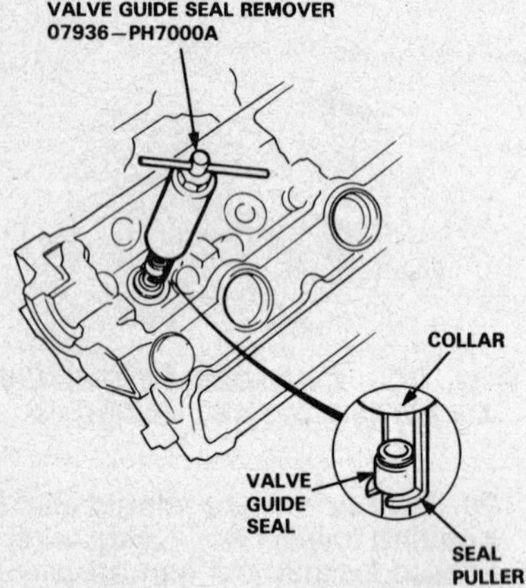

Fig. 24 Valve seal removal. 1987 Legend

4. Rotate crankshaft clockwise one full turn, then adjust cylinders Nos. 3, 5 and 6, ensuring timing marks are properly positioned, **Fig. 22.**

VALVE SPRINGS & SEALS

REPLACE

INTEGRA

1. Remove valve cover, then the bearing cap bolts. **Loosen bearing cap bolts in a criss-cross pattern, two turns at a time to prevent damaging rocker arms or valves.**
2. Compress valve springs using a suitable tool, then remove spring keepers and springs. **With piston at TDC, insert a spark plug air hold fitting to hold valves closed and allow removal of the keepers.**
3. Remove valve seals, **Fig. 23.**
4. Reverse procedure to install, noting the following:
   a. Lubricate valve stems prior to spring installation.
   b. Position valve springs with painted portion or closely wound coils toward cylinder head.
   c. With springs installed, lightly tap end of each valve stem several times to seat valves and keepers.

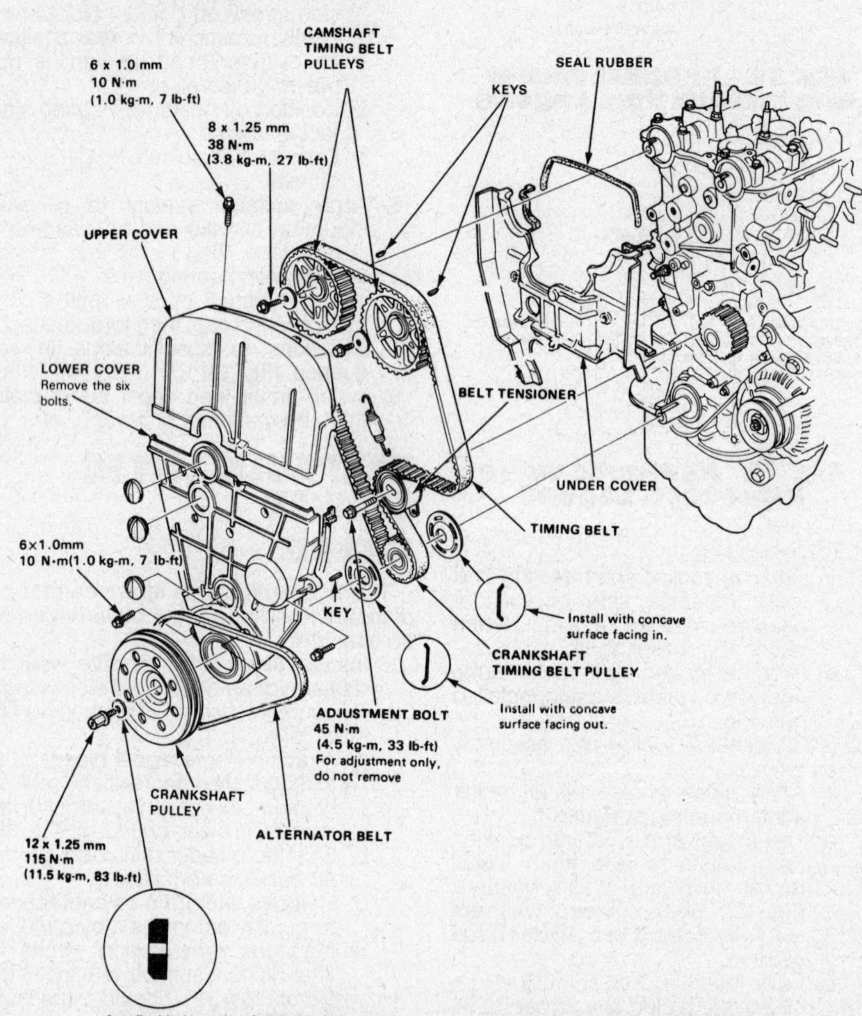

Fig. 25 Timing belt replacement. Integra

LEGEND

1. Remove valve cover and side cover, then the bearing cap, bearing cap pipe and camshaft.
2. Remove intake rocker arms, exhaust inside rocker arms and pushrods.
3. Remove rocker shaft and exhaust rocker arms.
4. Compress valve springs using a suitable tool, then remove spring keepers and springs. **With piston at TDC, insert a spark plug air hold fitting to hold valves closed and allow removal of the keepers.**
5. Remove valve seals, **Fig. 23.** On 1986 models, remove seals using tool No. 07GAC-PH70100 or equivalent. On 1987 models, remove seals using tool No. 07936-PH7000A, **Fig. 24,** as follows:
   a. Turn nut on tool counterclockwise until it contacts handle.
   b. Slide seal puller fully out of collar.

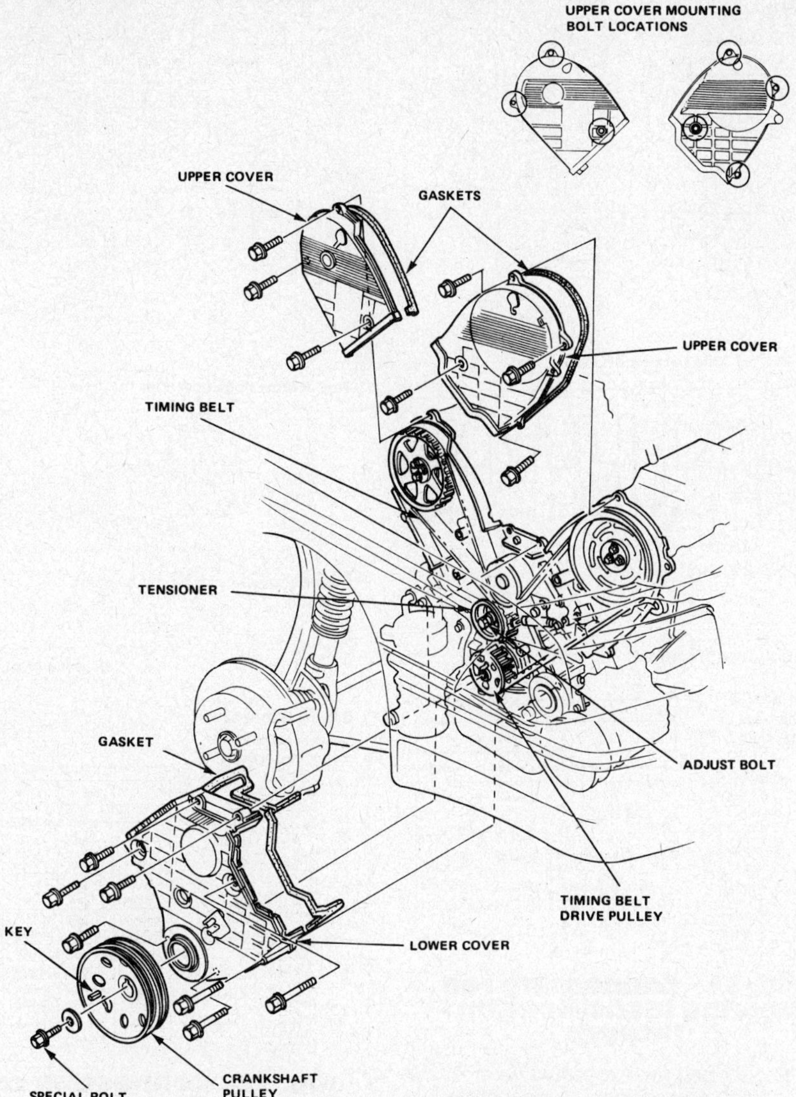

Fig. 26 Timing belt replacement. Legend

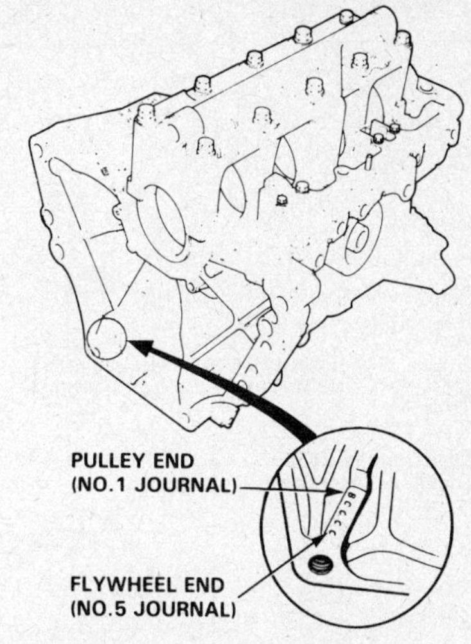

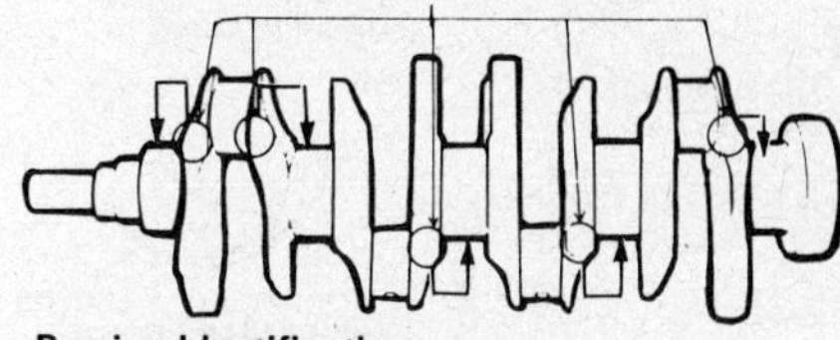

Bearing Identification

Color code is on the edge of the bearing.

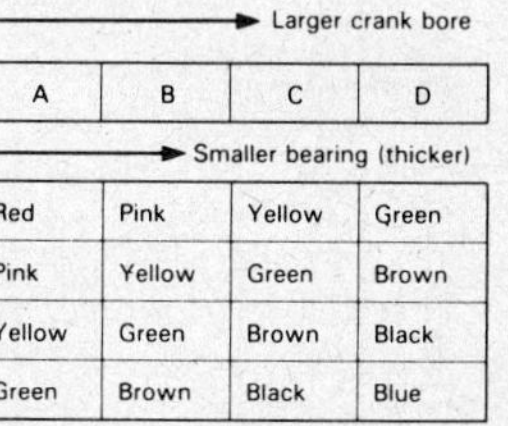

→ Larger crank bore; → Smaller bearing (thicker); ↓ Smaller main journal; ↓ Smaller bearing (thicker)

	A	B	C	D
1	Red	Pink	Yellow	Green
2	Pink	Yellow	Green	Brown
3	Yellow	Green	Brown	Black
4	Green	Brown	Black	Blue

Fig. 29 Main bearing identification. Integra

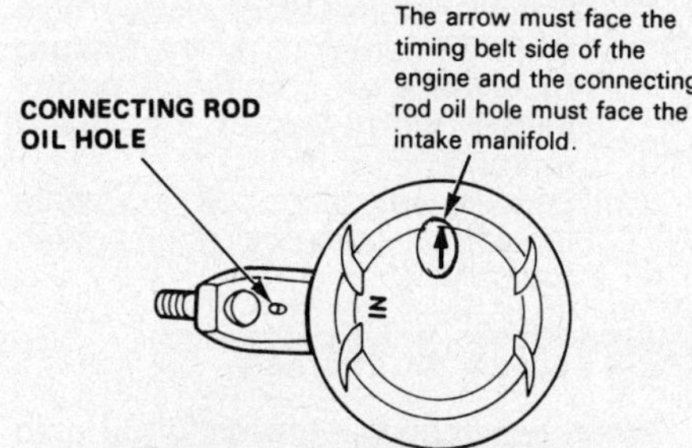

Fig. 27 Piston & connecting rod assembly. Integra

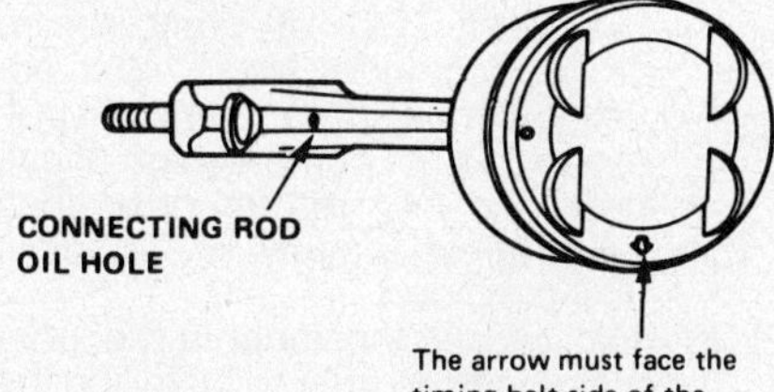

Fig. 28 Piston & connecting rod assembly. Legend

c. Hold collar against nut and insert seal puller under valve guide seal.
d. Slide collar over seal puller to rest on valve spring seat.
e. While holding handle stationary, rotate nut on tool clockwise until seal is removed from guide.
f. Back off nut and slide seal puller down to remove old seal from tool.

6. Reverse procedure to install, noting the following:
   a. Lubricate valve stems prior to spring installation.
   b. Position valve springs with painted portion or closely wound coils toward cylinder head.
   c. With springs installed, lightly tap end of each valve stem several times to seat valves and keepers.

VALVE GUIDES

REPLACE

Heat cylinder head to 300°F before removing or installing valve guides.

1. Drive valve guide out of bottom of cylinder head using a suitable tool.
2. Chill replacement guides in freezer for approximately one hour prior to installation.
3. Using suitable valve guide installation tool, drive valve guide into place until tool bottoms.

TIMING BELT

REPLACE

INTEGRA

1. Refer to **Fig. 25** and perform steps 1 through 18 under "Cylinder Head, Replace."
2. Inspect belt for excessive wear or oil soaking and replace as necessary.
3. Install timing belt with cylinder No. 1 at TDC of compression stroke, **Fig. 8.**
4. Adjust belt tension as follows:
   a. Ensure cylinder No. 1 is at TDC of compression stroke.

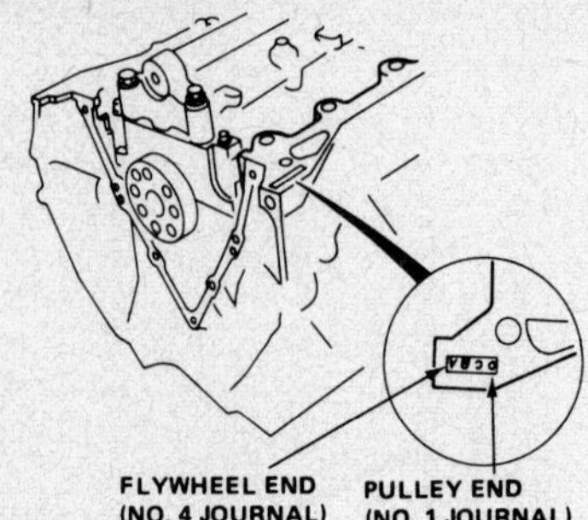

Main Journal Code Locations (Numbers)

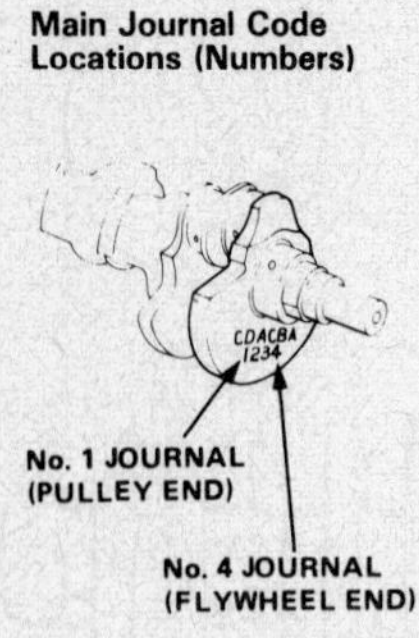

Bearing Design

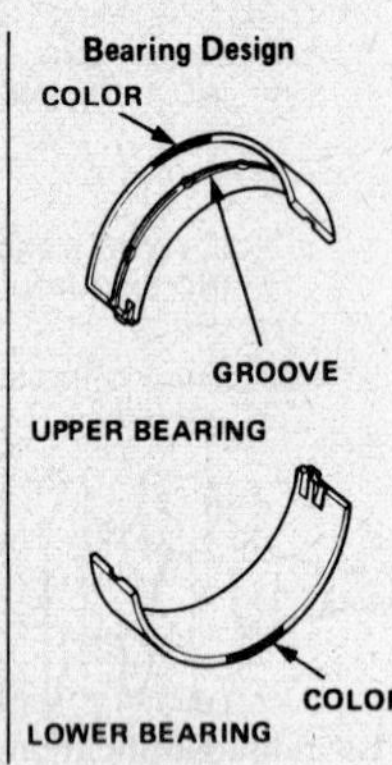

Bearing Identification

Color code is on the edge of the bearing

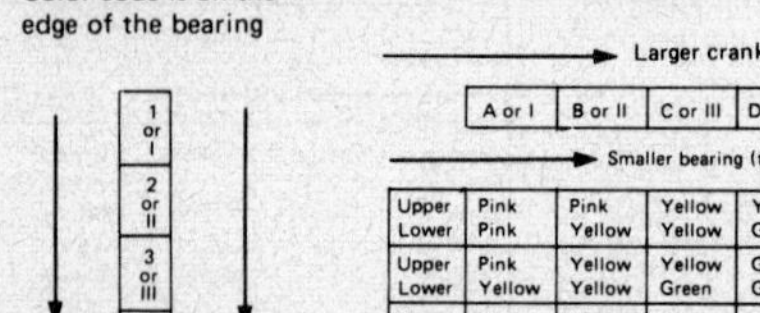

Larger crank bore →

Smaller bearing (thicker) →

		A or I	B or II	C or III	D or IIII
1 or I	Upper Lower	Pink Pink	Pink Yellow	Yellow Yellow	Yellow Green
2 or II	Upper Lower	Pink Yellow	Yellow Yellow	Yellow Green	Green Green
3 or III	Upper Lower	Yellow Yellow	Yellow Green	Green Green	Green Brown
4 or IIII	Upper Lower	Yellow Green	Green Green	Green Brown	Brown Brown
5 or IIIII	Upper Lower	Green Green	Green Brown	Brown Brown	Brown Black
6 or IIIIII	Upper Lower	Green Brown	Brown Brown	Brown Black	Black Black

Fig. 30 Main bearing identification. Legend

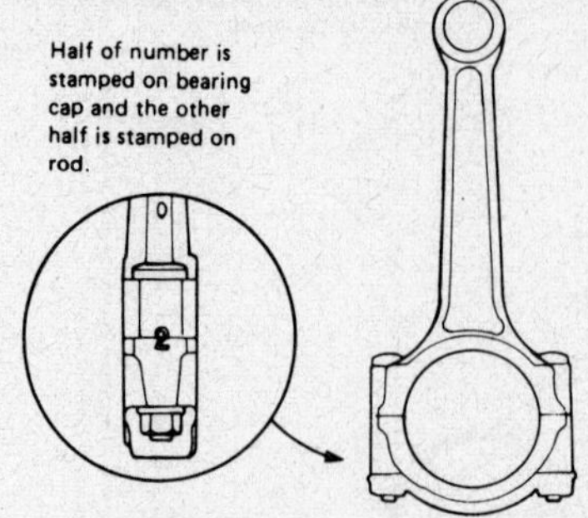

Half of number is stamped on bearing cap and the other half is stamped on rod.

Rod Journal Code Locations (Letters)

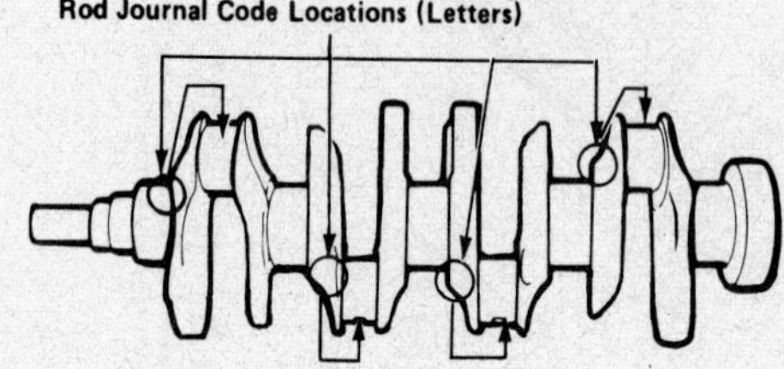

Bearing Identification

Color code is on the edge of the bearing.

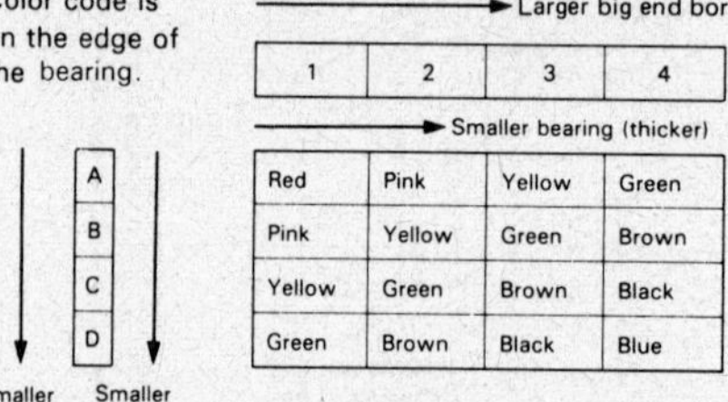

Larger big end bore →

Smaller bearing (thicker) →

	1	2	3	4
A	Red	Pink	Yellow	Green
B	Pink	Yellow	Green	Brown
C	Yellow	Green	Brown	Black
D	Green	Brown	Black	Blue

Fig. 31 Connecting rod bearing identification. Integra

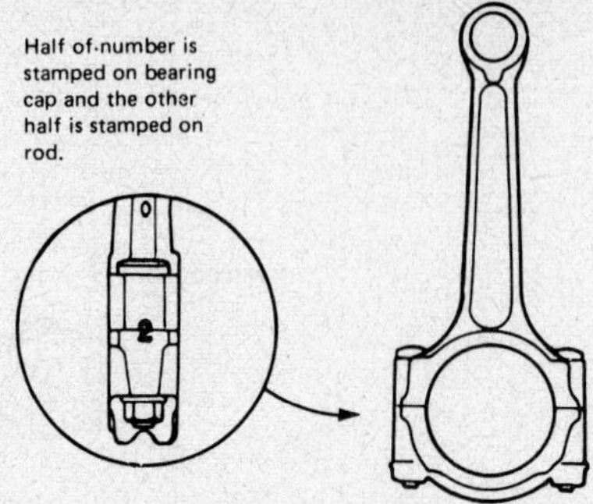

Half of number is stamped on bearing cap and the other half is stamped on rod.

Rod Journal Code Locations (Letters)

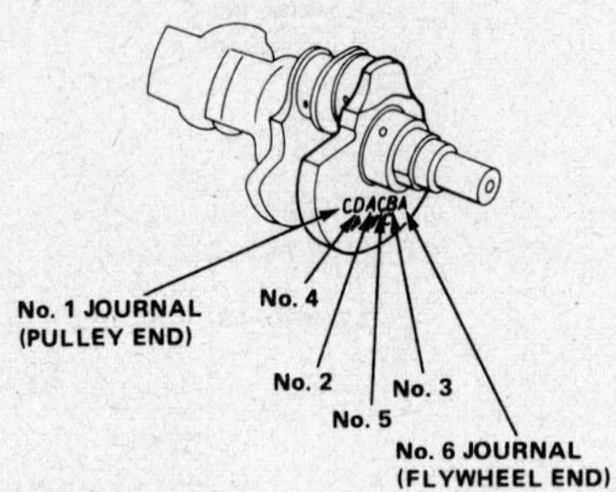

Bearing Identification

Color code is on the edge of the bearing

Smaller rod journal ↓ Smaller bearing (thicker) ↓

Larger big end bore →

Smaller bearing (thicker) →

	1 or I	2 or II	3 or III	4 or IIII
A or I	Pink Pink	Pink Yellow	Yellow Yellow	Yellow Green
B or II	Pink Yellow	Yellow Yellow	Yellow Green	Green Green
C or III	Yellow Yellow	Yellow Green	Green Green	Green Brown
D or IIII	Yellow Green	Green Green	Green Brown	Brown Brown
E or IIIII	Green Green	Green Brown	Brown Brown	Brown Black
F or IIIIII	Green Brown	Brown Brown	Brown Black	Black Black

Fig. 32 Connecting rod bearing identification. Legend

b. Loosen adjusting bolt, then rotate crankshaft counterclockwise three teeth on camshaft pulley to tension timing belt and tighten adjusting bolt.

c. If necessary, re-torque pulley bolt to 83 ft. lbs.

LEGEND

1. Remove pulley cover and harness cover from above timing belt upper cover.
2. Remove engine sub-harness clamp.
3. Support engine using a suitable hoist.
4. Remove engine support bolts, then loosen side mount rubber and raise the side mount bracket.
5. Remove lower splash guard attaching bolts and the guard.
6. Remove A/C compressor drive belt, alternator drive belt and power steering pump drive belt.
7. Remove front and rear upper covers, then the crankshaft pulley attaching bolts and pulley.
8. Remove lower cover, then loosen adjusting bolt and remove timing belt, **Fig. 26.**
9. Inspect belt for excessive wear or oil soaking and replace as necessary.
10. Reverse procedure to install, noting the following:
    a. Remove all spark plugs, then advance crankshaft approximately 15° from TDC of compression stroke of cylinder No. 1. After adjusting front and rear camshaft pulleys to TDC of compression of cylinder No. 1, return crankshaft pulley approximately 15° to adjust TDC position.
    b. Position belt tensioner in the loosening position prior to installing the belt.
    c. Advance rear camshaft pulley approximately 1/2 tooth from TDC position, then install timing belt over pulleys in the following sequence: crankshaft pulley, front camshaft pulley, water pump pulley, tensioner and rear camshaft pulley.
    d. Loosen adjusting bolt, then retighten it after tensioning the belt.
    e. Rotate crankshaft clockwise five or six revolutions to ensure proper installation of belt on pulleys.
11. Following installation, adjust belt tension as follows:
    a. Position cylinder No. 1 at TDC position of compression stroke, **Fig. 11.**
    b. Rotate crankshaft clockwise nine teeth on camshaft pulley. **Ensure blue mark on crankshaft pulley aligns with pointer on lower cover.**
    c. Loosen adjusting bolt to create tension on timing belt, then tighten the bolt.

PISTONS & RODS

When assembling connecting rod onto piston, the oil hole in the connecting rod must be on the same side as the mark on the piston head, **Figs. 27 and 28.** On Integra models, when installing piston and connecting rod assemblies into engine, the arrow on piston head must face timing belt side of engine and connecting rod oil hole must face intake manifold. On Legend models, when installing connecting rod and piston assemblies into engine, the arrow on piston head must face rear side of engine.

MAIN & ROD BEARINGS

Marks are stamped on the end of the en-

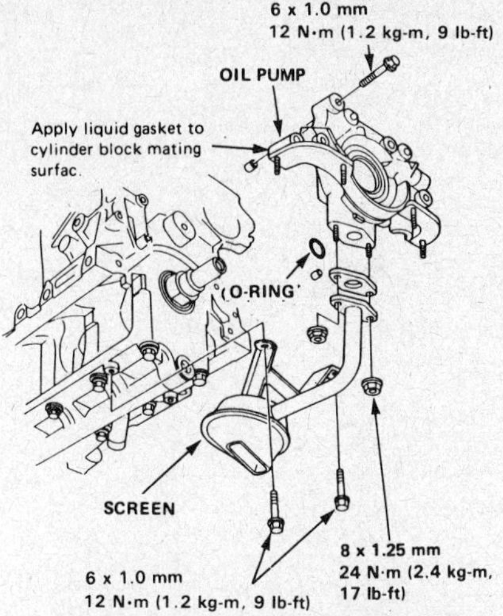

Fig. 33 Oil pump replacement. Integra

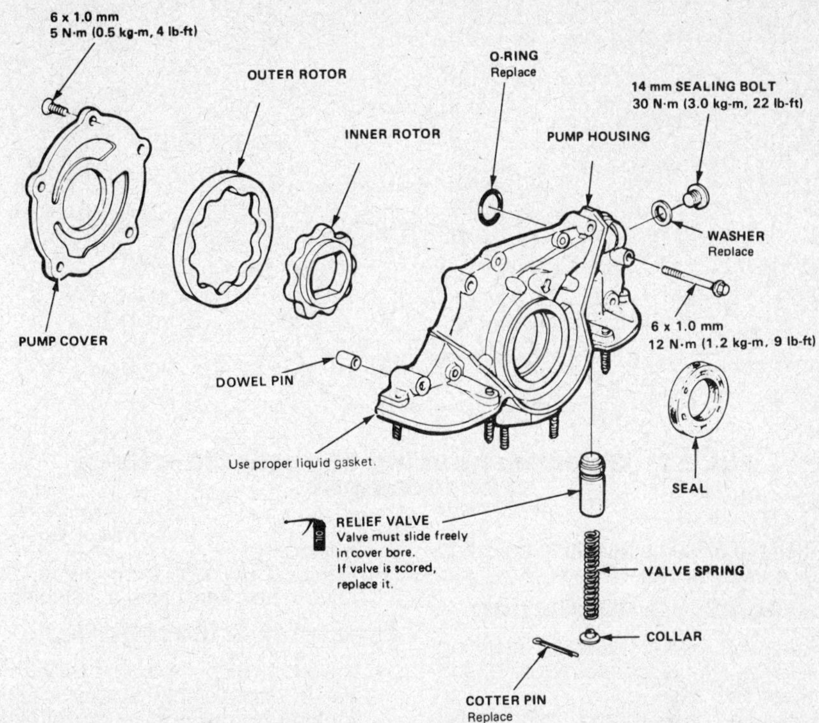

Fig. 34 Exploded view of oil pump assembly. Integra

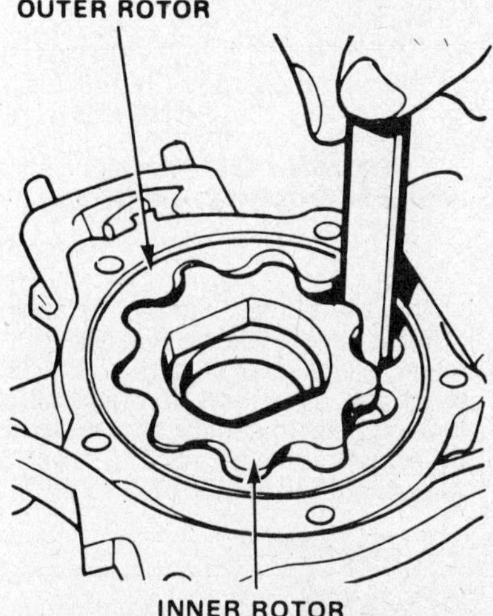

Fig. 35 Oil pump outer rotor radial clearance measurement

gine block as a code for each of the main journal bores, **Figs. 29 and 30.** Use these marks in conjunction with numbers stamped on crankshaft to select correct bearings.

Numbers are stamped on the side of each connecting rod to code the size of the big end. Use these numbers in conjunction with letters stamped on crankshaft, **Figs. 31 and 32,** to select correct bearings.

OIL PUMP SERVICE

INTEGRA

Removal

1. Drain engine oil into a suitable container.
2. Rotate crankshaft until "T" mark on pulley aligns with index mark on cover.
3. Remove valve cover, timing belt upper cover, alternator drive belt, crankshaft pulley and timing belt lower cover.
4. Release timing belt tensioner, then remove timing belt and driven pulley.
5. Remove oil pan attaching bolts and the oil pan.
6. Remove oil screen, then the oil pump attaching bolts and oil pump, **Fig. 33.**

Disassembly & Inspection

1. Remove pump housing attaching screws, then separate housing and cover, **Fig. 34.**
2. Measure outer pump rotor radial clearance, **Fig. 35.** Clearance must not exceed .008 inch.
3. Measure outer pump rotor axial clearance, **Fig. 36.** Clearance must not exceed .006 inch.
4. Measure radial clearance between housing and outer rotor, **Fig. 37.** Clearance must not exceed .008 inch.
5. Inspect both rotors and pump housing for wear or damage and replace as necessary.
6. Remove oil seal from pump, then drive in new seal using a suitable tool.

Assembly & Installation

1. Assemble oil pump in the reverse order of disassembly. **Apply suitable locking compound to pump housing screws prior to installation.**
2. Ensure oil pump rotates freely.
3. Apply clean engine oil to seal lip, then install dowel pins and new O-ring on cylinder block.
4. Ensure mating surfaces are clean and dry, then apply suitable sealant to cylinder block mating surface.
5. Apply suitable sealant to inner threads of bolt holes, then install oil pump. Torque attaching bolts to specifications, **Fig. 33.**
6. Install oil pump screen and torque attaching bolts to specifications. **Do not fill engine with oil for at least 30 minutes after assembly.**

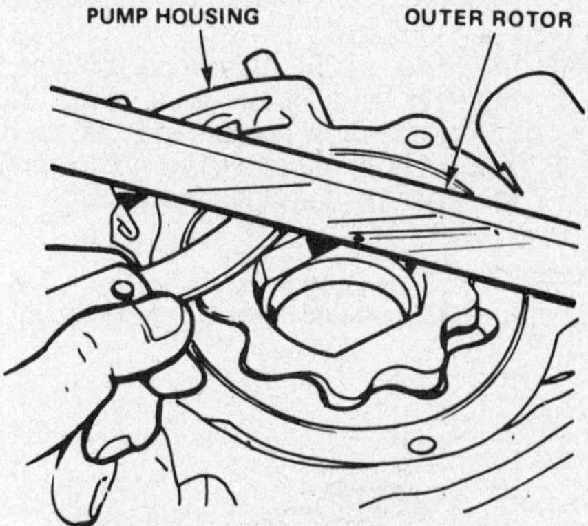

Fig. 36 Oil pump outer rotor axial clearance measurement

LEGEND

Removal

1. Drain engine oil into a suitable container.
2. Rotate crankshaft until "TDC" mark on pulley aligns with index mark on cover.
3. Remove timing belt upper cover, then the alternator drive belt, power steering pump drive belt and A/C compressor drive belt.
4. Remove engine splash guard, then the crankshaft pulley and timing belt lower cover.
5. Release timing belt tensioner, then remove timing belt and driven pulley.
6. Remove oil filter, then the oil pan attaching bolts and oil pan.
7. Remove oil screen and baffle plate,

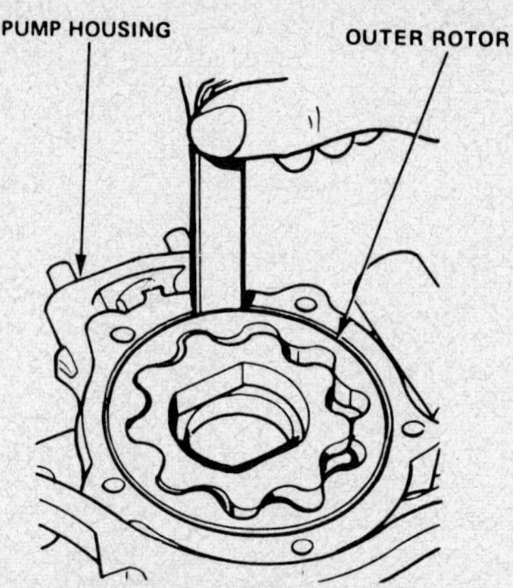

Fig. 37 Oil pump housing to rotor clearance measurement

then the oil pump attaching bolts and oil pump, **Fig. 38.**

Disassembly & Inspection

1. Remove pump housing attaching screws, then separate housing and cover, **Fig. 39.**
2. Measure outer pump rotor radial clearance, **Fig. 35.** Clearance must not exceed .008 inch.
3. Measure outer pump rotor axial clearance, **Fig. 36.** Clearance must not exceed .005 inch.
4. Measure radial clearance between housing and outer rotor, **Fig. 37.** Clearance must not exceed .008 inch.
5. Inspect both rotors and pump housing for wear or damage and replace as necessary.
6. Remove oil seal from pump, then drive in new seal using a suitable tool.

Assembly & Installation

1. Assemble oil pump in the reverse order of disassembly. **Apply suitable locking compound to pump housing screws prior to installation.**
2. Ensure oil pump rotates freely.
3. Apply clean engine oil to seal lip, then install dowel pins and new O-ring on cylinder block.
4. Ensure mating surfaces are clean and dry, then apply suitable sealant to cylinder block mating surface.
5. Apply suitable sealant to inner threads of bolt holes and to bolt threads, then install oil pump. Torque attaching bolts to specifications, **Fig. 38.**
6. Install oil pass pipe and joint, baffle plate and oil screen, torquing all attaching bolts to specifications. **Do not fill engine with oil until at least 30 minutes after assembly.**

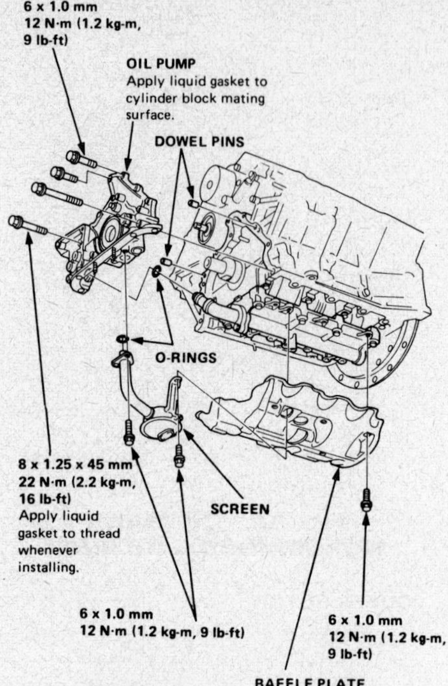

Fig. 38 Oil pump replacement. Legend

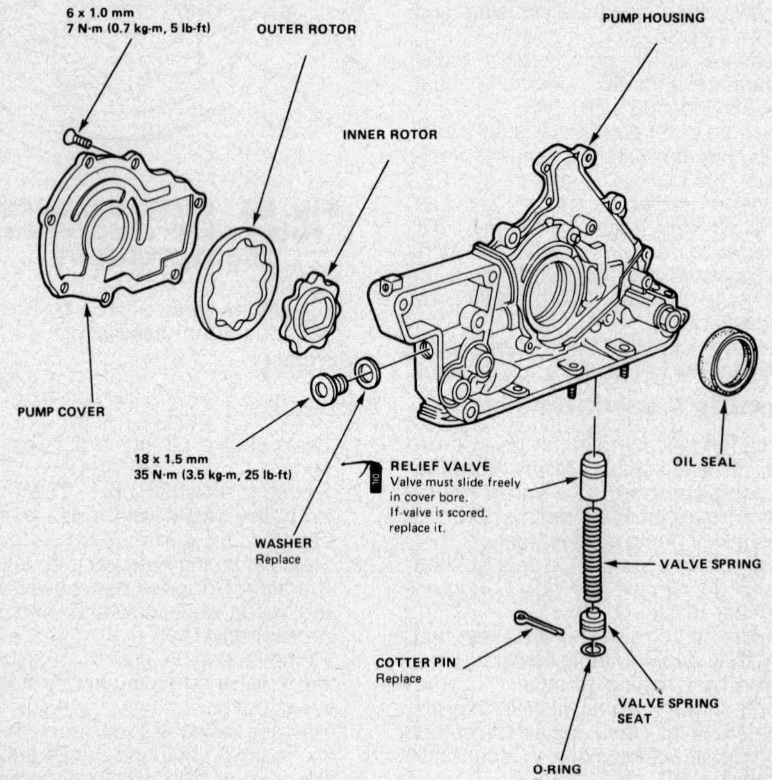

Fig. 39 Exploded view of oil pump assembly. Legend

FUEL PUMP

REPLACE

INTEGRA

1. Disconnect battery ground cable, then relieve fuel system pressure by loosening the service bolt on top of fuel filter, **Fig. 1,** one complete revolution.

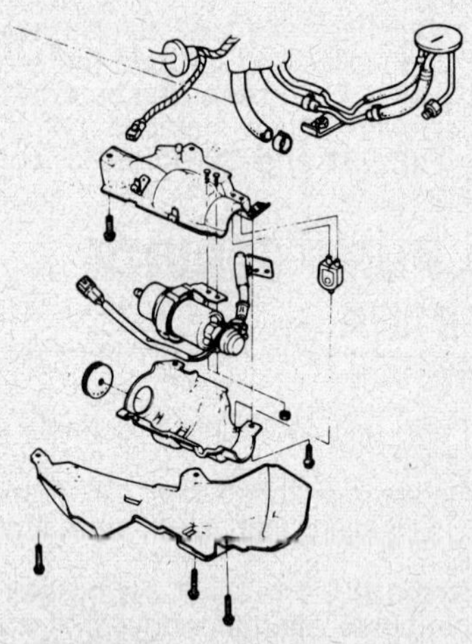

Fig. 40 Fuel pump replacement. Integra

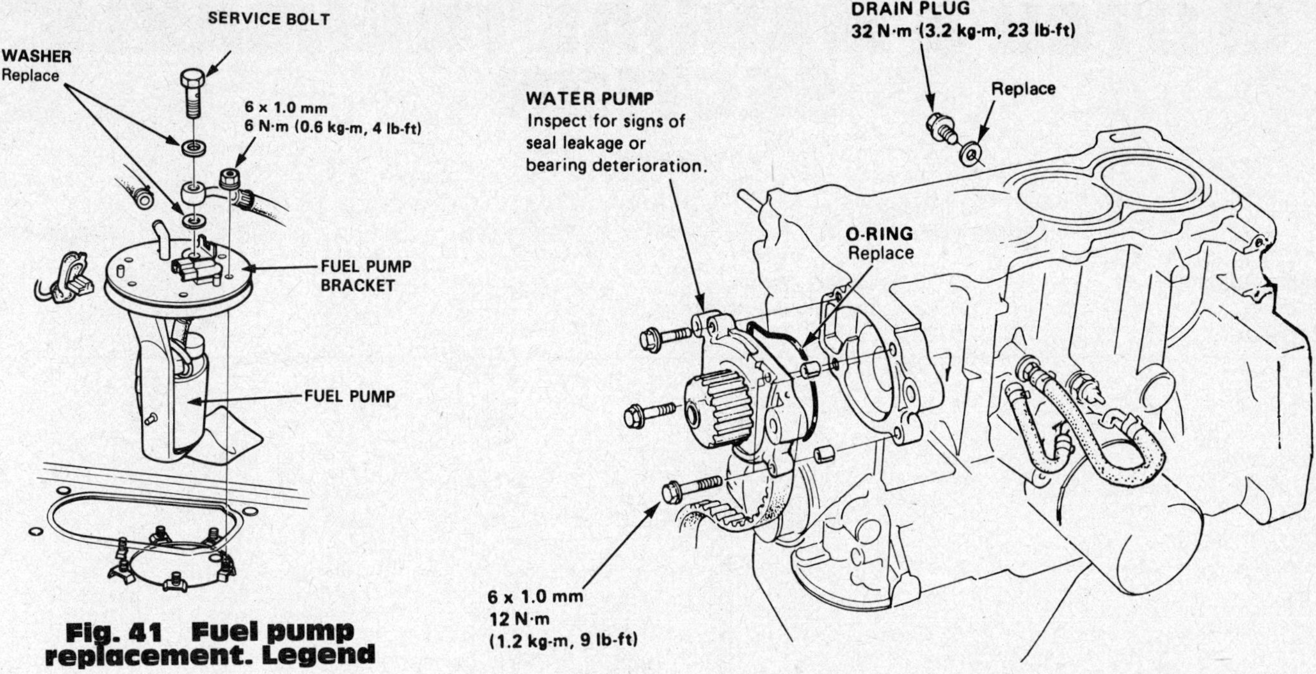

Fig. 41 Fuel pump replacement. Legend

Fig. 42 Water pump replacement. Integra

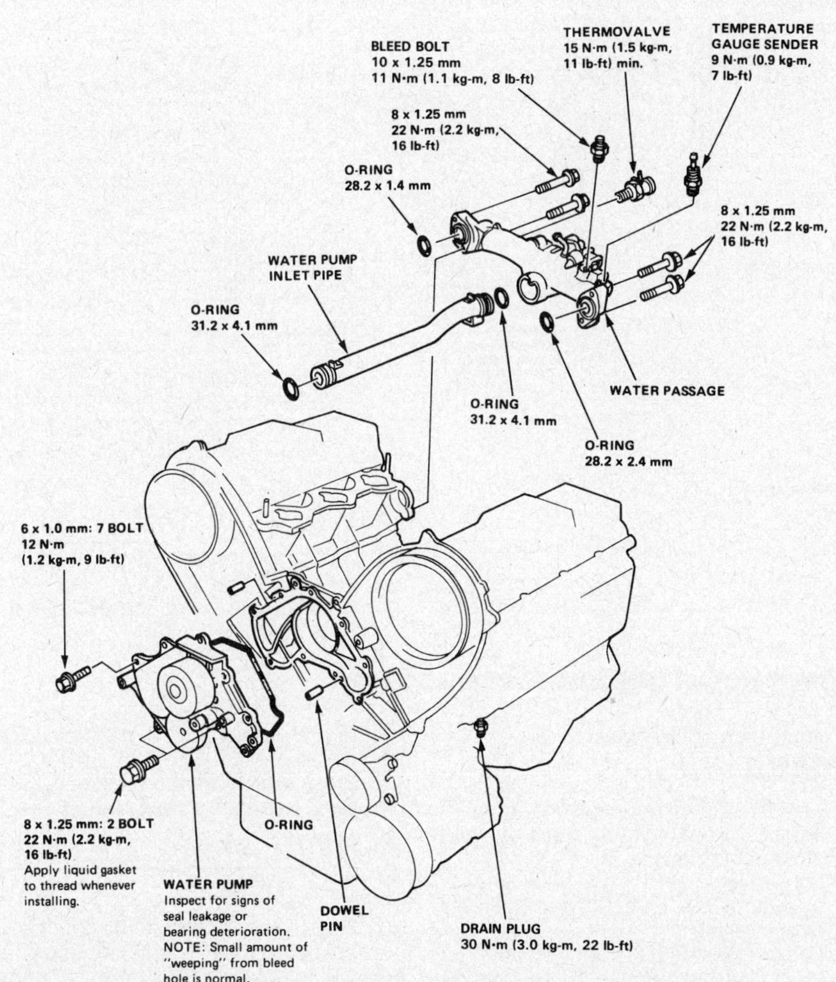

Fig. 43 Water pump replacement. Legend

2. Block front wheels, then raise and support rear of vehicle.
3. Remove fuel pump cover, then the fuel pump attaching bolts and the pump with bracket, **Fig. 40.**
4. Disconnect fuel lines and electrical connector from pump, then remove pump from vehicle.
5. Remove fuel line and pulsation damper from pump. **The fuel pump must not be disassembled.**
6. Reverse procedure to install, noting the following:
   a. Torque pulsation damper attaching nut to 20 ft. lbs.
   b. Thoroughly clean flared fittings of fuel lines before reconnecting them.
   c. Following installation, run engine and check fuel pump fittings for leaks.

LEGEND

1. Disconnect battery ground cable, then relieve fuel system pressure by loosening the service bolt on top of fuel filter, **Fig. 1,** one complete revolution.
2. Remove fuel pump access cover from luggage compartment.
3. Disconnect fuel lines and electrical connector from fuel pump.
4. Remove fuel pump mounting nuts and the fuel pump, **Fig. 41.**
5. Reverse procedure to install.

WATER PUMP REPLACE

Refer to **Figs. 42 and 43** when replacing water pump.

CLUTCH & MANUAL TRANSAXLE SECTION

INDEX

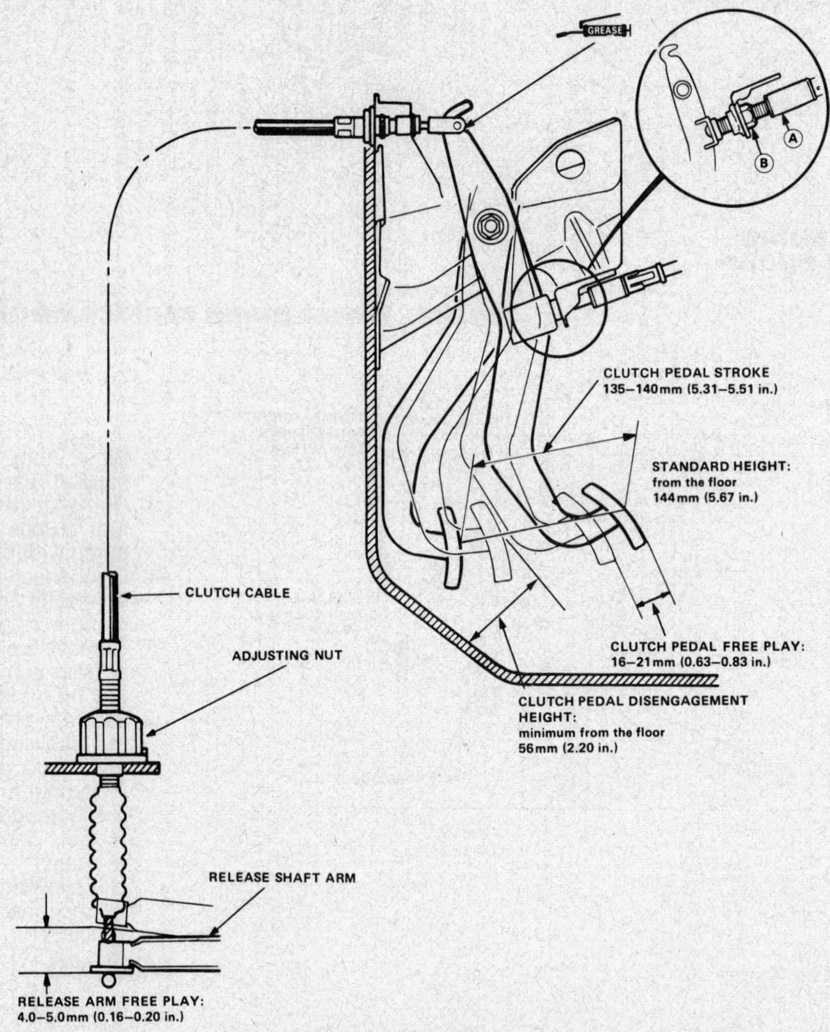

Fig. 1 Clutch pedal adjustments. Integra

CLUTCH

ADJUST

INTEGRA

1. Measure clutch pedal disengagement height and freeplay, **Fig. 1.**
2. Adjust freeplay to specifications by turning adjusting nut as necessary.
3. Ensure specified release arm freeplay exists following adjustment.
4. On models equipped with cruise control, turn adjuster (A), **Fig. 1,** until clutch pedal stroke is within specifications, then tighten locknut (B).

LEGEND

1. Measure clutch pedal disengagement height, pedal height, freeplay and stroke at pedal, **Fig. 2.**
2. Loosen locknut (A), then back off pedal switch until it no longer contacts clutch pedal.
3. Loosen locknut (B), then turn pushrod in or out as necessary to provide specified stroke and pedal height measurements.
4. Tighten locknut (B), then screw in pedal switch until it contacts clutch pedal.
5. Turn switch in an additional 1/4-1/2 turn, then tighten locknut (A).

CLUTCH

REPLACE

1. Remove transaxle assembly as described under "Transaxle, Replace."
2. On Integra models, remove release fork and bearing attaching bolt, then the fork and bearing assembly.
3. On Legend models, remove damper

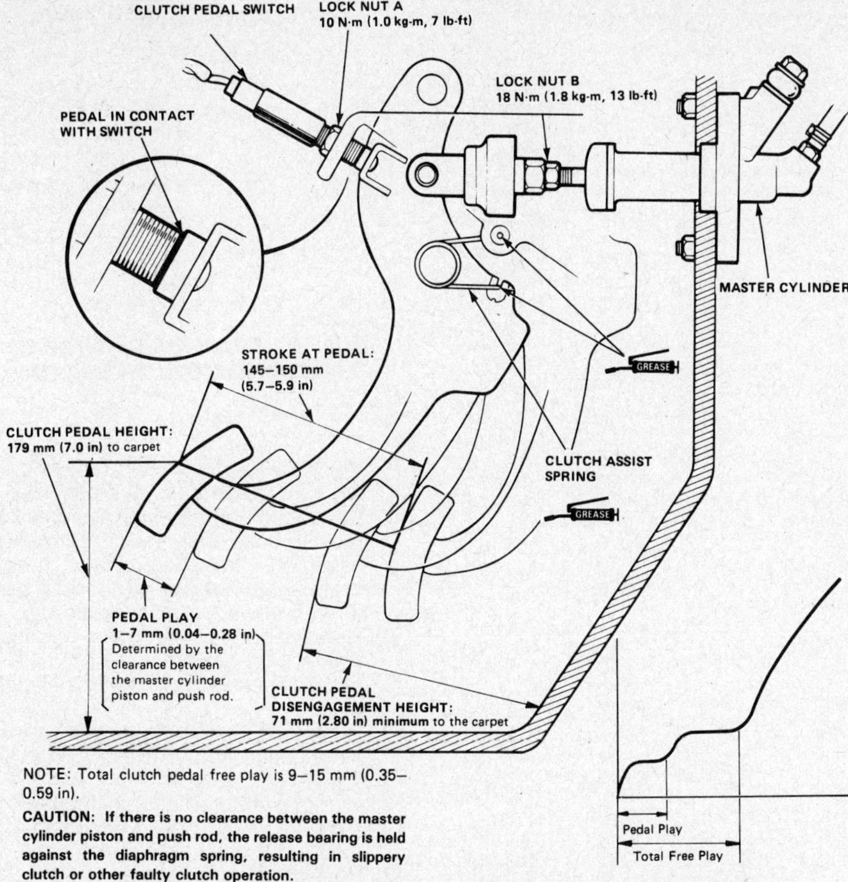

NOTE: Total clutch pedal free play is 9–15 mm (0.35–0.59 in).

CAUTION: If there is no clearance between the master cylinder piston and push rod, the release bearing is held against the diaphragm spring, resulting in slippery clutch or other faulty clutch operation.

Fig. 2 Clutch pedal adjustments. Legend

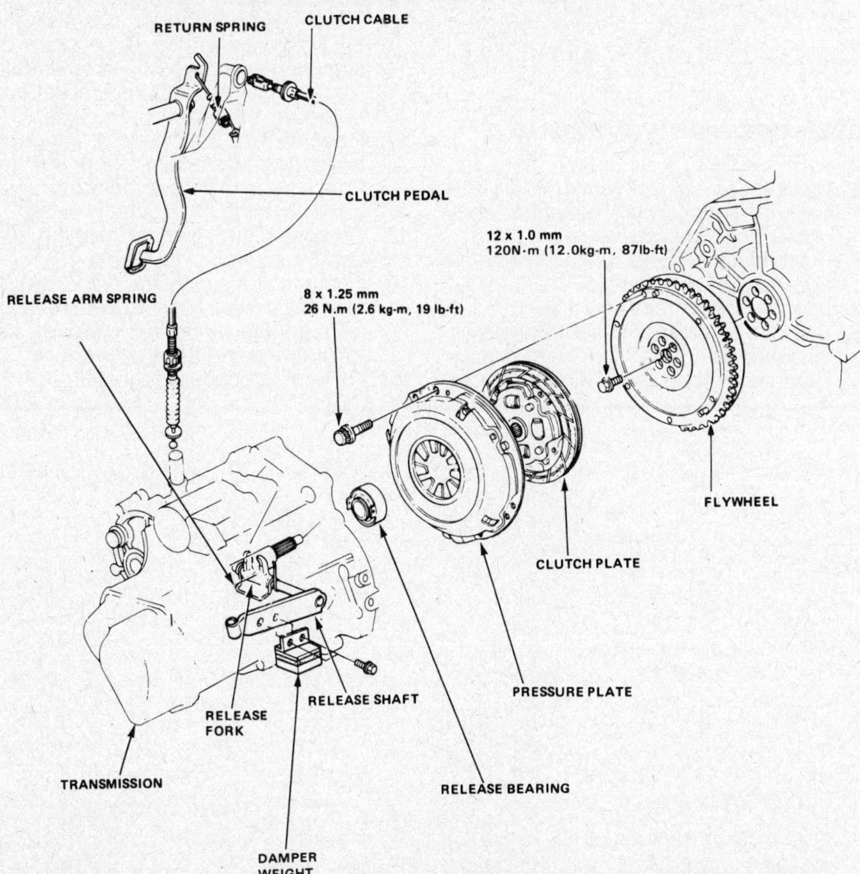

Fig. 3 Exploded view of clutch assembly. Integra

and boot from clutch case, then the release fork and bearing attaching bolt and fork and bearing assembly.

4. On all models, check release bearing for excessive play or roughness and replace if necessary.
5. Lock flywheel using a suitable ring gear holder.
6. Loosen pressure plate attaching bolts two turns at a time in crossing pattern to prevent warpage, then remove attaching bolts and the pressure plate, **Figs. 3 and 4.**
7. Remove clutch disc from flywheel.
8. Reverse procedure to install, noting the following:
   a. Lock flywheel using a suitable ring gear holder, then install clutch disc and pressure plate with flywheel dowels properly aligned with holes in plate.
   b. Install pressure plate attaching finger tight, then install suitable clutch disc alignment tool and torque bolts to specifications. **Torque bolts two turns at a time in a criss-cross pattern to prevent warpage.**

TRANSAXLE
REPLACE
INTEGRA

1. Disconnect battery ground cable from battery and transaxle.
2. Release steering lock and place gear selector in Neutral position.
3. Disconnect battery positive cable from starter motor, black/white wire from starter solenoid and green/black and yellow wires from back-up lamp switch.
4. Disconnect speedometer cable from transaxle.
5. Disconnect clutch cable from release arm.
6. Raise and support vehicle.
7. Drain transaxle oil, then reinstall drain plug and washer.
8. Remove both front driveshafts and intermediate shaft as described in the "Drive Axle Section."
9. Thread a 10 mm bolt into engine block. Attach one end of a suitable lifting chain to bolt and opposite end to engine hanger plate, then lift engine slightly to relieve weight from mounts.
10. Remove engine under cover and splash shield, then disconnect exhaust header pipe from manifold.
11. Disconnect shift lever torque rod from clutch housing.
12. Drive out shift rod spring pin and disconnect the rod.
13. Remove front transaxle mount to engine stiffener attaching bolts.
14. Remove intake manifold bracket and rear engine mount bracket.
15. Remove transaxle housing to engine torque bracket attaching bolts.
16. Remove starter motor attaching bolts and the starter motor.
17. Remove remaining transaxle attaching bolts.
18. Separate transaxle from engine until transaxle clears dowel pins, then

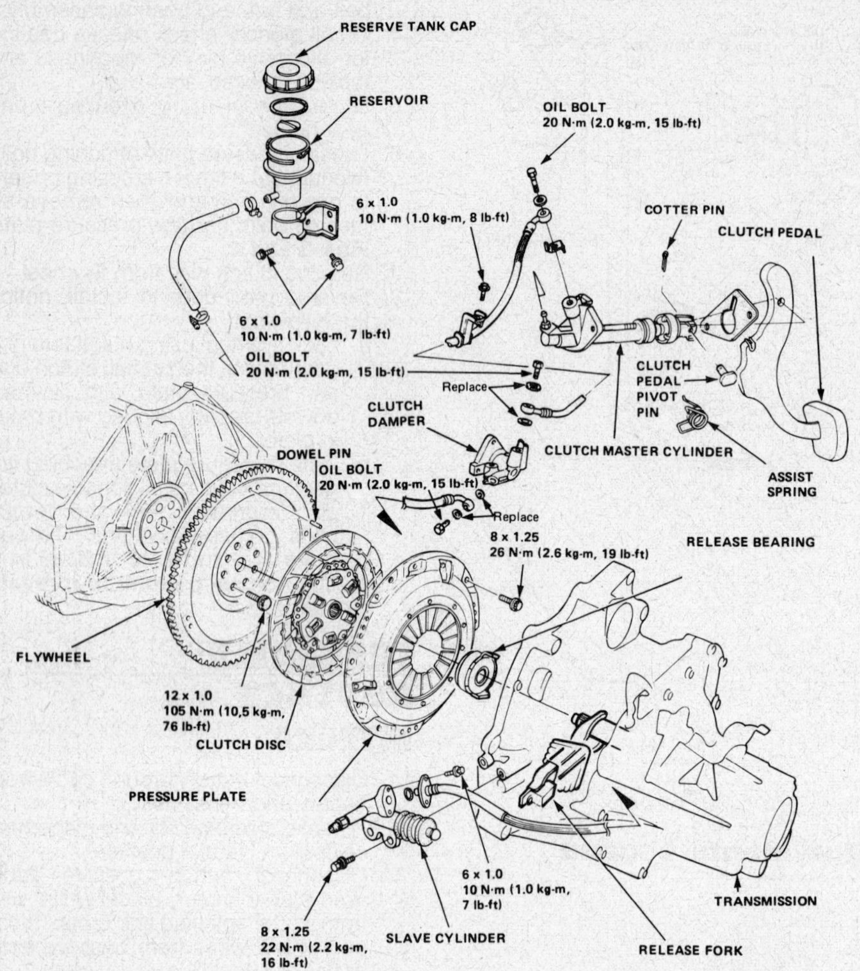

Fig. 4 Exploded view of clutch assembly. Legend

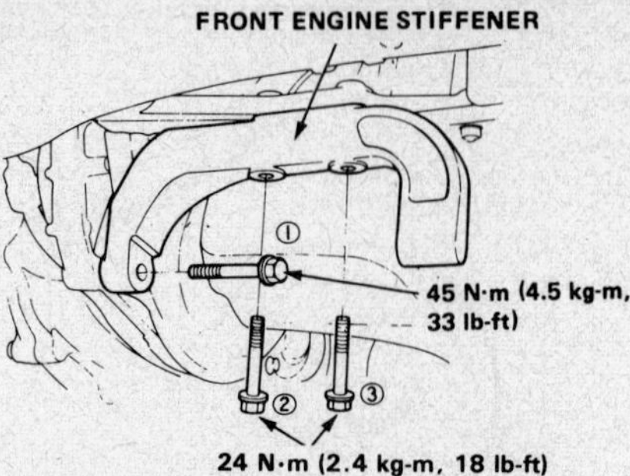

Fig. 5 Engine stiffener installation. Integra

carefully lower assembly from vehicle.

19. Reverse procedure to install. Torque engine stiffener attaching bolts to specifications in sequence shown in **Fig. 5.**

LEGEND

1. Disconnect battery ground and positive cables from battery.
2. Disconnect starter wiring, then the back-up lamp switch electrical connector from engine.
3. Disconnect engine wiring harness from transaxle housing.
4. Loosen bolts at battery base.
5. Remove air cleaner assembly with air intake hose.
6. Remove clutch slave cylinder attaching bolts, then the clutch slave cylinder with clutch hose and pushrod.
7. Remove clutch damper assembly attaching bolts, then the clutch damper assembly from transaxle hanger bracket. **Do not operate clutch pedal with slave cylinder removed.**
8. Remove power steering speed sensor with sensor hose.
9. Drain transaxle oil, then reinstall drain plug.
10. Remove both front driveshafts and intermediate shaft as described in the "Drive Axle Section."
11. Remove shift rod and shift extension.
12. Remove two bolts attaching the torque rod bracket to clutch case.
13. Position a suitable jack securely beneath transaxle.
14. Remove sub-frame center beam.
15. Attach engine hanger set plates or equivalent to engine and support engine using suitable hoist equipment.
16. Remove center stopper bracket from transaxle, then the clutch cover.
17. Remove two rear engine mounting bolts from transaxle, then the two front engine mounting bolts from transaxle housing.
18. Remove starter motor attaching bolts and the starter.
19. Remove remaining transaxle mounting bolts, then pull transaxle away from engine to clear dowel pins and lower transaxle from vehicle.
20. Reverse procedure to install.

BRAKE SECTION

INDEX

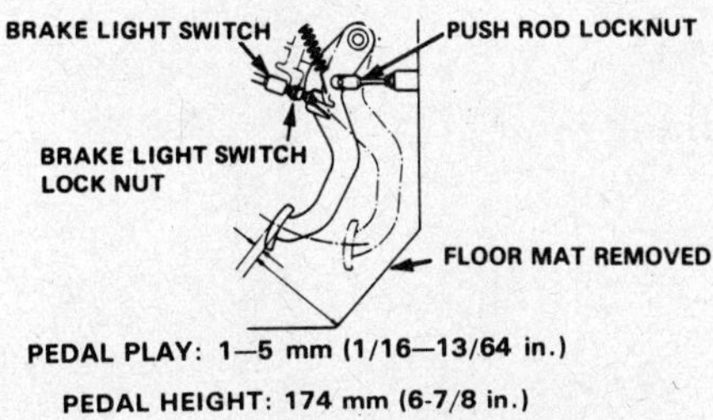

Fig. 1 Brake pedal height & freeplay adjustments

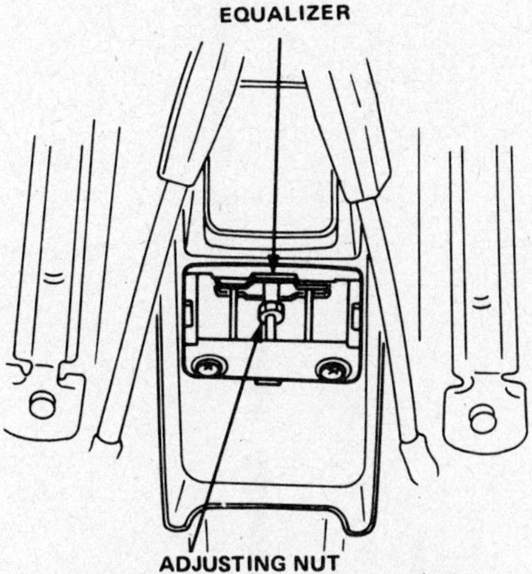

Fig. 4 Parking brake adjusting nut. Integra

BRAKE PEDAL HEIGHT ADJUST

1. Loosen brake light switch locknut, then back off switch until it breaks contact with brake pedal, **Fig. 1.**
2. Loosen pushrod locknut, then turn pushrod in or out as necessary until pedal height measures $6\frac{7}{8}$ inches on Integra models, or $6\frac{11}{16}$ inches on Legend models.
3. Turn in brake light switch until plunger is full depressed, then back switch off $\frac{1}{2}$ turn and tighten locknut.
4. With engine stopped, ensure brake pedal freeplay is within specifications, **Fig. 1. Ensure brake lights go out with brake pedal released.**

PARKING BRAKE ADJUST

After servicing rear brakes, depress brake pedal several times to set self-adjusting brakes before adjusting parking brake cable. On Legend models, actuate brake pedal with engine running and parking brake cable adjustment nut loosened.

1. Block front wheels, then raise and support rear of vehicle.
2. Ensure rear caliper is in contact with pin, **Figs. 2 and 3.**
3. Pull parking brake lever up one notch, then tighten equalizer adjusting nut, **Figs. 4 and 5,** until rear wheels drag slightly when turned.
4. Release parking brake lever and ensure rear wheels do not drag when turned. **When properly adjusted, rear brakes should be fully applied when parking lever has traveled 4-8 clicks on Integra models, or 7-11 clicks on Legend models.**

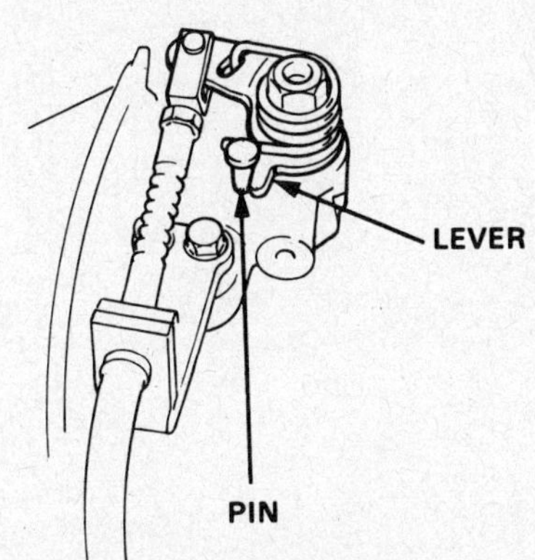

Fig. 2 Parking brake cable attachment. Integra

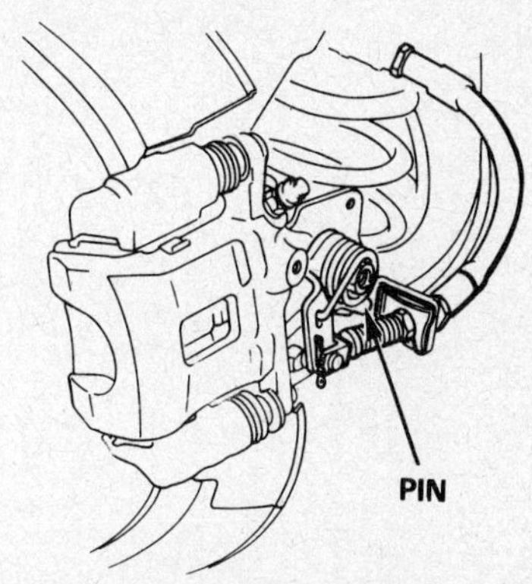

Fig. 3 Parking brake cable attachment. Legend

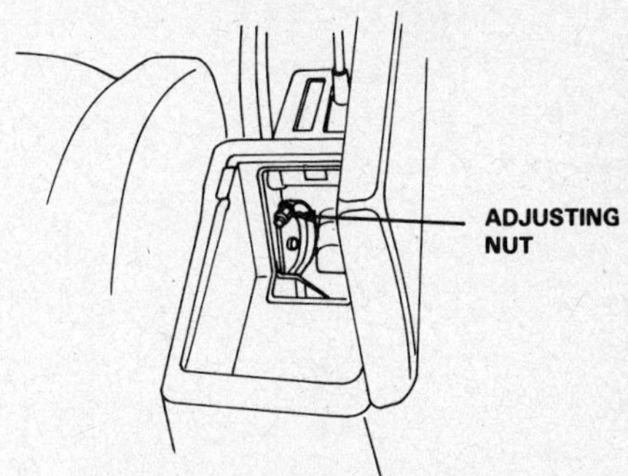

Fig. 5 Parking brake adjusting nut. Legend

MASTER CYLINDER REPLACE

1. Disconnect primary and secondary brake lines from master cylinder.
2. Disconnect fluid level sensor electrical connector, if equipped.
3. Remove master cylinder attaching bolts and the master cylinder.
4. Reverse procedure to install.

BRAKE PADS REPLACE

FRONT

1. Raise and support front of vehicle and remove wheels.
2. Remove caliper pin bolt, then pivot caliper up away from pads.
3. Remove brake pad shims and the pads, **Figs. 6, 7 and 8.**
4. Clean caliper and inspect for excessive wear or damage.
5. Install pad retainers, then the pad shims and pads, **Figs. 6, 7 and 8.**
6. Back out bleed screw and push in piston to allow caliper to fit over pads, then tighten bleed screw.
7. Pivot caliper into position, then install pin bolt and torque to 33 ft. lbs. on Integra models, or 24 ft. lbs. on Legend models.

REAR

1. Raise and support rear of vehicle and remove wheels.
2. Remove caliper shield, then disconnect parking brake cable from caliper.
3. Unfasten caliper and position aside, leaving brake line attached.
4. Remove brake pads and, on Legend models, the shims, **Figs. 9 and 10.**
5. Clean caliper and inspect for excessive wear or damage.
6. Install pad retainers, then the pads

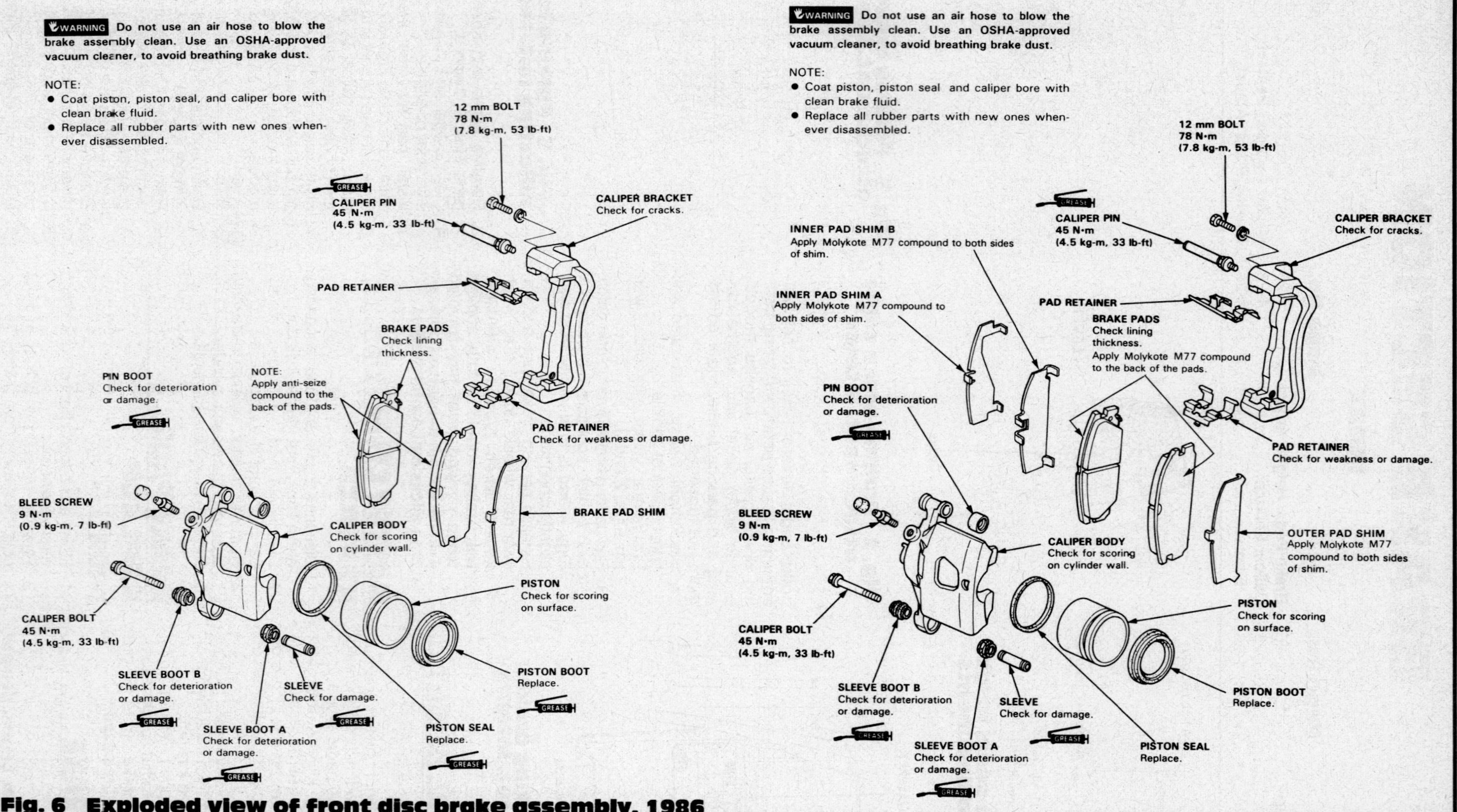

Fig. 6 Exploded view of front disc brake assembly. 1986 Integra

Fig. 7 Exploded view of front disc brake assembly. 1987 Integra

WARNING Do not use an air hose to blow the brake assembly clean. Use an OSHA-approved vacuum cleaner, to avoid breathing brake dust.

CAUTION:

- Do not spill brake fluid on the car; it may damage the paint; if brake fluid does contact the paint, wash it off immediately with water.
- To prevent spills, cover the hose joints with rags or shop towels.
- Clean all parts in brake fluid and air dry; blow out all passages with compressed air.
- Before reassembling, check that all parts are free of dust and other foreign particles.
- Replace parts with new ones whenever specified to do so.
- Make sure no dirt or other foreign matter is allowed to contaminate the brake fluid.
- Do not mix different brands of brake fluid as they may not be compatible.
- Do not reuse the drained fluid.

NOTE:

- Coat piston, piston seal, and caliper bore with clean brake fluid.
- Replace all rubber parts with new ones whenever disassembled.

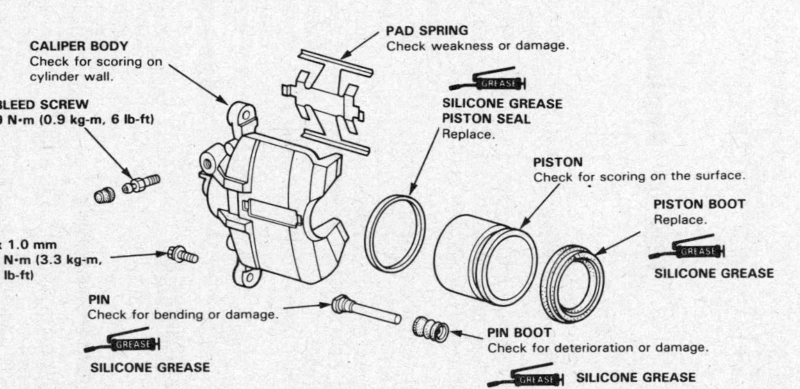

Fig. 8 Exploded view of front disc brake assembly. Legend

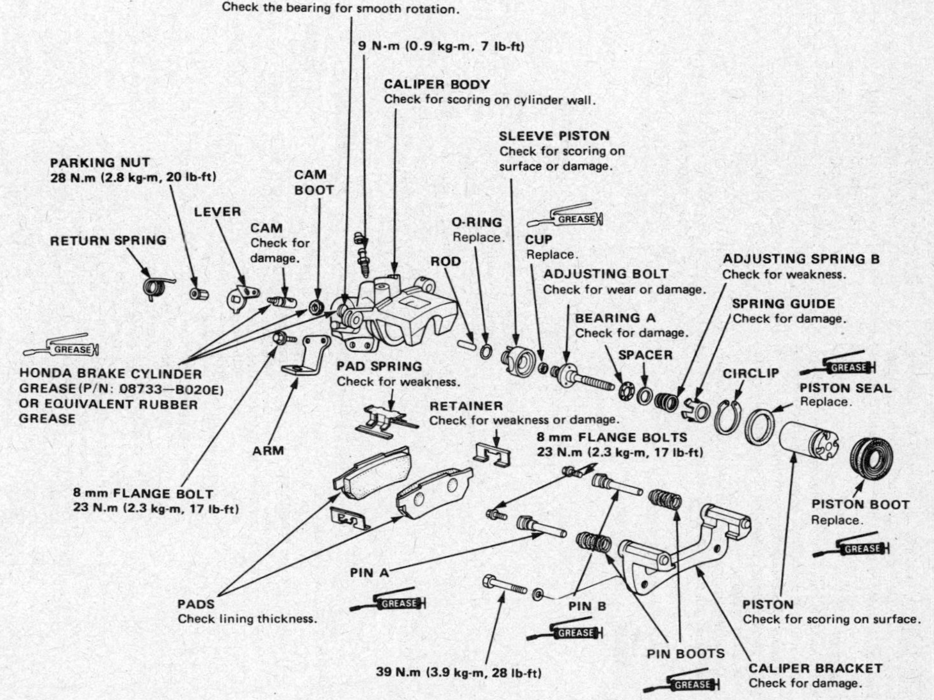

Fig. 9 Exploded view of rear disc brake assembly. Integra

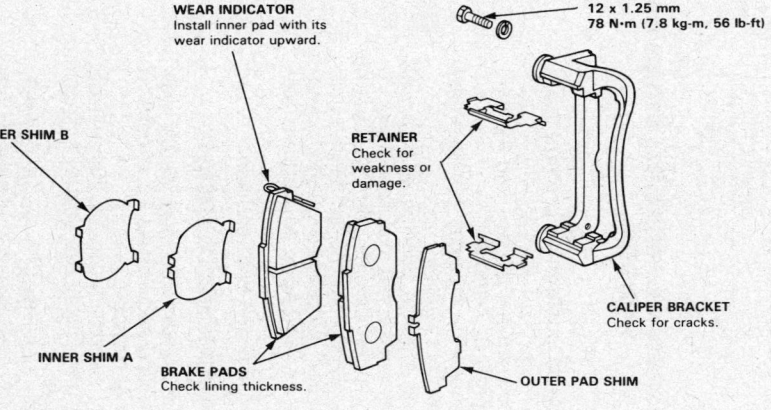

WARNING Do not use an air hose to blow the brake assembly clean. Use an OSHA-approved vacuum cleaner, to avoid breathing brake dust.

CAUTION:
- Do not spill brake fluid on the car; it may damage the paint; if brake fluid does contact the paint, wash it off immediately with water.
- To prevent spills, cover the hose joints with rags or shop towels.
- Clean all parts in brake fluid and air dry; blow out all passages with compressed air.

GREASE : RUBBER GREASE

GREASE : SILICONE GREASE

- Before reassembling, check that all parts are free of dust and other foreign particles.
- Replace parts with new ones whenever specified to do so.
- Make sure no dirt or other foreign matter is allowed to contaminate the brake fluid.
- Do not mix different brands of brake fluid as they may not be compatible.
- Do not reuse the drained fluid.

NOTE:
- Coat piston, piston seal, and caliper bore with clean brake fluid.
- Replace all rubber parts with new ones whenever disassembled.

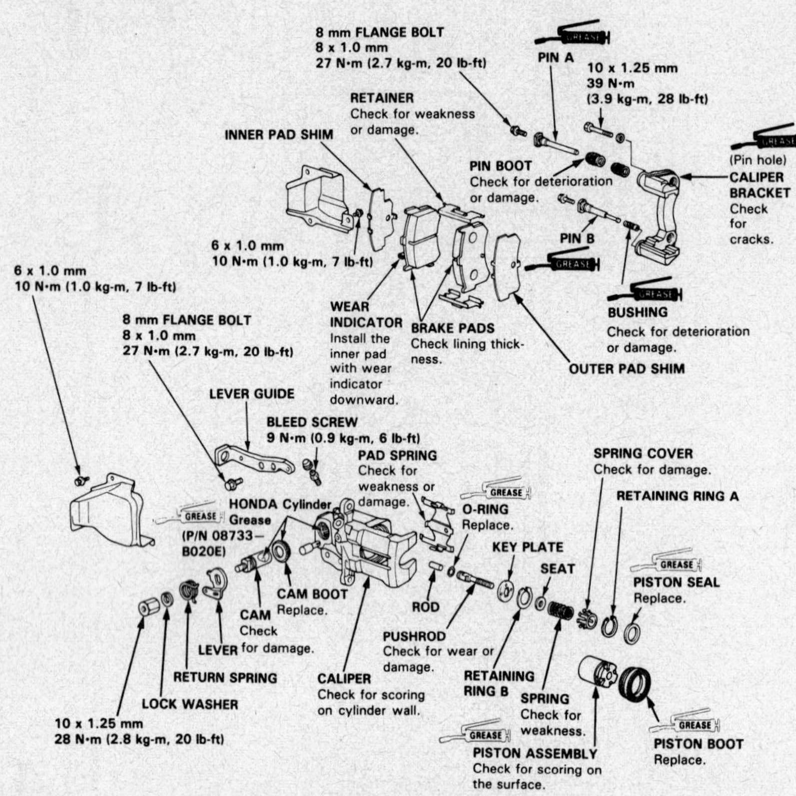

Fig. 10 Exploded view of rear disc brake assembly. Legend

and shims, if equipped, **Figs. 9 and 10.**

7. Rotate caliper piston into position in cylinder, then turn back piston to align cutout in piston with projection on inner pad.
8. Install caliper, torquing attaching bolts to 17 ft. lbs. on Integra models, or 20 ft. lbs. on Legend models. **Ensure piston boot is not twisted when installing caliper.**
9. Connect parking brake cable to caliper.
10. Install caliper shield, torquing attaching bolts to 7 ft. lbs.

CALIPER SERVICE

FRONT

Removal & Disassembly

1. Raise and support front of vehicle and remove wheels.
2. Remove banjo bolt and disconnect brake line from caliper. **Secure hose in raised position to prevent leakage.**
3. Remove caliper pin bolt and the caliper, **Figs. 6, 7 and 8.**
4. On Legend models, remove pad spring from caliper.
5. On all models, position a block of wood or shop rag in caliper opposite piston, then carefully remove piston by applying compressed air into fluid inlet port. **Use only as much air pressure as is needed to remove piston.**
6. Remove piston boot and seal.

Assembly & Installation

1. Clean caliper bore and piston with brake fluid and inspect for excessive wear or damage.
2. Apply suitable grease to new piston seal, then install the seal in cylinder groove.
3. Install piston boot, then apply clean brake fluid to piston and cylinder and install piston. **Ensure dished end of piston faces inward.**
4. On Legend models, install pad spring in caliper.
5. On all models, install caliper in reverse order of removal.

REAR

Removal & Disassembly

1. Raise and support rear of vehicle and remove wheels.
2. Remove caliper shield, then disconnect parking brake cable from caliper.
3. Remove banjo bolt and disconnect brake line from caliper. **Secure hose in raised position to prevent leakage.**
4. Remove caliper mounting bolts and the caliper, **Figs. 9 and 10.**
5. Remove pad spring from caliper.
6. Remove piston and piston boot using needle-nose pliers. **Rotate piston as it is removed.**
7. On Integra models, remove circlip, washer, adjusting spring and adjusting nut from piston.

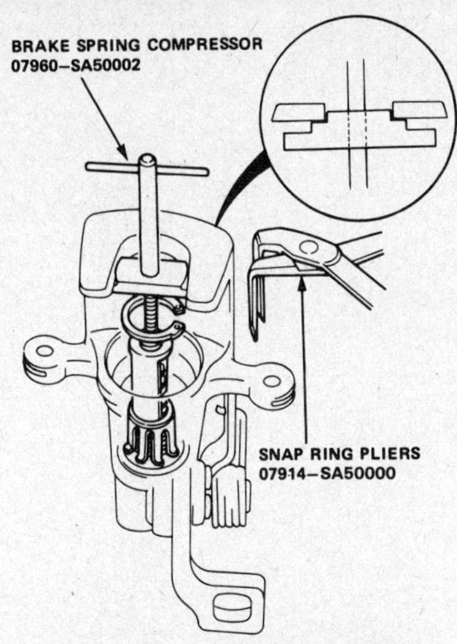

Fig. 11 Brake spring removal. Integra

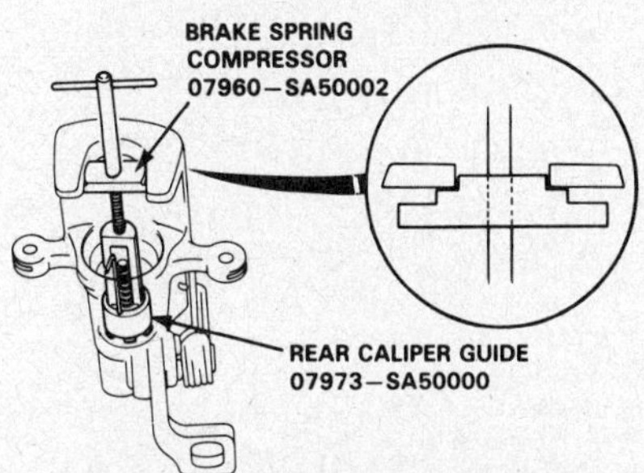

Fig. 12 Brake spring removal. Legend

8. On Legend models, remove retaining ring, spacer, wave washer, spacer, ball bearing, adjuster nut and cup from piston.
9. On all models, carefully pry piston seal out of caliper bore.
10. Position brake spring compressor tool between caliper body and spring cover, **Figs. 11 and 12.**
11. Turn shaft of tool to compress adjusting spring, then remove circlip or retaining ring.
12. On Integra models, remove spring cover, adjusting spring, spacer, bearing, adjusting bolt, sleeve piston and rod.
13. On Legend models, remove spring compressor, then the spring cover, spring, seat, retaining ring, key plate, pushrod and rod from caliper. Remove O-ring from pushrod.
14. On all models, remove return spring, parking nut, spring washer, lever, cam and cam boot.

Assembly & Installation

1. Pack needle bearing with suitable grease.
2. Apply suitable grease to cam boot, then install the boot in caliper.
3. Install cam, ensuring hole in cam faces cylinder.
4. Install lever, spring washer and parking nut. Torque nut to 20 ft. lbs., then install return spring.
5. Install rod in cam, then position new O-ring on sleeve piston or pushrod.
6. On Integra models, install sleeve piston. **Ensure hole in bottom of piston is properly aligned with rod in cam and two pins on piston are aligned with holes in caliper.**
7. On Legend models, install pushrod and key plate in cylinder. **Ensure hole in pushrod aligns with rod, cut-out in key plate aligns with square portion of pushrod and lug on key plate aligns with hole in cylinder.**
8. On Integra models, install new cup with cup groove facing bearing side on adjusting bolt, then position bearing, spacer, adjusting spring and spring cover on adjusting bolt. Install adjusting bolt assembly into caliper cylinder.
9. On Legend models, depress pushrod and install retaining ring, then the seat, spring and spring cover on pushrod.
10. On all models, position rear caliper guide tool No. 07973-SA50000 on Integra models or No. 07GAE-SD40200 on Legend models, or equivalent in cylinder, ensuring cutout on tool aligns with tab on spring cover.
11. Install brake spring compressor tool, **Figs. 13 and 14,** and compress spring until tool bottoms out. **Ensure rear caliper guide slides freely with spring.**
12. Remove rear caliper guide tool and ensure flared end of spring cover is below circlip groove.
13. Install circlip, then remove spring compressor. **Ensure circlip is properly seated in groove.**
14. On Integra models, install adjusting nut, adjusting spring, washer and circlip into piston.
15. On Legend models, position cup on adjuster not with grove facing bearing, then install adjuster nut, bearing, spacers wave washer and retaining ring into piston.
16. Apply suitable grease to new piston seal and piston boot, then install the seal and boot into caliper.
17. Apply suitable grease to outer surface of piston, then install piston while rotating it clockwise.
18. Install pad spring in caliper.
19. Install caliper in reverse order of removal.

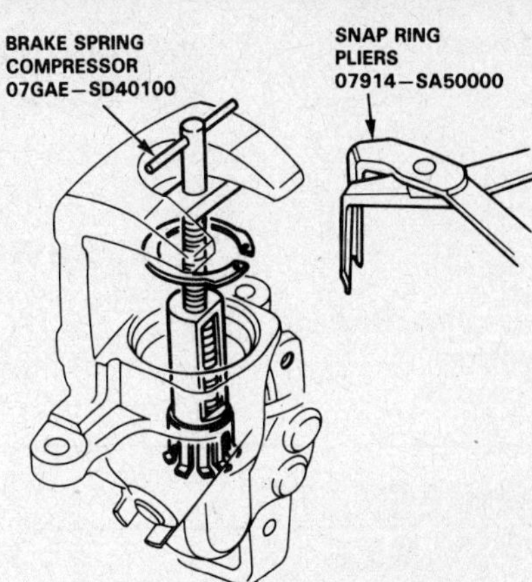

Fig. 13 Brake spring installation. Integra

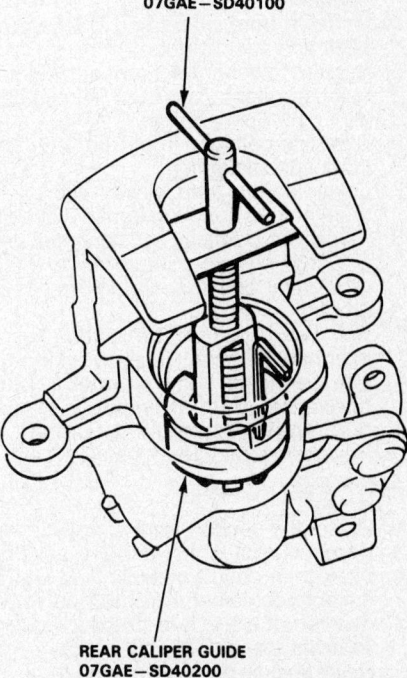

BRAKE SPRING COMPRESSOR
07GAE–SD40100

REAR CALIPER GUIDE
07GAE–SD40200

Fig. 14 Brake spring installation. Legend

DRIVE AXLE SECTION

INDEX

DRIVESHAFT REPLACE

INTEGRA

1. Loosen front wheel spindle nut.
2. Raise and support front of vehicle.
3. Drain transaxle fluid into a suitable container.
4. Remove front wheel and tire assemblies and spindle nuts.
5. Support lower control arm at ball joint using a suitable jack, then remove ball joint cotter pin and nut.
6. Separate ball joint from front hub using a suitable puller.
7. Lower control arm slowly with jack, then remove front hub from driveshaft.
8. Pry inboard CV joint out approximately 1/2 inch using a suitable tool to force differential side gear spring clip out of groove.
9. Remove driveshaft from differential of intermediate shaft. **To prevent damage to seals, hold inboard joint horizontal until driveshaft clears differential or intermediate shaft.**
10. Reverse procedure to install.

LEGEND

1. Raise and support front of vehicle.
2. Remove front wheel and tire assemblies, then drain transaxle fluid into a suitable container. **If removing right driveshaft only, it is not necessary to drain transaxle.**
3. Raise spindle nut lock tab and remove the nut.
4. Remove damper fork bolt and pinch bolt, then the damper fork.
5. Remove steering knuckle to lower control arm castellated nut cotter pin and the nut.
6. Separate lower control arm from steering knuckle using a suitable puller.
7. Pull steering knuckle outward and tap driveshaft outboard joint from steering knuckle.
8. Pry driveshaft out with a screwdriver to force set ring at driveshaft end past the groove.
9. Pull inboard CV joint and remove driveshaft and CV joint as an assembly. **Pull shaft straight out to prevent damaging seals.**
10. Reverse procedure to install.

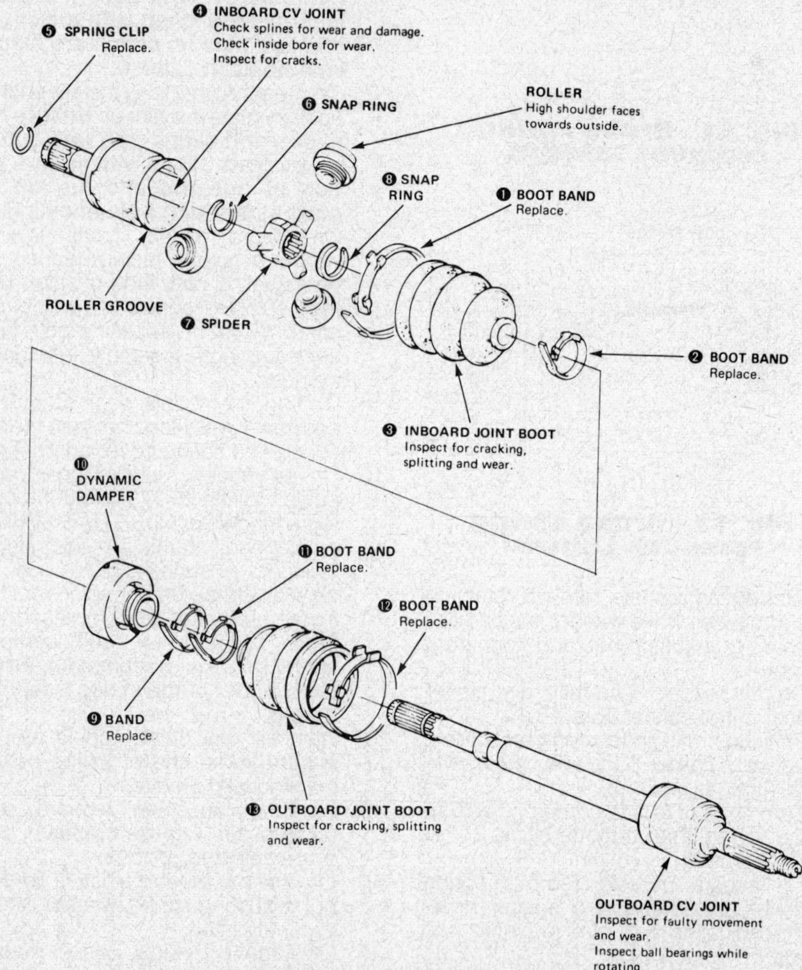

Fig. 1 Exploded view of driveshaft assembly. Integra

DRIVESHAFT SERVICE

1. Disassemble driveshaft assembly referring to, **Figs. 1 and 2. Mark rollers and roller grooves for assembly reference.**
2. Assemble driveshaft assembly in the reverse order of disassembly, noting the following:
   a. Pack bearings, joint boot cavity and both CV joints with suitable grease prior to installation.
   b. Install rollers and bearing races on spider shafts, then position spider assembly into inboard CV joint. **On Legend models, position rollers on spider with their high shoulders facing outward.**
   c. Avoid getting grease or oil on rubber components.
   d. On Integra models, position new boot bands on small ends of boots so they are centered between protrusions at each end of driveshaft, then expand and contract boots until they return to normal shape and length.
   e. On all models, adjust length of driveshafts to specifications, **Figs. 3 and 4.**
   f. Install new boot bands on boots. **Bend both sets of locking tabs, then lightly tap down doubled over portion of bands.**
   g. On Integra models, install dynamic

GREASE Thoroughly pack the inboard joint and both joint boots with high quality molybdenum disulfide grease when reassembling.

Grease Quantity:
Inboard Joint: 100–110 g
Outboard Joint: 130–140 g

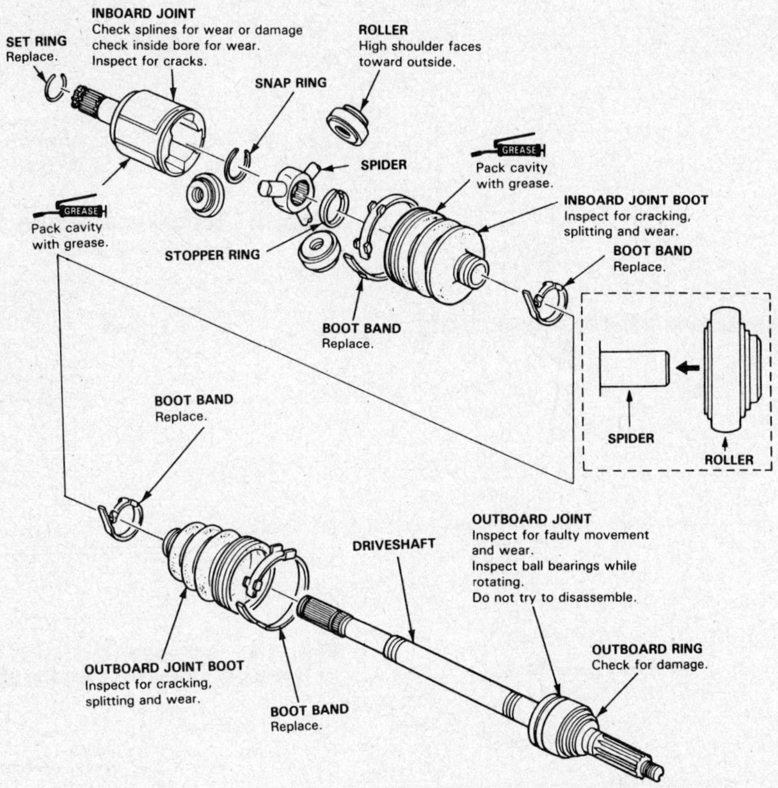

Fig. 2 Exploded view of driveshaft assembly. Legend

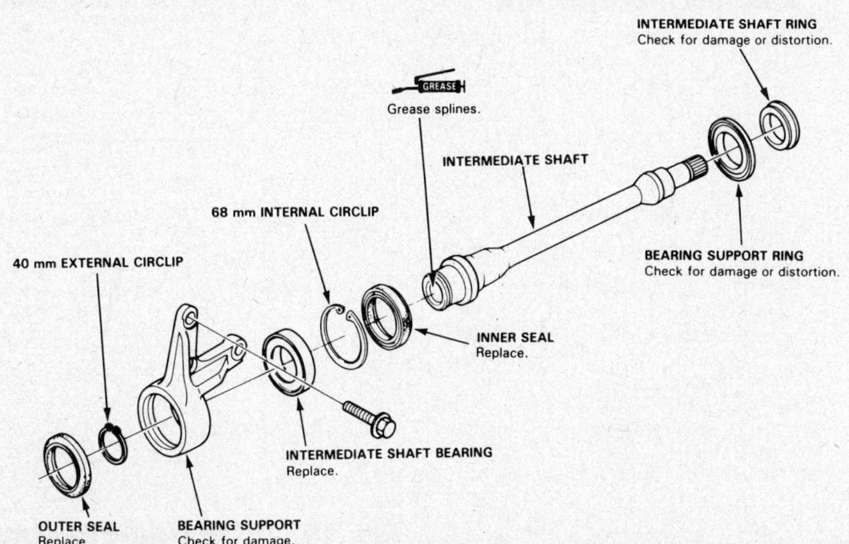

Fig. 6 Exploded view of intermediate shaft assembly. Integra

damper at specified dimension, **Fig. 5.**

h. On Integra models, install new spring clip in groove of CV joint sub-axle. **Ensure clip locks properly into differential or intermediate shaft groove.**

i. On Legend models, install new set ring into driveshaft groove, then position inboard end of driveshaft

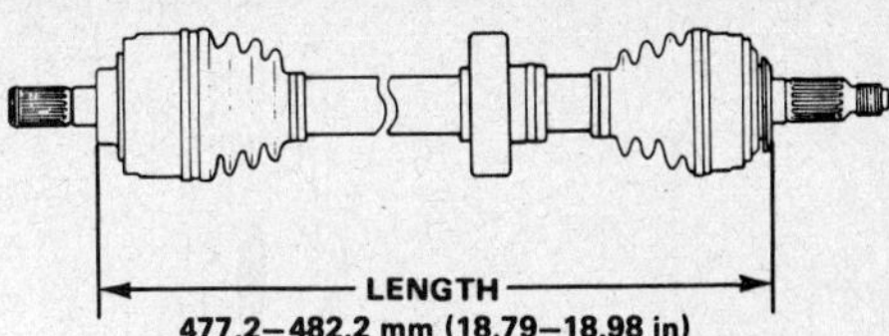

Fig. 3 Driveshaft length adjustment. Integra

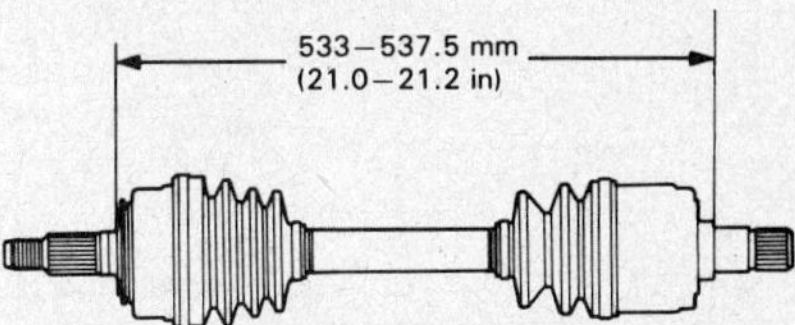

Fig. 4 Driveshaft length adjustment. Legend

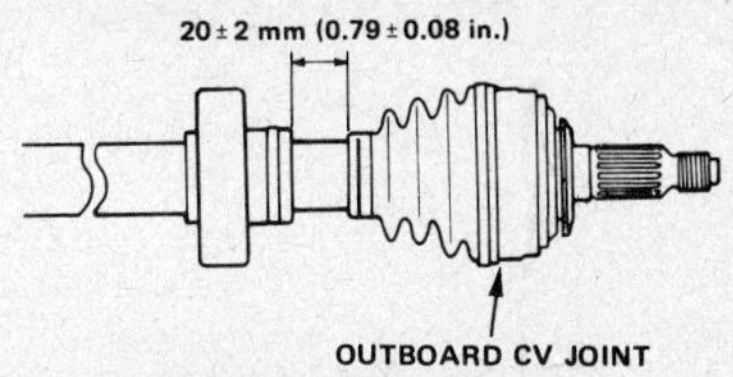

Fig. 5 Driveshaft dynamic damper installation. Integra

into differential. **Ensure driveshaft locks in differential side gear groove and CV joint sub-axle bottoms in differential or intermediate shaft.**

INTERMEDIATE SHAFT REPLACE

1. Raise and support front of vehicle.
2. Drain transaxle fluid into a suitable container.
3. Remove intermediate shaft bearing support attaching bolts.
4. Lower bearing support and remove intermediate shaft from differential. **To prevent damage to differential oil seal, hold intermediate shaft horizontal until it clears differential.**
5. Reverse procedure to install. **On Integra models, torque bearing support attaching bolts to 29 ft. lbs. On Legend models, torque three 8 mm bolts to 16 ft. lbs. and one 10 mm bolt to 28 ft. lbs.**

INTERMEDIATE SHAFT SERVICE

DISASSEMBLY

1. On Legend models, remove heat shield from bearing support.
2. On all models, remove outer seal and circlip from bearing support, **Figs. 6 and 7.**
3. Press intermediate shaft out of shaft bearing, **Fig. 8.**
4. Remove inner seal and circlip from shaft bearing.
5. Press shaft bearing out of bearing support, **Fig. 9.**

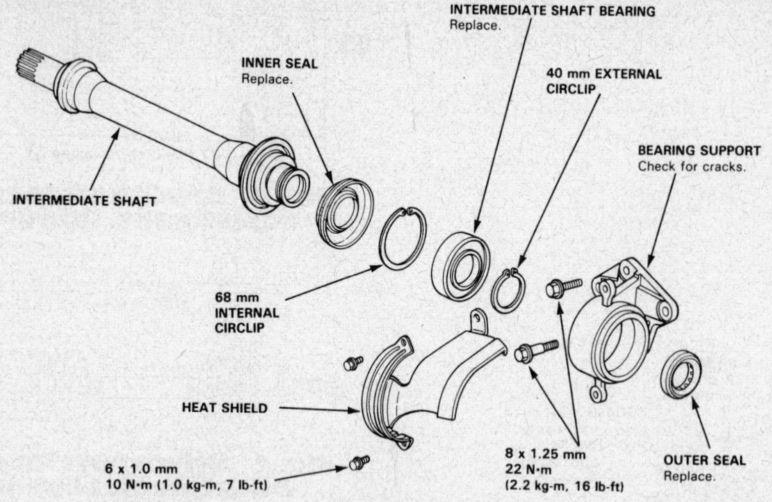

Fig. 7 Exploded view of intermediate shaft assembly. Legend

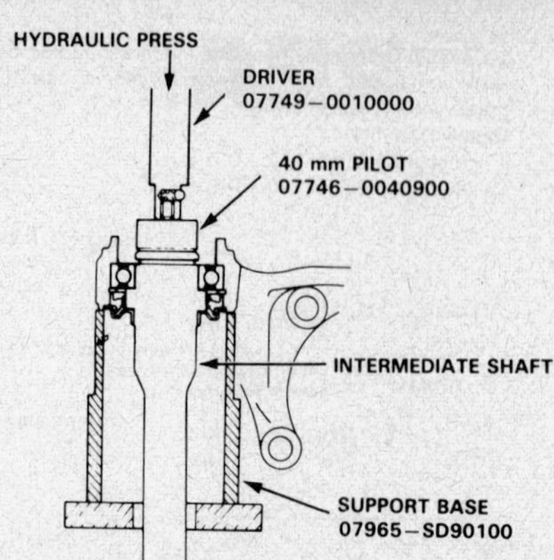

Fig. 8 Intermediate shaft removal

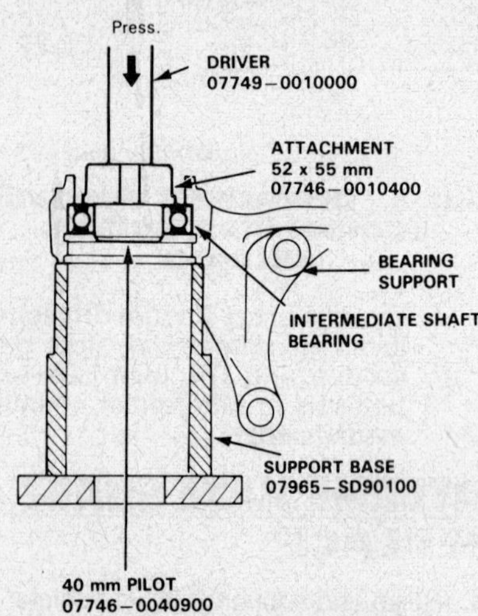

Fig. 9 Intermediate shaft bearing removal

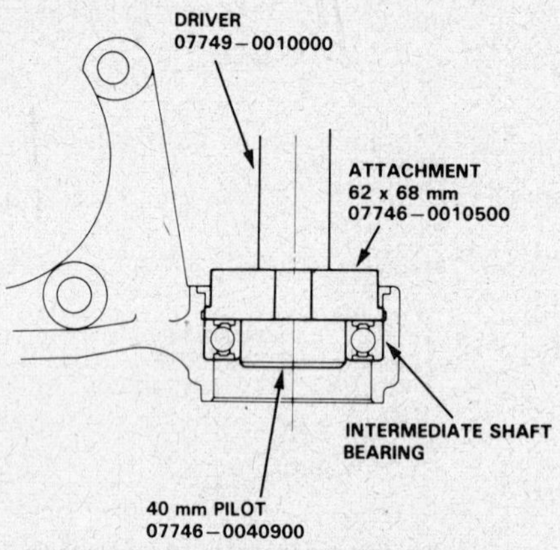

Fig. 10 Intermediate shaft bearing installation

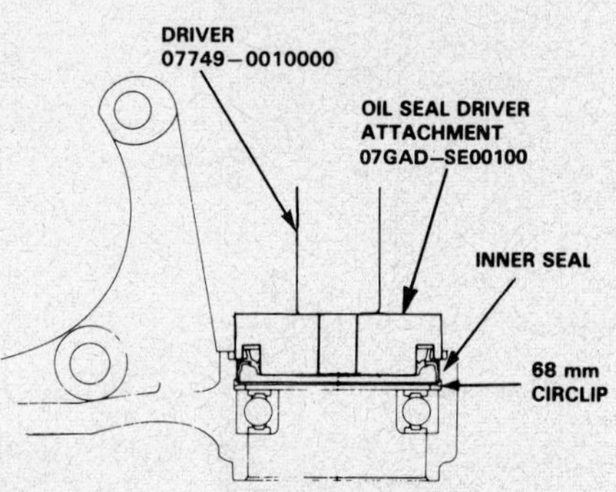

Fig. 11 Intermediate shaft inner seal installation

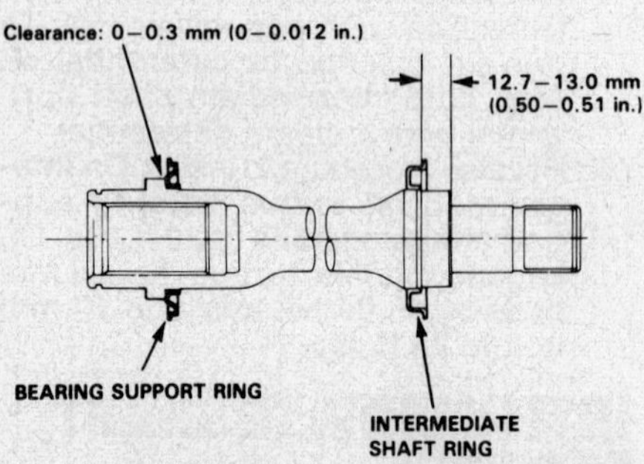

Fig. 12 Intermediate shaft ring & bearing support ring installation. Integra

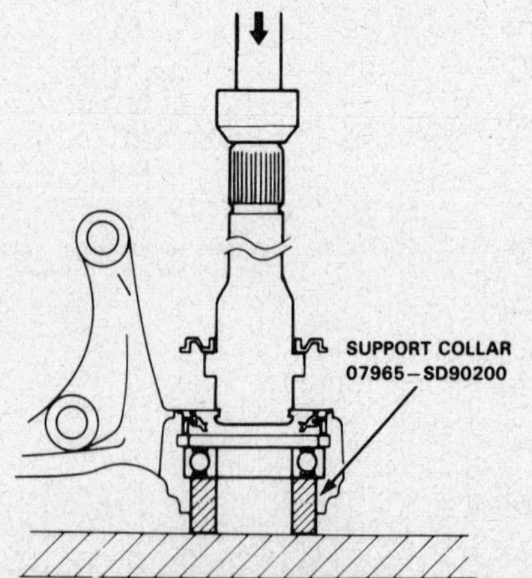

Fig. 13 Intermediate shaft installation

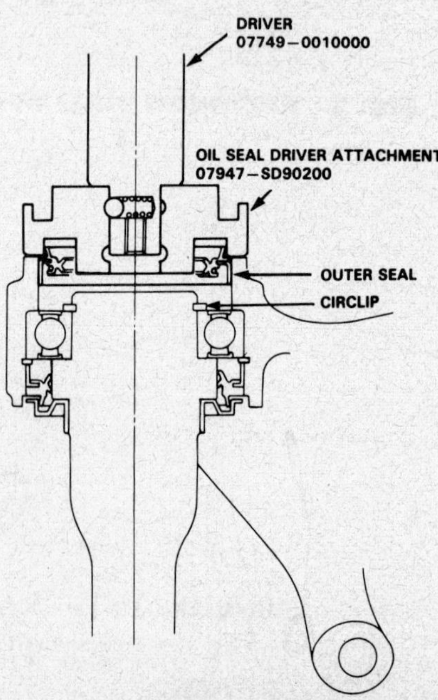

Fig. 14 Intermediate shaft outer seal installation

ASSEMBLY

1. Press shaft bearing into bearing support, **Fig. 10.**
2. Install inner circlip into bearing support groove. **Ensure tapered end of circlip faces out.**
3. Press inner seal into bearing support, **Fig. 11.**
4. On Integra models, install shaft ring and bearing support ring on shaft to specified clearances, **Fig. 12.**
5. On all models, press shaft into shaft bearing, **Fig. 13.**
6. Install outer circlip into shaft groove. **Ensure tapered end of circlip faces out.**
7. Press outer seal into bearing support, **Fig. 14.**
8. In Legend models, install bearing support heat shield, torquing bolts to 7 ft. lbs.

REAR SUSPENSION SECTION

INDEX

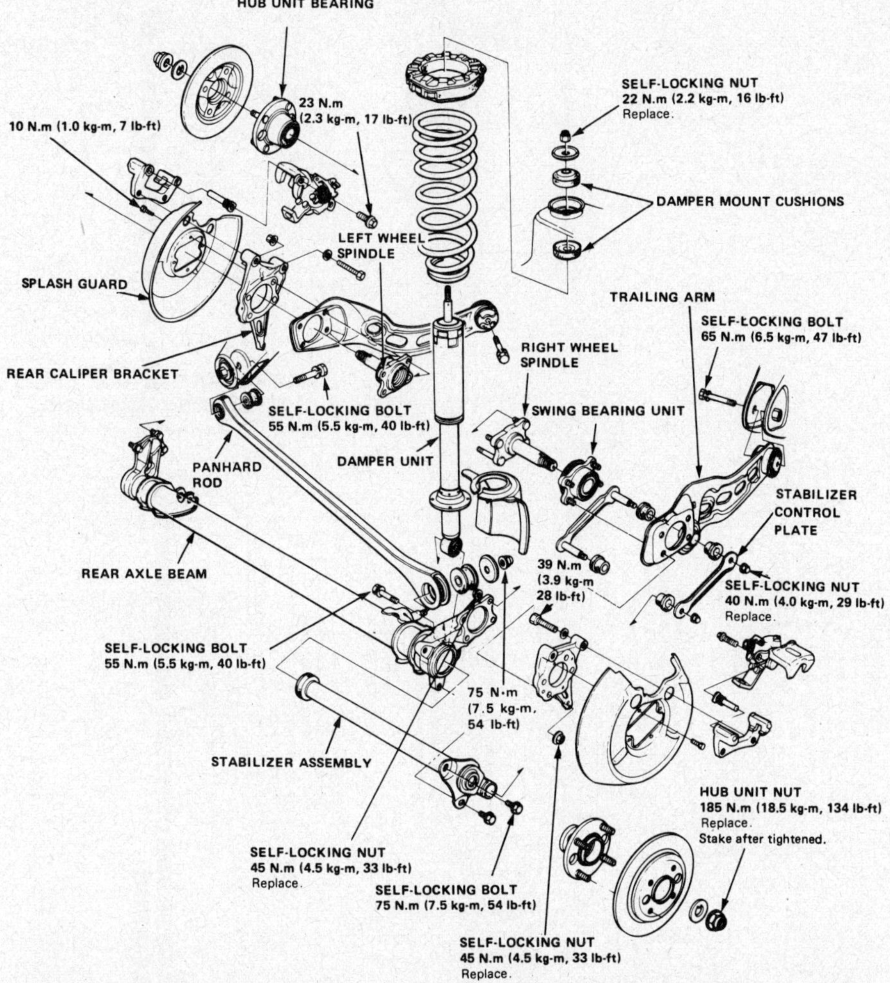

Fig. 1 Exploded view of rear suspension components. Integra

SHOCK ABSORBER REPLACE

INTEGRA

1. Raise and support rear of vehicle and remove wheel and tire assembly.
2. Support rear axle beam with a suitable jack.
3. Remove shock absorber access cover, then the shock self-locking nut, **Fig. 1.**
4. Slowly lower jack and remove self-locking bolt, shock absorber assembly and spring seat.
5. Reverse procedure to install. Torque self-locking bolt to 40 ft. lbs. and self-locking nut to 17 ft. lbs. on 1986 models, or 16 ft. lbs. on 1987 models.

LEGEND

1. Raise and support rear of vehicle.
2. Raise lower control arm slightly with a suitable jack.
3. Slowly lower jack and remove upper shock mount retaining nuts.
4. Remove shock absorber lower attaching bolt and the shock absorber, **Fig. 2.**
5. Remove shock mount self-locking nut and the mount from shock absorber.
6. Reverse procedure to install. Torque mount self-locking nut to 54 ft. lbs., mount retaining nuts to 16 ft. lbs. and lower attaching bolt to 47 ft. lbs.

HUB & ROTOR REPLACE

INTEGRA

1. Raise and support rear of vehicle and remove wheel and tire assembly.
2. Remove brake caliper and brake disc, then the hub cap, hub nut and hub assembly, **Fig. 1.**
3. Reverse procedure to install. Torque hub nut to 134 ft. lbs.

LEGEND

1. Remove hub carrier assembly as shown in **Fig. 2.**
2. Remove hub cap and spindle nut, then the splash guard attaching bolts from hub carrier, **Fig. 3.**
3. Separate hub assembly from hub carrier, **Fig. 4.**
4. Reverse procedure to install. Press hub assembly into hub carrier as shown, **Fig. 5.**

SWING BEARING REPLACE

INTEGRA

1. Raise and support rear of vehicle and remove wheel and tire assembly.
2. Remove splash guard and caliper bracket.
3. Remove stabilizer control plate, then unfasten trailing arm from swing bearing housing unit, **Fig. 1.**
4. Remove rear wheel spindle from axle beam, then separate spindle from swing bearing housing, **Fig. 6.**
5. Remove swing bearing inner race using a suitable puller.
6. Reverse procedure to install. Press wheel spindle into bearing as shown in **Fig. 7.**

CAUTION: Install the spring with the wider-diameter coils down and the spring end pointing toward the hub.

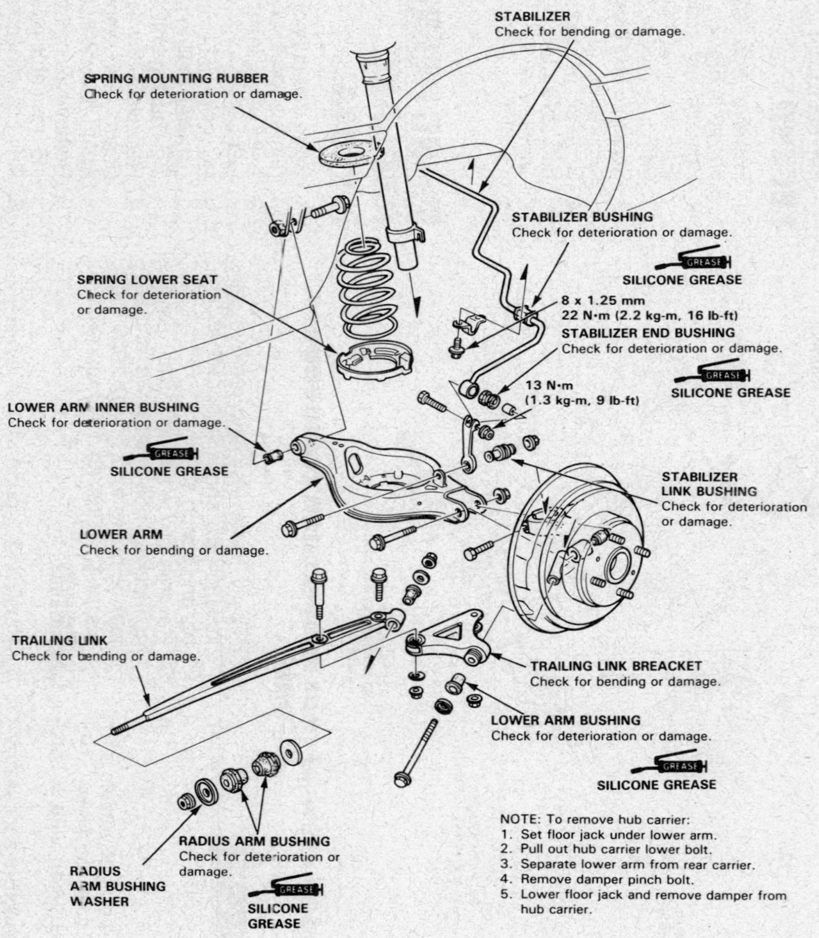

STABILIZER
Check for bending or damage.

SPRING MOUNTING RUBBER
Check for deterioration or damage.

STABILIZER BUSHING
Check for deterioration or damage.
SILICONE GREASE

SPRING LOWER SEAT
Check for deterioration or damage.

8 x 1.25 mm
22 N·m (2.2 kg-m, 16 lb-ft)

STABILIZER END BUSHING
Check for deterioration or damage.
SILICONE GREASE

13 N·m
(1.3 kg-m, 9 lb-ft)

LOWER ARM INNER BUSHING
Check for deterioration or damage.
SILICONE GREASE

STABILIZER LINK BUSHING
Check for deterioration or damage.

LOWER ARM
Check for bending or damage.

TRAILING LINK
Check for bending or damage.

TRAILING LINK BREACKET
Check for bending or damage.

LOWER ARM BUSHING
Check for deterioration or damage.
SILICONE GREASE

RADIUS ARM BUSHING
Check for deterioration or damage.
SILICONE GREASE

RADIUS ARM BUSHING WASHER

NOTE: To remove hub carrier:
1. Set floor jack under lower arm.
2. Pull out hub carrier lower bolt.
3. Separate lower arm from rear carrier.
4. Remove damper pinch bolt.
5. Lower floor jack and remove damper from hub carrier.

Fig. 2 Exploded view of rear suspension components. Legend

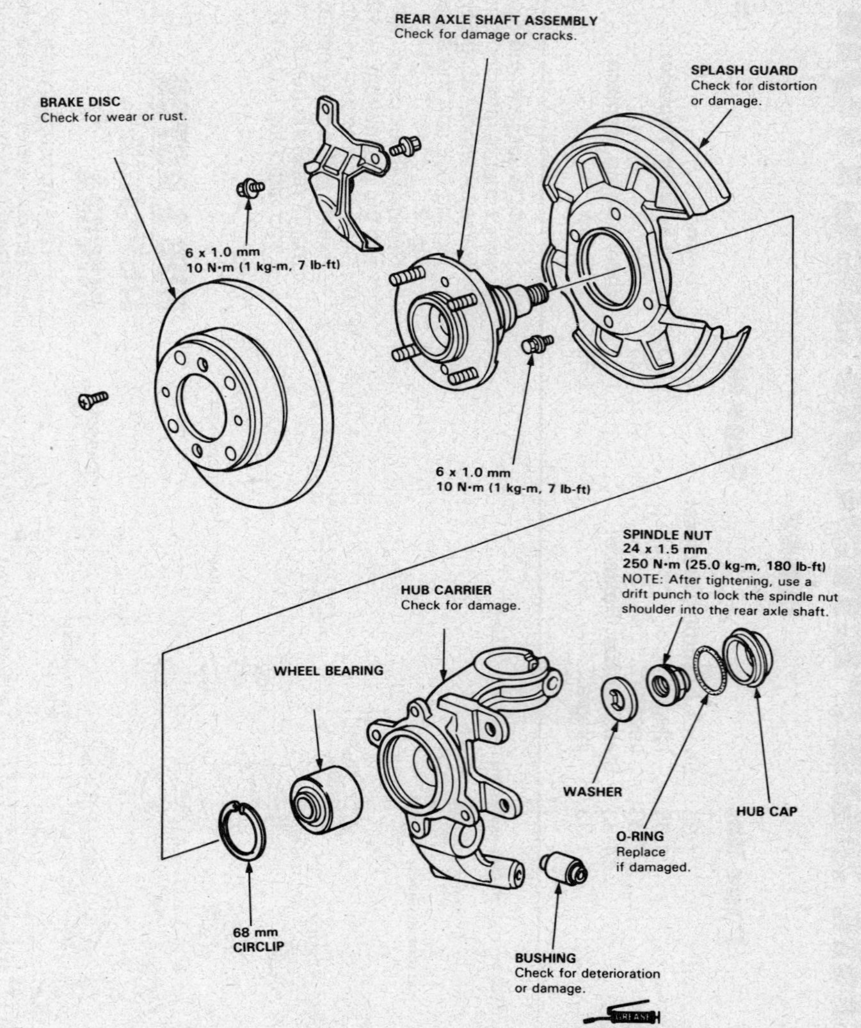

Fig. 3 Exploded view of hub carrier & rear axle shaft. Legend

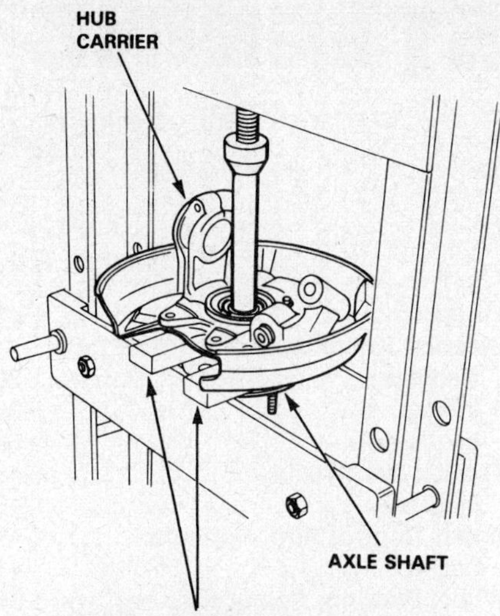

Fig. 4 Hub assembly removal. Legend

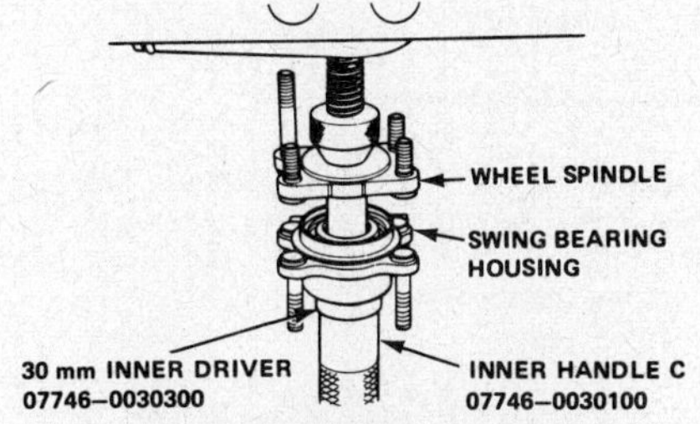

Fig. 7 Swing bearing housing installation. Integra

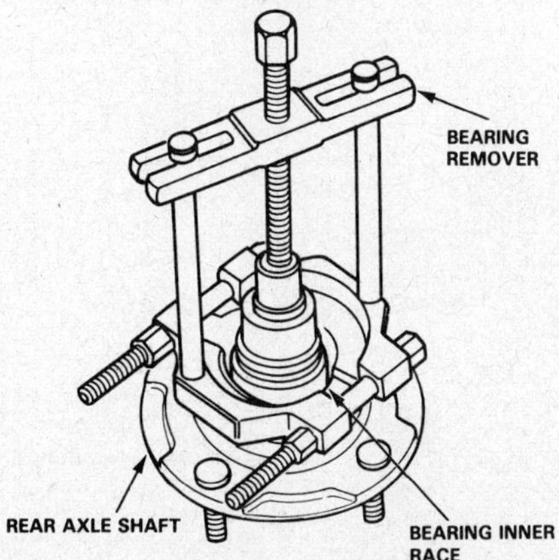

Fig. 9 Wheel bearing inner race removal. Legend

STABILIZER BAR

REPLACE

INTEGRA

1. Raise and support rear of vehicle and remove rear wheels.

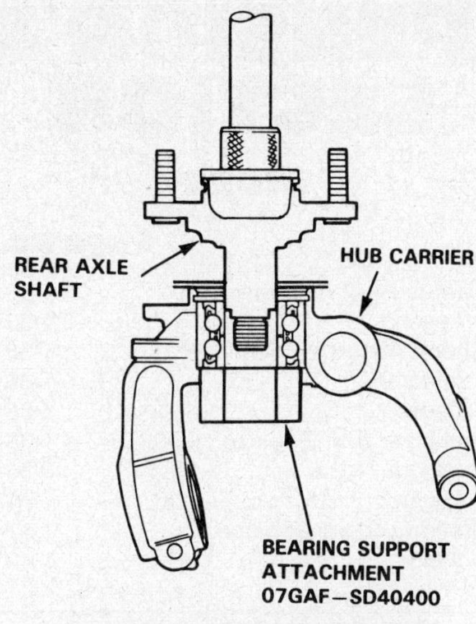

Fig. 5 Hub assembly installation. Legend

2. Remove right and left caliper brackets, **Fig. 1.**
3. Remove stabilizer control arm.
4. Remove stabilizer assembly mounting bolt, then the right axle beam cap.
5. Lower stabilizer assembly from vehicle.
6. Reverse procedure to install.

LEGEND

Refer to **Fig. 2** when replacing stabilizer bar.

COIL SPRING

REPLACE

LEGEND

1. Raise and support rear of vehicle.
2. Raise lower control arm slightly with a suitable jack.
3. Remove hub carrier lower bolt.
4. Loosen lower control arm outer attaching bolt and remove lower arm inner attaching bolt, **Fig. 2.**
5. Slowly lower jack and remove coil spring.
6. Reverse procedure to install, noting the following:
   a. Install spring with lower end of spring outside.
   b. Torque all fasteners with vehicle at rest on a level surface.
   c. Torque lower arm attaching bolts to 40 ft. lbs. and hub carrier lower bolt to 54 ft. lbs.

WHEEL BEARING

REPLACE

LEGEND

1. Remove hub carrier assembly as

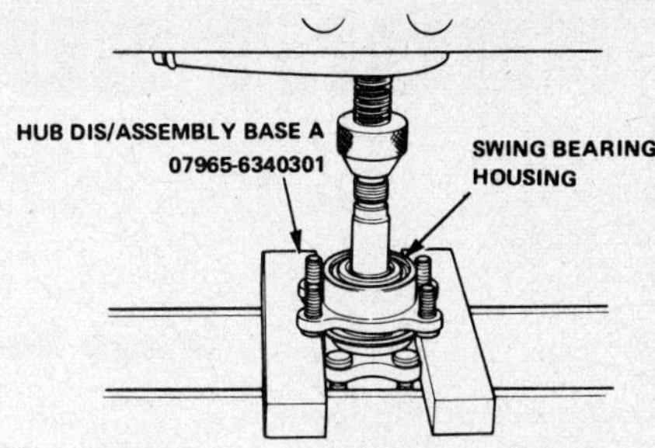

Fig. 6 Swing bearing housing removal. Integra

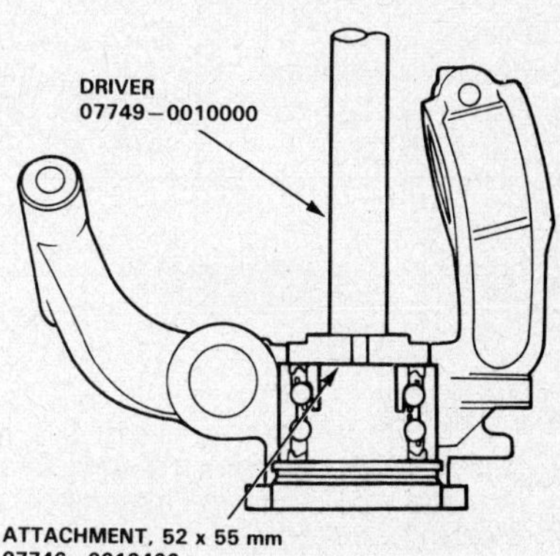

Fig. 8 Wheel bearing removal. Legend

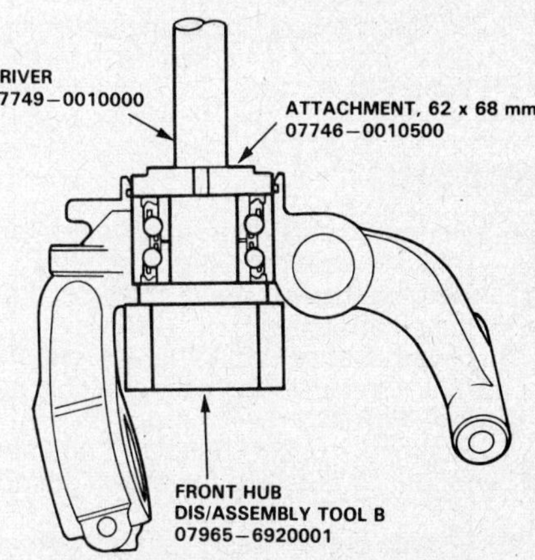

Fig. 10 Wheel bearing installation. Legend

shown in **Fig. 2.**

2. Remove splash guard and circlip from hub carrier, **Fig. 3.**
3. Remove bearing from rear hub, then the bearing inner race from axle shaft, **Figs. 8 and 9.**
4. Press new bearing into hub carrier as shown, **Fig. 10.**

FRONT SUSPENSION & STEERING SECTION

INDEX

SHOCK ABSORBER REPLACE

INTEGRA

1. Raise and support front of vehicle and remove wheel and tire assembly.
2. Remove brake hose clamp bolt, then position a suitable jack to support lower control arm.
3. Remove self-locking bolt, the slowly lower jack and remove it from knuckle.
4. Remove upper self-locking nut, then compress spring and remove shock absorber assembly.
5. Reverse procedure to install. Torque attaching nut and bolt to specifications, **Fig. 1.**

LEGEND

1. Raise and support front of vehicle and remove wheel and tire assembly.
2. Remove brake hose clamps from shock absorber.
3. Remove shock absorber lower pinch bolt, then the damper fork bolt and fork, **Fig. 2.**
4. Remove upper shock absorber mounting nuts and the shock absorber.
5. Install upper base studs through mounting holes, ensuring alignment tab on shock body faces toward inside, then install base mounting nuts hand tight.
6. Install damper fork over drive axle and lower, then slide fork over lower end of shock absorber, aligning tab on shock with slot in fork.
7. Install damper fork retaining bolt and pinch bolt hand tight.
8. Position suitable jack under knuckle hub, then raise knuckle until weight of vehicle is supported by damper assembly.
9. With weight of vehicle supported by damper, torque damper fork retaining bolt, damper fork pinch bolt and shock absorber base nuts to specifications, **Fig. 3.**

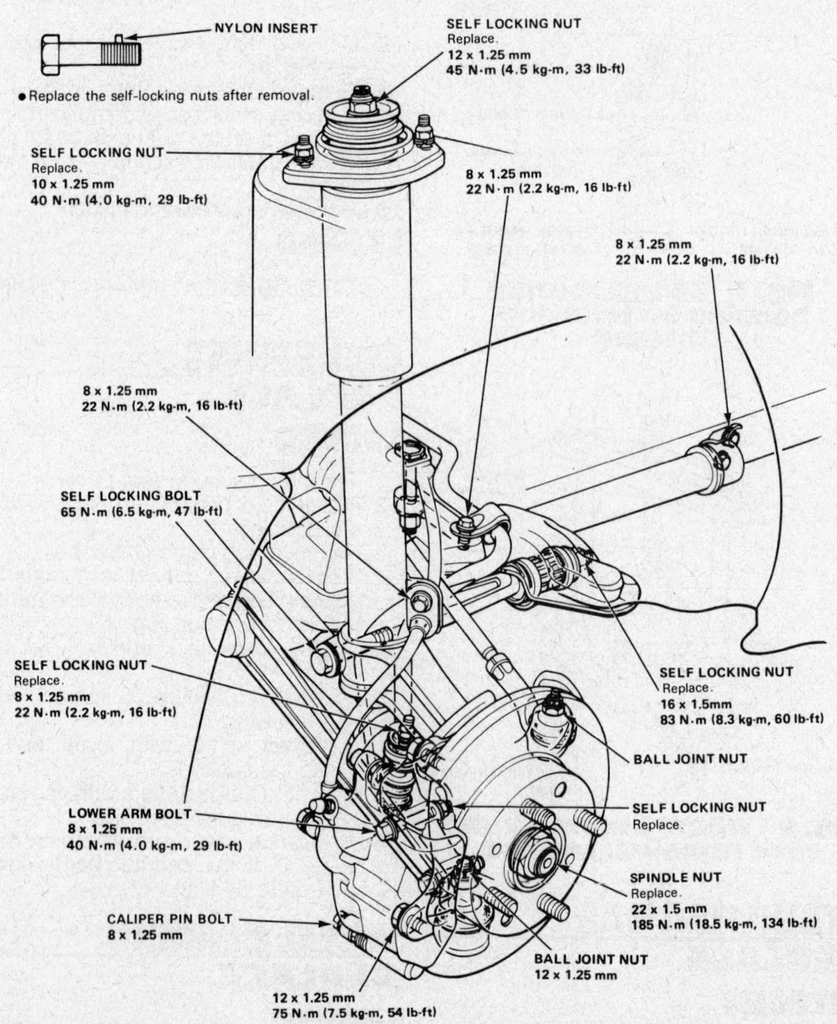

Fig. 1 Cross sectional view of front suspension. Integra

CAUTION:
- The radius rod bushings can easily be misinstalled; the thick radius rod bushing should be installed in the front position.
- R or L mark is stamped on the rear end of the radius arm to prevent misinstallation.

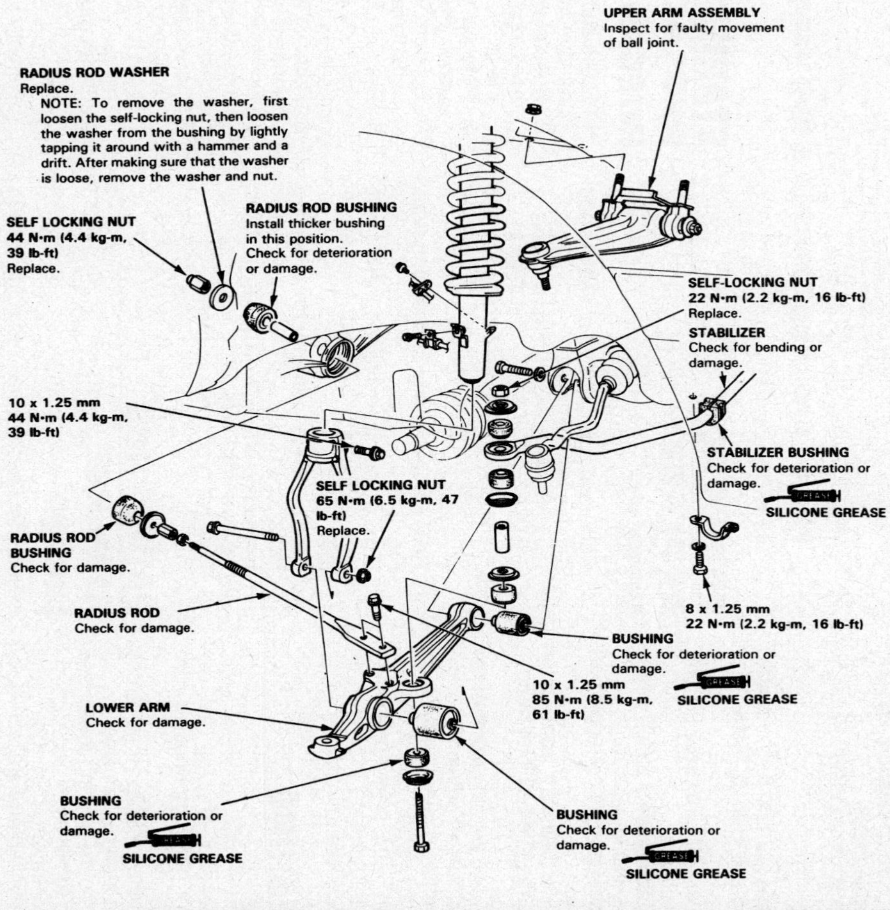

UPPER ARM ASSEMBLY
Inspect for faulty movement of ball joint.

RADIUS ROD WASHER
Replace.
NOTE: To remove the washer, first loosen the self-locking nut, then loosen the washer from the bushing by lightly tapping it around with a hammer and a drift. After making sure that the washer is loose, remove the washer and nut.

SELF LOCKING NUT
44 N·m (4.4 kg-m, 39 lb-ft)
Replace.

RADIUS ROD BUSHING
Install thicker bushing in this position.
Check for deterioration or damage.

SELF-LOCKING NUT
22 N·m (2.2 kg-m, 16 lb-ft)
Replace.

STABILIZER
Check for bending or damage.

10 x 1.25 mm
44 N·m (4.4 kg-m, 39 lb-ft)

STABILIZER BUSHING
Check for deterioration or damage.
SILICONE GREASE

SELF LOCKING NUT
65 N·m (6.5 kg-m, 47 lb-ft)
Replace.

RADIUS ROD BUSHING
Check for damage.

RADIUS ROD
Check for damage.

8 x 1.25 mm
22 N·m (2.2 kg-m, 16 lb-ft)

BUSHING
Check for deterioration or damage.
SILICONE GREASE

10 x 1.25 mm
85 N·m (8.5 kg-m, 61 lb-ft)

LOWER ARM
Check for damage.

BUSHING
Check for deterioration or damage.
SILICONE GREASE

BUSHING
Check for deterioration or damage.
SILICONE GREASE

Fig. 2 Exploded view of front suspension components. Legend

CAUTION:
- Replace the self-locking nuts after removal.
- Replace the self-locking bolts if you can easily thread a nut past their nylon locking inserts.

NOTE: Wipe off the grease before tightening the nut at the ball joint.

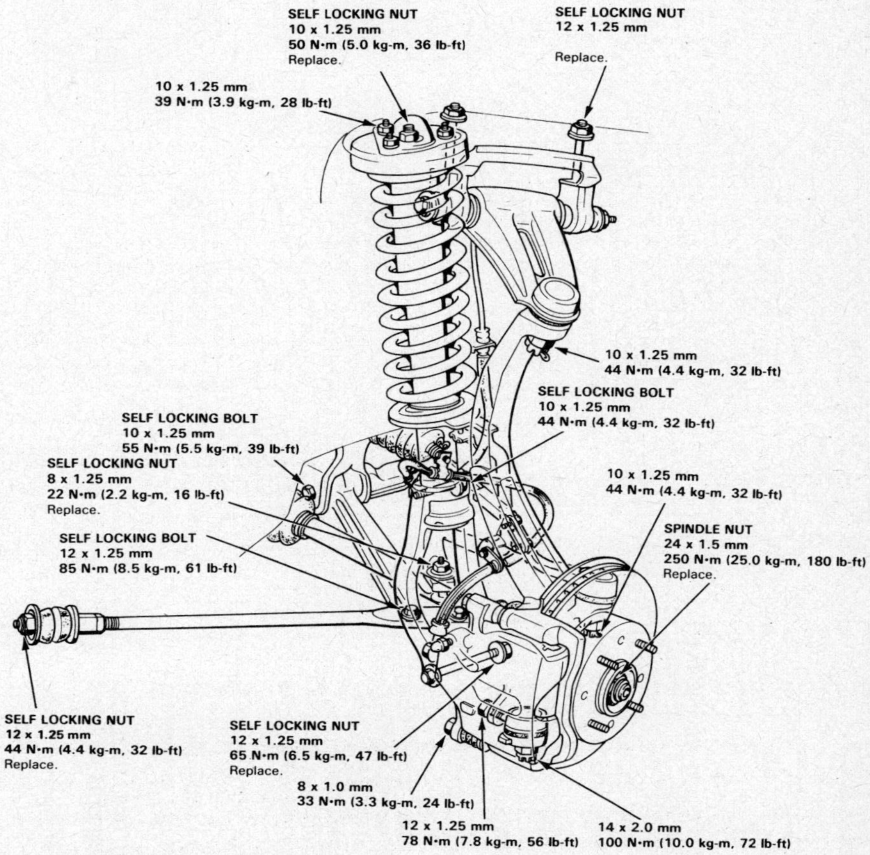

SELF LOCKING NUT
10 x 1.25 mm
50 N·m (5.0 kg-m, 36 lb-ft)
Replace.

SELF LOCKING NUT
12 x 1.25 mm
Replace.

10 x 1.25 mm
39 N·m (3.9 kg-m, 28 lb-ft)

10 x 1.25 mm
44 N·m (4.4 kg-m, 32 lb-ft)

SELF LOCKING BOLT
10 x 1.25 mm
44 N·m (4.4 kg-m, 32 lb-ft)

SELF LOCKING BOLT
10 x 1.25 mm
55 N·m (5.5 kg-m, 39 lb-ft)

SELF LOCKING NUT
8 x 1.25 mm
22 N·m (2.2 kg-m, 16 lb-ft)
Replace.

10 x 1.25 mm
44 N·m (4.4 kg-m, 32 lb-ft)

SPINDLE NUT
24 x 1.5 mm
250 N·m (25.0 kg-m, 180 lb-ft)
Replace.

SELF LOCKING BOLT
12 x 1.25 mm
85 N·m (8.5 kg-m, 61 lb-ft)

SELF LOCKING NUT
12 x 1.25 mm
44 N·m (4.4 kg-m, 32 lb-ft)
Replace.

SELF LOCKING NUT
12 x 1.25 mm
65 N·m (6.5 kg-m, 47 lb-ft)
Replace.

8 x 1.0 mm
33 N·m (3.3 kg-m, 24 lb-ft)

12 x 1.25 mm
78 N·m (7.8 kg-m, 56 lb-ft)

14 x 2.0 mm
100 N·m (10.0 kg-m, 72 lb-ft)

CAUTION: Before tightening the bolts or nuts connected to rubber mounts or bushings, the vehicle should be on the ground.

Fig. 3 Cross sectional of front suspension. Legend

STEERING KNUCKLE, HUB & ROTOR

REPLACE

INTEGRA

1. Remove spindle nut locking device, then loosen spindle nut, **Fig. 4.**
2. Loosen wheel lug nuts.
3. Raise and support front of vehicle, then remove front wheels and spindle nut.
4. Unfasten caliper and position aside, leaving brake line attached. **Do not allow caliper assembly to hang from brake hose.**
5. Remove brake disc attaching screws, then thread two 81.2512 mm bolts into attaching screw holes to pull disc from hub. **When tightening screws, turn only two turns at a time to prevent cocking the brake disc.**
6. Remove tie rod end cotter pin and nut.
7. Remove tie rod end using suitable tie rod end remover.
8. Support lower control arm using a suitable jack.
9. Remove lower ball joint cotter pin and nut, then pry ball joint out of steering knuckle.
10. Remove self-locking bolt, then tap steering knuckle down until it clears the damper.
11. Pull driveshaft out of steering knuckle, then remove the hub and knuckle assembly.
12. Remove splash guard attaching screws and the splash guard.
13. Remove hub from steering knuckle using a suitable press.
14. Reverse procedure to install.

LEGEND

1. Perform steps 1 through 7 under "Steering Wheel, Hub & Rotor, Replace, Integra."
2. Remove lower ball joint cotter pin and loosen nut halfway.
3. Using a suitable jawed puller, separate ball joint and lower arm.
4. Remove upper ball joint cotter pin and nut.
5. Separate upper ball joint from upper arm using a suitable ball joint remover.
6. Remove steering knuckle and hub assembly by sliding off driveshaft.
7. Remove splash guard attaching screws and the splash guard, **Fig. 5.**
8. Remove hub from steering knuckle using a suitable press.
9. Reverse procedure to install.

WHEEL BEARING

REPLACE

1. Remove steering knuckle as described under "Steering Knuckle, Hub & Rotor, Replace."
2. Remove bearing circlip, then press bearing from steering knuckle.
3. Remove outboard bearing inner race with bearing remover.
4. Install replacement bearings and races with a suitable press.
5. Install circlip, then press in wheel hub.

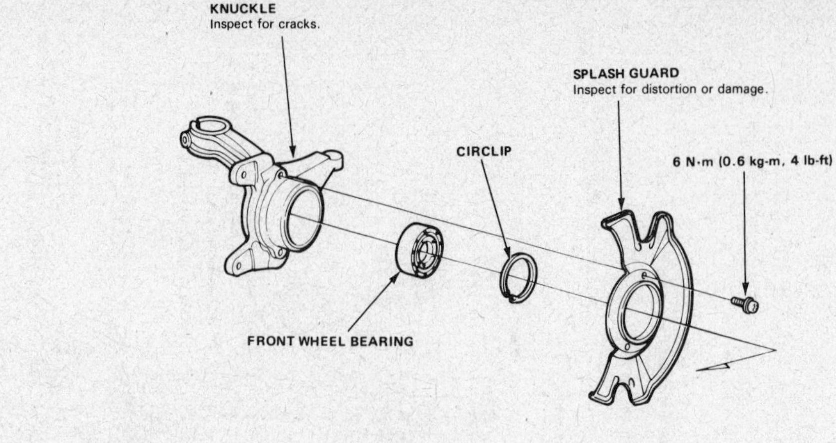

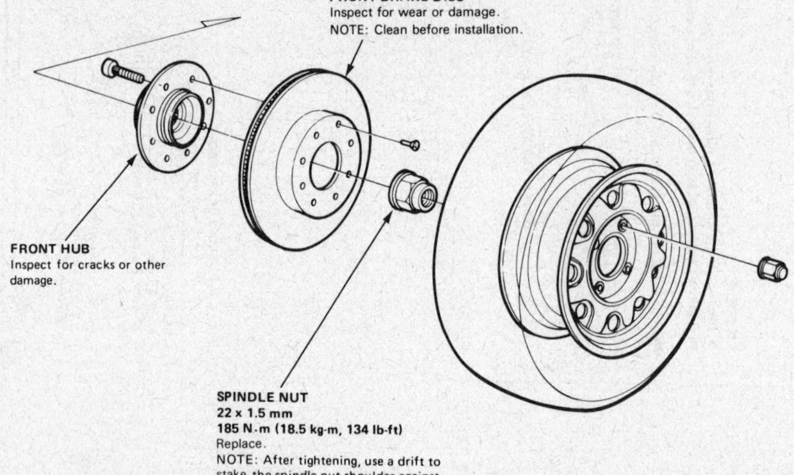

Fig. 4 Steering knuckle & hub assembly. Integra

RADIUS ARM

REPLACE

INTEGRA

1. Raise and support front of vehicle and remove front wheels.
2. Support lower control arm using a suitable jack.
3. Remove lower ball joint cotter pin and nut, then pry ball joint out of steering knuckle.
4. Remove radius arm self-locking nuts, **Fig. 6.**
5. Remove stabilizer bar self-locking nut, then separate radius arm from stabilizer spring.
6. Remove lower control arm attaching bolts.
7. Pull radius arm down and forward and remove from vehicle.
8. Reverse procedure to install.

RADIUS ROD

REPLACE

LEGEND

Refer to **Fig. 2** when replacing radius rod.

STABILIZER BAR

REPLACE

INTEGRA

1. Raise and support front of vehicle and remove front wheels.
2. Support weight of engine with a chain hoist or other suitable lifting equipment.
3. Remove steering gear as described under "Steering Gear, Replace."
4. Support lower control arm using a suitable jack.
5. Remove lower ball joint cotter pin and nut, then pry ball joint out of steering knuckle.
6. Remove torque tube holder, then disconnect exhaust pipes A and B.
7. On models equipped with manual transaxle, disconnect shift rod and extension from transaxle.
8. On models equipped with automatic transaxle, remove shift cable guide from floor and pull shift cable down by hand.
9. On all models, remove engine mount bracket nuts.
10. Support center of rear beam with a suitable jack, then remove beam attaching bolts and pry beam loose.

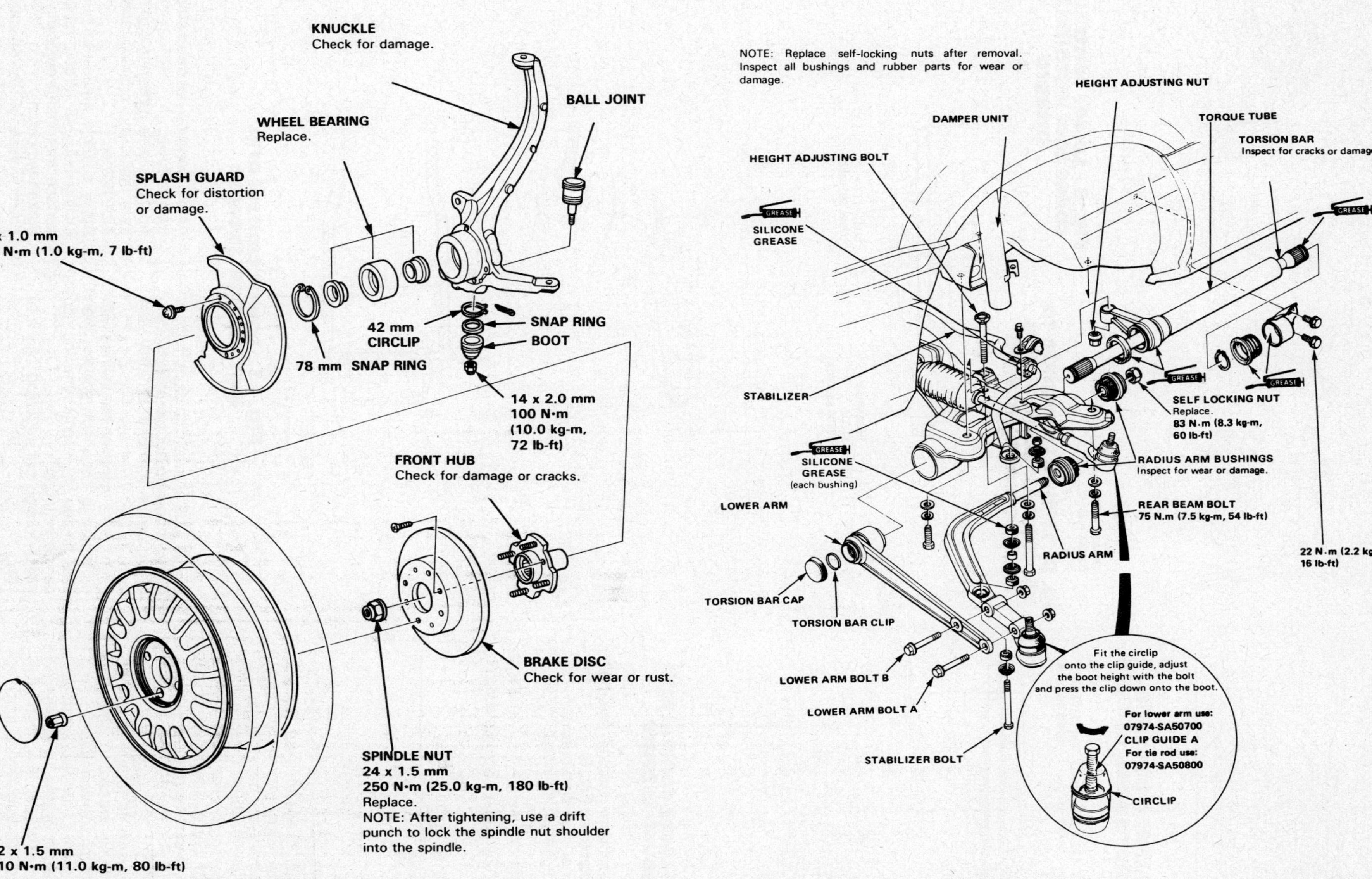
KNUCKLE
Check for damage.
BALL JOINT
WHEEL BEARING
Replace.
SPLASH GUARD
Check for distortion
or damage.
6 x 1.0 mm
10 N·m (1.0 kg-m, 7 lb-ft)
42 mm
CIRCLIP
SNAP RING
BOOT
78 mm SNAP RING
14 x 2.0 mm
100 N·m
(10.0 kg-m,
72 lb-ft)
FRONT HUB
Check for damage or cracks.
BRAKE DISC
Check for wear or rust.
SPINDLE NUT
24 x 1.5 mm
250 N·m (25.0 kg-m, 180 lb-ft)
Replace.
NOTE: After tightening, use a drift
punch to lock the spindle nut shoulder
into the spindle.
12 x 1.5 mm
110 N·m (11.0 kg-m, 80 lb-ft)

Fig. 5 Steering knuckle & hub assembly. Legend

NOTE: Replace self-locking nuts after removal.
Inspect all bushings and rubber parts for wear or
damage.
HEIGHT ADJUSTING NUT
DAMPER UNIT
TORQUE TUBE
TORSION BAR
Inspect for cracks or damage.
HEIGHT ADJUSTING BOLT
GREASE
SILICONE
GREASE
STABILIZER
SELF LOCKING NUT
Replace.
83 N.m (8.3 kg-m,
60 lb-ft)
RADIUS ARM BUSHINGS
Inspect for wear or damage.
SILICONE
GREASE
(each bushing)
LOWER ARM
REAR BEAM BOLT
75 N.m (7.5 kg-m, 54 lb-ft)
RADIUS ARM
22 N.m (2.2 kg-m,
16 lb-ft)
TORSION BAR CAP
TORSION BAR CLIP
LOWER ARM BOLT B
LOWER ARM BOLT A
STABILIZER BOLT
Fit the circlip
onto the clip guide, adjust
the boot height with the bolt
and press the clip down onto the boot.
For lower arm use:
07974-SA50700
CLIP GUIDE A
For tie rod use:
07974-SA50800
CIRCLIP

Fig. 6 Exploded view of front suspension components. Integra

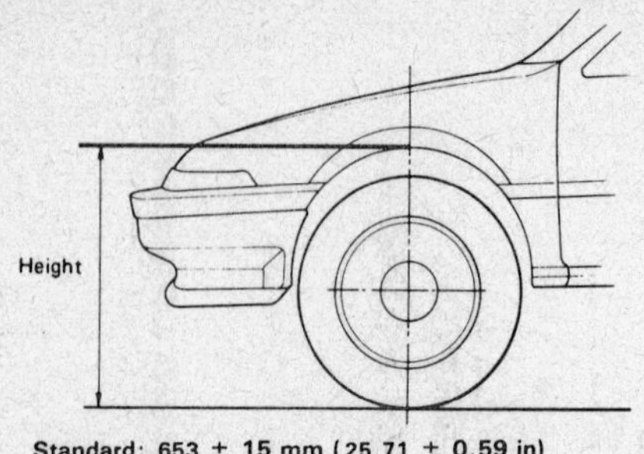

Fig. 7 Torsion bar spring height adjustment. Integra

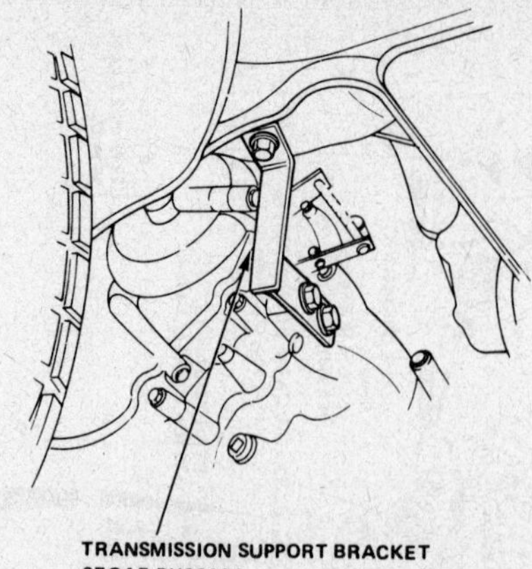

Fig. 8 Lifting transaxle to allow lower control arm replacement. Integra

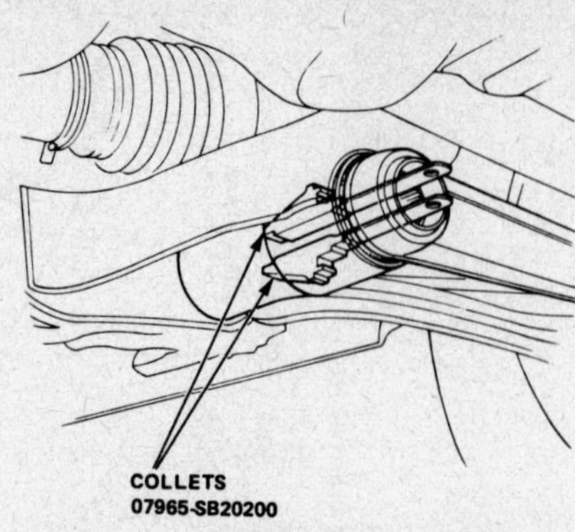

Fig. 9 Lower control arm collet tool installation. Integra

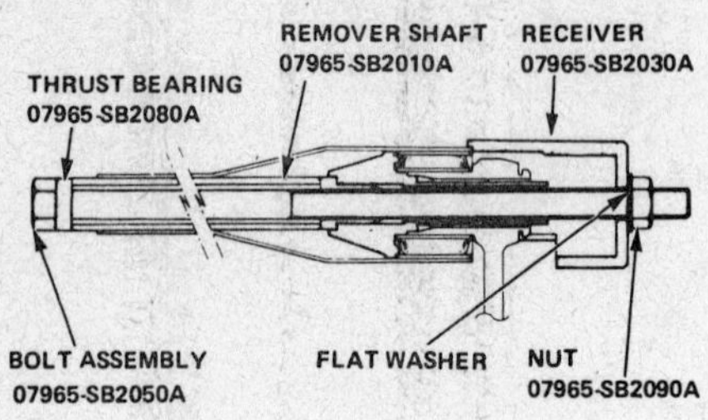

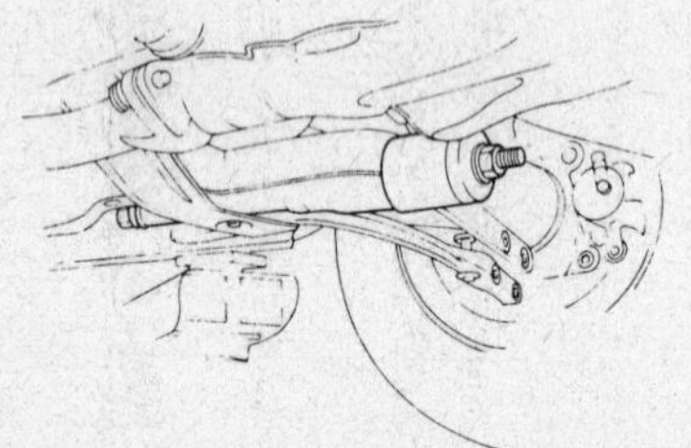

Fig. 10 Lower control arm removal. Integra

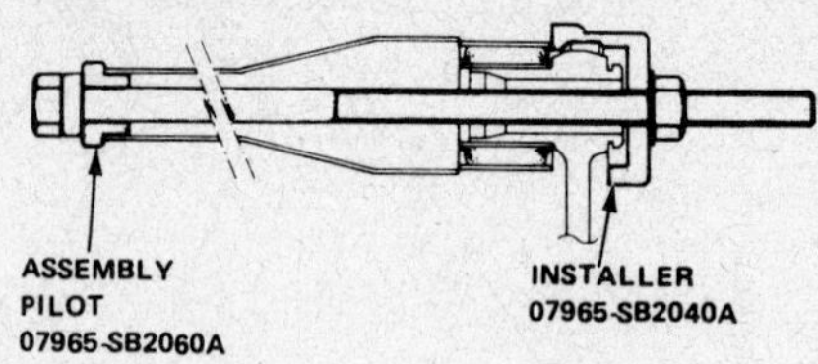

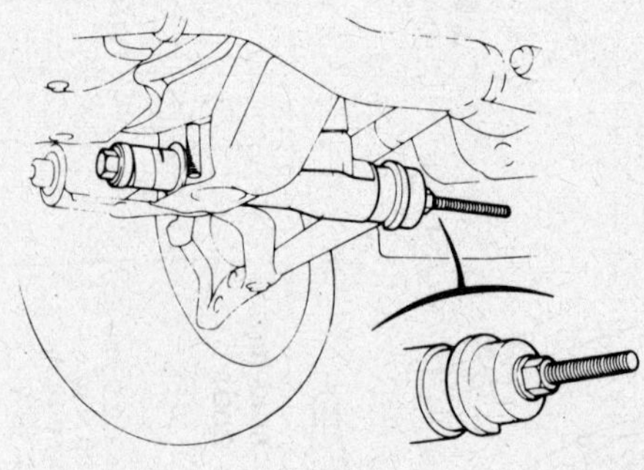

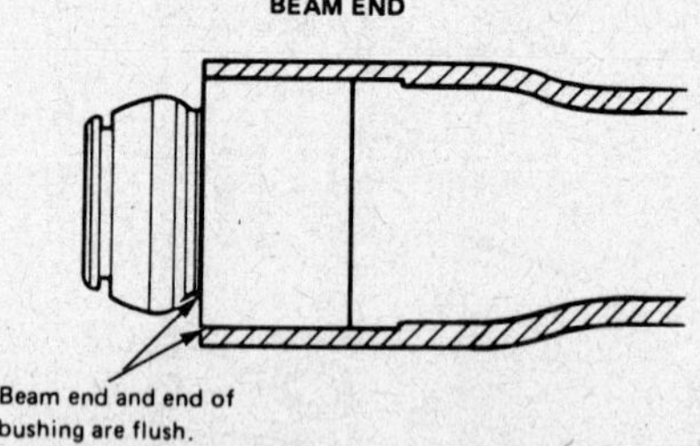

Fig. 11 Lower control arm installation. Integra

11. Remove stabilizer bracket and bolt, then the stabilizer, **Fig. 6.**
12. Remove rear mounting bracket.
13. Reverse procedure to install.

LEGEND

Refer to **Fig. 2** when replacing stabilizer bar.

TORSION BAR REPLACE

INTEGRA

Removal

1. Raise and support front of vehicle.
2. Remove height adjusting nut, then the torque tube holder and circlip, **Fig. 6.**
3. Remove torsion bar cap, then tap torsion bar forward out of torque tube and remove torsion bar clip.
4. Tap torsion bar backward out of torsion tube, then remove torque tube.

Installation

1. Install new seal on torque tube, then apply suitable grease to seal and torque tube sliding surface.
2. Install torque tube on rear beam.
3. Apply suitable grease to splines on both ends of torsion bar, then slide torsion bar into torque tube from the rear.
4. Align punch mark or projection on torque tube splines with paint mark or cutout in torsion bar bar splines, then insert torsion bar approximately .394 inch.
5. Align cutout in torsion bar splines with projection in lower arm splines, then slide torsion bar in until retaining clip can be installed.
6. Install torsion bar retaining clip and cap.
7. Install circlip on back of torsion bar. **Slide torsion bar forward to eliminate clearance between circlip and torque tube.**
8. Apply suitable grease to cap bushing, then install the bushing and torque tube holder.
9. Apply suitable grease to height adjusting nut and torque tube sliding surface, then install adjusting nut and tighten temporarily.
10. Lower vehicle to rest on a level surface, then adjust torsion bar spring height to specifications, **Fig. 7.**

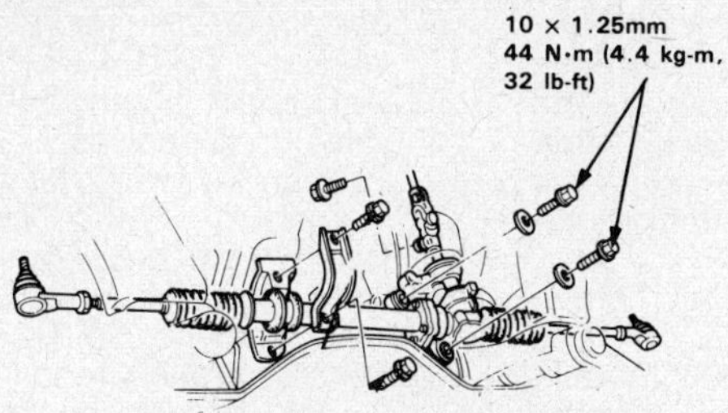

Fig. 12 Steering gear replacement. Integra

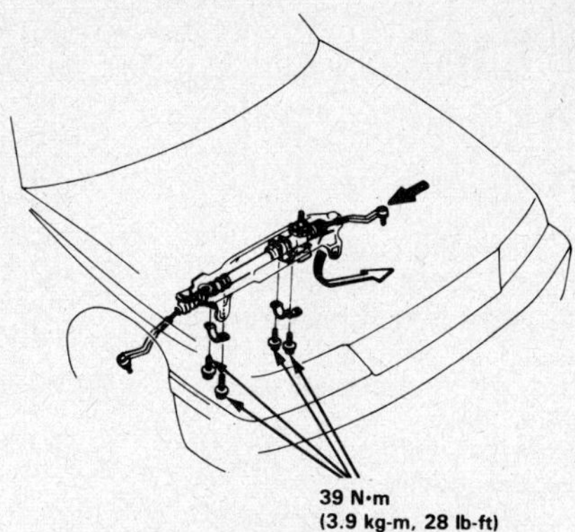

Fig. 13 Steering gear replacement. Legend

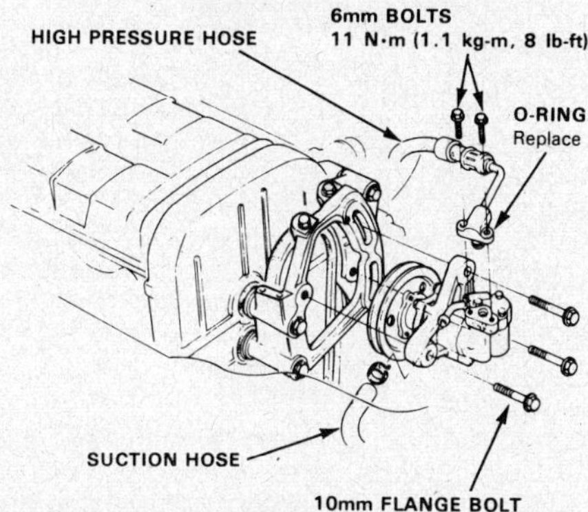

Fig. 14 Power steering pump replacement. Integra

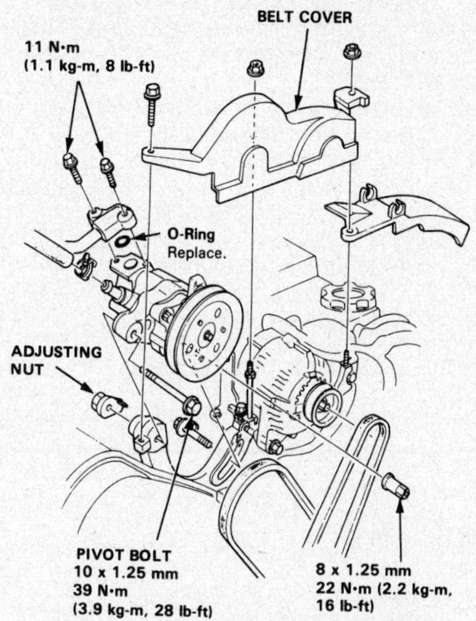

Fig. 15 Power steering pump replacement. Legend

LOWER CONTROL ARM REPLACE

INTEGRA

Removal

1. Remove torsion bar and torque bar as described under "Torsion Bar, Replace."
2. Remove lower control arm to radius arm attaching nuts and bolts.
3. Remove power steering pump bracket and, on models equipped with cruise control, the cruise control actuator.
4. If replacing left side control arm, proceed as follows:
   a. Remove alternator adjusting bolt and push alternator up against engine block.
   b. Lift engine and position engine mount spacer into mount to raise oil pan clear of control arm.
5. If replacing right side control arm on models equipped with automatic transaxle, proceed as follows:
   a. Remove battery and battery tray.
   b. Raise transaxle slightly and remove transaxle mount.
   c. Install transaxle support bracket, **Fig. 8,** to provide clearance for control arm removal.
6. Insert collets into lower control arm 180° apart, **Fig. 9.**
7. Slide remover shaft into bushing, **Fig. 10.**
8. Position thrust bearing on remover shaft bolt, then slide bolt through shaft.
9. Install receiver tool, **Fig. 10,** over bolt and lower and install flat washer and nut.
10. Hold nut with a suitable wrench and turn bolt clockwise to remove lower control arm from beam end, **Fig. 6,** then remove tools from beam.

Installation

1. Draw reference line through center of alignment lug cast on lower control arm and onto the bushing.
2. With thrust bearing and flat washer installed on bolt, slide assembly pilot into position, **Fig. 11,** then install tool into back of bushing hole in beam.
3. Position lower control arm on bolt and align reference mark with notch on beam bushing mount.
4. Position installer tool, flat washer and nut on bolt.
5. Hold nut with a suitable wrench and turn bolt clockwise to pull control arm into position. **Draw control arm on until edge of bushing's steel outer sleeve is flush with end of beam, then remove tools from beam.**
6. Remove any tools previously installed to lift engine or transaxle and install any components that were removed.
7. Reverse remainder of removal procedure to complete installation.

LEGEND

Refer to **Fig. 2** when replacing lower control arm.

UPPER CONTROL ARM REPLACE

LEGEND

Refer to **Fig. 2** when replacing upper control arm.

LOWER BALL JOINT REPLACE

LEGEND

1. Remove steering knuckle as described under "Steering Knuckle, Hub & Rotor, Replace."
2. Remove ball joint boot snap ring and the boot.
3. Remove circlip, then press ball joint out of steering knuckle using a suitable tool.
4. Reverse procedure to install.

STEERING GEAR REPLACE

INTEGRA

1. Remove steering joint cover.
2. Remove steering shaft connector attaching bolts, then pull connector up off pinion shaft.
3. Raise and support front of vehicle and remove front wheels.
4. Remove cotter pins and loosen tie rod end ball joint nuts halfway.
5. Break ball joints loose using a suitable ball joint remover, then remove nuts and lift tie rod ends from steering knuckles.
6. On models equipped with manual transaxle, remove shift extension from transaxle case, then slide pin retainer aside and drive out spring pin to disconnect shift rod.
7. On models equipped with automatic transaxle, remove shift cable guide from floor and pull shift cable down by hand.
8. On all models, drain power steering fluid into a suitable container.
9. Disconnect exhaust header pipe from manifold.
10. Thoroughly clean steering gear unit and surrounding area, then disconnect three hydraulic lines from valve body housing.
11. Remove steering gear attaching bolts and the gear, **Fig. 12. Lower unit until end of pinion shaft clears hole in channel, then rotate it forward until shaft is pointing rearward. Slide gear to the right until tie rod clears rear beam, then lower unit from vehicle.**
12. Reverse procedure to install. Torque bracket bolts to 27 ft. lbs. on 1986 models, or 29 ft. lbs. on 1987 models.

LEGEND

1. Remove steering joint cover, then disconnect steering shaft from steering gear.
2. Drain power steering fluid into a suitable container, then remove steering gear shield.
3. Thoroughly clean steering gear unit and surrounding area.
4. Raise and support front of vehicle and remove front wheels.
5. Disconnect tie rods from steering knuckles using a suitable tool.
6. On models equipped with manual transaxle, remove shift extension from transaxle case, then remove spring pin to disconnect gearshift rod from transaxle case.
7. On models equipped with automatic transaxle, disconnect control cable from clamp, then remove center beam attaching bolts and the beam. **The self-locking bolts must be replaced if a nut can easily be threaded past nylon locking inserts.**
8. Disconnect exhaust header pipe from manifold.
9. Disconnect four hydraulic lines from valve body housing.
10. Position tie rod as far as possible to the right.
11. Remove steering gear unit attaching bolts, then slide unit to the right and lower from vehicle, **Fig. 13.**
12. Reverse procedure to install.

POWER STEERING PUMP REPLACE

INTEGRA

1. Disconnect and cap hoses from power steering pump reservoir.
2. Remove power steering pump attaching bolts, then the pump pulley and pump, **Fig. 14.**
3. Reverse procedure to install. Torque pump attaching bolts to 33 ft. lbs. on 1986 models, or 29 ft. lbs. on 1987 models.

LEGEND

1. Remove belt cover, then drain power steering fluid into a suitable container.
2. Disconnect and cap hoses from power steering pump reservoir.
3. Loosen pump pivot bolt and remove pump drive belt.
4. Remove power steering pump attaching bolt and nut and the pump, **Fig. 15.**
5. Reverse procedure to install.

WHEEL ALIGNMENT SECTION

INDEX

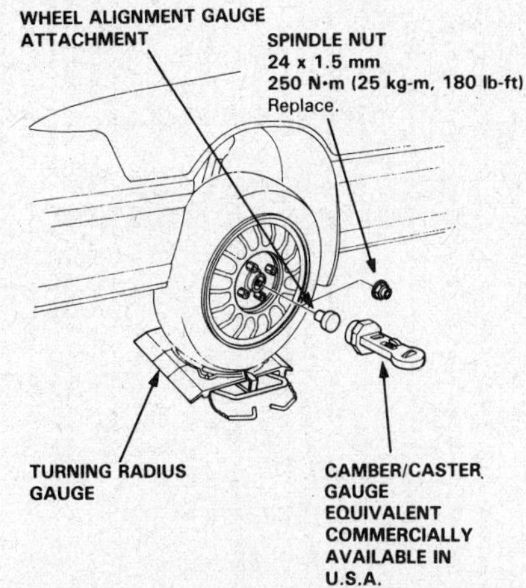

Fig. 1 Caster angle check

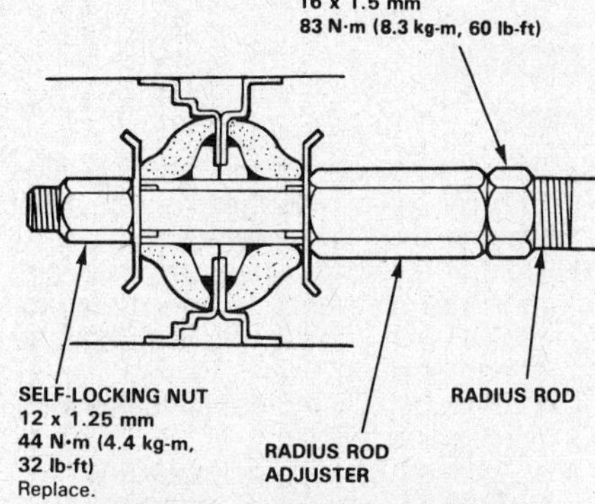

Fig. 2 Caster angle adjustment. Legend

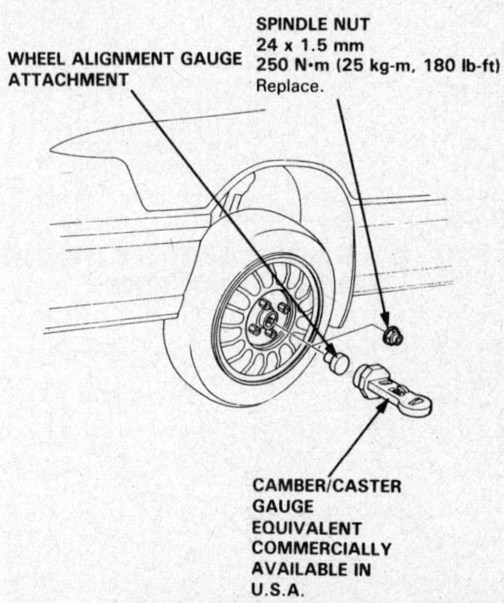

Fig. 3 Camber angle check. Exc. Legend rear camber

CASTER INSPECTION & ADJUSTMENT

Ensure tires are properly inflated prior to checking or adjusting caster angles.

INTEGRA

Caster angle is not adjustable, however, the following procedure may be used to ensure caster is within specifications.

1. Raise front of vehicle and position turning radius gauges under front wheels, then lower vehicle.
2. Remove spindle nut and install suitable caster gauge and adapter, **Fig. 1.**
3. Apply front brakes and turn wheels 20° inward.
4. Position caster gauge at 0°, then return wheels to straight-ahead position and note gauge reading. If caster angle is not within specifications, inspect suspension components for damage and repair as necessary, then recheck caster.

LEGEND

1. Raise front of vehicle and position turning radius gauges under front wheels, then lower vehicle.
2. Raise rear of vehicle and position wooden boards with a thickness equal to the turning radius gauge under rear wheels, then lower vehicle.
3. Remove spindle nut and install suitable caster gauge and adapter, **Fig. 1.**
4. Apply front brakes and turn wheels 20° inward.
5. Position caster gauge at 0°, then return wheels to straight-ahead position and note gauge reading. If caster angle is not within specifications, proceed as follows:
   a. Loosen radius rod attaching bolts at lower control arm.
   b. Loosen radius rod adjuster locknut and self-locking nut on end of radius rod, **Fig. 2.**
   c. Turn radius rod adjuster in to increase caster or out to decrease caster as necessary. **One complete revolution of the adjuster moves radius rod .049 inch and changes caster 14/60°.**
   d. Tighten radius rod attaching bolts, adjuster locknut and self-locking nut, then recheck caster angle.

CAMBER INSPECTION

Front and rear camber angles are not adjustable, however, the following procedures may be used to ensure camber is within specifications. **Ensure tires are properly inflated prior to checking camber angles.**

INTEGRA

1. Remove spindle nut and install suitable camber gauge and adapter, **Fig. 3,** with wheels in straight-ahead position.
2. Note gauge reading with bubble centered on the gauge. If camber is not within specifications, inspect suspension components for damage and repair as necessary, then recheck camber.

LEGEND

Front

1. Remove spindle nut and install suitable camber gauge and adapter, **Fig. 3,** with wheels in straight-ahead position.
2. Note gauge reading with bubble centered on the gauge. If camber is not within specifications, inspect suspension components for damage and repair as necessary, then recheck camber.

Rear

1. Remove two lug nuts and install adapter and camber gauge on hub carrier, **Fig. 4. Ensure adapter is installed parallel to hub carrier by using a depth gauge through the three holes in adapter.**
2. Note gauge reading with bubble centered on the gauge. If camber is not within specifications, inspect suspension components for damage and repair as necessary, then recheck camber.

TOE-IN INSPECTION & ADJUSTMENT

Ensure tires are properly inflated prior to checking or adjusting toe-in.

INTEGRA

Front

1. Raise front of vehicle and position turning radius gauges under front wheels, then lower vehicle.
2. Center steering wheel spokes and measure difference in toe measurements with wheels in the straight-ahead position.
3. If toe-in does not meet specifications, proceed as follows:
   a. Loosen tie rod locknuts and turn both tie rods, **Fig. 5,** in the same di-

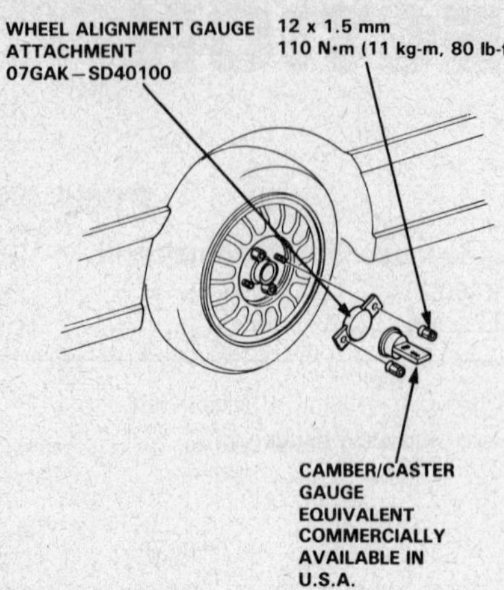

Fig. 4 Rear camber angle check. Legend

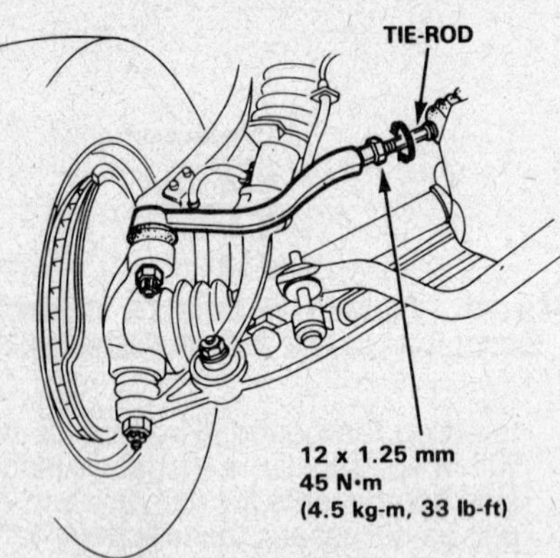

Fig. 6 Front toe-in adjustment. Legend

rection until front wheels are in the straight-ahead position.

b. Turn both tie rods an equal amount until toe-in meets specifications, then tighten tie rod locknuts. **Ensure tie rod boots are not deformed after adjustment.**

Rear

Rear wheel toe-in is not adjustable, however, the following procedure may be used to ensure toe-in is within specifications.

1. Raise rear of vehicle and position turning radius gauges under rear wheels, then lower vehicle.
2. Measure toe-in with parking released.
3. If toe-in does not meet specifications, inspect suspension components for damage and repair as necessary, then recheck toe-in.

LEGEND

Front

1. Raise front of vehicle and position turning radius gauges under front wheels, then lower vehicle.
2. Center steering wheel spokes and measure difference in toe measurements with wheels in the straight-ahead position.
3. If toe-in does not meet specifications, proceed as follows:
   a. Loosen tie rod locknuts and turn both tie rods, **Fig. 6,** in the same direction until front wheels are in the straight-ahead position.
   b. Turn both tie rods an equal amount until toe-in meets specifications, then tighten tie rod locknuts. **Ensure tie rod boots are not deformed after adjustment.**

Rear

1. Raise rear of vehicle and position turning radius gauges under rear wheels, then lower vehicle.
2. Center steering wheel spokes and measure difference in toe measurements with parking brake released and wheels in the straight-ahead position.
3. If toe-in does not meet specifications, proceed as follows:
   a. Loosen locknuts, **Fig. 7,** and turn adjusting bolt as necessary until toe-in meets specifications.
   b. Install new locknuts and tighten while holding adjusting bolt in position.

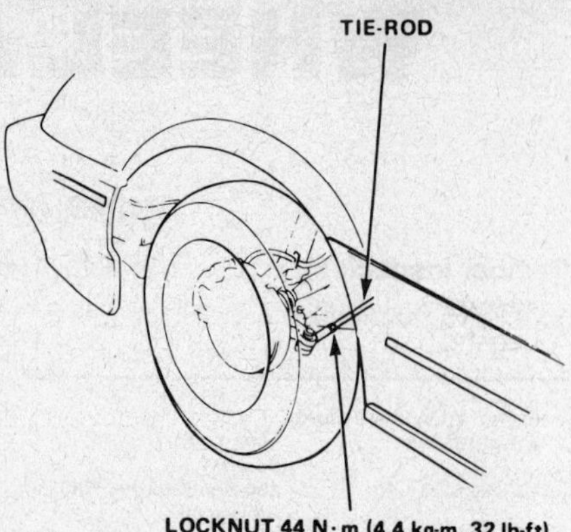

Fig. 5 Front toe-in adjustment. Integra

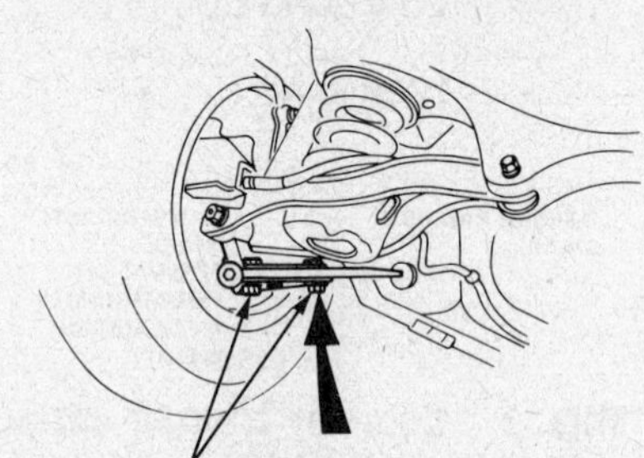

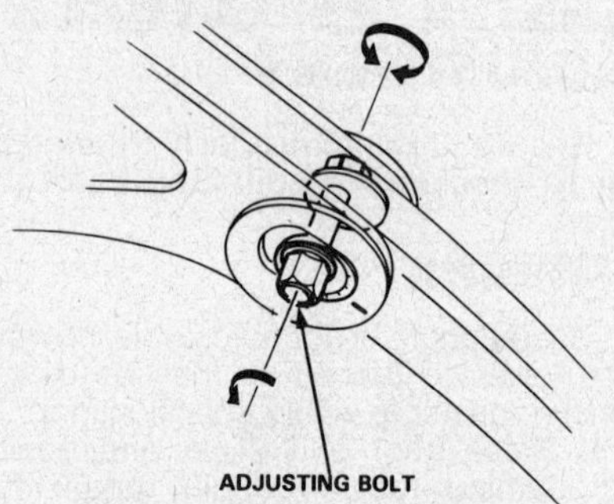

Fig. 7 Rear toe-in adjustment. Legend

AUDI (Germany)

INDEX OF SERVICE OPERATIONS

General Engine Specifications

Year	Model	Engine Code	Fuel System	Bore And Stroke (In)	Piston Displacement Cubic Inches (cc)	Compression Ratio	Maximum Brake HP @ RPM	Maximum Torque Lb. Ft. @ RPM
1983	4000 ①	WT	Fuel Inj.	3.13 X 3.40	105 (1715)	8.2	74 @ 5000	89.6 @ 3000
	4000 ① ④	WT	Fuel Inj.	3.13 X 3.15	96.9 (1587)	23.0	52 @ 4800	71.5 @ 2000
	Coupe ②	—	Fuel Inj.	3.12 X 3.40	130.8 (2144)	8.2	100 @ 5100	112.4 @ 3000
	Quattro ② ⑤	—	Fuel Inj.	3.12 X 3.40	130.8 (2144)	7.0	156 @ 5500	181 @ 3000
	5000 ②	—	Fuel Inj.	3.12 X 3.40	130.8 (2144)	8.2	100 @ 5100	112.4 @ 3000
	5000 ② ④ ⑤	—	Fuel Inj.	3.12 X 3.40	130.8 (2144)	23.0	84 @ 4500	127 @ 2800
1984	4000 ①	JN	Fuel Inj.	3.19 X 3.40	109 (1800)	9	88 @ 5500	96 @ 3250
	4000 ②	WE	Fuel Inj.	3.19 X 3.40	136 (2200)	8.5	115 @ 5500	126 @ 3000
	5000 ②	WU	Fuel Inj.	3.19 X 3.40	131 (2100)	8.2	100 @ 5500	107 @ 3000
	5000 ② ⑤	KH	Fuel Inj.	3.19 X 3.40	131 (2100)	8	140 @ 5500	149 @ 2500
	Coupe GT ②	KX	Fuel Inj.	3.19 X 3.40	131 (2100)	8.2	100 @ 5100	112.4 @ 3000
	Quattro Coupe ②	WU	Fuel Inj.	3.19 X 3.40	131 (2100)	7	160 @ 5500	181 @ 3000
1985	4000S ①	MG	Fuel Inj.	3.19 X 3.40	109 (1800)	10	102 @ 5500	105 @ 3250
	4000S ②	JT	Fuel Inj.	3.19 X 3.40	136 (2220)	8.5	115 @ 5500	126 @ 3000
	Quattro Turbo ②	WX	Fuel Inj.	3.19 X 3.40	131 (2100)	7	160 @ 5500	170 @ 3000
	5000S ②	KZ	Fuel Inj.	3.19 X 3.40	136 (2220)	8.5	110 @ 5500	122 @ 2500
	5000S Turbo ②	MC	Fuel Inj.	3.19 X 3.40	131 (2100)	8.3	140 @ 5500	149 @ 2500
	5000S Wagon ②	KZ	Fuel Inj.	3.19 X 3.40	136 (2220)	8.5	110 @ 5500	122 @ 2500
	Coupe GT ②	KX	Fuel Inj.	3.19 X 3.40	136 (2220)	8.5	110 @ 5500	110.6 @ 2500
1986	4000S ①	MG	Fuel Inj.	3.19 X 3.40	109 (1800)	10	102 @ 5500	111 @ 3250
	4000CS Quattro ②	JT	Fuel Inj.	3.19 X 3.40	136 (2220)	8.5	115 @ 5500	126 @ 3000
	5000S ②	KZ	Fuel Inj.	3.19 X 3.40	136 (2220)	8.5	110 @ 5500	122 @ 2500
	5000S ② ⑥	MC	Fuel Inj.	3.19 X 3.40	136 (2220)	7.8	158 @ 5500	166 @ 2500
	5000CS Quattro ② ⑥	MC	Fuel Inj.	3.19 X 3.40	136 (2220)	7.8	158 @ 5500	166 @ 2500
	5000CS Quattro Wagon ② ⑤	MC	Fuel Inj.	3.19 X 3.40	136 (2220)	7.8	158 @ 5500	166 @ 2500
	Coupe GT ②	KX	Fuel Inj.	3.19 X 3.40	136 (2220)	8.5	110 @ 5500	122 @ 2500
1987	4000S ①	—	Fuel Inj.	3.19 X 3.40	109 (1800)	10	102 @ 5500	111 @ 3250
	4000CS Quattro ②	—	Fuel Inj.	3.19 X 3.40	136 (2220)	8.5	115 @ 5500	126 @ 3000
	Coupe GT ②	—	Fuel Inj.	3.19 X 3.40	136 (2220)	8.5	110 @ 5500	122 @ 2500
	5000S ②	—	Fuel Inj.	3.19 X 3.40	136 (2220)	8.5	110 @ 5500	122 @ 2500
	5000S Wagon ②	—	Fuel Inj.	3.19 X 3.40	136 (2220)	8.5	110 @ 5500	122 @ 2500
	5000CS ② ⑤	—	Fuel Inj.	3.19 X 3.40	136 (2220)	7.8	158 @ 5500	166 @ 2500
	5000CS Quattro ② ⑤	—	Fuel Inj.	3.19 X 3.40	136 (2220)	7.8	158 @ 5500	166 @ 3000
	5000CS Quattro Wagon ② ⑤	—	Fuel Inj.	3.19 X 3.40	136 (2220)	7.8	158 @ 5500	166 @ 3000

①—4 cylinder engine.
②—5 cylinder engine.
③—California models 100 @ 5500.
④—Diesel.
⑤—Turbocharged model.

Distributor Specifications

If unit is checked on vehicle, double the RPM and degrees to get crankshaft figures.

Distributor Part No.	Centrifugal Advance Degrees @ RPM of Distributor			Vacuum Advance		Distributor Retard
	Advance Starts	Intermediate Advance	Full Advance	Inches of Vacuum to Start Plunger	Max. Adv. Dist. Eg. @ Vacuum	Max. Ref. Dist. Deg. @ Vacuum
035905205J	0 @ 525	11 @ 1250	15 @ 3500	4.4	7 @ 7.6	5 @ 7.6
049505205A	0 @ 613	12 @ 2000	14 @ 2500	8.9	6 @ 11.2	4.5 @ 9.6
049905206B	0 @ 613	8.75 @ 1100	14 @ 2500	3.8	5.5 @ 7.4	—
049905205Q	0 @ 613	8.75 @ 1100	14 @ 2500	3.8	5.5 @ 7.4	4.5 @ 6.5
035905206R	0 @ 700	12 @ 1600	14 @ 3500	3.8	6 @ 7.4	—
035905205B	0 @ 500	10 @ 1250	11.5 @ 2250	7.1	3 @ 9.1	4.5 @ 6.9
035905205G	0 @ 625	11 @ 2450	13.5 @ 3500	3.8	6 @ 6.8	4.5 @ 6.8
035905205E	0 @ 625	11 @ 2450	13.5 @ 3500	3.2	6 @ 6.8	—
035905206A	0 @ 625	12 @ 1600	14 @ 3500	5.2	6 @ 7.4	4.5 @ 6.8
035905205L	0 @ 625	12 @ 1600	14 @ 3500	8.6	3 @ 10.8	4.5 @ 9.3
035905205H	0 @ 588	2 @ 700	3.5 @ 1000	7.9	6.5 @ 5.9	9 @ 8.4
035905206J	0 @ 588	2 @ 700	2.5 @ 1000	7.9	6.5 @ 5.9	9 @ 8.4
035905205AM	0 @ 650	10 @ 1400	11.75 @ 2750	—	—	—
035905205AJ	①	①	①	①	①	①
035905206AF	①	①	①	①	①	①
026905205S	①	①	①	①	①	①
026905205L	0 @ 588	8.5 @ 1300	12 @ 2250	4.1	6 @ 7.4	—

①—Nonadjustable.

Alternator & Regulator Specifications

Alternator				Regulator		
Model	Rated Hot Output Amps	Output @ 14 Volts 2200 RPM	Output @ 14 Volts 6000 RPM	Model	Regulated Voltage	Load Current Amps
K1-14V-35A22	35	23	35	0192052004	13.7–14.5	5–7
K1-14V-55A22	55	36	55	0192052004	13.7–14.5	5–7
65 amp	65	①	—	—	13.5–14.5	—

①—Minimum output reading at 3000 RPM, gasoline engine models, 49 amps; diesel engine models, 58 amps.

Starting Motor Specifications

Model	No Load Test			Torque Test			Brush Spring Tension Ounces
	Amperes (Max.)	Volts	RPM (Min.)	Amperes (Max.)	Volts	Torque Ft. Lbs. (Min.)	
0001211209	55	11.5	6000	410	8.5	8.31	40–45

Valve Specifications

Year	Model	Valve Lash		Valve Angle		Valve Spring Installed Height (In.)	Valve Spring Pressure Lbs. @ In.	Stem Clearance (Max.)		Stem Diameter	
		Intake	Exhaust	Seat	Face			Intake	Exhaust	Intake	Exhaust
1983	5000	.006–.010①	.014–.018①	45°	45°	—	—	.039	.051	.314	.313
1983	4000	.006–.010①	.014–.018①	45°	45°	—	—	.039	.051	.314	.313
1984	Quattro Coupe	—	—	45°	45°	—	—	.039	.051	.314	.313
1984–85	4000S	—	—	45°	45°	—	—	.039	.051	.314	.313
1984–87	4000S②	—	—	45°	45°	—	—	.039	.051	.314	.313
1984–87	5000S	—	—	45°	45°	—	—	.039	.051	.314	.313
1984–87	5000S Turbo	—	—	45°	45°	—	—	.039	.051	.314	.313
1984–87	Coupe GT	—	—	45°	45°	—	—	.039	.051	.314	.313
1985–87	Quattro Turbo	—	—	45°	45°	—	—	.039	.051	.314	.313

①—Cold. Intake, .008–.012; Exhaust, .016–.020, hot.

②—4 cylinder engine.

Engine Tightening Specifications

Torque specifications are for clean and lightly lubricated threads only. Dry or dirty threads produce increased friction which prevents accurate measurement of tightness.

Year	Model	Spark Plugs Ft. Lbs.	Cylinder Head Bolts Ft. Lbs.	Intake & Exhaust Manifold Ft. Lbs.	Camshaft Bearing Cap Bolts Ft. Lbs.	Connecting Rod Cap Bolts Ft. Lbs.	Main Bearing Cap Bolts Ft. Lbs.	Flywheel to Crankshaft Ft. Lbs.	Camshaft Drive Belt Sprockets Ft. Lbs.
1983	4000	14	⑤⑨	16	14	33	47	58⑧	—
	4000②	51③	⑤⑩	16	—	⑦	47	33⑧	—
	5000④	14	⑥⑨	18	14	36	47	58	—
	5000 Turbo④	14	⑥⑨	18	14	36	47	58	—
	Coupe④	14	⑥⑨	16	14	36	47	58	—
	Quattro④	14	—	—	—	—	—	—	—
1984	4000	14	⑨	17	14	⑦	47	①⑧	58
	4000④	14	⑨	17	14	⑦	47	①	58
	5000④	14	⑨	18	14	⑪	47	①	56
	5000 Turbo④	14	⑨	18	14	⑪	47	①	56
	Coupe GT④	14	⑨	17	14	⑦	47	①	58
	Quattro Coupe④	14	⑨	17	14	⑦	47	①	58
1985	4000S	14	⑨	17	14	⑦	47	①⑧	58
	4000S④	14	⑨	17	14	⑦	47	①	58
	Quattro Turbo④	14	⑨	17	14	⑦	47	①	58
	5000S④	14	⑨	18	14	⑪	47	①	56
	5000S Turbo④	14	⑨	18	14	⑪	47	①	56
	5000S Wagon④	14	⑨	18	14	⑪	47	①	56
	Coupe GT④	14	⑨	17	14	⑦	47	①	58
1986–87	4000S	14	⑨	17	14	⑦	47	①⑧	58
	4000CS Quattro Turbo④	14	⑨	17	14	⑦	47	①	58
	5000S④	14	⑨	18	14	⑪	47	①	56
	5000CS Turbo④	14	⑨	18	14	⑪	47	①	56
	5000CS Quattro Turbo④	14	⑨	18	14	⑪	47	①	56
	5000CS Quattro Turbo Wagon④	14	⑨	18	14	⑪	47	①	56
	Coupe GT④	14	⑨	17	14	⑦	47	①	58

cont.

ENGINE TIGHTENING SPECIFICATIONS—Continued

①—Bolt without shoulder, 54 ft. lbs.; bolt with shoulder, 72 ft. lbs.
②—Diesel engine.
③—Fuel injectors.
④—5 cylinder engine.
⑤—On gasoline engines with cylinder head bolts other than M11, or diesel engines with cylinder head bolts other than M12: torque in sequence to 29, 43 & 54 ft. lbs., then additional ¼ turn on gasoline engine or additional ½ turn on diesel engine. Warm up then stop engine and tighten additional ¼ turn in sequence. After 1000 miles, tighten ¼ turn in sequence.
⑥—Engines with cylinder head bolts other than M11; torque in sequence to 29, 43 & 54 ft. lbs., then additional ¼ turn in sequence.
⑦—Torque to 22 ft. lbs., then tighten nut additional ¼ turn.
⑧—Drive belt sprocket on crankshaft, 145 ft. lbs. on later models.
⑨—Engines with M11 cylinder head bolts: with engine cold, torque in sequence to 29 & 43 ft. lbs., then additional ½ turn.
⑩—Engines with M12 cylinder head bolts: with engine cold, torque in sequence to 29 & 43 ft. lbs., then additional ½ turn. Warm up then stop and tighten additional ¼ turn in sequence. After 1000 miles,tighten ¼ turn in sequence.
⑪—Bolt without notches, 36 ft. lbs.; bolt with notches, 22 ft. lbs. plus ¼ turn.

Pistons, Rings, Pins, Crankshaft & Bearing Specifications

Year	Model	Piston Clearance Top Of Skirt	Ring End Gap			Rod Bearings		Main Bearings			
			Top	Second	Oil	Shaft Diameter	Bearing Clearance	Shaft Diameter	Bearing Clearance	Thrust Bearing No.	Shaft End Play
1983	5000	.001–.003	.010–.020	.010–.020	.010–.020	1.81	.0006–.002	2.283	.0006–.003	4	.003–.007
1983–84	5000①	.011–.027	.012–.020	.012–.020	.010–.016	1.880–1.881	.0005–.0024	2.281–2.282	.0006–.0029	4	.003–.007
1983–87	4000	.0011–.0027	.012–.018	.012–.018	.012–.018	1.809–1.810	.0011–.0034	2.124–2.125	.001–.003	3	.003–.007
1983–87	4000②	.001–.003	.010–.020	.010–.020	.010–.020	1.811	.0006–.002	2.283	.0006–.003	4	.003–.007
1983	4000①	.0011–.0027	.012–.020	.012–.020	.010–.016	1.880–1.881	.0011–.0034	2.124–2.125	.001–.003	3	.003–.007
1983–87	Coupe②	.0011–.0027	.010–.020	.010–.020	.010–.020	1.809–1.810	.0006–.002	2.282–2.283	.0006–.003	4	.003–.007
1984	5000 Turbo②	.0011–.0027	.010–.020	.010–.020	.010–.020	1.809–1.810	.0006–.002	2.282–2.283	.0006–.003	4	.003–.007
	Quattro Coupe②	.0010–.0016③	.010–.020	.010–.020	.010–.020	—	.0006–.002	2.282–2.283	.0006–.003	4	.003–.007
1985	Quattro Turbo②	.0011–.0027	.010–.020	.010–.020	.010–.020	1.809–1.810	.0006–.002	2.282–2.283	.0006–.003	4	.003–.007
	5000S Turbo②	.0010–.0016③	.010–.020	.010–.020	.010–0.20	—	.0006–.002	2.282–2.283	.0006–.003	4	.003–.007
1985–87	5000S②	.0010–.0016③	.010–.020	.010–.020	.010–.020	—	.0006–.002	2.282–2.283	.0006–.003	4	.003–.007
1986–87	4000CS Quattro②	.0011–.0027	.010–.020	.010–.020	.010–.020	1.809–1.810	.0006–.002	2.282–2.283	.0006–.003	4	.003–.007
	5000CS Turbo②	.0010–.0016③	.010–.020	.010–.020	.010–.020	—	.0006–.002	2.282–2.283	.0006–.003	4	.003–.007
	5000CS Turbo Quattro②	.0010–.0016③	.010–.020	.010–.020	.010–.020	—	.0006–.002	2.282–2.283	.0006–.003	4	003–.007

①—Diesel.
②—5 cylinder engine.
③—Measure ⅜ inch from lower edge at 90° to piston pin.

Wheel Alignment Specifications

Year	Model	Caster Angle, Degrees		Camber Angle, Degrees		Toe-In Degrees
		Limits	Desired	Limits	Desired	
1983	5000	①	①	−1 to 0	−1/2	−1/6 to +1/12
1983–87	4000	0 to +1	+1/2	−1 1/6 to −1/6	−2/3	0 to +1/3
1983–87	4000②	③	③	−1 1/6 to −1/6	−2/3	0 to +1/3
1983–87	Coupe	③	③	−1 1/6 to −1/6	−2/3	0 to +1/3
1983–84	Quattro	+5/6 to +2 1/6	+1 1/2	−1 1/3 to −1/3	−5/6	0 to +1/12
1984–87	5000	−1/6 to +1 1/2	+2/3	−1 to 0	−1/2	−1/6 to +1/12
	5000 Turbo	−1/6 to +1 1/2	+2/3	−1 to 0	−1/2	−1/6 to +1/12
1985	Quattro Turbo	+5/6 to +2 1/6	+1 1/2	−1 1/3 to −1/3	−5/6	−1/6 to +1/12
1986–87	4000 Quattro	+11/12 to +1 11/12	+1 5/12	−1 1/4 to −1/4	−3/4	0 to +1/3
	5000 Quattro	−1/3 to +1 2/3	+2/3	−1 to 0	−1/2	−1/12 to +1/6

①—Vehicles up to VIN No. 43A0016066; limits −5/6 to +1/2, desired −1/6. Vehicles from VIN No. 43A0016066; limits +1/2 to +1 5/6, desired +1 1/16.

②—5 cylinder.

③—Vehicles less link rod between wishbone & stabilizer bar; limits 0 to +1, desired +1/2. Vehicles with link rod between wishbone & stabilizer bar; limits +11/12 to +1 11/12, desired +1 5/12.

Brake Specifications

Year	Model	Wheel Cylinder Bore			Master Cylinder Bore	Rear Drums		Rear Disc Brake Rotor				Front Disc Brake Rotor			
		Front Disc	Rear Drum	Rear Disc		Nominal Diameter	Maximum Diameter	Nominal Thickness	Minimum Thickness	Runout (T.I.R.)	Paralelism	Nominal Thickness	Minimum Thickness	Runout (T.I.R.)	Paralelism
1983	5000	—	11/16	—	—	9.005	9.094	—	—	—	—	.866	.807	.002	.0008
1983	4000	—	—	—	—	—	7.894	—	—	—	—	.472	.413	—	.002
	Quattro	—	—	—	—	—	—	—	—	—	—	.866	.807	.002	.0008
1984	4000②	—	—	—	—	—	7.894	—	—	—	—	.472	.413	.002	—
	4000	—	—	—	—	—	7.894	—	—	—	—	.787	.728	.0011	.0003
	5000	—	11/16	—	—	9.055	9.075	—	—	—	—	.866	.807	.002	—
	5000①	—	—	—	—	—	—	.394	.335	.002	.0008	.866	.807	.002	—
	Coupe GT	—	—	—	—	—	7.894	—	—	—	—	.787	.728	.0011	.0003
	Quattro	—	—	—	—	—	—	.394	.335	.002	.0008	.787	.728	.0011	.0003
1985	4000S②	—	—	—	.81	—	7.894	—	—	—	—	.787	.728	.0011	.0003
	4000S	—	—	—	.81	—	7.894	—	—	—	—	.787	.728	.0011	.0003
	Quattro①	—	—	—	—	—	—	.394	.335	.002	.0008	.866	.807	.002	.0008
	5000S	—	11/16	—	—	9.055	9.075	—	—	—	—	.866	.807	.002	—
	5000S①	—	—	—	—	—	—	.394	.335	.002	.0008	.866	.807	.002	—
	Coupe GT	—	—	—	.81	—	7.894	—	—	—	—	.787	.728	.0011	.0003
1986–87	4000S②	—	—	—	.81	—	7.894	—	—	—	—	.787	.728	.0011	.0003
	4000CS Quattro	—	—	—	—	—	—	.394	.335	.002	.0008	.787	.728	.0011	.0003
	5000S	—	11/16	—	—	9.055	9.075	—	—	—	—	.866	.807	.002	—
	5000CS①	—	—	—	—	—	—	.394	.335	.002	.0008	.866	.807	.002	—
	5000CS Quattro ①	—	—	—	—	—	—	.394	.335	.002	.0008	.866	.807	.002	—
	Coupe GT	—	—	—	.81	—	7.894	—	—	—	—	.787	.728	.0011	.0003

①—Turbocharged model.

②—4 cylinder engine.

Cooling System & Capacity Data

Year	Model	Coolant Capacity Qts. ①	Radiator Cap Relief Pressure Lbs.	Thermostat Opening Temperature Degrees F.	Fuel Tank Gals.	Engine Oil Refill Qts. ②	Transmission 4 Speed Pints ③	5 Speed Pints ③	Automatic Pints ④	Differential ⑤
1983	4000 4E	8.5	17–14	—	15.8	4.7⑧	3.6	—	6.4	1.6⑦
	4000 Diesel	8.5	17–19	—	15.8	⑨	3.6	—	6.4	1.6⑦
	5000	8.5	17–19	194–216	19.8	5.3⑧	5.2	5.2	6.4	—
	5000 Turbo	10	17–19	194–216	19.8	5.3⑧	5.2	5.2	6.4	—
	Coupe	7.4	17–19	—	15.8	5.3⑧	—	5⑥	6.4	1.6⑦
	Quattro	9.8	17–19	—	23.8	4.5⑧	—	—	6.4	—
1984	4000	6.9	17–19	194	15.8	4.7⑧	—	4.2	6.4	—
	5000	8.5	17–19	188	21.1	5.3⑧	—	5.4	6.4	—
	5000 Turbo	8.5	17–19	188	21.1	5.3⑧	—	5.4	6.4	—
	Coupe GT	7.4	17–19	189	15.8	5.3⑧	—	5	6.4	—
	Quattro	8.45	17–19	189	18.5	3.7⑧	—	7	6.4	—
	Coupe	9.8	17–19	189	23.8	4.5⑧	—	7	6.4	—
1985	4000S	6.9	17–19	194	15.8	3.7	—	4.2	6.4	—
	Quattro Turbo	9.8	17–19	189	23.8	4.5	—	7	6.4	—
	5000S	8.5	17–19	188	21	5.3	—	5.4	6.4	—
	5000S Turbo	8.5	17–19	188	21	5.3	—	5.4	6.4	—
	5000S Wagon	8.5	17–19	188	21	5.3	—	5.4	6.4	—
	Coupe GT	7.4	17–19	189	15.8	4	—	5	6.4	—
1986–87	4000S	6.9	17–19	194	15.8	3.7	—	4.2	6.4	—
	4000CS Quattro	8.5	17–19	189	18.51	4	—	7	6.4	—
	5000S	8.5	17–19	188	21	5.3	—	5.4	6.4	—
	5000CS Turbo	8.5	17–19	188	21	5.3	—	5.4	6.4	—
	5000CS Quattro	8.5	17–19	188	21	5.3	—	5.4	6.4	—
	5000CS Quattro Wagon	8.5	17–19	188	21	5.3	—	5.4	6.4	—
	Coupe GT	7.4	17–19	189	15.8	4	—	5	6.4	—

①—Incl. expansion tank.
②—Incl. filter.
③—SAE 80W/90 API/GL-4.
④—Refill capacity. Dextron II.
⑤—SAE 90 API/GL-5.
⑥—Transaxle.
⑦—With automatic transmission.
⑧—Total capacity.
⑨—Total capacity, w/auto. trans., 5 qts.; w/manual trans., 3.2 qts.

ELECTRICAL SECTION

INDEX

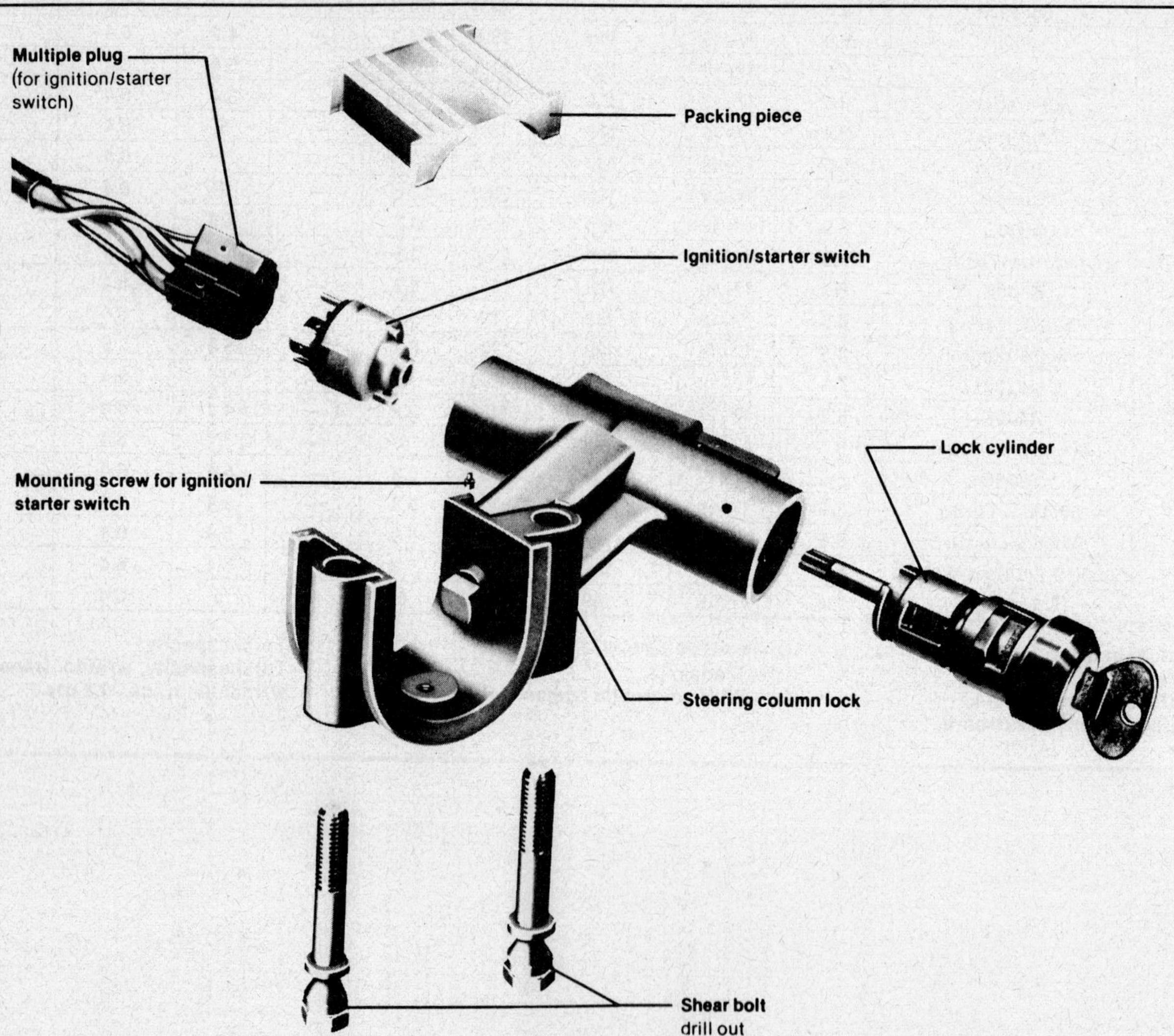

Fig. 1 Disassembled view of ignition switch & steering lock assembly. 1983 5000 models.

ALTERNATOR IN-VEHICLE TESTING

OUTPUT TEST

1. Connect suitable alternator test equipment as per manufacturer's instructions.
2. Switch off all electrical accessories, then start engine and run at 3000 RPM.
3. Adjust load maximum ammeter reading while maintaining voltage of at least 12 volts.
4. If ammeter reading is more than 16 amps below alternator reading, replace regulator and retest.
5. If ammeter reading is still too low, replace alternator.

REGULATOR TEST

1. With tester still connected, turn off all electrical components.
2. Run engine at 3000 RPM until voltage stops rising. If voltage is not 13.5-14.5 volts, replace regulator and repeat test.

DIODE TEST

1. With tester still connected, run engine at 3000 RPM and adjust load according to tester manufacturer's instructions.

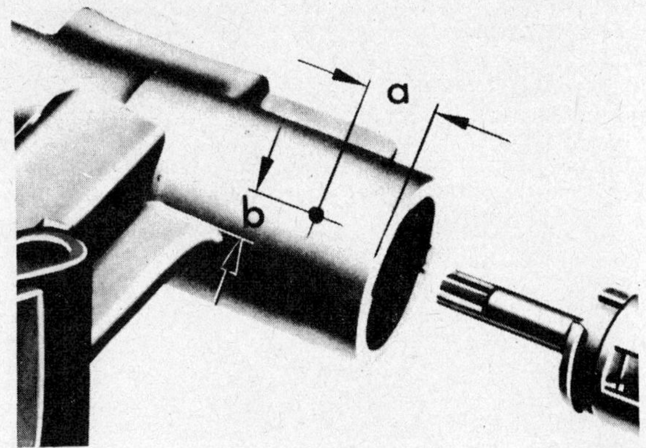

Fig. 2 Ignition lock cylinder removal drill dimensions

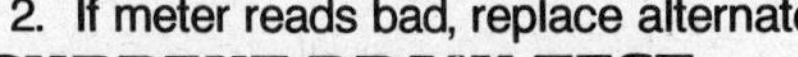

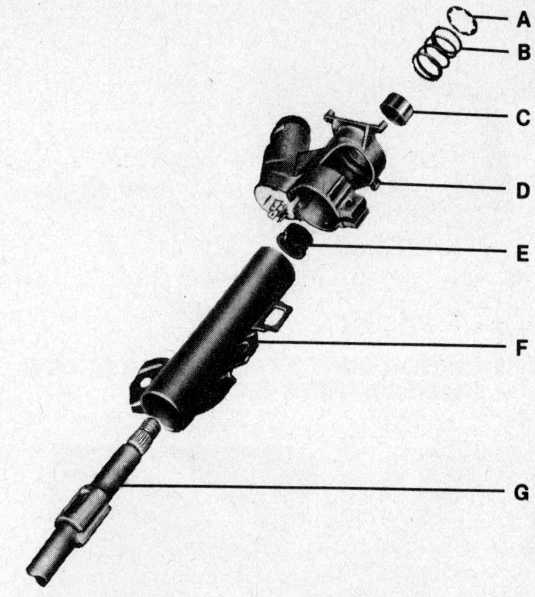

Fig. 3 Ignition switch & steering lock installation. 4000, Coupe & Quattro

2. If meter reads bad, replace alternator.

CURRENT DRAIN TEST

1. Turn off ignition switch, radio and all lights, but leave rear window defogger switch and A/C switches on.
2. Disconnect battery ground cable.
3. Connect test light between ground cable and negative battery terminal.
4. If test light burns brightly, something is switched on or shorted.
5. Locate problem by removing fuses from fuse box one at a time until light goes out.
6. If no faults are found in fused circuits, disconnect cables from non-fused circuits until test light goes out.

STARTER

REPLACE

1. Disconnect battery ground cable.
2. Remove screws securing wiring harness connectors and nut securing positive battery cable and disconnect wires and cable from solenoid switch.
3. Remove nuts or bolts securing starter to engine and remove starter motor from vehicle.
4. Reverse procedure to install.

IGNITION LOCK & SWITCH

REPLACE

1983 5000

1. Disconnect battery ground cable.
2. Lower air conditioning ducts as required and remove combination switch assembly.
3. Disconnect wiring harness connector from switch, **Fig. 1**.
4. Support steering column and drill out two shear bolts using a 5/16 inch drill bit.
5. Remove steering lock and switch assembly from vehicle.
6. Remove screw from bottom of lock housing and remove ignition switch.
7. Drill hole in lock housing as shown in **Fig. 2**, using a 1/8 inch drill bit.
8. Insert punch into hole to depress spring, turn ignition key slightly to right and pry lock cylinder from housing.
9. Noting correct key position, insert new lock cylinder into housing until spring snaps into position.
10. Insert ignition switch into housing, making sure switch aligns with hole in housing and engages lock mechanism, then secure switch with set screw.
11. Remove shear bolts from upper steering column support.
12. Install housing on steering column, making sure projection on housing engages hole in steering column.
13. Install two new shear bolts and temporarily secure housing. Check operation of steering lock mechanism.
14. Tighten shear bolts until heads shear off.
15. Reinstall steering column covers and air conditioning ducts as required.

4000, COUPE & QUATTRO MODELS

1. Disconnect battery ground cable.
2. Remove two screws securing steering column cover and remove cover.
3. Remove steering wheel, horn contact and spring.
4. Disconnect wiring harness connectors from combination switch, remove three screws securing switch to column and remove combination switch.
5. Pry off lock washer "A", **Fig. 3**, relieving spring tension carefully. Pull out contact ring "C", **Fig. 3**, and remove bolt securing ignition lock assembly to tube.
6. Remove ignition lock and switch assembly from tube "F", **Fig. 3.**
7. Drill hole in lock housing as shown in **Fig. 2**, using a 1/8 inch drill bit.
8. Insert punch into hole to depress spring, turn ignition key slightly to right, and pry lock cylinder from housing.
9. Noting correct key position, insert new lock cylinder into housing until spring snaps into position.
10. Remove screw, **Fig. 4**, and ignition switch from housing.
11. Push new steering lock and ignition switch assembly "D", **Fig. 3**, onto steering column tube to stop and install retaining bolt.
12. Push support ring "E", **Fig. 3**, onto steering shaft "G", and fit shaft into tube "F".
13. Push contact ring "C" onto steering shaft to stop and install spring "B", **Fig. 3**, and lock washer "A", fully compressing spring.
14. Reverse procedure to install combination switch, steering wheel and covers.

1984–87 5000 MODELS

To remove ignition switch, proceed as follows:

1. Disconnect battery ground cable.
2. Pull off horn pad, then remove steering wheel.
3. Remove instrument cluster attaching bolts.
4. Disconnect speedometer cable at transmission.
5. Pull instrument cluster forward and detach speedometer cable at speedometer.
6. Disconnect electrical connectors at instrument cluster and remove instrument cluster.
7. Remove locking compound and remove ignition switch attaching bolt.
8. Disconnect electrical connector and remove ignition switch.
9. Reverse procedure to install.

To remove ignition lock, proceed as follows:

1. Disconnect battery ground cable.
2. Pull off horn pad and remove steering wheel.

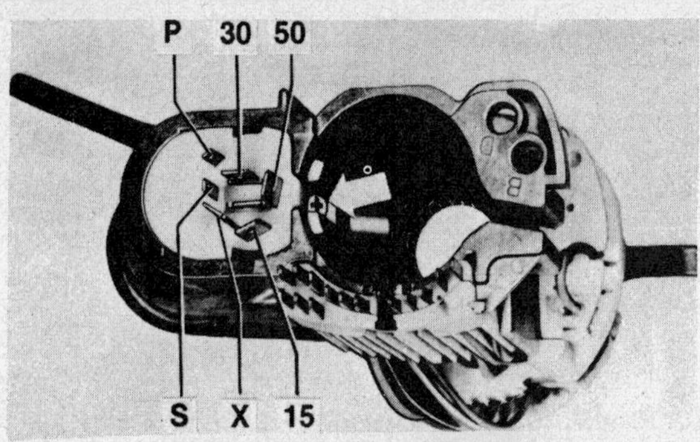

Fig. 4 Ignition switch retaining screw (arrow). 4000 & Coupe

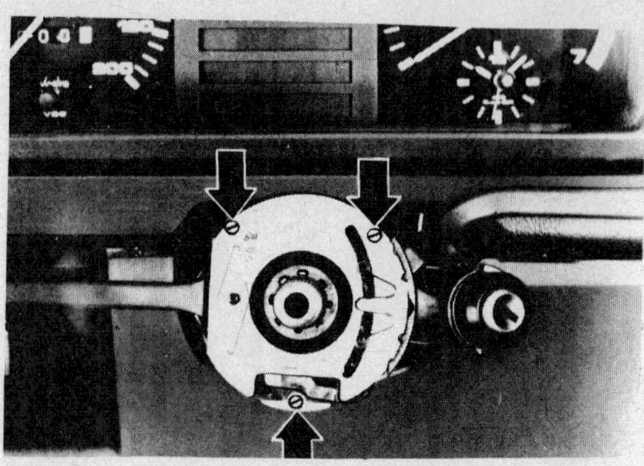

Fig. 5 Combination switch removal. 4000, Coupe & Quattro

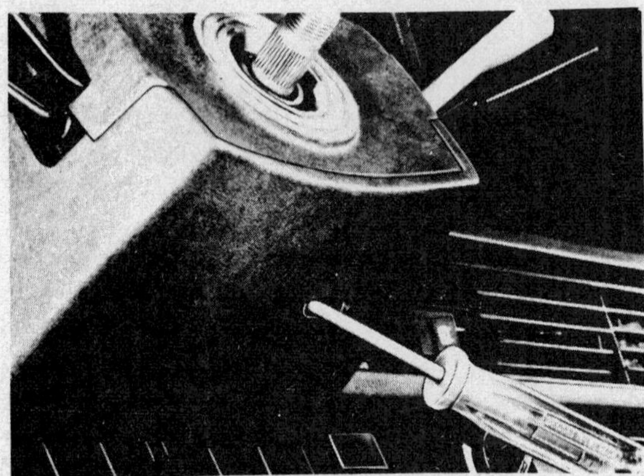

Fig. 6 Combination switch housing removal. 5000 models

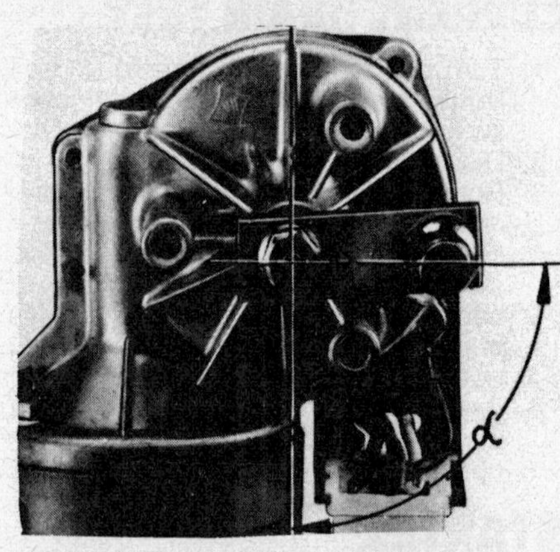

Fig. 7 Wiper crank park position L=90°. 5000

3. Loosen steering column switch clamp, disconnect electrical connectors, and remove steering column switch.
4. Remove instrument cluster attaching screws.
5. Disconnect speedometer cable at transmission.
6. Pull instrument cluster forward and disconnect speedometer cable at speedometer.
7. Disconnect electrical connectors of instruments and remove instrument cluster.
8. Using 1/8 inch bit, drill out steering column shear bolt.
9. Loosen steering column bolts.
10. Remove left lower dash panel, then the left air deflector.
11. Slide steering column tube with steering column downward, then remove steering lock from steering column clamp.
12. Using 1/8 inch bit, drill hole in lock housing as shown, **Fig. 2.**
13. Push retaining spring in with suitable punch and remove lock cylinder.
14. Reverse procedure to install.

HEADLAMP SWITCH REPLACE

4000 & COUPE

1. Remove instrument cluster cover as outlined under, "Instrument Cluster, Replace."

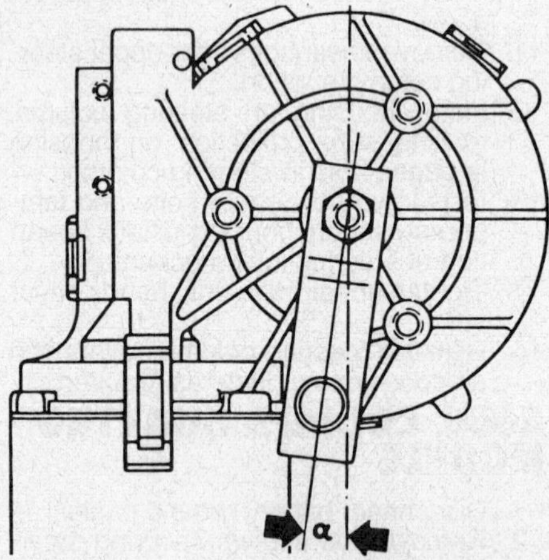

Fig. 8 Wiper crank park position α=8°. 4000 & Coupe

2. Disconnect wiring harness connector from rear of switch.
3. Depress clips on switch retainer and remove switch from cluster.
4. Reverse procedure to install.

COMBINATION SWITCH REPLACE

The steering column combination switch includes the turn signal switch, windshield wiper/washer switch, dimmer switch, and on some models, the main headlamp switch. On some models, individual switches can be replaced, while on others, the combination switch must be replaced.

4000, COUPE & QUATTRO

1. Remove horn cover prying off by hand, remove nut and washer securing steering wheel, and remove steering wheel, spring and horn contact.
2. Remove screws securing lower steering column cover and remove cover.
3. Remove screws securing combination switch to steering lock housing, **Fig. 5**, disconnect switch from wiring harness and remove switch.
4. Reverse procedure to install.

5000 MODELS

1. Disconnect battery ground cable.
2. Remove horn cover prying by hand, remove nut and washer securing steering wheel and remove steering wheel.
3. Remove screw securing combination switch housing through access hole, **Fig. 6.**
4. Pull housing and switch assembly forward to clear steering shaft and disconnect wiring harness connectors.
5. Switches can be removed from housing by removing retaining screws.
6. Reverse procedure to install.

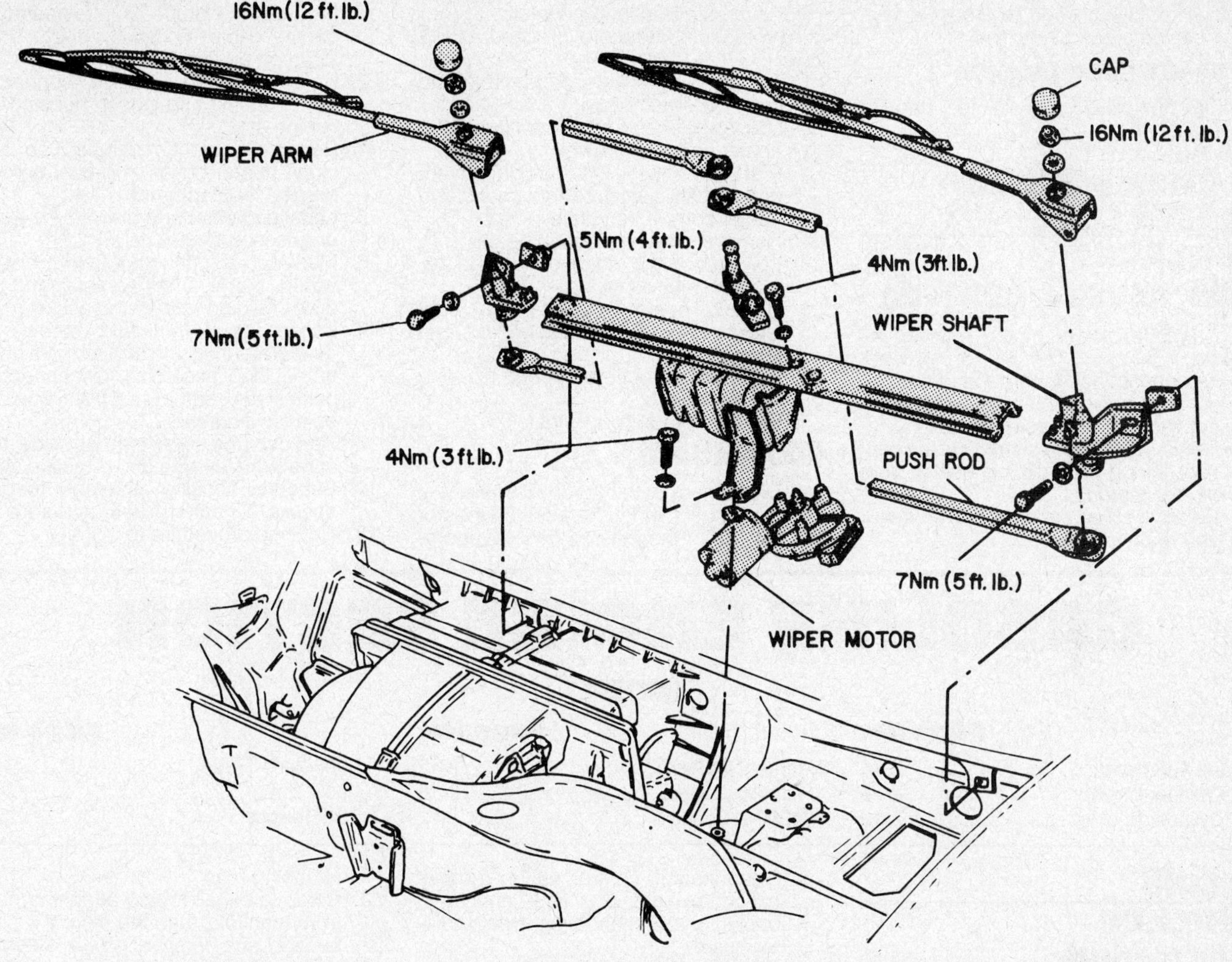

Fig. 9 Disassembled view of windshield wiper assembly. 1984–87 models

INSTRUMENT CLUSTER REPLACE

4000, COUPE & QUATTRO

1. Disconnect battery ground cable.
2. Remove screws and trim strip and the instrument cluster cover.
3. Disconnect wiring harness connectors and speedometer cable from rear of instrument cluster.
4. Remove switches and screws securing instrument cluster to dash.
5. Remove instrument cluster from dash.
6. Reverse procedure to install.

5000 MODELS

1983

1. Disconnect battery ground cable.
2. Remove instrument panel trim and the screws securing cluster cover.
3. Remove upper portion of cluster cover, then remove lower portion.
4. Remove screws securing instrument cluster to dash and pull forward to gain access.
5. Disconnect wiring harness connectors and speedometer cable from instrument cluster and remove cluster.
6. Reverse procedure to install.

1984–87

1. Disconnect battery ground cable.
2. Pull off horn pad, then remove steering wheel.
3. Remove instrument cluster attaching bolts.
4. Disconnect speedometer cable at transmission.
5. Pull out instrument cluster and disconnect speedometer cable at speedometer.
6. Disconnect electrical connectors at instruments and remove instrument cluster.
7. Reverse procedure to install.

WINDSHIELD WIPER MOTOR & LINKAGE REPLACE

WIPER MOTOR

4000, Coupe, Quattro & 1983 5000

1. Disconnect battery ground cable and disconnect wiring harness connector at motor.
2. Remove nut securing crank to wiper motor, while holding crank and remove crank.
3. Remove bolts securing wiper motor to support and remove motor.
4. Connect new motor to harness, run two revolutions and turn wiper switch to off position. Wiper motor should stop in park position.
5. Reverse procedure to install wiper motor, making sure crank is installed in proper position, **Figs. 7 and 8.**

1984–87 5000 Models

When removing wiper motor on 1984-87 5000 models, refer to **Fig. 9.**

LINKAGE

4000, Coupe, Quattro & 1983 5000

1. Remove wiper motor as outlined above.
2. Lift wiper arm off glass and lift cap over retaining nut while lowering arm.
3. Remove nut and washer securing wiper arm.
4. Remove nuts, washer and spacers securing pivot to cowl.
5. Remove bolt securing wiper frame

and remove linkage as an assembly.
6. Reverse procedure to install.

1984–87 5000 Models

When removing wiper linkage, refer to **Fig. 9.**

BLOWER MOTOR & HEATER CORE REPLACE

4000, COUPE & QUATTRO

To remove blower motor, proceed as follows:

1. Disconnect battery ground cable.
2. Remove cowl air plenum, disconnecting vacuum lines as needed.
3. Remove ballast resistor and disconnect wiring harness connector from blower motor.
4. Remove screw securing blower motor and remove blower.
5. Reverse procedure to install.

To remove heater core, proceed as follows:

1. Disconnect battery ground cable and drain cooling system.
2. Loosen clamps and carefully remove heater hoses at firewall.
3. Remove console, left and right covers under dash, heater control knobs and heater control trim plate.
4. Remove screws securing heater control and center dash cover and remove center cover.
5. Remove heater core cover on right side by depressing retaining tabs and prying.
6. Remove heater core through opening left by cover.
7. Reverse procedure to install.

5000 MODELS

1. Disconnect battery ground cable.
2. Disconnect wiring harness connector for A/C thermostat "A", evaporator/heater clamp "B", temperature control cable "C" and vacuum hose for fresh air flap "D".
3. Remove wiring harness connector from housing and loosen housing retaining strap.
4. Remove coolant reservoir cap and pinch heater hoses at heater core in engine compartment.
5. Loosen clamps and disconnect heater hoses at heater core.
6. Mark and disconnect vacuum hoses, wiring harness connectors and air ducts leading to housing assembly.
7. Loosen four mounting screws at evaporator housing and remove heater housing assembly, disconnecting cables and harnesses from housing as it is withdrawn.
8. Remove one screw on right side, two screws on left side and retaining clips.
9. Separate housing assembly to gain access to heater blower and core.
10. Reverse procedure to install.

GASOLINE ENGINE SECTION

INDEX

ENGINE REPLACE

4000 & COUPE

4 Cylinder Engine W/Automatic Transmission

1. Disconnect battery ground cable.
2. On vehicles with air conditioning, proceed as follows:
   a. Remove clips and screw securing grill, then the grill.
   b. Remove condenser to radiator attaching bolts.
   c. Remove air duct from throttle valve housing and the hose from air duct to auxiliary air regulator.
   d. Remove fuel distributor, air flow sensor, fuel injectors and air cleaner as an assembly, leaving fuel lines connected and capping injectors and cold start valve.
   e. Remove engine stop attaching bolts and the stop.
   f. Loosen nuts attaching outer half of crankshaft pulley and remove drive belt.
   g. Discharge refrigerant, then remove air conditioner hoses and plug openings.
   h. Disconnect compressor clutch wire.
   i. Remove crankcase vent hose connection at valve cover and position air conditioner hoses out of way.
   j. Remove two upper and three lower compressor mounting bolts and the compressor.
3. Open heater control valve, remove cap from expansion tank, and drain coolant by disconnecting lower radiator hose.
4. Remove upper and lower radiator hoses.
5. Disconnect electrical connectors for radiator fan and thermo switch.
6. Remove radiator rubber mounts, then the radiator, fan and fan shroud as an assembly.
7. Disconnect engine electrical connectors as necessary.
8. Remove control pressure regulator, leaving fuel lines connected.
9. Disconnect alternator wiring and position out of way.
10. Disconnect electrical connectors of oil pressure switch and coolant temperature sender.
11. Disconnect wiring at ignition coil terminals 1 and 4.
12. Remove heater hose adjacent to ignition coil.
13. Disconnect vacuum hose at retard connection on ignition distributor.
14. Disconnect hoses at intake manifold.
15. Remove throttle cable and the rubber air duct.
16. On vehicles less air conditioning, remove fuel injectors and cold start valve, leaving fuel lines connected and capping injectors and cold start valve.
17. Disconnect hose between auxiliary air regulator and air duct.
18. On all vehicles, remove upper engine to transmission mounting bolts.
19. Remove left and right engine mount attaching nuts.
20. Remove exhaust pipe attaching nuts from manifold, then the pipe.
21. Loosen and remove power steering drive belt, then remove power steering pump, leaving hoses attached, and position out of way.
22. Remove bolts attaching inspection plate and the plate.
23. Disconnect and tag starter electrical connections.
24. Remove starter mounting bolts and the starter.
25. Working through starter mounting hole, remove torque converter attaching bolts.
26. Remove bolts from exhaust pipe hanger and catalytic converter/muffler flange.
27. Remove engine stop attaching bolts and the stop, if not previously removed.
28. Install transmission support bar VW758/1 or equivalent with slight preload.
29. Attach suitable lifting device to engine and lift engine enough to take weight off engine mounts.
30. Adjust support bar to contact transmission housing.
31. Remove engine to transmission attaching bolts and pry engine and transmission apart.
32. Lift engine out of vehicle.
33. Reverse procedure to install, noting the following:
    a. Tighten engine mount and subframe bolts with engine running at idle.

b. Torque bolts and/or nuts as follows: cold start valve, 7 ft. lbs., control pressure regulator, 14 ft. lbs., engine cover plate, 7 ft. lbs., engine to transmission attaching bolts, 40 ft. lbs., engine mount attaching bolts, 25 ft. lbs., engine stop to block attaching bolts, 18 ft. lbs., exhaust pipe hanger, 18 ft. lbs., exhaust pipe to manifold attaching bolts, 22 ft. lbs., power steering pump, 14 ft. lbs., radiator mounting bolts, 7 ft. lbs., starter mounting bolts, 14 ft. lbs., and torque converter mounting bolts, 22 ft. lbs.
c. On vehicles equipped with air conditioning, adjust compressor drive belt by varying number of shims behind outer half of pulley.
d. Torque air conditioner compressor bracket to engine upper bolts to 22 ft. lbs. and lower bolts to 18 ft. lbs.

4 Cylinder Engine W/Manual Transmission

1. Disconnect battery ground cable.
2. Open heater control valve, remove expansion tank cap, and drain cooling system by disconnecting lower hose.
3. Remove upper and lower radiator hoses and disconnect wiring harness connectors from radiator fan and thermo switch.
4. On air conditioned vehicles, remove clips and grille. Remove bolts securing condenser to radiator.
5. Remove upper and lower rubber mounts, then radiator as an assembly with fan and fan shroud.
6. Disconnect clutch cable from transmission and support bracket.
7. Label, then disconnect all electrical connectors from engine.
8. Remove control pressure regulator, leaving fuel lines connected.
9. Remove hose and rear cover on alternator, where equipped, and disconnect wiring harness connections to alternator.
10. Disconnect wiring and heater hoses.
11. Label, then disconnect all vacuum hoses from engine.
12. Remove throttle cable.
13. On air conditioned models, remove air duct from throttle valve housing, air hose at auxiliary air regulator and remove fuel distributor, airflow sensor, fuel injectors, and air cleaner as an assembly.
14. On non-air conditioned models remove fuel injectors and cold start valve. **Leave all fuel lines connected. Protect injectors and cold start valve with caps.**
15. Disconnect hose from auxiliary air regulator.
16. Remove air conditioning compressor as follows:
    a. Remove front engine mount bolts and remove mount.
    b. Loosen nuts on outer half of crankshaft pulley, and remove air conditioning compressor drive belt.
    c. Discharge refrigerant, and disconnect lines from compressor and support bracket. Plug all open lines and ports.
    d. Disconnect wiring harness connector at compressor clutch and crankcase vent hose at valve cover.
    e. Remove upper and lower compressor mount bolts and remove air conditioning compressor from vehicle.
17. Remove upper three bolts securing engine to transmission.
18. Remove nuts securing right and left engine mounts.
19. Disconnect exhaust pipe at manifold and front support and remove pipe.
20. Remove bolts securing flywheel inspection plate and remove plate.
21. On non-air conditioned models, remove bolts securing front engine mount and remove mount.
22. Disconnect wiring harness and battery cable connectors at starter and remove starter.
23. Remove lower two bolts securing engine to transmission, and loosen nuts securing engine mounts to subframe.
24. Support transmission and attach suitable lifting equipment to engine.
25. Raise engine, pry engine and transmission apart, and lift and guide engine from vehicle.
26. Reverse procedure to install, leaving engine mount bolts hand tight. Torque front engine mount bolts to 18 ft. lbs., and left and right bolts to 25 ft. lbs. with engine running at idle.

5 Cylinder Engine W/Automatic Transmission

1. Disconnect battery ground cable.
2. Open heater control valve, remove expansion tank cap, and drain cooling system by disconnecting hose at bottom of radiator.
3. Remove engine/transmission bolt securing coolant pipe, loosen clamp, and disconnect hose from pipe.
4. Remove upper radiator shroud, disconnect radiator hoses and cooling fan connections.
5. Remove bolts securing radiator and remove as an assembly with cooling fan.
6. Disconnect vacuum hoses at brake booster and cruise control transducer.
7. Loosen power steering pump and remove belt. Remove mounting bolts and remove power steering pump, leaving hoses connected.
8. Loosen clamp and remove hose from thermostat housing.
9. Disconnect wiring harness connectors at oil pressure switch and control pressure regulator, remove harness clamps and lay wiring aside.
10. Remove throttle pushrod.
11. Remove control pressure regulator, leaving hoses connected.
12. Loosen clamp and disconnect coolant hose at rear of cylinder head from pipe.
13. Remove bolts securing alternator and lower alternator onto lower radiator cover.
14. Remove alternator bracket and front stop from engine.
15. Loosen clamps and remove air duct.
16. Label, then disconnect all electrical connectors and vacuum hoses from engine.
17. Remove fuel injectors and cold start valve. **Leave all fuel lines connected. Protect injectors and cold start valve with caps.**
18. Remove fuel distributor with air flow sensor plate and disconnect fuel feed and return lines.
19. Disconnect PCV hose at valve cover, release upper air filter housing clips, and remove bolt securing air filter housing.
20. Disconnect wiring harness connectors at points indicated.
21. Disconnect heater hoses and transmission cooler lines, and remove hose flange "C" from engine block.
22. Remove cover from right engine mount, loosen nuts on right and left engine mounts, and remove ground strap from engine mount.
23. Remove all upper engine to transmission bolts except one bolt that is accessible.
24. Disconnect wiring harness connector at oil temperature switch and compressor clutch.
25. Loosen air conditioning compressor adjusting bolts, remove front clamping bolt, and remove bracket on front of engine.
26. Remove upper compressor mounting bolts and remove compressor, leaving hoses connected.
27. Disconnect wiring harness and battery cable connectors from starter motor.
28. Remove both front subframe bolts.
29. Disconnect exhaust pipe at manifold and front bracket and remove pipe.
30. Remove bolts securing starter, then the starter motor.
31. Remove three bolts securing torque converter to drive plate through starter hole.
32. Remove lower bolts securing engine to transmission.
33. Disconnect shift rod at transmission.
34. Support transmission and attach suitable lifting equipment to engine.
35. Remove remaining bolt securing engine to transmission, raise engine and pry engine from transmission.
36. Continue to lift engine, while turning to left, and guide engine from vehicle.
37. Reverse procedure to install, leaving engine mount bolts hand tight. Torque engine mount bolts to 32 ft. lbs. with engine running at idle.

5 Cylinder Engine W/Manual Transmission

1. Disconnect battery ground cable.
2. Open heater control valve, remove expansion tank cap, and drain coolant by disconnecting lower radiator hose at radiator.
3. Loosen clamp and remove coolant hose from pipe, then remove engine to transmission attaching bolt securing pipe.
4. Remove upper radiator shroud and upper radiator hose.
5. Disconnect vacuum hose at brake booster.
6. Remove belt cover from power steer-

ing pump, then the power steering pump attaching bolts.
7. Disconnect vacuum hose at cruise control vacuum unit, if equipped.
8. Loosen and remove drive belts, then remove power steering pump, leaving hoses connected, and lay pump in cowl.
9. Disconnect coolant hose at thermostat housing.
10. Disconnect electrical connectors at oil pressure switch and control pressure regulator and position wiring out of way.
11. Disconnect clutch cable.
12. Remove upper engine to transmission attaching bolts, except one that is accessible.
13. Remove control pressure regulator, leaving fuel lines attached.
14. Loosen clamp and disconnect coolant hose from pipe adjacent to control pressure regulator.
15. Remove lower grill.
16. Remove engine stop bolts and the engine stop.
17. Remove upper and lower timing belt covers.
18. Attach tool 2084 or equivalent to crankshaft pulley.
19. Attach tool 2079 or equivalent to crankshaft bolt through grille panel opening and remove crankshaft bolt.
20. Remove two drive belt pulley bolts and loosen other two.
21. Tap two remaining bolts lightly and remove bolts, then remove pulley. **Leave drive belt sprocket attached to crankshaft.**
22. Remove adjusting bolt from alternator bracket.
23. Remove upper alternator bolt and lower alternator into lower radiator cover, leaving wires connected.
24. Remove alternator bracket from engine.
25. Loosen clamps and remove air duct.
26. Remove distributor vacuum unit hoses and disconnect coil high tension lead, electrical connector at cold start valve and wiring harness.
27. Pull out fuel injectors and remove cold start valve and wiring harness.
28. Remove fuel distributor with air flow sensor plate.
29. Disconnect fuel feed and return lines.
30. Disconnect PCV hose at valve cover, release upper air filter housing clips, and remove bolt securing air filter housing.
31. Disconnect wiring harness connectors.
32. Remove cover from right engine mount, loosen nuts on left and right engine mounts, and remove ground strap from engine mount.
33. On vehicles equipped with air conditioning, proceed as follows:
    a. Loosen compressor drive belt adjusting bolts.
    b. Disconnect oil temperature switch electrical connector.
    c. Loosen bolt accessible through front grille opening.
    d. Remove bracket from engine block and disconnect compressor clutch electrical connector.
    e. Remove upper compressor attaching bolts and tie compressor out of way, leaving hoses attached.
34. Disconnect starter electrical connectors and position out of way.
35. Remove two front subframe bolts.
36. Remove nuts attaching exhaust pipe to manifold and the exhaust pipe hanger bolt.
37. Remove starter, then the lower engine to transmission attaching bolts.
38. Install transmission supporting tool VW785/1 or equivalent, attach suitable engine lifting device, and adjust support tool to contact transmission.
39. Remove remaining upper engine to transmission attaching bolt and the left side engine bracket.
40. Lift engine slightly, pry engine and transmission apart, and lift engine out while turning to left.
41. Reverse procedure to install, noting the following:
    a. Coat mainshaft splines with suitable lubricant.
    b. When installing drive belt pulley, align with mark on drive belt sprocket.
    c. Coat threads and contact surface of crankshaft bolt with suitable locking compound.
    d. Torque bolts and/or nuts as follows: A/C compressor to engine, 29 ft. lbs., alternator to engine and bracket, 14 ft. lbs., cold start valve, 7 ft. lbs., control pressure regulator, 14 ft. lbs., crankshaft bolt, 253 ft. lbs., engine stop on body/block, 32 ft. lbs., engine mounts, 32 ft. lbs., engine to transmission bolts, M8 14 ft. lbs., M10 32 ft. lbs., and M12 43 ft. lbs., exhaust pipe to manifold, 22 ft. lbs., exhaust pipe support, 22 ft. lbs., power steering pump, 14 ft. lbs., starter, 14 ft. lbs., subframe to body, 51 ft. lbs., and drive belt pulley, 14 ft. lbs.

5000 LESS TURBO

1. Disconnect battery ground cable.
2. Remove cap from expansion tank, and disconnect hose from bottom of tank. Drain into a suitable container.
3. On air conditioned vehicles, put temperature lever in cold position. On models without air conditioning, open heater valve.
4. Disconnect hose and drain coolant. Disconnect all other hoses from radiator.
5. Remove control pressure regulator, cold start valve, and fuel injectors. **Leave all fuel lines connected. Protect injectors and cold start valve with caps.**
6. Disconnect air duct and vacuum hoses from throttle valve and remove air cleaner cover with filter.
7. Disconnect hood latch cable from guide bracket.
8. On air conditioned vehicles, remove grille and bolts securing condenser.
9. Remove upper radiator shroud, where equipped, disconnect wiring harness connectors from cooling fan and thermo switch, and remove radiator as an assembly with cooling fan.
10. Remove bolts securing power steering pump and pump, leaving hoses connected.
11. Remove vacuum amplifier, ignition coil and EGR control valve.
12. Remove windshield washer and power steering reservoirs from holders.
13. Remove distributor cap, wires and distributor rotor. Tape dust cover in place.
14. Disconnect throttle cable on manual transmission models, and remove throttle rod on automatic transmission models.
15. Disconnect wiring harness connectors at distributor, oil pressure sending unit, water temperature sending unit, and air conditioning compressor clutch.
16. Remove bolts securing air conditioning compressor and compressor, leaving hoses connected.
17. Disconnect exhaust pipe from manifold and front bracket.
18. Remove front engine mount.
19. Remove alternator, leaving wiring harness connected.
20. Disconnect wiring harness and battery cable connectors from starter, then remove starter motor.
21. On automatic transmission models, remove bolts securing torque converter to drive plate through starter motor hole.
22. Remove lower bolts securing engine to transmission.
23. Support transmission and remove upper bolts securing engine to transmission.
24. Attach suitable lifting equipment to engine.
25. Remove left engine bracket and nut securing right bracket to engine mount.
26. Raise engine slightly until lower pulley is opposite grille opening.
27. Separate engine from transmission, raise engine, and turn to right while lifting.
28. Reverse procedure to install, note the following:
    a. On vehicles with manual transmission, coat mainshaft splines with suitable lubricant.
    b. Tighten engine mounts to subframe while engine is idling.
    c. Ensure that metal lip on gasket between exhaust manifold and exhaust pipe faces exhaust pipe.
    d. Torque bolts and/or nuts as follows: A/C compressor to engine, 29 ft. lbs., alternator to engine and bracket, 14 ft. lbs., cold start valve, 7 ft. lbs., control pressure regulator, 14 ft. lbs., crankshaft bolt, 253 ft. lbs., engine stop on body/block, 32 ft. lbs., engine mounts, 32 ft. lbs., engine to transmission bolts, M8 14 ft. lbs., M10 32 ft. lbs., and M12 43 ft. lbs., exhaust pipe to manifold, 22 ft. lbs., exhaust pipe support, 22 ft. lbs., power steering pump, 14 ft. lbs., starter, 14 ft. lbs., subframe to body, 51 ft. lbs., and drive belt pulley, 14 ft. lbs.

5000 TURBO

1. Disconnect battery ground cable.

2. Remove cap from expansion tank and drain coolant by disconnecting lower radiator hose.
3. Remove bolt from coolant pipe.
4. Remove upper radiator hose, disconnect radiator thermoswitch electrical connector and disconnect heater hose at engine.
5. Disconnect vacuum hose at brake booster.
6. Remove belt cover from power steering pump, loosen and remove power steering drive belt, remove power steering pump, leaving hoses connected, and lay pump in cowl.
7. Disconnect electrical connectors from oil pressure switch, temperature sending unit and control pressure regulator.
8. Remove control pressure regulator, leaving fuel lines attached, and loosen vacuum hose adjacent to control pressure regulator.
9. Disconnect accelerator cable and linkage.
10. Remove windshield washer reservoir.
11. Disconnect electrical connectors at throttle valve switch, cold start valve, auxiliary air regulator, boost pressure safety switch, ignition coil, 2-way valve, thermo time switch, and ignition distributor.
12. Disconnect vacuum hoses at thermo pneumatic valve, and the vacuum hose at distributor retard.
13. Remove distributor cap.
14. Disconnect vacuum hoses at intake manifold and delay valve.
15. Remove cold start valve and pull out fuel injectors, leaving fuel lines connected.
16. Remove intake air duct and hose/pipe connection to turbocharger.
17. Disconnect fuel return line.
18. Disconnect fuel supply line at gas filter, then remove the filter.
19. Remove fuel distributor and air flow sensor as an assembly.
20. Remove A/C compressor mounting bolts and tie compressor out of way, leaving hoses connected.
21. Remove front engine mount.
22. Remove upper engine to transmission attaching bolts except the easiest one to reach.
23. Disconnect exhaust pipe at turbocharger and remove heat shield.
24. Disconnect exhaust pipe at wastegate, remove transmission bracket, and disconnect exhaust pipe at catalytic converter.
25. Remove starter and position out of way, leaving wiring connected.
26. Disconnect oil temperature switch electrical connector.
27. On vehicles equipped with automatic transmission, remove torque converter mounting bolts through starter mounting hole.
28. Remove air guide cover for oil cooler and the air guide hose for engine mount.
29. Disconnect oil lines at oil cooler, then remove lower engine to transmission attaching bolts.
30. Remove alternator with bracket and position out of way, leaving wiring connected.
31. Remove left and right engine mount nuts.
32. Install transmission support tool VW785/1 or equivalent with slight preload.
33. Attach suitable lifting device to engine.
34. Loosen ground strap on and remove left engine bracket.
35. Remove remaining upper engine to transmission attaching bolt.
36. Lift engine until wastegate is above water cowl panel, then turn disc of supporting tool until it touches transmission housing.
37. Turn engine toward right while lifting, then turn engine 90° and lift out.
38. On vehicles equipped with automatic transmission, secure torque converter using tool VW540 or equivalent.
39. Reverse procedure to install, noting the following:
    a. Tighten engine mounts to side frame while engine is idling.
    b. Ensure that metal lip on gasket between manifold and exhaust pipe faces exhaust.
    c. Torque bolts and/or nuts as described under "5000 Less Turbo."

QUATTRO COUPE

1. Disconnect battery ground cable.
2. Open heater control valve, remove cap from expansion tank, and drain coolant by disconnecting lower radiator hose.
3. Remove intake hose from injector cooling blower motor.
4. Remove upper radiator cover screws and the cover, then the upper radiator hose.
5. Disconnect coolant fan electrical connector, then remove coolant hose between radiator and expansion tank.
6. Remove bleeder hose to auxiliary radiator, then disconnect thermoswitch electrical connector.
7. Remove radiator mountings, then the right side and bottom radiator covers.
8. Remove windshield washer reservoir.
9. Disconnect refrigerant lines at A/C condenser, then remove radiator and condenser as an assembly.
10. Remove upper compressor mounting bracket attaching bolts and the compressor to bracket attaching bolts, then remove compressor and bracket.
11. Remove power steering pump and its drive belt, positioning pump out of way without disconnecting hoses.
12. Disconnect coolant hose at thermostat housing.
13. Disconnect electrical connectors at oil pressure switch, temperature gauge sender, and control pressure regulator.
14. Remove injector cooling air distributor, hose and motor.
15. Remove control pressure regulator, leaving fuel lines attached.
16. Remove throttle cable.
17. Remove holder for injector lines and pull out injectors.
18. Disconnect electrical connector and remove cold start valve, leaving fuel line connected.
19. Disconnect electrical connectors of the two throttle valve switches and intake temperature switch, then disconnect air intake hose and position wiring out of way.
20. Disconnect electrical connector of auxiliary air regulator, the vacuum hoses, engine breather hose, and the electrical connector of the injector cooling fan and position wiring out of way.
21. Disconnect vacuum hoses of two way valve.
22. Remove thermo pneumatic valve, leaving vacuum hoses connected.
23. Remove RPM sensor, then disconnect speedometer cable at transmission.
24. Remove distributor and the No. 4 ignition wire from the distributor.
25. Disconnect electrical connector for Hall sender at distributor, then the connectors for the thermotime switch and overheating warning lamp.
26. Disconnect heater hoses from engine.
27. Disconnect hydraulic brake booster with reservoir from motor mount, leaving lines connected.
28. Disconnect electrical connectors for differential lock control lights and back-up light switch.
29. Disconnect tie rod bracket on steering rack.
30. Disconnect shift linkage.
31. Remove clutch slave cylinder, leaving hydraulic line connected, then the bracket and pin from the transmission. **Do not operate clutch pedal after removing slave cylinder.**
32. Disconnect ground strap from left engine mount and the vacuum hose from the auxiliary air valve.
33. Remove oil cooler air duct, then the intercooler.
34. Disconnect alternator electrical connectors.
35. Remove oil cooler, leaving lines connected, then disconnect starter electrical connectors.
36. Disconnect exhaust pipe at flange.
37. Remove transmission cover plates and right side transmission mount.
38. Disconnect axle shafts at transmission.
39. Disconnect differential lock cable by removing front and rear circlip, pushing back boot, and disconnecting cable from mounting.
40. Remove transmission mounting bolt, then the transmission mounts.
41. Remove attaching bolts for ball joints.
42. Disconnect rear subframe mounts.
43. Remove front subframe mounting bolts, then remove subframe and press ball joint out of strut.
44. Attach suitable lifting device to engine lift points and lift slightly.
45. Remove side engine mounts and lower engine and transmission assembly.
46. Raise and support vehicle and remove assembly from under vehicle, then separate engine from transmission.
47. Reverse procedure to install, torquing nuts and/or bolts as follows:
    a. Cold start valve and M6 intercool-

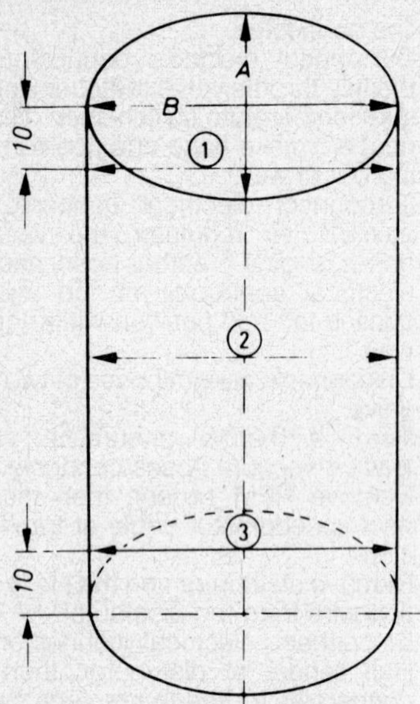

— measure at points 1, 2 and 3 first in direction **A** then direction **B**

1 = 10 mm (3/8 in.) from top

2 = middle of cylinder wall

3 = 10 mm (3/8 in.) from bottom

• piston to cylinder clearance; new part 0.025 mm (0.001 in.) wear limit: 0.08 mm (0.003 in.)

Fig. 1 Cylinder bore checking dimensions

er, 7 ft. lbs.

b. Control pressure regulator, hydraulic brake servo to engine mount, ground strap to engine mount, and M8 intercooler, 14 ft. lbs.
c. Exhaust pipe flange, 18 ft. lbs.
d. M8 engine to transmission, exhaust pipe to transmission mount, and oil cooler, 22 ft. lbs.
e. Tie rod bracket to steering rack and engine mount to body, 29 ft. lbs.
f. M10 engine to transmission, driveshaft to transmission, and transmission mount, 32 ft. bs.
g. Ball joint to strut, 36 ft. lbs.
h. M12 engine to transmission, 43 ft. lbs.
i. Subframe to body, 51 ft. lbs.
j. Axle shafts to transmission, 58 ft. lbs.

ENGINE OVERHAUL

When conducting the following engine disassembly and assembly procedures, place disassembled components neatly on a clean workbench or equivalent. Lubricate all seals, or when specified to do so. Note location of the different size attaching bolts used and do not interchange or use substandard bolts. Ensure to correctly align timing marks when removing the timing belt, camshaft and cylinder head assembly use caution as not to disturb the alignment marks during assembly. Due to the overhead camshaft design of the 4 and 5 cylinder engines, do not rotate crankshaft when these components are removed or serious engine damage will result.

	Piston Diameter	Cylinder Bore
Standard	3.1291 inches (79.48mm)	3.1303 inches (79.51mm)
	3.1295 inches (79.49mm)	3.1307 inches (79.52mm)
	3.1299 inches (79.50mm)	3.1311 inches (79.53mm)
1st Oversize	3.1390 inches (79.73mm)	3.1402 inches (79.76mm)
	3.1394 inches (79.74mm)	3.1405 inches (79.77mm)
	3.1398 inches (79.75mm)	3.1409 inches (79.78mm)
2nd Oversize	3.1488 inches (79.98mm)	3.1500 inches (80.01mm)
	3.1492 inches (79.99mm)	3.1504 inches (80.02mm)
	3.1496 inches (80.00mm)	3.1508 inches (80.03mm)
3rd Oversize	3.1685 inches (80.48mm)	3.1697 inches (80.51mm)
	3.1689 inches (80.49mm)	3.1701 inches (80.52mm)
	3.1693 inches (80.50mm)	3.1705 inches (80.53mm)

Fig. 2 Piston & cylinder dimension chart. 1983 4 cylinder engine

4 CYLINDER ENGINE

REAR CRANKSHAFT OIL SEAL, REPLACE

1. Remove transmission from vehicle.
2. Remove flywheel.
3. Using suitable tool, remove oil seal.
4. Reverse procedure to install, coating sealing lips of new seal with oil.

FRONT CRANKSHAFT OIL SEAL, REPLACE EXC. LATE MODELS W/1700cc ENGINE

1. Remove fan belt, then the upper drive belt cover.
2. Set crankshaft at TDC.
3. Remove fan belt pulley and loosen drive belt sprocket. To remove drive belt sprocket bolt and pulley, have assistant engage 4th gear and apply service brake.
4. Remove water pump pulley, then the lower drive belt cover.
5. Loosen drive belt and remove belt and drive belt sprocket as an assembly.
6. Reverse procedure to install noting the following:
   a. Coat sealing lips of new seal with oil.
   b. Using sprocket bolt washer between bolt head and tool 10-203 or equivalent, press seal to a depth of .079 inch below outer edge of cover.

FRONT CRANKSHAFT OIL SEAL, REPLACE LATE MODELS W/1700cc ENGINE

1. Follow same procedure as for earlier models, noting the following:
   a. Insert bolt of tool 3083 or equivalent in crankshaft to guide seal extractor tool 2085 or equivalent and remove old oil seal.
   b. Slide sleeve of tool 3083 or equivalent onto crankcase journal.
   c. Dip new seal in engine oil and slide over sleeve.
   d. Slide thrust sleeve over guide sleeve and press in seal with thrust sleeve and bolt until fully seated.

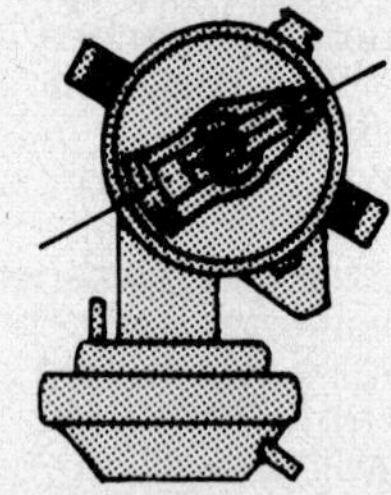

Fig. 3 Setting distributor to adjust valve timing. 4 cylinder engine

MAIN & ROD BEARINGS

Main bearing clearance should be .001-.003 inch, crankshaft end play should be .003-.007 inch measured at main bearing No. 3, connecting rod bearing clearance should be .0011-.0034 inch, and connecting rod side clearance should not exceed .015 inch. Main bearing journals are available in undersizes of 2.1248, 2.1051 and 2.0953 inches. Connecting rod journals are available in undersizes of 1.8000, 1.7902 and 1.7803 inches. Main and connecting rod bearing shells are available in .010, .020 and .030 inch undersizes.

PISTON & ROD ASSEMBLY

Connecting rods are installed so that forged marks point toward front of engine. Pistons are installed with arrow pointing toward timing gear.

PISTONS, PINS & RINGS

Piston ring end gap should be .012-.018 inch. Piston ring side clearance should be .0008-.002 inch. When installing piston rings, ensure that "TOP" mark faces up, that recessed edge on outside of center ring faces piston pin, and that ring end gaps are spaced 120° apart. When checking cylinder clearance, refer to **Fig. 1.** Available piston and cylinder sizes for 1983 are shown in **Fig. 2.** For 1984-87 models, piston diameters are as follows: standard, 3.1882 inches (80.98 mm); 1st oversize, 3.1980 inches (81.23 mm); 2nd oversize, 3.2079 inches (81.48 mm) and cylinder bore diameters are as follows: standard, 3.1894 inches (81.01 mm); 2nd oversize, 3.2090 inches (81.51 mm).

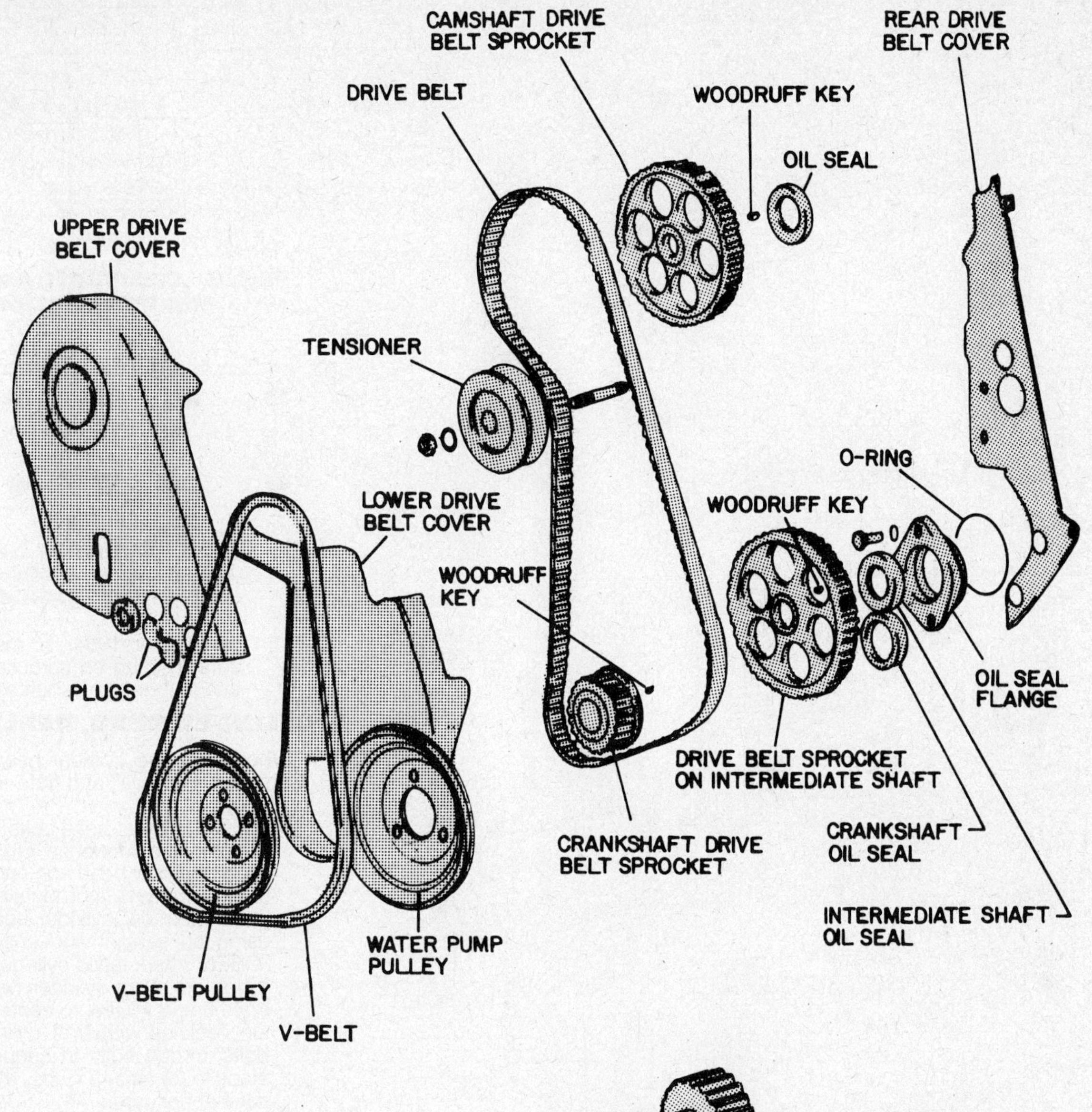

Fig. 4 Camshaft & crankshaft drive exploded view. 1983 4 cylinder engine shown, 1984–87 similar

VALVE TIMING, ADJUST

Adjust valve timing whenever drive belt is removed or replaced. If timing belt requires removal, do not rotate crankshaft with belt removed.

1. Rotate crankshaft until No . 1 cylinder is positioned at TDC. This is accomplished by aligning pointer on crankcase alignment tab with "O" mark on flywheel assembly. **Both intake and exhaust valve for No. 1 cylinder should be in the closed position.**
2. Rotate intermediate shaft until distributor rotor points to mark on distributor housing as shown in **Fig. 3.**
3. Ensure all marks are correctly aligned, then carefully tighten distributor attaching bolts. After tightening attaching bolts, ensure crankshaft and intermediate shaft are still correctly aligned.
4. Turn camshaft until mark is in line with upper edge of rear drive belt cover.

VALVES, ADJUST

1984-87 vehicles use hydraulic valve lifters.

1. Run engine until coolant temperature is approximately 95°F.
2. Disconnect accelerator linkage.
3. Remove upper drive belt cover and the cylinder head cover.
4. Turn crankshaft pulley bolt clockwise until cam lobes of cylinder to be adjusted point up.
5. Using a suitable feeler gauge measure valve clearances.
6. On engines with mechanical valve lifters, clearance should be .008-.012 inch for intake valve or .016-.020 inch for exhaust valve. If clearance obtained is not as specified, replace adjusting disc with thinner or thicker disc as necessary.
7. On engines with hydraulic valve lifters, clearance should be .006-.010 inch for intake valve or .014-.018 inch for exhaust valve. A noisy hydraulic valve lifter will indicate excessive clearance, replace valve lifter(s) as required.

CAMSHAFT, REPLACE

When replacing camshaft, refer to **Figs.**

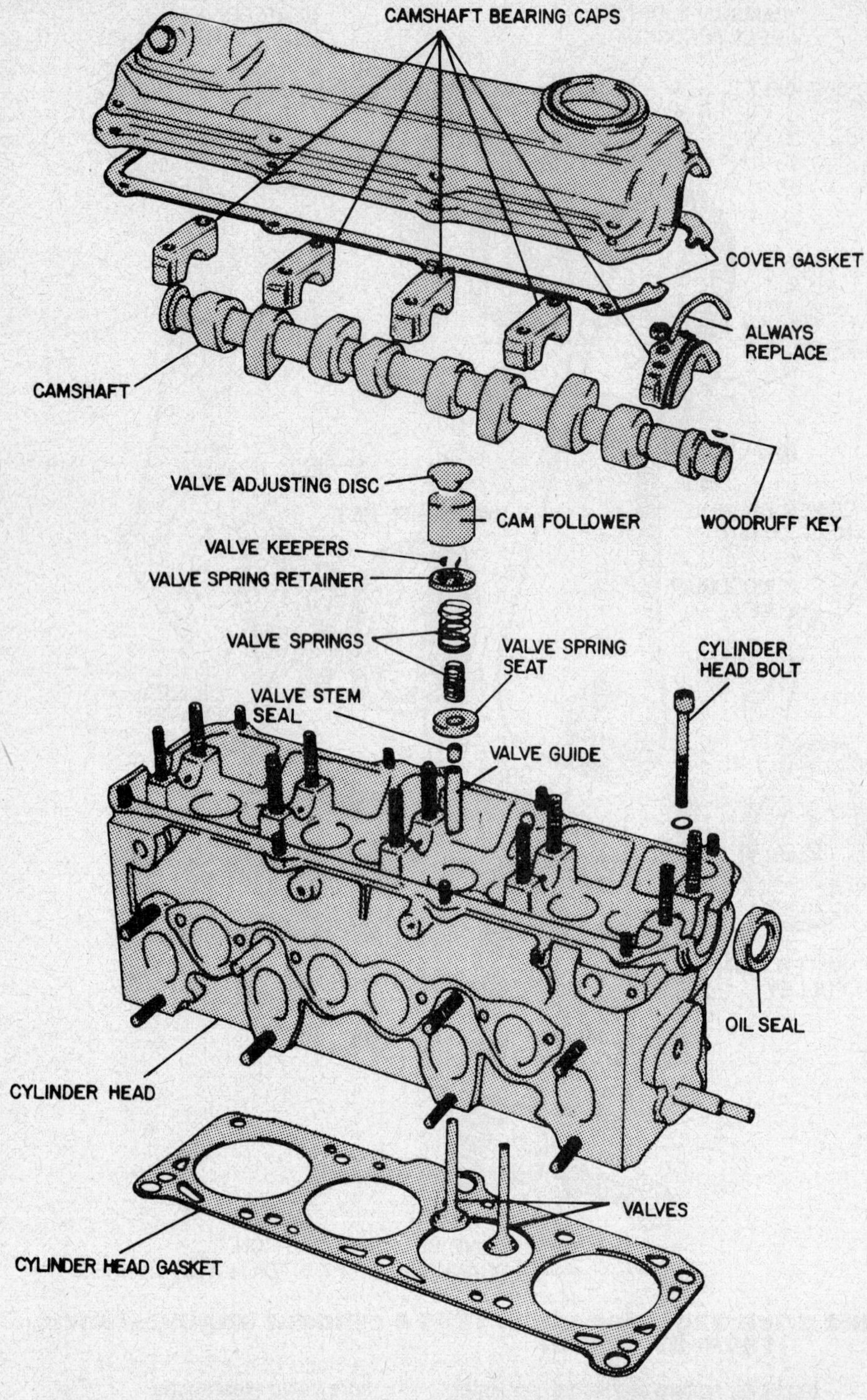

Fig. 5 Cylinder head exploded view. 1983 4 cylinder engine shown, 1984–87 similar

4 and 5, noting the following:

1. Ensure that camshaft end play does not exceed .006 inch with cam followers or hydraulic lifters removed.
2. When removing camshaft bearing caps on 1983 models, first remove caps 1, 3 and 5, then diagonally loosen caps 2 and 4. On 1984-87 models, first remove caps 1, 3 and 4, then loosen cap 2.
3. When installing camshaft bearing caps, note the following:
   a. Lubricate bearing surfaces and camshaft journals.
   b. Install caps in proper order, observing off center position, **Fig. 6.**
   c. On 1983 models, lightly and carefully tighten caps 2 and 4 diagonally before installing caps 5, 1 and 3, then torque all bearing cap nuts to 14 ft. lbs.
   d. On 1984-87 models, lightly and carefully tighten bearing cap 2 before installing caps 4, 1 and 3, then torque all bearing cap nuts to 14 ft. lbs.
   e. When installing crankshaft drive belt sprocket on late model 1700cc engines or 1984-87 models, ensure that lug on sprocket is fitted into slot on crankshaft assembly.

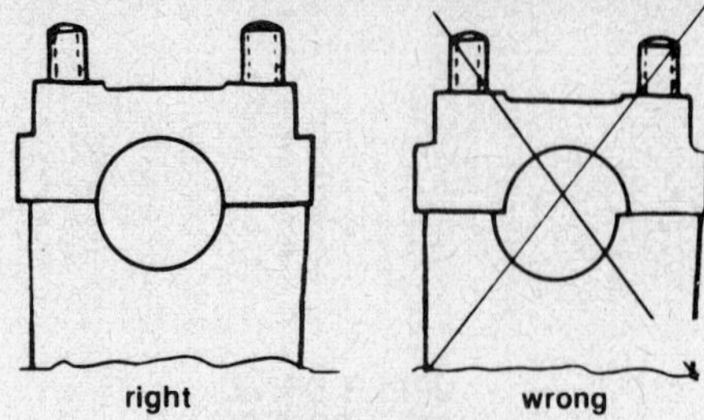

Fig. 6 Camshaft bearing cap installation

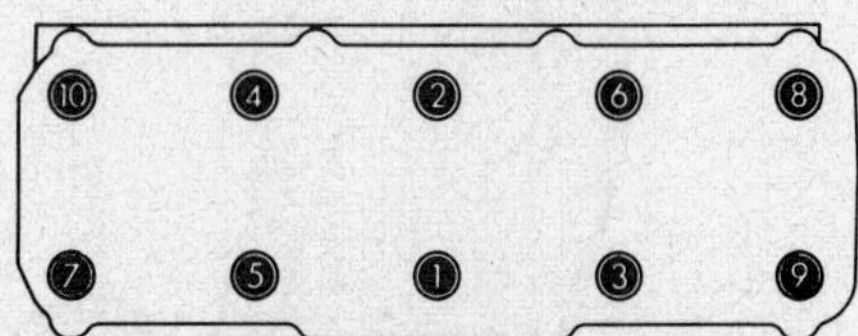

Fig. 7 Cylinder head tightening sequence. 4 cylinder engine

CYLINDER HEAD, REPLACE

When replacing cylinder head, refer to "Camshaft, Replace" and note the following:

1. Loosen cylinder head bolts in reverse of tightening sequence, **Fig. 7.**
2. Clean cylinder head and engine block mating surfaces thoroughly.
3. Install new dry cylinder head gasket using no sealant and ensuring that "OBEN" mark faces cylinder head.
4. When installing cylinder head, insert bolts 8 and 10 first to center head.
5. On vehicles with M11 cylinder head bolts, torque bolts in sequence in 3 steps to 29 and 43 ft. lbs., then an additional half turn.
6. On vehicles with cylinder head bolts other than M11, torque bolts in sequence in 4 steps to 29, 43, and 54 ft. lbs., then an additional quarter turn.

VALVE GUIDES

Worn valve guides can be removed using tool 10-206 or equivalent. Press worn guides out from combustion chamber side of cylinder head. Coat new guides with engine oil and press into cold cylinder head from camshaft side. Press guides in as far as they will go. Ream guides by hand using proper cutting lubricant. Once valve guide shoulder is seated, do not use more than one ton pressure or guide shoulder may break.

OIL PAN, REPLACE

1. Remove oil pan drain plug and drain oil.
2. Support engine using tool 10-222 or equivalent.
3. Remove cover plate from under engine.
4. Remove four bolts from subframe, then lower subframe.

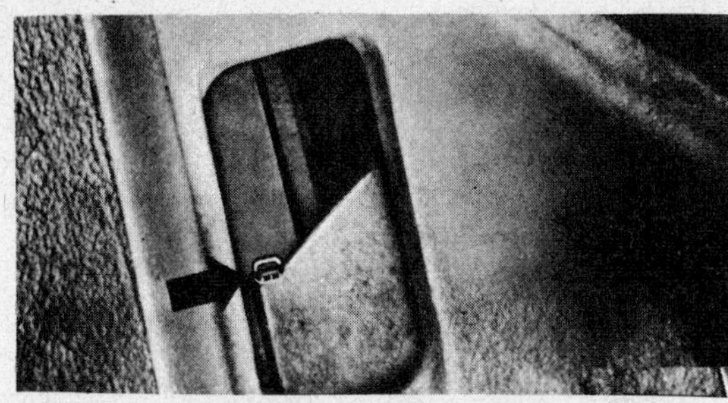

Fig. 8 Crankshaft timing marks. 5 cylinder engine

Fig. 9 Crankshaft timing marks. 5 cylinder engine

Fig. 10 Cylinder head bolt torque sequence. 5 cylinder engines

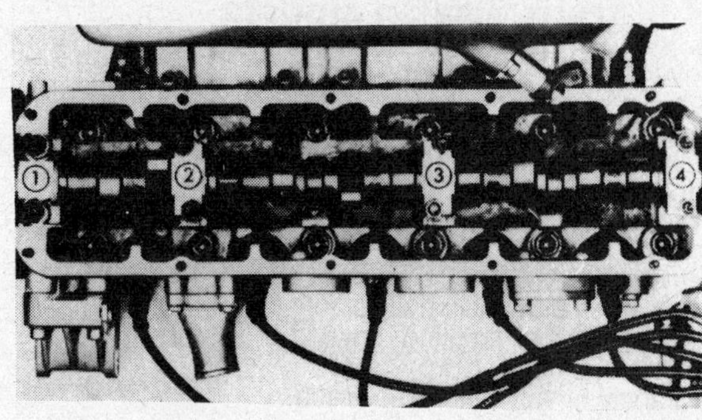

Fig. 11 Camshaft bearing cap removal

5. Remove oil pan.
6. Reverse procedure to install, torquing oil pan attaching bolts to 7 ft. lbs. and the drain plug to 22 ft. lbs.

WATER PUMP, REPLACE

1. Drain cooling system.
2. Loosen alternator adjusting bolt, then remove alternator drive belt.
3. Remove water pump pulley attaching bolts, then the pulley.
4. Remove water pump to housing attaching bolts and the water pump.
5. Reverse procedure to install.

5 CYLINDER ENGINE

DISASSEMBLY

1. Drain engine oil and coolant into a suitable container. Remove all engine accessories, brackets and mounts, camshaft cover, and timing belt cover.
2. Rotate engine until mark on flywheel, **Fig. 8,** is aligned with mark on clutch housing, and mark on camshaft sprocket, **Fig. 9,** is aligned with upper edge of gasket surface on cylinder head.
3. Loosen bolts securing water pump to engine block and rotate pump counterclockwise to loosen belt.
4. Remove timing belt, bolts securing water pump and water pump. **Do not rotate crankshaft or camshaft independently as engine damage may result.**
5. Remove bolts securing cylinder head working from outside toward center in reverse of tightening sequence, **Fig. 10.**

Crankshaft & Cylinder Block Disassembly

1. Remove bolt securing crankshaft pulley, pulley and belt drive sprocket.
2. Remove oil pan, oil pump pickup and pickup tube.
3. Remove bolts securing oil pump, then the pump.
4. Using a suitable punch, mark connecting rods and caps with matching marks to aid assembly.
5. Remove connecting rod cap retaining nuts and remove cap and bearing.
6. Remove piston/connecting rod assemblies through cylinder head side of block, using a suitable drift. **Keep pistons, connecting rods, rod caps and bearings in correct order.**
7. Remove piston rings using a ring expander.
8. Remove piston pin retainers, piston pins and pistons from connecting rods.
9. Measure pistons approximately 5/8 inch from lower edge at 90° angle to piston axis.
10. Measure cylinder bores as shown in **Fig. 1.** If difference between measurements exceeds piston clearance specifications, new pistons must be fitted to bores.
11. Mark position of flywheel in relation to crankshaft and remove flywheel.
12. Remove bolts securing rear engine cover and remove rear cover and seal.
13. Note markings on main bearing caps, remove bolts securing main bearing caps, and remove caps along with lower main bearings.
14. Remove crankshaft from cylinder block and remove upper main bearings. **Keep main bearings and bearing caps in correct order.**

Cylinder Head Disassembly

1. Diagonally loosen camshaft bearing caps 2 and 4, **Fig. 11,** and remove caps.
2. Diagonally remove camshaft bearing caps 1 and 3, **Fig. 11,** and remove caps.
3. Remove camshaft and followers, or hydraulic lifters, keeping followers lifters in correct order.
4. Using suitable tool, compress valve springs and remove locks.
5. Remove valve springs, retainers and spring seats.
6. Remove valves and valve stem seals.
7. Press worn valve guides out of cylinder head from combustion chamber side.

ASSEMBLY

Cylinder Head Assembly

1. Coat new guides with oil and press into cylinder head from camshaft side as far as they will go.
2. Ream new guides to specifications using a hand reamer.
3. Insert valve in cylinder head and install valve stem seal using a suitable tool.
4. Install valve spring seat, valve springs and spring retainer. Compress valve springs and install locking collets.
5. Place cam followers or hydraulic lift-

Fig. 12 Flywheel installation. Automatic transmission models

Fig. 13 Piston installation

Fig. 14 Connecting rod installation marks

ers over valve springs and install camshaft.

6. Lubricate camshaft bearing caps and journals and install bearing caps, noting off center bearing position, **Fig. 6.**
7. First lightly tighten nuts of bearing caps 2 and 4, **Fig. 11,** diagonally, then tighten all nuts to 14 ft. lbs.
8. Rotate camshaft until valve is fully closed, cam lobe pointing upward, and check clearance.
9. If clearance is not within specifications on models less hydraulic lifters, adjustment disc in top of cam follower will have to be replaced.
10. Depress cam follower using suitable tools and remove adjusting disc.
11. Measure disc and replace with one of the correct size to restore proper clearance.

Crankshaft & Cylinder Block Assembly

1. Install upper main bearings in cylinder block. Upper main bearings contain oil grooves, and thrust bearing is No. 4 from drive belt end of engine.
2. Lubricate crankshaft journals and upper main bearings with assembly lubricant and install crankshaft.
3. Install nongrooved lower main bearings into main bearing caps and lubricate bearings with assembly lubricant.
4. Install main bearing caps in correct order with reference number toward oil filter side of engine.
5. Torque main bearing cap bolts to specification evenly, working from center toward outside.
6. Check that crankshaft rotates smoothly and end play is within specifications.
7. Install new seal in rear cover and install cover and seal assembly.
8. Align reference marks between flywheel and crankshaft and install flywheel.
9. On automatic transmission models, notch on outer washer (1), **Fig. 12,** must face converter. Distance between drive plate must measure .677-.741 inch, and can be adjusted by thickness of shim (2), **Fig. 12.**
10. Install new seal in oil pump and install oil pump making sure crankshaft engages oil pump gears correctly.
11. Install oil pump pickup and oil pan, using new gaskets.
12. Insert piston pin through piston and connecting rod and secure with pin retainers.
13. Install piston rings using a ring expander. "Top" marking must face piston crown, recessed edge on outside of center ring must face piston pin.
14. Insert bearing half in connecting rod big end and lubricate bearing and crankshaft journal with assembly lubricant.
15. Install piston/connecting rod combination with arrows on piston crown, **Fig. 13,** toward drive belt side and marks on connecting rod, **Fig. 14,** toward oil filter side of engine.
16. Insert bearing half in connecting rod cap, lubricate bearing, and install cap.
17. Torque connecting rod cap retaining nuts to specifications.
18. Install belt drive sprocket and crankshaft pulley, torquing bolt to 235 ft. lbs.

FINAL ASSEMBLY

1. Align timing marks on camshaft and cylinder head, **Fig. 9,** and on flywheel and clutch housing, **Fig. 8,** before installing cylinder head.
2. Install cylinder head and torque bolts to specifications in sequence, **Fig. 10.**
3. Install water pump with bolts hand tight.
4. With timing marks aligned, install camshaft drive belt and adjust tension by rotating water pump clockwise. Tighten water pump bolts.
5. Belt is properly adjusted when it can be twisted 90°, by hand, in run between camshaft and water pump sprockets.
6. Reverse procedure to install remaining components.

TURBOCHARGER

The turbocharger is an exhaust driven device which compresses the air/fuel mixture that is used to increase engine power on a demand basis, allowing a smaller, more economical engine to be used.

A turbine in the exhaust gas flow is connected through a shaft to the impeller (compressor). During normal, steady operation, the turbine does not rotate with sufficient speed to boost pressure to compress the air/fuel mixture. As speed increases, the mixture is compressed, allowing the denser mixture to enter the combustion chambers and develop more engine power during the combustion cycle.

The intake manifold pressure (boost) is controlled by a wastegate valve which is used to bypass a portion of the exhaust gases around the turbine at a predetermined point in the cycle, limiting the boost pressure.

DIESEL ENGINE SECTION

INDEX

ENGINE

REPLACE

4000

1. Disconnect battery ground cable.
2. Remove engine and transmission cover plates.
3. Open heater control valve, remove cap from expansion tank, and drain coolant by disconnecting lower hose at thermostat housing and lower radiator hose at radiator.
4. On vehicles equipped with air conditioning, remove radiator cowl attaching bolts, cowl and both fans as an assembly. Remove front grille and condenser from radiator.
5. On vehicles less air conditioning, disconnect electrical connectors at thermoswitch and fan, then remove radiator with fan.
6. On all vehicles, disconnect fuel supply and return lines at injection pump.
7. Disconnect accelerator cable at injection pump and detach bracket from pump body.
8. Disconnect cold start cable at pin and remove retaining washer from bracket.
9. Disconnect electrical connector at fuel shut off solenoid.
10. Remove gearshift light switch, with wiring, from bracket.
11. Disconnect electrical connectors of oil pressure switch, both coolant temperature sensors, all glow plugs and thermoswitch.
12. Disconnect coolant hose located between coolant temperature sensors.
13. Loosen clutch cable at bracket and unhook cable from clutch lever.
14. Remove upper engine mount attaching bolts.
15. Disconnect vacuum pump to reservoir vacuum hose at reservoir.
16. Remove alternator, then the engine stop attaching bolts and engine stop.
17. On vehicles equipped with air conditioning, proceed as follows:
    a. Remove compressor pulley attaching bolts, then the compressor drive belt.
    b. Remove compressor brackets from engine, then tie compressor out of way so that hoses are not under tension.
18. Disconnect exhaust pipe at manifold.
19. Disconnect starter cable at starter and detach at intermediate plate.
20. Disconnect exhaust pipe at hanger.
21. Remove starter and place on engine carrier.
22. Remove two lower engine to transmission attaching bolts, then the flywheel cover plate bolts.
23. Install transmission support tool VW785/1B or equivalent.
24. Attach suitable lifting device to engine and lift engine/transmission assembly until transmission housing touches steering rack.
25. Adjust transmission support tool so that it contacts transmission.
26. Remove three upper engine to transmission attaching bolts then pry engine and transmission apart.
27. Lift engine out of engine compartment.
28. Reverse procedure to install, torquing bolts and/or nuts as follows:
    a. Cover plate to engine/transmission, radiator mounts, and transmission cover to 7 ft. lbs.
    b. A/C compressor pulley, alternator, and starter to 14 ft. lbs.
    c. Engine stop on body/block and exhaust pipe hanger to 18 ft. lbs.
    d. A/C compressor bracket and exhaust pipe to 22 ft. lbs.
    e. Engine mounts to 25 ft. lbs.
    f. Engine to transmission to 40 ft. lbs.

5000

1. Remove air cleaner and disconnect battery ground cable.
2. Remove grille and cover plates underneath engine and transmission.
3. Remove windshield washer and power steering reservoirs from bracket and position aside.
4. Disconnect hood release cable from bracket.
5. Remove expansion tank cap, disconnect hoses 1 and 2 and drain coolant.
6. Remove upper radiator hose and loosen power steering pump.
7. Remove power steering belt, then the power steering pump leaving hoses connected.
8. On air conditioned models, remove bolts securing condenser and position aside.
9. Disconnect wiring harness connectors from cooling fan and overheating fuse. Remove radiator.
10. Remove upper part of fuel filter (1) and detach accelerator cable.
11. Disconnect wiring harness connectors from coolant and engine temperature sensors.
12. Disconnect fuel return pipe at injection pump and idle speed control cable from injection pump lever.
13. Remove cover from right engine mount and front mount from crossmember.
14. Remove alternator bracket and disconnect exhaust pipe at manifold and front bracket.
15. Disconnect wiring harness and battery cable connectors from starter motor.
16. On air conditioned models, remove four bolts securing compressor mount, then the compressor and mount leaving hoses connected.
17. Disconnect ground strap.
18. Remove lower bolts securing engine to transmission and remove flywheel cover from transmission.
19. Support transmission and attach suitable lifting equipment to engine.
20. Remove left engine mount bracket and nut securing right mount to engine bracket.
21. Raise engine and transmission until transmission contacts steering housing, and support transmission.
22. Remove upper bolts securing engine to transmission and pry engine and transmission apart.
23. Turn engine toward the right while lifting and remove from vehicle.
24. Reverse procedure to install, torquing bolts and/or nuts as follows:
    a. Alternator to engine and bracket, M8 engine to transmission attaching bolts, power steering pump, starter, and fan belt pulley to 14 ft. lbs.
    b. Coolant pipe flange to engine, exhaust pipe to manifold, and exhaust pipe bracket to 22 ft. lbs.
    c. A/C compressor to engine to 29 ft. lbs.
    d. Engine stop on body/block, engine mounts, and M10 engine to transmission attaching bolts to 32 ft. lbs.
    e. M12 engine to transmission attaching bolts to 43 ft. lbs.
    f. Subframe to body to 80 ft. lbs.

ENGINE OVERHAUL

4000

FRONT CRANKSHAFT OIL SEAL, REPLACE EXC. TURBO DIESEL

1. Using seal extractor tool 2085 or equivalent, unscrew inner part of tool approximately .12 inch out of outer part, then lock in position by tightening knurled screw.
2. Guide extractor by screwing sprocket bolt in until it protrudes approximately .79 inch.
3. Lubricate threaded head of oil seal

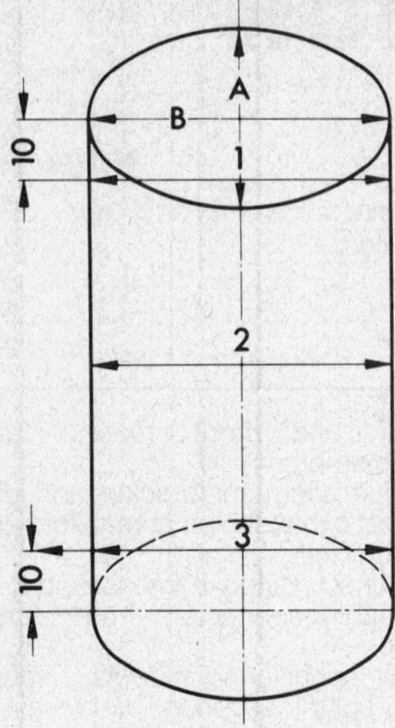

— measure at points 1, 2 and 3 first in direction A then direction B
1 = 10 mm (3/8 in.) from top
2 = middle of cylinder wall
3 = 10 mm (3/8 in.) from bottom
• piston to cylinder clearance
new part: 0.03 mm (0.011 in.)
wear limit: 0.07 mm (0.027 in.)

Fig. 1 Cylinder bore checking dimensions

extractor, place extractor in position, and screw into oil seal as far as possible while pushing inward.

4. Loosen knurled screw and turn inner part of tool against crankshaft until seal is pulled out.
5. Clamp extractor in vise and remove oil seal with pliers.
6. Using tool 10-203 or equivalent, press tool in to depth of 3/32 inch, then install new seal flush with front cover.

FRONT CRANKSHAFT OIL SEAL, REPLACE TURBO DIESEL

When replacing this oil seal, refer to "Front Crankshaft Oil Seal, Replace. Late Models W/1700cc Engine" in "Gasoline Engine Section."

REAR CRANKSHAFT OIL SEAL, REPLACE

When replacing this oil seal, refer to "Rear Crankshaft Oil Seal, Replace" for 4 cylinder gasoline engine.

MAIN & ROD BEARINGS

No. 1 main bearing cap is at front of engine and No. 5 cap is at rear. When installing bearing shells, install shells less lubrication groove in bearing cap and shells with lubrication groove in block. Ensure that shells are properly seated. Check crankshaft end play at No. 3 bearing. Clearance should be .003-.007 inch.

	Piston Diameter	Cylinder Bore
Standard	3.0110 inches (76.48mm)	3.0122 inches (76.51mm)
	3.0114 inches (76.49mm)	3.0126 inches (76.52mm)
	3.0118 inches (76.50mm)	3.0130 inches (76.53mm)
1st Oversize	3.0209 inches (76.73mm)	3.0220 inches (76.76mm)
	3.0213 inches (76.74mm)	3.0224 inches (76.77mm)
	3.0216 inches (76.75mm)	3.0228 inches (76.78mm)
2nd Oversize	3.0307 inches (76.98mm)	3.0319 inches (77.01mm)
	3.0311 inches (76.99mm)	3.0323 inches (77.02mm)
	3.0315 inches (77.00mm)	3.0327 inches (77.03mm)
3rd Oversize	3.0504 inches (77.48mm)	3.0516 inches (77.51mm)
	3.0508 inches (77.49mm)	3.0520 inches (77.52mm)
	3.0512 inches (77.50mm)	3.0524 inches (77.53mm)

Fig. 2 Piston dimension chart

PISTON & ROD ASSEMBLY

When removing piston, mark number on piston to match cylinder number. When installing piston, ensure that arrow points toward front of engine. Place mating marks on connecting rods and caps before removing. When installing connecting rod, ensure that casting marks and bearing shell retaining lug face intermediate shaft. When removing piston pin, remove circlips, heat piston to approximately 140°F as necessary, and drive out pin using tool VW222a or equivalent.

PISTONS, PINS & RINGS

When installing piston rings, ensure that "TOP" mark faces up. Side clearance of oil scraper ring should be .006 inch and side clearance of other rings should be .008 inch. When measuring piston ring end gap, push ring down squarely into cylinder approximately 9/16 inch from top edge. End gap should be .039 inch. Ensure that ring gaps are offset 120°. When checking cylinder clearance, refer to **Fig. 1.** Available piston and cylinder sizes are shown in **Fig. 2.**

TIMING BELT, REPLACE

1. Remove timing belt cover and the valve cover.
2. Turn engine to TDC on cylinder No. 1 and fix camshaft in position using tool 2065A or equivalent. Align tool as follows:
   a. Turn camshaft until one end of tool touches cylinder head.
   b. Measure gap at other end of tool with feeler gauge.
   c. Insert feeler gauge whose thickness is 1/2 that of measured gap between tool and cylinder head.
   d. Turn camshaft so that tool rests on feeler gauge.
   e. Insert feeler gauge whose thickness is that of gauge in step c between other end of tool and cylinder head.
3. Using tool 2064 or equivalent, lock injection pump sprocket in place.
4. Ensure that marks on sprocket, bracket and pump body are aligned, then loosen tensioner.
5. Remove fan belt pulley from crankshaft, then remove timing belt.
6. Ensure that TDC mark on flywheel is aligned with reference mark.
7. Loosen camshaft sprocket bolt 1/2 turn, then loosen gear from camshaft end by tapping with rubber mallet.
8. Install drive belt and remove tool 2064 from injection pump sprocket.
9. Tighten belt by turning tensioner to right.
10. Using tool VW210 or equivalent, ensure that scale reads 12-13 midway between camshaft sprocket and injection pump sprocket.
11. Torque camshaft sprocket bolt to 33 ft. lbs.
12. Remove tool from camshaft, then turn crankshaft two turns clockwise.
13. Using rubber hammer strike belt once midway between camshaft sprocket and injection pump sprocket, then recheck belt tension.
14. Check injection pump timing.

INJECTION PUMP, REPLACE

1. Remove timing belt as previously described.
2. Remove rear timing belt cover.
3. Remove injection pump.
4. Reverse procedure to install.

CAMSHAFT, REPLACE

1. Remove timing belt as previously described.
2. Remove bearing caps 1, 3 and 5, then diagonally loosen caps 2 and 4.
3. Reverse procedure to install, noting the following:
   a. Lubricate bearing surfaces and camshaft journals.
   b. Install caps in proper order, observing off center bearing position.
   c. Lightly tighten bearing caps 2 and 4 diagonally, then install caps 5, 1 and 3.
   d. Torque all camshaft bearing cap bolts to 14 ft. lbs.

CYLINDER HEAD, REPLACE

1. Remove timing belt as previously described.
2. Remove camshaft as previously described.
3. Loosen cylinder head bolts in reverse order of tightening sequence.
4. Select proper replacement gasket as described for 5 cylinder diesel engine, **Fig. 3.**
5. Install new gasket with "OBEN" mark

Piston Height Inches	Identification Notches in Gasket
.026-.031	1
.032-.035	2
.036-.040	3

Fig. 3 Head gasket selection chart

facing cylinder head.

6. On engine with M12 cylinder head bolts, torque in sequence as follows:
   a. Torque in three steps to 29 and 43 ft. lbs., then additional 1/2 turn.
   b. Install camshaft and timing belt as previously described.
   c. Run engine until oil temperature reaches 212°F., then tighten in sequence an additional 1/4 turn without loosening.
   d. After 1000 miles, torque additional 1/4 turn without loosening.
7. On engine with cylinder head bolts other than M12, torque in sequence as follows:
   a. Torque in three steps to 29, 43 and 54 ft. lbs.
   b. Torque additional 1/2 turn.
   c. Install camshaft and timing belt as previously described.
   d. Run engine until it reaches operating temperature, then stop engine and torque bolts an additional 1/4 turn in sequence.
   e. After 1000 miles, torque additional 1/4 turn without loosening.

VALVES, ADJUST

1. Run engine until coolant temperature reaches 95°F., then remove valve cover.
2. Turn camshaft by pushing vehicle in 4th gear until cam lobes of valve to be adjusted face up. **When adjusting valves, pistons must not be at TDC. Turn crankshaft approximately 1/4 turn past TDC.**
3. If intake valve clearance is not .008-.012 inch and/or exhaust valve clearance is not .016-.020 inch, install replacement valve adjusting disc to bring clearance to mid-range. **Thickness of valve adjusting disc is etched on underside of disc. When installing, ensure that markings face toward cam follower.**

VALVE GUIDES

Worn valve guides can be removed using tool 10-206 or equivalent. Press worn guides out from combustion chamber side of cylinder head. Coat new guides with engine oil and press into cold cylinder head from camshaft side. Press guides in as far as they will go. Ream guides by hand using proper cutting lubricant.

OIL PAN, REPLACE

1. Remove oil pan drain plug and drain oil.
2. Support engine using tool 10-222 or equivalent.
3. Remove cover plate from under engine.
4. Remove four bolts from subframe, then lower subframe.
5. Remove oil pan.
6. Reverse procedure to install, torquing oil pan attaching nuts to 7 ft. lbs. and the drain plug to 22 ft. lbs.

WATER PUMP, REPLACE

1. Drain cooling system.
2. Loosen alternator adjusting bolt, then remove alternator drive belt.
3. Remove water pump pulley attaching bolts, then the pulley.
4. Remove water pump to housing attaching bolts and the water pump.
5. Reverse procedure to install.

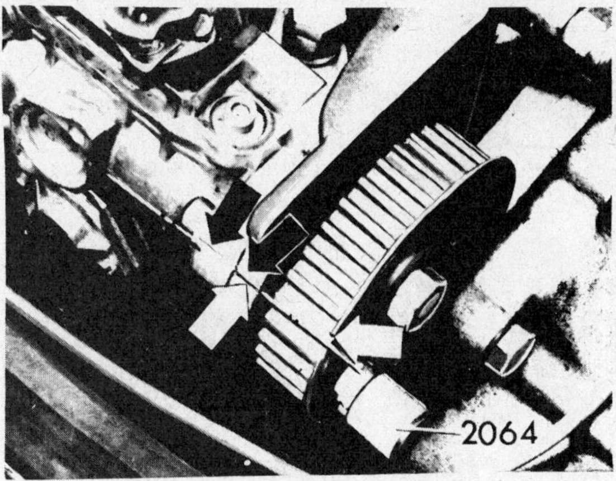

Fig. 4 Injector pump timing marks

5000

DISASSEMBLY

1. Drain engine oil and coolant. Remove engine accessories, brackets and mounts, camshaft cover, vacuum pump pulley and belt, and both timing belt covers.
2. Rotate engine to TDC for No. 1 cylinder, aligning timing marks between flywheel and clutch housing and between injector pump sprocket and housing, **Fig. 4.**
3. Lock injector pump sprocket, inboard half of vacuum pump pulley, and injector pump drive sprocket with proper tools.
4. Remove center bolt from injector pump drive sprocket and remove inner pulley, injector pump drive belt and sprocket.
5. Lock camshaft with proper tool.
6. Remove bolts securing crankshaft pulley and water pump, and remove pulley, water pump and camshaft drive belt.
7. Remove camshaft sprocket and rear belt cover.
8. Remove fuel pipe assemblies from injector pump and injectors.
9. Remove injector pump pulley using a suitable puller. Remove bolts securing injector and vacuum pumps and remove pumps. Remove pump brackets.
10. Remove fuel injectors from cylinder head, using suitable tool.
11. Remove bolts securing cylinder head, in reverse of tightening sequence, **Fig. 5.**
12. Remove cylinder head from cylinder block.

Crankshaft & Cylinder Block Disassembly

1. Remove oil pan. Remove bolts, oil pump pickup and pickup tube.
2. Remove bolts securing oil pump, then the pump.
3. Mark connecting rods and rod caps with matching marks to aid reassembly.
4. Remove connecting rod cap retaining nuts, rod cap, and bearing.
5. Remove piston/connecting rod assemblies through cylinder head side of block, using a suitable drift. **Keep pistons, connecting rods, rod caps, and bearings in correct order.**
6. Remove piston rings using a ring expander.
7. Press out piston pins and remove pistons from connecting rod.
8. Measure pistons approximately 9/16 from lower edge at 90° angle to pin axis.
9. Measure cylinder bores as shown in **Fig. 1.** If difference between measurements exceeds piston clearance specifications, new pistons must be fitted to bores.
10. Mark position of flywheel in relation to crankshaft and remove flywheel.
11. Remove bolts, rear engine cover and seal.
12. Note position of marks on main bearing caps. Remove bolts, main bearing caps and lower bearings.
13. Remove crankshaft from cylinder block and remove upper main bearings. **Keep main bearings and caps in correct order.**

Cylinder Head Disassembly

1. Remove camshaft bearing caps 1and 4.
2. Loosen nuts retaining bearing caps 2 and 3 diagonally and remove bearing caps and camshaft.
3. Remove cam followers and keep them in order.
4. Using suitable tool, depress valve springs and remove locks.
5. Remove valve springs, retainers, and

Fig. 5 Cylinder head bolt tightening sequence

Fig. 6 Piston installation

spring seats.
6. Remove valves and valve stem seals.
7. Press worn valve guides out through combustion chamber side.

ASSEMBLY

Cylinder Head Assembly

1. Coat new guides with oil and press into cold cylinder head from camshaft side as far as they will go.
2. Ream new guides to fit using a hand reamer.
3. Insert valves into cylinder head and install valve stem seal using a suitable tool.
4. Install valve spring seat, valve springs and spring retainer. Compress valve springs and install locking collets.
5. Place cam followers over valve springs and install camshaft.
6. Lubricate camshaft bearing caps and journals and install bearing caps, noting offset bearing position on No. 2 and 3.
7. Tighten bearing caps 2 and 3 diagonally and then tighten bearing caps 1 and 4. Torque bearing cap nuts to 14 ft. lbs.

Crankshaft & Cylinder Block Assembly

1. Install upper main bearings in cylinder block. Upper main bearings contain oil grooves, and thrust bearing is No. 4 from drive belt side of engine.
2. Lubricate crankshaft journals and upper main bearings with assembly lubricant and install crankshaft.
3. Install nongrooved lower main bearings into main bearing caps and lubricate bearings with assembly lubricant.
4. Install main bearing caps in correct order with reference number toward oil filter side of engine.
5. Torque main bearing cap bolts to specifications evenly, working from center toward outside.
6. Check that crankshaft rotates smoothly and end play is within specifications.
7. Install new seal in rear cover and install cover.
8. Align reference marks between crankshaft and flywheel and install flywheel.
9. Install pistons on connecting rods and press fit piston pins. Arrows on pistons face drive belt side of engine, **Fig. 6**, while casting marks on connecting rods, **Fig. 7**, face oil filter side of engine.
10. Install piston rings using a piston ring expander. "Top" marking on rings must face piston crown.
11. Insert bearing half in connecting rod big end and lubricate bearing and crankshaft journal.
12. Install piston/connecting rod combination into correct cylinder, making sure piston and rod face correctly.
13. Insert bearing half in matching connecting rod cap, lubricate bearing, and install cap.
14. Torque connecting rod cap nuts to specifications.
15. Install new seal in oil pump housing and install oil pump, making sure crankshaft engages oil pump gears correctly.
16. Install oil pump pickup and oil pan, using new gaskets.
17. Rotate engine until No. 1 cylinder is at TDC, and mark on flywheel is aligned with reference mark.

Final Assembly

1. Measure projection of piston above block deck surface and select a suitable head gasket.
2. Rotate camshaft until both valves for No. 1 cylinder are closed and install tool to lock position of camshaft.
3. With No. 1 piston at TDC, install cylinder head and correct gasket, and torque bolts to specifications in sequence, **Fig. 5.**
4. Install water pump loosely and install crankshaft pulley and sprocket and camshaft sprocket along with camshaft drive belt.
5. Tension drive belt by rotating water pump and torque water pump, camshaft sprocket, and crankshaft sprocket bolts to specifications. **Make sure crankshaft stays in TDC position while installing and tensioning belt.**
6. Install injectors, injector pump, fuel pipes, and vacuum pump, leaving injector pump bolts hand tight.
7. Install injector pump sprocket and align marks on sprocket, injector pump, and mounting plate, **Fig. 4**, and install setting pin.
8. Remove camshaft fixture and install drive sprocket and drive belt.
9. Tighten drive sprocket bolt so that drive sprocket can be turned by hand.
10. Adjust pump drive belt tension, check timing marks, and tighten sprocket and pump bolts.
11. Adjust injection pump timing.
12. Reverse procedure to install remaining engine accessories.

TURBOCHARGER

DESCRIPTION

The turbocharger is an exhaust driven device which compresses the air/fuel mixture that is used to increase engine power on a demand basis, allowing a smaller, more economical engine to be used.

A turbine in the exhaust gas flow is connected through a shaft to the impeller (compressor). During normal, steady operation, the turbine does not rotate with sufficient speed to boost pressure to compress the air/fuel mixture. As speed increases, the mixture is compressed, allowing the denser mixture to enter the combustion chambers and develop more engine power during the combustion cycle.

The intake manifold pressure (boost) is controlled by a wastegate valve which is used to bypass a portion of the exhaust gases around the turbine at a predetermined point in the cycle, limiting the boost pressure.

SERVICE

When servicing the turbocharger, observe the following precautions:

1. Thoroughly clean all connections and areas near connections before disconnecting.
2. Place removed parts on clean surface and cover with paper or plastic.
3. Components that have been opened or disassembled must be covered or carefully sealed if repair cannot be carried out immediately.
4. Install only clean components. Unpack replacement parts immediately before installation and do not use parts that have been stored loose.
5. When fuel system is open, do not

Fig. 7 Connecting rod installation identification mark

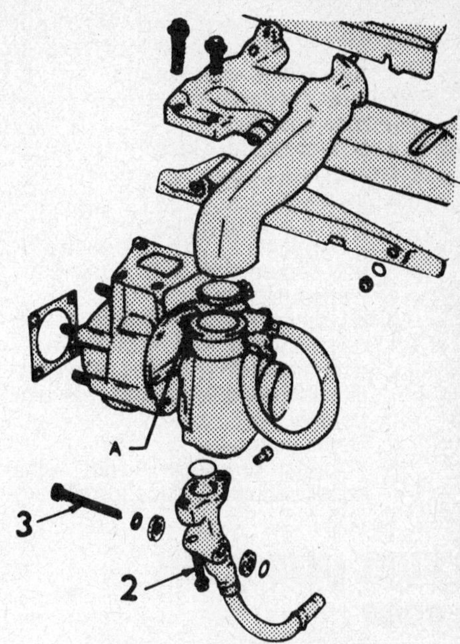

Fig. 8 Installing turbocharger. 4000

work with compressed air or move vehicle unless absolutely necessary.

6. Ensure that diesel fuel does not drip on coolant hoses. Replace hoses damaged by diesel fuel.

4000

Turbocharger, Replace

1. Disconnect battery ground cable.
2. Remove engine/transmission cover plate.
3. Loosen left and right stabilizer bar clamps and push stabilizer bar down.
4. Loosen oil return line on turbocharger and the engine support.
5. Remove turbocharger heat shield attaching nuts and the oil return line.
6. Remove hoses between turbocharger and intake manifold and turbocharger and air cleaner.
7. Disconnect oil supply line, then the exhaust pipe at turbocharger.
8. Remove turbocharger to exhaust manifold attaching bolts and the turbocharger.
9. Reverse procedure to install, noting the following:
   a. Install bolts, **Fig. 8,** hand tight, then torque as follows: (1) 50 ft. lbs., (2) and (3) 18 ft. lbs.
   b. Before connecting oil supply line to turbocharger, fill oil supply line connection (A), **Fig. 8,** with engine oil.
   c. After installing turbocharger, run for approximately one minute with engine at idle speed to allow turbocharger to be supplied with sufficient quantity of engine oil.

Testing

1. When performing testing, note the following:
   a. Bring engine to operating temperature.
   b. Ensure that there are no leaks on intake or exhaust side.
   c. Measure boost pressure at full throttle on road test or on a dynamometer.
   d. Ensure that test time does not exceed ten seconds per measurement.
2. Using T-fitting, install pressure gauge in hose between intake manifold and injection pump and position gauge so that it can be read from driver's seat.
3. Measure boost pressure with engine at full throttle as follows:
   a. On dynamometer, with manual transmission measure at 4000 RPM in 3rd gear, with automatic transmission measure at 4000 RPM in 2nd range.
   b. On road test, with manual transmission measure in 2nd gear while slowing and holding speed to 35 mph with brake, with automatic transmission measure in 1st range while slowing and holding speed to 35 mph with brake. **To make boost pressure reading easier during road test, pull valve outward to hold indicated reading on gauge.**
4. If boost pressure exceeds 9.3-10.2 psi, replace turbocharger.
5. If boost pressure is less than 9.3-10.2 psi, proceed as follows:
   a. Disconnect blow-off valve hose from intake air hose.
   b. Plug air hose with 1 inch plug and secure plug with clamp.
   c. Repeat step 3.
   d. If boost pressure is within specifications, replace blow-off valve.
   e. If boost pressure is not within specifications, replace turbocharger.

5000

Turbocharger, Replace

1. Remove air cleaner assembly.
2. Disconnect battery cables at battery and remove battery.
3. Remove right side engine mount heat shield, engine cover plate, and alternator.
4. Disconnect exhaust pipe at turbocharger and remove exhaust bracket from transmission.
5. Disconnect oil supply line at turbocharger.
6. Loosen lower hose clamp of hose connection to intake manifold.
7. Remove oil return line and air tube.
8. Remove four attaching nuts between turbocharger and exhaust manifold, loosening two rear nuts from above.
9. Remove turbocharger.
10. Reverse procedure to install, noting the following:
    a. Install turbocharger and tighten attaching nuts sufficiently so that air hose on intake manifold can be attached to turbocharger, then torque nuts to specifications.
    b. Fill connection branch of turbocharger with engine oil and connect oil supply line.
    c. After installing turbocharger, run engine approximately one minute at idle speed so oil supply of turbocharger is properly distributed.

Testing

1. When performing testing, note the following:
   a. Ensure that there are no leaks at intake or exhaust gas side.
   b. Measure boost pressure with engine at full throttle on road test or on a dynamometer.
   c. Ensure that test time does not exceed ten seconds per measurement.
2. Using T-fitting, install suitable pressure gauge in hose between intake pipe and fuel injection pump, then position gauge so that it can be read from driver's seat.
3. Open gauge stop valve by pushing inward.
4. Measure boost pressure with engine at full throttle as follows:
   a. On dynamometer, with manual transmission measure at 4000 RPM in 3rd gear, with automatic transmission measure at 4000 RPM in second range.
   b. On road test, with manual transmission measure in 2nd gear while slowing vehicle to 37 mph with brake, with automatic transmission measure in 1st range while slowing vehicle to 37 mph with brake. **To make boost pressure reading**

easier during road test, pull gauge stop valve outward to lock reading on gauge.

5. If boost pressure exceeds 9-10 psi, replace wastegate.
6. If boost pressure is less than 9-10 psi, proceed as follows:
   a. Disconnect blow-off valve hose from intake air hose.
   b. Plug air hose with one inch plug and secure plug with clamp.
   c. Repeat step 4.
   d. If boost pressure is within specifications, replace blow-off valve.
   e. If boost pressure is less than specifications, replace wastegate temporarily.
   f. Repeat step 4.
   g. If boost pressure is not within specifications, replace turbocharger.

FUEL INJECTION

4000

Injection Timing, Adjust

Fully depress cold start device when checking or adjusting injection timing.

1. Remove plug from injection pump cover.
2. Install adapter and 0-.118 inch dial gauge in place of plug and preload gauge to approximately .097 inch.
3. Slowly turn engine counterclockwise until dial gauge needle stops moving, then zero dial gauge.
4. Turn engine clockwise until TDC mark on flywheel is aligned with boss on bellhousing. Dial gauge should read .0346-.0366 inch.
5. If necessary, loosen bolts on mounting plate and support.
6. Set lift by turning pump until gauge reads .0331-.0346 inch.
7. Tighten pump mounting bolts and recheck injection timing.
8. Install new seal on center plug and torque plug with copper seal to 10-14 ft. lbs. or plug with bronze seal to 14-18 ft. lbs.

Engine Speed, Adjust

1. Start engine and run until oil temperature reaches 104°F.
2. Using test VW1367 or equivalent, connect TDC sensor of tester into pickup in bellhousing.
3. If idle speed is not 920-980 RPM, loosen locknut, adjust idle speed screw, and tighten locknut.
4. If maximum speed is not 5300-5400 RPM, loosen locknut, adjust maximum speed screw, and tighten locknut.

Accelerator Cable, Adjust

1. Check and adjust idle speed and maximum speed as previously described.
2. Set accelerator pedal in full throttle position.
3. Adjust accelerator cable by inserting clip in appropriate slot so that lever in injection pump rests against maximum speed stop but is not under tension.

Injection Pump, Replace

1. Turn engine until TDC mark on flywheel is in line with boss on bellhousing.
2. Disconnect battery ground cable.
3. Lock camshaft with setting bar, then remove timing belt.
4. Lock pump sprocket with pin 2064 or equivalent.
5. Slightly loosen injection pump sprocket retaining nut, then remove pin.
6. Attach puller 3032 or equivalent so jaws are at right angles to cross bar and point in direction of spindle rotation, then carefully apply tension with puller.
7. Hit puller spindle head with light hammer taps until sprocket loosens from injection pump shaft taper.
8. Remove puller and nut, then the sprocket by hand.
9. Disconnect all fuel pipes from pump, covering unions with clean cloth.
10. Disconnect lines at injectors and remove lines.
11. Disconnect fuel shutoff solenoid electrical connector at injection pump, then the accelerator and cold start cables.
12. Remove bolt from injection pump mounting plate, but do not loosen bolts on fuel distributor head.
13. Remove bolts from front injection pump mounting plate support, then the pump.
14. Reverse procedure to install, noting the following:
    a. When installing pump, align marks on pump and mounting plate.
    b. Torque pump bolts and fuel line unions to 18 ft. lbs. and pump sprocket to 33 ft. lbs.
    c. Adjust injection timing as previously described.
    d. Ensure that pump run-out does not exceed .0079 inch.

Injector, Replace

1. Clean all injector pipe fittings.
2. Remove injector pipes.
3. Disconnect fuel return hoses.
4. Remove injectors with suitable tools.
5. Remove and discard heat shields.
6. Install new heat shields.
7. Install injectors and torque to 51 ft. lbs.
8. Install injector pipes and torque to 18 ft. lbs.
9. Connect fuel return hoses.
10. Start engine and accelerate several times to clear air bubbles, then check for leaks.

5000

Injection Pump, Replace

1. Remove vacuum pump pulley and fan belt, then the injection pump drive belt cover.
2. Set crankshaft to TDC on No. 1 cylinder by aligning marks on flywheel and clutch housing.
3. Secure injection pump sprocket with setting pin 2064 or equivalent.
4. Secure vacuum pump belt pulley and injection pump drive sprocket with tool 3036 or equivalent.
5. Loosen and remove drive sprocket attaching bolt, then remove drive sprocket with timing belt.
6. Slightly loosen injection pump sprocket attaching nut, then remove setting pin.
7. Attach puller 3032 or equivalent so that jaws are at right angles to cross bar and point in direction of spindle rotation, then carefully apply tension with puller.
8. Lightly tap puller spindle with hammer until sprocket loosens.
9. Remove puller and attaching nut, then the injection pump sprocket.
10. Disconnect injector pipes, fuel supply and return lines, and shutoff solenoid electrical connector at injection pump, then the accelerator cable.
11. Remove coolant hoses from cold start device.
12. Remove four bolts from injection pump mounting plate and one bolt from support bracket, then remove injection pump. **To remove rear attaching bolt at mounting plate, use 6 mm hex key socket with 8.6 inch extension.**
13. Install injection pump, aligning marks on pump and mounting plate.
14. Install attaching bolts loosely.
15. Align rear support so that it contacts cylinder block and injection pump free of tension and tighten in this position.
16. When installing injection pump sprocket, ensure that run-out of sprocket does not exceed .0079 inch.
17. Install injection pump sprocket, turning to align marks on gear and mounting plate.
18. Lock pump with tool 2064 or equivalent and torque attaching nut to 33 ft. lbs.
19. Install timing belt with injection pump drive sprocket on camshaft.
20. Tighten drive sprocket attaching bolt so that drive sprocket can still be turned manually.
21. Using tool VW210 or equivalent, check timing belt tension.
22. If scale of tool does not read 12-13, adjust drive belt tension by loosening bolts and moving mounting plate with pump.
23. Ensure that TDC mark on flywheel is aligned with reference mark.
24. Secure injection pump drive sprocket with setting bar and torque sprocket attaching bolt to 72 ft. lbs.
25. Remove tool 2064.
26. Connect coolant hoses to cold start device.
27. Loosen cold start device cable by loosening screw on slip collar. Do not loosen cable clamping nut.
28. Hold cold start lever to left while turning collar 1/4 turn to allow cable clamp to slide to left in collar slot.
29. Install adapter 2066 or equivalent and small dial indicator with .0984 inch preload in place of plug on injection pump.
30. Remove cover plate below engine.
31. Slowly turn crankshaft counterclockwise until dial indicator needle stops moving.
32. Zero dial indicator with approximately .03937 inch preload.

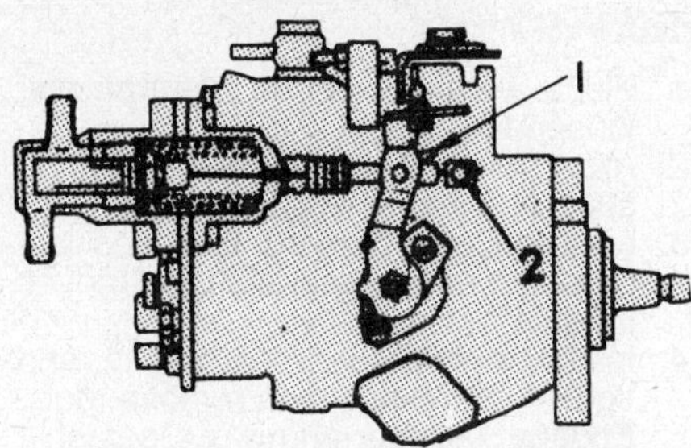

Fig. 9 Fast idle linkage screw location. 5000

33. Turn crankshaft clockwise until TDC mark on flywheel is aligned with reference mark. Dial indicator should read .0315-.0354 on vehicles less turbocharger or .0346-.0386 inch on turbocharged vehicles.
34. If necessary, loosen injection pump bolts and set lift by turning injection pump. Set to .0327-.0343 inch on vehicles less turbocharger or .0358-.0374 inch on turbocharged vehicles.
35. Torque injection pump attaching bolts to 18 ft. lbs.
36. Tension cold start device cable by rotating slip collar back 1/4 turn and tightening screw previously loosened.
37. Connect hoses to cold start device.
38. Connect injector pipes, fuel supply and return lines, and shutoff solenoid electrical connector.
39. Torque unions and injector pipes to 18 ft. lbs.
40. Install timing belt cover.
41. Adjust idle and maximum speeds and fast idle linkage.

Injection Timing, Adjust

1. Set engine to TDC on cylinder No. 1 by aligning marks on flywheel and clutch housing.
2. Loosen cold start device cable by first loosening screw on slip collar. Do not loosen cable clamping nut.
3. Hold cold start lever to left and turn slip collar 1/4 turn to allow cable clamp to slide to left in collar slot.
4. Install adapter 2066 or equivalent and small dial indicator with .0984 inch preload on injection pump cover.
5. Slowly turn crankshaft counterclockwise until dial indicator needle stops moving.
6. Zero dial indicator with approximately .03937 inch preload.
7. Turn crankshaft clockwise until TDC mark on flywheel is aligned with reference mark. Dial indicator should read .0315-.0354 inch on vehicles less turbocharger or .0346-.0386 inch on turbocharged vehicles.
8. If necessary, loosen injection pump bolts and set lift by turning injection pump. Set to .0327-.0343 inch on vehicles less turbocharger or .0358-.0374 inch on turbocharged vehicles.
9. Tension cold start device cable by rotating slip collar back 1/4 turn and tightening screw previously loosened.

Idle Speed, Adjust

1. Measure engine speed with tester VW1367 through TDC sensor or equivalent.
2. Run engine until oil temperature reaches 122-158°F.
3. Turn idle speed control knob on instrument panel counterclockwise to stop.
4. Connect tester according to manufacturer's instructions.
5. Adjust speed, by turning idle adjusting screw, to 700-800 RPM on vehicles less turbocharger or 720-820 RPM on turbocharged vehicles.
6. Lock screw and seal with paint.

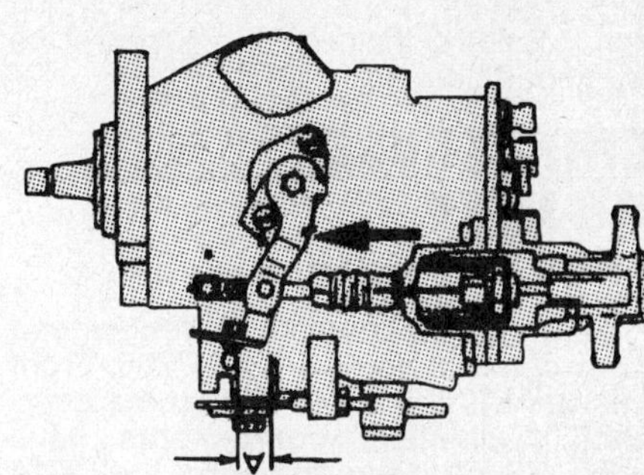

Fig. 10 Adjusting fast idle linkage. 5000

Fast Idle Linkage, Adjust

1. Loosen screw (1) of fast idle linkage and rotate clamp 90°, **Fig. 9.** Do not loosen screw (2).
2. Push fast idle linkage against stop in direction of stop, **Fig. 10.**
3. Measure gap (A) between linkage ball and top linkage arm. If gap is not 1/2 inch, adjust.
4. Rotate clamp back 90° into proper position and retighten screw (1).

Maximum Speed, Adjust

1. Run engine until oil temperature reaches 122-158°F.
2. Connect tester VW1367 or equivalent according to manufacturer's instructions.
3. Open throttle fully and adjust maximum speed by turning maximum speed screw. Set speed to 5350-5450 RPM on vehicles less turbocharger or 5050-5150 RPM on turbocharged vehicles.
4. Lock screw and seal with paint.

Injectors, Replace

Refer to "Injector, Replace" under "4000."

CLUTCH & MANUAL TRANSMISSION SECTION

INDEX

CLUTCH

ADJUST

4000 & COUPE W/013 OR 014 TRANSMISSION

Turn adjusting nuts at bracket on transmission case so that clutch pedal freeplay is 9/16 inch.

4000 & COUPE W/093 TRANSMISSION

Adjust by moving clip in slots of cable guide sleeve so that clutch pedal freeplay is 9/16 inch.

4 SPEED 5000 MODELS

This model has a hydraulic nonadjustable type clutch release mechanism. The position of the clutch pedal should be .375 inch above the brake pedal for ideal operation. Position of the pedal is adjusted at the master cylinder adjusting fork.

SHIFT LEVER

ADJUST

4000 & COUPE

Gearshift mechanism is redesigned from chassis No. 3-5 2 044 765. From chassis No. 3-5 2 044 957, some gearshift mechanism components have been altered. New adjusting tool 3014 is required which replaces old tool 3009. New tool 3014 can be used from chassis No. 3-5 2 044 765.

1. Place shift lever in neutral.
2. Loosen clamp nut.
3. Check that shift finger slides freely on shift rod.
4. Remove gearshift lever knob and shift boot.
5. Align centering holes of gearshift lever housing and gearshift lever bearing housing.
6. Install tool with locating pin toward front.
7. Push gearshift lever into left cutout of slide.
8. Secure tool position by tightening lower knurled screw.
9. Move slide with gear lever to left side until it stops and tighten upper knurled screw.
10. Push gear shift lever into right cutout of slide (3-4 position).
11. Align shift rod/shift finger (transmission in Neutral) and tighten clamp nut.
12. Remove tool.
13. Engage 1st gear.
14. Press gearshift lever to left side until it stops.
15. When gearshift lever is released, it must spring back approximately 0.2-0.4 inch. If not, correct by moving gearshift lever housing very slightly sideways in elongated holes.
16. Check that all gears engage easily without jamming. Check function of reverse gear stop.

5 SPEED 4000 & COUPE

1. Place shift lever in neutral.
2. Loosen clamp nut, then ensure that shift finger slides freely on shift rod.
3. Remove shift lever knob and shift boot, then loosen bolts slightly.
4. Align centering holes of gearshift lever housing and gearshift lever bearing housing, then tighten bolts.
5. Using tool 3057 or equivalent, install tool so that locating pin is in front centering hole.
6. Place shift lever in right cut out of slide, then tighten lower knurled nut on tool.
7. Move slide with shift lever to right stop and tighten upper knurled nut on tool.
8. Push shift lever into left cut out of slide.
9. Adjust shift rod and shift finger (transmission in neutral), then tighten clamp nut.
10. Remove tool.
11. Engage 1st gear, press shift lever to right stop, and release lever. Lever should spring back to right.
12. Engage 5th gear, press shift lever to right stop, and release lever. Lever should spring back to left.
13. If lever does not spring back approximately same distance in steps 11 and 12, move shift lever housing slightly in slots sideways.
14. Ensure that all gears engage easily without jamming.
15. Install shift boot and shift lever knob.

4 SPEED 5000 MODELS

1. Place shift lever in neutral.
2. Adjust selector shaft lever on transmission so that distance from rear of selector shaft knob to front of transmission case is 4.095 inches.
3. Adjust selector lever flush with selector shaft, then tighten clamp bolt.
4. Adjust length of adjusting rod so that distance between center point of end holes is 5 9/32 inches.
5. Push front shift rod on to selector lever ball and install adjusting rod.
6. Ensure that seam of plastic stop bracket on shift lever aligns with center hole of left stop pad with shift lever at 1st/2nd gear gate in neutral position.
7. Loosen four bolts, align holes of stop plate and bearing support, and tighten bolts.
8. Loosen clamp between front and rear shift rods, then ensure that rear shift rod moves freely.
9. Using tool 2073 or equivalent, install tool by inserting pins of tools into open holes on left stop pad, then lock shift lever.
10. Ensure that front shift rod is in neutral position, adjusting as necessary, then tighten clamp.
11. Remove tool.
12. Engage 1st gear, push shift lever to left side to stop, and release shift lever.
13. If shift lever does not move to right 1/4 to 3/8 inch, adjust by moving slightly sideways in slots.
14. Shift through all gears, ensuring that gears engage easily without jamming.
15. Install shift lever knob and boot, ensuring that boot contacts shift knob.

5 SPEED 5000 MODELS

1983

1. Place transmission in neutral.
2. Loosen four bolts, align holes of stop plate and bearing support, and tighten four bolts.
3. Loosen clamp between front and rear rods, then ensure that rear shift rod move freely.
4. Install tool 3048 or equivalent, fitting locating pins into holes of stop plates.
5. Ensure front gear shift rod remains in neutral position, tighten shift rod clamp and remove tool.
6. Shift through all gears and ensure that gears engage easily without jamming.
7. Adjust stop plate mounting, if necessary.
8. Install gearshift lever boot and knob, ensuring that boot contacts knob.

1984–87

1. Place transmission in neutral and loosen four bolts.
2. Align holes of stop plate and bearing support, then tighten bolts.
3. Loosen clamp between front and rear rods and ensure rear shift rod moves freely.
4. Install tool 3048 or equivalent and tighten clamp nut, then remove tool.
5. Engage 1st gear and press gearshift lever to left stop.
6. Release gearshift lever and ensure lever springs back to right.
7. Engage 5th gear and press gearshift lever to right stop.
8. Release gearshift lever and ensure lever springs back to left.
9. If lever does not spring back approximately same distance in steps 12 and 15, move gearshift lever housing slightly sideways in slot.
10. Ensure all gears engage easily without jamming, especially reverse gear.
11. On later models, adjust projecting portion of bearing pin to 11/16 inch.
12. Readjust stop plate mounting as necessary.
13. Install gearshift lever boot and knob, ensuring boot contacts shift knob.

QUATTRO COUPE & TURBO

1. Place shift lever in neutral.
2. Adjust length of adjusting rod so that distance between center point of end holes is 5.275 inch.
3. Loosen clamp nut, ensuring that shift rods move freely.
4. Loosen bolts slightly, align centering holes of gearshift lever housing and stop plate, and tighten bolts.
5. Install tool 3048 or equivalent, tighten clamp nut, and remove tool.
6. Engage 1st gear, press shift lever to left stop, and release shift lever.
7. Engage 5th gear, press shift lever to right stop, and release shift lever.
8. If lever does not spring back approximately the same distance in steps 6 and 7, move gearshift lever housing slightly in slots sideways.
9. Ensure that all gears engage easily without jamming.

TRANSMISSION

REPLACE

4 SPEED 4000 & COUPE

1. Disconnect battery ground cable.
2. Disconnect electrical connectors for back-up lights and the cable strap adjacent to master cylinder.
3. Remove upper engine to transmission attaching bolts.
4. Disconnect speedometer cable.
5. Disconnect clutch cable at clutch lever.
6. Disconnect exhaust pipe at manifold.
7. Remove engine stop attaching bolts.
8. Disconnect front exhaust pipe at front muffler.
9. Remove driveshafts from transmission.
10. Remove transmission cover plate and the starter.

11. Remove bolt from shift rod coupling, pry off linkage coupling, and pull shift rod coupling off shift rod.
12. On early models, proceed as follows:
    a. Loosen rear attaching bolt of right side transmission support.
    b. Remove two front attaching bolts of right side transmission support.
    c. Pivot transmission support toward rear of vehicle.
    d. Remove attaching bolts of front bracket for right side transmission support.
13. On late models, proceed as follows:
    a. Loosen rear attaching bolt of right side transmission support.
    b. Remove front attaching bolt of right side transmission support.
    c. Pivot transmission support toward rear of vehicle.
    d. Remove attaching bolts of front bracket for right side transmission support.
14. Remove lower engine to transmission attaching bolts.
15. Pry transmission away from engine at front, then remove transmission.
16. Reverse procedure to install noting the following:
    a. Ensure that all engine and transmission mounts are properly aligned and free of tension.
    b. Adjust gearshift lever as necessary.
    c. Coat mainshaft splines with suitable lubricant.
    d. Ensure that intermediate shaft is properly seated.
    e. Position transmission on dowel sleeves.
    f. Secure bolt on shift rod coupling with wire.
    g. Torque transmission cover plate attaching bolts and shift rod coupling bolts to 7 ft. lbs.
    h. Torque starter attaching bolts to 14 ft. lbs.
    i. Torque engine stop to block attaching bolts, front bracket to transmission attaching bolts, muffler to catalytic converter attaching bolts, rubber mount to bracket attaching bolts on late model vehicles, and rubber mounting on early model vehicles to 18 ft. lbs.
    j. Torque exhaust pipe to manifold attaching bolts to 22 ft. lbs.
    k. Torque rubber mount to body attaching bolts to 29 ft. lbs. on early model vehicles.
    l. Torque driveshaft to flange attaching bolts to 33 ft. lbs.
    m. Torque rubber mount to bracket attaching bolts on early model vehicles and transmission to engine attaching bolts to 40 ft. lbs.
    n. Torque subframe support to body attaching bolts to 51 ft. lbs.
    o. Torque rubber mount to body attaching bolts to 80 ft. lbs. on late model vehicles.

4000 & COUPE W/013 5 SPEED TRANSMISSION

1. Disconnect battery ground cable.
2. Remove upper engine to transmission attaching bolts.
3. Disconnect speedometer cable and unhook clutch cable.
4. Disconnect exhaust pipe at manifold.
5. Remove engine stop attaching bolts.
6. Remove front muffler and exhaust pipe.
7. Disconnect driveshafts at transmission.
8. Disconnect electrical connectors for back-up lights.
9. Remove transmission cover plate attaching bolts and the lower starter attaching bolt.
10. Remove shift rod coupling bolt at rear of shift rod, pry off shift rod coupling ball, and pull shift rod coupling off of shift rod.
11. Position suitable jack under transmission and lift transmission slightly.
12. Loosen rear attaching bolt of right hand transmission support.
13. Remove front attaching bolt of right hand transmission support.
14. Pivot transmission support toward rear of vehicle.
15. Remove rubber mount from bracket at front of right hand transmission support.
16. Remove front bracket attaching bolts.
17. Remove lower engine to transmission attaching bolts, then pry transmission from engine.
18. Lower transmission and remove from beneath vehicle.
19. Reverse procedure to install, noting the following:
    a. Coat mainshaft splines with suitable lubricant.
    b. Ensure that cover plate is properly seated.
    c. Ensure that engine and transmission mounts are properly aligned and free of tension.
    d. Adjust shifting mechanism as necessary.
    e. Torque cover plate to transmission attaching bolts and shift rod coupling attaching bolt to 7 ft. lbs.
    f. Torque starter mounting bolts to 14 ft. lbs.
    g. Torque engine stop to block attaching bolts, front bracket to transmission attaching bolts, muffler to catalytic converter attaching bolts, and rubber mount to bracket attaching bolts to 18 ft. lbs.
    h. Torque exhaust pipe to manifold attaching bolts to 22 ft. lbs.
    i. Torque driveshaft to flange attaching bolts to 33 ft. lbs.
    j. Torque transmission to engine attaching bolts to 40 ft. lbs.
    k. Torque subframe/support to body attaching bolts to 51 ft. lbs.
    l. Torque rubber mount to body attaching bolts to 80 ft. lbs.

4000 & COUPE W/093 5 SPEED TRANSMISSION

1. Disconnect battery ground cable.
2. Remove upper engine to transmission attaching bolts.
3. Install engine support tools 10-222 and 10-222/1 or equivalents to hold engine in place.
4. Remove air cleaner assembly.
5. Disconnect speedometer cable and unhook clutch cable.
6. Disconnect driveshafts at transmission.
7. Remove front exhaust pipe.
8. Remove bolts of bracket on steering rack after loosening locknuts.
9. Disconnect electrical connectors from back-up lights.
10. Remove cover plate, lower engine to transmission attaching bolts and the starter.
11. Position suitable jack under transmission and lift transmission slightly.
12. Remove shift rod coupling bolt at rear of shift rod, pry off shift rod coupling ball, and pull shift rod coupling off of shift rod.
13. Loosen transmission support on body, then remove front attaching bolt from right side transmission support and pivot transmission support toward rear of vehicle.
14. Remove transmission bracket attaching bolts and the rubber mount.
15. Pry transmission away from engine, then lower transmission and remove from under vehicle.
16. Reverse procedure to install, noting the following:
    a. Coat mainshaft splines with suitable lubricant.
    b. Ensure that cover plate is properly seated.
    c. Ensure that engine and transmission mounts are properly aligned and free of tension.
    d. Tighten steering rack bracket bolts with wheels of vehicle on ground.
    e. Adjust shifting mechanism as necessary.
    f. Torque cover plate to transmission attaching bolts and shift rod coupling bolts to 7 ft. lbs.
    g. Torque starter attaching bolts to 14 ft. lbs.
    h. Torque bracket to transmission attaching bolts and muffler to catalytic converter attaching bolts to 18 ft. lbs.
    i. Torque exhaust pipe to manifold attaching bolts to 22 ft. lbs.
    j. Torque driveshaft to flange attaching bolts and steering rack bracket bolts to 33 ft. lbs.
    k. Torque transmission to engine attaching bolts to 40 ft. lbs.
    l. Torque subframe/support to body attaching bolts to 51 ft. lbs.
    m. Torque rubber mount to body attaching bolts to 80 ft. lbs.

5000 MODELS

1. Disconnect battery ground cable.
2. On vehicles with diesel engine, remove air cleaner assembly.
3. On all vehicles, remove windshield washer reservoir.
4. Remove upper engine to transmission attaching bolts.
5. Disconnect speedometer cable, then remove spring clip from clutch slave cylinder.
6. Drive out lock pin for clutch slave cylinder, **Fig. 1**, then remove clutch slave cylinder, leaving lines attached.
7. Attach tool No. 10-222 or equivalent and support engine, **Fig. 2.**

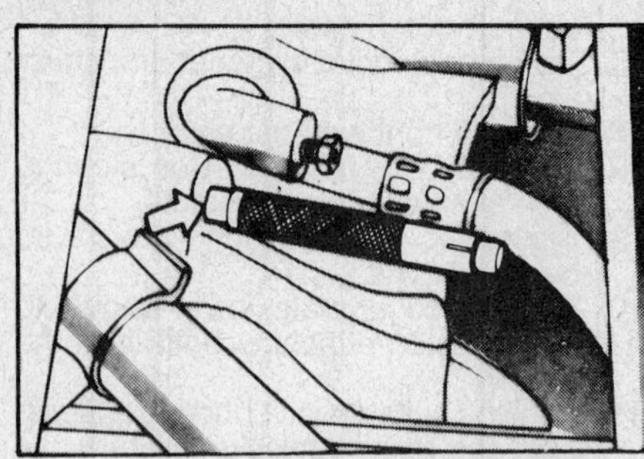

Fig. 1 Removing clutch slave cylinder lock pin

8. On vehicles with diesel engine, remove splash shield from beneath engine and transmission.
9. On all vehicles, remove front exhaust pipe.
10. Remove right side guard plate, then disconnect driveshafts at flanges and rest driveshafts on top of subframe.
11. Disconnect electrical connectors from back-up light switch.
12. Pry off shift and adjusting rods.
13. Remove lower engine to transmission attaching bolts, then the starter.
14. Remove guard plate from subframe.
15. Install tools US618/1 or equivalents on suitable jack and lift transmission slightly.
16. Remove both rear subframe attaching bolts.
17. Remove both transmission support bolts from subframe.
18. Remove right side transmission bracket.
19. Pull transmission off dowel sleeves, then lower transmission and remove from under vehicle.
20. Reverse procedure to install, noting the following:
    a. Coat mainshaft splines with suitable lubricant.
    b. Install transmission on engine dowels and install lower engine to transmission attaching bolts.
    c. Check gear shift adjustments.
    d. Torque bracket to transmission attaching bolts and transmission support to subframe mounting bolts to 29 ft. lbs.
    e. Torque driveshaft to flange attaching bolts to 33 ft. lbs.
    f. Torque transmission to engine mounting bolts to 40 ft. lbs.
    g. Torque subframe to body attaching bolts to 80 ft. lbs.

QUATTRO COUPE

1. Disconnect battery ground cable.
2. Disconnect RPM sensor.
3. Remove upper engine to transmission attaching bolts.
4. Disconnect speedometer cable.
5. Disconnect tie rod coupling from steering rack, first removing self locking nuts below tie rod coupling, then the mounting bolts.
6. Drive out clutch slave cylinder lock pin, then remove clutch slave cylinder, leaving hydraulic lines attached.
7. Disconnect back-up light switch and the shift linkage.
8. Attach tool No. 10-222 or equivalent and support engine, **Fig. 2**.
9. Remove deflector for axle shaft and right transmission mount, then the right transmission mount.
10. Disconnect exhaust pipe at flange and the right axle shaft at transmission.
11. Remove left transmission mount, then disconnect left axle shaft at transmission.
12. Disconnect driveshaft at rear of transmission.
13. Disconnect differential lock cable.
14. Remove transmission cover plate.
15. Turn spindle of tool 10-222 to raise engine slightly.
16. Place suitable jack under transmission.
17. Remove lower engine to transmission attaching bolts.
18. Remove transmission from under vehicle.
19. Reverse procedure to install, noting the following:
    a. Ensure that engine and transmission mounts are free of tension.
    b. Adjust shift linkage as necessary.
    c. Coat driveshaft and axle shaft flanges with suitable lubricant.
    d. Torque exhaust pipe to flange attaching bolts to 18 ft. lbs.
    e. Torque exhaust pipe to transmission mount attaching bolts to 22 ft. lbs.
    f. Torque tie rod coupling to steering rack attaching bolts and transmission mount to transmission attaching bolts to 29 ft. lbs.
    g. Torque transmission mount to subframe attaching bolts and driveshaft attaching bolts to 32 ft. lbs.
    h. Torque engine to transmission mounting bolts to 43 ft. lbs.
    i. Torque axle shaft to transmission mounting bolts to 58 ft. lbs.

QUATTRO TURBO

1. Disconnect battery ground cable.
2. Disconnect RPM sensor.
3. Remove upper engine to transmission attaching bolts.
4. Disconnect speedometer cable.
5. Disconnect tie rod coupling from steering rack, first removing self locking nuts below tie rod coupling, then the mounting bolts.
6. Drive out clutch slave cylinder lock pin and remove clutch slave cylinder, leaving hydraulic line connected.
7. Disconnect electrical connector for back-up light switch, then the shift linkage.
8. Install tool 10-222 or equivalent to support engine.
9. Remove deflector for axle shaft and right transmission mount, then the right transmission mount.

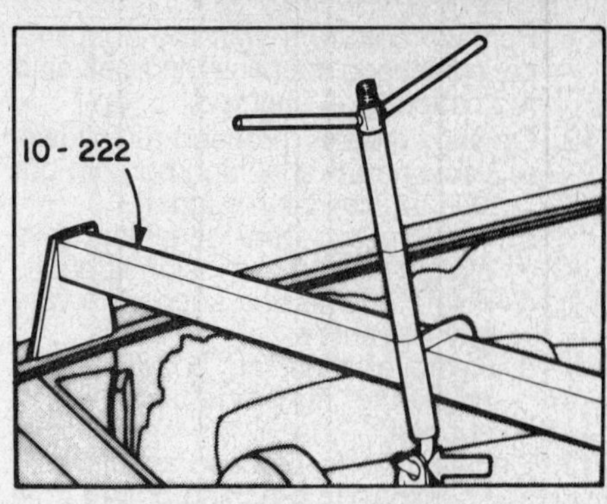

Fig. 2 Engine support tool No. 10-222

10. Disconnect exhaust pipe at flange and the right axle shaft at transmission.
11. Remove left transmission mount, then disconnect left axle shaft at transmission.
12. Disconnect driveshaft at rear of transmission.
13. Disconnect differential lock cable.
14. Remove transmission cover plate.
15. Turn spindle on tool 10-222 to raise engine slightly.
16. Place suitable jack under transmission and remove lower engine to transmission attaching bolts.
17. Remove transmission toward rear of vehicle, ensuring transmission clears axle shafts, driveshaft, tie rods and shift linkage.
18. Reverse procedure to install, noting the following:
    a. Ensure engine to transmission mounts are free of tension.
    b. Adjust shift linkage as necessary.
    c. Clean driveshaft and axle shaft flanges and lightly coat with suitable lubricant.
    d. If lifting eye is still in place on transmission housing near starter, it may be necessary to hacksaw it off to facilitate assembly of exhaust pipe.
    e. Torque engine to transmission attaching bolts to 43 ft. lbs.
    f. Torque tie rod coupling to steering rack and the transmission mount to transmission attaching bolts to 29 ft. lbs.
    g. Torque axle shaft to transmission attaching bolts to 58 ft. lbs.
    h. Torque exhaust pipe to transmission mount attaching bolts to 22 ft. lbs.
    i. Torque transmission mount to subframe and the driveshaft to transmission attaching bolts to 32 ft. lbs.
    j. Torque exhaust pipe to flange attaching bolts to 18 ft. lbs.

REAR AXLE & SUSPENSION SECTION

INDEX

REAR AXLE

REPLACE

4000 & COUPE

1. Raise and support rear of vehicle, then remove wheel and tire assemblies.
2. Detach muffler hanger bands, then lower and support muffler and tail pipe.
3. Remove parking brake cable to equalizer nut, then pry cable sleeve from bracket.
4. Remove both parking brake cables at brackets, then disconnect brake hoses at brake line brackets and cap hoses and lines.
5. Remove nuts from bolts attaching trailing arms to body, **Fig. 1.** Do not remove bolts at this time.
6. Disconnect spring from brake pressure regulator.
7. Remove bolts attaching diagonal arms to axle, then remove bolts attaching strut to axle.
8. Slide out trailing arm to body attaching bolts, then carefully remove axle from vehicle.
9. Reverse procedure to install. After positioning axle in vehicle, install both trailing arm bolts finger tight. Install wheel and tire assemblies and lower vehicle. Torque trailing arm attaching bolts to 72 ft. lbs., then raise vehicle and install remaining components. Torque strut attaching bolts to 43 ft. lbs. and diagonal arm attaching bolts to 51 ft. lbs. After completing installation, bleed brake system and adjust parking brake.

1983 5000

Exc. Turbo

1. Loosen lug nuts, then raise and support rear of vehicle.
2. Remove bolts attaching diagonal arms to body.
3. Disconnect right and left hand brake hoses at brake line brackets.
4. Disconnect spring from parking brake equalizer.
5. Remove retaining strap from right hand side of fuel tank, then detach parking brake cable from guide on fuel tank.
6. Loosen left hand parking brake cable bolt, remove parking brake cable to equalizer nut and disconnect parking brake cable.
7. Remove rear portion of exhaust system, then lower vehicle.
8. Remove upper shock absorber attaching nuts, then raise vehicle body until springs can be removed from axle.
9. Raise and support rear of vehicle and remove wheel and tire assemblies, **Fig. 2.**
10. Remove trailing arm to body attaching bolts, then carefully remove axle from vehicle.
11. Reverse procedure to install. After positioning axle in vehicle, install trailing arm attaching bolts and hand tighten, then install wheel and tire assemblies. Lower vehicle and install both spring damper rings on springs. Raise vehicle body and position springs between body mounting and axle, then lower body to seat springs and install upper shock absorber mounting nuts. Raise vehicle and check to ensure that springs are properly positioned, then lower vehicle and torque trailing arm bolts to 51 ft. lbs. Raise vehicle and install remaining components. Torque attaching bolts to 65 ft. lbs. and shock absorber lower mounting bolts to 40 ft. lbs. After completing installation, bleed brake system and adjust parking brake.

Turbo

1. Loosen lug nuts, then raise and support rear of vehicle.
2. Remove bolts attaching diagonal arm to body, then detach spring from parking brake pressure regulator.
3. Loosen lower shock absorber attaching bolt. Do not remove bolt at this time.
4. Loosen parking brake cable to equalizer nut, then detach parking brake cable at coupling.
5. Remove parking brake cable bracket from body, then detach cable from axle brackets and pull boot and slide cable from guide.
6. Disconnect brake hoses at brake line support brackets and cap lines and hoses.
7. Loosen trailing arm to body attaching bolts, **Fig. 3**, then lower vehicle. Do not remove trailing arm bolts at this time.
8. Remove both lower shock absorber attaching bolts, then raise vehicle until rear wheels are off floor. Remove wheel and tire assemblies and rear coil springs.
9. Further raise and support rear of vehicle, then remove trailing attaching bolts and carefully remove axle from vehicle.
10. Reverse procedure to install. After positioning rear axle in vehicle, install trailing arm attaching bolts and hand tighten. Install wheel and tire assemblies, then lower vehicle. Install damper rings on coil springs, then raise vehicle body slightly and position springs and damper between body mounting and rear axle. Gradually lower vehicle to seat springs, then install lower shock absorber attaching bolts and torque to 33 ft. lbs. Check to ensure springs are properly positioned. Install remaining components. Torque trailing arm attaching bolts to 69 ft. lbs. and diagonal arm attaching bolts to 65 ft. lbs. with weight of vehicle resting on wheels.

QUATTRO COUPE & QUATTRO TURBO

1. Loosen wheel bolts.
2. Remove axle nut cover, then the axle nut.
3. Raise and support vehicle.
4. Remove wheel bolts and wheel.
5. Disconnect axle shaft from final drive flange and position aside.
6. Press off tie rod end using suitable tool. **Axle shafts are diagonally interchangeable; left rear is identical with right front and right rear is identical with left front.**
7. Remove ball joint clamp bolt.
8. Disconnect brake hose at bracket.
9. Pry ball joint out of hub and move strut toward outside.
10. Press out stub axle from hub, ensur-

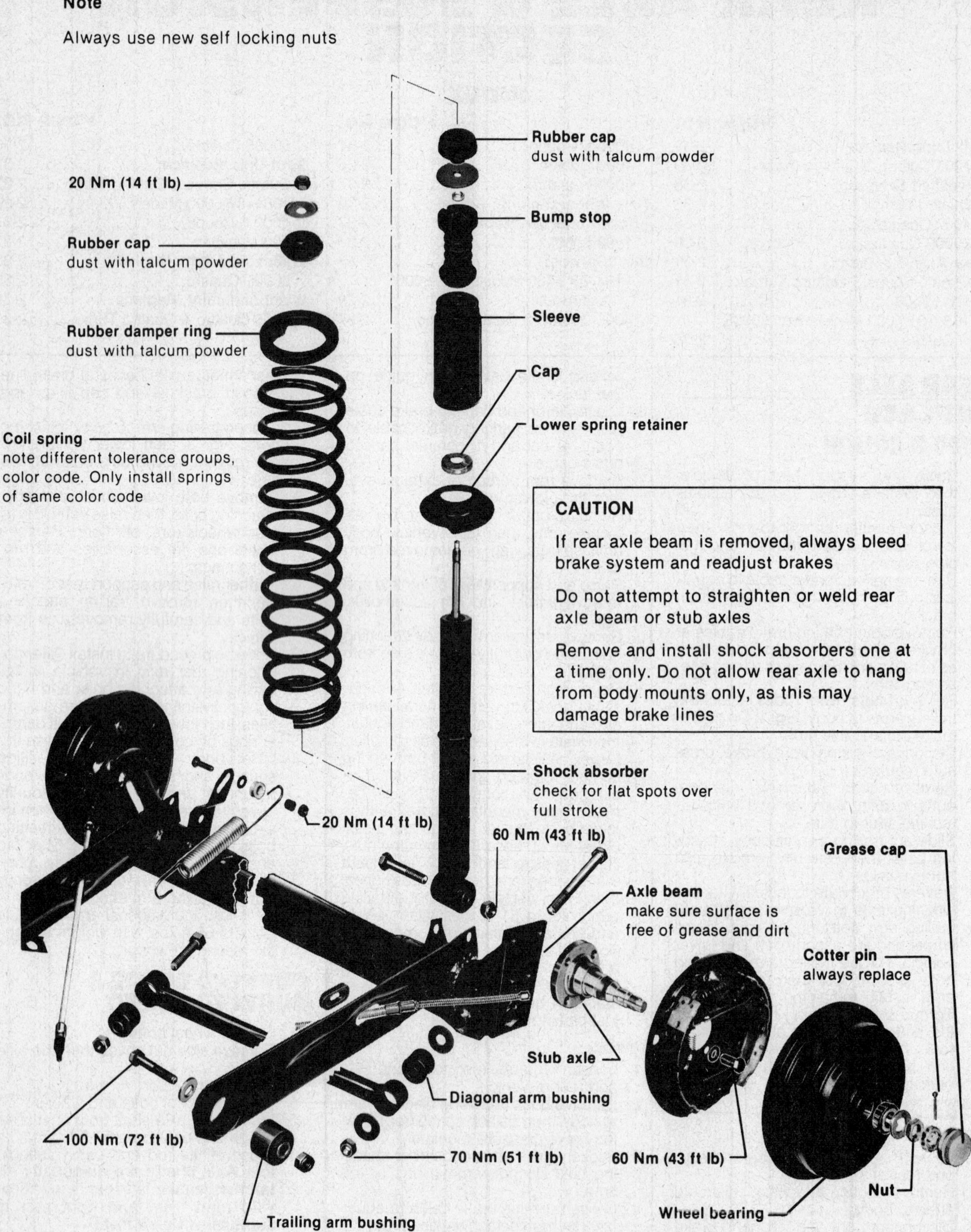
Note
Always use new self locking nuts
Rubber cap
dust with talcum powder
20 Nm (14 ft lb)
Bump stop
Rubber cap
dust with talcum powder
Sleeve
Rubber damper ring
dust with talcum powder
Cap
Lower spring retainer
Coil spring
note different tolerance groups, color code. Only install springs of same color code
CAUTION
If rear axle beam is removed, always bleed brake system and readjust brakes
Do not attempt to straighten or weld rear axle beam or stub axles
Remove and install shock absorbers one at a time only. Do not allow rear axle to hang from body mounts only, as this may damage brake lines
Shock absorber
check for flat spots over full stroke
20 Nm (14 ft lb)
60 Nm (43 ft lb)
Grease cap
Axle beam
make sure surface is free of grease and dirt
Cotter pin
always replace
Stub axle
Diagonal arm bushing
100 Nm (72 ft lb)
70 Nm (51 ft lb)
60 Nm (43 ft lb)
Nut
Wheel bearing
Trailing arm bushing

Fig. 1 Rear axle & suspension. 4000 & Coupe

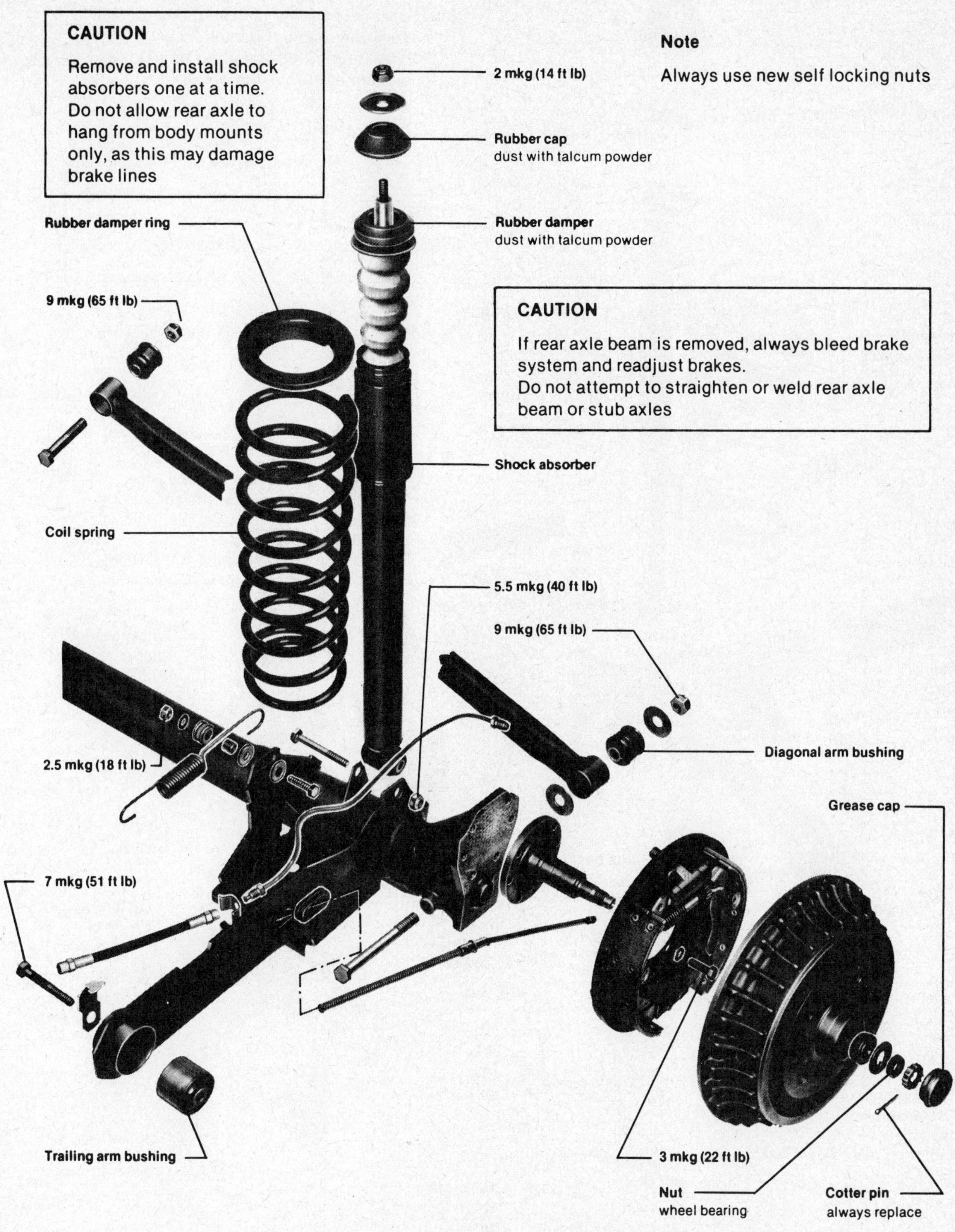
CAUTION
Remove and install shock absorbers one at a time. Do not allow rear axle to hang from body mounts only, as this may damage brake lines
2 mkg (14 ft lb)
Note
Always use new self locking nuts
Rubber cap
dust with talcum powder
Rubber damper ring
Rubber damper
dust with talcum powder
9 mkg (65 ft lb)
CAUTION
If rear axle beam is removed, always bleed brake system and readjust brakes.
Do not attempt to straighten or weld rear axle beam or stub axles
Shock absorber
Coil spring
5.5 mkg (40 ft lb)
9 mkg (65 ft lb)
2.5 mkg (18 ft lb)
Diagonal arm bushing
Grease cap
7 mkg (51 ft lb)
Trailing arm bushing
3 mkg (22 ft lb)
Nut
wheel bearing
Cotter pin
always replace

Fig. 2 Rear axle & suspension. 1983 5000 exc. Turbo

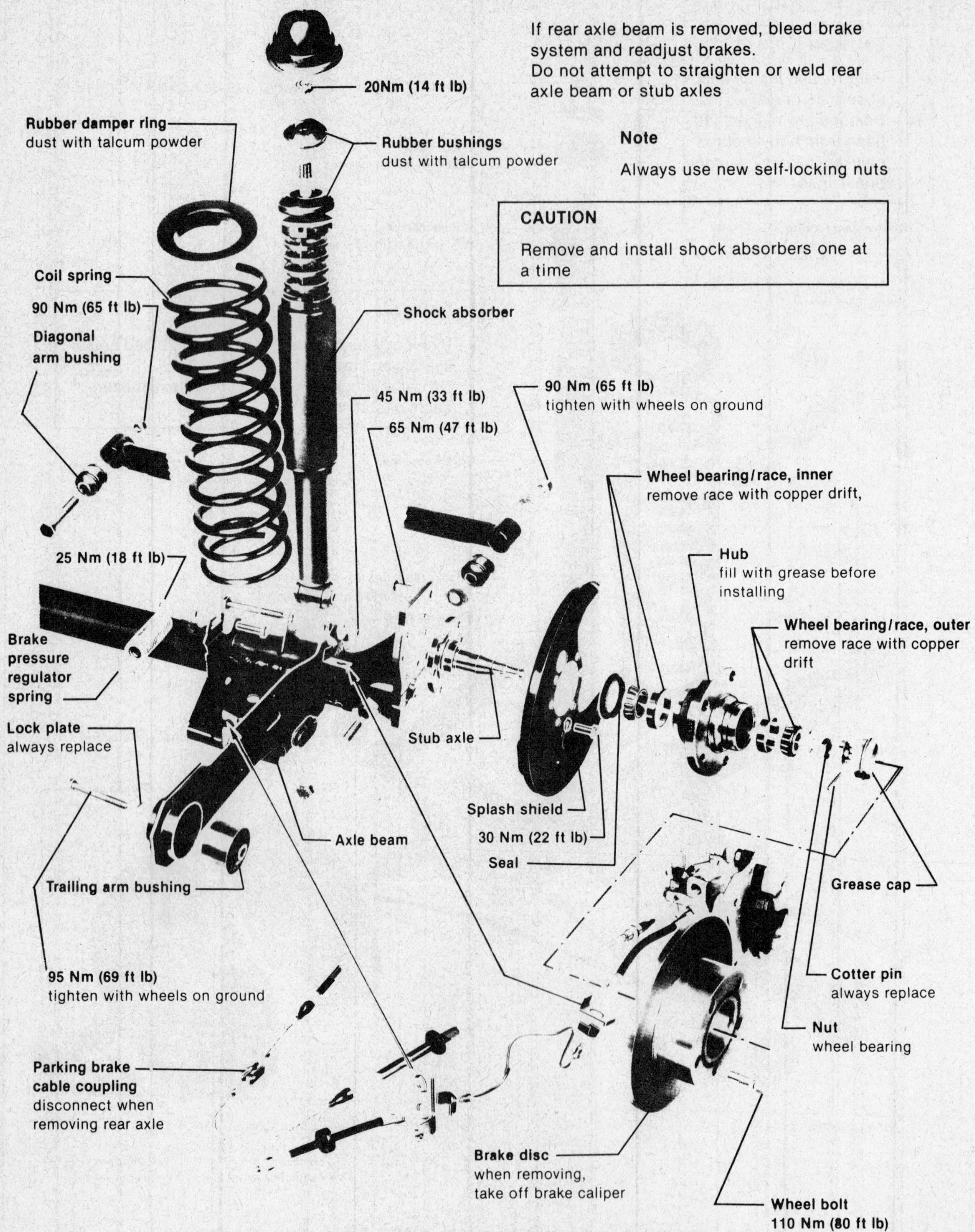
If rear axle beam is removed, bleed brake system and readjust brakes.
Do not attempt to straighten or weld rear axle beam or stub axles
Note
Always use new self-locking nuts
CAUTION
Remove and install shock absorbers one at a time
20Nm (14 ft lb)
Rubber damper ring dust with talcum powder
Rubber bushings dust with talcum powder
Coil spring
90 Nm (65 ft lb)
Diagonal arm bushing
Shock absorber
45 Nm (33 ft lb)
65 Nm (47 ft lb)
90 Nm (65 ft lb) tighten with wheels on ground
Wheel bearing/race, inner remove race with copper drift,
25 Nm (18 ft lb)
Hub fill with grease before installing
Wheel bearing/race, outer remove race with copper drift
Brake pressure regulator spring
Lock plate always replace
Stub axle
Splash shield
Axle beam
30 Nm (22 ft lb)
Seal
Trailing arm bushing
Grease cap
95 Nm (69 ft lb) tighten with wheels on ground
Cotter pin always replace
Nut wheel bearing
Parking brake cable coupling disconnect when removing rear axle
Brake disc when removing, take off brake caliper
Wheel bolt 110 Nm (80 ft lb)

Fig. 3 Rear axle & suspension. 5000 Turbo

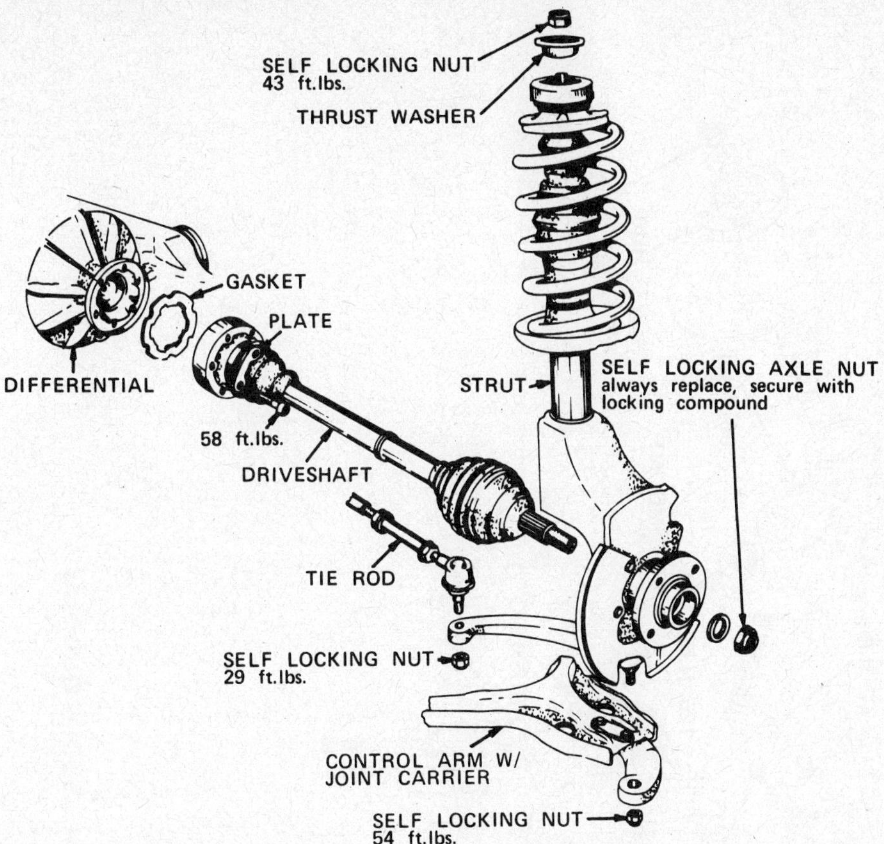

Fig. 4 Rear driveshaft & suspension strut. 4000 Quattro

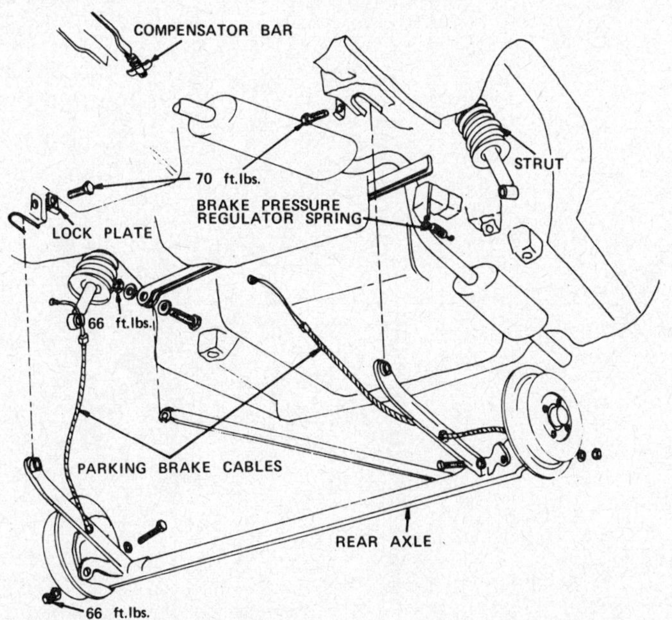

Fig. 5 Rear axle assembly. 1984–87 5000 models exc. 5000S Quattro

ing that there is sufficient clearance between inner constant velocity joint and final drive housing. **Use only mechanical or hydraulic puller to remove stub axle. Never use hot air blower or flame to heat stub axle.**

11. Reverse procedure to install, noting the following:
    a. Replace gasket on inner constant velocity joint.
    b. Ensure that splines on stub axle and wheel hub are free of oil, grease and old locking compound.
    c. Apply bead of suitable locking compound approximately 13/64 inch wide around splines and allow to harden for at least one hour.
    d. Install stub axle.
    e. Torque ball joint clamp nut to 47 ft. lbs., axle shaft to final drive attaching bolts to 58 ft. lbs., wheel bolts to 80 ft. lbs., and axle nut to 203 ft. lbs.

4000 QUATTRO

1. Remove axle nut, wheel bolts and wheel.
2. Loosen driveshaft at differential flange, **Fig. 4. Remove and install axle nut only with wheels on ground. Do not move vehicle without driveshaft or outer constant velocity joint installed.**
3. Remove ball joint attaching nut and, using suitable tool, press ball joint out of joint carrier.
4. Loosen control arm attaching bolts at subframe and swing control arm downward.
5. Using suitable tool, remove tie rod.
6. Pull off brake hose and parking brake cable with rubber grommet.
7. Using suitable puller, press driveshaft out of hub. **Always remove stub axle with mechanical or hydraulic hub puller only. Do not heat wheel bearing housing.**
8. Angle driveshaft upward alongside differential.
9. Reverse procedure to install, noting the following:
    a. Ensure splines on stub axle and wheel hub are free of oil, grease and old locking compound.
    b. Apply suitable locking compound around splines in a bead not more than 1/4 inch wide. Allow locking compound to harden for at least one hour.
    c. Replace gasket on inner CV joint.
    d. Torque axle shaft to transmission attaching bolts to 58 ft. lbs., rear axle nut to 203 ft. lbs. and the wheel bolts to 80 ft. lbs.

1984–87 5000 MODELS EXC. 5000S QUATTRO

1. Raise and support vehicle, then remove rear wheel and tire assemblies.
2. Remove parking brake cable adjusting nut, **Fig. 5.**
3. Disconnect parking brake cable at coupling.
4. Remove clip and unhook right side parking brake cable.
5. Remove clips and unhook left side parking brake cable.
6. Remove bracket with pressure accumulator, leaving fuel lines connected.
7. Disconnect both brake hoses and plug lines.
8. Remove diagonal arm.
9. Unhook brake pressure regulator spring.
10. Support axle with suitable jack.
11. Remove lower shock absorber attaching bolts.
12. Remove trailing arm bolts on both sides.
13. Lower and remove rear axle.
14. Reverse procedure to install, noting the following:
    a. After placing rear axle in position, install both trailing arm bolts and

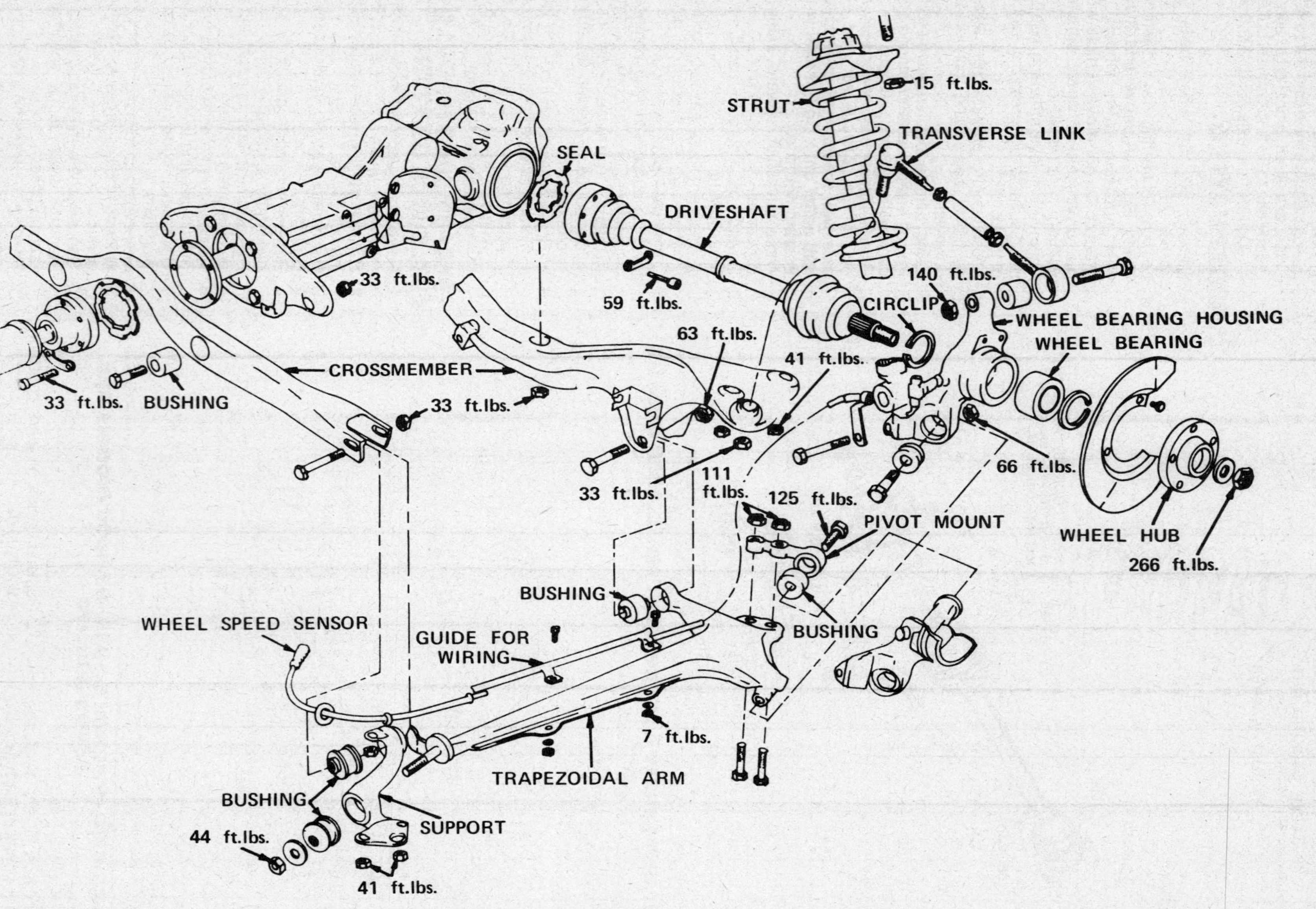

Fig. 6 Rear axle & suspension. 5000S Quattro

tighten lightly.
  b. Lift rear axle and install lower shock absorber attaching bolts.
  c. Install diagonal arm, brake hoses and pressure regulator spring.
  d. Bleed brake system.
  e. Install parking brake cable and adjust parking brake.
  f. Tighten bolts for trailing arm and shock absorbers with wheels standing on ground.

5000S QUATTRO

1. Remove wheel trim and loosen lug nuts.
2. Remove axle nut, **Fig. 6. Remove and install axle nut only with wheels on ground. Do not move vehicle without driveshaft or outer constant velocity joint installed.**
3. Remove wheel and tire assembly.
4. Remove caliper attaching bolt and caliper, suspending caliper from body with wire.
5. Remove brake disc.
6. Remove bolts from driveshaft flange. **When removing right side driveshaft, remove fuel tank cover plate.**
7. When working on left side, remove transverse link to wheel bearing housing attaching nut and the transverse link.
8. Remove trapezoidal arm to crossmember attaching nut and bolt, then press arm downward to remove.
9. Using suitable puller, press out driveshaft from hub. **Always remove stub axle with mechanical or hydraulic hub puller. Do not heat wheel bearing housing.**
10. Reverse procedure to install, noting the following:
    a. Ensure splines of driveshaft and wheel hub are free of oil, grease and old locking compound.
    b. Apply suitable locking compound to splines of outer joint over an area of approximately 3/16 inch.
    c. Install driveshaft.
    d. Apply suitable locking compound to threads of driveshaft to wheel hub nut. Allow locking compound to harden for at least one hour.
    e. Torque brake caliper attaching bolt to 48 ft. lbs., wheel hub to driveshaft nut to 266 ft. lbs., trapezoidal arm to crossmember bolt to 63 ft. lbs. and the transverse link to wheel bearing housing bolts to 148 ft. lbs.

SHOCK ABSORBER REPLACE

1983 5000

If vehicle is to be raised to remove shock absorber, spring tensioner 3004 must be used to support rear axle before removing any of the shock absorber attaching nuts or bolts. If vehicle is not to be raised, the spring tensioner tool is not required.

1. Open trunk and loosen carpet trim, then remove stem from shock absorber upper mounting stud.
2. Remove nut and bushing from shock absorber upper mounting, then remove shock absorber lower attaching bolt and remove shock absorber, **Figs. 2 and 3.**
3. Reverse procedure to install. Torque shock absorber upper attaching nut to 14 ft. lbs. and lower attaching bolt to 43 ft. lbs.

STRUT UNIT REPLACE

4000 & COUPE

Do not remove both strut units at the same time. Replace one side, then the other.

1. Loosen trunk sheet metal trim, then remove cap and retaining nut from upper strut unit attachment.
2. Raise and support rear of vehicle, then remove strut unit lower attachment retaining bolt and remove strut unit, **Fig. 1.**
3. Reverse procedure to install. Torque upper strut mounting nut to 14 ft. lbs. and lower attaching bolt to 43 ft. lbs.

Strut Unit Service

Before removing strut unit upper retaining nut, compress coil spring using a suitable spring compressor. When servicing strut unit, refer to Fig. 1.

QUATTRO COUPE & QUATTRO TURBO

1. Loosen wheel bolts.
2. Remove axle nut cover, then the axle nut.
3. Raise and support vehicle.
4. Remove wheel bolts and wheel.
5. Press off tie rod end using suitable tool.
6. Remove caliper attaching bolts.
7. Disconnect brake hose at bracket.
8. Remove caliper and tie out of way, leaving brake lines attached.
9. Remove brake disc.
10. Remove ball joint clamp bolt.
11. Pry ball joint out of hub.
12. Press out stub axle from hub.
13. Remove fuel tank cover.
14. Remove sunroof storage holder.
15. Remove strut attaching nut, holding suspension strut from below to keep from falling, then remove suspension strut assembly.
16. Reverse procedure to install, noting the following:
    a. Apply bead of suitable locking compound approximately 13/64 inch wide around splines and allow to harden for at least one hour.
    b. Install stub axle.
    c. Torque tie rod nut and suspension strut to body attaching nut to 43 ft. lbs., ball joint clamp nut and brake caliper mounting bolts to 47 ft. lbs., wheel bolts to 80 ft. lbs., and the axle nut to 203 ft. lbs.

4000 QUATTRO

1. Remove axle nut and loosen lug nuts.
2. Raise and support vehicle, then remove wheel and tire assembly.
3. Remove ball joint attaching nut and, using suitable tool, press ball joint out of carrier.
4. Loosen control arm attaching bolts at subframe and swing arm downward.
5. Using suitable tool, remove tie rod.
6. Pull out brake hose and parking brake cable with rubber grommet.
7. Remove caliper attaching bolts and the caliper, suspending caliper from body with wire.
8. Remove brake disc.
9. Using suitable puller, press driveshaft from hub.
10. Secure suspension strut from below.
11. Remove rear seat bench and back rest.
12. Pull rear shelf lining forward.
13. Remove upper shock absorber nut, holding piston rod with suitable tool.
14. Remove strut from vehicle.
15. Reverse procedure to install, noting the following:
    a. Torque shock absorber nut to 43 ft. lbs. while holding piston rod with suitable tool.
    b. Ensure splines on driveshaft and wheel hub are free of oil, grease and old locking compound.
    c. Apply suitable locking compound around splines in a bead not more than 1/4 inch wide. Allow locking compound to harden for at least one hour.

1984–87 5000 MODELS

1. Raise and support vehicle, then remove wheel and tire assembly.
2. Support axle with suitable jack.
3. Remove lower shock absorber mounting bolt.
4. Remove upper strut to flange attaching nuts, then the strut.
5. Reverse procedure to install. Torque flange to strut attaching nuts to 15 ft. lbs. Torque lower shock absorber attaching bolt to 66 ft. lbs. with wheels resting on ground.

STRUT SERVICE

4000 QUATTRO & QUATTRO TURBO

When working on strut assembly on these vehicles, gap on tool VW340/5 must be enlarged to 2 3/16 inch.

1. Install tool VW340/5 or equivalent so that spring cannot jump out.
2. Compress spring with spring tensioner until upper spring retainer is free of tension.
3. Hold shock absorber shaft with suitable tool and remove slotted nut.
4. Remove strut bearing and spring retainer.
5. Remove spring tensioner.
6. Remove remaining strut components.
7. Remove shock absorber threaded cap and the shock absorber.
8. Reverse procedure to assemble. Torque shock absorber threaded cap to 130 ft. lbs. and the upper spring retainer nut to 36 ft. lbs.

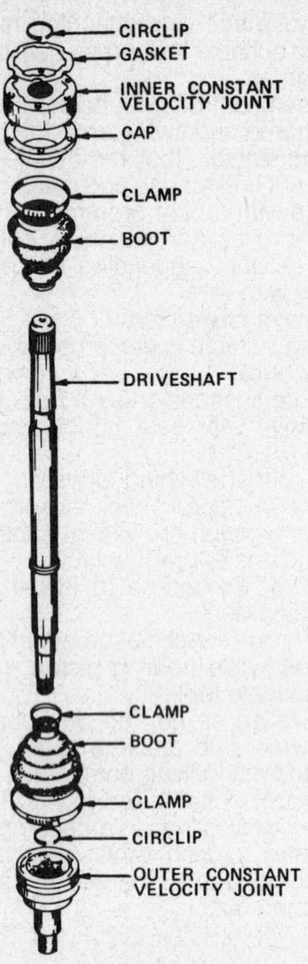

Fig. 7 Exploded view of rear driveshaft. 4000 Quattro

1984–87 5000 MODELS EXC. 5000S QUATTRO

When disassembling strut, compress spring with tool US1117 or equivalent and remove nut from shock absorber using tool 3017A or equivalent. When assembling, note the following:

1. Push protective cap over shock absorber.
2. Push bump stop into protective sleeve and attach to rubber damper ring.
3. Dust rubber cap and rubber damper ring with talcum powder.
4. Hole in upper retainer ring must be centered.
5. Lower end of left side coil spring must point toward rear and lower end of right side must point toward front.

5000S QUATTRO

When disassembling strut, use tool VW340 or equivalent to compress spring. When assembling, note assembling instructions under "1984-87 5000 Models Exc. 5000S Quattro". Additionally, ensure two lugs of damper ring are seated against spring and that stop for coil spring is aligned with hole for shock absorber mounting.

DRIVESHAFT SERVICE

QUATTRO TURBO

Driveshafts are diagonally interchangeable. When servicing these driveshafts, refer to "Front Suspension & Steering Section."

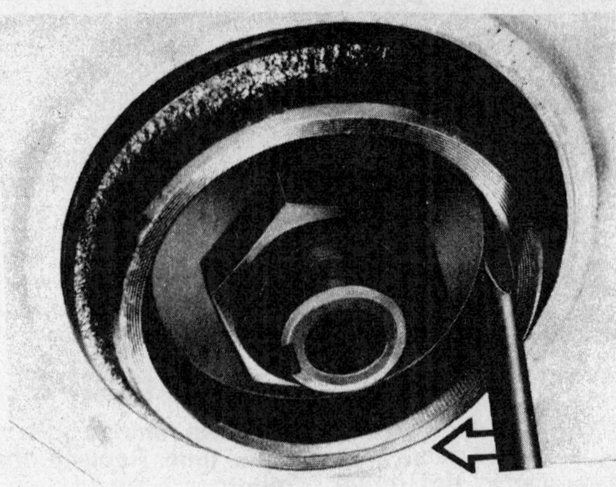

Fig. 8 Checking wheel bearing adjustment

4000 QUATTRO

1. When disassembling driveshaft, **Fig. 7**, note the following:
   a. Length of left driveshaft is 19.63 inches and length of right driveshaft is 21.39 inches.
   b. Always use suitable pliers to loosen or tighten clamps.
   c. When removing outer CV joint, spread circlip and drive joint off of shaft by tapping lightly against hub with copper drift.
   d. When removing inner CV joint circlip, use suitable tool.
   e. When removing inner CV joint protective cap, drive off joint with suitable drift.
   f. Use tools VW411 and VW402, or equivalents, to press off inner CV joint.
2. When disassembling outer CV joint, proceed as follows:
   a. Mark position of hub in relation to cage and housing.
   b. Swivel hub and cage to remove balls.
   c. Turn two larger openings of cage until level with joint edge, then remove cage with hub.
   d. Swing hub until one segment can be pushed into larger rectangular opening of cage, then tilt hub out. **Six balls of each joint belong to one tolerance group, always replace hub, outer ring, ball cage and balls together.**
   e. Check housing, hub, cage and boss for pitting. Replace joint if excessive radial clearance in joint is noticeable when shifting gears.
3. When assembling outer CV joint, reverse disassembly procedure and note the following:
   a. Fill joint with 60 grams of grease (half the amount supplied in repair kit).
   b. Install cage with hub into housing, installing balls from opposite side, and ensure marked positions of hub, cage and housing are aligned.
   c. Install new circlip into joint hub.
   d. Fill joint with remaining grease.
4. When disassembling inner CV joint, proceed as follows:
   a. Pivot ball hub and cage out of outer ring and push out.
   b. Remove balls. **Six balls of one joint belong to one tolerance group. Always replace hub, outer ring, ball cage and balls together.**
   c. Align two grooves and take ball hub out of ball cage.
   d. Check housing, hub, cage and boss for pitting. Replace joint if excessive radial clearance in joint is noticeable when shifting gears.
5. When assembling inner CV joint, proceed as follows:
   a. Install 60 grams of grease supplied with repair kit into each side of joint.
   b. Install ball hub along both grooves in ball cage.
   c. Push balls into cage.
   d. Install ball hub into proper outer ring, ensuring chamfer on inside diameter of ball hub points to contact shoulder on driveshaft and to larger diameter of outer ring.
   e. Insert hub with cage and balls into outer ring vertically.
   f. Ensure wide ball groove in outer ring and narrow groove in hub are together on one side when hub is swung into outer ring.
   g. When pivoting ball hub with cage and balls in outer ring, hub should be pivoted out of cage until balls are spaced to fit grooves.
   h. Press cage firmly until hub swings fully into position. **Joint is correctly assembled when ball hub can be moved in and out over full range of axial movement by hand.**
6. When assembling driveshaft, note the following:
   a. Always install new circlips and boot clamps.
   b. Check boots for cracks, replacing as necessary. Inner boot has breather hole. When installing do not install small clamp.
   c. When installing outer boot, lift

small diameter end of boot if folded inward.

d. When installing CV joint circlip, press joint onto shaft with suitable tools until circlip can be pressed into groove. **Chamfer on inside diameter of ball hub must face contact shoulder on driveshaft.**

e. Seal protective cap against inner CV joint with suitable locking compound.

5000S QUATTRO

For service procedures on these driveshafts, refer to "Front Suspension & Steering Section."

WISHBONE JOINT
REPLACE
4000 QUATTRO & QUATTRO TURBO

1. Raise and support vehicle, then remove wheel and tire assembly.
2. Remove ball joint attaching nut and, using suitable tool, press ball joint out of joint carrier.
3. Loosen control arm mounting bolts at subframe and swing control arm downward.
4. Reverse procedure to install.

BALL JOINT
REPLACE
4000 QUATTRO & QUATTRO TURBO

1. Remove wishbone joint as previously described.
2. Remove bolts from wheel bearing housing.
3. Insert two M8 40 mm bolts approximately one inch into wheel bearing housing.
4. Push preassembled tool 40-204A or equivalent over ball joint.
5. Attach joint mounting nut with large washer onto joint and tighten as far as possible.
6. Pull out ball joint by turning installed bolts counterclockwise one at a time. **Before driving ball joint into place, align holes with wheel bearing housing.**
7. Using tool VW415a or equivalent, drive ball joint into wheel bearing housing until seated.
8. Torque ball joint bolts to 29 ft. lbs.
9. Swivel control arm into place and torque ball joint nut to 54 ft. lbs.
10. Tighten control arm mountings with vehicle wheels resting on ground.

TRAPEZOIDAL ARM
REPLACE
5000S QUATTRO

1. Raise and support vehicle, then remove wheel and tire assembly.
2. Remove fasteners securing guide for wheel speed sensor wiring and remove guide.
3. Remove bolt at front attaching wheel bearing housing to trapezoidal arm.
4. Remove bolt at rear securing trapezoidal arm to wheel bearing housing.
5. Remove bolt attaching trapezoidal housing to crossmember.
6. Disconnect brake pressure regulator spring.
7. Remove nut at front support and pull trapezoidal arm out.
8. Reverse procedure to install, noting the following:
   a. Apply suitable locking compound to bolts securing wheel bearing housing to trapezoidal arm.
   b. Torque wheel speed sensor guide to arm fasteners to 7 ft. lbs.
   c. Torque trapezoidal arm to wheel bearing housing bolts to 125 ft. lbs.
   d. Torque trapezoidal arm to crossmember attaching bolt to 63 ft. lbs.
   e. Torque trapezoidal arm to support attaching bolts to 44 ft. lbs.

REAR WHEEL BEARING
ADJUST

1. Raise and support rear of vehicle.
2. Remove grease cap and cotter pin, then while rotating wheel, tighten bearing adjusting nut until it is firmly seated against bearing.
3. Back off adjusting nut and check wheel bearing clearance. Wheel bearing clearance is correct when bearing thrust washer can be moved slightly with a screwdriver and finger pressure, **Fig. 8.**
4. After completing adjustment, install cotter pin, grease cap and lower vehicle.

FRONT SUSPENSION & STEERING SECTION

INDEX

DRIVESHAFT
REPLACE
4000 & COUPE
Models Less Stabilizer Link Rod

1. Remove wheel cover and remove nut securing axle shaft in hub.
2. Raise and support front of vehicle and remove front wheels.
3. Remove screws securing drive shaft flange to transmission.
4. Mark position of ball joint on control arm and disconnect ball joint from control arm.
5. Remove drive shaft from hub and remove from vehicle while holding pivot mounting outward.
6. Install axle shaft end of drive shaft through front hub and position shaft in installed position.
7. Bring ball joint into position as marked with tool, **Fig. 1,** and torque nuts to 47 ft. lbs.
8. Install bolts securing drive shaft flange to transmission and torque to 33 ft. lbs.
9. Install wheels and lower vehicle to ground.
10. Install nut securing axle shaft in front hub and torque to 167 ft. lbs.

Models With Stabilizer Link Rod

1. Remove wheel cover, then the axle nut.
2. Loosen lug nuts, then raise and support vehicle and remove wheel.
3. Disconnect driveshaft at transmission flange and angle driveshaft upward along side transmission.
4. Using suitable puller, press driveshaft out of hub and remove driveshaft. **Use only mechanical or hydraulic hub puller to remove stub axle. Do not heat wheel bearing housing or wheel bearing. When installing driveshaft, ensure that splines on**

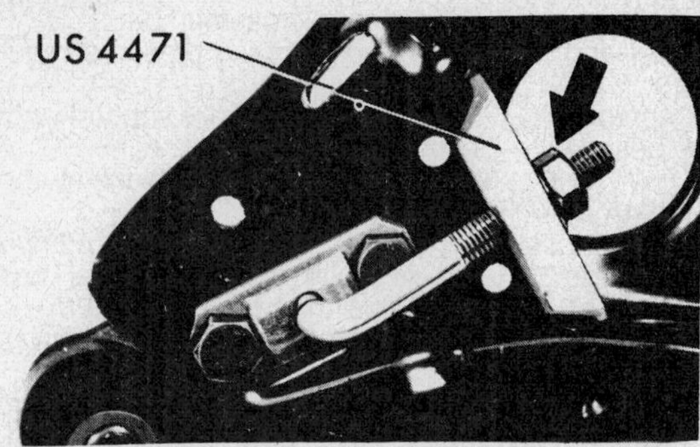

Fig. 1 Ball joint installation. 4000 & Coupe models

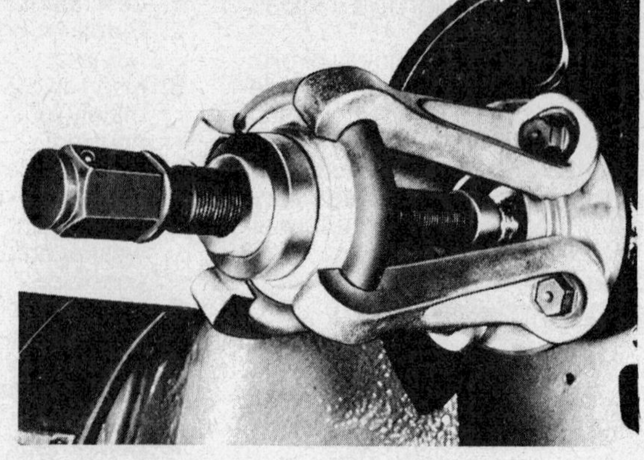

Fig. 2 Driveshaft removal. 5000 models

driveshaft and wheel hub are free of oil, grease and old locking compound.

5. Reverse procedure to install, noting the following:
   a. Apply a bead of suitable locking compound not more than 1/4 inch wide around splines of driveshaft and allow to harden for at least one hour.
   b. Replace gasket on inner constant velocity joint.

5000 MODELS

1. Remove wheel cover and remove nut securing axle shaft in hub.
2. Raise and support vehicle and remove wheels. Remove shield in right side drive shaft.
3. Remove screws securing drive shaft flange to transmission.
4. On automatic transmission models, remove stabilizer bar clamps and disconnect ball joint from hub.
5. Press axle shaft from hub, **Fig. 2**.
6. Raise transmission end of shaft and guide axle shaft out of hub. On automatic transmission models, pull suspension strut outward to remove drive shaft.
7. Reverse procedure to install, torque axle shaft nut to 203 ft. lbs. and transmission flange bolts to 32 ft. lbs., 58 ft. lbs. on turbocharged models.

QUATTRO COUPE & QUATTRO TURBO

1. Remove wheel cover and loosen lug nuts, then remove dust cap and the axle nut.
2. Raise and support vehicle, then remove lug nuts and wheel.
3. Remove right backing plate.
4. Disconnect axle shaft at transmission flange and position out of way.
5. Using suitable puller, press out stub axle from hub. **Use only mechanical or hydraulic puller to remove stub axle. Never use hot air blower or flame to heat stub axle.**
6. Reverse procedure to install, noting the following:
   a. Replace gasket on inner constant velocity joint. **Ensure that splines on stub axle and wheel hub are free of oil, grease and old locking compound.**
   b. Apply bead of suitable locking compound approximately 13/64 inch wide around splines and install stub axle. Allow locking compound to harden for at least one hour.
   c. Torque axle shaft to transmission attaching bolts to 58 ft. lbs., lug nuts to 80 ft. lbs., and axle nut to 203 ft. lbs.

DRIVESHAFT SERVICE

4000 MODELS

Two types of driveshafts are used on these vehicles. All 4 cylinder models and 5 cylinder models up to VIN No. DA077974 use driveshafts referred to as type A. 5 cylinder models from VIN No. DA077974 use driveshafts referred to as type B. Driveshaft length varies from side to side and differs according to engine and transmission type. Driveshaft lengths are as follows: 4 cylinder w/manual transmission, left side-20.87 inches, right side-20.87 inches; 4 cylinder w/automatic transmission, left side-23.21 inches, right side-19.28 inches; 5 cylinder w/manual transmission exc. 4000 Quattro, left side-22.95 inches, right side-19.63 inches; 5 cylinder w/automatic transmission exc. 4000 Quattro, left side-22.95 inches, right side-19.05 inches; 4000 Quattro, left side-21.32 inches, right side-19.53 inches.

1. When disassembling drive shaft, note the following:
   a. Always use suitable pliers when loosening or tightening boot clamps.
   b. When removing outer CV joint on type A driveshafts, spread circlip and drive joint off shaft by tapping lightly with copper drift against hub.
   c. When removing outer CV joint on type B driveshaft, drive joint off shaft by tapping with copper drift or mallet against hub.
   d. Always use suitable pliers when removing inner CV joint circlip.
   e. To remove protective cap from inner CV joint, drive off joint with drift.
   f. When removing inner CV joint, press off with suitable tools.
2. To disassemble outer CV joint, proceed as follows:
   a. Mark position of hub in relation to cage and housing.
   b. Swivel hub and cage while removing balls one after the other.
   c. Turn two larger openings of cage until level with joint edge, then remove cage with hub.
   d. Swing hub until one segment can be pushed into larger rectangular opening of cage, then tilt hub out. **Six balls of each joint belong to one tolerance group. Always replace hub, outer ring, ball cage and balls together.**
   e. Check housing, hub, cage and balls for pitting. If excessive radial clearance in joint is noticeable when shifting gears, replace joint.
3. When assembling outer CV joint, proceed as follows:
   a. Fill joint with 45 grams of grease included with repair kit.
   b. Install cage with hub into housing, install balls from opposite side, and ensure marked position of hub, cage and housing match.
   c. Install new circlip on shaft.
   d. Fill joint with remaining 45 grams of grease.
4. When disassembling inner CV joint, proceed as follows:
   a. Pivot ball hub and cage out of outer ring and push out, then pull out balls. **Six balls of each joint belong to one tolerance group. Always replace hub, outer ring, ball cage and balls as an assembly.**
   b. Align two grooves and take ball hub out of ball cage.
   c. Check housing, hub, cage and balls for pitting. If excessive radial clearance in joint is noticeable when shifting gears, replace joint.
5. When assembling inner CV joint, proceed as follows:
   a. Fill joint with 45 grams of grease, supplied with repair kit, on each side.
   b. Install ball hub along both grooves in ball cage.
   c. Push balls into cage and insert ball hub into proper outer ring, ensuring chamfer on inside diameter of ball hub points to contact shoulder on driveshaft and to larger diameter of outer ring.

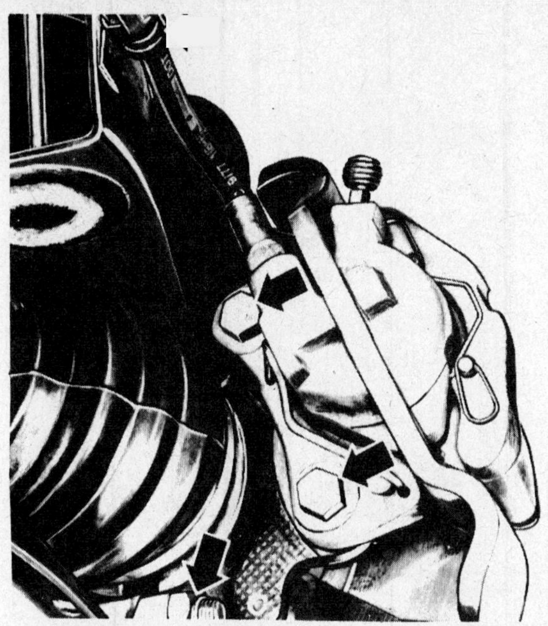

Fig. 3 Caliper & ball joint removal. 4000, Coupe & Quattro Coupe models

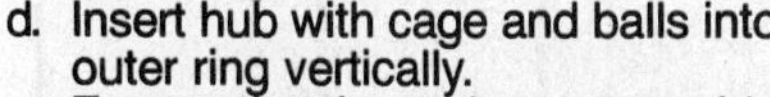

d. Insert hub with cage and balls into outer ring vertically.
e. Ensure that in each case a wide ball groove in outer ring and a narrow groove in hub are together on one side when hub is swung into outer ring. When pivoting ball hub with cage and balls in outer ring, hub should be pivoted out of cage until balls are spaced to fit grooves.
f. Press cage firmly until hub swings fully into position.
g. Joint is correctly assembled when ball hub can be moved in and out over full range of axial movement by hand.

6. When assembling driveshaft, note the following:
   a. Always use new circlips and boot clamps.
   b. Check boots for cracks, replacing as necessary.
   c. Type A driveshaft uses either of two types of dished washer for inner CV joint, install same type as that removed.
   d. Use concave washer without internal splines for inner CV joint end on type A driveshaft and concave washer with internal splines for type B driveshaft.
   e. When installing outer CV joint on type B driveshaft, place new circlip into groove of driveshaft and drive outer axle shaft onto driveshaft with plastic hammer until circlip is seated.
   f. When installing inner CV joint circlip, use suitable tools to press joint onto shaft until circlip can be pressed into groove.

5000 MODELS

Repair procedures for these driveshafts are the same as for those used on type B driveshafts used on 4000 models. Later model driveshafts used on 1983 5000 models incorporate a cooling fan for the inner CV joint. When servicing early production driveshafts, cooling fans should be installed on inner CV joints. On vehicles with automatic transmission, install cooling fan only on right side driveshaft. Driveshaft lengths are as follows: 1983 w/manual transmission, right side-21.80 inches, left side 21.80 inches; 1983 w/automatic transmission, right side-20.94 inches, left side-23.06 inches; 1984-87 w/manual transmission, right side-21.69 inches, left side 21.69 inches; 1984-87 w/automatic transmission, right side-20.83 inches, left side-22.945 inches.

SUSPENSION STRUT REPLACE

4000 & COUPE

Vehicles Less Stabilizer Link Rod

1. Remove wheel cover and remove nut securing axle shaft in hub.
2. Raise and support front of vehicle and remove wheels.
3. Remove bolts and clamp indicated by arrows, **Fig. 3,** and remove caliper leaving hydraulic line connected.
4. Disconnect tie rod from steering knuckle and remove stabilizer bar clamps and bar.
5. Push control arm down and remove axle shaft from hub.
6. Remove nut from top of shock absorber while supporting strut from below. Remove strut from vehicle.
7. Reverse procedure to install, and check front suspension alignment.

Vehicles With Stabilizer Link Rod

1. Remove wheel cover and loosen lug nuts, then remove dust cover and the axle shaft nut.
2. Raise and support vehicle, then remove wheel.
3. Remove bolts and clamps indicated by arrows, **Fig. 3,** and remove caliper, leaving brake hoses connected.
4. Remove brake disc.
5. Press off tie rod end.
6. Remove lower link rod attaching nut, then pry down on control arm to remove ball joint from wheel bearing housing.
7. Using suitable puller, press out driveshaft from hub and remove driveshaft.
8. Remove upper strut attaching nut while holding piston rod.
9. Reverse procedure to install, noting the following:
   a. Torque shock absorber nut, while holding piston, to 43 ft. lbs. **Splines on driveshaft and wheel hub must be free of oil, grease and old locking compound.**
   b. Apply bead of suitable locking compound no more than 1/4 inch wide around splines and allow locking compound to harden for at least one hour.
   c. Replace gasket on inner constant velocity joint.

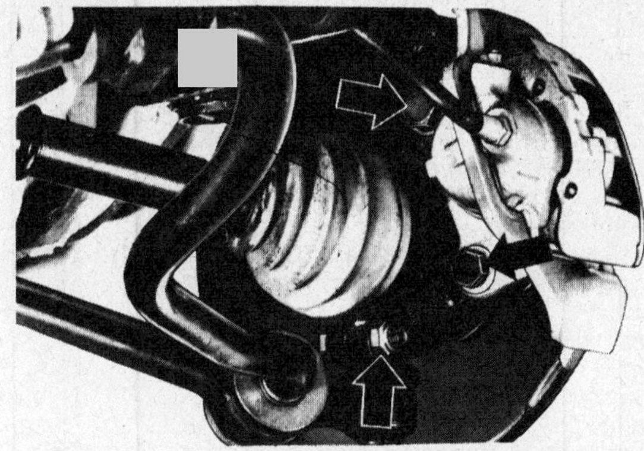

Fig. 4 Caliper & ball joint removal. 5000 models

5000 MODELS

1. Remove wheel cover and remove nut securing axle shaft in front hub.
2. Raise and support front of vehicle and remove wheels.
3. Remove stabilizer bar clamps on both sides.
4. Remove bolts indicated by arrows, **Fig. 4,** and remove caliper, leaving hydraulic line connected.
5. Disconnect tie rod from steering knuckle.
6. Press axle shaft from hub, **Fig. 2,** and remove ball joint from hub.
7. Remove nuts securing top of strut while supporting strut from below. Remove strut from vehicle.
8. Reverse procedure to install, and check front suspension alignment.

QUATTRO COUPE & QUATTRO TURBO

1. Remove wheel cover and loosen lug nuts, then remove dust cover and the

axle shaft nut.
2. Raise and support vehicle, then remove wheel.
3. Press off tie rod end.
4. Remove bolts and clamps indicated by arrows, **Fig. 3,** then remove brake caliper, leaving brake hoses attached.
5. Remove brake disc.
6. Remove stabilizer bar. **Wheels must be on ground when installing stabilizer bar.**
7. Remove ball joint from hub by prying downward.
8. Using suitable puller, press out stub axle from hub.
9. Remove upper suspension strut attaching nut, while holding strut from below, then remove strut assembly.
10. Reverse procedure to install, noting the following:
    a. Replace gasket on inner constant velocity joint. **Splines on stub axle and wheel hub must be free of oil, grease and old locking compound.**
    b. Apply bead of suitable locking compound approximately 13/64 inch wide around splines and install stub axle. Let locking compound harden for at least one hour.
    c. Torque stabilizer bar attaching bolts to 18 ft. lbs., suspension strut to body bolts to 43 ft. lbs., ball joint clamp nut to 47 ft. lbs., brake caliper attaching bolts to 83 ft. lbs., and the axle nut to 203 ft. lbs.

SUSPENSION STRUT REPAIR

4000, COUPE, QUATTRO COUPE & QUATTRO TURBO MODELS

1. Remove strut assembly as outlined under "Suspension Strut, Replace."
2. Compress coil spring with suitable spring compressor, **Fig. 5,** until upper spring retainer is free.
3. Hold shock absorber shaft and remove retaining nut, bearing, retainer, bump stop, and sleeve, **Fig. 6.** Remove compressed coil spring carefully and lay aside.
4. Remove threaded cap from top of strut tube and remove shock absorber cartridge, **Fig. 6.**
5. Reverse procedure to assemble, torque fasteners to specifications, **Fig. 6. Torque values for Quattro Turbo are as follows: slotted nut, 36 ft. lbs.; threaded cap, 130 ft. lbs.**

5000 MODELS

1983

1. Remove strut assembly as outlined under "Suspension Strut, Replace."
2. Mount assembly in vise and compress coil spring, **Fig. 7,** until upper spring retainer is free.
3. Mark position and remove upper spring mounting and retainer, damping ring, and bump stop, **Fig. 8.** Remove compressed coil spring carefully and lay aside.

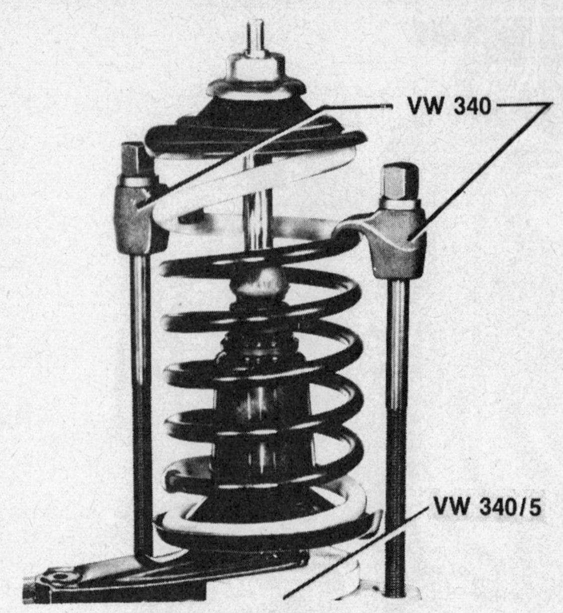

Fig. 5 Coil spring removal. 4000, Coupe & Quattro Coupe models

4. Remove threaded cap from top of strut tube, and remove shock absorber cartridge, **Fig. 8.**
5. Reverse procedure to assemble, torque fasteners to specifications, **Fig. 8.**

1984–87

1. Remove axle nut and washer.
2. Remove spring strut cover.
3. Remove upper shock absorber attaching nut.
4. Mark position of spring strut mounting, then remove mount.
5. Turn steering so piston rod of shock absorber is aligned in center of upper spring retainer, then insert piece of wood between spring and wheel housing to hold in position.
6. Attach tool 2070/1 or equivalent to shock absorber piston and tighten spindle until seated.
7. Tighten tool plate mounting nuts, then the spindle nut until seated.
8. Raise and support vehicle, then remove wheel and tire assembly.
9. Press off tie rod end with suitable tool.
10. Remove caliper mounting bolts and caliper, then suspend caliper from body with wire, leaving brake lines connected.
11. Remove brake disc.
12. Remove ball joint clamp bolt.
13. Remove stabilizer bar clamps on both sides.
14. Remove ball joint from hub by prying down on control arm.
15. Using suitable tool, press out stub axle from hub and remove axle shaft. **Always remove stub axle with mechanical or hydraulic hub puller. Do not apply heat to wheel bearing housing.**
16. Remove three tool plate attaching nuts while holding suspension strut from below.
17. Pull strut off of driveshaft.
18. Clamp strut in suitable vise.
19. Pull boot off cover, then loosen spindle nut while holding spindle.
20. Remove tool and disassemble strut.
21. Remove threaded cap using tool 2069 or equivalent, then pull out shock absorber.
22. Reverse procedure to assemble, noting the following:
    a. Ensure splines on CV joint and wheel hub are free of oil, grease and old locking compound.
    b. Apply suitable locking compound around splines in a bead not more than 1/4 inch wide.
    c. Allow locking compound to harden for at least one hour.
    d. Torque threaded cap to 133 ft. lbs.
    e. Torque shock absorber upper mounting nut to 44 ft. lbs., using tool 3078 or equivalent.
    f. Torque strut mounting bracket attaching bolts to 22 ft. lbs.
    g. Check front wheel alignment, adjusting as necessary.

POWER STEERING PUMP REPLACE

4000 MODELS

1. Disconnect battery ground cable.
2. Loosen drive belt adjusting bolt and swing pump downward, then remove drive belt.
3. Remove power steering pump pulley.
4. Disconnect pressure and suction hoses at pump.
5. Remove pump to mounts attaching bolts and remove pump.
6. Reverse procedure to install, noting the following:
    a. Torque pump to mounts attaching bolts to 14 ft. lbs.
    b. Torque pressure and suction hos-

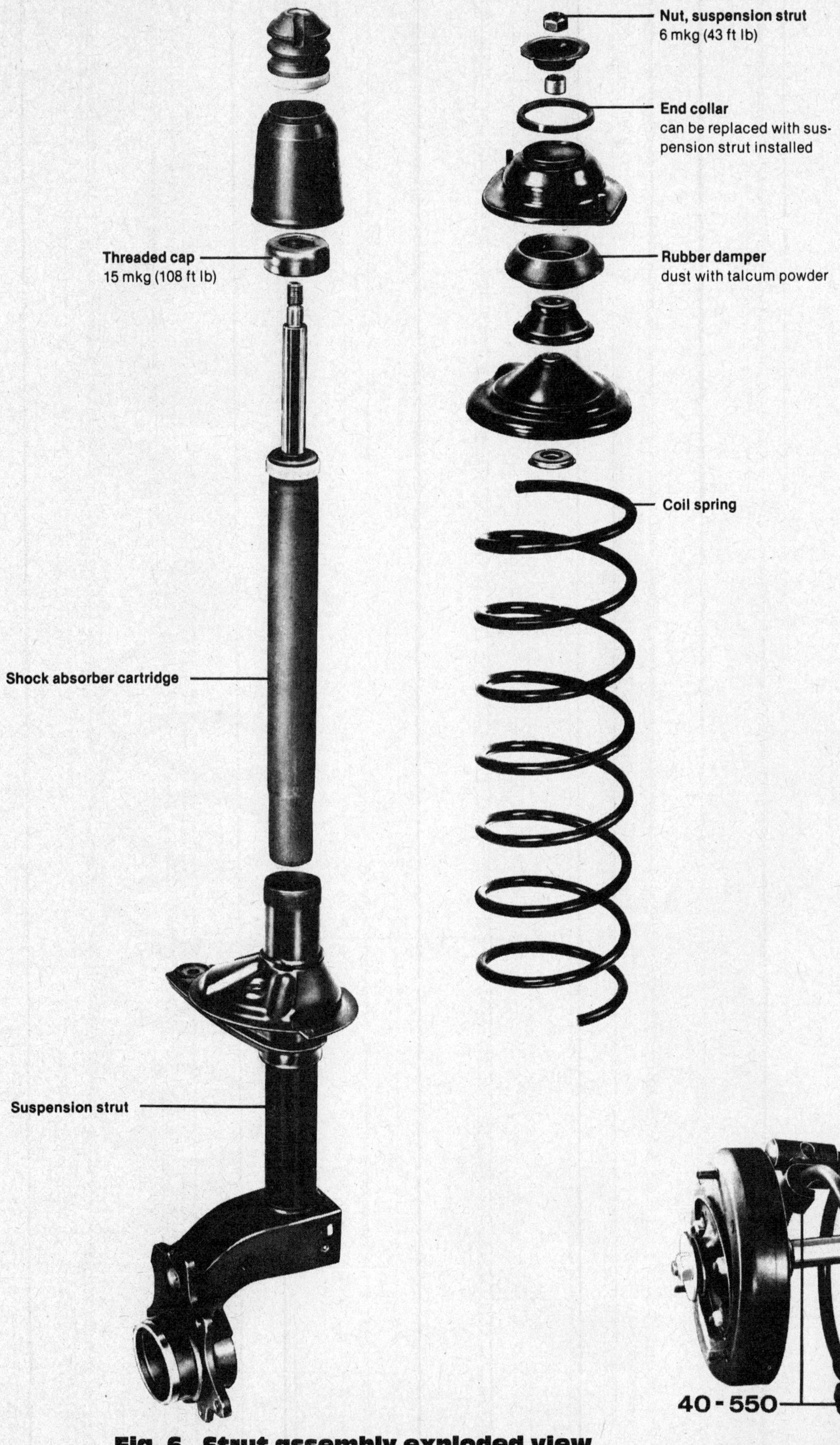

Nut, suspension strut
6 mkg (43 ft lb)

End collar
can be replaced with suspension strut installed

Threaded cap
15 mkg (108 ft lb)

Rubber damper
dust with talcum powder

Coil spring

Shock absorber cartridge

Suspension strut

Fig. 6 Strut assembly exploded view. 4000 models shown, Coupe & Quattro Coupe similar

Fig. 7 Coil spring removal. 5000 models

Note

Readjust camber and toe after replacing shock absorber. When replacing suspension strut mounting or coil spring always mark position of eccentric bolt

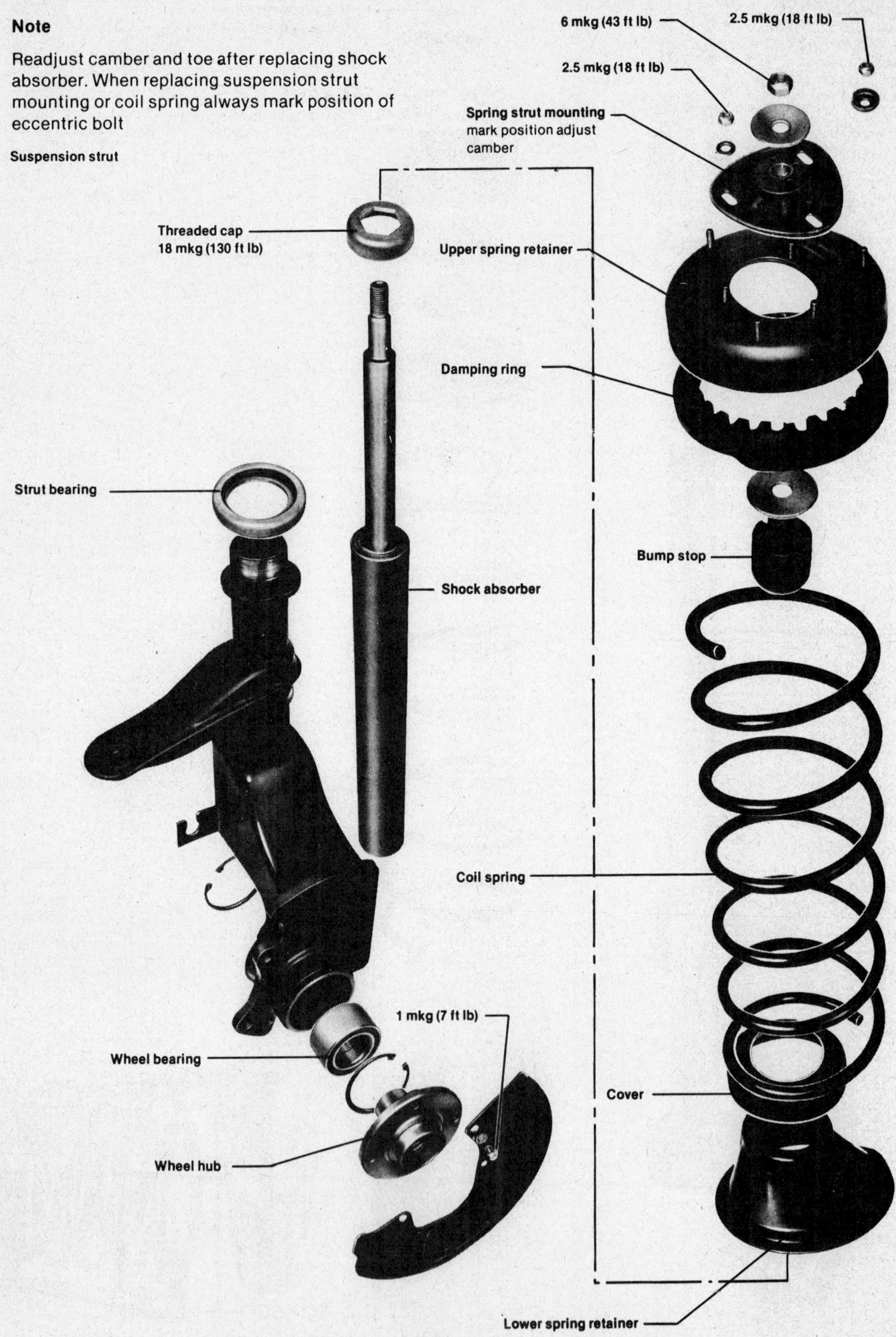

Fig. 8 Strut assembly exploded view. 5000 models

es to 29 ft. lbs.

c. Ensure mark "4-Z" or "5-Z" is on outer face of pulley.
d. Torque pulley attaching bolts to 14 ft. lbs.
e. Adjust drive belt with adjuster bolt.

5000 MODELS

When replacing power steering pump on 1983 models refer to "4000 Models".

When replacing pump on 1984-87 models, it is not necessary to remove power steering pump pulley. On 1984-87 models, torque pump to mounts attaching bolts to 15 ft. lbs., pressure accumulator feed pipe to pump bolt to 11 ft. lbs., pressure line attaching bolt to 18 ft. lbs. and the return line attaching bolt to 30 ft. lbs.

WHEEL ALIGNMENT SECTION

INDEX

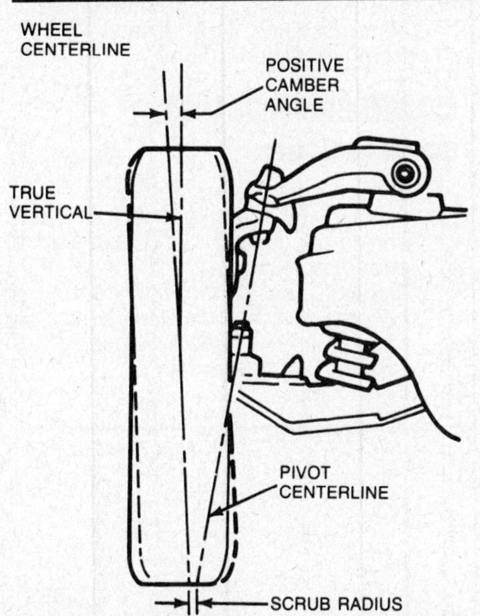

Fig. 1 Camber description

Fig. 2 Caster description

Fig. 3 Toe description

FRONT WHEEL ALIGNMENT PRECAUTIONS

Do not attempt to check and adjust front wheel alignment without first conducting a preliminary inspection of the front suspension components.

When checking/adjusting front axle wheel alignment, the following conditions are important and should be adhered to:

1. Front axle wheel alignment should not be checked until vehicle has accumulated approximately 1000-2000 miles and coil springs have properly settled.
2. Vehicle should be at gross vehicle weight or curb load weight when the checking or adjusting procedure is made.
3. Tire pressures should be to specification.
4. Test surface should be level and horizontal.
5. The steering gear should be correctly adjusted.
6. Steering linkage should be free of play.

FRONT WHEEL ALIGNMENT DESCRIPTION

CAMBER

Camber is the amount of centerline of the wheel is tilted inward or outward from true vertical, **Fig. 1.** If a wheel tilts outward, camber angle is positive. If the top of a wheel tilts inward, camber angle is negative.

CASTER

Caster is the forward or rearward tilt of the top of the front wheel spindle, **Fig. 2.** If the top of the spindle tilts to the rear, caster is positive. If the top of the spindle tilts to the front, caster is negative.

TOE

Toe should only be checked and adjusted after the caster and camber have been adjusted to specification.

Check toe with the front wheels in the straight ahead position. Lock steering wheel in place and measure distance between extreme front and also between the extreme rear of both front wheels. The difference between these two distances is the toe-in or toe-out dimensions, **Fig. 3.**

FRONT WHEEL ALIGNMENT ADJUSTMENTS

CAMBER, ADJUST

1983 4000 & Coupe

1. Loosen both ball joint mounting bolts on control arm and install tools US4490 and VW582, or equivalents.
2. Tighten tensioner nut to break joint loose from control arm.
3. Loosen tensioner nut until wheel has negative camber. **When nut is loosened, weight of vehicle on wheels will move wheel to negative camber position.**
4. Adjust camber to specification, torque mounting bolts to 47 ft. lbs. and remove tools.

1984–87 4000 Models Exc. Quattro

1. Loosen both ball joint mounting nuts on control arms.
2. Check that ball joint breaks loose from control arm. If not, bounce vehicle lightly, wheel will move to negative camber position.
3. Install tools US4490 and VW552, or equivalents.
4. Tighten tension nut on tool VW552 to adjust camber to specification.

5. Torque outboard ball joint mounting nut to 47 ft. lbs.
6. Recheck camber and correct as necessary, then remove tools.
7. Torque inboard ball joint mounting nut to 47 ft. lbs.

4000 Quattro

1. Loosen both ball joint mounting nuts on control arm.
2. Using tool 3098 or equivalent, move ball joint until camber is within specifications.
3. Torque mounting nuts to 47 ft. lbs., recheck camber, and adjust as necessary.

5000 Models

Camber is adjusted by moving suspension strut in slots.

TOE, ADJUST

All 4000 Models

On 4 cylinder vehicles, toe is adjusted on one side only by turning tie rod. The following procedure must be used when adjusting 5 cylinder vehicles.

1. Remove lower gear box cover plate attaching bolt.
2. Turn steering gear to center position.
3. Attach center tool 3075 or equivalent with bracket over mounting nut on left tie rod.
4. Remove bolt from spacer on chain of centering tool.
5. Insert bolt removed in step 4 through hole marked with "L" on centering tool and tighten to steering gear.
6. Measure and divide total toe in half.
7. Loosen clamps and outer locknut on both tie rods.
8. Turn tie rods until toe is within specifications.
9. Tighten clamps and locknuts on tie rods, check and position steering wheel in center position as necessary, remove centering tool and torque lower gear box cover plate attaching bolt to 14 ft. lbs.

1983 5000 Models

Toe is adjusted by turning tie rod ends.

1984–87 Models

1. Attach centering tool 3076 or equivalent into holes on top of steering unit and tie rod carrier.
2. Measure and divide total toe in half.
3. Adjust toe by turning tie rods.

REAR WHEEL ALIGNMENT ADJUSTMENTS

TOE, ADJUST

4000 Quattro

1. Loosen tie rod sleeve clamp nuts.
2. Adjust toe by turning sleeve either clockwise or counterclockwise.
3. Recheck adjustment.
4. With toe correctly adjusted, torque clamp nuts to 29 ft. lbs.

5000 Models

1. Install centering tool 3076 or equivalent into steering unit and tie rod carrier alignment holes.
2. Measure and divide total toe measurement in half.
3. Loosen clamps and outer locknut on both tie rods.
4. Turn both tie rods until specified toe is obtained. Correct toe should be $1/12$ to $5/12$ of an inch.
5. Tighten clamp and locknuts on tie rods.
6. Check and position steering wheel in center position, if necessary.
7. Remove centering tool.

CAMBER, ADJUST

5000 Models

1. Loosen suspension strut bolts.
2. Install suitable socket wrench to suspension strut nut and move in slots to correct position.
3. Tighten nuts and check camber. If necessary, adjust camber to specification. Camber should be minus $1/6$ to minus $5/6$ inches.

DISC BRAKES SECTION

INDEX

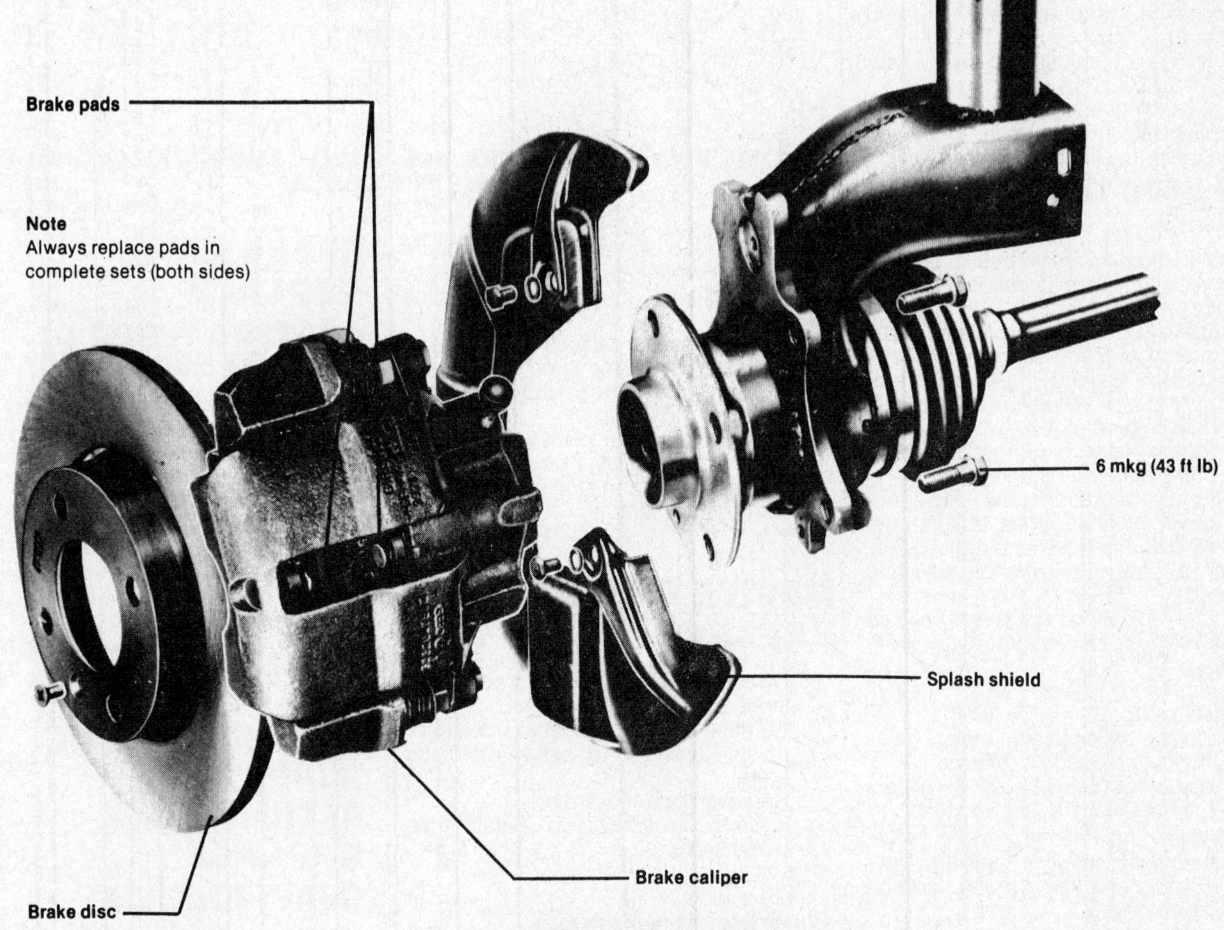

Fig. 1 Front disc brake assembly. 1984 4000 models exc. 1984 Coupe

PARKING BRAKE

ADJUST

1983 QUATTRO TURBO

1. Ensure parking brake cable is not under tension as follows:
   a. Press parking brake levers alternately against their stops with screwdriver.
   b. If parking brake lever on opposite caliper is pulled away from stop, cable is under tension.
2. If cable is under tension, proceed as follows:
   a. Loosen parking brake cable adjusting nut until both levers contact stop.
   b. Depress brake pedal with moderate force approximately 40 times.
   c. Ensure both wheels rotate freely.
3. Loosen parking brake cable adjusting nut until levers just move away from their stops.
4. Loosen adjusting nut two additional turns.
5. Press parking brake levers alternately against their stops with screwdriver.
6. If parking brake lever on opposite cali-

per is pulled away from stop, cable is under tension.
7. If cable is under tension, loosen parking brake cable adjusting nut until both levers contact their stops.
8. Apply and release parking brake, then ensure both wheels turn freely.

QUATTRO COUPE & QUATTRO TURBO EXC. 1983

1. Perform steps 1 and 2 under "1983 Quattro Turbo."
2. Tighten parking brake cable adjusting nut. **It may be necessary to disconnect driveshaft at rear differential to gain access to parking brake cable.**
3. Tighten nuts at calipers until both caliper brake levers just move away from stop.
4. Loosen nuts two turns.
5. Push caliper brake levers against stops.
6. If opposite side caliper lever is pulled away from stop, cable is too tight.
7. Loosen cable adjusting nut until both levers rest against stops.
8. Apply and release parking brake, then ensure both wheels rotate freely and parking brake linkage moves freely.

1983 5000 TURBO MODELS

1. Using screwdriver, push parking brake levers at rear calipers against stops.
2. If lever at opposite side moves away from stop, proceed as follows:
   a. Loosen parking brake cable adjusting nut until levers at rear calipers rest on stops.
   b. Attach 1/4 inch (6 mm) diameter drift between coil and roller.
   c. Firmly depress brake pedal approximately 40 times, ensure both wheels turn freely and remove drift.
3. Tighten parking brake cable adjusting nut.
4. Tighten adjusting nuts at rear calipers until levers just move away from stops.
5. Using screwdriver, push levers against stops.
6. If lever on opposite side moves away from stop, proceed as follows:
   a. Loosen adjusting nuts at calipers until both levers rest on stops.
   b. Apply and release parking brake, then ensure both wheels turn freely and parking brake linkage moves freely.

1984–87 5000 TURBO MODELS

1. Using screwdriver, push caliper brake levers against stops.
2. If lever on opposite side moves away from stop, proceed as follows:
   a. Loosen parking brake cable adjusting nut until both levers rest against stops.
   b. Insert screwdriver between end of rear spring and the roller.
   c. Apply brake pedal approximately 40 times with equal force.
   d. Remove screwdriver and ensure both wheels turn freely.
3. Tighten parking brake cable adjusting nut.
4. Tighten caliper adjusting nuts until both levers just move off stops.
5. Loosen caliper adjusting nuts two turns.
6. Using screwdriver, push caliper levers against stops. If lever on opposite side moves away from stop, parking brake cable is too tight.

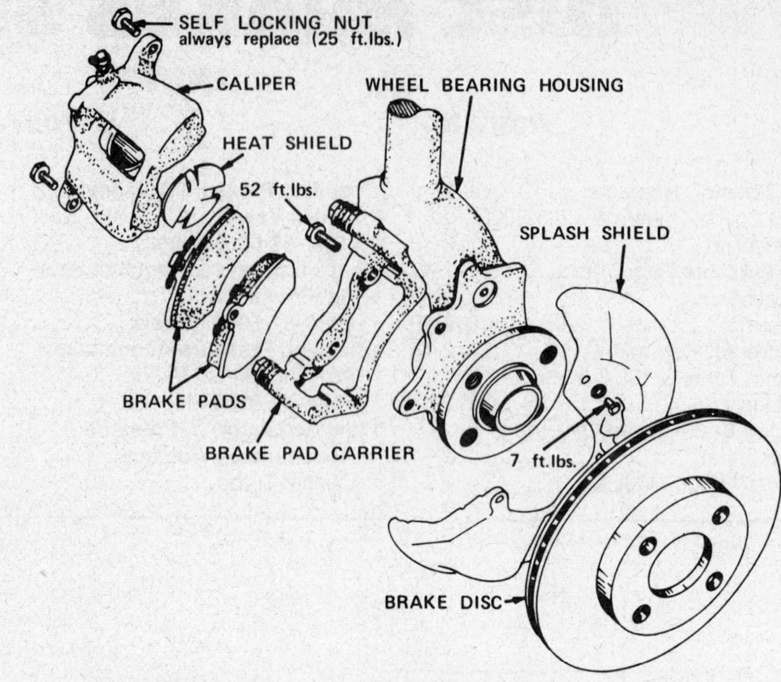

Fig. 2 Front disc brake assembly. 1985–87 4000 models & 1984 Coupe

MASTER CYLINDER REPLACE

1. Disconnect brake lines at master cylinder.
2. Remove master cylinder to booster or master cylinder to servo attaching bolts.
3. Remove master cylinder.
4. Reverse procedure to install, then bleed system.

BRAKE BOOSTER REPLACE

4000, COUPE, QUATTRO & 1983 5000 MODELS

1. Remove master cylinder as previously described.
2. Disconnect vacuum line(s) at booster.
3. Remove brake booster attaching bolts.
4. Disconnect booster pushrod at brake pedal.
5. Reverse procedure to install.

BRAKE SERVO REPLACE

QUATTRO TURBO & 1984–87 5000 MODELS

1. Relieve brake system pressure by firmly depressing brake pedal approximately 20 times.
2. Remove master cylinder as previously described.
3. Disconnect pressure and return lines at brake servo.
4. Remove pushrod clevis pin, servo attaching bolts and the servo.
5. Reverse procedure to install, using new gaskets on servo pressure and return lines and torquing lines to 19-25 ft. lbs.

FLOW REGULATOR W/PRESSURE ACCUMULATOR REPLACE

QUATTRO TURBO

1. Relieve brake system pressure by firmly depressing brake pedal approximately 20 times.
2. Disconnect at flow regulator; pressure line from power steering pump, pressure line to power steering unit and return line to oil reservoir.
3. Disconnect low pressure warning switch electrical connectors at flow regulator.
4. Remove attaching nuts at upper mounting plates, then the flow regulator with pressure accumulator.
5. Reverse procedure to install, using

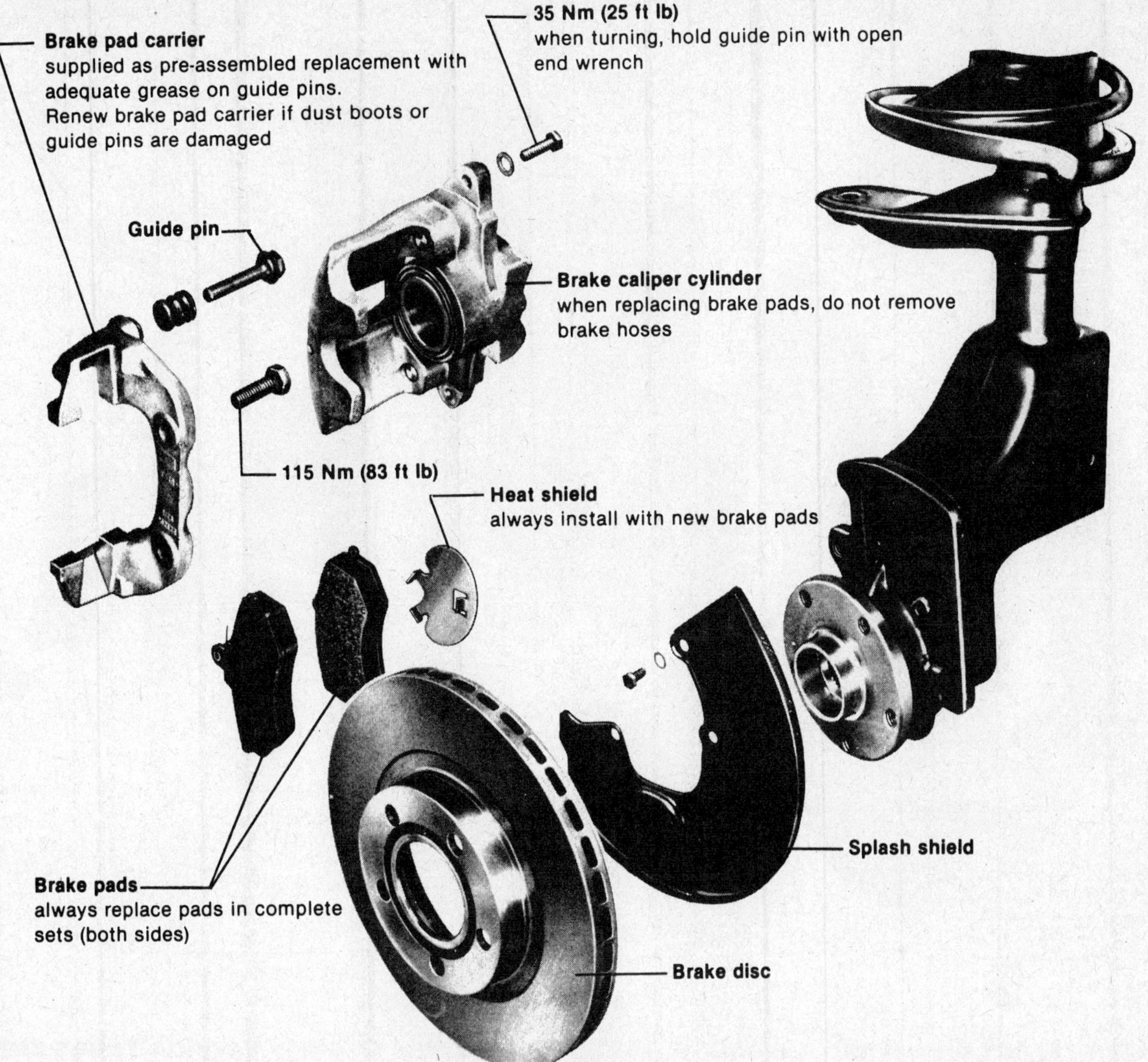

Fig. 3 Front disc brake assembly. 5000 models w/Girling Caliper, Quattro & Quattro Turbo

new gaskets for hollow bolts.

6. Torque lines as follows: pressure line from pump, 22-29 ft. lbs.; pressure line to brake unit, 18-25 ft. lbs; pressure line to steering unit, 32-35 ft. lbs.; return line to oil reservoir, 11-13 ft. lbs.

BRAKE PRESSURE REGULATOR

CHECKING

1983–85 4000 & Coupe & 1983 5000 Models

Brake pressure regulator is mounted on right rear (4000 and Coupe) or left rear (5000) of body and operated by spring attached to rear axle.

1. Firmly depress pedal once.
2. Release pedal suddenly and ensure lever on pressure regulator moves. It is normal for small amounts of brake fluid to escape through vent hole. If in doubt, proceed to step 3.
3. Connect tool US1016 according to manufacturer's instructions and bleed tool.
4. Depress brake pedal until front axle pressure gauge reads 1450 psi and hold for 5 seconds.
5. If rear pressure reading varies more than 145 psi within 5 seconds, replace pressure regulator.

Quattro & Quattro Turbo

1. Raise and support vehicle.
2. Remove bleeder screws and connect adapters to left front and rear brake calipers.
3. Connect gage US1016 or equivalent and bleed both hoses and gages with bleeder valves on gages.
4. Unlock parking brake cable on rear brake caliper.
5. Depress brake pedal until gage for front axle reads 725 psi and ensure gage for rear axle reads 508-566 psi.
6. Further depress brake pedal until gage on front axle reads 1450 psi and ensure gage for rear axle reads 841-899 psi.
7. If pressures cannot be maintained, replace regulator.
8. Bleed brake system.

1984–87 5000 Models Exc. Turbo & Quattro

1. Firmly depress brake pressure once.
2. Release pedal suddenly and ensure lever on pressure regulator moves.
3. Raise and support vehicle so that load is taken off rear axle.
4. Press brake pressure regulator lever toward rear.
5. Loosen nut at front of spring and attach spring, without play or tension, to plastic roller.
6. Torque nut to 18 ft. lbs.

1984–87 5000 Turbo

1. Firmly depress brake pedal once.
2. Release pedal suddenly and ensure lever on pressure regulator moves.

5000S Quattro

1. Remove bleeder screws from rear

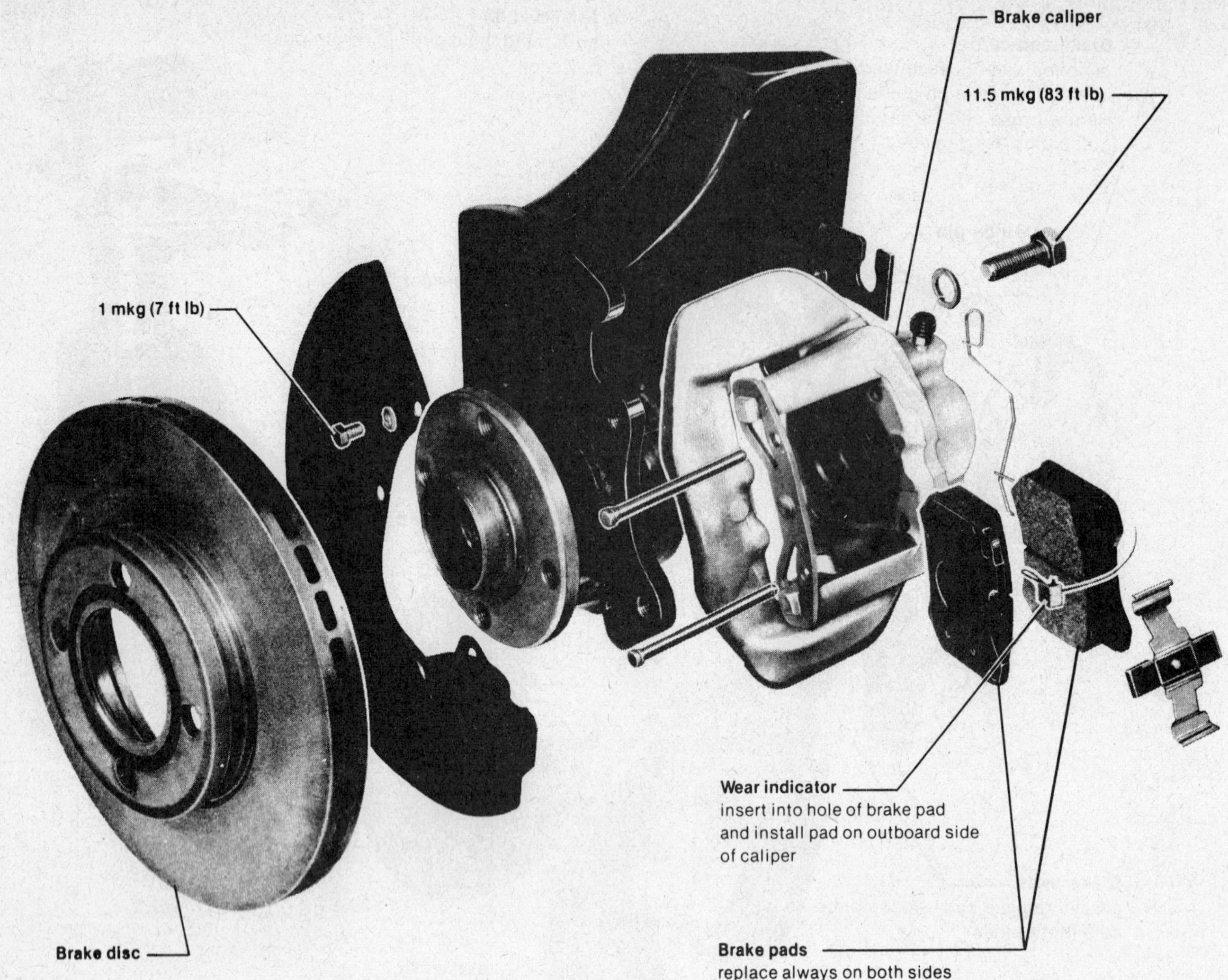

Fig. 4 Front disc brake assembly. 1983 5000 models w/early version Teves caliper

brake calipers.

2. Connect gage US1016 or equivalent and bleed both hoses and gages with bleeder valve on gages.
3. Have person (approximately 165 lbs.) sit on drivers's seat.
4. Apply parking brake.
5. Raise and support right side of vehicle so that it is 14-18 inches (350-450 mm) from ground as measured at wheel house opening.
6. Depress brake pedal until left rear gage reads approximately 580 psi.
7. If right rear gage does not read 290-362 psi, replace brake pressure regulator.

ADJUSTING

1983–84 4000 & Coupe & 1984–87 5000 Models Exc. Turbo & Quattro

Vehicle must be empty and resting on wheels with fuel tank full.

1. Remove bleeder screw and connect adapter to left front brake caliper and right rear wheel cylinder.
2. Connect gage US1016 or equivalent and bleed both hoses and gages with bleeder valve on gages.
3. Bounce car several times at rear.
4. Firmly depress brake pedal several times.
5. Depress brake pedal until gage on left caliper reads 725 psi and ensure gage on right wheel cylinder reads 457-566 psi on 4000 models or 741-616 psi on 5000 models.
6. Further depress brake pedal until gage on left caliper reads 1450 psi and ensure gage on right wheel cylinder reads 725-914 psi on 4000 models or 782-1037 psi on 5000 models.
7. If pressure at rear axle is too high, release spring tension by loosening bolt and moving forward, then tighten bolt.
8. If pressure is too low, move bolt rearward. **Do not adjust pressure regulator with brake pedal depressed.**
9. Recheck pressure and, if pressures cannot be properly adjusted, replace regulator.
10. Bleed brake system.

1985–87 4000 & Coupe

1. Ensure brake system is properly filled and bled.
2. Press lever on brake pressure regulator toward rear of vehicle to stop.
3. Loosen nut and adjust spring between brake pressure regulator and plastic roller behind nut so no play exists.
4. Torque nut to 18 ft. lbs.
5. If necessary, pressure test adjustment can be performed as described for 1983-84 models, noting the following:
   a. When gage on left caliper reads 725 psi, gage on right wheel cylinder should rear 741-616 psi.
   b. When gage on left caliper reads 1450 psi, gage on right wheel cylinder should read 783-1037 psi.

1983 5000 Models

1. Place vehicle on a drive on type lift.
2. Remove bleeder valves and connect adapters to left front brake caliper and right rear wheel cylinder.
3. Connect gage US1016 or equivalent.
4. Bleed both hoses and gages with bleeder valve on gages.
5. Firmly depress brake pedal several times.
6. Depress brake pedal until gage on left caliper reads 725 psi and ensure gage on cylinder reads 493-566 psi.
7. Further depress brake pedal until

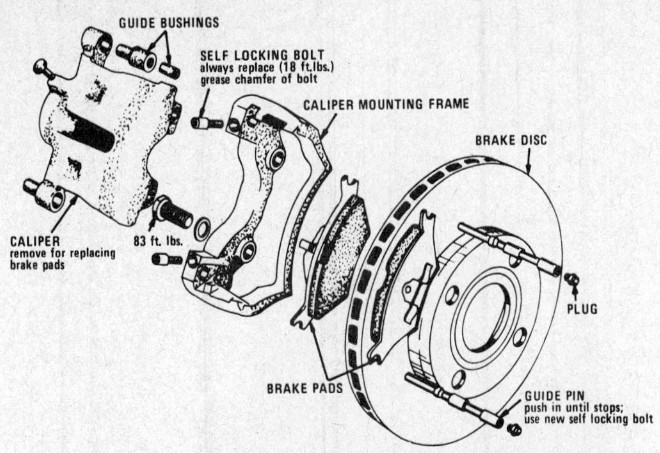

Fig. 5 Front disc brake assembly. 1983 5000 models w/late version Teves caliper

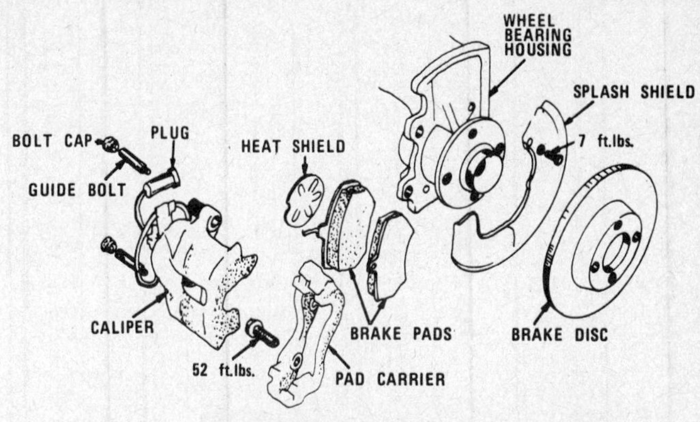

Fig. 6 Front disc brake assembly. 1984–87 5000 models w/Teves caliper

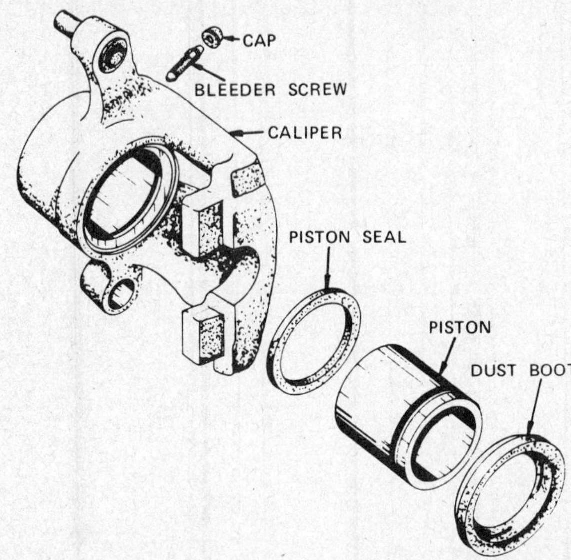

Fig. 7 Front caliper assembly. 1983 5000 models w/late version Teves caliper

gage on caliper reads 1450 psi and ensure gage on cylinder reads 827-899 psi.

8. If pressure at rear axle is too high, release spring tension by loosening bolt and moving it forward.
9. If pressure is too low, move bolt rearward.
10. Tighten bolt.
11. Recheck pressures. If pressures cannot be adjusted, replace regulator.
12. Bleed brake system.

1984–87 5000S Turbo

Vehicle must be empty and resting on wheels with fuel tank full.

1. Remove bleeder screw and connect adapter to left front brake caliper and right rear wheel cylinder.
2. Connect gage US1016 or equivalent and bleed both hoses and gages with bleeder valves on gages.
3. Bounce vehicle at rear several times.
4. Firmly depress brake pedal several times.
5. Depress brake pedal until gage on front axle reads 725 psi and ensure gage on rear axle reads 507-652 psi.
6. Further depress brake pedal until gage on front axle reads 1450 psi and ensure gage on rear axle reads 826-1058 psi.
7. Raise and support vehicle so load is removed from rear axle.
8. Push brake pressure regulator down to stop.
9. Loosen nut at lower end of spring.
10. Insert 10 mm diameter drill bit between spring and plastic roller.
11. Torque nut to 18 ft. lbs.
12. Lower vehicle to ground and repeat steps 6 and 7.
13. If pressure at rear axle is too low, increase brake regulator spring tension.
14. If pressure at rear axle is too high, decrease brake regulator spring tension.
15. If proper readings cannot be obtained, replace brake pressure regulator.

CHECKING PRESSURE ACCUMULATOR GAS PRESSURE

1984–87 5000 MODELS

Gas pressure of new accumulator should be 1276-1334 psi at 68°F. with minimum pressure of 435 psi at 68°F.

1. With engine off, depress brake pedal approximately 20 times to reduce brake system pressure.
2. Disconnect electrical connector and remove warning light switch.
3. Attach suitable pressure gage with hollow bolt and copper washers to brake servo unit. Attach thick copper washer between brake servo unit and banjo fitting and the thin copper washer between hollow bolt and banjo fitting.
4. Start engine and let idle unit pressure gage reads approximately 2030 psi.
5. Turn ignition off.
6. Pump brake pedal until pressure drops slowly. Pressure reads at point where gage needle drops rapidly to zero is gas pressure of pressure accumulator.
7. If pressure is less than 435 psi, replace accumulator.

CHECKING BRAKE SERVO OPERATING PRESSURE

1984–87 5000 MODELS

1. With engine off, depress brake pedal approximately 20 times to reduce brake system pressure.
2. Disconnect electrical connector at and remove warning light switch.
3. Attach suitable pressure gage with hollow bolt and copper washers to brake servo unit. Attach thick copper washer between brake servo unit and banjo fitting and the thin copper washer between hollow bolt and banjo fitting.
4. Start engine and let idle until pressure gage reading exceeds 2030 psi.
5. If specified pressure is not reached,

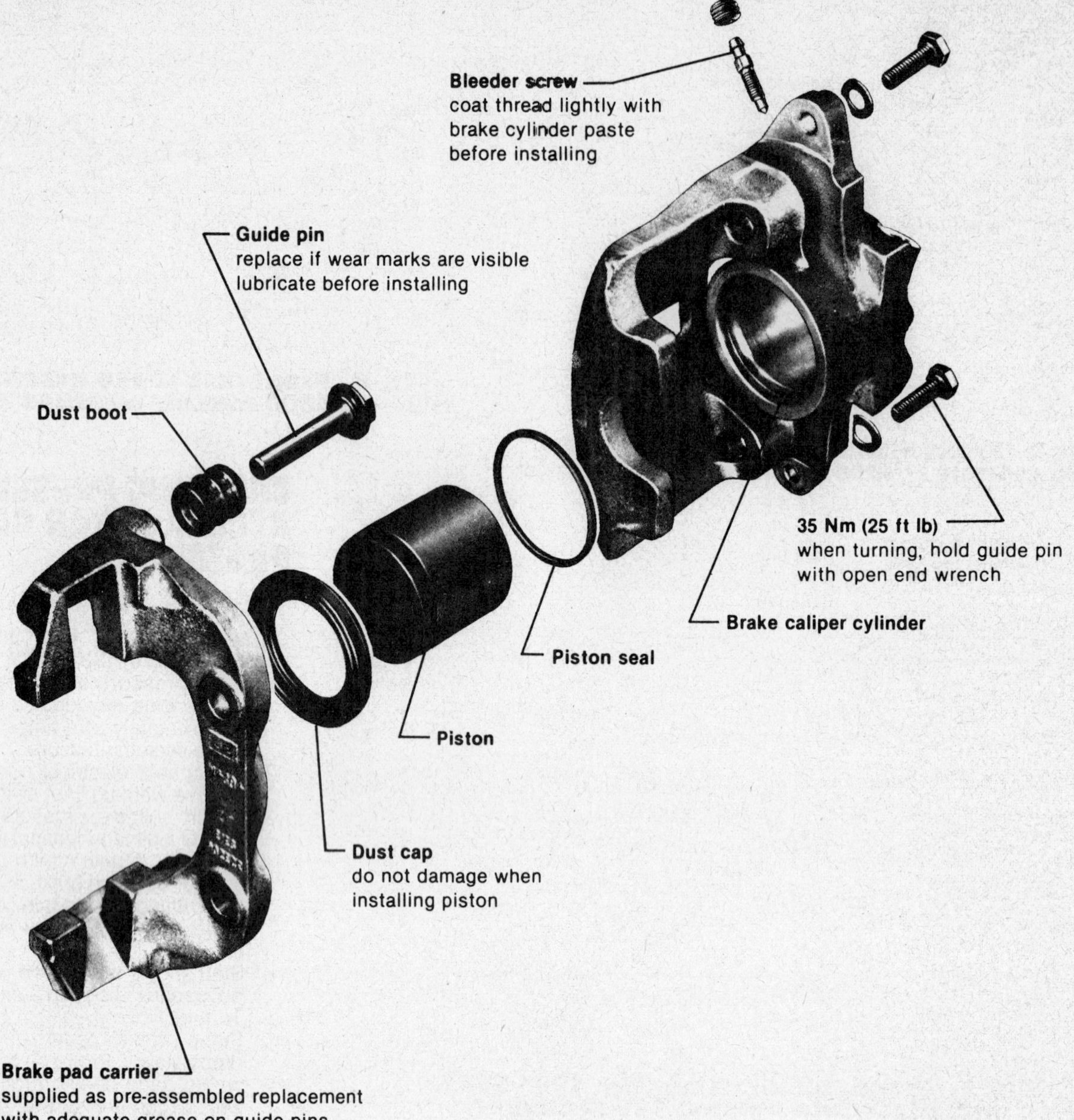

Fig. 8 Front caliper assembly. 5000 models w/Girling caliper & 1983–84 4000 models exc. 1984 Coupe

check delivery rate of central hydraulic pump as follows. **Turn ignition off and leave pressure gage connected.**

a. Disconnect pressure line at hydraulic pump.
b. Connect hose of pressure limiter VW1354 or equivalent to pump, using existing hollow bolt.
c. Remove cap from fluid reservoir.
d. Place end of pressure limiter hose into reservoir.
e. Start engine and let idle until line is bled, then turn ignition off.
f. Insert hose in measuring jar, then start engine, run at idle and check delivery rate.
g. If delivery rate is not at least .3 qt. per minute, replace hydraulic pump.
h. If delivery rate is within specifications but operating pressure is not, replace pressure accumulator.

CHECKING PRESSURE ACCUMULATOR CHECK VALVE

1984–87 5000 MODELS

1. With engine off, depress brake pedal approximately 20 times to reduce brake system pressure.
2. Disconnect electrical connector at and remove warning light switch.
3. Attach suitable pressure gage with hollow bolt and copper washers to brake servo unit. Attach thick copper washer between brake servo unit and banjo fitting and the thin copper washer between hollow bolt and banjo fitting.
4. Start engine and idle until pressure gage reads approximately 2030 psi, then turn Ignition off.
5. Pump brake pedal until pressure drops to 1957 psi.
6. If pressure drops below 1885 psi within 5 minutes, replace pressure accumulator.

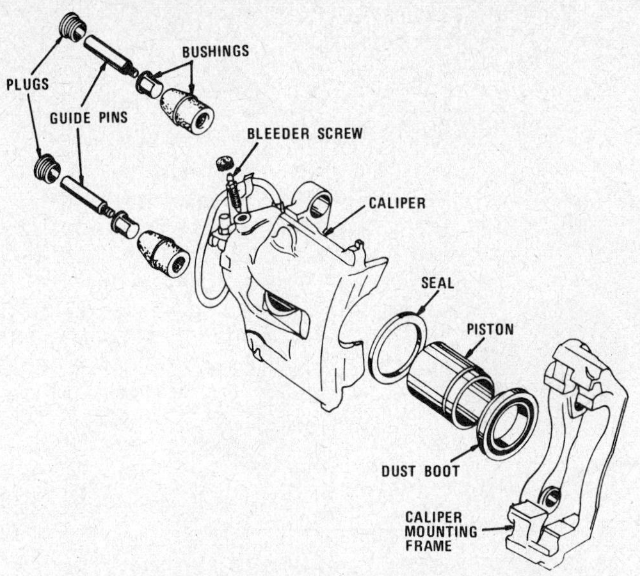

Fig. 9 Front caliper assembly. 1985–87 4000 models & 1984 Coupe

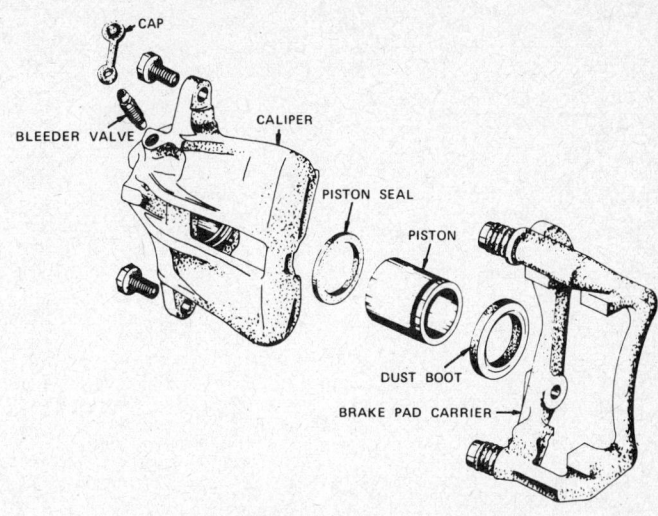

Fig. 10 Front caliper assembly. 1984–87 5000 models w/Teves caliper

CHECKING PRESSURE ACCUMULATOR PRESSURE RELIEF VALVE

1984–87 5000 MODELS

1. Ensure pump delivery rate is within specifications. Refer to "Checking Brake Servo Operating Pressure", step 5.
2. With engine off, depress brake pedal approximately 20 times to reduce brake system pressure.
3. Disconnect electrical connector at and remove warning light switch.
4. Attach suitable pressure gage with hollow bolt and copper washers to brake servo unit. Attach thick copper washer between brake servo unit and banjo fitting and the thin copper washer between hollow bolt and banjo fitting.
5. Start engine and let idle until pressure gage reading exceeds 2030 psi.
6. If more than 2030 psi cannot be achieved, replace pressure accumulator and recheck system pressure.

FRONT DISC BRAKE SERVICE

BRAKE PADS, REPLACE

1983 5000 Models W/Girling Calipers & All 4000 Models

1. Raise and support front of vehicle, then remove wheel and tire assembly.
2. Using open end wrench to hold guide pin head, remove lower caliper mounting bolt, **Figs. 1 through 3.**
3. Swing caliper upward and lift brake pads from holder.
4. Install replace brake pads, and heat shield(s) if used, then swing caliper downward and install lower mounting bolt. Use an open end wrench to hold guide pin in position when tightening lower mounting bolt. Torque bolt to 25 ft. lbs.
5. Depress brake pedal several times to position caliper piston and seat brake pads.

1983 5000 Models W/Early Version Teves Caliper

1. Raise and support vehicle, then remove wheel and tire assembly.
2. Disconnect wear indicator electrical connector.
3. Remove retaining clip and drive out brake pad retaining pins, **Fig. 4.**
4. Remove inner brake pad.
5. To remove outer pad, press floating frame and brake cylinder outward.
6. Press piston to end position.
7. Adjust piston position as necessary and install replacement pads.
8. Install wear indicator contact in outside pad.
9. Install retaining pins and clips.
10. Depress brake pedal several times to adjust position of caliper piston and seat brake pads.

1983 5000 Models W/Late Version Teves Caliper

1. Raise and support vehicle, then remove wheel and tire assembly.
2. Remove plug, then the bolt, **Fig. 5.**
3. Remove guide pins, using 4.7 inch long 8 mm threaded bolt to pull out pins.
4. Remove caliper from frame and position aside.
5. Remove pads, outer pad first.
6. Bottom piston in housing.
7. Install replacement pads, inner pad first, ensuring peg at back plate on outer pad fits into holes of brake caliper.
8. Push guide pins into housing as far as they will go, then torque bolt to 18 ft. lbs. and install plug.
9. Depress brake pedal several times to position caliper and seat pads.

1984–87 5000 Models W/Girling Caliper

1. Raise and support vehicle, then remove wheel and tire assembly.
2. Pull plug connector out of clip, then press connector on knurled surface to separate.
3. Remove lower caliper mounting bolt, **Fig. 3,** holding guide pin with open end wrench.
4. Swing caliper up and lift out pads.
5. Bottom piston in caliper housing.
6. Install brake pad and heat shield with shield facing piston.
7. Swing caliper down and install new lower self locking mounting bolts. Torque bolts to 26 ft. lbs. while holding guide pin with open end wrench.
8. Connect plug connector and attach to retaining clip.

1984–87 5000 Models W/Teves Caliper

1. Raise and support vehicle, then remove wheel and tire assembly.
2. Pull plug connector out of clip and press connector plug on knurled surface to separate.
3. Remove both bolt caps, then both guide bolts, **Fig. 6.**
4. Remove brake caliper housing, then the pads.
5. Bottom piston in caliper.
6. Install replacement pads.
7. Torque brake caliper housing guide pins to 18 ft. lbs., then install bolt caps.
8. Connect plug connector and attach to retaining clip.

CALIPER OVERHAUL

5000 Models W/Girling Or Late Version Teves Caliper & All 4000 Models

1. Place wooden block between caliper piston and caliper housing, then apply

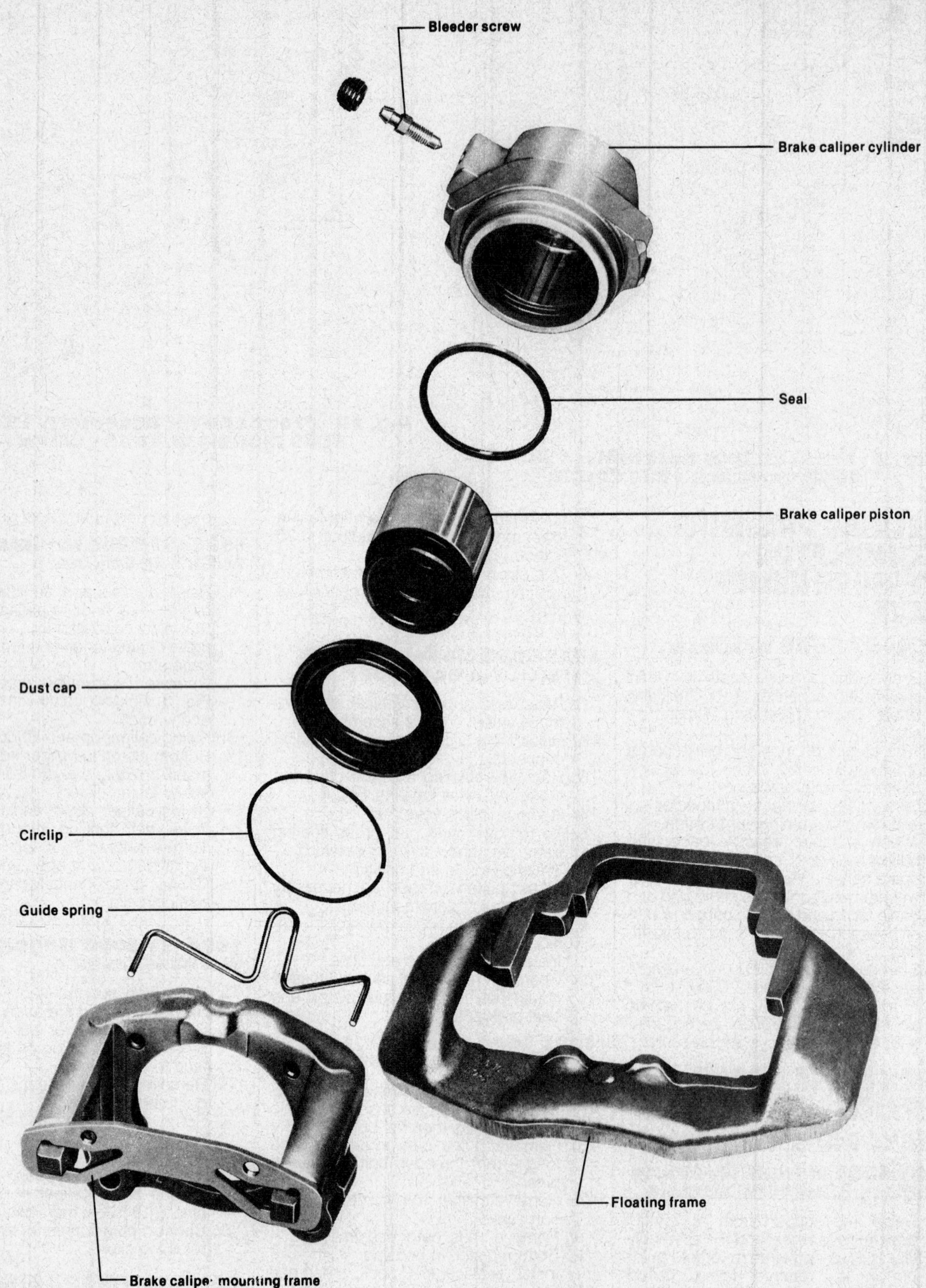

Fig. 11 Front caliper assembly. 1983 5000 models w/early version Teves caliper

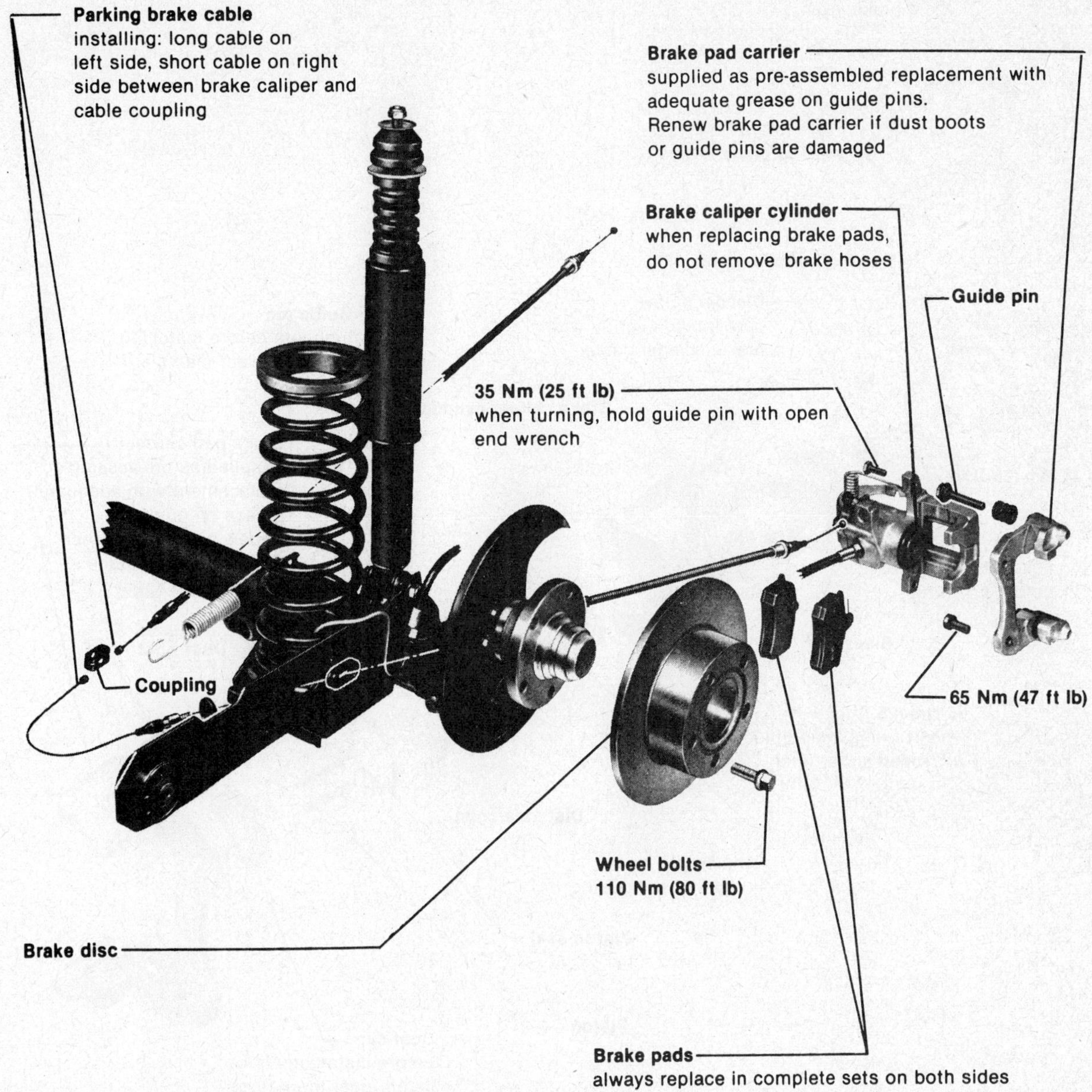

Fig. 12 Rear disc brake assembly. 4000 Quattro, Quattro Turbo & 5000 Turbo

air pressure to brake line bore to force piston from housing.

2. Remove piston seal from caliper piston bore using a plastic rod, **Figs. 7 through 10.**
3. Slide dust cap onto piston, then lubricate piston and caliper piston bore with clean brake fluid.
4. Install piston seal into caliper bore and lubricate with clean brake fluid.
5. Install piston into caliper bore and insert inner lip of dust seal into groove on caliper.
6. Press caliper piston into caliper as far as possible, ensuring outer lip of dust cap slips into groove in piston.

1983 5000 Models W/Early Version Teves Caliper

1. Remove floating frame from brake caliper, **Fig. 11**, by positioning a wooden block in floating frame and driving caliper off with a brass drift.
2. Position caliper piston against wooden work bench, then apply air pressure to brake hose fitting to force piston from caliper bore.
3. Using plastic rod, remove piston seal from caliper bore.
4. Install replacement piston in caliper bore and coat seal with clean brake fluid.
5. Install piston into caliper bore and insert inner lip of dust seal into groove on caliper.
6. Press caliper piston into caliper bore as far as possible.

REAR DISC BRAKE SERVICE

BRAKE PADS, REPLACE

4000 Quattro, Quattro Turbo & 5000 Turbo

1. Raise and support vehicle, then remove wheel and tire assembly.

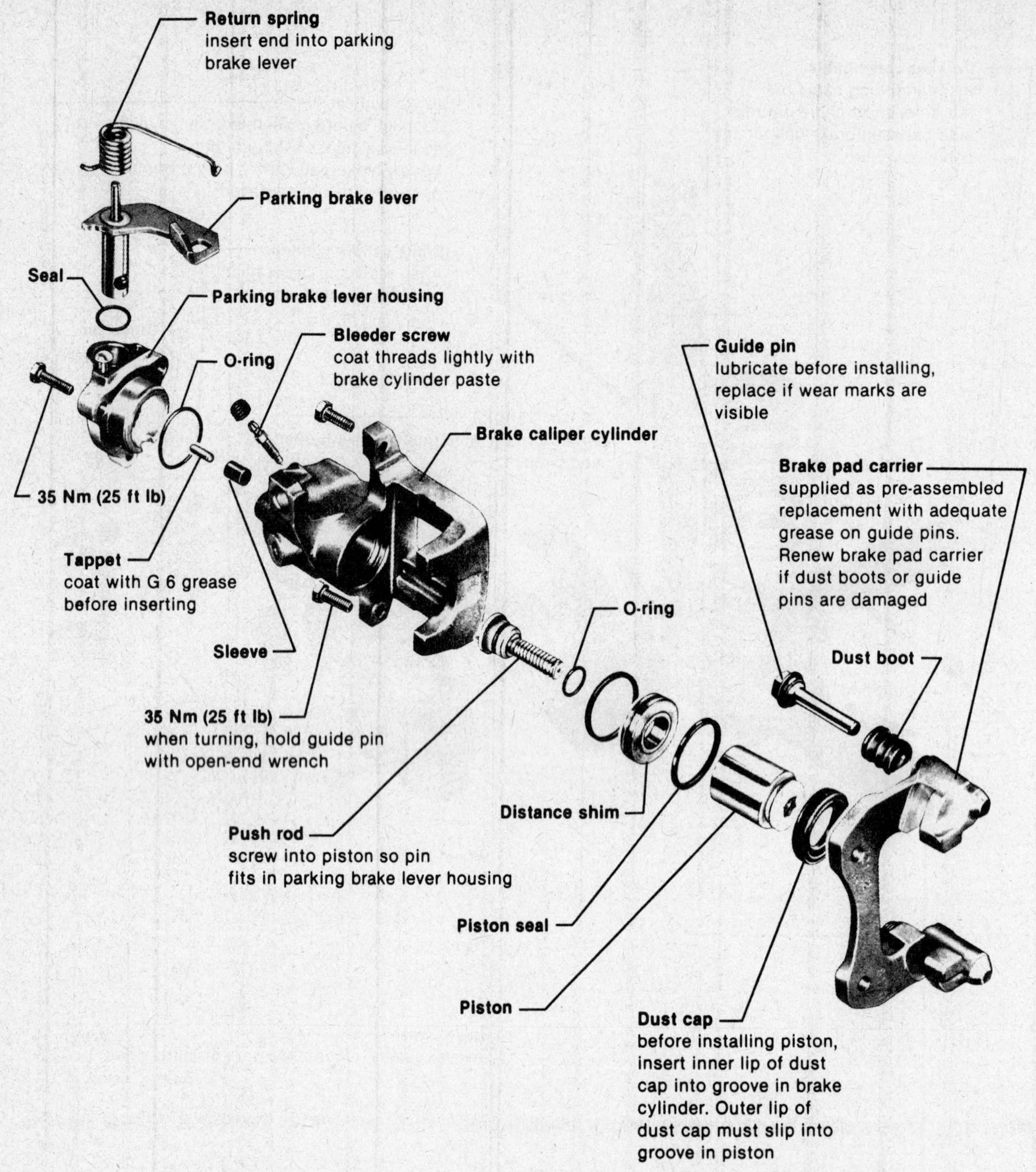

Fig. 13 Rear caliper assembly. 4000 Quattro, Quattro Turbo & 5000 Turbo

2. While holding guide pin head with an open end wrench, remove caliper upper and lower mounting bolts, **Fig. 12.**
3. Lift caliper assembly upward from rotor and secure to frame with wire.
4. Remove brake shoes from holder.
5. Using an Allen wrench, turn caliper piston to right and push into caliper bore.
6. Install brake pads onto holder, then install caliper over rotor.
7. Install caliper attaching bolts and torque to 25 ft. lbs. When tightening caliper attaching bolts, use an open end wrench to hold guide pin head in position.

CALIPER OVERHAUL

1. Remove parking brake lever housing.
2. Push caliper piston into caliper and out through rear of bore.
3. Remove piston seal using plastic rod, **Fig. 13.**
4. Install replacement piston seal into caliper bore. Lubricate seal with clean brake fluid.
5. Lubricate piston and caliper bore with clean brake fluid, then push piston into bore.
6. Position caliper with bleeder screw facing upward, then connect bleeder hose and open bleeder screw. Fill caliper with clean brake fluid through bleeder screw, then close bleeder valve.

DRUM BRAKES SECTION

INDEX

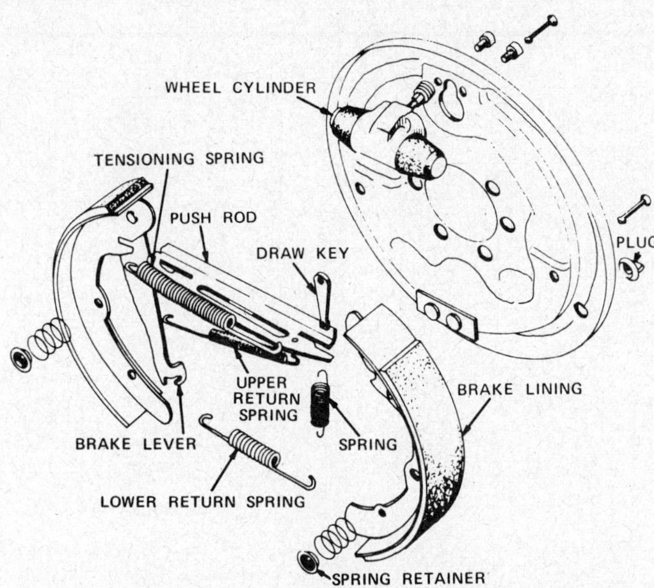

Fig. 1 Drum brake assembly. 4000 models

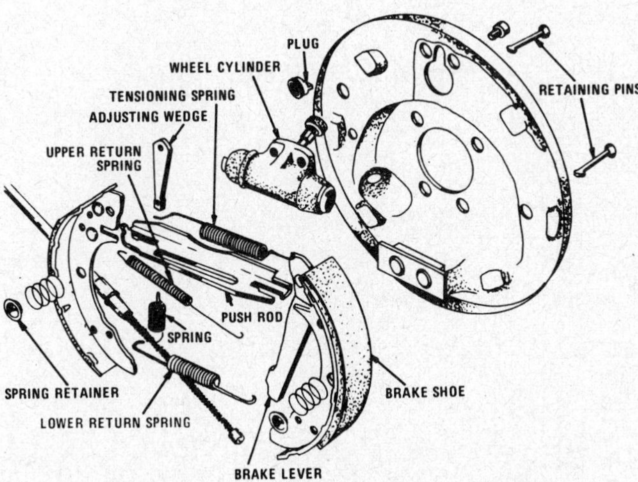

Fig. 2 Drum brake assembly. 5000 models

REAR DRUM BRAKES

ADJUST

A brake adjuster lug is used on all models. The brakes are automatically adjusted when the brake pedal is depressed.

PARKING BRAKE

ADJUST

4000 & COUPE

1. Release parking brake lever, then firmly depress service brake pedal once to seat brake shoes.
2. Set parking brake lever on second tooth of ratchet, then raise and support rear of vehicle.
3. Tighten nut at parking brake equalizer until rear wheels can just be rotated by hand.
4. Release parking brake and check to ensure wheels can be rotated freely by hand.
5. Apply grease to parking brake cable equalizer, then lower vehicle.

1983 5000 MODELS EXC. TURBO

1. Release parking brake lever.
2. Firmly depress service brake pedal once.
3. Pull parking brake onto third tooth.
4. Tighten adjusting nut until both wheels can be turned by hand.
5. Release parking brake lever and ensure both wheels turn freely.
6. With ignition switch in "ON" position, ensure brake warning light illuminates when parking brake lever is pulled to first notch and goes out when lever is fully released.

1984–87 5000 MODELS EXC. TURBO

1. Release parking brake lever.
2. Loosen parking brake cable adjusting nut.
3. Firmly depress service brake pedal once.
4. Pull parking brake lever to third notch.
5. Tighten adjusting nut until both rear wheels can just be turned by hand.
6. Release parking brake and ensure both wheels turn freely.
7. Lubricate equalizer with suitable grease.

BRAKE BOOSTER

REPLACE

Refer to Disc Brake Section.

BRAKE SERVO

REPLACE

Refer to Disc Brake Section.

MASTER CYLINDER

REPLACE

Refer to Disc Brake Section.

BRAKE SHOES
REPLACE

1. Raise and support vehicle, then remove wheel and tire assembly.
2. Remove dust cap, cotter pin, wheel nut cover and wheel nut, then the thrust washer and outer wheel bearing.
3. Working through wheel bolt hole, pry adjusting wedge up against stop with screwdriver and remove brake drum.
4. Remove caps from shoe retaining springs, **Figs. 1 and 2.**
5. Unhook lower return spring.
6. Lift shoes out from support.
7. Disconnect parking brake cable from lever.
8. Clamp shoes in suitable vise.
9. Unhook upper return and adjusting wedge springs.
10. Unhook tension spring.
11. Install tension spring and place shoe on pushrod.
12. Insert adjusting wedge with lug toward backing plate.
13. Install shoe with lever in pushrod.
14. Connect upper return spring.
15. Hook parking brake cable on lever.
16. Place shoes on wheel cylinder piston.
17. Connect lower return spring and lift shoes onto lower support.
18. Connect adjusting wedge spring.
19. Install shoe retaining springs and caps.
20. Install brake drum, then adjust wheel bearing as described in "Rear Axle & Suspension Section."

BMW (Germany)

INDEX OF SERVICE OPERATIONS

General Engine Specifications

Year	Engine Cubic Inch/cc	Fuel System	Bore x Stroke	Compression Ratio	Net HP @ RPM	Maximum Torque Lbs. Ft. @ RPM	Normal Oil Pressure Psi
1983	4-107/1766	Fuel Injection	3.5 x 2.8	8.8	101 @ 5800	100 @4500	57–71
	6-164/2693	Fuel Injection	3.3 x 3.2	9.0	121 @ 4250	170 @ 3250	57–85
	6-196/3210	Fuel Injection	3.5 x 3.386	8.8	181 @ 6000	195 @ 4000	57–71
1984	4-107/1766	Fuel Injection	3.5 x 2.8	9.3	101 @ 5800	103 @ 4500	57–71
	6-164/2693	Fuel Injection	3.3 x 3.2	9.0	121 @ 4250	170 @ 3250	57–85
	6-196/3210	Fuel Injection	3.5 x 3.386	8.8	181 @ 6000	195 @ 4000	57–71
1985	4-107/1766	Fuel Injection	3.5 x 2.8	8.8	101 @ 5800	103 @ 4500	57–71
1985–86	6-164/2693	Fuel Injection	3.31 x 3.19	9.0	121 @ 4250	170 @ 3250	57–85
	6-209/3430	Fuel Injection	3.62 x 3.86	8.0	182 @ 5400	214 @ 4000	57–71
1986	6-149/2400 ①	Fuel Injection	3.15 x 3.19	22	114 @ 4800	155 @ 2400	58
1987	4-140/2302 ②	Fuel Injection	3.68 X 3.31	10.5	143 @ 6750	166 @ 4750	57–85
	6-152/2494	Fuel Injection	3.31 x 2.95	8.8	168 @ 5800	164 @ 4300	57–85
	6-164/2693	Fuel Injection	3.31 x 3.19	9.0	121 @ 4250	170 @ 3250	57–85
	6-209/3430	Fuel Injection	3.62 x 3.86	8.0	182 @ 5400	214 @ 4000	57–71
	6-211/3453 ③	Fuel Injection	3.68 x 3.31	9.8	256 @ 6500	243 @ 4500	57–85

①—Diesel engine.
②—S14, "M3" series performance engine.
③—S38, "M5 & M6" series performance engine.

Alternator & Regulator Specifications

Year	Alternator				Regulator	
	Model	Rated Hot Output Amps	Output @ 14 Volts		Model	Voltage @ 2000 RPM
			Amps @ RPM	Amps @ RPM		
1983	0 120 489 718	65	43.3 @ 2100	65 @ 6000	1 192 052 006	13.7–14.5
1983–87	—	65	—	—	—	13.5–14.2 ①
	—	80	—	—	—	13.5–14.2 ①
1987	—	90	—	—	—	13.5–14.2 ①

①—At 1500 RPM (Engine), 86°–140° F, charge rate approx. 5 amperes.

Starting Motor Specifications

Year	Engine	Model No.	Rotation	Brush Spring Tension Ounces	No Load Test			Torque Test		
					Amperes (Max.)	Volts	RPM (Max.)	Amperes (Max.)	Volts	Torque Ft. Lbs. (Min.)
1983–85	4-107	0 001 311 125	R	.512	—	12.5	—	—	—	—
1983–87	Exc. 4-107	—	R	.512	—	12.5	—	—	—	—

Valve Specifications

Year	Model	Valve Lash		Valve Angles		Valve Spring Installed Height	Valve Spring Pressure Lbs. @ In.	Stem Clearance		Stem Diameter	
		Int.	Exh.	Seat	Face			Intake	Exhaust	Intake	Exhaust
1983	320i	.008–.010 H	.008–.010 H	45	45½	—	154 @ 1.122	.0010–.0022	.0016–.0027	.3149	.3149
1983–85	318i	.010 H	.010 H	45	45½	—	—	.006①	.006①	—	—
1983–87	325 & 528e	.012	.012	45	45½	—	—	.006①	.006①	—	—
	533/535i 633/635CSi 733/735i	.014	45	45½	—	—	.006①	.006①	—	—	
1986	524TD②	.012C	.012C	45	45	—	—	.010①	.010①	—	—
1987	M3	.014H	.014H	45	—	—	—	.025③	.031③	.276	.276
	M5, M6	.015H	.015H	45	—	—	—	.025③.031 ③	.276	.276	

①—Maximum. ②—Diesel. ③—Tilt clearance.

Pistons, Pins, Rings, Crankshaft & Bearings

Year	Model	Piston Clearance Top of Skirt	Ring End Gap		Wristpin Diameter	Rod Bearings		Main Bearings			
			Comp.	Oil		Shaft Diameter	Bearing Clearance	Shaft Diameter	Bearing Clearance	Thrust on Bear. No.	Shaft Endplay
1983	320i	.0018	①	.010	.8661	1.8898	.0009–.0031	2.1653	②	3	.0033–.0068
1983	528e	.0004–.0015	.012	.010	.8661	1.7717	.0012–.0028	2.3622	.0012–.0028	4	.0031–.0064
1983–84	533i, 633CSi & 733i	.0008–.002	①	.010	.8661	③	④	⑤	⑥	4	.0033–.0069
1983–85	318i	.0008–.002	①	.010	.8661	③	④	⑦	⑥	3	.0033–.0069
1983–87	528e	.0004–.0016	.012	.010	.8661	⑧	④	⑤	⑥	4	.0031–.0064
1984–87	325	.0004–.0016	.012	.010	.8661	⑧	④	⑤	⑥	4	.0031–.0064
1985–87	535i, 635CSi & 735i	.0008–.002	①	.010	.8661	③	④	⑤	⑥	4	.0069
1986	524TD⑨	⑩	.008	.010	—	—	—	⑪	.0008–.0018	6	.003–.006
1987	M3	.0012–.0024	.012	.010	—	1.8890	④	⑫	⑥	—	.0033–.0068
	M5, M6	.0012–.0024	.012	.010	—	1.8890	④	⑬	⑥	—	.0033–.0068

①—Top, .012 inch; 2nd, .008 inch.
②—Red, .0012–.0027 inch; blue, .0012–.0026 inch.
③—Exc. double class, 1.8898 inch; double class, 1.8888–1.8894 inch.
④—Exc. double class, .0012–.0028 inch; double class, .0008–.0022 inch.
⑤—Double class, 2.3622 inch. Triple class: yellow, 2.3616–2.3618 inch; green, 2.3613–2.3615 inch; white, 2.3611–2.3613 inch.
⑥—Double class, .0012–0028 inch; triple class, .0008–.0018 inch.
⑦—Double class, 2.1654 inch. Triple class: yellow, 2.1647 inch; green, 2.1644 inch; white, 2.1642 inch.
⑧—Exc. double class, 1.7717 inch; double class, 1.8888–1.8894 inch.
⑨—Diesel.
⑩—Alcan-Nural pistons, .0010–.0021; KS pistons, .0016–.0027; Mahle pistons, .0018–.0029.
⑪—Refer to Diesel Engine Section.
⑫—Double class, 2.1653. Triple class: yellow, 2.1647–2.1649; green, 2.1644–2.1646; white, 2.1642–2.1644.
⑬—Double class, 2.3622. Triple class: yellow, 2.3615–2.3618; green, 2.3612–2.3615; white, 2.3610–2.3612.

Engine Tightening Specifications

***Torque specifications are for clean and lightly lubricated threads only.Dry or dirty threads produce increased friction which prevents accurate measurement of tightness.**

Year	Engine	Spark Plugs Ft. Lbs.	Cylinder Head Bolts Ft. Lbs.	Intake Manifold Ft. Lbs.	Exhaust Manifold Ft. Lbs.	Camshaft Bearing Caps Ft. Lbs.	Camshaft Sprocket Bolts Ft. Lbs.	Rocker Arm Nuts Ft. Lbs.	Rocker Arm Cover Ft. Lbs.	Connecting Rod Cap Bolts Ft. Lbs.	Main Bearing Cap Bolts Ft. Lbs.	Flywheel To Crankshaft Ft. Lbs.	Vibration Damper or Pulley Ft. Lbs.
1983–84	6-196	18–22	④	22–24	22–34	—	99–107①	7	7–8	38–41	42–46	71–81⑤	311–325
1983–85	4-107	18–22	④	22–24	22–24	—	5	7	70–8	38–41	42–46	71–81⑤	130–144
1983–87	6-164	18–22	②	22–24	22–24	—	39–47⑥	7	7–8	③	42–46	71–81⑤	283–311
1985–87	6-209	18–22	④	22–24	22–24	—	99–107①	7	7–8	38–41	42–46	71–81⑤	311–325
1986	6-149⑦	—	⑧	14–17	14–17	⑩	44	—	6–7	⑨	43–48	77–85	282–311
1987	4-140	15–21	⑪	7	7	15–17	7	—	—	⑬	⑭	71–81⑤	311–325
	6-152	15–21	②	22–24	22–24	—	39–47⑥	7	7–8	③	42–46	71–81⑤	283–311
	6-211	15–21	⑪	⑫	7	15–17	7	—	—	⑬	⑭	71–81⑤	311–325

①—Camshaft flange nut.
②—Torque in 3 steps: 1st, 22–25 ft. lbs.; 2nd, 43–47 ft. lbs.; 3rd, tighten additional 20–30°.
③—Torque in 2 steps: 1st, 14 ft. lbs.; 2nd, tighten additional 70°.
④—Torque in 4 steps: 1st, 25–29 ft. lbs.; 2nd, 42–45 ft. lbs.; 3rd, wait 15 min. & tighten 30–36°; 4th, wait 2.5 min. & tighten 20–30°.
⑤—Using new micro-encapsulated bolts.
⑥—DME adapter plate.
⑦—Diesel engine.
⑧—Torque in four steps: 1, 22-29 ft. lbs. 2, 36-43 ft. lbs.; 3, torque bolts an additional 70° from step 2; 4, start engine and allow to run 25 minutes, then torque bolts an additional 90° from step 3.
⑨—Torque in two steps: 1, 14 ft. lbs.; 2, torque bolts and additional 70° from step 1.
⑩—Torque 6 mm nuts to 7 ft. lbs. and 8 mm nuts to 16 ft. lbs.
⑪—Torque in 3 steps: 1st, 35–37 ft. lbs.; 2nd, 57–59 ft. lbs.; 3rd, wait 15 minutes & torque to 71–73 ft. lbs.
⑫—M6 bolts, 7 ft. lbs.; M8 bolts, 14–17 ft. lbs.
⑬—Torque in 3 steps: 1st, 7 ft. lbs.; 2nd, 22 ft. lbs.; 3rd, tighten an additional 60–62° from that in step 2.
⑭—Torque in 2 steps: 1st, 16 ft. lbs.; 2nd, tighten an additional 47–53° from that in step 1.

Brake Specifications

Year	Model	Brake Drum I.D.	Wheel Cylinder Bore			Master Cylinder Bore	Disc Brake Rotor				
							Nominal Thickness		Minimum Thickness		Runout (T.I.R.)
			Front Disc	Rear Disc	Rear Drum		Front	Rear	Front	Rear	
1983	320i	9.842	1.890	—	.750	.812	.866	—	.827	—	.008
1983–87	528e	—	—	—	—	—	—	—	.803	.331	.008
1983–84	533i	—	—	—	—	—	—	—	.803	.331	.008
	633CSi & 733i	—	—	—	—	—	—	—	.921	.331	.008
1983–85	318i	—	—	—	—	—	—	—	.437	.331	.008
1984–87	325	—	—	—	—	—	—	—	.803	.331	.008
1985–87	535i, 635CSi & 735i	—	—	—	—	—	—	—	.921	.331①	.008
1986	524TD	—	—	—	—	—	—	—	.803	.331	.008
1987	M3	—	—	—	—	—	—	—	.921	.409	.008
	M5, M6	—	—	—	—	—	—	—	1.118	.331	.008

①—1987 735i, .409 inch.

ear Axle Sp cifications

Year	Model	Carrier Type	Ring Gear & Pinion Backlash		Pinion Bearing ① Preload			Differential Bearing ① Preload	
			Method	Adjustment	Method	With Seal Inch-Lbs.	Less Seal Inch-Lbs.	Method	Adjustment
1983–87	All ①	Removable	Shim	.0024–.0051	Sleeve	24	22	Shim	4–6 ②
1987	735i	Removable	Shim	.0024–.0051	Sleeve	③	④	Shim	—
	M3	Removable	Shim	.0024–.0051	Sleeve	③	④	Shim	—
	M5, M6	Removable	Shim	.0024–.0051	Sleeve	⑤	⑥	Shim	—

①—Exc. "M" series & 1987 735i.
②—Greater than measured pinion rotating torque.
③—With FAG or Timken bearings, 23 inch lbs. With SKF bearing, 18 inch lbs. With Koyo bearing, 19 inch lbs.
④—With FAG or Timken bearings, 21 inch lbs. With SKF bearing, 16 inch lbs. With Koyo bearing, 17 inch lbs.
⑤—With FAG or Timken bearings, 34 inch lbs. With SKF bearing, 29 inch lbs. With Koyo bearing, 33 inch lbs.
⑥—With FAG or Timken bearings, 32 inch lbs. With SKF bearing, 27 inch lbs. With Koyo bearing, 31 inch lbs.

Front Wheel Alignment Specifications

Year	Model	Caster Angle, Degrees		Camber Angle, Degrees				Toe-In Inch
				Limits		Desired		
		Limits	Desired	Left	Right	Left	Right	
1983	320i	+7 1/6 to +8 5/6	+8 1/3	−1/2 to +1/2	−1/2 to +1/2	0	0	.060
1983–84	533i	+7 1/2 to +8 1/2 ①	+8 ①	−5/6 to +1/6	−5/6 to +1/6	−1/3	−1/3	.079 ②
	633 CSi	+7 1/2 to +8 1/2 ①	+8 ① −5/6 to +1/6	−5/6 to +1/6	−1/3	−1/3	.079 ②	
	733i	+8 1/2 to +9 1/2 ①	+9 ①	−1/2 to +1/2	−1/2 to +1/2	0	0	.020 ③
1983–85	318i	+8 to +9 ①	+8 1/2 ①	−1 1/6 to −1/6	−1 1/6 to −1/6	−2/3	−2/3	.079 ②
1983–87	528e	+7 1/2 to +8 1/2 ①	+8 ①	−5/6 to +1/6	−5/6 to +1/6	−1/3	−1/3	.079 ②
1984–87	325	+8 to +9 ①	+8 1/2 ①	−1 1/6 to −1/6	−1 1/6 to −1/6	−2/3	−2/3	.079 ②
1985–87	535i	+7 1/2 to +8 1/2 ①	+8 ①	−5/6 to +1/6	−5/6 to +1/6	−1/3	−1/3	.079 ②
	635 CSi	+7 1/2 to +8 1/2 ①	+8 ①	−5/6to +1/6	−5/6 to +1/6	−1/3	−1/3	.079 ②
	735i	+8 1/2 to +9 1/2 ①	+9 ①	−1/2 to +1/2	−1/2 to +1/2	0	0	.020 ③
1987	M3	+8 19/30 to +9 19/30 ①	+9 2/15 ①	−1 3/15 to −3/15	−1 3/15 to −3/15	−7/10	−7/10	.079
	M5, M6	—	—	—	—	—	—	—

①—With 10° wheel lock. ②—With TRX tires, .083 inch. ③—With TRX tires, .024 inch.

Rear Wheel Alignment Specifications

Year	Model	Camber Degrees		Toe-In Inch
		Limits	Desired	
1983	320i	$-1\frac{7}{10}$ to $-2\frac{13}{15}$	$-2\frac{11}{30}$	.080
1983–84	533i	$-1\frac{5}{6}$ to $-2\frac{5}{6}$	$-2\frac{1}{3}$	.079①
	633CSi	$-1\frac{5}{6}$ to $-2\frac{5}{6}$	$-2\frac{1}{3}$	.079①
	733i	$-1\frac{5}{6}$ to $-2\frac{5}{6}$	$-2\frac{1}{3}$	.079①
1983–85	318i	$-1\frac{1}{3}$ to $-2\frac{1}{3}$	$-1\frac{5}{6}$	.079①
1983–87	528e	$-1\frac{5}{6}$ to $-2\frac{5}{6}$	$-2\frac{1}{3}$	.079①
1984–87	325	$-1\frac{1}{3}$ to $-2\frac{1}{3}$	$-1\frac{5}{6}$	.079①
1985–87	535i	$-1\frac{5}{6}$ to $-2\frac{5}{6}$	$-2\frac{1}{3}$	.079①
	635CSi	$-1\frac{5}{6}$ to $-2\frac{5}{6}$	$-2\frac{1}{3}$	.079①
	735i	$-1\frac{5}{6}$ to $-2\frac{5}{6}$	$-2\frac{1}{3}$	.079①
1987	M3	$-1\frac{5}{6}$ to $-2\frac{5}{6}$	$-2\frac{1}{3}$	.114
	M5, M6	—	—	—

①—With TRX tires, .083 inch.

Cooling System & Capacity Data

Year	Engine or Model	Cooling Capacity Qts.		Radiator Cap Relief Pressure Lbs.	Thermo. Opening Temp. °F	Fuel Tank Gals.	Engine Oil Refill Qts. ①	Transmission Oil			Rear Axle Oil Pints
		Less A/C	With A/C					4 Speed Pints	5 Speed Pints	Auto. Trans. Qts.	
1983	320i	7.4	7.4	14	176	15.3	4	2.1	3.2	②	2.0
1983–84	533i	12.7	12.7	14.5	176	16.6	5.3	—	③	④	3.6
	633CSi	12.7	12.7	14.5	176	16.6	5.3	—	③	④	3.6
	733i	12.7	12.7	14.5	176	22.4	5.3	—	③	④	3.6
1983–85	318i	7.4	7.4	14.5	176	14.5	4	—	2.4	⑤	2.7
1983–87	528e	11.6	11.6	14.5	176	16.6	4	—	③	⑤	3.6
1984–87	325	11.6	11.6	14.5	176	14.5	4	—	2.4	⑤	3.6
1985–87	535i	12.7	12.7	14.5	176	16.6	5.3	—	③	④	3.6
	635CSi	12.7	12.7	14.5	176	16.6	5.3	—	③	④	3.6
	735i	12.7	12.7	14.5	176	22.4	5.3	—	③	④	3.6
1986	524TD	12.7	12.7	—	176	16.6	7.6	—	—	④	3.6
1987	M3	—	—	14.5	176	18.5	4.3	—	2.6	—	3.6
	M5, M6	—	—	14.5	176	16.6	5.3	—	—	—	4.0

①—Less filter.
②—Total capacity, 6 qts.; drain & refill, 2.1 qts.
③—Type 260, 2.65 pts.; type 265, 3.4 pts.
④—Total capacity, 7.25–7.65 qts.; drain & refill, 2.1 qts.
⑤—Total capacity, 3 spd., 6–6.4 qts.; 4 spd., 7.9 qts. Drain & refill: 3 spd., 2.1 qts.; 4 spd., 3.15 qts.

ELECTRICAL SECTION

INDEX

STEERING WHEEL

REPLACE

VEHICLES LESS SUPPLEMENTAL RESTRAINT SYSTEM (SRS)

1. Remove padded crash pad or, on one piece steering wheels, pry out BMW emblem with small screwdriver.
2. Mark installation position of steering wheel in relation to steering shaft.
3. When reinstalling steering wheel, note that wheel must be installed in straight ahead position so that marks on steering housing and steering shaft align. Replace self-locking nut and torque to 63-70 ft. lbs.

VEHICLES W/SUPPLEMENTAL RESTRAINT SYSTEM (SRS)

Vehicles with "SRS" designation are equipped with an air bag restraint system. Use extreme caution when working near steering wheel or column to avoid personal injury.

1. Disconnect battery ground cable.
2. Remove retaining screws and steering column lower case section, then disconnect plug electrical connector.
3. Working from behind steering wheel, remove the four steering wheel pad retaining screws.
4. Disconnect plug, then remove air bag and position aside with padded plate facing upward.
5. Position front wheels in straight ahead position, mark installation position of steering wheel in relation to steering shaft, then remove retaining nut and steering wheel.
6. Reverse procedure to install. Ensure lock pin in column engages hole in steering wheel.

ALTERNATOR IN-CAR TESTING

1. Connect suitable volt/ammeter, and oscilloscope if available, following manufacturer's instructions.
2. Start engine and run until it reaches normal operating temperature.
3. Switch on electrical accessories to create load and maintain engine speed of 900-1000 RPM.
4. Regulated voltage should be within specifications, charge rate should be greater than 15 amperes and scope pattern, if applicable, should show a ripple of less than 6%. **Refer to oscilloscope manufacturer's instructions to diagnose variances in scope pattern.**
5. If charge indicator lamp goes out while engine is running and scope pattern is acceptable, but regulated voltage is less than specified, or if regulated voltage is greater than specified, check for defective voltage regulator.
6. If voltage or amperage are not as specified, or if charge indicator remains illuminated, check for open or grounded D+ lead.
7. If wiring is satisfactory and charging system malfunction persists, repair or replace alternator as needed.
8. After performing test, turn off accessories and return engine to idle.

STARTER

REPLACE

320i

1. Remove mixture control unit intake cowl.
2. Disconnect battery ground cable. Disconnect wire at solenoid and ground wire at support bracket.
3. Detach support bracket at engine block. Remove starter and lift off with support bracket.
4. Reverse procedure to install.

318i & 325

1. Disconnect battery ground cable and drain cooling system.
2. Remove air flow sensor and air cleaner assembly.
3. Remove intake air collector lower bracket.
4. Mark position of starter leads, remove retaining nuts and disconnect electrical connectors from starter.
5. Remove starter bracket.
6. Disconnect heater hose above starter motor and remove coolant fitting from block.
7. Remove starter retaining nuts, then lift starter from engine compartment.
8. Reverse procedure to install, ensuring that trapped air is removed from cooling system by opening bleeder screw on pump housing during final filling.

528e

1. Disconnect battery ground cable and remove upper starter retaining bolt. **It may be necessary to bend a suitably sized box end wrench to remove and install starter upper retaining bolt.**
2. Raise and support vehicle, then remove starter rear bracket.
3. Mark position of starter leads, remove retaining nuts and disconnect electrical connectors from starter.
4. Remove starter lower mounting bolt and the starter motor.
5. Reverse procedure to install.

533/535i & 633/635CSi

1. Disconnect battery ground cable and drain cooling system.
2. Mark position of starter leads, remove

Fig. 1 Removing ignition switch. 320i models

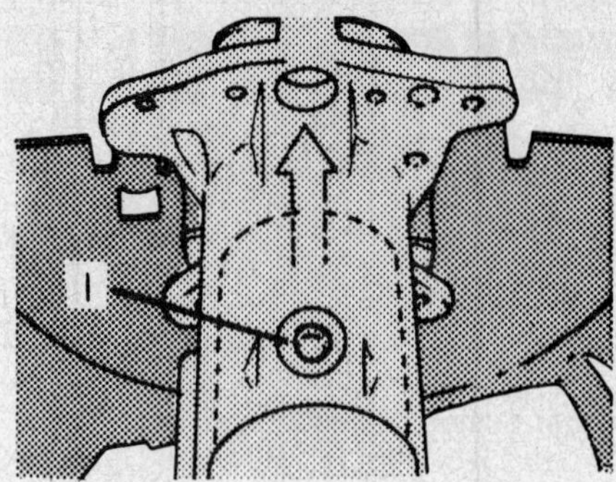

Fig. 2 Steering lock housing removal. 318i & 325

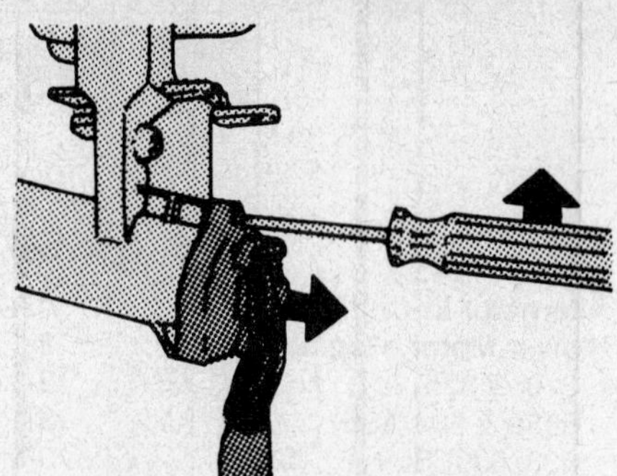

Fig. 3 Ignition switch removal. 318i & 325

retaining nut and disconnect electrical connectors from starter.
3. Disconnect coolant hose shrouding starter mounting bolts.
4. Remove starter mounting bolts and the starter motor.
5. Reverse procedure to install, ensuring that trapped air is removed from cooling system by opening bleed screw on pump housing during final filling.

733/735i

1. Disconnect battery ground cable.
2. Mark position of starter leads, remove retaining nut and disconnect electrical connectors from starter.
3. Remove starter retaining bolts and the starter. **It may be necessary to bend a suitably sized box end wrench to remove and install upper starter bolt.**
4. Reverse procedure to install.

STARTER MOTOR TROUBLESHOOTING

STARTER INOPERATIVE

1. Disconnect push on connector from starter solenoid and connect to B+ connector using suitable jumper wire.
2. If starter operates, check for open in wiring between starter switch and solenoid or defective starter switch.
3. If starter fails to operate, switch on headlamps and reconnect solenoid terminal to B+ connection while observing lights.
4. If headlamps dim, starter motor is shorted.
5. If headlamps do not dim, check for defective solenoid, open in starter windings or excessively worn starter brushes.

STARTER TURNS SLOWLY

1. Undercharged battery.
2. Worn or dirty armature bushings.
3. Defective armature or field coils.

SOLENOID CLICKS BUT STARTER DOES NOT OPERATE

1. Turn on headlamps and observe lights while operating starter.
2. If headlamps dim when starter is engaged, check for shorted armature or field coils.
3. If headlamps do not dim when starter is engaged, check for defective brushes or open in starter.
4. If starter tests satisfactorily, check for defective solenoid.

IGNITION SWITCH REPLACE

320i

1. Disconnect battery ground cable.
2. Remove lower casing under steering column.
3. Some models require lower left center instrument panel trim be removed.
4. With key set at "0" position, loosen setscrew and pull switch away, **Fig. 1.**
5. Disconnect switch from horn wires, multiple connectors and harness straps.
6. Remove switch.
7. Reverse procedure to install.

318i & 325

Removal

1. Disconnect battery ground cable and remove steering wheel.
2. Remove steering column lower cover.
3. Remove turn signal and windshield wiper switches.
4. Remove steering shaft snap ring collar, snap ring, washer, spring and locating ring, noting position for installation.
5. Pry up steering shaft bearing with screwdrivers, taking care not to damage bearing.
6. Disconnect ignition switch central connector from instrument panel harness.
7. Remove shear screw (1), **Fig. 2,** with chisel, then pull steering lock casing section from outer steering column tube.
8. Depress spring retainer and remove switch from lock housing, **Fig. 3.**
9. Depress steering lock retainer, turn key to lock position, then withdraw lock from housing.
10. Drill out rivets and remove carbon contact from lock.

Installation

1. Attach carbon contact to steering lock using suitable bolts and nuts.
2. Hold housing and turn key to lock position, then insert lock assembly into housing, ensuring that retainer engages lock housing.
3. Align switch and steering lock notches, then insert switch into rear of housing, ensuring that retaining hook engages notch in switch housing.
4. Position lock housing assembly over outer steering column tube, install new shear screw and tighten screw with suitable driver until head breaks off.
5. Connect ignition switch electrical connector to instrument panel harness.
6. Tap steering shaft bearing into place, using suitable spacer to prevent distortion.
7. Install lower spring washer with stem facing bearing, then the spring and upper washer.
8. Install snap ring using spacer 323052 and driver 323050 or equivalent, taking care not to compress steering column.
9. Install snap ring collar ensuring that notch in collar locks into snap ring.
10. Reverse remaining procedure to complete installation.

528e, 533/535i & 633/635CSi

Removal

1. Disconnect battery ground cable and remove steering wheel.
2. Remove left lower instrument panel trim and the lower steering column cover.
3. Remove retaining screws and disconnect headlamp and windshield wiper switches from column.
4. Pull flasher relay out of holder.
5. Remove 4 shear screws securing steering column bracket using suitable chisel.
6. Remove shear screw (1) and setscrew (3), **Fig. 4,** securing steering lock housing.
7. Hold down on steering column and withdraw steering lock assembly.
8. Disconnect ignition switch electrical connector.
9. Depress retainer and remove switch and/or lock, as needed, **Fig. 5.**

Installation

1. Ensure that lock and switch tabs are

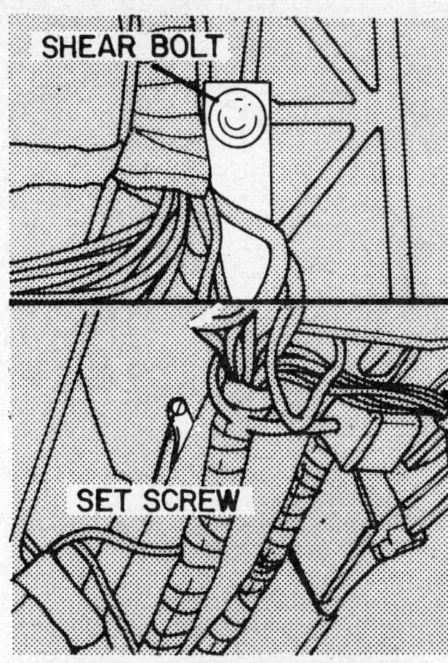

Fig. 4 Steering lock housing removal. 528e, 533/535i & 633/635CSi

Fig. 7 Neutral safety switch installation

aligned, then install switch into lock housing.
2. Connect switch electrical connector, hold down on column and install lock assembly.
3. Install setscrew and lock with paint, then install new lock housing shear screw, tightening screw until head breaks off.
4. Install 4 new shear screws securing steering column bracket and tighten screws until heads break off.
5. Reverse remaining procedure to complete installation.

733/735i

1. Disconnect battery ground cable and remove lower steering column cover.
2. Remove flasher relay from holder.
3. Remove screw securing switch (1), then withdraw switch (2), **Fig. 6.**
4. Disconnect main electrical connector from harness and single black wire to power saving relay, then remove

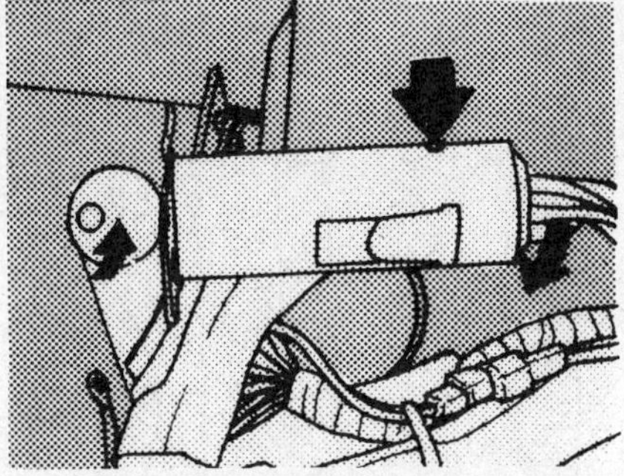

Fig. 5 Ignition switch removal. 528e, 533/535i & 633/635CSi

switch.
5. Reverse procedure to install, inserting switch into housing and turning key slowly until switch engages lock.

LIGHT SWITCH

REPLACE

318i/325

1. Unscrew light switch knob, while holding shaft with an appropriate punch inserted through hole in shaft.
2. Remove any panels which restrict access.
3. Loosen collar or escutcheon.
4. Pull switch through hole and disconnect from multiple plug.
5. Reverse procedure to install.

528e, 533/535i & 733/735i

1. Disconnect battery ground cable remove left lower instrument panel trim.
2. Remove nut from rear of switch, then pull switch out from front of instrument panel.
3. Disconnect electrical connector and remove switch.
4. Reverse procedure to install.

633/635CSi

1. Disconnect battery ground cable and remove left lower instrument panel trim.
2. Disconnect vacuum hoses and electrical connector from in-car temperature sensor.
3. Remove switch knob.
4. Remove bracket from behind switch and disconnect switch electrical connector.
5. Withdraw switch from rear of instrument panel.
6. Reverse procedure to install.

STOP LIGHT SWITCH

REPLACE

1. Remove necessary trim on certain series.
2. Pull off electrical connections to switch.
3. Loosen locknut and unscrew switch.
4. To replace, screw in switch and lock it so that a 0.197-0.236 inch (5-6 mm) of black contact button is visible.

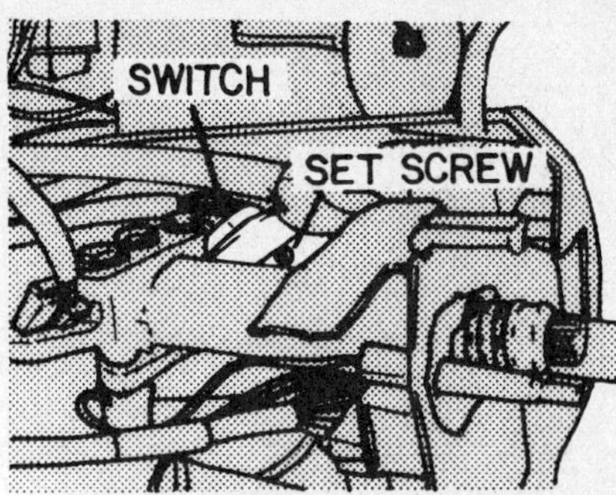

Fig. 6 Ignition switch removal. 733/735i

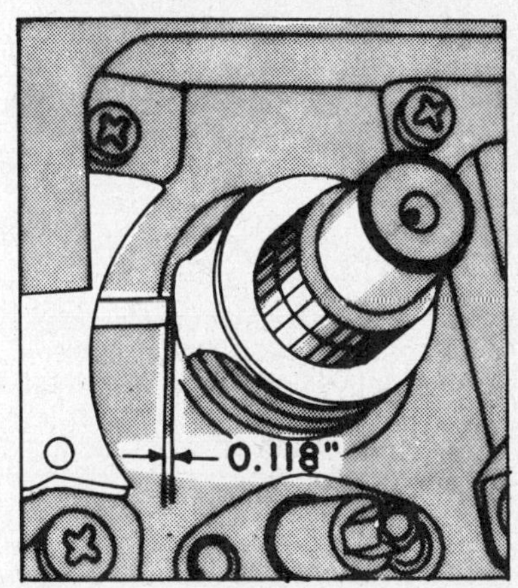

Fig. 8 Turn signal switch cancelling cam adjustment

5. Reinstall connectors and install trim.

NEUTRAL SAFETY SWITCH

REPLACE

1. Remove selector lever and base, then drive out pin and separate lower section from this assembly.
2. Remove central gate screw, then switch.
3. When installing switch, make sure that bosses or pins of switch fit into appropriate gate holes, **Fig. 7.**
4. Reassemble selector group.

TURN SIGNAL SWITCH

REPLACE

1. In all cases, remove necessary trim panels and steering wheel.
2. Disconnect battery ground cable.
3. Disconnect multi-pin plug from signal harness.
4. Disconnect all harness clips in area.
5. On all models, disconnect plug and remove switch.
6. Make sure wheels are pointing straight ahead before reassembling switch.
7. When installing switch, make sure that there is a gap of .012 inch between switch cam and reset dog, **Fig. 8.** On 320i models, be sure to secure ground wire on left side assembly screw.

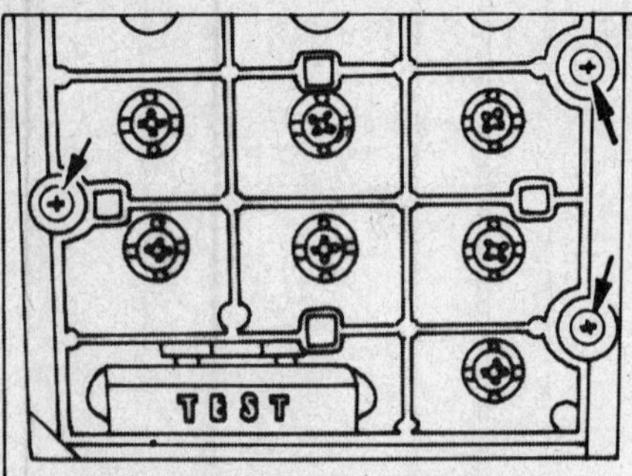

Fig. 9 Removing check control. 633/635CSi

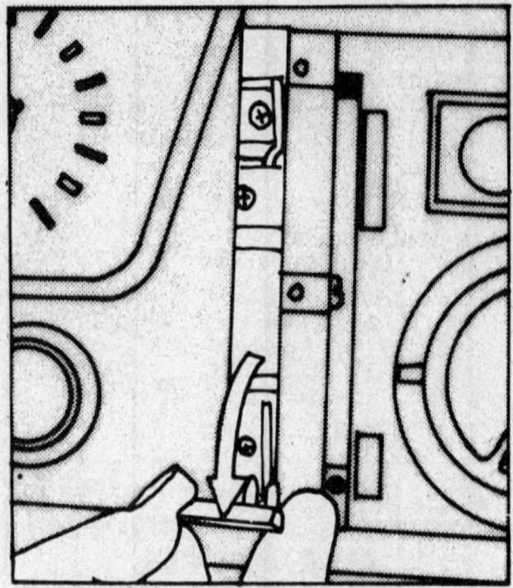

Fig. 10 Removing air control cover plate. 633/635CSi

Fig. 11 Removing panel trim screws. 733/735i

INSTRUMENT CLUSTER REPLACE

320i

1. Disconnect battery ground cable.
2. Remove steering wheel.
3. Remove center instrument panel trim.
4. Disconnect speedometer cable.
5. After removing knurled nut where required, pull instrument carrier.
6. Separate main plugs, tachometer wires and fog lamp indicator light wire, if equipped.
7. On some models equipped with automatic transmission, it may be necessary to disconnect wires at gearshift diagram and resistor.
8. Reverse procedure to install.

318i & 325

1. Disconnect battery ground cable and remove left lower instrument panel trim.
2. Remove nuts securing trim panel between cluster and steering column from the rear, then pull out trim panel.
3. Remove screws securing instrument cluster bezel and the bezel.
4. Remove screws securing cluster, then pull cluster away from instrument panel. **Remove steering wheel, as needed, to allow clearance for cluster removal.**
5. Release clip securing main harness connector, then disconnect main and accessory electrical connectors from cluster and remove cluster assembly.
6. Reverse procedure to install.

528e & 533/535i

1. Disconnect battery ground cable.
2. Remove left lower instrument panel trim and the steering wheel.
3. Remove cluster retaining screws and press cluster out from rear.
4. Disconnect electrical connector and remove instrument cluster.
5. Reverse procedure to install.

633/635CSi

1. Disconnect battery ground cable.
2. Remove left lower instrument panel trim and steering wheel.
3. Lift off check control lens, remove retaining screws and remove check control assembly, **Fig. 9.**
4. Remove fog lamp switch from instrument panel, leaving wiring connected.
5. Remove knobs as needed, then the trim plate between the A/C control and instrument cluster, **Fig. 10.**
6. Remove retaining screws from left and right sides of cluster.
7. Remove steering column racket bolts.
8. Disconnect speedometer cable, if equipped, press down on steering column and withdraw cluster.
9. Disconnect electrical connectors and remove cluster. **Release slide lock on main harness connector before pulling connector from cluster.**
10. Reverse procedure to install.

733/735i

1. Remove lower instrument panel trim and disconnect battery ground cable.
2. Remove screws, **Fig. 11.**
3. Loosen steering column support and pull out steering wheel to maximum length.
4. Disconnect central plugs and wires. Slide cluster out towards right.
5. Reverse procedure to install.

WINDSHIELD WIPER SWITCH REPLACE

1. Disconnect battery ground cable and remove steering wheel.
2. Remove left lower instrument panel trim and lower steering column cover. **On 633/635CSi, disconnect hoses from in-car temperature sensor and the sensor electrical connector.**
3. Release harness straps and disconnect switch electrical connector from harness.
4. Remove switch mounting screws and the switch.
5. Reverse procedure to install.

WINDSHIELD WIPER MOTOR REPLACE

528e & 533/535i

1. Disconnect battery ground cable and remove rubber seal between firewall and cowl panel.
2. Disconnect crank and drive arm, then loosen mounting screws.
3. Disconnect plug and remove motor.
4. Reverse procedure to install. Install motor crank in horizontal position facing left (off position).

318i & 325

1. Remove blower motor and wiper motor support bracket.
2. Disconnect wiper motor electrical connector and remove cowl grille.
3. Disconnect both linkage arms from left side of transmission.
4. Lift up covers, then remove wiper arm retaining nuts and the wiper arms.
5. Remove transmission shaft covers, retaining nuts and washers, then withdraw wiper motor and transmission assembly from cowl chamber.

733/735i

Removal

1. Remove mounting screws and cowl fresh air grille.
2. Remove 4 screws securing air intake cover, pull back rubber seal and washer hose, then tilt cover forward taking care not to damage vacuum hoses.
3. Remove wiper motor cover and disconnect electrical connector.
4. Remove wiper arm nuts and the wiper arms.
5. Remove covers, nuts, springs and spacers from transmission spindles, as equipped, noting position for installation.
6. Pull back rubber insulator, then disconnect right side transmission link.
7. Remove motor mounting bolts and insulators noting position of insulators, withdraw motor and bracket assembly, then disconnect transmission link from motor.
8. Remove wiper motor crank, bracket retaining bolts and the bracket.

Installation

1. Install bracket on motor and securely tighten retaining bolts.
2. Ensure that wiper motor is in park position, then install crank as shown in **Fig. 12,** and tighten nut securely holding crank to prevent motor shaft from turning.
3. Connect transmission link to wiper

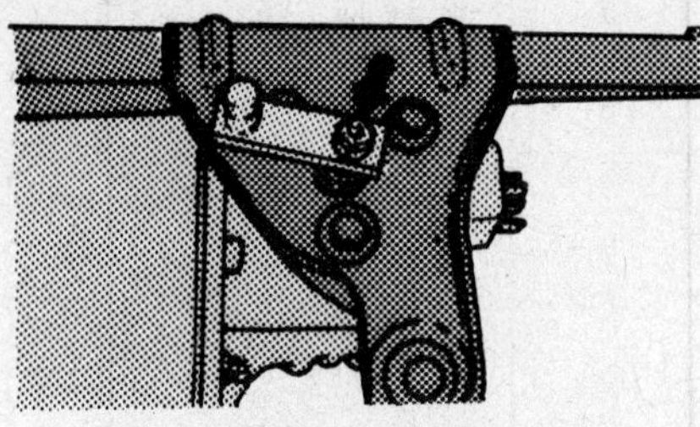
Fig. 12 Wiper motor crank installation. 733/735i

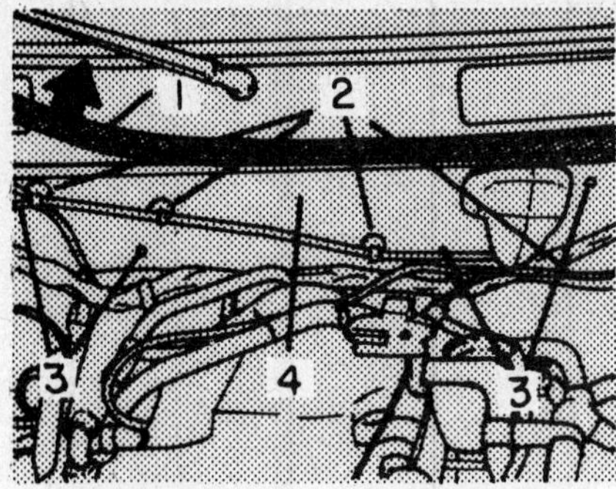

Fig. 13 Upper firewall removal. 318i & 325

Fig. 14 Upper firewall removal. 528e & 533/535i

motor crank, mount motor and bracket assembly in cowl, then install insulators and mounting bolts.
4. Connect right side transmission link, then reinstall rubber pad ensuring that pad supports motor properly.
5. Mount transmission spindles in cowl panel, install rings diaphragm springs and retaining nuts, then torque retaining nuts to 8-10 ft. lbs. **Do not over tighten spindle nuts, as cowl panel may be damaged.**
6. Reverse remaining procedure to complete installation.

RADIO
REPLACE
318i & 325

1. Remove radio knobs and hex nuts from radio shafts.
2. Remove front plate. Remove countersunk screws (2 per side) holding radio shelf into console side walls.
3. Pull shelf out. Disconnect all wiring and antenna cable.
4. Remove rear bracket holding radio to shelf and lift out radio.
5. Reverse procedure to install.

528e & 533/535i

1. Remove radio knobs, tone control, and right ornamental disc.
2. Remove nuts from shaft and remove radio trim plate.
3. Remove studs and brackets.
4. Pull radio out and disconnect all wiring and antenna cable.
5. Reverse procedure to install.

633/635CSi

1. Remove hazard warning switch and cigar lighter holder.
2. Remove left and right screws (2 per side) and pull radio and carrier out.
3. Disconnect all wiring and antenna cable.
4. Remove rear bracket holding radio to carrier.
5. Remove knobs, tone control, nut and trim plates. On mono and stereo radios, remove nuts from shafts. On cassette models, remove mounting bracket screws. Remove radio from carrier.
6. Reverse procedure to install.

BLOWER MOTOR
REPLACE
318i & 325

1. Disconnect battery ground cable.
2. Remove rear hood seal (1) from channel, cut harness strap (2), remove retaining bolts (3), then pull back upper firewall section (4), **Fig. 13.**
3. Open retaining straps and remove blower motor cover.
4. Disconnect electrical connectors noting position for installation.
5. Release motor clamp and remove motor and impeller assembly. **Do not remove impellers from motor, as they are balanced as an assembly.**
6. Reverse procedure to install.

528e & 533/535i

Heater Blower

1. Disconnect battery ground cable and remove rear hood seal from channel.
2. Remove upper firewall retaining screws, **Fig. 14,** then pull back firewall section to gain access to blower motor.
3. Release tabs securing blower motor cover, taking care not to break tabs, then remove cover.
4. Disconnect electrical connectors noting position for installation.
5. Release clamp securing motor, then remove motor & impeller assembly. **Do not separate impellers from blower motor as they are balanced as an assembly.**
6. Reverse procedure to install.

Evaporator Blower Motor

1. Disconnect battery ground cable and discharge A/C system.
2. Remove right and left lower instrument panel sections.
3. Disconnect electrical connectors from both electric window cutout switches.
4. On models with automatic temperature control, disconnect vacuum hose and electrical connector from passenger compartment temperature sensor.
5. Pull up parking brake lever insulator from center and remove insulator.
6. Lift up covers (1) from screws securing rear console section, remove screws (2), then pull back rear section to console, **Fig. 15.**
7. On models with manual transmission, unscrew shift knob and remove dust boot and shift lever insulator.
8. On models with automatic transmission, remove trim plate from right side of selector lever, housing screws and the selector lever housing, **Fig. 16.**
9. Remove ashtray, then the console retaining screws from ashtray well and from behind shift lever.
10. Pull switches from console, disconnect electrical connectors and remove switches, noting position for installation.
11. Open glove box and remove upper console retaining screws and screws from right and left sides of console.
12. Pull console assembly back and remove remaining screws.
13. Disconnect radio electrical connectors and antenna lead, then remove console assembly.
14. Remove evaporator trim panel and disconnect refrigerant lines from evaporator. **Plug lines and open fittings to prevent moisture and contaminants from entering A/C system.**
15. Disconnect electrical connectors from evaporator, noting position for installation.
16. Remove center bracket mounting bolts, side mounting screws and release retaining clamps, then remove evaporator assembly.
17. Release 7 clips securing blower motor cover and remove center retaining screw, then lift off evaporator cover along with blower motor.
18. Reverse procedure to install.

633/635CSi

Heater Blower Motor

1. Disconnect battery ground cable.
2. Remove screws securing cover and the cover, **Fig. 17.**
3. Release tabs securing blower motor cover and remove cover, taking care not to break tabs.
4. Disconnect electrical connectors noting position for installation, release clamp and remove motor and impeller assembly. **Do not separate impellers from motor as they are balanced as an assembly.**

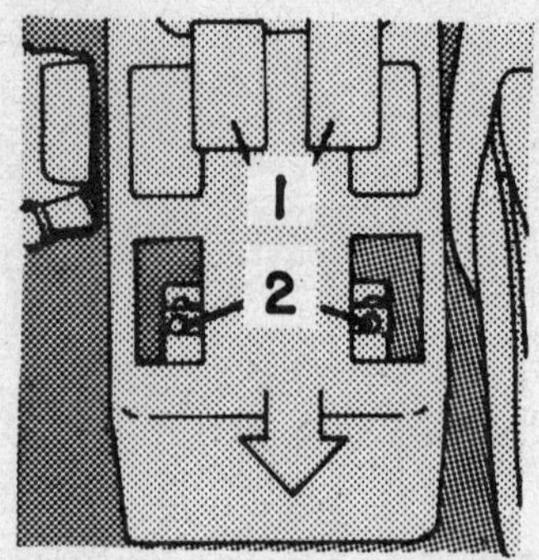

Fig. 15 Removing rear console section. 528e, 533/535i & 633/635CSi

5. Reverse procedure to install.

Evaporator Blower Motor

1. Disconnect battery ground cable and discharge A/C system.
2. Pry out trim plate between cluster and A/C control, switches and trim plates at either side above control, then remove switch and A/C control knobs.
3. Remove radio and bolts securing center trim plate, pull plate forward and disconnect panel lamps, then remove trim plate.
4. Disconnect electrical connector from heater temperature sensor and A/C control connector from main harness.
5. Disconnect cables from control assembly, noting position for installation, then remove A/C control.
6. Remove both instrument panel lower trim panels, then disconnect electrical connectors from electric window cut out switches.
7. Disconnect vacuum hose and electrical connector from in car temperature sensor.
8. Remove trim plate from headlamp aiming control, pull out bulb holders, then remove control retaining screws and the control.
9. Pull up parking brake lever insulator from center and remove insulator.
10. Remove covers (1) or switches from above rear console mounting nuts, then the nuts, and push rear console section toward rear of vehicle, **Fig. 15.**
11. On models with manual transmission, remove shift knob, dust boot and shift lever insulating pad.
12. On models with automatic transmission, remove trim plate from right side of selector lever, selector housing retaining screws and the housing.
13. Pull out console switches and disconnect electrical connectors.
14. Remove console retaining screw from behind shifter.
15. Open glove box door, disconnect retaining straps and remove glove box.
16. Remove right and left front console retaining screws.
17. Pull out switches along lower edge of console center panel and disconnect electrical connectors, noting position for installation.

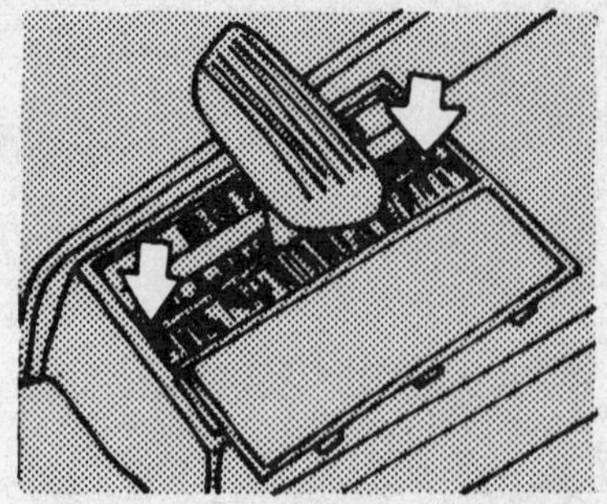

Fig. 16 Selector lever housing removal. 528e & 533/535i w/automatic transmission

18. Pull back console, disconnect necessary electrical connectors and remove console.
19. Remove side trim, impact switch and spacers, noting position for installation.
20. Disconnect refrigerant lines from evaporator, then plug lines and open fittings.
21. Remove blower relay and disconnect electrical connector from evaporator temperature sensor.
22. Remove center bracket bolt, side retaining screws and release clamps, then remove evaporator assembly.
23. Release 7 clamps securing and remove center bolt securing upper evaporator case, then remove upper case and blower motor assembly.
24. Reverse procedure to install.

733/735i

1. Remove cowl ventilation grille.
2. Remove rear hood seal from channel and the 12 screws securing air intake cover, then pull back cover.
3. Mark and disconnect hoses from vacuum servos.
4. Remove relay and bracket and the temperature sensor.
5. Release clamp securing blower motor cover, remove protective grille and slide cover to one side.
6. Remove blower motor assembly.
7. Reverse procedure to install.

HEATER CORE REPLACE

318i & 325

1. Disconnect battery ground cable and drain cooling system.
2. Remove rear ashtray and console retaining screw from ashtray well.
3. Pull back on console and remove center section from over parking brake lever.
4. On models with manual transmission, remove shift knob, boot and insulation sheet from around shift lever.
5. On models with automatic transmission, remove panel to right of selector lever, selector bezel screws and the bezel.
6. Remove power window switches and disconnect electrical connectors, if equipped.
7. Remove console retaining nut from behind shift lever.
8. Remove screws securing front ashtray, ashtray assembly and the cigar lighter.
9. Remove screws securing package tray from sides and lower edge of center cluster, then remove package tray.
10. Remove left lower instrument panel trim and the left and center connecting ducts.
11. Remove screw securing heater core tube clamps.
12. Remove bolts and disconnect heater core tubes from water valve.
13. Remove heater case cover and withdraw heater core.
14. Reverse procedure to install.

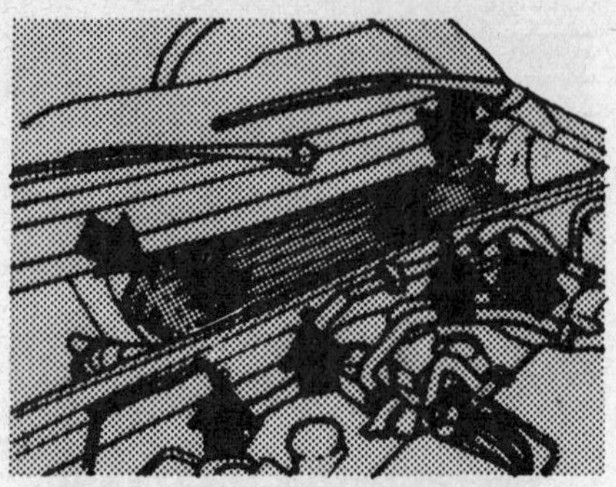

Fig. 17 Cowl intake cover removal. 633/635CSi

528e, 533/535i & 633/635CSi

1. Disconnect battery ground cable, drain cooling system and discharge A/C system.
2. Remove evaporator assembly as outlined in "Evaporator Blower Motor, Replace."
3. Remove upper firewall panel as outlined in "Heater Blower Motor, Replace."
4. Remove nuts securing heater housing to cowl panel and disconnect heater hoses.
5. Mark installation position and disconnect electrical connectors from heater housing.
6. Lift out air guides from heater housing.
7. Remove nuts securing heater housing to instrument panel support, then the heater housing assembly.
8. Remove air guides and blower cover from housing.
9. Release 13 retaining clips, then separate housing and remove core.
10. Reverse procedure to install, noting the following:
    a. Cement new seal to heater core prior to installation.
    b. Ensure that air distribution flaps are properly mounted when joining heater case.
    c. Ensure that trapped air is removed from cooling system by opening bleed screw on pump housing during final filling.

733/735i

1. Remove instrument panel trim and fresh air grille.
2. Remove rubber seal, if necessary, and the cowl cover and tilt cover forward.
3. Release cooling system pressure and disconnect coolant and vacuum hoses from heater.
4. Open duct mounting clamp. Disconnect central plug and remove duct cover downward.
5. Detach center strut. Remove insulation and disconnect refrigerant lines at heater/air conditioner. Disconnect wire.
6. Remove heater bolts from passenger compartment and spray wall. Remove heater toward inside.
7. Disconnect condensation hoses. Heater case can now be separated and core removed.
8. Reverse procedure to install.

GASOLINE ENGINE SECTION

INDEX

ENGINE REPLACE

320i

1. Remove transmission and radiator.
2. Remove air-flow sensor intake cowl and disconnect fuel lines noting their locations.
3. Disconnect plug from air flow sensor, lift harness out of holder and disconnect vacuum hoses.
4. Disconnect fuel line holder on air flow sensor and remove mixture control unit.
5. Disconnect accelerator cable and hose at throttle housing.
6. Disconnect pressure converter hoses noting colors, and heater hoses noting locations.
7. Disconnect coil wires and remove battery. Disconnect central electric plug.
8. Disconnect left engine mount and damper.
9. Disconnect right engine mount and lift out engine.
10. Reverse procedure to install.

318i & 325

Mark installation position of all hoses and electrical connectors prior to removal.

1. Disconnect positive and negative cables from battery, and drain cooling system.
2. Raise and support vehicle, remove transmission and disconnect exhaust system.
3. Remove bolts securing power steering pump and secure pump aside, leaving hoses connected.
4. Loosen A/C compressor tensioning bolts and remove upper bracket retaining bolts, then remove compressor and secure aside, leaving hoses connected.
5. Disconnect hoses from radiator, loosen fan shroud clamps and hang shroud over cooling fan.
6. Disconnect electrical connectors from radiator temperature switches, if equipped.
7. On models with automatic transmission, disconnect cooler lines from radiator, then plug lines and open fittings.
8. On all models, remove radiator mounting bolts, radiator and the fan shroud.
9. Remove hood support and gas pressure spring, then install suitable locks to secure hood in open position.
10. Remove screw securing harness ground near battery, open wire retaining straps, then disconnect electrical connectors from engine compartment temperature sensor (next to battery) and oxygen sensor.
11. Remove inner glove box trim panels, disconnect electrical connectors from idle and fuel injection control unit, then push harness out into engine compartment.
12. Disconnect primary and secondary leads from ignition coil and electrical connector from sensor below coil.
13. Disconnect electrical connectors from air cleaner intake duct and air flow sensor, and remove cap and relay next to sensor.
14. Loosen clamp securing duct to intake manifold, then remove air cleaner/flow sensor assembly.
15. Remove cap from relay board, then disconnect main harness connector behind relay board and connector to ignition control unit.
16. Disconnect vacuum hoses and electrical connector from firewall mounted distributor vacuum control switch.
17. Disconnect cables and vacuum hoses from throttle body and remove transmission cable bracket.
18. Disconnect and plug fuel hoses and remove "U" shaped bracket.
19. Disconnect coolant hoses between engine and body.
20. Disconnect engine to chassis ground straps, then remove engine mount nuts and engine damper assembly.
21. Attach suitable lifting equipment to engine, and remove engine assembly, securing wiring harnesses to engine to prevent damage.
22. Reverse procedure to install.

528e & 533/535i

Mark installation position of components, electrical connectors and hoses prior to removal.

1. Disconnect positive and negative cables from battery and harness lead from battery cable terminal, then drain cooling system.
2. Raise and support vehicle. Disconnect exhaust system and remove transmission, then drain engine block.
3. Lower vehicle, remove power steering pump retaining bolts and secure pump aside leaving hoses connected.
4. Disconnect lower radiator hose and electrical connectors from radiator temperature switches.
5. Remove screws securing fan shroud,

separate shroud from radiator, then disconnect upper radiator hose and expansion tank hose.
6. On models with automatic transmission, disconnect and plug cooler lines.
7. Remove radiator mounting bolts and disconnect hood cable, then lift radiator from engine compartment and remove fan shroud.
8. Loosen A/C compressor tensioner bolts and disconnect drive belt.
9. Remove A/C compressor bracket bolts, then secure compressor and bracket aside, leaving hoses connected.
10. Remove hood supports and install suitable locks to secure hood in open position.
11. Disconnect accelerator, cruise control and transmission cables from throttle lever and brackets, and vacuum hoses from throttle body.
12. Loosen clamp securing intake duct to throttle body, disconnect electrical connector and intake duct from air flow sensor, release harness retaining strap and remove air flow sensor.
13. Remove relay board covers and cap, relays and release harness retaining straps.
14. Disconnect and plug fuel lines, and the evaporative emission hose, then remove support bracket.
15. Disconnect heater hoses from engine.
16. Disconnect ground straps between engine and chassis.
17. Disconnect electrical connectors from idle and fuel injection control units, and check panel connector from engine control harness, release straps securing harness to firewall, and pull engine control harness out into engine compartment.
18. Disconnect vacuum hoses and electrical connectors from firewall mounted ignition control components, then secure harness to engine.
19. Remove motor mount nuts and disconnect remaining ground straps, then remove engine using suitable lifting equipment.
20. Reverse procedure to install.

633/635CSi

Mark installation position of all components, electrical connectors and hoses prior to removal.

1. Disconnect positive and negative cables from battery, positive harness lead from battery cable terminal and ground strap from body.
2. Lift off headlamp covers and disconnect electrical connector for hood lamp.
3. Disconnect windshield and headlamp washer hoses.
4. Mark installation position of bolts securing hinges to hood and remove 2 bolts from each hinge.
5. Remove retainers and disconnect hood supports.
6. Support hood, then remove remaining hinge bolts and the hood.
7. Remove expansion tank cap, open radiator drain, raise and support vehicle and remove block drain plug.
8. Disconnect exhaust system and remove transmission, then lower vehicle.
9. Secure fan pulley, then remove fan retaining nut and the fan and clutch assembly. **Retaining nut has lefthand threads.**
10. Disconnect lower radiator hose and electrical connectors to radiator temperature switches.
11. Remove fan shroud retaining screws and disconnect radiator inlet hoses.
12. On models with automatic transmission, disconnect and plug cooler lines.
13. On all models, remove left and right radiator mounting nuts, radiator and fan shroud.
14. Remove power steering pump retaining bolts and secure pump aside, leaving hoses connected.
15. Remove bolts securing A/C compressor to bracket, disconnect belt and secure compressor aside, leaving hoses connected.
16. Disconnect electrical connectors from air flow sensor, release harness from clips and pull out drain hose, loosen clamp securing duct to throttle body, then remove air flow sensor/air cleaner assembly.
17. Disconnect electrical connectors from idle and fuel injection control units, then pull harness into engine compartment.
18. Disconnect ground strap from firewall and electrical connector from oxygen sensor.
19. Release straps securing engine harness to firewall and secure harness to engine.
20. Disconnect primary and secondary leads from ignition coil, distributor leads from main harness and electrical connector from solenoid near coil, then secure harness to engine.
21. Remove lower relays from relay board and disconnect engine harness from connector under relay board.
22. Disconnect accelerator, cruise control and transmission control cables as equipped, and secure cables aside.
23. Disconnect expansion tank and heater hoses, and the fuel hoses, then plug hoses and remove support brackets as needed.
24. Disconnect all vacuum hoses from components chassis mounted components.
25. Remove upper radiator hose and connect suitable lifting equipment to engine.
26. Remove nuts securing left and right engine mounts, then lift engine from engine compartment.
27. Reverse procedure to install.

733/735i

Mark installation position of components, electrical connectors and hoses prior to removal.

1. Disconnect positive and negative cables from battery and harness lead from battery cable terminal.
2. Disconnect engine compartment lamp and supports from hood.
3. Mark installation position of hood hinges and insert a suitable insulator between hood and header panel.
4. Support hood, then remove hood hinge bolts and the hood.
5. Raise and support vehicle, disconnect exhaust system and remove transmission.
6. Open radiator drain and remove block drain plug, drain cooling system, then lower vehicle.
7. Secure fan pulley, then remove fan retaining nut and the fan and clutch assembly. **Pulley retaining nut has lefthand threads.**
8. Disconnect lower radiator hose and electrical connectors for radiator temperature sensors.
9. Disconnect upper radiator hoses and remove screws securing fan shroud.
10. On models with automatic transmission, disconnect and plug cooler lines.
11. Remove radiator mounting bolts, radiator and fan shroud.
12. Remove power steering pump bolts and secure pump aside leaving hoses connected.
13. Remove bolts securing A/C compressor to bracket, then secure compressor aside leaving hoses connected.
14. Remove battery.
15. Disconnect electrical connectors from air flow sensor and release harness from clips, loosen clamp securing duct to throttle body, then remove air flow sensor/air cleaner assembly.
16. Remove right radio speaker cover and disconnect glove box retaining straps.
17. Disconnect electrical connectors from idle and fuel injection control units and check panel and trip computer connectors from control harness.
18. Remove master relay and screw securing relay socket to firewall, disconnect oxygen sensor connector and remove harness lead from bracket, release harness retaining straps, then pull engine control harness through firewall into engine compartment and secure harness to engine.
19. Disconnect primary and secondary leads from ignition coil and distributor leads from body harness, then release wiring retainers.
20. Disconnect engine harness along with necessary relay sockets from connections at relay board and secure harness to engine.
21. Disconnect and plug fuel hoses.
22. Disconnect accelerator, cruise control and transmission cables, as equipped, and secure cables aside.
23. Disconnect heater hoses and all vacuum hoses between engine and body.
24. Remove upper radiator hose and connect suitable lifting equipment to engine.
25. Remove left and right engine mount nuts and the engine damper, then lift engine from vehicle.
26. Reverse procedure to install.

CYLINDER HEAD REPLACE

4-107/1766cc ENGINE

320i

1. Drain coolant, then disconnect battery

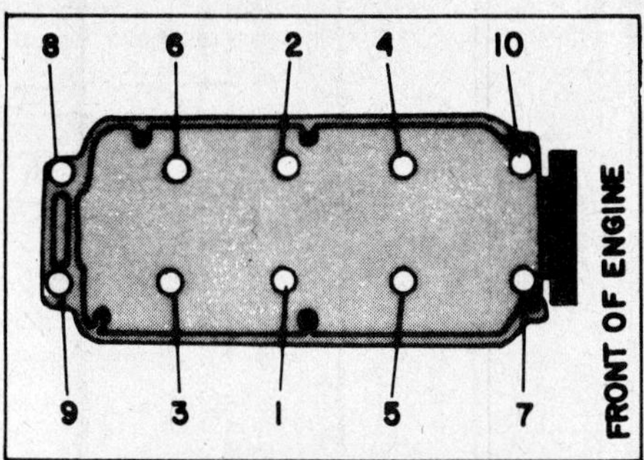

Fig. 1 Cylinder head bolt tightening sequence. 4-107/1766cc engine

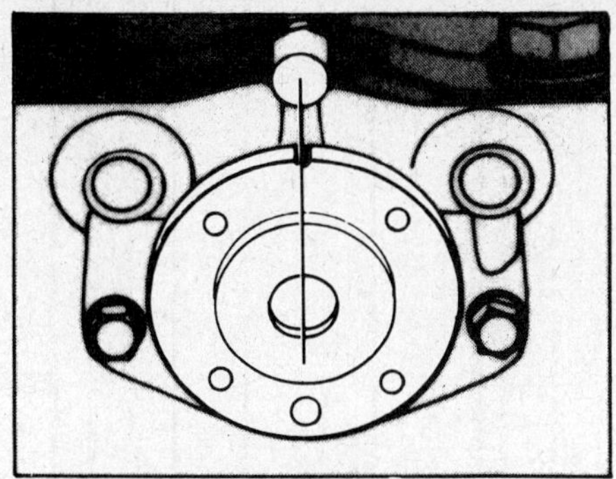

Fig. 2 Aligning camshaft Flange. 4-107/1766cc engine

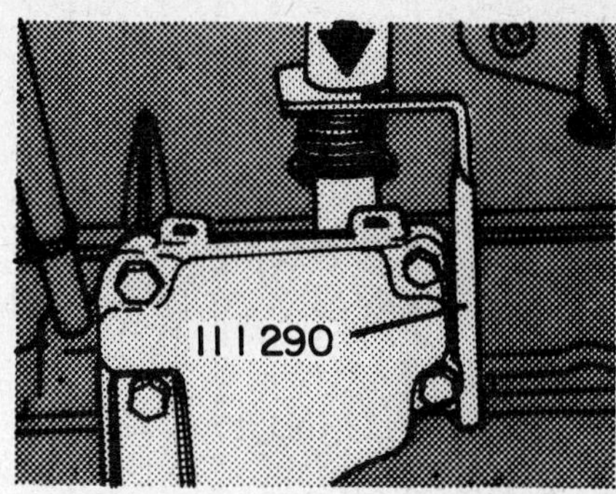

Fig. 3 Compressing crankcase ventilation tube

ground cable and remove cylinder head cover and intake cowl.

2. Disconnect vacuum hoses, accelerator cable, injection valve wires, temperature sensor and temperature timing wires. Disconnect water hoses at head, hoses at thermo valve, throttle housing and EGR valve.
3. Remove distributor cap, oil dipstick clamp and exhaust pipe.
4. Disconnect wire plugs at cold start valve, auxiliary air valve and timing valve, distributor and oil pressure sending switch.
5. Rotate crankshaft so that No. 1 piston is at TDC on compression stroke, remove upper timing case cover, chain tensioner piston and camshaft sprocket retaining bolts, then disconnect sprocket from camshaft.
6. Loosen cylinder head retaining bolts in reverse of sequence shown in **Fig. 1**, then remove cylinder head and gasket.
7. Ensure that gasket surfaces are clean and free from old gasket material and that No. 1 piston is at TDC, align notch in camshaft hub with cast tab on cylinder head, **Fig. 2**, then install cylinder head.
8. Torque cylinder head bolts to specifications in sequence shown in **Fig. 1.**
9. Ensure that dowel pin hole in camshaft sprocket is properly aligned, then mount sprocket and timing chain, tighten sprocket bolts and install tensioner piston.
10. Reverse remaining procedure to complete installation.

318i

1. Disconnect battery ground cable, then raise and support vehicle.
2. Disconnect exhaust pipe from manifold and remove clamp securing pipe to transmission.
3. Remove block drain bolt near exhaust manifold, drain cooling system into suitable container, then lower vehicle.
4. Disconnect electrical connectors from air cleaner inlet and air flow sensor, loosen clamp securing duct to throttle body and remove air flow sensor/air cleaner assembly.
5. Disconnect cables from throttle lever and remove throttle lever bracket.
6. Disconnect coolant and vacuum hoses, and the electrical connector from throttle body noting installation position, then remove support bracket.
7. Disconnect and plug fuel lines, then remove support bracket.
8. Mark and disconnect distributor vacuum hoses from firewall switch and the brake booster hose from intake manifold.
9. Disconnect necessary electrical connectors from cylinder head mounted sensors, switches and the fuel injectors noting installation position, disconnect starter solenoid lead, release harness straps and secure wiring harness aside.
10. Disconnect spark plug wires and distributor electrical connector, then remove distributor cap and wires as an assembly.
11. Disconnect heater hoses from firewall connection.
12. Rotate engine until No. 1 cylinder is at TDC on compression stroke, then remove distributor.
13. Remove upper timing case cover, timing chain tensioner piston and camshaft sprocket retaining bolts, then separate sprocket and timing chain from camshaft and position aside.
14. Remove cylinder head retaining bolts in sequence shown in **Fig. 1**, then the cylinder head and gasket.
15. Ensure that gasket surfaces are clean and free from old gasket material and that No. 1 piston is at TDC.
16. Align notch in camshaft flange with cast tab on cylinder head, **Fig. 2**, then install cylinder head.
17. Torque cylinder head bolts to specifications in 4 steps, noting the following:
    a. Install timing chain and adjust valve clearances to specifications between second and third steps.
    b. Perform fourth step (tightening to specified angle) after engine has been run long enough to reach normal operating temperature.
    c. Torque bolts in sequence shown in **Fig. 1.**
18. Ensure that camshaft is properly positioned and dowel pin hole in sprocket is aligned, install sprocket and tighten retaining bolts, then reverse remaining procedure to complete installation.

6-164/2693cc ENGINE

325

1. Disconnect battery ground cable and remove radiator/expansion tank cap.
2. Raise and support vehicle, remove drain plug from engine block and drain cooling system into suitable container.
3. Disconnect exhaust pipe from manifold and remove clamp securing pipe to transmission, then lower vehicle.
4. Disconnect accelerator, cruise control and transmission control cables, as equipped, and secure cables aside.
5. Mark and disconnect vacuum hoses from throttle body, loosen clamp securing intake duct and remove throttle body support bracket.
6. Disconnect electrical connectors from throttle body and air flow sensor, release harness straps and remove air flow sensor/air cleaner assembly.
7. Remove diagnosis connector and disconnect coolant hoses from water outlet housing and heater core.
8. Depress crankcase ventilation tube and lock with bracket 111290 or equivalent, **Fig. 3.**
9. Disconnect and plug fuel lines.
10. Disconnect electrical connectors from speed and reference transmitters, noting position for installation, then remove bracket.
11. Disconnect electrical connectors from fuel injectors, pressure and temperature sensors and necessary switches, release harness straps and secure harness aside.
12. Disconnect high tension leads from ignition coil and spark plugs, then remove cylinder head cover.
13. Rotate crankshaft until No. 1 cylinder is at TDC on compression stroke, then remove distributor cap assembly and distributor rotor.
14. Loosen adapter (12), remove cover (13), bolts (14) and nut (15), then remove housing (16), **Fig. 4.**
15. Loosen camshaft belt tensioner bolts, compress tensioner, then retighten bolts and remove belt from camshaft sprocket. **Do not rotate camshaft or crankshaft with timing belt removed.**
16. Loosen cylinder head bolts in reverse of sequence shown in **Fig. 5**, then remove cylinder head.
17. Ensure that gasket surfaces are clean and free from old gasket material, then align crankshaft and camshaft timing marks to set No. 1 cylinder at TDC as shown in **Fig. 6.**

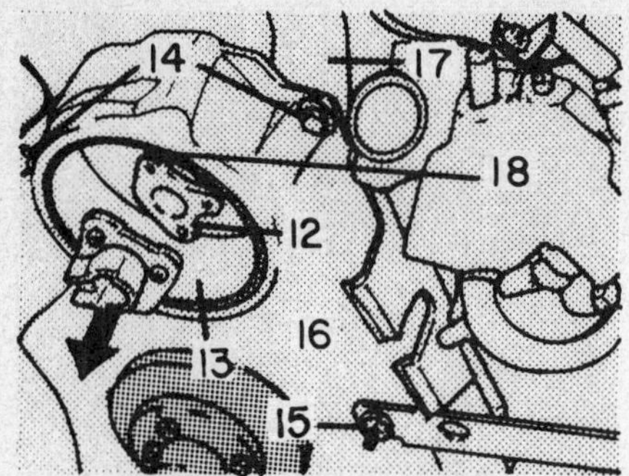

Fig. 4 Removing distributor housing

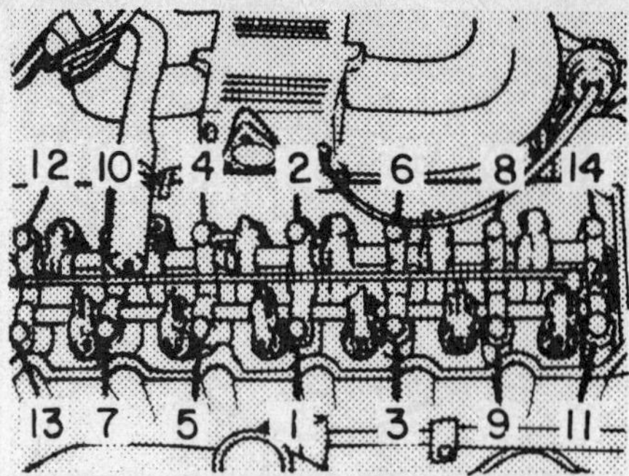

Fig. 5 Cylinder head bolt tightening sequence. 6-164/2693cc engine

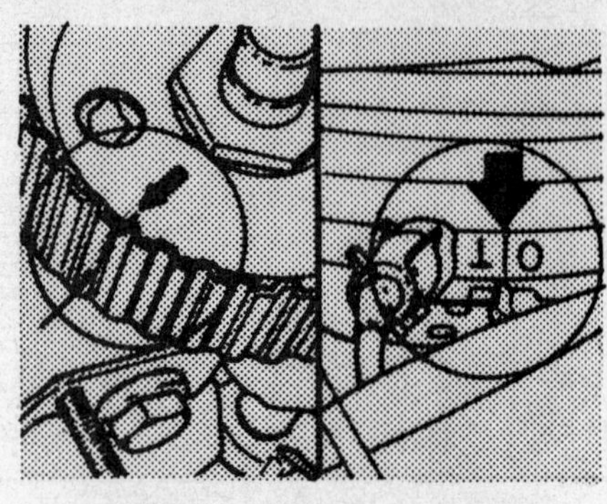

Fig. 6 Timing mark alignment (balancer installed). 6-164/2693cc engine

18. Install cylinder head gasket and cylinder head, then torque retaining bolts to specifications in 3 steps. **Perform final tightening step (tightening to specified angle) after engine has been run long enough to reach normal operating temperature.**
19. Install and tighten timing belt as outlined in "Timing Belt, Replace."
20. Reverse remaining procedure to complete installation.

528e

1. Disconnect battery ground cable and remove radiator/expansion tank cap.
2. Raise and support vehicle, remove cylinder block drain plug and drain cooling system into suitable container.
3. Disconnect exhaust pipes from manifold, remove clamp securing pipes to transmission and lower vehicle.
4. Disconnect accelerator, cruise control and transmission control cables from throttle body, as equipped.
5. Mark and disconnect necessary vacuum hoses, disconnect throttle switch and air flow meter electrical connectors, and loosen clamp securing intake duct to throttle body.
6. Remove air cleaner/air flow sensor assembly.
7. Disconnect coolant hoses from water outlet bracket, disconnect and plug fuel return hose, then remove fuel line bracket and diagnosis socket retaining screws.
8. Loosen bracket retaining screw, then disconnect coolant bypass hose.
9. Compress crankcase ventilation tube and secure with bracket 111290 or equivalent, **Fig. 3.**
10. Remove reference and speed transmitter bracket retaining screws, disconnect and plug fuel supply lines, then disconnect electrical connectors from fuel injectors and nearby electrical components.
11. Disconnect electrical connectors from temperature and pressure sensors, ignition coil, solenoids and switches noting installation position, release harness straps and secure harness aside.
12. Disconnect high tension leads from ignition coil and spark plugs and remove screws securing spark plug wire tube.
13. Disconnect vent hose and remove bracket, cylinder head cover nuts and the cylinder head cover.
14. Rotate crankshaft until No. 1 piston is at TDC on compression stroke, then remove distributor cap and spark plug wire assembly.
15. Loosen adapter (12), remove cover (13), bolts (14) and nut (15), then remove distributor housing (16), **Fig. 4.**
16. Loosen bolts securing timing belt tensioner, compress tensioner and retighten bolts, then remove belt from camshaft sprocket. **Do not rotate camshaft or crankshaft with timing belt removed.**
17. Loosen cylinder head bolts in reverse of sequence shown in **Fig. 5**, then remove cylinder head and gasket.
18. Ensure that gasket surfaces are clean and free from old gasket material, then align crankshaft and camshaft timing marks as shown in **Fig. 6.**
19. Install cylinder head and torque bolts to specifications, in 3 steps, tightening bolts in sequence shown in **Fig. 5. Perform final tightening step (tightening to torque angle) after engine has been run long enough to reach normal operating temperature.**
20. Install and adjust timing belt as outlined in "Timing Belt, Replace," then reverse remaining procedure to complete installation.

6-196/3210cc & 6-209/3430cc ENGINES

1. Disconnect battery ground cable and remove radiator/expansion tank cap.
2. Raise and support vehicle, remove cylinder block drain plug and drain cooling system into suitable container.
3. Disconnect exhaust pipes from manifold, remove clamp securing pipes to transmission and lower vehicle.
4. Disconnect accelerator, cruise control and transmission control cables, as equipped, and secure cables aside.
5. Mark and disconnect necessary vacuum hoses, disconnect electrical connectors from throttle switch and air flow sensor, and loosen clamp securing intake duct to throttle body.
6. Loosen vent pipe and disconnect vent hose, then remove air cleaner/air flow sensor assembly.
7. Remove relay board cover and cap, then remove relays and disconnect electrical connectors as needed to separate engine harness and relay board.
8. Disconnect electrical connectors and coolant hoses from water outlet housing, then disconnect and plug fuel return and feed hoses.
9. Disconnect heater and expansion tank hoses and water valve vacuum hose.
10. Remove bolt securing starter harness bracket, then disconnect electrical connectors from starter and alternator and adjacent electrical components.
11. Remove bolts securing ignition lead tube, diagnosis socket and DME connector bracket. **Note installation position and connector color of DME connector, and speed and reference transmitters to ensure proper installation.**
12. Disconnect breather hose, then remove cylinder head cover.
13. Disconnect electrical connectors from fuel injectors and cold start valve, idle control, oil pressure switch and other necessary switches and sensors noting installation position, release harness retainers, then secure harness aside.
14. Rotate crankshaft until No. 1 piston is at TDC on compression stroke, then remove timing case cover assembly as follows:
    a. Remove thermostat housing cover, gasket and the thermostat.
    b. Remove bolts securing distributor cap, then the cap and spark plug wire assembly.
    c. Remove retaining bolts, then the upper timing case cover.
15. Remove timing chain tensioner piston assembly and camshaft sprocket re-

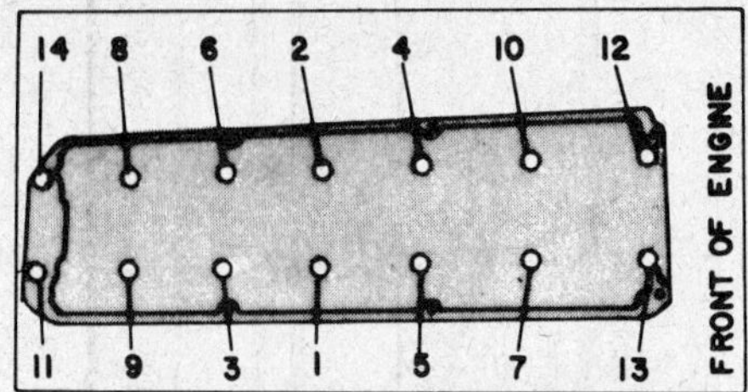

Fig. 7 Cylinder head bolt tightening sequence. 6-196/3210cc & 6-209/3 430cc engines

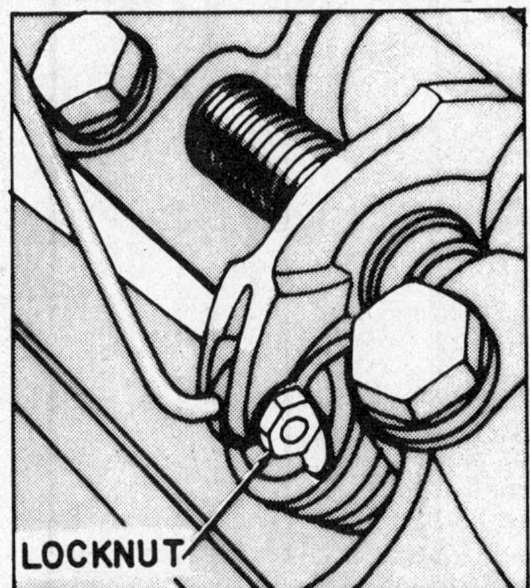

Fig. 10 Adjusting valve clearance

taining bolts, then separate sprocket and chain from camshaft flange and position aside. **Do not rotate crankshaft or camshaft with timing chain disconnected.**

16. Remove cylinder head bolts in reverse of sequence shown in **Fig. 7.**
17. Install dowel pins 111063 or suitable equivalents, **Fig. 8**, to prevent rocker shafts from rotating, then remove cylinder head.
18. Ensure that No. 1 piston is at TDC and that camshaft flange dowel pin is at 7:30 position with sprocket bolt bores aligned with projection on cylinder head, **Fig. 9**, then install cylinder head.
19. Torque cylinder head bolts to specifications in 4 steps, tightening bolts in sequence shown in **Fig. 7. Perform final tightening step (tightening to specified angle) after engine has been run long enough to reach normal operating temperature.**
20. Mount camshaft sprocket and timing chain, ensuring that crankshaft and camshaft remain properly timed, then repeat remaining procedure to complete installation.

VALVES
ADJUST

1. The valves should be adjusted in firing order at TDC, i.e., 1-3-4-2 or 1-5-3-6-2-4.

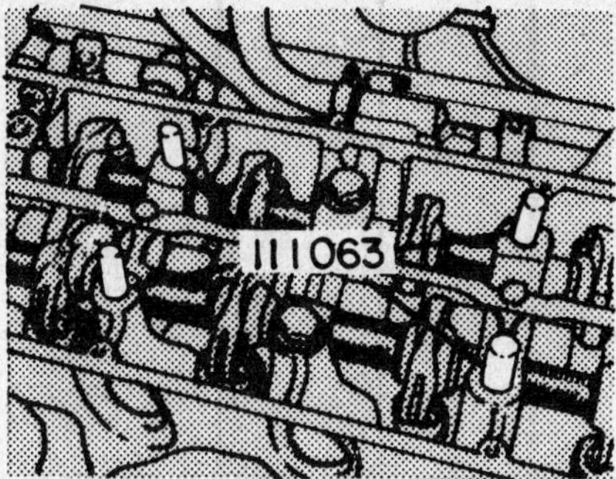

Fig. 8 Rocker arm locking dowel installation

2. Loosen eccentric nut and rotate eccentric with adjusting tool to clearances shown in specifications, **Fig. 10.**

ROCKER ARM SHAFT
REPLACE

4-107/1766cc, 6-196/3210cc & 6-209/3430 cc ENGINES

1. Remove camshaft, slide rocker arms and thrust rings back and remove circlips, **Fig. 11.**
2. On 4 cylinder engines, remove distributor flange. On 6 cylinder engines, remove rear cover, plugs from shaft bores and rocker shaft dowel pins, as equipped.
3. On 4 cylinder engines, drive shaft out using punch 113040 or equivalent. On 6 cylinder engines, remove shafts with slide hammer puller 113060 or equivalent. **Note installation position of rocker arms, springs and washers, Fig. 12, as rocker shafts are withdrawn.**
4. Replace worn components and reverse order to install, noting the following:
   a. Align shafts so that head bolts can be inserted through slots in shafts, then insert dowel pins to secure position.
   b. On 4 cylinder engines, note that rear end of intake rocker shaft is BMW (Germany) 30 open and rear end of exhaust rocker shaft is closed.
   c. Replace gaskets for end covers or distributor flange as needed.

6-164/2693cc ENGINE

1. Remove cylinder head and mount in suitable fixture to prevent damaging valves.
2. Remove camshaft sprocket assembly, press adapter from sprocket and reinstall adapter on camshaft.
3. Adjust all valves for greatest possible clearance.
4. Remove front and rear plugs from above rocker shafts, and the guide plates, noting installation position of plates.
5. Remove spring clamps.
6. Rotate camshaft until valves for cylinder No. 6 are in overlap position to relax spring tension on exhaust rocker shaft, then withdraw exhaust side shaft.
7. Rotate camshaft toward exhaust side until intake rockers are as loose as possible, then withdraw intake rocker shaft.
8. Replace worn components as needed, then reverse procedure to install, noting the following:
   a. Install shafts so that large oil holes face valve guides and small oil holes and guide plate notches face inward.
   b. Ensure that straight surfaces of spring clamps fit into grooves in rocker shafts.
   c. Ensure that guide plates are fully seated in rocker shaft grooves.

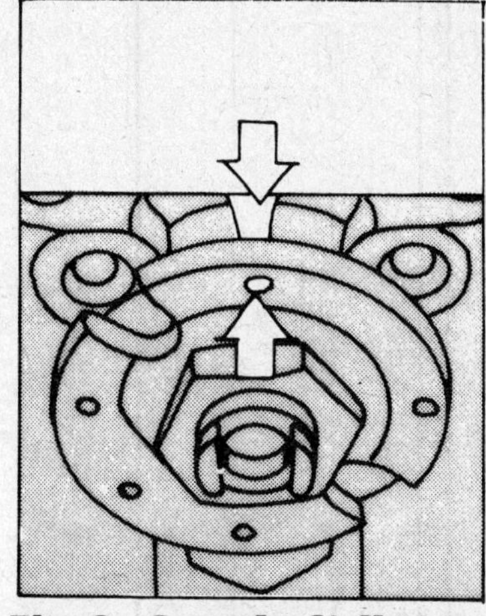

Fig. 9 Camshaft flange alignment. 6-196/3210cc & 6-209/3430cc engines

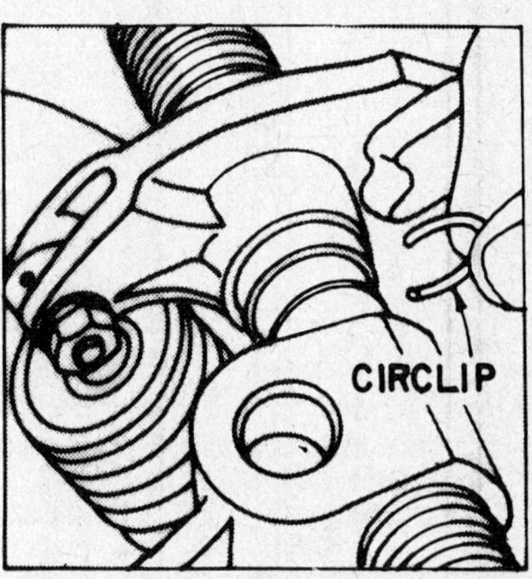

Fig. 11 Removing rocker shaft circlip

TIMING CASE COVER
REPLACE

6-196/3210cc & 6-209/3430cc ENGINES

1. Disconnect battery ground cable and

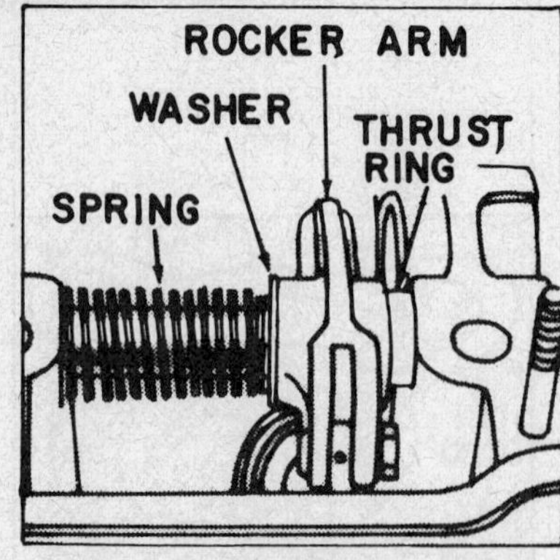

Fig. 12 Rocker shaft assembly. 4-107/1766cc, 6-196/3210cc & 6-209/3430cc engines

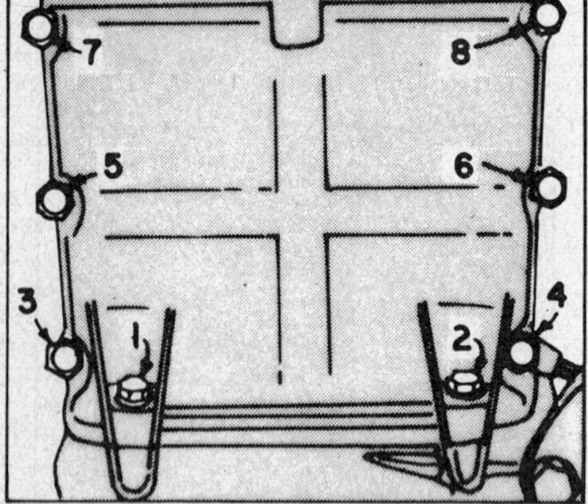

Fig. 15 Upper timing case cover bolt tightening sequence. 4-107/1766cc engine

drain cooling system.

2. Disconnect air flow sensor electrical connector, loosen clamp securing intake duct to throttle body and release wiring and hoses from clamps on sensor body.
3. On 533/535i, loosen breather pipe and disconnect vent hose.
4. On all models, remove air flow sensor/air cleaner assembly.
5. Remove nuts securing ignition lead tube, cable brackets and intake plenum braces to cylinder head cover, as equipped, then loosen nuts securing brackets to plenum.
6. Disconnect breather hose and remove cylinder head cover.
7. Secure pulley, then remove engine cooling fan nut, and the fan and clutch assembly. **Fan retaining nut has left hand threads.**
8. Release tension on accessory drive belts, lock flywheel using suitable tool, then remove crankshaft balancer nut and pull balancer from crankshaft.
9. Remove thermostat housing cover, thermostat and gasket.
10. Loosen distributor cap bolts and position cap aside.
11. Remove upper timing cover retaining bolts and the upper cover.
12. Remove alternator and power steering pump from brackets and position aside.

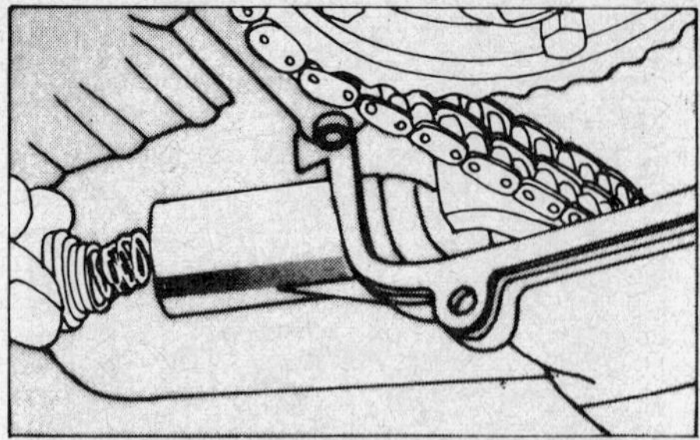

Fig. 13 Removing timing chain tensioner piston

13. Remove alternator and power steering pump brackets.
14. Remove tensioner piston plug, spring and the piston, **Fig. 13.**
15. Remove lower cover retaining bolts and front oil pan bolts, then loosen but do not remove remaining pan bolts.
16. Pry oil pan away from cover taking care not to damage pan gasket, then remove cover. If oil pan gasket is damaged, pan must be removed and the gasket must be replaced.
17. Reverse procedure to install, noting the following:
    a. Coat oil pan sealing surface with suitable sealer, and tighten oil pan bolts before tightening lower cover retaining bolts. **Ensure that chain tensioner is properly positioned in oil pocket before installing lower cover.**
    b. Apply suitable sealer to joints between upper cover and cylinder head and tighten bolts in sequence shown in **Fig. 14.**

4-107/1766cc ENGINE

1. Disconnect battery ground cable and drain coolant, then remove cylinder head cover and disconnect exhaust pipe.
2. Remove upper timing cover.
3. Remove water pump, alternator, chain tensioner, air pump and tension strut with bracket.
4. Remove lower cover, then lock flywheel.
5. Remove nut and vibration damper.
6. Unbolt lower timing cover and remove from vehicle.
7. Reverse procedure to install. Tighten upper timing cover bolts in sequence, **Fig. 15.**

TIMING CHAIN REPLACE

4-107/1766cc, 6-196/3210cc & 6-209/3430cc ENGINES

1. Remove upper and lower timing case covers.
2. Set No. 1 piston at TDC position.
3. Remove tensioner, **Fig. 13,** safeties, bolts and cam sprocket.
4. On 4 cylinder models, remove snap ring at lower end of chain guide rail and unscrew pivot pin at top end until

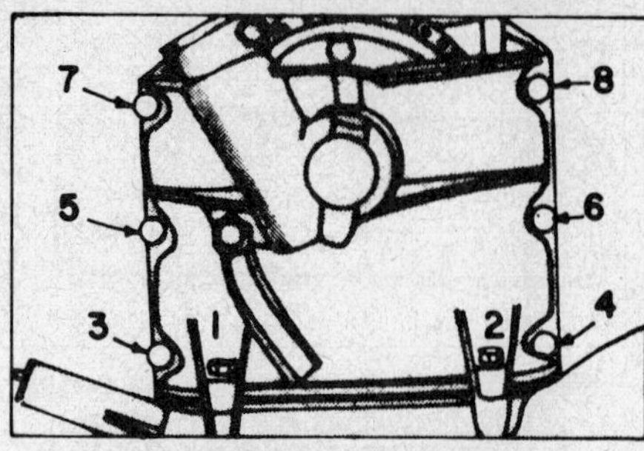

Fig. 14 Upper timing case cover bolt tightening sequence. 6-196/3210cc & 6-209/3430cc engines

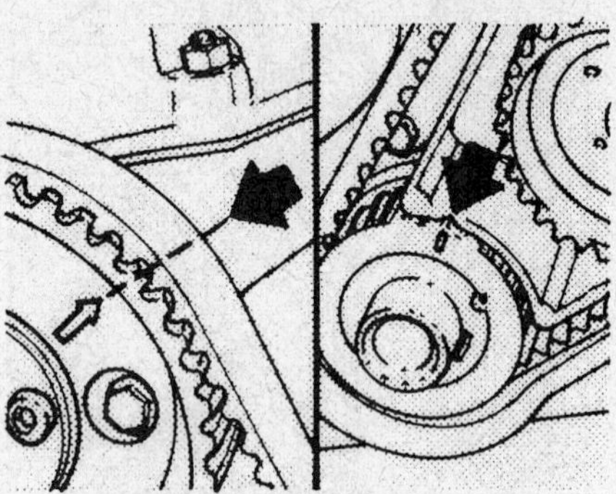

Fig. 16 Timing mark alignment (balancer removed). 6-164/2693cc engine

front edge of guide touches inside edge of head gasket extension that protrudes out in that area. Remove upper end of chain from cam sprocket, pull guide outward and to right, then remove chain from guide.

5. On six cylinder models, remove chain from lower sprocket and swing chain out of guide to right. On 4 cylinder models, remove guide rail, if necessary.
6. When replacing chain, reverse procedure, but align cam flange with notch facing up in line with projection above it and with bore hole facing down on 4 cylinder models, **Fig. 12.** On six cylinder models, dowel pin should be at 7:30 on clock and sprocket bore must be in line with threaded bore in flange and projection, **Fig. 9.**

TIMING BELT REPLACE

6-164/2693cc ENGINE

1. Disconnect battery ground cable and drain cooling system.
2. Disconnect lower radiator hose and electrical connectors from radiator switches.
3. Disconnect upper radiator hoses and transmission cooling lines, if equipped, then plug lines.
4. Remove radiator mounting bolts and the radiator.
5. Remove distributor cap and position aside, then remove rotor and distributor adapter, **Fig. 4.**

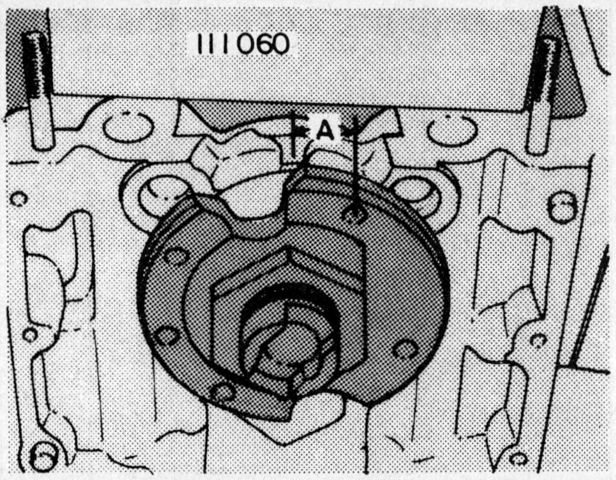

Fig. 17 Aligning camshaft for removal. 6-196/3210cc & 6-209/3430cc engines

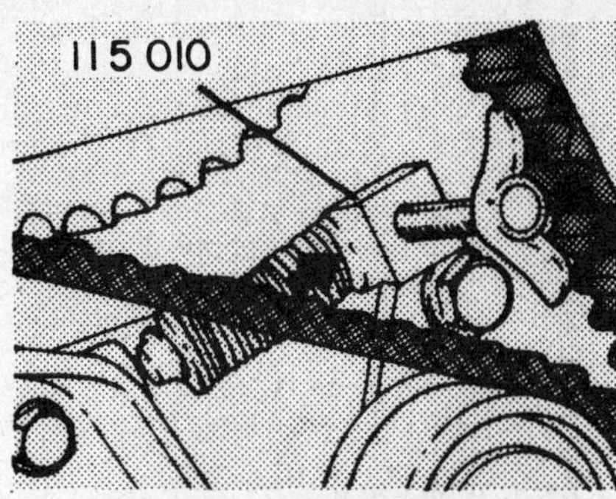

Fig. 18 Compressing timing belt tensioner spring. 6-164/2693cc engine

6. Loosen and remove accessory drive belts, then remove timing belt guard.
7. Rotate crankshaft until No. 1 cylinder is at TDC on compression stroke and timing marks are aligned, **Fig. 6.**
8. Remove bolts securing vibration damper to hub, then the damper and pulley assembly.
9. Lock position of damper hub using 112150 or equivalent, then remove center bolt.
10. Remove washer from bolt, reinstall bolt tightening it approximately 3 turns, then remove hub using suitable puller.
11. Loosen bolts securing timing belt tensioner, compress tensioner, then retighten bolts.
12. Mark running direction of belt, then remove belt.
13. Install drive belt starting on crankshaft sprocket, and proceeding opposite engine's direction of rotation.
14. Ensure that belt is properly installed, and that timing marks are properly aligned, **Fig. 16.**
14. Ensure that belt is properly installed, and that timing marks are properly aligned, **Fig. 16.**
15. Loosen timing belt tensioner bolts turn crankshaft one revolution in normal direction of rotation and ensure that timing marks are still aligned, **Fig. 16.**
16. Turn crankshaft several more revolutions, then tighten tensioner bolts.
17. Reverse remaining procedure to complete installation.

CAMSHAFT

REPLACE

4-107/1766cc ENGINE

1. Remove cylinder head and distributor, air injection pipes and exhaust manifold.
2. Remove oil spray tube, noting location of seals, then remove cold start valve.
3. Adjust valves to maximum clearance. Install tool 11 1 040 and preload rocker arms.
4. Check endplay between guide plate and camshaft. Endplay should not exceed 0.0051 inch (0.13 mm).
5. Remove guide plate and carefully withdraw camshaft.
6. Reverse procedure to install. Note that guide plate is installed properly when camshaft turns easily. Notch in camshaft flange aligns with tab on cylinder head, **Fig. 2.**

6-164/2693cc ENGINE

1. Remove cylinder head and rocker shafts as outlined.
2. Remove end cover and withdraw camshaft from cylinder head.
3. Inspect seals and replace as needed.
4. Reverse procedure to install, ensuring that maximum axial camshaft play is .008 inch.

6-196/3210cc & 6-209/3430cc ENGINES

1. Remove cylinder head. Remove EGR valve with tool 11 7 000 or equivalent. Remove oil spray tube, noting location of seals.
2. Adjust valves to maximum clearance, then turn camshaft from cylinder 1 TDC position to position shown in **Fig. 17.** A = 0.590 inch (15 mm).
3. Install tool 11 1 060 moving intake valve rocker arms of cylinders 2 and 4 forward approximately 0.275 inch (7 mm). First tighten exhaust side nuts then intake side nuts in order to prevent contact between valve heads.
4. Check endplay between camshaft and guide plate. Endplay should not exceed 0.0071 inch (0.18 mm).
5. Remove bolts through flange notches and withdraw camshaft.
6. Reverse procedure to install. Guide plate is installed correctly when camshaft turns easily. Turn camshaft so cylinder No. 6 valves are in overlap position, with threaded bore aligned with cast tab as shown in **Fig. 9.**

REAR OIL SEAL

REPLACE

1. Drain oil from pan, then remove transmission and flywheel.
2. Loosen oil pan and carefully pull down while separating oil pan gasket with a knife.
3. Remove clutch end cover bolts around perimeter of crankshaft flange exercising care where it meets extension of oil pan gasket.
4. Remove and replace sealing ring with appropriate driver.
5. Reverse procedure to install. Apply suitable sealer to lower mating surface areas.

OIL PAN

REPLACE

4-107/1766cc ENGINE

320i

1. Drain oil.
2. Remove steering gear from front axle beam.
3. Remove oil pan attaching bolts and oil pan.
4. Reverse procedure to install.

318i

1. Disconnect battery ground cable and remove dipstick.
2. Raise and support vehicle and drain engine oil.
3. Remove lower oil pan retaining bolts and the lower oil pan section.
4. Remove bolts securing oil pump drive sprocket and separate sprocket from pump.
5. Remove oil pump retaining bolts and the oil pump.
6. Disconnect ground strap from upper pan section.
7. Remove upper oil pan retaining bolts and the upper oil pan section.
8. Reverse procedure to install, coating end and timing cover joining surfaces with suitable sealer.

6-164/2693cc ENGINE

1. Disconnect battery ground cable, then raise and support vehicle.
2. Remove splash shield on 325e, then disconnect sensor electrical connector and drain oil.
3. Remove transmission cover reinforcement plate.

4. Remove oil pan retaining bolts, then lower oil pan.
5. Remove oil pump retaining bolts, and disconnect pump, then remove oil pan.
6. Remove oil pan gasket, coating both end cover joining surfaces with suitable sealer, then position oil pan and pump under crankcase.
7. Install oil pump, guiding driveshaft into bearing.
8. Position oil pan on crankcase, install retaining bolts and evenly torque bolts to 7-8 ft. lbs.

6-196/3210cc & 6-209/3430cc ENGINES

1. Disconnect battery ground cable and partially drain cooling system.
2. Remove alternator and power steering pump from mounting brackets and secure aside.
3. Remove alternator and power steering pump brackets, then raise and support front of vehicle.
4. Drain engine oil, then remove transmission cover reinforcement plate, engine mount retaining nuts and the oil pan retaining bolts.
5. Disconnect upper radiator hose, connect suitable lifting equipment and raise engine.
6. Lower oil pan and rotate crankshaft to position connecting rods for cylinders 5 and 6 to highest point.
7. Remove oil pan.
8. Reverse procedure to install, coating timing and end cover joining surfaces with suitable sealer.

OIL PUMP REPLACE

4-107/1766cc, 6-196/3210cc & 6-209/3430cc ENGINES

1. Drain oil and remove oil pan.
2. Remove oil pump sprocket. On 4 cylinder models remove two bolts holding pump. On 6 cylinder models, remove oil pump and rear pickup holder bolts.
3. Remove oil pump.
4. Reverse procedure to install. Using shims, adjust chain to yield under slight pressure.

6-164/2693cc ENGINE

Refer to "Oil Pan, Replace" procedure for oil pump replacement.

WATER PUMP REPLACE

4-107/1766cc, 6-196/3210cc & 6-209/3430cc ENGINES

1. Disconnect battery ground cable, drain cooling system, and remove engine cooling fan and clutch assembly. **Cooling fan retaining nut has left hand threads.**
2. Release drive belt tension, then remove water pump pulley.
3. Disconnect coolant hoses and remove water pump.
4. Reverse procedure to install.

6-164/2693cc ENGINE

1. Disconnect battery ground cable and drain cooling system.
2. Disconnect distributor cap and position aside, then remove rotor.
3. Remove distributor adapter assembly, **Fig. 4.**
4. On models with A/C, disconnect fan shroud from radiator, then on all models, remove cooling fan and clutch assembly. **Fan retaining nut has left hand threads.**
5. Release drive belt tension and remove water pump pulley.
6. Remove belt tensioner nut and the timing belt cover.
7. Compress timing belt tensioner spring and secure with pin 115010 or equivalent, **Fig. 18. Ensure that engine is not rotated with tensioner spring compressed.**
8. Disconnect coolant hoses and remove water pump.
9. Reverse procedure to install.

COOLING SYSTEM BLEEDING

Whenever the cooling system is opened or drained to perform service operations, trapped air must be bled from system to ensure proper coolant circulation and to prevent engine damage.

1. Place heater control in warmest position, fill cooling system until no more coolant can be added, then start engine.
2. Set engine to run at fast idle and continue filling cooling system.
3. Open bleed screw on water pump or thermostat housing, maintain coolant level in expansion tank, then close bleed screw when escaping coolant is free from air bubbles.
4. Ensure that coolant level in expansion tank is correct, install cap and return engine to normal idle speed.

FUEL PUMP REPLACE

1. Disconnect battery ground cable.
2. Disconnect wires from fuel pump. Disconnect and plug fuel hoses.
3. Remove pump and expansion tank (if so equipped) as assembly. Then detach hose and separate fuel pump from expansion tank.
4. Reverse procedure to install.

DIESEL ENGINE SECTION

INDEX

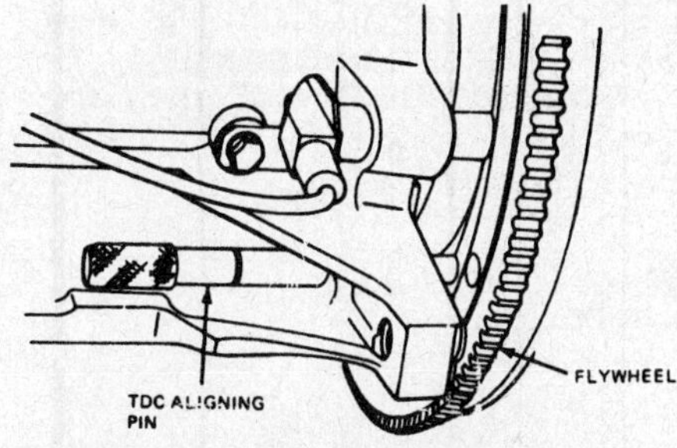

Fig. 1 TDC aligning pin installed

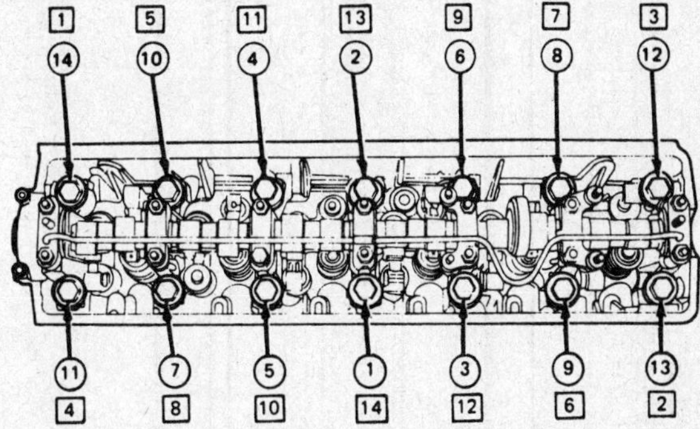

☐REMOVAL ○INSTALLATION

Fig. 2 Cylinder head bolt removal & installation

ENGINE
REPLACE

1. Support engine with suitable jack and remove transmission.
2. Disconnect power steering pump and A/C compressor and position aside. Do not disconnect hoses or lines from pump or compressor.
3. Drain coolant, disconnect transmission cooling lines, then remove radiator.
4. Disconnect hood ground wire, remove hood struts, then support hood using suitable tools.
5. Disconnect battery cables.
6. Disconnect wires and plugs from preheater time control unit, lift off cover, then remove attaching bolts and control unit.
7. Remove reservoir tank, then disconnect and mark all remaining wires and lines that will interfere with engine removal.
8. Disconnect wire harness at body and ground strap at engine.
9. Disconnect accelerator cable, cruise control cable, fuel hoses and exhaust pipes as needed.
10. Disconnect hoses from heater core, then remove air cleaner assembly.
11. Disconnect and plug lines to oil cooler. **When installing engine, fill cooler with specified oil to prevent engine damage.**
12. Working from passenger compartment, disconnect plug from control unit located in glove box, then pull engine wire harness into engine compartment.
13. Attach tool 11 0 020 or equivalent to engine, remove engine mount to body retaining nuts and bolts, then lift and remove engine from vehicle.
14. Reverse procedure to install.

CYLINDER HEAD
REPLACE

1. Disconnect battery ground cable and drain cooling system.
2. Disconnect heater hose, then remove accessory drive belts.
3. Remove valve cover.
4. Disconnect coolant temperature switch and glow plug electrical connectors.
5. Disconnect breather hose and bracket.
6. Remove oil dipstick tube to intake manifold attaching clamp and position tube aside.
7. Disconnect boost pressure switch electrical connector.
8. Disconnect radiator hose from cylinder head, then the idle boost coolant hose.
9. Remove vacuum pump from cylinder head.
10. Disconnect No. 1 injector nozzle to injection pump leak hose.
11. Using tool T84P-9395-B or equivalent, disconnect injection pump. Cap nozzles and lines to prevent dirt entry.
12. Disconnect turbocharger oil lines.
13. Rotate crankshaft pulley until No. 1 cylinder is at TDC, compression stroke, then install TDC aligning pin between cylinder block flange and flywheel, **Fig. 1.**
14. Loosen camshaft drive sprocket retaining bolt, then camshaft drive belt tensioning roller nut and bolt. Remove drive belt.
15. Loosen cylinder head attaching bolts following sequence shown in **Fig. 2**, then remove cylinder head.
16. Clean cylinder head and crankcase sealing surfaces using suitable spray solvent. **Do not score or scratch sealing surfaces, since leakage may occur due to high compression pressures.**
17. Check cylinder head for warpage. If warpage exceeds .006 inch, replace cylinder head.
18. Select cylinder head gasket thickness as follows:
    a. Mount dial indicator D82L-4201-A and height gauge D84P-6100-A so that indicator pointer is on top of No. 1 piston.
    b. Rotate crankshaft until piston is at TDC.
    c. Zero indicator on crankcase, then move indicator pointer to front of piston. Record measurement. Move pointer to rear of piston and again record measurement. Average the two measurements.
    d. Repeat steps a through c for remaining pistons.
    e. Using measurement of highest piston, select the correct cylinder head gasket using chart shown, **Fig. 3.**
19. Clean carbon and oil deposits from head bolts. **Keep oil and/or antifreeze from entering cylinder head bolt holes, since damage to crankcase may result. If either enters bolt holes, blow out using compressed air.**
20. Position head gasket onto crankcase, then install cylinder head.
21. Install and torque cylinder head bolts in sequence shown, **Fig. 2.**
22. Reverse steps 1 through 13 to complete installation, noting the following:

a. Torque turbocharger oil lines to 14-17 ft. lbs.
b. Torque injection line fittings to nozzles and pump to 14-18 ft. lbs.
c. Torque vacuum pump-to-cylinder head attaching bolts to 6-7 ft. lbs.
d. After installation is complete, start and run engine for 15 minutes, checking for any fuel, coolant or oil leaks. Repair as necessary.
e. After running engine for 25 minutes, stop engine and remove valve cover. Using a suitable breaker bar, tighten cylinder head bolts an additional quarter turn (90 degrees). Adjust valves to specifications, then install valve cover.

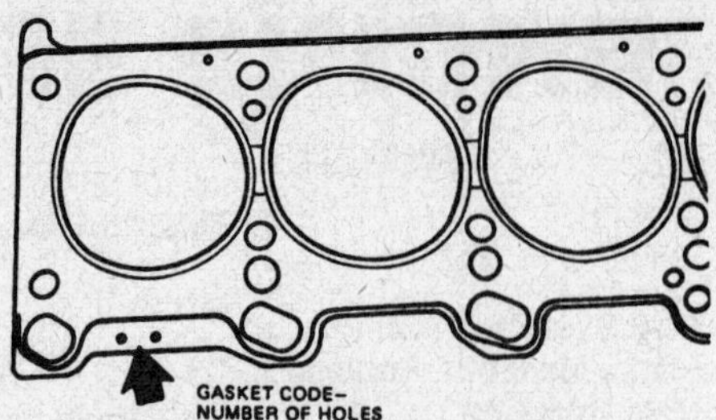

HIGHEST PISTON PROTRUSION OF ALL 6 PISTONS mm	CYL. HEAD GASKET CODE NO. OF HOLES	THICKNESS OF CYL. HEAD GASKET mm
0.60 – 0.70	1	1.4
0.70 – 0.85	2	1.5
0.85 – 1.00	3	1.6

Fig. 3 Cylinder head gasket selection chart

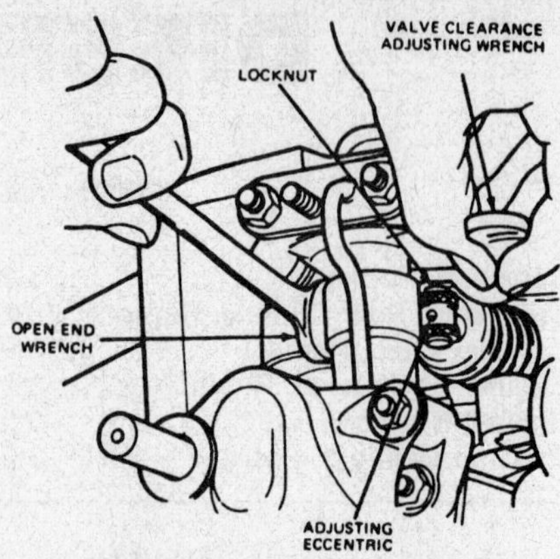

Fig. 4 Loosening adjustment eccentric

INTAKE MANIFOLD
REPLACE

1. Disconnect battery ground cable.
2. Disconnect turbocharger boost pressure indicator connector.
3. Remove oil dipstick tube to intake manifold attaching clamp and position tube aside.
4. Loosen turbocharger crossover pipe boot clamp.
5. Remove intake manifold to cylinder head attaching bolts, then the intake manifold.
6. Reverse procedure to install.

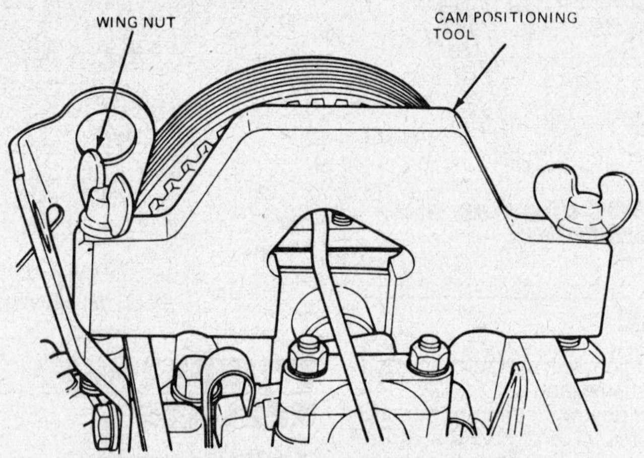

Fig. 5 Camshaft positioning tool installation

EXHAUST MANIFOLD
REPLACE

1. Disconnect battery ground cable, then remove air cleaner assembly.
2. Disconnect muffler inlet pipe from turbocharger outlet. Plug outlet to prevent dirt entry.
3. Disconnect EGR valve vacuum line.
4. Disconnect inlet duct from turbocharger. Plug inlet to prevent dirt entry.
5. Loosen turbocharger crossover pipe boot clamp, then remove oil feed tube to exhaust manifold retaining clamp.
6. Remove oil feed line to turbocharger attaching bolts. Plug oil feed line and oil inlet port on turbocharger to prevent contamination of turbocharger oiling system.
7. Disconnect oil return line from turbocharger oil drain port. Plug line and port to prevent contamination of turbocharger oiling system.
8. Remove exhaust manifold to cylinder head attaching bolts, then the exhaust manifold and turbocharger assembly. Plug crossover pipe to prevent dirt entry.
9. Reverse procedure to install. Torque manifold attaching bolts and oil feed line to 14-17 ft. lbs., oil return line to 29-36 ft. lbs. and muffler inlet pipe to turbocharger outlet bolts to 31-35 ft. lbs.

VALVE TIMING SPECS
INTAKE OPENS BEFORE TOP DEAD CENTER

Engine	Year	Degrees
6-149	1986	6

VALVE LIFT

Engine	Year	Intake	Exhaust
6-149	1986	.374	.376

ROCKER ARM
REPLACE

1. Remove valve cover and vacuum pump.
2. Rotate engine until cam lobe for rocker arm being replaced faces upward.
3. Remove rocker arm retaining clip.
4. Using suitable tool compress valve spring.
5. Remove rocker arm assembly. **Ensure valve spring retainers remain locked in valve stem.**
6. Reverse procedure to install. Coat barrel of pivot ball pin with Loctite 270 or equivalent, before installing rocker arm.
7. Adjust valve clearances as outlined in "Valves, Adjust" procedure.

VALVES
ADJUST

1. Remove valve cover.
2. Rotate engine until camshaft lobe of valve being adjusted faces upward.
3. Using suitable valve clearance adjusting tool and a 12 mm open end wrench, loosen adjusting eccentric locknut, **Fig. 4.**
4. Position feeler gauge, then rotate eccentric with a suitable punch until clearance is within specifications.
5. Tighten adjusting eccentric locknut.

TIMING BELT
REPLACE

1. Disconnect battery ground cable, then drain cooling system.
2. Disconnect upper radiator hose, then remove fan shroud.
3. Remove accessory drive belts, then the fan and clutch assembly.
4. Remove crankshaft pulley and vibration damper retaining bolts, then the

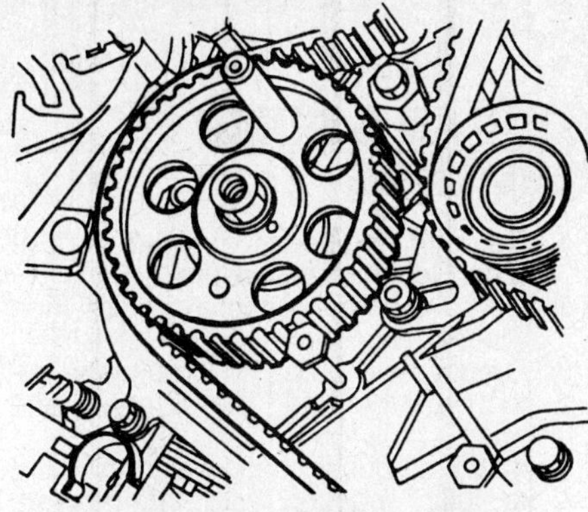

Fig. 6 Injection pump aligning pin installation

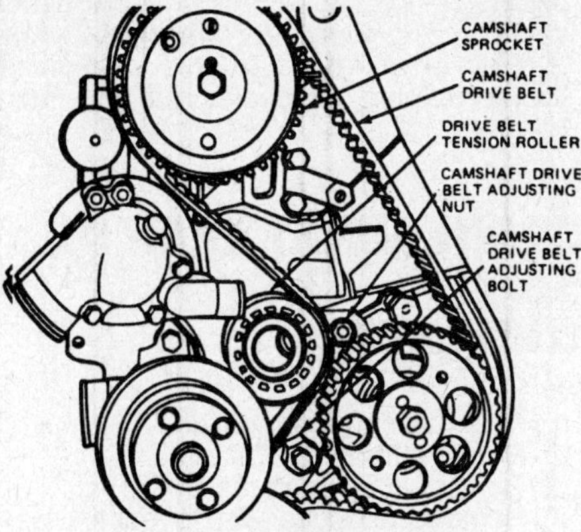

Fig. 7 Timing belt installation

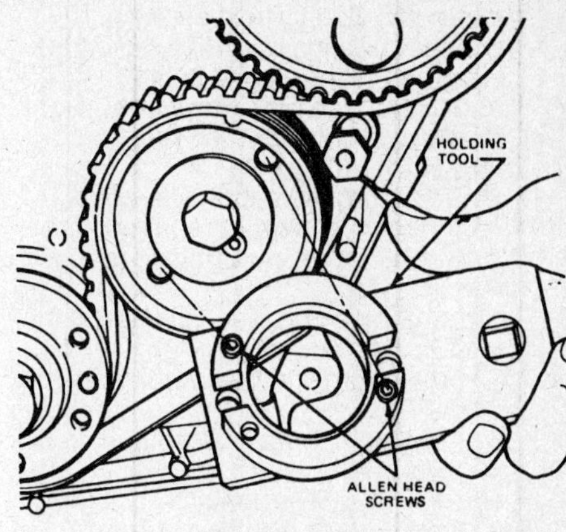

Fig. 8 Aligning Allen head screws

pulley and damper.
5. Disconnect heater hose from thermostat housing.
6. Remove timing belt cover-to-crankcase attaching bolts, then the cover.
7. Remove valve cover.
8. Rotate engine until No. 1 cylinder is at TDC compression stroke, then install TDC aligning pin, **Fig. 1.**
9. Install suitable camshaft positioning tool onto cylinder head, **Fig. 5. Flat side of nut or cam position tool should be facing down.**
10. Loosen camshaft sprocket bolt.
11. If old belt will be reinstalled/installed, mark direction of engine rotation on belt.
12. Loosen belt tensioner attaching bolts, then remove timing belt.
13. If using new belt or belt with less than 10,000 miles, insert .098 inch feeler gauge between camshaft positioning tool, **Fig. 5,** and right corner of cylinder head.
14. Install injection pump aligning pin through injection pump sprocket, **Fig. 6.**
15. Rotate camshaft sprocket clockwise against aligning pin, then install timing belt. Starting at crankshaft sprocket, route belt around intermediate shaft sprocket, injection pump sprocket, camshaft sprocket and tension roller, **Fig. 7. Ensure V side of belt is correctly positioned in pulley V.**
16. Hand tighten belt tensioner until all slack is removed from timing belt.
17. Remove injection pump aligning pin.
18. Torque belt tensioner to 35 ft. lbs. for belts with less than 10,000 miles, or 24 ft. lbs. for belts greater than 10,000 miles.
19. torque belt tensioner attaching bolts to 17 ft. lbs.
20. Torque camshaft sprocket bolt to 44 ft. lbs.
21. Reverse steps 1 through 9 complete installation. Torque crankshaft pulley and vibration damper retaining bolts to specification.
22. Adjust injection pump timing.

CAMSHAFT
REPLACE

1. Disconnect battery ground cable, then remove valve cover.
2. Remove vacuum pump, cooling fan and fan clutch.
3. Remove accessory drive belts and tensioner, then the camshaft drive belt cover.
4. Remove rocker arms as outlined previously.
5. Rotate engine until cylinder No. 1 is at TDC compression stroke, then install TDC aligning pin between cylinder block flange and flywheel, **Fig. 1.**
6. Loosen camshaft sprocket bolt, then the timing belt tensioner roller nut and bolt.
7. Remove camshaft sprocket retaining bolt and the sprocket.
8. Scribe alignment marks on camshaft bearing caps and cylinder head so that they can be installed in original position.
9. Remove bearing cap retaining nuts, then the bearing caps.
10. Remove camshaft.
11. Position camshaft onto cylinder head.
12. Install bearing caps and retaining nuts. Torque 6 mm nuts to 7 ft. lbs. and 8 mm nuts to 16 ft. lbs.
13. Loosely install camshaft sprocket, then install timing belt.
14. Torque camshaft sprocket retaining bolt to 44 ft. lbs.
15. Remove TDC alignment pin, then install rocker arms.
16. Install camshaft drive belt cover. Torque bolts to 6-7 ft. lbs.
17. Install accessory drive belt tensioner, drive belts, fan and fan clutch.
18. Install vacuum pump and rocker arm cover.
19. Connect battery ground, then run engine while checking for oil, intake air and coolant leaks.

ENGINE FRONT COVER
REPLACE

1. Perform steps 1 through 6 of "Timing Belt, Replace" procedure.
2. Remove intermediate shaft sprocket retaining bolt using suitable tool, **Fig. 8. Ensure Allen head screws are aligned with holes in intermediate shaft sprocket, Fig. 8.**
3. Remove vibration damper flange and sprocket retaining bolt. Using suitable puller remove flange and sprocket.
4. Remove the three oil pan to front cover attaching bolts, then loosen the remaining oil pan bolts.
5. Remove the six front cover to crankcase attaching bolts, then the front cover.
6. Clean front cover and crankcase mating surfaces.
7. Inspect and, if necessary, replace crankshaft and intermediate shaft oil seals.
8. Install new front cover gasket. Coat areas where front cover gasket meets oil pan gasket with a 1/4 inch bead of RTV sealant.
9. Position front cover onto crankcase and install attaching bolts. Torque 6 mm bolts to 7 ft. lbs. and 8 mm bolts to 16 ft. lbs.
10. Install the three front cover to oil pan attaching bolts. Torque all bolts to 7 ft. lbs.
11. Install vibration damper flange and sprocket onto crankshaft with shoulder facing toward front of vehicle.
12. Position intermediate shaft sprocket onto intermediate shaft, guiding locating pin into bore.
13. Install holding tool T84P-6316-A or equivalent, ensuring that Allen head screws in tool align with holes in intermediate shaft.
14. Install vibration damper flange and sprocket retaining bolt. Torque bolt to 282-311 ft. lbs.
15. Install intermediate shaft sprocket retaining bolt and torque to 44 ft. lbs.
16. Install and adjust timing belt as outlined previously.
17. Perform steps 1 through 6 of "Timing Belt, Replace" procedure in reverse sequence to complete installation.

FUEL SYSTEM BLEEDING

1. Ensure that vent screw is closed and that power is available to fuel shut-off solenoid.
2. Turn ignition "On" and allow pump to operate for approximately two minutes, then start engine. If engine runs correctly, system does not require bleeding. If engine does not run cor-

rectly, proceed to next step.

3. Loosen coupling nuts on injector nozzles, then crank engine until air is bled from lines. **Use extreme caution not to allow high pressure fuel to contact skin.**
4. Start engine. If engine runs correctly, no further bleeding is required. If engine does not run correctly, proceed to next step.
5. Crank engine and bleed system in the following locations:
   a. Fuel return line banjo bolt (labeled OUT).
   b. Injection pump distributor head plug bolt.
   c. Fuel shut-off solenoid.
   d. Fuel lines at injection pump.

PISTON & ROD ASSEMBLE

Pistons are supplied by three different manufacturers, Alcan-Nural, KS and Mahle. Both standard size and oversize pistons are available, however pistons can be replaced only in sets of six.

Numbers on connecting rod and bearing cap must be on same side when installing piston. Install piston with arrow facing toward front of engine.

MAIN BEARINGS

Main bearings are available in standard size and undersizes of .010 and .020 inch. The different main bearing thicknesses are identified by a color code on the edge of the bearing shell. The correct bearings to use for each journal are determined during production and are shown by paint marks in the crankcase for bearings in the block; and by paint marks on the crankshaft counterweights, for bearings in the main caps.

CRANKSHAFT REAR OIL SEAL REPLACE

1. Raise and support vehicle.
2. Remove transmission.
3. Remove drive plate assembly.
4. Remove the four oil pan to rear engine cover attaching bolts.
5. Loosen, but do not remove, the remaining oil pan bolts.
6. Remove rear cover attaching bolts, then the rear cover.
7. Clean crankcase and rear engine cover mating surfaces.
8. Press oil seal from rear cover using an arbor press.
9. Using seal replacer T84P-6701-A or equivalent, press new seal into rear cover.
10. Lubricate sealing lips with engine oil, then install new cover gasket onto crankcase.
11. Apply gasket sealer at points where rear cover gasket meets oil pan gasket.
12. Install rear cover onto crankcase. Torque 6 mm bolts to 7 ft. lbs. and 8 mm bolts to 16 ft. lbs.
13. Install the four oil pan to rear cover attaching bolts, then torque all oil pan bolts to 7 ft. lbs.
14. Install drive plate assembly.
15. Install transmission, then lower vehicle.
16. Start engine and check for oil leaks.

OIL PAN & PUMP REPLACE

1. Remove engine as outlined in "Engine, Replace" procedure.
2. Remove oil pan attaching bolts, then the oil pan.
3. Remove oil pump to crankcase attaching bolts, then the oil pump and shaft.
4. Install oil pump shaft, ensuring that it is fully engaged with intermediate shaft.
5. Install oil pump and attaching bolts, then torque bolts to 16 ft. lbs.
6. Clean oil pan and crankcase mating surfaces, then apply a 1/4 inch bead of RTV sealant on split lines of engine front and rear covers and crankcase.
7. Position new oil pan gasket onto oil pan, then install oil pan and attaching bolts. Torque bolts to 7 ft. lbs.

WATER PUMP REPLACE

1. Drain cooling system into suitable container.
2. Remove drive belts, then the cooling fan and clutch assembly.
3. Remove water pump pulley, the disconnect heater hose from thermostat housing.
4. Remove timing belt cover.
5. Remove water pump attaching bolts, then the water pump.
6. Reverse procedure to install.

CLUTCH & MANUAL TRANSMISSION SECTION

INDEX

CLUTCH PEDAL ADJUST

All models use hydraulic clutch release mechanisms with automatic wear compensation. No provision for clutch pedal adjustment is provided.

CLUTCH REPLACE

1. Disconnect battery ground cable, raise and support vehicle, then remove transmission and clutch housing dust cover.
2. On models with DME-Motronics system, note installation position of speed and reference mark transmitters, then remove transmitters from clutch housing. **Speed transmitter (black electrical connector) is installed facing ring gear, while reference transmitter (connector with gray ring) is installed facing flywheel reference pin. If sensors are not properly installed, engine will not start.**
3. Remove clutch housing and measure height of pressure plate fingers. If deviation is greater than .024 inch, pressure plate should be replaced.
4. Lock flywheel with holder 11 2 160 or equivalent. Remove pressure plate bolts 1-1½ turns at a time until tension is released.
5. Remove bolts, pressure plate, and clutch disc.
6. Check clutch disc for wear or cracks. Make sure torsional damper springs are tight and check lateral runout.
7. Inspect needle pilot bearing in crankshaft and check flywheel for cracks.
8. Inspect pressure plate for cracks, loose rivets, wear, and burnt spots. Check flatness of pressure surface.
9. Reverse procedure to install. Align clutch disc with tool 21 2 100 or equivalent. Apply suitable grease to transmission input shaft splines. Torque pressure plate bolts to 16-17 ft. lbs. (22-24 Nm).

TRANSMISSION REPLACE

320i

1. Remove upper mounting bolts, then

all brackets at flange and disconnect exhaust pipe at manifold. Unscrew lambda sensor.

2. Disconnect drive shaft, leaving special coupling on shaft. Disconnect center bearing and position drive shaft aside.
3. Disconnect back-up light switch wire, speedometer cable, harness from holders, and remove cover plate to gain access to driver's compartment.
4. Remove snap ring retainer, washer and disconnect selector linkage, then remove slave cylinder and lower cover of clutch housing.
5. Remove crossmember, then remove transmission toward rear.
6. When reinstalling transmission, preload driveshaft center bearing by 0.078 inches and replace coupling stop nuts.

318i

1. Disconnect battery ground cable, then raise and support vehicle.
2. Disconnect electrical connector to oxygen sensor. On 1984-85 models, remove oxygen sensor to prevent damage.
3. Disconnect exhaust pipes from manifold, remove necessary hangar bolts and clamps and remove exhaust system as an assembly.
4. Remove exhaust system heat shield.
5. Remove nuts, then the bolts securing propeller shaft to transmission flange.
6. Remove bolts securing center bearing support, bend propeller shaft down to disengage centering pin and secure shaft assembly aside. **During installation, preload center bearing assembly .079-.157 inch toward front of vehicle before tightening mounting bolts.**
7. Disconnect electrical connector from back-up lamp switch, remove bolts securing console, and clip and washer from selector rod, then withdraw rod from transmission.
8. Remove bolts securing clutch slave cylinder, then secure cylinder aside leaving hose connected.
9. Support transmission using suitable jack, remove bolts securing crossmember to body, then lower transmission.
10. Remove bolts securing transmission to engine, then the transmission.
11. Reverse procedure to install.

325

1. Remove shift knob, boot and insulation from around shift lever.
2. Pull out cover sleeve between body and console, then remove snap ring securing shift lever.
3. Disconnect battery ground cable, then raise and support vehicle.
4. Disconnect electrical connector from oxygen sensor and remove sensor.
5. Disconnect exhaust pipe from manifold, remove necessary hangars and clamps and remove exhaust system as an assembly.
6. Remove transmission tunnel brace and exhaust heat shield.
7. Remove nuts and bolts securing propeller shaft to transmission, then loosen threaded sleeve behind center bearing using wrench 261040 or equivalent.
8. Remove bolts securing center bearing and compress propeller shaft. **During installation, preload center bearing .079-.157 inch toward front of vehicle before tightening retaining bolts.**
9. Support transmission with suitable jack, remove bolts securing crossmember to body and lower transmission, then disconnect propeller shaft and secure aside.
10. Remove snap ring and washer, disconnect shift lever from selector rod, then push lever into passenger compartment and withdraw selector rod.
11. Remove bolts securing console to transmission.
12. Note installation position of speed and reference transmitters, then remove transmitters from clutch housing. **Speed transmitter (black electrical connector) is installed facing flywheel ring gear, while reference transmitter (gray identification ring) is installed facing reference pin on flywheel. If transmitters are improperly installed, engine will not start.**
13. Remove slave cylinder retaining bolts and secure cylinder aside leaving hose connected.
14. Disconnect electrical connector from back-up lamp switch and release wiring from retaining clips.
15. Remove transmission retaining bolts and the transmission.
16. Reverse procedure to install.

528e, 533/535i, 633/635CSi & 733/735i

1. Disconnect battery ground cable, then raise and support vehicle.
2. Disconnect electrical connector from oxygen sensor. On 633/635CSi and 733/735i, remove oxygen sensor to prevent damage.
3. Disconnect exhaust pipes from manifold, remove necessary clamps and hangars and remove exhaust system as an assembly.
4. Remove exhaust system heat shield.
5. Remove nuts and bolts securing propeller shaft to transmission and bolts securing center bearing, pull shaft down from center to disengage centering pin, then secure shaft aside. **During installation, preload center bearing .079-.157 inch toward front of vehicle before tightening retaining bolts.**
6. Remove bolts securing shift console to transmission, and selector rod snap ring and washer, then withdraw selector rod.
7. Remove flywheel dust shield and the speed and reference transmitter cover.
8. Note installation position of speed and reference transmitters, then remove transmitters from clutch housing. **Speed transmitter (black electrical connector) faces flywheel ring gear, while reference transmitter (gray identification ring) is installed facing reference pin on flywheel. If sensors are improperly installed, engine will not start.**
9. Support transmission and remove bolts securing crossmember to body.
10. Remove bolts securing clutch slave cylinder and secure cylinder aside leaving hose connected.
11. Disconnect electrical connector from back-up lamp switch and release wiring from retaining straps.
12. Place suitable block between engine and front crossmember and lower transmission until engine rests on block.
13. Remove transmission mounting bolts and the transmission.
14. Reverse procedure to install.

DISC BRAKES SECTION

INDEX

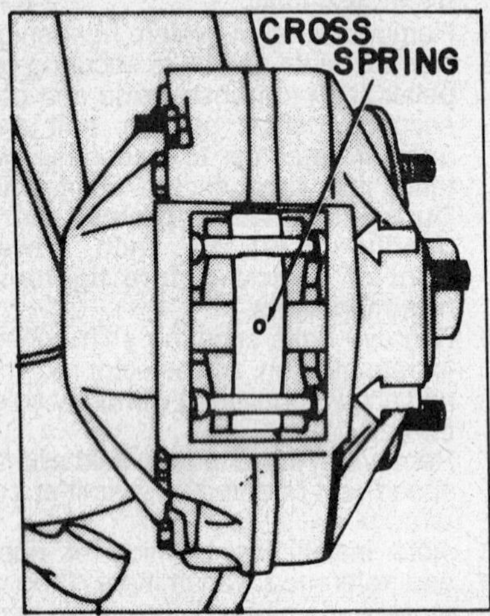

Fig. 1 Caliper retaining pins & spring

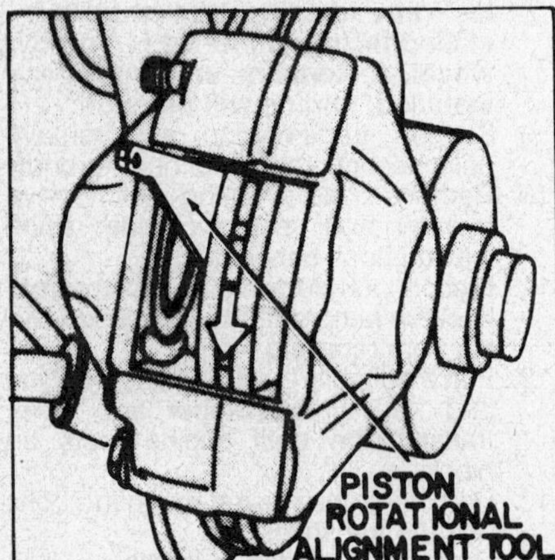

Fig. 4 Positioning piston in caliper

FRONT DISC BRAKE PADS

REPLACE

320i & 733/735i

1. Remove wheel and disconnect wear sensor, if equipped, then drive out pad retaining pins and remove cross spring, **Fig. 1.**
2. Remove pads with two hook extractor No. 34 1-010, or a two hook extractor with slide hammer, No. 34 1000. The hooks fit into ear holes of pads, **Fig. 2.**

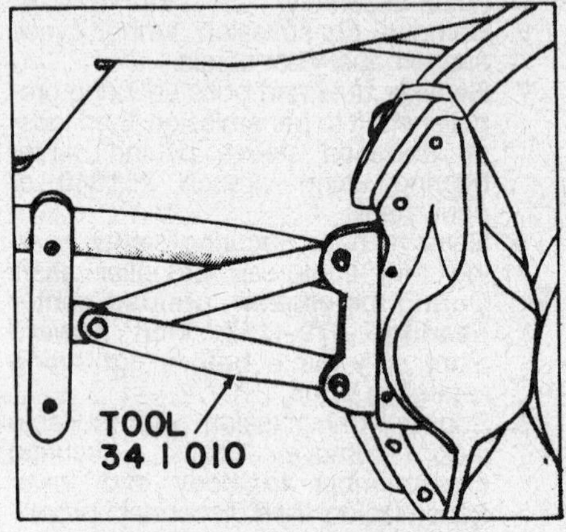

Fig. 2 Using tool to remove brake pads

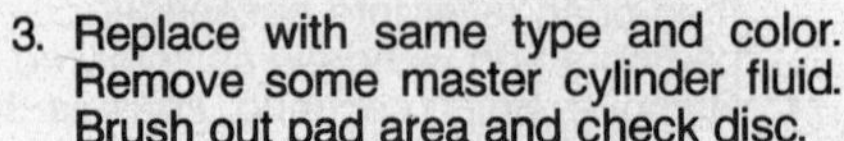

3. Replace with same type and color. Remove some master cylinder fluid. Brush out pad area and check disc.
4. Squeeze back pistons with an appropriate tool, **Fig. 3, then slide pads into place. On models with notched piston, rotate notch in piston to 20 degree position and check alignment as shown in Fig. 4.**
5. Install cross springs and retaining pins, then bleed brake system.

318i & 325

1. Remove wheels and disconnect wear sensor indicator connector from inboard pad.
2. Remove lower retaining bolt securing caliper to bracket and pivot caliper upward.
3. Note installation position of springs, then remove pads from caliper mounting bracket.
4. Transfer wear indicator to inner pad, ensuring that retaining clip is properly positioned.
5. Siphon off fluid from master cylinder, then press caliper pistons into bores fully, taking care not to damage dust boots.
6. Lower caliper assembly over pads and ensure that springs (4), **Fig. 5**, are properly positioned.
7. Install new lower caliper retaining bolt and torque to 22-25 ft. lbs.
8. Refill master cylinder and bleed system.

524TD, 528e, 533/535i & 633/635CSi

1. Remove wheels and disconnect electrical connectors from brake pad wear sensors.

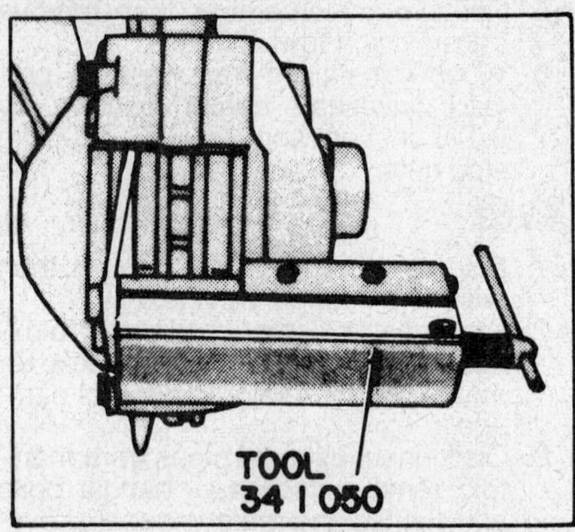

Fig. 3 Using tool to press piston against stop

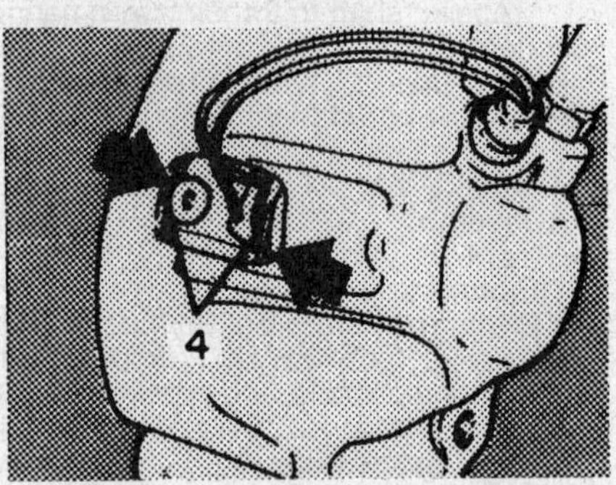

Fig. 5 Front caliper installation. 318i & 325

2. Pry caps off caliper guide bolts and remove bolts using suitable Allen key.
3. Pry outer pad retaining clamp from caliper, then remove caliper.
4. Remove outer pad from caliper bracket and inner pad and spring from caliper piston, noting position for installation.
5. Reverse procedure to install, torquing guide bolts to 22-25 ft. lbs.

REAR DISC BRAKE PADS

REPLACE

1. Remove wheels and disconnect electrical connector from wear sensor, if equipped.
2. Pry caps off caliper guide bolts and remove guide bolts.
3. Pry outer pad retaining clamp from caliper, then remove caliper.

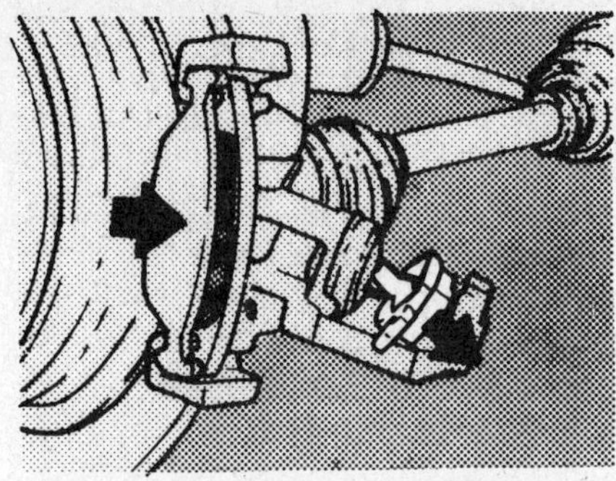

Fig. 6 Rear disc brake pad removal

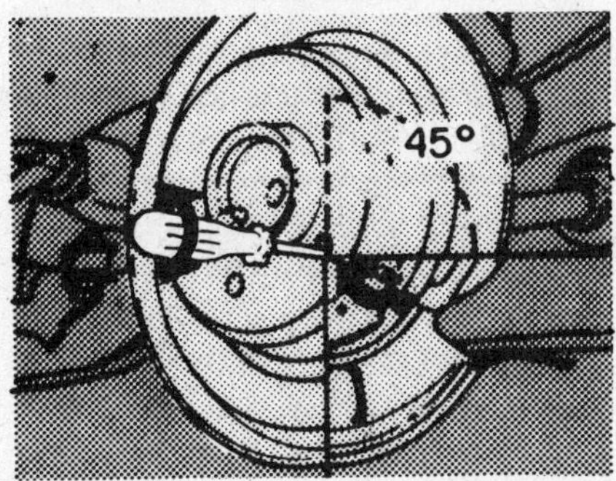

Fig. 9 Parking brake shoe adjustment. 500, 600 & 700 series

4. Remove outer pad from caliper bracket and inner pad and spring from caliper piston, **Fig. 6.**
5. Reverse procedure to install, torquing guide bolts to 22-25 ft. lbs.

CALIPER REPLACE

FRONT

318i, 320i, 325 & 733/735i

1. Remove wheel, then siphon some fluid from master cylinder.
2. Remove two mounting bolts and disconnect hydraulic line. Disconnect brake pad wear sensor wires, if equipped.
3. Reverse procedure to install. Do not switch right and left hand calipers, since bleeder valves must face up. Torque caliper bolts to 59-69 ft. lbs., then bleed brake system.

524TD, 528e, 533/535i & 633/635CSi

1. Dismount caliper as outlined in front brake pad replacement procedure.
2. Disconnect hydraulic line from caliper and plug line.
3. Reverse procedure to install. Use new sealing washers, if equipped, when installing hydraulic line, then bleed brake system.

REAR

1. Dismount caliper as outlined in rear brake pad replacement procedure.

Fig. 7 Guide bolt dowel sleeve installation

2. Disconnect hydraulic line from caliper and plug line.
3. Reverse procedure to install, then bleed brake system.

DISC BRAKE CALIPER OVERHAUL

320i (FRONT)

1. Remove brake pads, then snap out retaining ring and protective rubber.
2. With special pliers, lock in one piston, insert a .30 in. thick piece of wood into caliper gap and force piston out by injecting compressed air into hydraulic connection. Always protect any piston from damage.
3. Remove rubber sealing rings with a plastic tipped tool.
4. Clean all surfaces with brake fluid. **Never machine or hone any of these parts.**
5. When reinstalling pistons, use special 20 degree piston rotational alignment tool. The 20 degree portion must face incoming pad.

733/735i (FRONT)

1. Remove brake pads, then snap out retaining rings and remove dust boots.
2. Insert a .30 in. thick piece of wood into caliper gap and force piston out by injecting compressed air into hydraulic connection. Always protect piston from damage.
3. Plug open piston bore with a sealing plate, then press opposite piston from caliper through bleeder bore.
4. Repeat steps 2 and 3 for remaining pistons.
5. Remove rubber seal rings from caliper bores with a plastic tipped tool.
6. Clean caliper and pistons with alcohol, blow dry with compressed air and coat sealing surfaces with brake fluid.
7. Inspect pistons and replace if corroded, or if sealing surface is worn or damaged.
8. Inspect caliper body and replace if sealing grooves are worn or corroded, or if caliper is damaged or distorted. **Do not machine inner bore of caliper.**
9. Coat new piston seals with brake fluid and seat seals in caliper bore groove.
10. Install dust boot on piston, then seat piston in caliper bore, ensuring that piston enters bore straight.
11. Seat dust boots in groove, then install retaining rings.

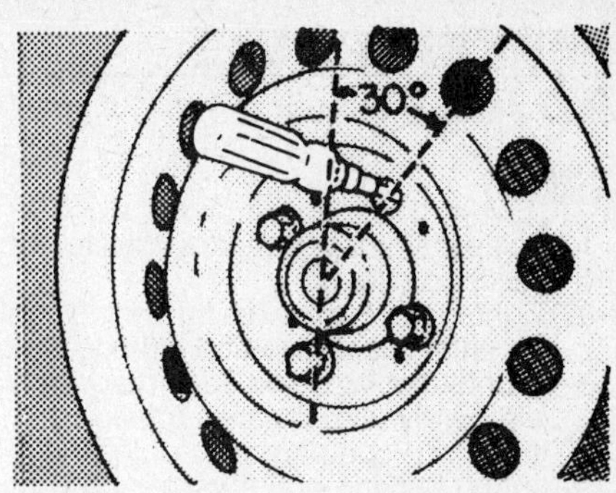

Fig. 8 Parking brake shoe adjustment. 318i & 325

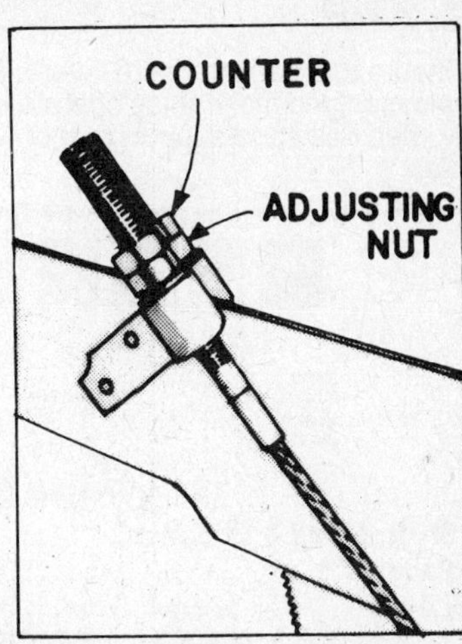

Fig. 10 Adjusting parking brake cable (Typical)

524TD, 528e, 533/535i & 633/635CSi (FRONT) & ALL REAR CALIPERS

1. Remove piston boot and snap ring.
2. Position suitable block of wood in caliper recess, then apply compressed air to fluid inlet to force piston from bore.
3. Remove bleeder screw.
4. Remove piston seal using suitable tool, taking care not to mar caliper bore.
5. Remove dowel sleeves (5) from guide bolt bores, **Fig. 7.**
6. Clean caliper and piston with alcohol, blow dry with compressed air and coat sealing surfaces with brake fluid.
7. Inspect piston and replace if corroded, or if sealing surface is worn or damaged.
8. Inspect caliper body and replace if sealing grooves are worn or corroded, or if caliper is damaged or distorted. **Do not machine inner bore of caliper.**
9. Coat new piston seal with brake fluid and seat seal in caliper bore groove.
10. Install dust boot on piston, then seat piston in caliper bore, ensuring that piston enters bore straight.
11. Seat dust boot in groove, then install retaining ring.
12. Install guide bolt dowel sleeves.
13. Ensure that bleeder valve is clear, then install valve.

PARKING BRAKE

ADJUST

320i

1. Raise and support rear of vehicle with parking brake off.
2. Tighten up rear brakes by turning right eccentric clockwise and left eccentric counterclockwise on each rear wheel, just barely allowing free rotation.
3. In driver's compartment, unlock locknut on parking brake cable and tighten adjusting nut until parking brake locks at less than five notches.

EXC. 320i

1. Ensure that parking brake lever is fully released and that cables operate freely, then raise and support rear of vehicle.
2. On models with wheel bolts, remove 1 wheel bolt from each wheel. On models with studs, remove rear wheels and secure brake discs using lug nuts and suitable spacers.
3. Rotate wheel until bolt hole is aligned with parking brake star adjuster. **Adjuster is located approximately 30 degrees behind the vertical axis of the wheel on 300 series vehicles, Fig. 8, or 45 degrees below horizontal axis of wheel toward rear of vehicle on 500, 600 and 700 series vehicles, Fig. 9.**
4. Insert screwdriver through bolt hole and tighten adjuster until wheel can just barely be rotated, then back off adjuster 3-4 notches for 300 series or 4-6 notches for 500, 600 and 700 series vehicles. **On 300 series vehicles, left adjuster is turned up to tighten, while right adjuster is turned down to tighten. On 500, 600 and 700 series vehicles, turning adjuster clockwise tightens the adjustment.**
5. Pull parking brake lever up 5 notches, then tighten adjusters, **Fig. 10**, until rear wheels can just barely be rotated.
6. Release brake lever and ensure that rear wheels rotate freely.

MASTER CYLINDER

REPLACE

1. On 320i models, remove mixture control unit.
2. Siphon fluid from reservoir, then disconnect and position various hydraulic output tubes out of way.
3. Unbolt master cylinder from booster.
4. Fill and pre-bleed master cylinder.
5. Reverse procedure to install, then bleed brake system.

REAR AXLE & SUSPENSION SECTION

INDEX

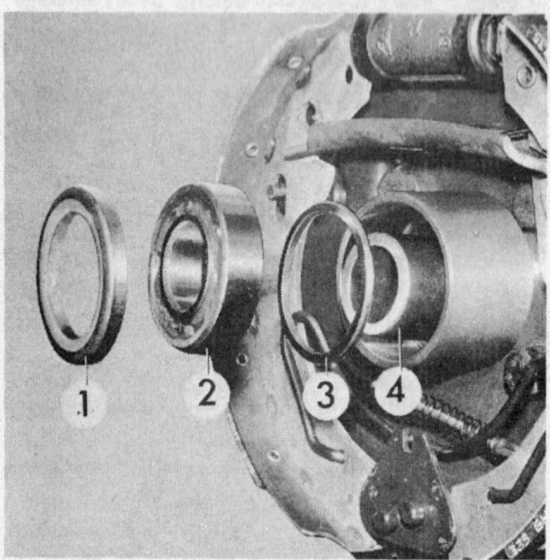

Fig. 1 Removing seal, bearing shim & spacer. 320i models

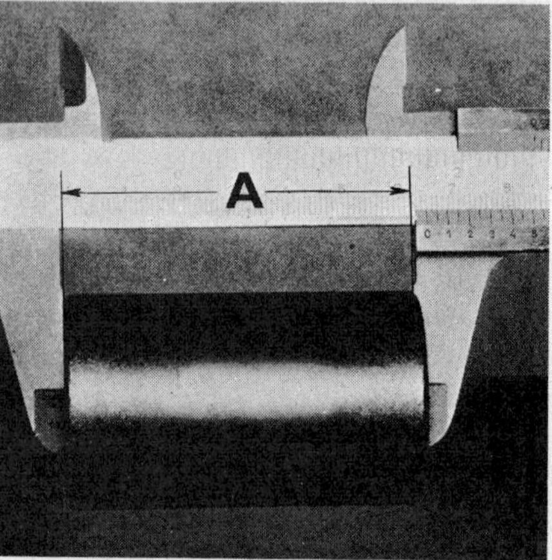

Fig. 2 Measuring spacer sleeve. 320i models

Fig. 3 Measuring distance between inner & outer bearing race contact surfaces. 320i models

AXLE SHAFT, SEALS & BEARINGS

REPLACE

320i

1. Raise and support rear of vehicle, then remove wheel, cotter pin, axle nut, small screw, two wheel bolts and the drum.
2. Using appropriate puller, remove drive flange, then disconnect outboard end of output shaft from inside stub axle flange and position aside.
3. Replace axle nut on stub axle backwards and drive out with a soft faced or plastic faced hammer.
4. Drive out seal and bearing, then remove shim or locating ring and spacer from hub, **Fig. 1.**
5. Inner bearing and seal can be driven out at this time.
6. When replacing, install inner seal and bearing first, then measure spacer length, **Fig. 2**, and inside hub distance from outer bearing race land to outer race of inner bearing, **Fig. 3.** Subtract second number from first, then subtract .004 inch for clearance to obtain shim or ring thickness required to fit bearings.

318i & 325

1. Raise and support rear of vehicle, then remove wheel and hub cover.
2. Pry out and discard lock plate, then remove output shaft retaining nut.
3. Remove nuts securing output shaft to rear axle drive flange, then suspend shaft from suspension.
4. Install suitable press using 2 wheel bolts, **Fig. 4**, then press shaft from hub.
5. Remove brake disc, then drive out hub using suitable drift.

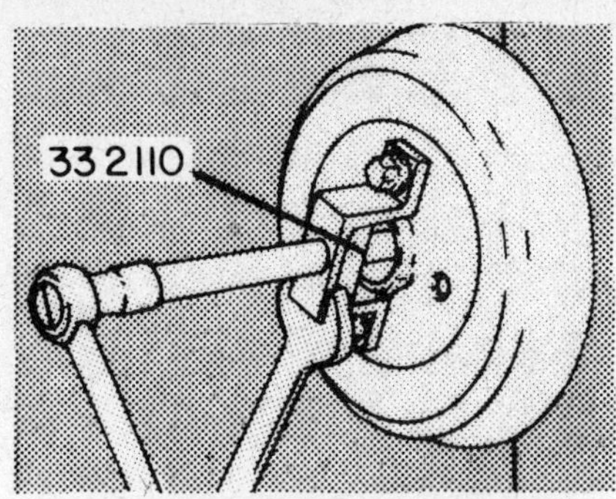

Fig. 4 Output shaft removal. 318i & 325

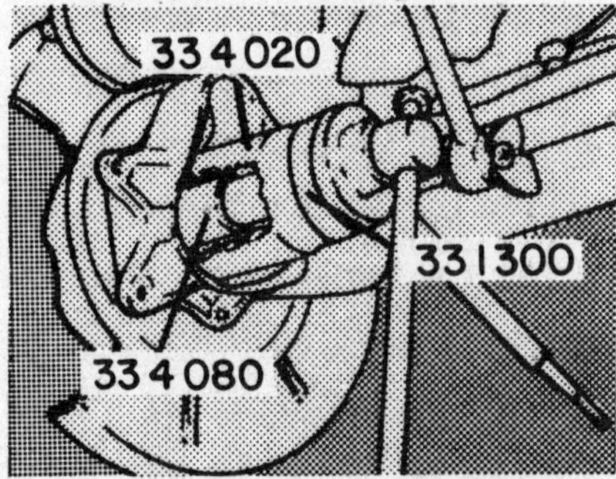

Fig. 6 Stub axle installation. 524TD, 528e, 533/535i, 633/635CSi & 733/735i

6. Remove snap ring securing bearing in housing.
7. Remove bearing from housing and inner race from hub using suitable pullers.
8. Press bearing into housing using forcing screw 334041, nut 334042 and spacer 334046 against bearing, and nut 334043 and spacer 334047 on rear side of housing or suitable equivalents.
9. Install bearing snap ring, then press hub into bearing using forcing screw 334041, nut 334042 and spacer 334047 against hub, nut 334043 and spacer 334045 on rear side of housing, or suitable equivalents.
10. Install brake disc and mount puller bracket 332110 using 2 wheel bolts.
11. Insert output shaft spline through hub, engage puller screw and pull shaft into hub, **Fig. 5.**
12. Connect output shaft to rear axle drive flange and torque bolts to 42-46 ft. lbs.
13. Install output shaft retaining nut, prevent hub assembly from turning and torque nut to 140-152 ft. lbs.
14. Install new lock plate and reverse remaining procedure to complete installation.

524TD, 528e, 533/535i, 633/635CSi & 733/735i

1. Raise and support rear of vehicle and remove wheel.
2. Remove bolts securing output shaft to stub axle drive flange and suspend shaft assembly from suspension member. **If output shaft is to be replaced, remove bolts securing shaft to rear axle drive flange and remove shaft assembly.**
3. Remove bolts securing brake caliper, secure caliper aside, then remove brake disc.
4. Install 2 wheel bolts and use suitable lever to prevent stub axle from turning, then remove lock plate and drive flange retaining nut.
5. Remove drive flange from stub axle using suitable puller.
6. Install drive flange retaining nut flush with end of stub axle, then drive axle from bearing using suitable driver.
7. Remove bearing race from stub axle, if necessary, using suitable puller, then inspect axle and drive flange and replace if damaged, distorted or excessively worn.
8. Remove snap ring securing bearing, then the bearing, using suitable puller.
9. Press bearing into housing using forcing screw and suitable spacers, then install snap ring, ensuring that snap ring is fully seated in groove.
10. Install stub axle into bearing using suitable puller, **Fig. 6. Do not drive axle into bearing, as bearing may be damaged.**
11. Install drive flange and retaining nut, then torque nut to 169-188 ft. lbs.
12. Reverse remaining procedure to complete installation, torquing output shaft bolts to 42-46 ft. lbs.

REAR COIL SPRING/SHOCK ABSORBER REPLACE

320i, 524TD, 528e, 533/535i, 633/635CSi & 733/735i

1. Raise and support rear of vehicle and trailing arm using a suitable jack. Remove lower shock end mounting bolt at arm, **Fig. 7.**
2. Remove centering plate from upper end in wheel house area.
3. Remove assembly.
4. Compress coil spring using suitable tool, then disassemble shock absorber from coil spring, **Fig. 8.**
5. When assembling, make sure spring ends line up with notches in rubber spring insulator.
6. Install assembly with damping ring on top end.

318i & 325

Shock Absorber

1. Raise and support rear of vehicle, and support trailing arm with suitable jack.

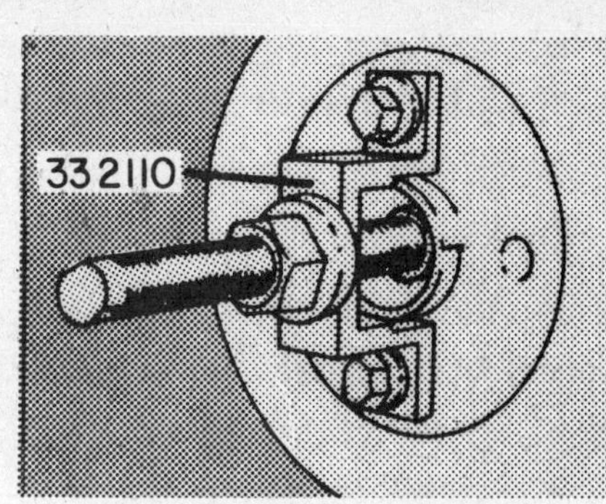

Fig. 5 Output shaft installation. 318i & 325

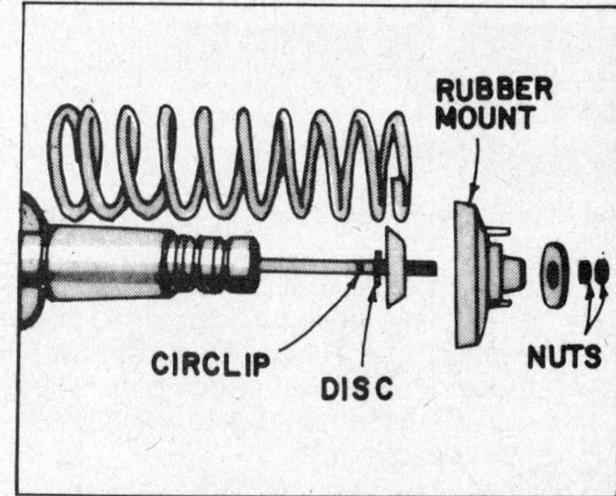

Fig. 7 Coil spring & shock absorber

2. Remove bolt securing shock absorber to trailing arm, **Fig. 9.**
3. Pull back trunk trim panel and remove 2 nuts securing upper shock absorber mount and the shock absorber assembly.
4. Reverse procedure to install.

Coil Spring

1. Raise and support rear of vehicle, and support trailing arm at outboard end with suitable jack.
2. Disconnect exhaust hanger and suspend resonator with piece of wire.
3. Remove bolts securing differential housing rubber mount on side to be serviced, pull down on mount and wedge with block of wood.
4. Disconnect shock absorber and stabilizer bar, if equipped, from trailing arm.
5. Slowly lower jack supporting trailing arm until spring tension is released, then remove coil spring. **Only lower trailing arm enough to allow spring to be removed. If arm is allowed to hang free, output shaft constant velocity joints will be damaged.**
6. Reverse procedure to install, ensuring that coil spring is properly positioned in mount. Torque shock absorber bolt to 52-63 ft. lbs. and rubber axle mount bolt to 58-63 ft. lbs.

FRONT SUSPENSION & STEERING SECTION

INDEX

WHEEL BEARINGS

ADJUST

320i & 733/735i

1. Remove wheel, bearing cap, and cotter pin.
2. Torque castle nut to 22-24 ft. lbs. (30-33 Nm) while turning hub to align bearing rollers and to force away grease which can affect play. Give hub an additional 2 turns without disturbing castle nut.
3. Loosen castle nut until hub can move axially. Torque castle nut to 2 ft. lbs. (3 Nm), then turn back to nearest slot and insert new cotter pin. Using screwdriver, check that notched washer turns freely in both directions.

EXC. 320i & 733/735i

Front wheel bearings on these models are permanently lubricated and sealed, and cannot be adjusted. If wheel bearing service is required, use replacement procedure outlined below.

1. Raise and support front of vehicle and remove wheels.
2. Remove bolts securing caliper bracket to spindle, then the caliper and bracket assembly.
3. Remove bolt securing brake rotor and the rotor.
4. Remove hub cover, chisel away staked portion of nut, then remove hub retaining nut.
5. Remove hub assembly using suitable puller.
6. If inner bearing race remains on spindle, remove race as follows:
   a. Remove nuts securing brake rotor dust shield and the dust shield.
   b. Push back hub dust shield, install guide sleeve to protect spindle threads, then remove bearing race using suitable puller.
   c. Inspect spindle if damaged or scored.
   d. Reinstall rotor dust shield.
7. Install dust guard, then press replacement hub assembly using tool 312120 for 318i and 325 or 312110 for 500 and 600 series models. **Bearing and hub assemblies should not be reused after removal.**
8. Install new retaining nut, torque nut to 188-231 ft. lbs. on 318i and 325 or 166-203 ft. lbs. for 500 and 600 series models. Stake nut into spindle, then reverse remaining procedure to complete installation.

HUB & BEARING

REPLACE

320i & 733/735i

1. Raise and support front of vehicle, then remove wheel.
2. Remove caliper mounting bolts, then suspend caliper with suitable wire.
3. Remove bearing cap, cotter pin, castle nut and notched washer, then the hub and rotor assembly.
4. Remove rotor to hub retaining bolt, then separate hub from rotor.
5. Remove outer bearing from hub, then pry out inner seal and remove inner bearing.
6. Drive out bearing races with suitable drift.
7. Clean hub in suitable solvent and check for wear or heat damage. Replace hub, if necessary.
8. Pack hub with suitable grease, then press new races into hub using suitable tools.
9. Pack inner bearing with suitable grease, then install into hub.
10. Coat inner seal lip with suitable grease, then install seal using tool 31 2 040 or equivalent.
11. Attach hub to rotor with retaining bolt, then install hub/rotor assembly onto spindle.
12. Pack outer bearing with suitable grease, then install bearing, washer and castle nut.
13. Adjust wheel bearings as outlined previously, then install bearing cap, brake caliper and front wheel.

EXC. 320i & 733/735i

The hub and bearing on these models are a matched set and should not be reused after removal. Refer to "Wheel Bearings, Adjust" for replacement procedure.

CONTROL ARMS

REPLACE

320i

1. Disconnect stabilizer bar at control arm and disconnect control arm from crossmember.
2. Remove cotter pin and castle nut. Press control arm off steering knuckle with tool No. 31 1 100 or equivalent.
3. Ball joint turning torque should be 1-3.5 ft. lbs. (1.5-5 Nm) and axial play should not exceed 0.055 inch (1.4 mm) or control arm must be replaced.
4. Reverse procedure to install noting the following torques: Ball joint to steering knuckle 44-50 ft. lbs. (60-70 Nm); control arm to crossmember 58-65 ft. lbs. (81-90 Nm); and stabilizer bar to control arm 34-37 ft. lbs. (47-52 Nm).

318i & 325

1. Raise and support front of vehicle and remove wheels.
2. Remove bolts securing rear control arm bracket to crossmember.
3. Remove nut securing stabilizer shaft link, then disconnect shaft.
4. Remove nut securing front control arm joint to crossmember, strike joint body with suitable hammer to loosen stud, then disconnect joint from crossmember.
5. Remove nut securing ball joint to spindle, then press joint from spindle using ball joint press 311110 or equivalent and remove control arm.
6. Reverse procedure to install noting the following:
   a. Replace nuts securing ball joints to spindle support and crossmember.
   b. Torque spindle support ball joint nut to 43-51 ft. lbs., crossmember ball joint nut to 55-69 ft. lbs., and the control arm bracket bolts and stabilizer link nut to 29-34 ft. lbs.

524TD, 528e, 533/535i & 633/635CSi

1. Raise and support front of vehicle and remove wheels.
2. Remove bolts securing tie rod to spring strut, then disconnect tie rod.
3. Remove cotter pin and castle nut securing ball joint, then press out ball joint stud.
4. Remove bolt and nut securing control arm to crossmember, then the crossmember.
5. Reverse procedure to install, noting the following:
   a. Ensure that locating key of strut, if

applicable, is properly engaged in slot in tie rod support, **Fig. 1**.

b. Torque nut securing control arm to crossmember to 52-63 ft. lbs., control arm ball joint nut to 44-51 ft. lbs. and tie rod to spring strut bolts to 40-48 ft. lbs. **Apply suitable thread locking compound to tie rod retaining bolts. Torque control arm retaining bolt nut with vehicle at normal ride height.**

733/735i

1. Remove front wheel and disconnect stabilizer bar link from control arm.
2. Disconnect control arm from crossmember.
3. Disconnect steering arm from MacPherson strut.
4. Remove cotter pin and castle nut. Using tool No. 31 1 110 or equivalent, press off control arm.
5. Condition of ball joints can be checked by measuring turning torque using a suitable torque wrench or by measuring axial play. Turning torque should be 0.4-1.8 ft. lbs. (0.5-2.5 Nm) at 10 RPM. Axial play of ball joint pin should not exceed 0.055 inch (1.4 mm). If ball joint fails to meet these specifications, control arm must be replaced.

MacPHERSON STRUT REPLACE

320i

1. Remove front wheel and disconnect brake line bracket from strut leaving brake lines connected.
2. Disconnect caliper and suspend. Remove cotter pin and castle nut and press off tie rod end with tool No. 32 2 050 or equivalent.
3. Remove cotter pin and castle nut. Using tool N 31 1 100 or equivalent, press control arm off steering arm.
4. Disconnect strut at spring tower in engine compartment.
5. Reverse procedure to install, noting the following. Torque strut to spring tower to 16-17 ft. lbs. (22-24 Nm); ball joint to steering arm 44-50 ft. lbs. (60-70 Nm); tie rod end 25-29 ft. lbs. (35-40 Nm); brake caliper to steering arm 58-69 ft. lbs. (80-95 Nm).

318i & 325

1. Raise and support front of vehicle and remove wheels.
2. Disconnect ground wire and brake pad sensor electrical connector, then release wiring from retaining clips.
3. Remove bolts securing brake caliper bracket, lift caliper assembly from spindle support and secure aside, leaving hose connected.
4. Disconnect stabilizer shaft from control arm connecting link.
5. Remove ball joint retaining nut, then press joint from spindle support.
6. Remove tie rod retaining nut, then separate tie rod from steering arm using suitable puller.

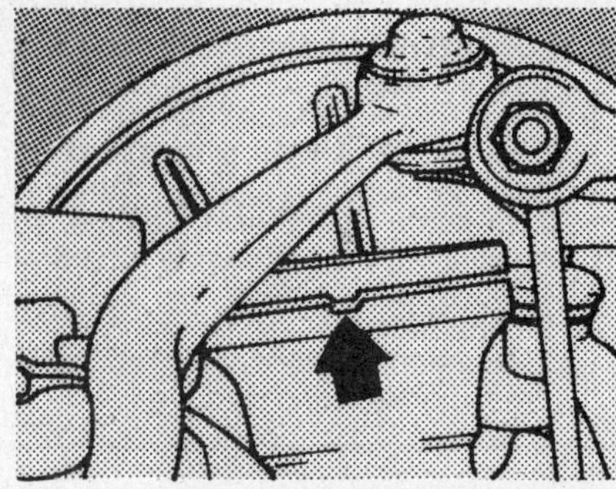

Fig. 1 Positioning locating key. 524TD, 528e, 533/535i & 633/635CSi

7. Pull out on spring strut assembly and disconnect lower ball joint.
8. Support strut assembly, then remove upper retaining nuts and the strut assembly.

524TD, 528e, 533/535i & 633/635CSi

1. Remove front wheel and disconnect brake line bracket at front strut.
2. Disconnect and support brake caliper leaving brake lines connected.
3. If applicable, remove safety wire from the three bolts at base of steering arm. Disconnect steering arm from base of strut.
4. Disconnect strut at top of spring tower in engine compartment and remove strut.
5. Reverse procedure to install noting the following: Torque strut to spring tower to 16-18 ft. lbs. (22-25 Nm); steering arm to strut to 33-34 ft. lbs. (45-60 Nm) and brake caliper to 58-69 ft. lbs. (80-95 Nm).

733/735i

1. Remove front wheel and disconnect stabilizer link from control arm.
2. Disconnect brake hose bracket from strut.
3. Disconnect brake pad wear indicator plug and ground wire. Disconnect and support caliper leaving hoses connected.
4. Remove three bolts and disconnect steering arm from base of strut.
5. Disconnect strut at spring tower in engine compartment and remove strut.
6. Reverse procedure to install, noting the following: Torque strut to spring tower bolts to 16-17 ft. lbs. (22-24 Nm); torque steering arm to strut bolts to 33-44 ft. lbs. (45-60 Nm). Steering arm bolts must be clean and coated with green Loctite No. 270 or equivalent. Torque brake caliper to 59-70 ft. lbs. (80-95 Nm) and stabilizer link to 18-20 ft. lbs. (25-28 Nm).

STEERING GEAR REPLACE

320i

1. Remove front wheels and press tie rod ends off steering arms using tool No. 32 2 050 or equivalent.
2. Disconnect and remove steering rack from front crossmember.
3. Loosen and remove U-joint clamp bolt and pull steering gear off steering spindle.
4. Reverse procedure to install, noting the following: Ridge on dust seal must be between marks on steering gear box; torque U-joint clamp bolt to 15-17 ft. lbs. (20-23 Nm); steering rack to 35-39 ft. lbs. (49-54 Nm); tie rod ends to 25-29 ft. lbs. (35-40 Nm).

318i & 325

1. Ensure that steering wheel is centered and front wheels are in straight ahead position, then raise and support vehicle and remove front wheels.
2. Scribe matching marks between steering shaft joint coupling and steering gear housing, loosen pinch bolt and pry coupling off steering gear spindle.
3. Disconnect fluid pressure and return hoses from steering gear, drain fluid into suitable container, then plug lines and open fittings. **Do not reuse power steering fluid.**
4. Remove nuts securing tie rods to spring struts and disconnect tie rods using suitable puller.
5. Remove bolts securing gear to crossmember and the steering gear.
6. Reverse procedure to install, noting the following:
   a. Replace self locking nuts during installation.
   b. Torque steering gear bolts to 29-34 ft. lbs. and tie rod retaining nuts to 25-29 ft. lbs.
   c. Ensure that steering shaft joint is properly aligned and that pinch bolt is engaged in groove, then torque nut to 16 ft. lbs.

524TD, 528e, 533/535i & 633/635CSi

1. Turn steering wheel to left lock in order to raise piston in steering box.
2. Drain power steering fluid and discard. Do not reuse.
3. Turn front wheels to right lock and after removing cotter pin and castle nut, press off center link from pitman arm with tool No. 32 2 070 or equivalent.
4. Steering wheel and front wheels should be aimed straight ahead. Mark alignment of steering shaft and coupling. Remove lower clamping bolt of steering coupling and slide coupling up. Disconnect hoses at steering box and plug openings.
5. Disconnect power steering box from crossmember and remove.
6. Reverse procedure to install noting the following: Torque steering box to crossmember bolts to 33-37 ft. lbs. (45-50 Nm). Make sure that coupling clamp bolt is in locking groove of shaft and torque to 16-17 ft. bs. (22-24 Nm). Use new self-locking nuts. Torque hose fitting to 33-37 ft. lbs. (45-50 Nm). Torque center link to pitman arm to 26-30 ft. lbs. (35-40 Nm). Bleed power steering by turning steer-

ing wheel from lock to lock with engine idling until no bubbles appear. Fluid level must remain constant at upper mark.

733/735i

1. Turn steering wheel to left lock in order to move piston up. Discharge hydraulic accumulator by pumping brake pedal 20 times.
2. Disconnect hose fittings at steering box and plug openings. Do not reuse drained fluid.
3. Using tool No. 31 1 110 or equivalent, press center link off pitman arm.
4. Remove lower coupling clamp bolt and push up coupling flange with steering column. Steering wheel and front wheels should be positioned straight ahead.
5. Disconnect steering box from crossmember and remove.
6. Reverse procedure to install, noting the following: Torque steering box to crossmember to 32-35 ft. lbs. (43-48 Nm). Make sure that lower coupling nut is located in steering shaft locking groove. Replace self-locking nuts and torque to 18-20 ft. lbs. (25-28 Nm). Torque center link to pitman arm to 26-30 ft. lbs. (35-40 Nm). Replace seals and torque hose fitting to 34-37 ft. lbs. (45-50 Nm).

WHEEL ALIGNMENT SECTION

INDEX

FRONT WHEEL ALIGNMENT

CASTER

Caster values are designed into the front suspension geometry and are not adjustable. If caster is not within specification, check for worn or damaged suspension components and replace as necessary.

CAMBER

Although designed into the front suspension geometry, camber can be altered up to plus or minus 1/2° by installing eccentric upper mounting plates on the strut assembly. These mounts are marked with a + or − at the bolt bores. Depending on the situation, press knurled bolts into the bolt bores as required using tool 31 3 130 or equivalent. After installation, ensure that bolts are vertical and completely flush with mount.

TOE-IN

Toe-in is adjusted by means of threaded sleeves on the tie rods. To adjust toe value, proceed as follows:

1. Position steering gear in straight ahead position.
2. Loosen tie rod sleeve retaining clamp nuts, then rotate both sleeves as required until toe value is within specification.
3. Ensure that tie rod end ball stud is vertically centered, then tighten clamp nuts.

REAR WHEEL ALIGNMENT

CAMBER & TOE-IN

Camber and toe values are designed into the rear suspension geometry and are not normally adjustable. However, eccentric trailing arm blocks are available on most models to modestly compensate for slight camber or toe deviations. If camber or toe-in values deviate radically from specification, check for the following conditions:

1. Damaged rear axle carrier mounts or carrier.
2. Damaged trailing arm blocks or trailing arm.
3. Damaged final drive mount.
4. Excessive suspension sag. Replace coil springs and recheck alignment.
5. Damaged floor assembly. Check and repair body if necessary, then recheck alignment.

DODGE / PLYMOUTH (Japan)

INDEX OF SERVICE OPERATIONS

Gen ral Engine Sp cifications

Year	Engine CID①/cc	Carb. Type	Bore X Stroke Inches (mm)	Comp. Ratio	Horsepower @ RPM	Torque Lbs. Ft. @ RPM	Normal Oil Pressure Lbs.
1983	4-86/1400	2 Barrel	2.91 X 3.23 (74 X 82)	8.8	64 @ 5000	78 @ 3000	64③
	4-97.5/1600	2 Barrel	3.03 X 3.39 (77 X 86)	8.5	72 @ 5000	85 @ 3000	64③
	4-122/2000	2 Barrel	3.34 X 3.46 (85 X 88)	8.5	90 @ 5000	107 @ 3500	49③
	4-143/2300④	Fuel Inj.	3.58 X 3.54 (91 X 90)	21	80 @ 4200	125 @ 2500	57③
	4-156/2600	2 Barrel	3.59 X 3.86 (91 X 98)	8.2	105 @ 5000	139@ 2500	57③
1984	4-86/1400	2 Barrel	2.91 X 3.23 (74 X 82)	8.8	64 @ 5000	78 @ 3000	64③
	4-97.5/1600⑦	2 Barrel	3.03 X 3.39 (77 X 86)	8.5	72 @ 5000	85 @ 3000	64③
	4-97.5/1600⑤	Fuel Inj.	3.03 X 3.39 (77 X 86)	7.6	102 @ 5500	122 @ 3000	64③
	4-122/2000	2 Barrel	3.34 X 3.46 (85 X 88)	8.5	88 @ 5000	108 @ 3500	7.1②
	4-143/2300④	Fuel Inj.	3.58 X 3.54 (91 X 90)	21	80 @ 4200	125 @ 2500	7.1②
	4-156/2600	2 Barrel	3.59 X 3.86 (91 X 98)	8.2	105 @ 5000	139@ 2500	7.1②
	4-156/2600	Fuel Inj.	3.59 X 3.86 (91 X 98)	7.0	145 @ 5500	185 @ 2500	21②
1985	4-90/1500	2 Barrel	2.97 X 3.23 (76 X 82)	9.4	68 @ 5500	82 @ 3500	11②
	4-97.5/1600⑤	Fuel Inj.	3.03 X 3.39 (77 X 86)	7.6	102 @ 5500	122 @ 3000	11②
	4-122/2000	2 Barrel	3.34 X 3.46 (85 X 88)	8.5	88 @ 5000	108 @ 3500	7.1②
	4-143/2300④	Fuel Inj.	3.59 X 3.54 (91 X 90)	21	80 @ 4200	125 @ 2500	7.1②
	4-156/2600⑦	2 Barrel	3.59 X 3.86 (91 X 98)	8.7	106 @ 5000	139 @ 2500	7.1②
	4-156/2600⑤	Fuel Inj.	3.59 X 3.86 (91 X 98)	7.0	145 @ 5000	185 @ 2500	21②
	4-156/2600⑥	Fuel Inj.	3.59 X 3.86 (91 X 98)	7.0	170 @ 5000	220 @ 2500	21②
1986	4-90/1500	2 Barrel	2.97 X 3.23 (76 X 82)	9.4	68 @ 5500	82 @3500	11②
	4-97.5/1600⑤	Fuel Inj.	3.03 X 3.39 (77 X 86)	7.6	102 @ 5500	122 @ 3000	11②
	4-122/2000	2 Barrel	3.35 X 3.46 (85 X 88)	8.5	88 @ 5000	108 @3500	7.1②
	4-156/2600⑦	2 Barrel	3.59 X 3.86 (91 X 98)	8.2	106 @ 5000	139 @ 2500	7.1②
	4-156/2600⑤	Fuel Inj.	3.59 X 3.86 (91 X 98)	7.0	145 @ 5000	185 @ 2500	11②
	4-156/2600⑥	Fuel Inj.	3.59 X 3.86 (91 X 98)	7.0	170 @ 5000	220 @ 2500	11②
1987	4-90/1500	2 Barrel	2.97 X 3.23 (76 X 82)	9.4	68 @ 5500	85 @3500	11②
	4-97.5/1600⑤	Fuel Inj.	3.03 X 3.39 (77 X 86)	7.6	102 @ 5500	122 @ 3000	11②
	4-122/2000⑧	2 Barrel	3.35 X 3.46 (85 X 88)	8.5	88 @ 5000	108 @3500	7.1②
	4-122/2000⑨	2 Barrel	3.35 X 3.46 (85 X 88)	8.5	90 @ 5500	109 @ 3500	7.1②
	4-156/2600⑦	2 Barrel	3.59 X 3.86 (91 X 98)	8.7	109 @ 5000	142 @ 3000	7.1②
	4-156/2600⑤	Fuel Inj.	3.59 X 3.86 (91 X 98)	7.0	145 @ 5000	185 @ 2500	11②
	4-156/2600⑥	Fuel Inj.	3.59 X 3.86 (91 X 98)	7.0	176 @ 5000	223 @ 2500	11②

①—Cubic inch displacement.
②—Minimum at idle.
③—At 2000 RPM.
④—Turbocharged diesel engine.
⑤—Turbocharged engine.
⑥—Turbocharged intercooled engine.
⑦—Exc. Turbocharged.
⑧—Colt Vista.
⑨—Ram 50.

Alternator & Regulator Specifications

Year	Alternator				Regulator	
			Output @ 14 Volts			
Year	Model No.	Rated Hot Output Amps.	2500 RPM Amps.	5000 RPM Amps.	Model	Constant Voltage Relay Voltage @ 68°F
1983	AQ2250G1	50	41	48	Integral	14.1–14.7
	A2T16371	45	37	44	Integral	14.1–14.7
	A2T16471	45	37	44	Integral	14.1–14.7
	100211-0320	45	—	—	①	13.9–14.9
1984	A5T15470	45	—	—	Integral	13.9–14.9
	A5T15370	45	—	—	Integral	13.9–14.9
	A3T32772	65	45②	—	Integral	14.1–14.7
	A5T15171	45	—	—	Integral	13.9–14.9
	A5T20571	50	—	—	Integral	13.9–14.9
1985	A3T34572	65	—	—	Integral	14.4–15
	A2T41791	65	—	—	Integral	14.4–15
	A1T40391	55	—	—	Integral	14.4–15
	A1T40491	50	—	—	Integral	14.4–15
	A2T41991	65	—	—	Integral	14.4–15
1986	A1T40391	55	—	—	Integral	14.4–15
	A1T40491	50	—	—	Integral	14.4–15
	A2T41991	65	—	—	Integral	14.4–15
	A2T43791	65	—	—	Integral	14.4–15
	A3T34572	65	—	—	Integral	14.4–15
	A5T15370	45	—	—	Integral	14.1–14.7
	5T15470	45	—	—	Integral	14.1–14.7
1987	A2T02271	45	31③	—	Integral	13.9–14.9
	A2T02471	45	31③	—	Integral	13.9–14.9
	A2T03477	50	35③	—	Integral	13.9–14.9
	A2T03691	60	42③	—	Integral	14.2–15.2
	A2T03792	65	45③	—	Integral	14.2–15.2
	A2T03892	75	52③	—	Integral	14.2–15.2
	A2T03972	65	45③	—	Integral	13.9–14.9
	A2T48691	65	45③	—	Integral	14.2–15.2
	A2T49972	75	52③	—	Integral	13.9–14.9

①—4-122/2000cc engine, Add-on type electronic voltage regulator; 4-156/2600cc and 4-143/2300cc engines, Built-in type electronic voltage regulator.

②—@ 1150 RPM.

③—Minimum.

Starting Motor Specifications

Year	Engine	Model No.	Rotation ①	Brush Spring Tension Ounces	No Load Test		
					Amperes (Max.)	Volts	RPM (Min.)
1983 ④	1400,1600 ②	M3T32581	C	53	60	11.5	6500
	1600 ③	M3T25781	C	53	60	11.5	6600
	2000,2600 ②	M3T25781	C	53	60	11.5	6600
	2000,2600 ③	—	C	53	90	11.5	3300
1983–84 ⑤	2000,2600 ②	M3T25882	C	—	60	11.5	6500
	2000,2600 ③	M2T53083	C	—	100	11.5	3000
	2300 ⑥	M2T56171	C	—	130	11	4000
1984	1400, 1600 ②	M3T32583	C	53	60	11.5	6500
	1600 ③	M3T25883	C	53	60	11.5	6600
	2000	M3T25783	C	53	60	11.5	6500
	2000	M2T53085	C	53	90	11.5	3300
	2600 ②	M3T25882	C	—	60	11.5	6500
	2600 ③	M2T53083	C	—	100	11.5	3000
1985	1500, 1600 ③	M2T40081	C	—	60	11.5	3900
	1500,1600 ②	M3T32592	C	—	60	11.5	6500
	2000 ③ ⑦	M3T25783	C	—	60	11.5	6500
	2000 ② ⑦	M2T53085	C	—	100	11.5	3000
	2000, 2300 ② ⑤	M3T25885	C	—	60	11.5	6600
	2000, 2300 ③ ⑤	M2T53086	C	—	90	11.5	3300
	2600 ②	M3T25882	C	—	60	11.5	6500
	2600 ③	M2T53083	C	—	100	11.5	3000
1986	1500, 1600 ②	M3T32592	C	—	60	11.5	6500
	1500, 1600 ③	M2T40081	C	—	60	11.5	3900
	2000 ② ⑦	M3T25783	C	—	60	11.5	6500
	2000 ③ ⑦	M2T53085	C	—	100	11.5	3000
	2000 ② ⑤	M3T25885	C	—	60	11.5	6600
	2000 ③ ⑤	M2T53086	C	—	90	11.5	3300
	2600 ② ④	M3T25882	C	—	60	11.5	6500
	2600 ③ ④	M2T53083	C	—	100	11.5	3000
	2600 ⑤	M2T53086	C	—	90	11.5	3300
1987	1500, 1600 ②	M3T32592	C	—	60	11.5	6500
	1500, 1600 ③	M3T41081	C	—	60	11.5	6500
	2000 ②	M3T41081	C	—	60	11.5	6600
	2000 ③	M1T70481	C	—	90	11	3000
	2600 ⑧	M2T53085	C	—	100	11.5	3000
	2600 ⑨	M1T70481	C	—	90	11	3000

①—As viewed from pinion side of starter motor.
②—Man. trans.
③—Auto. trans.
④—Exc. Ram 50.
⑤—Ram 50 only.
⑥—Turbocharged diesel engine.
⑦—Colt Vista only.
⑧—Conquest.
⑨—Ram 50 & Raider.

Valve Specifications

Year	Model	Valve Lash		Valve Angles		Valve Spring Installed Height	Valve Spring Pressure Lbs. @ In.	Stem Clearance		Stem Diameter	
		Int.	Exh.	Seat	Face			Intake	Exhaust	Intake	Exhaust
1983–84	1400	.006H①	.010H	45②	45②	1.417③	69 @1.417	.0012–.0024	.0020–.0035	.3150④	.3150
	1600	.006H①	.010H	45②	45②	1.469③	62 @ 1.469	.0012–.0024	.0020–.0035	.3150④	.3150
	2000,2600	.006H①	.010H	45②	45②	1.590③	62 @ 1.591	.0012–.0024	.0020–.0035	.3150④	.3150
1983–85	2300⑤	.010H	.010H	45	45	1.591	61 @ 1.591	.0012–.0024	.0020–.0035	.3150	.3150
1985	1500	.006H⑥	.010H	45②	45②	1.417	69 @ 1.417	.0012–.0024	.0020–.0035	.3150④	.3150
	1600	.006H⑥	.010H	45②	45②	1.469	62 @ 1.469	.0012–.0024	.0020–.0035	.3150④	.3150
	2000, 2600	⑥⑧	⑧	45⑦	45⑦	1.591	⑨	.0012–.0024	.0020–.0035	.3150⑦	.3150
1986	1500	.006H⑥	.010H	45②	45②	1.469	53 @ 1.469	.0008–.0020	.0020–.0035	.260④	.260
	2000, 2600	⑥⑧	⑧	45⑦	45⑦	1.591	72 @ 1.591	.0012–.0024	.0020–.0035	.3150⑦	.3150
1987	1500	.006H⑥	.010H	44②	45②	1.469	53 @ 1.468	.0008–.0020	.0020–.0035	.260④	.260
	1600	.006H⑥	.010H	45②	45②	1.469	62 @ 1.469	.0012–.0024	.0020–.0035	.3150④	.3150
	2000	⑥⑧	⑧	45⑦	45⑦	1.591	74 @ 1.591	.0012–.0024	.0020–.0035	.3150⑦	.3150
	2600	⑥⑧	⑧	45⑦	45⑦	⑩	⑩	.0012–.0024	.0020–.0035	.3150⑦	.3150

①—Jet valve lash .006 inch hot.
②—Jet valve face and seat angle, 45°.
③—Jet valve spring installed height, .846 inch.
④—Jet valve stem diameter, .1693 inch.
⑤—Turbocharged diesel engine.
⑥—Jet valve lash .010 inch hot.
⑦—Inspect jet valve face and body for seizure and damage. If defective, replace jet valve and body as an assembly.
⑧—These engines are equipped with automatic lash adjusters on the intake and exhaust valves. No adjustments provided.
⑨—Exc. Conquest, 72 @ 1.591; Conquest, 62 @ 1.591.
⑩—Installed height: Conquest, 1.6299 inches; Ram 50 & Raider, 1.591 inches. Spring Pressure: Conquest, 72 lbs. @ 1.6299 inches; Ram 50 & Raider, 72 lbs. @ 1.591 inches.

Pistons, Pins, Rings, Crankshaft & Bearings

Year	Engine	Piston Clearance Top of Skirt	Ring End Gap①		Wrist Pin Diameter	Rod Bearings		Main Bearings			
			Comp.	Oil		Shaft Diameter	Bearing Clearance	Shaft Diameter	Bearing Clearance	Thrust on Bear. No.	Shaft Endplay
1983	1400	.0008–.0016	.008	.008	⑥	1.6535	.0004–.0024	1.8898	.0008–.0028	3	.002–.007
	1600	.0008–.0016	.008	.008	⑥	1.7717	.0004–.0024	2.2441	.0008–.0028	3	.002–.007
	2000	.0008–.0016	②	.008	⑥	1.772	.0008–.0020	2.244	.0008–.0020	3	.002–.007
	2300⑤	.0016–.0024	.010	.010	1.425	2.087	.0008–.0024	2.5980	.0008–.0020	3	.0008–.0020
	2600③	.0008–.0016	.010	.0078	⑥	2.0866	.0008–.0028	2.3622	.0008–.0028	3	.002–.007
	2600④	.0008–.0016	.010	.008	⑥	2.0866	.0008–.0028	2.5984	.0008–.0028	3	.002–.007
1984	1400	.008–.0016	.008	.008	⑥	1.6535	.0004–.0024	1.8898	.0008–.0028	3	.002–.007
	1600⑩	.0008–.0016	.008	.008	⑥	1.7717	.0004–.0024	2.2441	.0008–.0028	3	.002–.007
	1600⑧	.0008–.0016	②	.008	⑥	1.7717	.0004–.0024	2.2441	.0008–.0028	3	.002–.007
	2000	.0008–.0016	②	.008	⑥	1.772	.0008–.0020	2.244	.0008–.0020	3	.002–.007
	2300⑤	.0016–.0024	.010	.010	1.425	2.087	.0008–.0024	2.598	.0008–.0020	3	.0008–.0020
	2600	.0008–.0016	⑨	.012	⑥	2.087	.0008–.0024	2.362	.0008–.0020	3	.0020–.0071
1985	1500	.0008–.0016	.008	.008	⑥	1.6535	.0004–.0024	1.8898	.0008–.0028	3	.002–.007
	1600	.0008–.0016	⑪	⑪	⑥	1.7717	.0004–.0024	2.2441	.0008–.0028	3	.002–.007
	2000	.0008–.0016	②	.008	⑥	1.772	.0008–.0020	2.244	.0008–.0020	3	.002–.007
	2300⑤	.0016–.0024	.010	.010	1.425	2.087	.0008–.0024	2.598	.0008–.0020	3	.0008–.0020
	2600	.0008–.0016	⑨	.012	⑥	2.087	.0008–.0024	2.362	.0008–.0020	3	.002–.007
1986	1500	.0008–.0016	.008	.008	⑥	1.6535	.0004–.0024	1.8898	.0008–.0028	3	.002–.007
	1600	.0008–.0016	②	.008	⑥	1.7717	.0004–.0024	2.2441	.0008–.0028	3	.002–.007
	2000	.0008–.0016	②	.008	⑥	1.772	.0008–.0020	2.244	.0008–.0020	3	.002–.007
	2600	.0008–.0016	⑨	.012	⑥	2.087	.0008–.0024	2.362	.0008–.0020	3	.002–.007

PISTONS, PINS, RINGS, CRANKSHAFT & BEARINGS—Continued

Year	Engine	Piston Clearance Top of Skirt	Ring End Gap ①		Wrist Pin Diameter	Rod Bearings		Main Bearings			
			Comp.	Oil		Shaft Diameter	Bearing Clearance	Shaft Diameter	Bearing Clearance	Thrust on Bear. No.	Shaft Endplay
1987	1500	.0008-.0016	.008	.008	⑥	1.6535	.0008-.0024	1.8898	.0008-.0028	3	.002-.007
	1600	.0012-.0019	②	.008	⑥	1.7717	.0008-.0019	2.2441	.0008-.0019	3	.002-.007
	2000	.0004-.0012	②	.008	⑥	1.772	⑦	2.244	.0008-.0020	3	.002-.007
	2600	.0008-.0016	⑨	.012	⑥	2.087	.0008-.0024	2.362	.0008-.0020	3	.002-.007

①—Fit rings in tapered bores for clearance listed in tightest portion of ring travel.
②—Top ring, .010; 2nd ring, .008.
③—Arrow Pickup, D-50 & Ram 50.
④—Except Arrow Pickup, D-50 & Ram 50.
⑤—Turbocharged diesel engine.
⑥—Wrist pins are full floating in pistons and press fit into rods. Pressure required to install pins is 1102 to 3306 lbs. on 1400, 1500 and 1600 models or 1653 to 3858 lbs. on 2000 and 2600 models.
⑦—Colt Vista, .0006-.0020 inch; Ram 50, .0008-.020 inch.
⑧—Turbocharged.
⑨—Top ring, .011; 2nd ring, .010.
⑩—Exc. turbocharged.
⑪—Man. Trans. models: Top ring, .010; 2nd ring, .008. Auto. Trans. models: Top ring, .008; 2nd ring, .008.

Engine Tightening Specifications

*Torque specifications are for clean and lightly lubricated threads only. Dry or dirty threads produce increased friction which prevents accurate measurement of tightness.

Year	Engine	Spark Plugs Ft. Lbs.	Cylinder Head Bolts Ft. Lbs.	Intake Manifold Ft. Lbs.	Exhaust Manifold Ft. Lbs.	Camshaft Bearing Caps Ft. Lbs.	Camshaft Sprocket Bolts Ft. Lbs.	Rocker Arm Nuts Ft. Lbs.	Rocker Arm Cover Ft. Lbs.	Connecting Rod Cap Nuts Ft. Lbs.	Main Bearing Cap Bolts Ft. Lbs.	Flywheel To Crankshaft Ft. Lbs.	Vibration Damper or Pulley Ft. Lbs.
1983-84	1400	15-21	51-54③	11-14	11-14	—	47-54	⑤	1-1.5	24-25	37-39	94-101	7.5-8.5
1983-85	1600	15-21	51-54③	11-14	11-14	14-15	44-57	—	4-5	24-25	37-39	94-101	7.5-8.5
	2000	15-21	65-72③	11-14	11-14	14-15	59-72	—	4-5	33-34	37-39	94-101	11-15
	2300①	—	76-83③	11-14	11-14	14-15	47-54	④	4-5	33-34	55-61	94-101	123-137
	2600	15-21	②③	11-14	11-14	14-15	37-43	—	4-5	33-34	55-61	94-101	80-94
1985	1500	15-21	51-54③	11-14	11-14	—	47-54	⑤	1-1.5	24-25	37-39	94-101	7.5-8.5
1986	1500	15-21	51-54③	11-14	11-14	—	47-54	⑤	1-1.5	24-25	37-39	94-101	51-72
	1600	15-21	51-54③	11-14	11-14	14-15	59-72	—	4-5	24-25	37-39	94-101	11-13
	2000	15-21	65-72③	11-14	11-14	14-15	59-72	—	4-5	37-39	37-39	94-101	80-94
	2600	15-21	②③	11-14	11-14	14-15	37-43	—	4-5	33-34	55-61	94-101	80-94
1987	1500	15-21	51-54③	11-14	11-14	—	47-54	⑤	1-1.5	24-25	37-39	94-101	51-72
	1600	15-21	51-54③	11-14	18-22	14-15	59-72	—	4-5	24-25	37-39	94-101	11-13
	2000	15-21	65-72③	11-14	11-14	⑥	58-72	—	4-5	37-39	37-39	94-101	80-94
	2600	15-21	②③	11-14	11-14	14-15	37-43	—	4-5	33-34	55-61	94-101	80-94

①—Turbocharged diesel engine.
②—Bolts 1 thru 10, 65-72 ft. lbs.; Bolt No.11, 11-15 ft. lbs.
③—Engine cold.
④—Rocker arm shaft mounting bolts, 25-28 ft. lbs.
⑤—Rocker arm shaft mounting bolts, 15-19 ft. lbs.
⑥—Colt Vista, 14-20 ft. lbs. Ram 50: 8 25 mm bolts, 15-19 ft. lbs.; 8 65 mm bolts, 14-15 ft. lbs.

Brake Specifications

Year	Model	Drum Brake I.D.	Wheel Cylinder Bore			Master Cylinder Bore	Disc Brake Rotor				
			Front Disc	Rear Disc	Rear Drum		Nominal Thickness Front	Nominal Thickness Rear	Min. Thickness Front	Min. Thickness Rear	Runout (T.I.R.)
1983	Colt	7	2.010	—	.75	.8125	.51	—	.45	—	.006
	Challenger, Sapporo⑤	9	2.12	—	.81	.875	.49	—	.43	—	.006
	Challenger, Sapporo⑥	—	2.12	1.50	—	.875	.49	.39	.43	.33	.006
	Ram 50①	9.5	2.125	—	.75	.875	.79	—	.72	—	.006
	Ram 50②	10	2.125	—	.8125	.875	.79	—	.72	—	.006
1984	Colt③	7	2.01	—	.75	.8175	.51	—	.45	—	.006
	Colt④	7	2.01	—	.75	.875	.70	—	.64	—	.006
	Colt Vista	8	2.12	—	.81	.87	.71	—	.65	—	.006
	Conquest	—	2.25	1.63	—	.94	—	—	.88	.65	.006
	Ram 50⑦	10	2.125	—	.8125	.875	.79	—	.72	—	.006
	Ram 50⑧	9.5	2.125	—	.75	.875	.79	—	.72	—	.006
1985–86	Ram 50⑦	10	2.125	—	.81	.875	.79	—	.72	—	.006
	Ram 50⑧	9.5	2.125	—	.75	.875	.79	—	.72	—	.006
1985–87	Colt③	7	2.01	—	.75	.81	.51	—	.45	—	.006
	Colt④	7	2.12	—	.75	.87	.71	—	.65	—	.006
	Colt Vista④	8	2.12	—	.81	.87	.71	—	.65	—	.006
	Colt Vista⑦	9	2.12	—	.75	.87	.94	—	.88	—	.004
	Conquest	—	2.25	1.63	—	.94	.94	.71	.88	.65	.006
1987	Ram 50⑦	10.0	2.25	—	.875	.93	—	—	.803	—	.006
	Ram 50⑧	10.0	2.25	—	.93	.875	—	—	.803	—	.006
	Ram Raider	10.0	2.125	—	.8125	.875	.79	—	.724	—	.006

①—Except Ram 50 with diesel engine & four wheel drive.
②—With diesel engine & four wheel drive.
③—Exc. turbocharged.
④—Turbocharged.
⑤—Models less 4 wheel disc brakes.
⑥—Models w/4 wheel disc brakes.
⑦—4 wheel drive models.
⑧—Models less 4 wheel drive.

Drive Axle Specifications

Year	Model	Carrier Type	Ring Gear & Pinion Backlash		Pinion Bearing Preload			Differential Bearing Preload	
			Method	Adjustment	Method	With Seal Inch Lbs.	Less Seal Inch Lbs.	Method	Adjustment
1983	Challenger, Sapporo	Removable	④	.004–.006	Shim	10–16	7–13	④	—
	Ram 50②	Removable	④	.005–.007	Shim	9–11	6–9	④	—
	Ram 50③	Integral	Shim	.005–.007	Shim	9–11	6–9	Shim	①
1984	Conquest	Removable	Shim	.004–.006	Shim	9–11	6–9	Shim	①
1984–85	Ram 50②	Removable	④	.005–.006	Shim	9–11	6–9	④	⑤
	Ram 50③	Integral	Shim	.005–.007	Shim	9–11	6–9	Shim	①
1985–87	Colt Vista 4 X 4②	Integral	Shim	.004–.006	Shim	8.6–11.3	6.1–8.6	Shim	①
	Conquest⑥	Removable	Shim	.004–.006	Shim	3–4	1.3–2.2	Shim	①
	Conquest⑦	Removable	Shim	.005–.007	Shim	3.5–4.3	1.3–2.2	Shim	①
1986–87	Ram 50②	Removable	④	.0043–.0063	Shim	5.6—-6.5	3.5–4.3	④	⑤
	Ram 50③	Removable	Shim	.004–.006	Shim	5.2-6.13	3.9-4.3	Shim	①
1987	Ram Raider②	Removable	④	.0043–.0063	Shim	5.6–6.5	3.5–4.3	④	⑤
	Ram Raider③	Removable	Shim	.0043–.0063	Shim	5.2–6.1	3.5–4.3	Shim	①

①—Zero clearance plus .002 inch installed on both sides of differential case.
②—Rear axle.
③—Four wheel drive front axle.
④—Threaded adjusters.
⑤—Tighten each adjuster one-half the distance between the centerlines of the lock plate holes.
⑥—Less limited slip differential.
⑦—With limited slip differential.

Wheel Alignment Specifications

Year	Model	Caster Angle, Degrees		Camber Angle, Degrees				Toe-In	
				Front		Rear			
		Limits	Desired	Limits	Desired	Limits	Desired	Front	Rear
1983	Colt	+1/2 to +1 1/6	+5/6	0 to +1	+1/2	—	—	①	—
	Challenger, Sapporo	+2 1/6 to +3 1/6	+2 2/3	+2/3 to +1 2/3	+1 1/6	—	—	0-.28	—
	Ram 50②	+1 1/2 to +3 1/2	+2 1/2	+1/2 to +1 1/2	+1	—	—	.08-.35	—
1983–86	Ram 50③	+1 to +3	+2	+1/2 to +1 1/2	+1	—	—	.08-.35	—
1984	Colt	+1/2 to +1 1/6	+5/6	0 to 1	+1/2	—	—	①	—
	Colt Vista	+3/10 to +1 3/10	+4/5	−1/12 to +11/12	5/12	—2-3°	0	−④	
	Conquest	—	+5 1/3	—	0	—	−1/3	0	−.08 to +.08
	Ram 50②	+1 1/2 to +3 1/2	+2 1/2	+1/2 to +1 1/2	+1	—	—	.08 to .35	—
1985	Colt	+13/60 to +1 13/60	+43/60	−1/2 to +1/2	0	—	−2/3	④	—
	Colt Vista⑤	+3/10 to +1 3/10	+4/5	−1/12 to +1/12	+5/12	−1 1/10 to 0	−5/12	④	—
	Colt Vista⑥	+3/10 to +1 3/10	+4/5	+2/6 to +1 1/3	+5/6	—	0	④	0
	Conquest	—	+5 1/3	—	0	—	0	0	−.08 to +.08
	Ram 50②	+1 1/2 to +3 1/2	+2 1/2	+1/2 to +1 1/2	+1	—	—	.08 to .35	—
1986	Colt	+13/60 to +1 13/60	+43/60	−1/2 to +1/2	0	—	−2-3	④	0
	Colt Vista⑤	+3/10 to +1 3/10	+4/5	−1/12 to +1/12	+5/12	—	−2/3	④	0
	Colt Vista⑥	+3/10 to +1 3/10	+4/5	+2/6 to +1 1/3	+5/6	—	0	④	0
	Conquest	—	+5 5/6	—	−1/2	—	0	0	−.08 to +.08
	Ram 50②	+1 1/2 to +3 1/2	+2 1/2	+1/2 to +1 1/2	+1	—	—	.08 to .35	—
1987	Colt	⑦	⑦	−1/2 to +1/2	0	—	−2/3	④	0
	Colt Vista⑤	+3/10 to +1 3/10	+4/5	−1/12 to +1 1/12	+5/12	—	−2/3	⑧	0
	Colt Vista⑥	+1/3 to +1 1/3	+5/6	+11/30 to +1 1/30	+13/15	—	0	⑨	0
	Conquest	—	+5 5/6	—	−1/2	—	0	0	−.08 to +.08
	Ram 50②	+2 to +4	+3	+1/10 to +1 1/10	+2/3	—	—	⑩	—
	Ram 50③	+1 to +3	+2	+1/2 to +1 1/2	+1	—	—	⑩5	—
	Ram Raider②	+3/10 to +1 3/10	+4/5	−1/12 to +1 1/12	+5/12	—	+2/3	⑧	0
	Ram Raider③	+1/3 to +1 1/3	+5/6	+11/30 to +1 1/30	+13/15	—	0	⑨	0

①—.16 inch in to .08 inch out.
②—Except 4 wheel drive.
③—4 wheel drive only.
④—.12 inch toe in to .12 inch toe-out.
⑤—2 wheel drive.
⑥—4 wheel drive.
⑦—Limits: less power steering, +1/2° to +1 1/2°; w/power steering, +2°10' to +2°10'. Desired: less power steering, +1°; w/power steering, +1°40'.
⑧—At center of tread, .12 inch toe-out to .12 inch toe-in; At rim of disc wheel, .06 inch toe-out to .06 inch toe-in.
⑨—At center of tread, .12 inch toe-out to .12 inch toe-in; At rim of disc wheel, .07 inch toe-out to .07 inch toe-in.
⑩—At center of tread, .08 to .35 inch; at rim of disc wheel, .04 to .18 inch.

Cooling System & Capacity Data

Year	Engine or Model	Cooling Capacity Qts.		Radiator Cap Relief Pressure Lbs.	Thermo. Opening Temp. °F.	Fuel Tank Gals.	Engine Oil Refill Qts.①	Transmission Oil			Rear Axle Oil Pints
		Less A/C	With A/C					4 Speed Pints	5 Speed Pints	Auto. Trans. Qts.②	
1983	1400 Colt Hatchback	4.7	4.7	13	190	10.6⑦	3.7	4.8	—	6	—
	1600 Colt Hatchback	4.7	4.7	13	190	10.6⑦	4.2	4.8	—	6	—
	2000 Ram 50④	9.5	9.5	13	190	15.1⑧	4.2	4.4	4.9	7.2	3.2
	2000 Ram 50③	9.5	9.5	13	190	18.0	5.2	4.6⑯	4.6⑯	7.2⑯	3.2⑰
	2300 Ram 50④	8.5	8.5	13	180	15.1⑧	5.0	4.4	4.9	7.2	3.2
	2300 Ram 50③	8.5	8.5	13	180	18.0	6.3	4.6⑯	4.6⑯	7.2⑯	3.2⑰
	2600 Challenger, Sapporo	9.7	9.7	13	190	15.8	4.5	—	4.8	7.2	2.7
	2600 Ram 50④	9.5	9.5	13	190	15.1⑧	5.2	4.4	4.9	7.2	3.2
	2600 Ram 50③	9.5	9.5	13	190	18.0	6.1	4.6⑯	4.6⑯	7.2⑯	3.2⑰

Continued

COOLING SYSTEM & CAPACITY DATA—Continued

Year	Engine or Model	Cooling Capacity Qts.		Radiator Cap Relief Pressure Lbs.	Thermo. Opening Temp. °F.	Fuel Tank Gals.	Engine Oil Refill Qts.①	Transmission Oil			Rear Axle Oil Pints
		Less A/C	With A/C					4 Speed Pints	5 Speed Pints	Auto. Trans. Qts.②	
1984	1400 Colt	5.0	5.0	13	190	10.6	3.7	4.8	—	6	—
	1600 Colt	5.0	5.0	13	190	10.6	4.2	4.8	—	6	—
	2000 Colt Vista	7.4	7.4	13	190	13.2	4.2	4.9	—	6.15	—
	2000 Ram 50④	9.5	9.5	13	190	15.1⑧	4.2	4.4	4.9	7.2	3.2
	2000 Ram 50③	9.5	9.5	13	190	18	5.2	4.6⑯	4.6⑯	7.2⑯	3.2⑰
	2300 Ram 50④	8.5	8.5	13	180	15.1⑧	5.9⑨	4.4	4.9	7.2	3.2
	2300 Ram 50③	8.5	8.5	13	180	18	6.4⑩	4.6⑯	4.6⑯	7.2⑯	3.2⑰
	2600 Conquest	9.7	9.7	13	190	19.8	4.5	—	2.4	7.4	—
	2600 Ram 50④	9.5	9.5	13	190	15.1⑧	5.2	4.4	4.9	7.2	3.2
	2600 Ram 50③	9.5	9.5	13	190	18	6.1	4.4⑯	4.9⑯	7.2⑯	3.2⑰
1985	Colt⑪	5.3	5.3	13	190	11.9	3.2	4.4	4.4	6.1	—
	Colt⑫	5.3	5.3	13	190	11.9	3.7⑬	—	4.8	6.1	—
	Colt Vista④	4.2	4.2	13	190	13.2	4.2	—	4.9	12.3	—
	Colt Vista③	4.2	4.2	13	190	14.5	4.2	—	4.4⑭	—	1.7
	Conquest	9.7	9.7	13	190	19.8	5.1	4.8	4.8	7.4	2.7
	2000 Ram 50	9.5	9.5	13	190	15.1⑧	4.2	4.4	4.9	7.2	3.2
	2300 Ram 50④	8.5	8.5	13	180	15.1⑧	5.9⑮	4.4	4.9	7.2	3.2
	2300 Ram 50③	8.5	8.5	13	180	18	6.4⑮	—	4.6⑯	7.2⑯	3.2⑰
	2600 Ram 50④	9.5	9.5	13	190	15.1⑧	5.2	4.4	4.9	7.2	3.2
	2600 Ram 50③	9.5	9.5	13	190	18	6.1	—	4.6⑯	7.2⑯	3.2⑰
1986	Colt⑪	5.3	5.3	13	190	11.9	3.7	4.4	4.4	6.1	—
	Colt⑫	5.3	5.3	13	190	11.9	4.5⑬	—	4.8	6.1	—
	Colt Vista④	7.4	7.4	13	190	13.2	4.2	—	4.9	12.3	—
	Colt Vista③	7.4	7.4	13	190	14.5	4.2	—	4.4⑭	—	1.7
	Conquest	9.7	9.7	13	190	19.8	5.1	—	4.8	7.4	2.7
	2000 Ram 50	9.5	9.5	13	190	15.1⑧	4.2	—	4.9	7.2	3.2
	2600 Ram 50④	9.5	9.5	13	190	15.1⑧	5.2	—	4.9	7.2	3.2
	2600 Ram 50③	9.5	9.5	13	190	18	6.1	—	4.6⑯	7.2⑯	3.2⑰
1987	Colt⑪	5.3	5.3	13	190	11.9	3.7	3.6	3.8	6.1	—
	Colt⑫	5.3	5.3	13	190	11.9	⑤	—	3.8	6.1	—
	Colt Vista④	7.4	7.4	13	190	13.2	4.2	—	5.3	6.1	—
	Colt Vista③	7.4	7.4	13	190	14.5	4.2	—	4.4⑭	—	1.5
	Conquest	9.2	9.2	13	190	19.8	5.0	—	4.8	7.4	2.7
	2000 Ram 50	7.4	7.4	13	190	⑥	4.2	—	4.9	6.3	2.7
	2600 Ram 50④	8.3	8.3	13	190	⑥	5.3	—	4.9	6.3	2.7
	2600 Ram 50③	8.3	8.3	13	190	⑱	6.1	—	4.7⑯	7.6⑯	⑲ ⑰
	Ram Raider	8.45	8.45	13	190	15.9	5.3	—	4.7	7.6	⑳

①—Includes filter.
②—Approximate, make final check with dipstick.
③—With four wheel drive.
④—Except four wheel drive.
⑤—Auto. trans. (w/oil cooler), 4.4 qts. Manual trans., 4.2 qts.
⑥—Standard body, 13.7 gals.; long body, 18.2 gals.
⑦—LS, RS & models w/optional fuel tank, 13.2 gals.
⑧—Models w/optional fuel tank, 18 gals.
⑨—California models, 6.3 qts.
⑩—California models, 6.8 qts.
⑪—Exc. Turbocharged.
⑫—Turbocharged.
⑬—Includes filter and oil cooler.
⑭—Transfer case, 1.5 pints.
⑮—Calif. models add .4 qt.
⑯—Transfer case, 4.6 pints.
⑰—Front axle, 2.3 pints.
⑱—Standard body, 15.7 gals.; long body, 19.8 gals.
⑲—Standard differential, 2.7 pts.; limited slip differential, 3.2 pts.
⑳—Rear axle: standard differential, 2.3 pts.; limited slip differential, 3.8 pts. 4 X 4 front axle, 2.3 pts.

LECTRICAL SECTION

INDEX

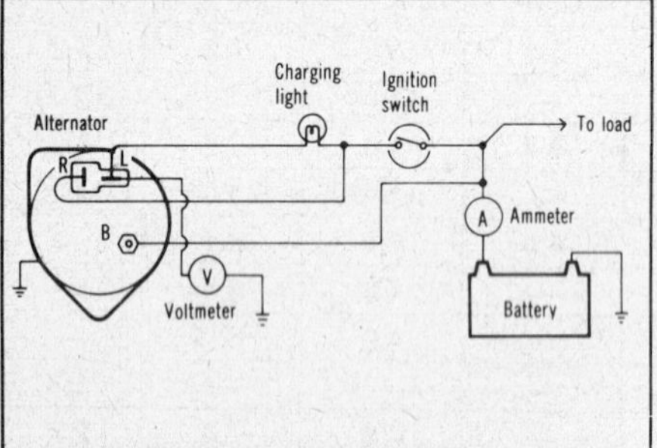

Fig. 1 Alternator charging voltage test connection

ALTERNATOR IN-VEHICLE TESTING

CHARGING VOLTAGE TEST

1. With ignition switch in the "Off" position, disconnect battery positive cable, then connect an ammeter between cable and battery positive post, **Fig. 1.**
2. Connect a voltmeter between alternator terminal L and ground. Ensure voltage reading is zero, **Fig. 1.** If a reading or needle deflection is indicated on the voltmeter, either the alternator or alternator wiring is defective.
3. Place ignition switch in the "On" position, then note voltmeter reading. Voltmeter should indicate a reading considerably less than battery voltage. If reading indicates battery voltage, the alternator may be defective.
4. Connect jumper cable between battery positive post and battery positive cable, then start engine. This will prevent starting current from being applied to ammeter.
5. Remove jumper cable connected between battery positive post and cable, then increase engine speed to 2000 to 3000 RPM and note ammeter reading. If reading is 5 amps or less, note voltage reading. If reading is above 5 amps, either continue to charge battery until reading drops to 5 amps or less or install a fully charged battery. The charging current may also be limited by installing a 1/4 ohm resistor in series with the battery.
6. Charging voltage should be as listed in the "Alternator and Regulator Specification Chart."

OUTPUT TEST

1. With ignition switch in the "Off" position, disconnect battery cables.
2. Disconnect wire from terminal B of alternator, then connect an ammeter between battery positive cable and alternator B terminal, **Fig. 2.**
3. Connect a voltmeter between B terminal and ground, **Fig. 2.**
4. Connect battery ground cable to battery ground post, then note voltmeter reading. The voltmeter should indicate battery voltage.
5. Connect a tachometer to engine, then start engine and turn on lights.
6. Operate engine at approximately 2500 RPM and note ammeter reading. After engine has been started, the ammeter reading will gradually decrease as the battery approaches a fully charged condition. Read the ammeter indication at its maximum value while increasing engine RPM. Refer to "Alternator and Regulator Specification Chart."

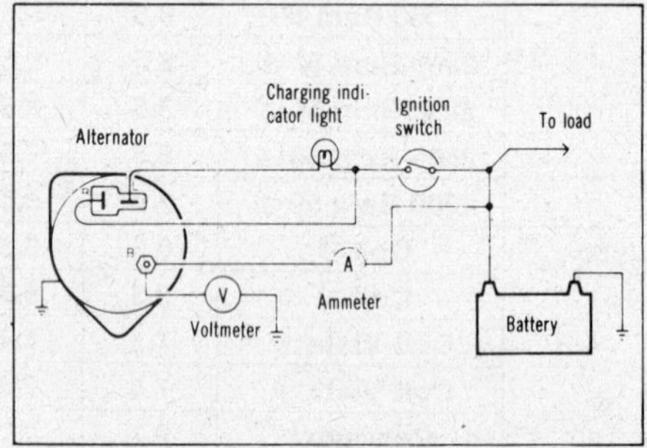

Fig. 2 Alternator output test connection

STARTER

REPLACE

1. Disconnect battery ground cable and remove air cleaner, as needed, to gain access to starter.
2. Disconnect starter wiring.
3. Remove starter mounting bolts, then the starter. On truck models, brake pipes, steering joint or A/C lines may prevent lifting starter from engine compartment. If so, remove splash shield and remove starter from under vehicle.
4. Before mounting starter, clean the mating surfaces of starter and the engine.
5. Install starter and tighten mounting bolts so the starter motor shaft is perfectly parallel with the central axis of the engine in all directions. Torque mounting bolts to 16-23 ft. lbs.
6. Connect starter wiring and battery ground cable.

IGNITION SWITCH

REPLACE

The ignition switch is mounted in the rear of the steering column lock. When the key is turned to "LOCK" position and pulled out, the lock pin automatically ejects from the cylinder and enters a groove in the steering shaft, locking the steering wheel.

The heads of the bolts securing the steering lock assembly shear off when the bolts are tightened. Replacement of the steering lock assembly may require that the steering column be removed, as these

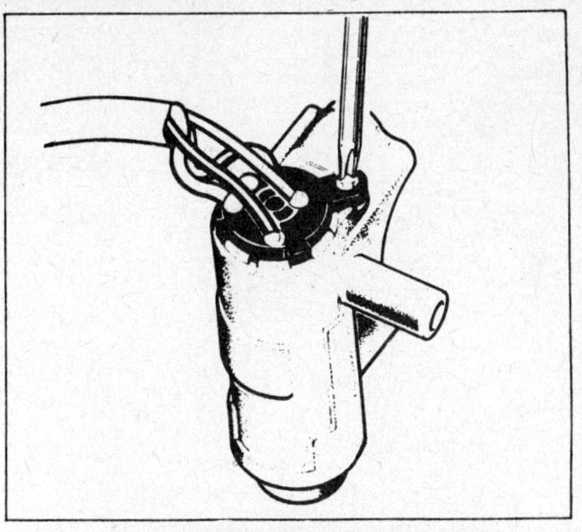

Fig. 3 Ignition switch removal

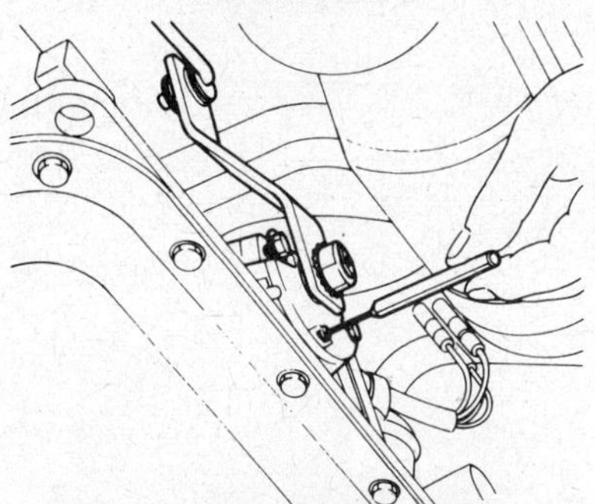

Fig. 6 Neutral safety switch adjustment. Conquest

bolts must be cut or slotted to permit removal with a screwdriver. When the lock assembly is installed, new shear bolts must be used and the bolts should be tightened until the bolt heads twist off.

However, the ignition switch can be serviced separately from the lock assembly using the following procedures.

EXC. CHALLENGER & SAPPORO

1. Disconnect battery ground cable, then remove upper and lower column covers.
2. Remove bands securing switch harness and disconnect electrical connector.
3. Loosen the bolt holding the switch, **Fig. 3,** and pull from lock assembly.
4. Reverse procedure to install, first inserting key to check for proper operation.

CHALLENGER & SAPPORO

1. Disconnect battery ground cable, then remove steering wheel using suitable puller. **Mark position of steering wheel prior to removal to ensure proper assembly.**
2. Place tilt handle in its lowest position, then remove steering column cover.
3. Remove ignition switch attaching screws, then the switch.
4. Remove key reminder switch attaching screws, then the switch.
5. Reverse procedure to install. When installing ignition switch, position switch wiring along column tube as close to the center of the steering column as possible.

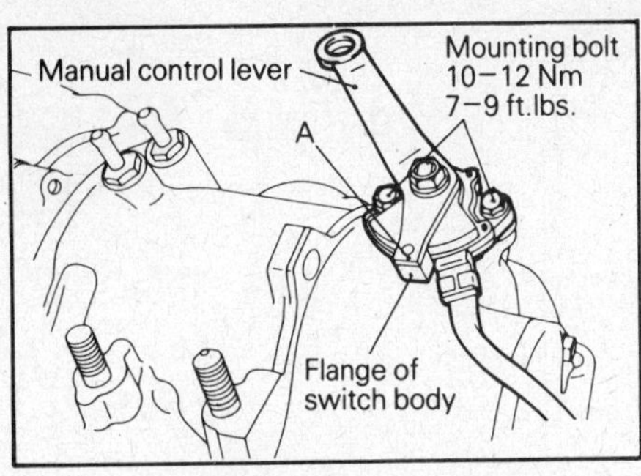

Fig. 4 Adjusting stop lamp switch clearance

LIGHT SWITCH REPLACE

EXC. 1985–87 COLT

On models equipped with dash mounted light switch, the switch is serviced with the instrument cluster. Refer to "Instrument Cluster, Replace" procedure.

On models equipped with turn signal mounted light switch, the switch is serviced with the turn signal/combination switch. Refer to "Turn Signal/Combination Switch, Replace" for procedure.

1985–87 COLT

1. Disconnect battery ground cable and remove lower steering column cover.
2. Remove strap securing switch harness to column, then disconnect light switch and wiper switch electrical connectors.
3. Remove upper steering column cover, place light switch in the Off position, then pull off switch knob.
4. Straighten switch claws, then remove switch from cover.
5. Reverse procedure to install.

STOP LAMP SWITCH REPLACE

The stop light switch also serves as a brake pedal stopper and is located under the instrument panel, behind the brake pedal. Disconnect the wire, then remove retaining nut from bracket and the switch. Reverse procedure to install. Ensure brake pedal height is correct, then adjust switch to obtain a clearance of .02 to .04 inch between switch housing and pedal stopper with pedal released, **Fig. 4.**

NEUTRAL SAFETY SWITCH REPLACE

COLT & COLT VISTA

1. Place selector lever in neutral position.
2. Hold transaxle shift lever and remove retaining nut, then remove manual lever.
3. Disconnect switch electrical connector and remove retaining screws, then remove switch from transaxle.

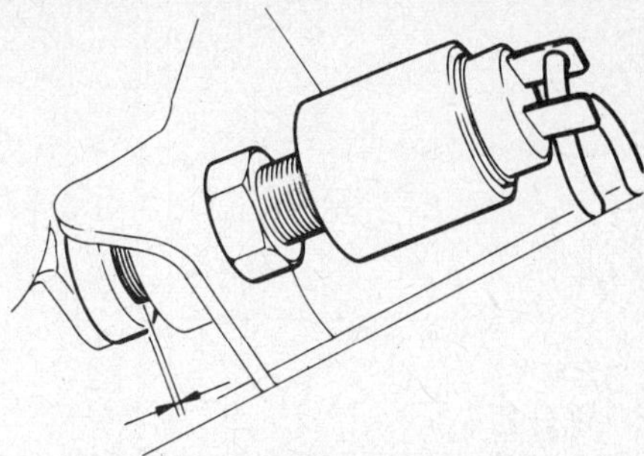

Fig. 5 Neutral safety switch adjustment. Colt & Colt Vista

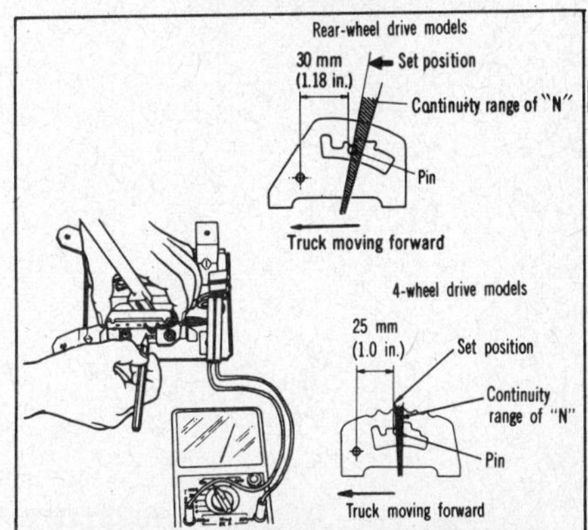

Fig. 7 Positioning selector lever for neutral safety switch installation. Challenger, Ram Raider, Sapporo & 1983–86 Ram 50

4. Install replacement switch over selector shaft, loosely install retaining screws and connect electrical connector.
5. Install manual lever and torque retaining nut to 13-15 ft. lbs., then adjust switch as follows:
   a. Ensure shift linkage is properly adjusted and transaxle lever is in neutral position.
   b. Rotate switch body until .472 inch wide end of manual lever (A) overlaps switch body as shown in **Fig. 5.**
   c. Hold switch in this position and torque retaining screws to 7-9 ft. lbs.
   d. Check operation of selector and switch, and ensure that starter only engages with selector in park or neutral.

CONQUEST

1. Place selector lever in neutral position, then raise and support vehicle.
2. Hold transmission selector lever and remove retaining nut, then remove manual lever.
3. Disconnect switch electrical connector and remove retaining screws, then remove switch from transmission.
4. Install replacement switch over selector shaft, loosely install retaining screws and connect electrical connector.
5. Install manual lever and torque retaining nut to 22-29 ft. lbs., then adjust switch as follows:

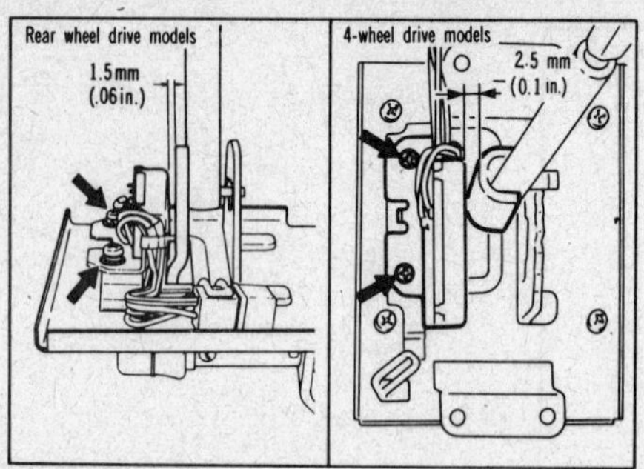

Fig. 8 Neutral safety switch clearance. Challenger, Ram Raider, Sapporo & 1983–86 Ram 50

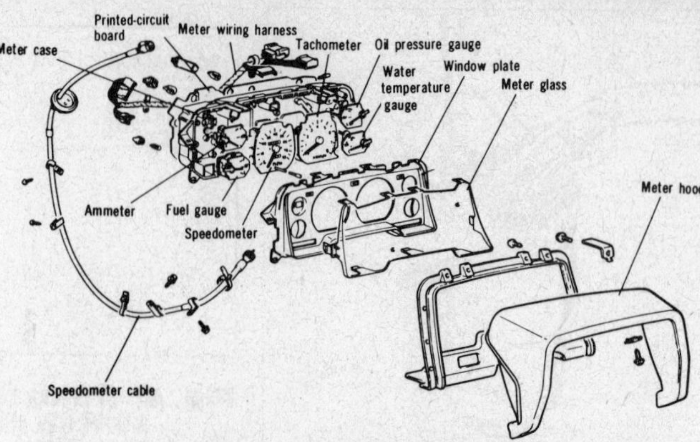

Fig. 9 Analog instrument cluster. Challenger & Sapporo

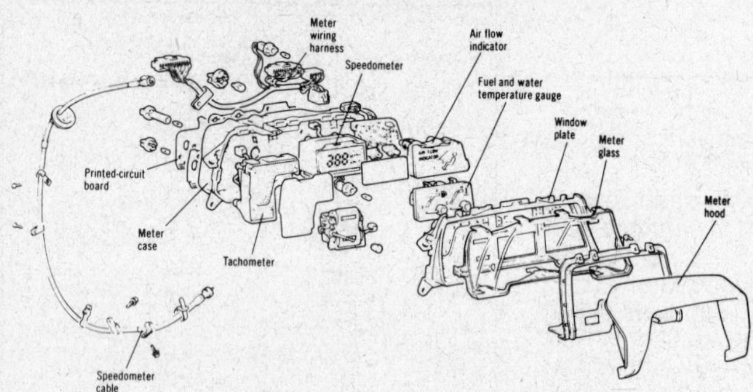
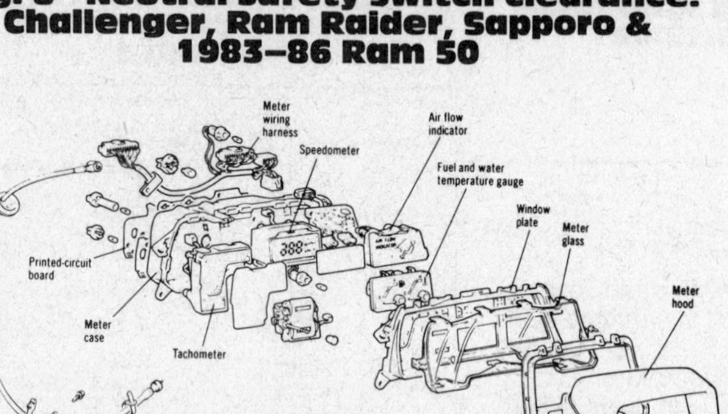

Fig. 10 Digital instrument cluster. Challenger & Sapporo

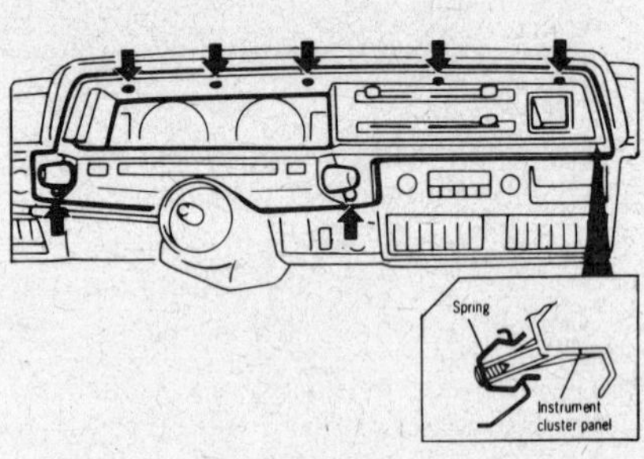

Fig. 11 Instrument cluster bezel removal. 1983–84 Colt Hatchback

a. Ensure shift linkage is properly adjusted and transaxle lever is in neutral (vertical) position, then remove screw from screw from switch alignment hole, **Fig. 6.**
b. Rotate switch body until .079 inch gauge rod can be inserted through alignment hole and switch rotor, then torque switch retaining screws to 4-5 ft. lbs.
c. Remove gauge pin and install screw, lower vehicle, then ensure that starter only engages with selector lever in park or neutral.

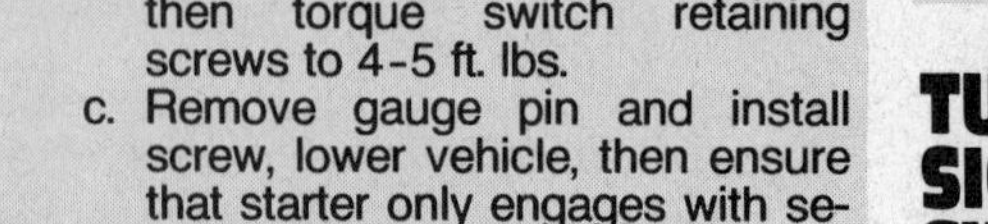

CHALLENGER, RAM RAIDER, SAPPORO & 1983–86 RAM 50

1. Loosen shift lever handle setscrew, then remove shift lever handle.
2. Remove shift position indicator attaching screws, then the position indicator by lifting upward.
3. Disconnect shift position indicator light from indicator assembly, then the neutral safety switch wiring.
4. Loosen neutral safety switch adjustment screws, then remove attaching screws and switch.
5. Reverse procedures to install, noting the following:
   a. Position selector lever as shown in **Fig. 7,** install switch on selector lever bracket leaving screws loose, then connect suitable ohmmeter to switch terminals.
   b. Move switch forward and backward through range of adjustment noting meter indication, and scribe alignment mark between switch and bracket in position where continuity is first indicated.
   c. Set clearance between switch and selector to .06 inch for 2 wheel drive models or .1 inch for 4 wheel drive models, ensure scribed marks are aligned, then tighten switch mounting screws.

TURN SIGNAL/COMBINATION SWITCH REPLACE

1. Disconnect battery ground cable.
2. Remove steering wheel using a suitable puller. Scribe alignment mark between steering wheel and shaft to ensure proper installation. On models with tilt steering columns, place column in lowest position during steering wheel removal.
3. Remove upper and lower steering column covers.
4. Remove wiring harness retaining straps, if equipped, then disconnect electrical connectors.
5. Remove column switch assembly.
6. Reverse procedure to install, noting the following:
   a. Ensure column switch is properly aligned with steering shaft center.
   b. Attach switch wiring along column tube as close to centerline as possible.
   c. Retain wiring using suitable retaining straps to prevent contact with other parts.

INSTRUMENT CLUSTER REPLACE

CHALLENGER & SAPPORO

1. Disconnect battery ground cable.
2. Remove four cluster bezel attaching screws, then the bezel, **Figs. 9 and 10.**
3. Remove two instrument cluster mounting nuts and screws.
4. Pull cluster slightly outward, then disconnect speedometer cable and all wire connectors. Remove cluster from panel.
5. Reverse procedure to install.

COLT

1983–84

1. Disconnect battery ground cable.
2. Remove steering wheel using a suitable puller.
3. Remove instrument cluster attaching screws, **Fig. 11,** then disconnect electrical connectors for light switch, wiper switch, clock and indicator lights.
4. Remove cluster panel, then the combination meter attaching screws.
5. Pull combination meter slightly outward, then disconnect speedometer cable and wire connectors.
6. Remove combination meter from vehicle, **Fig. 12.**
7. Reverse procedure to install.

1985–87

1. Disconnect battery ground cable.

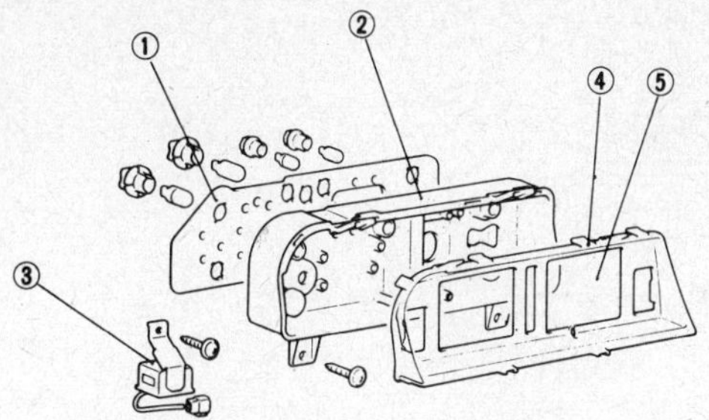

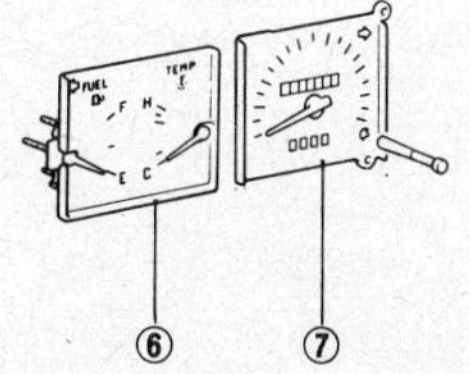

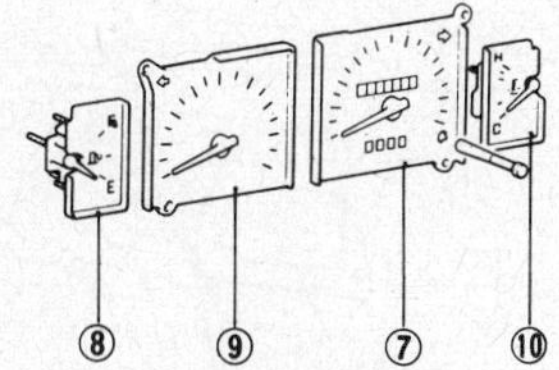

(1) Printed circuit board
(2) Meter case
(3) Buzzer
(4) Meter panel
(5) Meter glass
(6) Fuel and water temperature gauge (combination gauge)
(7) Speedometer
(8) Fuel gauge
(9) Tachometer
(10) Water temperature gauge

Fig. 12 Instrument cluster. 1983–84 Colt Hatchback

2. Remove steering column lower cover, then remove upper cover and position aside, leaving switches connected.
3. Remove 2 retaining screws from bottom of cluster bezel, release upper retaining clips and remove cluster bezel.
4. Remove instrument cluster attaching screws, then tilt cluster outwards and disconnect speedometer cable and electrical connectors, **Figs. 13 and 14.**
5. Remove instrument cluster.
6. Reverse procedure to install.

COLT VISTA

1. Disconnect battery ground cable and remove steering wheel using a suitable puller. Mark position of steering wheel and shaft to ensure proper assembly.
2. On 1984-86 models, remove ashtray.
3. On all models, remove cluster bezel cover using a suitable tool, then remove bezel attaching screws, **Fig. 15.**
4. Pull bezel outward slightly, then disconnect electrical connectors and remove bezel.
5. Remove instrument cluster retaining screws and pull cluster away from instrument panel.
6. Disconnect speedometer cable and electrical connectors, then remove instrument cluster.
7. Reverse procedure to install.

CONQUEST

1. Disconnect battery ground cable.
2. Remove instrument cluster bezel attaching screws, **Fig. 16.**
3. While pulling both edges at lower side of bezel outward, lift bezel upward and out.
4. Remove instrument cluster upper attaching nuts, then the lower attaching screws.
5. Pull lower part of case slightly outward, then disconnect speedometer cable.
6. Disconnect electrical connectors, then the wiring harness at body side of panel.
7. Remove instrument cluster from vehicle.
8. Reverse procedure to install.

RAM 50

1983–86

1. Disconnect battery ground cable.

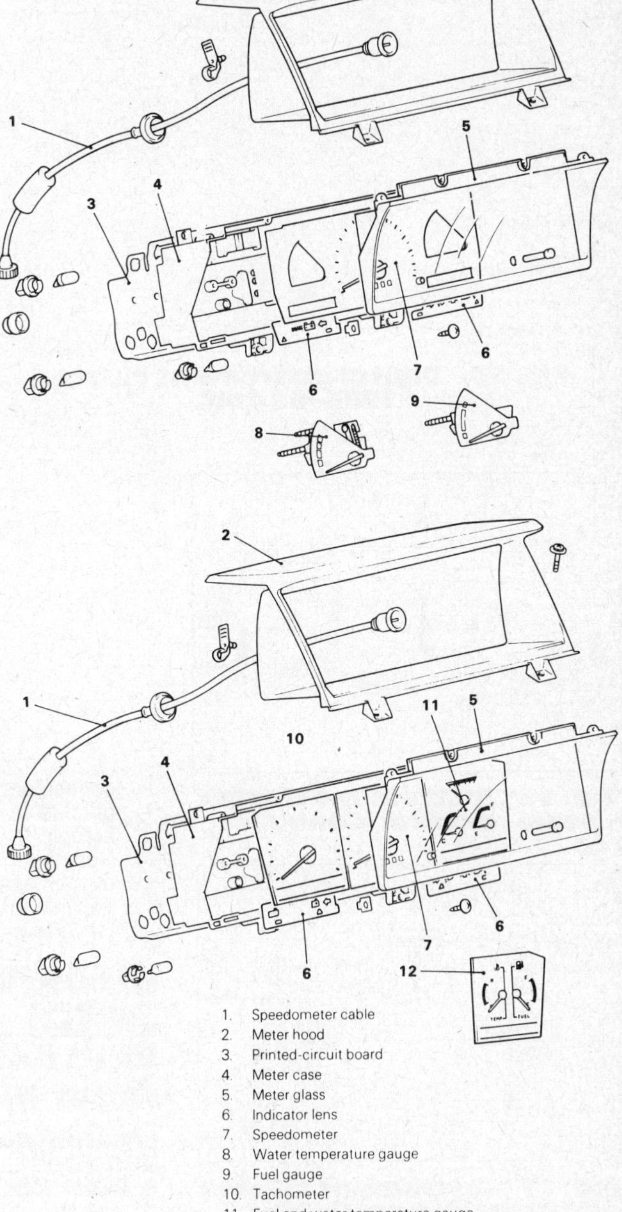

1. Speedometer cable
2. Meter hood
3. Printed-circuit board
4. Meter case
5. Meter glass
6. Indicator lens
7. Speedometer
8. Water temperature gauge
9. Fuel gauge
10. Tachometer
11. Fuel and water temperature gauge, and boost meter (combination meter)
12. Fuel and water temperature gauge (combination meter)

Fig. 13 Analog instrument cluster. 1985–87 Colt

2. Pull off radio and heater control knobs.
3. Remove adjusting nuts from radio and heater control stalks.
4. Remove ashtray, then the ashtray bracket.
5. Remove two cluster to dashboard attaching screws, then draw out cluster panel from lower left corner.
6. Disconnect cluster wiring and speedometer cable, then remove cluster.
7. Reverse procedure to install.

1987

1. Pry hazard warning switch or switch opening plug from cluster bezel.

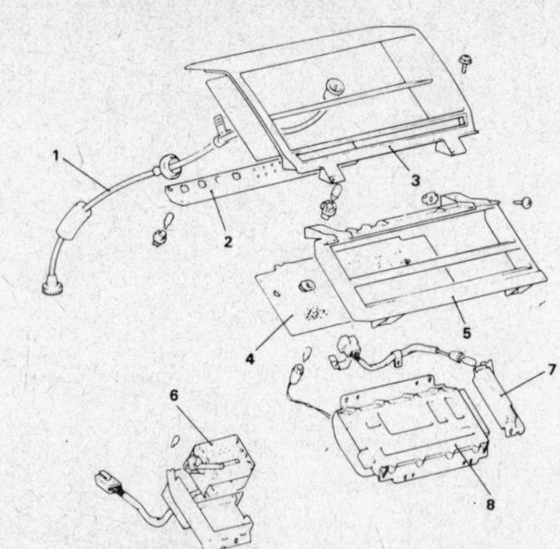

1. Speedometer cable
2. Printed film
3. Meter hood
4. Meter panel
5. Frame
6. Odometer
7. Light case
8. Liquid crystal display unit

Fig. 14 Digital instrument cluster. 1985–86 Colt

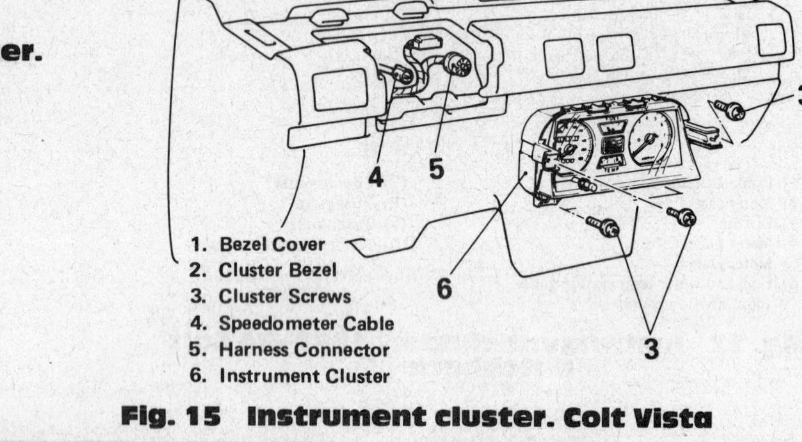

Fig. 15 Instrument cluster. Colt Vista

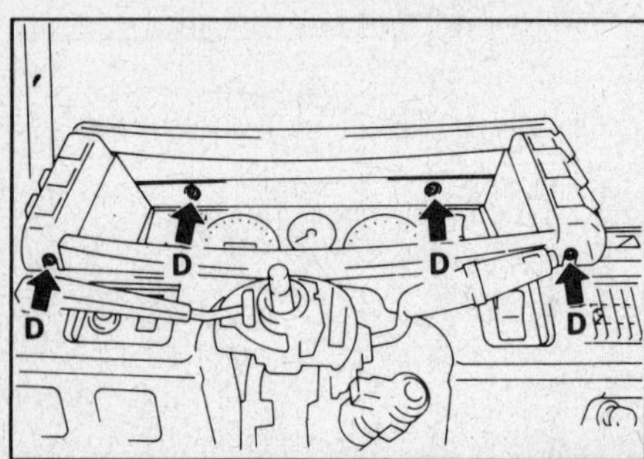

Fig. 16 Instrument cluster bezel removal. Conquest

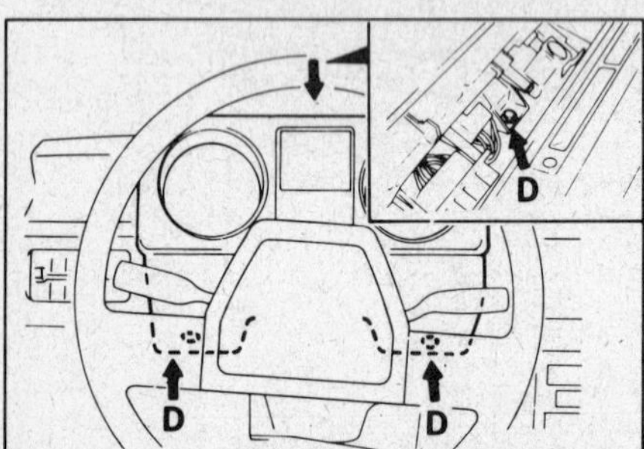

Fig. 17 Instrument cluster removal. Ram Raider

2. Position tilt wheel at lowest position, remove 4 cluster bezel retaining screws and the bezel.
3. Remove cluster retaining screws and pull cluster away from dash.
4. Disconnect electrical connectors and speedometer cable, pressing stopper on cable side of connection to disconnect cable, then remove cluster.
5. Reverse procedure to install.

RAM RAIDER

1. Place rag over joint between top of cluster cover and instrument panel, then pry cover away from panel with screwdriver.
2. Remove 2 screws from top and 1 screw from top of cluster, **Fig. 17**, then pull cluster away from dash.
3. Disconnect speedometer cable, cluster electrical connectors and electrical connectors from switches at bottom of cluster, then remove cluster assembly.
4. Remove individual components from cluster assembly as needed, noting position for installation.
5. Reverse procedure to install.

WINDSHIELD WIPER SWITCH

REPLACE

FRONT WIPER

Challenger, Colt Vista, Conquest, Sapporo, Ram 50 & Ram Raider

The windshield wiper switch is incorporated in the turn signal switch. Refer to "Turn Signal/Combination Switch, Replace."

1983–84 Colt Hatchback

1. Disconnect battery ground cable.
2. Remove instrument cluster panel as previously described.
3. Pull wiper switch outward, then remove wiper switch knob.
4. Remove attaching screws from wiper switch and electrical connector, then the switch from panel.
5. Reverse procedure to install.

1985–87 Colt

1. Disconnect battery ground cable and remove lower steering column cover.
2. Remove strap securing switch harness to column, then disconnect light switch and wiper switch electrical connectors.
3. Remove upper steering column cover, place wiper switch in the Off position, then pull off switch knob.
4. Straighten switch claws, then remove switch from cover.
5. Reverse procedure to install.

REAR WIPER

Exc. 1985–87 Colt

1. Insert suitable tool behind switch garnish, compress lock tab and pry switch and garnish assembly from instrument panel, taking care not to mar garnish or instrument panel.
2. Disconnect electrical connector and remove switch. On Conquest models, compress tabs on side of switch and remove switch from garnish.
3. Reverse procedure to install.

1985–87 Colt

The rear windshield wiper switch is incorporated in the front windshield wiper switch. Refer to "Windshield Wiper Switch, Replace" for procedure.

WINDSHIELD WIPER MOTOR

REPLACE

FRONT WIPER

1. Disconnect battery ground cable and remove wiper motor access hole cover, located on the lefthand side of the front deck, if applicable.
2. Raise covers and remove nuts securing wiper arms to pivot shafts, note installation position of arms, then remove wiper arms.

3. Remove cowl moldings, as needed, to gain access to pivot shaft fasteners.
4. Remove wiper pivot shaft attaching bolts or nuts, then push pivots inwards.
5. Remove wiper motor attaching bolts or nuts, pull motor out slightly and disconnect linkage. Mark relationship of wiper motor crank arm to driveshaft prior to disconnecting linkage to ensure proper stop angle after installation.
6. Remove wiper motor.
7. Reverse procedure to install. When installing crank arm on wiper motor, ensure reference marks made during removal are aligned, then install wiper arms as outlined in "Windshield Wiper Transmission, Replace."

REAR WIPER

Exc. Ram Raider

1. Disconnect battery ground cable.
2. Remove wiper arm from shaft, then remove wiper arm shaft locknut and washers, noting position for installation.
3. Remove liftgate trim panel, then disconnect wiper motor wire connector.
4. Remove wiper motor attaching screws, then the motor from liftgate.
5. Reverse procedure to install. Mount wiper arm so that when motor is in park position distance between tip of blade and lower window molding is 2.2-2.6 inches on Colt, .6-1 inch on Colt Vista or 1.8-2.2 inches on Conquest.

Ram Raider

1. Remove rear compartment inner door handle, door trim and water shield.
2. Remove wiper arm from shaft then remove wiper arm shaft locknut and washers, noting position for installation.
3. Remove wiper motor attaching screws, then the motor.
4. Reverse procedure to install. With motor in park position, wiper blade should be parallel with lower edge of window glass.

WINDSHIELD WIPER TRANSMISSION

REPLACE

EXC. 1983–84 COLT HATCHBACK

1. Remove wiper motor as outlined under "Windshield Wiper Motor, Replace."
2. Position wiper motor shaft at right angles to the linkage and remove linkage while holding shaft.
3. Reverse procedure to install, noting the following:
   a. Ensure shaft bracket positioning boss is properly located in access hole.
   b. Mount wiper arm so that when motor is in park position distance between wiper blade and bottom of windshield is .6 inch on left side and .8 inch on right side for 1985-87 Colt, 1.2 inch on left side and 1 inch on right side for Colt Vista, .5 inch on both sides for Conquest, .6-1 inch on both sides for Ram 50 and 1.5-1.9 inch on both sides for Ram Raider.

1983–84 COLT HATCHBACK

1. Remove wiper arm and blade assemblies from wiper arm shafts.
2. Remove cowl grille attaching screws, then the cowl grille.
3. Remove screws attaching wiper link shafts to cowl.
4. Disconnect wiper linkage from wiper motor crank arm, then lift wiper linkage from cowl.
5. Reverse procedure to install. Install wiper arms so that when blades are parked there is a clearance of .8 inch between blade and windshield lower molding.

RADIO

REPLACE

CHALLENGER & SAPPORO

1. Disconnect battery ground cable.
2. Remove radio control knobs and control shaft nuts, then the radio trim panel.
3. Remove console side covers from both sides.
4. Remove radio bracket to reinforcement attaching screws.
5. Disconnect antenna, feed, and speaker wiring from radio, then remove radio.
6. Remove bracket attaching screws, then bracket from radio.
7. Reverse procedure to install.

COLT

1983–84

1. Disconnect battery ground cable.
2. Disconnect antenna lead and wiring harness connector from radio.
3. Remove steering wheel using suitable puller.
4. Remove instrument cluster attaching screws, **Fig. 11**, then pull off heater control knobs.
5. Remove wiring harness from cluster, then the instrument cluster.
6. Remove instrument panel trim attaching screws.
7. Remove wiring harness from panel trim, then instrument panel trim. The radio ground wire is attached to the cigar lighter bracket.
8. Remove glove box lid.
9. Remove radio control knobs, then the radio attaching nuts behind them.
10. Remove radio attaching bolt from either side of radio.
11. Remove radio ground wire from cigar lighter bracket if not previously removed.
12. Remove radio assembly.
13. Reverse procedure to install.

1985–87

1. Disconnect battery ground cable.
2. Remove ashtray, parking brake lever cover and shift knob.
3. Remove floor console mounting screws, then the console.
4. Remove radio and console bracket mounting screws.
5. Remove radio bracket screws, then the radio.
6. Reverse procedure to install.

COLT VISTA

1984

1. Remove radio control knobs, then the control shaft attaching nuts.
2. Remove radio trim plate, then the side cover.
3. Disconnect electrical connector and antenna leads from rear of radio.
4. Remove radio to console reinforcement attaching screws, then the radio.
5. Reverse procedure to install.

1985–87

1. Disconnect battery ground cable.
2. Using a suitable thin edged tool, pry off radio panel.
3. Remove console side covers, then disconnect radio harness connector and antenna lead.
4. Remove radio mounting screws from console reinforcement bracket, then slide radio out of console.
5. Reverse procedure to install.

CONQUEST

1. Open rear console accessory box cover, then remove inner box.
2. Remove power window switch panel and cover, if equipped.
3. Remove rear console box attaching screws, then the box.
4. Insert a suitable screwdriver into space between cover and rear console tray, then twist screwdriver and remove tray.
5. Pull out ashtray.
6. Remove rear console tray attaching screws, then the rear console box.
7. Remove console side cover attaching screws from under instrument panel, then the side covers by pushing downward and slightly forward, and bracket.
8. Remove radio panel, then the radio from console box.
9. Reverse procedure to install.

RAM 50

1983–86

1. Disconnect battery ground cable.
2. Remove instrument cluster bezel as outlined in "Instrument Cluster, Replace."
3. Remove radio bracket to instrument panel attaching screws, then the bracket.
4. Pull radio slightly outward and disconnect antenna, speaker and feed leads, then remove radio from instrument panel.
5. Reverse procedure to install.

1987

1. Disconnect battery ground cable and pull off heater control knobs.

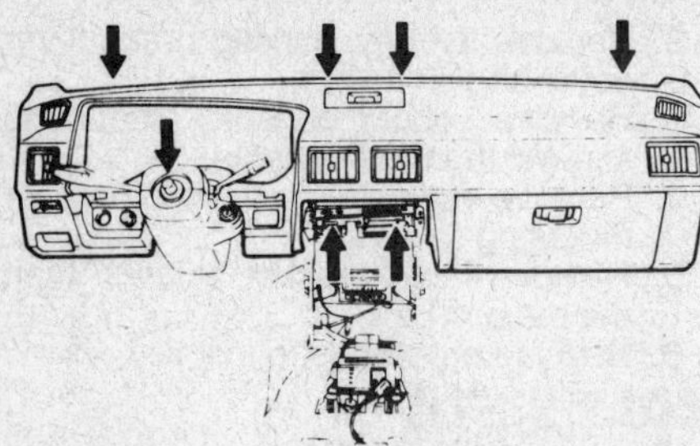

Fig. 18 Instrument panel pad removal. Challenger & Sapporo

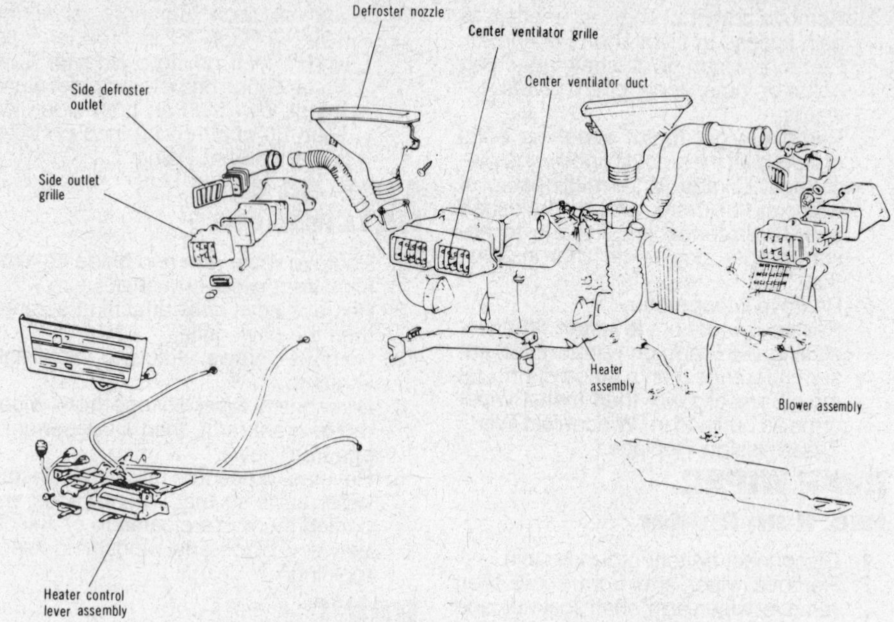

Fig. 19 Heater & blower housing. Challenger & Sapporo

2. Remove screws securing center trim panel, insert suitable tool between top of trim and instrument panel and pry trim away from instrument panel.
3. Remove radio bracket mounting screws and pull radio assembly away from instrument panel.
4. Disconnect antenna lead and electrical connectors, then remove radio assembly.
5. Reverse procedure to install.

RAM RAIDER

1. Disconnect battery ground cable, pull knobs from heater control, and pry hole covers from sides of console, taking care not to mar covers or console.
2. Remove screws securing console, pull console away from instrument panel and disconnect electrical connectors.
3. Remove radio panel and radio brackets, disconnect antenna lead and electrical connectors, and remove radio.

HEATER CORE REPLACE

CHALLENGER & SAPPORO

1. Disconnect battery ground cable, then position temperature control lever in the Hot position and drain cooling system.
2. Remove steering wheel using a suitable puller.
3. Loosen tilt lock lever and lower steering column to its lowest position.
4. Remove instrument cluster as described under "Instrument Cluster, Replace."
5. Remove inner box from center console storage compartment, then disconnect remote control mirror switch and the wire connector.
6. Remove center console storage compartment attaching screws, then disconnect wire connectors and remove storage compartment.
7. Remove heater control knobs, then pull control panel outward and disconnect wire connector.
8. Remove radio knobs and shaft nuts, then the radio panel.
9. Remove lower cover attaching screws, located beneath glove box, then the cover assembly.
10. Remove console side cover attaching screws from both side covers, then the covers.
11. Remove console attaching screws, then the console. On models with manual transmission, it will be necessary to remove the shift lever knob before removing the console assembly.
12. Remove instrument panel pad attaching nut covers at each side of instrument panel, then the attaching nuts.
13. Remove hood release cable knob, then the release cable to instrument panel pad attaching screws.
14. Remove defroster garnish panels from top of instrument panel pad.
15. Remove glove compartment plate to center instrument panel reinforcement attaching screws.
16. Remove instrument panel pad attaching screws, **Fig. 18.**
17. Disconnect wire connectors from clock, glove compartment, chime and dimmer control, then remove instrument panel pad.
18. Disconnect wire connectors from chime driver, defogger switch, defogger relay and radio, then the antenna lead from rear of radio.
19. Remove four center reinforcement attaching bolts, then the reinforcement.
20. From engine compartment, disconnect heater hoses from heater core. Install plugs in heater core fittings to prevent coolant spillage.
21. Remove all ducts from heater assembly, then disconnect all control cable and wire connectors from heater assembly, **Fig. 19.**
22. Remove heater assembly attaching screws, then the heater assembly.
23. Remove power relay attaching screw, then the power relay from heater case.
24. Remove heater core cover attaching screws, then the cover.
25. Slide heater core from heater case.
26. Reverse procedure to install.

COLT

1983–84 Hatchback

1. Disconnect battery ground cable.
2. Place temperature control cable in warm position, then drain cooling system.
3. Disconnect heater hoses at heater core.
4. Remove center console and parcel tray, if equipped.
5. Remove defroster and center ventilation ducts, then the steering wheel using a suitable puller.
6. Remove instrument cluster panel mounting screws, then the heater control lever knobs.
7. Disconnect the instrument cluster harness.
8. Remove instrument panel trim mounting screws.
9. Remove wiring harness from instrument panel trim, then the trim.
10. Disconnect radio ground wire from cigar lighter bracket, then remove glove box door.
11. Disconnect heater unit control cables, then the harness connector.
12. Remove heater assembly attaching bolts, then the heater assembly, **Fig. 20.**
13. Remove blower motor from heater assembly, the fan from motor.
14. Remove heater unit cover, then disconnect water valve to air mix damper connecting rod.
15. Remove screws from clamp and water valve, then the heater core from heater unit case, **Fig. 20.**
16. Remove water valve from heater core.

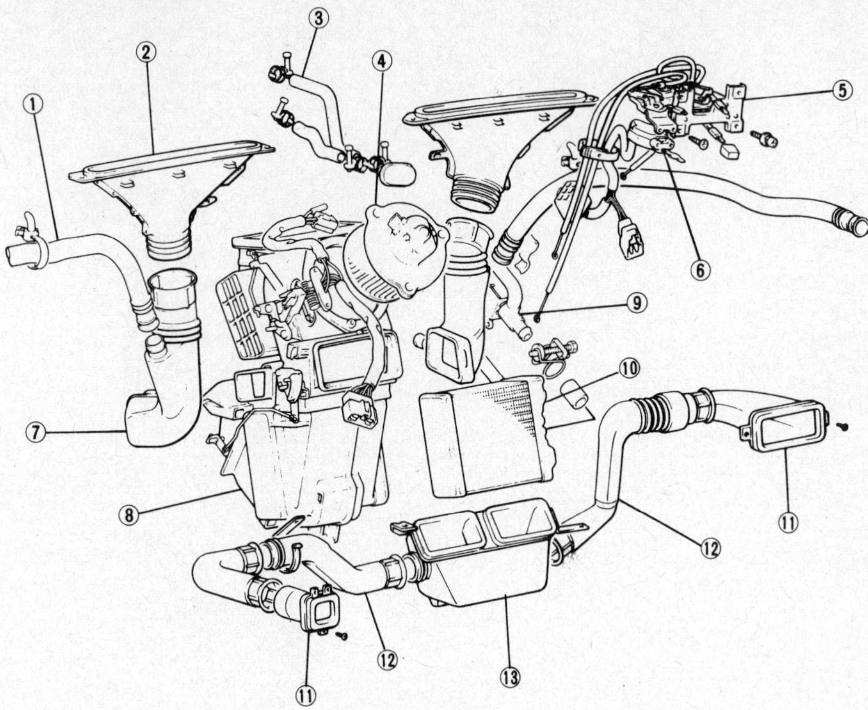

(1) Side defroster duct
(2) Defroster nozzle
(3) Heater hose
(4) Blower motor assembly
(5) Heater control assembly
(6) Heater blower switch
(7) Defroster duct
(8) Heater unit case
(9) Water valve assembly
(10) Heater core
(11) Side duct
(12) Air duct
(13) Center ventilator duct

Fig. 20 Heater & blower housing assemblies. 1983–84 Colt Hatchback

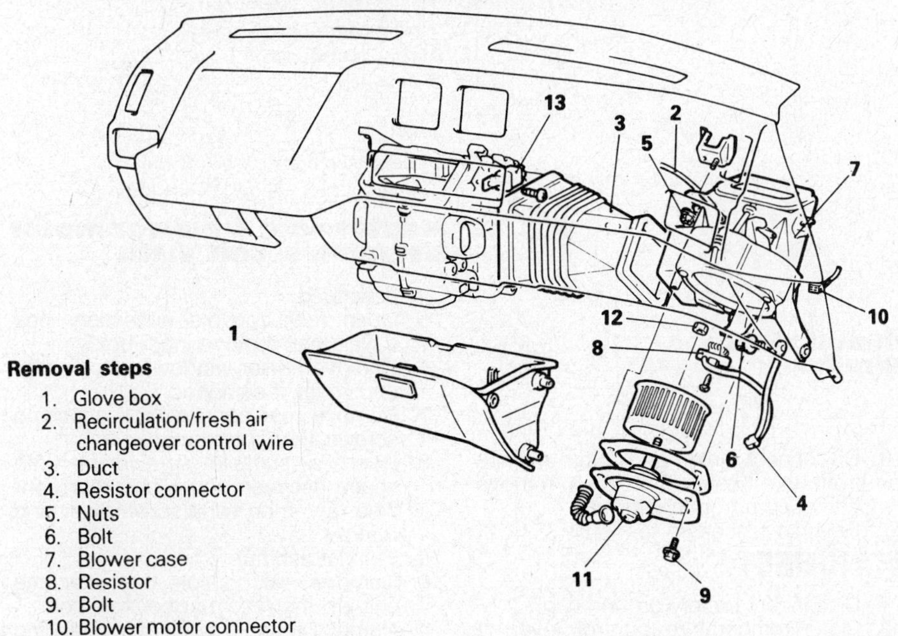

Fig. 21 Heater and blower housing assemblies. 1985–87 Colt, 1877 Ram 50 similar

17. Reverse procedure to install.

1985–87

1. Disconnect battery ground cable.
2. Set temperature lever at the extreme hot position, then drain engine coolant.
3. Remove steering wheel using suitable puller.
4. Remove glove compartment, ashtray lap heater duct or steering column lower trim and parcel tray (if equipped).
5. Remove steering column lower cover, then disconnect light switch and wiper switch wiring connectors.
6. Remove steering column upper cover.
7. Remove cluster bezel attaching screws, then the bezel, **Figs. 13 and 14.**
8. Remove instrument cluster attaching screws, then tilt cluster outwards and disconnect speedometer cable and electrical connectors.
9. Remove instrument cluster, then the steering column bracket.
10. Remove upper left hand side instrument corner panel.
11. Working from the back side of the heater control panel, push the right side control panel clip to the right while pushing control panel out of instrument panel. Allow control panel to hang.
12. Remove heater control panel mounting screws.
13. Remove instrument panel pad.
14. Remove instrument panel attaching bolts, then the instrument panel assembly. On some models it may be necessary to remove center console.
15. Remove heater to blower motor connecting duct, **Fig. 21,** and center ventilator duct.
16. Disconnect heater hoses at the heater unit side, then remove heater assembly.
17. Remove hose clamp and cut connecting hose between water valve and core, remove water valve, then detach heater core from heater unit.
18. Reverse procedure to install.

COLT VISTA

1. Disconnect battery ground cable.
2. Place temperature control lever in warm position, then drain cooling system.
3. Remove steering wheel using a suitable puller, then the ashtray.
4. Remove instrument cluster as outlined.
5. Remove outer passenger side defroster duct, then the outlet control wire at left side of heater unit.
6. Remove retaining clips from trim panels A and B, **Fig. 22,** then remove lower and upper glove compartments.
7. Disconnect the recirculation/fresh air control wire from left of blower assembly, then the blower harness connector.
8. Remove inner passenger side defroster duct, then the floor console side covers with duct.
9. On vehicles with manual transaxle, remove shift lever knob.

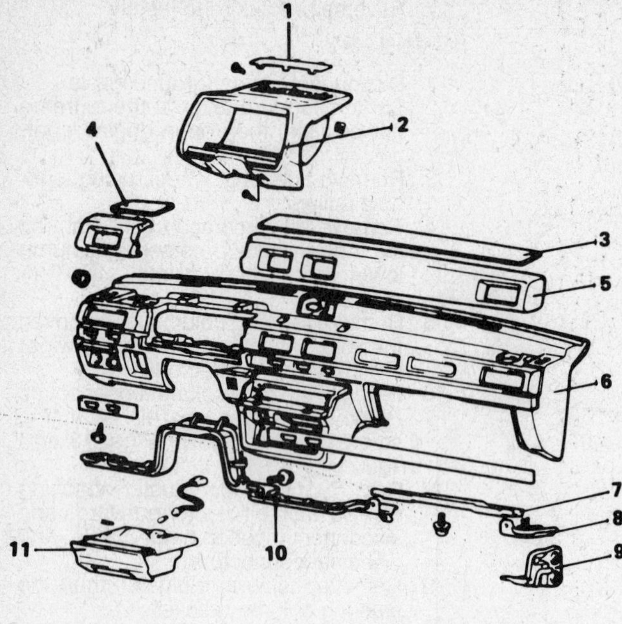

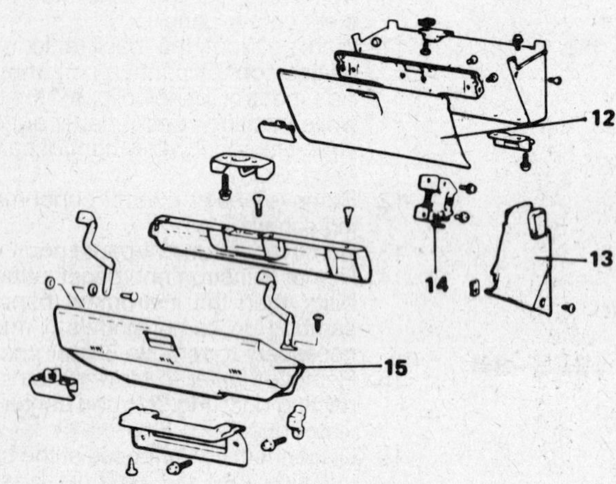

1. Meter hood cover
2. Meter hood
3. Trim panel A
4. Trim panel B
5. Instrument pad
6. Instrument panel
7. Center frame
8. Side frame
9. Side bracket
10. Frame
11. Ashtray
12. Upper glove box
13. Side cover
14. Bracket
15. Lower glove box

Fig. 22 Instrument panel exploded view. 1985–87 Colt Vista, 1987 similar

1. Heater relay
2. Heater unit
3. Duct
4. Blower case
5. Water control assembly
6. Heater core
7. Resistor
8. Fan
9. Fan motor assembly
10. Heater control assembly
11. Heater control panel cover
12. Heater control panel
13. Fan switch

Water hose clamp bolts : 1.3–1.8 Nm (.9–1.3 ft.lbs.)

Fig. 23 Heater core & blower motor assemblies. Colt Vista

10. On all vehicles, remove floor console.
11. Remove lap heater duct, then the fuse box.
12. Disconnect electrical connectors for instrument panel harness, body harness, brake switch and antenna feed wire.
13. Remove instrument panel attaching nuts and bolts, then the instrument panel.
14. Remove duct between heater unit and blower motor, then disconnect heater hoses at heater unit.
15. Remove heater unit, then the heater core cover, **Fig. 23.**
16. Disconnect links and pipe clamps from the heater unit, then remove heater core from heater unit.
17. Reverse procedure to install.

CONQUEST

1. Disconnect battery ground cable.
2. Place temperature control lever in warm position, then drain cooling system.
3. Disconnect heater unit hoses, then remove steering wheel using a suitable puller.
4. Remove steering column switch, then the instrument cluster as previously described.
5. Open rear console accessory box cover, then remove inner box.
6. Remove power window switch panel and cover, if equipped.
7. Remove rear console box attaching screws, then the rear box.
8. Insert a suitable screwdriver into space between cover and rear console tray, then twist screwdriver and remove tray.
9. Pull out ashtray.
10. Remove rear console tray attaching screws, then the rear console box.
11. Remove console side cover attaching screws from under instrument panel, then the side covers by pushing downward and slightly forward.
12. Remove under cover, then the inner glove box by pulling it forward and pressing sides inward.
13. Remove glove box door hinge retain-

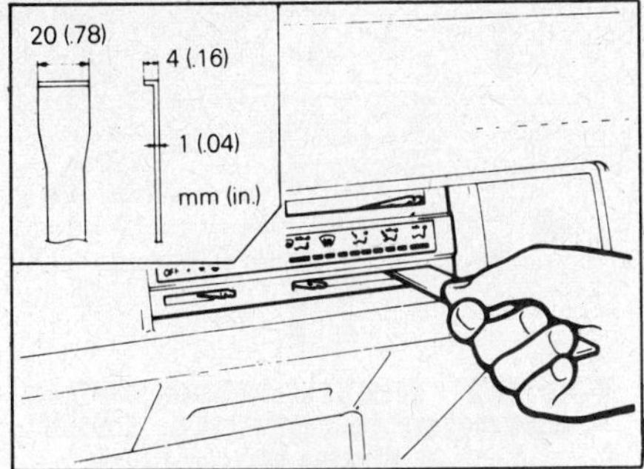

Fig. 24 Heater panel removal. Conquest

ing screws and hinge, then the ashtray.

14. Carefully remove left and right instrument panel side covers by inserting a suitable tool into space between instrument panel side cover and instrument pad.
15. Remove hood lock release handle, then the fuse block.
16. Remove passenger side defroster grille using a suitable screwdriver, then the heater control lever knobs.
17. Remove heater control panel using a suitable tool, **Fig. 24,** then disconnect electrical connector.
18. Remove instrument panel attaching screws and nuts.
19. Remove ashtray heat protector, then disconnect ashtray light connector.
20. Remove driver side defroster duct, then disconnect wiring harness for glove box, rear window defogger, cigar lighter, rear wiper and thermostat.
21. Remove clock from instrument pad, then disconnect electrical connector.
22. Pull instrument pad outward, then remove center reinforcement bolts.
23. Loosen main harness clamp, then remove instrument panel and center reinforcement.
24. Remove center ventilation, defroster and lap heater duct, then the heater control assembly, **Fig. 25.**
25. Remove heater unit, then the core.
26. Reverse procedure to install.

RAM 50

1983–86

1. Disconnect battery ground cable, then place temperature control lever in Off position and drain cooling system.
2. Remove parcel tray, center ventilation duct and grille and defroster duct.
3. Disconnect heater hoses from heater core. Plug heater core fittings to prevent coolant spillage.
4. Disconnect wire connector from blower motor, **Fig. 26.**
5. Remove bolts and nuts attaching heater assembly to dash panel, then the heater assembly.
6. Remove heater core from heater assembly.
7. Reverse procedure to install.

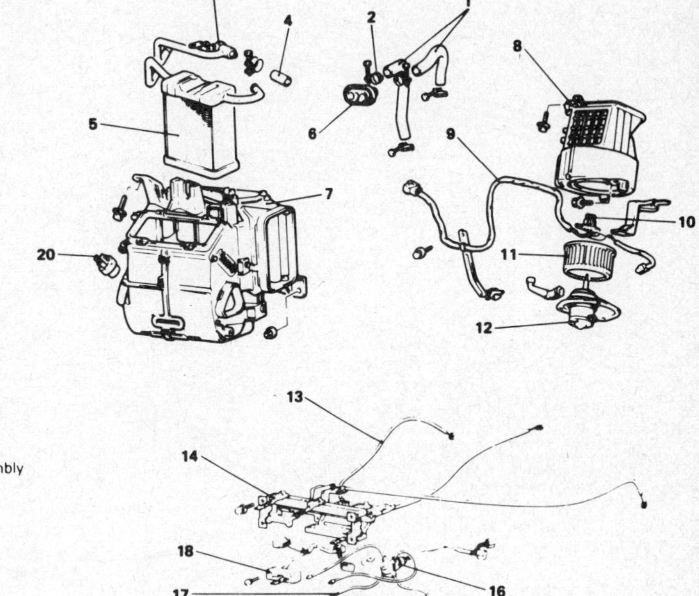

1. Water hose
2. Clamp
3. Water valve
4. Hose
5. Heater core
6. Grommet
7. Heater case
8. Blower case
9. Blower motor harness
10. Resistor
11. Fan
12. Blower motor
13. Heater control cable
14. Heater control lever
15. Heater control knob
16. Optical fiber lamp assembly
17. Optical fiber
18. Heater fan switch
19. Heater control panel
20. Heater relay

Fig. 25 Heater core & blower motor assemblies. Conquest

1987

1. Disconnect battery ground cable, place heater control in warm position and drain cooling system, then disconnect heater hoses at firewall.
2. Remove instrument cluster as outlined.
3. Remove fuse box cover and fuse box.
4. Remove glove box assembly, then the defroster duct.
5. Disconnect air select, mode selector and temperature cables.
6. Remove speaker grilles and the parcel box and/or clock, as equipped.
7. Pry up cover at center front of instrument panel to gain access to attaching nut.
8. Remove cover from center instrument panel brace, shift knob and center console.
9. Remove instrument panel retaining nuts and bolts, **Fig. 27,** disconnect necessary harness connectors, then remove instrument panel assembly. On models with tilt wheel, position wheel at lowest possible position.
10. Remove air ducts and center instrument panel brace.
11. Remove heater housing retaining nuts, bolt and the housing assembly, **Fig. 21.**
12. Remove hose cover from side of housing, then the hose clamp, connecting hose and heater core cover plate.
13. Withdraw heater core from housing.
14. Reverse procedure to install.

RAM RAIDER

1. Disconnect battery ground cable, place heater control in warm position and drain cooling system, then disconnect heater hoses at firewall.
2. Remove lap heater ducts, hood release cable bracket, and left and right defroster grilles.
3. Remove glove box assembly, then the instrument cluster.
4. Pull knobs from heater control and pry hole covers from sides of console, taking care not to mar covers or console.
5. Remove screws securing console, pull console away from instrument panel and disconnect electrical connectors.
6. Disconnect air select, mode select and temperature cables from heater assembly.
7. Remove horn pad, mark installation position of steering wheel, then remove steering wheel using suitable puller.
8. Remove center instrument panel brace, fuse box cover and the fuse box.
9. Remove instrument panel fasteners, **Fig. 28,** disconnect necessary electrical connectors and harness clamps, then remove instrument panel.
10. Remove air ducts, heater housing fasteners and the housing assembly.
11. Remove heater core from housing as follows:
    a. Remove water valve cover.
    b. Remove clamp securing core tubes and disconnect water valve link.
    c. Remove clamp and disconnect hose between water valve and core, remove retaining screw and remove water valve.
    d. Remove damper link from mode

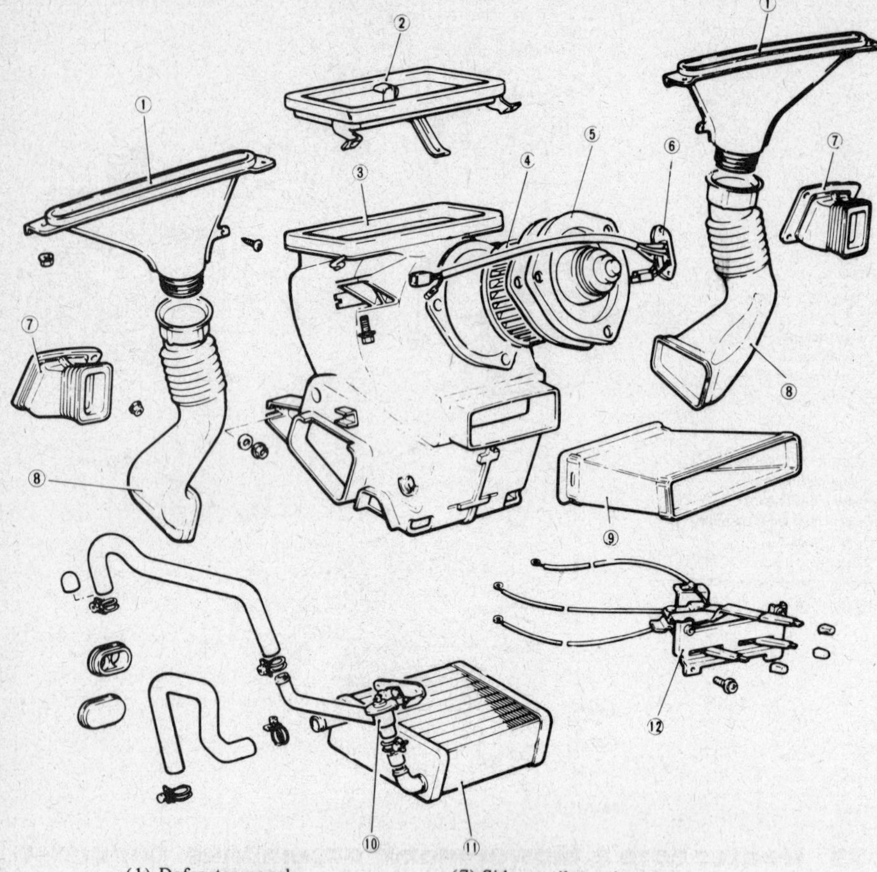

(1) Defroster nozzle
(2) Ventilator assembly
(3) Heater assembly
(4) Turbo fan
(5) Motor
(6) Heater resistor
(7) Side ventilator duct
(8) Defroster duct
(9) Center ventilator duct
(10) Water valve
(11) Heater core
(12) Heater control panel assembly

Fig. 26 Heater core & blower motor. 1983–86 Ram 50

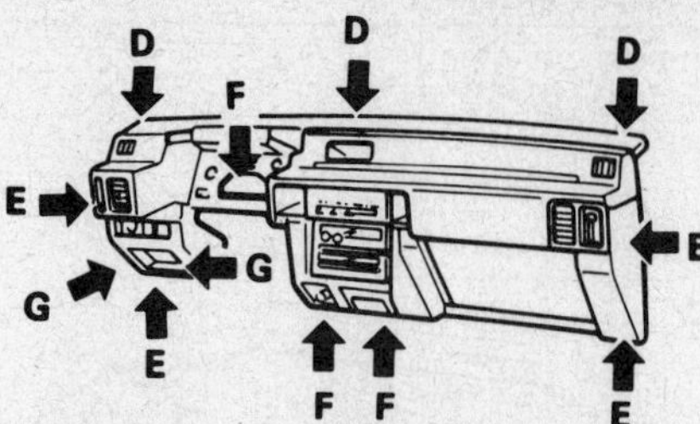

Fig. 27 Instrument panel fastener locations. 1987 Ram 50

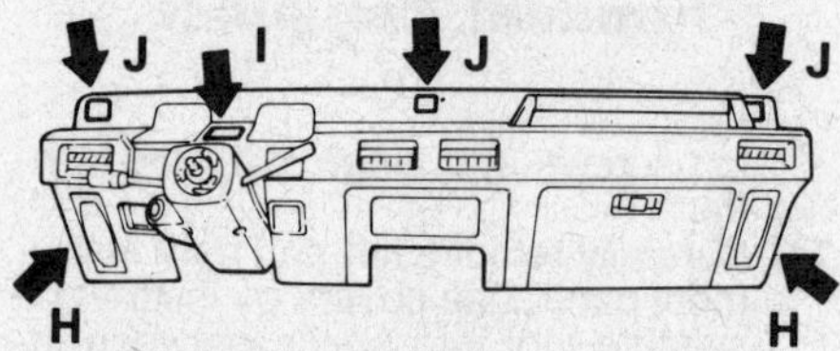

Fig. 28 Instrument panel fastener locations. Ram Raider

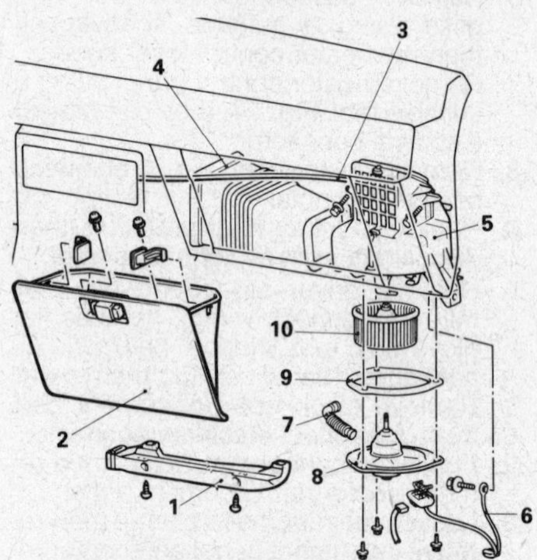

Fig. 29 Blower motor installation. Ram Raider

selector damper lever, move damper lever away from heater core opening as far as possible, then withdraw heater core from housing.

12. Reverse procedure to install.

BLOWER MOTOR REPLACE

CHALLENGER & SAPPORO

1. Disconnect battery ground cable.
2. Remove instrument panel lower cover assembly attaching screws, located beneath glove compartment, then the cover assembly.
3. Remove console side cover from passenger side of console.
4. Remove screw attaching glove compartment plate to center reinforcement.
5. Loosen glove compartment stops, then disconnect glove compartment wire connector.
6. Remove glove compartment plate to instrument panel attaching screws, then the glove compartment.
7. Disconnect ducts, blower switch wire connector and air control cables, **Fig. 19.**
8. Remove blower motor attaching bolts and nuts, then the blower motor assembly.
9. Reverse procedure to install.

COLT

1983–84 Hatchback

1. Perform steps 1 through 13 as described under "Heater Core, Replace."

1985–87

1. Disconnect battery ground cable.
2. Remove glove compartment.
3. Disconnect blower motor wiring connector.
4. Disconnect blower motor cooling tube.
5. Remove blower motor attaching screws, then the blower motor, **Fig. 21.**
6. Reverse procedure to install.

COLT VISTA

1. Disconnect battery ground cable.
2. Remove lower glove box attaching screws, then the lower glove box.
3. Remove upper glove box attaching screws, then the upper glove box.
4. Disconnect fan motor electrical connectors, then remove fan motor attaching bolts and fan motor.
5. Reverse procedure to install.

CONQUEST

1. Disconnect battery ground cable.
2. Remove instrument panel under cover, then the glove box door hinge retaining screws and door. Remove glove box.
3. Disconnect the recirculation/fresh air changeover cable from blower assembly, then remove blower assembly duct.

4. Disconnect heater fan switch connector.
5. Remove blower assembly attaching screws through the glove box opening, then the blower assembly.
6. Reverse procedure to install.

RAM 50

1983–86

1. Disconnect battery ground cable.
2. Remove instrument cluster outlined.
3. Disconnect cable between blower motor and heater unit at connector.
4. Working through instrument cluster panel mounting area, remove blower motor attaching bolts, **Fig. 26.**
5. Remove blower motor.
6. Reverse procedure to install.

1987

1. Disconnect battery ground cable.
2. Remove glove box stopper and frame.
3. Disconnect air select control cable, then remove duct between blower and heater housings, **Fig. 21.**
4. Remove blower attaching screws, blower assembly and gasket.
5. Reverse procedure to install. Place air select control in fresh air position, and move lever on intake housing against stop, then connect cable to lever and secure cable housing with clip.

RAM RAIDER

1. Disconnect battery ground cable.
2. Remove right lap heater and the glove box.
3. Disconnect air select control cable, then remove duct from between blower and heater housings.
4. Disconnect harness connector from blower housing, remove retaining bolts and ground strap, then lower blower housing from dash panel, **Fig. 29.**
5. Remove blower resistor and vent hose, then remove blower motor from housing.
6. Reverse procedure to install. Place air select control in recirculation position, connect control cable to damper lever and pull lever toward cable clamp, then secure cable housing with clamp.

GASOLINE ENGINE SECTION

INDEX

ENGINE REPLACE

CHALLENGER & SAPPORO

1. Remove battery from engine compartment.
2. Drain cooling system, then disconnect radiator and heater hoses.
3. Disconnect ground strap and wiring from ignition coil, vacuum control solenoid valve, alternator, starter, trans. switch, back-up lamp switch, temperature sender unit and oil pressure switch.
4. Remove air cleaner, then disconnect accelerator linkage from carburetor.
5. On models equipped, remove power steering pump and position aside.
6. Disconnect exhaust pipe from exhaust manifold, then detach muffler pipe bracket from transmission.
7. Disconnect fuel hose between fuel strainer and fuel pump return line.
8. On models equipped with auto. trans., disconnect oil cooler lines from radiator.
9. Remove fan shroud, radiator and radiator cowl, as equipped.
10. From vehicle passenger compartment, remove center console, then detach shift lever from transmission.
11. Remove hood from vehicle.
12. Disconnect speedometer cable from vehicle.
13. On models with manual transmission, disconnect clutch cable from release lever and bracket.
14. Drain transmission fluid.
15. If equipped, remove dynamic damper, then remove propeller shaft.
16. Support transmission using a suitable jack and remove front and rear insulator attaching bolts, then the rear engine support bracket.
17. Attach suitable engine lifting fixture to engine, then remove engine and transmission assembly from vehicle. Position cables of engine lifting fixture so that transmission will be lower than front of engine when assembly is raised from vehicle. If interference is encountered between bellhousing and relay rod during engine removal, raise rear of transmission until bellhousing is above relay rod.
18. Reverse the removal procedure noting the following:
    a. When installing the engine/transmission unit, place rags at rear of cylinder head to avoid damage to firewall.
    b. Lift the engine/transmission unit slightly higher than the mounting position, install the front insulators, then the rear insulators and related parts. **When installing the insulator, use caution not to twist the rubber or smear the rubber with gasoline or oil.**
    c. When installing a rolling stopper (a stop to restrict engine movement

on the mountings), to the front insulator, use care to provide clearance between the stopper and the side of the insulator.

d. To install rear engine support bracket to floor stringer of vehicle body, tighten attaching bolts to 7 ft. lbs., then check if flat of bolt is aligned with lock washer tang. If flat is not aligned, tighten bolt until flat is aligned with tang, then bend lock washer tang.

e. Check to ensure that clearance between rear support bracket and exhaust pipe is at least .75 inch.

COLT

1983–84 Hatchback

1. Remove battery and battery tray, then remove air cleaner assembly.
2. Detach purge control valve hose bracket from battery support, then disconnect hose from valve.
3. Remove windshield washer tank, cooling system reservoir and evaporative emissions canister.
4. Drain cooling system, then remove radiator and engine cooling fan.
5. Disconnect accelerator cable, clutch cable and speedometer cable.
6. Disconnect heater hoses from engine.
7. Disconnect PCV valve vacuum hose and on California models, disconnect high altitude compensator vacuum hose.
8. Disconnect carburetor bowl vent purge hose.
9. On models with automatic transaxle, disconnect selector lever control cable, throttle control cable and neutral safety switch wire connector at transaxle.
10. Disconnect wiring from starter motor, alternator, water temperature switch, ignition coil, high temperature sensor and oil pressure switch. Also disconnect coil high tension lead and engine ground cable.
11. On models with manual transaxle, disconnect back-up light switch wire connector at transaxle.
12. Remove ignition coil.
13. Raise and support front of vehicle, then drain fluid from transaxle.
14. Remove under cover, then detach lower arm ball joint and strut bar from lower arm. **Position lower ball joint on lower arm to prevent damage to dust boot.**
15. Insert a suitable pry bar between transaxle case and axle shaft joint outer case. Move pry bar to the right to withdraw left hand axle shaft, to the left to remove right hand right shaft from transaxle case. Support axle shafts at a suitable position. Cover transaxle axle shaft openings with a cloth. **When detaching axle shaft from transaxle case, do not insert pry bar more than .28 inch, otherwise oil seal may be damaged. Before the axle shaft is reinstalled, the shaft retainer ring should be replaced.**
16. Remove transaxle assist and control rods.
17. Disconnect exhaust pipe from exhaust manifold and suspend from frame with wire.
18. Remove front roll rod to bracket attaching bolt, then the rear roll stopper attaching bolt.
19. Support engine using a suitable engine lifting device.
20. Loosen transaxle mount bracket bolt, then remove engine mount bracket nuts.
21. Remove transaxle mount bolt and engine mount insulator bolts, then the transaxle mount insulator from fender shield.
22. Remove engine mount bracket from engine, then the engine and transaxle assembly from vehicle. When removing engine and transaxle assembly from vehicle, use care not to allow transaxle to come in contact with battery bracket.
23. Reverse procedure to install. Temporarily tighten front roll rod attaching bolts and nuts, then after the weight of the engine and transaxle has been placed on the insulators, tighten front roll rod bolt to 22-29 ft. lbs. and front roll rod to bracket bolts to 29-36 ft. lbs. This will prevent axial force from being applied to roll rods.

1985–87

1. Scribe reference marks between hood and hood hinges, then remove hood.
2. On models equipped with fuel injection, relieve fuel pressure as follows:
   a. Remove rear seat and pull back carpet.
   b. With engine running, disconnect fuel pump connector.
   c. Allow engine to deplete fuel supply, then turn ignition Off.
3. On all models, disconnect battery cables, then remove battery and battery tray.
4. Remove air cleaner and engine under cover.
5. Drain cooling system into suitable container.
6. On auto. trans. models, disconnect transaxle cooling hoses from transaxle.
7. Disconnect heater and the upper and lower radiator hoses from engine, then remove radiator.
8. Mark and disconnect necessary vacuum hoses and engine/transaxle wiring that would interfere with engine removal.
9. Disconnect accelerator cable and brake booster vacuum hose.
10. On models with manual transaxle, disconnect control cable.
11. On auto. trans. models, disconnect auto. trans. control cable. **Handle control cable very carefully so as not to bend inner cable.**
12. On all models, disconnect speedometer cable.
13. Remove power steering pump and hoses as an assembly leaving hoses connected, then use wire to secure pump.
14. Raise and support vehicle.
15. If equipped with A/C, remove compressor belt, then remove compressor mounting bolts and compressor leaving refrigerant lines connected. Disconnect compressor wiring, then use wire to secure compressor and hose assembly.
16. On man. trans. models, remove shift control rod and extension rod from transaxle. Use wire to secure rods out of the way.
17. Remove front exhaust pipe.
18. Drain engine oil into suitable container. On turbocharged engines, remove oil cooler lines from engine.
19. Disconnect stabilizer bar from lower control arm.
20. Loosen, but do not remove ball joint stud attaching nut, then disconnect ball joint from steering knuckle using tool MB991113.
21. Loosen, but do not remove tie rod end attaching nut, then disconnect tie rod end from steering knuckle using tool MB991113.
22. Drain transaxle oil.
23. On models equipped with drive shaft center bearing, remove snap ring securing center bearing, then using plastic hammer, lightly tap D.O.J. (double offset joint) outer race to remove drive shaft from transaxle. Remove center bearing.
24. On models not equipped with drive shaft center bearing, insert suitable pry bar between transaxle case and drive shaft, then pry drive shaft from transaxle case. **Do not insert pry bar too deep or oil seal will be damaged. Do not pull on drive axle and do not overextend CV joints, as joints will be damaged.**
25. Cover transaxle holes to prevent entry of dirt and replace drive axle circlips.
26. Use wire to secure drive shafts out of the way.
27. Attach suitable engine lifting device, then raise lift enough to tension equipment.
28. Remove front roll stopper insulator bolt, then the rear roll stopper insulator bolt.
29. Remove left mount insulator attaching nut. **Do not remove bolt.**
30. Raise engine/transaxle assembly enough to remove weight from mounts.
31. Remove blind cover from inside right fender shield, then remove transaxle mount bracket bolt.
32. Remove left mount insulator bolt, then while directing transaxle side down, remove engine/transaxle assembly from vehicle.
33. Reverse procedure to install.

COLT VISTA

Prior to engine removal on 1987 fuel injected models, start engine, disconnect electric fuel pump connector and allow engine to run out of fuel to relieve residual fuel system pressure. **Failure to relieve fuel system pressure prior to disconnecting fuel system components may cause fire or personal injury.**

2 Wheel Drive Models

1. Remove battery, then the engine

ground, radiator fan motor connector, engine harness connector and battery tray.
2. Remove battery tray installation bracket, then drain engine coolant and transmission fluid.
3. Discharge A/C refrigerant, then drain the power steering fluid.
4. Remove radiator reservoir tank, then the windshield washer reservoir.
5. Disconnect transaxle oil cooler hoses on vehicles equipped with automatic transaxles, then plug hose openings.
6. Disconnect upper and lower radiator hoses from engine side, then the heater hoses.
7. Remove firewall ground cable, then the air cleaner.
8. Disconnect brake booster vacuum hose, then the high tension cables from coil and spark plugs.
9. On vehicles with manual transaxles, disconnect clutch cable from transaxle.
10. On vehicles with automatic transaxles, disconnect control cable from transaxle and transaxle mounting bracket.
11. On all models, disconnect speedometer cable from transaxle, then the accelerator cable from engine.
12. Disconnect right fender engine ground, then the A/C hoses from compressor, if equipped. **Cap compressor and hose openings to prevent foreign matter from entering.**
13. Disconnect power steering hoses from pump, then the pressure switch connector, if equipped.
14. Disconnect alternator electrical connector, then the oil pressure switch.
15. Remove vacuum control unit and solenoid valve attaching screws, then disconnect electrical connector.
16. Disconnect purge control valve hoses, then loosen canister body clamp and remove hoses.
17. Disconnect fuel return hose from carburetor, then the main hose from fuel filter.
18. Raise and support vehicle, then disconnect and support front exhaust pipe.
19. On vehicles with manual transaxle, remove shift rod, then the extension and range selector cable.
20. On all models, disconnect left and right strut bars, then the stabilizer bars from lower arms.
21. Remove left and right lower arms to No. 2 crossmember attaching bolts, then the drive shaft from transaxle. **Plug case openings to prevent foreign matter from entering and replace driveshaft retaining ring after each removal.**
22. Secure lower arms and drive shaft to No. 2 crossmember, then attach a suitable lifting device to engine.
23. Slightly raise engine, then remove left mount insulator nut.
24. Remove front roll insulator nut and heat protector bolt then the rear roll insulator protector bolt.
25. Remove left mount insulator to fender attaching bolt, then the power steering oil reservoir, if equipped.
26. Remove cap from right inner fender shield, the insulator bracket attaching bolts and bracket, then remove, in sequence, the select control valve attaching bolts and valve, wiring connector and vacuum hoses.
27. Lift engine until no weight is applied to mountings, then remove insulator bolts from rear roll stopper, front roll bracket and left mount bracket.
28. Remove engine/transaxle assembly from vehicle.
29 Reverse procedure to install, noting the following:
   a. Torque transaxle insulator bracket attaching bolt to 22-29 ft. lbs. and transaxle mount insulator attaching bolt to 43-58 ft. lbs.
   b. Torque front roll insulator attaching bolt to 36-47 ft. lbs. and roll stopper bracket attaching bolt to 22-29 ft. lbs.
   c. Torque left mount bracket attaching nuts to 36-47 ft. lbs. and left mount insulator bolt to 43-58 ft. lbs.
   d. Torque rear roll insulator bolt to 22-29 ft. lbs. and rear roll stopper stay attaching bolt to 22-29 ft. lbs.

4 Wheel Drive Models

1. Disconnect battery cables, then remove battery, battery tray and battery tray support bracket.
2. Disconnect power steering and engine oil pressure switch connectors.
3. Disconnect alternator wiring, then remove the air cleaner.
4. Disconnect coil high tension lead, distributor wiring and engine ground strap from the firewall.
5. Remove windshield washer tank.
6. Disconnect power brake booster hose, then identify and remove all vacuum hoses and electrical connectors from engine.
7. Drain engine coolant into suitable container, then remove reservoir container.
8. Disconnect radiator upper and lower hoses from engine, then remove radiator assembly.
9. Disconnect heater hoses from engine, then the accelerator cable and speed control cable (if equipped) from carburetor.
10. Disconnect speedometer cable.
11. Discharge A/C system (if equipped), then disconnect A/C hoses from compressor. **Cap all open ends of A/C system to prevent entry of dirt and foreign matter.**
12. Disconnect power steering hose from pump, fuel return hose from carburetor and main fuel line at fuel filter.
13. Disconnect shift control cables from transaxle case, then raise and support vehicle.
14. Remove engine/transaxle lower protection plate and cover.
15. Drain transmission and transfer case oil into suitable container.
16. Disconnect front exhaust pipe from manifold.
17. Remove driveshaft, then the clutch slave cylinder. Disconnect clutch hydraulic tubes.
18. Remove front drive shafts as outlined under "Front Suspension & Steering Section."
19. Remove transfer extension stopper bracket.
20. Lower vehicle to floor, then remove top engine to body coupling bracket nuts. **Do not remove coupling bracket bolt at this time.**
21. Remove select control valves from transaxle insulator bracket, then the transaxle mounting insulator nut. Do not remove bolt at this time.
22. Remove front roll insulator installation nut, then the rear insulator to engine coupling nut.
23. Remove front grille, bridge panel and A/C condenser, if equipped.
24. Attach suitable engine lifting equipment to engine/transaxle assembly, then lift engine/transaxle assembly enough to relieve pressure on engine mounts. Remove mounting bolts.
25. Remove engine/transaxle assembly from vehicle.

CONQUEST

1984–86

1. Release residual fuel pressure as follows:
   a. Start engine, then disconnect electrical connector from fuel pump.
   b. When engine stops from lack of fuel, turn off ignition. **Failure to release pressure prior to disconnecting fuel lines may cause fire or personal injury.**
2. Disconnect battery ground cable, then drain cooling system.
3. Disconnect accelerator cable, heater hoses, brake booster vacuum hose, and the fuel hoses.
4. Disconnect coil high tension cable from distributor then the intake manifold ground cable connector.
5. Disconnect starter motor wiring harness, then the power steering pump.
6. Disconnect engine oil cooler hoses, then remove radiator assembly.
7. Disconnect alternator wiring harness, then the engine ground cable.
8. Disconnect ECI unit wiring harness, then the boost sensor hose.
9. Remove rear catalytic converter, then disconnect speedometer cable.
10. On models with automatic transmission, disconnect transmission oil cooler lines.
11. On all models, disconnect back-up light switch, then remove propeller shaft.
12. Disconnect oil pressure gauge wiring harness, then remove clutch release cylinder.
13. Remove engine mounting bolts, then the gearshift lever assembly.
14. Attach engine to a suitable lifting fixture, then remove engine/transmission assembly from vehicle.
15. Reverse procedure to install, noting the following:
   a. Torque front insulator stopper attaching bolt to 22-29 ft. lbs.
   b. Torque engine mounting front insulator attaching bolt to 22-29 ft. lbs.

c. Torque engine support bracket and heat insulator attaching bolt to 9.4-14 ft. lbs.
d. Torque distance piece, plate and lockwasher to cushion pad attaching bolt to 7.2ft. lbs.
e. Add coolant to cooling system, then fill transmission to specifications.
f. Adjust clutch and accelerator cable, then adjust hood alignment.

1987

1. Disconnect battery ground cable.
2. Drain cooling system, crankcase, transaxle and clutch release system, and remove engine under cover.
3. Mark position of hood hinges, then remove hood.
4. Release residual fuel pressure as follows:
   a. Remove high floor side panel from luggage compartment.
   b. Start engine and disconnect electrical connector from fuel tank sending unit (fuel pump connector).
   c. When engine stops from lack of fuel, turn off ignition. **Failure to release pressure prior to disconnecting fuel lines may cause fire or personal injury.**
5. Remove air cleaner and heat protector, then disconnect oxygen sensor electrical connector and remove intercooler inlet and outlet hoses, if equipped.
6. Disconnect brake booster hose and heater hoses.
7. Remove accessory drive belts. On models with A/C and/or power steering, remove compressor and power steering pump mounting bolts, then secure assemblies aside, leaving hoses connected.
8. Disconnect exhaust pipe from catalytic converter.
9. Disconnect and plug oil cooler and transaxle cooler lines, if equipped, disconnect radiator hoses, then remove radiator assembly.
10. Disconnect accelerator, cruise control and kickdown cables, as equipped.
11. Disconnect and plug fuel lines and clutch slave cylinder hose.
12. Disconnect coil high tension lead and speedometer cable.
13. Mark and disconnect necessary electrical connectors and vacuum hoses from both engine and transmission, then secure harnesses aside to prevent damage.
14. Remove shift knob and spool release lever, console cover, inner and rear console boxes, console side covers and the front console box, then remove shifter assembly.
15. Raise and support vehicle, mark installation position of propeller shaft companion flange, then remove propeller shaft.
16. Remove front engine mount nuts and loosen but do not remove rear mount nuts and bracket bolts.
17. Lower vehicle and attach suitable lifting equipment to engine.
18. Support transmission with suitable jack, then remove rear engine mount and bracket assembly.
19. Remove engine and transmission assembly from vehicle.
20. Reverse procedure to install. Torque rear mount bracket bolts to 7.2 ft. lbs, rear mount nuts to 14-17 ft. lbs., front mount nuts to 9-14 ft. lbs., and propeller shaft companion flange bolts to 36-43 ft. lbs.

RAM 50

1. Disconnect battery ground cable and drain cooling system.
2. Remove hood and the air cleaner.
3. Remove radiator shrouds, as needed, disconnect radiator hoses and remove radiator.
4. Disconnect heater hoses, then the brake booster vacuum hose.
5. Disconnect fuel hoses, then the accelerator cable.
6. Disconnect starter motor wiring harness, then the clutch cable from transmission.
7. Disconnect alternator wiring harness, then the engine ground cable.
8. Disconnect coil wiring, then the water temperature gauge connector.
9. Remove power steering pump, if equipped, then disconnect the oil pressure switch or oil pressure gauge unit harness.
10. On models less 4WD, remove under cover.
11. On 4WD models, remove engine under cover and skid plate, then the transfer case protector.
12. On all models, disconnect speedometer cable at transmission.
13. On 2WD models, disconnect back-up light switch harness. On 4WD models, disconnect back-up light switch harness and 4WD indicator light harness.
14. Remove drive shaft(s).
15. Remove gearshift lever assembly.
16. Support transmission with a suitable jack, then remove rear insulator and No. 2 crossmember.
17. On 4WD models, support transfer case with a suitable jack, then remove transfer case mounting bracket and support insulator from side frame plate. Remove side frame plate, then the transfer case mounting bracket from case.
18. On all models, remove engine mount attaching nuts from front insulators.
19. Attach suitable lifting fixture to engine, then remove engine/transmission assembly from vehicle.
20. Reverse procedure to install, noting the following:
   a. Torque front insulators to engine mounting bracket attaching bolts to 22-29 ft. lbs.
   b. Torque front insulators to engine support bracket attaching bolts to 10-14 ft. lbs.
   c. Torque No. 2 crossmember to side frame attaching bolts to 29-36 ft. lbs. on models less 4WD and 40-54 ft. lbs. on models W/4WD.
   d. Torque rear insulator to No. 2 crossmember attaching bolts to 11-14 ft. lbs. on models less 4WD and 22-30 ft. lbs. on models W/4WD.
   e. Torque rear insulator to transmission attaching bolts to 15-17 ft. lbs. on models less 4WD and 14-18 ft. lbs. on models W/4WD.
   f. On models W/4WD, torque plate to side frame, transfer case support insulator to mounting bracket and transfer case mounting bracket to transfer case attaching bolts to 14-18 ft. lbs.

RAM RAIDER

1. Disconnect battery ground cable and drain cooling system.
2. Mark installation position of hood hinges and remove hood.
3. Remove engine under cover and engine and transmission skid plates, then drain transmission.
4. On models equipped with A/C and/or power steering, discharge refrigerant and drain power steering system.
5. Remove air cleaner and disconnect control cables from throttle lever and brackets.
6. Disconnect radiator and recovery tank hoses, and remove upper and lower shrouds.
7. Disconnect and plug transmission cooler lines, if equipped, then remove radiator.
8. Disconnect brake booster hose and heater hoses.
9. Mark and disconnect necessary electrical connectors and vacuum hoses from engine and transmission, and secure harnesses aside to prevent damage.
10. Disconnect and plug power steering hoses, fuel inlet and outlet hoses and refrigerant lines, as equipped.
11. Remove bolt securing ground to left front of engine, then disconnect exhaust pipe from manifold.
12. Remove transmission/transfer case shifter assemblies and the front and rear propeller shafts, as equipped.
13. Disconnect speedometer cable, 4 wheel drive indicator and overdrive solenoid electrical connectors, and the oil cooler feed and return hoses at the front crossmember.
14. On manual transmission models, remove bolt securing clutch slave cylinder and secure cylinder aside.
15. On automatic transmission models, remove gear selector cross shaft, noting position of bushings, washers and springs for installation, then remove transmission control rod.
16. Support transmission with suitable jack, then remove rear mount support plates, transfer case mounting bracket and insulator, and the rear mount and crossmember assembly.
17. Attach suitable lifting equipment to engine, remove engine mount nuts and bolts securing mount insulators to frame, then lift engine and transmission assembly from vehicle.
18. Reverse procedure to install, noting the following:
   a. Torque engine mount insulator bolts to 22-29 ft. lbs. and mount nuts to 4-7 ft. lbs.

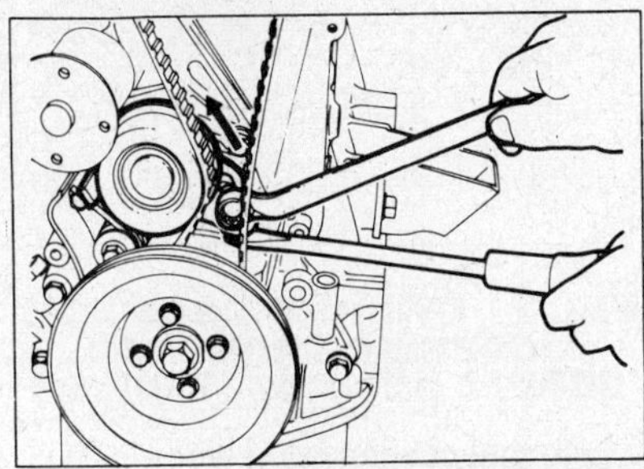

Fig. 1 Positioning timing belt tensioner toward water pump. 1400cc engine

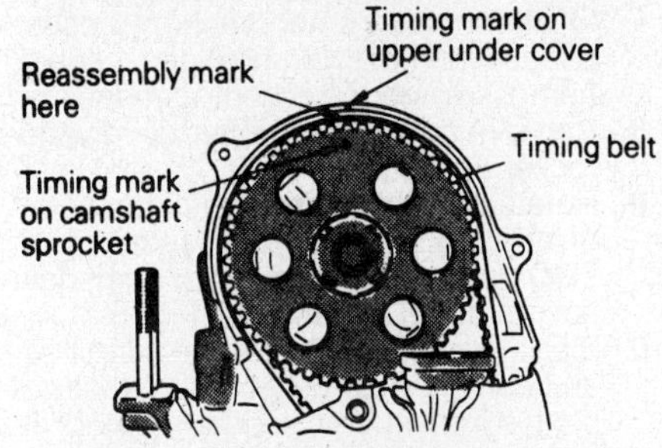

Fig. 4 Camshaft timing marks. 1600cc engines

b. Torque crossmember bolts to 50-54 ft. lbs., support plate bolts mount and transfer case bracket bolts to 13-18 ft. lbs., transfer case insulator nut top 22-30 ft. lbs.
c. Torque propeller shaft companion flange bolts to 36-43 ft. lbs.

CYLINDER HEAD REPLACE

1400cc ENGINE

1. Position No. 1 cylinder at top dead center compression stroke.
2. Drain cooling system, then disconnect upper radiator hose at engine.
3. Remove crankcase breather hose connected between rocker arm cover and air cleaner, then remove air cleaner assembly.
4. Disconnect vacuum hose, coolant hose, accelerator linkage and fuel line at carburetor.
5. Disconnect spark plug wires at spark plugs, then remove distributor assembly.
6. Remove carburetor assembly, then remove intake manifold.
7. Remove heat cowl and exhaust manifold.
8. Remove timing belt cover, then move timing belt tensioner toward water pump as far as possible and secure in this position, **Fig. 1.**
9. Remove timing belt from camshaft sprocket. **Do not remove belt from crankshaft sprocket. Do not rotate crankshaft or camshaft independently.**
10. Remove rocker arm cover, then remove cylinder head bolts in sequence shown in **Fig. 2,** using tool No. TW-

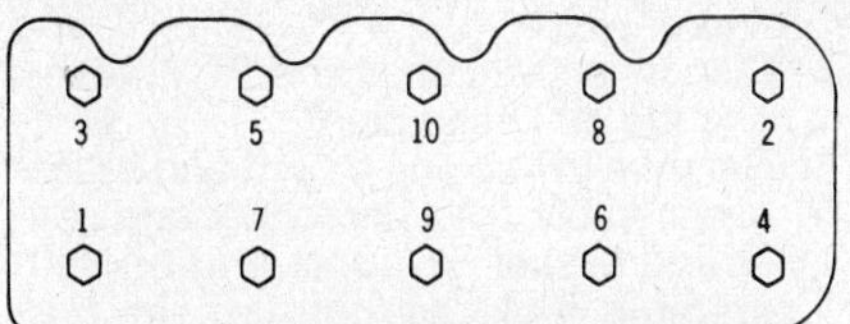

Fig. 2 Cylinder head bolt loosening sequence. 1400cc, 1600cc & 2000cc engines

10B. **Loosen cylinder head bolts evenly, in three steps, to avoid cylinder head warpage.**

11. Remove cylinder head assembly from engine, then clean cylinder head and cylinder block gasket surfaces.
12. Reverse procedure to install, noting the following:
    a. Do not apply sealer to cylinder head gasket or gasket surfaces.
    b. When installing intake manifold gasket, apply sealer to both sides of gasket at passage opening. Do not allow sealer to contact jet air passage.
    c. Prior to installing cylinder head on engine, ensure that crankshaft and camshaft timing marks are aligned as outlined in "Timing Belt, Replace."
    d. When tightening cylinder head bolts, refer to **Fig. 3** for tightening sequence and torque bolts in two steps to ensure proper cylinder head to cylinder block seating.
    e. Before installing timing belt, position belt tensioner toward water pump as far as possible. After installing timing belt check to ensure that tension side is tight, by turning camshaft sprocket slightly in the reverse direction of rotation and noting that all marks are aligned. Refer to "Timing Belt, Replace."
    f. After cylinder head has been installed, adjust timing belt tension and valve clearance as outlined.

1600cc ENGINE

Exc. Turbocharged Engine

1. Drain cooling system, then disconnect upper radiator hose from engine.
2. Remove canister purge hose and PCV valve breather hose, then the air cleaner assembly and disconnect fuel line at carburetor.
3. Disconnect vacuum hose at distributor and purge control valve.
4. Disconnect spark plug wires at spark plugs, then remove distributor.
5. Disconnect heater hose from intake manifold.
6. Disconnect coolant hose at carburetor.
7. Disconnect coolant temperature wire connector, then remove fuel pump.
8. Disconnect exhaust pipe from exhaust manifold, then remove exhaust manifold from cylinder head.
9. Remove intake manifold and carburetor as an assembly from cylinder head.

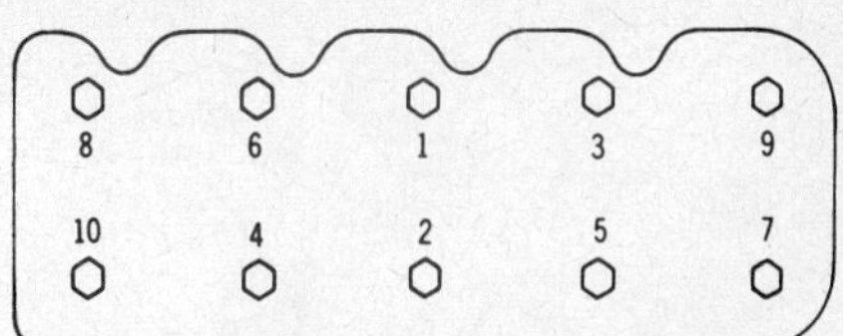

Fig. 3 Cylinder head bolt tightening sequence. 1400cc, 1600cc & 2000cc engines

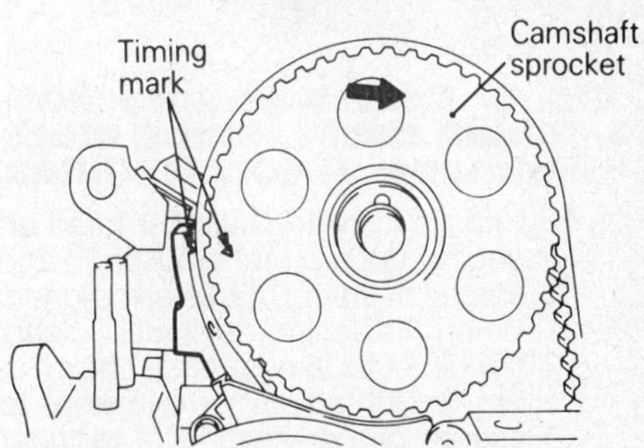

Fig. 5 Camshaft timing marks. 2000cc engine

10. Remove timing belt upper front cover, then rotate crankshaft to bring No. 1 cylinder to top dead center compression stroke. The No. 1 cylinder is at top dead center compression stroke when the mark on the upper timing under cover is aligned with the mark on the camshaft sprocket, **Fig. 4.**
11. Place an alignment mark on timing belt, in line with mark on camshaft sprocket, **Fig. 4.**
12. Remove camshaft sprocket attaching bolt, then detach sprocket from camshaft with timing belt attached. The timing belt lower cover incorporates a holder which will retain the camshaft sprocket in position. If clearance between camshaft sprocket and lower front cover is considerable, a piece of timing belt or other suitable spacer should be inserted between sprocket and holder. This is done to prevent the timing belt from becoming dislodged from the crankshaft sprocket or oil pump sprocket. **Use care not to rotate crankshaft after sprocket has been detached from camshaft.**
13. Remove three timing belt upper under cover bolts, then remove cover.
14. Remove rocker arm cover attaching bolts, then the rocker cover.
15. Remove cylinder head attaching bolts in sequence shown in **Fig. 2.** Loosen bolts evenly, in three steps, to prevent cylinder head warpage. Two dowel pins are used to locate the cylinder head on the cylinder block. When removing cylinder head use care not to disturb the camshaft sprocket and timing belt. After removing cylinder head, clean gasket surfaces on head and block.
16. Reverse procedure to install, noting the following;
    a. When applying sealer, use care not to allow sealer to contact jet air passage.

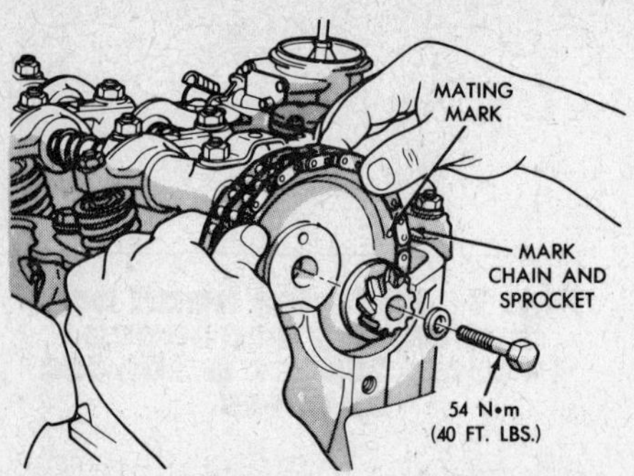

Fig. 6 Camshaft sprocket & timing chain timing mark alignment. 2600cc engines

b. Prior to installing cylinder head on engine, ensure that crankshaft and camshaft timing marks are aligned.
c. When installing cylinder head, tighten bolts in sequence shown in **Fig. 3.** Tighten bolts in two steps to ensure proper seating of cylinder head to cylinder block.
d. Before installing intake manifold gasket, apply sealer to both sides of gasket at water passage openings.
e. After cylinder head has been installed, adjust timing belt tension and valve clearance as outlined.

Turbocharged Engine

1. Relieve fuel pressure as follows:
   a. Remove rear seat and pull back carpet.
   b. With engine running, disconnect fuel pump connector.
   c. Allow engine to deplete fuel supply, then turn ignition Off. **Failure to release pressure prior to disconnecting fuel lines may cause fire or personal injury.**
2. Disconnect battery ground cable, remove left engine under cover and drain cooling system, then disconnect upper radiator hose.
3. Disconnect and plug oil return line from turbocharger.
4. Disconnect air flow sensor electrical connector, then remove air cleaner.
5. Remove bolts securing power steering pump to bracket and position pump aside, then remove pump bracket.
6. Remove alternator and position aside, then remove condenser fan motor, if equipped.
7. Disconnect hose from air injection tube, then remove air injection and dipstick tubes.
8. Mark and disconnect necessary electrical connectors and vacuum hoses, release harness from clips and secure aside.
9. Remove bolt securing engine ground to manifold.
10. Disconnect coil high tension lead and remove plug wires.
11. Remove solenoid valve bracket from above distributor.
12. Disconnect fuel hoses, heater and manifold water hoses and the brake booster hose.
13. Disconnect control cables from throttle body.
14. Disconnect breather and PCV hoses, and the air intake pipe.
15. Remove left engine mount and bracket assembly, then the rocker arm cover and gasket. **Support engine with suitable jack, as needed, to prevent engine from twisting in mounts.**
16. Remove timing belt upper front cover, then rotate crankshaft in normal direction of rotation to bring No. 1 cylinder to top dead center compression stroke. The No. 1 cylinder is at top dead center compression stroke when the mark on the upper timing under cover is aligned with the mark on the camshaft sprocket, **Fig. 4.**
17. Place an alignment mark on timing belt, in line with mark on camshaft sprocket, **Fig. 4.**
18. Remove camshaft sprocket attaching bolt, then detach sprocket from camshaft with timing belt attached. Position camshaft sprocket on lower belt cover or suspend sprocket and belt from hood to maintain proper timing alignment. **Do not rotate crankshaft after removing sprocket from camshaft.**
19. Remove timing belt upper under cover and turbocharger heat shield, if equipped.
20. Remove cylinder head attaching bolts in sequence shown in **Fig. 2.** Loosen bolts evenly, in three steps, to prevent cylinder head warpage. Two dowel pins are used to locate the cylinder head on the cylinder block. When removing cylinder head use care not to disturb the camshaft sprocket and timing belt. After removing cylinder head, clean gasket surfaces on head and block.
21. Reverse procedure to install, noting the following;
   a. Do not apply sealer to cylinder head gasket.
   b. Prior to installing cylinder head on engine, ensure that crankshaft and camshaft are aligned.
   c. When installing cylinder head, tighten bolts in sequence shown in **Fig. 3.** Tighten bolts in two steps to ensure proper seating of cylinder head to cylinder block.
   d. Before installing intake manifold gasket, apply sealer to both sides of gasket at water passage openings.
   e. After cylinder head has been installed, adjust timing belt tension and valve clearance as outlined.
   f. When installing rocker cover, apply 3M sealant 8660 or equivalent to semi-circular packing.

2000cc ENGINES

1. Disconnect battery ground cable and drain cooling system.
2. Remove air cleaner and disconnect control cables from throttle lever and bracket.
3. Disconnect exhaust pipe from manifold.
4. Disconnect upper radiator hose and heater hoses as needed.

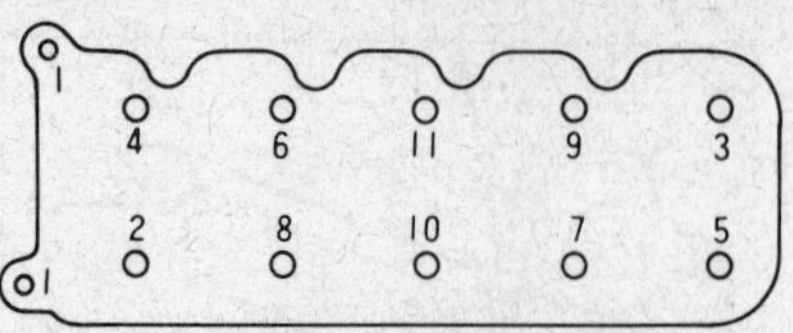

Fig. 7 Cylinder head bolt loosening sequence. 2600cc engines (Typical)

5. Disconnect spark plug wires.
6. Remove power steering pump mounting bolts and drive belt, then secure pump aside leaving hoses connected.
7. Mark and disconnect necessary electrical connectors and vacuum hoses, release harness clamps and secure harness aside to prevent damage.
8. Remove timing belt upper cover and rocker arm cover.
9. Rotate crankshaft in normal direction of rotation until No. 1 cylinder is at TDC and crankshaft and camshaft timing marks are aligned, **Fig. 5.**
10. Place chalk mark between timing belt and camshaft sprocket, remove camshaft sprocket bolt, separate sprocket from camshaft leaving belt in place on sprocket, then secure sprocket and belt on lower timing cover. Take care that sprocket does not disengage from belt and fall, and maintain tension on belt to maintain proper timing. **Do not rotate crankshaft after sprocket is removed from camshaft.**
11. Remove cylinder head attaching bolts in sequence shown in **Fig. 2.** Loosen bolts evenly, in three steps, to prevent cylinder head warpage, then remove cylinder head and gasket. Take care not to dislodge camshaft sprocket during cylinder head removal.
12. Reverse procedure to install, noting the following;
   a. Do not apply sealer to cylinder head gasket. Ensure that proper I.D. mark is on gasket and install with mark towards cylinder head.
   b. Prior to installing cylinder head on engine, ensure that crankshaft and camshaft timing marks are aligned.
   c. When installing cylinder head, tighten bolts in sequence shown in **Fig. 3.** Tighten bolts in two steps to ensure proper seating of cylinder head to cylinder block.
   d. After cylinder head has been installed, adjust timing belt tension and valve clearance as outlined.
   e. When installing rocker cover, apply 3M sealant 8660 or equivalent to semicircular packing.

2600cc ENGINES

Conquest

1. Release residual fuel pressure as follows:
   a. Start engine, then disconnect electrical connector from fuel pump.
   b. When engine stops from lack of fuel, turn off ignition. **Failure to release pressure prior to disconnecting fuel lines may cause fire or personal injury.**

2. Disconnect battery ground cable and drain crankcase and cooling system.
3. On models with A/C, loosen compressor drive belt tensioner and remove drive belt.
4. On all models, remove master cylinder and turbocharger heat shields and disconnect oxygen sensor lead from harness connector.
5. Remove air cleaner assembly.
6. On models with intercooler, proceed as follows:
   a. Disconnect intercooler hoses from turbocharger and air inlet tube.
   b. Disconnect boost sensor hose.
   c. Disconnect electrical connector from air intake temperature sensor on air intake tube.
7. On all models, disconnect upper radiator hose and remove air intake tube.
8. Remove secondary air cleaner, then disconnect PCV hose.
9. Disconnect control cables from throttle lever and brackets.
10. Remove bolt securing boost sensor tube.
11. Remove rocker arm cover, gasket and semi-circular packing.
12. Rotate crankshaft clockwise until No. 1 cylinder is at TDC on compression stroke and camshaft sprocket timing mark and plated link on timing chain are aligned as shown in **Fig. 6.**
13. Remove distributor cap and spark plug wires, mark position of distributor rotor and installation position of distributor, then remove distributor. **Do not rotate crankshaft with distributor removed.**
14. Disconnect fuel hoses, water hoses and brake booster hose.
15. Mark and disconnect necessary electrical connectors and vacuum hoses, release harness clips and secure harness aside to prevent damage.
16. Remove dipstick tube and O-ring seal, and plug opening.
17. Disconnect and plug turbocharger oil lines.
18. Disconnect water hoses from turbocharger, if equipped, and disconnect exhaust pipe.
19. Remove camshaft sprocket bolt and distributor drive gear.
20. Separate camshaft sprocket leaving timing chain on sprocket, then seat sprocket and chain assembly on sprocket holder inside timing cover. Maintain tension on chain and do not allow chain to come off sprocket. **Do not rotate crankshaft with camshaft sprocket removed.**
21. Remove cylinder head attaching bolts in sequence shown in **Fig. 7.** Loosen bolts evenly, in three steps, to prevent cylinder head warpage, then remove cylinder head and gasket. Take care not to dislodge camshaft sprocket during cylinder head removal.
22. Reverse procedure to install, noting the following;
   a. Do not apply sealer to cylinder head gasket. Apply a thin bead of sealer at joint between timing cover and cylinder block. Ensure that proper I.D. mark is on gasket and install with mark at front of engine and facing up.
   b. Prior to installing cylinder head on engine, ensure that crankshaft and camshaft timing marks are aligned.
   c. Tighten cylinder head bolts in sequence shown in **Fig. 8.** Tighten bolts in two steps to ensure proper seating of cylinder head to cylinder block.
   d. Install sprocket and chain on camshaft, then the distributor drive gear and sprocket bolt, and torque bolt to 37-43 ft. lbs. Ensure that timing marks are aligned, **Fig. 6.**
   e. Install distributor, aligning matching marks made during disassembly.
   f. When installing rocker cover, apply 3M sealant 8660 or equivalent to semi-circular packing.

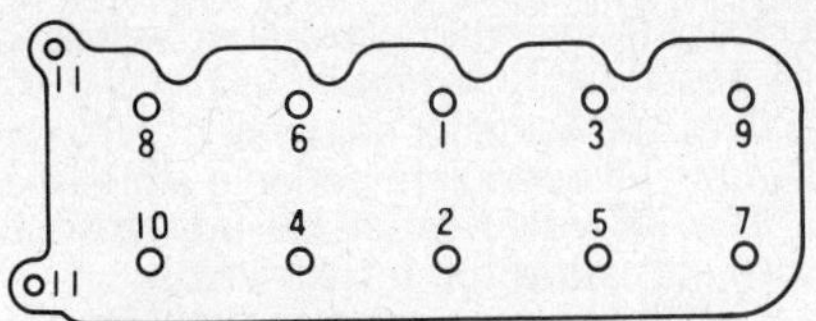

Fig. 8 Cylinder head bolt tightening sequence. 2600cc engines (Typical)

Ram 50 & Ram Raider

1. Disconnect battery ground cable and drain cooling system.
2. Remove air cleaner and disconnect control cables from throttle lever and brackets.
3. Disconnect radiator, breather and PCV hoses, and on Raider, disconnect power steering breather pipe.
4. On models with A/C, loosen compressor drive belt tensioner and remove drive belt.
5. On all models, mark and disconnect necessary electrical connectors, fuel and water hoses, and vacuum hoses, then release harness clips and secure harnesses aside to prevent damage.
6. Disconnect exhaust pipe from manifold.
7. Remove distributor cap and plug wires, and the rocker cover, gasket and semi-circular packing.
8. Rotate crankshaft clockwise until No. 1 cylinder is at TDC on compression stroke and camshaft sprocket timing mark and plated link on timing chain are aligned as shown in **Fig. 6.**
9. Mark position of distributor rotor and installation position of distributor, then remove distributor. **Do not rotate crankshaft with distributor removed.**
10. Remove camshaft sprocket bolt and distributor drive gear.
11. Separate camshaft sprocket leaving timing chain on sprocket, then seat sprocket and chain assembly on sprocket holder inside timing cover. Maintain tension on chain and do not allow chain to come off sprocket. **Do not rotate crankshaft with camshaft sprocket removed.**
12. Remove cylinder head attaching bolts in sequence shown in **Fig. 7.** Loosen bolts evenly, in three steps, to prevent cylinder head warpage, then remove cylinder head and gasket. Take care not to dislodge camshaft sprocket during cylinder head removal.
13. Reverse procedure to install, noting the following;
   a. Do not apply sealer to cylinder head gasket. Apply a thin bead of sealer at joint between timing cover and cylinder block.
   b. Prior to installing cylinder head on engine, ensure that crankshaft and camshaft timing marks are aligned.
   c. Tighten cylinder head bolts in sequence shown in **Fig. 8.** Tighten bolts in two steps to ensure proper seating of cylinder head to cylinder block.
   d. Install sprocket and chain on camshaft, then the distributor drive gear and sprocket bolt, and torque bolt to 37-43 ft. lbs. Ensure that timing marks are aligned, **Fig. 6.**
   e. Install distributor, aligning matching marks made during disassembly.
   f. When installing rocker cover, apply 3M sealant 8660 or equivalent to semi-circular packing.

1500cc ENGINES

Removal

1. Disconnect battery ground cable and drain cooling system.
2. Disconnect breather and secondary air hose, then remove air cleaner assembly, air intake duct and hot air duct.
3. Disconnect accelerator cable from throttle lever and brackets.
4. Disconnect upper radiator, heater and water hoses, fuel hoses and the brake booster hose.
5. On models with auto. trans., disconnect throttle cable from engine. On models with manual trans., disconnect clutch cable and secure aside.
6. Mark and disconnect necessary electrical connectors and vacuum hoses, release harness clips and secure harnesses aside to prevent damage.
7. Disconnect ignition coil high tension lead, then remove distributor cap and plug wires.
8. Support engine as needed, then remove left engine mount bracket from cylinder head.
9. Remove exhaust manifold covers and disconnect exhaust pipe from manifold.
10. Remove engine oil dipstick and plug opening.
11. Remove upper timing belt cover, rocker arm cover and the gasket.
12. Rotate crankshaft in normal direction of rotation to bring No. 1 cylinder to top dead center compression stroke. The No. 1 cylinder is at top dead center compression stroke when the mark on the upper timing under cover is aligned with the mark on the cam-

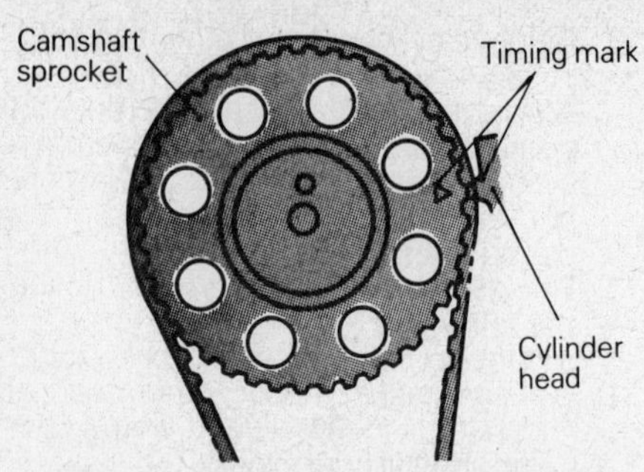

Fig. 9 Camshaft timing marks. 1500cc engine

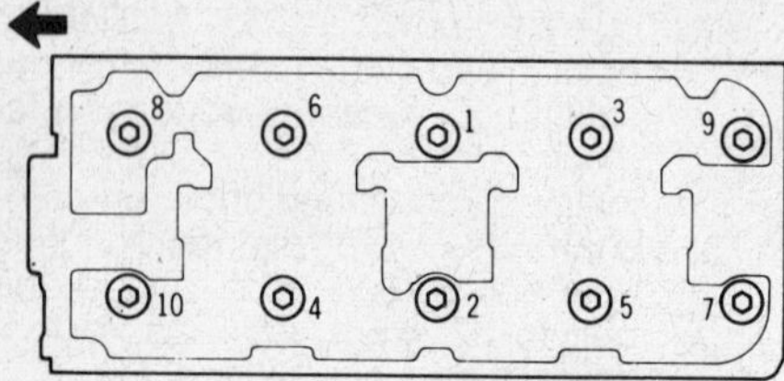

Fig. 11 Cylinder head bolt tightening sequence. 1500cc engine

shaft sprocket, **Fig. 9.**

13. Place an alignment mark on timing belt, in line with mark on camshaft sprocket timing mark, **Fig. 9.**
14. Remove camshaft sprocket attaching bolt, then detach sprocket from camshaft with timing belt attached. Position camshaft sprocket on lower belt cover or suspend sprocket and belt from hood to maintain proper timing alignment. **Do not rotate crankshaft after removing sprocket from camshaft.**
15. Remove cylinder head attaching bolts in sequence shown in **Fig. 10.** Loosen bolts evenly, in three steps, to prevent cylinder head warpage, then remove cylinder head and gasket. Take care not to dislodge camshaft sprocket during cylinder head removal.
16. Reverse procedure to install, noting the following;
    a. Do not apply sealer to cylinder head gasket. Install gasket with I.D. mark toward timing belt.
    b. Prior to installing cylinder head on engine, ensure that crankshaft and camshaft timing marks are aligned.
    c. Tighten cylinder head bolts in sequence shown in **Fig. 11.** Tighten bolts in two steps to ensure proper seating of cylinder head to cylinder block.
    d. After cylinder head has been installed, adjust timing belt tension and valve clearance as outlined.

VALVES

ADJUST

INTAKE & EXHAUST VALVES

On 1985-87 2000cc and 2600cc engines, the intake and exhaust valves are equipped with hydraulic lash adjusters with no provision for adjustment. However, the jet valve requires periodic adjustment.

The jet valve must be adjusted before adjusting the intake valve.

1. With engine at operating temperature, remove rocker arm cover.
2. Disconnect high tension lead from ignition coil.
3. While observing rocker arms on No. 4 cylinder, rotate crankshaft until the exhaust valve is closing and the intake valve has just started to open with crankshaft pulley mark aligned with TDC mark on timing chain case. At this position the No. 1 cylinder is at top dead center compression stroke. Check and adjust valve clearance for both intake and exhaust valves of No. 1 cylinder, intake valve of No. 2 cylinder and exhaust valve of No. 3 cylinder, as necessary, **Fig. 12.**
4. Rotate crankshaft 360 degrees and check and adjust valve clearance for exhaust valve of No. 2 cylinder, intake valve of No. 3 cylinder and intake and exhaust valves of No. 4 cylinder.
5. After completing adjustment, install rocker arm cover and connect ignition coil high tension lead.

JET VALVE

Exc. Models Equipped W/Hydraulic Lash Adjusters

Following procedure for intake and exhaust valve adjustment, position No. 1 cylinder at top dead center compression stroke. Loosen intake valve adjusting screw at least 2 turns, then loosen jet valve adjusting screw locknut. Rotate jet valve adjusting screw counterclockwise and insert a suitable feeler gauge blade as specified in Valve Specification Chart, between jet valve stem and adjusting screw, **Fig. 13.** Tighten jet valve adjusting screw until it contacts the feeler gauge blade, then while holding adjusting screw in position, tighten locknut. After jet valve adjustment has been completed, adjust intake valve clearance. Continue to follow intake and exhaust valve adjustment procedure and adjust jet valves as necessary.

Models Equipped W/Hydraulic Lash Adjusters

Following procedure for intake and exhaust valve adjustment, position No. 1 cylinder at top dead center compression stroke. Loosen jet valve adjusting screw locknut. Back off jet valve adjusting screw and insert a suitable feeler gauge as specified in "Valve Specification Chart" between jet valve stem and adjusting screw, **Fig. 13.** Tighten jet valve adjusting screw until it contacts the feeler gauge blade, then while holding screw in position, tighten locknut. Position remaining cylinders at top dead center and repeat jet valve adjustment procedure.

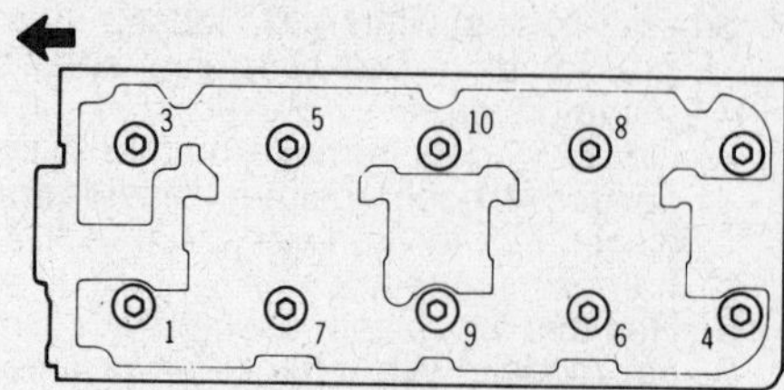

Fig. 10 Cylinder head bolt loosening sequence. 1500cc engine

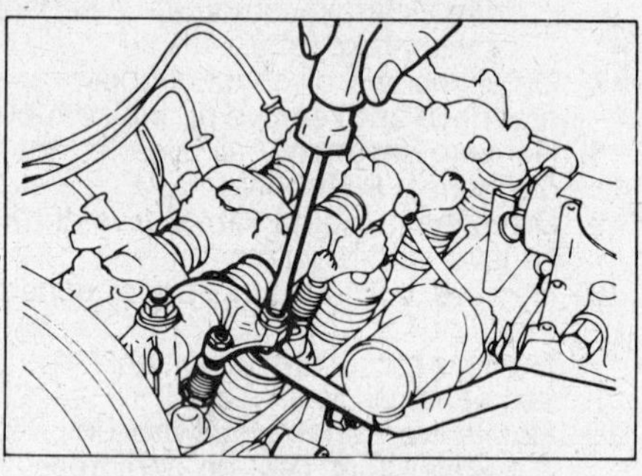

Fig. 12 Adjusting valve clearance (Typical)

CAMSHAFT, ROCKER ARMS & SHAFTS

REPLACE

1400cc ENGINE

Removal

1. Disconnect breather hose from air cleaner and rocker arm cover, then remove air cleaner.
2. Remove timing belt cover, position belt tensioner toward water pump as far as possible and secure in this position, then remove timing belt and camshaft sprocket as outlined in "Cylinder Head, Replace." **Do not rotate crankshaft after removing camshaft sprocket.**
3. Remove rocker arm cover.
4. Remove rocker arm shaft attaching bolts, then lift rocker shaft and arms as an assembly from cylinder head.
5. Remove rocker shaft bolts, rocker arms and springs from rocker shaft.
6. Remove rear cover from cylinder head, then remove camshaft thrust case retaining bolt and remove camshaft and thrust case from transaxle side of cylinder head, **Fig. 14.**

Installation

1. Install camshaft thrust case and thrust plate on end of camshaft, then install and tighten bolt. Check camshaft endplay using a feeler gauge, **Fig. 15.** Endplay should be .002-.008 inch. If endplay exceeds limits, replace thrust case and recheck endplay. If clear-

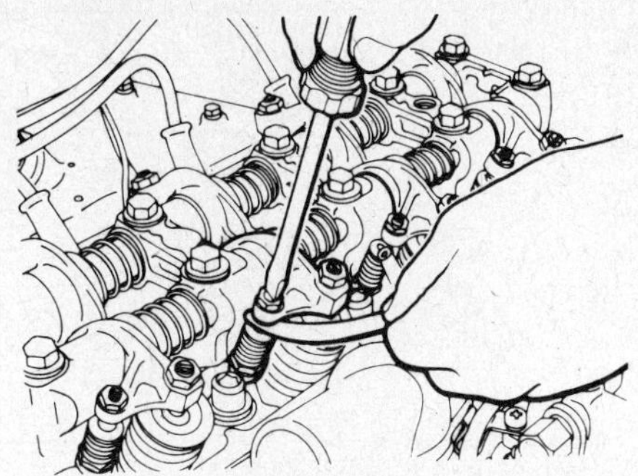

Fig. 13 Adjusting jet valve clearance

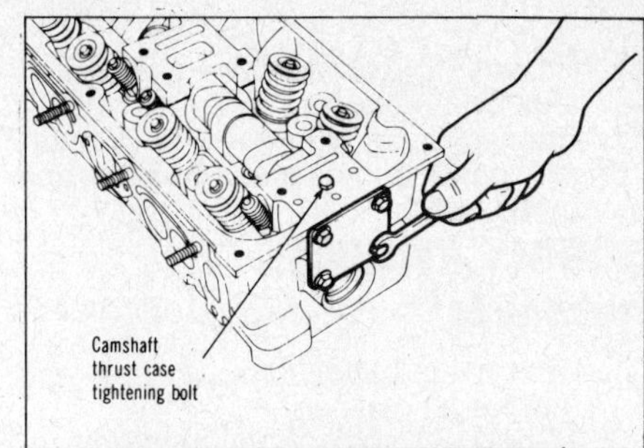

Fig. 14 Camshaft rear cover & thrust case bolt removal. 1400cc engine

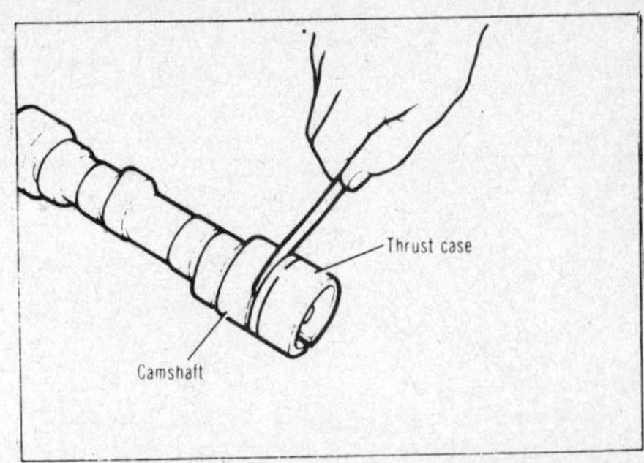

Fig. 15 Camshaft endplay check. 1400cc engine

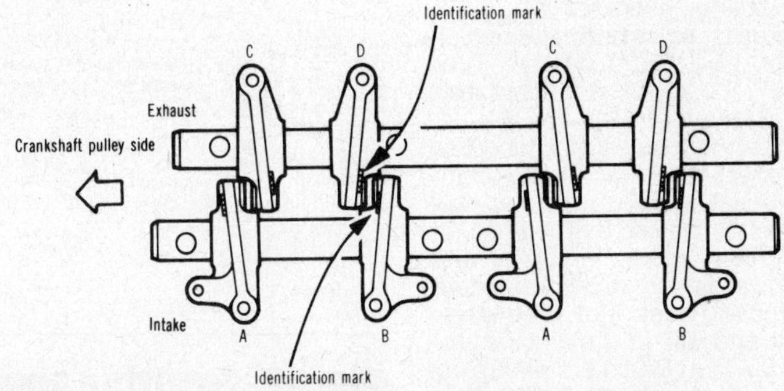

Fig. 16 Rocker arm & shaft assembly & installation. 1400cc engine

ance still exceeds limits, check rear camshaft journal for wear and replace camshaft, if necessary.

2. Lubricate bearing surfaces and thrust surfaces of camshaft with engine oil, then install camshaft from transaxle side of cylinder head. When installing camshaft, position thrust case so bolt hole is aligned with bolt hole in cylinder head, then install and tighten thrust case retaining bolt, **Fig. 14.**
3. Install timing belt under cover, ensure camshaft dowel pin hole is pointing up (TDC on compression stroke for No. 1 cylinder), then install camshaft sprocket and timing belt.
4. Release timing belt tensioner and ensure timing marks are properly aligned as outlined in "Timing Belt, Replace."
5. Install rocker arms and springs on rocker shaft, **Fig. 16.** Intake rocker arms have two adjusting screws, one for valve adjustment and the other for jet valve adjustment. Both intake and exhaust rocker have identification marks stamped on the side of the rocker arm at the valve end. Rocker arms marked 1-3 can be installed at cylinder locations 1 and 3. Rocker arms marked 2-4 can be installed at cylinder locations 2 and 4. Also note that rocker arm springs for exhaust rocker arms have a free length of 1.85 inch, while those for intake rocker arms have a free length of 3.03 inch.
6. Back-off rocker arm adjusting screws, install rocker arm and shaft assembly, and torque mounting bolts to 15-19 ft. lbs.
7. Align camshaft sprocket and crankshaft sprocket timing marks, referring to "Valves, Adjust" procedure. Set valve to a cold setting of .003 inch for intake and jet valves and .007 inch for exhaust valves.
8. Temporarily install rocker cover and gasket.
9. Start engine and allow to reach operating temperature. Adjust valves to warm clearance listed in "Valve Specifications Chart" as described under "Valves, Adjust."
10. Install rocker arm covers, then install timing belt cover.

1600cc ENGINE

Removal

1. Disconnect breather and purge hoses, then remove air cleaner.
2. Disconnect spark plug wires at spark plugs, then remove upper timing belt cover.
3. Rotate crankshaft until camshaft sprocket mark is aligned with mark on timing belt upper under cover, **Fig. 4.** This will position No. 1 cylinder at top dead center compression stroke.
4. Place alignment mark on timing belt in line with mark on camshaft sprocket.
5. Remove camshaft sprocket attaching bolt, then remove camshaft sprocket with timing belt attached to sprocket. The timing belt lower cover incorporates a sprocket holder which will hold camshaft sprocket in position. If clearance between sprocket and holder is excessive, insert a piece of timing belt approximately 2 inches long or other suitable material between sprocket and holder. This will prevent the timing belt from becoming dislodged from the crankshaft sprocket. **After sprocket has been removed from camshaft, use care not to rotate crankshaft.**
6. Remove camshaft spacer if equipped, then remove upper timing belt under cover.
7. Remove rocker arm cover and gasket, then remove camshaft bearing attaching bolts.
8. Remove rocker arms, rocker shafts and camshaft bearing caps as an assembly from cylinder head. Remove camshaft bearing cap bolts, then remove bearing caps, rocker arms and springs from rocker shafts.
9. On models less silent shaft, remove oil seal, distributor drive gear and camshaft as an assembly, then remove oil seal and distributor drive gear from camshaft.
10. On models with silent shaft, remove oil seal and distributor drive gear from camshaft, then remove camshaft from cylinder head.

Installation

1. Lubricate camshaft lobes and bearing surfaces with engine oil. Then position camshaft on cylinder head.
2. Check camshaft endplay, which should be .002 to .006 inch.
3. If removed, position distributor drive gear on camshaft.
4. On all models, position intake and exhaust rocker shafts into front camshaft bearing cap. Position shafts as shown in **Fig. 17.** Install bearing cap bolts retaining shafts in position.
5. Assemble rocker arms, spring and bearing caps. After installing rear camshaft bearing caps, insert bolts through rear bearing caps to retain rocker shaft components. When installing rocker arms, note that intake rocker arms have two adjusting screws.
6. Position camshaft so that camshaft key is 41° from cylinder head rocker arm cover mounting surface, as viewed front front of engine, **Fig. 18.**
7. On all models, position rocker arm assemblies on cylinder head, then install camshaft bearing cap attaching bolts. Torque camshaft bearing cap bolts to

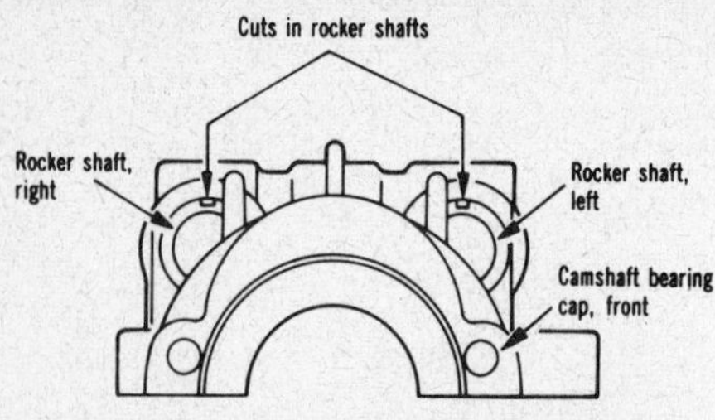

Fig. 17 Rocker arm shaft installation, 1600cc, 2000cc engines

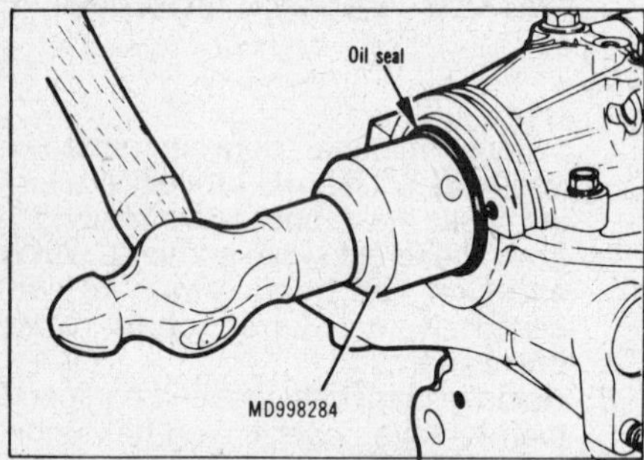

Fig. 19 Camshaft front oil seal installation. 1600cc engine

7 ft. lbs., starting at the center bearing cap and working outward and alternating from side to side. Torque bolts to a final toque of 14-15 ft. lbs. in the same sequence.

8. Lubricate camshaft front oil seal lips with engine oil, then install seal into camshaft front bearing bore using tool MD998284 or equivalent, **Fig. 19.** Tap seal into bore until tool contacts distributor drive gear.
9. Install upper timing belt under cover, then lubricate camshaft spacer with engine oil and install spacer on camshaft.
10. Pull camshaft sprocket upward and install on camshaft. If dowel hole on camshaft sprocket cannot be aligned with dowel on camshaft spacer, use a screwdriver at the two projections located to the rear of the No. 2 exhaust cam lobe to rotate the camshaft slightly to align dowel and dowel hole.
11. Install camshaft sprocket bolt and torque to 44-57 ft. lbs. on 1983-85 models or 59-72 ft. lbs. on 1986-87 models. **Check to ensure that crankshaft pulley, camshaft sprocket and timing belt to camshaft sprocket marks are aligned.**
12. Set valves to cold clearance of .003 inch for intake and jet valves and .007 inch for exhaust valves. Refer to "Valves, Adjust."
13. Temporarily install rocker arm cover.
14. Start engine and allow to reach operating temperature, then adjust valves to warm clearance, referring to "Valves, Adjust" and Valve Specifications Chart.
15. Remove rocker arm cover and apply sealer at locations indicated in **Fig. 20.**
16. Reinstall rocker arm cover and tighten attaching bolts.
17. Connect spark plug wires, then install air cleaner and connect breather and purge hoses.

2000cc ENGINES

Removal

1. Disconnect battery ground cable and remove air cleaner.
2. Disconnect spark plug wires and remove accessory drive belts, as needed.
3. Mark and disconnect necessary electrical connectors and vacuum hoses, then remove timing belt upper cover and rocker arm cover.
4. Rotate crankshaft in normal direction of rotation until No. 1 cylinder is at TDC and crankshaft and camshaft timing marks are aligned, **Fig. 5.**
5. Place chalk mark between timing belt and camshaft sprocket, remove camshaft sprocket bolt, separate sprocket from camshaft leaving belt in place on sprocket, then secure sprocket and belt on lower timing cover. Take care that sprocket does not disengage from belt and fall, and maintain tension on belt to maintain proper timing. **Do not rotate crankshaft after sprocket is removed from camshaft.**
6. Evenly loosen camshaft bearing cap/rocker arm retaining bolts in crossing pattern, remove bearing caps and rocker shafts as an assembly, then remove camshaft.
7. Disassemble components in numerical order, **Fig. 21,** noting position for installation.

Installation

1. Coat camshaft with suitable assembly lubricant and position cam in head, with camshaft aligned so that valves for No. 1 cylinder are closed (TDC on compression stroke).
2. Insert rocker shafts into front bearing cap, installing shaft with oil hole side down and noting that front end of shaft has a cut .16 inch wide, **Fig. 17.**
3. Apply engine oil to I.D. of rocker arms prior to assembly. Assemble rocker arms, springs and remaining bearing caps on rocker shafts, **Fig. 22,** in positions noted during disassembly.
4. On models with hydraulic lash adjusters, insert each adjuster into rocker arm taking care not to spill fluid from adjuster. Retain adjusters using suitable clips, **Fig. 23,** to prevent them from falling out during installation.
5. On all models, install assembly onto cylinder head and evenly tighten bolts in crossing pattern until bearing caps are seated. When caps are seated, torque bolts to specifications in crossing pattern.
6. Install sleeve over camshaft and press oil seal into place using suitable driver.
7. Install camshaft sprocket and timing belt, then ensure timing marks are properly aligned.

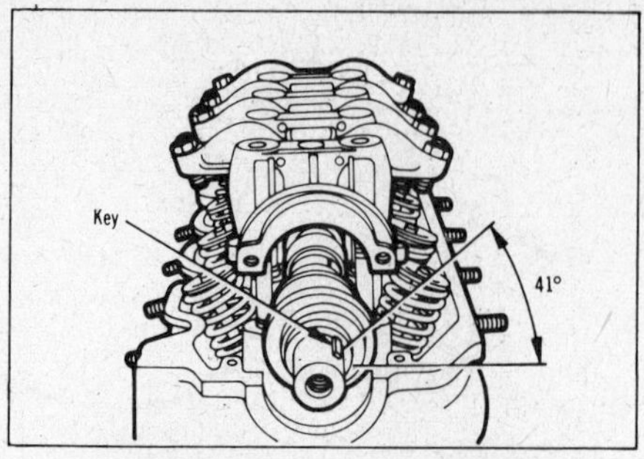

Fig. 18 Camshaft installation. 1600cc engine

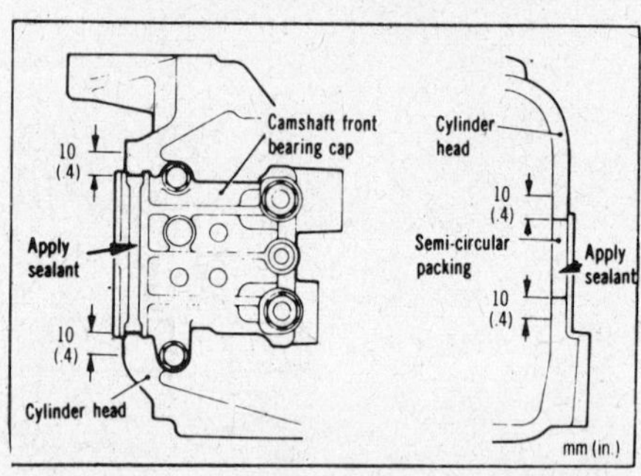

Fig. 20 Applying sealer for rocker cover installation. 1600cc engine

8. Adjust valves to specifications as outlined, then temporarily install rocker cover.
9. Reverse remaining procedure to complete installation, then check timing belt tension as outlined. After engine reaches normal operating temperature, recheck valve clearances and adjust as needed.
10. When installing rocker cover after checking valve clearances, apply suitable sealer to semi-circular packing and cylinder head, **Fig. 24,** then install rocker cover.

2600cc ENGINES

Removal

1. If rocker assembly and camshaft are being removed with cylinder head in place, proceed as follows:
   a. Remove necessary hoses cables and wiring to permit rocker cover removal, then remove cover and gasket.
   b. Rotate crankshaft clockwise until No. 1 cylinder is at TDC on compression stroke and camshaft sprocket timing mark and plated link on timing chain are aligned as shown in **Fig. 6.**
   c. Remove distributor cap and spark plug wires, mark position of distributor rotor and installation position of distributor, then remove distributor. **Do not rotate crankshaft with distributor removed.**
   d. Remove camshaft sprocket bolt and distributor drive gear.

(1) Oil filler cap
(2) Bolt (2)
(3) Washer (2)
(4) Oil seal (2)
(5) Rocker cover
(6) Rocker cover gasket
(7) Semi-circular packing
(8) Flange bolt (2)
(9) Flange bolt (10)
(10) Rocker arm and shaft assembly
-(1) Bearing cap, rear
-(2) Rocker arm "D" (2)
-(3) Spring (2)
-(4) Bearing cap, No. 4
-(5) Rocker arm "C" (2)
-(6) Spring (2)
-(7) Bearing cap, No. 3
-(8) Rocker arm "C" (2)
-(9) Spring (2)
-(10) Bearing cap, No. 2
-(11) Rocker arm "C" (2)
-(12) Spring
-(13) Wave washer
-(14) Nut (8)
-(15) Adjusting screw (8)
-(16) Rocker arm shaft, left
-(17) Rocker arm shaft, right
-(18) Bearing cap, front
(11) Camshaft

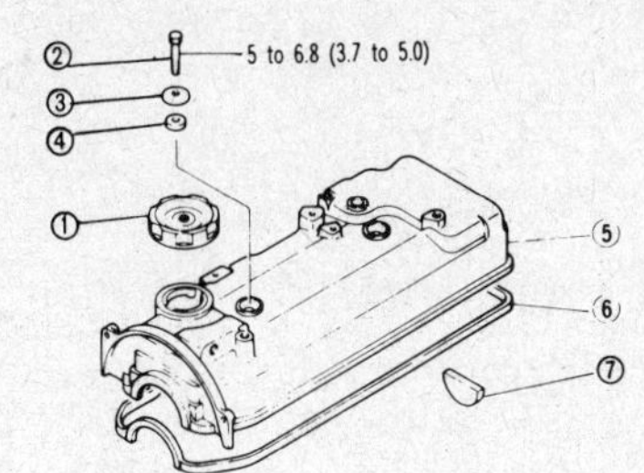

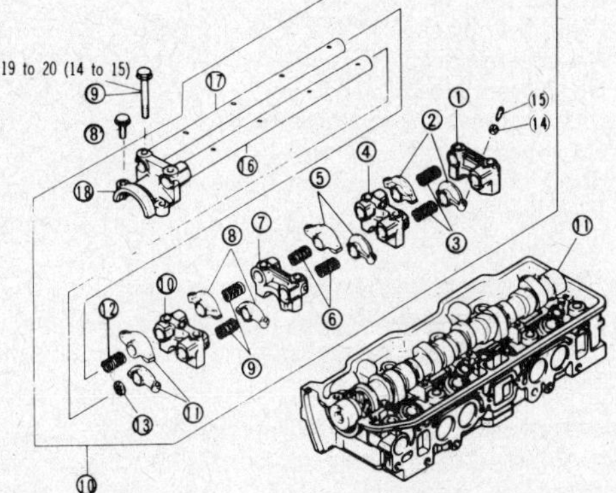

Tightening torque: Nm (ft-lbs.)

Fig. 21 Rocker arms, rocker shafts & camshaft exploded view. 2000cc engines

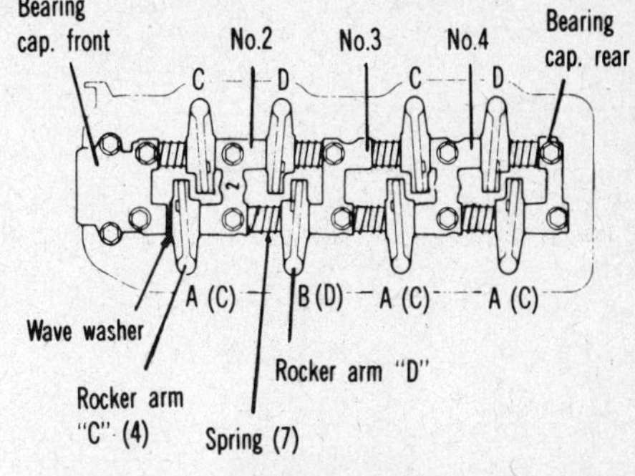

Fig. 22 Assembling rocker arms & rocker arm shafts. 2000cc engine

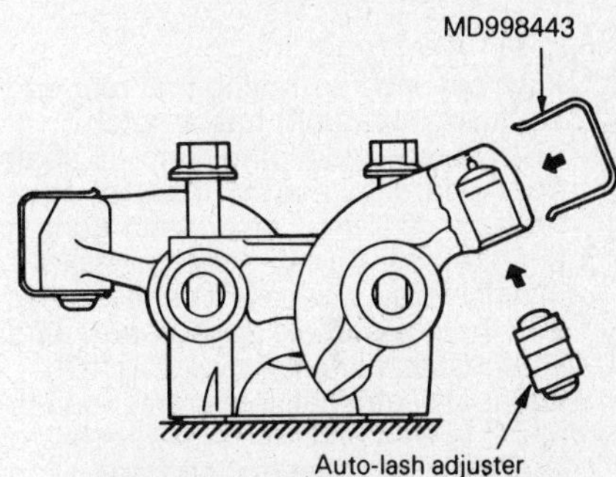

Fig. 23 Hydraulic lash adjuster & retaining clip installation. 1985–87 2000cc & 2600cc engines

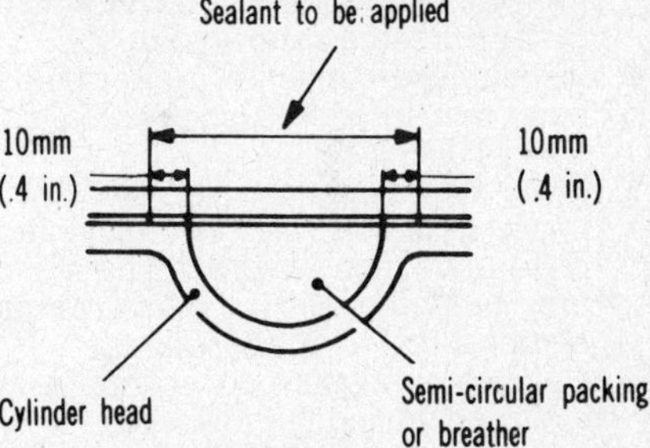

Fig. 24 Applying sealant to semi-circular packing

(1) Oil filler cap
(2) Bolt – 8 x 40 (2)
(3) Washer (2)
(4) Oil seal (2)
(5) Rocker cover
(6) Rocker cover gasket
(7) PCV valve
(8) Semi-circular packing
(9) Flange bolt (10)
(10) Flange bolt – 8 x 25 (2)
(11) Rocker arm and shaft assembly
-(1) Bearing cap, front
-(2) Wave washer (2)
-(3) Rocker arm "A" (4)
-(4) Adjusting screw (4)
-(5) Nut (4)
-(6) Adjusting screw (8)
-(7) Nut (8)
-(8) Rocker arm "C" (4)
-(9) Bearing cap, No. 2
-(10) Rocker arm spring (6)
-(11) Bearing cap, No. 3
-(12) Bearing cap, No. 4
-(13) Bearing cap, rear
-(14) Rocker arm shaft, left
-(15) Rocker arm shaft, right
(12) Circular packing
(13) Camshaft

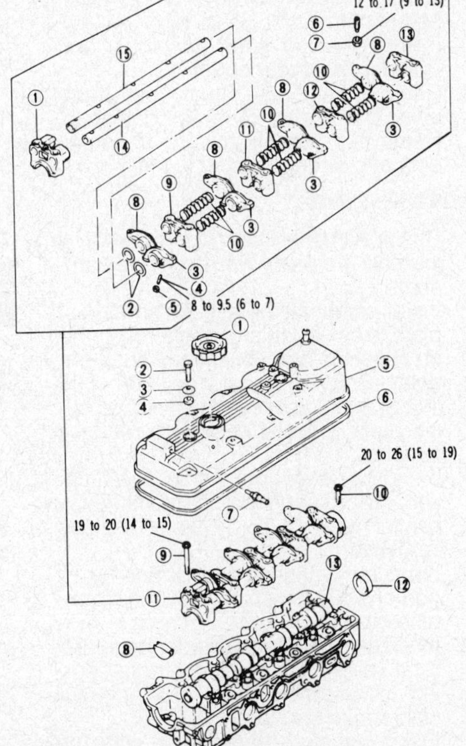

Tightening torque: Nm (ft-lbs.)

Fig. 25 Rocker arms, rocker shafts & camshaft exploded view. 2600cc engines

e. Separate camshaft sprocket leaving timing chain on sprocket, then seat sprocket and chain assembly on sprocket holder inside timing cover. Maintain tension on chain and do not allow chain to come off sprocket. **Do not rotate crankshaft with camshaft sprocket removed.**

2. Evenly loosen bolts securing camshaft bearing caps in crossing pattern, then remove caps, rockers and rocker shafts as an assembly. **On 1985-87 models with hydraulic lash adjusters, install suitable retainer clips over adjusters, Fig. 23, prior to removing rocker assembly.**
3. Remove parts in numerical order as shown, Fig. 25.

Installation

1. Insert left and right rocker shafts into

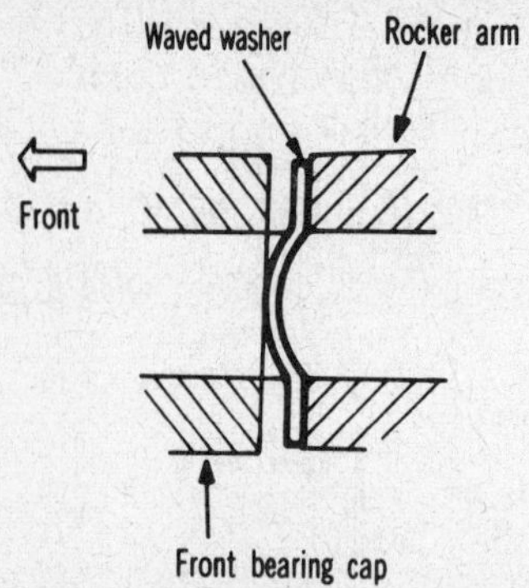

Fig. 26 Rocker shaft waved washer installation. 2600cc engines

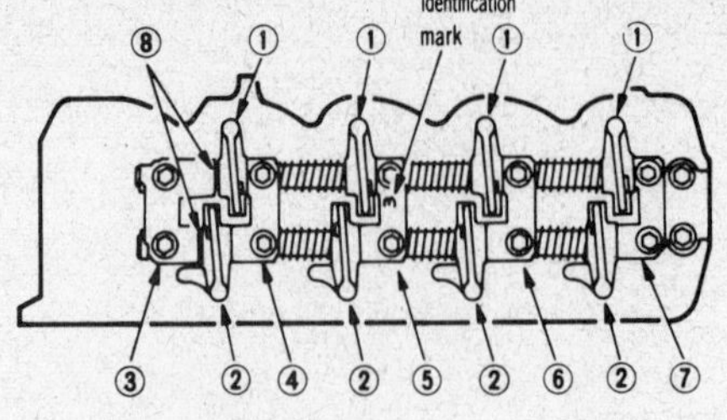

(1) Rocker arm "C"
(2) Rocker arm "A"
(3) Front bearing cap
(4) No. 2 bearing cap
(5) No. 3 bearing cap (Inscribed mark 3 on top surface)
(6) No. 4 bearing cap (Rocker screw hole on top surface)
(7) Rear bearing cap
(8) Waved washer

Fig. 27 Assembling rocker arms & rocker arm shafts. 2600cc engine

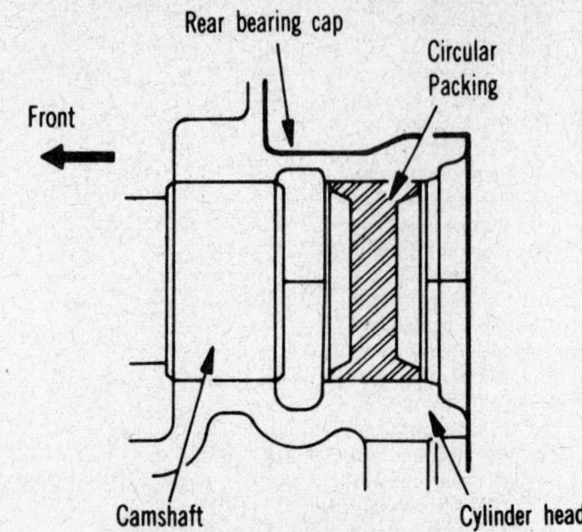

Fig. 28 Semicircular packing installation

front bearing cap, noting that rear end of intake shaft (left) has a notch.

2. Align mating mark of rocker arm shaft front end with mating mark of front bearing cap, then insert and tighten shaft to bearing cap attaching bolts.
3. Install waved washers as shown, **Fig. 26,** then assemble rocker arm and shaft assembly as shown, **Fig. 27.**
4. Lubricate camshaft lobes and bearing journals with engine oil, then position camshaft on cylinder head and align camshaft so that intake and exhaust valves for No. 1 cylinder will be fully closed (TDC on compression stroke for No. 1 cylinder).
5. Apply sealant to O.D. of circular packing, then assemble circular packing to cylinder head as shown, **Fig. 28.**
6. Install rocker assembly onto cylinder head, then torque bearing cap bolts to specifications.
7. Install camshaft sprocket and timing chain assembly, and the distributor drive gear, then ensure timing marks are properly aligned and torque sprocket bolt to specifications.
8. Reverse procedure to complete installation, noting the following:
   a. Install distributor, aligning matching marks made during disassembly.
   b. On 1983-84 models, adjust valve clearances as outlined.
   c. Install semi-circular packing to front of cylinder head, then apply a suitable sealant to top of packing.
   d. Install rocker cover and gasket, then torque to 3.7-5 ft. lbs.

1500cc ENGINE

Removal

1. Disconnect battery ground cable.
2. Disconnect breather hose and secondary air hose.
3. Remove air cleaner and the timing belt cover.
4. Rotate crankshaft in normal direction of rotation to bring No. 1 cylinder to top dead center compression stroke. The No. 1 cylinder is at top dead center compression stroke when the mark on the upper timing under cover is aligned with the mark on the camshaft sprocket, **Fig. 9.**
5. Move timing belt tensioner fully toward the water pump assembly and temporarily secure it.
6. Remove camshaft sprocket attaching bolt, then detach sprocket from camshaft with timing belt attached. Position camshaft sprocket on lower belt cover or suspend sprocket and belt from hood to maintain proper timing alignment. **Do not rotate crankshaft after removing sprocket from camshaft.**
7. Remove rocker cover, and note position of camshaft.
8. Remove rocker shaft assembly and cylinder head rear cover.
9. Remove camshaft thrust case tightening bolt, thrust case and camshaft. Remove assembly toward transaxle side of cylinder head.

Installation

1. Check camshaft journals for wear. If journals are badly worn, replace camshaft.
2. Install camshaft thrust case and thrust plate to camshaft end and firmly tighten attaching bolt. Check camshaft endplay. Endplay should be .002-.008 inch. If endplay exceeds specified value, replace thrust case and recheck endplay.
3. If endplay is still not within specification, check rear end of camshaft journal for wear. If badly worn, replace camshaft.
4. Lubricate camshaft journal and thrust portions of camshaft with clean engine oil.
5. Insert camshaft into cylinder head and rotate camshaft to position noted during disassembly (TDC on compression stroke for No. 1 cylinder).
6. Insert camshaft thrust case with the threaded hole facing upward. Align threaded hole with bolt hole in the cylinder head. Install and firmly tighten attaching bolt.
7. Install rear gasket and cover. Firmly tighten bolts.
8. Install camshaft oil seal. Lubricate external surface of seal completely with engine oil.
9. Ensure seal is completely seated.
10. Install camshaft sprocket and timing belt, and ensure timing marks are aligned, **Fig. 9.** Torque bolt to 47-54 ft. lbs.
11. Install rocker arm and shaft assembly.
12. Temporarily set valve clearances to specifications with the engine cold.
13. Install gasket in rocker cover groove, then temporarily install rocker cover.
14. Start and operate engine at idle speed until normal operating temperature is reached and adjust valve clearances. With engine hot, adjust jet valve clearance to specifications.
15. Install rocker cover.
16. Reverse remaining procedure to complete installation.

VALVE GUIDES REPLACE

1. Press old valve guide from cylinder head toward lower surface using pushrod from valve guide replacement kit, tool No. MD998115 and a suitable press.
2. Ream each valve guide bore in cylinder head to the O.D. of replacement valve guide, **Fig. 29.**
3. Press fit new valve guide into top of cylinder head using tool No. MD998115. This tool installs valve guide to a predetermined height. If a standard size valve guide has been removed, replacement valve guide should be oversized. New valve guide should be installed at room temperature.
4. After installation of new valve guides, insert valve and check for proper clearance. If clearance is not correct, ream guide until proper clearance is obtained. Refer to "Valve Specifications" for stem to guide clearance.

Engine	Valve Guide Oversize Inch (mm)	Valve Guide Mark	Valve Guide Cylinder Head Bore Inch (mm)
1400cc & 1500cc	.002 (.05)	5	.4766-.4770 (12.105-12.115)
	.010 (.25)	25	.4844-.4848 (12.305-12.315)
	.020 (.50)	50	.4943-.4947 (12.555-12.565)
1600, 2000 & 2600cc	.002 (.05)	5	.5138-.5145 (13.050-13.068)
	.010 (.25)	25	.5216-.5224 (13.250-13.268)
	.020 (.50)	50	.5315-.5323 (13.500-13.518)

Fig. 29 Valve guide & guide bore oversizes

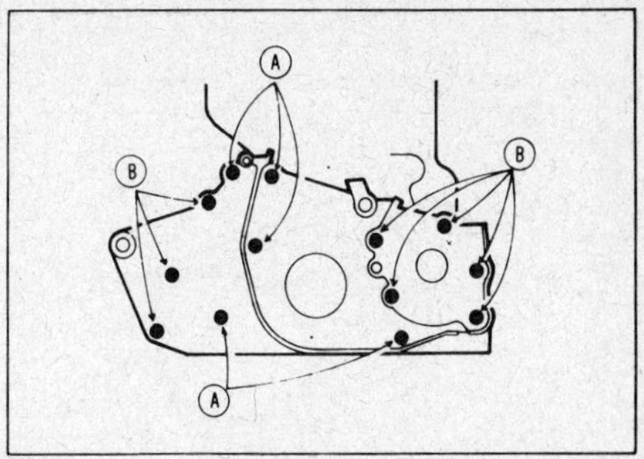

Fig. 30 Timing case cover bolt locations. 1600cc engine

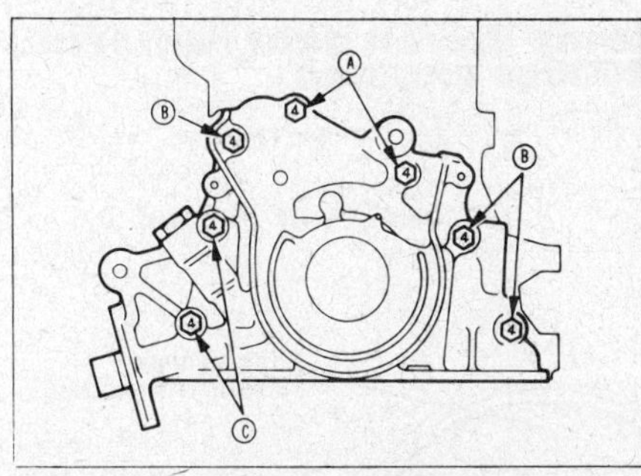

Fig. 31 Timing case cover bolt locations. 1400cc & 1500cc engine

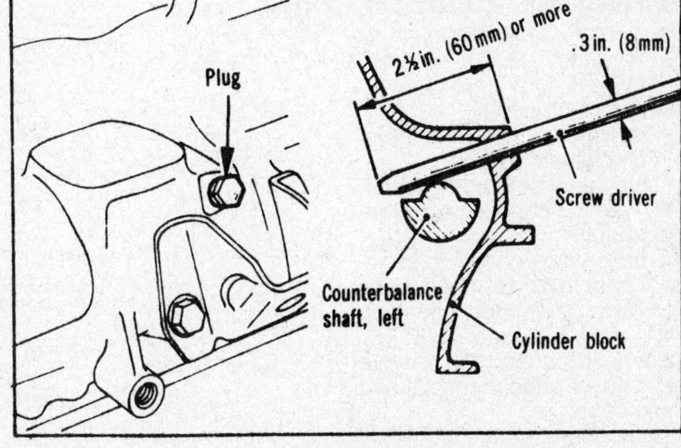

Fig. 32 Locking left silent shaft. 2000cc engines

TIMING CASE REPLACE

1600CC ENGINE

1. Remove timing belt as described under "Timing Belt or Chain, Replace."
2. Drain crankcase, then remove oil pan and oil pickup screen.
3. Remove oil pump cover, then remove eight front timing case to cylinder block attaching bolts and remove timing case and oil pump as an assembly.
4. Reverse procedure to install. When installing timing case attaching bolts, refer to **Fig. 30** and note that bolts to be installed in locations A are .31 X 1.38 inch (8 X 35 mm) and locations B are .31 X 1.57 inch (8 X 40 mm). Before installing oil pan, apply sealer at the four front timing case and rear oil seal case to cylinder block mating surfaces. Torque front timing case attaching bolts to 11-13 ft. lbs., oil pickup screen tube attaching bolts to 13-18 ft. lbs. and oil pan attaching bolts to 4.5-5.5 ft. lbs.

1400cc & 1500cc ENGINES

1. Remove timing belt as described under "Timing Belt, Replace."
2. Remove oil pan and oil screen, then the timing case.
3. Reverse procedure to install. When installing timing case attaching bolts, refer to **Fig. 31** and note that bolts to be installed in location A are 1.18 inch in length, bolts installed in location B are .79 inches in length and bolts installed in location C are 2.36 inches in length. When installing oil seal, lubricate seal lips with engine oil, then position seal on crankshaft and tap into timing case using tool No. MD998306. Before installing oil pan, apply sealer at the four front timing case and rear oil seal case to cylinder block mating surfaces. Torque front timing case attaching bolts to 9-10 ft. lbs. and oil pan attaching bolts to 4.5-5.5 ft. lbs.

2000cc ENGINES

1. Remove timing belt as described under "Timing Belt, Replace."
2. Remove camshaft sprocket, crankshaft sprocket and flange.
3. Remove timing belt tensioner.
4. Remove oil pump sprocket. When the oil pump sprocket nut is removed, first remove plug at bottom of left side of cylinder block, then insert a suitable screwdriver to keep the left counterbalance shaft in position, **Fig. 32.**
5. Loosen counterbalance shaft sprocket mounting bolt then remove tensioner "B," **Fig. 33,** and timing belt "B."
6. Remove crankshaft sprocket "B," **Fig. 33,** and the counterbalance shaft sprocket.
7. Remove timing belt upper under and lower under covers.
8. Remove water pump.
9. Remove cylinder head assembly.
10. Remove oil pan, oil screen and oil pump cover.
11. Insert a screwdriver through plug hole in left side of cylinder block to hold counterbalance shaft in position, then loosen oil pump driven gear mounting bolt, **Fig. 34.**
12. Remove timing case with left counterbalance shaft attached.
13. Reverse procedure to install. Refer to "Timing Belt or Chain, Replace" procedure for timing belt installation.

2600cc ENGINES

1. Disconnect battery cables, then drain cooling system.
2. Remove fan shroud, then disconnect upper and lower radiator hoses and remove radiator.
3. Raise and support front of vehicle, then remove lower splash shield.
4. Drain crankcase, then remove oil pan attaching bolts and oil pan.
5. Position No. 1 cylinder at top dead

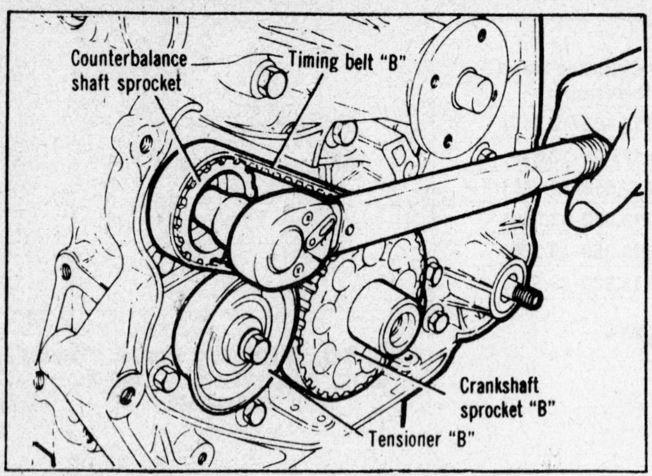

Fig. 33 Silent shaft timing belt (B) & tensioner. 2000cc engines

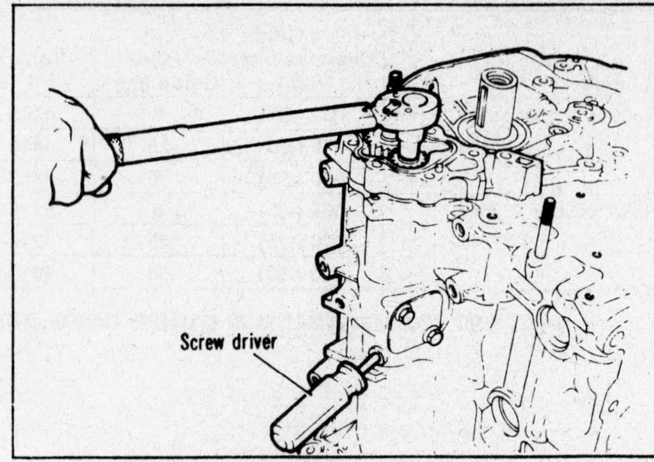

Fig. 34 Oil pump driven gear removal. 2000cc engines

center compression stroke.

6. Remove fan, water pump pulley, alternator and crankshaft pulley.
7. Remove air cleaner, then detach spark plug wire at spark plugs and remove distributor.
8. Remove rocker arm cover, then remove two front cylinder head bolts and air cleaner vent tube attaching bolt.
9. Disconnect heater hose, then remove timing case cover attaching bolts and timing case cover.
10. Reverse procedure to install. Apply sealer to timing case cover to cylinder head mating surfaces. Also apply sealer to oil pan side of oil pan gasket and to the four timing case covers and rear seal case to cylinder block mating surfaces.

TIMING BELT OR CHAIN REPLACE

1600cc ENGINES

Removal

1. Disconnect battery ground cable and remove left engine under cover.
2. Disconnect accelerator cable and breather hose and remove air intake pipe from between turbocharger and throttle body.
3. Remove distributor cap and spark plug wires as an assembly.
4. Remove accessory drive belts.
5. Support engine as needed, then remove left engine mount bracket.
6. Remove power steering pump and water pump pulleys.
7. Disconnect PCV hose, then remove rocker cover, gasket and packing, and the timing belt upper cover.
8. After removing rocker cover, back off all valve adjusting screws until tip of each screw protrudes less than .08 inch (2 mm) from rocker arm. **This is essential to provide enough "freeplay" at camshaft to allow correct valve timing during timing belt installation.**

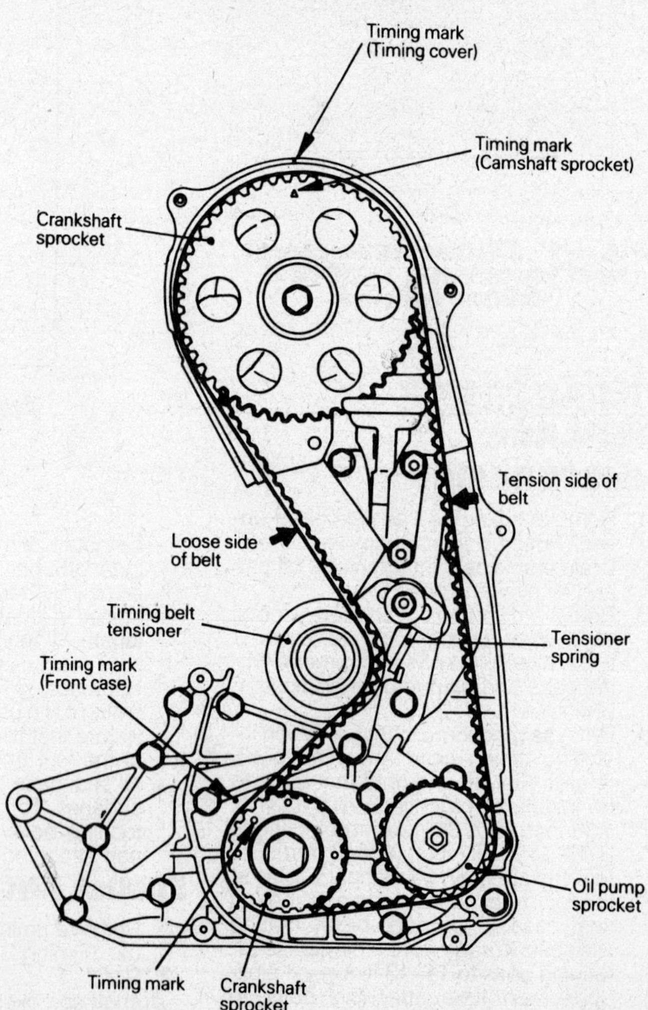

Fig. 35 Timing belt, tensioner and sprockets. 1600cc engine

9. Remove damper pulley, crankshaft pulley and lower timing belt cover.
10. Rotate crankshaft clockwise until crankshaft and camshaft timing marks are aligned as shown in **Figs. 35 and 36.**
11. Loosen belt tensioner bolts, move tensioner toward water pump to relieve tension on belt, then tighten tensioner bolts.
12. Remove timing belt. If belt is to be reused, place chalk mark on back of belt

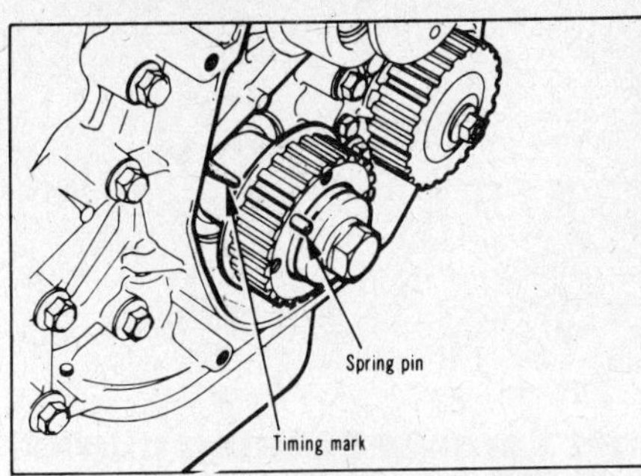

Fig. 36 Crankshaft timing mark detail. 1600cc engines.

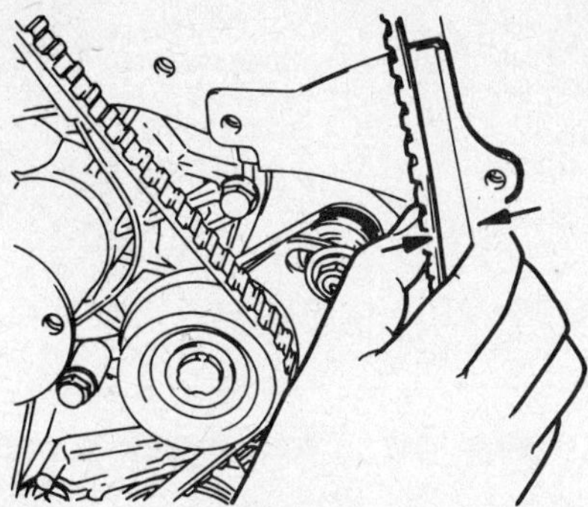

Fig. 37 Checking timing belt tension. 1600cc & 2000cc engines

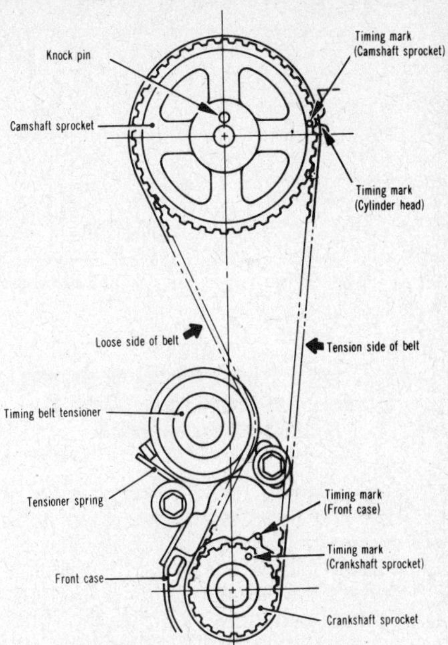

Fig. 38 Camshaft & crankshaft sprocket timing marks. 1400cc engine

indicating direction of rotation. To ensure proper operation, reused belt must be installed in original position.

13. Remove crankshaft sprocket, camshaft sprocket and timing belt tensioner as needed.
14. Inspect belt and replace if any of the following conditions are noted:
    a. Hardened back surface rubber with back surface glossy, non-elastic and so hard that no mark is produced when fingernail is forced into surface.
    b. Cracked back surface rubber.
    c. Cracked or separated canvas.
    d. Cracks at tooth bottom or side of belt.

Installation

1. Install spacer, flange and crankshaft sprocket. Torque sprocket attaching bolt to 44 to 50 ft. lbs.
2. Apply a thin coat of engine oil to outer surface of camshaft spacer, then position spacer on camshaft.
3. Install camshaft sprocket and torque attaching bolt to 44 to 57 ft. lbs.
4. Install tensioner spring, then install tensioner and tighten nut. Check to ensure that straight end of tensioner spring is against side of water pump body, while bent end of spring is against the tensioner tang. Rotate lower portion of tensioner to align bolt holes, then install bolt.
5. Loosen tensioner adjusting nut, then push tensioner toward water pump as far as possible and tighten nut to hold tensioner in this position.
6. Ensure sprocket timing marks are aligned, **Fig. 35.**
7. Install timing belt over crankshaft sprocket, then over oil pump sprocket and camshaft sprockets, keeping tension side of belt tight as belt is installed, **Fig. 35** If used belt is installed, ensure belt is installed in original direction.
8. Adjust belt tension as follows:
    a. Apply counterclockwise force to camshaft sprocket to tighten belt tension side and ensure all timing marks remain aligned, then loosen tensioner nut and bolt. This will allow the tensioner spring to move the tensioner against the timing belt.
    b. Install crankshaft pulley to prevent timing belt from becoming misaligned, then rotate crankshaft clockwise until camshaft sprocket timing mark is two teeth away from mark on belt cover. This operation sets proper belt tension. **Do not rotate crankshaft counterclockwise or push on belt to check tension.**
    c. Using hand pressure, push tensioner toward mounting nut to ensure that belt is in mesh with camshaft sprocket, tighten tensioner nut, then tighten tensioner pivot bolt. If pivot bolt is tightened before nut, tensioner may rotate with bolt releasing tension on timing belt.
    d. Press outward on belt in run between oil pump and camshaft sprockets, as shown in **Fig. 37,** and check clearance between belt and timing belt cover. Clearance should be approximately .23 inch.
9. Rotate crankshaft clockwise 2 revolutions and ensure timing marks are correctly aligned.
10. Reverse remaining procedure to complete installation, then adjust valves as outlined.

1400cc ENGINES

Removal

1. Remove water pump pulley and belt, then the timing belt cover.
2. Rotate crankshaft in normal direction of rotation until crankshaft and camshaft timing marks are aligned as shown in **Fig. 38.**
3. Loosen tension nut and bolt, move tensioner toward water pump as far as possible, then secure in this position by tightening tensioner nut.
4. Remove timing belt from camshaft sprocket, then the sprocket.
5. Remove crankshaft pulley, then place mark on timing belt to indicate portion of belt toward front of engine and remove timing belt.
6. Remove crankshaft sprocket attaching bolts, then the sprocket and flange, if necessary.
7. Remove timing belt tensioner, if necessary.
8. Inspect timing belt and camshaft and crankshaft sprockets for wear and damage.

Installation

1. Install flange and crankshaft sprocket, then torque sprocket attaching bolt to 37 to 43 ft. lbs.
2. Install camshaft sprocket then torque attaching bolt to 47 to 54 ft. lbs.
3. Align camshaft sprocket and crankshaft sprocket timing marks, **Fig. 38.**
4. Install timing belt tensioner, spring and spacer, then tighten tensioner bolts. Position lower end of tensioner spring against timing case flange.
5. Loosen tensioner bolts and position tensioner toward water pump as far as possible.
6. Install timing belt over crankshaft sprocket, then position belt over camshaft sprocket. Check to ensure that tension side of belt is tight by rotating camshaft sprocket slightly in the reverse direction of rotation and noting that all timing marks are aligned.
7. Install crankshaft pulley and pin, then insert attaching bolts and torque to 7.5 to 8.5 ft. lbs.
8. Loosen tensioner mounting bolt, then the tensioner adjusting bolt. This will apply tension to loose side of belt. Check to ensure that timing belt is properly positioned on sprockets.
9. Tighten tensioner adjusting bolt, then the mounting bolt.
10. Rotate crankshaft one revolution clockwise in direction of rotation, then align crankshaft and camshaft timing marks. Crankshaft should rotate smoothly. **Do not rotate crankshaft in the opposite direction of rotation.**
11. Loosen tensioner mounting bolt, then the tensioner adjusting bolt.
12. Tighten tensioner adjusting bolt, then the tensioner mounting bolt. Torque bolts to 15-18 ft. lbs.

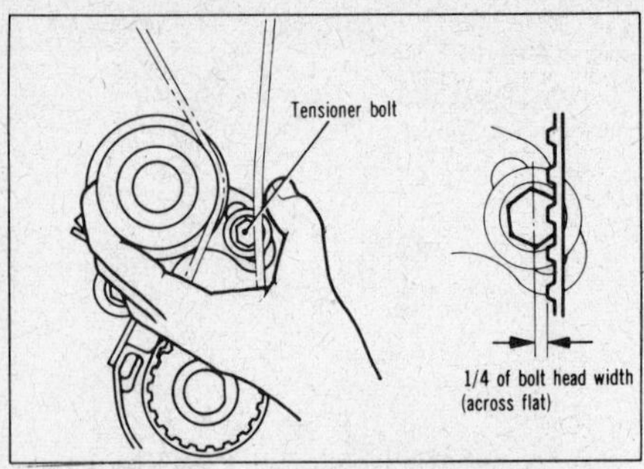

Fig. 39 Checking timing belt tension. 1400cc & 1500cc engines

13. Grasp timing belt at tension side of belt and tensioner pulley, then push inward on belt applying approximately 11 lbs. of force. If timing belt tension is correct, the cog end of the belt should be approximately 1/4 of the tensioner adjusting bolt width away from the center of the bolt, **Fig. 39.**
14. Install timing belt cover, then the water pump pulley and drive belt.

1500cc ENGINE

Removal

1. Disconnect breather and secondary air hoses, then remove air cleaner assembly, air intake duct and heated air duct.
2. Disconnect accelerator cable and oxygen sensor lead, and remove spark plug wires.
3. Remove accessory drive belts.
4. Support engine as needed, then remove left engine mount bracket.
5. Remove power steering pump and water pump pulleys.
6. Remove rocker arm cover, gasket and packing, and the upper timing belt cover.
7. After removing rocker cover, back off all valve adjusting screws until tip of each screw protrudes less than .08 inch (2 mm) from rocker arm. **This is essential to provide enough "free-play" at camshaft to allow correct valve timing during timing belt installation.**
8. Remove damper pulley, crankshaft pulley and the lower timing belt cover.
9. Rotate crankshaft in normal direction of rotation until timing marks are aligned, **Fig. 40, loosen belt tensioner bolts and move timing belt tensioner fully toward the water pump, then tighten bolts to hold tensioner.**
10. Remove timing belt. If the timing belt is to be reused, place an arrow mark indicating turning direction (direction of engine rotation) to ensure that the belt is installed in the same direction as before.
11. Remove camshaft sprocket, crankshaft sprocket and flange, and timing belt tensioner as needed.
12. Inspect belt and replace if any of the following conditions are noted:
    a. Hardened back surface rubber. With back surface glossy, non-elastic and so hard that no mark is produced when fingernail is forced into surface.
    b. Cracked back surface rubber.
    c. Cracked or separated canvas.
    d. Cracks at tooth bottom or side of belt.

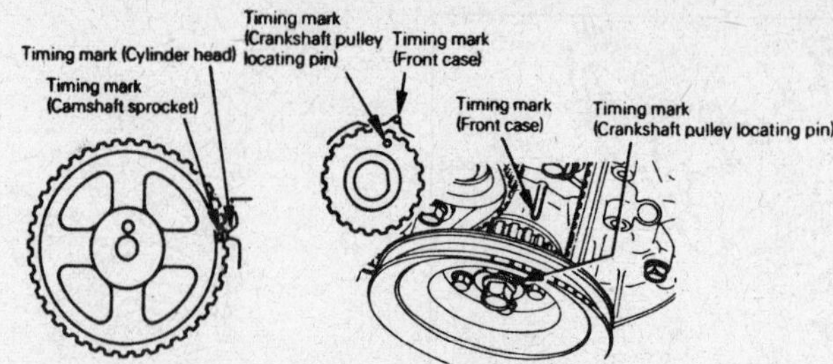

Fig. 40 Camshaft & crankshaft sprocket timing marks. 1500cc engine

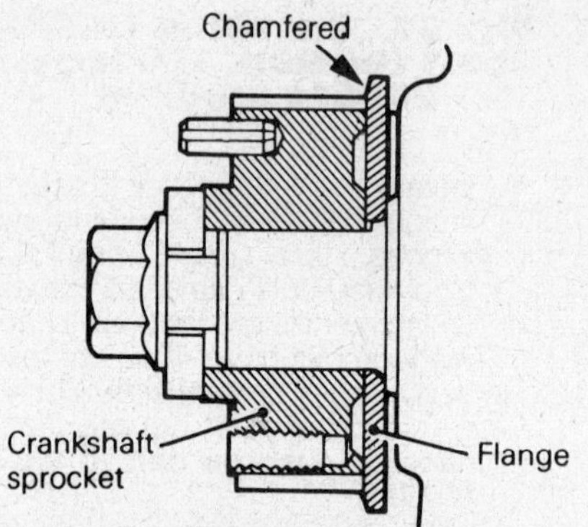

Fig. 41 Installing flange & crankshaft sprocket. 1500cc engine

Installation

1. Install flange and crankshaft sprocket as shown in **Fig. 41.**
2. Torque crankshaft sprocket bolt to 37-43 ft. lbs.
3. Install camshaft sprocket and torque bolt to 47-54 ft. lbs.
4. Install timing belt tensioner as follows:
    a. Mount tensioner, spring and spacer, then temporarily tighten pivot bolt.
    b. Temporarily tighten the adjusting bolt, then install bottom end of the spring into front case.
    c. Secure tensioner to the position nearest the water pump.
5. Ensure timing marks are aligned, **Fig. 40.**
6. Install timing belt over crankshaft sprocket, then the camshaft sprocket, keeping tension side of belt tight as belt is installed. If used belt is installed, ensure belt is installed in original direction.
7. Apply counterclockwise force to camshaft sprocket to tighten tension side of belt, ensuring that timing marks remain aligned.
8. Install crankshaft pulley to prevent belt from slipping off sprocket, then adjust belt tension as follows:
    a. Loosen tensioner bolts to allow tensioner to bear against belt, then tighten adjusting bolt and pivot bolt. **Tighten adjusting bolt first to prevent tensioner from rotating away from belt.**
    b. Rotate crankshaft clockwise one full revolution, then realign crankshaft sprocket timing mark with pointer. **Crankshaft must be rotated smoothly, in clockwise direction. Do not apply any force other than spring force of tensioner to timing belt.**
    c. Loosen tensioner pivot and adjusting bolts. then tighten adjuster bolt and pivot bolt. **Tighten adjusting bolt first to prevent tensioner from rotating away from belt.**
    d. Check belt tension by holding belt as shown in **Fig. 39**, and applying thumb pressure to tension side of belt. Tension is correct when tooth of belt covers approximately 1/4 the width of the tensioner adjuster bolt.
    e. Rotate crankshaft clockwise, one full revolution and ensure that timing marks line up.
9. Reverse remaining procedure to complete installation, then adjust valve clearances as outlined.

2000cc ENGINES

Removal

1. Remove crankshaft pulley(s), then the timing belt upper and lower front covers.
2. Rotate crankshaft in normal direction of rotation and align timing marks as shown in **Fig. 42,** then remove crankshaft sprocket attaching bolt.
3. Loosen main tensioner pivot and disengage spring from boss on water pump, then remove tensioner assembly.
4. Remove main timing belt from crankshaft, camshaft and oil pump sprockets. If belt is to be reused, place chalk mark on belt indicating direction of rotation.
5. Remove camshaft sprocket, then the crankshaft sprocket and flange.
6. Remove plug from lower left hand side of cylinder block, then insert a screwdriver into hole to hold silent shaft in position while removing oil pump sprocket nut, **Fig. 32.** Use a screwdriver with shaft diameter of .3 inch which can be inserted at least 2.4 inches.

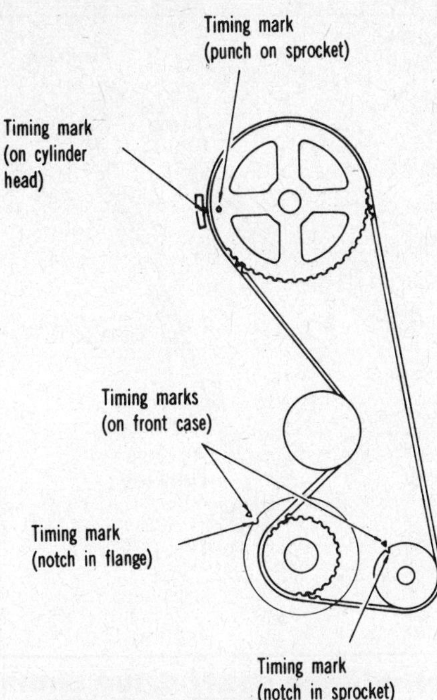

Fig. 42 Crankshaft, camshaft & oil pump timing marks. 2000cc engine

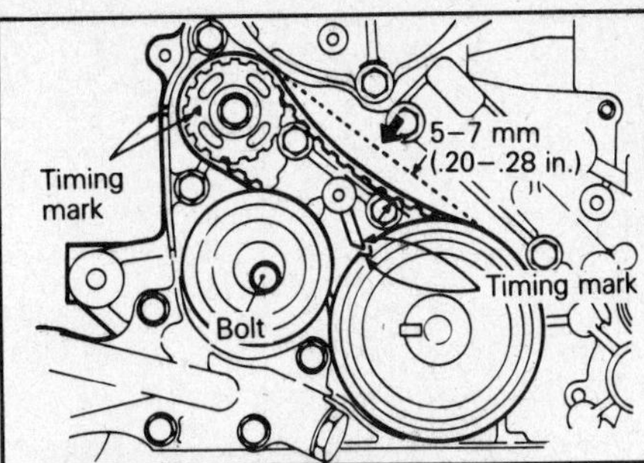

Fig. 43 Aligning silent shaft & crankshaft sprocket timing marks. 2000cc engines

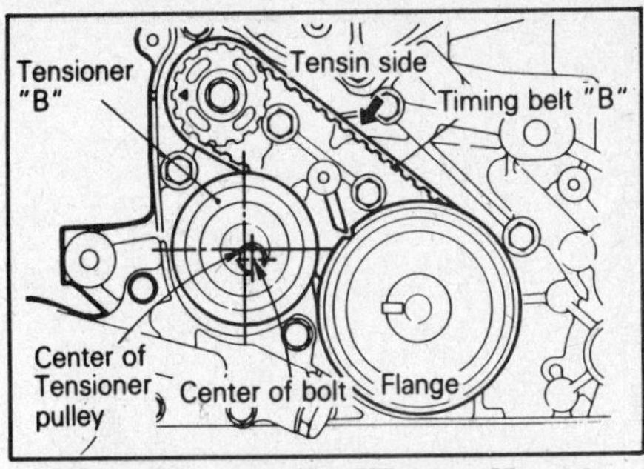

Fig. 44 Installing silent shaft belt tensioner. 2000cc engines

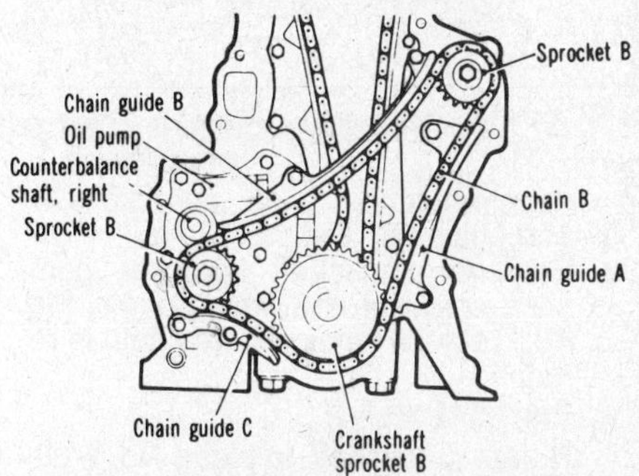

Fig. 45 Counterbalance shaft drive system. 2600cc engine

7. Loosen right hand silent shaft sprocket bolt until it can be rotated by hand, then remove silent shaft belt tensioner and silent shaft timing belt. If belt is to be reused, place chalk mark on belt indicating direction of rotation.
8. Remove crankshaft sprocket, then the right hand silent shaft sprocket and spacer.
9. Inspect timing belts, sprocket and tensioners for wear and damage.

Installation

1. Install crankshaft sprocket inner sprocket with raised lip toward inside.
2. Coat silent shaft spacer with oil and install spacer with chamfer toward inside, then install right hand silent shaft sprocket and tighten attaching bolt.
3. Install and adjust silent shaft timing belt (B) as follows:
   a. Align crankshaft and silent shaft sprocket timing marks with marks on timing case, **Fig. 43.**
   b. Install silent shaft timing belt (B) over crankshaft and silent shaft sprockets. When installing timing belt, ensure tension side of belt has no slack. If used belt is installed, ensure belt is installed in original position.
   c. Install silent shaft belt tensioner (B), assembling tensioner so that pulley is to left of installation bolt and pulley flange faces front of engine, **Fig. 44.**
   d. Raise tensioner toward belt by hand and apply sufficient pressure so that tension side of belt is taut, then tighten tensioner bolt. **Ensure tensioner does not rotate with bolt as it is tightened, as excessive tension will be placed on belt.**
   e. Ensure timing marks are still aligned and check belt tension. There should be approximately .20-.28 inch (5-7 mm) slack on tension side of belt when belt is moved by hand.
4. Install crankshaft sprocket flange with raised side facing out, then install crankshaft sprocket.
5. Install oil pump sprocket and align timing mark, **Fig. 42.** With oil pump sprocket timing marks aligned, insert a screwdriver with a shaft diameter of .3 inch into hole in left hand side of cylinder block, **Fig. 32.** If screwdriver can be inserted 2.4 inches or more, alignment is correct. If screwdriver can be inserted only 1 inch, rotate oil pump sprocket one revolution and realign timing marks. Check to ensure that screwdriver can be inserted 2.4 inches or more. This check is performed to ensure that silent shaft and oil pump sprocket are properly positioned. Leave screwdriver inserted in hole until after timing belt has been installed.
6. Torque oil pump sprocket bolt to 25-28 ft. lbs. and ensure that timing marks remain aligned.
7. Install main timing belt tensioner, attach top side of tensioner spring to protrusion on water pump, move tensioner as far as possible toward water pump and tighten tensioner bolts.
8. Install camshaft sprocket and align timing marks, **Fig. 42.**
9. Install and adjust main timing belt as follows:
   a. Install timing belt, first over the crankshaft sprocket, then the oil pump and camshaft sprockets, holding belt tight so there is no slack on tension side of belt. Apply counterclockwise force on camshaft sprocket to aid in tensioning belt, and ensure that all timing marks remain aligned.
   b. Loosen tensioner bolts, allowing tensioner to spring to apply force to timing belt.
   c. Remove screwdriver from hole in left side of block, then rotate crankshaft clockwise until mark on camshaft sprocket is moved 2 teeth away from mark on cylinder head. **Do not rotate crankshaft counterclockwise or place pressure on belt to test tension.**
   d. Press tensioner toward belt until timing belt is fully seated on camshaft sprocket, then tighten tensioner adjuster bolt and pivot bolt. Belt should engage approximately 225° of crankshaft sprocket. When tightening tensioner bolts, always tighten adjuster bolt first, then the pivot bolt, to prevent tensioner from rotating out of position.
   e. Press belt toward outer edge of cover between oil pump and camshaft sprockets, squeezing belt and edge of cover with thumb and forefinger, then check clearance between back of belt and cover. Belt tension is correct when clearance is approximately .55 inch (14 mm).
   f. Rotate crankshaft clockwise, 2 full turns, align crankshaft timing mark with mark on cover, and ensure oil pump and camshaft sprocket timing marks are properly aligned, **Fig. 42.**
10. Ensure camshaft sprocket bolt is properly tightened, the reverse remaining procedure to complete installation.

2600cc ENGINES

Removal

1. Remove timing chain case as outlined under "Timing Case, Replace."
2. Remove chain guides "A," "B" and "C," **Fig. 45.**
3. Remove sprocket "B" locking bolts, **Fig. 45.**
4. Remove crankshaft sprocket "B,"

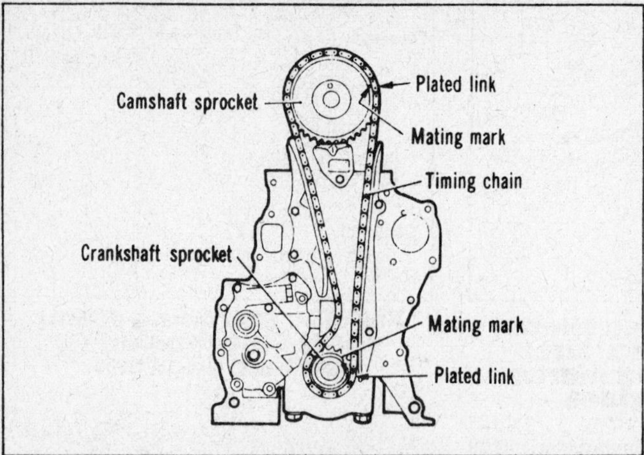

Fig. 46 Timing chain installation. 2600cc engines

counterbalance shaft sprocket "B" and chain "B," **Fig. 45.**

5. Remove crankshaft sprocket, camshaft sprocket and timing chain, **Fig. 46,** Depress tensioner as chain is removed.

Installation

1. Rotate crankshaft to place No. 1 piston at top dead center, compression stroke.
2. Install camshaft sprocket and crankshaft sprocket on timing chain. When the sprockets are installed, ensure the mating marks of the chain and sprockets are properly aligned. The mating marks on the sprockets are punched marks on the corresponding teeth. The marks on the chain are two plated links, **Fig. 46.**
3. Install camshaft sprocket on camshaft and align the keyway of the crankshaft sprocket with the key of the crankshaft, then install sprocket on crankshaft. Ensure timing marks are properly aligned.
4. Install crankshaft sprocket "B," **Fig. 45,** on the crankshaft.
5. Install two counterbalance shaft sprockets "B" on chain "B," aligning the mating marks. The mating marks on sprockets are punched marks on the corresponding teeth. The mating marks on the chain are three plated links, **Fig. 47.**
6. Install chain "B" on crankshaft sprocket, then the two counterbalance shaft sprockets "B" and tighten the lock bolts.
7. Install chain guides "A," "B" and "C," **Fig. 47,** and loosely install mounting bolts.
8. Tighten chain guides "A" and "C" mounting bolts.
9. Shake right and left sprockets "B" to collect chain slack at point "P," **Fig. 47.** Adjust position of chain guide "B" so when the chain is pulled in direction of arrow "Y," **Fig. 47,** the clearance between chain guide "B" and the links of chain "B" will be .04-.14 inch. Tighten chain guide "B" mounting bolts.
10. Install timing case gasket and case.
11. Install oil screen and oil pan.
12. Install crankshaft pulley.

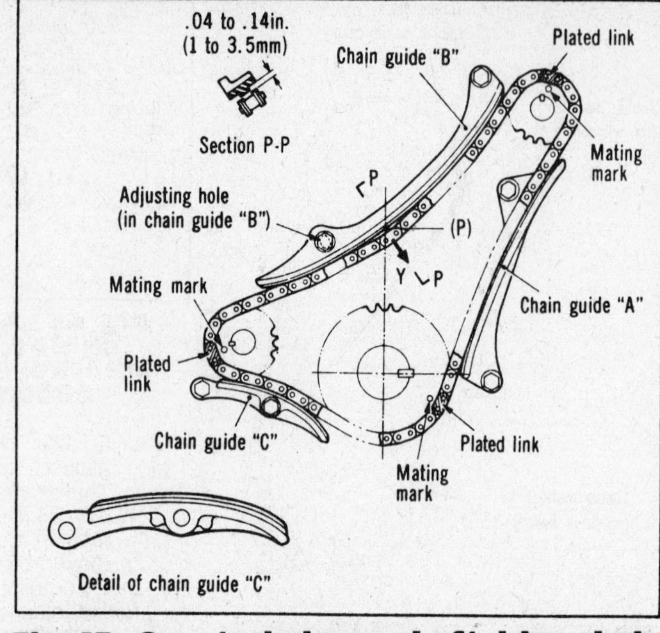

Fig. 47 Counterbalance shaft drive chain & tensioner installation. 2600cc engines

TIMING BELT OR CHAIN TENSION

ADJUST

On 1500, 1600, 2000 & 2600cc engines, the timing belt or chain tension may be adjusted without removing the timing cover through adjustment ports located on the cover. For all other engines, refer to "Timing Belt Or Chain, Replace" procedure to adjust tension.

2600cc ENGINES

1. Remove adjusting port cover located at center timing chain cover under water pump.
2. Loosen timing chain guide retaining bolt (B), **Fig. 48.**
3. With finger, push downward on timing chain guide projection as far as possible and torque retaining bolt (B) to 11-16 ft. lbs. Then install timing port cover and gasket. **Use only finger pressure to push downward on timing chain guide projection. Do not use a screwdriver or other tool to push downward on guide, as timing chain tension will be excessive.**

1500, 1600 & 2000cc ENGINES

1. On Colt models, turn steering wheel all the way to left lock, support engine with suitable jack and remove left engine mount bracket to provide clearance to rotate crankshaft.
2. Remove timing belt upper front cover and the spark plugs.
3. Rotate crankshaft clockwise (normal direction of rotation) and inspect timing belt. If belt is satisfactory, continue rotating crankshaft until No. 1 Cylinder is at TDC on compression stroke and timing mark on camshaft sprocket is aligned with mark on belt cover or cylinder head.
4. Rotate crankshaft clockwise until mark on camshaft sprocket is 2 teeth away from mark on cover or cylinder head, **Fig. 49.** This causes spring pressure of No. 2 exhaust valve to apply specific tension to tension timing belt. **Do not rotate crankshaft counterclockwise, as belt tension will be adversely affected.**
5. Remove accessory drive belts and pulleys as needed, then the two adjusting port covers, inserting a screwdriver into slot on timing belt cover and prying timing port covers off.
6. Insert 14 mm socket through adjusting port, loosen timing belt tensioner nut and bolt 1/2-3/4 turn. **Do not loosen bolt or nut more than 3/4 turn, as fastener may fall out into cover.**
7. Check to ensure that tensioner is not sticking, by inserting a screwdriver through opening on top of lower timing belt cover and pushing tensioner toward timing belt. Release tensioner and remove screwdriver. Spring tension of the timing belt tensioner will automatically adjust the timing belt.
8. Tighten tensioner adjuster bolt, then the pivot bolt. Always tighten slotted adjuster bolt or nut first to prevent tensioner from rotating out of position.
9. Install adjusting port covers, then install timing belt upper front cover.

PISTON & ROD ASSEMBLY

This piston and rod is assembled with the indented arrow on the piston and the embossed numeral on the rod facing toward front of engine, **Fig. 50.**

PISTON, PINS & RINGS

Pistons and rings are available in standard size and oversizes of .010, .020, .030 and .039 inch. Oversize pins are not available.

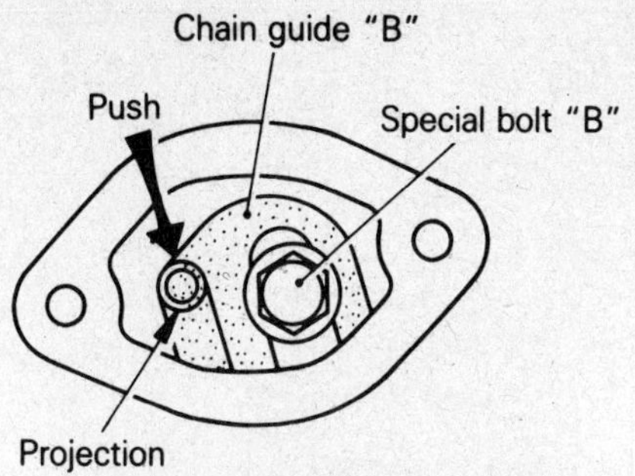

Fig. 48 Counterbalance shaft timing chain adjustment. 2600cc engines

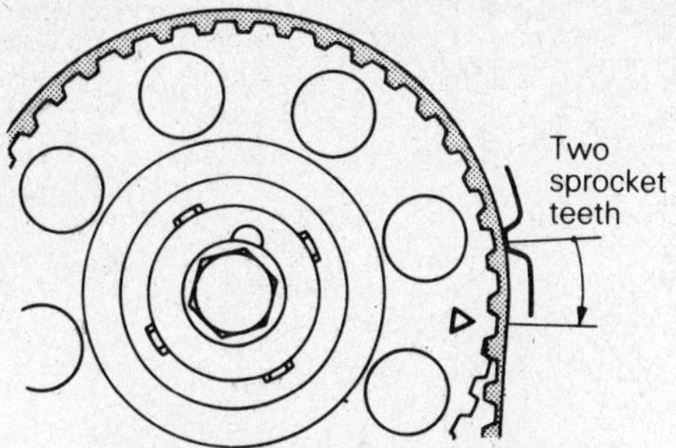

Fig. 49 Positioning camshaft sprocket for timing belt adjustment. 1500cc engine, 1600cc & 2000cc engines similar

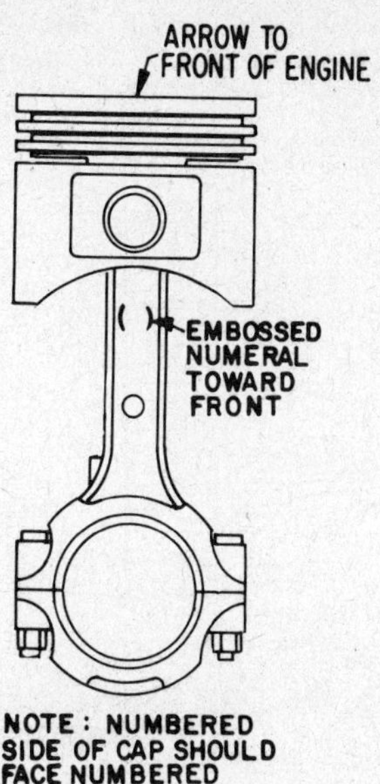

Fig. 50 Piston & rod assembly

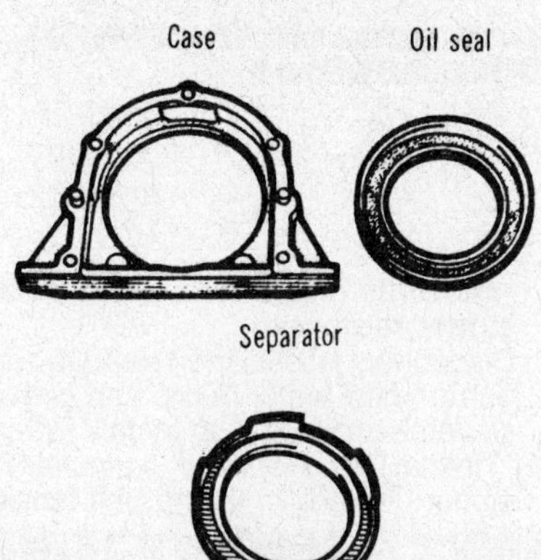

Fig. 51 Disassembled view of rear seal

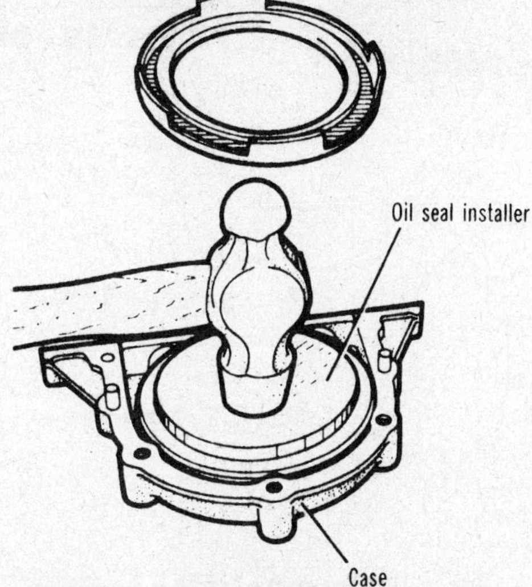

Fig. 52 Installing rear seal into case

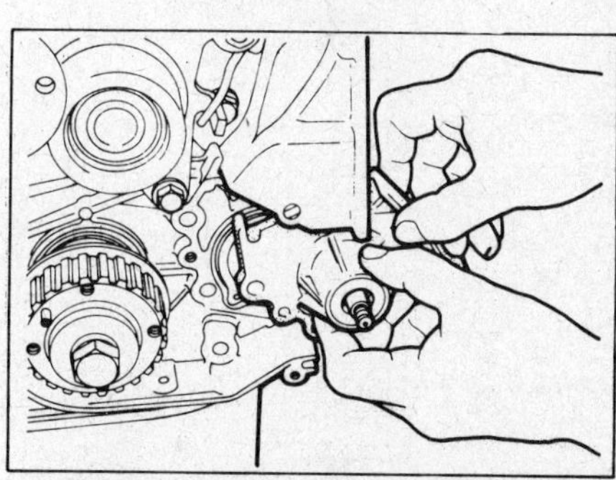

Fig. 53 Removing oil pump cover. 1600cc engine

MAIN & ROD BEARINGS

Main and rod bearings are available in undersizes of .010, .020 and .030 inch.

The main bearing caps are installed with arrows facing front of engine.

REAR OIL SEAL

REPLACE

1. Remove transmission, clutch assembly and flywheel or flex plate, as equipped.
2. Remove rear oil seal case and separate into three parts: oil seal, separator and case, **Fig. 51.**
3. Drive in oil seal from inside of case, using suitable tool, **Fig. 52.** Ensure the oil seal plate fits properly in the inner contact surface of the seal case, if equipped.
4. Install separator with the oil hole facing the bottom of the case, if equipped.
5. Apply engine oil to oil seal lips.
6. Install the oil seal case in the cylinder block.

OIL PAN

REPLACE

On some models it may be necessary to remove engine from vehicle to gain access to oil pan.

1. Raise and support vehicle, remove engine splash pan, if equipped, then drain crankcase.
2. Remove the oil pressure sender unit, if necessary, and on turbocharged models, disconnect oil drain hose and remove oil drain pipe.
3. Remove the oil pan bolts and oil pan.
4. Remove oil pump pickup if necessary.
5. Reverse procedure to install.

OIL PUMP

REPLACE

To remove oil pump pickup, refer to "Oil Pan, Replace."

1400cc & 1500cc ENGINES

1. Remove timing case as described under "Timing Case, Replace."
2. Remove oil pump cover, then the inner and outer gears from front case. Mark outer gear surface facing timing case so it can be installed in the same direction.
3. Remove relief valve plug, spring and valve.
4. Reverse procedure to install. Lubricate oil pump internal components with engine oil before installing. Torque oil pump cover attaching bolts to 6 to 7 ft. lbs. After installing oil pump cover, check to ensure that oil pump gears rotate smoothly. Torque relief valve plug to 29-36 ft. lbs.

1600cc ENGINES

1. Remove timing case as described under "Timing Case, Replace."
2. Remove relief plug, spring and plunger, then the bolt and oil pump cover, **Fig. 53.**
3. Remove rotor from oil pump housing.
4. Reverse procedure to install. Lubricate oil pump internal components with engine oil. Torque oil pump sprocket attaching nut to 25-28 ft. lbs.

2000cc ENGINES

The oil pump is of the gear type, **Fig. 54.** The oil pump is also used to drive the left counterbalance shaft. The oil pump drive gear has a sprocket driven by a timing belt. The counterbalance shaft is mounted to the oil pump driven gear and rotates in the opposite direction of crankshaft rotation.

1. Remove timing case as outlined under "Timing Case, Replace" procedure.

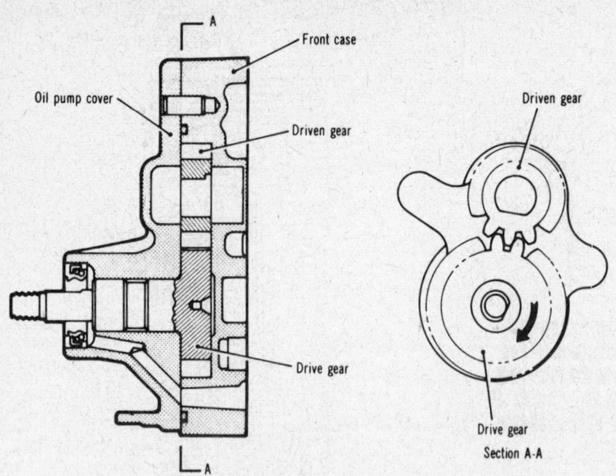

Fig. 54 Oil pump assembly. 2000cc engines

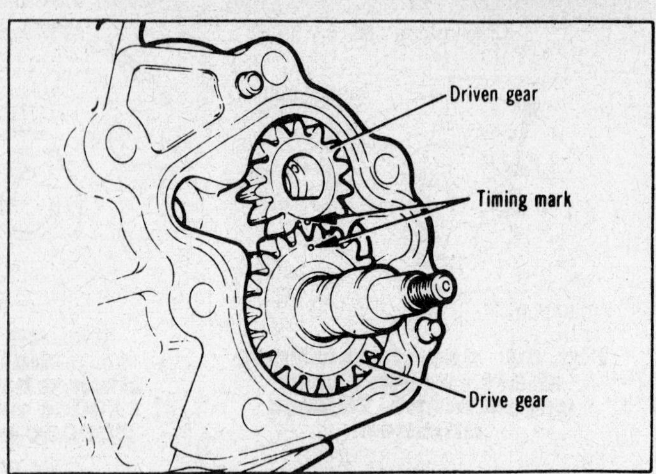

Fig. 55 Oil pump gear timing marks. 2000cc engines

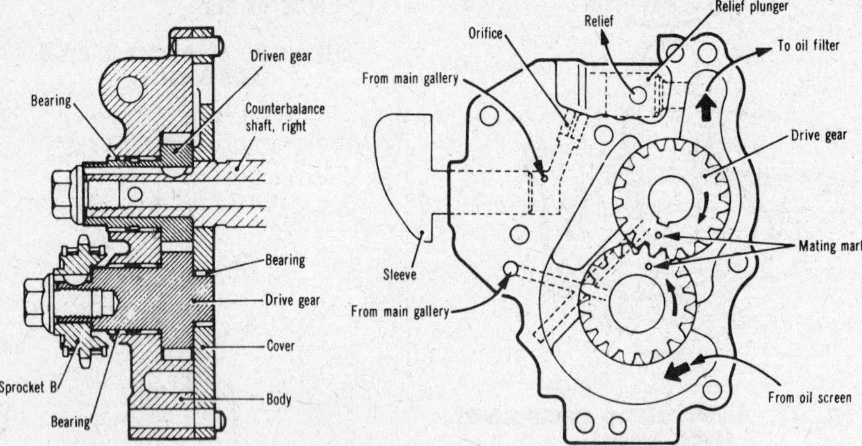

Fig. 56 Oil pump assembly. 2600cc engines

2. Remove oil pump gears and left counterbalance shaft from case.
3. Install oil pump gear in timing case, aligning timing marks, **Fig. 55.**
4. Insert left counterbalance shaft into driven gear.
5. Install timing case.

2600cc ENGINES

The oil pump is of the gear type, **Fig. 56,** and is also used to drive the right counterbalance shaft. The oil pump drive gear has a sprocket driven by a chain. The counterbalance shaft is mounted to the oil pump driven gear and rotates in the opposite direction of crankshaft rotation.

1. Remove timing chain as outlined under "Timing Belt or Chain, Replace" procedure.
2. Remove bolt locking oil pump driven gear to right balancer shaft, then the oil pump mounting bolts.
3. Remove the oil pump assembly.
4. When installing the oil pump, be sure that the keyway of the oil pump driven gear fits the woodruff key at the end of the balancer shaft and that the key does not go out of the keyway. After the oil pump assembly has been correctly installed, firmly tighten the oil pump mounting bolts. Next, tighten the balancer shaft and driven gear mounting bolts. If the fit of the woodruff key and driven gear is too tight, first insert the balancer shaft into the oil pump, temporarily tighten the bolt and insert the balancer shaft and oil pump as an assembly in the cylinder block. **Fill the oil pump with a sufficient amount of engine oil (more than .6 cu. in.) prior to installation.**

WATER PUMP REPLACE

1400cc ENGINES

1. Disconnect battery ground cable and drain cooling system.
2. Remove accessory drive belts, water pump pulley and the timing belt cover.
3. Rotate crankshaft in normal direction of rotation until crankshaft and camshaft timing marks are aligned as shown in **Fig. 38.**
4. Loosen tension nut and bolt, disengage tensioner spring from water pump and remove belt tensioner. **Do not rotate crankshaft with belt tensioner removed.**
5. Disconnect hoses, then remove water pump bolts, water pump and gasket.
6. Reverse procedure to install. Refer to "Timing Belt, Replace" to install tensioner and adjust timing belt tension.

1500cc & 1600cc ENGINES

1. Disconnect battery ground cable and drain cooling system.
2. On models with power steering, remove power steering pump and bracket leaving hoses connected, and secure pump aside.
3. Remove timing belt as outlined in "Timing Belt, Replace."
4. Remove alternator brace and disconnect hoses from water pump.
5. Remove water pump bolts, water pump, gasket and O-ring.
6. Reverse procedure to install.

2000cc ENGINES

1. Disconnect battery ground cable and drain cooling system.
2. Remove fan shroud, then disconnect lower radiator hose.
3. Remove drive belt cooling fan and pulley.
4. Place No. 1 piston at top dead center, compression stroke.
5. Remove camshaft pulley, timing belt covers, timing belt, camshaft sprocket, upper under cover and timing belt tensioner.
6. Remove water pump mounting bolts and the water pump.
7. Reverse procedure to install.

2600cc ENGINES

1. Drain cooling system, then disconnect battery ground cable.
2. Remove fan shroud, then disconnect lower radiator hose.
3. Remove drive belt, cooling fan and pulley.
4. Remove water pump mounting bolts and the water pump.
5. Reverse procedure to install.

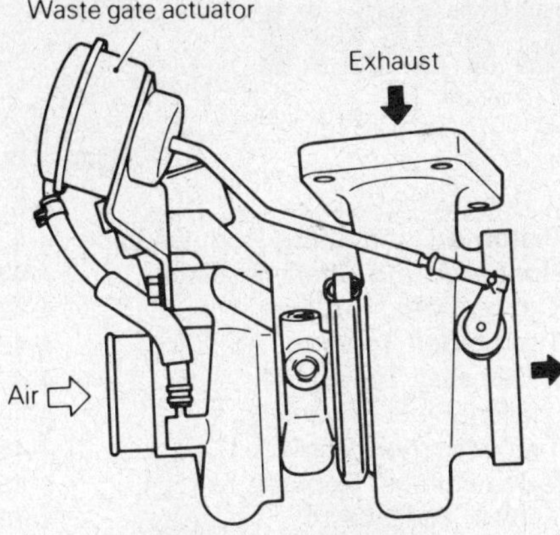

Fig. 57 Typical turbocharger.

FUEL PUMP REPLACE

EXC. FUEL INJECTED ENGINES

1. Remove air cleaner and position No. 1 cylinder at top dead center compression stroke.
2. Disconnect fuel lines from fuel pump.
3. Remove fuel pump mounting bolts or nuts, then the fuel pump.
4. Remove fuel pump pushrod, if equipped.
5. Remove fuel pump insulator and gaskets.
6. Reverse procedure to install. Tighten fuel pump mounting bolts or nuts alternately and evenly.

COLT W/1600cc TURBO

1. Relieve fuel system pressure as follows:
   a. Remove rear seat cushion and pull back carpet.
   b. Start engine and disconnect fuel pump connector.
   c. When engine stops from lack of fuel, turn off ignition and disconnect battery ground cable.
2. Remove fuel tank cap, raise and support rear of vehicle and drain fuel into suitable container.
3. Disconnect filler hose from tank, support tank with suitable jack and remove nuts securing tank straps.
4. Lower fuel tank, then mark and disconnect fuel hoses, vapor hoses and electrical connectors.
5. Remove nuts securing fuel pump assembly, then the fuel pump and gasket.
6. Reverse procedure to install.

1987 COLT VISTA

1. Relieve fuel system pressure as follows:
   a. Start engine and disconnect electric fuel pump connector. Connector is located inside rear compartment.
   b. When engine stops from lack of fuel, turn off ignition and disconnect battery ground cable.
2. Push fuel pump/sending unit lead and grommet through floor and remove fuel tank cap.
3. Raise and support rear of vehicle, drain fuel tank into suitable container and disconnect filler hose.
4. On 2 wheel drive models, remove spare tire carrier assembly.
5. Support tank with suitable jack and remove nuts securing tank straps.
6. Lower tank, mark and disconnect fuel hoses, vapor hoses and electrical connectors, then remove tank.
7. Remove nuts or bolts securing pump, then withdraw pump assembly from tank.
8. Reverse procedure to install.

CONQUEST

1. Remove high floor side panel from luggage compartment floor, then the fuel pump connector access panel.
2. Start engine, then disconnect fuel pump and gauge sending unit electrical connectors.
3. When engine stops from lack of fuel, turn off ignition and disconnect battery ground cable.
4. Remove fuel tank cap, raise and support rear of vehicle and drain fuel into suitable container.
5. Remove left rear wheel and fuel pipe cover, then mark and disconnect fuel and vapor hoses.
6. Disconnect fuel filler and breather hoses from tank.
7. Support fuel tank and remove retaining bolts, then lower tank from vehicle.
8. Remove fuel pump from tank.
9. Reverse procedure to install.

TURBOCHARGER

The turbocharger, **Figs. 57 and 58,** is an exhaust driven device which compresses the air being delivered to the engine through the intake system. The turbocharger is used to increase engine power on a demand basis, allowing a smaller more economical engine to be used.

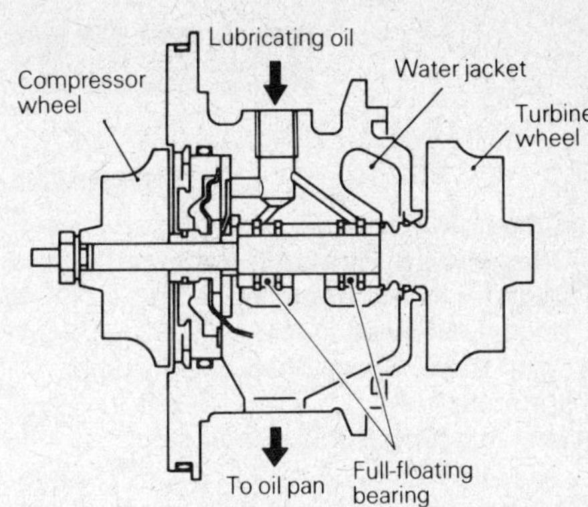

Fig. 58 Turbocharger cross sectional view

Exhaust gasses flow through a turbine which is connected through a shaft to the impeller (compressor). During normal, steady operation, the turbine does not rotate fast enough to boost pressure. As speed increases, the mixture is compressed, allowing a denser mixture to enter the combustion chambers and develop more engine power during the combustion process.

The intake manifold pressure (boost pressure) is controlled by a wastegate valve which is used to bypass a portion of the exhaust gasses around the turbine at a predetermined point in the cycle, limiting boost pressure.

The turbocharger shaft bearings are lubricated by engine oil pressure, and on some models the turbocharger center section is water cooled. Due to the extreme high heat and high RPM operating conditions, a constant supply of clean oil is essential to proper turbocharger operation and service life. The engine should never be shut off immediately after driving, as flow of oil to the turbocharger bearings will be stopped while the shaft is still rotating, and excessive heat build-up during the "hot soak" period after engine shut down will cause residual oil on the turbocharger bearings to carbonize. Rather the engine should be allowed to idle for several minutes after driving to allow the turbocharger to cool and to maintain oil pressure until the turbine shaft slows down or stops.

DIESEL ENGINE SECTION

INDEX

ENGINE
REPLACE

1. Disconnect battery ground cable, then drain engine oil.
2. Remove hood and air cleaner duct.
3. Disconnect heater hoses, accelerator cable and throttle cable.
4. Remove fuel filter, then disconnect water level sensor connector and fuel lines.
5. Remove power steering oil pump, if equipped.
6. Disconnect glow cable and gauge unit harness connector.
7. Remove clutch release cylinder from transmission.
8. Disconnect engine ground cable, then the starter motor and alternator wiring harness.
9. Disconnect engine oil cooler hoses and brake booster vacuum hose.
10. Disconnect oil pressure switch harness, then remove front exhaust pipe and radiator assembly.
11. Remove under cover and, on four wheel drive models, remove under skid plate and transfer case protector.
12. Disconnect speedometer cable.
13. Disconnect back-up light switch harness and, on four wheel drive models, 4WD indicator light switch harness.
14. Paint mating marks on differential drive flange and transmission yoke. On four wheel drive models, place transmission in 2H and place hubs in free position.
15. Remove propeller shaft.
16. Support transmission with suitable jack, then remove gearshift lever assembly.
17. Remove rear insulator from transmission, then the No. 2 crossmember.
18. On four wheel drive models, support transfer case with suitable jack. Remove transfer case support insulator and mounting bracket. Remove plate from side frame.
19. On all models, remove engine mounting nuts from front insulators.
20. Attach suitable lifting device to engine and raise engine and transmission assembly diagonally from engine compartment.
21. Reverse procedure to install, noting the following:
    a. Torque front insulators to engine mounting bracket attaching bolts to 22-29 ft. lbs.
    b. Torque front insulators to engine support bracket attaching bolts to 10-14 ft. lbs.
    c. Torque No. 2 crossmember to side frame attaching bolts to 40-54 ft. lbs.
    d. Torque rear insulator to No. 2 crossmember attaching bolts to 40-54 ft. lbs.
    e. Torque plate to side frame attaching bolts to 14-18 ft. lbs.
    f. Torque rear insulator to transmission attaching bolts to 14-18 ft. lbs.
    g. Torque transfer case support insulator to transfer case mounting bracket attaching bolts to 22-30 ft. lbs.
    h. Torque transfer case mounting bracket to transfer case attaching bolts to 14-18 ft. lbs.

TIMING BELTS
REPLACE

Refer to **Fig. 1** and remove parts in numerical order as shown. Perform steps 1 through 4 before starting removal procedure.

1. Rotate crankshaft until piston of No. 1 cylinder is at top dead center. No. 1 cylinder will be at top dead center when all timing marks are aligned as shown in **Fig. 2.**
2. Mark timing belts to show direction of rotation for reinstallation.
3. Slightly loosen tensioners for each drive belt and slide toward water pump and secure in this position.
4. Remove two silent shaft sprockets. Hold shafts as shown in **Fig. 3** to prevent rotation when loosening sprocket nut and bolt.
5. Reverse procedure to install. Install crankshaft sprocket B, flange and sprocket as shown in **Fig. 4**. Install injection pump sprocket and install flange to injection pump sprocket, **Fig. 5.** Install spacer on left silent shaft with chamfered end toward oil seal. Tighten silent shaft sprockets nut and bolt with shafts held in position as shown in **Fig. 3.**
6. Move tensioner B fully toward water pump and secure.
7. Align timing marks of silent shaft sprockets and crankshaft sprocket. Install timing belt B with no slack on tension side. Push down on B belt with finger at point A as in **Fig. 6.**
8. Place tensioner B again timing belt B so belt has slight spring tension. Tighten tensioner B nut and bolt. **Tighten nut first, then bolt.**
9. Check deflection of timing belt B, **Fig. 7.** Deflection should be from .16-.20 inch.
10. Move tensioner fully toward water pump and secure.
11. Align timing marks of three sprockets, **Fig. 8,** and install timing belt. When installing timing belt onto sprocket make sure tension side is not slack. Install belt onto crankshaft sprocket, injection pump sprocket and camshaft sprocket in that order. Reinstall belt in original direction of drive.
12. Loosen tensioner mounting bolts and allow tensioner to apply tension to belt by spring force. Check belt at camshaft sprocket for correct engagement.
13. Torque tensioner mounting bolts. Torque slot side bolt before torquing fulcrum side bolt.
14. Check all timing marks for proper alignment.
15. Rotate crankshaft clockwise through two camshaft teeth. Reverse direction of crankshaft until timing marks are realigned.
16. Check belt deflection halfway between camshaft sprocket and injection pump sprocket. Timing belt deflection should be .16-.20 inch.

TIMING BELT TENSION
ADJUST
CAMSHAFT TIMING BELT

1. Remove timing belt upper cover. Turn crankshaft until No. 1 cylinder is at top dead center on compression stroke and timing marks on all sprockets are aligned.
2. Loosen timing belt tensioner mounting bolts and allow tensioner to be pushed by tensioner spring into auto-

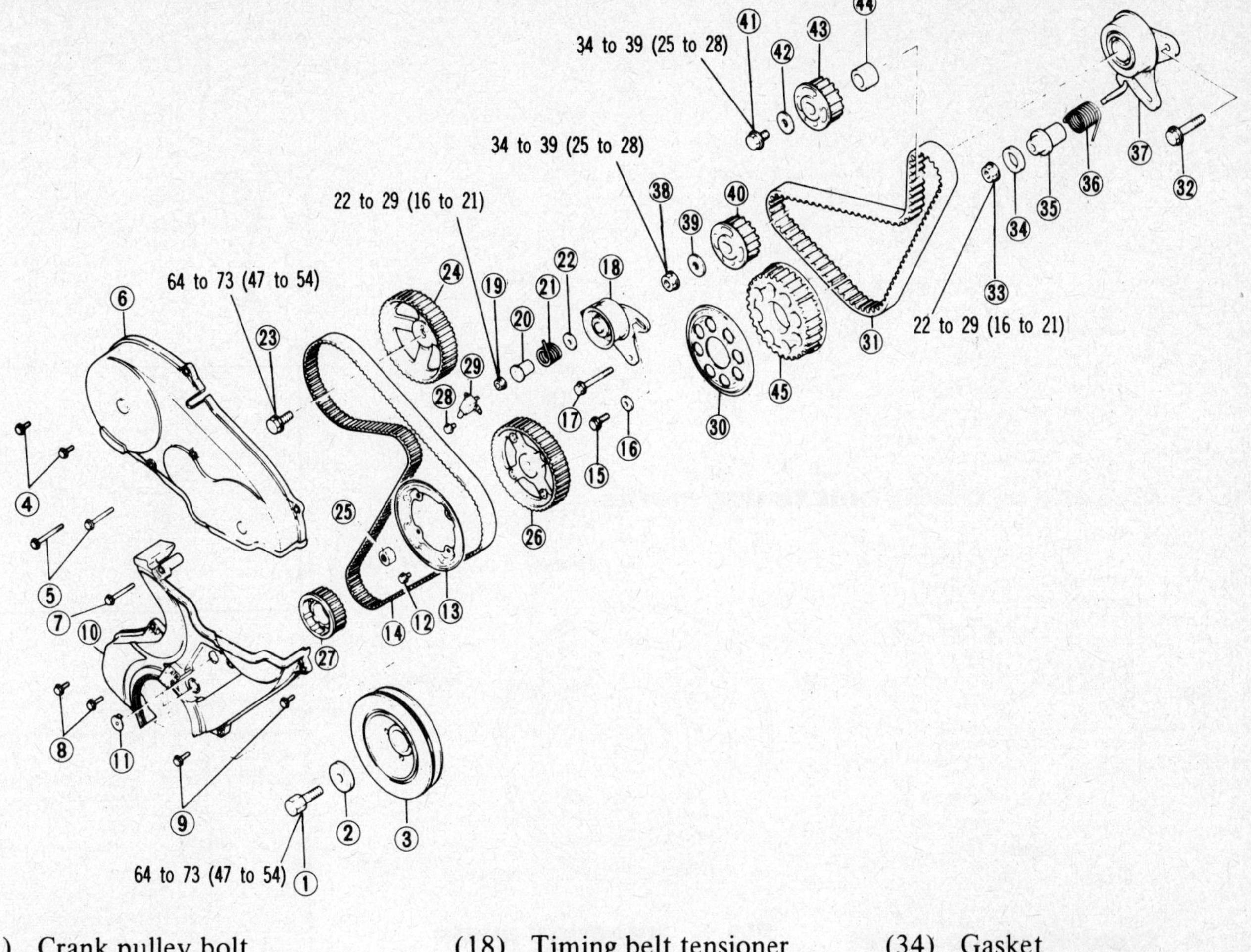

(1) Crank pulley bolt
(2) Special washer
(3) Dumper pulley
(4) Flange bolt (2)
(5) Flange bolt (2)
(6) Timing belt front upper cover
(7) Flange bolt
(8) Flange bolt (2)
(9) Flange bolt (3)
(10) Timing belt front lower cover
(11) Access cover
(12) Flange bolt (4)
(13) Flange
(14) Timing belt
(15) Flange bolt
(16) Washer
(17) Flange bolt
(18) Timing belt tensioner assembly
(19) Flange nut
(20) Tensioner spacer
(21) Tensioner spring
(22) Plain washer
(23) Flange bolt
(24) Camshaft sprocket
(25) Nut
(26) Injection pump sprocket
(27) Crankshaft sprocket
(28) Flange bolt (2)
(29) Switch assembly
(30) Flange
(31) Timing belt "B"
(32) Flange bolt
(33) Flange nut
(34) Gasket
(35) Tensioner spacer
(36) Tensioner spring "B"
(37) Timing belt tensioner assembly "B"
(38) Flange nut
(39) Washer
(40) Counterbalance shaft sprocket
(41) Flange bolt
(42) Washer
(43) Counterbalance shaft sprocket
(44) Spacer
(45) Crankshaft sprocket "B"

Fig. 1 Exploded view of timing belts

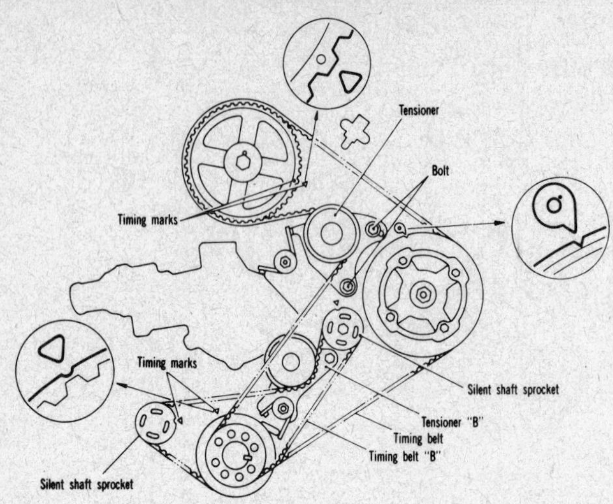

Fig. 2 Aligning of timing belt timing marks

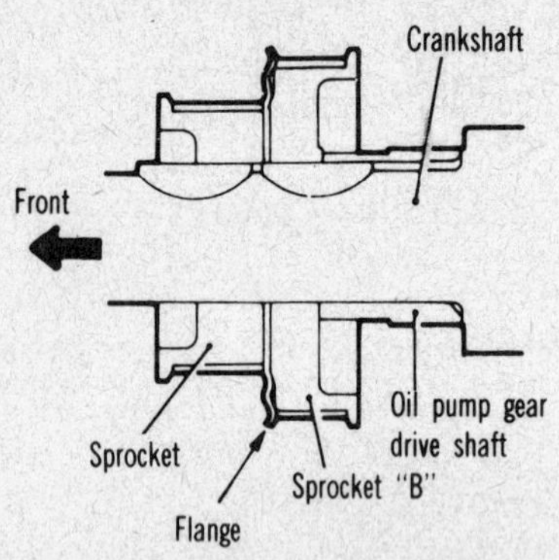

Fig. 4 Crankshaft sprocket & flange installation

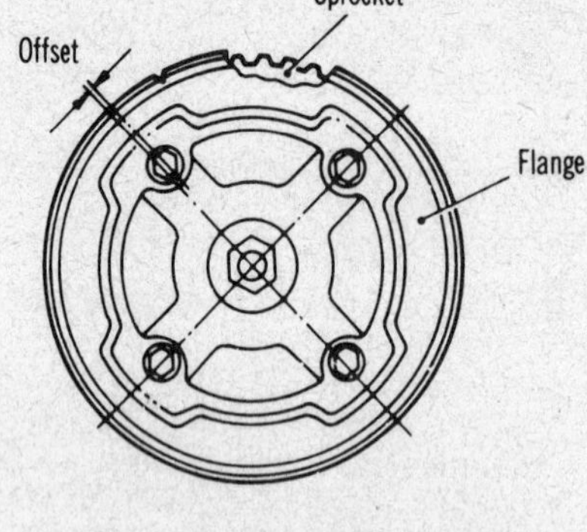

Fig. 5 Injection pump sprocket & flange installation

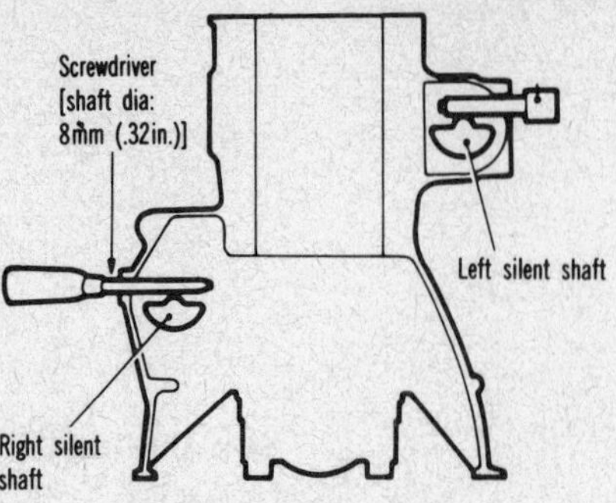

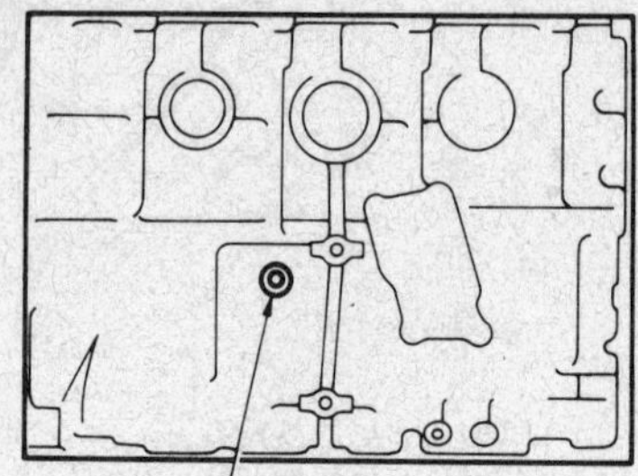

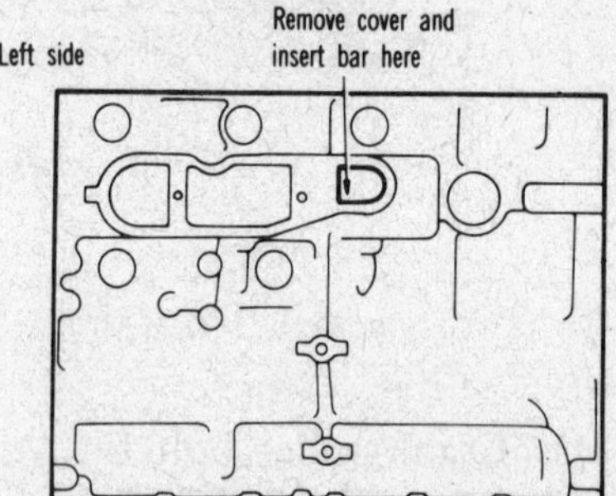

Fig. 3 Preventing silent shaft rotation

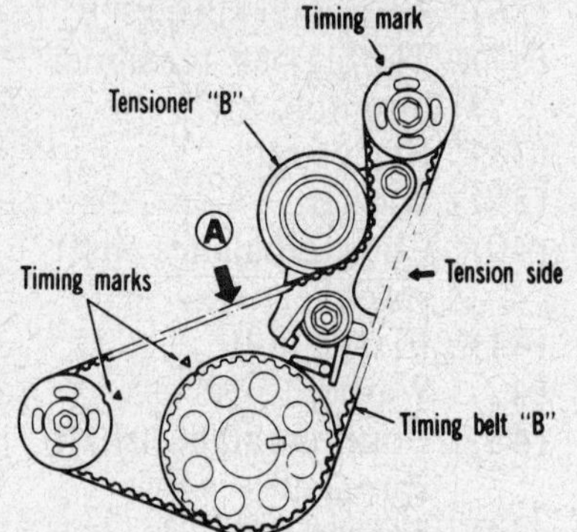

Fig. 6 Timing belt B tension adjustment

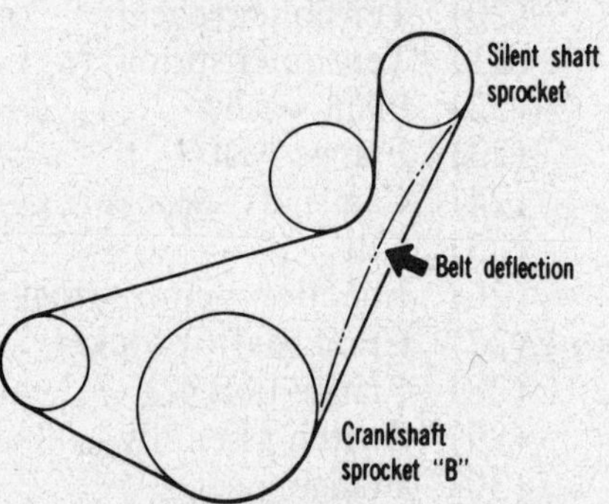

Fig. 7 Deflection test of timing belt B

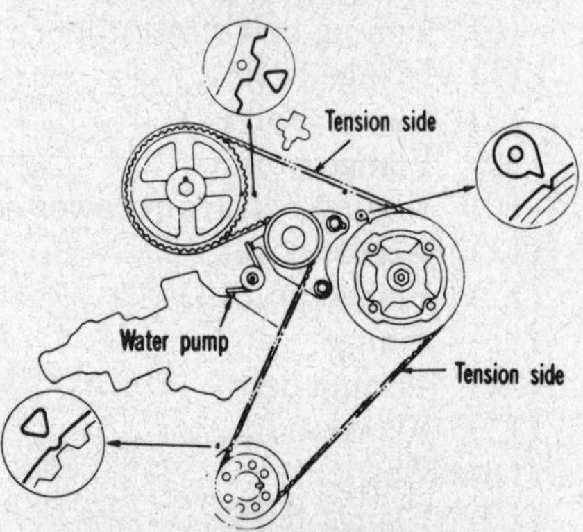

Fig. 8 Timing belt installation & sprocket timing mark alignment

matic tensioning of timing belt.

3. Rotate crankshaft until two teeth of camshaft sprocket pass timing mark and hold in this position, **Fig. 9**, then torque tensioner mounting bolts. **Torque upper side bolt first, then torque lower side bolt.**
4. Turn crankshaft in counterclockwise direction until all sprocket timing marks are in alignment. Check belt deflection halfway between camshaft sprocket and injection pump sprocket. Deflection should be .16-.20 inch.
5. On 1983 models, depress timing belt switch knob until it is flush with base and mount timing belt upper cover, **Fig. 10.**

SILENT SHAFT DRIVE BELT

1. Turn crankshaft until No. 1 cylinder is at top dead center on compression stroke.
2. Pry up on access cover with screwdriver at position shown in **Fig. 11** and remove cover.
3. Loosen tensioner B mounting bolts and allow tensioner to properly tension belt B.
4. Torque tensioner B mounting bolts. Torque lower bolt to 16-21 ft. lbs. and upper bolt to 15-19 ft. lbs. **Torque lower nut before torquing upper nut.**
5. Install front access cover. Slide cover down along two embossed lines of front lower cover, **Fig. 11.**

ROCKER ARM & SHAFT REPLACE

1. Turn crankshaft until piston of No. 1

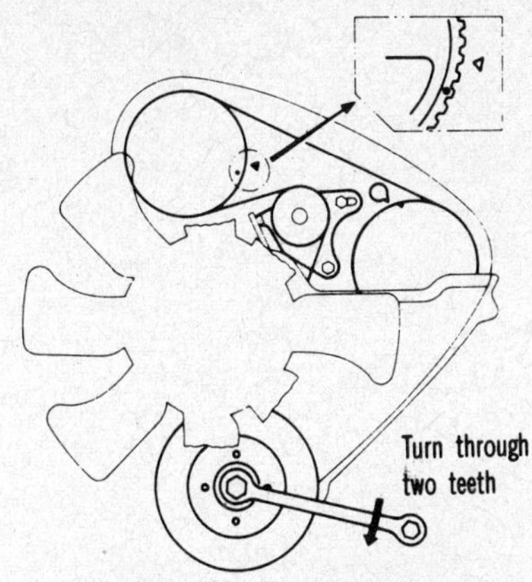

Fig. 9 Positioning crankshaft for torquing of tensioner mounting bolts

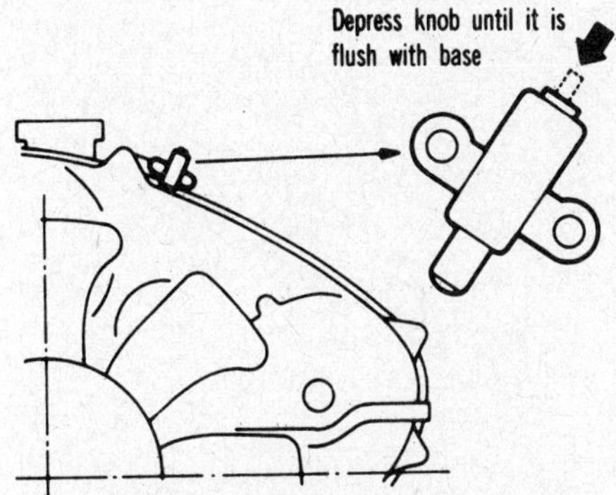

Fig. 10 Setting of timing bolt switch knob

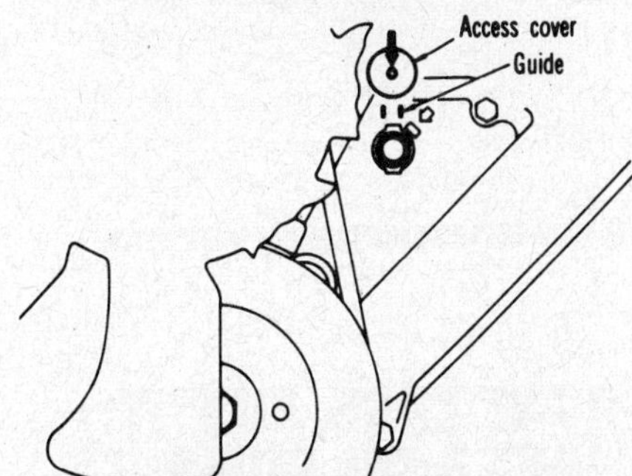

Fig. 11 Access cover removal hole & front cover guide lines

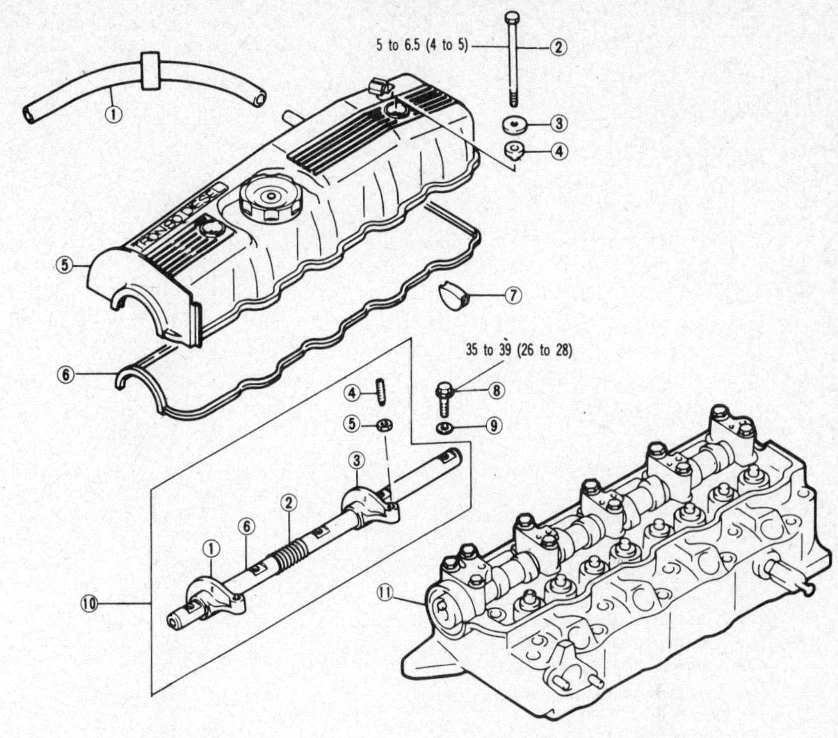

(1) Breather hose
(2) Bolt (2)
(3) Washer (2)
(4) Oil seal (2)
(5) Rocker cover
(6) Rocker cover gasket
(7) Semi-circular packing
(8) Flange bolt (5)
(9) Washer (5)
(10) Rocker arm and shaft assembly
(10) -(1) Exhaust rocker arm (4)
-(2) Rocker shaft spring (4)
-(3) Inlet rocker arm (4)
-(4) Rocker arm adjusting screw (8)
-(5) Nut (8)
-(6) Rocker arm shaft
(11) Cylinder head

Fig. 12 Exploded view of rocker arm & shaft

cylinder is at top dead center of compression stroke.

2. Remove parts in numerical order as shown in **Fig. 12.**
3. Reverse procedure to install. Before assembly, apply engine oil to inside diameter of rocker arm. Install rocker arm shaft with oil holes facing downward. End of shaft with one oil hole is front end. Apply sealant to areas shown in **Fig. 13.** Torque rocker arm cover bolts to 4-5 ft. lbs.

CAMSHAFT REPLACE

1. Turn crankshaft until No. 1 piston is at top dead center of compression stroke.
2. Remove parts in numerical order shown in **Fig. 14.**
3. Reverse procedure to install. Calculate endplay by measuring distance A and B, **Fig. 15.** Subtract measurement A from B. This is endplay. Maximum allowable endplay is .0020-.0071 inch. Install camshaft bearing caps from front in numerical order, starting with front bearing cap, **Fig. 14.** Rear bearing cap has no identification number stamped on it. Apply engine oil to oil seal lip and drive oil seal in using tool No. MD998381. Check timing mark alignment on crankshaft and injection pump sprockets before installing camshaft sprocket.

TURBOCHARGER REPLACE

Refer to **Fig. 16** and remove parts in numerical order as shown. Reverse procedure to install. Pour new engine oil into turbocharger before installing oil pipe flare nut.

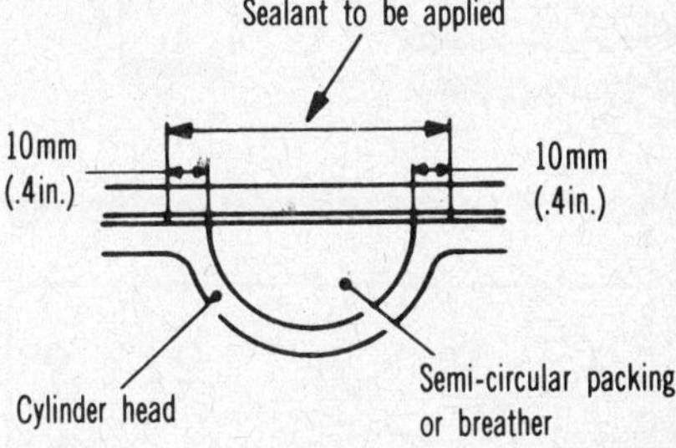

Fig. 13 Rocker arm cover sealant application areas

CYLINDER HEAD REPLACE

1. Remove fuel injection pipes. Refer to "Fuel Injection Pipe, Replace."
2. Remove fuel injectors. Refer to "Fuel Injectors, Replace."

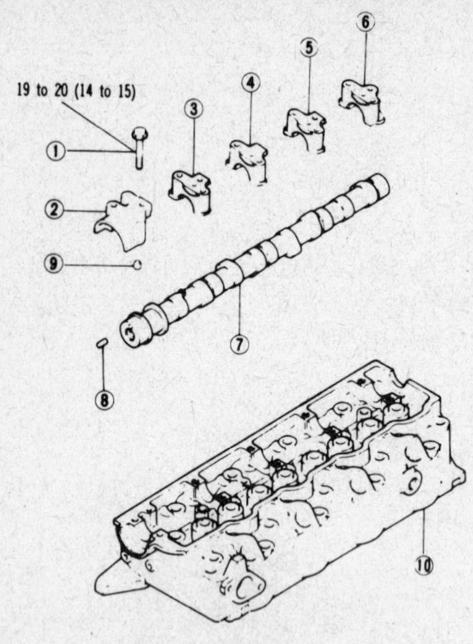

(1) Flange bolt (11)
(2) Camshaft bearing cap, front
(3) Camshaft bearing cap, No. 2
(4) Camshaft bearing cap, No. 3
(5) Camshaft bearing cap, No. 4
(6) Camshaft bearing cap, rear
(7) Camshaft
(8) Spring pin
(9) Knock bushing (10)
(10) Cylinder head

Fig. 14 Exploded view of camshaft & bearing caps

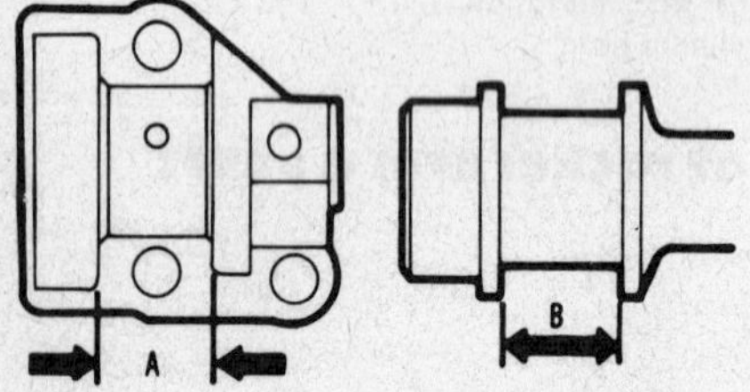

Fig. 15 Camshaft endplay

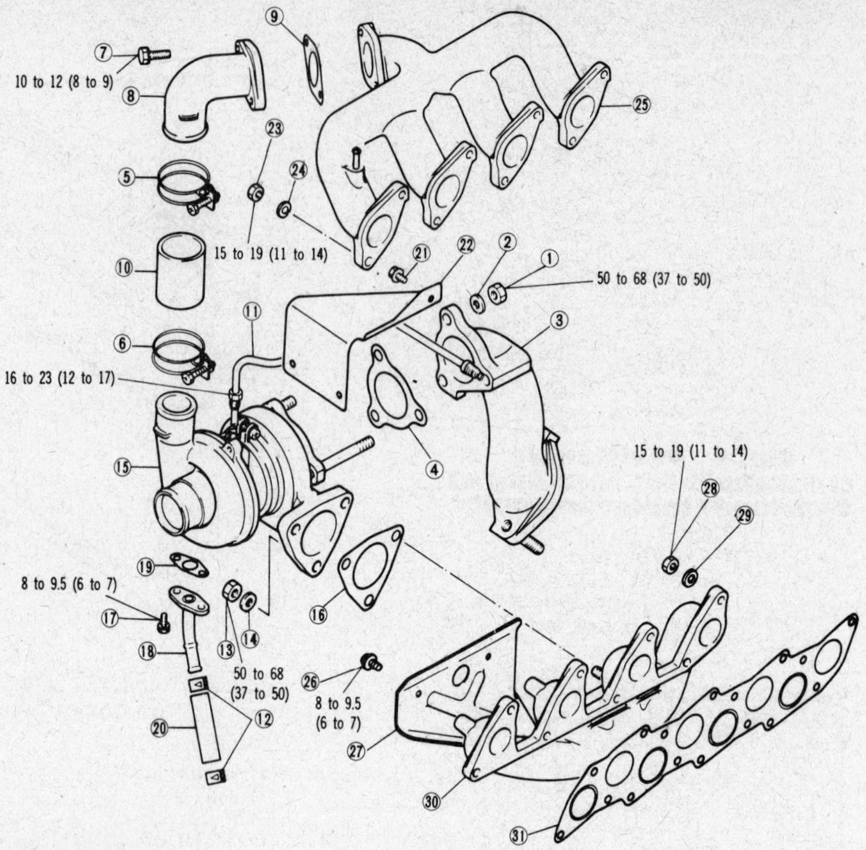

(1) Nut (3)
(2) Plain washer (3)
(3) Exhaust fitting
(4) Gasket
(5) Hose clamp
(6) Hose clamp
(7) Bolt (2)
(8) Inlet fitting
(9) Gasket
(10) Air hose
(11) Oil pipe
(12) Hose clip
(13) Nut (3)
(14) Plain washer (3)
(15) Turbocharger
(16) Gasket
(17) Bolt (2)
(18) Oil return pipe
(19) Gasket
(20) Oil hose
(21) Bolt (3)
(22) Heat protector
(23) Nut (8)
(24) Spring washer (8)
(25) Inlet manifold
(26) Flange bolt (3)
(27) Heat protector
(28) Nut (8)
(29) Plain washer (8)
(30) Exhaust manifold
(31) Gasket

Fig. 16 Exploded view of turbocharger system

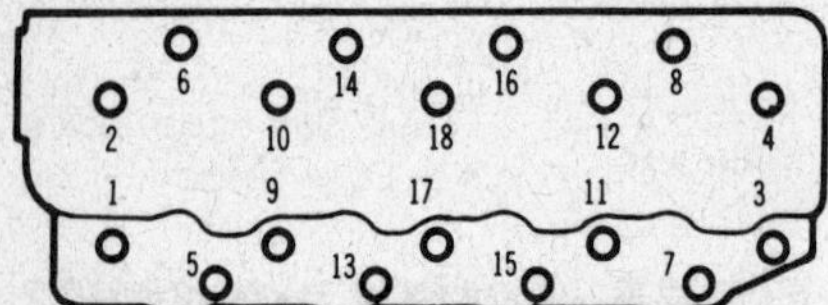

Fig. 17 Cylinder head bolt loosening sequence

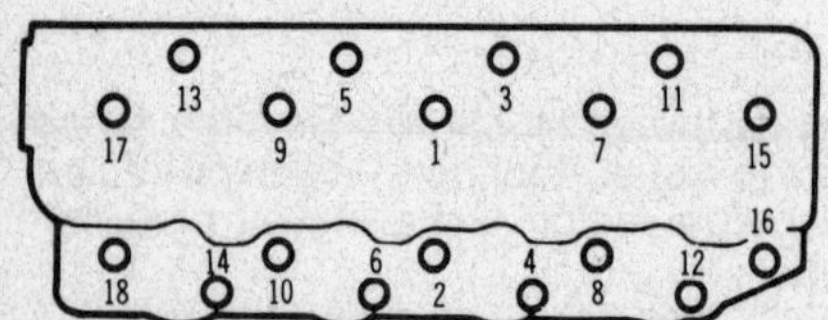

Fig. 18 Cylinder head bolt tightening sequence

3. Disconnect breather hose from valve cover and remove valve cover.
4. Remove timing belts. Refer to "Timing Belt, Replace."
5. Remove rocker arm. Refer to "Rocker Arm, Replace."
6. Remove camshaft. Refer to "Camshaft, Replace."
7. Remove water outlet fitting from cylinder head.
8. Remove cylinder head bolts in two steps in sequence shown in **Fig. 17.**
9. Reverse procedure to install. Torque cylinder head bolts to 76-83 ft. lbs. for cold engine and 84-90 ft. lbs. for hot engine in sequence shown in **Fig. 18.** Torque all bolts to 1/2 specified torque first, then finish torquing to full torque specifications.

VALVES
REPLACE

Refer to **Fig. 19** and remove parts in numerical order as shown. Reverse procedure to install.

FRONT CASE, SILENT SHAFT & OIL PUMP
REPLACE

Refer to **Fig. 20** and remove parts in numerical order as shown. Before removing inner oil gear from outer oil gear place identification marks on gears for reference at installation. Before loosening silent shaft driven gear retaining bolt, remove plug on right side of cylinder block and insert screwdriver to prevent rotation of right silent shaft, **Fig. 21.** Use tool No. MD998251 to remove right silent shaft rear bearing and tool No. MD998250 to install right silent shaft rear bearing.

Reverse procedure to install, observing following procedures:

1. Press fit oil seal into front lower case. Install drive gear shaft using tool MD998385.

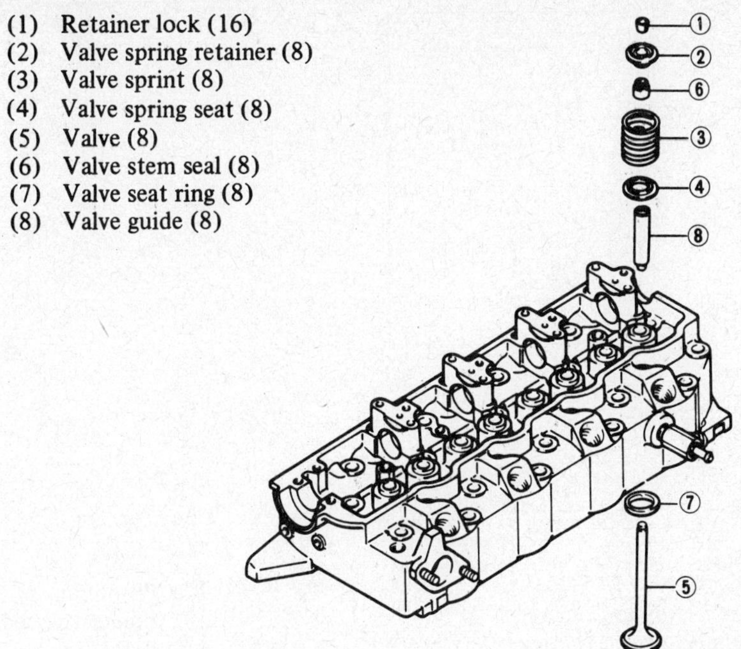

Fig. 19 Exploded view of valve train components

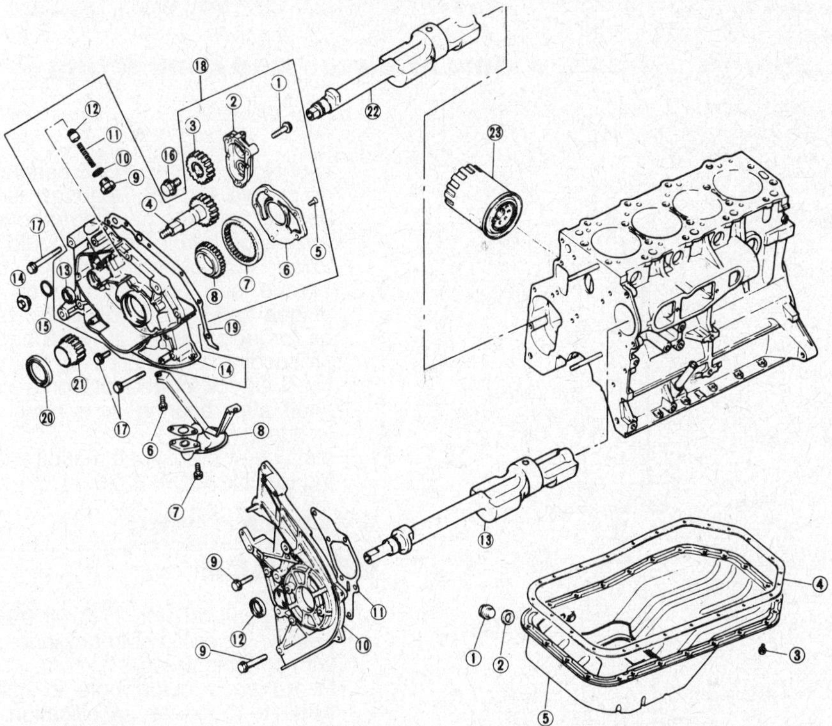

(1) Oil drain plug	(14) Plug cap	(18) -(9) Plug
(2) Gasket	(15) O-ring	-(10) Gasket
(3) Bolt (24)	(16) Flange bolt	-(11) Relief valve spring
(4) Oil pan gasket	(17) Flange bolt (7)	-(12) Relief valve
(5) Oil pan	(18) Front lower case assembly	-(13) Oil seal
(6) Bolt (2)	(18) -(1) Flange bolt (3)	-(14) Front lower case
(7) Bolt (2)	-(2) Silent shaft gear cover	(19) Front lower case gasket
(8) Oil screen	-(3) Silent shaft driven gear	(20) Front oil seal
(9) Flange bolt (3)	-(4) Silent shaft drive gear	(21) Oil pump gear drive shaft
(10) Front upper case	-(5) Machine screw (5)	(22) Right silent shaft
(11) Front upper case gasket	-(6) Oil pump cover	(23) Oil filter
(12) Oil seal	-(7) Oil pump outer gear	
(13) Left silent shaft	-(8) Oil pump inner gear	

Fig. 20 Exploded view of front case, silent shafts & oil pump

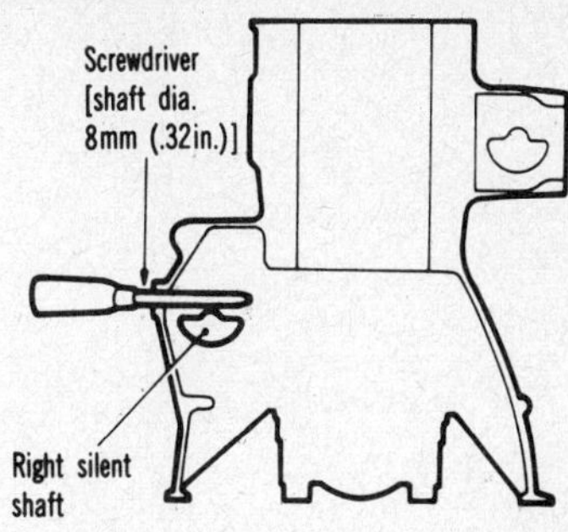

Cylinder block right side

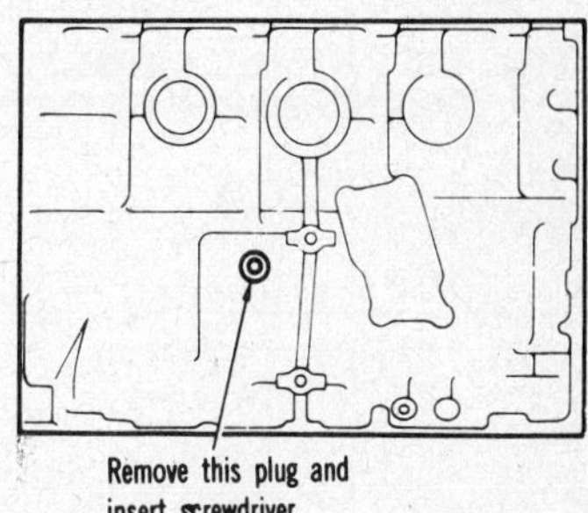

Fig. 21 Preventing right silent shaft rotation

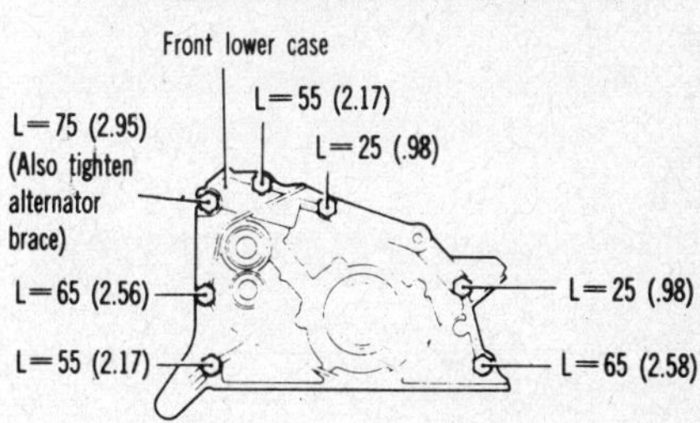

L=Bolt length mm (in.)

Fig. 22 Front lower case bolt identification

2. Check alignment marks on back of silent shaft drive and driven gears before installation. Marks are in alignment when they come together.
3. Install right silent shaft into front lower case and temporarily torque flange bolt. Apply oil to silent shaft journal.
4. Place new front lower case gasket on cylinder block. Install front lower case while inserting silent shaft into cylinder block. Torque flange bolts to 9-10 ft. lbs. Refer to **Fig. 22** for bolt identification.
5. Insert screwdriver through plug hole in right side of cylinder block before torquing silent shaft driven gear bolt, **Fig. 21.**
6. Use tool No. MD998382 and tool No. MD998383 for crankshaft front oil seal installation.
7. Torque front upper case flange bolts to 9-10 ft. lbs. and refer to **Fig. 23** for bolt identification.
8. Apply sealant to four places indicated in **Fig. 24** when installing oil pan gasket.

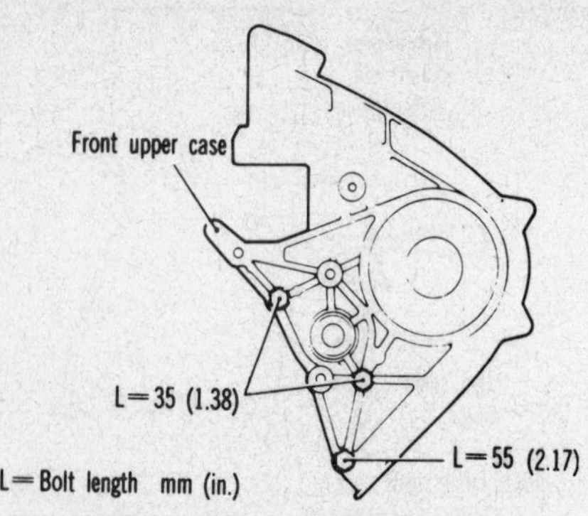

Fig. 23 Front upper case bolt identification

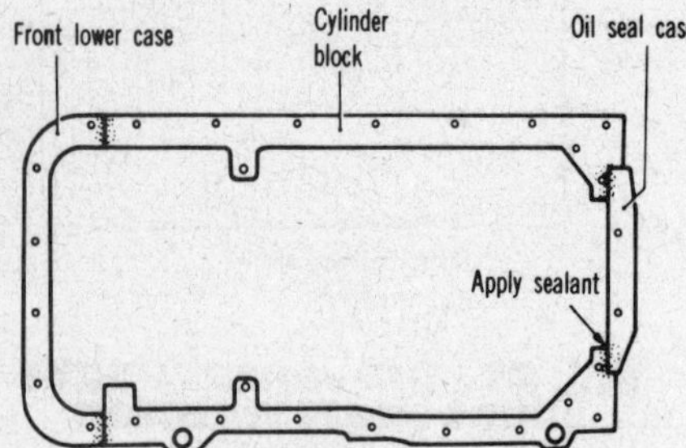

Fig. 24 Oil pan sealant application points

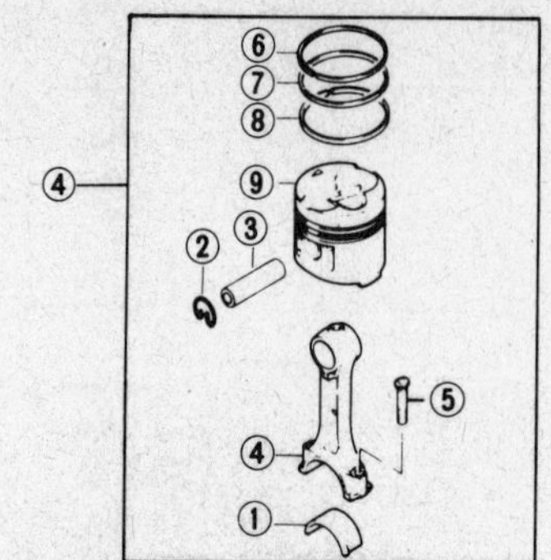

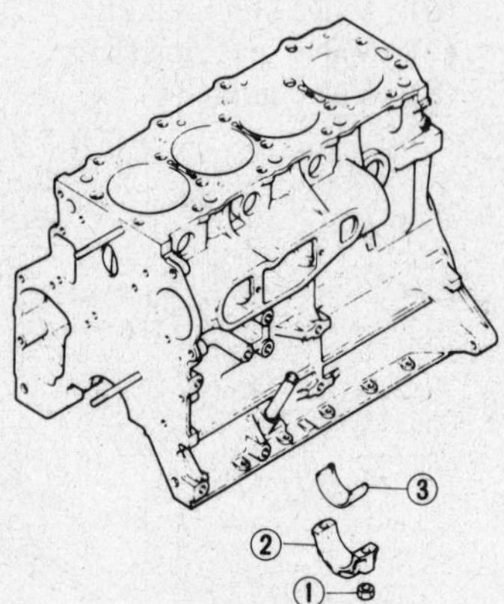

(1) Nut (8)
(2) Connecting rod cap (4)
(3) Connecting rod bearing (4)
(4) Piston and connecting rod assembly (4)
(4) -(1) Connecting rod bearing (4)
-(2) Snap ring (8)
(4) -(3) Piston pin (4)
-(4) Connecting rod (4)
-(5) Bolt (8)
-(6) Piston ring No. 1 (4)
-(7) Piston ring No. 2 (4)
-(8) Oil ring (4)
-(9) Piston (4)

Fig. 25 Exploded view of piston and connecting rod

PISTON & CONNECTING ROD

REPLACE

Refer to **Fig. 25** and remove parts in numerical order as shown. Number all connecting rods and caps before disassembly so cap can be mated to same rod at reassembly. Use tool No. MD998386 for removal of bushing in connecting rod piston pin end. Use same tool to install new bushing. Make sure oil hole in bushing lines up with oil hole in connecting rod, **Fig. 26.**

Reverse procedure to install, observing following procedures:

1. Assemble piston and connecting rod with front mark of piston and identification mark of connecting rod facing in same direction.
2. Assemble bearing cap to connecting rod using numbers applied before disassembly. If new connecting rods are used, position cap so bearing stopper notches are on same side.

CRANKSHAFT & FLYWHEEL

REPLACE

Refer to **Fig. 27** and remove parts in numerical order as shown. Identify main bearings so they can be reinstalled with same bearing cap. Reverse procedure to install, observing following procedures:

1. Bearings can be identified in following manner. Bearings for cylinder block side will have grooves running through the center on all bearings except No. 3 bearing. No. 3 bearing has no groove, **Fig. 28.** Bearings used on bearing cap side have no grooves.
2. Arrows on bearing caps should point toward front of engine when installed.
3. Torque cap bolts in two or three stages to 55-61 ft. lbs. Caps should be torqued starting at No. 3 cap and proceeding to No. 2, No. 4, No. 1 and No. 5. Check for free rotation of crankshaft after bearing caps have been torqued.
4. Install new crankshaft rear oil seal using tool No. MD998376.

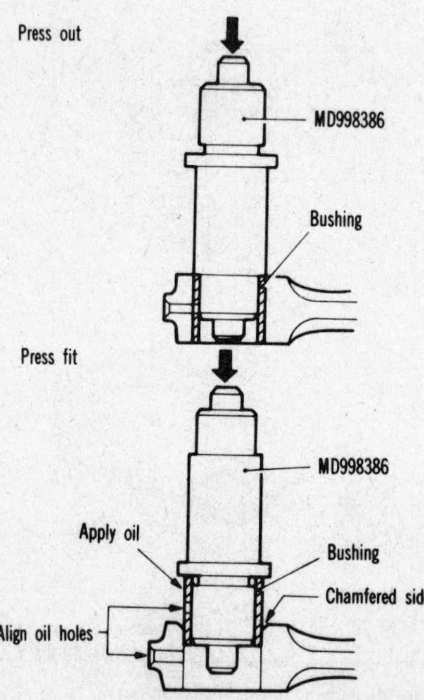

Fig. 26 Replacing connecting rod piston pin bushing

VALVE GUIDES

REPLACE

1. Using pushrod of tool No. MD998115, push valve guide out of cylinder head with suitable press.
2. Ream each guide hole in cylinder head to oversize specification. **Fig. 29.**
3. Install new valve guide from top of cylinder head using tool No. MD998115. Valve guide should protrude from cylinder head .591 inch.
4. Measure inside diameter of new guide. Ream out if necessary.

GLOW PLUG SYSTEM

DESCRIPTION

The quick glow system has two main circuits to maintain the glow plug at a constant temperature and to shorten prestart time, **Fig. 30.** One circuit is used to

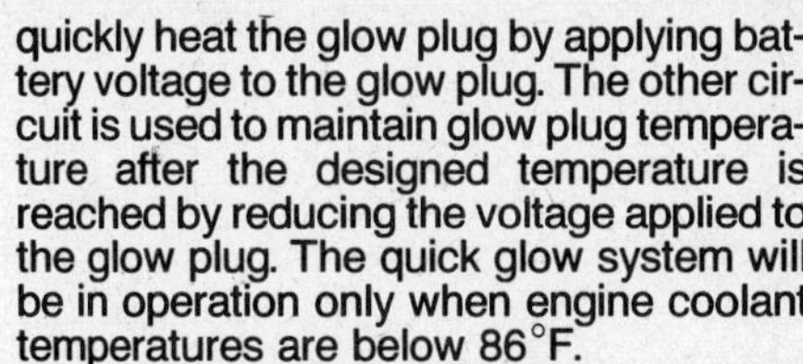

quickly heat the glow plug by applying battery voltage to the glow plug. The other circuit is used to maintain glow plug temperature after the designed temperature is reached by reducing the voltage applied to the glow plug. The quick glow system will be in operation only when engine coolant temperatures are below 86°F.

SYSTEM DIAGNOSIS

Refer to **Figs. 30 through 34** for quick glow system diagnosis procedures.

COMPONENTS TESTS

Glow Plug

Check resistance between glow plug terminal and body, **Fig. 35.** resistance should be .1 ohm at 68°F.

Glow Plug Relay

Connect 6 volt power source to relay coil terminal and check for continuity between relay B terminals, **Fig. 36.** Continuity should exist, if not, replace relay.

Dropping Resistor

Connect ohmmeter between dropping resistor terminals and note reading, **Fig. 37.** Resistance should be 130m ohms.

FUEL INJECTION PUMP REPLACE

If fuel injection pump is found to be defective, it should be replaced.

REMOVAL

1. Remove timing belt cover upper cover, then remove nut and washer attaching injection pump sprocket. Use care not to allow nut and washer to drop into lower cover.
2. Rotate crankshaft to bring No. 1 cylinder TDC compression stroke, aligning timing marks, **Fig. 38.**
3. Using a suitable puller, detach sprocket from pump driveshaft. Do not remove sprocket, but position in timing belt lower cover with timing belt attached. **When disengaging sprocket from pump shaft use care not to damage timing belt. After sprocket has been removed from pump shaft, do not rotate crankshaft.**

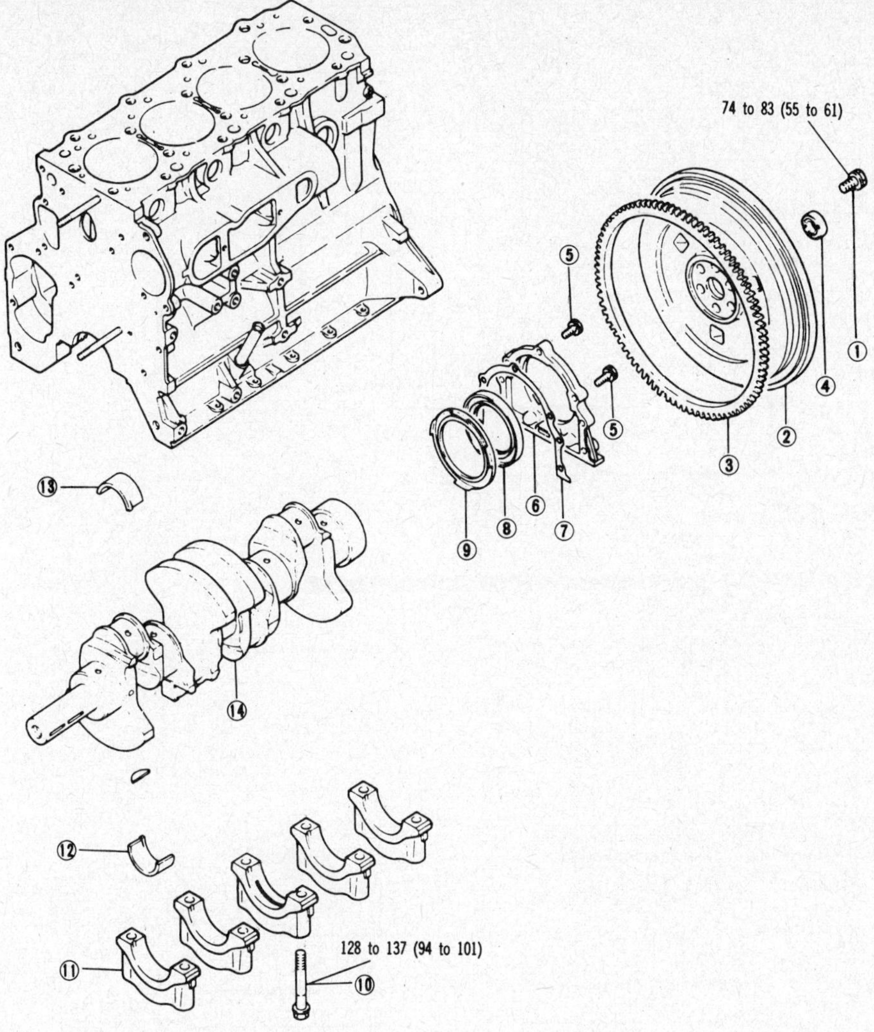

(1) Flywheel bolt (6)
(2) Flywheel
(3) Ring gear
(4) Ball bearing
(5) Flange bolt (5)
(6) Rear seal case
(7) Gasket
(8) Rear seal
(9) Oil separator
(10) Bearing cap bolt (1)
(11) Bearing cap (5)
(12) Bearing (5)
(13) Bearing (5)
(14) Crankshaft

Fig. 27 Exploded view of crankshaft & flywheel

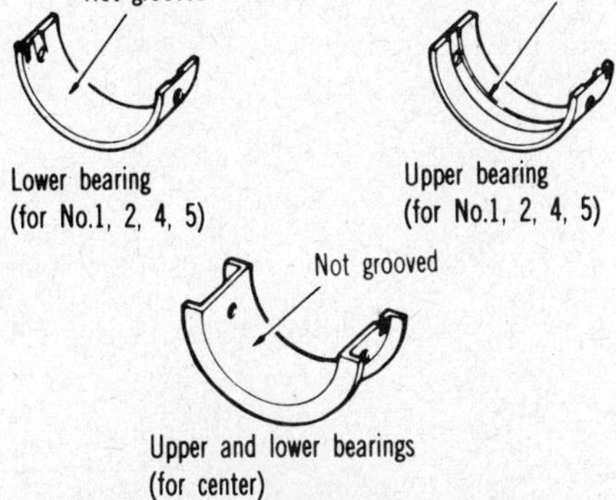

Fig. 28 Main bearing identification

Engine	Valve Guide Oversize Inch (mm)	Valve Guide Mark	Valve Guide Cylinder Head Bore Inch (mm)
2345cc	.002 (.05)	5	.5138-.5145 (13.050-13.068)
	.010 (.25)	25	.5217-.5224 (13.250-13.268)
	.020 (.50)	50	.5315-.5322 (13.500-13.518)

Fig. 29 Valve guide & guide bore oversizes

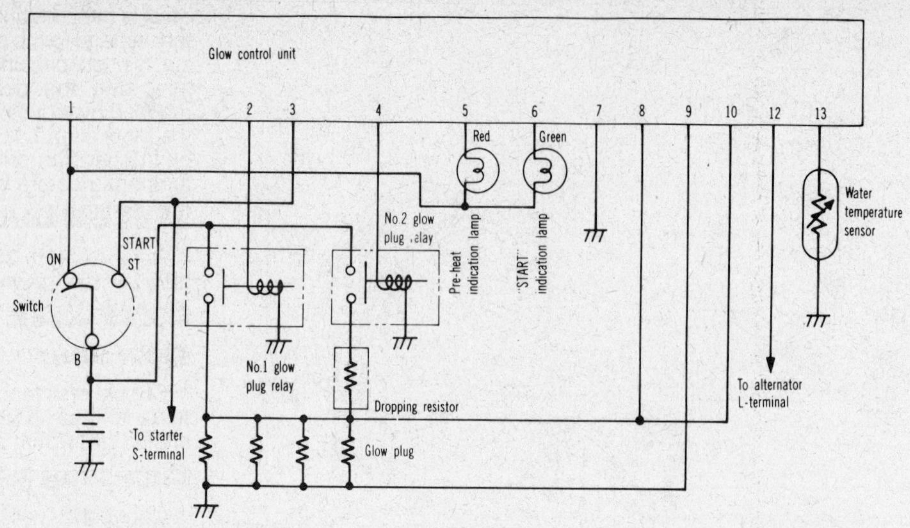

Fig. 30 Quick Glow System electrical schematic

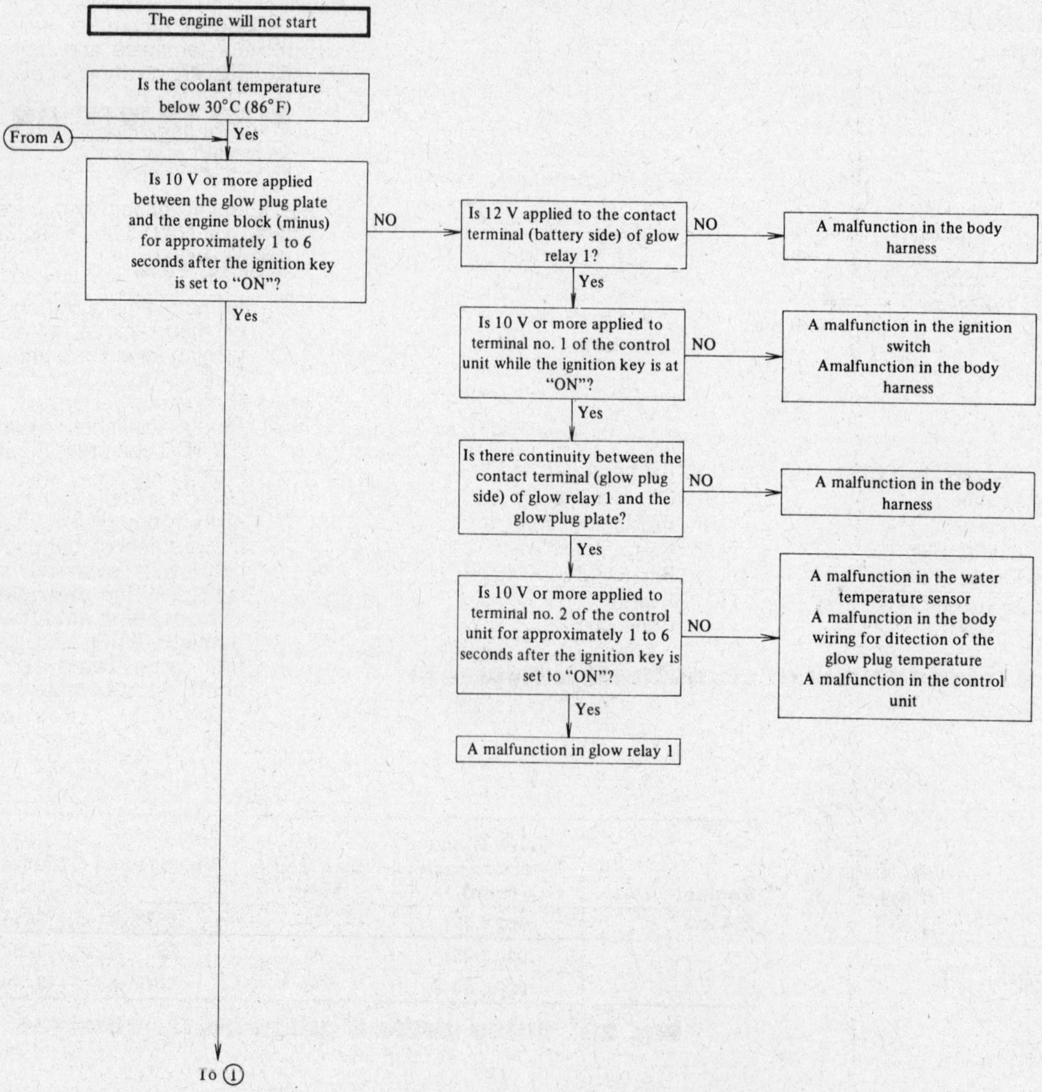

The engine will not start

↓

Is the coolant temperature below 30°C (86°F)

From A → Yes ↓

Is 10 V or more applied between the glow plug plate and the engine block (minus) for approximately 1 to 6 seconds after the ignition key is set to "ON"?

- NO → Is 12 V applied to the contact terminal (battery side) of glow relay 1?
  - NO → A malfunction in the body harness
  - Yes ↓ Is 10 V or more applied to terminal no. 1 of the control unit while the ignition key is at "ON"?
    - NO → A malfunction in the ignition switch / Amalfunction in the body harness
    - Yes ↓ Is there continuity between the contact terminal (glow plug side) of glow relay 1 and the glow plug plate?
      - NO → A malfunction in the body harness
      - Yes ↓ Is 10 V or more applied to terminal no. 2 of the control unit for approximately 1 to 6 seconds after the ignition key is set to "ON"?
        - NO → A malfunction in the water temperature sensor / A malfunction in the body wiring for ditection of the glow plug temperature / A malfunction in the control unit
        - Yes ↓ A malfunction in glow relay 1
- Yes ↓ To ①

Fig. 31 Quick Glow System diagnosis chart (Part 1 of 4)

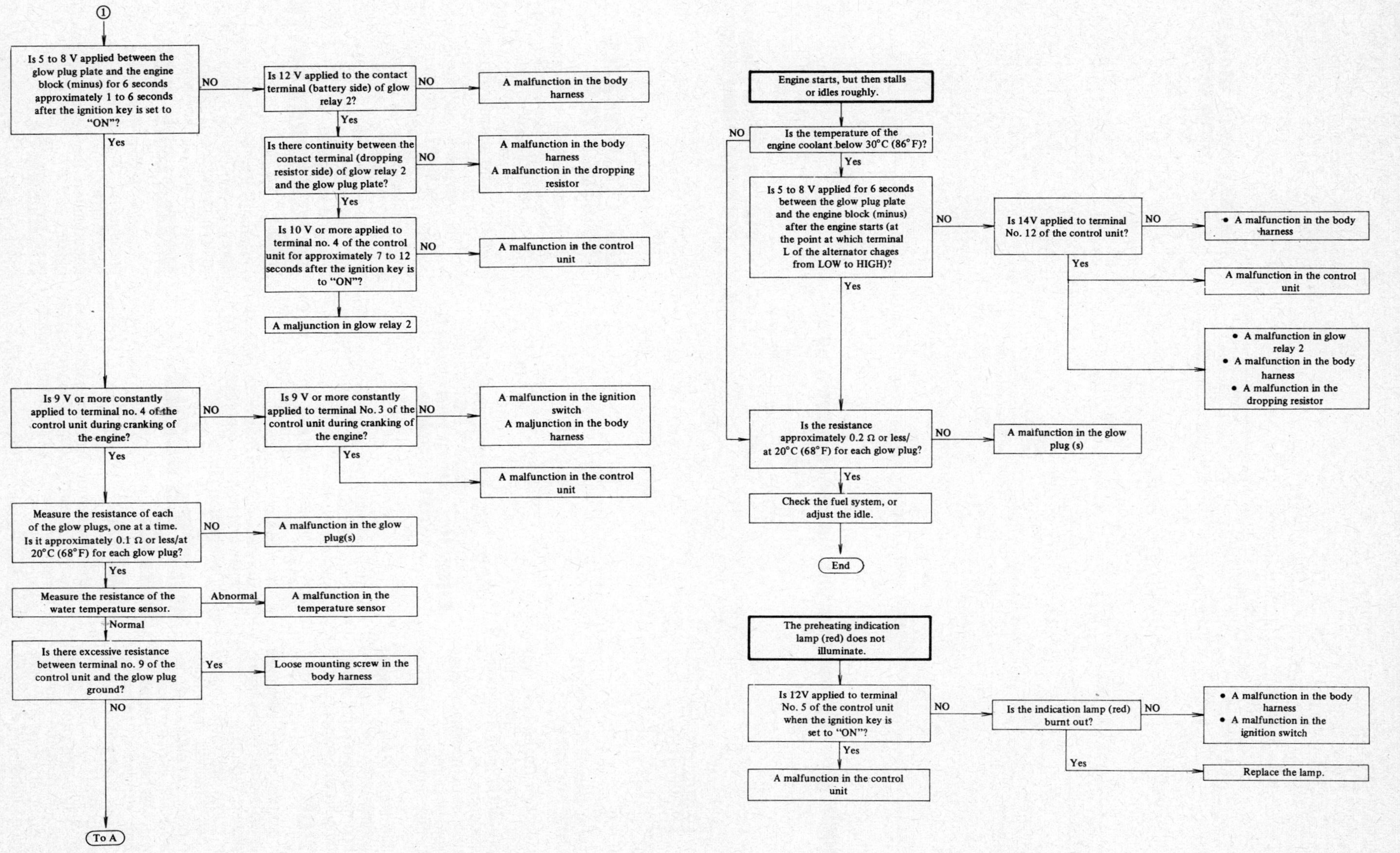

Fig. 32 Quick Glow System diagnosis chart (Part 2 of 4)

Fig. 33 Quick Glow System diagnosis chart (Part 3 of 4)

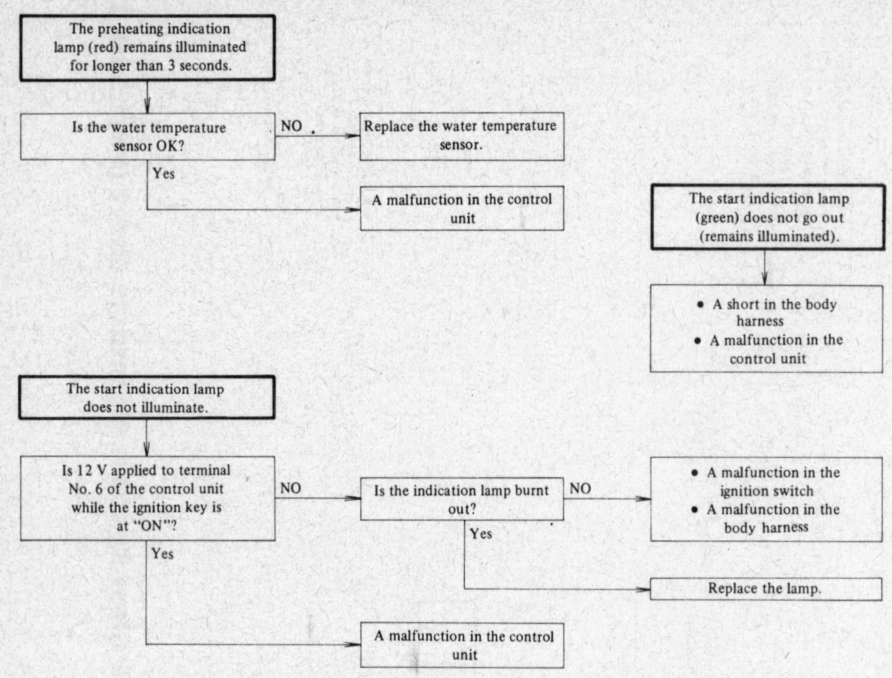

Fig. 34 Quick Glow System diagnosis chart (Part 4 of 4)

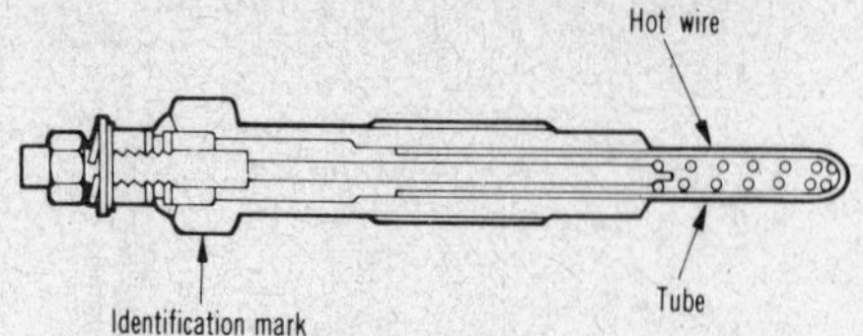

Fig. 35 Quick Glow System glow plug

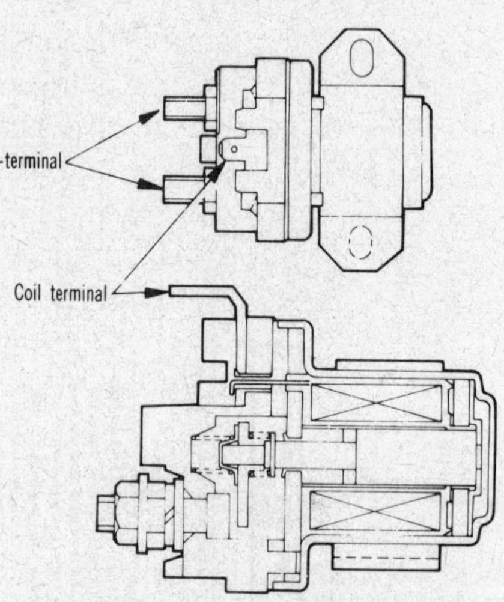

Fig. 36 Glow plug relay terminal identification

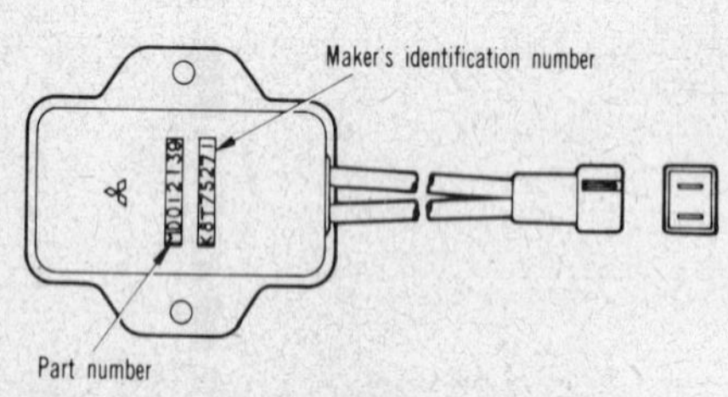

Fig. 37 Quick Glow System dropping resistor

4. Disconnect coolant hoses from wax element, then position hose high enough to prevent coolant from draining from cylinder head.
5. Disconnect boost compensator hose from fuel injection pump.
6. Disconnect fuel injection lines at pump.
7. Remove injection pump support bracket attaching bolts, then remove injection pump mounting nuts and lift pump assembly from engine.

INSTALLATION

1. Check to ensure that camshaft sprocket and crankshaft pulley timing marks are aligned, **Fig. 38.**
2. Lift injection pump sprocket upward with timing belt attached, then position injection pump on engine and insert pump driveshaft into sprocket tapered hole. **When installing injection pump driveshaft to pump sprocket, ensure that shaft key is properly positioned.**
3. Tighten the two injection pump mounting bolts and nuts, then tighten nut attaching pump sprocket to pump.
4. Install injection lines on injection pump and torque to 17-26 ft. lbs.

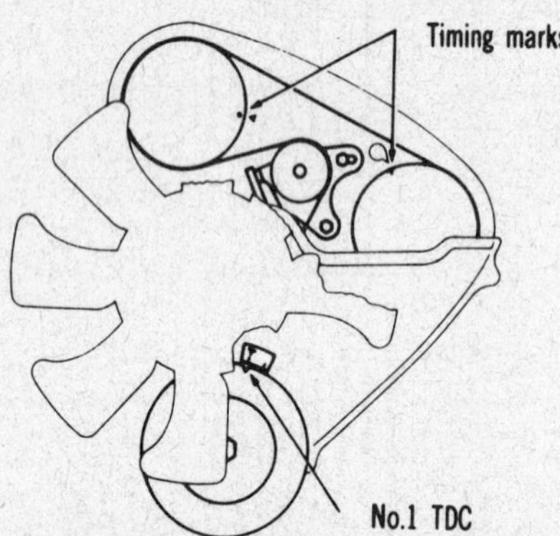

Fig. 38 Alignment of timing marks for fuel injection pump removal & installation

5. Adjust timing belt as described in Engine Section under "Timing Belt, Replace."
6. Adjust injection pump timing to 2° ATDC at .039 inch plunger stroke, then bleed fuel system.
7. Connect coolant hoses to wax element and boost compensator hose to fuel injection pump.

INJECTION NOZZLE SERVICE

REMOVAL

1. Using a spanner wrench to hold injection nozzle in position, disconnect fuel injection and return lines from nozzle, **Fig. 39.**
2. Using tool No. MD998387, remove injection nozzle from cylinder head.

INJECTION NOZZLE PRESSURE TEST

1. Position injection nozzle on a suitable injection pressure tester, **Fig. 40.**
2. Operate injection pressure tester at approximately 60 cycles per minute and note pressure gauge readings. The reading should increase gradually, with pointer oscillating when nozzle is injecting. The pressure gauge reading at the point where the gauge pointer starts to oscillate should be 1707-1849 psi. If pressure is below the service limit of 1565 psi or less, then nozzle must be disassembled and inspected.

NOZZLE SPRAY PATTERN TEST

Refer to **Fig. 41** when checking nozzle spray pattern. If an unacceptable spray pattern is obtained, the nozzle should be disassembled and inspected.

NOZZLE LEAK TEST

Operate tester, **Fig. 40** to maintain a pressure of 1422 to 1565 psi and check nozzle tip for leaks. If a leaking condition is encountered, the nozzle tip should be replaced.

DISASSEMBLY

1. Position nozzle holder body in a soft jawed vise, then remove retainer nut

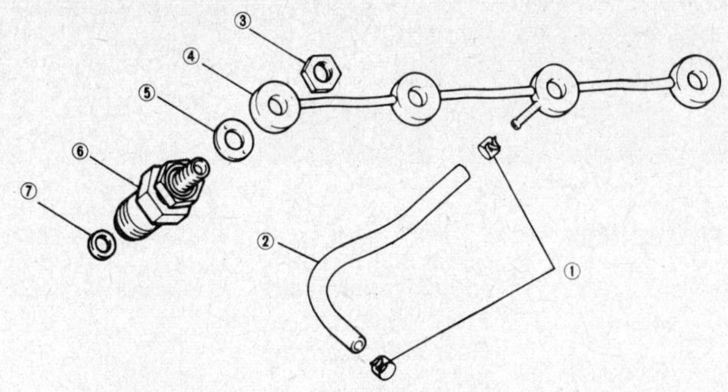

Fig. 39 Injection nozzle & fuel return lines

Fig. 40 Checking injector nozzle pressure

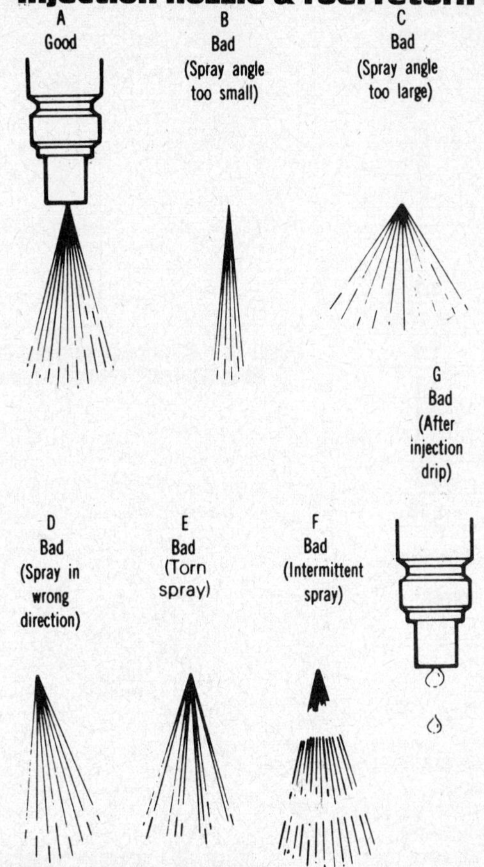

Fig. 41 Injector nozzle spray patterns

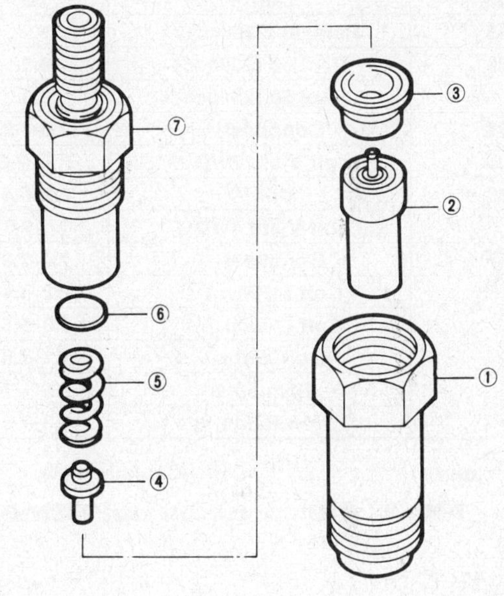

Fig. 42 Disassembled view of injector nozzle

using tool No. MD998387.

2. Disassemble injection nozzle, **Fig. 42.** Use a piece of wood to remove carbon from nozzle component, then clean components in a suitable cleaning solvent. After cleaning immerse components in light oil. Use care not to damage nozzle tip needle tip valve.

INSPECTION

1. Position nozzle tip and plunger in fuel oil, then lift plunger upward and allow plunger to slide downward into nozzle tip, **Fig. 42.**
2. Plunger should slide smoothly within the nozzle tip, if not replace nozzle assembly.
3. Also check plunger tip for damage and replace as necessary.

ASSEMBLY

1. Clean all components with fuel oil before assembling.
2. Assemble fuel injection nozzle components, **Fig. 42.**
3. Position nozzle holder body in soft jawed vise.
4. Using tool No. MD998387, tighten injection nozzle retaining nut.

INJECTION NOZZLE PRESSURE ADJUSTMENT

1. Position injection nozzle on a suitable injection pressure tester and check pressure as described under "Nozzle Pressure Test."
2. Injection pressure should be 1707-1849 psi.
3. If pressure is not within limits, adjust by changing the thickness of the internal shim. An increase of .004 inch in shim thickness will increase pressure by 142 psi.

INSTALLATION

1. Clean nozzle mounting area of cylinder head.
2. Install a replacement nozzle tip gasket.
3. Install injection nozzle on cylinder head and torque using tool No. MD998387 to 44 to 50 ft. lbs.
4. Connect return line, **Fig. 39** and fuel injection line to nozzle using a spanner wrench to hold nozzle in position while tightening line nut. Torque fuel return line nuts to 33-39 ft. lbs. Torque fuel injection line nuts to 17-26 ft. lbs.

CLUTCH & MANUAL TRANSMISSION SECTION

INDEX

Year	Model	Pedal Height (A) Inch	Freeplay (B) Inch	Release Point (C) Inch①
1983	Challenger & Sapporo②	7.5	.6–.8	1.5
1983–84	Colt②	7.2	.8–1.2	1.3
1983–85	Ram 50 (2300cc)③	6.9	.4–.5	.9
1983–86	Ram 50 (2000cc)	6.5	.8–1.4	.9
	Ram 50 (2600cc)	6.9	.8–1.4	.9
1984–85	Conquest③	7.0-7.2	.2–.4	—
1984–86	Colt Vista 2WD②	7.1--7.3	.6–.8	2.2
1985–86	Colt②	6.2–6.4	.8–1.2	3.1
	Colt Vista 4WD③	7.1-7.3	4.9-5.1	2.17
1985–87	Conquest③	7.4–7.6	.2–.5	1.4
1987	Colt (1500cc)②	6.2–6.4	.8–1.2	3.1
	Colt (1600cc)③	6.3–6.5	.24–.55	3.1
	Colt Vista③	7.1–7.3	.24–.51	2.17
	Ram 50②	6.5–6.7	.8–1.4	2.4
	Ram Raider③	7.3–7.5	.31–.63	1.38

①—Minimum. ②—Cable release. ③—Hydraulic release.

Fig. 1 Clutch pedal adjustment specifications

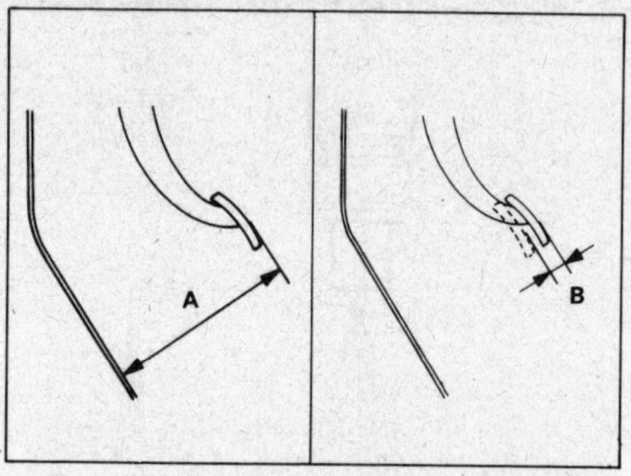

A B

Fig. 2 Clutch pedal height & freeplay measurement

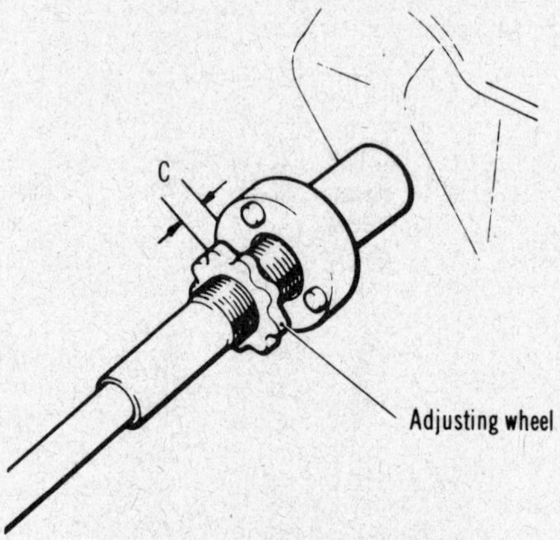

C
Adjusting wheel

Fig. 3 Clutch cable adjustment

CLUTCH PEDAL

ADJUST

Refer to **Fig. 1** for clutch pedal height, freeplay and pedal height specifications.

GASOLINE ENGINE MODELS

Models W/Cable Release System

1. Measure clutch pedal height (A), **Fig. 2.** If height is not within specifications, adjust with pedal stopper bolt. If pedal height is not within specifications on models without stopper bolt, check pedal stop and pedal support for damage and wear and repair as needed.
2. Measure clutch pedal freeplay (B), **Fig. 2.** If freeplay is not within specifications, adjust as follows:
   a. Pull outer cable away from cable retainer at toe board and turn adjusting wheel until clearance (C), **Fig. 3,** is .12-.16 inch for Challenger, Sapporo and Ram 50, .2-.24 inch for Colt or 0-.04 inch for Colt Vista.
   b. Depress clutch pedal several times and recheck pedal freeplay.
   c. Repeat adjustment as needed until freeplay is within specifications.
3. After adjusting pedal height and freeplay, measure height of clutch pedal from floorboard at clutch release point (D), **Fig. 4.**
4. If release point is less than value specified in chart, check clutch assembly and release mechanism and repair as needed.

Models W/Hydraulic Release System

1. Measure clutch pedal height (A), **Fig. 2.**
2. Check clutch pedal clevis pin play. It should be .04-.12 inch, measured at pedal.
3. If clutch pedal height is not within specifications, turn either the clutch switch or adjusting bolt to bring height within specifications. If clevis pin play is not within specifications, adjust clutch master cylinder pushrod as necessary to bring play within specifications. **Do not press pushrod into master cylinder when adjusting clevis pin clearance.**
4. Check clutch pedal freeplay and clutch release point. If either dimension is not within specifications, hydraulic system requires bleeding or clutch is faulty.

DIESEL ENGINE MODELS

1. Slightly loosen adjusting bolt.
2. Loosen jam nut on operating rod, then turn pushrod to adjust distance between top of pedal and toe board to 6.9 inches.
3. Holding yoke in position, tighten jam nut to secure yoke to rod.
4. Set adjusting bolt to prevent it from depressing pedal lever.

Distance between the clutch pedal and the firewall when the clutch is disengaged

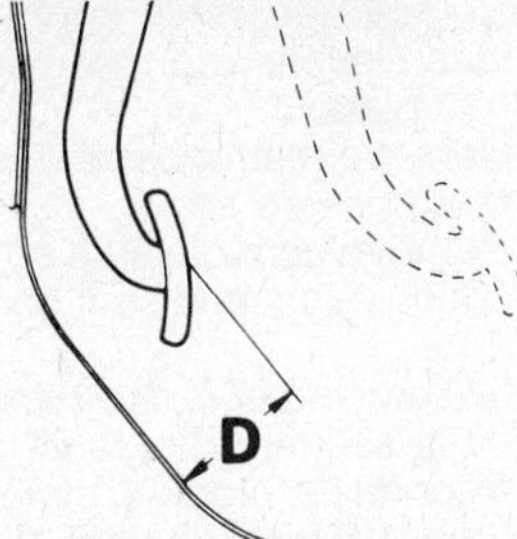

Fig. 4 Clutch release point measurement

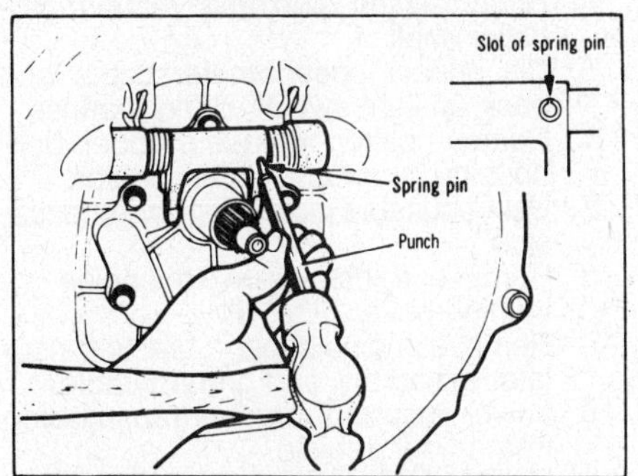

Fig. 5 Clutch release lever & shaft installation

5. Ensure clutch freeplay is .4-.5 inch and that clutch pedal stroke is 5.9 inches.
6. If clutch pedal freeplay and clutch pedal stroke are not within specifications, bleed system.

CLUTCH REPLACE

EXC. COLT VISTA W/4 WHEEL DRIVE

1. Remove transmission as described under "Transmission, Replace."
2. With suitable clutch disc guide inserted in center hole to prevent clutch disc from dropping, evenly loosen bolts holding clutch cover assembly in a crossing pattern, then remove clutch cover assembly.
3. Remove clutch disc.
4. Remove return clip on transmission side, then remove release bearing carrier and bearing.
5. Using a suitable punch, remove shift arm spring pin and control lever shaft assembly, then remove clutch shaft arm, two felt packings and return springs.
6. Insert clutch control lever and shaft assembly into transmission case from left side, then install clutch shift arm, two felt packings and two return springs onto shaft. Apply grease to inside surface of bushing and oil seal lips. Apply engine oil to felt packings.
7. Align lock pin holes of shift arm and control shaft, then drive in two spring pins using lock pin installer MD998245. When driving in spring pins, ensure spring pin slot direction is at right angles to centerline of control shaft, **Fig. 5.**
8. Apply suitable grease to clutch disc spline and main drive gear spline.
9. Using suitable clutch disc guide tool, install clutch disc and clutch cover on flywheel. Install clutch disc with manufactures stamped mark facing pressure plate. When installing clutch cover, align flywheel and clutch cover notches to ensure proper balance.
10. Install release bearing and carrier, then install return clip. Apply grease to inside diameter of carrier and fill groove with grease.
11. Install transmission, then adjust clutch pedal as described under "Clutch Pedal, Adjust."

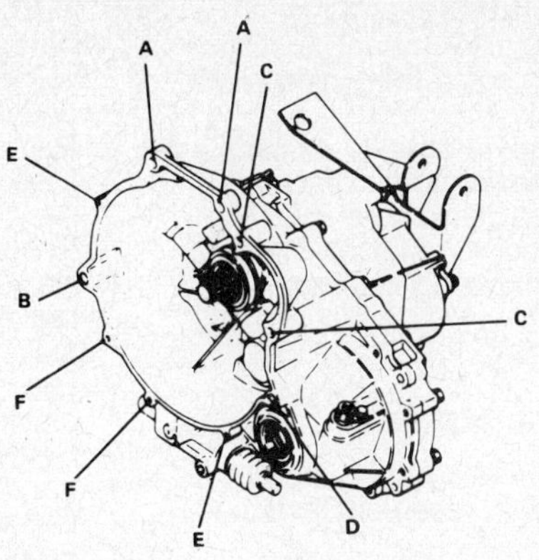

	Nm	ft.lbs.	O.D. x Length mm (in.)	Bolt indentification
A	43–55	31–40	⑦ 10 x 40 (1.6)	⑦ A x B
B	43–55	31–40	⑦ 10 x 65 (2.6)	
C	22–32	16–23	⑦ 10 x 55 (2.2)	A
D	30–34	22–25	⑩ 10 x 60 (2.4)	B
E	10–12	7–9	⑦ 8 x 14 (0.6)	
F	15–22	11–16	⑦ 8 x 20 (0.8)	

Fig. 6 Transmission to engine bolt torque specifications.

COLT VISTA W/4 WHEEL DRIVE

1. Remove clutch slave cylinder hydraulic line.
2. Remove transaxle as described under "Manual Transmission, Replace."
3. Remove return clip, then the release bearing.
4. With suitable clutch disc guide inserted in center hole to prevent clutch disc from dropping, loosen bolts holding clutch cover assembly one at a time diagonally and remove clutch cover assembly.
5. Remove clutch disc.
6. Reverse procedure to install, noting the following:
   a. Apply suitable grease to clutch linkage that encounters metal to metal contact.
   b. Apply grease to groove of inner surface of release bearing.
   c. Apply coating of grease to end of slave cylinder pushrod.
   d. After installing transaxle, adjust clutch as described under "Clutch Pedal, Adjust," then bleed hydraulic system and check for leakage.

MANUAL TRANSMISSION REPLACE

FRONT WHEEL DRIVE UNITS

EXC. COLT VISTA

1. Disconnect battery ground cable, then remove the battery and battery tray.
2. On turbocharged models, remove air cleaner case, then the actuator mounting bolts, actuator to shaft coupling pin and the actuator. **Do not reuse actuator collar.**
3. On models equipped with 5 speed, disconnect select control valve connector.
4. Remove speedometer and clutch release cables.
5. Disconnect back-up light switch and starter wiring.
6. Remove top engine to transaxle attaching bolts, then the starter motor.
7. Raise and support vehicle, then remove under cover.
8. Drain transaxle oil into suitable container.
9. Disconnect shift linkage and extension rod.
10. Disconnect stabilizer bar from lower control arms.
11. Remove right and left side drive shafts. Refer to Front Suspension and Steering Section for procedure.
12. Support lower part of transaxle with suitable jack. **Support a wide area of transaxle so oil pan is not partially supported.**
13. Remove bellhousing cover, then remaining engine to transmission at-

taching bolts.
14. Remove transaxle mount insulator bolt, then blind cover from inside right fender shield.
15. Remove transaxle bracket assembly, then the transaxle mount bracket.
16. Remove transaxle from vehicle.
17. Reverse procedure to install. Refer to **Fig. 6** for torque specifications.

COLT VISTA

2 Wheel Drive Models

1. Remove battery and battery tray.
2. Remove radiator reservoir tank and air cleaner.
3. Disconnect clutch cable, speedometer cable and back-up lamp wiring harness from transaxle.
4. Disconnect electrical connectors from starter, then remove 5 upper transaxle to engine attaching bolts.
5. Remove select control valve and switch harness, then the starter.
6. Disconnect engine wiring harness, then the battery cable at transaxle.
7. Raise and support vehicle, then remove front wheels and drain transaxle oil.
8. Remove extension, shift control rod and selector control cable from under engine compartment.
9. Remove stabilizer bar and strut bar from lower arm.
10. Remove drive shafts. Refer to Front Suspension and Steering Section for procedure.
11. Using a suitable jack, support lower part of transaxle over a wide area so as not to damage oil pan.
12. Remove bellhousing cover.
13. Remove lower transaxle to engine attaching bolts, then the transaxle mount insulator bolt.
14. Slide transaxle to the right, then lower and remove from vehicle.
15. Reverse procedure to install, noting the following:
    a. Torque bolts as follows: transaxle mounting bracket bolt, 22-30 ft. lbs.; 814 mm bellhousing cover to transaxle attaching bolts, 7-9 ft. lbs.; 820 mm bellhousing cover to transaxle attaching bolts, 11-16 ft. lbs.; extension to transaxle bolt, 43-51 ft. lbs.; starter mounting bolt, 16-23 ft. lbs.; back-up lamp switch, 22 ft. lbs.; drain plug, 22-25 ft. lbs.; filler plug, 7-8 ft. lbs.; driveshaft nuts, 144-188 ft. lbs.; and engine to transaxle attaching bolts as shown, **Fig. 6.**
    b. Fill transaxle to specifications with suitable fluid.
    c. Adjust clutch cable, gearshift lever, and range selector lever.

4 Wheel Drive Models

1. Disconnect battery ground cable.
2. Remove radiator reservoir tank, then disconnect speedometer cable, back-up light harness and shift linkage.
3. Remove select control valves and connectors.
4. Remove transaxle electrical harness connectors.
5. Disconnect clutch hydraulic line from transaxle bracket, then remove slave cylinder. Cap lines to prevent leakage and entry of dirt.
6. Remove vacuum reservoir tank.
7. Disconnect starter motor wiring harness, then remove five upper engine to transaxle attaching bolts.
8. Raise and support vehicle, then remove front tires, lower plate and cover.
9. Drain transmission and transfer case oil into suitable container.
10. Remove rear drive shaft, then the transfer case extension housing.
11. Remove front drive shafts. Refer to Front Suspension and Steering Section for procedure.
12. Disconnect right side lower control arm strut bar, then remove right fender under cover.
13. Support transaxle with suitable jack.
14. Remove remaining transaxle to engine attaching bolts, then the bellhousing cover attaching bolts.
15. Remove transaxle mounting bracket insulator bolt, then the transaxle mounting bracket bolts.
16. Move transaxle/transfer case assembly towards right side of vehicle.
17. Tilt right side of transfer case downwards until transfer case is moved to upper part of the cylinder tube of rack housing, then rotate transaxle/transfer case assembly to the left and remove from vehicle.
18. Reverse procedure to install noting the following:
    a. Torque attaching bolts to specifications given in **Fig. 6.**
    b. After installation, bleed hydraulic clutch assembly.
    c. Refill transaxle and transfer case.

REAR WHEEL DRIVE UNITS

CHALLENGER & SAPPORO

1. Disconnect battery ground cable.
2. Remove air cleaner and place gearshift lever in any position except reverse. Place clean rag between firewall and rocker arm cover.
3. Raise vehicle and support with suitable safety stands.
4. Remove starter and disconnect clutch cable from clutch control lever. Remove cable from transmission case.
5. Remove four bolts attaching bellhousing cover and the cover.
6. Disconnect back-up light switch wire harness and speedometer cable at transmission.
7. Remove propeller shaft assembly and plug extension housing.
8. Support rear of engine and transmission with suitable jacks and remove engine support rear bracket.
9. Tilt transmission assembly rearward slightly and remove control housing.
10. Remove remaining transmission bolts and withdraw transmission from engine.
11. Lower transmission on transmission jack and remove from under engine.
12. Reverse procedure to install. Torque transmission mounting bolts to 31-40 ft. lbs. and starter mounting bolts to 16-24 ft. lbs.

CONQUEST

1. Disconnect battery ground cable.
2. Remove gearshift lever assembly as follows:
    a. Remove gearshift knob, spool release levers and rear console box trim plate.
    b. Remove rear console liner and the rear console box.
    c. Remove console side covers, front console box and shift boot retainer ring.
    d. Ensure shifter is in neutral, remove bolts securing gearshift assembly, disconnect stopper plate from extension housing, then lift gearshift assembly off extension housing.
3. Place a suitable insulator at rear of cylinder head to prevent damage, then raise and support vehicle.
4. Drain transmission, then remove propeller shaft.
5. Disconnect speedometer cable and back-up light switch wiring harness.
6. Remove clutch release cylinder, bellhousing cover and starter motor.
7. Using suitable jack, support transmission.
8. Remove transmission to engine attaching bolts.
9. Remove engine support bracket, insulator assembly, and ground cable.
10. Lower jack and remove transmission from under vehicle.
11. Reverse procedure to install, torquing bolts as follows: starter motor mounting bolts, 16-23 ft. lbs.; engine to transmission mount bolts, 31-40 ft. lbs.; drain plug, 44 ft. lbs.; oil filter plug, 22-25 ft. lbs.; back-up light switch, 22 ft. lbs.; under cover attaching bolts 6-7 ft. lbs.; and speedometer sleeve clamp bolt, 7.5-9 ft. lbs.

RAM 50

1. Disconnect battery ground cable.
2. Remove air cleaner and the starter motor.
3. Remove upper transmission attaching bolts from bellhousing.
4. Working from inside vehicle, remove lock screws, then lift console box upward and remove it. If vehicle does not have a console, lift carpet upward over center tunnel.
5. Remove lock screws, then lift dust cover retaining plate upward and remove it.
6. Turning dust cover upward, remove four attaching bolts at lower part of extension housing and remove gearshift lever assembly. **Remove gearshift lever with lever placed in second speed on four speed transmission models or first speed on five speed transmission models.**
7. Raise and support vehicle, then drain transmission fluid.
8. Remove speedometer cable, then disconnect transmission switch and back-up light switch wiring from transmission.
9. Remove bolts from rear propeller shaft, then withdraw propeller shaft from transmission.

10. On 4 wheel drive models, remove transfer plate skid plate, then the front propeller shaft.
11. On all models, disconnect front exhaust pipe.
12. Disconnect clutch cables on gasoline engine models. On diesel engine models, remove clutch release cylinder. Support rear of engine with jack. On four wheel drive models, remove transfer case mounting bracket.
13. With transmission supported on a transmission jack, remove No. 2 crossmember.
14. Remove bellhousing cover.
15. Remove retaining bolts from transmission and draw transmission rearward from engine. **Be careful not to twist front end of the main drive gear.**
16. Reverse procedure to install, noting the following:
    a. When installing control lever assembly, place shift lever in second speed position on four speed transmission models or in first speed position on five speed transmission models, so that nylon bushing hole is vertical. **During this operation, use care to prevent dirt from entering transmission at control housing mounting section.**
    b. When assembling bellhousing cover, ensure cover is not bent. A bent cover will not make proper contact with cylinder block and transmission, resulting in entry of mud into transmission.
    c. Install gearshift lever dust cover snugly into hole in tunnel and attach retaining plate with screws.
    d. Adjust clutch pedal as described under "Clutch Pedal, Adjust."
    e. Fill transmission with specified amount of fluid.

RAM RAIDER

1. Disconnect battery ground cable.
2. Remove transmission and transfer case shift lever knobs, then the console.
3. Raise and support vehicle, remove transfer case skid plate, then drain transmission and transfer case.
4. Mark positions of propeller shaft companion flanges, remove retaining bolts, then remove front and rear propeller shafts.
5. Disconnect front exhaust pipe and remove bellhousing cover.
6. Disconnect speedometer cable and electrical connectors from transmission and transfer case.
7. Remove bolt securing clutch slave cylinder, then secure cylinder aside leaving hose connected.
8. Support transmission assembly with suitable jack, then remove transfer case bracket and the No. 2 crossmember.
9. Remove bolts securing transmission to engine, separate transmission taking care not to twist or damage input shaft.
10. Remove transmission and transfer case as an assembly, tilting front of transmission downward and lowering assembly toward front of vehicle.
11. Reverse procedure to install. Torque companion flange bolts to 36-43 ft. lbs.

TRANSFER CASE

REPLACE

EXC. COLT VISTA

1. Disconnect back-up light switch electrical connector.
2. Remove steel ball, if equipped.
3. Raise and support vehicle.
4. Remove plug from right side of transfer case assembly, then the select spring and select plunger.
5. Remove control lever assembly and gasket.
6. On 5 speed manual transmission, remove plugs from the top of the adapter, then withdraw resistance spring, steel ball, neutral return springs and plungers.
7. Remove transfer case to transmission adapter attaching bolts.
8. Drive out spring pin from change shifter assembly, if equipped.
9. Remove four bolts and two nuts attaching transfer case to adapter assembly.
10. Remove transfer case assembly from adapter and shifter from control shaft, if equipped.
11. Reverse procedure to install.

COLT VISTA

1. Raise and support vehicle.
2. Drain fluid from transfer case.
3. Disconnect propeller shaft from transfer case assembly.
4. Remove transfer case extension housing attaching bolts, then the extension housing.
5. Remove transfer case installation bolt, then the transfer case assembly.
6. Reverse procedure to install.

DISC BRAKES SECTION

INDEX

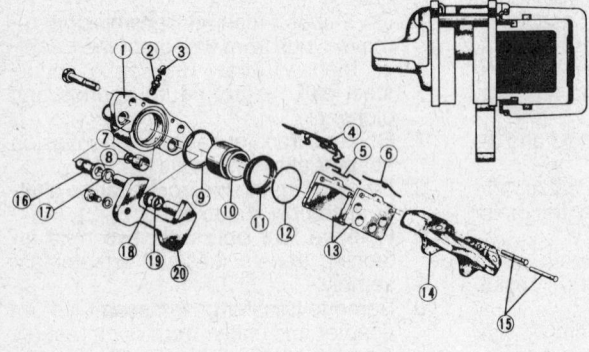

(1) Caliper, inner
(2) Bleeder screw
(3) Bleeder screw cap
(4) Pad protector
(5) K-spring
(6) M-clip
(7) Torque plate pin cap
(8) Cap plug
(9) Piston seal
(10) Piston
(11) Dust seal
(12) Retaining ring
(13) Pad assembly
(14) Caliper, outer
(15) Pad retaining pin
(16) Torque plate pin bushing
(17) Spacer
(18) Wiper seal retainer
(19) Wiper seal
(20) Torque plate

Fig. 1 Two piece pin type caliper exploded view

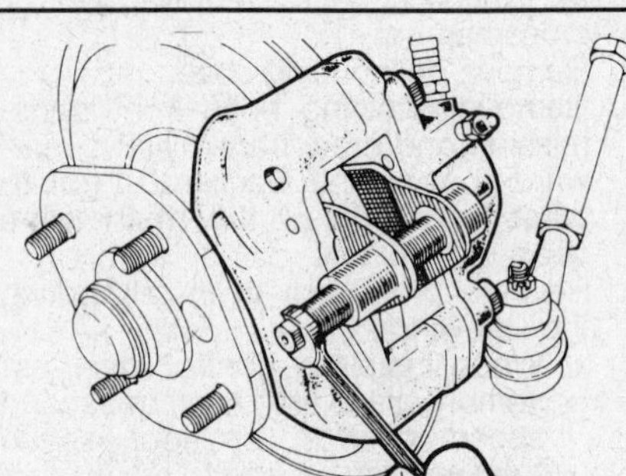

Fig. 2 Brake pad installation. Two piece pin type caliper

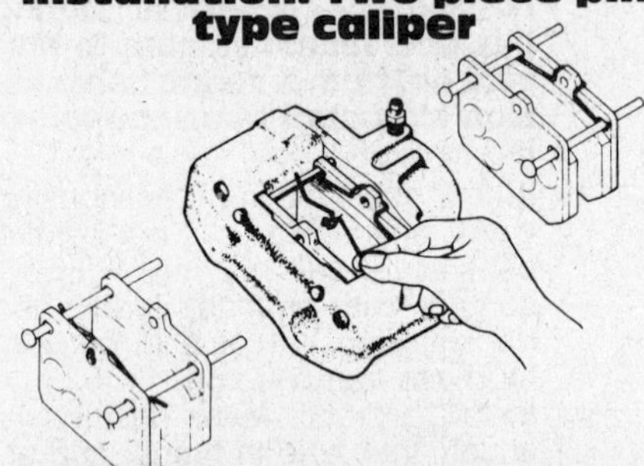

Fig. 3 Installing K-spring & M-clip. Two piece pin type caliper

FRONT DISC BRAKE SERVICE

TWO PIECE PIN TYPE CALIPER

Brake Pad Removal

1. Remove the wheel.
2. Remove the protector, **Fig. 1,** by prying up the edge of the clip at the center of the pad protector with a screwdriver.
3. Holding the center of the M-clip with fingers, detach the M-clip from the pad and the ends from the retaining pins.
4. Pull the retaining pins from the caliper assembly and remove the K-spring.
5. Remove the brake pad assembly by holding the backing plate area of the pad with pliers.

Caliper Removal

1. Remove the brake pads as outlined previously.
2. Remove the brake hose clip from the strut area, then disconnect the brake hose from the caliper.
3. Remove the caliper assembly by loosening torque plate and adapter mounting bolts.

Caliper Overhaul

1. Loosen caliper attaching bridge bolts and separate the outer caliper from the inner caliper.
2. After the removal of the dust seal, remove the piston by applying compressed air at the brake hose fitting. **Do not apply high pressure suddenly since the piston may cause personal injury.**
3. Remove the piston seal, using care not to damage the cylinder.
4. Clean all parts using clean brake fluid.
5. Apply rubber grease to the piston seal and apply brake fluid to the cylinder bore. Insert the piston seal into the piston carefully to prevent distortion.
6. Whenever the torque plate has been removed from the inner caliper, it is necessary to clean the torque plate shaft and the shaft bore of the caliper and apply suitable grease to the rubber bushing, wiper seal inner surface and torque plate shaft before assembly. Apply sufficient grease to the threaded portion of the torque plate shaft.
7. Tighten the inner and outer caliper bridge bolts to 58-69 ft. lbs.

CALIPER INSTALLATION

1. Install caliper on adapter.
2. Torque the caliper assembly (torque plate) to the adapter bolts to 58-72 ft. lbs.
3. Torque the brake hose to 9-12 ft. lbs.

BRAKE PAD INSTALLATION

1. Spread the piston, using the special tool, Piston Spreader (C-3992) or equivalent, then insert the brake shoe through the shim, **Fig. 2.**
2. Install the K-spring and M-clip, **Fig. 3.**
3. Install the pad protector.

ONE PIECE PIN TYPE CALIPER

COLT TURBO & COLT VISTA

Brake Pads, Replace

1. Remove approximately 1/3 of brake fluid from master cylinder.
2. Raise and support front of vehicle, then remove tire and wheel assembly.
3. Remove lock pin, **Fig. 4,** then lift caliper assembly upwards. Support caliper assembly with suitable piece of wire to prevent damage to brake hose.
4. Remove inner shim, anti-squeak shim and brake pad assemblies from support mounting.
5. Press caliper piston into caliper bore with suitable tool.
6. Install pad clips "B" and "C", **Fig. 4,** pad assemblies, inner shims and anti-squeak shims into support mounting.
7. Lower caliper body, then install lock pin. Refer to **Fig. 4,** for torque specifications.
8. Depress brake pedal several times to seat pads, then check and replenish brake fluid as necessary.
9. Install wheel and tire assembly and lower vehicle.

Caliper, Replace

1. Raise and support vehicle, then remove wheel and tire assembly.
2. Disconnect brake hose at caliper strut, then at the brake caliper.
3. Remove support mounting to steering knuckle attaching bolts, then the front brake assembly.

1. Lid
2. Lock pin
3. Sleeve
4. Caliper body
5. Guide pin boot
6. Piston
7. Lock pin boot
8. Piston seal
9. Piston boot
10. Boot ring
11. Inner shim
12. Pad assembly
13. Pad clip B
14. Pad clip C
15. Anti-squeak shim
16. Guide pin
17. Sleeve
18. Support mounting
19. Brake disc
20. Hub

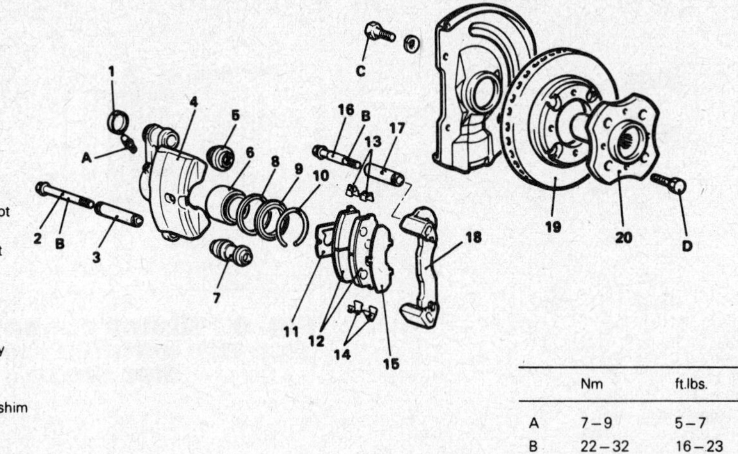

	Nm	ft.lbs.
A	7–9	5–7
B	22–32	16–23
C	80–100	58–72
D	50–60	36–43

Fig. 4 One piece pin type caliper exploded view. Colt Turbo & Colt Vista

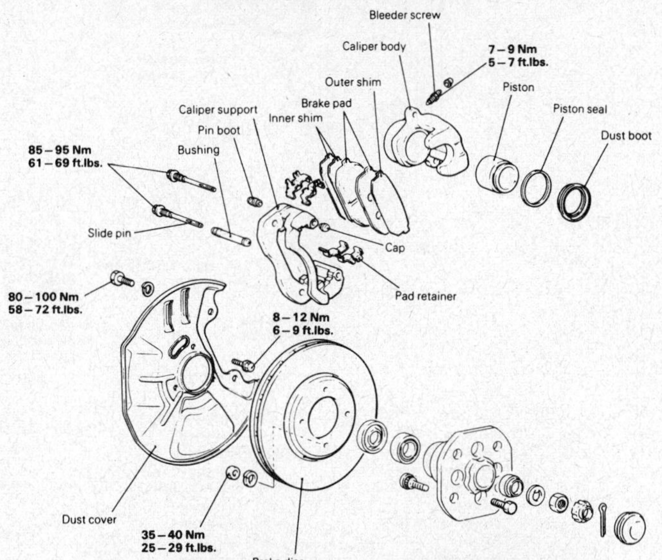

Fig. 5 One piece pin type caliper exploded view. Conquest

1. Sleeve bolt B
2. Sleeve
3. Caliper
4. Bushing
5. Sleeve bolt A
6. Pin boot
7. Piston
8. Piston seal
9. Dust boot
10. Inner shim
11. Pad assembly
12. Pad liner
13. Outer shim
14. Torque member
15. Brake disc
16. Hub

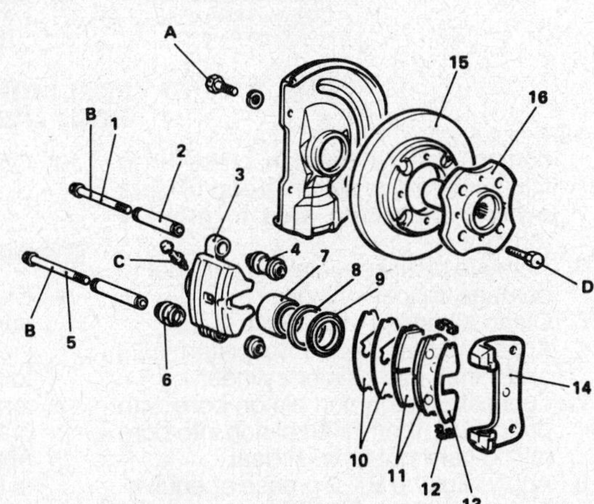

	Nm	ft.lbs.
A	80–100	58–72
B	22–32	16–23
C	7–9	5–7
D	50–60	36–43

Fig. 6 One piece pin type caliper exploded view. Colt exc. Turbo

4. Remove brake pads, then separate caliper body from support mounting.
5. Reverse procedure to install. Refer to **Fig. 4,** for torque specifications.

Caliper Overhaul

1. Remove caliper as described under "Caliper, Replace."
2. Remove boot ring from caliper body.
3. Place shop towel in saddle of caliper body, then apply compressed air to brake fluid inlet to force piston from bore. Remove piston. **Keep hands away from front of piston during removal. Apply compressed air slowly to ease piston from bore.**
4. Remove piston seal using caution not to scratch cylinder walls.
5. Clean piston and cylinder wall surfaces with brake fluid or alcohol.
6. Remove sleeve and boot from caliper body.
7. Inspect cylinder and piston for wear, damage and/or corrosion. Inspect caliper body and sleeve for wear.
8. Apply brake fluid to caliper body cylinder walls.
9. Apply an even coat of brake grease to piston seal, then install seal in caliper bore.
10. Carefully install caliper piston. Ensure seal does not twist during installation.
11. Apply brake grease to piston boot, then install boot and boot ring.
12. Apply brake grease to lock pin and guide pin sleeves.
13. Install caliper assembly. Refer to **Fig. 4,** for torque specifications.

CONQUEST & COLT EXC. TURBO

Brake Pad, Replace

1. Raise and support vehicle, then remove wheel assembly.
2. Remove lower caliper slide pin, **Figs. 5 and 6,** then lift caliper up and suspend it with wire.
3. Remove brake pads along with inner and outer shims.
4. Reverse procedure to install. Refer to **Figs. 5 and 6,** for torque specifications.

Caliper, Replace

1. Raise and support vehicle, then remove wheel assembly.
2. Disconnect brake hose at caliper strut, then at brake caliper.
3. Remove caliper support to steering knuckle attaching bolts, then front brake assembly.
4. Remove brake pads and shims, then separate caliper body from caliper support.
5. Reverse procedure to install. Refer to **Figs. 5 and 6,** for torque specifications.

Caliper Overhaul

1. Remove caliper assembly as outlined under "Caliper, Replace."
2. Remove bushing from caliper support using slide pin, then cap and pin boot.
3. Position a shop towel in caliper body, then apply compressed air through the brake hose fitting hole to remove

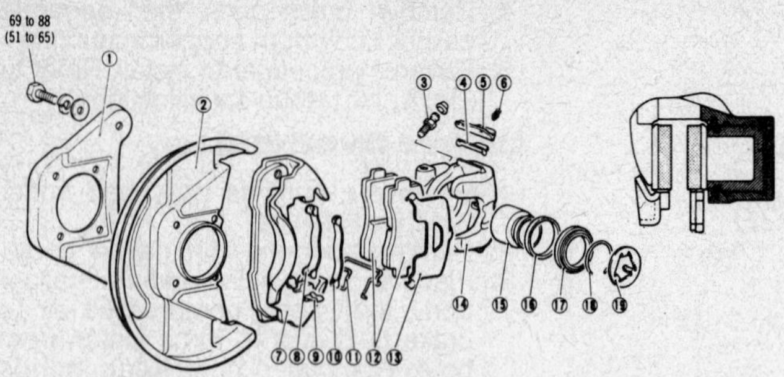

(1) Disc brake adapter
(2) Dust cover
(3) Bleeder screw
(4) Pad support plate
(5) Stopper plug
(6) Spigot pin
(7) Caliper support
(8) Pad clip (inner)
(9) Pad clip B
(10) Pad clip (outer)
(11) Anti-rattle spring
(12) Brake pad
(13) Anti-squeak shim, outer
(14) Caliper body
(15) Piston
(16) Piston seal
(17) Dust boot
(18) Boot ring
(19) Anti-squeak shim, inner

Fig. 7 Sliding type caliper exploded view. Front disc brake

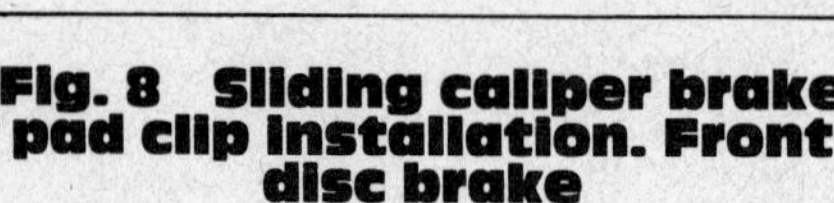

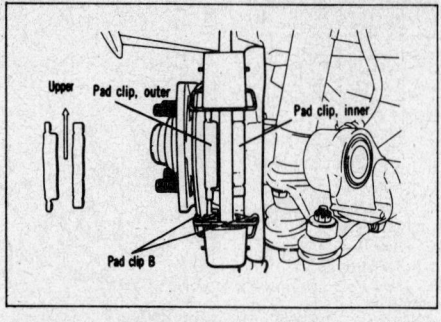

Fig. 8 Sliding caliper brake pad clip installation. Front disc brake

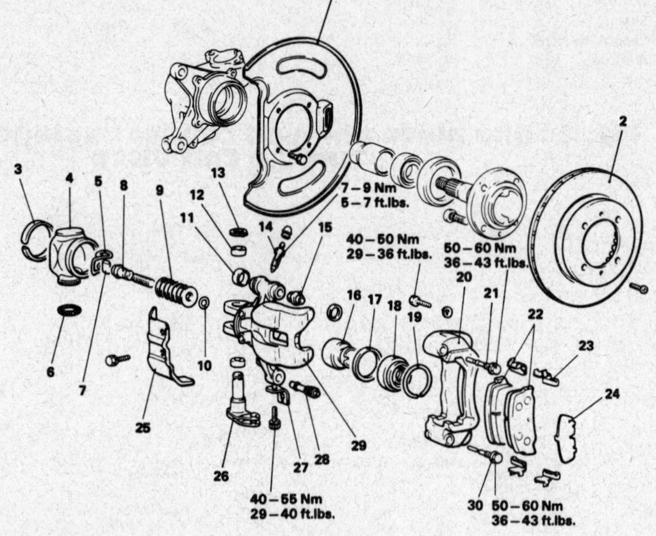

1. Dust cover
2. Brake disc
3. Cap ring
4. Lever cap
5. Return spring
6. Garter spring
7. Connecting link
8. Spindle
9. Spring washer
10. Spindle seal
11. Lid
12. Bearing
13. Retaining ring
14. Bleeder screw
15. Guide pin boot
16. Piston assembly
17. Piston seal
18. Piston boot
19. Boot ring
20. Caliper support
21. Guide pin
22. Brake pad
23. Pad clip
24. Outer shim
25. Dust cover
26. Parking lever assembly
27. Parking cable bracket
28. Lock pin boot
29. Caliper body
30. Lock pin

Fig. 9 Pin type caliper exploded view. Rear disc brake

piston and dust boot.

4. Using a suitable screwdriver, remove piston seal.
5. Inspect cylinder and piston for wear or damage and/or corrosion. Inspect caliper body and sleeve for wear.
6. Install new piston seal into cylinder. The piston seal in repair kit is coated with a special grease, do not wipe it off.
7. Apply suitable grease to lip of cylinder, then brake fluid to external surface of piston.
8. Install new dust boot onto piston.
9. Position end of dust boot into caliper body groove and install piston into caliper by hand. Take care not to damage piston. Ensure that end of dust boot is fitted into piston groove.
10. Apply a suitable grease to contact surface of slide pin, seat surface of cap for caliper support, and inside surface of pin boot.
11. Install cap and pin boot to caliper support, then apply suitable grease to inside surface of bushing.
12. Apply a suitable adhesive to lip of slide pin bushing, then install bushing into caliper support using slide pin.
13. Apply brake fluid to threads of slide pin and a suitable grease to shank of slide pin, then install caliper body to caliper support.
14. Install caliper assembly. Refer to **Figs. 5 and 6,** for torque specifications.

SLIDING TYPE CALIPER

CALIPER & BRAKE PAD REMOVAL

1. Remove wheel, then retainer clip and stopper plug, **Fig. 7.**
2. Loosen caliper mounting and remove caliper.
3. Remove anti-squeak shims, then brake pad from caliper support.

CALIPER SERVICE

1. Remove brake pads as previously outlined.
2. Remove hose clip from strut area and disconnect brake hose from caliper, then remove caliper.
3. Remove dust boot, then cover outer surface of caliper with cloth. Apply compressed air through brake hose fitting to remove piston. **Keep fingers away from piston area to prevent injury.**
4. Remove piston seal taking care not to damage caliper cylinder.
5. Clean all parts using brake fluid.
6. Apply rubber grease to piston seal and install into caliper cylinder.
7. Lubricate piston and piston bore with brake fluid, then insert piston into bore taking care not to twist seal.
8. Apply Niglube RX-2 grease or equivalent to dust boot attaching groove in caliper, then insert dust boot.
9. Install brake pad, then apply Plastilube #2 or equivalent grease to stopper plug and caliper sliding surface. Install caliper and retainer clip.
10. Connect and tighten brake hose, then bleed brakes.

BRAKE PAD INSTALLATION

1. Clean exposed part of piston, then push piston into original position using hammer handle. If piston is difficult to move, open bleeder screw and piston will move easily. Be sure to bleed brakes.
2. Apply Plastilube grease or equivalent to both faces of outer pad anti-squeak shim, then install both brake pads with anti-squeak shims into caliper support. Install clip B and inner and outer clips in proper directions, **Fig. 8.**
3. Install caliper, then stopper plug and retainer clip.

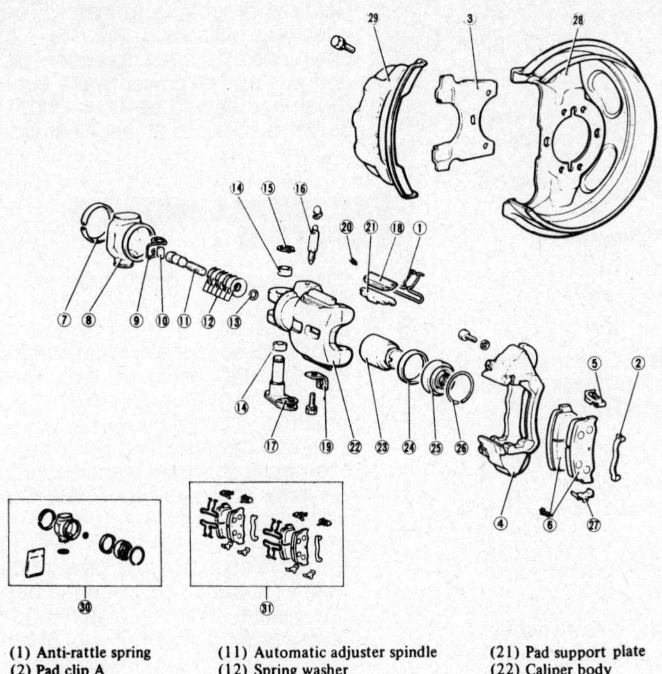

(1) Anti-rattle spring
(2) Pad clip A
(3) Dust cover
(4) Caliper support
(5) Pad clip B
(6) Brake Pad
(7) Cap ring
(8) Lever cap
(9) Spring
(10) Connecting link
(11) Automatic adjuster spindle
(12) Spring washer
(13) Automatic adjuster seal
(14) Needle bearing
(15) Retaining ring
(16) Bleeder screw
(17) Lever assembly
(18) Stopper plug
(19) Bracket
(20) Spigot pin
(21) Pad support plate
(22) Caliper body
(23) Piston
(24) Piston seal
(25) Piston boot
(26) Boot ring
(27) Pad clip C
(28) Dust cover
(29) Dust cover
(30) Seal & boot kit
(31) Pad kit

Fig. 10 Sliding type caliper exploded view. Rear disc brake

REAR DISC BRAKE SERVICE

PIN TYPE CALIPER

Brake Pads, Replace

1. Raise and support vehicle, then remove wheel assembly.
2. Disconnect parking brake cable.
3. Remove lower caliper lock pin, then lift caliper upward and support it with wire.
4. Remove brake pads and shims, **Fig. 9.**
5. Reverse procedure to install. Refer to **Fig. 9** for torque specifications.

Caliper, Replace

1. Raise and support vehicle, then remove wheel assembly.
2. Disconnect brake hose, then parking brake cable from brake assembly.
3. Remove brake assembly attaching bolts, then brake assembly.
4. Remove brake pads and shims, then separate caliper body from caliper support, **Fig. 9.**
5. Reverse procedure to install. Refer to **Fig. 9** for torque specifications.

Caliper Overhaul

1. Remove caliper assembly as outlined.
2. Using a suitable screwdriver, remove cap ring and garter spring from lever cap.
3. Remove lever cap from caliper groove, then retaining ring and pull out parking lever assembly.
4. Unscrew spindle from caliper body, then remove boot ring.
5. Push out piston from caliper body using a suitable screwdriver.
6. Using a suitable screwdriver, remove piston seal. Take care not to damage caliper bore.
7. Using tool No. MB990665 or equivalent, and a suitable vise, remove bearings from caliper.
8. Remove guide pin boot and lock pin boot from caliper body.
9. Inspect cylinder and piston for wear or damage and/or corrosion. Inspect caliper body and sleeve for wear.
10. Apply a suitable grease to caliper bearings.
11. Using a suitable vise and tool No. MB990665 or equivalent, press bearings in until it is flush with caliper body.
12. Install new piston seal into cylinder, then coat piston seal and inside surface of cylinder.
13. Install piston assembly into cylinder.
14. Apply suitable grease to dust boot fitting groove in caliper body, then install new dust boot and boot ring.
15. Coat spindle seal with brake fluid, then install washers on spindle.
16. Coat contact surface of caliper body and spring washers with suitable grease, then screw spindle into caliper body until it rotates freely.
17. Using tool No. MB990666 or equivalent and a suitable vise, compress spring washers and screw spindle into caliper.
18. Position connecting link and return spring onto spindle and install lever cap to parking lever assembly, then install assembly into caliper body. Hold parking lever assembly with retaining ring.
19. Apply suitable grease to lever cap and lip, then install lever cap to caliper body.
20. Coat contact point of caliper support guide pin and inside of lock pin boot with suitable grease, then install caliper body to caliper support.
21. Install caliper assembly. Refer to **Fig. 9** for torque specifications.

SLIDING TYPE CALIPER

Brake Pad Removal

1. Raise and support rear of vehicle, then remove wheel and tire assembly.
2. Remove caliper support dust cover, then disconnect parking brake cable from parking lever and bracket, **Fig. 13.**
3. Remove retainer clips, then using pliers, remove stopper plugs.
4. Remove caliper assembly and suspend from chassis using a wire hook to prevent brake hose from becoming damaged.
5. Remove brake pads from caliper support.

Caliper Removal

1. Raise and support rear of vehicle, then remove wheel and tire assembly.
2. Remove dust cap from caliper bleeder valve, then loosen bleeder valve and allow brake fluid to drain. When draining brake fluid, attach a length of hose or vinyl tubing to bleeder valve and allow fluid to drain into a suitable container. Do not reuse fluid that has been drained.
3. Detach brake hose clip, then disconnect brake hose from caliper.
4. Disconnect parking brake cable from lever and bracket.
5. Remove retainer clips, then using pliers, remove stopper plugs.
6. Remove caliper assembly.

Caliper Overhaul

1. Remove snap ring and spring, then remove lever cap from caliper body groove.
2. Remove parking brake lever with lever cap from caliper body.
3. Rotate auto adjuster spindle counterclockwise and remove from caliper.
4. Using a screwdriver, remove caliper piston dust boot snap ring, then push piston and boot from caliper body.
5. Press bearing from caliper using tool No. MB990665, if necessary.
6. Using a screwdriver, remove piston seal from caliper bore. Use care when removing seal not to damage caliper bore.
7. Clean brake components with clean brake fluid.

8. Apply Niglube RX-2 or equivalent to inner surface of adjuster spindle bearing, then using tool No. MB990665, press bearing into spindle bore until stamped surface of bearing is flush with caliper body.
9. Install caliper piston seal into caliper bore, then apply Rubber Grease H151-59 or equivalent to inner surface of caliper bore.
10. Install caliper piston into caliper bore using care not to twist piston seal.
11. Apply Niglube RX-2 grease or equivalent to piston boot groove on caliper body, then install piston boot and snap ring.
12. Position seal on adjuster spindle, then lubricate seal with clean brake fluid.
13. Install lock washers on adjuster spindle as shown in **Fig. 11,** then apply Niglube RX-2 or equivalent to contact surfaces of lock washer and caliper. Thread adjuster into piston.
14. After pressing in lock washers using tool No. MB990666, use a screwdriver to rotate and press in adjuster spindle.
15. Position lever cap onto parking lever, then install parking brake lever on caliper body.
16. Apply Niglube RX-2 grease or equivalent to inner surfaces of lever cap, then install lever cap over caliper body.

Caliper & Brake Pad Installation

1. Using tool No. MB990652, push back on caliper piston while turning slightly clockwise to position piston in caliper. The groove on the piston must be positioned so that projection on rear of brake pad fits securely into groove.
2. Install brake pad clips and brake pads on caliper support.
3. Position caliper onto caliper support and install stopper plugs and retainer clips.

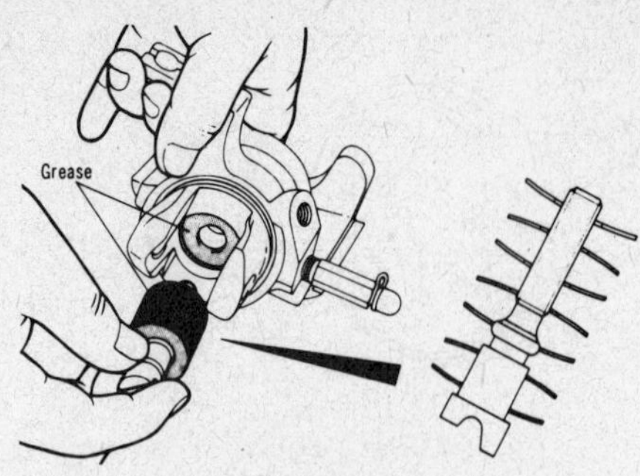

Fig. 11 Adjuster spindle washer installation. Sliding type caliper

4. Connect parking brake cable and brake hose to caliper, then bleed brake system and adjust parking brake.
5. Install dust cover, then install wheel and tire assembly.

MASTER CYLINDER REPLACE

CHALLENGER & SAPPORO

1. Disconnect connector and tube from brake master cylinder.
2. Remove reservoir bracket bolts.
3. Remove brake master cylinder attaching bolts and remove master cylinder along with reservoir and hoses.
4. Drain brake fluid from reservoir and disconnect hoses from master cylinder.
5. Reverse procedure to install. Torque attaching bolts to 6-9 ft. lbs. Check clearance between primary piston and pushrod of power brake booster. Clearance should be .004-.020. Turn pushrod screw to adjust clearance.

EXC. CHALLENGER & SAPPORO

1. Disconnect the brake tube from the master cylinder.
2. On 1983-84 Colt Hatchback, disconnect level sensor electrical connector.
3. On models equipped with manual brakes remove clevis pin connecting pushrod to brake pedal.
4. Remove the attaching bolts from the toe-board or power brake assembly.
5. Reverse procedure to install. Torque attaching bolts to 6-9 ft. lbs. Torque brake tube flare nut to 9.5-12 ft. lbs. If the car is equipped with power brakes, check clearance between the back of the master cylinder piston and the power brake pushrod. It should be 0 to .03 in. If clearance is not correct, adjust the length of the pushrod.

POWER BRAKE UNIT REPLACE

1. Remove master cylinder as outlined previously.
2. Disconnect vacuum hose from power brake unit.
3. Remove pin connecting power brake rod with brake pedal.
4. Remove power brake unit attaching nuts and the power brake unit.
5. Reverse procedure to install.

DRUM BRAKES SECTION

INDEX

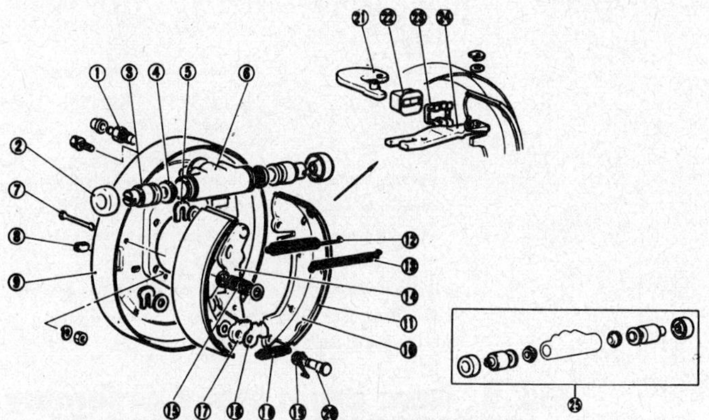

(1) Bleeder screw
(2) Wheel cylinder boot
(3) Wheel cylinder piston
(4) Wheel cylinder cup
(5) Retainer
(6) Wheel cylinder body
(7) Shoe hold-down pin
(8) Adjusting wheel cover
(9) Backing plate
(10) Brake shoe assembly
(11) Brake lining
(12) Shoe return spring (upper)
(13) Strut to shoe spring
(14) Adjusting lever
(15) Shoe hold-down spring
(16) Shoe return spring (lower)
(17) Adjusting latch
(18) Stopper
(19) Latch spring
(20) Pin
(21) Parking brake extension lever
(22) Parking brake extension lever cup
(23) Parking brake extension lever retainer
(24) Parking brake strut
(25) Wheel cylinder kit

Fig. 1 Rear drum brake assembly exploded view. Challenger & Sapporo

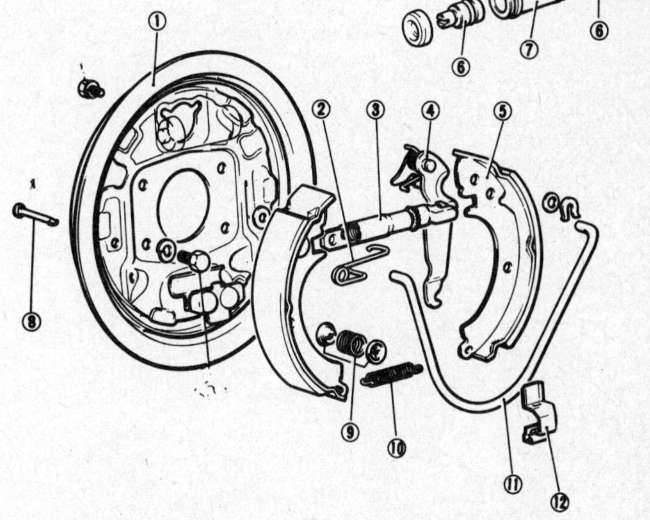

(1) Backing plate
(2) Spring
(3) Adjuster
(4) Parking lever
(5) Shoe and lining assembly
(6) Piston
(7) Wheel cylinder body
(8) Shoe hold spring pin
(9) Shoe hold-down spring
(10) Shoe to shoe spring
(11) Shoe return spring
(12) Clip spring

Fig. 2 Rear drum brake assembly exploded view. Colt

DRUM BRAKE SERVICE

For drum brake service procedures, refer to **Figs. 1 through 5.**

SERVICE BRAKE ADJUSTMENTS

These brakes are equipped with self adjusting mechanisms, therefore periodic adjustments are not necessary. If stopping power is insufficient, or if brake pedal travel is excessive, brakes should be cleaned and inspected, and the self-adjusting mechanisms should be checked.

After performing brake service, adjust brake shoes as follows:

1. Ensure shoes are centered on backing plate and measure width of brake shoes using suitable caliper. On Colt Vista models, also measure inside diameter of brake drum.
2. Adjust width of brake shoes to approximately 7.06 inches for Colt or 9.97 inches for Ram 50 and Ram Raider. On Colt Vista, adjust brake shoes to a width approximately .060 inch less than inside diameter of brake drum.
3. Install brake drums and adjust parking brake as outlined.
4. After adjusting parking brake, release parking brake lever and ensure that shoe actuating lever is not being pulled by parking brake cable. **If shoe actuating lever is pulled by parking brake cable, self-adjusters will not operate.**

MASTER CYLINDER & POWER BRAKE UNIT REPLACE

Refer to "Disc Brakes Section" for replacement procedures.

PARKING BRAKE ADJUSTMENTS

CHALLENGER & SAPPORO

Models W/Rear Drum Brake

1. Release parking brakes fully.
2. Check to ensure rubber hanger to bracket clearance complies with dimension shown in **Fig. 6.**
3. Adjust extension lever to stop clearance to .1 inch (2.5 mm) or less by using cable adjusting nuts, **Figs. 6 and 7.** Loosen both rubber hanger attaching bolt and adjusting nuts, then move rubber hanger to right. First, set left cable and tighten rubber hanger, then tighten right cable and set right cable.
4. Check for parking brake lever travel of 5-6 notches. If travel is excessive, rear brake automatic adjusters are malfunctioning.

Models w/Rear Disc Brake

1. Release parking brake fully and depress brake pedal twice.
2. Adjust parking brake cable using adjusting nut located on rear axle housing. Adjust sufficiently so inner cable does not slacken.
3. Check parking brake lever travel. Travel should be 5-6 notches.

2WD

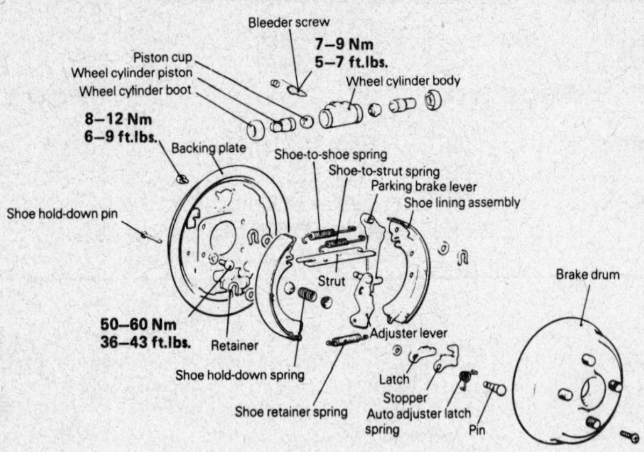

4WD

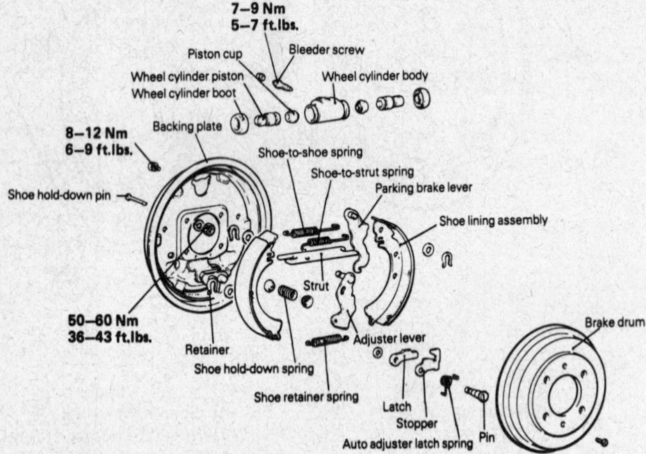

Fig. 3 Rear drum brake assembly exploded view. Colt Vista

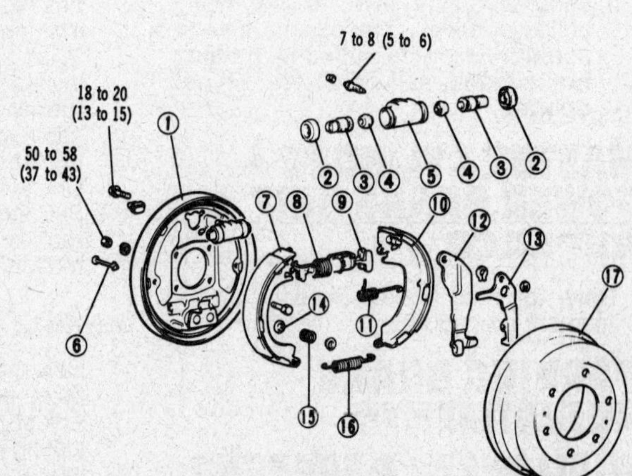

(1) Backing plate
(2) Wheel cylinder boot
(3) Wheel cylinder piston
(4) Wheel cylinder piston cup
(5) Wheel cylinder body
(6) Shoe hold-down pin
(7) Shoe and lining assembly
(8) Shoe return spring
(9) Brake shoe adjuster
(10) Shoe and lever assembly
(11) Adjusting spring
(12) Parking brake lever
(13) Autoadjuster lever
(14) Shoe hold-down cup
(15) Shoe hold-down spring
(16) Shoe retaining spring
(17) Brake drum

Fig. 5 Rear drum brake assembly exploded view. Ram Raider & 1984–87 Ram 50

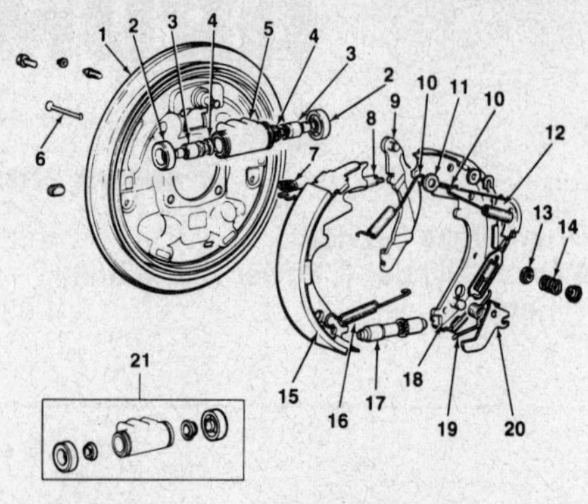

1. Backing plate
2. Dust boot
3. Piston
4. Cup
5. Wheel cylinder body
6. Shoe holddown pin
7. Anti-rattle spring
8. Parking brake strut
9. Parking brake lever
10. Brake shoe return spring
11. Brake shoe adjusting cable
12. Brake shoe adjusting cable guide
13. Shoe holddown spring cup
14. Shoe holddown spring
15. Brake shoe primary lining
16. Brake shoe adjusting lever spring
17. Brake shoe adjuster
18. Secondary shoe and lining assembly
19. Spring
20. Brake shoe automatic adjuster lever
21. Rear wheel cylinder repair kit

Fig. 4 Rear drum brake assembly exploded view. 1983 Ram 50

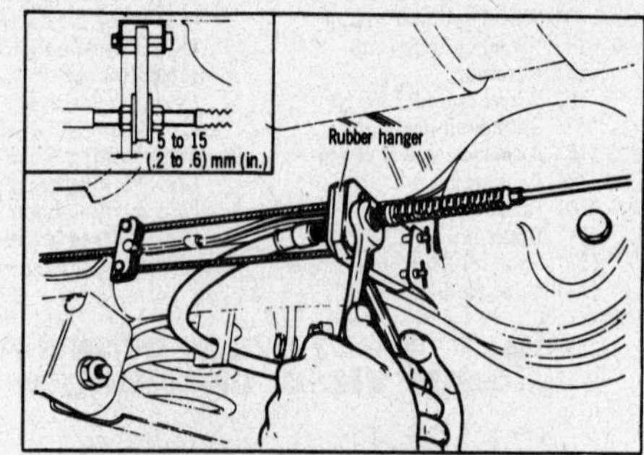

Fig. 6 Parking brake hanger to bracket clearance adjustment. Challenger & Sapporo w/rear drum brakes

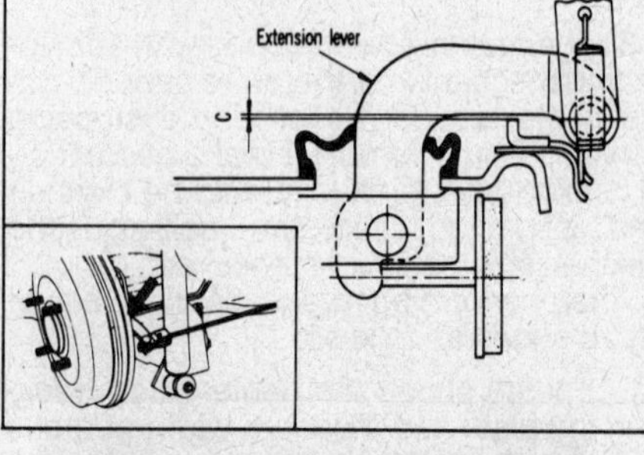

Fig. 7 Parking brake extension lever to stop clearance adjustment. Challenger & Sapporo w/rear drum brakes

1983–84 COLT

1. Check for parking brake lever travel of 6-7 notches. If travel is excessive, adjust right and left cable length by using adjusting nuts, **Fig. 8.** If rear cable is excessively taut when lever is returned, the adjuster lever will not engage adjuster and rear brake automatic adjuster will malfunction.

COLT VISTA & 1985–86 COLT

1. Apply parking brake lever with a force of approximately 45 lbs. while counting number of clicks. Lever should click 5-7 times.
2. If not within specifications, release parking brake lever and remove center console, if equipped.
3. Loosen adjusting nut on parking brake lever to free parking brake cables, then depress brake pedal several times to ensure shoe to drum clearance is properly maintained by self-adjusters.
4. Tighten adjusting nut until brake lever can be raised 5-7 notches with a force of approximately 45 lbs. **If adjusting nut is tightened excessively, self-adjuster mechanism will be inoperative.**
5. After adjustment, raise rear of vehicle and ensure brakes do not drag with parking brake lever released.

CONQUEST

1. Apply parking brake while counting number of clicks.

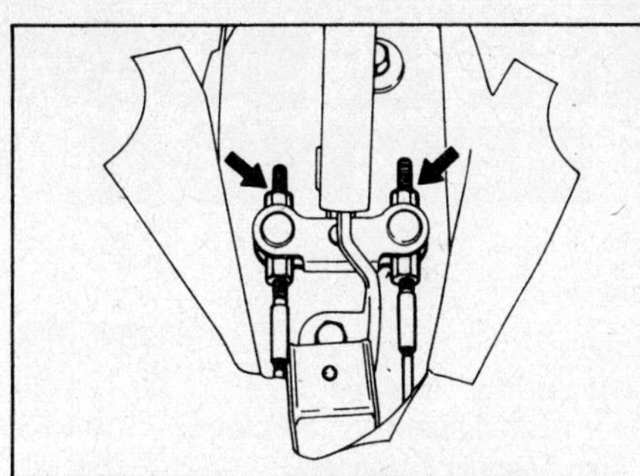

Fig. 8 Parking brake adjustment. 1983–84 Colt

2. Lever should click 4-5 times. If not within specifications, remove console and release parking brake lever, then turn adjusting nut located behind parking brake lever as necessary to bring parking brake within specifications.

RAM 50

1. Apply parking brake with a force of approximately 66 lbs. while counting number of clicks. Lever should pull out 16-17 notches.
2. If pull stroke is not as specified, loosen cable adjuster to release parking brake cable then depress brake pedal several times to ensure shoe to drum clearance is properly maintained by self-adjusters.
3. Tighten adjusting nuts or turnbuckle until brake lever stroke is 16-17 notches with a pulling force of approximately 66 lbs. **If adjusting nut is tightened excessively, self-adjuster mechanism will be inoperative.**
4. After adjustment, ensure that brake equalizer on 1983–86 2 wheel drive models is nearly parallel with centerline of vehicle. On 1983-86 4 wheel drive models and all 1987 models, ensure equalizer and joint are at right angles to each other.

RAM RAIDER

1. Apply parking brake lever with a force of approximately 45 lbs. while counting number of clicks. Lever should click 4-6 times.
2. If not within specifications, release parking brake lever and raise vehicle.
3. Loosen adjusting nut on parking brake lever to free parking brake cables, then depress brake pedal several times to ensure shoe to drum clearance is properly maintained by self-adjusters.
4. Tighten adjusting nut until brake lever can be raised 4-6 notches with a force of approximately 45 lbs. **If adjusting nut is tightened excessively, self-adjuster mechanism will be inoperative.**
5. After adjustment, raise rear of vehicle and ensure brakes do not drag with parking brake lever released.

REAR AXLE & SUSPENSION SECTION

INDEX

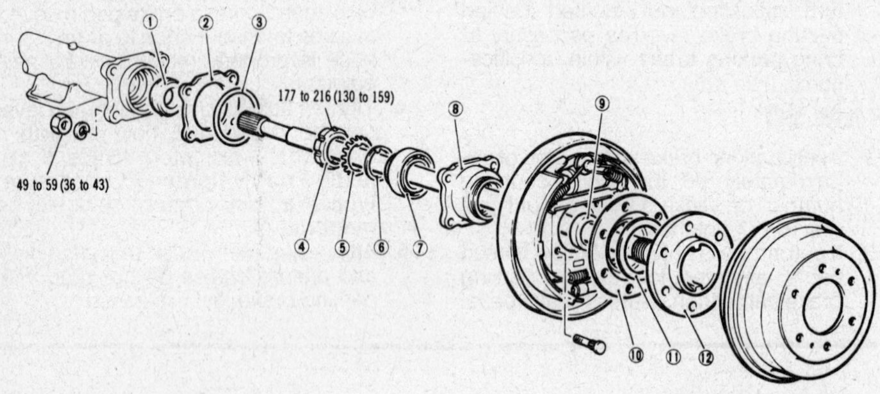

(1) Rear axle shaft oil seal (Inner)
(2) Shim
(3) O Ring
(4) Lock nut
(5) Lock washer
(6) Washer
(7) Rear axle shaft bearing
(8) Bearing case
(9) Rear axle shaft oil seal (Outer)
(10) Dust cover
(11) Packing
(12) Rear axle shaft

Fig. 1 Rear axle shaft assembly exploded view. Ram 50 & Ram Raider

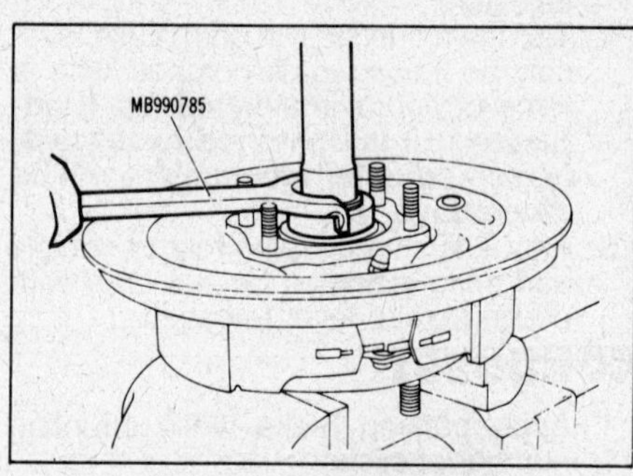

Fig. 2 Axle shaft bearing locknut removal & installation. Ram 50 & Ram Raider

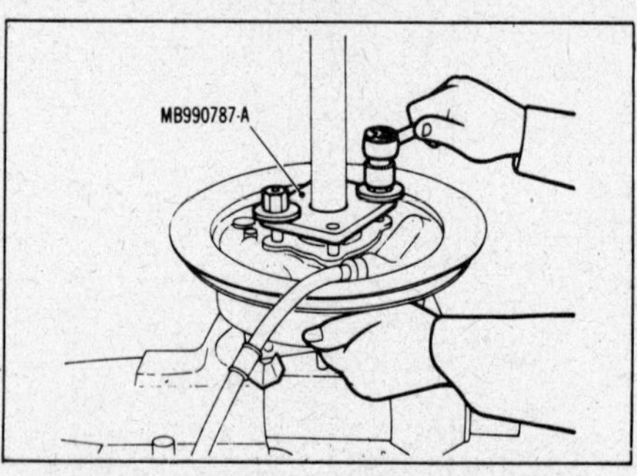

Fig. 3 Rear axle shaft bearing case removal. Ram 50 & Ram Raider

REAR AXLE SHAFT SERVICE

RAM 50 & RAM RAIDER

Removal

1. Raise and support rear of vehicle, then remove rear wheel and brake drum.
2. Disconnect rear parking brake cable at equalizer and remove cable retaining bolts and heat shields as needed.
3. Disconnect brake tube from wheel cylinder and plug line and open fitting.
4. Remove 4 nuts securing bearing case, then remove axle shaft, bearing case and brake backing plate as an assembly, **Fig. 1.** Use suitable slide hammer, if necessary, to free assembly from axle housing.
5. Remove O-ring and shims for preloading bearing. Retain shims for reassembly.
6. Disengage lock washer then remove locknut using tool No. MB990785 as in **Fig. 2.**
7. Reinstall locknut on axle shaft approximately 3 turns, then install tool No. MB990787-A and washers as in **Fig. 3.** Turn nuts with equal pressure to ensure smooth removal of bearing and remove bearing case from shaft.
8. Using hammer and suitable drift, remove bearing outer race from bearing case.
9. Remove inner axle shaft oil seal from housing using suitable puller, and drive outer seal from bearing housing.

Installation

1. Apply wheel bearing grease to outer surface of bearing outer race and to lip of outer oil seal, then drive them into bearing case.
2. Place backing plate, bearing case and bearing over rear axle shaft, then apply bearing grease to bearing rollers and install bearing race.
3. Install washer, lock washer and locknut. Torque locknut to 130-159 ft. lbs. (177-216 Nm) using tool No. MB990785, then bend tab on lock washer into groove on locknut. If lock washer does not engage with locknut, slightly retighten locknut.
4. Apply bearing grease to lip of inner oil seal and drive seal into rear axle housing using tool No. C-4572.
5. Adjust axial play of rear axle shaft as follows:

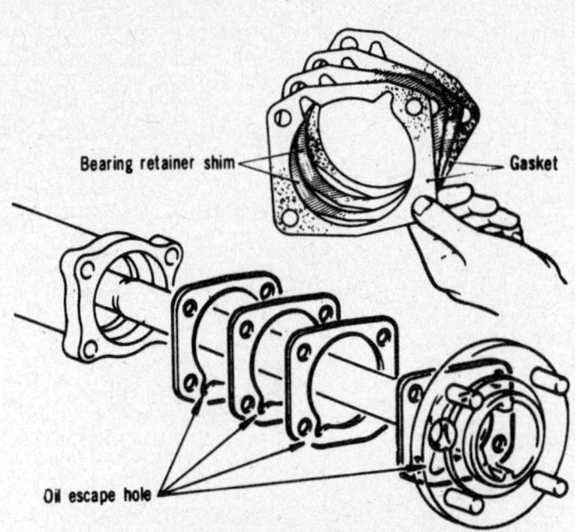

Fig. 4 Rear axle shaft bearing shims. Challenger & Sapporo

a. Remove any rust or old sealer from mating surface of bearing case and housing.
b. Insert 1 mm shim and O-ring into left side of housing, and apply silicone rubber sealant to mating face of bearing case, **Fig. 1.**
c. Install left side axle shaft into left side housing and torque bearing case nuts to 36-43 ft. lbs. (49-59 Nm).
d. Install right side axle shaft into right side housing, without shim or O-ring, and temporarily torque bearing case nuts to .4 ft. lbs. (.6 Nm). Measure and record gap between bearing case and housing using feeler gauge.
e. Remove axle shaft from housing, then select a shim with thickness of measured gap of step "d" and a shim with thickness from .05-.20 mm (.002-.007 inch). Insert selected shims and O-ring into housing and apply silicone sealer to mating face of bearing case.
f. Install right side axle shaft into right side housing and torque bearing case nuts to 36-43 ft. lbs. (49-59 Nm). Then, using a dial indicator, check axial play as in **Fig. 5.** The axial play should be .002-.007 inch (.05-.20 mm). If specified play is not obtained, change thickness of selected shims and reassemble.

6. Connect brake tube to wheel cylinder and install rear brake drum and wheel.

1983 CHALLENGER & SAPPORO

Removal

1. Raise vehicle and remove wheel and brake drum, or the caliper support with parking brake cable, caliper assembly and brake hose. Secure caliper assembly aside and remove brake disc.
2. Using hole provided in rear axle flange, remove bolts attaching bearing outer retainer to axle housing.
3. Remove rear axle shaft using suitable puller.
4. Remove oil seal from axle housing.
5. Remove bearing inner retainer by grinding down a portion of retainer to thickness of .04-.06 inch. Cut bearing retainer at ground portion to remove.
6. Press bearing from axle shaft.

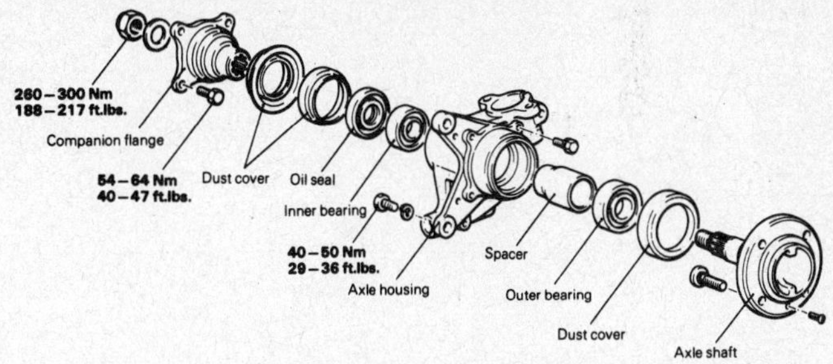

Fig. 5 Axle housing exploded view. Conquest

Installation

1. Install bearing outer retainer with chamfered edge facing splined end of shaft, bearing and bearing inner retainer onto rear axle shaft, then, press bearing inner retainer onto shaft until its face is firmly against bearing.
2. Apply grease to rear axle housing oil seal, then install seal into housing until it is seated against housing.
3. Apply additional grease to oil seal lip and to oil seal surface which contacts bearing inner retainer.
4. Install rear axle shaft into housing, without gasket or shims, and torque bolts in crossing pattern to 25-36 ft. lbs. (34-49 Nm).
5. For vehicles with rear drum brakes, remove rear brake shoes from backing plate.
6. On all models, adjust axial play of rear axle shaft as follows:
   a. Measure clearance between bearing outer retainer and backing plate using feeler gauge, and select gasket(s) and shim(s) so clearance will be .0-.25 mm (0-.01 inch).
   b. Remove rear axle shaft and alternately install selected gasket(s) and shim(s) with oil escape holes facing downward.
   c. Install rear axle shaft into housing and torque bolts in crossing pattern to 25-–36 ft. lbs. (34-49 Nm). Then, using dial indicator, check axial play. The axial play should be .03 inch (.8 mm). If specified play is not obtained, change thickness of shim(s) and reassemble, **Fig. 4.**
7. For vehicles with rear drum brakes, install brake shoes and drum. For vehicles with rear disc brakes, install brake disc, caliper support, caliper and brake hose. Torque caliper support bolts to 29-36 ft. lbs. (39-49 Nm).

CONQUEST

1. Raise and support rear of vehicle.
2. Remove rear wheel and tire assembly, then disconnect parking brake cable from rear brake caliper.
3. Remove rear caliper assembly, caliper support and rotor. Support caliper assembly with suitable piece of wire to prevent damage to brake hose.
4. Remove four drive axle to companion flange attaching bolts, then disconnect the drive axle.
5. Remove axle housing from lower control arm and strut assembly.
6. Position axle housing in suitable vise, then loosen companion flange nut and washer.
7. Using suitable hammer free axle shaft from bearings, then remove nut, companion flange and axle shaft, **Fig. 5.**
8. Remove dust covers, then using tool C-4381 and bearing puller C-293-PA, remove rear axle bearings.
9. Press fit new outer bearing to axle shaft. The seal side of outer bearing should face the flange side of the axle shaft.
10. Apply suitable grease to axle housing inside surface, then press fit inner bearing with seal side facing companion flange.
11. Install oil seal with suitable seal installer until seal contacts edge of axle housing.
12. Install axle housing, the apply suitable oil to seal lip.
13. Assemble axle housing using **Fig. 9** for reference and torque specifications.
14. Measure axle axial endplay with dial indicator. If endplay exceeds .031 inch, replace bearing.

COLT VISTA W/4 WHEEL DRIVE

1. Raise and support rear of vehicle.
2. Remove rear wheel and tire assembly, then the brake drum.
3. Remove three bolts securing drive axle to companion flange, then disconnect drive axle.
4. Remove companion flange nut and washer, **Fig. 6.**
5. Using suitable axle puller, remove axle shaft from inner arm.
6. Remove inner arm from rear suspension.
7. Using suitable press, remove dust covers and wheel bearings from axle shaft and inner arm.
8. Install replacement outer dust cover on axle shaft using suitable tool and plastic hammer. Install dust cover with concave side facing towards companion flange side of axle shaft.
9. Apply suitable grease to outer bearing seal inner lip circumference, the install outer bearing with suitable press. Install bearing with seal surface facing

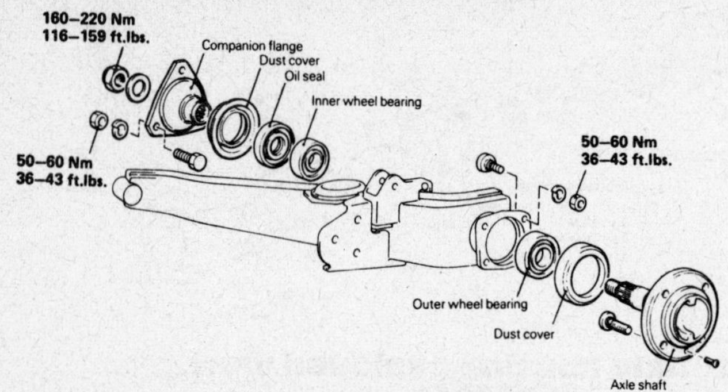

Fig. 6 Axle housing exploded view. Colt Vista w/4 Wheel Drive

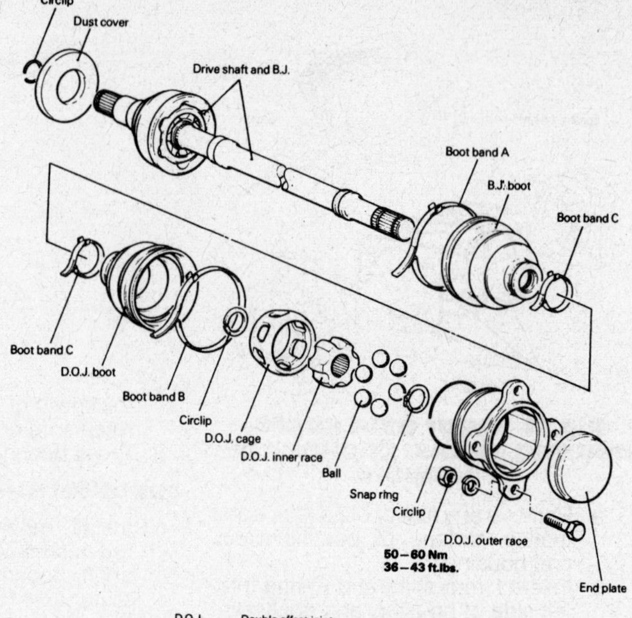

Fig. 7 Drive axle assembly. Models w/independent rear suspension

companion flange side of axle shaft.

10. Using suitable press, install replacement inner bearing in inner arm, then using suitable seal installer and plastic hammer, install replacement oil seal.
11. Press axle shaft into inner arm.
12. Assemble axle housing using **Fig. 6** for reference and torque specifications.
13. Measure axle axial endplay with dial indicator. If endplay exceeds .031 inch, replace bearing.

DRIVE AXLE SERVICE

MODELS EQUIPPED W/INDEPENDENT REAR SUSPENSION

Removal

1. Raise and support rear of vehicle, then drain differential lubricant.
2. Remove axle shaft to companion flange attaching bolts, then on Colt Vista Models, remove axle shaft from differential by prying with screwdriver. On Conquest models, use suitable axle puller to remove axle from differential.
3. If necessary, renew axle shaft oil seal.

Cleaning & Inspection

1. Remove axle shaft boot bands, then remove Double Offset Joint (D.O.J.) circlip from outer race. Separate axle shaft from D.O.J., **Fig. 7.**
2. On Conquest models, proceed as follows:
   a. Remove D.O.J. balls from cage by prying out with screwdriver.
   b. Push D.O.J. cage towards Birfield Joint (B.J.), then remove D.O.J. snap ring from axle shaft and remove inner race and cage from axle shaft.
   c. Wrap vinyl tape around axle shaft splines, then remove D.O.J. and B.J. boots. Do not disassemble B.J.
3. On Colt Vista models, proceed as follows:
   a. Remove snap ring from axle shaft, then the D.O.J. inner race, cage and balls as a unit.
   b. Clean D.O.J. as a unit in suitable solvent. If balls fall out of D.O.J., reinstall them with D.O.J. outer race.
   c. Wrap vinyl tape around axle shaft splines, then remove D.O.J. and B.J. boots.
   d. Wipe grease from B.J. Do not disassemble B.J.
4. On all models, inspect axle shaft for damage, corrosion and bending. Inspect axle splines for wear and damage. Inspect B.J. and D.O.J. for signs of water and dirt entry and replace as necessary.
5. Wrap vinyl tape around D.O.J. side of axle shaft splines, the slide boots and small boot bands over tape into position.
6. On Conquest models, proceed as follows:
   a. Install D.O.J. cage onto axle shaft in such a way that smaller diameter of cage is installed first.
   b. Install circlip on axle shaft, then the D.O.J. outer race. Install snap ring on axle shaft.
   c. Apply grease from repair kit to D.O.J. inner race and cage, then fit together.
   d. Apply grease from repair kit to D.O.J. ball friction areas and balls, then insert balls in D.O.J.
   e. Apply 1.8-2.8 oz. of repair kit grease to D.O.J. outer race, then install axle into D.O.J. outer race.
   f. Apply 1.8-2.8 oz. of repair kit grease to D.O.J. inner and outer race.
   g. Install D.O.J. outer race circlip.
   h. Install D.O.J. boot and secure large end with boot band. Measuring from large boot band, install small boot band 3.1 inches down axle shaft.
   i. Pack 3.5-5.3 oz. of repair kit grease into B.J. boot, then install boot with boot bands.
   j. Wipe off excess grease.
7. On Colt Vista models, proceed as follows:
   a. Fill inside of B.J. and B.J. boot with 3.2-3.3 oz. of repair kit grease, then install B.J. boot with boot bands.
   b. Apply repair kit grease to D.O.J. assembly, then install D.O.J. onto axle shaft and secure with snap ring.
   c. Apply repair kit grease to D.O.J. outer race, then install axle shaft into D.O.J. and apply more grease. The amount of grease recommended for this operation is 2.3-3.3 oz.
   d. Install axle shaft circlip.
   e. Install D.O.J. boot and secure large end with boot band. Measuring from large boot band, install small boot band 3.1 inches down axle shaft.
   f. Wipe off excess grease.

Installation

1. Install dust cover and new circlip on B.J. side of axle shaft.
2. Install axle shaft to differential carrier and companion flange.
3. Insert companion flange to axle shaft boots from companion flange side, then install nuts and torque to 36-43 ft. lbs.

REAR HUB & WHEEL BEARINGS

REPLACE

EXC. REAR WHEEL DRIVE MODELS

1. Raise and support rear of vehicle and remove wheel.

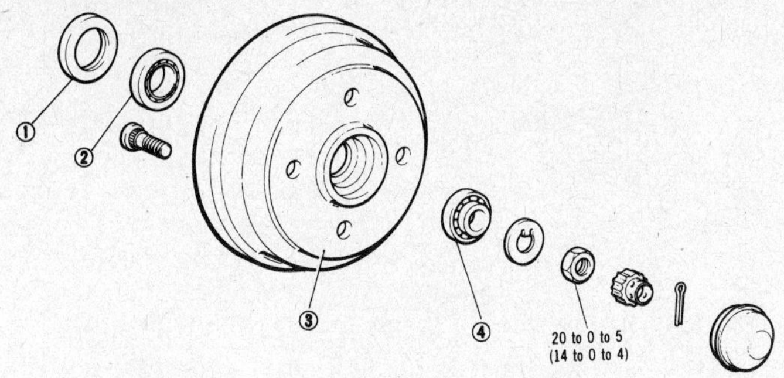

(1) Oil seal
(2) Inner bearing
(3) Brake drum
(4) Outer bearing

Fig. 8 Rear hub & bearings. Colt Vista w/2 wheel drive & 1983–84 Colt

2. Remove dust cap, then on all except 1985-87 Colt remove cotter pin and pin retainer, **Fig. 8.**
3. Remove bearing retaining nut, washer and the outer bearing, then pull hub and drum assembly from spindle.
4. Pry oil seal from rear of hub and remove inner bearing.
5. Drive bearing inner races from hub using suitable drift.
6. Clean hub and bearings with suitable solvent and blow dry with compressed air. Inspect components noting the following:
   a. Check fit of bearing outer races in hub. If bearings have "spun" and races are loose in hub, hub should be replaced.
   b. Inspect bearings and replace if damaged, scored or excessively worn.
   c. On 1985–87 Colt, install bearing retaining nut on spindle until nut is .08-.12 inch from inner end of threads, then measure torque necessary to loosen nut. If loosening torque is not at least 48 ft. lbs., replace nut.
7. Press new races into hub using suitable drivers.
8. Pack inner and outer bearings with suitable grease, working grease into rollers from wide end of bearing with palm of hand. Keep bearings covered until installation.
9. Pack center of hub with grease, install inner bearing in hub, then press new oil seal into hub and coat seal lips with grease.
10. Mount hub and drum on spindle, install outer bearing, washer and nut, as equipped, then adjust wheel bearings as outlined.

REAR WHEEL DRIVE MODELS

Refer to "Rear Axle Shaft, Replace."

REAR WHEEL BEARING

ADJUST

COLT VISTA W/2 WHEEL DRIVE & 1983–84 COLT

1. Raise and support rear of vehicle, then remove wheel and tire assembly.
2. Remove dust cap from brake drum, then remove cotter pin and adjusting nut retainer, **Fig. 8.**
3. Torque wheel bearing adjusting nut to 14 ft. lbs. and rotate drum several turns to seat bearings, then loosen adjusting nut.
4. Torque adjusting nut to 4 ft. lbs. for Colt and 1984-86 Colt Vista or 7 ft. lbs. on 1987 Colt Vista, rotate drum several times, then retorque nut to 4 ft. lbs. for all except 1987 Colt Vista or 7 ft. lbs. for 1987 Colt Vista.
5. Install nut retainer and cotter pin. If cotter pin holes are not aligned reposition retainer. If holes cannot be aligned, the adjusting nut may be backed off a maximum of 15° to align holes.
6. Install dust cap on brake drum, then install wheel and tire assembly.

1985–87 COLT

1. Raise and support rear of vehicle and remove wheel.
2. Ensure parking brake is fully released.
3. Check wheel bearing endplay with suitable dial indicator. Maximum allowable endplay is .008 inch.
4. Check hub and drum starting torque by rotating hub with suitable spring scale. Maximum allowable starting torque is 10.8 lbs.
5. If endplay or starting torque exceed limits, loosen bearing retaining nut, the retorque nut to 72-108 ft. lbs.
6. If endplay or starting torque are still not within limits, replace wheel bearings as needed.

REAR AXLE ASSEMBLY

REPLACE

EXC. MODELS EQUIPPED W/INDEPENDENT REAR SUSPENSION

1. Raise vehicle and support at frame. Support rear axle with a suitable jack.
2. Remove wheels and propeller shaft. Place matching mark on propeller shaft flange yoke and companion yoke for reassembly.
3. Disconnect brake hose from brake line.

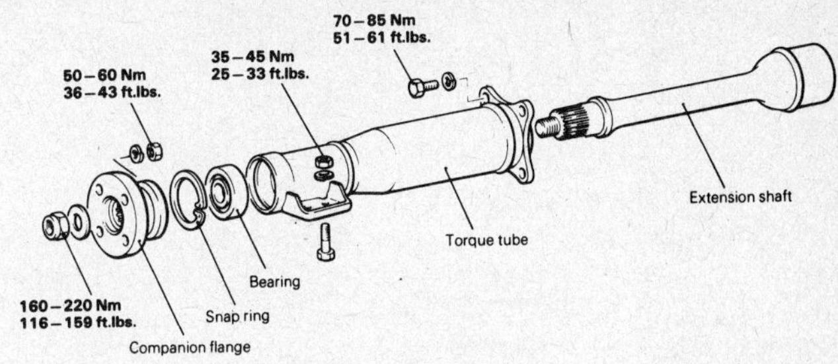

Fig. 9 Torque tube assembly. Conquest

4. Disconnect parking brake cable from both wheels and remove the parking brake cable lever on axle housing.
5. Remove shock absorbers.
6. Remove coil springs (if so equipped) or leaf springs as outlined.
7. If equipped with coil springs, remove lower control arm, assist link and upper control arm.
8. Remove rear axle assembly from vehicle.
9. Reverse procedure to install.

DIFFERENTIAL ASSEMBLY

REPLACE

MODELS EQUIPPED W/INDEPENDENT REAR SUSPENSION

Conquest

1. Drain gear oil into suitable container.
2. Remove drive axles as outlined.
3. Remove torque tube as follows:
   a. Remove driveshaft.
   b. Apply parking brake, then loosen torque tube companion flange attaching nut, **Fig. 9. Loosen nut only. Do not remove.**
   c. Remove torque tube to differential attaching bolts, then the torque tube to front support attaching bolts.
   d. Using a suitable slide hammer, remove extension shaft spline from spline coupling.
   e. Remove slide hammer, then pull torque tube assembly out towards rear.
4. Remove rear support insulator to crossmember attaching nuts, then the rear support to rear support insulator attaching nuts.
5. Raise differential carrier assembly with suitable jack, then disconnect differential carrier from rear support insulators.
6. Remove carrier.

Colt Vista W/4 Wheel Drive

1. Drain gear oil into suitable container.
2. Remove drive axles as outlined.
3. Disconnect driveshaft from companion flange.
4. Remove differential front support bracket to crossmember attaching bolt.
5. Remove differential rear support to differential carrier attaching bolts,

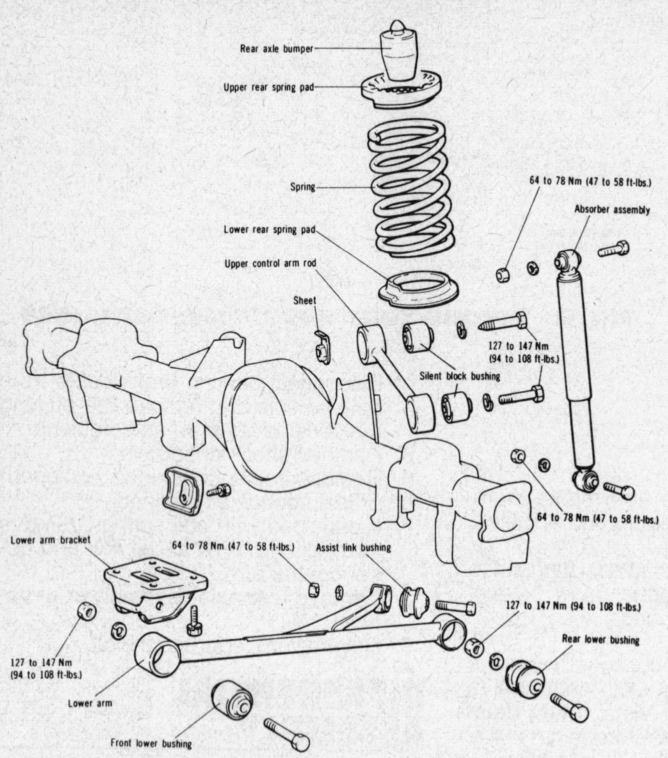

Fig. 10 Coil spring rear suspension. Challenger & Sapporo

(1) Shock absorber
(2) Spring upper seat
(3) Coil spring
(4) Spring lower seat
(5) Bump stopper
(6) Plain washer
(7) Washer B
(8) Fixture assembly, R.H.
(9) Washer C
(10) Suspension arm, R.H.
(11) Stabilizer bar
(12) Dust cover
(13) Clamp
(14) Bushing A
(15) Bushing B
(16) Rubber stopper
(17) Suspension arm, L.H.
(18) Washer A
(19) Fixture assembly, L.H.

Fig. 11 Coil spring rear suspension. Colt & Colt Vista w/2 wheel drive

then remove differential carrier.

6. Remove front support bracket and differential cover.

SHOCK ABSORBER REPLACE

CHALLENGER & SAPPORO

1. Raise rear of vehicle and position jack stands under frame side rails.
2. Position a suitable jack under center of rear axle to support axle assembly.
3. Remove wheel and tire assembly, then disconnect shock absorber at upper and lower mounting and remove from vehicle, **Fig. 10.**
4. Reverse procedure to install. Torque upper and lower mounting nuts to 47-58 ft. lbs.

COLT & COLT VISTA W/2 WHEEL DRIVE

1. Raise rear of vehicle and position jack stands under frame side rails.
2. Remove wheel and tire assembly.
3. Using a suitable jack, support lower suspension arm, then disconnect shock absorber from upper and lower mounting and remove from vehicle, **Fig. 11.**
4. Reverse procedure to install. Torque upper and lower shock absorber mounting nuts to 47-58 ft. lbs.

CONQUEST

1. Raise and support rear of vehicle, then remove wheel and tire assembly.
2. Disconnect rear brake hose at shock assembly, then separate drive axle from companion flange.
3. Remove shock assembly to axle housing attaching bolts, then the shock assembly from axle housing. Push axle housing down while opening coupling with a suitable tool.
4. Remove shock assembly attaching bolts from under side trim in rear hatch area, then the shock assembly from rear wheel housing.
5. Compress coil spring using tool L-4514 or equivalent, then remove top end nut.
6. Remove shock insulator, spring seat, dust cover, rubber helper, then the seat.
7. Reverse procedure to install. Torque top end nut to 51-65 ft. lbs. Torque shock insulator attaching bolts to 18-25 ft. lbs. Torque shock assembly to axle housing attaching bolts to 36-51 ft. lbs.

RAM 50 & RAM RAIDER

1. Raise rear of vehicle and position jack stands under frame side sills.
2. Remove wheel and tire assembly, then disconnect shock absorber at upper and lower mounting and remove from vehicle, **Fig. 12.**
3. Reverse procedure to install. Torque upper and lower mounting nuts to 13-18 ft. lbs.

LEAF SPRING REPLACE

1. Raise rear of vehicle and position jack stands under frame side rails, then remove wheel and tire assembly. Lower jack and allow vehicle to rest on jack stands.
2. Disconnect parking brake cable bracket from leaf spring.
3. Disconnect shock absorber from upper and lower mounting.
4. Loosen U-bolt nuts, then raise rear axle housing until axle clears U-bolt seat, and remove U-bolt seat.
5. Remove spring pin from spring front mounting and shackle pin from spring rear mounting, then remove leaf spring assembly, **Fig. 12.**

COIL SPRING REPLACE

CHALLENGER & SAPPORO

1. Position a suitable jack under center of axle housing and raise rear of vehicle, then position jack stands under frame side rails to support body.
2. Remove wheel and tire assembly, then detach parking brake cable from extension lever.
3. Raise jack slightly, then disconnect shock absorber from upper and lower mounting, **Fig. 10.**
4. Carefully lower jack until spring tension is relieved, then remove coil springs. **When lowering axle housing, use care not to damage brake lines or hoses.**
5. Reverse procedure to install. Adjust parking brake as described under "Parking Brake, Adjust" in the Brake Section.

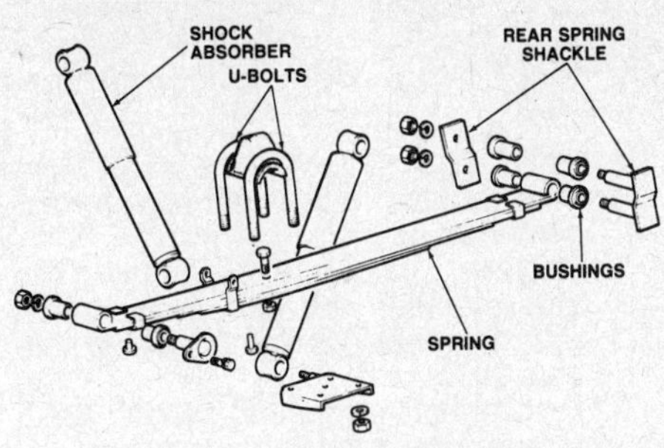

Fig. 12 Leaf spring rear suspension. Ram 50 & Ram Raider

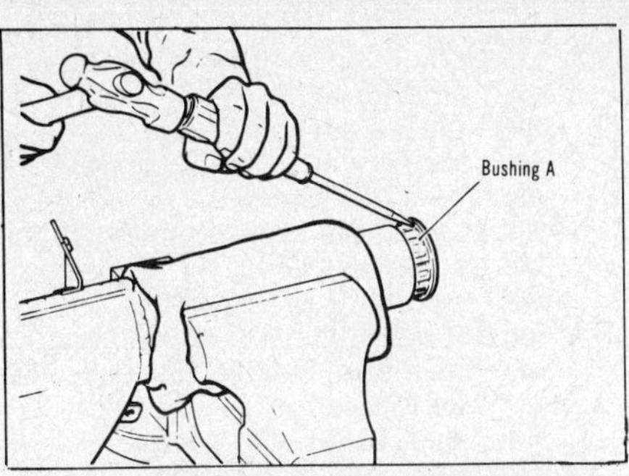

Fig. 13 Removing bushing "A" from left suspension arm. Colt & Colt Vista w/2 wheel drive

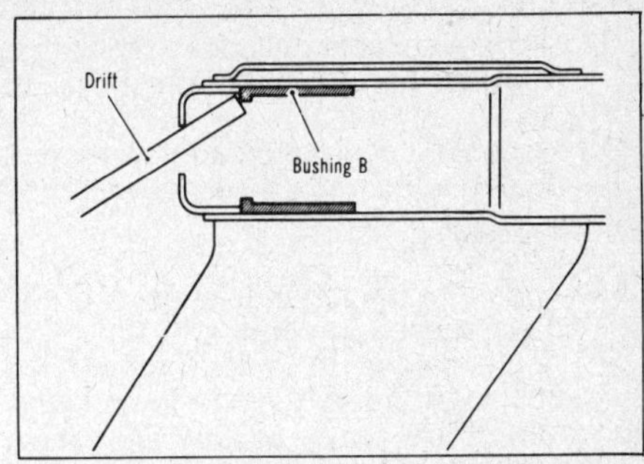

Fig. 14 Removing bushing "B" from left suspension arm. Colt & Colt Vista w/2 wheel drive

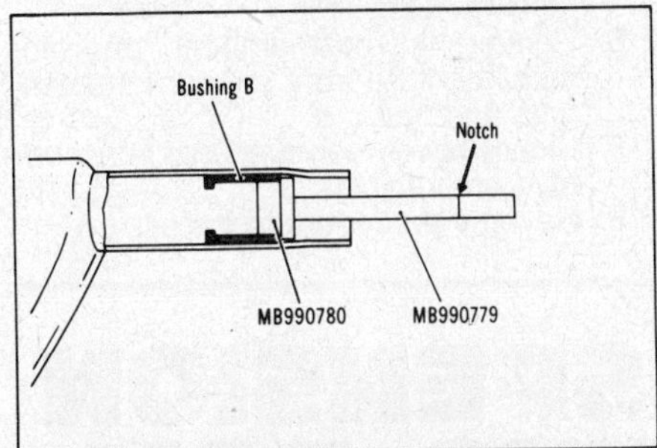

Fig. 15 Installing bushing "B" into left suspension arm. Colt & Colt Vista w/2 wheel drive

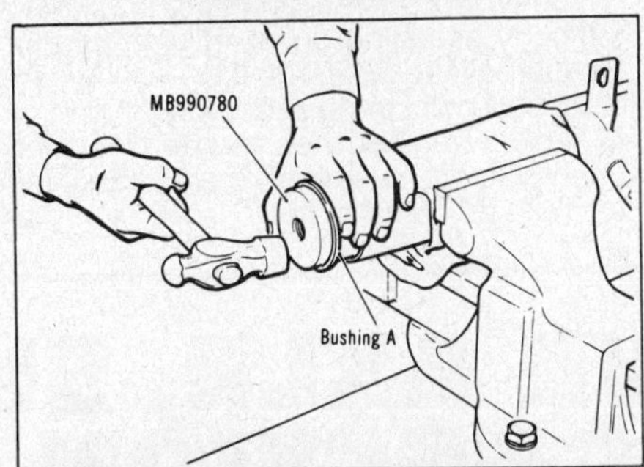

Fig. 16 Installing bushing "A" into left suspension arm. Colt & Colt Vista w/2 wheel drive

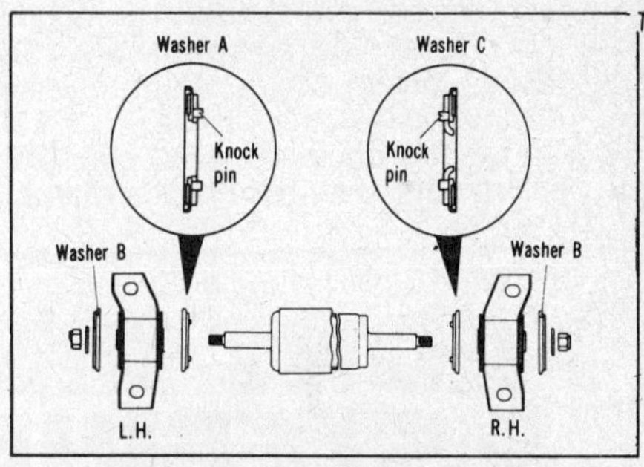

Fig. 17 Installing mounting bracket components. Colt & Colt Vista w/2 wheel drive

COLT & COLT VISTA W/2 WHEEL DRIVE

1. Raise rear of vehicle and position jack stands under frame side rails to support body.
2. Remove wheel and tire assembly, then remove rear drum brake assembly.
3. Disconnect muffler from exhaust pipe, then remove muffler assembly.
4. Position a suitable jack under suspension arm, then raise suspension arm slightly.
5. Disconnect shock absorber from upper and lower mounting, **Fig. 11.**
6. Carefully lower jack to relieve spring tension, then remove coil spring. When removing spring, note location of upper and lower spring seats.
7. Reverse procedure to install. After completing installation, bleed brake system and adjust rear wheel bearings.

CONTROL ARMS REPLACE

CHALLENGER & SAPPORO

1. Position a suitable jack under center of rear axle housing and raise rear of vehicle. Then position jack stands under frame rails to support body. After supporting body on jack stands, raise rear axle housing slightly.
2. Remove wheel and tire assembly, then on models equipped with rear drum brakes, detach parking brake rear cable from lower control arm.
3. Remove upper control arm attaching bolts, then remove control arm, **Fig. 10.**
4. Remove lower control arm to axle housing and body attaching bolts, then remove lower control arm.
5. Check upper and lower control arms and bushings for wear and damage.
6. Reverse procedure to install. Torque lower control arm lower bracket and axle housing outer bracket bolts to 94-108 ft. lbs. Torque lower control arm inner axle housing bracket bolt to 47-58 ft. lbs. Torque upper control arm attaching bolts to 94-108 ft. lbs. **Before torquing upper control arm to axle housing bracket attaching bolts, ensure tang on control arm attaching nut is against tang on axle housing bracket.**

CONQUEST

1. Raise and support rear of vehicle, then remove wheel and tire assembly.
2. Disconnect parking brake cable from lower control arm, then remove the stabilizer bar.
3. Remove lower control arm to axle housing attaching bolts, then the lower arm to front support attaching bolts.
4. Remove lower control arm to crossmember attaching bolts, then the lower control arm from vehicle.
5. Reverse procedure to install. Apply a coat of suitable grease to shaft cutout between lower control arm and axle housing. Install shaft with identification mark facing downward.

SUSPENSION ARM REPLACE

COLT & COLT VISTA W/2 WHEEL DRIVE

Removal

1. Remove coil springs as outlined.
2. Disconnect brake hose at suspension arm assembly.
3. Remove suspension arm bracket attaching bolts at each side of arm, then remove right and left hand suspension arms as an assembly, **Fig. 11.**

Disassembly

Before disassembly, place alignment marks on suspension arms and components so they can be assembled in the same position.

1. Remove nut at each end of the suspension arm assembly, then remove mounting brackets and bushings, **Fig. 11.**
2. Remove dust cover retaining band, then on models equipped with a stabilizer bar, place an alignment mark at each end of the stabilizer bar in line with punch mark on stabilizer bracket.
3. Separate suspension arm assembly into right and left hand suspension arms, leaving the dust cover attached to the right hand suspension arm.
4. Remove rubber stopper from right hand suspension arm.
5. Using a screwdriver, remove bushing A from left hand suspension arm, **Fig. 13.**

6. Using a suitable drift, drive bushing B from left hand suspension arm, **Fig. 14.**
7. Inspect all components for wear and damage and replace as necessary.

Assembly

1. Apply grease to inner surface of left hand suspension arm.
2. Apply grease to outer surfaces of bushings, then using tools Nos. MB990779 and MB990780, drive bushing B in until tool contacts end of left suspension arm. Using tool No. MB990780, drive bushing A into left suspension arm, **Figs. 15 and 16.**
3. Position dust cover on right suspension arm, then coat suspension arm with grease from shoulder at mounting bracket end approximately 15.7 inches toward center of arm and install rubber stopper.
4. On models equipped, align stabilizer bar and stabilizer bar bracket marks.
5. Carefully push left and right suspension arms together, while wiping excess grease as necessary, then align suspension arm and component alignment marks.
6. Install washers and mounting brackets as shown in **Fig. 17.** Loosely install mounting bracket nuts. Do not tighten nuts until suspension assembly has been installed and vehicle lowered to floor.
7. Pack dust cover with grease, then install cover retaining clamp.

Installation

1. Position suspension arm assembly to body, then install mounting bracket to body attaching bolts. Torque attaching bolts to 36-51 ft. lbs.
2. Install coil spring assembly.
3. Lower vehicle, then torque mounting bracket to suspension arm attaching nuts to 47-54 ft. lbs.

CONQUEST

1. Raise and support rear of vehicle, then remove rear wheel and tire assemblies.
2. Secure shock assembly to crossmember with wire, then support rear suspension assembly with a suitable jack.
3. Disconnect propeller shaft from torque tube, then remove center exhaust pipe and main muffler.
4. Disconnect parking brake cable from rear disc brake and lower control arm.
5. Disconnect brake hose at rear floor, then remove the shock absorber attaching nuts.
6. Remove crossmember attaching nuts, then the front support attaching nuts and bolts.
7. Slowly lower rear suspension assembly from vehicle.
8. Reverse procedure to install.

FRONT DRIVE AXLE, SUSPENSION & STEERING SECTION, EXC. RAM 50 4 X 4 & RAM RAIDER 4 X 4

INDEX

WHEEL BEARINGS ADJUST

REAR WHEEL DRIVE MODELS EXC. RAM 50 4 X 2

After installing the bearings and wheel hub, tighten the nut to 14.5 ft. lbs. to seat all parts then loosen the nut. Tighten the nut to 4 ft. lbs. and after installing the cap, install the cotter pin. If the holes do not align after shifting the position of the installed cap, loosen the nut until a flute on the nut aligns with cotter pin hole in the spindle. Do not back off the nut more than 15 degrees.

RAM 50 4 X 2

Install hub bearings on spindle, then install hub nut and torque to 22 ft. lbs. to seat bearings. Loosen hub nut, then torque nut to 6 ft. lbs. Install nut retainer cap and cotter pin. If cotter pin holes are not aligned, loosen nut to align holes. The nut may be loosened to a maximum of 30° to align cotter pin holes. Check to ensure hub assembly rotates freely without play.

HUB, ROTOR & WHEEL BEARINGS REPLACE

FRONT WHEEL DRIVE MODELS

Refer to "Front Wheel Drive Hub & Knuckle, Replace."

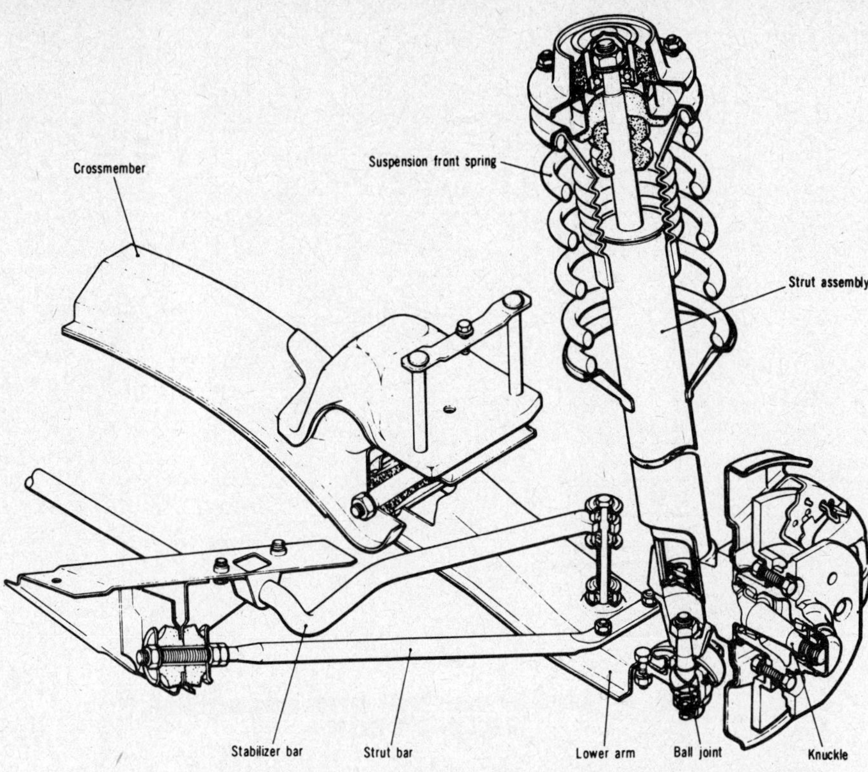

Fig. 1 Front suspension. Challenger & Sapporo

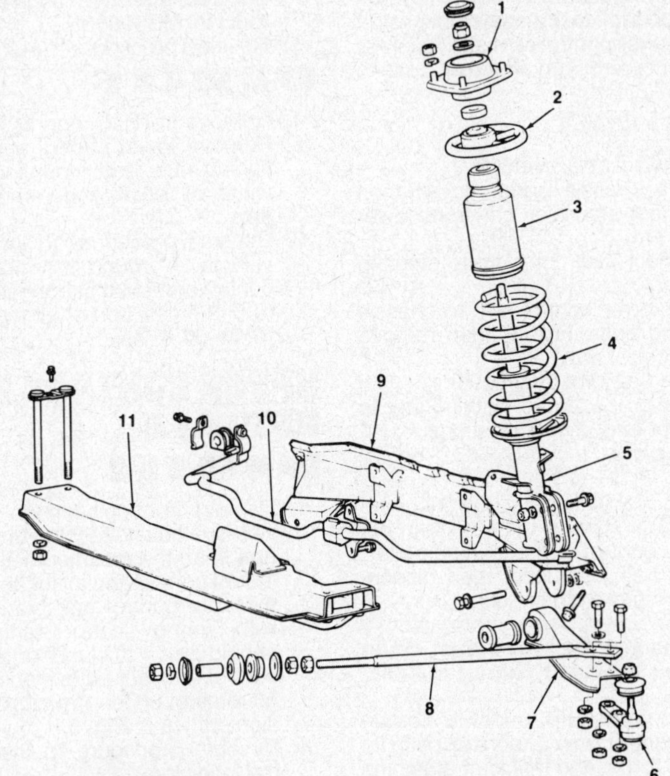

1. Strut Insulator
2. Upper Spring Seat
3. Bumper Rubber
4. Spring
5. Strut Assembly
6. Lower Ball Joint
7. Lower Arm
8. Strut Bar
9. No. 2 Crossmember
10. Stabilizer
11. No. 1 Crossmember

Fig. 2 Front suspension. 1983–84 Colt

REAR WHEEL DRIVE MODELS

Challenger, Conquest & Sapporo

1. Raise and support front of vehicle and remove wheel.
2. Remove bolts securing caliper support to steering knuckle, remove caliper and support as an assembly leaving hose connected and suspend caliper from front spring, taking care not to damage brake hose.
3. Remove hub cap, cotter pin, and pin retainer.
4. Remove hub nut, washer and outer bearing, then remove hub and rotor assembly from spindle.
5. Scribe matching marks between hub and rotor. On models less intercooler, remove bolts securing brake rotor to hub, then separate hub and rotor. On models with intercooler, remove retaining clips and bolts, then separate rotor from hub.
6. Remove oil seal and inner bearing, then drive bearing outer races from hub using suitable drift.
7. Clean hub and bearings with suitable solvent and blow dry with compressed air. Inspect components noting the following:
   a. Check fit of bearing outer races in hub. If bearings have "spun" and races are loose in hub, hub should be replaced.
   b. Inspect bearings and replace if damaged, scored or excessively worn.
8. Install inner and outer bearing outer races in hub using suitable driver, then pack center of hub with grease.
9. Install brake rotor on hub and align matching marks. On models less intercooler torque nuts to 25-29 ft. lbs. On models with intercooler, install hub bolts and secure rotor with retaining clips.
10. Pack wheel bearings, working grease through rollers from wide end of bearing with palm of hand. Keep bearings covered until installation.
11. Install inner wheel bearing in hub, then press new seal into hub using suitable driver.
12. Coat seal lips with grease, mount hub assembly on spindle.
13. Install outer bearing, washer and nut, then adjust wheel bearings as outlined.
14. Install caliper assembly and torque caliper support bolts to 51-65 ft. lbs.

Ram 50 4 X 2

1. Raise and support front of vehicle and remove wheel.
2. Remove bolts securing caliper support to steering knuckle, remove caliper and support as an assembly leaving hose connected and suspend caliper from front spting, taking care not to damage brake hose.
3. Remove hub cap and cotter pin.
4. Remove hub nut, washer and outer bearing, then remove hub and rotor assembly from spindle.

5. Scribe matching marks between hub and rotor, remove bolts securing brake rotor to hub, then separate hub and rotor.
6. Remove oil seal and inner bearing, then drive bearing outer races from hub using suitable drift.
7. Clean hub and bearings with suitable solvent and blow dry with compressed air. Inspect components noting the following:
   a. Check fit of bearing outer races in hub. If bearings have "spun" and races are loose in hub, hub should be replaced.
   b. Inspect bearings and replace if damaged, scored or excessively worn.
8. Install inner and outer bearing outer races in hub using suitable driver, then pack center of hub with grease.
9. Install brake rotor on hub, align matching marks then torque nuts to 34-37 ft. lbs.
10. Pack wheel bearings, working grease through rollers from wide end of bearing with palm of hand. Keep bearings covered until installation.
11. Install inner wheel bearing in hub, then press new seal into hub using suitable driver.
12. Coat seal lips with grease, mount hub assembly on spindle.
13. Install outer bearing, washer and nut, then adjust wheel bearings as outlined.
14. Install caliper assembly and torque caliper support bolts to 51-65 ft. lbs. on 1983-84 models or 58-72 ft. lbs. on 1985-87 models.

LOWER CONTROL ARM REPLACE

CHALLENGER & SAPPORO

1. Raise and support front of vehicle, then remove wheel and tire assembly.
2. Remove bolts and nuts attaching stabilizer bar, strut bar and ball joint to lower control arm, **Fig. 1.**
3. Remove idler arm support from body, then move steering linkage rearward.
4. Remove lower control arm to crossmember mounting bolt, and lower control arm.
5. Reverse procedure to install. When tightening stabilizer bar to lower control arm locknut, tighten nut until clearance between end of bolt and locknut end surface is .59-.67 inch. Torque lower control arm to crossmember mounting bolt to 58-69 ft. lbs., stabilizer bar to lower control arm nut to 7-14 ft. lbs., strut bar to lower control arm and ball joint to lower control attaching bolts to 43-51 ft. lbs.

1983–84 COLT

1. Remove bolts attaching ball joints to lower control arm, **Fig. 2.**
2. Remove bolts attaching strut bar to lower control arm.
3. Remove lower control arm to crossmember mounting bolt, and lower control arm.
4. Reverse procedure to install. Torque lower control to crossmember, strut bar to lower control arm and ball joint to lower control arm attaching bolts to 69 to 87 ft. lbs.

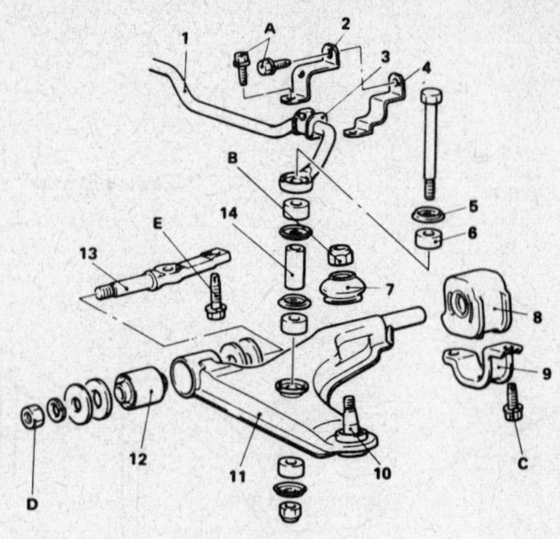

1. Stabilizer bar
2. Upper fixture
3. Stabilizer bushing
4. Lower fixture
5. Joint cup
6. Stabilizer rubber
7. Dust cover
8. Lower arm bushing (B)
9. Bushing support bracket
10. Ball joint assembly
11. Lower arm
12. Lower arm bushing
13. Lower arm shaft
14. Collar

	Nm	ft.lbs.
A	17–26	12–19
B	60–72	43–52
C	60–80	43–58
D	95–120	69–87
E	160–190	116–137

Fig. 3 Lower control arm assembly. 1985–87 Colt

1985–87 COLT

1. Raise and support vehicle.
2. Remove chassis under cover, then disconnect stabilizer bar from lower control arm.
3. Disconnect ball joint from steering knuckle.
4. Loosen lower control arm to chassis attaching bolts, **Fig. 3,** then remove lower control arm.
5. Replace ball joint dust cover.
6. Reverse procedure to install. Refer to **Fig. 3** for torque specifications.

COLT VISTA

1. Remove stabilizer bar to lower control arm attaching bolts, then the strut bar to lower control arm attaching bolts.
2. Loosen ball joint stud, then disconnect ball joint from knuckle.
3. Remove lower arm from No. 2 crossmember. **Ball joint dust cover must be replaced during installation.**
4. Reverse procedure to install. Torque lower control arm attaching bolts to 87-108 ft. lbs. and ball joint attaching nut to 43-52 ft. lbs.

CONQUEST

1. Remove stabilizer bar and strut bar attaching bolts.
2. Disconnect tie rod from knuckle arm.
3. Remove MacPherson strut as outlined.
4. Remove lower control arm and knuckle arm from crossmember, then the ball joint from the knuckle arm using tool No. MB990635.
5. Reverse procedure to install.

RAM 50 4 X 2

1. Remove front coil spring, **Fig. 4.**
2. Remove lower control arm shaft retaining nuts and mounting nut, then withdraw shaft and remove control arm.
3. Reverse procedure to install. Lower vehicle to ground, then torque lower control arm shaft flange retaining nuts to 6-9 ft. lbs. and shaft mounting nut to 40-54 ft. lbs.

UPPER CONTROL ARM REPLACE

RAM 50 4 X 2

1. Remove front coil spring.
2. Remove bolts attaching upper control arm shaft to crossmember.
3. Mount control arm in suitable vise and measure control arm starting torque with spring scale. Starting torque should be 14 ft. lbs. Prior to installing control arm, adjust to standard caster by rotating upper arm shaft to dimension shown in **Fig. 5.**
4. Reverse procedure to install noting the following:
   a. Install camber adjusting shims between upper control arm shaft and crossmember.
   b. When installing control arm shaft to crossmember, install attaching bolts through crossmember, then through shaft.
   c. Torque upper control arm shaft to crossmember attaching bolts to 72-87 ft. lbs.

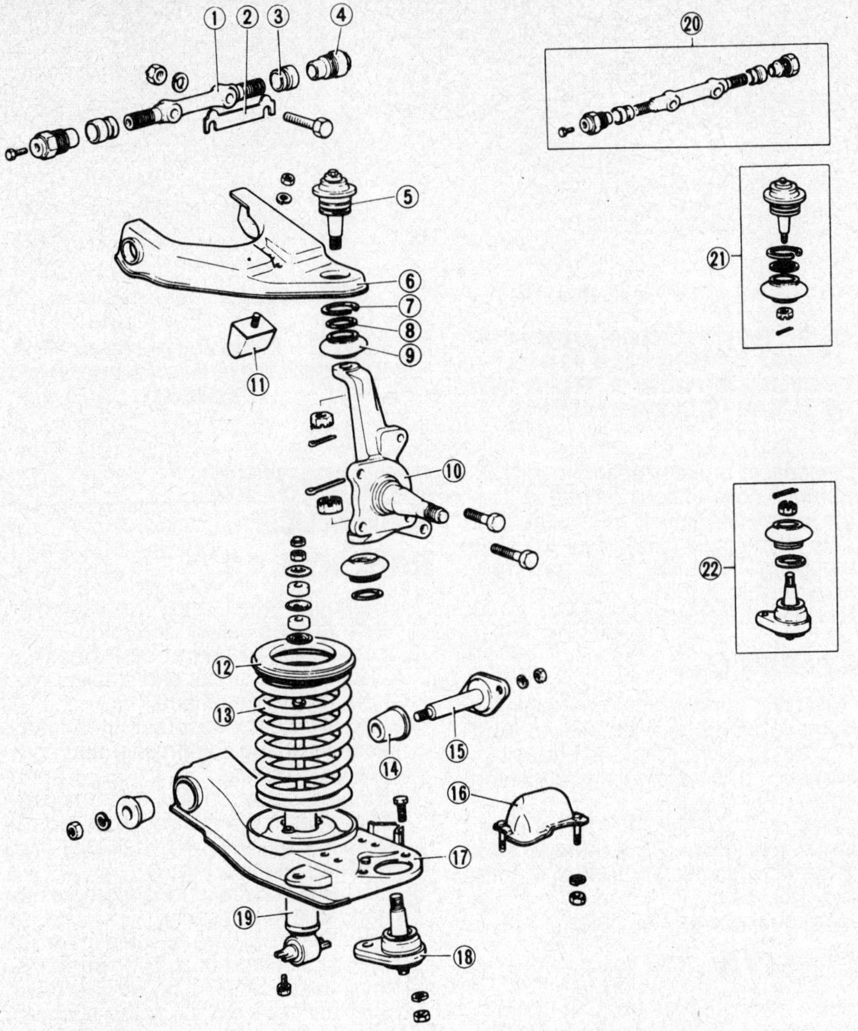

(1) Upper arm shaft
(2) Camber adjusting shim
(3) Dust seal
(4) Pivot bushing
(5) Upper ball joint
(6) Upper arm
(7) Snap ring
(8) Ring
(9) Dust cover
(10) Knuckle
(11) Rebound stop
(12) Spring seat
(13) Front coil spring
(14) Lower arm bushing
(15) Lower arm shaft
(16) Bump stop
(17) Lower arm
(18) Lower ball joint
(19) Shock absorber
(20) Upper arm bush and shaft kit
(21) Upper ball joint kit
(22) Lower ball joint kit

Fig. 4 Front suspension. Ram 50 4 X 2 w/2 wheel drive

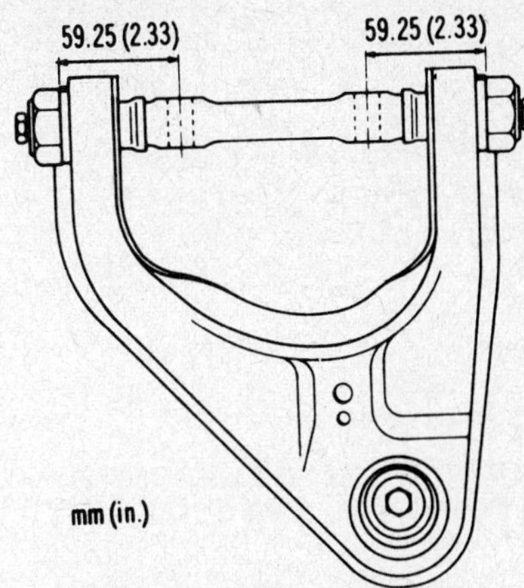

Fig. 5 Measuring & adjusting upper control arm. Ram 50 4 X 2 w/2 wheel drive

BALL JOINT REPLACE

UPPER BALL JOINT

Ram 50 4 X 2

1. Remove upper control arm.
2. Remove snap ring and dust cover from ball joint, then using tools Nos. MB990799 and MB990800, press ball joint from arm.
3. Using a torque wrench, check torque required to start upper ball joint in motion. The torque required should be .6-2.5 ft. lbs. Inspect ball joint cover for wear and damage.
4. If ball joint is to be reused, lubricate with grease.
5. Align ball joint and control alignment marks, then press ball joint into control arm using tools Nos. MB990799 and MB990800. The initial pressure to install the ball joint to a depth of .12-.24 inch is 1550 lbs. or above. **If standard pressure is not obtained when pressing in ball joint, replace ball joint and/or control arm as necessary.**
6. Using snap ring pliers, position snap ring into groove on ball joint case.
7. Install dust cover and ring into groove on ball joint.
8. Install upper control arm as outlined.

LOWER BALL JOINT

Challenger & Sapporo

1. Raise and support front of vehicle, then remove wheel and tire assembly.
2. Remove caliper and caliper support assembly. Suspend caliper assembly from coil spring using a wire hook to prevent damage to brake hose.
3. Remove attaching nut, then disconnect tie rod end from steering knuckle using puller C-3894-A.
4. Remove bolts attaching steering knuckle arm to strut assembly, then separate knuckle arm from strut using a soft faced mallet.
5. Using a screwdriver, remove ball joint dust cover.
6. Using a torque wrench, measure torque required to start rotation of ball joint stud. Torque required to start ball joint movement should be 3.6-5.8 ft. lbs.
7. Apply grease to inner surface of ball joint dust cover, then apply sealer to internal circular surface of dust cover.
8. Install ball joint dust cover using a suitable tool.
9. Install ball joint on steering knuckle arm by tightening attaching nuts to 43-52 ft. lbs.
10. Apply a suitable sealer to knuckle arm to strut contact surface, then install and torque knuckle arm to strut assembly attaching bolts to 58-78 ft. lbs.
11. Connect tie rod end to knuckle arm and torque stud nut to 25-33 ft. lbs., then install cotter pin.
12. Install caliper and caliper support as outlined.
13. Install ball joint to lower control arm attaching bolts and torque to 43-51 ft. lbs.

1983-84 Colt

1. Remove lower ball joint to lower control arm attaching bolts.
2. Loosen ball joint to steering knuckle nut, then using a suitable chisel between ball joint and steering knuckle, free ball joint stud from knuckle.
3. Remove ball joint stud nut and ball joint.
4. Using a torque wrench measure ball joint starting and rotating torque. Starting torque should be 9 ft. lbs. and rotating torque should be 2.2-4.3 ft. lbs. Check ball joint boot for wear and damage.

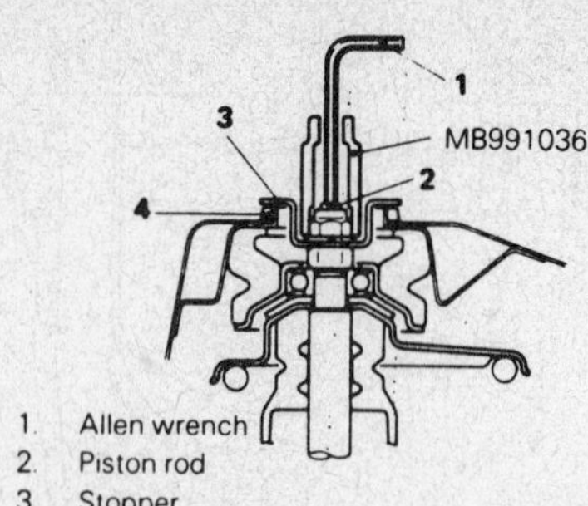

Fig. 6 Strut assembly removal. 1985–87 Colt

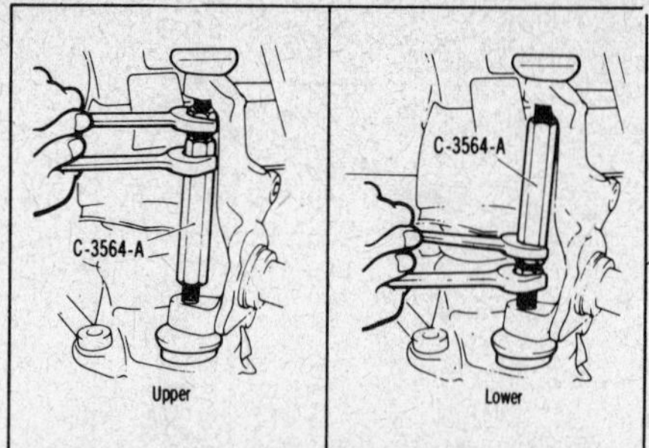

Fig. 7 Separating upper & lower ball joints from steering knuckle. Ram 50 4 X 2 w/2 wheel drive

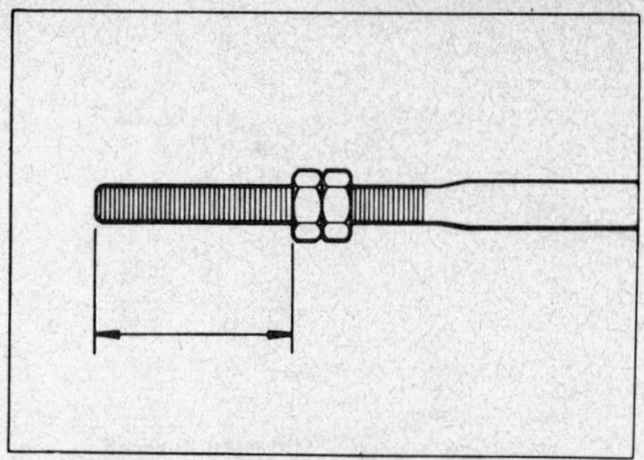

Fig. 8 Positioning strut bar bushing retaining nuts (Typical)

5. Install ball joint and stud nut onto steering knuckle, then install ball joint to lower control arm attaching bolts. Torque ball joint stud nut to 40-51 ft. lbs. and ball joint to lower control arm attaching bolts to 69-87 ft. lbs.

1985–87 Colt

With load removed from lower ball joint, check starting torque with inch lb. wrench. If starting torque is not 21.7-86.8 inch lbs., replace lower control arm and ball joint as an assembly. Refer to "Lower Control Arm, Replace" for procedure.

Colt Vista & Conquest

To replace lower ball joints, refer to "Lower Control Arm, Replace."

Ram 50 4 X 2

1. Remove lower control arm as outlined.
2. Remove snap ring and dust cover from ball joint.
3. Remove ball joint to lower control arm attaching bolts, then remove ball joint.
4. Check ball joint for axial play. Ball joint axial play should not exceed .02 inch.
5. Lubricate ball joint with grease, then install ball joint dust cover and snap ring.
6. Position ball joint on lower control arm, then install attaching bolts and torque to 22-30 ft. lbs.
7. Install lower control arm as outlined.

MacPHERSON STRUT REPLACE

CHALLENGER & SAPPORO

1. Raise and support front of vehicle, then remove wheel and tire assembly.
2. Disconnect brake hose at strut and body mounting bracket.
3. Remove caliper assembly, disc brake rotor, dust cover and disc brake adapter.
4. Remove four nuts attaching strut insulator to upper mounting, then remove bolts attaching strut to knuckle arm and remove strut assembly from vehicle, **Fig. 1.**
5. Reverse procedure to install.

1983–84 COLT

1. Raise and support front of vehicle, then remove wheel and tire assembly.
2. Disconnect brake hoses from strut.
3. Remove bolts attaching strut assembly to steering knuckle, then the four nuts attaching strut insulator to upper mounting. Remove strut assembly from vehicle, **Fig. 2.**
4. Reverse procedure to install.

1985–86 COLT

1. Raise and support front of vehicle.
2. Remove brake hose bracket to strut attaching screws, then the bracket.
3. Remove strut to knuckle attaching bolts.
4. Remove dust cover from top of strut.
5. Using tool MB991036, remove strut assembly attaching nuts, **Fig. 6,** then the strut.
6. Reverse procedure to install.

COLT VISTA

1. Raise and support front of vehicle, then remove wheel and tire assembly.
2. Remove brake hose bracket from strut assembly, then the strut assembly from knuckle.
3. Remove strut insulator to strut housing panel attaching bolts, then remove strut from wheel housing.
4. Reverse procedure to install.

CONQUEST

1. Raise and support front of vehicle.
2. Remove wheel, tire, brake caliper, rotor and dust cover from steering knuckle.
3. Remove knuckle arm to strut attaching bolts, then separate knuckle arm and strut.
4. Remove strut to wheelhouse attaching nuts, then the strut.
5. Reverse procedure to install.

SHOCK ABSORBER REPLACE

RAM 50 4 X 2

Disconnect shock absorber at upper and lower mountings, then remove shock absorber from vehicle. When installing, torque shock absorber upper attaching bolts to 9-13 ft. lbs. and lower attaching bolts to 6-9 ft. lbs.

COIL SPRING REPLACE

RAM 50 4 X 2

1. Remove wheel and tire assembly, then remove caliper and rotor.
2. Loosen nut at end of strut bar, then disconnect strut bar and stabilizer bar from lower control arm.
3. Remove shock absorber, then install suitable spring compressor and compress coil spring.
4. Remove cotter pin and nut from lower control arm, then using tool No. C-3564A, separate lower ball joint from steering knuckle, **Fig. 7.**
5. Carefully loosen spring compressor and remove coil spring.
6. Reverse procedure to install. Torque lower ball joint nut to 87-130 ft. lbs., then install cotter pin. Torque brake strut bar nut to 54-61 ft. lbs. and strut bar to lower control arm attaching bolts to 51-61 ft.lbs. Torque stabilizer bar bolts to 18-5 ft. lbs.

STABILIZER & STRUT BAR REPLACE

CHALLENGER, SAPPORO & RAM 50 4 X 2

1. Raise and support front of vehicle, then remove wheel and tire assembly.
2. Disconnect stabilizer bar and strut bar from lower control arm.
3. Remove strut bar bracket to body attaching bolts, then remove stabilizer bar and strut bar from strut bar bracket. When removing strut bar bushings note position and direction of bushings and washers for reassembly.
4. Reverse procedure to install, noting the following:
   a. When assembling strut bar to bracket, refer to **Fig. 8,** and set clearance between end of strut bar and retaining nut. Clearance should be 3.2 inches for Challenger and Sapporo, 3.8 inches for 1983-84 Ram 50 4 X 2 or 2.9 inches for 1985-87 Ram 50 4 X 2.
   b. After installing strut bar bushings, temporarily tighten outer retaining

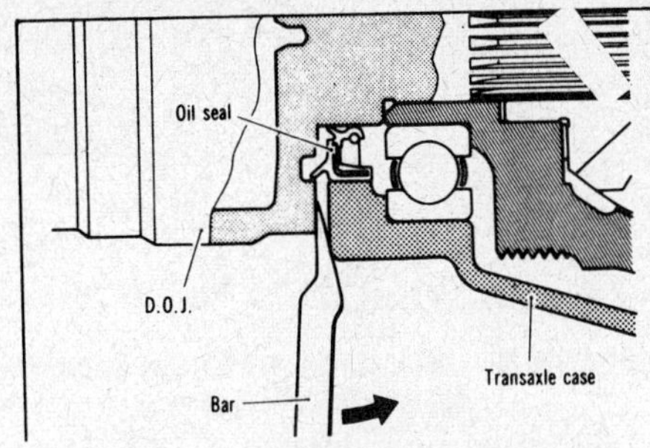

Fig. 9 Removing front drive axle from transaxle case

nut, as nut will be tightened to specified torque after vehicle has been lowered.

c. When connecting stabilizer bar to lower control arm, set clearance between end of bolt and retaining nut to .59-.67 inch for Challenger and Sapporo or .87-.94 inch for Ram 50 4 X 2.
d. Tighten components to the following torque: Stabilizer bar bracket bolts, 6-8 ft. lbs. Stabilizer bar to lower control arm: Challenger & Sapporo, 7-14 ft. lbs.; Ram 50 4 X 2, 18-25 ft. lbs. Strut bar to bracket nuts, 54-61 ft. lbs. Strut bar to lower control arm: Challenger and Sapporo, 43-51 ft. lbs.; Ram 50 4 X 2, 51– -61 ft. lbs. Strut bar bracket to frame, 25-33 ft. lbs.

1983–84 COLT

1. Raise and support front of vehicle, then remove wheel and tire assembly.
2. Remove under cover, then remove strut bar and stabilizer bar and lower ball joint.
3. When removing strut bar, note position and location of bushings and washers.
4. Reverse procedure to install, noting the following:
   a. Before installing bushings on strut bar, position inner retaining nuts 3.17 inches from end of bar, **Fig. 11.**
   b. When installing ball joint to lower control arm, a flat washer must be installed under bolt not retaining the strut bar.
   c. Strut bar to be installed on the right hand side can be identified by a yellow mark.
   d. After lowering vehicle, torque stabilizer bar and strut bar components to the values shown below in ft. lbs.
   Ball joint to lower control arm: 69-87
   Stabilizer bar to crossmember: 22-29
   Stabilizer bar to strut bar: 3.6-4.3
   Strut bar to crossmember: 54-61
   Strut bar to lower control arm: 69-87

CONQUEST

1. Disconnect strut bars from lower control arms, then from strut bar bracket.
2. Disconnect stabilizer bar from lower control arm, then from frame.
3. Remove strut bar and/or stabilizer bar from vehicle.
4. Reverse procedure to install. Tighten stabilizer bar bushing attaching nuts until distance from top of threads to top of nuts is .59-.67 inch.
5. Tighten strut bar attaching nut until distance between the end of strut bar and the front surface of the locknut is 3.09 inches, **Fig. 8.**

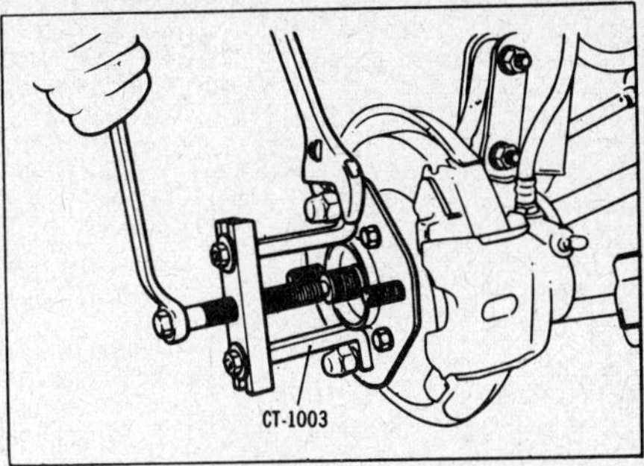

Fig. 10 Pressing front drive axle from hub

COLT VISTA

1. Disconnect stabilizer bar from lower control arm, then from frame.
2. Disconnect strut bars from lower control arms, then from frame.
3. Remove strut bar and/or stabilizer bar from vehicle.
4. Reverse procedure to install. Tighten stabilizer bar to frame bushing attaching nuts until distance from top of threads to top of nuts is .31-.39 inch. Tighten stabilizer bar to lower arm bushing attaching nuts until distance from top of threads to top of nuts is .31-.39 inch on two wheel drive models, or .51-.59 inch on four wheel drive models.
5. Tighten strut bar attaching nut until distance between the end of strut bar and the front surface of the locknut is 3.07 inches, **Fig. 8.**

STABILIZER BAR REPLACE

1985–87 COLT

1. Raise and support vehicle, then re-

1. Cardan joint assembly
2. Dust seal
3. Bearing bracket
4. Bearing retainer
5. Center bearing
6. Oil seal
7. Oil seal retainer
8. O-ring
9. Snap ring
10. D.O.J. outer race
11. Center bearing assembly
12. Circlip
13. Snap ring
14. D.O.J. inner race
15. D.O.J. cage
16. Ball
17. D.O.J. boot
18. D.O.J. boot band
19. Boot band(small)
20. B.J. boot band
21. B.J. boot
22. B.J. Assembly
23. Dust cover

	Nm	ft.lbs.
A	40–55	29–39
B	200–260	145–188

B.J.–Birfield joint
D.O.J.–Double offset joint

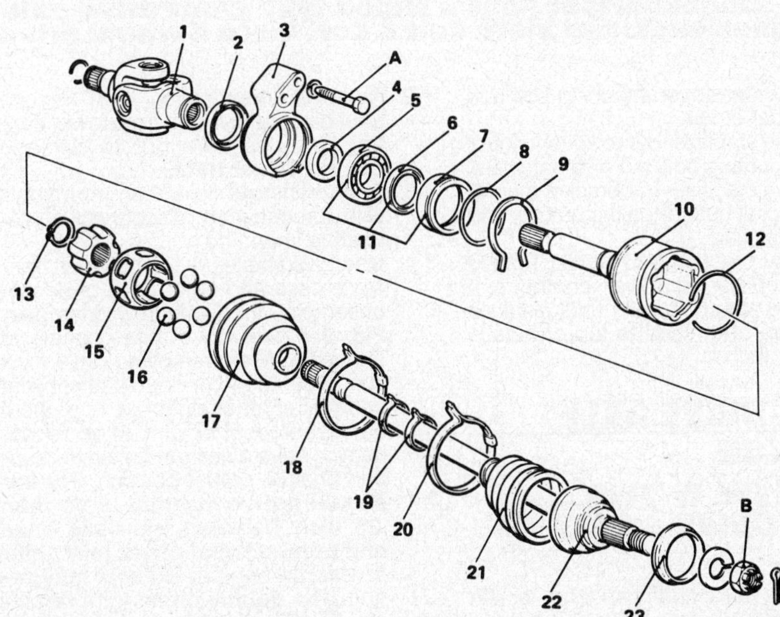

Fig. 11 Double offset joint drive axle exploded view. Colt Vista w/four wheel drive

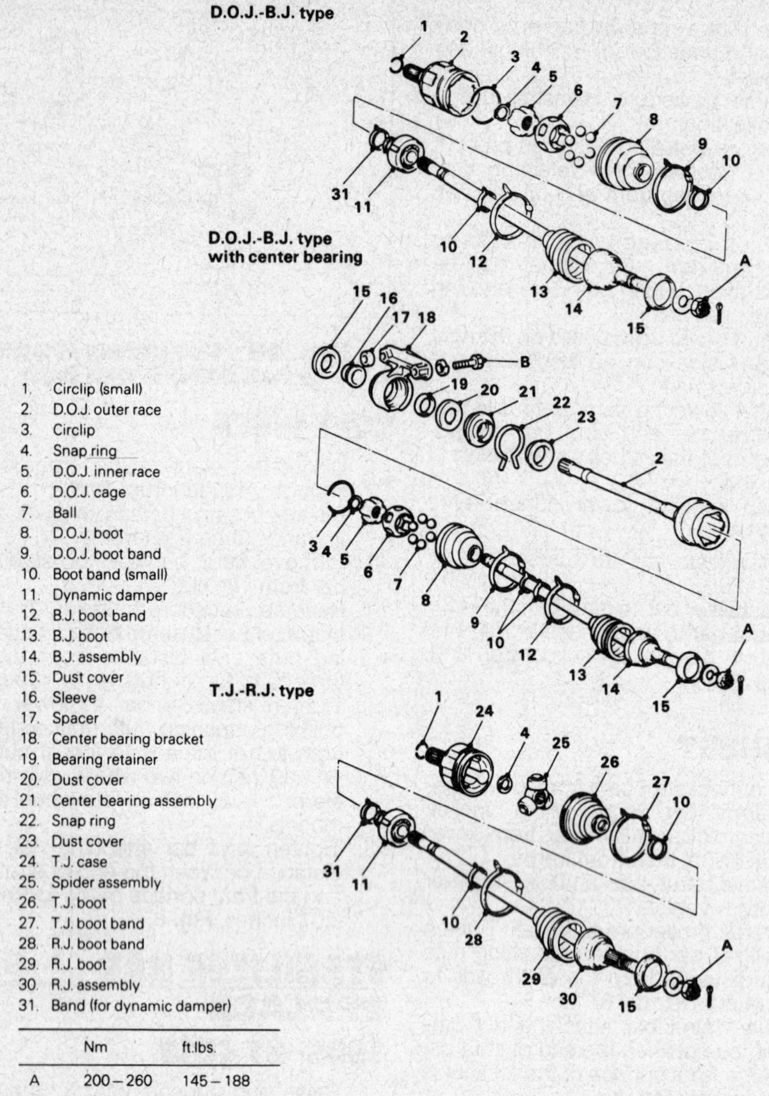

	Nm	ft.lbs.
A	200–260	145–188
B	35–40	25–29

Fig. 12 Double offset joint & tripod type front drive axle assemblies exploded view. Colt & Colt Vista 2 wheel drive

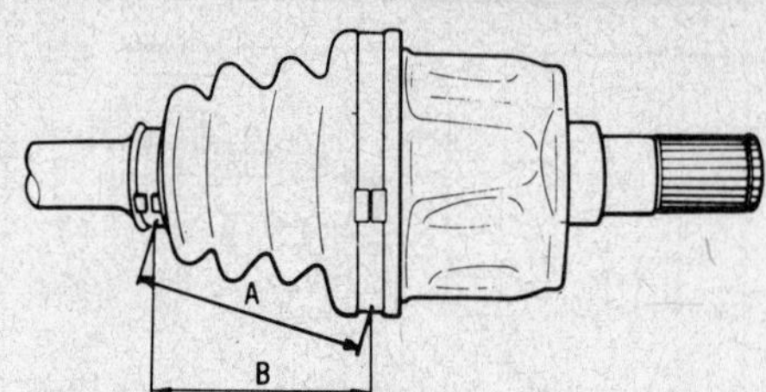

Fig. 13 Double offset boot installation

move under cover attaching bolt and the under cover.

2. Remove stabilizer bar to lower control arm mounting bolt, nut and hardware.
3. Remove stabilizer bar bracket mounting bracket bolts, then the bracket and stabilizer bar.
4. Reverse procedure to install. Tighten stabilizer bar to lower control arm bushing attaching nuts until distance from top of threads to top of nuts is .83-.91 inch.

FRONT DRIVE AXLE

REPLACE

COLT VISTA W/TWO WHEEL DRIVE & 1983–84 COLT

1. Remove hub dust cap and loosen drive axle nut, then raise and support front of vehicle and remove wheel and tire assembly.
2. Remove under cover, then remove strut bar and ball joint from lower control arm. **Use care not to damage ball joint dust boot.**
3. Drain transaxle fluid, then on models with turbocharger, disconnect center bearing snap ring.
4. Insert a suitable pry bar between transaxle case and outer case of double offset joint, then withdraw drive axle, **Fig. 9.** Cover drive axle opening in transaxle. When removing drive axle, support at tripod or double offset joint and pull shaft straight out to prevent damage to boot or joint. After disconnecting drive axle from transaxle, support shaft in proper position. **Pry bar should not be inserted more than .28 inch between transaxle case and outer case of offset joint, otherwise damage to oil seal may result. The double offset joint retainer ring should be replaced whenever the drive axle is removed from transaxle case.**
5. Press drive axle, from hub using tool No. CT-1003, **Fig. 10,** then on models with turbochargers, lightly tap on double offset joint outer race with a suitable mallet to remove. **When pressing drive axle from hub, use care to prevent the spacer from moving out of position.**
6. Reverse procedure to install. Position drive axle so that raised inner diameter of washer is facing nut, then install and torque drive axle nut to 145-188 ft. lbs.

COLT VISTA W/FOUR WHEEL DRIVE

The following procedure is only for the left side drive axle. Refer to Colt Vista Less Four Wheel Drive for right side drive axle replacement procedure.

1. Remove center cap and drive axle nut.
2. Raise and support vehicle, then remove front wheel.
3. Drain transmission fluid.
4. Disconnect lower arm ball joint and knuckle coupling, then remove strut bar and stabilizer bar from lower arm.
5. Remove center bearing snap ring from bearing bracket.
6. Lightly tap double offset joint outer race with a wooden hammer and disconnect drive axle from cardan joint assembly.
7. Disconnect drive axle from bearing bracket.
8. Remove drive axle from hub.
9. Remove bearing bracket attaching bolts, then the bearing bracket.
10. Lightly tap yoke of cardan joint with a wooden hammer and remove it from transaxle assembly.
11. Reverse procedure to install. Torque bearing bracket bolts to 29-39 ft. lbs. Torque drive axle nut to 145-188 ft. lbs. After installation, ensure boot length is 3.23-3.47 inch.

1985–87 COLT

1. Remove hub nut cotter pin, hub nut and washer, then raise and support vehicle.
2. Remove lower ball joint from steering knuckle using tool No. MB991113 or equivalent.
3. Remove tie rod from steering knuckle using tool No. MB991113 or equivalent.
4. On drive axles equipped with center bearing, remove center bearing snap ring.

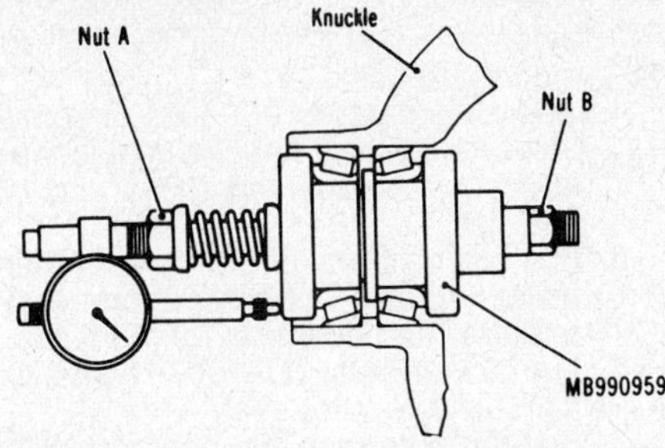

Fig. 14 Determining front wheel bearing preload. Colt

Dial Indicator Reading Inch (mm)	Bearing Preload Adjusting Spacer Thickness Inch (mm)	Identification Color
.020 to .023 (.52 to .58)	.2236 (5.68)	Pink
.023 to .025 (.58 to .64)	.2260 (5.74)	Green
.025 to .028 (.64 to .70)	.2283 (5.80)	Red
.028 to .030 (.70 to .76)	.2307 (5.86)	White
.030 to .032 (.76 to .82)	.2330 (5.92)	None
.032 to .035 (.82 to .88)	.2354 (5.98)	Yellow
.035 to .037 (.88 to .94)	.2378 (6.04)	Blue
.037 to .039 (.94 to 1)	.2402 (6.10)	Orange
.039 to .042 (1 to 1.06)	.2425 (6.16)	Light Green
.042 to .044 (1.06 to 1.12)	.2449 (6.22)	Brown
.044 to .046 (1.12 to 1.18)	.2472 (6.28)	Gray
.046 to .049 (1.18 to 1.24)	.2496 (6.34)	Navy Blue
.049 to .051 (1.24 to 1.30)	.2520 (6.40)	Vermillion
.051 to .054 (1.30 to 1.36)	.2543 (6.46)	Purple

Fig. 15 Front wheel bearing preload spacer selection chart. 1983–84 Colt

5. On drive axles not equipped with center bearing, insert pry bar between transaxle case and drive shaft, then pry drive axle from transaxle case, **Fig. 9.** Remove drive axle from hub using tool No. CT-1003 or equivalent, **Fig. 10. Do not pull on drive axle or joints will be damaged. Do not insert pry bar further than necessary or damage to oil seal will result.**
6. On drive axle equipped with center bearing, remove shaft from transaxle by lightly tapping Double Offset Joint (D.O.J.) with plastic hammer, then drive the drive axle from hub by lightly tapping with plastic hammer. **Do not pull on drive axle or joints will be damaged.**

FRONT AXLE SERVICE

COLT & COLT VISTA W/TWO WHEEL DRIVE

DOUBLE OFFSET JOINT TYPE DRIVESHAFT

When servicing the drive axle, do not disassemble the Birfield bell type constant velocity joint, as components on this type joint are precision fitted.

Disassembly

1. Remove double offset joint boot band, then remove snap ring using a suitable screwdriver, **Figs. 11 and 12.**
2. Remove drive axle from double offset joint, then clean grease from shaft and joint.
3. Remove snap ring, then remove double offset joint inner race, cage and bearings as an assembly. Clean bearing assembly and disassemble bearing if necessary.
4. Wind tape around drive axle splines, then remove Birfield joint boot band and slide boot from drive axle. When inspecting Birfield joint, note amount of grease removed for reassembly.

Assembly

A special grease containing Molybdenum is used to lubricate the drive axle double offset joint and the Birfield joint. This special grease is included in the drive axle repair kit and must be used.

1. Apply gear oil to drive axle, then install double offset joint and Birfield joint boots. Wrap tape around drive axle splines to prevent damage to boots.
2. Apply special Molybdenum grease to double offset joint inner race and cage, then assemble race and cage, aligning raised portions on race with bearing holes on cage.
3. Apply special Molybdenum grease to cage, then position ball bearings into cage.
4. Install inner race cage and bearings on drive axle with chamfered side of cage facing splined end of shaft, then install snap ring.
5. Apply 1.4-2.1 ounces of special Molybdenum grease to double offset joint outer race, then position outer race on drive axle.
6. Apply an additional .7-1.4 ounce of special Molybdenum grease to outer race, then install clip.
7. Add amount of special Molybdenum grease to Birfield joint as removed during disassembly and inspection.
8. Install boots and boot bands for each joint. When installing boot bands for double offset joint, position bands, **Fig. 13,** so that dimension A is 2.9-3.3 inches and dimension B is 2.7-3.1 inches on 1983 models. On 1984-85 models, position bands so that dimension A is 3.2 inches on models less turbocharger or 3.3 inches on models with turbocharger.

TRIPOD JOINT TYPE DRIVESHAFT

Disassembly

When servicing the drive axle, do not disassemble the Rzeppa type constant velocity joint, as components of this type joint are precision fitted.

1. Remove boot clamps, then remove boot from tripod joint housing and position on drive axle, **Figs. 11 and 12.**
2. Pull drive axle from tripod joint housing, then remove snap ring and lift tripod joint spider from housing. Clean tripod joint spider and check for wear and damage. Also check joint needle roller bearings for smooth operation. **Do not disassemble tripod joint spider.**
3. Wind tape around drive axle splines, then remove bands for Rzeppa type joint and remove boots from drive axle. If Rzeppa joint is to be reused, do not wipe away grease. Check grease for contamination and clean and replace grease only if necessary. Note amount of grease removed for use during reassembly.

Assembly

A special grease is used to lubricate the drive axle tripod joint and Rzeppa joint. This grease is included in the drive axle repair kit and must be used.

1. Apply grease to drive axle, then install boots.
2. Position tripod joint spider on drive axle, then install snap ring.
3. Apply 2.8-3.2 ounces of special grease to tripod joint housing, then insert drive axle and spider into housing.
4. Apply another 2.8-3.2 ounces of special grease to tripod joint housing.
5. Apply as much special grease as removed to Rzeppa joint, if necessary.
6. Install bands and boots for each joint. When installing boot bands for tripod joint, bands must be positioned 3.1 inches apart (dimension A), **Fig. 13.**

COLT VISTA W/FOUR WHEEL DRIVE

The following procedure is only for the left side drive axle. Refer to Colt Vista Less Four Wheel Drive for service procedure on right side drive axle.

CENTER BEARING, REPLACE

1. Remove double offset joint outer race from drive axle.
2. Using a suitable grinder, partially grind the certain point of the circumference of the bearing retainer to a thickness of .04-.06 inch.
3. Using a suitable hammer and chisel, break then remove bearing retainer. When the break is made in the bearing retainer, tap the chisel in between the bearing and bearing retainer and pry to remove the bearing retainer. **Do not damage the drive axle in any way.**
4. Remove center bearing assembly using tool MB990560 or equivalent and a press.
5. To install proceed as follows:
   a. After passing the snap ring through the double offset joint outer race, use tool MB990560 or equivalent and a press to install center bearing assembly onto the shaft of the double offset joint outer race.
   b. Face polished surface of the bearing retainer toward the bearing side and, after placing it onto the shaft of the double offset joint outer face, use the tool mentioned previously and the press to install bearing retainer.
   c. Install drive axle onto double offset joint outer race.

CENTER BEARING DUST SEAL, REPLACE

1. Using a suitable screwdriver, remove dust seal from bearing bracket assembly.
2. Using tools MB990938 and 990930 or equivalents and a mallet, press dust seal in until seal is flush with bearing bracket end.
3. Coat inside circumference of seal with suitable grease.

FRONT WHEEL DRIVE HUB & KNUCKLE SERVICE

COLT & COLT VISTA W/TWO WHEEL DRIVE

REMOVAL & INSTALLATION

1. Remove front drive axle as outlined. Retain bearing spacers for use during reassembly.
2. Remove front brake assembly from hub, then using suitable puller, disconnect tie rod end from steering knuckle.
3. Disconnect steering knuckle from strut, then remove knuckle and hub as an assembly.
4. Reverse procedure to install. After installing brake assembly, bleed brake system.

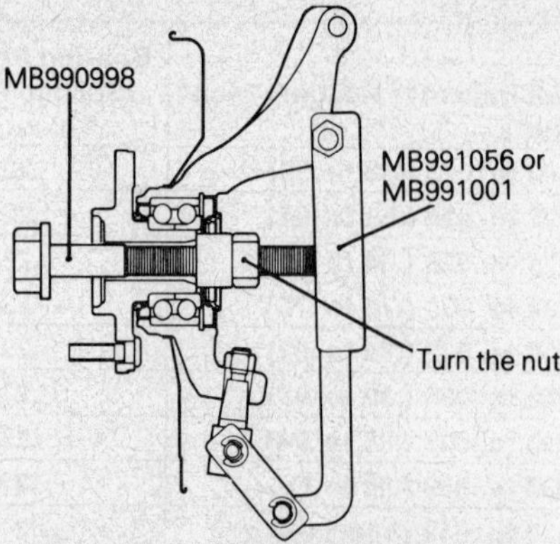

Fig. 16 Installing tools onto knuckle & hub. Colt Vista w/four wheel drive

DISASSEMBLY

1. On 1983-84 models except 1984 Colt turbo, remove hub assembly and inner bearing inner race from steering knuckle. It may be necessary to position steering knuckle in a vise and drive hub from knuckle using a soft faced mallet.
2. On 1984 Colt turbo and all 1985-87 models, remove hub assembly from knuckle using tool No. MB990998 and knuckle arm bridge tool No. MB991001. Do not strike hub and knuckle with a hammer or damage to bearing may result.
3. On 1983-84 models except 1984 Colt Turbo, remove hub bearing spacer.
4. On all models, remove disc brake rotor from hub.
5. Remove outer bearing inner race using a suitable drift, then the inner and outer oil seals.
6. Remove bearing outer races using a suitable drift, then inspect bearings, hub, races and steering hub for wear and damage.
7. Ensure proper fit of knuckle to outer race and hub to inner race and replace as necessary.

ASSEMBLY

1983–84 Exc. 1984 Colt Turbo

1. Using a hammer and suitable drift, install inner and outer bearing outer races onto steering knuckle.
2. Select the proper front wheel bearing preload spacer as follows:
   a. Position tool No. MB990959 and dial indicator to steering knuckle, **Fig. 20,** then tighten tool nuts finger tight.
   b. Tighten nut B, **Fig. 14,** approximately 5 turns, then rotate tool several turns to seat bearings.
   c. Zero dial indicator, then loosen nut B, **Fig. 14,** until dial indicator needle stops, and note reading.
   d. Refer to **Fig. 15,** and select the proper spacer. Tool No. MB990959 incorporates a dummy spacer finished to a thickness of 5 mm.
3. Remove tool No. MB990959, dial indicator and bearing inner races from steering knuckle.
4. Apply lubricant No. 2525035 or equivalent to steering knuckle inside wall surfaces, bearing and races and oil seal lips.
5. Position disc brake rotor to hub, then install attaching bolts and torque alternately and evenly to 29-36 ft. lbs.
6. Using tool Nos. DT-1007-D and C-4171, install outer seal.
7. Support outer bearing inner race with tool No. MB990776-A, then press hub assembly onto steering knuckle.
8. Insert selected spacer into steering knuckle. Then press inner bearing into hub in the same manner as described in previous step.
9. Using tools Nos. DT-1007-D and C-4171, install inner oil seal.

1984 Colt Turbo & 1985–87 All

1. Lubricate outside surface of bearing outer races using a suitable lubricant, then install inner and outer bearing outer races into knuckle using a suitable drift.
2. Lubricate knuckle, oil seals and bearings using a suitable lubricant, then install hub and brake disc. Torque attaching bolts to 36-43 ft. lbs.
3. Place outside bearing inner race on outer race, then install outside oil seal using seal installer tool. Pressure required to install oil seal is 880 lbs.
4. Install inner bearing into knuckle. Torque hub and knuckle to 145-188 ft. lbs.
5. Install tool No. MB990998, then measure hub bearing starting torque. Starting torque should be 18.2 inch lbs. on 1984 models or, 11.3 or less inch lbs. on 1985-87 models. Endplay should be .005 inch on 1984 models or .008 inch on 1985-87 models. If bearing preload or axial endplay specifications cannot be obtained, recheck assembly of bearing, knuckle and hub.
6. Remove tool No. MB990998, then install inside oil seal.
7. Reverse removal procedure, noting the following:
   a. Torque drive axle nut to 145 to 188 ft. lbs.
   b. Torque knuckle to strut attaching bolts to 54 to 65 ft. lbs.
   c. Torque lower arm to ball joint nut to 69 to 87 ft. lbs.
   d. Torque lower arm to strut bar nut to 69 to 87 ft. lbs.
   e. Torque knuckle to tie rod attaching bolts to 11 to 25 ft. lbs.
   f. Measure brake disc runout.

COLT VISTA W/FOUR WHEEL DRIVE

BEARING REPLACEMENT

1. Attach tools as shown in **Fig. 16** onto knuckle and hub.
2. Secure knuckle assembly in a vise.
3. Tighten nut and remove hub from knuckle, **Fig. 17.**
4. Crush oil seal in two places (opposite

1. Oil seal (drive shaft side)
2. Snap ring
3. Wheel bearing
4. Knuckle
5. Dust cover
6. Oil seal (hub side)
7. Hub
8. Brake disc

	Nm	ft.lbs.
A	75–90	54–65

Fig. 17 Hub & Knuckle assembly. Colt Vista w/four wheel drive

each other) so that tabs of puller tool will be caught on the outside bearing inner race.
5. Using a suitable puller, remove outside bearing inner race from hub.
6. Remove oil seal (hub side) from hub.
7. Remove brake disc from hub.
8. Remove oil seal (drive axle side) from knuckle.
9. Remove snap ring from knuckle.
10. Remove bearing.
11. Coat knuckle and bearing contact surfaces with suitable grease.
12. Using a suitable tool, press in the bearing.
13. Install snap ring, then drive oil seal (hub side) into knuckle by using tools C-4171 and C-3972-A until seal is flush with knuckle end surface.
14. Coat oil seal with suitable grease.
15. Mount hub onto knuckle. Torque hub to knuckle to 145-188 ft. lbs.
16. Rotate the hub to seat the bearing.
17. Using a suitable torque wrench, measure turning torque. Turning torque should be 15.6 inch lbs. or less.
18. If turning torque is zero, measure hub axial play using a dial indicator. Axial play should be .008 inch. If turning torque and axial play are not as specified, repeat steps 1 through 17.
19. Remove tools from hub or knuckle assembly.
20. Drive oil seal (drive axle side) into the knuckle until it contacts snap ring.
21. Coat seal lip with suitable grease.
22. Torque knuckle mount attaching bolt to 54-65 ft. lbs.

STEERING GEAR REPLACE

MANUAL STEERING

Exc. Colt & Colt Vista

1. Remove the clamp bolt connecting the steering shaft with the steering gear housing mainshaft.
2. Using Pitman and idler arm puller (C-3894), disconnect the pitman arm and the relay rod.
3. Remove the steering gear assembly from the body frame.
4. Using the pitman arm puller (Special Tool CT-1106), remove the pitman arm from the cross shaft.
5. Reverse procedure to install.

Colt & Colt Vista

1. Raise and support front of vehicle, then remove wheel and tire assembly.
2. Remove clamp bolt securing joint with pinion shaft.
3. Remove tie end stud nut, then using suitable puller disconnect tie rod from steering knuckle.
4. Remove steering gear clamp bolts from crossmember, then remove steering gear.
5. Reverse procedure to install.

POWER STEERING

Exc. Conquest, Colt Vista & 1985–87 Colt

1. Disconnect steering shaft from steering gear mainshaft.
2. Remove retaining nuts, then disconnect tie rod from relay rod and pitman arm from relay rod using puller C-3894A.
3. Disconnect pressure and return hoses from steering gear, then remove steering gear mounting bolts and steering gear. On Challenger and Sapporo it may be necessary to position fuel line aside to permit steering gear removal. On Pickup models with automatic transmission, it may be necessary to disconnect throttle linkage and remove splash shield. On Pickup models with manual transmission, it may be necessary to remove starter motor to permit steering gear removal.
4. Reverse procedure to install.

Colt Vista

1. Raise and support front of vehicle, then remove wheel and tire assemblies.
2. Disconnect tie rod from knuckle using tool No. C-3894-A.
3. Disconnect joint assembly from gear box, then drain power steering fluid.
4. Disconnect pressure and return hoses from power steering gear.
5. Remove crossmember support bracket attaching bolts, then the support bracket from No. 2 crossmember.
6. Remove steering gear attaching bolts, then the steering gear.
7. Reverse procedure to install.

Conquest

1. Raise and support front of vehicle, then remove wheel and tire assembly.
2. Remove steering shaft to steering gear mainshaft retaining clamp, then disconnect pressure and return hoses from steering gear.
3. Disconnect pitman arm from relay rod using tool No. MB990635, then remove steering gear assembly.
4. Remove pitman arm from steering gear using tool No. C-3894-A.
5. Reverse procedure to install.

1985–87 Colt

1. Raise and support front of vehicle.
2. Remove return hose from reservoir and allow fluid to drain into suitable container.
3. Remove steering shaft to gear box pinion coupling bolt.
4. Remove tie rod ends from steering knuckles using tool No. MB991113 or equivalent.
5. Remove pressure and return lines from steering gear box.
6. Remove clamp from lower steering column dust cover.
7. Remove steering gear bracket bolts, then the brackets.
8. Remove mounting rubber, then the gear box assembly.
9. Reverse procedure to install. When installing mounting rubber, apply adhesive to joints to prevent opening.

FRONT DRIVE AXLE, SUSPENSION & STEERING SECTION, RAM 50 4 X 4 & RAM RAIDER 4 X 4

INDEX

UPPER & LOWER CONTROL ARMS

REPLACE

1. Remove front wheel, brake caliper assembly and front hub assembly.
2. Remove dust covers from anchor arm assemblies, **Fig. 1.**
3. Place alignment mark on torsion bar with mark on anchor arm B.
4. Remove anchor arm assembly, then remove torsion bar from anchor arm assembly B.
5. Remove stabilizer bar from lower arm, then remove shock absorber.
6. Remove cotter pins and nuts from upper and lower ball joint studs at tie rod end.
7. Disconnect tie rod from knuckle using tool C3894-A.
8. Separate upper ball joint from knuckle using tool No. MB990635.
9. Separate upper ball joint from knuckle using tool No. C3894-A.
10. Remove bolts connecting upper arm shaft to arm post of side frame, then remove upper arm assembly.
11. Remove two bolts attaching lower arm then remove lower arm.
12. Reverse procedure to install, noting the following:
    a. Refer to **Fig. 1** for torque specifications.
    b. Torque shock absorber lower mounting bolts to 6 to 8 ft. lbs. On 1983-84 models, tighten shock absorber upper mounting nut until protrusion of stud above bottom of nut is .8 inch. On 1985-87 models, tighten shock absorber upper mounting nut until protrusion of stud above top of nut is .5 inch for 1985 models or .27-.31 inch for 1986 Ram 50 and 1987 Ram Raider. On 1987 Ram 50, tighten nut to end of threads. On all models, install jam nut and torque to 9-13 ft. lbs.
    c. Refer to **Fig. 2** and check dimension A when torsion bar and anchor arm are assembled. Standard value is 5.6-5.8 inch for left side and 5.4-5.6 inch for right side on Ram 50, or 5.32-5.64 inches for left side and 4.9-5.2 inches for right side on Ram Raider.
    d. Torque anchor bolt until protrusion is to specification shown in **Fig. 2** for Ram 50 or **Fig. 3** for Ram Raider.
    e. On 1983-84 models, tighten stabilizer bar to lower arm nut until protrusion of stud above bottom of nut is .63-.71 inch. On 1985-87 models, tighten stabilizer bar to lower arm nut until protrusion of stud above top of nut is .24-.31 inch.
    f. With installation procedure complete and vehicle lowered to ground, torque lower arm to bracket of side frame to 102-115 ft. lbs. Measure distance A, **Fig. 4.** Measured distance should be 2.8 inch. If measurement is out of specification, turn adjusting nut of torsion bar anchor bolt until measurement comes into specification.

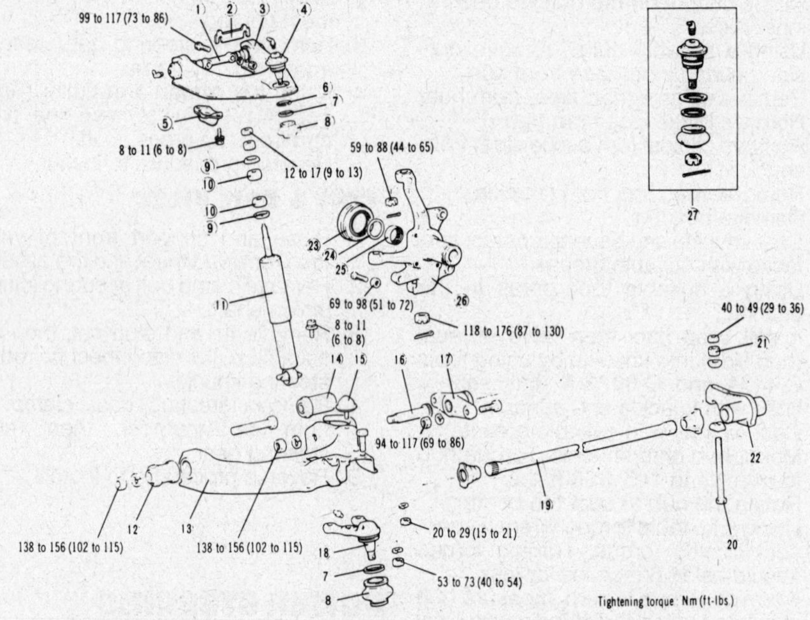

(1) Upper arm shaft	(10) Bushing	(19) Torsion bar
(2) Camber adjusting shim	(11) Shock absorber	(20) Anchor bolt
(3) Upper arm	(12) Bushing (B)	(21) Adjusting nut
(4) Upper ball joint	(13) Lower arm	(22) Anchor arm assembly
(5) Rebound stop	(14) Bushing (A)	(23) Oil seal
(6) Snap ring	(15) Bump stop	(24) Spacer
(7) Ring	(16) Lower arm shaft	(25) Needle bearing
(8) Dust cover	(17) Anchor arm (B)	(26) Knuckle
(9) Joint cup (A)	(18) Lower ball joint	(27) Upper ball joint kit

Fig. 1 Front suspension exploded view

BALL JOINT

REPLACE

The following procedures are given for control arms removed from vehicle.

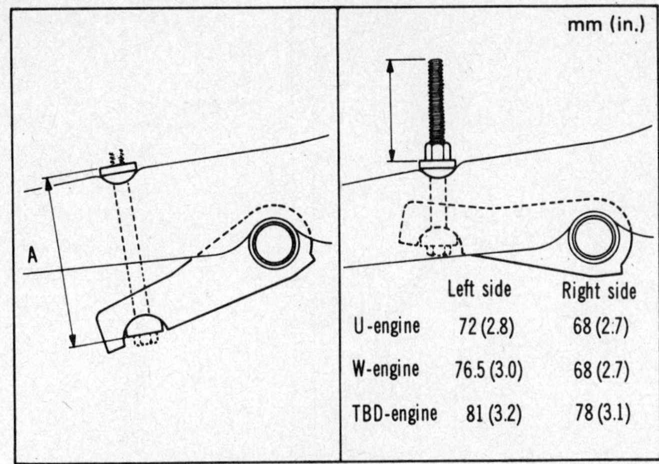

Fig. 2 Torsion bar anchor bolt installation. Ram 50 4 X 4, Ram Raider similar

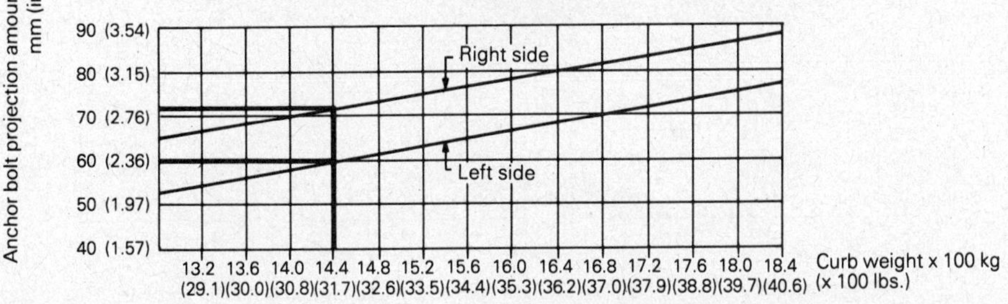

Fig. 3 Torsion bar anchor bolt specifications. Ram Raider

UPPER BALL JOINT

1. Remove rebound stop. Remove ring, dust cover and snap ring from upper ball joint.
2. Remove upper ball joint using tool Nos. MB990799 and MB990800.
3. Reverse procedure to install. Align ball joint and control alignment marks and press ball into upper arm using tool Nos. MB990799 and MB990800. Initial pressure to install ball joint to a depth of .12-.24 inch is 1500 lbs. minimum. If minimum ball joint pressure is not obtained when pressing in ball joint, replace ball joint or upper arm as necessary.

LOWER BALL JOINT

1. Remove four lower ball joint retaining nuts and remove lower ball joint.
2. Reverse procedure to install. Torque lower ball joint to lower arm nuts to 40-54 ft. lbs.

SHOCK ABSORBER REPLACE

1. Detach shock absorber from upper and lower mounting, then remove shock absorber.
2. Reverse procedure to install. Torque shock absorber lower mounting bolts to 6 to 8 ft. lbs. On 1983-84 models, tighten shock absorber upper mounting nut until protrusion of stud above bottom of nut is .8 inch. On 1985-87 models, tighten shock absorber upper mounting nut until protrusion of stud above top of nut is .5 inch for 1985 models or .27-.31 inch for 1986 Ram 50 4 X 4 and 1987 Ram Raider. On 1987 Ram 50 4 X 4, tighten nut to end of threads. On all models, install jam nut and torque to 9-13 ft. lbs.

STABILIZER BAR REPLACE

1. Remove stabilizer bar from stabilizer link assembly and lower arm.
2. Reverse procedure to install, noting the following:
   a. On 1983-84 models tighten stabilizer link to No. 1 crossmember until protrusion of stud above bottom of nut is .63-.71 inch. On 1985-87 models tighten stabilizer link to No. 1 crossmember until protrusion of stud above top of nut is .24-.31 inch.
   b. On 1983-84 models, tighten stabilizer bar to lower arm nut until protrusion of stud above bottom of nut is .63-.71 inch. On 1985-87 models, tighten stabilizer bar to lower arm nut until protrusion of stud above top of nut is .24-.31 inch.

FRONT SUSPENSION CROSSMEMBER REPLACE

1. Install suitable jack under differential carrier.
2. Remove front suspension crossmember from differential carrier assembly and from support bracket of side frame, **Fig. 5.**
3. Reverse procedure to install. Torque front suspension crossmember to support bracket of side frame bolt to 73-86 ft. lbs. Torque front suspension crossmember to bracket bolt to 22-30 ft. lbs.

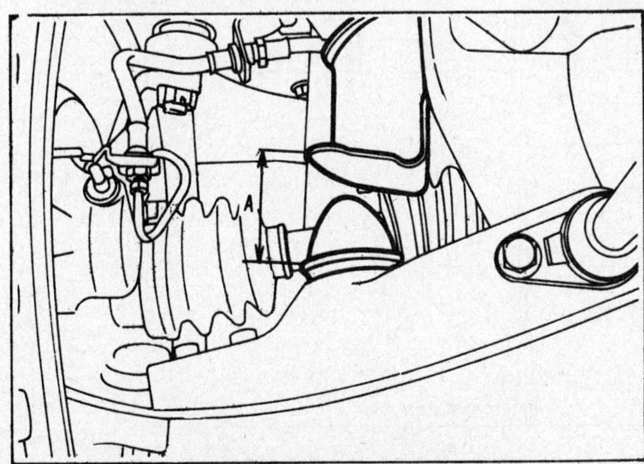

Fig. 4 Dimension between bump stop and bump stop bracket

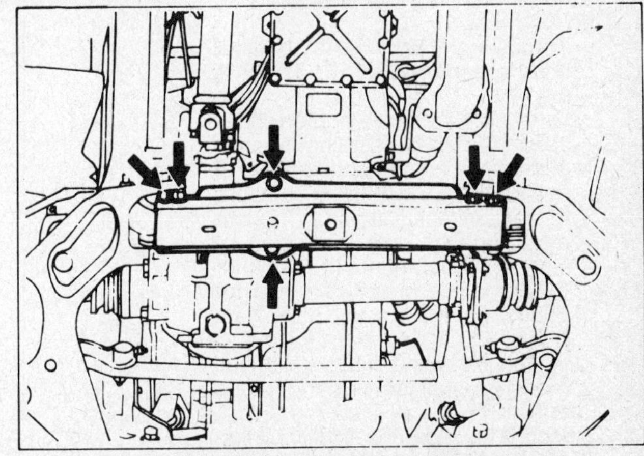

Fig. 5 Location front suspension crossmember bolts

STEERING KNUCKLE
REPLACE

1. Raise and support front of vehicle, and place suitable jack under lower control arm to relieve spring tension from knuckle.
2. Remove hub assembly as outlined, then remove brake rotor dust cover.
3. Remove cotter pin and retaining nut, then disconnect tie rod from knuckle using suitable puller.
4. Remove cotter pins and nuts, disconnect upper and lower ball joints, then remove knuckle.
5. Reverse procedure to install. Refer to **Fig. 1** for torque specifications.

DRIVE AXLE SERVICE
REMOVAL & INSTALLATION

1. Remove wheel and brake caliper assembly, leaving brake hose connected, and hang caliper from body or suspension arm. **Do not allow caliper to hang by brake hose.**
2. Remove hub cover assembly, then remove snap ring from drive axle, **Fig. 6.**
3. Remove knuckle and front hub assembly as a unit. **Support lower control arm with suitable jack prior to disconnecting ball joints from steering knuckle.**
4. To remove left drive axle, slowly lower jack supporting control arm, then pull drive axle from differential carrier.
5. To remove right drive axle, raise right lower control arm with jack and proceed as follows:
   a. Remove upper mounting nuts from right shock absorber, then remove shock absorber from arm post of side frame. **Do not remove lifting device from lower arm until shock absorber has been reconnected.**
   b. Remove four nuts connecting right drive axle to inner shaft assembly, then remove right drive axle.
6. Remove inner shaft from differential shaft carrier assembly.
7. Remove dust seal.
8. Reverse procedure to install noting the following:
   a. Torque right drive axle to inner shaft assembly bolts to 37-43 ft. lbs.
   b. On 1983-84 models, tighten shock absorber upper mounting nut until protrusion of stud above bottom of nut is .8 inch. On 1985-87 models, tighten shock absorber upper mounting nut until protrusion of stud above top of nut is .5 inch for 1985 models or .27-.31 inch for 1986 Ram 50 4 X 4 and 1987 Ram Raider. On 19887 Ram 50 4 X 4, tighten nut to end of threads. On all models, install jam nut and torque to 9-13 ft. lbs.
   c. Mount knuckle and front hub assembly together and check drive axle endplay as follows: Install

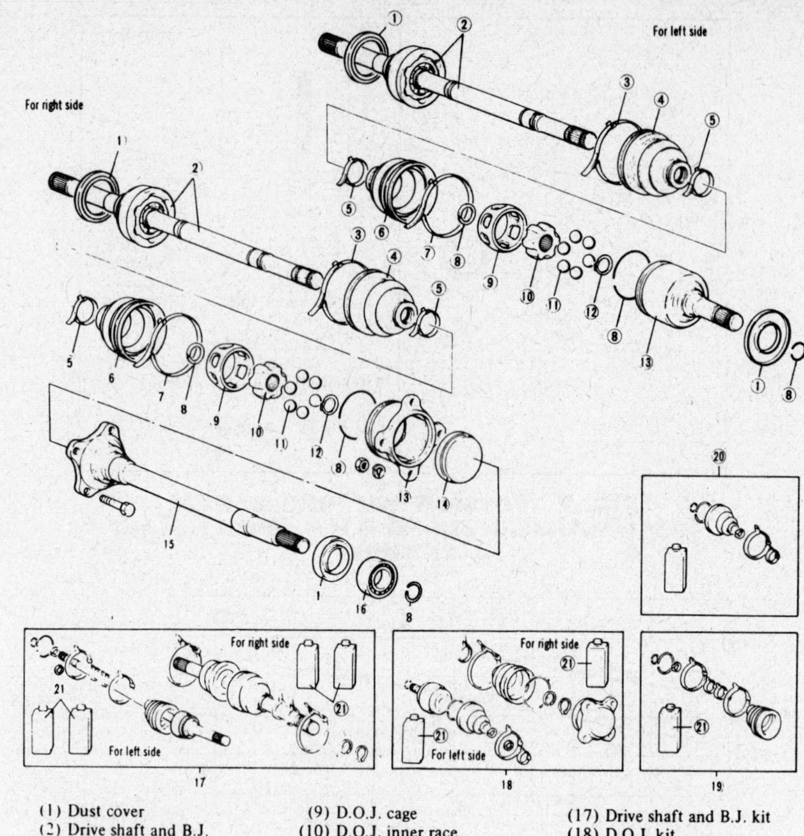

(1) Dust cover
(2) Drive shaft and B.J.
(3) Boot band (A)
(4) B.J. boot
(5) Boot band (C)
(6) D.O.J. boot
(7) Boot band (B)
(8) Circlip
(9) D.O.J. cage
(10) D.O.J. inner race
(11) Ball
(12) Snap ring
(13) D.O.J. outer race
(14) End plate
(15) Inner shaft
(16) Bearing
(17) Drive shaft and B.J. kit
(18) D.O.J. kit
(19) B.J. boot kit
(20) D.O.J. boot kit
(21) Grease

Abbreviation:
D.O.J. – Double offset joint
B.J. – Birfield joint

Fig. 6 Drive axle assembly exploded view

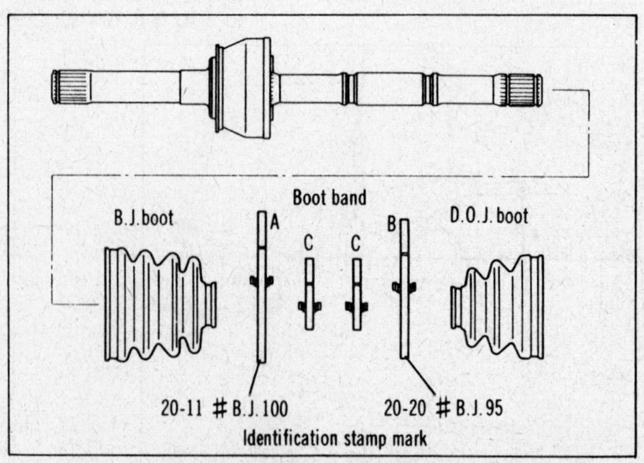

Fig. 7 Driveshaft boot and band identification

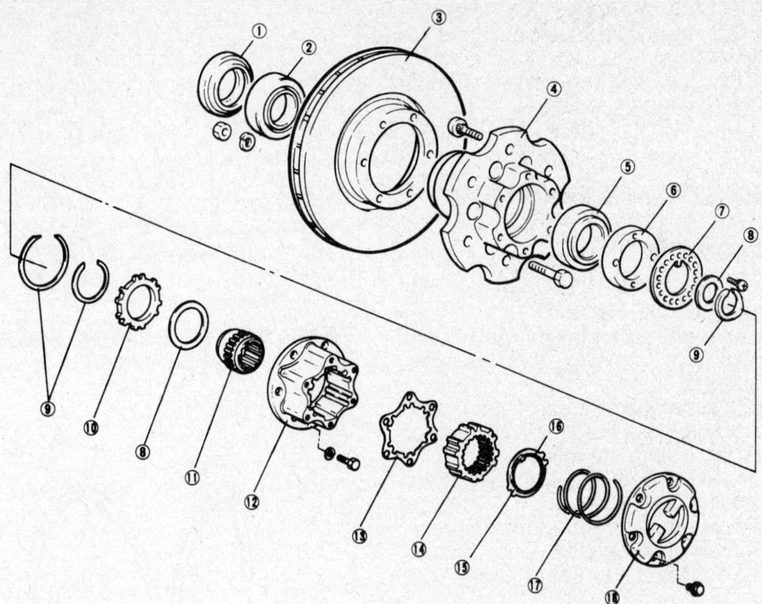

(1) Oil seal
(2) Wheel bearing (Inner)
(3) Brake disc
(4) Front hub
(5) Wheel bearing (Outer)
(6) Lock nut
(7) Lock washer
(8) Spacers
(9) Snap rings
(10) Free wheeling hub ring
(11) Inner hub
(12) Free wheeling hub body
(13) Packing
(14) Clutch
(15) Follower
(16) Tension spring
(17) Compression spring
(18) Free wheeling hub cover

Fig. 8 Hub & wheel bearing assembly exploded view. Shown w/manual locking hub

(1) Housing C-ring
(2) Brake (B)
(3) Brake (A)
(4) Brake spring
(5) Housing snap ring
(6) Retainer (B) C-ring
(7) Drive gear
(8) Retainer (A)
(9) Drive gear snap ring
(10) Slide gear C-ring
(11) Cam
(12) Spring holder
(13) Shift spring
(14) Slide gear
(15) Return spring
(16) Retainer (B)
(17) Retainer bearing
(18) Free wheeling hub body
(19) O-ring
(20) Free wheeling hub cover

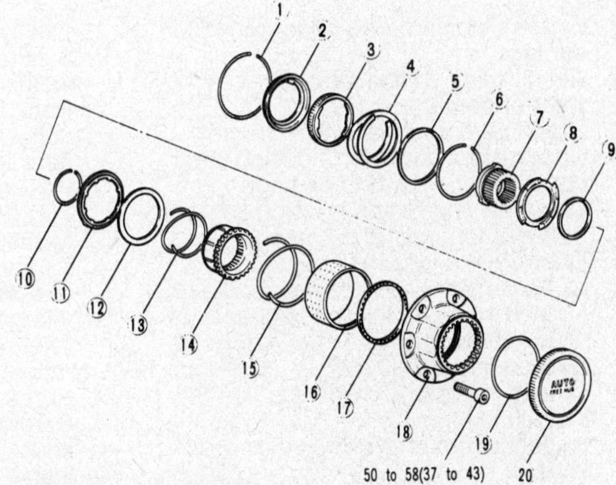

Fig. 9 Automatic (free wheeling) locking hub

snap ring onto drive axle. Position dial indicator on end of drive axle and turn drive axle in axial direction. Drive axle endplay should be .008-.020 inch. Install proper spacer to bring endplay into specification.

DISASSEMBLY

1. Remove boot bands from Birfield joint and double offset joint boots. Discard bands and replace with new bands at reassembly.
2. Remove circlip from double offset joint outer race.
3. Remove drive axle from double offset joint outer race.
4. Clean grease from outer race, then remove balls from cage.
5. Turn double offset joint cage 30 degrees from position at which balls were installed and push cage down toward Birfield joint until it is off inner race.
6. Remove inner race snap ring, inner race and cage from end of drive axle.
7. Remove snap ring from drive axle, then remove double offset joint boot and Birfield boot. Tape end of drive axle so splines do not damage boots as they are removed.
8. Remove dust cover. **Do not disassemble Birfield joint.**
9. Using suitable tool and press, remove bearing from inner shaft.

INSPECTION

1. Inspect outer race of double offset joint for excessive wear or damage.
2. Inspect bearing for damage to races.
3. Inspect drive axle and inner shaft for damage to splines.
4. Inspect drive and inner shaft for bending or other damage.
5. Inspect Birfield joint for damage to balls, water contamination, rust and other foreign material.
6. Inspect dust cover for proper shape and damage.
7. Inspect Birfield joint and double offset joint boots for deterioration, tears or cracks.
8. Inspect double offset joint inner race, balls and cage for damage, wear or rust.

ASSEMBLY

1. Press dust cover onto inner shaft.
2. Press inner bearing onto shaft using tool No. MD990560.
3. Press dust covers onto Birfield joints and double offset joints.
4. Apply grease to drive axle.
5. Install Birfield joint boot, all boot bands and double offset joint boot on drive axle and Birfield joint, **Fig. 7.**
6. Install double offset joint cage onto drive axle with smaller diameter end of cage toward Birfield joint. Install snap ring, inner race and circlip onto drive axle.
7. Apply grease to double offset joint inner race and cage, then fit balls into cage.
8. Apply 2-3 ounces of grease to outer race, then install race on drive axle.
9. Apply 2-3 ounces of grease to outer race, then install circlip.
10. Apply as much grease as was removed from Birfield joint during inspection, then install boot. Birfield joint boot should measure 3 inches in length from outer band to inner band.

HUB, ROTOR & WHEEL BEARING SERVICE

REMOVAL

1. Remove wheel and tire assembly, then remove brake caliper assembly leaving brake hose connected. Suspend caliper assembly from frame using a wire hook to prevent damage to brake hose.
2. Place hub in free position, then remove free wheeling hub cover, **Figs. 8 and 9.** On models with automatic locking hubs, ensure hub is in "free wheeling" position by placing transfer case lever in 2H position and moving in reverse 4-7 feet. If cover cannot be removed by hand, loosen cover with suitable strap wrench, taking care not to damage cover.

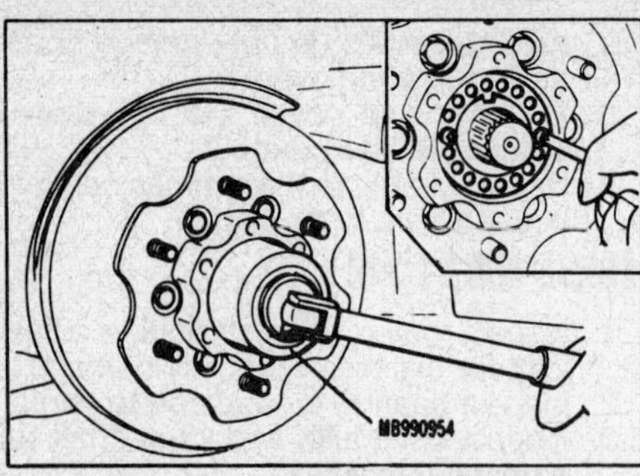

Fig. 10 Spindle nut removal & installation

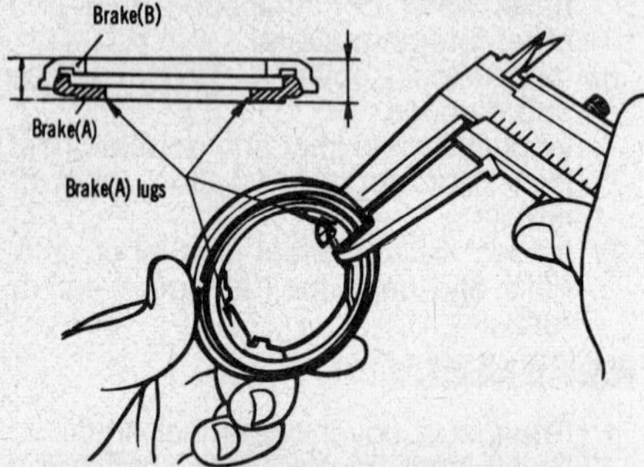

Fig. 12 Measuring brake assembly. Automatic locking hub

3. Remove snap ring securing drive axle, then the adjusting shims.
4. Remove free wheeling hub assembly from front hub, using tool MD998360 or equivalent to remove bolts securing automatic locking hub.
5. Remove lock washer, then remove hub locknut using tool No. MB990954, **Fig. 10.**
6. Pull front hub with brake disc from knuckle, using care not to drop outer wheel bearing inner race.
7. Remove grease from inside front hub, then using a suitable drift, drive bearing races from hub.
8. Place alignment marks on brake disc and hub, then separate hub and disc as necessary.

INSPECTION

HUB, SPINDLE & BEARINGS

1. Clean components with suitable solvent and blow dry with compressed air.
2. Inspect spindle for wear and damage and measure spindle bearing seating area diameter, **Fig. 11.** Diameter should be 1.7805 to 1.7812 inch.
3. Inspect bearings for damage excessive wear, overheating and scoring, and replace as needed.
4. Check fit of bearing outer races in hub. If races are loose, hub should be replaced.

MANUAL LOCKING HUB

1. Inspect hub ring, inner hub and hub body, and the clutch, **Fig. 8.** If components are damaged or worn, assembly should be replaced.
2. Inspect tension spring and compression spring, and replace if collapsed or deteriorated.
3. Check operation of control handle and replace as needed.

AUTOMATIC LOCKING HUB

Disassembly

1. Press in on brake B, then remove housing C-ring, **Fig. 9.**
2. Remove brake B, brake B and brake spring from housing, then remove housing snap ring.
3. Mount assembly in press, lightly compress drive gear, then remove retainer B C-ring, noting the following:
   a. Place protective cloth under cover mating surface.
   b. Because return spring is approximately 1.57 inches long, ensure press stroke is more than 1.57 inches.
   c. Do not apply more than 441 lbs. pressure to drive gear.
   d. After removing C-ring, slowly reduce press force until return spring relaxes completely.
4. Remove retainer B, return spring, slide gear assembly and drive gear assembly from housing, **Fig. 9.**
5. Remove and discard drive gear snap ring.
6. Press in on slide gear cam and remove slide gear C-ring.

Inspection

1. Check slide and drive gear splines for damage.
2. Check cam portion of retainer A for wear or damage.
3. Check cam for wear and damage.
4. Check slide gear and housing tooth surfaces for wear and damage.
5. Check retainer B and housing contact surfaces for wear and damage.
6. Check brake wear as follows:
   a. Assemble brake A and brake B, then measure thickness of assembly at two lugs on brake A, **Fig. 12.**
   b. Standard thickness is .413 inch and minimum thickness is .378 inch.
7. Inspect return and shift springs as follows:
   a. Measure free length of spring as shown in **Fig. 13.**
   b. Minimum return spring free length is 1.38 inches.
   c. Minimum shift spring free length is 1.18 inches.
8. Replace any components that are damaged, excessively worn, or that are not within specifications.

Assembly

Apply Mopar grease 2525035 or equivalent to mounting surfaces of all components and reverse disassembly procedure, noting the following:

1. Pack grooves of retainer B with specified grease.

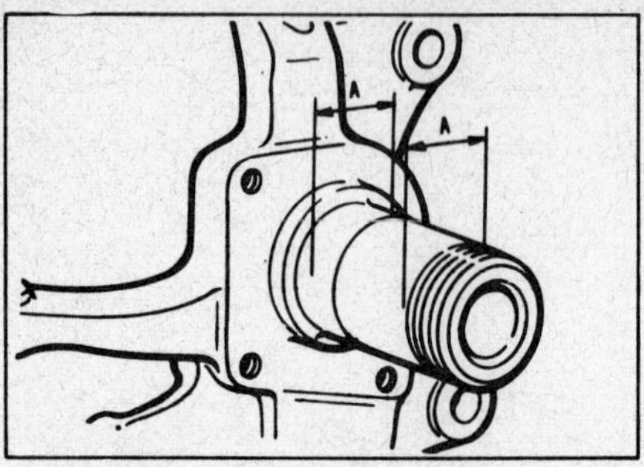

Fig. 11 Checking spindle for wear

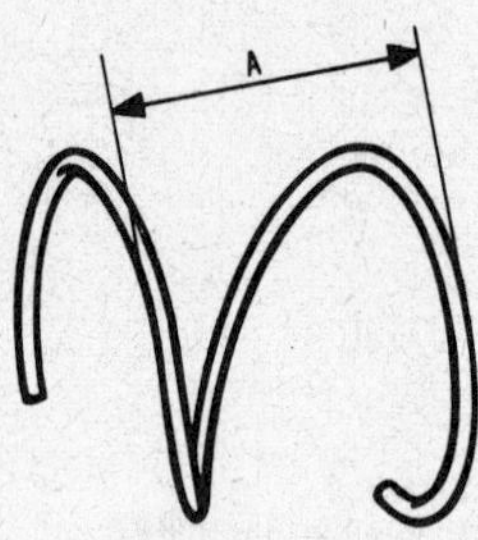

Fig. 13 Measuring spring free length. Automatic locking hub

2. Install return spring with smaller diameter coil toward cam.
3. Pack grooves of brake B with specified grease.

INSTALLATION

1. Drive outer races into front hub using a suitable drift, then evenly coat inner wall of front hub with grease.
2. Pack inner and outer bearings with suitable grease. Apply grease to oil seal lip.
3. Position inner bearing and oil seal on hub, then install oil seal using tool No. MB990985.
4. If removed, install brake disc on front hub, **Fig. 8,** tightening attaching bolts alternately and evenly to 36-44 ft. lbs. After assembling, check brake disc runout. Brake disc runout should not exceed .006 inch.
5. Carefully install front hub on steering knuckle spindle.
6. Install outer bearing on spindle, then install spindle nut.
7. Adjust wheel bearings as follows:
   a. Torque bearing locknut to 94-145 ft. lbs. while rotating hub to seat bearings.
   b. Loosen spindle nut and retighten to 18 ft. lbs., then back off 30°.
   c. Install lock washer. If hole in lock washer is not aligned with hole in spindle nut, the nut may be loosened up to an additional 20° to obtain proper alignment.
   d. Using a suitable spring scale or torque wrench, measure force required to rotate front hub, **Fig. 14.**
   e. The force required to rotate the front hub assembly should be 1.1-4.0 lbs. (spring scale) or 3-11

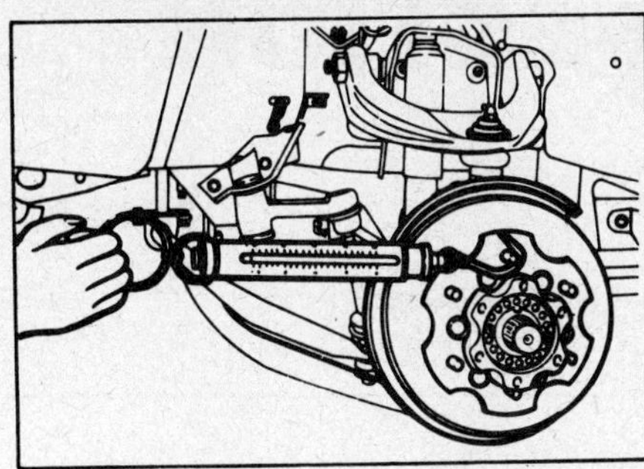

Fig. 14 Checking front hub rotating torque

inch lbs. (torque wrench), and endplay should be less than .002 inch. If rotating force is not within specifications, repeat adjustment.

f. When adjustment is correct, secure washer with retaining screws.

8. On models with automatic locking hubs, measure brake contact surface depth as follows:

a. Measure dimension A, **Fig. 15,** in two places using suitable depth gauge.

b. Average of two readings should be .46-.48 inch. If depth is greater than specified, install suitable shims. If depth is less than specified, recheck hub and bearing installation.

9. Apply grease to inner surface of free wheeling hub body assembly.
10. Apply semi-dry sealant to front hub surface to which the free wheeling hub body assembly is attached.
11. Align tab on free wheel hub with groove on spindle, install free wheeling hub body assembly on front hub, then torque attaching bolts to 37-43 ft. lbs.
12. Reverse remaining procedure to complete installation.

STEERING GEAR REPLACE

1. Disconnect steering shaft from steering gear main shaft.

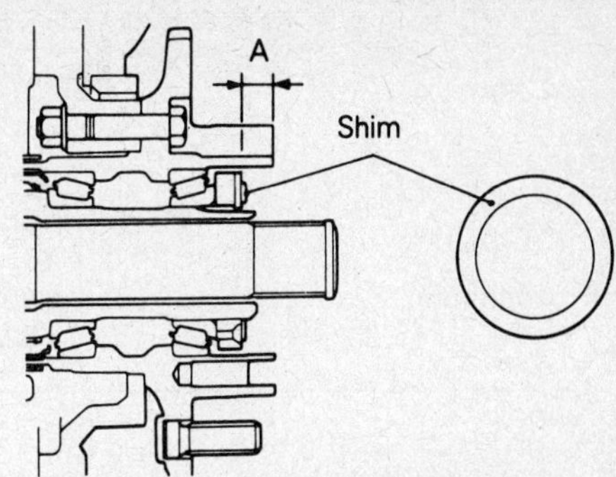

Fig. 15 Measuring brake contact surface depth. Automatic locking hub

2. Disconnect tie rod from relay rod and pitman arm from relay rod using tool No. C3894A.
3. Remove air cleaner and disconnect pressure and return hose from steering gear. Remove under cover.
4. Remove starter from transmission.
5. Remove steering gear. Use tool No. CT1106 if pitman arm is removed.
6. Reverse procedure to install. Torque pressure hose to 40-47 ft. lbs., return hose to 29-36 ft. lbs., tie rod socket and relay rod connection to 26-32 ft. lbs. and steering gear to 40-47 ft. lbs.

W L ALIG M T S CTIO

INDEX

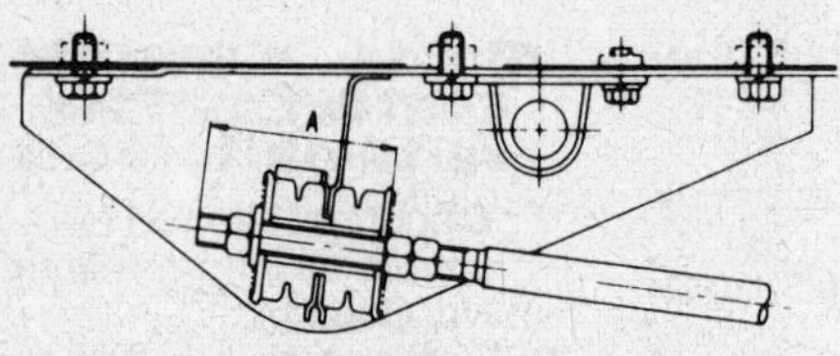

Fig. 1 Caster adjustment. Exc. Ram 50, Ram Raider & 1985–87 Colt

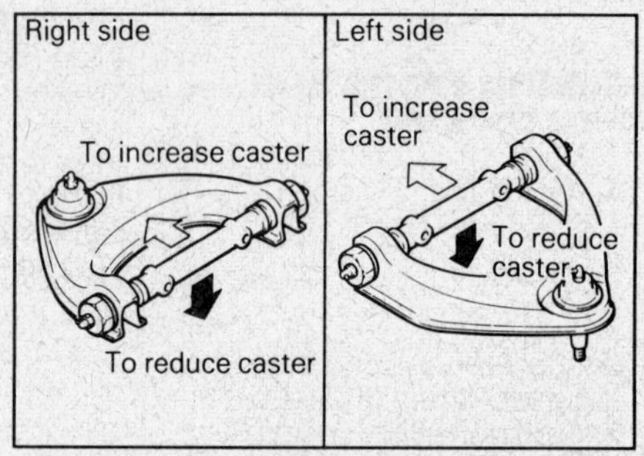

Fig. 2 Caster adjustment. Ram Raider & 1983–86 Ram 50

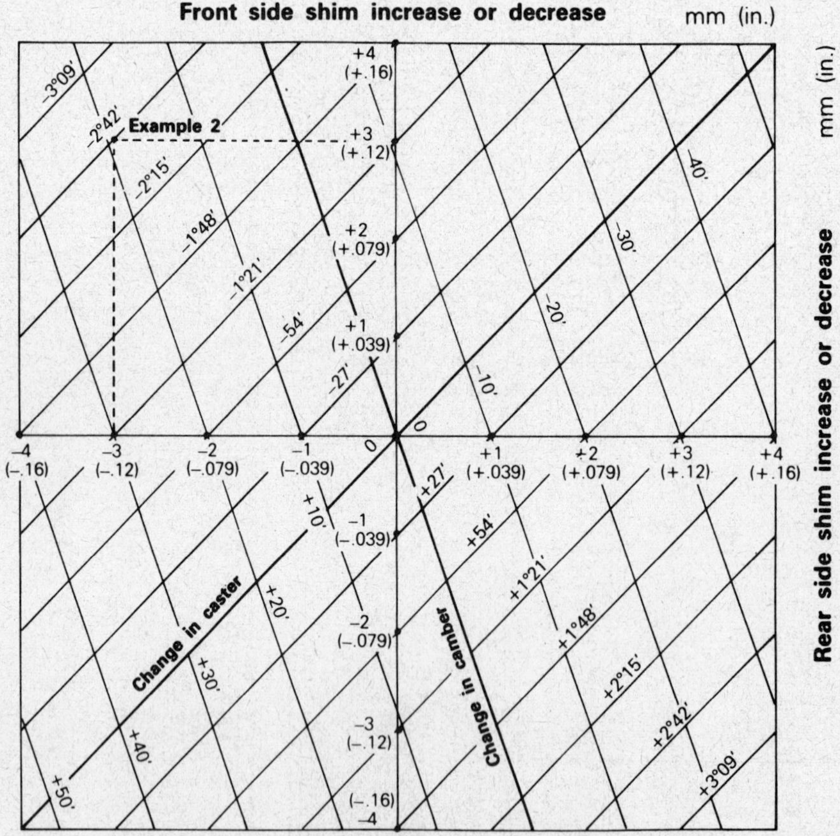

Fig. 3 Caster & camber adjusting shim selection chart. 1987 Ram 50

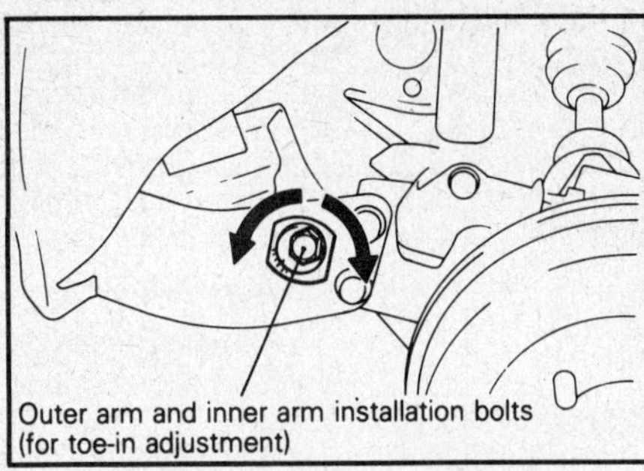

Fig. 4 Rear toe adjustment. Colt Vista

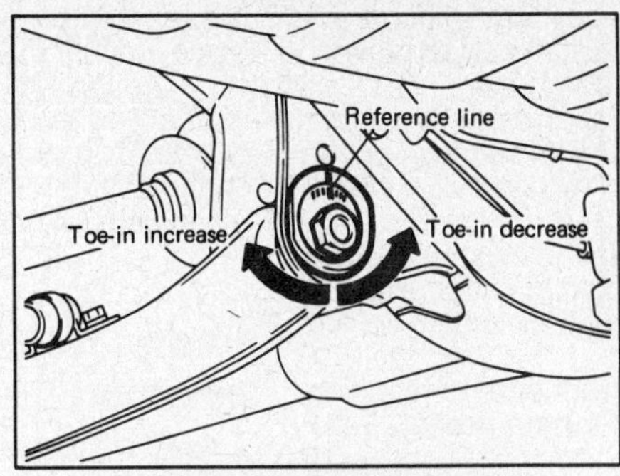

Fig. 5 Rear toe adjustment. Conquest

PRELIMINARY CHECK

1. Road test vehicle noting any abnormal steering or handling characteristics.
2. Ensure tires are the proper type, correctly inflated and that tires on each axle are the same size.
3. Inspect ball joints, suspension arms, bushings and tie rods, and repair or replace any component that is damaged or excessively worn.
4. Ensure wheel runout is not excessive, and that wheel bearings are properly adjusted.
5. Jounce vehicle several times to settle suspension.
6. Place vehicle on suitable alignment rack following manufacturer's instructions. On Ram 50 and Ram Raider models, remove hub cap and cotter pin (2WD) or free wheeling hub (4WD), and attach alignment gauges to wheel hub.
7. Check and correct alignment angles in the following sequence: Rear toe and camber, caster, front camber and front toe.
8. Correct any angle that is not within specifications. If no adjustment is possible, check for damaged or worn suspension components and/or damaged or distorted chassis and correct as needed.

ADJUSTMENTS

CASTER

ALL EXC. RAM 50, RAM RAIDER & 1985–87 COLT

Caster normally requires no adjustment. However, slight adjustments can be made by moving the strut bar nut, **Fig. 1.** After adjustment, ensure that variation between left and right sides is less than 1/2°.

RAM RAIDER & 1983–86 RAM 50

Caster is adjusted by turning the upper control arm shaft as follows:

1. Remove upper control arm.
2. Rotate upper control arm shaft to alter caster setting, **Fig. 2.** One half turn of the upper control arm shaft will cause the upper arm shaft to move approximately .049 inch forward or rearward, resulting in approximately 17 minute (17/60°) change in caster setting.
3. Reinstall control arm and recheck caster.
4. Repeat adjustment until caster is within specifications. Maximum variation between left and right sides should be less than 1/2°.

1985–87 COLT

Caster is pre-set at the factory and is not adjustable. If caster is out of specifications, replace bent or otherwise damaged parts.

1987 RAM 50

Caster and camber are adjusted together by adding or removing shims from between the upper control arm shaft and crossmember.

1. Check alignment angles following equipment manufacturer's instructions.
2. If caster and/or camber are not within specifications, loosen nuts securing upper control arm shaft to crossmember.
3. Increase or decrease thickness of shims between control arm shaft and crossmember, noting the following:
   a. Refer to chart, **Fig. 3,** to select proper shims.
   b. Do not use more than 4 shims at one location.
   c. Difference in shim thickness between front and rear bolts must not exceed .16 inch (4 mm).

CAMBER

FRONT

Exc. Ram 50 & Ram Raider

The specified camber is built into the steering knuckle, which is part of the strut assembly, and no adjustment is provided.

1983–86 Ram 50 W/2 Wheel Drive

1. Using tool No. MB990805 to hold upper arm shaft to crossmember bolt in position, remove nut from engine compartment side and adjust the number of shims between upper arm shaft and crossmember.
2. The normal shim pack thickness is .16 inch. A change of .024 inch in thickness of the shim pack will provide a change of approximately 2/15 degree in camber adjustment.

Ram Raider & 1983–86 Ram 50 W/4 Wheel Drive

Adjust number of shims between upper arm shaft and arm post of side frame. The normal shim package thickness is .12 inch. A change of .039 inch in thickness of shim pack will provide a change of approximately 13 minutes in camber adjustment. Camber adjusting shims are available in thicknesses of .039 and .079 inch.

1987 Ram 50

Refer to caster adjustment for procedure.

REAR

Rear camber is pre-set during vehicle assembly and cannot be adjusted. If camber is not within specifications, check for worn or damaged suspension component, and damaged or deformed floor pan or body and repair as needed.

TOE-IN

FRONT

Except Challenger, Sapporo & Colt Vista

On Colt models, remove outer bellows clip from tie rod before adjusting toe. After completing adjustment, reinstall clamp.

The amount of toe-in of the left front wheel is reduced by turning the tie rod turnbuckle toward the front of the car and the amount of toe-in on the right front wheel is reduced by turning it toward the rear of the the car. After adjustment, the difference in length between the two tie rods should not exceed .2 inch (5 mm).

Challenger & Sapporo

1. While holding tie rod end in position, loosen left tie outer locknut.
2. Position a wooden block between lower control arm and inner end of left tie rod, then loosen inner locknut.
3. Adjust tie rod by rotating the left tie rod, then torque locknuts to 36-40 ft. lbs.
4. After completing adjustment, tighten tie rod locknuts and measure difference in length between both tie rods. The difference in length between left and right tie rods should not exceed .2 inch. If difference exceeds .2 inch, adjust right hand tie rod as follows:
   a. Remove wheel and tire assembly, then remove brake caliper and support with brake hose attached.

Suspend caliper assembly from frame using a wire hook, to prevent damage to brake hose.

b. Remove tie rod end cotter pin and nut, then using a suitable puller, disconnect tie rod end from steering knuckle.
c. Loosen tie rod end locknut and adjust tie rod length by rotating tie rod end. Then torque locknut to 36-40 ft. lbs.
d. Connect tie rod end to steering knuckle, then torque nut to 25-33 ft. lbs.
e. Reinstall caliper assembly and wheel.

Colt Vista

Adjust toe-in by removing the left and right tie rod turnbuckle retaining clips, then turning the left and right turnbuckles the same amount in opposite directions. To reduce toe-in, turn the left turnbuckle toward the front of the vehicle and the right turnbuckle toward the rear of the vehicle. For each half turn of the turnbuckle, toe-in will be adjusted by approximately .24 inch.

REAR

Exc. Colt Vista & Conquest

Rear toe is pre-set during vehicle assembly and cannot be adjusted. If toe is not within specifications, check for worn or damaged suspension components, and damaged or deformed floor pan or body and repair as needed.

Colt Vista

Toe is adjustable by rotating the outer and inner arm mounting bolts. If toe-in is not within specifications, rotate left and right outer arm and inner arm bolts, each by the same amount, to perform adjustment. An adjustment of approximately .08 inch (2 mm) will be made when the outer arm and inner arm bolts are turned the equivalent of 1 alignment mark, **Fig. 4.**

Conquest

Toe-in is adjusted by rotating the lower control arm mounting bolts, **Fig. 5**, as follows:

1. Loosen locknut while holding mounting bolt.
2. Rotate mounting bolts until toe is within specifications. Movement of 1 graduation, **Fig. 5,** will change toe by approximately .08 inch (2 mm). **Rotate left and right mounting bolts equally.**
3. Tighten locknut and recheck setting.
4. Repeat adjustment until toe setting is equal for both wheels and total toe is within specifications.

HONDA (Japan)

INDEX OF SERVICE OPERATIONS

General Engine Specifications

Year	Model	Engine CID ①/cc	Carburetor	Bore and Stroke Inches (mm)	Compression Ratio	Net Brake HP @ RPM	Net Torque Lbs. Ft. @ RPM	Normal Oil Pressure PSI
1983	Accord	4-107/1751	3 Barrel	3.031 x 3.701 (77 x 94)	8.8	75 @ 4500	96 @ 3000	54–65③
	Civic 1300	4-81/1335	3 Barrel	2.83 x 3.23 (72 x 82)	9.3	60 @ 5500	68 @ 4000	48–60③
	Civic 1500	4-91/1488	3 Barrel	2.91 x 3.41 (74 x 86.5)	9.3	67 @ 5000	79 @ 3500	48–60③
	Prelude	4-112/1830	Two 1 Bbls.②	3.15 x 3.58 (80 x 91)	9.4	100 @ 5500	104 @ 4000	54–65③
1984	Accord	4-112/1830	3 Barrel	3.15 x 3.58 (80 x 91)	9.0	86 @ 5800	98.6 @ 3500	54–65③
	Civic 1300	4-82/1342	3 Barrel	2.91 x 3.07 (74 x 78)	10.0	60 @ 5500	73 @ 3500	48–60③
	Civic 1500	4-91/1488	3 Barrel	2.91 x 3.41 (74 x 86.5)	9.2	76 @ 6000	83.9 @ 3500	48–60③
	Prelude	4-112/1830	Two 1 Bbls.	3.15 x 3.58 (80 x 91)	9.4	100 @ 5500	104 @ 4000	54–65③
1985	Accord	4-112/1830	3 Barrel	3.15 x 3.58 (80 x 91)	9.0	86 @ 5800	99 @ 3500	54–65③
	Accord Sei	4-112/1830	Fuel Injection	3.15 x 3.58 (80 x 91)	8.8	101 @ 5800	109 @ 2500	54–65③
	Civic 1300	4-82/1342	3 Barrel	2.91 x 3.07 (74 x 78)	10	60 @ 5500	73 @ 3500	48–60③
	Civic 1500	4-91/1488	3 Barrel	2.91 x 3.41 (74 x 86.5)	9.2	④	⑤	48–60③
	CRX	4-91/1488	3 Barrel	2.91 x 3.41 (74 x 86.5)	9.6	76 @ 6000	84 @ 3500	48–60③
	CRX (HF)	4-91/1488	3 Barrel	2.91 x 3.41 (74 x 86.5)	10	58 @ 4800	79 @ 2500	48–60③
	CRX (Si)	4-91/1488	Fuel Injection	2.91 x 3.41 (74 x 86.5)	8.7	91 @ 5500	—	48–60③
	Prelude	4-112/1830	Two 1 Bbls.	3.15 x 3.58 (80 x 91)	9.4	100 @ 5500	10 @ 4000	54–65③
1986	Accord	4-119/1955	3 Barrel	3.25 x 3.58 (82.7 x 91)	9.1	98 @ 5500	109 @ 3500	54–65③
	Accord LXi	4-119/1955	Fuel Injection	3.25 x 3.58 (82.7 x 91)	8.8	110 @ 5500	114 @ 4500	54–65③
	Civic 1300	4-82/1342	3 Barrel	2.91 x 3.07 (74 x 78)	10	60 @ 5500	73 @ 3500	48–60③
	Civic 1500	4-91/1488	3 Barrel	2.91 x 3.41 (74 x 86.5)	9.2	④	⑤	48–60③
	Civic Si	4-91/1488	Fuel Injection	2.91 x 3.41 (74 x 86.5)	8.7	91 @ 5500	92 @ 4500	48–60③
	CRX	4-91/1488	3 Barrel	2.91 x 3.41 (74 x 86.5)	9.2	76 @ 6000	84 @ 3500	48–60③
	CRX (HF)	4-91/1488	3 Barrel	2.91 x 3.41 (74 x 86.5)	9.6	58 @ 4500	79 @ 2500	48–60③
	CRX (Si)	4-91/1488	Fuel Injection	2.91 x 3.41 (74 x 86.5)	8.7	91 @ 5500	93 @ 4500	48–60③
	Prelude	4-112/1829	Two 1 Bbls.	3.15 x 3.58 (80 x 91)	9.1	100 @ 5500	107 @ 4000	54–65③
	Prelude Si	4-119/1955	Fuel Injection	3.26 x 3.58 (82.7 x 91)	8.8	110 @ 5500	114 @ 4500	54–65③
1987	Accord DX	4-119/1955	3 Barrel	3.25 x 3.58 (82.7 x 91)	9.1	98 @ 5500	109 @ 3500	54–65③
	Civic 1300	4-82/1342	3 Barrel	2.91 x 3.07 (74 x 78)	10	60 @ 5500	73 @ 3500	48–60③
	Civic 1500	4-91/1488	3 Barrel	2.91 x 3.41 (74 x 86.5)	9.2	④	⑤	48–60③
	CRX (HF)	4-91/1488	3 Barrel	2.91 x 3.41 (74 x 86.5)	9.3	58 @ 4500	79 @ 2500	48–60③
	CRX (Si)	4-91/1488	Fuel Injection	2.91 x 3.41 (74 x 86.5)	8.7	91 @ 5500	93 @ 4500	48–60③
	Prelude Si	4-119/1955	Fuel Injection	3.26 x 3.58 (82.7 x 91)	8.8	110 @ 5500	114 @ 4500	54–65③

—Not available.
①—Cubic inch displacement.
②—With additional 1 barrel carburetor to feed prechambers.
③—At 3000 RPM.
④—Exc. 4WD Wagon, 76 @ 6000; 4WD Wagon, 74 @ 6000.
⑤—Exc. 4WD Wagon, 84 @ 3500; 4WD Wagon, 83 @ 3500.

Alternator & Regulator Specifications

Year	Model	Alternator				Voltage Regulator		
		Rated Hot Output	Field Current 12 Volts @ 80 °F	OUtput @ 14 Volts		Air Gap In.	Point Gap In.	Voltage @ 125°F
				2000 RPM	5000 RPM			
1983	Accord	60	—	43	60	—	—	13.8–14.4
	Civic	45	—	35	52	—	—	13.5–14.5
	Prelude	60	—	43	60	—	—	13.8–14.4
1984	Accord	65	—	40	65	—	—	—
	Civic	②	—	25	55	—	—	—
	Prelude	60	—	45	60	—	—	13.8–14.4
1985	Accord	65	—	40⑤	65⑤	—	—	—
	Civic	55	—	③⑤	④⑤	—	—	—
	Prelude	60	—	43	60	—	—	—
1985–87	Accord	65	—	45③	65③	—	—	13.9–15.1
	Civic, CRX④	55	—	25③	54③	—	—	—
	CRX HF	60	—	30③	59③	—	—	—
1986–87	Prelude⑤	60	—	43	60	—	—	13.8–14.4
	Prelude①	65	—	43③	65③	—	—	13.9–15.1

—Not available.
①—Fuel injected engine.
②—Exc. Coupe, 45 amps.; Coupe, 55 amps.
③—Output @ 13.5 volts.
④—Exc. HF.
⑤—Carbureted engine.

Starting Motor Specifications

Year	Model	Brush Spring Tension Lbs.	No Load Test			Torque Test		
			Amperes	Volts	RPM	Amperes	Volts	Torque Ft. Lbs.
1983	Accord	3–4.5	90	11.5	3500	350	8.5	9.8
	Civic	3.2–4.5⑥	90①	11.5②	3000③	230④	8	4.7⑤
	Prelude	4.6	90	11.5	3500	350	8.5	13.5
1984	Accord	⑦	—	—	—	350	8.0	—
	Civic	⑧	—	—	—	350	8.0	—
	Prelude	⑦	—	—	—	350	8.0	—
1985–86	Accord, Prelude	⑦	—	—	—	350	8.0	—
	Civic, CRX	⑥⑨	—	—	—	⑩	⑪	—
1987	Accord, Prelude	⑦	—	—	—	350	8.0	—
	Civic, CRX	⑨	—	—	—	⑩	⑪	—

—Not available
①—Calif., Nippondenso model 50; Hitachi model 70.
②—Calif., 11.
③—Calif., Nippondenso model 5000; Hitachi model 6000.
④—Calif., 200.
⑤—Calif., 3.3.
⑥—Calif., Nippondenso models, 2.2–3.0 lbs.; Hitachi models, 3.2–3.9 lbs.
⑦—With Mitsuba starter, 4.6 lbs.; with ND starter, 3.7 lbs.
⑧—Calif. models with ND starter, 2.6 lbs., with Hitachi starter, 3.5 lbs.; Fed. & High Alt. models with ND starter, 3.8 lbs., with Mitsuba starter, 4.6 lbs.
⑨—Hitachi starter, 3.5 lbs.; Mitsuba starter, 4.6 lbs.; ND 0.8 Kw starter, 2.6 lbs.; ND 1.0 Kw and 1.4 Kw starters, 3.8 lbs.
⑩—0.8 Kw starter, 200 amps; 1.0 Kw starter, 230 amps; 1.4 Kw starter, 350 amps.
⑪—0.8 Kw and 1.4 Kw starters, 8 volts; 1.0 Kw starter, 8.5 volts.

Piston, Pins, Rings, Crankshaft & Bearings

			Ring End Gap ① ②			Rod Bearings		Main Bearings			
Year	Model	Piston Clearance ①	Comp.	Oil	Wristpin Diameter	Shaft Diameter	Bearing Clearance	Shaft Diameter	Bearing Clearance	Thrust on Bear. No.	Shaft Endplay
1983	Accord	.0004	.006	.012	.7076	1.6526–1.6535	.0008–.0015	1.9687–1.9697	.0010–.0022	4	.004–.014
	Civic 1300	.0004	.006	.012	.6692	1.5739–1.5748	.0008–.0015	1.9676–1.9685	.0009–.0017	4	.004–.014
	Civic 1500	.0004	.006	.012	.6692	1.6526–1.6535	.0008–.0015	1.9687–1.9803	.0010–.0022	4	.004–.014
	Prelude	.0005	.008	.008	.7873	1.7707–1.7717	.0008–.0015	1.9687–1.9697	.0008–.0019	3	.004–.014
1984	Accord	.0008	.008	.008	.7873	1.7707–1.7717	.0008–.0015	1.9685–1.9694	.0010–.0022	3	.004–.014
	Civic 1300	.0004	.006	.008	.7479	1.4951–1.4961	.0008–.0015	1.7707–1.7717	.0009–.0016	4	.004–.014
	Civic 1500	.0004	.006	.008	.7479	1.6526–1.6535	.0008–.0015	1.9676–1.9685	.0009–.0016	4	.004–.014
	Prelude	.0008	.008	.008	.7873	1.7707–1.7717	.0008–.0015	1.9673–1.9683	.0010–.0022	3	.004–.014
1985	Accord	.0008	.008	.008	.7873	1.7707–1.7717	.0008–.0015	1.9685–1.9694	.0010–.0022	3	.004–.014
	③	.0004	.006	.008	.7479	1.4951–1.4961	.0008–.0015	1.7707–1.7717	.0009–.0017	4	.004–.014
	Civic, CRX ④	.0004	.006	.008	.7479	1.6526–1.6535	.0008–.0015	1.9676–1.9685	.0009–.0017	4	.004–.014
	Prelude	.0008	.008	.008	.7873	1.7707–1.7717	.0008–.0015	1.9673–1.9683	.0010–.0022	3	.004–.014
1986	Accord	.0008	⑤	.008	.7873	1.7707–1.7717	.0008–.0015	1.9673–1.9683	⑥	3	.004–.014
	③	.0004	.006	.008	.7479	1.4951–1.4961	.0008–.0015	1.7707–1.7717	.0009–.0017	4	.004–.014
	Civic, CRX ④	.0004	.006	.008	.7479	1.6526–1.6535	.0008–.0015	1.9679–1.9685	.0009–.0017	4	.004–.014
	Prelude ⑦	.0008	.008	.008	.7873	1.7707–1.7717	.0008–.0015	1.9673–1.9683	.0010–.0022	3	.004–.014
	Prelude ⑧	.0008	⑤	.008	.7873	1.7707–1.7717	.0008–.0015	1.9673–1.9683	⑥	3	.004–.014
1987	Accord	.0008	⑤	.008	.7873	1.7707–1.7717	.0008–.0015	⑨	⑥	3	.004–.014
	③	.0004	.006	.008	.7479	1.4951–1.4961	.0008–.0015	1.7707–1.7717	.0009–.0017	4	.004–.014
	Civic, CRX ④	.0004	.006	.012	.7479	1.6526–1.6535	.0008–.0015	1.9679–1.9685	.0009–.0017	4	.004–.014
	Prelude ⑦	.0008	⑩	.008	.7873	1.7707–1.7717	.0008–.0015	1.9673–1.9683		3	.004–.014
	Prelude ⑧	.0008	⑪	.008	.7873	1.7707–1.7717	.0008–.0015	1.9673–1.9683	⑥	3	.004–.014

—Not available.
①—Minimum.
②—Measured with ring .6–.8 inch from bottom of bore.
③—Civic 1300 & CRX HF.
④—Exc. Civic 1300 & CRX HF.
⑤—Top, 0.008 inch; second, 0.010 inch.
⑥—Exc. journal No. 3, 0.0010–0.0022 inch; journal No. 3, 0.0013–0.0024 inch.
⑦—Carbureted engine.
⑧—Fuel injected engine.
⑨—Journal No. 1, 1.9676–1.9685 inch; journal No. 3, 1.9671–1.9680 inch; journal Nos. 2, 4 and 5, 1.9673–1.9683 inch.
⑩—Top, .006 inch; second, .008 inch.
⑪—Top, .008 inch; second, .012 inch.

Valve Specifications

Year	Model	Valve Lash			Valve Angles		Valve Spring Inst Height Inches	Valve Spring Pressure Lbs. @ In.	Stem Clearance			Stem Diameter		
		Int.	Exh.	Aux.	Seat	Face			Intake	Exhaust	Auxiliary	Intake	Exhaust	Auxiliary
1983	Civic 1300 & 1500	.006	.008	.006	45	45	⑥	⑩	.0008–.002	.0025–.0037	.0009–.0023	.2591–.2594	.2574–.2578	.2587–.2593
	Accord	.006	.011	.006	45	45	⑨	⑩	.001–.002	.002–.004	.0009–.0023	.2748–.2751	.2732–.2736	.2587–.2593
	Prelude	.006	.011	.006	45	45	⑪	⑫	.001–.002	.002–.004	.001–.002	.2591–.2594	.2732–.2736	.2587–.2593
1984	Accord	.006	.011	.006	45	45	⑧	①	.001–.002	.002–.004	.001–.002	.2591–.2954	.2732–.2736	.2587–.2593
	Civic 1300 & 1500	.008	.010	.008	45	45	1.69	⑦	.001–.002	.002–.003	.001–.002	.2591–.2594	.2579–.2583	.2587–.2593
	Prelude	.006	.011	—	45	45	②	③	.001–.002	.002–.004	—	.2591–.2594	.2732–.2736	—
1985	Accord④	.006	.011	.006	45	45	—	—	.001–.002	.002–.004	.001–.002	.2591–.2594	.2732–.2736	.2587–.2593
	Accord⑤	.006	.011	—	45	45	—	—	.001–.002	.002–.004	—	.2591–.2594	.2732–.2736	—
	Civic 1300 & 1500 ④	.008	.010	.008	45	45	—	—	.001–.002	.002–.003	.001–.002	.2591–.2594	.2579–.2583	.2587–.2593
	CRX 1500 HF④	.008	.010	.008	45	45	—	—	.001–.002	.002–.003	.001–.002	.2591–.2594	.2579–.2583	.2587–.2593
	CRX 1500 Si⑤	.008	.010	—	45	45	—	—	.001–.002	.002–.003	—	.2591–.2594	.2579–.2583	—
	Prelude⑤	.006	.011	—	45	45	—	—	.001–.002	.002–.004	—	.2591–.2594	.2732–.2736	—
1986	Accord	.006	.011	—	45	45	—	—	.001–.002	.002–.004	—	.2591–.2594	.2732–.2736	—
	Civic, CRX④	.008	.010	.008	45	45	—	—	.001–.002	.002–.003	.001–.002	.2591–.2594	.2576–.2583	.2587–.2593
	Civic, CRX⑤	.008	.010	—	45	45	—	—	.001–.002	.002–.003	—	.2591–.2594	.2576–.2583	—
	Prelude	.006	.011	—	45	45	—	—	.001–.002	.002–.004	—	.2591–.2594	.2732–.2736	—
1987	Accord	.006	.011	—	45	45	—	—	.001–.002	.002–.004	—	.2591–.2594	.2732–.2736	—
	Civic, CRX④	.008	.010	.008	45	45	—	—	.002–.004	.004–.006	.001–.002	.2591–.2594	.2576–.2583	.2587–.2593
	Civic, CRX⑤	.008	.010	—	45	45	—	—	.002–.004	.004–.006	—	.2591–.2594	.2576–.2583	—
	Prelude	.006	.011	—	45	45	—	—	.001–.002	.002–.004	—	.2591–.2594	.2732–.2736	—

①—Intake valve spring, 228.2 @ 1.66 inch. Exhaust valve: inner spring, 10.9 @ 1.46 in.; outer spring, 36.5 @ 1.67 inch. Auxiliary valve spring, 22.45 @ .98 in.

②—Intake valve spring, 1.66 inch. Exhaust valve: inner spring, 1.46 in.; outer spring, 1.67 in.

③—Intake valve spring, 52 @ 1.66 inch. Exhaust valve: inner spring, 10.9 @ 1.46 in.; outer spring, 36.6 @ 1.67 in.

④—Carbureted engine.

⑤—Fuel injected engine.

⑥—Intake & exhaust inner spring, 1.402 inch; intake & exhaust outer spring, 1.488 inch; 1983 1500 & 1300 auxiliary valve spring, .984 inch.

⑦—1300 models, 31.45 @ 1.69; 1500 models, 43 @ 1.69.

⑧—Intake valve spring, 1.66 inch; exhaust valve inner spring, 1.46 inch; exhaust valve outer spring, 1.67 inch; auxiliary valve spring, .98 inch.

⑨—Intake & exhaust inner valve spring, 1.402 inch; intake & exhaust outer valve spring, 1.488 inch; all 1983 models, .98 inch.

⑩—Intake & exhaust inner valve spring, 8.8 @ 1.402; intake & exhaust outer valve spring, 28.25 @ 1.488; 1983 models, 15.45 @ .98.

⑪—Intake valve spring, 1.66 inch; exhaust valve inner spring, 1.46 inch; exhaust valve outer spring, 1.67 inch; auxiliary valve spring, 1.67 inch; auxiliary valve spring, .98 inch.

⑫—Intake valve spring, 52.7 @ 1.66; exhaust valve inner spring, 10.9 @ 1.46; exhaust valve outer spring, 34.5 @ 1.67; auxiliary valve spring, 22.45 @ .98 inch.

Final Drive Gear Specifications

Year	Model	Carrier Type	Final Driven Gear Backlash		Differential Side Clearance ④		Pinion To Side Gear Backlash	
			Method	Clearance In.	Method	Clearance In.	Method	Clearance In.
1983	Civic	①	—	.006–.008	③	.006 Max.	②	.002–.006
1983–84	Accord, Prelude	①	—	.006–.008	③	.006 Max.	②	.002–.006
1984	Civic	①	—	.0029–.0052	③	.006 Max.	②	.002–.006
1985	Accord	①	—	.006–.008	③	.006	②	.002–.006
	Civic, CRX	①	—	⑤	③	.006	②	.002–.006
	Prelude	①	—	.006–.008	③	.006	②	.002–.006
1986–87	Accord	①	—	.0033–.0059	③	.006	②	.002–.006
	Civic, CRX	①	—	.0029–.0052	③	.006	②	.002–.006
	Prelude	①	—	.006–.008	③	.006	②	.002–.006

—Not available.
①—Integral with trans.
②—Thrust washers.
③—Selective fit snap ring.
④—Measured between snap ring & outer bearing race.

Rear Axle Specifications

Year	Model	Carrier Type	Ring Gear & Pinion Backlash (Inch)		Pinion Bearing Preload (Inch Lbs.)		Differential Bearing Preload (Inch Lbs.)	
			Method	Adjustment	Method	Adjustment	Method	Adjustment
1985–87	Civic Wagon 4WD	Removable	Shim	.0043–.0063	Spacer	10–13	Shim	3.4–5.2

Engine Tightening Specifications

*Torque specifications are for clean and lightly lubricated threads only. Dry or dirty threads produce increased friction which prevents accurate measurement of tightness.

Year	Model	Spark Plugs Ft. Lbs.	Cylinder Head Bolts Ft. Lbs.	Intake Manifold Ft. Lbs.	Exhaust Manifold Ft. Lbs.	Camshaft Carrier Bolts Ft. Lbs.	Connecting Rod Cap Bolts Ft. Lbs.	Main Bearing Cap Bolts Ft. Lbs.	Flywheel to Crankshaft Ft. Lbs.
1983	Accord	13	44	16	16	①	21	48	⑥
	Civic	13	44	16	16	④	21	⑤	③
	Prelude	13	49	16	20	①	23	48	⑥
1984	Accord & Prelude	13	49	16	22	①	23	48	⑥
	Civic	13	44	16	23	16	20	36	②
1985	Accord	13	49	16	23	①	23	48	⑥
	Civic, CRX	13	43	16	17	16	20	36	⑥
	Prelude	13	49	16	20	①	23	48	⑥
1986–87	Accord	13	49	16	23	①	23	49	⑥
	Civic, CRX	13	43	16	23	16	20	33 ⑦	⑥
	Prelude	13	49	16	23	①	23	49	⑥

①—6 mm bolts, 9 ft. lbs; 8 mm bolts 16 ft. lbs.
②—Auto. trans., 54 ft. lbs.; man. trans., 86 ft. lbs.
③—Auto. trans., 35 ft. lbs.; man. trans., 51 ft. lbs.
④—M6 bolts, 8 ft. lbs.; M8 bolts, 16 ft. lbs.
⑤—1300 models, 29 ft. lbs.; 1500 models, 33 ft. lbs.
⑥—Auto trans., 54 ft. lbs.; man. trans, 76 ft. lbs.
⑥—1987 Civic, 36 ft. lbs.

Brake Specifications

Year	Model	Brake Drum Inside Diameter ①	Disc Brake Rotor Specifications					
			Nominal Thickness		Minimum Thickness		Thickness Variation (Parallelism)	Run Out (T.I.R.)
			Front	Rear	Front	Rear		
1983	Accord	7.91	.670	—	.600	—	.0006	.006
	Civic 1300	7.13	⑤	—	⑥	—	.0006	.006
	Civic 1500	②	.470	—	.390	—	.0006	.006
	Prelude	7.91	.750	—	.670	—	.0006	.006
1984	Accord	7.91	.750	—	.670	—	.0006	.006
	Civic 1300	7.13	⑦	—	③	—	.0006	.006
	Civic 1500	②	.670	—	.590	—	.0006	.006
	Prelude	—	.750	.390	.670	.310	.0006	.004
1985	Accord	7.91	.750	—	.670	—	.0006	.004
	Civic 1300	7.13	.470	—	390	—	.0006	.004
	Civic 1500, CRX④	②	.670	—	.590	—	.0006	.004
	CRX HF	7.13	.430	—	.350	—	.0006	.004
	Prelude	—	.750	.390	.670	.310	.0006	.004
1986–87	Accord	7.91	.750	—	.670	—	.0006	.006
	Civic 1300	7.13	.470	—	390	—	.0006	.004
	Civic 1500, CRX④	②	.670	—	.590	—	.0006	.004
	CRX HF	7.13	.430	—	.350	—	.0006	.004

—Not available.
①—Service limit.
②—Exc. Wagon, 7.13 inches; Wagon, 7.91 inches.
③—Coupe, .350 inch; Hatchback, .390 inch.
④—Exc. CRX HF.
⑤—Exc. 4 speed manual trans., .470 inch; 4 speed manual trans., .430 inch.
⑥—Exc. 4 speed manual trans., .390 inch; 4 speed manual trans., .350 inch.
⑦—Coupe, .430 inch; Hatchback, .470 inch.

Wheel Alignment Specifications

Year	Model	Caster Angle, Degrees		Camber Angle, Degrees				King Pin Inclination	Toe-Out Inch	
				Limits		Desired				
		Limits	Desired	Front	Rear	Front	Rear		Front	Rear
1983	Accord	+5/12 to +2 5/12	+1 5/12	−1 to +1	−1 to +1	0	0	12 1/2°	0	0
	Civic 1300, 1500	+1 1/20 to +3 1/20	+2 1/20	−1 to +1	−3/4 to +1/4	0	−1/4	12 1/3°	0	−.078
	Civic①	+1 1/20 to +3 1/20	+2 1/20	−1 to +1	−3/4 to +1/4	0	−1/4	12 1/3°	0	−.078
	Civic②	+3/10 to +2 3/10	+1 3/10	−1 to +1	−1 to +1	0	0	12 1/3°	0	0
	Prelude	−1/2 to + 1/2	0	−1 to +1	—	0	—	6 51/60°	0	−.078
1984	Accord	+5/12 to +2 5/12	+1 5/12	−to +1	—	0	—	12 1/2°	0	0
	Civic① ③	+1 1/3 to +3 1/3	+2 1/3	−1 to +1	−1/2 to −1	0	−3/4	12 5/6°	0	−.078
	Civic②	+1 1/12 to +3 1/12	+2 1/12	−1 to +1	−1/2 to −1	0	−3/4	12°	0	−.078
	Civic④	+1 5/12 to +3 5/12	+2 5/12	−1 to +1	−1/2 to −1	0	−3/4	12 11/12°	0	−.078
	Prelude	−1/2 to + 1/2	0	−1 to +1	—	0	—	6 51/60°	0	−.078
1985	Accord	+1/2 to +2 1/2	+1 1/2	0	0	0	0	12 1/2°	0	.08
	Civic CRX Si	+1 5/12 to +3 5/12	+2 5/12	−5/6 to +1 1/6	−1 to −1/2	−1/6	−3/4	13°	0	.08
	Civic 4WD Wagon	+11/12 to +2 11/12	+1 11/12	−1/3 to +1 2/3	—	+2/3	—	11 5/12°	0	—
	Civic Wagon Exc. 4WD	+1 to +3	+2	−1 to +1	−1 to −1/2	0	−3/4	12°	0	2
	Civic Exc. CRX Si & Wagon	⑤	⑥	−1 to +1	−1 to −1/2	0	−3/4	13°	0	2
	Prelude	0	0	0	0	0	0	7°	0	.08
1986–87	Accord	−1/2 to +1 1/2	+1/2	−1 to +1	−1 to +1	0	0	6 5/6°	0	−0
	Civic Exc. Wagon	⑤	⑥	−1 to +1	−1 to −1/2	0	−3/4	13°	0	−.08
	Civic Wagon Exc. 4WD	+1 to +3	+2	−1 to +1	−1 to −1/2	0	−3/4	12°	0	−.08
	Civic 4WD Wagon	+11/12 to +2 11/12	+1 11/12	−1/3 to +1 2/3	−1 to +1	+2/3	0	11 5/12°	0	0
	CRX	+1 5/12 to +3 5/12	+2 5/12	−1 1/6 to −5/6	−1 to −1/2	−1/6	−3/4	13°	0	−.079
	Prelude	−1/2 to +1/2	0	−1 to +1	−1 to +1	0	0	6 5/6°	0	−.079

Continued

WHEEL ALIGNMENT SPECIFICATIONS—Continued

—Not available.
①—Sedan.
②—Station Wagon.
③—Hatchback.
④—Coupe.
⑤—Without power steering, +1½° to +3½°; with power steering, +2° to +4°.
⑥—Without power steering, +2½°, with power steering, +3°.

Cooling System & Capacity Data

Year	Model	Cooling Capacity Qts.	Radiator Cap Relief Pressure, Lbs.	Thermo. Opening Temp.	Fuel Tank Gals.	Engine Oil Refill Qts. w/filter	Transmission Oil		
							4 Speed Pts.	5 Speed Pts.	Auto. Trans. Pts.
1983	Accord	6②	11–14	203	15.8	3.2	—	5.0	6.0
	Civic 1300	4.8②	11–15	203	10.8	3.7	5.6	5.6	—
	Civic 1500	5.8②	11–15	203	10.8	3.7	5.6	5.2	5.2
	Prelude	①⑤	11-15	203	15.8	4.2	—	5.0	6.0
1984	Accord	5.6②	11–15	203	15.8	4.2	—	5.0	6.0
	Civic 1300	4.8①	11–15	196	⑥	3.7	4.8	4.8	—
	Civic 1500	6.0①	11–15	196	⑥	3.7	4.8	4.8	6.0
	Prelude	①⑤	11–15	203	15.8	4.2	—	5.0	6.0
1985	Accord, Prelude	7.2①	11–15	203	15.9	3.7	—	5.0	6.0
	Civic 1300	4.8①	11–15	196	11.9	3.7	4.8	4.8	6.0
	Civic 1500, CRX⑦	6.0①	11–15	196	⑧	3.7	4.8	4.8	6.0
	CRX HF	4.8①	11–15	196	10.0	3.7	—	4.8	—
1986–87	Accord	⑨	11–15	203	15.9	3.7	—	5.2 ⑩	6.4
	Civic 1300	4.8①	11–15	196	11.9	3.7	4.8	4.8	5.0
	Civic 1500, CRX⑦	6.0①	11–15	196	⑧	3.7	4.8	4.8	5.0
	CRX HF	4.8①	11–15	196	10.0	3.7	—	4.8	—
	Prelude	③	11–15	203	15.9	3.7	—	④	⑪

—Not available.
①—Including reserve tank.
②—Not including reserve tank.
③—Exc. carbureted engine w/auto. trans., 7.2 qts.; carbureted engine w/auto. trans., 8.0 qts.
④—Carbureted engine, 5.0 pts.; fuel injected engine, 5.2 pts.
⑤—Man. Trans., 7.2 qts.; Auto. Trans., 8.0 qts.
⑥—Coupe, 10.8 gals.; Hatchback, 11.9 gals.; Sedan & Wagon, 12.1 gals.
⑦—Exc. CRX HF.
⑧—CRX, 10.8 gals.; Civic Hatchback, 11.9 gals.; Civic Sedan & Wagon, 12.1 gals.
⑨—Man. Trans., 6.8 qts.; Auto trans., 7.2 qts.
⑩—1987, 5.0 pts.
⑪—Carbureted engine, 6.0 pts.; fuel injected engine, 6.4 pts.

ELECTRICAL SECTION

INDEX

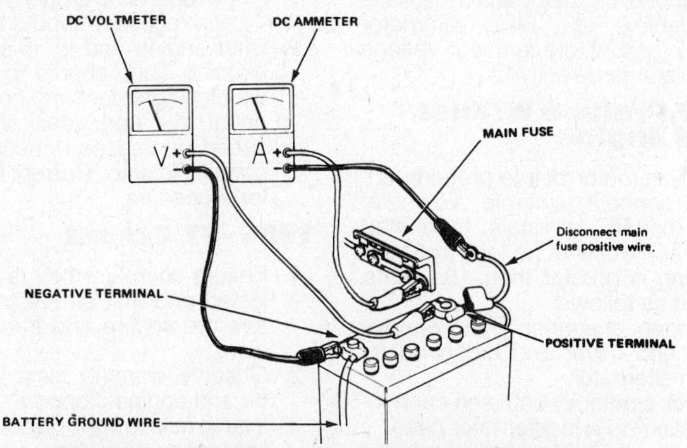

Fig. 1 Connections for alternator performance tests. 1983 models exc. Accord & Prelude

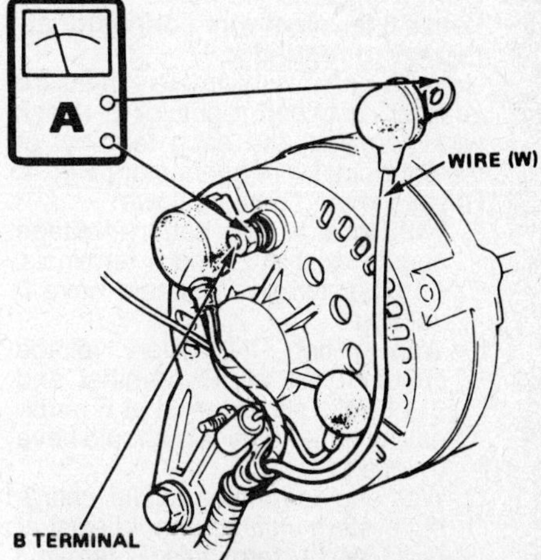

Fig. 2 Connections for alternator performance tests. 1983 Accord & Prelude (1984–87 models similar)

ALTERNATOR IN-VEHICLE TESTING

CURRENT OUTPUT TEST

1983 Civic

1. Connect voltmeter and ammeter as in **Fig. 1**
2. Detach connector from voltage regulator, then connect jumper wire from positive battery terminal to white/red wire to bypass regulator.
3. Start engine and check that output is within specifications. If output is correct, go on to "Voltage Regulator Test."
4. If output is not correct, reconnect regulator connector and detach connector from alternator. Then connect jumper wire from positive battery terminal to white/red pin of alternator.
   a. If output is now correct, check white/red wire between alternator and regulator for open circuit.
   b. If still no output, check alternator white wire between alternator and 55 amp fuse. If there is continuity, repair or replace alternator.

1983 Accord & Prelude & 1984–87 All

1. Connect ammeter as shown in **Fig. 2**, and connect suitable voltmeter across battery terminals.
2. Start engine, turn on headlamps and rear defroster, and set blower fan on high speed.
3. Observe current output on ammeter and voltage reading at battery to compare reading to specifications. **Do not allow voltage reading at battery to exceed 19 volts. If voltage reading is over 19 volts, stop engine and replace voltage regulator.**
4. If readings are not within specifications, inspect charging system and perform "Voltage Regulator Test," repair system as needed, then repeat test.
5. If current output is still not within specifications, repair or replace alternator.

VOLTAGE REGULATOR TEST

1983 Civic

All lights and accessories must be OFF during this test.

1. Connect voltmeter and ammeter as in **Fig. 1.**
2. With engine running, remove negative battery terminal cable.
3. If engine stops immediately, reconnect battery cable and start engine. Then check voltage at black/yellow wire of regulator connector.
   a. If no voltage, check for continuity between 10 amp regulator/fuel pump fuse and connector at regulator.
   b. If voltage is present, check white/red wire for system voltage at all connectors between regulator and alternator. If voltage is present at alternator, check alternator output current. If no voltage at white/red wire at regulator, replace regulator.
4. Vary engine speed from 2000-4000 RPM and check for voltage from 13.5-14.5 volts. If voltage is not within specifications, adjust regulator as follows:
   a. Remove regulator cover without letting it contact any internal parts and reconnect regulator connector.
   b. Bend adjusting tab on voltage relay, **Fig. 3**, upward to increase voltage, or downward to decrease voltage, using long-nose pliers.
   c. Install cover and recheck voltage. If voltage cannot be adjusted, replace regulator.

1983 Accord & 1983–87 Prelude w/Carbureted Engine

1. On Accord models, remove relay box attaching bolts, then the box.

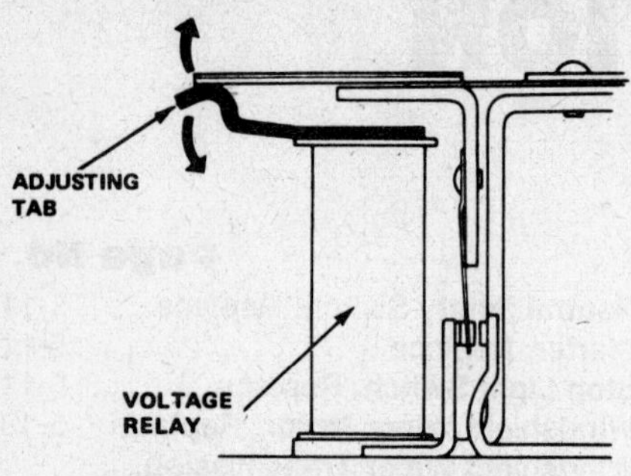

Fig. 3 Adjustment of voltage regulator. 1983 models exc. Accord & Prelude

2. On all models, remove regulator. **Leave 6 terminal wire connector attached to regulator.**
3. Using a suitable voltmeter, measure voltages between regulator E (black wire) terminal and each terminal of the 6 terminal wire connectors, **Fig. 4.** Results should be as follows:
   a. With ignition Off, battery voltage should exist at B and F terminals. All other terminals should have 0 voltage.
   b. With ignition ON, battery voltage should exist at IG terminal and 9-11 volts should exist at F terminal. All other terminals should have 0 voltage.
   c. With engine running at idle, charging system voltage should exist at B, IG and L terminals, P terminal should have approximately 7.5 volts and F terminal should have 5-7.5 volts.
   d. With engine running at 1000 RPM, measure voltage at terminal F. Voltage should be approximately 9 volts. Raise engine speed to 2000 RPM, voltage at terminal F should increase to 11 volts. Raise engine speed to 3000 RPM, voltage at terminal F should increase to 12 volts.
4. If measurements do not fall within the specifications above, check for loose harness coupler, broken wires or blown fuse.
5. If voltage during test 3d is out of specifications, replace regulator.

1986–87 Accord

1. Connect ammeter and voltmeter as outlined in "Current Output Test."
2. With engine running, insert short screwdriver through brush holder screw opening in rear of alternator, **Fig. 5.**
3. While touching brush holder screw, ground screwdriver against alternator cover, and note amperage readings at various speeds. Ground brush holder screw for as short a time as possible. **Do not allow system voltage to exceed 19 volts as electrical system components may be damaged.**
4. Compare current output with specifications, noting the following:
   a. If output is not within specifications and 12 volts is available at the alternator black/yellow wire terminal, alternator is defective.
   b. If output is within specifications when brush holder screw is grounded, regulator and 12 volts is available at the alternator black/yellow wire terminal, voltage regulator is defective.

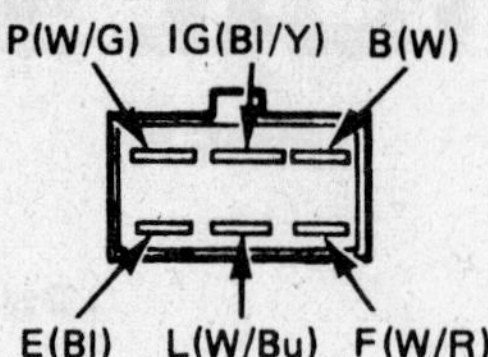

Fig. 4 Voltage regulator test connections. 1983 Accord & 1983–87 Prelude w/carbureted engine

1986–87 Prelude W/Fuel Injected Engine

1. Ensure alternator belt is properly adjusted, connect suitable voltmeter across battery terminals, then start engine and observe no load voltage.
2. If reading is greater than 15.1 volts, proceed as follows:
   a. Remove alternator, then remove rear end cover and brush holder from alternator.
   b. Check continuity between each rotor slip ring and alternator case.
   c. If continuity exists, alternator is defective. If no continuity exists, regulator is defective.
3. If no load voltage is approximately 12 volts, proceed as follows:
   a. Stop engine and ensure B+ terminal at alternator (large diameter wire secured by stud and nut) is properly connected.
   b. Disconnect plug on electrical connector from alternator.
   c. With ignition on, check for voltage at black/yellow wire terminal in connector.
   d. If no voltage is present, check circuit between connector and fuse no. 4 and repair as needed.
   e. If battery voltage is present, check for defective voltage regulator, rectifier or stator and repair as needed.

CHARGE WARNING LAMP TEST

1984–87 Exc. 1986–87 Accord

These models use a voltage regulator that is integral with the alternator. No provision for on-vehicle testing is provided. The following procedure is for testing the charge warning light, but can be helpful for diagnosing the voltage regulator.

1. Turn ignition switch to the On position, the charge warning light should glow. If not, unplug the voltage regulator connector from the alternator and connect the white/blue wire pin to ground, then proceed as follows:
   a. If charge warning light does not glow, check fuses, warning light bulb, wire connectors and related wires for an open circuit. Repair as necessary.
   b. If the charge warning light glows, the regulator warning light relay is not operating properly and the voltage regulator should be replaced.
2. Start engine and let idle, the charge warning light should go off. If the warning light does not go off, or stays on at idle and goes off as engine speed increases, check alternator output. Refer to "Current Output Test" for procedure.

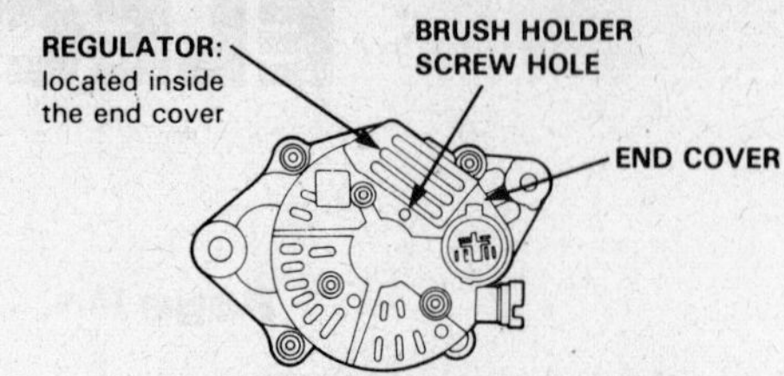

Fig. 5 Grounding brush holder screw to test alternator output

1986–87 Accord

1. Ensure alternator belt is properly adjusted and that all electrical connectors are secure and free from corrosion.
2. Observe warning lamp with ignition on and engine stopped.
3. If lamp fails to light, disconnect electrical connector from alternator and short the white/blue wire terminal in connector to ground.
4. If lamp still does not light, check the following:
   a. Blown no. 1 fuse in dash fuse panel or defective bulb.
   b. Open in black/yellow wire between warning lamp and fuse panel, or between fuse panel and ignition switch.
   c. Open in white/blue wire between alternator and warning lamp.
   d. Poor ground connections.
5. If lamp lights in step 3, check for defective regulator or poor internal connections in alternator.
6. With engine running at idle, charge warning lamp should be off.
7. If lamp remains on, proceed as follows:
   a. Check for blown No. 8 fuse in relay panel or open in white/green wire between relay box and alternator, and repair as needed.
   b. Check alternator output as outlined and repair system if output is not within specifications.
   c. If output is satisfactory but lamp remains on with engine running, proceed with remaining tests.
8. On carbureted engines, proceed as follows:
   a. Stop engine and disconnect choke heater connector. If lamp goes out with engine running, check for defective choke heater.
   b. Stop engine and disconnect 7 terminal connector from EFE heater control. If lamp goes out, check for

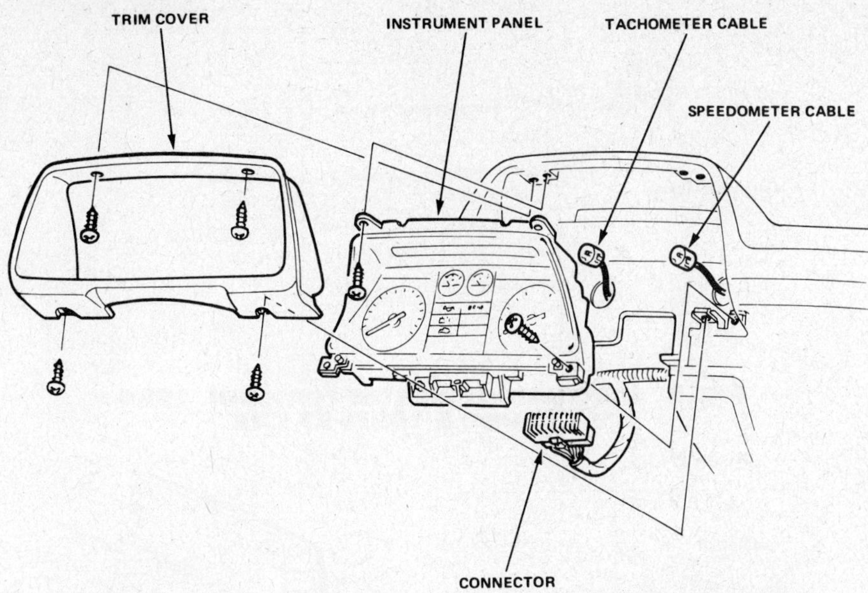

Fig. 6 Instrument cluster assembly. 1983 Civic

defective EFE heater control.

c. If lamp remains on, check for short to ground in blue/white wire between charge warning lamp and choke heater or EFE control unit.

9. On fuel injected engines, proceed as follows:
   a. Stop engine and disconnect electrical connector from alternator.
   b. Turn on ignition and observe lamp.
   c. If lamp, voltage regulator is defective. If lamp remains on, check for short to ground in harness between alternator and charge warning lamp.

STARTER
REPLACE

1. Disconnect battery ground cable.
2. Disconnect all electrical leads at starter.
3. Loosen left and right mounting bolts and remove starter.
4. Reverse procedure to install.

IGNITION LOCK
REPLACE

1. Remove lower steering column cover.
2. Disconnect ignition switch connector.
3. Center punch each of the two shear screw heads, then using a suitable drill and drill bit, remove screw heads and the switch.
4. Install new switch without ignition key inserted.
5. Hand tighten shear screws, insert ignition key, and check for proper operation of wheel lock.
6. Tighten shear screws until hex heads twist off.
7. Reconnect switch connector.
8. Position switch wiring and install lower steering column cover.

IGNITION SWITCH
REPLACE

The following procedure applies to models without the ignition switch built into the ignition lock. For models with the ignition switch built into the ignition lock, the entire lock must be replaced. Refer to "Ignition Lock, Replace" for procedure.

1. Remove the lower steering column cover.
2. Disconnect the ignition switch connector.
3. Insert key and place in the "LOCK" or "O" position.
4. Remove two switch setscrews, then the switch.
5. Reverse procedure to install.

COMBINATION SWITCH
REPLACE

1. Disconnect battery ground cable.
2. Remove steering wheel.
3. Remove steering column upper and lower attaching screws, then remove covers.
4. On models equipped with cruise control, remove cruise control slip ring.
5. Remove turn signal cancelling sleeve.
6. Disconnect wiring harness from switch.
7. Remove screws securing combination switch, then remove switch.
8. Reverse procedure to install.

STOP LIGHT SWITCH
REPLACE

1. Disconnect wiring at switch.
2. Loosen locknut and remove switch.
3. Reverse procedure to install, allowing 0.039-0.196 inch (1-5 mm) brake pedal freeplay.

NEUTRAL SAFETY SWITCH
REPLACE

1. Remove floor console cover.
2. Disconnect electrical connector.
3. Place shift lever in Neutral.
4. Remove the two bolts holding switch to selector lever control assembly and remove switch.
5. To install, position switch slider to Neutral position on all except Accord and Prelude models. On Accord and Prelude models, position switch slider in Park position.
6. Ensure gear selector lever is in Neutral position on all except Accord and Prelude models. On Accord and Prelude models, position gear selector lever in Park position.
7. Position switch with selector lever actuator rod inserted in its slot in switch slider.
8. Hook forward end of switch bracket over forward end of selector lever control assembly and tighten attaching bolts.
9. Plug in electrical connector.
10. Install console cover.

WINDSHIELD WIPER/WASHER SWITCH
REPLACE

The following procedure applies to 1983-85 Prelude models which utilize a removable wiper/washer switch. On all other models, the wiper/washer switch is integral with the combination switch. Refer to "Combination Switch, Replace" for procedure.

1. Remove steering column upper cover.
2. Disconnect electrical connector.
3. Remove wiper/washer switch.
4. Reverse procedure to install.

INSTRUMENT CLUSTER
REPLACE
CIVIC & CRX
1983

1. Lower steering column assembly
2. Remove four screws attaching trim cover and remove.
3. Working behind dashboard, remove speedometer cable and tachometer cable (if equipped) from cluster assembly.
4. Remove instrument cluster mounting screws, then pull cluster assembly partially away from dashboard.
5. Remove upshift indicator connector (if equipped) and instrument connector, **Fig. 6.**
6. Remove instrument cluster assembly.
7. Reverse procedure to install.

1984 Coupe & 1985–87 CRX

1. Remove dashboard lower panel under instrument panel, **Fig. 7.**
2. Remove heater control knob and lower panel, then the heater control mounting screws.

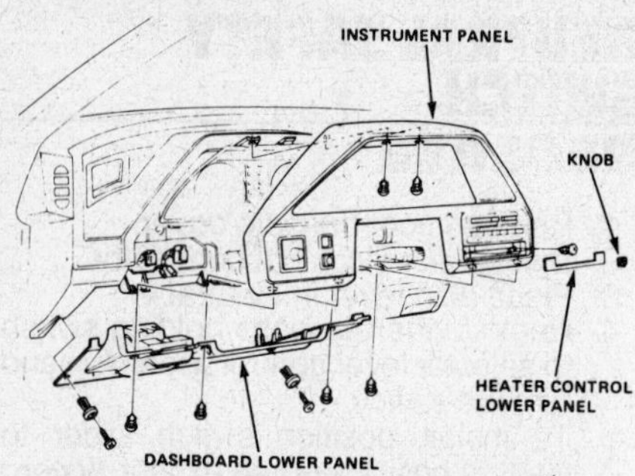

Fig. 7 Instrument panel removal. 1984 Civic Coupe & 1985–87 CRX

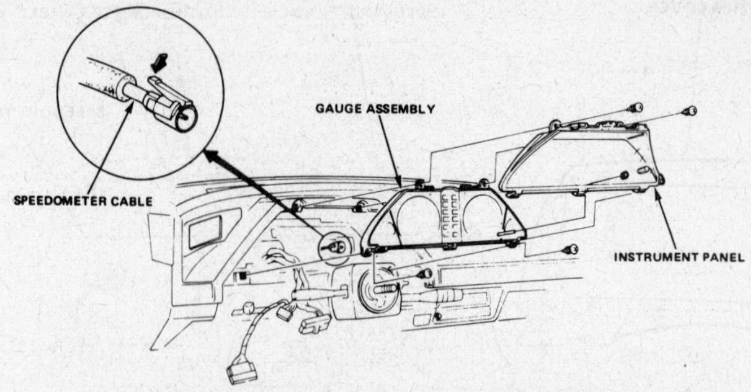

Fig. 8 Instrument cluster removal. 1984 Civic Coupe & 1985–87 CRX

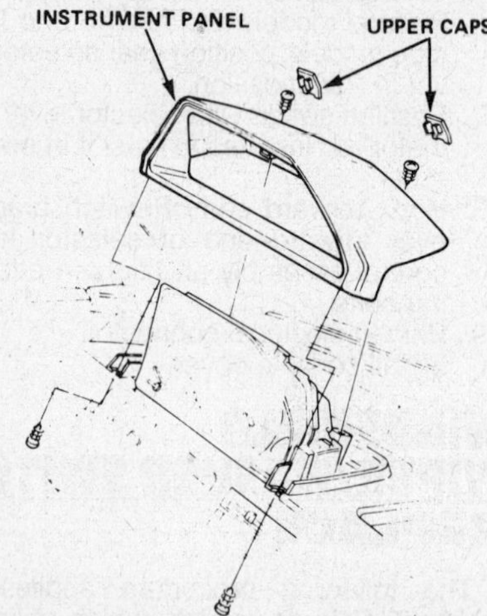

Fig. 9 Instrument panel removal. 1984–87 Civic Hatchback & Sedan

3. Remove instrument panel upper attaching screws.
4. Pull instrument panel slightly away from dashboard, then disconnect electrical connectors and remove panel.
5. Remove four instrument cluster attaching screws, then pull instrument cluster assembly slightly away from dashboard and remove wire connectors.
6. Remove speedometer cable then the instrument cluster, **Fig. 8.**
7. Reverse procedure to install.

1984–87 Hatchback & Sedan

1. Remove instrument panel upper caps, then four mounting screws and the panel, **Fig. 9.**
2. Remove four instrument cluster attaching screws, the lift cluster assembly to gain access to wiring connectors and speedometer cable.
3. Remove wire connectors and speedometer cable, then the instrument cluster assembly.
4. Reverse procedure to install.

1984–87 Wagon

1. Remove dashboard lower panel, **Fig. 10.**
2. Working under dashboard, remove four instrument panel attaching bolts, then disconnect wire connectors and speedometer cable.
3. Remove instrument panel with instrument cluster attached.
4. Remove cluster to panel attaching screws, then the instrument cluster assembly.

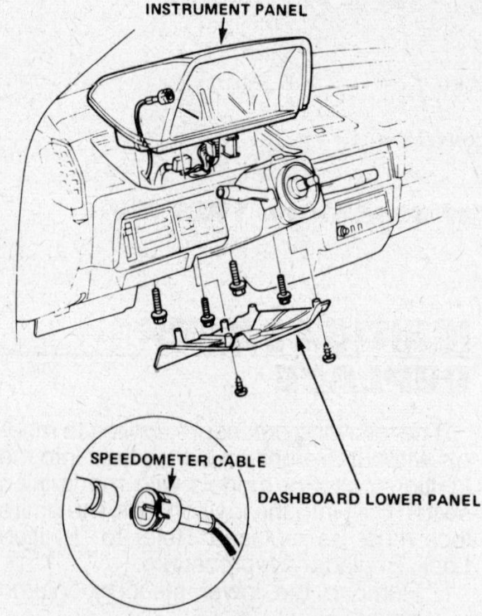

Fig. 10 Instrument panel removal. 1984–87 Civic Wagon

ACCORD

1983

1. Lower steering column assembly.
2. Remove three screws attaching instrument panel, disconnect wire harness and remove panel.
3. Remove four cluster mounting screws. Allow cluster assembly to move forward and disconnect speedometer cable.
4. Disconnect instrument wire harness and remove assembly.
5. Reverse procedure to install.

1984–85

1. Disconnect battery ground cable and remove steering wheel.
2. Remove 3 retaining screws from under upper side of instrument cluster bezel, spray suitable vinyl protector between instrument panel and bezel, then remove bezel. **It may be necessary to pry the bezel upward and insert a suitable puller behind the lower edge of the bezel, Fig. 11, in order to free the bezel from the instrument panel.**

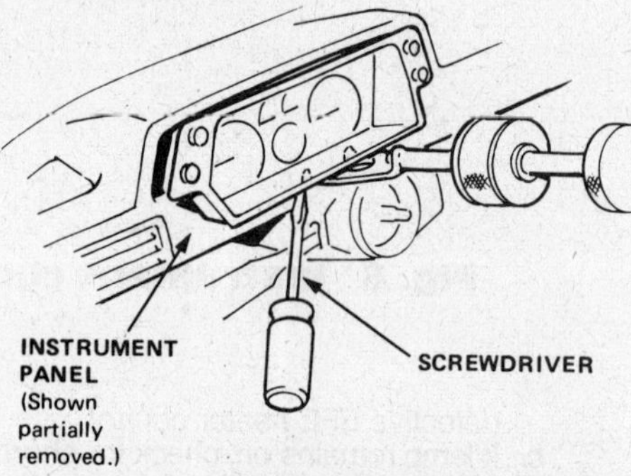

Fig. 11 Instrument cluster bezel removal. 1984–85 Accord

3. Remove 4 screws securing instrument cluster and pull cluster away from instrument panel.
4. Disconnect speedometer cable and electrical connectors, then remove instrument cluster.
5. Reverse procedure to install.

1986–87

1. Disconnect battery ground cable.
2. Pry each switch from instrument cluster bezel, inserting a thin flat blade screwdriver under the center of each switch to release the switch retainer, then remove switches.
3. Remove upper cap from cluster bezel, bezel retaining screws and the instrument cluster bezel, **Fig. 12.**
4. Remove 4 screws securing instrument cluster, then pull cluster away from instrument panel.
5. Disconnect speedometer cable and electrical connectors, then remove instrument cluster.
6. Reverse procedure to install.

PRELUDE

1. Lower steering column, then remove dashboard lower panel under instrument panel.
2. Remove four instrument panel attaching screws, **Fig. 13,** then pull instrument panel away from dashboard and disconnect wire connectors. Remove panel.

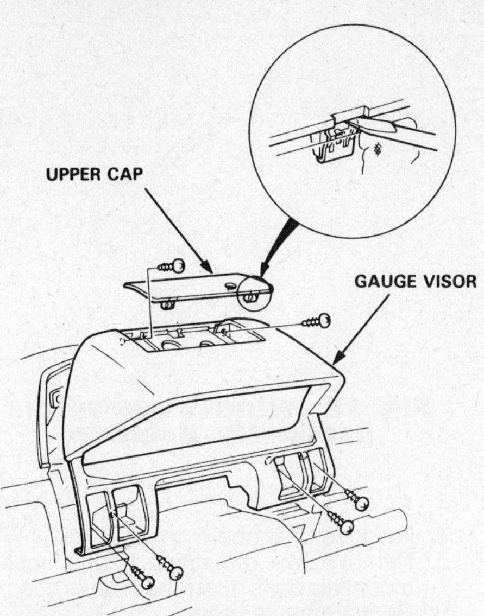

Fig. 12 Instrument cluster removal. 1986–87 Accord

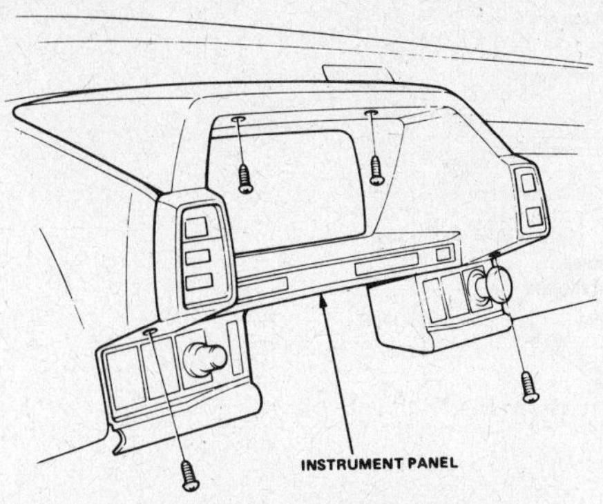

Fig. 13 Instrument panel removal. Prelude

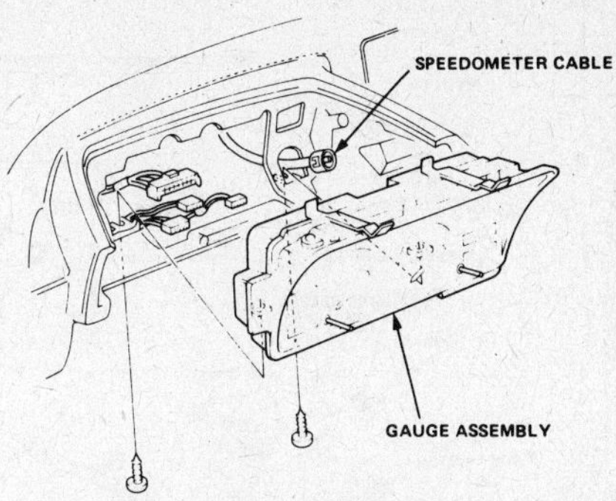

Fig. 14 Instrument cluster removal. Prelude

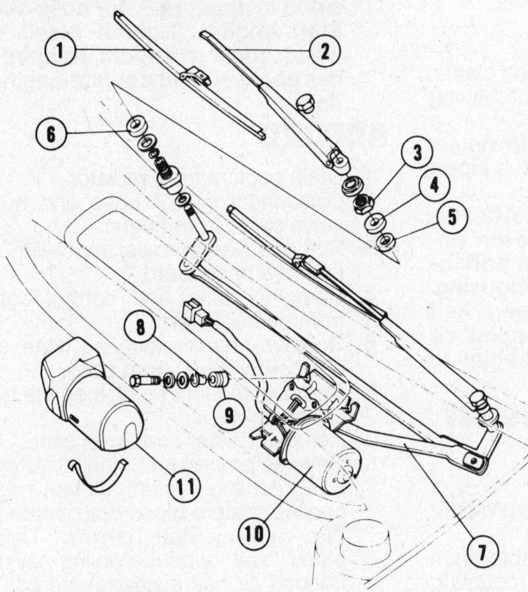

Fig. 15 Windshield wiper assembly. 1983 Civic (Typical)

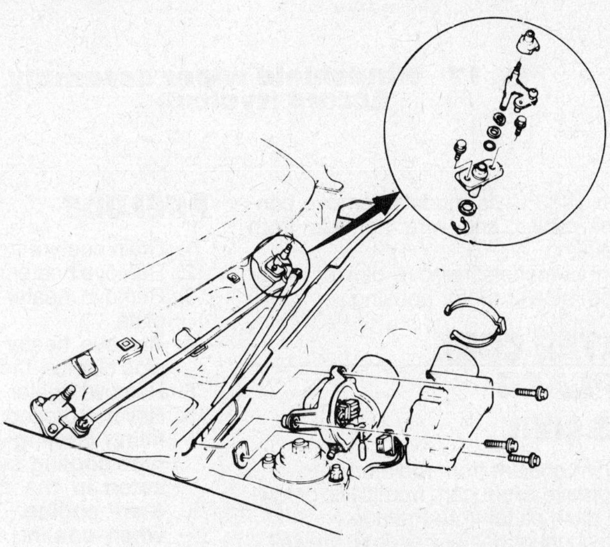

Fig. 16 Windshield wiper assembly. 1984–87 Civic & 1985–87 CRX

3. Remove two instrument cluster attaching screws, then lift gauge assembly to gain access to wire connectors and speedometer cable.
4. Disconnect wire connectors and speedometer cable, then remove instrument cluster, **Fig. 14.**

WINDSHIELD WIPER MOTOR
REPLACE

On some models, it may be necessary to remove the wiper arm retaining nuts and the wiper arms prior to removing air scoop.

1. Unsnap clips carefully with a screwdriver and remove air scoop complete with hood sealing rubber.
2. Remove lower connecting rod from wiper motor pivot arm.
3. Disconnect wiring harness at motor.
4. Loosen attaching bolts and remove wiper motor together with its cover from cowl. **On some models, it may be necessary to remove motor cover (if equipped) to gain access to motor attaching bolts.**
5. Separate cover (if equipped and not previously removed) from wiper motor.
6. Reverse procedure to install.

WINDSHIELD WIPER TRANSMISSION
REPLACE

Refer to **Figs. 15 through 18,** and replace all or part of the linkage in the sequence indicated.

BLOWER MOTOR
REPLACE

On some models, the evaporator must be removed before removing blower motor.

1. Disconnect battery ground cable.
2. Remove glove compartment and passengers tray, if equipped.
3. Remove blower duct.
4. On all exc. 1983 Civic models, remove wire connector from blower motor.
5. On all models, remove vacuum hose from blower housing, if equipped.
6. Remove three blower motor housing attaching bolts, then the blower motor housing.

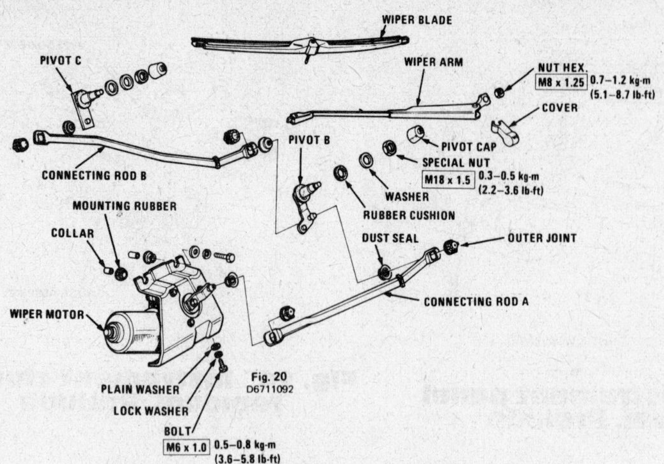

Fig. 17 Windshield wiper assembly. Accord (typical)

Fig. 18 Windshield wiper assembly. Prelude

7. On 1983 Civic models, remove control cables and wire harness from housing.
8. On all models, remove blower motor from blower motor housing.

HEATER CORE REPLACE

1983 CIVIC

1. Drain coolant from radiator.
2. Remove dashboard from Civic or lower dash panel from Prelude.
3. Disconnect heater hoses at firewall.
4. Remove heater lower mount nut on firewall.
5. Remove heater duct. Also, on models with air conditioning, remove evaporator duct bands and move evaporator aside.
6. Remove control cables from heater.
7. Remove heater upper mount bolts, then heater assembly.
8. Reverse procedure to install. Check control cables for proper operation.

PRELUDE

1. Drain coolant from radiator.
2. Remove heater pipe cover and clamp.
3. Remove heater core cover retaining plate.
4. Remove heater core pipe to heater pipe clamps, then separate the pipes.
5. Remove heater core.
6. Reverse procedure to install. **After refilling cooling system, loosen engine cooling system bleed bolt located in the thermostat housing. Start engine. Tighten bleed bolt when cooling system trapped air has escaped and coolant begins to flow.**

1984–87 CIVIC & 1985–87 CRX

1. Drain coolant from radiator.
2. Disconnect heater hoses from heater core.
3. Disconnect heater valve cable, then remove heater case lower mounting nut.
4. Remove dashboard assembly.
5. Remove two remaining heater case mounting bolts, then the heater case.
6. Remove heater core.
7. Reverse procedure to install. **After refilling cooling system, loosen engine cooling system bleed bolt located in upper radiator hose outlet. Start engine. Tighten bleed bolt when cooling system trapped air has escaped and coolant begins to flow.**

ACCORD

1. Drain coolant from radiator.
2. Disconnect heater hose and heater valve cable from heater.
3. Remove heater lower mounting nut, then the dashboard.
4. Remove ducts and control cables from heater levers.
5. Remove heater mounting bolts, then pull heater away from body.
6. Remove vacuum hose, then the heater assembly.
7. Remove heater core from case.
8. Reverse procedure to install. After refilling cooling system, loosen engine cooling system bleed bolt, located on the engine. Start engine. Tighten bleed volt when cooling system trapped air has escaped and coolant begins to flow.

ENGINE SECTION

INDEX

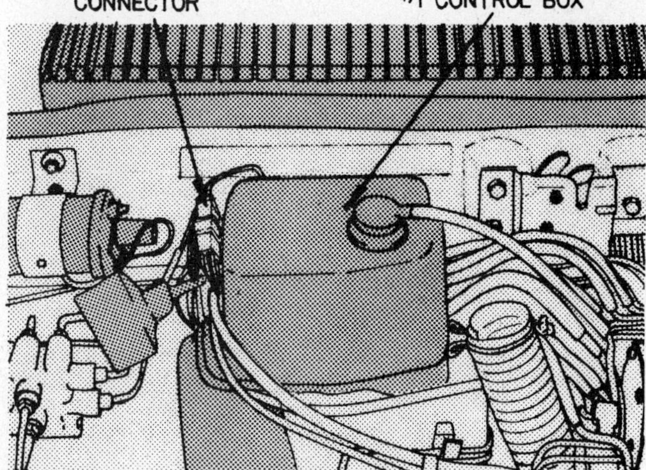

Fig. 1 Control Box No. 1. 1983 Civic (1984–85 similar)

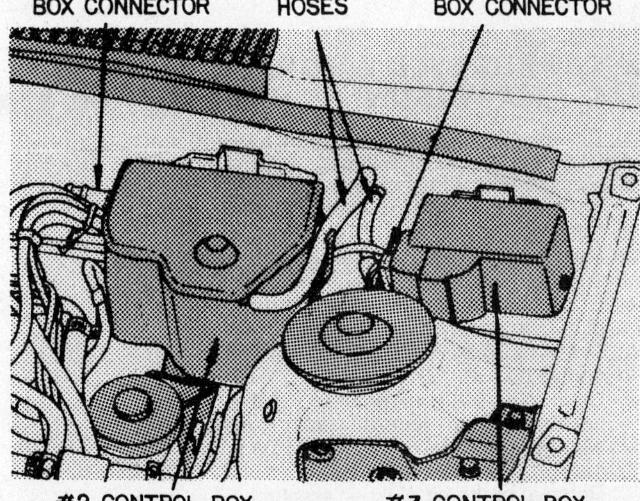

Fig. 2 Control Box Nos. 2 & 3. 1983 Civic

ENGINE REPLACE

1983 CIVIC

1. Disconnect and remove both battery cables.
2. Remove hold-down bracket, battery and tray.
3. Remove grille, then the hood.
4. Drain coolant from radiator, then disconnect radiator and heater hoses from engine.
5. Drain engine and transmission oil.
6. On 1983 1300 5 speed models, remove hose from top of air cleaner.
7. Remove air filter cover and filter.
8. Disconnect following control cables, hoses and wires from engine:
   a. Air intake duct, hot air duct and air control diaphragm hose.
   b. On 1983 1300 5 speed models, remove air and control valves from brackets.
   c. Air temperature sensor wire, automatic choke and fuel cut off valve wires.
   d. Remove condensation chamber, vacuum hose supports and air cleaner.
   e. Brake booster vacuum hose and fuel filter hose.
   f. Engine ground cable, oil pressure sensor and alternator harness connectors. **On vehicles with A/C disconnect compressor wire connector.**
   g. Coil wire, ignition wires at coil, condenser ground and engine compartment harness connectors.
   h. On 1983 1300 5 speed models, disconnect 5th/reverse connector.
   i. Throttle and choke cables from carburetor.
   j. Disconnect control box Nos. 1, 2 and 3 connectors and hoses, **Figs. 1 and 2.**
   k. Purge control diaphragm vacuum hose and charcoal canister hose from carburetor. **On vehicles with A/C, remove vacuum hoses from idle control solenoid.**
   l. On Calif. and High Altitude models, disconnect three air jet hoses from air jet controller.
   m. Tachometer, if equipped.
   n. On automatic transmission models, remove oil cooler hoses to radiator.
   o. On manual transmission models, remove clutch cable.
   p. Speedometer cable and antiafterburn valve. **On vehicles with A/C, remove compressor and bracket.**
9. Raise vehicle and support with safety stands, then remove front wheels.
10. Remove right and left ball joint with suitable tool.
11. Pry constant velocity valve joint out

approx. 1/2 inch (13 mm) and pull subaxle out of transmission case, then repeat on opposite side.
12. On manual transmission models, disconnect gearshift rod at transmission, then gearshift extension at engine.
13. On automatic transmission models, remove shift lever at shift console.
14. Disconnect exhaust pipe from manifold.
15. Attach suitable hoist to engine, then raise engine slightly to remove load on engine mounts.
16. Remove nuts securing front and rear engine mounts.
17. Remove bolts and push left engine support into shock mount bracket as far as possible.
18. Remove torque rod.
19. Remove engine from vehicle.
20. Reverse procedure to install, noting the following:
    a. Refer to **Fig. 3** for engine mount torque specifications.
    b. When installing driveshafts, be sure driveshaft clicks into groove in differential.
    c. Adjust all control cables to carburetor and transmission as necessary.

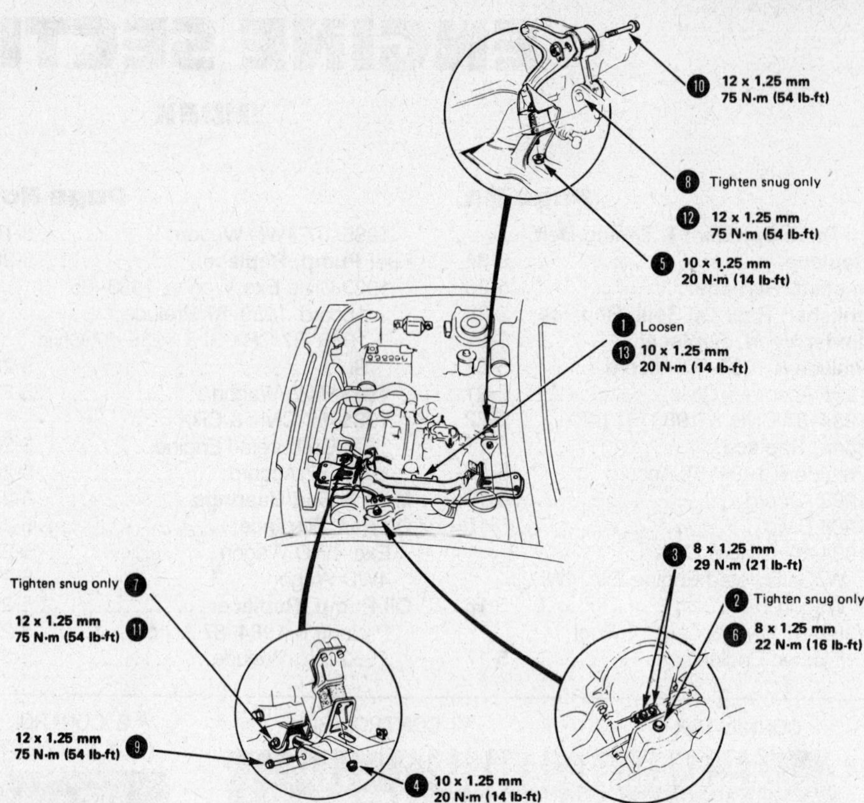

Fig. 3 Engine mount torque sequence. 1983 Civic

1984–87 CIVIC & CRX W/CARBURETED ENGINE EXC. 4WD WAGON

1. Disconnect ground cable from battery, then the positive cable.
2. Mark position of hood hinges, disconnect washer hoses, then remove hood.
3. Remove engine and wheelwell splash shields.
4. Drain engine oil, then reinstall drain plug using new sealing washer.
5. Drain radiator coolant into suitable container.
6. Drain transaxle lubricant into suitable container, then reinstall drain plug with new washer and torque to 29 ft. lbs.
7. Remove entire air cleaner assembly.
8. Disconnect engine compartment subharness connector located near right front shock tower.
9. Remove engine secondary ground cable located on valve cover.
10. Disconnect brake booster vacuum hose, then on models equipped with A/C, disconnect idle control solenoid valve.
11. Disconnect control box No. 1 connector, **Fig. 1**, then lift control box off the mounting bracket and allow it to hang near engine.
12. Disconnect purge control solenoid valve vacuum hose from charcoal canister.
13. On Calif. and High Alt. models, remove air jet controller and Nos. 2 and 3 control boxes if necessary, located near left front shock tower.
14. On 1985 models with power steering, remove power steering mount bolts and V-belt from power steering pump, then without disconnecting hose, pull pump away from its mounting bracket.

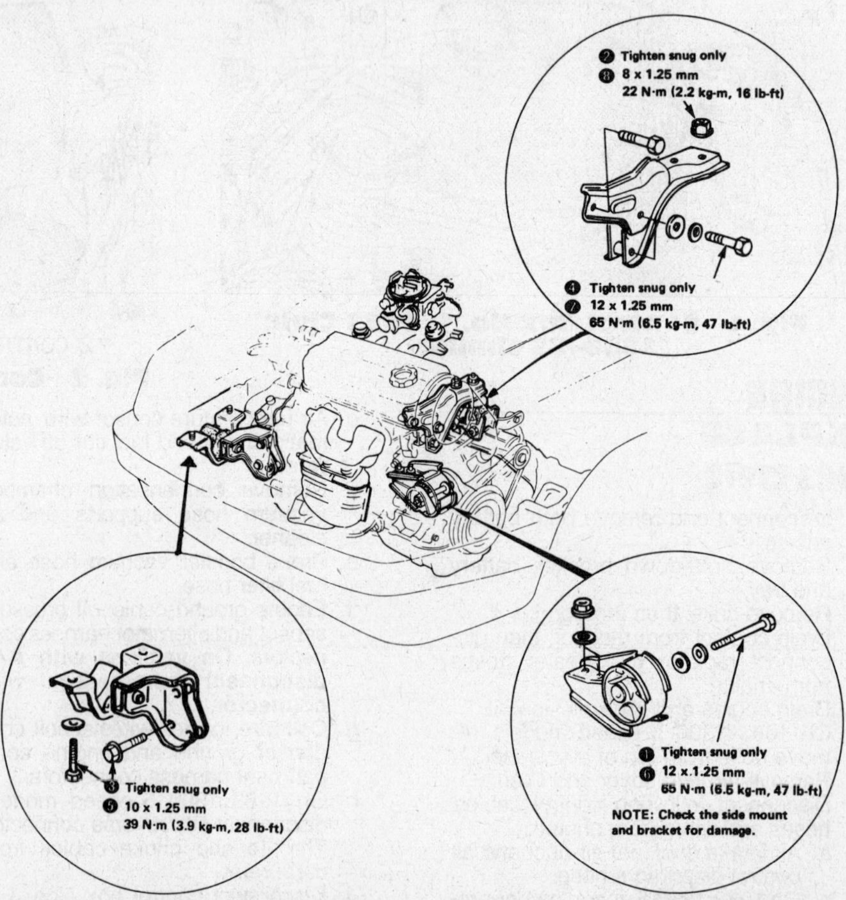

Fig. 4 Engine mount torque sequence. 1984–87 Civic

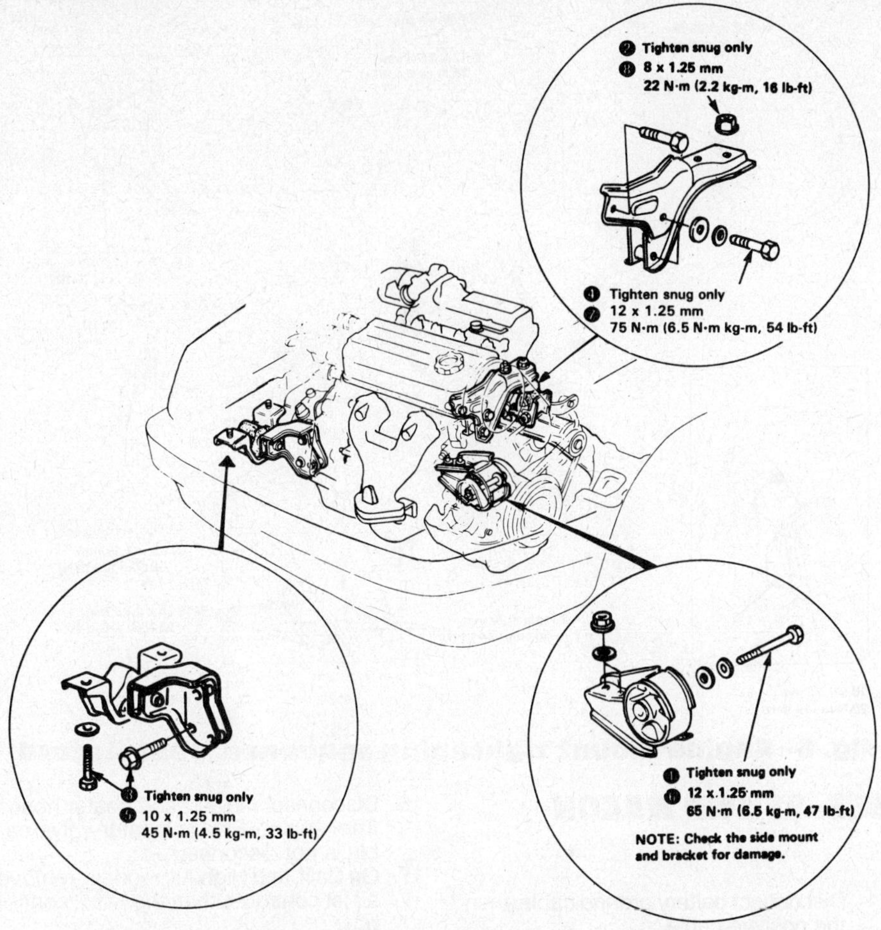

Fig. 5 Engine mount torque sequence. CRX

15. On all models, remove battery and battery tray.
16. Remove throttle cable from carburetor. **To prevent kinking, do not bend throttle cable while removing it. If cable should become kinked, replace it.**
17. Remove fuel hoses from fuel pump, then remove fuel pump and cover.
18. Disconnect spark plug wires, then remove distributor assembly.
19. Mark heater hoses to ensure correct assembly, then remove heater and radiator hoses. **Do not disconnect heater valve cable.**
20. On vehicles equipped with manual transaxle, proceed as follows:
    a. Loosen clutch cable adjusting nut, then disconnect clutch cable from release arm.
    b. Disconnect transmission ground cable, then the shift lever torque rod from clutch housing.
    c. Slide shift lever coupler spring pin retainer aside, then using a suitable 8 mm punch, drive out shift lever coupler retaining spring pin and remove linkage.
21. On vehicles equipped with automatic transaxle, proceed as follows:
    a. Disconnect transaxle oil cooler hoses from transaxle and allow to drain. Position hoses aside.
    b. Remove center console, then position shift lever in Reverse and remove lock pin from end of shift cable.
    c. Working underneath vehicle, remove cable mounting bolts from shift cable holder and cable guide.
    d. Remove throttle control cable.
22. On all models, remove cable clip from speedometer cable holder, then the speedometer cable. **Do not remove speedometer cable holder as drive gear may fall into transaxle housing.**
23. Remove exhaust header pipe.
24. Remove right and left side ball joints, then pry right and left side CV joints out of transaxle.
25. Attach suitable hoist to engine, then raise engine slightly to remove load on engine mounts.
26. Remove rear transaxle mount bracket, then remove transaxle mount transaxle mount bolts.
27. Remove engine side mount bolt.
28. On vehicles equipped with A/C, proceed as follows:
    a. Loosen A/C belt, then remove compressor mounting bolts and lift compressor from mounting bracket with hoses attached and wire it aside.
    b. Remove compressor lower mounting bracket.
29. On all models, remove alternator belt and alternator.
30. Ensure all connections which would restrict engine removal are removed.
31. Lift engine and transaxle assembly approximately six inches, then repeat step 30.
32. Remove engine and transaxle assembly. **After engine removal, coat all machined surfaces with clean engine oil or grease to prevent rust and corrosion. Tie plastic bags over driveshaft ends.**
33. Reverse procedure to install, noting the following:
    a. Tighten engine mount bolts in 2 steps using sequence shown in **Figs. 4 and 5. When tightening engine mounts, ensure bushings are not twisted or offset. Failure to tighten mounts in proper sequence may cause excessive vibration.**
    b. When installing driveshafts, use new spring clips and ensure driveshafts click into groove in differential.
    c. After refilling cooling system, loosen bleed bolt located on upper radiator hose outlet. Start engine. Tighten bleed bolt when cooling system trapped air has escaped and coolant begins to flow.
    d. Adjust all control cables to carburetor and transaxle as necessary.

1985–87 CIVIC & CRX W/FUEL INJECTED ENGINE

1. Disconnect battery ground cable, then the positive cable.
2. Mark position of hood hinges, disconnect washer hoses, then remove hood.
3. Remove engine and wheelwell splash shields.
4. Drain engine oil, then reinstall drain plug using new sealing washer.
5. Drain radiator coolant into a suitable container.
6. Drain transaxle lubricant into a suitable container, then reinstall drain plug with new washer and torque to 29 ft. lbs.
7. Disconnect air intake duct and vacuum hose.
8. Relieve fuel pressure slowly, by loosening the service bolt on the fuel filter approximately one turn. **Place a shop towel over the fuel filter to prevent pressurized fuel from spraying over the engine.**
9. Disconnect fuel return hose from the pressure regulator, then the special nut and fuel hose.
10. Disconnect engine compartment subharness connector, then the engine secondary ground cable.
11. Disconnect brake booster vacuum hose.
12. On models equipped with A/C, remove idle control solenoid valve.
13. On all models, remove throttle cable by loosening locknut and throttle cable adjusting nut. **To prevent kinking, do not bend throttle cable while removing it. If cable should become kinked, replace it.**
14. Disconnect No. 1 control box connector, then lift control box off its mounting and allow it to hang near engine.

15. Disconnect ignition wires at spark plugs, then remove the distributor.
16. Disconnect radiator and heater hoses from engine. Ensure heater valve cable is not disconnected.
17. Loosen clutch cable adjusting nut, then disconnect clutch cable from release arm.
18. Disconnect transmission ground cable, then the shift lever torque rod from the clutch housing.
19. Slide shift rod spring retainer to one side and drive out spring pin using a suitable punch, then disconnect shift rod.
20. Remove speedometer cable attaching clip, then pull speedometer cable out of holder. **Ensure speedometer gear does not fall into transmission housing.**
21. Remove seven exhaust header pipe attaching bolts, then the header pipe. Apply suitable penetrating oil to studs to facilitate removal.
22. Remove right and left side ball joint, then pry right and left side CV joint out of transaxle.
23. Attach suitable hoist to engine, then raise engine slightly to remove load on engine mounts.
24. Remove rear transaxle mount bracket, then the front transaxle mount attaching bolts.
25. Remove engine side rubber mount attaching bolt.
26. On models equipped with A/C, proceed as follows:
    a. Loosen belt adjusting bolt and idler pulley nut.
    b. Remove compressor mounting bolts, then lift compressor out of bracket with hoses attached and wire it aside.
    c. Remove lower compressor mounting bracket.
27. On all models, remove alternator.
28. Ensure all connections which would restrict engine removal are removed.
29. Lift engine and transaxle assembly approximately six inches, then repeat step 28.
30. Remove engine and transaxle assembly. **After engine removal, coat all machined surfaces with clean engine oil or grease to prevent rust and corrosion. Tie plastic bags over driveshaft ends.**
31. Reverse procedure to install, noting the following:
    a. Tighten engine mount bolts in 2 steps using sequence shown in **Fig. 5 When tightening engine mounts, ensure bushings are not twisted or offset. Failure to tighten mounts in proper sequence may cause excessive vibration.**
    b. When installing driveshafts, use new spring clips and ensure driveshafts click into groove into differential.
    c. After refilling cooling system, loosen bleed bolt and start engine. Tighten bleed bolt when cooling system trapped air has escaped and coolant begins to flow.
    d. Adjust all control cables as required.

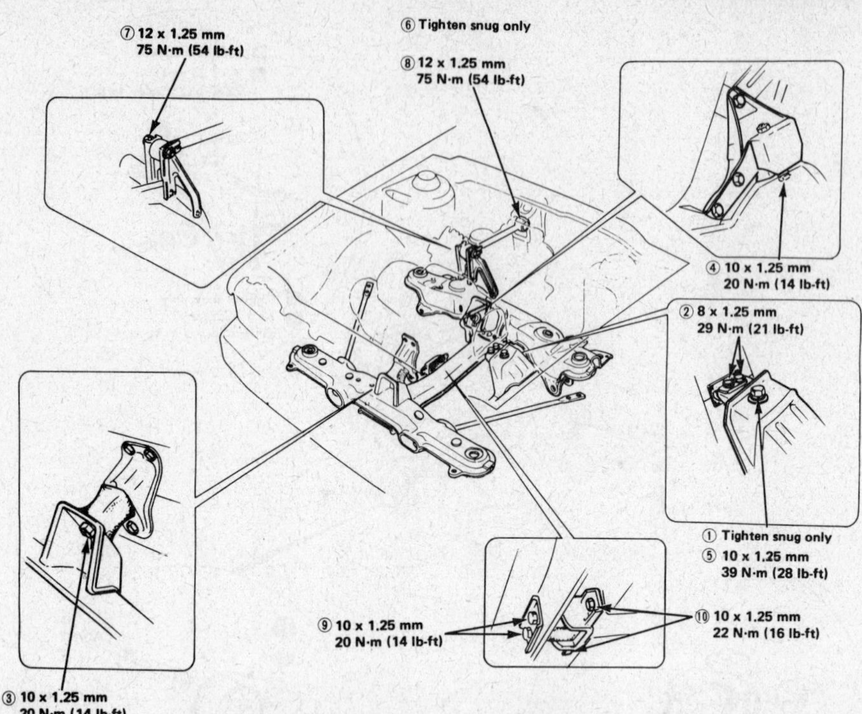

Fig. 6 Engine mount tightening sequence. 1983 Accord

1985–87 4WD WAGON

1. Disconnect battery ground cable, then the positive cable.
2. Scribe reference marks in the hood hinge area, then remove hood.
3. Remove engine and wheelwell splash shields.
4. Drain engine oil, then reinstall drain plug using new sealing washer.
5. Drain radiator coolant into a suitable container.
6. Drain transaxle lubricant into a suitable container, then reinstall drain plug with new washer and torque to 29 ft. lbs.
7. Remove air cleaner assembly.
8. Disconnect engine compartment subharness connector, then the engine secondary ground cable and coil wires.
9. On models equipped with A/C, remove idle control solenoid valve.
10. On all models, disconnect No. 1 control box connector, then lift control box off its mounting and allow it to hang near engine.
11. Disconnect purge control solenoid valve vacuum hose at charcoal canister.
12. On all models, remove throttle cable by loosening locknut and throttle cable adjusting nut. **To prevent kinking, do not bend throttle cable while removing it. If cable should become kinked, replace it.**
13. Disconnect fuel hose at fuel pump.
14. Loosen clutch cable adjusting nut, then disconnect clutch cable from release arm.
15. Disconnect transmission ground cable.
16. Disconnect radiator and heater hoses from engine. Ensure heater valve cable is not disconnected.
17. On Calif. and High Alt. models, remove air jet controller, then the No. 2 control box.
18. On all models, disconnect brake booster vacuum hose from intake manifold, then remove cable bracket.
19. Disconnect shift control cables.
20. Remove exhaust header pipe attaching bolts, then the header pipe. Apply suitable penetrating oil to studs to facilitate removal.
21. Disconnect drive shaft at transmission.
22. Remove speedometer cable attaching clip, then pull speedometer cable out of holder. Ensure speedometer gear does not fall into transmission housing.
23. Remove right and left side ball joint, then pry right and left side CV joints out of transaxle.
24. Attach suitable hoist to engine, then raise engine slightly to remove load on engine mounts.
25. Remove rear transaxle mount bracket, then the front transaxle mount attaching bolts.
26. Remove engine side rubber mount attaching bolt.
27. On models equipped with A/C, proceed as follows:
    a. Loosen belt and adjusting bolt and idler pulley nut.
    b. Remove compressor mounting bolts, then lift compressor out of bracket with hoses attached and wire it aside.
    c. Remove lower compressor mounting bracket.
28. On all models, remove alternator.
29. Ensure all connections which would

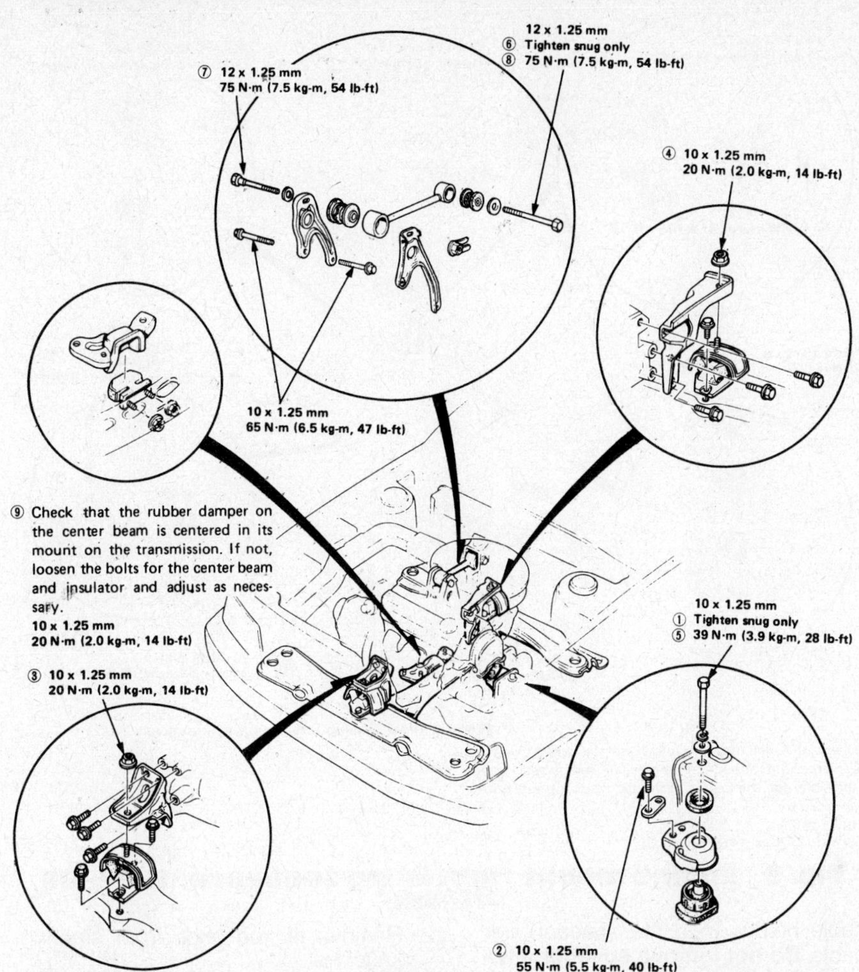

Fig. 7 Engine mount tightening sequence. 1984–85 Accord

restrict engine removal are removed.

30. Lift engine and transaxle assembly approximately six inches, then repeat step 29.
31. Remove engine and transaxle assembly. **After engine removal, coat all machined surfaces with clean engine oil or grease to prevent rust and corrosion. Tie plastic bags over driveshaft ends.**
32. Reverse procedure to install, noting the following:
    a. Refer to **Fig. 4** for engine mount torque specifications.
    b. When installing driveshafts, use new spring clips and ensure driveshafts click into groove into differential.
    c. After refilling cooling system, loosen bleed bolt and start engine. Tighten bleed bolt when cooling system trapped air has escaped and coolant begins to flow.
    d. Adjust all control cables as required.

1983 ACCORD

1. Disconnect and remove both battery cables. On Prelude models, remove battery and tray.
2. Remove grille and hood.
3. Drain engine coolant, then disconnect radiator and heater hoses from engine.
4. Drain engine and transmission fluid.
5. Remove air filter cover and filter.
6. Disconnect and/or remove the following cables, hoses and wires, if equipped:
    a. Air intake ducts and air control diaphragm.
    b. Condensation chamber, vacuum hose supports and air cleaner housing.
    c. Air temperature sensor wire, purge control solenoid hose and brake booster hose.
    d. Ground cables, starter cable, A/C compressor wire (if equipped) and ignition system secondary wiring.
    e. Oil pressure sender wire, engine compartment and alternator harness connectors, fuel cut-off solenoid valve wire and electric choke wire.
    f. Fuel and charcoal canister lines at carburetor and A/C vacuum hoses from idle control solenoid.
    g. Throttle cable and heater valve cable.
    h. Vacuum hose thermovalve and delay valve, control box numbers 1, 2 and 3 connectors and hoses and the three air jet hoses from air jet controller.
    i. Speedometer cable and antiafterburn valve.
7. On Accord models with manual transmission, disconnect clutch cable; on Prelude models with manual transmission, remove clutch slave cylinder with line attached.
8. On models with manual transmission, disconnect gearshift rod at transmission, then gearshift extension at engine.
9. On models with automatic transmission, remove shift lever at shift console.
10. On models with A/C, discharge system and remove compressor. On Prelude models with A/C, also remove alternator.
11. Raise and support vehicles with safety stands, then remove front wheels.
12. Disconnect exhaust pipe from manifold.
13. On Prelude models, remove engine shields, then the stabilizer bar.
14. Remove right and left ball joints using suitable tool.
15. Pry constant velocity valve joint out about 1/2 inch (13 mm) and pull subaxle out of transmission case, then repeat on other side.
16. Attach suitable hoist to engine, then raise engine slightly to remove load from mounts and remove nuts securing front and rear engine mounts.
17. Remove bolts and push left engine support into shock mount bracket as far as possible, then remove torque tube.
18. Remove engine from vehicle.
19. Reverse procedure to install, noting the following:
    a. Refer to **Fig. 6** or engine mount torque specifications.
    b. When installing driveshafts, be sure driveshaft clicks into groove in differential.
    c. Adjust all control cables to carburetor and transmission as necessary.

PRELUDE & 1984–87 ACCORD

1. Disconnect battery ground cable, then positive cable.
2. On Prelude models, remove left and right side manual headlight retracting knob covers, then rotate knobs to bring headlights to open position.
3. On Prelude models, remove grille attaching screws, then the grille.
4. On all models, scribe reference in the hood hinge area, then remove hood assembly.
5. Remove engine splash shield (if equipped).
6. On all models, drain engine oil, then reinstall drain plug using new washer.
7. Drain radiator coolant into suitable container.
8. Drain transaxle lubricant, then reinstall drain plug using new washer. Torque drain plug to 29 ft. lbs.
9. On models equipped with fuel injected engine, proceed as follows:
    a. Remove air intake duct, then the engine secondary ground cable.
    b. Disconnect air cleaner connecting tube assembly and all necessary vacuum tubes.

c. Remove air cleaner case attaching nuts, then the air cleaner case.
d. Remove throttle cable by loosening locknut and adjusting nut.
e. Disconnect ground cable at fuse box, then the engine compartment sub-harness connector and clamp.
f. Disconnect high tension wire and ignition primary leads at the ignition coil.
g. Disconnect radio condenser electrical connector.
h. Relieve fuel pressure slowly, by loosening service bolt on fuel filter approximately one turn. **Place a shop towel over the fuel filter to prevent pressurized fuel from spraying over the engine.**
i. Disconnect fuel return hose from pressure regulator, then remove the special nut and fuel hose.
j. Disconnect emission hoses from the tubing manifold.
k. Disconnect No. 2 control box connectors, then lift box off its bracket and position aside.
l. Disconnect brake booster vacuum hose.

10. On models equipped with carbureted engine, proceed as follows:
    a. Disconnect vacuum hoses as necessary, then remove air cleaner assembly.
    b. Disconnect ignition coil primary and secondary wiring.
    c. On Accord models equipped with A/C, remove idle control solenoid valve hoses.
    d. On all models, remove air intake duct, hot air duct, power steering hose clamp bolt (if equipped), power brake booster vacuum hose, engine secondary ground cable and engine compartment wire harness connector(s).
    e. Disconnect throttle cable from carburetor linkage. **To prevent kinking, do not bend throttle cable while removing it. If cable should become kinked, replace it.**
    f. Disconnect control box No. 1 connector, then lift control box off the mounting bracket and allow it to hang near engine.
    g. Disconnect charcoal canister purge control solenoid valve vacuum hose.
    h. Disconnect fuel hose from fuel filter.
    i. Remove air jet controller (if equipped).
11. On all models, mark heater hoses to ensure correct assembly, then remove heater and radiator hoses. **Do not disconnect heater valve cable.**
12. On models equipped with manual transaxle, loosen clutch cable adjusting nut, then disconnect clutch cable from release arm.
13. On models equipped with automatic transaxle, disconnect transaxle cooler hoses and allow to drain. Position hoses aside.
14. On all models, remove transaxle ground cable and starter cable.
15. Remove cable clip from speedometer

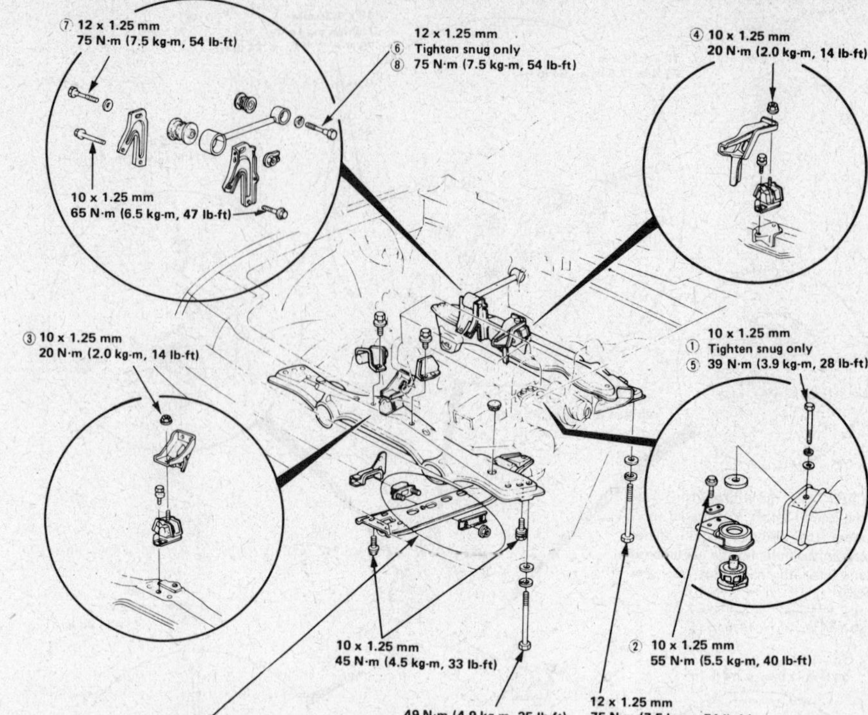

⑨ Check that the rubber damper on the center beam is centered in its mount on the transmission. If not, loosen the bolts for the center beam and insulator and adjust as necessary.
10 x 1.25 mm
20 N·m (2.0 kg-m, 14 lb-ft)

Fig. 8 Engine mount tightening sequence. 1984–85 Prelude

cable holder, then the speedometer cable. **Do not remove speedometer cable holder as drive gear may fall into transaxle housing.**

16. On models equipped with power steering, remove speed sensor with hoses attached and position aside, then remove power steering pump attaching bolts and position pump aside.
17. On Accord models, remove sub-frame center beam, then loosen radius rod nuts. Remove exhaust header pipe.
18. On all models equipped with A/C, disconnect compressor clutch lead wire then, remove compressor with pressure and return lines attached and position aside. **It is not necessary to discharge A/C system.**
19. On Prelude models equipped with manual transaxle, remove shift rod yoke attaching bolts, then disconnect shift lever torque rod from clutch housing.
20. On Accord models equipped with manual transaxle, disconnect shift lever torque rod from clutch housing, then remove shift rod yoke attaching
21. On all models equipped with automatic transaxle, remove center console, then place shift lever in Reverse and remove the lock pin from end of shift cable. Remove cable mounting bracket bolts, then the cable. Remove throttle control cable from transaxle. **When removing throttle control cable, loosen lower locknut only. If upper locknut is loosened, the transaxle shift points will be changed.**
22. Remove tie rod ends from steering knuckles.
23. Remove right and left side ball joints, then pry right and left side CV joints out of transaxle. **Do not pull on axle shafts to remove them.**
24. On models equipped with fuel injected engine, disconnect sub-engine harness connectors and clamp.
25. On Prelude models, remove exhaust header pipe.
26. Disconnect cruise control vacuum hoses and linkage (if equipped).
27. Attach suitable hoist to engine, then raise engine slightly to remove load on engine mounts.
28. On Prelude models with carbureted engine, proceed as follows:
    a. Disconnect control box No. 2 connector, then lift control box off the mounting bracket and allow it to hang freely near engine.
    b. If equipped with A/C, remove idle control solenoid valve.
    c. Remove air chamber.
29. On all models, remove three motor mount bolts, then push motor mount into motor mount tower.
30. Remove front and rear engine mount nuts.
31. Disconnect alternator wiring harness, then remove alternator assembly.
32. Remove rear torque rod to engine mounting bolt, then loosen torque rod to frame mounting bolt and swing torque rod out of the way.
33. Ensure all connections that would restrict engine/transaxle removal are removed.

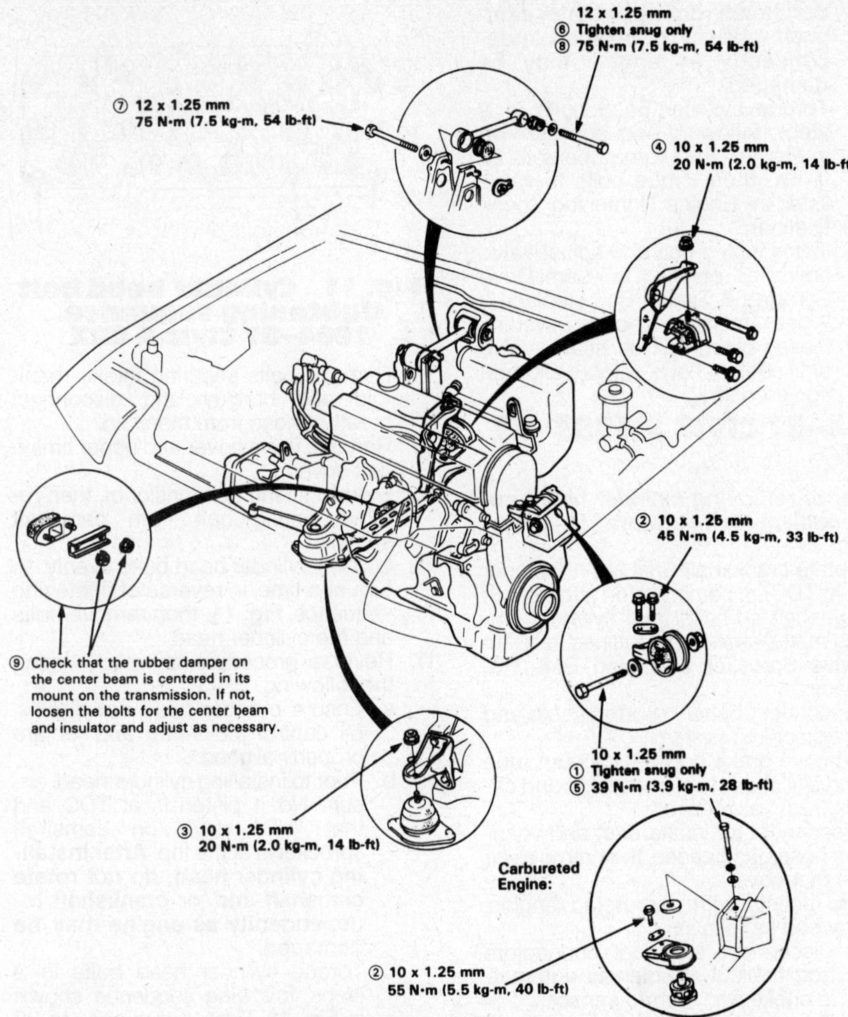

Fig. 9 Engine mount tightening sequence. 1986–87 Accord & Prelude

34. Lift engine/transaxle assembly approximately six inches and repeat step 33.
35. Remove engine/transaxle assembly. **After engine/transaxle removal, coat all machine surfaces with clean engine oil or grease to prevent rust and corrosion. Tie plastic bags over driveshaft ends.**
36. Reverse procedure to install, noting the following:
    a. Refer to **Figs. 7 through 9** for engine mount torque specifications.
    b. When installing driveshafts, use new spring clips and ensure driveshafts click into groove in differential.
    c. After refilling cooling system, loosen bleed bolt located on thermostat housing. Start engine. Tighten bleed bolt when cooling system trapped air has escaped and coolant begins to flow.
    d. Adjust all control cables to carburetor and transaxle as necessary.

CYLINDER HEAD REPLACE

1983 ACCORD & CIVIC

1. Disconnect battery ground cable, then drain coolant from radiator.
2. Remove air cleaner.
3. Disconnect wires from temperature gauge sending unit, fuel cut-off solenoid valve, automatic choke and, on air conditioned models, idle cut-off solenoid valve.
4. Disconnect fuel lines and throttle cable from carburetor, then identify and disconnect all hoses from carburetor. Remove carburetor.
5. Disconnect upper radiator hose, heater inlet hose and bypass inlet hose from cylinder head.
6. Disconnect exhaust pipe from manifold.
7. Remove bolt holding alternator bracket to cylinder head, then loosen alternator adjusting bolt.
8. On air conditioned models, remove compressor drive belt and loosen adjusting nut. Remove compressor mounting bolts and move compressor aside, secure compressor in place, then remove compressor bracket from cylinder head.
9. On 1300cc engines, remove anti-afterburn valve and bracket from cylinder head.
10. Disconnect tachometer cable and radio noise suppressor wire from distributor, if equipped.
11. On Accord and Prelude, disconnect brake booster vacuum hoses at carburetor.
12. Remove valve and timing belt covers.
13. Loosen timing belt adjusting and pivot bolts, then remove belt from camshaft sprocket.
14. Remove oil pump gear cover, then remove oil pump shaft from cylinder head.
15. Loosen cylinder head bolts in criss-cross pattern starting with outside bolt, then remove cylinder head.
16. Remove manifolds from cylinder head.
17. Reverse procedure to install, noting the following:
    a. Be sure top dead center mark on crankshaft pulley is aligned with index mark on timing belt cover.
    b. Torque cylinder head bolts in criss-cross pattern starting with inside bolt to 43 ft. lbs. (6 kg-m).
    c. Align marks on camshaft sprocket as outlined in step 4 of "Cam Drive Sprocket & Timing Belt, Replace" procedure.

PRELUDE & 1984–87 ACCORD

Prior to removing cylinder head, ensure coolant temperature is below 100°F.

1. Rotate crankshaft until No. 1 cylinder is at TDC on compression stroke, with camshaft sprocket and flywheel timing marks aligned as outlined in "Cam Drive Sprocket Timing Belt, Replace."
2. Disconnect battery ground cable and drain cooling system.
3. Remove brake booster vacuum tube and disconnect secondary ground cable from valve cover.
4. Disconnect electrical connector from radio condenser and primary and secondary wiring from remote mounted ignition coil, as equipped.
5. On models with carbureted engine, proceed as follows:
    a. Remove air cleaner, noting position of all vacuum hoses for installation.
    b. Disconnect electrical connectors from fuel cut-off solenoid, electric choke and temperature gauge sending unit.
    c. Disconnect fuel lines and throttle cable from carburetor.
    d. Disconnect electrical connector from distributor and remove vacuum hoses, noting position for installation.
    e. Mark installation position, then disconnect No. 1 control box hoses from vacuum manifold.
    f. Disconnect air jet controller hoses.
6. On models with fuel injected engine, proceed as follows:
    a. Remove air cleaner cover.
    b. Relieve fuel pressure by placing shop towel over service bolt on fuel filter and loosening bolt approximately 1 turn.
    c. Disconnect fuel supply and return hoses, then plug hoses.
    d. Disconnect throttle cable and canister vent hose from throttle body.

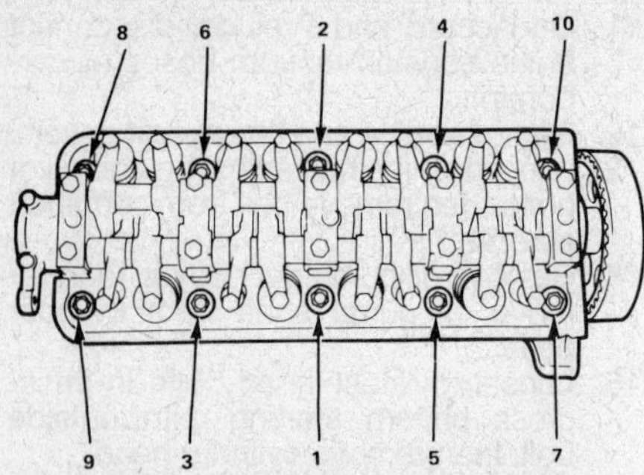

Fig. 10 Cylinder head bolt tightening sequence. Prelude & 1984–87 Accord

e. Disconnect engine sub-harness electrical connectors from cylinder head and intake manifold mounted components, noting position for installation.
f. Release 4 sub-harness retaining clamps and secure harness aside.
g. Disconnect electrical connector to oxygen sensor.

7. Disconnect upper radiator, heater and bypass hoses from cylinder head, and the hose between the thermostat housing and intake manifold.
8. On 1985 Accord with fuel injection and all 1986-87 models, disconnect connecting pipe to valve body hose and bypass outlet hose.
9. On all models, remove power steering pump and secure aside, leaving hoses connected.
10. Remove hose clamp bolt and power steering pump bracket from cylinder head.
11. On 1983-85 Prelude, disconnect electrical connector from control box No. 2, remove control from bracket and suspend control along side carburetor.
12. Remove air chamber, disconnect A/C idle control solenoid hoses and remove cruise control actuator, as equipped.
13. Working from under vehicle, remove engine splash shield, as needed, then disconnect header pipe from exhaust manifold and bracket and pull pipe clear of manifold.
14. Remove air cleaner base mounting bolts and disconnect breather hose from intake manifold.
15. Remove valve cover and upper timing belt cover.
16. Loosen timing belt tensioner and remove timing belt.
17. Loosen cylinder head bolts evenly, 1/3 turn at a time, in reverse of tightening sequence, **Fig. 10,** then remove bolts and the cylinder head.
18. Reverse procedure to install, noting the following:
    a. Ensure cylinder head dowel pins, oil control jet O-ring and jet are properly aligned.
    b. Prior to installing cylinder head, ensure No. 1 piston is at TDC and that "UP" mark or round timing reference mark on camshaft sprocket is at the top. **After installing cylinder head, do not rotate camshaft and/or crankshaft independently as engine may be damaged.**
    c. Torque cylinder head bolts in 2 steps, following sequence shown in **Fig. 10.** First torque bolts to 22 ft. lbs., then torque bolts to value listed in "Engine Tightening Specifications."
    d. Install timing belt and adjust valve timing as outlined in "Cam Drive Sprocket & Timing Belt, Replace."
    e. When refilling cooling system, loosen bleed bolt on heater valve until coolant flows without air, then tighten bolt

1984–87 CIVIC & 1985–87 CRX

Prior to removing cylinder head, ensure coolant temperature is below 100°F.

1. Rotate crankshaft until No. 1 cylinder is at TDC on compression stroke, with camshaft sprocket and flywheel timing marks aligned as outlined in "Cam Drive Sprocket & Timing Belt, Replace."
2. Disconnect battery ground cable and drain cooling system.
3. Remove brake booster vacuum tube and disconnect secondary ground cable from valve cover.
4. Disconnect air intake duct and vacuum hoses, as needed, then remove air cleaner cover.
5. On models with carbureted engine, proceed as follows:
    a. Disconnect electrical connectors from fuel cut-off solenoid, automatic choke and thermo sensor.
    b. Disconnect fuel lines.
    c. On California and High Altitude models, disconnect hoses from air jet controller.
6. On models with fuel injection, proceed as follows:
    a. Relieve fuel pressure by placing shop towel over service bolt on fuel filter and loosening bolt approximately 1 turn.
    b. Disconnect fuel supply and return hoses, then plug hoses.
    c. Disconnect engine sub-harness electrical connectors from intake manifold and cylinder head mounted components, noting position for installation.
    d. Disconnect electrical connector to oxygen sensor.
7. Disconnect wires from spark plugs, then remove distributor assembly.
8. Disconnect throttle cable.
9. Disconnect No. 1 control box vacuum hoses from vacuum manifold and vacuum hoses from charcoal canister, noting position for installation.
10. On models with A/C, disconnect hoses from idle-up solenoid.
11. Disconnect upper radiator hose and the bypass and heater inlet hoses, and remove hose between thermostat housing and intake manifold.
12. Remove bolts securing exhaust manifold and bracket, then remove manifold.

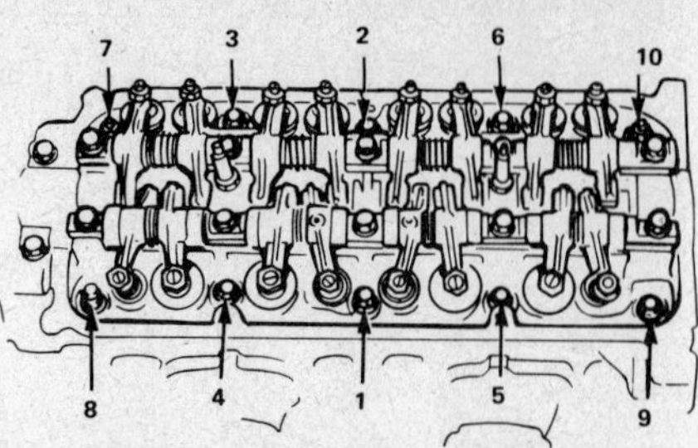

Fig. 11 Cylinder head bolt tightening sequence. 1984–87 Civic & CRX

13. Remove bolts securing intake manifold and bracket and disconnect breather hose from manifold.
14. Remove valve cover and upper timing belt cover.
15. Loosen timing belt tensioner, then remove timing belt from camshaft sprocket.
16. Loosen cylinder head bolts evenly, 1/3 turn at a time, in reverse of tightening sequence, **Fig. 11,** then remove bolts and the cylinder head.
17. Reverse procedure to install, noting the following:
    a. Ensure cylinder head dowel pins, oil control jet O-ring and jet are properly aligned.
    b. Prior to installing cylinder head, ensure No. 1 piston is at TDC and that "UP" mark on camshaft sprocket is at the top. **After installing cylinder head, do not rotate camshaft and/or crankshaft independently as engine may be damaged.**
    c. Torque cylinder head bolts in 2 steps, following sequence shown in **Fig. 11.** First torque bolts to 22 ft. lbs., then torque bolts to value listed in "Engine Tightening Specifications."
    d. Install timing belt and adjust valve timing as outlined in "Cam Drive Sprocket & Timing Belt, Replace."
    e. When refilling cooling system, loosen bleed bolt on heater valve until coolant flows without air, then tighten bolt.

ROCKER ARMS REPLACE

1983 EXC. PRELUDE

1. Remove camshaft drive sprocket as outlined, then disconnect battery ground cable. **While timing belt is removed, do not allow camshaft or crankshaft to rotate independently, as engine may be damaged.**
2. Evenly loosen camshaft holder/rocker arm shaft retaining bolts in crossing pattern, then remove rocker arm shaft assemblies.
3. Remove camshaft holder attaching bolts then the rocker arm shafts, bearing caps and rocker arms.
4. Compress serrated, two-piece retaining spring pin with pliers and pry spring pin pieces up a little at a time, **Fig. 12. Removing either spring pin releases rocker arms and springs.**

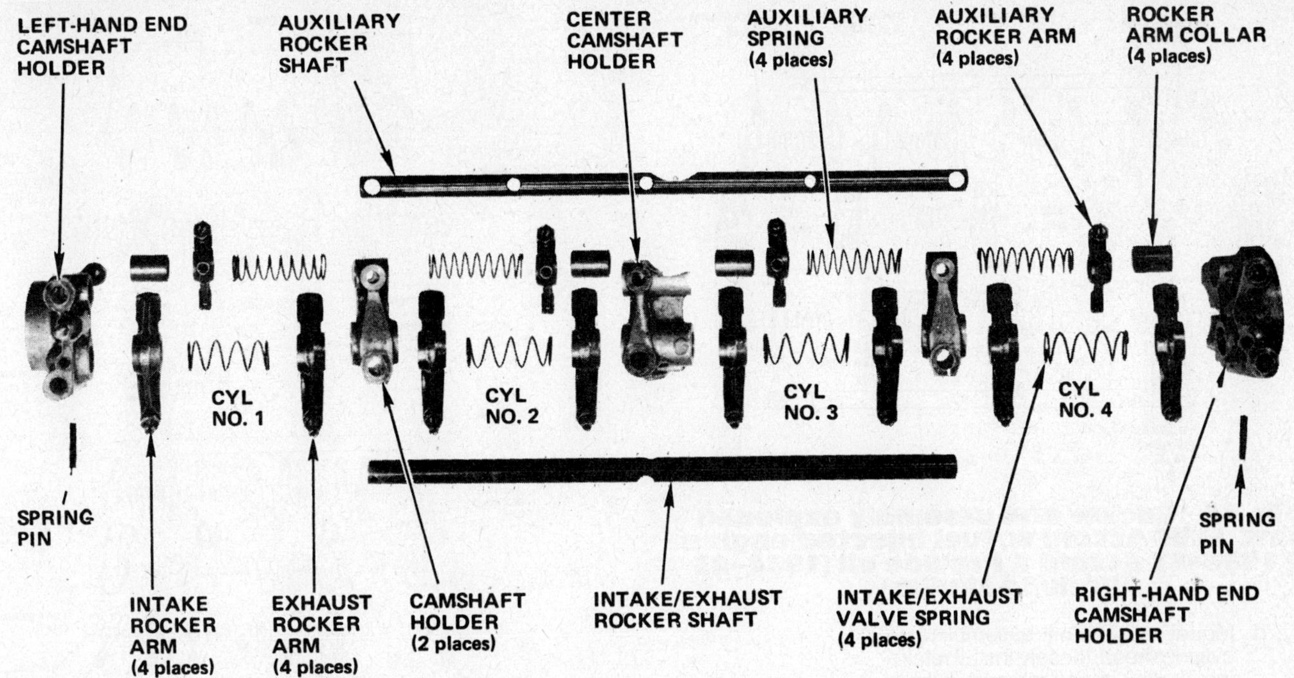

Fig. 12 Rocker arm assembly exploded view. 1983 exc. Prelude

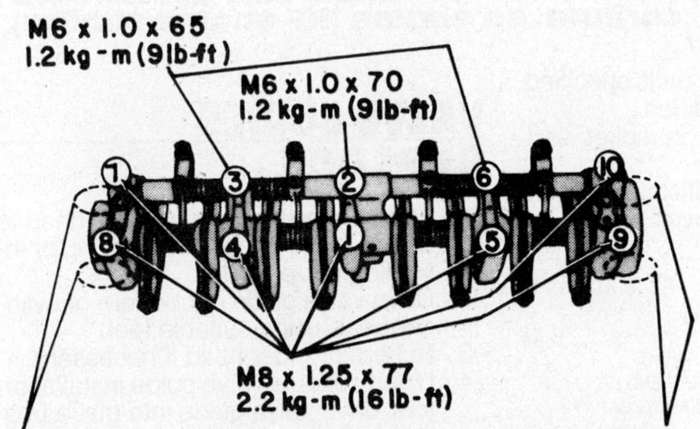

Fig. 13 Rocker shaft retaining bolt tightening sequence. 1983 exc. Prelude

5. Disassemble one or all parts of rocker arm assembly as necessary as shown in **Fig. 12**. Identify parts as they are removed to ensure reinstallation in original position.
6. Measure outside diameter of intake/exhaust rocker shaft and auxiliary rocker shaft at each arm location, then measure inside diameter of rocker arm. Difference between diameters should not exceed 0.003 inch (0.08 mm). If over limit, replace both the rocker shaft and the applicable rocker arm.
7. Loosen valve adjusting nuts and back off adjusting screws before installing rocker arms.
8. Ensure crankshaft timing marks are properly aligned and that camshaft keyway is facing up.
9. Lubricate camshaft surfaces and apply suitable sealant to areas shown in **Fig. 13**
10. Install rocker arm assemblies, then tighten bolts evenly in sequence shown in **Fig. 13** until specified torque is obtained.
11. Install camshaft drive sprocket and timing belt as outlined.
12. Adjust valves to specifications, the install cylinder head cover.

1983 PRELUDE & 1984–87 ALL

1. Remove camshaft drive sprocket as outlined, then disconnect battery ground cable. **While timing belt is removed, do not allow camshaft or crankshaft to rotate independently, as engine may be damaged.**
2. Evenly loosen camshaft holder/rocker arm shaft retaining bolts in crossing pattern, then remove rocker arm shaft assemblies.
3. Remove bolts, then lift off camshaft holder, rocker arm shafts and rocker arms.
4. Disassemble one or all parts of rocker arm assembly as necessary as shown in **Figs. 14 through 17. Prior to removal, identify all parts so they can be installed in their original locations.**
5. Using suitable micrometer, measure outside diameter of both rocker arm shafts at each rocker arm location, then measure the inside diameter of each respective rocker arm. Difference between diameters should not exceed .003 inch (0.08 mm). If difference exceeds specifications, replace applicable rocker arm shaft and rocker arm.
6. Loosen valve adjustment locking nuts, then back off valve adjusting screws.
7. Ensure crankshaft timing marks are properly aligned and that keyway on camshaft is facing up, then lubricate camshaft surfaces with engine oil.
8. On Civic & CRX models, proceed as follows:
   a. Apply suitable sealer to cylinder head mating surfaces of camshaft holders 1 and 5.
   b. Position camshaft holders on cylinder head.
   c. Assemble rocker shafts, using rubber bands to retain rocker arms in position.

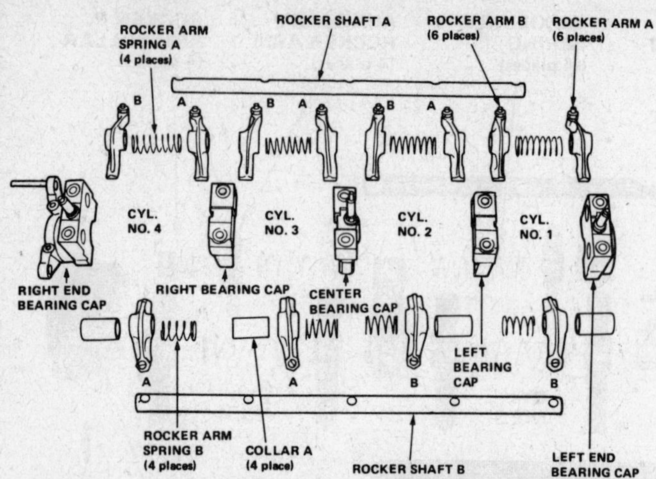

Fig. 14 Rocker arm assembly exploded view. 1985 Accord w/fuel injected engine & 1986–87 Accord & Prelude all (1984–85 Prelude similar)

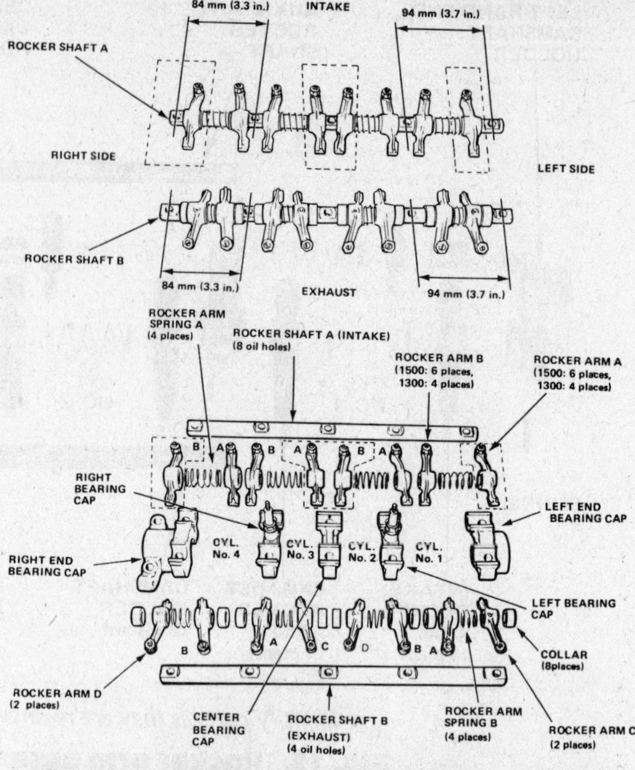

Fig. 16 Rocker arm assembly exploded view. 1984–87 Civic & CRX w/standard carbureted engine (HF engine similar)

d. Mount rocker shaft assemblies on cylinder head, loosely install retaining bolts, then remove rubber bands. **Ensure collars do not ride up over camshaft holders.**

e. Tighten retaining bolts evenly, 1-2 turns at a time, using sequence shown in **Fig. 18,** until specified torque.

9. On Accord and Prelude models, proceed as follows:
   a. Assemble rocker shafts, position rocker shaft assembly on cylinder head, then loosely install retaining bolts.
   b. Tighten retaining bolts evenly, 1-2 turns at a time, using sequence shown in **Fig. 19,** until specified torque value is obtained.
10. Install camshaft drive sprocket and timing belt as outlined.
11. Adjust valves to specifications, then install cylinder head cover.

VALVE GUIDES
REPLACE

1. For best results, heat cylinder head to 300°F (150°C) before removing or installing valve guides.
2. Drive valve guide out bottom of cylinder head using suitable tool.
3. Reheat cylinder head if necessary.
4. Using suitable valve guide installation tool, drive valve guide into place until tool bottoms.

CAM DRIVE SPROCKET & TIMING BELT
REPLACE

1. If necessary, loosen alternator and remove alternator drive belt.
2. Remove valve cover.
3. Remove upper timing belt cover.
4. Rotate crankshaft until No. 1 cylinder is at TDC (top dead center) compression stroke, then align camshaft sprocket timing marks as shown in **Figs. 20 through 24. Crankshaft may be rotated with engine installed in vehicle using a socket wrench inserted through access hole in the front of left fender well.**
5. Working through lower belt cover, loosen belt tensioner adjuster and pivot bolts on 1983 models or adjustment bolt on 1984-87 models. **Do not remove adjuster and pivot bolts (1983) or adjustment bolt (1984-87).**

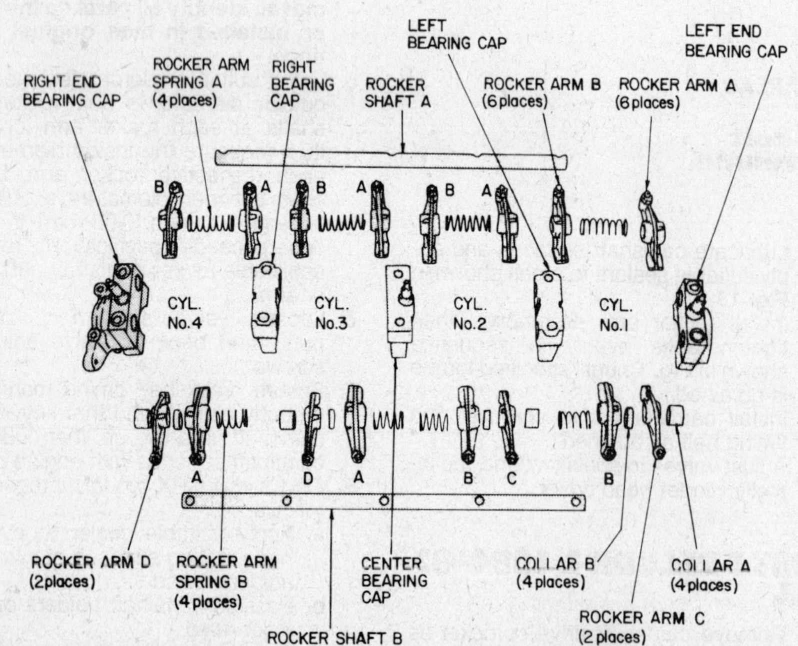

Fig. 15 Rocker arm assembly. 1983 Prelude & 1984–85 Accord w/carbureted engines

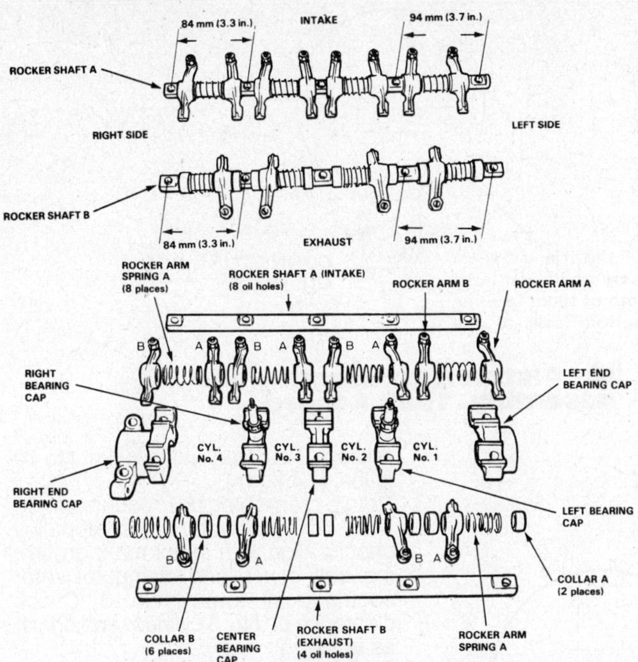

Fig. 17 Rocker arm assembly exploded view. 1985–87 Civic & CRX w/fuel injected engine

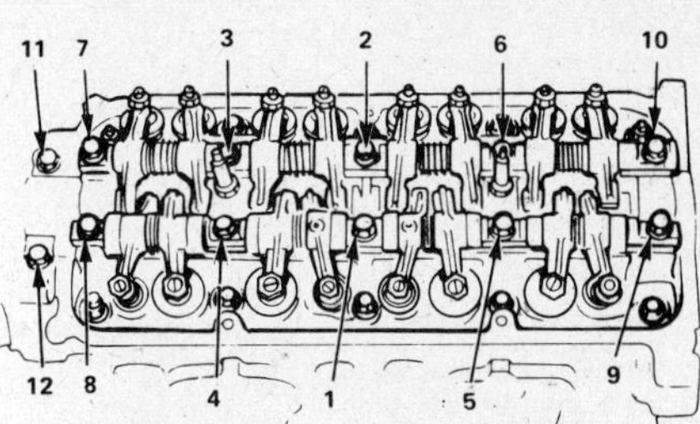

Fig. 18 Camshaft holder/rocker arm shaft bolt tightening sequence. 1984–87 Civic & CRX

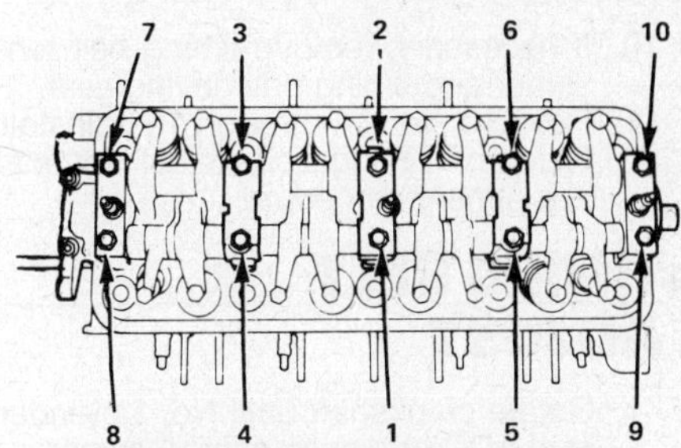

Fig. 19 Camshaft holder/rocker arm shaft bolt tightening sequence. 1983 Prelude & 1984–87 Accord

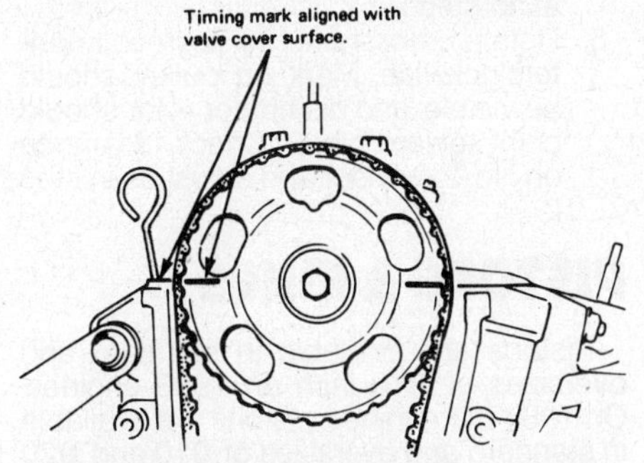

Fig. 20 Camshaft sprocket timing marks. 1983 Civic 1300

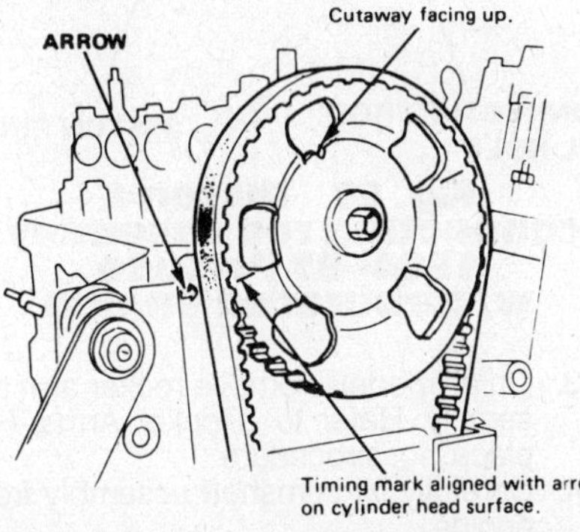

Fig. 21 Camshaft sprocket timing marks. 1983 Civic 1500 & 1983 Accord

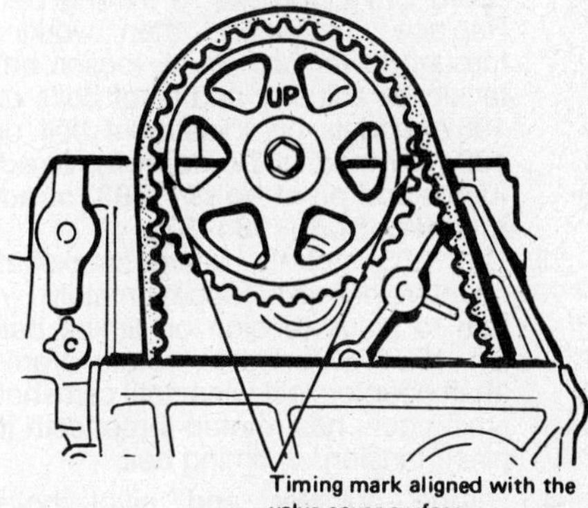

Fig. 22 Camshaft sprocket timing mark. 1984–87 Civic & CRX

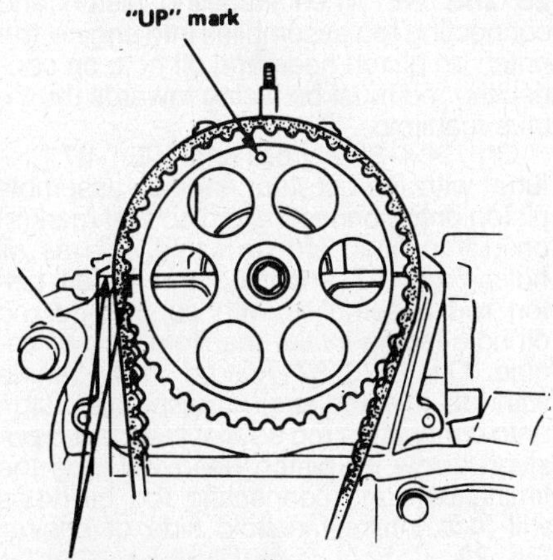

Fig. 23 Camshaft sprocket timing mark. Prelude w/carbureted engine & 1984–85 Accord

6. Mark direction of rotation on timing belt and draw it carefully off the driven or camshaft sprocket. **Avoid crimping or bending timing belt and avoid letting it contact oil or gasoline. If belt is oil soaked, it must be replaced.**
7. Remove driven gear from camshaft by loosening attaching bolt. Be careful not to lose the special washer and key.
8. Remove crankshaft pulley from crankshaft end by loosening the attaching bolt. Be careful not to lose the key. **On some models with external mount water pump pulley, it may be necessary to remove the water pump pulley prior to removing the lower cover.**
9. Remove lower cover but leave the loosened adjustment and pivot bolts in place, and then remove timing belt.

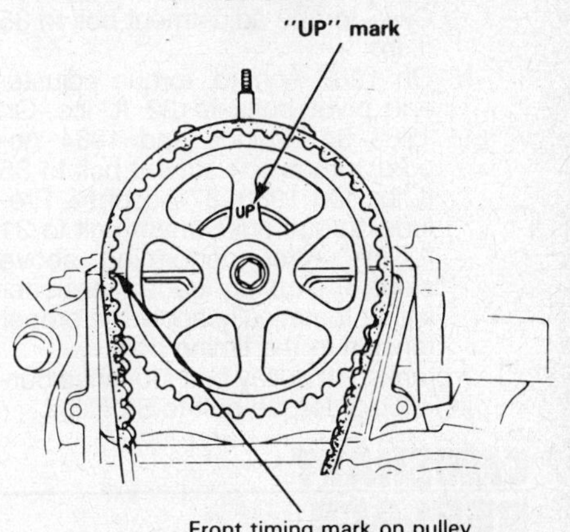

Fig. 24 Camshaft timing mark. 1986–87 Accord & Prelude exc. Prelude w/carbureted engine

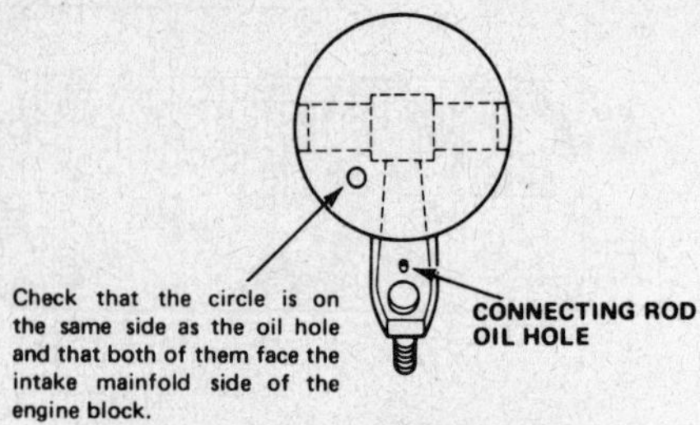
Check that the circle is on the same side as the oil hole and that both of them face the intake manifold side of the engine block.
CONNECTING ROD OIL HOLE

Fig. 25 Piston & connecting rod assembly. 1983 exc. Accord

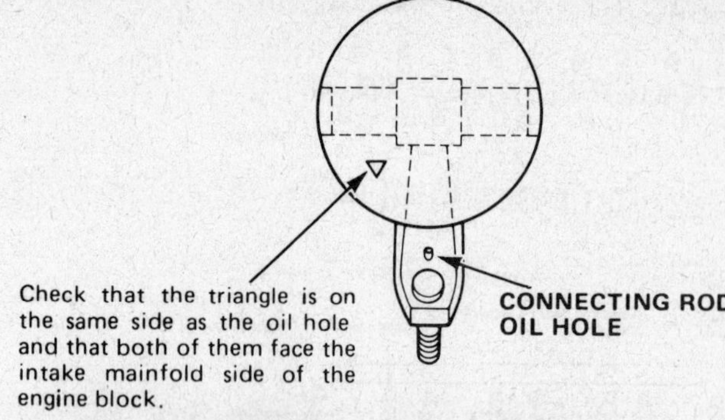
Check that the triangle is on the same side as the oil hole and that both of them face the intake mainfold side of the engine block.
CONNECTING ROD OIL HOLE

Fig. 26 Piston & connecting rod assembly. 1983 Accord

10. If necessary, remove timing belt tensioner and timing belt driving gear.
11. Reverse steps 4 through 10 to install. Refer to "Timing Belt, Adjust" for final adjustment procedure.

TIMING BELT

ADJUST

1. Rotate crankshaft until No. 1 cylinder is at TDC (top dead center) compression stroke. **Crankshaft may be rotated by using a suitable socket wrench inserted through access hole in left front fender well.**
2. Perform steps 1 through 3 under "Cam Drive Sprocket & Timing Belt, Replace" procedure, then working through lower belt cover, loosen belt tensioner adjuster and pivot bolts on 1983 models or adjustment bolt on 1984-87 models. **Do not remove adjuster and pivot bolts (1983) or adjustment bolt (1984-87).**
3. On 1983 models, rotate crankshaft counterclockwise approximately 1/4 turn to place tension on timing belt. On 1984-87 models, rotate crankshaft counterclockwise until camshaft timing gear has rotated three teeth to place tension on timing belt.
4. Torque adjuster and pivot bolts (1983) or adjustment bolt (1984-87) as follows:
   a. On 1983 Civic, torque adjuster and pivot bolts to 32 ft. lbs. On 1984-87 Civic, torque adjustment bolt to 35 ft. lbs.
   b. On 1983 Accord, torque adjuster and pivot bolts to 22 ft. lbs. On 1983-84 Prelude and 1984 Accord, torque adjustment bolt to 35 ft. lbs. On 1986-87 Accord & Prelude, torque adjustment bolt to 31 ft. lbs. After performing above steps, the spring loaded tensioner will automatically apply the proper tension to the timing belt.
5. If crankshaft pulley bolt loosened during step 3, torque bolt to 83 ft. lbs.

CAMSHAFT

REPLACE

1. Remove camshaft driven sprocket as described under "Cam Drive Sprocket & Timing Belt, Replace" procedure.
2. On 1983 models, remove oil pump gear cover, gear shaft and gear.

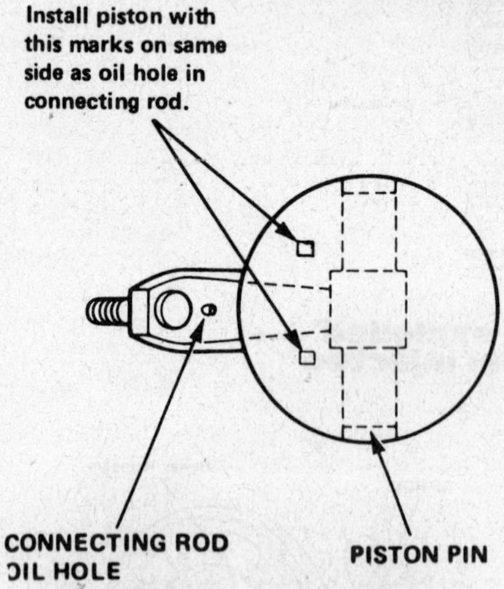

Install piston with this marks on same side as oil hole in connecting rod.

CONNECTING ROD OIL HOLE

PISTON PIN

Fig. 27 Piston & connecting rod assembly. 1984–87 Prelude w/carbureted engine

3. On all models, remove rocker arm assembly. Refer to "Rocker Arms, Replace" for procedure.
4. Carefully lift camshaft assembly from engine.
5. Reverse procedure to install, noting the following:
   a. Lubricate camshaft assembly prior to installation.
   b. After camshaft and rocker arms are installed, install new camshaft seal with spring side facing out using suitable seal installation tool.
   c. Adjust timing belt. Refer to "Timing Belt, Adjust" for procedure.

VALVES

ADJUST

Valves should be adjusted cold. Refer to "Valve Specifications" table for clearances.

1. Set No. 1 piston at top dead center with mark on camshaft pulley at top and TDC groove on back of pulley aligning with cylinder head surface. Also, distributor rotor should point toward No. 1. plug wire terminal
2. Loosen locknut and turn adjustment screw until feeler slides back and forth with slight amount of drag. Then torque intake and exhaust valve locknut to 14 ft. lbs. (2 kg-m) and, if equipped, auxiliary valve locknut to 10 ft. lbs. (1.4 kg-m).
3. Rotate crankshaft 180° counterclockwise. TDC groove on camshaft pulley should align with index mark on timing belt cover, and distributor rotor should point toward No. 3. Check clearance on No. 3 cylinder and adjust as in step 2.
4. Rotate crankshaft 180° counterclockwise. TDC groove should align with cylinder head surface, and distributor rotor should point toward No. 4. Check clearance on No. 4 cylinder and adjust as in step 2.
5. Rotate crankshaft 180 degrees counterclockwise. Mark on pulley should be visible, and distributor rotor should point toward No. 2. Check clearance on No. 2 cylinder and adjust as in step 2.

PISTONS & RINGS

Pistons are available in standard and oversizes of .010 inch on 1983 engines. On 1984-87 engines, pistons are available in standard and oversizes of .010 and .020 inch.

On 1983 engines, when assembling connecting rod onto piston, the oil hole in the connecting rod must be on the same side as the mark on the piston head, **Figs. 25 and 26.** When installing piston and connecting rod assemblies into engine, the notch on piston head and oil hole on connecting rod must be facing towards the intake manifold.

On 1984-85 Accord and 1984-87 Prelude with carbureted engine, assemble piston onto connecting rod so that mark(s) on piston head are on same side as oil hole, **Figs. 27 and 28,** and install piston/rod assemblies with connecting rod oil hole facing intake manifold side of engine. On 1986-87 Accord and Prelude with fuel injected engine, assemble piston onto connecting rod so that in installed position arrow on piston head will face the timing belt and connecting rod oil holes will face intake manifold side of engine, **Fig. 29.**

On 1984-87 Civic and CRX, assemble pistons onto connecting rods with valve depressions on opposite side from connecting rod oil hole, **Fig. 30.** Also note that pistons must be properly matched with connecting rods so that in installed position valve depressions face as shown in

Install piston with this mark on same side as oil hole in connecting rod.

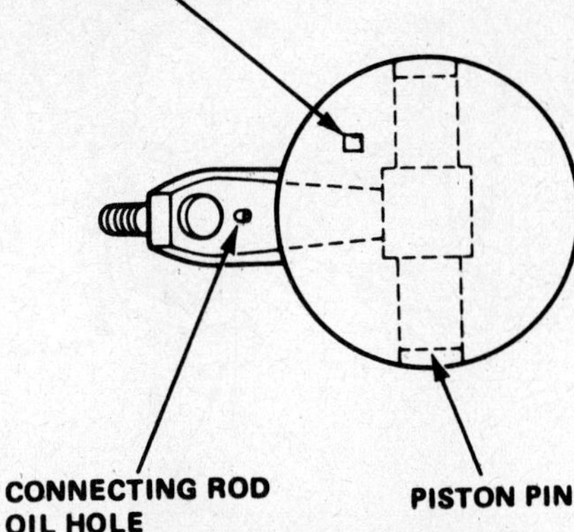

Fig. 28 Piston & connecting rod assembly. 1984–85 Accord

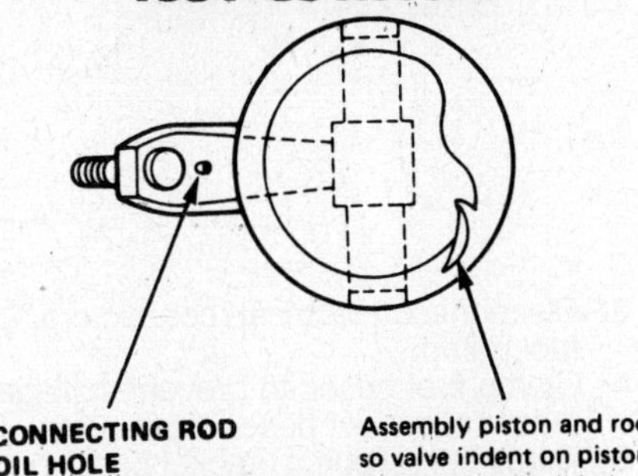

Fig. 30 Piston & connecting rod assembly. 1984–86 Civic & CRX

Fig. 31, and connecting rod oil holes face intake manifold side of engine.

MAIN & ROD BEARINGS

Main bearings are color coded on their edge according to the following table of tolerances:

COLOR	TOLERANCE
Red	−0.0001 to −0.0002 in. (−0.002 to 0.005 mm)
Pink	+0.00004 to −0.0001 in. (+0.001 to −0.002 mm)
Yellow	+0.0002 to −0.00004 in. (+0.004 to −0.001 mm)
Green	+0.00003 to −0.0002 in. (+0.007 to −0.004 mm)
Brown	+0.00004 to −0.0003 in. (+0.010 to −0.007 mm)
Black	+0.00005 to −0.0004 in. (+0.013 to −0.010 mm)
Blue	+0.00006 to −0.0005 in. (+0.016 to −0.013 mm)

Connecting rod bearings are color coded on their edge according to the following table of tolerances:

Red	−0.0002 to −0.0003 in. (−0.005 to 0.008 mm)
Pink	+0.0001 to −0.0002 in. (−0.002 to −0.005 mm)
Yellow	+0.00004 to −0.0001 in. (+0.001 to −0.002 mm)
Green	+0.00002 to −0.00004 in. (+0.004 to −0.001 mm)
Brown	+0.0003 to +0.0002 in. (+0.007 to +0.004 mm)
Black	+0.0004 to +0.0003 in. (+0.0.010 to +0.007 mm)
Blue	+0.0005 to +0.0004 in. (+0.013 to −0.010 mm)

OIL PAN

REPLACE

EXC. 4WD WAGON

1. On manual transmission models, remove flywheel cover. On automatic transmission models, remove driven plate cover.
2. Remove oil pan attaching bolts and nuts, then the oil pan.
3. Reverse procedure to install. Tighten retaining bolts in crossing pattern moving outward from center. On 1983-85 Accord and Prelude, torque retaining bolts to 10 ft. lbs. and retaining nuts to 7 ft. lbs. On 1983-85 Civic, 1985 CRX and all 1986 models, torque retaining bolts and nuts to 7 ft. lbs. On 1987 Accord and Prelude, torque retaining bolts and nuts to 10 ft. lbs. On 1987 Civic and CRX, torque retaining bolts and nuts to 9 ft lbs.

4WD WAGON

1. Remove engine splash shield, then drain engine and transmission oil.
2. Remove exhaust header pipe, then disconnect propeller shaft at transmission.
3. Remove transmission splash shield, then the transfer left side cover from the transfer case.
4. Remove driven gear from transfer case, then the transfer case from clutch housing.
5. Remove clutch case cover.
6. Remove oil pan attaching bolts, then the oil pan.
7. Reverse procedure to install, noting the following:
   a. Apply liquid gasket to the clutch housing mating surface of the transfer case.
   b. Apply suitable sealant to the inner threads of the oil pan attaching bolts.
   c. Tighten attaching bolts alternately on each side, moving out from the center. Torque attaching bolts to 7 ft. lbs.

OIL PUMP

REPLACE

1983 EXC. PRELUDE

1. Remove camshaft/valve cover.
2. Remove oil pump gear cover.
3. Raise vehicle and remove oil pan.
4. Loosen attaching bolts and remove oil pump cover, oil pressure relief valve, valve spring, pin and collar.
5. Drive lock pin from oil pump shaft and remove inner and outer pump rotors.
6. Lower vehicle and lift oil pump gear and shaft from the cylinder head.
7. Reverse procedure to install.

The arrow must face the timing belt side of the engine and the connecting rod oil hole must face the intake manifold.

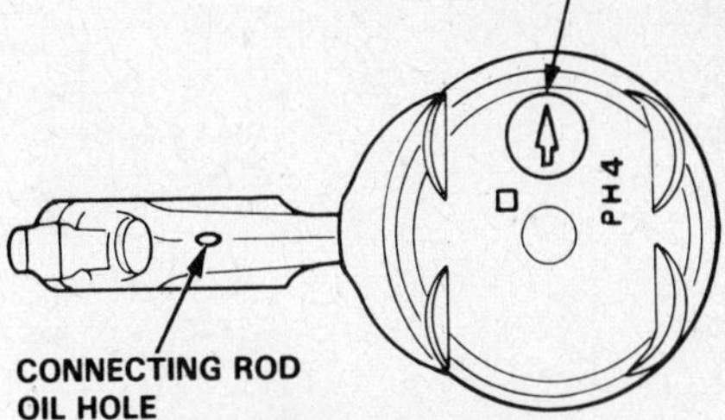

Fig. 29 Piston & connecting rod assembly. 1986–87 Accord & 1986–87 Prelude w/fuel injection engine

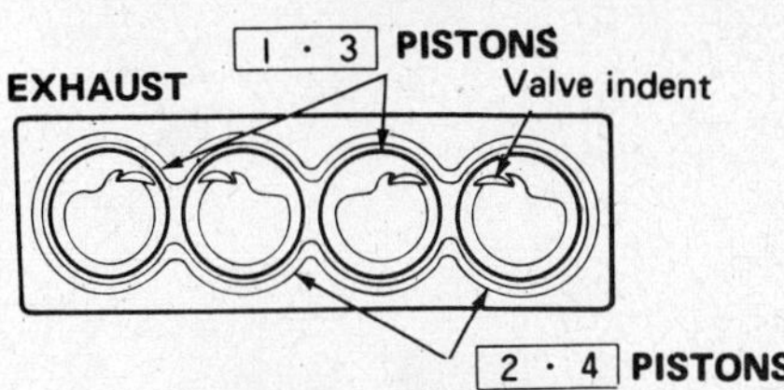

Fig. 31 Piston & connecting rod installation. 1984–87 Civic & CRX

PRELUDE & 1984–87 ACCORD

1. Drain engine oil into suitable container.
2. Remove timing belt. Refer to "Cam Drive Sprocket & Timing Belt, Replace" procedure.
3. Remove oil pump drive pulley attaching nut, then the drive pulley. **The oil pump drive pulley nut has lefthand threads.**
4. Remove oil pump attaching nut and bolts, then the oil pump, **Fig. 32.**
5. Reverse procedure to install. Torque pump attaching bolts and nut to 9 ft. lbs. and oil pump pulley attaching nut to 22 ft. lbs.

1984–87 CIVIC & CRX

1. Drain engine oil into suitable container.
2. Remove timing belt. Refer to "Cam Drive Sprocket & Timing Belt, Replace" procedure.
3. Remove timing belt tensioner and timing belt driving gear.
4. Remove oil pan and oil pump pickup screen.
5. Remove oil pump attaching bolts, then the oil pump, **Fig. 33.**
6. Reverse procedure to install. Torque oil pump and screen attaching bolts to 9 ft. lbs. and oil pump screen attaching nuts to 18 ft. lbs.

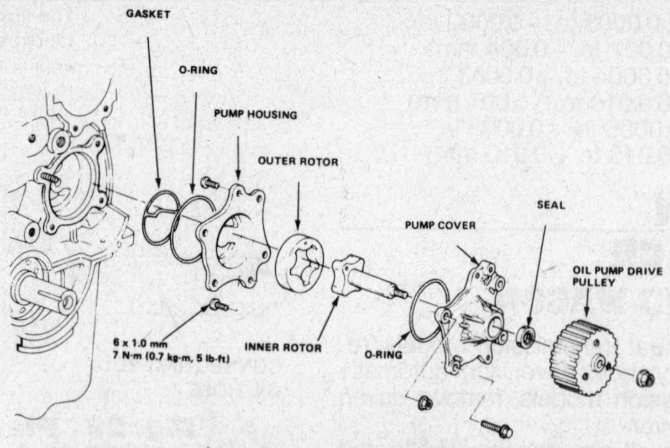

Fig. 32 Oil pump assembly. Prelude & 1984–87 Accord

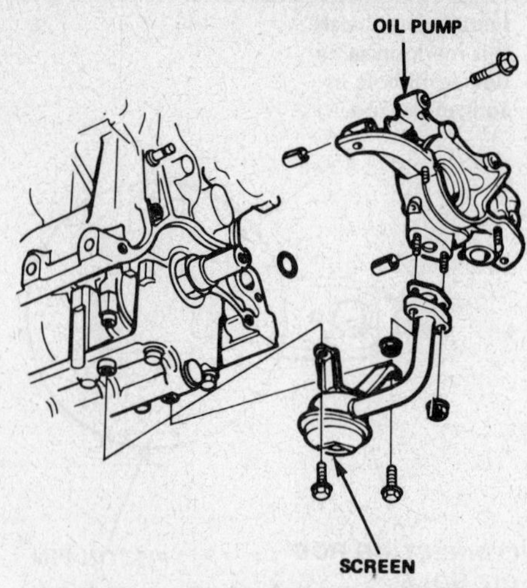

Fig. 33 Oil pump assembly. 1984–87 Civic & CRX

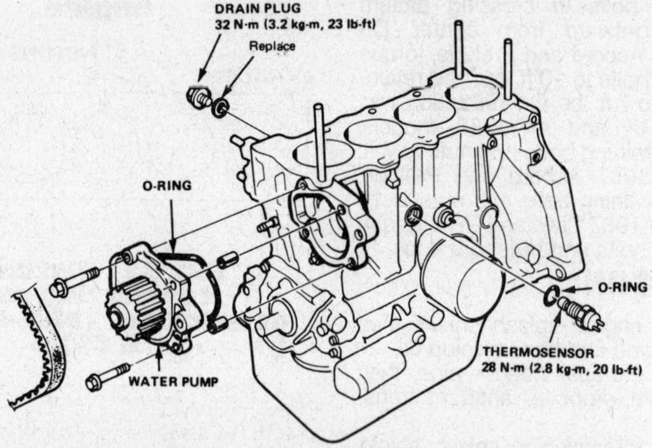

Fig. 34 Water pump assembly. 1984–87 Civic & CRX

CRANKSHAFT REAR OIL SEAL

REPLACE

1. Remove engine/transmission assembly.
2. Remove transmission, then the flywheel housing and flywheel.
3. Remove oil pan.
4. Remove oil seal, using seal removal tool.
5. Clean seal seating surfaces thoroughly, apply a light coat of oil to the crankshaft and the lip of the seal and position seal with the part number side facing out.
6. Drive seal until it bottoms against block using suitable seal installer tool.
7. Install oil pan and then install engine and transmission assembly in vehicle.
8. Fill crankcase and check for leaks.

TIMING BELT GEAR OIL SEAL

REPLACE

1. Remove cam drive sprocket as outlined in "Cam Drive Sprocket & Timing Belt, Replace."
2. Pry seal from its seat in the crankcase.
3. Clean seal seating surfaces thoroughly, apply a light coat of oil to crankshaft and lip of seal and position seal with part number side facing out.
4. Drive seal until it bottoms in the crankcase.
5. Install cam drive gears, timing belt, and adjust timing belt as outlined in "Cam Drive Sprocket & Timing Belt, Replace."

FUEL PUMP

REPLACE

Prior to disconnecting fuel lines on models with fuel injected engines, relieve fuel system pressure as follows:

1. Disconnect battery ground cable.
2. Place shop towel over 6 mm service bolt located on top of fuel filter.
3. Slowly loosen service bolt one full turn.

1983 CIVIC EXC. WAGON, 1983–85 ACCORD, 1983–87 PRELUDE, 1985–87 CRX Si & 1986–87 CIVIC Si

1. Disconnect battery ground cable.
2. Raise and support rear of vehicle, then remove left rear wheel and fuel pump cover, as needed.
3. Disconnect electrical connectors to fuel pump.
4. Clamp fuel hoses to prevent spillage, then disconnect hoses from pump.
5. Remove fuel pump bracket bolts, then the fuel pump and bracket assembly.
6. Reverse procedure to install.

1983 CIVIC WAGON

1. Disconnect battery ground cable.
2. Raise and support rear of vehicle.
3. Remove bolts securing fuel pump to rear of tank, then lower pump and bracket assembly. **Do not remove bracket from tank.**
4. Clamp fuel hoses to prevent spillage, then disconnect hoses and electrical connectors from pump, and remove pump.
5. Reverse procedure to install.

1984–87 CIVIC & CRX W/CARBURETED ENGINE

1. Clamp fuel lines to prevent fuel leakage, then disconnect fuel lines at fuel pump. **Use caution not to damage fuel lines during removal.**
2. Remove fuel pump from engine.
3. Reverse procedure to install. Torque fuel pump attaching bolts to 17 ft. lbs.

1986–87 ACCORD

1. Disconnect battery ground cable.
2. Remove left access cover in luggage area.
3. Disconnect electrical connector and fuel lines from pump.
4. Remove fuel pump mounting bolts, the withdraw pump from fuel tank, taking care not to spill fuel in luggage area. **Fuel pump removal can be aided by loosening fuel tank mounting nuts and lowering tank.**
5. Reverse procedure to install, ensuring that fuel pump and access cover

seals are properly positioned.

WATER PUMP REPLACE

When refilling cooling system, loosen bleed bolt on heater valve or water outlet, as equipped, and allow coolant to flow out until stream is free from bubbles.

EXC. 1984–87 CIVIC & CRX

1. Drain cooling system, then remove alternator belt.
2. Loosen clamps and remove upper coolant hose at pump, along with bracket.
3. Loosen attaching bolts and remove the water pump pulley.
4. Loosen attaching bolts and remove water pump, along with O-ring.
5. Reverse procedure to install, replacing the O-ring with a new one.

1984–87 CIVIC & CRX

1. Drain cooling system into suitable container.
2. Remove timing belt. Refer to "Cam Drive Sprocket & Timing Belt, Replace" for procedure.
3. Remove water pump attaching bolts, then the water pump, **Fig. 34.**
4. Reverse procedure to install. Torque water pump attaching bolts to 9 ft. lbs.

CLUTCH & MANUAL TRANSMISSION SECTION

INDEX

CLUTCH ADJUST

1. Turn cable adjusting nut located on cable casing near transaxle, **Fig. 1,** until freeplay at release arm is 13/64-1/4 inch on Accord and Prelude models, 3/16-7/32 inch on 1983 Civic models, or 5/32-13/64 inch on all other models.
2. After adjusting release arm freeplay, check clutch pedal height at the clutch release point and clutch pedal freeplay. **It may be necessary to pull back carpet to obtain accurate pedal release height measurement.**
3. Minimum pedal height above floor at clutch release point should be as follows:

1983 Civic	1 3/16 inches
1983 Accord	1 1/4 inches
1983 Prelude	1 1/4 inches
1984-85 Accord	3.4 inches
1984-85 Prelude	1.85 inches
1984-87 Civic Exc. Wagon	3.3 inches
1984-87 Civic Wagon	3.1 inches
1985-87 CRX	2.4 inches
1986 Accord	2.9 inches
1986 Prelude	3.4 inches
1987 Accord & Prelude	2.3 inches

4. Clutch pedal free travel should be as follows:

1983 Accord	3/8-1 3/16 inches
1983 Civic	0.9-1.1 inches
1983-85 Prelude	7/8-1 1/8 inches
1984-85 Accord	7/8-1 1/8 inches
1984-86 Civic	0.4-1.18 inches
1984-87 CRX	0.4-1.18 inches
1987 Civic	0.6-0.8 inch
1986-87 Accord & Prelude	0.6-1.0 inch

5. If specified clearances cannot be obtained, inspect clutch and release mechanism and repair as needed.

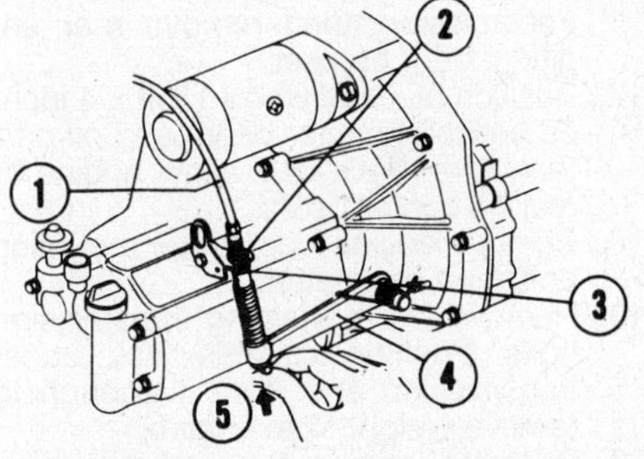

① Clutch control cable
② Adjusting nut
③ Lock nut
④ Clutch release lever
⑤ Clutch release lever play

Fig. 1 Typical clutch release mechanism

CLUTCH REPLACE

1. Remove transmission as described under "Manual Transmission, Replace."
2. Remove release bearing arm to shaft attaching bolt, then the release bearing assembly.
3. Remove release bearing clip, then the bearing from arm.
4. Check release bearing for excessive play and roughness and replace if necessary.
5. Lock flywheel with a suitable ring gear holder.
6. On models equipped with a two-piece pressure plate, separate clutch diaphragm spring from pressure plate, if necessary, by removing stopper springs.
7. On all models, loosen pressure plate attaching bolts one turn at a time to prevent warping pressure plate, then remove attaching bolts and pressure plate.
8. Remove clutch disc from flywheel.
9. Reverse procedure to install. Torque 6 mm pressure plate attaching bolts to 7-9 ft. lbs. and 8 mm bolts to 19 ft. lbs. in a criss-cross pattern, two turns at a time to prevent warpage. On models equipped with a two-piece pressure plate, ensure mark on pressure plate is aligned with flywheel. On one-piece pressure plate, align flywheel dowel pins with alignment holes in pressure plate. On all models, use suitable clutch disc alignment tool before tightening pressure plate bolts.

MANUAL TRANSMISSION REPLACE

1983 CIVIC 4 SPEED

1. Disconnect battery ground cable.
2. Release steering lock and place gear shift lever in neutral.
3. Disconnect the following engine compartment electrical connectors:
   a. Battery positive cable from starter.
   b. Black/white wire from starter solenoid.
   c. Yellow/green wire from temperature gauge sending unit.
   d. Black/yellow and yellow wires from ignition timing thermosensor.
   e. Green/black and yellow wires from back-up light switch.
4. Remove speedometer cable retaining clip. **Do not disassemble speedometer gear holder.**

5. Disconnect clutch cable at release arm.
6. Remove transmission side starter bolt and top transmission mounting bolt.
7. Remove forward bolt for rear torque arm bracket.
8. Raise and support vehicle.
9. Drain oil, then reinstall washer and drain plug.
10. Remove front wheels.
11. Remove nut and washer from end of each stabilizer bar. Remove both mounting brackets, then remove bar.
12. Disconnect right and left lower arm ball joints and tie rod end ball joints, or remove pivot bolts from lower control arms instead.
13. Rotate right side steering knuckle fully outward. With screwdriver positioned against inboard constant velocity joint, pry right axle out of transmission housing approximately 1/2 inch to force its spring clip out of groove inside differential gear splines, then remove completely. Repeat on other side.
14. Disconnect shift lever torque rod from clutch housing.
15. Slide pin retainer rearward, then remove spring pin using suitable punch. Disconnect shift rod.
16. Position suitable jack under engine oil pan and raise engine enough to remove weight from mounts. **Place piece of wood on jack to prevent oil pan damage.**
17. Remove front and rear torque rods, then remove rear torque rod brackets.
18. Remove engine damper bracket from transmission.
19. Position block of wood 1 x 2 x 4 inches between center beam and oil pan, then lower jack, allowing engine to rest on center beam.
20. Remove engine-side starter mounting bolt, then the starter.
21. Remove two remaining engine to transmission bolts, then position suitable jack under transmission and raise enough to remove weight from engine.
22. Separate transmission from engine until mainshaft clears clutch pressure plate. Lower jack and remove transmission from vehicle.
23. Reverse procedure to install.

1983 CIVIC 5 SPEED

1. Disconnect battery ground cable from battery and transmission.
2. Release steering column lock and place gear selector in neutral range.
3. Disconnect all electrical connectors from starter and transmission.
4. Disconnect clutch cable from transmission by removing outer cable circlip at firewall and disconnecting inner cable end from clutch arm. Raise and support vehicle.
5. Remove speedometer cable retaining clip. Do not disassemble speedometer gear holder.
6. Remove transmission side starter mounting bolt and upper transmission mounting bolt.
7. Remove front bolt from rear torque arm bracket.
8. Drain transmission and reinstall drain plug. Remove both front wheels.
9. Remove stabilizer bar attaching bolts, then the stabilizer bar.
10. Disconnect both lower arm ball joints and tie rod end ball joints using suitable removal tool. The lower control arm pivot bolts may be removed and lower control arm lowered instead of disconnecting ball joints.
11. Rotate right side steering knuckle fully outward. Position screwdriver against inboard constant velocity joint and pry axle out of transmission housing 1/2 inch. This will force the spring clip out of groove in differential gear splines. Continue removing axle from transmission housing. Repeat procedure for left side axle shaft.
12. Disconnect shift lever torque rod from clutch housing.
13. Remove shift rod spring pin using suitable punch, then disconnect shift rod.
14. Position suitable jack under engine oil pan and raise engine until weight is removed from mounts. Use block of wood on lifting pad to prevent damage to oil pan.
15. Remove front and rear torque rods and rear torque rod brackets.
16. Remove engine damper bracket from transmission, then remove rear engine mount bracket.
17. Position block of wood 1 x 2 x 4 inches between center beam and oil pan, then lower jack and allow engine to rest on center beam.
18. Remove engine side starter mounting bolt, then the starter.
19. Remove two remaining transmission bolts. Position suitable jack under transmission and raise it enough to remove weight from engine.
20. Separate engine from transmission until mainshaft clears pressure plate, then lower transmission and remove from vehicle.
21. Reverse procedure to install.

1984–87 CIVIC & CRX EXC. 4WD WAGON

1. Perform steps 1 through 6 as outlined in "1983 Civic 4 Speed" removal.
2. Raise and support front of vehicle and remove front wheels.
3. Attach a suitable chain hoist to engine, then raise engine just enough to take weight off mounts.
4. Drain transaxle, then reinstall drain plug.
5. Position jack under right lower ball joint, disconnect ball joint from steering knuckle and slowly lower jack to relieve spring tension. Repeat procedure for left ball joint. **Ensure jack is positioned securely under lower control arm.**
6. Remove engine and right wheelwell splash shields.
7. Disconnect and remove exhaust header pipe.
8. Rotate right steering knuckle outward as far as possible, pry right inner constant velocity joint approximately 1/2 inch from transaxle to release spring retainer, then disconnect right driveshaft from transaxle. **Do not pull driveshaft from transaxle without first releasing spring retainer as constant velocity joints will be damaged.**
9. Disconnect shift lever torque rod from clutch housing.
10. Slide shift rod pin retainer back, drive out pin securing shift rod and disconnect rod from transaxle.
11. Support transaxle with a suitable jack and remove bolts from front transaxle mount and bolts securing engine torque bracket to transaxle.
12. Remove bolts securing rear transaxle bracket to clutch housing and remaining bolts securing transaxle to engine.
13. Separate transaxle from engine until mainshaft clears clutch pressure plate.
14. Pry left inner constant velocity joint approximately 1/2 inch out of transaxle to release spring retainer, then disconnect left driveshaft while lowering transaxle from vehicle.
15. Reverse procedure to install.

CIVIC 4WD WAGON

Transaxle must be removed with engine, refer to "Engine Section" for procedure.

1. Remove starter motor, then the three engine attaching bolts.
2. Remove transaxle attaching bolts, then the half shaft and transaxle assembly.
3. Reverse procedure to install.

ACCORD

1. Disconnect ground cable at battery and at transmission.
2. Release steering lock and place gear selector in neutral position.
3. Disconnect engine compartment wiring as follows:
   a. Battery positive cable from starter motor.
   b. Black/white wire from starter solenoid.
   c. Green/black and yellow wires from back-up light switch.
   d. Red and blue wires from distributor (1983).
4. Release engine sub-wire harness from clamp at clutch housing.
5. Disconnect clutch cable at release arm.
6. Remove transmission side starter mounting bolt and two upper transmission mounting bolts.
7. Raise and support vehicle.
8. Drain transmission oil, then reinstall drain plug and washer.
9. Remove front wheels.
10. Place suitable jack securely beneath transmission.
11. Remove speedometer drive holder attaching bolt and pull assembly out of transmission.
12. Disconnect shift lever torque rod from clutch housing.
13. Remove bolt from shift rod clevis.
14. Using suitable tools, disconnect lower ball joints and tie rod end ball joints.

15. Turn each steering knuckle fully outboard, then, using screwdriver, pry constant velocity joint out approximately 1/2 inch, then pull sub-axle out of transmission housing. Repeat on opposite side.
16. Remove right side radius rod.
17. Remove torque arm bracket bolts from clutch housing.
18. Remove damper bracket from center beam.
19. Remove clutch housing bolts from both transmission mounting brackets.
20. Remove clutch cover.
21. Remove engine side starter mounting bolt and the starter.
22. Remove front transmission mounting bolt.
23. Pull transmission away from engine block enough to clear dowel pins, then lower transmission and remove from under vehicle.
24. Reverse procedure to install.

PRELUDE

1. Disconnect ground cable at battery and at transmission.
2. Release steering lock and place selector lever in neutral.
3. Disconnect engine compartment wiring as follows:
   a. Battery positive cable from starter motor.
   b. Black/white wire from starter solenoid.
   c. Green/black and yellow wires from back-up light switch.
4. Release engine sub-wire harness from clamp at clutch housing.
5. Disconnect clutch cable at release arm.
6. Remove two upper transmission mounting bolts.
7. Raise and support vehicle.
8. Drain transmission oil, then reinstall drain plug and washer.
9. Remove front wheels.
10. Place suitable jack securely beneath transmission.
11. Remove speedometer drive holder attaching bolt and pull assembly out of transmission.
12. Disconnect shift lever torque rod from clutch housing.
13. Remove bolt from shift rod clevis.
14. Using suitable tools, disconnect tie rod ball joints from steering knuckles.
15. Remove lower arm ball joint bolt from right side lower control arm, disconnect ball joint from knuckle with suitable puller, and remove damper fork bolt.
16. Turn either steering knuckle fully outboard, then, using screwdriver, pry constant velocity joint out approximately 1/2 inch, then pull stub axle out of transmission housing. Repeat procedure on other side.
17. Remove right side radius rod.
18. Remove torque arm bracket bolts from clutch housing.
19. Remove damper bracket from transmission.
20. Remove clutch housing bolts from front transmission mount.
21. Remove clutch housing bolts from rear transmission mounting bracket.
22. Remove clutch cover.
23. Remove starter mounting bolts and the starter.
24. Remove front transmission mounting bolt.
25. Pull transmission away from engine block enough to clear dowel pins, then lower transmission and remove from beneath vehicle.

DISC BRAKES SECTION

INDEX

BRAKE PEDAL HEIGHT ADJUST

1. Pull up floor mat or carpeting and measure distance between top of pedal and floor as shown in **Fig. 1.**
2. Brake pedal height should be as follows:

1983 Civic	7.25 inches
1983-85 Accord	7.36 inches
1983-87 Prelude	7.00 inches
1984-87 Civic Exc. Wagon	6.80 inches
1984-87 Civic Wagon	6.60 inches
1985-87 CRX	6.80 inches
1986-87 Accord	8.07 inches

3. If brake pedal height is not as specified, loosen locknut on brake lamp switch and back-off switch until it no longer contacts pedal arm.
4. Loosen locknut on pedal pushrod, **Fig. 1,** rotate pushrod to adjust pedal height, then tighten locknut while holding position of pushrod.
5. Tighten stop lamp switch against pedal arm stop until brake pedal free travel is zero, back switch off 1/2 turn, then tighten switch locknut.
6. Ensure pedal free travel is .04-.2 inch and that stop lamps go out when pedal is released.

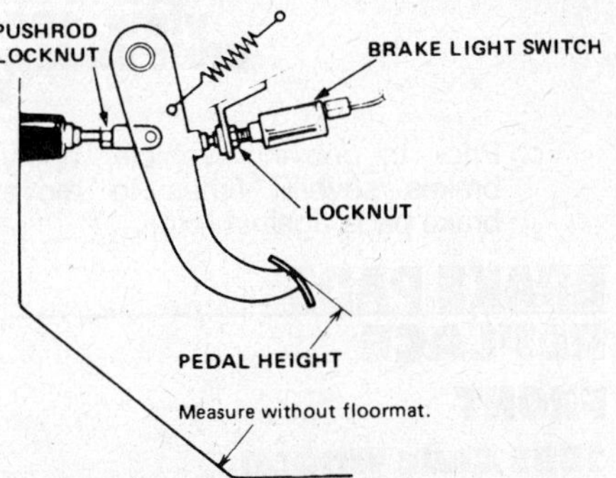

Fig. 1 Typical brake pedal height adjustment

PARKING BRAKE ADJUST

1. Raise rear wheels off ground.
2. Loosen equalizer adjusting nut.
3. Pull parking brake lever up one notch.
4. Tighten equalizer adjusting nut until rear wheels drag slightly when turned.
5. Release brake lever and check that rear wheels do not drag when turned. Readjust if necessary.

MASTER CYLINDER REPLACE

1. Disconnect primary and secondary brake lines.
2. Disconnect wires to fluid level sensors.
3. Remove two attaching bolts holding master cylinder to the vacuum booster unit, and remove master cylinder.
4. Reverse procedure to install, bleeding brakes as necessary.

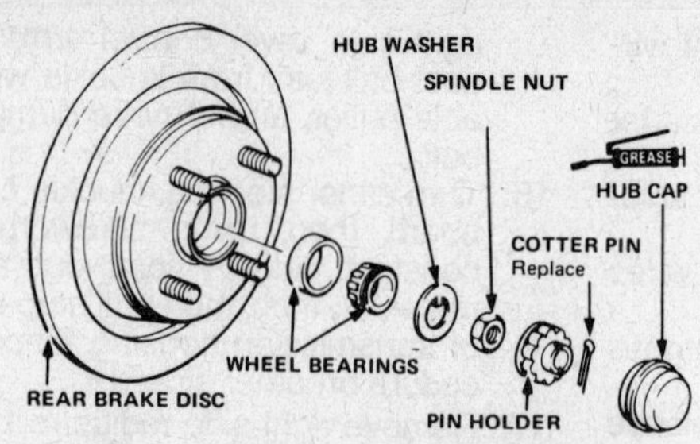

Fig. 2 Rear brake disc & hub assembly. 1984–87 Prelude

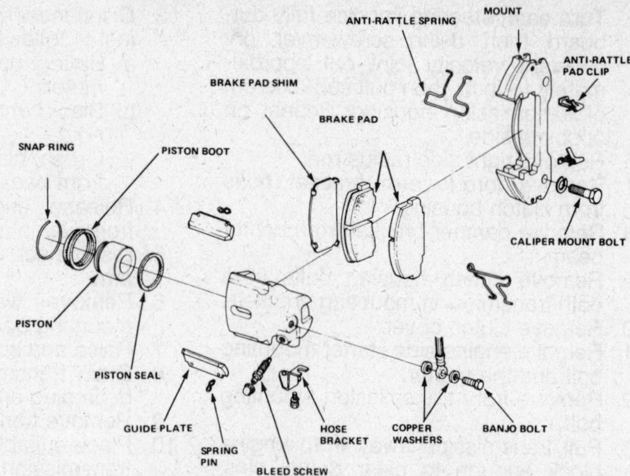

Fig. 3 Front disc brake caliper exploded view. 1983 Civic Wagon

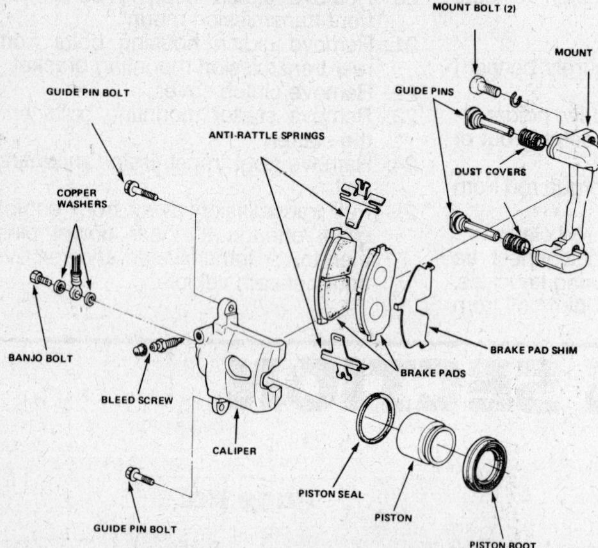

Fig. 4 Front disc brake caliper exploded view. 1984 Civic 1300 Coupe & 1985–87 CRX HF

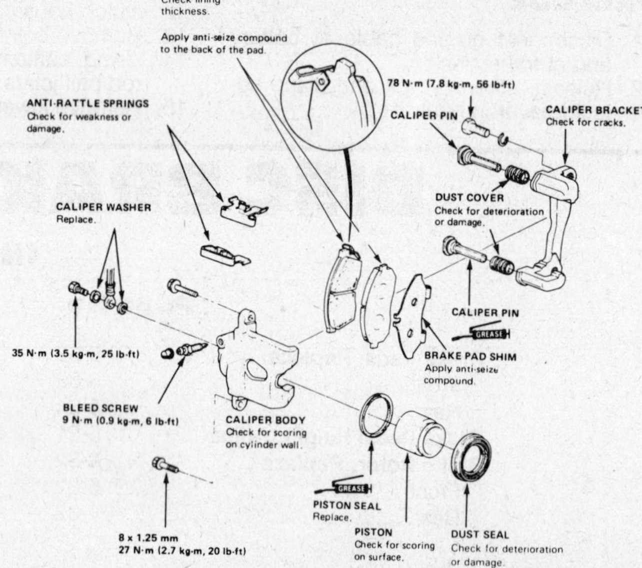

Fig. 5 Front disc brake caliper exploded view. 1984 Civic 1500 Coupe & 1984–87 Civic Sedan & Hatchback (1983 Civic Sedan & Hatchback similar)

BRAKE ROTOR REPLACE

FRONT

1. Raise and support front of vehicle and remove wheel and tire assembly.
2. Unfasten caliper and position aside, leaving brake line attached.
3. Remove two disc retaining screws.
4. Install two 8 x 1.25 x 12 mm bolts into threaded holes and turn bolts evenly to pull rotor off.
5. Reverse procedure to install.

REAR

1984–87 Prelude

1. Raise and support rear of vehicle, then remove rear wheels.
2. Remove caliper bolts and position caliper aside without disconnecting brake hose.
3. Remove rear grease cap, cotter pin, and pin holder, **Fig. 2**
4. Remove spindle nut, then brake rotor.
5. Reverse procedure to install, noting the following:
   a. Ensure wheel bearings are properly lubricated, then adjust as outlined in Rear Suspension Section.
   b. Install caliper as outlined in "Caliper, Replace."
   c. Prior to moving vehicle, apply brakes several times to move brake pads against rotor.

BRAKE PADS REPLACE

FRONT

1983 Civic Wagon

1. Raise and support front of vehicle and remove wheels.
2. Remove 2 spring pins from each guide plate, **Fig. 3,** then remove guide plates from between caliper and bracket noting installation position.
3. Remove caliper body from bracket and secure aside.
4. Remove outer pad along with pad shim.
5. Remove inner pad anti-rattle clips and the inner pad.
6. Loosen bleed screw and compress caliper piston so caliper will fit over pads, then tighten bleed screw.
7. Reverse procedure to install.

Civic Exc. Wagon & 1985–87 CRX HF

1. Raise and support front of vehicle and remove wheels.
2. Remove lower guide pin bolt and pivot caliper up away from pads.
3. Remove brake pads, spring plate, shim and anti-rattle springs, as equipped, **Figs. 4 and 5,** noting installation position.
4. Position anti-rattle springs on bracket, then install brake pads. **Ensure wear sensor is positioned toward inside, if equipped.**
5. Install shim on outer brake pad, then install spring plate, if equipped.
6. Loosen caliper bleed screw and compress piston so caliper will fit over pads, then tighten bleed screw.

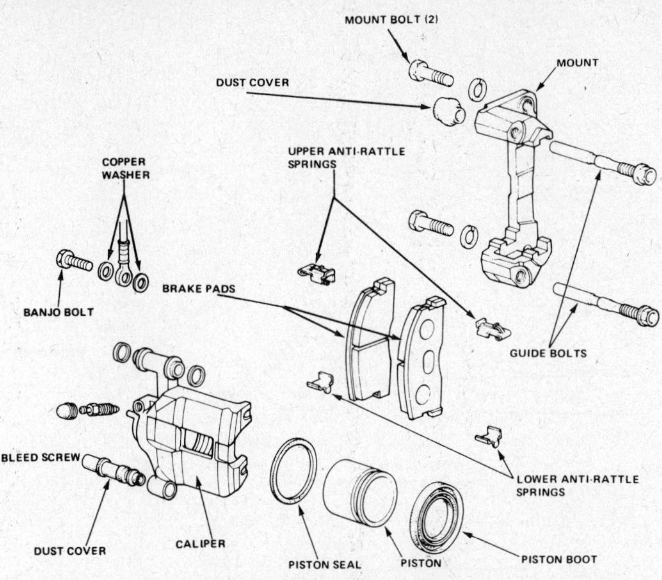

Fig. 6 Front disc brake caliper exploded view. 1983 Prelude

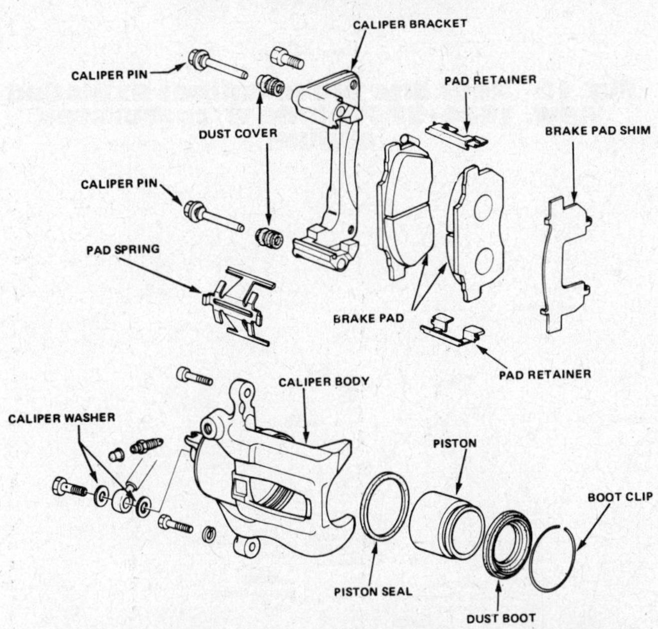

Fig. 8 Front disc brake caliper exploded view. Prelude w/carbureted engine, 1984–87 Civic Wagon & 1985–87 CRX Exc. HF

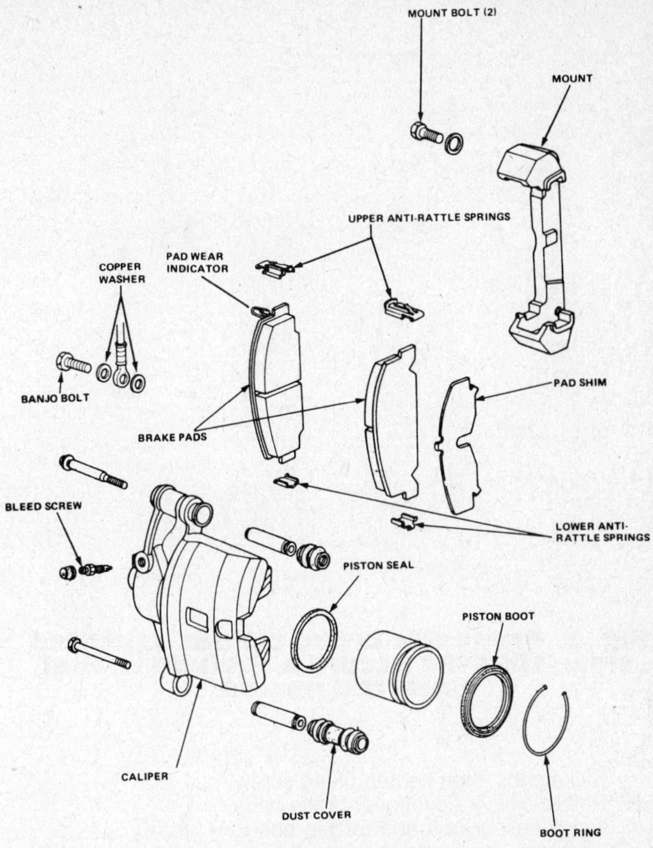

Fig. 7 Front disc brake caliper exploded view. 1984–85 Prelude

4. Remove pad spring from caliper and retainers from mounting bracket, noting installation position.
5. Apply suitable anti-seize compound to outer edges of brake pad backing and apply thin film of high temperature brake grease to back of pad.
6. Position pad retainers in caliper bracket, then install brake pads and shim. **Install inner pad with wear indicator toward inside.**
7. Loosen caliper bleed screw and compress piston so caliper will fit over brake pads, then tighten bleed screw.
8. Position pad spring in caliper, rotate caliper over brake pads and install caliper pin, then torque pin to 13 ft. lbs.

7. Rotate caliper down over pads, install guide pin bolt and torque bolt to 20 ft. lbs.

1983–85 Accord

1. Raise and support vehicle and remove wheels.
2. Remove lower caliper guide bolt, **Figs. 6 and 7**, then pivot caliper up and away from pads.
3. Remove brake pads and anti-rattle springs from caliper bracket, noting installation position.
4. Position anti-rattle springs and new pads in caliper bracket and install pad shims, if equipped. **Install inner pad with wear indicator, if equipped, toward inside.**
5. Loosen caliper bleed screw and compress piston so caliper will fit over pads, then tighten bleed screw.
6. Rotate caliper down into position, install guide bolt and torque bolt to 13 ft. lbs. on Prelude models or 20 ft. lbs. on Accord models.

Prelude w/Carbureted Engine, 1984–87 Civic Wagon & 1985–87 CRX Exc. HF

1. Raise and support front of vehicle and remove wheels.
2. Remove caliper pin A, **Fig. 8,** and rotate caliper up away from pads.
3. Remove shim and brake pads from mounting bracket.

1986–87 Accord & Prelude w/Fuel Injected Engine

1. Raise and support front of vehicle and remove wheels.
2. Remove bolts securing brake hose clamp to steering knuckle.
3. Remove caliper bolt, **Fig. 9,** and pivot caliper up away from brake pads.
4. Remove pad shim, pad retainers and brake pads, noting installation position.
5. Apply anti-seize compound to back of brake pads and both sides of pad shim.
6. Position pad retainers in caliper bracket, then install brake pads and outer pad shim. **Install brake pad with wear indicator on inside.**
7. Loosen caliper bleed screw and compress piston so caliper will fit over

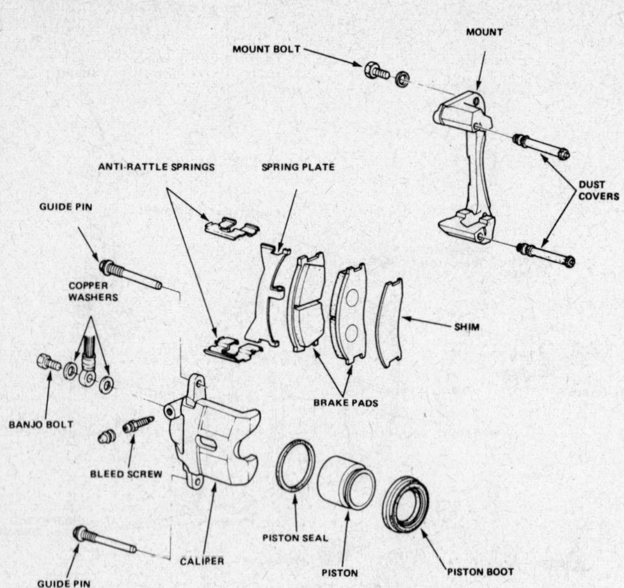

Fig. 9 Front disc brake caliper exploded view. 1986–87 Accord & Prelude w/fuel injected engine

brake pads, then tighten bleed screw.

8. Rotate caliper down over brake pads, install caliper bolt and torque bolt to 33 ft. lbs.

REAR

1984–87 Prelude

1. Raise and support rear of vehicle, then remove rear wheels.
2. Remove caliper shield, then the parking brake cable.
3. Remove caliper guide pins, then the caliper, **Figs. 10 and 11.**
4. Remove brake pads and guides.
5. Clean caliper thoroughly of rust and dirt.
6. Install brake pads and guides in caliper bracket.
7. Rotate caliper piston fully clockwise into caliper bore. Align piston cut-out with inner brake pad tab by turning piston counterclockwise.
8. Install brake caliper, parking brake cable and caliper shield.
9. Depress brake pedal several times to seat pads, then check brake fluid and replenish as necessary.
10. Install rear wheels and lower vehicle.

CALIPER REPLACE

FRONT

1983 Civic Wagon

1. Raise and support front of vehicle and remove wheels.
2. Remove bolt securing brake hose bracket and the brake hose banjo bolt, disconnect nose and secure hose in raised position.
3. Remove 2 spring pins from each guide plate, **Fig. 3,** then remove guide plates from between caliper and

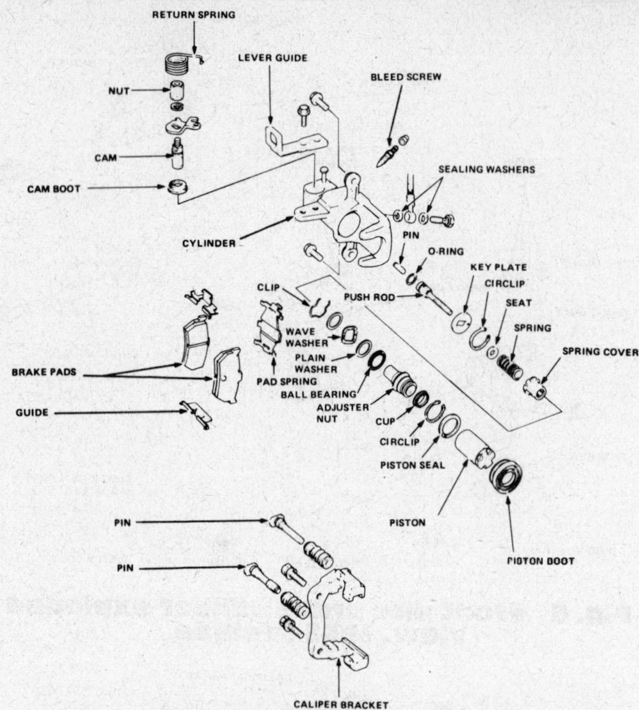

Fig. 10 Rear disc brake caliper exploded view. 1984–87 Prelude w/carbureted engine

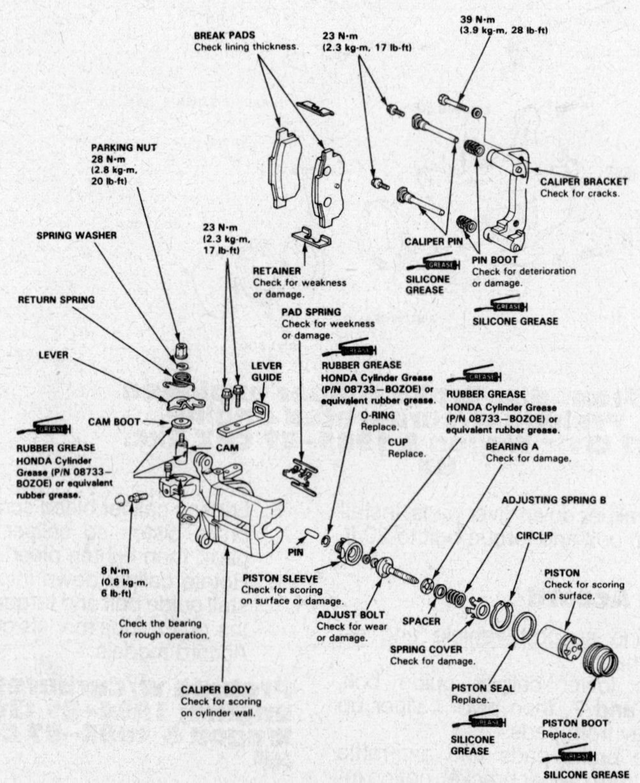

Fig. 11 Rear disc brake caliper exploded view. 1986–87 Prelude w/fuel injected engine

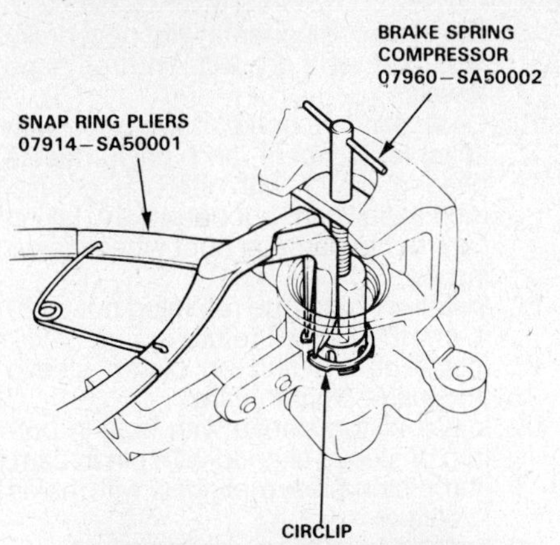

Fig. 12 Rear caliper adjusting spring removal. 1984–87 Prelude

bracket noting installation position.
4. Remove caliper body from bracket.
5. Remove brake pads as outlined.
6. Remove caliper bracket retaining bolts and the bracket.
7. Install mounting bracket and torque bolts to 56 ft. lbs.
8. Install brake pads as outlined, ensure caliper piston is fully seated, then position caliper over brake pads.
9. Insert guide plates between caliper and bracket and secure with new spring pins.
10. Install brake hose using new sealing washers, torque banjo bolt to 25 ft lbs. and hose bracket screw to 7 ft. lbs, then bleed brake system.

Exc. 1983 Civic Wagon, 1986–87 Accord & Prelude w/Fuel Injected Engine

1. Raise and support front of vehicle and remove wheels.
2. Remove brake hose bracket bolt, if equipped and the brake hose banjo bolt, disconnect brake hose and secure hose in raised position.
3. Remove caliper guide pins or guide pin bolts, **Figs. 4 through 8,** then remove caliper.
4. Remove brake pads, shims, retainers and/or anti-rattle springs as outlined.
5. Remove caliper bracket retaining bolts and the caliper bracket.
6. Install mounting bracket and torque bolts to 56 ft. lbs.
7. Install brake pads as outlined, ensure caliper piston is fully seated, then position caliper over brake pads.
8. Install guide pin retaining bolts or guide pins and torque to 20 ft. lbs. on all except Prelude or 13 ft. lbs. for Prelude models.
9. Install brake hose using new sealing washers, torque banjo bolt to 25 ft. lbs. and hose bracket screw to 7 ft. lbs, then bleed brake system.

1986 Accord & 1986 Prelude w/Fuel Injected Engine

1. Raise and support front of vehicle and remove wheels.
2. Remove brake hose bracket bolt and the brake hose banjo bolt, disconnect brake hose and secure hose in raised position.
3. Remove caliper retaining bolt, **Fig. 9,** rotate caliper up away from pads and pull caliper off pin.
4. Remove brake pads, shims and retainers as outlined.
5. Remove caliper bracket retaining bolts and the caliper bracket.
6. Install mounting bracket and torque bolts to 53 ft. lbs.
7. Install brake pads as outlined.
8. Ensure caliper piston is fully compressed and press caliper onto caliper pin.
9. Rotate caliper down over pads, install caliper bolt and torque bolt to 33 ft. lbs.
10. Install brake hose using new sealing washers, torque banjo bolt to 25 ft. lbs. and hose bracket screw to 7 ft. lbs., then bleed brake system.

REAR

1984–87 Prelude

1. Raise and support rear of vehicle and remove wheels.
2. Remove caliper dust shield and disconnect parking brake cable.
3. Remove brake hose banjo bolt, **Figs. 10 and 11,** disconnect brake hose and secure in raised position.
4. Remove caliper and brake pads as outlined in "Brake Pads, Replace."
5. Reverse procedure to install using new sealing washers when connecting brake hose. Torque brake hose banjo bolt to 25 ft. lbs. and caliper retaining bolts to 22 ft. lbs. on models with carbureted engine or 17 ft. lbs. on models with fuel injected engine, then bleed brake system.

CALIPER OVERHAUL

FRONT

1. Remove caliper and bracket as outlined, then clean dirt and rust from bracket and outside caliper.
2. Remove boot retaining ring and pad spring, if equipped, **Figs. 3 through 9.**
3. Place block of wood or shop rag in the caliper opposite piston, then carefully remove piston by applying compressed air to fluid inlet port. **Use only enough air pressure to ease piston from caliper bore.**
4. Remove piston dust boot.
5. Remove piston seal using nonmetallic tool and take care not to mar caliper bore.
6. Remove bleed screw from caliper.
7. Remove guide pin dust boots and sleeves from mounting bracket or caliper, as equipped.
8. Clean piston and caliper bore with brake fluid and wipe dry with lint free shop towels.
9. Inspect caliper, piston, mounting bracket for damage and excessive wear, and replace as needed.
10. Lubricate piston seal and caliper bore with new brake fluid and work seal into caliper groove.
11. Lubricate piston and dust seal with new brake fluid and slide seal over bottom end of piston.

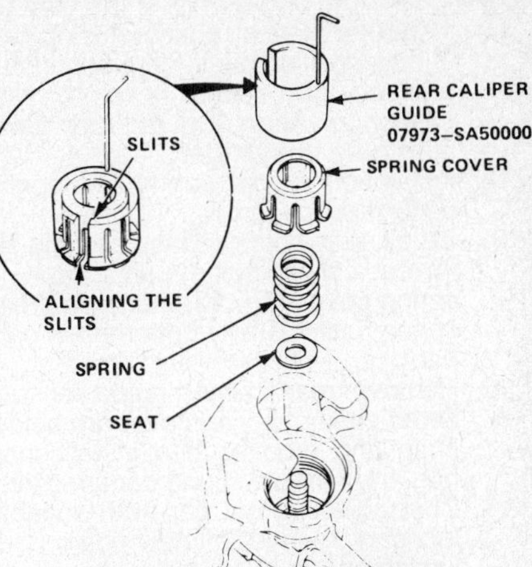

Fig. 13 Rear caliper adjusting spring installation. 1984–87 Prelude w/carbureted engine

12. Hold piston slightly above caliper bore, then seat bottom ridge of boot in caliper.
13. Ensure piston is square with bore, then press piston into bore and ensure dust boot lip seats in piston groove.
14. Install new dust boot retaining ring, guide pin sleeves and dust boots and pad spring, as equipped.
15. Ensure bleeder is clear and free from foreign material, then install bleeder and torque to 6 ft. lbs.

REAR

1984–87 Prelude w/Carbureted Engine

1. Remove caliper and bracket as outlined, then clean dirt and rust from bracket and outside of caliper.
2. Rotate caliper piston counterclockwise and remove piston and dust boot.
3. Pry out retaining clip, then remove washers, bearing adjusting nut and seals from piston, **Fig. 10.**
4. Remove piston seal from caliper, taking care not to damage caliper bore.
5. Mount suitable spring compressor in caliper, **Fig. 12,** compress adjusting spring cover, and remove circlip.
6. Slowly release spring compressor, then remove spring cover, spring and seat, **Fig. 10.**
7. Remove pushrod retaining ring, key plate pushrod and O-ring from caliper body, then remove pin from cam.
8. Remove parking brake cam return spring, retaining nut, lever cam and cam dust boot.
9. Clean all components with new brake fluid and wipe dry with lint free shop towels.
10. Coat parking brake cam boot with suitable lubricant and pack needle bearing cavity with silicone grease, then install cam boot and cam, taking care not to damage boot when inserting cam.
11. Install lever, torque retaining nut to 20 ft. lbs. then install return spring.

12. Install key plate on pushrod using new O-ring, position pin in cam and install pushrod, then secure assembly with snap ring. **Align lug on key plate with hole in cylinder.**
13. Install spring seat, spring, and spring cover over pushrod.
14. Install spring compressor, aligning slit in rear caliper guide with groove in spring cover, **Fig. 13,** then compress spring until it is fully bottomed in caliper.
15. Remove rear caliper guide, ensure flared ends of spring cover are below snap ring groove, then install snap ring and remove spring compressor.
16. Coat adjusting nut cap with suitable lubricant, then install new cup on adjusting nut.
17. Install ball bearing, wave washer and flat washer on adjusting nut, insert assembly into piston, then secure with retaining clip.
18. Coat piston seal and dust boot with suitable lubricant, then install seals in caliper.
19. Coat outside of piston with suitable lubricant, then install piston on pushrod, rotating piston clockwise until fully seated.

1986–87 Prelude w/Fuel Injected Engine

1. Remove caliper and bracket as outlined, then clean dirt and rust from bracket and outside of caliper.
2. Rotate caliper piston counterclockwise and remove piston and dust boot.
3. Remove snap ring, washer, adjusting spring A and adjusting nut from piston, **Fig. 11.**

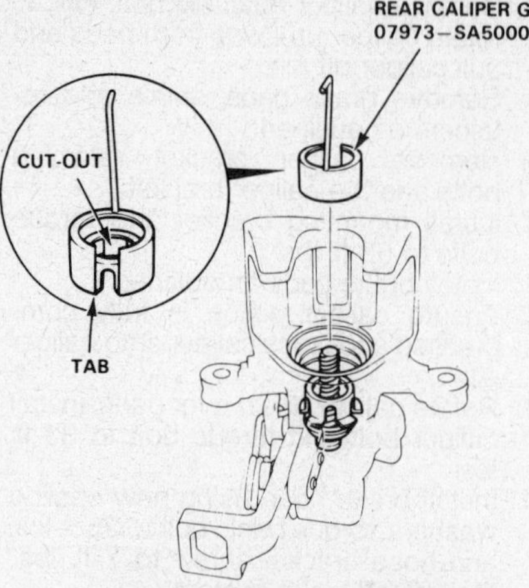

Fig. 14 Rear caliper adjusting spring installation. 1986–87 Prelude w/ fuel injected engine

4. Remove piston seal from caliper, taking care not to damage caliper bore.
5. Mount suitable spring compressor in caliper, **Fig. 12,** compress adjusting spring and remove circlip.
6. Slowly release spring compressor, then remove cover, adjusting spring B, spacer, bearing and adjusting bolt, **Fig. 11.**
7. Remove piston sleeve, then remove pin from cam.
8. Remove parking brake lever return spring, retaining nut, lever cam and dust boot.
9. Clean all components with new brake fluid and wipe dry with lint-free shop towels.
10. Coat parking brake cam boot with suitable lubricant and pack needle bearing cavity with silicone grease, then install cam boot and cam, taking care not to damage boot when inserting cam.
11. Install lever, torque retaining nut to 20 ft. lbs. then install return spring.
12. Install new O-ring on piston sleeve and insert pin into cam.
13. Install piston sleeve with hole in bottom of sleeve aligned with pin in cam, and piston sleeve aligned with holes in caliper.
14. Install new cup on adjusting bolt with groove facing bearing side of bolt.
15. Install bearing, spacer, spring and spring cap over adjusting bolt, then position assembly in caliper.
16. Install spring compressor, aligning slit in rear caliper guide with tab on spring cover, **Fig. 14,** then compress spring until it is fully bottomed in caliper.
17. Remove rear caliper guide, ensure flared ends of spring cover are below snap ring groove, then install snap ring and remove spring compressor.
18. Install adjusting nut, spring A and washer in piston and secure assembly with snap ring.
19. Coat new piston seal and dust boot with silicone grease and install seals in caliper, ensuring that seals are properly seated in caliper grooves.
20. Coat outside of piston with suitable lubricant, then install piston on adjusting bolt, rotating piston clockwise until fully seated.

DRUM BRAKES SECTION

INDEX

BRAKE PEDAL HEIGHT ADJUST

Refer to the "Disc Brakes Section" for pedal height adjustment procedure.

PARKING BRAKE ADJUST

Refer to the "Disc Brakes Section" for parking brake adjustment procedure.

DRUM BRAKES ADJUST

These models have self-adjusting mechanisms which automatically adjust brake lining to drum clearance each time the brake pedal is depressed and released. If excessive pedal travel or poor braking performance is caused by improperly adjusted rear brakes, the drums should be removed and the self-adjusting mechanisms should be checked and repaired as needed.

Prior to adjusting the parking brake, the brake pedal should be depressed and released several times to ensure the rear brake shoes are properly adjusted.

BRAKE SHOES REPLACE

Mark installation position of all components prior to removal to ensure proper assembly. Components that are to be reused should be installed in original position.

1983 CIVIC

1. Raise and support rear of vehicle and remove wheels.
2. Fully loosen parking brake equalizer adjusting nut.
3. Remove rear wheel bearing cap and seal, cotter pin and pin holder, rear axle washer and the spindle nut.
4. Remove brake drum and hub assembly, taking care not to drop wheel bearings.
5. Note installation position of upper and lower return springs, **Fig. 1,** then remove return springs and spring securing tensioner ratchet.
6. Compress each brake shoe retainer

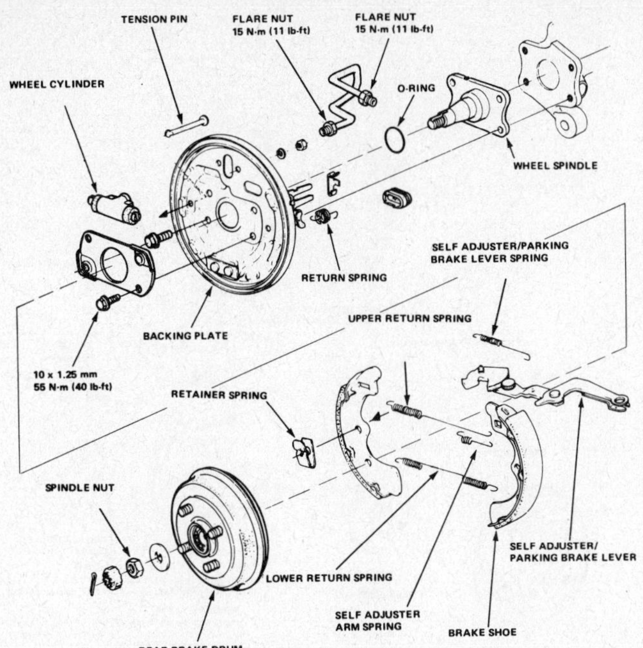

Fig. 1 Rear drum brake assembly exploded view. 1983 Civic

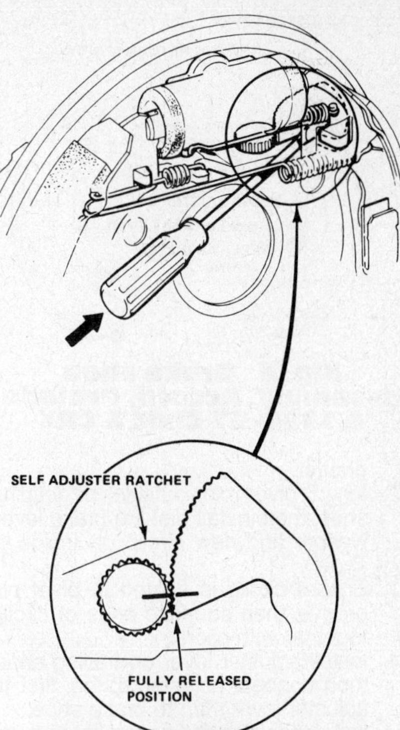

Fig. 2 Releasing self adjuster. 1983 Civic

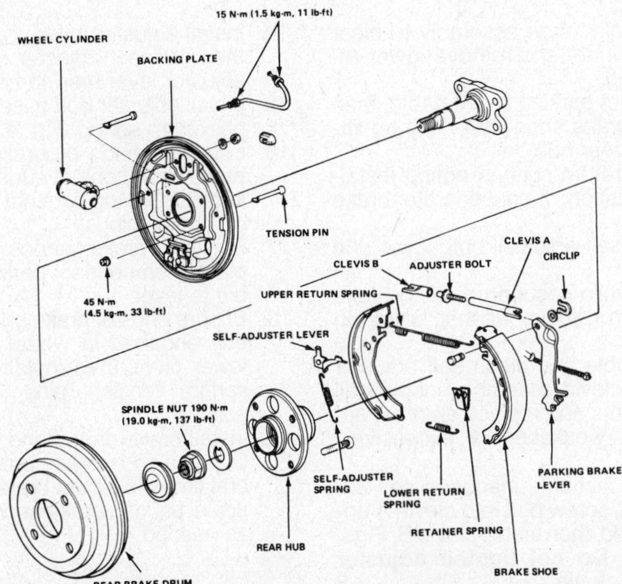

Fig. 3 Rear drum brake assembly exploded view. 1984–87 Civic & CRX & 1987 Accord (1983 Prelude & 1983–86 Accord similar)

spring while holding tension pin, rotate spring to align notch with pin, then remove spring.

7. Mark installation position of brake shoes, then remove brake shoes and self-adjuster/parking brake lever assembly.
8. Lubricate ends of brake shoes and brake shoe contact surfaces of backing plate.
9. Position brake shoes and self adjuster lever of backing plate, then install brake shoe retaining springs. **When installing new brake shoes, manufacturer's number should face toward outside.**
10. Install self adjuster spring and brake shoe retaining springs in positions noted during disassembly.
11. Move self-adjuster mechanisms to fully released position as shown in **Fig. 2.**
12. Reverse remaining procedure to complete installation, noting the following:
    a. Ensure tension pins are properly seated in brake shoe clamping springs and that brake shoe return springs are properly installed, **Fig. 1.**
    b. Inspect wheel bearings and grease seal, replace as needed, and adjust bearings as outlined in "Rear Suspension Section."
    c. Adjust parking brake cable as outlined.

1983 PRELUDE & 1983–85 ACCORD

1. Raise and support rear of vehicle and remove wheels.
2. Fully loosen parking brake equalizer adjusting nut.
3. Remove rear wheel bearing cap and seal, cotter pin and pin holder, rear axle washer and spindle nut.
4. Remove brake drum and hub assembly, taking care not to drop wheel bearings.
5. Compress each retainer spring, **Fig. 3,** rotate spring until slot is aligned with tension pin, then remove retainer spring and tension pin.
6. Lower brake shoes and pull assembly away from backing plate, disconnect parking brake cable from lever and remove brake shoe assembly.
7. Remove return springs noting installation position, then separate brake shoes.
8. Remove self-adjuster bolt, lever and spring.
9. Pry off circlip securing parking brake lever, then remove washer, pivot pin and lever.
10. Disassemble and clean self adjuster bolt and clevis assembly, inspect all components and replace any that are damaged, weakened or excessively worn.
11. Lubricate friction surfaces of self adjuster bolt, screw bolt into clevis A until bottomed, then install clevis B, **Fig. 3. Do not tighten adjuster bolt into**

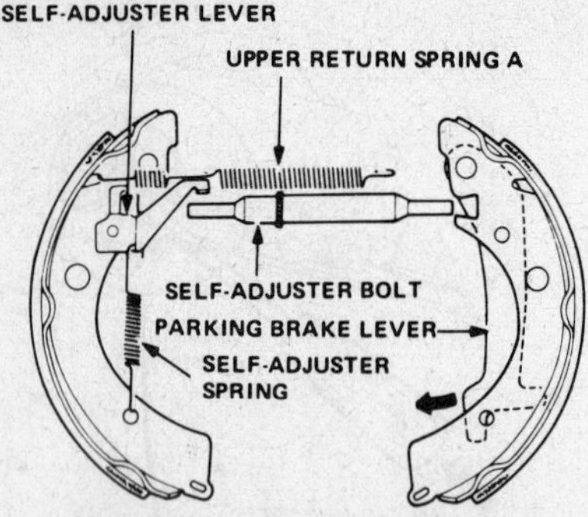

Fig. 4 Brake shoe assembly. Accord, Prelude & 1984–87 Civic & CRX

clevis.

12. Insert pivot pin outside of leading shoe, then install parking brake lever, washer and new circlip on inside of shoe.
13. Ensure circlip is seated in pivot pin groove, then squeeze ends of circlip together with pliers.
14. Install adjuster lever on trailing shoe, then connect adjuster spring, first to adjuster lever then to brake shoe.
15. Install adjuster bolt assembly and upper return spring, **Fig. 4.**
16. Lubricate ends of brake shoes and brake shoe contact surfaces on backing plate, taking care not to get grease on brake linings.
17. Position brake shoes on backing plate, then connect parking brake cable to lever.
18. Ensure ends of brake shoes are properly engaged in wheel cylinder and lower pivot, then install lower return spring, tension pins and retainer springs.
19. Install brake drum and adjust wheel bearings as outlined in "Rear Suspension Section."
20. Depress and release brake pedal several times to adjust brake shoes, then adjust parking brake and bleed brakes as needed.

1984–87 CIVIC & CRX & 1986–87 ACCORD

1. Raise and support rear of vehicle and remove wheels.
2. Fully loosen parking brake equalizer adjusting nut.
3. Remove brake drums.
4. Compress each retainer spring, **Figs. 3 and 5,** rotate spring until slot is aligned with tension pin, then remove retainer spring and tension pin.

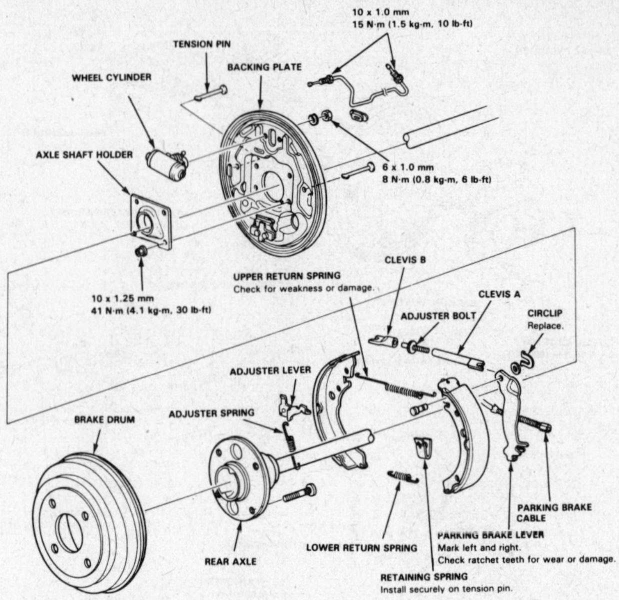

Fig. 5 Rear drum brake assembly exploded view. 1985–87 Civic 4WD Wagon

5. Lower brake shoe assembly to clear wheel cylinder and remove lower return spring.
6. Disconnect parking brake cable, then remove brake shoe assembly by lifting it up over hub.
7. Remove return springs noting installation position, then separate brake shoes.
8. Remove self-adjuster bolt, lever and spring.
9. Pry off circlip securing parking brake lever, then remove washer, pivot pin and lever.
10. Disassemble and clean self adjuster bolt and clevis assembly, inspect all components and replace any that are damaged, weakened or excessively worn.
11. Lubricate friction surfaces of self adjuster bolt, screw bolt into clevis A until bottomed, then install clevis B, **Figs. 3 and 5. Do not tighten adjuster bolt into clevis.**
12. Insert pivot pin outside of leading shoe, then install parking brake lever, washer and new circlip on inside of shoe.
13. Ensure circlip is seated in pivot pin groove, then squeeze ends of circlip together with pliers.
14. Install adjuster lever on trailing shoe, then connect adjuster spring, first to adjuster lever then to brake shoe.
15. Install adjuster bolt assembly and upper return spring, **Fig. 4.**
16. Lubricate ends of brake shoes and brake shoe contact surfaces on backing plate, taking care not to get grease on brake linings.
17. Position brake shoes on backing plate, then connect parking brake cable to lever.
18. Ensure ends of brake shoes are properly engaged in wheel cylinder and lower pivot, then install lower return spring, tension pins and retainer springs.
19. Install brake drums and wheels.
20. Depress and release brake pedal several times to adjust brake shoes, then adjust parking brake and bleed brakes as needed.

MASTER CYLINDER REPLACE

Refer to the "Disc Brakes Section" for master cylinder replacement procedure.

DRIVE AXLE & PROPELLER SHAFT SECTION

INDEX

a − (b + c) = X

Example

a: 17.92 mm
b: 2.60 mm
c: 15.20 mm
17.92 − (2.60 + 15.20) = 0.12
One 0.1 mm shim is required.

X	Shims required
−0.16−0.10 mm (−0.0063−0.0039 in.)	None
0.10−0.25 mm (0.0039−0.0098 in.)	Use one 0.1 mm shim
0.25−0.40 mm (0.0098−0.0157 in.)	Use one 0.25 mm shim

Fig. 1 Rear axle shim selection. Civic 4WD Wagon

DRIVE AXLE

REPLACE

FRONT

Replacement procedures for left and right driveshafts are the same.

1. Drain transaxle, then reinstall drain plug.
2. After removing spindle nut locking device, loosen spindle nut. **On models equipped with staked spindle nut, loosen nut with suitable wrench to overcome nut lock. Nut must be replaced during installation.**
3. Raise and support front of vehicle, then remove front wheel assembly and spindle nut.
4. On Prelude and 1986-87 Accord, remove damper fork through bolt, pinch bolt and the damper fork.
5. On all models, separate lower ball joint from steering knuckle. **On models equipped with front stabilizer bar, remove stabilizer bar attaching bolts prior to separating lower ball joint from steering knuckle.**
6. Pull hub outward, separating hub assembly from driveshaft.
7. Using a blunt screwdriver or other suitable tool, pry CV joint out approximately 0.5 inch (12 mm) to force spring clip past differential side gear spline groove.
8. Pull driveshaft assembly out of transaxle and vehicle.

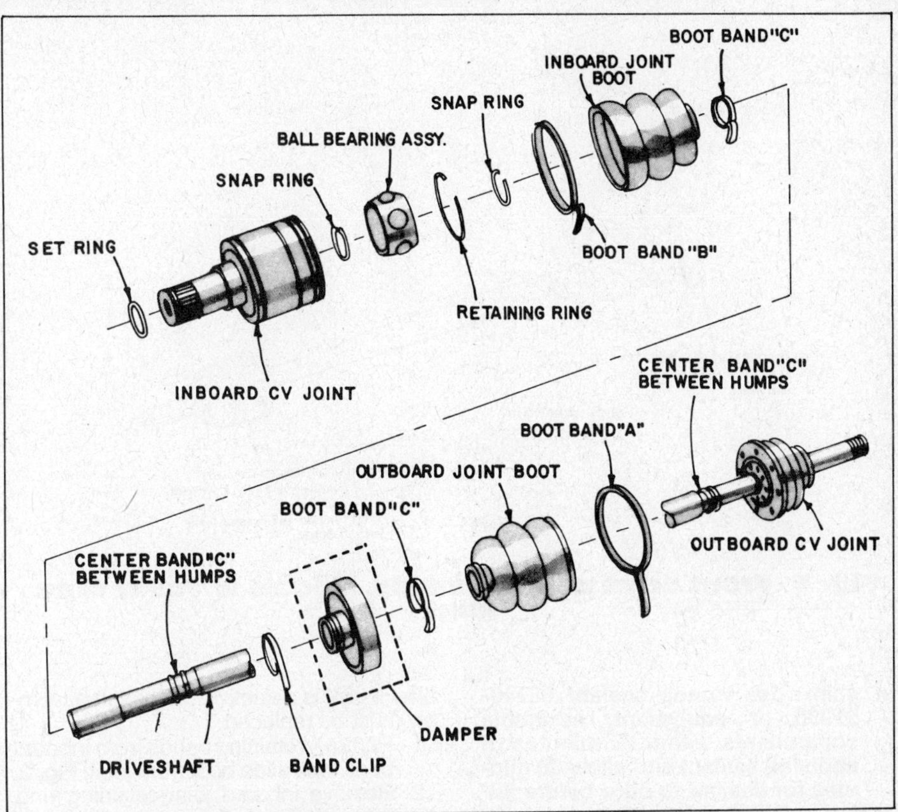

Fig. 2 Front drive axle assembly. Models w/ball type joint (Note: damper not used on all models)

REAR

Civic 4WD Wagon

1. Raise and support rear of vehicle.
2. Remove wheel and brake drum.
3. Disconnect brake line from wheel cylinder, then plug line and open cylinder port.
4. Remove brake shoes and disconnect parking brake cable from backing plate.
5. Remove 4 nuts securing axle retainer.
6. Remove axle assembly from housing using suitable slide hammer attached to opposite wheel lugs.
7. Pry axle seal from housing, taking care not to damage housing.
8. Install new seal in housing using suitable driver, then coat seal lip with grease.
9. If axle shaft, bearing or backing plate is replaced, select adjusting shim as follows:
   a. Measure and record width of axle bearing outer race.
   b. Measure and record thickness of backing plate at mounting surface.
   c. Measure and record depth of bearing pocket from edge of axle housing surface to bearing seating surface.
   d. Add dimensions obtained in steps b and c and subtract sum from dimension measured in step a. Refer to **Fig. 1**, and select appropriate shim.
10. Apply thin coat of suitable sealer to housing flange and shim contact faces of backing plate and axle shaft retainer. **Do not apply sealant to lower holes of flange or raised portion of**

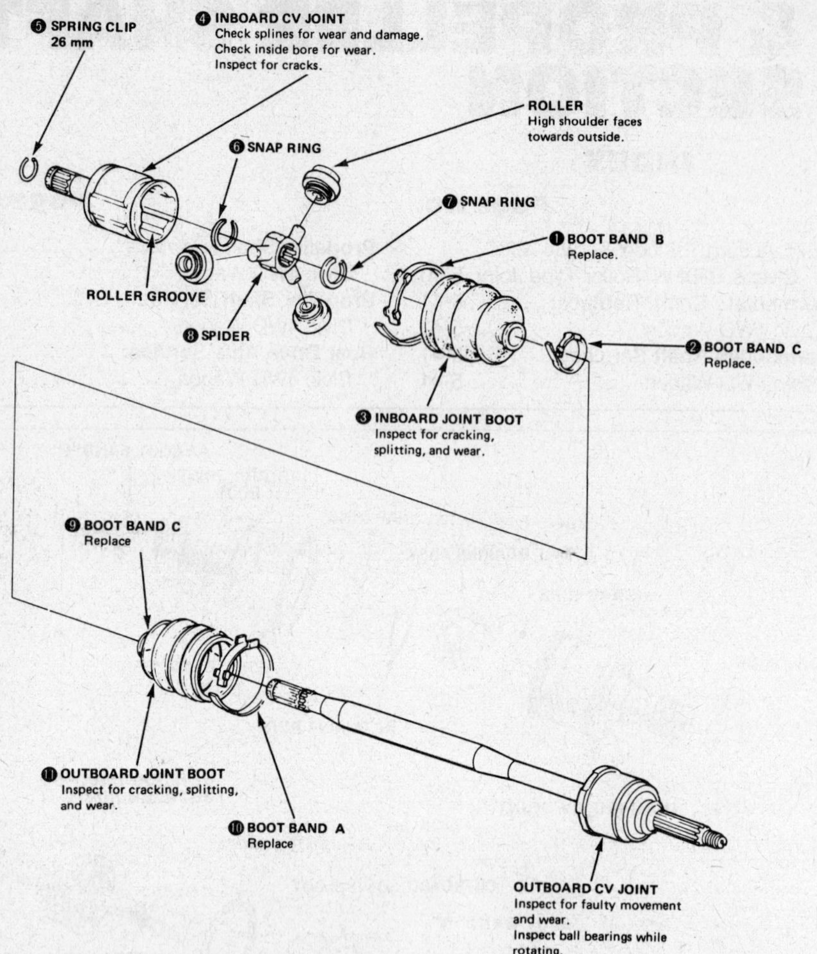

Fig. 3 Front drive axle assembly. Models w/roller type joint

shim. Use Honda sealant 08740-99986 or equivalent, assemble components within 20 minutes of applying sealant and allow 30 minutes for sealant to cure before filling housing.

11. Apply sealant to inner corner of bearing seating surface in housing, then position backing plate and shim on axle housing.
12. Insert axle assembly into housing, then align axle splines with differential side gear splines, and axle retainer with studs on housing.
13. Seat bearing in housing using suitable slide hammer bearing against axle flange.
14. Torque retaining nuts to 30 ft. lbs., repeat remaining procedure to complete installation, then bleed brakes and fill axle housing to specified level.

FRONT DRIVE AXLE SERVICE

EXC. ACCORD, PRELUDE, & 1984–87 CIVIC & CRX W/ROLLER TYPE JOINT

The outboard joint cannot be disassembled. If joint is defective, driveshaft assembly must be replaced.

1. Remove retaining bands from inboard boot, then slide boot from joint, **Fig. 2.**
2. Remove inboard joint retaining ring, then inboard housing and shaft end snap ring.
3. Hold bearing cage and then, with upward-downward motion, move driveshaft to press balls out of cage.
4. Remove inner snap rings and bearing race.
5. Check driveshaft runout, then ball bearings, inner retainer and bearing cage for wear. Remove excess grease from outboard joint, then bend joint to expose cage and ball bearings. Check internal parts for wear, pitting or contamination.
6. Reverse procedure to assemble, noting the following:
   a. Pack molybdenum disulfide grease into outboard joint.
   b. Pack each bearing slot of inboard joint with molybdenum disulfide grease, then fill inboard housing until 1/3 full and also coat housing walls. Install driveshaft and continue adding grease.
   c. After installing boot bands, stake with punch to prevent slippage.

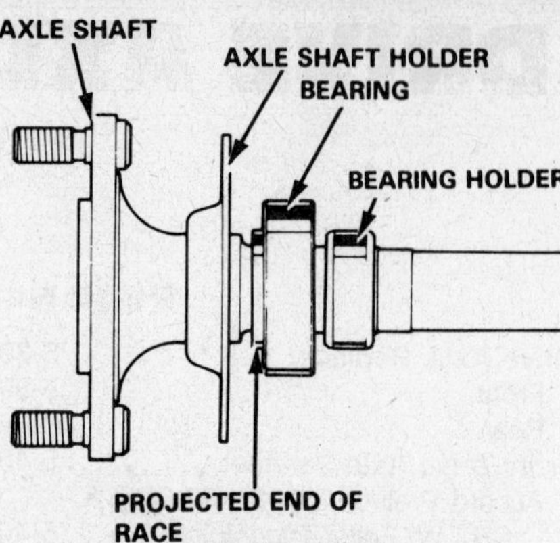

Fig. 4 Rear axle shaft bearing installation. Civic 4WD Wagon

ACCORD, PRELUDE & 1984–87 CIVIC & CRX W/ROLLER TYPE JOINT

Prior to disassembly, mark rollers and roller grooves.

1. To disassemble driveshafts, follow numbered sequence shown in **Fig. 3. Prior to disassembly, mark rollers and grooves to ensure proper component installation during assembly.**
2. To assemble, reverse numbered sequence shown in **Fig. 3,** noting the following:
   a. Pack inboard and outboard joints with molybdenum disulfide grease.
   b. Install rollers on spider shafts, then slide spider assembly into inboard shaft joint. **Avoid getting grease on rubber parts.**
   c. Position boots and install small end bands, then expand and compress boots until they return to their normal shape and length.
   d. Install large end bands.

REAR DRIVE AXLE SERVICE

CIVIC 4WD WAGON

1. Separate backing plate and shim from axle shaft holder if necessary.
2. Grind away part of bearing holder until thickness is approximately .02 inch.
3. Secure axle shaft in vise, then break off retaining collar using suitable chisel. **Take care not to damage axle shaft when grinding and removing bearing retainer.**
4. Press bearing off axle using suitable separator plates, taking care not to damage axle shaft retainer.
5. Mount axle shaft in suitable centering tool and check runout with dial indicator.
6. Inspector splines, bearing surface and seal surfaces.
7. Axle shaft should be replaced if damaged, scored or if runout exceeds .04 inch.
8. Inspect axle shaft retainer and replace if damaged or worn.

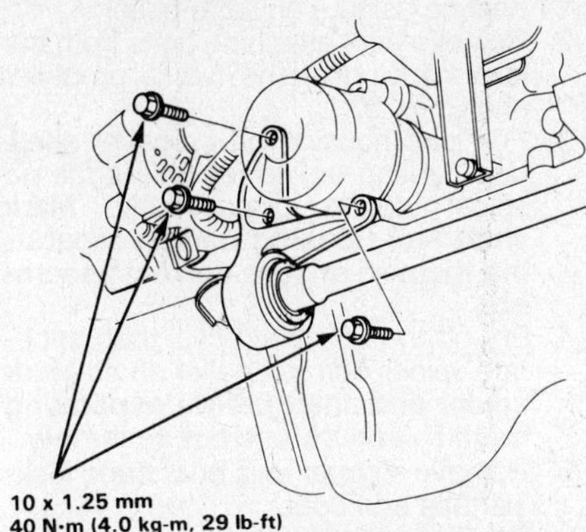

Fig. 5 Intermediate shaft removal. Civic 4WD Wagon

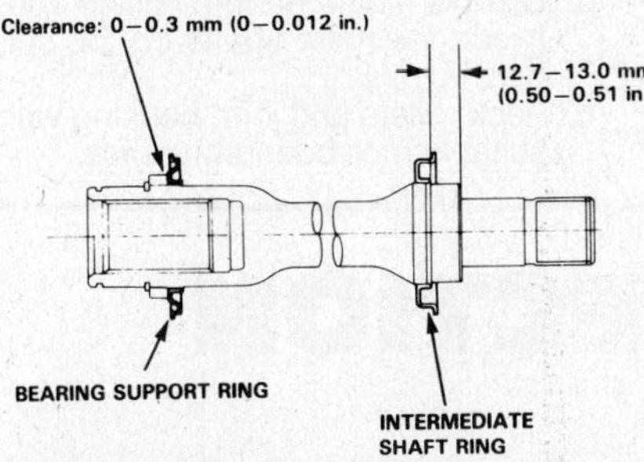

Fig. 7 Intermediate shaft ring & bearing support ring installation. Civic 4WD Wagon

9. Ensure all components are clean and free from foreign material, then install axle shaft retainer, bearing and new bearing retainer on axle shaft as shown in **Fig. 4.**
10. Press bearing and retainer onto shaft until projected end of bearing race is seated against shoulder on shaft.

INTERMEDIATE SHAFT REPLACE

CIVIC 4WD WAGON

1. Drain transaxle fluid, then remove three intermediate shaft attaching bolts, **Fig. 5.**
2. Lower bearing support case, then remove intermediate shaft from differential. **To prevent damage to the differential oil seal, hold intermediate shaft horizontal until it is clear of differential.**
3. Reverse procedure to install. Torque intermediate shaft attaching bolts to 29 ft. lbs.

INTERMEDIATE SHAFT SERVICE

CIVIC 4WD WAGON

1. Remove intermediate shaft outer seal, then the 40 mm external clip, **Fig. 6.**
2. Press intermediate shaft out of the shaft bearing, then remove shaft inner seal.

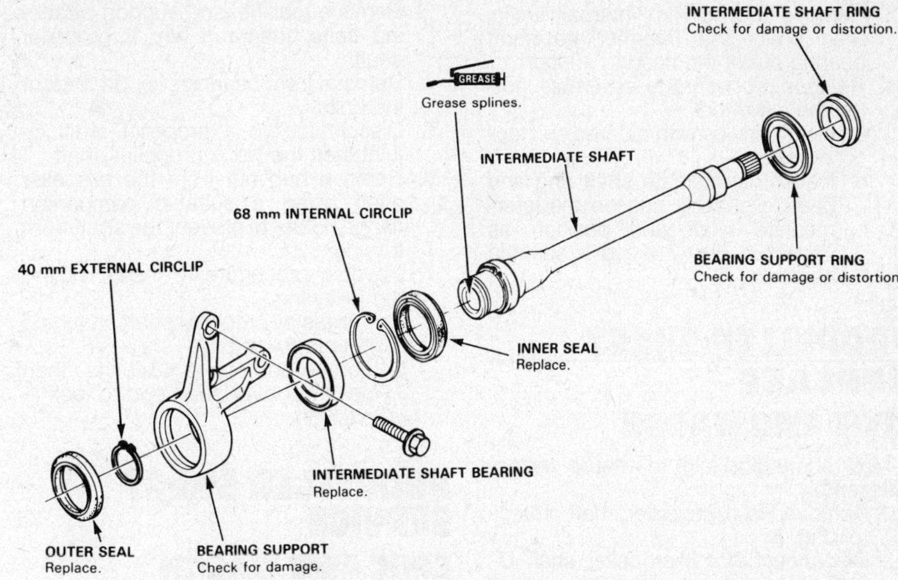

Fig. 6 Intermediate shaft assembly. Civic 4WD Wagon

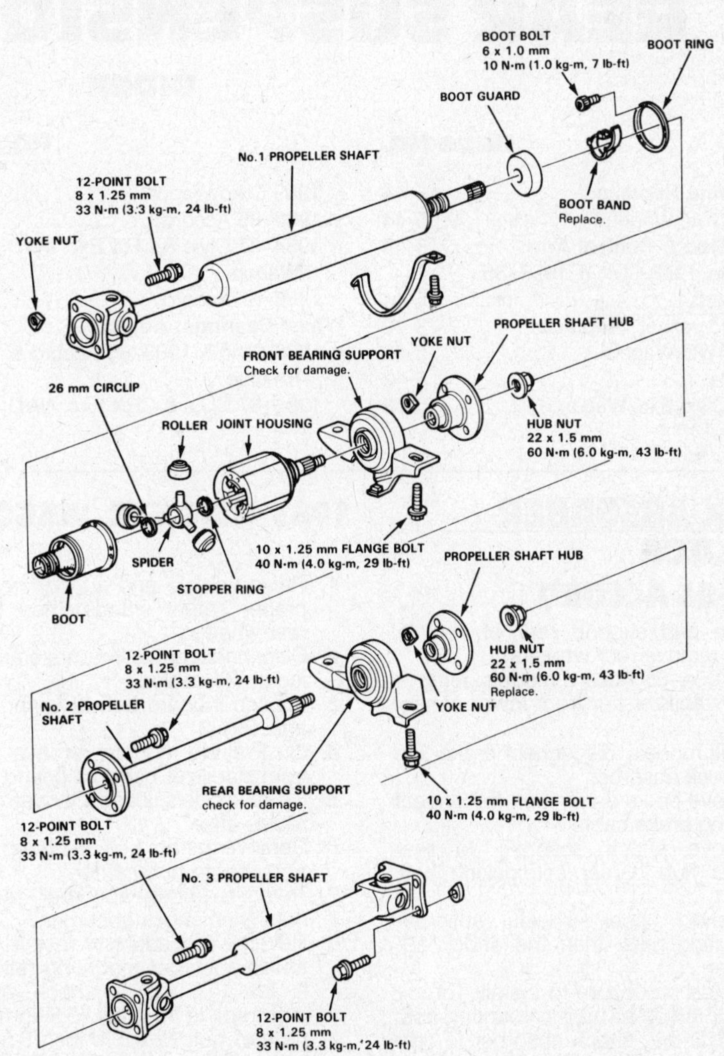

Fig. 8 Propeller shaft assembly. Civic 4WD Wagon

3. Remove the 68 mm internal circlip, then press the intermediate shaft bearing out of the bearing support.
4. Reverse procedure to assemble, noting the following:
   a. Install circlips with tapered end facing out.
   b. Install intermediate shaft ring and bearing support ring on the intermediate shaft and position as shown in **Fig. 7** using a suitable hammer.

PROPELLER SHAFT REPLACE

CIVIC 4WD WAGON

Mark shafts and joint to ensure correct reassembly.

1. Remove No. 1 propeller shaft protector, **Fig. 8.**
2. Disconnect No. 3 propeller shaft U-joint, then remove No. 3 propeller shaft.
3. Remove rear bearing support attaching bolts, then the No. 2 propeller shaft.
4. Remove front bearing support attaching bolts.
5. Disconnect No. 1 propeller shaft U-joint then the No. 1 propeller shaft.
6. Remove hub nut from the propeller shaft using a suitable companion flange holder to prevent the shaft from turning.
7. Reverse procedure to install, noting the following:
   a. Torque all propeller shaft attaching nuts to 24 ft. lbs.
   b. Torque hub nut to 43 ft. lbs., then peen nut over shaft end to lock in position.

PROPELLER SHAFT SERVICE

CIVIC 4WD WAGON

1. Remove center bearing support from bearing using a suitable puller.
2. Remove boot attaching bolts from the joint housing of the No. 1 propeller shaft, **Fig. 8.**
3. Pull joint housing off propeller shaft. Use caution not to let rollers fall off spider during disassembly. **Mark shaft and housing before separating them to ensure correct assembly.**
4. Pry off the 26 mm circlip, then separate spider from propeller shaft. **Mark spider and shaft before separating them to ensure correct assembly.**
5. Remove stopper ring, boot band locking tabs and boot.
6. Reverse procedure to assemble, noting the following:
   a. Position boot on shaft so the raise area of the boot is aligned with the shaft groove.
   b. Do not interchange rollers between the roller shafts on the spider.
   c. Pack rollers and joint housing with suitable molybdenum grease.

REAR SUSPENSION SECTION

INDEX

Page No.

SHOCK ABSORBER REPLACE

1983–85 ACCORD

1. Raise and support rear of vehicle, then remove rear wheel(s).
2. On 1984-85 Accord models, remove rear stabilizer bar from lower control arm.
3. On all models, disconnect brake line at shock absorber.
4. Remove brake drum, then disconnect parking brake cable.
5. Remove shock absorber to rear wheel hub carrier self-locking bolt, **Fig. 1.**
6. Remove upper shock absorber mounting nuts, then the shock absorber.
7. Reverse procedure to install. Torque shock absorber upper mounting nuts to 16 ft. lbs., shock absorber to rear wheel hub carrier self-locking bolt to 40 ft. lbs., on 1984-85 Accord, stabilizer bar to lower control arm attaching bolt, 16 ft. lbs.

1983 CIVIC EXC. WAGON

1. Raise vehicle and support rear with proper safety stands, then remove rear wheels.
2. Disconnect brake line, hose and parking brake cable.
3. Loosen inboard bolt of lower control arm, **Fig. 2**
4. On Prelude models, remove locknut from stabilizer bar connecting link.
5. On all models, loosen forward bolt of radius arm.
6. Remove pinch bolt securing shock absorber to hub carrier.
7. Remove shock absorber mounting nuts, then shock absorber.
8. Reverse procedure to install. Torque shock absorber mounting nuts to 16 ft. lbs. (2.2 kg-m), shock absorber pinch bolt to 40 ft. lbs. (5.5 kg-m), radius arm bolt to 61 ft. lbs. (8.5 kg-m), lower control arm bolt to 40 ft. lbs. (5.5 kg-m), and if so equipped, stabilizer connecting link nut to 16 ft. lbs. (2.2 kg-m).

1983 CIVIC WAGON

1. Raise vehicle and support rear with safety stands.
2. Remove shock absorber upper and lower mounting bolts, then shock absorber, **Fig. 3.**
3. Reverse procedure to install. Torque mounting bolts to 32 ft. lbs. (4.4 kg-m).

PRELUDE

1. Raise and support rear of vehicle, then remove rear wheel(s).
2. On 1983 models, separate brake hose from brake line and remove from clip.
3. On 1984-87 models, remove brake hose clamp bolt.
4. On all models, remove stabilizer bar from lower control arm.
5. Loosen lower arm bolt, **Fig. 4.**
6. Loosen radius rod nut and rear hub carrier to lower control arm bolt.
7. Remove shock absorber locking bolt, then remove shock absorber from rear hub carrier.

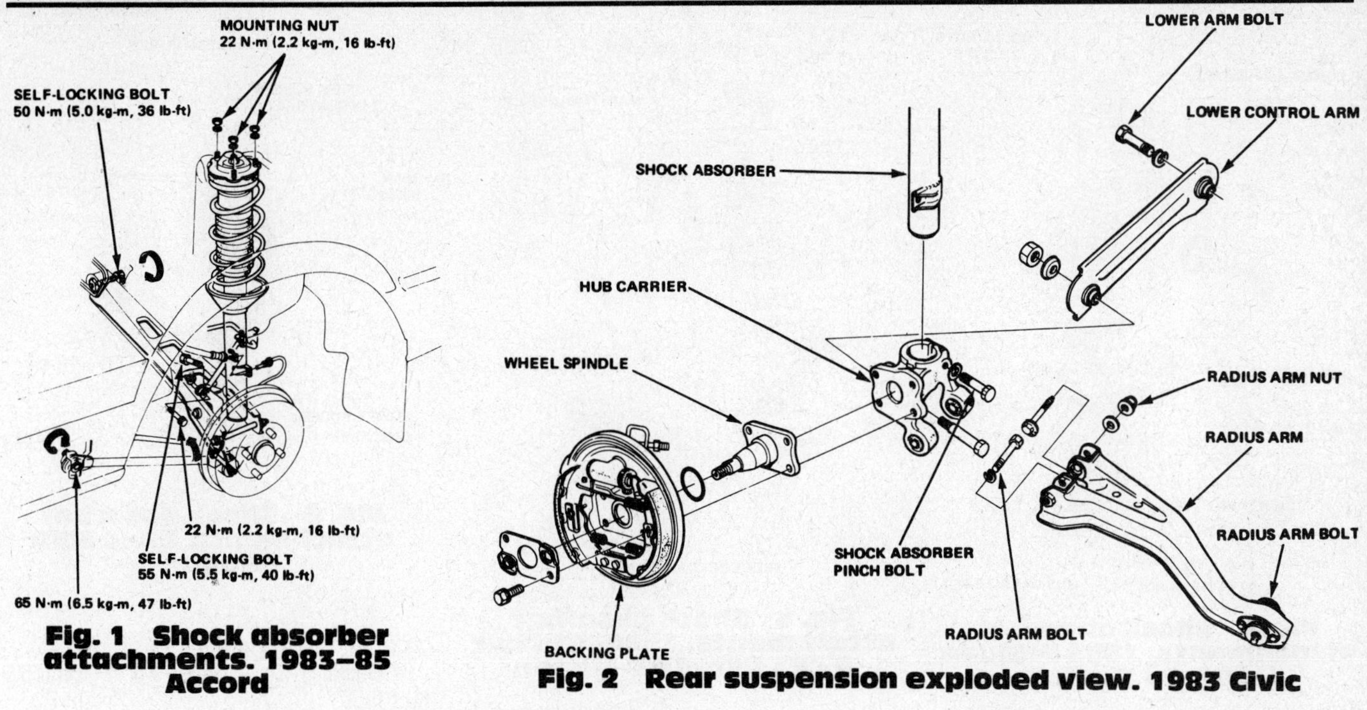

Fig. 1 Shock absorber attachments. 1983–85 Accord

Fig. 2 Rear suspension exploded view. 1983 Civic

Fig. 3 Rear suspension exploded view. 1983 Civic Station Wagon

8. Remove upper shock absorber mounting nuts, then the shock absorber.
9. Reverse procedure to install. Torque shock absorber upper mounting nuts to 16 ft. lbs., lower arm bolt and shock absorber locking bolt to 40 ft. lbs., rear hub carrier to lower control arm bolt to 60 ft. lbs., radius rod nut to 47 ft. lbs. and stabilizer bolt to 16 ft. lbs.

1984–87 CIVIC & CRX EXC. 4WD WAGON

1. Raise and support rear of vehicle. Remove rear wheel(s).
2. Position a suitable jack under rear axle beam, **Fig. 5.**
3. Working inside vehicle, remove shock absorber maintenance lid, then the self-locking nut, **Fig. 5.**
4. Remove self-locking bolt, shock absorber assembly and spring cushion.
5. Reverse procedure to install. Torque shock absorber upper self-locking nut to 16 ft. lbs. and self-locking bolt to 40 ft. lbs.

CIVIC 4WD WAGON

1. Raise and support rear of vehicle, then remove rear wheels.
2. Position a suitable floor jack under rear axle housing.
3. Working from inside of vehicle, remove shock absorber access cover, **Fig. 6,** then the cap and 10 mm attaching nuts.
4. Lower floor jack and remove shock absorber spring and upper and lower spring seats.
5. Remove 12 mm self-locking bolt, then the shock absorber.
6. Reverse procedure to install. Torque 12 mm self locking bolt to 60 ft. lbs., upper 10 mm attaching nut to 16 ft. lbs. and lower 10 mm attaching nut to 14 ft. lbs.

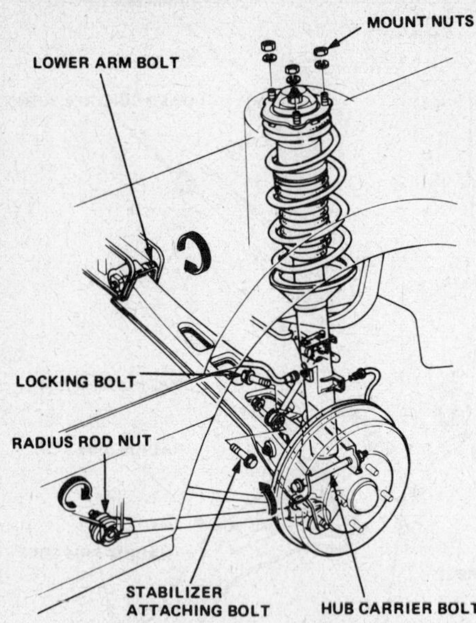

Fig. 4 Shock absorber attachments. 1983 Prelude (1984–87 similar)

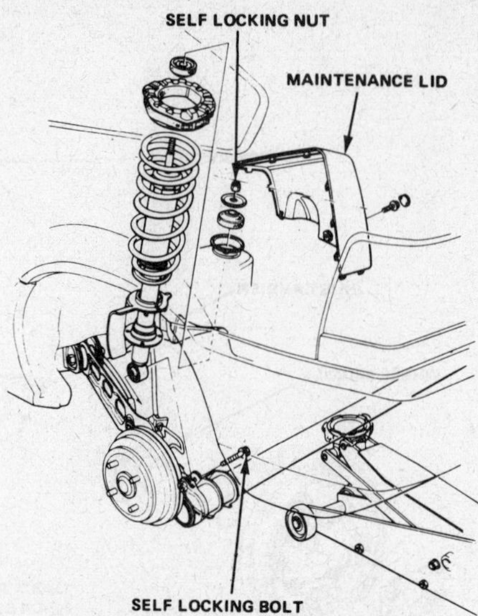

Fig. 5 Shock absorber attachments. 1984–87 Civic & CRX Exc. 4WD Wagon

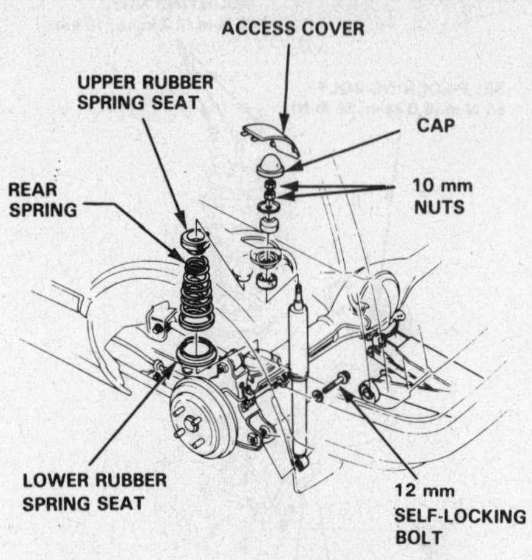

Fig. 6 Shock absorber attachments. Civic 4WD Wagon

1986–87 ACCORD

1. Remove damper upper cover at rear seat lining.
2. Raise and support rear of vehicle.
3. Remove stabilizer bar from lower control arm.
4. Remove 2 upper base mounting nuts.
5. Remove lower damper assembly.
6. Lower suspension arms and remove damper mounting bolt.
7. Reverse procedure to install. Install mounting bolts hand tight, load suspension with weight of vehicle, then torque lower mounting bolt to 40 ft. lbs. and upper base nuts to 28 ft. lbs.

LEAF SPRING

REPLACE

1983 CIVIC WAGON

1. Raise vehicle and support rear with safety stands.
2. Remove rear wheels and brake drums.
3. Disconnect brake lines and parking brake equalizer cables at backing plate, then remove backing plate.
4. Disconnect parking brake cable from equalizer and pull free of brackets on rear axle and left spring clamp.
5. Support center or rear axle with suitable jack and remove lower shock absorber mounting bolts.
6. Remove leaf spring pin nuts, then spring pins from front end of leaf springs, **Fig. 3.**
7. Remove shackles from rear of leaf springs, then lower jack and rear suspension assembly.
8. Remove U-bolts to detach leaf springs from rear axle.
9. Reverse procedure to install, noting the following:
   a. Install leaf springs with arrow mark facing forward.
   b. With shackle and spring pin nuts loosely installed, jack axle up and down several times to seat spring rubber bushings.
   c. Lower vehicle to ground and torque bolts as specified in **Fig. 3.**

RADIUS ROD & CONTROL ARM

REPLACE

PRELUDE, 1983 CIVIC & 1983–85 ACCORD

1. Raise and support rear of vehicle, then remove rear wheels and brake drums or discs.
2. Disconnect brake line and parking brake cable.
3. Remove backing plate assembly.
4. On models so equipped, remove stabilizer bar locknuts and mounting bolts, then stabilizer bar.
5. Remove radius arm nuts and bolts, then radius arm, **Figs. 1, 2 and 4.**
6. Remove shock absorber pinch bolt, then separate hub carrier from shock absorber.
7. Remove lower control arm bolts, then control arm.
8. Reverse procedure to install. Torque fasteners to specifications shown below.

Torque Specifications

Lower control arm bolts: 40 ft. lbs. (5.5 kg-m).

Shock absorber pinch bolt: 40 ft. lbs. (5.5 kg-m).

Radius arm to frame bushing bolt: 64 ft. lbs. (8.5 kg-m).

Radius arm to hub carrier inner bolt: 40 ft. lbs. (5.5 kg-m).

Radius arm to hub carrier outer bolt: 74 ft. lbs. (10.2 kg-m).

Backing plate bolts: 40 ft. lbs. (5.5 kg-m).

Stabilizer bar bolts: 16 ft. lbs. (2.2 kg-m).

WHEEL BEARINGS

ADJUST

1983 CIVIC & 1983–85 ACCORD & PRELUDE

1. Raise and support rear of vehicle, then remove wheels, grease cap, cotter pin and pin holder.
2. Torque spindle nut to 18 ft. lbs.
3. Rotate drum or disc several revolutions, then loosen spindle nut.
4. Torque spindle nut to 4 ft. lbs.
5. Install pin holder so that slot is as close as possible to hole in spindle.
6. Tighten spindle nut just enough to align pin holder slot with hole in spindle, then install cotter pin and grease cap.
7. Check hub and drum assembly rotating torque with suitable spring scale. **Ensure parking brake is fully released and that brakes are not dragging.**
8. If rotating torque is not 0.9-4 lbs., check for improperly tightened spindle nut or damaged bearings and correct as needed.

1984–87 CIVIC & CRX EXC. 4WD WAGON & 1986–87 ACCORD

Wheel bearings and hub on these models are an integral assembly and bearings cannot be adjusted. If hub endplay exceeds 0.002 inch with spindle nut properly tightened (134 ft. lbs.), hub and bearing assembly should be replaced.

1986–87 PRELUDE

1. Raise and support rear of vehicle, remove wheels, then remove brake pads as outlined in "Disc Brakes Section."

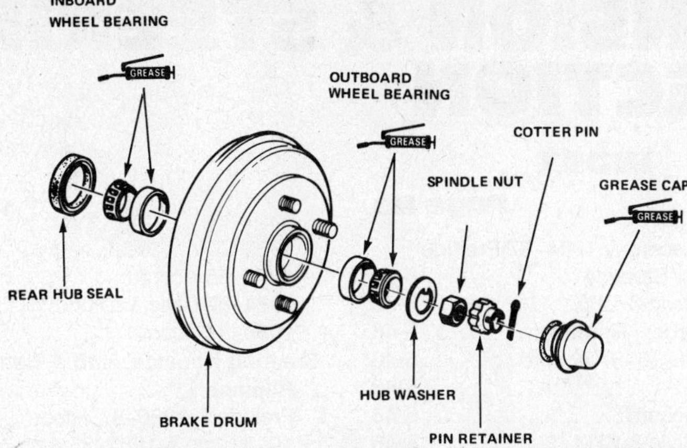

Fig. 7 Hub & bearing assembly exploded view. 1983 Civic (1983 Accord & Prelude similar)

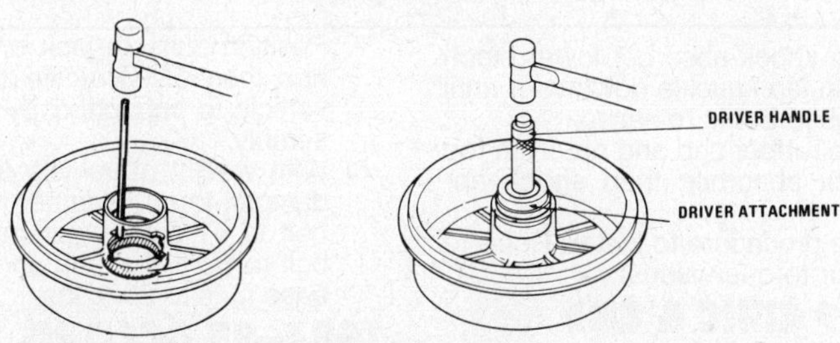

Fig. 8 Typical wheel bearing outer race replacement

2. Remove grease cap, cotter pin, pin holder and pin holder.
3. Lubricate spindle threads, install spindle nut and torque nut to 18 ft. lbs.
4. Rotate brake disc several revolutions, then torque spindle nut to 18 ft. lbs.
5. Repeat step 3 until nut torque holds at 18 ft. lbs.
6. Loosen spindle nut until it just breaks free, but does not turn (0 ft. lbs.), then torque nut to 40 ft. lbs.
7. Install pin holder with slot as close as possible to hole in spindle, tighten nut just enough to align slot, then install cotter pin and grease cap.
8. Check rotating torque of disc and hub assembly with suitable spring scale.
9. If reading is not 0.9-4 lbs., check for improperly tightened spindle nut or damaged bearings.
10. Reinstall brake pads and wheels, depress and release brake pedal several times to seat pads against brake disc, then lower vehicle.

WHEEL BEARINGS REPLACE

1983 CIVIC & PRELUDE & 1983–85 ACCORD

1. Raise and support rear of vehicle, then remove wheels, grease cap, cotter pin and pin holder, **Fig. 6.**
2. Remove spindle nut and washer, then the drum and hub assembly, taking care not to drop outer bearing.
3. Remove outer bearing from hub, drive out rear grease seal using suitable punch, then remove rear bearing.
4. Clean bearings, hub cavity, spindle, washer, nut, pin holder and grease cap with suitable solvent and blow dry with compressed air. **Keep solvent away from brake linings and drum contact surface. Do not spin dry bearings as bearings will be damaged.**
5. Inspect bearings and races, and replace if damaged, scored, pitted or excessively worn.
6. If bearings are to be replaced, proceed as follows:
   a. Drive races from hub, positioning suitable drift in slots behind each race.
   b. Position new race squarely in hub and seat race in hub using suitable driver.
   c. Pack bearings with grease, working grease through wide end of bearing with palm of hand, then coat outer surfaces of rollers with grease.
7. Pack bearings with grease, working grease through wide end in bearing with palm of hand, then coat outer surfaces of rollers with grease.
8. Pack grease in hub cavity behind inner and outer bearing races.
9. Place inner bearing in hub, install new grease seal using suitable driver, then coat seal lip with thin film of grease.
10. Mount hub and drum assembly on spindle, install outer bearing, washer and nut, then adjust bearings as outlined.
11. Pack grease cap approximately 1/4 full of grease, install new seal, if equipped, then install grease cap.

1984–87 CIVIC & CRX EXC. 4WD WAGON & 1986–87 ACCORD

1. Raise and support rear of vehicle, then remove wheel and brake drum.
2. Remove grease cap, spindle nut and washer.
3. Remove hub and bearing unit from spindle.
4. Reverse procedure to install. Torque spindle nut to 134 ft. lbs., then stake shoulder of nut into groove in spindle.

1984–87 PRELUDE

1. Raise and support vehicle, the remove caliper and mounting bracket as outlined in "Disc Brakes Section." **It is not necessary to disconnect brake hose from caliper.**
2. Remove grease cap, cotter pin, retainer, nut and washer, then remove disc and hub assembly, taking care not to drop outer bearing.
3. Remove outer bearing from hub, drive out rear grease seal using suitable punch, then remove rear bearing.
4. Clean bearings, hub cavity, spindle, washer, nut, pin holder and grease cap with suitable solvent and blow dry with compressed air. **Keep solvent away from brake contact surface. Do not spin dry bearings as bearings will be damaged.**
5. Inspect bearings and races, and replace if damaged, scored, pitted or excessively worn.
6. If bearings are to be replaced, proceed as follows:
   a. Drive races from hub, positioning suitable drift in slots behind each race, **Fig. 8.**
   b. Position new race squarely in hub and seat race in hub using suitable driver, **Fig. 8.**
7. Pack bearings with grease, working grease through wide if bearing with palm of hand, then coat outer surfaces of rollers with grease.
8. Pack grease in hub cavity behind inner and outer bearing races.
9. Place inner bearing in hub, install new grease seal using suitable driver, then coat seal lip with thin film of grease.
10. Mount hub assembly on spindle, install outer bearing, washer and nut, then adjust bearings as outlined.
11. Pack grease cap approximately 1/4 full of grease, install new seal, if equipped, then install new grease cap.
12. Install caliper assembly and wheels, depress and release brake pedal several times to seat pads against rotor, then lower vehicle.

FRONT SUSPENSION & STEERING SECTION

INDEX

DESCRIPTION

1983 CIVIC & 1983–85 ACCORD

These models use a conventional MacPherson strut damper and spring to support the upper end of the steering knuckle/hub assembly and a lower control arm to support the lower end of the hub, **Figs. 1 and 2.** All models are equipped with a stabilizer bar, and Accord models include radius rods between the lower control arms to the sub-frame. The radius rods increase vehicle stability by positively locating the control arm during the full range of travel, while the stabilizer bar links the lower control arms to the chassis in order to minimize body lean during cornering.

PRELUDE & 1986–87 ACCORD

These models use upper and lower control arms to support the knuckle/hub assembly and radius rods to locate the lower control arms, **Fig. 3.** The strut damper and spring assembly is connected between the chassis and lower control arm, and serves only to dampen motion. A stabilizer bar is used to link the lower control arms and chassis in order to minimize body lean during cornering.

1984–87 CIVIC & CRX

This front suspension consists of modified MacPherson struts supporting the upper end of the steering knuckle with the lower end being supported by a lower arm, **Fig. 4.** A torsion bar, integral with the front of the lower arm acts in place of a coil spring.

SHOCK ABSORBER REPLACE

1983 CIVIC

1. Raise vehicle and support with safety stands, then remove front wheels.
2. Remove brake hose clamp from shock absorber, **Fig. 1.**
3. Remove caliper assembly and secure out of way.
4. Remove shock absorber lower pinch bolt, then tap knuckle downward until shock absorber is released.
5. Remove rubber cap and nut from top of shock absorber, then shock absorber.
6. Reverse procedure to install. Refer to **Fig. 1** for torque values.

1984–87 CIVIC & CRX

1. Raise and support front of vehicle, then remove front wheels.
2. Remove brake hose clamp attaching bolt.
3. Place a suitable floor jack under lower arm and raise slightly to restrain lower arm. **Ensure jack is positioned securely under lower control arm at the ball joint to prevent torsion bar tension from causing steering knuckle to jump when shock absorber is removed.**
4. Remove shock absorber to lower arm pinch bolt, **Fig. 4,** then slowly lower jack.
5. Remove upper shock absorber mounting nuts, then remove shock absorber.
6. Reverse procedure to install. Torque upper shock absorber mounting nuts to 28 ft. lbs. and shock absorber to lower arm pinch bolt to 47 ft. lbs.

PRELUDE & 1986–87 ACCORD

1. Raise and support front of vehicle and remove wheels.
2. Remove damper fork pinch bolt, fork retaining bolt and the damper fork, **Fig. 3.**
3. Remove upper strut base mounting nuts and the strut assembly.
4. Insert upper base studs through mounting holes ensuring that alignment tab on shock body faces toward inside, then install base mounting nuts hand tight.
5. Install damper fork over drive axle and lower arm, then slide fork over lower end of shock absorber, aligning tab on shock with slot in fork.
6. Install damper fork retaining bolt and pinch bolt hand tight.
7. Position suitable jack under knuckle hub, then raise knuckle until weight of vehicle is supported by damper assembly.
8. With weight of vehicle supported by damper, torque damper fork retaining bolt to 47 ft. lbs., damper fork pinch bolt to 32 ft. lbs. and shock absorber base nuts to 29 ft. lbs.

1983–85 ACCORD

1. Raise vehicle and support with safety stands, then remove front wheels.
2. Remove brake hose clamp from shock absorber, **Fig. 2.**
3. Remove caliper assembly and secure out of way.
4. Remove stabilizer bar.
5. Remove shock absorber lower pinch bolt, then tap knuckle downward until shock absorber is released.
6. Remove rubber cap and nuts from top of shock absorber, then shock absorber.
7. Reverse procedure to install. Refer to **Fig. 2** for torque values.

BALL JOINTS REPLACE

1983 CIVIC & 1983–85 ACCORD

Ball joint and lower control arm are replaced as an assembly.

1. Raise and support front of vehicle and remove wheels.
2. Remove ball joint stud pinch bolt, then separate ball joint from knuckle.
3. Remove bolts securing stabilizer bar and radius rod to lower control arm, as equipped.
4. Remove lower control arm pivot bolt and the lower control arm.
5. Reverse procedure to install. Torque bolts to specifications shown in **Figs. 1 and 2.**

1984–87 CIVIC & CRX

1. Raise and support front of vehicle, then remove front wheels.
2. Support lower control arm with a suitable floor jack. **Ensure jack is posi-**

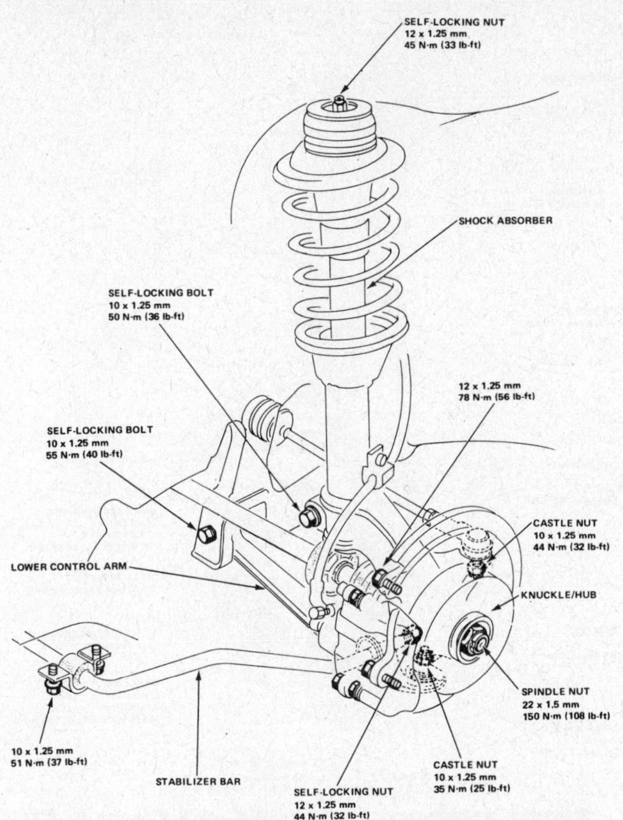

Fig. 1 Front suspension. 1983 Civic

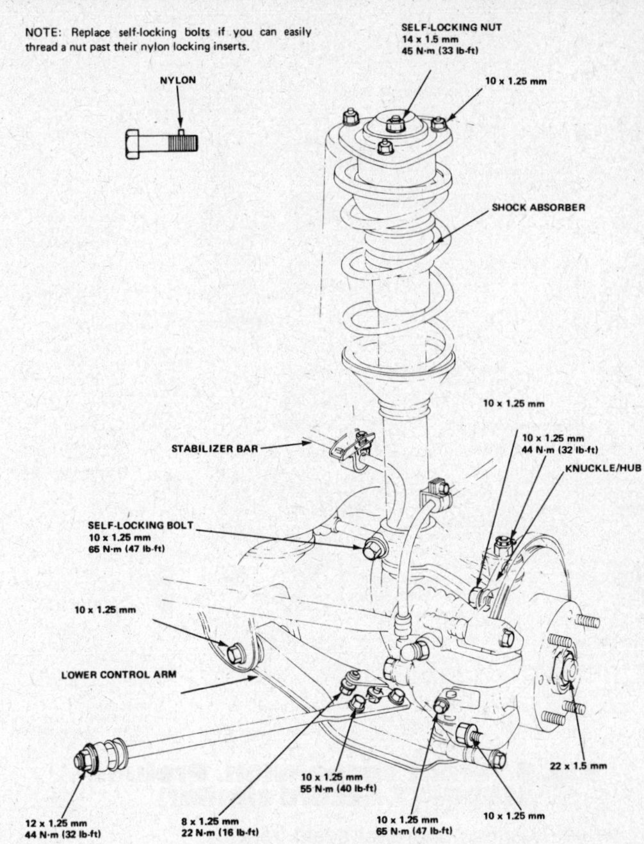

Fig. 2 Front suspension. 1983—85 Accord

tioned securely under lower control arm at the ball joint to prevent torsion bar tension causing steering knuckle to jump when lower ball joint is removed.

3. Remove ball joint cotter pin and nut.
4. Pry ball joint from steering knuckle. If necessary, a ball joint removal tool may be used. Lower floor jack slowly.
5. Remove radius arm self locking nut, **Fig. 4,** then the radius arm/ball joint to torsion arm self locking bolts.
6. Remove radius arm/ball joint assembly.
7. Replace ball joint.
8. Reverse procedure to install. Refer to **Fig. 4** for torque specifications.

PRELUDE

Lower

1. Remove steering knuckle. Refer to "Steering Knuckle, Hub & Bearing, Replace" for procedure.
2. Remove lower ball joint dust cover snap ring, then the dust boot.
3. Remove ball joint snap ring, then using ball joint removal and installation tool 07965-SB00100 and ball joint removal base 07965-SB00200, press ball joint out of steering knuckle.
4. Press replacement ball joint into steering knuckle with hand.
5. Press ball joint into steering knuckle using ball joint removal and installation tool 07965-SB00100 and ball joint installation base 07965-SB00300.
6. Install ball joint snap ring.
7. Install dust cover and snap ring.

Upper

1. Raise and support front of vehicle, then remove front wheels.
2. Remove upper ball joint shield.
3. Remove upper ball joint cotter pin and nut, then using a suitable ball joint removal tool, remove ball joint from steering knuckle.
4. Remove upper ball joint to upper arm attaching bolts, then the ball joint.
5. Reverse procedure to install. Refer to **Fig. 2** for torque specifications.

1986–87 ACCORD

Lower

Refer to procedure for Prelude.

Upper

1. Raise and support front of vehicle and remove wheels.
2. Remove cotter pin and nut securing upper ball joint to knuckle, then separate joint from knuckle using suitable tool.
3. Remove nuts securing upper control arm and the control arm. **Ball joint and control arm are replaced as an assembly.**
4. Reverse procedure to install. Torque upper control arm nuts to 53 ft. lbs. and ball joint nut to 32 ft. lbs.

STEERING KNUCKLE, HUB & BEARING REPLACE

1983 CIVIC & 1983–85 ACCORD

1. Raise vehicle and place on safety stands.
2. Remove front wheel.
3. Remove spindle nut locking device, then remove spindle nut.
4. Loosen the two mounting bolts and remove the front brake caliper as an assembly.
5. If knuckle is to remain on vehicle, use suitable slide hammer to remove wheel hub.
6. Detach bolt at lower arm then remove tie rod ball joint.
7. Remove pinch bolt securing knuckle to shock absorber.
8. Using hammer, tap knuckle off shock absorber.
9. Slide driveshaft out of hub.
10. Remove knuckle, hub, backing plate and front brake disc as an assembly.
11. Loosen attaching bolts and remove hub.
12. Loosen attaching bolts and remove front brake disc.
13. Loosen attaching bolts and remove backing plate.
14. Loosen attaching screws and remove front bearing retainer.
15. Using a hydraulic press and suitable tool set, press inner and outer front

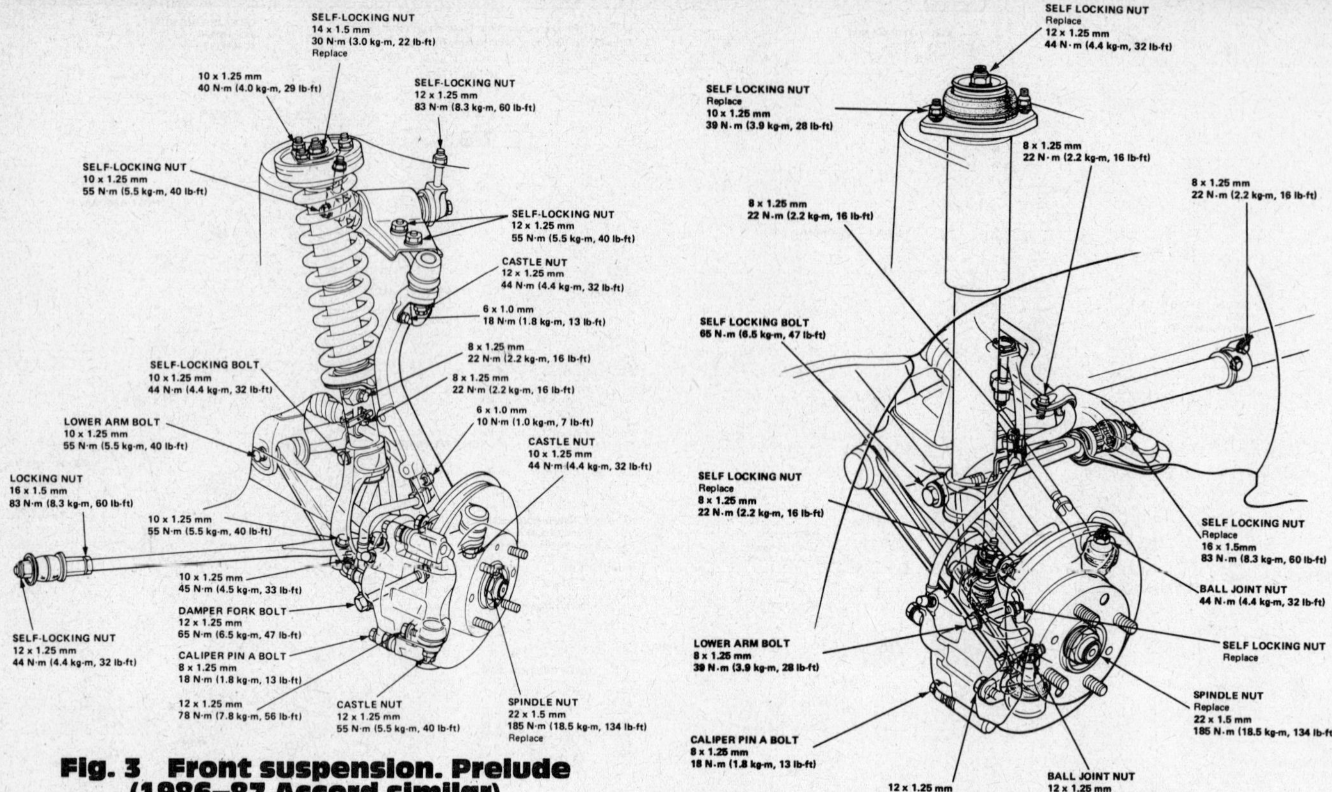

Fig. 3 Front suspension. Prelude (1986–87 Accord similar)

Fig. 4 Front suspension. 1984–87 Civic & CRX

wheel bearings and dust seals from knuckle.

16. Install new bearings with part numbers on both facing inward, using a hydraulic press and suitable tool set.
17. Reverse procedure above for remainder of assembly, making sure that aligning dowel at the bottom of the shock absorber seats properly and that the lower arm pivot bolt is tightened only when car is raised slightly off safety stand by a jack placed under the knuckle. Tighten lower arm pivot bolt to 25-36 ft. lbs. (3.5-5.0 kg-m) and use a new lock tab to secure.

1984–87 CIVIC & CRX

1. Remove spindle nut locking device, then loosen spindle nut.
2. Loosen wheel lug nuts.
3. Raise and support front of vehicle, then remove front wheels and spindle nut.
4. Remove brake caliper and wire aside. **Do not allow caliper assembly to hang from brake hose.**
5. Remove brake disc attaching screws, then thread two 8 x 1.25 x 12 mm bolts into attaching screw holes to pull disc from hub. **When tightening screws, turn only two turns at a time to prevent cocking the brake disc.**
6. Remove tie rod end cotter pin and nut.
7. Remove tie rod end using suitable tie rod end remover.
8. Place a suitable floor jack under lower arm and raise slightly to restrain lower arm. **Ensure jack is positioned securely under lower arm at the ball joint to prevent torsion bar tension causing steering knuckle to jump when lower ball joint is removed.**
9. Remove ball joint cotter pin and nut.
10. Pry ball joint from steering knuckle. If necessary, a ball joint removal tool may be used.
11. Remove shock absorber to lower arm pinch bolt, **Fig. 4,** then slowly lower jack.
12. To remove knuckle assembly, tap down with suitable brass or lead hammer until knuckle clears shock absorber.
13. Pull driveshaft out of knuckle, then remove hub/knuckle assembly.
14. Remove two splash guard to knuckle attaching screws, then the splash guard.
15. Remove hub from steering knuckle with a suitable press.
16. Remove bearing circlip, then press bearings from steering knuckle.
17. Remove outboard bearing inner race with bearing remover.
18. Install replacement bearings and races with suitable press. Install circlip.
19. Press in wheel hub.
20. Reverse remaining procedure to install. Refer to **Fig. 4** for torque specifications.

PRELUDE & 1986–87 ACCORD

1. Remove spindle nut locking device, then loosen spindle nut.
2. Loosen wheel lug nuts.
3. Raise and support front of vehicle, then remove front wheels and spindle nut.
4. Remove caliper and wire aside. **Do not allow caliper assembly to hang from brake hose.**
5. Remove brake disc attaching screws, then thread two 8 x 1.25 x 12 mm bolts into attaching screw holes to pull disc from hub. **When tightening screws, turn only two turns at a time to prevent cocking the brake disc.**
6. Remove tie rod end cotter pin and nut.
7. Remove tie rod end using suitable tie rod end remover.
8. Remove lower ball joint cotter pin, then loosen ball joint nut half way.
9. Using a suitable jawed puller, separate ball joint and lower arm.
10. Remove upper ball joint shield, then cotter pin and nut.
11. Separate upper ball joint from upper arm using a suitable ball joint remover.
12. Remove steering knuckle and hub assembly by sliding off driveshaft.
13. Remove two splash guard to knuckle attaching screws.
14. Remove hub from steering knuckle using a suitable press.
15. Remove remaining splash guard to knuckle attaching screw, then the splash guard.
16. Remove outboard dust seal and snap ring from steering knuckle, then the outboard inner bearing race and bearing.
17. Flip knuckle over, then remove inboard dust seal, inboard inner bearing race and bearing.
18. Using a suitable press, remove bearing outer race from steering knuckle.
19. Remove outboard bearing inner race with bearing remover.
20. Remove outboard dust seal from hub.
21. Reverse procedure to install. Refer to **Fig. 3,** for torque specifications.

STEERING GEAR REPLACE

Prior to removing steering gear on models with power steering, proceed as follows:

1. Disconnect fluid return hose from pump reservoir and place end of hose in suitable container.
2. Start engine, then turn steering wheel from lock to lock several times.
3. When fluid stops running from hose, stop engine.
4. Reconnect hose to pump.
5. After installing gear, fill reservoir and repeat step 2 to bleed air from system, filling reservoir as needed.

1983–85 ACCORD

Manual Steering

1. Remove bottom bolt from steering shaft coupler, then disconnect coupler from pinion shaft.
2. Raise and support front of vehicle and remove wheels.
3. Remove cotter pins and retaining nuts, then disconnect tie rods from steering knuckles using suitable puller.
4. Remove sub-frame center beam.
5. On models with manual transmission, proceed as follows:
   a. On 1983 models, place selector in low or third gear, remove bolt from shift rod yoke and disconnect shift linkage, then disconnect shift lever torque arm from transmission,
   b. On 1984-85 models, disconnect shift rod extension from transmission.
6. On 1984-85 models with automatic transmission, disconnect shift cable guide from floor and pull shift cable guide down by hand.
7. On all models, remove nuts securing exhaust pipe to manifold and exhaust pipe bracket nuts, then lower exhaust pipe.
8. Push rack all the way to the right, then remove steering gear brackets.
9. Lower steering gear until pinion shaft clear opening in frame and rotate steering gear forward until pinion shaft points toward the rear.
10. Move steering gear to the right until the left tie rod clears the exhaust pipe, then lower steering gear and remove from left side of vehicle.
11. Reverse procedure to install. Torque bracket bolts to 16 ft. lbs., tie rod nuts to 32 ft. lbs. and coupler pinch bolt to 22 ft. lbs. **When installing center beam, ensure insulator is centered with mount on transmission.**

Power Steering

1. Turn steering wheel all the way to the left.
2. Remove boot from base of steering column, loosen upper and lower steering shaft coupler pinch bolts, then disconnect coupler from steering gear.
3. Raise and support front of vehicle, then remove wheels and steering gear shield.

Fig. 5 Typical rack guide screw adjustment

4. Remove cotter pins and retaining nuts, then disconnect tie rods from steering knuckles using suitable puller.
5. Remove sub-frame center beam.
6. On 1983 models with 5 speed transmission, place selector in low or third, remove bolt from shift rod clevis and disconnect shift rod, then disconnect shift lever torque arm from transmission.
7. On models with automatic transmission, proceed as follows:
   a. On 1983 models, remove control cable cushion from retaining bracket.
   b. On 1984-85 models, remove control cable holder.
8. On all models, remove nuts securing exhaust pipe to manifold and exhaust pipe bracket nuts, then lower exhaust pipe.
9. Clean dirt from steering gear control unit, disconnect fluid lines, then plug lines and open fittings.
10. Remove bracket bolts, then lower steering gear until pinion shaft clears opening in frame and rotate steering gear forward until pinion shaft points toward the rear.
11. Move steering gear to the right until the left tie rod clears the exhaust pipe, then lower steering gear and remove from left side of vehicle.
12. Reverse procedure to install. Torque bracket bolts to 16 ft. lbs., tie rod nuts to 32 ft. lbs. and coupler pinch bolts to 22 ft. lbs.

1986–87 ACCORD

1. Turn steering wheel all the way to the left.
2. Remove steering gear joint cover from floor panel at base of steering column, then disconnect steering shaft from gear.
3. Remove steering gear shield and clean dirt from control unit and fluid line connections.
4. Raise and support front of vehicle and remove wheels.
5. Remove cotter pins and retaining nuts, then disconnect tie rods from steering knuckles using suitable puller.
6. On models with manual transmission, remove shift extension and disconnect shift rod from transmission case.
7. On models with automatic transmission, remove bolt securing control cable clamp to floor panel.
8. On all models, remove sub-frame canter beam.
9. Remove nuts securing exhaust pipe to manifold and exhaust pipe bracket nuts, then lower exhaust pipe.
10. Disconnect fluid lines from control unit, then plug lines and open fittings.
11. Remove steering gear mounting bolts, slide gear to right so tie rod clears bottom of beam, then remove steering gear.
12. Reverse procedure to install. Torque steering gear bolts to 16 ft. lbs., center beam bolts to 37 ft. lbs. and tie rod nuts to 32 ft. lbs.

1983 CIVIC

1. Raise and support front of vehicle and remove wheels.
2. Remove cotter pins and retaining nuts, then disconnect tie rods from steering knuckles using suitable puller.
3. Remove bottom bolt from steering shaft coupler, then the steering gear bracket bolts.
4. Lower steering gear straight down until pinion shaft is free from coupler, rotate gear 180°, then remove gear through opening in left side of vehicle.
5. Reverse procedure to install. Torque tie rod nuts to 32 ft. lbs. and coupler pinch bolt to 22 ft. lbs.

1984–87 CIVIC & CRX

Manual Steering

1. Remove bottom bolt from steering shaft coupler, then disconnect coupler from steering gear.
2. Raise and support front of vehicle and remove wheels.
3. Remove cotter pins and retaining nuts, then disconnect tie rods from steering knuckles using suitable puller.
4. On models with manual transmission, disconnect shift lever torque rod from clutch housing, slide pin retainer aside and drive out spring pin, then disconnect shift rod.
5. On models with automatic transmission, remove shift cable guide and pull cable down by hand.
6. Remove nuts bolts and springs joining exhaust header pipe to intermediate pipe, then pull intermediate pipe down by hand.
7. Push rack all the way to the right, then remove steering gear brackets.
8. Lower steering gear until pinion shaft clears opening in frame and rotate steering gear forward until pinion shaft points toward the rear.
9. Move steering gear to the right until the left tie rod clears the exhaust pipe, then lower steering gear and remove from left side of vehicle.
10. Reverse procedure to install. Torque steering gear mounting bolts to 29 ft. lbs., tie rod nuts to 32 ft. lbs. and coupler pinch bolt to 22 ft. lbs.

Power Steering

1. Turn steering wheel all the way to the left.
2. Remove bottom bolt from steering

shaft coupler, then disconnect coupler from steering gear.
3. Raise and support front of vehicle and remove wheels.
4. Remove cotter pins and retaining nuts, then disconnect tie rods from steering knuckles using suitable puller.
5. Remove shift cable holder and pull cable down by hand.
6. Remove nuts bolts and springs securing exhaust header pipe to intermediate pipe, then remove intermediate pipe.
7. Clean dirt away from gearbox and fluid lined, disconnect fluid lines, then plug lines and open fittings.
8. Remove steering gear mounting bolts.
9. Move steering gear to the right until the left tie rod clears the exhaust pipe, then lower steering gear and remove from left side of vehicle.
10. Reverse procedure to install. Torque 8 mm steering gear mounting bolts to 27 ft. lbs., 10 mm mounting bolts to 32 ft. lbs., tie rod nuts to 32 ft. lbs. and coupler pinch bolt to 22 ft. lbs.

PRELUDE

Manual Steering

1. Remove bottom bolt from steering shaft coupler, then disconnect coupler from pinion shaft.
2. Raise and support front of vehicle and remove wheels.
3. Remove cotter pins and retaining nuts, then disconnect tie rods from steering knuckles using suitable puller.
4. Remove sub-frame center beam.
5. On models with manual transmission, disconnect shift rod extension from transmission.
6. On models with automatic transmission, remove shift cable guide from floor and pull cable down by hand.
7. On all models, remove nuts securing exhaust pipe to manifold and exhaust pipe bracket nuts, then lower exhaust pipe.
8. Push rack all the way to the right, then remove steering gear brackets.
9. Lower steering gear until pinion shaft clear opening in frame and rotate steering gear forward until pinion shaft points toward the rear.
10. Move steering gear to the right until the left tie rod clears the exhaust pipe, then lower steering gear and remove from left side of vehicle.
11. Reverse procedure to install. Torque bracket bolts to 16 ft. lbs., tie rod nuts to 32 ft. lbs. and coupler pinch bolt to 22 ft. lbs. **When installing center beam, ensure insulator is centered with mount on transmission.**

Power Steering

1. Turn steering wheel all the way to the left.
2. Remove boot from base of steering column, loosen upper and lower steering shaft coupler pinch bolts, then disconnect coupler from steering gear.
3. Raise and support front of vehicle, then remove wheels and steering gear shield.
4. Remove cotter pins and retaining nuts, then disconnect tie rods from steering knuckles using suitable puller.
5. Remove sub-frame center beam.
6. Remove transmission control cable holder.
7. Remove nuts securing exhaust pipe to manifold and exhaust pipe bracket nuts, then lower exhaust pipe.
8. Clean dirt from steering gear control unit, disconnect fluid lines, then plug lines and open fittings.
9. Remove steering gear bracket bolts, pull steering gear down until pinion shaft clears frame, move gear to the right until left tie rod drops free, then remove gear from left of vehicle.
10. Reverse procedure to install. Torque bracket bolts to 16 ft. lbs., tie rod nuts to 32 ft. lbs. and coupler pinch bolts to 22 ft. lbs.

RACK GUIDE SCREW ADJUST

1983 CIVIC & PRELUDE & 1983–85 ACCORD W/MANUAL STEERING

1. Loosen rack guide screw locknut with suitable tool, **Fig. 5.**
2. Tighten guide screw until it compresses spring and lightly seats against guide, then back screw off approximately 1/8 turn (45°) on models with manual steering or 1/5 turn (70°) on models with power steering.
3. Hold position of adjusting screw and torque locknut to 18 ft. lbs.

1983–87 ACCORD & 1984–87 PRELUDE W/POWER STEERING

1. Loosen rack guide screw locknut with suitable tool, **Fig. 5.**
2. Tighten guide screw until it compresses spring and lightly seats against guide, then loosen screw.
3. Torque screw to 2.9 ft. lbs. on 1986-87 Accord, or 2 ft. lbs. on all other models, then back screw off approximately 1/10 turn (35°) on 1984-85 models or 1/12 turn (25°) on 1986-87 models.
4. Hold position of adjusting screw and torque locknut to 18 ft. lbs.

1984–87 CIVIC & CRX

1. Loosen rack guide screw locknut with suitable tool, **Fig. 5.**
2. Torque guide screw to 3 ft. lbs on all except Civic with variable ratio manual steering or 4 ft. lbs. on 1986-87 Civic with variable ratio manual steering.
3. Loosen guide screw as follows:
   a. On all except 1986-87 Civic with manual steering, back guide screw off approximately 1/10 turn (35°).
   b. On 1986-87 Civic with constant ratio manual steering back guide screw off approximately 1/12 turn (25°).
   c. On 1986-87 Civic with variable ratio manual steering, back screw off approximately 15°.
4. Hold position of adjusting screw and torque locknut to 60 ft. lbs. on 1986-87 Civic with variable ratio manual steering, or 18 ft. lbs. on all other models.

WHEEL ALIGNMENT SECTION

INDEX

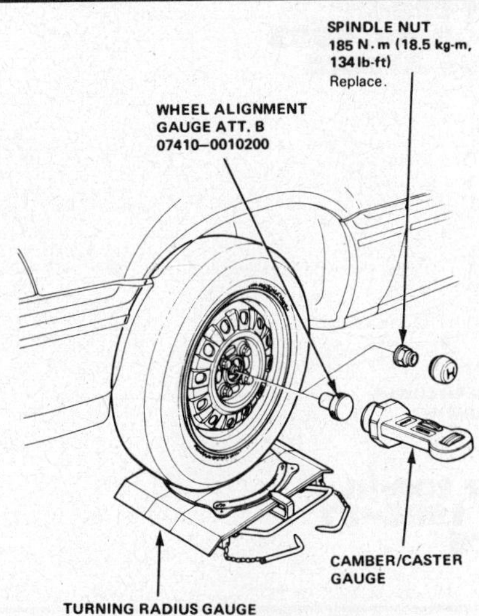

Fig. 1 Caster angle inspection

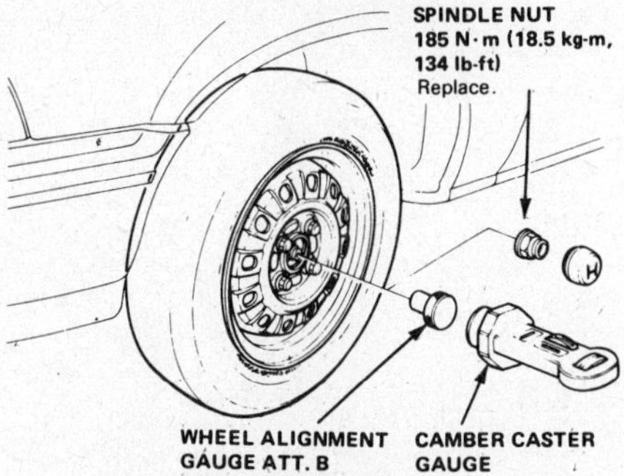

Fig. 3 Camber angle inspection

CASTER INSPECTION & ADJUSTMENT

Ensure tires are properly inflated prior to checking or adjusting caster angles.

EXC. PRELUDE & 1986–87 ACCORD

Caster angle is not adjustable, however, the following procedure may be used to ensure caster is within specifications.

1. Raise front of vehicle and position turning radius gauges under front wheels, then lower vehicle.
2. Remove spindle nut and install suitable caster gauge and adapter, **Fig. 1.**
3. Apply front brakes and turn wheels 20° inward.
4. Position caster gauge at 0°, then return wheels to straight-ahead position and note gauge reading. If caster angle is not within specifications, inspect suspension components for damage and repair as necessary, then recheck caster.

PRELUDE & 1986–87 ACCORD

1. Check caster angle as described under "Exc. Prelude & 1986-87 Accord."
2. If caster adjustment is necessary, loosen radius rod adjuster locknut and self-locking nut on end of radius rod, **Fig. 2.**
3. Turn radius rod adjuster in to increase caster or out to decrease caster as necessary. **One complete revolution of the adjuster moves radius rod .049 inch and changes caster 2/15°.**
4. Tighten radius rod adjuster locknut and self-locking nut, then recheck caster angle.

CAMBER INSPECTION & ADJUSTMENT

Ensure tires are properly inflated prior to checking or adjusting camber angles.

EXC. PRELUDE

Camber angles are not adjustable, however, the following procedure may be used to ensure camber is within specifications.

1. Remove spindle nut and install suitable camber gauge and adapter, **Fig. 3.** with wheels in straight-ahead position.
2. Note gauge reading with bubble centered on the gauge. If camber is not within specifications, inspection suspension components for damage and repair as necessary, then recheck camber.

PRELUDE

1. Check camber angle as described under "Exc. Prelude."
2. If camber adjustment is necessary, loosen upper arm attaching nuts, **Fig. 4,** then hold wheel by hand and adjust camber to 0° on gauge.
3. Tighten upper arm attaching nuts, then recheck camber angle.

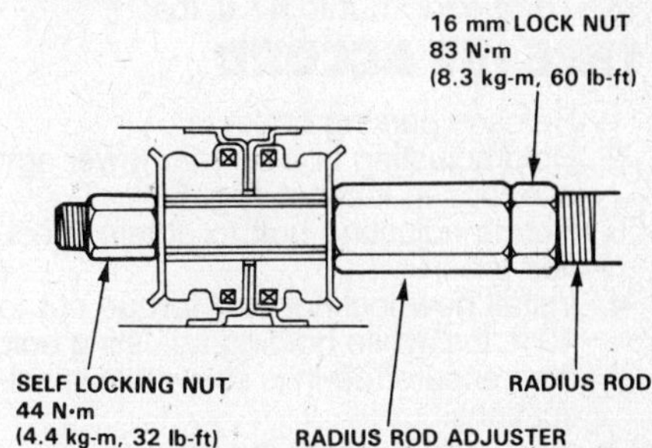

Fig. 2 Caster adjustment. Prelude & 1986–87 Accord

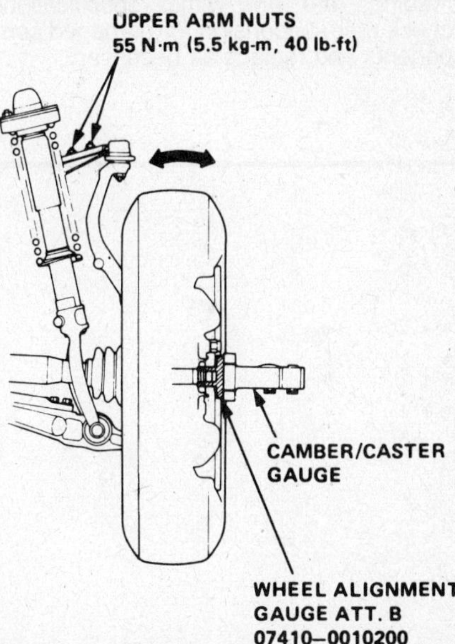

Fig. 4 Camber adjustment. Prelude

FRONT TOE-IN INSPECTION & ADJUSTMENT

Ensure tires are properly inflated prior to checking or adjusting toe-in.

1. Center the steering wheel, then loosen tie rod locknuts.
2. Turn both tie rods in the same direction until both front wheels are positioned straight ahead.
3. Adjust toe to specifications by turning both tie rods in the same direction, then tighten tie rod locknuts. **On 1983 Civic models, turn left side tie rod until toe-out reading is within specifications, then repeat on right side.**

REAR TOE-IN INSPECTION & ADJUSTMENT

PRELUDE, 1983 CIVIC & 1983–85 ACCORD

Ensure tires are properly inflated prior to checking or adjusting toe-in.

1. Release parking brake.
2. Loosen locknut in rear radius arm pivot bolt, then turn adjusting bolt, **Fig. 5**, until toe-in is within specifications.
3. Torque locknut to 47 ft. lbs.

1986–87 ACCORD

1. Release parking brake.
2. Hold adjusting bolt on rear lower arm and loosen locknut, **Fig. 6.**
3. Rotate adjusting bolt to obtain specified toe-in.
4. Install new locknut and torque nut to 40 ft. lbs. while holding adjusting bolt, then ensure toe-in is still within specifications.

1984–87 CIVIC & CRX

Rear wheel toe-in is not adjustable. If readings are not within specifications, check rear suspension for damaged components and replace as necessary.

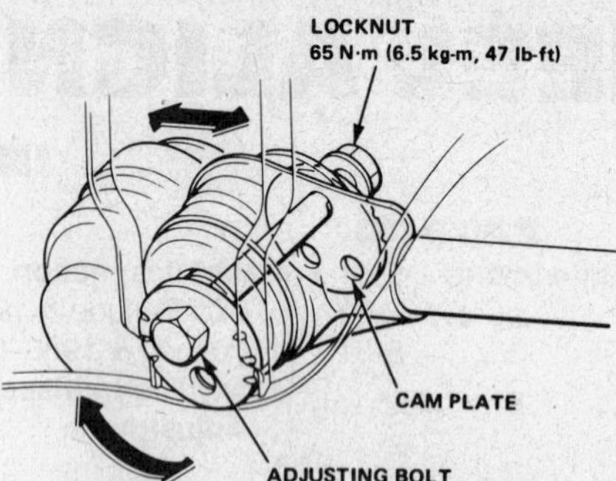

Fig. 5 Rear toe-in adjustment. Prelude, 1983 Civic & 1983–85 Accord

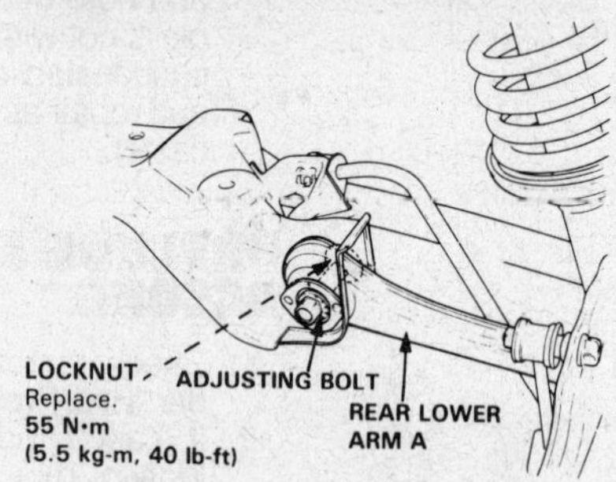

Fig. 6 Rear toe-in adjustment. 1986–87 Accord

HYUNDAI (Korea)

INDEX OF SERVICE OPERATIONS

General Engine Specifications

Year	Engine Displacement cu. in./liters	Fuel System	Bore & Stroke	Compression Ratio	Maximum Net H.P. @ RPM	Maximum Torque Ft. Lbs. @ RPM
1986–87	4-90/1.5L	2 Barrel①	2.97 X 3.23	9.4	68 @ 5500	82 @ 3500

①—Mikuni feedback carburetor.

Valve Specifications

Year	Engine	Valve Lash		Valve Angles		Valve Spring Free Length	Valve Spring Pressure Lbs. @ In.	Stem Clearance		Stem Diameter	
		Int. (hot)	Exh. (hot)	Seat	Face			Intake	Exhaust	Intake	Exhaust
1986–87	4-90/1.5L	.006①	.010	45	45	②	③	.0012–.0024	.0020–.0035	.260	.260

①—Jet valve lash, .010 inch.
②—Intake and exhaust valves, 1.756 inch; Jet valve, 1.165 inch.
③—Intake and exhaust valves, 53 @ 1.469 inch; Jet valve, 6 @ .846 inch.

Pistons, Pins, Rings, Crankshaft & Bearings

Year	Engine	Piston Clearance	Ring End Gap		Wristpin Diameter	Rod Bearings		Main Bearings		Thrust on Bear. No.	Shaft End Play
			Comp.	Oil		Shaft Diameter	Bearing Clearance	Shaft Diameter	Bearing Clearance		
1986–87	4-90/1.5L	.0008–.0016	.008	.008	—	1.6535	.0004–.0024	1.8898	.0008–.0028	3	.002–.007

Engine Tightening Specifications

***Torque specifications listed are in Ft. Lbs. and are for clean and lightly lubricated threads only. Dry or dirty threads produce increased friction which prevents acccurate measurement of tightness.**

Year	Engine	Spark Plugs	Cylinder Bolts Head	Manifold Nuts or Bolts	Rocker Shaft Bracket Bolts	Camshaft Sprocket Bolt	Oil Pan Bolts	Connecting Rod Cap Bolts	Main Bearing Cap Bolts	Flywheel to Crankshaft	Vibration Damper or Pulley
1986–87	4-90/1.5L	15–21	①	11–14	15–19	47–54	5–6	24–25	37–39	94–101	9–11

①—With engine cold, torque to 51–54 ft. lbs.; with engine hot, torque to 58–61 ft. lbs.

Alternator & Regulator Specifications

Year	Alternator			Regulator	
	Make	Rated Hot Output Amps.	Hot Output Amps. @ 2500 RPM	Type	Regulated Voltage
1986–87	Bosch	55	—	Integral	14.4–14.6

Starter Motor Specifications

Year	Engine	Starter	Free Speed Test		
			Amps.①	Volts	RPM②
1986–87	4-90/1.5L	All	60	11.5	③

①—Maximum.
②—Minimum.
③—With manual trans., 6500; with auto trans., 6600.

Brake Specifications

Year	Model	Brake Drum Inside Diameter	Wheel Cylinder Bore Diameter		Master Cylinder Bore Diameter	Disc Brake Rotor Specifications			
			Disc Brake	Rear Drum Brake		Nominal Thickness	Minimum Refinish Thickness	Thickness Variation Parallelism	Lateral Run-out (T.I.R.)
1986–87	Excel	7.100	2.010	.750	.810	.510	.450	—	.006

Front Wheel Alignment Specifications

Year	Model	Caster Angle, Degrees		Camber Angle, Degrees		Toe-in Inch	King Pin Inclination
		Limits	Desired	Limits	Desired		
1986–87	Excel	+1/2 to +1 1/6	+5/6	0 to +1	+1/2	−.08 to +.16	+12 7/10

Rear Wheel Alignment Specifications

Year	Model	Camber Angle, Degrees		Toe-In, Inches
		Limits	Desired	
1986–87	Excel	−1 1/3 to −1/6	−2/3	—

Cooling System & Capacity Data

Year	Model	Cooling Capacity Qts.	Radiator Cap Relief Pressure, Lbs.	Thermo. Opening Temp.	Fuel Tank Gals.	Engine Oil Refill Qts. w/filter	Transmission Oil		
							4 Speed Pts.	5 Speed Pts.	Auto Trans. Qts.
1986–87	Excel	5.3	13	190	①	4.2	4.4	4.4	6.0

①—Exc. GLS w/auto trans., 10.6; GLS w/auto. trans., 13.2

ELECTRICAL SECTION

INDEX

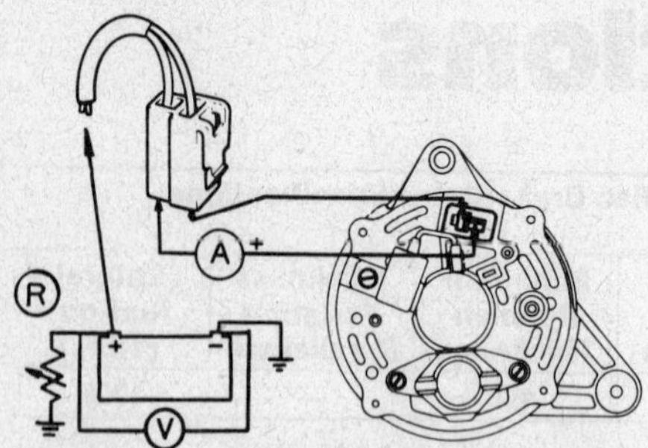

Fig. 1 Alternator output test connections

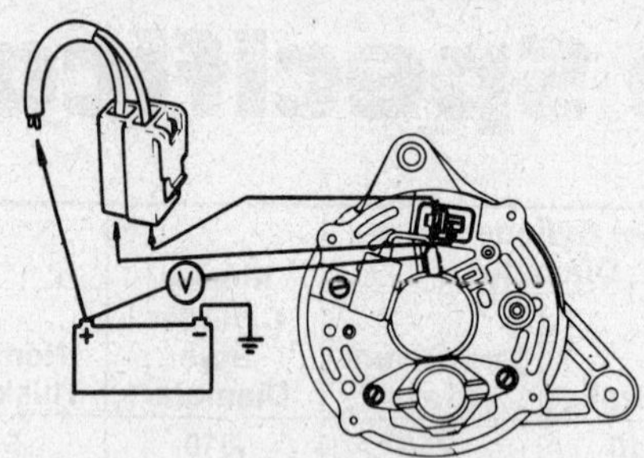

Fig. 2 Positive side voltage drop test connections

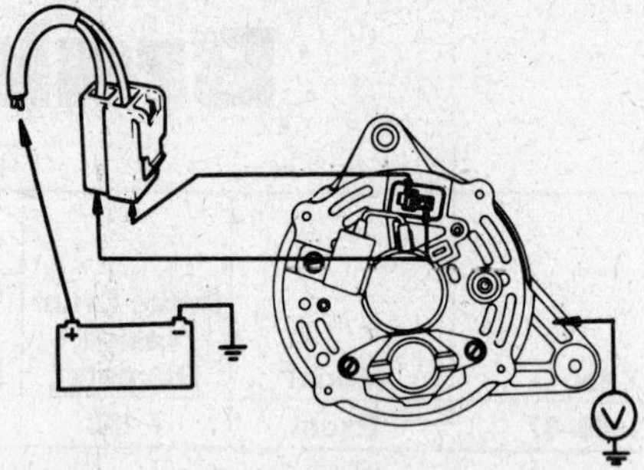

Fig. 3 Negative side voltage drop test connections

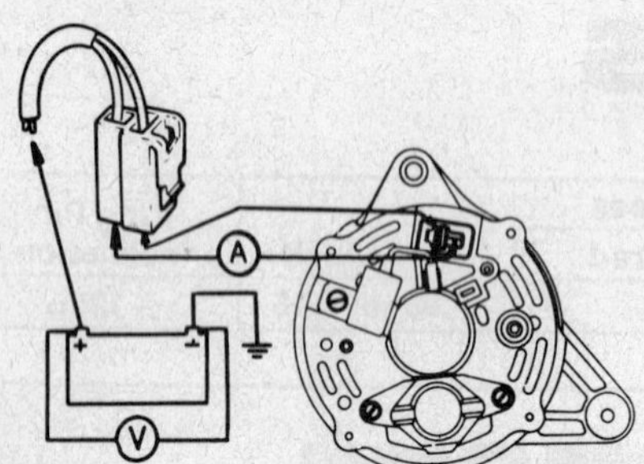

Fig. 4 Control voltage test connections

ALTERNATOR TESTING

Ensure that alternator drive belt is properly adjusted and battery is fully charged before performing the following procedures.

CIRCUIT CONTINUITY TEST

1. Disconnect battery ground cable.
2. Disconnect "L" and "R" terminals from alternator, then reconnect battery ground cable and place ignition switch in On position.
3. Connect positive lead of a suitable voltmeter to disconnected terminal and negative lead to ground. Observe voltmeter. Voltmeter should read battery voltage. Repeat procedure for remaining terminal. If voltmeter reading is not as specified, check for short or open in circuit.

OUTPUT TEST

1. Connect ammeter (A), voltmeter (V) and 30 amp resistor (R) to circuit as shown in **Fig. 1.**
2. Switch on all accessories, then start engine and allow to run at 3,000 RPM.
3. Vary resistance to increase current load and observe test equipment.
4. Rated output should be reached without voltage dropping below 13 volts.

CIRCUIT VOLTAGE DROP TEST

1. To test positive side voltage drop, proceed as follows:
   a. Reconnect "L" and "R" terminals at alternator, then connect voltmeter (V) to circuit as shown in **Fig. 2.**
   b. Switch on all accessories, then start engine and allow to run at 3,000 RPM.
   c. Observe voltmeter.
   d. If voltmeter reading obtained in previous step is greater than .5 volt, check positive side of charging circuit for excess resistance and repair as necessary.
2. To test negative side voltage drop, proceed as follows:
   a. With "L" and "R" terminals still connected to alternator, connect voltmeter (V) to circuit as shown in **Fig. 3.**
   b. Switch on all accessories, then start engine and allow to run at 3,000 RPM.
   c. Observe voltmeter.
   d. If voltmeter reading obtained in previous step is greater than .25 volt, check negative side of charging circuit for excess resistance and repair as necessary.

CONTROL VOLTAGE TEST

1. Connect ammeter (A) and voltmeter (V) to circuit as shown in **Fig. 4.**
2. Start engine, allow to run at 3,000 RPM, then observe ammeter.

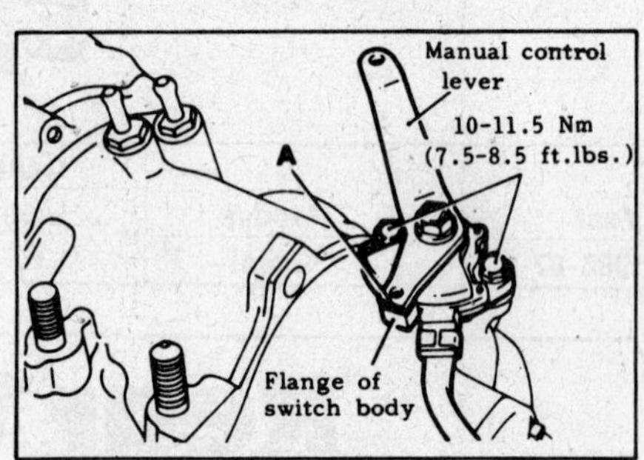

Fig. 5 Adjusting neutral start (inhibitor) switch

3. When ammeter reading falls to between 3 and 5 amps, observe voltmeter reading.
4. Voltmeter reading obtained in previous step should be 13.7 to 14.5 volts. If readings obtained are not within specification, replace voltage regulator.

STARTER REPLACE

1. Disconnect battery ground cable.
2. Disconnect starter electrical connections.
3. Remove starter retaining bolts, then the starter.
4. Reverse procedure to install.

STOPLIGHT SWITCH REPLACE

The stoplight switch is located on the brake pedal support.

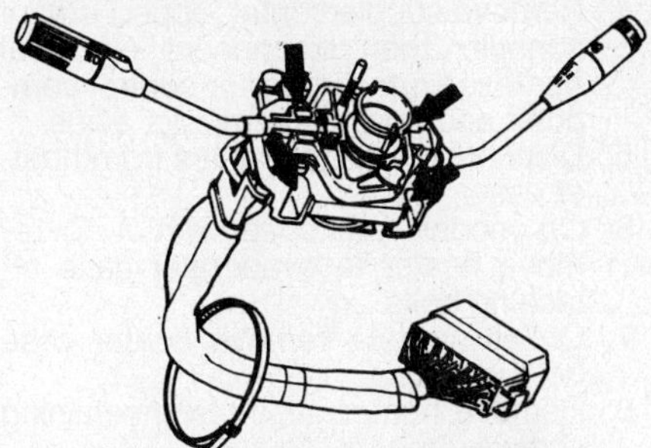

Fig. 6 Multi-function switch retaining screw location

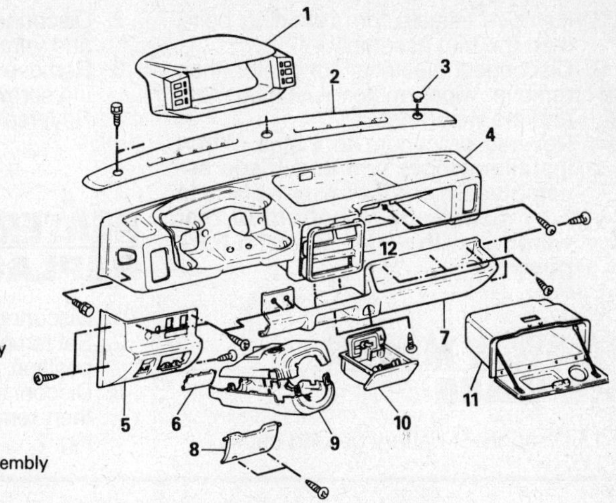

1. Cluster housing assembly
2. Crash pad upper cover
3. Upper cover pad
4. Crash pad main assembly
5. Lower crash pad side assembly
6. Fuse box cover
7. Lower crash pad main assembly
8. Shroud under cover
9. Steering column shroud
10. Ash tray
11. Glove box housing
12. Crash pad main facia panel assembly

Fig. 7 Instrument panel assembly

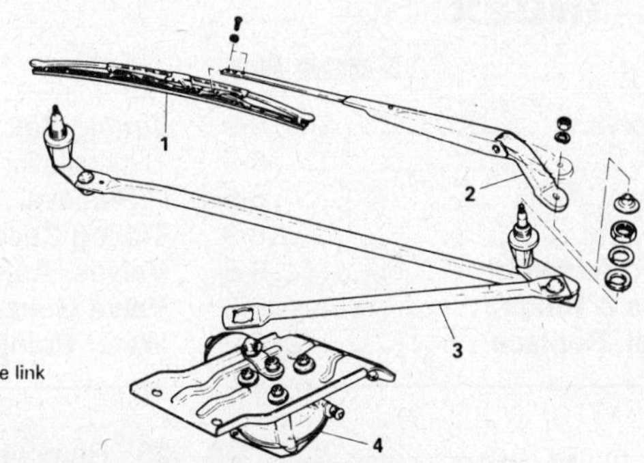

1. Windshield wiper blade
2. Windshield wiper arm
3. Windshield wiper spindle link
4. Windshield wiper motor

Fig. 8 Front wiper motor & linkage assembly

1. Disconnect switch electrical connectors.
2. Loosen switch retaining locknut, then remove switch from vehicle.
3. Reverse procedure to install. Adjust switch until clearance between outer case of switch and brake pedal arm is .02-.04 inch, then tighten locknut.

NEUTRAL START (INHIBITOR) SWITCH

REPLACE

1. Place manual control lever in Neutral position, then remove control lever retainer and control lever.
2. Disconnect electrical harness, then remove switch retaining bolts and switch assembly.
3. Reverse procedure to install, then adjust switch as follows:
   a. With manual control lever in Neutral position, turn switch body until wide end (A) of control lever, **Fig. 5**, overlaps switch body flange.
   b. Hold switch body in position, then torque retaining bolts to 8 ft. lbs.

MULTI-FUNCTION SWITCH

REPLACE

The lighting, dimmer, turn signal/hazard and wiper/washer switches are all incorporated into the multi-function switch assembly.

1. Disconnect battery ground cable.
2. Remove horn button cover, scribe alignment marks on steering wheel and shaft, then remove steering wheel using suitable puller.
3. Remove steering column trim shroud attaching screws, then the trim shrouds.
4. Remove switch retaining screws, **Fig. 6**, disconnect switch harness connector, then pull switch assembly from steering column.
5. Reverse procedure to install.

INSTRUMENT PANEL

REPLACE

1. Disconnect battery ground cable.
2. Remove horn button cover, scribe alignment marks on steering wheel and shaft, then remove steering wheel using suitable puller.
3. Remove steering column trim shroud attaching screws, then the trim shrouds, **Fig. 7**.
4. Remove glove box, then the steering column shroud under cover.
5. Remove lower crash pad cover.
6. Remove hood release handle retaining screws, then the handle.
7. Remove lower instrument panel side panel retaining screws, disconnect electrical connector, then pull panel outward and remove from vehicle.
8. Remove cigar lighter and ashtray.
9. Remove lower instrument panel assembly retaining screws, pull assembly outward to disconnect electrical connector, then remove lower instrument panel from vehicle.
10. Remove instrument cluster retaining screws, pull cluster outward to disconnect electrical connectors and speedometer cable, then remove cluster from vehicle.
11. Remove radio knobs and front trim panel, disconnect antenna cable and wiring, then remove radio retaining screws and radio.
12. Disconnect control wires from heater control assembly, then remove heater bracket to instrument panel retaining bolts.
13. Remove instrument panel upper cover pads, then the retaining bolts.
14. Remove remaining instrument panel retaining bolts and the instrument panel.
15. Reverse procedure to install.

FRONT WIPER MOTOR & LINKAGE

REPLACE

1. Remove wiper arm and blade assembly.
2. Remove cowl top cover retaining bolts, then the top cover.
3. Remove retaining nuts, then the linkage assembly, **Fig. 8.**
4. Disconnect electrical connector, then remove wiper motor retaining nuts and the wiper motor.
5. Reverse procedure to install. **When installing wiper arm and blade assembly, ensure that wiper blade is 1 1/2 inches above bottom of windshield, with wiper motor in Park position.**

REAR WIPER MOTOR

REPLACE

1. Remove wiper arm and blade assembly.

2. Remove tailgate trim retaining bolts, then the trim assembly.
3. Disconnect electrical connector, then remove wiper motor retaining nuts and the wiper motor.
4. Reverse procedure to install. **When installing wiper arm and blade assembly, ensure that wiper blade is 1 1/2 inches above bottom of rear window, with wiper motor in Park position.**

BLOWER MOTOR REPLACE

1. Disconnect battery ground cable.
2. Disconnect wire harness connector and ventilation tube at blower motor.
3. Remove blower motor to case attaching screws, then the blower motor.
4. Reverse procedure to install.

HEATER CORE REPLACE

1. Disconnect battery ground cable.
2. Set temperature control lever to "Hot" position, then drain cooling system.
3. Disconnect heater hoses from core, then remove lower instrument panel, Fig. 7.
4. Remove supplemental (upper) end of console, then disconnect electrical harness from carburetor control computer and position computer aside.
5. Disconnect control cables from heater case.
6. On models equipped with A/C, remove heater to evaporater case attaching bolts.
7. On all models, remove heater case from vehicle.
8. Remove heater case cover retaining screws, then the cover.
9. Remove hoses, clamps and water valve from case.
10. Pulling outward, remove heater core from case.
11. Reverse procedure to install.

ENGINE SECTION

INDEX

ENGINE REPLACE

The engine and transaxle are removed as an assembly.

1. Disconnect battery cables and remove battery.
2. Remove air cleaner.
3. Disconnect back-up lamp and engine harness electrical connectors.
4. On models equipped with 5-speed transaxle, disconnect select control valve electrical connector.
5. On all models, disconnect alternator and oil pressure switch electrical connectors.
6. Drain cooling system.
7. On models equipped with automatic transaxle, disconnect cooling lines from radiator.
8. On all models, disconnect upper and lower radiator hoses from engine, then remove radiator attaching bolts and the radiator.
9. Disconnect high tension leads and electrical connections from distributor and ignition coil.
10. Disconnect engine ground, then the brake booster vacuum hose.
11. Disconnect fuel supply, return and vapor hoses from engine.
12. Disconnect heater hoses and accelerator cable from engine.
13. Disconnect clutch or selector control lever cable from transaxle.
14. Disconnect speedometer cable from transaxle.
15. Remove A/C compressor mounting bracket, if equipped, and position compressor aside.

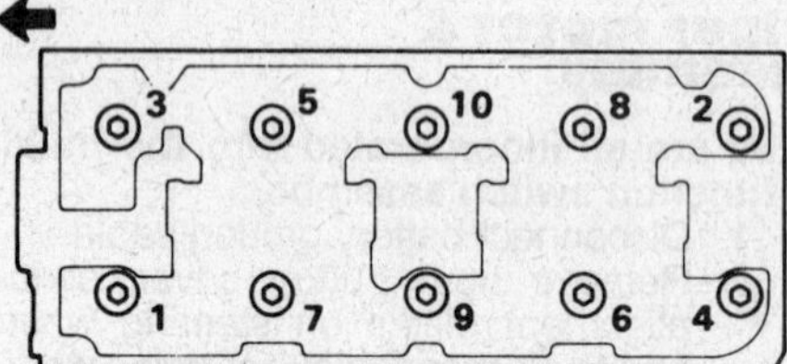

Fig. 1 Cylinder head bolt loosening sequence

16. Raise and support vehicle, then drain transaxle.
17. Disconnect exhaust pipe from manifold. Support pipe from underside of vehicle with suitable wire.
18. On models equipped with manual transaxle, disconnect shift control and extension rods from transaxle.
19. On all models, disconnect ball joint and strut bar from control arms and driveshafts from transaxle. Plug openings in transaxle to prevent dirt entry, then support control arms and driveshafts from underside of vehicle with suitable wire.
20. Attach suitable lifting equipment to engine, then raise engine slightly.
21. Disconnect engine mounts from engine.
22. Ensure that all remaining cables, hoses, harnesses and connectors that will interfere with engine removal are disconnected.
23. Remove cover from right front fender shield, then disconnect transaxle mountings.
24. Direct transaxle side of engine/transaxle assembly downward, then raise hoist and remove assembly from vehicle.
25. Reverse procedure to install.

CYLINDER HEAD REPLACE

1. Disconnect battery ground cable.
2. Drain coolant, then disconnect upper radiator hose.
3. Remove breather hose and air cleaner.
4. Disconnect all electrical connectors, hoses and vaccum lines that will interfere with cylinder head removal.
5. Disconnect high tension leads from spark plugs, then remove distributor.
6. Remove carburetor, intake manifold, heat cowl and exhaust manifold from cylinder head.
7. Remove timing belt cover.
8. Move timing belt tensioner fully toward water pump and temporarily secure it.
9. Remove timing belt from camshaft sprocket. Do not remove belt from crankshaft sprocket.
10. Remove rocker cover.
11. Using tool 09221-11000 or equivalent, loosen and remove cylinder head attaching bolts in sequence shown in **Fig. 1.**
12. Remove cylinder head from vehicle

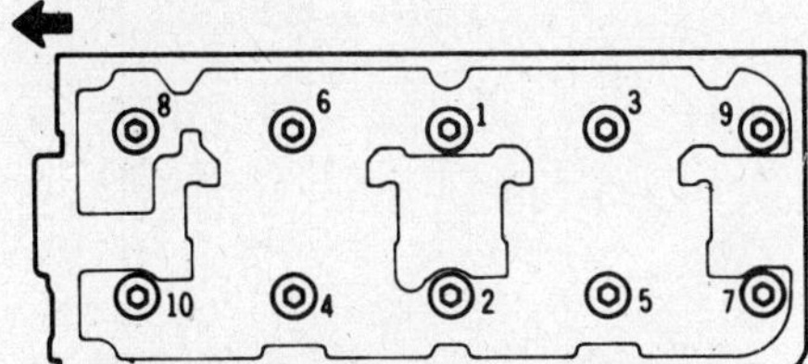

Fig. 2 Cylinder head bolt tightening sequence

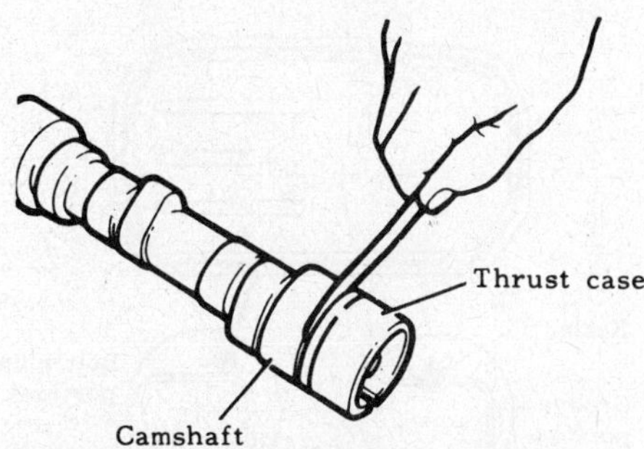

Fig. 3 Checking camshaft end play

and gasket from cylinder block.

13. Reverse procedure to install. When installing cylinder head, torque cylinder head attaching bolts to 25 ft. lbs. in sequence shown in **Fig. 2.** Then retorque bolts in sequence to final specification. After cylinder head has been installed, ensure timing belt is correctly installed and positioned, then adjust timing belt tension and valve clearances.

VALVES

ADJUST

The jet valve must be adjusted prior to adjusting the intake valve.

1. With engine at normal operating temperature, remove rocker arm cover.
2. Disconnect high tension lead from ignition coil.
3. Position No. 1 piston at TDC compression stroke, then back off intake valve adjusting screws of No. 1 and 2 cylinders approximately 2 turns.
4. With engine in this firing position, adjust the following valves:
   a. No. 1 and 2 jet and intake valves and No. 1 and 3 exhaust valves.
   b. To adjust valves, loosen adjusting screws, then turn screws until specified feeler gauge can be positioned between valve stem and screw.
   c. While holding adjusting screw in position, tighten locknut.
5. Rotate engine 360° to place No. 4 piston at TDC compression stroke, then back off intake valve adjusting screws of No. 3 and 4 cylinders approximately 2 turns.
6. With engine in this firing position, adjust No. 3 and 4 jet and intake valves and No. 2 and 4 exhaust valves as outlined above.
7. After adjustment is completed, install rocker arm cover and connect ignition coil high tension lead.

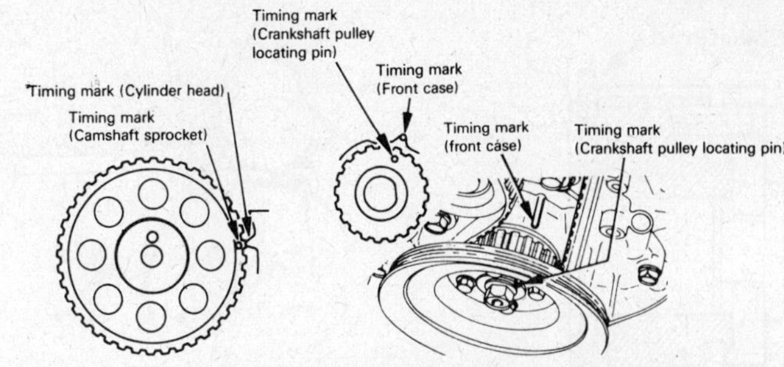

Fig. 4 Camshaft and crankshaft sprocket timing marks

CAMSHAFT, ROCKER ARMS & SHAFTS

REPLACE

REMOVAL

1. Disconnect battery ground cable.
2. Disconnect breather and secondary air hoses, then remove air cleaner.
3. Remove timing belt cover.
4. Move timing belt tensioner fully toward water pump, then secure in place.
5. Remove timing belt from camshaft sprocket. Do not remove belt from crankshaft sprocket.
6. Remove camshaft sprocket and rocker cover.
7. Remove rocker shaft assembly and cylinder head rear cover.
8. Remove camshaft thrust case tightening bolt, then the thrust case and camshaft assembly. Remove assembly from transaxle side of cylinder head.

INSTALLATION

1. Check camshaft journals for wear. If journals are badly worn, replace camshaft.
2. Install camshaft thrust case and thrust plate to camshaft end, then tighten attaching bolt securely. Check camshaft endplay with suitable feeler gauge as shown in **Fig. 3.** Endplay should be .002-.008 inch. If endplay exceeds specifications, replace thrust case and recheck endplay.
3. Lubricate camshaft journals and thrust surfaces with engine oil, then install camshaft into cylinder head.
4. Install camshaft thrust case with threaded hole facing upward. Align threaded hole with bolt hole in cylinder head, then install and firmly tighten attaching bolt.
5. Install rear cover and gasket. Firmly tighten bolts.
6. Install camshaft oil seal. Lubricate external surface of seal with engine oil to facilitate installation.
7. Install camshaft sprocket.
8. Install rocker arm and shaft assembly.
9. Align camshaft and crankshaft sprocket timing marks as shown in **Fig. 4.** When marks are properly aligned, the No. 1 piston will be at TDC of compression stroke.
10. Install timing belt. Adjust tension as outlined under "Timing Belt, Replace" procedure.
11. Temporarily set valve clearances with engine cold. **With engine cold, valve clearances should be set as follows: intake and jet valves, .003 inch; exhaust valves, .007 inch.**
12. Install new gasket into rocker cover groove, then temporarily install rocker cover.
13. Start engine and allow to reach normal operating temperature, then readjust valve clearances.
14. Install rocker cover.
15. Install timing belt cover.

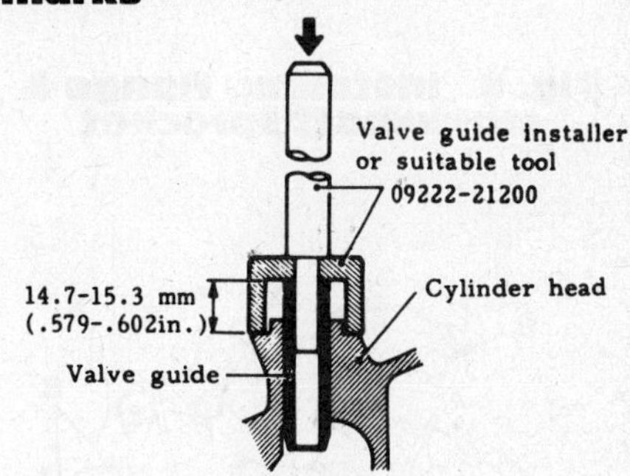

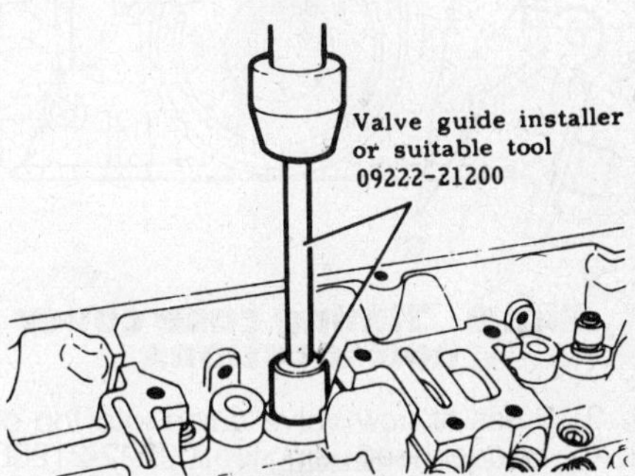

Fig. 5 Installing valve guides

VALVE GUIDES

REPLACE

1. Press old valve guide from cylinder head toward lower surface, using tool 09222-21200 or equivalent.
2. Ream each valve guide bore in cylinder head to the O.D. of replacement valve guide.

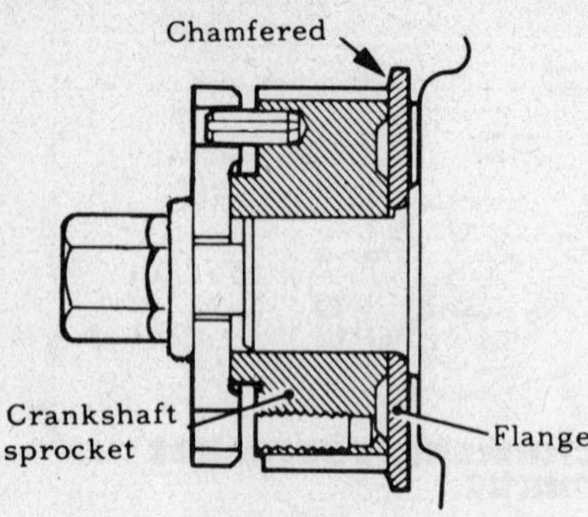

Fig. 6 Installing flange & crankshaft sprocket

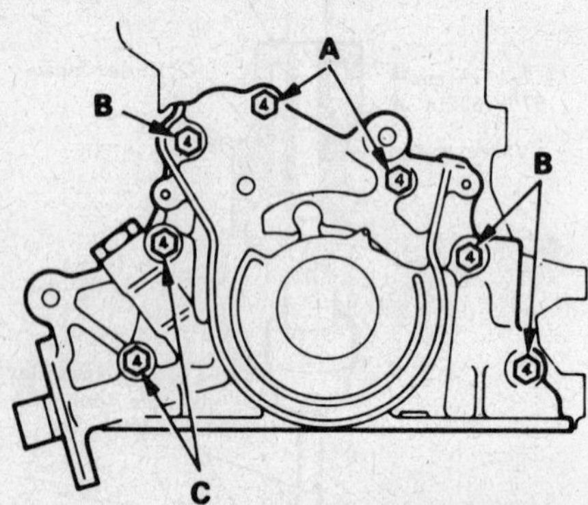

Fig. 9 Timing case cover bolt locations

3. Press fit new valve guide into top of cylinder head using tool 09222-21200 or equivalent, Fig. 5. **Tool 09222-21200 installs valve guide to a predetermined height. If this tool is not available, ensure that distance between cylinder head and top of guide is .579-.602 inch, Fig. 5. If a standard size valve guide has been removed, the replacement guide should be oversized. Ensure that valve guides are installed at room temperature.**
4. After installation of new guides, install valves and ensure ease of movement, then check for correct valve contact and seating.

TIMING BELT REPLACE

REMOVAL

1. Remove fan, spacer, water pump pulley and drive belt.
2. Remove timing belt cover.
3. Move timing belt tensioner fully toward water pump and secure in place.
4. Remove timing belt from camshaft sprocket.
5. Remove camshaft sprocket retaining bolt, then the sprocket.
6. Remove crankshaft pulley.
7. Remove timing belt. If belt is to be reused, scribe an arrow on belt indicating rotation for later installation.

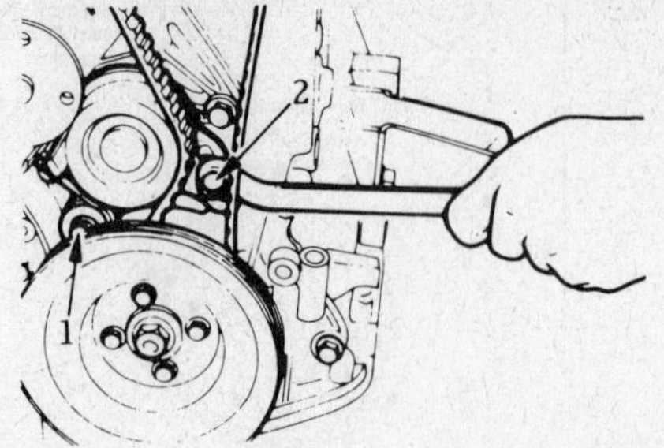

Fig. 7 Tensioner mounting bolts

8. Remove crankshaft sprocket retaining bolt, then the sprocket and flange.
9. Remove timing belt tensioner.

INSTALLATION

1. Install flange and crankshaft sprocket as shown in **Fig. 6,** then torque sprocket bolt to 37-43 ft. lbs.
2. Install camshaft sprocket and torque bolt to 47-54 ft. lbs.
3. Align crankshaft and camshaft timing marks as shown, **Fig. 4.**
4. Install timing belt tensioner as follows:
   a. Mount tensioner, spring and spacer, then temporarily tighten attaching bolt.
   b. Temporarily tighten the tensioner long hole side washer and bolt, then install bottom end of spring into front case.
   c. Secure tensioner to a position nearest water pump.
5. Install timing belt onto crankshaft and camshaft sprockets.
6. With timing belt installed, ensure that tension side is tight and all timing marks are aligned when camshaft sprocket is rotated in reverse direction.
7. Install crankshaft pulley, ensuring that sprocket pin engages hole in pulley. Torque pulley attaching bolts to 8 ft. lbs.
8. Loosen tensioner mounting bolts 1 and 2 in order shown, **Fig. 7.** This will allow spring tension only. Ensure timing belt is not out of position and has not jumped a sprocket tooth.
9. Tighten tensioner bolts 2 and 1 in that order. Do not tighten bolt 1 first.
10. Turn crankshaft one complete revolution clockwise, until crankshaft sprocket timing mark aligns with TDC position.
11. Loosen tensioner attaching bolts 1 and 2 in that order, then torque bolts 2 and 1 in order to 15-18 ft. lbs.
12. Recheck belt tension. When tensioner and the tension side of timing belt are pushed inward with moderate force, the timing belt cog end should be approximately 1/4 of the tensioner mounting bolt head width away from bolt head center as shown, **Fig. 8.**
13. Install timing belt cover.
14. Install water pump pulley, spacer, fan and drive belt.

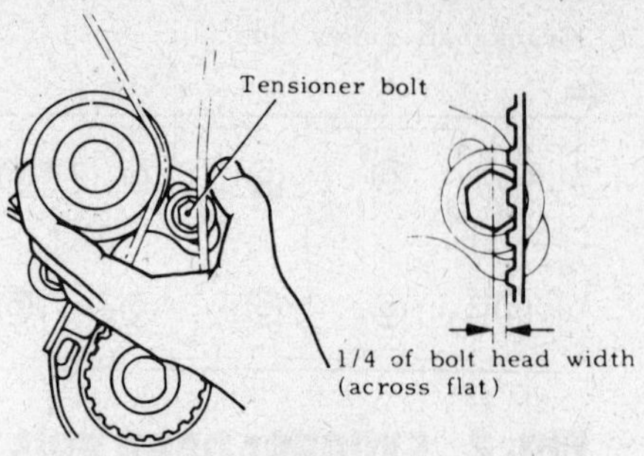

Fig. 8 Final belt tension check

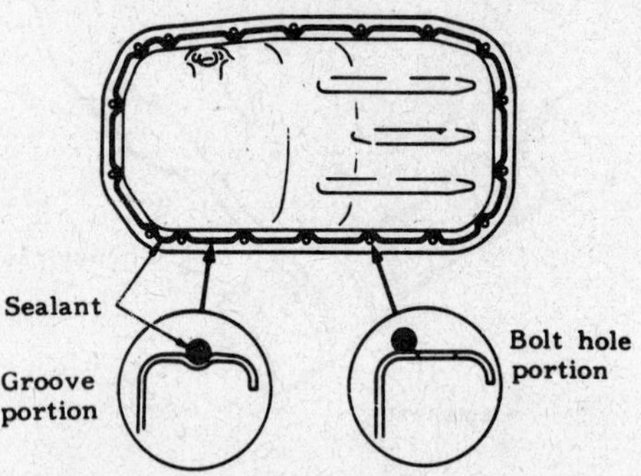

Fig. 10 Applying sealer to oil pan flange

TIMING CASE REPLACE

1. Remove timing belt as outlined under "Timing Belt, Replace" procedure.
2. Remove oil pan and screen.
3. Remove attaching bolts, then the timing case.
4. Reverse procedure to install. When installing timing case attaching bolts, refer to **Fig. 9** and note that bolts to be installed in location A are .79 inch in length, bolts installed in location B are 1.18 inches in length and bolts installed in location C are 2.36 inches in length. Torque attaching bolts to 10 ft. lbs. When installing oil seal, lubricate seal lips with engine oil, then position seal over crankshaft snout. Drive seal into timing case using tool 09214-21000 or equivalent. Before installing oil pan, apply sealer to pan flange as shown in **Fig. 10,** then torque attaching bolts to 5 ft. lbs.

PISTON & ROD ASSEMBLY

Assemble piston to rod so that indented arrow on piston and embossed numeral on rod are facing upward when piston is held horizontally.

PISTONS, PINS & RINGS

Pistons and rings are available in standard size and oversizes of .010, .020, .030 and .039 inch. Oversized pins are not available.

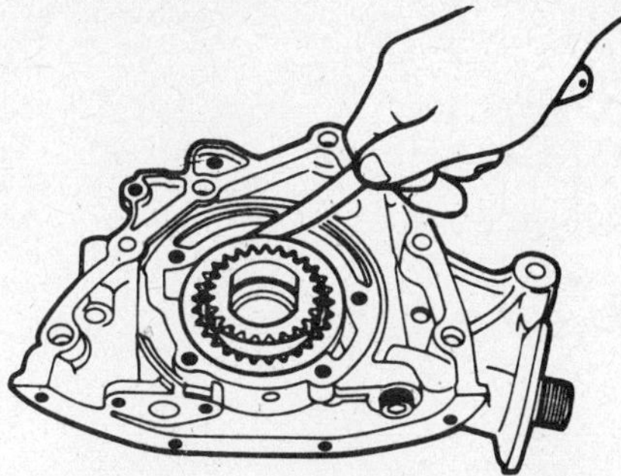

Fig. 11 Checking outer gear to case clearance

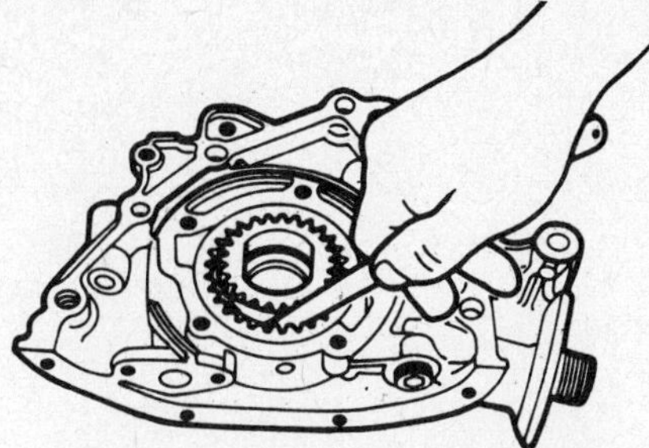

Fig. 12 Checking outer gear tooth to crescent clearance

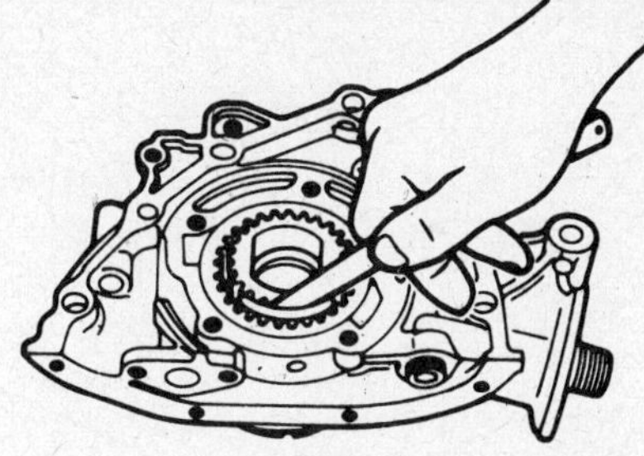

Fig. 13 Checking inner gear tooth to crescent clearance

MAIN & ROD BEARINGS

Main and rod bearings are available in standard size and undersizes of .010, .020 and .030 inch.

When installing main caps, ensure that arrows on caps face toward front of engine.

REAR OIL SEAL
REPLACE

1. Remove transaxle.
2. Remove flywheel.
3. Remove rear plate, seal case and seal.
4. Using tool 09231-11000 or equivalent, press new seal into case, ensuring seal does not cock to one side.
5. Install seal case and new gasket, then coat seal lips with engine oil.
6. Install rear plate and flywheel.
7. Install transaxle.

OIL PUMP SERVICE
REMOVAL

1. Remove timing case as outlined under "Timing Case, Replace" procedure.
2. Remove oil pump cover.
3. Remove inner and outer gears from case, noting location of mating marks to aid in installation.
4. Remove plug, spring and relief valve from case.

INSPECTION

1. Check gear teeth and timing case for excessive wear or damage.
2. Check clearance between outer gear circumference and timing case as shown in **Fig. 11.** Clearance should be .0039-.0079 inch.
3. Check clearance between outer gear tooth and crescent as shown in **Fig. 12.** Clearance should be .0087-.0134 inch.
4. Check clearance between inner gear tooth and crescent as shown in **Fig. 13.** Clearance should be .0083-.0126 inch.
5. Check endplay of inner and outer gears. Endplay should be .0016-.0039 inch.
6. If damage or values other than those specified are noted, replace parts as necessary.

INSTALLATION

1. Install inner and outer gears into timing case, ensuring mating marks are properly aligned.
2. Install oil pump cover and torque retaining bolts to 7 ft. lbs.
3. Install relief valve, spring and plug. Torque plug to 33 ft. lbs.
4. Install timing case.

WATER PUMP
REPLACE

1. Drain cooling system, then remove drive belt.
2. Remove water pump pulley.
3. Remove timing belt cover and tensioner.
4. Remove water pump mounting bolts, then the alternator support brace.
5. Remove water pump assembly.
6. Reverse procedure to install. When installing water pump mounting bolts, torque bolts marked "4" to 10 ft. lbs. and bolts marked "7" to 17 ft. lbs. Install timing belt tensioner, then adjust belt tension as outlined under "Timing Belt, Replace" procedure.

CLUTCH & MANUAL TRANSAXLE SECTION

INDEX

CLUTCH PEDAL
ADJUST

1. Turn adjusting bolt on pedal support so that distance between pedal pad and toe board is approximately 7.4 inches.
2. Working from engine compartment, pull on clutch outer cable, then adjust clearance between adjusting nut and holder as shown in **Fig. 1**, until clearance is .20-.25 inch.
3. After performing above procedures, clutch pedal free play (b), **Fig. 2,** should be .80-1.20 inches, while pedal stroke (C) should be 5.70 inches. If clutch pedal stroke is greater than specified value, check for defective clutch assembly.

CLUTCH
REPLACE

1. Remove transaxle as outlined under "Transaxle, Replace" procedure.
2. Insert tool 09411-11000 or equivalent into center spline to support clutch disc.

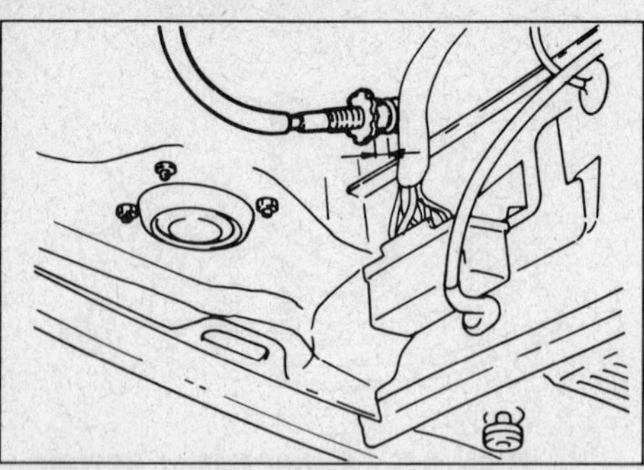

Fig. 1 Adjusting clearance between adjusting nut and holder

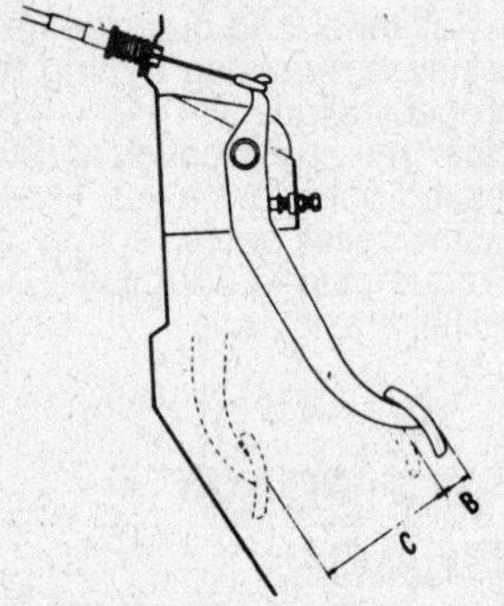

Fig. 2 Clutch pedal free play & stroke adjustment

3. Diagonally loosen pressure plate attaching bolts until all spring pressure is relieved, then remove pressure plate and clutch disc.
4. Reverse procedure to install. Torque attaching bolts to 13 ft. lbs.

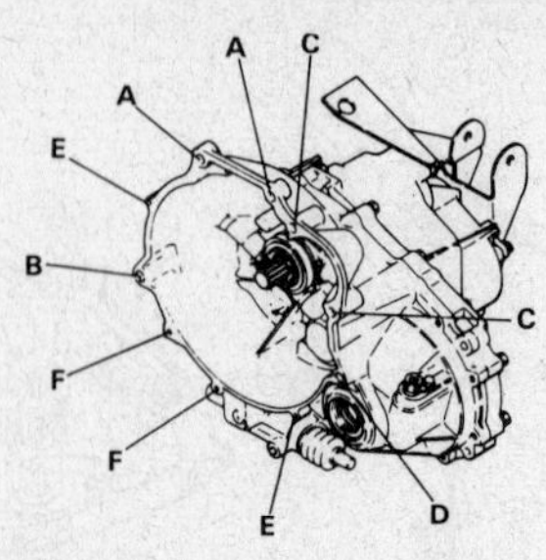

	Nm	kg.cm	ft.lb.	O.D. × Length mm (in)	Bolt identification
A	43-55	430-560	31-40	(7) 10 × 40 (1.6)	(7) A × B
B	43-55	430-560	31-40	(7) 10 × 65 (2.6)	
C	22-32	220-330	16-23	(7) 10 × 55 (2.2)	
D	30-34	300-350	22-25	(10) 8 × 60 (2.4)	
E	10-12	100-120	7-9	(7) 8 × 14 (.6)	
F	15-22	150-220	11-16	(7) 8 × 20 (.8)	

Fig. 3 Transaxle mounting bolt torque specifications

TRANSAXLE REPLACE

1. Disconnect battery cables and remove battery.
2. On models equipped with 5 speed units, disconnect select control valve connector.
3. On all models, disconnect speedometer and clutch cables, then the back up lamp switch electrical connector.
4. Disconnect starter motor electrical connections, then remove upper transaxle to engine mounting bolts.
5. Remove starter motor mounting bolts and the starter motor.
6. Raise and support vehicle.
7. Remove under cover, then drain transaxle.
8. Working from engine compartment, disconnect extension and shift rods from transaxle.
9. Disconnect stabilizer bar from control arm, then remove control arm at body mount.
10. Remove driveshafts from transaxle and support with suitable wire.
11. Support transaxle with suitable jack, then remove bellhousing cover.
12. Remove remaining transaxle to engine mounting bolts.
13. Remove transaxle mount insulator bolt.
14. Remove cover from right front fender shield, then remove transaxle bracket and mount assembly.
15. Slide transaxle assembly to the right, then lower and remove from underside of vehicle.
16. Reverse procedure to install, noting the following:
    a. Torque bracket and mount assembly bolts to 22-30 ft. lbs., 814 mm bell housing cover attaching bolts to 7-9 ft. lbs., 820 mm bell housing cover bolts to 11-16 ft. lbs., extension rod to transaxle bolt to 43-51 ft. lbs., shift rod to transaxle bolt to 24 ft. lbs., and all transaxle to engine mounting bolts as shown in **Fig. 3.**
    b. Refill transaxle with suitable oil, then torque drain plug to 25 ft. lbs.
    c. Adjust clutch pedal as outlined previously.

DISC BRAKES SECTION

INDEX

COMPONENTS

1. Bleeder screw
2. Caliper, inner
3. Piston seal
4. Piston
5. Dust seal
6. Retaining ring
7. Cap plug
8. Torque plate pin cap
9. Oil seal retainer
10. Wiper seal
11. Torque plate
12. Pad assembly
13. Anti-squeak shim
14. Pad retaining pin
15. Torque plate pin bushing
16. K-spring
17. Pad protector
18. M-clip
19. Caliper, outer
20. Dust cover
21. Brake disc

	Nm	kg.cm	ft.lbs.
A	7-9	71-92	5-7
B	59-78	602-796	43-58
C	78-93	796-949	58-69

Fig. 1 Exploded view of disc brake assembly

BRAKE PADS REPLACE

1. Raise and support vehicle, then remove wheel/tire assembly.
2. Remove pad protector by prying upward at center with screwdriver or equivalent tool.
3. Remove M-clip and K-spring from pad retaining pins, **Fig. 1.**
4. Remove brake pad retaining pins from caliper, then pull brake pads from caliper assembly and remove anti-squeak shim from outer pad.
5. Bottom piston in caliper using suitable tool.
6. Install anti-squeak shim onto outer pad, then install pads and retaining pins into caliper.
7. Install M-clip and K-spring onto retaining pins, then place pad protector into position on retaining pins.

CALIPER SERVICE

REMOVAL

1. Remove brake pads as outlined previously.
2. Working at strut, disconnect brake tube from hose.
3. Remove brake hose clip, then disconnect brake hose from strut.
4. Remove caliper to steering knuckle mounting bolts, then the caliper assembly.

DISASSEMBLY

1. Remove retaining bolts, separate inner and outer caliper, then remove torque plate from inner caliper, **Fig. 1.**
2. Remove dust seal retaining ring and the dust seal.
3. Protect fingers with shop towel, then blow piston from caliper bore with compressed air.
4. Pry piston seal from caliper bore using suitable tool. Use caution to prevent scoring of bore.

ASSEMBLY

1. Clean all parts with new brake fluid.
2. Inspect caliper bore, piston and torque plate for damage or excessive wear. Replace parts as necessary.
3. Lubricate new piston seal with suitable grease and caliper bore with clean brake fluid, then install seal into bore.
4. Press piston into caliper bore. Ensure piston does not cock to one side during installation.
5. Lubricate torque plate and bushings with suitable grease, then install torque plate onto inner caliper.
6. Assembly inner and outer calipers and torque retaining bolts to 58-69 ft. lbs.

INSTALLATION

1. Install caliper assembly onto steering knuckle and torque mounting bolts to 43-58 ft. lbs.
2. Install brake hose onto strut with retaining clip.
3. Connect brake hose to brake tube, install brake pads, then bleed brake system.

MASTER CYLINDER REPLACE

1. Disconnect electrical connector from fluid level sensor.
2. Disconnect brake lines from master cylinder.
3. Remove master cylinder to brake booster attaching nuts, then the master cylinder.
4. Reverse procedure to install. Check clearance between primary piston and push rod of brake booster. Clearance should be .016-.031 inch. If clearance is not as specified, turn adjusting screw on push rod as required. Torque attaching nuts to 6-9 ft. lbs., then bleed brake system.

POWER BRAKE BOOSTER REPLACE

1. Remove master cylinder as outlined previously.
2. Disconnect vacuum hose from booster.
3. Remove pin connecting booster rod to brake pedal.
4. Remove brake booster attaching nuts, then the brake booster.
5. Reverse procedure to install.

DRUM BRAKES SECTION

INDEX

BRAKE SHOES

REMOVAL

1. Raise and support vehicle, then remove wheel/tire assembly.
2. Remove brake drum.
3. Remove clip from shoe-to-shoe spring.
4. Remove shoe retainer, shoe-to-shoe and shoe hold-down springs, **Fig. 1.**
5. Remove shoes and adjuster as an assembly.
6. Disconnect parking brake lever from secondary shoe.

INSPECTION

1. Check backing plate for wear or damage. Replace as necessary.
2. Check wheel cylinder for fluid leakage. Repair or replace cylinder as necessary.
3. Check shoe-to-shoe spring for sagging or insufficient tension. Replace spring as necessary.
4. Check inside diameter of brake drum. If I.D. is greater than 7.20 inches, drum is beyond wear limit and should be replaced.

INSTALLATION

1. Apply suitable grease to backing plate shoe contact surfaces.
2. Install primary shoe and hold-down spring.
3. Connect parking brake lever to secondary shoe, then install shoe and hold-down spring.
4. Install adjuster and remaining springs, then the shoe-to-shoe clip.
5. Adjust shoe outside diameter to 7.06-7.07 inches, then install brake drum.
6. Bleed brake system, if necessary, then adjust brakes.

1. Backing plate
2. Spring
3. Adjuster
4. Parking lever
5. Shoe and lining assembly
6. Piston
7. Wheel cylinder body
8. Shoe hold spring pin
9. Shoe hold-down spring
10. Shoe retainer spring
11. Shoe to shoe spring
12. Clip spring
13. Bleeder screw
14. Wheel cylinder boot

	Nm	kg.cm	ft.lbs.
A	8-12	82-122	6-9
B	7-9	71-92	5-7
C	29-39	296-398	22-29

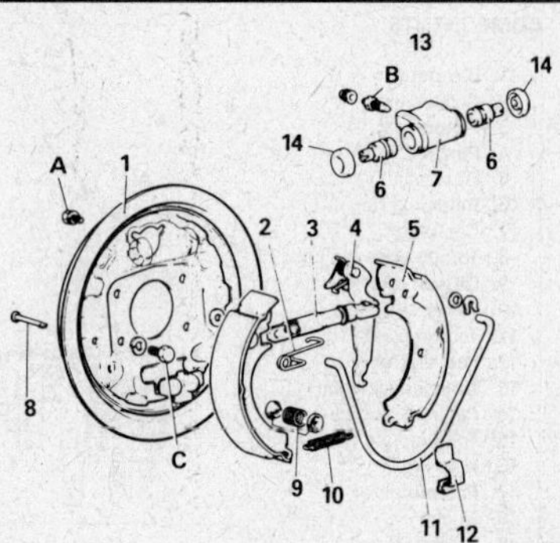

Fig. 1 Exploded view of drum brake assembly

MASTER CYLINDER

REPLACE

Refer to Disc Brakes Section.

POWER BRAKE BOOSTER

REPLACE

Refer To Disc Brakes Section.

SERVICE BRAKES

ADJUST

The automatic self-adjusting mechanism operates whenever the parking brake lever and brake pedal are alternately applied. To adjust brakes, proceed as follows:

1. Pull up, then return parking brake lever to normal position.
2. Depress and release brake pedal.
3. Repeat steps 1 and 2 several times until shoe clearance is sufficient and no brake drag is evident.

PARKING BRAKE

ADJUST

Service brakes must be properly adjusted before attempting to adjust parking brake lever.

1. Pull parking brake lever upward with a force of approximately 44 lbs. A stroke of 5-7 notches on lever is acceptable.
2. If lever stroke is not as specified, turn cable adjusting nut as required.

REAR AXLE & SUSPENSION SECTION

INDEX

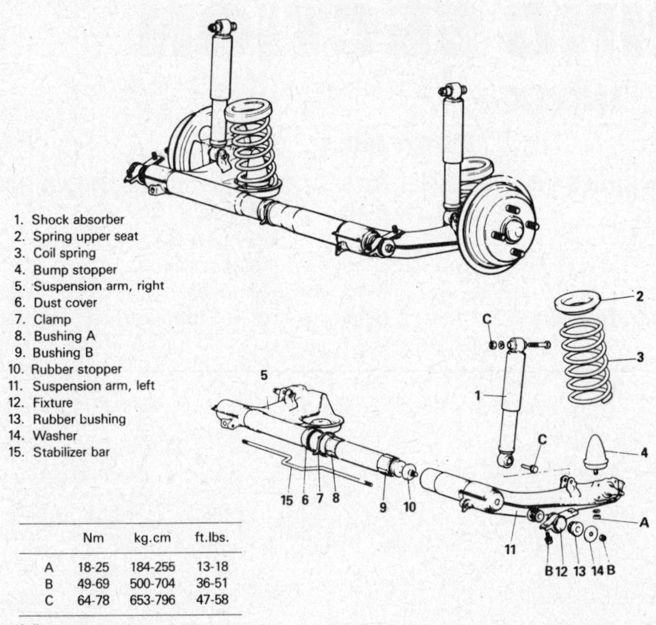

Fig. 1 Exploded view of rear axle & suspension

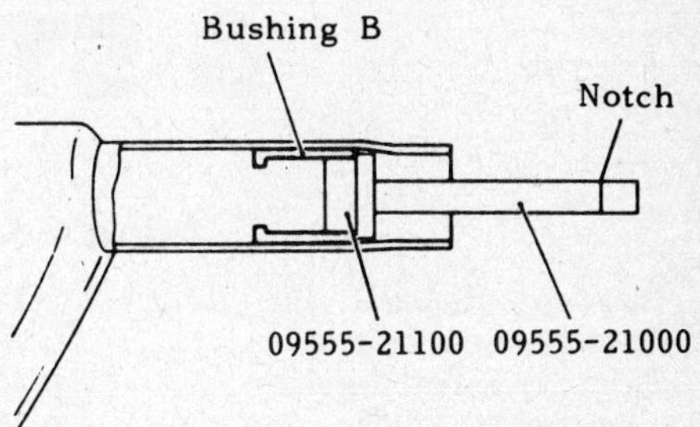

Fig. 2 Installing bushing "B" into left suspension arm

WHEEL BEARINGS

ADJUST

1. Raise and support vehicle, then remove wheel/tire assembly.
2. Remove grease cap, cotter pin and adjusting nut retaining cap.
3. Loosen adjusting nut, then torque nut to 14 ft. lbs.
4. Back off adjustment, then retorque adjusting nut to 4 ft. lbs.
5. Install adjusting nut retaining cap, cotter pin, and grease cap. **If holes in retaining cap are out of alignment with hole in stub axle, loosen adjusting nut approximately 15° until holes are aligned, then reinstall retaining cap and cotter pin.**
6. Reinstall wheel/tire assembly.

SHOCK ABSORBER

REPLACE

1. Raise and support vehicle at side frame.
2. Remove wheel/tire assembly, then support suspension arm with suitable jack.
3. Remove upper and lower retaining nuts and bolts, then the shock absorber.
4. Reverse procedure to install. Torque retaining nuts and bolts to specifications as shown in **Fig. 1.**

COIL SPRING

REPLACE

1. Remove shock absorber as outlined previously.
2. With jack positioned under suspension arm, lower jack and remove coil spring and spring seats.
3. Reverse procedure to install. **The upper and lower spring seats are not interchangeable. Ensure that seats are correctly positioned before installing spring.**

REAR AXLE ASSEMBLY

REMOVAL

When removing rear suspension assembly, ensure that front of vehicle is adequately supported to prevent tilting during removal procedure.

1. Remove brake drums and rear brake assemblies.
2. Remove muffler.
3. Remove coil spring as outlined previously.
4. Temporarily reinstall shock absorbers, then disconnect brake hoses from suspension arms.
5. Remove shock absorbers and suspension to body retaining bolts, then the rear suspension assembly.

DISASSEMBLE

Before disassembly, scribe alignment marks on fixtures and suspension arms to ensure components are assembled in same position. On models equipped with stabilizer bar, scribe alignment marks on bar and stabilizer bracket.

1. Remove stabilizer bar from brackets, if equipped.
2. Remove nuts on both ends of suspension arms, then remove washers, fixtures and rubber bushings, **Fig. 1.**
3. Remove dust cover clamp, then separate suspension into right and left arms. **Leave dust cover attached to right suspension arm to protect lip from damage during disassembly.**
4. Remove rubber stopper, then using suitable screwdriver, remove bushing "A" from left suspension arm, **Fig. 1.**
5. Using hammer and suitable drift, drive bushing "B" from left suspension arm.
6. Inspect all components for excessive wear or damage, replacing parts as necessary.

ASSEMBLE

1. Apply suitable grease to inside of left suspension arm, outer edge of right suspension arm and to outside surfaces of bushings "A" and "B".
2. Using tools 09555-21100 and 09555-21000 or equivalents, drive bushings "B" and "A" in that order into left suspension arm. **When installing bush-**

ing "B", drive bushing inward until notch on tool 09555-21000 reaches end of arm, Fig. 2.

3. Install rubber stopper into right suspension arm. **If dust cover if being replaced, install cover up to center position of right suspension arm.**
4. Slowly push right and left suspension arms together, wiping away excess grease.
5. Install stabilizer bar, if equipped, aligning marks made before disassembly.
6. Install rubber bushings, fixtures, washers and retaining nuts, aligning all marks made during disassembly. Do not tighten retaining nuts at this time. **Ensure that washers are installed with tooth faced end positioned against bushings.**
7. Pack grease in dust cover and lips, then install dust cover and retain with clamp.

INSTALLATION

Reverse removal procedure to install, torquing all nuts and bolts to specification, **Fig. 1.** After vehicle is lowered to floor, torque suspension arm fixture and shock absorber retaining nuts and bolts to specified values.

FRONT SUSPENSION, DRIVE AXLE & STEERING SECTION

INDEX

CONTROL ARM

REPLACE

1. Disconnect strut bar from control arm.
2. Remove ball joint to control arm retaining nuts and bolts, then separate ball joint from control arm. **Do not separate ball joint from steering knuckle unless damage to ball joint or dust cover is evident.**
3. Remove control arm to crossmember retaining nut and bolt, then the control arm.
4. Inspect control arm and bushings, replacing parts as necessary.
5. Install control arm, then the retaining nut and bolt onto crossmember. Do not tighten nut at this time.
6. Install ball joint to control arm, then torque retaining nuts and bolts to 69-87 ft. lbs.
7. Loosely install strut bar.
8. Lower vehicle to floor, then torque control arm to crossmember and strut bar to control arm retaining nuts and bolts to 69-87 ft. lbs.

BALL JOINT

REPLACE

1. Disconnect strut bar from control arm.
2. Remove ball joint to control arm retaining nuts and bolts, then separate ball joint from control arm.
3. Remove ball joint stud nut, then separate ball joint from steering knuckle using suitable tool.
4. Install ball joint to control arm, then torque retaining nuts and bolts to 69-87 ft. lbs.
5. Install ball joint stud into steering knuckle, then torque ball joint stud nut to 43-52 ft. lbs.
6. Loosely install strut bar to control arm, then lower vehicle to floor and torque

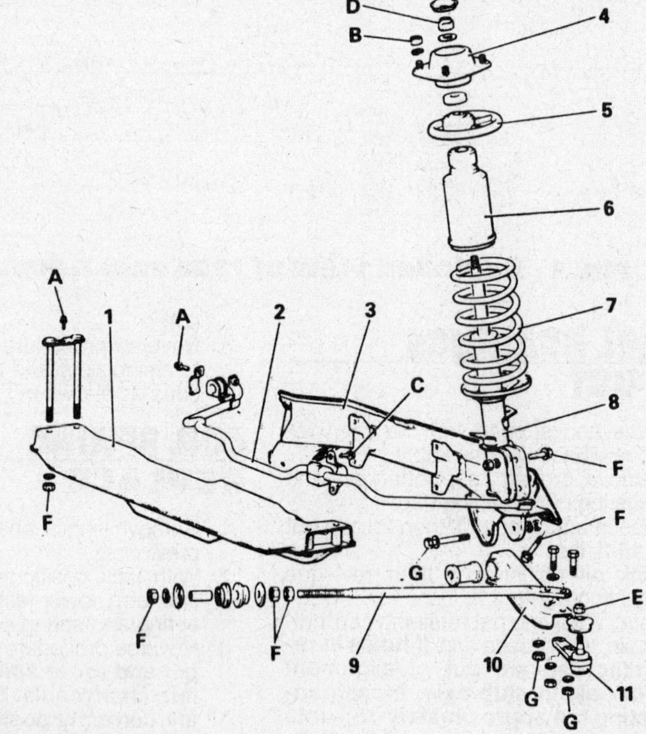

1. Crossmember (No. 1)
2. Stabilizer bar
3. Crossmember (No. 2)
4. Strut insulator
5. Spring seat (upper)
6. Bump rubber
7. Spring
8. Strut
9. Strut bar
10. Lower arm
11. Ball joint assembly

	Nm	kg.cm	ft.lbs.
A	5-6	51-61	4-5
B	10-15	102-153	7-11
C	29-39	296-398	22-29
D	39-49	398-500	29-36
E	59-71	602-724	43-52
F	74-88	755-898	54-65
G	93-118	949-1204	69-87

Fig. 1 Exploded view of front suspension

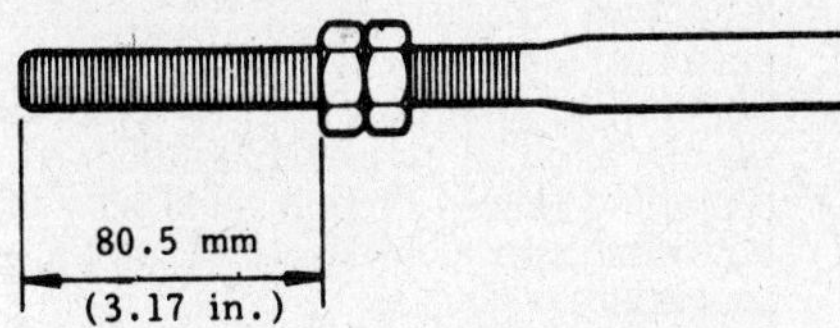

Fig. 2 Strut bar adjusting and locknut dimensions

strut bar to control arm retaining nuts and bolts to 69-87 ft. lbs.

MacPHERSON STRUT SERVICE

REMOVAL

1. Raise and support vehicle, then remove wheel/tire assembly.
2. Detach brake hose from strut assembly.
3. Remove strut to steering knuckle and strut to wheel house retaining nuts and bolts, then remove strut assembly from vehicle.

DISASSEMBLY

1. Compress coil spring using suitable tool.
2. Pry off insulator cap from insulator.
3. Hold upper spring seat from rotating, then remove insulator retaining nut and washer. Discard nut.
4. Remove insulator, spring seat, spring and bumper rubber, **Fig. 1.**
5. Mount strut assembly in vise, then remove oil seal and retaining nut using tool 09546-21000 or equivalent. Discard nut.
6. Drain fluid, then remove O-ring from strut tube. Discard O-ring.
7. Pull piston rod and guide upward and remove from strut tube.

ASSEMBLY

1. Apply shock fluid to sliding surfaces of piston rod and strut tube, then install piston rod into tube.
2. Fill strut tube with approximately 240 cc of shock fluid, then slide piston guide over rod.
3. Lubricate and install new O-ring into strut tube.
4. Lubricate oil seal with shock fluid, then install oil seal and retaining nut into strut tube. Tighten nut until bottom edge contacts tube.
5. Compress coil spring and install spring onto strut assembly, ensuring painted mark on spring faces toward steering knuckle.
6. Install bumper rubber, spring seat, insulator and washer.
7. Align D-shaped hole in spring seat with dent on piston rod, then install retaining nut. While preventing spring seat from rotating, torque retaining nut to 29-36 ft. lbs.
8. Pack grease into cavity, then install insulator cap.

INSTALLATION

1. Install strut assembly into wheel house.
2. Torque strut to wheel house retaining nuts to 7-11 ft. lbs. and strut to steering knuckle retaining nuts and bolts to 54-65 ft. lbs.
3. Reattach brake hose to strut assembly, then bleed brake system and install wheel/tire assembly.

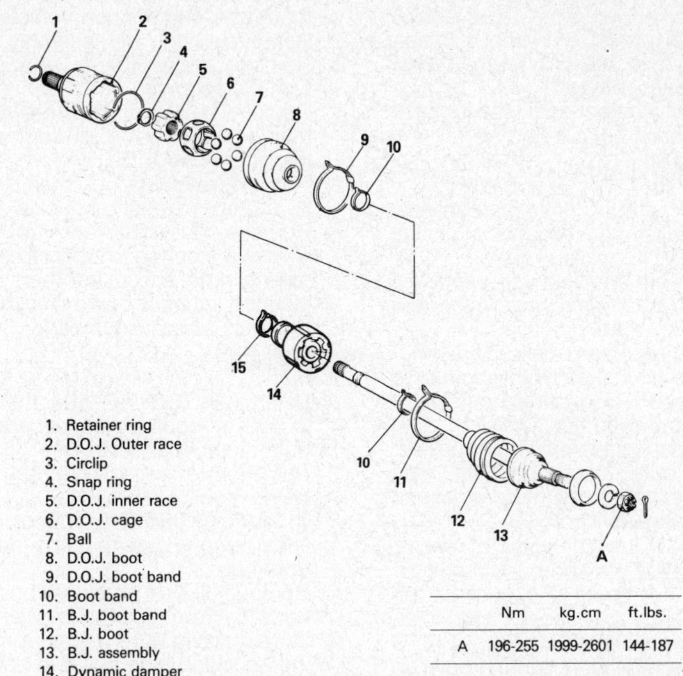

1. Retainer ring
2. D.O.J. Outer race
3. Circlip
4. Snap ring
5. D.O.J. inner race
6. D.O.J. cage
7. Ball
8. D.O.J. boot
9. D.O.J. boot band
10. Boot band
11. B.J. boot band
12. B.J. boot
13. B.J. assembly
14. Dynamic damper
15. Dynamic damper band

	Nm	kg.cm	ft.lbs.
A	196-255	1999-2601	144-187

Fig. 3 Exploded view of front driveshaft

STRUT & STABILIZER BAR

REPLACE

1. Raise and support vehicle.
2. Remove strut bar to control arm a strut bar to crossmember attaching nuts and bolts.
3. Remove stabilizer bar bracket to strut bar attaching nuts and bolts, then the strut bar.
4. Remove stabilizer bar to crossmember attaching nuts and bolts, then the stabilizer bar. **The right and left strut bars are not interchangeable. The left strut bar has a white marked area on its surface. Ensure that strut bars are correctly positioned before installation.**
5. Position inner locknut and adjusting nut onto new strut bar according to dimensions shown in **Fig. 2.**
6. Install strut and stabilizer bars, then loosely install attaching nuts and bolts. Do not tighten nuts and bolts at this time.
7. Lower vehicle to floor, then proceed as follows:
   a. Torque strut bar to crossmember attaching nut to 54-61 ft. lbs., strut bar to control arm attaching nuts and bolts to 69-87 ft. lbs., stabilizer bar to crossmember attaching nuts and bolts to 22-29 ft. lbs. and stabilizer bar bracket to strut bar attaching nuts and bolts to 4-5 ft. lbs.
8. Check and adjust wheel alignment to specification.

FRONT DRIVESHAFT SERVICE

REMOVAL

1. Remove dust cover, cotter pin, driveshaft retaining nut and washer, then raise and support vehicle.
2. Remove wheel/tire assembly and under cover.
3. Separate ball joint and strut bar from control arm.
4. Drain transaxle fluid.
5. Insert a suitable pry bar between transaxle case and double offset joint (D.O.J.), then pry driveshaft from case. **When inserting pry bar, ensure bar contacts rib of transaxle case and that bar point does not damage oil seal.**
6. Using tool 09526-11001 or equivalent, disengage driveshaft from hub and remove from vehicle. Remove retainer ring from groove on D.O.J. side of driveshaft.

DISASSEMBLY

1. Remove D.O.J. boot band, then disengage boot from D.O.J. outer race, **Fig. 3.**
2. Using screwdriver or similar tool, remove circlip.
3. Disengage D.O.J. outer race from driveshaft, then remove snap ring.
4. Remove inner race, cage and balls as an assembly, then clean assembly with suitable solvent.
5. Remove Birfield joint (B.J.) boot band.

6. Remove D.O.J. and B.J. boots. If boots are to be reused, wrap tape around driveshaft splines to prevent damage to boots. **The birfield joint should not be disassembled.**
7. Inspect all components and replace as necessary.

ASSEMBLY

1. Wrap tape around driveshaft splines, apply grease to driveshaft, then install B.J. and D.O.J. boots.
2. Using grease supplied with repair kit, lubricate D.O.J. inner race, cage and balls.
3. Install D.O.J. cage, balls and inner race onto driveshaft, with chamfered side of race facing toward outside of shaft. Install snap ring.
4. Using grease supplied with repair kit, lubricate outer race, then install race onto driveshaft. Apply more grease to race, then install circlip.
5. Lubricate B.J. with suitable grease, then install boots and boot bands.
6. Install D.O.J. boots and boot bands. Ensure bands are 3 inches apart to allow for expansion of air in boot.
7. Install new retainer ring into groove on D.O.J. side of driveshaft.

INSTALLATION

Reverse removal procedure to install and note the following:

1. Torque ball joint and strut bar to control arm retaining nuts and bolts to 69-87 ft. lbs.
2. Install new washer and retaining nut onto driveshaft, then lower vehicle to floor and torque retaining nut to 144-187 ft. lbs. Install cotter pin.

STEERING KNUCKLE, HUB & BEARING SERVICE

REMOVAL

1. Remove dust cover, cotter pin, driveshaft retaining nut and washer, then raise and support vehicle.
2. Remove wheel/tire assembly.
3. Remove brake caliper and support with suitable wire.
4. Remove ball joint stud retaining nut, then separate ball joint from steering knuckle.
5. Remove retaining nut, then separate tie rod from steering knuckle.
6. Remove driveshaft from hub.
7. Remove steering knuckle to strut retaining nuts and bolts, then remove steering knuckle, brake disc, hub and bearings as an assembly.

SERVICE

1. Using tools 09517-21500 and 09517-21600 or equivalents, separate hub from steering knuckle.
2. Remove brake disc from hub.
3. Using tools 09532-11000, 09532-11301 and 09517-21100 or equivalents, remove outer bearing inner race from hub.
4. Remove oil seal and inner bearing inner race from steering knuckle.
5. Drive bearing outer races from steering knuckle using suitable drift. **If either inner or outer races require replacement, they must be replaced as a set.**
6. Apply suitable grease to outer surface of bearing outer race, then drive race into steering knuckle.
7. Install brake disc to hub and torque retaining bolts to 36-43 ft. lbs.
8. Apply suitable grease to bearings and inside surface of hub, then position outer bearing inner race into steering knuckle.
9. Drive hub side oil seal into steering knuckle, then apply suitable grease to seal lip and hub contact areas.
10. Install inner bearing into knuckle.
11. Using tool 09517-21500 or equivalent, assemble hub to steering knuckle. Torque nut on tool to 144-188 ft. lbs., then rotate hub to seat bearing.
12. Measure bearing starting torque. Starting torque should be 11 inch lbs. If starting torque is 0 inch lbs., measure hub axial play. Axial play should be .004 inch with tool nut torqued to specification as in previous step.
13. If starting torque or hub axial play is not within specification, repeat service procedures.
14. Remove service tool, then apply suitable grease to bearing and inside surface of steering knuckle.
15. Drive driveshaft side oil seal into steering knuckle until it contacts bearing outer race, then apply suitable grease to lip of seal.

INSTALLATION

Reverse removal procedure to install. Torque brake caliper to steering knuckle retaining bolts to 43-58 ft. lbs., strut to steering knuckle retaining nuts and bolts to 54-65 ft. lbs. and tie rod to knuckle retaining nut to 11-25 ft. lbs. Lower vehicle to floor, then torque ball joint stud to knuckle retaining nut to 43-52 ft. lbs. and driveshaft retaining nut to 144-187 ft. lbs.

STEERING GEAR REPLACE

1. Raise and support vehicle.
2. Remove both wheel/tire assemblies.
3. Disconnect joint coupling from steering gear.
4. Remove tie rod to steering knuckle retaining nut, then separate tie rod from knuckle.
5. Remove steering gear to crossmember retaining nuts, then the steering gear assembly.
6. Reverse procedure to install. Torque steering gear to crossmember retaining nuts to 22-29 ft. lbs., joint coupling bolt to 11-14 ft. lbs. and tie rod to steering knuckle retaining nut to 11-25 ft. lbs.

WHEEL ALIGNMENT SECTION

INDEX

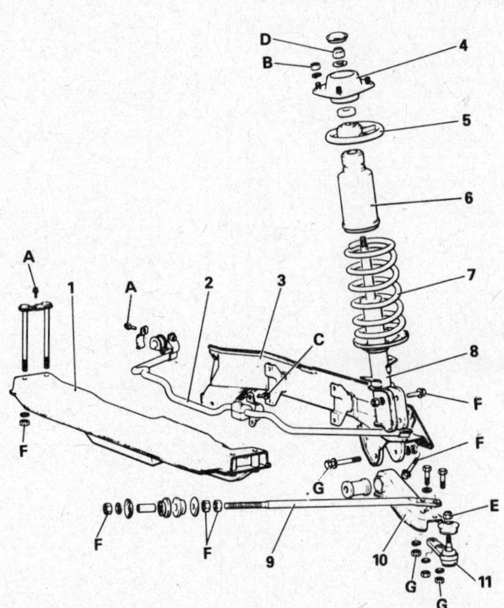

1. Crossmember (No. 1)
2. Stabilizer bar
3. Crossmember (No. 2)
4. Strut insulator
5. Spring seat (upper)
6. Bump rubber
7. Spring
8. Strut
9. Strut bar
10. Lower arm
11. Ball joint assembly

	Nm	kg.cm	ft.lbs.
A	5-6	51-61	4-5
B	10-15	102-153	7-11
C	29-39	296-398	22-29
D	39-49	398-500	29-36
E	59-71	602-724	43-52
F	74-88	755-898	54-65
G	93-118	949-1204	69-87

Fig. 1 Exploded view of front suspension

FRONT ALIGNMENT

CAMBER

Camber is pre-set to specifications and is not adjustable. If camber setting is not within specification, check for damaged or bent suspension components.

CASTER

Caster on these vehicles generally requires no adjustment. However, slight adjustments can be made by turning the adjusting nut on the strut bar, **Figs. 1 and 2,** clockwise or counterclockwise as required.

TOE-IN

Toe-In is adjusted by turning the tie-rod turnbuckles, **Fig. 3.** Changes achieved by turning the tie-rods for both left and right wheels simultaneously one turn, will result in a toe change of approximately .47 inch. To adjust toe-in, proceedas follows:

1. Remove outer bellows clip to prevent damage to bellows.
2. Loosen locknuts, then turn right and left tie-rods an equal amount as required.
3. After adjustment is completed, torque locknuts to 36-40 ft. lbs., then reinstall bellows clip.

STEERING ANGLE

Steering angle **Fig. 4,** requires no adjustment. If there is a difference in steering angle between right and left wheels, change length of right and left tie rods. Steering angle should be 34°10'-37°10' for inner wheel, 29°17' for outer wheel.

REAR ALIGNMENT

CAMBER

Camber is set at the factory and cannot be adjusted. Ensure assembly is free of worn, loose or damaged parts prior to measurement of rear wheel alignment. Camber should be −0°40'.

TOE-IN

Toe-In is set at the factory and cannot be adjusted. Ensure assembly is free of worn, loose or damaged parts prior to measurement of rear wheel alignment. Toe-In should be 0 inches.

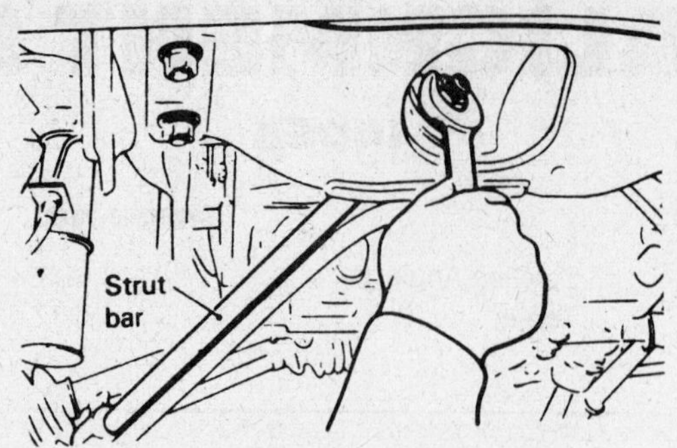

Fig. 2 Adjusting caster

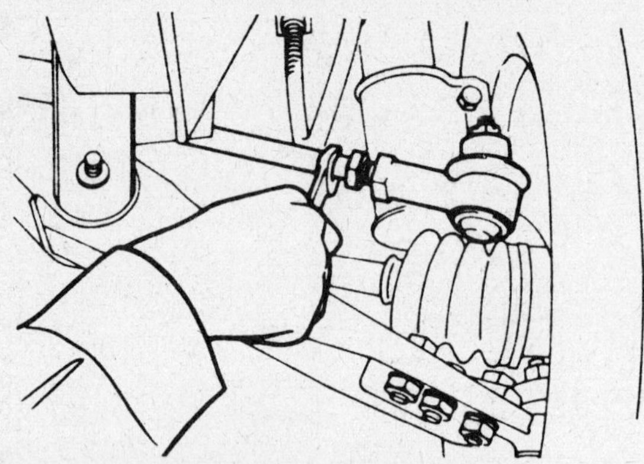

Fig. 3 Adjusting toe-in

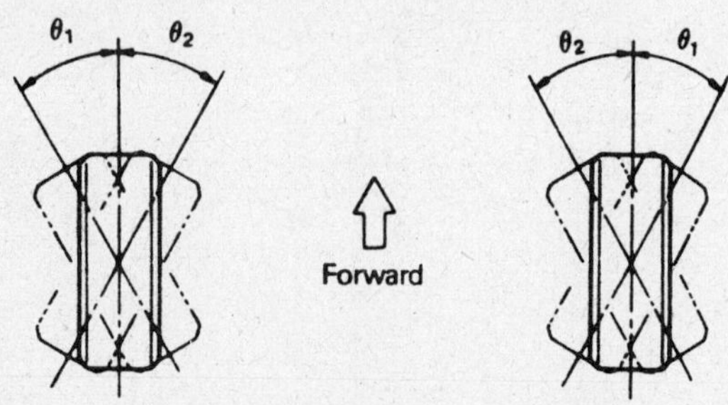

Fig. 4 Steering angle

ISUZU (Japan)

INDEX OF SERVICE OPERATIONS

General Engine Specifications

Year	Engine CID①/L	Engine Model	Carb. Type	Bore & Stroke Inches (mm)	Comp. Ratio	Horsepower @ RPM	Torque Ft. Lbs. @ RPM	Normal Oil Pressure Lbs.
1983–84	4-110.8/1.8	G180Z	2 Barrel	3.31 x 3.23 (84 x 82)	8.5	80 @ 4800	95 @ 3000	57
	4-110.8/1.8②③	4FB1	Fuel Inj.	3.31 x 3.23 (84 x 82)	22.0	51 @ 5000	72 @ 2000	64
	4-136.6/2.2②④	C223	Fuel Inj.	3.46 x 3.62 (88 x 92)	21.0	58 @ 4300	93 @ 2200	—
	4-119/1.9④	G200Z	2 Barrel	3.42 x 3.23 (87 x 82)	8.4	82 @ 4600	101 @ 3000	57
	4-119/1.9⑤	G200Z	Fuel Inj.	3.42 x 3.23 (87 x 82)	9.2	90 @ 5000	108 @ 3000	57
1984	4-119/1.9⑥	G200Z	2 Barrel	3.42 x 3.23 (87 x 82)	8.4	82 @ 4600	101 @ 3000	57
1985	4-110.8/1.8	G180Z	2 Barrel	3.31 x 3.23 (84 x 82)	8.5	78 @ 4800	95 @ 3000	63.5
	4-110.8/1.8②③	4FB1	Fuel Inj.	3.31 x 3.23 (84 x 82)	22.0	51 @ 5000	72 @ 3000	—
	4-119/1.9④	G200Z	2 Barrel	3.42 x 3.23 (87 x 82)	8.4	82 @ 4600	101 @ 3000	64
	4-119/1.9⑤	G200Z	Fuel Inj.	3.29 x 3.23 (87 x 82)	9.2	90 @ 5000	108 @ 3000	57
	4-136.6/2.2②④	C223	Fuel Inj.	3.46 x 3.62 (88 x 92)	21.0	58 @ 4300	93 @ 2200	—
1986–87	4-90/1.5③	4XCI-U	2 Barrel	3.03 x 3.11 (77 x 79)	9.6	70 @ 5400	87 @ 3400	50
	4-119/1.9④	G200Z	2 Barrel	3.42 x 3.23 (87 x 82)	8.4	—	—	57
	4-119/1.9⑤	G200Z	Fuel Inj.	3.43 x 3.29 (87 x 82)	9.2	90 @ 5000	108 @ 3000	57
	4-121.7/2.0⑤⑦	4ZCI-T	Fuel Inj.	3.46 x 3.29 (88 x 82)	7.9	140 @ 5400	166 @ 3000	57
	4-138/2.2④⑥	4ZDI	2 Barrel	3.52 x 3.54 (83.9 x 90)	8.3	—	—	57
	4-136.6/2.2②④⑥⑦	C223	Fuel Inj.	3.46 x 3.62 (88 x 92)	21.0	—	—	—

①—Cubic inch displacement.
②—Diesel.
③—I-Mark only.
④—Pickup only.
⑤—Impulse only.
⑥—Trooper II.
⑦—Turbocharged.

Alternator & Regulator Specifications

Year	Alternator: Model No.	Alternator: Rated Hot Output Amps.	Alternator: Field Current 12 Volts @ 80°F	Alternator: Output @ 14 Volts 2500 RPM Amps.	Alternator: Output @ 14 Volts 5000 RPM Amps.	Regulator: Model	Pilot Lamp Relay: Air Gap In.	Pilot Lamp Relay: Point Gap In.	Pilot Lamp Relay: Closing Voltage	Constant-Voltage Relay: Air Gap In.	Constant-Voltage Relay: Point Gap In.	Constant-Voltage Relay: Voltage @ 68°F
1983–85	021000-7030①②	—	—	—	50	External	—	—	4–5.8	—	—	—
	121000-0300①②	—	—	—	50	External	—	—	4–5.8	—	—	—
	LT140-126①③	—	—	—	40	—	—	—	—	—	—	—
	LT150-144①③	—	—	—	50	—	—	—	—	—	—	—
	LT150-131B①③	—	—	—	50	—	—	—	—	—	—	—
	②④	50	—	—	—	Integral	—	—	—	—	—	14.0–14.6
	②③④	40	—	—	—	Integral	—	—	—	—	—	14.0–14.6
	③④⑥	50	—	—	—	Integral	—	—	—	—	—	14.0–14.6
1983–86	⑦⑩	60	—	—	—	Integral	—	—	—	-	—	13.8–14.4
1984–85	⑧	50	—	—	—	External	—	—	—	-	.015	13.8–14.8
1986–87	⑧	—	—	—	50	Integral	—	—	—	—	—	—
	①③⑨	—	—	—	50	Integral	—	—	—	—	—	—
	①③⑩	—	—	—	50	External	—	—	—	—	—	—
	③④⑪	—	—	—	50	Integral	—	—	—	—	—	—
	⑦⑫	60	—	—	—	Integral	—	—	—	—	—	14.05–15.03
	②	60⑬	—	—	—	Integral	—	—	—	—	—	14.2–14.8

①—Gasoline engine only.
②—I-Mark only.
③—Pickup only.
④—Diesel engine.
⑤—Two wheel drive.
⑥—Four wheel drive.
⑦—Impulse only.
⑧—Trooper II.
⑨—With engine model 4ZD-I.
⑩—With engine model G200Z.
⑪—With engine model C223.
⑫—With engine model 4ZCI-T.
⑬—Less A/C 50 amps.

Starting Motor Specifications

Year	Engine	Model No.	Rotation	Brush Spring Tension Lbs.	No Load Test			Torque Test		
					Amperes (Max.)	Volts	RPM (Min.)	Amperes (Max.)	Volts	Torque Ft. Lbs. (Min.)
1983–85	G180Z	S114-271	—	3.53	70	12	6000	200	7.4	3.6
	4FB1①	S13-62A②	—	6.6	—	—	—	—	—	—
	C223①	②	—	—	120	11.5	4000	—	—	—
1983–86	G200Z③	—	—	3.53	—	—	—	200	9.2	3.4
1983–86	G200Z④	—	—	3.53	60	11.5	6000	200	9.2	3.4
1984–85	G200Z⑤	—	—	3.53	—	—	—	200	9.2	3.4
1986–87	C223①③⑤	②	—	—	—	—	—	—	7.5	9.4
	4ZDI③⑤	—	—	—	—	—	—	230	8	4.7
	4ZCI-T④	—	⑥	—	90	11.5	3000	230	8	4.7
	4XCI-U	—	⑥	—	50	11	5000	260⑦	9.5	3.5⑧

①—Diesel engine.
②—Reduction gear starter.
③—Pickup.
④—Impulse.
⑤—Trooper II.
⑥—Clockwise when viewed from pinion side.
⑦—With auto. trans. 270.
⑧—With auto trans. 5.1.

Valve Specifications

Year	Model	Valve Lash		Valve Angles		Valve Spring Installed Height	Valve Spring Pressure Lbs. @ In.	Stem Clearance		Stem Diameter	
		Int.	Exh.	Seat	Face			Intake	Exhaust	Intake	Exhaust
1983–85	G180Z	.006C	.010C	45°	45°	—	②	.0009–.0022	.0015–.0031	.3102	.3091
	4FB1①	.010	.014	45°	45°	—	③	.0015–.0027	.002–.003	.313	.313
	C223①	.016C	.016C	45°	45°	—	④	.0015–.0027	.0025–.0037	.3150	.3150
1983	G200Z	.006C	.010C	45°	45°	—	⑤	.0009–.0022	.0015–.0031	.3102	.3091
1984–86	G200Z	.006C	.010C	45°	45°	—	55.4 @ 1.60	.0009–.0022	.0015–.0031	.3102	.3091
1986–87	C223①	.015C	.015C	45°	45°	—	—	.0015–.0027	.0025–.0037	.3103	.3091
	4ZDI	.006C	.010C	45°	45°	—	—	.009–.0022	.0015–.0031	.3102	.3091
	4ZCI-T	.006C	.010C	45°	45°	—	—	.009–.0022	.0015–.0031	.3102	.3091
	4XCI-U	.006C	.010C	45°	45°	—	—	.009–.0022	.0018–.00248	.2716	.2716

①—Diesel engine.
②—Outer, 35 lbs. @ 1.61 inch; inner, 20 lbs. @ 1.5 inch.
③—Outer, 35 lbs. @ 1.61 inch; inner, 20 lbs. @ 1.52 inch.
④—Outer, 44 lbs. @ 1.54 inch; inner, 13 lbs. @ 1.46 inch.
⑤—Outer, 37 lbs. @ 1.614 inch; inner, 21.5 lbs. @ 1.516 inch.

Pistons, Pins, Rings, Crankshaft & Bearings

Year	Model	Piston Clearance	Ring End Gap①		Wristpin Diameter	Rod Bearings		Main Bearings			
			Comp.	Oil		Shaft Diameter	Bearing Clearance	Shaft Diameter	Bearing Clearance	Thrust on Bearing No.	Shaft End Play
1983–85	G180Z	②	.012–.018	.008–.035	—	1.9262–1.9268	.0007–.0030	2.2016–2.2022	.0008–.0025	3	.0024–.0094
	4FB1③	.005–.045④	.0078–.0157	.0078–.0157	.984	1.925–1.926	.0016–.0027	2.201–2.2022	.0012–.0027	3	.0024–.0094
	C223③	.0062–.0070④	.0079–.0158	.0079–.0158	1.0630	2.0835–2.0839	.0016	2.3591–2.3594	.0011–.0033	3	.0039
1983–86	G200Z	②	.014–.020	.008–.035	.866	1.9262–1.9268	.0007–.0030	2.2016–2.2022	.0008–.0025	3	.0024–.0094
1986–87	C223③⑤	.0014–.0022④	⑦	⑧	⑨	2.0835–2.0839	.0016	2.3591–2.3594	.0011–.0033	3	.0039

Continued

PISTONS, PINS, RINGS, CRANKSHAFT & BEARINGS—Cont.

Year	Model	Piston Clearance	Ring End Gap①		Wristpin Diameter	Rod Bearings		Main Bearings			
			Comp.	Oil		Shaft Diameter	Bearing Clearance	Shaft Diameter	Bearing Clearance	Thrust on Bearing No.	Shaft End Play
	4ZDI	.0018–.0026④	⑥	.008–.028	.906	1.9276–1.9282	.0007–.0029	2.2032–2.2038	.0008–.0025	3	.0024–.0099
	4ZCI-T⑤	.0018–.0026④	⑥	.008–.028	.906	1.9276–1.9282	.0007–.0029	2.2032–2.2038	.0008–.0025	3	.0024–.0099
	4XCI-U	.011–.019	.0098–.0138	.0039–.0236	.7085–.7088	1.5720–1.5726	.0079–.0138	1.8865–1.8873	.00079–.00199	3	.0024–.0095

①—Fit rings in bores for clearance listed in tightest portion of ring travel.
②—.0018–.0026. Measure piston 1.575 inch below piston head, at a right angle to piston pin.
③—Diesel engine.
④—Measure piston at a right angle to piston pin hole, on level with piston pin.
⑤—Turbocharged.
⑥—1st ring, .012–.015; 2WD ring, .010–.016 in.
⑦—Less turbocharger, 1st ring .0018–.0028 inch; 2nd ring .0012–.0021 inch: with turbocharger, 1st ring .0047–.0061 inch; 2nd ring .0020–.0033 inch.
⑧—Less turbocharger, .0008–.0021 inch; with turbocharger, .0012–.0028 inch.
⑨—Less turbocharger, 1.0630 inch; with turbocharger, 1.1417 inch.

Gasoline Engine Tightening Specifications

*Torque specifications are for clean and lightly lubricated threads only. Dry or dirty threads produce increased friction which prevents accurate measurement of tightness.

Year	Engine	Spark Plugs Ft. Lbs.	Cylinder Head Bolts Ft. Lbs.	Intake Manifold Ft. Lbs.	Exhaust Manifold Ft. Lbs.	Camshaft Bearing Caps Bolts Ft. Lbs.	Camshaft Sprocket Bolts Ft. Lbs.	Rocker Shaft Nuts Ft. Lbs.	Rocker Arm Cover Ft. Lbs.	Connecting Rod Cap Nuts Ft. Lbs.	Main Bearing Cap Bolts Ft. Lbs.	Flywheel To Crankshaft Ft. Lbs.	Vibration Damper or Pulley Ft. Lbs.
1983–85	G180Z	18–22	72	—	—	—	58	16	4	43	72	69①	87
1983	G200Z	18–23	72	—	—	—	58	16	4	43	72	69	87
1984–86	G200Z	18–22	②	16	16	—	58	16	4	43	72	76	87
1986–87	4ZDI	14	④	16	16	—	44	17	7	43	72	44	87
	4ZCI-T③	14	65	16	16	—	43.4	16	7	43	72	43	87
	4XCI-U	18–22	58	17	17	—	7.2	16	7	25	68	21	108.5

①—1984–85 models, 76 ft. lbs.
②—Tighten in three steps to 44, 65 and 80 ft. lbs.
③—Turbocharged.
④—Tighten in three steps to 58, 65 and 80 ft. lbs.

Diesel Engine Tightening Specifications

*Torque specifications are for clean and lightly lubricated threads only. Dry or dirty threads produce increased friction which prevents accurate measurement of tightness.

Year	Engine	Glow Plugs Ft. Lbs.	Cylinder Head Bolts Ft. Lbs.	Intake Manifold Ft. Lbs.	Exhaust Manifold Ft. Lbs.	Camshaft Bearing Caps Bolts Ft. Lbs.	Camshaft Sprocket Bolts Ft. Lbs.	Rocker Arm Nuts Ft. Lbs.	Rocker Arm Cover Ft. Lbs.	Connecting Rod Cap Bolts Ft. Lbs.	Main Bearing Cap Bolts Ft. Lbs.	Flywheel To Crankshaft Ft. Lbs.	Vibration Damper or Pulley Ft. Lbs.	Injection Pump Pulley Ft. Lbs.
1983–85	4FB1	47–61	①	25–32	11–18	—	43–50	15–22	6–8	54–61	65–72	36–43②	98–119	43–50
	C223	51–58	③	10–17	10–17	—	72–87	9–17	6–13	58–65	116–130	65–72②	124–151	42–52
1986–87	C223	51–58	③	10–17④	10–17④	—	72–87	9–17	6–13	58–65	116–130	83–90	124–151	42–52

①—New bolts, 98 ft. lbs.; used bolts, 105 ft. lbs.
②—Apply Loctite to threads, do not lubricate bolts.
③—New bolts, 54–61 ft. lbs.; used bolts, 61–69 ft. lbs. On turbocharged models, torque bolts an additional 120–150 degrees.
④—On turbocharged models, 13–17 ft. lbs.

Cooling System & Capacity Data

Year	Model	Cooling Capacity Qts.		Radiator Cap Relief Pressure Lbs.	Thermo. Opening Temp. °F	Fuel Tank Gals.	Engine Oil Refill Qts. ①	Transmission Oil			Differential Capacity, Pints
		Auto Trans.	Man. Trans.					4 Speed Pints	5 Speed Pints	Auto. Tans. Qts. ②	
1983	I-Mark③	7.1	7.2	15	180	13.7	3.8	2.64	3.28	6.7	2.5
	Pickup③	6.4	6.8	15	180	⑤	3.8	2.7⑥	2.7	7.0	2.7⑦
	I-Mark④	7.3	7.4	15	180	13.7	5.5	2.64	3.28	6.7	2.5
	Pickup④	—	8.5	15	180	⑤	5.1	2.7⑥	2.7	—	2.7⑤
1983–86	Impulse	6.7	6.6	15	180	15.1	3.8	—	3.28	6.7	2.1⑪
1984–85	Trooper II	—	8.5	15	180	13.2	3.7	5.3⑧	—	—	⑨
	I-Mark③⑭	7.1	7.2	15	180	13.7	3.8	2.64	3.28	6.7	2.1
	Pickup③	8.2	8.5	15	180	⑤	3.7	2.64⑥	3.28	6.3	2.7⑦
	I-Mark④⑭	7.3	7.4	15	180	13.7	5.2	2.64	3.28	6.7	2.1
	Pickup④	11.2	9.5	15	180	⑤	6.0	2.64⑥	3.28	6.3	2.7⑦
1986–87	I-Mark⑮	5.7	5.7	16	176	15.1	3.4	—	2.70	6.3	—
	Pickup③	6.6	6.6	15	180	—	5.1	2.62	3.28⑥	⑩	2.7⑦
	Pickup④	11.2	9.5	15	180	—	6.0	2.62	3.28⑥	⑩	2.7⑦
	Trooper II	—	8.5⑫	15	180	21.9	4.4⑬	—	9.75⑧	—	⑨

①—Includes filter.
②—Approximate. Make final check with dipstick.
③—Gasoline engine.
④—Diesel engine.
⑤—Short wheelbase, 13.2 gal.; long wheelbase, 19.1 gal.
⑥—On 44 models, transfer case & transmission capacity is 5.2.
⑦—On 44 models, front axle, 1.7 pts.; rear axle, 2.7 pts.
⑧—Includes transfer case.
⑨—Front axle, 2.1 pts.; rear axle, 3.2 pts.
⑩—On models equipped with C223 Engine, 6.3; with 4ZD1 Engine, 6.7
⑪—1985–86 models, 3.1.
⑫—With diesel engine, 10.
⑬—With diesel engine, 6.0.
⑭—Exc. FWD
⑮—FWD models.

Brake Specifications

Year	Model	Drum Brake I.D.	Wheel Cylinder Bore		Master Cylinder Bore	Disc Brake Rotor Specifications		
			Front Disc	Rear Drum	Power	Nominal Thickness	Minimum Thickness	Runout (T.I.R.)
1983–85	I-Mark all models②	9	—	1.0	.875	.394	.338	—
	Pickup all models	10	—	1.0	.875	.492	.453	.005
1983–87	Impulse	—	2.12	1.50①	.870	.709	.654	.005
1984–85	Trooper II	10	—	.875	.874	.705	.654	.005
1986–87	I-Mark③	7.2	—	.698	.825	.433	.378	.006
	Pickup & Trooper II	10	—	.875	.874	.705	.668	.005

①—Rear caliper.
②—Exc. FWD.
③—W/FWD.

Rear Axle Specifications

Year	Model	Carrier Type	Ring Gear & Pinion Backlash		Pinion Bearing Preload			Differential Bearing Preload		
			Method	Adjustment	Method	New Bearings	Used Bearings	Method	New Bearings Inch Lbs.	Used Bearings Inch Lbs.
1983–85	I-Mark	Integral	Shim	.005–.007	Spacer	6–13①	5–8①	Shim	20–30	10–20
1983	Pickup	Removable	Shim	.005–.007	Spacer	17②	7–9②	Shim	⑥	⑥
1983–87	Impulse	Integral⑤	Shim	.005–.007	Spacer	6–11③	6–11③	Shim	26–47④	26–47④
1984–87	Trooper II	Removable	Shim	.005–.007	Spacer	6–10	6–10	Shim	⑥	⑥
1984–87	Pickup	Removable	Shim	.005–.007	Spacer	5.6–10	5.6–10	Shim	⑥	⑥

①—Inch pounds.
②—Pounds measured at pinion flange using a spring scale.
③—Models equipped with 4ZC1-T Engine, 5.6–10 in. lbs.
④—Models equipped with 4ZC1-T engine, slip fit plus .002 inch preload on each side.
⑤—Models equipped with 4ZC1-T engine, removable.
⑥—Slip fit plus .002 inch preload on each side.

Front Drive Axle Specifications

Year	Model	Carrier Type	Ring Gear & Pinion Backlash		Pinion Bearing Preload①			Differential Bearing Preload		
			Method	Adjustment	Method	New Bearings	Used Bearings	Method	New Bearings Inch Lbs.	Used Bearings Inch Lbs.
1983–85	Pickup 44	Removable	Shim	.004–.006	Spacer	17 lbs.	7–9 lbs.	Shim	—	—
1984–87	Trooper II	Removable	Shim	.005–.007	Spacer	5–10	5–10	Shim	②	②
1986–87	Pickup 44	Removable	Shim	.005–.007	Spacer	5–10	5–10	Shim	②	②

①—Measured at pinion flange using a spring scale.
②—Slip fit plus .002 inch preload on each side.

Wheel Alignment Specifications

Year	Model	Caster Angle Degrees		Camber Angle Degrees				Toe-In Inch	Kingpin Inclination
				Limits		Desired			
		Limits	Desired	Left	Right	Left	Right		
1983–85	I-Mark①	3 2/3 to 6 1/6	5 1/6°	−13/15 to +19/30	−13/15 to +19/30	2/15	2/15	.08–.16	7 13/15°
1981	Pickup	0 to +1	+1/2	0 to +1	0 to +1	+1/2	+1/2	0 to 1/4	7° to 8°
1983–87	Impulse	3 1/2 to 6	4 3/4	−1 to +1/2	−1 to +1/2	−1/2	−1/2	.06	8°
1984–85	Trooper II	0 to 1	+1/2	1/12 to 1 1/12	1/2 to 1 1/12	+7/12	+7/12	0	7 5/12°
1984–87	Pickup 42③	0 to 1	+1/2	0 to 1	0 to 1	+1/2	+1/2	.08	7° to 8°
	Pickup 44④	−1/16 to +5/16	+1/3	−1/12 to +1 1/12	−1/12 to +1 1/12	+7/12	+7/12	0	6 11/12 to 7 11/12
1986–87	I-Mark②	1 3/4 to 2 3/4	2 1/4	−2/3 to +1 1/3	−2/3 to +1 1/3	+2/3	+2/3	0	11 5/6
	Trooper II	+1/2	+1/2	+7/12	+7/12	+7/12	+7/12	0	7 5/12°

①—Exc. FWD
②—FWD models
③—42 models
④—44 models

ELECTRICAL SECTION

INDEX

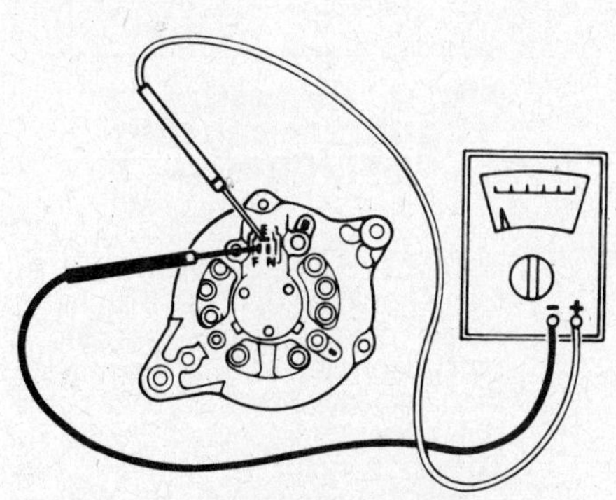

Fig. 1 Testing rotor coil resistance

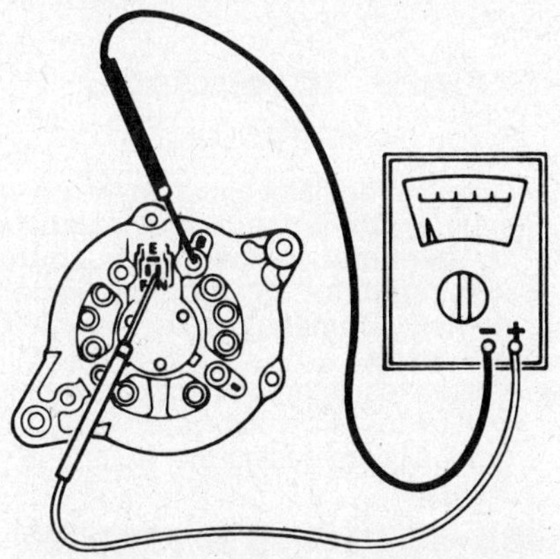

Fig. 2 Positive diode test connections (Typical)

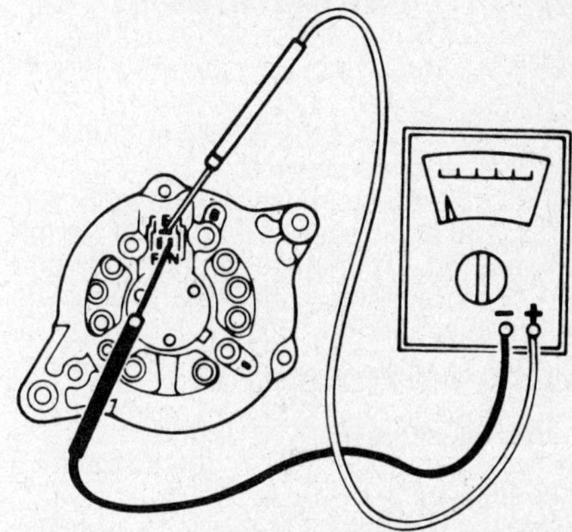

Fig. 3 Negative diode test connections

ALTERNATOR TESTING

DIESEL ENGINES

Special equipment is required to test these alternators. Follow manufacturer's instructions.

GASOLINE ENGINES

I-Mark Exc. FWD

Alternator must be removed from vehicle for testing.

1. Check rotor coil resistance using and ohmmeter across terminals F and E, **Fig. 1.** Reading should be 4.2 ohm. If resistance is zero, a short is indicated. If resistance is infinite, poor brush contact, broken lead wire or an open rotor coil is indicated.
2. Connect positive lead of ohmmeter to B terminal and negative lead to N terminal, **Fig. 2.** If continuity exists between terminals, one or more of the three positive diodes are shorted.
3. Connect positive lead of ohmmeter to N terminal and negative E terminal, **Fig. 3.** If continuity exists between terminals, then one or more of the three negative diodes are shorted.

I-Mark W/FWD

Special equipment is required to test these alternators. Follow manufacturer's instructions.

Impulse

Special equipment is required to test these alternators. Follow manufacturer's instructions.

1983–85 Pickup

Alternator must be removed from vehicle for testing.

1. Connect an ohmmeter between "E" and "F" terminals, **Fig. 1.**
2. If resistance is higher than 5 ohms, poor continuity exists between brushes and commutator.
3. If no continuity exists between "E" and "F" terminals, check for open in rotor coil circuit, sticking brush or broken lead wire.
4. If resistance is lower than 5 ohms, this may be an indication of rotor coil layer short of circuit being grounded.
5. Connect positive lead of ohmmeter to "N" terminal and negative lead to "A" terminal, **Fig. 2.** If continuity exists between terminals, one or more of the three positive diodes are shorted.
6. Connect positive lead of ohmmeter to E terminal and negative lead to "N" terminal, **Fig. 3.** If continuity exists between terminals, then one or more of the three negative diodes are shorted.

1986–87 Pickup

Special equipment is required to test these alternators. Follow manufacturer's instructions.

1984–85 Trooper II

1. Measure resistance across terminals "F" and "E," **Fig. 4.** Resistance should be 5 ohms.
2. If resistance is greater than 5 ohms, there is poor contact between brushes and commutator.
3. If there is no continuity, rotor coil circuit is open, one of the brushes is sticking or the lead wire is broken.
4. A resistance of less than 5 ohms indicates a short in the rotor coil layer or a short in the circuit being grounded.
5. Connect tester positive lead to "N" terminal and negative lead to "A" terminal, **Fig. 5.** If there is no continuity,

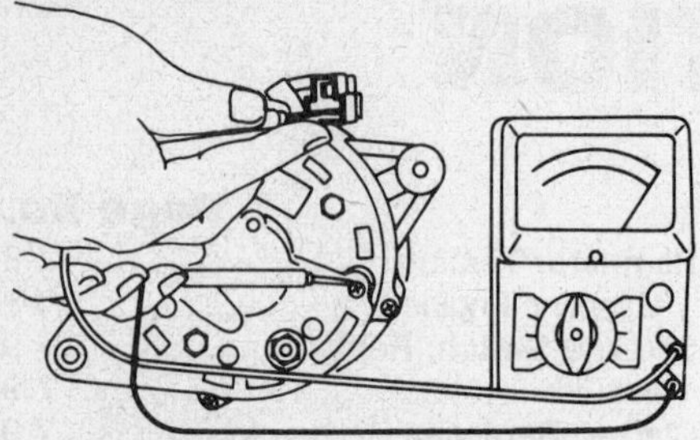

Fig. 4 Checking contact between brushes and commutator

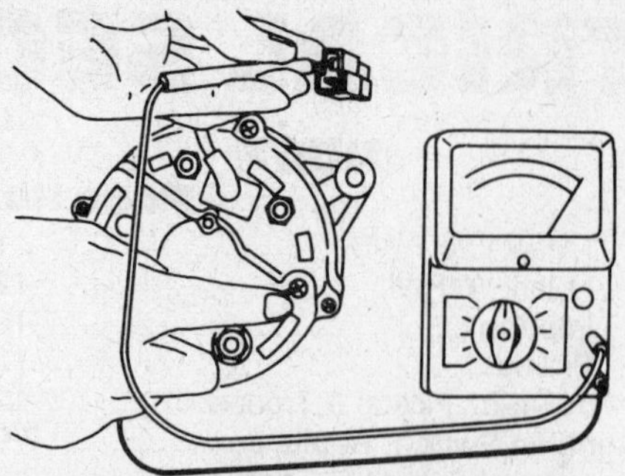

Fig. 5 Testing positive diodes

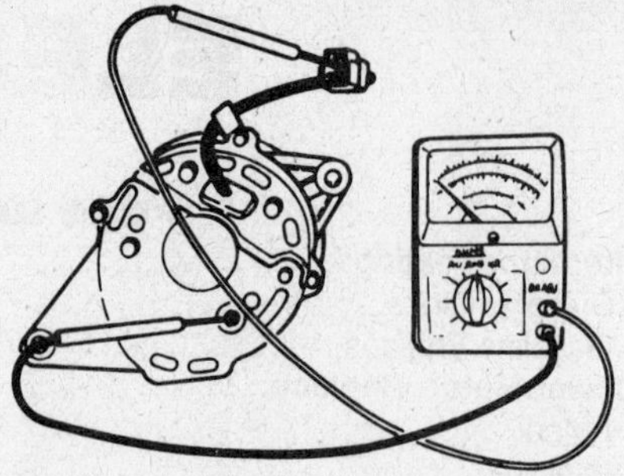

Fig. 6 Testing negative diodes

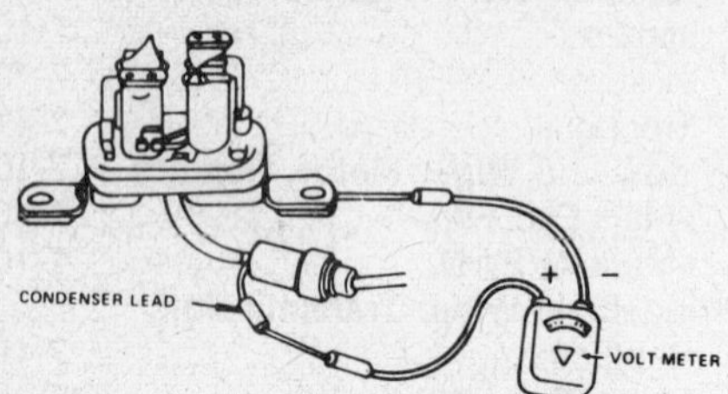

Fig. 7 Regulator test connections

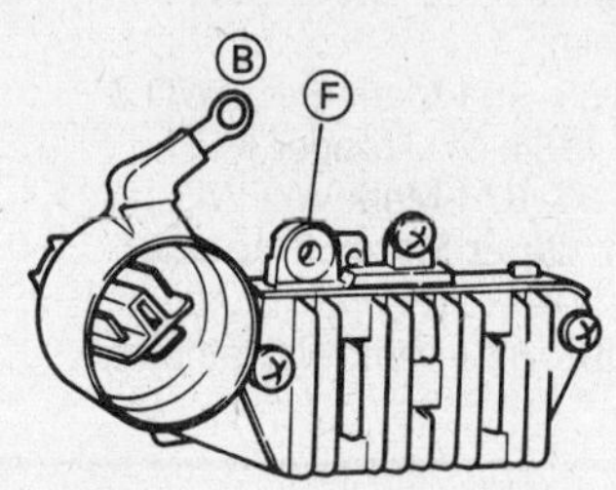

Fig. 8 IC regulator

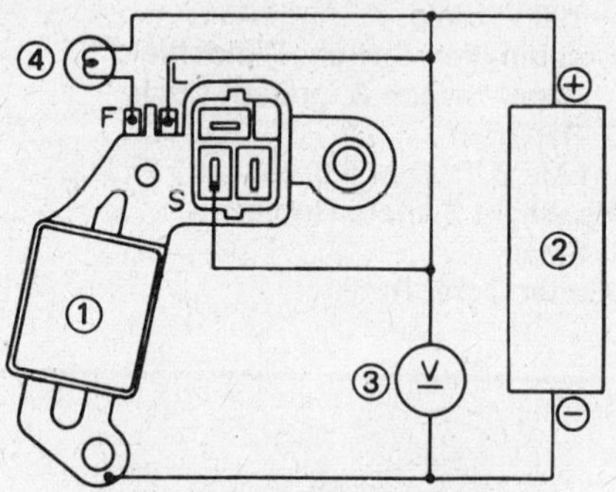

Fig. 9 Installing IC regulator testing components

one or more of the diodes on the positive side are shorted.

6. Connect tester positive lead to "E" terminal and negative lead to "N" terminal, **Fig. 6.** If there is no continuity, one or more of the diodes on the negative side is shorted.

1986–87 Trooper II

Special equipment is required to test these alternators. Follow manufacturer's instructions.

REGULATOR TESTING

GASOLINE ENGINES

1983–85 I-Mark, Exc. FWD.

1. Turn off all accessories, disconnect blower relay. Connect a voltmeter between condenser lead and ground, **Fig. 7.**
2. Normal operation of the regulator is indicated when the voltage is in the range of 13.8 to 14.8 volts.

1985–87 I-Mark W/FWD

1. Using a suitable ohmmeter, check for continuity between terminals "B" and "F," **Fig. 8**
2. When polarity is changed, there should be continuity in one direction and no continuity in opposite direction. If not, replace IC regulator.

1983–87 Impulse

The following instruments are required to perform the regulator test: Variable DC power source, voltmeter and test lamp. Connect components mentioned as shown in Fig. 9

1. Take measurements at the following points with instruments connected to the regulator assembly as shown in **Fig. 10.**
2. Connect regulator circuit to the power source. **Do not connect regulator "L" terminal to the power source with regulator "S" terminal disconnected. Damage to the regulator will result.**
3. Ensure test light is off at approximately 13.8 to 14.4 volts, when tested by gradually increasing the voltage from 10 volts.

1983–85 Pickup & 1984–85 Trooper II

Test regulator when it is cold. Do not test immediately after driving.

1. Connect ammeter and voltmeter as shown in **Fig. 11.**
2. Start engine and run at 2500 RPM for several minutes, then ensure that ammeter reading is 5 amps or less. **Ensure that battery is fully charged or incorrect ammeter reading may result.**
3. Lower engine speed to idle, then gradually increase speed to 2500 RPM and note voltmeter reading.
4. If voltmeter does not read 13.8-14.8 volts, adjust regulator as follows:
   a. Disconnect electrical connectors at voltage regulator and remove regulator cover.
   b. If voltage is too high, adjust regulator by bending core arm (D) **Fig. 12.** If voltage is too low, bend core arm up. If voltage cannot be corrected by bending core arm, continue to step c.
   c. Disconnect battery ground cable, then depress armature until moving point contacts (E) side point. Bend point arm (E) to obtain an armature gap of .012 inch.
   d. Release armature and adjust gap between (F) side point and moving point by bending point arm (F). Gap should be .012-.018 inch.
   e. Adjust point gap by loosening 3 mm upper contact attaching screw, then moving upper contact up or down as required. Gap should be .012-.016 inch.
   f. Readjust voltage with adjustment screw. When specified adjustment is obtained, secure adjusting screw by tightening locknut.
   g. Install regulator cover and connect electrical connectors, then recheck voltage.

1986–87 Pickup & Trooper II

To perform regulator tests, the following measuring instruments will be needed: resistor (10 ohms, 3 watts)...R1, variable resistor (0-300 ohms, 3 watts)...Rv, battery (12 volts, 2 pieces)...BAT1, BAT2, DC voltmeter (0-30).

1. Connect instruments as shown in **Fig. 13.**
2. Measure voltage at BAT1 (V1). Voltmeter reading should be 10-13 volts.
3. Measure voltage between terminals "F" and "E" (V2). Voltmeter reading should be approximately 2 volts.
4. Measure voltage between BAT1 and BAT2 (V3) with terminal "S" disconnected. Voltmeter reading should be 20-26 volts.
5. Measure voltage between terminals "E" and "F" while varying resistance gradually with variable resistor. Voltage should increase from 2 volts to 10-13 volts without any interruption. If voltage increase is interrupted, replace regulator.

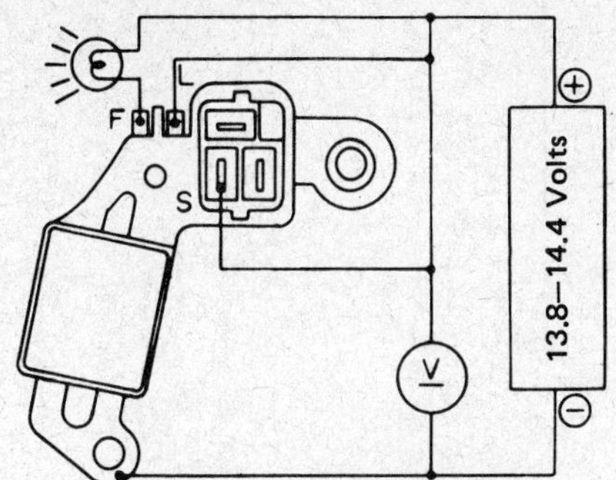

Fig. 10 Testing IC regulator

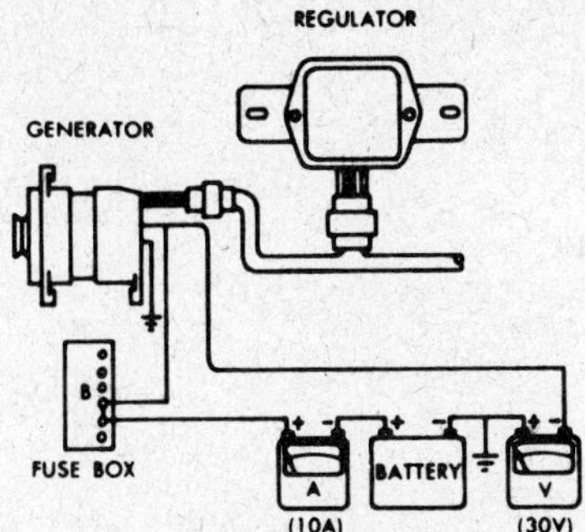

Fig. 11 Regulator test connections

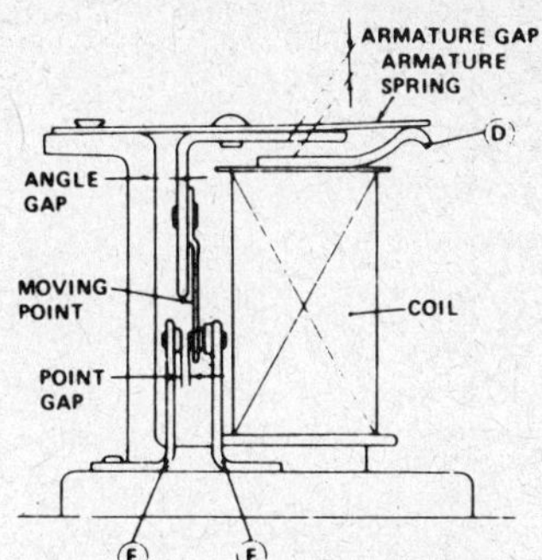

Fig. 12 Adjusting regulator

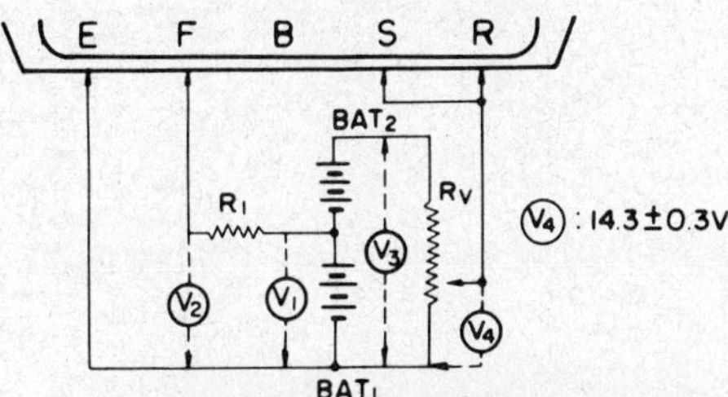

Fig. 13 IC regulator testing

6. Measure voltage between intermediate tap on variable resistor and terminal "E" (V4) without actuating the variable resistor. Voltmeter should read 14.0-14.6 volts, or regulator must be replaced.
7. Connect instruments as shown in **Fig. 14.**
8. Measure voltage between terminals "B" and "E" while gradually increasing voltage with variable resistor. Voltage should increase from approximately 2 volts to 10-13 volts. If voltage does not vary, replace regulator.
9. Check voltage between intermediate tap of variable resistor and terminal "E" without acuating variable resistor. Voltmeter should read 14.5-16.6 volts, or regulator must be replaced.

STARTER

REPLACE

1. Disconnect battery ground cable.
2. On gas engine models, remove EGR pipe.
3. Disconnect wiring from solenoid, remove bolts and nuts, then starter assembly.
4. Reverse procedure to install.

COMBINATION SWITCH, WINDSHIELD WIPER SWITCH & IGNITION LOCK

REPLACE

I-MARK, TROOPER II & 1984–87 PICKUP

1. Disconnect battery ground cable.
2. Remove steering wheel center pad.
3. Using steering wheel puller J-29752, remove steering wheel.
4. Remove screws securing upper and lower steering column covers. Disconnect electrical connectors.
5. Remove windshield wiper/washer switch and/or combination turn signal, headlight dimmer and hazard warning switch by removing retaining screws.
6. Remove lock cylinder housing by removing snap ring and washer followed by attaching bolts.
7. Reverse procedure to install.

COMBINATION SWITCH

REPLACE

1983 PICKUP

1. Disconnect battery ground cable.
2. Remove two screws securing the horn pad and remove, disconnect horn electrical lead. Remove steering wheel nut and lockwasher.
3. Using steering wheel puller J-24292-A, remove the steering wheel.
4. Remove five screws securing the upper and lower column shrouds and disconnect switch wiring connector.
5. Remove two switch to column flange screws and remove switch.
6. Reverse procedure to install.

IGNITION SWITCH

REPLACE

IMPULSE

1. Disconnect battery ground cable.
2. Remove horn pad attaching bolts, then the horn pad, disconnecting electrical connector.
3. Remove steering wheel retaining bolt and washer.
4. Using puller tool J-29752 or equivalent, remove steering wheel assembly.
5. Remove turn signal switch retaining screws, then the turn signal switch.
6. Remove ignition switch cover.
7. Remove steering shaft retaining ring, then the washer and spring assembly.
8. Remove ignition switch retaining bolts and the ignition switch.
9. Reverse procedure to install.

1983 PICKUP

1. Disconnect battery ground cable.

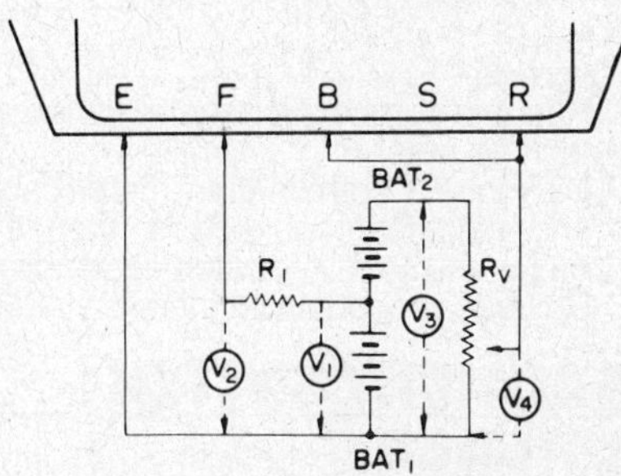

Fig. 14 IC regulator testing

2. Remove five screws securing the upper and lower column shrouds and disconnect switch wiring connector.
3. Remove switch ornament.
4. Remove switch ring nut and switch.
5. Reverse procedure to install.

TURN SIGNAL SWITCH

REPLACE

IMPULSE

1. Disconnect battery ground cable.
2. Remove horn pad attaching bolts, then the horn pad, disconnecting electrical connector.
3. Remove steering wheel retaining bolt and washer.
4. Using puller tool J-29752 or equivalent, remove steering wheel assembly.
5. Remove turn signal switch retaining screws, then the switch.
6. Reverse procedure to install.

SATELLITE SWITCH

REPLACE

IMPULSE

1. Disconnect battery ground cable.
2. Remove horn pad attaching bolts, then the horn pad, disconnecting electrical connector.
3. Remove steering wheel retaining bolt and washer.
4. Using puller tool J-29752 or equivalent, remove steering wheel assembly.
5. Remove upper and lower steering wheel cowl attaching screws and the cowls.
6. Remove hood of combination meter.
7. Remove combination meter retaining

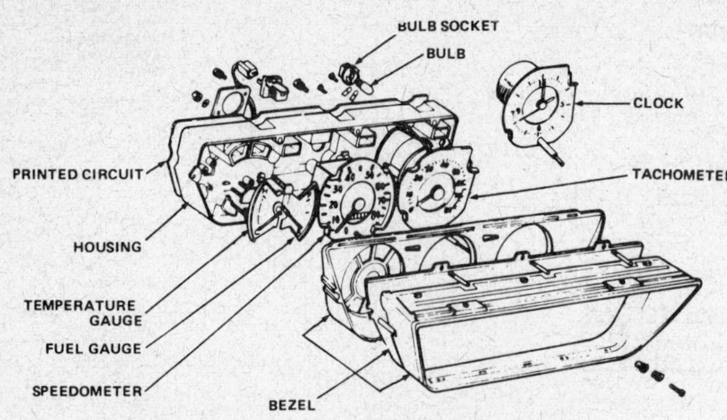

Fig. 15 Instrument cluster, disassembled (Typical)

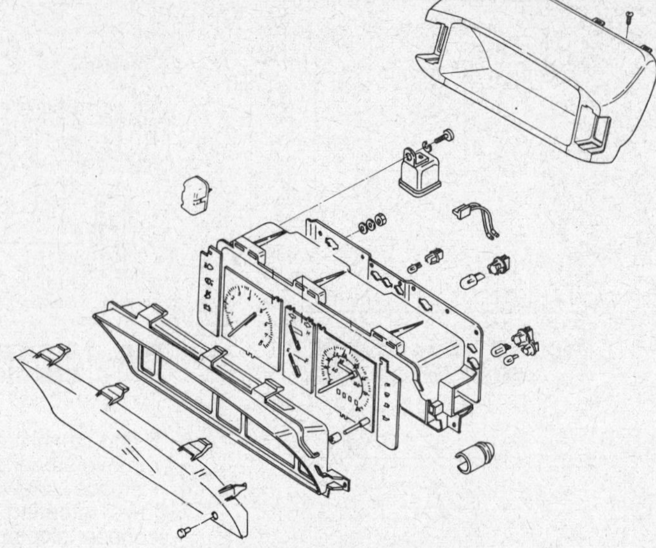

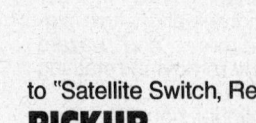

Fig. 16 Exploded view of meter assembly

screws.
8. Remove combination meter flange attaching nuts.
9. Disconnect combination meter cable and electrical connectors, then the meter and satellite switch assemblies.
10. Reverse procedure to install.

HEADLIGHT SWITCH REPLACE

I-MARK

1. Loosen knob setscrew and remove.
2. Remove switch body retaining locknut and switch assembly.
3. Disconnect switch wiring connector.
4. Reverse procedure to install.

INSTRUMENT CLUSTER REPLACE

1983–85 I-MARK EXC. FWD & 1984–87 TROOPER II

1. Disconnect ground cable from battery.
2. Remove steering wheel as described in "Combination Switch, Windshield Wiper Switch & Ignition Lock, Replace."
3. Disconnect speedometer cable from speedometer and remove wing nut.
4. Remove cluster attaching screws.
5. Carefully pull the cluster rearward and rotate sideways, disconnect the round six and twelve pole connectors. Remove cluster, Fig. 15. **On diesel engine equipped models, disconnect the harness connected to the speedometer reed switch at the connector.**
6. Reverse procedure to install.

1985–87 I-MARK W/FWD

1. Disconnect battery ground cable.
2. Remove meter hood attaching screws, **Fig. 16**, then meter hood.
3. Remove windshield wiper and light switch electrical connectors.
4. Remove meter assembly attaching screws, then meter assembly.
5. Reverse procedure to install.

IMPULSE

When removing instrument cluster, refer to "Satellite Switch, Replace."

PICKUP

1983

1. Remove radio knobs and nuts, then radio bezel.
2. Remove instrument cluster panel attaching screws, then panel.
3. Remove instrument cluster attaching screws and pull assembly outward.
4. Disconnect speedometer cable and electrical connectors, then remove instrument cluster.
5. Reverse procedure to install.

1984–87

1. Disconnect battery ground cable.
2. Disconnect speedometer cable.
3. Remove instrument cluster attaching screws, then pull instrument cluster assembly outward.
4. Disconnect electrical connectors, then remove cluster assembly.
5. Reverse procedure to install.

WINDSHIELD WIPER MOTOR REPLACE

I-MARK EXC. FWD

1. Disconnect battery ground cable.
2. Working from under instrument panel, remove nut and crankarm from motor.
3. Disconnect wire connectors.
4. Remove three nuts securing motor and remove.
5. Reverse procedure to install.

I-MARK W/FWD

1. Disconnect battery ground cable.
2. Remove wiper arm locknuts, then wiper arms.
3. Working from under the hood, remove wiper motor attaching bolts.
4. Disconnect wiper motor linkage from wiper motor, then motor.
5. Reverse procedure to install.

WINDSHIELD WIPER TRANSMISSION REPLACE

I-MARK EXC. FWD

1. Disconnect battery ground cable.
2. Remove wiper arms and nuts securing pivots to the body.
3. Remove steering wheel, instrument cluster and glove box.
4. Working through instrument cluster opening, carefully pry linkage loose from wiper transmission and remove three screws securing linkage to cowl.
5. Reach through glove box, pry linkage from wiper transmission using a screwdriver, remove two screws securing linkage to cowl. Remove transmission.
6. Reverse procedure to install.

WINDSHIELD WIPER MOTOR & TRANSMISSION REPLACE

IMPULSE

1. Remove wiper arm and blade assembly.
2. Remove wiper motor to body attaching bolts.
3. Remove bracket assembly with pivot assembly, link, and motor assembly.
4. Remove wiper link with pivot assembly from motor.
5. Reverse procedure to install.

PICKUP

1. Remove the access hole covers on the engine side of the dash panel.
2. Remove wiper arm covers and nuts, remove wiper arms.
3. Remove pivot covers and pivot nuts. Push the pivots into the dash panel.
4. Remove four bolts securing the wiper motor. Disconnect wire connectors

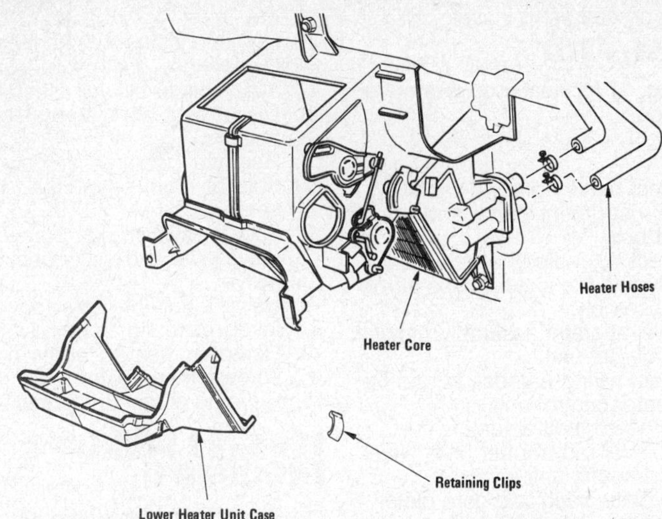

Fig. 17 Removal & installation of heater core

and remove the wiper motor assembly together with the linkage.
5. Reverse procedure to install.

TROOPER II

1. Disconnect battery ground cable.
2. Remove wiper arm assembly attaching nut and the wiper arm assembly.
3. Remove pivot link nut.
4. Remove center work hole cover.
5. Remove left work hole cover from engine compartment side of dash panel.
6. Disconnect wiper motor electrical connector.
7. Remove wiper motor assembly with link assembly.
8. Separate link assembly from wiper motor assembly.
9. Reverse procedure to install.

REAR WIPER MOTOR REPLACE

1985–87 I-MARK W/HATCHBACK

1. Disconnect battery ground cable.
2. Remove hatchback trim.
3. Remove wiper arm nut, then wiper arm assembly.
4. Remove wiper motor attaching nuts and bolts, disconnect electrical connector, then the motor.
5. Reverse procedure to install.

IMPULSE

1. Disconnect battery ground cable.
2. Remove trim cover.
3. Remove wiper arm nut, then wiper arm assembly.
4. Remove seal, locknut and collar from motor.
5. Disconnect electrical connector, then wiper motor mounting bolt.
6. Remove wiper motor, collar to washer.
7. Reverse procedure to install.

BLOWER MOTOR REPLACE

I-MARK

1. Disconnect battery ground cable.
2. Disconnect blower motor wiring.
3. Vehicles equipped with A/C, remove rubber hose.
4. Remove screws and caps securing blower motor.
5. Remove blower motor.
6. Reverse procedure to install.

IMPULSE

1. Disconnect battery ground cable.
2. Remove instrument panel and compartment box.
3. Disconnect A/C pipes at evaporator assembly and the water hoses at heater assembly.
4. Remove the evaporator assembly, then the blower unit.
5. Remove blower unit cover to case attaching bolts, then both cover halves with linings.
6. Remove motor assembly.
7. Reverse procedure to install.

1983 PICKUP

1. Disconnect battery ground cable.
2. Remove screw securing right side vent duct, then withdraw duct downward.
3. Compress the duct between the blower motor and the heater assembly and remove.
4. Disconnect blower motor wiring.
5. Remove the three nuts securing the blower motor to the dash panel.
6. Pull the blower motor in rearward to clear the stud bolts on the dash panel, then down.
7. Reverse procedure to install.

1984–87 PICKUP & TROOPER II

1. Disconnect battery ground cable.
2. Remove steering wheel.
3. Remove instrument panel.
4. Remove evaporator to compressor and receiver tank attaching flare nuts.
5. Disconnect vacuum hose at evaporator assembly.
6. Disconnect evaporator relay electrical connectors.
7. On models with diesel engines disconnect heater hoses at heater control unit.
8. Disconnect air ducts from heater control unit.
9. Disconnect heater unit relay electrical connectors.
10. Remove heater unit attaching nuts.
11. Remove heater unit assembly.
12. Disconnect electrical connectors and vacuum hose at blower unit.
13. Remove blower unit attaching nuts and the blower unit.
14. Separate blower unit case halves.
15. Remove blower motor assembly.
16. Separate blower motor from assembly.
17. Reverse procedure to install.
18. Adjust water valve link rod as follows:
    a. Set air mix door in stop position in counterclockwise direction.
    b. Move water valve lever to stop position in clockwise direction.
    c. Attach link rod to swivel joint with screw.
19. Install mode and temperature cables as follows:
    a. Attach control assembly to instrument panel.
    b. Connect cable with mode selector lever and heater assembly lever set in "OFF" position, then secure outer tube with cable clip.
    c. Connect cable with temperature lever and heater lever set in "HOT" position and secure outer tube with cable clip.
    d. Check all doors and water valve. If doors or valve do not close properly, loosen cable clamp screw at control and adjust cable length as necessary.
20. Ensure that defroster door is in defroster position when control lever is moved to "DEF" and "HEAT" positions.
21. Check heat door by ensuring that air is directed to floor out lets in "HEAT" and "BI-LEVEL" positions.
22. Check vent door by ensuring that air is directed out the center and side outlets in "VENT" and "BI-LEVEL" positions.
23. Check air mix door by ensuring that hot air is delivered and the water valve is fully open with temperature control lever in "HOT" position, or water valve is fully closed when temperature control lever is in "COLD" position.

HEATER CORE REPLACE

I-MARK EXC. FWD

1. Disconnect battery ground cable.
2. Drain cooling system.
3. Disconnect heater hoses at core and plug core tubes to prevent spillage of

coolant when removing heater assembly.
4. Remove outer blower unit case cover and disconnect the fresh-air door bowden cable.
5. Disconnect the temperature cable at water valve.
6. Remove steering wheel.
7. Remove instrument cluster.
8. Disconnect wiring for console gauges and remove console retaining screws, shift lever leather and console.
9. Remove heater control and radio face plate.
10. Remove glove box.
11. Remove radio.
12. Disconnect selector mode cable from driver's side of heater unit assembly.
13. Carefully pull the temperature and fresh-air door cables through the cowl and remove control panel through the cluster opening.
14. Remove instrument panel assembly.
15. Remove heater unit assembly through bolt located at the rear and bottom of heater unit assembly.
16. Remove four attaching nuts holding heater unit and blower unit together and remove heater unit assembly.
17. Remove bolts holding heater unit case halves together and the heater core.
18. Reverse procedure to install.

I-MARK W/FWD

Refer to **Fig. 17** for heater core removal and installation.

IMPULSE

1. Disconnect battery ground cable.
2. Remove instrument panel and compartment box.
3. Disconnect A/C pipes at evaporator assembly and the water hoses at the heater assembly.
4. Remove evaporator assembly, blower unit and heater unit.
5. Disconnect wiring harness at and remove heater control unit.
6. Remove heater unit actuator.
7. Remove lever rod, shutter lever, lever cable and heater unit lever.
8. Remove plate lining and core plate.
9. Remove heater core attaching screws and the heater core.
10. Reverse procedure to install.

PICKUP

1983

1. Disconnect battery ground cable.
2. Drain cooling system and disconnect hoses from heater core. **Plug core tubes to prevent spillage into vehicle.**
3. Remove instrument panel assembly.
4. Disconnect duct connecting heater assembly to blower assembly.
5. Disconnect all related electrical connectors.
6. Remove heater assembly attaching nuts at dash panel, then heater assembly.
7. Loosen swivel joint screw on water valve lever and disconnect valve from swivel.
8. Using a suitable screwdriver, remove lever operating air mix door.
9. Remove heater core hold down screws, then heater core.
10. Reverse procedure to install.

1984–87 PICKUP & TROOPER II

1. Disconnect battery ground cable.
2. Remove heater unit as described under "Blower Motor, Replace."
3. Remove defroster door spring.
4. Remove defroster door rod and lever.
5. Remove battery relay.
6. Remove A/C resistor.
7. Remove heater core plate and seal.
8. Remove water valve rod and the heater core.
9. Reverse procedure to install.

GASOLINE ENGINE SECTION

INDEX

Page No.

ENGINE REPLACE

I-MARK EXC. FWD

1. Remove hood, then disconnect battery ground cable.
2. Remove undercover, fan shroud and radiator.
3. Drain oil and cooling system.
4. Remove air cleaner assembly from engine.
5. Mark then disconnect all electrical connectors, cables and vacuum hoses from engine.
6. Disconnect front exhaust pipe from exhaust manifold.
7. Loosen clutch control cable adjusting nut.
8. Disconnect and plug heater hose from heater.
9. Disconnect control cable from heater temperature control valve.
10. Remove control valve attaching screws, then the control valve assembly.
11. Raise and support vehicle.
12. Remove engine mount nut.
13. Install tool J-26555 or equivalent onto engine. **Use exhaust manifold stud**

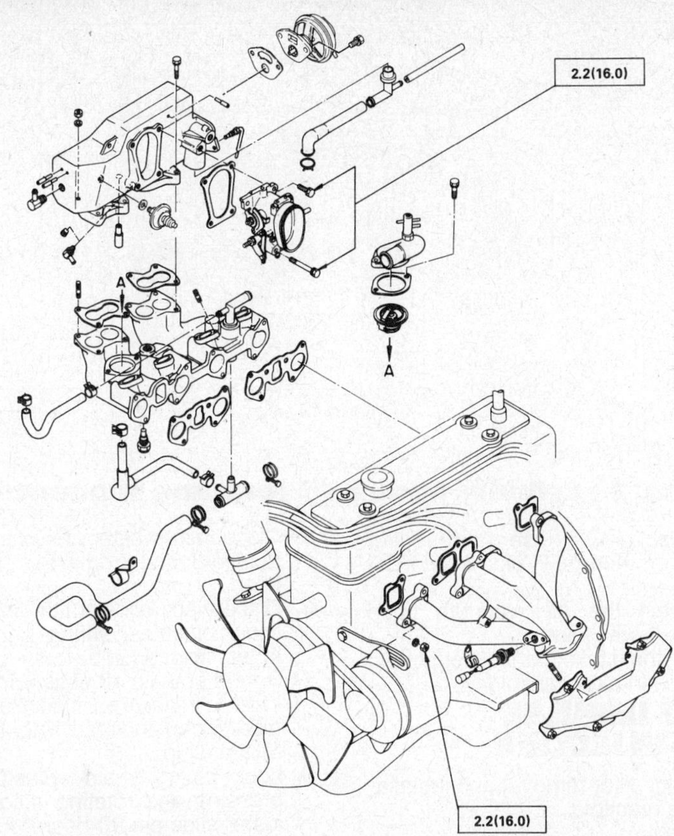

Fig. 1 Removal & installation of intake & exhaust manifolds. 1984–87 Impulse w/fuel injection

bolts to attach tool onto engine.
14. Disconnect engine ground strap from cylinder block.
15. Disconnect back-up light switch electrical connector from transmission.
16. Disconnect ECS hose from oil pan.
17. Remove engine stop plate attaching bolts, then the stop plate.
18. Position a suitable jack under engine, then raise engine slightly.
19. Remove left side engine mount stop plate attaching bolts, then the stop plate.
20. Remove gearshift lever assembly.
21. Remove parking brake return spring, then disconnect brake cable.
22. Disconnect propeller shaft from transmission.
23. Remove clutch return spring, then disconnect clutch control cable from lever.
24. Remove front exhaust pipe bracket from transmission.
25. Remove front exhaust pipe assembly from vehicle.
26. Disconnect speedometer cable from transmission.
27. Install suitable engine lifting equipment onto engine.
28. Remove rear engine mount bolts.
29. Remove engine and transmission assembly from vehicle.
30. Reverse procedure to install.

1985–87 I-MARK W/FWD

1. Remove hood, then disconnect battery ground cable.
2. Drain oil from transaxle case and engine.
3. Drain cooling system.
4. If equipped with A/C, discharge refrigerant from system.
5. Disconnect fuel pump hoses. Cap all openings to prevent entry of dirt and dust.
6. Remove air cleaner assembly.
7. Disconnect power steering hoses.
8. If equipped with A/C, disconnect A/C hose assembly.
9. Disconnect upper and lower radiator hoses, then the two heater hoses.
10. If equipped with automatic transmission, disconnect cooler hoses.
11. Disconnect brake booster hose.
12. Mark, then disconnect all electrical connectors, cables and vacuum hoses from engine.
13. Remove driveshafts as follows:
    a. Raise and support vehicle.
    b. Remove front wheels, then disconnect tie rods from steering knuckles using tool J-21687-02 or equivalent.
    c. Disconnect lower arm end ball joints from lower arm.
    d. Loosen nuts attaching strut to the body, but do not remove them.
    e. Using a suitable screwdriver, pry out driveshafts.
14. Remove front exhaust pipe assembly from vehicle.
15. Install suitable engine lifting equipment onto engine.
16. Raise engine to remove weight from engine mounts, then remove torque rod from body side.
17. Remove front and rear engine mounting through bolts.
18. Remove engine along with transaxle assembly.

TROOPER II & PICKUP

1. Remove hood, then disconnect battery ground cable.
2. Remove undercover, radiator and fan.
3. Drain oil and cooling system.
4. Remove air cleaner assembly from engine.
5. Mark then disconnect all electrical connector, linkages, cables and vacuum hoses from engine.
6. Disconnect front exhaust pipe from exhaust manifold.
7. Loosen clutch control cable adjusting nut.
8. Disconnect and plug heater hoses from heater.
9. On California models, disconnect hose from air switching valve and vacuum switching valve.
10. Remove engine mount nut.
11. Disconnect engine ground strap.
12. Raise and support vehicle.
13. Disconnect back-up light switch electrical connector from transmission.
14. Remove engine mount nuts.
15. Raise engine slightly, then remove left side engine mount stop plate.
16. On 4 4 models, remove transmission from vehicle.
17. Remove parking brake return spring, then disconnect brake cable from bracket.
18. On two wheel drive models, disconnect propeller shaft from transmission.
19. Remove clutch return spring and clutch control cable.
20. Remove front exhaust pipe bracket from transmission.
21. Disconnect speedometer cable from transmission.
22. Position a suitable jack under engine, then raise engine slightly.
23. Remove rear engine mounting bolts.
24. Install suitable engine lifting equipment onto engine.
25. Remove engine and transmission assembly from vehicle.
26. Reverse procedure to install.

IMPULSE

1. Scribe reference marks in hood hinge area, then remove hood.
2. Disconnect battery cables.
3. Drain cooling system, then remove intake air duct.
4. Disconnect upper radiator hose.
5. Remove engine under cover.
6. On automatic transmission models, disconnect and cap transmission fluid cooler lines.
7. Carefully discharge refrigerant from A/C system.
8. Disconnect receiver to A/C line, then the compressor hose.
9. Remove condenser assembly and position aside.
10. Mark then disconnect all electrical connectors, vacuum hoses and fuel lines from engine.
11. Disconnect accelerator cable from mounting bracket.
12. Disconnect wire harness from fender skirt and cylinder head mounting clips.

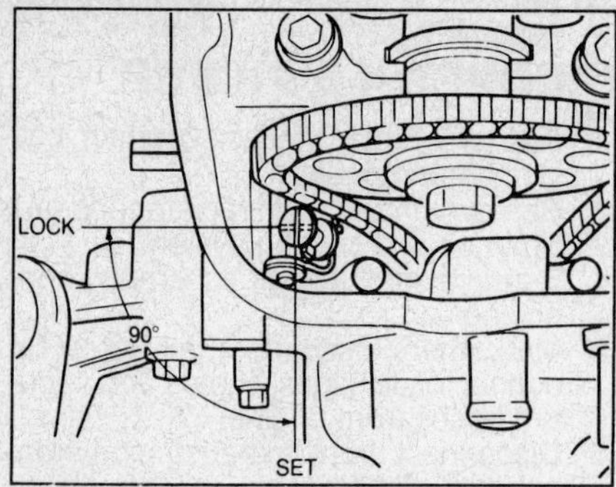

Fig. 2 Locking timing chain adjuster

13. On automatic transmission models, remove transmission selector lever pin.
14. Disconnect ignition coil wire.
15. Raise and support vehicle.
16. Disconnect cable and electrical wires from starter motor.
17. Disconnect engine to crossmember ground strap.
18. Remove right side engine mount nuts.
19. Disconnect and cap power steering lines from power steering pump, if equipped.
20. Disconnect propeller shaft from transmission. Cap transmission output shaft to prevent fluid leakage.
21. Disconnect speedometer cable from transmission.
22. On manual transmission models, remove clutch slave cylinder and position aside.
23. Remove catalytic converter mounting bracket and strap.
24. Disconnect front exhaust pipe from exhaust manifold.
25. Remove rear engine mount bracket bolts, then the bracket.
26. Install suitable engine lifting equipment onto engine.
27. Remove engine and transmission assembly from engine.
28. Separate engine from transmission.
29. Reverse procedure to install.

INTAKE MANIFOLD

REPLACE

I-MARK, PICKUP & TROOPER II

1. Disconnect battery ground cable and drain cooling system.
2. Remove air cleaner assembly.
3. Disconnect radiator upper hose from intake manifold.
4. Disconnect fuel hose, vacuum hose and heater hoses from manifold, then heater hoses from the dashboard.
5. Disconnect the accelerator control cable from carburetor.
6. Disconnect distributor vacuum hose from distributor, then thermo-unit wiring at connector.
7. Disconnect the automatic choke and solenoid wiring at connectors.
8. On some 1983-87 models, disconnect ground wire at connector, canister hose and EFE heater wiring at connector.

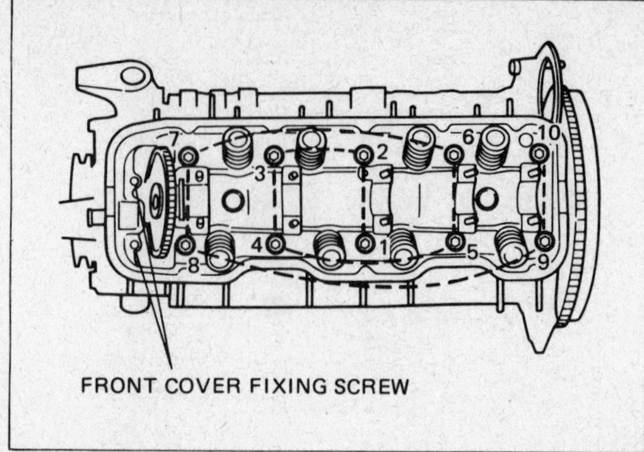

Fig. 3 Cylinder head bolt torquing sequence

9. Disconnect PCV hose from rocker arm cover, then EGR pipe from EGR valve.
10. Disconnect the AIR vacuum hose from the 3-way joint.
11. Remove the intake manifold attaching nuts, then intake manifold.

1984–87 IMPULSE W/FUEL INJECTION

Refer to **Fig. 1** for removal and installation of intake manifold.

EXHAUST MANIFOLD

REPLACE

I-MARK, PICKUP & TROOPER II

1. Disconnect battery ground cable.
2. Remove bolts attaching the air cleaner, then loosen clamp bolt.
3. Lift air cleaner assembly slightly, then remove the hot air hose.
4. Remove manifold cover attaching bolts, then the manifold cover.
5. Remove EGR pipe clip from upper portion of transmission, and disconnect EGR pipe from exhaust manifold.
6. On some 1983-87 models, disconnect oxygen sensor wiring at connector.
7. Remove exhaust pipe to manifold attaching nuts, then disconnect exhaust pipe from manifold.
8. Remove exhaust manifold attaching nuts, then the exhaust manifold.

1984–87 IMPULSE W/FUEL INJECTION

Refer to **Fig. 1** for removal and installation of exhaust manifold.

CYLINDER HEAD

REPLACE

I-MARK & 1983 PICKUP

1. Disconnect battery ground cable.
2. Remove cam cover and EGR pipe clamp bolt from rear of cylinder head.
3. Raise and support vehicle, then disconnect exhaust pipe from manifold.
4. Lower vehicle and drain cooling system.
5. Disconnect heater hoses from intake manifold and from rear of cylinder head.
6. Disconnect accelerator linkage, fuel lines, electrical wiring and vacuum hoses from engine.
7. Rotate crankshaft until number 4 cylinder is in firing position. Remove distributor cap and mark rotor to housing relationship.
8. Lock timing chain adjuster by depressing and rotating automatic adjuster slide pin 90 degrees clockwise **Fig. 2.**
9. On 1983-87 models, remove camshaft sprocket and fuel pump drive cam to camshaft bolt. On all models, do not remove the sprocket from chain.
10. Disconnect AIR hose and check valve from exhaust manifold.
11. Remove cylinder head to timing cover attaching bolts, then cylinder heat bolts.
12. Remove cylinder head, intake and exhaust manifold as an assembly from engine.
13. Reverse procedure to install. Torque cylinder head bolts in sequence, **Fig. 3.** Refer to engine tightening specifications for torque valves.

1984–87 PICKUP, IMPULSE & TROOPER II

Refer to **Fig. 4** for removal and installation of cylinder head. Refer to engine tightening specifications for torque valves.

VALVES

ADJUST

1. Remove cam cover.
2. Torque rocker arm shaft bracket nuts to 16 ft. lbs.
3. Position No. 1 piston at top dead center, compression stroke. In this position, adjust the following valves to specifications: No. 1 cylinder, intake and exhaust; No. 2 cylinder, intake; No. 3 cylinder, exhaust.
4. Rotate crankshaft 360 degrees and adjust the following valves: No. 2 cylinder, exhaust; No. 3 cylinder, intake; No. 4 cylinder, intake and exhaust.
5. Install cam cover.

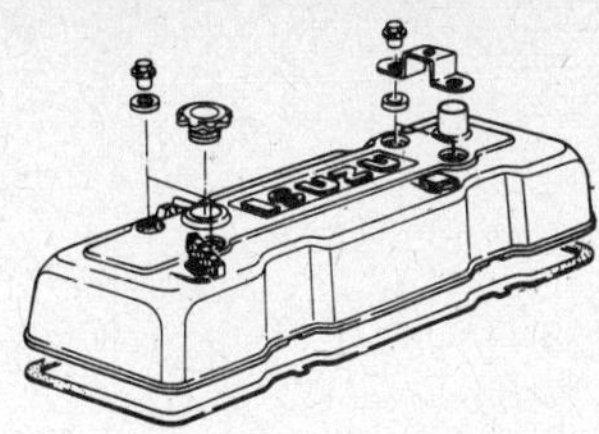
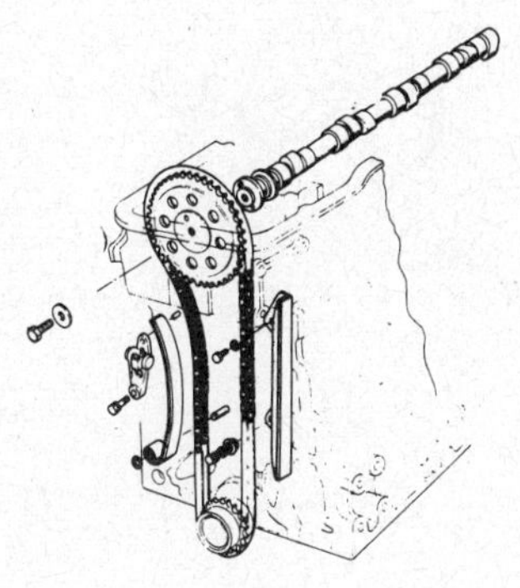
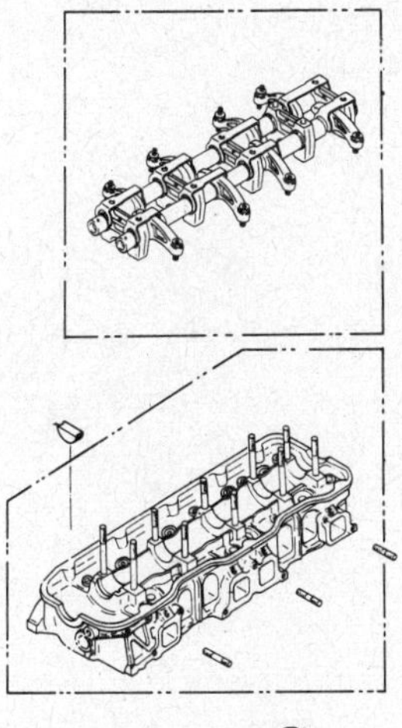
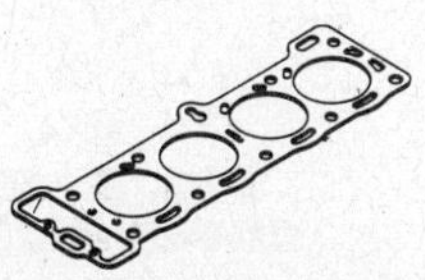

Fig. 4 Removal & installation of cylinder head & rocker arm assembly. 1984–87 Impulse, Pickup & Trooper II (Typical)

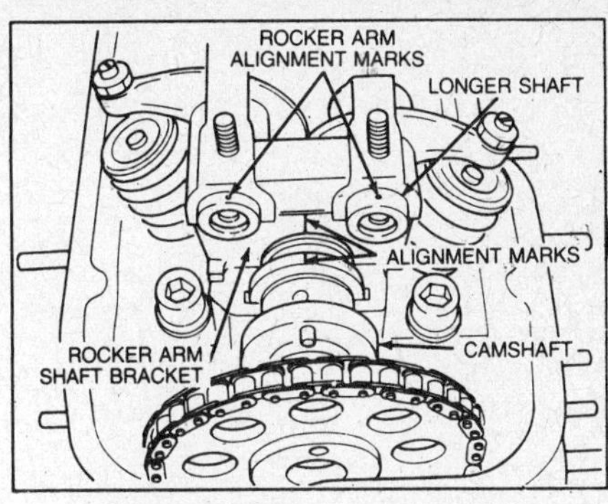

Fig. 5 Rocker arm shaft installation

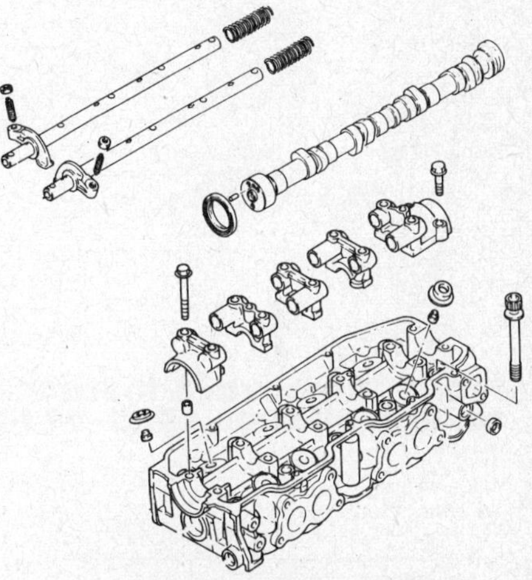

Fig. 6 Removal & installation of rocker arm assembly. 1985–87 I-Mark W/FWD

ROCKER ARMS & SHAFTS

I-MARK EXC. FWD, 1983 PICKUP

Removal

1. Remove cam cover.
2. Alternately loosen rocker arm shaft bracket nuts and remove nuts from brackets.
3. Remove spring from rocker arm shaft, then the rocker arm brackets and arms.

Installation

1. Lubricate rocker arms, shafts and valve stems with engine oil.
2. Install the longer rocker shaft on the exhaust valve side and the shorter rocker shaft on the intake valve side, **Fig. 5**, with aligning marks facing front.
3. Install rocker arm shaft brackets and rocker arms on the rocker arm shafts so that the cylinder number (on the upper face of the brackets) is facing toward front of engine.
4. Align the mark on the No. 1 rocker arm shaft bracket with the mark on the rocker arm shafts.
5. The exhaust side rocker arm shaft should protect a greater distance from the face of the No. 1 rocker shaft bracket outer face than the intake side rocker arm shaft when the rocker arm shaft stud holes are aligned with the rocker arm shaft bracket stud holes.
6. Position rocker arm shaft springs between rocker arm shaft bracket and rocker arm.
7. Ensure punch mark on rocker arm shaft is facing upward. Install rocker arm shaft bracket assembly onto cylinder head studs. Align mark on camshaft with mark on No. 1 rocker arm shaft bracket.
8. Torque rocker arm shaft stud nuts to 16 ft. lbs. **Hold the rocker arm springs in position while torquing the stud nuts to prevent spring damage.**
9. Adjust valves and install cam cover.

1985–87 I-MARK W/FWD

Refer to **Fig. 6** for removal and installation of rocker arm assembly.

1984–87 IMPULSE, PICKUP & TROOPER II

Refer to **Fig. 4** for removal and installation of rocker arm assembly.

FRONT OIL SEAL REPLACE

I-MARK EXC. FWD, 1983 PICKUP

1. Disconnect battery ground cable and drain cooling system.
2. Disconnect radiator hoses and remove radiator assembly.
3. Remove drive belts and engine fan, then A/C compressor and power steering pump if equipped.
4. Remove crankshaft pulley center bolt, pulley and balancer assembly. Remove A/C pulley and power steering pulley if equipped.
5. Pry seal from timing cover using a suitable screwdriver.
6. Install new seal using tool J-26587 or equivalent.

1985–87 I-MARK W/FWD

Refer to **Fig. 7** for removal and installation of front oil seal.

1984–87 IMPULSE, PICKUP & TROOPER II

Refer to **Fig. 8** for removal and installation of front oil seal.

FRONT COVER REPLACE

I-MARK EXC. FWD & 1983 PICKUP

Removal

1. Disconnect battery ground cable.
2. Remove cylinder head as outlined under "Cylinder Head Replace."

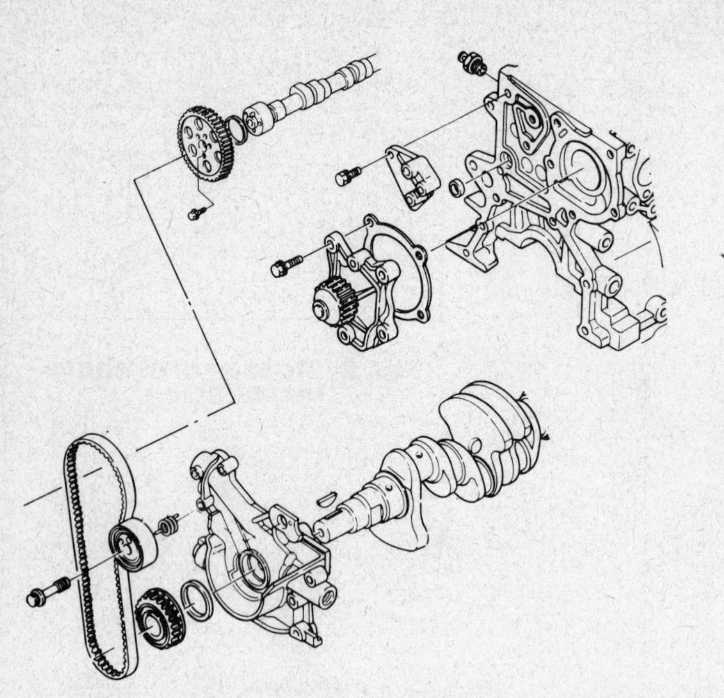

Fig. 7 Removal & installation of front cover & oil seal. 1985–87 I-Mark W/FWD

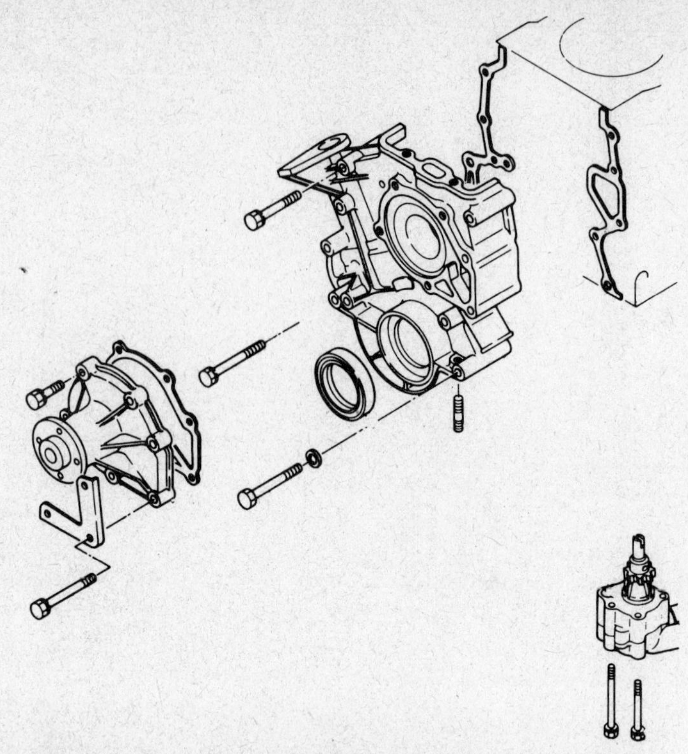

Fig. 8 Removal & installation of front cover & oil seal. 1984–87 Impulse, Pickup & Trooper II

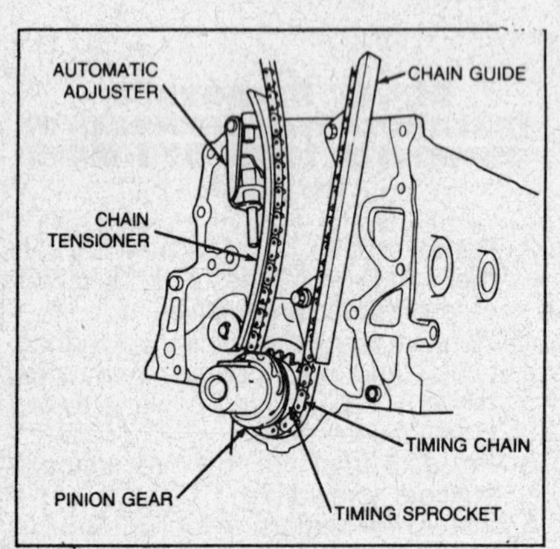

Fig. 9 Timing chain removal

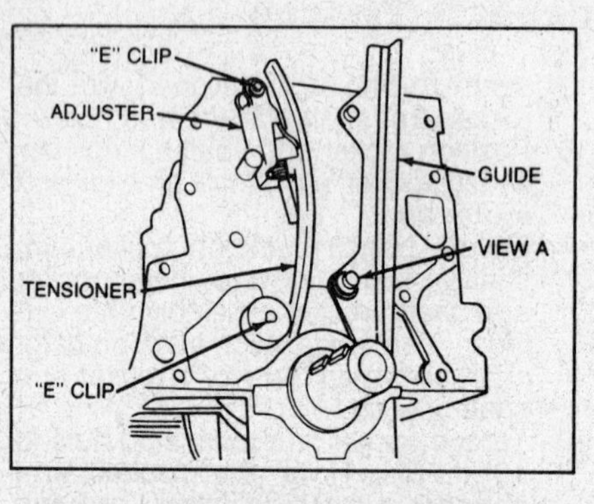

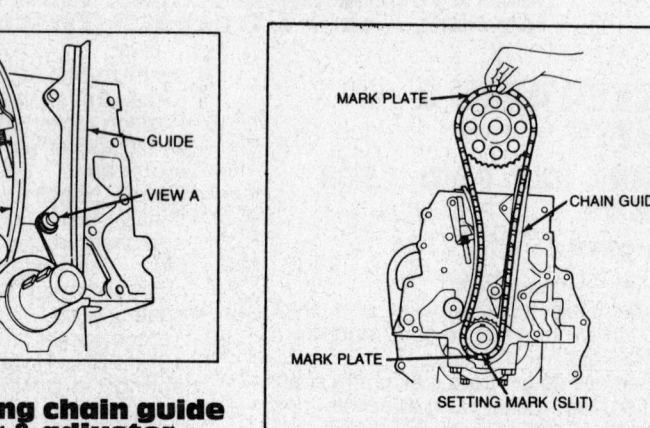

Fig. 10 Timing chain guide tensioner & adjuster

Fig. 11 Timing chain alignment

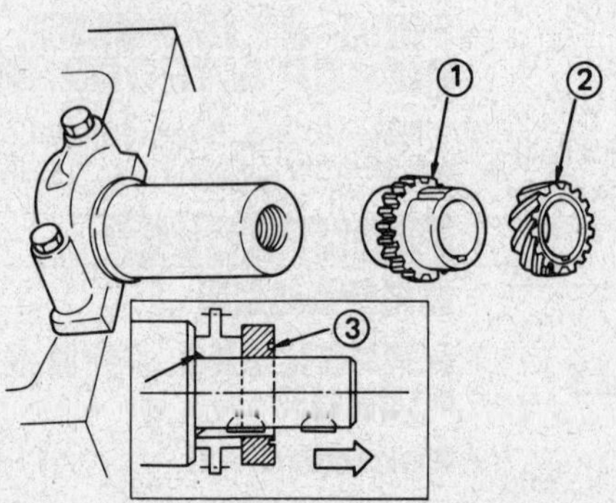

Fig. 12 Replacing crankshaft gear

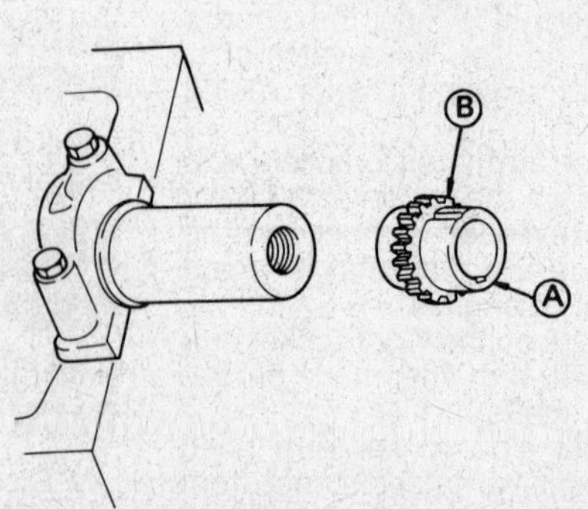

Fig. 13 Key groove "A" on timing gear

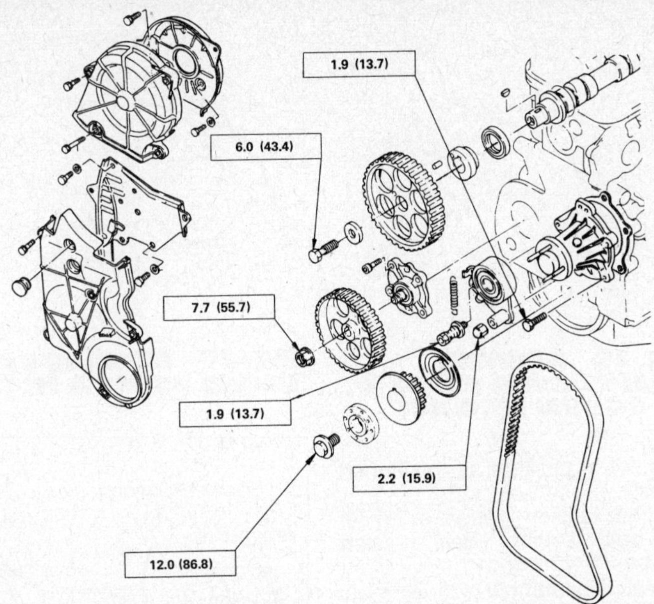

Fig. 14 Timing belt cover, belt & sprocket assembly exploded view

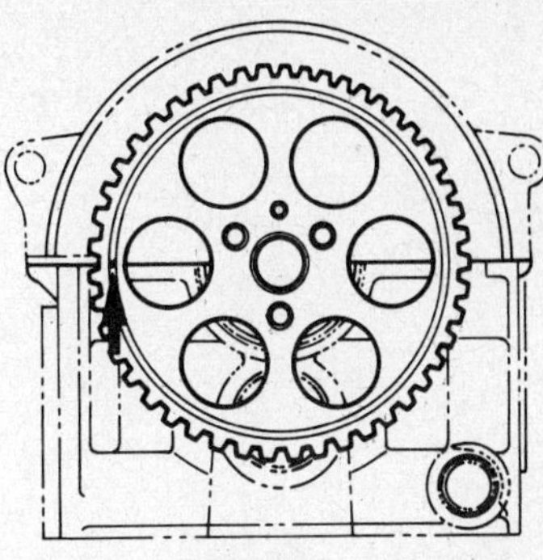

Fig. 15 Aligning camshaft pulley

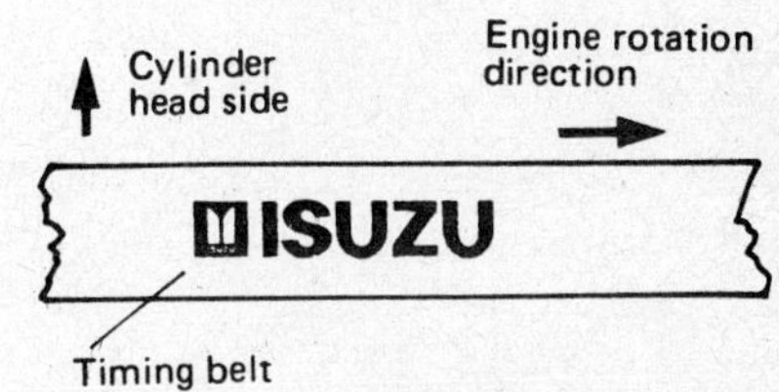

Fig. 17 Installing timing belt

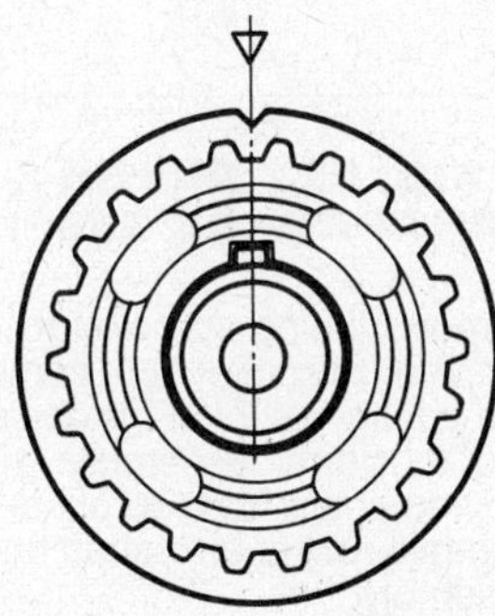

Fig. 16 Installing crankshaft pulley

3. Remove oil pan as outlined under "Oil Pan Replace."
4. Remove oil pickup tube from oil pump, then crankshaft pulley as outlined under "Front Oil Seal Replace."
5. Remove AIR pump drive belt.
6. If equipped with A/C, remove compressor and compressor mounting brackets.
7. Remove distributor cap, then distributor.
8. Remove front cover attaching bolts, then front cover.

Installation

1. Install new gasket onto cylinder block.
2. Align oil pump drive gear punch mark with oil filter side of cover, then align the center of dowel pin with alignment mark on oil pump case.
3. Rotate crankshaft until Nos. 1 and 4 cylinders are at top dead center.
4. Install front cover by engaging pinion gear with oil pump drive gear on crankshaft.
5. Check that punch mark on oil pump drive gear is turned to the rear, viewed through the clearance between front cover and cylinder block.
6. Check that slit at the end of oil pump shaft is parallel with front face of cylinder block and is offset forward.
7. Install front cover and tighten front cover bolts.
8. Reverse steps 1 thru 8 under "Front Cover, Replace."
9. Check engine timing.
10. Check for leaks.

1985–87 I-MARK W/FWD

Refer to **Fig. 7** for removal and installation of front cover.

1985–87 IMPULSE, PICKUP & TROOPER II

Refer to **Fig. 8** for removal and installation of front cover.

TIMING CHAIN REPLACE

I-MARK EXC. FWD & 1983 PICKUP

1. Remove front cover assembly as outlined under "Front Cover Replace."
2. Remove timing chain from crankshaft sprocket, **Fig. 9.**
3. Remove E-clips, then chain adjuster and tensioner, **Fig. 10**. Inspect components for wear or damage. Also inspect chain guide and oil jet, view "A", **Fig. 10.**
4. Install timing sprocket and pinion gear with groove side toward front cover. Align key grooves with key on crankshaft, then drive into position using tool J-26587.
5. Turn crankshaft so key is turned toward cylinder head side with No. 1 and 4 pistons at top dead center.
6. Install timing chain by aligning mark plate on chain with mark on crankshaft timing sprocket. The side of the chain with the mark plate is located on the front side and the side of chain with the most links between mark plates is located on the chain guide side, **Fig. 11.**
7. Install camshaft timing sprocket so marked side of sprocket faces forward and the triangular mark aligns with the chain mark plate. **Keep the timing chain engaged with camshaft timing sprocket until the camshaft timing sprocket is installed on camshaft.**
8. Install front cover assembly as outlined previously.

1984–87 IMPULSE & PICKUP W/4-119 ENGINE & 1984–85 TROOPER II W/4-119 ENGINE

1. Remove front cover assembly as outlined under "Front Cover Replace."
2. Remove E-clips and bolts, then chain adjuster assembly.
3. Remove timing chain.
4. If crankshaft gear requires replacement, install gear with chamfered side towards cylinder body and oil groove in pinion must be turned toward front of engine, **Fig. 12.**
5. Bring No. 1 and No. 4 piston to TDC. The key groove "A", **Fig. 13,** on timing gear should be turned toward cylinder head side and setting mark "B" (slit) to the oil pan side.
6. Install timing chain.

TIMING BELT REPLACE

1985–87 I-MARK W/FWD

1. Disconnect battery ground cable.
2. Remove drive and accessories as needed, then remove timing belt cover, **Fig. 14.**
3. Ensure mark on cam pulley is aligned with upper surface of cylinder head,

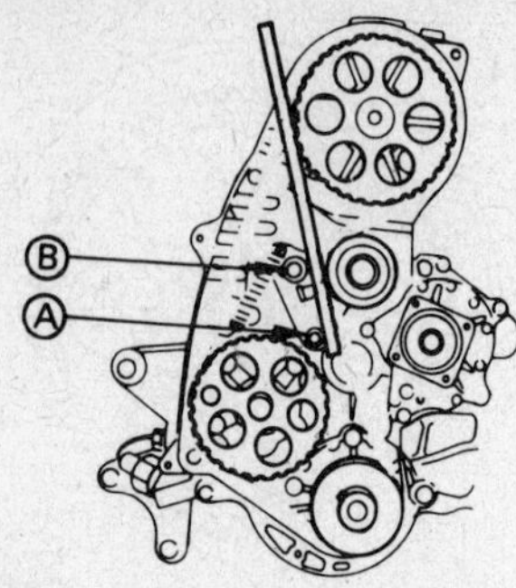

Fig. 18 Timing belt removal

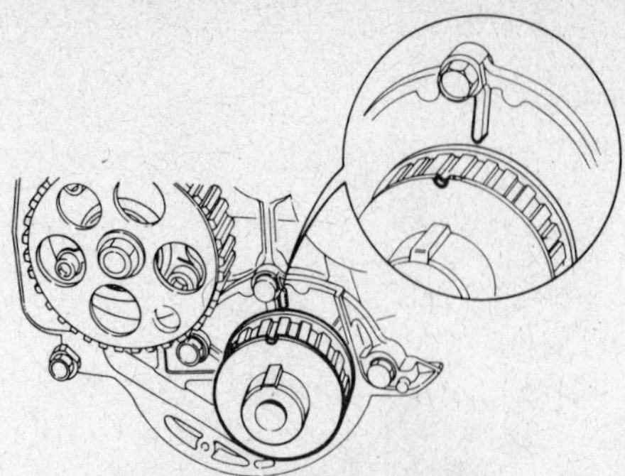

Fig. 19 Aligning crankshaft timing pulley & front oil seal retainer

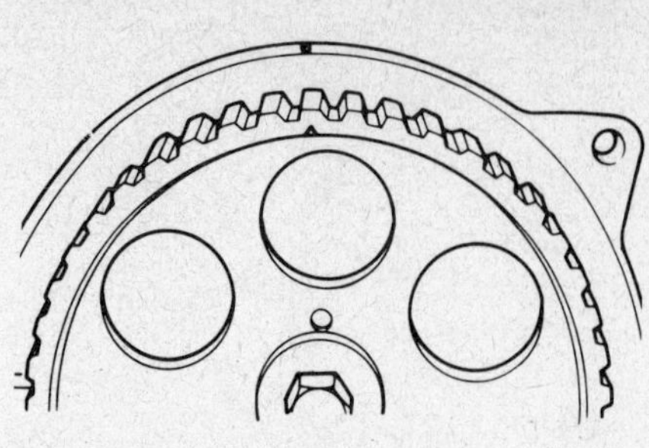

Fig. 20 Aligning camshaft timing pulley & front plate

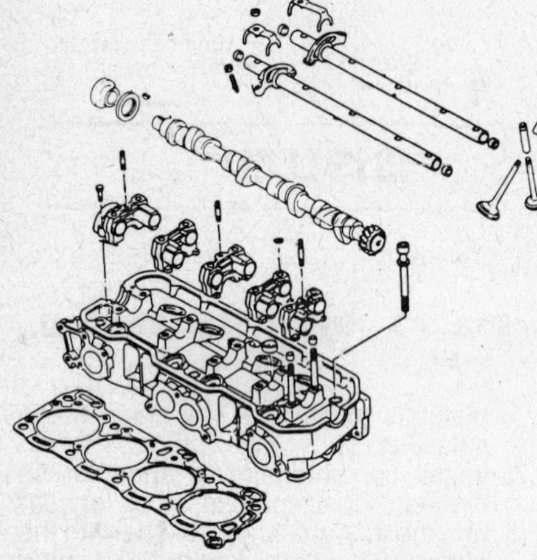

Fig. 21 Removal & installation of camshaft

and dowel pin on camshaft is positioned at the top, **Fig. 15.**

4. Ensure crankshaft pulley is aligned as shown in **Fig. 16.**
5. Remove tension pulley, water pump pulley, camshaft timing pulley and crankshaft timing pulley.
6. Inspect timing belt and replace if cracked or worn.
7. Set timing belt letter mark in the direction of engine rotation, **Fig. 17.**
8. Install timing belt in the following order: crankshaft timing pulley, camshaft timing pulley, water pump pulley and tension pulley. Ensure both gears are aligned correctly. **There must be no slack in belt after installation. The teeth of belt and teeth of pulley must be in perfect alignment.**
9. Loosen tension pulley bolt.
10. Install a suitable hex wrench into tension pulley hexagonal hole and hold pulley, while temporarily tightening the bolt.
11. Turn crankshaft two complete reverse revolutions and align crankshaft timing pulley groove with mark on oil pump.
12. Loosen tension pulley bolt and apply tension to belt, then insert hex wrench into tension pulley hexagonal hole. Hold pulley and torque bolt to 37 ft. lbs.
13. Move crankshaft back to about 50 degrees BTDC and once again perform the normal operation. Ensure crankshaft is set in position as mentioned previously.
14. Using belt tension gauge J-35779, check belt tension. Belt tension should be 34-42 lbs.
15. Check valve clearance.

1985–87 IMPULSE W/4-121.7/2.0L ENGINE & 1986–87 PICKUP TROOPER II W/4-138/2.2L ENGINE

Refer to **Fig. 14** for removal and installation of timing belt.

1. Disconnect battery ground cable.
2. Align crankshaft timing pulley and camshaft timing pulley, **Figs. 19 & 20.**
3. Remove tension spring.
4. Loosen bolt "B", then draw tension pulley toward water pump side, **Fig. 18.**
5. Remove timing belt.
6. Install tension spring, and temporarily tighten bolt "B", **Fig. 18.**
7. Install timing belt and loosen bolt "B" to allow tension spring to tighten belt. Ensure marks on gears are still properly aligned.
8. Temporarily tighten bolt "B", then turn crankshaft two revolutions in the opposite direction of normal rotation. Ensure that matchmarks are aligned.
9. Loosen bolt "B" and tighten belt with tension pulley, then torque bolt "B" to 14 ft. lbs.
10. Install timing belt cover and torque to 6 ft. lbs.

CAMSHAFT REPLACE

I-MARK EXC. FWD & 1983 PICKUP

Removal

1. Remove cam cover.
2. Rotate camshaft until No. 4 cylinder is in firing position. Remove distributor cap and mark rotor to housing position.
3. Lock timing chain adjuster by depressing and turning the automatic adjuster slide pin 90 degrees in the clockwise direction, **Fig. 2. After locking chain adjuster, ensure chain is free.**

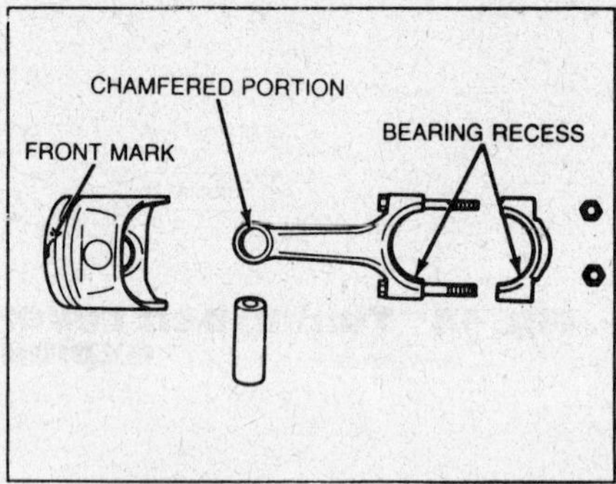

Fig. 22 Piston & connecting rod assembly

4. Remove timing sprocket to camshaft bolt, then sprocket from camshaft. Retain timing sprocket on chain damper and tensioner assembly without removing chain from sprocket.
5. Remove rocker arm, shaft and bracket assembly.
6. Remove camshaft assembly.

Installation

1. Lubricate camshaft and journals of cylinder head with engine oil.
2. Install camshaft assembly.
3. Install rocker arm, shaft and bracket assembly.
4. Align mark on No. 1 rocker arm shaft bracket with mark on camshaft. Ensure crankshaft pulley groove is aligned with TDC mark on front cover.
5. Assemble timing sprocket to camshaft by aligning sprocket with pin on camshaft. **Use caution not to remove chain from sprocket.**
6. Install sprocket retaining bolt and washer. Remove half-moon seal from front of head and torque bolt to 58 ft. lbs.
7. Set automatic adjuster by rotating adjuster slide pin 90 degrees counterclockwise with a screwdriver, **Fig. 2. When the automatic adjuster is set, ensure timing chain is properly tensioned.**
8. Check distributor rotor and mark on distributor housing that they are aligned with the No. 4 piston in the firing position. The timing mark on crankshaft pulley should also align with TDC mark on front cover.
9. Install distributor cap, adjust valves and install cam cover.

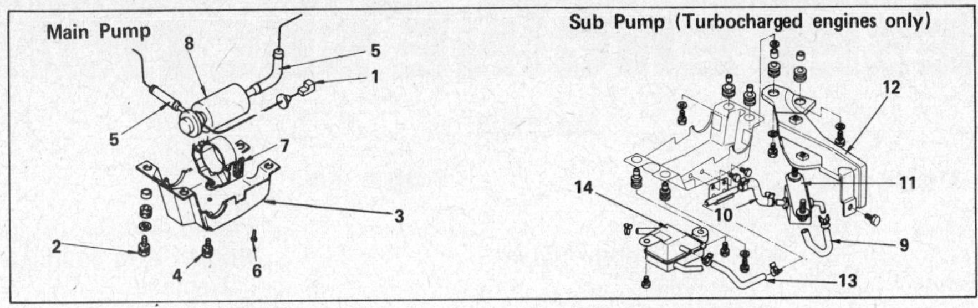

1. Electrical Connector
2. Guard Bolt
3. Guard Bracket
4. Guard Bolt
5. Fuel Hose
6. Bracket Screw
7. Fuel Pump Bracket
8. Fuel Pump
9. Sub Pump To Return Line Hose
10. Sub Pump To Vapor Separator Hose
11. Sub Pump Assembly
12. Sub Pump Assembly Bracket
13. Vapor To Sub Pump Hose
14. Vapor Separator

Fig. 23 Removal & installation of fuel pump

1985–87 I-MARK W/FWD

Refer to **Fig. 6** for removal and installation of camshaft.

1984–87 IMPULSE, PICKUP & 1984–85 TROOPER W/4-119

Refer to **Fig. 4** for removal and installation of camshaft.

1985–87 IMPULSE W/4-121.7 ENGINE & 1986 PICKUP & TROOPER II

Refer to **Fig. 21** for removal and installation of camshaft.

PISTON & RODS

Assemble piston to rod so the mark on the piston is facing toward front of engine, **Fig. 22**, and the face of the connecting rod with cylinder number mark is facing toward the starter side of the engine.

OIL PAN REPLACE

1. Remove engine as described under "Engine, Replace."
2. Remove oil pan attaching bolts, then oil pan.
3. Reverse procedure to install.

FUEL PUMP REPLACE

1983–85 I-MARK EXC. FWD, 1983–86 PICKUP W4-119 ENGINE & 1984–85 TROOPER II

1. Disconnect battery ground cable.
2. Remove distributor assembly.
3. Disconnect distributor cap wires.
4. Disconnect rubber hoses at fuel pump.
5. Remove engine hanger.
6. Remove fuel pump attaching bolt, then the fuel pump.
7. Reverse procedure to install.

1986–87 PICKUP & TROOPER II W/4-138 ENGINE

1. Remove air cleaner assembly.
2. Remove intake manifold as described under "Intake Manifold, Replace."
3. Remove fuel pump attaching nuts, then fuel pump.
4. Reverse procedure to install.

1985–87 I-MARK W/FWD

1. Disconnect fuel pump hoses.
2. Remove fuel pump, attaching nuts, then fuel pump, insulator and packing.
3. Reverse procedure to install.

1984–87 IMPULSE

Refer to **Fig. 23** for removal and installation of fuel pump.

WATER PUMP REPLACE

1983–85 I-MARK EXC. FWD, 1983 PICKUP

1. Disconnect battery ground cable.
2. Remove lower cover attaching bolts, then lower cover.
3. Drain cooling system.
4. On models less A/C, remove engine fan.
5. On models with A/C, proceed as follows:
   a. Remove air pump and alternator mounting bolts, then the fan and air pump drive belt.
   b. Remove engine fan and pulley assembly.
   c. Remove bolts attaching fan set plate and fan pulley.
6. On all models, remove water pump attaching bolts, then water pump.
7. Reverse procedure to install.

1984–87 IMPULSE, PICKUP & TROOPER II W/4-119 ENGINE

1. Disconnect battery ground cable.
2. Drain cooling system.
3. Remove cooling fan, then cooling fan belt.
4. Remove water pump pulley, then water pump and gasket.
5. Reverse procedure to install.

1985–87 IMPULSE W/4-121.7 & 1986–87 PICKUP & TROOPER II W/4-138 ENGINE

Refer to **Fig. 17** for removal and installation of water pump assembly.

1985–87 I-MARK W/FWD

Refer to **Fig. 7** for removal and installation of water pump assembly.

TURBOCHARGER

The turbocharger is an exhaust driven device which compresses the air charge being delivered to the engine through the intake system. The turbocharger increases engine power on a demand basis. Exhaust gases flow through a turbine which is connected through a shaft to the impeller wheel (compressor). During normal operation, the turbine does not rotate fast enough to boost air pressure. As turbine speed increases, the air is compressed allowing a denser mixture to enter the combustion chambers, in turn developing more engine power during the combustion process. Intake manifold pressure (boost pressure) is controlled by a wastegate valve which is used to bypass a portion of the exhaust gases around the turbine wheel at a predetermined point in the cycle, limiting boost pressure.

DIESEL ENGINE SECTION

INDEX

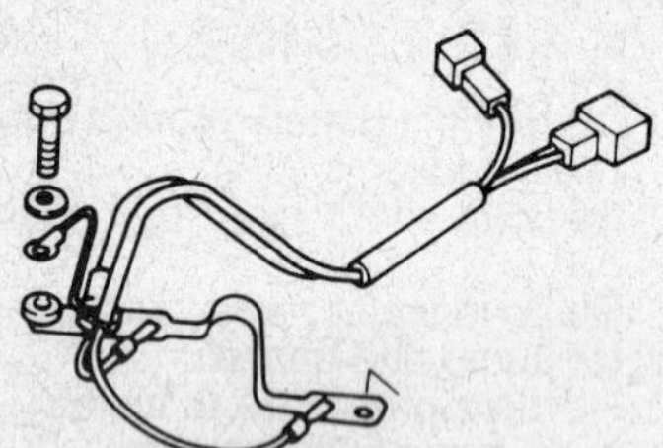

Fig. 1 Sensing resistor assembly

ENGINE REPLACE

I-MARK

1. Scribe a reference mark in the area of hinges and remove hood.
2. Remove battery cables, battery clamp and battery.
3. Remove under cover and drain coolant.
4. Disconnect radiator hoses, remove fan shroud and radiator.
5. Remove air connecting hose.
6. Disconnect heater hoses at thermostat housing and water inlet pipe.
7. Disconnect the Q.S.S.I. thermo switch, fast idle thermo switch, thermo unit wiring at the connector on the thermostat housing.
8. Disconnect alternator wiring and vacuum pump hose connections.
9. Remove vacuum hose from fast idle actuator.
10. Disconnect exhaust pipe from manifold and separate pipe from manifold, then remove nuts connecting exhaust front pipe to mounting bracket, separate pipe from bracket and remove front pipe.
11. Disconnect accelerator cable from injection pump lever.
12. Disconnect fuel cut solenoid valve switch at wire connector. Disconnect tachometer wire at connector.
13. Disconnect starter motor connections and oil pressure switch connections.
14. Disconnect fuel hoses at injection pump.
15. Disconnect sensing resistor wiring at connector.
16. Disconnect back-up light switch and top/third switch.
17. Remove clutch cable and return spring from transmission.
18. Remove speedometer cable from transmission.
19. Remove driveshaft.
20. Remove console, pry off gearshift dust boot. Remove gearshift.
21. Remove exhaust rear mounting bracket. Disconnect rear engine mount.
22. Using a suitable hoist, raise engine slightly.
23. Remove engine mount nuts and engine damper from the frame.
24. Remove engine and transmission as an assembly.
25. Reverse procedure to install.

EXC. I-MARK

4x2 Models

1. Disconnect battery ground cable.
2. Remove hood, battery and air cleaner assembly.
3. Drain cooling system by removing under cover and opening drain plugs on radiator and cylinder block.
4. Remove air cleaner assembly.
5. Disconnect upper radiator hose at engine, then remove fan and shroud and disconnect lower radiator hose at engine.
6. Remove radiator grille, then radiator.
7. Disconnect accelerator cable from injection pump.
8. If equipped with A/C, disconnect compressor control cable.
9. Disconnect fuel lines from injection pump, battery ground cable from engine, transmission wiring, vacuum hose from fast idle actuator, connector at fuel cut solenoid, sensing resistor connector, thermoswitch connector and A/C compressor connector.

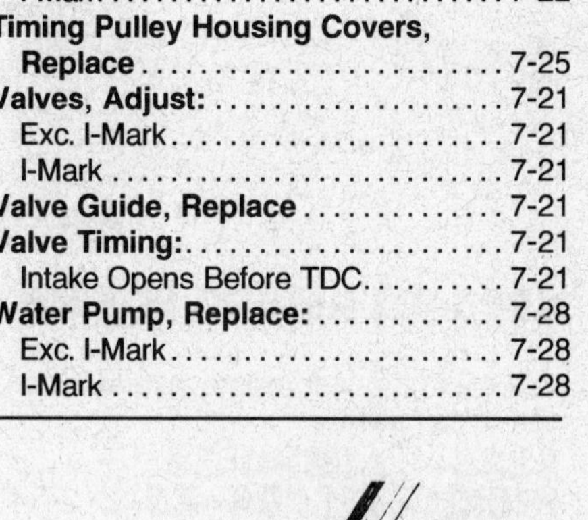

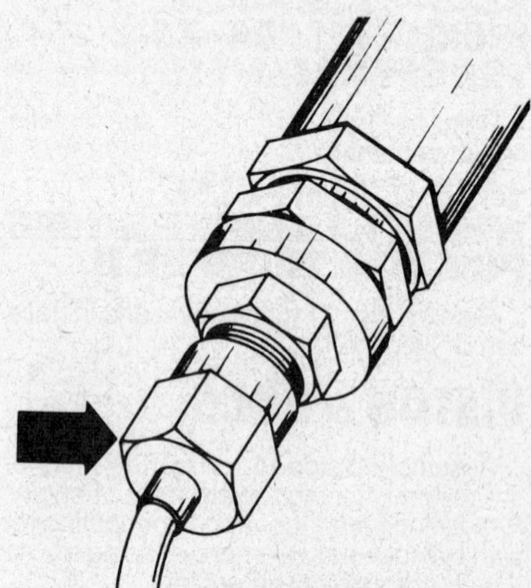

Fig. 2 Fuel injection pipe sleeve nut

10. Disconnect heater hoses at dash panel, power brake vacuum hose at pump and alternator wiring at connector.
11. Disconnect exhaust pipe from exhaust manifold, then remove exhaust pipe bracket from engine backing plate.
12. Disconnect wiring from starter motor.
13. Slide gear shift lever boot upwards, then remove retaining bolts and lever.
14. Disconnect speedometer cable and ground cable from transmission, then remove propeller shaft.
15. Remove return spring from clutch fork, then disconnect clutch cable from fork and pull it out through stiffener plate.
16. Remove the two brackets to transmission rear mount bolts and nuts.
17. Raise engine and transmission as necessary, then remove the 4 crossmember to frame bracket bolts.
18. Remove rear mounting nuts from transmission rear extension, then dis-

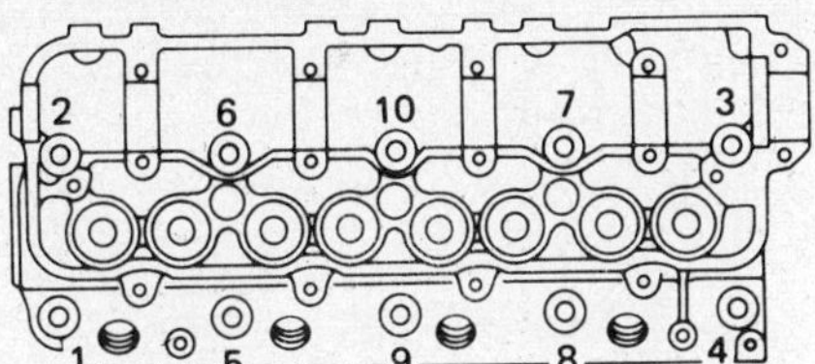

Fig. 3 Cylinder head loosening sequence

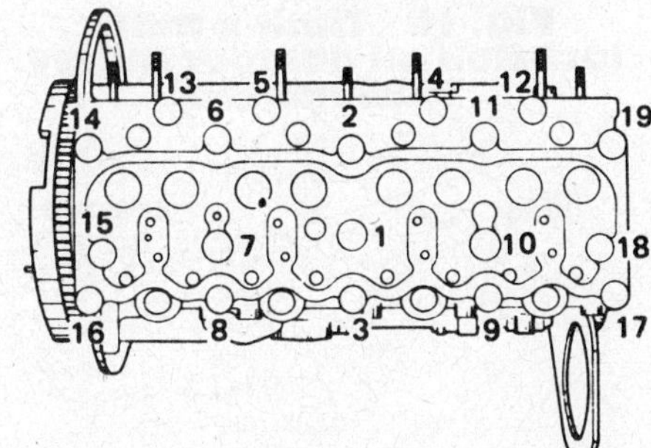

Fig. 6 Cylinder head bolt torque sequence

connect electrical connectors at CRS switch and back-up lamp switch.

19. Raise engine slightly, then remove engine mounting nuts and bolts.
20. Carefully remove engine using a suitable hoist.
21. Reverse procedure to install.

4x4 Models

1. Follow steps 1 through 11 under "42 Models."
2. Slide transmission and transfer case shift lever boot upwards, then remove shift lever bolts.
3. Remove return spring from transfer case gear shift lever, then levers.
4. Remove transmission. Refer to "Clutch & Manual Transmission Section" for procedure.
5. Raise engine slightly. Then remove engine mount bolts.
6. Carefully remove engine using a suitable hoist.
7. Reverse procedure to install.

CYLINDER HEAD

REPLACE

I-MARK

1. Drain coolant into a suitable container.
2. Remove camshaft. Refer to "Camshaft, Replace" for procedure.
3. Remove sensing resistor, **Fig. 1.**
4. Remove fuel injection clips and pipes, **Fig. 2.**
5. Remove fuel leak off hose clip, then remove hose.
6. Disconnect exhaust pipe from manifold.
7. Disconnect joint bolt attaching oil feed pipe to cylinder head.
8. Remove heater hose from thermostat housing.

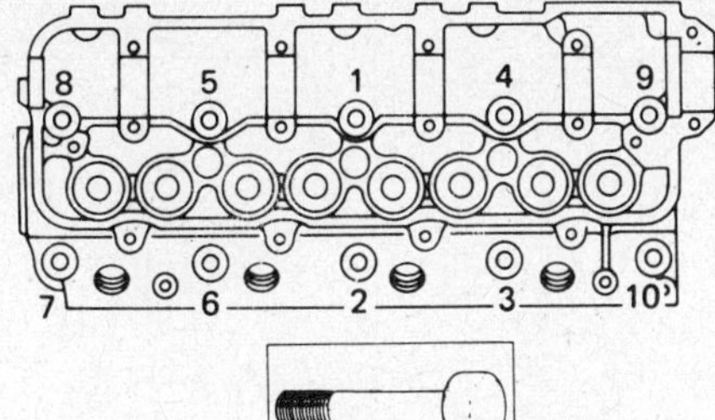

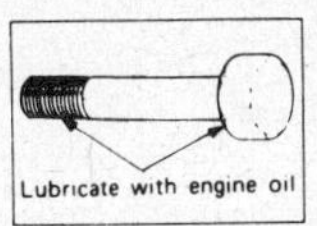

Fig. 4 Cylinder head tightening sequence

9. Remove ten cylinder head bolts in sequence shown in **Fig. 3.** Remove cylinder head and gasket.
10. Reverse procedure to install, tighten cylinder head bolts in sequence shown in **Fig. 4.**

EXC. I-MARK

1. Remove intake and exhaust manifolds.
2. Drain cooling system, then disconnect the upper radiator hose at engine.
3. Remove fan and shroud.
4. Remove sleeve nuts, then disconnect injection pipes.
5. Remove nozzle holder fixing nuts, then nozzle holder assembly.
6. Remove rocker arm assembly as outlined under "Rocker Arm Shaft Assembly, Replace."
7. Remove pushrods.
8. Remove joint bolt, then disconnect leak-off pipe.
9. Remove cylinder head attaching bolts in sequence shown in **Fig. 5**, then the cylinder head.
10. Reverse procedure to install. Torque bolts to an initial torque of 40-47 ft. lbs. (5.5-6.5 kg-m) in sequence shown in **Fig. 6.** Then torque bolts to a final torque of 54-61 ft. lbs. (7.5-8.5 kg-m) if new bolts are used, or 61-69 ft. lbs. (8.5-9.5 kg-m) if the original bolts are used.

VALVE TIMING

INTAKE OPENS BEFORE TDC

1983-85 110.8 engine, 32°.
1983-87 136.6 engine, 16°.

VALVES

ADJUST

I-MARK

1. Remove cam cover.
2. Inspect the rocker arm shaft bracket bolts for looseness, retorque as necessary.
3. Bring No. 1 cylinder to TDC on compression stroke.
4. Adjust valve clearances of cylinder No. 1, intake valve of No. 2 and exhaust valve of No. 3. Turn crankshaft one full revolution to bring cylinder No. 4 TDC on compression stroke. Adjust clearances of cylinder No. 4, exhaust valve of No. 2 and intake valve of No. 3.
5. Reinstall cam cover.

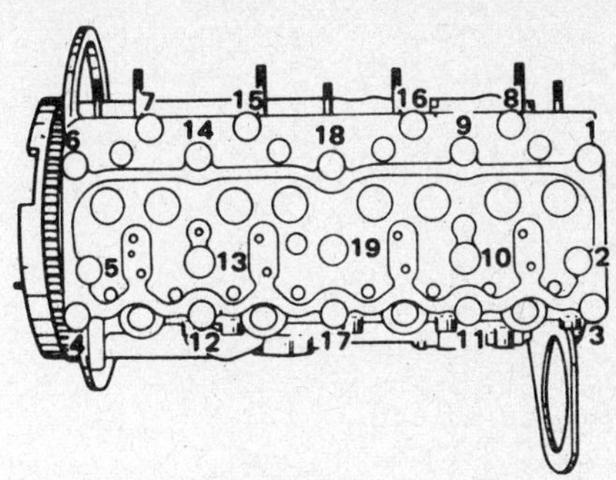

Fig. 5 Cylinder head bolt removal sequence

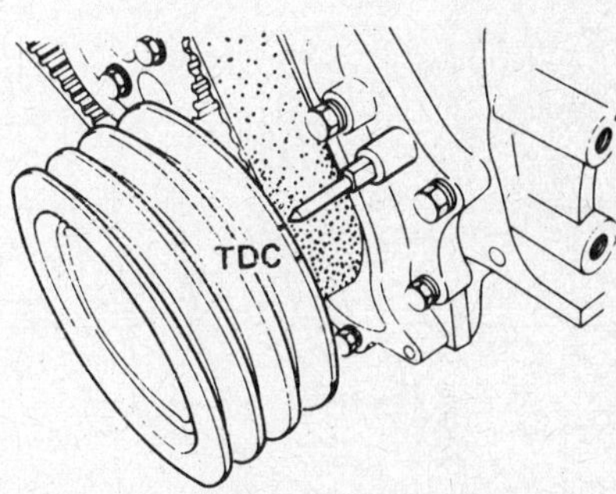

Fig. 7 TDC timing mark

EXC. I-MARK

1. Make sure that rocker arm shaft assembly bolts are torqued to specifications.
2. Bring No. 1 piston to top dead center compression stroke by turning crankshaft until timing mark on pulley aligns with pointer, **Fig. 7**
3. Adjust the intake valve of Nos. 1 and 2 cylinders and exhaust valve of Nos. 1 and 3 cylinders to specifications.
4. Rotate engine one complete revolution to bring No. 4 piston to top dead center compression stroke.
5. Adjust the intake valve of Nos. 3 and 4 cylinders and exhaust valve of Nos. 2 and 4 cylinders to specifications.

VALVE GUIDE

REPLACE

1. Using tool No. J-26512 drive out the valve guide from the lower face of the cylinder head.
2. Apply engine oil to outer circumference of valve guide, then using tool No. J-26512, drive the guide into position from the upper face of the cylinder head, **Fig. 8. Always replace valve guide land valve as a set.**

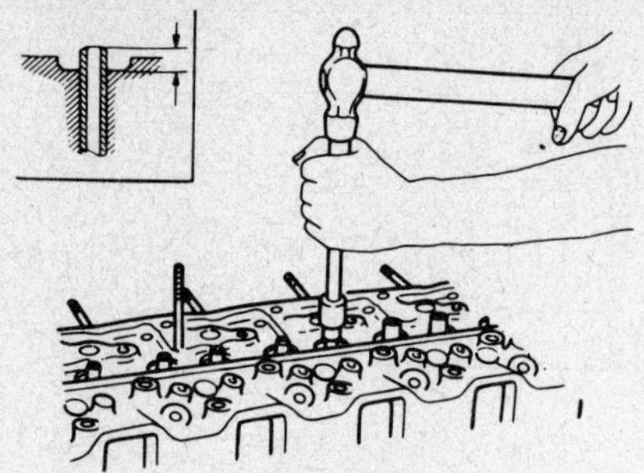

Fig. 8 Installing valve guides

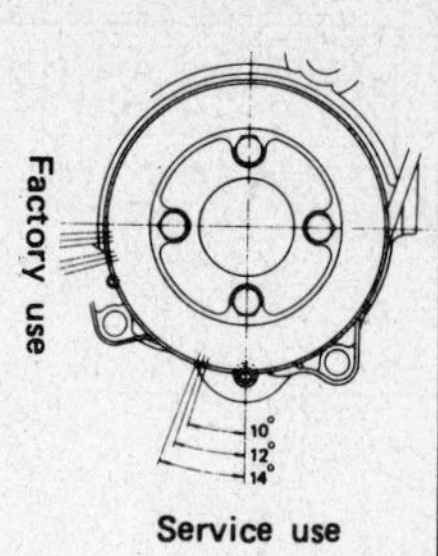

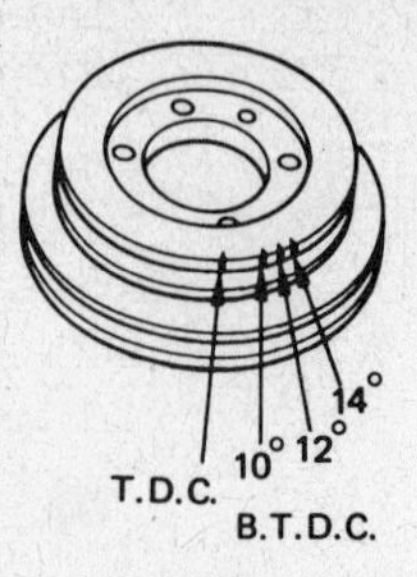

Fig. 9 Timing mark location on damper pulley. 1984 models

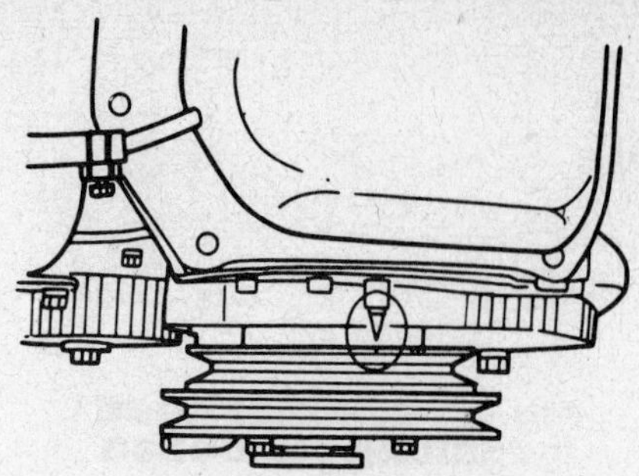

Fig. 10 Timing mark location on damper pulley. 1985 models

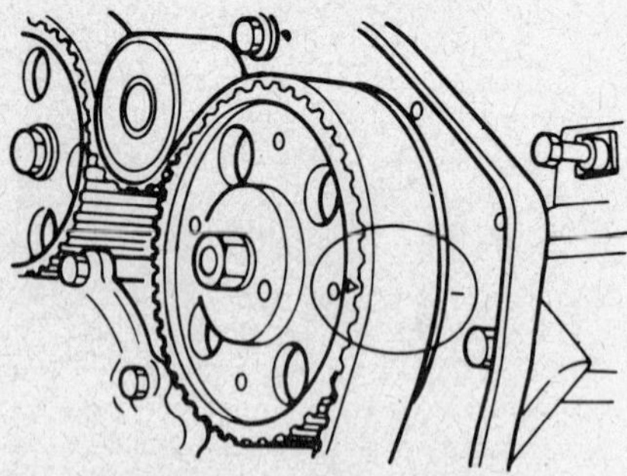

Fig. 11 Injection pump pulley installation

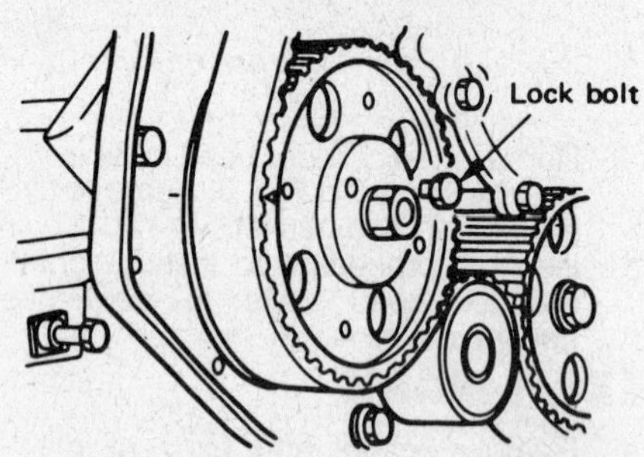

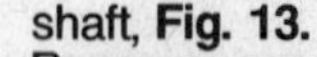

Fig. 12 Injection pump pulley installation

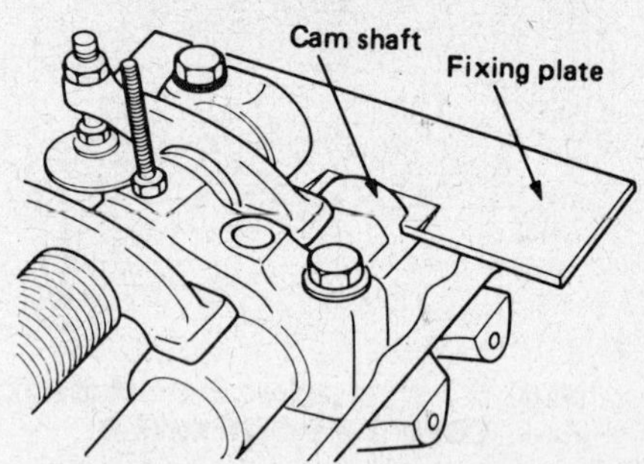

Fig. 13 Camshaft installation

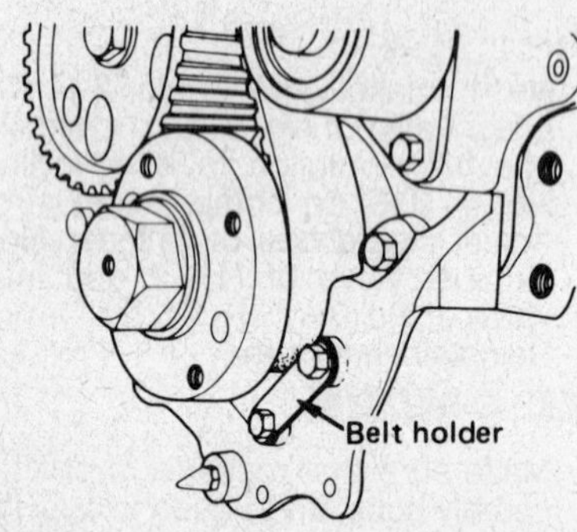

Fig. 14 Timing belt holder

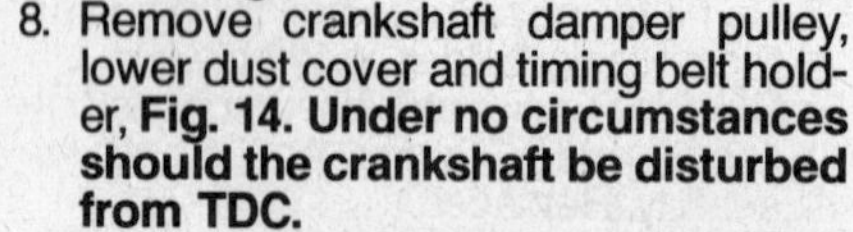

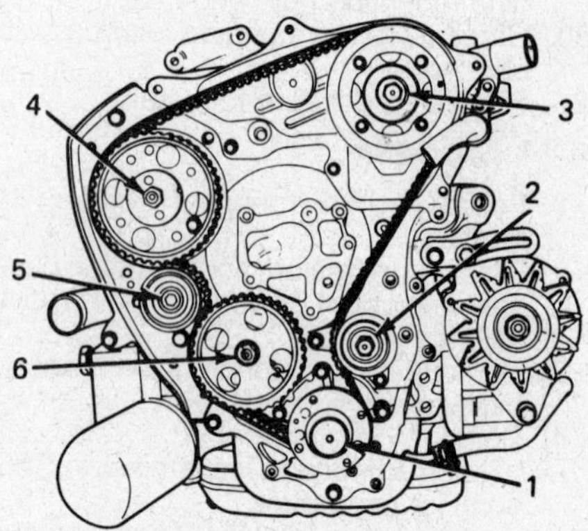

Fig. 15 Timing belt installation sequence

TIMING BELT

REPLACE

I-MARK

1. Disconnect battery ground cable.
2. Remove under cover and drain coolant.
3. Remove fan shroud, alternator belt, cooling fan and water pump pulley.
4. Remove ten bolts securing upper dust cover, remove dust cover.
5. Remove bypass hose.
6. Bring cylinder No. 1 to TDC, **Figs. 9 and 10,** ensure that setting mark on injection pump pulley is in alignment with front plate, then fix the pulley with 8 mm 1.25 pitch bolt, **Fig. 11 and 12.**
7. Remove cam cover and loosen valve adjustment screws so rocker arms are in a free state. Fix the camshaft by installing fixing plate, tool No. J-29761 into the slit in rear end of the camshaft, **Fig. 13.**
8. Remove crankshaft damper pulley, lower dust cover and timing belt holder, **Fig. 14. Under no circumstances should the crankshaft be disturbed from TDC.**
9. Remove tension pulley spring, then loosen tension pulley and plate bolts, remove timing belt.
10. Remove camshaft pulley bolt, using a suitable puller remove camshaft pulley, then reinstall pulley and bolt. Tighten bolt just enough to allow the pulley to be turned smoothly by hand.
11. Install new timing belt using sequence shown in **Fig. 15.** Ensure that belt cogs are properly installed in pulleys. Do not disturb crankshaft setting.
12. Concentrate belt looseness on tension pulley, depress tension pulley with finger and install tension spring. Semi-tighten bolts in numerical sequence 1 and 2 to prevent movement of tension pulley, **Fig. 16.**
13. Tighten camshaft pulley bolt.
14. Remove injection pump pulley lock bolt and camshaft fixing plate.
15. Install crankshaft damper pulley, ensure No. 1 cylinder is at TDC.
16. Ensure injection pump pulley mark is in alignment with mark on plate and fixing plate fits smoothly into the rear slit of the camshaft. Remove plate.
17. Loosen tensioner plate bolts and pulley. Concentrate looseness of belt on tensioner, then tighten the bolts in numerical sequence 1, 2 and 3, **Fig. 17.** Torque bolts 1 and 2, 11 to 18 ft. lbs. Bolt 3, 47 to 61 ft. lbs.
18. Using a belt tension gauge, check tension between camshaft pulley and injection pump pulley. Tension should be 47 to 64 lbs.
19. Remove crankshaft damper and install timing belt holder.
20. Adjust valves. Refer to "Valves, Adjust" for procedure.
21. Reverse steps 1 through 8 to reassemble.

EXC. I-MARK

1. Remove timing pulley housing cover. Refer to "Timing Pulley Housing Cover, Replace" for procedure.
2. Remove injection pump timing pulley flange bolts, then remove flange.
3. Remove tension spring, **Fig. 18.** Do not use excessive force.
4. Remove tension pulley nut, **Fig. 19** then remove tension pulley and tension center.

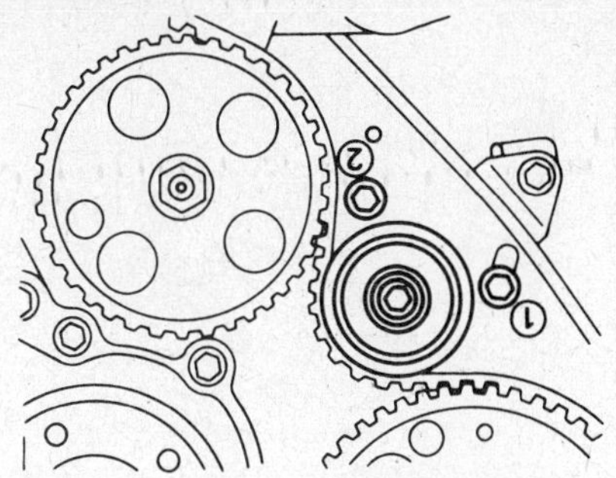

Fig. 16 Semi-tightening sequence of tension pulley

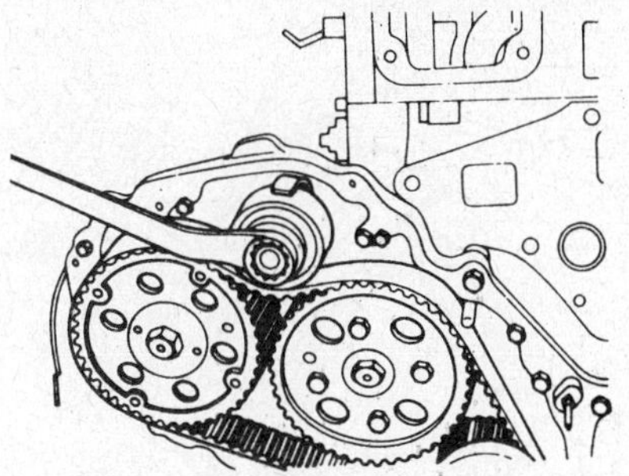

Fig. 19 Removing tension pulley nut

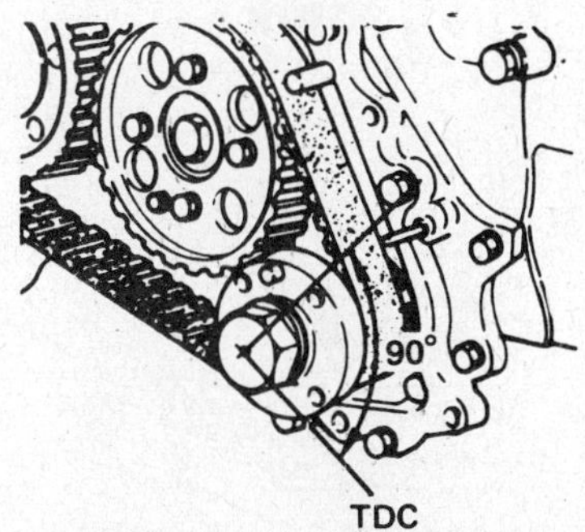

Fig. 22 Positioning crankshaft to set injection pump

5. Remove timing belt. Do not twist or kink belt or allow it to come in contact with water, dirt, oil or other foreign material. **Do not attempt to readjust a used belt which has become loose through service.**
6. Before installing belt, make sure that marks on crank pulley, injection pump timing pulley and cam shaft timing pulley are aligned as shown in **Fig. 20**. Install belt around the crankshaft pulley camshaft timing pulley and then the injection pump timing pulley. **Use care to avoid damaging belt during installation.**
7. Install tension center and tension pulley, making sure that end of tension center is properly contacting the two pins on timing housing, **Fig. 21**. Adjust tension pulley to remove slack from belt.
8. Hand tighten nut so that tension pulley is free to slide, then install tension

Fig. 17 Torquing tension pulley bolt sequence

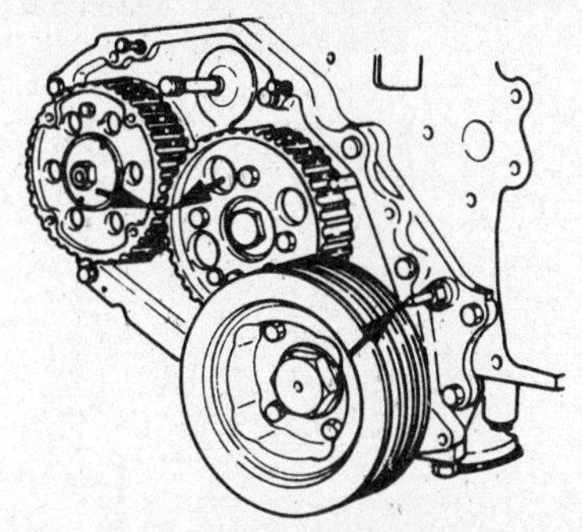

Fig. 20 Crankshaft pulley, injection pump pulley and camshaft pulley timing marks

spring, **Fig. 18**, and torque pulley nut to 22-36 ft. lbs. (3-5 kg-m).

9. Turn crankshaft 2 turns in normal direction of rotation to allow belt to seat then turn crankshaft an additional 1/4 turn beyond TDC to set the injection pump, **Fig. 22. Do not turn crankshaft in reverse direction of rotation.**
10. Completely loosen pulley nut to allow pulley to take up slack in belt, then torque nut to 78-95 ft. lbs. (10.8-13.2 kg-m).
11. Install flange on injection pump pulley. The hole in the outer circumference of flange should be aligned with triangular shaped timing mark on camshaft pulley, **Fig. 23.**
12. Turn crankshaft 2 turns in normal direction of rotation until No. 1 piston is at TDC compression stroke. Triangular shaped timing mark on camshaft timing pulley should be aligned with hole in flange, **Fig . 25.**
13. Using tension gauge J-26486 or equivalent, check timing belt tension between injection pump pulley and crankshaft pulley. Tension should be 33-55 lbs. (15-25 kg).
14. Adjust valves. Refer to "Valves, Adjust" for procedure.
15. Reverse removal procedure to install remaining parts.

INJECTION TIMING ADJUST

I-MARK

1. Check that alignment mark on injec-

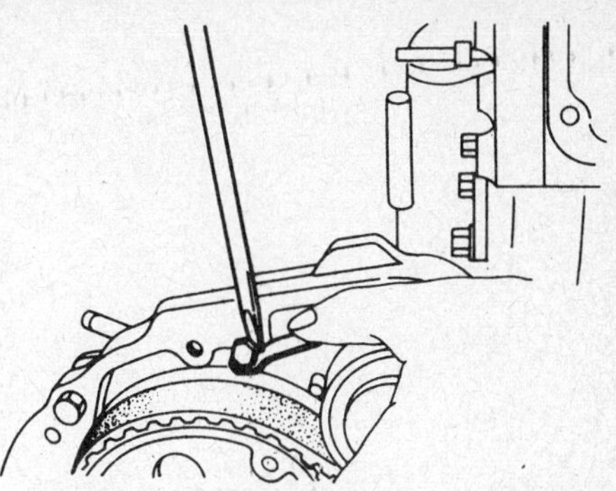

Fig. 18 Removing tension spring

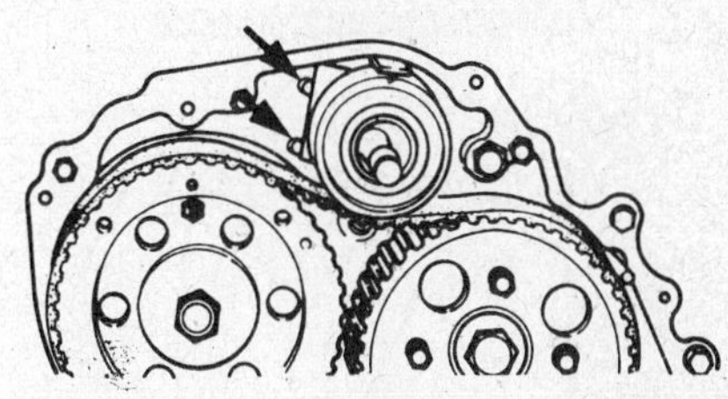

Fig. 21 Installing tension center and tension pulley

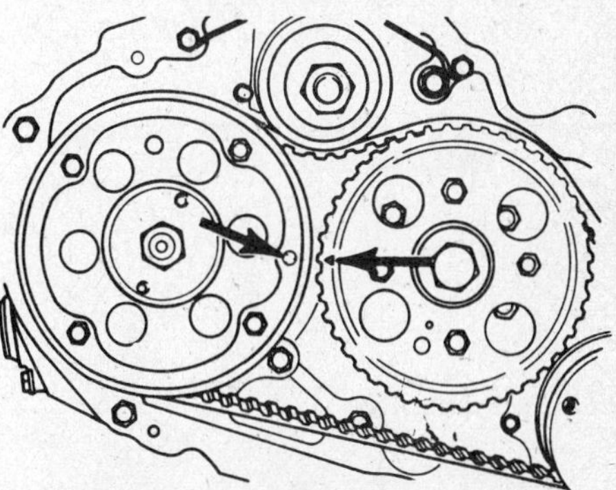

Fig. 23 Injection pump flange & camshaft timing pulley alignment marks

tion pump flange is aligned with alignment mark on front plate, **Fig. 24.**

2. Bring cylinder No. 1 to TDC on compression stroke by turning crankshaft until timing mark on pulley aligns with pointer. **The damper pulley has eleven notched lines as shown in Figs. 9 and 10. Four lines on one side, seven elsewhere. The four lines are intended for service use while the other seven are for factory use only.**
3. Remove upper dust cover, ensure the injection pump belt is properly tensioned and the timing marks are aligned. See "Timing Belt, Replace."
4. Remove the cam cover and rear plug, ensure that the fixing plate fits smoothly into the camshaft rear slit, then remove the fixing plate. See "Timing Belt, Replace."
5. Disconnect injection pipe from injection pump, then remove distributor head screw and gasket. Install static timing gauge J-28827 on 1983-85 models, **Fig. 25.** Set the gauge lift approximately .040 inch (1 mm) from the plunger.

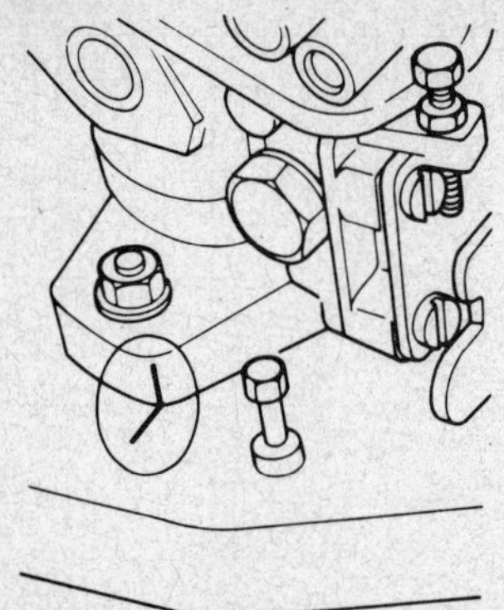

Fig. 24 Injection pump flange to front plate alignment mark

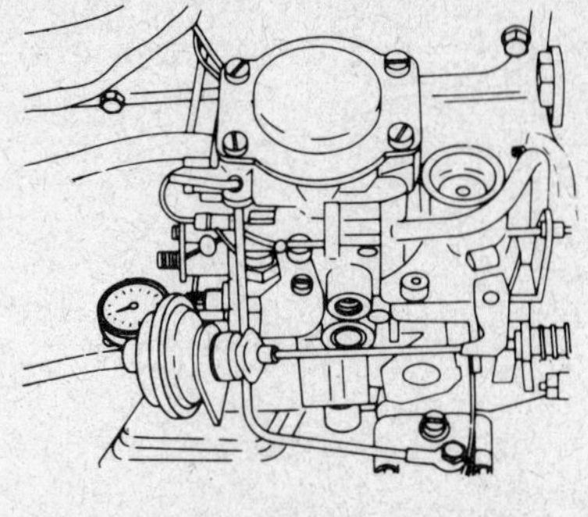

Fig. 25 Static timing gauge, J29763 or J-28827 installed

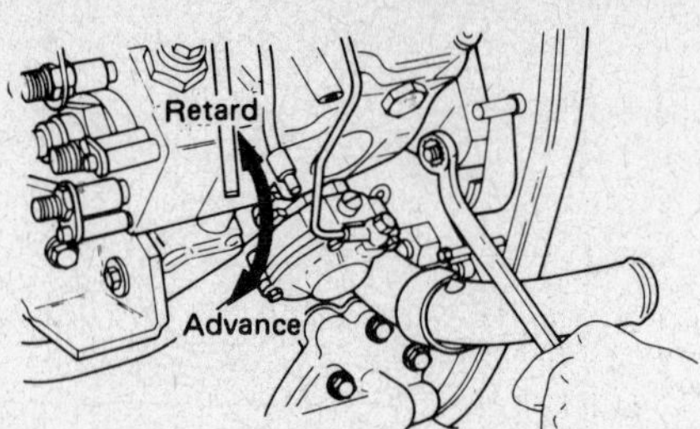

Fig. 26 Injection pump flange nuts

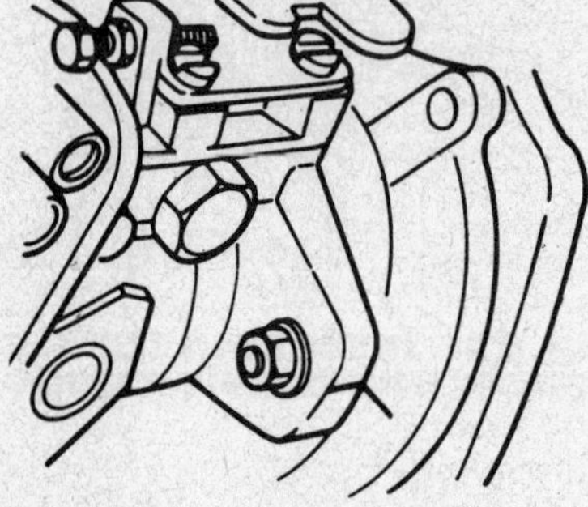

Fig. 27 Injection pump alignment marks

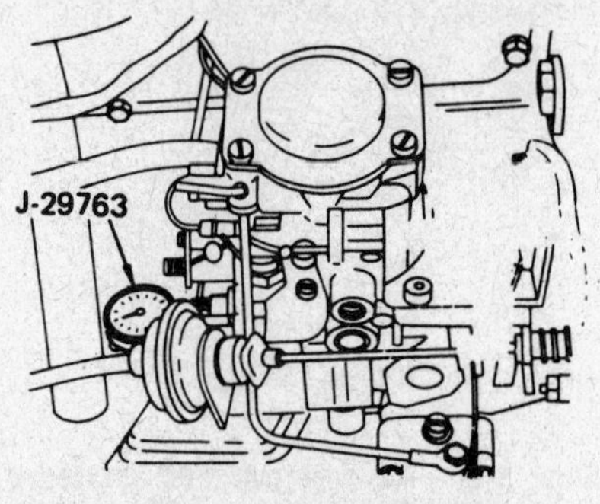

Fig. 28 Static timing gauge J-29763 installed on pump

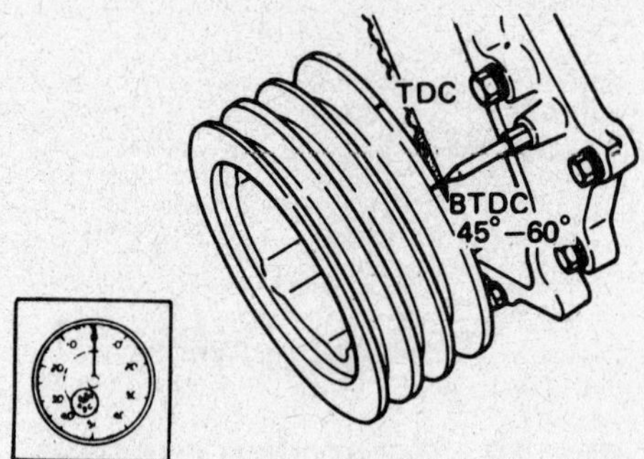

Fig. 29 45-60° BTDC timing mark

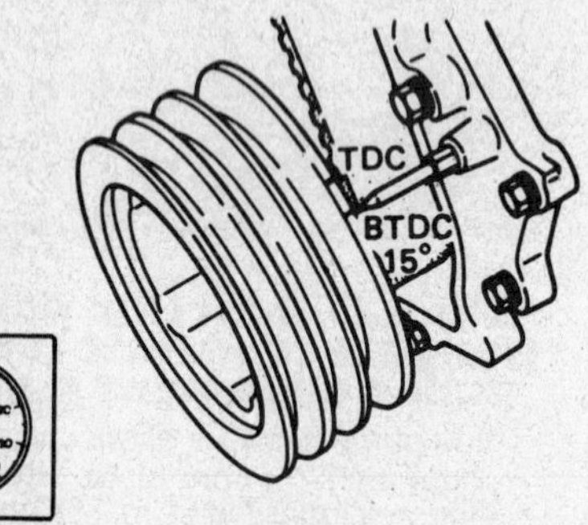

Fig. 30 15° BTDC timing mark

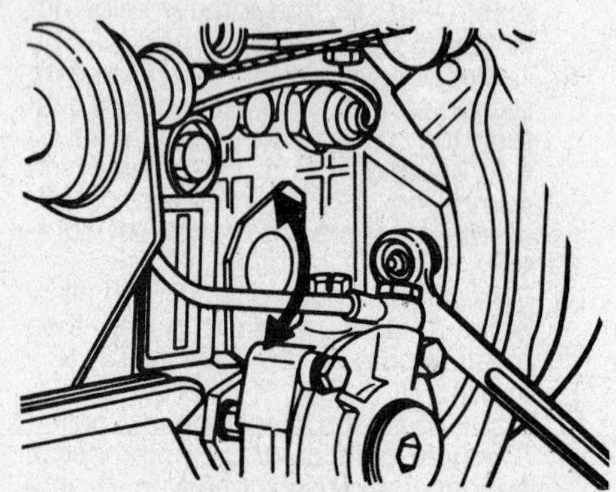

Fig. 31 Adjusting injection timing

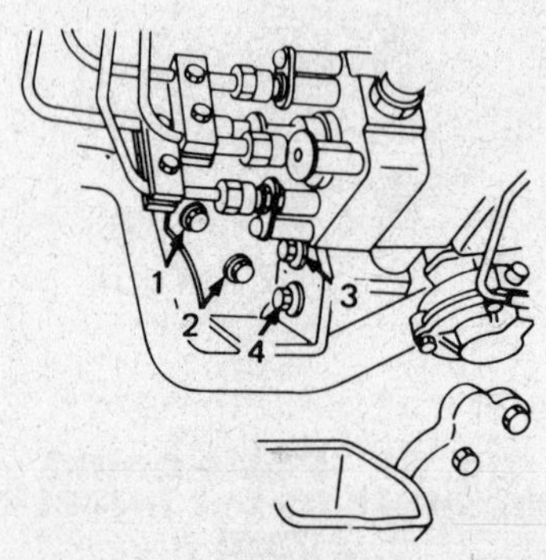

Fig. 32 Injection pump rear bracket tightening sequence

6. Bring No. 1 piston to a point 45-60 degrees BTDC by turning the crankshaft, set dial indicator to zero. Turn crankshaft slightly in both directions, ensuring gauge indication is stable.
7. Turn crankshaft in normal direction of rotation until the 18 degree mark on 1981 models or 12 degree mark on 1982-85 models on the damper is aligned with the timing pointer, **Figs. 10, 11 and 12.** Note reading on dial indicator. If reading is not .020 inch (.5 mm), hold crankshaft in position and loosen two nuts on injection pump flange, **Fig. 26.** Move pump until reading on dial indicator is .020 inch (.5 mm), then tighten nuts.

EXC. I-MARK

1. Check that alignment mark on injection pump flange is aligned with alignment mark on injection pump front bracket, **Fig. 27.**
2. Bring No. 1 cylinder to top dead center compression by turning crankshaft until timing mark on pulley aligns with pointer, **Fig. 7.**
3. Remove timing pulley housing and check that timing belt is properly tensioned, and that timing marks are aligned, **Fig. 23.**
4. Disconnect injection pipe from injection pump and remove distributor head screw. Install static timing gauge J-29763, **Fig. 28** then set lift to approximately .040 inch (1 mm) from plunger.
5. Bring No. 1 piston to 45-60° before top dead center by turning crankshaft, **Fig. 29**, then set dial indicator to zero. Turn crankshaft slightly in both directions and check that gauge indication is stable.
6. Turn crankshaft in normal direction of rotation and note reading on dial indicator when the 15° timing mark on pulley is aligned with pointer, **Fig. 30.** If dial indicator reading is not .020 inch (.5 mm), hold crankshaft at the 15° mark and loosen the two nuts on injection pump flange, **Fig. 31**. Move pump until reading on dial indicator is .020 inch (.5 mm), then tighten nuts.

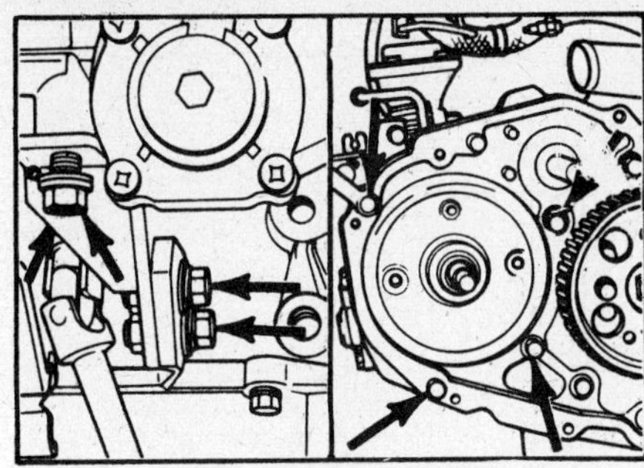
Fig. 33 Injection pump retaining bolts and nuts

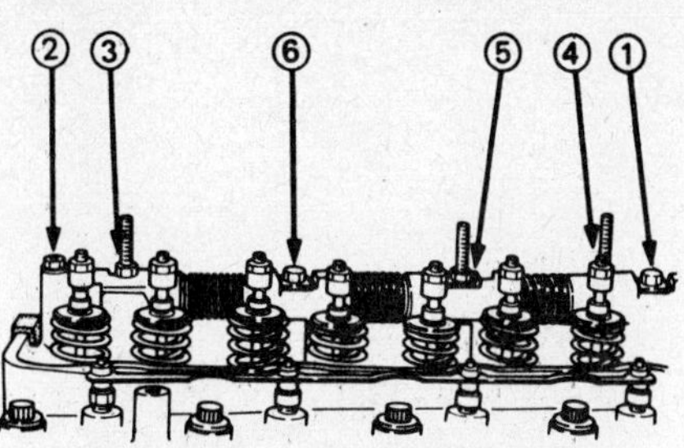

Fig. 34 Rocker arm bracket bolt loosening sequence. 4-110.8 engine

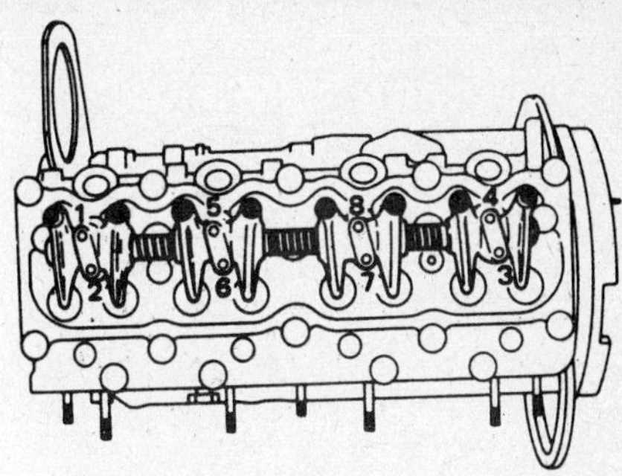
Fig. 35 Rocker arm shaft bolts removal sequence. 4-136.6

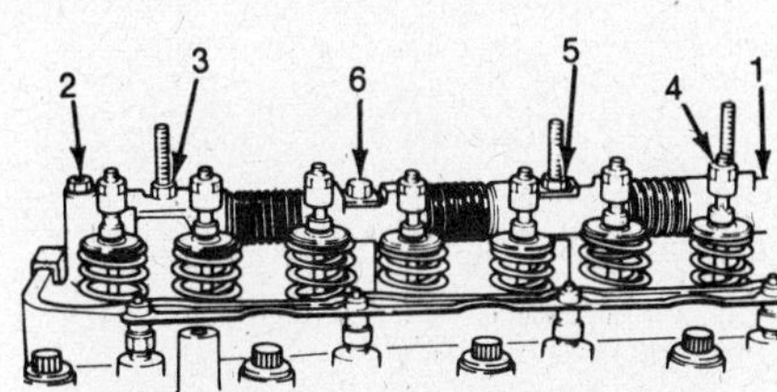

Fig. 36 Rocker arm bracket bolt tightening sequence. 4-110.8 engine

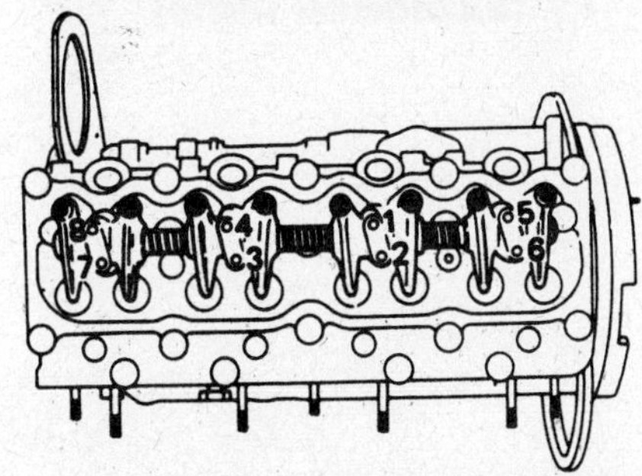
Fig. 37 Rocker arm shaft bolts installation sequence. 4-136.6 engine

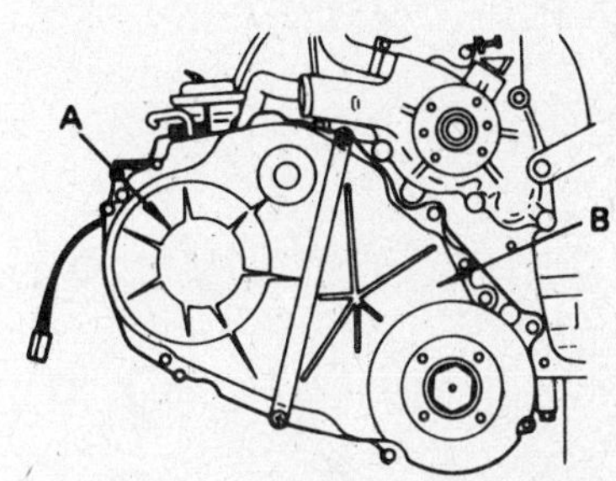

Fig. 38 Timing pulley housing covers

INJECTION PUMP
REPLACE
I-MARK

1. Remove timing belt. See "Timing Belt, Replace."
2. To prevent rotation of injection pump pulley during disassembly, thread a 8 mm 1.25 pitch bolt through the pulley into the housing, **Fig. 12.**
3. Remove injection pump pulley bolt.
4. Remove bolt installed in step two, then using a suitable puller remove injection pump pulley.
5. Disconnect fuel cut solenoid valve switch wiring and tachometer pickup sensor wiring at connector.
6. Disconnect accelerator cable from pump lever. If equipped with automatic transmission, remove throttle valve control cable.
7. Disconnect vacuum hose from fast idle actuator.
8. Disconnect fuel hoses from injection pump.
9. Remove six screws attaching injection pipe clips and remove.
10. Remove injection pipes.
11. Remove injection pump rear bracket, then control lever spring.
12. Remove attaching nuts and pump with fast idle device installed.
13. Install injection pump with fast idle device installed by aligning notched line on pump flange with the line on the front plate, **Fig. 24.**
14. Install rear bracket bolts following sequence in **Fig. 32.**
15. Install the injection pump pulley by aligning it with key groove, torque nut to 43 to 50 ft. lbs. Hold pulley from rotating by installing a bolt as described in step 2.
16. Refer to "Timing Belt, Replace" for reassembly procedures.

EXC. I-MARK

1. Remove battery and under cover.
2. Drain cooling system and disconnect upper radiator hose at engine.
3. Remove cooling fan and shroud and disconnect lower radiator hose at engine.
4. Remove air conditioner compressor, if used.
5. Remove fan belt and crankshaft pulley.
6. Remove timing pulley housing covers. Refer to "Timing Pulley Housing Covers, Replace" for procedure.
7. Remove tension spring, **Fig. 18**, tension pulley nut, **Fig. 19**, tension center, pulley and timing belt.
8. Disconnect engine control cable and wiring harness from fuel cut-off solenoid.
9. Disconnect fuel hoses and injection pipes. Use a back-up wrench to hold delivery holder when loosening sleeve nuts on injection pump side.
10. Install a 6 mm bolt with a pitch of 1.25 into threaded hole in timing pulley to prevent pulley from turning, then remove bolts retaining injection pump timing pulley and remove pulley using suitable puller.
11. Remove injection pump flange retaining nuts and rear bracket bolts, **Fig. 33**, then remove injection pump.
12. Install injection pump with marks on flange and front bracket aligned, **Fig. 27.**
13. Install injection pump timing pulley and torque bolt to 42-52 ft. lbs. (5.8-7.2 kg-m).
14. Rotate crankshaft until No. 1 piston is at TDC compression stroke, **Fig. 7,** and marks on timing pulley are aligned, **Fig. 20.**
15. Install timing belt. Refer to "Timing Belt, Replace" for procedure.
16. Check injection timing. Refer to "Injection Timing, Adjust" for procedure.

ROCKER ARM SHAFT ASSEMBLY
REPLACE

1. Remove cam cover.
2. Using sequence shown in **Fig. 34 and 35,** remove rocker arm shaft bracket bolts and nuts, then remove rocker arm shaft and rocker arm assembly.
3. Prior to installation, apply a generous amount of engine oil to the rocker arm shaft, rocker arms and valve stem end caps.
4. Install rocker arm shaft assembly and tighten bolts in sequence as shown in **Fig. 36 and 37.**
5. Adjust valves. Refer to "Valves, Adjust" for procedure.

TIMING PULLEY HOUSING COVERS
REPLACE

1. Remove radiator, drive belts, fan and crankshaft pulley.
2. Remove cover retaining bolts and covers, **Fig. 38.**
3. Reverse procedure to install.

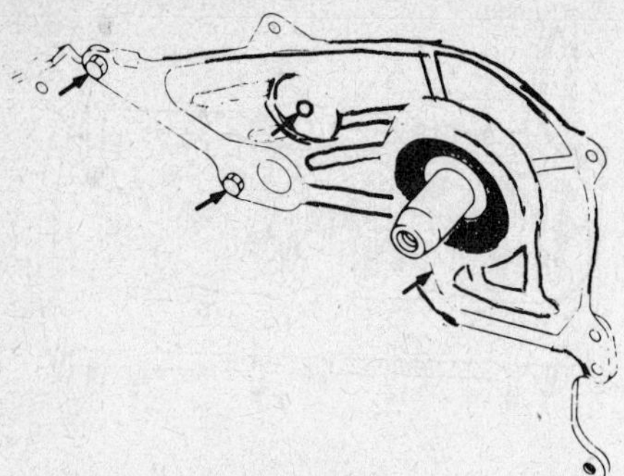

Fig. 39 Removing front head plate

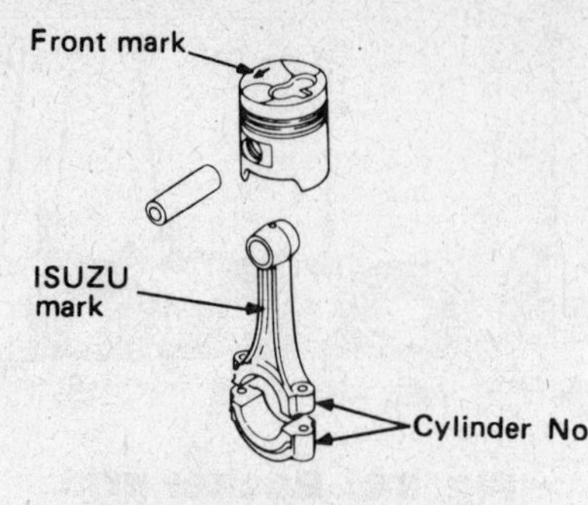

Fig. 40 Piston & connecting rod assembly (Exploded view)

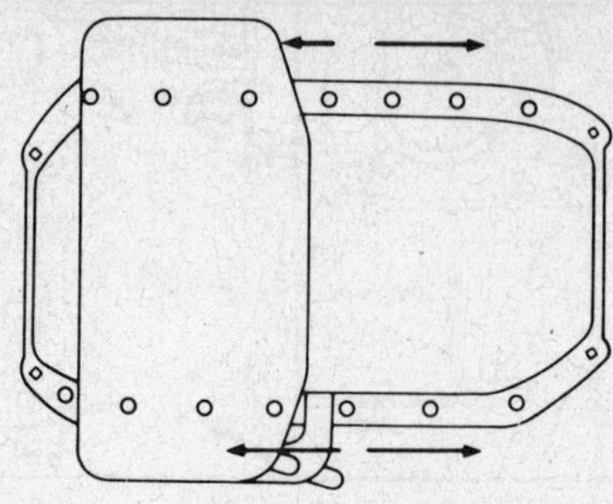

Fig. 41 Oil pan tightening sequence

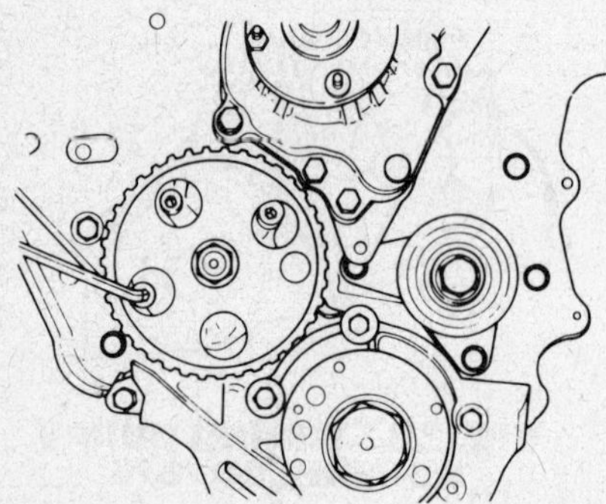

Fig. 42 Removing oil pump

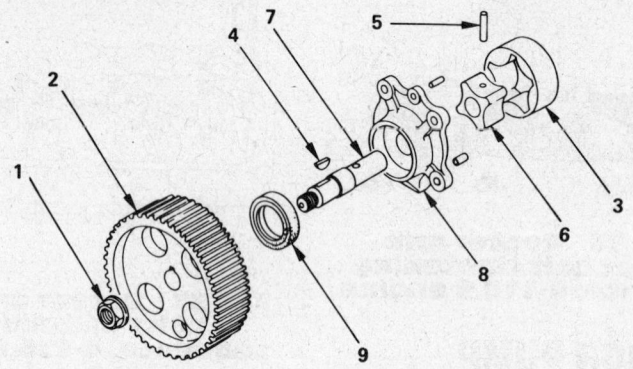

1. Nut
2. Oil pump pulley
3. Vane
4. Key
5. Pin
6. Rotor
7. Shaft
8. Housing
9. Oil seal

Fig. 43 Oil pump, disassembled

CAMSHAFT

REPLACE

I-MARK

1. Remove cam cover.
2. Remove timing belt as described in "Timing Belt, Replace."
3. Remove camshaft gear as described in "Timing Belt, Replace."
4. Remove rocker arm shaft assembly as described in "Rocker Arm Shaft Assembly, Replace."
5. Remove bolts attaching front head plate and remove, **Fig. 39.**
6. Remove the camshaft bearing cap bolts, then remove bearing caps with cap side bearing.
7. Remove camshaft oil seal followed by the camshaft.
8. Install camshaft oil seal, camshaft, and rocker arm shaft assembly. Torque camshaft bearing cap bolts to 15-22 ft. lbs. Begin at center bolt and work outward, alternating sides. Loosen rocker arm adjustment screws so that rocker arms are free of contact with valve train. Reverse procedure from step five to reinstall.

CRANKSHAFT FRONT OIL SEAL

REPLACE

I-MARK

1. Remove timing belt. Refer to "Timing Belt, Replace."
2. Remove crankshaft hub center bolt and washer.
3. Using a suitable puller, remove hub from crankshaft.
4. Using suitable puller, remove crankshaft timing belt pulley.
5. Pry out front oil seal using a suitable size screwdriver.
6. Apply clean engine oil to inner and outer surfaces of new seal, using a suitable seal installer, install the oil seal.
7. Position crankshaft timing belt pulley flange into seal, align pulley groove with crankshaft key. Drive pulley onto crankshaft using suitable driver.
8. Align crankshaft hub keyway with crankshaft key, install center bolt. Torque to 98 to 119 ft. lbs.
9. Reinstall timing belt. Refer to "Timing Belt, Replace."

EXC. I-MARK

1. Remove timing belt as outlined under "Timing Belt, Replace".
2. Install a 6 mm bolt with a pitch of 1.25 into threaded hole in timing pulley housing, through hole in pulley, to prevent turning of pulley. Remove camshaft timing pulley using a suitable puller.
3. Remove oil seal retaining bolts, then retainer.
4. Remove oil seal from retainer.
5. Remove crankshaft pulley bolt, then crankshaft center and timing pulley using a suitable puller.
6. Remove front oil seal dust cover, then oil seal.
7. Coat lipped portion of seal with oil, then install seal using tool J-24250 or equivalent.
8. Reverse procedure to install noting the following:
   a. Using tool J-24254 or equivalent, install camshaft oil seal into retainer.
   b. Install oil seal retainer and cam center with camshaft timing pulley. Torque bolts to 72-87 ft. lbs. (10-12 kg-m).

CRANKSHAFT REAR OIL SEAL

REPLACE

1. Remove the clutch pressure plate assembly.
2. Remove the six flywheel attaching bolts, then the flywheel.
3. Using a suitable screwdriver, pry out the rear seal.
4. Apply clean engine oil to all sides of

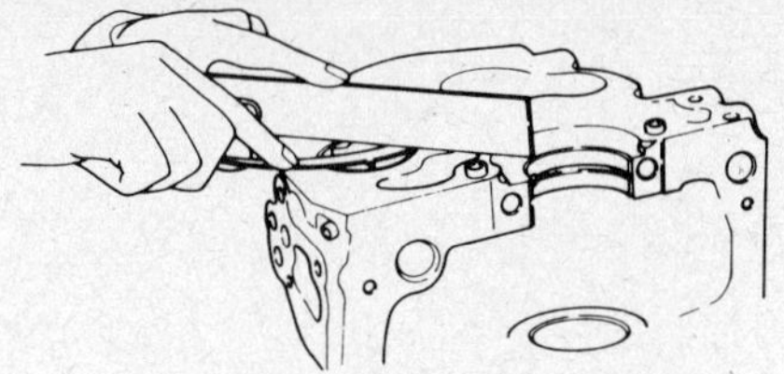

Fig. 44 Measuring vane and cylinder clearance in direction of thrust

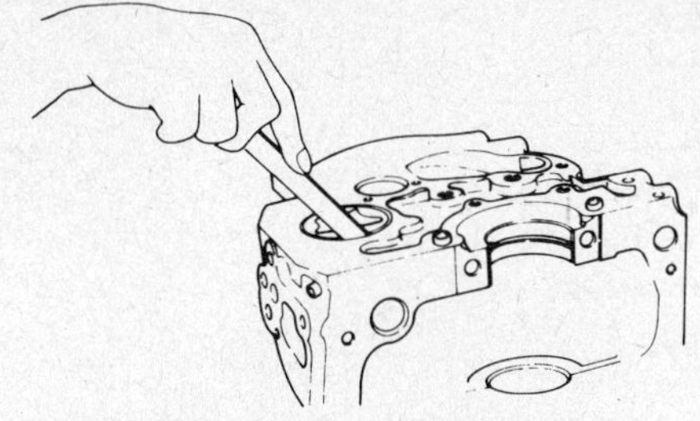

Fig. 45 Measuring vane and cylinder body clearance

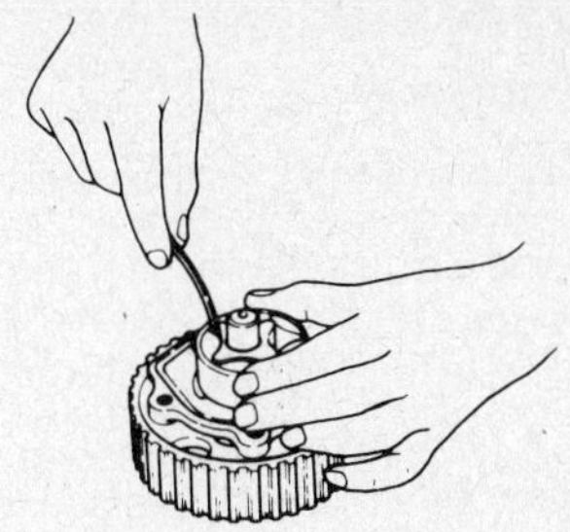

Fig. 46 Measuring vane and rotor clearance

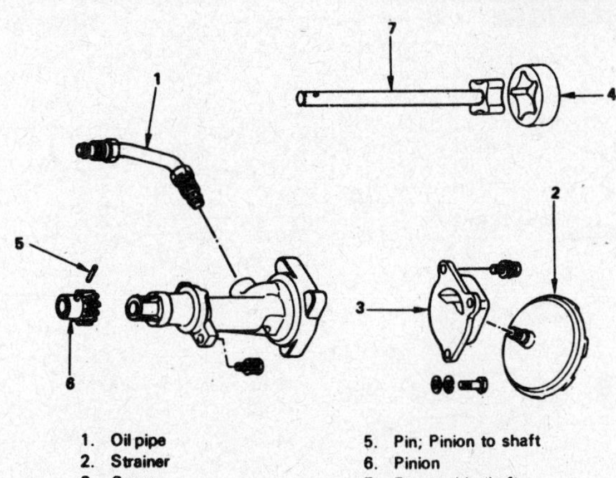

Fig. 47 Oil pump assembly (Exploded view). 4x2 models

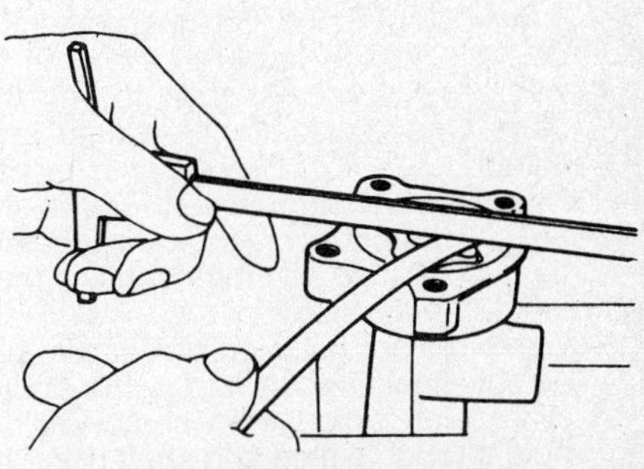

Fig. 48 Checking vane and rotor to cover clearance. 4x2 models

new seal.

5. Install the oil seal in the oil seal retainer using tool No. J-29818.
6. Position flywheel on crankshaft hub. Using new bolts, apply Loctite to threads and install flywheel. On models equipped with 4-110.8 engine, torque bolts to 36-43 ft. lbs. On models equipped with 4-136.6, torque bolts to 65-72 ft. lbs.
7. Reverse procedure to install remaining parts.

PISTON AND CONNECTING ROD

Install piston on connecting rod so that the combustion chamber on piston head is on the same side with the cylinder mark side (side with bearing stopper) of the connecting rod big end. The front of the piston should be on the same side as the "Isuzu" mark on the connecting rod, **Fig. 40.**

OIL PAN

REPLACE

I-MARK

1. Remove engine assembly. Refer to "Engine, Replace" for procedure.
2. Remove fourteen bolts and four nuts attaching oil pan and remove.
3. Discard old gasket, clean mounting surfaces. Install new gasket using a suitable sealing compound on oil pan, and install.
4. Following tightening sequence shown in **Fig. 41**, torque bolts 4 to 6 ft. lbs.

OIL PAN & CRANKCASE

REPLACE

EXC. I-MARK

1. Remove engine as outlined under "Engine, Replace."
2. Remove oil pan to crankcase attaching bolts, then oil pan. To remove crankcase, remove crankcase to engine attaching bolts.
3. Reverse procedure to install.

OIL PUMP

REPLACE

I-MARK

1. Remove timing belt. Refer to "Timing Belt, Replace."
2. Remove four Allen bolts securing oil pump, remove oil pump and pulley as an assembly, **Fig. 42.**
3. Refer to "Oil Pump, Inspection & Service."
4. Prior to installation apply a generous amount of clean engine oil to vane, install with taper side towards the cylinder body.
5. Install new pump O-ring, lubricate with motor oil and install in the housing groove. Lubricate oil pump rotor and install pump body together with pulley.
6. Reverse procedure to install. Torque mounting bolts to 11-18 ft. lbs.

EXC. I-MARK

1. Remove engine as outlined under "Engine, Replace".
2. Remove crankcase as outlined under "Oil Pan & Crankcase, Replace."
3. Remove the oil pipe sleeve nut and the two oil pump attaching bolts, then oil pump.
4. Refer to "Oil Pump, Inspection & Service."
5. Reverse procedure to install.

OIL PUMP INSPECTION & SERVICE

I-MARK

1. Disassemble pump as shown in **Fig. 43.**
2. Inspect all parts for any signs of abnormal wear or damage.
3. Measure outside diameter of pulley flange. Diameter should be 1.1-1.1035 inch (27.94-28.03 mm).
4. Using a straightedge and feeler gauge, check clearance between vane and cylinder body in direction of thrust, **Fig. 44.** Clearance should be .0011-.0027 inch (.03-.07 mm).
5. Check clearance between vane and cylinder body, **Fig. 45.** Clearance should be .0094-0141 inch (.24-.36 mm).
6. Check clearance between vane and rotor, **Fig. 46.** Clearance should be .0051-.0059 (.13-.15 mm).
7. Reassemble as shown in **Fig. 43.**

EXC. I-MARK

4x2 Models

1. Remove oil strainer, then remove cover bolts and cover, **Fig. 47.**
2. Using a straightedge and feeler gauge, check clearance between vane, rotor and cover, **Fig. 48.** Clearance should be .0008-.0028 inch (.02-07 mm). If clearance is greater than .0059 (.15 mm), replace the rotor, vane, shaft and pin.
3. Check clearance between rotor and vane, **Fig. 49**. Clearance should be no greater than .0055 inch (.14 mm). If it is, replace rotor, vane, shaft and pin.
4. Check clearance between vane and pump body, **Fig. 50.** Clearance should be .0079-.0106 inch (.2-.27 mm). If clearance is greater than the maximum limit, replace entire pump assembly.
5. Check clearance between rotor shaft and pump body. If clearance is greater than .0079 inch (.04 mm), replace entire pump assembly.
6. When replacing pinion and shaft assembly, install shaft into pump body and install pinion onto shaft. Drill a hole through pinion and shaft using a 5 mm drill. Install pin and secure.
7. Reverse procedure to assemble pump.

4x4 Models

1. Remove oil strainer, cover bolts and cover, **Fig. 51.**
2. Check clearance between pump body inner wall and gear tip, **Fig. 52**. clearance should be .0049-.0055 inch (.125 mm). If clearance exceeds the maximum limit, replace drive gear, shaft pin.
3. Check clearance between pump body and end of gear, **Fig. 53.** Clearance should be .0016-.0037 inch (.04-094 mm). If clearance exceeds the maximum limit, replace pump assembly.
4. Reverse procedure to assemble pump.

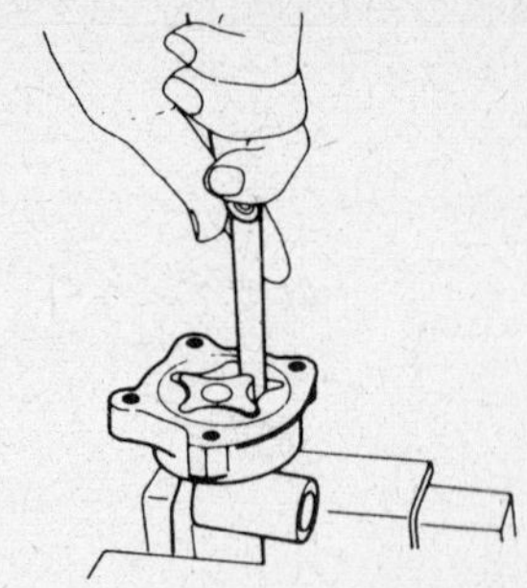

Fig. 49 Checking vane to rotor clearance. 4x2 models

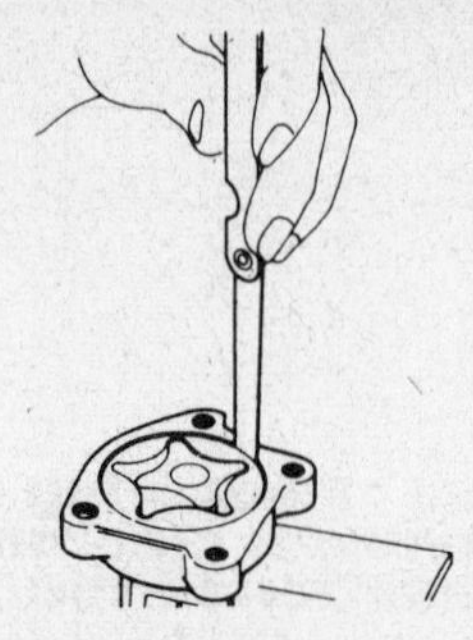

Fig. 50 Checking vane to pump body clearance. 4x2 models

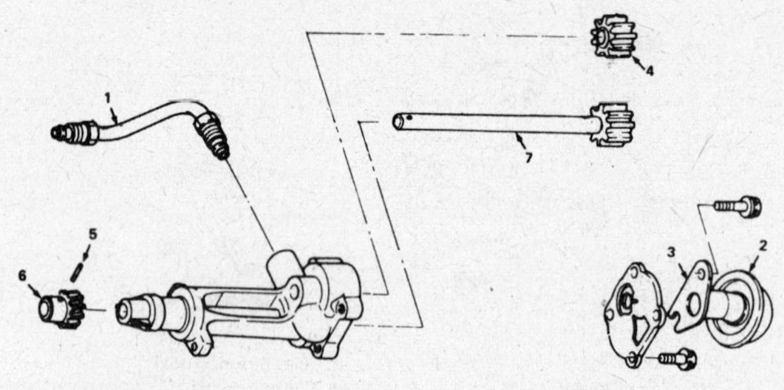

1. Oil pipe
2. Strainer
3. Cover
4. Driven gear
5. Pin; Pinion to shaft
6. Pinion
7. Drive gear with shaft

Fig. 51 Oil assembly (Exploded view). 4x4 models

OIL COOLER

REPLACE

I-MARK

1. Disconnect battery ground cable.
2. Remove oil cooler drain plug, allow cooler to drain.
3. Remove rubber hoses.
4. Remove two joint bolts securing cooler, **Fig. 54.** Remove cooler.
5. Install new joint bolt gaskets and install cooler.
6. Reverse steps 1 to 3 to install. Torque joint bolts to 33 ft. lbs.

EXC. I-MARK

1. Place a pan under oil filter to catch any oil and water that may flow out of filter.
2. Drain cooling system.
3. Remove oil cooler water drain plug and allow coolant to drain.
4. Disconnect oil cooler hoses at cooler side.
5. Remove oil filter.
6. Remove nut retaining oil cooler assembly, then remove oil cooler.
7. Reverse procedure to install. Use a new O-ring and torque nut to 54-61 ft. lbs. (7.5-8.5 kg-m).

WATER PUMP

REPLACE

I-MARK

1. Disconnect battery ground cable.
2. Drain cooling system.
3. Remove four nuts securing cooling fan and pulley assembly and remove. Remove nut belt.
4. Remove crankshaft damper pulley.
5. Remove front engine dust covers.
6. Remove bypass hose.
7. Remove five water pump attaching bolts and remove pump.
8. Reverse procedure to install. Torque mounting bolts to 11-18 ft. lbs.

EXC. I-MARK

1. Remove radiator and crankshaft pulley.
2. Remove fan pulley.
3. Remove water pump attaching bolts, then water pump.
4. Reverse procedure to install.

DIESEL FUEL INJECTION

DESCRIPTION

The diesel powered I-Mark and Pickup vehicles utilize four stroke cycle diesel engines using belt driven Bosch VE type injection pumps turning at camshaft speed to detect and inject the proper amount of fuel at the proper time, **Fig. 55**. The pumps major components are the feed pump, cam disc and plunger, control sleeve, delivery nozzles and injectors, governor, aneroid compensator, automatic timer, cold start device, fuel cut solenoid and the lubrication system, **Fig. 56.**

Feed Pump

The fuel in the fuel tank is drawn in and delivered through a water separator to the injection pump by means of the feed pump built into the injection pump. The feed pump is a rotary vane type consisting of four vanes driven by the injection pump driveshaft. The pressurized fuel is then delivered into the injection pump housing. Any excess volume of fuel is returned to the feed pump by an internal regulating valve.

Cam Disc And Plunger

The cam disc and plunger is attached to

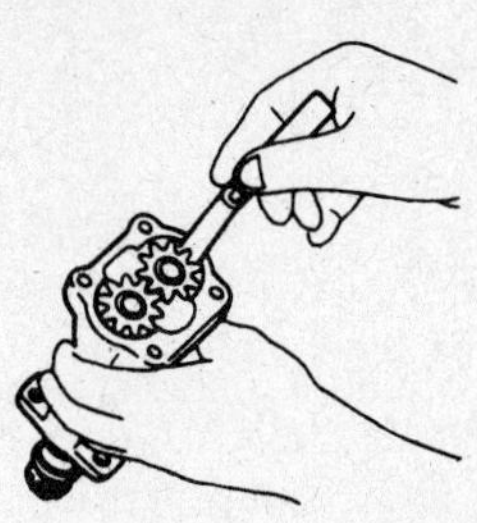

Fig. 52 Checking clearance between gear tip & pump body. 4x4 models

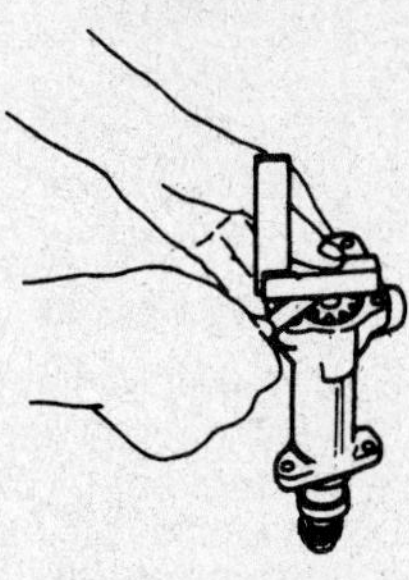

Fig. 53 Checking gears to cover clearance. 4x4 models

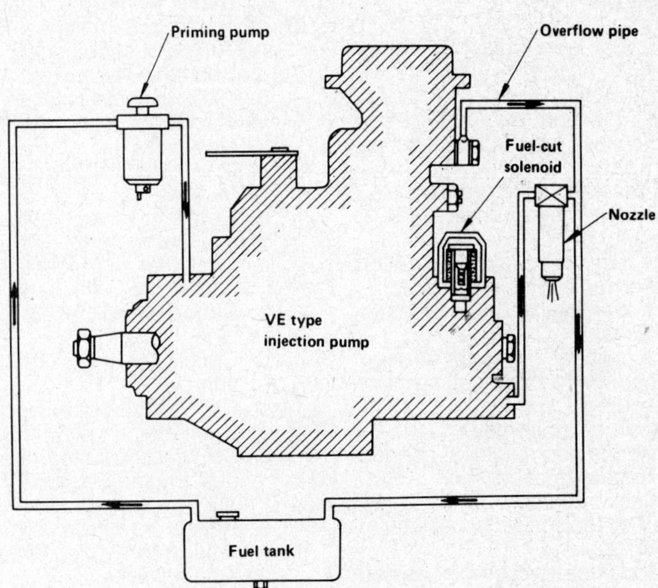

Fig. 55 VE type fuel injection, schematic

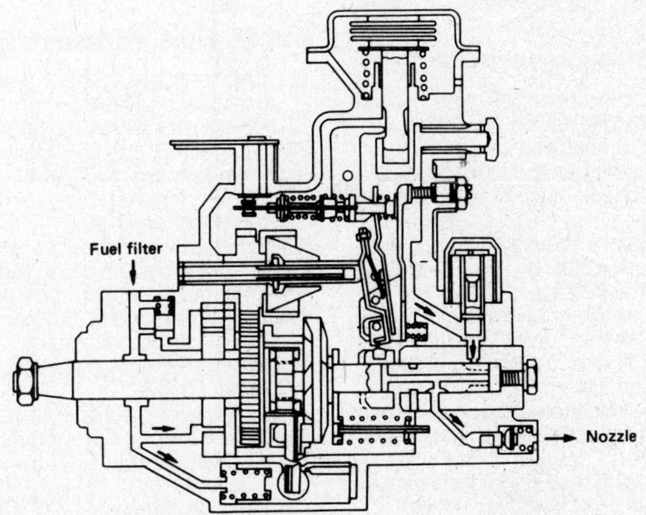

Fig. 56 Sectional view, VE type injection pump

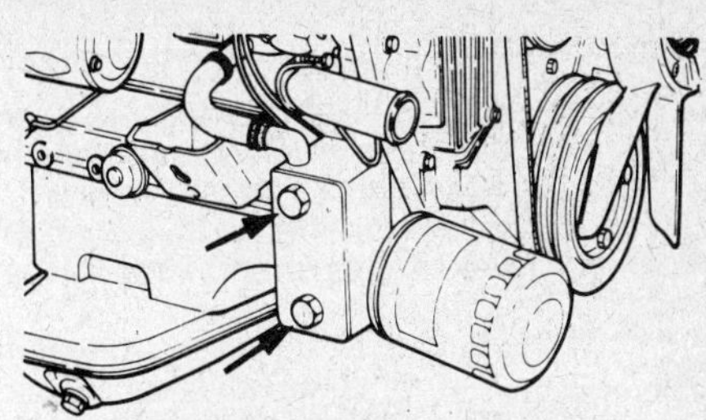

Fig. 54 Oil cooler installation

the injection pump driveshaft through a drive disc. The cam disc is spring loaded and held against a roller, as the cam disc is rotated the high points on the cam disc contact the roller, forcing the cam disc outward. This in turn forces the plunger outward and into the plunger barrel. The plunger barrel is connected to the pump housing by an inlet port where pressurized fuel is stored. The plunger barrel is located in the distributor head and is also referred to as the high pressure chamber. The plunger is connected to the cam disc by a drive pin and rotates with the cam disc, and is provided with a fuel intake slit and a fuel distribution slit. As the plunger rotates in the plunger barrel, the intake slit aligns with the intake port, pressurized fuel in the pump housing is taken into the high pressure chamber. As the plunger rotates, the intake port closes, and the action of the cam disc forces the plunger in and the fuel to pressurize. When the plunger distributor slit meets the outlet passage, pressurized fuel is allowed to flow to one of four delivery valves, as the plunger continues moving in, the fuel cut-off port aligns with the pump housing so that pressurized fuel within the plunger is released into the pump housing.

Control Sleeve

The control sleeve is mounted on the plunger to control the volume of fuel delivery. This is accomplished by regulating the effective stroke of the plunger through moving the fuel cut-off port, thereby releasing the plunger pressure into the pump housing rather than into a delivery valve. The effective stroke decreases as the control sleeve is moved away from the high pressure chamber, causing a reduction in the volume of injection. The effective stroke increases as the control sleeve is moved towards the high pressure chamber, causing the injection volume to increase.

Delivery Nozzles And Injectors

The delivery nozzles are located in the delivery head. There is one delivery valve for each cylinder and each valve consists of a spring loaded check valve designed to open when fuel pressure is behind them, and to provide a drip free seal when pressure drops off. The delivery valves are connected to the injection valves by steel lines, when injection pressure reaches a predetermined level, (I-Mark 1707 psi, Pickup 1494 psi) the injection valves open, admitting fuel into the combustion chamber.

Governor

The governor flyweight holders are gear driven by the pump driveshaft which causes the flyweights to open outward.

The ball head pin is fitted to lower part of governor lever assembly and fitted to the hole in the control sleeve.

When the engine is stationary, the start lever is forced against the governor sleeve by the start spring action causing the control sleeve to move to the fuel increase position on the pivot point. As the engine is started and accelerator pedal is released, the control lever returns to normal idling position. The flyweights are forced outward by centrifugal force forcing the governor sleeve to move right and control sleeve to move left. However, movement of these parts are regulated by the start idling spring action. As a result, the control spring is moved to a point until these forces are balanced, to hold the engine running at idle.

As the control lever is moved to a position of medium speed, the yoke is pulled to the left and causes the tension of the spring inside to increase. When the tension of the spring overcomes the tension of the damper spring, it acts to pull the tension lever to the left for fuel increase, thereby causing RPM's to build up, and the flyweights to open outward. The resulting increase in centrifugal force causes the partial load spring within the yoke to be compressed until a balance is obtained between the centrifugal force and spring tension, causing a reduction in fuel volume.

When the control lever is moved until it is set against the maximum speed stopper, the yoke is pulled to the extreme left to compress the damper and partial load springs fully and causes the tension lever to be pulled to the left until it comes in contact with the aneroid compensator lever. When the tension lever is pulled to this position, damper spring tension, partial load spring tension and governor spring tension overcomes the centrifugal force created by the flyweights, causing the governor to idle, maintaining rated full-load maximum speed. When the full load adjusting bolt is turned in, the corrector lever pivots to the left on the axis MI., causing the control sleeve to move to the right and increase the volume of injection.

Aneroid Compensator

The aneroid compensator serves to control the volume of fuel delivery according to altitude (above sea level) thereby to prevent deterioration in exhaust emissions and exhaust smoke.

Automatic Timer

The automatic timer makes use of change in the delivery pressure of the feed pump to control fuel injection timing.

Cold Start Device (CSD)

The cold start device (CSD) is a system designed to facilitate cold engine starting. The CSD is installed on the automatic timer pressure side to keep fuel injection timing advanced during cold starts.

Fuel Cut Solenoid

The fuel cut solenoid is installed in the fuel inlet port of the high pressure chamber to cut the fuel supply when the ignition is switched off.

Lubrication System

The injector pump is lubricated and cooled by fuel. When the cam disc and plunger pass the fuel cut-off port, the excess pressurized fuel is fed into the pump housing and is then returned to the fuel tank through the overflow valve, lubricating the internal parts.

FUEL INJECTION DIAGNOSIS

Hard Starting

1. Out of fuel.
   a. Check fuel level, adjust as necessary.
2. Injection timing.
   a. Check injection pump alignment mark to block mark, adjust if necessary.
3. Fuel not reaching injector nozzles.
   a. Check for air in fuel lines, bleed as necessary.
   b. Check fuel cut solenoid operation, repair or replace as necessary.
   c. Check fuel filter and fuel pipes for blockages.
   d. Check delivery valves for sticking.
   e. Overhaul or readjust setting of injector pump.
4. Pre-heat circuit inoperative.
   a. Check fuse and electrical connections, repair as necessary.
5. Faulty injection nozzles.
   a. Repair or replace as necessary.
6. Low compression.
   a. Check compression, repair as necessary.
7. Excessive valve clearance.
   a. Adjust valves.
8. Valve train trouble.
   a. Check timing belt and camshaft installation, repair as necessary.
9. Injection pump faulty.
   a. Readjust or overhaul injection pump.

Engine Idling Unstable

1. Incorrect idle speed, on A/C models check fast idle device operation.
   a. Reset to specified range.
2. Check accelerator cable for binding or twisting, check accelerator lever for looseness.
   a. Repair as necessary.
3. Check for water or air in fuel filter/water separator.
   a. Drain water if necessary.
   b. Prime system using fuel filter hand pump, find air source and repair.
4. Injection timing.
   a. Check injection pump alignment mark to block mark, adjust as necessary.
5. Check engine mounts for loosening or cracks.
   a. Tighten or replace as necessary.
6. Faulty injection nozzles.
   a. Repair or replace as necessary.
7. Low compression.
   a. Check compression, repair as necessary.
8. Excessive valve clearance.
   a. Adjust valves.
9. Valve train trouble.
   a. Check timing belt and camshaft installation, repair as necessary.
10. Injection pump faulty.
   a. Overhaul or readjust setting of injection pump.

Lack Of Engine Power & Excessive Fuel Consumption

1. Check air cleaner for restrictions.
   a. Clean or replace element as necessary.
2. Check accelerator linkage for binding or twisting.
   a. Repair or replace as necessary.
3. Check maximum speed stop bolt and full load adjust bolt seals.
   a. Repair as necessary.
   b. Check if accelerator control lever is in contact with maximum speed stop bolt.
4. Check exhaust pipe and muffler for restrictions.
   a. Repair or replace as necessary.
5. Check fuel system.
   a. Check for air in fuel lines, bleed as necessary.
   b. Check for collapsed or loose fuel pipes.
   c. Check for tank breather restrictions.
   d. Check for proper fuel quality.
3. Injection timing.
   a. Set injection timing, refer to text under "Engine Section."
4. Faulty injection nozzles.
   a. Repair or replace as necessary.
5. Excessive valve clearances.
   a. Adjust valves.
6. Low compression.
   a. Check compression, repair as necessary.
7. Delivery valves.
   a. Check delivery valves for sticking.
8. Injection pump.
   a. Readjust or overhaul injection pump.

Excessive Exhaust Smoke

1. Engine not thoroughly warmed up.
   a. Allow engine to warm up.
2. Check air cleaner for restrictions.
   a. Clean or replace element as necessary.
3. Check for water or air in fuel filter/water separator.
   a. Drain water if necessary.
   b. Prime system using fuel filter hand pump, find air source and repair.
4. Check full load adjust bolt seal.
   a. Repair as necessary.
5. Check exhaust pipe and muffler for restrictions.
   a. Repair or replace as necessary.
6. Check for proper fuel quality.
   a. Drain and refill tank with proper fuel.
7. Injection timing.
   a. Set injection timing, refer to text under "Engine Section."
8. Faulty injection nozzles.
   a. Repair or replace as necessary.

9. Excessive valve clearances.
   a. Adjust valves.
10. Low compression.
   a. Check compression, repair as necessary.
11. Valve train trouble.
   a. Check timing belt and camshaft installation, repair as necessary.
12. Delivery valves.
   a. Check delivery valves for sticking.
3. Valve guides and seats.
   a. Check condition of valve guides and seats, repair as necessary.
14. Injection pump faulty.
   a. Readjust or overhaul injection pump.

Abnormal Engine Noise

1. Engine knocking.
   a. Ensure engine is thoroughly warmed up.
   b. Check injection timing (refer to text under "Engine Section").
   c. Check injection nozzles.
   d. Check compression.
   e. Check that fuel is the proper quality.
   f. Readjust or replace injection pump.
2. Noise indicating gas leakage.
   a. Check exhaust pipe for loose connections or leakage.
   b. Check glow plug and nozzle installation.
   c. Check cylinder head gasket for leakage.
   d. Check, and if necessary, adjust valve clearances.
   e. Check compression.
3. Continuous noise.
   a. Check fan belt tension.
   b. Check cooling fan for looseness.
   c. Check water pump bearing.
   d. Check alternator and vacuum pump operation.
   e. Check, and if necessary, adjust valve clearances.

CLUTCH & MANUAL TRANSMISSION SECTION

INDEX

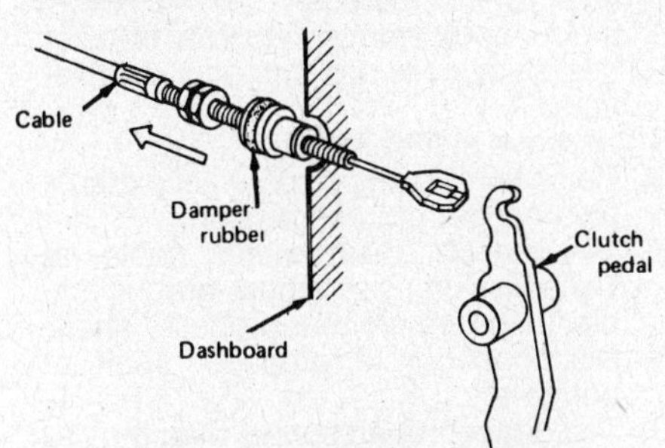

Fig. 1 Clutch cable

CLUTCH PEDAL ADJUST

I MARK

1. Loosen lock and adjusting nuts on clutch cable.
2. Pull cable toward front of vehicle and take up slack.
3. Turn adjusting nut inward until clutch pedal free travel is approximately 5/8 inch.
4. Tighten locknut.

IMPULSE

Clutch pedal free play and pedal stroke are self-adjusted on these models.

PICKUP & TROOPER II

Exc. Diesel Models

1. With clutch switch contacting pedal bracket, adjust the clutch pedal height until flush with the brake pedal.
2. Pull outer cable forward and turn adjusting nut until washer damper rubber is contacting dash board, **Fig. 1.**
3. Depress and release clutch pedal repeatedly.
4. Pull outer cable forward again and fully tighten adjusting nut, then back off nut and adjust free play to 0.2 inch (5 mm), **Fig. 2.**
5. Release cable and retighten locknut.

Diesel Models

1. Pull outer cable all the way forward and turn in adjusting nut until washer damper contacts dashboard, **Fig. 1.**
2. Depress and release clutch pedal several times.
3. Pull outer cable forward again and fully tighten adjusting nut until .2 inch (5 mm) is obtained, **Fig. 2.**
4. Release outer cable and tighten locknut.

CLUTCH REPLACE

I MARK

Removal

1. Remove transmission as outlined elsewhere in this section.
2. Mark relationship of clutch assembly to flywheel to facilitate installation.
3. Install alignment tool, then remove six retaining bolts.
4. Remove release bearing to yoke retaining springs, then the release bearing with support.
5. Remove release yoke from transmission ball stud.

Installation

1. Apply a suitable lubricant to ball stud, then install release yoke.
2. Apply a suitable lubricant to support, then assemble release bearing and support to release yoke with retaining springs.
3. Install clutch assembly in original position using alignment tool, then insert attaching bolts and torque to 14 ft. lbs.
4. Install transmission.

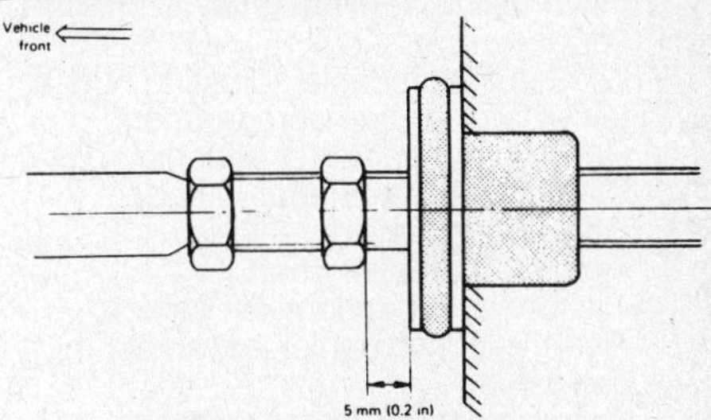

Fig. 2 Clutch cable adjustment

IMPULSE

1. Remove transmission as described elsewhere in this section.
2. Mark clutch assembly to flywheel for installation in original position.
3. Remove pressure plate assembly attaching bolts and the pressure plate assembly.
4. Remove clutch driven disc assembly.
5. Remove shift collar retaining spring.
6. Remove shift collar and bearing.
7. Remove clutch shift fork assembly.
8. Reverse procedure to install, noting the following:
   a. Torque pressure plate assembly attaching bolts to 12-14 ft. lbs. in proper sequence, **Fig. 3.**
   b. Lubricate clutch shift fork assembly with suitable grease.

PICKUP & TROOPER II

1. Raise vehicle and remove transmission.
2. Mark relationship between clutch assembly and flywheel to aid assembly.
3. Gradually loosen the six clutch cover

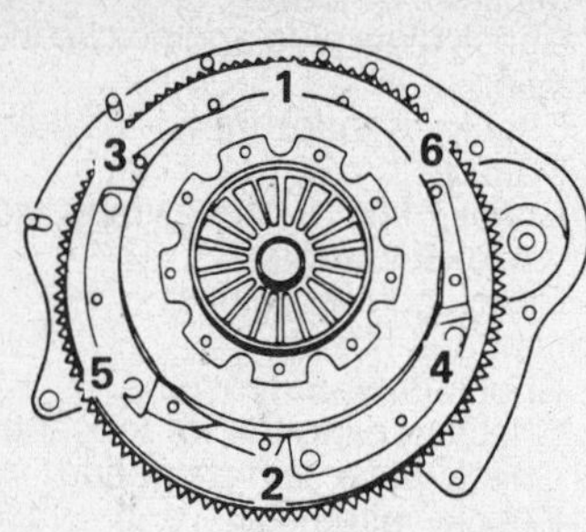

Fig. 3 Pressure plate attaching bolt tightening sequence

to flywheel attaching bolts until spring pressure is released.
4. Support clutch pressure plate and cover assembly with a dummy shaft, then remove the attaching bolts and clutch assembly.
5. Reverse procedure to install. Torque clutch attaching bolts to 13 ft. lbs.

TRANSMISSION REPLACE

I MARK

1. Disconnect battery ground cable.
2. From inside vehicle, remove shift lever assembly.
3. Loosen clutch cable adjusting nuts at left side of engine compartment.
4. Remove upper starter attaching bolts, then disconnect starter wiring.
5. Raise and support vehicle.
6. Remove propeller shaft.
7. Disconnect speedometer cable.
8. Remove clutch cable heat shield, then the cable.
9. Remove starter lower attaching bolt, then the starter.
10. Disconnect exhaust pipe from manifold.
11. Remove flywheel inspection cover.
12. Remove rear transmission support attaching bolt.
13. Support transmission, then remove rear transmission support from frame.
14. Lower transmission approximately 4 inches.
15. Disconnect back-up lamp, then the CRS switch wires.
16. Remove transmission housing to engine block attaching bolts.
17. Move transmission rearward, then lower from vehicle.
18. Reverse procedure to install, noting the following:
    a. Apply a suitable lubricant to drive gear shaft prior to installation.
    b. Adjust clutch lash.
    c. Fill transmission to level of filler hole with specified lubricant.

IMPULSE

1. Disconnect battery ground cable.
2. Raise and support vehicle.
3. Drain transmission oil.
4. Remove gearshift knob, then the shift lever cover assembly and the console assembly.
5. Remove front exhaust pipe.
6. Disconnect propeller shaft from transmission.
7. Disconnect speedometer cable at transmission.
8. Disconnect clutch slave cylinder.
9. Remove transmission case undercover.
10. Position suitable jack under transmission, remove rear engine attaching nuts, and lower transmission slightly, then remove quadrant box cover to transmission attaching bolts.
11. Disconnect all electrical connectors at transmission.
12. Remove control box assembly.
13. Remove transmission to engine attaching bolts, being careful not to drop starter.
14. Lower transmission and remove from under vehicle.
15. Reverse procedure to install, noting the following:
    a. When installing transmission, position transmission with speedometer cable fitting face turned downward and slide assembly forward, guiding gear shaft into pilot bearing.
    b. Install quadrant box cover with new gasket and tighten attaching bolts before installing rear engine mount.
    c. When installing propeller shaft, install bolts from extension shaft side and torque to 18-22 ft. lbs.
    d. Install drain plug, then remove filler plug and fill transmission with suitable fluid. Torque drain and filler plugs to 22-36 ft. lbs.
    e. Torque rear engine mount attaching nuts to 14-22 ft. lbs. and bend up washer tabs.

PICKUP & TROOPER II

Exc. 4x4 Models

1. Disconnect battery ground cable.
2. Slide gearshift lever boot upward and remove lever.
3. Remove starter and position aside.
4. Raise vehicle and disconnect exhaust pipe hanger from transmission. Drain transmission.
5. Disconnect speedometer cable.
6. Remove propeller shaft.
7. Remove return spring from clutch fork.
8. Remove bolts securing the flywheel cover.
9. Remove frame bracket to transmission rear mount bolts, **Fig. 4.**
10. Raise engine and transmission slightly to remove the crossmember to frame bracket bolts.
11. Remove rear mount bolts from transmission rear cover.

Fig. 4 Frame to rear mount attaching bolt location

12. Lower the engine and transmission assembly and support rear of engine.
13. Disconnect electrical connectors from CRS and back-up lamp switches.
14. Remove transmission to engine attaching bolts and lower transmission from vehicle.
15. Reverse procedure to install.

4x4 Models

1. Disconnect battery ground cable.
2. Drain transmission fluid.
3. Slide transmission and transfer gearshifts lever boots upward and remove lever attaching bolts.
4. Disconnect return spring from transfer gearshift lever and remove both levers.
5. Remove starter motor.
6. Raise vehicle and disconnect exhaust pipe hanger at transmission.
7. Disconnect speedometer cable at transmission. Disconnect ground cable, then remove rear propeller shaft.
8. Disconnect front propeller shaft at both ends.
9. Disconnect return spring, then the cable from clutch fork position cable aside.
10. Remove lower bolts from flywheel stone guard then remove bolts securing frame bracket to rear transmission mount, **Fig. 4.**
11. Remove rear mounting bolts from transfer case.
12. Remove bolts attaching side case and remove case. **Use care not to misplace detent spring and detent ball during disassembly.**
13. Remove stud bolt from transfer case, then lower engine and transmission. Support rear of engine using suitable jack.
14. Disconnect electrical connectors at coasting richer system switch and back-up lamp switch.
15. Remove bolts retaining shifter cover, then remove cover and gasket from top of transfer case.
16. Remove engine to transmission attaching bolts, then lower transmission from vehicle.
17. Reverse procedure to install.

DISC BRAKE SECTION

INDEX

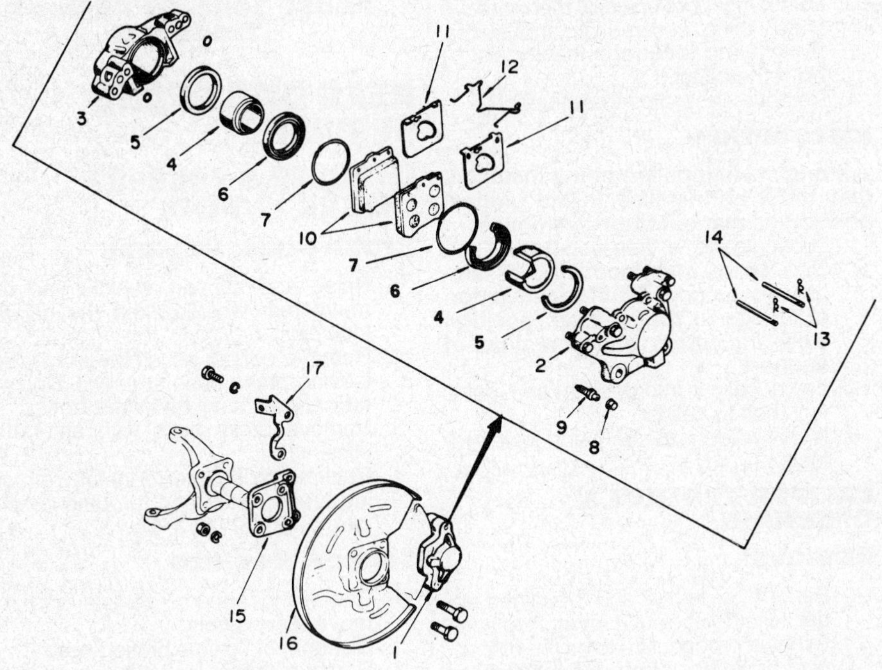

1. CALIPER ASSEMBLY
2. INNER CALIPER
3. OUTER CALIPER
4. PISTON
5. PISTON SEAL
6. DUST SEAL
7. DUST SEAL RING
8. BLEEDER CAP
9. BLEEDER
10. PAD ASSEMBLY
11. PAD SHIM
12. M TYPE SPRING
13. CLIP
14. PIN
15. ADAPTER
16. DUST COVER
17. BRACKET

Fig. 1 Exploded view of disc brake. I-Mark

FRONT DISC BRAKE SERVICE

I-MARK

BRAKE SHOE, REPLACE

Removal

1. Raise and support front of car, then remove front wheels.
2. Remove clips, pins, "M" type spring, shims and brake shoes, **Fig. 1.**
3. Remove any dirt or foreign material from brake shoe recess of caliper.
4. Visually inspect piston seal for leakage.

Installation

1. Apply P.B.C. grease, included in shoe repair kit to vertical edges of shoes.
2. Push pistons into bores, using Tool J-22430. While pressing piston into bores, open bleeder valve slightly to prevent brake fluid from overflowing reservoir. Tighten bleeder valve when pistons are bottomed.
3. Assemble anti-rattle shims to brake shoes with arrow mark facing directions for normal disc rotation and install into caliper.
4. Install "M" type spring, pins and clips, **Fig. 1**
5. Install wheels and lower vehicle.

CALIPER, REPLACE

1. Raise and support front of vehicle and remove wheel.
2. Disconnect caliper brake pipe from brake hose and cap or tape or cap ends to protect against dirt.
3. Remove caliper attaching bolts. This will allow the brake hose and bracket to hand fully. Remove caliper assembly. Reverse procedure to install. Bleed brakes before installing wheel. Torque caliper attaching to 36.2 ft. lbs. and the brake pipe flare nut to 11.6 ft. lbs.

CALIPER OVERHAUL

Disassembly

1. Remove dust seal ring and the dust seal from each piston.
2. Install clamp J-22429 on mounting half of caliper and remove rim half piston by applying compressed air at the brake line connection.
3. Install clamp J-22429 on rim half of caliper and remove mounting half piston by applying compressed air at the brake line connection.
4. Remove fluid seals from annular grooves in caliper piston bores, **Fig. 1. The caliper is of an integral design and cannot be disassembled. The entire caliper assembly should be replaced if brake fluid is found to be leaking from the caliper joint. Never attempt to loosen bridge bolts, since breakage of brake fluid at the mating surface may result.**

Inspection

1. Check caliper and adapter plates for distortion or cracking and replace, if necessary.
2. Inspect cylinder bores and pistons for wear, scuffing or corrosion and replace, if necessary.

Assembly

1. Apply special rubber grease (included in caliper seal repair kit) to the seal and cylinder wall, then insert new piston seal into the cylinder. **Do not use lubricants other than those included in repair kit.**
2. Carefully install piston to bottom of cylinder bore using finger pressure only to avoid scratching cylinder wall, piston or seal.
3. Install dust seal and seal ring.

IMPULSE

BRAKE PADS, REPLACE

1. Raise and support vehicle and remove front wheels.
2. Remove upper and lower caliper mounting bolts, then remove caliper

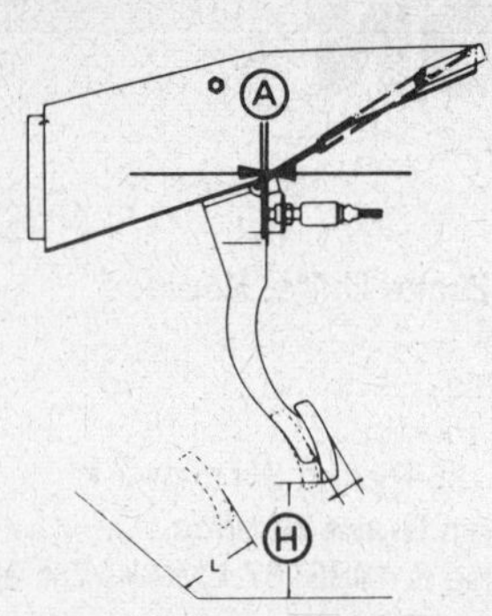

Fig. 2 Adjusting brake pedal. Impulse

from disc, leaving brake hose attached. **Do not let caliper hang by brake hose.**
3. Remove brake pads, with shims, from support bracket.
4. Apply thin coat of suitable grease to rear face of new brake pad and install shim.
5. Push in caliper piston and install pads.
6. Install caliper assembly, torquing attaching bolts to 25-28 ft. lbs.

CALIPER, REPLACE

1. Raise and support vehicle and remove front wheels.
2. Disconnect flexible brake hose at caliper and cap hose openings.
3. Remove upper and lower caliper mounting bolts, then remove caliper from disc.
4. Reverse procedure to install, torquing caliper attaching bolts to 25-28 ft. lbs. and the brake hose to 10-13 ft. lbs.

CALIPER, OVERHAUL

1. Remove caliper as previously described.
2. Remove boot guide pin and boot lock pin.
3. Remove breather with cap.
4. Remove dust boot using small screwdriver.
5. Remove piston boot.
6. Install block of wood into caliper and remove piston by applying compressed air through opening for brake hose.
7. Reverse procedure to assemble, using new guide pin boot, lock pin boot, piston ring boot and caliper to piston seal supplied with overhaul kit, and note the following:
   a. Using special grease supplied with overhaul kit, lubricate ring seal and cylinder wall, then insert ring seal into cylinder bore.
   b. When installing piston into cylinder bore, use finger pressure only.
   c. Using special grease supplied with overhaul kit, lubricate boot fitting face of piston before installing piston boot.
   d. Fill guide pin boot with grease before installing on caliper.
   e. Apply grease to inner face of lock pin boot after applying grease into lock pin hose in caliper.
   f. Install guide pin boot after applying grease into lock pin hole in caliper.
   g. Install new gaskets for flexible brake hoses.
   h. Torque breather to 4.5-6.5 ft. lbs. and install cap.
   i. Torque flexible brake hose to 24-27 ft. lbs.

1983–87 PICKUP & 1984–87 TROOPER II

BRAKE SHOE & LINING, REPLACE

Removal

1. Raise vehicle and remove wheel assembly.
2. Remove lock bolt from caliper.
3. Position caliper upward, then remove shoe, lining assemblies and shims. **Mark lining locations if they are to be reinstalled.**
4. Remove shoe clips from support.

Installation

If original linings are being installed, they must be installed in the original position as marked during removal.

1. Lubricate shims, then install new shoe clips, shims, shoe and lining assemblies to support. **During installation of linings to the support, position wear indicators to lower side of support.**
2. Lower caliper into position and install lock bolt to caliper.
3. Install wheel assembly and lower vehicle.

CALIPER REPLACE & OVERHAUL

Removal

1. Perform steps 1, 2 and 3 outlined under "Brake Shoe & Lining, Replace," removal procedure. However, disconnect brake hose from caliper and cap openings in hose and caliper.
2. Remove caliper from vehicle.

Overhaul

1. Remove dust seal from caliper with a suitable tool.
2. Place a block of wood into caliper and force piston from caliper with compressed air applied to the fluid port.
3. Remove piston square sealing ring.
4. Inspect cylinder bore and piston for wear, scuffing or corrosion. Stains and minor corrosion in the cylinder bore may be removed with crocus cloth. Thoroughly clean caliper after using crocus cloth.
5. Lubricate cylinder bore and piston square seal, then install piston seal into bore.
6. Install piston into caliper.
7. Lubricate piston and install dust seal onto piston and install dust seal onto piston and caliper.

Installation

1. Perform steps 1 and 3 outlined under "Brake Shoe & Lining, Replace" Installation procedure.
2. Connect brake hose to caliper, then bleed brake system.
3. Install wheel assembly and lower vehicle.

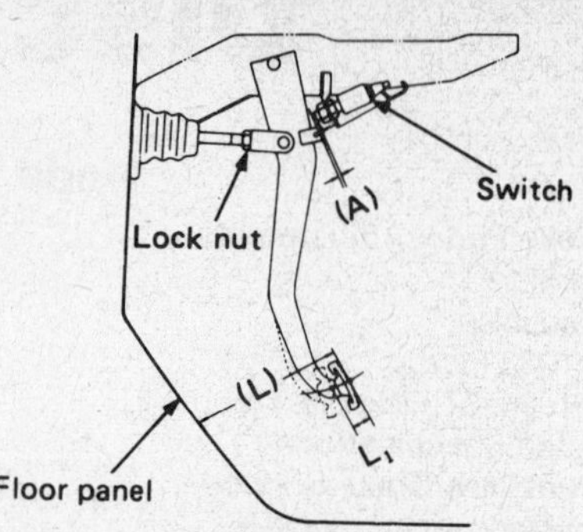

Fig. 3 Adjusting brake pedal. 1984–87 Pickup & Trooper II

REAR DISC BRAKE SERVICE

IMPULSE & 1985–87 I-MARK W/FWD

Brake Pads, Replace

1. Raise and support vehicle and remove rear wheels, then the caliper lock pin.
2. Remove caliper assembly from disc, leaving brake hose attached. **Do not let caliper hang by brake hose.**
3. Remove brake pads with anti-rattle clips.
4. Reverse procedure to install, retracting brake piston and torquing caliper lock pin to 13-16 ft. lbs.

Caliper, Replace

1. Raise and support vehicle and remove rear wheels.
2. Disconnect flexible brake hose.
3. Remove caliper lock pin.
4. Remove caliper assembly from disc.
5. Reverse procedure to install, torquing caliper lock pin to 13-16 ft. lbs. and the flexible brake hose to 9-14 ft. lbs.

Caliper, Overhaul

1. Remove caliper as previously described.
2. Remove guide pin boot, then the sleeve and sleeve boot.
3. Remove piston boot ring using small screwdriver.
4. Remove piston dust boot.
5. Insert suitable piece of wood into caliper and force piston out by applying compressed air through brake hose opening in caliper.
6. Remove caliper to piston seal.
7. Remove breather with cap.
8. Reverse procedure to assemble, installing new guide pin boot, sleeve boot, piston boot ring, piston boot, and caliper piston seal supplied with overhaul kit, and note the following:
   a. Using special rubber grease supplied with rear kit, lubricate ring seal and cylinder bore.
   b. When inserting piston into cylinder bore, use finger pressure only.
   c. Using special grease, lubricate piston boot before installing into cylinder bore and apply grease to foot

fitting face of piston.
d. Fill sleeve boot and guide pin boot with grease before installing on caliper.
e. Install guide pin boot after applying grease into lock pin hole in caliper.
f. Torque breather to 4.5-6.5 ft. lbs. and install cap.

BRAKE PEDAL ADJUSTMENTS

I-MARK

1. Adjust setting of brake pedal by turning the pushrod as necessary, so that the distance between upper face of brake pedal and floor mat as adjusted to approximately 6¾ inch.
2. Push the brake pedal by turning the stop light switch so brake pedal free play is eliminated.
3. When the adjustment is completed, tighten the clevis locknut and light switch locknut.

IMPULSE

1. Adjust master-vac push rod so that distance between upper face of floor carpet and lower face of brake pedal (H), **Fig. 2**, is approximately 5.63 inches.
2. Adjust brake switch so that clearance between brake switch and brake pedal (A) is .0039 inch.
3. Turn brake switch to ½ turn so that clearance (H) is adjusted to 5.52 inches.
4. Bleed brake system, then ensure that brake pedal free play is .24-.39 inch and that pedal stroke is not more than 2.95 inches.

1983 PICKUP

1. Disconnect the battery ground cable.
2. With brake pedal fully released, measure distance from the surface of the foot pad to the toe pan. Distance should be 6.5-6.9 inches on 1983 models.
3. If an adjustment is necessary, disconnect stop lamp switch wiring harness, then loosen switch locknut and remove switch.
4. Loosen pushrod locknut, then rotate pushrod in the appropriate direction until specified pedal height is achieved.
5. Install stop lamp switch. Adjust clearance between switch housing and brake pedal tab to .02-.04 inch. Tighten switch locknut.
6. Connect stop lamp switch harness and battery ground cable.

1984–87 PICKUP & TROOPER II

1. Measure brake pedal height and free play, **Fig. 3**, with brake pedal fully released.
2. Pedal height should measure 6.5-6.9 inches on Pickup models, or 7.8-8.2 inches on Trooper II models. Pedal free play should measure .24-.35 inch on Pickup models, or .28-.39 inch on 1984-85 Trooper II models and .24-.31 on 1986-87 Trooper II models.
3. If measurements are not within specifications, adjust brake pedal as follows:
   a. Disconnect stop light switch.
   b. Loosen pushrod locknut.
   c. Rotate pushrod as needed to bring pedal height within specifications, then torq ue locknut to 13-16 ft. lbs.
   d. Install stop light switch. Adjust clearance between switch housing and brake pedal to .02-.04 inch.
   e. Check that pedal free play is within specifications.

MASTER CYLINDER REPLACE

I-MARK

Removal

1. Disconnect front and rear brake pipes from master cylinder.
2. Remove nuts securing the master cylinder to brake booster and support bracket.
3. Remove bolts securing fluid reservoir bracket, then the master cylinder assembly with the fluid reservoir and rubber hoses.

Installation

1. Place master cylinder fluid reservoir and rubber hoses in position with the fluid reservoir bracket.
2. Install nuts securing master cylinder to brake booster and support bracket.
3. Connect front and rear brake pipes to master cylinder.
4. Torque the master-cylinder-to-brake-booster bolt to 10 ft. lbs.
5. Torque brake line flare nut to 12 ft. lbs.
6. Bleed brake system.

IMPULSE

Removal

1. Loosen front master cylinder brake pipe attaching nut, then remove brake pipe. **During removal of brake pipe, use care to prevent spillage of brake fluid onto painted surfaces.**
2. Remove master cylinder to master vac attaching bolts, then the master cylinder assembly from vehicle.

Installation

1. Align master cylinder assembly and new gasket with attaching bolt holes in vehicle.
2. Insert master cylinder to master vac attaching bolts, then torque bolts to 8 to 11 ft. lbs.
3. Install brake pipe assembly, then torque attaching nut to 9 to 14 ft. lbs.

1983 PICKUP

1. Disconnect battery ground cable.
2. Disconnect lines from master cylinder. Plug opened lines to prevent entry of dirt.
3. Remove master cylinder bracket bolt, then remove master cylinder to power cylinder nuts and washers and remove master cylinder. **Use care to avoid spilling fluid onto painted surfaces.**
4. Reverse procedure to install.

1984–87 PICKUP & TROOPER II

1. Disconnect brake lines from master cylinder. Plug lines to prevent contamination.
2. Remove master cylinder-to-power brake unit retaining nut, then lift master cylinder from engine compartment.
3. Reverse procedure to install. Torque master cylinder retaining nut to 8-11 ft. lbs. and brake line fittings to 6.5-11 ft. lbs.

POWER BRAKE UNITS REPLACE

I-MARK

1. Remove master cylinder as outlined previously.
2. Remove vacuum hose clip and hose from the check valve.
3. Pull out clevis pin and separate clevis from brake pedal arm.
4. Remove master-vac to spacer retaining nuts and the master-vac assembly.
5. Reverse procedure to install after measuring the distance between the master cylinder mounting face on the master-vac and the end of the pushrod.

IMPULSE

Removal

1. Loosen air duct hose clamp, then pull hose from fitting and position aside.
2. Loosen vacuum hose clamp, then remove vacuum hose.
3. Remove brake pipe. **During removal of brake pipe, use care to prevent spillage of brake fluid onto painted surfaces.**
4. Remove retaining clip from brake pedal jaw joint pin from upper portion of brake pedal.
5. Remove master vac to master cylinder attaching bolts, then separate master vac from master cylinder.
6. Remove master cylinder assembly as previously described, then the master vac assembly from vehicle

Installation

1. Install master vac assembly into vehicle, then measure distance from master vac flange fact to pushrod end. Distance should be .732 inch. Adjust to specifications using locknut at end of pushrod and pushrod gauge tool No. J-29759. Torque locknut to 8 to 11 ft. lbs.
2. Install master cylinder assembly as previously described.
3. Assemble master vac to master cylinder assembly, then insert attaching bolts and torque to 8 to 11 ft. lbs.
4. Install jaw joint pin, then insert new retaining pin.
5. Install brake pipe, then torque fitting to 9 to 14 ft. lbs.

6. Install vacuum hose, then tighten retaining clamp.
7. Install air duct hose, then tighten hose clamp.

1983 PICKUP

1. Disconnect battery ground cable.
2. Disconnect brake lines from master cylinder. Cap all openings to prevent entry of foreign matter from entering the system.
3. Loosen vacuum line clamp at power cylinder check valve, then move vacuum line out of way.
4. Disconnect brake pedal return spring.
5. Remove cotter pin and washer, then push rod clevis to brake pedal pin.
6. Remove power cylinder to dash panel attaching nuts, then power cylinder and master cylinder as an assembly.
7. Reverse procedure to install.

1984–87 PICKUP & TROOPER II

1. Remove vacuum hose clamp, then disconnect vacuum hose from power brake unit.
2. Disconnect brake lines from master cylinder.
3. Unhook brake pedal return spring from pushrod.
4. Remove snap ring from pushrod-to-brake pedal pin, then slide pin out of pedal.
5. Remove attaching nuts, then the power brake unit and master cylinder assembly.
6. Separate master cylinder from brake unit.
7. Reverse procedure to install, noting the following:
   a. Prior to installation of the master cylinder, measure distance from flange surface of power brake unit to end of pushrod. If projection does not measure .709– -.171 inch, adjust with locknut at end of pushrod, then torque locknut to 13- 16 ft. lbs.
   b. Torque power brake unit attaching nuts to 18-21 ft. lbs.
   c. Torque brake line fittings to 6.5-11 ft. lbs.

DRUM BRAKES SECTION

INDEX

BRAKE SHOES REPLACE

1983 I-MARK

1. Raise and support vehicle.
2. Remove wheel and brake drum assembly.
3. Remove return springs, shoe holding pins, cups, and springs.
4. Position the automatic adjuster all the way in direction of expansion and disconnect the strut, then remove the primary shoe.
5. Disconnect parking brake cable from parking brake lever, then remove the secondary shoe.
6. Reverse procedure to install.

1983 PICKUP

1. Raise and support vehicle.
2. Remove rear wheel assembly.
3. Disconnect parking brake cable from actuating lever.
4. Remove drum to hub retaining screws, then drum.
5. Remove brake shoe hold down springs, then depress spring retainer while rotating 90 degrees to align slot in retainer with flanged end of pin.
6. Remove the lower pull back spring and expand brake shoes until they disengage from the actuator assembly, then remove shoes along with upper pull back spring.
7. Reverse procedure to install.

1984–87 PICKUP & TROOPER II

Refer to **Fig. 1** for brake shoe removal and installation.

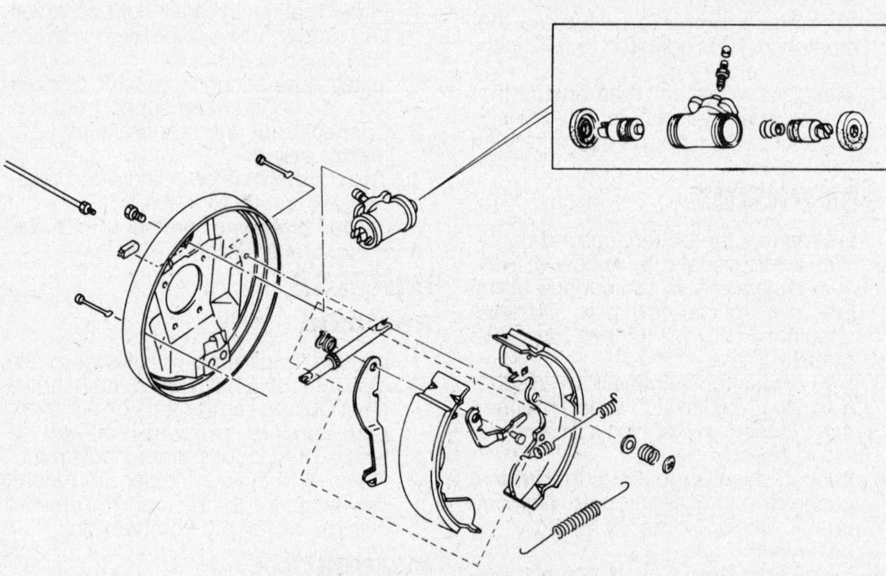

Fig. 1 Removal & installation of brake shoes. 1984–87 Pickup & Trooper II

MASTER CYLINDER REPLACE

Refer to Disc Brakes Section.

POWER BRAKES UNITS REPLACE

Refer to Disc Brakes Section.

SERVICE BRAKE ADJUST

I-MARK

1. Raise and support rear of vehicle.
2. Mark relationship of wheel to axle flange assembly and remove rear wheels.
3. Remove brake drum, using a brake

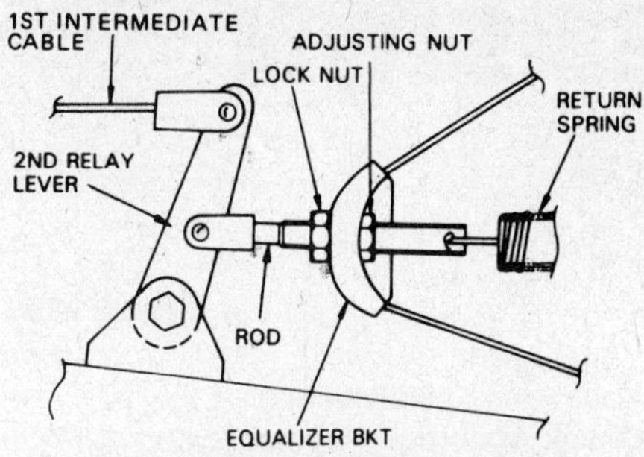

Fig. 2 Adjusting parking & service brake. 1984–87 Pickup & Trooper II

adjuster gauge, measure the inside diameter of brake drum.

4. Using measurement obtained in step 3 on gauge, adjust rear brake shoes using a screwdriver by moving auto adjuster lever towards secondary shoe for increase in diameter. Move auto adjuster towards primary shoe to decrease diameter.
5. Install brake drum and wheel assembly.
6. Lower vehicle.

1983 PICKUP

1. Raise and support rear of vehicle, remove rear wheels.
2. Remove flange to drum retaining screw, remove brake drums disconnect rear brake cable.
3. Using a brake adjusting gauge, measure the brake drum inside diameter.
4. Transfer measurement obtained in step 3 to brake shoes by using brake shoe star wheel adjuster until the gauge just slides over the linings.
5. Connect parking brake cable, install brake drum and flange to drum retaining screw.
6. Lower vehicle, while the vehicle is stationary, operate the parking brake repeatedly while depressing the brake pedal until a sufficient pedal stroke is obtained.

1984–87 PICKUP & TROOPER II

All brakes are self-adjusting. The front brakes are adjusted as the vehicle moves slowly back and forth while applying the service brakes. The rear brakes are adjusted as the parking brake is applied and released. However, the following preliminary rear brake adjustment should perform after the brakes have been relined or replaced.

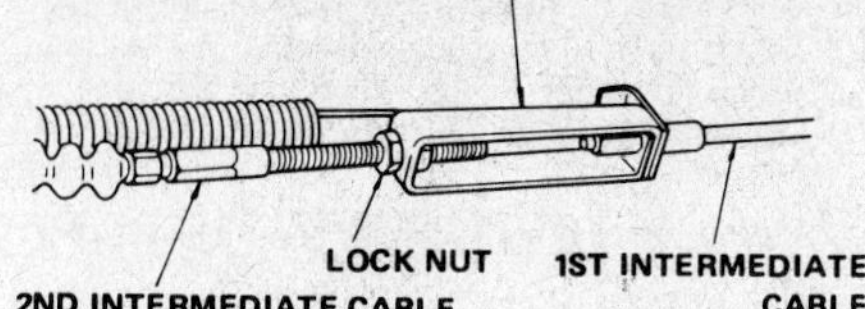

Fig. 3 Parking brake cable adjuster

1. Ensure parking brake is fully released.
2. Rotate adjusting nut on second relay lever rod, **Fig. 2**, until all slack is removed from cable. Secure adjusting nut in this position with locknut.
3. Apply approximately 66 lbs. of force to pull parking brake lever to the fully applied position three or four times.
4. Check that total travel of parking brake lever is 12-14 notches. If lever travel is not within specifications, the adjusting nut must be reset.

PARKING BRAKE ADJUST

I MARK

1. Fully release the parking brake lever; check parking brake cable for free movement.
2. Remove the cable play by turning the brake lever rod against nut.
3. When adjustment is completed, check that the travel of the parking brake lever is set firmly. If the travel of the parking brake lever is more than eight clicks, readjust with the lever rod adjust nut.

IMPULSE

1. Insert screwdriver or brake tool through service hole on backing plate and turn adjuster until brake shoe contact can be felt when manually turning wheel, then back off six notches.
2. Adjust parking brake cable so that lever travel is 11-12 notches when lever is pulled with a force of 66 lbs.
3. Ensure that brakes do not drag.

1983 PICKUP

The service brake must be properly adjusted before adjusting parking brake.

1. Raise and support vehicle.
2. Release parking brake, loosen the

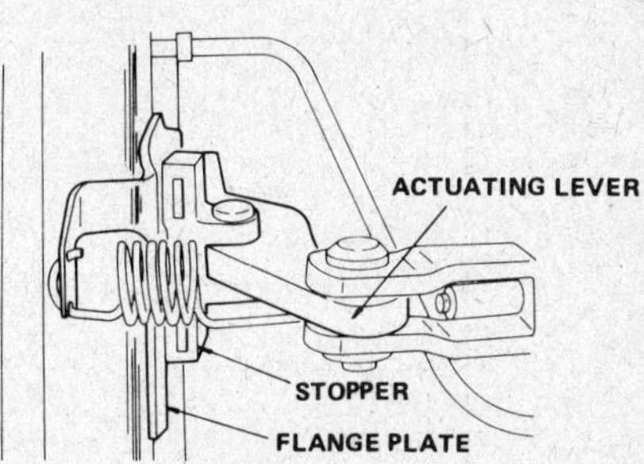

Fig. 4 Actuating lever & flange plate assembly

brake cable adjuster locknut, **Fig. 3.**

3. Turn the parking brake cable adjuster clockwise until actuating lever stopper on each rear wheel is lifted off the flange plate completely, **Fig 4.**
4. Turn the brake cable adjuster in the opposite direction until the actuating lever stopper on each wheel brake makes contact with the flange plate.
5. Tighten the cable adjuster locknut, then apply and release the parking brake 3 or 4 times.
6. Repeat steps 2 and 3. Bring actuating lever stopper on each flange plate by turning the cable adjuster counterclockwise, when slack in the actuating lever is removed, turn the stopper an additional 1½ to 2 turns. Tighten the cable adjuster locknut.
7. Parking brake lever stroke should be 12 to 13 notches to firmly set the parking brake, release parking brake fully and rotate rear wheels. No drag should be present.
8. Lower vehicle floor.

1984–87 PICKUP & TROOPER II

Refer to "Service Brake, Adjust", "1984-87 Pickup & Trooper II" for information regarding parking brake adjustment on these models.

BRAKE PEDAL ADJUSTMENTS

Refer to Disc Brakes Section.

REAR AXLE & SUSPENSION SECTION

INDEX

AXLE SHAFT REPLACE

I-MARK EXC. FWD

Removal

1. Raise and support rear of vehicle.
2. Remove wheel and brake drum.
3. Remove rear axle shaft retaining plate and, with a suitable puller, remove axle shaft.
4. Remove retaining ring with a chisel.
5. Press bearing from axle shaft.

Installation

1. Check radial runout of axle shaft at ball bearing seat and lateral runout of axle shaft flange near largest diameter. Allowable radial runout is .002 inch and allowable lateral runout is .004 inch. An axle shaft that exceeds these tolerances, or one that has been damaged during removal, must be replaced.
2. Press on bearing so oil seal groove on bearing faces shaft splines.
3. Press on retainer ring so shoulder faces bearing.
4. Check axle shaft end play as follows:
   a. Using a depth gauge, measure depth of rear axle bearing seat in axle housing with backing plate and gaskets in place.
   b. Measure width of bearing outer race. The difference between the two measurements indicates the required thickness of the shims. The maximum allowable end play is .002 in. If necessary to reduce end play, add .004 shims behind bearing as necessary. A slight crush fit (to .006 in.) is desirable.
5. Coat rear axle shaft splines with hypoid gear lubricant prior to installation.
6. Insert axle shaft into housing. Using a mallet, drive axle shaft completely into housing.
7. Install lock washers and nuts. Torque bolts to 20 ft. lbs.
8. Lower rear of vehicle.

IMPULSE

1. Raise and support vehicle and remove rear wheels.
2. Remove caliper assembly, then the brake disc.
3. Remove axle plate to axle housing attaching bolts.
4. Disconnect parking brake cable.
5. Remove rear axle shaft assembly with suitable puller.
6. Remove parking brake plate assembly.
7. Remove rear axle sleeve.
8. Remove rear axle shaft bearing by applying pressure on shaft using a bench press and tool J-33949 or equivalent.
9. Remove rear axle bearing ring.
10. Remove rear axle bearing retainer.
11. Reverse procedure to install, noting the following:
    a. Ensure that axle shaft runout does not exceed .004 inch and that axle shaft flange runout does not exceed .006 inch.
    b. Install O-ring on outer circumference of bearing outer race and install bearing with O-ring turned to splined end of shaft.
    c. Install sleeve with flanged side facing ball bearing and press bearing assembly in with bench press and tool J-22912-01 or equivalent.
    d. Torque parking brake plate to axle housing attaching bolts to 26-29 ft. lbs.
    e. Torque caliper assembly attaching bolts to 35-38 ft. lbs.

PICKUP & TROOPER II

Removal

1. Raise vehicle on hoist.
2. Remove rear wheel and brake drum.
3. Remove brake shoes and disconnect parking brake inner cable, **Fig. 1.**
4. Disconnect brake line from wheel cylinder.
5. From inboard side of brake backing plate, remove the four nuts from bearing holder through bolts.
6. Pull out axle shaft assembly. Do not strike backing plate in an attempt to remove axle shaft. Use tool J-5748 if necessary.
7. Flatten locking tab on lock washer, then mount axle shaft in vise, clamping vise jaws around locknut. **Do not tighten vise excessively.**
8. Place tool J-24246 onto studs and secure with two wheel nuts, then turn axle shaft from locknut.
9. Remove locknut, washer, bearing and holder, then using a press, remove brake backing plate from axle shaft. **Only a small amount of force is required to remove bearing from shaft. Make sure to support backing plate solidly and hold onto axle shaft to prevent it from falling.**
10. Remove oil seal from bearing holder and drive out bearing outer race using a drift.
11. Reverse steps 7 thru 10 to reassemble shaft. Torque locknut to 190 ft. lbs.

Installation

If both axle shafts have been serviced, the following steps should be used for installation. If only one shaft has been serviced, skip step 1.

1. Insert a .079 inch shim between the bearing holder and axle tube end-flange. Slide the axle shaft assembly into the axle tube and tighten the four bearing holder-to-flange bolts evenly to 55 ft. lbs.
2. Push the opposite axle shaft, assembled without shims, into the axle tube until it comes into contact with thrust block in the differential. Measure the clearance between the bearing holder and flange, **Fig. 2.** Add .012 inch to this measurement to obtain the correct shim size.
3. Withdraw the axle shaft, and install correct thickness shims between bearing holder and flange face. Torque to 55 ft. lbs.
4. Reverse steps 1 thru 6 of disassembly procedure. Torque through bolts to 52 ft. lbs.
5. Bleed brake system.

REAR AXLE REPLACE

I-MARK EXC. FWD

Removal

1. Raise rear of vehicle with a suitable jack under differential carrier and position jack stand under jack bracket on

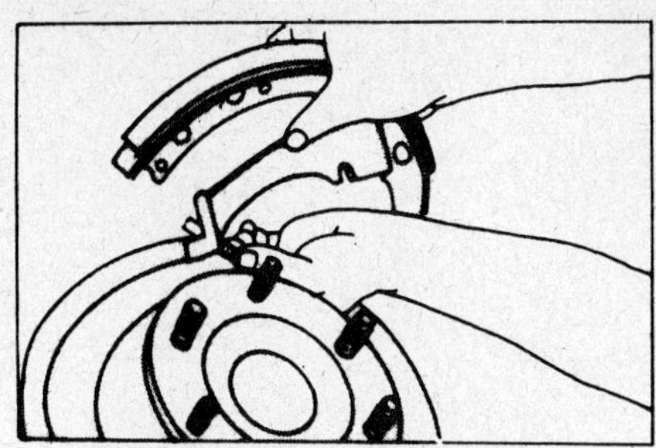

Fig. 1 Disconnecting parking brake inner cable

each side of vehicle. Remove rear wheel assemblies and one brake drum.
2. Disconnect parking brake cable equalizer and return spring from brake rod.
3. Disconnect parking brake cable from actuator lever and backing plate at wheel with brake drum removed. Disconnect cable from lower control arm brackets and pull loose end over exhaust system.
4. Disconnect shock absorbers at lower end.
5. Disconnect track rod at left end.
6. On vehicles equipped with a stabilizer rod, disconnect the shackles at rear axle housing.
7. Disconnect universal joint from pinion flange and support propeller shaft aside after marking mating areas. If propeller shaft is removed, install plug in rear of transmission to prevent loss of lubricant.
8. Disconnect brake hose from brake pipe at differential and remove retaining clip.
9. Lower rear axle assembly to remove coil springs.
10. Remove central joint support bracket to underbody retaining bolts.
11. Disconnect lower control arms at rear axle assembly and roll the assembly from under vehicle.

Installation

1. Roll rear axle assembly under car on floor jack and loosely attach lower control arms to rear axle housing.
2. Attach central joint support to underbody with bolts only finger tight.
3. Lower rear axle assembly, install lower damper rings in spring seats, coil springs and upper damper rings on springs. Make certain the damper rings and springs are properly positioned.
4. Install track rod on axle housing.
5. Place a load of approximately 350 lbs. in luggage compartment and raise rear axle far enough for underbody to clear jack stands.
6. Torque central joint support to underbody bolts to 36 ft. lbs.
7. Torque lower control arm to axle housing bolts to 29 ft. lbs.
8. Torque track rod to rear axle attaching nut to 54 ft. lbs. and remove added weight.
9. Install shock absorbers and tighten nuts to 29 ft. lbs.
10. If vehicle is equipped with stabilizer rod, connect shackles to axle housing. Tighten to 25 ft. lbs.
11. Connect brake hose to brake pipe and install retaining clip.
12. Route parking brake cable over exhaust system and connect to lower control arm brackets, parking brake actuating lever and brake backing plate. Install brake drum.
13. Align mating marks and connect propeller shaft to pinion flange. Tighten universal joint attaching bolts to 18 ft. lbs. Bend respective lock plate tabs to secure nuts or bolts.
14. Connect parking brake cable equalizer and return spring to brake rod and adjust parking brake.
15. Bleed rear brake system and fill master cylinder.
16. Install wheel assemblies and torque lug nuts to 65 ft. lbs.
17. Remove jack stands and lower vehicle.

IMPULSE

1. Remove axle shafts as previously described.
2. Remove parking brake cable adjusting nut and rear cable from front cable, then the clip attaching parking brake cable to body.
3. Remove propeller shaft.
4. Remove center exhaust pipe.
5. Remove stabilizer bar to rear axle attaching bolts and the stabilizer shackles, then disconnect rear brake flexible hose.
6. Remove lower shock absorber mounting bolts.
7. Remove lateral rod assembly.
8. Remove insulator and spring assemblies.
9. Remove rear control arm to axle attaching bolts.
10. Remove bridge to body attaching bolts.
11. Remove rear axle assembly from under vehicle.
12. Remove extension housing to axle case attaching bolts and detach extension housing.
13. Reverse procedure to install, noting the following:
   a. Before connecting extension housing to axle case, ensure that a new washer and bumper rubber have been fitted into hole in splines at carrier side of housing.
   b. Torque extension housing to axle attaching bolts to 19-22 ft. lbs.
   c. Torque bridge to body attaching bolts to 19-22 ft. lbs.
   d. Torque control arm to axle attaching bolts to 44-50 ft. lbs.
   e. Install insulator to spring seat on axle case by aligning projected portion of damper rubber with end of the coil spring.
   f. Torque lateral rod assembly attaching bolts to 43-51 ft. lbs.
   g. Torque lower shock absorber mounting bolts to 27-30 ft. lbs.
   h. Ensure that coil spring is installed in driveshaft and install attaching bolts from extension shaft side, torquing to 18-22 ft. lbs.

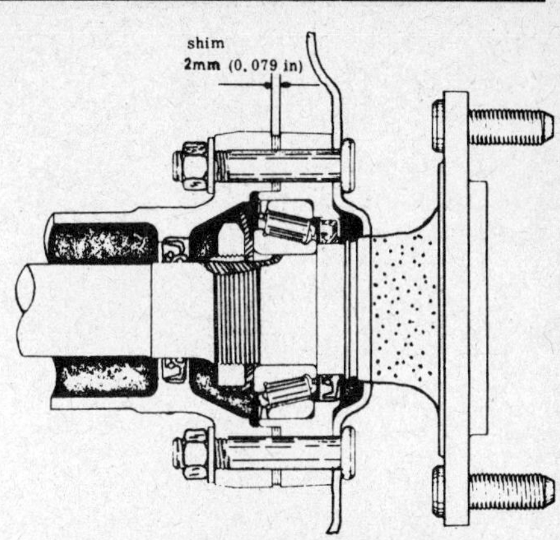

Fig. 2 Measuring axle shaft clearance

   i. Connect brake flexible hose.

CARRIER REPLACE

EXC. 1985–87 I-MARK W/FWD

Removal

1. Remove wheels and brake drums.
2. Disconnect brake pipes at both rear wheel cylinder. **Cover ends of brake pipes to prevent foreign material into system.**
3. Disconnect emergency brake cable brackets at rear spring.
4. Remove bolts from each end flange.
5. Disengage axle shafts from carrier assembly and partially withdraw shafts from axle tube. **It is not necessary to remove axle shaft.**
6. Disconnect the propeller shaft at the companion flange and remove propeller shaft.
7. Remove the nuts mounting the differential carrier assembly to the axle housing and remove the carrier, **Fig. 3.**

Installation

1. Clean the faces of the rear axle case and differential carrier and install gasket.
2. Mount the carrier assembly to the rear axle case and torque nuts to 35 ft. lbs.
3. Install the axle shaft assemblies.
4. Install propeller shaft and torque companion flange bolts to 18 ft. lbs.
5. Fill the rear axle case with hypoid gear lubricant, slightly below the filler hole.

SHOCK ABSORBER REPLACE

I-MARK EXC. FWD

Removal

1. Raise vehicle and remove wheel.
2. Disconnect lower end of shock absorber from axle, **Fig. 4.**
3. Remove fuel tank cover from inside trunk and disconnect upper end of shock absorber.
4. Remove shock absorber from vehicle.

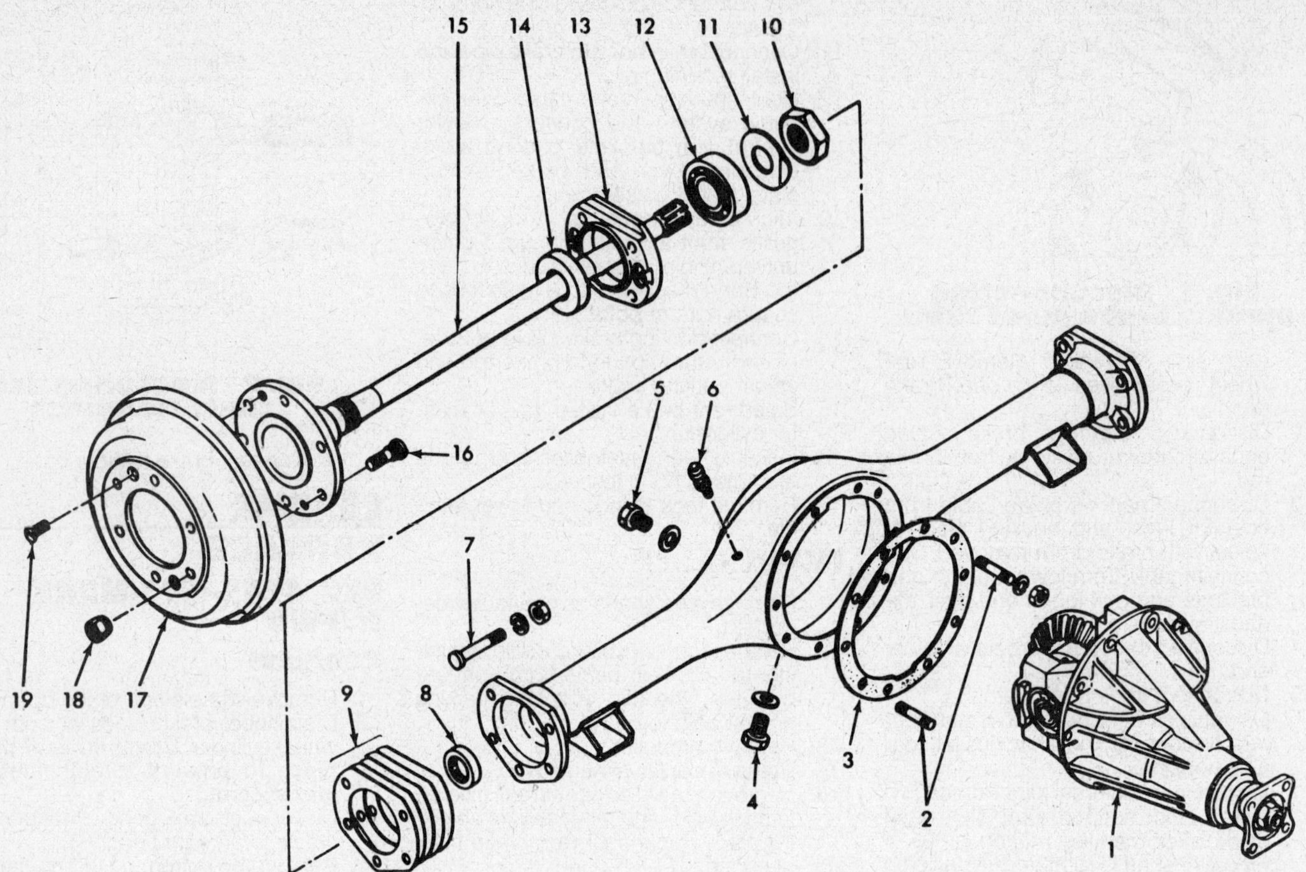

1. Differential Carrier and Case Assembly
2. Mounting Bolt
3. Gasket
4. Drain Plug
5. Filler Plug
6. Vent
7. Through Bolt
8. Oil Seal
9. Shims
10. Lock Nut
11. Lock Washer
12. Axle Shaft Bearing
13. Bearing Holder
14. Grease Seal
15. Axle Shaft
16. Wheel Stud
17. Brake Drum
18. Wheel Nut
19. Drum to Flange Screw

Fig. 3 Differential case and carrier assembly

Installation

1. Attach shock absorber upper mounting.
2. Install fuel tank cover.
3. Attach lower end of shock absorber to axle. Torque nut to 29 ft. lbs.
4. Install wheel and torque nuts to 50 ft. lbs.
5. Lower vehicle.

1985–87 I-MARK W/FWD

Refer to **Fig. 5** for removal and installation of shock absorber.

IMPULSE

1. Raise and support rear axle with a suitable jack.
2. Remove lower shock absorber attaching bolt and grommet, **Fig. 6.**
3. Remove upper mounting nut, washers and grommets, then the shock absorber.
4. Reverse procedure to install. Torque lower attaching bolt to 29 ft. lbs.

PICKUP & TROOPER II

1. Raise vehicle and support with jack stands placed under frame near rear end of spring brackets.
2. Remove upper and lower shock absorber retaining nuts and remove shock absorber.
3. Reverse procedure to install.

COIL SPRING REPLACE

I-MARK EXC. FWD.

Removal

1. Raise vehicle and remove wheel.
2. Raise rear axle with a suitable jack.
3. Disconnect lower end of shock absorber from rear axle, **Fig. 4.**
4. Lower jack supporting rear axle until the coil spring can be removed.
5. Remove coil spring.

Installation

1. Install coil spring.
2. Raise rear axle with the jack.
3. Connect lower end of shock absorber to rear axle.
4. Remove jack under rear axle.
5. Install wheel and torque nuts to 50 ft. lbs.
6. Lower vehicle.

IMPULSE

1. Disconnect shock absorber lower mounting bolts.
2. Remove stabilizer bar as outlined under "Stabilizer Bar, Replace" procedure.
3. Remove lateral rod as outlined under "Lateral Rod, Replace" procedure.
4. Lower axle housing and remove coil spring from vehicle.
5. Reverse procedure to install.

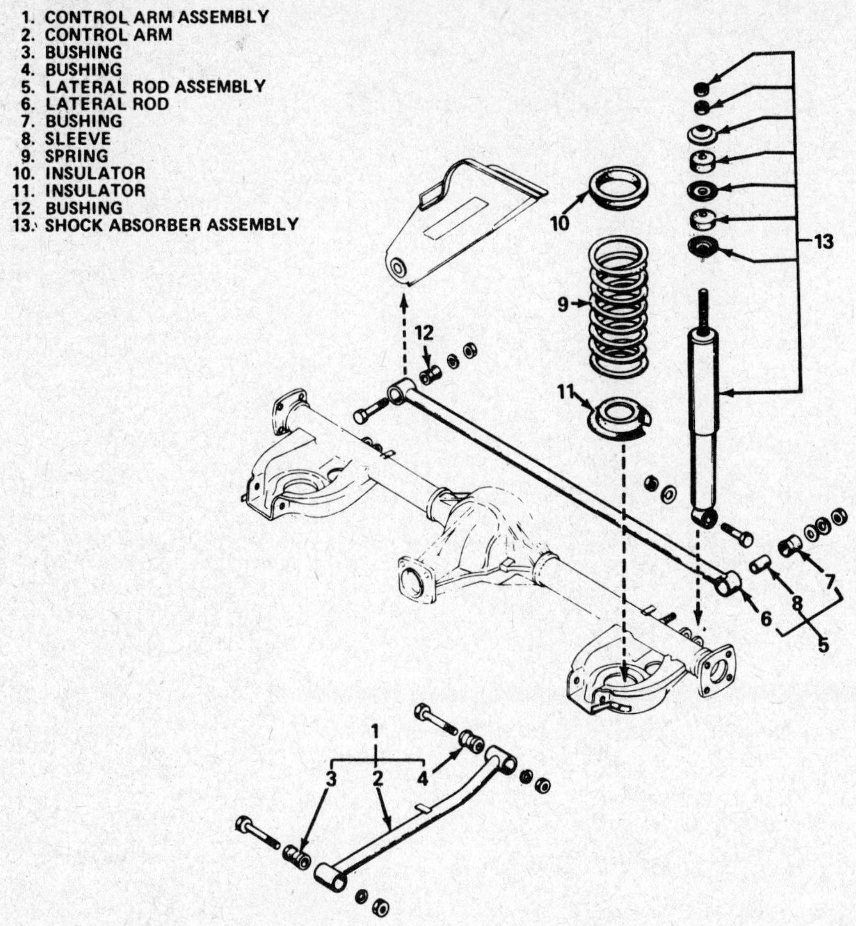

1. CONTROL ARM ASSEMBLY
2. CONTROL ARM
3. BUSHING
4. BUSHING
5. LATERAL ROD ASSEMBLY
6. LATERAL ROD
7. BUSHING
8. SLEEVE
9. SPRING
10. INSULATOR
11. INSULATOR
12. BUSHING
13. SHOCK ABSORBER ASSEMBLY

Fig. 4 Exploded view of rear suspension. I-Mark Exc. FWD

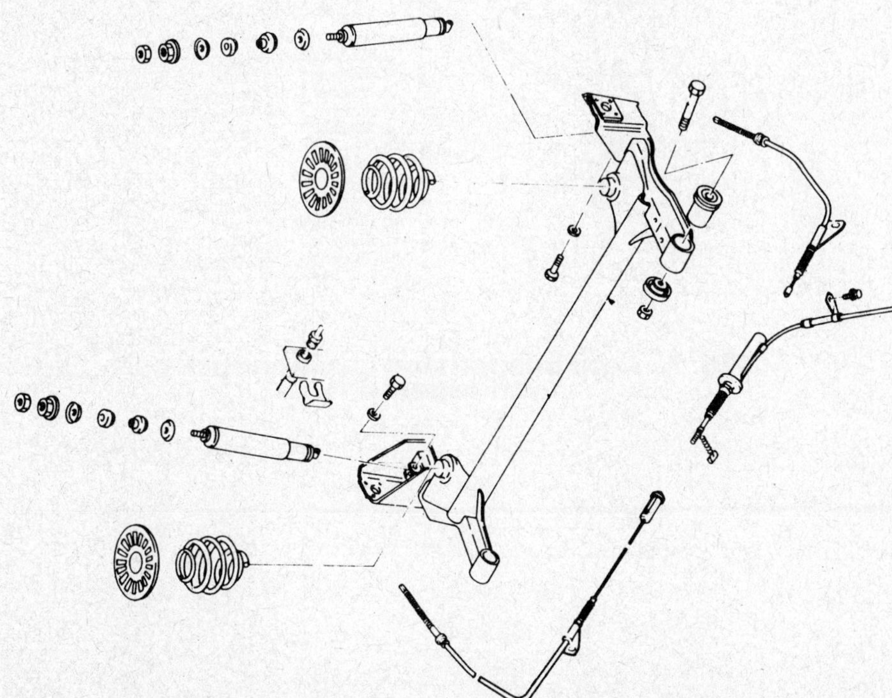

Fig. 5 Exploded view of rear suspension. 1985–87 I-Mark W/FWD

LEAF SPRING
REPLACE
PICKUP & TROOPER II

1. Remove the shock absorbers, **Fig. 7.**
2. Remove the parking brake cable clips.
3. Remove the "U" bolts.
4. Jack up the rear axle slightly to separate it from the leaf spring assemblies.
5. Remove the front and rear shackle bolt nuts and drive out rear shackle bolt.
6. Drive out the front shackle bolt and remove the leaf spring assembly rearward.
7. Remove the shackle bolt from the rear springs bracket and remove the shackle.
8. Reverse procedure to install. Torque "U" bolts to 40 ft. lbs. and shackle bolt nuts to 70 ft. lbs.

STABILIZER BAR
REPLACE
IMPULSE

1. Raise and support rear of vehicle.
2. Remove stabilizer bar to axle attaching bolts, **Fig 3.**
3. Remove stabilizer bar to underbody attaching bolts.
4. Remove stabilizer bar from vehicle.
5. Reverse procedure to install.

LATERAL ROD
REPLACE
I-MARK
Removal

1. Raise vehicle and remove rear wheels.
2. Remove lower shock absorber bolt.
3. Remove bolt securing lateral rod to body, **Fig. 4.**
4. Remove nut securing lateral rod to axle case.
5. Remove lateral rod assembly.

Installation

1. Attach lateral rod to axle case and to body.
2. Torque lateral rod to body bolt to 43 ft. lbs.
3. Torque lateral rod to axle case nut to 54 ft. lbs.
4. Install lower shock absorber bolt. Torque nut to 29 ft. lbs.
5. Install wheels and torque nuts to 50 ft. lbs.
6. Lower vehicle.

IMPULSE

1. Raise and support rear of vehicle, then remove rear wheels.
2. Remove lateral rod to underbody attaching nut, washer and bolt.
3. Remove rod to axle housing attaching nut, washer and cover, then the lateral rod.
4. Reverse procedure to install.

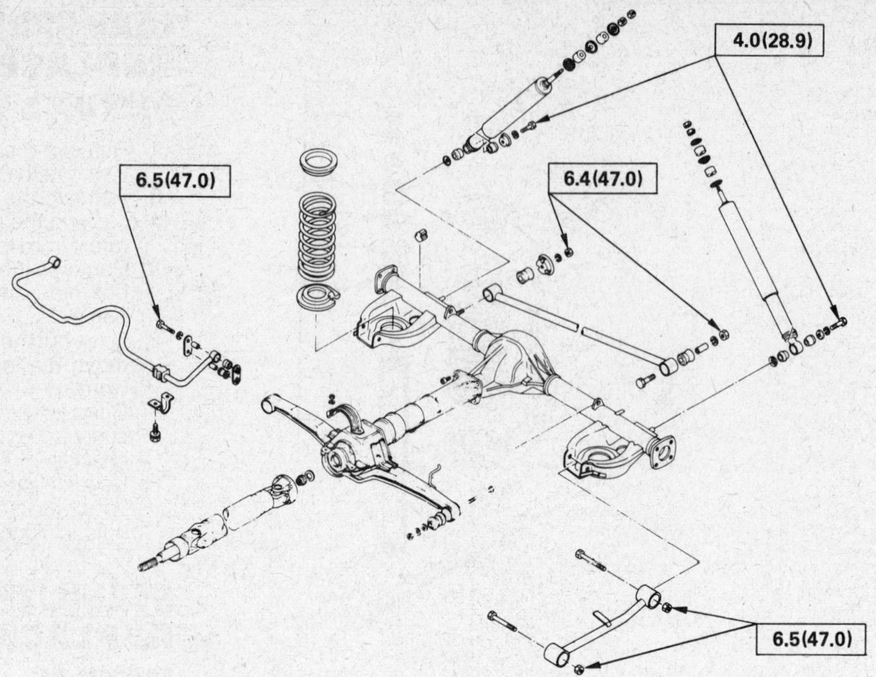

Fig. 6 Exploded view of rear suspension. Impulse

CONTROL ARM REPLACE

I-MARK EXC. FWD

Removal

1. Raise vehicle and remove rear wheel.
2. Remove bolt connecting the control arm to axle case, **Fig. 4.**
3. Remove bolt connecting the control arm to the body.
4. Remove control arm assembly.

Installation

1. Attach control arm assembly to the body and to axle case. Torque bolts to 29 ft. lbs.
2. Install wheels and torque nuts to 50 ft. lbs.

IMPULSE

1. Raise and support rear of vehicle and axle housing assembly.
2. Remove control arm to axle housing attaching bolt and nut.
3. Remove control arm to underbody attaching bolt and nut, then the control arm.
4. Reverse procedure to install. Torque attaching nuts to 47 ft. lbs.

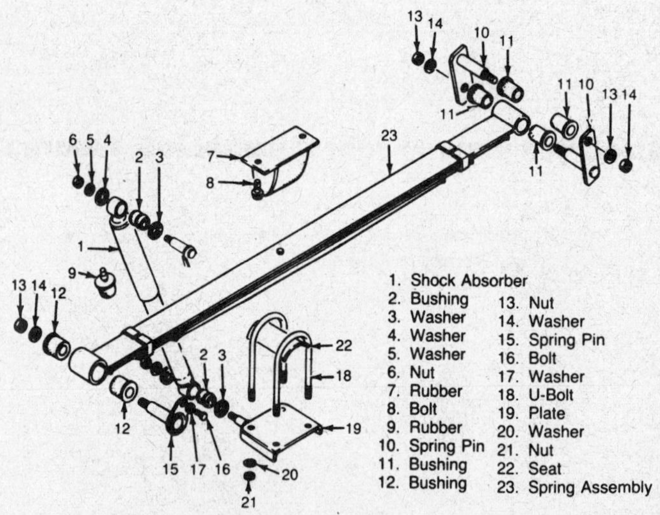

Fig. 7 Rear suspension components part arrangement

FRONT SUSPENSION & STEERING SECTION, EXC. 1985–87 I-MARK W/FRONT WHEEL DRIVE

INDEX

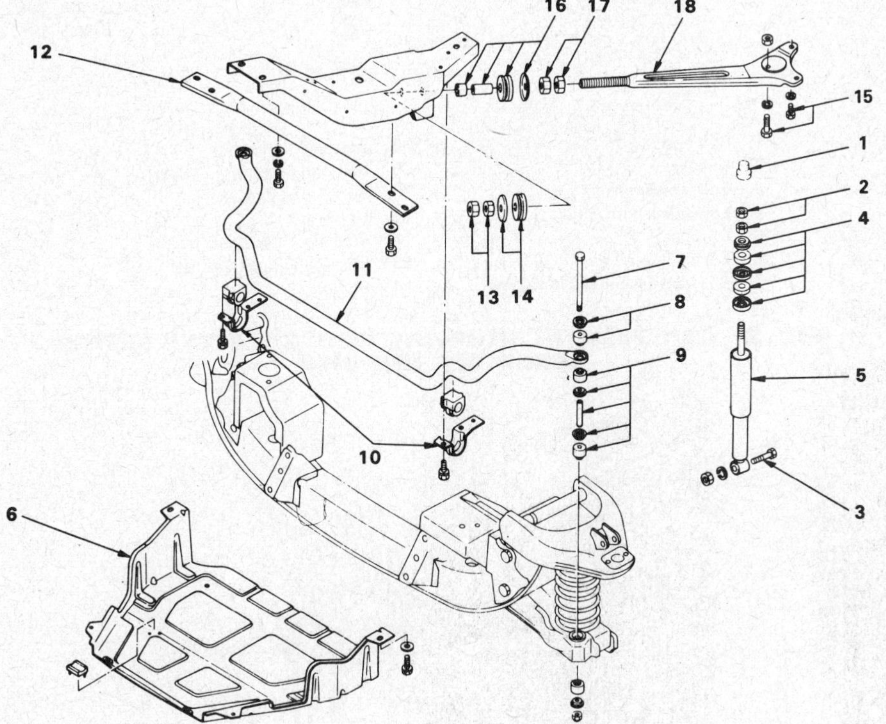

1. Cap ; shock absorber
2. Nuts ; hexagon, shock absorber
3. Bolt ; shock absorber to upper link
4. Bumper rubbers and washers
5. Shock absorber
6. Cover ; under, engine room
7. Bolt ; stabilizer bar to lower link
8. Retainer and grommet
9. Retainer, grommet and tube
10. Bracket ; stabilizer bar to body
11. Stabilizer bar
12. Bar ; cross, strut bar
13. Nuts ; strut bar
14. Cushion rubber and washer
15. Bolts ; strut bar to lower link
16. Cushion rubber, washer and tube
17. Nuts ; strut bar
18. Strut bar

Fig. 1 Shock absorber, strub bars & stabilizer bar assembly. Impulse

SHOCK ABSORBER, STRUT BAR & STABILIZER BAR

I-MARK

Shock Absorber, Replace

1. Raise and support vehicle, then remove wheel.
2. Disconnect shock absorber from upper control arm.
3. Remove shock absorber nuts from engine compartment.
4. Remove shock absorber from vehicle.
5. Reverse procedure to install, noting the following:
   a. Torque upper control arm to shock absorber attaching nut to 29 ft. lbs.
   b. Install wheel, then torque retaining nuts to 50 ft. lbs.

IMPULSE

Shock Absorber, Replace

1. Raise and support front of vehicle.
2. Remove shock absorber cap, **Fig. 1.**
3. Remove shock absorber nuts.
4. Remove shock absorber to upper link bolt.
5. Remove rubber bumpers and washers.
6. Remove shock absorber.
7. Reverse procedure to install. Torque shock absorber to upper link bolt to 27-30 ft. lbs.

Stabilizer Bar, Replace

1. Raise and support front of vehicle.
2. Remove engine undercover.
3. Remove stabilizer bar to lower link bolt.
4. Remove retainer and grommet.
5. Remove tube retainer and grommet.
6. Remove stabilizer bar to body bracket.
7. Remove stabilizer bar.
8. Reverse procedure to install.

Strut Bar, Replace

1. Raise and support front of vehicle.

2. Remove cross strut bar.
3. Remove strut bar attaching nuts.
4. Remove rubber cushion and washer.
5. Remove strut bar to lower link bolts.
6. Remove tube cushion and washer.
7. Remove remaining strut bar attaching nuts, then the strut bar.
8. Reverse procedure to install. Torque strut bar nuts to 65-80 ft. lbs.

CONTROL ARMS, STEERING KNUCKLE & COIL SPRINGS

IMPULSE

For control arms, steering knuckle and coil spring service, refer to **Fig. 2**. Note the following:

1. When removing rod end, use tool No. J-21687-02 to secure rod end.
2. When removing steering knuckle, proceed as follows:
   a. Compress coil springs using tool No. J-33992 or equivalent to disconnect the upper and lower link balls from the steering knuckle.
   b. Set guide link plate 4, **Fig. 3** with its tool number facing outward. The guide link plate has a stamped mark R for right or L for left in addition to the tool number.
   c. Set hook 1, **Fig. 4** onto the third coil from the top of spring.
   d. Set plate to lower link A using alignment hole in guide link plate 4. **Install a suitable chain through one coil nearest top of spring and connect other end to the upper control arm to prevent spring from coming out.**
   e. Tighten compressor tool screw 6, **Fig. 5**, after tightening rod 3 on each side evenly.
   f. Disconnect upper link B.
   g. Compress coil spring until top end releases from cushion C, **Fig. 6** at center of upper link B, then remove coil spring.
   h. Remove lower link bolt D, **Fig. 6**, then remove coil spring together with lower link A.
   i. Loosen rod 3, **Fig. 6** on each side alternately and evenly, then separate coil spring from lower link.
3. During installation, torque upper link bolt to 44-50 ft. lbs. Torque lower link bolt to 58-65 ft. lbs. Torque upper link to steering knuckle nuts to 54-65 ft. lbs.

1. Rod end
2. Knuckle
3. Bolt ; lower link
4. Lower link with spring
5. Damper
6. Spring
7. Ball joint assembly ; lower link
8. Bushing ; lower link
9. Ball joint assembly ; upper link
10. Bolt ; upper link
11. Upper link
12. Bushing ; upper link, front
13. Bushing ; upper link, rear
14. Bumper

Fig. 2 Control arm, steering knuckle & coil spring assembly. Impulse

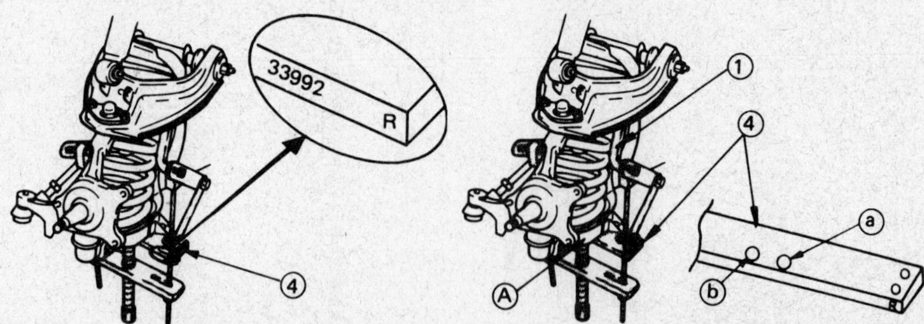

Fig. 3 Installing guide link plate

Fig. 4 Installing hook 1 onto third coil from top of spring

TORSION BAR, STRUT BAR, STABILIZER BAR & SHOCK ABSORBER

4x4 MODELS

Torsion Bar, Replace

1. Raise and support front of vehicle.
2. Remove adjustment bolt and seat, **Fig. 7**.
3. Remove height control arm.
4. Remove torsion bar and rubber seat.
5. Reverse procedure to install.

Strut Bar, Replace

1. Raise and support front of vehicle.
2. Remove rubber bushing and washer.
3. Remove bolts, nuts, washers, bushings and strut bar.
4. Reverse procedure to install.

Stabilizer Bar, Replace

1. Raise and support front of vehicle.
2. Remove rubber bushing and washer.
3. Remove bracket.
4. Remove stabilizer bar.
5. Reverse procedure to install.

Shock Absorber, Replace

1. Raise and support front of vehicle.
2. Remove nut, rubber bushing and washer.
3. Remove bolt, nut and washer.
4. Remove shock absorber.
5. Reverse procedure to install.

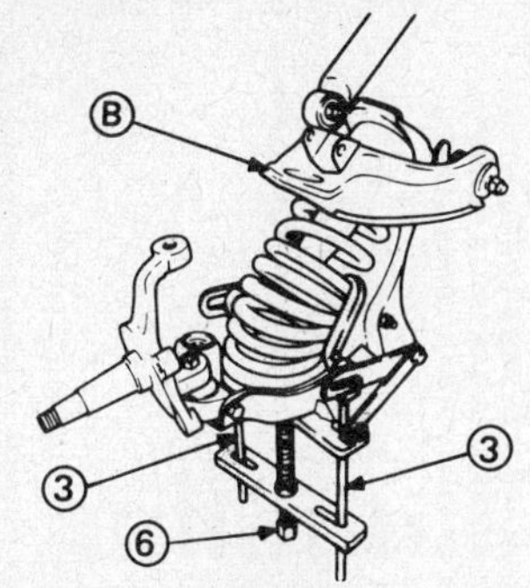

Fig. 5 Tightening compressor tool screw 6

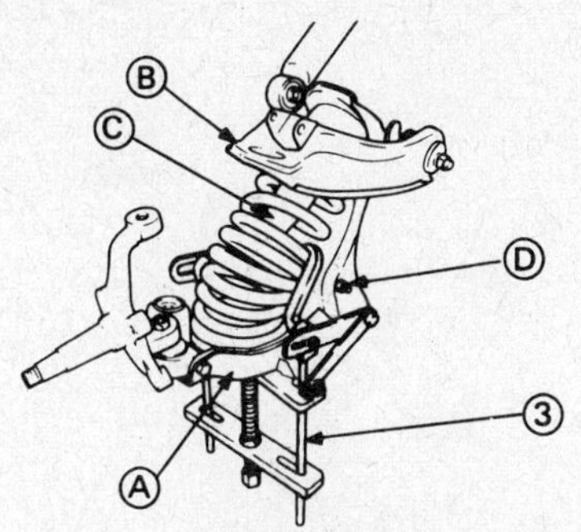

Fig. 6 Compressor tool components

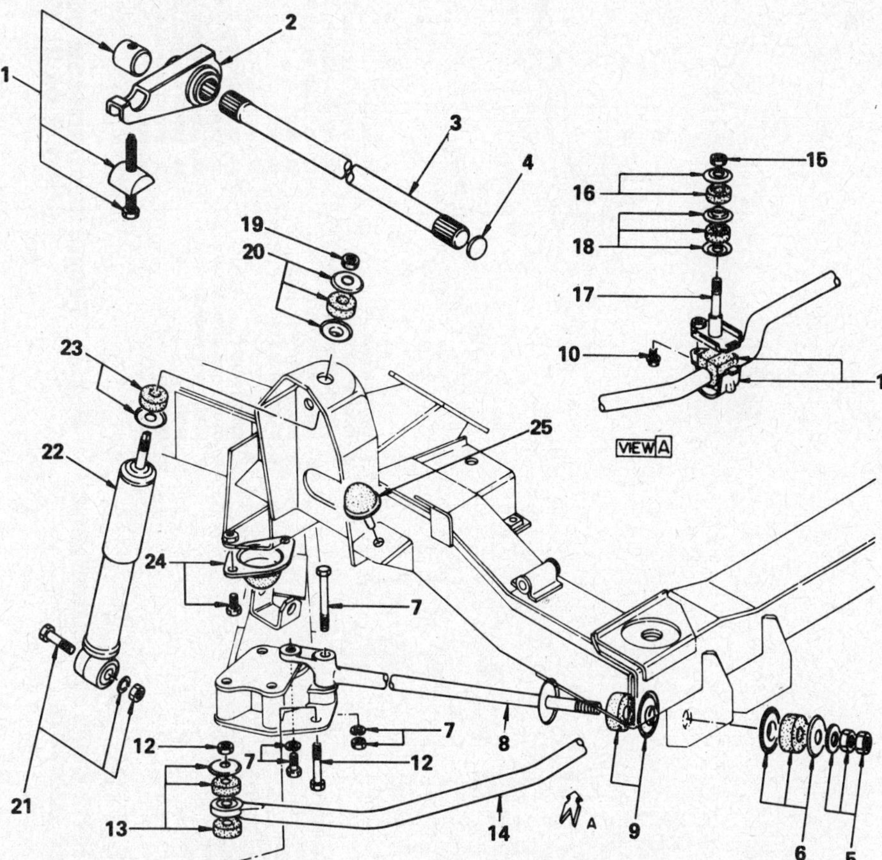

1. Adjust bolt and seat
2. Height control arm
3. Torsion bar
4. Rubber seat
5. Nut and washer
6. Rubber bushing and washer
7. Bolt, nut, and washer
8. Strut bar
9. Rubber bushing and washer
10. Bolt
11. Bracket and rubber bushing
12. Bolt, nut, and washer
13. Rubber bushing and washer
14. Stabilizer bar
15. Nut
16. Rubber bushing and washer
17. Bracket
18. Rubber bushing and washer
19. Nut
20. Rubber bushing and washer
21. Bolt, nut, and washer
22. Shock absorber
23. Rubber bushing and washer
24. Lower control arm bumper
25. Upper control arm

Fig. 7 Torsion bar, strut bar, stabilizer bar & shock absorber assembly 4x4 models

EXC. 4x4 MODELS

Torsion Bar Replace

1. Remove the height control arm adjusting bolt.
2. Scribe location and remove the height control arm from the torsion bar and third crossmember.
3. Scribe location and withdraw the torsion bar from the lower control arm.
4. Grease torsion bar ends and height control arm. Reverse removal procedure to install the torsion bar, **Fig. 8.**
5. Turn adjuster bolt to location marked upon removal.

Torsion Bar Adjustment

1. With vehicle on a level surface, rock vehicle up and down to settle suspension.
2. Loosen nuts at front strut bar.
3. Measure clearance between rubber bumper and the lower control arm. The proper clearance should be 7/8 inch.
4. To adjust height, turn adjusting bolt inward to raise height or outward to decrease height.
5. Tighten strut bar nuts.

Strut Bar Replace

1. Remove the frame side bracket by removing the strut bar nuts, washer and rubber bushings.
2. Remove the two bolts fastening the strut bar to the lower control arm and remove the strut bar.
3. Reverse procedure for installation of strut bar. Refer to **Fig. 8** for proper bushing positions and tighten to specification. Strut bar to lower control arm, torque 45 ft. lbs. Strut bar to frame, torque nut 15 ft. lbs.; locknut 50 ft. lbs.

Stabilizer Bar Replace

1. Raise and support vehicle.
2. Disconnect stabilizer bar from lower control arms.
3. Remove stabilizer bar brackets and remove stabilizer.
4. Reverse procedure to install.

Front Shock Absorber

1. With an open end wrench hold the shock absorber upper stem from turning, and then remove the upper stem retaining nut, retainer and rubber grommet.
2. Remove bolt retaining the lower shock absorber pivot to the lower control arm and remove shock absorber assembly.
3. Reverse procedure for installation. Refer to **Fig. 8** for bushing position.

STEERING KNUCKLE, UPPER & LOWER LINKS

TROOPER II

Steering Knuckle, Replace

1. Raise and support front of vehicle.
2. Remove back plate and knuckle arm, **Fig. 9.**

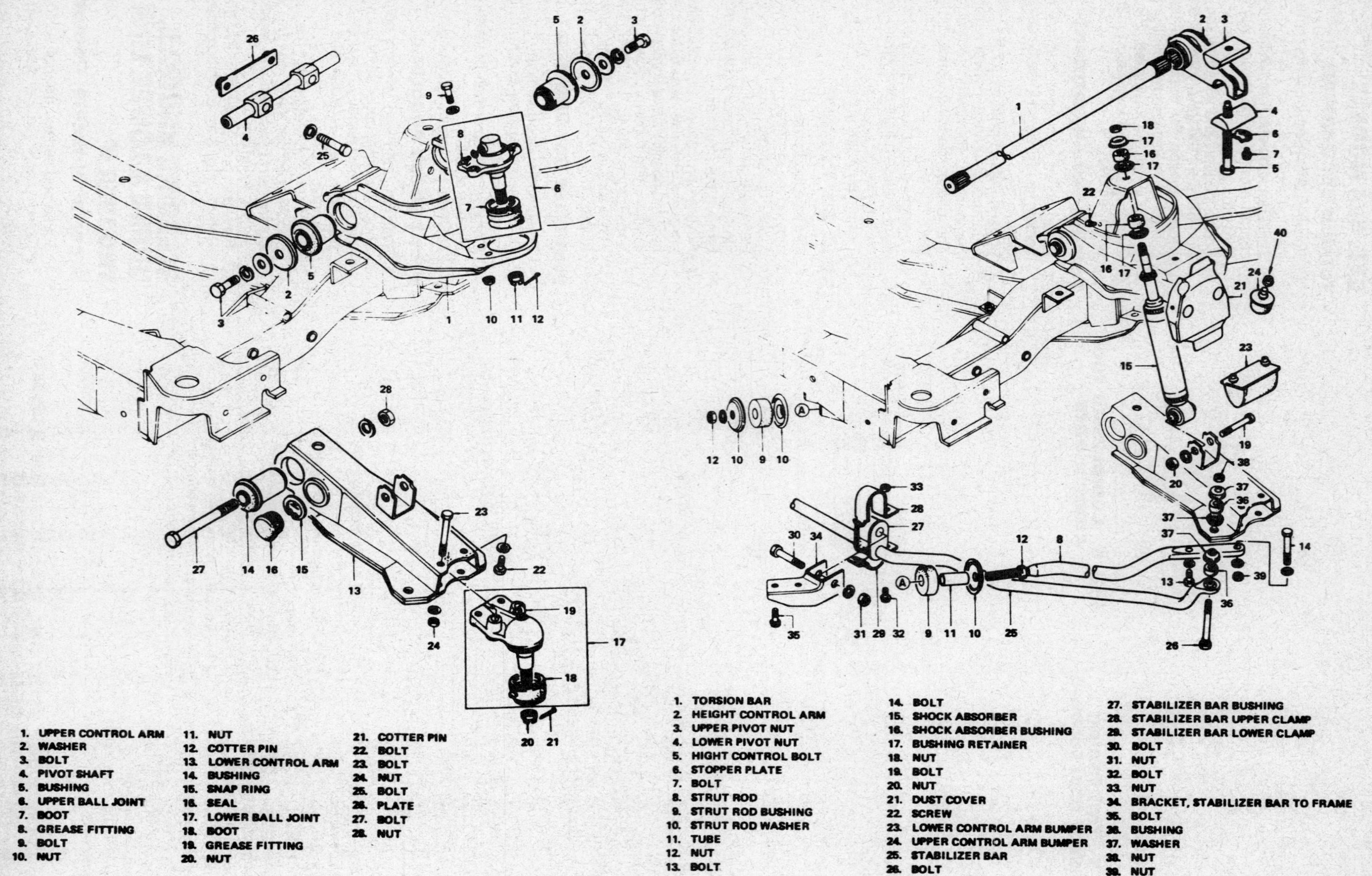

1. UPPER CONTROL ARM
2. WASHER
3. BOLT
4. PIVOT SHAFT
5. BUSHING
6. UPPER BALL JOINT
7. BOOT
8. GREASE FITTING
9. BOLT
10. NUT
11. NUT
12. COTTER PIN
13. LOWER CONTROL ARM
14. BUSHING
15. SNAP RING
16. SEAL
17. LOWER BALL JOINT
18. BOOT
19. GREASE FITTING
20. NUT
21. COTTER PIN
22. BOLT
23. BOLT
24. NUT
25. BOLT
26. PLATE
27. BOLT
28. NUT

Fig. 8 Front suspension component part arrangement (Part 1 of 2). Exc. 4x4 models

1. TORSION BAR
2. HEIGHT CONTROL ARM
3. UPPER PIVOT NUT
4. LOWER PIVOT NUT
5. HIGHT CONTROL BOLT
6. STOPPER PLATE
7. BOLT
8. STRUT ROD
9. STRUT ROD BUSHING
10. STRUT ROD WASHER
11. TUBE
12. NUT
13. BOLT
14. BOLT
15. SHOCK ABSORBER
16. SHOCK ABSORBER BUSHING
17. BUSHING RETAINER
18. NUT
19. BOLT
20. NUT
21. DUST COVER
22. SCREW
23. LOWER CONTROL ARM BUMPER
24. UPPER CONTROL ARM BUMPER
25. STABILIZER BAR
26. BOLT
27. STABILIZER BAR BUSHING
28. STABILIZER BAR UPPER CLAMP
29. STABILIZER BAR LOWER CLAMP
30. BOLT
31. NUT
32. BOLT
33. NUT
34. BRACKET, STABILIZER BAR TO FRAME
35. BOLT
36. BUSHING
37. WASHER
38. NUT
39. NUT
40. NUT

Fig. 8 Front suspension component part arrangement (Part 2 of 2). Exc. 4x4 models

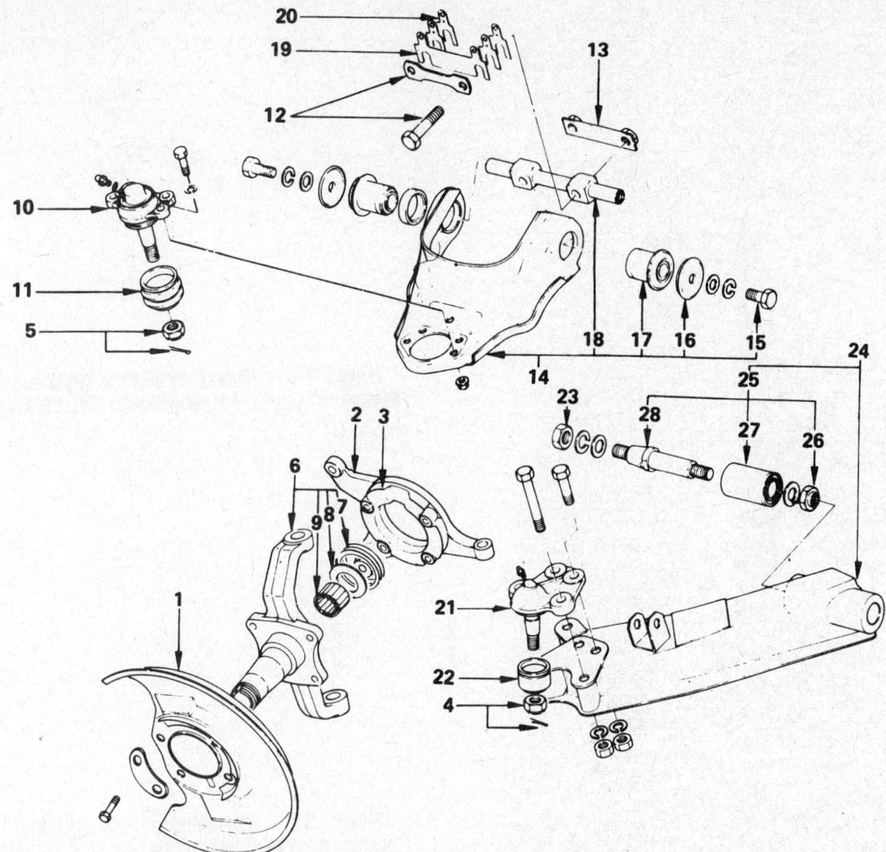

1. Back plate
2. Knuckle arm
3. Dust shield
4. Nut and cotter pin
5. Nut and cotter pin
6. Knuckle
7. Oil seal
8. Washer
9. Needle bearing
10. Upper end
11. Boot
12. Bolt and plate
13. Nut assembly
14. Upper link assembly
15. Bolt and washer
16. Plate
17. Bushing
18. Fulcrum pin
19. Camber shims
20. Caster shims
21. Lower end
22. Boot
23. Nut and washer
24. Lower link assembly
25. Bushing and pin
26. Nut and washer
27. Bushing
28. Fulcrum pin

Fig. 9 Steering knuckle, upper & lower link assembly. Trooper II

3. Remove dust shield, nut and cotter pin.
4. Remove steering knuckle.
5. Reverse procedure to install. Torque steering knuckle nuts to 72-80 ft. lbs.

Upper Link, Replace

1. Raise and support vehicle.
2. Remove upper end and boot.
3. Remove bolt and plate assembly.
4. Remove nut assembly, then the upper link.
5. Reverse procedure to install. Torque bolts to 80-94 ft. lbs. Torque bolt and plate assembly to 72-80 ft. lbs. Torque upper link nuts to 17-20 ft. lbs.

Lower Link, Replace

1. Raise and support vehicle.
2. Remove lower end and boot assembly.
3. Remove nut, washer and lower link assembly.
4. Reverse procedure to install. Torque nuts to 72-80 ft. lbs.

UPPER CONTROL ARM REPLACE

I-MARK

Removal

1. Raise vehicle and remove wheel.
2. Remove upper brake caliper bolt and slide hose retaining clip back approximately 1/4-1/2 inch.
3. Remove lower shock absorber bolt and push shock absorber upward.
4. Raise lower control arm until level and place support under outer end of control arm.
5. Loosen upper ball joint castle nut until top of nut is flush with the top of the ball joint. Using Tool J-26407-1, disconnect the upper ball joint from the steering knuckle, **Fig. 10.**
6. Remove through bolt connecting upper control arm to the crossmember.
7. Remove upper control arm.

Installation

1. Install ball joint in upper control arm.
2. On installation of the upper control arm, make sure the smaller washer is on the inner face of the front arm and the larger washer is on the inner face of the rear arm.
3. Attach upper control arm to crossmember. Do not fully tighten bolt.
4. Attach upper ball joint to steering knuckle and torque castle nut to 40 ft. lbs.
5. Torque through bolt connecting upper control arm to the crossmember to 43 ft. lbs.
6. Install lower shock absorber bolt. Torque bolt to 29 ft. lbs.
7. Slide hose retaining clip in place and install the upper brake caliper bolt. Torque bolt to 36 ft. lbs.
8. Install wheel and torque to 50 ft. lbs.

UPPER BALL JOINT REPLACE

I-MARK

Removal

1. Raise vehicle and remove wheel.
2. Remove upper brake caliper bolt and slide hose retaining clip back approximately 1/4 to 1/2 in.
3. Remove lower shock absorber bolt and push shock absorber upward.
4. Raise lower control arm until level and place support under outer end of control arm.
5. Loosen upper ball joint castle nut until top of nut is flush with top of ball joint. Using Tool J-26407-1, disconnect upper ball joint from the steering knuckle, **Fig. 10.**
6. Remove two bolts connecting upper ball joint to control arm.
7. Remove upper ball joint.

Installation

1. Install upper ball joint in control arm so the cut-off portion is facing outward.
2. Install two bolts connecting upper ball joint to control arm. Torque nuts to 29 ft. lbs.
3. Attach upper ball joint to steering knuckle and torque castle nut to 40 ft. lbs.
4. Install lower shock absorber bolt. Torque to 29 ft. lbs.
5. Slide hose retaining clip in place and install the upper brake caliper bolt. Torque bolt to 36 ft. lbs.
6. Install wheel and torque nuts to 50 ft. lbs.

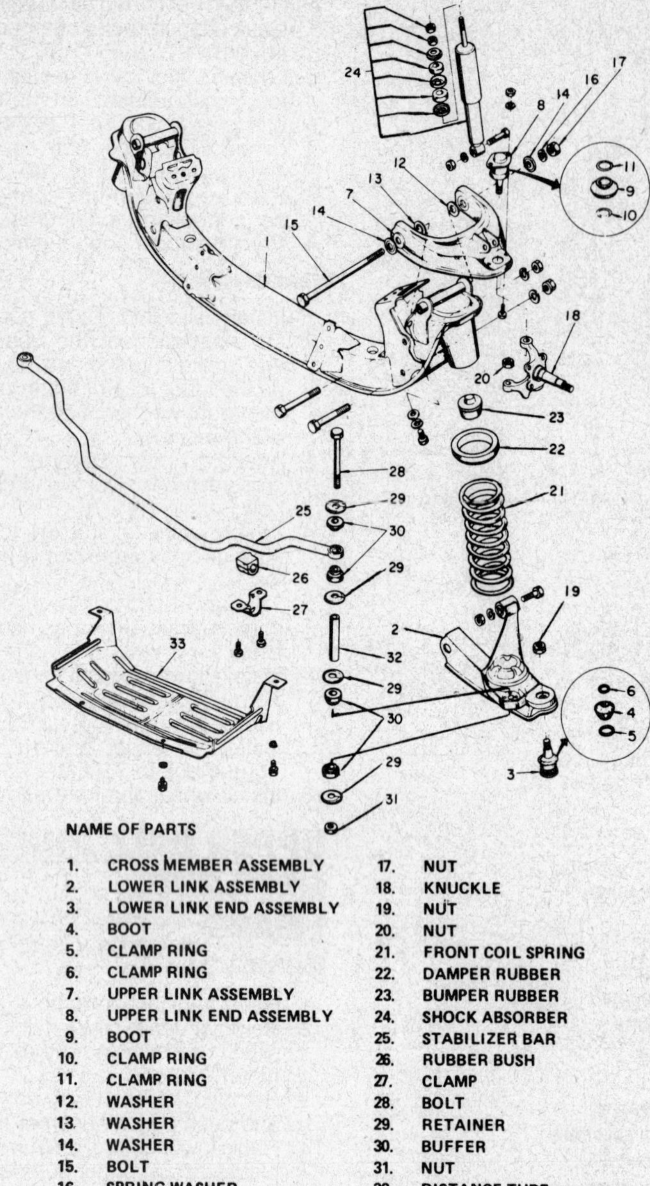

Fig. 10 Front suspension. I-Mark

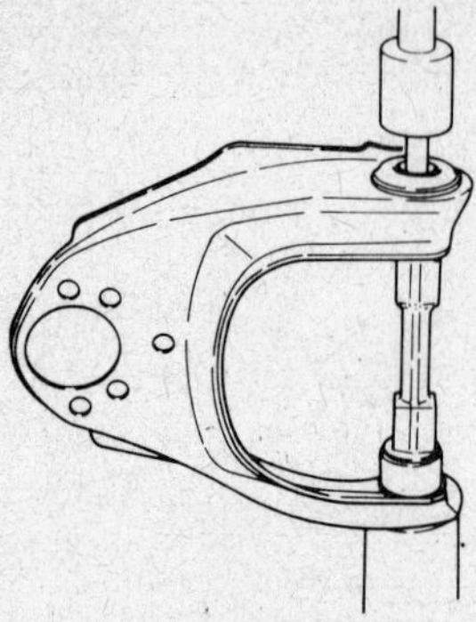

Fig. 11 Removing pivot arm shaft bushing. Pickup

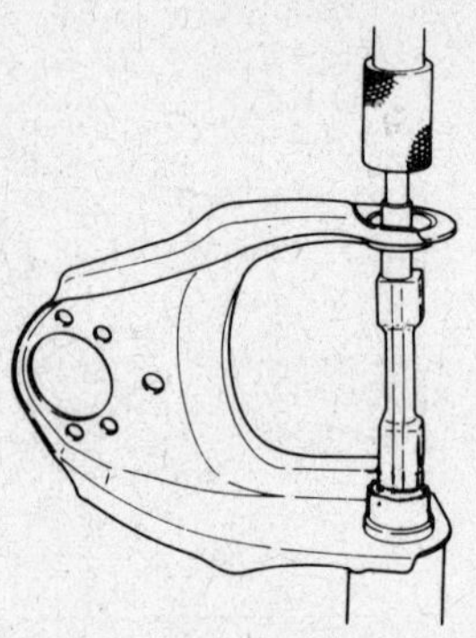

Fig. 12 Removing pivot arm shaft bushing. Pickup

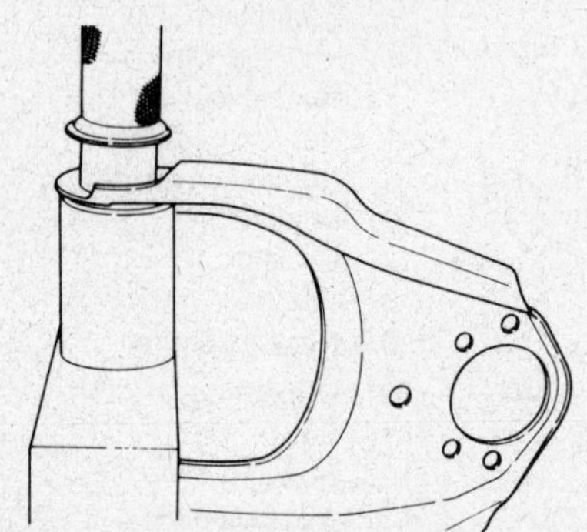

Fig. 13 Installing pivot arm shaft bushing. Pickup

UPPER CONTROL ARM, BALL JOINT & PIVOT SHAFT

REPLACE

PICKUP

The upper control arm and ball joint are replaced as an assembly.

1. Raise and support front of vehicle under the lower control arms, remove wheel assembly.
2. Remove shock absorber dust cover.
3. Remove cotter pin and castellated nut from upper ball joint, separate upper control arm from the knuckle, **Fig. 8. Wire the knuckle assembly to the frame or other support, to prevent assembly from hanging by the brake flexible line.**
4. Remove the two upper pivot mounting bolts, then the upper shock retaining nut, retainer and grommet. Compress the shock absorber.
5. Remove the upper control arm from the bracket.

Pivot Shaft, Replace

1. Remove the bolts, lock washers, washers and plates from each side of the pivot shaft.
2. Remove the bushings and pivot shaft from the upper control arm using tool J-29775, **Figs. 11 and 12.**
3. Install new pivot shaft and bushing on the upper control arm using tool J-29775, **Figs. 13 and 14.** Install plates, washers, lock washers and bolts, torque bolts to 87 ft. lbs.
4. Install ball joint stud through the steering knuckle, install castellated nut and torque to 75 ft. lbs. (plus additional torque to align cotter pin) and install cotter pin.
5. Install upper control arm on chassis frame. Torque upper pivot mounting bolts to 75 ft. lbs.
6. Install wheel assembly and lower vehicle.

LOWER CONTROL ARM

REPLACE

I-MARK

Removal

1. Raise vehicle and remove wheel.

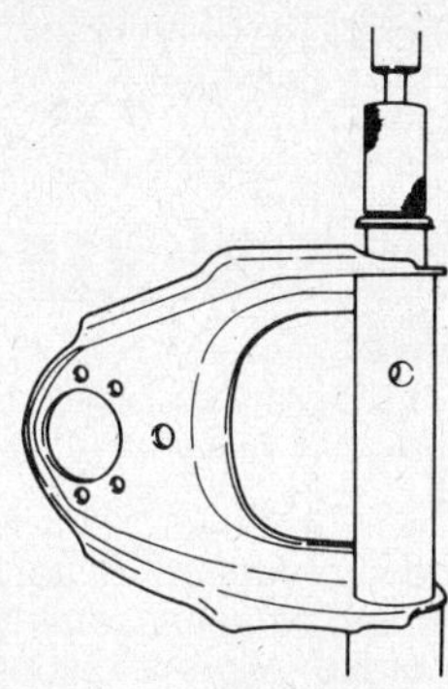

Fig. 14 Installing pivot arm shaft bushing. Pickup

2. Remove tie rod end cotter key and castle nut. Using Tool J-21687-1, disconnect tie rod end from steering knuckle.
3. Remove lower shock absorber bolt and push shock absorber upward.
4. Remove stabilizer bar bolt and grommet assembly from lower control arm.
5. Remove upper brake caliper bolt and slide hose retaining clip back approximately 1/4-1/2 inch.
6. Place spring compressor over upper control arm and let hang.
7. Raise lower control arm until level and place support under outer end of control arm.
8. Loosen lower ball joint castle nut until top of nut is flush with the top of the ball joint. Using Tool J-26407-1, disconnect the lower ball joint from the steering knuckle.
9. Remove hub assembly and steering knuckle from lower ball joint and secure, with a wire or equivalent, to the side.
10. Install spring compressor between first exposed coil of spring.
11. Compress spring until spring clears lower spring seat.
12. Remove support under lower control arm.
13. Remove bolts connecting lower control arm to crossmember and the body.
14. Remove lower control arm.

Installation

1. Install ball joint in lower control arm.
2. Install bolts connecting front of control arm to crossmember and rear of control arm to body. Do not fully tighten bolts.
3. Raise lower control arm until level and place support under outer extreme of control arm.
4. Remove spring compressor.
5. Attach hub assembly and steering knuckle to lower ball joint. Torque castle nut to 72 ft. lbs.
6. Attach upper ball joint to steering knuckle. Torque castle nut to 40 ft. lbs.
7. Torque bolts connecting lower control arm to crossmember and body to 43 ft. lbs.
8. Install stabilizer bar bolt and grommet assembly to lower control arm. Tighten the nut to the end of the threads on the bolt.
9. Install lower shock absorber bolt. Torque bolt to 29 ft. lbs.
10. Slide hose retaining clip in place and install upper brake caliper bolt. Torque bolt to 36 ft. lbs.
11. Attach tie rod end to steering knuckle. Torque castle nut to 29 ft. lbs. Install new cotter key.
12. Install wheel and torque nuts to 50 ft. lbs.

PICKUP

Removal

1. Remove the wheel and tire assembly.
2. Remove the strut bar and withdraw the stabilizer from the rod.
3. Remove the torsion bar.
4. Remove the lower shock absorber bolt.
5. Take out the two bolts retaining the lower ball joint and disconnect the lower ball joint from the lower control arm.
6. Remove the retaining bolts and the lower control arm, **Fig. 8.**

Installation

1. Fasten the lower ball joint to the lower control arm and torque retaining bolts to 45 ft. lbs.
2. Mount the lower control arm to the chassis frame. Drive the bolt into position and torque to 90 ft. lbs.
3. Install torsion bar.
4. Install the strut bars in position after removing jack. **Leave the strut bar to frame nuts finger tight until the vehicle height is adjusted.**

LOWER BALL JOINT REPLACE

I-MARK

Removal

1. Raise vehicle and remove wheel.
2. Remove tie rod end cotter key and castle nut. Using Tool J-21687-1, disconnect tie rod end from steering knuckle.
3. Remove stabilizer bar bolt and grommet assembly from lower control arm.
4. Remove upper brake caliper bolt and slide hose-retaining clip back approximately 1/4-1/2 inch.
5. Remove lower shock absorber bolt and push shock absorber upward.
6. Place spring compressor over upper control arm and let hang.
7. Place support under outer extreme of lower control arm, and loosen lower ball joint castle nut until top of nut is flush with top of ball joint.
8. Using Tool J-26407-1, disconnect the lower ball joint from the steering knuckle.
9. Remove hub assembly and steering knuckle from lower ball joint and secure, with a wire or equivalent, aside.
10. Install spring compressor between first exposed coil of spring and compress spring.
11. Remove support under lower control arm.
12. Remove lower ball joint from control

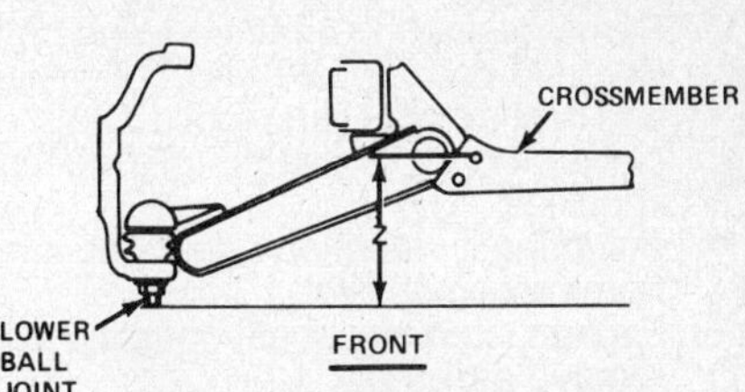

Fig. 15 Torsion bar adjustment, all models. Pickup

arm, using tools J-9519 as installer and J-9519-4 as receiver.

Installation

1. Install new ball joint in lower control arm using Tools J-9519 as installer and J-9519-4 as receiver. Do not strike ball joint bottom.
2. Place support under outer end of lower control arm.
3. Remove spring compressor.
4. Attach hub assembly and steering knuckle to lower ball joint. Torque castle nut to 72 ft. lbs.
5. Slide hose retaining clip in place and install upper brake caliper bolt. Torque nut to 72 ft. lbs.
6. Install stabilizer bar bolt and grommet assembly to lower control arm. Tighten the nut to the end of the threads on the bolt.
7. Attach tie rod end to steering knuckle. Torque castle nut to 29 ft. lbs. Install new cotter key.
8. Install lower shock absorber bolt. Torque to 29 ft. lbs.
9. Install wheel and torque nuts to 50 ft. lbs.

COIL SPRING REPLACE

I-MARK

Removal

1. Raise vehicle and remove wheel.
2. Remove tie rod end cotter key and castle nut. Using Tool J-21687-1, disconnect tie rod end from steering knuckle.
3. Remove lower shock absorber bolt and push shock absorber upward.
4. Remove stabilizer bar bolt and grommet assembly from lower control arm.
5. Remove upper brake caliper bolt and slide hose retaining clip back approximately 1/4-1/2 inch.
6. Place spring compressor over upper control arm and let hang.
7. Raise lower control arm until level and place support under outer end of control

STEERING GEAR REPLACE

I-MARK

Removal

1. Raise vehicle and remove undercover.

2. Remove steering shaft coupling bolt.
3. Remove both tie rod end cotter pins and castle nuts. Using tool J-21687-1, disconnect tie rod ends from steering knuckles.
4. Disconnect steering gear housing from crossmember.
5. Expand steering shaft coupling and remove assembly.
6. Remove tie rod assemblies from steering gear.

Installation

1. Attach tie rod assemblies to steering gear.
2. Prior to installation of steering gear assembly, set steering gear to high point by positioning front wheels straight ahead with steering wheel centered.
3. Attach steering coupling to steering wheel.
4. Attach steering gear housing to crossmember. Torque bolts to 29 ft. lbs.
5. Install steering shaft coupling bolt. Torque bolt to 19 ft. lbs.
6. Attach both tie rod ends to steering knuckles. Torque castle nuts to 29 ft. lbs. Install new cotter pins.
7. Check and adjust toe-in.
8. Install under cover.

TORSION BAR SUSPENSION

PICKUP

All models are equipped with the short and long arm independent type front suspension, utilizing height control arms. The control arms are attached to the chassis with bolts and bushings at their inner pivot points and to the steering knuckles, at their outer points, **Fig. 8.** The fore and aft movement of the front suspension is controlled by strut bars.

TORSION BAR ADJUSTMENT

1. With vehicle on a level surface, rock vehicle up and down to settle suspension.
2. Loosen nuts at front strut bar.
3. On all models except 4x4, measure clearance between rubber bumper and the lower control arm. The proper clearance Z, should be 6.1 inch. for base model, 7.5 inch for long wheel base model, **Fig. 15.**
4. On 44 models measure dimension Z, **Fig. 15** which should be 5.0 inches.
5. To adjust height, turn adjusting bolt inward to raise height or outward to decrease height.
6. Tighten strut bar nuts.

STEERING KNUCKLE REPLACE

PICKUP

Removal

1. Raise and support front of vehicle, remove tire and wheel assembly.
2. Remove brake caliper and support assembly, followed by hub and rotor.
3. Remove two bolts retaining the tie rod end link and move the link aside. Remove the remaining two bolts and remove the dust shield and adapter.
4. Remove the cotter pins and nuts from the lower and upper ball joints.
5. Disconnect knuckle from ball joints and remove knuckle.

Installation

1. Reverse procedure to install steering knuckle. Torque dust shield and adapter to 29 ft. lbs., torque ball joints to 75 ft. lbs. plus any additional torque to align cotter pins. Adjust wheel bearings as previously described.

FRONT SUSPENSION & STEERING SECTION, 1985–87 I-MARK W/FRONT WHEEL DRIVE

INDEX

DESCRIPTION

The front suspension, **Fig. 1,** is of the MacPherson strut, independent type. A strut support anchors the upper end of the strut to the body. The lower end of the strut is connected to the upper end of the steering knuckle. The lower end of the steering knuckle is attached to the ball joint, which is mounted to the suspension control arm.

STRUT SERVICE

REMOVAL

1. Remove both strut-to-body attaching nuts.
2. Raise and support front of vehicle.
3. Remove wheel and tire assembly.
4. Remove brake hose clip from strut, then disconnect hose from caliper.
5. Pull brake hose back through opening in strut bracket, then cap hose and open port in caliper to prevent contamination.
6. Remove both strut-to-knuckle attaching nuts and bolts, then the strut assembly, **Fig. 1.**

DISASSEMBLY

1. Secure strut spring compressor in a vise or suitable holding fixture.
2. Install strut into compressing tool, **Fig. 2,** and compress spring just enough to release spring tension.
3. Remove nut from strut shaft, then release spring and disassemble strut, **Fig. 1.**

INSPECTION

1. Ensure the following items meet specified measurements: piston diameter, 1.18 inch; stroke, 5.75 inches; compressed length, 14.65 inches; extended length, 20.39 inches; coil spring free length 13.33 inches with auto, trans. and A/C, 13.7 inches with man. trans. less A/C, or 13.5 inches on other models.
2. Check shock for oil leaks and defective operation.
3. Check coil spring for wear, cracks or distortion.
4. Check upper strut mounting for abnormal noise, binding or defective turning, or any other defects.

ASSEMBLY

1. Assemble strut in compressor tool, **Fig. 2,** ensuring "IN" marking on inside of spring upper seat faces inside of vehicle.
2. Compress spring just enough to allow installation of shaft nut.
3. Install shaft nut and tighten until shaft begins to rotate.
4. Release spring compressing tool, then torque shaft nut to 43 ft. lbs.

INSTALLATION

1. Install strut-to-knuckle attaching bolts and torque to 80 ft. lbs.

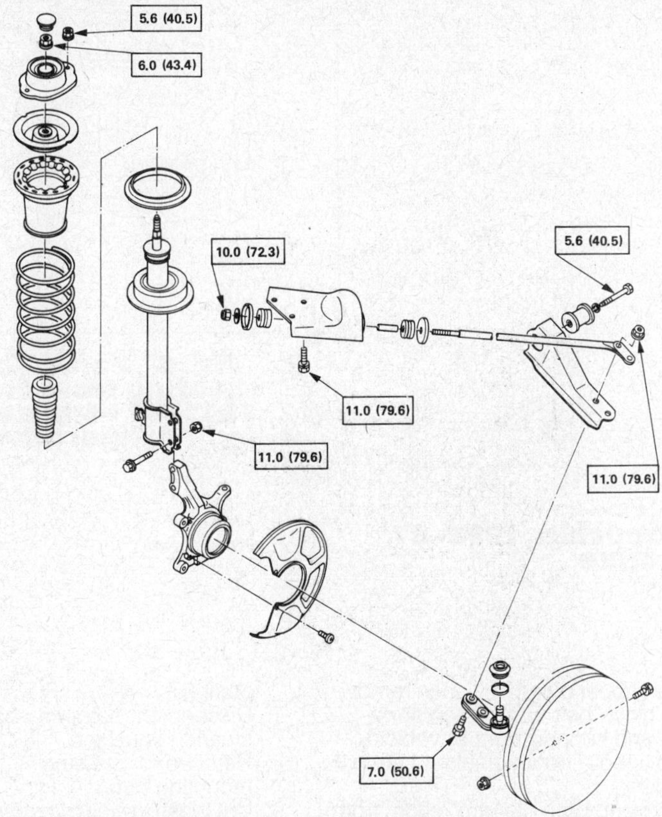

Fig. 1 Front suspension components. 1985–87 I-Mark w/front wheel drive

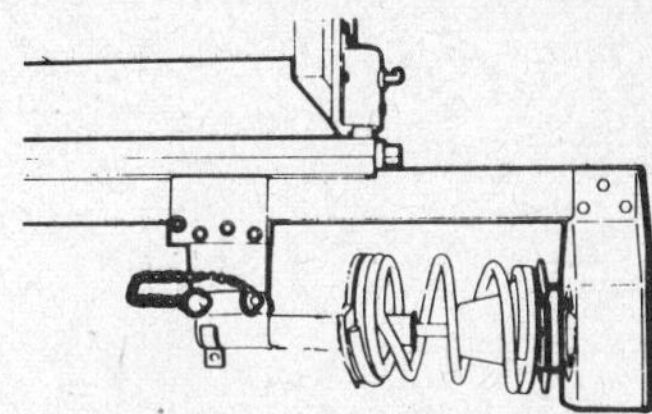

Fig. 2 Strut installed in compressor tool

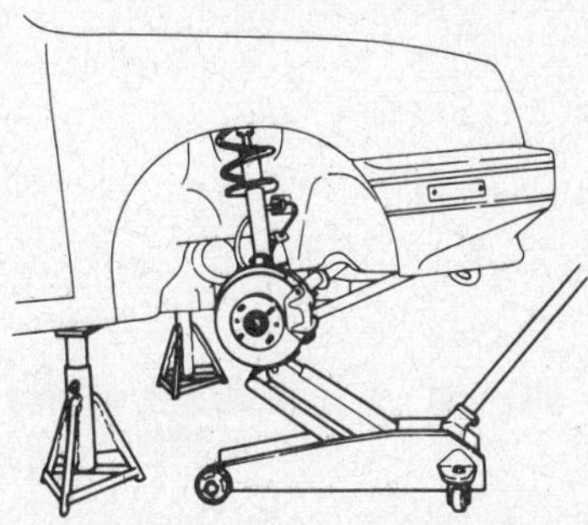

Fig. 3 Setting control arm height. 1985–87 I-Mark w/front wheel drive

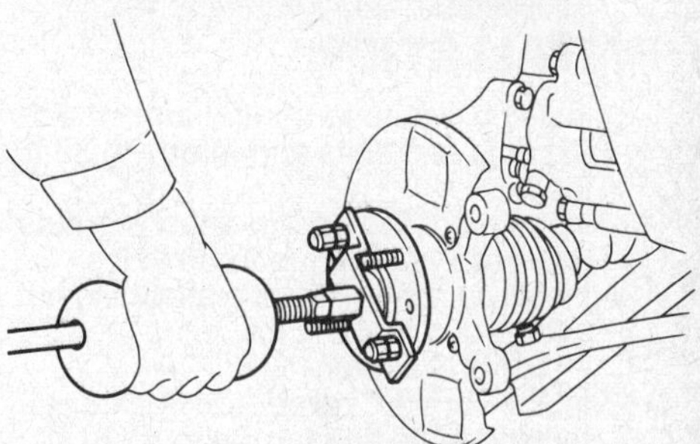

Fig. 4 Removing hub assembly. 1985–87 I-Mark w/front wheel drive

2. Route flex hose back through strut bracket opening. Connect fitting to caliper and torque to 13 ft. lbs.
3. Install wheel and tire assembly.
4. Lower vehicle to height where upper mount can be aligned with holes in body, then install and torque nuts to 41 ft. lbs.
5. Lower vehicle to ground and tighten wheel nuts.

CONTROL ARM

REPLACE

1. Raise and support front of vehicle.
2. Remove lower control arm-to-tension rod attaching nuts and bolts.
3. Remove control arm-to-body attaching bolt and nut.
4. Remove control arm, **Fig. 1.**
5. Reverse procedure to install, noting the following.
   a. Replace self-locking nuts when installing arm.
   b. When attaching control arm to body, first jack up lower part of arm to 15.18 inches, **Fig. 3,** then torque attaching bolts to specifications, **Fig. 1**

LOWER BALL JOINT

REPLACE

1. Raise and support front of vehicle.
2. Remove wheel and tire assembly.
3. Remove 2 nuts and bolts attaching ball joint, tension rod and control arm.
4. Remove ball joint-to-knuckle pinch bolt, then the ball joint, **Fig. 1.**
5. Reverse procedure to install. Torque knuckle-to-ball joint nut to 51 ft. lbs. and ball joint, tenison rod and control arm attaching nuts to 80 ft. lbs.

TENSION ROD

REPLACE

1. Raise and support front of vehicle.
2. Remove stabilizer bar-to-tension rod bracket and insulator attaching nuts and bolts, if equipped.
3. Remove tension rod-to-body attaching nut and washer.
4. Remove tension rod-to-control arm attaching nuts and bolts and the tension rod, **Fig. 1.**
5. Reverse procedure to install, using new self-locking nut. Torque tension rod-to-body nut to 72 ft. lbs. and tension rod-to-control arm bolts to 80 ft. lbs.

STEERING KNUCKLE & HUB SERVICE

REMOVAL

1. Raise and support front of vehicle.
2. Remove wheel and tire assembly.
3. Remove brake hose retaining clip from strut, then disconnect hose from caliper.
4. Unfasten caliper from steering and support caliper.
5. Remove rotor, then the hub using tools J-34866 and J-2619-01 or equivalents, **Fig. 4.**
6. Remove splash shield.
7. Remove tie rod using suitable tool.
8. Remove 2 ball joint-to-control arm and tension rod attaching nuts and bolts.
9. Remove steering knuckle-to-strut attaching nuts and bolts and the steering knuckle, **Fig. 1.**

DISASSEMBLY

1. Remove inner seal, snap rings and inner bearing race from steering knuckle, **Fig. 5.**
2. Press hub bearing from knuckle, **Fig. 6.**
3. Press outer bearing race from hub. **The hub bearing, both inner and outer seals and races must not be reused.**

ASSEMBLY

1. Install outer snap ring to knuckle.
2. Install hub bearing assembly using a suitable press.
3. Install inner snap ring, then the inner

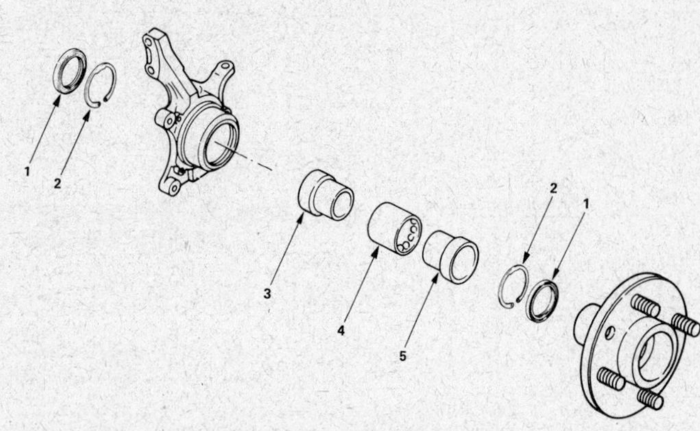

Fig. 5 Exploded view of steering knuckle. 1985–87 I-Mark w/front wheel drive

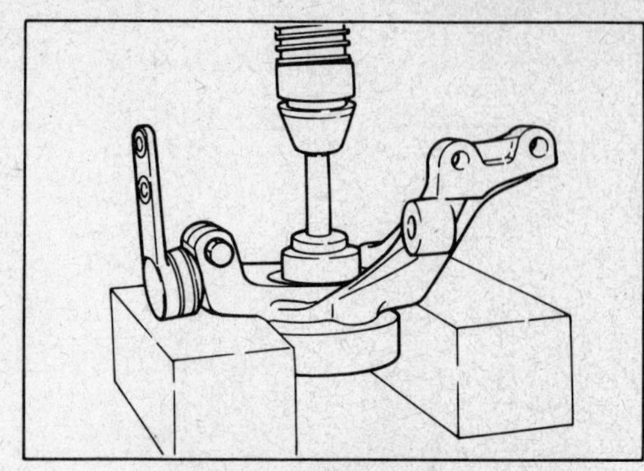

Fig. 6 Removing hub bearing from knuckle. 1985–87 I-Mark w/front wheel drive

and outer seals using tool J-35302 or equivalent.

INSTALLATION

1. Install ball joint-to-control arm attaching nuts and bolts and torque to 80 ft. lbs.
2. Install strut-to-knuckle attaching nuts and bolts and torque to 80 ft. lbs.
3. Install tie rod-to-knuckle attaching nut and torque to 42 ft. lbs.
4. Install brake rotor.
5. Install brake caliper-to-knuckle attaching bolts and torque to 41 ft. lbs.
6. Install brake hose to caliper and torque fitting to 13 ft. lbs.
7. Install wheel and tire assembly, then lower vehicle.
8. Apply suitable grease to axle shaft threads and nut, then install axle-to-hub attaching nut, washer and cotter pin. Torque nut to 137 ft. lbs.
9. Tighten wheel nuts, then bleed brake system.

MANUAL STEERING GEAR

REPLACE

1. Remove intermediate shaft cover.
2. Loosen upper pinch bolt, then remove lower pinch bolt from pinion shaft.
3. Raise and support front of vehicle.
4. Remove both front wheel and tire assemblies.
5. Disconnect both tie rod ends from steering knuckles using tool No. J-21687-02 or equivalent.
6. Remove steering gear-to-body mounting nuts.
7. Remove band from left boot, then slide boot off steering gear.
8. Straighten lock washer between inner tie rod and rack, then separate tie rod from rack.
9. Reverse procedure to install.

POWER STEERING GEAR

REPLACE

1. Remove intermediate steering protector.
2. Loosen upper and remove lower intermediate shaft pinch bolts.
3. Position suitable container below gear.
4. Clean area around pressure and return hoses at gear valve.
5. Raise and support front of vehicle.
6. Remove both front wheel and tire assemblies.
7. Disconnect both tie rod ends from steering knuckles.
8. Remove steering gear-to-dash mounting nuts.
9. Cut plastic retaining straps from power steering pipes and hose.
10. Disconnect inner boot band from right back boot.
11. Pull boot back to provide access inner tie rod.
12. Straighten lock washer between inner tie rod and rack, ten separate tie rod from rack.
13. Reverse procedure to install.

POWER STEERING PUMP

REPLACE

1. Position suitable container below pump.
2. Remove pressure hose clamp.
3. Disconnect pressure and return hoses from pump.
4. Remove adjusting bolt, pivot bolt and drive belt.
5. Remove pump and pump bracket.
6. Remove pulley from pump.
7. Reverse procedure to install. Torque pressure hose fitting to 20 ft. lbs.

FRONT DRIVE AXLE SECTION, PICKUP & TROOPER II

INDEX

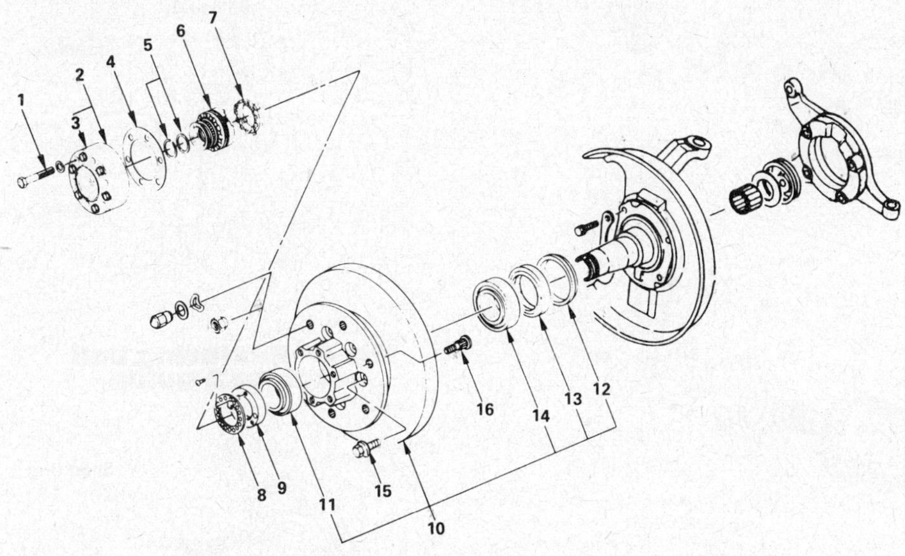

1. Bolt
2. Housing assembly
3. Driven clutch assembly
4. Spacer
5. Snap ring and shims
6. Drive clutch assembly
7. Inner cam
8. Lock washer
9. Hub nut
10. Hub and disc assembly
11. Outer bearing and outer race
12. Retaining ring
13. Oil seal
14. Inner bearing and outer race
15. Bolt
16. Wheel pin

Fig. 1 Front wheel hub & steering knuckle assembly

DESCRIPTION

This front wheel drive assembly, **Figs. 1 and 2**, incorporates a free wheeling hub at each wheel which allows the operator to manually engage and disengage the hub from the axle shafts. Each axle shaft is made up of a splined center shaft with a double offset joint (D.O.J.) on the inboard side and a Birfield joint (B.J.) on the outboard side.

WHEEL BEARINGS ADJUST

1. Place transfer shift lever in 2H position and free wheeling hub knob in FREE position.
2. Raise vehicle and remove free wheeling hub cover then remove snap ring and shims from end of spindle.
3. Remove free wheeling hub body then remove lock washer.
4. Rotate wheel while tightening hub nut with tool J-29020 until wheel cannot be turned then turn hub 2-3 turns and adjust nut to be finger tight.
5. With no free play present measure drag on wheel bearings with an accurate spring scale hooked to a wheel hub stud. Pull the scale in a tangent direction to achieve a drag reading of 2.6-4.0 lbs. as wheel begins to rotate. **Check to see brake pads are not contacting rotor when measuring wheel bearing drag.**
6. Install lock washer and free wheeling hub body after lubricating then pull axle shaft outward and measure clearance between free wheeling hub body and snap ring.
7. Install shim to adjust clearance to between 0-.039 inch. Shims are available in .008, .010, .020, and .040 inch thicknesses.
8. Install snap ring and reverse remaining part of disassembly procedure aligning stopper nails to grooves of hub body.

FREE WHEELING HUB REPLACE

Refer to steps 1-3 and 6-8 of "Wheel Bearings Adjust" for removal and replacement procedure.

FREE WHEELING HUB OVERHAUL

DISASSEMBLY

Cover Assembly

1. Push follower towards knob, turn clutch assembly clockwise then remove clutch assembly from knob, **Fig. 1.**
2. Remove snap ring then remove knob from cover taking care not to lose detent ball.
3. Remove detent ball and spring from knob, then remove X-ring from knob by pressing with your fingers. **Do not use screwdriver to remove X-ring or damage may result.**
4. Remove compression spring from follower and retaining spring from follower hanger then remove follower from clutch assembly.
5. Remove retaining spring from clutch assembly by turning counterclockwise.

Body Assembly

1. Remove snap ring then remove inner assembly from body.
2. Separate ring, inner clutch and spacer by removing snap ring.

ASSEMBLY

Cover Assembly

1. Apply grease onto X-ring and install into knob groove.
2. Apply grease to outer circumference of knob and inner circumference of cover with detent ball in place. When assembling knob to cover, line up detent ball with either groove in cover.
3. Install snap ring to knob with smoother face of snap ring facing knob.
4. Apply grease to cam portion of knob and install gasket, then place knob in FREE position.
5. Install retaining spring to clutch spring groove so that end of the spring matches end of cut portion of clutch spring groove.
6. Install follower to clutch so follower nail contacting cam will come closer

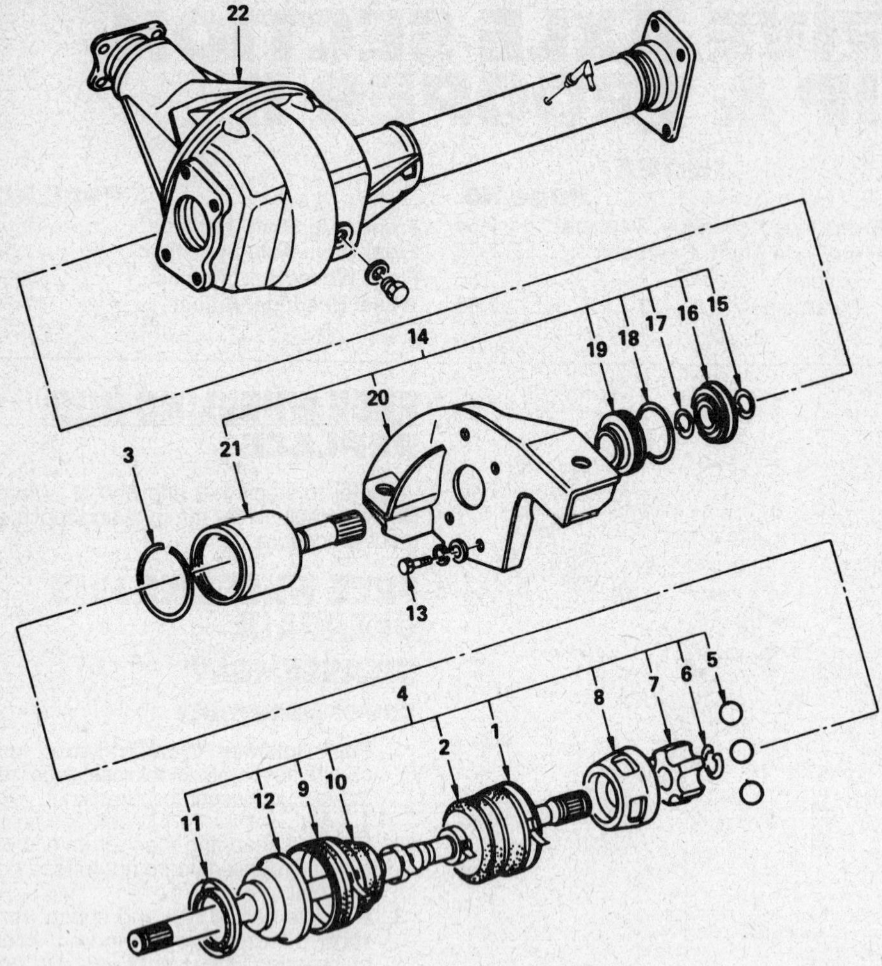

1. Band
2. Bellows
3. Circlip
4. BJ shaft assembly
5. Ball
6. Snap ring
7. Ball retainer
8. Ball guide
9. Band
10. Bellows
11. Dust seal
12. BJ shaft
13. Bolt
14. DOJ case assembly
15. Snap ring
16. Bearing
17. Snap ring
18. O-ring
19. Oil seal
20. Bracket
21. DOJ case
22. Axle case and differential

Fig. 2 Front drive axle assembly

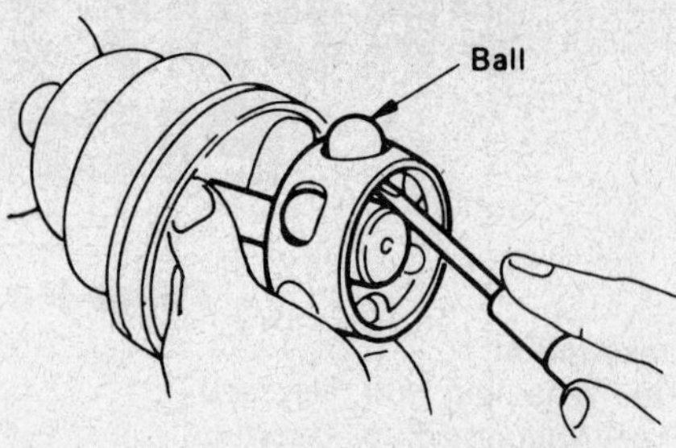

Fig. 3 Removing DOJ balls

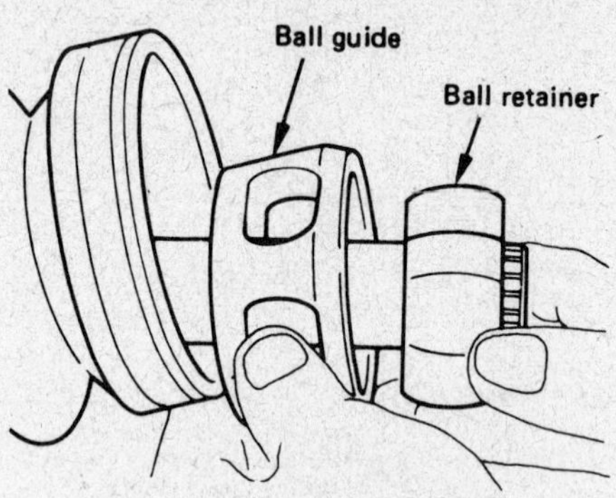

Fig. 4 Replacing ball retainer & guide

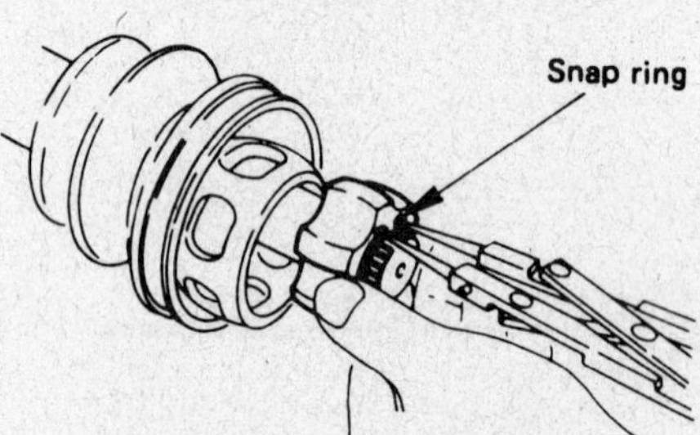

Fig. 5 Removing or installing snap ring

to bent portion of retaining spring by lining up follower stopper nail with outer teeth of clutch, then hook retaining spring onto upper portion of follower nails.

7. Install compression spring with smaller diameter side facing follower.
8. Line up nail contacting cam to handle groove, then assemble clutch and knob by pushing and turning clutch counterclockwise to knob.

Body Assembly

1. Apply grease to face of spacer and inside face of ring, then install spacer and ring to inner clutch and secure with snap ring.
2. Apply grease to splined portion of body, then install inner assembly to body from flange side and secure with snap ring.

FRONT WHEEL HUB REPLACE

1. Raise vehicle and remove tire and wheel assembly.
2. Remove free wheeling hub assembly as described under "Free Wheeling Hub, Replace".
3. Remove disc brake support and caliper assembly then secure on frame with wire.
4. Remove lock washer and hub nut using front hub nut wrench then remove hub and rotor assembly.
5. Separate hub from rotor if replacing either component.
6. Reverse procedure to install. Refer to "Wheel Bearings, Adjust" for wheel bearing adjustment procedure.

FRONT AXLE ASSEMBLY REPLACE

1. Raise and support vehicle so weight is removed from front springs then disconnect propeller shaft from front axle differential.
2. Remove wheels and skid plate then loosen torsion bar height control arm bolts completely.
3. Remove strut bars then disconnect stabilizer bar from lower control arms.
4. Remove disc brake caliper assemblies and secure to frame with wire.
5. Remove lower ball joints and tie rod ends from steering knuckle.
6. Remove upper control arm pivot shaft bolts and note position of wheel alignment shims to insure proper installation.

7. Remove lower shock absorber bolts then remove nuts holding lower control arms to frame brackets. Place lower control arms under frame.
8. Remove free wheeling hub as described under "Free Wheeling Hub, Replace" then remove hub and rotor assembly along with upper control arm and steering knuckle.
9. Remove pitman arm using tool J-5504-1 or equivalent and idler arm using tool J-5825 or equivalent then remove steering linkage.
10. Place suitable jack under center of front axle and remove bolts holding axle support brackets to frame then lower axle assembly being careful not to damage axle shaft joints.
11. Reverse procedure to install.

FRONT AXLE SHAFT

REPLACE

1. Remove front axle assembly as described under "Front Axle Assembly, Replace" and drain differential case then remove mounting brackets from case and pull axle shaft assemblies.
2. Reverse procedure to install. Torque case bracket bolts to 43 ft. lbs.

FRONT AXLE SHAFT OVERHAUL

DISASSEMBLY

Double Offset Joint (DOJ)

1. Remove DOJ inner and outer boot clamps then slide boot towards BJ assembly.
2. Remove circular clip and withdraw shaft then remove six balls with a screwdriver, **Fig. 3.**
3. Rotate case half a pitch so ball guide lines up with projected portion of ball retainer then slide towards boot to remove.
4. Remove snap ring holding ball retainer on center shaft then remove ball retainer along with cage and boot, **Figs. 4 and 5.**
5. Inspect all parts for abnormal wear, cracks and damage.

Birfield Joint (BJ)

The BJ assembly is non-serviceable with the exception of boot replacement.

1. Disassemble and remove DOJ assembly from center shaft.
2. Remove boot clamps and slide boot towards inboard side of center shaft to remove.
3. Inspect all parts for abnormal wear, cracks and damage.

ASSEMBLY

Birfield Joint (BJ)

1. Slide boot onto center shaft from inboard side taking care not to damage it.
2. Fill boot half way with suitable lubricant and lubricate ball grooves.
3. Position boot over BJ assembly making sure boot is not collapsed, then install boot clamps.

Double Offset Joint (DOJ)

1. Install small boot clamp center shaft then install boot and slide towards BJ assembly.
2. Install case small diameter side first onto center shaft then install ball retainer and secure with snap ring, **Fig. 5.**
3. Line up ball guide of cage with projected portion of ring on ball retainer, then turn cage half pitch. Align track on ball retainer with cage window and place six balls in position, **Fig. 4.**
4. Slide case over ball cage and install circular clip so that clip ends are away from ball groove then lubricate joint sufficiently.
5. Fill boot half way with suitable lubricant and install over DOJ assembly making sure it does not collapse, then install boot clamps.

FRONT DRIVE AXLE SECTION, 1985–87 I-MARK W/FRONT WHEEL DRIVE

INDEX

Page No.

DRIVE AXLE

REPLACE

1. Remove wheel cover, cotter pin and drive shaft nut.
2. Raise and support vehicle, then remove front wheel and tire assembly.
3. Drain transaxle oil into suitable container.
4. Using a suitable screwdriver or tire iron, pry inboard joint away from transaxle to disengage axle spline snap ring from differential side gear, **Fig. 1.** Do not attempt to remove axle shaft at this time.
5. Remove steering knuckle and hub assembly. Refer to Front Suspension and Steering Section for procedure.
6. Remove drive shaft from differential side gear by pulling inboard joint away from transaxle. **Do not pull on axle shaft. After axle shaft removal, do not allow axle boots to contact other parts as damage may occur.**
7. Reverse procedure to install. Torque drive shaft nut to 137 ft. lbs. and install cotter pin. If cotter pin cannot be installed, drive shaft nut can be tightened up to an additional 1/6 turn.

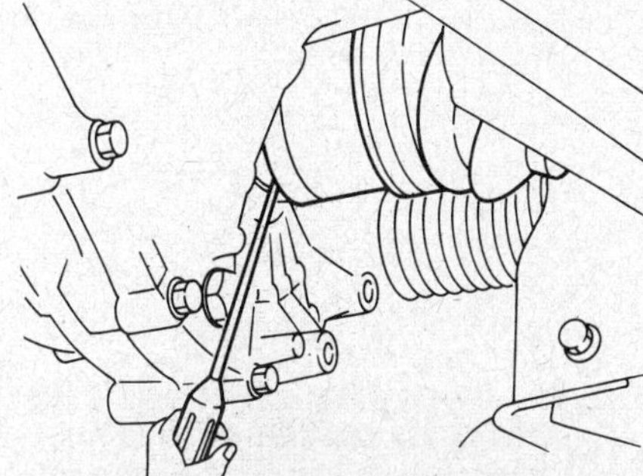

Fig. 1 Disengaging axle spline snap ring from differential side gear

DRIVE AXLE SERVICE

DISASSEMBLY

Double Offset Joint

1. Secure axle assembly, **Fig. 2,** in a suitable soft-jawed vise.
2. Remove boot band from differential side joint, **Fig. 3.**
3. Move boot slightly and remove circular clip, **Fig. 4.**
4. Separate case from shaft and remove 6 balls with a suitable screwdriver, **Fig. 5.**
5. Turn ball guide on an angle and move into center shaft side.
6. Remove snap ring from shaft, **Fig. 6,** then slide out ball guide and retainer.
7. Remove boot from shaft.

Birfield Joint

The Birfield joint must be serviced as an assembly only. However, the boot may be

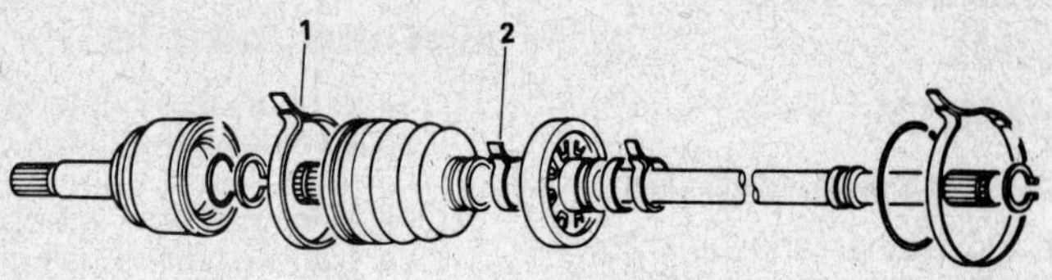

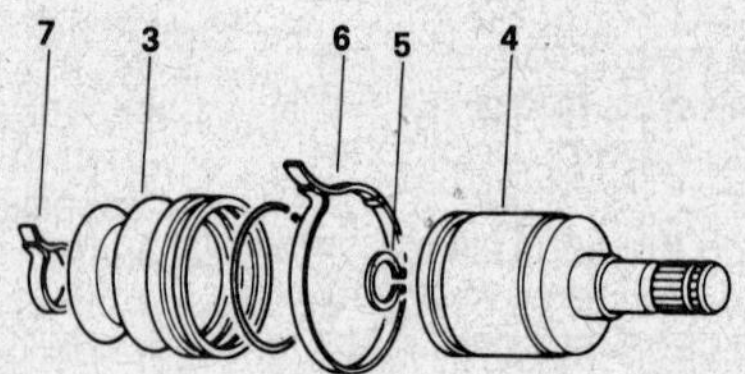

1. Circular clip
2. Clip
3. Boot
4. Double off-set joint shaft
5. Circular clip
6. Band
7. Clip

Fig. 2 Front drive shaft assembly

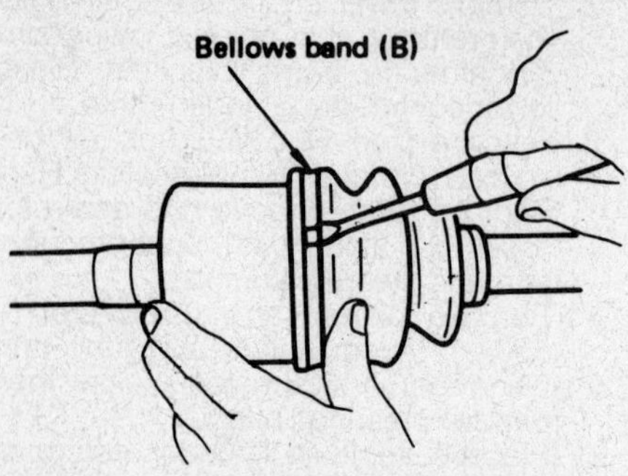

Fig. 3 Removing boot band

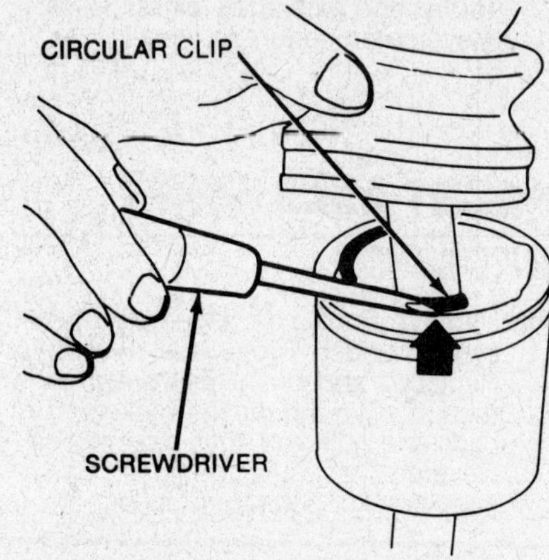

Fig. 4 Removing circular clip from outer case

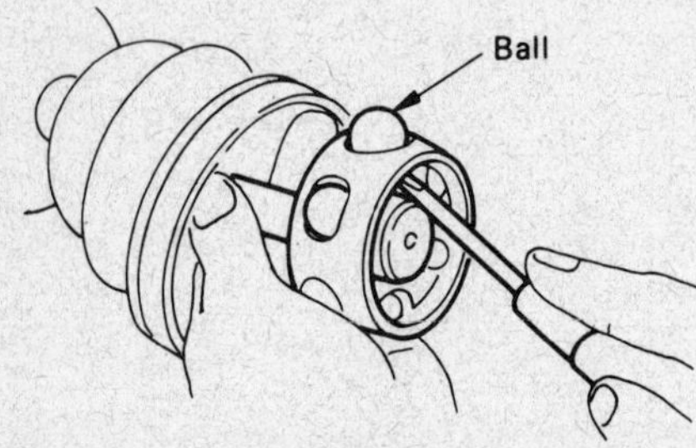

Fig. 5 Removing balls from joint

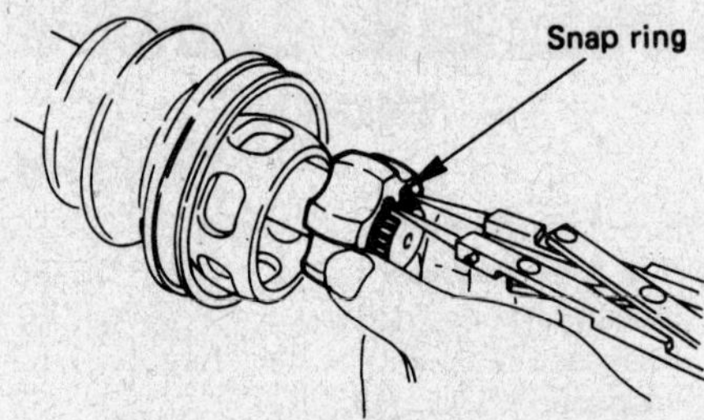

Fig. 6 Removing shaft snap ring

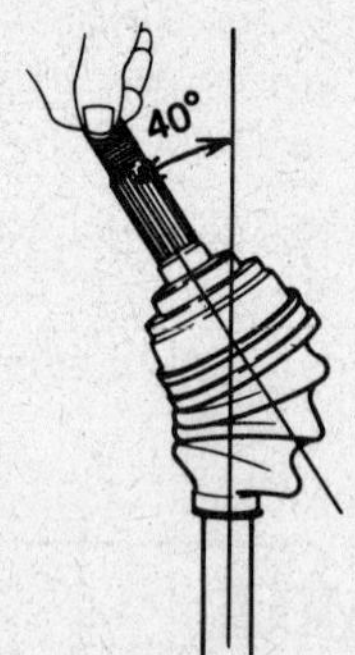

Fig. 7 Inspecting Birfield joint

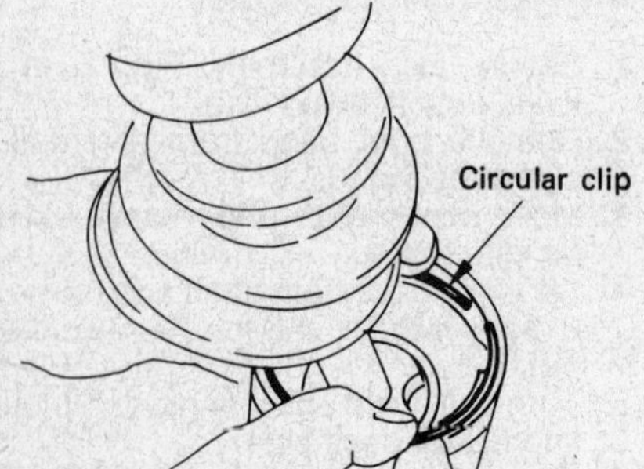

Fig. 8 Installing circular clip in outer case

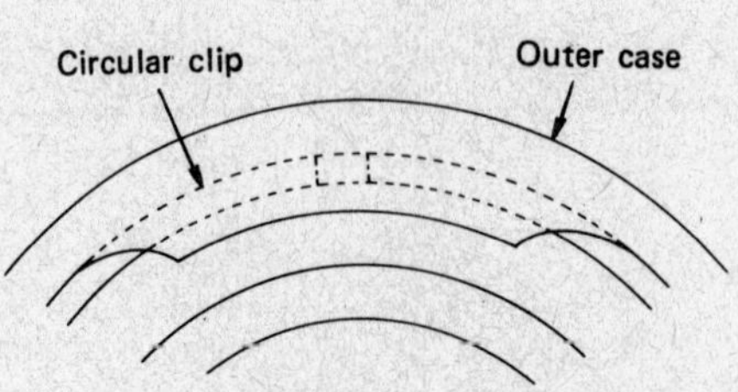

Fig. 9 Aligning circular clip ends in outer case

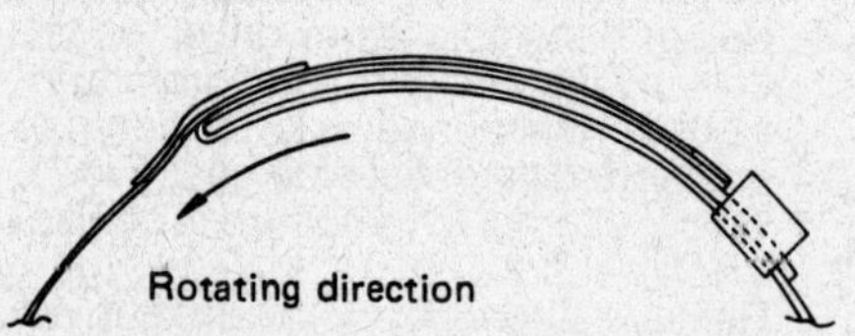

Fig. 10 Installing boot band

removed in the same manner as described for the Double Offset type joint.

INSPECTION

1. Visually inspect all components and replace those showing signs of damage or excessive wear.
2. Check Birfield joint by bending joint approximately 40° and rotating the shaft to ensure smooth and normal rotation, **Fig. 7.**

ASSEMBLY

Double Offset Joint

1. Assemble in the reverse order of disassembly, noting the following:
   a. Use care to avoid damaging boot when installing boot on shaft.
   b. Install and align circular clip as shown, **Figs. 8 and 9.**
   c. To install boot band, first insert a screwdriver into end of boot, then install band as shown, **Fig. 10.** Ensure band end clip is securely tightened around the band and boot is not twisted.

WHEEL ALIGNMENT SECTION

INDEX

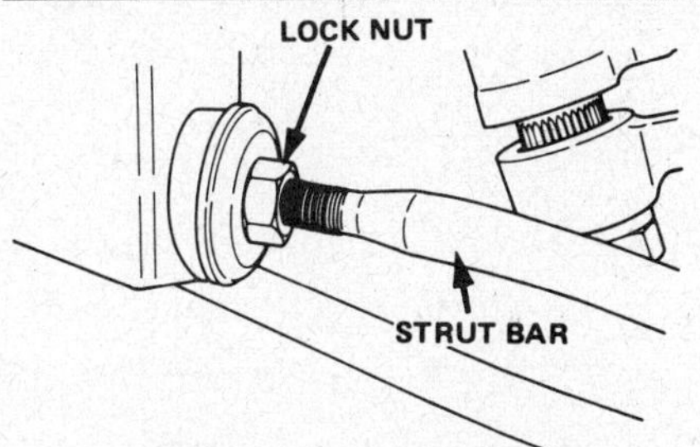

Fig.1 Caster angle adjustment. 1983 Pickup

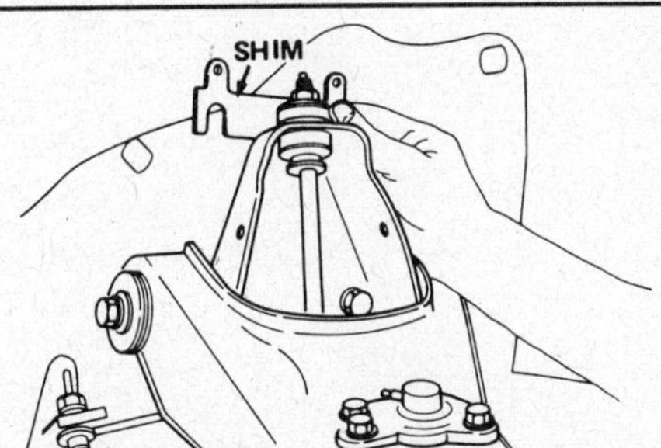

Fig.2 Adjusting camber & caster angle

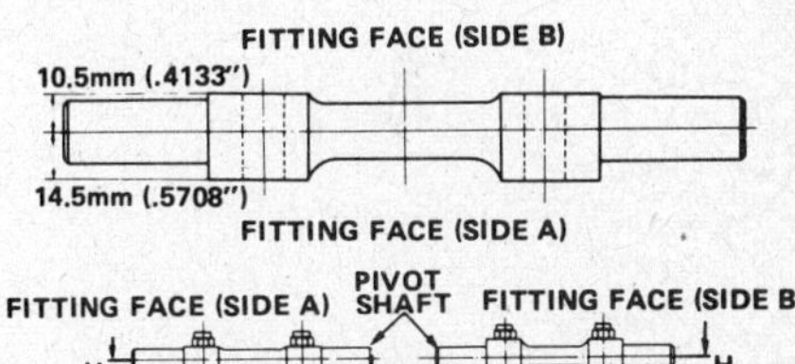

Fig.3 Pivot shaft adjustment. 1983 Pickup

Number of Shims	Distance Between Pivot Center and Fitting Face; H, Inch (mm)	
	Pivot Shaft Fitting Face (Side A)	Pivot Shaft Fitting Face (Side B)
0	0.57 (14.5)	0.41 (10.5)
1	0.63 (16.1)	0.48 (12.1)
2	0.70 (17.7)	0.54 (13.7)
3	0.76 (19.3)	0.60 (15.3)
4	0.82 (20.9)	0.67 (16.9)
5	—	0.73 (18.5)
6	—	0.79 (20.1)

Fig. 4 Shim selection chart. Pickup

EXC. 1985–87 I-MARK W/FRONT WHEEL DRIVE

PICKUP & TROOPER II

Caster & Camber

Caster angle is adjusted by varying length of the strut by means of the strut bar locknut, **Fig. 1.**

Camber & caster angle is adjusted by varying thickness of shim, **Fig. 2,** and on 1983 models, inverting the pivot shaft as shown in **Fig. 3.**

a. The distance between pivot shaft center and fitting face; H, can be adjusted 0.16 inch (4.0 mm) by inverting the pivot shaft.
b. The distance between the pivot shaft center and fitting shaft (side A or B) can be adjusted using shims selected by referring to the selection chart, **Fig. 4.**

I-MARK

Caster, Adjust

Caster angle is preset and cannot be adjusted.

Camber, Adjust

Camber angle can be increased approximately 1 degree by removing the upper ball joint, rotating it 1/2 turn, then reinstalling it with flat of upper flange on the inboard side of the control arm.

Toe-In, Adjust

Toe-In is adjusted by the position of the tie rod. To adjust the toe-in setting, loosen the nuts at the steering knuckle end of tie rod, then loosen rubber cover at other end. Tighten cover and locking nuts.

Wheel Bearing, Adjust

1. Remove grease cap, cotter pin, then the spindle nut.
2. Torque spindle nut to 21 ft. lbs. while rotating wheel to seat bearings.
3. Back off spindle nut 1/4 turn. If slot and cotter key hole are not aligned, back off nut until next slot in nut is in alignment with hole in spindle. Do not tighten spindle nut to bring slot in nut into alignment with hole in spindle. Install new cotter pin. A properly adjusted wheel bearing has a small amount of end play and a loose nut.

IMPULSE

Caster, camber and kingpin inclination are preset and cannot be adjusted.

1985–87 I-MARK W/FRONT WHEEL DRIVE

DESCRIPTION

The front suspension is of the MacPherson strut, independent type. A strut support anchors the upper end of the strut to the body. The lower end of the strut is connected to the upper end of the steering knuckle. The lower end of the steering knuckle is attached to the ball joint, which is mounted to the suspension control arm.

CASTER & CAMBER

Caster and camber angles are preset and cannot be adjusted. If caster and/or camber are out of specifications, the cause must be found. If worn or damaged suspension components are the cause, they should be replaced. If problem is body related, the body should be repaired as needed.

TOE-IN ADJUSTMENT

Toe-in is adjusted by altering tie rod length. To perform adjustment, loosen small end boot clamps and slide from the boot. Loosen right and left tie rod end locknuts, then turn both tie rods the same amount to bring toe-in within specifications. Ensure right and left tie rods are equal in length, then tighten locknuts. When adjustment is complete, ensure boots are not twisted.

JAGUAR (England)

INDEX OF SERVICE OPERATIONS

General Engine Specifications

Year & Model	Engine	Fuel System	Bore & Stroke Inches (millimeters)	Compression Ratio
1983–87, XJ6	6-258/4235cc	Fuel Injected	3.62 x 4.17 (90 x 106)	8.1
1983–87, XJ-S H.E.	V12-326/5343cc	Fuel Injected	3.543 x 2.756 (90 x 70)	11.5

Alternator & Regulator Specifications

		Alternator				Regulator	
Year	Engine	Make	Model	Field Winding Resistance ohm (68°F)	Maximum Output	Model	Cut in Voltage @ RPM
1983–87	6-258/4355cc	Lucas	18ACR①	3.2	45	—	13.5 @ 2100
		Lucas	20ACR②	3.6	66	—	13.5 @ 2100
		Lucas	25ACR②	3.6	66	—	13.5 @ 2100
		Motorola	9AR2512P②	3.6	70	—	14 @ 1050
1983–87	V12-326/5343cc H.E.	Lucas	25ACR③	3.6	66	—	13.5 @ 1500
		Lucas	A133④	2.43	75	Lucas 11TR	13.5 @ 1500

①—Vehicles less air conditioning.
②—Vehicles with air conditioning.
③—Early model V12-326/5343cc H.E. engine.
④—Late model V12-326/5343cc H.E. engine.

Valve Specifications

	Valve Lash		Valve Angles		Stem Clearance		Stem Diameter	
Year & Model	Intake	Exhaust	Seat	Face	Intake	Exhaust	Intake	Exhaust
1983–87, XJ6	.013C	.013C	45	45	.001–.004	.001–.004	.3100–.3125	.3100–.3125
1983–87, XJ-S H.E.	.011C	.011C	44.5	44.5	.002–.0023	.002–.0023	.3092–.3093	.3092–.3093

Pistons, Pins, Rings, Crankshaft & Bearings

		Ring End Gap				Rod Bearings		Main Bearing	
Year & Engine	Piston Clearance Bottom of Skirt①	No. 1 Comp.	No. 2 Comp.	Oil	Wrist Pin Diameter	Shaft Diameter	Bearing Clearance	Shaft Diameter	Shaft End Play
1983–87, 6-258/4235cc	.0007–.0013	.015–.020	.009–.014	.015–.045	②	2.2330–2.2335	.0010–.0027	2.7503	.004–.006
1983–87, V12-326/5343cc	.0012–.0017	.014–.020	.010–.015	.015–.045	③	2.441–2.447	.0015–.0034	3.0007–3.0012	.004–.006

①—Measured midway down the bore.
②—Marked red, .8751–.8752; marked green, .8750–.8751.
③—Marked red, .9375; marked green, .9373.

Engine Tightening Specifications

Torque specifications are for clean & lightly lubricated threads only. Dry dirty threads produce increased friction which prevents accurate measurement of tightness.

Year	Engine	Cylinder Head Bolts Ft. Lbs.	Camshaft Cap Bolt Ft. Lbs.	Camshaft Cover Bolts Ft. Lbs.	Connecting Rod Cap Bolt Ft. Lbs.	Main Bearing Cap Bolt Ft. Lbs.	Flywheel to Crankshaft Ft. Lbs.
1983–87	6-258/4235cc	52–54	9	5–6	35.7–37.5	68.4–72	63.4–66.6
1983–87	V12-326/5343cc	①	9	8.3	40–41	②	63.3–66.6

①—7/16" bolts, 52; 3/8" bolts, 28.
②—1/2" bolts, 59.4–62.5; 3/8" bolts, 27–28.

Cooling System & Capacity Data

Year & Model	Cooling Capacity Qts.	Radiator Cap Relief Pressure, lbs.	Thermostat Opening Temp.	Fuel Tank Gals.	Engine Oil Qts. ①	Transmission Oil			Axle Oil Pints
						4 Speed Pts.	Overdrive Pts.	Auto. Trans. Pts.	
1983–87, XJ6	19.25	—	—	③	8.7	—	—	16.75	3.25
1983–87, XJ-S H.E.	21.5	②	—	24	11.6	—	—	19	3.25

①—With filter change.
②—Engine filler cap, 20 lbs.; expansion tank cap, 15 lbs.
③—Left tank, 12.6 gal.; right tank, 12.6 gal.

Brake Specifications

Year	Model	Disc Brake Rotor Nominal Thickness		Master Cylinder Bore Diameter
		Front	Rear	
1983–87	XJS	.95	①	.875
1983–87	XJ6	.95	.50	.937

①—Standard, .5"; Optional with overdrive, .95".

Wheel Alignment Specifications

Year & Model	Front & Rear Wheel Alignment	Caster Angle, Degrees		Camber Angle, Degrees				Toe-in Inch
				Limits		Desired		
		Limits	Desired	Left	Right	Left	Right	
1983–87, XJS	Front	+3¼ to +3¾	+3½	+¼ to +¾	+¼ to +¾	+½	+½	1/16
	Rear	—	—	−½° to −1°	−½° to −1°	−¾°	−¾°	−1/32 to +1/32
1983–87, XJ6	Front	+2 to +2½	+2¼	+¼ to +¾	+¼ to +¾	+½	+½	1/16 to 1/8
	Rear	—	—	−½° to −1°	−½° to −1°	−¾°	−¾°	−1/32 to +1/32

ELECTRICAL SECTION

INDEX

ALTERNATOR IN-VEHICLE TESTS

XJ-S

Test 1

1. Remove connections from alternator and switch ignition on.
2. Connect a voltmeter between ground and each of the disconnected leads in turn.
3. The voltmeter should indicate battery voltage.
4. If the voltmeter reads zero when connected to indicator light terminal and ground, check indicator light bulb and all connections to the indicator light.
5. If voltmeter reads zero when connected to the main output terminal and ground, check wiring and connections to starter solenoid and battery.
6. If voltmeter reads zero when connected to stator terminal and ground, check wiring and battery connections. Alternator output is based directly on battery condition. If battery sensor circuit is broken, there will be no output from the alternator. **Some alternators are not equipped with a stator terminal. A plug will be inserted in the opening.**

Test 2

1. Replace connections to alternator and switch ignition on.
2. Connect voltmeter between suitable ground and indicator light terminal.
3. Voltmeter should indicate 1.5-2.0 volts. If the reading is zero, check surge-protection diode. If reading is 12 volts, proceed to test 3.

Test 3

1. Connect voltmeter between suitable ground and green lead. Switch ignition on.
2. Voltmeter should indicate approximately .5 volt. If reading is 12 volts, control box should be replaced. If the reading is .5 volt but on test 2 the reading was 12 volts, check alternator brushes and rotor.

Test 4

1. Connect voltmeter between battery positive terminal and alternator main output terminal.
2. Start engine and run it at 3000 RPM. The voltmeter reading should not exceed .5 volts. If reading is higher, check wiring from alternator to battery for loose or dirty connections.

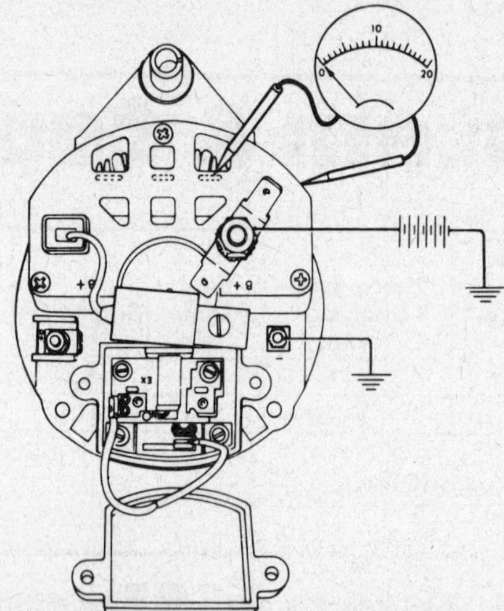

Fig. 1 Checking alternator voltage polarity. XJ6

Test 5

1. Start and run engine at 3000 RPM. Check for voltage at alternator main output terminal and indicator light terminal.
2. The difference should not exceed .5 volt. If it does exceed .5 volt, replace the rectifier pack.

Test 6

1. Disconnect battery ground cable.
2. Connect ammeter between starter solenoid and alternator main output cable.
3. Connect voltmeter across battery terminals and reconnect battery ground cable.
4. Start and run engine at 3000 RPM until ammeter indicates 10 amps.
5. Voltmeter reading should be within 13.6 to 14.4 volts. If reading is outside limit, change control box.

XJ6

1. With ignition switched off, connect voltmeter between first phase window and ground, **Fig. 1,** then between field winding and B terminal. Ensure correct polarity reading on voltmeter. Any reading other than zero indicates a defective positive rectifier diode.
2. With ignition switched off, check voltage at B terminal and at battery positive terminal, **Fig. 2.** If voltage at B terminal is lower than battery voltage, or fluctuates, check for broken wires, faulty connections or corroded terminals.
3. With ignition switched on, but engine not running. Check voltage at the slip ring. Place lead of voltmeter on field terminal EX. If reading on voltmeter is higher than 2 volts, field circuit is defective. Remove brush holder by disconnecting green regulator lead from EX terminal. Remove screws and washers securing brush holder to alternator. New brushes protrude approximately .35 inch from brush holder. Brush holder should be replaced if new brush protrudes less than .15 inch. Check regulator circuit by disconnecting green lead from EX terminal and measuring voltage across windings. Voltage should not exceed 2 volts. If voltage exceeds limit, replace alternator.
4. With ignition switched on, and engine running above idle, check voltage at output terminal and at battery positive terminal. Voltage should be 14.2 volts at 77°F. If battery voltage is 0.3 volts higher than B terminal voltage, check for broken wires and corrosion.
5. With field lead and regulator disconnected, and output terminal shorted to EX terminal, ignition switched on, and engine running above idle, check voltage between output B terminal and ground. If voltage rises 14-16 volts, replace regulator.

STARTER REPLACE

XJ-S

1. Disconnect battery ground cable.
2. Drain power steering system.
3. Remove bolts securing lower column universal joint to its respective columns on both ends.
4. Remove the heat shield protecting rubber boot which covers inner tie rod joint.
5. Remove bolt that holds lower steering column to steering gear.
6. Disengage lower column upper uni-

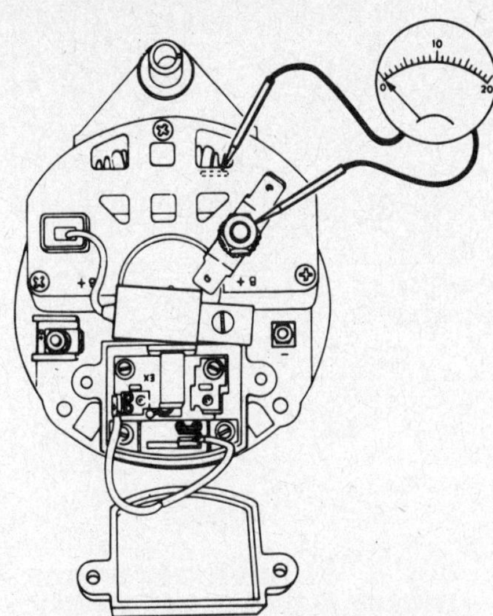

Fig. 2 Checking voltage at alternator positive terminal. XJ6

versal joint from bottom of steering column.
7. Loosen securing clip still holding upper universal joint and remove joint from lower column.
8. Disengage lower column from steering gear and ease it out through the bulkhead.
9. Release clip holding power steering feed and return lines to bridge piece and rack tube assembly.
10. Disconnect feed and return lines from steering gear. Plug lines and nipples on steering gear, and position lines clear of bridge piece and rack tube assembly.
11. Remove bolts holding exhaust pipe to intermediate pipe, then disengage the two pipes.
12. Remove screws attaching front exhaust heat shield to underbody and remove heat shield.
13. Loosen bottom screws that secure steering rack assembly to front suspension, remove bolt that holds rack and heat shield mounting bracket to suspension, and lower rack carefully. Be sure to retrieve pack washers from top mounting joint of steering rack.
14. Remove exhaust pipe.
15. Remove nuts that hold heat shield over starter motor and clip that retains cable. Remove heat shield.
16. Remove nut which holds alternator-to-starter motor cable at starter. Disconnect cable.
17. Disconnect starter solenoid-to-terminal post connector at terminal post. Tie solenoid cable using cord to a suitable support and disconnect cable at bulkhead fitting. Make sure cord is long enough to be pulled up through engine compartment.
18. Remove bolts that hold starter motor to bellhousing.
19. Detach string holding solenoid cable and pull entire assembly up through engine compartment.

Fig. 3 Ignition switch removal

20. Remove string from cable and remove heat shield bracket and support piece from starter motor.
21. Reverse procedure to install. Be sure to fill and bleed the power steering system.

XJ6

1983–87

1. Disconnect battery ground cable.
2. Remove bolt securing starter lead and transmission breather tube to the starter mounting bracket.
3. Disconnect starter lead from starter terminal on fire wall.
4. Remove top bolt attaching starter mounting bracket to bellhousing.
5. Using a suitable lift, raise vehicle.
6. Remove lower securing bolt and remove the starter and mounting bracket as an assembly.
7. Remove starter lead from starter solenoid.
8. Remove mounting bracket from starter.
9. Reverse procedure to install.

IGNITION SWITCH

REPLACE

XJ-S

1. Disconnect battery ground cable.
2. Remove underside dash casing on driver's side of vehicle by detaching fasteners holding casing to panel.
3. Remove screw that holds instrument shroud to panel and to instrument module casing.
4. Loosen screws that hold shroud to lower mounting bracket, and ease shroud out of its spot. This allows access to screw holding ignition switch.
5. Loosen this screw, and ease the switch and harness out of mount, **Fig. 3.**
6. Remove rubber retainer and disconnect harness connector to release ignition switch.

XJ6

1. Disconnect battery ground cable.
2. Remove driver's side dash liner.
3. Remove snap ring from rear of ignition and steering lock assemblies. Remove screw from ignition and steering lock assemblies if equipped.
4. Disconnect switch from ignition harness at electrical connector.
5. Reverse procedure to install.

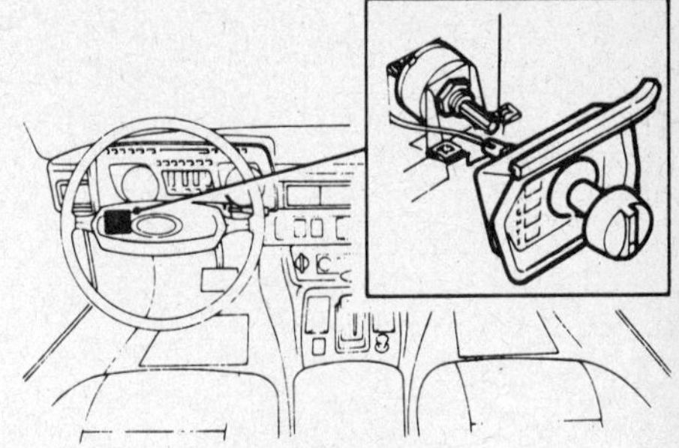

Fig. 4 Headlight switch removal

HEADLIGHT SWITCH

REPLACE

1. Disconnect battery ground cable.
2. Remove underside dash casing on driver's side of vehicle by detaching fasteners holding casing to panel.
3. Remove screw that holds instrument shroud to panel and to instrument module casing.
4. Loosen screws that hold shroud to lower mounting bracket and ease the shroud clear to gain access to the spring-loaded pin retaining knob.
5. Depress pin and remove knob, which permits removal of shroud, **Fig. 4.**
6. Remove nut holding headlight switch to mounting bracket.
7. Remove switch from bracket and disconnect wiring harness at connector to free switch.

STOPLIGHT SWITCH

REPLACE

1. Disconnect battery ground cable.
2. Disconnect electrical connectors from switch terminals.
3. Remove switch attaching bolt holding nut.
4. Remove switch.
5. After replacing switch, leave switch attaching bolt loose.
6. Adjust position of switch so stoplights operate when brake pedal is depressed and go off when pedal is fully released. **The ignition switch must be on while adjustments are being made.**
7. Tighten switch attaching bolt.

COMBINATION SWITCH

REPLACE

1. Disconnect battery ground cable.
2. Loosen steering wheel adjustment ring and extend it to its maximum travel.
3. Remove screws attaching steering column lower shroud. Then remove shroud.
4. Remove steering wheel as follows:
   a. Remove steering wheel horn pad.
   b. Adjust wheels to straight ahead position, then remove ignition key and lock steering wheel.

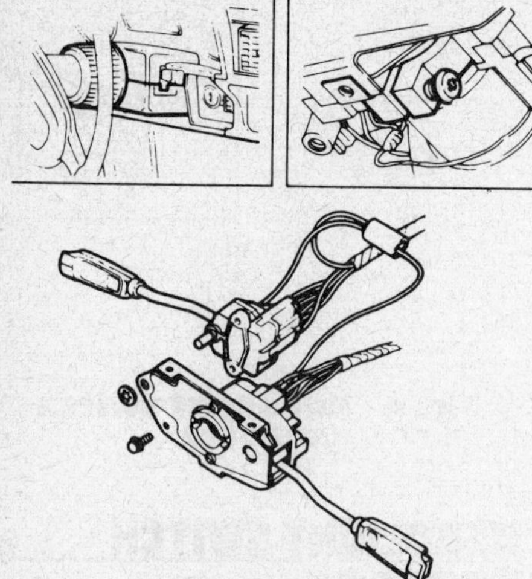

Fig. 5 Combination switch removal

c. Remove horn contact rod from upper column.
d. Remove nut attaching steering wheel to upper column and gently tap steering wheel loose.

5. Remove screw that holds upper shroud to bracket on steering column.
6. Loosen screw holding switch assembly to steering column and withdraw switch assembly and upper shroud. Separate shroud and switch assembly, **Fig. 5.**
7. Disconnect wiring harness at connectors.
8. Remove nuts and screws holding switch mounting plate and disconnect ground cable at snap connector.
9. Remove windshield wiper-washer switch from assembly. **Do not try to separate the turn signal-high beam-hazard flasher switch from mounting bracket. If switch is faulty, a new switch and bracket assembly will have to be installed.**

NEUTRAL SAFETY SWITCH

REPLACE

1. Disconnect battery ground cable.
2. Remove electric window control panel.
3. Remove transmission selector lever knob.
4. Remove screws and console center panel.
5. Remove bolts and transmission selector cover.
6. Disconnect electrical connection from neutral safety switch and remove switch.
7. Reverse procedure to install.

INSTRUMENT CLUSTER

REPLACE

XJ-S

1. Disconnect battery ground cable.
2. Remove underside dash casing on driver's side of vehicle by detaching fasteners holding casing to panel.
3. Remove center securing strip and screw from instrument cluster trim.
4. Remove screws holding side trim pieces, then remove trim.
5. Pry off covers from instrument cluster securing screw.
6. Remove screws holding instrument cluster to panel.
7. Disconnect speedometer cable from angle drive at rear of speedometer.
8. Pull cluster forward and disconnect cable harness at connectors.
9. Loosen steering wheel adjustment ring and extend to maximum travel.
10. Remove instrument cluster from housing.

XJ6

1. Disconnect battery ground cable.
2. Depress and rotate tachometer counterclockwise until tachometer studs release fascia locking ring, and remove tachometer from fascia.
3. Remove nut and lock washer from oil pressure bracket.
4. Remove oil pressure gauge from fascia, and disconnect electrical connectors from oil pressure gauge.
5. Depress and rotate speedometer counterclockwise until speedometer studs release from locking tabs.
6. Disconnect electrical connectors from speedometer, and remove speedometer cable.
7. Rotate speedometer trip reset connector counterclockwise until connector releases locking tabs.
8. Remove nut and lock washer from coolant temperature gauge bracket, and pull gauge out of fascia.
9. Disconnect electrical connectors from temperature gauge.
10. Remove nut and lock washer from fuel gauge bracket, and pull gauge from fascia.
11. Disconnect electrical connectors from back of gauge.
12. Reverse procedure to install.

BLOWER MOTOR

REPLACE

RIGHT HAND BLOWER ASSEMBLY

1. Disconnect battery ground cable and remove dash liner and console side casing.
2. Remove glove box liner and take out nuts holding mounting plate to blower assembly and lower plate. Pull the plate clear.
3. Disconnect sensor hose from blower assembly duct, the pliable duct from side of air conditioner, the blower harness at block connector and the vacuum line from valve on blower assembly.
4. Wedge open recirculation valve in base of blower assembly and remove bolts securing blower assembly to mounting brackets.
5. Ease blower assembly from position and detach the duct by removing tape.

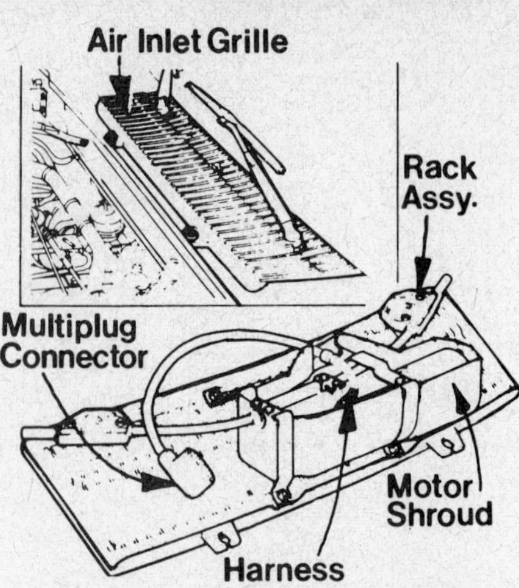

Fig. 6 Windshield wiper motor & grille assembly

LEFT HAND BLOWER ASSEMBLY

1. Disconnect battery ground cable and remove dash liner and console side casing.
2. Remove nuts holding bottom of fuse box mounting plate to blower assembly. Loosen nuts holding top of fuse box mounting plate.
3. Ease fuse box clear of blower assembly.
4. Disconnect pliable duct side of air conditioner, blower harness at block connector, and vacuum line from valve servo on blower.
5. The remainder of the procedure is the same as that outlined in steps 4 and 5, "Right Hand Blower Assembly, Replace".

WINDSHIELD WIPER MOTOR

REPLACE

XJ-S

1. Disconnect battery ground cable.
2. Remove windshield wiper arms.
3. Remove air inlet grille retaining nuts, bolts and washers, **Fig. 6.**
4. Raise grille which is attached to windshield wiper assembly.
5. Disconnect washer tube at jet and disconnect multiplug connector at bulkhead.
6. Remove grille and wiper assembly.
7. Remove nuts that secure motor mounting bracket to grille, then remove bolts that hold bracket to motor. Remove bracket.
8. Turn over grille-motor assembly and remove gearbox spindle nuts.
9. Invert grille-motor assembly again, then remove motor and drive rack assembly.
10. Remove rack cover plate retaining bolts. Lift off cover and remove rack assembly.
11. Take off motor shroud and disconnect harness at gearbox connector. The motor is now free.

12. Reverse procedure to install.

XJ6

1. Disconnect and remove battery.
2. Remove windshield wiper arms from spindles.
3. Remove cable rack conduit from wiper motor.
4. Remove nuts and washers from wiper motor clamp, then tilt wiper motor toward engine compartment and disconnect multiplug connector.
5. Remove wiper motor and drive rack assembly, pulling drive rack from conduit.
6. Reverse procedure to install.

ENGINE SECTION

INDEX

ENGINE REPLACE

XJ-S

1. Remove hood and lower grille.
2. Disconnect battery cables, drain coolant and depressurize fuel system.
3. Discharge air conditioning system and disconnect hoses; immediately seal all connections.
4. Remove engine compartment stays.
5. Disconnect cables from temperature sensors.
6. Disconnect cold-start relay harness, throttle switch-and-trigger unit cable and kickdown switch cable.
7. Remove ground lead to a right-hand intake manifold and main harness. Withdraw the harness.
8. Disconnect cables at cold start injection relay and right-hand water rail feed pipe from heater valve.
9. Disconnect brake vacuum hoses, heater vacuum hose, throttle cable and cables to starter solenoid and starter motor.
10. Remove air cleaners.
11. Remove fuel pipes and plug connections.
12. Disconnect cooling system hoses.
13. On models with automatic transmission, remove transmission oil cooler hoses and plug connections.
14. Disconnect and remove alternator harness.
15. Detach radiator fittings and disconnect A/C receiver-drier outlet line.
16. Remove fan cowl.
17. Remove radiator top rail together with evaporator and receiver-drier.
18. Attach engine support tool MS 53A.
19. Disconnect coolant sensor.
20. Remove radiator and fan.
21. Disconnect exhaust pipes and remove left and right front heat shields.
22. Remove intermediate and rear heat shields.
23. Raise engine at rear engine mounting plate so you can remove collision plate at transmission and rear engine mounting stud.
24. Remove rear engine mounting plate and lower jack.
25. Withdraw propeller shaft from output flange.
26. On models with manual transmission, remove gearshift knob and console retainer. Place gear shift into first gear position and disconnect clutch slave cylinder hose and plug connections.
27. On models with automatic transmission, remove selector cable and selector lever from shaft.
28. Disconnect speedometer cable and unhook ground strap from side of torque converter/bellhousing.
29. Remove steering heat shields and left-side exhaust manifold heat shield.
30. Disconnect EGR lines from exhaust manifold and exhaust pipes.
31. Disconnect and move power steering oil cooler away from engine.
32. Disconnect power steering pump.
33. Using a suitable jack, support transmission.
34. Attach lifting chains to engine front and rear lifting eyes. **Removing engine will be facilitated if rear lifting chains are approximately 6 inches (154mm) longer than front chains.**
35. Remove engine from engine compartment.

XJ6

1. Remove hood, air cleaner, disconnect battery cables and drain cooling system.
2. Vehicles equipped with air conditioning, note the following. **Carefully discharge refrigerant from air conditioning system.**
   a. Disconnect, seal and remove fuel lines from heat exchanger.
   b. Remove screws and heat exchanger.
3. Remove fender support bars.
4. Disconnect all radiator hoses.
5. Remove nut and washers securing front engine mounts to brackets.
6. Drain fluid from power steering pump reservoir.
7. Disconnect and seal supply and return power steering lines from pump.
8. Loosen power steering pump mounting bolts, then push pump as close to engine as possible.
9. Disconnect electrical connectors from alternator and engine harness.
10. Disconnect brake vacuum line from intake manifold.
11. Remove vacuum line bracket, then pull heater and air conditioning vacuum line from check valves.
12. Remove bolts and exhaust pipes from exhaust manifolds.
13. Disconnect solenoid cable from electrical connector.
14. Remove heater hoses from heater core.
15. Disconnect inner and outer throttle cables from engine.
16. Disconnect choke cables from carburetors, and hoses from purge canister.
17. Remove banjo bolt from clutch master cylinder reservoir.
18. Vehicles equipped with manual transmission, remove overdrive switch and knob from gearshift lever.
19. Vehicles equipped with automatic transmission, remove center nut from transmission support mounting plate. Remove nuts and washers securing transmission bracket.
20. Remove bolts and heat shield.
21. Using a suitable jack, support transmission.
22. Remove transmission support mounting plate attaching bolts, washers, rubber rings and support mounting plate.
23. Remove nuts securing propeller shaft to transmission output flange.
24. Vehicles equipped with manual transmission, disconnect transmission harness from electrical connector.
25. Vehicles equipped with automatic transmission, note the following:

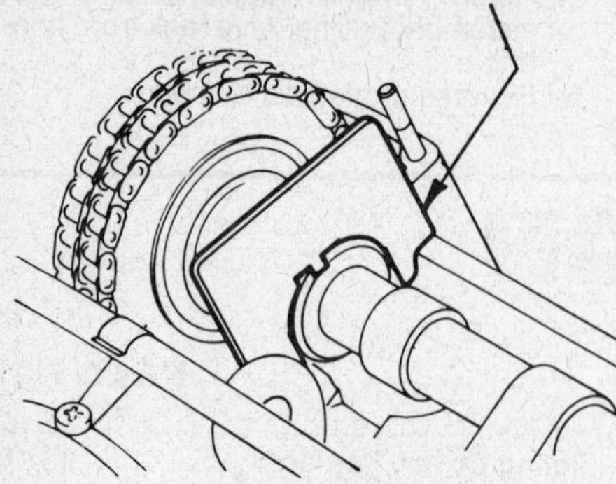

Fig. 1 Valve timing gauge installed

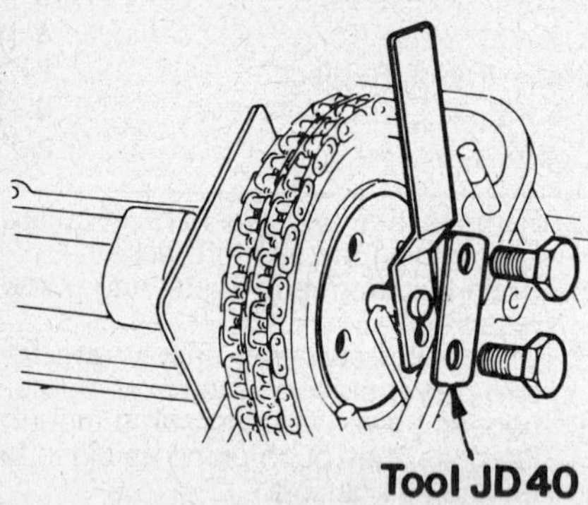

Fig. 3 Retaining tool installation. XJ-S

a. Remove nut and ball peg from shift lever cable.
b. Remove bolt, washer and shift cable.

26. Disconnect speedometer cable from transmission.
27. Position a suitable jack under transmission oil pan.
28. Using a hoist, support engine, then lower rear of vehicle.
29. Carefully remove engine from compartment.
30. Reverse procedure to install.

CYLINDER HEAD REPLACE

XJ-S

LEFT SIDE (B BANK)

Except H.E. Engine

1. Disconnect battery.
2. Remove left and right-side camshaft covers.
3. Disconnect and remove thermostat housing from engine.
4. Remove bolts securing fan and Torquatrol unit to spindle.
5. Rotate engine until valve timing gauge C.3993 can be fitted in the slot in the right-side ("A" bank) camshaft front flange, **Fig. 1.**
6. Remove rubber grommet from timing gear cover.
7. Insert blade of timing chain tensioner retractor and release tool JD.50 through hole to release locking catch on timing chain tensioner.
8. Using timing chain tensioner retractor and release tool JD.50, retract timing chain tensioner. The locking catch will engage when tensioner is properly retracted, **Fig. 2.**
9. Disconnect camshaft sprocket from camshaft and fit sprocket retaining tool JD.40, **Fig. 3.**
10. Remove steering linkage heat shield.
11. Remove front heat shield, exhaust pipe heat shield, and exhaust pipe to exhaust manifold.
12. Disconnect EGR line and remove exhaust manifold heat shield.
13. Remove rear exhaust manifold.
14. On models with automatic transmission, disconnect transmission dipstick tube.
15. Disconnect fuel hoses from cooler and plug connections.
16. Disconnect and move amplifier away from cylinder head.
17. Remove camshaft oil feed bolt.
18. Remove three nuts holding cylinder head to timing cover and progressively loosen cylinder head nuts working from center out.
19. Lift off cylinder head and place it on blocks of wood to avoid damage to valves, which protrude below cylinder head face when open. **Do not remove valve timing gauge from "A" bank camshaft.**
20. Rotate camshaft until timing gauge C.3993 can be fitted in slot in left side camshaft. **The mating surface of cylinder head and block must be cleaned before proceeding.**
21. Fit cylinder head gasket, making sure that side marked "TOP" is in topmost position. **Do not use jointing compound or grease.**
22. Fit cylinder head, tightening retaining bolts in order shown in **Fig. 4** to a torque of: 27.5 ft. lbs. (3.7 kg/m) for $3/8$ inch nuts; 52 ft. lbs. (7.2 kg/m) for $7/16$ inch nuts.
23. Tighten cylinder head to timing cover nuts to a torque of 9 ft. lbs. (1.2kg/m).
24. Remove sprocket retaining tool JD.40 and check alignment of retaining bolt holes. Be sure camshaft and sprocket holes are aligned.
25. Rotate coupling to line up bolt holes, and bolt coupling to camshaft.
26. Refit retaining clip and remove gauge C.3993 from left side camshaft and rotate engine until remaining camshaft sprocket retaining bolts can be fitted.
27. Continue by reversing operations above not already performed, completing reassembly by adjusting fan belt tension, checking ignition timing and assuring that engine meets emission control standards.

H.E. Engine

1. Disconnect battery ground cable and drain coolant from system.
2. Remove both air cleaner elements and covers.
3. Remove ignition amplifier.
4. Remove both intake manifolds and gaskets.

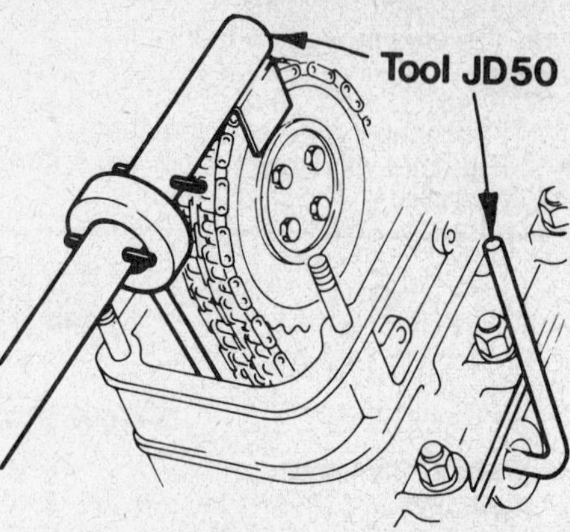

Fig. 2 Retracting timing chain tensioner. XJ-S

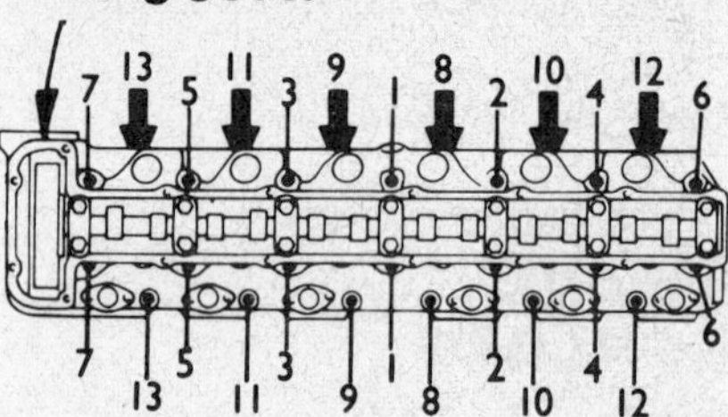

Fig. 4 Cylinder head bolt tightening sequence. XJ-S

5. Remove both camshaft covers and gaskets. Remove left side fender brace.
6. Disconnect fuel return hose from fuel cooler and position fuel cooler aside.
7. Disconnect spark plug lead wires from spark plugs.
8. Disconnect left side top hose from the thermostat housing and disconnect left side hose from the water rail.
9. Loosen clip securing coolant cross pipe hose to water rail.
10. Remove bolts securing water rail.
11. Remove engine lifting eyes and disconnect water rail and gaskets from coolant cross pipe and remove rail.
12. Disconnect camshaft oil feed pipe from left side cylinder head.
13. Remove exhaust manifold heat shield, and engine dipstick and tube assembly.
14. Raise front of vehicle and support with suitable stands.
15. Working from under the vehicle, remove left side down pipe heat shield and disconnect pipe from exhaust manifold. Remove rear manifold lower securing nuts.
16. Lower vehicle and remove rear exahust manifold. Loosen fan belt and remove fan/Torquatrol assembly from pulley, position aside.
17. Disconnect expansion hose from coolant filler pipe neck.
18. Rotate engine using crankshaft pulley nut and position camshaft 180° BTDC.
19. Bend back tab washers and loosen accessible camshaft sprocket retaining bolts.

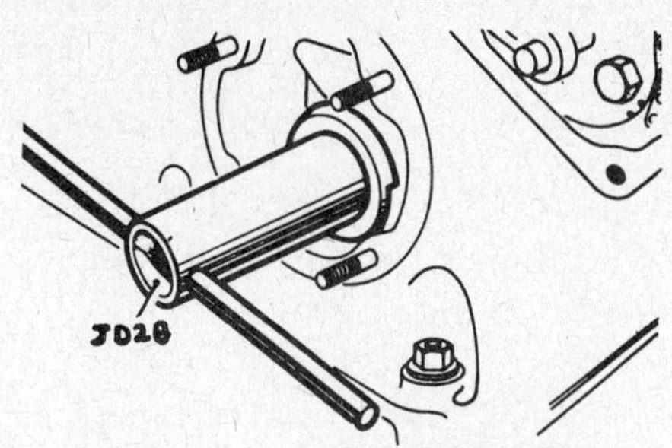

Fig. 5 Loosening idler sprocket locknut. XJ6

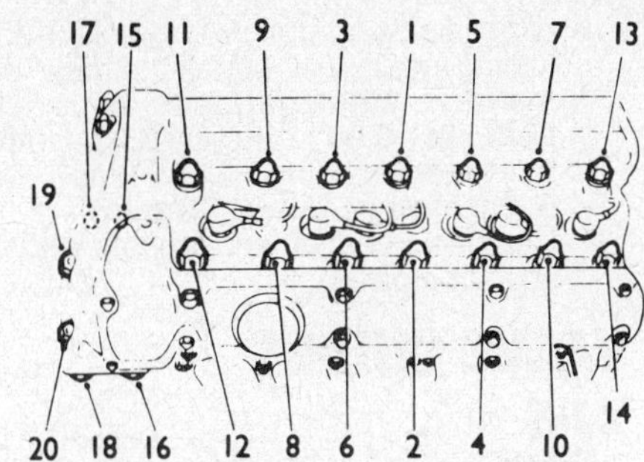

Fig. 6 Cylinder head bolt tightening sequence. XJ6

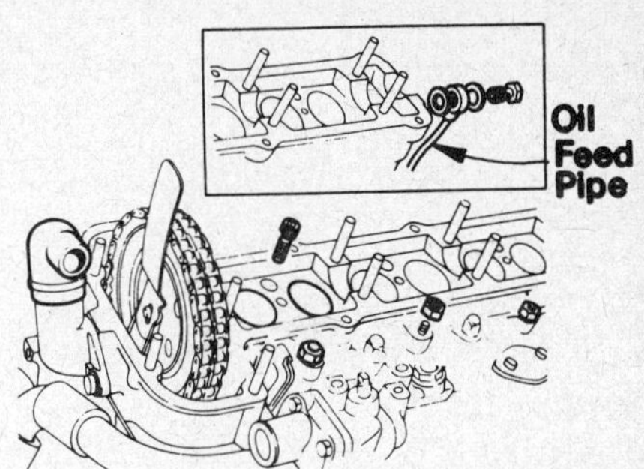

Fig. 7 Removing oil supply line. XJ-S

20. Rotate engine until valve timing gauge C3993 can be fitted, **Fig. 1.**
21. Bend back tab washers and loosen remaining camshaft sprocket bolts.
22. Remove rubber grommet from front timing chain cover and using tool JD 50 release tension on timing chain, **Fig. 2.**
23. Remove camshaft sprocket retaining bolts and tab washers.
24. Place sprocket onto chain guide and retain using tool JD 40, **Fig. 3. Do not rotate engine again until camshaft sprocket is replaced on camshaft.**
25. Starting at the center and working outward remove cylinder head nuts.
26. Remove cylinder head and gasket.
27. Reverse procedure to install and tighten cylinder head bolts in sequence shown in, **Fig. 4.**

RIGHT SIDE (A BANK)

Except H.E. Engine

The procedure is similar to that explained above for the left side (B bank) cylinder head except as follows:

1. The air conditioner compressor must be disengaged and swung clear of cylinder head.
2. It is not necessary to remove left hand camshaft cover.
3. The starter motor and starter motor heat shield have to be removed. **Do not rotate the engine until cylinder liner retaining tool JD.41 has been fitted to the cylinder head studs.**
4. If crankshaft or camshaft are moved, or cylinder head overhauled and/or piston decarbonization has been carried out, you will have to perform the following steps before refitting the cylinder head and completing reassembly as outlined above:
   a. Remove distributor cover and attach a clock gauge to the cylinder head stud.
   b. Rotate the engine using clock gauge to set No. 1 piston at TDC, then remove gauge.
   c. Turn camshaft until valve timing gauge C.3993 can be fitted into slot in camshaft front flange.
   d. Remove cylinder liner retaining tool JD.41 and continue as above.

H.E. Engine

1. Disconnect battery ground cable.
2. Remove right air cleaner cover and element.
3. Remove right intake manifold and gasket.
4. Loosen A/C compressor drive belt and position auxiliary pulley bracket away from cylinder head.
5. Loosen clip securing coolant cross pipe to right side water rail.
6. Disconnect thermotive switch and coolant temperature sensor lead wires.
7. Disconnect top hose from thermostat housing.
8. Remove A/C compressor securing bolts and position compressor aside.
9. Disconnect spark plug lead wires from spark plugs.
10. Disconnect harness and throttle cable from right side fender brace and remove brace.
11. Remove harnesses from air valve cross pipe and disconnect cross pipe from left side manifold.
12. Disconnect all vacuum hoses from cross pipe and note position of each vacuum hose for installation.
13. Disconnect water valve hose from right water rail.
14. Remove automatic transmission dip stick tube assembly, lifting eye bracket and right side water rail assembly.
15. Disconnect right side camshaft oil feed pipe and remove camshaft cover.
16. Disconnect exhaust manifold heat shield and down pipe from manifold.
17. Remove front exhaust manifold.
18. Remove upper and lower rear manifold front securing nuts.
19. Raise and support front of vehicle.
20. Working from under vehicle, remove starter motor heat shield and spacer.
21. Working from under vehicle, remove remaining lower rear manifold attaching nuts and lower vehicle.
22. Remove remaining upper rear manifold attaching nuts.
23. Remove right side upper engine mounting nut.
24. Using a suitable jack lift engine enough to facilitate removal of exhaust manifold, lower engine.
25. Loosen fan belt and remove fan/Torquatrol assembly from pulley, position aside.
26. Disconnect expansion hose from coolant filler neck.
27. Rotate engine using crankshaft pulley nut and position camshaft 180° BTDC.
28. Bend back tab washers and loosen accessible camshaft sprocket retaining bolts.
29. Rotate engine until valve timing gauge C3993 can be fitted, **Fig. 1.**
30. Bend back tab washers and loosen remaining camshaft sprocket bolts.
31. Remove rubber grommet from front timing chain cover and using tool JD 50 release tension on timing chain, **Fig. 2.**
32. Remove camshaft sprocket retaining bolts and tab washers.
33. Place sprocket onto chain guide and retain using tool JD 40, **Fig. 3. Do not rotate engine again until camshaft sprocket is replaced on camshaft.**
34. Starting at the center and working outward remove cylinder head nuts.
35. Remove cylinder head and gasket.
36. Reverse procedure to install and tighten bolts in sequence shown in **Fig. 4.**

XJ6

1. Disconnect battery ground cable, remove air cleaner and drain cooling system.
2. Remove fender support bars.
3. Vehicles equipped with automatic transmission model 65, disconnect inner, outer and kickdown cables from linkage brackets. **Vehicles equipped with air conditioning system, carefully discharge refrigerant from system.**
4. Mark and disconnect all lines and hoses from engine.
5. Loosen power steering pump bolts, and remove pump drive belt.
6. Remove nuts and exhaust manifolds from cylinder head.
7. Remove distributor cap, leads and spark plugs.
8. Remove dome nuts, countersunk screws and camshaft covers.
9. Remove nuts and breather housing from cylinder head.
10. Loosen locknut on idler sprocket shaft, then position tool No. JD2B or equivalent, **Fig. 5**, on serrated adjuster plate. Rotate tool clockwise to relieve timing chain tension.
11. Push tangs downward and remove camshaft sprocket retaining bolts.
12. Rotate engine and remove remaining bolts. **Engine should not be rotated while camshaft sprockets are removed and cylinder head is in place.**
13. Remove sprockets from camshaft

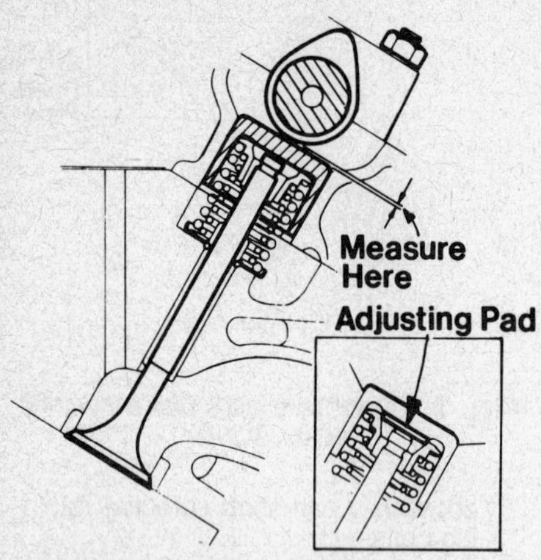

Fig. 8 Valve adjustment

and slide them up the support brackets.

14. Remove fourteen cylinder head dome nuts, and six nuts securing front of cylinder head.
15. Using a suitable lifting assembly, lift cylinder head from cylinder block.
16. Reverse procedure to install, noting the following:
    a. Thoroughly clean cylinder head and engine block mating surfaces.
    b. Install a new gasket with word "TOP" facing upward.
    c. Rotate crankshaft to set No. 6 cylinder at TDC compression stroke, with distributor arm pointing approximately forward of engine.
    d. Torque dome nuts in order shown in **Fig. 6**, to 54 ft. lbs.
    e. Firmly tighten remaining nuts.

ROCKER ARM SERVICE

1. Remove camshaft.
2. Remove oil feed pipe to rocket arm bolt, disconnect breather pipe and progressively loosen retaining nuts and cap screws, working from center out, **Fig. 7.**
3. Lift off rocker arm. **Record from order in which tappets and pads are removed to facilitate valve adjustment.**
4. Clean rocker arm and cylinder head mating surfaces and smear surfaces with a suitable lubricant.
5. Refit rocker arm, tightening retaining nuts and cap screws from center out.
6. Lubricate tappets and adjusting pads with clean engine oil.
7. Complete reassembly.

VALVES

ADJUST

1. Tighten bearing caps evenly to a torque of 9 ft. lbs. (1.2 kg/m).
2. Check and record clearance between each tappet and heel of each cam. Correct clearance is .012 to .014 in. (.305 to .355 mm) for both intake and exhaust, **Fig. 8.**
3. Subtract correct valve clearance from dimension you obtain and select adjusting pads that equal the new dimension. **Adjusting pads are available in 0.001 inch (0.03 mm) increments from 0.085 inch to 0.110 inch (2.16 to 2.79 mm).**
4. Remove camshaft and tappets, and fit adjusting pads.

VALVE GUIDES

XJ-S

Valve guides are available in two oversize dimensions. The first, having two identification grooves, has a 0.506 in. to 0.507 inch (12.85 mm to 12.88 mm) diameter. The second, having three grooves, has a 0.511 inch to 0.512 inch (12.98 mm to 13.00 mm) diameter.

When new guides are fitted, they should be one size larger than the old guides. Cylinder head bores will require reaming as follows:

a. First oversize (two grooves) −.505 inch + .0005 inch − .0002 inch (12.83 mm + .012 mm − .005 mm).
b. Second oversize (Three grooves) −.510 inch + .0005 inch − .0002 inch (12.95 mm + .012 mm − .0005 mm).

XJ6

Valve guides are available in three oversize dimensions. The first has one machined groove, and has a 0.503-0.504 inch diameter. The second, has two grooves, and has a 0.506-0.507 inch diameter. The third, has three grooves, and a 0.511-0.512 inch diameter.

TIMING COVER

REPLACE

XJ-S

1. Remove engine and transmission assembly from vehicle, then remove cylinder heads, oil pan assembly, alternator, power steering pump, emission control air pump, air conditioning compressor and water pump.
2. Remove brackets attached to area of disassembly.
3. Remove bolts holding timing cover to block.
4. Remove timing cover. Discard oil seal.
5. Clean mating surfaces.
6. Lubricate new oil seal in clean engine oil and press into timing cover.
7. Smear both sides of a new gasket with joint compound and place on timing cover.
8. Position timing cover and continue reassembly in reverse of disassembly.

XJ6

1. Remove engine and transmission assembly from vehicle.
2. Remove cylinder heads and oil pan assembly.
3. Remove water pump and crankcase breather.
4. Remove crankshaft vibration damper, cone and woodruff key.
5. Remove bolts, timing chain cover, O-ring and gasket.

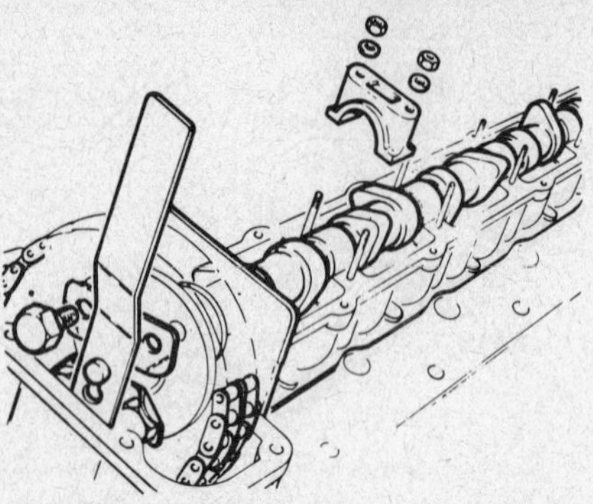

Fig. 9 Camshaft removal. XJ-S

6. Reverse procedure to install. Clean mating surfaces, then install a new O-ring and gasket.

TIMING CHAIN

REPLACE

XJ-S

1. Remove timing cover.
2. Fit retaining tool JD 39 in position on pulley shaft and disconnect timing chain from camshaft and pulley shaft sprockets.
3. Remove crankshaft sprocket and chain. **Do not rotate the engine.**

XJ6

1. Remove timing cover.
2. Remove oil thrower from crankshaft.
3. Remove bolts, timing chain tensioner and chain guides. Remove cone filter from tensioner.
4. Loosen bolts and washers securing timing chain assembly, then remove crankshaft and chain assembly, **Fig. 5.**
5. Remove timing chain spacers, dampers and retainer.
6. Remove camshaft sprockets from timing chain.
7. Remove nut, washer and idler shaft. Remove plate, plunger and spring from idler shaft opening.
8. Remove nuts and washers, then separate front from rear mounting bracket.
9. Remove timing chains from intermediate and idler sprockets.
10. Remove idler shaft, sprocket and bushing from rear mounting bracket.
11. Remove snap ring, intermediate shaft, sprockets, bushing and shim from rear mounting bracket.
12. Reverse procedure to install. Check timing chains and sprockets for signs of wear and corrosion. Replace all damaged parts.

CAMSHAFT

REPLACE

XJ-S

1. Remove camshaft cover.
2. Insert timing chain tensioner retractor tool JD 50 through hole in timing cov-

er and retract timing chain tensioner until locking catch engages on step, **Fig. 9.**

3. Remove camshaft sprocket retaining bolts.
4. Rotate engine until timing gauge C.3993 can be inserted in camshaft slot.
5. Remove two remaining bolts in camshaft sprocket and attach retaining tool JD 40. **Do not rotate engine while the camshaft is disconnected.**

XJ6

1. Remove bolts and camshaft covers.
2. Remove nuts and breather housing from front of cylinder head.
3. Loosen nut on idler shaft sprocket. Push down locking tabs, and remove camshaft sprocket bolts.
4. Rotate engine until valve timing gauge can be inserted in camshaft slot, **Fig. 1.**
5. Using tool No. JD2B or equivalent, insert tool through camshaft opening. Rotate tool clockwise, to relieve camshaft chain tension. **Do not rotate engine with camshafts removed.**
6. Evenly loosen camshaft bearing cap nuts, starting with center nut and working outward. **If original camshaft bearings are to be installed, note location of camshaft bearings for proper installation.**
7. Remove camshaft from cylinder head.
8. Reverse procedure to install. Torque nuts to 9 ft. lbs.

PISTONS, PINS & RINGS

Pistons and rings are available in standard size only. If cylinder wear is excessive, replace the cylinder bore liners.

Pistons and wrist pins are a matched assembly. Parts should not be interchanged.

OIL PAN
REPLACE

XJ-S

1. Drain engine oil.
2. Remove screws and serrated washers holding oil pan, then lower pan.

XJ6

1. Remove front shock absorber and coil spring assemblies from vehicle.
2. Drain engine oil.
3. Remove nuts, washers and oil return line.
4. Vehicles equipped with automatic transmission only, remove nuts, bolts, washers and transmission oil cooler line brackets.
5. Remove bolts, lockwashers and oil pan.
6. Reverse procedure to install.

OIL PUMP
REPLACE

XJ-S

Removing oil pump is an extensive task, requiring almost complete disassembly of engine. It is therefore recommended that oil pump be inspected for wear and damage whenever it is accessible for other reasons.

XJ6

1. Refer to "Oil Pan, Replace" procedure and remove oil pan.
2. Disconnect supply and return line clips from brackets.
3. Push down locking tabs, and remove bolts securing oil supply line.
4. Pull both lines from oil pump.
5. Push down locking tabs, and remove bolts, oil pump, line bracket and drive coupling.
6. Reverse procedure to install.

WATER PUMP
REPLACE

XJ-S

1. Remove drive belt.
2. Remove fan, Torquatrol unit, adjuster assembly and idler pulley housing.
3. Remove power steering, air pump and air conditioner compressor belts.
4. Remove thermostatic switch housing and bottom hose.
5. Remove water pump retaining hardware and water pump.

XJ6

1. Drain cooling system.
2. Remove fan cowl.
3. Loosen fan and power steering pump bolts, then remove drive belts.
4. Remove support strap bolt from water pump.
5. Remove nut, bolt, washers and air pump delivery line from exhaust manifold cowl.
6. Loosen air pump belt adjuster nuts and remove belt.
7. Remove bolts, washers, bracket and air pump from cylinder block.
8. Remove bolts and the header tank.
9. Loosen nut on radiator bottom hose.
10. Remove distributor cap.
11. Loosen bolts on heater supply line bracket.
12. Loosen bolt on throttle housing outlet bracket, if equipped.
13. Remove bolts, then break seal and remove water pump from cylinder block.
14. Reverse procedure to install.

FUEL PUMP
REPLACE

1. Depressurize the fuel system as described in "Fuel Injection Section," if equipped, then disconnect battery.
2. Remove spare tire.
3. Remove fuel pump cover.
4. Remove intake and outlet hoses.
5. Remove fuel pump retaining band from mounting.
6. Remove electrical connector.
7. Place a receptacle to catch spilled fuel and release hoses.
8. Separate fuel pump retaining band and remove two foam rubber insulation bands.
9. Reverse procedure to install.

CLUTCH, MANUAL TRANSMISSION & OVERDRIVE SECTION

INDEX

CLUTCH
ADJUST

These models are equipped with a self-adjusting clutch mechanism. Therefore, no adjustments are necessary. Anytime clutch hydraulic lines are disconnected for servicing clutch assembly components, the entire system must be bled using the following procedure.

1. Attach one end of bleed tube to slave cylinder bleed nipple and immerse other end of tube in container of clean, suitable brake fluid.
2. Loosen slave cylinder bleed nipple and pump clutch pedal slowly up and down, pausing between each stroke.
3. Continue this operation until all air bubbles are removed from system.
4. Fill reservoir to proper level, then replace reservoir cap.

MANUAL TRANSMISSION
REPLACE

1. Remove engine and transmission from vehicle.
2. Remove clutch.
3. Remove clutch fork assembly.
4. Remove and discard locking wire.
5. Knock back locking tabs and remove screws holding bellhousing to transmission. Discard tabs.
6. Remove bellhousing, discarding gasket and oil seal.
7. Coat a new oil seal with clean engine oil.
8. Push oil seal into bellhousing so lip of seal is toward transmission.
9. Coat a new gasket with grease. Place gasket on front of transmission.
10. Cover splines of input shaft with adhesive tape to keep shaft from damaging oil seal and slide bellhousing over shaft.
11. Install new lock plates and tighten screws diagonally to prevent distortion.
12. Turn up tabs of lock plates and wire lock the screws.
13. Complete reassembly by reversing steps 1 through 3 above.

OVERDRIVE
REPLACE

1. Disconnect battery ground cable and drain transmission oil.
2. Disconnect exhaust pipe from exhaust manifold.
3. Remove intermediate heat shield.
4. Support engine at rear mount using suitable jack, then remove bolts, nuts, washers and spacers, attaching engine mounting bracket to body and base plate.
5. Lower jack to release tension, then remove nuts and washers attaching rear engine center bolt.
6. Remove rear heat shield from engine mounting base plate.
7. Remove mounting base plate to body, attaching screws and the mounting base plate.
8. Disconnect speedometer drive gear from overdrive unit.
9. Disconnect drive shaft from overdrive unit.
10. With rear of engine supported, carefully lower rear of engine as far as possible without allowing it to contact steering rack. Do not let engine rest on steering rack or on air conditioner expansion valve, if equipped. Ensure that clutch supply hose does not bend or kink.
11. Disconnect overdrive solenoid electrical connector.
12. Remove nuts and washers, securing overdrive unit rear casing to transmission adapter plate studs.
13. Pull overdrive unit rearward until it clears studs and transmission shaft splines.
14. Remove overdrive oil pump drive cam from transmission output shaft.
15. Reverse procedure to install. Place transmission in first gear before installing overdrive unit.

FRONT SUSPENSION & STEERING SECTION

INDEX

HUB & ROTOR
REPLACE

1. Raise and support vehicle and remove wheel.
2. Remove five bolts and washers holding hub assembly to brake disc.
3. Remove hub grease cap and split pin.
4. Remove nut and washer from stub axle. Remove hub by hand.
5. To reassemble, pack hub with specified grease and refit to stub axle.
6. Fit bearing, nut and washer to stub axle and tighten nut to give end float of .05-.15mm (.002- .006 inch). **End-float is measured by fitting a dial test indicator with the button against the hub.**
7. Fit new split pin, grease cap and ensure vent hole is clear.
8. Replace wheel.

WHEEL BEARINGS
ADJUST

Wheel bearings are adjusted by tightening the adjusting nut to eliminate all play and then backing the nut off slightly to provide play of .002-.005 inch (.05-.15mm).

UPPER BALL JOINT
REPLACE

1. Remove the wheel and turn the steering wheel to full lock position.
2. Reinforce brake hose to relieve strain.
3. Remove upper ball joint hardware.
4. Release ball joint from axle carrier with taper separator tool JD.24.
5. Hold the ball joint against taper fit washer and tighten retaining nut to 35-50 ft. lbs. (4.84-6.91 kgf/m). **The bolts holding the ball joint to the wishbone must be replaced with heads facing forward.**
6. Reassemble in reverse of disassembly, tightening fasteners to 26-32 ft. lbs. (3.60-4.42 kgf/m).

LOWER BALL JOINT
ADJUST

1. Raise the car, remove wheel and place a jack under front spring seat, and lift to relieve pressure on axle carrier.
2. Remove tie rod ball joint fasteners, and separate tie rod from steering arm using steering joint taper separator tool JD.24.
3. Remove all other hardware, leaving ball joint free. **Shims are added to obtain correct adjustment. However, excessive wear must not be compensated for by shims. Worn parts must be replaced.**
4. Remove shims one by one until ball pin is tight in socket with screws tightened to 15-20 ft. lbs (2.10-2.75 kgf/m). **Shims are available in .002 and .004 inch (0.5 and 0.10mm).**
5. Remove screws, ball pin cap, shims and socket. Add shims to value of .004-.006 (0.10-0.15mm).
6. Grease ball pin and socket lightly. Refit the socket ball pin cap and washers.
7. Torque to 15-20 ft. lbs. (2.1-2.75 kgf/m). When correctly adjusted, hub and axle carrier may be pivoted with very slight drag.
8. Apply grease to ball joint and replace tie rod.
9. Tighten tie rod nut to 35-50 ft. lbs. (4.84-6.91 kgf/m).
10. Loosen spring compressor tool and remove spring.
11. When installing, lighten hardware to 27-32 ft. lbs. (3.74-4.42 kgf/m).

UPPER CONTROL ARM
REPLACE

1. Raise up front of car and place stand beneath spring seat pan.
2. Remove two nuts, bolts and plain washers securing upper ball joint to

upper control arm.
3. Tie stub axle carrier to road spring turret to prevent damage to brake flexible hose.
4. Remove two bolts, special washers and nylon nuts securing upper control arm fulcrum shaft to road spring turret.
5. Reverse procedure to install.

LOWER CONTROL ARM REPLACE

1. Raise and support vehicle.
2. Remove front suspension unit and invert.
3. Remove self-locking nut and washer, securing steering tie rod ball joint.
4. Seperate rod from steering arm using tool JD 24.
5. Remove three bolts, nuts and washers securing steering rack to front suspension crossmember.
6. Remove front spring.
7. Remove two nuts, bolts and plain washers securing upper ball joint to upper control arm.
8. Remove self-locking nut and washers and seperate lower ball joint from control arm.
9. Remove split pin at fulcrum shaft nut and remove nut and plain washer.
10. Drift fulcrum shaft from crossmember and recover two washers.
11. Reverse procedure to install. **Do not fully tighten fulcrum shaft nut until full weight of vehicle is on suspension.**
12. Fully tighten fulcrum shaft nut to correct torque and fit new split pin.
13. Check front wheel alignment.

POWER STEERING GEAR REPLACE

1. Remove lower steering column.
2. Drain fluid from steering pump.
3. Disconnect and plug all fluid supply lines, **Fig. 1.**

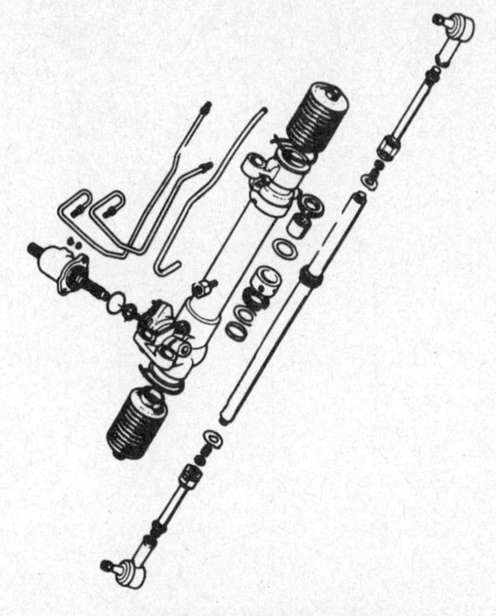

Fig. 1 Disassembled view of steering gear

4. Using ball joint separator tool No. JD24 or equivalent, separate left and right tie rods.
5. Remove steering gear from front suspension.
6. Reverse procedure to install, noting the following:
   a. Shims are installed between gear and mounting bracket to obtain a 0.05 inch gap on either side of gear and mounting bracket. On XJ6 models a 0.10-0.12 inch gap is required.
   b. Using tool No. JD36A or equivalent, align front wheels.
7. Align front wheels as follows:
   a. Loosen locknuts on outer ends of each tie rod.
   b. Remove hose clips securing outer ends of boots to tie rods.
   c. Equally rotate tie rods until desired wheel alignment.
   d. Secure track rod end and torque locknuts to 60-70 ft. lbs.

POWER STEERING PUMP REPLACE

1. Remove cover from front of air cleaner on 6 cylinder models, and remove left hand air cleaner on 12 cylinder models.
2. Detach and plug pipes, slacken pivot and trunnion bolts.
3. Remove adjusted rod bolt to pump.
4. Press pump towards engine, lift belt off pulley.
5. Remove pivot bolt and lift pump and bracket away from engine.
6. Detach pump from bracket.

SHOCK ABSORBER REPLACE

1. From beneath hood, remove hardware from shock absorber front mounting.
2. Raise vehicle.
3. Remove locking nut and bolt from bottom of shock.
4. Remove shock absorber from vehicle.
5. Install shock absorber and torque lower mounting bolt to 32-36 ft. lbs. (4.42-4.98 kgf/m) and upper mounting bolt to 27-32 ft. lbs. (3.73-4.42 kgf/m).

COIL SPRING REPLACE

1. Raise vehicle and remove wheel.
2. Fit spring compressor tool JD 6D with adapter JD 6D-1 to spring and compress sufficiently to relieve load on seat fastener.
3. Remove bolts and spring plate assembly.
4. Loosen spring compressor tool and remove spring.
5. Install and torque bolts to 27-32 ft. lbs. (3.74-4.42 kgf/m).

WHEEL ALIGNMENT SECTION

INDEX

FRONT

INSPECTION

1. Inflate tires to correct pressures.
2. Set front wheels in straight ahead position.
3. Remove grease nipple from rack adjuster pad. **Fig. 1.**
4. Insert centralizing tool and adjust position of rack until reduced tip of tool enters locating hole in rack, **Fig. 1.**
5. Check alignment by using light beam equipment or an approved track setting gauge.
6. Remove steering levers.
7. Accurately check dimensions of each lever against those in **Fig. 2.**
8. Replace any lever that does not meet specifications.

ADJUSTMENT

Always adjust alignment settings in the following order: caster, camber, then toe.

Caster

Caster angle is adjusted by loosening the four upper wishbone-to-ball joint nuts and refitting shims from one side of the ball joint to the opposite side. Placing the front shims to the rear position decreases caster angle, while placing rear shims to the front position increases caster angle. The rate of alteration is approximately 1/4 degree for each 1/16 inch (1.6mm) shim.

Camber

Camber angle is adjusted by loosening the two nuts holding the end of the upper wishbone away from the ball joint at the trunnion. Add or remove an equal number of shims from both spots. Removing shims decreases camber angle, while adding shims increases camber angle. The rate of alteration is approximately 1/4 degree for 1/16 inch (1.6mm) shim.

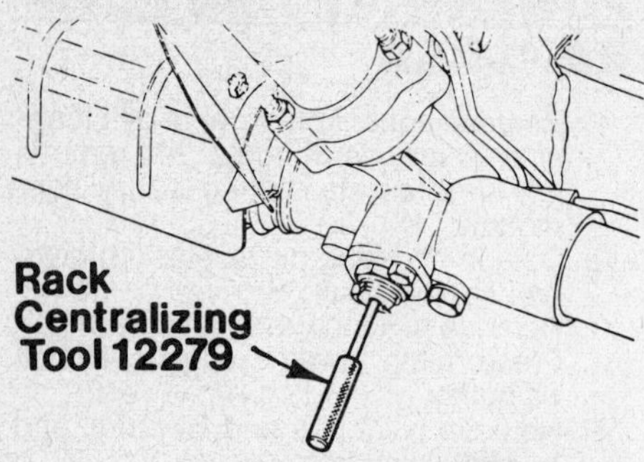

Fig. 1 Toe-in adjustment

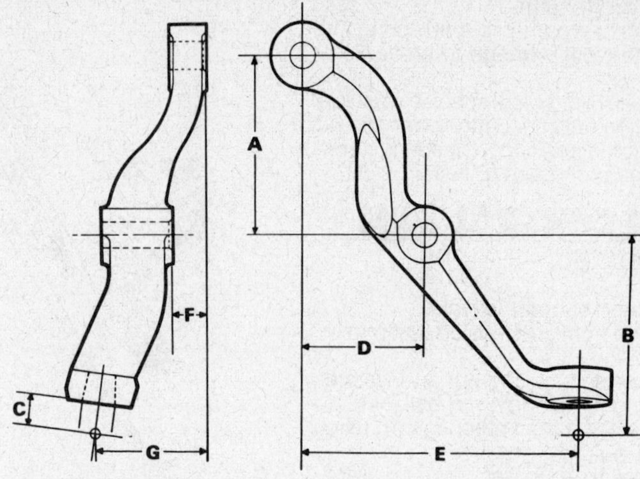

DIMENSIONS—STEERING LEVER, Fig. 5

'A' 82,5 mm to 82,6 mm (3.248 in to 3.252 in)
'B' 101,85 mm to 102,36 mm (4.01 in to 4.03 in)
'C' 22,23 mm (0.875 in)
'D' 58,93 mm to 59,44 mm (2.32 in to 2.34 in)
'E' 135,38 mm to 135,89 mm (5.33 in to 5.35 in)
'F' 17,78 mm to 18,03 mm (0.70 in to 0.71 in)
'G' 54,36 mm to 54,86 mm (2.14 in to 2.16 in)

Fig. 2 Steering lever dimensions

Toe-In

1. With tires inflated properly and wheels in a straight-ahead position, remove the grease fitting from the steering rack adjuster nut and insert rack centralizing tool 12279 into the hole, **Fig. 2.**
2. Slowly turn the steering wheel until the tool locates itself in the recess in the rear of the rack.
3. Check toe-in.
4. If adjustment is necessary, loosen the locknuts at the outer ends of the tie rods and loosen the clips holding the tie rod retaining bracket.
5. Turn tie rods by an equal amount until alignment of wheels is correct.
6. Tighten locknuts while holding track rod end spanner flats.
7. Recheck alignment.
8. Ensure boots are not twisted and tighten clips.
9. Remove centralising tool and refit grease nipple.

REAR

CAMBER

Check

1. Ensure car is on level surface and tire pressure is correct.
2. Install one end of setting link tool JD 25 in lower hole of rear mounting. Depress body until other end of setting link can be slid over outer wishbone fulcrum nut. Repeat on other side of car.
3. Set camber gauge against each rear tire and read off camber angle. The correct reading should be ½°-1°.
4. If these limits are not met, note deviation and adjust camber angle.
5. If results are satisfactory, remove setting links.

Adjust

1. Raise rear of vehicle and support body.
2. Remove wheel.
3. Remove lower wishbone outer fulcrum grease nipple.
4. Release clip securing inner universal joint cover. Slide cover clear of joint.
5. Remove four steel locknuts securing drive shaft flange to brake disc.
6. Separate drive shaft from disc to enable shims to be fitted. **Addition of one shim, .5 mm (.020 inch) will alter camber position ¼°.**
7. Add or remove shims as required.
8. Replace drive shaft, cover, nipple and wheel.
9. Remove vehicle from stands and recheck camber angle.

SUSPENSION HEIGHT

Check

1. Ensure radiator is topped with coolant.
2. Ensure engine sump is filled to correct level with specified lubricant.
3. Ensure tire pressures are correct
4. Ensure fuel tank is full (24 U.S. imperial gallons).
5. Measure distance between lower surface of rear crossmember and ground at both sides of car. Distance should be 182.6-195.4 mm (7.20-7.70 inches).
6. If dimension is not correct, check all bushes and bearing points of rear suspension. If cause is not discovered, all four springs must be replaced as a set.

REAR AXLE SECTION

INDEX

DESCRIPTION

The standard rear axle unit is a Salisbury 4 HU final drive incorporating a "Powr Lok" differential. The unit is rigidly attached to a fabricated sheet steel crossbeam which is flexibly mounted to the body structure by four rubber and metal sandwich mounts.

AXLE SHAFT, OIL SEAL & BEARINGS

REPLACE

1. Remove output shaft assembly. Clean assembly and clamp caliper mounting bracket in a vise.
2. Using special spanner SL 15 or SL 15A, turn down tabs of lock washer and remove nut from shaft.
3. Separate shaft and caliper mounting bracket, collecting inner bearing and cone. Mark bearing and cone to facilitate reassembly.
4. Discard spacer and pry oil seal from caliper mounting bracket. Discard oil seal and retrieve outer bearing and cone.
5. Thoroughly clean caliper mounting bracket and inspect axle shaft bearings. Replace bearings if they are damaged.
6. Apply grease to outer bearing assembly and place it in position.
7. Press on a new oil seal, making sure that spring-loaded sealing edge is adjacent to bearing and that sealing edges are loaded with grease.
8. With caliper mounting bracket held in a vise, check to ensure that four brake disc bolts are in position on axle shaft flange. Place shaft through seal and outer bearing assembly.
9. Install a spacer, inner bearing assembly (greased) and lock washer.
10. Place shaft nut in place and tighten by hand.
11. Check torque needed to turn shaft in caliper mounting bracket. Set torque screwdriver initially to a setting of 4 in. lbs. (0.05 kgf/m). The setting should be increased progressively until the torque requirement is established at the point when the shaft starts to turn.
12. Using spanner SL.15 and a pry bar at disc attachment bolts to oppose torque, tighten shaft nut just enough to almost eliminate play from the bearings and remeasure torque as measured in step 11. **The torque needed to turn the shaft should be unchanged. If it has increased, loosen the nut slightly and recheck.**
13. Tighten shaft nut just slightly, but not more than 3/16 in. (5 mm) and test torque needed to turn shaft. If torque exceeds 2.5 to 3 in. lbs. (0.03-0.035 kgf/m) the torque recorded before in step 11, correct bearing pre-load has been established. If this figure has not been attained, continue to tighten axle shaft nut in small increments, measuring torque after each increment, until desired specification has been reached. **If torque required to turn shaft is 4 in. lbs. (0.045 kgf/m) more than that attained in initial tightening sequence in step 11, you will have to disassemble unit, discard spacer and reassemble using a new spacer.**
14. Complete reassembly, which is done in reverse of diassembly.

COIL SPRING & SHOCK ABSORBER

REPLACE

1. Remove rear wheel.
2. Remove washers and nuts holding bottom of shock absorber to wishbone.
3. Remove shock absorber lower mounting pin, spacer and retaining bracket.
4. Remove fasteners holding upper part of shock absorber to crossmember.
5. Remove shock absorber and coil spring assembly.
6. Separate the two, using hand press SL 14 and adapter JD 11B.

REAR HUB & CARRIER ASSEMBLY

REPLACE

1. Raise and support vehicle.
2. Remove wheel.
3. Remove fulcrum shaft grease nipple.
4. Remove split pin, nut and plain washer from splined end of half shaft and fit thread protector JD 1C-7 over end of shaft.
5. Fit hub puller, JD 1D to rear hub and secure.
6. Remove hub and carrier from half shaft. Remove hub puller and thread protector.
7. Remove spacer from half shaft.
8. Inspect inner oil seal track and renew if necessary.
9. Drift out fulcrum shaft from control arm.
10. Remove hub and carrier assembly from car. Temporarily secure retaining washers and shims using adhesive tape.
11. Reverse procedure to install, using a small amount of Loctite on half shaft splines.

BRAKE SECTION

INDEX

FRONT BRAKE PADS
REPLACE

1. Remove wheel assembly.
2. Remove clips holding pad retaining pins.
3. Remove upper pin only and then the anti-chatter springs.
4. Remove lower pin.
5. Pull pads from caliper.

REAR BRAKE PADS
REPLACE

1. Remove wheel assembly.
2. Remove clips holding pad retaining pins.
3. Remove mounting pins and pull pads from caliper. **If thickness of pads, front or rear, is less than 0.125 inch (3.17mm) new pads should be installed.**

PARKING BRAKE PADS
REPLACE

1. Remove handbrake caliper as follows:
   a. Raise carpet for access to cable adjusting nuts.
   b. Ensure handbrake is released, then loosen cable adjusting nuts.
   c. Remove nuts and bolts securing tie plate to differential, **Fig. 1,** then tie plate.
   d. Using a suitable pry bar, move caliper arm towards driveshaft and disconnect cable from arm.
   e. Remove rubber boot from cable at caliper arm.
   f. Disconnect springs from caliper arms and position handbrake cable away from calipers.
   g. Remove locking tabs securing caliper mounting bolts, then mounting bolts, tab washer and retraction plate.
   h. Remove caliper.
2. Remove nut and spring washer securing pads to brake pad carriers, then pads.

FRONT CALIPER
REPLACE

1. Disconnect and plug brake line.

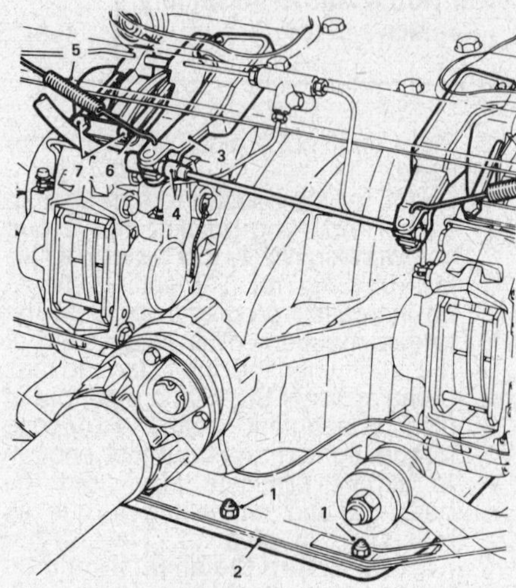

1. TIE PLATE BOLTS
2. TIE PLATE
3. CALIPER ARM
4. RUBBER BOOT
5. CALIPER SPRING
6. LOCKING TABS
7. CALIPER MOUNTING BOLTS

Fig. 1 Removing tie plate

2. Remove lock wire from caliper mounting bolts.
3. Remove caliper mounting bolts, noting position of shims located between steering arm and caliper.
4. Remove caliper.
5. When reassembling, torque caliper mounting bolts to 55 ft. lbs. (7.5 kg/m).

REAR CALIPER
REPLACE

1. Remove handbrake caliper.
2. Loosen brake line connection at three-way connector, then disconnect brake line at caliper and swing line clear of caliper. Be sure to plug brake lines.
3. Remove lock wire holding caliper mounting bolts.
4. Remove caliper mounting bolts.
5. Slide caliper around disc and remove through gap left by removing bracket.
6. When reassembling, torque caliper mounting bolts to 55 ft. lbs. (7.5 kg/m).

FRONT & REAR CALIPER
OVERHAUL

1. Remove pads.
2. Remove spring clips holding piston dust covers.
3. Remove piston dust covers.
4. Fit piston clamp 18G672 to any half of caliper and carefully feed compressed oil into caliper fluid inlet port.
5. Remove pistons from caliper.
6. Carefully pry seals from recesses in caliper cylinder bore. **Under no circumstances must the two halves of the caliper be separated. Use extreme caution not to damage the cylinder bore when removing seals.**
7. Coat new seals with brake lubricant.
8. Using your fingers only, fit new seals into recesses in caliper cylinder bore.
9. Coat pistons with brake lubricant and reinsert them into caliper cylinder bores.
10. Fit rear dust covers and push pistons in.
11. Position dust covers over caliper rim and secure with spring clips.
12. Complete reassembly in reverse of disassembly.

PARKING BRAKE
ADJUST

1. Raise carpeting to rear of the driver's seat to gain access to adjusting nuts.
2. Loosen cable locknut.
3. Tighten adjusting nut so that when parking brake is released there is a slight amount of cable play. **If all play is removed, parking brake caliper may bind.**
4. Tighten cable locknut.

MASTER CYLINDER
REPLACE

1. Remove cover from brake fluid reservoir cap and disconnect wires from brake fluid level indicator.
2. Remove reservoir cap and filter.
3. With a syringe, draw fluid from master cylinder.
4. Disconnect brake lines from master cylinder and plug them.
5. Remove master cylinder from power booster.

MAZDA (Japan)

INDEX OF SERVICE OPERATIONS

General Engine Specifications

Year	Model	Carburetor	Bore & Stroke Inch (mm)	Piston Displacement Cubic Inches (cc)	Compression Ratio	Maximum Brake HP @ RPM	Maximum Torque Ft. Lbs. @ RPM	Normal Oil Pressure Psi
1983–84	B2000①	2 Barrel	3.15 x 3.86 (80 x 98)	120 (1970)	8.6	③	④	50–64
	B2200 Diesel	Diesel Fuel Inj. Pump	3.50 x 3.50 (89 x 89)	135 (2209)	21.1	58 @ 4000	88 @ 2500	57
	RX-7 (12A)②	4 Barrel	—	70 (1146)	9.4	100 @ 6000	105 @ 4000	64–78
1983–85	GLC①	2 Barrel	3.03 x 3.15 (77 x 80)	91 (1490)	9.0	68 @ 5000	82 @ 3000	50–60
	626①	2 Barrel	3.39 x 3.39 (86 x 86)	122 (1998)	8.6	84 @ 4800	110 @ 2500	43–57
1984–85	RX-7 (13B)②	Electronic Fuel Inj.	—	80 (1308)	9.4	135 @ 6000	133 @ 2750	64–78
1985	626 Diesel	Diesel Fuel Inj. Pump	3.39 x 3.39 (86 x 86)	122 (1988)	22.7	—	—	58–70
1986	323	2 Barrel	3.07 x 3.29 (78 x 83.6)	97 (1597)	9.3	—	—	43–57
	323	Electronic Fuel Inj.	3.07 x 3.29 (78 x 83.6)	97 (1597)	9.3	82 @ 5000	92 @ 2500	43–57
	626 Non-Turbo	Electronic Fuel Inj.	3.39 x 3.39 (86 x 86)	122 (1998)	8.6	93 @ 5000	115 @ 2500	43–57
	626 Turbo	Electronic Fuel Inj.	3.39 x 3.39 (86 x 86)	122 (1998)	7.8	120 @ 5000	150 @ 3000	43–57
	RX-7②	Electronic Fuel Inj.	—	80 (1308)	9.4	146 @ 6500	138 @ 3500	64–78
	B2000	2 Barrel	3.39 x 3.39 (86 x 86)	122 (1998)	8.6	—	—	43–57
1987	323	2 Barrel	3.07 x 3.29 (78 x 83.6)	97 (1597)	9.3	—	—	50–64
	323	Electronic Fuel Inj.	3.07 x 3.29 (78 x 83.6)	97 (1597)	9.3	82 @ 5000	92 @ 2500	50–64
	626 Non-Turbo	Electronic Fuel Inj.	3.39 x 3.39 (86 x 86)	122 (1998)	8.6	93 @ 5000	115 @ 2500	43–57
	626 Turbo	Electronic Fuel Inj.	3.39 x 3.39 (86 x 86)	122 (1998)	7.8	120 @ 5000	150 @ 3000	43–57
	RX-7 Non-Turbo ②	Electronic Fuel Inj.	—	80 (1308)	9.4	146 @ 6500	138 @ 3500	64–78
	RX-7 Turbo②	Electronic Fuel Inj.	—	80 (1308)	8.5	182 @ 6500	183 @ 3500	64–78
	B2200	2 Barrel	3.39 x 3.70 (86 x 94)	133 (2184)	8.6	—	—	43–57
	B2600	2 Barrel	3.59 x 3.86 (91.1 x 98)	156 (2555)	8.7	—	—	78

①—Piston Engine.
②—Rotary Engine.
③—Exc. Calif., 77 @ 4300; California, 72 @ 4300.
④—Exc. Calif., 109 @ 2400; California, 105 @ 2400.

Alternator & Regulator Specifications

Year	Model	Alternator		Regulator Voltage @ 2500 RPM⑧
		Rated Output Amps.	Output @ 14V, 2500 RPM Amps⑧	
1983	GLC	50	30	14.1–14.7
1983	RX-7	50	36①	—
1983–84	B2000	50	23①	14.1–14.7
	B2200	40	28①	14.1–14.7
1983–85	626	65	30	14.4–15
1984–85	GLC	50	30	14.4–15
	RX-7②	55	51	—
	RX-7③	60	53	—
1985	626④	65	30	⑤
1986	B2000	55	21	14.4–15
1986–87	323⑥	55	42	14.4–15
	323⑦	60	45	14.4–15
	626	65	51	14.4–15
	RX-7	70	55	14.4–15
1987	B2200 & B2600	55	50	14.2–15.2

—Not Available.
①—At 13.5 volts.
②—12A engine.
③—13B engine.
④—Diesel engine.
⑤—With glow plugs operating, 12.7–13.3; with glow plugs not operating, 14.1–14.7.
⑥—Carbureted model.
⑦—Fuel injected model.
⑧—Engine RPM.

Starter Motor Specifications

Year	Model	No Load Test			Torque Test			Min. Brush Length In.	Brush Spring Tension Ounces
		Amps	Volts	RPM	Amps	Volts	Torque Ft. Lbs.		
1983–84	GLC	53	11.5	6800	310	5	5.4	.45	46–60
	B2000	53	11.5	6800	310	5	5.4	.45	49–63
	B2200	180	11	3800	1050	2	21.6	.45	49–63
1983–85	RX-7①	60	11.5	6500	420	5	6.9	.45	49–92
	RX-7②	100	11.5	3500	1100	4	22.4	.45	59–78
	626①	60	11.5	6500	310	5	5.4	.31	—
	626②	60	11.5	6600	310	5	5.4	.31	—
1985	626④	130 max.	11	4500	1020 max.	2.5	21.7	.45	—
1986	B2000	60	11.5	6500	430	5	7.2	.67	—
1986–87	323	60	11.5	6500	—	—	—	.45	—
	626	60	11.5	6500	—	5	③	.45	32
	RX-7①	90	11	3000	780	4	13	.69	50–83
	RX-7②	90	11	3000	980	4	16.6	.69	50–83
1987	B2200①	60	11.5	6600	570	5	9.3	.45	58–79
	B2200②	90	11	3000	780	4	13	.39	65–86
	B2600	90	11	3000	780	4	13	.39	65–86

—Not Available.
①—Manual trans.
②—Automatic trans.
③—Less Turbo, 7.2 ft. lbs.; Turbo, 9.3 ft. lbs.
④—Diesel engine.

Valve Specifications-Piston Engine

		Valve Lash		Valve Angles		Valve Spring Pressure Lbs. @ Inches		Stem Clearance		Stem Diameter	
Year	Model	Intake Inch	Exhaust Inch	Seat	Face	Inner	Outer	Intake Inch	Exhaust Inch	Intake Inch	Exhaust Inch
1983–84	626	①	①	45	45	—	—	.0010–.0024	.0010–.0024	.3164	.3162
	B2000	①	①	45	45	—	—	.0007–.0021	.0007–.0023	.3150	.3150
	B2200	.012	.012	③	③	25.4 @ 1.49	35.8 @ 1.59	.0015–.0046	.0002–.0051	.3150	.3150
1983–85	GLC	②	②	45	45	—	—	.0007–.0021	.0007–.0021	.3164	.3163
1985	626④	①		45	45	⑤	—	.0010–.0024	.0010–.0024	.3164	.3162
	626⑥	.008–.012	.012–.016	45	45	⑦	—	.0016–.0031	.0020–.0031	.3138–.3144	.3136–.3142
1986	323	⑧	⑧	45	45	⑨	—	.0018–.0051	.0019–.0053	.274–.275	.274–.275
	626	⑩	⑩	45	45	⑪	⑫	.0010–.0024	.0010–.0024	.3161–.3167	.3159–.3165
	B2000	.012H	.012H	45	45	⑪	⑫	.0010–.0024	.0010–.0024	.3161–.3167	.3159–.3165
1987	323	⑧	⑧	45	45	⑨	—	.0010–.0024	.0012–.0026	.2744–.2750	.2742–.2748
	626	⑩	⑩	45	45	⑪	⑫	.0010–.0024	.0010–.0024	.3161–.3167	.3159–.3165
	B2200	0	0	45	45	⑫	⑫	.0010–.0024	.0012–.0026	.3161–.3167	.3159–.3165
	B2600	0⑬	0⑬	45	45	—	—	.0010–.0023	.0020–35	.313–.314	.312–.313

—Not Available.
①—Valve side, .012H; cam side, .009H.
②—Valve side, intake, .010H, exhaust,.012H; cam side, intake, .007H, exhaust, .009H.
③—Intake 45°; Exhaust 30°.
④—Gasoline engine.
⑤—Spring rate, 101 lb./inch.
⑥—Diesel engine.
⑦—Spring rate, 211 lb./inch.
⑧—Valve side, .012H; cam side, .007H.
⑨—Spring rate, 157 lbs./inch.
⑩—Valve side, .012H; cam side, .008H.
⑪—Spring rate, 95 lbs./inch.
⑫—Spring rate, 96 lbs./inch.
⑬—Jet valve .010H.

Pistons, Pins, Rings, Crankshaft & Bearings-Piston Engine

			Ring End Gap①			Rod Bearings		Main Bearings			
Year	Model	Piston Clearance Top of Skirt Inch	Comp. Inch	Oil Inch	Wristpin Diameter Inch	Shaft Diameter Inch	Bearing Clearance Inch	Shaft Diameter Inch	Bearing Clearance Inch	Thrust On Bearing No.	Shaft End Play Inch
1983–84	B2000	.0019–.0025	.008	.012	.7874	2.0866	.0011–.0030	2.4804	.0012–.0030	5	.003–.009
	B2200	.0021–.0031	②	.014	1.1024	2.0866	.0014–.0030	2.5591	.0016–.0036	3	.006–.015
1983–85	GLC	.0010–.0026	.008	.012	.7867	1.5729	.0009–.0019	1.9664	.0009–.0017	5	.004–.006
	626	.0014–.0030	③	.012	.8653	2.0050	.0010–.0026	2.359	.0012–.0019	3	.003–.007
1985	626④	.0012–.0020	.0079–.0157	.0079–.0157	.9840–9843	2.0055–2.0063	—	2.360–2.361	.0012–.0024	3	.0016–.0110
1986	323	.0015–.0020	③	.012	.7865	1.7696	.0011–.0027	1.9665	.0011–.0027	—	.0031–.0071
	626	.0014–.0030	③	.012	.8652	2.0055	.0010–.0026	2.3595	.0012–.0019	—	.0031–.0071
	B2000	.0014–.0030	③	.012	.8652	2.0055	.0010–.0026	2.3600	.0012–.0019	—	.0031–.0071
1987	323	.0015–.0020	.006–.012	.008–.028	.7865	1.7696	.0011–.0027	1.9665	.0009–.0017	—	.0031–.0111
	626	.0014–.0030	⑤	.012–.035	.8652	2.0055	.0010–.0026	2.3595	.0012–.0019	—	.0031–.0071
	B2200	.0014–.0030	⑤	.012–.035	.8652	2.0055	.0011–.0026	2.3592	.0012–.0019	—	.0031–.0071
	B2600	.0008–.0016	⑥	.012–.024	.8663	2.0855	.0008–.0024	2.3618	.0008–.0020	-	.0020–.0071

①—Fit rings in tapered bores for clearance listed in tightest portion of ring travel.
②—Top ring, .016; second ring, .012.
③—Top ring, .008; second ring, .006.
④—Diesel engine.
⑤—Top ring, .014; second ring, .012.
⑥—Top ring, .018; second ring, .016.

Apex Seal Specifications-Rotary Engine

Year	Engine	Apex Seal				Apex Seal Spring	
		Length Inch	Width Inch	Height Standard Inch	Height Minimum Inch	Standard Height Inch	Minimum Height Inch
1983–85	12A	2.7481	.1181	.3347	.2756	.2727	.2165
1984–85	13B	3.1418	.1181	.3347	.2756	.2244	.1496
1986–87	13B	3.1450	.07575	.315	.256	①	②

①—Long spring standard height, .246 inch; short spring standard height, .130 inch.

②—Long spring minimum height, .181 inch; short spring minimum height, .067 inch.

Corner, Side & Oil Seal Specifications-Rotary Engine

Year	Corner Seal			Side Seal			Oil Seal		
	Outside Diameter Inch	Height Inch	Minimum Protrusion Inch	Thickness Inch	Height Inch	Minimum Protrusion Inch	Height Inch	Maximum Contact Width	Minimum Protrusion Inch
1983–85	.4331	.2756	.0197	.0394	.1378	.0197	.2205	.0197	.0197
1986–87	.43305	.272	.020	.0265	.1131	.020	.224	.020	.020

Rotor & Housing Specifications-Rotary Engine

Year	Engine	Housing						Rotor	
		Rotor		Intermediate		Front & Rear			
		Width Inches	Distortion Max. Inch	Distortion Max. Inch	Wear Max. Inch	Distortion Max. Inch	Wear Max. Inch	Rotor Width Inch	Side Clearance Inch
1983–85	12A	2.7559	.0024	.0016	.0039	.0016	.0039	2.7481	.0047–.0075
1984–85	13B	3.1497	.0024	.0016	.0039	.0016	.0039	3.1438	.0047–.0083
1986–87	13B	3.14925	—	.0016	.0039	.0016	.0039	3.143	.0047–.0083

—Not available.

Seal Clearances—Rotary Engine

Year	Model	Side Seal				Apex Seals			
		To Rotor Groove		To Corner Seal		To Side Housing		To Rotor Groove	
		Desired Inch	Max. Inch	Desired Inch	Max. Inch	Desired Inch	Max. Inch	Desired Inch	Max. Inch
1983–85	RX-7	.0012–.0031	.0039	.0020–.0059	.0157	—	—	.0020–.0035	.0059
1986	RX-7	.0011–.0031	.0039	.0020–.0059	.016	—	—	.0024–.0040	.0059
1987	RX-7	.0011–.0031	.0039	.0020–.0059	.016	—	—	①	.0059

—Not available.
①—Less Turbo, .0024–.0040 inch; Turbo, .0020–.0040 inch.

Eccentric Shaft Specifications-Rotary Engine

Year	Model	Eccentric Shaft End-Play		Max. Shaft Runout Inch	Journal Diameter		Oil Clearance	
		Desired Inch	Maximum Inch		Main Bearing Inch	Rotor Bearing Inch	Main Bearing Inch	Rotor Bearing Inch
1983–85	RX-7	.0016–.0028	.0035	.0024	1.6929	2.9134	.0016–.0031	.0016–.0031
1986–87	RX-7	.0016–.0028	.0035	.0047	1.69205	2.9125	.0016–.0031	.0016–.0031

Camshaft Specifications-Piston Engine

Year	Model	Cam Lobe Height		Bearing Clearance			Journal Diameter			Basic Cam Circle @ Inches	Max. Runout @ Inches	End Play @ Inches	
		Intake @ Inches	Exhaust @ Inches	Front @ Inches	Center @ Inches	Rear @ Inches	Front @ Inches	Center @ Inches	Rear @ Inches			New	Used
1983–84	B2000	1.7731	1.7718	.0007–.0027	.0011–.0031	.0007–.0027	1.7717	1.7717	1.7717	1.4961	.0012	.001–.007	.008
	B2200	1.6767	1.6767	.0024–.0047	.0024–.0047	.0024–.0047	2.0473	2.0374	2.0177	—	.0031	.0008–.0071	.012
1983–85	GLC	1.7368	1.7368	.0014–.0030	.0026–.0042	.0014–.0030	1.6519	1.6507	1.6519	—	.0012	.001–.007	.008
	626	1.5023	1.5024	.0014–.0033	.0026–.0045	.0014–.0033	1.257	1.256	1.257	—	.0012	.003–.006	.008
1986	B2000	1.5040	1.5040	.0014–.0033	.0026–.0045	.0014–.0033	1.257	1.2568	1.2575	—	.0012	.003–.006	.008
1986–87	323	1.441	1.441	.001–.003	.003–.005	.001–.003	1.7105	1.7095	1.7105	—	.0012	.0020–.0071	.0079
	626	1.5040	1.5040	.0014–.0033	.0026–.0045	.0014–.0033	1.257	1.2568	1.2575	—	.0012	.003–.006	.008
1987	B2200	1.498	1.498	.0014–.0033	.0026–.0045	.0014–.0033	1.258	1.2568	1.2579	—	.0012	.003–.006	.008
	B2600	1.669	1.669	.002–.004	.002–.004	.002–.004	1.336	1.336	1.336	—	.0008	.0008–.0070	.008

—Not available.

Tightening Specifications—Piston Engine

*Torque specifications are for clean and lightly lubricated threads only. Dry or dirty threads produce increased friction which prevents accurate measurement of tightness.

Year	Model	Spark Plugs Ft. Lbs.	Cylinder Head Bolts Ft. Lbs.	Intake Manifold Ft. Lbs.	Exhaust Manifold Ft. Lbs.	Rocker Arm Shaft Bracket Ft. Lbs.	Rocker Arm Cover Ft. Lbs.	Connecting Rod Cap Bolts Ft. Lbs.	Main Bearing Cap Bolts Ft. Lbs.	Flywheel to Crankshaft Ft. Lbs.	Vibration Damper or Pulley Ft. Lbs.
1983–84	B2000	11–17	(2)	14–19	16–21	(2)	1.1–1.4	30–33	61–65	112–118	101–108
	B2200	7–11 (4)	80–85	12–17	12–17	80–85	2.2–3.3	50–54	80–85	95–137	145–181
1983–85	GLC	11–17	56–59	14–19	14–17	56–59	—	22–25	48–51	(1)	80–87
	626	11–17	(3)	14–19	16–21	13–19.5	2.2–2.9	37–41	61–65	71–76	80–87
1985	626 (5)	11–17	(3)	14–19	16–21	13–19.5	2.2–2.9	37–41	61–65	71–76	(6)
	626 (7)	11–15 (4)	(8)	12–17	16–20	—	5–7	51–54	61–65	130–137	(9)
1986	323	11–17	56–60	14–19	12–17	14–17	3.5–6.5	37–41	40–43	71–76	(10)
	626, B2000	10.8–16.6	59–64	13.7–18.8	15.9–21	13–19.5	2.2–2.9	37–41	61–65	71–76	(11)
1987	323	11–17	50–60	14–19	12–17	16–21	3.5–6.5	37–41	40–43	71–76	(12)
	626	11–17	59–64	14–19	16–21	13–20	2.2–2.9	37–41	61–65	71–76	(13)
	B2200	11–17	59–64	14–19	16–21	13–20	2.9–4.3	48–51	61–65	71–76	(14)
	B26000	11–17	(15)	11–14	11–14	-	3.6–5	33–35	54–61	94–101	80–94

—Not available.

(1)—Man. trans., 60–65 ft. lbs; auto. trans., 51–61 ft. lbs.

(2)—Cold, 65–69 ft. lbs.; warm, 69–72 ft. lbs.

(3)—Cold, 59–64 ft. lbs.; warm, 69–80 ft. lbs.

(4)—Glow plug.

(5)—Gasoline engine.

(6)—Timing belt sprocket, 108–116 ft. lbs.; Crankshaft pulley, 8–11 ft.lbs.

(7)—Diesel engine.

(8)—Tighten in 3 steps; 1, 27.7 ft. lbs.; 2, additional 1/4 turn; 3, additional 1/4 turn.

(9)—Timing belt sprocket, 116–123 ft. lbs.; Crankshaft pulley, 17–24 ft.lbs.

(10)—Timing belt sprocket, 80–94 ft. lbs.; Crankshaft pulley, 36–45 ft. lbs.

(11)—On 626 models, torque timing belt sprocket, 108–112 ft. lbs. and crankshaft pulley, 9.0–12.6 ft. lbs.; On B2000 models, torque timing belt sprocket, 116–123 ft. lbs. and crankshaft pulley, 9.0–12.6 ft. lbs.

(12)—Timing belt pulley, 80–94 ft. lbs.; Crankshaft pulley, 9–13 ft. lbs.

(13)—Timing belt pulley, 116-123 ft. lbs.; Crankshaft pulley, 35–48 ft. lbs.

(14)—Timing belt pulley, 108–116 ft. lbs.; Crankshaft pulley, 9.4–12.3 ft. lbs.

(15)—65–72 ft. lbs. w/engine cold; 72–79 ft. lbs. w/engine hot.

Tightening Specifications-Rotary Engine

*Torque specifications are for clean and lightly lubricated threads only. Dry or dirty threads produce increased friction which prevents accurate measurement of tightness.

Year	Model	Spark Plug Ft. Lbs.	Tension Bolts Ft. Lbs.	Eccentric Shaft Pulley Bolt Ft. Lbs.	Intake Manifold Ft. Lbs.	Exhaust Manifold Ft. Lbs.	Flywheel/Counterweight Lock Nut Ft. Lbs.
1983-85	RX-7	9-11	①	72-87	14-19	23-34	289-362
1986-87	RX-7	9.4-13	23-29	80-98	14-19	23-34	290-360

①—1983-85 12A engine, 23-27 ft. lbs.;
1983-85 13B engine, 23-29 ft. lbs.

Front Wheel Alignment Specifications

Year	Model	Caster Angle, Degrees		Camber Angle, Degrees		Toe-In Inch	King Pin Inclination
		Limits	Desired	Limits	Desired		
1983	626	+7/12° to +2 1/12°	+1 1/3°	−1/6° to +5/6°	+1/3°	①	+12 11/12°
	RX-7	②	③	+1/2° to +1 1/2°	+1	0 to .24	+10 11/15°
1983-84	B2000	—	+1	+5/12° to +1 1/4°	+ 5/6°	0 to .24	+8 1/4°
	B2200	—	+1°	+5/12° to +1 1/4°	+5/6°	0 to .24	+8 1/4°
1983-85	GLC	+1 1/6° to +2 2/3°	+1 11/12°	+5/12° to +1 5/12°	+11/12	①	+12 1/6°
1984-85	626	+11/12° to +2 5/12°	+1 2/3°	−1/6° to +5/6°	+1/3°	①	+12 11/12°
	RX-7	②	③	④	⑤	0 to .24	⑥
1986	B2000	—	⑦	+5/12° to +1 1/4°	+3/4°	0 to .24	+8 1/4°
1986-87	323	+5/6° to +2 1/3°	+1 7/12°	+1/20° to +1 11/20°	+4/5°	−.04 to .20	+12 11/30°
	626	+11/12° to +2 5/12°	+1 2/3°	−1/6° to +5/6°	+1/3°	0 to .24	+12 11/12°
	RX-7	—	+4 2/3°	—	+1/3°	0 to .24	+13 3/4°
1987	B2200	⑧	⑦	+/12° to +1 1/4°	+3/4°	0 to .24	+8 1/4°
	B2600 2WD	+1/12° to +1 7/12°	+1 5/6°	+5/12° to +1 1/4°	+1/4°	0 to .24	+8 1/4°
	B2600 4WD	+1 1/4° to +2 3/4°	+2°	+2/3° to +1 1/2°	+1°	0 to .24	+10 1/3°

①—.12 inch out to .12 inch in.
②—Left side, +3 1/6° to +4 1/6°; Right side, +3 2/3° to +4 2/3°.
③—Left side, +3 2/3°; Right side, +4 1/6°.
④—Models with 13 inch wheels, +1/2° to +1 1/2°; models with 14 inch wheels, +1/12° to +1 1/12°.
⑤—Models with 13 inch wheels, +1°; models with 14 inch wheels, +7/12°.
⑥—Models with 13 inch wheels, +10 11/15°; models with 14 inch wheels, +11 1/3°.
⑦—Manual steering, +5/6°; power steering, +1 5/6°
⑧—Manual steering, +1/12° to +1 7/12°; power steering, +1 1/12° to +2 7/12°

Rear Wheel Alignment Specifications

Year	Model	Camber Angle, Degrees		Toe-In Inch
		Limits	Desired	
1983–85	GLC	—	—	−.12 to +.12
1983–86	626	—	—	−.118 to +.118
1986	323	−3/4° to +3/4°	0°	−.12 to +.12
1986–87	RX-7	+7/30° to +1 7/30°	+°11/15°	−.12 to +.12
1987	323	−3/4° to +3/4°	0°	①
	626	—	—	−.12 to +.12

①—323 exc. Wagon, −.12 to +.12 inch; 323 Wagon, −.04 to +.20 inch.

Brake Specifications

Year	Model	Brake Drum Inside Diameter	Wheel Cylinder Bore Diameter		Master Cylinder Bore Diameter	Disc Brake Rotor Specifications			
			Disc Brake	Rear Drum Brake		Nominal Thickness	Minimum Refinish Thickness	Thickness Variation Parallelism	Lateral Run-out (T.I.R.)
1983–84	626	7.874	2.1260	3/4	7/8	.5500	.4900	—	.0040
	RX-7	7.874	①	3/4	13/16	②	③	—	.0039
	B2000	10.236	2.1248	7/8	7/8	.4724	.4331	—	.0039
	B2200	10.236	2.1248	7/8	13/16	.7874	.7480	—	.0039
1983–85	GLC	7.09	2.1248	11/16	13/16	.4300	.3900	—	.0040
1985	626④	7.87	2.125	3/4	7/8	.5500	.4700	—	.0040
	626⑤	7.87	2.125	3/4	7/8	.7800	.7100	—	.0040
	RX-7	7.87	①	3/4	13/16	⑥	⑦	—	.0039
1986	323	7.87	⑧	3/4	7/8	⑨	⑩	—	.0030
	626	7.87	2.125	3/4	7/8	.7800	.7100	—	.0040
	RX-7	—	⑪	—	7/8	⑫	⑬	—	.004
	B2000	10.24	2.125	3/4	7/8	.7800	.7100	—	.0020
1987	323 Exc. Wagon	7.87	⑧	11/16	7/8	⑨	⑩	—	.003
	323 Wagon	9.00	2.00	11/16	7/8	.71	.63	—	.003
	626	7.87	2.125	3/4	7/8	.78	.71	—	.004
	RX-7	—	⑪	—	7/8	⑫	⑬	—	.004
	B2200	10.24	2.125	11/16	7/8	.79	.71	—	.0006
	B2600 2WD	10.24	2.125	11/16	7/8	.79	.71	—	.0006
	B2600 4WD	10.24	2.125	3/4	7/8	.87	.79	—	.0006

—Not available.
①—Front, 2.0 inch; rear, 1.3752 inch.
②—Front, .7087 inch; rear, .3937 inch.
③—Front, .6693 inch; rear, .3543 inch
④—Gasoline engine models.
⑤—Diesel engine models.
⑥—Front disc, .7087 inch; rear solid disc .3937 inch; rear ventilated disc, .866 inch.
⑦—Front disc, .6693 inch; rear solid disc .3543 inch; rear ventilated disc, .787 inch.
⑧—Front, 2 inches; rear, 1.19 inches.
⑨—Front disc, .7100 inch; rear disc, .3900 inch.
⑩—Front disc, .6300 inch; rear disc, .3500 inch.
⑪—Front w/14 inch wheels, 2.0 inch; front w/15 inch wheels, 1.42 inch; rear, 1.37 inch.
⑫—Front disc, .87 inch; rear disc w/14 inch wheels, .40 inch; rear disc w/15 inch wheels, .79 inch.
⑬—Front disc, .79 inch; rear disc w/14 inch wheels, .31 inch; rear disc w/15 inch wheels, .71 inch.

Cooling System & Capacity Data

Year	Model	Cooling Capacity Qts.		Radiator Cap Relief Pressure, Lbs.	Thermo. Opening Temp. F.	Fuel Tank Gals.	Engine Oil Refill Qts.	Transmission Oil			Rear Axle Oil Pints
		Less Heater	With Heater					4 Speed Pints	5 Speed Pints	Auto. Trans. Qts. ①	
1983–84	626	—	7.4	13	191	15.6	4.8	—	7	6	—
	RX-7	9	10	13	180	16.4	⑦	—	4.2	⑧	2.6
	B2000	7	7.6	13	180	②	4.1	3	3.6	6.6	2.8
	B2200	10.6	11.1	13	180	②	⑨	3	3.6	—	2.8
1983–85	GLC	5.3	5.8	13	180	⑥	3.9	6.8	6.8	6	—
1985	626⑩	7.4	7.4	13	190	15.6	4.8	—	7	6	—
	626⑪	9.5	9.5	13	190	15.6	6.7	—	7	6	—
	RX-7	9	10	13	180	16.4	⑦	—	4.2	7.9	⑫
1986	323	⑬	⑭	13	⑮	11.9	3.6	6.8	6.8	6	—
	626	7.4	7.4	13	190	15.9	4.5	—	7.2	6	—
	RX-7	7.7	7.7	13	180	16.6	③	—	4.2	7.9	2.8
	B2000	7.9	7.9	13	190	⑯	4.5	3	3.6	—	2.8
1987	323	⑬	⑭	13	⑮	11.7	3.6	6.8	6.8	6	—
	626	7.4	7.4	13	190	15.9	4.5	—	7.2	6.3	—
	RX-7	⑰	⑰	13	180	16.6	③	—	5.2	7.9	2.8
	B2200	7.3	7.9	13	190	④	4.5	3.6	4.2	7.9	2.8
	B2600	7.9	7.9	13	190	⑤	⑱	—	⑲ ⑳	7.9⑳	㉑

①—Approximate, make final check with dipstick.
②—Short body, 14.8 gals.; long body, 17.4 gals.
③—Oil pan, 4.7 qts.; full capacity, 6.1 qts.
④—Short body, 14.8 gals.; long body, 17.2 gals.
⑤—Short body, 18.8 gals.; long body, 17.5 gals.
⑥—Sedan & Hatchback, 11.1 gals.; Sta. Wagon, 11.9 gals.
⑦—Except fuel injected engine: oil pan, 4.4 qts.; full capacity, 4.9 qts. Fuel injected engine: oil pan, 4.9 qts.; full capacity, 6.1 qts.
⑧—1983, 6.6 qts.; 1984, 7.9 qts.
⑨—Oil pan, 5.3 qts.; full capacity, 6.1 qts.
⑩—Gasoline engine.
⑪—Diesel engine.
⑫—Standard differential, 2.6 pts; limited slip differential, 3.4 pts.
⑬—W/manual transmission, 4.8 qts; w/automatic transmission, 5.8 qts.
⑭—W/manual transmission, 5.3 qts; w/automatic transmission, 6.3 qts.
⑮—Sub unit, 185°F; main unit, 190°F.
⑯—Standard tank, 14.3 gals; optional tank, 15.6 gals.
⑰—Less Turbo, 7.7 qts.; w/Turbo, 9.2 qts.
⑱—2WD models, 4.4 qts.; 4WD models, 5.1 qts.
⑲—2WD models, 6 pts.; 4WD models, 6.8 pts.
⑳—Transfer case capacity, 4.2 pts.
㉑—2WD models, 2.8 pts.; 4WD models front axle, 2.6 pts.; 4WD models rear axle, 3.6 pts.

ELECTRICAL SECTION

INDEX

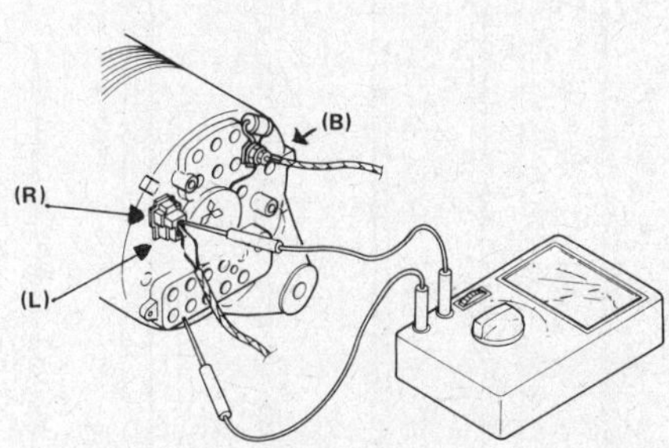

Fig. 1 Alternator terminal location. Typical

ALTERNATOR ON VEHICLE TESTING

1983–85 EXC. 1984–85 RX-7

1. With ignition switch off, connect voltmeter between alternator terminal "B" and ground, **Fig. 1,** and observe reading. Reading should be battery voltage.
2. Connect voltmeter between alternator terminal "R" and ground on 1983 RX-7 and "L" and ground on all models. Observe reading. Voltmeter should read zero volts. If not, replace alternator.
3. Turn on ignition, then connect voltmeter between alternator terminal "L" and ground. Observe reading. Voltmeter should read 1-3 volts. If voltmeter reads zero volts, the alternator, regulator and/or the wiring harness is defective. If voltmeter reads close to battery voltage, proceed to next step.
4. Ground "F" terminal at rear of alternator, **Fig. 2,** then observe "L" terminal voltage. If voltage reads significantly less than battery voltage, replace regulator. If voltage reads at, or near, battery voltage, replace alternator.

1984–85 RX-7 & 1986 B2000

Battery Discharges

1. With engine idling, measure voltage of alternator B terminal, then measure B terminal voltage at engine speed of approximately 2000 RPM. Compare voltage at idle to voltage at 2000 RPM. If voltage does not change, proceed to step 2. If voltage at 2000 RPM is higher, proceed to step 6.
2. Stop engine and place ignition switch to On position, then check voltage at alternator L terminal. If voltage is 0-1 volt, proceed to step 3. If voltage is same as battery voltage, proceed to step 5. If voltage is 1-3 volts, proceed to step 6.
3. Short circuit alternator B and R terminals using suitable jumper wires, then repeat step 2. If voltage is 0-1 volt, proceed to step 4. If voltage is 1-3 volts, correct poor ground at chassis side.
4. On RX-7 models, disconnect alternator electrical connector, then check continuity between L and R terminals using a suitable meter. If meter indicates 35-100 ohms, IC regulator is defective. If no continuity is present, IC regulator is defective.
5. On all models, with engine stopped and ignition switch in On position, measure voltage at alternator F terminal. If voltage is same as battery voltage, IC regulator is defective. If voltage is 0-.5 volts, check for poor brush contact or defective field coil. If voltage is .5-2 volts, (+) diode has short circuit. **When measuring voltage at F terminal, ensure voltmeter test leads do not touch.**
6. Disconnect alternator B terminal electrical connector, then connect ammeter between wiring and terminal. Start engine and suddenly increase engine speed to 2500-3000 RPM, then immediately read maximum indication of meter. If meter reads 70% or less of idle output, alternator is defective. If meter reads 70%-90% of idle output, proceed to step 7. If meter reads 90% or more of idle output, alternator is satisfactory. **Test should be performed with all electrical loads left on.**
7. Check for poor contact between alternator B terminal and battery positive terminal, then slightly discharge battery and repeat step 6. If meter reads 90% or less of idle output, remove alternator from vehicle and inspect carefully. If meter reads 90% or more of idle output, alternator is satisfactory.
8. Disconnect battery positive terminal and connect suitable ammeter between cable and battery. Before starting engine, short circuit ammeter terminals so starter current will flow to ammeter.
9. Start engine and read ammeter reading at engine speed of 2500 RPM. If meter reads less than 5 amps, measure L terminal voltage. If meter reads 5 amps or more, either charge battery until it becomes less than 5 amps or replace with new battery and measure again. If voltage is 14.7 volts on RX-7

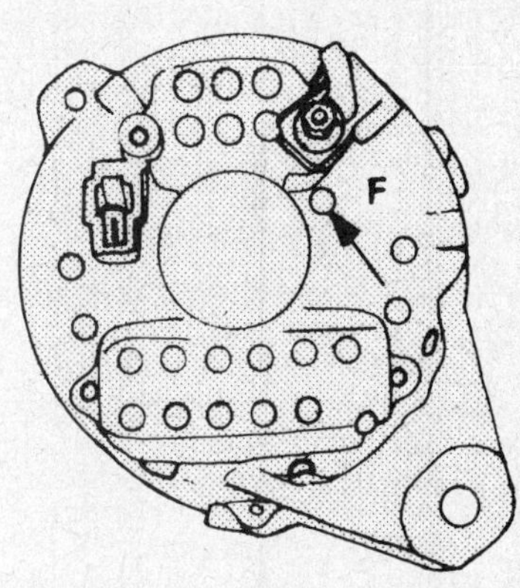

Fig. 2 Location of test terminal "F". Typical

or 14.2 volts on B2000, IC regulator is satisfactory. If voltage is not 14.7 volts on RX-7 or 14.2 volts on B2000, alternator is defective.

Battery Overcharged

1. Measure voltage at alternator B terminal, then slowly increase engine RPM. If voltage is less than 15.5 volts, proceed to step 2. If voltage is 15.5 volts or more, alternator or IC regulator is defective.
2. Measure and compare voltage at IC regulator F terminal at idle and 3000 RPM. If voltage is higher at 3000 RPM, proceed to step 3. If voltage is not higher at 3000 RPM, alternator or IC regulator is defective. **F terminal voltage may not become high when battery is discharging.**
3. With battery fully charged, measure alternators L terminal voltage when engine speed is at 2500 RPM. If voltage is 14.7 volts on RX-7 or 14.2 volts on B2000, alternator is satisfactory. If voltage is not 14.7 volts on RX-7 or 14.2 volts on B2000, alternator is defective.

1986-87 323, 626 & RX-7

Battery Discharges

1. Inspect output current as follows:
   a. Start engine and allow to idle.
   b. Turn on all lights and accessories.
   c. Disconnect alternator B terminal electrical connector, then connect suitable ammeter between wire and terminal. **Use caution not to ground B terminal.**
   d. Read meter at engine speed of 2500-3000 RPM. If meter reads 90% or less of idle output on 1986 RX-7 and 1986-87 323, 51 amps or less of idle output on 1986 626 models or 55 amps or less of idle output on 1987 626 and RX-7, proceed to step 2. If meter reads 90% or more of idle output on 1986 RX-7 and 1986-87 323, 51 amps or more of idle output on 1986 626 models or 55 amps or more of idle output on 1987 626 and RX-7, alternator is satisfactory.
2. Inspect output voltage as follows:
   a. Turn all electrical loads off.
   b. Disconnect alternator B terminal electrical connector, then connect suitable ammeter between wire and terminal. **Use caution not to ground B terminal.**
   c. Charge battery until charging rate indication becomes less than 5 amps or replace with new battery.
   d. Read meter at engine speed of 2500 RPM. If meter reads less than 5 amps, proceed to step e. If meter reads more than 5 amps, there is a short circuit in vehicle.
   e. Connect alternator B terminal.
   f. Measure L terminal voltage at an engine speed of 2500 RPM. If voltage is 14.4-15 volts at 68° F on all 1986 models and 1987 323 or 14.2-15.2 volts at 68° F on 1987 626 and RX-7, proceed to step 3. If voltage is less than 14.4-15 volts at 68° F on all 1986 models and 1987 323, stator coil or diodes are defective. If voltage is less than 14.2-15.2 volts at 68° F, check for poor connection at battery terminals, B terminal and 2 prong connector or for defective stator coil or diodes.
3. Inspect IC regulator power source as follows:
   a. Disconnect alternator terminal R connector.
   b. Place ignition switch to On position, then measure R terminal voltage at connector. If battery voltage is present, proceed to step 4. If meter reads less than battery voltage, check for defective wiring harness.
4. Inspect rotor coil as follows:
   a. Place ignition switch to Off position. Disconnect alternator B terminal connector on all 1986 models and 1987 323 and RX-7. Disconnect alternator B terminal and L and R connector to alternator.
   b. Measure resistance between alternator L and F terminals at alternator. If meter reads 2-2.6 ohms on 1986 323 and 1986-87 RX-7 or 3-6 ohms on 1986-87 626 and 1987 323, proceed to step 5. If meter reads other than 2-2.6 ohms on 1986 323 and 1986-87 RX-7 or 3-6 ohms on 1986-87 626 or 1987 323, field rotor or slip ring is defective.
5. Inspect alternator L terminal voltage as follows:
   a. Connect alternator B terminal connector on all 1986 models and 1987 323 and RX-7. Connect alternator B terminal and L and R connector to alternator. On all models, place ignition switch to On position.
   b. Measure alternator L terminal voltage. If meter reads 1-3 volts on all 1986 models and 1987 323, stator coil and diodes are defective. If meter reads 1-3 volts on 1987 626 and RX-7, alternator is satisfactory. If meter reads over 3 volts, IC regulator or field coil is defective.

Battery Overcharged

1. Inspect output voltage as follows:
   a. Turn off all electrical loads.
   b. Disconnect alternator B terminal electrical connector, then connect suitable ammeter between wire and terminal.
   c. Charge battery until charging rate indication becomes less than 5 amps or replace with new battery.
   d. Read meter at engine speed of 2500 RPM. If meter reads less than 5 amps, proceed to e.
   e. If terminal B is less than 5 amps, measure voltage at L terminal at engine speed of 2500 RPM. If meter reads more than 15 volts at 68° F on all 1986 models and 1987 323 or 15.2 volts or more at 68° F on 1987 626 and RX-7, proceed to step 2. If meter reads 14.4-15 volts at 68° F on all 1986 models and 1987 323 or 14.2-15.2 volts at 68° F on 1987 626 and RX-7, alternator is satisfactory.
2. Inspect IC regulator power source as follows:
   a. Disconnect alternator R connector on all 1986 models and 1987 323 and RX-7 or alternator L and R connector on 1987 626, then place ignition switch to On position.
   b. Measure L and/or R terminal voltage at connector, then reconnect connector(s). If meter reads battery voltage, proceed to step 3. If meter reads less than battery voltage, wiring harness is defective.
3. Inspect rotor coil as follows:
   a. Place ignition switch to Off position, then disconnect alternator B terminal on all 1986 models and 1987 323 and RX-7 or alternator B terminal and L and R terminals at alternator on 1987 626.
   b. Measure resistance between alternator L and F terminals. If meter reads 3-6 ohms on 1986-87 323 and 626 or 2-2.6 ohms on 1986-87 RX-7 models, IC regulator is defective. If meter reads other than 3-6 ohms on 1986-87 323 and 626 or 2-2.6 ohms on 1986-87 RX-7 models, rotor coil or slip ring is defective.

1987 B2200 & B2600

Battery Discharges

1. Perform alternator quick test as follows:
   a. Disconnect alternator R and L connectors.
   b. Connect adapter harness 49U018003 or equivalent to alternator.
   c. Connect checker lamp 49F018001 or equivalent to adapter harness.
   d. Connect adapter harness red clip to battery positive terminal, then ensure that red and green lamp illuminate.
   e. Start engine, then ensure both lamps go off. If lamps go off, proceed to step 2. If lamps do not go off, proceed to step 4.
2. Inspect IC regulator power source as follows:
   a. Place ignition switch in Off position, then disconnect alternator terminal R connector.
   b. Place ignition switch to On position, then measure R terminal voltage at connector. If battery voltage is present, proceed to step 3. If meter reads less than battery voltage, check for defective wiring harness.
3. Inspect output current as follows:
   a. Start engine and allow to idle.
   b. Turn on all lights and accessories and depress brake pedal.
   c. Disconnect alternator B terminal electrical connector, then connect suitable ammeter between wire and terminal. **Use caution not to ground B terminal.**
   d. Read meter at engine speed of 2500-3000 RPM. If meter reads 50 amps or less of idle output, pro-

ceed to step 4. If meter reads 50 amps or more of idle output, alternator is satisfactory.

4. Inspect output voltage as follows:
   a. Turn all electrical loads off and release brake pedal.
   b. Charge battery until charging rate indication becomes less than 5 amps or replace with new battery.
   c. Read meter at engine speed of 2500 RPM. If meter reads less than 5 amps, proceed to step d. If meter reads more than 5 amps, proceed to step 4.
   d. Connect alternator B terminal.
   e. Measure L terminal voltage at an engine speed of 2500 RPM. If voltage is 14.2-15.2 volts at 68° F, proceed to step 5. If voltage is less than 14.2-15.2 volts at 68° F, check for poor connection at battery terminals, B terminal and 2 prong connector or for defective stator coil or diodes.
5. Inspect rotor coil as follows:
   a. Place ignition switch to Off position, then disconnect alternator B terminal and L and R connectors at alternator.
   b. Measure resistance between alternator L and F terminals. If meter reads 3-6 ohms, proceed to step 6. If meter reads other than 3-6 ohms, rotor coil or slip ring is defective.
6. Inspect alternator L terminal voltage as follows:
   a. Connect alternator B terminal and L and R connectors at alternator.
   b. Place ignition switch to On position, then measure alternator L terminal voltage. If meter read 1-3 volts, alternator is satisfactory. If meter reads over 3 volts, IC regulator or rotor coil is defective.

Battery Overcharged

1. Inspect output voltage as follows:
   a. Turn off all electrical loads.
   b. Disconnect alternator B terminal electrical connector, then connect suitable ammeter between wire and terminal.
   c. Charge battery until charging rate indication becomes less than 5 amps or replace with new battery.
   d. Read meter at engine speed of 2500 RPM. If meter reads less than 5 amps, proceed to e.
   e. If terminal B is less than 5 amps, measure voltage at L terminal at engine speed of 2500 RPM. If meter reads more than 15.2 volts at 68° F, alternator is defective. If meter reads 14.2-15.2 volts, alternator is satisfactory.

STARTER
REPLACE

1. Disconnect battery ground cable.
2. Raise and support vehicle.
3. Disconnect starter motor electrical connectors.
4. Remove starter motor bolts and starter motor from vehicle. On some vehicles equipped with automatic transmissions, remove starter motor bracket, bolts and starter motor from vehicle.
5. Reverse procedure to install.

IGNITION LOCK
REPLACE

RX-7

1. Disconnect battery ground cable.
2. Remove horn cap assembly.
3. Mark steering column shaft and steering wheel, and remove steering wheel. **Do not strike the steering column shaft end with a hammer. Striking the shaft will damage the steering bearing or collapsible steering shaft.**
4. Remove steering column cover.
5. If necessary, remove air duct and disconnect electrical connectors from combination switch.
6. Remove combination switch assembly from steering column.
7. Using a hammer and chisel, gently tap a groove into the ignition lock body attaching bolts. Using a screwdriver, loosen bolts and remove ignition lock from steering column.
8. Reverse procedure to install.

GLC

1. Disconnect battery ground cable.
2. Remove instrument panel lower cover.
3. Remove horn cap assembly.
4. Mark steering column shaft and steering wheel, then remove steering wheel.
5. Disconnect combination switch coupler, then remove combination switch.
6. Remove steering column assembly from vehicle.
7. Position steering column in a suitable vise, then using a hammer and chisel, gently tap a groove into the ignition lock body attaching bolts. Using a screwdriver, loosen bolts and remove ignition lock from steering column.
8. Reverse procedure to install.

626

1. Disconnect battery ground cable.
2. Remove steering column cover.
3. Disconnect ignition switch coupler.
4. Remove horn cap cover.
5. Mark steering column shaft and steering wheel, then remove steering wheel.
6. Using a hammer and chisel, gently tap a groove into the ignition lock body attaching bolts. Using a screwdriver, loosen and remove ignition lock from steering column.
7. Reverse procedure to install.

323

1. Disconnect battery ground cable.
2. Remove horn cap and steering wheel locknut.
3. Mark steering column shaft and steering wheel assembly, then remove steering wheel.
4. Remove steering column covers, then disconnect necessary electrical connectors.
5. Using a suitable hammer and chisel, tap a groove into the steering lock installation screw head.
6. Using a suitable screwdriver, remove the screw and steering lock assembly.
7. Reverse procedure to install.

B2000, B2200 & B2600

1. Disconnect battery ground cable.
2. Remove steering column upper and lower cover attaching screws, then the covers.
3. Disconnect ignition switch electrical connector.
4. Using a suitable hammer and chisel, tap a groove into the steering lock body to column shaft attaching bolts.
5. Using a suitable screwdriver, loosen the bolts, then remove steering lock assembly.
6. Reverse procedure to install.

COMBINATION SWITCH
REPLACE

1. Disconnect battery ground cable.
2. Mark steering column shaft and steering wheel, and remove steering wheel and steering column covers.
3. Disconnect combination switch electrical connectors, and remove stop ring from steering column shaft.
4. Remove combination switch from steering column.
5. Reverse procedure to install.

INSTRUMENT CLUSTER
REPLACE

1983–84 B2000 & B2200

1. Disconnect battery ground cable.
2. Remove horn cap assembly.
3. Scribe marks on steering column shaft and steering wheel, then remove steering wheel.
4. Remove steering column cover.
5. Working from underneath instrument panel, disconnect speedometer cable from cluster.
6. Remove instrument cluster hood.
7. Remove instrument cluster to dash panel attaching screws, then pull cluster outward and disconnect cluster electrical couplers.
8. Remove instrument cluster from vehicle.
9. Reverse procedure to install.

1983–85 626

Exc. Models W/Cluster Switches

1. Disconnect battery ground cable.
2. Remove cluster cover attaching screws (1), then disconnect cluster light electrical connector (2), **Fig. 3.**
3. Remove cluster cover (3), then the cluster attaching screws (4).
4. Pull cluster outward, then disconnect electrical connectors (5) and remove cluster (6) from vehicle.
5. Reverse procedure to install.

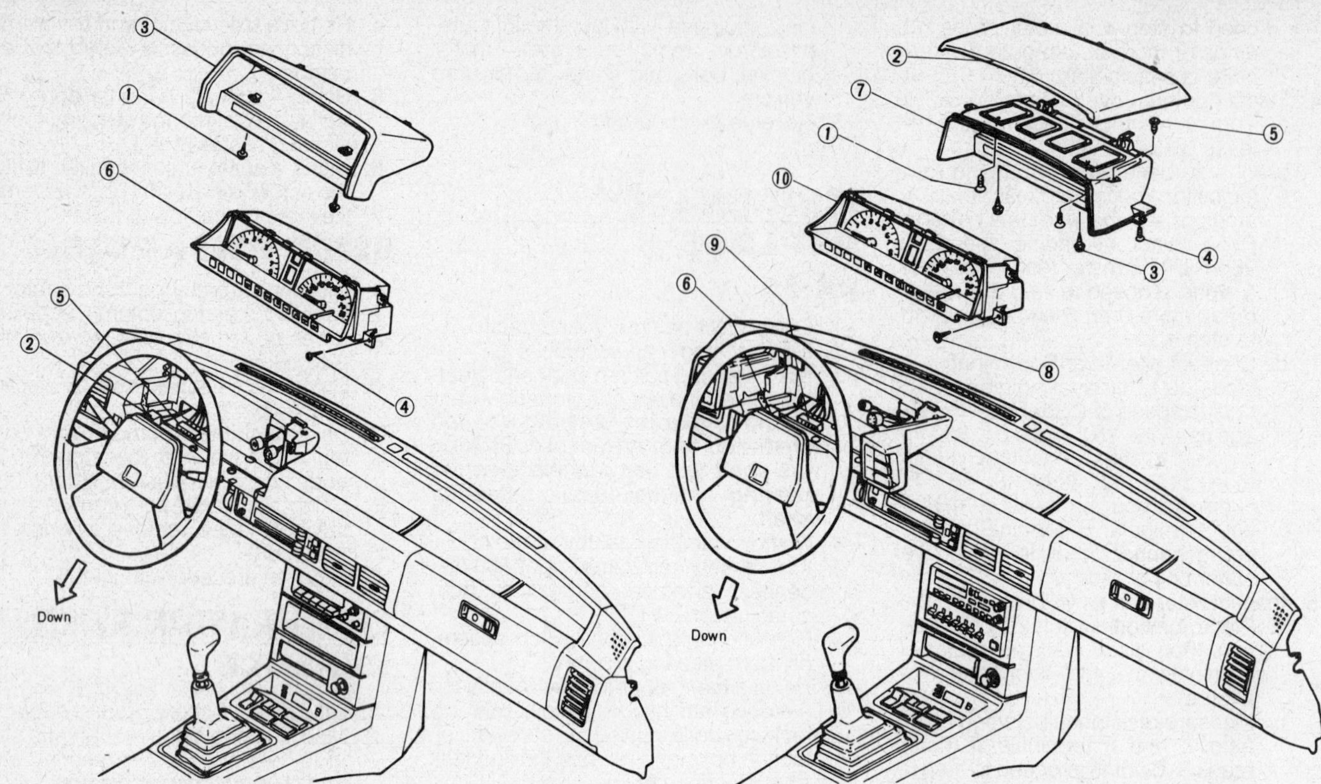

Fig. 3 Instrument cluster, replace. 1983–85 626 less cluster switches

Fig. 4 Instrument cluster, replace. 1983–85 626 w/cluster switches

Models W/Cluster Switches

1. Disconnect battery ground cable.
2. Remove cluster upper cover attaching screws (1) and the upper cover (2), **Fig. 4.**
3. Remove cluster cover attaching screws (3), (4) and (5), then disconnect cluster light electrical connector (6).
4. Remove cluster cover (7), then the cluster attaching screws (8).
5. Pull cluster outward, then disconnect electrical connectors (9) and remove cluster (10) from vehicle.
6. Reverse procedure to install.

1986–87 626 W/ANALOG OR DIGITAL INSTRUMENT CLUSTER

Refer to **Figs. 5 and 6,** when replacing the instrument cluster assembly.

1983–85 GLC

1. Disconnect battery ground cable.
2. Scribe marks on steering column shaft and steering wheel, then remove steering wheel.
3. Remove cluster cover attaching screws and the cover.
4. Disconnect speedometer cable from cluster.
5. Twist upper portion of cluster and pull cluster outward.
6. Disconnect electrical connector and remove cluster from vehicle.
7. Reverse procedure to install.

1983 RX-7

1. Disconnect battery ground cable.

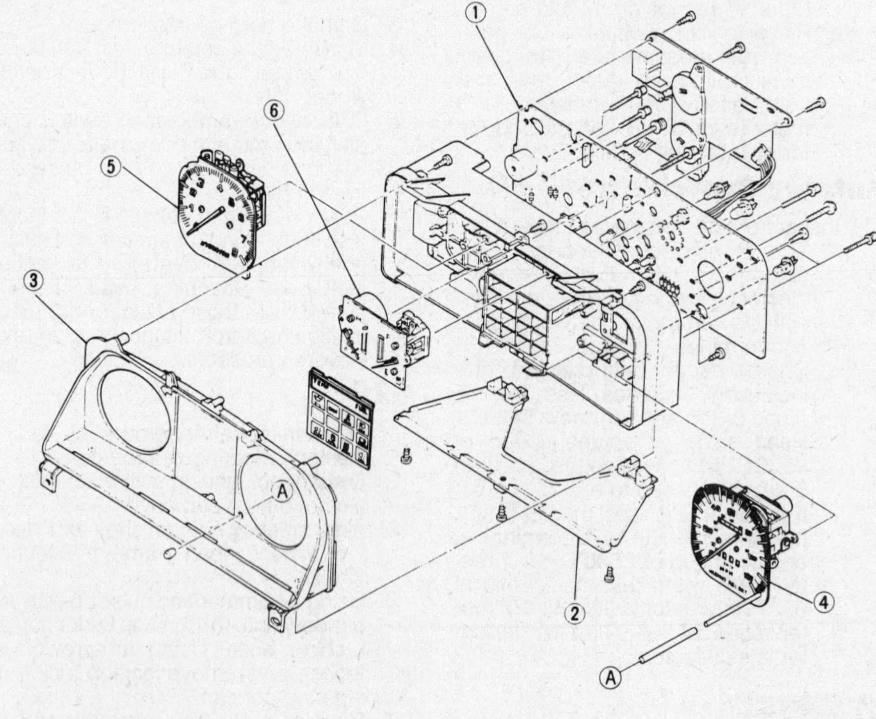

1. Printed circuit board
2. Lighting plate
3. Window plate
4. Speedometer
5. Tachometer
6. Fuel and water temp. gauge

Fig. 5 Instrument cluster, replace. 1986–87 626 w/analog instrument cluster

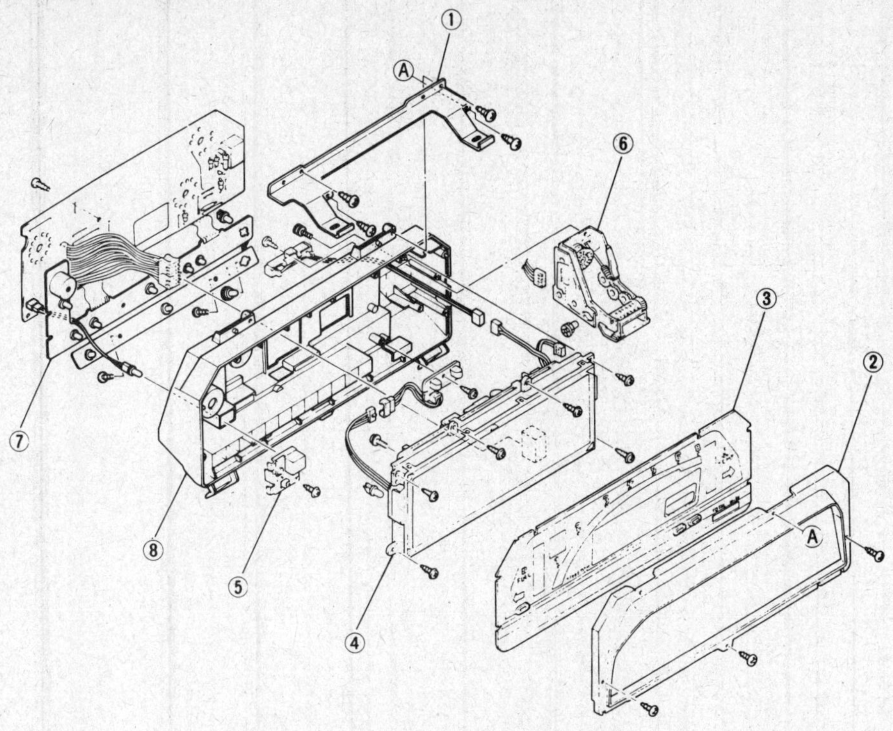

1. Bracket
2. Hood
3. Front lens
4. Meter unit
5. Speed sensor
6. Odometer
7. Printed plate
8. Meter case

Fig. 6 Instrument cluster, replace. 1986–87 626 w/digital instrument cluster

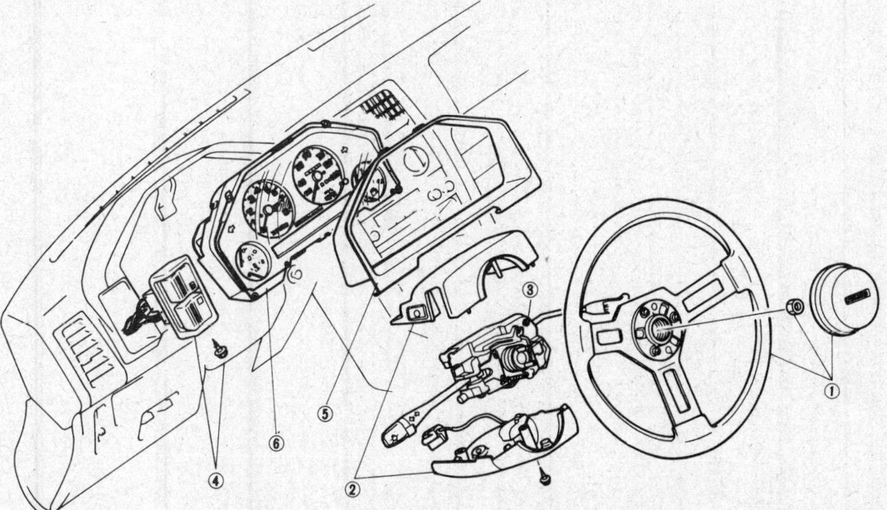

Fig. 7 Instrument cluster, replace. 1984–85 RX-7

2. Disconnect speedometer cable from speedometer.
3. Pull out steering wheel center cap, and remove the steering wheel.
4. Remove light switch knob and steering column cover. **Before removing column cover from combination switch lever, separate hole cover from column cover.**
5. Remove screws and cluster hood.
6. Remove screws and pull cluster assembly slightly from dashboard.
7. Disconnect electrical connectors from cluster and remove from dashboard.
8. Reverse procedure to install.

1984–85 RX-7

1. Disconnect battery ground cable.
2. Remove horn cap and steering wheel (1), **Fig. 7.**
3. Remove steering column covers (2), then the combination switch (3) and cluster switches (4), **Fig. 7.**
4. Remove cluster cover (5), then pull cluster outward, disconnect electrical connectors and remove cluster (6) from vehicle.
5. Reverse procedure to install.

1986–87 RX-7

Refer to **Fig. 8** when replacing the instrument cluster assembly.

1986–87 323

Refer to **Fig. 9** when replacing the instrument cluster assembly.

1986 B2000 & 1987 B2200 & B2600

Refer to **Fig. 10** when replacing the instrument cluster assembly.

RADIO

REPLACE

1983–85 GLC

1. Disconnect battery ground cable.
2. Remove radio control knobs.
3. Remove radio mounting bolts and pull radio outward.
4. Disconnect antenna feed and multiplug connector from radio, then remove radio from dashboard.
5. Reverse procedure to install.

HEATER CORE

REPLACE

1983–85 GLC

1. Disconnect battery ground cable, then drain cooling system.
2. Remove crash pad and instrument panel frame.
3. Disconnect defroster hose, then set heater control lever to "DEF" position and disconnect "DEF" wire.
4. Set heater control lever to "HOT" position and disconnect "HOT" wire.
5. Disconnect heater hose at engine, then remove heater core.
6. Reverse procedure to install.

323

Refer to **Fig. 11** when replacing heater core assembly.

626

Refer to **Fig. 12** when replacing heater core assembly.

RX-7

Refer to **Fig. 13** when replacing heater core assembly.

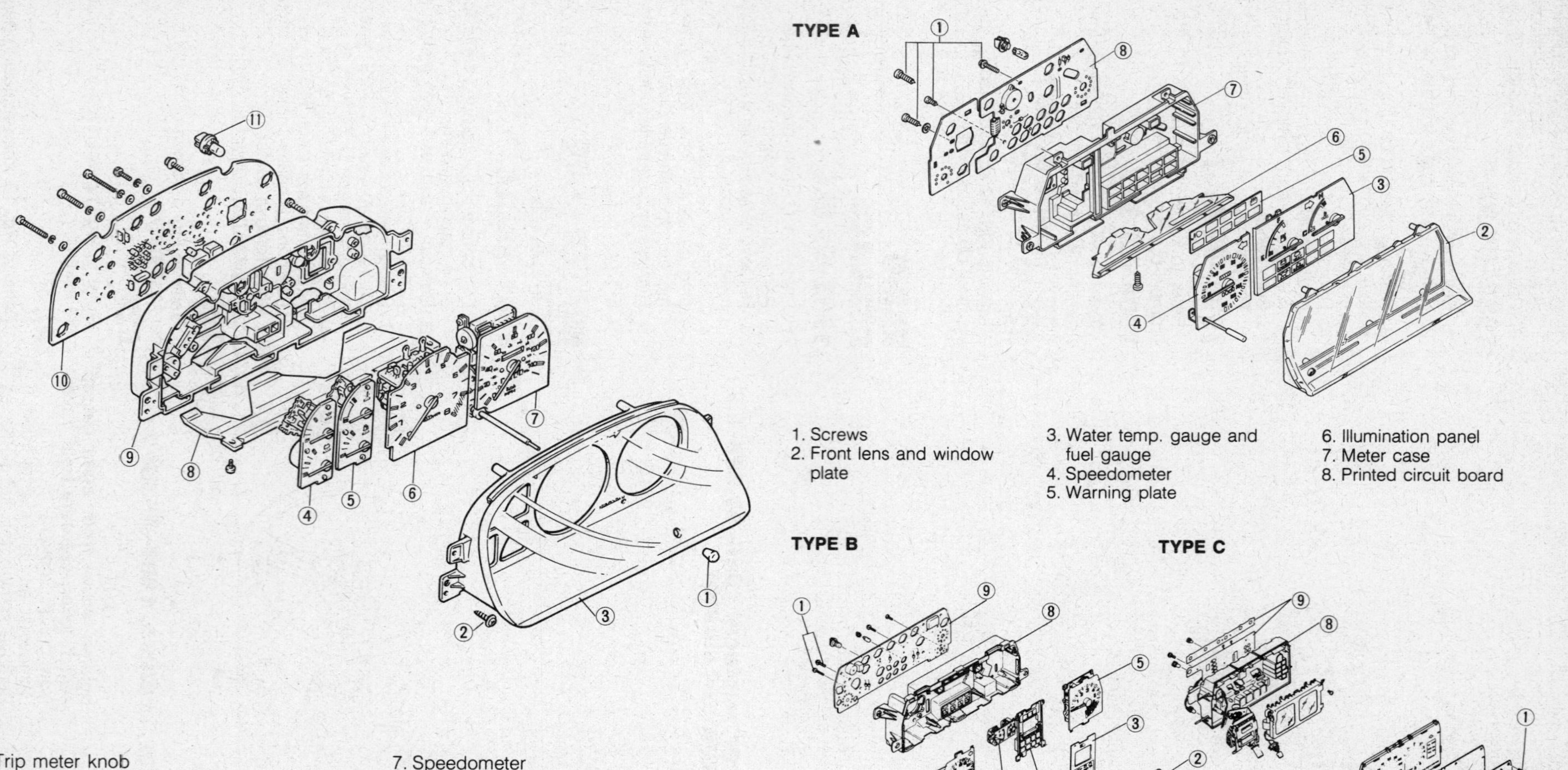

1. Trip meter knob
2. Screws
3. Front lens & window plate
4. Voltmeter & oil pressure gauge
5. Fuel & water temp. gauge
6. Tachometer
7. Speedometer
8. Plate
9. Meter case
10. Printed plate
11. Bulb & socket

Fig. 8 Instrument cluster, replace. 1986–87 RX-7

TYPE A

1. Screws
2. Front lens and window plate
3. Water temp. gauge and fuel gauge
4. Speedometer
5. Warning plate
6. Illumination panel
7. Meter case
8. Printed circuit board

TYPE B / TYPE C

1. Screws
2. Front lens and window plate
3. Warning plate
4. Warning case
5. Tachometer
6. Speedometer
7. Water temp gauge and fuel gauge
8. Meter case
9. Printed circuit board

Fig. 9 Instrument cluster, replace. 1986–87 323

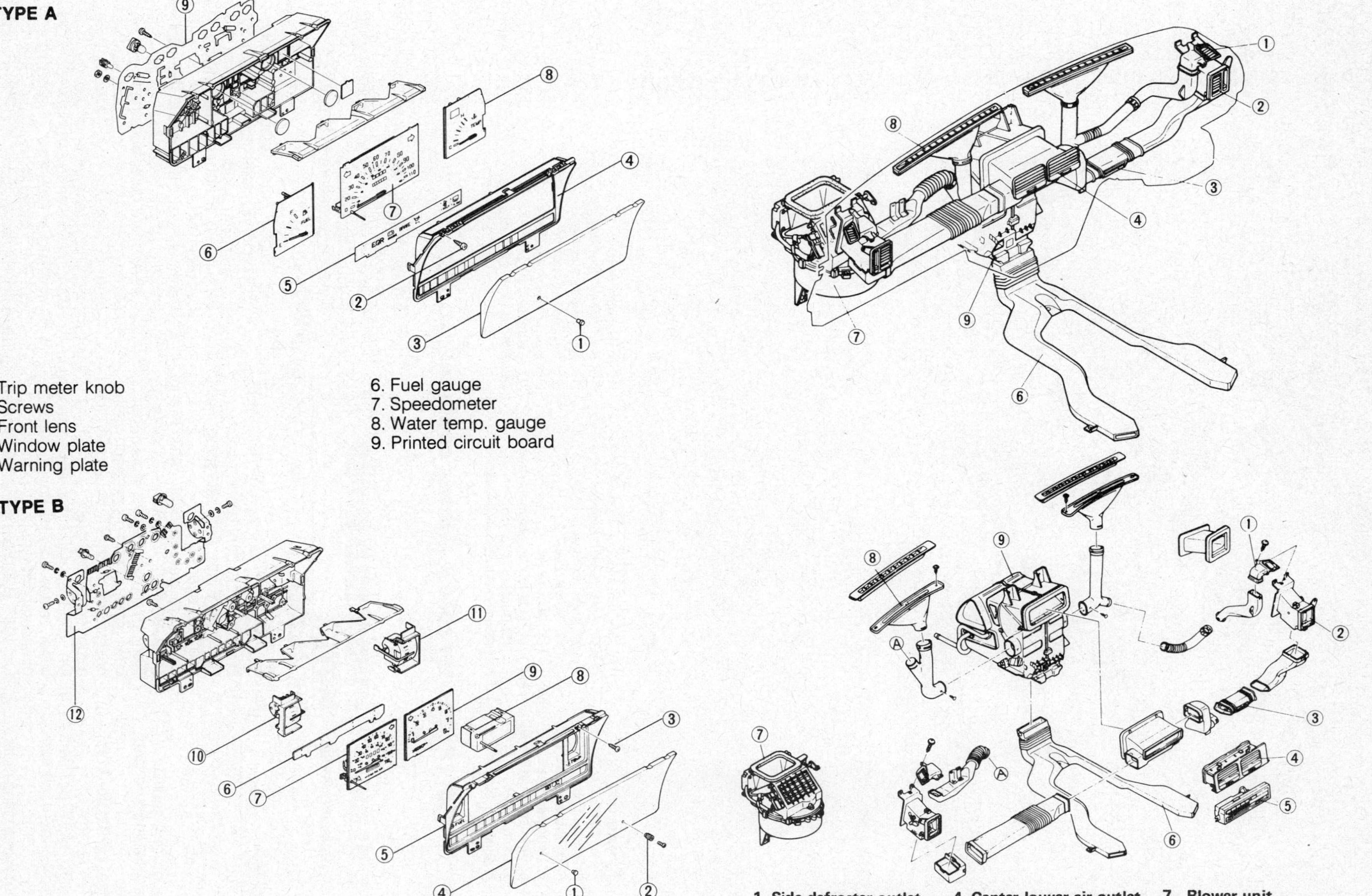

1. Trip meter knob
2. Screws
3. Front lens
4. Window plate
5. Warning plate
6. Fuel gauge
7. Speedometer
8. Water temp. gauge
9. Printed circuit board

1. Trip meter knob
2. Clock adjust knob
3. Screw
4. Front lens
5. Window plate
6. Warning plate
7. Speedometer
8. Digital clock
9. Tachometer
10. Fuel gauge
11. Water temp. gauge
12. Printed circuit board

Fig. 10 Instrument cluster, replace. 1986 B2000 & 1987 B2200 & B2600

1. Side defroster outlet
2. Side louver air outlet
3. Lower louver
4. Center louver air outlet
5. Heater control panel
6. Rear heater duct
7. Blower unit
8. Front defroster air outlet
9. Heater unit

Fig. 11 Heater core & related components. 323

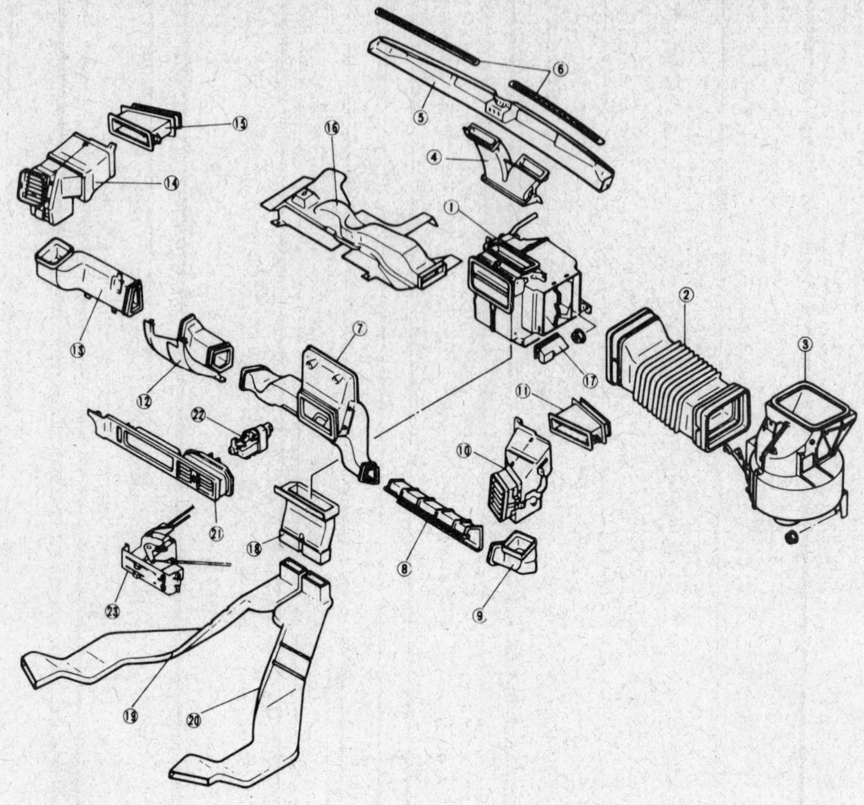

1. Heater unit
2. Air duct
3. Blower unit
4. Defroster duct
5. Defroster nozzle
6. Defroster nozzle grille
7. Center duct
8. Dust no. 1
9. Duct no. 2
10. Side louver assembly (left)
11. Duct no. 3
12. Blower duct
13. Duct no. 4
14. Side louver assembly (right)
15. Duct no. 5
16. Louver panel assembly
17. Assist side duct
18. Rear heater duct (front)
19. Rear heater duct (right)
20. Rear heater duct (left)
21. Center louver assembly
22. Swing louver
23. Control knob assembly

Fig. 12 Heater core & related components. 626

B2000, B2200 & B2600

Refer to **Fig. 14** when replacing heater core assembly.

BLOWER MOTOR REPLACE

1983–85 GLC

1. Disconnect battery ground cable.
2. Remove dashboard undercover and right defroster hose.
3. Disconnect electrical connector from blower motor.
4. Set the control lever to "HOT" position and disconnect temperature control wire.
5. Remove blower motor mounting bolts and the blower motor.
6. Reverse procedure to install.

WINDSHIELD WIPER MOTOR REPLACE

EXC. RX-7

1. Disconnect battery ground cable.
2. Remove wiper arm attaching bolts and the wiper arms.
3. On all models except B2000 and 1983-85 GLC, remove cowl plate attaching screws. Move front side of cowl plate up and disconnect washer hose from nozzle, if necessary, then remove the cowl plate.
4. On 1983-85 GLC models, remove wiper motor access cover from engine compartment.
5. On 1987 B2200 and B2600 models, remove seal cover attaching bolts, then the seal cover.
6. On all models, disconnect electrical connector from motor.
7. Remove wiper motor attaching bolts and the wiper motor.
8. Reverse procedure to install.

RX-7

1. With wiper motor operating, disconnect battery ground cable when wiper blades reach upper limit of travel.
2. Remove wiper arm attaching nuts and the wiper arms.
3. Remove seal caps, then the wiper linkage shaft retaining nuts, cup washers and outer bushings.
4. Remove cowl plate attaching screws, then disconnect washer hose from nozzle and remove cowl plate.
5. Disconnect wiring connections from wiper motor, then remove wiper motor and link assembly retaining bolts.
6. Remove wiper motor and link assembly from vehicle.
7. Reverse procedure to install.

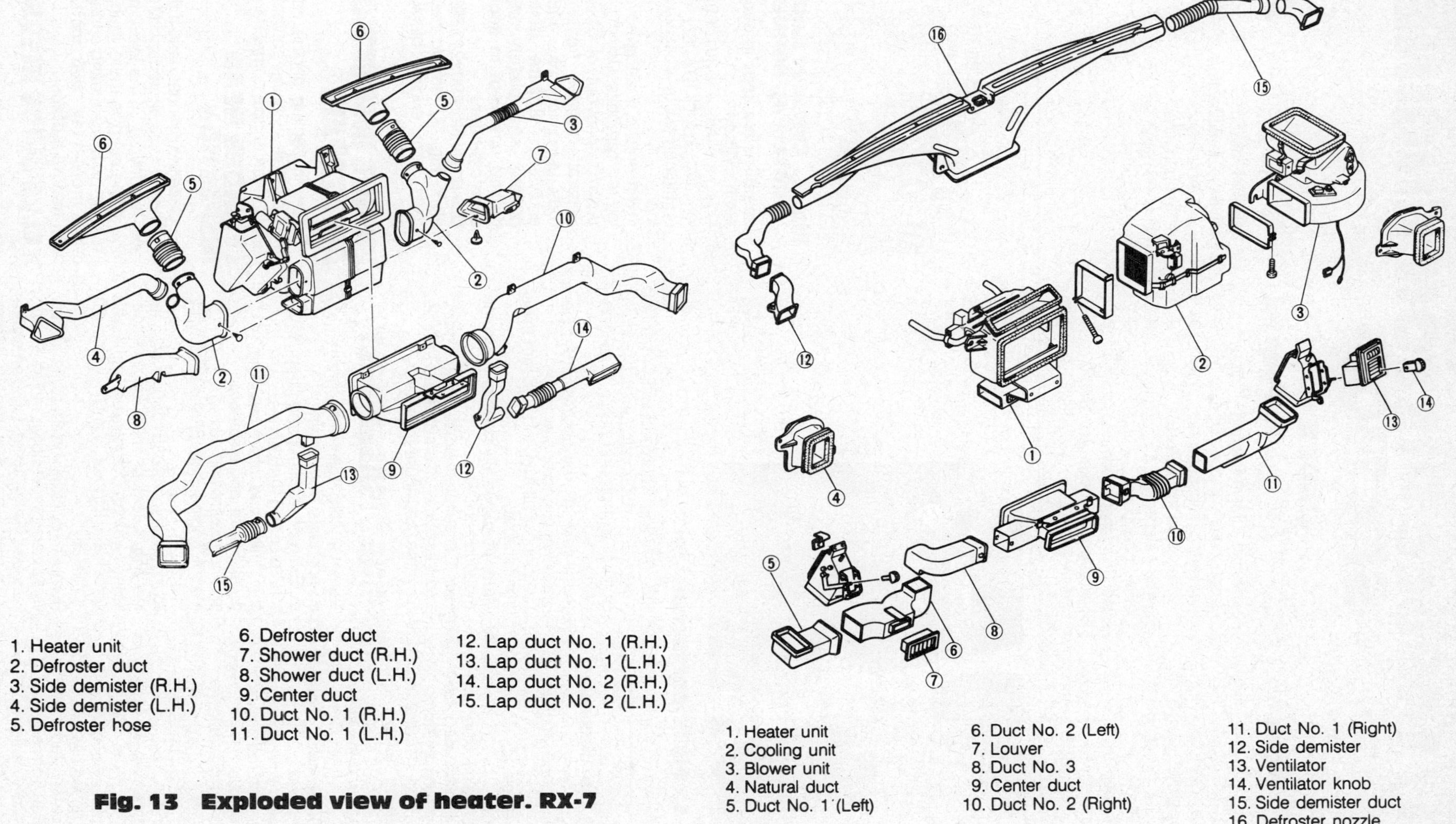

1. Heater unit
2. Defroster duct
3. Side demister (R.H.)
4. Side demister (L.H.)
5. Defroster hose
6. Defroster duct
7. Shower duct (R.H.)
8. Shower duct (L.H.)
9. Center duct
10. Duct No. 1 (R.H.)
11. Duct No. 1 (L.H.)
12. Lap duct No. 1 (R.H.)
13. Lap duct No. 1 (L.H.)
14. Lap duct No. 2 (R.H.)
15. Lap duct No. 2 (L.H.)

Fig. 13 Exploded view of heater. RX-7

1. Heater unit
2. Cooling unit
3. Blower unit
4. Natural duct
5. Duct No. 1′(Left)
6. Duct No. 2 (Left)
7. Louver
8. Duct No. 3
9. Center duct
10. Duct No. 2 (Right)
11. Duct No. 1 (Right)
12. Side demister
13. Ventilator
14. Ventilator knob
15. Side demister duct
16. Defroster nozzle

Fig. 14 Heater core & related components. B2000, B2200 & B2600

4-91/1490cc PISTON ENGINE SECTION

INDEX

Fig. 1 Flywheel locking tool

ENGINE

REPLACE

Engine and transaxle assemblies are removed as a unit.

1. Remove hood and disconnect battery ground cable.
2. Raise and support vehicle.
3. Remove undercover.
4. Drain engine oil, transaxle fluid and coolant. **Remove radiator cap before draining the cooling system.**
5. Remove engine and transaxle crossmember, then using suitable lifting equipment, raise engine slightly.
6. Remove both front wheels and steering knuckles.
7. Disconnect and remove both driveshafts from transaxle.
8. On vehicles equipped with manual transaxle, disconnect shift rod and extension bar from transaxle.
9. On all vehicles, remove radiator lower water hose.
10. Remove front and rear transaxle mounting rubbers.
11. Disconnect exhaust pipe from front catalytic converter.
12. Remove bolts and transaxle bracket.
13. Remove air cleaner assembly.
14. Disconnect all distributor, starter motor and alternator wires from engine.
15. Disconnect accelerator cable from engine.
16. Remove speedometer cable from transaxle. **Ensure speedometer drive gear is free of dust and dirt.**
17. On vehicles equipped with manual transaxle, disconnect clutch cable, bracket and ground cable from transaxle.
18. On all vehicles, remove radiator upper water hose, and heater hose.
19. Disconnect all fuel and vacuum lines from engine.
20. Remove purge canister and engine mounting bracket.
21. Using a suitable hoist, raise engine and transaxle assembly from vehicle.
22. Reverse procedure to install.

ENGINE DISASSEMBLY

1. Remove the following preliminary components from engine:
   a. Exhaust manifold and fan pulley.
   b. Water and fuel pumps.
   c. Oil filter and intake manifold.
   d. Alternator and distributor.
   e. Thermostat and cover.
2. Mount engine onto a suitable work stand.
3. Using tool No. 49E301060 or equivalent, **Fig. 1**, lock flywheel. Using a suitable wrench, remove camshaft sprocket locknut and camshaft sprocket.
4. Remove cylinder head bolts in reverse sequence shown in **Fig. 2**, and remove cylinder head. **Loosen cylinder head bolts a few turns at a time.**
5. Using tool Nos. 490636100A and 490221222A or equivalents, remove valve assembly. **Ensure valve assemblies are kept in sequence for each cylinder.**

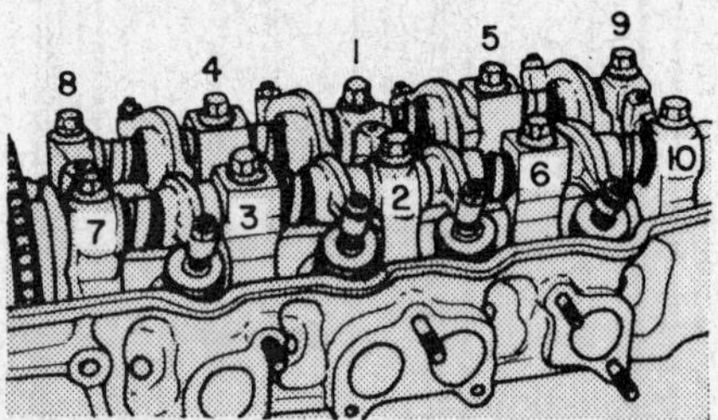

Fig. 2 Cylinder head bolt tightening sequence

6. Using tool No. 49E301060 or equivalent, **Fig. 1**, lock flywheel and remove crankshaft pulley bolts, then the pulley.
7. Invert engine, then remove connecting rod cap bolts. Using a wood drift, push pistons out of cylinder block. Separate pistons from connecting rods using tool No. 49813040, or equivalent. **Ensure disassembled pistons and piston rings, if removed, are kept in sequence for each cylinder.**
8. Using tool No. 490221270B or equivalent, **Fig. 3**, remove main bearing caps from engine block. Remove crankshaft.

ENGINE INSPECTION AND REPAIR

Before inspecting engine components, use a suitable cleaning solvent and thoroughly clean engine components.

CYLINDER HEAD INSPECTION

Replace the cylinder head if there is any evidence of wear or damage. Measure cylinder head warp on the lower mating surface. If the warp is more than .006 inch, (.15mm), grind the mating surface. **Do not grind more than .008 inch, (0.2mm) from mating surface.**

VALVE GUIDE INSPECTION

Measure the clearance between the valve and guide. If the clearance exceeds .0079 inch, (0.20mm), replace the valve, guide or both. To replace the valve guide,

Fig. 3 Removing main bearing cap

remove valve seal from valve guide. Using tool No. 490221251A or equivalent, knock valve guide out toward the opposite side of the combustion chamber. Using tool described, install clip onto new valve guide. Using a hammer and suitable drift, install new valve guide into cylinder head.

VALVE INSPECTION

Minor damage to the valves can be corrected by grinding. Using a micrometer, measure valve stem diameter. Minimum valve stem diameter should be .0394 inch, (1.0mm). Limit of diameter reduction for the intake valve should not exceed .3142 inch, (7.980mm), and for exhaust valve .3140 inch, (7.975mm). If the thickness of the valve stem is less than specified limit, replace the valve as required.

VALVE SPRING INSPECTION

Check the valve spring for cracks and damage, replace as required. Measure free length of spring. Free length should be 1.654 inch, (42.0mm). If free length of spring is less than specified limit, replace the valve spring as required.

Using a straightedge, check right angle limit. Right angle limit should be less than 0.118 inch, (3mm) per 3.937 inch, (100mm). If right angle is more than specified limit, replace valve spring.

VALVE SEAT INSPECTION

If the surface on the valve seat which is in contact with the valve face is damaged, repair by grinding as follows:

1. Make sure clearance between valve guide and stem is correct.
2. Cut the valve seat surface with a 90° grinder so the width of surface in contact with the valve becomes 0.055 inch, (1.4mm), **Fig. 4.**
3. Ensure area in contact with the valve is at center of the valve face.
4. Improve valve and valve seat fit by using a suitable lapping compound and lapping the valve.
5. Check valve seat wear. If the valve seat has worn less than .020-.059 inch, (0.5-1.5mm), position washers

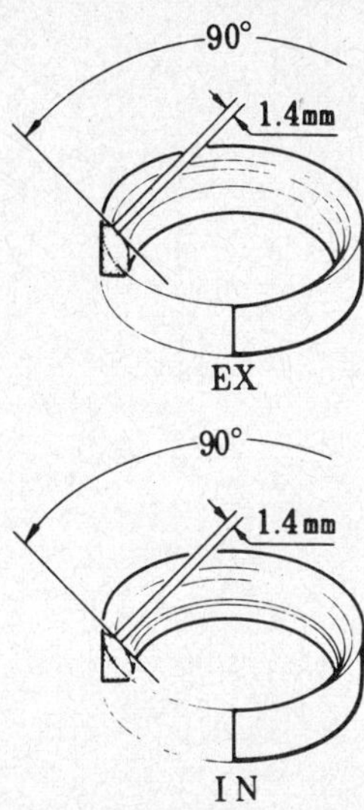

Fig. 4 Intake and exhaust valve seat dimensions

equal to the depth in wear onto the valve spring seat. If the wear depth is more than .059 inch, (1.5mm), replace as required.

ROCKER ARM & ROCKER ARM SHAFT INSPECTION

Replace rocker arm or cam if contact surfaces are damaged or worn. Measure rocker arm and shaft clearance. Clearance limit should be .0039 inch, (0.10mm). If clearance is not within specified limit, replace rocker arm shaft assembly.

CYLINDER BLOCK INSPECTION

Check cylinder block for cracks and wear. Replace if necessary. Measure upper surface area for warping. Warp limit should not exceed .006 inch, (.15mm). If warping is more than specified limit, grind the mating surface. **Do not grind more than .008 inch, (0.2mm) from mating surface.**

Check cylinder walls for scratches or burns. Rebore the walls as required. Standard bore diameter is 3.0201-3.0268 inch, (77.0-77.019mm). Maximum bore difference is .0059 inch, (.15mm). Inner diameter error of each cylinder is .0035 inch, (0.09mm) or less. After boring cylinder walls select oversize pistons according to the maximum wear on the cylinder bore. The following oversize pistons are available:.010 inch, (.25mm).020 inch, (.50mm).

PISTON INSPECTION

Check the pistons for burns or scratches on the outside circumference of the piston. Using a micrometer, measure piston diameter under the oil ring groove, at right angles with the piston pin location. Piston diameter should be 3.0297-3.0305 inch, (76.954-76.974mm). Measure clearance between piston and cylinder wall, which should be .0059 inch, (.15mm).

PISTON RING INSPECTION

Check piston rings for wear. Replace

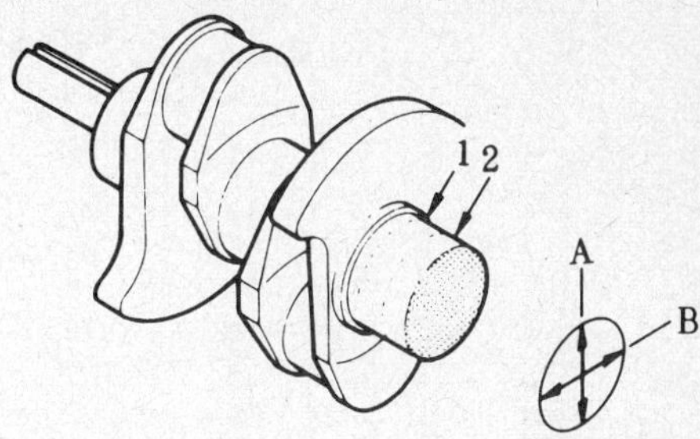

Fig. 5 Checking locations for crankshaft wear

any broken ring. Push piston rings into the cylinder bore, and measure piston ring end gap. End gap limit is .039 inch, (1.0mm). Measure piston ring and ring groove clearance. **Measure the clearance around the total circumference of the ring groove.**

Ring groove and ring clearance limit is .006 inch (.15mm).

CONNECTING ROD & BEARING INSPECTION

Check connecting rod for any bending or twisting. Maximum allowable twist is .002 inch, (.04mm) per 3.937 inch, (100mm).

CRANKSHAFT & MAIN BEARING INSPECTION

Check crankshaft for evidence of wear and damage. Check for clogged oil passages. Using a dial indicator, check crankshaft runout. Runout should not exceed .0012 inch, (.03mm). Measure uneven wear on the journal and pin, at the four indicated locations (A and B), **Fig. 5.** Maximum uneven wear allowed is .002 inch, (.05mm). If wear exceeds specified limit, replace the bearing with an undersized bearing and grind the crankshaft to properly fit the undersized bearing. Check crankshaft bearings for peeling, damage or seizure and replace bearings as required.

CAMSHAFT INSPECTION

Check camshaft for evidence of wear and damage, and replace if necessary. Using a dial indicator, measure runout. Runout should not exceed .0012 inch, (.03mm). If runout exceeds specified limit, replace camshaft. Using a micrometer, measure cam lobe height. Standard cam lobe height is 1.7337 inch, (44.114mm). Measure uneven wear on the camshaft journals at the four indicated locations, **Fig. 6.** Maximum uneven wear allowed is .0020 inch, (.05mm). Standard journal diameter front and rear should be 1.6486-1.6492 inch, (41.949-41.965mm). Center journal diameter should be 1.6474-1.6480 inch, (41.919-41.935mm).

FLYWHEEL INSPECTION

Check the flywheel for cracks and wear, and replace if necessary. Position flywheel onto a flat surface, and measure warp. Flywheel warp should not exceed .008 inch, (.20mm). If flywheel warp exceeds speci-

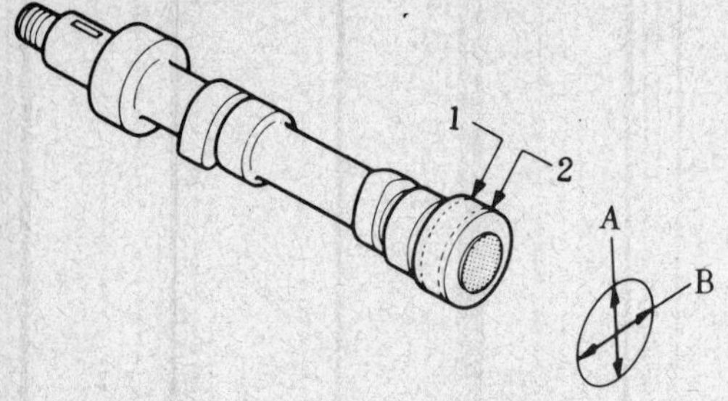

Fig. 6 Checking location for camshaft wear

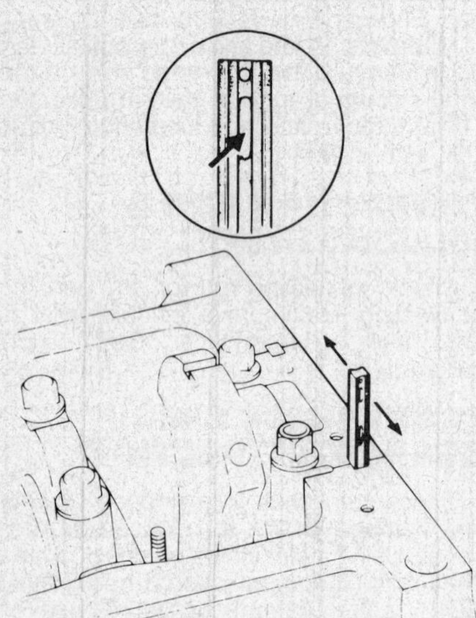

Fig. 9 Installing side seal

fied limit replace flywheel. Replace flywheel ring gear as follows:

1. Using a suitable torch, heat ring gear.
2. Using a hammer, tap circumference of ring gear and remove from flywheel.
3. Heat the new ring gear to 480°-570° F, (250-300° C), and install onto flywheel. **Ensure chamfered side of ring gear faces the engine.**

CHAIN, CHAIN ADJUSTER, BLADE, DAMPER & SPROCKET INSPECTION

Check each component for wear and damage, replace components if necessary.

Check contacting position of stopper and sleeve. If protrusion is between 13 and 18 notches, **Fig. 7,** the chain has stretched excessively and must be replaced.

ENGINE ASSEMBLY

Ensure all engine components are thoroughly cleaned prior to assembly. Lubricate all mating surfaces with clean engine oil. During assembly ensure all gaps and endplays are accurate.

1. Install piston onto connecting rod. Lubricate piston pin with clean engine oil.

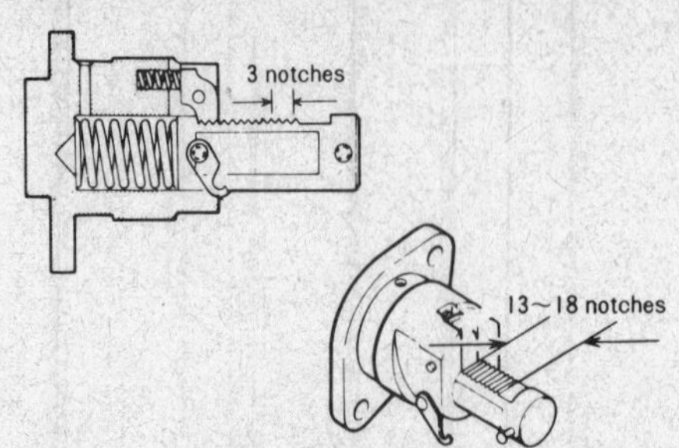

Fig. 7 Timing chain stretch check

2. Using an arbor press, press piston pin into piston. **Pressing load is 1,100-3,300 lbs., (500-1500kg). If pressing load is other than specified limit, replace piston pin or connecting rod.**
3. Install oil ring upper and lower plates and the spacer onto piston. Install compression rings, making sure "R" marks face upward.
4. Set open end of each ring in the position shown in **Fig. 8.**
5. Install crankshaft and pistons into cylinder block. Make sure "F" marks stamped on pistons face toward crankshaft pulley.
6. Install the crankshaft thrust washer into cylinder block, with groove facing outward.
7. Using Plastigage, measure oil clearance between crankshaft journal and main bearing. Clearance limit should be .0031 inch, (.08mm). If clearance exceeds specified limit, grind the crankshaft and use an undersize bearing. Note the following:

Under Size	Finished Size
.010 inch, (.25 mm)	1.9528-1.9534 inch, (49.6-49.7mm)
.020 inch, (.50 mm)	1.9430-1.9436 inch, (49.4-49.5mm)
.030 inch, (.75 mm)	1.9332-1.9338 inch, (49.1-49.2mm)

Match installation of main bearing caps with cap number and arrow mark shown on the bearing caps.

8. Install side seal into cylinder block, making sure seal hole, **Fig. 9,** is facing either inside or outside of cylinder block.
9. Using a dial indicator, check crankshaft endplay. Endplay should be .0039-.0059 inch, (.10-.15mm). Endplay limit is .0118 inch, (.30mm). If endplay exceeds specified limit, use oversize washers and install onto crankshaft. The following oversize washers are available: .010 inch, (.25mm), .020 inch, (.50mm) and .030 inch, (.75mm).
10. Using Plastigage, check clearance between crank pin and connecting rod bearing as follows:
    a. Install and torque connecting rod cap bolts to 22-25 ft. lbs., (30-35 Nm). **When installing the connecting rod bearing cap onto the connecting rod, ensure mark on bearing cap aligns with mark on connecting rod**

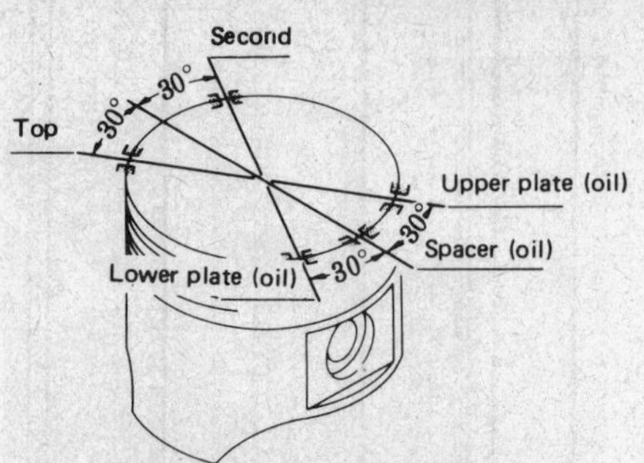

Fig. 8 Positioning piston rings onto piston

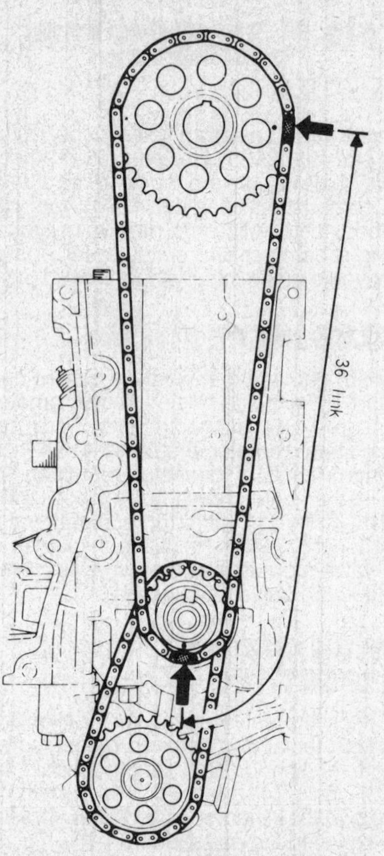

Fig. 10 Aligning timing marks on timing chain and crankshaft sprocket with engine inverted

    b. Measure clearance, which should not exceed .0039 inch (0.1mm).
    c. If clearance exceeds specified limit, grind crankshaft and use an undersize bearing. The following undersize bearings are available:

Under Size	Finished Size
.010 inch, (.25 mm)	1.5598-1.5604 inch, (39.690-39.706mm)
.020 inch, (.50 mm)	1.5500-1.5506 inch, (39.440-39.456mm)
.030 inch, (.75 mm)	1.5402-1.5408 inch, (39.190-39.206mm)

11. Using a feeler gauge, measure connecting rod endplay. Endplay should be .012 inch, (.3mm).
12. Install sprocket onto crankshaft, then install oil pump, pump sprocket and chain into cylinder block. Engage oil

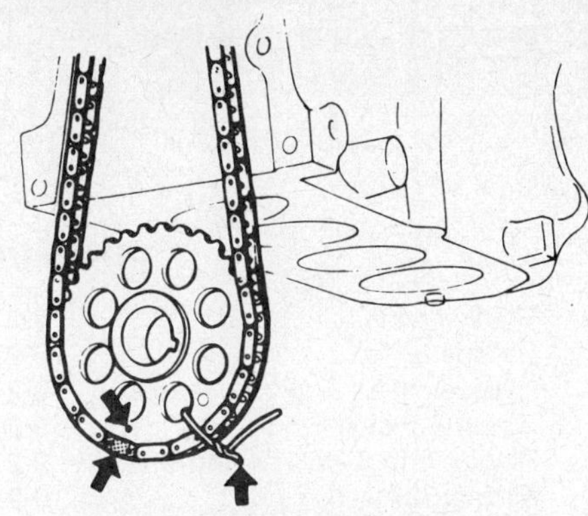
Fig. 11 Securing timing chain and sprocket with engine inverted

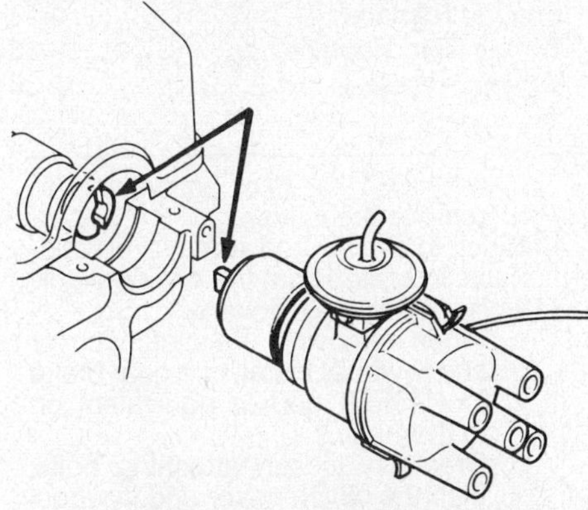
Fig. 13 Aligning distributor shaft notch with camshaft groove

pump and crankshaft sprockets with chain.

13. Align crankshaft and camshaft sprocket timing marks with colored links on timing chain, **Fig. 10.**
14. Using a piece of wire, tie the timing chain and camshaft sprocket to prevent movement, **Fig. 11.**
15. Using sealer No. 852777739 or equivalent, apply sealer onto oil pan flange and install onto engine. Wait approximately 30 minutes then torque oil pan bolts to 5-9 ft. lbs., (7-12 Nm).
16. Install timing chain cover gasket and timing chain cover onto engine. Cut off any excessive portion of the timing chain cover gasket from both ends of timing chain cover.
17. Install flywheel assembly onto crankshaft. Using tool No. 49E301060 or equivalent, lock flywheel and torque flywheel bolts to 60-65 ft. lbs., (81-89 Nm) on models with manual transaxle or 51-61 ft. lbs. (70-85Nm) on models with automatic transaxle.
18. Using sealer No. 852777739 or equivalent, apply sealer onto crankshaft pulley bolt and torque bolt to 80-87 ft. lbs., (118-120 Nm).
19. Using tool Nos. 490636100A and 490221222A or equivalents, install valves into cylinder head.
20. Install valve rocker arms onto the rocker arm shaft. **Ensure there is at least .039 inch, (1mm) of off-set between center of rocker arm adjusting screw and exhaust valve stem.**
21. Install cylinder head and cylinder head bolts. Torque cylinder head bolts in sequence, **Fig. 2.** Torque bolts to 56-59 ft. lbs., (74-80 Nm).
22. Using Plastigage, measure oil clearance between camshaft and bearing cap. Oil clearance should be .0059 inch, (.15mm).
23. Using tool No. 49E301060 or equivalent, lock flywheel and torque camshaft sprocket nut to 51-58 ft. lbs., (70-79 Nm).
24. Check camshaft endplay (clearance between camshaft sprocket and thrust plate). Endplay should be .008 inch, (.20mm). If endplay exceeds specified limit, replace the thrust plate.
25. Install the chain tensioner into the timing chain cover as follows:
    a. Push sleeve completely into chain tensioner body and lock with pin, **Fig. 12.**
    b. Install chain tensioner into timing chain cover. **When the engine is cranked, the pin will unlock, forcing the sleeve outward, completing the timing chain adjustment.**
26. Rotate crankshaft until No. 1 cylinder is at TDC of the compression stroke. **Ensure mark on crankshaft aligns with mark (T) on the timing chain cover.**
27. Using clean engine oil, lubricate distributor shaft O-ring. Turn and install distributor shaft onto camshaft. Ensure distributor shaft notch engages groove on camshaft, **Fig. 13.**

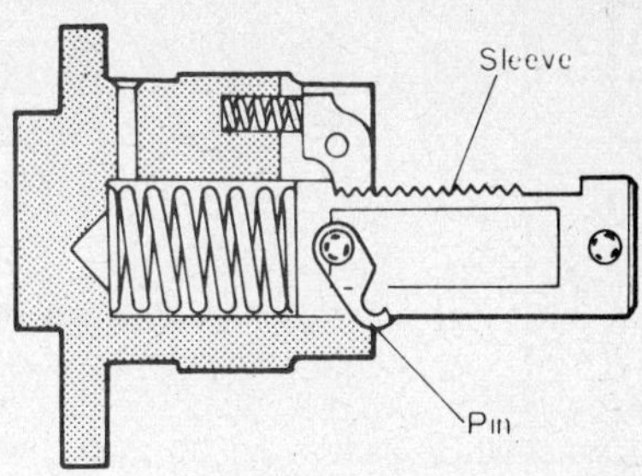

Fig. 12 Chain tensioner assembly

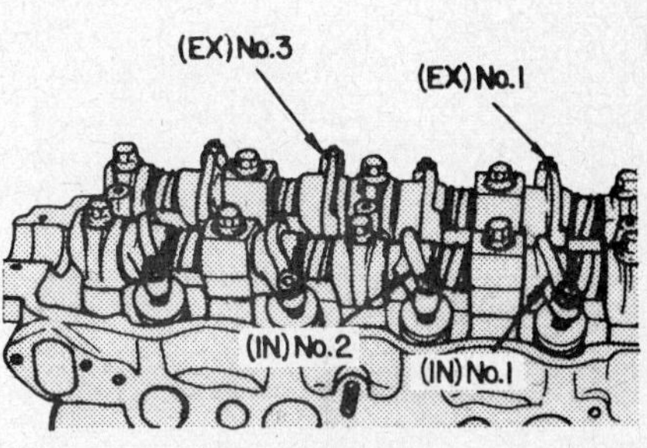

Fig. 14 Adjusting valve clearances

FINAL ASSEMBLY

1. Install thermostat and cover.
2. Install alternator.
3. Install oil filter and intake manifold.
4. Install water and fuel pumps.
5. Install exhaust manifold and fan pulley.

VALVES ADJUST

With No. 1 cylinder at TDC of its compression stroke, adjust valves in sequence as shown, **Fig. 14.** Rotate crankshaft 360° and adjust remaining valves. Note the following valve clearance limits:

	Intake Valve	Exhaust Valve
Valve Side	.010 inch, (.25mm)	.012 inch, (.30mm)
Cam Side	.007 inch, (.18mm)	.009 inch, (.23mm)

4-97/1597cc PISTON ENGINE SECTION

INDEX

ENGINE REPLACE

1. Disconnect battery cable.
2. Drain engine oil, transaxle oil and coolant into suitable containers.
3. Remove battery and battery carrier.
4. Remove air cleaner assembly.
5. Mark, then disconnect all electrical connectors from the engine.
6. Remove cooling fan and radiator assembly.
7. Disconnect accelerator cable and cruise control cable, if equipped.
8. Disconnect speedometer cable.
9. On fuel injected models, slowly and carefully discharge pressure from fuel system.
10. On all models, disconnect and cap fuel lines and hoses.
11. Disconnect heater hoses from engine.
12. Disconnect brake vacuum hose and three-way solenoid valve hose.
13. Disconnect canister purge hose.
14. Disconnect engine ground strap.
15. Disconnect upper and lower radiator hoses.
16. Disconnect exhaust pipe from exhaust manifold.
17. Remove secondary air pipe, if equipped.
18. Remove A/C compressor, if equipped.
19. Remove power steering pump, if equipped.
20. Mark driveshaft alignment, then disconnect driveshafts. **Do not use a lead pencil or a sharp tool to place alignment marks on driveshaft assemblies.**
21. Disconnect clutch control cable, if equipped.
22. Disconnect shift control rod.
23. Remove engine under cover and side cover.
24. Remove engine mount bolts.
25. Remove engine from vehicle.
26. Reverse procedure to install.

DISASSEMBLY

1. With engine placed on a suitable work stand, remove the following components from the engine:
   a. Exhaust manifold and gasket.
   b. Alternator.
   c. Spark plug wires, spark plugs and distributor.
   d. Intake manifold assembly and gasket.
   e. Fuel pump and gasket, if equipped with carburetor.
   f. Oil filter and oil pressure switch.
2. Refer to **Fig. 1** and remove components indicated from the front of the engine, and note the following:
   a. When removing the timing belt, remove the tensioner spring after loosening the tensioner lock bolt.
   b. Mark direction of rotation on the timing belt. **Use a piece of chalk to place direction mark on the timing belt. Do not use a pencil or pen to place mark on belt.**
   c. Remove timing belt.
   d. When removing crankshaft pulley and timing belt pulley, place ring gear brake tool 49E301060 or equivalent on to flywheel. Remove crankshaft pulley and timing belt pulley.
3. Refer to **Fig. 2** and remove components indicated from cylinder head and note the following:
   a. When removing the rocker arm and rocker shaft assembly, loosen attaching bolts gradually in sequence shown in **Fig. 3.**
   b. Remove rocker arm and shaft assembly. **Do not interchange the various components of the rocker arm and shaft assembly.**
   c. When removing the cylinder head assembly, loosen the cylinder head attaching bolts in sequence shown in **Fig. 4.**
   d. When removing the valves from the cylinder head, use valve spring lifter and pivot tools 490636100A and 49S120222 or equivalents to remove the valves.
4. Refer to **Fig. 5** and remove components indicated from the engine block, while noting the following:
   a. When removing the clutch cover and flywheel, install ring gear brake tool 49E301060 or equivalent on to flywheel.
   b. Gradually loosen attaching bolts, then the clutch cover and flywheel assembly.
5. Refer to **Fig. 6** and remove components indicated from engine block.

ENGINE INSPECTION & REPAIR

CYLINDER HEAD

Replace cylinder head assembly if there is any evidence of wear or damage. Measure cylinder head for distortion on the lower mating surfaces along the areas indicated in **Fig. 7.** Cylinder head distortion should not exceed .006 inch. If cylinder head distortion exceeds .006 inch, grind cylinder head or replace as necessary. Do not grind more than .008 inch from cylinder head.

VALVE & VALVE GUIDE

Inspect valve and valve guide for excessive wear or damage. Check valve head thickness. Intake valve head thickness should be .039 inch. Exhaust valve head thickness should be .051 inch. Measure valve stem diameter and valve stem clearance. If measurements obtained are not to specifications, replace valve and/or valve guide.

VALVE SPRING

Inspect each valve spring for cracks or damage. Check spring free length and spring angle. Spring free length should be 1.673 inch for 1986 models or 1.171 inch for 1987 models. Check spring angle limit as shown in **Fig. 8.** Angle limit should be .055 inch for 1986 models or .059 inch for 1987 models. Replace valve spring if mea-

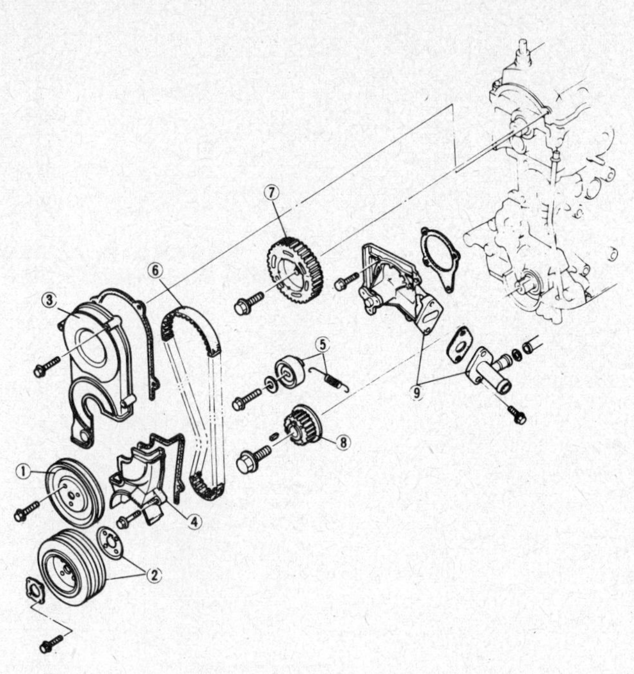

1. Waterpump pulley
2. Crankshaft pulley and baffle plate
3. Timing belt cover, upper
4. Timing belt cover, lower
5. Timing belt tensioner and spring
6. Timing belt
7. Camshaft pulley
8. Timing belt pulley
9. Water pump and water inlet pipe

Fig. 1 Exploded view of front engine components

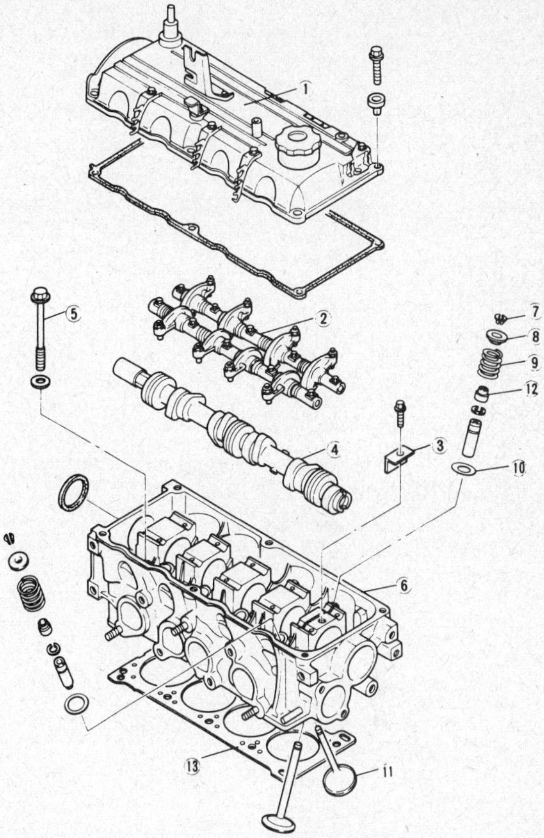

1. Cylinder head cover
2. Rocker arm and rocker shaft assembly
3. Thrust plate
4. Camshaft
5. Cylinder head bolts
6. Cylinder head
7. Spring retainers
8. Upper spring seats
9. Valve springs
10. Lower spring seats
11. Valves
12. Valve seals
13. Cylinder head gasket

Fig. 2 Exploded view of cylinder head & components

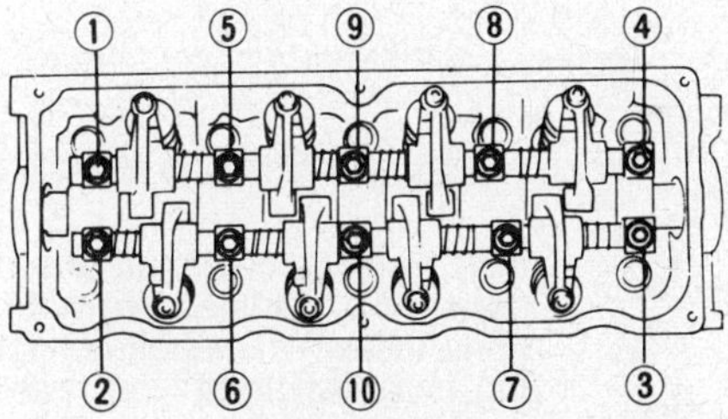

Fig. 3 Rocker arm & shaft attaching bolt loosening sequence

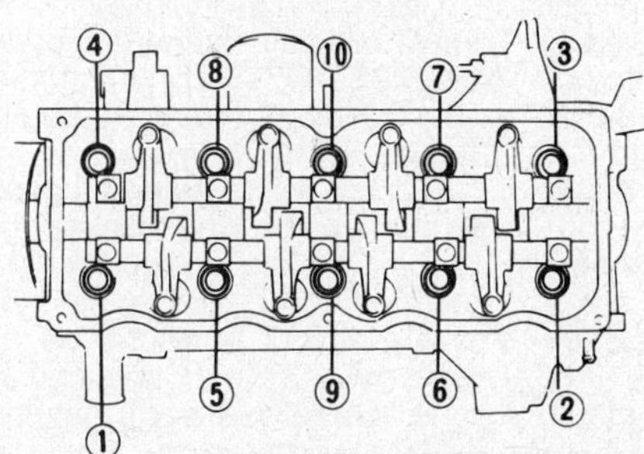

Fig. 4 Cylinder head bolt loosening sequence

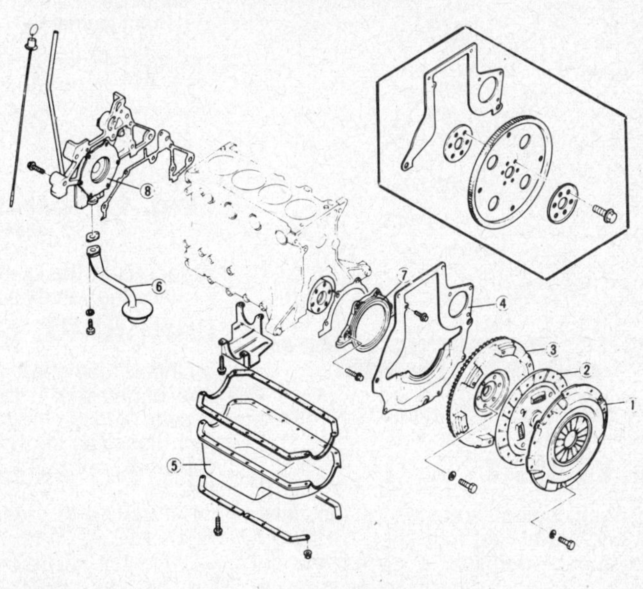

1. Clutch cover
2. Clutch disc
3. Flywheel
4. End plate
5. Oil pan
6. Oil strainer
7. Rear cover
8. Oil pump

Fig. 5 Exploded view of oil pump, oil pan, clutch cover & flywheel

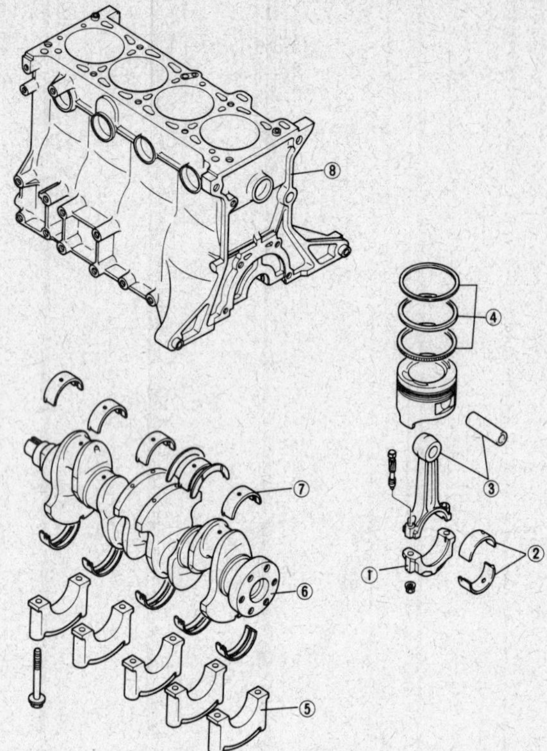

1. Connecting rod caps
2. Connecting rod bearings
3. Connecting rod and piston pin
4. Piston rings
5. Main bearing caps
6. Crankshaft
7. Main bearings
8. Cylinder block

Fig. 6 Exploded view of crankshaft & piston assembly

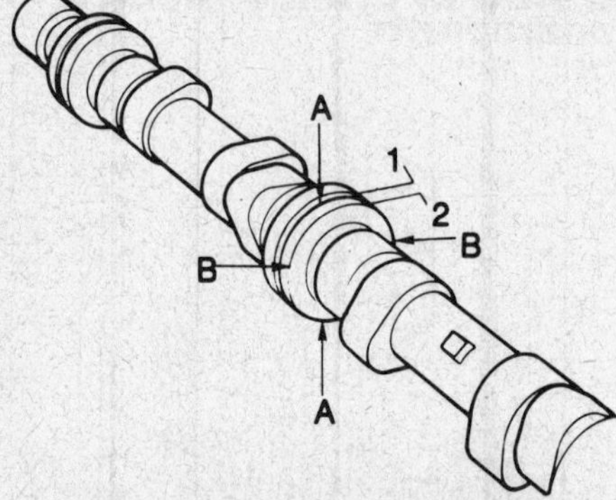

Fig. 10 Measuring wear of camshaft journal

surements obtained exceed specifications.

VALVE SEAT

Inspect contact surfaces of the valve seat and valve face for excessive roughness and/or damage. If necessary, cut valve seat using a suitable valve seat cutter or grinder of 15, 35, 45, 70 and 75 degrees, **Fig. 9.** Intake and exhaust seat angle should be 45 degrees. Valve seat contact width should be .043-.067 inch. Use suitable compound to seat the valve and valve seat. Ensure that the contact surface is at the center of the valve face. Replace the valve seal if the valve was cut.

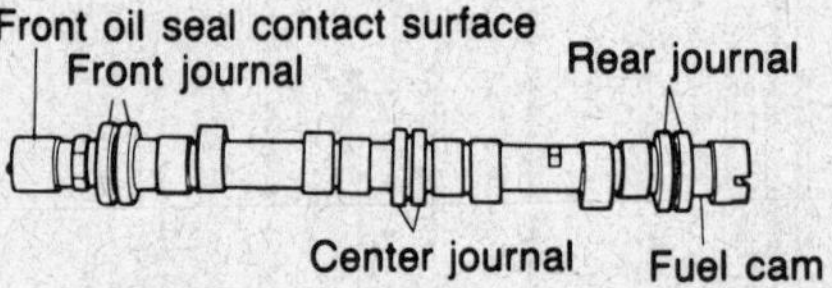

Fig. 11 Camshaft journal areas

CAMSHAFT

Check camshaft assembly for wear and/or damage. Replace camshaft, if necessary. Measure camshaft journal wear at four places as shown in **Figs. 10 and 11.** Camshaft journal diameters should be as follows:

1. Front and rear journal diameter, 1.7103-1.7112 inch.
2. Center journal (measured at three places), 1.6870-1.7091 inch.
3. Front oil seal contact surface, 1.1796-1.1811 inch.
4. Elliptical limit, .020 inch.

Inspect fuel cam for excessive wear and/or damage. Measure fuel cam height. Fuel cam height should be 1.331-1.346 inch. Replace camshaft assembly if measurements obtained are not to specifications. Inspect camshaft deflection by placing camshaft front and rear journals on suitable V-blocks. Using a suitable dial indicator, place dial indicator pointer on to camshaft center journal assembly. Rotate camshaft and measure deflection. Camshaft deflection should be .0012 inch. If not, replace camshaft assembly.

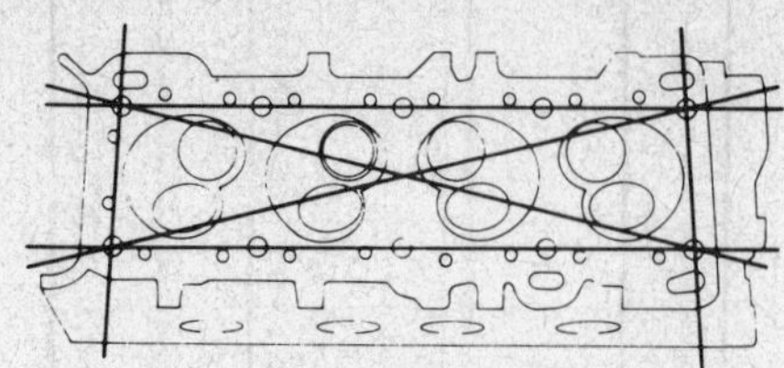

Fig. 7 Checking cylinder head for warpage

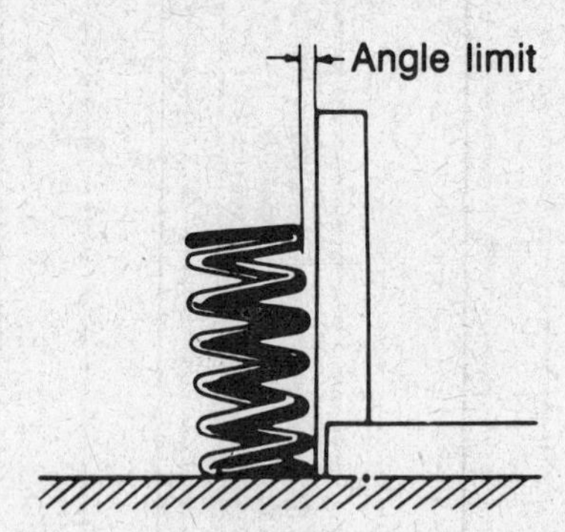

Fig. 8 Checking valve spring angle limit

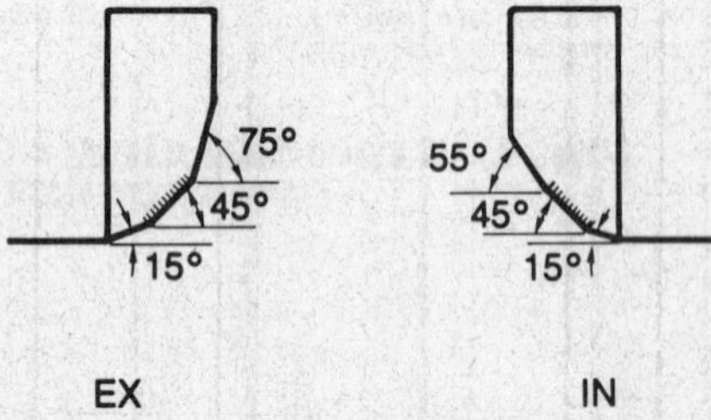

Fig. 9 Valve seat angles

Using a dial indicator, measure camshaft endplay. Camshaft endplay should be .002-.007 inch. If endplay exceeds specifications, replace camshaft or cylinder head assembly.

Using a micrometer, measure camshaft journal and bearing oil clearance. Remove any oil, grease or dirt from the camshaft journals and bearings. Measure oil clearances at four locations on each journal. Note measurement obtained. Measure the inner diameter of each bearing at four locations. Front and rear oil clearance should be .0014-.0033 inch. Oil clearance maximum limit is .0059 inch. If oil clearance exceeds specifications, replace cylinder head and/or camshaft assembly.

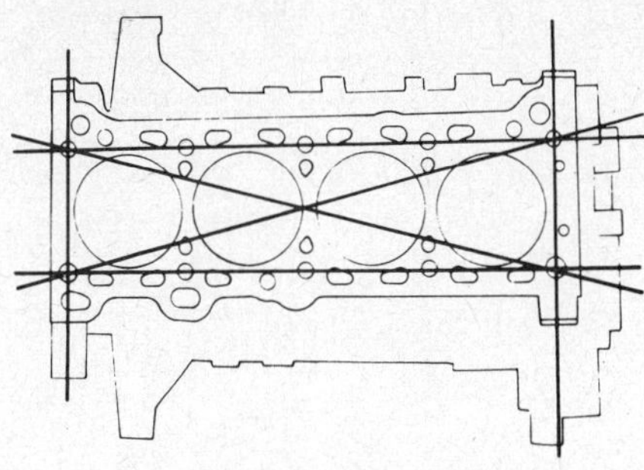

Fig. 12 Checking cylinder block for warpage

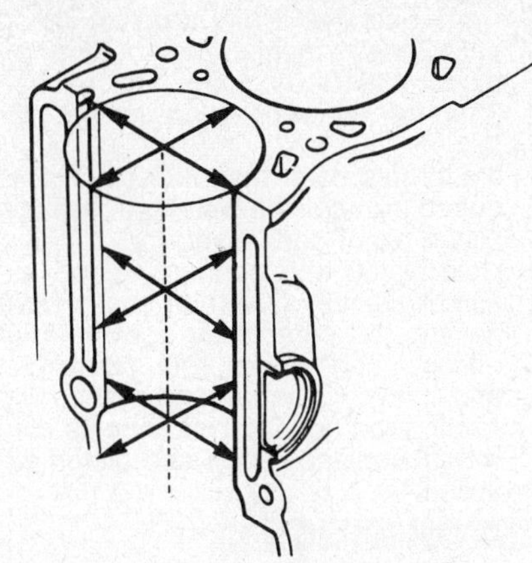

Fig. 13 Measuring cylinder bore at six locations

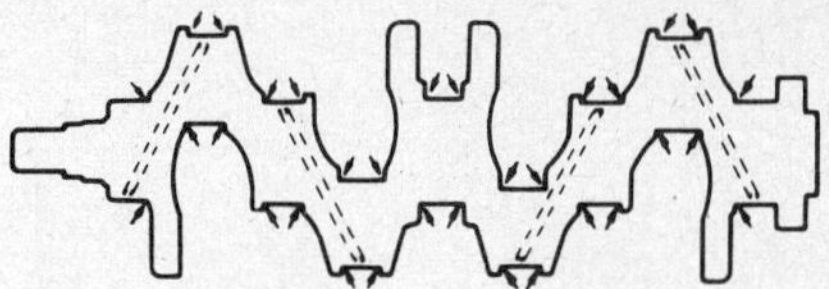

Fig. 14 Checking crankshaft fillet R dimension

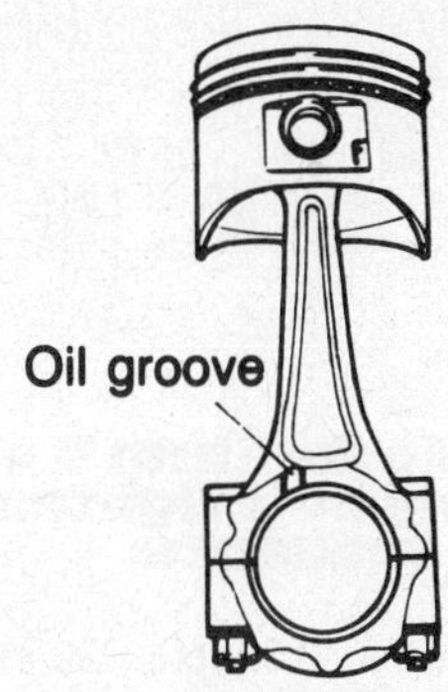

Fig. 15 Piston & rod assembly

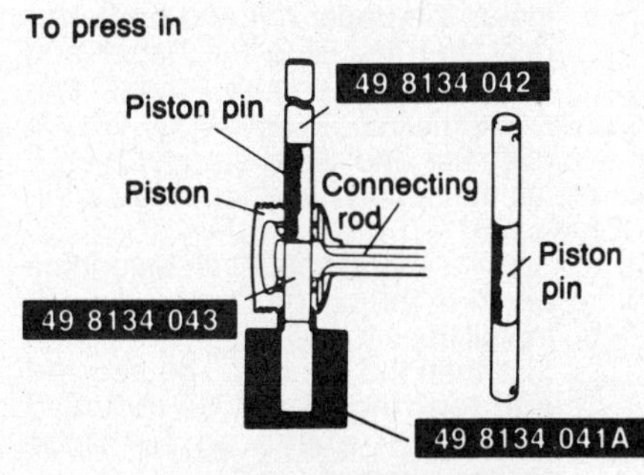

Fig. 16 Piston pin installation

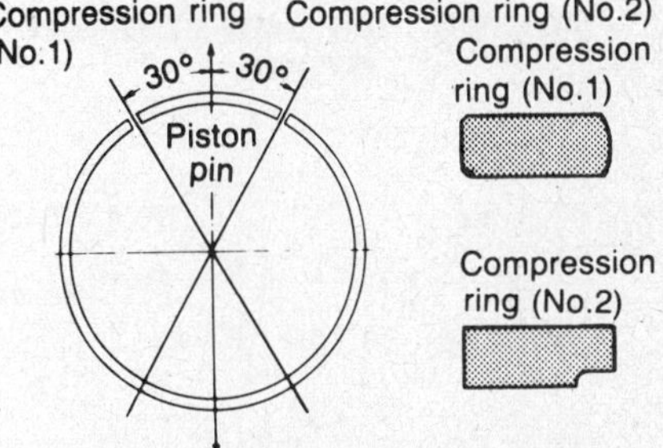

Fig. 17 Positioning piston rings

ROCKER ARM & ROCKER ARM SHAFT

Inspect contact surfaces of rocker arm and rocker arm shaft for excessive wear and/or damage. Replace rocker arm and rocker arm shaft, if necessary. Using a micrometer, measure clearance between rocker shaft and rocker arms. Clearance should be .004 inch. The oil holes on the rocker arm shaft must be assembled in the down position.

CYLINDER BLOCK

Inspect cylinder block for leakage damage, cracks and cylinder wall scoring. Repair or replace cylinder block, if necessary.

Measure cylinder block top surface distortion (warpage) in six directions as shown in **Fig. 12.** Distortion limit should be .006 inch. If distortion exceeds specified limit, grind top surface of cylinder block or replace cylinder block assembly. When grinding, do not grind more than .008 inch from top surface of cylinder block assembly.

Check cylinder walls. If upper portion of cylinder wall(s) indicate uneven wear, use a suitable ridge reamer to repair.

Measure cylinder diameter at six locations indicated in **Fig. 13.** Standard cylinder diameter should be 3.0709-3.0717 inch. Cylinder diameter limit should be 3.0776 inch. Cylinder diameter difference should be .0007 inch. If the difference between the maximum and minimum range of the standard cylinder diameter exceeds the limit, rebore cylinder. **The cylinder boring size should be based on the size of an oversize piston to be used.**

PISTON & PISTON RING

Inspect outer circumferences of all pistons for seizure or scoring. Replace, if necessary. Measure outer diameter of each piston and ensure clearance between piston and cylinder is correct. Standard diameter should be 3.0691-3.0699 inch for 1986 models or 3.0691-3.0694 inch on 1987 models. Standard piston and cylinder clearance should be .006 inch. Oversize piston and piston ring should be .010 inch oversize or .020 inch oversize.

Inspect piston rings for excessive wear and/or damage. Replace, if necessary. Insert piston ring into cylinder bore by hand and push inward using a piston. Using a suitable feeler gauge, measure piston ring end gap (clearance). Top ring clearance should be .008-.016 inch for 1986 models or .006-.012 inch for 1987 models. Second ring clearance should be .006-.012 inch. Oil ring clearance should be .012-.035 inch for 1986 models or .008-.028 inch on 1987 models.

Measure clearance of the piston ring and groove around the entire circumference. Top and second ring clearance should be .001-.003 inch.

CONNECTING ROD

Check connecting rods for bends or twists. Replace connecting rod(s) if bends or twists are excessive.

CRANKSHAFT

Check crankshaft journals and pins for damage, scoring or oil hole restrictions. Using a suitable dial indicator, check crankshaft deflection. Deflection should not exceed .0016 inch. Measure each journal diameter and crankpin. Main journal diameter should be 1.9662-1.9668 inch. Crankpin diameter should be 1.7693-1.7699 inch. If crankshaft wear exceeds standard limit, grind crankshaft to match an undersized bearing, with attention to each crank fillet R dimension, **Fig. 14.** Crankshaft grinding limit is .0295 inch. Undersize bearings available are .010 inch, .020 inch and .0295 inch. Crankshaft fillet R dimension is .012 inch.

TIMING BELT

Replace timing belt if there is any oil grease or moisture on it. Check timing belt from damage, wear, peeling, cracks or evidence or hardening. Replace, if necessary. **Never forcefully twist the timing belt or turn the timing belt inside out or bend it. Ensure not to allow oil, grease or moisture to contact timing belt assembly.**

TIMING BELT TENSIONER

Check rotation of the timing belt tensioner for smoothness or abnormal noise. Replace timing belt, if necessary. **Do not clean the timing belt tensioner with cleaning fluids. If timing belt is dirty, use a soft shop towel to wipe it clean and avoid scratching it.**

CAMSHAFT PULLEY & TIMING BELT PULLEY

Inspect pulley teeth for excessive wear and/or damage. Replace pulley, if necessary. **Do not clean the pulley with cleaning fluids. If pulley if dirty, use a soft shop towel to wipe it clean.**

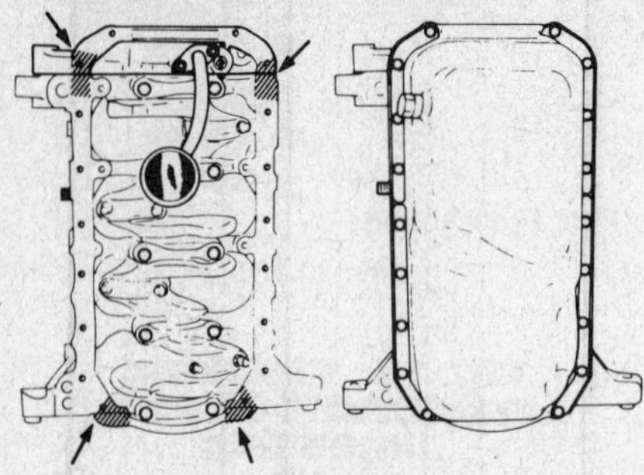

Fig. 18 Oil pan sealant areas

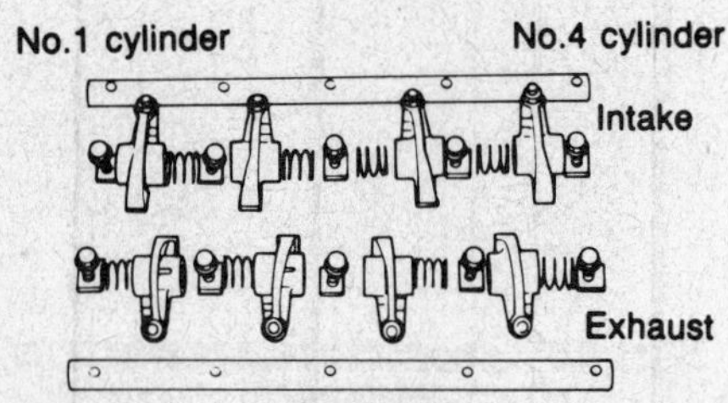

Fig. 20 Rocker arm & shaft assembly

UPPER & LOWER TIMING BELT COVERS

Inspect timing belt covers for excessive wear and/or damage. Replace covers, if necessary.

ASSEMBLY

VALVE, VALVE SEAL & SPRING

1. Apply clean engine oil to the inner surfaces of the new valve seal, then install valve seal on to the valve guide.
2. Install lower spring seat, then the valve. Install valve spring and upper spring sear into the cylinder head assembly. **Install spring with its narrow pitch end toward the cylinder head.**
3. Compress valve spring, then install spring retainer.

CONNECTING ROD

1. Align oil groove in the large end of the connecting rod opposite the F mark on the piston, **Fig. 15.**
2. Apply a clean coat of engine oil on to the circumference of each piston pin and to the small end of each connecting rod.
3. Place piston pin setting tools 498134041A, 498134042 and 498134043 or equivalents into position as shown in **Fig. 16.**
4. Insert the piston pin from the direction of the F mark on the piston.
5. Press upper portion of 498134042 with a suitable press to force the pin inward.
6. The piston pin should be pressed inward until the lower end of guide 498134043 meets the bottom of block 498134043. Do not exceed 3300 lbs. When pressing pin into piston.
7. If a force greater than 3300 lbs, is required to install the piston pin, replace piston pin or connecting rod.
8. Hold piston and connecting rod assembly. Move crankshaft end of connecting rod completely upward, then release connecting rod crankshaft end. If the crankshaft end of the connecting rod does not drop by its own weight, replace piston and piston pin assembly.

PISTON RINGS

1. Install the three-piece oil rings on to the pistons as follows:
   a. Apply clean engine oil to the oil ring spacer and rails.
   b. Install the oil ring spacer.
   c. Install the upper rail and the lower rail. After installing the upper and lower rails, ensure they turn smoothly in both directions. Do not align the end gaps, stagger them.
2. Install the second and top ring as follows:
   a. Apply a liberal coat of clean engine oil on to the piston rings.
   b. Install the second ring to the piston first, then the top one. **The second and top rings must be installed with the R marks on the rings facing upward.**
   c. Position the opening of each ring as shown in **Fig. 17.**

CRANKSHAFT

1. Inspect oil clearances on the crankshaft and main bearings.
2. Remove any foreign material and oil from the journal and bearing.
3. Install the main bearings and the crankshaft.
4. Position Plastigage on top of each journal (in the journal axial direction), away from the oil hole.
5. Set the main bearing caps according to the cap number and forward mark and tighten cap bolts. Torque bolts to 40-43 ft. lbs.
6. Remove main bearing cap and measure oil clearance. Oil clearance should be .0011-.0027 inch for 1986 models or .0009-.0017 inch for 1987 models. If oil clearance exceeds specifications, grind crankshaft and use undersize main bearings. Undersize main bearings are available in undersizes of .010 inch, .020 inch and .030 inch.
7. Apply clean engine oil to mian bearing and bearing journals.
8. Install the thrust bearings to the cylinder block side.
9. Install the crankshaft, and main bearing caps according to the cap number and forward direction mark on cap.
10. Check crankshaft endplay. Endplay should be between .0031-.0111 inch. If endplay exceeds specified amount, adjust endplay by using thrust bearings. Standard thickness available is .0984-.1004 inch. Undersize widths available are .010 inch, .020 inch and .030 inch. **Oil groove of the thrust bearing must face the crankshaft.**

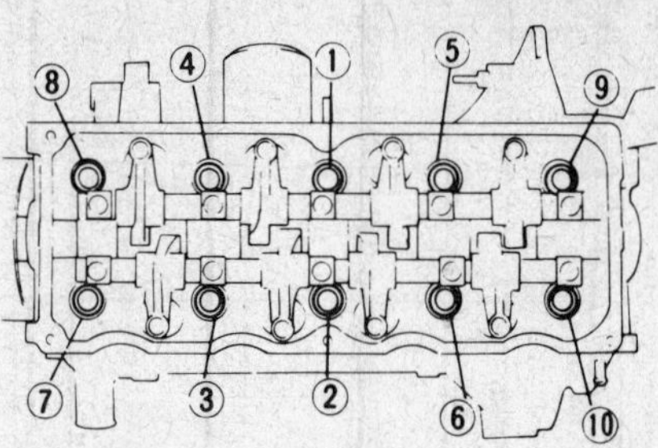

Fig. 19 Cylinder head bolt tightening sequence

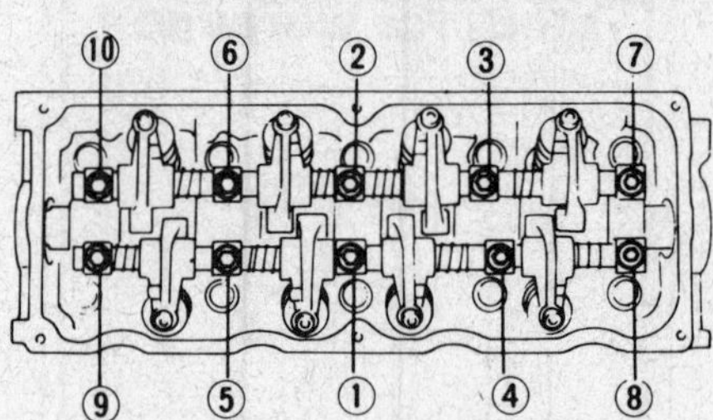

Fig. 21 Rocker arm & shaft attaching bolt tightening sequence

PISTON & CONNECTING RODS

1. Apply clean engine oil to the cylinder walls, piston and piston rings.
2. Insert each piston and connecting rod into the cylinder block. **Install pistons with F mark on piston facing front of cylinder block.**

CONNECTING ROD CAP

1. Inspect and adjust the connecting rod bearing and crankshaft pin journal oil clearance by using the same procedure used for the crankshaft and main bearing oil clearance.
2. Torque connecting rod cap bolts to 37-41 ft. lbs. Align match marks on cap and on connecting rod when installing connecting rod cap.
3. Standard oil clearance is .0011-.0027 inch.
4. Undersize connecting rod bearings available are .010 inch, .020 inch and .030 inch.
5. Check side clearance of the connecting rod. Clearance should be 012 inch.
6. Apply clean engine oil to the crankpin journal and connecting rod bearing.
7. Install the connecting rod cap to align the match mark. Torque bolts to 37-41 ft. lbs.

REAR COVER & END PLATE

1. Apply clean engine oil to the rear cover, oil seal and oil seal lip.
2. Using a suitable press, install oil seal into the rear cover.
3. Install the rear cover along with a new gasket.

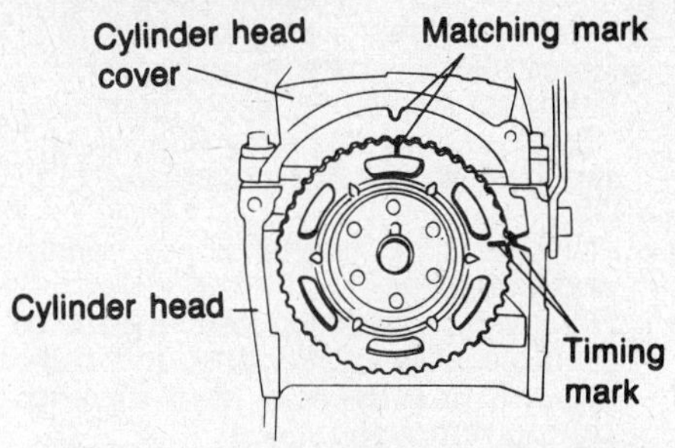

Fig. 22 Aligning camshaft pulley

4. Torque rear cover attaching bolts to 69-95 inch lbs.
5. Cut away seal portion protruding from the rear cover assembly.
6. Install end plate assembly.
7. Torque end plate attaching bolts to 65-95 inch lbs.

OIL PUMP, STRAINER, BAFFLE PLATE & OIL PAN

1. Remove any dirt or grease from pump contact surfaces.
2. Apply clean engine oil to the oil pump seal lip.
3. Install a new gasket. **When installing gasket, do not allow gasket sealer to block pump oil hole.**
4. Install oil pump. Torque oil pump attaching bolts to 14-19 ft. lbs.
5. Install oil strainer and a new gasket. Torque oil strainer attaching bolts to 69-95 inch lbs.
6. Install oil baffle plate, if equipped. Torque oil baffle plate attaching bolts to 14-19 ft. lbs.
7. Apply suitable sealer to cylinder block as shown in **Fig. 18.**
8. Install gasket and oil pan. Torque oil pan attaching bolts to 52-78 inch lbs. for 1986 models or 69-78 inch lbs. for 1987 models.

FLYWHEEL, CLUTCH DISC & COVER

1. Using a suitable drift and hammer, tap flywheel pilot bearing into flywheel.
2. Apply sealer 853077743 or equivalent, on to flywheel bolts. **If original flywheel bolts are used, clean threads to remove old sealant, apply new sealant and torque attaching bolts to 71-75 ft. lbs. If old sealant cannot be removed, install new bolts.**
3. Install flywheel and torque attaching bolts to 71-75 ft. lbs.
4. Install clutch disc and clutch cover, using clutch disc centering tool 49SE01301 or equivalent.
5. Torque clutch cover attaching bolts to 13-20 ft. lbs.

WATER PUMP

1. Remove any dirt or old gasket from water pump mounting surface.
2. Place a new water pump gasket into position.
3. Install water pump. Torque pump attaching bolts to 14-29 ft. lbs. for 1986 models or 14-19 ft. lbs. for 1987 models.

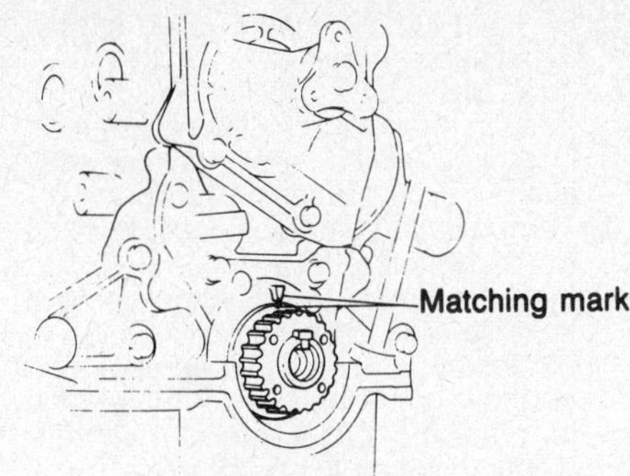

Fig. 23 Aligning timing belt pulley

CYLINDER HEAD & CAMSHAFT

1. Thoroughly remove all dirt and grease from top of cylinder block.
2. Place a new cylinder head gasket in position.
3. Install cylinder head. Torque cylinder head bolts gradually and in sequence shown in **Fig. 19** to 63-67 ft. lbs. for 1986 models or 56-60 ft. lbs. for 1987 models.
4. Apply clean engine oil to camshaft journals and bearings, the install camshaft.

ROCKER ARM & SHAFT

1. Assemble rocker arm and rocker shaft assembly as shown in **Fig. 20.**
2. Ensure both rocker arm shaft oil holes face downward. **The installation bolt holes are different for the exhaust and intake sides.**
3. There are two types of rocker arms with different offsets. The rocker arms used for the No. 1 and No. 2 cylinders are the same for exhaust and intake, No. 3 and No. 4 also use the same rockers.
4. Install rocker arm and rocker shaft assembly. Torque attaching bolts gradually and in sequence shown in **Fig. 21** to 14-17 ft. lbs. for 1986 models or 16-21 for 1987 models.

CAMSHAFT OIL SEAL

1. Apply a thin coat of engine oil to camshaft oil seal and into the cylinder head.
2. Using a suitable drift and hammer, tap camshaft oil seal into the cylinder head.

TIMING BELT PULLEY, CAMSHAFT PULLEY, TIMING BELT TENSIONER & TIMING BELT

1. Install timing belt pulley and key.
2. Apply sealer 853077743 or equivalent, on to timing belt pulley bolt. Torque attaching bolt to 80-94 ft. lbs.
3. Slowly turn crankshaft so that timing mark on oil pump body is aligned with groove mark.
4. Install camshaft pulley on to dowel pin and with pin groove facing upward.

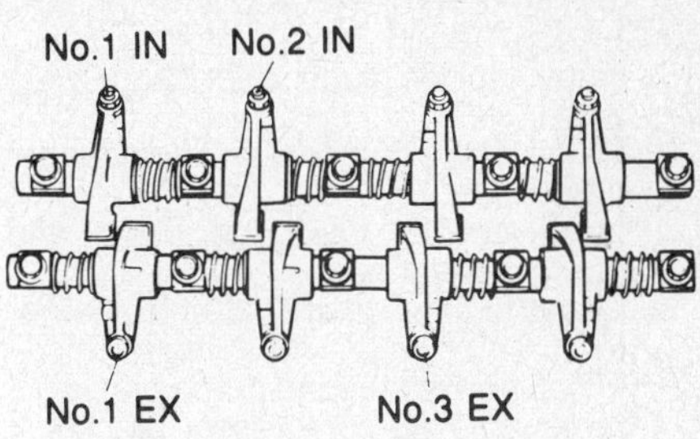

Fig. 24 Valve clearances adjust

Ensure that dowel pin on camshaft also faces upward.

5. Tighten camshaft pulley bolt. Hold camshaft using a suitable wrench. Torque attaching bolt to 36-45 ft. lbs.
6. Ensure timing mark on cylinder head and timing mark on camshaft pulley are aligned properly.
7. Install timing belt tensioner and tensioner spring.
8. Temporarily secure tensioner so spring is completely extended.
9. Install timing belt. **The timing belt must be installed in the direction of previous rotation if the original belt is used.**
10. Loosen tensioner lock bolt.
11. Turn crankshaft twice in the direction of rotation and align timing marks.
12. Ensure timing marks are correctly aligned.
13. Torque timing belt tensioner lock bolt to 14-19 ft. lbs.
14. Measure tension between crankshaft pulley and camshaft pulley. Tension should be 22 lbs.
15. Install timing belt cover gaskets and covers. Torque cover attaching bolts to 69-95 inch. lbs.

CRANKSHAFT PULLEY

1. Install crankshaft pulley and baffle plate.
2. Torque crankshaft pulley attaching bolts to 11-13 ft. lbs.

FUEL PUMP

Carbureted Models Only

1. Apply clean engine oil to the fuel cam contact surface.
2. Install fuel pump, insulator and gasket.
3. Torque fuel pump attaching bolts to 17-22 ft. lbs.

FINAL ASSEMBLY

1. Install oil pressure switch.
2. Install engine hanger.
3. Install thermostat and thermostat cover.
4. Install distributor as follows:
   a. Apply clean engine oil to distributor O-ring and place on to distributor.
   b. Apply clean engine oil to distributor drive gear, then align distributor blade with oil holes.
   c. Install distributor into cylinder head with No. 1 piston at TDC of compression stroke.

d. Temporarily tighten distributor hold down bolt.
5. Install spark plugs and spark plug wires.
6. Install intake manifold and coolant bypass hose.
7. Install coolant inlet pipe, upper and lower radiator hose.
8. Install exhaust manifold and alternator.
9. Install power steering pump bracket, if removed, A/C compressor bracket, if removed and engine mount.

TIMING BELT
REPLACE

1. Disconnect battery ground cable.
2. Remove engine side cover attaching bolts, then the engine side cover.
3. Remove A/C and power steering drive belts, if equipped.
4. Remove alternator and alternator drive belt.
5. Remove water pump pulley, then the crankshaft pulley and baffle plate.
6. Remove upper and lower timing belt cover.
7. Turn crankshaft to align matching mark of camshaft pulley with cylinder head and cylinder head cover timing mark, **Fig. 22.**
8. Mark direction of rotation on timing belt to ensure correct position during installation.
9. Remove timing belt tensioner and spring, then the timing belt.
10. Inspect timing belt, timing belt pulley, camshaft pulley and timing belt tensioner and spring. Replace defective parts as required.
11. Ensure timing mark on timing belt pulley is aligned with case matching mark, **Fig. 23.**
12. Ensure matching mark on camshaft pulley is aligned with cylinder head cover matching mark, **Fig. 22.**
13. Install timing belt tensioner and spring, then temporarily secure spring in fully extended position.
14. Install timing belt. **Timing belt must be install in same direction of previous rotation.**
15. Remove all spark plugs, then loosen tensioner lock bolt.
16. Turn crankshaft twice in direction of rotation, then align matching marks.
17. If timing marks are not correctly aligned, repeat steps 11 through 16.
18. Torque timing belt tensioner lock bolt to 14-19 ft. lbs.
19. Measure timing belt tension using a suitable tool. If timing belt tension is not 22 lbs., loosen tensioner lock bolt and turn crankshaft twice in direction of rotation. Torque timing belt tensioner lock bolt to 14-19 ft. lbs.
20. Install lower and upper timing belt cover, then the cover attaching bolts. Torque attaching bolts to 69-95 inch lbs.
21. Install spark plugs.
22. Install baffle plate, crankshaft pulley and water pump pulley, then the alternator and drive belt.
23. Install A/C and power steering drive belt, if equipped, then the engine side cover.

CYLINDER HEAD
REPLACE

1. Disconnect battery ground cable.
2. Drain engine coolant into a suitable container.
3. Remove air cleaner assembly, then the oil level dip stick.
4. Remove accelerator cable and cruise control cable, if equipped.
5. Disconnect and plug fuel hoses, then remove fuel pump, if equipped with carburetor.
6. Disconnect heater hoses, brake vacuum hose and canister hose.
7. Disconnect spark plug wires and all engine electrical connectors, then remove distributor.
8. Remove secondary air pipe, if equipped with carburetor.
9. Remove front engine hanger and ground wire.
10. Remove upper radiator hose, then the water bypass hose and bracket.
11. Remove intake manifold assembly, then the exhaust manifold insulator and exhaust manifold.
12. Remove engine side cover, then the upper and lower timing belt cover.
13. Turn crankshaft to align matching mark on camshaft pulley with matching mark on cylinder head cover, **Fig. 22.**
14. Remove timing belt tensioner, spring and timing belt.
15. Remove camshaft pulley. **Insert a suitable screwdriver through pulley slot to prevent it from turning during removal.**
16. Remove rear engine hanger, then the cylinder head cover.
17. Remove cylinder head attaching bolts, then the cylinder head assembly.
18. Remove thermostat assembly.
19. Reverse procedure to install, noting the following:
    a. Torque cylinder head bolts gradually and in sequence shown in **Fig. 19** to 63-67 ft. lbs. for 1986 models or 56-60 ft. lbs. for 1987 models.
    b. Install camshaft pulley onto dowel pin and keyway with matching mark straight up. Ensure timing marks on camshaft pulley and cylinder head align.
    c. Torque camshaft pulley attaching bolt to 36-46 ft. lbs.
    d. Install timing belt, refer to "Timing Belt, Replace" procedure.
    e. Adjust valve clearance, refer to "Valve Adjust" procedure.
    f. Apply suitable sealant to cylinder head cover before installing gasket.

VALVES ADJUST

1. With No. 1 piston at TDC of compression stroke, adjust valves indicated in **Fig. 24.**
2. Turn crankshaft one complete revolution to bring No. 4 piston to TDC of compression stroke and adjust remaining valves.
3. Adjust intake and exhaust valves to .012 inch.
4. After adjustment, install cylinder head cover gasket and cover. Torque cover attaching bolts to 43-78 inch lbs.

4-120/1970cc GASOLINE ENGINE SECTION

INDEX

ENGINE

REPLACE

1. Disconnect battery ground cable.
2. Scribe hood hinge locations and remove hood.
3. Drain cooling system and engine oil.
4. Remove air cleaner, then disconnect primary wire coupler from distributor and the high tension cable from ignition coil.
5. Disconnect wire from alternator terminal "B" and pull electrical connector off rear of alternator.
6. Disconnect engine ground wire from right side of engine mount.
7. Disconnect electrical connectors from water temperature gauge unit and oil pressure switch.
8. Disconnect bullet connectors from slow fuel cut valve solenoid and automatic choke heater.
9. Disconnect electrical connectors from starter motor terminals "B" and "S."
10. Disconnect throttle linkage and fuel lines from carburetor.
11. Disconnect power brake unit vacuum line from intake manifold.
12. Disconnect vacuum sensing tubes from intake manifold and carburetor.
13. Disconnect heater hoses from intake manifold.
14. Disconnect all hoses and lines from radiator, then remove radiator from vehicle.
15. Remove exhaust pipe hanger from transmission bracket.
16. Disconnect exhaust pipe from exhaust manifold.
17. Remove starter motor.
18. Remove engine-to-transmission attaching bolts and support transmission with a suitable jack.
19. Attach suitable lifting equipment to engine, then carefully lift engine from vehicle.
20. Disconnect air hoses from air pump outlet and check valve.
21. Disconnect vacuum sensing tube and air hose from anti-afterburn valve, then remove valve, if equipped.
22. Remove air bypass valve, EGR valve and servo diaphragm, as equipped.
23. Remove air manifold, heat insulator and exhaust manifold.
24. Remove cylinder head port liners, if equipped.
25. Reverse procedure to install.

ENGINE DISASSEMBLY

PRELIMINARY COMPONENTS

1. Remove distributor.
2. Remove alternator.
3. Remove air pump.
4. Remove oil filter.
5. Remove fan and pulley.
6. Remove water pump.
7. Remove thermostat.

MANIFOLD & CARBURETOR ASSEMBLY

1. Disconnect the vacuum sensing tube (distributor-carburetor) from carburetor.
2. Disconnect the ventilation hose from the ventilation valve at intake manifold.
3. Remove the bolts attaching intake manifold to the cylinder head and remove intake manifold and carburetor assembly.

REMOVING CYLINDER HEAD

1. Remove the attaching nuts and the rocker arm cover and gasket.
2. Remove two semicircular oil seals.
3. Install the flywheel brake (49 0221 030A) or other suitable tool to the flywheel.
4. Remove the locknut and washer and slide the distributor drive gear off the camshaft.
5. With the spanner (49 0164 631A) or other suitable tool, loosen the locknut holding the camshaft sprocket.
6. Remove the bolt that attaches the cylinder head to the timing chain cover.
7. Loosen the cylinder head bolts in the reverse order of tightening, **Fig. 1. To**

Fig. 1 Cylinder head bolt tightening sequence

Fig. 2 Removing rear main bearing cap

avoid cylinder head distortion, loosen the bolts a few turns at a time until they are all loose.

8. Remove the rocker arm assembly.
9. Pull the camshaft rearward and separate the camshaft from the camshaft sprocket. Remove the camshaft sprocket.
10. Remove the camshaft bearing halves from the cylinder head.
11. Remove the cylinder head and gasket. **When removing only the camshaft or the cylinder head, the timing chain should be lifted upward to prevent the slipper head of the chain adjuster from flying out and causing a difficulty in adjusting the timing chain.**

VALVE & VALVE SPRING

1. Remove the carbon inside the combustion chamber.
2. Using suitable spring compressor, compress valve springs.
3. Remove the taper sleeves, upper spring seat, valve springs and lower spring seat.
4. Remove the valve, then place the taper sleeves, upper spring seats, valve springs, lower spring seats and valves in order for reassembling.

CRANKSHAFT PULLEY

1. Install the brake (49 0221 030A) or other suitable tool to the flywheel.
2. Remove the pulley bolt and pull the pulley off the front end of the crankshaft.

CLUTCH ASSEMBLY

1. Install the brake (49 0221 030A) or other suitable tool to the flywheel.
2. Remove the bolts holding the clutch cover to the flywheel and remove the clutch cover and pressure plate assembly and clutch disc.
3. Remove the bolts attaching the flywheel to the rear end of the crankshaft.
4. Remove the brake and flywheel.

OIL PAN

1. Invert the cylinder block.
2. Remove the nuts and bolts that attach the oil pan to the cylinder block.
3. Remove the oil pan and gasket.

CHAIN COVER

1. Remove the bolts and nuts that attach the timing chain cover to the cylinder block.
2. Remove the chain cover and gaskets.
3. Remove the oil thrower from the crankshaft.

CHAIN ADJUSTER, CHAIN GUIDE STRIP & VIBRATION DAMPER

Remove the screws and bolts, and then remove the chain adjuster, chain guide strip and vibration damper.

TIMING CHAINS & SPROCKETS

1. Remove locknut and lock washer attaching oil pump sprocket.
2. Remove the crankshaft sprocket, oil pump drive chain and oil pump sprocket.
3. Remove the timing chain and crankshaft sprocket.
4. Remove the key from the crankshaft.

OIL PUMP & OIL STRAINER

1. Remove the nuts attaching the oil strainer to the oil pump and remove the oil strainer and O-ring.
2. Remove the bolts and the oil pump, O-ring and adjusting washers from the cylinder block.

PISTON & CONNECTING ROD

1. Remove the bolts from each connecting rod and remove the bearing caps.
2. Push the piston and connecting rod assembly out of the cylinder block with the handle end of a hammer until the piston rings are free from the cylinder bore. Remove the piston and connecting rod assembly from the top of the block.
3. To separate the piston and connecting rod assembly, remove the clips and the piston pin with the installer (49 0223 061). If tight, heat the piston with a piston heater.

CRANKSHAFT

1. Remove bolts that attach main bearing caps to cylinder block.
2. Remove main bearing caps and thrust washers. When removing the rear main bearing cap, use puller (49 0221 270B), **Fig. 2.**
3. Take out oil seal from crankshaft rear end.
4. Remove crankshaft from cylinder block.

INSPECTION & REPAIR

CYLINDER HEAD INSPECTION

Remove all carbon in the combustion chamber and exhaust port. Be sure that the water passages are open. Inspect the tapped openings. Repair or replace any damaged threads or broken studs.

Check for cylinder head distortion by placing a straightedge on the cylinder head surface. Measure the clearance between the straightedge and the cylinder head surface with a feeler gauge. If the distortion exceeds .006 inch (.15mm), grind with a surface grinder.

MANIFOLD INSPECTION

Check the intake and exhaust manifold for distortion. To check, place the manifold on a surface plate and check the clearance between the manifold and surface plate with a feeler gauge. If excessive distortion is found, correct it by grinding. Do not grind more than .006 inch, (0.15mm) from manifold mating surface.

VALVE SPRING INSPECTION

Examine the springs for corrosion or any damage, and replace as necessary. Measure the free length and the fitting pressure. Replace with new springs if the free length is decreased under 1.425 inch (36.2mm) on the outer spring and 1.406 (35.7mm) in on the inner spring, or if the fitting load is reduced under 26.7 lbs. (12.1 kg) on the outer spring and 17.9 lbs. (8.1 kg) on the inner spring. Refer to specifications.

VALVE INSPECTION

Remove all carbon from the valves. Visually inspect all valves for warp, cracks or excessive burning and replace if any of these conditions are found.

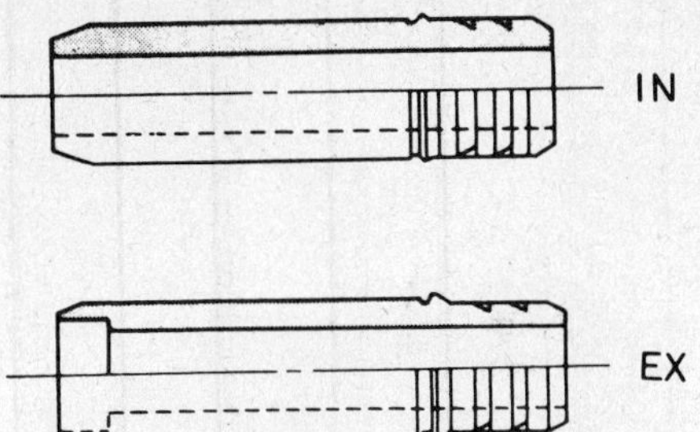

Fig. 3 Intake & exhaust valve guide identification

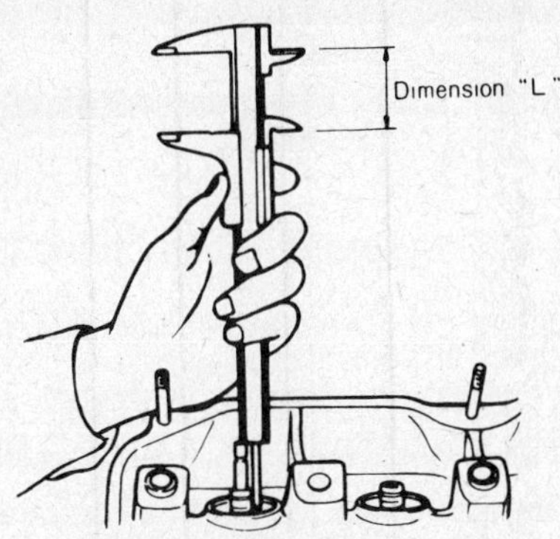

Fig. 5 Checking valve sinking

Replace any worn, pitted or corroded valves that cannot be cleaned or refaced.

Measure the diameter of the valve stem at two or three places along the length of the stem with a micrometer. Replace if the stem diameter is less than 0.3142 in. (7.980mm) on the inlet valve and 0.3140 in. (7.975mm) on the exhaust valve.

CHECKING VALVE STEM TO GUIDE CLEARANCE

The standard clearance between the valve stem and guide is, under the condition of the guide being fitted with the cylinder head, 0.0007-0.0021 in. (0.018-0.053mm) on the inlet side and 0.0007-0.0023 in. (0.018-0.058mm) on the exhaust side.

To check this clearance, place the valve in each guide. Check the clearance with a suitably mounted dial indicator, or feel the clearance by moving the stem back and forth. If the clearance is 0.008 in. (0.20mm) or more, replace the valve guide and valve.

REPLACING VALVE GUIDE

1. Press out the old guide with the puller and installer (49 0221 251A).
2. Press in new guide squarely with same tool until ring on guide touches cylinder head. **Intake and exhaust valve guides are different as shown in Fig. 3.**
3. Install the new valve seal onto the valve guide with the pusher (49 0223 160B), **Fig. 4.**

REFACING VALVE

Reface the valves with a valve refacer, following the instructions of the valve refacer manufacturer. Take off only the minimum of metal required to clean the valve faces.

If the outer edge of the valve (valve margin) becomes less than 0.039 in. (1.0mm) from excessive grinding, the valve must be replaced.

INSPECTING & REFACING VALVE SEAT

Inspect the valve seats for cracks, burrs, ridges or improper angle and width. If necessary to reface the valve seats, use a valve seat grinder or valve seat cutter and grind to a 45 degree angle. Do not grind any more than is necessary to clean up the valve seat.

If the valve guides are to be replaced, this must be done before refacing the valve seat. The valve seat is shrink fitted in the cylinder head and cannot be replaced.

CHECKING VALVE FACE & VALVE SEAT CONTACT

After the valve or valve seat is ground, check the contact between the valve and valve seat as follows:

1. Apply a thin coat of Prussian Blue on the valve face and insert the valve into the valve seat.
2. Move the valve up and down with hand pressure, rotating the valve.
3. Remove the valve and observe the transfer of Prussian Blue to the valve seat. An even transfer indicates accurate valve and valve seat refacing. If uneven, the valve must be lapped into the valve seat, using a suitable lapping compound.
4. Check the valve seat width with a scale. The valve seat width is 0.055 in. (1.4mm) on both, intake and exhaust, valve seats. If the valve seat width is too wide, it can be reduced from inside with a 30° seat cutter, and from outside with a 150° seat cutter.

CHECKING VALVE SEAT SINKING

When the valve and the valve seat have been refaced several times or they must be cut deeply for adequate reconditioning, the valve sinks below the standard position. Accordingly, the spring pressure under the fitting condition falls. Check the sinking of the valve seat by using a vernier calipers as shown in **Fig. 5.** Sinking of the intake valve seat should measure 1.61 inch (40.9mm). Sinking of the exhaust valve seat should measure 1.49 inch (37.9mm). If the sinking exceeds 0.020 in. (0.5mm), washers of sufficient thickness to compensate the sinking must be placed under the springs so as to maintain the specified spring pressure. If it is more than 0.059 in. (1.5mm), replace the valve.

INSPECTION OF ROCKER ARM & SHAFT

The standard clearance between the rocker arm bore and shaft is 0.0011-0.0032 in. (0.027-0.081mm). Measure clearance and if it is more than 0.004 in. (0.10mm), replace the rocker arm or shaft.

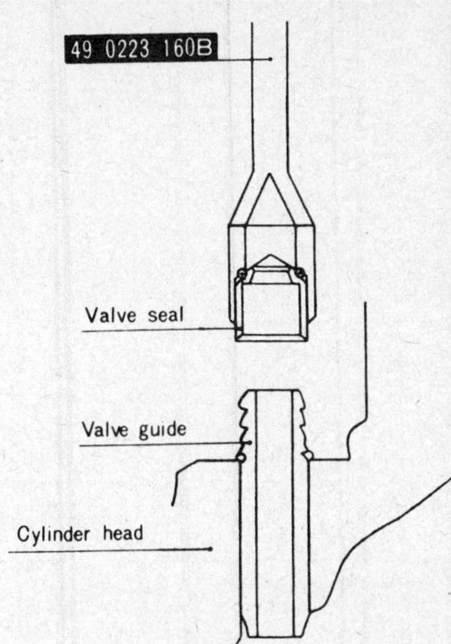

Fig. 4 Installing valve guide seal

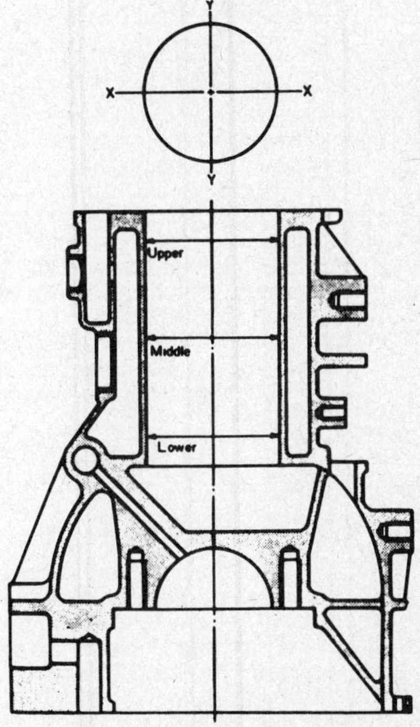

Fig. 6 Cylinder bore checking locations

CYLINDER BLOCK INSPECTION

Clean the cylinder block with a suitable solvent. Special care must be taken when cleaning the oil passages, coolant passages and cylinder bore to remove all sludge, dirt and carbon deposit. After cleaning, use compressed air to dry the block thoroughly.

Examine the cylinder block for cracks and any damage. Examine all machined surfaces of the block for burrs and scores. Check the cylinder block for distort ion in the same way, as described under "Cylinder Head Inspection."

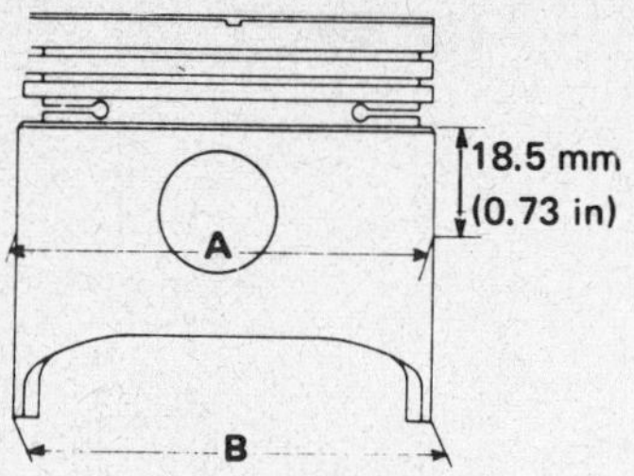

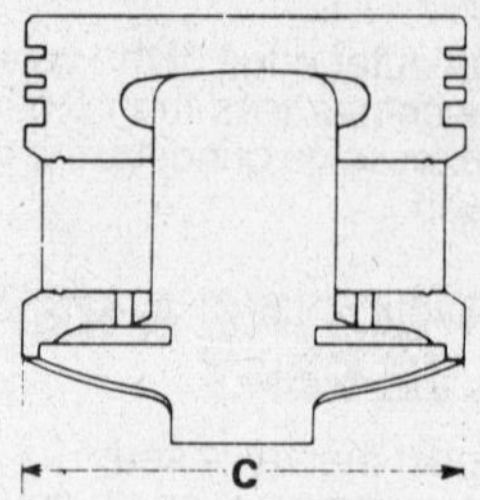

A: 79.954 ± 0.01 mm (3.1478 ± 0.0004 in)
B: 79.980 mm (3.1489 in)
C: 79.550 mm (3.1319 in)

Fig. 7 Piston dimensions

Fig. 8 Checking crankshaft runout

INSPECTING CYLINDER BORE

Check the cylinder bores for wear, scratching and distortion. Measure the diameter of the cylinder bore by using a cylinder gauge.

This measurement should be taken in the X-X direction and the Y-Y direction at each of the 3 sections, upper, middle and lower, of one cylinder, as shown in **Fig. 6.** The difference between the minimum and maximum values of the 6 measured values is the amount of wear. If the wear of cylinder bore is 0.0059 in. (0.15mm) or more, it should be honed or rebored. Honing and reboring should be made to correspond to piston and rings oversize and to the recommended piston clearance of .0014-.0030 inch (.036-.075mm).

If any one of the cylinder bores requires reboring, the remaining ones also require reboring. Reboring must not go beyond 0.040 in. (1.00mm)

The following oversize pistons and rings are available, 0.010 inch (0.025mm) or 0.020 inch (0.050mm).

PISTON INSPECTION

Carefully inspect the piston and replace if it is severely scored, scratched or burned. Measure the diameter of the piston without the piston pin fitted by means of a micrometer. The standard diameter piston is shown in **Fig. 7.** If the wear is severe, replace the piston.

PISTON CLEARANCE

Check the clearance between each piston and cylinder by measuring the diameter of the piston and cylinder. Measure the piston diameter at right angle to the piston pin and 0.67 in. (17mm) below the ring groove. The standard clearance is .0019-.0025 inch (.048-.063mm). If the clearance exceeds 0.006 in. (0.15mm), rebore the cylinders and use the oversize pistons and rings, referring to "Inspecting Cylinder Bore."

PISTON RING GROOVE INSPECTION

Remove the carbon from the piston ring grooves by using a ring groove cleaner or a broken piece of piston ring. With a feeler gauge, check the side clearance of the piston rings at several places. If it is improper, replace the piston rings. The standard clearances are as follows:

	Side Clearance
Top Ring	.0012-.0028 in. (.030-.070mm)
Second Ring	.0012-.0025 in. (.030-.064mm)

CHECKING PISTON RING END GAP

Place the piston ring in the cylinder bore below the ring travel, using a piston head to push the ring in squarely. Check the piston ring end gap with a feeler gauge. The end gap should be 0.008-0.016 in. (0.2-0.4mm) for the top and second ring, and 0.012-0.035 in. (0.3-0.9mm) for oil ring.

CHECKING PISTON PIN FIT

Check fit of piston pin and connecting rod small end bushing to be 0.0004-0.0012 in. (0.01-0.03mm). Replace if they are worn heavily.

REPLACING SMALL END BUSHING

1. Press out the old bushing with a suitable mandrel.
2. Press fit the new bushing, being sure to align the holes of the bushing and connecting rod.
3. Finish the bushing with a reamer or a pin hole grinder to the correct fit. **The fit is correct when the piston pin slides through the bushing with some pressure but without any noticeable looseness.**

CONNECTING ROD BEARING

The connecting rod bearings are aluminum-lined and of the interchangeable type.

When properly installed, the bearings provide proper clearance without filing, scraping or shimming.

Each bearing consists of two halves and should be replaced as a set. The connecting rod bearing sets are available in the standard size and undersize of 0.010, 0.020 and 0.030 in. (0.25, 0.50 and 0.75mm).

Inspect the bearing carefully and replace if it is worn, scored or flaked.

CHECKING CONNECTING ROD BEARING CLEARANCE

The connecting rod bearing clearance should be 0.0011-0.0030 in. (0.027-0.077mm). Check the bearing clearance by using a Plastigage as follows:

1. Clean the surfaces of the bearing and crankpin.
2. Place the Plastigage on the crankpin.
3. Install the bearing cap and tighten the bolts to 30-34 ft. lbs. (40-43Nm) to flatten the Plastigage to a width which indicates the bearing clearance.
4. Remove the cap and measure the width of the Plastigage, using the scale printed on the envelope.

CHECKING CONNECTING ROD SIDE PLAY

Check the connecting rod side play with a feeler gauge. The side play should be between 0.004-0.008 in. (0.11-0.21mm).

CHECKING CONNECTING ROD ALIGNMENT

Check the connecting rod for bend or twist using a suitable alignment fixture. Follow the instructions of the fixture manufacturer. If the bend or twist exceeds .0008 per 1.9685 inches (.02mm per 50mm), the connecting rod must be straightened or replaced.

CHECKING MAIN JOURNAL & CRANKPIN

Clean the crankshaft thoroughly with a suitable solvent and blow out the oil passages with compressed air. Inspect the crankshaft for cracks or scratches and the oil passages for clogs. Measure the diameter of each crankpin and main journal with a micrometer. If the wear is more than 0.0020 in. (0.05mm), the crankshaft should be ground to the undersize of 0.010, 0.020 and 0.030 in. (0.25, 0.50 and 0.75mm). Refer to specifications for standard diameters of crankpins and main journals.

Fig. 9 Checking camshaft runout

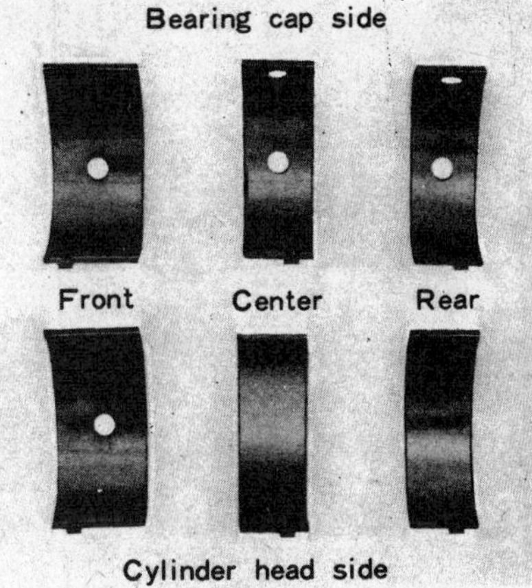

Fig. 10 Camshaft bearing identification

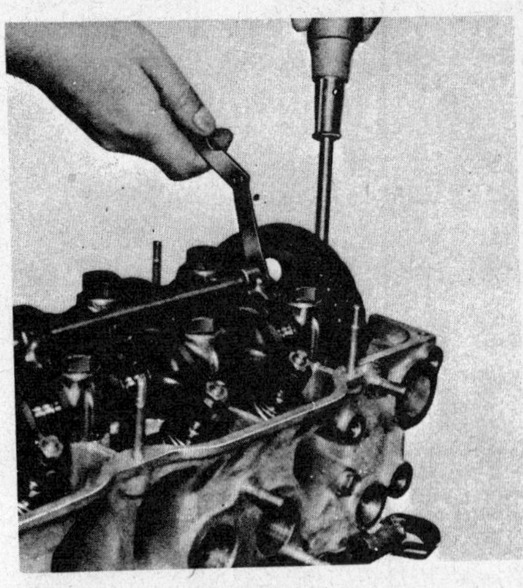

Fig. 11 Checking camshaft endplay

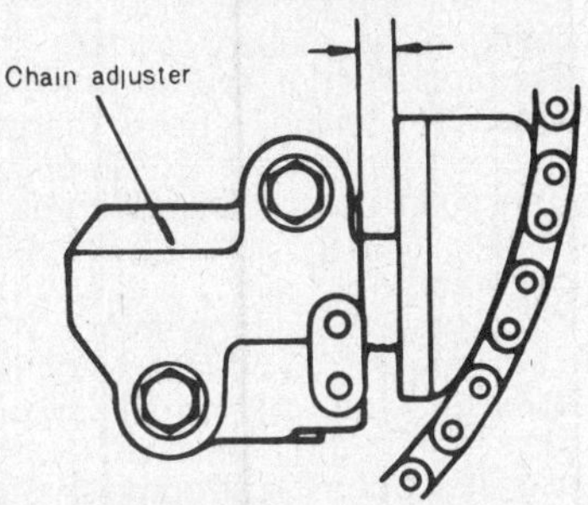

Fig. 12 Checking timing chain stretch

CHECKING CRANKSHAFT ALIGNMENT

To check alignment, mount crankshaft on V-blocks and install a dial indicator, **Fig. 8.** Slowly rotate crankshaft and note reading on dial indicator. The maximum allowable runout is 0.0012 in. (0.03mm). If necessary, correct with a press.

MAIN BEARING

The main bearings are of the aluminum-lined and interchangeable type. They are classified into 3 types according to the shape. When correctly installed, it provides proper clearance without filing, scraping or shimming. Each bearing consists of two halves and should be replaced as a set with the same type bearing as removed. The main bearings are available in the standard size and undersizes of 0.010, 0.020 and 0.030 in. (0.25, 0.50 and 0.75mm). Inspect the bearings carefully for wear, scoring, flaking or any damage. If any of these conditions exist, replace with new bearings.

CHECKING MAIN BEARING CLEARANCE

Check the main bearing clearance by using a Plastigage in the same manner as for the connecting rod bearing clearance.

Note the following differences:

1. The main bearing clearance is 0.0012-0.0020 inch (0.031-0.050mm).
2. The tightening torque for bearing cap bolts is 61-65 ft. lbs., (82-88 Nm).

CHECKING CRANKSHAFT ENDPLAY

The end thrust of the crankshaft is taken by the thrust washers at the rear of the crankshaft.

The standard endplay of the crankshaft is 0.003-0.009 in. (0.08-0.24mm).

Check the endplay with a dial indicator or a feeler gauge. Correct if the endplay exceeds 0.012 in. (0.3mm). The endplay can be adjusted by the thrust washer. Thrust washers are available in the oversizes of 0.010, 0.020 and 0.030 in. (0.25, 0.50 and 0.75mm).

CAMSHAFT INSPECTION

Check to see that the cam faces and journals are smooth and are not scored or worn.

Measure the cam height with a micrometer and replace the camshaft if it is not within the specification. Measure the diameter of the camshaft journals. When they are worn more than 0.0020 in. (0.05mm), grind the journals to the undersize of 0.010, 0.020 or 0.030 in. (0.25, 0.50 or 0.75mm).

CHECKING CAMSHAFT RUNOUT

Check the camshaft runout with a dial indicator, **Fig. 9.** The maximum permissible runout is 0.0012 inch (0.03mm). If necessary, correct the camshaft with a press.

CAMSHAFT BEARING

The camshaft bearings are the interchangeable type. They are classified into 3 types, **Fig. 10.** When correctly installed, it provides proper clearance without filing, scraping or shimming.

Each bearing consists of two halves and should be replaced as a set with the same type bearing as removed. The camshaft bearings are available in the standard size and undersizes of 0.010, 0.020 and 0.030 in. (0.25, 0.50 and 0.75mm). Inspect the bearings carefully for wear, scoring, flaking or any damage. If any of these conditions exist, replace with new bearings.

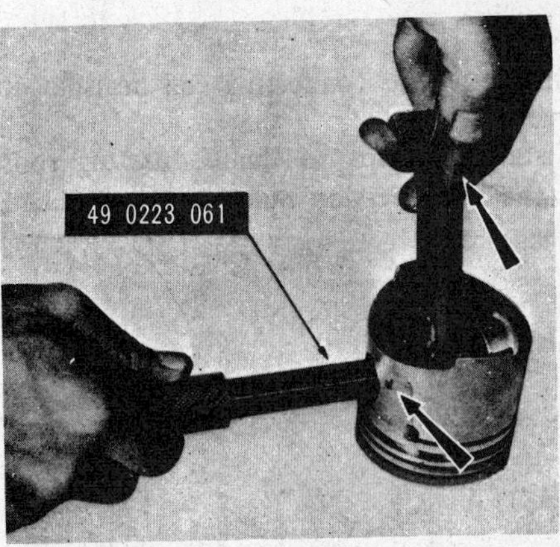

Fig. 13 Piston and connecting rod assembly

CHECKING CAMSHAFT BEARING CLEARANCE

Check the camshaft bearing clearance by using a Plastigage in the same manner as the connecting rod bearing clearance. Refer to specifications.

CHECKING CAMSHAFT ENDPLAY

The end play of the camshaft is determined by the clearance between the sprocket surface and the thrust plate surface. Measure this clearance with a feeler gauge, **Fig. 11.** This clearance should be 0.001-0.007 inch (0.02-0.18mm). If the endplay is excessive, replace with a new thrust plate.

CHECKING TIMING CHAIN FOR STRETCH

Before disassembly, check timing chain stretch. To check stretch, readjust chain tension and check protrusion amount of slipper head, **Fig. 12.** If it exceeds .67 inch (17mm), replace the timing chain.

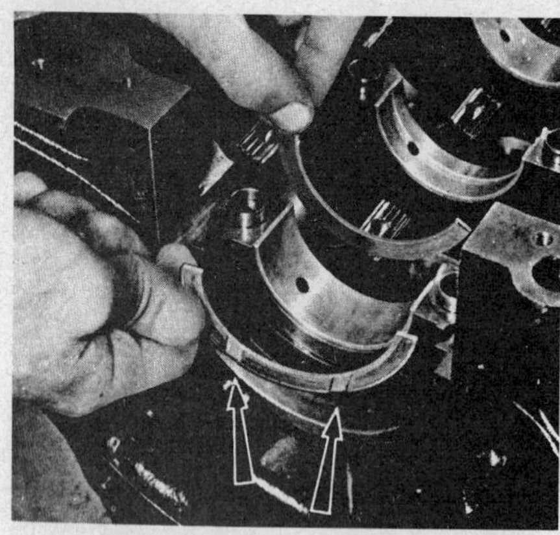

Fig. 14 Install thrust washer into engine block

Fig. 15 Install rear oil seal

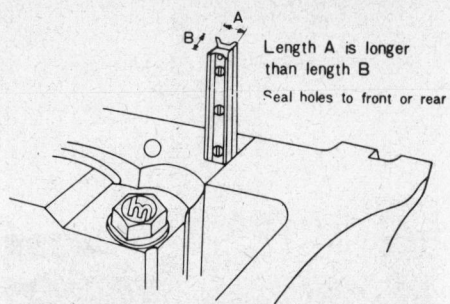

CHECKING TIMING CHAIN, OIL PUMP DRIVE CHAIN & SPROCKETS

Check each chain for broken links. Check the sprockets for cracks and worn or damaged teeth. If any defects are found, replace with new parts.

CHECKING CHAIN ADJUSTER

Check the slipper head on the chain adjuster for wear or damage and the adjuster spring for loss of tension. If they are defective, replace with a new adjuster assembly.

CHECKING CHAIN GUIDE STRIP & VIBRATION DAMPER

Check the chain strip and chain vibration damper for wear or any damage and replace if they are defective.

ENGINE ASSEMBLY

PISTON & CONNECTING ROD

1. Install the piston pin clip in the groove on one side of the piston.
2. Place the connecting rod in the piston and align the hole of the connecting rod with the hole of the piston.
3. Insert the piston pin with the installer (49 0223 061) until the piston pin clip can be fitted. Preheat the piston if tight.
4. Fit the piston pin clip in the groove. **Care must be taken during the installation that relative positions of the oil hole on the connecting rod big end and the F mark on the piston are in accordance with Fig. 13.**

PISTON RING

1. Fit the expander in the bottom ring groove and install the oil ring on it with a suitable installer.
2. Install the second ring, then the top ring. **Be sure to install the rings with the inscription mark upward as the faces of the top and second rings are tapered. Do not expand the rings more than necessary to install. Also be careful not to burr the piston with the end of the rings.**

PISTON & CONNECTING ROD ASSEMBLY

1. Place the piston rings at about 120° apart so that the gap is not located on the thrust side and the piston pin side.
2. Lubricate the entire assembly with engine oil.
3. Using a suitable piston installer, insert the piston and connecting rod assembly from the top of the cylinder block by tapping the piston lightly with a plastic hammer. **Insert the piston to the cylinder so that F mark on the piston is directed to the front of the engine.**
4. Invert cylinder block.
5. Fit connecting rod bearing halves into their respective locations.

CRANKSHAFT

1. Clean contact surfaces of cylinder block, main bearings and crankshaft.
2. Fit the five sets of main bearings properly to cylinder block and bearing caps respectively.
3. Fit the half of the thrust washers to the cylinder block with oil grooved surface facing crankshaft thrust side, **Fig. 14.**
4. Lubricate main bearing surfaces with engine oil.
5. Place crankshaft in cylinder block, being careful not to drop thrust washers.
6. Fit oil seal to rear end of crankshaft after applying grease to seal lip, **Fig. 15.**
7. Insert the rod-shaped oil seals (side seals) into grooves on both sides of rear main bearing cap. **The side seals should be installed as shown in Fig. 16.**
8. Fit the half of the thrust washers to the rear main bearing cap with grooves toward crankshaft thrust side.
9. Install main bearing caps. **The main bearing caps are marked with a number which shows the order of their arrangement.**
10. Tighten bolts to 61-65 ft. lbs. (8.4-9.0m-kg).

Fig. 16 Installing side seal

TIMING CHAIN, OIL PUMP DRIVE CHAIN & SPROCKETS

1. Place timing chain on crankshaft sprocket and camshaft sprocket with timing marks aligned, **Fig. 17.**
2. Being careful not to change the relations of timing chain, camshaft sprocket and crankshaft sprocket, fit crankshaft sprocket onto crankshaft so as to flush the sprocket with end of crankshaft.
3. Install key on oil pump shaft.
4. Fit oil pump drive chain onto oil pump sprocket and crankshaft sprocket, then slide in the crankshaft sprocket, aligning key on the oil pump shaft with keyway of pump sprocket.
5. Check slack of drive chain by pressing a finger as shown in **Fig. 18.** If slack exceeds 0.157 in. (4.0mm), install adjusting shims between cylinder block, **Fig. 19,** and oil pump body and adjust slack to be within 0.157 in. (4.0mm). The thickness of the adjusting shims is 0.006 in. (0.15mm).
6. Tighten nut for oil pump sprocket to 22-25 ft. lbs. (3.0-3.5m-kg) and bend tab of lockwasher.
7. Align keyways of crankshaft and sprocket and install the key.

CONNECTING ROD BEARING CAP

1. Fit connecting rod bearing halves into their respective caps.
2. Lubricate connecting rod bearing surfaces with engine oil.
3. Install caps to the connecting rods, ensuring identification numbers are matched, **Fig. 20.**
4. Torque bolts 36-40 ft. lbs. (5.0-5.5 m-kg).
5. Turn crankshaft and ensure rotation is light and smooth.

OIL PUMP & STRAINER

1. Fit O-ring to outlet hole on oil pump and install oil pump to cylinder block, aligning dowel pins, **Fig. 21.**
2. Tighten attaching bolts.
3. Place O-ring on oil pump and install oil strainer to the oil pump. Tighten the nuts.

CHAIN GUIDE STRIP & VIBRATION DAMPER

1. With adjuster spring compressed fully, install chain adjuster guide (49 0660

Fig. 17 Installing timing chain, oil pump drive chain and sprockets

Fig. 18 Checking oil pump drive chain stretch

Fig. 19 Installing oil pump drive chain adjusting shims

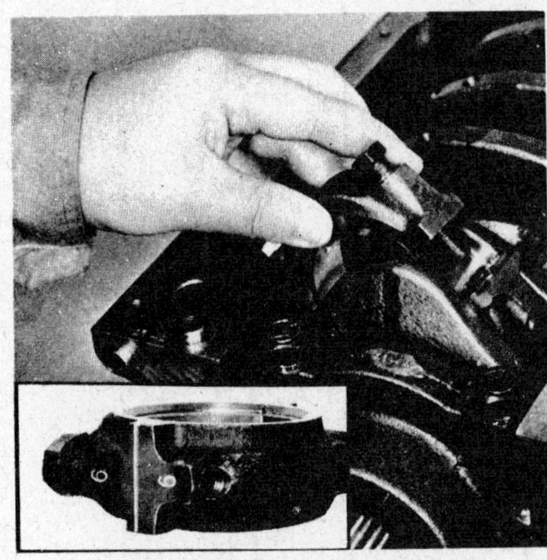

Fig. 20 Installing connecting rod cap. Note identification numbers must be on same side

Fig. 21 Installing O-ring

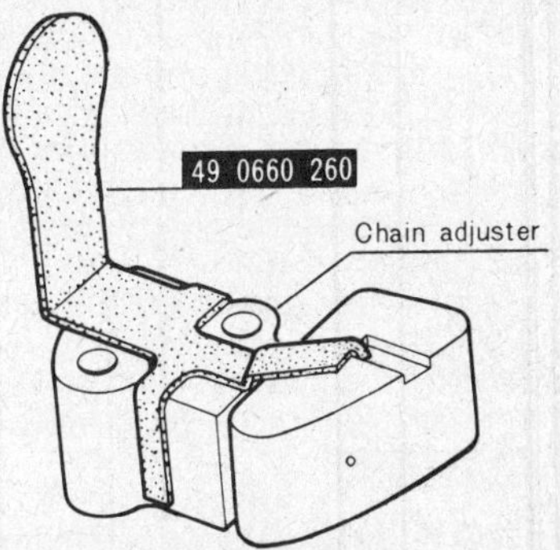

Fig. 22 Installing chain adjuster guide

260) to adjuster, **Fig. 22.**

2. Do not remove tool until chain adjustment is finished.
3. Install and tighten attaching bolts, while holding tool in place. Do not remove plate until timing chain is adjusted.
4. Install chain vibration damper to cylinder block and tighten attaching screws.
5. Install chain guide strip. Do not tighten attaching screws as tension is adjusted by the strip, which is explained under "Adjusting Timing Chain."

TIMING CHAIN COVER

1. Fit oil thrower to crankshaft with edge turned outward.
2. Fit oil deflector and oil seal into timing chain cover, then fill oil seal lip with grease.
3. Place gaskets on cylinder block and install chain cover, aligning dowel pins. Tighten the bolts.
4. Cut off excess gaskets along mounting surfaces of oil pan and cylinder head.

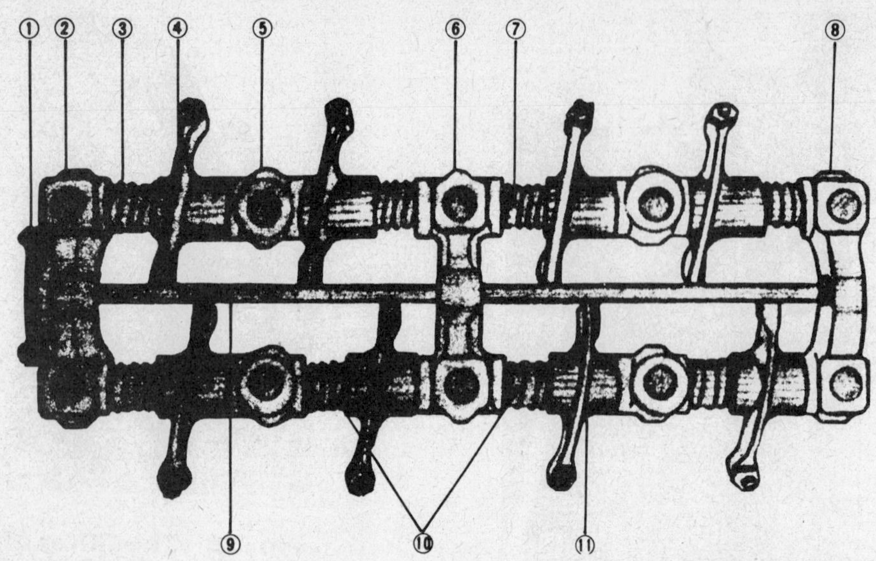

Fig. 23 Rocker arms & shaft assemblies

OIL PAN, FLYWHEEL & CLUTCH

1. Before installing oil pan, make a final internal inspection.
2. Apply a thin coat of gasket paste onto oil pan.
3. Place a new gasket on cylinder block.
4. Install oil pan and tighten bolts and nuts little by little in turn.
5. Install flywheel and clutch.

CRANKSHAFT PULLEY

1. Lock flywheel with brake (49 0221 030A) or other suitable tool.
2. Install crankshaft pulley to crankshaft so that key groove of pulley aligns with key on crankshaft.
3. Tighten pulley bolt to 101-108 ft. lbs. (14.0-15.0 m-kg).

CYLINDER HEAD

1. Hold the camshaft sprocket and chain securely and invert the cylinder block.
2. Place the sprocket and the chain on the top of the chain guide strip and the vibration damper. **Ensure that alignment marks of the camshaft sprocket and the chain are aligned properly.**
3. Place a new gasket on the cylinder block.
4. Position the cylinder head on the cylinder block, aligning the dowels.

CAMSHAFT

1. Fit the three sets of the camshaft bearings properly to the cylinder head and the bearing caps respectively.
2. Lubricate the bearing surfaces with engine oil.
3. Install the camshaft to the sprocket, aligning the key and fit the camshaft journals onto the respective bearings.

ASSEMBLING ROCKER ARMS

Assemble the rocker arms in the formation shown in **Fig. 23.** Care must be taken on the following points:

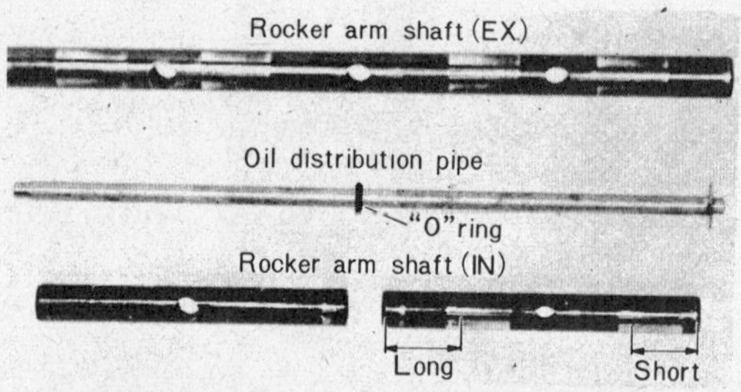

Fig. 24 Rocker arm shafts

1. The rocker arm shaft supporters are interchangeable for intake and the exhaust valves, however, the intake and exhaust rocker arms are not interchangeable.
2. The rocker arm shafts for the intake and the exhaust valves are not interchangeable. Two shafts are installed on the intake side and one on the exhaust side. The two shafts for the intake side are interchangeable.
3. When installing rocker arm shafts on intake side, ends with longer distance between oil hole and tip are turned toward inside each other, as shown in **Fig. 24.**
4. The center bearing cap is installed with the oil hole facing the intake side.
5. The oil pipe is installed with the oil ejection hole facing the camshaft. In order to avoid vibration of the pipe after it has been installed, the O-ring on the pipe is pressed into the hole for the pipe on the center bearing cap.

INSTALLING ROCKER ARM ASSEMBLY

1. Position rocker arm assembly on the cylinder head, with dowels properly aligned.
2. Tighten the cylinder head bolts temporarily.
3. Move the rocker arm supporters and offset each of the rocker arms 0.04 in. (1mm) from the valve stem center as shown in **Fig. 25.**
4. Tighten the cylinder head bolts evenly to 56-60 ft. lbs. (7.7-8.3m-kg) in the sequence shown in **Fig. 1.**
5. Lock the flywheel with the brake (49 0221 030A) and tighten the camshaft sprocket lock nut to 51-58 ft. lbs. (7.0-8.0 m-kg) with the spanner (49 0164 631A). Bend the tab of the lock washer.
6. Aligning the key groove with the pin, install the distributor drive gear to the camshaft. Tighten the lock nut to 51-58 ft. lbs. (7.0-8.0 m-kg) and bend the tab of the lock washer.

ADJUSTING TIMING CHAIN

1. Slightly rotate the crankshaft in normal direction of rotation.
2. Press the top of the chain guide strip with a lever through the hole of the chain cover and tighten the guide strip attaching screws with a screwdriver inserted through two holes on the timing chain cover, **Fig. 26.**
3. Remove the guide which was installed to the chain adjuster. The timing chain now has the proper tension and no further manual adjustment is required.
4. Install the blind plugs and aluminum washers to the two holes on the timing chain cover.
5. Install the blind cover and gasket for the chain adjuster to the chain cover and tighten the nuts.

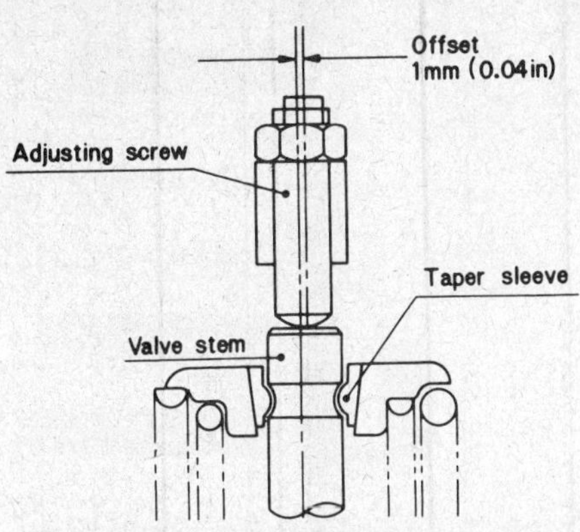

Fig. 25 Rocker arm offset

MANIFOLD & CARBURETOR ASSEMBLY

1. Place the gasket on the cylinder head and install intake manifold and carburetor assembly.
2. Tighten the attaching nuts.
3. Connect the vacuum tube to the carburetor.
4. Connect the water hose to intake manifold.
5. Connect the water bypass hose to the thermostat case.
6. Connect the ventilation hose to the ventilation valve at intake manifold.

ROCKER ARM COVER

1. Apply rubber sealer to the semicircular oil seals and fit them, with the "OUT" mark facing outward, to the front and rear of the cylinder head.
2. Place the gasket on the cylinder head.
3. Install the rocker arm cover and tighten the attaching nut to 0.15-0.2 m-kg (1.1-1.4 ft. lbs.).

FINAL ASSEMBLY

1. Install thermostat.
2. Install water pump.
3. Install fan and pulley.
4. Install oil filter.
5. Install air pump.
6. Install alternator.
7. Install distributor.

ADJUSTING VALVE CLEARANCE

Prior to adjusting valve clearances, ensure flat surface on rocker arm ball is facing downward.

1. Loosen lock nut and insert specified feeler gauge between rocker arm and valve stem, or between rocker arm and cam. Refer to "Valve Specifications" for proper clearances.

Fig. 26 Adjusting timing chain tension

2. Turn adjusting screw until specified clearance is obtained, then tighten lock nut and recheck clearance. **Whenever engine is overhauled, warm up engine and readjust valve clearance after torquing cylinder head bolts to specifications.**

4-122/1998cc & 4-133/2184cc GASOLINE ENGINE SECTION

INDEX

ENGINE REPLACE

626

1. Disconnect battery ground cable.
2. Scribe hood hinge locations and remove hood.
3. Remove air cleaner, then disconnect fuel lines and fuel pump, as required.
4. Disconnect accelerator cable, then the speedometer cable from transaxle.
5. On models equipped with manual transaxle, disconnect clutch cable or clutch release cylinder, as required.
6. On models equipped with automatic transaxle, disconnect transaxle control cable.
7. On all models, disconnect engine ground wire.
8. Disconnect power brake unit vacuum hose, then remove 3-way valve vacuum switch and bracket.
9. Disconnect heater hoses from engine, then remove duty solenoid valve and vacuum sensor, as required.
10. Disconnect all electrical connectors from engine and transaxle necessary for engine removal.
11. Disconnect carbon canister air vent hose and vacuum hoses.
12. Remove electric fan and radiator, then the windshield washer fluid tank.
13. On models equipped with air conditioning, remove washer fluid sub-tank, then the alternator. Unfasten air conditioning compressor and position aside.
14. On all models, raise and support front of vehicle.
15. Remove front wheels and splash

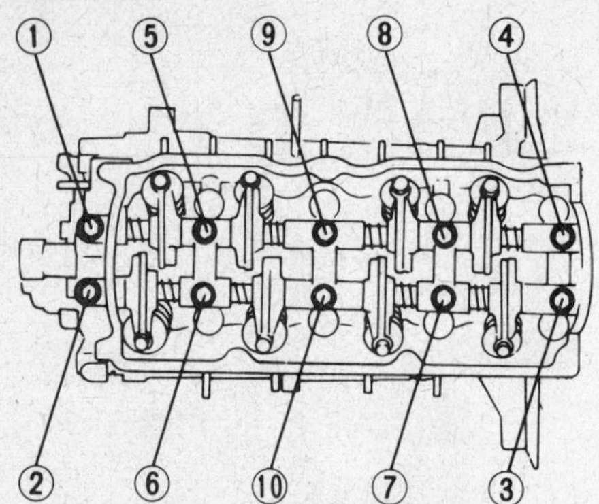

Fig. 1 Rocker shaft bolt loosening sequence

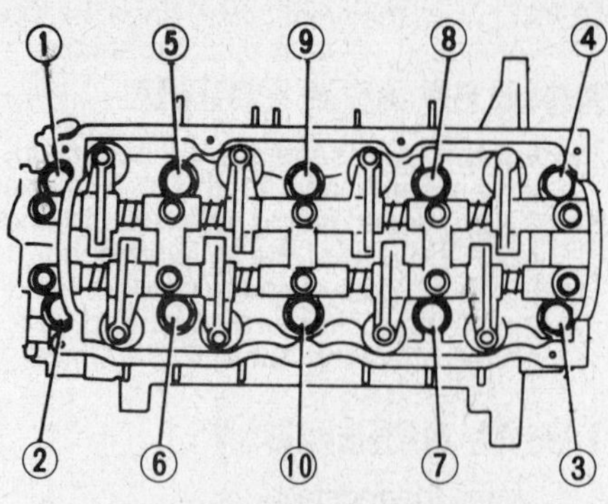

Fig. 2 Cylinder head bolt loosening sequence

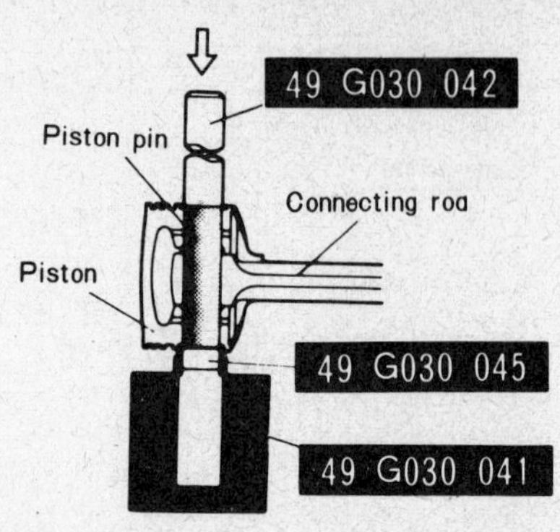

Fig. 3 Piston pin removal

shields.

16. On models equipped with power steering, unfasten steering pump and position aside.
17. On all models, disconnect driveshafts from transaxle.
18. On models equipped with manual transaxle, disconnect shift rod and extension bar.
19. On all models, disconnect exhaust manifold from head joint.
20. Remove torque stopper rubber cap and attaching bolts from right wheelhouse. Remove remaining attaching bolts from engine compartment and lift torque stoppers out of vehicle.
21. Support engine and transaxle with a suitable jack and remove engine and transaxle mounting nuts.
22. Attach suitable lifting equipment to engine, then carefully lift engine and transaxle assembly from vehicle.
23. Reverse procedure to install.

1986 B2000 & 1987 B2200

1. Disconnect battery ground cable.
2. Drain engine oil and coolant.
3. Remove air cleaner assembly and oil level gauge.
4. Remove cooling fan and radiator cowling.
5. Disconnect accelerator cable, then the cruise control cable, if equipped.
6. Disconnect and cap fuel hose.
7. Disconnect heater and brake vacuum hoses.
8. Remove three-way solenoid valves and vacuum sensor assembly. Do not disconnect vacuum lines.
9. Remove duty solenoid valve assembly. Do not disconnect vacuum lines.
10. Remove vacuum switch. Do not disconnect vacuum lines.
11. Disconnect and cap carbon canister lines.
12. Disconnect engine harness coupler and engine ground.
13. Disconnect upper and lower radiator hoses.
14. Remove radiator assembly.
15. Remove secondary air pipe assembly.
16. Disconnect exhaust pipe from exhaust manifold.
17. Remove A/C compressor and position aside, if equipped.
18. Remove power steering pump, if equipped.
19. Remove starter motor, gusset plates and rear under cover.
20. Position a suitable jack under transmission assembly, then remove engine to transmission attaching bolts.
21. Remove engine mount nuts, then the engine from vehicle.
22. Reverse procedure to install.

ENGINE DISASSEMBLY

1. Remove torque stopper housing, then the engine mounts.
2. Remove alternator with mounting bracket, then the A/C compressor, power steering pump and cooling fan bracket, as required.
3. Remove lower inlet pipe assembly with water hose.
4. Remove engine oil dipstick, then the secondary air pipes, if equipped.
5. Remove ignition wires, spark plugs and distributor.
6. Remove thermostat and coolant outlet.
7. On 626 models, remove insulator assembly, then the front catalytic converter and exhaust pipe.
8. On all models, remove exhaust manifold, oxygen sensor and turbocharger, as required.
9. Remove coolant bypass hose, then the intake manifold assembly.
10. Remove oil filter, oil pressure switch and knock sensor, if equipped.
11. Install ring gear brake (49 E301 060) to flywheel, then remove crankshaft pulley.
12. Remove upper and lower timing belt covers.
13. Loosen timing belt tensioner lock bolt, then remove tensioner spring, tensioner and timing belt.
14. Remove idler pulley, if equipped, then the camshaft pulley while preventing it from turning with a suitable tool.
15. Remove front housing assembly, then the water pump and timing belt pulley.
16. Remove valve cover, then the rear housing assembly and fuel pump, as required.
17. Remove rocker shaft assembly. Loosen attaching bolts in several steps in sequence, **Fig. 1.**
18. Remove camshaft, then the cylinder head assembly. Loosen cylinder head attaching bolts in several steps in sequence, **Fig. 2.**
19. Remove valve retainers, then the upper valve seats and valve springs.
20. Remove valves, then the lower valve spring seats.
21. Remove valve guides and clips, then the cylinder head gasket.
22. On models equipped with manual transaxle, remove clutch cover assembly, clutch and flywheel.
23. On models equipped with automatic transaxle, remove backing plate, drive plate assembly and adapter. **Use ring gear brake (49 E301 060) to remove clutch cover assembly and flywheel or drive plate.**
24. On all models, remove end plate, then the No. 3 engine bracket from front of engine, if equipped.
25. Remove oil pan, oil strainer and oil pump.
26. Remove rear cover assembly.
27. Remove connecting rod bearing caps and bearings.
28. Push piston and connecting rod assemblies out of cylinder block. Remove piston pins from pistons, **Fig. 3.**
29. Remove piston rings using a suitable ring expander.
30. Remove main bearing caps, then the crankshaft and pilot bearing.
31. Remove pilot bearing from crankshaft using needle bearing puller (49 1285 071).
32. Remove upper and lower main bearings.

INSPECTION & REPAIR

Thoroughly clean and dry all engine components prior to inspection.

CYLINDER HEAD INSPECTION

Replace cylinder head if any wear or damage is evident. Measure cylinder head distortion using suitable tools If distortion exceeds .006 inch (.15mm), grind the mating surface. Do not grind off more than .008 inch (.20mm) from cylinder head.

VALVE INSPECTION

Inspect valve stem for wear or damage and replace as necessary. Check valve face for damage or roughness. Minor dam-

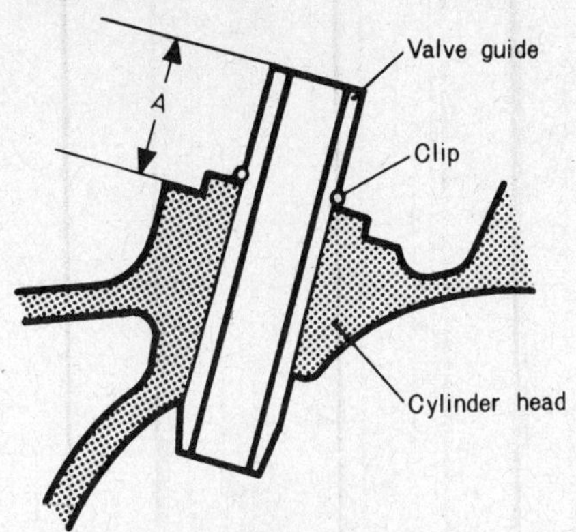

Fig. 4 Valve guide installation

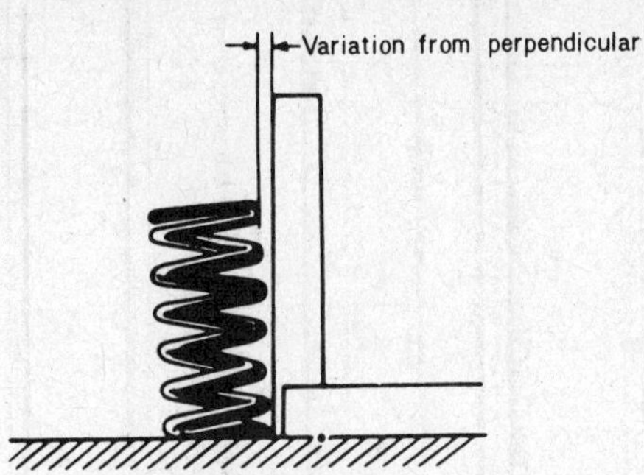

Fig. 5 Valve spring angle limit

Fig. 6 Valve seat height measurement

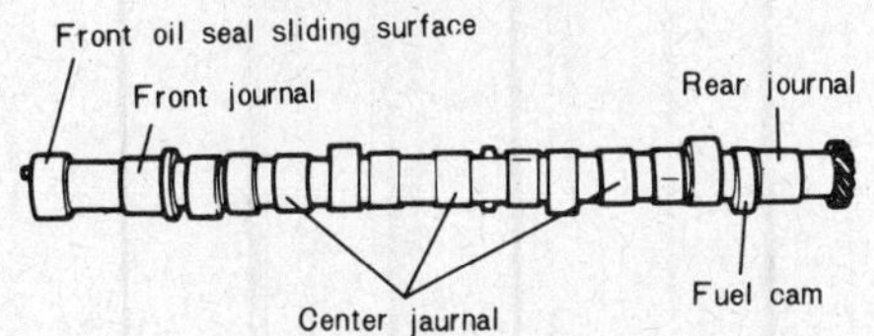

Fig. 7 Camshaft inspection

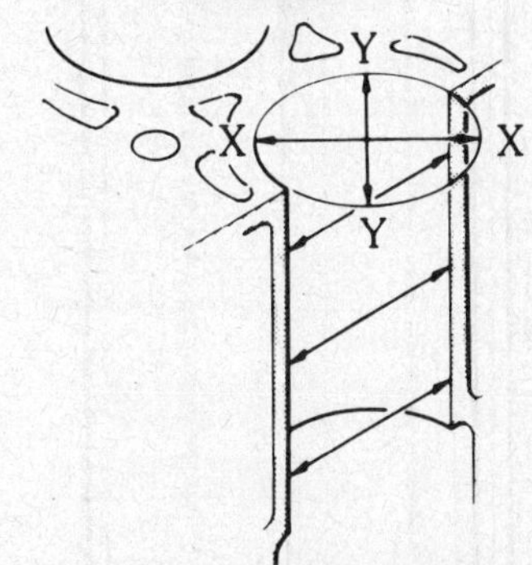

Fig. 8 Cylinder bore measurement

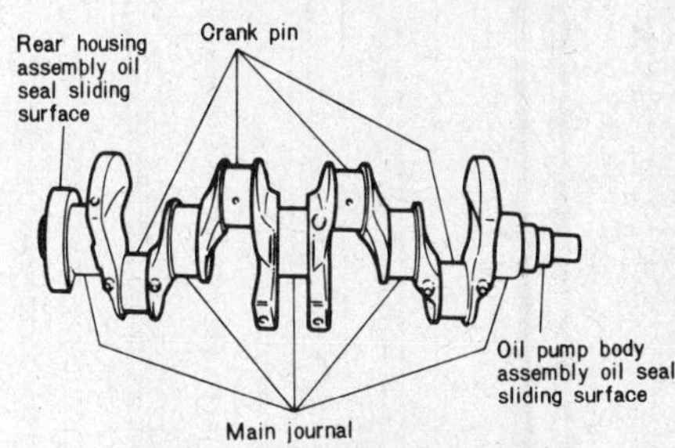

Fig. 9 Crankshaft inspection

age can be corrected by refacing the valve. Measure valve head thickness and stem diameter. If valve head thickness exceeds .020 inch (.5mm) on intake valve, or .039 inch (1mm) on exhaust valve, replace valve. On 1983-86 626, if valve stem diameter is less than .3142 inch (7.980mm) on intake valve or .3140 inch (7.975mm) on exhaust valve, replace valve. On 1986 B2000, 1987 626 or 1987 B2200, if valve stem diameter is less than .3161 inch (8.030mm) on intake valve or .3159 inch (8.025mm) on exhaust valve, replace valve.

VALVE GUIDE INSPECTION

Measure clearance between valve stem and guide. If clearance exceeds .008 inch (.2mm), replace valve guide. To replace valve guide, use tool No. 49 0221 251A and knock guide out from side opposite combustion chamber. Install clip onto new guide, then drive guide into cylinder head using removal tool. The clip must just contact cylinder head, .752-.772 inch (19.1-19.6mm) from end of valve guide, **Fig. 4.**

VALVE SPRING INSPECTION

Inspect valve springs for cracks or other damage and replace as necessary. Measure free length of springs. Free length of outer spring should measure 1.984 inch (50.4mm) for 1983-85 626 & 1987 B2200, 2.047 inch (52mm) for 1986 B2000 or 2 inch (50.8mm) for 1986-87 626 and inner spring 1.744 inch (44.3mm) for 1983-85 626, 1.732 inch (44mm) for 1986 B2000 or 1.681 inch (42.7mm) for 1986-87 626 and 1987 B2200. Replace springs not meeting specifications. Measure angle limit of springs, **Fig. 5.** If spring varies more than .07 inch (1.8mm) for 1983-86 626 and 1986 B2000, .06 inch (1.5mm) for 1987 626 and B2200 inner spring or .07 inch (1.8mm) for 1987 626 and B2200 outer spring, it must be replaced.

VALVE SEAT INSPECTION

If the valve seat surface which is in contact with the valve face is damaged, it may be repaired by grinding. Ensure valve seat surface which contacts valve is centered in valve face. Measure valve seat height, **Fig. 6,** which should be 1.831 inch (46.5mm). On all 1983-86 models, if height is .0196-.0590 inch (.5-1.5mm) less than specification, insert a washer onto spring seat. On all 1983-86 models, if height is more than .0590 inch (1.5mm) less than specification, replace cylinder head. On 1987 models, if height is 1.850-1.890 inch (47-48mm), insert a washer onto spring seat area. On 1987 models, if height is more than 1.890 inch (48mm), replace cylinder head.

Install valve seat using tool No. 49 G030 160.

CAMSHAFT INSPECTION

Check camshaft for wear or damage and replace as necessary. Measure cam height and journal diameter and replace the camshaft if not within specifications. Measure front oil seal sliding surface and fuel cam, **Fig. 7.** Oil seal sliding surface should measure 1.337-1.338 inch (33.961-34.000mm) and fuel cam should measure no less than 1.4645 inch (37.2mm). If measurements are not within specifications, replace camshaft. Ensure camshaft runout does no exceed .0012 inch (.03mm) and camshaft endplay is not more than .008 inch (.20mm).

ROCKER ARM & ROCKER ARM SHAFT INSPECTION

Replace rocker arm or cam if mating surfaces are worn or damaged. Measure clearance between rocker arm and shaft. If clearance exceeds .004 inch (.10mm), replace rocker arm shaft assembly.

CYLINDER BLOCK INSPECTION

Check block for cracks or other damage and replace if necessary. Measure cylinder block distortion. If distortion exceeds .006 inch (.15mm), grind the mating surface.

Inspect cylinder walls for scoring or indications of seizure and rebore or replace as necessary. Uneven wear on upper portion of cylinder wall may be repaired with a ridge reamer. Measure cylinder bore in six places indicated in **Fig. 8.** Standard bore diameter is 3.3859-3.3865 inches (86.000-86.019mm). Bore must not be worn more than .0059 inch (.150mm) and difference between bores must not exceed .0007 inch (.019mm). If necessary, rebore cylinder and install .010 inch (.25mm) or .020 inch (.50mm) oversize piston.

PISTON & PISTON RING INSPECTION

Check outer circumference of piston for scoring or indications of seizure and replace if necessary. Measure piston diameter at right angle to piston pin and below oil ring groove. Standard piston diameter is 3.3837-3.3845 inches (85.944-85.964mm). Ensure clearance between piston and cylinder wall does not exceed .006 inch (.15mm).

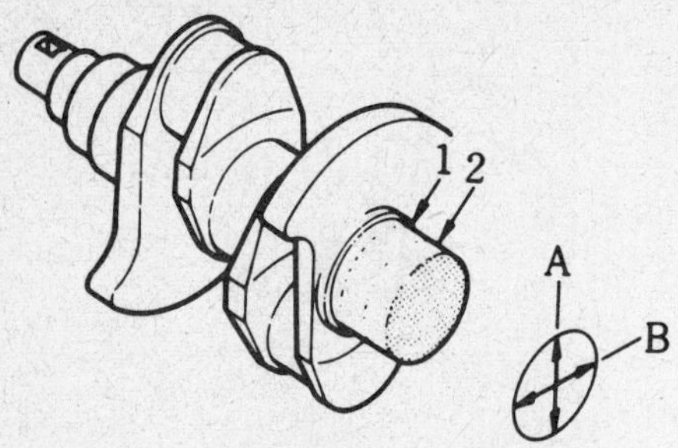

Fig. 10 Checking locations for crankshaft wear

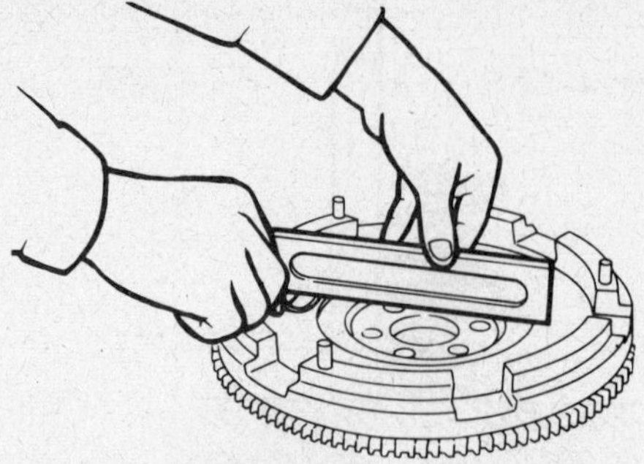

Fig. 11 Flywheel distortion check

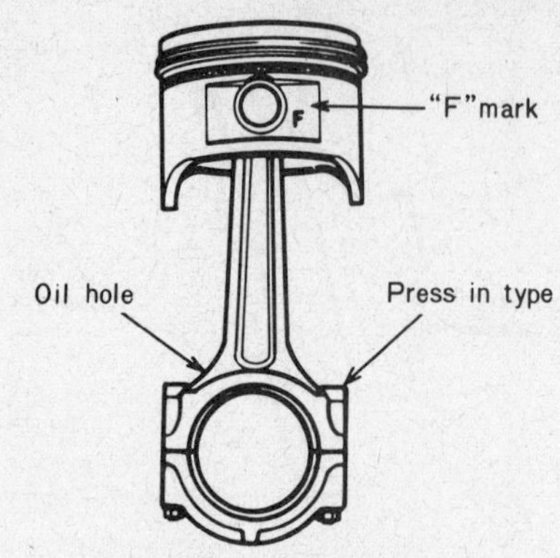

Fig. 12 Piston & connection rod assembly

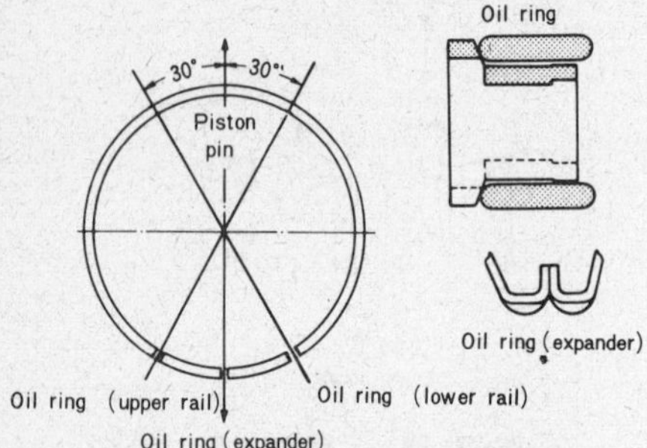

Fig. 13 Oil ring installation

Replace worn, damaged or broken piston rings. Slide ring into cylinder head and ensure ring gap does not exceed .039 inch (1mm). Measure ring clearance in piston around entire circumference of ring groove. Maximum ring clearance is .006 inch (.15mm).

CONNECTING ROD INSPECTION

Check connecting rod for bending or twisting. Maximum allowable twist is .016 inch (.04mm) per 3.94 inches (100mm).

CRANKSHAFT INSPECTION

Check crankshaft for wear, damage or clogged oil passages. Replace crankshaft if runout exceeds .0012 inch (.03mm). Compare crankshaft measurement, **Fig. 9**, to the following specifications: main journal diameter, 2.3597-2.3605 inches (59.937-59.955mm); crank pin diameter, 2.0055-2.0061 inches (50.940-50.955mm); rear housing assembly oil seal sliding surface, 3.5412-3.5434 inches (89.946-90.000mm); oil pump body assembly oil seal sliding surface, 1.3371-1.3386 inch (33.961-34.000mm). Measure uneven wear on journal and pin at four indicated positions, **Fig. 10.** Wear should not exceed .002 inch (.05mm). If wear exceeds limits, the crankshaft may be ground to a maximum of .0295 inch (.75mm) and an undersize bearing installed. Undersize bearings are available in the following sizes: .010 inch (.25mm), .020 inch (.50mm) and .030 inch (.75mm).

FLYWHEEL INSPECTION

Check flywheel for wear or damage and replace if necessary. Measure flywheel warp using a suitable straightedge, **Fig. 11.** Warp must not exceed .008 inch (.20mm). Inspect ring gear teeth for wear or damage and replace if necessary. To remove ring gear, heat gear with torch and tap off flywheel. Prior to installing new ring gear, heat gear to 480-570°F (250-300°C). Ensure beveled side of ring gear faces engine.

ENGINE ASSEMBLY

PISTON & CONNECTING ROD

1. Align oil hole in large end of connecting rod opposite the F mark on piston, **Fig. 12.**
2. Press piston pin into piston using tools 49G030042, 49G030043 and 49G030041 or equivalents. **Insert the piston pin from the direction of the F mark on the piston. The piston pin should be pressed in, until lower portion of guide (tool 49G030043) meets bottom of block (tool 49G030041). Do not exceed 3300 lbs. when pressing pin into piston. If a force greater than 3300 lbs. is required, replace piston pin or connecting rod. After pressing pin into piston, hold piston head and raise crankshaft end of connecting rod until rod contacts piston. With connecting rod contacting piston, release crankshaft end of connecting rod. If connecting rod does not drop by its own weight, replace piston and connecting rod assembly. Repeat this procedure for all piston and connecting rod assemblies.**
3. Install oil ring spacer, then the upper and lower side rails onto piston, **Fig. 13.**
4. Install compression rings (lower ring first), ensuring R marks face upward. Position rings as shown in **Fig. 14.**
5. Apply clean engine oil to piston, rings and cylinder walls, then install piston and connecting rod assemblies into cylinder block. **The F mark on piston must face front of engine.**

CRANKSHAFT

1. Install main bearings into cylinder block and bearing caps. **The shape of center main bearing on cylinder block side is different from that of the other main bearings.**
2. Measure oil clearance between crankshaft journal and main bearing using Plastigage as follows:
   a. Clean bearing and crankshaft journal.
   b. Position Plastigage on top of journal in axial direction of journal.
   c. Install main bearing cap and torque bolts to specifications.
   d. Remove cap and measure oil clearance.
   e. Clearance should measure .0012-.0019 inch (.031-.049mm) and must not exceed .0031 inch (.08mm).
   f. If clearance is not within specifications, grind crankshaft and install suitable undersize bearings. Bearings are available in undersizes of .010 inch (.25mm), .020 inch (.50mm) and .030 inch (.75mm).
3. Apply clean engine oil to bearings and journals, then install crankshaft and main bearing caps. Torque cap bolts to specifications.
4. Measure crankshaft endplay. Endplay should be .0012-.0051 inch (.03-.13mm) for 1983-85 626 and 1986 B2000 or .0031-.0071 inch (.08-.18mm) on 1986-87 626 and 1987 B2200 and must not exceed .012 inch (.30mm) on all models. If endplay is greater than specifications, install correct undersize bearing needed to bring endplay within allowable limits. **Thrust bearings are available in undersizes of .010 inch (.25mm), .020 inch (.50mm) and .030 inch (.75mm).**
5. On models equipped with manual transaxle, install pilot bearing as follows:

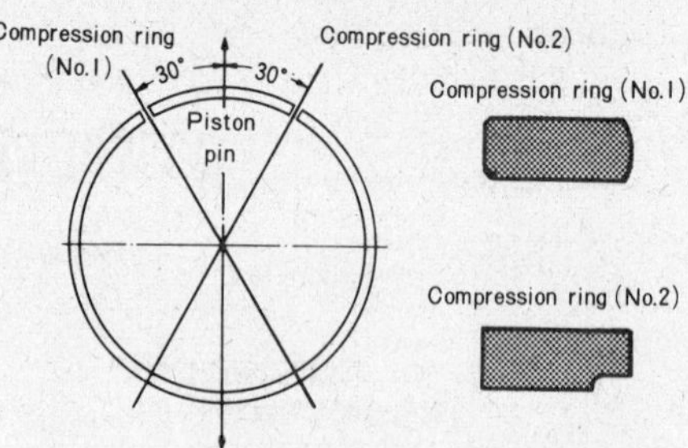

Fig. 14 Compression ring installation

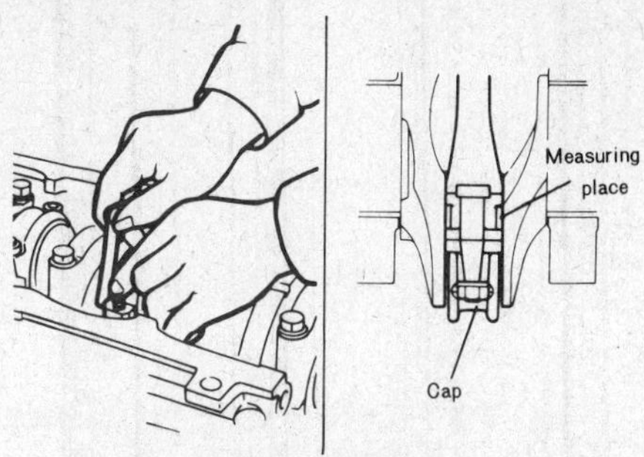

Fig. 15 Connecting rod endplay check

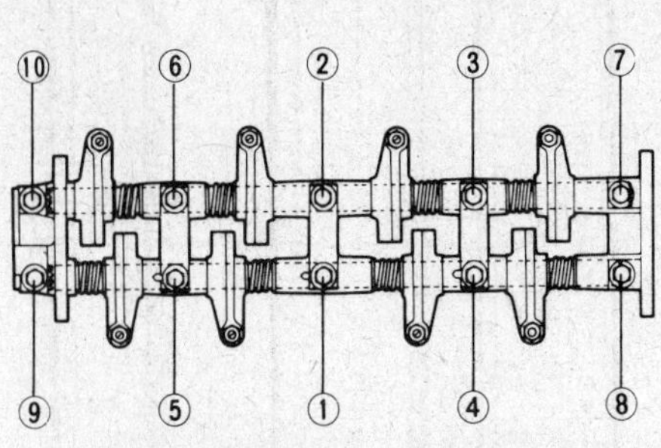

Fig. 16 Cylinder head bolt tightening sequence

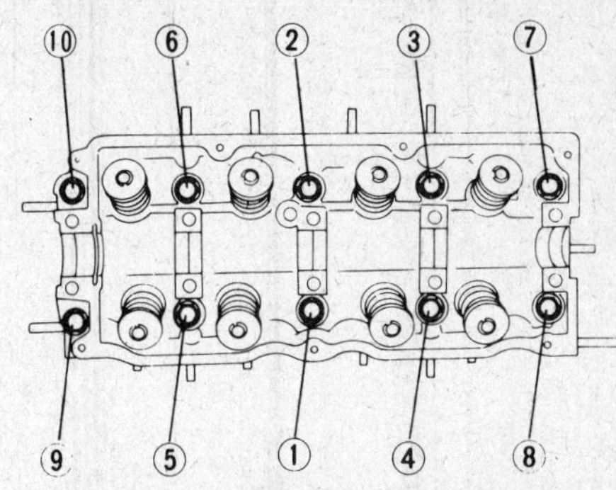

Fig. 17 Rocker shaft bolt tightening sequence

a. Apply clean engine oil to crankshaft and outer surface of bearing.
b. Position a pipe with an outside diameter of 1.18-1.34 inch against outer bearing race and drive bearing into place.
c. Apply suitable grease to bearing.

6. On all models, measure clearance between connecting rod bearing and crankshaft pin journal using Plastigage as described in step 2. Clearance should measure .0010-.0026 inch (.027-.067mm) and must not exceed .0039 inch (.10mm). If clearance is not within specifications, install undersize bearings as needed. Bearings are available in undersizes of .010 inch (.25mm), .020 inch (.50mm) and .030 inch (.75mm).
7. Install connecting rod bearing caps and torque attaching bolts to specifications.
8. Measure connecting rod endplay, **Fig. 15.** Endplay must not exceed .012 inch (.30mm).

REAR COVER & END PLATE

1. Apply clean engine oil to rear cover and oil seal, then press seal into cover.
2. Install tubular pin into cylinder block.
3. Apply clean engine oil to seal lip, then install rear cover to cylinder block. Torque cover attaching bolts to 6-9 ft. lbs. (8-12 Nm).
4. Trim gasket protruding between oil pan and rear cover, then install end plate and torque attaching bolts to 14-22 ft. lbs. (19-31 Nm) for all models exc. 1987 B2200 or 14-19 ft. lbs. (19-25 Nm) for 1987 B2200.

OIL PUMP, OIL STRAINER & OIL PAN

1. Apply suitable lithium based grease to O-ring, then install O-ring into oil pump body.
2. Apply suitable sealant to oil pump mating surface, then slide tubular pin into pump and install pump. Torque attaching bolts to 14-19 ft. lbs. (19-26 Nm) for 8mm bolts or 27-38 ft. lbs. for 10mm bolts.
3. Install baffle plate, if equipped, then the oil strainer. Torque attaching bolts to 6-9 ft. lbs. (8-12 Nm).
4. Apply a bead of suitable sealant to oil pan mating surface, then install oil pan. Torque attaching bolts to 5-9 ft. lbs. (7-12 Nm).

FLYWHEEL, CLUTCH & WATER PUMP

1. Install flywheel or drive plate assembly and torque attaching bolts to specifications. Lock assembly with ring gear brake (49 E301 060) when tightening bolts.
2. Install clutch disc and cover. Torque attaching bolts to 16-24 ft. lbs. (22-33 Nm).
3. On 626 models, install No. 3 engine bracket and torque attaching bolts to 27-38 ft. lbs. (38-53 Nm).
4. On all models, install water pump with a new gasket and torque attaching bolts to 14-19 ft. lbs. (19-26 Nm).

CYLINDER HEAD & ROCKER SHAFT ASSEMBLY

1. Install cylinder head assembly with new gasket. Torque attaching bolts to specifications in sequence, **Fig. 16.**
2. Install camshaft and check oil clearance as follows:
   a. Clean bearing and camshaft journal.
   b. Position Plastigage on top of journal in axial direction of journal.
   c. Install bearing cap and torque to specifications.
   d. Remove cap and measure oil clearance.
   e. Clearance should measure .0014-.0033 inch (.035-.085mm) at No. 1 and 5 bearings, or .0026-.0059 inch (.065-.115mm) at No. 2 and 4 bearings, and must not exceed .0059 inch (.15mm) at any bearing.
   f. If clearances are not within specifications, replace cylinder head and camshaft cap.
3. Apply clean engine oil to camshaft and bearings, then install camshaft. Ensure camshaft knock pin is at 12 o'clock position.
4. Apply clean engine oil to rocker shaft components and assemble rocker shaft assembly. **Rocker arm shafts are not interchangeable. Rocker arms Nos. 1 and 3 are identical and Nos. 2 and 4 are also identical.**
5. Apply suitable sealant to front and rear rocker shaft-to-cylinder head mating surface, then install rocker shaft assembly. Torque attaching bolts to specifications in sequence, **Fig. 17.**

FRONT HOUSING & TIMING BELT

1. Apply clean engine oil to front housing and oil seal mating surfaces, then press seal into housing.
2. Install front housing assembly with a new gasket. Torque attaching bolts to 14-19 ft. lbs. (19-26 Nm).
3. Install timing belt pulley with semicircular key. Torque pulley retaining bolt to 80-87 ft. lbs. (110-120 Nm) for 1983-84 models, 108-112 ft. lbs (150-160 Nm) for 1985 models, 117-125 ft. lbs. (160-170 Nm) for 1986 626, 108-116 ft. lbs. (147-157 Nm) for 1986 B2000 and 1987 B2200 or 116-123 ft. lbs. (157-167 Nm) for 1987 626, after reversing direction of ring gear brake. **Ensure reference mark on oil pump body aligns with semicircular key.**
4. Install camshaft pulley and torque retaining bolt to 35-48 ft. lbs. (48-66 Nm). **Camshaft pulley must be installed so that "A" or "triangle" mark on pulley is at 12 o'clock position and aligns with mark on front housing.**
5. Install timing belt tensioner, tensioner spring and idler, if equipped. Slide tensioner as far as possible toward intake side, then tighten lock bolt to temporarily hold in place.
6. Install timing belt. Adjust belt tension as follows:
   a. Loosen tensioner lock bolt and apply spring tension to belt.
   b. Release ring gear brake.
   c. Rotate timing belt pulley two complete revolutions in normal direction of rotation.
   d. Align timing marks, then torque tensioner lock bolt to 28-38 ft. lbs. (38-53 Nm). **If original timing belt is being reinstalled, measure belt deflection, Fig. 18.** If deflection is not .47-.55 inch (12-14mm) for 1983-86 626 or .43-.51 inch (11-13mm) for 1986 B2000 and 1987 626, repeat tension adjustment procedure.
7. Install lower timing belt cover, then the upper cover using new gaskets. Torque attaching bolts to 5-7 ft. lbs. (7-10 Nm).

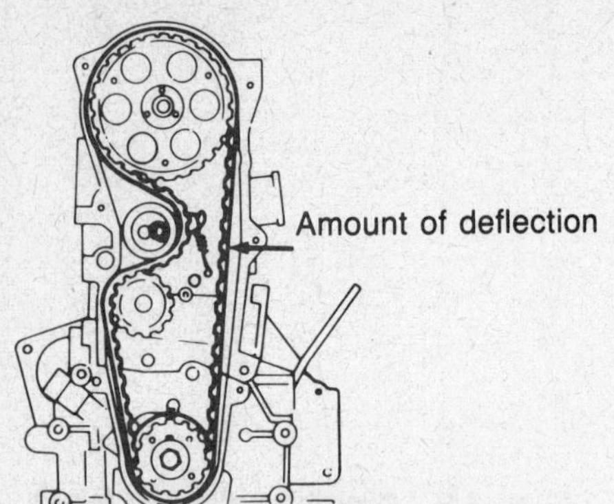

Fig. 18 Timing belt deflection check

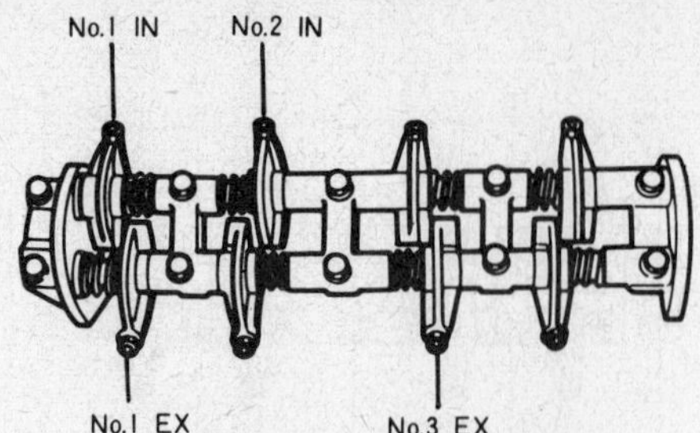

Fig. 19 Valve cover sealant application

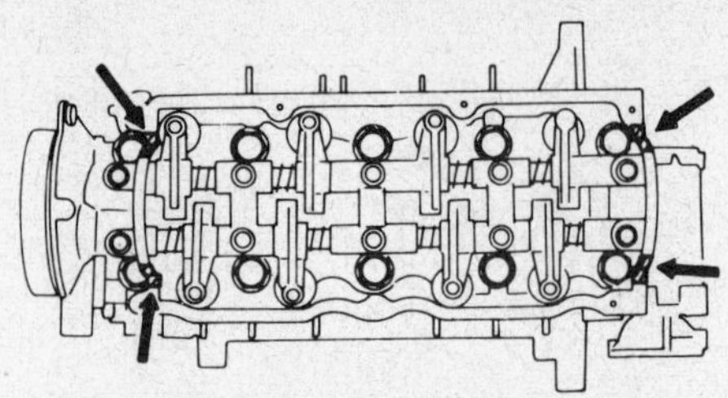

Fig. 20 Valve adjustment sequence

FUEL PUMP & REAR HOUSING

1. Apply clean engine oil to fuel pump cam sliding surface.
2. Install fuel pump with insulator and two gaskets. Torque attaching bolt to 14-19 ft. lbs. (19-26 Nm).
3. Install rear housing assembly with a new gasket. Torque attaching bolts to 14-19 ft. lbs. (19-26 Nm).
4. Install crankshaft pulley and torque retaining bolt to specifications.

VALVE COVER

1. Position gasket on valve cover, then apply suitable sealant to areas indicated in **Fig. 19.**
2. Install valve cover and torque attaching bolts to specifications.
3. Install filler cap and ventilation hose.

FINAL ASSEMBLY

1. Install oil pressure switch and oil filter.
2. Install front engine hanger, then the rear hanger and clip.
3. Install thermostat, then the coolant outlet with a new gasket. Ensure printed side of coolant outlet gasket faces toward rear of housing, then torque retaining bolt to 14-22 ft. lbs. (19-31 Nm).
4. Install upper water hose, ensuring reference marks on hose and coolant outlet align.
5. Apply clean engine oil to distributor O-ring and drive gear and install O-ring.
6. Install distributor assembly and loosely tighten attaching bolts. Ensure reference marks on distributor housing and drive gear align and are facing straight up.
7. Install spark plugs and ignition wires. Torque spark plugs to specifications.
8. Install intake manifold assembly with a new gasket and torque attaching bolts to specifications.
9. Install water bypass hose assembly and torque to 13-22 ft. lbs. (19-31 Nm).
10. Install inlet pipe assembly with new gaskets. Torque retaining bolt at water pump to 14-19 ft. lbs. (19-26 Nm) and retaining bolt at engine bracket to 28-38 ft. lbs. (38-53 Nm) **Reference marks on inlet pipe assembly and lower water hose must be properly aligned.**
11. Install exhaust manifold with new gasket and torque attaching bolts to specifications.
12. Install alternator, brackets and drive belt. With a force of 22 lbs. applied to a point midway between crankshaft pulley and alternator pulley, drive belt deflection should measure .24-31 inch (6-8mm) for a new belt or .39-.47 inch (10-12mm) for a used belt.
13. Install insulator on No. 3 engine bracket, power steering pump bracket and A/C compressor bracket, as required.
14. Install engine torque stopper casing assembly and torque to 44.8-55.7 ft. lbs. (62-77 Nm).

ADJUSTING VALVE CLEARANCE

1. Position No. 1 cylinder at TDC and adjust the following valves to specifications: Nos. 1 and 2 intake and Nos. 1 and 3 exhaust, **Fig. 20.**
2. Release ring gear brake and rotate crankshaft forward one complete revolution, then adjust remaining valves.

TIMING BELT REPLACE

1983–87 626

1. Disconnect battery ground cable.
2. Remove A/C, power steering and alternator drive belt, as required.
3. Remove upper and lower timing belt cover, then the crankshaft pulley assembly.
4. Turn crankshaft to align "A" mark of camshaft pulley with front housing timing mark, **Fig. 21.**
5. Mark a direction arrow on the timing belt to ensure correct position during installation.
6. Remove tensioner lock bolt, then the tensioner, spring and timing belt.
7. Inspect timing belt, timing belt tensioner and spring, timing belt pulley and camshaft pulley. Replace defective parts as required.
8. Align timing mark on timing belt pulley with matching mark on case, **Fig. 22.**
9. Ensure that "A" mark of camshaft pulley is aligned with front housing timing mark, **Fig. 21.**
10. Install timing belt tensioner and spring, then temporarily secure tensioner in fully extended position.
11. Install timing belt. **Ensure to install timing belt in same direction as removed.**
12. Loosen tensioner lock bolt so tension spring applies tension.
13. Turn crankshaft twice in direction of rotation, then align matching marks.
14. If marks are not correctly aligned, repeat steps 8 through 13.
15. Torque timing belt tensioner lock bolt to 28-38 ft. lbs (37-52 Nm).
16. Check timing belt deflection, **Fig. 18.** If deflection is not .47-.55 inch (12-14mm) for 1983-86 626 or .43-.51 inch (11-13mm) for 1987 626, repeat steps 12 through 15.
17. Install lower and upper timing belt cover. Torque cover attaching bolts to 61-87 inch lbs. (7-10 Nm).
18. Install crankshaft pulley assembly, then the drive belts, as required. Torque pulley attaching bolts to 9-12 ft. lbs. (13-17 Nm).

1986 B2000 & 1987 B2200

1. Disconnect battery ground cable.
2. Drain engine coolant, then remove cooling fan and radiator cowling.
3. Remove distributor, then the alternator and alternator drive belt.
4. Remove secondary air pipe assembly, then the cooling fan bracket.
5. Remove A/C compressor and power steering drive belts, as required.
6. Remove crankshaft pulley and baffle plate, if equipped.
7. Remove upper and lower timing belt cover.
8. Turn crankshaft to align "A" or "triangle" mark of camshaft pulley with front housing timing mark, **Figs. 21 and 22.**
9. Mark a direction arrow on the timing belt to ensure correct position during installation.
10. Remove tensioner lock bolt, then the tensioner, spring and timing belt.
11. Inspect timing belt, timing belt tensioner and spring, timing belt pulley and camshaft pulley. Replace defective parts as required.
12. Align timing mark on timing belt pulley with matching mark on case, **Fig. 23.**
13. Ensure that "A" or "triangle" mark of camshaft pulley is aligned with front housing timing mark, **Figs. 21 and 22.**
14. Install timing belt tensioner and spring, then temporarily secure tensioner in fully extended position.

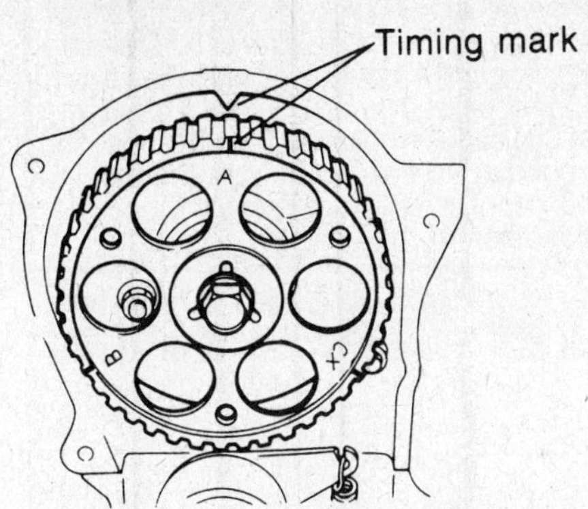

Fig. 21 Aligning camshaft pulley. 626 & B2000

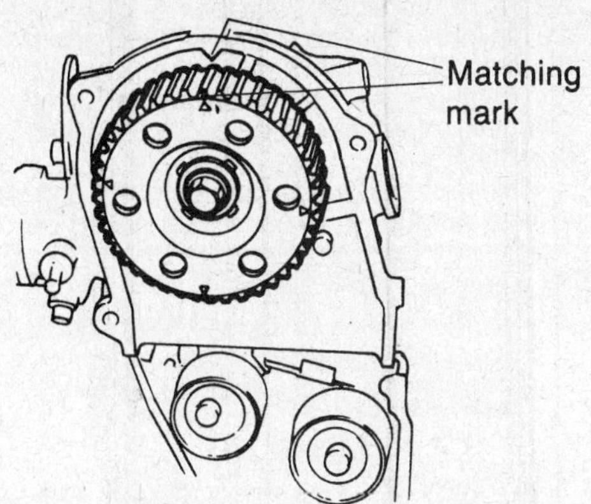

Fig. 22 Aligning camshaft pulley. 1987 B2200

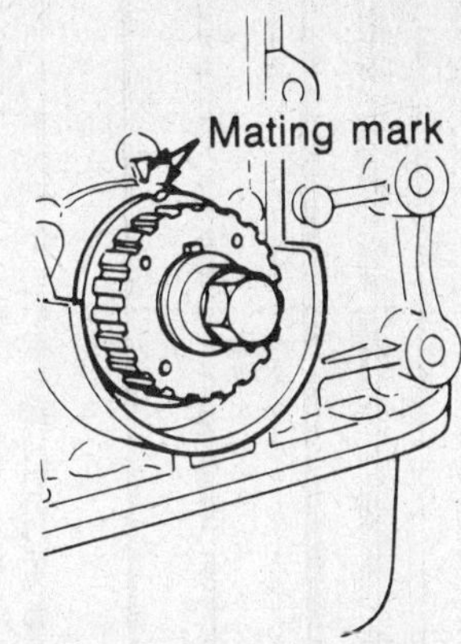

Fig. 23 Aligning timing belt pulley

15. Install timing belt. **Ensure to install timing belt in same direction as removed.**
16. Loosen tensioner lock bolt so tension spring applies tension.
17. Turn crankshaft twice in direction of rotation, then align matching marks.
18. If marks are not correctly aligned, repeat steps 12 through 17.
19. Torque timing belt tensioner lock bolt to 28-38 ft. lbs (37-52 Nm).
20. Check timing belt deflection, **Fig. 18.** If deflection is not .43-.51 inch (11-13mm), repeat steps 16 through 19.
21. Install lower and upper timing belt cover. Torque cover attaching bolts to 61-86 inch lbs. (7-10 Nm).
22. Install crankshaft pulley and baffle plate. Torque pulley attaching bolts to 9-13 ft. lbs. (13-17 Nm).
23. Install cooling fan bracket. Torque bracket attaching bolts to 27-46 ft. lbs. (37-63 Nm).
24. Install coolant bypass pipe, cooling fan pulley, cooling fan, radiator cowling, alternator and alternator drive belt.
25. Install A/C compressor and power steering pump drive belt, as required.
26. Install secondary air pipe assembly, then the distributor in front housing.
27. Fill radiator with suitable coolant.

CYLINDER HEAD REPLACE

1983–85 626

1. Disconnect battery ground cable.
2. Turn crankshaft so that No. 1 cylinder piston is at top dead center, then drain engine coolant.
3. Remove air cleaner assembly, then the distributor.
4. Remove thermostat, then the fuel pump.
5. Remove accelerator cable.
6. Remove intake manifold and carburetor assembly.
7. On models equipped with A/C, remove alternator and alternator bracket.
8. On models equipped with A/C, remove compressor.
9. On all models, remove engine ground wire.
10. Remove upper timing belt cover, then the timing belt.
11. Remove secondary air pipes, then the oxygen sensor electrical connector.
12. Remove manifold insulator assembly, then disconnect exhaust pipe from exhaust manifold.
13. Remove cylinder head rear housing and gasket.
14. Remove valve cover and gasket.
15. Gradually loosen and remove cylinder head attaching bolts in sequence shown in **Fig. 2.**
16. Remove cylinder head and exhaust manifold, then the cylinder head gasket.
17. Reverse procedure to install. Torque cylinder head attaching bolts to specifications in sequence, **Fig. 16.**

1986 B2000 & 1987 B2200

1. Disconnect battery ground cable.
2. Drain engine coolant, then remove air cleaner assembly.
3. Remove cooling fan and radiator cowling.
4. Remove oil level dip stick, then the accelerator cable and cruise control cable, as required.
5. Disconnect and plug fuel hoses.
6. Disconnect brake vacuum hose, then the 3-way solenoid valves and vacuum sensor assembly. **Do not disconnect vacuum tubes.**
7. Disconnect duty solenoid valves assembly, then the vacuum switch. **Do not disconnect vacuum tubes.**
8. Disconnect canister hoses, then the engine harness electrical connector.
9. Disconnect coil wire and spark plug wires, then remove distributor assembly.
10. Remove secondary air pipe assembly and front engine hanger.
11. Remove upper radiator hose and water bypass hoses and brackets.
12. Remove intake manifold and carburetor assembly.
13. Remove exhaust manifold insulator, then the exhaust manifold.
14. Remove timing belt upper cover, then turn crankshaft to align "A" or "triangle" mark on camshaft pulley with front housing timing mark.
15. Remove timing belt tensioner, spring and timing belt.
16. Remove camshaft pulley, then the engine ground and rear engine hanger.
17. Remove valve cover, then gradually loosen and remove cylinder head attaching bolts in sequence shown in **Fig. 2.**
18. Remove cylinder head, then the front cover and thermostat assembly.
19. Reverse procedure to install, noting the following:
    a. Torque cylinder head attaching bolts to specifications in sequence, **Fig. 16.**
    b. Install camshaft pulley onto dowel pin and keyway with "A" or "triangle" mark at 12 o'clock position. Torque camshaft pulley attaching bolts to 35-48 ft. lbs. (47-65 Nm).

1986–87 626

1. Disconnect battery ground cable.
2. Drain engine coolant, then remove accelerator cable.
3. Remove secondary air pipe assemblies.
4. Remove distributor assembly, then the rear housing.
5. Remove air hose and oil pipe, as required.
6. Remove insulator Nos. 1, 2 and 3, then the bracket.
7. Remove front catalytic converter.
8. Remove oil return hose, then the water inlet and outlet hoses.
9. Remove EGR pipe, then the exhaust manifold, gasket and turbocharger assembly, as required.
10. Remove intake manifold assembly and gasket.
11. Remove timing belt cover, then turn crankshaft to align "A" mark on camshaft pulley with front housing timing mark.
12. Remove timing belt tensioner, spring and timing belt.
13. Remove valve cover, then gradually loosen and remove cylinder head attaching bolts in sequence shown in **Fig. 2.**
14. Remove cylinder head and gasket.
15. Reverse procedure to install. Torque cylinder head attaching bolts to specifications in sequence, **Fig. 16.**

TURBOCHARGER

The turbocharger system used on some 1986-87 626 models comprise of the turbocharger, wastegate valve and actuator, pressure switch, warning buzzer, indicator light and the fuel injection control unit.

The turbocharger assembly utilizes the energy of the exhaust gasses to pressurize the intake air, which supplies more than the normal amount of air to the combustion chamber. As a result of the increased charged, a higher output and torque can be obtained.

The wastegate valve and actuator control the amount fo exhaust gas acting on the turbine wheel, corresponding to a turbocharged boost pressure. To prevent the vehicle from operating with the pressure (boost pressure) of the intake air at 11 psi or higher, an indicator light flashes, corresponding to the signal from the fuel injection control unit, indicating the over boost condition to the vehicle operator.

4-156/2555cc GASOLINE ENGINE SECTION

INDEX

ENGINE REPLACE

1. Disconnect battery ground cable.
2. Remove engine under cover, then drain engine oil and coolant.
3. Remove air cleaner, then the accelerator cable.
4. Remove radiator upper and lower hose, then the cooling fan.
5. Remove radiator cowling and radiator.
6. Remove 3-way solenoid valve and vacuum switch assembly, then the canister hoses.
7. Remove high altitude control valve, then disconnect engine harness electrical connector.
8. On models equipped with automatic transmission, remove oil cooler pipe retainers and oil cooler pipes.
9. On all models, remove exhaust pipe, then the secondary air pipe.
10. Remove engine ground wire, then disconnect heater hoses.
11. Disconnect coil wire and spark plug wires, then remove starter.
12. Remove A/C compressor and power steering pump, then with hoses still connected, position aside.
13. Remove gusset plates, then the rear under cover.
14. Support transmission using a suitable jack, then remove transmission attaching bolts.
15. Disconnect and plug fuel hoses, then remove brake vacuum hose.
16. Support engine using a suitable jack, then remove engine mounting nuts and lower engine from vehicle.
17. Reverse procedure to install.

DISASSEMBLY

1. With engine placed on suitable work stand, remove the following components from the engine:
   a. Oil dipstick and pipe.
   b. Water bypass hose.
   c. Intake manifold, gasket and carburetor assembly.
   d. Nos. 1 and 2 air control valve and air injection pipe.
   e. Exhaust manifold insulator, exhaust manifold and gasket.
   f. Distributor, coil wire and spark plug wires.
   g. A/C compressor bracket and power steering oil pump strap, if equipped.
   h. Alternator assembly.
   i. Engine mounting brackets.
2. Refer to **Fig. 1** and remove components from cylinder head in indicated order, noting the following:
   a. Before removing rocker arm and rocker shaft assembly, place suitable hydraulic lash adjuster holder in position to prevent adjuster from falling.
   b. When removing rocker arm and shaft assembly, do not take rocker arm shaft bolts out of shaft.
   c. Remove jet valve using jet valve socket wrench 49U012007 or equivalent.
3. Refer to **Fig. 2** and remove components form front of engine in indicated order.
4. Refer to **Fig. 3** and remove timing chain case and timing chain assembly in indicated order, noting the following:
   a. When removing parts connected to crankshaft, install ring gear brake 49WD37060 or equivalent to prevent crankshaft from turning.
   b. Remove oil pump by removing attaching bolts, then pushing in and holding chain tensioner head, **Fig. 4.**
   c. Remove thrust plate by installing two 8mm bolts into threaded holes of flange and turning bolts equally to remove thrust plate.
5. Refer to **Fig. 5** and remove crankshaft and piston assembly in indicated order, noting the following:
   a. Before removing connecting rod, punch alignment marks on connecting rod cap and rod.
   b. Remove piston pins using a press and suitable tools.

ENGINE INSPECTION & REPAIR

CYLINDER HEAD

1. Inspect cylinder head for water leakage, fuel leakage, damage or cracks. Replace as required.
2. Measure cylinder head distortion. If distortion exceeds .008 inch (.20mm), grind cylinder head surface or replace as required. Do not grind more than .008 inch (.20mm) from cylinder head.
3. Measure manifold contact surface distortion. If distortion exceeds .002 inch (.05mm), grind surface or replace cylinder head.

VALVE GUIDE

1. Inspect valves for damage, bending or scores. Replace as required.
2. Measure valve length and margin. Intake valve length is 4.248 inch (107.9mm) and margin is .047 inch (1.2mm). Exhaust valve length is 4.165 inch (105.8mm) and margin is .079 inch (2mm). Replace valve as required.
3. Measure outer diameter of each valve stem. Intake valve stem diameter should be .313-.314 inch

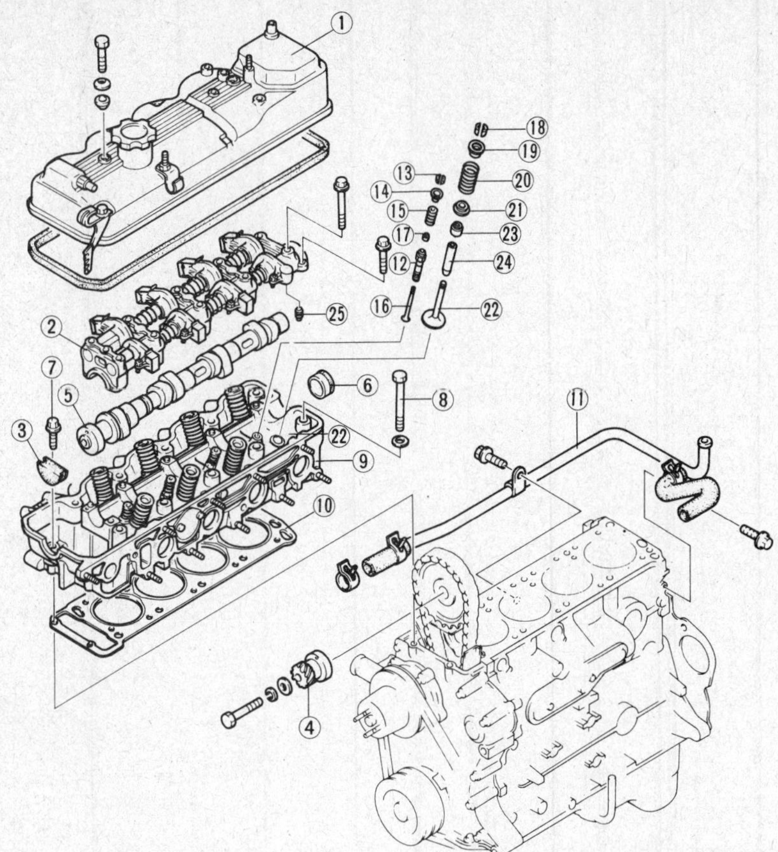

1. Cylinder head cover
2. Rocker arm and shaft assembly
3. Semi-circular packing
4. Distributor drive gear
5. Camshaft
6. Circular packing
7. Timing chain cover attaching bolt
8. Cylinder head bolt
9. Cylinder head
10. Cylinder head gasket
11. Water by-pass pipe
12. Jet valve assembly
13. Jet valve retainer
14. Jet valve spring upper seat
15. Jet valve spring
16. Jet valve
17. Jet valve seal
18. Valve retainer
19. Valve spring upper seat
20. Valve spring
21. Valve spring lower seat
22. Valve
23. Valve seal
24. Valve guide
25. Hydraulic lash adjuster

Fig. 1 Exploded view of cylinder head assembly

(7.960-7.975mm). Exhaust valve stem diameter should be .312-.313 inch (7.930-7.950mm). Replace valve as required.

4. Measure valve guide inner diameter. Valve guide inner diameter should be .315-.316 inch (8.00-8.02mm). Replace valve as required.
5. Measure oil clearance by subtracting outer diameter of valve stem from inner diameter of valve guide. Replace valve or guide if clearance exceeds .0079 (.20mm).

VALVE SPRING

1. Inspect each valve spring for cracking or damage. Replace spring as required.
2. Check spring free length and angle. Spring length should be 1.921 inch (48.8mm). Spring angle should not exceed .067 inch (1.7mm). If valve spring measurements are not as specified, replace spring.

JET VALVE

1. Ensure jet valve slides smoothly with no play in jet body. If valve is not satisfactory, replace valve and body as an assembly. **Do not attempt to adjust fit of jet valve in valve body.**
2. Check jet valve face and jet body seat for sticking or damage. If valve is not satisfactory, replace valve and body as an assembly.
3. Check jet valve spring for deterioration, cracks and damage. Replace spring as required.

CAMSHAFT

1. Check camshaft for wear or damage, then measure cam lobe height. If cam lobe height is less than 1.650 inch (42mm), replace camshaft.
2. Check camshaft runout. If runout exceeds .0008 inch (.02mm), replace camshaft.
3. Measure outer diameter of each camshaft journal. If journal diameter is not 1.336-1.337 inch (33.94-33.95mm), replace camshaft.
4. Measure inner diameter of each camshaft bearing on cylinder head. Diameter should be 1.339-1.340 inch (34-34.03mm).
5. Check camshaft bearing oil clearance by subtracting outer diameter of camshaft journal from inner diameter of camshaft bearing. If clearance exceeds .0059 inch (.15mm), replace camshaft or cylinder head as required.

ROCKER ARM & SHAFT

1. Check rocker arm assembly for cracking, wear or damage. Replace as required.
2. Ensure rocker arm and shaft oil holes are not clogged. Clean as required.
3. Check oil clearance between rocker arms and shafts. If oil clearance exceeds .04 inch (.10mm), replace rocker arm or shaft as required.

CYLINDER BLOCK

1. Check cylinder for leakage, damage or cracks. Replace block as required.
2. Measure distortion of top surface of cylinder block. If distortion exceeds .0039 inch (.10mm), replace cylinder block. **Do not grind surface of cylinder block.**
3. Measure inner diameter of cylinder. If cylinder inner diameter is not as specified, bore cylinder to accept and oversize piston.

PISTON & PISTON RING

1. Check piston for cracking, braking, heat damage or wear. Replace piston as required. Pistons are available in .010 inch, .020 inch, .030 inch and .040 inch oversize.
2. Check piston rings for excessive wear and damage. Replace rings as required. Piston rings are available in .010 inch, .020 inch, .030 inch and .040 inch oversize.
3. Install piston ring into cylinder bore by hand and push inward using a piston. Using a suitable feeler gauge, measure piston ring end gap clearance. If end gap is not as specified, replace piston rings.
4. Measure clearance between piston ring grooves and piston ring using a suitable feeler gauge. If clearance exceeds .010 inch (.25mm), replace piston or rings as required.

CONNECTING ROD

Check connecting rods for bends or twists. Replace connecting rod(s) if bends or twists are excessive.

CRANKSHAFT

1. Check crankshaft for cracking or damage. Replace as required.
2. Check crankshaft deflection using a suitable dial gauge and V-blocks. If deflection exceeds .0012 inch (.03mm), replace crankshaft.
3. Measure main journal and crankpin diameter for wear. If journal or crank pin diameter are not as specified, replace or grind crankshaft to match an undersized bearing.

BALANCE SHAFT

1. Check journals for wear, damage or seizure. If excessive damage or seizure is present, check bearing. Replace balance shaft and/or bearing as required.
2. Check shaft oil passages for clogging. Clean or replace as required.
3. Check balance shaft oil clearance. Rear clearance should be .0024-.0039 inch (.06-.10mm) and front clearance should be .0008-.0024 inch (.02-.06mm). If clearance is not as specified, replace balance shaft and/or bearings as required.

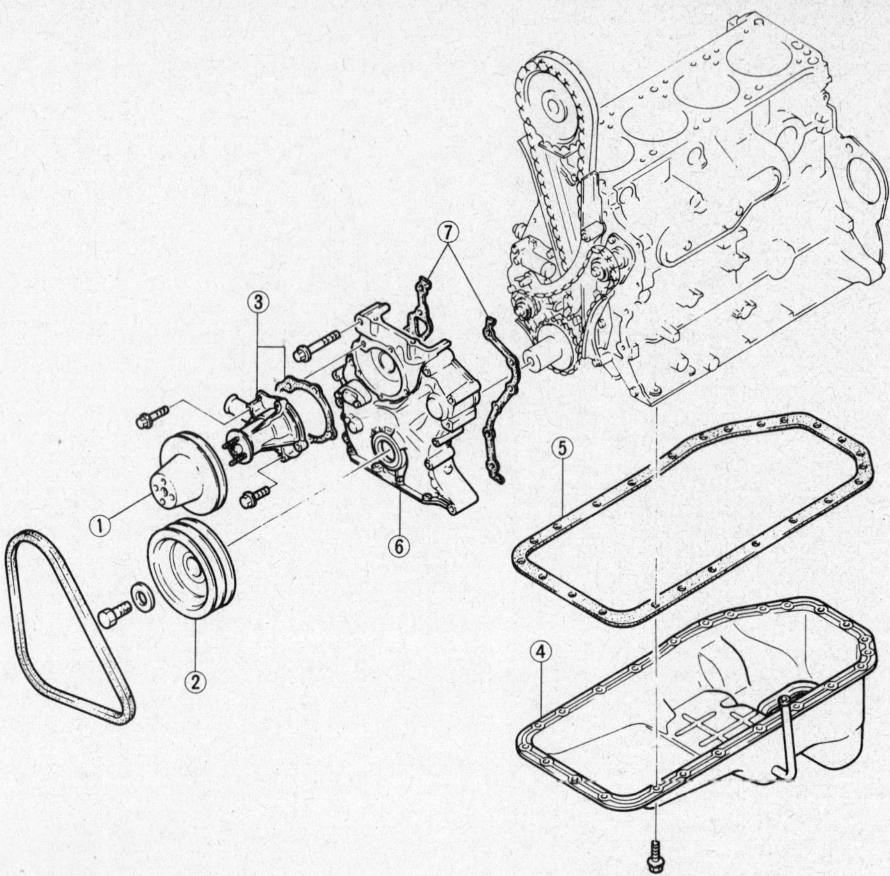

Fig. 2 Exploded view of front engine components

ASSEMBLY

VALVE SEAL & VALVE

1. Apply suitable oil to valve guides, then install lower spring seats.
2. Install valve seals on valve guides using valve seal pusher tool 49WD37160 or equivalent.
3. Apply suitable grease to valve stem, then install valve in cylinder head.
4. Install valve springs and upper spring seats. Ensure valve spring blue identification mark faces the upper valve spring seat.
5. Compress valve spring using a suitable tool, then install valve retainers. Lightly tap end of valve stem with plastic hammer to seat retainers.

JET VALVE

1. Install new jet valve seal using a suitable tool.
2. Apply suitable oil to jet valve stem, then install jet valve into body. Ensure valve slides smoothly. **Use caution not to damage valve seal lip.**
3. Install jet valve spring and spring seat in body.
4. Compress spring using a suitable tool, then install valve retainers. **Use caution not to damage valve stem by spring seat.**
5. Install new O-ring into groove of jet valve body, then apply suitable oil to jet valve threads and seat surface.
6. Screw jet valve assembly into cylinder head, then torque to 13-15 ft. lbs. using suitable tools.

CRANKSHAFT

1. Install main bearings as shown in **Fig. 6. Ensure bearings are in correct location or damage may occur.**
2. Check main bearing clearance using Plastigage. If clearance is not as specified, replace bearing caps.
3. After checking and correcting oil clearance, apply suitable oil to main bearings and main journals, then install crankshaft.
4. Install main bearing caps and cap attaching bolts, then move crankshaft back and forth to ensure proper seating. Torque cap attaching bolts to 54-61 ft. lbs.
5. Ensure crankshaft turns easily, then measure crankshaft endplay. If endplay exceeds .010 inch, replace bearings.

PISTON & CONNECTING ROD

1. Align connecting rod oil hole with mark on top of piston as shown in **Fig. 7.**
2. Apply suitable oil to piston pin and small end of connecting rod.
3. Install piston pin using a press and suitable tools. If pin cannot be installed with a pressure of 1650-3850 lbs., replace piston pin and/or connecting rod.
4. Apply suitable oil to piston ring grooves, then install piston ring spacer, upper side rail and lower side rail. Ensure upper and lower side rails turn smoothly in both directions.
5. Install No. 2 piston ring, with "2T" identification mark facing up, using a suitable tool.
6. Install No. 1 piston ring, with "TT" identification mark facing up, using a suitable tool.
7. Apply engine oil to piston and rings, then position rings as shown in **Fig. 8. Ensure ring gaps are not positioned in thrust or pin direction.**
8. Apply suitable oil to cylinder wall, then install pistons and connecting rods into cylinder using a suitable tool. **Ensure triangle mark on top of piston point toward front.**
9. Install connecting rod caps, aligning matching marks, then the cap attaching bolts.

REAR OIL SEAL CASE

1. Apply suitable oil to lip of case oil seal, then install oil seal in oil seal case using suitable tools.
2. Install oil separator in oil case with 4mm diameter hole in 6 o'clock position.
3. Install oil seal case and gasket to rear surface of cylinder block, then the oil seal case attaching bolts. Torque attaching bolts to 87-104 inch lbs.

END PLATE, PILOT BEARING, FLYWHEEL & CLUTCH COVER

1. Install end plate, gasket and end plate attaching bolts. Torque attaching bolts to 52-69 inch lbs.
2. Press pilot bearing into flywheel using suitable tools. Ensure bearing is fully seated.

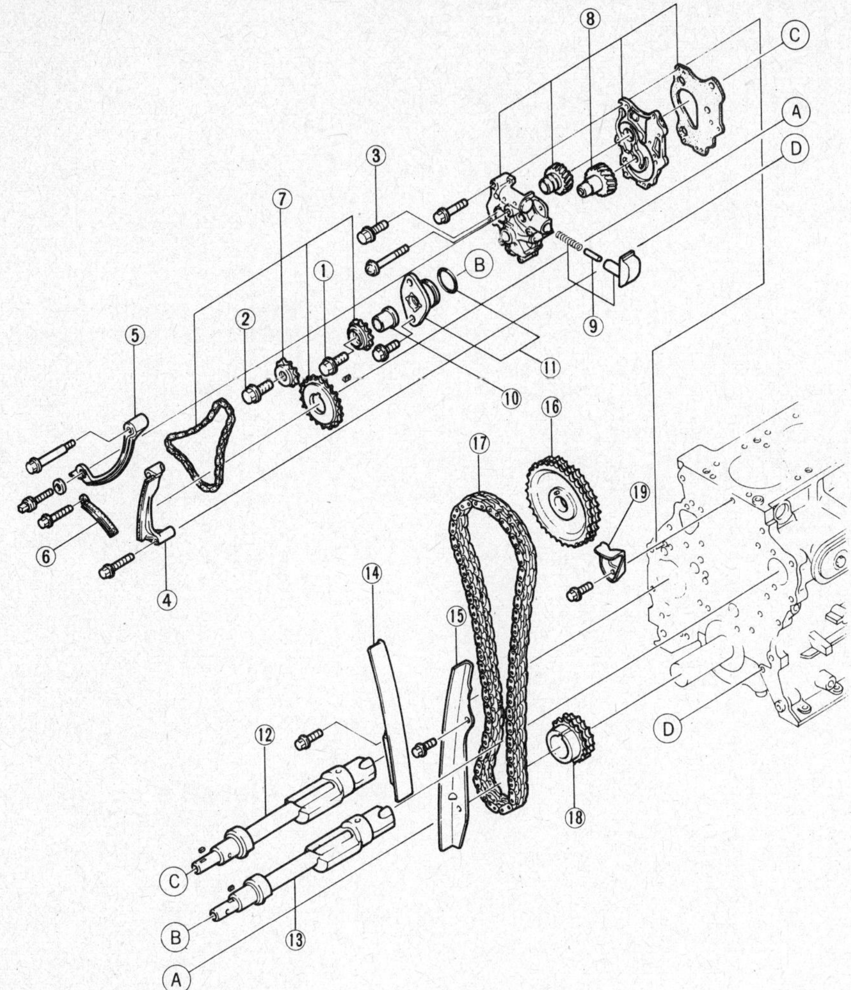

1. Left balance shaft sprocket bolt
2. Oil pump sprocket bolt
3. Right balance shaft sprocket bolt
4. Chain guide A
5. Chain guide B
6. Chain guide C
7. Balance shaft and oil pump drive sprockets and chain
8. Oil pump
9. Chain adjuster
10. Spacer
11. Thrust plate
12. Right balance shaft
13. Left balance shaft
14. Chain guide
15. Chain guide (tension side)
16. Camshaft sprocket
17. Valve timing chain
18. Crankshaft sprocket
19. Camshaft sprocket holder

Fig. 3 Exploded view of timing chain case & timing chain

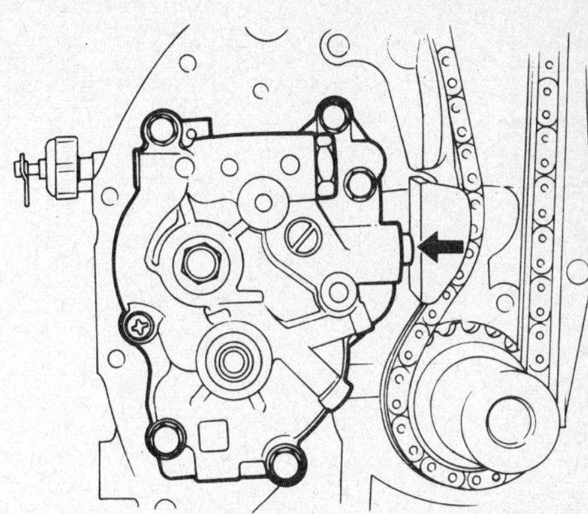

Fig. 4 Removing oil pump

3. Turn flywheel until No. 1 piston is at TDC, then install flywheel to crankshaft.
4. Install ring gear brake, then torque flywheel attaching bolts to 94-101 ft. lbs.
5. Install clutch disc, spring washers and clutch cover using suitable tools. Torque clutch cover attaching bolts to 12 ft. lbs.

TIMING CHAIN & SPROCKET

1. Install sprocket holder, then the timing chain guides. Torque guide attaching bolts to 87-104 inch lbs.
2. Align plated links of timing chain with timing marks on sprockets, **Fig. 9.**
3. Slide crankshaft sprocket onto crankshaft and place camshaft sprocket on sprocket holder.

LEFT BALANCE SHAFT

1. Apply suitable oil to journal of shaft, then install balance shaft into cylinder block. **Use caution not to damage bearing.**
2. Install new O-ring into groove of thrust plate, then apply suitable oil around O-ring.
3. Install thrust plate using two 6mm x 50mm bolts as guides to ensure proper alignment.
4. Remove two guides, then install thrust plate attaching bolts. Torque bolts to 87-95 inch lbs.

RIGHT BALANCE SHAFT

1. Install oil pump gears in oil pump body with timing marks aligned, **Fig. 10.**
2. Install oil pump cover and cover attaching screw to body, then apply approximately 10cc of suitable oil in delivery port.
3. Install balance shaft into oil pump driven gear and torque to 43-50 ft. lbs.
4. Apply suitable oil to balance shaft journal, then install balance shaft, oil pump assembly and chain adjuster into cylinder block. Push in and hold chain adjuster head to facilitate installation. **Use caution not to damage bearing.**
5. Torque oil pump attaching bolts to 69-78 inch lbs.

OIL PUMP & BALANCE SHAFT DRIVE CHAIN

1. Install balance shaft drive sprocket on crankshaft, **Fig. 11.**
2. Assemble balance shaft sprockets to balance shaft drive chain. Ensure timing marks are in alignment with polished links. **Note that right and left sprockets are installed in opposite directions, Fig. 12.**
3. Holding assembled sprockets and balance shaft drive chain, align timing mark on crankshaft sprocket with balance shaft drive chain, then install oil pump drive and right balance shaft. Hand tighten bolts.
4. Temporarily install chain guides A, B and C.
5. Tighten chain guides A and C, then torque balance shaft sprocket bolt to 43-50 ft. lbs. and oil pump sprocket bolt to 22-29 ft. lbs.
6. Rotate both balance shaft sprockets to position chain slack between left balance shaft sprocket and oil pump sprocket, **Fig. 13.**
7. Adjust position of chain guide B so that when chain is pulled in direction of arrow, **Fig. 13,** clearance between chain guide B and links of chain is .04-.14 inch (1-3.5mm).
8. After adjustment is complete, torque upper bolt to 69-78 inch lbs. and lower bolt to 11-15 ft. lbs.

TIMING CHAIN CASE

1. Apply suitable oil to oil seal lip, then install crankshaft front oil seal in timing chain case.
2. Install timing chain case and gasket. Torque case attaching bolts 9-10 ft. lbs.

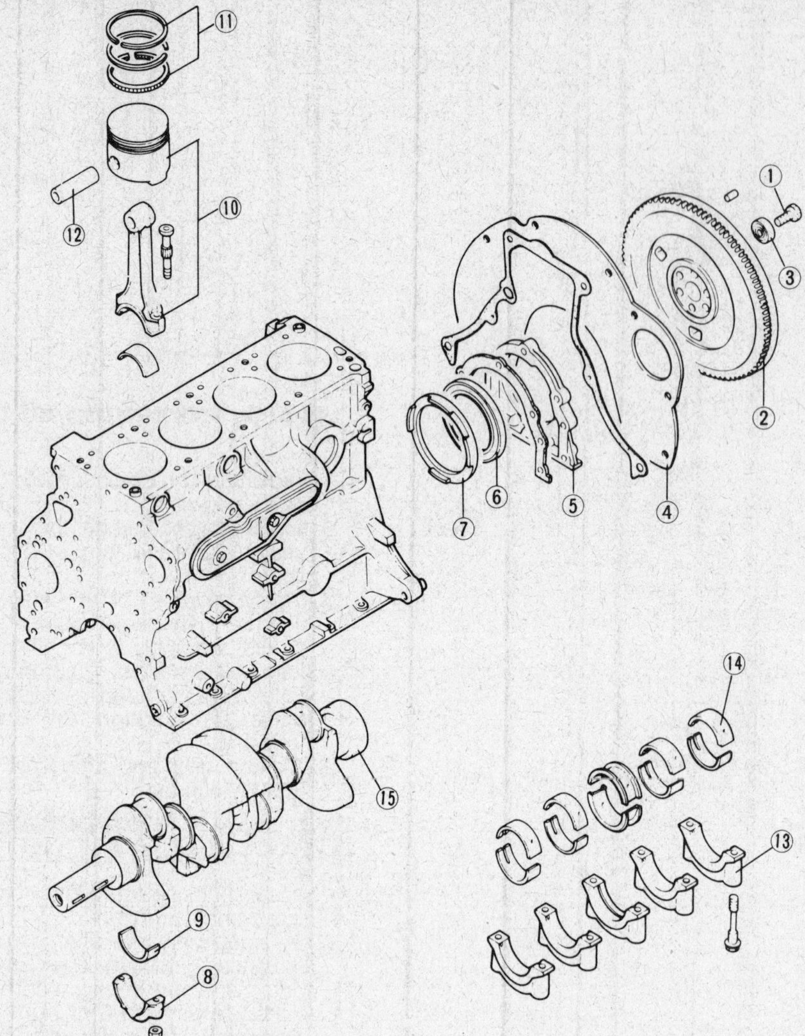

1. Flywheel bolt
2. Flywheel
3. Pilot bearing
4. End plate
5. Oil seal case
6. Oil seal
7. Oil separator
8. Connecting rod bearing cap
9. Connecting rod bearing
10. Connecting rod and piston
11. Piston rings
12. Piston pin
13. Main bearing caps
14. Main bearings
15. Crankshaft

Fig. 5 Exploded view of crankshaft & piston assembly

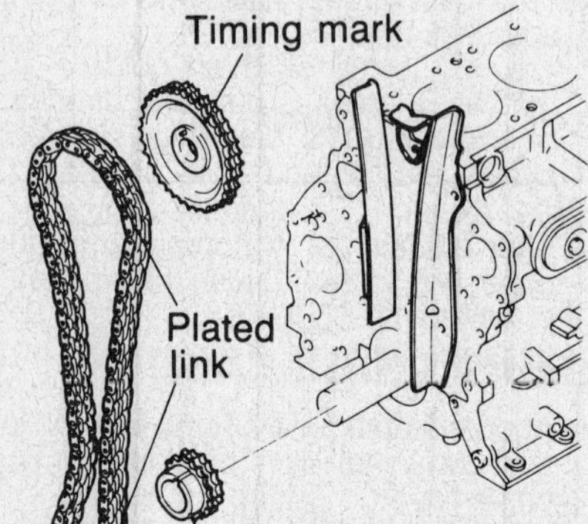

Fig. 9 Aligning timing chain & sprockets

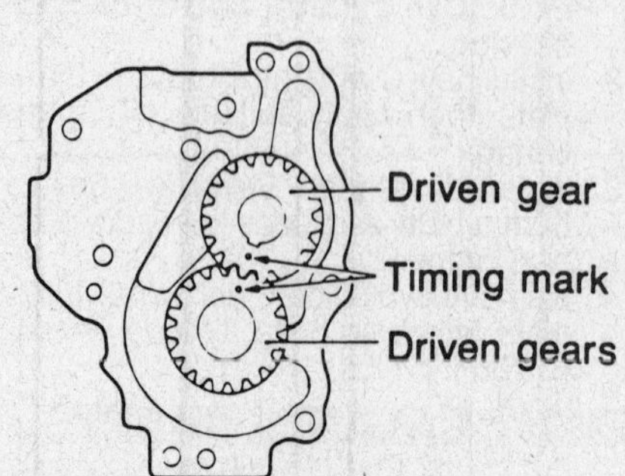

Fig. 10 Aligning oil pump gears

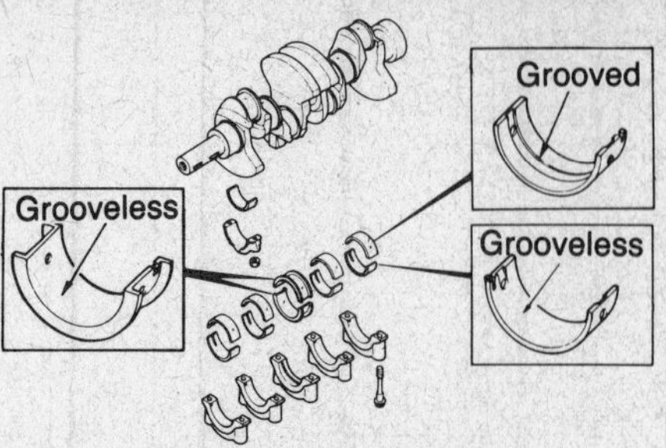

Fig. 6 Installing crankshaft main bearings

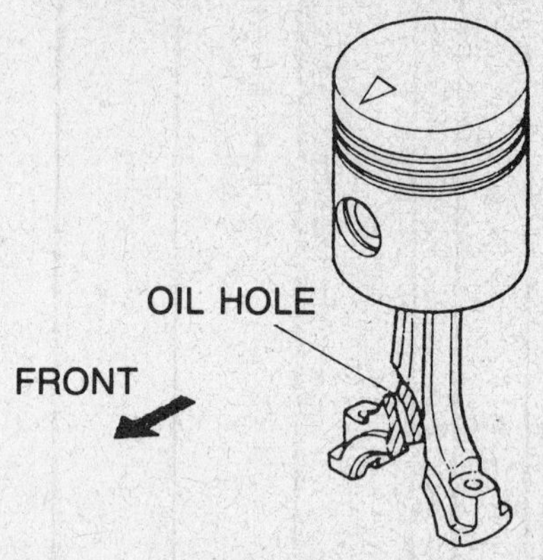

Fig. 7 Piston & connecting rod assembly

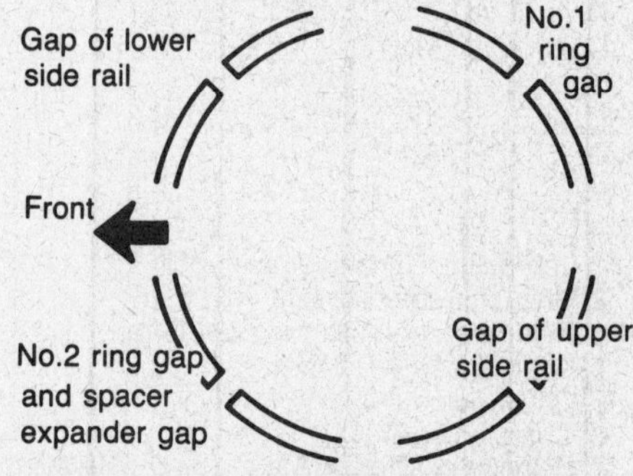

Fig. 8 Installing piston rings

OIL STRAINER, OIL PAN & CRANKSHAFT PULLEY

1. Install oil strainer and gasket to oil pump cover, then the strainer attaching bolts. Torque bolts to 11-16 ft. lbs.

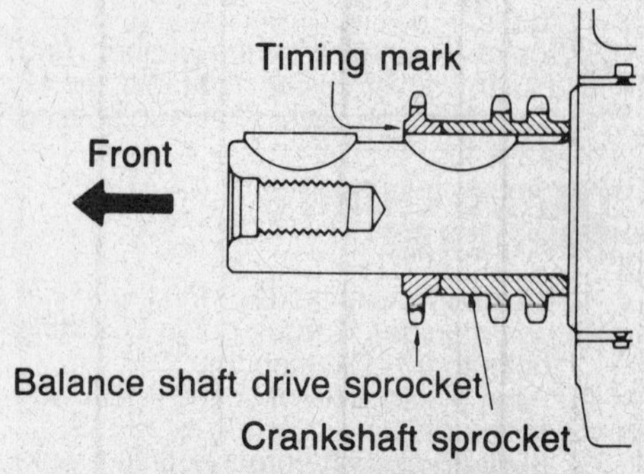

Fig. 11 Installing balance shaft drive sprocket

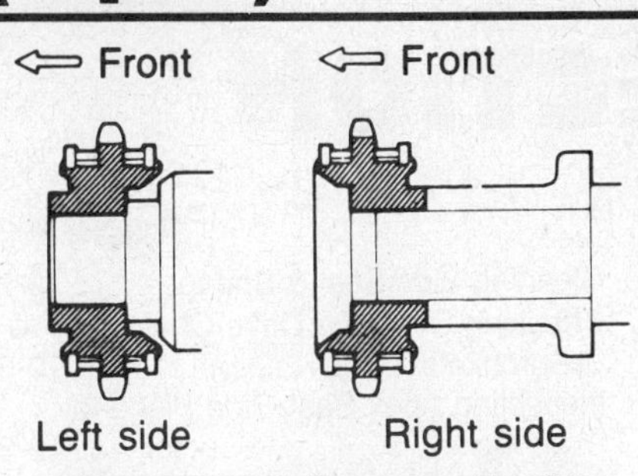

Fig. 12 Balance shaft drive sprocket alignment

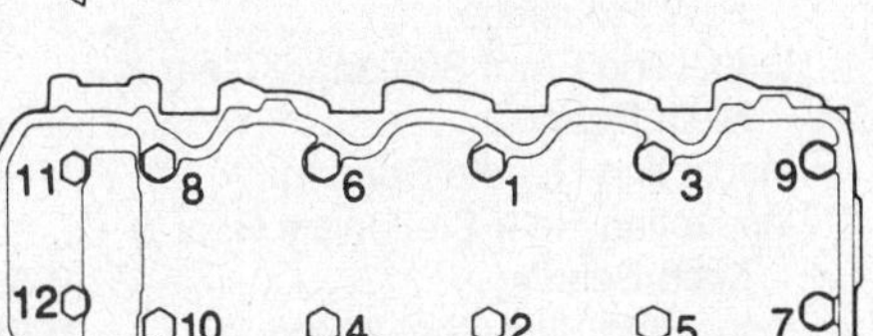

Fig. 15 Cylinder head bolt torquing sequence

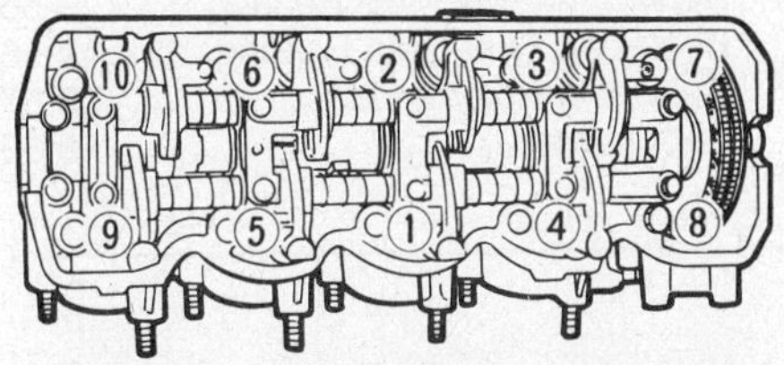

Fig. 17 Camshaft bearing cap bolt torquing sequence

2. Apply suitable sealant to oil pan as shown in **Fig. 14,** then install oil pan gasket.
3. Install oil pan and gasket assembly, then the oil pan attaching bolts. Torque bolts to 52-61 inch lbs.
4. Install crankshaft pulley and attaching bolt on crankshaft. Torque attaching bolt to 80-94 ft. lbs. and remove ring gear brake.

CYLINDER HEAD

1. Remove dirt or grease from cylinder head surface, then apply suitable sealant to cylinder block and chain contact surfaces.
2. Install cylinder head gasket with identification mark facing cylinder head.
3. Install cylinder head and cylinder head attaching bolts. Torque bolts to specifications and in sequence shown in **Fig. 15.**

ROCKER ARM & SHAFT ASSEMBLY

1. Apply suitable oil to all moving parts, then install right and left rocker arm shafts to front camshaft cap.
2. Align mating mark on front of rocker arm shaft with mating mark on front of camshaft cap, **Fig. 16.**
3. Assembly intake and exhaust rocker arms, springs, wave washers and camshaft caps. Ensure wave washer faces toward front of engine.

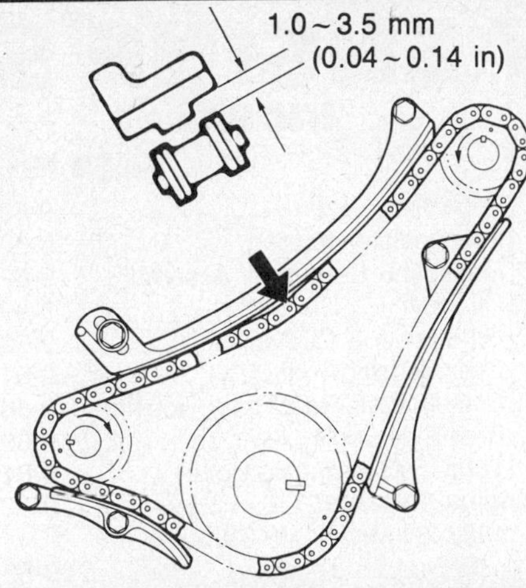

Fig. 13 Adjusting oil pump & balance shaft drive chain

4. Install hydraulic lash adjusters under rocker arms, then place a suitable lash adjuster holder in position on rocker arm to prevent adjusters from falling out.

CAMSHAFT

1. Apply suitable oil to camshaft journals and install onto cylinder head. **When installing camshaft, align dowel pin on camshaft sprocket with hole in camshaft.**
2. Apply suitable sealant on circular packing, then install packing on end of cylinder head.
3. Install rocker arm and rocker shaft assembly on cylinder head.
4. Torque camshaft bearing cap bolts to specifications and in sequence shown in **Fig. 17.**
5. Align and install distributor drive gear to camshaft, **Fig. 18.** Torque drive gear attaching bolt to 36-43 ft. lbs.
6. Adjust jet valve at TDC of compression stroke for each cylinder to .010 inch.
7. Apply suitable sealant to valve cover, then install valve cover and cover attaching bolts.

FINAL ASSEMBLY

1. Install water pump, gasket and water pump attaching bolts. Torque bolts to 104-122 inch lbs.
2. Install oil pressure switch and oil filter.
3. Install intake manifold, gasket and carburetor assembly.
4. Connect fuel hoses, then install distributor, spark plug wires and coil wires.
5. Install exhaust manifold assembly, then the alternator and cooling fan.
6. Install engine mount bracket.

TIMING CHAIN REPLACE

1. Remove air cleaner assembly, then the spark plugs.
2. Remove valve cover, then turn crankshaft until timing chain polished link is at top. **Stuff rags between camshaft sprocket and cylinder head to prevent objects from falling into engine.**
3. Remove timing chain polished link using link remover 494120110 or equivalent.
4. Install a master joint link through end of used chain and end of new chain.
5. Attach polished link and secure with clip.
6. Install wooden wedges between timing chain and cylinder head, then turn crankshaft slowly to engage new timing chain into camshaft sprocket wheel.
7. Remove old chain, then install intermediate link plate in center of the new chain.
8. Align chain holes, then install master joint link and polished link.
9. Secure joint link with clip. Install clip so open end faces a counterclockwise position.
10. Install cylinder head cover, spark plugs and air cleaner assembly.

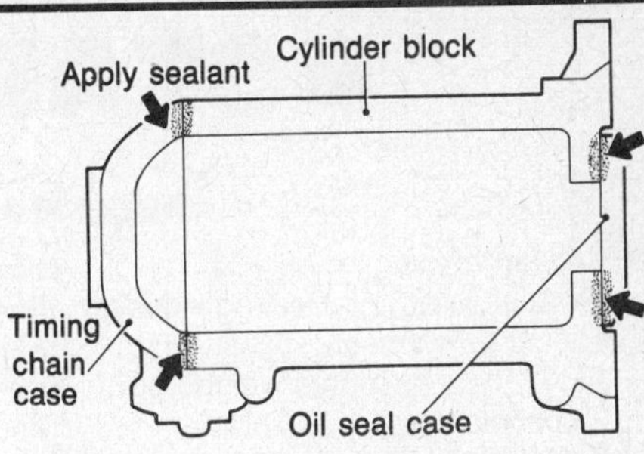

Fig. 14 Installing oil pan

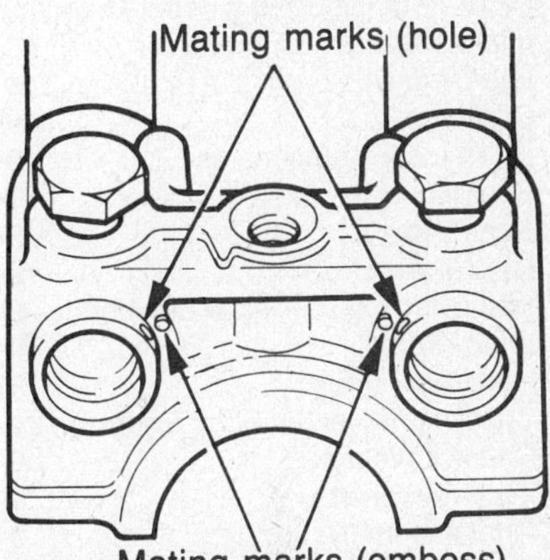

Fig. 16 Install rocker arm shaft

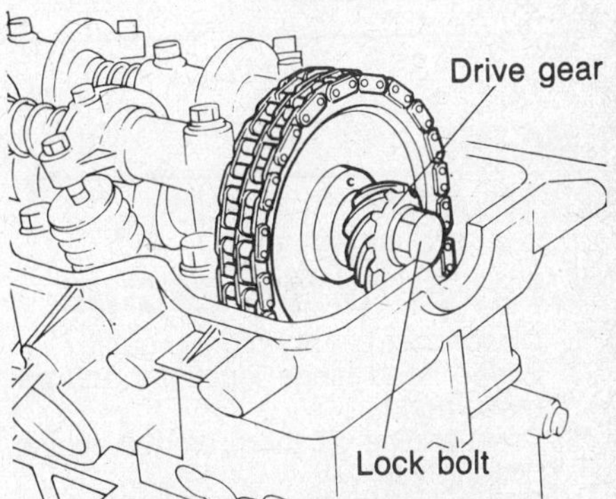

Fig. 18 Installing distributor drive gear

ROTARY ENGINE SECTION

INDEX

ENGINE

REPLACE

1983–84 MODELS W/CARBURETED ENGINE

1. Disconnect battery ground cable.
2. Scribe hood hinge locations and remove hood.
3. Drain engine oil, then remove engine undercover.
4. Disconnect high tension wires from ignition coils.
5. Disconnect pickup coil wiring and condenser lead.
6. Disconnect electrical connectors from level sensor, water temperature gauge unit and oil thermo sensor, as equipped.
7. Disconnect evaporative hose, then the vacuum sensing tube from vacuum diaphragm, if equipped.
8. Disconnect electrical connector from coolant level sensor lead.
9. Disconnect coolant reservoir hose, then remove air cleaner.
10. Disconnect electrical connector from No. 2 water temperature switch, if equipped.
11. Drain cooling system by disconnecting lower hose from radiator.
12. Disconnect upper radiator hose and transmission oil cooler lines, if equipped, from radiator.
13. Remove cooling fan and fan drive assembly, then the radiator and shroud.
14. Disconnect vacuum line from power brake unit, then the air pipe from rear of intake manifold.
15. Disconnect electrical connectors from choke heater lead, power valve solenoid, coasting richer solenoid, antiafterburn valve solenoid, idle switch, MAB solenoid valve, idle richer solenoid and port air solenoid valve, as equipped.
16. Remove transmission to engine attaching bolts.
17. Disconnect accelerator cable, choke cable and hot start assist cable from carburetor.
18. Disconnect cruise control cable, if equipped.
19. Disconnect sub-zero start assist fluid hose from carburetor, if equipped.
20. Remove wire from alternator terminal B and disconnect electrical connector from rear of alternator.
21. Disconnect electrical connectors from No. 1 water temperature switch, air vent solenoid valve, vacuum switch and 3-way valve, as equipped.
22. Remove engine ground wire, then disconnect heater hoses from engine.
23. Remove starter motor.
24. Remove transmission to engine attaching bolts.
25. Remove exhaust pipe front cover.
26. Loosen exhaust pipe-to-exhaust manifold attaching nuts.
27. Support catalytic converter to prevent it from dropping.
28. Support front of transmission with a suitable jack and remove attaching nuts from right and left engine mounts.
29. Attach suitable lifting equipment to engine, then pull engine forward until it clears the clutch shaft and carefully lift engine from vehicle.
30. Reverse procedure to install.

1984–85 MODELS W/FUEL INJECTED ENGINE

1. Disconnect battery ground cable.
2. Scribe hood hinge locations and remove hood.
3. Disconnect ignition wires from distributor, then remove distributor cap and rotor.
4. Disconnect oil level gauge, oil pressure gauge and oil temperature gauge electrical connectors.
5. Disconnect accelerator cable, then the fuel lines and evaporator hose.
6. Unfasten A/C compressor and power steering pump and position aside.
7. Remove power steering pump bracket.
8. Disconnect oil line from lower left side of engine and drain oil into a suitable container.
9. Remove starter harness bracket, then disconnect heater hose from left side of engine.
10. Disconnect water temperature gauge unit electrical connector.
11. Remove air cleaner assembly, then disconnect hoses from radiator.
12. Remove cooling fan and fan shroud.
13. Disconnect radiator water temperature switch and coolant level sensor electrical connectors.
14. Remove radiator attaching bolts and the radiator.
15. Disconnect front oil cooler hose.
16. Disconnect cruise control cable, then

the metering oil pump connecting rod.
17. Disconnect water lines from intake plenum.
18. Disconnect air hoses from right side of engine.
19. Disconnect vacuum sensing tubes from intake plenum.
20. Disconnect intake air temperature sensor, air supply valve and throttle sensor electrical connectors from intake plenum.
21. Disconnect terminal cover wire from intake plenum, then remove the plenum assembly.
22. Disconnect electrical connectors for the following:
    a. Oxygen sensor.
    b. Injectors.
    c. Water temperature sensor.
    d. Vacuum control solenoid valve.
    e. Pressure regulator control solenoid valve.
    f. Vent solenoid and vacuum solenoid valve.
    g. Engine ground.
    h. Alternator.
23. Raise and support front of vehicle.
24. Remove exhaust pipe front cover, then the catalytic converter insulator.
25. Remove exhaust pipe bracket and the exhaust pipe.
26. Remove starter motor.
27. On models equipped with automatic transmission, remove upper plate, then the torque converter attaching bolts.
28. On all models, support transmission with a suitable jack and remove transmission attaching bolts.
29. Remove engine mount attaching bolts, then lower the vehicle.
30. Attach suitable lifting equipment to engine, then lift engine and remove from vehicle.
31. Reverse procedure to install.

1986–87 MODELS W/FUEL INJECTED NON-TURBO ENGINE

1. Disconnect battery ground cable.
2. Scribe hood hinge locations and remove hood.
3. Drain engine oil and coolant, then remove air intake pipe.
4. Remove relief silencer hose, then the air cleaner assembly.
5. Remove cooling fan and radiator hoses, then the heater return hose.
6. Disconnect coolant level sensor and radiator switch electrical connector.
7. Remove ATF hose, if equipped, then the radiator and cowling.
8. Disconnect accelerator cable, then the cruise control cable and vacuum hose, if equipped.
9. Disconnect brake vacuum hose, BAC air hose and boost sensor vacuum hose.
10. Disconnect engine harness electrical connectors.
11. Disconnect spark plug wires, then the crank angle sensor, alternator and oil pressure gauge electrical connectors.
12. Disconnect engine ground, then the canister hose and heater hose.
13. Disconnect and plug fuel inlet and return hoses.
14. Disconnect oil cooler pipe and bracket and A/T pipe bracket, if equipped.
15. Remove power steering pump and A/C compressor with hoses still connected, then secure pump and compressor to one side, as required.
16. Remove compressor and pump drive belts, then the dust cover.
17. Raise and support vehicle, then remove engine under cover and exhaust pipe under cover.
18. Remove catalytic converter insulator, then the secondary air pipe and hose.
19. Remove exhaust pipe bracket and exhaust pipe.
20. Remove starter attaching bolts, then the starter.
21. On models equipped with automatic transmission, remove torque converter attaching bolts.
22. On all models, support engine assembly using a suitable jack, then remove transmission to engine attaching bolts.
23. Remove engine mount, then lower engine from vehicle.
24. Reverse procedure to install.

1987 MODELS W/FUEL INJECTED TURBO ENGINE

1. Disconnect battery ground cable.
2. Scribe hood hinge locations and remove hood.
3. Drain engine oil and coolant, then remove air intake pipe.
4. Remove air cleaner assembly, then the battery and box.
5. Remove cooling fan and radiator hoses, then the heater return hose.
6. Disconnect coolant level sensor and radiator switch electrical connector.
7. Remove radiator and cowling, then the intercooler.
8. Disconnect accelerator cable, then the cruise control cable, if equipped.
9. Disconnect brake vacuum hose, pressure sensor vacuum hose and relief silencer hose.
10. Disconnect RH split air pipe, then the oxygen sensor electrical connector.
11. Remove insulator covers, then the front converter upper nut.
12. Disconnect engine harness electrical connectors.
13. Remove power steering pump and A/C compressor with hoses still connected, then secure pump and compressor to one side, as required.
14. Remove compressor and pump drive belts.
15. Disconnect spark plug wires, then the crank angle sensor, alternator and oil pressure gauge electrical connectors.
16. Disconnect engine ground, then the canister hose and heater hose.
17. Disconnect and plug fuel inlet and return hoses.
18. Disconnect heater hose, then the oil cooler pipe and bracket, if equipped.
19. Disconnect clutch release cylinder, if equipped.
20. Raise and support vehicle, then remove engine under cover.
21. Remove catalytic converter insulator, then the split air pipe.
22. Remove exhaust pipe bracket, then the catalytic converter.
23. Remove exhaust pipe and front converter.
24. Remove starter attaching bolts, then the starter.
25. Support engine assembly using a suitable jack, then remove transmission to engine attaching bolts.
26. Remove engine mount, then lower engine from vehicle.
27. Reverse procedure to install.

DISASSEMBLY

PRELIMINARY COMPONENTS

Exc. Fuel Injected Engine

1. Remove deceleration control vale.
2. Remove vacuum control valve.
3. Remove EGR valve and solenoid.
4. Remove air pump.
5. Remove alternator.
6. Remove thermal reactor or exhaust manifold.
7. Remove distributor.
8. Remove engine mount.
9. Remove oil filter, cover and/or oil cooler.

Fuel Injected Engine, Exc. 1986–87 Models

1. Remove engine mount.
2. Remove air pump.
3. Remove alternator.
4. Remove attaching bolts from emission control valve mounting bracket located on top of engine.
5. Remove delivery pipe attaching bolts.
6. Remove emission control valve mounting bracket and delivery pipe as an assembly.
7. Remove fuel injection nozzles.
8. Remove metering oil pump lines.
9. Remove intake manifold and gasket.
10. Remove auxiliary port valves.
11. Remove exhaust manifold covers, exhaust manifold and gasket.
12. Remove distributor.
13. Remove oil filter and body.
14. Remove eccentric shaft pulley.

Fuel Injected Engine, 1986–87 Models

1. Remove A/C compressor and power steering pump bracket.
2. Remove left engine mount.
3. Remove spark plugs and oil level gauge.
4. Remove oil filter and filter body.
5. Remove oil pressure gauge.
6. Remove crank angle sensor.
7. Remove air pump drive belt, air pump and air pump bracket.
8. Remove alternator drive belt and alternator.
9. Remove clutch cover and clutch disc.
10. Remove metering oil connecting rod, throttle and dynamic chamber.
11. On non-turbocharged models, proceed as follows:
    a. Remove exhaust absorber plate, exhaust manifold and insulator.
    b. Remove fuel injector and delivery pipe.
    c. Remove air hose, manifold oil nozzle and metering oil tube.

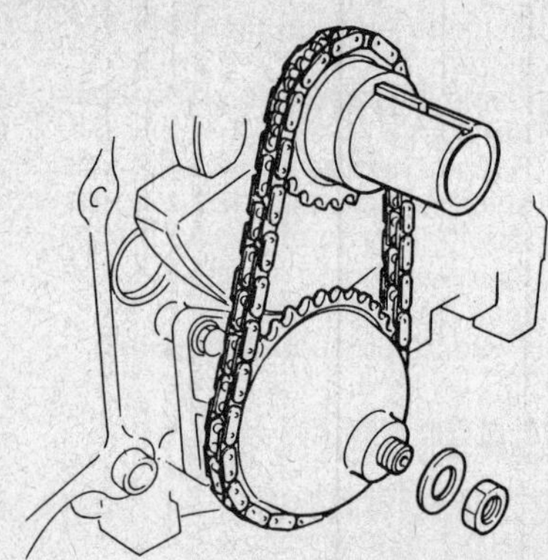

Fig. 1 Removing oil pump drive

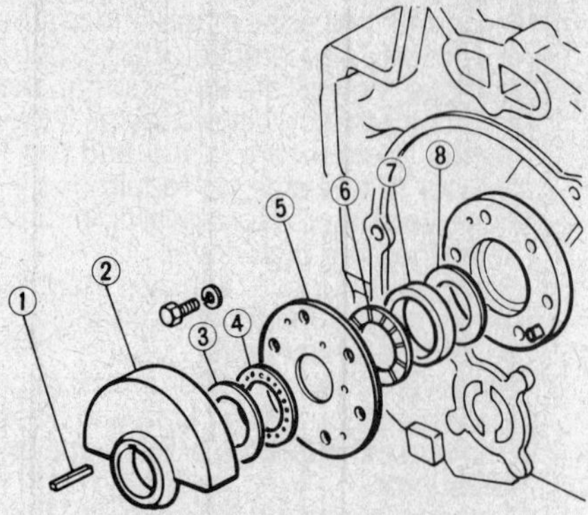

Fig. 2 Balance weight and bearing housing assemblies (Typical)

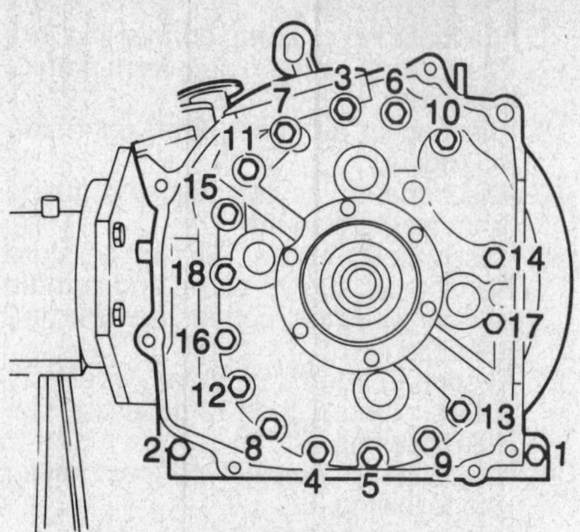

Fig. 3 Rear housing tension bolts removal sequence

d. Remove intake manifold, housing oil nozzle and metering oil tube.
e. Remove metering oil pump and eccentric shaft pulley.
f. Remove water pump, engine harness and vacuum lines.
g. Remove EGR valve.

12. On turbocharged models, proceed as follows:
    a. Remove secondary vacuum piping.
    b. Remove primary fuel injector and distribution pipe.
    c. Remove air control valve, then the switching actuator.
    d. Remove water pipe, then the turbocharger and insulator.
    e. Remove air hose, housing oil nozzle and manifold oil nozzle.
    f. Remove intake manifold, exhaust manifold and insulator.
    g. Remove metering oil pump and eccentric shaft pulley.
    h. Remove water pump, then the dynamic chamber bracket.
    i. Remove engine harness, vacuum piping and oil inlet pipe.

INTAKE MANIFOLD & CARBURETOR

Exc. Fuel Injected Engine

1. Disconnect the vacuum sensing tube from the vacuum control unit on the distributor.
2. Disconnect the connecting rod from metering oil pump lever and remove the washer.
3. Disconnect the oil hoses from metering oil pump outlets.
4. Disconnect the air outlet hose from air control valve.
5. Remove the bolts and nuts attaching the thermal reactor or exhaust manifold cover to the engine, and remove the covers.
6. Remove the nuts attaching intake manifold to the engine, and remove intake manifold and carburetor assembly.
7. Remove the manifold gasket and O-rings.

WATER PUMP

1. Remove the pulley from power steering oil pump by removing the attaching bolts (if equipped).
2. Remove the nuts and bolts that attach the water pump to the front housing.
3. Remove the alternator and air pump straps, and then the water pump.

REMOVING OIL PAN & OIL STRAINER

1. Invert the engine on the engine stand.
2. Remove the bolts attaching the oil pan, and remove the oil pan.
3. Remove the bolts attaching the oil strainer, and remove the oil strainer and gasket.

ECCENTRIC SHAFT PULLEY

1. Turn the engine on the engine stand so that the top of the engine is up.
2. On the engine equipped with manual transmission, attach the brake (49 F011 101) to the flywheel. On the engine equipped with automatic transmission, attach the stopper (49 1881 055) to the counter weight.
3. On 1983-85 models, remove the eccentric shaft pulley bolt, then the pulley.
4. On 1986-87 models, proceed as follows:
   a. Remove eccentric shaft lock bolt.
   b. Remove washer and O-ring from lock bolt.
   c. Remove eccentric shaft bypass valve and spring.
   d. Remove eccentric shaft pulley.

FRONT COVER

1. Turn the engine on the engine stand so that the front end of the engine is up.
2. On 1986-87 models, remove oil pressure control valve.
3. On all models, remove the front cover attaching bolts, and the front cover and gasket.
4. Remove the O-ring from the oil passage on the front housing.

OIL PUMP

1. Slide the distributor drive gear off the shaft.
2. Straighten the tab of the lock washer and remove the nut and lock washer from the oil pump sprocket.
3. Slide the oil pump sprocket and eccentric shaft sprocket together with the drive chain off the eccentric shaft and oil pump shaft simultaneously, **Fig. 1.**
4. On models equipped with turbocharger, remove oil pump baffle plate.
5. On all models, remove oil pump.

BALANCE WEIGHT & BEARING HOUSING

1. Remove the key from eccentric shaft, **Fig. 2.**
2. Slide the balance weight, thrust washer, needle bearing and spacer, if equipped, off the shaft.
3. Remove the bolts attaching the bearing housing, and slide the bearing housing, needle bearing, spacer and thrust plate off the shaft.

CLUTCH & FLYWHEEL

Manual Transmission

1. Turn the engine on the engine stand so that the top of the engine is up.
2. Attach the brake (49 1881 060) to the flywheel.
3. Remove the clutch cover attaching bolts, and remove the clutch cover assembly and clutch disc.
4. Straighten the tab of the lock washer and remove the flywheel nut, using the box wrench (49 0820035).
5. Remove flywheel using puller No. 49 0823 300A or equivalent.
6. Remove the key from the eccentric shaft.

DRIVE PLATE & COUNTERWEIGHT

Automatic Transmission

1. Attach suitable counterweight stopper to the rear housing.
2. Remove the drive plate attaching bolts, then the drive plate and retainer.
3. Straighten the tab of the lock washer and remove the counter weight nut using the box wrench (49 0820 035).
4. Remove the counter weight by using the puller (49 0839305A), turning the handle of the puller and lightly hitting the head of the puller.
5. Remove key from eccentric shaft, then the counter weight stopper.

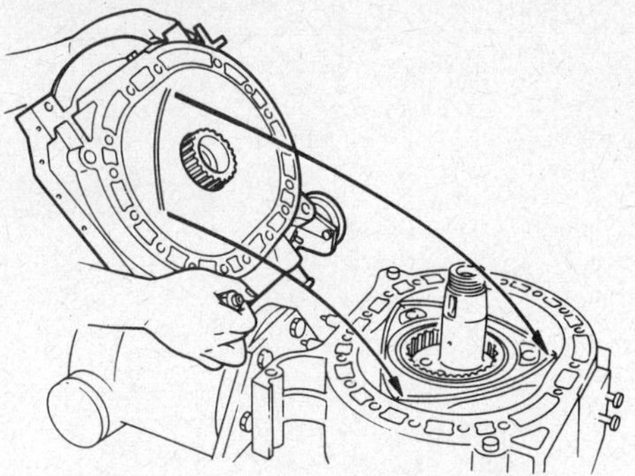

Fig. 4 Removing rear housing

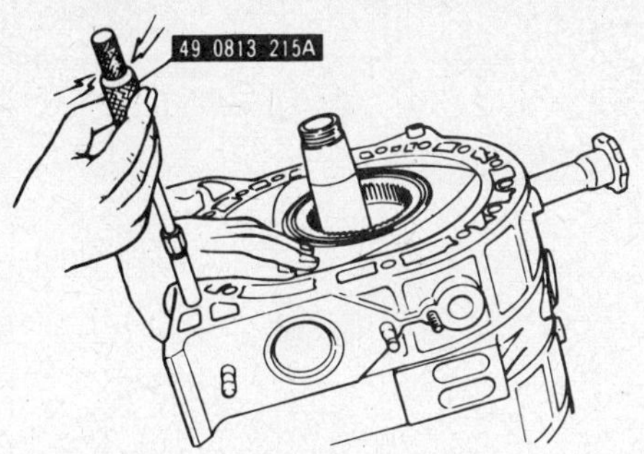

Fig. 5 Removing tubular dowel

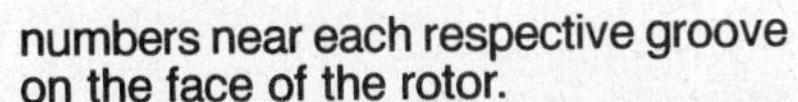

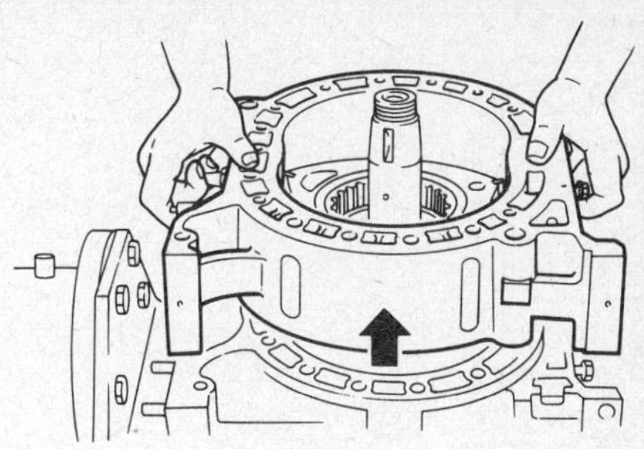

Fig. 6 Removing rear rotor housing

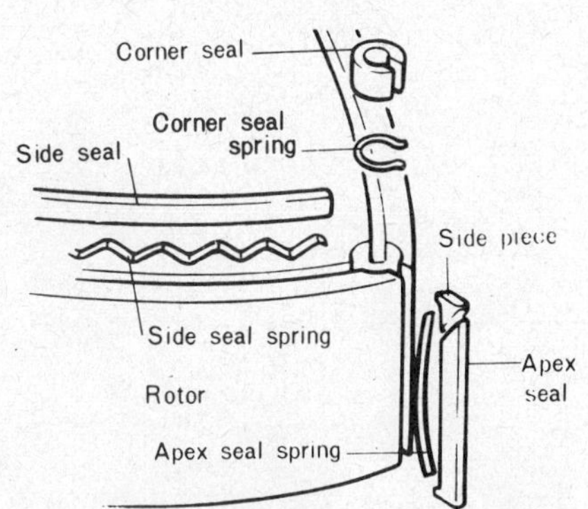

Fig. 7 Removing rear rotor side pieces

REAR HOUSING

1. Turn the engine on the engine stand so that the rear of the engine is up.
2. Loosen the tension bolts in sequence shown in **Fig. 3.** Loosen bolts in several steps. **Note that some engines do not have the No. 6 tension bolt.**
3. Remove rear housing from shaft, **Fig. 4.**
4. Remove seals remaining on rotor sliding surface of rear housing and place them back into their original positions.

REAR ROTOR HOUSING

1. Remove the two sealing rubbers and O-ring from the rear side of the rear rotor housing.
2. Attach the puller (49 0813 215A), and pull the tubular dowels off the rear rotor housing while holding the rotor housing down by hand to prevent it from moving up, **Fig. 5.**
3. Lift the rear rotor housing away from the rotor, **Fig. 6,** being careful not to drop the apex seals on the rear rotor. Remove the two sealing rubbers and O-ring from the front side of the rear rotor housing. Discard the used sealing rubbers and O-ring, then use new sealing rubbers and O-ring.

REAR ROTOR

1. Remove the side pieces, **Fig. 7,** each apex seal and spring from the rear rotor and place them in the seal case (49 0813 250), in accordance with the numbers near each respective groove on the face of the rotor.
2. Remove the all corner seals, corner seal springs, side seals and side seal springs from the rear side of the rotor, and place them in the seal case.
3. Remove the rear rotor away from the eccentric shaft and place it internal gear side down on a clean rubber pad or cloth.
4. Remove each seal and spring on the other side of the rear rotor.
5. Place a suitable protector onto the inner oil seal lip to protect the oil seal lip and remove the outer oil seal with remover (49 0813 225). Do not exert strong pressure at only one place to prevent deformation of the oil seal.
6. Remove the inner oil seal with oil seal remover. **Discard the used O-rings and use new O-rings when the engine is reassembled.**
7. Remove the oil seal springs from each respective groove.
8. Remove the oil seals and springs on the other side of the rear rotor.
9. Apply identification mark onto the rear rotor, so that when reassembling the engine the rotor can be installed in its original position.

INTERMEDIATE HOUSING

1. Holding the intermediate housing down by hand, pull the tubular dowel off the intermediate housing using the puller (49 0813 215A), **Fig. 5.**
2. Lift the intermediate housing off the shaft, being careful not to damage the shaft. The intermediate housing should be removed by sliding it beyond the rear rotor journal on the eccentric shaft while holding the intermediate housing up and at the same time pushing up the eccentric shaft.

ECCENTRIC SHAFT

Remove the eccentric shaft being careful not to damage the rotor bearing and main bearing.

FRONT ROTOR HOUSING & FRONT ROTOR

Remove the front housing and the front rotor assembly in the same manner as the rear rotor housing and rotor.

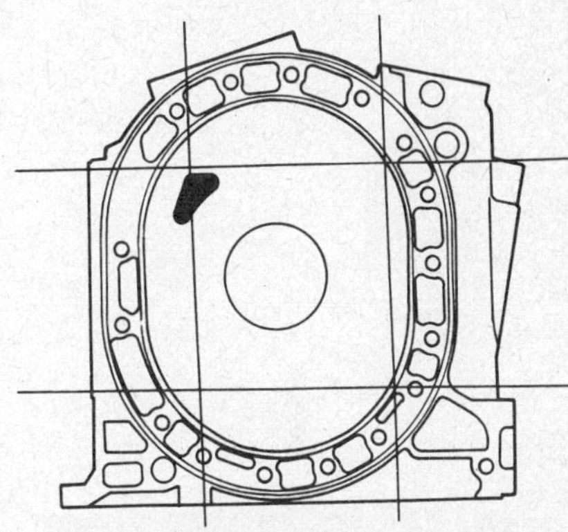

Fig. 8 Checking housing for distortion

INSPECTION & REPAIR

CLEANING INTERMEDIATE & REAR HOUSINGS

1. Remove all carbon on the housings with an extra-fine emery paper. If using a carbon scraper, be careful not to damage the finished surfaces of the housings.
2. Remove the sealing agent from housings by using a cloth or a brush soaked in a solution of ketone or thinner.

CLEANING ROTOR HOUSING

Before cleaning, check for traces of gas or water leakage along the inner margin of each side face of the rotor housing.

1. Remove all carbon from the inner surface of the rotor housing by wiping with cloth. Soak the cloth in a solution of ketone or thinner if it is difficult to remove the carbon.
2. Remove all deposits and rust from the cooling water passages on the housing.
3. Remove the sealing agent by wiping with a cloth or brush soaked in a solution of ketone or thinner.

CLEANING ROTOR

Remove the carbon from rotor by using a carbon remover or emery paper. Carbon in the seal grooves of the rotor should be removed with a carbon remover being

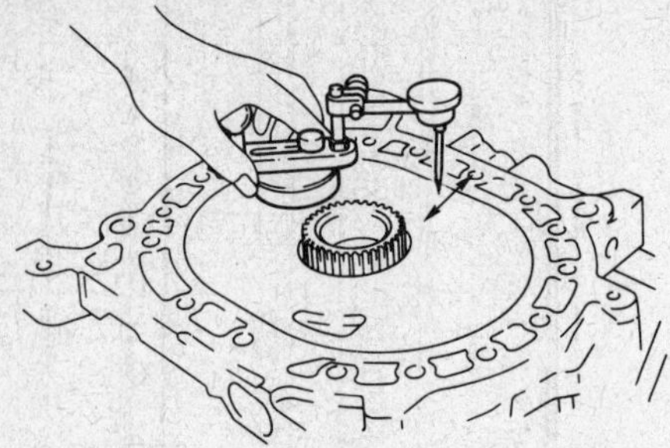

Fig. 9 Checking housing for wear

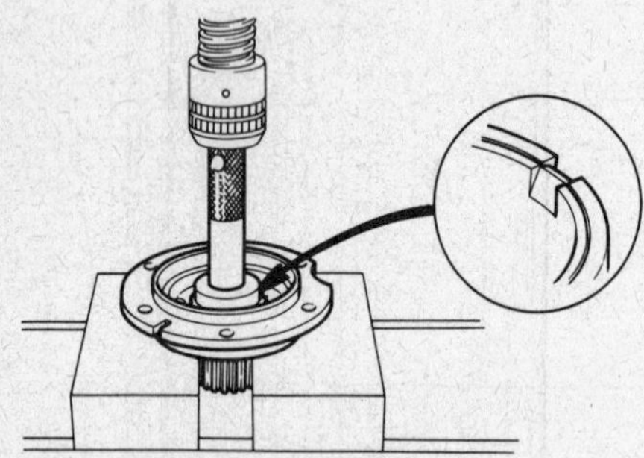

Fig. 12 Installing front stationary gear

careful not to damage the grooves. Wash the rotor in cleaning solution and dry by blowing with compressed air.

CLEANING APEX SEAL, SIDE PIECE & SPRING

Remove all carbon from the apex seal, side piece and spring, being careful not to damage the apex seal and side piece.

Never use emery paper as it will damage the apex seal and side piece. Wash them with cleaning solution.

CLEANING SIDE SEAL & SPRING

Remove all carbon from the side seal and spring with a carbon remover.

CLEANING CORNER SEAL & SPRING

Remove the carbon from the corner seal and spring.

INSPECTING FRONT, INTERMEDIATE & REAR HOUSINGS

1. Check for housing distortion by placing a straightedge on the housing surface. Measure the clearance between the straight edge and the housing surface with a feeler gauge, as shown in **Fig. 8.** If the distortion exceeds 0.0016 in. (0.04mm), reface or replace the housing.
2. Check for wear on the rotor sliding surfaces of the housing and joint surfaces with rotor housing as shown in **Fig. 9.** If the wear exceeds 0.0039 inch (0.10mm), reface or replace the

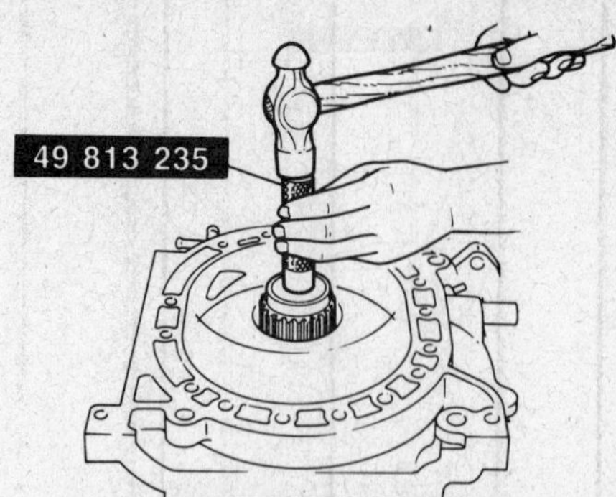

Fig. 10 Removing front stationary gear

housing. The side housings (front housing, intermediate housing and rear housing) can be reused by grinding them, if the required finish can be maintained.

INSPECTING FRONT STATIONARY GEAR & MAIN BEARING

1. Check the stationary gear for cracked, scored, worn or chipped teeth.
2. Check the main bearing for wear, scratching, flaking or any damage.
3. Check the main bearing clearance by measuring the inner diameter of the main bearing and outer diameter of the eccentric shaft main journal. Standard clearance is .0016-.0028 inch (.04-.07mm) on 1983 models or .0016-.0031 inch (.04-.08mm) on 1984-87 models. If bearing clearance exceeds .0039 inch (.10mm), replace the main bearing.

REPLACING FRONT MAIN BEARING

1. Remove the stationary gear and main bearing assembly from the front housing, using the puller and installer (49 0813 235), as shown in **Fig. 10.**
2. Using the main bearing replacer without adapter ring, press the main bearing out of the stationary gear.
3. Using the main bearing replacer with adapter ring, and aligning the tang of the bearing and the slot of the stationary gear, press fit the main bearing into the stationary gear until the adapter touches the stationary gear flange, **Fig. 11.**
4. Press in the stationary gear to the front housing with the main bearing replacer, aligning the slot of the stationary gear flange and the dowel pin on the housing, as shown in **Fig. 12.**

INSPECTING REAR STATIONARY GEAR & MAIN BEARING

Check the rear stationary gear and main bearing according to "Front Stationary Gear & Main Bearing."

REPLACING REAR MAIN BEARING

1. Remove the bolts attaching the stationary gear to the rear housing.

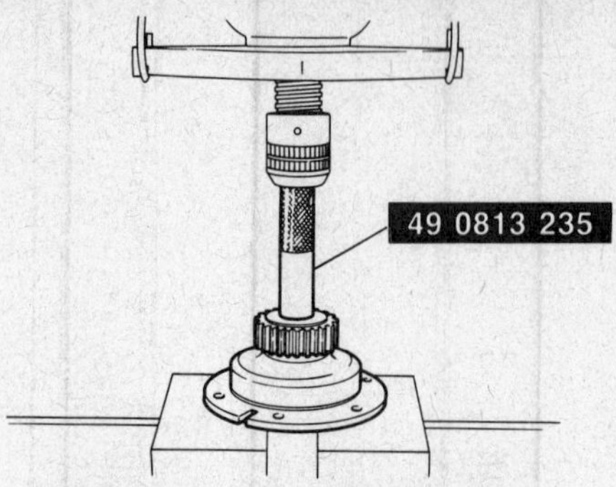

Fig. 11 Removing and installing main bearing

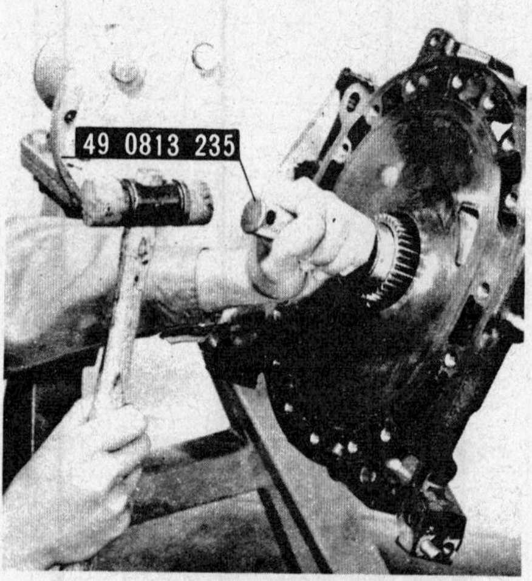

Fig. 13 Removing rear stationary gear

2. Using the puller & installer (49 0813 235), remove the stationary gear from the rear housing, **Fig. 13.**
3. Check the O-ring on the stationary gear for damage. Replace the O-ring if necessary.
4. Using the main bearing replacer without adapter ring, press the main bearing out of the stationary gear.
5. Use the main bearing replacer with adapter ring, and aligning the tang of the bearing and the slot of the stationary gear, press fit the main bearing into the stationary gear until the adapter touches the stationary gear flange.
6. Apply a thin coat of Vaseline on the O-ring and place it in the groove of the stationary gear.
7. Apply sealing agent onto the stationary gear flange.
8. Install the stationary gear to the rear housing, being careful not to damage the O-ring and aligning the slot of the stationary gear with the dowel pin on the rear housing, **Fig. 14.**
9. Tighten the bolts attaching the stationary gear.

Fig. 14 Installing rear stationary gear

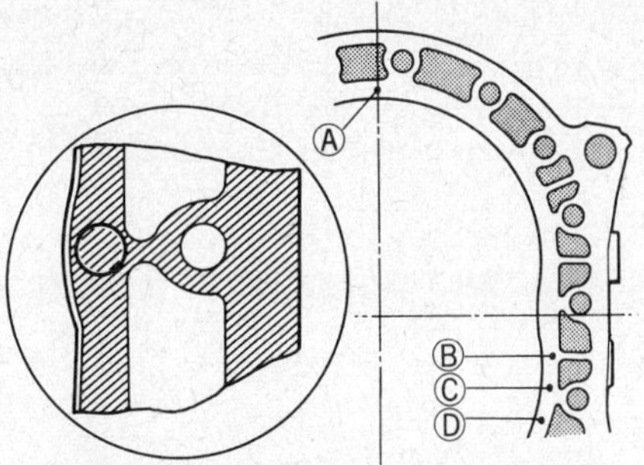

Fig. 15 Checking rotor housing width points

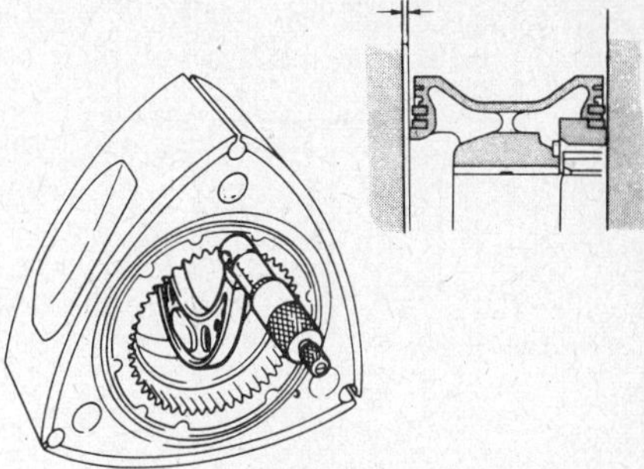
Fig. 16 Checking rotor width

4. The difference between maximum width of rotor and width of point A of rotor housing, **Fig. 15.** Clearance should be .0047-.0074 inch (.12-.19mm) on 1983-85 RX-7 models less fuel injected engine or .0047-.0083 inch (.12-.21mm) on 1984-87 RX-7 models with fuel injected engine.
5. If the clearance is more than the specification, replace the rotor assembly. If the clearance is less than the specification, it indicates that the internal gear has come out, so strike the internal gear lightly with plastic hammer, being careful not to damage, then recheck the clearance between the side housing and the rotor.
6. Check the corner seal bores for wear with the gauge (49 0839 165), **Fig. 17,** noting the following:
   a. If neither end of the gauge goes into the bore, use the original corner seal.
   b. If the not-go-end of the gauge does not go into the bore while the go-end does, replace with a new corner seal.
   c. If both ends of the gauge go into the bore, replace the rotor.

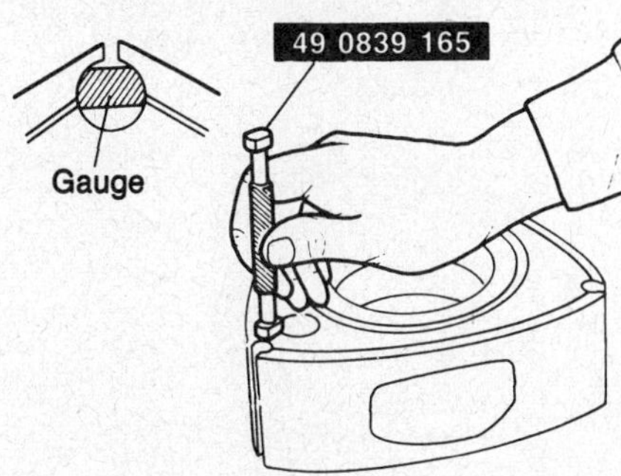

Fig. 17 Checking corner seal bore

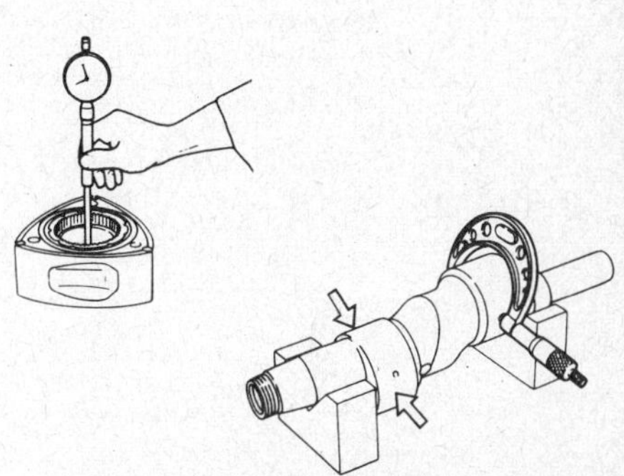
Fig. 18 Checking rotor bearing clearance

INSPECTING ROTOR HOUSING

1. Check the chromium plated surface on the rotor housing for scoring, flaking or any damage. If any of these conditions exists excessively, replace the rotor housing.
2. Check the rotor housing width at points close to the trochoid surface by using a micrometer. The measurements should be taken at four points, as shown in **Fig. 15.** If the difference between the value of point A and the minimum value among the points B, C and D exceeds 0.0024 in. (0.06mm), the rotor housing should be replaced with a new one.

INSPECTING ROTOR

1. Carefully inspect the rotor and replace if it is severely worn or damaged.
2. Check the internal gear for cracked, scored, worn or chipped teeth.
3. Check the clearance between the side housing and the rotor by measuring the rotor housing width and rotor width. The rotor width should be measured at three points, as shown in **Fig. 16.**

INSPECTING ROTOR BEARING

1. Check the rotor bearing for wear, flaking, scoring or any damage. If any of these conditions are found, replace the bearing.
2. Check the rotor bearing clearance by measuring the inner diameter of the rotor bearing and outer diameter of the eccentric shaft rotor journal, as shown in **Fig. 18.** The standard clearance is 0.0016-0.0031 in. (0.04-0.08mm). Replace the bearing if it is more than 0.0039 in. (0.10mm).

REPLACING ROTOR BEARING

1. Place the rotor on the support so that the internal gear is facing downward. Using the puller and installer (49 0813 240) without adapter ring, press the bearing out of the rotor, being careful not to damage the internal gear.
2. Place the rotor on the support with internal gear faced upward, and place the new rotor bearing on the rotor so that the bearing lug is in line with the slot of the rotor bore.
3. Remove the screws attaching the adapter ring to the replacer. Using the replacer and adapter, press fit the new bearing until the bearing is flush with the rotor boss.

INSPECTING ROTOR OIL SEAL & SPRING

1. Check the oil seal for wear or any damage. If the lip width of the oil seal is more than 0.02 in. (0.5mm), replace the oil seal.
2. Check the free movement of the oil seal in the rotor groove by pressing with finger.
3. Check the oil seal protrusion as shown in **Fig. 19** and replace the oil seal spring if the protrusion is less than 0.02 in. (0.5mm).

INSPECTING APEX SEAL, SIDE PIECE & SPRING

1. Check the apex seal and side piece for wear, crack or any damage. If any of these conditions is found, replace the seal. Check the spring for wear.
2. Measure the height of the apex seal with a micrometer at two positions shown in **Fig. 20.** Replace if the height is less than 0.276 in. (7.0mm) for 1983-85 models or 0.256 in. (6.5mm) for 1986-87 models. **On 1986-87 models, replace short apex seal spring, if apex seal height is below 0.295 in. (7.5mm).**
3. Place two apex seals together, top-to-top, and measure warpage using a feeler gauge. Repeat with all three

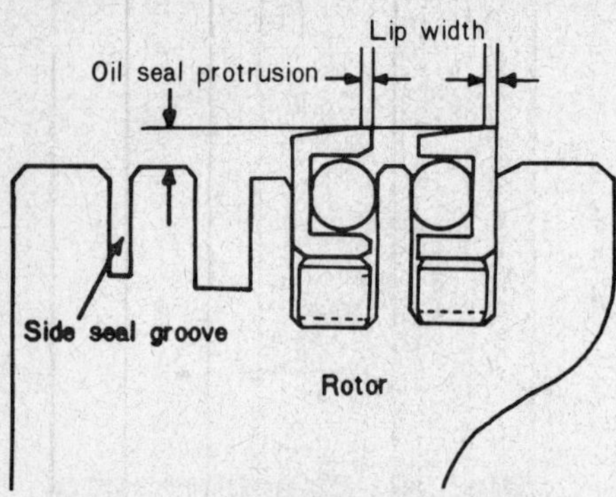

Fig. 19 Checking oil seal protrusion

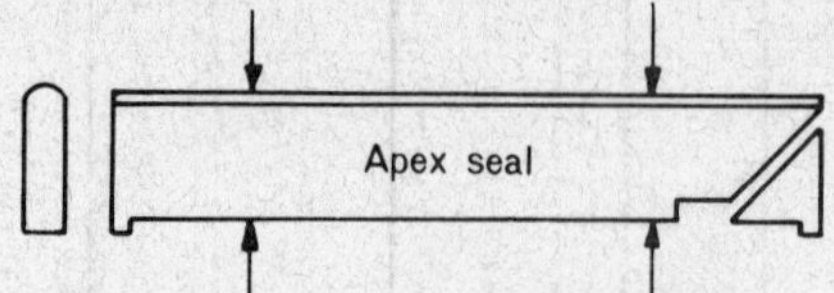

Fig. 20 Apex seal height

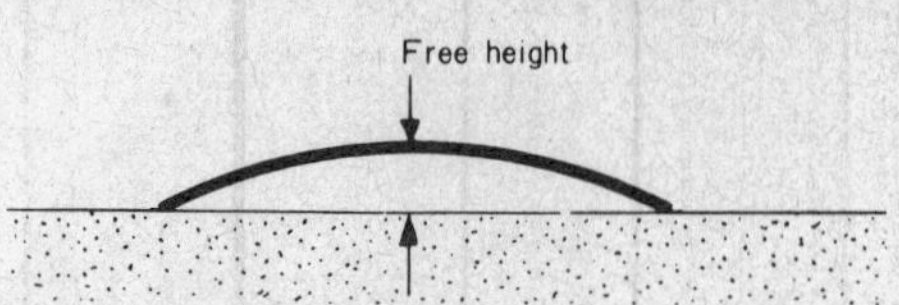

Fig. 21 Checking apex seal spring

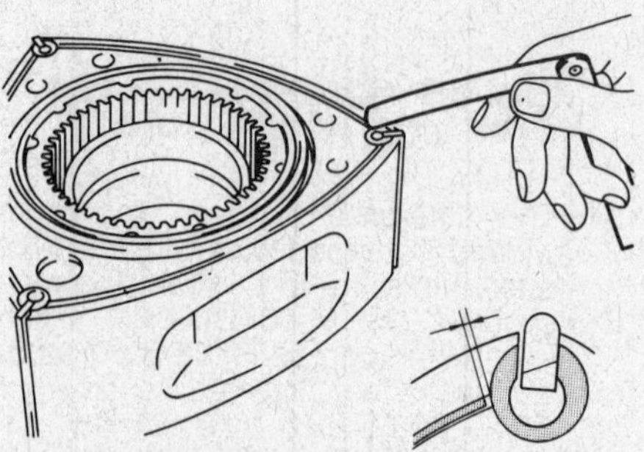

Fig. 23 Checking side seal to corner seal clearance

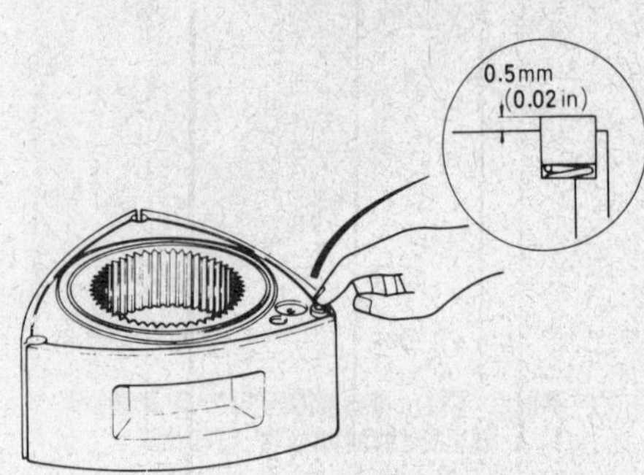

Fig. 24 Checking corner seal protrusion

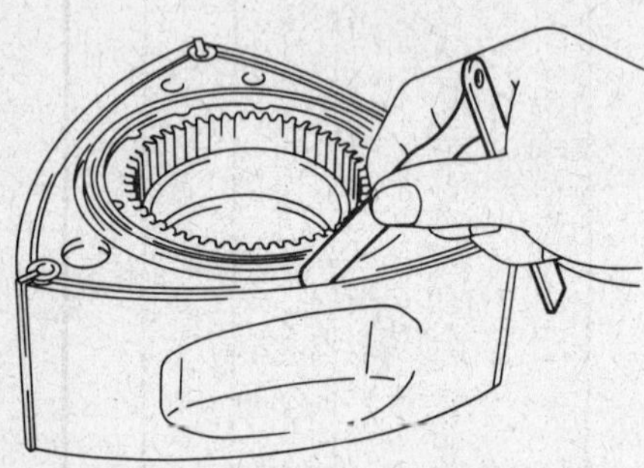

Fig. 22 Checking side seal clearance

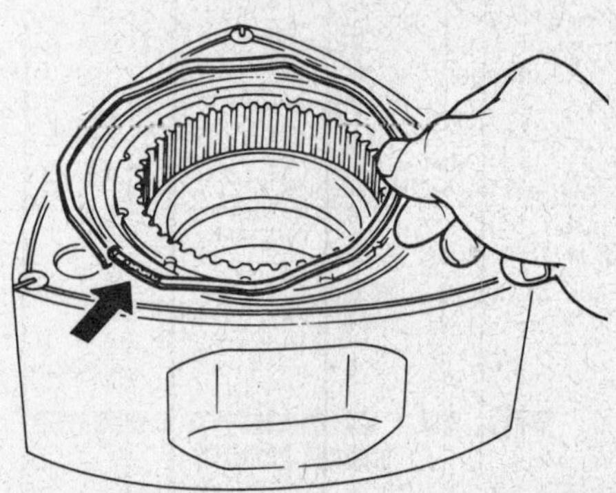

Fig. 26 Stopper hole of oil seal ring

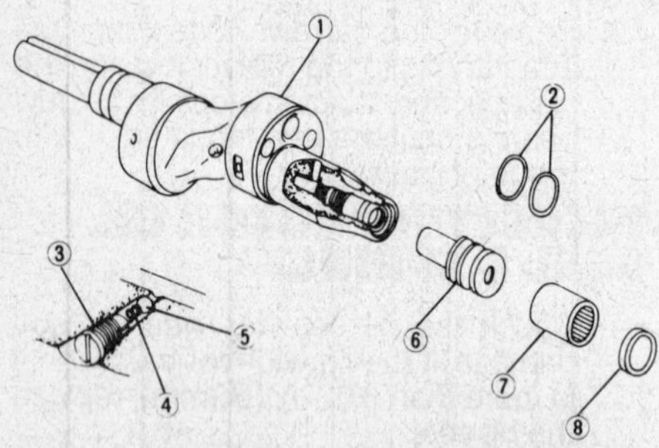

1. Eccentric shaft
2. "O" ring
3. Plug
4. Spring
5. Steel ball
6. Blind plug
7. Pilot bearing
8. Oil seal

Fig. 25 Eccentric shaft and related components

seals. If clearance exceeds .0024 in. (.06mm), replace all three rotor apex seals.

4. Check the clearance between the apex seal and the groove. To check the clearance, place the apex seal in its respective groove on the rotor and measure the clearance between the apex seal and the groove with a feeler gauge. The feeler gauge should be inserted until the tip of the gauge reaches the bottom of the groove. The standard clearance is 0.0020-0.0035 in. (0.05-0.090mm) for 1983-85 models or 0.0024-0.0040 in. (.062-.102mm) for 1986-87 models. If the clearance is more than 0.15 mm (0.0006 in), replace the apex seal.
5. Check the free height of apex seal spring, **Fig. 21.** Free height should measure .2165 inch (5.5mm) on 1983-84 models with 12A engine, .1496 inch (3.8mm) on 1984-85 models with 13A engine, .181 inch (4.6mm) for long spring on 1986–87 models or .118 inch (3mm) for short spring on 1986-87 models.

INSPECTING SIDE SEAL & SPRING

1. Check the free movement of the side seal in the rotor groove by pressing with finger.
2. Check the side seal protrusion from the rotor surface and replace the side seal spring if the protrusion is less than 0.02 in. (0.5mm).
3. Check clearance between side seal and the groove with a feeler gauge, **Fig. 22.** Standard clearance is .0011-.0031 inch (.03-.08mm). If clearance exceeds .0039 inch (.10mm), replace side seal.
4. Using a feeler gauge, check the clearance between the side seal and the corner seal with these seals installed on the rotor, **Fig. 23.** If the clearance exceeds 0.016 in. (0.4mm), replace the side seal. **When the side seal is replaced, adjust the clearance between the side seal and the corner seal by grinding the one end of the side seal along the round shape of the corner seal with a fine file so that the clearance will be 0.002-0.006 in. (0.05-0.15mm).**

INSPECTING CORNER SEAL & SPRING

1. Check the corner seal for wear, crack or any damage. If any of these conditions is found, replace the seal. Check the spring for wear.
2. Check the free movement of the corner seal in the rotor groove by pressing with finger.
3. Check the corner seal protrusion, **Fig. 24,** from the rotor surface and replace the corner seal spring if the protrusion is less than 0.02 in. (0.5mm).

INSPECTING ECCENTRIC SHAFT

1. Check the shaft for cracks, scratches, wear or any damage. Be sure that the oil passages are open.
2. Check the shaft for runout. To check, mount the shaft on V-blocks and install a dial indicator. Slowly rotate the shaft and note the reading on the indicator. If the run out is more than 0.0024 in. (0.06mm) for 1983-85 models or 0.0047 in. (.12mm) for 1986-87 models, replace the shaft with a new one.
3. Check the blind plug in the shaft end for oil leakage or looseness. If any oil leakage is found, remove the blind plug with a hexagonal Allen key and replace the O-ring, **Fig. 25.**

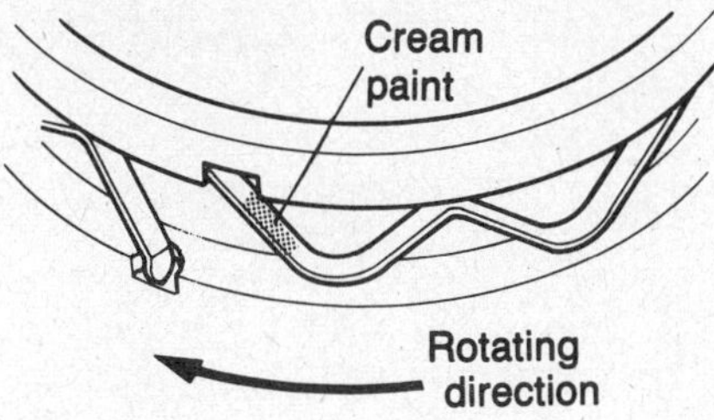

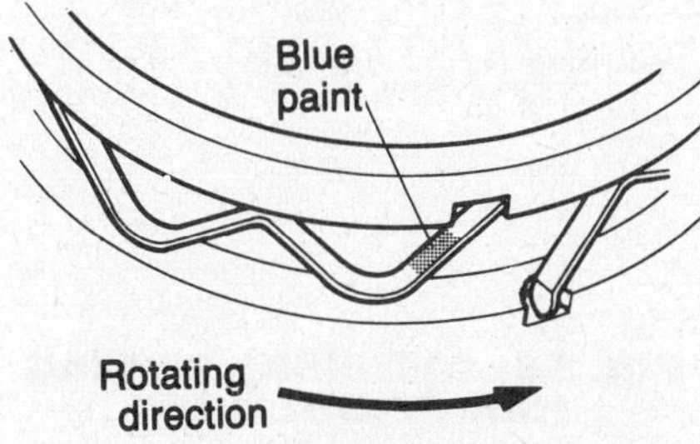

Fig. 27 Installing oil seal springs

4. The oil jets are installed in the eccentric shaft. The oil jets open when engine speed increases and oil pressure rises. Check for spring weakness, sticking or damage of the steel ball.

INSPECTING NEEDLE BEARING

Check needle bearing for wear or damage. Inspect bearing housing and thrust plate for wear or any damage.

INSPECTING ECCENTRIC SHAFT FRONT & REAR OIL SEALS

Check the front oil seal fitted into the front cover and the rear oil seal fitted into the rear stationary gear. If it is worn or damaged, replace the oil seal as follows:

1. Remove the oil seal by using a suitable tool.
2. Clean the oil seal mounting bore.
3. Position a new oil seal on its mounting bore and place a block of wood on the oil seal. Install the oil seal while tapping the wooden block with a hammer until it is firmly seated. **Do not coat the outer surface of the oil seal with any lubricant or sealing agent. Do not tap the oil seal directly with a hammer.**

CHECKING OIL PUMP DRIVE CHAIN SPROCKETS

Check the oil pump drive chain for broken links. Check the eccentric shaft sprocket and oil pump sprocket for cracks and worn or damaged teeth. If any defects are found, replace with new parts.

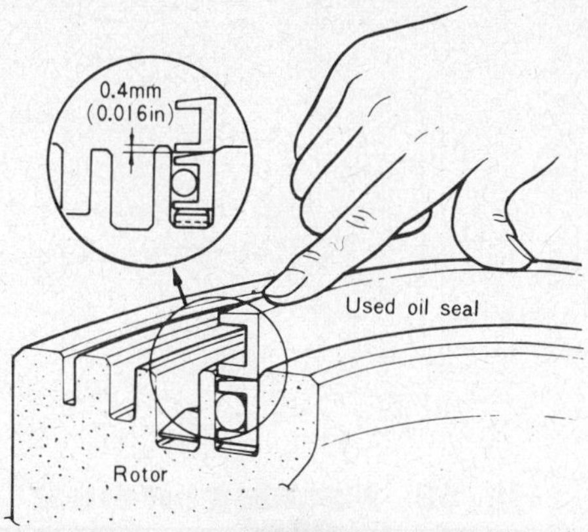

Fig. 28 Installing inner oil seal

ENGINE ASSEMBLY

OIL SEAL

1. Place the rotor on a rubber pad or cloth.
2. Install the oil seal springs in their respective grooves on the rotor with each round edge of the spring fitted in the stopper hole in the oil seal grooves as shown in **Fig. 26. The oil seal springs have been painted in cream or blue color. The cream-painted springs should be fitted on the front faces of both front and rear rotors. While the blue-painted springs should be fitted on the rear faces, Fig. 27.**
3. Install a new O-ring in each oil seal.
4. Place the inner oil seal in the oil seal groove so that the square edge of the spring fits in the stopper notch of the oil seal.
5. Press the inner oil seal by using a used inner oil seal so that the lip surface of the oil seal sinks into a position approximately 0.016 in. (0.4mm) below the surface of the rotor, as shown in **Fig. 28.**
6. Place the outer oil seal to the oil seal groove so that the square edge of the spring fits in the stopper notch of the oil seal.
7. Push the oil seal slowly with fingers. **When replacing the oil seal, confirm the smooth movement of the oil seal by placing the oil seal on the oil seal spring in the groove before inserting the O-ring. Be careful not to deform the lip of the oil seal.**
8. Apply sufficient engine oil onto each oil seal, and confirm the smooth movement of each oil seal by pressing the oil seal.
9. Install the oil seal springs and oil seals on the other side of the rotor.

FRONT SIDE SEALS

1. Place front rotor on rubber pad or cloth with internal gear upward.
2. Install apex seals without spring and side piece into their respective grooves so that side piece positions to the rear side of rotor, **Figs. 29 and 30.**

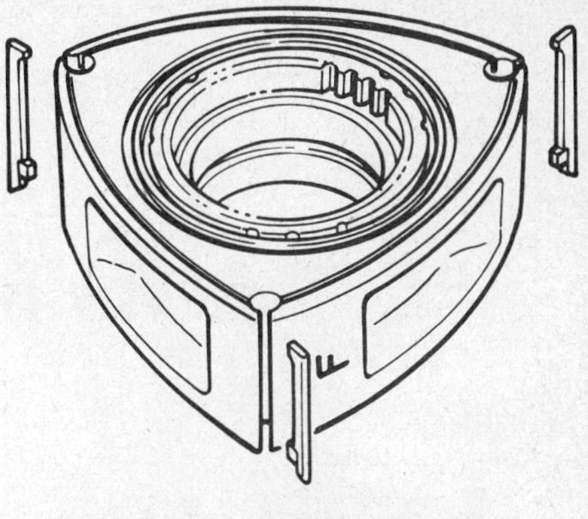

Fig. 29 Installing apex seal

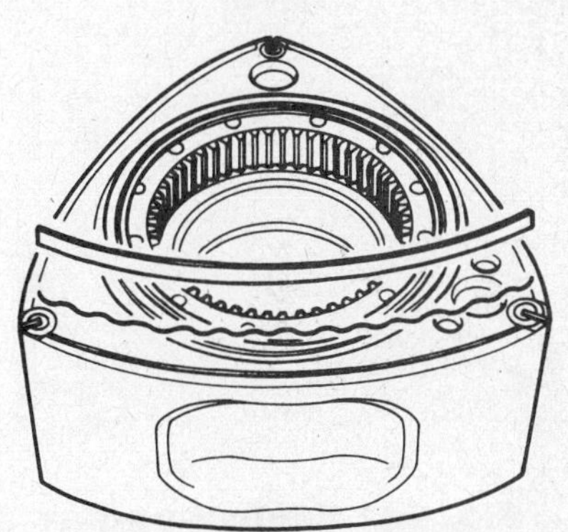

Fig. 30 Installing side seal

3. Apply engine oil onto each seal, and confirm the smooth movement of each seal by pressing its head.

FRONT ROTOR

1. Mount the front housing on the engine stand.
2. Apply engine oil onto the internal gear of the rotor.
3. Place the front rotor assembly on the front housing taking care not to drop the seals into the port, **Fig. 31.**
4. Mesh the internal gear and stationary gear so that one of the rotor apexes is set to any one of the four places shown in **Fig. 32.**

ECCENTRIC SHAFT

1. Lubricate the front rotor journal and main journal on the shaft with engine oil.
2. Insert the eccentric shaft, being careful not to damage the rotor bearing and main bearing, **Fig. 33.**

FRONT ROTOR HOUSING

1. Apply sealing agent onto the front side of the front rotor housing, as shown in **Fig. 34.**
2. Apply Vaseline onto new O-ring and sealing rubbers to prevent them from coming off, and place the O-ring and sealing rubbers on the front side of the front rotor housing.
   a. On 1983-85 models, the wider iine of the inner sealing rubber should face to combustion chamber and

Fig. 31 Installing front rotor

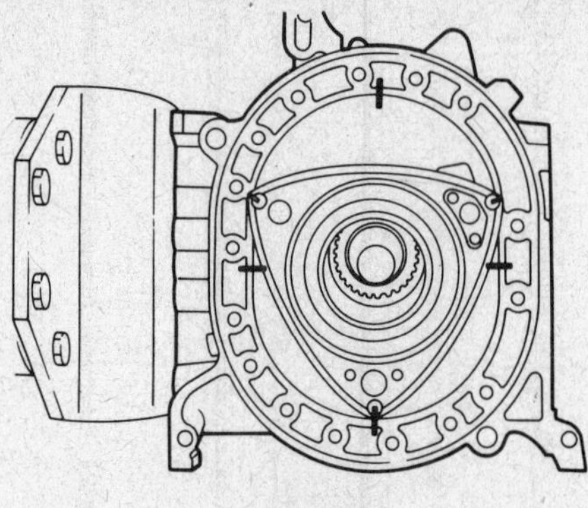

Fig. 32 Meshing internal gear

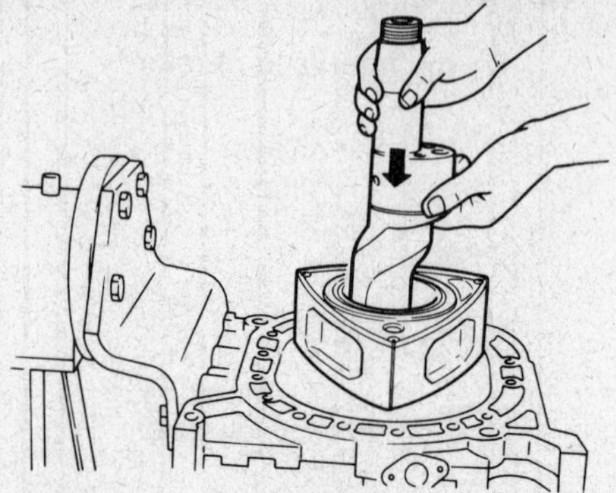

Fig. 33 Installing eccentric shaft

Fig. 34 Typical sealer application areas

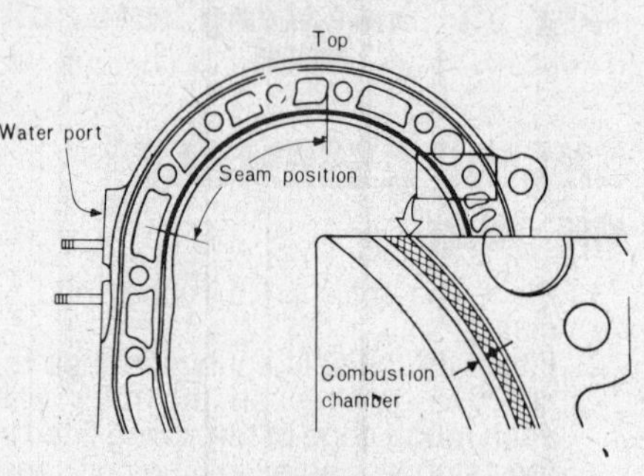

Fig. 35 Positioning inner seal rubber

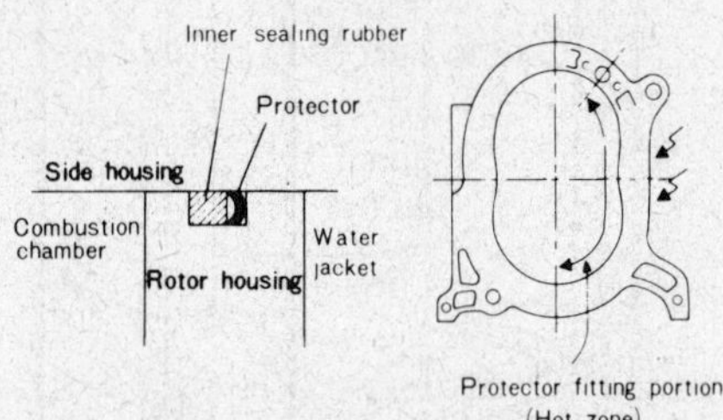

Fig. 36 Installing sealing rubber protector

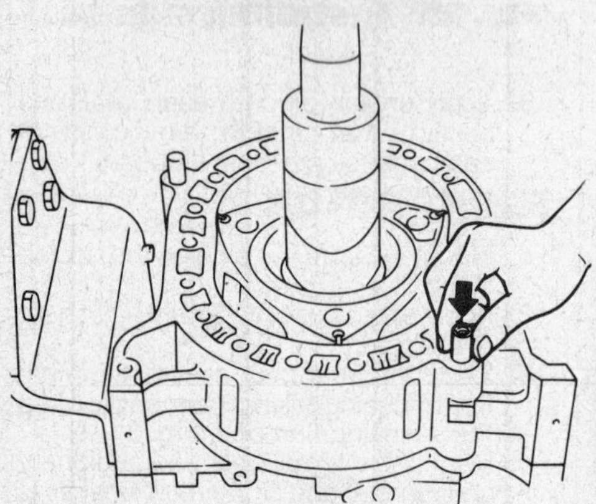

Fig. 37 Installing tubular dowels

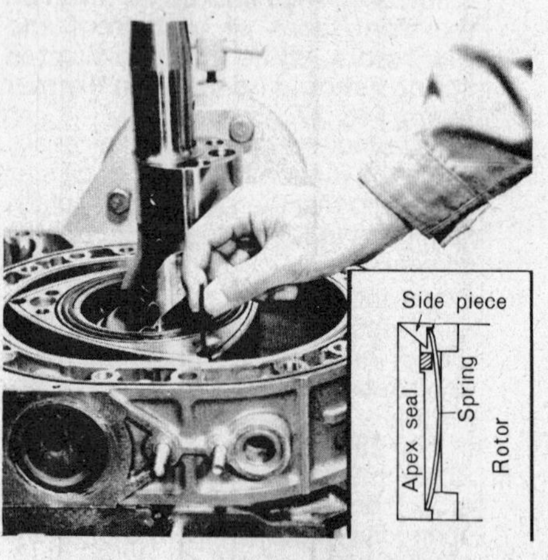

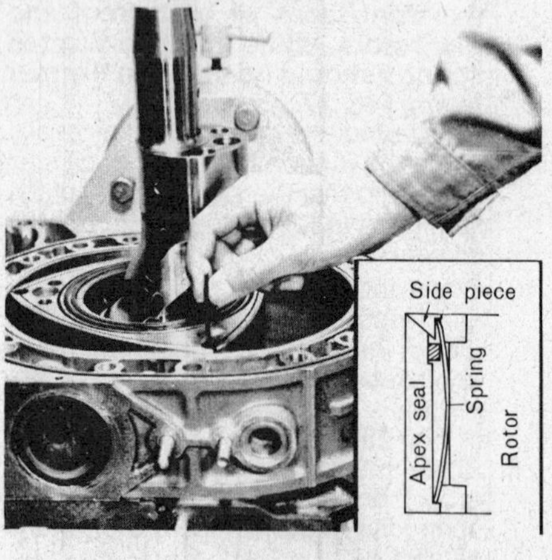

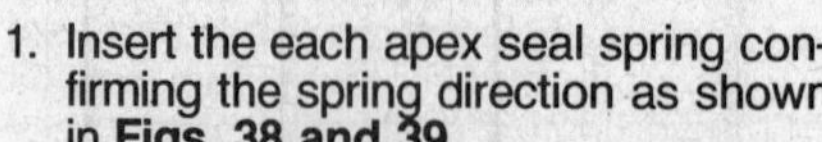

Fig. 38 Installing apex seal spring. 1983–85

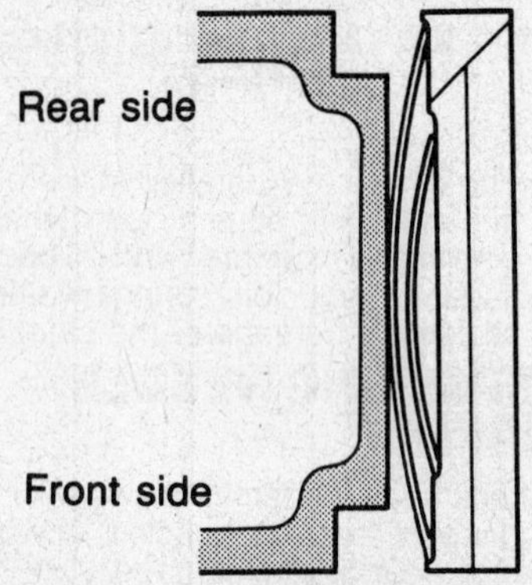

Fig. 39 Installing apex seal spring. 1986–87

the seam of the sealing rubber should be placed at the position as shown in **Fig. 35.** Do not stretch the sealing rubbers.

b. On 1983-85 models, when engine overhauling, install the protector behind the inner sealing rubber, as shown in **Fig. 36,** to improve the durability of the sealing rubber.

3. Invert the front rotor housing and install it onto the front housing, being careful not to drop the sealing rubbers and O-ring.
4. Apply engine oil onto the tubular dowels and insert the tubular dowels through the front rotor housing holes into the front housing holes, as shown in **Fig. 37.**

REAR SIDE SEALS

1. Insert the each apex seal spring confirming the spring direction as shown in **Figs. 38 and 39.**
2. Install the corner seal springs and corner seals into their respective grooves.
3. Install the side seal springs and side seals into their respective grooves, as shown in **Fig. 40.**
4. Fit each side piece to its original position, and confirm that the spring is set correctly on the side piece.
5. Apply engine oil onto each seal, and confirm the smooth movement of each seal by pressing its head.
6. Apply the sealing agent on the rear side of the front rotor housing, as instructed under "Front Rotor Housing."
7. Place new O-ring, sealing rubbers and protector on the rear side of the front rotor housing, as instructed under "Front Rotor Housing."
8. Apply engine oil onto the sliding surface of the front rotor housing. And make sure that the front rotor housing is free of any foreign matter.

INTERMEDIATE HOUSING

1. Turn the front housing so that the top of the housing inclines to upward.
2. Pull the eccentric shaft about 1 in. (25mm), but do not pull over 1.5 in. (35mm).
3. Install the intermediate housing through the eccentric shaft on the front rotor housing.

REAR ROTOR & REAR ROTOR HOUSING

1. Turn the engine on the engine stand

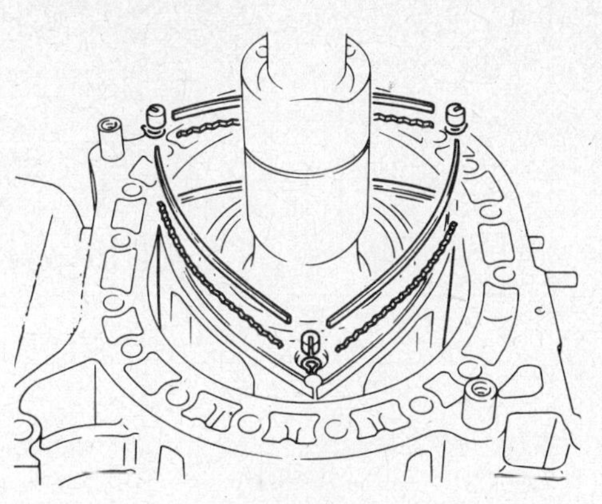

Fig. 40 Installing side seal & springs

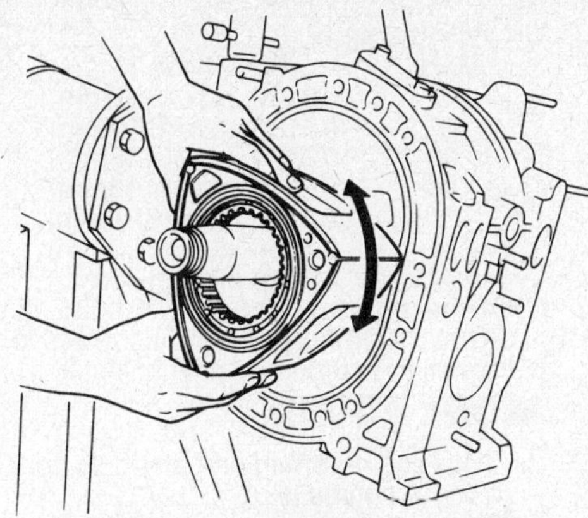

Fig. 41 Installing rear rotor

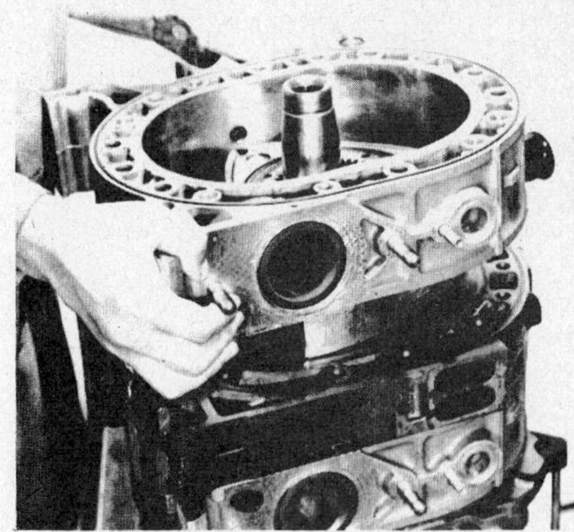

Fig. 42 Installing rear housing (Typical)

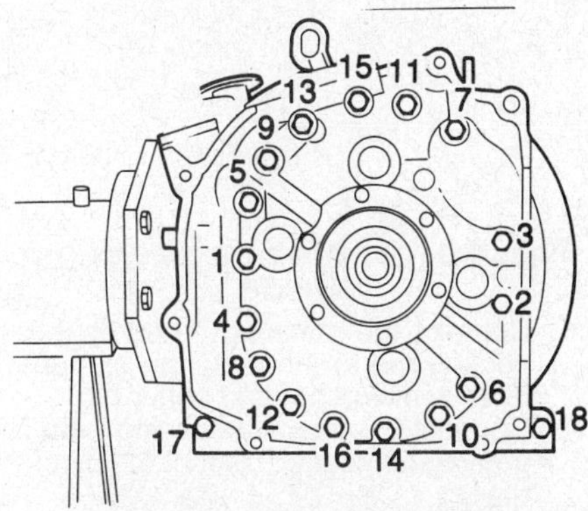

Fig. 43 Tension bolt tightening sequence

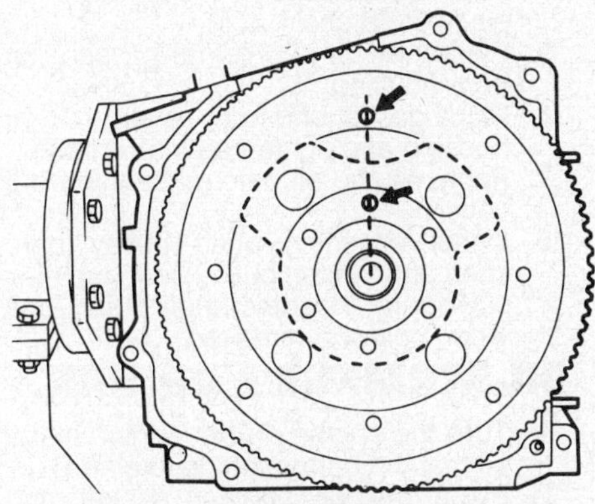

Fig. 44 Installing drive plate

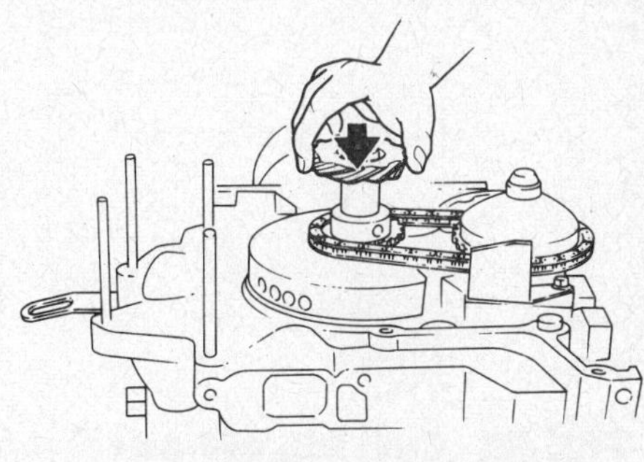

Fig. 45 Installing distributor drive gear

so that the rear of the engine is up.
2. Install the rear rotor and rear rotor housing, **Figs. 41 and 42.**

REAR HOUSING

1. Apply sufficient engine oil onto the stationary gear and main bearing.
2. Install the rear housing on the rear rotor housing, **Fig. 41.**

TORQUING TENSIONING BOLTS

1. Install a new sealing washer to each tension bolt.
2. Apply engine oil onto bolt threads.
3. Install tension bolts and torque in sequence, **Fig. 43,** in several steps to 23-29 ft. lbs. on models with fuel injected engine or 23-27 ft. lbs. on all other models. **Note that some engines will not have the No. 11 tension bolt. Also on 1986–87 models, the bolt marked "m" is for the No. 17 bolt position.**
4. Turn the eccentric shaft and make sure that the rotation is light and smooth. Replace the sealing washer in the tension bolt when the engine is overhauled.

FLYWHEEL

Manual Transmission

1. Turn the engine so that the top of the engine is up.
2. Apply engine oil to the oil seal in the rear housing.
3. Fit the key into keyway on the eccentric shaft.
4. Install the flywheel to the rear end of the eccentric shaft, aligning the keyway of the flywheel with the key.
5. Apply sealing agent to both sides of the flywheel lock washer and place it in position. Install the nut.
6. Install the suitable flywheel brake and with the box wrench (49 0820 035) tighten the nut to 290-360 ft. lbs. (40.0-50.0 m-kg).
7. Bend the tab of the lockwasher.
8. Install the clutch disc and clutch cover assembly on the flywheel.

COUNTER WEIGHT

Automatic Transmission

1. Turn the engine so that the top of the engine is up.
2. Apply engine oil to the oil seal in the rear housing.
3. Fit the key into keyway on the eccentric shaft.
4. Install counter weight to the rear end of the eccentric shaft, aligning the keyway of the counter weight with the key.
5. Apply sealing agent to inner side of the locknut and place it in position.
6. Install the stopper (49 1881 055) and with the box wrench (49 0820 035) tighten the nut to 40.0-50.0 m-kg (289-362 ft. lbs.).
7. Bend the tab of the lockwasher.
8. Install the drive plate on the counter weight as shown in **Fig. 44** and tighten the attaching bolts.

CHECKING ECCENTRIC SHAFT ENDPLAY

1. Turn the engine on the engine stand so that the front of the engine is up.
2. Fit the thrust plate with the chamfer downward, and slide the spacer and needle bearing onto the eccentric shaft, then apply sufficient engine oil onto them.
3. Place the bearing housing on the front housing. Tighten the attaching bolts with washers. **If the bearing housing has not been removed from the front housing, special care should be taken when installing the spacer, so that the center of the needle bearing in the bearing housing comes to the center of eccentric shaft, and the spacer should be seated to the thrust plate.**
4. Slide the needle bearing onto the shaft, and apply engine oil onto it.
5. Slide the balance weight together with the thrust washer onto the shaft.
6. Fit the key into keyway on the oil pump shaft.
7. Fit the oil pump drive chain onto the oil pump sprocket and eccentric shaft sprocket, and install them to the eccentric shaft and oil pump shaft, aligning the key and keyway, **Fig. 1.**
8. Align the keyways of the eccentric shaft sprocket and balance weight,

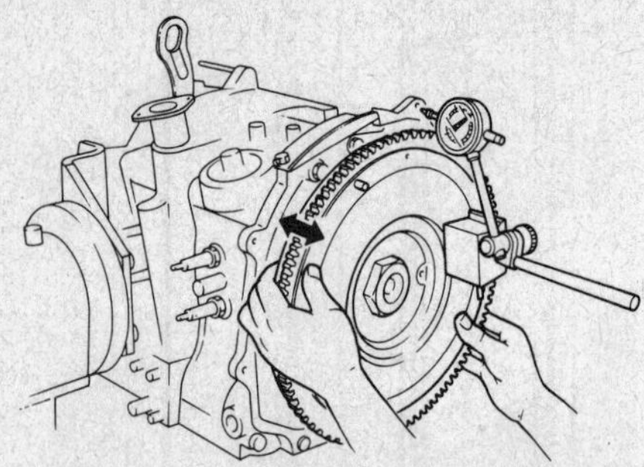

Fig. 46 Checking eccentric shaft endplay

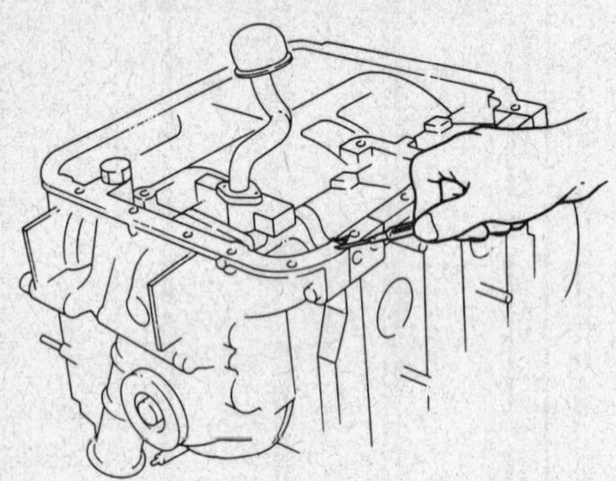

Fig. 48 Cutting off excess gasket

and install the key.

9. Slide the distributor drive gear onto the eccentric shaft with "F" mark toward the front of engine, **Fig. 45.**
10. Install the eccentric shaft pulley onto the shaft aligning the keyway of the pulley with the key.
11. Install the pulley bolt and washer.
12. Turn the engine on the engine stand so that the top of the engine is up.
13. To check the eccentric shaft endplay, position a dial indicator on the rear housing so as to contact the feeler with the flywheel or the counter weight as shown in **Fig. 46.**
14. Move the flywheel fore and aft, and note the reading of the indicator. The standard endplay is 0.0016-0.0028 in. (0.04-0.07mm).
15. If the endplay is more than 0.0035 in. (0.09mm), adjust it by grinding the spac er, **Fig. 47,** on the surface plate using an emery paper or by replacing the spacer with a thinner one.
6. If the endplay is less than 0.0016 in. (0.04mm), replace with a thicker spacer.

The spacers are available in the following thicknesses:

Identification Mark	Thickness
S	0.3197 inch, (8.12mm)
T	0.3189 inch, (8.10mm)
X	0.3181 inch, (8.08mm)
K	0.3173 inch, (8.06mm)
Y	0.3165 inch, (8.04mm)
V	0.3158 inch, (8.02mm)
Z	0.3150 inch, (8.00mm)

17. If the endplay is 0.0016-0.0035 in. (0.04-0.09mm), proceed as follows to install the oil pump chain adjuster.

FRONT COVER

1. Turn engine on engine stand so that front of engine is up.
2. Remove eccentric shaft pulley.
3. Tighten oil pump sprocket nut and bend tab of lock washer.
4. Check oil pump drive chain slack. If slack exceeds .047 in. (12mm), replace drive chain.
5. Place new O-ring on oil passage of front housing.
6. Place gasket and front cover on front housing and tighten attaching bolts.
7. Apply engine oil onto oil seal in front cover.
8. Install eccentric shaft pulley onto shaft and tighten pulley bolt. Use new washer in eccentric shaft pulley bolt when pulley is removed.

OIL STRAINER & OIL PAN

1. Turn the engine on the engine stand so that the bottom of the engine is up.
2. Place the oil strainer gasket and strainer gasket and strainer on the front housing and tighten the attaching bolts.
3. Cut off the excess gaskets along the mounting surface of the oil pan, as shown in **Fig. 48.**
4. Apply the 0.16-0.24 in. (4-6mm) diameter continuous bead of sealer (Part number 0398 77 739) on the mounting surface of the oil pan as shown in **Fig. 49.** Be sure there are no gaps in the sealer bead.
5. Position the oil pan on engine.
6. Install bolts and torque alternately and evenly to 6-8 ft. lbs.

MANIFOLD & CARBURETOR ASSEMBLY

Exc. Fuel Injected Engine

1. Place the O-rings and gasket in position.
2. Install intake manifold and carburetor assembly and tighten the attaching nuts.
3. Install the thermal reactor covers and tighten the attaching bolts and nuts.
4. Connect the air outlet hose valve to the air control valve.
5. Connect the oil hoses to metering oil pump outlets.

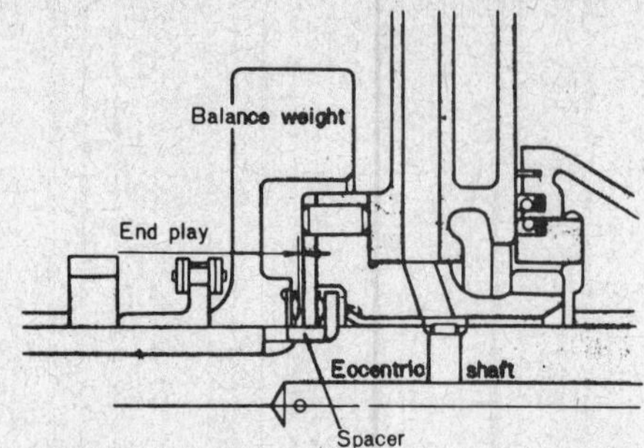

Fig. 47 Eccentric shaft end play

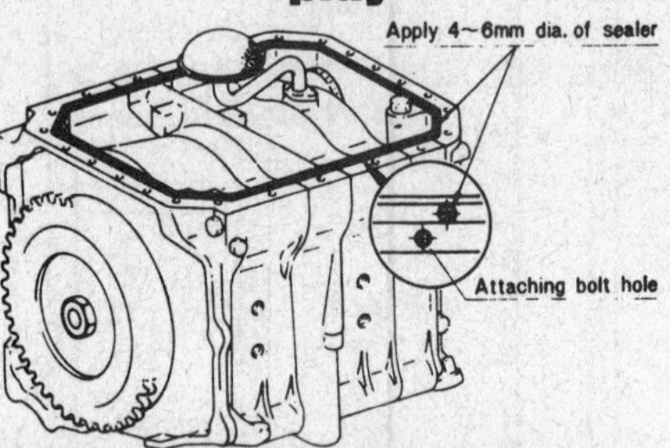

Fig. 49 Sealer application areas

6. Connect the metering oil pump connecting rod to the metering oil pump lever with washer and cotter pin.
7. Connect the vacuum sensing tube to the vacuum control unit of the distributor.

FINAL ASSEMBLY

Install components removed as described under "Preliminary Components" in the disassembly procedure in the reverse order of removal to complete engine assembly.

TURBOCHARGER

Some 1987 RX-7 models are equipped with a dual chamber scroll turbocharger. In this turbocharger design, the primary and secondary chambers are separated by an integrally cast wall, with an intake vacuum-activated valve spring serving as a gate to open or close the secondary chamber. At low engine speeds, the smaller primary chamber concentrates exhaust gases and increases their velocity. This results in a significant improvement in throttle response and engine torque. At engine speeds above 2500 RPM or under certain load conditions, the larger secondary chamber opens, directing additional exhaust gases across the entire face of the turbine blades, providing increased engine horsepower and RPM. An air-to-air intercooler is positioned directly above the engine plenum chamber to cool incomming pressurized air.

626 DIESEL ENGINE SECTION

INDEX

ENGINE
REPLACE

1. Disconnect battery ground cable.
2. Remove hood.
3. Remove oil filler cap and radiator cap.
4. Raise and support vehicle.
5. Remove both front wheels.
6. Drain engine oil and coolant. Drain enough transaxle oil to avoid leakage when driveshafts are removed.
7. Disconnect starter motor wiring.
8. Disconnect wiring from oil pressure switch.
9. Disconnect lower radiator hose.
10. Remove rubber exhaust supports.
11. Remove exhaust pipe with bracket.
12. Disconnect shift linkage and support rod from transaxle.
13. Separate right and left tie rod ends.
14. Remove clinch bolt and nut and pull lower control arm down to disconnect ball joint from steering knuckle. Repeat on opposite side.
15. Insert suitable lever between right driveshaft and joint shaft, **Fig. 1,** and uncouple driveshaft and joint shaft. Pull front hub forward and separate driveshaft from joint shaft.
16. Remove 3 nuts from engine mount.
17. Lower vehicle.
18. Remove air cleaner assembly.
19. Disconnect Q.S.S. relay and glow plug relay from air cleaner bracket and remove bracket, **Fig. 2.**
20. Disconnect clutch release cylinder.
21. Remove engine harness bracket.
22. Disconnect engine ground strap from transaxle case.
23. Disconnect speedometer cable from transaxle case.
24. Insert suitable lever between driveshaft and transaxle and uncouple driveshaft end. Take care not to damage transaxle oil seal.
25. Install differential side gear holder 49 G030 455, or equivalent, on transaxle case.

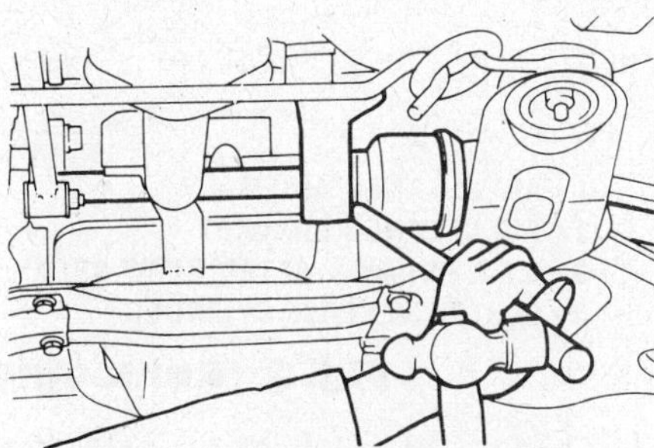

Fig. 1 Removing right hand drive shaft

26. Disconnect electric cooling fan wiring connector, **Fig. 3.**
27. Disconnect back up lamps connector.
28. Disconnect 2 fuel hoses from fuel injection pump.
29. Disconnect glow plug wiring connector.
30. Disconnect RPM sensor connector.
31. Disconnect fuel cut valve connector.
32. Disconnect water temperature sensor connector from thermostat body.
33. Disconnect upper radiator hose from thermostat cover.
34. Disconnect coolant level sensor connector, coolant temperature switch coupler and ground wire.
35. Disconnect coolant overflow hose from radiator.
36. Remove radiator and mounting snubbers.
37. Disconnect accelerator cable from fuel injection pump.
38. Disconnect CSD cable from fuel injection pump, **Fig. 3.**
39. Disconnect alternator harness.
40. Disconnect brake vacuum hose from pipe.
41. Disconnect 2 coolant hoses from oil cooler.
42. Disconnect oil bypass hoses from oil cooler.
43. Disconnect engine ground cable from body.
44. Remove torque limiter.
45. Remove engine and transaxle from vehicle.
46. Reverse procedure to install.

ENGINE DISASSEMBLY
EXTERNAL COMPONENTS

1. Remove dipstick and tube assembly, **Fig. 4.**
2. Remove oil pressure gauge.
3. Disconnect 2 vacuum pump oil hoses from side of engine.
4. Remove alternator drive belt by loosening 2 alternator mounting bolts.
5. Remove alternator and mounting brackets.
6. Mount engine on suitable stand.
7. Remove engine lifting eyes.
8. Remove engine mount located below crankshaft pulley.
9. Remove exhaust manifold heat shield.
10. Remove coil cooler inlet hose and pipe.
11. Remove intake manifold.
12. Remove oil filter, oil return pipe, and oil cooler assembly.

TIMING BELT ASSEMBLY

1. Install ring gear brake 49 V101 060 or equivalent.
2. Remove crankshaft pulley, **Fig. 5.**
3. Remove right and left timing belt covers.
4. Remove valve cover.
5. Loosen belt tensioner lock bolt. Push tensioner away from belt as far as possible, then tighten tensioner lock bolt.
6. Remove timing belt. If belt is to be reused, draw arrow on belt indicating direction of rotation.
7. Hold camshaft with 29mm wrench, and loosen front camshaft pulley lock bolt.
8. Using suitable puller, pull camshaft sprocket from camshaft. Do not strike camshaft sprocket with hammer.

9. Remove seal plate, **Fig. 5.**
10. Remove stopper casing, **Fig. 5.**
11. Remove brake vacuum pipe.
12. Remove water pump.
13. Remove timing belt crankshaft sprocket.

INJECTION PUMP TIMING BELT ASSEMBLY

1. Remove injection pump rear timing belt cover, **Fig. 6.**
2. Loosen tensioner lock bolt, rotate as far clockwise as possible, then tighten lock bolt.
3. Remove rear timing belt. If belt is to be reused, draw arrow indicating direction of rotation.
4. Remove tensioner and spring.
5. Using 29mm wrench, hold camshaft and loosen rear camshaft sprocket lock bolt.
6. Using puller 49 S120 215A, or equivalent, pull rear camshaft sprocket from camshaft. Do not strike sprocket with hammer.
7. Install two M81.2545mm bolts through holes in injection pump sprocket and thread into fuel injection pump bracket to prevent sprocket from turning while loosening lock bolt.
8. Loosen fuel injection pump sprocket lock bolt. Remove two bolts installed in step 7.
9. Using sprocket puller 49 S120 215A, or equivalent, pull sprocket from injection pump shaft.
10. Remove rear seal plate.
11. Remove fuel injection pipes.
12. Using universal wrench, remove fuel injection pump, **Fig. 7.**
13. Remove fuel injection pump bracket.

CYLINDER HEAD

1. Remove fuel return pipe, **Fig. 8.**
2. Remove fuel injection nozzles, washers and corrugated washers.
3. Remove glow plugs and cable.
4. Loosen camshaft cap nuts in sequence shown in **Fig. 9.**
5. Remove camshaft.
6. Remove adjusting discs and tappets.
7. Loosen cylinder head bolts in sequence shown in **Fig. 10.**
8. Using plastic hammer, tap cylinder head to assist in removal.
9. Using suitable valve spring compressor, remove valves, spring seats and valve cotters.
10. Remove lower spring seats, then valve seals using valve seal remover 49 S120 170.
11. Using suitable mandrel, remove combustion chamber inserts from bottom surface of cylinder head.

OIL PUMP & FLYWHEEL

1. Install ring gear brake on flywheel. Remove clutch cover, clutch disc and flywheel, **Fig. 11.**
2. Remove oil pan and pickup.
3. Remove rear cover assembly.
4. Remove oil pump body assembly.

CRANKSHAFT & PISTONS

1. Remove connecting rod bearing caps, **Fig. 12.**

1 - AIR CLEANER ASSEMBLY
2 - AIR CLEANER BRACKET
3 - Q.S.S. RELAY & AFTER GLOW RELAY
4 - CLUTCH RELEASE CYLINDER
5 - ENGINE HARNESS BRACKET
6 - ENGINE GROUND CABLE
7 - SPEEDOMETER CABLE

Fig. 2 Removing air cleaner and wiring

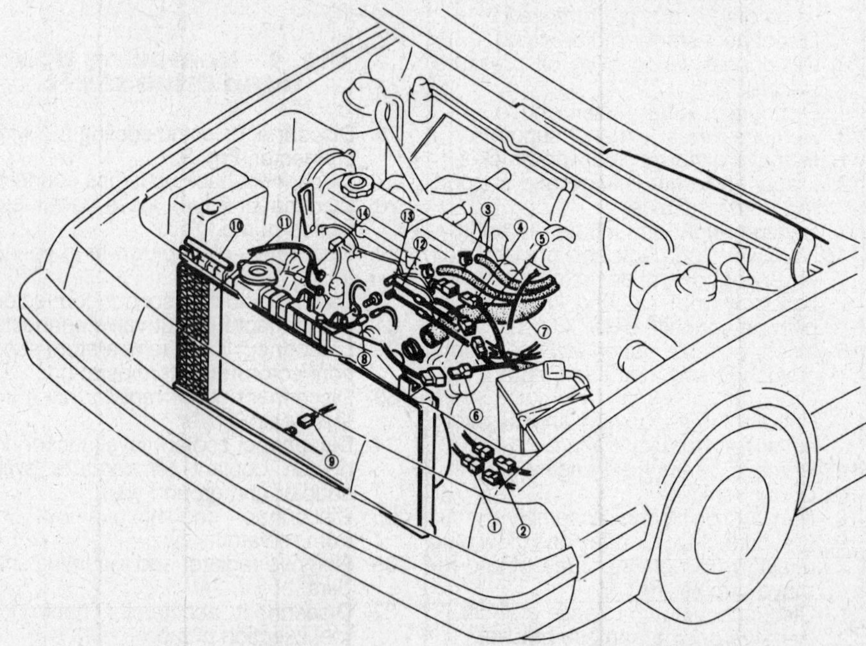

1 - ELECTRIC COOLING FAN COUPLER
2 - BACK-UP LAMP SWITCH COUPLER
3 - FUEL HOSE
4 - GLOW PLUG COUPLER
5 - FUEL-CUT VALVE COUPLER
6 - WATER TEMPERATURE SENSOR COUPLER
7 - UPPER RADIATOR HOSE
8 - COOLANT LEVEL SENSOR COUPLER
9 - WATER TEMPERATURE SWITCH COUPLER
10 - SUB TANK HOSE
11 - RADIATOR
12 - ACCELERATOR WIRE
13 - C.S.D. WIRE
14 - ALTERNATOR HARNESS

Fig. 3 Disconnecting engine wiring

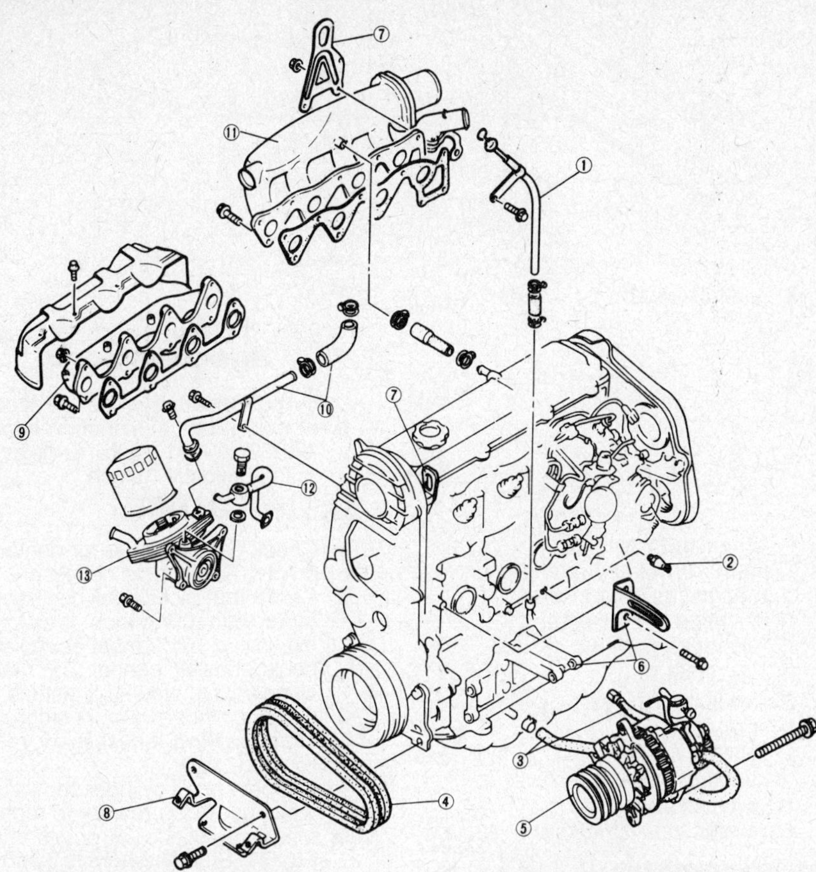

1 - OIL LEVEL GAUGE ASSEMBLY
2 - OIL PRESSURE SWITCH
3 - VACUUM PUMP HOSES
4 - V-BELT
5 - ALTERNATOR
6 - ALTERNATOR STRAP & BRACKET
7 ENGINE HANGERS
8 - NO. 3 ENGINE MOUNT
9 - EXHAUST MANIFOLD
10 - OIL COOLER INLET HOSE & PIPE
11 - INTAKE MANIFOLD
12 - OIL COOLER RETURN PIPE
13 - OIL COOLER ASSEMBLY

Fig. 4 Engine external components

2. Remove piston assembly from engine block.
3. Remove connecting rod bearings.
4. Disassemble piston and connecting rod assembly into following components:
   a. Snap rings.
   b. Piston pins.
   c. Connecting rod.
   d. Piston.
   e. Piston rings.
5. Remove main bearing caps.
6. Remove crankshaft.
7. Remove main bearings and thrust bearings.
8. Using needle bearing puller 49 1285 071 or equivalent, remove pilot bearing from crankshaft end.
9. Remove oil jets and oil jet valves.

INSPECTION & REPAIR

CYLINDER HEAD

1. Inspect for coolant leakage, fuel leakage, damage and cracks. Replace cylinder head as necessary.
2. Check that distortion does not exceed .004 inch, in 6 planes shown in **Fig. 13.** If distortion is excessive, replace cylinder head. Do not attempt to mill head.
3. Check that manifold contact surface distortion does not exceed .008 inch. Mill or replace head as necessary.

COMBUSTION CHAMBER INSERT

1. Check combustion chamber insert projection, **Fig. 14.** Chamber must not project less than .0016 inch or project more than .0024 inch. If either limit is exceeded, replace insert or cylinder head as necessary.

VALVE SEATS

1. Using straight edge and feeler gauge, measure valve recession from cylinder head surface. If valve has receded .061-.100 inch, install an equivalent shim under valve seat. If valve has receded more than .100 inch, replace cylinder head.
2. Check valve seat for roughness or damage. Check contact width by applying red lead to valve seat and pressing valve against seat.
3. Use 15, 45, or 60 degree valve seat cutter to remove roughness or scars. Maintain minimum valve seat contact width of .067-.091 inch, **Fig. 15.**
4. Seat valve by applying thin coat of engine oil and small amount of compound to seat surface. Lightly tap while turning valve.

VALVES

1. Inspect each valve and replace any that show valve stem wear, damage, bending or nicks. Intake valve stem diameter should be .3138-.3144 inch; exhaust valve stem diameter should be .3136-.3142 inch.
2. Check valve faces for roughness or damage. Reface or replace valve as necessary.

VALVE GUIDES

1. Check difference between valve guide inner diameter and valve stem diameter. Replace valve guide if clearance exceeds .004 inch, **Fig. 16.**
2. Drive valve guide out through top of cylinder head, away from combustion chamber, **Fig. 17.**
3. Install clip on new valve guide, and tap valve guide in from top of cylinder head until clip barely contacts cylinder head, **Fig. 18.** Note that exhaust valve guides are shorter than intake valve guides. After guide is installed, check valve guide clearance again.

VALVE SPRINGS

1. Inspect each valve spring for cracks or other damage.
2. Check that free length of each spring is 1.764 inches. Check that variation from perpendicular does not exceed .062 inch.

TAPPET & ADJUSTING DISC

1. Check that tappet outer diameter is 1.3763-1.3771 inches. If not, replace tappet.
2. Check that inner diameter of tappet bore is 1.3776-1.3787 inches. Clearance between tappet and bore should be .0008-.0024 inch and must not exceed .0040 inch.

CAMSHAFT

1. Measure camshaft lobe height. Standard intake lobe height is 1.744 inches, and must be no less than 1.728 inches. Standard exhaust lobe height is 1.783 inches, and must be no less than 1.768 inches.
2. Measure journal wear at four places as shown in **Fig. 19.** Standard journal diameter is 1.258-1.259 inches and should be no less than 1.254 inches.
3. Check that camshaft run out does not exceed .0040 inch.
4. Remove tappets and adjusting discs noting their locations. Clean oil and dirt from camshaft and cylinder head journal. Set plastic gauge on camshaft journal. Install camshaft journal cap and torque to 15-20 ft. lbs. Remove camshaft cap and check clearance. Clearance should be .00098-.0026 inch and must not exceed .0039 inch. If clearance is excessive, camshaft or

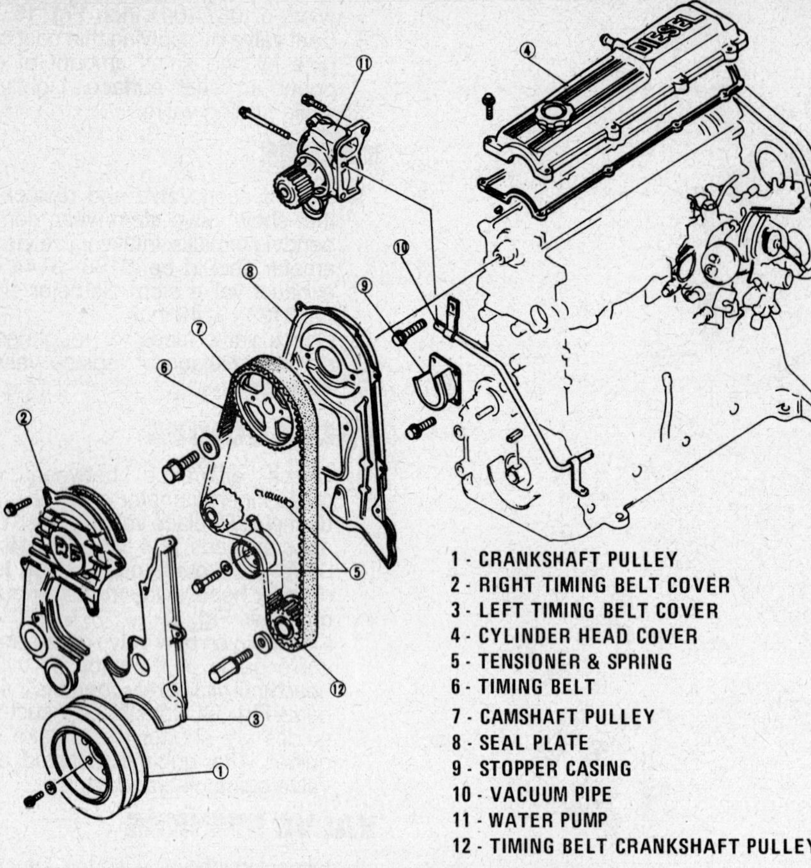

Fig. 5 Timing belt assembly

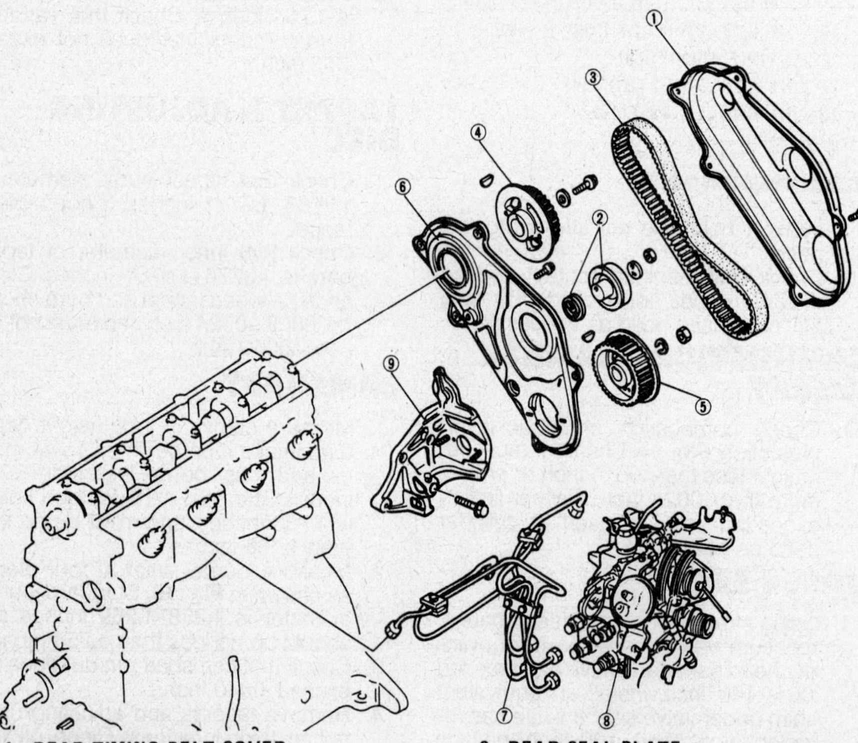

Fig. 6 Injection pump timing belt assembly

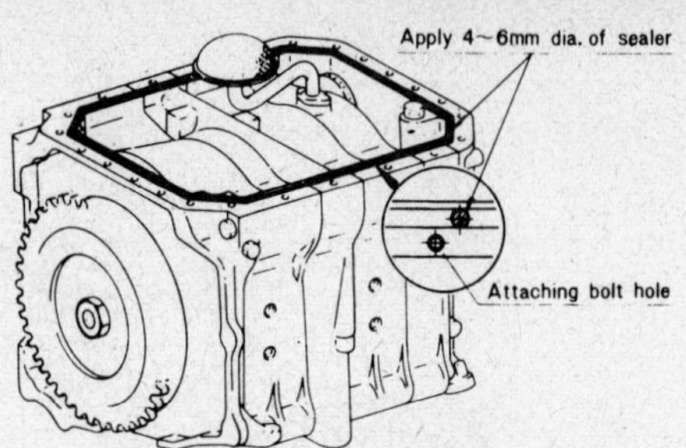

Fig. 7 Removing fuel injection pump

cylinder head must be replaced.

5. Check that camshaft endplay is .00079-.00591 inch. Endplay must not exceed .0079 inch.

ENGINE BLOCK

1. Check each cylinder for damage and cracks. Replace as necessary.
2. Check that block deck distortion is no more than .0040 inch. If distortion is excessive, block must be replaced as deck surface cannot be machined since valves would hit pistons.
3. Check cylinder walls for signs of seizing or scoring. If necessary, rebore or replace block.
4. If upper part of cylinder shows uneven wear, use ridge reamer to repair.
5. Measure cylinder at points shown in **Fig. 20.** Standard bore is 3.386-3.387 inches and must be no less than 3.39 inch. Difference between cylinder bore measurements should not exceed .0009 inch. Pistons are available in .010 and .020 inch oversizes.

PISTONS & RINGS

1. Inspect piston circumference for scoring or seizing. Replace as necessary.
2. Measure piston outside diameter in thrust direction, **Fig. 21.** Standard piston diameter is 3.384-3.385 inch. Piston to bore clearance should not exceed .006 inch. If piston is replaced, replace piston rings also. Piston rings are available in .010 and .020 oversizes.
3. Inspect piston rings for damage, abnormal wear, or breakage. Replace as required.
4. Insert piston in bore and push in using a piston. Check that ring end gap does not exceed .039 inch.
5. Check that piston ring side clearance does not exceed .008 inch.

CONNECTING RODS

1. Check that connecting rod bend does not exceed .006 inch per 3.94 inches.
2. Check that connecting rod twist does not exceed .006 inch per 3.94 inches.
3. Measure clearance between outer diameter of piston pin and inner diameter of bushing. Standard bushing diameter is .9846-.9854 inch. Clearance between pin and bushing must not exceed .002 inch.
4. If necessary, replace connecting rod bushing using a press and a pipe 1.06-1.88 inch in diameter. Oil new bushing and connecting rod. Align

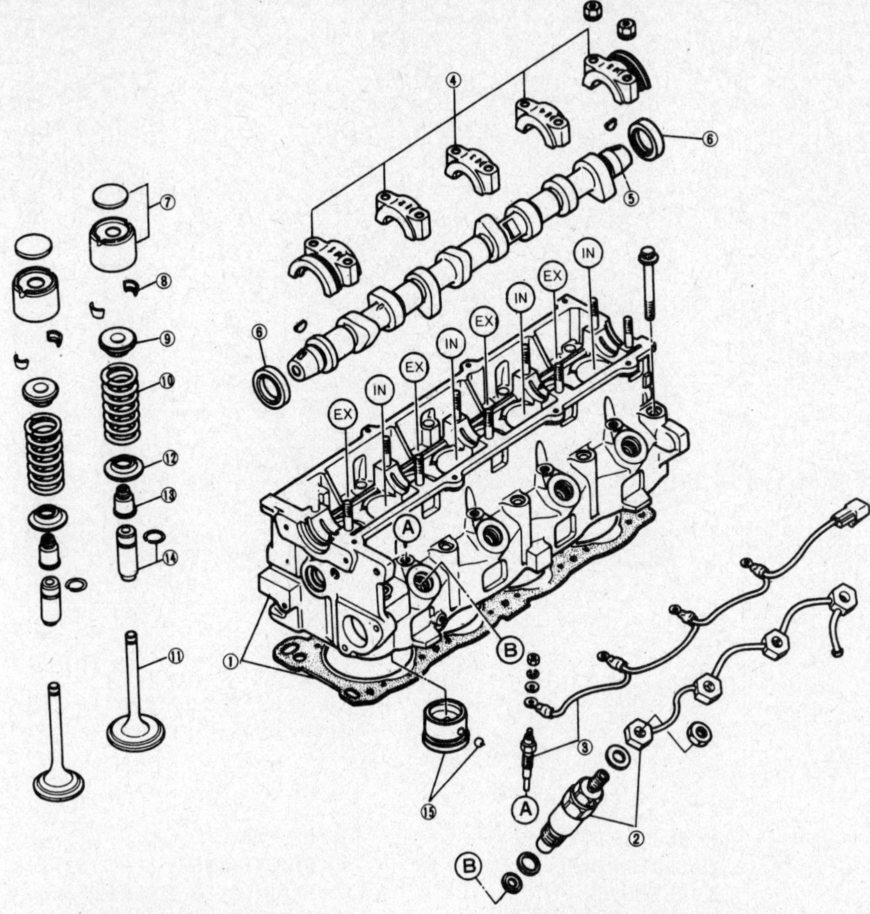

1 - CYLINDER HEAD & GASKET
2 - INJECTION PIPE & NOZZLE
3 - GLOW PLUG
4 - CAMSHAFT CAP
5 - CAMSHAFT
6 - OIL SEAL
7 - TAPPET & ADJUSTING DISC
8 - VALVE COTTER
9 - UPPER VALVE SPRING SEAT
10 - VALVE SPRING
11 - VALVE
12 - LOWER VALVE SPRING SEAT
13 - VALVE SEAL
14 - VALVE GUIDE & CLIP
15 - COMBUSTION CHAMBER INSERT

Fig. 8 Exploded view of cylinder head

bushing oil hole and connecting rod oil hole and press bushing in. Ream out bushing to correct diameter.

CRANKSHAFT

1. Check main and rod journals for damage, scoring, and clogged oil holes.
2. Check that crankshaft run out does not exceed .002 inch.
3. Measure journal diameters:
   a. Main journals, 2.360-2.361 inches.
   b. Connecting rod journals, 2.0055-2.0063 inches.
   c. Oil seal surface of crankshaft flange, 3.541-3.543 inches. Wear should not exceed .0020 inch on any journal. If wear is excessive, crankshaft must be reground. Do not remove more than .0295 inch. Bearings are available in .010, .020, and .0295 inch undersizes.
4. When grinding crankshaft, maintain a fillet R dimension of .102-.118 inch.

MAIN & CONNECTING ROD BEARINGS

1. Check main and connecting rod bearings inside surfaces for streaking, flaking, pin holes, etc. If any damage is found, replace all bearings as set.

TIMING BELTS

Inspect timing belts for following conditions and replace belt(s) as necessary. **Never twist or kink timing belt. Do not allow oil, grease, or moisture on timing belt.**

1. Premature breakage – check for proper installation. Check that timing belt cover gaskets are installed and not damaged.
2. Cracked, damaged or missing teeth.
3. Noticeable wear or cracks on belt face.
4. Wear or damage on one side only.
5. Noticeable wear on belt teeth.

TIMING BELT TENSIONER

Check rotation of tensioner pulley. Check for play or abnormal noise. Replace as necessary. Do not immerse tensioner in cleaning fluid. If dirty, clean with rag to avoid scratching tensioner.

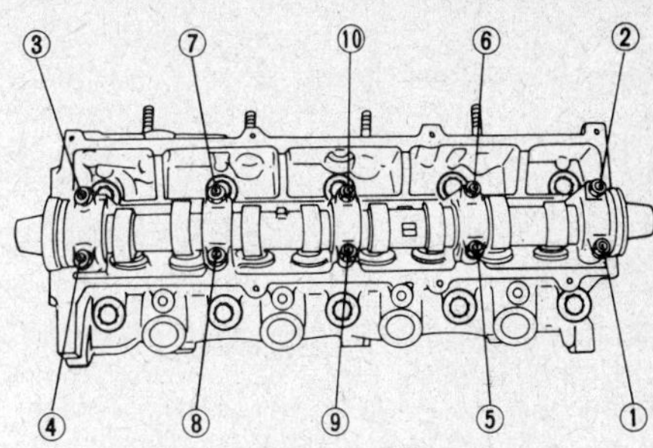

Fig. 9 Camshaft caps loosening sequence

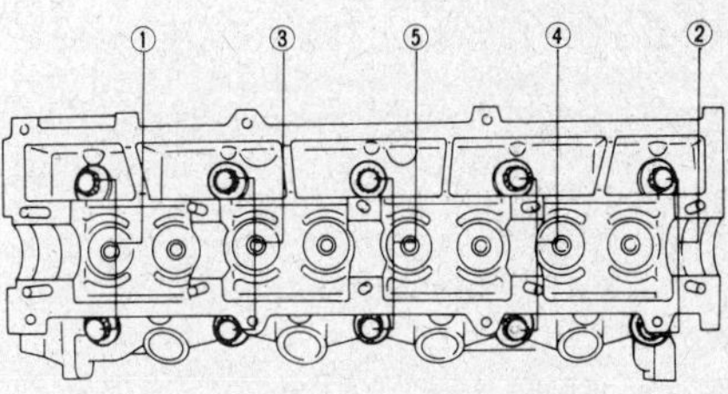

Fig. 10 Cylinder head bolt loosening sequence

TIMING BELT SPROCKETS

Inspect sprocket teeth for wear, deformation, or other damage. Replace if necessary. Make sure sprocket is free of oil and grease.

TIMING BELT COVERS

1. Inspect each timing cover for deformation or cracks. Replace, if necessary.
2. Inspect gasket for deformation, cracks, or hardening. Replace, if necessary.

ENGINE ASSEMBLY

Before assembling engine note the following:

1. Make sure all parts are clean before installation.
2. Apply new engine oil to all sliding and rotating parts.
3. Do not reuse gaskets or oil seals.
4. Check all critical clearances, end plays, and oil clearances.
5. Tighten critical fasteners to specified torques.
6. Replace any plain bearings that are damaged in any way.

CYLINDER HEAD ASSEMBLY

1. Apply engine oil to valve guides.
2. Using valve seal installer 49 S120 160, or equivalent, install valve seals.
3. Install valves as follows:
   a. Install lower spring seat.
   b. Coat valve stems with molybdenum disulphide grease. Insert valve.
   c. Install valve spring and spring seat.
   d. Using valve spring compressor 49 0636 100A and pivot 49 S120 222, or equivalents, compress valve spring and install valve keeper.

4. Install valve tappets and adjusting discs as follows:
   a. Apply engine oil to tappet and insert in bore.
   b. Insert adjusting discs.

PISTON & CONNECTING ROD

1. Assemble piston and connecting rod as follows:
   a. Align oil hole in big end of connecting rod with F mark on piston, **Fig. 22.**
   b. Coat small end of connecting rod with motor oil.
   c. Insert snap ring into one piston pin hole.
   d. Heat piston to 122-167 degrees F and install connecting rod and piston pin. Install remaining snap ring.
2. Apply liberal coat of motor oil and install piston rings as follows:
   a. Install in sequence, oil ring expander, oil ring, second ring, and top ring.
   b. Align ring gaps as shown in **Fig. 23.**
3. Install pistons and connecting rods as follows:
   a. Install connecting rod bearing in connecting rod and apply coat of oil.
   b. Clean inner surface of cylinder and apply coat of engine oil.
   c. Using suitable piston installer, insert each piston and connecting rod into cylinder block with F mark on piston facing towards front of engine block.

CRANKSHAFT ASSEMBLY

1. Install oil jets in cylinder block and torque to 9-13 ft. lbs.
2. Make sure back surfaces of main bearings are clean and install.
3. Using Plastigage, check main bearing clearance. Torque main bearing cap bolts to 61-65 ft. lbs. Standard clearance is .0012-.0019 inch. Clearance must not exceed .0031 inch.
4. If clearances are excessive, replace bearings with new bearings and recheck.
5. If clearances are still excessive, crankshaft must be reground and undersize bearing installed.
6. Coat main bearings and journals with motor oil and set crankshaft in journals.
7. Apply motor oil to thrust bearing and install in center journal so oil groove faces toward crankshaft, **Fig. 12.**
8. Position main bearing cap, and push crankshaft forwards. Then pull crankshaft back, and torque main cap bolts to 61-65 ft. lbs.
9. Check end play. Standard end play is .0016-.0110 inch. Endplay must not exceed .0118 inch. Also check that crankshaft turns easily.
10. If endplay is not correct, replace thrust bearing. Standard size thrust bearing thickness is 0787-.0807 inch. Oversize thrust bearing thickness is .0858-.0878 inch. Replace rear thrust bearing first. If endplay is still not correct, replace front thrust bearing.

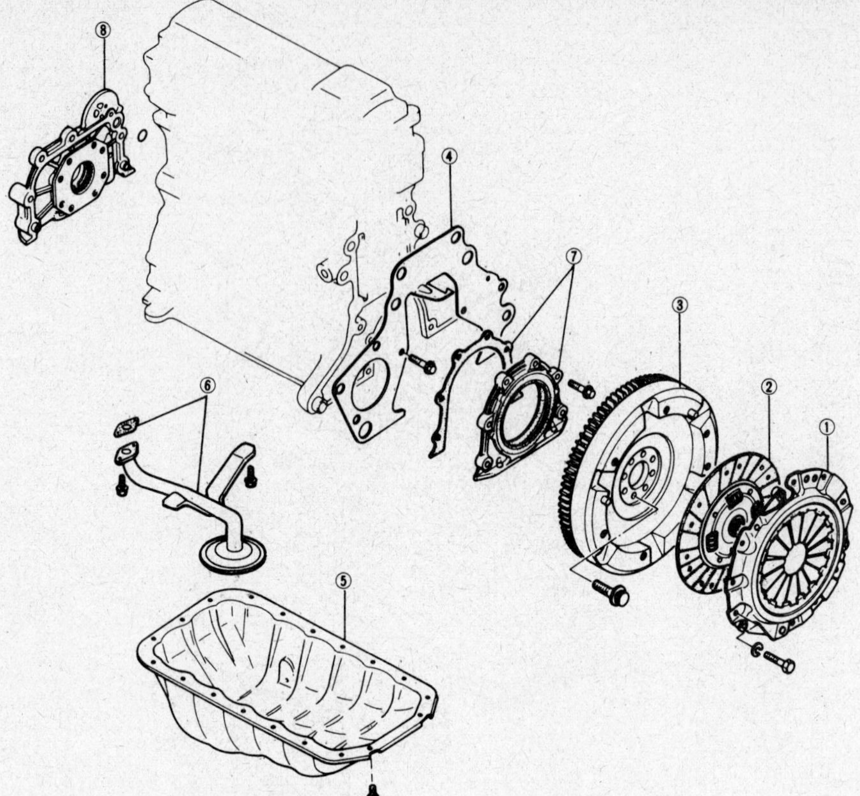

Fig. 11 Exploded view of oil pump, oil pan & flywheel assembly

11. Coat outside of pilot bearing and pilot bearing bore with motor oil. Set suitable pipe against outer bearing race and tap pilot bearing into crankshaft.
12. Apply grease to pilot bearing.
13. Using Plastigage, check connecting rod bearing clearance. Standard clearance is .0012-.0024 inch. Clearance must not exceed .0031. Undersize bearings are available in .010, .020, and .030 inch sizes.
14. Measure connecting rod side clearance. Standard clearance is .0043-.0102 inch. Side clearance must not exceed .014 inch.
15. Apply motor oil to connecting rod bearing. Install connecting rod cap taking care to align connecting rod and cap mating marks, and torque to 51-54 ft. lbs.

REAR OIL SEAL RETAINER

1. Apply motor oil to oil seal and retainer.
2. Press oil seal into rear cover.
3. Install bearing retainer and gasket and torque to 5-7 ft. lbs., **Fig. 11.**

OIL PUMP BODY ASSEMBLY

1. Apply lithium base grease to O-ring, and position in oil pump body, **Fig. 11.**
2. Apply motor oil to oil seal lip.
3. Apply sealant to oil pump flange and install oil pump. Torque mounting bolts to 12-17 ft. lbs.

OIL PUMP PICKUP & PAN

1. Install oil pump pickup on oil pump body and torque bolts to 5-7 ft. lbs.
2. Trim rear oil seal retainer gasket flush with oil pan mounting flange. Take care not to scratch oil seal retainer.
3. Apply continuous .08-.16 inch thick bed of sealer to oil pan flange inside of bolt holes. If oil pan gasket is used, apply sealant only to seams where rear oil seal retainer and oil pump meet engine block.
4. Torque oil pan bolts to 5-7 ft. lbs.

END PLATE, FLYWHEEL & CLUTCH

1. Install end plate and torque bolts to 12-17 ft. lbs.
2. Install flywheel and apply sealant to bolts and torque to 130-137 ft. lbs.
3. Clean clutch disc and splines. Apply thin coat of molybdenum sulphide grease to splines.
4. Install clutch disc and cover using suitable aligning tool. Torque clutch cover bolts to 16-24 ft. lbs.

TIMING BELT CRANKSHAFT SPROCKET

1. Install timing belt sprocket with key

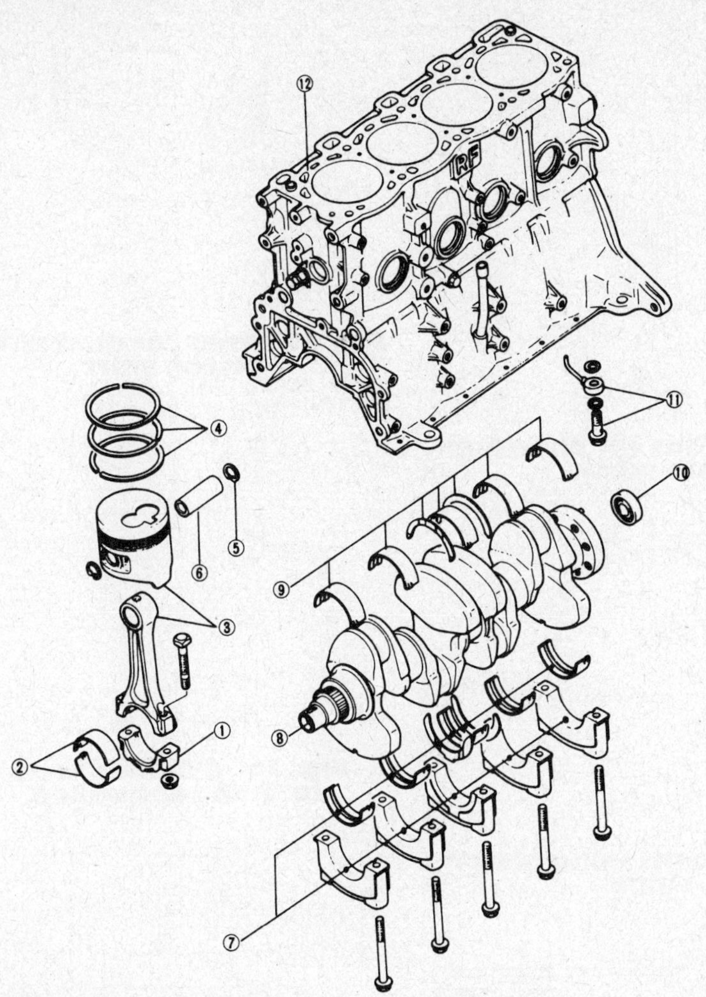

1 - CONNECT ROD BEARING CAP
2 - CONNECTING ROD BEARING
3 - CONNECTING ROD & PISTON
4 - PISTON RING
5 - SNAP RING
6 - PISTON PIN
7 - MAIN BEARING CAP, MAIN BEARING & THRUST BEARING
8 - CRANKSHAFT
9 - MAIN BEARING & THRUST BEARING
10 - PILOT BEARING
11 - OIL JET & OIL JET VALVE
12 - CYLINDER BLOCK ASSEMBLY

Fig. 12 Exploded view of crankshaft & cylinder block assembly

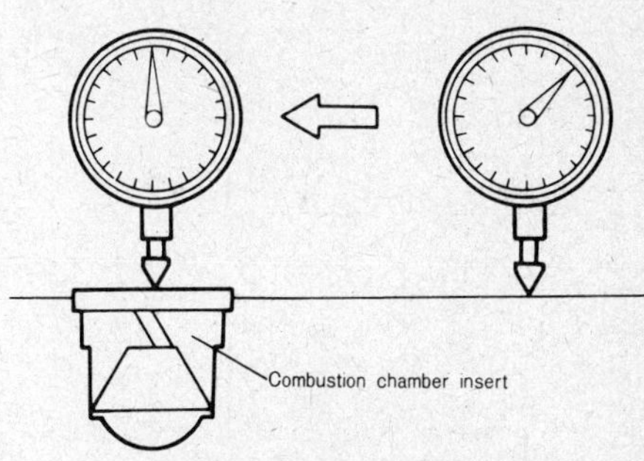

Fig. 13 Checking cylinder head flatness

Fig. 14 Checking combustion chamber insert projection

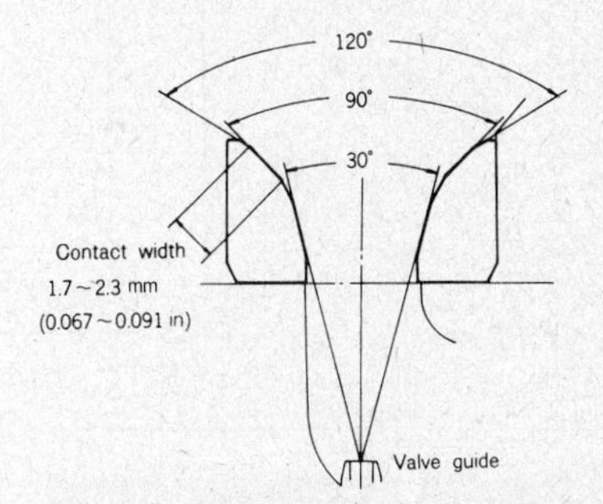

Fig. 15 Valve seat cutting angles

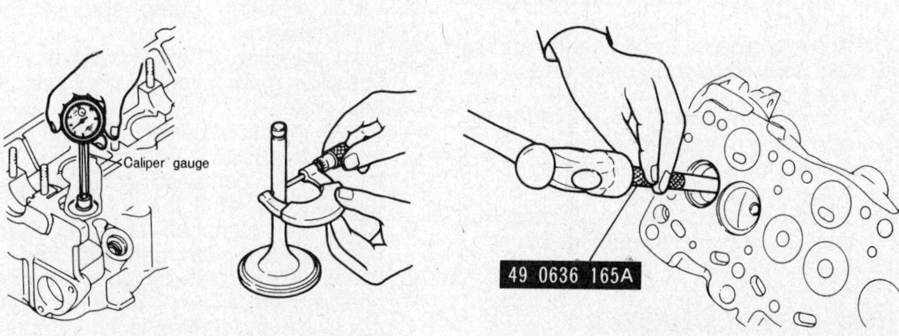

Fig. 16 Determining valve stem clearance

Fig. 17 Driving out valve guide

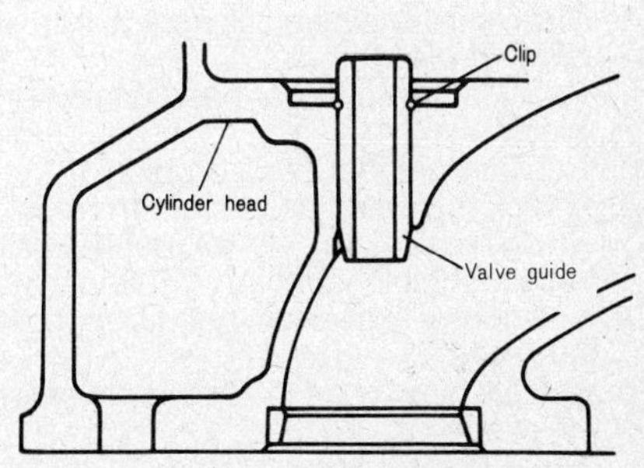

Fig. 18 Installing new valve guide

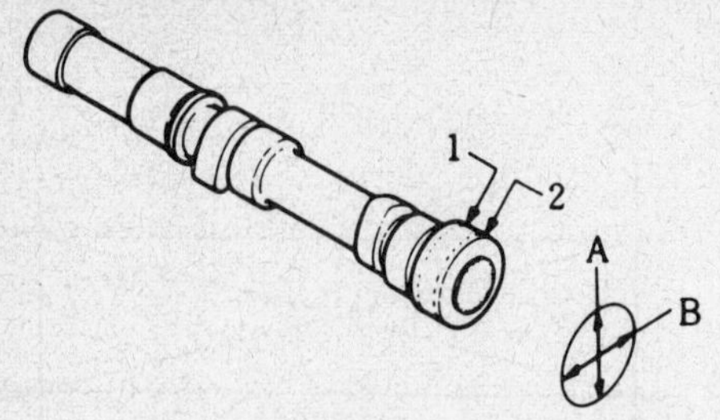

Fig. 19 Checking camshaft wear

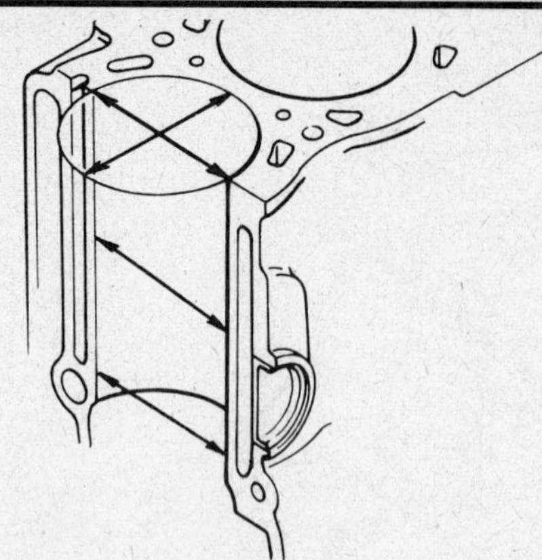

Fig. 20 Areas for checking bore wear

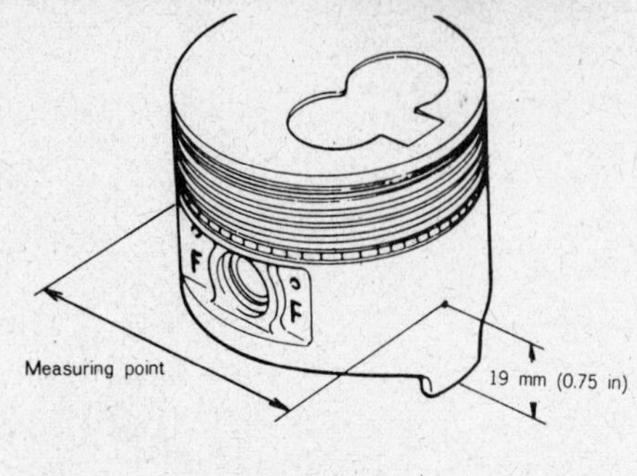

Fig. 21 Area for measuring piston skirt

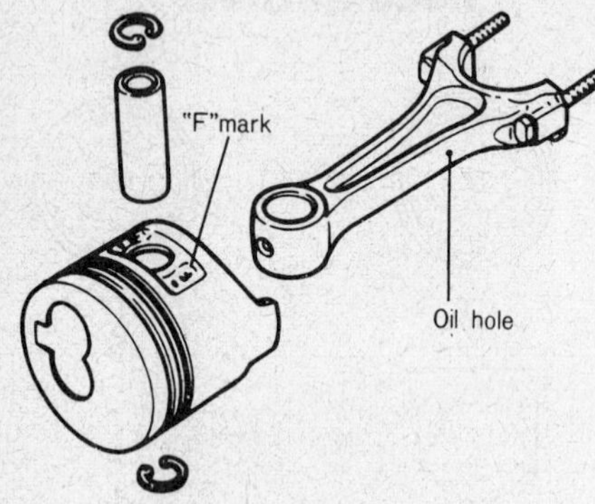

Fig. 22 Piston & connecting rod alignment

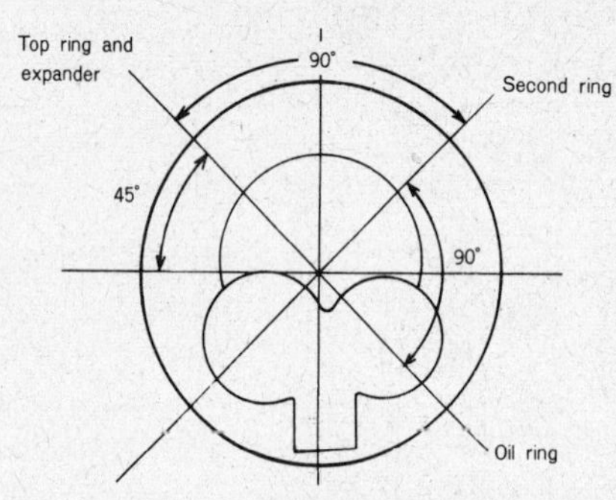

Fig. 23 Positioning piston rings

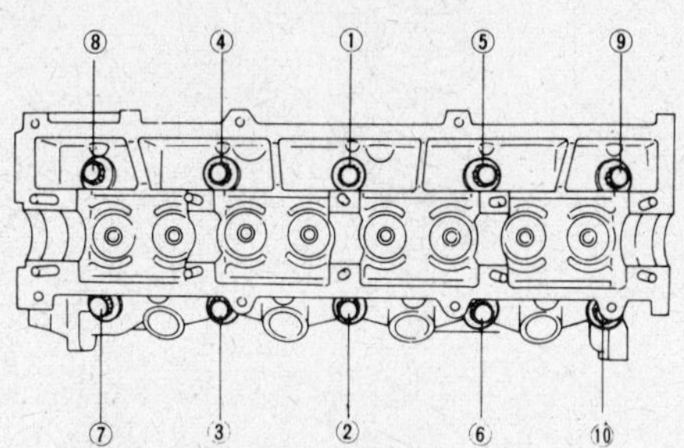

Fig. 24 Cylinder head torquing sequence

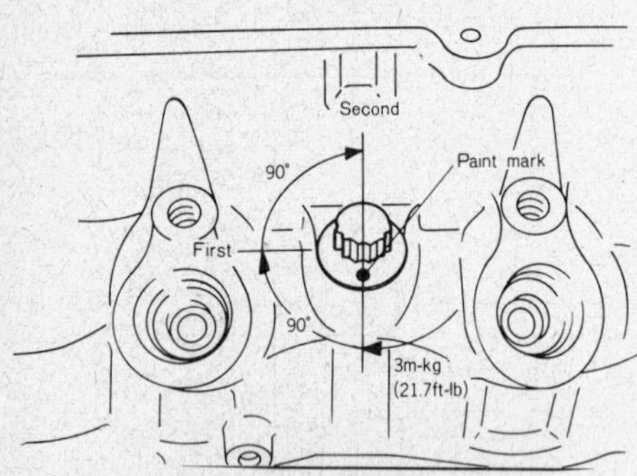

Fig. 25 Cylinder head angle tightening

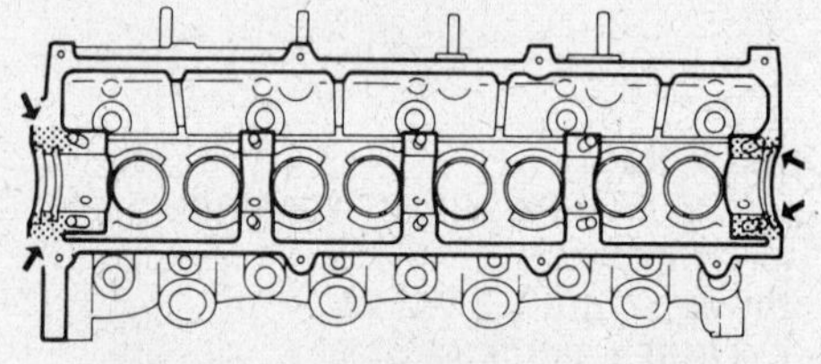

Fig. 26 Applying sealer prior to installing caps

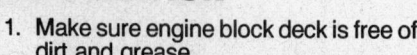

Fig. 27 Tightening camshaft caps

and torque bolt to 116-123 ft. lbs.

2. Turn crankshaft so No. 1 cylinder is at TDC, then turn crankshaft about 45 degrees in clockwise direction.

CYLINDER HEAD INSTALLATION

1. Make sure engine block deck is free of dirt and grease.
2. Position new cylinder head gasket on block.
3. Position cylinder head on block.
4. Check that head bolt length from bellow head is 4.437-4.460 inches. Bolt must not be longer than 4.508 inches. If length is excessive, head bolt must be replaced.
5. Torque head bolts to 22 ft. lbs. in order shown in **Fig. 24.**
6. Make paint marks on bolt heads as shown in **Fig. 25.**
7. Tighten each head bolt an additional 1/4 turn, **Fig. 25**, following torque sequence in **Fig. 24.** Then tighten each head bolt an additional 1/4 turn in sequence.
8. Apply motor oil to camshaft and journals.
9. Apply sealant as shown in **Fig. 26.**
10. Position camshaft in head with keyway facing up. Position camshaft caps on studs.
11. Apply engine oil to oil seal lip and insert seal. Repeat on other end of cylinder head.
12. Torque camshaft nut to 15-20 ft. lbs. according to sequence in **Fig. 27.**
13. Install glow plugs and torque to 11-15 ft. lbs. Install cable.
14. Install new corrugated washers so red paint mark is facing up, **Fig. 28.**
15. Install injection nozzles and torque to 43-51 ft. lbs.

INJECTION PUMP & BRACKET

1. Install injection pump bracket and torque bolts to 23-24 ft. lbs.
2. Align injection pump with mating mark and torque 2 nuts to 12-17 ft. lbs.
3. Install fuel injection pipes, and torque to 13-17 ft. lbs.
4. Tighten clip channels.

REAR TIMING MECHANISM

1. Install rear seal plate and torque bolts to 5-7 ft. lbs.
2. Install injection pump sprocket on pump shaft.
3. Turn injection pump sprocket until sprocket mark aligns with mark on seal plate.
4. Install injection pump sprocket and torque to 43-52 ft. lbs.
5. Install rear camshaft sprocket and torque to 41-48 ft. lbs.
6. Align rear camshaft sprocket mark with rear seal plate mark, **Fig. 29.**
7. Install timing belt tensioner, spring and locknut. Turn tensioner fully clockwise and tighten locknut temporarily.
8. Install rear timing belt on injection pump sprocket, then rear camshaft sprocket.

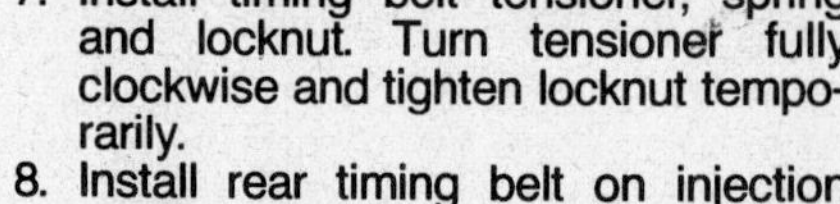

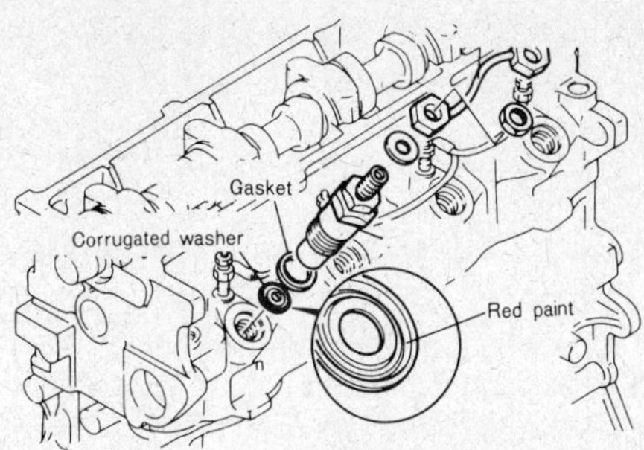

Fig. 28 Installing injectors

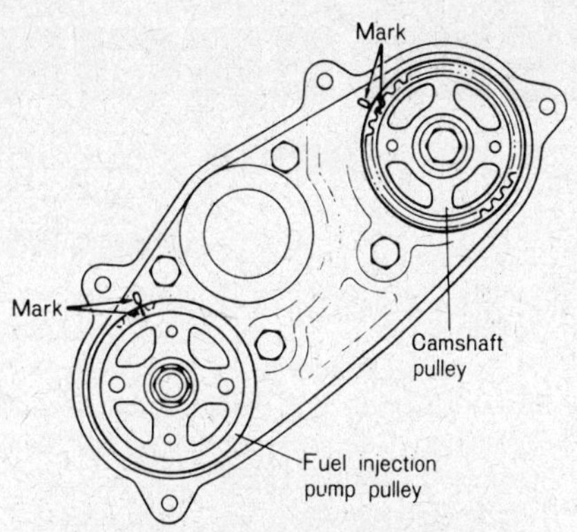

Fig. 29 Aligning rear camshaft sprocket mark w/rear seal plate mark

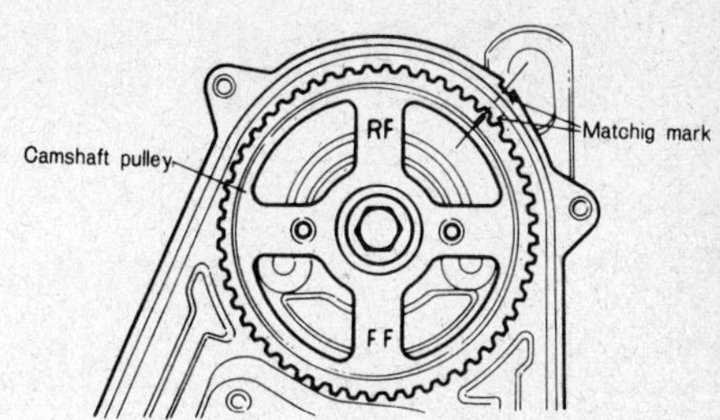

Fig. 30 Aligning front camshaft sprocket

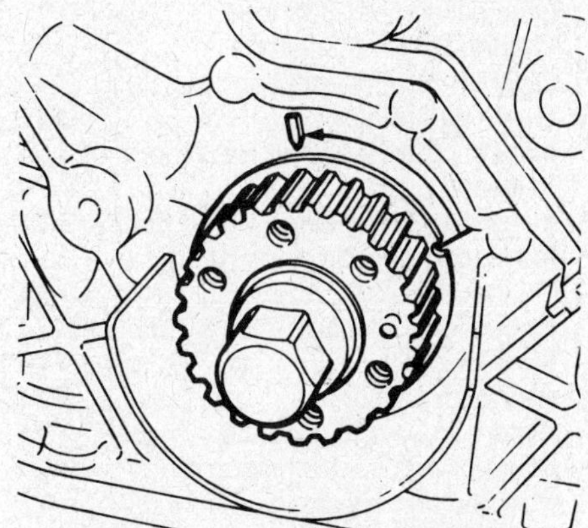

Fig. 31 Aligning front crankshaft sprocket

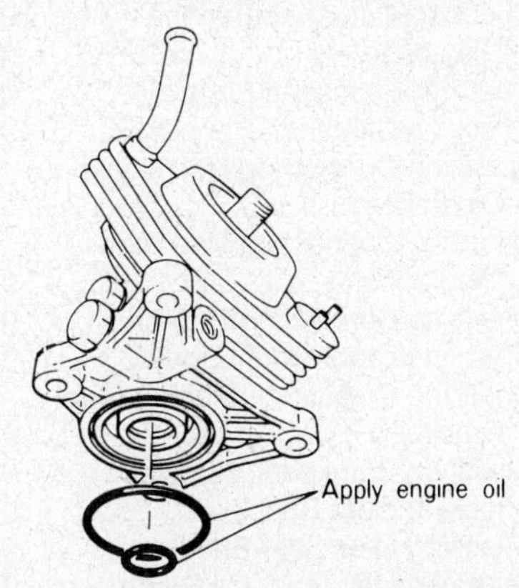

Fig. 32 Installing O-rings in oil cooler

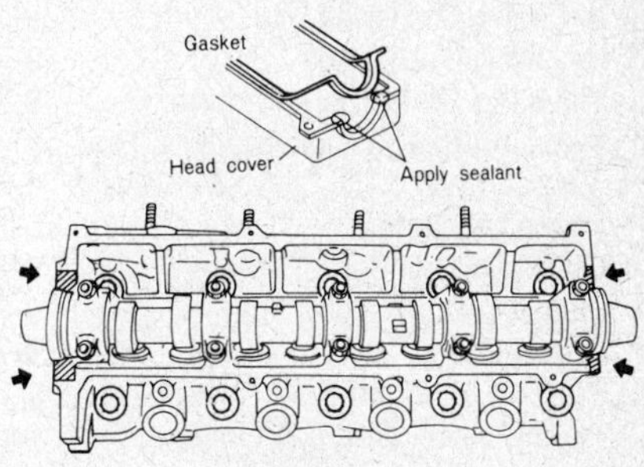

Fig. 33 Applying sealant to valve cover

9. Loosen lock nut and allow tensioner spring to apply tension to timing belt.

FRONT TIMING MECHANISM

1. Install water pump, and torque mounting bolts to 23-34 ft. lbs.
2. Install brake vacuum pipe.
3. Install torque stop casing and torque to 23-34 ft. lbs.
4. Install seal plate and spacer and torque 6-8 ft. lbs.
5. Install front camshaft sprockets on camshaft, **Fig. 30.** Hold camshaft with 29mm wrench and torque bolt to 41-48 ft. lbs.
6. Turn crankshaft back about 45 degrees to timing mark on oil pump housing, **Fig. 31.**
7. Install tensioner pulley and spring. Position tensioner over towards water pump and tighten locknut temporarily.
8. Install front timing belt.
9. Loosen tensioner lock bolt so tension is applied to timing belt.
10. Turn crankshaft clockwise twice to equalize tension on timing belt. Do not turn in reverse direction.
11. Torque front tensioner lock bolt to 23-34 ft. lbs.
12. Torque rear tensioner lock bolt to 14-20 ft. lbs.
13. Recheck timing marks on crankshaft and front camshaft sprocket, fuel injection pump sprocket and rear camshaft sprocket.
14. Timing belts should be tensioned so that front belt deflects .413-472 inch, and rear belt deflects .374 inch.
15. Install left, right, and rear timing covers. Torque mounting bolts to 5-7 ft. lbs.
16. Install No. 3 engine mount bracket and torque to 23-34 ft. lbs.
17. Install crankshaft pulley and torque bolts to 17-24 ft. lbs.

OIL COOLER ASSEMBLY

1. Apply coat of engine oil to center of oil cooler fitting on engine block.
2. Apply motor oil to 2 new O-rings and install in oil cooler assembly, **Fig. 32.**
3. Install oil cooler assembly and torque to 23-34 ft. lbs.
4. Install oil return pipe and torque to 17-26 ft. lbs.
5. Install oil filter.

INTAKE & EXHAUST MANIFOLD

1. Position intake manifold gasket.
2. Install intake manifold and torque to 12-17 ft. lbs.
3. Install oil cooler inlet pipe and torque to 6-8 ft.lbs. Torque inlet pipe bracket to 14-19 ft. lbs.
4. Install exhaust manifold and gasket, and torque to 16-20 ft. lbs.
5. Install 2 engine hangers.

NO. 3 ENGINE MOUNT

1. Install No. 3 engine mount and torque 16-24 ft. lbs.

CYLINDER HEAD COVER

1. Apply sealant to shaded area, **Fig. 33.**
2. Install cylinder head cover and torque to 5-7 ft. lbs.
3. Install PCV hose.

ALTERNATOR

1. Install alternator strap and bracket, and torque to 23-34 ft. lbs.
2. Install alternator and drive belt. Torque 8mm bolt to 14-22 ft. lbs., front 10mm bolt to 28-38 ft. lbs., and rear 10mm bolt to 23-34 ft. lbs.
3. Install 2 alternator oil hoses.
4. Install oil pressure switch.
5. Install dipstick.

B2200 DIESEL ENGINE SECTION

INDEX

ENGINE

REPLACE

1. Disconnect battery ground cable and remove hood.
2. Remove air cleaner.
3. Drain cooling system and oil pan.
4. Disconnect all wiring connections that will interfere with engine removal.
5. Disconnect accelerator cable from injection pump.
6. Disconnect fuel and overflow pipes.
7. Disconnect heater hoses, then the upper and lower hoses from radiator.
8. Remove exhaust pipe to manifold attaching bolts, then position exhaust pipe aside.
9. Remove clutch hydraulic cylinder.
10. Remove cooling fan and radiator cowl.
11. Remove radiator to radiator support attaching bolts, then the radiator.
12. Remove oil cooler.
13. Remove exhaust pipe hanger, then support transmission with suitable jack.
14. Remove engine to transmission support bolts.
15. Remove engine mount bracket nuts and bolts, then install suitable engine hoist.
16. Pull engine forward until transmission input shaft clears clutch assembly, then raise and remove engine from vehicle.
17. Reverse procedure to install.

ENGINE DISASSEMBLY

PRELIMINARY COMPONENTS

1. Remove starter.
2. Remove vacuum sensing tube.
3. Remove alternator.
4. Remove fan and pulley.
5. Remove thermostat housing.
6. Remove water pump.

INJECTION PUMP

1. Remove fuel cut solenoid coupler.
2. Disconnect injection pipes and fuel hoses.
3. Remove drive gear cover retaining nuts, then the cover.
4. Remove drive gear locknut, spring washer and lock plate.
5. Remove injection pump to case attaching nuts and bolts, then using extractor tool 49 SE01 157 or equivalent, **Fig. 1,** remove injection pump from engine.

INTAKE MANIFOLD

1. Disconnect vacuum sensing tube at manifold.
2. Remove intake manifold to cylinder head attaching bolts, then the intake manifold.

REMOVING CYLINDER HEAD

1. Remove injectors and glow plugs from cylinder head.
2. Remove valve cover to cylinder head attaching bolts and the valve cover.
3. Remove rocker shaft and cylinder head bolts in reverse order of sequence shown in **Fig. 2.**
4. Remove rocker shaft, valve caps and push rods, then the cylinder head and gasket.

VALVE & VALVE SPRING

1. Using a suitable spring compressor, compress valve spring.
2. Remove the taper sleeves, upper spring seat, valve springs and lower spring seat.
3. Remove valve from cylinder head.

CRANKSHAFT PULLEY

1. Install flywheel brake 49 E301 060 or equivalent, onto flywheel ring gear.
2. Remove pulley retaining bolt and

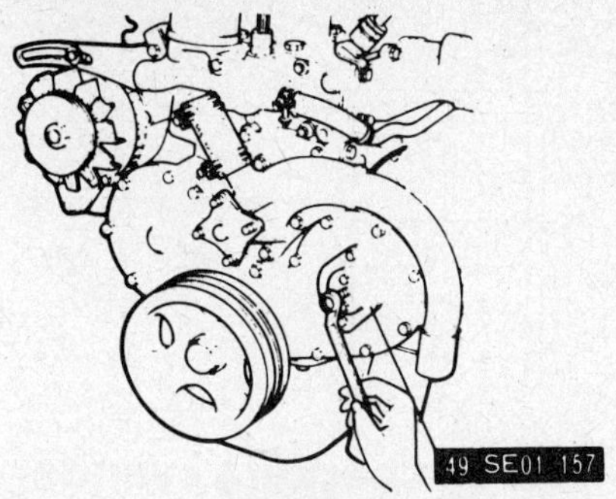

Fig. 1 Removing injection pump

Fig. 2 Cylinder head bolt tightening sequence

washer, then pull crankshaft pulley off the front end of the crankshaft.

CLUTCH ASSEMBLY

1. Install flywheel brake as described previously.
2. Remove clutch cover to flywheel retaining bolts, then the clutch cover, pressure plate and disc.
3. Remove flywheel to crankshaft retaining bolts, then the flywheel brake and flywheel.
4. Remove end plate.

OIL PAN

1. Invert cylinder block.
2. Remove oil pan to cylinder block attaching bolts.
3. Remove oil pan and gasket.

OIL PUMP & STRAINER

1. Remove set screw from side of cylinder block.
2. Remove oil pipe attaching bolts.
3. Remove oil pump and strainer.

TIMING GEAR COVER

1. Remove timing gear cover to case attaching bolts.
2. Remove timing gear cover and gasket.

CAMSHAFT, CRANKSHAFT, IDLER & INJECTION PUMP GEARS

1. Remove oil slinger and washers from crankshaft snout.
2. Using puller set 49 0839 425C or equivalent, remove crankshaft timing gear, **Fig. 3.**

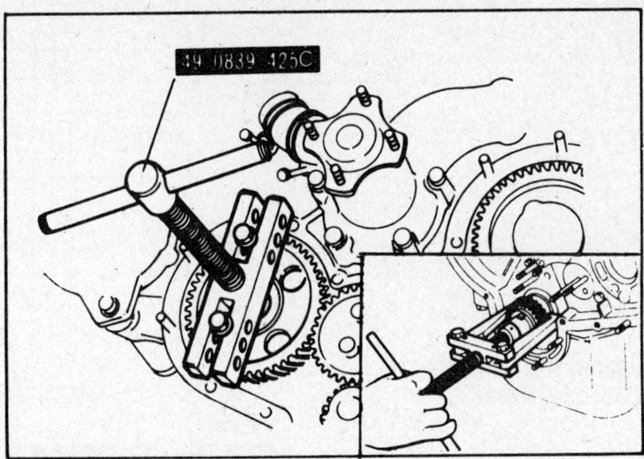

Fig. 3 Removing timing gears

3. Position a clean rag between camshaft and idler gears, then remove cam gear lock bolt and washers.
4. Using puller set 49 0839 425C or equivalent, remove cam gear from camshaft, **Fig. 3.**
5. Remove idler gear to spindle retaining nuts and washers, then remove idler gear and spindle assemblies.
6. Remove injection pump drive gear.
7. Remove timing gear case to cylinder block attaching bolts, then the timing case.

CAMSHAFT

1. Remove tappets from cylinder block.
2. Remove camshaft thrust plate to cylinder block retaining bolts and washers, then pull camshaft from block.

PISTON & CONNECTING ROD

1. Remove connecting rod bearing cap retaining nuts and bolts, then separate bearing cap from connecting rod.
2. Using the wooden handle end of a hammer, push the piston and connecting rod assembly outward until piston rings clear cylinder bore. Remove piston and connecting rod assembly through top of cylinder block.
3. To separate piston from connecting rod, remove piston pin retaining clips, then press pin from piston using a suitable driver.

CRANKSHAFT

1. Remove rear oil seal cap retaining bolts, then the cap and seal.
2. Remove main bearing cap to cylinder block retaining bolts, then the main bearing caps and thrust washers.
3. Lift crankshaft from cylinder block.

INSPECTION & REPAIR

CYLINDER HEAD INSPECTION

Visually inspect cylinder head for cracks or damage. Repair or replace as necessary.

Check for cylinder head distortion by placing a straightedge on the cylinder head mating surface. Measure the clearance between the straightedge and cylinder head surface with a feeler gauge Maximum permissible distortion is .004 inch across length and .010 inch across width. If distortion exceeds specifications, replace cylinder head.

VALVE SPRING INSPECTION

Examine valve springs for corrosion or damage. Replace if necessary. Measure free length of inner and outer springs. Minimum free length should be 1.654 inch for inner spring and 1.717 inch for outer spring. If measured length is less than specified, replace valve spring(s).

VALVE INSPECTION

Visually inspect valves for warping, cracks or excessive pitting. If damage is excessive, replace valve.

Measure valve stem diameter at several places with a micrometer. If valve stem diameter is less than .3102 inch for intake valve or .3097 inch for exhaust valve, replace valve(s).

CHECKING VALVE STEM TO GUIDE CLEARANCE

Position valve in guide, then mount a dial indicator so that pointer contacts valve stem. Move valve fore and aft and measure stem to guide clearance. Maximum allowable clearance for both intake and exhaust valves is .005 inch. If clearance is not within specifications, replace valve and guide.

PUSHROD INSPECTION

Visually inspect both ends of pushrod for wear or damage. If damage is excessive, replace pushrod. Measure push rod deflection by positioning rod on a surface plate and measuring curvature with feeler gauge. Maximum allowable deflection is .0075 inch. If deflection is greater than specified limit, replace pushrod.

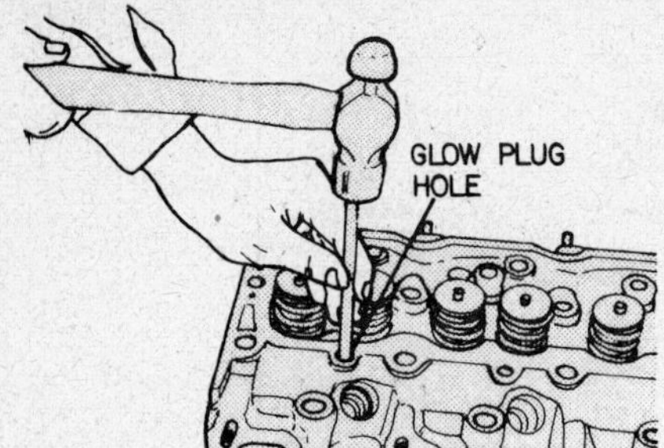

Fig. 4 Removing pre-chamber insert

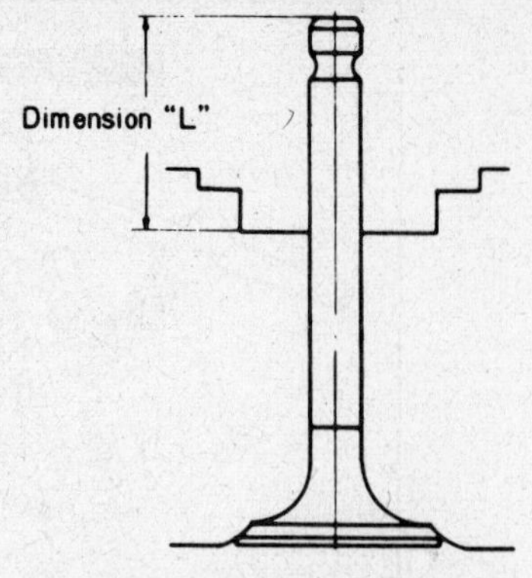

Fig. 5 Checking valve stem protrusion

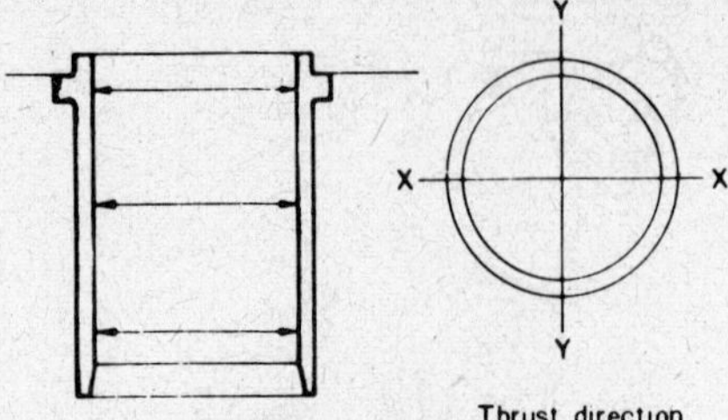

Fig. 6 Checking cylinder liner for wear

INSPECTING & REPAIRING PRE-CHAMBER INSERT

Visually inspect insert for cracks or breakage. If damage is evident, replace insert as follows:

1. Position metal rod into glow plug hole, then strike rod firmly with hammer until insert is pushed out of cylinder head, **Fig. 4.**
2. Install new insert, making sure projected portion of welsh washer faces head gasket side of head. Stake welsh washer by striking lightly with a suitable punch.

REPLACING VALVE GUIDE

1. Using service tool 49 0636 165A or equivalent, drive old guide out toward combustion chamber side of cylinder head.
2. Working from combustion chamber side of head, install and drive new guide into guide boss until guide protrudes exactly .650 inch above cylinder head.

REFACING VALVE

Reface the valves with a valve refacer, following the instructions of the valve refacer manufacturer. The intake valve face has a 45° angle, while the exhaust valve face has an angle of 30°. Take off only enough metal to assure a clean valve face. Make sure that the valve face contact area (valve margin) has a minimum width of .079 inch.

INSPECTING & REPAIRING VALVE SEAT

Visually inspect valve seat for cracks, burrs, ridges or improper angle or width. If it is necessary to cut the valve seat, use a valve seat cutter and cut intake valve seats to a 45° angle and exhaust valve seats to a 30° angle. Remove only enough metal to assure a smooth surface area.

After the valve seat is cut, check the contact area between the valve and seat as follows:

1. Apply a thin coat of Prussian Blue to valve seat, then press valve against seat.
2. Remove valve and observe the transfer of prussian blue to valve face. An even transfer indicates accurate valve and seat refacing. If transfer is uneven, hand lap the valve into the seat using suitable lapping compound.
3. Check valve seat width. Contact area should be located in center of valve face and seat, and seat width should be .079 inch for both intake and exhaust seats. If seat width is not as specified, service as required.

CHECKING VALVE STEM PROTRUSION

After valve and seat have been refaced, check the distance that valve stem protrudes above cylinder head, **Fig. 5.** Dimension "L" should be 1.890 inch. If dimension "L" is up to .020 inch greater than specified, no correction is necessary. If dimension "L" is .021-.059 inch greater than specified, install washers under lower spring seat to bring protrusion to stated value. If dimension "L" is .060 inch or greater than specified value, replace valve.

INSPECTION OF ROCKER ARM & SHAFT

The standard clearance between rocker arm bushing and shaft is .0028 inch. If clearance is greater than specified, replace rocker arm bushing or shaft.

CYLINDER BLOCK INSPECTION

Check cylinder block for cracks, cuts or damage and cooling and oil passages for blockage. Repair or replace as necessary. Check cylinder block for distortion. Maximum permissible distortion across width should be .0039 inch. Maximum permissible distortion across length should be .0098 inch. If distortion exceeds allowable limit, repair or replace cylinder block.

INSPECTING & REPLACING CYLINDER LINER

Inspect the cylinder liner for wear and out of round at locations shown in **Fig. 6.** The cylinder liner bore should be 3.5001 inches. If wear or out of round is greater than .007 inch, replace cylinder liner as follows:

1. Using service tool 49 0636 015 and a suitable press, drive liner out of cylinder block bore toward deck side of block.
2. Apply engine oil to cylinder block bore and outer surface of liner, then press new liner into bore. Make sure that liner protrudes .026-.031 inch above deck surface. **Pressing force should not exceed 6,600 lbs. If pressing force exceeds limits, find and correct cause of fitting problem.**
3. Check that cylinder liner bore is within specifications.

PISTON INSPECTION

Visually inspect piston for scores, deep scratches or heat damage. Replace, if necessary. Measure piston diameter at top of skirt and perpendicular to piston pin with a micrometer. Piston diameter should be 3.4989 ±.0005 inch. If diameter is not within specifications, replace piston.

PISTON TO LINER CLEARANCE

Measure piston diameter and cylinder liner bore as outlined previously. Compare measurements. Piston to liner clearance should be .0021-.0031 inch. If clearance exceeds specifications, replace piston or cylinder liner.

PISTON RING GROOVE INSPECTION

Remove carbon from ring groove by using a ring groove cleaner or a broken piece of ring. Using a feeler gauge, check piston ring to groove side clearance. Side clearance limit is .012 inch. If side clearance is greater than specified limit, replace piston ring.

CHECKING PISTON RING END GAP

Place the piston ring in the cylinder bore below the ring travel, using a piston head to push the ring in squarely. Check the piston ring end gap with a feeler gauge. The end gap should be .015-.021 inch for the top ring, .011-.016 for second ring and .013-.021 inch for oil ring.

CHECKING PISTON PIN FIT

Check the clearance between the piston and the connecting rod small end bushing. Maximum allowable clearance is .0020 inch. If clearance exceeds specifications, replace the piston pin or small end bushing.

REPLACING CONNECTING ROD SMALL END BUSHING

1. Press out old bushing with a suitable mandrel.

Fig. 7 Measuring camshaft endplay

2. Press fit the new bushing into the connecting rod, making sure oil holes in bushing and connecting rod are in alignment.
3. Finish the new bushing with a reamer to the desired clearance.

CONNECTING ROD BEARING

Visually inspect the connecting rod bearing for peeling, deep scores or heat damage. Replace, if necessary.

CHECKING CONNECTING ROD BEARING CLEARANCE

The connecting rod bearing clearance should be .0014-.0030 inch. Check the clearance by using Plastigage as follows:

1. Clean the surfaces of the bearing and crankpin.
2. Position a piece of Plastigage on the crankpin, then install the bearing cap and torque to specifications.
3. Remove the bearing cap and measure the width of the Plastigage. Compare width of Plastigage with the scale printed on the Plastigage envelope.

CHECKING CONNECTING ROD SIDE CLEARANCE

Check connecting rod side clearance with a feeler gauge. Side clearance should be .009-.013 inch. If side clearance is beyond specifications, replace connecting rod.

CHECKING CONNECTING ROD TWIST

Check the connecting rod for bend or twist by using a suitable connecting rod aligner. Maximum allowable twist is .002 inch per 3.9371 inches of rod. Repair, if necessary.

CHECKING CRANKSHAFT MAIN JOURNAL & CRANKPIN

Clean the crankshaft thoroughly with a suitable solvent and blow out the oil passages with compressed air. Inspect the crankshaft for cracks or scratches and the oil passages for clogs. Measure diameter of each crankpin and main journal with a micrometer. If the wear is more than 0.0020 in. (0.05mm), the crankshaft should be ground to the undersize of 0.010, 0.020 and 0.030 in. (0.25, 0.50 and 0.75mm). Refer to specifications for standard diameters of crankpins and main journals.

CHECKING CRANKSHAFT RUNOUT

To check runout, mount the crankshaft on the V-blocks and install a dial indicator. Slowly rotate the crankshaft and note the reading on the dial indicator. The maximum allowable run out is .0019 inch. If necessary, correct with a press.

MAIN BEARING

Visually inspect main bearing for peeling, deep scores or heat damage. Replace, if necessary.

CHECKING MAIN BEARING CLEARANCE

The main bearing clearance should be .0016-.0036 inch. Check the clearance by using Plastigage as follows:

1. Clean the surfaces of the bearing and main journal.
2. Position a piece of Plastigage on the main journal, then install the bearing capand torque to specifications.
3. Remove the bearing cap and measure the width of the Plastigage. Compare width of Plastigage with the scale printed on the Plastigage envelope.

CHECKING CRANKSHAFT ENDPLAY

The end thrust of the crankshaft is taken by the thrust washers at the #3 main bearing. The standard endplay should be .0055-.0153 inch.

To measure crankshaft endplay, mount a dial indicator at rear of crankshaft, then move shaft fore and aft. Observe reading. If endplay is beyond specifications, replace thrust washer with available oversize washer.

CAMSHAFT INSPECTION

Visually inspect lobes and journals for scoring, wear or heat damage. Measure cam lift with a micrometer and, if not within specifications, replace camshaft. If cam journals are worn greater than .0003 inch, replace camshaft.

CHECKING CAMSHAFT RUNOUT

To check run out, mount camshaft in V-blocks, then install dial indicator and rotate camshaft. The maximum allowable run out is .0003 inch. If run out exceeds limit, replace camshaft.

CHECKING CAMSHAFT ENDPLAY

The endplay of the camshaft is determined by the clearance between the sprocket surface and the thrust plate surface. Measure this clearance with a feeler gauge as shown in **Fig. 7.** This clearance should be .0008-.0071 inch. If the endplay is excessive, replace with a new thrust plate.

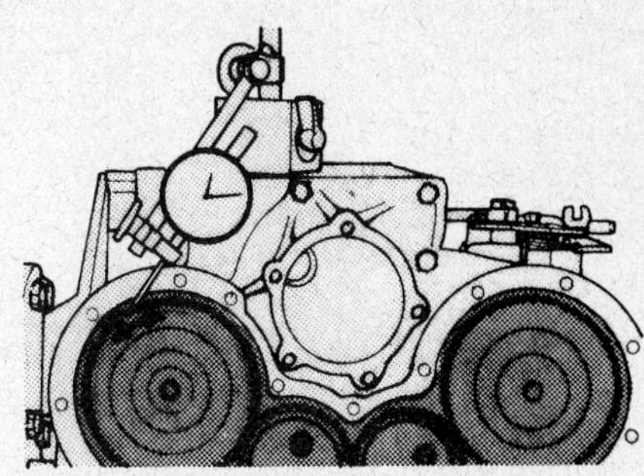

Fig. 8 Measuring gear backlash

CHECKING CAMSHAFT BEARING CLEARANCE

Using suitable micrometers, measure camshaft journal outside diameter and camshaft bearing inner diameter. Compare measurements. Maximum allowable bearing clearance is .0057 inch. If bearing clearance exceeds specifications, replace camshaft or cylinder block.

GEAR INSPECTION

Visually inspect gears for cracks, damage or missing teeth. Replace, if necessary.

CHECKING GEAR BACKLASH

Mount a dial indicator to gear being checked, then move gear clockwise and counterclockwise, **Fig. 8.** The maximum allowable gear backlash is .0118 inch. If backlash exceeds allowable limit, replace gear(s).

CHECKING IDLER GEAR ENDPLAY

Measure endplay with feeler gauge positioned between the gear and thrust plate. Gear endplay should be .0079-.0118 inch. If end play exceeds specifications, replace thrust plate or gear.

CHECKING IDLER GEAR OIL CLEARANCE

Measure inner diameter of idler gear bushing and outer diameter of spindle, **Fig. 9.** Compare measurements. The maximum allowable oil clearance is .0059 inch. If clearance exceeds allowable limit, replace idler gear bushing. To replace idler gear bushing, proceed as follows:

1. Using a suitable mandrel, press bushing from idler gear.
2. Press in new bushing using suitable mandrel.
3. Using a suitable reamer, ream bushing to desired fit.

ENGINE ASSEMBLY

PISTON & CONNECTING ROD

1. Assemble piston to rod as shown in **Fig. 10.**

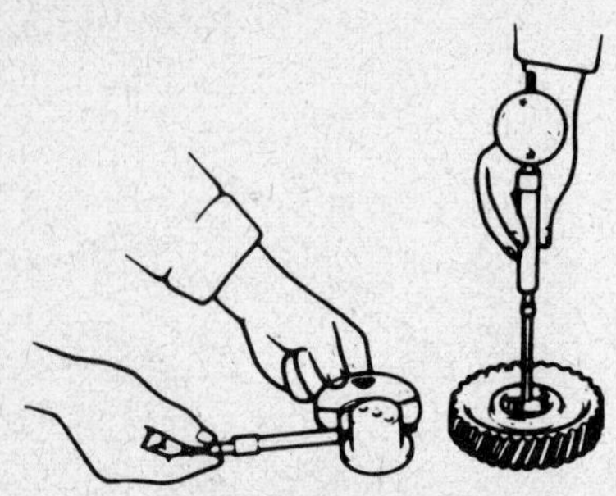

Fig. 9 Checking idler gear oil clearance

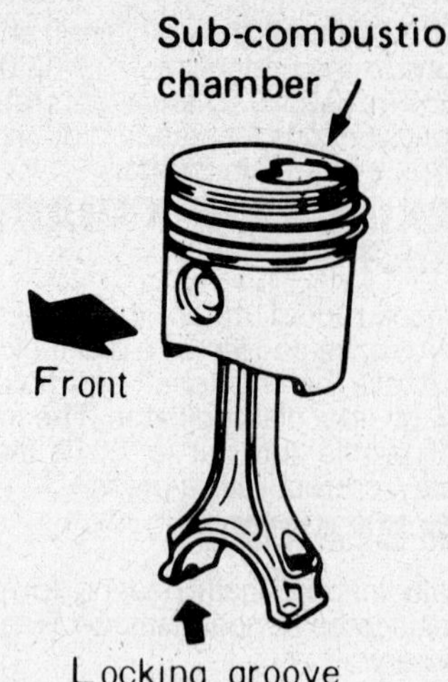

Fig. 10 Assembling piston to connecting rod

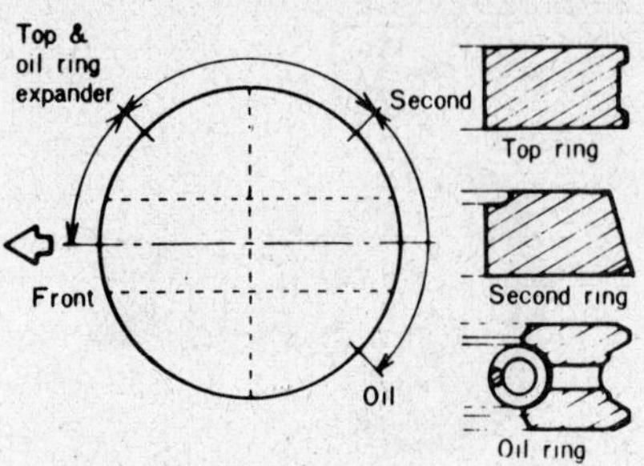

Fig. 11 Positioning ring end gaps

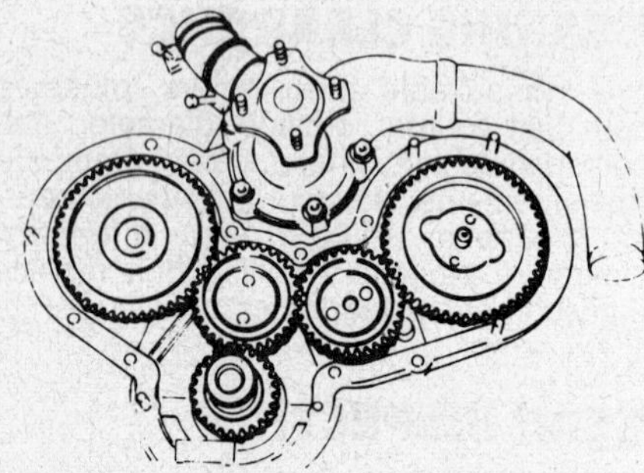

Fig. 12 Aligning timing gear marks

2. Install piston pin retaining clip into one end of piston groove, then press pin in until it contacts clip.
3. Install remaining clip into piston groove.

PISTON RINGS

1. Install oil ring expander and rails into oil ring groove.
2. Install second, then the top compression ring. When installing compression rings, make sure markings on rings face upward.
3. Position ring end gaps as shown in **Fig. 11.**

INSTALLING CRANKSHAFT

1. Clean contact surfaces of cylinder block, main bearings and crankshaft.
2. Install the five sets of main bearings to the cylinder block and bearing caps.
3. Coat crankshaft journals and main bearings with fresh engine oil. **Only coat the outer surface of bearing with engine oil. The bearing cap side of the main bearings should be kept dry.**
4. Gently place crankshaft into cylinder block.
5. Install thrust washers onto No. 3 main bearing cap, making sure oil grooves face outward.
6. Install main bearing caps, making sure arrows on caps are facing towards front of engine.
7. Torque main bearing caps to specifications.
8. Coat rear oil seal outer lip with engine oil, then install oil seal and retaining bolts.

INSTALLING PISTON & CONNECTING ROD ASSEMBLY

1. Lubricate entire assembly with fresh engine oil.
2. Compress rings using suitable ring compressor, then install piston and rod assembly into cylinder block by tapping piston head with a wooden drift. Install piston by positioning as shown, **Fig. 10.**
3. Install connecting rod bearing halves into their respective locations in rods and bearing caps.
4. Lubricate outer surface of bearings and the crankshaft journals with fresh engine oil, then install connecting rod bearing caps to connecting rod, making sure weight marks on cap and rod align.
5. Torque bearing caps to specification.
6. Turn crankshaft to make sure rotation is smooth and no binding exists.

INSTALLING CAMSHAFT

1. Coat camshaft journals and lobes with fresh engine oil.
2. Carefully slide camshaft into cylinder block.
3. Install thrust plate and thrust plate retaining bolts. Torque bolts to 15 ft. lbs.

INSTALLING OIL PUMP & STRAINER

1. Position oil pump into cylinder block.
2. Install oil pipe onto pump cover and cylinder block using new gaskets, then tighten retaining bolts.
3. Install oil pump set screw and locknut at side of cylinder block.

TIMING CASE, GEARS & COVER

1. Install timing case to cylinder block, then torque retaining bolts to 15 ft. lbs.
2. Install crankshaft timing gear onto crankshaft, making sure keyway aligns with key, then install washers and oil slinger. **When installing timing gears, align timing marks on gears as shown in Fig. 12.**
3. Install camshaft gear, washers and lock bolt onto camshaft, then torque lock bolt to 48 ft. lbs.
4. Install injection pump drive gear.
5. Install idler gear spindles, then the idler gears, thrust plates, lock washers and retaining nuts. Torque retaining nuts to 20 ft. lbs.
6. Install timing cover using a new gasket, then torque retaining bolts to 15 ft. lbs.

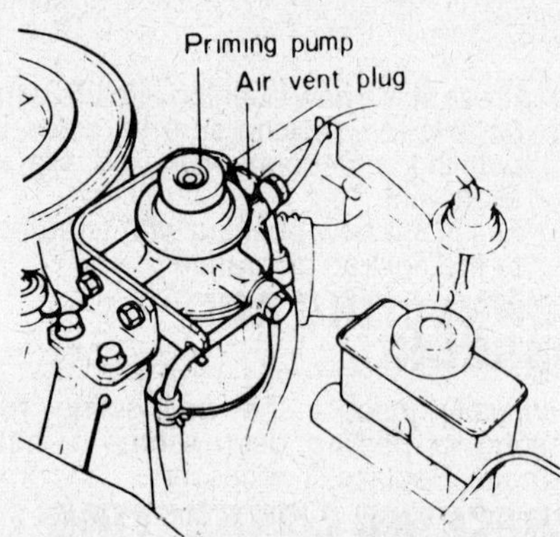

Fig. 13 Fuel filter priming pump and air vent location

OIL PAN, FLYWHEEL & CLUTCH

1. Install new oil pan gasket set, applying suitable sealer to cylinder block, timing case and contact area of gasket.
2. Install oil pan, then the oil pan attaching bolts. Torque attaching bolts to 7 ft. lbs.
3. Install end plate and torque end plate retaining bolts to 29 ft. lbs.
4. Install flywheel to crankshaft, then torque retaining bolts to 95-137 ft. lbs.
5. Install clutch assembly.

CRANKSHAFT PULLEY

1. Install flywheel brake 49 E301 060 or equivalent, onto flywheel ring gear.
2. Install pulley, washer and retaining bolt, then torque retaining bolt to 145-181 ft. lbs. **When installing crankshaft pulley, make sure keyway in pulley aligns with crankshaft key.**

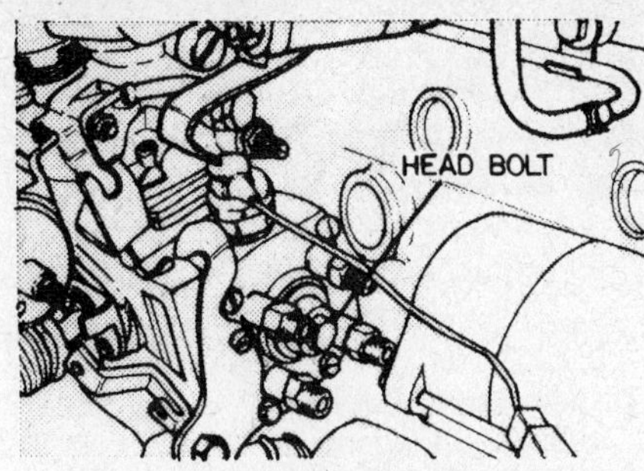

Fig. 14 Injection pump head bolt location

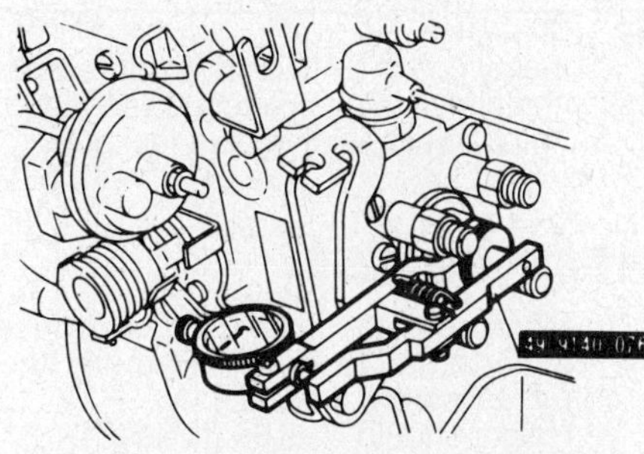

Fig. 16 Injection pump plunger measuring tool

CYLINDER HEAD & ROCKER ASSEMBLY

1. Lubricate and install tappets into their respective bores.
2. Position new cylinder head gasket onto cylinder block, then install cylinder head, making sure dowels are correctly aligned.
3. Lubricate and install pushrods, valve caps and the rocker assembly.
4. Install rocker shaft and cylinder head bolts, then torque bolts to 80-85 ft. lbs., in sequence shown in **Fig. 2.**

INTAKE MANIFOLD

1. Install intake manifold to cylinder head using a new gasket.
2. Torque intake manifold retaining bolts to 12-17 ft. lbs.

INJECTION PUMP

1. Position injection pump into timing case, making sure key on pump shaft aligns with keyway in drive gear.
2. Install injection pump to case attaching bolts and nuts.
3. Install drive gear lock plate, spring washer and locknut. Torque locknut to 29-51 ft. lbs.
4. Install drive gear cover and cover retaining nuts.
5. Install injectors and glow plugs into cylinder head. Torque injectors to 43-51 ft. lbs. and glow plugs to 7-11 ft. lbs.
6. Connect injection pipes to injectors and torque flare nuts to 18-22 ft. lbs.
7. Connect fuel hoses and fuel cut solenoid coupler.

FINAL ASSEMBLY

1. Install water pump.
2. Install thermostat housing.
3. Install fan and pulley.
4. Install alternator.
5. Connect vacuum sensing tube.
6. Install starter.

PURGING AIR FROM FUEL SYSTEM

Whenever the injection pump has been removed, the fuel system should be bled as follows:

1. Loosen the fuel filter air vent plug, then press the priming pump up and down until a steady flow of fuel flows from vent plug, **Fig. 13.** Close the vent plug while keeping priming pump depressed.
2. Loosen the injection pump head bolt, **Fig. 14,** then crank engine until fuel flows from head bolt. Torque head bolt to 12 ft. lbs.
3. Disconnect injection pipes at injectors, then crank engine until fuel flows from injection pipes.Reconnect injection pipes and torque to 18-22 ft. lbs.

ADJUSTING VALVE CLEARANCE

1. Start engine and allow it to reach normal operating temperature.
2. Loosen cylinder head bolts in reverse order of sequence shown in **Fig. 2.**
3. Torque cylinder head bolts to specification in sequence, **Fig. 2.**
4. Position No. 1 cylinder at TDC of compression stroke, then adjust the following valves to specification: Intake valves 1,2; Exhaust valves 1,3.
5. Rotate the crankshaft 360°, then adjust the following valves to specification: Intake valves 3,4; Exhaust valves 2,4.
6. Install valve cover and torque retaining bolts to 2-3 ft. lbs.

INJECTION PUMP TIMING

To check injection pump timing, proceed as follows:

1. Disconnect injection pipes from injection pump.
2. Remove head bolt from injection pump, **Fig. 14,** then align timing mark (2° ATDC) with pointer as shown, **Fig. 15.**
3. Mount measuring tool 49 9140 076 or equivalent, into head bolt hole, making sure that tip of dial indicator pointer contacts the plunger end of the pump, **Fig. 16.** Dial gauge should indicate approximately .080 inch.
4. Slowly rotate crankshaft counterclockwise until original timing position

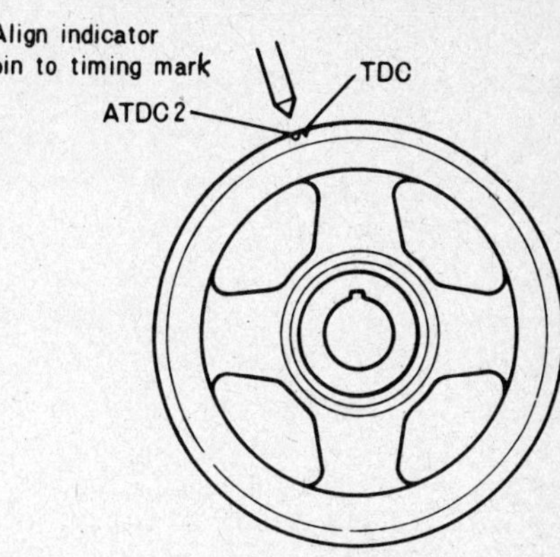

Fig. 15 Aligning timing mark with pointer

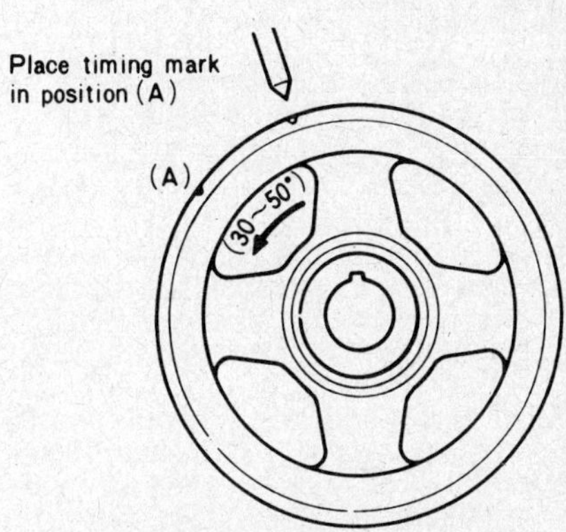

Fig. 17 Changing crankshaft pulley position

(2°ATDC) is approximately 30°-50° to the left of pointer, **Fig. 17.** Make sure dial indicator pointer stops moving, then zero indicator. **To ensure that dial indicator pointer does not deviate from zero, turn crankshaft slightly to the left and right and observe pointer.**

5. Turn crankshaft clockwise until original timing mark aligns with pointer, **Fig. 15.** Observe reading of dial gauge. Dial gauge should indicate .040 ±.0008 inch. If reading is as specified, injection pump timing is correct. If not, proceed to next step.
6. To adjust injection pump timing, loosen injection pump retainers and proceed as follows:
   a. If dial gauge reading in Step 5 is greater than specified, rotate injection pump in reverse direction of engine rotation, until dial gauge indicates as specified in Step 5.
   b. If dial gauge reading in Step 5 is less than specified, rotate injection pump in direction of engine rotation, until dial gauge indicates as specified in Step 5.
7. Tighten injection pump retaining bolts and nuts.
8. Purge air from system.

CLUTCH & MANUAL TRANSMISSION SECTION

INDEX

CLUTCH PEDAL

ADJUST

EXC. GLC, 1986–87 323, 1986–87 626, 1986–87 RX-7 & 1987 B2200 & B2600

1. Freeplay of the clutch pedal before the push rod contacts the master cylinder piston, on all except 626, RX-7, B2000 & B2200 models, should be .040-.120 inch.
2. Clutch pedal height should measure as follows: RX-7, 7.5 inches; 1983-85 626, 8.43 inches; 1983-85 B2000, 8.07 inches; B2200, 8.45 inches.
3. Clutch pedal freeplay should measure .08-.12 inch on 1983-85 626 models, or .02-.12 inch on all other models.
4. Adjust clutch pedal height by loosening locknut and turning stop bolt on clutch switch until specified height is reached.
5. On all except 1983-85 626 models, adjust clutch pedal freeplay by loosening locknut and turning push rod until specified freeplay is obtained.
6. On 1983-85 626 models, adjust clutch pedal freeplay by loosening locknut, then depressing lever and turning adjusting nut until clearance is as specified. Tighten locknut after making any adjustments.

GLC

1. Adjust pedal height by loosening locknut and turning adjusting bolt or switch at clutch pedal. Pedal height should be 9.05 inches.
2. Tighten the locknut after adjustment is completed.
3. To adjust pedal freeplay, loosen locknut (C) at clutch release lever, **Fig. 1,** then turn adjusting nut (B) until clearance between roller and release lever (A) is .08-.12 inch with release lever depressed and roller pulled as shown, **Fig. 1.** This permits correct freeplay of .43-.67 inch to be obtained.
4. Tighten locknut.

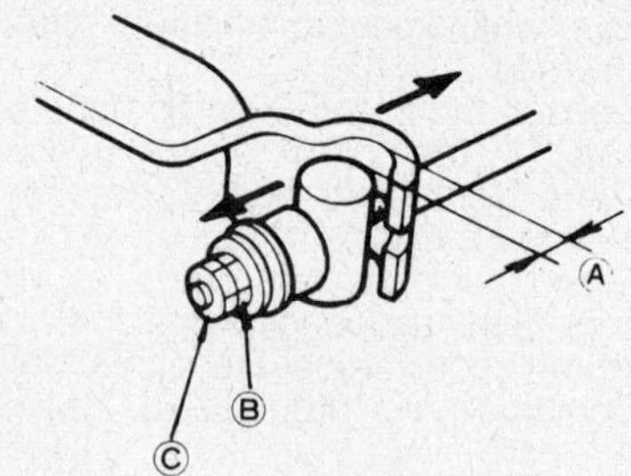

Fig. 1 Adjusting clutch pedal freeplay. 1983–85 GLC

2. If not, adjust pedal height by loosening locknut and turning clutch switch until specified height is obtained.
3. Depress pedal by hand and measure pedal freeplay. Ensure freeplay is .35-.59 inch. If not, adjust clearance by depressing release lever and pulling pin away from lever. Turn adjusting nut until a clearance of .06-.10 inch is obtained.
4. After adjustment, ensure that when the clutch is disengaged, the distance between floor and upper center of pedal pad is approximately 3.3 inches or more.

1986–87 323

1. Measure distance from upper center of pedal pad to firewall and ensure distance (height) is 8.44-8.64 inches.

1986–87 626

1. Measure distance from upper surface of pedal pad to the firewall. Ensure measurement is 8.43 inches.
2. If not, adjust by loosening locknut and turning stopper adjuster bolt until specified height is obtained.
3. Depress pedal lightly by hand and measure clutch pedal play. Clutch pedal play. Clutch pedal play should be .43-.67 inch on fuel injected models and .20-.51 on turbocharged models.
4. If not, press release lever and, when the roller is pulled, turn adjusting nut until a clearance of .08-.12 inch is obtained between release lever and roller on fuel injected models. On turbocharged models, adjust by loosening the locknut and turning the pushrod. Ensure that the distance from floor to the center of the upper surface of the pedal pad is 2.4 inches or more when the clutch is completely disengaged.
5. After adjustment, tighten locknut.

1986–87 RX-7

1. Measure distance from upper surface of pedal pad to firewall. Remove carpet assembly, if necessary.
2. Height should be 8.66 inches.
3. If not, adjust clutch pedal height by loosening locknut and turning the clutch switch until specified height is obtained.
4. Depress clutch pedal lightly by hand and measure clutch pedal freeplay. Freeplay should be .02-.12 inch.
5. If not, adjust freeplay by loosening locknut and turning push rod assembly until specified value is obtained.
6. After adjustment, tighten locknut.
7. Ensure distance from the floor to the center of the upper surface of pedal pad is 3.23 inches.
8. With pedal height and pedal freeplay adjusted correctly, ensure pedal assist spring is at correct length. Measure assist spring length. Length should be 1.54 inch. If not, turn assist spring locknut until correct length is obtained.

1987 B2200 & B2600

1. Measure distance from upper surface of pedal pad to firewall.
2. Height should be 8.43-8.63 inches for B2200 or 8.82-9.02 inches for B2600.
3. If height is not as specified, adjust loosening locknut and turning the clutch stopper bolt until specified height is obtained.
4. Depress clutch pedal lightly by hand and measure clutch pedal freeplay. Freeplay should be .024-.071 inch.
5. If freeplay is not as specified, adjust loosening locknut and turning pushrod assembly until specified value is obtained.
6. After adjustment, tighten locknut.
7. Ensure distance from the floor to the center of the upper surface of pedal pad is 4.37 inches for B2200 or 4.76 inches for B2600 when clutch is fully disengaged.

TRANSMISSION REPLACE

1983–85 RX-7

1. Disconnect battery ground cable.
2. Remove clutch release cylinder.
3. Remove transmission to engine attaching bolts from rear of engine.
4. On models with carbureted engine, remove air cleaner assembly.
5. Remove gear shift lever knob, boot and boot plate, then the gearshift lever and retainer assembly.
6. Raise and support vehicle.
7. Remove front and rear undercovers.
8. Remove catalytic converter undercover.
9. Disconnect air pipe from catalytic converter and remove converter brackets.
10. Remove rear exhaust pipe and catalytic converter assembly.
11. Remove front exhaust pipe and catalytic converter assembly.
12. Remove floor undercovers.
13. Drain transmission fluid, then clean and reinstall drain plug.
14. Remove driveshaft.
15. Remove starter motor.
16. Remove transmission-to-engine attaching bolts.
17. Disconnect all electrical connectors from transmission, then support transmission with a suitable jack.
18. Disconnect speedometer cable, then remove transmission support-to-body attaching nuts.
19. Slide transmission rearward until main driveshaft clears clutch disc, then carefully lower transmission from vehicle.
20. Reverse procedure to install.

1986–87 RX-7

1. Disconnect battery ground cable.
2. Raise and support vehicle, then drain transmission fluid.
3. Remove console box, then the gear shift lever.
4. Remove clutch release cylinder.
5. Remove exhaust pipe, then the engine and transmission under covers.
6. Remove propeller shaft.
7. Disconnect speedometer cable, then all transmission electrical connectors.
8. Remove starter motor.
9. Position suitable jack under transmission, then remove transmission crossmember.
10. Remove engine to transmission attaching bolts, then lower transmission from vehicle.
11. Reverse procedure to install.

1983–84 B2000 & B2200

1. Disconnect battery ground cable, then place gear shift lever in Neutral position.
2. Remove gearshift lever boot, then the gearshift retainer cover and gasket.
3. Pull gearshift lever, wave washer, shim and bushing straight up and away from gearshift lever retainer.
4. Raise and support vehicle, then drain transmission fluid.
5. Remove driveshaft, then the exhaust pipe hanger to clutch housing attaching bolt.
6. Remove clutch release cylinder and place to one side.
7. Disconnect all electrical connectors from transmission, then remove starter.
8. Remove speedometer cable from extension housing.
9. Position suitable jack under rear of engine, protecting oil pan with wooden block.
10. Remove transmission to rear end of cylinder block attaching bolts, then support transmission using suitable jack.
11. Remove transmission support, then the crossmember attaching bolts and crossmember.
12. Separate clutch housing from locating dowels, then slide transmission rearward until main drive shaft spline clears clutch disc.
13. Lower transmission from vehicle.
14. Reverse procedure to install.

1986 B2000 & 1987 B2200

1. Disconnect battery ground cable.
2. Raise and support vehicle, then drain transmission fluid.
3. Remove console box, then the gear shift lever.
4. Remove propeller shaft.
5. Disconnect speedometer cable, then all transmission electrical connectors.
6. Remove parking brake cable return springs, then the parking brake cables.
7. Remove clutch release cylinder, then the transmission gusset plate.
8. Remove exhaust pipe, then the starter motor.
9. Position suitable jack under transmission, then remove transmission crossmember.
10. Remove engine to transmission attaching bolts, then lower transmission from vehicle.
11. Reverse procedure to install.

1987 B2600

1. Disconnect battery ground cable.
2. Raise and support vehicle, then drain transmission fluid.
3. Remove shift lever knobs, then the console box assembly.
4. Remove shift lever insulator plate and boot.
5. Remove shift lever assembly attaching bolts, then the shift lever assembly.
6. Remove upper transmission bracket attaching bolt.
7. Remove rear under cover, then the transfer case cover.
8. Remove exhaust pipe, then the front and rear propeller shafts.
9. Disconnect speedometer cable, then all transmission electrical connectors.
10. Remove front converter installation spring and nut.
11. Remove clutch release cylinder.
12. Position suitable jack under transmission, then remove gusset plates.
13. Lower transmission approximately 1 inch, then remove clutch housing under cover.
14. Remove transmission crossmember.
15. Remove transmission to engine attaching bolts, then lower transmission from vehicle.
16. Reverse procedure to install.

1983 GLC WAGON

1. Disconnect battery ground cable, then shift transmission to Neutral and remove shift lever.
2. Raise and support vehicle, then remove two upper bolts from clutch housing.
3. Drain transmission and remove drive shaft.
4. Disconnect speedometer cable, and all electrical connectors from transmission.
5. Disconnect exhaust pipe hanger from bracket on clutch housing.
6. Remove exhaust pipe support bracket from clutch housing, then disconnect clutch cable from clutch release lever.
7. Remove clutch housing undercover.
8. Remove starter motor, then the exhaust pipe hanger from extension housing.
9. Install suitable jack under engine, protecting oil pan with a block of wood.
10. Disconnect transmission support member, then install suitable jack under transmission.
11. Remove transmission to engine attaching bolts, then lower transmission from vehicle.
12. Reverse procedure to install.

TRANSAXLE REPLACE

1983–85 GLC

1. Disconnect battery ground cable and speedometer cable.
2. Remove clutch cable brackets and disconnect clutch cable from release lever.
3. Remove water pipe bracket and harness clip.
4. Raise and support front of vehicle.
5. Completely drain oil from transaxle.
6. Remove front wheels, undercover and side covers from vehicle.
7. Remove ball joint from lower control arm.
8. Pull driveshafts out from transaxle. The driveshaft can be removed by pulling the brake caliper toward the operator. Pull the shaft straight out of the axle and do not damage oil seal. **Ensure the driveshaft ball joint is not bent severely.**
9. Using engine support 49E301025 or equivalent, connect onto engine lifting eyes. Using a suitable hoist, raise engine.
10. Disconnect shift control and shift rod from transaxle.
11. Remove extension bar from transaxle.
12. Remove bolts and crossmember.
13. Disconnect four rubber mounts and transaxle case from transaxle.
14. Remove starter motor.

15. Using a suitable jack, support transaxle.
16. Remove transaxle mounting bolts and the transaxle.
17. Reverse procedure to install.

626

1. Disconnect battery ground cable and drain transaxle fluid.
2. Disconnect speedometer cable from transaxle.
3. Remove clutch cable bracket attaching bolts, then disconnect clutch cable from release lever.
4. Disconnect ground wire and wire harness clip.
5. Remove starter, then install engine support 49 G030 025 or equivalent and attach to engine.
6. Remove 4 transaxle to engine attaching bolts, then raise and support vehicle.
7. Remove front wheels, then the right and left splash shields.
8. Remove stabilizer bar control link.
9. Remove transaxle undercover, then the right and left control arms by pulling arms downward to separate them from knuckles. **Use caution to avoid damaging ball joint dust boots.**
10. Remove right driveshaft as follows:
    a. Pull front hub outward, then install suitable pry bar between hub and transaxle.
    b. Tap pry bar until driveshaft disconnects from transaxle side gear.
    c. Pull front hub outward, then pull driveshaft out from transaxle and set aside. **Use caution not to damage driveshaft oil seal when removing driveshaft from transaxle.**
11. Remove right driveshaft as follows:
    a. Install suitable pry bar between drive shaft and joint shaft, then tap pry bar until driveshaft coupling opens.
    b. Pull front hub outward, then pull driveshaft out from joint shaft and set aside.
    c. Remove joint shaft bracket attaching bolts, then pull joint bracket from transaxle as a complete assembly.
12. Remove crossmember and lower control arm attaching bolts, then lower crossmember and lower control arm from vehicle as an assembly.
13. Separate shift control rod from shift rod.
14. Remove extension bar from transaxle, then the transaxle undercover.
15. Attach suitable rope to transaxle mount bracket in two places, then secure rope to engine support.
16. Install suitable jack under transaxle. Note which part of transaxle contacts jack, as transaxle is not well balanced.
17. Remove 2 transaxle to engine attaching bolts, then remove transaxle from vehicle by lowering floor jack and loosening rope at the same time.
18. Remove transaxle mount bracket from transaxle.
19. Reverse procedure to install.

323

1. Disconnect battery ground cable.
2. Remove air cleaner assembly.
3. Loosen front wheel lug nuts.
4. Disconnect speedometer cable from transaxle.
5. Disconnect clutch cable from release lever and remove clutch cable bracket mounting bolts.
6. Remove ground wire attaching bolt.
7. Remove water pipe bracket.
8. Remove secondary air pipe and EGR pipe bracket.
9. Remove wire harness clip.
10. Disconnect Neutral start and back-up light switch electrical connectors.
11. Disconnect body ground electrical connector.
12. Remove two upper transaxle to engine attaching bolts.
13. Position engine support tool 49E30125A or equivalent, on to engine hanger.
14. Raise and support vehicle.
15. Drain fluid from transaxle.
16. Remove front wheels.
17. Remove undercover and side covers.
18. Remove front stabilizer bar.
19. Remove lower control arm ball joints and steering knuckle clinch bolts. Pull lower arms downward, then separate lower arms from steering knuckles. **Take care not to damage ball joint dust boots.**
20. Separate driveshaft by pulling the front hub outward. Do not use excessive force at once, gradually increase force applied. Use caution to prevent overextending CV joints. Support driveshaft using a suitable piece of wire or string.
21. Remove crossmember attaching bolts, then the crossmember.
22. Separate shift control rod from transaxle.
23. Remove extension bar from transaxle.
24. Disconnect starter positive cable from start motor, then remove starter motor.
25. Remove end plate.
26. Gradually lean engine assembly toward transaxle to lower transaxle assembly by loosening engine support hook bolt.
27. Support transaxle with a suitable jack.
28. Remove No. 2 engine bracket.
29. Remove remaining transaxle to engine attaching bolts.
30. Remove transaxle from vehicle.
31. Reverse procedure to install.

DISC BRAKES SECTION, EXC. 1986–87 RX-7

INDEX

B2000

B2200

1. Caliper assembly
2. Bleeder cap
3. Bleeder screw
4. Caliper body
5. Piston seal
6. Piston
7. Dust boot
8. Boot retainer
9. Shim
10. Brake shoe and lining assembly
11. Locking clip
12. Stopper plate
13. Spring
14. Caliper bracket
15. Anti-rattle spring clip
16. Anti-rattle spring

Fig. 1 Disc brake assembly. 1983–84 B2000 & B2200

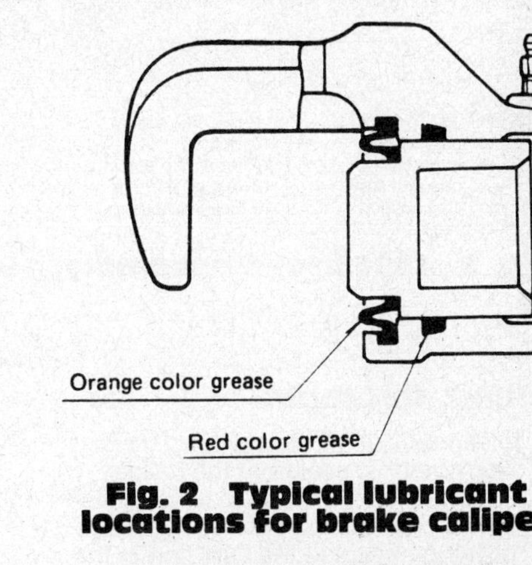

Fig. 2 Typical lubricant locations for brake caliper

FRONT DISC BRAKE SERVICE

1983–84 B2000 & B2200

Brake Pads, Replace

1. Raise and support front of vehicle, then remove the front wheel.
2. On B2000, remove locking clips and stopper plates, **Figs. 1.**
3. On B2200 models, remove the sliding pins, **Fig. 1.**
4. On all models, remove the caliper and anti-rattle spring, then pull out the brake shoes and shims.
5. Remove the rubber cap from the bleeder screw, and connect a drain tube onto the bleeder screw. Submerge the other end of the tube into a suitable container.
6. Open the bleeder screw and press the piston into the cylinder.
7. Tighten the bleeder screw and remove the tube and retracting tool.
8. Install new brake pads and shims on the caliper.
9. On B2000 models, install the anti-rattle spring, caliper, stopper plates and locking pins. On B2200 models, install the anti-rattle spring and the sliding pins.
10. Install the front wheel and lower the vehicle.

Caliper, Replace

1. Raise and support the front end of the vehicle.
2. Remove the front wheel.
3. Remove the pad and lining assembly as described previously.
4. Disconnect the brake fluid pipe from the caliper and plug the end of the fluid pipe to prevent entrance of dirt and loss of fluid.
5. Remove the caliper.
6. If necessary, remove the caliper bracket by removing the two bolts.
7. Reverse procedure to install. When installing caliper, lubricate caliper and mounting at positions shown in **Fig. 2.**

Caliper Overhaul

1. Clean outside of the caliper.
2. Remove retainer and dust boot from the caliper.
3. Place a piece of wood in front of piston to prevent damage to piston. Apply air pressure to the fluid port in the caliper to remove the piston. **If piston is seized and cannot be forced from the caliper, tap lightly around the piston while applying air pressure.**
4. Remove piston seal from caliper bore.
5. Apply brake fluid to piston seal and install it into groove of caliper bore. Ensure seal does not become twisted and that it is seated fully in the groove.
6. Lubricate piston and caliper bore.
7. Insert piston into caliper bore.
8. Install dust boot by setting flange squarely in inner groove of caliper bore. Install dust boot retainer.

1986 B2000

Brake Pads, Replace

1. Raise and support vehicle, then remove front wheel.
2. Remove main lock pin bolt and sub lock pin bolt, **Fig. 3.**
3. Remove caliper assembly, then the disc pads and shims from mounting support.
4. Reverse procedure to install.

Caliper, Replace

1. Raise and support vehicle, then remove front wheel.
2. Remove brake hose attaching bolt, then disconnect and cap brake hose from caliper.
3. Remove main lock pin bolt and sub lock pin bolt, **Fig. 3.**
4. Remove caliper assembly, then the disc pads, shims and mounting support.
5. Reverse procedure to install.

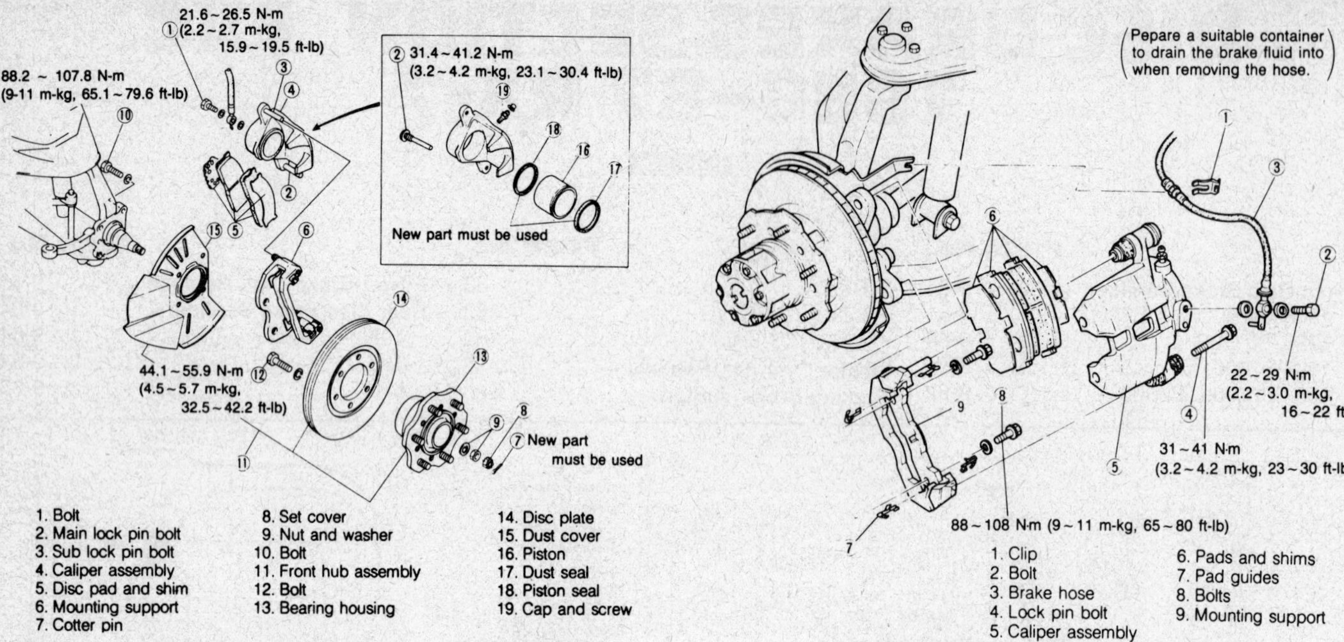

Fig. 3 Disc brake assembly. 1986 B2000

Fig. 4 Disc brake assembly. 1987 B2200 & B2600

Caliper, Overhaul

1. Clean outside of the caliper.
2. Remove dust seal from the caliper.
3. Place a piece of wood in front of piston to prevent damage to piston. Apply air pressure to the fluid port in the caliper to remove the piston. **If piston is seized and cannot be forced from the caliper, tap lightly around the piston while applying air pressure.**
4. Remove piston seal from caliper bore.
5. Apply brake fluid to piston seal and install it into groove of caliper bore. Ensure seal does not become twisted and that it is seated fully in the groove.
6. Lubricate piston and caliper bore.
7. Insert piston into caliper bore.
8. Install dust seal into groove of caliper bore.

1987 B2200 & B2600

Brake Pads, Replace

1. Raise and support vehicle, then remove front wheel.
2. Remove lock pin bolt, then the caliper assembly, **Fig. 4.**
3. Remove brake pads and shims from mounting support.
4. Reverse procedure to install.

Caliper, Replace

1. Raise and support vehicle, then remove front wheel.
2. Remove brake hose clip and attaching bolt, then disconnect and cap brake hose from caliper.
3. Remove lock pin bolt, then the caliper assembly, **Fig. 4.**
4. Reverse procedure to install.

Caliper, Overhaul

Refer to "1986 B2000" under "Caliper, Overhaul" procedure.

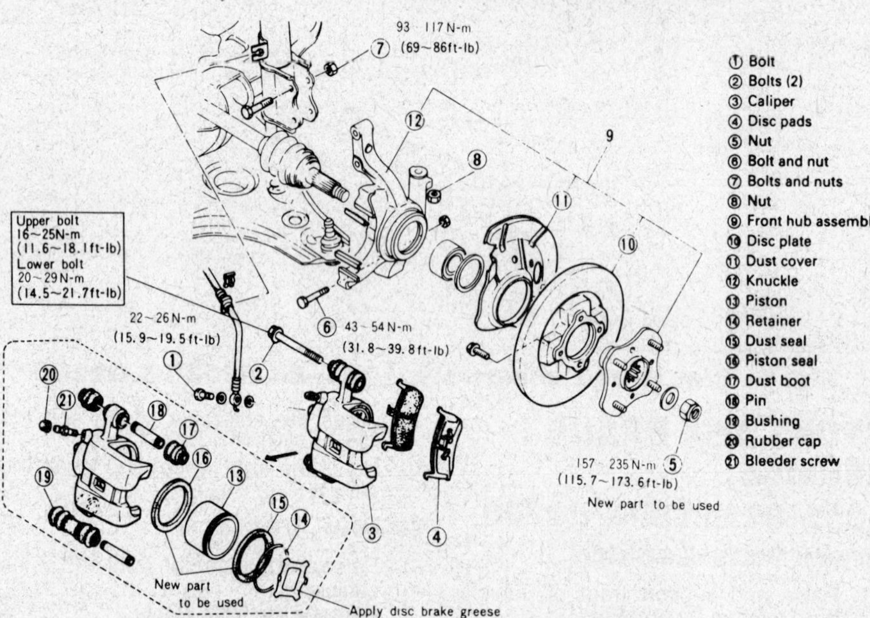

Fig. 5 Disc brake assembly. 626

626

Brake Pads, Replace

1. Raise and support front of vehicle.
2. Remove front wheel.
3. Remove caliper attaching bolts, then the caliper, **Fig. 5.**
4. Remove brake pads and shims.
5. Reverse procedure to install, noting the following:
   a. If difficulty is encountered when installing brake pads, remove rubber cap from bleeder screw and connect a vinyl hose to the screw. Place opposite end of hose into a suitable container. Open bleeder screw and press piston into cylinder using tool No. 490221600C or equivalent. Tighten bleeder screw, then remove hose and tool.

Caliper, Replace

1. Raise and support front of vehicle.
2. Remove front wheel.
3. Using tool No. 490259770A or equivalent, disconnect and plug brake line.
4. Remove caliper attaching bolts, then the caliper, **Fig. 5.**
5. Reverse procedure to install.

Caliper, Overhaul

1. Position a thick piece of wood into the caliper pit, and gradually blow compressed air from the fluid pipe hole and remove piston. **If the piston is seized and cannot be forced from**

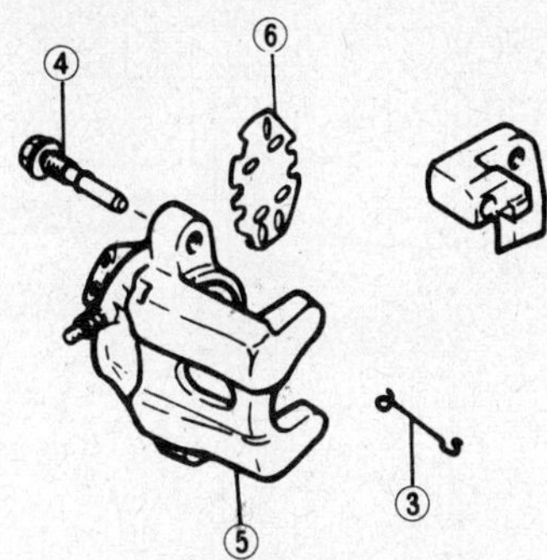

Fig. 6 Brake caliper. 1983–85 GLC

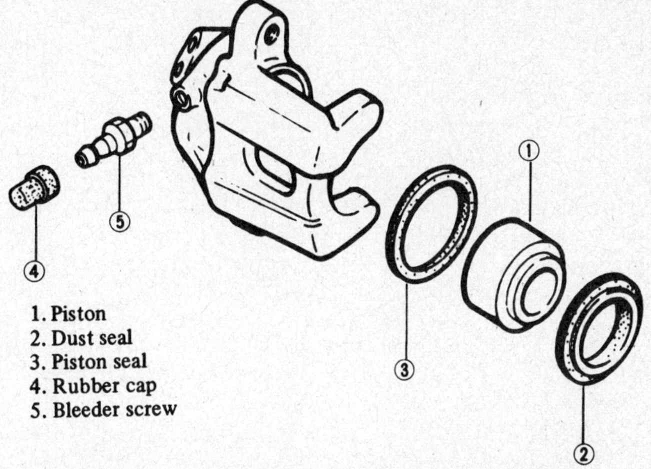

Fig. 7 Disassembled view of brake caliper components. 1983–85 GLC

the caliper, gently tap around the piston while applying air pressure.

2. Remove bleeder screw from caliper, if necessary.
3. Remove piston retainer and dust seal, **Fig. 5.**
4. Remove piston seal, dust boot, rubber caps and bushing.
5. Thoroughly clean disassembled components using clean brake fluid or alcohol and blow drying them with compressed air. **Do not use petroleum based solvents to clean the caliper components.**
6. Replace rubber caps, bushing, dust boot, piston seal and dust seal.
7. Ensure the piston seal does not twist and is seated correctly in the seal groove.
8. Lubricate the caliper, bushings and dust seal with suitable caliper grease.
9. Install retainer, then using compressed air, install piston into caliper.

RX-7

Brake Pads, Replace

1. Raise and support front of vehicle.
2. Remove front wheel.
3. Remove caliper lower attaching bolt and swing caliper upward. Remove spring, brake pads and shims.
4. Reverse procedure to install. If difficulty is encountered when installing brake pads, proceed as follows:
   a. Remove rubber cap from bleeder screw.
   b. Connect one end of a vinyl hose to screw and place opposite end in a suitable container.
   c. Open bleeder screw and press piston into cylinder using tool No. 490221600C or equivalent.
   d. Tighten bleeder screw, then remove hose and tool.

Caliper, Replace

1. Raise and support front of vehicle.
2. Remove front wheel.
3. Loosen brake line at caliper.
4. Remove caliper lower attaching bolt. Swing caliper upward, then slide caliper out toward inside of vehicle.
5. Disconnect and plug brake line from caliper.
6. Reverse procedure to install.

Caliper Overhaul

1. Clean outside of caliper.
2. Remove dust boot retainer and the dust boot.
3. Place a piece of wood in front of piston to avoid damage, then apply compressed air to fluid pipe hole and remove the piston. **If piston is seized and cannot be forced from caliper, tap lightly around piston while applying air pressure.**
4. Remove bleeder cap and screw.
5. Thoroughly clean caliper components using clean brake fluid or alcohol and dry with compressed air. **Do not use petroleum based solvents to clean brake components.**
6. Reverse steps 1 through 4 to assemble caliper, noting the following:
   a. Replace dust boot and piston seal.
   b. Ensure piston seal seats properly in seal groove.
   c. Lubricate caliper bore and piston with clean brake fluid.
   d. Apply suitable grease to areas indicated in **Fig. 2.**

1983–85 GLC

Brake Pads, Replace

1. Raise and support front of vehicle.
2. Remove front wheel.
3. Using a suitable screwdriver remove brake hose clip and disconnect brake hose from shock absorber.
4. Remove caliper return spring.
5. Remove slide pin from caliper, and secure caliper with a piece of wire.
6. Remove brake pad, shim and spring.
7. Check the brake pads for wear and replace brake pad if wear is excessive.
8. Reverse procedure to install. Note the following:
   a. Using a suitable grease, lubricate contact surface between pad mounting support and caliper assembly.
   b. Lubricate both surfaces of the outer and inner shims.
   c. Position brake hose into the shock absorber groove and lock with clip.
   d. Lubricate slide pin and bushing.
   e. Bleed the brakes. Pump the brake pedal two or three times and check brake efficiency.

Caliper, Replace

1. Raise and support front of vehicle.
2. Remove front wheel and disconnect brake hose from caliper.
3. Remove return spring (3), **Fig. 6,** slide pin (4), caliper assembly (5) and shim (6).
4. Reverse procedure to install.

Caliper Overhaul

1. Disassemble in order shown in **Fig. 7.**
2. Remove piston from caliper, by wrapping the outer side of caliper with a shop cloth and blowing compressed air a little at a time, through the brake hose connecting hole.

323

Brake Pads, Replace

Replace left and right brake pads at the same time. Do not replace brake pads for one side of the vehicle only.

1. Raise and support front of vehicle.
2. Remove tire and wheel assemblies.
3. Remove caliper attaching bolts, then the caliper assembly. Suspend caliper using a suitable piece of wire.
4. Remove brake pads.
5. Reverse procedure to install.

Caliper, Replace

1. Raise and support front of vehicle.
2. Remove tire and wheel assemblies.
3. Disconnect and cap brake line.
4. Remove caliper attaching bolts, then the caliper assembly.
5. Reverse procedure to install.

Caliper, Overhaul

1. With caliper removed from vehicle, remove piston, snap ring, dust seal, piston seal, cap and screw, as required.
2. When removing piston from caliper, place a suitable piece of wood into caliper assembly.
3. Blow compressed air through the flexible hose connection hole to force piston out of caliper assembly. **Apply air pressure gradually to prevent piston from jumping out.**

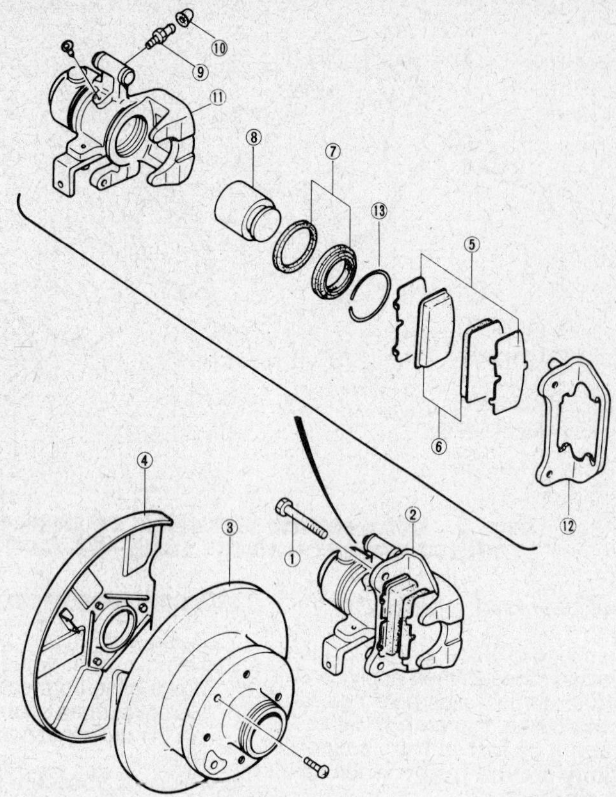

Fig. 8 Rear disc brake assembly exploded view. 1983–85 RX-7

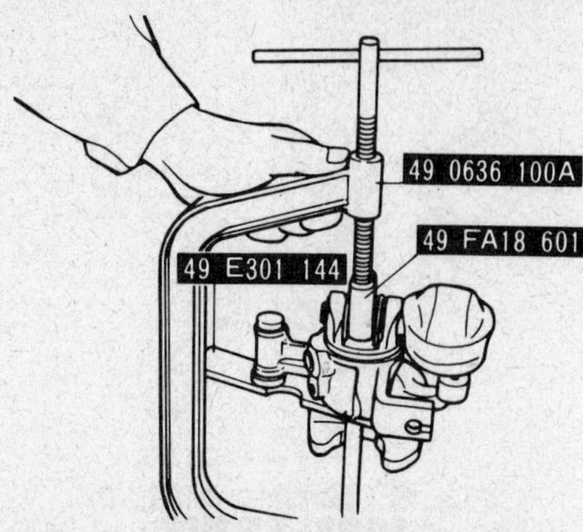

Fig. 9 Caliper disassembly. 1983–85 RX-7 rear disc brake

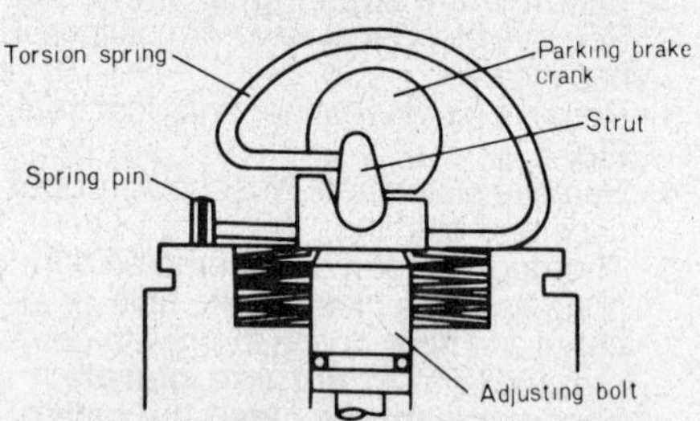

Fig. 10 Caliper assembly. 1983–85 RX-7 rear disc brake

REAR DISC BRAKE SERVICE

1983–85 RX-7

Brake Pads, Replace

1. Raise and support rear of vehicle.
2. Remove rear wheel.
3. Disconnect parking brake cable from caliper.
4. Remove caliper lower attaching bolt and swing caliper upward.
5. Remove spring, brake pads and shims.
6. Reverse procedure to install, noting the following:
   a. Turn piston clockwise using tool No. 49FA18602 or equivalent until piston is fully seated in caliper.
   b. Ensure stopper groove on piston is perpendicular to caliper mounting points.
   c. Ensure dowel on brake pad is properly seated in piston stopper groove.
   d. Torque caliper attaching bolt to 22-30 ft. lbs.

Caliper, Replace

1. Raise and support rear of vehicle.
2. Remove rear wheel.
3. Loosen brake line at caliper.
4. Remove caliper lower attaching bolt and swing caliper upward, then slide caliper out toward inside of vehicle.
5. Reverse procedure to install.

Caliper Overhaul

1. Clean outside of caliper.
2. Remove dust boot retainer and the dust boot, **Fig. 8**.
3. Screw piston out of caliper using tool No. 49FA18602 or equivalent.
4. Remove piston seal, boot retainer, boot and snap ring.
5. Compress conical spring in caliper, **Fig. 9,** and remove parking brake crank, torsion spring and strut.
6. Remove adjusting bolt and conical spring.
7. Remove needle roller bearings, if necessary, using a suitable press.
8. Thoroughly clean caliper components using clean brake fluid or alcohol and dry with compressed air. **Do not use petroleum based solvents to clean caliper components.**
9. Inspect components for wear or damage and replace as necessary.
10. Ensure endplay of piston and sleeve nut does not exceed .012-.020 inch (.3-.5mm).
11. Reverse steps 1 through 7 to assemble caliper, noting the following:
    a. Replace dust boot and piston seal.
    b. Ensure piston seal seats properly in seal groove.
    c. Apply white color grease to caliper mounting pin and attaching bolt.
    d. Apply orange color grease to bearings, adjusting bolt, strut and piston boot.
    e. Apply pink color grease to piston seal.
    f. Apply clean brake fluid to caliper bore and piston.
    g. Install needle bearing so arrow on bearing faces outward.
    h. Install adjusting bolt, strut and torsion spring into caliper as shown in **Fig. 10.**
    i. Install piston as described under "Brake Pads, Replace."

323

Brake Pads, Replace

Replace right and left brake pads at the same time. Do not replace one side only.

1. Raise and support rear of vehicle.
2. Remove tire and wheel assemblies.
3. Remove guide pin bolts, then the caliper assembly. Suspend caliper assembly using a suitable piece of wire.
4. Remove brake pads.
5. Reverse procedure to install.

Caliper, Replace

1. Raise and support rear of vehicle.
2. Remove tire and wheel assemblies.
3. Disconnect and cap brake line.
4. Remove caliper guide pin bolts.
5. Remove caliper assembly from vehicle.
6. Reverse procedure to install.

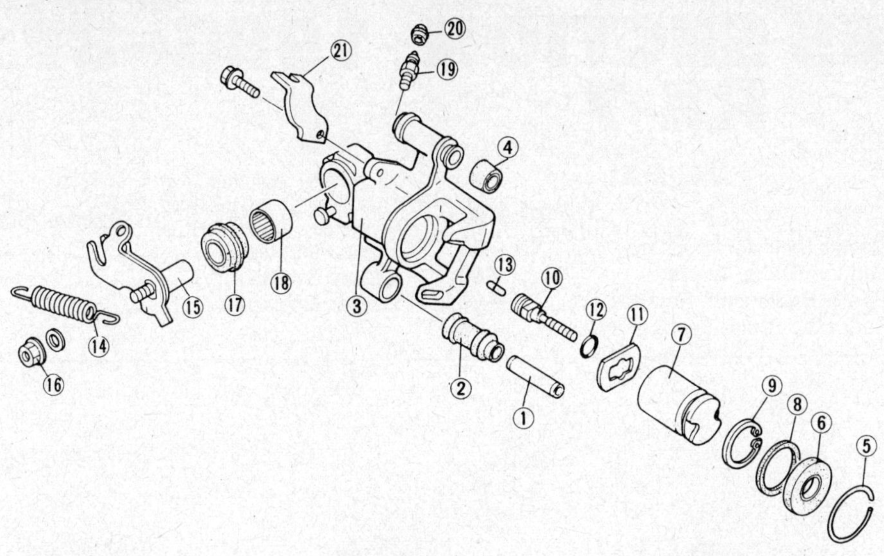

1. Guide pin
2. Guide pin boot
3. Caliper
4. Boot
5. Retainer
6. Dust seal
7. Piston
8. Piston seal
9. Snap ring
10. Adjuster spindle
11. Stopper
12. O-ring
13. Connecting ring
14. Spring
15. Spindle lever
16. Nut
17. Boot
18. Needle bearing
19. Bleeder screw
20. Rubber cap
21. Bolt
22. Bracket

Fig. 11 Exploded view of rear disc brake caliper. 323

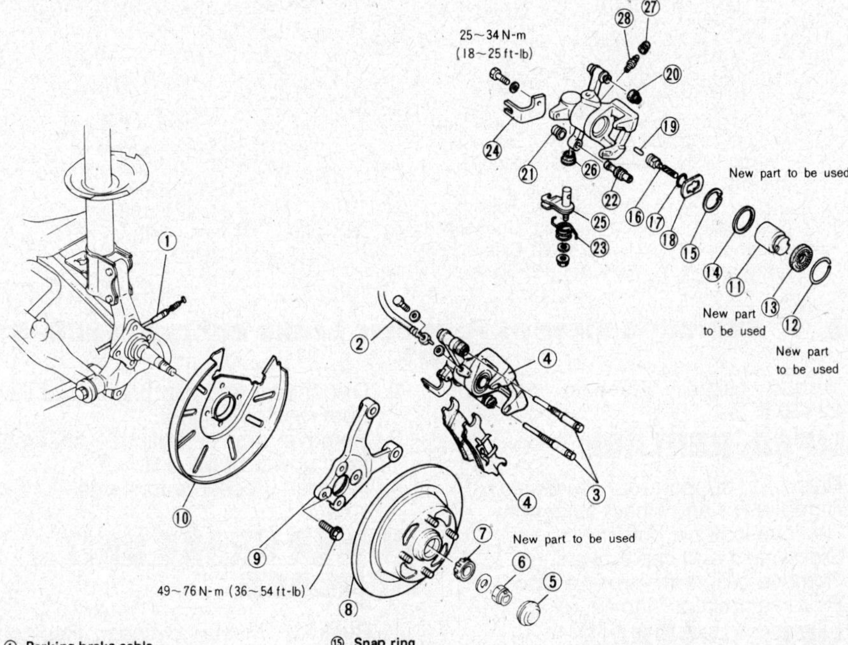

① Parking brake cable
② Brake hose
③ Guide pin and cover
④ Caliper and pad assembly
⑤ Hub cap
⑥ Lock nut
⑦ Bearing
⑧ Disc plate
⑨ Mounting support
⑩ Dust cover
⑪ Piston
⑫ Retainer
⑬ Dust seal
⑭ Piston seal
⑮ Snap ring
⑯ Adjuster spindle
⑰ O-ring
⑱ Stopper
⑲ Connecting link
⑳ Dust boot
㉑ Cover
㉒ Guide pin bushing
㉓ Return spring
㉔ Bracket
㉕ Spindle lever
㉖ Dust boot
㉗ Cap
㉘ Bleeder screw

Fig. 12 Exploded view of rear disc brake caliper. 626

Caliper Overhaul

When overhauling caliper assembly, refer to **Fig. 11.** When assembling caliper assembly, reverse numerical disassembly sequence.

626

Brake Pads, Replace

1. Raise and support rear of vehicle.
2. Remove tire and wheel assembly.
3. Remove caliper attaching bolts.
4. Suspend caliper with a suitable piece of wire.
5. Remove brake pads from caliper assembly.
6. Reverse procedure to install.

Caliper, Replace

1. Raise and support rear of vehicle.
2. Remove tire and wheel assembly.
3. Disconnect and cap brake lines.
4. Remove caliper guide pin bolts and cover.
5. Remove caliper assembly.
6. Reverse procedure to install.

Caliper Overhaul

When overhauling caliper assembly, refer to **Fig. 12.** Reverse numerical disassembly sequence for assembly.

MASTER CYLINDER REPLACE

1. Disconnect the oil level sensor coupler.
2. Using tool No. 490259770A or equivalent, disconnect and cap brake fluid lines from master cylinder.
3. Remove proportioning by-pass valve attaching bolts and valve, if equipped.
4. Remove master cylinder assembly from power brake unit.
5. Reverse procedure to install.

POWER BRAKE UNIT REPLACE

1. Refer to "Master Cylinder, Replace" and remove master cylinder.
2. Disconnect vacuum hose from power brake unit.
3. Disconnect push rod fork from brake pedal and remove power brake unit from vehicle.
4. Reverse procedure to install.

PARKING BRAKE ADJUST

For parking brake adjust procedure, refer to "Drum Brake Section."

DISC BRAKES SECTION, 1986–87 RX-7

INDEX

FRONT DISC BRAKE SERVICE

BRAKE PADS, REPLACE

Replace left and right brake pads at the same time. Do not replace one wheel side only.

1. Raise and support front of vehicle.
2. Remove tire and wheel assembly.
3. Remove lock pin bolt and lift caliper assembly with brake line connected, from disc assembly.
4. Remove brake pads from caliper assembly.
5. Reverse procedure to install. When installing new brake pads, push caliper piston inward using tool 490221600C or equivalent. Torque lock bolt to 23-30 ft. lbs.

CALIPER, REPLACE

1. Raise and support front of vehicle.
2. Remove tire and wheel assembly.
3. Remove lock pin bolt.
4. Disconnect and cap brake line.
5. Lift caliper assembly from brake disc.
6. Reverse procedure to install.

CALIPER OVERHAUL

1. With caliper removed from vehicle, remove caliper clip and dust seal.
2. Remove piston, piston seal, cap and bleeder screw.
3. When removing piston from caliper, place a piece of wood into the caliper assembly. Using compressed air, blow air through the flexible hose connection hole to force out the piston from the caliper assembly. **Apply air pressure gradually to prevent the piston from jumping out.**

REAR DISC BRAKE SERVICE

BRAKE PAD, REPLACE

Replace left and right brake pads at the same time. Do not replace one wheel side only.

1. Raise and support front of vehicle.
2. Remove tire and wheel assembly.
3. Remove lock pin bolt, then lift caliper from brake disc.
4. Remove V-spring and brake pads.
5. Reverse procedure to install. When installing brake pads, rotate piston clockwise with tool 49FA18602 or equivalent, and install new pads.

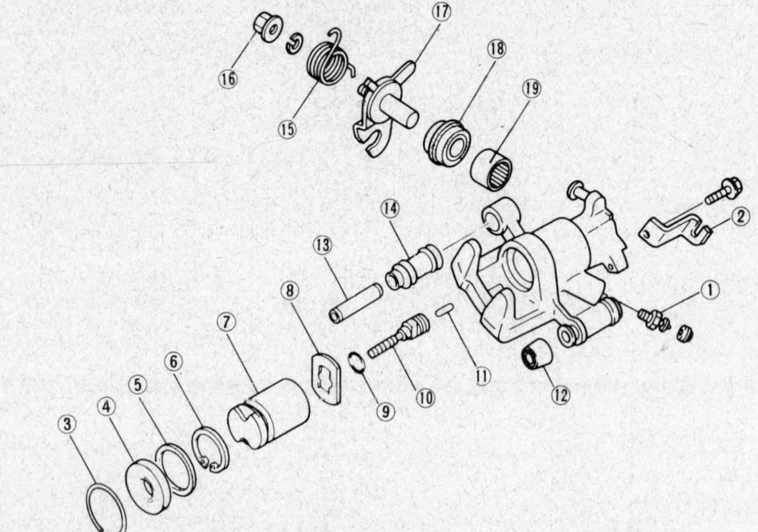

1. Air bleeder screw
2. Parking brake cable bracket
3. Clip
4. Dust seal
5. Piston
6. Piston seal
7. Snap ring
8. Stopper
9. "O" ring
10. Adjuster spindle
11. Connecting link
12. Sleeve boot
13. Guide pin
14. Guide pin boot
15. Spring
16. Nut
17. Spindle lever
18. Dust boot
19. Bearing

Fig. 1 Exploded view of rear disc brake caliper. 1986–87 RX-7

Torque caliper attaching bolt to 22-30 ft. lbs.

CALIPER, REPLACE

1. Raise and support rear of vehicle.
2. Remove tire and wheel assembly.
3. Remove lock pin bolt.
4. Disconnect and cap brake lines.
5. Remove caliper from brake disc.
6. Reverse procedure to install.

CALIPER OVERHAUL

When overhauling caliper, refer to **Fig. 1.** When removing piston from caliper assembly, remove retainer and dust seal. Turn piston counterclockwise using tool 49FA18602 or equivalent and screw out piston from caliper assembly. Remove snap ring from caliper. Reverse numerical sequence in **Fig. 1** for assembly.

MASTER CYLINDER

REPLACE

1. Disconnect the oil level sensor coupler.
2. Disconnect and cap brake fluid lines from master cylinder.
3. Remove master cylinder assembly from power brake unit.
4. Reverse procedure to install.

POWER BRAKE UNIT

REPLACE

1. Refer to "Master Cylinder, Replace" and remove master cylinder.
2. Disconnect vacuum hose from power brake unit.
3. Disconnect push rod fork from brake pedal.
4. Remove power brake attaching nuts, then the power brake unit from vehicle.
5. Reverse procedure to install.

PARKING BRAKE

ADJUST

For parking brake adjust procedure, refer to "Drum Brake Section."

DRUM BRAKE SECTIO

INDEX

Page No.

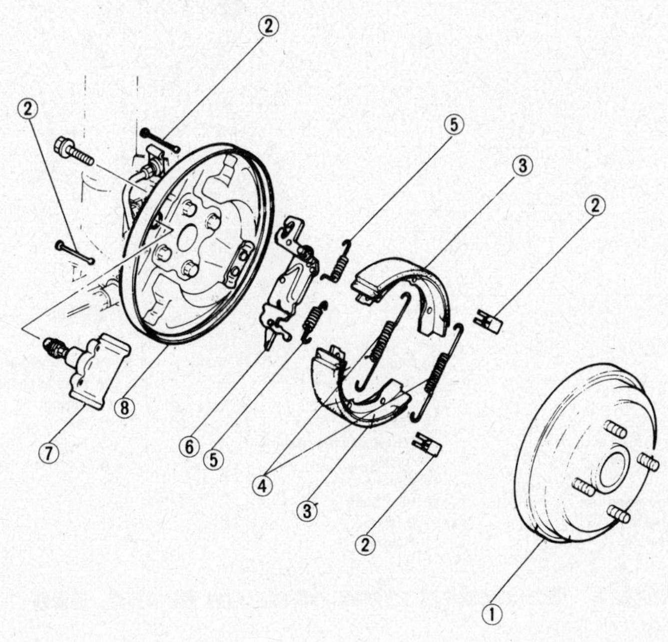

1. Brake drum
2. Hold pin and hold spring
3. Trailing and leading shoe
4. Return springs
5. Anti-rattle springs
6. Adjuster
7. Wheel cylinder assembly
8. Backing plate

Fig. 1 Exploded view of drum brake. 323

DRUM BRAKE SERVICE

For Brake Drum, Replace and Brake Shoes, Replace Procedures, refer to **Figs. 1 through 6** for exploded view of drum brake assemblies.

MASTER CYLINDER REPLACE

For master cylinder replace, refer to "Disc Brake" section under "Master Cylinder, Replace" procedure.

POWER BRAKE UNIT REPLACE

For power brake unit replace, refer to "Disc Brake" section under "Power Brake Unit, Replace" procedure.

PARKING BRAKE ADJUST

1. Ensure parking brake is completely released.
2. Block front wheels, then raise and support rear of vehicle.
3. Adjust parking brake lever screw or nut until wheels are locked when the brake lever is pulled the number of notches specified below:
   a. 1983-84 B2000 and B2200, 5-10 notches.
   b. 1983-85 GLC, 5-9 notches.
   c. 1983-85 RX-7, 6-8 notches.
   d. 1983-87 626, 7-9 notches.
   e. 1986-87 323, 7-11 notches on drum brake models, 9-15 notches on disc brake models.
   f. 1986 B2000, 11-13 notches.
   g. 1986-87 RX-7, 4-5 notches.
   h. 1987 B2200 and B2600, 7-12 notches.
4. After parking brake is adjusted properly, apply parking brake several times, then release and ensure rear wheels rotate freely without any drag.
5. Ensure parking brake warning light, if equipped, illuminates when the brake lever is pulled one notch.

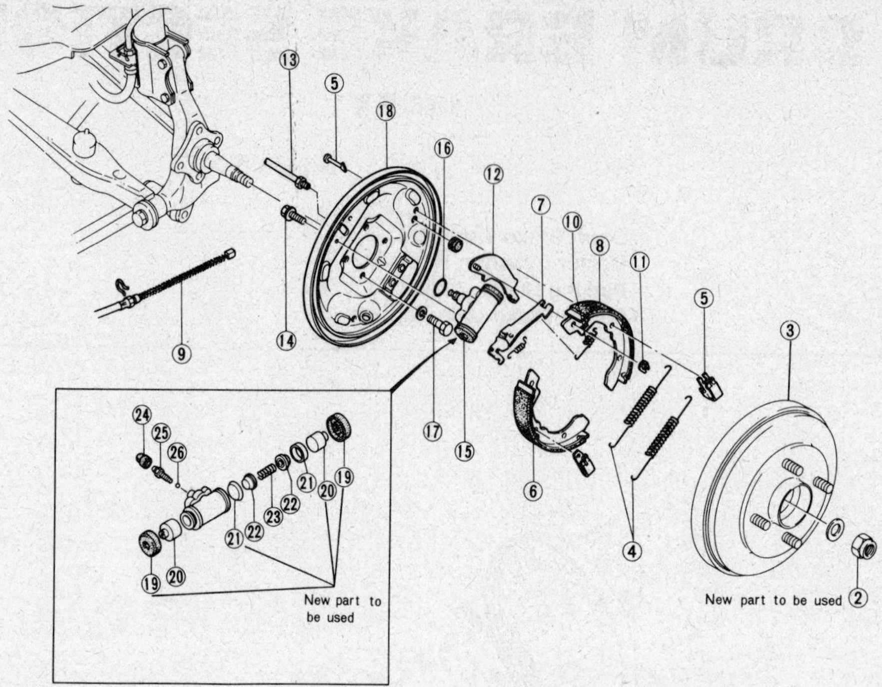

① Hub cap
② Nut
③ Brake drum
④ Return springs
⑤ Hold pins and hold springs
⑥ Leading shoe
⑦ Adjuster
⑧ Trailing shoe assembly
⑨ Parking brake wire
⑩ Anti-rattle spring
⑪ Clip
⑫ Operating lever
⑬ Brake-line pipe
⑭ Bolts
⑮ Wheel cylinder assembly
⑯ Gasket
⑰ Bolts
⑱ Back plate
⑲ Dust boots
⑳ Pistons
㉑ Piston cups
㉒ Feeling blocks
㉓ Spring
㉔ Rubber cap
㉕ Bleeder screw
㉖ Steel ball

Fig. 2 Exploded view of drum brake. 626

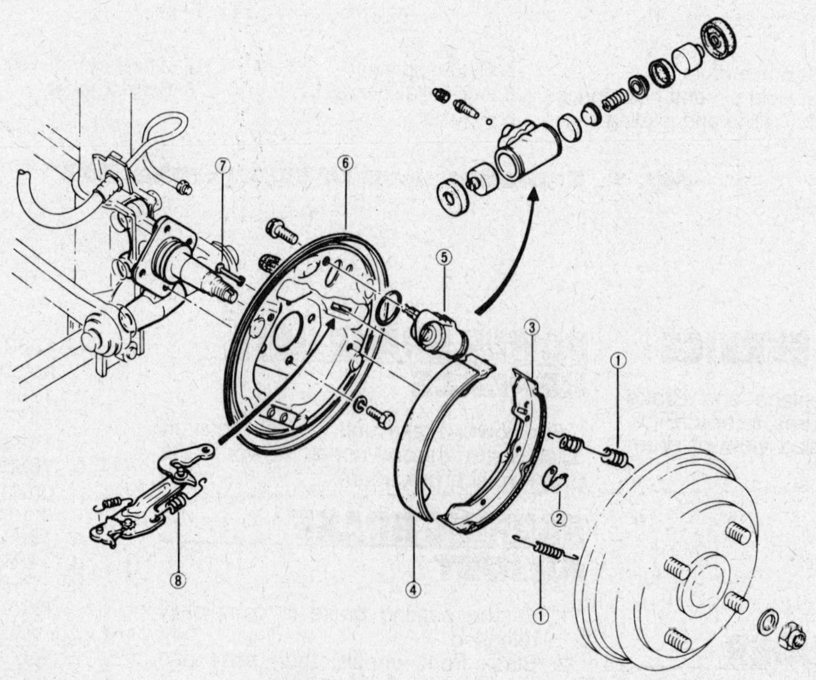

1. Return spring
2. Holding spring
3. Leading shoe
4. Trailing shoe
5. Wheel cylinder
6. Backing plate
7. Holding pin
8. Anti-rattle spring

Fig. 3 Exploded view of drum brake. 1983–85 GLC

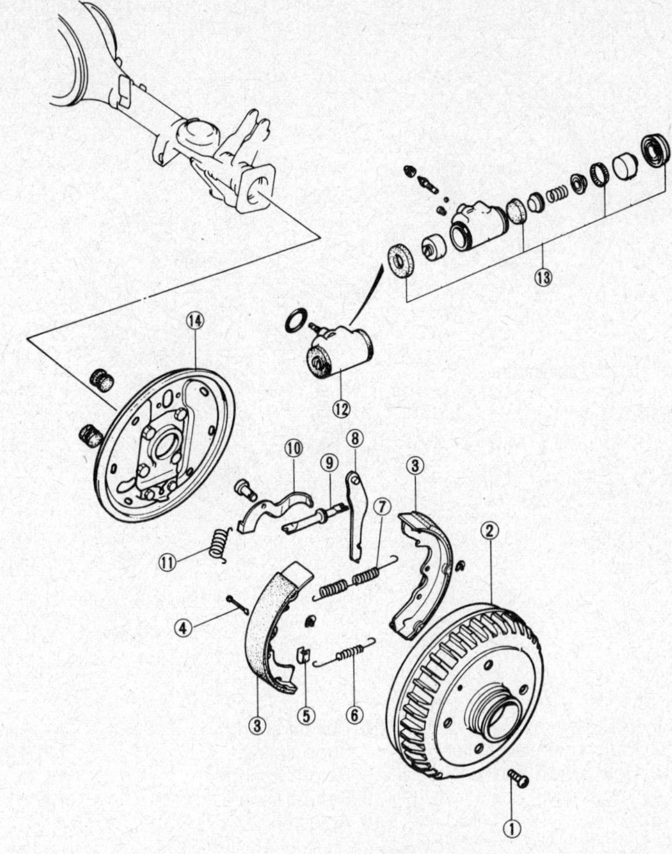

1	Screw	8	Operating lever
2	Brake drum	9	Adjuster
3	Brake shoe	10	Lever
4	Pin	11	Spring
5	Spring	12	Wheel cylinder
6	Lower return spring	13	Cup & Boot set
7	Upper return spring	14	Back plate

Fig. 4 Exploded view of drum brake. RX-7

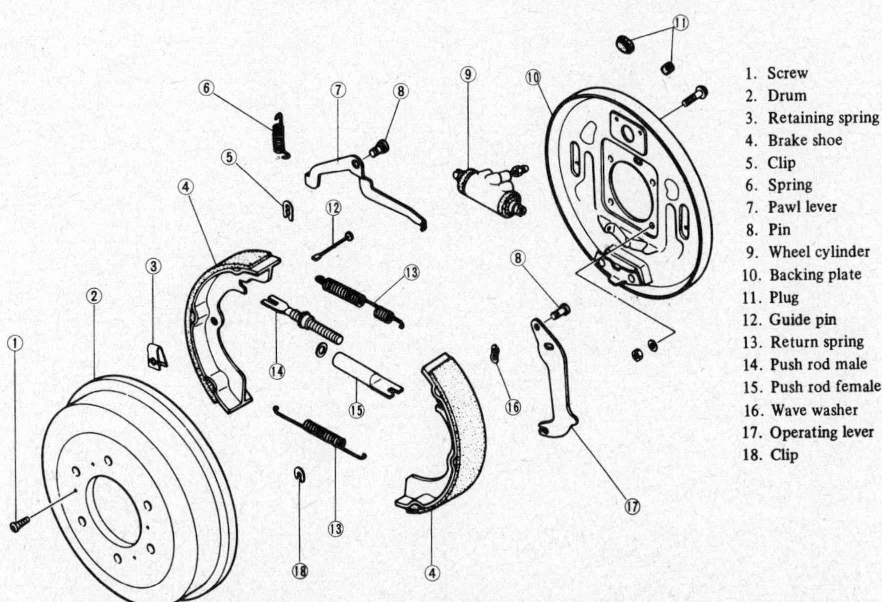

Fig. 5 Exploded view of drum brake. 1983–84 B2000 & B2200, 1986 B2000 & 1987 B2200 & B2600 w/2WD

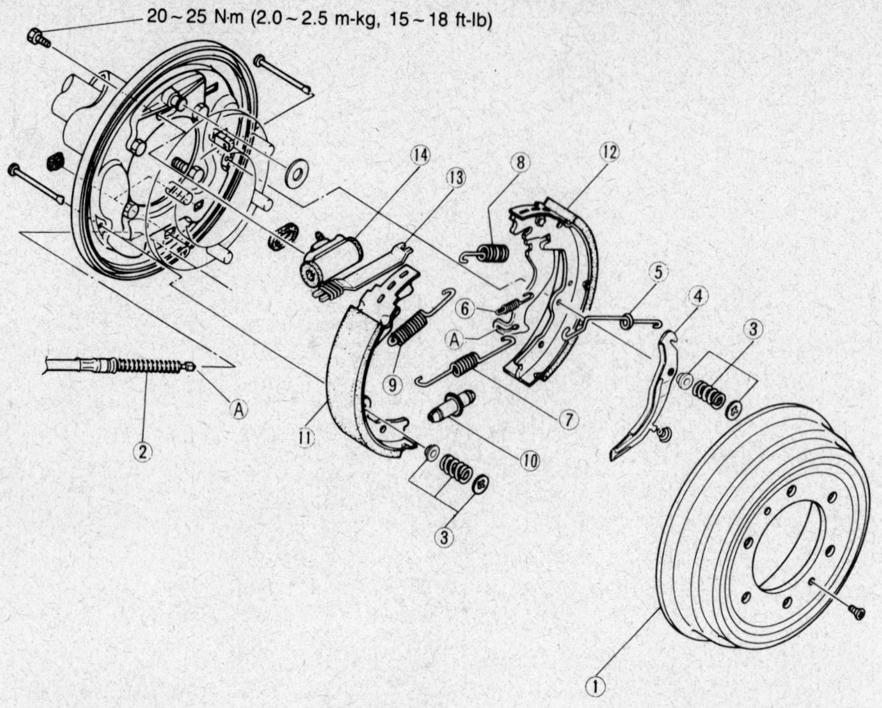

1. Brake drum
2. Parking brake cable
3. Hold spring and sleeve
4. Adjust lever
5. Link
6. Pull-off spring
7. Shoe spring
8. Return spring
9. Return spring
10. Adjuster
11. Primary brake shoe
12. Secondary brake shoe
13. Strut
14. Wheel cylinder assembly

Fig. 6 Exploded view of drum brake. 1987 B2600 w/4WD

REAR AXLE & SUSPENSION EXCEPT 1986-87 RX-7

INDEX

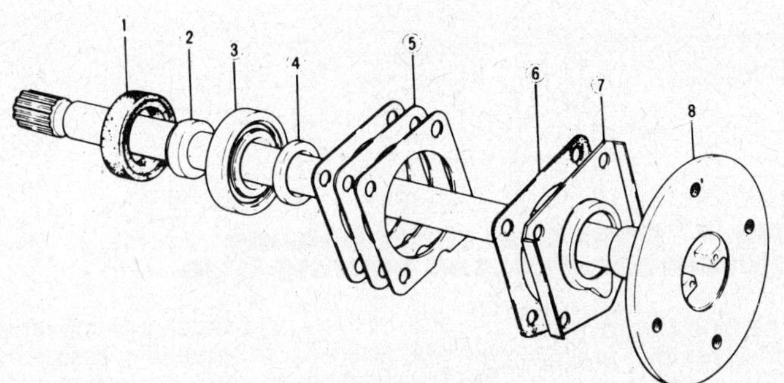

Fig. 1 Axle shaft components. Models w/pressed bearings

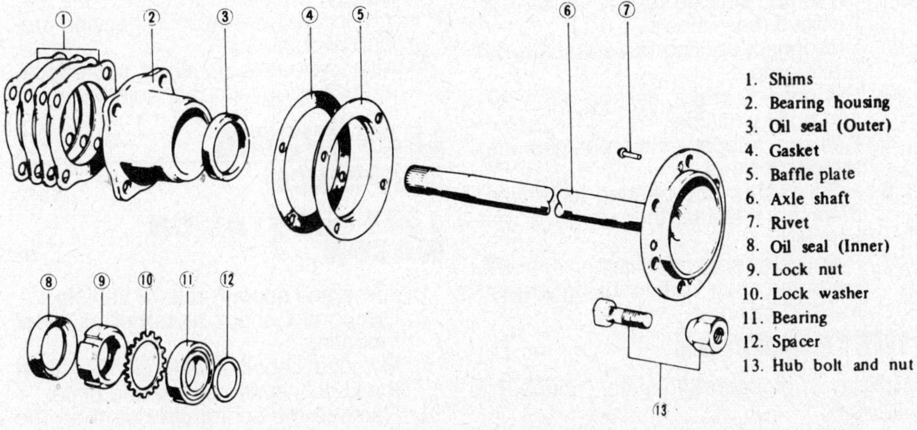

Fig. 2 Axle shaft components. Exc. 1986 B2000 & 1987 B2200 & B2600 models w/bearing housing

AXLE SHAFT

REPLACE

MODELS WITH PRESSED BEARINGS

1. Raise and support rear of vehicle.
2. Remove the rear wheel and brake drum.
3. Remove the brakes shoes assembly.
4. Remove the bolts holding the brake backing plate and bearing retainer to the axle housing. **On RX-7 and 1983-84 Pickup models, disconnect brake line and parking brake cable, then remove axle shaft and backing plate as an assembly.**
5. Remove the axle shaft assembly, **Fig. 1** with a suitable puller.
6. Remove the oil seal from the axle housing, if necessary.

MODELS WITH BEARING HOUSING

1. Raise and support rear end of the vehicle.
2. Remove the wheel, then the center cap adapter from the rear axle shaft flange, if equipped.
3. Remove brake drum.
4. Remove the brake shoe assembly.
5. Remove the parking brake cable retainer.
6. Disconnect the brake fluid pipes at the wheel cylinders.
7. Remove the nuts holding the backing plate and bearing housing to the axle housing.
8. Pull the axle shaft, backing plate, bearing housing assembly and shims off the axle housing **Figs. 2 and 3.**

R AR AXLE SHAFT B ARING

R PLACE

MODELS WITH PRESSED B ARINGS

1. Using an arbor press and suitable bearing replacer tool, **Fig. 4,** remove bearing and bearing retaining collar from axle shaft. **If pressure necessary to remove the bearing from the axle shaft exceeds 10 tons, or if bearing removal tool is not available, grind the bearing retaining collar and cut it with a chisel. Use caution to avoid to damaging axle shaft.**
2. Remove the bearing retainer from the axle shaft. Clean and inspect bearing retaining collar, spacer and axle shaft for wear and corrosion. Replace any damaged component as required.
3. Reverse procedure to install. During installation, position bearing onto axle shaft with sealed side of bearing facing toward the axle shaft flange. Do not attempt to press on both the bearing and bearing retaining collar at the same time. **If the bearing retaining collar requires less than 3 tons of pressure to install it onto the axle shaft, replace the bearing retaining collar.**

MODELS WITH BEARING HOUSING

1. Straighten lock washer locking tabs.
2. Using a suitable spanner wrench, remove lock nut and washer from axle shaft.
3. Using a suitable pulling tool, remove bearing and housing from axle shaft.
4. Remove bearing and race, spacer and oil seal(s), if damaged, from housing.
5. Reverse procedure to install.

DIFFERENTIAL CARRIER

R PLACE

1. Raise and support rear of vehicle.
2. Drain the oil by removing the drain plug.
3. Remove the rear axle shafts.
4. Mark the companion flange and propeller shaft for correct reassembly, then disconnect the propeller shaft.
5. Remove differential carrier to axle housing attaching bolts, then the differential carrier.
6. Reverse procedure to install.

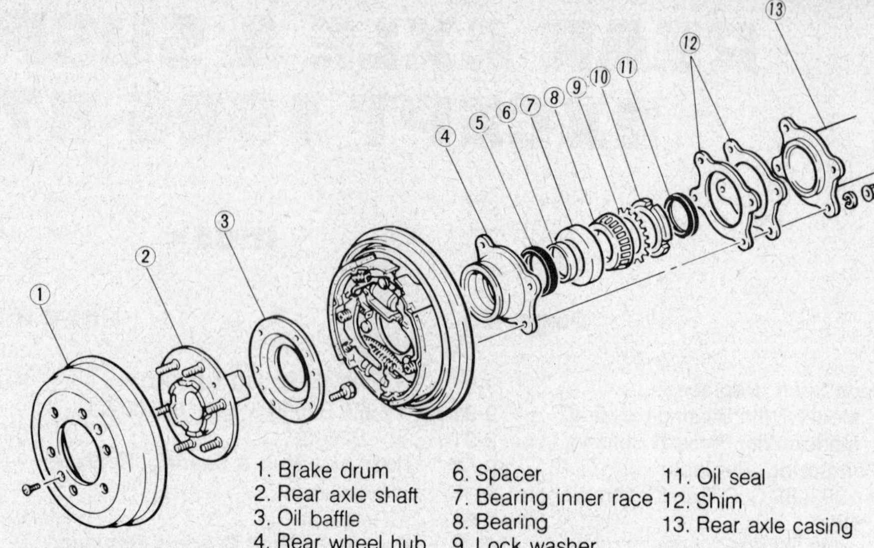

Fig. 3 Axle shaft components. 1987 B2200 & B2600 models w/bearing housing (1986 B2000 similar)

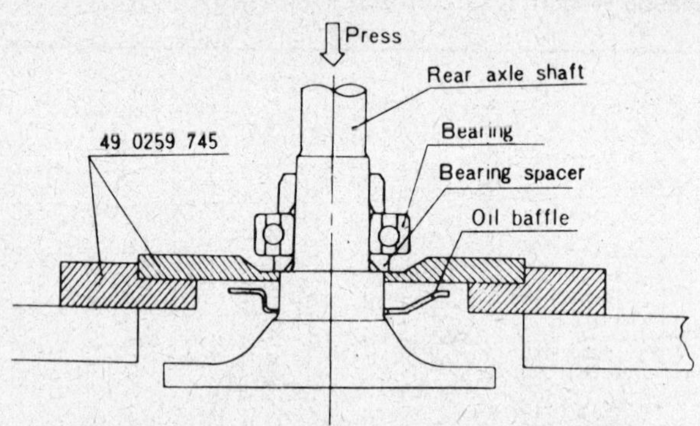

Fig. 4 Rear axle shaft bearing replacement. Pressed bearing type

R AR AXLE HUB & B ARING

R PLACE

R MOVAL

Models W/Drum Brakes

1. Raise and support rear of vehicle.
2. Remove rear wheels.
3. Remove hubcap, then unstake and remove locknut.
4. Hold washer and bearing to prevent them from falling, then remove brake drum.
5. Remove oil seal, then the inner and outer bearing using a brass rod and hammer.

Models W/Disc Brakes

1. Raise and support rear of vehicle.
2. Remove rear wheels.
3. Disconnect parking brake cable from brake caliper.
4. Disconnect brake caliper assembly and position aside.
5. Remove hubcap, then unstake and remove locknut.
6. Hold washer and bearing to prevent them from falling, then remove rear axle hub.
7. Remove oil seal and washer, then the inner and outer bearing using a brass rod and hammer.

INSTALLATION

Reverse procedure to install, noting the following:

1. Replace inner and outer bearings as a set.
2. Fill space between bearing rollers, inner and outer bearings, inner bearing and oil seal and outer bearing and lock washer with suitable grease.
3. To adjust bearing preload, torque new locknut to 18-22 ft. lbs., then turn wheel and hub to properly seat bearings. Loosen locknut slightly until it can be turned by hand, then measure oil seal drag using a suitable spring scale. If oil seal drag is not .9-2.2 lbs., turn locknut slowly until specified preload is obtained.
4. After preload is obtained, stake locknut with groove in rear spindle.

LEAF SPRING

REPLACE

1983 GLC STATION WAGON

1. Raise and support rear of vehicle.
2. Disconnect shock absorber at lower mounting.
3. Remove U-bolt attaching nuts, then the U-bolt, spring clamp and plate.
4. Remove the spring pin nut, then the spring pin plate to frame attaching nuts and bolts, **Fig. 5.** Remove spring pin and disconnect front end of spring from vehicle.

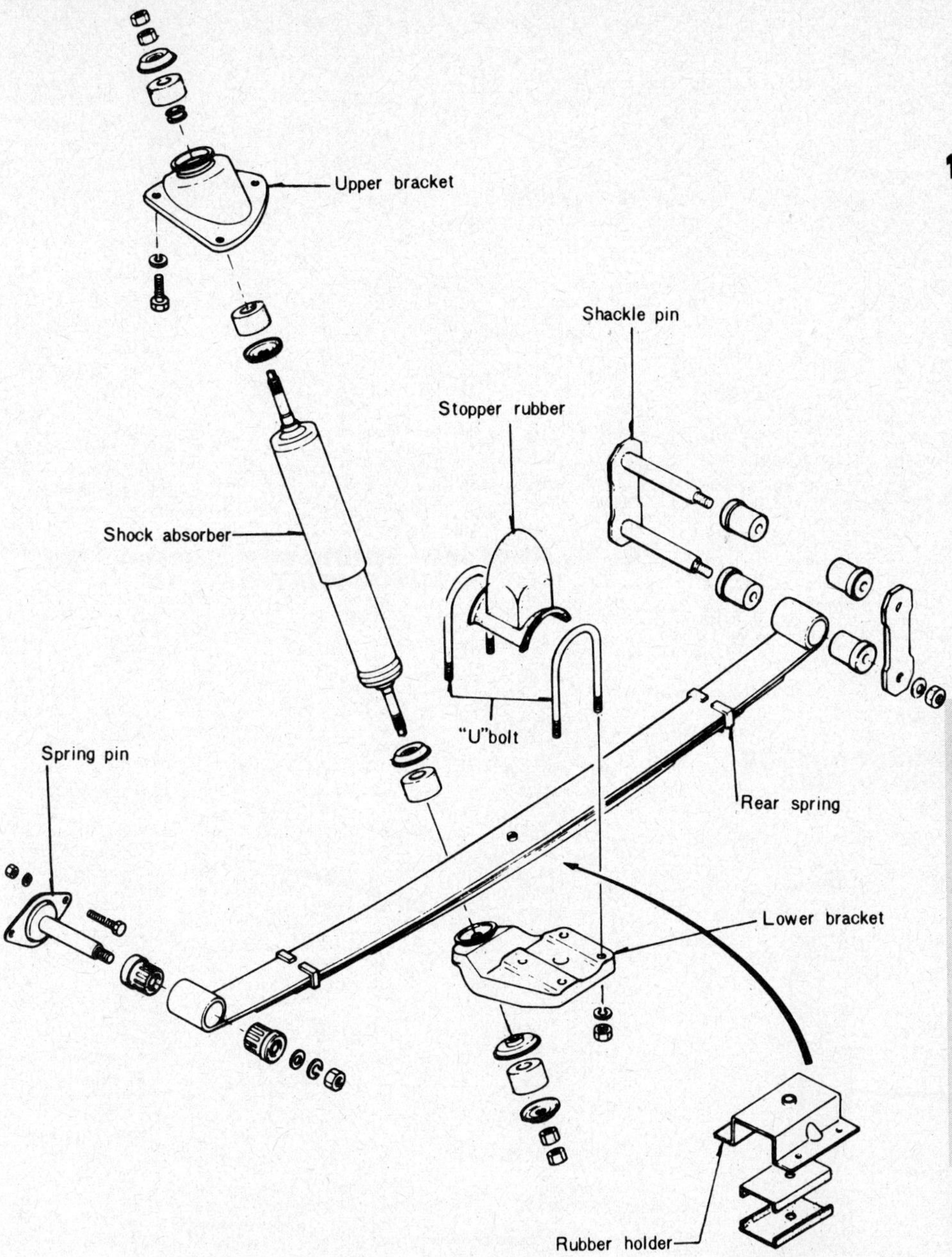

Upper bracket
Shackle pin
Stopper rubber
Shock absorber
"U"bolt
Spring pin
Rear spring
Lower bracket
Rubber holder

Fig. 5 Rear leaf spring suspension. GLC Station Wagon

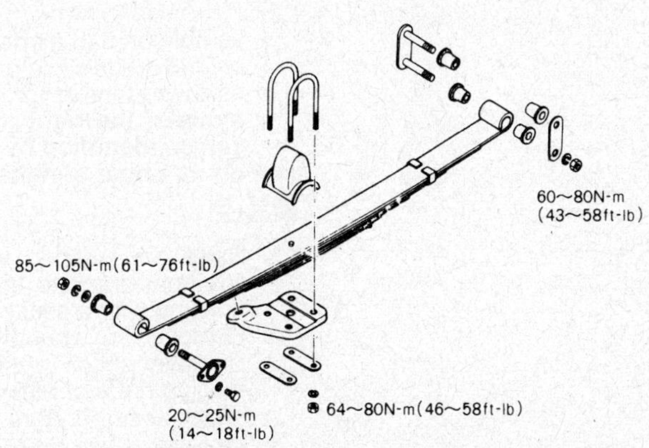

Fig. 6 Rear leaf spring suspension. 1983–84 B2000 & 2200

5. Remove shackle pin nuts, **Fig. 5**, then the shackle pin and plate. Disconnect rear end of spring from vehicle.
6. Remove leaf spring from vehicle.
7. Reverse procedure to install. Torque shackle, U-bolt and spring pin attaching nuts to 28 ft. lbs.

1983–84 B2000 & B2200

1. Raise rear end of vehicle and place a stand under frame side rail, permitting spring to hang free.
2. Support rear axle in this position with jack.
3. Remove rear wheel.
4. Disconnect rear shock absorber at lower mounting point.
5. Remove U-bolt nuts and spring clamp, **Fig. 6.**
6. Remove spring pin nut and the two bolts and nuts attaching the spring pin plate to the frame bracket.
7. Remove spring pin and the front end of spring from vehicle. Remove rubber bushings.
8. Remove shackle pin nuts and the shackle plate. Remove rear end of the spring from vehicle. Remove rubber bushings.
9. Reverse procedure to install.

1986 B2000 & 1987 B2200 & B2600

1. Raise rear end of vehicle and place a stand under frame side rail, permitting spring to hang free.
2. Support rear axle casing in this position using a suitable jack.
3. Remove rear wheel, then the shock absorber attaching nuts and shock absorber, **Figs. 7 and 8.**
4. Remove U-bolt attaching nuts, then the U-bolts, set plate and stopper rubber.
5. Remove spring pin.
6. Remove shackle pin and shackle plate.
7. Remove leaf spring assembly and bushings from vehicle.

COIL SPRING REPLACE

1983–87 626 & 1986–87 323

1. Raise and support rear of vehicle.
2. Remove shock absorber lower attaching bolts and nuts, **Figs. 9 and 10.**
3. Remove brake hose clip from lower shock absorber mounting.
4. Remove mounting block attaching nuts. The rear seat and trim should be removed to gain access to mounting block nuts.
5. Remove shock absorber assembly and secure in a suitable vise.
6. Loosen nut at upper end of shock absorber, then compress spring using suitable spring compressors and remove the nut.
7. Remove shock absorber mounting block, then the spring seat, dust boot and oil spring.
8. Reverse procedure to install. Position mounting block and shock absorber

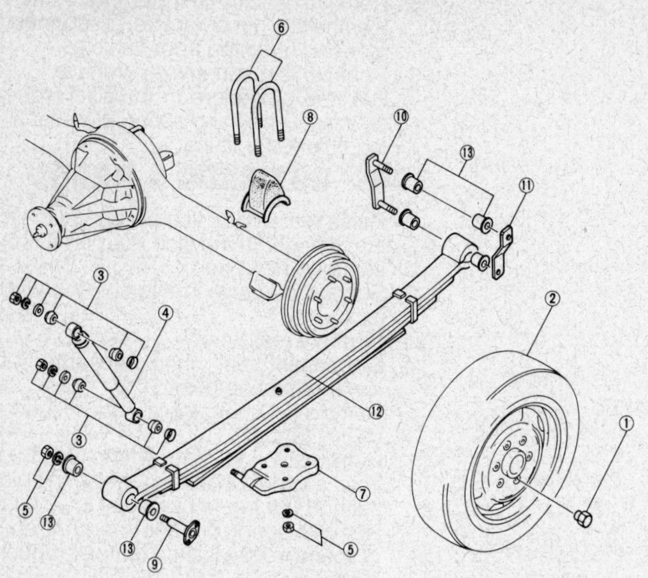

1. Wheel lug nut
2. Wheel and tire
3. Nut, washer, retainer and bushing
4. Shock absorber
5. Nut and washer
6. U-bolts
7. Set plate
8. Stopper rubber
9. Spring pin
10. Shackle pin
11. Shackle plate
12. Leaf spring assembly
13. Bushings

Fig. 7 Rear leaf spring suspension. 1986 B2000 & 1987 B2200 & B2600 w/2WD

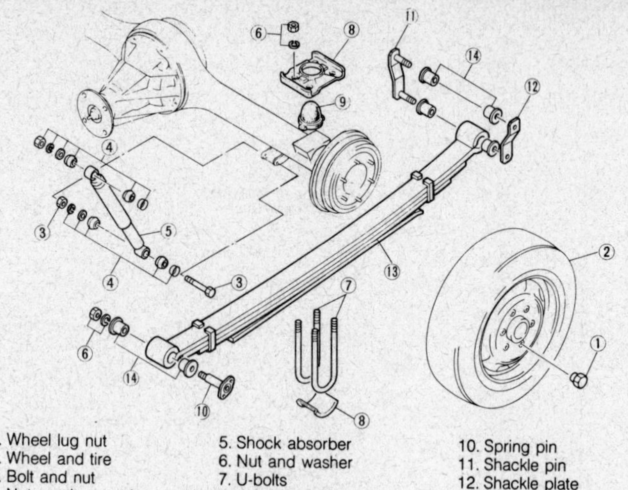

1. Wheel lug nut
2. Wheel and tire
3. Bolt and nut
4. Nut, washer, retainer and bushing
5. Shock absorber
6. Nut and washer
7. U-bolts
8. Set plate
9. Stopper rubber
10. Spring pin
11. Shackle pin
12. Shackle plate
13. Leaf spring assembly
14. Bushings

Fig. 8 Rear leaf spring suspension. 1987 B2600 w/4WD

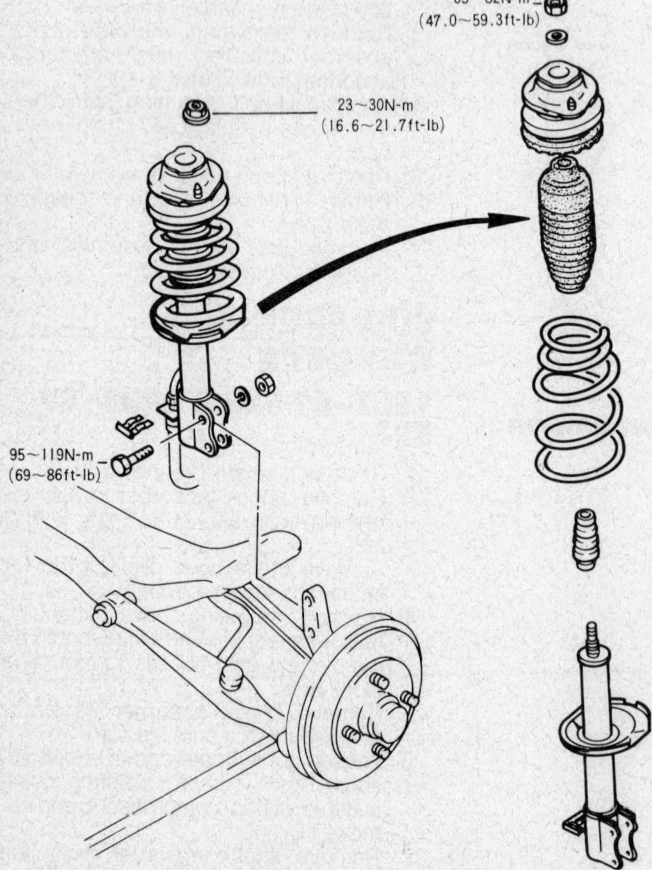

Fig. 9 Coil spring & shock absorber replacement. 1983–87 626

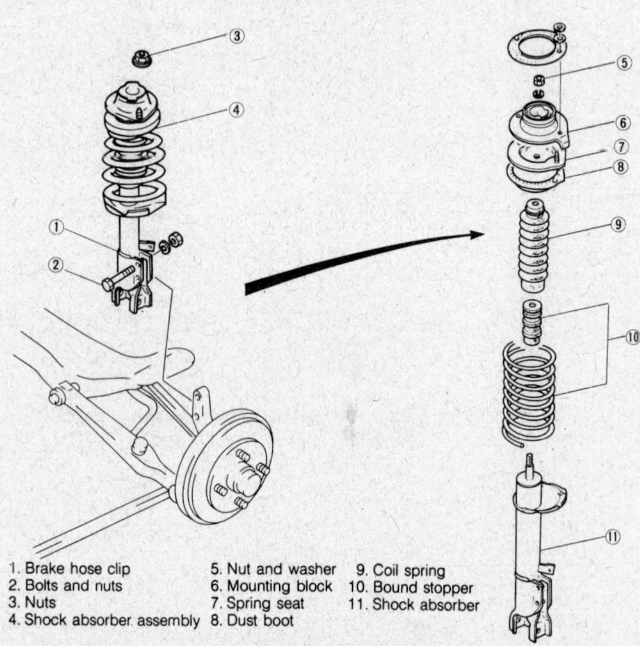

1. Brake hose clip
2. Bolts and nuts
3. Nuts
4. Shock absorber assembly
5. Nut and washer
6. Mounting block
7. Spring seat
8. Dust boot
9. Coil spring
10. Bound stopper
11. Shock absorber

Fig. 10 Coil spring & shock absorber replacement. 1986–87 323

so hole on 626 models or white mark on 323 models in mounting block faces toward inside of vehicle. **On 626 models, the right mounting block can be identified by the white paint on its upper surface.**

RX-7

1. Raise and support vehicle at lower link front brackets, then support axle housing with a suitable jack.
2. Remove rear wheel.
3. Remove shock absorber lower attaching nut and bolt, then disconnect shock absorber from axle housing.
4. Remove rear lower link attaching nut and bolt.
5. Remove upper link to axle housing attaching nut and bolt.

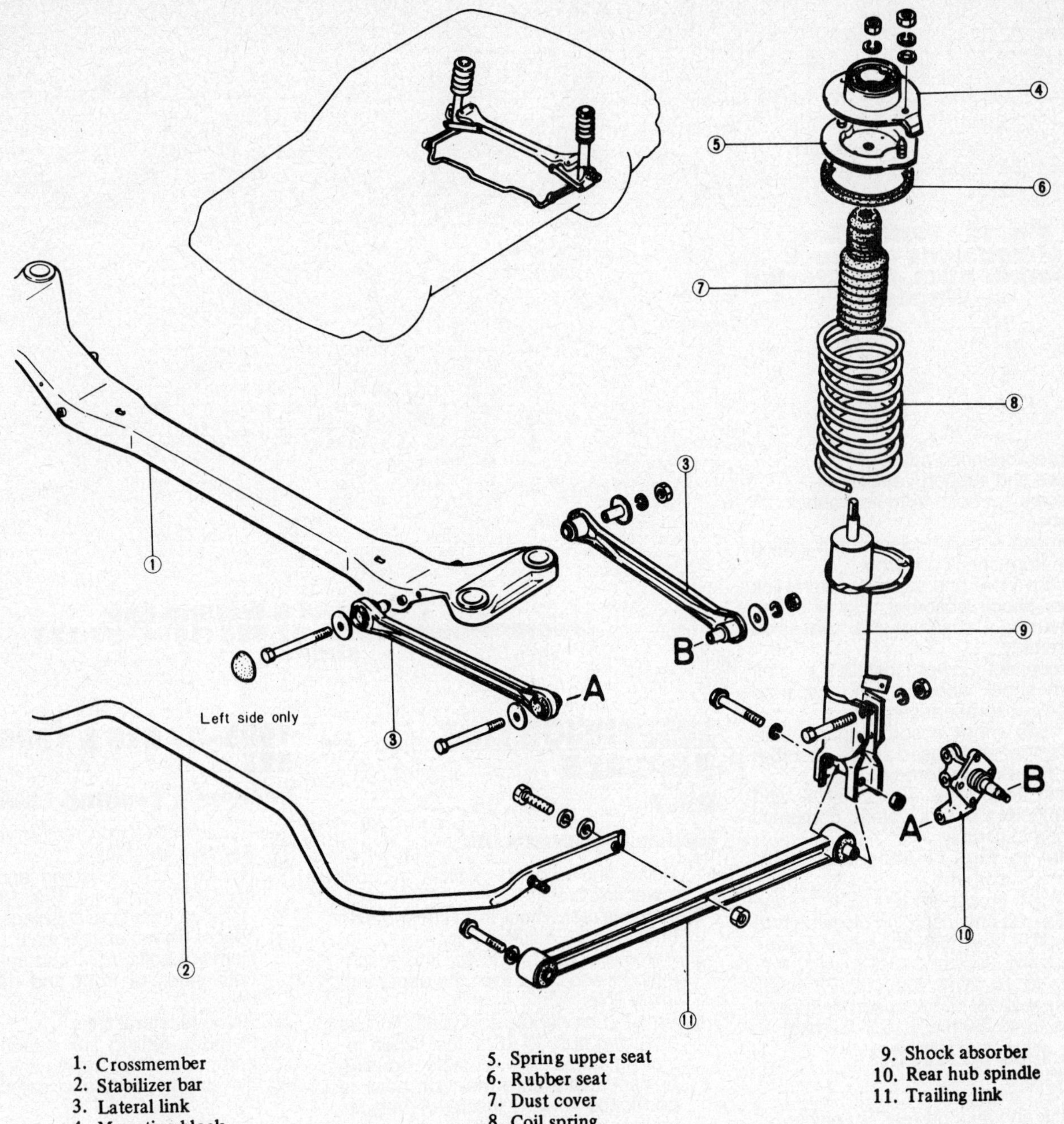

Fig. 11 Rear suspension exploded view. 1983–85 GLC Exc. Station Wagon

6. Remove stabilizer link to stabilizer bar attaching nuts, if equipped, then disconnect stabilizer bar from link.
7. Remove right and left "Watt" link to axle housing bracket attaching nuts, then slowly lower jack to relieve spring pressure. Remove spring and rubber seat.
8. Reverse procedure to install. Torque upper and lower link attaching nuts and bolts to 66 ft. lbs. and Watts link attaching nuts and bolts to 53 ft. lbs.

1983–85 GLC EXC. STATION WAGON

Refer to "Shock Absorber, Replace" procedure.

SHOCK ABSORBER REPLACE

1983–87 626 & 1986–87 323

1. Perform steps 1 through 7 as described under "Coil Spring, Replace," procedure for "1983-87 626 & 1986-87 323."
2. Remove bound stopper and shock absorber, **Figs. 9 and 10.**
3. Reverse procedure to install. Position mounting block and shock absorber so hole on 626 models or white mark on 323 models in mounting block faces toward inside of vehicle. **On 626 models, the right mounting block can be identified by the white paint on its upper surface.**

RX-7

1. Raise and support rear of vehicle.
2. Remove rear wheels.
3. Remove side trim from trunk and shock absorber upper nut.
4. Remove lower shock absorber nut and shock absorber from vehicle.
5. Reverse procedure to install.

1983–85 GLC EXC. STATION WAGON

1. Remove trunk side trim and shock ab-

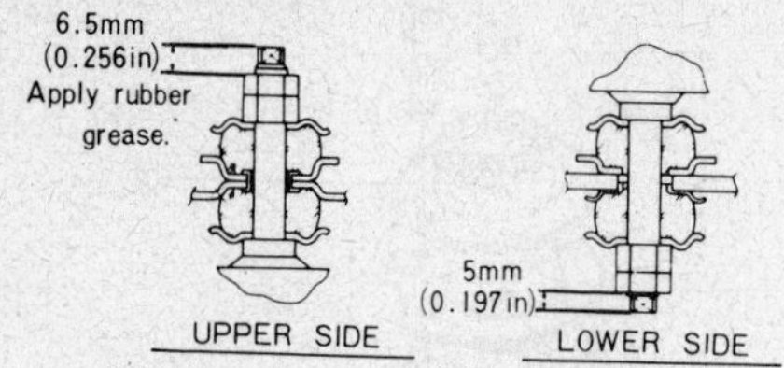

Fig. 12 Tightening dimensions of shock absorber nuts. GLC Station Wagon

sorber mounting nuts.
2. Raise and support vehicle.
3. Disconnect hose from rear shock absorber.
4. Remove nuts and disconnect trailing arm from shock absorber.
5. Remove bolt and separate lateral link from shock absorber, **Fig. 11.** Remove shock absorber and drum as an assembly.
6. Disconnect lower installation unit from shock absorber and separate shock absorber assembly.
7. Position shock absorber into a suitable vise, and loosen shock absorber top nut. **Do not remove nut.**
8. Using tool Nos. 490223640A and 490370641 or equivalent, compress spring assembly.
9. Refer to **Fig. 11** and disassemble shock absorber.
10. Reverse procedure to install. Torque piston rod and mounting block bolts to 41-60 ft. lbs., (5.6-8.2 mkg). Torque mounting block and suspension tower nuts to 16-20 ft. lbs. (2.2-2.7 mkg). Torque lower shock absorber support nuts to 40-50 ft. lbs. (5.5-6.9mkg).

1983 GLC STATION WAGON

1. Raise and support rear of vehicle.
2. Remove the three shock absorber upper bracket to body attaching bolts.
3. Remove lock nut, then the retaining nut at shock absorber lower bracket.
4. Compress shock absorber and remove from vehicle.
5. Remove upper bracket to shock absorber lock and retaining nuts, then separate upper bracket from shock.
6. Reverse procedure to install, noting the following points:
   a. Apply suitable grease to upper bracket bushing contact surface.
   b. Tighten shock absorber nuts to dimension shown in **Fig. 12.**

B2000, B2200 & B2600

1. Remove nuts, washers, and rubber bushings from upper and lower ends of shock absorber.
2. Compress shock absorber and remove from vehicle.
3. Reverse procedure to install.

Fig. 13 Lateral & trailing link replacement. 1983–87 626 (1986–87 323 similar)

SUSPENSION LINK REPLACE

RX-7

Upper & Lower Link

1. Raise and support vehicle at front lower link bracket.
2. Remove rear wheel, then support axle housing with a suitable jack.
3. Remove upper and lower link attaching nuts and bolts, then the upper and lower links.
4. Reverse procedure to install. Torque attaching nuts to 66 ft. lbs. When installing upper link to axle housing bracket, make sure that bolt head is positioned toward inside of vehicle. Lower vehicle to curb load position before tightening nuts to specified torque.

Watts Link

1. Raise and support vehicle at lower suspension link bracket.
2. Support axle housing with a suitable jack.
3. Remove watt link to frame attaching nuts and bolts.
4. Remove watt link bracket to axle housing attaching nut.
5. Remove watt link and bracket from vehicle.
6. Reverse procedure to install, noting the following;
   a. Install watt link with painted mark positioned toward outside of vehicle.
   b. Lower vehicle, then torque watt link to frame attaching nuts to 53 ft. lbs. and watt link bracket to axle housing attaching nuts to 66 ft. lbs.

1983–87 626 & 1986–87 323

Lateral & Trailing Link

1. Raise and support rear of vehicle.
2. Remove fuel tank.
3. Remove nuts, bushing and retainer from rear lateral link, **Fig. 13.**
4. Remove retainers, bushings, bolt and spacer from stabilizer bar.
5. Remove bolts, nuts and spacer from both sides of front and rear lateral links.
6. Remove lateral links.
7. Remove trailing link attaching bolts and nut and the trailing link.
8. Reverse procedure to install.

LATERAL LINK REPLACE

1983–85 GLC EXC. STATION WAGON

1. Raise and support rear of vehicle and remove rear wheels.
2. Remove nut and rear hub spindle from lateral link **Fig. 11.**
3. Remove mounting bolt and nut from crossmember.
4. Remove lateral link assembly from vehicle. To remove left front lateral link, loosen crossmember mounting nuts, lower cross member and remove lateral link.
5. Reverse procedure to install. Torque attaching bolts 69-86 ft. lbs. (9.5-11.9 mkg).

TRAILING LINK
REPLACE
1983–85 GLC EXC. STATION WAGON

1. Raise and support rear of vehicle and remove rear wheels.
2. Remove stabilizer mounting bolt and nut.
3. Remove lower shock absorber mounting nut.
4. Remove nuts and trailing link from body, **Fig. 11.**
5. Reverse procedure to install. Torque trailing link to stabilizer bar bolts to 23-34 ft. lbs. (3.2-4.7 mkg). Torque trailing link to body bolts to 43-54 ft. lbs. (6.0-7.5 mkg). Torque trailing link to rear hub spindle bolt to 40-50 ft. lbs. (5.5-6.9 mkg).

STABILIZER BAR
REPLACE
RX-7, 626, 323 & 1982–84 B2000 & B2200

1. Raise and support rear of vehicle.
2. Remove bolts from both ends of stabilizer bar.
3. Remove stabilizer bar mounting bracket, if necessary.
4. Remove stabilizer bar support plates (if equipped), rubber bushings and stabilizer bar from vehicle.
5. Reverse procedure to install.

1983–85 GLC EXC. STATION WAGON

1. Raise and support rear of vehicle and remove rear wheels.
2. Remove nuts, bolts and stabilizer bar from vehicle.
3. Reverse procedure to install. Torque stabilizer bar to trailing link nuts and bolts to 23-34 ft. lbs., (3.2-4.7 mkg).

REAR AXLE & SUSPENSION, 1986–87 RX-7

INDEX

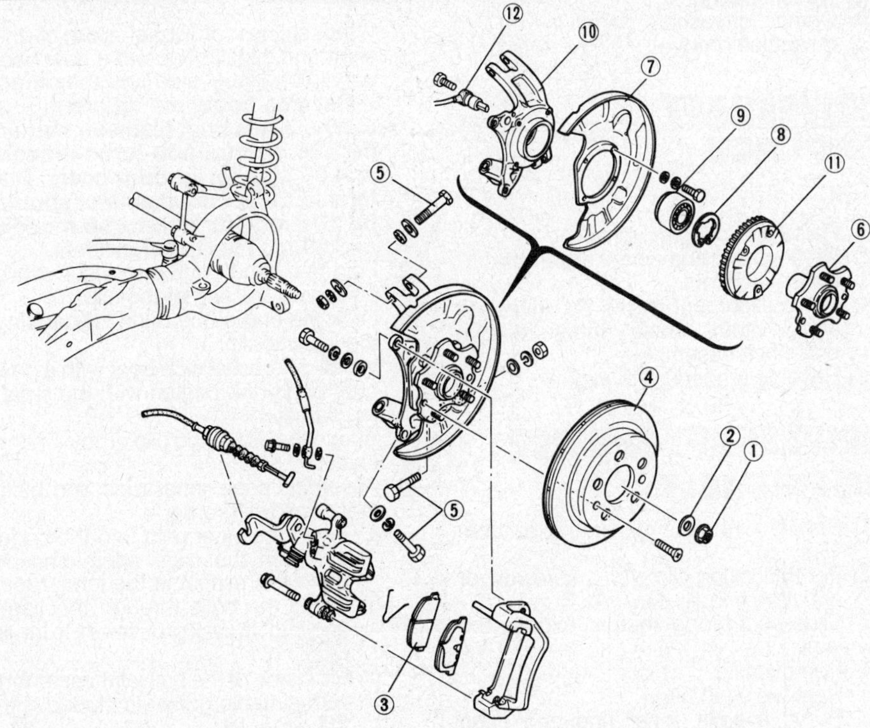

1. Lock nut
2. Washer
3. Caliper assembly
4. Disc plate
5. Bolts
6. Wheel hub
7. Dust cover
8. Retaining ring
9. Wheel bearing
10. Bearing housing
11. Sensor rotor (for ABS)
12. Speed sensor (for ABS)

Fig. 1 Rear axle hub, bearing & related components. 1986–87 RX-7

REAR AXLE HUB & BEARING
REPLACE
REMOVAL

1. Disconnect battery ground cable.
2. Raise and support rear of vehicle.
3. Remove tire and wheel assembly.
4. Uncrimp locknut.
5. Depress brake pedal to hold hub, then remove hub nut, **Fig. 1.**
6. Remove brake caliper assembly and suspend caliper with wire.
7. Remove set screws and disc plate.
8. Remove knuckle assembly.
9. Loosen dust cover.
10. Position hub assembly into a suitable press, and remove hub.
11. Using a suitable press and tools 49F026102 and 490636145 or equivalents, remove wheel bearing inner race.
12. Using suitable snap ring pliers, remove axle flange snap ring.
13. Using a suitable press and tool 49F027007 or equivalent, remove wheel bearing outer race.
14. On models with anti-lock brake system, remove sensor rotor and speed sensor.

INSPECTION

1. Check wheel hub for excessive wear and/or damage. Replace, if necessary.

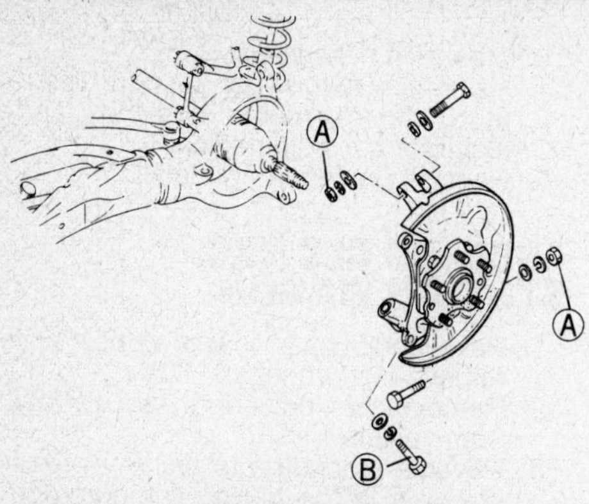

Fig. 2 Mounting bolts A & B. 1986–87 RX-7

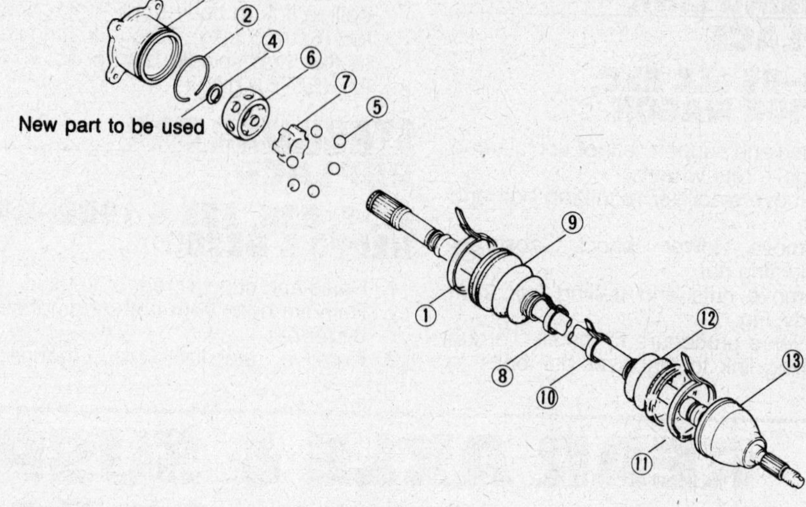

1. Boot band
2. Clip
3. Outer ring
4. Snap ring
5. Balls
6. Inner ring
7. Cage
8. Boot band
9. Boot
10. Boot band
11. Boot band
12. Boot
13. Shaft and ball joint assembly

Fig. 3 Exploded view of driveshaft assembly. 1986–87 RX-7

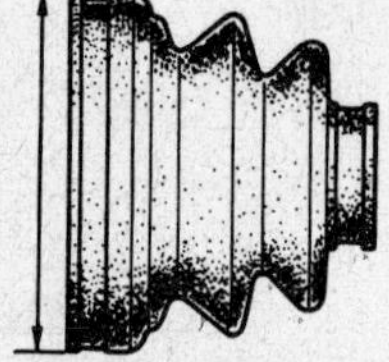
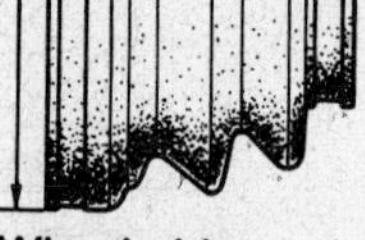

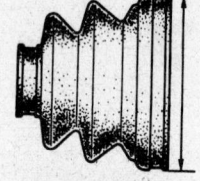

Fig. 4 Wheel & differential side boots. 1986–87 RX-7

2 Check bearing housing for cracks.
3. Check dust cover for warpage.
4. Check wheel lug bolts for excessive wear and/or damage. Replace wheel lug bolts by using a suitable press, if necessary. **Do not reuse wheel lug bolts once they have been removed or serious injury/vehicle damage may result.**
5. Replace any worn or damaged component as required.

ASSEMBLY

1. Using a suitable press and tools 49F026102 and 490259748 or equivalents, press new wheel bearing into the bearing housing.
2. Install snap ring and dust cover.
3. Using a suitable press and tool 49F026102 or equivalent, press in wheel hub.
4. Mount wheel hub and knuckle on to driveshaft, then place knuckle on to rear axle casing.
5. Torque bolts A to 46-69 ft. lbs., bolts B to 82-111 ft. lbs., **Fig. 2.**
6. On models with anti-lock brake system, install speed sensor and adjust clearance between speed sensor and sensor rotor. Clearance should be .016-.039 inch.
7. On all models, install disc plate and caliper assembly. Torque caliper attaching bolts to 33-40 ft. lbs.
8. Depress brake pedal to secure disc plate, then torque locknut to 174-231 ft. lbs.
9. Using a dial indicator, measure wheel bearing play. Wheel bearing play should be .004 inch or less. If play exceeds specified amount, replace wheel bearing.
10. Crimp driveshaft locknut on to driveshaft groove.

DRIVESHAFT REPLACE

1. Raise and support vehicle.
2. Remove tire and wheel assembly.
3. Loosen locknut.
4. Place alignment marks on driveshaft and output shaft, then remove driveshaft assembly.
5. Reverse procedure to install.

DRIVESHAFT SERVICE

DISASSEMBLY

1. Secure joint assembly into a suitable vise.
2. Pry up locking clip with a screwdriver and remove clip ban, **Fig. 3.**
3. Slide boot along shaft to expose the joint.
4. Remove clip.
5. Remove snap ring.
6. Remove balls, inner ring and cage from shaft as an assembly.
7. Insert a suitable screwdriver between the inner ring and cage to remove the balls.
8. Turn cage approximately 30 degrees and separate it from the inner ring.
9. Wrap spline shaft with tape, then remove boot.

ASSEMBLY

1. Wrap splines of wheel side of the shaft and install boot and a new boot band. **The wheel side and the differential side boots are different, Fig. 4. Wheel side boot diameter should be 3.88 inch for non-turbo models or 4.06 inch for turbo models. Differential side boot diameter should be 3.76 inch for non-turbo models or 3.90 inch for turbo models.**
2. Fold the band back over itself while pulling on the end of the clip.
3. Lock the end of the band by bending the locking clip.
4. Install differential side boot with a new boot band (the portion with the smaller diameter).
5. Attach the clip to the clip groove in the shaft.
6. Assembly cage, inner race and balls in the following order:
   a. Insert the inner race into the cage, and turn the cage approximately 30° with respect to the inner race.
   b. Install the balls through the cage and into the ball groove of the inner race.
   c. Fill inside of the ball joint assembly with suitable grease included with the repair kit.
7. Install cage on to the shaft.
8. Install snap ring into shaft snap ring groove.
9. Install differential side boot on to the outer race and the boot groove of the shaft assembly.
10. Secure boot with a new boot band.
11. After assembly driveshaft should

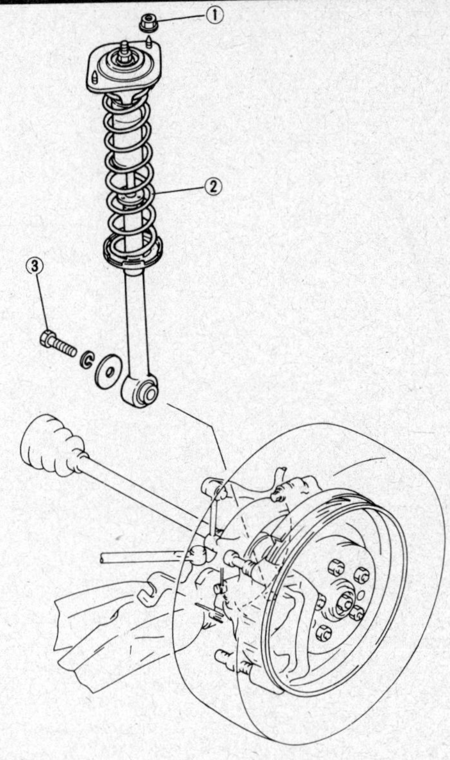

Fig. 5 Shock absorber & spring assembly. 1986–87 RX-7

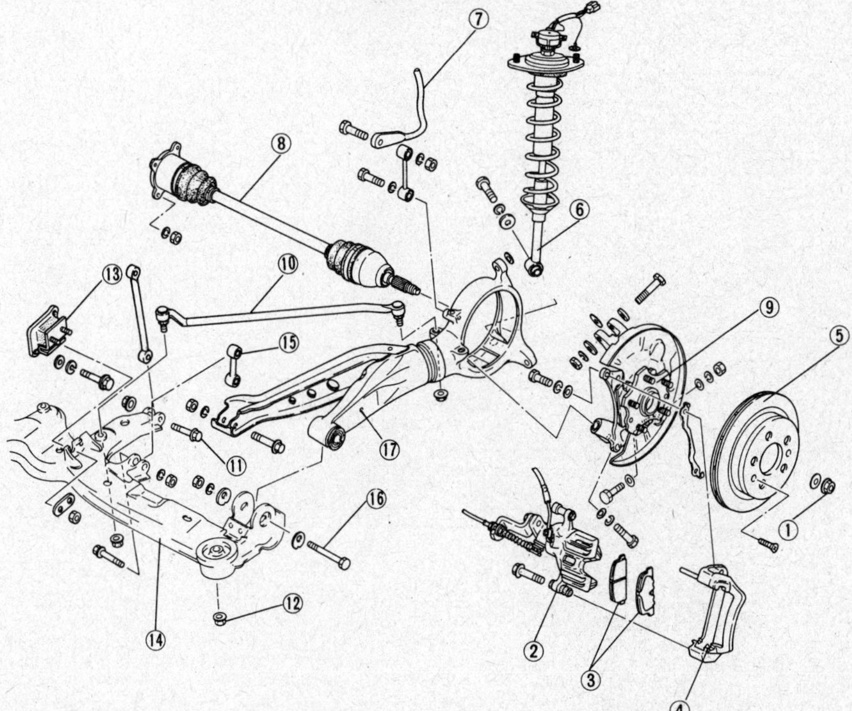

Fig. 6 Exploded view of trailing arm & related components. 1986–87 RX-7

measure 24.80-26.22 inches in length for non-turbo models or 24.17-25.63 inches in length for turbo models.

SHOCK ABSORBER & SPRING

REPLACE

When removing and installing shock absorber and spring, refer to **Fig. 5.** Reverse numerical removal sequence for installation.

TRAILING ARM

REPLACE

When removing and installing trailing arm assembly, refer to **Fig. 6.** Reverse numerical removal sequence for installation.

LATERAL LINK

REPLACE

When removing and installing lateral link assembly, refer to **Fig. 7.** Reverse numerical removal sequence for installation.

BALL JOINT

REPLACE

TRAILING ARM SIDE

1. Remove attaching nuts.
2. Using tool 49F032101 or equivalent, remove ball joint from trailing arm.
3. Reverse procedure to install.

SUBFRAME SIDE

1. Remove attaching nut.
2. Using a suitable drift and hammer, separate ball joint from the subframe.
3. Reverse procedure to install.

BALL JOINT PRELOAD

ADJUST

1. Attach preload attachment 490180510B or equivalent on to the ball stud.
2. Using a suitable scale, measure preload by pulling on scale handle and while ball stud is rotating. Scale reading obtained should be 1.1-2.6 lbs. Measure preload after shaking ball joint stud 3 or 4 times.

CONTROL LINK

REPLACE

When removing or installing control link assembly, refer to **Fig. 8.** Reverse numerical removal sequence for installation.

SUBLINK

REPLACE

When removing or installing sublink assembly, refer to **Fig. 9.** Reverse numerical removal sequence for installation.

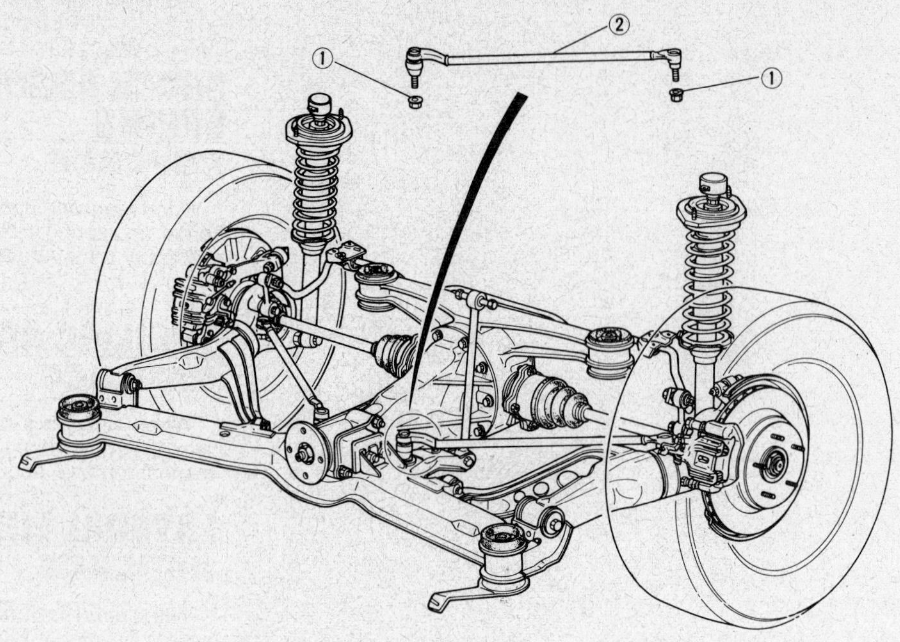

1. Nut 2. Lateral link

Fig. 7 Lateral link assembly. 1986–87 RX-7

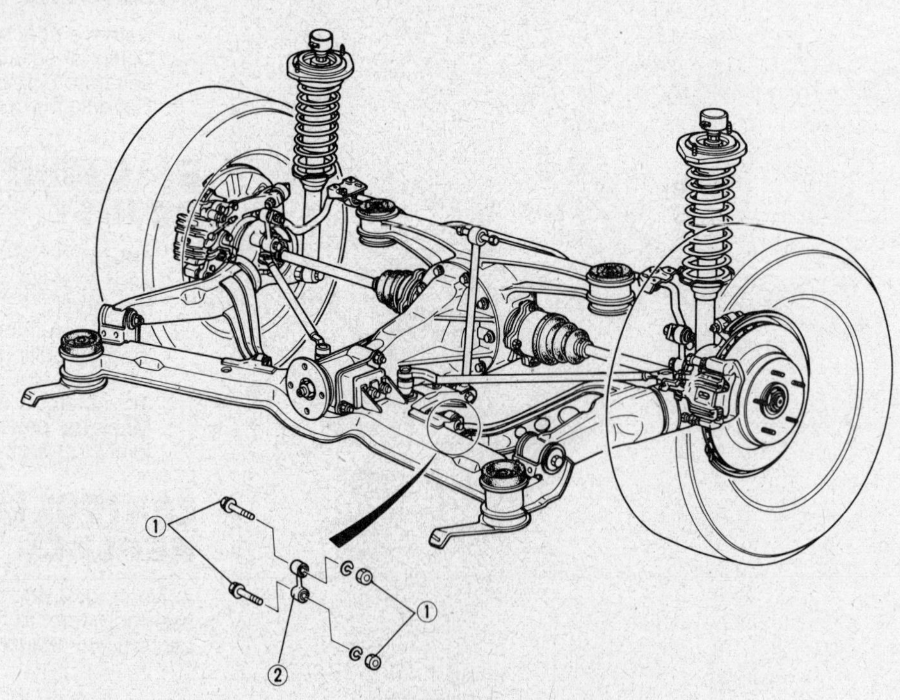

1. Bolt and nut 2. Control link

Fig. 8 Control link assembly. 1986–87 RX-7

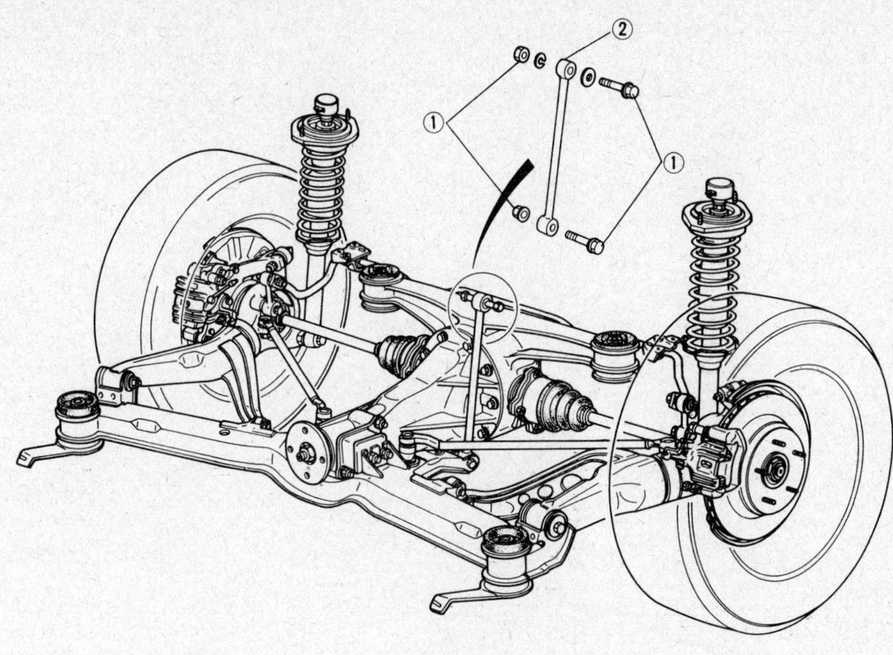

1. Bolt and nut
2. Sublink

Fig. 9 Sublink assembly. 1986–87 RX-7

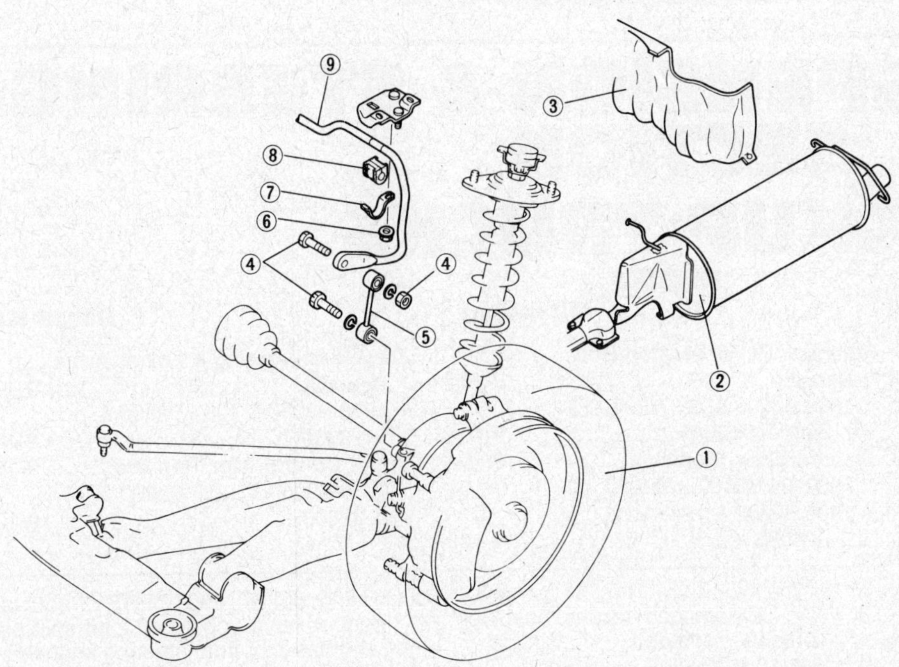

1. Wheel
2. Silencer
3. Fuel tank protector
4. Bolt and nut
5. Control link
6. Nut
7. Stabilizer bracket
8. Bushing
9. Stabilizer

Fig. 10 Stabilizer bar assembly. 1986–87 RX-7

STABILIZER BAR
REPLACE

When removing or installing stabilizer bar assembly, refer to **Fig. 10.** Reverse numerical removal sequence for installation.

SUBFRAME
REPLACE

When removing or installing subframe assembly, refer to **Fig. 11.** Reverse numerical removal sequence for installation.

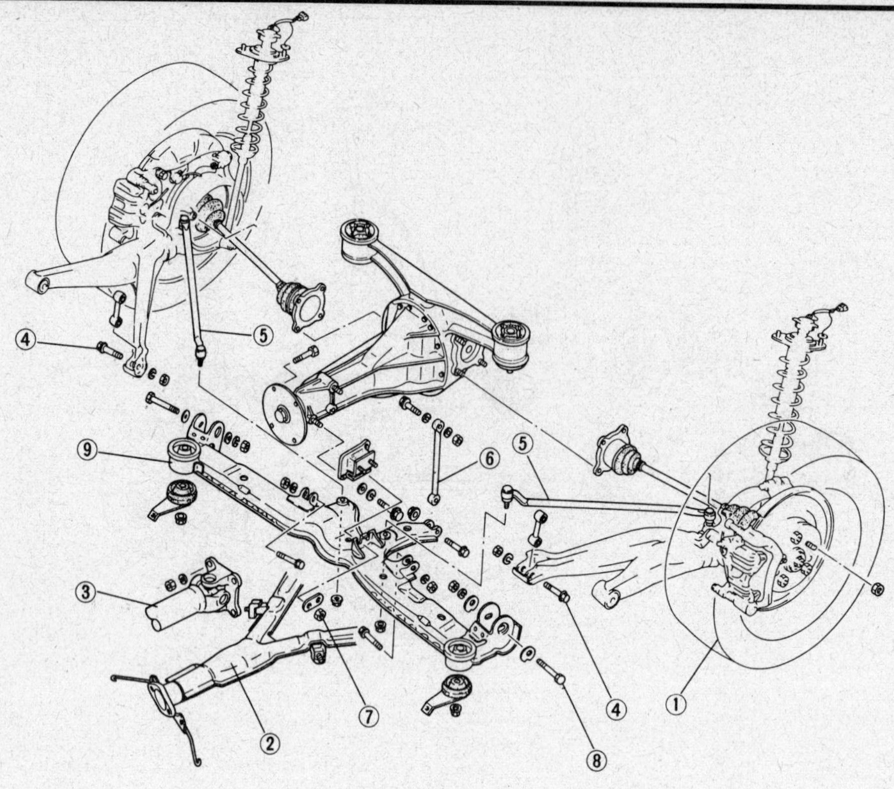

1. Wheel
2. Exhaust pipe
3. Propeller shaft
4. Bolt
5. Lateral link
6. Sublink
7. Nut
8. Bolt
9. Subframe

Fig. 11 Subframe assembly. 1986–87 RX-7

FRONT SUSPENSION & STEERING SECTION, PICKUP TRUCKS

INDEX

SHOCK ABSORBER REPLACE

1. Loosen the nuts that attach the upper end of the shock absorber to the crossmember.
2. Remove the rubber bushes and washers.
3. Loosen the bolts that attach the lower end of the shock absorber to the lower arm.
4. Remove the shock absorber from under the lower arm, **Figs. 1, 2 and 3.**
5. Worn or damaged rubber bushings should be discarded.
6. Reverse procedure to install.

FRONT SUSPENSION REPLACE

1983–84 B2000 & B2200

1. Raise and support front of vehicle.
2. Remove front wheels.
3. Remove front shock absorbers.
4. Using tool No. 490727575 or equivalent, remove upper ball joint split pin and ball joint from steering knuckle.
5. Remove upper control arm retaining bolts, nuts, shims and upper control arm from vehicle.
6. Remove ball joint nuts, bolts and ball joint from upper arm.
7. Remove stabilizer bar retaining nut, washers, bushings and stabilizer bar from lower arm.
8. Position a suitable jack under lower arm and raise lower arm slightly to re-

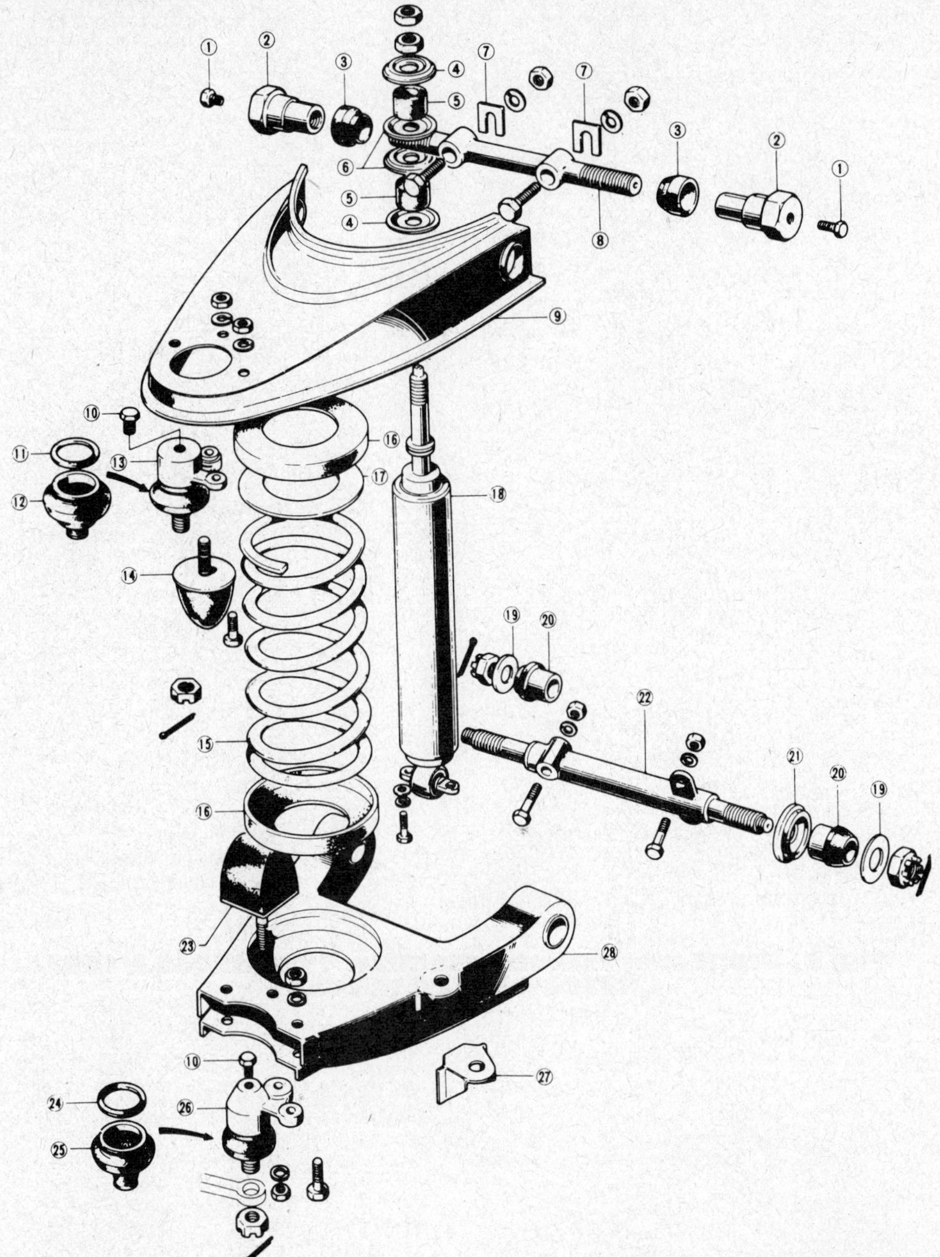

1. Plug
2. Thread bush
3. Dust seal
4. Retainer
5. Bush
6. Retainer
7. Adjusting shim
8. Upper arm shaft
9. Upper arm
10. Plug
11. Set ring
12. Dust seal
13. Ball joint assembly
14. Stopper
15. Coil spring
16. Seat
17. Adjusting plate
18. Shock absorber
19. Washer
20. Bush
21. Stopper
22. Lower arm shaft
23. Stopper
24. Set ring
25. Dust seal
26. Ball joint
27. Bracket
28. Lower arm

Fig. 1 Front suspension exploded view. 1983–84 models

lieve spring pressure.

9. Using tool No. 490727575 or equivalent, remove lower ball joint split pin, nut and ball joint from steering knuckle.
10. Lower jack and lower control arm and remove coil spring from vehicle.
11. Remove lower arm bolts, nuts and lower arm from vehicle.
12. Remove ball joint from lower arm.
13. Reverse procedure to install.

TORSION BAR SPRING & LOWER ARMS

REPLACE

1986 B2000 & 1987 B2200 & B2600

Refer to **Figs. 4 and 5** for torsion bar spring and lower control arm exploded view. When replacing assembly, note the following:

1. On 2WD models, before removing anchor bolt, place alignment marks on threads of anchor bolt.
2. On 4WD models, before removing anchor bolt, place alignment marks on threads of anchor arm.
3. On all models, remove anchor bolt.
4. Place alignment marks on torsion bar spring and anchor arm and on the torsion bar spring and torque plate. Remove torsion bar spring.
5. Using tool 490727575 or equivalent, separate ball joint from knuckle arm.
6. Using tool 49UB39615 or equivalent, separate lower arm from front suspension bracket bushing.
7. Install stabilizer bar control link nut so that end of bolt projects .55 inch from edge of locknut.
8. Adjust vehicle height as follows:
   a. With vehicle on level surface ensure tire pressure is satisfactory, then measure distance from center of wheel to fender brim.
   b. Ensure that difference between left and right side is .30 inch or less on 2WD models or .39 inch or less on 4WD models. If difference is not satisfactory, adjust anchor bolt until specified height difference is obtained.
9. If anchor bolt was not marked during disassembly, install torsion bar spring as follows:
   a. On 2WD models, install anchor arm to torsion bar spring so that there is approximately 4.92 inches between anchor arm tip and crossmember.
   b. On 4WD models, install torsion bar spring so that there is approximately 1.18 inch from body bracket to tip of anchor arm.
   c. On 2WD models, tighten anchor bolt until anchor arm contacts the anchor bolt swivel, then tighten anchor bolt an additional 1.77 inch.
   d. On 4WD models, lower vehicle and ensure vehicle is level with relation to ground. If vehicle height is high, loosen anchor bolt. If vehicle height is low, tighten anchor bolt.

UPPER CONTROL ARM

REPLACE

1986 B2000 & 1987 B2200 & B2600

Refer to **Fig. 6** for upper control arm and component exploded view. When removing assembly, note the following:

1. Using tool 490118850C or equivalent, separate upper arm ball joint from knuckle arm.
2. Remove nuts and bolts attaching upper arm shaft to the support bracket. Remove upper arm shaft. **When removing the nuts, note the number and position of the adjusting shims so that correct wheel alignment is obtained when assembled.**

STABILIZER BAR & T ..SION ROD
R PLACE
1986 B2000 & 1987 B2200 & B2600 W/2WD

Refer to **Fig. 7** for stabilizer bar and tension rod exploded view. When removing tension rod, loosen tension rod front bushing then pull tension rod outward. **Do not change the position of the double nut located at the rear of the tension rod bushing. Doing this may affect correct caster readings.**

STABILIZER BAR
R PLACE
1987 B2600 W/4WD

Refer to **Fig. 8** for stabilizer bar exploded view.

CH CKING FRONT SUSPENSION
1983–84 B2000 & B2200

1. Check upper and lower control arms for cracks, bending or twisting.
2. Inspect coil springs for damage or fatigue.
3. Check ball joint dust seal for cuts or damage. Replace, if necessary.
4. Check endplay of upper and lower ball joint. If endplay exceeds .040 inch, replace ball joint.

ST ERING GEAR
R PLACE
1983–84 B2000 & B2200

1. Disconnect battery ground cable, then remove horn cap.
2. Scribe marks on steering wheel and column shaft, then remove steering wheel retaining nut and the steering wheel.
3. Remove steering column cover, then the stop ring, cancel cam and spring from column shaft.
4. Disconnect combination switch wiring, then remove the combination switch.
5. Remove steering column support bracket retaining screws.
6. Remove floor cover and insulator pad from steering column.
7. Remove set plate bolts, then pull column jacket from steering shaft.
8. Remove yoke joint to worm shaft retaining bolt, then the steering shaft.
9. Remove air cleaner assembly.
10. If equipped with column shift, remove selection and shift rod from lower bracket, then disengage steering gear from bracket.

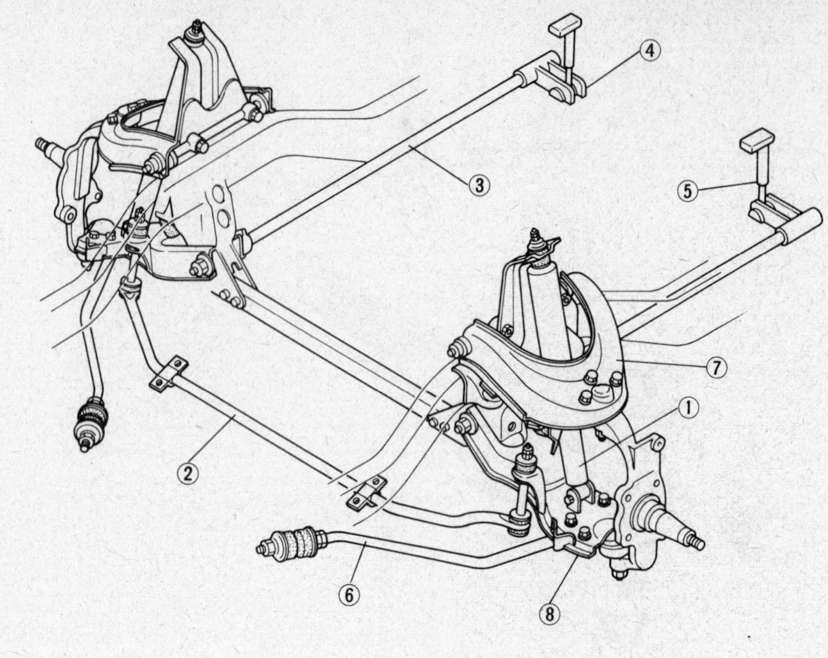

1. Shock absorber
2. Stabilizer
3. Torsion bar spring
4. Anchor arm
5. Anchor bolt
6. Tension rod
7. Upper arm
8. Lower arm

Fig. 2 Front suspension assembly. 1986 B2000 & 1987 B2200 & B2600 w/2WD

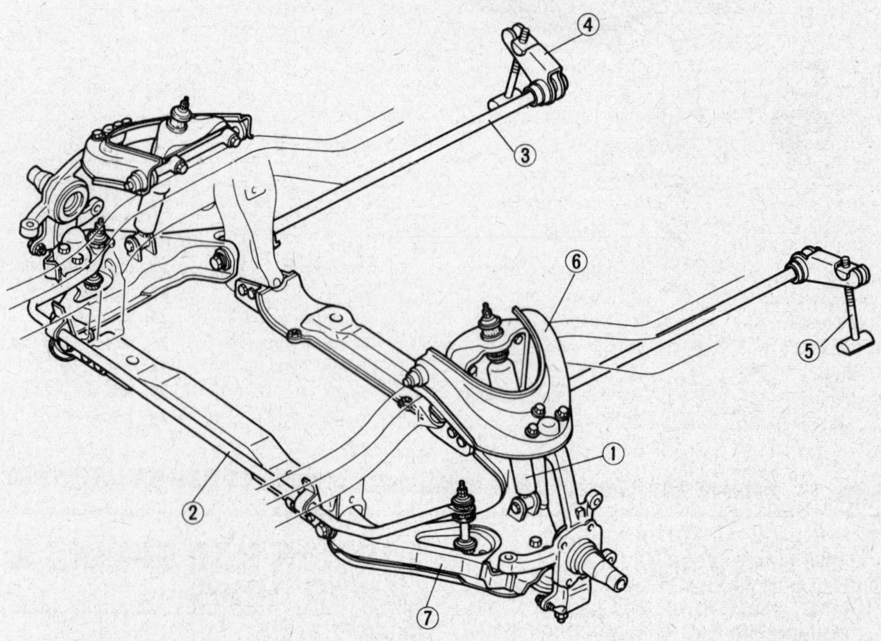

1. Shock absorber
2. Stabilizer
3. Torsion bar spring
4. Anchor arm
5. Anchor bolt
6. Upper arm
7. Lower arm

Fig. 3 Front suspension assembly. 1987 B2600 w/4WD

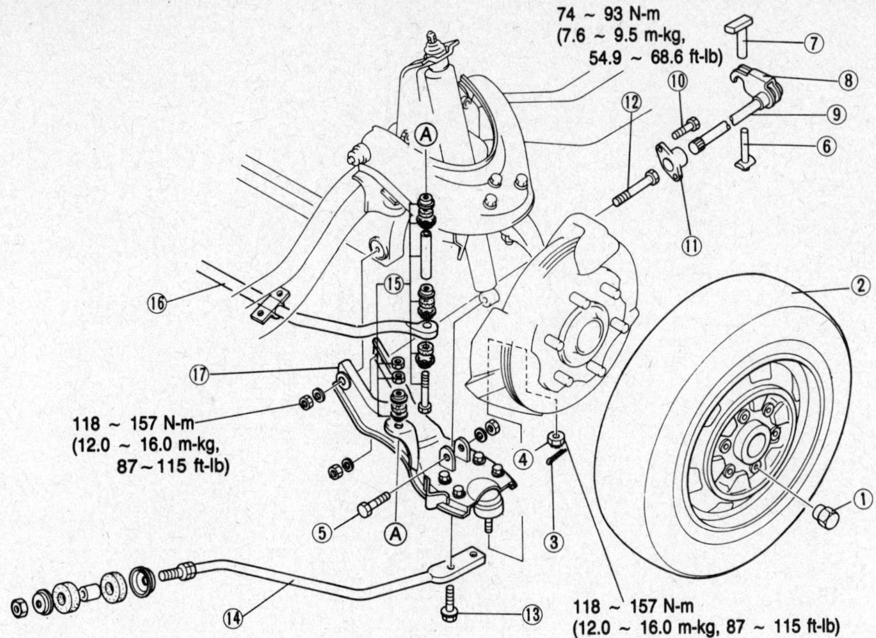

1. Lug nut
2. Wheel and tire
3. Cotter pin
4. Nut
5. Bolt
6. Anchor bolt
7. Anchor swivel
8. Anchor arm
9. Torsion bar spring
10. Bolt
11. Torque plate
12. Bolt
13. Bolt
14. Tension rod
15. Bolt, bushing, retainer and nut
16. Stabilizer
17. Lower arm assembly

Fig. 4 Torsion bar spring & lower control arm. 1986 B2000 & 1987 B2200 & B2600 w/2WD

11. Disconnect brake lines and remove master cylinder.
12. Using a suitable puller, disconnect center link from pitman arm, then remove pitman arm.
13. Remove steering gear to frame retaining bolts and nuts, then the steering gear.
14. Reverse procedure to install.

1986 B2000 & 1987 B2200 & B2600

1. Disconnect battery ground cable, then raise and support vehicle.
2. Remove nuts and cotter pins from tie rods, center link and idler arm.
3. Remove outer tie rod ends, tie rods, tie rod nuts and inner tie rod ends.
4. Remove center link.
5. Remove idler arm and bushings, then the idler arm bracket attaching bolts and idler arm bracket.
6. On models equipped with power steering, disconnect and cap pressure and return pipes from steering gear.
7. On all models, remove pitman arm attaching nut, then the pitman arm.
8. Remove steering gear attaching nuts, then the steering gear.
9. Reverse procedure to install.

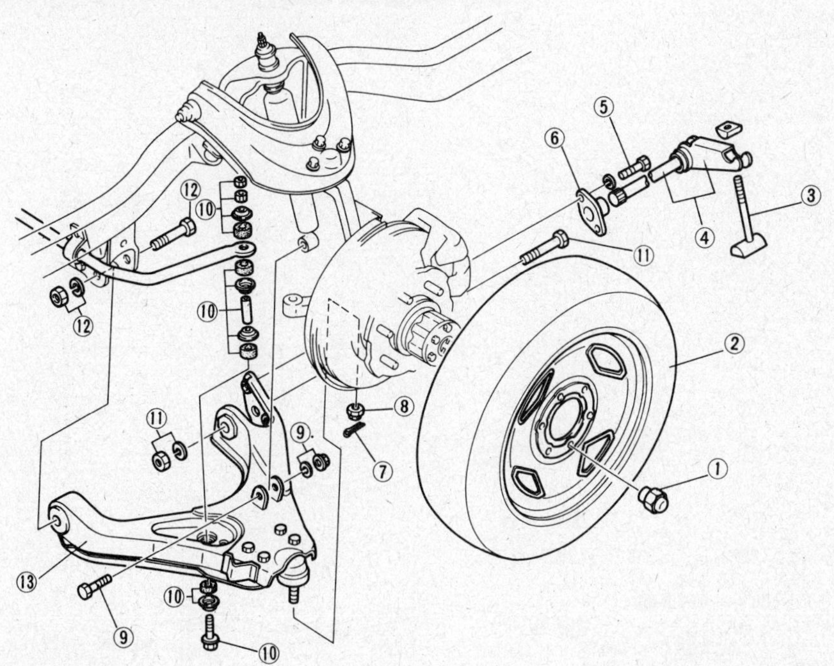

1. Lug nut
2. Wheel and tire
3. Anchor bolt
4. Torsion bar spring and anchor arm
5. Bolts
6. Torque plate
7. Cotter pin
8. Nut
9. Bolt and nut
10. Bolt, bushing, retainer and nut
11. Bolt and nut
12. Bolt and nut
13. Lower arm assembly

Fig. 5 Torsion bar spring & lower control arm. 1987 B2600 w/4WD

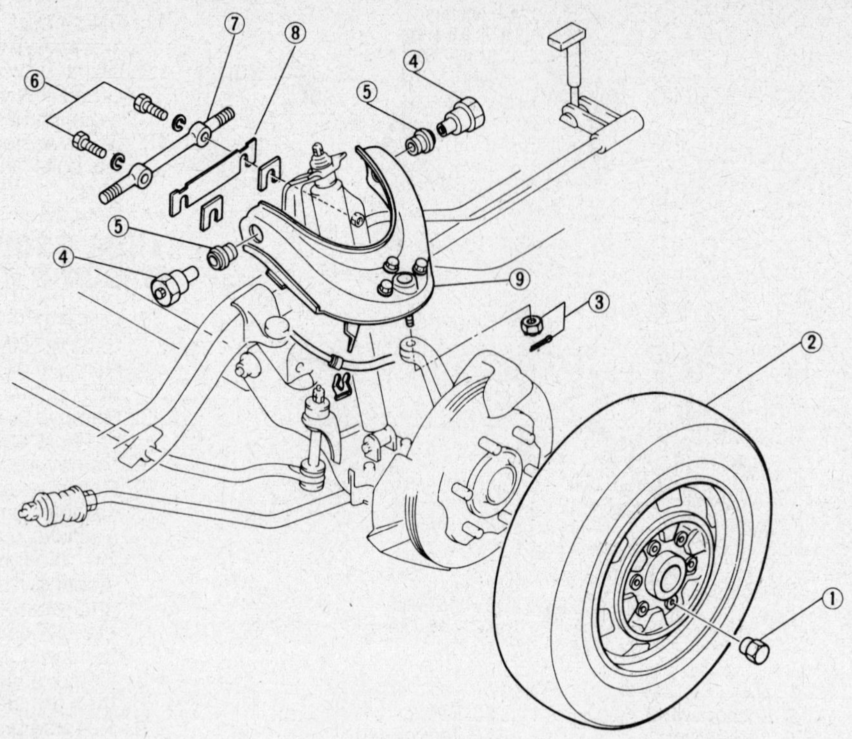

1. Lug nut
2. Wheel and tire
3. Cotter pin and nut
4. Bushing
5. Dust seal
6. Bolts
7. Upper arm shaft
8. Shim
9. Upper arm assembly

Fig. 6 Upper control arm assembly. 1986 B2000 & 1987 B2200 & B2600

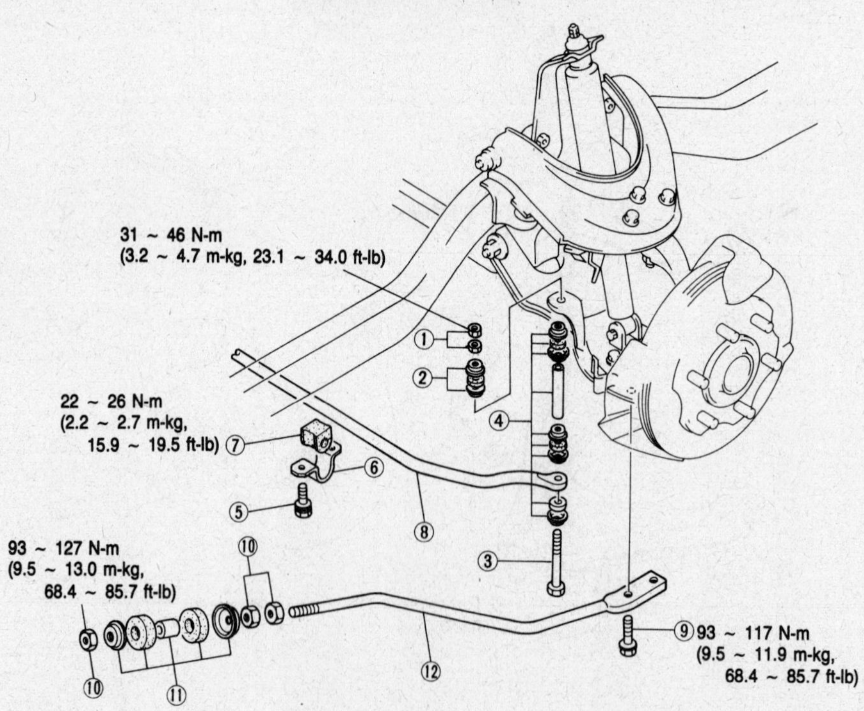

1. Nuts
2. Retainer and bushings
3. Bolt
4. Bushings, retainer and control link
5. Bolt
6. Stabilizer bracket
7. Bushing
8. Stabilizer
9. Bolt
10. Nut
11. Retainer, bushings and spacer
12. Tension rod

Fig. 7 Stabilizer bar & tension rod assembly. 1986 B2000 & 1987 B2200 & B2600 w/2WD

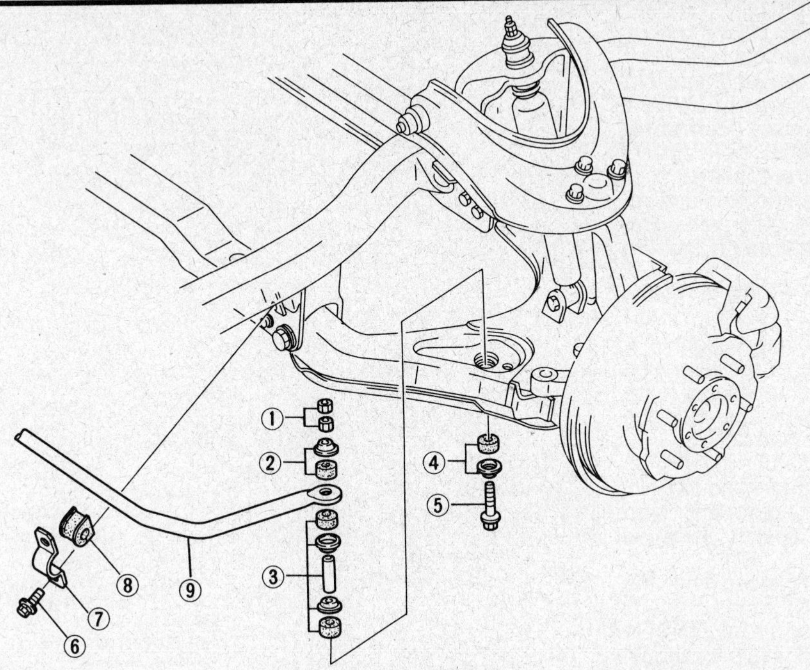

1. Nuts
2. Retainer and bushing
3. Bushings, retainers and control link
4. Bushing and retainer
5. Bolt
6. Bolt
7. Stabilizer bracket
8. Bushing
9. Stabilizer

Fig. 8 Stabilizer bar assembly. 1987 B2600 w/4WD

FRONT SUSPENSION & STEERING SECTION, GLC

INDEX

SUSPENSION ARM REPLACE

1983 GLC STATION WAGON

Remove the suspension arm in sequence shown in **Fig. 1.** Reverse sequence to install.

1983–85 GLC EXC. STATION WAGON

1. Raise and support vehicle.
2. Remove steering knuckle to ball joint retaining bolt. Separate knuckle from ball joint.
3. Remove suspension arm to body attaching nuts and bolts, **Fig. 2,** then the suspension arm.
4. Reverse procedure to install. Torque ball joint to steering knuckle bolt to 36 ft. lbs., spindle to body bolts to 78 ft. lbs. and rear side bracket to body bolts to 49 ft. lbs.

FRONT HUB & KNUCKLE REPLACE

1983–85 GLC EXC. STATION WAGON

1. Raise and support front of vehicle.
2. Remove front wheels.
3. Using a suitable hammer and chisel, remove driveshaft nut tab.
4. Apply the brakes and loosen driveshaft nut.
5. Using tool No. 490118850C or equivalent, separate tie rod end from knuckle, **Fig. 3. Temporarily leave nut in position. If tie rod end does not separate from knuckle, use a soft faced mallet and lightly tap knuckle and ball joint.**
6. Remove clip and disconnect brake line from shock absorber.
7. Remove brake assembly from knuckle and secure with a piece of wire.
8. Remove nuts and bolts from ball joint and knuckle nuts and bolts from shock absorber. **Hold knuckle assembly by hand to prevent it from falling.**
9. Remove knuckle and ball joint assembly from driveshaft. **During removal of ball joint and knuckle assembly, be careful not to scratch the oil seal.**
10. Separate ball joint from knuckle assembly.

11. Using tool No. 49B001726 or equivalent, **Fig. 4**, remove wheel hub.
12. Using an arbor press and tool No. B49F401368 or equivalent, remove outer bearing inner race. **During removal of inner race, hold wheel hub to prevent it from falling.**
13. Using a suitable hammer and drift, remove outer bearing outer race. **Remove bearing races only if bearing is to be replaced.**
14. Reverse procedure to install, noting the following:
    a. Clean components thoroughly.
    b. Check components for wear and damage. Use fine sandpaper to remove minor rust spots. Replace bearing races as one set.
15. Check bearing preload as follows:
    a. Install bearing, spacer and tool No. 49B001727 or equivalent onto knuckle, using spacer removed previously.
    b. Measure bearing preload when the spacer selector is torqued to 145 ft. lbs., (20 mkg). Using a spring scale measure preload. Preload should be 1.7-6.9 inch lbs., (2-8 mkg) measure when torque force is started, and 0.5-1.9 lbs., measured at caliper mounting hole of knuckle, **Fig. 5.**
    c. When tightening, increase the torque by 36.2 ft. lbs., (5 mkg) at a time. Ensure knuckle can be turned by hand each time torque is applied.
    d. Refer to **Fig. 6** and select proper spacer to keep the preload to specification. **Increase spacer thickness when preload is high and decrease it when preload is low. Changing the spacer thickness by 1, changes bearing preload by 1.7-3.5 inch. lbs., (2-4 cm-kg). The spacer mark is stamped on the outer diameter of the spacer.**
16. Torque the following to specified limits:
    a. Knuckle and shock absorber nuts to 58-86 ft. lbs., (8.0-11.9 mkg).
    b. Knuckle and lower arm ball joint nuts to 32.5-39.8 ft. lbs., (4.4-5.5 mkg).
    c. Lower arm and lower arm ball joint nuts to 69-86 ft. lbs., (9.5-11.9 mkg).
    d. Knuckle and brake assembly nuts to 41-48 ft. lbs., (5.6-6.6 mkg).
    e. Drive shaft locknut to 116-174 ft. lbs., (16-24 mkg).
    f. Knuckle and tie rod end nuts to 21-32.5 ft. lbs., (3-4.5mkg).
    g. Wheel set nut to 65-80 ft. lbs., (9-11 mkg).

BALL JOINT SERVICE

1983 GLC STATION WAGON

1. Check dust boot for wear, flaws or damage.
2. To check ball joint for wear, raise vehicle until wheels clear ground. Grip the tire and move fore and aft as shown in

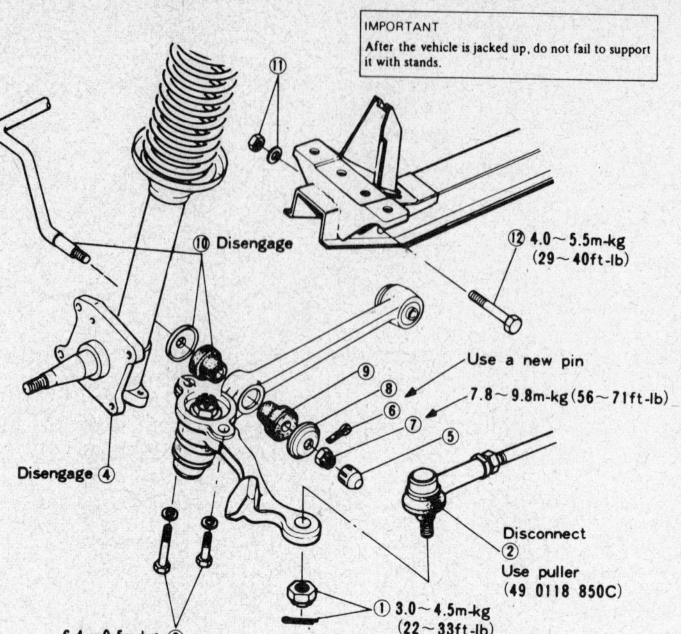

Fig. 1 Suspension arm removal. 1983 GLC wagon

Fig. 7. If endplay is more than .040 inch, replace the ball joint/suspension arm assembly as shown in **Fig. 8.**

1983–85 GLC EXC. STA. WAGON

1. Check ball joint dust boot for wear, flaws or damage.
2. To check ball joint for wear, proceed as follows:
    a. Disconnect ball joint from suspension arm.
    b. Attach a suitable spring scale to ball joint, then pull scale rearward and observe the effort required to revolve joint. Scale should read 63-109 oz. If reading is not as specified, replace ball joint.
3. To replace ball joint, proceed as follows:
    a. Remove ball joint to steering knuckle retaining bolt, then separate ball joint from knuckle.
    b. Remove ball joint to suspension arm retaining bolts, then the ball joint.
    c. Reverse procedure to install.

SHOCK ABSORBER REPLACE

1983 GLC STA. WAGON

Removal

1. Remove brake disc.
2. Remove upper mounting block to body attaching nuts.
3. Remove caliper bracket bolts, then the caliper bracket.
4. Disconnect brake line from shock by removing retaining clip.
5. Remove steering knuckle to shock assembly retaining bolts.
6. Remove shock absorber and spring assembly from vehicle.

Disassembly

1. Using a suitable spring compressor, compress spring and remove parts as shown in **Fig. 9.**
2. Clamp shock absorber in a suitable vise, then remove cap nut and seal assembly from reservoir tube, **Fig. 10.**
3. Remove O-ring from piston rod guide, then pull piston rod and pressure tube assembly from reservoir tube. **Do not remove base valve from pressure tube or piston from piston rod.**

Inspection

Inspect reservoir tube, cap nut and seal assembly, piston rod, piston rod guide, pressure tube and O-ring for damage or wear. Replace, if necessary.

Assembly

1. Install piston rod and tube into reservoir tube.
2. Fill reservoir tube with 250cc of shock absorber fluid, then install piston rod guide into pressure tube.
3. Position new O-ring between piston guide and reservoir tube, then apply grease to seal lip.
4. Install cap nut and oil seal assembly and partially tighten cap nut.
5. Extend piston rod to its maximum length, then torque cap nut to 72-94 ft. lbs.
6. Compress spring, then install parts as shown, **Fig. 9.**

Installation

Reverse removal procedure to install. Torque mounting block nuts to 18 ft. lbs., caliper bracket bolts to 29 ft. lbs. and steer-

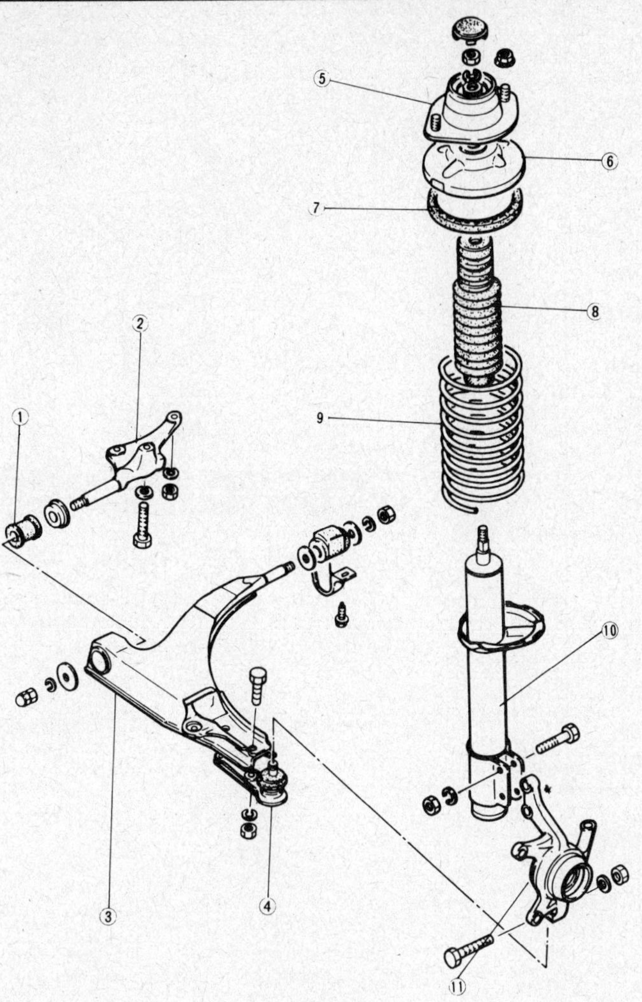

Fig. 2 Front suspension exploded view. 1983–85 GLC exc. Station Wagon

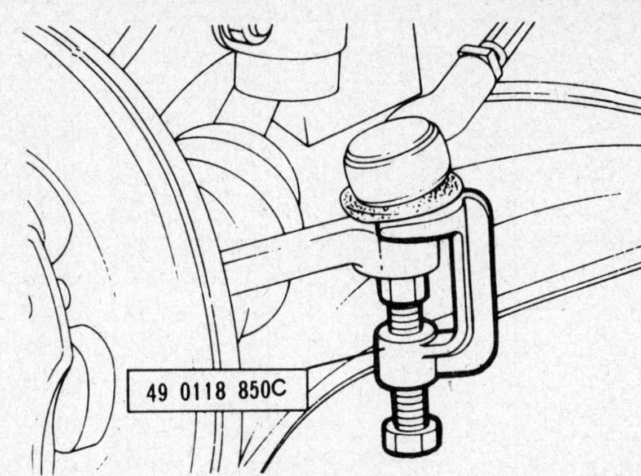

Fig. 3 Separating tie rod from steering knuckle

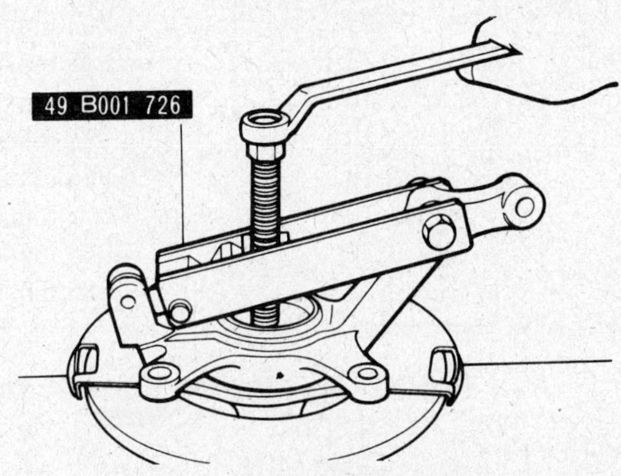

Fig. 4 Removing wheel hub

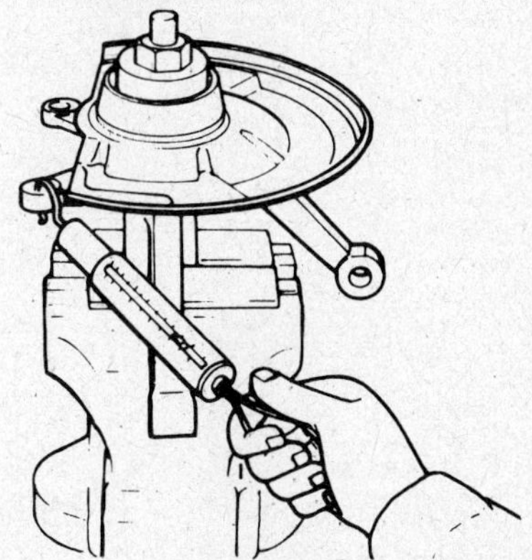

Fig. 5 Measuring bearing preload

ing knuckle to shock assembly bolts to 69 ft. lbs.

1983–85 GLC EXC. STA. WAGON

1. Raise and support front of vehicle.
2. Remove wheel and disconnect brake hose from shock absorber.
3. Remove knuckle, rubber mounts, nuts and shock absorber assembly from vehicle, **Fig. 2.**
4. Position shock absorber into a suitable vise, and loosen shock absorber top nut. **Do not remove nut.**
5. Using tool Nos. 490223640B and 490370641 or equivalent, compress spring assembly.
6. Disassemble shock absorber by referring to **Fig. 11.**
7. Reverse procedure to install. Torque mounting block and suspension tower bolts to 17-22 ft. lbs. (2.3-3.0 mkg). Torque shock absorber to lower mount bolt to 58-86 ft. lbs. (8.0-11.9 mkg). Torque piston rod and mounting block bolt to 41-50 ft. lbs. (56-69 mkg).

MANUAL STEERING GEAR

REPLACE

1983 GLC STA. WAGON

1. Disconnect battery ground cable, then raise and support vehicle. Remove horn cap.
2. Scribe a mark on steering wheel and column shaft, then remove steering wheel retaining nut and the steering wheel.
3. Remove steering column covers, then disconnect combination switch wiring.
4. Remove stop ring from steering shaft.
5. Remove combination switch retaining screw, then the combination switch.
6. Remove bushing from steering shaft.
7. Remove support bracket to dash panel retaining screws, then the support bracket.
8. Turn ignition to "ON" position, then remove column jacket and steering lock assembly.

Stamped mark	Thickness
1	6.285 mm (0.2474 in)
2	6.325 mm (0.2490 in)
3	6.365 mm (0.2506 in)
4	6.405 mm (0.2522 in)
5	6.445 mm (0.2538 in)
6	6.485 mm (0.2554 in)
7	6.525 mm (0.2570 in)
8	6.565 mm (0.2586 in)
9	6.605 mm (0.2602 in)
10	6.645 mm (0.2618 in)
11	6.685 mm (0.2634 in)
12	6.725 mm (0.2650 in)
13	6.765 mm (0.2666 in)
14	6.805 mm (0.2682 in)
15	6.845 mm (0.2698 in)
16	6.885 mm (0.2714 in)
17	6.925 mm (0.2730 in)
18	6.965 mm (0.2746 in)
19	7.005 mm (0.2762 in)
20	7.045 mm (0.2778 in)
21	7.085 mm (0.2794 in)

Fig. 6 Available spacer thicknesses chart

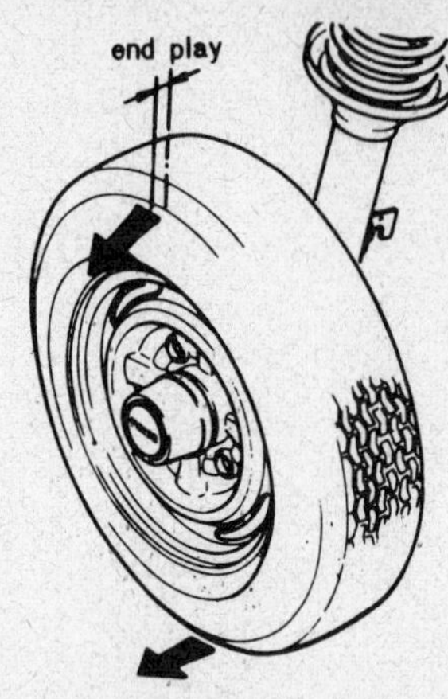

Fig. 7 Ball joint inspection. 1983 GLC Station Wagon

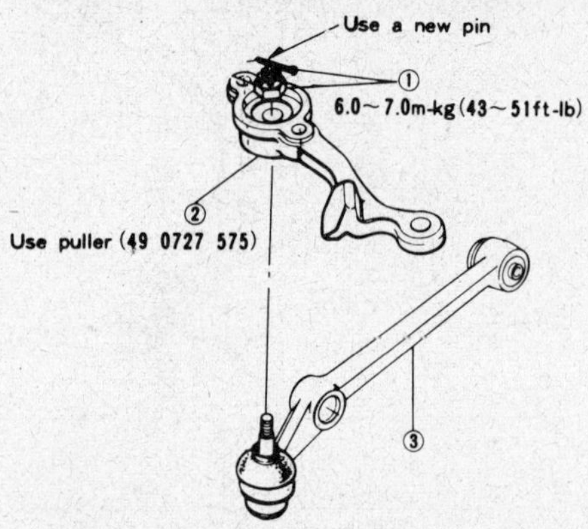

Fig. 8 Suspension arm and ball joint installation. 1983 GLC Wagon

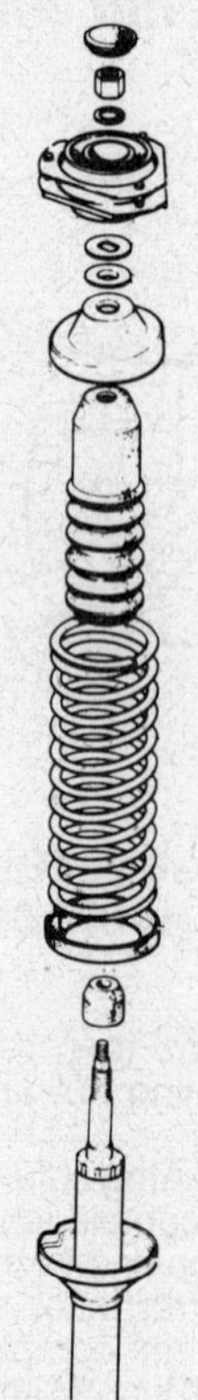

Fig. 9 Shock absorber assembly. 1983 GLC Station Wagon

9. Remove pitman arm to center link attaching nut, then using a suitable puller, separate center link from pitman arm.
10. Remove steering gear to frame attaching bolts, then the steering gear.
11. Reverse procedure to install. Torque steering gear to frame attaching bolts to 32-40 ft. lbs., pitman arm to center link nut to 22-33 ft. lbs. and support bracket to dash panel screws to 12-17 ft. lbs.

1983–85 GLC EXC. STATION WAGON

1. Raise and support vehicle, then remove front wheels.
2. Remove tie rod to steering knuckle retaining nuts, then separate tie rods from steering knuckles.
3. Remove intermediate shaft to pinion assembly boot clamp, then pull boot upward and remove pinch bolt and spring washer.
4. Remove steering gear assembly mounting bracket retaining bolts, **Fig. 12,** then remove steering gear through driver's side opening.
5. Reverse procedure to install. Torque mounting bracket to body retaining bolts to 23-34 ft. lbs., intermediate shaft to pinion assembly pinch bolt to 13-20 ft. lbs. and tie rod to steering knuckle retaining nuts to 22-33 ft. lbs.

POWER STEERING GEAR REPLACE

1983–85 GLC

1. Disconnect pressure and return lines from steering gear.
2. Raise and support front of vehicle and remove front wheels.
3. Separate tie rod ends from steering knuckles.

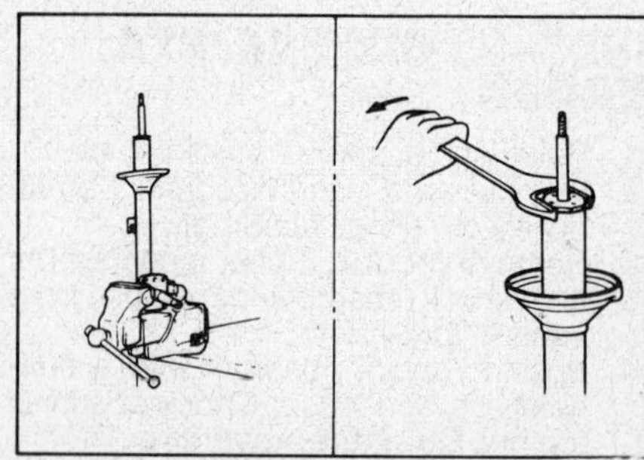

Fig. 10 Removing cap nut & oil seal from reservoir tube

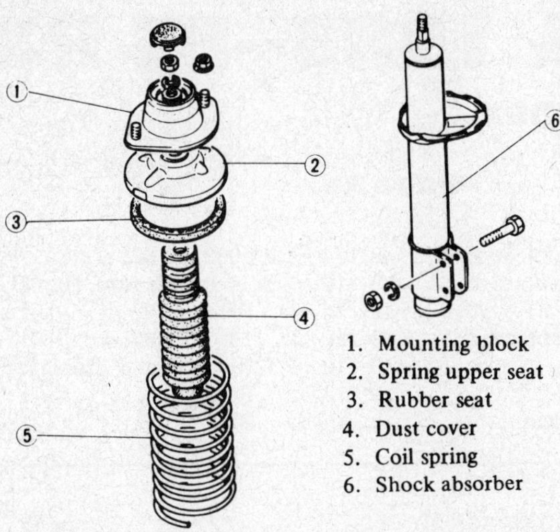

Fig. 11 Shock absorber assembly. 1983–85 GLC Exc. Station Wagon

4. Remove intermediate shaft to pinion assembly boot clamp, then pull boot upward and remove bolt.
5. Remove heat insulator, then the bracket bolt and steering gear.
6. Reverse procedure to install. Torque mounting bracket to body bolts to 23-34 ft. lbs., intermediate shaft to pinion assembly bolt to 13-20 ft. lbs. and tie rod to steering knuckle retaining nuts to 22-33 ft. lbs.

POWER STEERING PUMP REPLACE

1983–85 GLC

1. Disconnect air cleaner duct, then remove power steering pump drive belt.
2. Disconnect pressure switch electrical connector from pump.
3. Disconnect pressure and return lines from pump.
4. Remove pump attaching bolts and the pump.
5. Reverse procedure to install.

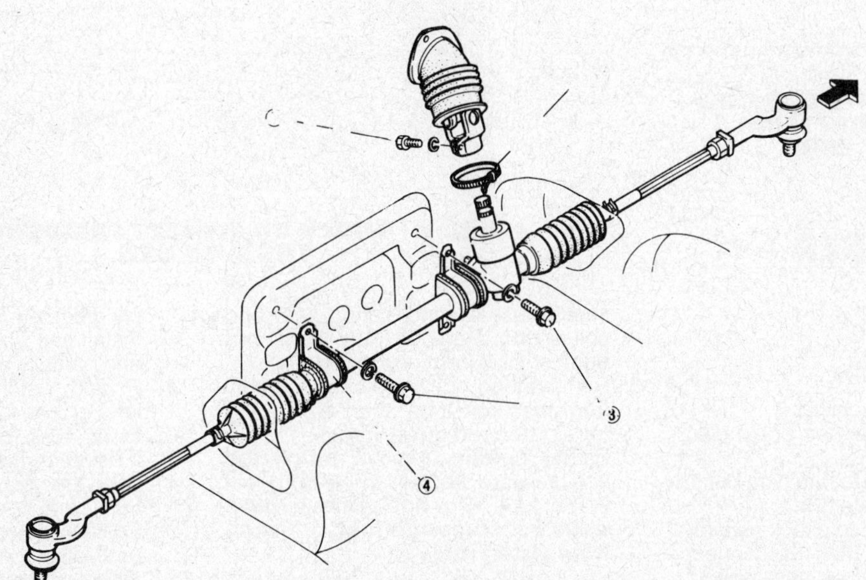

Fig. 12 Manual steering gear replacement. 1983–85 GLC Exc. Station Wagon

FRONT SUSPENSION & STEERING SECTION, 626 & 1983–85 RX-7

INDEX

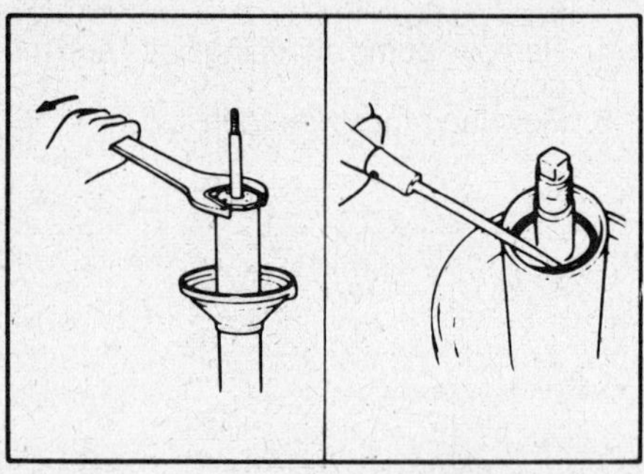

Fig. 1 Removing cap nut, seal and O-ring from reservoir tube

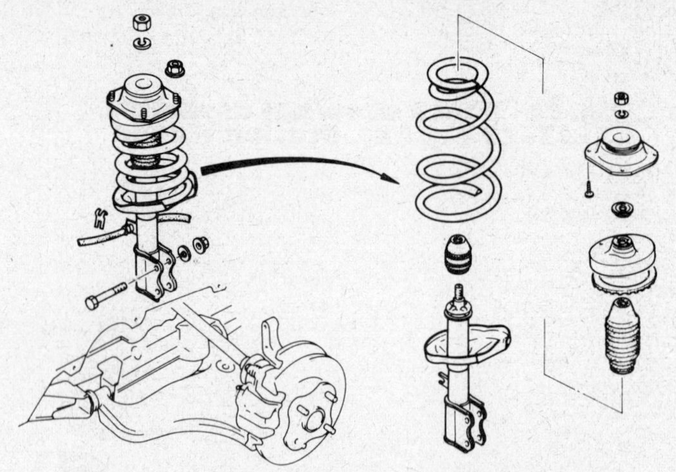

Fig. 2 Shock absorber replacement. 1983–87 626

SHOCK ABSORBER REPLACE

RX-7

Removal

1. Raise and support vehicle.
2. Remove wheels, then the brake disc and hub assembly.
3. Remove backing plate retaining bolts, then the backing plate.
4. Remove brake hose to shock assembly retaining clip, then disconnect brake hose from shock assembly, if necessary.
5. Remove steering knuckle to shock assembly retaining bolts.
6. Scribe a mark on the suspension tower and mounting block to aid installation, then remove mounting block attaching nuts.
7. Remove shock absorber and spring assembly from vehicle. Remove adjusting plate, if equipped, from mounting block.

Disassembly

1. Using a suitable spring compressor, compress spring and position shock assembly in a vise and loosen locknut several turns.
2. Remove the locknut and washer, then the mounting block, thrust bearing seat, thrust bearing, spring seat and coil spring. Remove dust boot and bumper stop from piston rod.
3. Remove cap nut and seal assembly from reservoir tube, then pry O-ring from piston rod guide, **Fig. 1.**
4. Pulling upward, remove piston rod and pressure tube assembly from reservoir tube. **Do not remove base valve from pressure tube or piston from piston rod.**

Inspection

Inspect reservoir tube and mounting block for damage or wear, thrust bearing for roughness, coil spring for signs of fatigue and cap nut and seal assembly for damaged threads or seal lip. Replace, if necessary.

Assembly

A cartridge type replacement damper is available. If this replacement damper is used, proceed to Step 6.

1. Install pressure tube and piston rod into reservoir tube.
2. Fill reservoir tube with 225cc of shock absorber fluid.
3. Position new O-ring between piston rod guide and reservoir tube, then apply grease to oil seal lip.
4. Install cap nut and oil seal assembly and partially tighten cap nut.
5. Extend piston rod to its maximum length, then lower and torque cap nut to 36-43 ft. lbs.
6. If using cartridge type damper, install cartridge and torque cap nut to 58-108 ft. lbs.
7. Position bumper stop and dust boot onto piston rod, then compress coil spring. Install spring, spring seat, thrust bearing, thrust bearing seat and the mounting block. Install washer and locknut, then partially tighten locknut.

Installation

Reverse removal procedure to install. Align marks on suspension tower and mounting block. Torque mounting block locknut to 47-59 ft. lbs., mounting block to suspension tower attaching nuts to 17-22 ft. lbs. and steering knuckle to shock assembly retaining bolts to 51 ft. lbs.

After installing shock absorber assembly, measure clearance between floor and each headlight. The difference between each side should not exceed .590 inch. Adjust clearance differences by positioning adjusting plates onto mounting blocks. Do

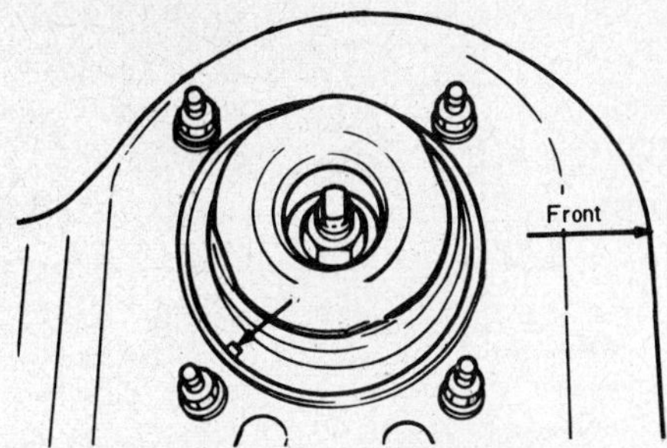

Fig. 3 Shock absorber mounting block positioning. 1983–87 626

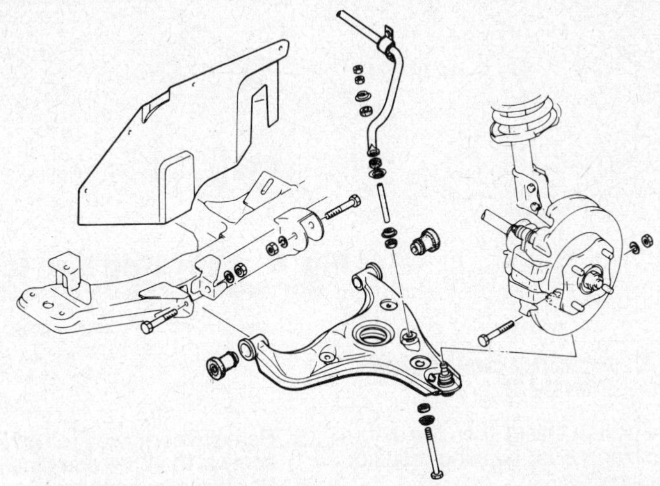

Fig. 4 Suspension arm & stabilizer bar replacement. 1983–87 626

not use more than two adjusting plates at one side.

1983–87 626

1. Raise and support front of vehicle and remove front wheel.
2. Remove brake hose clip from lower shock absorber mounting.
3. Remove shock absorber lower attaching bolts and nuts, **Fig. 2.**
4. Remove mounting block attaching nuts, then the shock absorber and spring assembly.
5. Position assembly in a suitable vise and loosen locknut several turns.
6. Compress spring using a suitable spring compressor, then remove locknut, mounting block, bearing, spring upper seat, spring seat, coil spring, dust boot and shock absorber.
7. Reverse procedure to install, noting the following:
   a. Install mounting block so reference mark on upper surface is positioned as shown in **Fig. 3.**
   b. Torque locknut at upper end of shock absorber to 47-59 ft. lbs. for 1984-84 models or 22-27 ft. lbs. on 1986-87 models.
   c. Torque mounting block attaching nuts to 17-22 ft. lbs. for 1984-84 models or 22-27 ft. lbs. on 1986-87 models.

SUSPENSION ARM REPLACE

1983–87 626

1. Raise and support front of vehicle and remove front wheel.
2. Disconnect stabilizer bar from suspension arm, **Fig. 4.**
3. Remove suspension arm attaching bolts and nuts.
4. Remove ball joint attaching bolt and nut, then the suspension arm.
5. Reverse procedure to install, noting the following:
   a. Torque ball joint attaching bolt to 32-40 ft. lbs. (4.4-5.5 mkg).
   b. Temporarily tighten suspension arm attaching bolts, then lower vehicle and torque bolts to 69-86 ft. lbs. (9.5-11.9 mkg).

RX-7

1. Raise and support front of vehicle.
2. Remove front wheels.
3. Remove bolts and knuckle arm from steering knuckle.
4. Using tool No. 490118850C or equivalent, disconnect tie rod from steering knuckle.
5. Remove bolts and disconnect stabilizer bar and tension rod.
6. Using tool No. 490727575 or equivalent, disconnect knuckle arm from suspension arm.
7. Remove bolts and suspension arm from vehicle.
8. Reverse procedure to install. Torque the following to specified limits:
   a. Ball joint to knuckle arm, 43-51 ft. lbs., (6.0-7.0 mkg).
   b. Suspension arm to crossmember, 29-40 ft. lbs., (4.0-5.5 mkg).
   c. Tension rod to suspension arm, 40 ft. lbs., (5.5-6.9 mkg).
   d. Knuckle arm to shock absorber, 43-51 ft. lbs., (6.0-7.0 mkg).

BALL JOINT SERVICE

To check ball joint, position suspension arm in a suitable vise and proceed as follows:

1. On RX-7 models, attach steering knuckle arm to ball joint, then rotate stud several turns to tighten it. Attach a suitable spring scale to tie rod connection hole in steering knuckle arm, **Fig. 5.**
2. On 1983-87 626 models, install tool No. 490180510B to ball joint stud and attach a suitable spring scale to tool, **Fig. 6.**
3. On all models, pull spring scale rearward and note reading. If reading is less than 14 oz. on RX-7 models, or 4.4-7.7 lbs. on 1983-87 626 models, replace ball joint and suspension arm. The ball joint cannot be separated from the suspension arm. If ball joint wear is excessive, replace the suspension arm/ball joint assembly.

TENSION ROD & STABILIZER BAR REPLACE

RX-7

1. Raise and support front of vehicle.
2. Remove engine undercover.
3. Remove tension rod nuts and tension rod.
4. Remove nuts from both ends of stabilizer bar and from right and left control links.
5. Remove stabilizer bar support plates and rubber bushings.
6. Remove right and left mounting brackets, tension rod and stabilizer bar from vehicle.
7. Reverse procedure to install. Note the following:
   a. Check tension rod and stabilizer bar components for cracks, warp and wear. Replace any damaged components as required.
   b. During installation of tension rod, install front end of tension rod onto the mounting bracket and tighten nut "A" to specification shown in **Fig. 7.** Torque nut "B" to 80-108 ft. lbs., (11.0-15.0 mkg). Torque tension arm to suspension nuts to 40-50 ft. lbs., (5.5-6.9 mkg) and stabilizer support plate bolts to 27-34 ft. lbs., (3.4-4.7 mkg).

STABILIZER BAR REPLACE

1983–87 626

1. Raise and support front of vehicle and remove front wheel.
2. Disconnect stabilizer bar from suspension arm, **Fig. 4.**

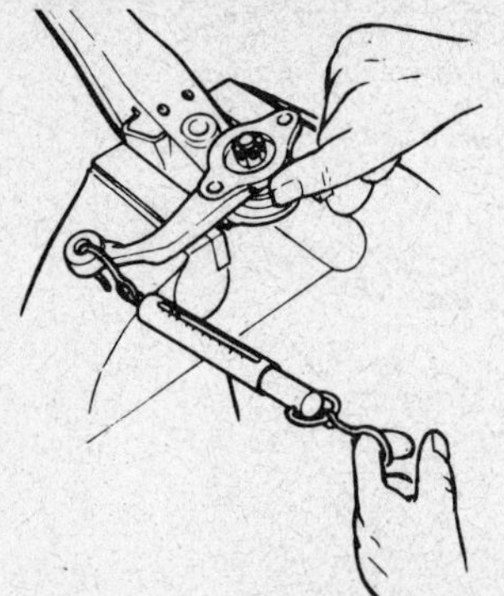

Fig. 5 Checking ball joint for wear. RX-7

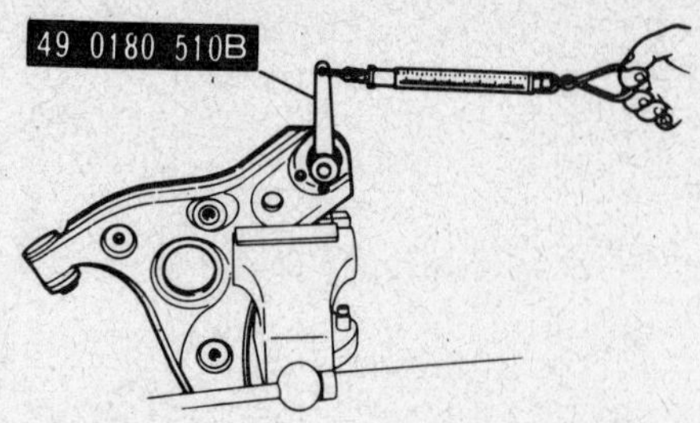

Fig. 6 Checking ball joint for wear. 1983–87 626

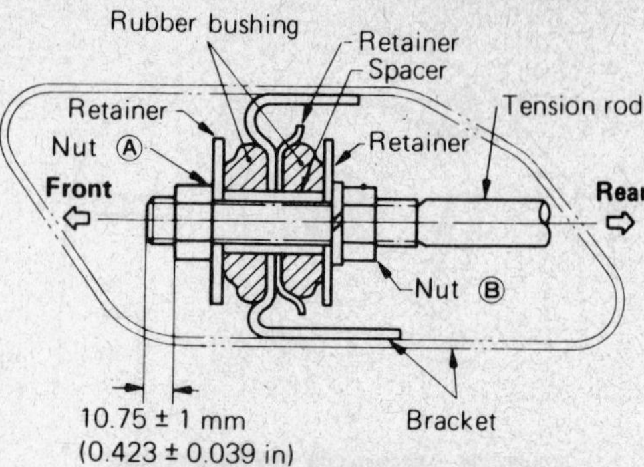

Fig. 7 Tightening tension rod nut "A"

3. Remove splash shield, then the stabilizer bushing bolts, bushing, bracket and stabilizer bar.
4. Reverse procedure to install, noting the following:
   a. Align rubber bushing with white reference line on stabilizer bar and install with notch facing rearward.
   b. Mount upper end of stabilizer bar first and tighten it temporarily, then mount lower end to suspension arm.
   c. Tighten stabilizer bar to suspension arm attaching nut so thread protrusion ensures 1 inch (25.5mm).

MANUAL STEERING GEAR

REPLACE

1983–87 626

1. Raise and support front of vehicle and remove front wheels.
2. Remove steering shaft to pinion coupling attaching bolt.
3. Remove cotter pins and nuts from tie rod ends.
4. Remove splash shield, then disconnect tie rods from steering knuckles using tool No.490118850C or equivalent.
5. Remove steering gear attaching bolts, then the steering gear and linkage.
6. Reverse procedure to install. Torque tie rod to 58-72 ft. lbs.

RX-7

1. Disconnect battery ground cable, then remove horn cap.
2. Mark steering wheel and column shaft, then remove steering wheel retaining nut and the steering wheel.
3. Remove steering column cover retaining screws, then the covers.
4. Remove air duct, then disconnect combination switch wiring connections.
5. Remove combination switch retaining screws, then the combination switch.
6. Position a suitable protector under the steering lock assembly, then using a chisel and hammer, remove steering lock body to column jacket retaining bolts. Remove steering lock assembly from vehicle.
7. Remove column jacket fixing bracket, then mark hood hinge locations and remove hood.
8. Raise and support vehicle, then disconnect center link from pitman arm using a suitable puller.
9. Using a suitable puller, disconnect pitman arm from steering gear sector shaft.
10. Remove steering gear housing retaining bolts, then the steering gear housing through the engine compartment.
11. Reverse procedure to install. When installing the steering lock assembly, tighten the new shear bolts until the heads of the bolts snap off.

POWER STEERING GEAR

REPLACE

1983–87 626

1. Raise and support front of vehicle and remove front wheels.
2. Remove steering shaft to pinion coupling attaching bolt.
3. Remove cotter pins and nuts from tie rod ends.
4. Remove splash shield, then disconnect tie rods from steering knuckles using tool No. 490118850C or equivalent.
5. Disconnect pressure and return lines from steering gear.
6. Remove steering gear attaching bolts, then the steering gear and linkage.
7. Reverse procedure to install. Torque tie rod to 58-72 ft. lbs.

1984–85 RX-7

1. Disconnect battery ground cable, then remove horn cap.
2. Mark steering wheel and column shaft, then remove steering wheel retaining nut and the steering wheel.
3. Remove steering column cover, then the heater duct.
4. Remove steering column support bracket, then the set plate, steering gear clamp bolt and coupling bolt.
5. Raise and support vehicle.
6. Disconnect center link from pitman arm using tool No. 490118850C or equivalent.
7. Remove steering gear attaching bolts, then disconnect pressure and return lines from steering gear.
8. Remove steering gear attaching nuts, then the steering gear from vehicle.
9. Reverse procedure to install.

POWER STEERING PUMP

REPLACE

1983–87 626

1. Raise and support front of vehicle and remove right wheel.
2. Remove power steering pump pulley attaching bolt, then alternator and drive belt.
3. Remove steering pump pulley.
4. Remove hose clamps and disconnect hoses from steering pump.
5. Remove steering pump attaching bolts and the pump.
6. Reverse procedure to install.

1984–85 RX-7

1. Disconnect pressure and return lines from power steering pump.
2. Remove steering pump drive belt and pulley.
3. Unfasten A/C compressor and position aside, leaving refrigerant lines attached.
4. Remove steering pump attaching bolts and the pump.
5. Reverse procedure to install.

FRONT SUSPENSION & STEERING SECTION, 1986–87 RX-7

INDEX

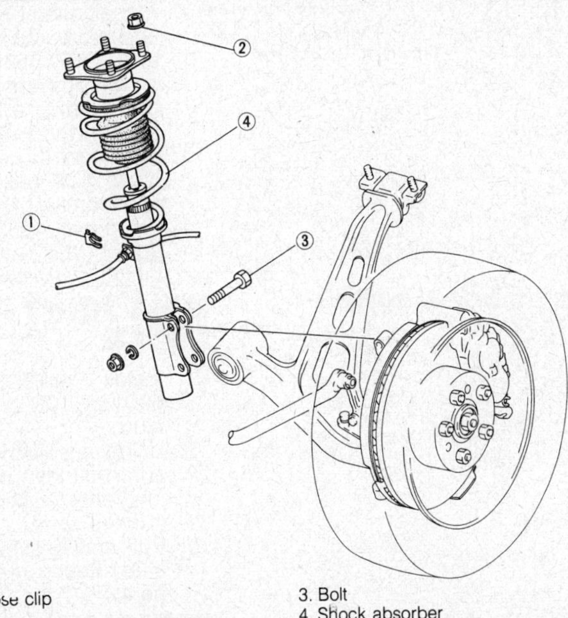

1. Brake hose clip
2. Nut
3. Bolt
4. Shock absorber

Fig. 1 Shock absorber & spring assembly. 1986–87 RX-7

SHOCK ABSORBER & COIL SPRING REPLACE

REMOVAL

1. Raise and support vehicle.
2. Remove components in numerical sequence shown in **Fig. 1.**
3. When removing shock absorber, note the following:
   a. Remove disc brake caliper attaching bolt.
   b. Suspend caliper assembly using a suitable piece of wire. Do not disconnect brake lines.
   c. Remove shock absorber attaching bolts and nuts, then the shock absorber assembly.

DISASSEMBLY

1. Disassemble shock absorber and related components in numerical sequence shown in **Fig. 2.**
2. When removing coil spring and mounting blocking proceed as follows:
   a. Loosen piston rod upper attaching nut several turns. **Do not remove piston rod upper nut.**
   b. Using tools 490223640B and 490370641 or equivalents, compress coil spring assembly, then remove attaching nut.
   c. Remove coil spring assembly.

INSPECTION

Check shock absorber for oil leakage or for abnormal noise. Check shock absorber control rod for smooth rotation. Replace any worn or damaged component as required.

ASSEMBLY

Reverse numerical sequence shown in **Fig. 2** and note the following:

1. Using tools 490223640B and 490370641 or equivalents, compress coil spring assembly.
2. Install mounting block into a suitable vise.
3. Torque piston rod upper attaching nut to 47-59 ft. lbs. Ensure spring is properly seated in the upper and lower seats.

INSTALLATION

Install shock absorber and spring assembly into vehicle by reversing numerical sequence shown in **Fig. 1.** When installing mounting block, place mounting block on to suspension tower so that the white mark on the mounting block is between the front and inside positions on mounting block, **Fig. 3.**

LOWER CONTROL ARM SERVICE

REMOVAL

Remove lower control arm and attaching components in numerical sequence shown in **Fig. 4.**

INSPECTION

Check lower control arm for wear or damage. Check control arm bushings for deterioration or wear. Check ball joint preload, adjust if necessary. Check dust boot for damage.

FRONT BUSHING, REPLACE

1. Place tools 49G030627A and 49G030625A or equivalents, against front bushing.
2. With assembly placed into a suitable press, press out the bushing from control arm.
3. Install new bushing, an press bushing approximately halfway into control arm.
4. Place tools 49G030627A, 49G030625A and 490823146 on to bushing.
5. Place assembly into a suitable press, and press bushing into control arm.

REAR BUSHING, REPLACE

1. Place tools 490710520, 49G030627A and 49G030625A or equivalents, against lower arm.

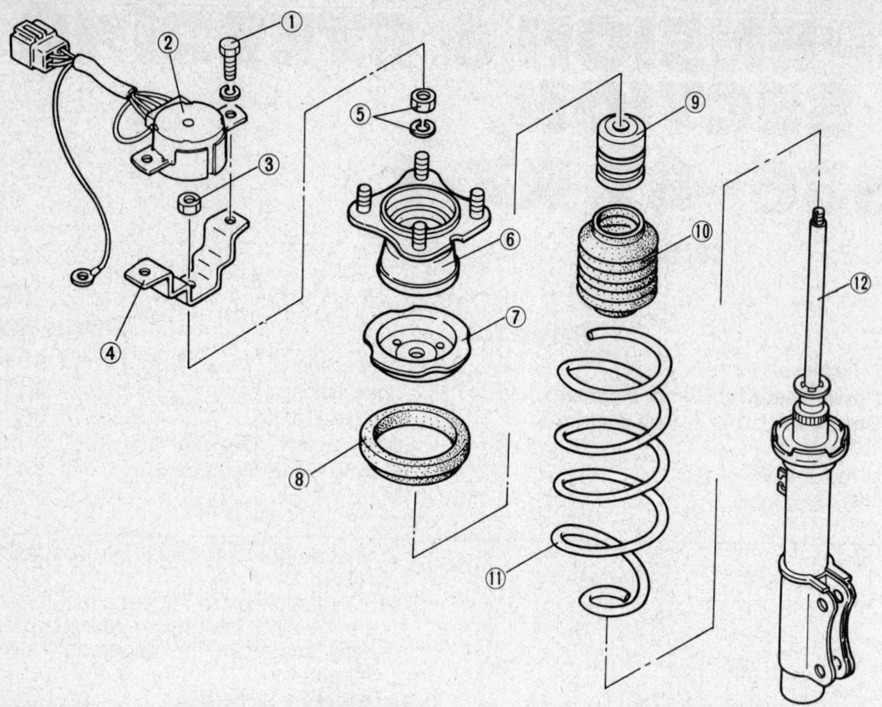

Fig. 2 Exploded view of shock absorber & spring assembly. 1986–87 RX-7

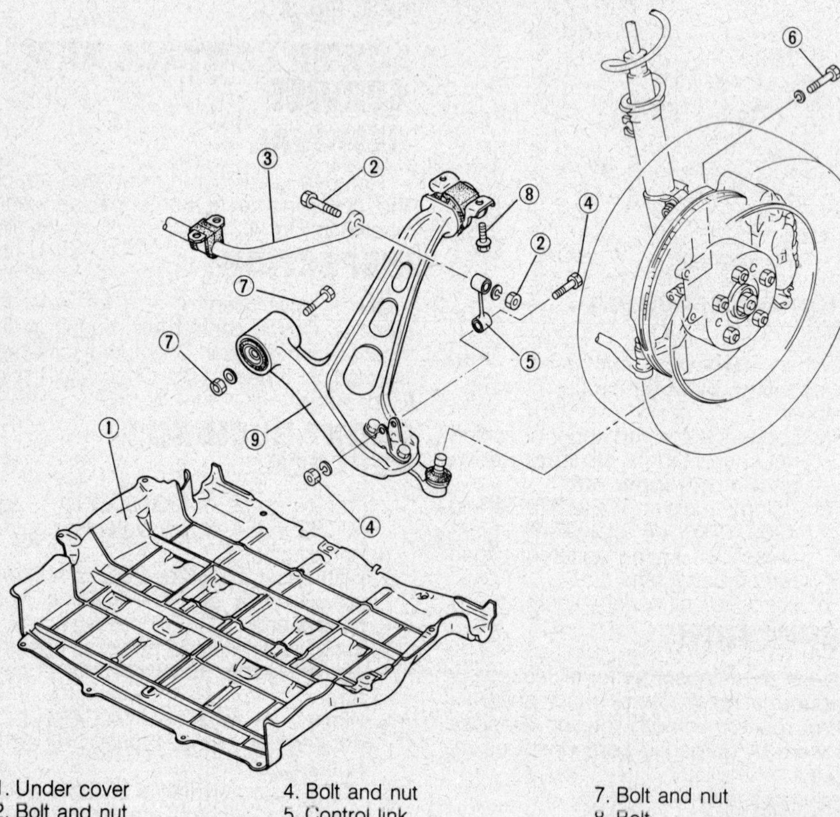

Fig. 4 Lower control arm & related components. 1986–87 RX-7

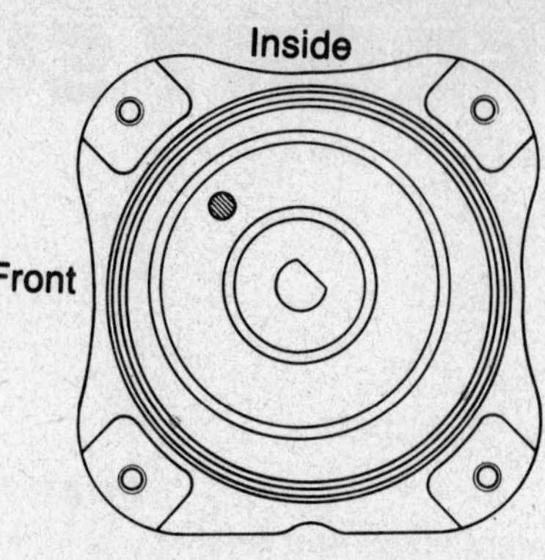

Fig. 3 Positioning mounting block. 1986–87 RX-7

2. Place assembly into a suitable press, and press out bushing. **When using tool 490710520, do not over tighten clamp nuts on tool or damage to the control arm may result. Hand tighten the tool's clamp nuts only.**
3. With control arm placed in a press, press new bushing into control arm approximately halfway in.
4. Place tool 490823146 or equivalent, against the new bushing, then press bushing into control arm.

BALL JOINT PRELOAD CHECK

1. Install preload attachment tool 490180510B or equivalent on to ball stud.
2. Using a suitable spring scale, measure ball joint preload. Measure preload after shaking ball joint stud 3 or 4 times.
3. Pull spring scale and with ball joint stud rotating, reading obtained should be 4.4-7.7 lbs.

INSTALLATION

Install control arm assembly by reversing numerical sequence shown in **Fig. 4.**

STABILIZER BAR REPLACE

Remove stabilizer bar by following numerical sequence shown in **Fig. 5.** Install stabilizer bar by reversing numerical sequence. When installing stabilizer bar, note the following:

1. Install stabilizer bar bushing so that bushing seam faces front of vehicle.
2. Align bushing with stabilizer installation mark (white line on stabilizer bar).
3. Install stabilizer bracket and temporarily tighten attaching bolts.
4. Lower vehicle, then with vehicle completely unloaded, torque attaching bolt to 13-20 ft. lbs.

STEERING GEAR REPLACE

1. Remove battery cover, then disconnect battery ground cable.

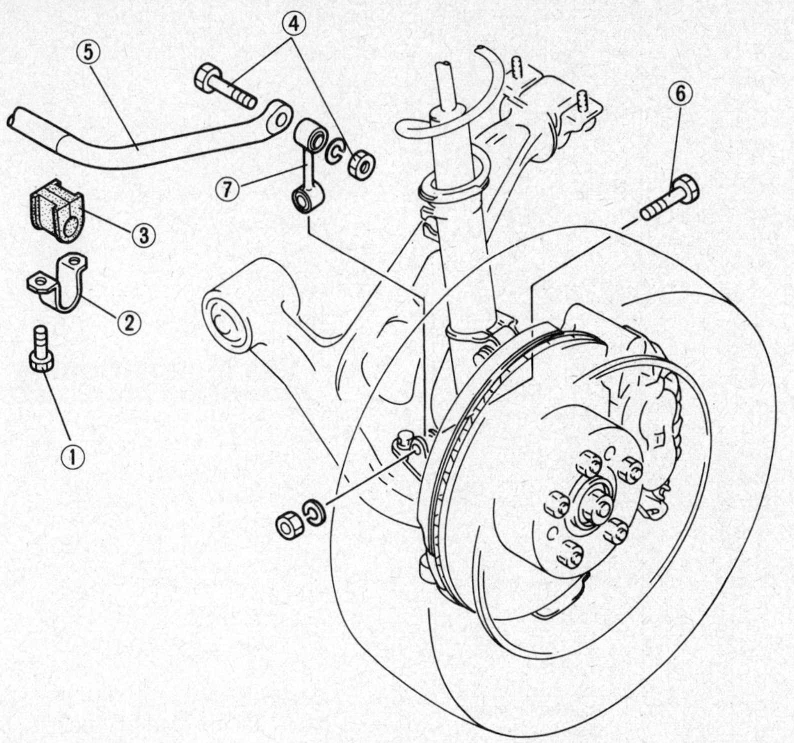

1. Bolt
2. Stabilizer bracket
3. Bushing
4. Bolt and nut
5. Stabilizer
6. Bolt and nut
7. Control link

Fig. 5 Stabilizer bar assembly. 1986–87 RX-7

2. Remove cooling fan, then the radiator cover and radiator.
3. Raise and support vehicle, then remove stabilizer bar.
4. On models equipped with power steering, disconnect and cap pressure and return lines at steering gear.
5. On all models, remove tie rod end attaching bolts, then disconnect tie rod end, using a suitable tool.
6. Remove steering gear attaching bolts, then the steering gear and linkage from vehicle.
7. Reverse procedure to install.

POWER STEERING PUMP REPLACE

1. Disconnect and cap pressure and return lines from power steering pump.
2. Remove steering pump drive belt and pulley.
3. Remove remaining hoses from pump.
4. Remove steering pump attaching bolts and the pump.
5. Reverse procedure to install.

FRONT SUSPENSION & STEERING SECTION, 323

INDEX

SHOCK ABSORBER & SPRING REPLACE

1. Raise and support front of vehicle.
2. Remove shock absorber and spring attaching components as shown in **Fig. 1.**
3. Check shock absorber for oil leakage or abnormal noise.
4. Check shock absorber for loose attaching nuts and bolts.
5. Check mounting block for deterioration or damage.
6. Check bound stopper for wear and/or damage.
7. Replace any worn or damaged part as required.
8. Install shock absorber and spring assembly as shown in **Fig. 1.**
9. When installing mounting block on to vehicle, ensure white paint mark mounting is facing inside of vehicle, **Fig. 2.**
10. Torque piston rod and mounting block attaching bolts to 16.6-21.7 ft. lbs. on 1986 models or 41-50 ft. lbs. on 1987 models.

LOWER CONTROL ARM SERVICE

REMOVAL

Raise and support vehicle. Remove control arm as shown in **Fig. 1.**

LOWER CONTROL ARM BUSHING, REPLACE

1. Place control arm into a suitable vise.
2. Using a hacksaw, cut away projecting portion of the lower arm bushing.

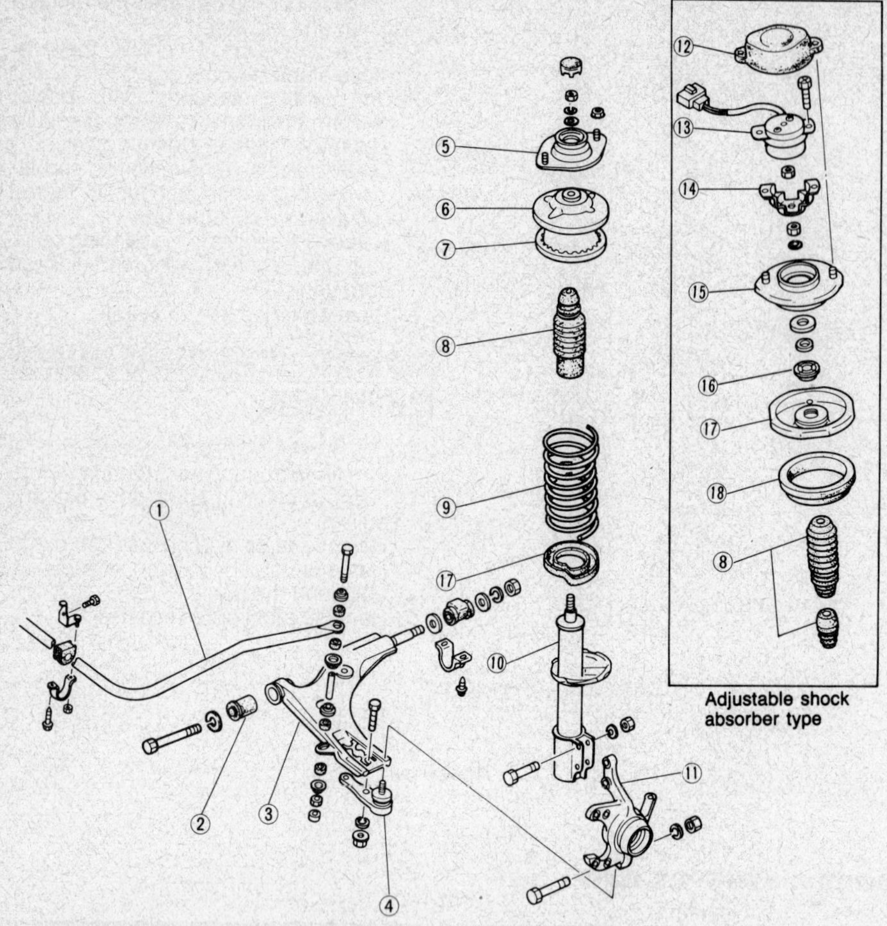

1. Stabilizer
2. Rubber bushing
3. Lower arm
4. Lower arm ball joint
5. Rubber mounting
6. Spring upper seat
7. Rubber seat
8. Bound stopper and dust boot
9. Coil spring
10. Shock absorber
11. Knuckle
12. Actuator cap
13. Actuator
14. Brackets
15. Rubber mounting
16. Bearing
17. Spring upper seat
18. Rubber seat

Fig. 1 Exploded view of front suspension assembly. 323

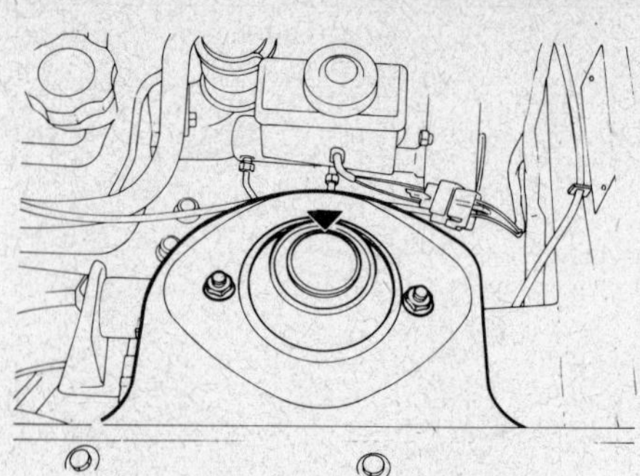

Fig. 2 Positioning mounting block. 323

3. Place tool 49B092625 or equivalent, on to lower control arm bushing.
4. Place assembly into a suitable vise. Tighten vise handle, and remove bushing from control arm.
5. Place tool 49B0926625 or equivalent, on to the new bushing. Repeat step 4 to install busing into control arm.

BALL JOINT PRELOAD CHECK

Install preload attachment tool 4901805108 or equivalent on to ball joint stud. Attach a suitable spring scale to preload attachment tool, then pull on spring scale. Reading obtained should be 15.6-26.9 inch. lbs.

INSTALLATION

Install lower control arm assembly on to vehicle as shown in **Fig. 1.**

STABILIZER BAR
REPLACE

1. Raise and support vehicle.
2. Remove stabilizer bar from vehicle as shown in **Fig. 1.**
3. Check stabilizer bar and bushing for wear or damage. Replace any component, if necessary.
4. Install stabilizer bar into vehicle as shown in **Fig. 1.**
5. When installing stabilizer bar bushing, mount bushing so that the bushing seam faces rear of chassis. Mount bracket side of the stabilizer first and temporarily tighten it. After mounting the control link side and with vehicle completely unloaded, torque attaching bolts to 23-34 ft. lbs. Tighten stabilizer bar attaching but so there is .43 inches of thread exposed at the top of the control link.

STEERING GEAR
REPLACE

1. Disconnect battery ground cable, raise and support vehicle.
2. Remove steering shaft universal joint attaching bolt.
3. Remove tie rod end attaching bolt, then separate tie rod end from lower control arm using a suitable tool.
4. On models equipped with power steering, disconnect and cap pressure and return hoses at steering gear.
5. On all models, remove steering gear attaching bolts, then the steering gear and linkage assembly.
6. Reverse procedure to install.

POWER STEERING PUMP
REPLACE

1. Disconnect and cap pressure and return lines from power steering pump.
2. Loosen belt tension bolt, then remove pump attaching bolt.
3. Remove pump drive belt and pulley, then the power steering pump from vehicle.
4. Reverse procedure to install.

WHEEL ALIGNMENT SECTION

INDEX

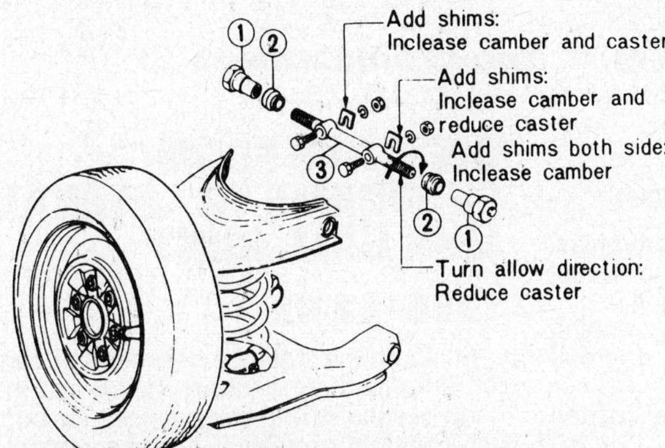

Fig. 1 Adjusting caster & camber. 1983-84 B2000 & B2200

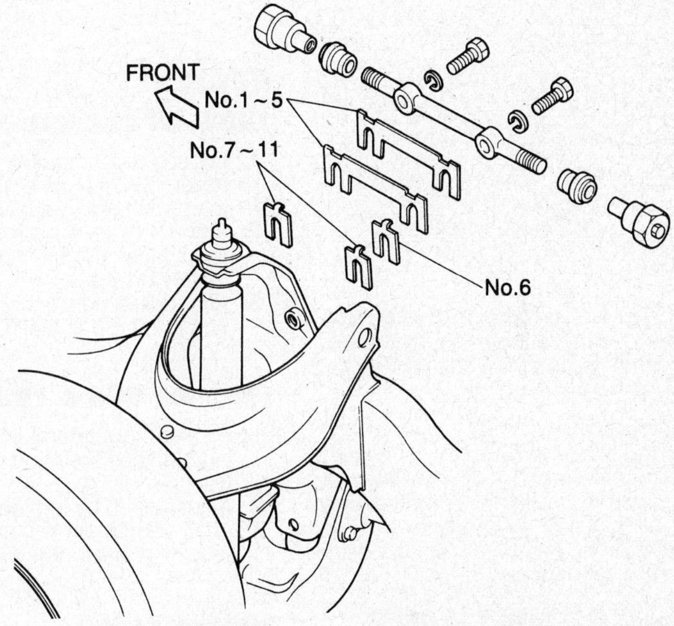

Fig. 2 Adjusting caster & camber. 1986 B2000 & 1987 B2200 & B2600

PRELIMINARY CHECKS

1. Ensure tire pressure is as specified by manufacturer.
2. Inspect ball joints and steering linkage for excessive looseness. Repair as required.
3. Ensure vehicle is level and has no luggage or passenger load.
4. Ensure difference in height from center of wheel to fender brim between right and left sides is equal.

CASTER

1983-85 GLC & 1986-87 323

Caster is not adjustable and is set to specifications during production. Whenever caster is moved out of specified angle, check all parts of front suspension and body alignment. Repair or replace defective part(s) as required.

1983-87 626 & RX-7

Caster and camber are adjusted at the same time. Refer to "Camber" adjustment procedure under "1983-87 626 & RX-7."

B2000, B2200 & B2600

Caster and camber are adjusted at the same time. Refer to "Camber" adjustment procedure under "B2000, B2200 & B2600."

CAMBER

FRONT

1983 GLC Wagon

Camber is not adjustable and is set to specifications during production. Whenever camber is moved out of specified angle, check all parts of front suspension and body alignment. Repair or replace defective part(s) as required.

1983-85 GLC Exc. Wagon & 1986-87 323

1. Raise and support front of vehicle, then open hood.
2. Remove two shock absorber mounting block to fender attaching nuts.
3. Push mounting block downward and turn it until specified angle is obtained. **When triangle mark on mounting block is rotated from engine to the outside, camber changes to negative side. When mark is moved back, camber changes to positive side.**
4. Install and tighten two shock absorber mounting block to fender attaching nuts.

1983-87 626 & RX-7

1. Raise and support front of vehicle, then open hood.
2. Remove four shock absorber mounting block to fender attaching nuts.
3. Push mounting block downward and turn it until specified angles are obtained.
4. Install four shock absorber mounting block to fender attaching bolts. Torque bolts to 22-27 ft. lbs.

B2000, B2200 & B2600

Caster and camber angles are adjusted by adding or subtracting shims. Refer to **Figs. 1 and 2** for adjustment shim locations, noting the following:

1. On 1986 B2000 & 1987 B2200 and B2600, shims Nos. 1 through 5 are used at left and right sides, shims Nos. 7 through 11 are used at front and rear left and right sides and shim No. 6 (models equipped with power steering) is used at rear left and right sides, **Fig. 3.**
2. To change camber on 1986 B2000 & 1987 B2200 and B2600, shim thicknesses (front and rear) of 1mm results in a change of $1/4°$. To change caster, a shim thickness of 1mm results in a change of $1/2°$.

No.	Thickness mm (in)	No.	Thickness mm (in)
1	1.0 (0.004)	7	1.0 (0.004)
2	1.6 (0.063)	8	1.6 (0.063)
3	2.0 (0.079)	9	2.0 (0.079)
4	3.2 (0.126)	10	3.2 (0.126)
5	4.0 (0.157)	11	4.0 (0.157)
6	2.0 (0.079)		

Fig. 3 Shim thickness chart

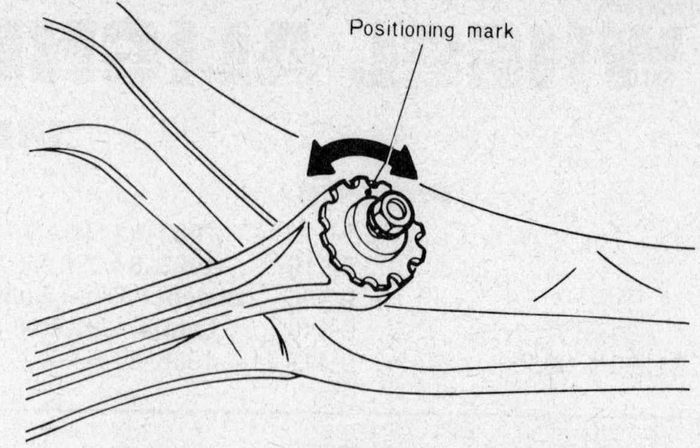

Fig. 4 Toe-in adjustment

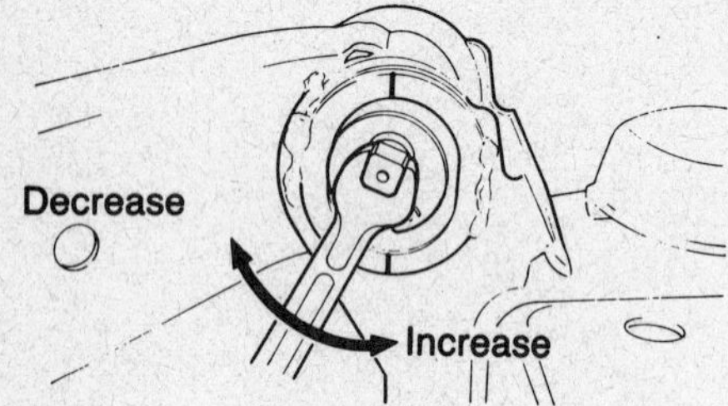

Fig. 5 Adjusting distance from subframe to lateral link ball joint. 1986–87 RX-7

REAR

Camber is not adjustable and is set to specifications during production. Whenever camber is moved out of specified angle, check all parts of rear suspension and body alignment. Repair or replace defective part(s) as required.

TOE-IN ADJUSTMENT

FRONT

1. Loosen left and right tie rod locknuts.
2. Turn both tie rods the same amount until specified adjustment is obtained. **Both tie rods have right hand threads.**
3. Torque tie rod lock nut to 25-29 ft. lbs. on GLC and 323 models or 51-58 ft. lbs. on 626, RX-7 and Pickup models.
4. If boot is twisted, loosen boot band and straighten.

REAR

1983–85 GLC Exc. Wagon

1. Loosen crossmember and lateral link assembly mounting bolt and adjust toe-in by turning spacer, **Fig. 4.**
2. Amount of toe-in adjusted by turning the spacer by one notch is approximately 0.1 inch.
3. After adjustment is completed, tighten bolt to 69-86 ft. lbs.

1983–87 626 & 1986–87 323

1. Loosen front lateral link inner attaching nut, then retorque nut to 52-63 ft. lbs.
2. Adjust toe-in by turning spacer, **Fig. 4.**
3. After adjustment is completed, torque attaching nut to 69-86 ft. lbs.

1986–87 RX-7

1. Turn the left and right adjusting cams by the same amount and adjust toe-in until specified value is obtained, **Fig. 5.**
2. To decrease the toe-in turn adjusting cam clockwise for the right arm or counterclockwise for the left arm.
3. To increase the toe-in, turn the adjusting cam counterclockwise for the right arm or clockwise for the left arm. Amount of toe-in change should be .09 inch for one wheel.

DISTANCE FROM SUBFRAME TO LATERAL LINK BALL JOINT

1986–87 RX-7

Measure the distance between the center of the subframe rubber mount and the center of the lateral link ball joint for both left and right of vehicle. If measurements obtained are within .2 inch or each other, distance is correct. If not, adjust as follows:

1. To increase the distance, turn adjusting cam as follows:
   a. Right arm—turn adjusting cam clockwise, **Fig. 5.**
   b. Left arm—turn adjusting cam counterclockwise, **Fig. 5.**
2. To decrease the distance, turn adjusting cam as follows:
   a. Right arm—turn adjusting cam counterclockwise, **Fig. 5.**
   b. Left arm—turn adjusting cam clockwise, **Fig. 5.** Amount of trailing arm movement is .07 inch.

KING PIN INCLINATION

King pin inclination is not adjustable and is set to specifications during production. Whenever king pin inclination is moved out of specified angle, check all parts of front suspension and body alignment. Repair or replace defective part(s) as required.

MERCEDES-BENZ (Germany)

INDEX OF SERVICE OPERATIONS

Model & Engine Identification Chart

Year	Vehicle Series	Vehicle Model	Engine Series
1983	123	240D	616
	123	300CD Turbo, 300D Turbo, 300TD Turbo	617
	126	300SD Turbo	617
	107	380SL	116
	126	380SEC, 380SEL	116
1984–85	201	190D 2.2	601
	201	190E 2.3	102
	123	300CD Turbo, 300D Turbo, 300TD Turbo	617
	126	300SD Turbo	617
	126	380SE	116
	107	380SL	116
	126	500SEC	117
	126	500SEL	117
1986–87	201	190D 2.5	—
	201	190E 2.3	—
	201	190E 2.3-16	—
	—	300E	—
	—300D Turbo	—	
	—	300SLD Turbo	—
	—	300TD Turbo	—
	126	420SEL	—
	126	560SEC	—
	126	560SEL	—
	107	560SL	—

General Engine Specifications

Year	Engine CID/cc	Engine Model	Bore and Stroke Inches (mm)	Compression Ratio	Maximum Brake HP @ RPM	Maximum Torque Ft. Lbs. @ RPM
1983	4-146.4/2399CC	616	3.58 x 3.64 (90.9 x 92.4)	21	65 @ 4200	97 @ 2400
	5-183/2998cc	617	3.58 x 3.64 (90.9 x 92.4)	21.5	①	②
	8-234.3/3839cc	116	3.46 x 3.11 (88 x 78.9)	8.3	155 @ 4750	196 @ 2750
1984	4-134.1/2197cc	601	3.43 x 3.64 (87 x 92.4)	22	72 @ 4200	96 @ 2800
	4-140.3/2299cc	102	3.76 x 3.16 (95.5 x 80.3)	8	113 @ 5000	133 @ 3500
	5-183/2998cc	617	3.58 x 3.64 (90.9 x 92.4)	21.5	①	②
	8-234.3/3839cc	116	3.46 x 3.11 (88 x 78.9)	8.3	155 @ 4750	196 @ 2750
	8-303.5/4974cc	117	—	8	184 @ 4500	247 @ 2000
1985	4-134.1/2197cc	601	3.43 x 3.64 (87 x 92.4)	22	72 @ 4200	96 @ 2800
	4-140.3/2299cc	102	3.76 x 3.16 (95.5 x 80.3)	8	120 @ 5000	136 @ 3500
	5-183/2998cc	617	3.58 x 3.64 (90.9 x 92.4)	21.5	①	②
	8-234.3/3839cc	116	3.46 x 3.11 (88 x 78.9)	—	—	—
	8-303.5/4974cc	117	—	8	184 @ 4500	247 @ 2000
1986	4-140.3/2299cc	—	3.76 x 3.16 (95.5 x 80.3)	8	121 @ 5000	136 @ 3500
1986–87	4-140.3/2299cc	—	3.76 x 3.16 (95.5 x 80.3)	9.7	167 @ 5800	162 @ 4750
1986–87	5-152.4/2497cc	—	3.43 x 3.31 (87 x 84)	22	93 @ 4600	122 @ 2800
1986–87	6-180.8/2962cc	—	3.48 x 3.16 (88.5 x 80.3)	9.2	177 @ 3200	188 @ 4400
1986	6-182.9/2997cc	—	3.43 x 3.31 (87 x 84)	22	③	④
1986–87	8-256.1/4196cc	—	3.62 x 3.10 (92 x 78.9)	9	201 @ 5200	228 @ 3600
1986–87	8-338.5/5547cc	—	3.80 x 3.73 (96.5 x 94.8)	9	238 @ 4800	287 @ 3500
1986–87	8-338.5/5547cc	—	3.80 x 3.73 (96.5 x 94.8)	9	227 @ 4750	279 @ 3250
1987	4-140.3/2299cc	—	3.76 x 3.16 (95.5 x 80.3)	9	130 @ 5100	146 @ 3500
	6-182.9/2997cc	—	3.43 x 3.31 (87 x 84)	22	143 @ 4600	195 @ 2400

Continued

GENERAL ENGINE SPECIFICATIONS—Continued

①—Exc. 300SD, 120 @ 4350; 300SD, 110 @ 4200.
②—Exc. 300SD, 170 @ 2400; 300SD, 168 @ 2400.
③—Exc. 300SDL Calif. models, 148 @ 4600; 300SDL Calif. models, 143 @ 4600.
④—Exc. 300SDL Calif. models, 201 @ 2400; 300SDL Calif. models, 195 @ 2400.

Alternator Specifications

Year	Model①	Rated Output
1983	K114V55A20	55
	N114V80A19	80
1984–87	K114V55A20	55
	K114V^{2}55A20	55
	K114V^{2}65A21	65
	N114V80A19	80

①—Bosch designation.

Starting Motor Identification

Year	Model
1983	GF12V1.5KW
	JF12V2.3KW
1984–87	EV12V2.2KW
	GF12V1.5KW
	JF12V2.3KW

①—Bosch designation.

Valve Specifications

Year	Engine	Valve Lash		Valve Angles		Valve Spring Installed Height	Valve Spring Pressure Lbs. @ In.	Stem Clearance		Stem Diameter, Standard	
		Int.	Exh.	Seat	Face			Intake	Exhaust	Intake	Exhaust
1983	4-146.4①	.004C	.010C	30	30	—	②	—	—	.3906-.3913	.3906-.3913
	5-182.9①	.004C	.012C	30	30	—	②	—	—	.3906-.3913	.3906-.3913
	8-234.3	Hydraulic		45	45	—	③	—	—	.3526-.3531	.3518-.3528
1984-87	4-134.1①	Hydraulic		45	45	—	159 @ 1.063	—	—	.3132-3138	.3522-.3528
	4-140.3	Hydraulic④		45	45	—	⑤	—	—	.3132-3128	.3519-.3528
	5-182.9①	.004C	.012C	30	30	—	②	—	—	.3906-3913	.3906-.3913
	8-234.3	Hydraulic		45	45	—	③	—	—	.3526-3531	.3518-.3528
	8-303.5	Hydraulic		45	45	—	③	—	—	.3526-.3531	.3518-.3528

—Not available.
①—Diesel engine.
②—Spring No. 1800530620, 106 @ 1,177; spring No. 6150530120, 126 @ 1.102.
③—Inner, 53 @ .846; outer, 196 @ 1.201.
④—Engines with mechanical lifters: intake, .006C; exhaust, .012C.
⑤—Engines with mechanical lifters, 175 @ 1.197; engines with hydraulic lifters, 187 @ 1.201.

Pistons, Rings, Pins, Crankshaft & Bearings Specifications

Year	Engine	Piston Clearance, Inch	Ring End Gap, Inch		Piston Pin Diameter Inch	Rod Bearings, Inch		Main Bearings, Inch	
			Comp.	Oil		Shaft Diameter	Bearing Clearance	Shaft Diameter	Bearing Clearance
1983	4-146.4①	.0007-.0015	.008	.010	1.023-1.224	2.0453-2.0457	.0012-.0029	2.7540-2.7543	.0012-.0029
	5-183①	.0017-.0025	⑤	.008	1.102-1.103	2.0453-2.0457	.0012-.0029	2.7540-2.7543	.0012-.0029
	8-234.3	.0003-.0007	.014	.010	.905-.906	③	.0012-.0027	2.5177-2.5183	.0016-.0035
1984-87	4-134.1①	.0007-.0017	.008	.008	1.062-1.063	1.8878-1.8884	.0012-.0029	2.815-2.2821	.0012-.0029
	4-140.3	.0006-.0016	④	.010	.944-.945	1.8880-1.8884	.0012-.0020	2.2815-2.2821	.0010-.0018
	5-183①	.0017-.0025	②	.008	1.102-1.103	2.0453-2.0457	.0012-.0029	2.7540-2.7543	.0012-.0029
	8-234.3	.0003-.0007	.014	.010	.905-.906	③	.0012-.0027	2.5177-2.5183	.0016-.0035
	8-303.5	.0003-.0007	.014	.010	.905-.906	③	.0012-.0027	2.5177-2.5183	.0016-.0035

—Not available.
①—Diesel engine.
②—Upper, .008 inch; lower, .006 inch.
③—Exc. engines 116.962 and 116.962 and 116.963, 2.0451-2.0459 inches; engines 116.962 and 116.963, 1.8876-1.8884 inches.
④—Exc. 1985 lower ring, .012 inches; 1985 lower ring, .010 inches.

Engine Tightening Specifications

Year	Engine	Spark Plugs or Glow Plugs Ft. Lbs.	Cylinder Head Bolts Ft. Lbs.①	Camshaft Bearing Caps Ft. Lbs.	Rocker Arm Mount Ft. Lbs.	Cylinder Head Cover Ft. Lbs.	Connecting Rod Cap Bolts Ft. Lbs.	Main Bearing Cap Bolts Ft. Lbs.	Flywheel to Crankshaft Bolts Ft. Lbs.	Crankshaft Front Bolt Ft. Lbs.
1983	4-146.4⑥	37	⑤	18	28	11	30-37③	66	22-30③	199-243
	5-183⑥	37	⑤	18	28	11	30-37③	66	22-30③	199-243
	8-234.3	18-22	②	37	—	2.2	30-37③	④	22-30③	199-243
1984-87	4-134.1⑥	15	18	18	—	7.4	22-26③	66	22-30③	277-302
	4-140.3	11	⑦	—	15	11	30-37③	66	22-30③	221
	5-183⑥	37	⑤	18	28	11	30-37③	66	22-30③	199-243
	8-234.3	18-22	②	37	—	2.2	30-37③	④	22-30③	199-243
	8-303.5	18-22	②	37	—	2.2	30-37③	④	22-30③	199-243

—Not available.
①—Coat all threads and contact area of bolts and washers with oil.
②—Torque bolts in steps indicated: Step 1 to 22 ft. lbs.; Step 2 to 44 ft. lbs., allow a setting period of 10 minutes and torque bolts to 44 ft. lbs.
③—After torquing bolts to specified torque, turn wrench in direction of tightening an additional 90–100°.
④—Studs to 22 ft. lbs., bolts, to 37 ft. lbs.
⑤—Hexagon socket cylinder head bolts, torque bolts in steps indicated: Step 1 to 52 ft. lbs.; Step 2 to 66 ft. lbs.; Step 3 to 74 ft. lbs. Twelve point socket cylinder head bolts, torque bolts in steps indicated: Step 1 to 29 ft. lbs; Step 2 to 52 ft. lbs.; Steps 3 and 4, turn bolts an additional 90°.
⑥—Diesel engine.
⑦—Torque bolts to 52 ft. lbs., then an additional 180° in two steps

Brake Specifications

Year	Model	Brake Caliper Piston Diameter		Master Cylinder Bore Diameter	Disc Brake Rotor Specifications					
					Nominal Thickness		Minimum Thickness		Lateral Runout	
		Front	Rear		Front	Rear	Front	Rear	Front	Rear
1983	240D	2.362	1.496	②	.4961	.3937	.4173	.3268	.0047	.0047
	300CD, D, TD Turbo	2.362	1.496	②	.4961	.3937	.4173	.3268	.0047	.0047
	300SD Turbo	2.362	1.496	②	.8661	.3937	.7638	.3268	.0047	.0047
	300SEC, SEL	2.362	1.496	②	.8661	.3937	.7638	.3268	.0047	.0047
	380SL	2.362	1.496	②	.8661	.3937	.7874	.3268	.0047	.0047
1984–87	190D 2.2	2.126	1.378	③	.4331	.3543	.3543	.2953	.0047	.0059
	190E 2.3	2.126	1.378	③	.4331	.3543	.3543	.2953	.0047	.0059
	300CD, D TD Turbo	2.362	①	②	.4961	.3937	.4173	.3268	.0047	.0047
	300SD Turbo	2.362	1.496	②	.8661	.3937	.7368	.3268	.0047	.0047
	380SE	2.362	1.496	②	.8661	.3937	.7638	.3268	.0047	.0047
	380SL	2.362	1.496	②	.8661	.3937	.7874	.3268	.0047	.0047
	500SEC	2.362	1.496	②	.8661	.3937	.7638	.3268	.0047	.0047
	500SEL	2.362	1.496	②	.8661	.3937	.7638	.3268	.0047	.0047

①—300CD, D, 1.496; 300TD, 1.654.
②—Stepped diameter master cylinder, front wheel brake, .9374"; rear wheel brake, .750".
③—Stepped diameter master cylinder, front wheel brake, .875"; rear wheel brake, .6875".

Wheel Alignment Specifications

Year	Model	Caster Angle, Degrees				Camber Angle, Degrees		Toe-In Inch
		Measured in Straight		Measured Over Lock				
		Limits	Desired	Limits	Desired	Limits	Desired	
1983	240D	+8 1/4 to +9 1/4	+8 3/4	+7 3/4 to +8 3/4	+8 1/4	−1/3 to +1/6	0	1/8
	300CD, D, TD Turbo	+8 1/4 to +9 1/4	+8 3/4	+7 3/4 to +8 3/4	+8 1/4	−1/3 to +1/6	0	1/8
	300SD Turbo	+9 1/4 to 10 1/4	+9 3/4	+8 3/4 to +9 3/4	+9 1/4	−1/6 to +1/6	0	2/3
	380SEC, SEL	+9 1/4 to 10 1/4	+9 3/4	+8 3/4 to +9 3/4	+9 1/4	−1/6 to +1/6	0	2/3
	380SL	+3 1/3 to +4	+3 2/3	+2 11/12 to +3 7/12	+31-4	−1/3 to +1/6	0	5/64
1984–87	190D 2.2	—	—	—	—	—	—	—
	190E 2.3	—	—	—	—	—	—	—
	300CD, D TD Turbo	+8 1/4 to +9 1/4	+8 3/4	+7 3/4 to +8 3/4	+8 1/4	−1/3 to +1/6	0	1/8
	300SD Turbo	+9 1/4 to 10 1/4	+9 3/4	+8 3/4 to +9 3/4	+9 1/4	−1/6 to +1/6	0	2/3
	380SE	—	—	—	—	—	—	—
	380SL	+3 1/4 to +4	+3 2/3	+2 11/12 to +3 7/12	+3 1/4	−1/3 to +1/6	0	5/64
	500SEC	—	—	—	—	—	—	—
	500SEL	—	—	—	—	—	—	—

Cooling System & Capacity Data

Year	Model	Cooling System Capacity Qts.	Radiator Cap Relief Pressure, Lbs.	Thermo. Opening Temp. °F	Fuel Tank, Gals.	Engine Oil Refill Qts. ①	Transmission Oil			Rear Axle Oil, Pts.
							Manual Trans. Pts.		Auto. Trans. Qts.	
							4 Speed	5 Speed		
1983	240D	10.6	14	176	24.1②	6.9	3.4	—	5.1	2.1
	300CD, D, TD Turbo	13.2	14	176	②④	7.9	—	—	6.6	2.1
	300SD Turbo	13.2	14	176	23.6②	8	—	—	6.6	2.1
	380SEC, SEL	13.2	14	183	27.1②	9	—	—	6.6	2.7
	380SL	13.2	14	183	25.5②	8.8	—	—	③	2.7
1984–85	190D 2.2	9	⑥	185	16.5②	6.9	—	3.2	6.2	1.5
	190E 2.3	9	⑤	189	16.5②	4.8	—	3.2	6.2	1.5
	300CD, D, TD Turbo	13.2	14	176	②④	7.9	—	—	6.6	2.1
	300SD Turbo	13.2	14	176	23.6②	8	—	—	6.6	2.1
	380SE	13.2	14	183	27.1②	8.5	—	—	6.6	2.7
	380SL	13.2	14	183	25.5②	8.8	—	—	③	2.7
	500SEC	13.7	14	183	27.1②	8.5	—	—	8.1	2.7
	500SEL	13.7	14	183	27.1②	8.5	—	—	8.1	2.7
1986–87	190D 2.5	8.5	—	—	16.3②	—	—	—	—	—
	190E 2.4	9	—	—	16.3②	—	—	—	—	—
	190E 2.3-16	8.5	—	—	21②	—	—	—	—	—
	300E	8.5	—	—	20.9②	—	—	—	—	—
	300D Turbo	10.6	—	—	20.9②	—	—	—	6.6	2.1
	300SDL Turbo	10.6	—	—	27.1②	—	—	—	—	—
	420SEL	13.7	—	—	27.1②	—	—	—	—	—
	560SEC	13.7	—	—	27.1②	—	—	—	—	—
	560SEL	13.7	—	—	27.1②	—	—	—	—	—
	560SL	13.7	—	—	25.5②	—	—	—	—	—

—Not available.
①—Including filter.
②—Includes reserve.
③—Trans. model W3A040, 8.5; trans. model W4A040, 6.5.
④—300CD, D, 23.9; 300TD, 21.4.
⑤—Code 100, 14; code 120, 17.
⑥—New, 17; used, 14.

ELECTRICAL SECTION

INDEX

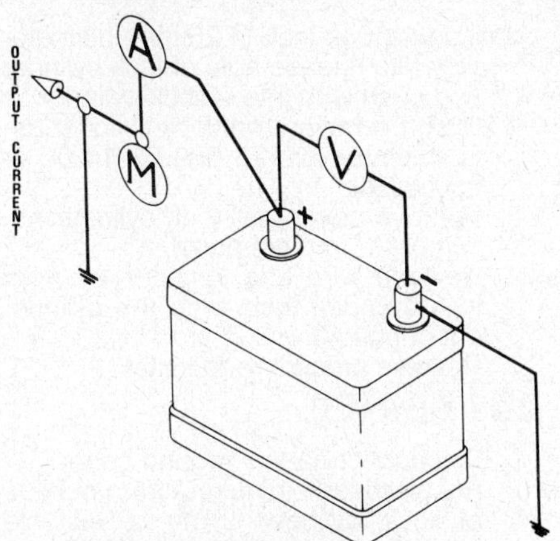

Fig. 1 Alternator test connections

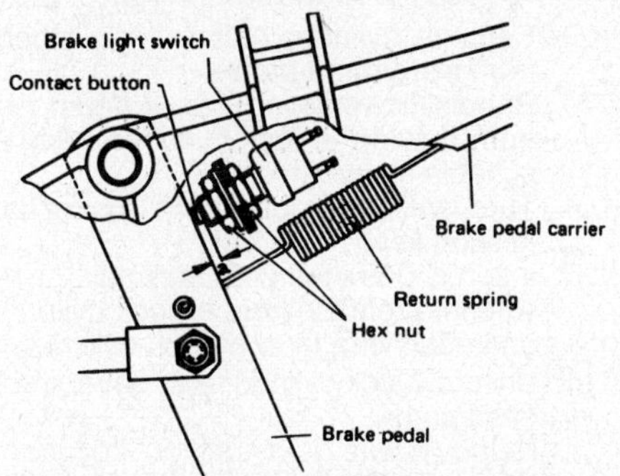

Fig. 2 Brake light switch adjustment. 107 & 123 Series (126 Series similar)

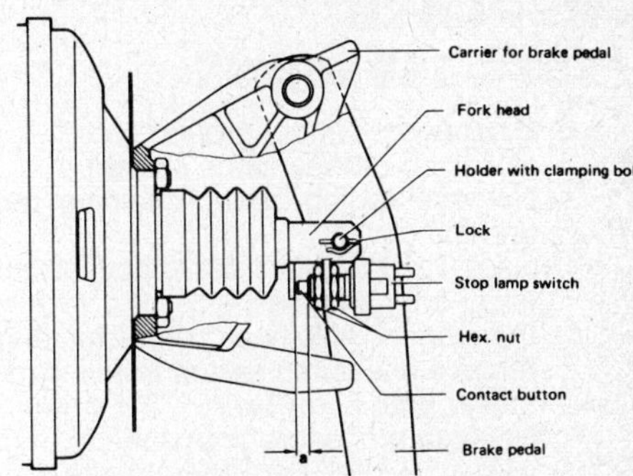

Fig. 3 Brake light switch adjustment. 201 Series

ALTERNATOR IN-VEHICLE TESTING

1. Ensure all battery and alternator connections are satisfactory and drive belt and battery are in good condition.
2. Connect voltmeter across battery terminals and run engine at 3000 RPM with no additional load placed on electrical system. Voltmeter should indicate 13-14.5 volts after two minutes of operation.
3. With voltmeter still connected across battery terminals, connect ammeter to charging circuit as shown in **Fig. 1.**
4. Run engine at 2400-2550 RPM with all electrical accessories turned on to ensure maximum charging current is reached. Also, ensure regulated voltage does not drop below 12.7 volts. **After engine has been started, the ammeter reading will gradually decrease as the battery approaches a fully charged condition. Read the ammeter indication at its maximum value while increasing engine RPM.**

STARTER

REPLACE

201 SERIES W/DIESEL ENGINE

1. Disconnect battery ground cable.
2. Remove air cleaner assembly.
3. Remove rear sound insulator, then disconnect starter wiring.
4. Remove starter attaching bolts and the starter.
5. Reverse procedure to install.

201 SERIES W/GASOLINE ENGINE

1. Disconnect battery ground cable.
2. Remove air cleaner assembly, then the intake manifold support.
3. Disconnect spring between throttle valve housing and intake manifold support.
4. On models equipped with cruise control, remove actuator from stud to allow removal of the starter.
5. On all models, remove starter support bracket from starter and engine block.
6. Remove starter-to-transmission attaching bolts, then separate drag link from pitman arm.
7. Remove battery positive cable and disconnect starter wiring from junction box.
8. Turn steering wheel fully to the right and unfasten starter.
9. Disconnect wiring from starter and remove starter from vehicle.
10. Reverse procedure to install.

BRAKE LIGHT SWITCH

ADJUST

107, 123 & 126 SERIES

1. Ensure dimension "a", **Fig. 2,** measures .236-.315 inch (6-8 mm).
2. If dimension "a" is not within specification, adjust by turning the two hex nuts, **Fig. 2,** as necessary. **When properly adjusted, the brake light should illuminate with a pedal travel of .197-.591 inch (5-15 mm) travel.**

201 SERIES

1. Ensure brake pedal travel, dimension "a", in **Fig. 3,** measures .118-.787 inch (3-20 mm) before center of pedal plate touches switch contact button.
2. If pedal travel is not within specifications, adjust by turning the two hex nuts, **Fig. 3,** as necessary.

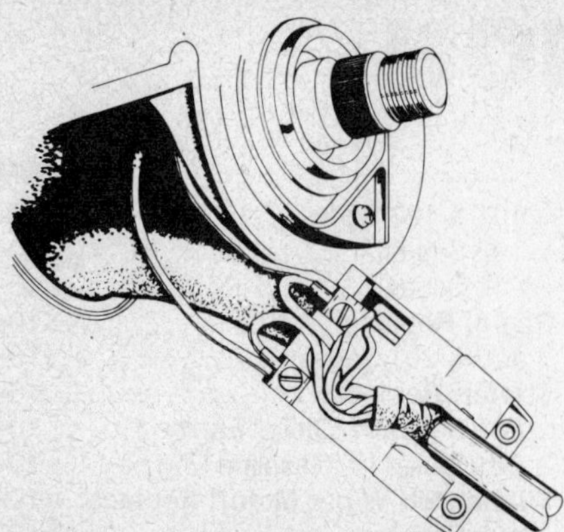

Fig. 4 Combination switch replacement. 107 Series

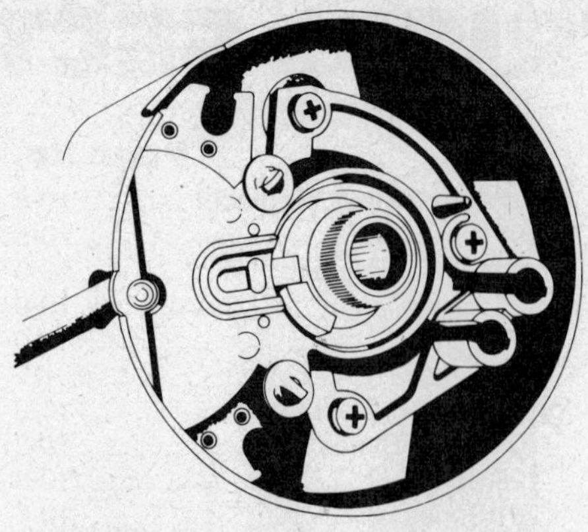

Fig. 5 Combination switch replacement. 126 Series

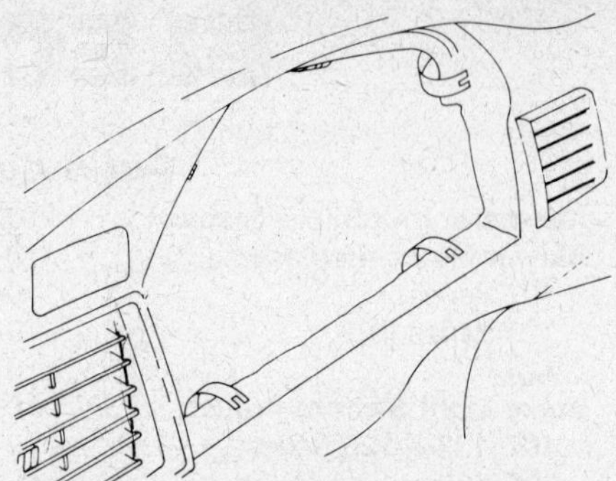

Fig. 6 Instrument cluster replacement. 126 & 201 Series

HEADLAMP SWITCH
REPLACE
107 & 123 SERIES

1. Disconnect battery ground cable.
2. Pull knob off headlamp switch.
3. Remove switch cover retaining nut and the cover.
4. Remove instrument panel cover from lower left hand side.
5. Disconnect electrical connector and remove headlamp switch from instrument panel.
6. Reverse procedure to install.

COMBINATION SWITCH
REPLACE
107 SERIES

The steering wheel does not have to be removed to replace the combination switch.

1. Disconnect battery ground cable.
2. Remove rubber sleeve from combination switch.
3. Remove two combination switch attaching screws.
4. Pull combination switch out slightly, then disconnect the two screw type and one plug type electrical connectors and remove switch from vehicle, **Fig. 4.**
5. Reverse procedure to install.

126 SERIES

1. Disconnect battery ground cable.
2. Remove steering wheel.
3. Remove instrument panel lower cover.
4. Remove three combination switch attaching screws, **Fig. 5.**
5. Disconnect 14 terminal electrical connector under instrument panel.
6. Remove combination switch from vehicle.
7. Reverse procedure to install.

IGNITION LOCK
REPLACE
107 & 123 SERIES
Models w/Screw Type Lock Cover

1. Disconnect battery ground cable.
2. Remove cylinder collar, if equipped, from instrument panel.
3. Pry plastic retaining ring, if equipped, from outside of lock cylinder using a suitable screwdriver.
4. Turn ignition to position "1" using the ignition key.
5. Insert a .049 inch (1.25 mm) diameter wire into release hole of lock cylinder and push wire in to unlock cylinder.
6. Unscrew lock cylinder and cover from dash panel.
7. Remove wire and ignition key from lock cylinder, then slide the cylinder out of cover.
8. Reverse procedure to install.

Models w/Chrome Plated Plug Type Lock Cover

1. Disconnect battery ground cable.
2. Turn ignition to position "1" using the ignition key.
3. Lift cover up to bottom edge of key, then turn key to "0" position and remove key and cover. **If necessary, pull cover to bottom edge of key using a .039 inch (1 mm) diameter wire hooked between ring and cover.**
4. Insert key back into lock cylinder and turn to the "1" position.
5. Turn key against detent to the right and remove lock cylinder from dash panel.
6. Reverse procedure to install.

Models w/Plastic Plug Type Lock Cover

1. Disconnect battery ground cable.
2. Remove cylinder collar, if equipped, from instrument panel.
3. Pull cover off lock cylinder using a .039 inch (1 mm) diameter piece of wire bent to an approximately .059 inch (1.5 mm) angle at one end.
4. Turn ignition to position "1" using the ignition key.
5. Turn key against detent to the right and remove lock cylinder from dash panel
6. Reverse procedure to install.

126 SERIES

1. Disconnect battery ground cable.
2. Turn ignition to position "1" using the ignition key.
3. Insert a .049 inch (1.25 mm) diameter wire into release hole of lock cylinder and push wire into unlock cylinder.
4. Unscrew cover from lock cylinder using sleeve No. 126 589 07 14 00 or equivalent.
5. Remove cover and lock cylinder assembly from dash panel.
6. Remove wire and ignition key from lock cylinder, then slide the cylinder out of cover.
7. Reverse procedure to install.

201 SERIES

1. Disconnect battery ground cable.
2. Pry plastic retaining ring from outside of lock cylinder using a suitable screwdriver.
3. Turn ignition to position "1" using the ignition key.
4. Insert both ends of a .078 inch (2 mm) diameter wire into release holes of lock cylinder and push wire in to unlock cylinder.
5. Remove lock cylinder and cover as an assembly from dash panel.
6. Remove wire and ignition key from lock cylinder, then slide the cylinder out of cover.
7. Reverse procedure to install.

INSTRUMENT CLUSTER
REPLACE
107 & 123 SERIES

1. Disconnect battery ground cable.
2. Remove steering wheel.
3. Remove rubber molding securing instrument cluster in dash.
4. Pull instrument cluster out slightly and disconnect speedometer cable, all electrical connectors and oil pressure gauge line from rear of cluster.
5. Remove instrument cluster from vehicle.
6. Reverse procedure to install.

126 SERIES

1. Disconnect battery ground cable.
2. Remove steering wheel.
3. Insert pulling hook (tool No. 125 589 03 33 00), curved end down, between instrument cluster and instrument panel.

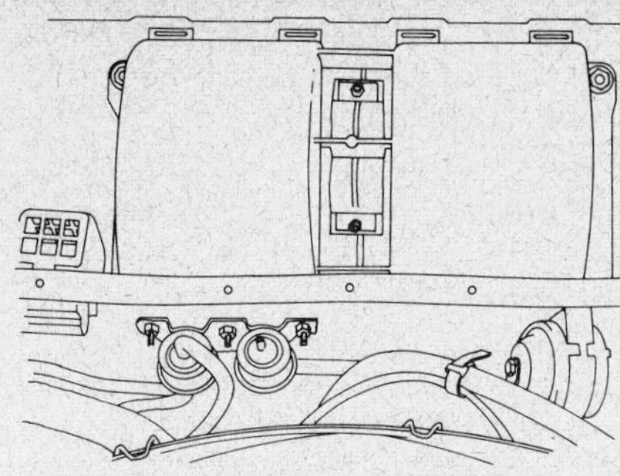

Fig. 7 Blower motor replacement. 107 Series

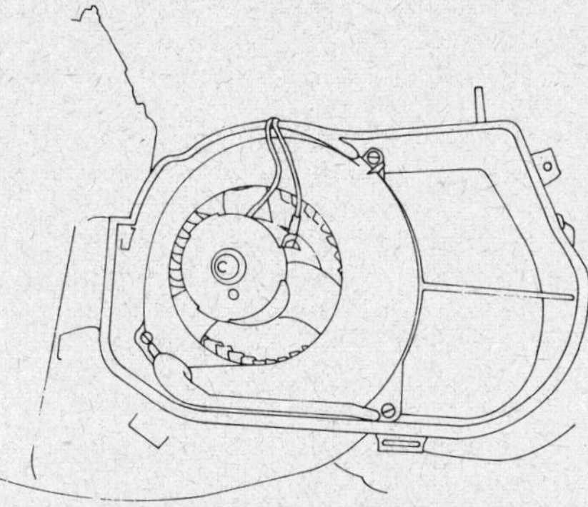

Fig. 9 Blower motor replacement. 126 Series

4. Turn tool 1/4 turn counterclockwise, then pull tool out until it rests against recess on instrument cluster.
5. Release instrument cluster from holder using the pulling hook. **The instrument cluster is secured by five spring clips on the instrument panel, Fig. 6.**
6. Disconnect speedometer cable, all electrical connectors and the oil gauge pressure line from rear of cluster, then remove cluster from vehicle.
7. Reverse procedure to install.

201 SERIES

1. Disconnect battery ground cable.
2. Remove instrument panel cover from lower left hand side.
3. Disconnect flexible hose from below left side duct.
4. Disconnect speedometer cable from rear of cluster.
5. Remove five spring clips securing instrument cluster, then push cluster out from rear, **Fig. 6.**
6. Disconnect all electrical connectors and the oil pressure gauge line from rear of cluster, then remove cluster from vehicle.
7. Reverse procedure to install.

RADIO

REPLACE

126 & 201 SERIES

1. Disconnect battery ground cable.
2. Open ashtray and remove two radio bracket attaching screws.
3. Disconnect electrical connectors and antenna lead from back of radio.
4. Remove radio through front of dash panel.
5. Reverse procedure to install.

WINDSHIELD WIPER MOTOR

REPLACE

123 SERIES

1. Disconnect battery ground cable.
2. Remove both right and left wiper arms.
3. Remove right side air intake grille.
4. Remove transmission-to-grille caps and bearing nuts, then the left side air intake grille.
5. Remove wiper assembly cover plate center cap, rivets and screws, then the cover plate.
6. Disconnect wiper linkage from wiper motor.
7. Remove water drain from right hand bearing shaft.
8. Disconnect wiper motor electrical connector in engine compartment.
9. Unfasten plug on electrical connector, then pull wiring through firewall.
10. Remove wiper motor attaching screws and the wiper motor.
11. Reverse procedure to install.

126 SERIES

1. Disconnect battery ground cable.
2. Remove air intake grille, then the three wiper housing attaching screws.
3. Disconnect front and rear electrical connectors from wiper motor.
4. Remove wiper motor and linkage as an assembly, then unfasten motor from linkage.
5. Reverse procedure to install.

201 SERIES

1. Disconnect battery ground cable.
2. Remove air intake grille, then the wiper assembly attaching screws.
3. Remove fuse box cover, then unfasten fuse box and disconnect wiper motor connector from rear of box.
4. Remove complete wiper system assembly from vehicle.
5. Remove wiper motor from wiper assembly.
6. Reverse procedure to install.

BLOWER MOTOR

REPLACE

107 SERIES

1. Disconnect battery ground cable.
2. Remove blower motor cover attaching screws and the cover.
3. Remove blower motor attaching nuts.
4. Disconnect blower motor resistor electrical connector from firewall, then remove the resistor.
5. Remove blower motor, **Fig. 7.**
6. Reverse procedure to install.

123 SERIES

1. Disconnect battery ground cable.
2. Remove lower right hand instrument panel cover.

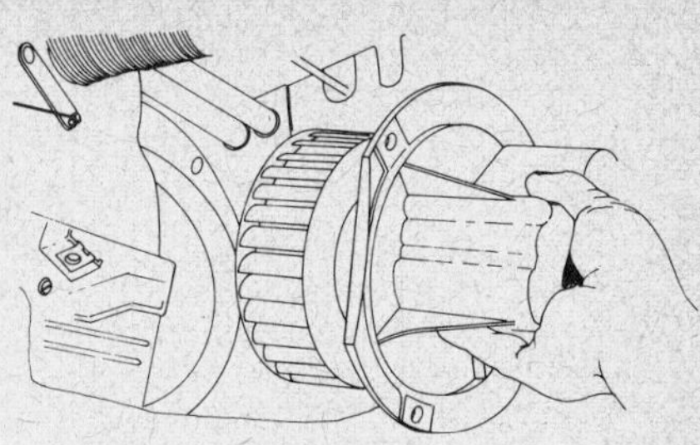

Fig. 8 Blower motor replacement. 123 Series

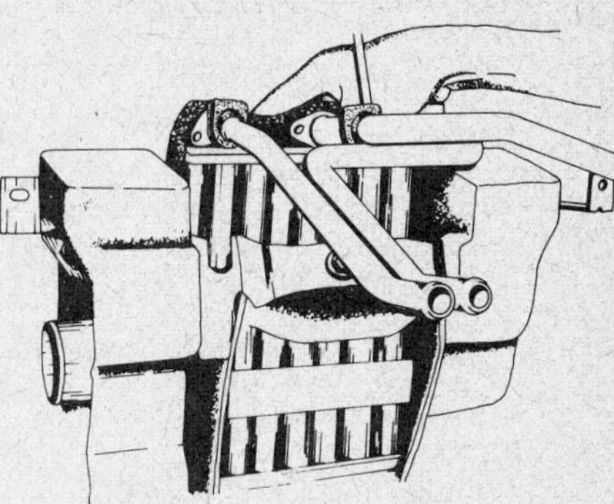

Fig. 10 Heater core replacement (Typical)

3. Disconnect electrical connector from blower motor.
4. Remove contact plate screw, then lift the plate and disconnect blower motor resistor wires.
5. Remove blower motor attaching screws and the blower motor, **Fig. 8.**
6. Reverse procedures to install.

126 SERIES

1. Disconnect battery ground cable.
2. Remove lower right hand instrument panel cover.
3. Remove blower motor cover attaching screws and the cover.
4. Disconnect blower motor electrical from blower housing.
5. Remove blower motor attaching bolts and the blower motor, **Fig. 9.**
6. Reverse procedures to install.

HEATER CORE

REPLACE

107 SERIES

1. Disconnect battery ground cable.
2. Drain approximately 3 quarts of coolant from the cooling system.
3. Remove both left and right air intake grilles.
4. Disconnect heater hose from heater case.
5. Remove steering wheel.
6. Remove both front seats and floor mats.
7. Remove ashtray with bracket.
8. Remove shift lever cover attaching screws and the cover.
9. Remove both right and left instrument panel lower covers.

10. Remove carpet attaching screws and loosen carpet on center console.
11. Remove center console screws from firewall, then pull out heater control lever.
12. Pry control lever moldings out of console using a plastic wedge.
13. Remove center console front cover, then the radio assembly.
14. Remove remaining center console attaching screws, then disconnect all cables from the console.
15. On models equipped with automatic transmission, loosen gate plate on floor shift.
16. On all models, remove center console from vehicle.
17. Remove rear view mirror from passenger compartment.
18. Loosen steering column shroud on crossmember and foot plate.
19. Remove glove box, then the instrument cluster.
20. Pull air duct for center nozzles from heater case.
21. Disconnect air vent control linkage from flap.
22. Disconnect flexible air hose from both sides of lower air duct.
23. Disconnect control cable from flap in air duct and remove the retaining duct.
24. Loosen rotary light switch on instrument panel.
25. Remove knob and rubber disc from parking brake release lever.
26. Disconnect rear window defogger switch electrical connector.
27. Remove both right and left side window moldings from windshield.
28. Remove two upper retaining bolts from heater case center support.
29. Remove remaining instrument panel retaining nuts and screws.
30. Bend upper right hand side of instrument panel downward and remove panel assembly from vehicle.
31. Disconnect electrical connector, then remove heater case center support.
32. Remove both right and left side air ducts.
33. Remove support between center air duct and transmission tunnel.
34. Loosen nut on both connecting levers, then disconnect the levers from shaft.
35. Remove four clamps from front and rear sides of heater case.
36. Disconnect all electrical connectors from heater case.
37. Pull center duct and control levers rearward, or to the right on models with automatic transmission.
38. Loosen cable harness clamps from heater on heater case crossmember.
39. Remove electronic fuel injection control unit.
40. Remove both upper heater case attaching nuts, then pull case back until heater hoses are disconnected from firewall.
41. Remove heater case from right side under the crossmember.
42. Remove retaining clips and shims from front of heater case.
43. Remove heater case front cover, then lift the heater core from case, **Fig. 10.**
44. Reverse procedure to install.

123 SERIES

1. Disconnect battery ground cable.
2. Remove both front floor mats.
3. Remove switches or cover plates from both sides of center console cover to provide access to cover attaching screws.
4. Remove center console cover attaching screws and the cover.
5. Remove gearshift lever cover, then the radio assembly.
6. Pull off control knobs from heater and blower controls and vent lever.
7. Remove retaining nuts from control shafts.
8. Remove cover plate from center console.
9. Remove center console attaching bolts and the console.
10. Remove both right and left instrument panel lower covers.
11. Push drivers seat to the rearmost position.
12. Drain approximately 2 quarts of coolant from the cooling system.
13. Disconnect heater hoses from heater case.
14. Remove glove box, then disconnect glove box light electrical connectors.
15. Remove rear compartment heater air duct attaching screws from both sides.
16. Remove air ducts from transmission tunnel.
17. Disconnect flexible air hoses from heater case.
18. Disconnect connecting duct between heater case and center nozzles.
19. Disconnect control lever from fresh air flap.
20. Unfasten heater case support brace from transmission tunnel.
21. Remove heater case-to-instrument panel attaching screw.
22. Remove plug, then open clamps on heater case.
23. Disconnect cable between heater control unit and water valve.
24. Disconnect cable between blower switch and main air flap.
25. Remove attaching nut from upper right hand heater case bracket.
26. Disconnect ignition switch electrical connectors.
27. Remove attaching nut from upper left hand heater case bracket.
28. Remove both screws from lower case bracket, then close the fresh air flap.
29. Lower heater case to rest on transmission tunnel, then pull case rearward until heater hoses are disconnected from firewall.
30. Remove heater case assembly from vehicle.
31. Remove heater case front cover attaching screws and clamps, then the cover.
32. Slide right and left clamps to bottom of heater case and remove the clamps.
33. Remove both rubber seals from water pipes, then lift heater core from heater case, **Fig. 10.**
34. Reverse procedure to install.

126 SERIES

1. Disconnect battery ground cable.
2. Remove heater case assembly.
3. Remove center air outlet cover retaining clips and the cover from heater case.
4. Disconnect heater control cable and place heater vents in the open position.
5. Remove retaining bracket from evaporator housing.
6. Remove heater core bracket and the heater core from case, **Fig. 10.**
7. Reverse procedure to install.

102 GASOLINE ENGINE SECTION

INDEX

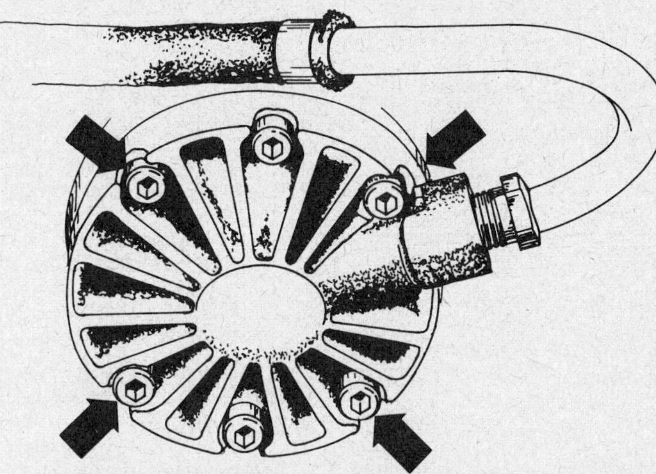

Fig. 1 Automatic level control oil pump bolt location

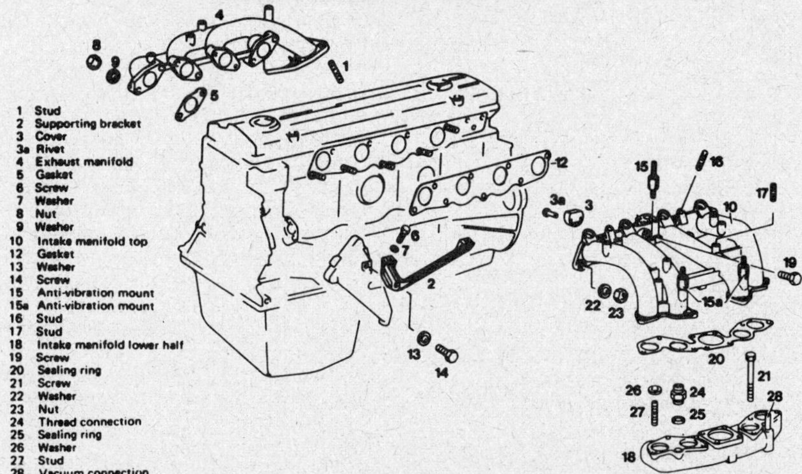

Fig. 2 Intake & exhaust manifold replacement

ENGINE

REPLACE

The engine and transmission are removed as an assembly.

1. Lift hood to a 90 degree angle and engage left hand locking lever.
2. Disconnect battery cables and position aside. **When disconnecting battery positive cable, also remove rubber protective strip from fire wall.**
3. Drain cooling system.
4. On models equipped with automatic transmission, disconnect oil cooler lines from radiator.
5. On all models, disconnect upper and lower coolant hoses from radiator.
6. Disconnect fan shroud attaching clips and position over fan, then remove radiator.
7. On models equipped with A/C, drain refrigerant from system, then disconnect and cap refrigerant lines from compressor.
8. On models equipped with automatic level control, unfasten pressure oil pump by removing bolts indicated by arrows, **Fig. 1**, then position pump aside with oil lines connected.
9. On all models, drain fluid from power steering pump tank, then disconnect hoses from power steering pump.
10. Disconnect accelerator linkage, then all electric, coolant, oil, fuel and vacuum lines leading to the engine.
11. Remove screws securing test socket to holder, then disconnect TDC transmitter wire from test socket.
12. Remove engine damper attaching screws, then the damper.
13. On models equipped with automatic transmission, remove engine stop adjusting bolt, bracket bolts and stop.
14. On all models, disconnect speedometer cable holding strap from link. then disconnect engine ground.
15. Disconnect propeller shaft from transmission and slide back as far as possible.
16. Disconnect exhaust pipe from exhaust manifold.
17. Remove front exhaust side support attaching nuts and bolts and swivel the support downward.
18. Disconnect speedometer cable from transmission. **Cap speedometer cable bore in transmission to prevent entry of dirt.**
19. Disconnect, then cap hydraulic line between clutch slave cylinder and master cylinder.
20. Label, then disconnect transmission shift rods from shift levers.
21. Install suitable engine lifting equipment to engine lifting points.
22. Remove rear engine mount and carrier.
23. Remove engine carrier attaching bolts from below both front engine mounts.
24. Raise engine and transmission at approximately a 45° angle and remove assembly from vehicle.
25. Reverse procedure to install.

INTAKE MANIFOLD

REPLACE

1. Disconnect battery ground cable.
2. Remove air cleaner assembly, then disconnect all fuel lines from fuel distributor and injectors.

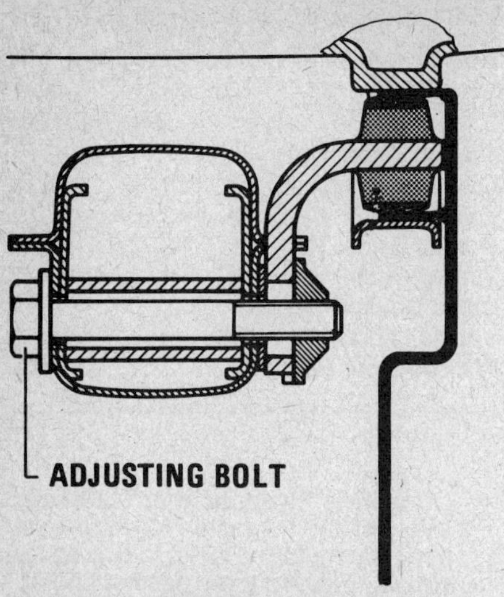

Fig. 3 Front engine stop adjustment

3. Remove regulator holder, then loosen hose clamp on rubber sleeve between throttle valve housing and air guide housing.
4. Remove rubber insulator nuts, then disconnect electrical connectors from mixture controller and air guide housing.
5. Remove mixture controller and air guide housing together with the idle speed air hose.
6. Disconnect two hoses from idle speed air distributor.
7. Remove injector holders, then disconnect return spring and linkages from throttle body.
8. Disconnect all remaining electrical connectors, vacuum lines, coolant lines and linkages from intake manifold.
9. Remove intake manifold support bracket.
10. Remove intake manifold attaching bolts and the manifold, **Fig. 2.**
11. Reverse procedure to install.

EXHAUST MANIFOLD REPLACE

1. Disconnect exhaust pipe from exhaust manifold.
2. Remove exhaust manifold attaching nuts and the manifold, **Fig. 2.**
3. Reverse procedure to install, using a new gasket.

FRONT ENGINE STOP SERVICE

The engine stop, located between the oil pan and crossmember, is not used on models equipped with manual transmission.

REPLACEMENT

1. Turn steering wheel fully to either side.
2. Remove lower engine cover.
3. Remove engine stop adjusting bolt, attaching bolts and clamp, then the stop attaching bolt.
4. Reverse procedure to install. Torque attaching bolts to 18 ft. lbs. (25 Nm) and the adjusting bolt to 96 ft. lbs. (130 Nm).

ADJUSTMENT

1. Turn steering wheel fully to either side.
2. Completely back out adjusting bolt, **Fig. 3,** then break engine stop free from crossmember.
3. Completely back out adjusting bolt on rear engine mount.
4. Insert adjusting gauge No. 201589042300 into the stop, then manually shake engine from side to side.
5. Torque adjusting bolt on rear engine mount to 22 ft. lbs. (30 Nm) and adjusting bolt on the stop to 96 ft. lbs. (130 Nm).
6. Remove adjusting gauge from engine stop.

CYLINDER HEAD REPLACE

The engine must be cold when removing the cylinder head.

1. Disconnect battery ground cable.
2. Lift hood to a 90° angle and engage left hand locking lever.
3. Remove air cleaner assembly, then drain cooling system.
4. On models equipped with automatic level control, unfasten pressure oil pump by removing bolts indicated by arrows, **Fig. 1,** then position pump aside with oil lines connected.
5. On all models, disconnect accelerator linkage and all fuel, coolant, vacuum and electric lines necessary for cylinder head removal.
6. Remove intake manifold support bracket attaching nuts or bolts.
7. Remove oil dipstick tube from cylinder head, then the dipstick.
8. On models equipped with A/C, remove refrigerant line brackets from cylinder head.
9. On models equipped with automatic transmission, remove transmission oil dipstick tube from cylinder head.
10. On all models, remove alternator drive belt, then position alternator and aside.
11. Disconnect exhaust pipe from exhaust manifold.
12. Remove cylinder head cover attaching bolts and the cover.
13. Turn crankshaft in normal direction of rotation until No. 1 piston is at TDC of compression stroke.
14. Carefully remove cap, seal and compression spring from chain tensioner.
15. Mark relationship between camshaft sprocket and timing chain for assembly reference.
16. Remove camshaft sprocket attaching bolts and the sprocket. **On models equipped with automatic level control, the drive sleeve for the pressure oil pump must also be removed from the camshaft.**
17. Remove slide rail from cylinder head.
18. Remove cylinder head bolt in reverse sequence of tightening, **Fig. 4.**
19. Remove M8 bolts from end of cylinder head, then lift head from engine.
20. Reverse procedure to install, noting the following:
    a. Use a new gasket when installing the cylinder head.
    b. Measure length "L" of cylinder head bolts, **Fig. 5,** prior to installation. If length exceeds 4.803 inches (122 mm), the bolts must be replaced.
    c. Install camshaft sprocket with wide flange facing camshaft. Torque sprocket bolt to 59 ft. lbs. (80 Nm).
    d. Ensure valve timing marks are properly aligned.

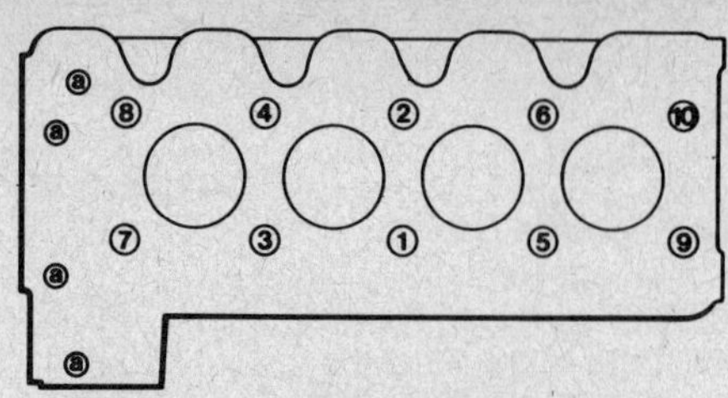

Fig. 4 Cylinder head bolt tightening sequence

ROCKER ARMS REPLACE

1. Remove air cleaner assembly, then the cylinder head cover.
2. Disconnect electrical connectors from ignition distributor, then turn crankshaft in normal direction of rotation until No. 1 piston is at TDC of compression stroke.
3. Mark relationship between camshaft sprocket and timing chain for assembly reference.
4. Carefully remove cap, seal and compression spring from chain tensioner.
5. On models equipped with automatic level control, remove pressure oil pump by loosening bolts indicated by arrows, **Fig. 1,** then position pump aside with oil lines connected.
6. Remove camshaft sprocket attaching bolt and sprocket. **On models equipped with automatic level control, the drive sleeve for the pressure oil pump must also be removed from camshaft.**
7. Fully back out all valve adjusting screws, then disconnect oil line from cylinder head.
8. Remove rocker arm bearing bracket attaching bolts and the brackets.
9. On models equipped with hydraulic valve lifters, remove ball sockets.
10. On all models, remove rocker arm shafts and the rocker arms from brackets.
11. Reverse procedure to install, noting the following:
    a. Torque cylinder head oil line attaching bolts to 15 ft. lbs. (21 Nm) in a crisscross pattern.
    b. Install rocker arm bearing brackets so that oil line mountings face rearward, and code numbers on brackets are at the right and aligned with

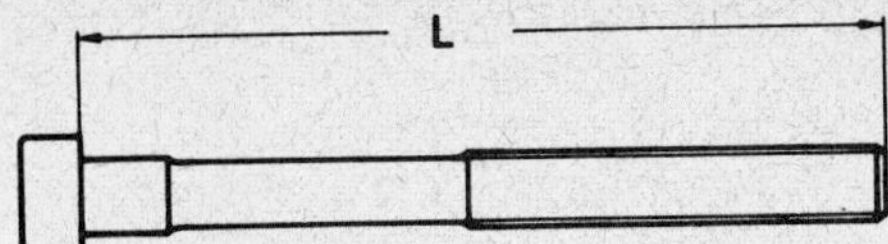

Fig. 5 Measuring cylinder head bolt length

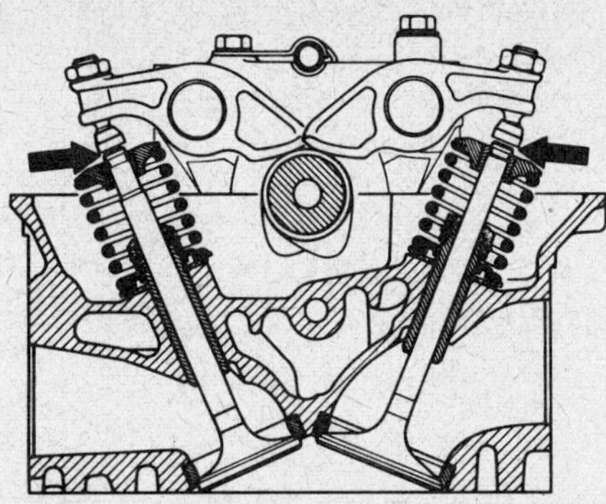

Fig. 6 Checking intake & exhaust valve clearance

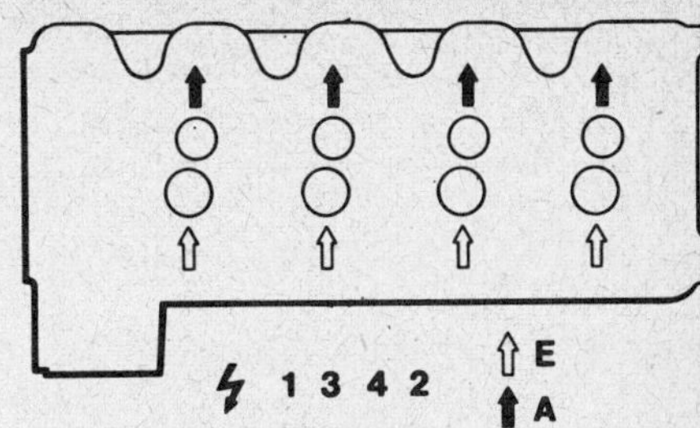

Fig. 7 Intake & exhaust valve arrangement

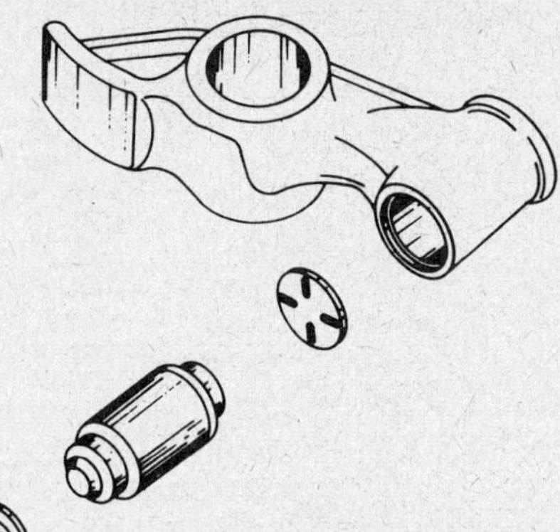

Fig. 8 Hydraulic valve lifter replacement

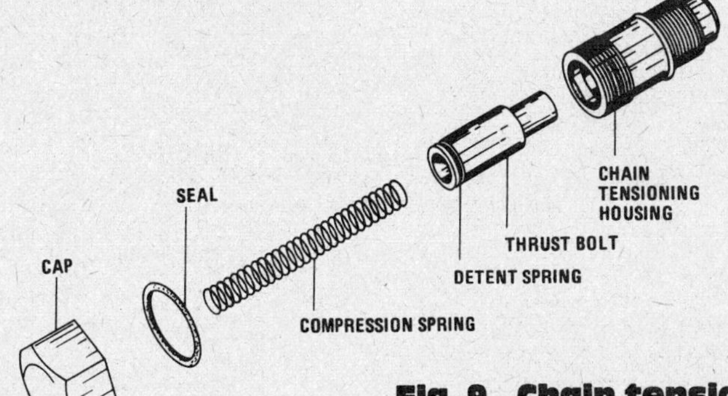

Fig. 9 Chain tensioner exploded view

number cast on cylinder head.

c. On models equipped with hydraulic valve lifters, install bearing bracket No. 1 first, then the camshaft sprocket and brackets No. 3, 4 and 2 in that order.
d. Install camshaft sprocket with wide flange facing camshaft. Torque sprocket bolt to 59 ft. lbs. (80 Nm).
e. Torque chain tensioner closing nut to 52 ft. lbs. (70 Nm).
f. On models equipped with automatic level control, torque pressure oil pump bolts to 10 ft. lbs. (13 Nm).
g. Ensure valve timing marks are properly aligned.

VALVES

ADJUST

Engines equipped with hydraulic valve lifters require no valve adjustment. When checking valve clearances, the engine may be rotated either manually or with a remote starter switch only after the distributor wiring has been disconnected. When rotating engine manually, do not crank in reverse (opposite normal direction of rotation), or by the camshaft sprocket bolt or serious engine damage will result.

1. Remove air cleaner assembly, then the cylinder head cover.
2. Measure valve clearance between end of valve stem and ball socket of adjusting screw, **Fig. 6.** To adjust valve clearance, loosen adjusting screw locknut. Turn adjusting screw, as necessary, and torque locknut to 15 ft. lbs. (20 Nm). **Refer to Fig. 7** for valve arrangement. Arrow marked E, indicates intake. Arrow marked A, indicates exhaust.

HYDRAULIC VALVE LIFTERS

REPLACE

1. Remove air cleaner assembly, then the cylinder head cover.
2. Remove rocker arm bearing bracket, then drive valve lifter out of rocker arm, **Fig. 8.**
3. Fill new valve lifter with clean engine oil. Work plunger up and down and refill.
4. Install new lifter with original disc up to stop on circlip in rocker arm.
5. Install rocker arm bearing bracket, ball socket, cylinder cover and air cleaner.

VALVE GUIDES

REPLACE

1. Clean valve guides and measure with .315 inch (8 mm) check plug No. 102589002300 for intake valves and .354 inch (9 mm) check plug No. 117589032300 for exhaust valves. If "no-go" end of plug can be inserted, remove valve guide with .315 inch (8 mm) knock-out plug No. 102589061500 for intake valves or .354 inch (9 mm) knock-out plug No. 110589021500 for exhaust valves.
2. If oversize valve guides must be installed, hone the bore with the applicable hand reamers and broaches:
   a. For first repair stage, intake and exhaust, .553 inch (14.035 mm) - 110589035300.
   b. For second repair stage, intake and exhaust, .559 inch (14.2 mm) - 115589005300 (broach) and 102589026300 (guide sleeve-intake) or 102589006300 (guide sleeve-exhaust).
3. Clean the bore, then cool valve guide in liquid nitrogen for three minutes or heat cylinder head in water to approximately 176°F. (80 degrees C).
4. Lubricate valve guide and install using a knock-in plug until circlip seats against cylinder head. Use .315 inch (8 mm) plug No. 102589041500 for intake valves and .354 inch (9 mm) plug No. 102589051500 for exhaust valves.

CHAIN TENSIONER

REPLACE

1. Remove alternator drive belt and alternator bracket, then position aside.
2. Carefully remove chain tensioner cap, seal and compression spring, **Fig. 9.**
3. Remove chain tensioner housing, then slide plunger out of the housing.
4. Reverse procedure to install. Torque chain tensioner housing to 7 ft. lbs. (10 Nm) and tensioner cap to 52 ft. lbs. (70 Nm).

TIMING CHAIN

REPLACE

1. Remove air cleaner assembly, then the cylinder head cover.
2. Remove spark plugs, then the chain tensioner, **Fig. 10.**
3. Separate timing chain using a suitable cutting tool or by grinding off both pins of one link.

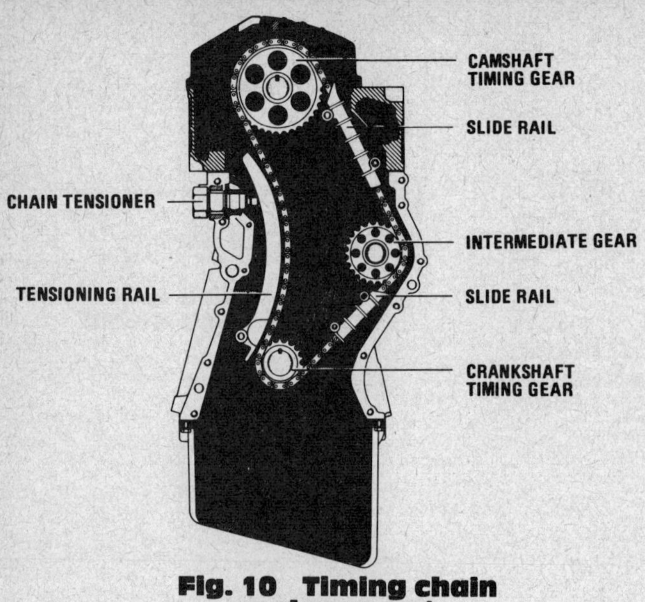

Fig. 10 Timing chain replacement

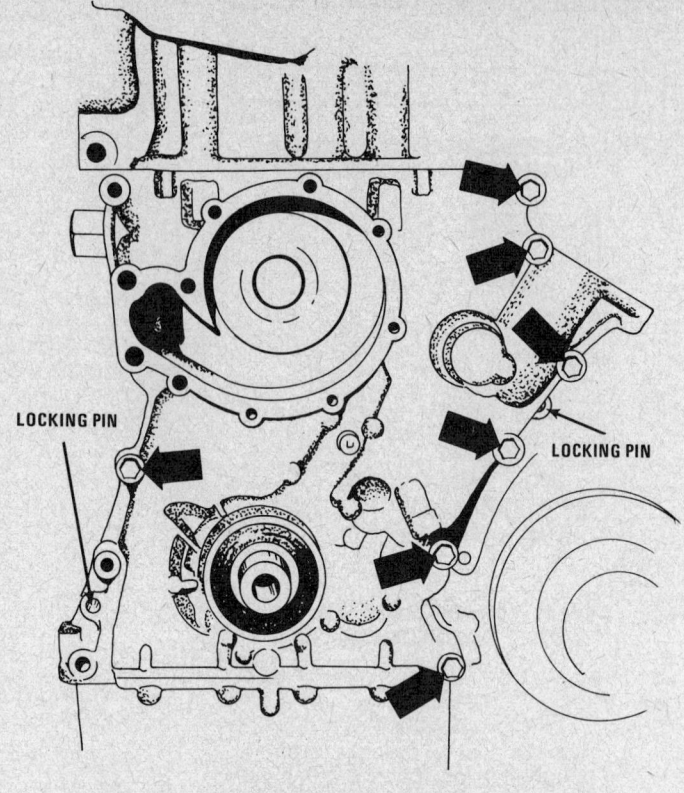

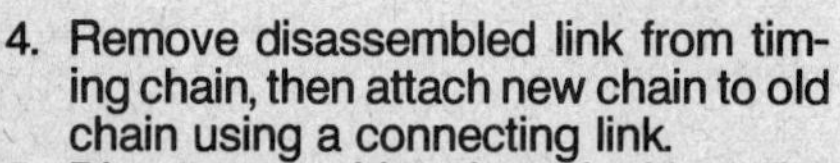

4. Remove disassembled link from timing chain, then attach new chain to old chain using a connecting link.
5. Disconnect wiring from ignition distributor.
6. Rotate crankshaft slowly in normal direction of rotation while simultaneously pulling up on old chain until connecting link comes to rest on top point of camshaft sprocket. **The timing chain must remain properly meshed in camshaft sprocket as crankshaft is turned.**

CAMSHAFT
REPLACE

1. Remove air cleaner assembly, then the cylinder head cover.
2. Disconnect wiring from ignition distributor, then rotate crankshaft in normal direction of rotation until No. 1 piston is at TDC of compression stroke.
3. Mark relationship between camshaft sprocket and timing chain for assembly reference.
4. Carefully remove chain tensioner cap, seal and compression spring.
5. On models equipped with automatic level control, remove pressure oil pump by loosening bolts indicated by arrows, **Fig. 1**, then position pump aside with oil lines connected.
6. On all models, remove camshaft sprocket attaching bolt and the sprocket.
7. Remove rocker arm bearing brackets, then carefully lift camshaft out of engine.
8. Remove woodruff key and spacer from camshaft.
9. Reverse procedure to install, noting the following:
   a. Install camshaft sprocket with wide flange facing camshaft. Torque sprocket bolt to 59 ft. lbs. (80 Nm).
   b. Torque chain tensioner closing nut to 52 ft. lbs. (70 Nm).
   c. On models equipped with automatic level control, torque pressure oil pump bolts to 10 ft. lbs. (13 Nm).
   d. Ensure valve timing marks are properly aligned.

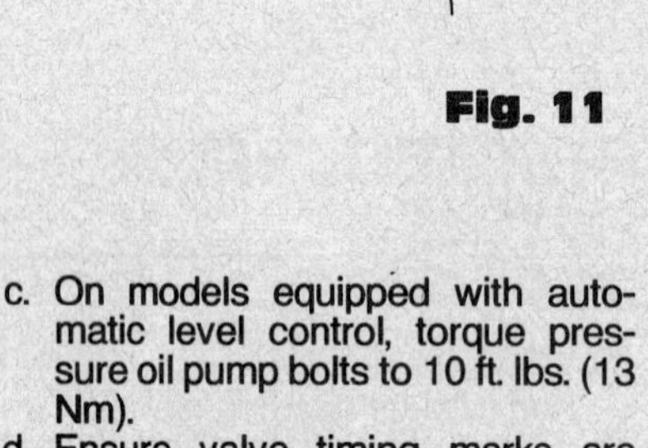

Fig. 11 Front cover replacement

FRONT COVER
REPLACE

1. Lift hood to a 90° angle and engage left hand locking lever.
2. Disconnect battery ground cable.
3. Drain cooling system and engine oil.
4. Remove air cleaner assembly.
5. On models equipped with automatic transmission, disconnect oil cooler lines from radiator.
6. On all models, disconnect upper and lower coolant hoses from radiator.
7. Disconnect fan shroud clips and position over fan, then remove radiator.
8. On models equipped with A/C, loosen compressor and position aside, leaving refrigerant lines connected.
9. On all models, disconnect wiring from ignition distributor, then rotate crankshaft in normal direction of rotation until No. 1 piston is at TDC of compression stroke.
10. Remove vibration damper and crankshaft pulley.
11. Remove TDC transmitter, then the distributor.
12. Disconnect accelerator linkage, then remove torsion bar bracket attaching bolts from both sides and swivel torsion bar downward.
13. On models equipped with automatic transmission, remove front engine stop, then disconnect and cap oil cooler lines from transmission.
14. Remove attaching bolts from front exhaust pipe lateral support bracket and swivel bracket downward.
15. Disconnect exhaust pipe from exhaust manifold.
16. Remove rear engine mount attaching bolts.
17. Remove engine carrier attaching bolts from below both front engine mounts.
18. Remove oil pan attaching bolts and lower pan to rest on frame crossmember.
19. Attach suitable hoist equipment to engine lifting points and raise engine as far as possible.
20. Remove oil intake pipe holder attaching bolts.
21. Remove two forward bolts from top of timing chain case.
22. Drive front cover locking pins rearward, then remove seven remaining attaching bolts and the front cover, **Fig. 11. When removing front cover, apply a slight downward pressure on the cover to avoid damaging the cylinder head gasket. If sticking spacer behind the front cover prevents removal of the cover, pry seal out of cover, then remove the spacer using a suitable puller.**
23. Reverse procedure to install, using new seals and gaskets. Torque front cover attaching bolts to 17 ft. lbs. (23 Nm) after driving locking pins into position.

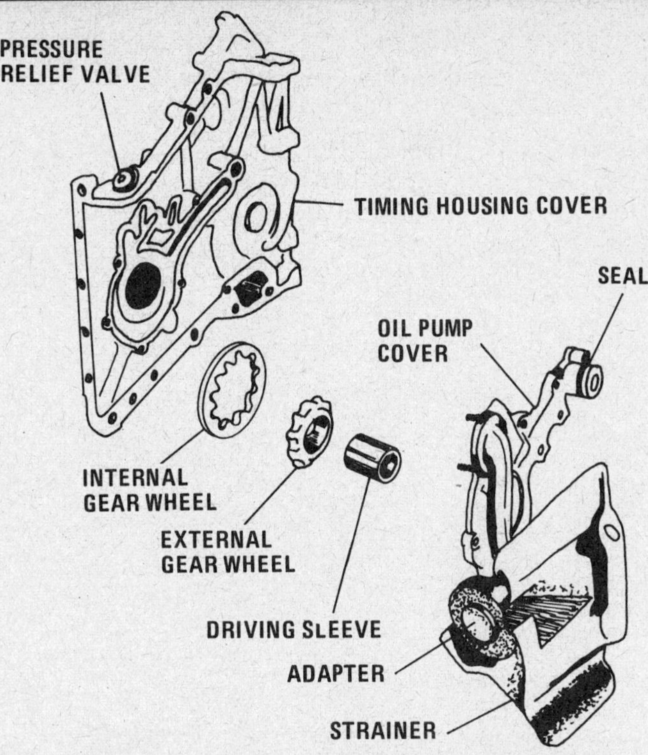

Fig. 12 Oil pump replacement

OIL PAN
REPLACE

1. Drain engine oil, then remove engine as described under "Engine, Replace."
2. Remove oil pan attaching bolts and the oil pan.
3. Reverse procedure to install, using a new gasket. Torque oil pan attaching bolts to 7 ft. lbs. (10 Nm).

OIL PUMP
REPLACE

1. Remove front cover as described under "Front Cover, Replace."
2. Remove attaching bolts, then the oil suction pipe with strainer and the oil pump cover, **Fig. 12.**
3. Remove oil pump gears from front cover.
4. Remove oil pump drive sleeve, if necessary. **If drive sleeve cannot be removed manually, remove crankshaft sprocket together with the sleeve.**
5. Reverse procedure to install.

FRONT OIL SEAL
REPLACE

1. Remove vibration damper and crankshaft pulley.
2. Carefully pry seal out of front cover using a suitable screwdriver.
3. Remove all burrs from oil seal bore.
4. Install new spacer, if necessary.
5. Fill new seal behind lip with suitable grease, then install seal using tool No. 102589001400 or equivalent.
6. Install crankshaft pulley and vibration damper.

REAR OIL SEAL
REPLACE

1. Remove transmission, then the flywheel or converter drive plate.
2. Carefully pry seal out of rear cover using a suitable screwdriver.
3. Clean seal bore, then mount insertion sleeve of installation tool No. 102589004300 to crankshaft.
4. Fill sleeve with suitable grease and position over sleeve.
5. Install up to stop using outer portion of installation tool.
6. Install converter drive plate or flywheel and the transmission.

BELT TENSION DATA

	New Lbs.	Used Lbs.
A/C Compressor	110	88-99
Alternator	66	44-55
Power Steering Pump	110	88-99
Water Pump	66	44-55

WATER PUMP
REPLACE

1. Drain cooling system, then remove air cleaner assembly.
2. Disconnect upper and lower coolant hoses from radiator.
3. Disconnect fan shroud clips and position over fan, then remove radiator.
4. Disconnect coolant lines from water pump.
5. Remove fan assembly, then the water pump drive belt and pulley. **If water pump pulley cannot be pulled off by hand, remove center screw and force pulley off with an M10 1 45 bolt.**
6. Disconnect electrical connector from water pump magnetic clutch and remove the clutch.
7. Loosen alternator and bracket and position aside.
8. Loosen coolant bypass line clamp, then remove water pump attaching bolts and the water pump.
9. Reverse procedure to install, noting the following:
   a. Torque water pump attaching bolts to 7 ft. lbs. (10 Nm).
   b. If pulley center screw was removed, apply suitable locking compound to new screw and torque to 11 ft. lbs. (15 Nm).

FUEL PUMP
REPLACE

1. Disconnect battery ground cable, then remove fuel tank filler cap to relieve excess fuel pressure.
2. Remove plastic shroud covering fuel filer and pump.
3. Pinch off fuel suction line with a suitable clamp.
4. Disconnect fuel lines and electrical connector from fuel pump.
5. Loosen fuel pump attaching screws and the fuel pump.
6. Reverse procedure to install.

103 GASOLI[illegible] [illegible]ol[illegible] S[illegible]CTIO[illegible]

INDEX

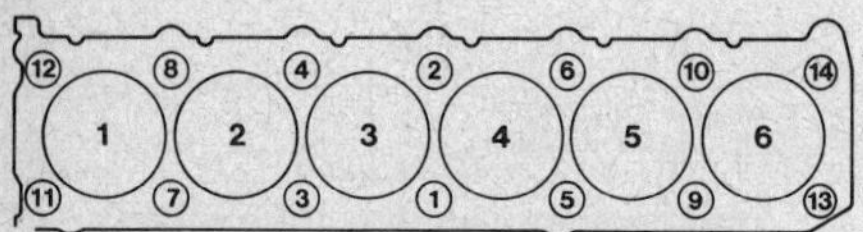

Fig. 1 Cylinder head tightening sequence

CYLINDER HEAD REPLACE

REMOVAL

Remove cylinder from engine only when engine is cold or cylinder head warpage may result.

1. Disconnect battery ground cable.
2. Remove engine compartment panels.
3. Drain coolant from radiator and engine assembly.
4. Remove air filter assembly.
5. Remove valve cover, ignition cables and distributor cap.
6. Remove distributor rotor.
7. Remove distributor driver and protective cover.
8. Remove front cover attaching screws, then the front cover.
9. Turn crankshaft in normal direction of engine rotation, until No. 1 cylinder is at TDC of compression stroke.
10. Loosen chain tensioner plug, then remove compression spring.
11. Remove threaded ring.
12. Using a M 8 screw, insert screw into chain tensioner bore and remove chain tensioner.
13. Mark position of camshaft sprocket in relation to camshaft. Apply a paint dot adjacent to bore in camshaft sprocket with dowel pin.
14. Mark chain link and camshaft sprocket with paint dots.
15. Remove camshaft sprocket attaching bolts, then the camshaft sprocket.
16. Using a suitable tool, remove slide rail bolt.
17. Remove oil dipstick guide tube bracket.
18. Remove intake manifold support from the top and bottom.
19. Loosen hose clamp from coolant pump hose.
20. Remove exhaust system from flanges.
21. Remove automatic transmission dipstick tube.
22. Disconnect all electrical connectors from cylinder head.
23. Relieve possible fuel system pressure by opening and closing fuel tank cap briefly, then pinch off fuel return and supply lines.
24. Disconnect accelerator pedal bowden cable.
25. Remove cylinder head attaching bolts, then the cylinder head and gasket.

INSTALLATION

1. Install new cylinder head gasket. **Install coolant hose onto cylinder head connecting pipe before placing cylinder head onto block.**
2. Install cylinder head. Ensure head is placed correctly over dowel pins.
3. Measure the 12 point socket head cylinder head bolts from the bottom of the bolt head to the bolt end tip. Measure length should be 4.13 inch (105 mm) for new bolts or 4.26 inch for used bolts.
4. Lubricate cylinder head bolt threads and cylinder head mating surface using clean engine oil, then insert bolts.
5. Tighten cylinder head attaching bolts in sequence shown in **Fig. 1** in three steps. First, torque cylinder head bolts in sequence to 52 ft. lbs. (70 Nm). Second, torque cylinder head attaching bolts an additional 90°. Third, torque cylinder head attaching bolts an additional 90°.
6. Mount camshaft sprocket, aligning the paint dots previously applied. Torque attaching bolts to 8 ft. lbs. (11 Nm).
7. The chain tensioner must be disassembled prior to installation. Pull thrust bolt (4) toward the right and out

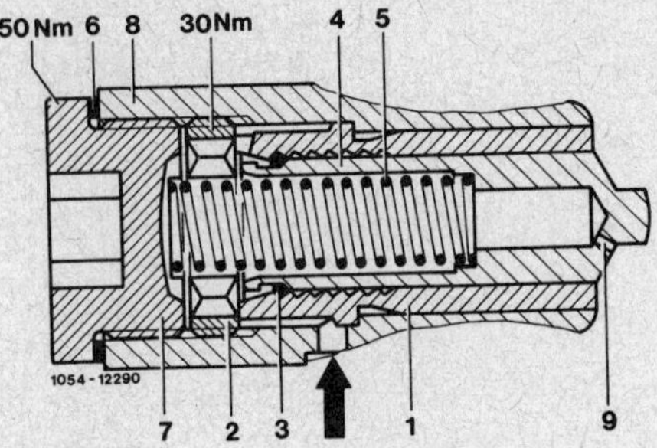

1 Chain tensioner housing
2 Threaded ring
3 Detent spring
4 Thrust bolt
5 Compression spring
6 Seal ring
7 Plug
8 Timing chain housing cover
9 Throttle bore

Fig. 2 Sectional view of chain tensioner

from the housing (1), **Fig. 2.** Tighten threaded ring (2) to 22 ft. lbs. (30 Nm). Insert thrust bolt (4) with detent spring (3). Mount compression spring (5) and plug (7) with seal ring (6). Torque plug (7) to 36 ft. lbs. (50 Nm).
8. Ensure alignment marks on camshaft bearing cap and camshaft are properly aligned. No. 1 piston should be at TDC of compression stroke.
9. Clean sealing surface on cylinder head, timing chain housing cover and cylinder head front cover. Apply a small quantity of sealing compound, part No. 0019894520 or 0029870020 or equivalents, on right and left side into groove of timing chain housing cover.
10. Install new gasket into groove.
11. Coat cylinder head front cover (surface contacting cylinder head) with sealing compound, part No. 0019894520 or 0029870020 or equivalents.
12. Install front cover. Torque the two lower attaching screws to 16 ft. lbs. (21 Nm).
13. Install protective cover, seal and driver into distributor. **The groove on driver must engage over camshaft pin.** Torque attaching screw to 16 ft. lbs. (21 Nm).
14. Reverse removal procedure to complete installation.

110 GASOLINE ENGINE SECTION

INDEX

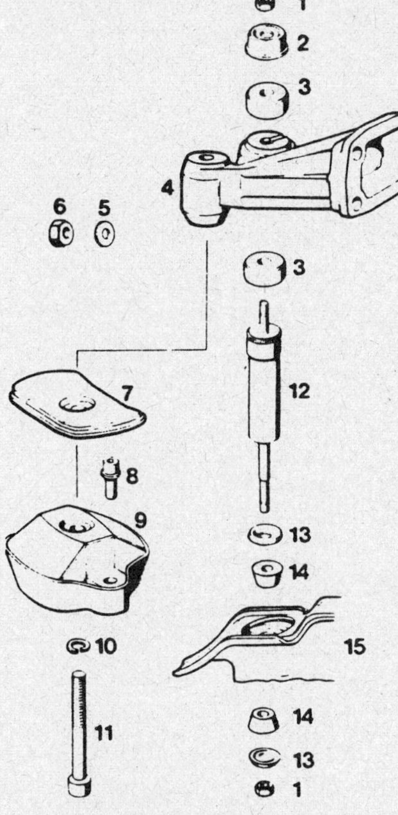

1 Nut M 6
2 Disc 44 mm dia.
3 Rubber pad 36 mm dia.
4 Engine carrier
5 Washer A 10.5 (six)
6 Nut M 10 (eight)
7 Guard
8 Combination bolt M 8 x 18
9 Engine mount 123 241 10 13 (right)
Engine mount 123 241 12 13 (left)
10 Lockwasher 12
11 Bolt M 12 x 35
12 Engine damper
13 Disc 30 mm dia.
14 Rubber pad 27 mm dia.
15 Holder

Fig. 1 Front engine mount disassembled view. 123 series

ENGINE MOUNTS REPLACE

123 SERIES

1. Remove bolt from underside of vehicle.
2. Remove nut from bottom of engine damper.
3. Position a wooden block under oil pan, and using suitable lifting equipment, raise engine.
4. Remove bolts (8) and engine mount, **Fig. 1.**
5. Reverse procedure to install. Torque bolt (11) to 55 ft. lbs., (75 Nm). **Left and righthand engine mounts are different.**

ENGINE REPLACE

Engine and transmission are removed as an assembly. **If engine removal is necessary, due to bearing damage, flush out the oil cooler and oil lines and thoroughly clean out the oil filter housing.**

1. Disconnect battery ground cable.
2. On 123 series vehicles, lift hood to a 90 degree angle and engage left hand locking lever.
3. On all models, drain cooling system.
4. Disconnect and cap air oil cooler and transmission oil cooler lines from radiator.
5. Remove radiator and air oil cooler as an assembly.
6. Remove fan and fan clutch.
7. On models equipped with A/C, unfasten A/C compressor and position aside, leaving refrigerant lines attached.
8. On models equipped with automatic level control, disconnect lines from oil pressure pump, then remove pump attaching bolts indicated by arrows, **Fig. 2**, and the pump.
9. On all models, drain fluid from power steering pump tank, then disconnect hoses from power steering pump.

Fig. 2 Screw location for removing level control oil pump

10. Disconnect starter motor and alternator wiring.
11. Disconnect all electrical connectors from engine.
12. Remove longitudinal control shaft, **Fig. 3.**
13. Disconnect all remaining electric, coolant, oil and vacuum lines leading to the engine.
14. Remove screws securing test socket to holder, then disconnect TDC transmitter wire from test socket.
15. Disconnect exhaust pipes from exhaust manifold and the exhaust strut from transmission.
16. Remove both right and left side engine dampers.
17. Remove engine mount attaching bolts from bottom of vehicle.
18. Remove rear engine carrier and mount.
19. Disconnect speedometer cable from transmission.
20. Disconnect driveshaft from transmission.
21. Disconnect all electrical connectors and linkages from transmission.
22. Raise engine and transmission at approximately a 45° angle and remove assembly from vehicle.

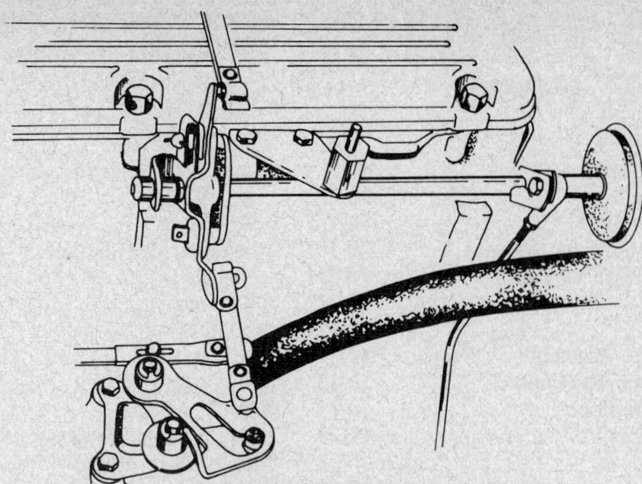

Fig. 3 Longitudinal control shaft, removal

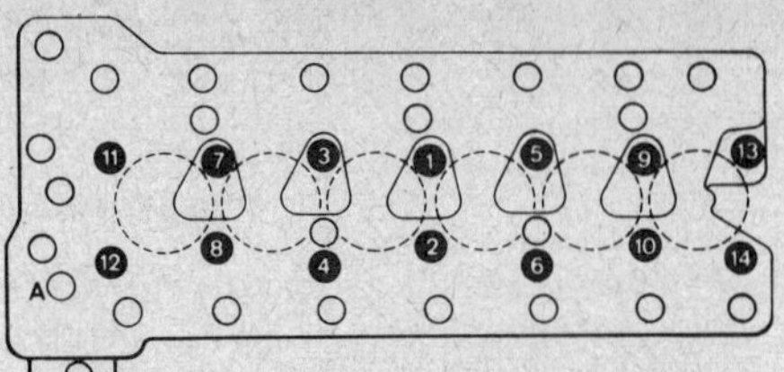

Fig. 4 Cylinder head bolt tightening sequence

23. Reverse procedure to install.

INTAKE MANIFOLD

REPLACE

1. Disconnect battery ground cable.
2. Remove air cleaner assembly, then drain cooling system.
3. Disconnect and cap all fuel lines from intake manifold.
4. Disconnect all electrical connectors, vacuum lines and linkages from intake manifold.
5. Disconnect heater hose, then remove decel shutoff valve from intake manifold.
6. Remove attaching screws and nuts from intake manifold and manifold support.
7. Remove engine mount and damper attaching bolts.
8. Raise engine using suitable lifting equipment and remove intake manifold.
9. Reverse procedure to install.

EXHAUST MANIFOLD

REPLACE

1. Disconnect exhaust pipe from exhaust manifold. **It may be necessary to heat the exhaust pipes to ease separation. In this case, a protective shield must be positioned between the exhaust pipes and floor of vehicle to prevent damage.**
2. Remove exhaust manifold attaching nuts and the exhaust manifold.
3. Reverse procedure to install.

CYLINDER HEAD

REPLACE

Remove cylinder head only with engine cold.

REMOVAL

1. Drain coolant from radiator.
2. Vehicles equipped with air conditioning, remove compressor and position aside. Do not disconnect refrigerant lines.
3. Remove screws and both camshaft housing covers.
4. Vehicles equipped with level control, remove oil pressure pump and position aside, **Fig. 2.**
5. Remove vacuum pump.
6. Vehicles equipped with carburetors, disconnect carburetor and intake pipe hot water lines.
7. Disconnect all electrical connectors, hoses, fuel and vacuum lines from the cylinder head, intake pipe and carburetor.
8. Remove the longitudinal regulating shaft.
9. Disconnect oil return lines from cylinder head.
10. Remove thermostat housing hose from water pump.
11. Disconnect water pump bypass hose.
12. Disconnect oil dipstick tube from cylinder head and bend it aside.
13. Disconnect exhaust pipes from exhaust manifold and transmission. Vehicles equipped with carburetors, loosen pre-heat cowl.
14. Using a suitable screwdriver, remove all spring clamps.
15. Using tool No. 110589046100 or equivalent, remove rocker arms.
16. Using tool No. SW27 001589650900 or equivalent, rotate crankshaft. **Do not rotate engine on camshafts or in reverse.**
17. Position No. 1 cylinder at TDC. Ensure marks on camshaft sprockets and housing align.
18. Using camshaft holder tool to prevent camshaft rotation, apply counterpressure to camshaft and remove both camshaft sprocket bolts.
19. Using tool No. 115589193300 or equivalent, remove bearing pins and upper slide rail.
20. Remove chain tensioner.
21. Push both camshafts rearward and remove camshaft sprockets.
22. Using tool No. 115589193300 or equivalent, remove bearing pins and guide wheel.
23. Using tool No. 115589193300 or equivalent, remove bearing pins and cylinder head guide rail.
24. Remove cylinder head bolts in reverse order of tightening sequence shown in **Fig. 4.**
25. Using a suitable tool, remove both M8 bolts from the timing case.
26. Lift timing chain, and position tensioning rail toward center of engine.
27. Using a suitable hoist, remove cylinder head from engine block.

Fig. 5 Positioning of wooden blocks

INSTALLATION

1. Clean cylinder head and crankcase mating surfaces thoroughly.
2. Install a new cylinder head gasket. **Two dowel pins are incorporated onto the crankcase to properly position the cylinder head.**
3. Position two wooden blocks onto the cylinder head gasket. The first block at the front should be upright, **Fig. 5.**
4. Position cylinder head onto the wooden blocks, and install timing chain and tensioning rail.
5. Raise front of cylinder head and remove front wooden block toward exhaust side. Lower cylinder head, until it seats properly over dowel pin.
6. Raise rear of cylinder head and remove rear block toward exhaust side. Lower cylinder head, until it seats properly over rear dowel pin.
7. Lubricate and install cylinder head bolts. **Camshaft housing clearance for the .875 inch (22 mm) diameter washer for cylinder head bolt No. 14 has been extended. The former .796 inch (20 mm) diameter washer must be installed on older camshaft housings, Fig. 6.**
8. Tighten cylinder head bolts in sequence shown on **Fig. 4** and in two steps as follows: step 1, 52 ft. lbs. (70 Nm); step 2, 74 ft. lbs. (100 Nm).

Fig. 6 Removing camshaft housing bolt No. 14

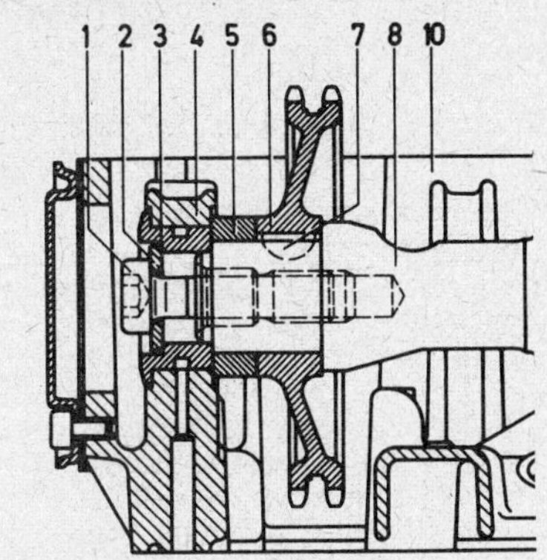

Intake

1 Expansion bolt
2 Washer
3 Spacer
4 Bearing
5 Spacer
6 Camshaft sprocket
7 Woodruff key
8 Camshaft
10 Camshaft housing

Fig. 8 Intake camshaft components

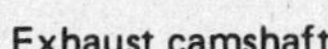

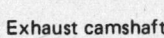

Exhaust camshaft

1 Expansion bolt
2 Washer
3 Spacer
4 Bearing
6 Camshaft sprocket
7 Woodruff key
9 Camshaft
10 Camshaft housing

Fig. 9 Exhaust camshaft components

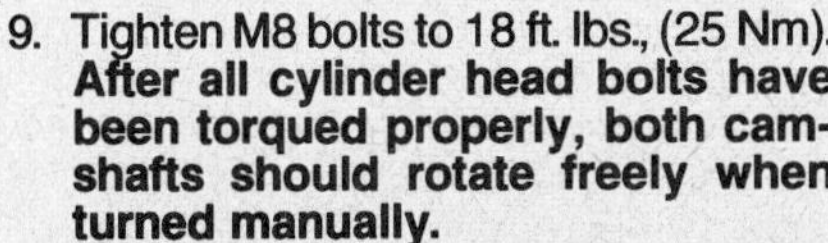

9. Tighten M8 bolts to 18 ft. lbs., (25 Nm). **After all cylinder head bolts have been torqued properly, both camshafts should rotate freely when turned manually.**
10. Lift timing chain, and using suitable tool, install slide rail (2A), **Fig. 7.** Using tool No. 115589193300 or equivalent, install slide rail bearing pins and align slide rail laterally.
11. Lift timing chain, and install guide wheel (4), **Fig. 7.** Using tool No. 115589193300 or equivalent, install guide rail bearing pins.
12. Install intake side camshaft sprocket (6) and spacer (5), **Fig. 8.** Using clean engine oil, lubricate and install spacer (3) onto bearing (4), **Fig. 8.**
13. Install exhaust side camshaft sprocket (6), **Fig. 9**, and timing chain. Using clean engine oil, lubricate and install spacer (3) onto bearing (4), **Fig. 9.**
14. Loosely install fastening bolt and washer.
15. Ensure adjustment marks on both camshafts sprockets and housing align, **Fig. 10. Engines on which the vibration damper incorporates a "010" mark in addition to a TDC mark, the TDC mark is located next to the pin on the vibration damper.**
16. Install sliding rail into camshaft housing properly to prevent timing chain from becoming loose.
17. Install and tighten rigid chain tensioner.

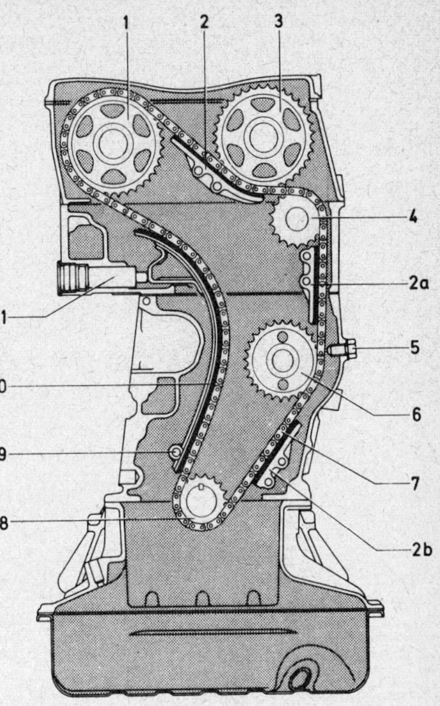

1 Exhaust camshaft sprocket
2– 2b Sliding rail
3 Intake camshaft sprocket
4 Guide wheel
5 Lock bolt
6 Intermediate wheel
7 Timing chain
8 Crankshaft sprocket
9 Tensioning rail bearing pin
10 Tensioning rail
11 Hydraulic chain tensioner

Fig. 7 Timing chain & chain driven components

18. Using tool No. SW27 001589650900 or equivalent, rotate crankshaft and position No. 1 cylinder at TDC.
19. Using a suitable tool, apply counterpressure to camshaft and torque fastening bolt to 59 ft. lbs., (80 Nm).
20. Install rocker arms and spring clamps.
21. Install chain tensioner.
22. Adjust valve clearances to specification.
23. Reverse removal steps 1 though 11 to complete installation procedure.
24. Operate engine until coolant temperature is 176°F, (80°C) then loosen cylinder head bolts by 1/4 turn and torque to 74 ft. lbs. Torque M8 bolts to 18 ft. lbs. **If self-adjusting cylinder head gasket is installed, retorquing cylinder head bolts after 300-630 miles of driving is not required.**

ROCKER ARMS

REPLACE

REMOVAL

1. Remove all rocker arm tensioning springs with a screwdriver, **Fig. 11.**
2. Crank engine with tool combination SW27 (001589650900) until the cam tip is facing up. **Do not crank the engine using the expanding screws of the camshaft gear. Do not turn the engine in reverse.**

Fig. 10 Aligning marks on camshaft with marks on housing

Fig. 11 Removing rocker arm tension springs

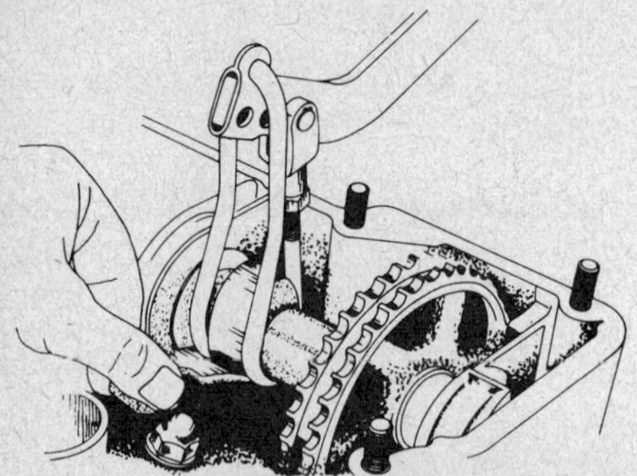

Fig. 12 Removing rocker arm using tool No. 110589046100

3. Remove the rocker arms using remover and installer 110589046100, Fig. 12.

INSTALLATION

There are two rocker arm versions, **Fig. 13**. One has a .275 inch (7 mm) guide surface; the other has a .55 inch (14mm) guide surface. When making repairs, exchange the rocker arms of the .275 inch (7 mm) version for rocker arms of the .55 inch (14 mm) version. **Rocker arms and tensioning springs of engines 110 and engines 116 & 117 may not be interchanged.**

1. Check to see that oil splash holes in rocker arms are unobstructed.
2. Lubricate the rocker arm supports with oil.
3. Install rocker arms.
4. Push tensioning springs into ring grooves of adjusting screws.
5. Adjust valve clearance.

VALVES

ADJUST

If adjustment cannot be made, install thinner thrust pieces. Thrust pieces are available in .098, .137 & .177 inch, (2.5, 3.5 and 4.5 mm) thicknesses, **Fig. 14**. If torque valve of valve adjusting screw is below 20 Nm (2 kpm), replace the screw or threaded bushing.

1. Force off tensioning springs and remove rubber gaskets.
2. Measure valve clearance between the slide surface of the rocker arm and basic cam circle of the camshaft, **Fig. 15.**
3. Crank the engine with tool SW27 (001589650900) or contact handle 001589462108. Adjust valves following the firing order of the engine, **Fig. 16.**
4. Adjust valve clearance by turning the valve adjusting screw with valve adjusting wrench SW17 (110589000100). Valve clearance is set correctly when the feeler gauge indicates a tight fit.

VALVE GUIDES

REPLACE

1. Remove valve guide with knock-out plug .354-.443 inch, (9 mm – 110589021500; 11 mm – 110589031500).
2. Check the basic bore in the cylinder head. If valve guides of standard dimension can be installed, knock in the valve guide with knock-in plug until the circlip is seated on the cylinder head. .354-.443 inch, (9 mm knock-in plug – 116589201500; 11 mm knock-in plug – 116589191500.)
3. If valve guides of a repair stage (oversize) must be installed, refinish the basic bore to the applicable dimension.
4. Clean the bore and heat the cylinder head in water to 176°F (80 deg. C.) If possible, cool the valve guide with dry ice.
5. Coat the valve guides with parafin and knock them in with the knock-in plug (see above) until the circlips rest on the cylinder head.

CAMSHAFT HOUSING

REPLACE

REMOVAL

1. Loosen air conditioner compressor

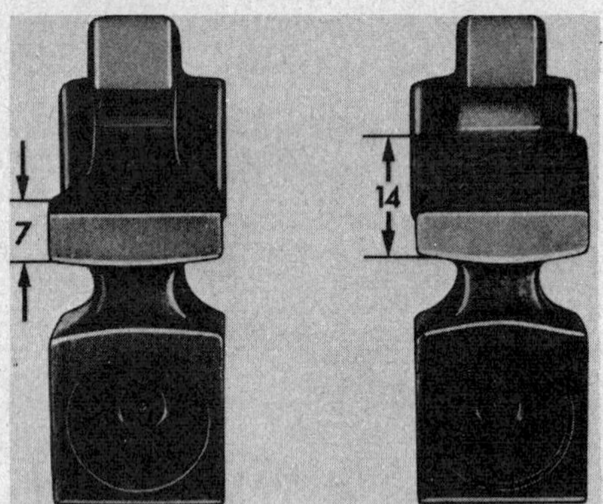

Fig. 13 Two types of rocker arms used

and move it aside with refrigerant lines still connected.

2. On cars with level control, remove the oil pressure pump and place it to one side with lines still connected, **Fig. 2.**
3. Remove the vacuum pump.
4. Drain coolant.
5. Remove the radiator hose.
6. Remove the cylinder head cover.
7. Unscrew the cover on the front of the camshaft housing.
8. Remove all tensioning springs.
9. Remove all rocker arms using remover and installer 110589046100.
10. Apply counterpressure only to the right-hand (exhaust) camshaft with holding wrench 116589010100 and loosen fastening screws.
11. Crank engine using special tool SW27 (001589650900), and set piston 1 to ignition TDC and both camshafts to their marks.
12. Remove the chain tensioner.
13. Remove the slide rail in the camshaft housing. Knock out bearing bolts with impact puller 115589193300.
14. Loosen the rear right-hand cover on the camshaft housing and push the right-hand camshaft toward the rear by means of remover and installer

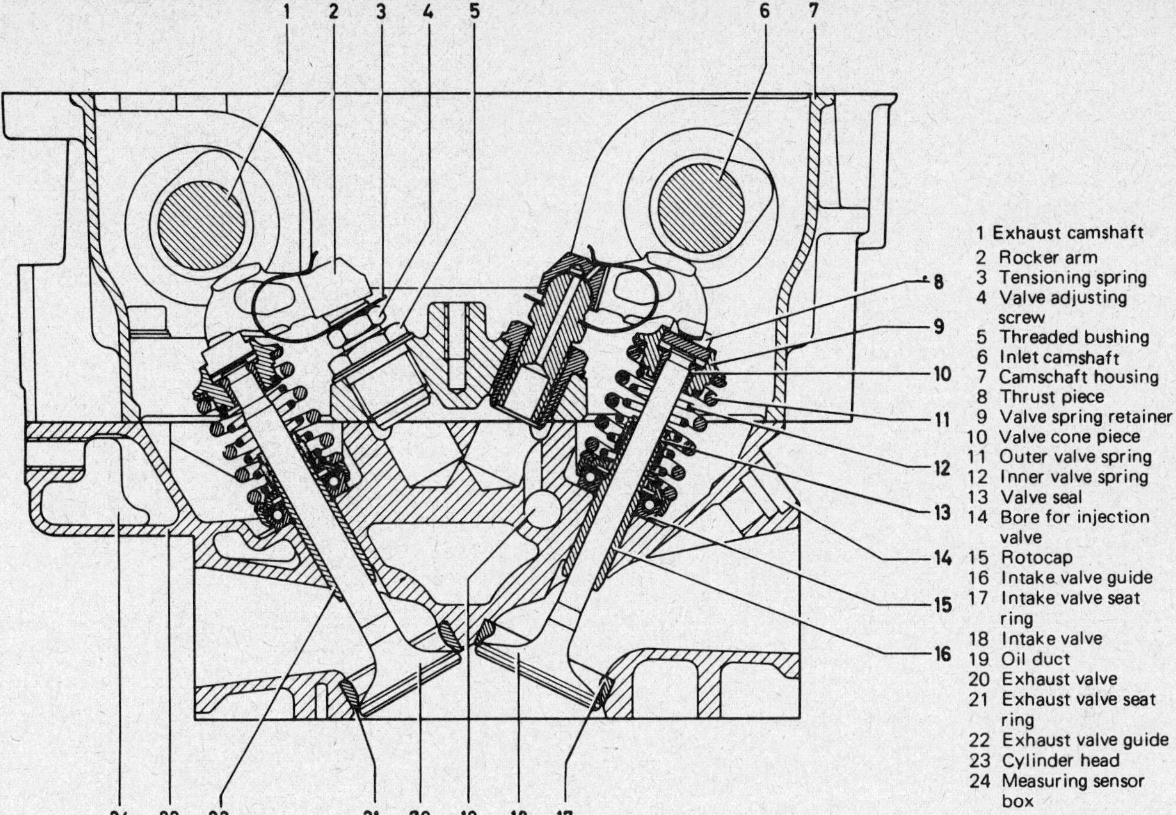

Fig. 14 Valve train components

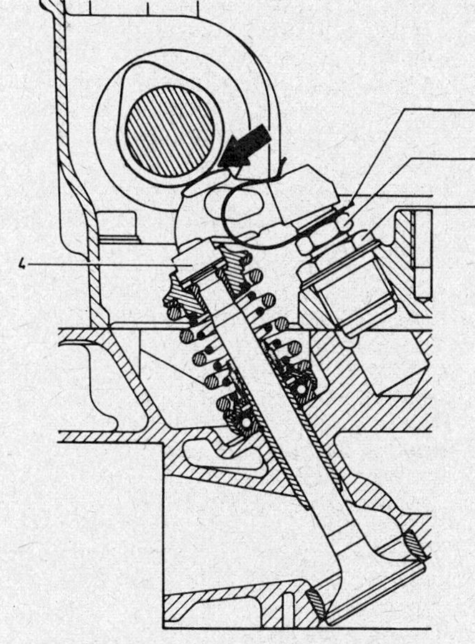

1 Tensioning spring
2 Valve adjusting screw
3 Threaded bushing
4 Thrust piece

Fig. 15 Valve adjustment

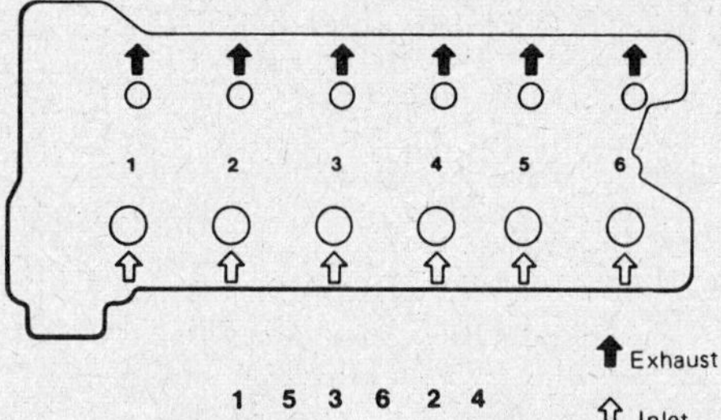

Fig. 16 Valve arrangement

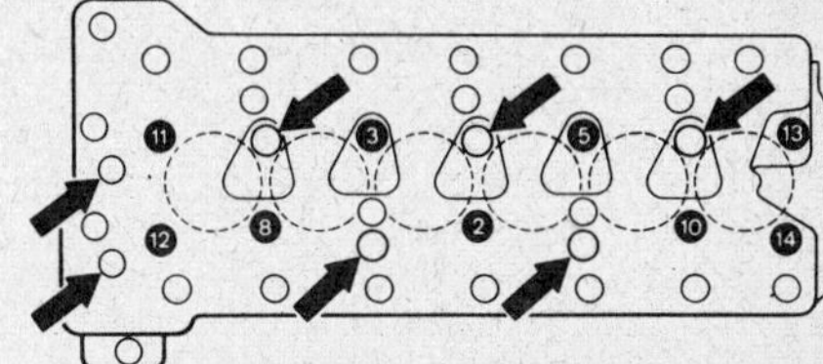

Fig. 17 Bolt pattern for camshaft housing replacement

110589033300 while supporting the camshaft gear.

15. Remove the camshaft gear.
16. Reintroduce the camshaft into the bearing points.
17. Unscrew bolts M8 and cylinder head bolts in reverse order of the tightening sequence, **Fig. 17. Do not loosen the five lower cylinder head bolts or the two M8 bolts shown in Fig. 17.**
18. Remove the camshaft housing containing the camshafts, **Fig. 18.**

INSTALLATION

1. Clean the cylinder head and camshaft housing mating surfaces.
2. Insert steel sheet 1100160480. Do not use sealing compound.
3. Place the camshaft housing in position.
4. Lubricate the camshaft bearings with engine oil. Install camshaft and camshaft bearings.
5. Lubricate the cylinder head bolts at threads and screw head base. Insert.
6. Tighten the cylinder head bolts in step-sequence as follows: 1st step: starting with bolt No. 2 to 52 ft. lbs. (70 Nm), **Fig. 17;** 2nd step: starting with bolt No. 1 to (81 ft. lbs. 110 Nm), **Fig. 17.** For this purpose, loosen slightly the five lower cylinder head bolts individually before retightening, **Fig. 17.**
7. Tighten M8 bolts from inside out to 18 ft. lbs. (25 Nm). **When all bolts have been tightened, both camshafts should rotate easily when turned manually.**
8. Mount the righthand camshaft gear, observing the adjusting mark on both camshafts. **On engines on which the vibration damper carries a "010" mark for BDC in addition to TDC, the TDC mark is next to the pin in the vibration damper.**
9. Install the slide rail. Ensure the timing chain doesn't jump across.
10. Mount the rigid chain tensioner. Apply tension manually.
11. Lubricate the spacers and slide into camshaft housing.
12. Crank the engine with tool SW27 (001589650900). Check both adjust-

Fig. 18 Camshaft housing

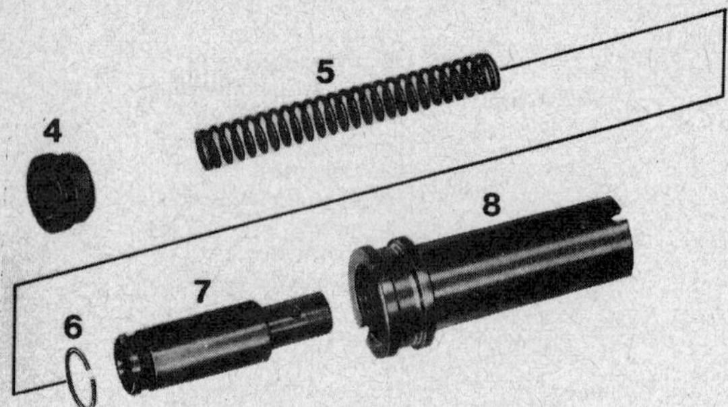

4 Oil nozzle with 1.1 mm bore
5 Spring
6 Snap ring
7 Pressure pin
8 Housing

Fig. 20 Second production model chain tensioner

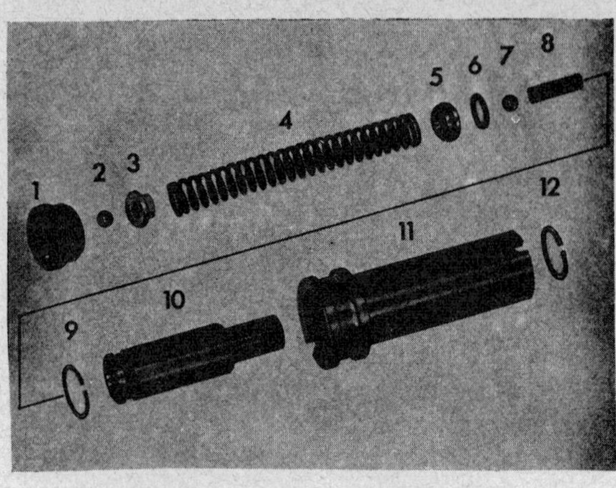

1 Ball seat ring with 3.0 mm bore
2 Ball
3 Ball cage
4 Spring
5 Valve disc
6 O-ring
7 Ball
8 Spring
9 Snap ring
10 Pressure pin
11 Housing
12 Snap ring

Fig. 19 First production model chain tensioner

ing marks. **If the camshaft housing has been face ground, adjust timing.**

13. Tighten the camshaft gear fastening screw to 59 ft.lbs. (80 Nm) while applying counterpressure to the camshaft using holding wrench 116589010100.
14. Install the chain tensioner.
15. Reverse remainder of removal procedure to complete installation.

CAMSHAFTS REPLACE

Camshafts can be removed with the engine installed in the vehicle together with the camshaft housing only. If the camshaft has to be replaced, the rocker arms also have to be replaced.

REMOVAL

1. Remove camshaft housing, **Fig. 18.**
2. Unscrew both rear covers on the camshaft housing.
3. Unscrew the fastening screw of the lefthand camshaft while applying counterpressure with holding wrench 116589010100.
4. Push the camshaft toward the rear and remove the camshaft gear. Remove the spacer ring of the intake camshaft.
5. Remove both camshafts toward the rear.

INSTALLATION

1. Lubricate the camshaft bearings with engine oil.
2. Reinsert the intake camshaft, camshaft gear and spacer ring.
3. Lubricate the spacer sleeve with engine oil. Insert. **When making repairs, use fastening screws with washers. Fastening screws and cup springs should no longer be used.**
4. Tighten the camshaft gear fastening screw to 59 ft.lbs. (80 Nm) while applying counterpressure to the camshaft with holding wrench 116589010100.
5. Introduce the exhaust camshaft into lubricated bearing points, but do not reassemble the gear which is slipped on after the camshaft housing has been mounted.
6. Mount both rear covers. **Do not tighten the righthand (exhaust end) cover. The camshaft must first be pushed back when mounting the timing chain.**
7. Mount the camshaft housing and complete reassembly.

CHAIN TENSIONER

REMOVAL

Chain tensioners are available in two production types, which are interchangeable. **Fig. 19** shows first production model, and **Fig. 20** shows second production model. First production models, incorporate a .118 inch, (3.0 mm) oil jet bore, while second production models do not incorporate valves and have .043 inch, (1.1 mm) oil jet bore. **Without counterpressure from clamping rail, pressure pin (10), Fig. 21, and snap ring (9) will be forced up to the stop by spring (4). The pressure pin cannot be pressed back beyond position "A," Fig. 22. The chain tensioner must be disassembled before each installation to movethe pressure pin to position "A."**

1. Remove battery. Vehicles equipped with air conditioning, remove compressor and position aside. Do not disconnect refrigerant lines.
2. Using a suitable tool, remove chain tensioning housing plug. **If a second production model chain tensioner is incorporated, remove camshaft sprocket or tensioning rail, then spring (5).**
3. Using a suitable tool, loosen ball locating ring (oil jet) approximately two turns.
4. Using a suitable screwdriver, remove threaded ring.
5. Using tool No. 000589050700 or equivalent, remove chain tensioner. **If the chain tensioner sticks, loosen ball seat ring. Remove ball, ball cage and compression spring. Install a M181.5 screw into chain tensioner housing, which will allow a greater force for removal of chain tensioner.**
6. Securely clamp chain tensioner into holder tool No. 110589023100 or equivalent.
7. Using a suitable tool, loosen ball seat ring (oil nozzle). **Ball seat ring is under spring tension.**
8. Remove spring (4), ball cage (3), ball (2) and valve disc (5).
9. Remove ball (7) and spring (8) from pressure limit valve.
10. Remove snap ring (12), and pressure pin.

INSTALLATION

First Production

1. Install snap ring (12) into clamp housing (11).
2. Install pressure pin (10) and snap ring (9) into clamp housing, **Fig. 19.**

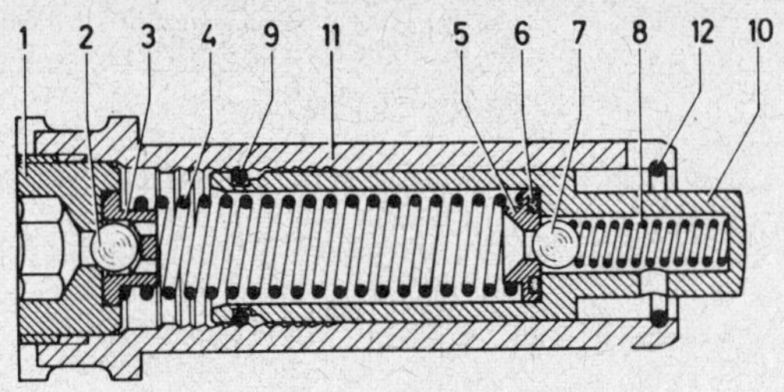

1 Ball locating ring
2 Ball
3 Ball cage
4 Spring
5 Valve disc
6 O-ring
7 Ball
8 Spring
9 Snap ring
10 Pressure pin
11 Housing
12 Snap ring

Fig. 21 Chain tensioner components

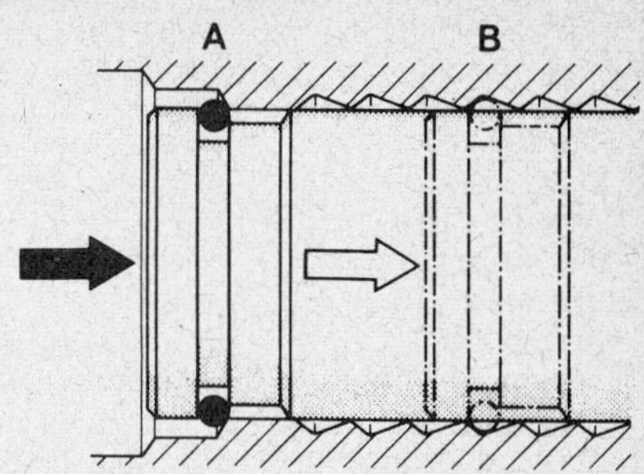

Fig. 22 Positioning chain tensioner into working position

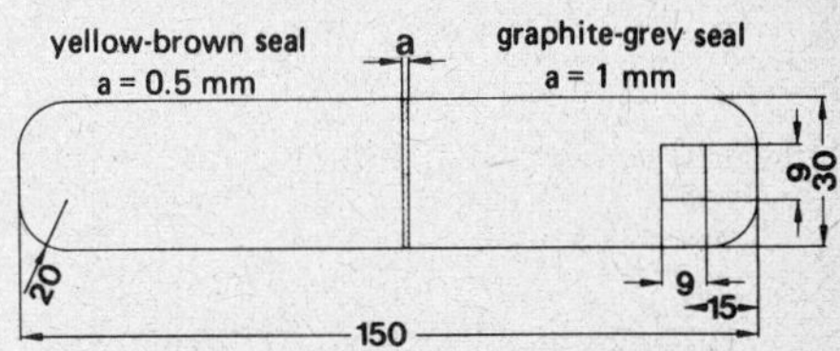

Fig. 23 Dimensions for fabricating tool for cutting oil pan radial seal

3. Install pressure limit valve spring (8) and ball (7).
4. Install spring (4), valve disc (5) and O-ring (6) into clamp housing.
5. Position ball cage (3) and ball (2) onto spring (4).
6. Install ball locating ring (1) onto ball cage. Compress spring (4) and screw locating ring onto clamp housing approximately two turns. **Do not tighten ball locating ring.**
7. Using a suitable tool, install chain tensioner into cylinder head. **Do not apply heavy force when installing chain tensioner.**
8. Install and torque threaded ring (15) to 37 ft. lbs., (50 Nm).
9. Torque ball locating ring to 18 ft. lbs., (25 Nm).
10. Install chain tensioner housing plug and torque to 37 ft. lbs., (50 Nm).

Second Production

1. Position housing (8) into cylinder head.
2. Install and torque threaded ring (3) to 37 ft. lbs., (50 Nm).
3. Install pressure pin (7), snap ring (6) and spring (5) into housing, **Fig. 20**, and torque oil jet (4) to 18 ft. lbs., (25 Nm). The pressure pin should jump forward and make an audible click.
4. Install chain tensioner housing plug and seal, and torque to 37 ft. lbs., (50 Nm).

TIMING CHAIN

REPLACE

REMOVAL

1. Remove spark plugs and cylinder head cover.
2. Remove the rocker arm of the right-hand (exhaust) camshaft.
3. Remove the chain tensioner.
4. Insert rigid chain tensioner 110589033100 and apply tension.
5. Cover the chain box with a rag and cut the timing chain with chain separating device 116589033500.

INSTALLATION

1. Attach a new timing chain and one link to the old timing chain.
2. Slowly crank the engine on the crankshaft with special tool SW17 (001589650900). Crank in the direction of rotation while simultaneously pulling up the old chain until the link comes to rest against the upper point of the right-hand camshaft gear. **The timing chain should always be in mesh while turning both camshaft gears.**
3. Disconnect the old timing chain and connect the ends of the new timing chain with a link. Mount lockwashers.
4. Crank engine and check the adjusting marks.
5. Install the chain tensioner and complete reassembly.

OIL PAN

REPLACE

REMOVAL

123 Series

1. Refer to "Engine, Replace" procedure and remove engine from vehicle.
2. Remove oil filter, lines and disconnect oil return line.
3. Loosen alternator bracket strut from oil pan, and remove pan.

INSTALLATION

123 Series

1. Clean the oil pan and engine mating surfaces.
2. Replace rear oil seal. Work it into place using a well oiled hammer handle. **The seal has to be cut about .0196 inch (.5 mm) above mating surface. Fabricate gauge shown in Fig. 23 for this purpose.**
3. Apply sealer to mating surfaces and install oil pan using new gasket.
4. Reverse remainder of procedure to install oil pan.

OIL PUMP

REPLACE

During repairs or when installing an oil pump drive, part No. 1100500206, replace with oil pump part No. 1101802701 (production model C). Production model C oil pumps incorporate a 2.36 inch, (60 mm) oil strainer and two screw on holders. Install oil pump only in combination with a 72.5 psi, (5 bar) main oil duct pressure relief valve. Some production models A & B oil pumps used, are provided with a 4.3 inch, (110 mm) oil strainer and one screw on holder. All engines starting with engine production No. 464130 are equipped with model C oil pumps. Oil pump 1101802601 is installed as standard equipment for fuel pumps without drive cam. As a replacement part only, oil pump 1101802701 with drive cam is available.

1. Remove fuel pump if vehicle is equipped with carburetor.
2. Remove oil pan lower half.
3. Remove attaching screw on cylinder crankcase and bearing cap.
4. Remove oil pump.
5. Reverse procedure to install. **For installation of oil pump 1101802701, install crankshaft bearing bolt 1080110071 onto first crankshaft bearing cap, and torque bolt to 74 ft. lbs., (80 Nm).**

FRONT OIL SEAL

REPLACE

REMOVAL

1. Drain cooling system, then remove radiator and fan.
2. Remove crankshaft pulley and vibration damper.
3. Remove crankshaft bolt while holding crankshaft with tool No. 100589004000 or equivalent.

4. Mark relationship between crankshaft and balance disc, then remove the disc using a suitable puller.
5. Carefully pry seal out using a suitable screwdriver.
6. Remove spacer ring, if necessary, using a suitable puller.

INSTALLATION

1. Remove all burrs from oil seal bore.
2. Fill new seal behind lip with suitable grease. **If original seal had been leaking at outer shoulder, apply suitable sealing compound to outer shoulder joint area. Leave seal in installation tool for 3 hours to allow complete hardening.**
3. Install new seal using tool No. 110589076100 or equivalent. **If sealant is used on new seal, the installation tool must remain in place for 10-15 minutes before removal.**
4. Install spacer ring. **If original spacer ring is being reused, invert the ring so that worn surface is at the rear.**
5. Position balance disc on crankshaft with dowel pin bores properly aligned.
6. Pull balance disc onto crankshaft using an M18x.5x45 bolt with a spring washer, then install dowel pins.
7. Install four spring washers on crankshaft bolt with concave surfaces facing bolt head.
8. Install crankshaft bolt and torque to 295 ft. lbs. (400 Nm) while holding crankshaft with tool No. 100589004000 or equivalent.
9. Reverse remainder of removal procedure to complete installation.

REAR OIL SEAL
REPLACE
REMOVAL

Do not replace crankshaft rear oil seal part No. 0009976941, with part No. 009979041.

1. Refer to "Engine, Replace" procedure and remove engine.
2. Remove oil pan, crankshaft and rear oil seal.

INSTALLATION

1. Using an oiled hammer handle, position new rear oil seal into crankcase and oil pan. **The new rear oil seal has to be cut approximately .0196 inch, (0.5 mm) above the mating surface. Fabricate gauge, Fig. 23, for this purpose.**
2. Lubricate rear oil seal with clean engine oil, and install crankshaft.
3. Install oil pan, and ensure crankshaft rotates freely.

BELT TENSION DATA

	New Lbs.	Used Lbs.
A/C Compressor	110	88-99
Air Pump	66	44-55
Alternator	66	44-55
Air Pump		44-55
Power Steering Pump	110	88-99
Water Pump	66	44-55

WATER PUMP
REPLACE

1. Drain cooling system, then remove radiator.
2. Remove fan and fan clutch.
3. Remove drive belts, then the pulley and vibration damper.
4. Remove water pump attaching bolts and the water pump.
5. Reverse procedure to install.

FUEL PUMP
REPLACE

1. Disconnect battery ground cable.
2. Remove fuel pump cover, then pinch off fuel suction hose with a suitable clamp.
3. On early production models, disconnect fuel lines from fuel pump.
4. On late production models, disconnect fuel lines from fuel filter, fuel reservoir and fuel pump.
5. On all models, disconnect electrical connector from fuel pump.
6. Remove fuel pump attaching screws and the fuel pump.
7. Reverse procedure to install.

116 (3.8L) & 117 (4.5 & 5.0L) GASOLINE ENGINE SECTION

INDEX

ENGINE
REPLACE

The engine and transmission are removed as an assembly.

1. Disconnect battery ground cable.
2. On 107 series vehicles, mark hood hinge locations and remove hood.
3. On 126 series vehicles, lift hood to a 90° angle and engage left hand locking lever.
4. On all models, drain cooling system. **The two drain plugs are located at the right and left side of engine block. Do not confuse crankshaft bearing capscrews with the plugs.**
5. On models equipped with A/C, carefully discharge refrigerant from system, then disconnect and cap refrigerant lines from compressor.
6. On 107 series vehicles with 116 engine and all 126 series vehicles, remove radiator and fan.
7. On all 107 and 126 series vehicles, remove complete exhaust system.

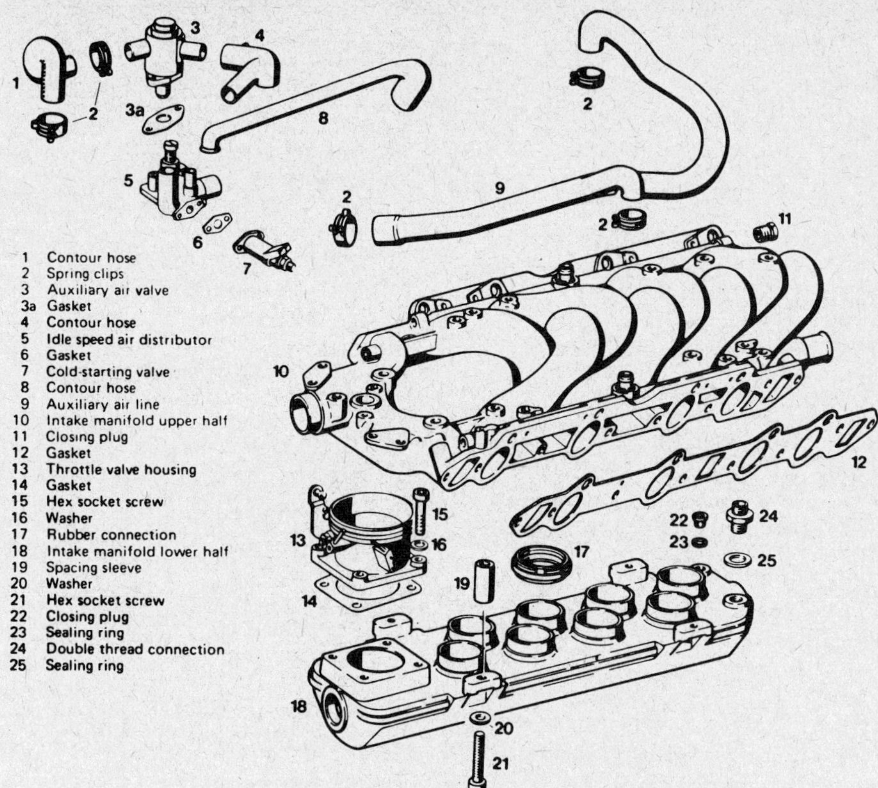

Fig. 1 Intake manifold replacement

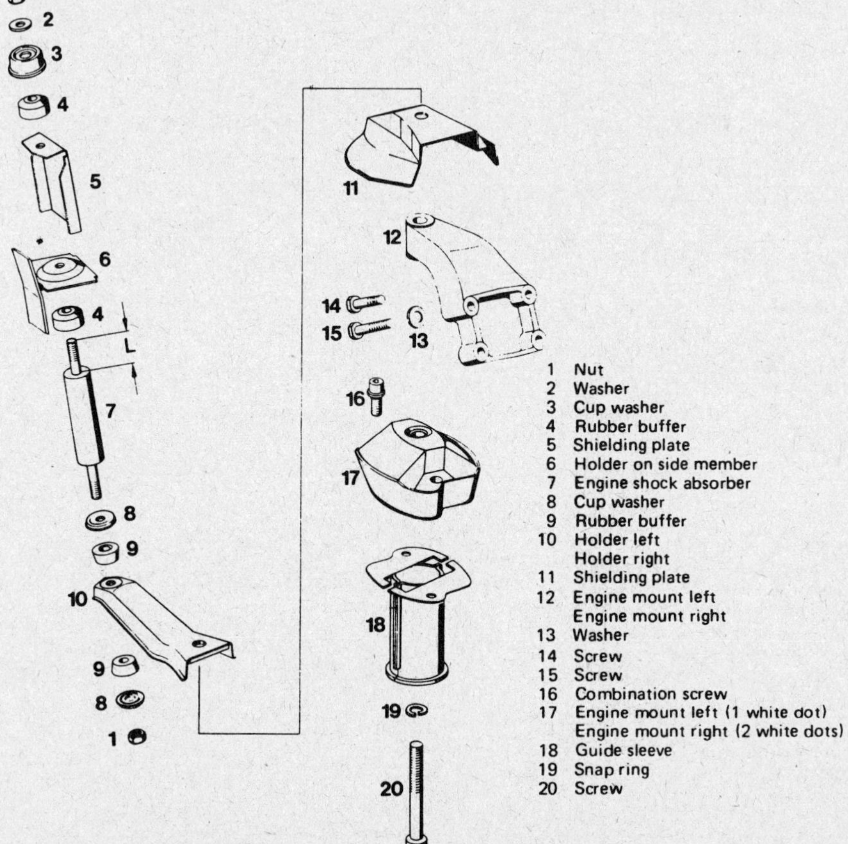

Fig. 2 Front engine mount exploded view. 380SL & SLC

8. On 107 series vehicles, disconnect drag link from righthand ball joint.
9. On all models, drain fluid from power steering pump tank, then disconnect hoses from power steering pump.
10. Disconnect all remaining electric, coolant, oil, fuel and vacuum lines leading to the engine.
11. Disconnect TDC transmitter wire from test socket.
12. On 107 series vehicles with 116 engine and all 126 series vehicles, disconnect accelerator linkage from throttle body.
13. On all models, remove left and right engine mount attaching bolts.
14. Remove both right and left side engine dampers.
15. Attach suitable hoist equipment to engine lifting points.
16. Remove rear engine mount together with carrier of closing plate.
17. Disconnect driveshaft from transmission.
18. Disconnect all electrical connectors and linkages from transmission.
19. Raise engine and transmission at approximately a 45° angle and remove assembly from vehicle.
20. Reverse procedure to install.

INTAKE MANIFOLD
REPLACE

1. Disconnect battery ground cable.
2. Drain a portion of coolant from the cooling system.
3. Disconnect and cap all fuel lines from intake manifold.
4. Disconnect all electrical connectors, vacuum lines, coolant lines and linkages from intake manifold.
5. On 107 series vehicles with 117 (4.5L) engine, remove idle speed air distributor.
6. On all models, remove intake manifold attaching bolts and the manifold, **Fig. 1.**
7. Reverse procedure to install.

EXHAUST MANIFOLD
REPLACE
107 SERIES

1. Disconnect exhaust pipe from exhaust manifolds.
2. Disconnect ignition wires from spark plugs, then remove heat shields from exhaust manifolds.
3. Remove engine mount attaching bolts, then the engine damper together with mounting bracket and heat shield.
4. Remove air cleaner assembly, then the lefthand exhaust manifold attaching nuts, bolts and manifold.
5. Remove windshield washer reservoir, then loosen coolant reservoir and position aside.
6. Remove battery together with the bracket and shield assembly.
7. Remove righthand exhaust manifold attaching nuts, bolts and the manifold.
8. Reverse procedure to install.

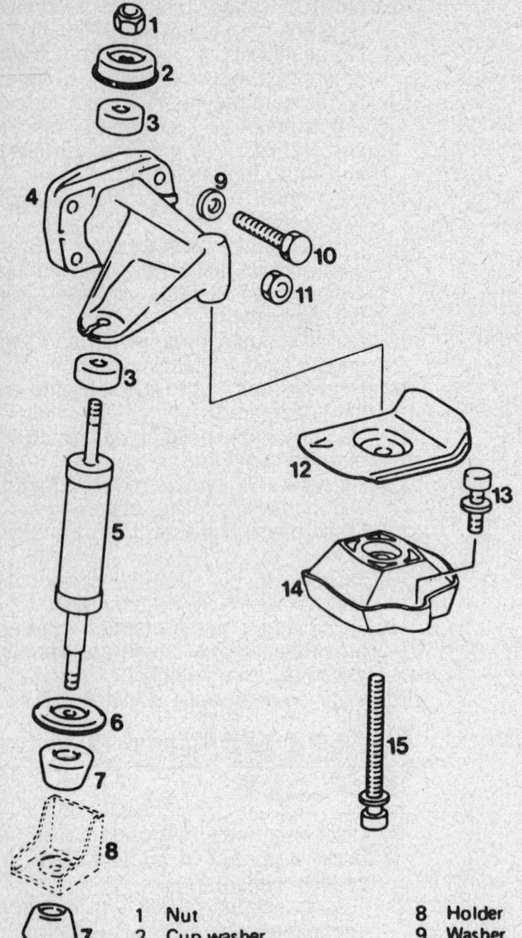

1	Nut	8	Holder
2	Cup washer	9	Washer
3	Rubber buffer	10	Screw
4	Engine mount	11	Nut
5	Engine shock absorber	12	Shielding plate
6	Cup washer	13	Combination screw
7	Rubber buffer	14	Engine mount
		15	Screw

Fig. 3 Front engine mount exploded view. 380SE, SEC, SEL & 500 SEC, SEL

126 SERIES

1. Disconnect exhaust pipe from exhaust manifold.
2. Disconnect ignition wires from spark plugs, then remove heat shields from exhaust manifolds.
3. Remove lefthand exhaust manifold attaching nuts, bolts and the manifold.
4. Remove air filter assembly, then the righthand exhaust manifold attaching nuts, bolts and the manifold.
5. Reserve procedure to install.

ENGINE MOUNTS

REPLACE

380SL & SLC

1. Remove through bolt from bottom of engine mount, **Fig. 2.**
2. Remove mount-to-crossmember attaching bolts.
3. Raise and support engine using suitable jack.
4. Remove engine mount from vehicle.
5. Reverse procedure to install. Torque mount through bolt to 55 ft. lbs. (75 Nm).

380SE, SEC, SEL & 500SEC, SEL

1. Remove through bolt from bottom of mount, **Fig. 3.**
2. Remove shock absorber lower attaching nut.
3. Raise and support engine using suitable jack.
4. Remove engine mount attaching bolt and the mount.
5. Reverse procedure to install. Torque mount through bolt to 52 ft. lbs. (70 Nm).

CYLINDER HEAD

REPLACE

REMOVAL

The engine must be cold when removing cylinder head.

Exc. 107 Series W/117 (4.5L) Engine

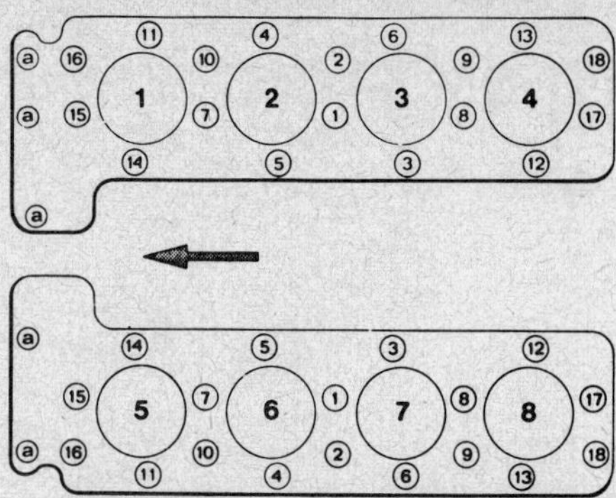

Fig. 4 Cylinder head bolt tightening sequence

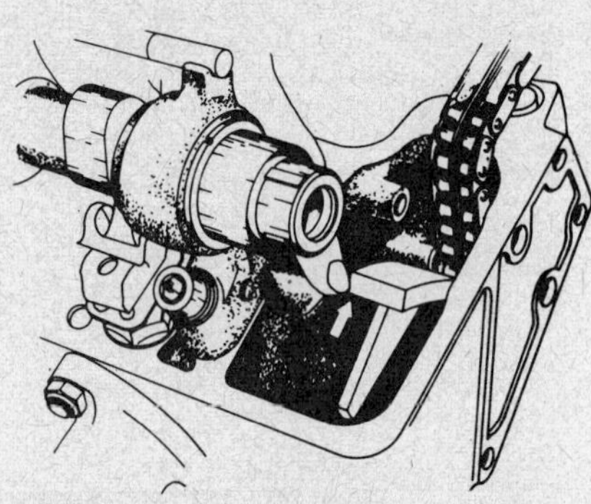

Fig. 5 Tensioning rail

1. Drain cooling system. **The two drain plugs are located at the right and left side of engine block. Do not confuse crankshaft bearing capscrews with the plugs.**
2. Disconnect fuel injection lines and remove injection nozzles from cylinder head to be replaced.
3. Remove all intake manifold attaching bolts from both cylinder heads, then rotate engine until pointer aligns with TDC mark on timing plate.
4. Mark relationship between camshaft sprocket and chain with two dots of paint.
5. Remove camshaft sprocket retaining bolt and the sprocket while holding camshaft with a suitable wrench.
6. When removing right hand cylinder head, proceed as follows:
   a. Remove alternator with mounting bracket.
   b. Remove chain tensioner, then the inner slide rail.
7. When removing left hand cylinder head, proceed as follows:
   a. Remove power steering pump and position aside, leaving fluid lines attached.
   b. Remove ignition distributor assembly.
   c. Pull out bearing bolts using a suitable puller, then remove inner slide rail from cylinder head.
8. When removing either cylinder head, disconnect exhaust pipe from exhaust manifold.
9. Remove cylinder head bolts in reverse sequence of tightening, **Fig. 4,** then lift cylinder head from engine.

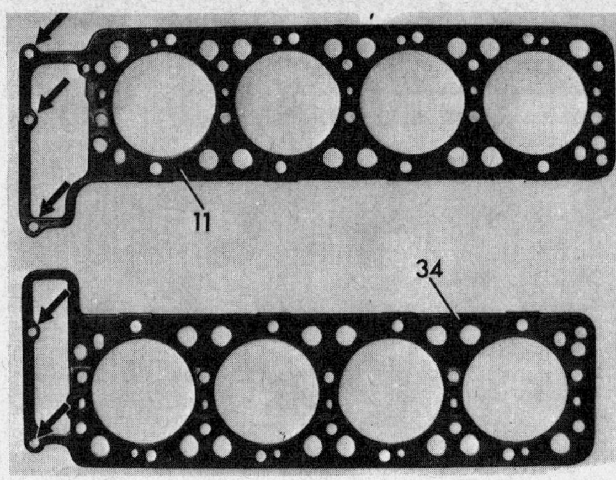

11 Righthand cylinder head gasket
34 Lefthand cylinder head gasket

Fig. 6 Cylinder head gasket identification

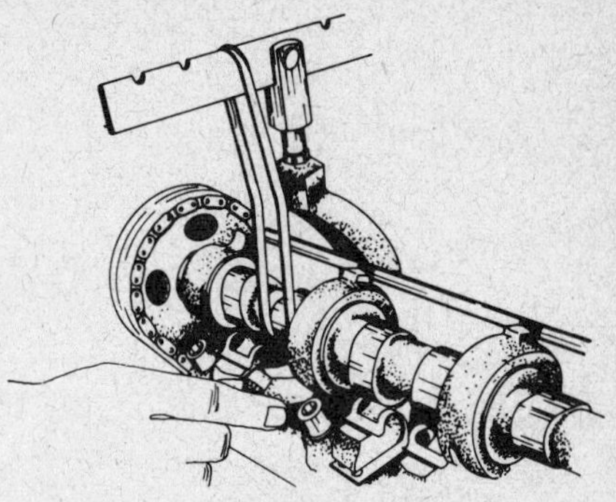

Fig. 7 Removing rocker arms using tool No. 123589036100

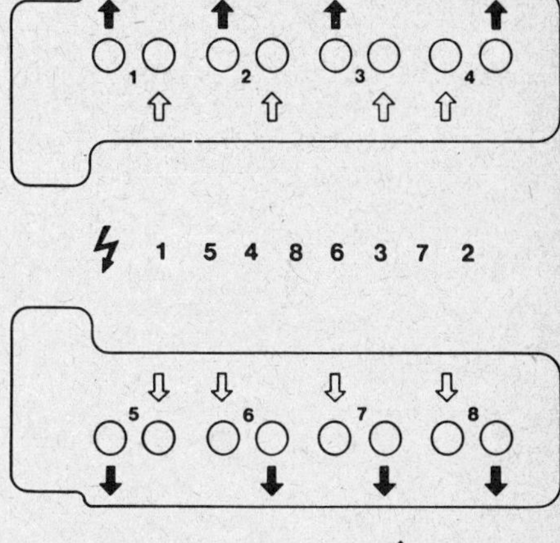

Fig. 8 Valve arrangement

When removing right hand cylinder head, push the tensioning rail with timing chain toward center of engine to prevent tensioning rail from binding.

107 Series W/117 (4.5L) Engine

1. Drain cooling system.
2. Remove battery if removing right hand cylinder head.
3. Disconnect fuel injection lines and remove injection nozzles from cylinder head to be replaced.
4. Disconnect accelerator linkage.
5. Remove intake manifold assembly.
6. When removing righthand cylinder head, remove alternator with mounting bracket, then the automatic transmission oil dipstick tube.
7. When removing lefthand cylinder head, remove ignition distributor and the power steering pump.
8. When removing either cylinder head, disconnect exhaust pipe from exhaust manifold.
9. Disconnect exhaust gas recirculation line from cylinder head.
10. Remove chain tensioner, then the slide rail.
11. Mark relationship between camshaft sprocket and chain with two dots of paint.
12. Remove cylinder head bolts in reverse sequence of tightening, **Fig. 4**, then lift cylinder head from engine. **When removing righthand cylinder head, push the tensioning rail with timing chain toward center of engine to prevent tensioning rail from binding, Fig. 5.**

INSTALLATION

1. Install new cylinder head gasket(s). **Do not mix up left and right cylinder head gaskets. The lefthand cylinder head gasket has two fastening holes in the timing chain housing, Fig. 6. The righthand cylinder head gasket has three fastening holes in the timing chain housing.**
2. Position the cylinder head. Lubricate cylinder head bolts liberally on threads and bolt head contact surfaces.
3. Tighten the cylinder head bolts in the sequence shown in **Fig. 4** to specifications.
4. Continue to reassemble the cylinder head in a reverse manner to that of removal.
5. Check valve clearance.
6. Retighten cylinder head bolts with the engine warmed to 176°F (80°C) to 44 ft. lbs. (60 Nm). **On 116 engine, torque cylinder head bolts in sequence shown on Fig. 4, and in steps as follows:** step 1, 22 ft. lbs. (30 Nm); step 2, 44 ft. lbs. (60 Nm). After a setting period of 10 minutes and with engine cold, slightly loosen cylinder head bolts and retorque to 44 ft. lbs. (60 Nm).
7. Retighten cylinder head bolts once more after the car has been driven 186-631 miles (300-1,000 km) and recheck valve clearance.

ROCKER ARMS

REPLACE

Install rocker arms at the same point where they are removed. If rocker arms are replaced, also replace the respective camshaft.

REMOVAL

1. Remove tensioning springs.
2. Disconnect ignition coil and fuel pump electrical connector and crank engine with a remote starter switch.
3. With the respective cam facing away from the rocker arm, remove the rocker arm, **Fig. 7.**

INSTALLATION

1. Lubricate the bearing surface of the rocker arm.
2. Install the rocker arm.
3. Push the tensioning spring into the ring groove of the adjusting screw.
4. Adjust valve clearance.

VALVES

ADJUST

117 (4.5L) ENGINE

If adjustments can no longer be made, install thinner thrust pieces. Thrust pieces are available in .098, .137 and .177 inch (2.5, 3.5 and 4.5 mm) thicknesses. If the torque of the valve adjusting screw cannot be obtained at 15 ft. lbs. (20 Nm), replace the valve adjusting screw or threaded bushing. Note the layout of the intake and exhaust valves, **Fig. 8.**

1. Measure the valve clearance between the slide surface of the rocker arm and basic cam circle of the camshaft. Valve clearance is correct when the gauge indicates a tight fit.
2. Adjust valve clearance by turning the valve adjusting screw with valve adjusting wrench 116589020100. **The engine may be cranked using spe-**

Fig. 9 Measuring valve guide clearance

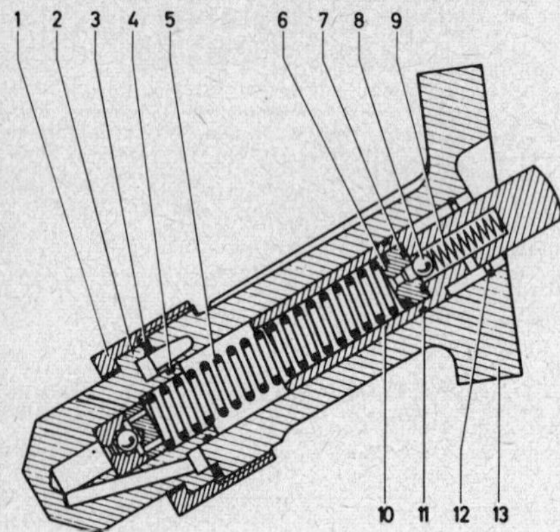

1 Closing nut
2 Closing cap
3 Sealing ring
4 Sealing ring
5 Compression spring
6 Valve disc
7 Sealing ring
8 Ball
9 Compression spring
10 Pressure bolt
11 Sealing ring
12 Circlip
13 Housing

Fig. 10 Sectional view of chain tensioner. 117 (4.5L) engine

cial tool 001589650900 applied to the crankshaft. Do not rotate the engine in reverse.

VALVE GUIDES
REPLACE

1. On 117 (4.5L) engine, clean valve guides and measure with .354 inch (9 mm) check plug No. 117789032300 for intake valves and .443 inch (11 mm) check plug No. 117589042300 for exhaust valves, **Fig. 9.** If "no-go" end of plug can be inserted remove valve guide with .354 inch (9 mm) knock-out plug No. 110589021500 for intake valves or .433 inch (11 mm) knock-out plug No. 110589031500 for exhaust valves.
2. On 116 and 117 (5.0L) engine, clean valve guides and measure with .354 inch (9 mm) check plug No. 117589032300 for intake and exhaust valves, **Fig. 9,** If "no-go" end of plug can be inserted, remove valve guide with .354 inch (9 mm) knock-out plug No. 110589021500 for intake and exhaust valves.
3. If oversize valve guides must be installed, hone the bore with the applicable hand reamers and broaches:

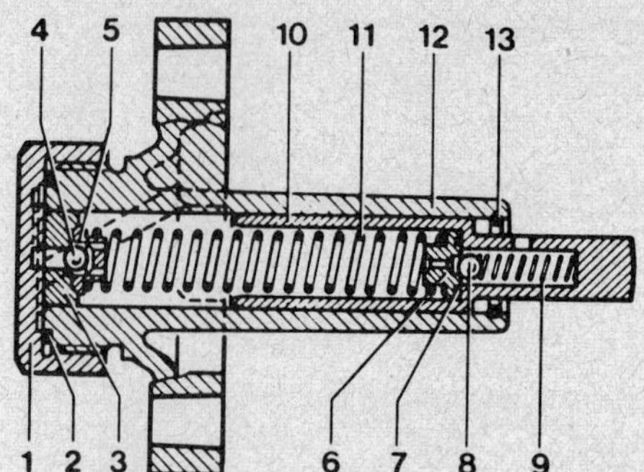

1 Closing nut
2 Aluminum sealing ring
3 Ball seat ring
4 Ball
5 Ball cage
6 Valve disc
7 O-ring
8 Ball
9 Compression spring
10 Thrust bolt
11 Compression spring
12 Housing
13 Circlip

Fig. 11 Sectional view of chain tensioner. 116 engine & 117 (5.0L) engine

   a. For first repair stage, intake .553 inch (14.035 mm)—110589035300.
   b. For first repair stage, exhaust .592 inch (15.035 mm)—110589025300.
   c. For second repair stage, intake .559 inch (14.2 mm)—115589005300 (broach) and guide sleeve No. 102589006300.
   d. For second repair stage, exhaust .598 inch (15.2 mm)—110589005300 (broach) and 117589006300 (guide sleeve).
4. Clean the bore, then cool valve guide in liquid nitrogen for three minutes or heat cylinder head in water to approximately 176 degrees F (80 degrees C).
5. Lubricate valve guide and install using a knock-in plug until circlip seats against cylinder head. On 117 (4.5L) engine, use .354 inch (9 mm) plug No. 110589001500 for intake valves and .433 inch (11 mm) plug No. 110589011500 for exhaust valves. On 116 engine and 117 (5.0L) engine, use .354 inch (9 mm) plug No. 110589001500 for intake and exhaust valves.

CHAIN TENSIONER
REPLACE

117 (4.5L) ENGINE

1. Remove chain tensioner attaching bolts and the tensioner, **Fig. 10.**
2. Insert replacement tensioner into a vessel filled with clean engine oil, ensuring tensioner is held vertically in a downward position in oil at least to the flange.
3. Actuate pressure bolt to fill tensioner with oil and vent the tensioner. Ensure tensioner allows compression only very slowly, uniformly and with considerable effort.
4. Install chain tensioner, using a new gasket. Torque attaching bolts to 18 ft. lbs. (25 Nm). **The pressure bolt of the chain tensioner should rest against the lug of the tensioning rail.**

116 ENGINE & 117 (5.0L) ENGINE

1. Remove chain tensioner attaching bolts and the tensioner, **Fig. 11.**
2. Install new tensioner using a new gasket. Torque attaching bolts to 18 ft. lbs. (25 Nm). **The pressure bolt of the chain tensioner should rest against the lug of the tensioning rail.**

TIMING CHAIN
REPLACE

1. Remove spark plugs, right hand rocker arms and chain tensioner.
2. Separate timing chain using a suitable cutting tool or by grinding off both pins of one link.
3. Remove disassembled link from timing chain, then attach new chain to old chain using a connecting link.
4. Rotate crankshaft slowly in normal direction of rotation while simultaneously pulling up on old timing chain until connecting link comes to rest on top point of right hand camshaft gear. **The timing chain must remain properly meshed in camshaft sprocket as crankshaft is turned.**
5. Disconnect old timing chain and connect ends of new chain with a connecting link.
6. Check valve timing and adjust as necessary.
7. Install chain tensioner, rocker arms and spark plugs.

FRONT COVER
REPLACE

1. Disconnect battery ground cable.
2. Drain cooling system and engine oil.
3. Remove all drive belts, then the radiator and fan.
4. Remove alternator with mounting bracket.
5. Remove ignition distributor, then remove air pump, A/C compressor and vacuum pump, as equipped.
6. Remove power steering pump and position aside, leaving lines connected. Remove power steering pump mounting bracket, if necessary.
7. Remove crankshaft pulley and vibration damper.
8. On models with 117 (4.5L) engine, remove oil damper with bracket, then the oil dipstick and tube. **Do not loosen plugs in oil damper.**
9. On models with 116 engine and 117 (5.0L) engine, remove warm-up com-

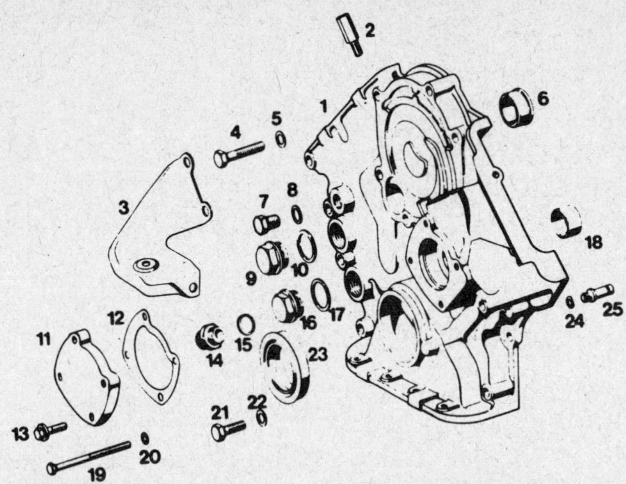

1 Timing housing cover
2 Threaded bolts for adjusting lever of ignition distributor
3 Holder for engine shock absorber
4 Screw
5 Washer
6 Bearing bushing guide wheel
7 Closing plug
8 Sealing ring
9 Closing plug
10 Sealing ring
11 End cover
12 Gasket
13 Combination screw
14 Screw connection
15 Sealing ring
16 Closing plug
17 Sealing ring
18 Bearing bushing for intermediate sprocket shaft
19 Screw
20 Washer
21 Screw
22 Washer
23 Radial sealing ring
24 Spring washer
25 Bearing bolt

Fig. 12 Front cover replacement. (Typical)

pensator.

10. On all models, remove water pump.
11. Loosen upper oil pan half attaching screws and remove oil pump.
12. Remove M8 bolts from end of each cylinder head.
13. Disconnect and remove TDC transmitter from front cover.
14. Remove front cover attaching bolts, then pry out front crankshaft seal.
15. Disconnect oil pump chain from crankshaft sprocket and remove front cover, **Fig. 12.**
16. Reverse procedure to install. Apply suitable lubricant to cylinder head gaskets and sealant to all sealing surfaces prior to installation.

CAMSHAFT

REPLACE

REMOVAL

1. Remove the rocker arms.
2. Set the piston on the first cylinder to ignition TDC using special tool 116589020100.
3. Secure the timing chain and camshaft gear with binding wire so the timing chain won't skip.
4. Remove the camshaft gear.
5. Remove the camshaft, camshaft bearing and oil line as an assembly.

INSTALLATION

1. Place the camshaft and camshaft bearing on the cylinder head and tighten progressively from the inside out. **Concerning the camshaft in the lefthand bank, the outer fastening bolt of the rear camshaft bearing must be inserted into the camshaft bearing before mounting the camshaft.**
2. Mount the oil pipe, placing connecting pieces into position and then checking the three inner connecting pieces to assure unobstructed passage through the oil line before knocking the camshaft bearings into place. Replace the oil pipe if the oil bores are obstructed. **Replace all plastic connections.**
3. Mount the compensating washer so the keyway at the notch is in mesh with the woodruff key of the camshaft, **Fig. 13.**
4. Mount rocker arms and tensioning springs.
5. Adjust valve clearance.
6. If installing a new camshaft, check timing. Refer to "Valve Timing Specifications" chart.

OIL PAN

REPLACE

107 SERIES

1. Remove radiator shroud and fan.
2. Remove front axle assembly.
3. Remove A/C compressor with mounting bracket and belt tensioner.
4. Remove supporting angle bracket, if equipped, from transmission.
5. Remove oil dipstick tube holder.
6. Remove oil pan attaching bolts and the oil pan.
7. Reverse procedure to install, using a new oil pan gasket.

126 SERIES

1. Remove A/C compressor with mounting bracket and belt tensioner.
2. Disconnect throttle linkage, then remove lower half of oil pan.
3. Remove oil dipstick tube, then the oil pump.
4. Removing attaching bolts from upper half of oil pan.
5. Remove two engine mount attaching bolts, then loosen both engine dampers.
6. Remove radiator shroud.
7. Attach suitable lifting equipment to engine, then raise engine and remove oil pan.
8. Reverse procedure to install, using a new oil pan gasket.

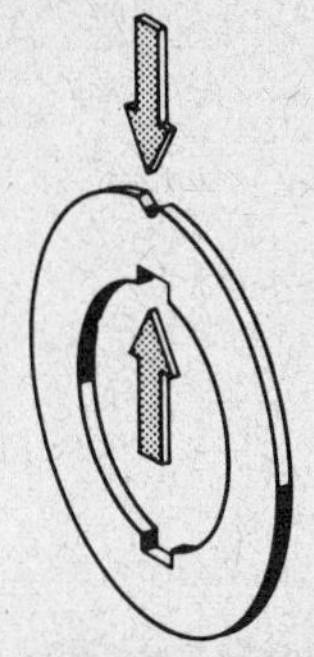

Fig. 13 Correct positioning for installing compensating washer

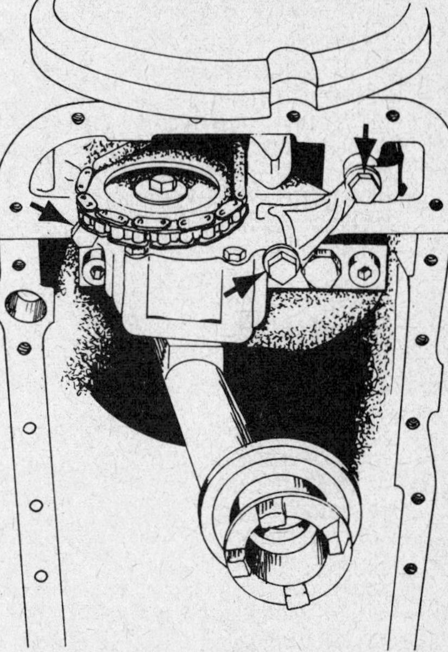

Fig. 14 Bolt locations for oil pump removal

OIL PUMP

REPLACE

This is a chain-driven sprocket type oil pump. When changing the oil pump, be sure the new pump has the same number of teeth on the sprocket.

1. Drain engine oil, then remove oil pan or lower half of oil pan depending on application.
2. Place counterweight of first crankpin in horizontal position to allow removal of oil pump.
3. On all except 107 series vehicles with 116 engine, proceed as follows:
   a. Remove three oil pump attaching bolts, **Fig. 14.**

b. Loosen drive sprocket bolt, then tilt oil pump rearward and remove the bolt.
c. Pry sprocket from oil pump and remove the pump.
d. Remove sprocket from drive chain.

4. On 107 series vehicles with 116 engine, remove three oil pump attaching bolts, **Fig. 14.** Tilt oil pump forward, lift chain from sprocket and remove oil pump.
5. Reverse procedure to install.

FRONT OIL SEAL
REPLACE

1. Remove hub, vibration damper and crankshaft pulley.
2. Carefully pry seal out using a suitable screwdriver.
3. Remove all burrs from oil seal bore.
4. Fill new seal behind lip with suitable grease, then install seal using tool No. 110589076100 or equivalent.
5. Reverse remainder of procedure to complete installation.

REAR OIL SEAL
REPLACE

1. Remove transmission, then the flywheel or converter drive plate.
2. Carefully pry seal out from around crankshaft flange.
3. Mount insertion sleeve of seal installation tool No. 117589004300 to crankshaft.
4. Fill seal with suitable grease and position over sleeve.
5. Install seal up to stop using the installation tool.
6. Install converter drive plate or flywheel and the transmission.

BELT TENSION DATA

	New Lbs.	Used Lbs.
A/C Compressor	110	88-99
Air Pump	66	44-55
Alternator	66	44-55
Power Steering Pump	66	44-45
Water Pump	66	44-55

WATER PUMP
REPLACE
EXC. 107 SERIES W/117 (4.5L) ENGINE

1. Drain cooling system, then remove water pump drive belt.
2. Disconnect heater hose from water pump.
3. Remove fan shroud and position aside.
4. Remove fan, fan clutch and fan cover.
5. Remove ignition distributor.
6. Disconnect electrical connection, then remove inlet connector from water pump.
7. On models equipped with automatic level control, remove hollow screw from oil pump and position high pressure line aside.
8. On all models, remove vibration damper.
9. Remove water pump attaching bolts and the water pump.
10. Reverse procedure to install, using new gasket.

107 SERIES W/117 (4.5L) ENGINE

1. Drain cooling system, then remove air cleaner assembly.
2. Remove water pump drive belt, then disconnect upper coolant hose from radiator and thermostat housing.
3. Remove fan and fan clutch, then disconnect lower coolant hose from thermostat housing and radiator.
4. Remove inlet connector from water pump.
5. Remove ignition distributor.
6. Remove water pump attaching bolts and the water pump. **Rotate vibration damper as necessary to gain access to all water pump attaching bolts.**
7. Reverse procedure to install.

FUEL PUMP
REPLACE

1. Disconnect battery ground cable.
2. Remove fuel pump cover, then pinch off fuel suction hose with a suitable clamp.
3. On all engines except late production 117 (4.5L), disconnect fuel lines from fuel pump.
4. On late production 117 (4.5L) engine, disconnect fuel lines from fuel filter, fuel reservoir and fuel pump.
5. On all models, disconnect electrical connector from fuel pump.
6. Remove fuel pump attaching screws and the fuel pump.
7. Reverse procedure to install.

601 DIESEL ENGINE SECTION

INDEX

ENGINE
REPLACE

The engine and transmission are removed as an assembly.

1. Open, then raise hood to a 90° angle.
2. Loosen noise suppresser lining attaching screws, then remove lining from under vehicle.
3. Completely drain cooling system.
4. Remove air hose and air cleaner cover.
5. Disconnect battery positive cable and position aside.
6. Remove radiator from vehicle.
7. Carefully discharge refrigerant from A/C system, then disconnect and cap refrigerant lines, if equipped.
8. On models with level control, loosen level control pressure oil pump attaching bolts. Refer to **Fig. 1**, for pressure oil pump bolt locations, then remove pump and position aside. Do not disconnect pressure line.
9. Drain fluid from power steering pump, then disconnect and cap pump lines.
10. While pushing on angle lever slotted guide piece, disconnect and remove bowden wire.
11. Mark, disconnect and/or cap all electrical connectors, vacuum lines oil and fuel lines from engine assembly.
12. Remove engine mount-to-crossmember attaching bolts.
13. Remove engine mount stop attaching bolts, then the engine stop.
14. Remove two lower starter motor attaching screws, then disconnect bracket and tachometer drive and position aside. Remove ground strap from engine and/or transmission assembly.
15. Disconnect RPM sensor from oil pan, if equipped.
16. Disconnect exhaust pipe from exhaust manifold.
17. Loosen lateral exhaust system support attaching bolts, then swivel exhaust pipe bracket downward.
18. Disconnect driveshaft from transmission, then remove slide piece and intermediate bearing bracket attaching screws. Slide driveshaft rearward as far as possible.

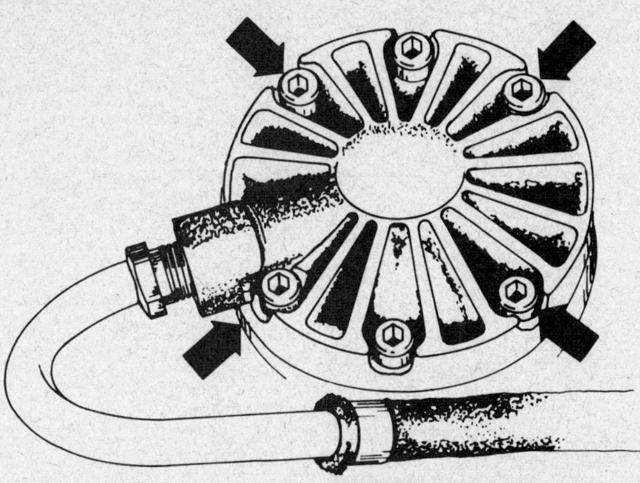

Fig. 1 Level control oil pump bolt locations

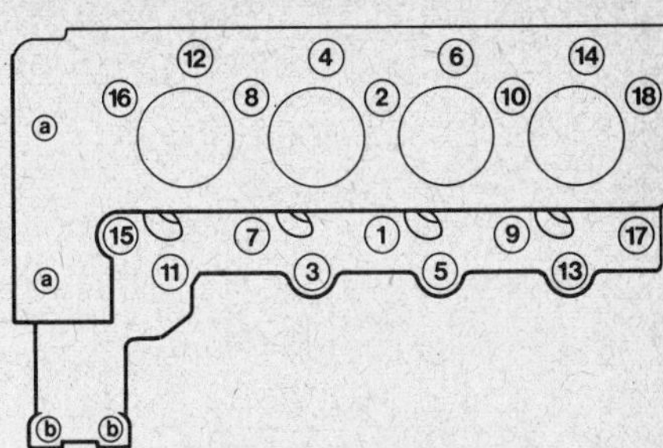

Fig. 2 Reversing cylinder head bolt tightening sequence

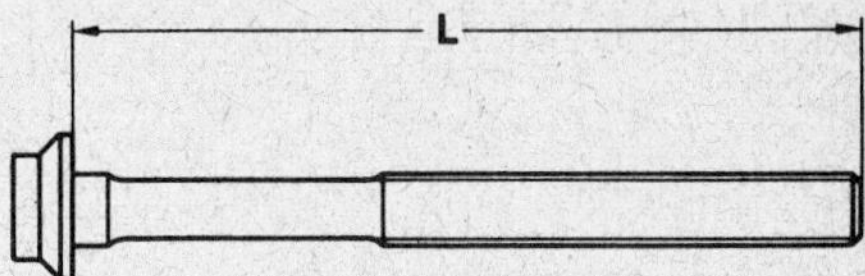

Fig. 3 Cylinder head bolt L dimension

19. Remove heat guide plate from vehicle floor, if necessary.
20. Disconnect tachometer cable from transmission rear cover.
21. Disconnect clutch master cylinder to slave cylinder oil line.
22. Remove shift rods from transmission shift levers.
23. Install suitable engine lifting equipment onto engine lifting eyes.
24. Remove rear engine crossmember and rear engine mount.
25. Remove both front engine carrier mount attaching bolts.
26. Gradually lift engine and transmission assembly from vehicle.
27. Reverse procedure to install.

CYLINDER HEAD REPLACE

The cylinder head should be removed with the engine cold and together with the exhaust manifold assembly.

1. Open and raise hood to a 90° position.
2. Completely drain cooling system.
3. Disconnect battery ground cable.
4. Remove radiator from vehicle.
5. Remove air cleaner assembly.
6. Loosen necessary attaching bolts, then remove drive belts.
7. On vehicles with level control, loosen level control pressure oil pump attaching bolts, **Fig. 1,** then position pump aside. Do not disconnect pressure lines.
8. Remove oil dipstick guide tube.
9. Disconnect coolant hoses and water temperature switch electrical connector.
10. Disconnect engine regulator bowden wire.
11. Using suitable tools, pinch fuel lines, then remove fuel filter.
12. Disconnect EGR hose from EGR valve, if equipped.
13. Remove exhaust flange from exhaust manifold.
14. Mark cylinder number, then remove fuel injection lines. Cap all open fittings.
15. Remove intake manifold and cylinder head cover.
16. Remove heater feed line lock.
17. Remove oil filter pipe elbow.
18. Mark cylinder number, then disconnect glow plug wires.
19. Place No. 1 cylinder to TDC of compression stroke. **Do not place a wrench on camshaft sprocket attaching bolt to place No. 1 cylinder at TDC. Do not turn engine (crankshaft) in reverse direction. Always turn engine (crankshaft) in normal direction of engine rotation.**
20. Remove chain tensioner assembly.
21. Mark camshaft sprocket and timing chain for installation alignment. **Use white paint to place alignment marks on sprocket and chain assembly. Do not use a lead pencil, pen or a sharp metal tool of any kind to place alignment marks.**
22. Remove camshaft sprocket attaching bolt.
23. Lift camshaft sprocket and chain assembly, then lower sprocket and chain assembly into timing chain lower cover.
24. Alternately and evenly loosen camshaft bearing cap attaching bolts, then carefully remove camshaft from engine.
25. Using a suitable puller, knock out slide rail attaching bolts, then remove guide rail assembly from engine.
26. Using a suitable screwdriver, remove both M8 attaching screws from cylinder head.
27. Loosen cylinder head attaching screws in reverse of tightening sequence shown in **Fig. 2. Cylinder head attaching screws 2, 8, 10 and 16 are located in the camshaft bearing bracket shafts.**
28. Remove cylinder head assembly from cylinder block.
29. Reverse procedure to install, noting the following:
    a. Install a new cylinder head gasket.
    b. Install cylinder head, noting location of cylinder head clamping sleeve.
    c. Measure length L, **Fig. 3,** of new cylinder head attaching screw.
    d. M 10 80 bolt, length L when new should be 3.14 inch (80 mm). Maximum length of this bolt should be 3.29 inch (83.6 mm).
    e. M 10 102 bolt, length L when new should be 4 inches (102 mm). Maximum length of this bolt should be 4.15 inches (105.6 mm).
    f. M 10 115 bolt, length L when new should be 4.52 inches (115 mm). Maximum length of this bolt should be 4.66 inches (118.6 mm).
    g. Lubricate cylinder head attaching screw threads and insert into cylinder head.
    h. Torque cylinder head attaching screws in sequence shown in **Fig. 2. Torque cylinder head attaching screws to initial torque and angle torque rotation. For this purpose, place an adjustable torque wrench is released position (locked) into the plug-in ratchet. Position the adjustable torque wrench with the plug-in ratchet lengthwise (in relation to the engine) and keep turning until it is transverse (in relation to the engine).**
    i. Torque cylinder head bolts (first stage) to 18 ft. lbs. (25 Nm).
    j. Torque cylinder head bolts (second stage) to 29.5 ft. lbs. (40 Nm).
    k. Allow cylinder head bolts to set for 10 minutes.
    l. Torque cylinder head bolts (third stage) and additional 90°.
    m. Torque cylinder head bolts (fourth stage) an additional 90°.
    n. Torque both M8 cylinder head attaching screws to 18 ft. lbs. (25 Nm).
    o. When installing camshaft sprocket, ensure alignment marks placed during removal are aligned properly. Ensure dowel pin on camshaft flange engages dowel pin hole on camshaft sprocket.

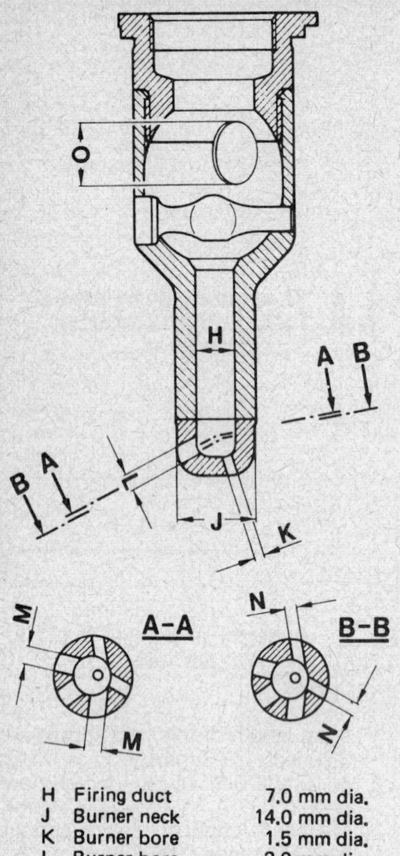

Fig. 4 Sectional view of pre-combustion chamber, firing duct, burner bores & glow plug bores

PRE-COMBUSTION CHAMBER

REPLACE

REMOVAL

The pre-combustion chambers are identified at the upper flange with the code numbers 601/07. Six burner bores of different diameters are located on the prechamber lower half (burner neck) at different levels and angle positions, **Fig. 4.** The firing duct portion has a .275 inch (7 mm) diameter and the burner neck has a .551 inch (14 mm) diameter. Also, the prechamber floor is designedas a spherical depression providing uniform wall thicknesses in range of the burner bores.

1. Mark, disconnect and cap fuel injection lines from fuel injection nozzles.
2. Loosen fuel injection line brackets from intake manifold.
3. Loosen bowden wire bracket from engine regulator and position aside.
4. Loosen nozzle holder bracket, then remove pencil element glow plugs, **Fig. 5.**
5. Remove threaded ring.
6. Using tool 601589063300 or equivalent, remove pre-combustion chambers from cylinder head bores and cover cylinder head cover bores.

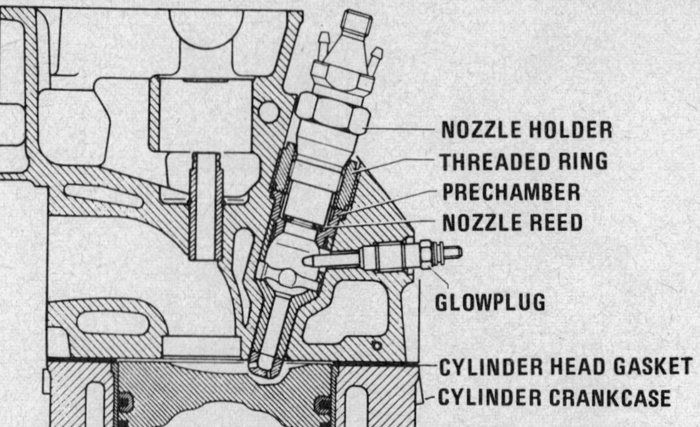

Fig. 5 Sectional view of cylinder crankcase, pencil element glow plug, pre-combustion chamber, nozzle reed & nozzle holder

INSTALLATION

If the original pre-combustion chambers are to be installed, ensure chambers are in perfect condition or driveability problems will result. Ensure ball pin end is not burnt or covered with carbon deposits. If burner tops are burned or cracks have developed in the pre-combustion chamber lower portion, remove intake manifold and check for traces of oil leakage. Any oil leakage traces, should be serviced (repaired and/or worn or damaged components replaced) before installing an original or new pre-combustion chamber. If oil moistened spots or deposits are found check vacuum pump for damage. If damaged, replace fuel injection pump vacuum control unit. Check the vacuum control unit vacuum lines. The vacuum lines (scored or blackened by excessive oil leakage) will indicate which of the two components of the vacuum unit has failed.

1. If the cylinder head assembly has been ground, distance C, **Fig. 6,** must be maintained to .292-.318 inches (7.6-81 mm).
2. If the distance is not maintained, select appropriate sealing ring and insert between cylinder head and pre-combustion chamber.
3. Install pre-combustion chamber into cylinder head. Ensure lug on pre-combustion chamber is pointing toward cylinder head recess.
4. Lubricate threaded ring and install into cylinder head assembly. Torque threaded ring to 66-81 ft. lbs. (90-110 Nm).
5. Install glow plugs and connect glow plug wires.
6. Insert new nozzle reed.
7. Completely install nozzle holder and torque to 52-59 ft. lbs. (70-80 Nm).
8. Connect fuel return hoses on to injection lines.
9. Install fuel injection lines.
10. Install bowden wire holder on to engine regulator.

TIMING CHAIN

REPLACE

A timing chain with connecting link is available for repairs. If only an endless timing chain is available, the chain can be opened prior to installation. During a engine overhaul, an endless timing chain must be installed only. Check camshaft and crankshaft sprockets for score marks and pitting. Replace, if necessary. Replacement part for timing chains with connecting links are available. The bushing chain with connecting link part No. 0019971694 and connecting link part No. 0009971198 is available. When repairing a timing chain, the connecting link is held in place by a locking spring. The outer flanges connecting link is pressed on by means of tool 000589574300.

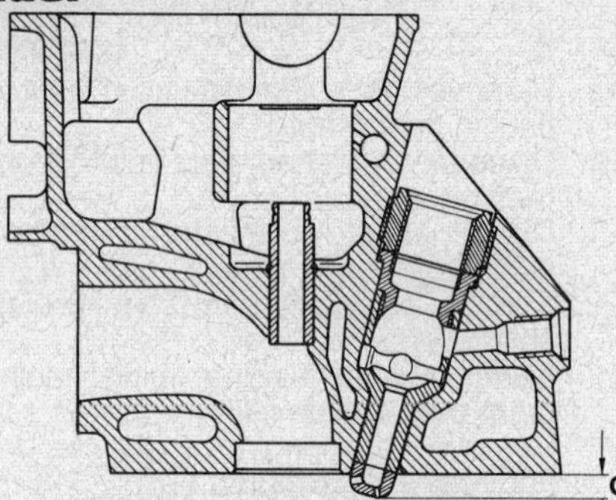

Fig. 6 Cylinder head parting surface to pre-combustion chamber tip clearance

1. Remove injection nozzles.
2. Remove cylinder head cover.
3. Remove chain tensioner.
4. Remove fan and fan cover.
5. Cover chain box with a clean shop towel, then cut through both chain bolts on one link of timing chain.
6. Connect new timing chain with connecting link onto the old chain, while pushing out the opened link.
7. Slowly rotate crankshaft in direction of engine rotation, while simultaneously pulling up the old timing chain until the connecting link comes to rest against the upper post point of camshaft timing gear. **The timing chain should remain in mesh while rotating the camshaft and crankshaft sprockets.**
8. Remove the old timing chain and connect ends of new timing chain with a connecting link. Secure camshaft sprocket.

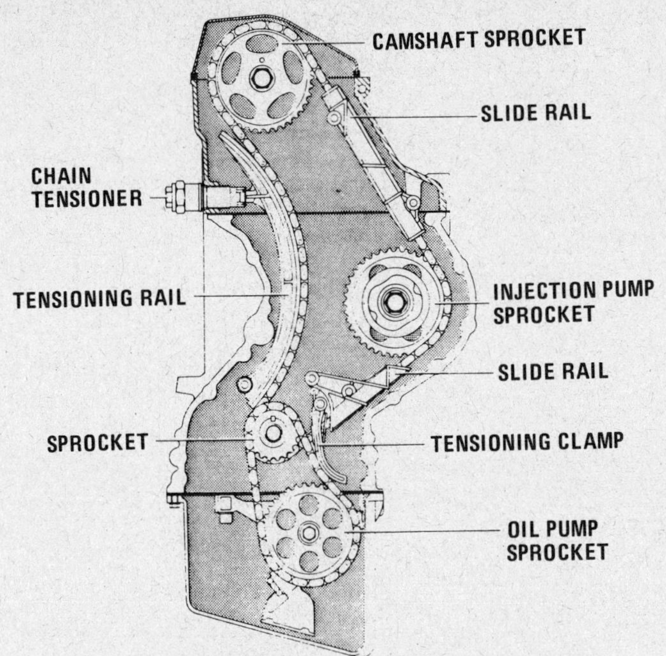

Fig. 7 Timing chain, chain tensioner & tensioning rail assembly

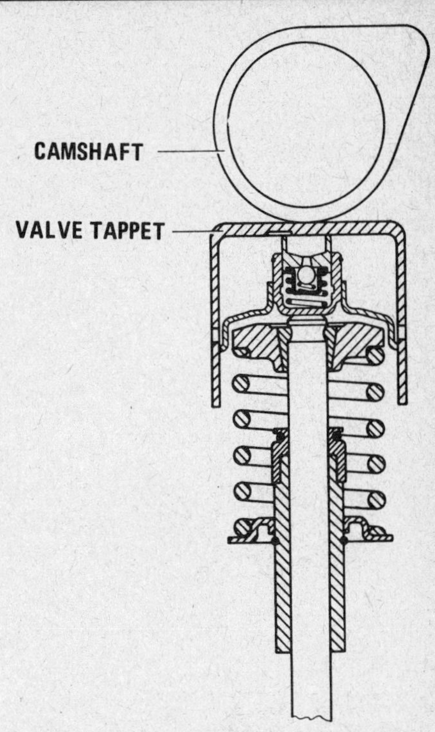

Fig. 8 Sectional view of camshaft & valve tappet

9. Insert connecting link from the rear into the timing chain.
10. Put separately enclosed outer flange of connecting link (with punched in IWIS identification) into a suitable pressing tool.
11. Place pressing tool onto connecting link end and press on flange assembly.
12. Force locking spring in opposite direction of engine rotation into chain pin grooves.
13. Install chain tensioner.
14. Rotate crankshaft and check alignment marks. **Ensure alignment marks are properly aligned. The No. 1 piston should be at TDC of compression stroke if alignment marks are correctly aligned. If alignment marks are not aligned, check crankshaft and injection pump timing.**
15. Install cylinder head cover, fan and fan cover.

CHAIN TENSIONER
REPLACE

1. Remove cylinder head cover.
2. Remove fan and fan cover.
3. Remove chain tensioner, **Fig. 7** from engine.
4. Reverse procedure to install. When installing tensioner, proceed as follows:
   a. Place chain tensioner with thrust pin facing downward into a container of SAE 10 engine oil. Ensure flange is submerged in oil.
   b. Press thrust bolt 7-10 times slowly downward against stop.
   c. Install chain tensioner and sealing ring.
   d. Thrust pin on chain tensioner should rest against tensioning rail lug.

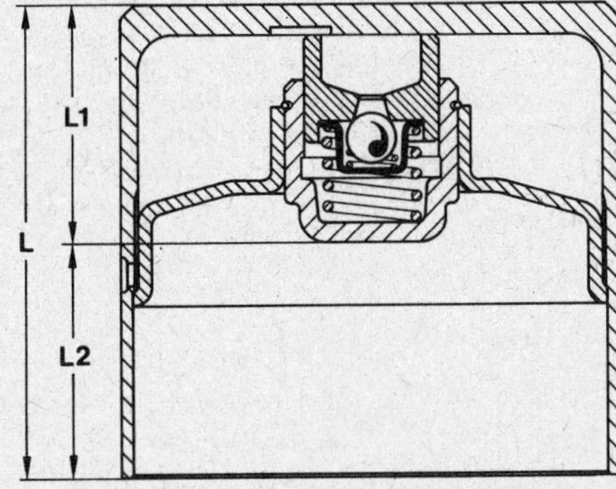

Fig. 9 Measuring valve tappet dimensions

CAMSHAFT
REPLACE

1. Remove cylinder head cover.
2. Turn crankshaft until No. 1 piston is at TDC of compression stroke.
3. Remove timing chain tensioner.
4. Place alignment marks on camshaft sprocket and timing chain for installation alignment. **Use white paint to place alignment marks.**
5. Remove camshaft sprocket.
6. Remove camshaft.
7. Reverse procedure to install. Torque cylinder head cover attaching bolts to 7 ft. lbs. (10 Nm). Torque camshaft sprocket attaching bolt to 33 ft. lbs. (45 Nm). Torque camshaft bearing cap attaching bolts to 18 ft. lbs. (25 Nm).

VALVE CHECK

1. Start and operate engine at approximately 3000 RPM for 5 minutes.
2. Remove cylinder head cover.
3. Place lobe of valve tappet on base circle with lobe pointing upward, **Fig. 8.**
4. Using a suitable tool, push or try to push valve tappet manually. **If compared with the other valves, the valve tappet drops quickly or if the valve tapped has excessive play in relation to base circle of lobe, perform step 6, then 8. If the valve tappet has play, or if the sinking time (when tappet is pushed) is too short, check basic position steps 5 through 7.**
5. Using a dial indicator placed on measuring bridge tool 601589082100 or equivalent, measure and note cylinder head parting surface to valve tappet dimension. Place measuring bridge over tappet to be checked on the cylinder head parting surface. **If necessary, measure this dimension on all the valves.**
6. Remove fan and fan cover.
7. Remove camshaft assembly.
8. Measure cylinder head parting surface to valve tappet dimension. The difference between dimension obtained in step 5 and step 8 is the initial stroke (installation position). The nominal value when valve tappet is new should be .0098-.0629 inch (.25-1.6 mm). The nominal value on a used valve tappet should be .0098-.0984 inch (.25-2.5 mm).
9. If the valve tappet sinks quickly or if the nominal dimension in step 8 is not obtained or exceeded, remove valve tappet.
10. Measure and note valve tappet dimension L, **Fig. 9.**
11. Measure and note valve tappet dimension L2, **Fig. 9.** Dimension L1 (dimension between L and L2) should be .708-.748 inch (18-19 mm).

12. If dimension L1 is higher or lower, remove guide sleeve. Using suitable pliers, remove guide sleeve from valve tappet. Do not damage guide sleeve.
13. Pull thrust bolt out of guide sleeve and remove compression spring.
14. Using compressed air, blow out all dirt from components. Blow through the valve tappet at the oil feed hole.
15. Remove snap ring from guide sleeve, then bend snap ring edges slightly and install into guide sleeve.
16. Assemble guide sleeve, compression spring and thrust pin into tappet.
17. Fill thrust pin with clean engine oil. Press on ball valve and close ball valve. Add oil, if necessary. Using a suitable tool, apply force on ball valve. No oil should flow out of ball. If oil flows out, replace valve tappet.
18. Fill valve tappet with clean engine oil and install vented thrust pin with guide sleeve into valve tappet. Push guide sleeve into valve tappet until snap ring engages ring groove.
19. Check dimension L1, refer to steps 9 and 10.
20. Loosen closing plug on oil duct on cylinder head and check oil supply.
21. Lubricate, then install valve tappets.
22. Install camshaft, cylinder head cover, fan and fan cover.
23. Operate engine and check for proper operation.

CAMSHAFT TIMING CHECK

During check, ensure alignment marks on camshaft sprocket flange and cylinder head are properly aligned. In this position the No. 1 cylinder is at TDC of compression stroke. Camshaft timing is measured at .078 inch (2 mm) of valve tappet travel.

1. Remove cylinder head cover.
2. Remove injection nozzles.
3. Turn crankshaft in direction of engine rotation, until the cam top of the second cam lobe is pointing upward.
4. Position dial indicator holder tool 363589022100 or equivalent, above intake valve of No. 1 cylinder.
5. Install dial indicator onto holder with dial indicator pointer seated on valve tappet under approximately .118 inch (3 mm) of preload (indicated by the smaller of the two dial indicator needles).
6. Set dial indicator to zero (indicated by the larger of the two dial indicator needles).
7. Continue turning the crankshaft in direction of engine rotation until small needle on dial indicator has moved back .078 inch (2 mm) to .039 inch (1 mm) of valve lift.
8. In this position, the valve on the balancing disc should be the same as the specified intake valve opening value. Intake valve opening on a new timing chain should be 11° or 12° on a used timing chain.
9. Install injection nozzles and cylinder head cover.

CONNECTING RODS & PISTONS

Connecting rod bearing and connecting rod bushing bores are similar in width. A weight compensation is attached at the left and right of the connecting rod bearing cap. Only connecting rods of similar weight may be installed in one engine. Connecting rods which have become overheated as a result of bearing damage (blue coloring) may no longer be used. Connecting rod and bearing caps are marked together. There should be no transverse score marks and notches on the connecting rod shaft.

A group code letter A, X or B, piston code number 05 or 06 and the driving direction (arrow) are punched into the piston crown. The group code letter is also stamped into the cylinder crankcase parting surface. For repairs only, pistons with group code letters X are available. These pistons are also for installation in cylinder bores with group code letters A or B. The following engine, piston code number, group letter and normal piston and cylinder diameter dimensions are available:

1. Engine 601.911:
   a. Piston code number, 01.
   b. Group code letter, A, X or B.
   c. Normal piston diameter for group A pistons should be 3.42-3.424 inch (86.970-86.976 mm).
   d. Normal piston diameter for group X pistons should be above 3.424-3.425 inches (86.975-86.983 mm).
   e. Normal piston diameter for group X pistons should be above 3.4244-3.4247 inches (86.982-86.988 mm).
   f. Normal cylinder diameter for group A pistons should be 3.425-3.4254 inches (87-87.006 mm).
   g. Normal cylinder diameter for group X pistons should be above 3.4254-3.4256 inches (87.006-87.012 mm).
   h. Normal cylinder diameter for group B pistons should be above 3.4256-3.4258 inches (87.012-87.018 mm).
2. Engine 610.921:
   a. Piston code number, 04.
   b. Group code letter, A, X or B.
   c. For normal piston and cylinder diameters, refer to 601.911 engine step 1.

OIL PAN & OIL PUMP
REPLACE

1. Remove engine noise shield.
2. Drain oil from engine.
3. Loosen engine shock absorber (mount) to crossmember attaching bolts.
4. Remove engine stop and bracket assembly.
5. On models with RPM sensor, disconnect RPM sensor electrical connector from oil pan.
6. Disconnect ground strap from transmission.
7. Remove engine carrier front engine mount attaching bolts.
8. Loosen right and left torsion bar ends from side member.
9. Install suitable engine lifting equipment onto front engine eye.
10. Lift engine enough to facilitate oil pan removal.
11. Loosen oil pan attaching bolts, then remove oil pan from vehicle.
12. Loosen oil pump attaching bolts, then remove oil pump from engine.
13. Reverse procedure to install. Torque oil pan to crankcase M6 attaching bolts to 7 ft. lbs. (10 Nm). Torque oil pan to crankcase M8 attaching bolts to 18 ft. lbs. (25 Nm).

WATER PUMP
REPLACE

1. Drain cooling system.
2. Disconnect all hoses and electrical connectors from water pump.
3. Remove fan and fan cover.
4. Remove drive belt.
5. Remove pulley attaching bolts, then the pulley.
6. Disconnect magnet cable from carrier.
7. Remove water pump together with magnet carrier.
8. Reverse procedure to install.

FUEL PUMP
REPLACE

1. Remove air cleaner cover.
2. Disconnect and cap all fuel lines, vacuum lines and electrical connectors from fuel pump.
3. Loosen attaching nuts, then remove fuel pump.
4. Reverse procedure to install.

616 & 617 DIESEL ENGINE SECTION

INDEX

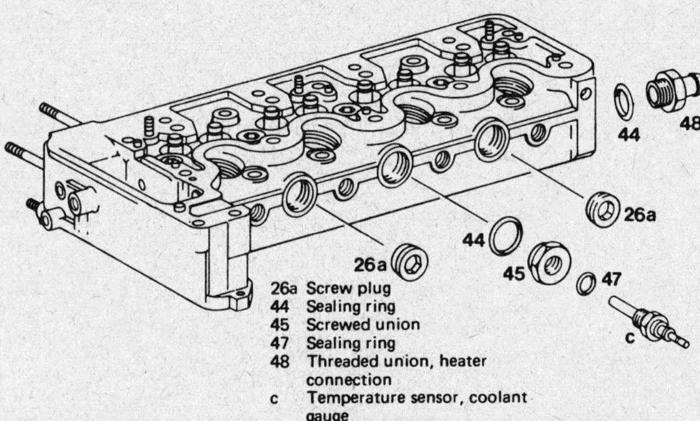

1st version cylinder head, w/pre-glow system and pre-glow indicator. 616 engine

616 & 617 EXC. TURBOCHARGED ENGINE

REPLACE

The engine and transmission are removed as an assembly.

1. Disconnect battery ground cable.
2. On vehicle series 123, open engine hood to 90° position and engage left-hand locking lever into latch.
3. Completely drain and remove radiator from vehicle.
4. Vehicles equipped with 616 engine, remove upper half of air filter. Vehicles equipped with injection pumps and mechanical governors, remove air filter.
5. Vehicles equipped with air conditioning, remove compressor and bracket, and position aside. Do not disconnect refrigerant lines. **If refrigerant lines have to be disconnected, carefully discharge refrigerant from air conditioning system.**
6. Vehicles equipped with level control, remove bolts, **Fig. 1** and oil pump.
7. Drain fluid from power steering pump reservoir and disconnect hoses.
8. Loosen control linkage, and disconnect all coolant, vacuum, oil, fuel and electrical lines from engine.
9. Remove clip and longitudinal control shaft, if equipped.
10. On vehicle series 115 and 123 equipped with automatic transmissions, loosen engine shock absorbers. On vehicle model 300D, remove engine shock absorbers from body.
11. Remove self locking nut and adjusting screw. On vehicle model 240D, lift retainer and remove adjusting screw.
12. Loosen exhaust pipes from exhaust manifold and transmission lateral support.
13. Remove engine support bolts from front engine mount.
14. Disconnect drive shaft from transmission.
15. Disconnect all electrical connections, cooling lines and shift rods from transmission.
16. Remove rear engine support and mount.
17. Using suitable lifting equipment, remove engine and transmission assembly from vehicle at about 45°. **If engine replacement is necessary due to bearing damage, flush oil cooler, oil hoses and filter housing before installing engine.**
18. Reverse procedure to install.

617 TURBOCHARGED ENGINE

REPLACE

Engine and transmission are removed as an assembly.

1. Remove hood, and disconnect battery ground cable.
2. Completely drain coolant from radiator and crankcase.
3. Remove radiator and fan guard.
4. Disconnect PCV and vacuum lines from intake duct.
5. Disconnect electrical connector from temperature switch, then remove air filter and intake duct.
6. Remove regulating linkage and longitudinal regulating shaft and position aside.
7. Loosen and slightly lift oil filter cover.
8. Drain power steering pump reservoir and disconnect hoses.
9. On vehicles equipped with air conditioning, remove compressor and position aside. Do not disconnect refrigerant lines.
10. Disconnect heater water hoses, fuel and vacuum lines.
11. Disconnect glow plug cable harness from preheat relay.
12. Remove TDC test socket, and disconnect TDC transmitter from test socket.
13. Disconnect electrical connector from alternator, and battery positive cable from starter.
14. Loosen oil pressure indicator from oil filter.
15. Loosen exhaust pipe from exhaust end of turbocharger.
16. Loosen exhaust pipe supporting clamp from transmission.
17. Loosen engine support bolts and engine mount.
18. Loosen both engine shock absorbers from crossmember.
19. Remove drive shaft intermediate bearing shield plate.
20. Loosen drive shaft clamp nut and drive shaft from transmission.

21. Loosen all electrical connections and remove selector rod from transmission.
22. Remove rear engine support and mount.
23. Using suitable lifting equipment, remove engine and transmission assembly from vehicle at about 45°. **If installation of a new engine is necessary due to bearing damage, flush oil cooler, all hoses and filter housing.**
24. Reverse procedure to install.

CYLINDER HEAD REPLACE

EXC. 617 TURBOCHARGED ENGINE

Remove cylinder head only when engine is cold.

1. Remove hood. On vehicle series 123, position hood 90° and engage left-hand lock into latch.
2. Disconnect battery ground cable and drain coolant from crankcase.
3. Vehicles equipped with oil bath air cleaner, remove fan and water pump pulleys, and air cleaner.
4. Vehicles equipped with 617 engine, remove adapter from air cleaner.
5. Vehicles equipped with level control, remove bolts, **Fig. 1,** oil pump and position aside. Do not disconnect oil lines.
6. Vehicle series 123 equipped with power steering, drain power steering fluid and remove power steering pump, oil dipstick bracket and fuel filter.
7. Vehicle series 123 less power steering, disconnect first injection nozzle line, then remove bolts and fuel filter. Do not disconnect any other fuel lines from fuel filter.
8. Disconnect all electrical connections, hot water, fuel and vacuum lines from cylinder head and intake pipe.
9. Loosen exhaust pipe from exhaust manifold and transmission.
10. On engines 616 equipped with dry air cleaners, remove intake pipe support from intake pipe.
11. Disconnect throttle linkage and remove longitudinal control spindle.
12. Disconnect and plug fuel injection lines.
13. Disconnect and plug three water hoses at thermostat housing.
14. Remove vent line between cylinder head and water pump housing.
15. Remove cylinder head cover.
16. Engines equipped with tension rail (A), **Fig. 2,** remove thermostat housing and chain tensioner.
17. Using a suitable tool to secure camshaft sprocket, remove camshaft sprocket bolt.
18. Rotate camshaft until rocker arms are free from load, and remove both rocker arm assemblies.
19. Using tool No. 116589203300 or equivalent, rotate crankshaft, and position No. 1 cylinder at TDC.
20. Mark camshaft sprocket and timing chain, **Fig. 3.**

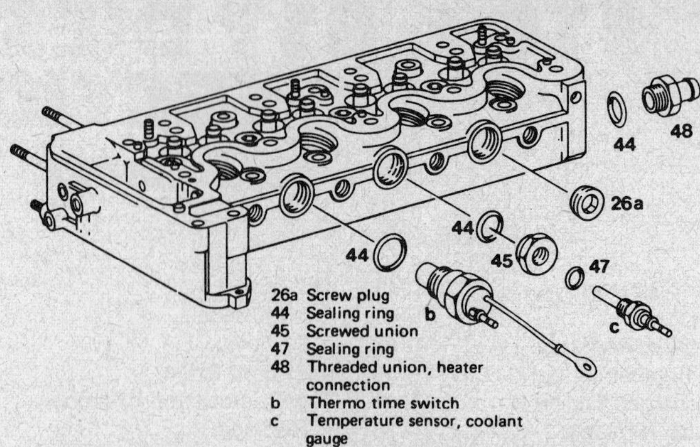

2nd version cylinder head, w/pre-glow system & starting standby indicator. 616 engine

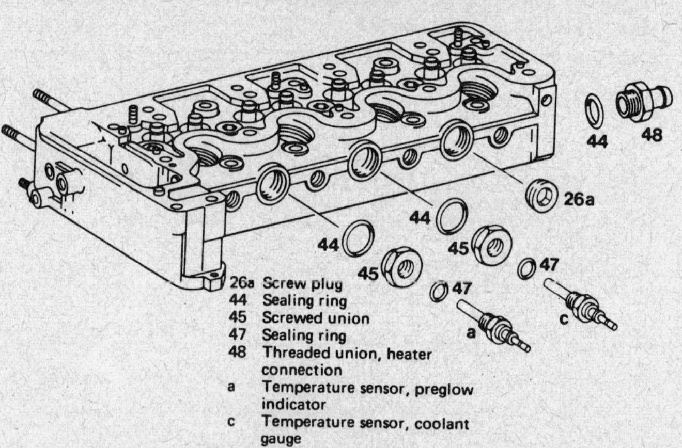

3rd version cylinder head, w/key starting system. 616 engine

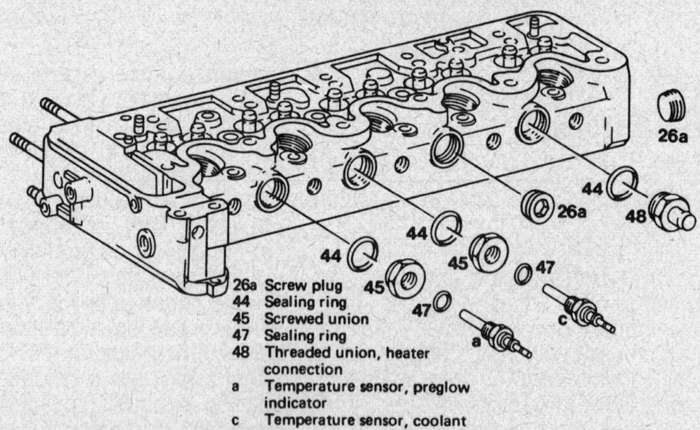

Cylinder head assembly. 617 & 617 turbocharged engine

21. Using tool No. 116589203300 or equivalent, remove bearing pin and slide rail from cylinder head.
22. Engines equipped with tension rail (B), **Fig. 2,** loosen thrust pin on chain tensioner and remove camshaft sprocket. Do not remove tension rail.
23. Engines equipped with tension rail (A), remove crankshaft pulley. Using tool No. 116589203300 or equivalent, remove bearing pin and tension rail. **If bearing pin cannot be removed with tool No. 116589203300, use tool No. 115589203300.**
24. Reverse tightening sequence, **Figs. 4 and 5,** and remove cylinder head bolts.
25. Using a suitable tool, remove M8 bolts.
26. Remove No. 4 and 5 cylinder head bolts, and injection nozzles.
27. Using suitable lifting equipment, remove cylinder head from engine block.
28. Twelve point socket cylinder head bolts are to be measured for correct length. Use new cylinder head bolts if measurements exceed the following

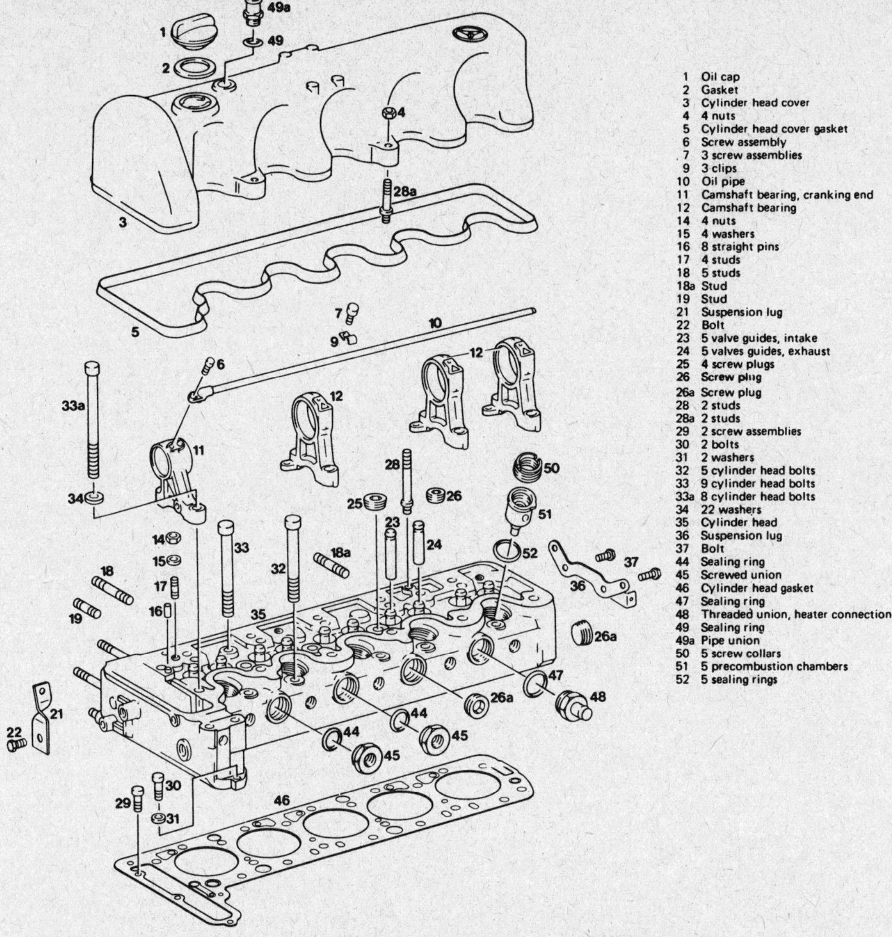

Exploded view of cylinder head & related components. 617 & 617 turbocharged engine

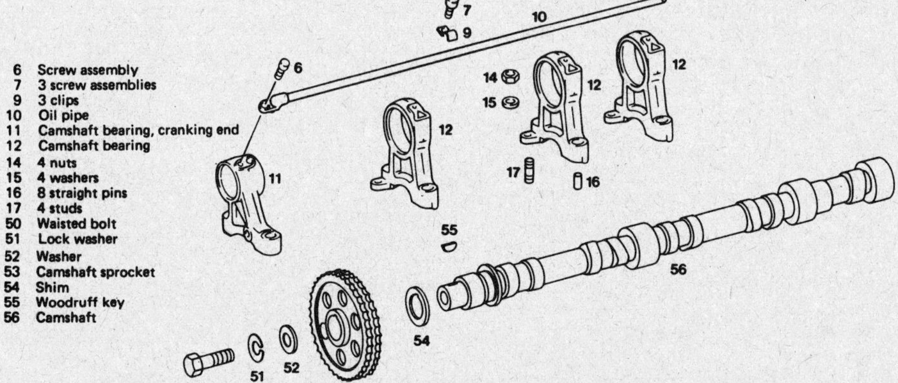

Exploded view of camshaft, bearings & camshaft sprocket assembly 616, 617 & 617 turbocharged engine

specifications: if maximum length of bolt is 4.0 inch (104 mm), replace with 4.1 inch (105.5 mm) bolt; if maximum length of bolt is 4.6 inch (119 mm), replace with 4.7 inch (120.5 mm) bolt; if maximum length of bolt is 5.6 inch (144 mm), replace with 5.7 inch (145 mm) bolt.

29. Reverse procedure to install. Torque cylinder head bolts in sequence shown on **Figs. 4 and 5** and in steps as follows: step 1, 30 ft. lbs. (40 Nm); step 2, 51 ft. lbs. (70 Nm). Allow a setting time of approximately 10 minutes, then: step 3, turn bolts and additional 90°; step 4, turn bolts and additional 90°.
30. Using a suitable wrench, tighten M8 bolts.

617 TURBOCHARGED ENGINE

Remove cylinder head only when engine is cold. **No re-torquing of cylinder head bolts is required during first inspection 310-630 miles, (500-1000 Km), and in the event of repair, after driving 310-630 miles (500-1000 Km).**

1. Drain coolant from crankcase.
2. Disconnect bleed and vacuum hoses from intake duct, and electrical connector from temperature switch.
3. Remove air filter and intake duct.
4. Disconnect three water hoses from thermostat housing, and heater supply hose from cylinder head.
5. Remove bleed hose between cylinder head and water pump housing.
6. Loosen and slightly lift oil filter cover.
7. Loosen exhaust pipe from turbocharger and transmission.
8. Vehicles equipped with automatic transmission, loosen transmission oil dipstick guide tube from boost air pipe.
9. Remove oil supply line from turbocharger.
10. Loosen regulating linkage from cylinder head and position aside. Remove longitudinal regulating shaft from firewall.
11. Remove and plug fuel injection line.
12. Remove cable harness and glow plugs from temperature transmitter. Remove pressure switch from boost air pipe.
13. Disconnect fuel return line from first injection nozzle.
14. Remove power steering pump, bracket, fuel filter and position aside.
15. Plug oil return line. Remove air filter holder and turbocharger assembly.
16. Loosen exhaust manifold support nut and remove cylinder head cover.
17. Using a suitable tool to secure camshaft, loosen camshaft sprocket fastening bolt.
18. Rotate camshaft until rocker arms are free of load, and remove both rocker arm assemblies.
19. Using tool No. 001589650900 or equivalent, rotate crankshaft until No. 1 cylinder is at TDC.
20. Mark camshaft sprocket and timing chain, **Fig. 3.**
21. Loosen chain tensioner closing bolt and remove compression spring.
22. Using tool No. 116589203300 or equivalent, remove bearing pin and slide rail from cylinder head.
23. Remove camshaft sprocket.
24. Reverse tightening sequence, **Fig. 5,** and remove cylinder head bolts.
25. Remove injection nozzles and five adjacent cylinder head bolts.
26. Using a suitable tool, remove M8 bolts.
27. Using suitable lifting equipment, remove cylinder head from cylinder block.
28. Pull out chain tensioner thrust bolts in an inward direction.
29. Reverse procedure to install. Install new cylinder head and turbocharger gaskets. Torque cylinder head bolts in sequence shown on **Fig. 5,** and in steps as follows: step 1, 51 ft. lbs. (70 Nm); step 2, 74 ft. lbs. (100 Nm).
30. Using a suitable tool tighten M8 bolts. Torque chain tensioner closing plug to 66 ft. lbs. (90 Nm). Operate engine until coolant temperature is 176°F (80°C). Loosen cylinder head bolts in

Fig. 1 Locations of bolts for removing pressure oil pump

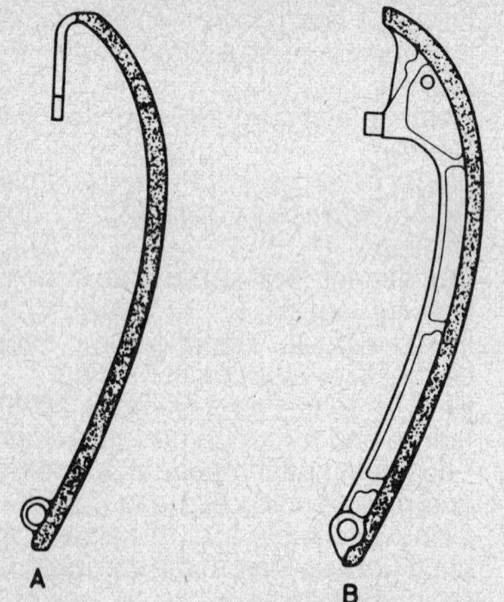

Fig. 2 Tensioning rail identification, early (A), late (B)

sequence by 1/4 turn and torque bolts to 74 ft. lbs. (100 Nm).

31. Using a suitable tool, tighten M8 bolts.

PRE-COMBUSTION CHAMBER

REPLACE

REMOVAL

616 & 617 Engines

1. Remove cylinder head cover.
2. Vehicles equipped with automatic transmission and vacuum controlled modulation pressure, disconnect vacuum hoses from switch over valve. **The vacuum hoses and hose unions are color coded. Do not mix up vacuum hose.**
3. Vehicles equipped with longitudinal control spindles, disconnect all control rods. Remove clip and push longitudinal control spindle backward. Remove bracket and disconnect idle control cable with plastic sleeve.
4. Remove fuel injection lines and disconnect fuel return line from injection nozzle.
5. Using a suitable tool, remove nozzle holder assembly.
6. Remove glow plugs (81), **Fig. 6.**

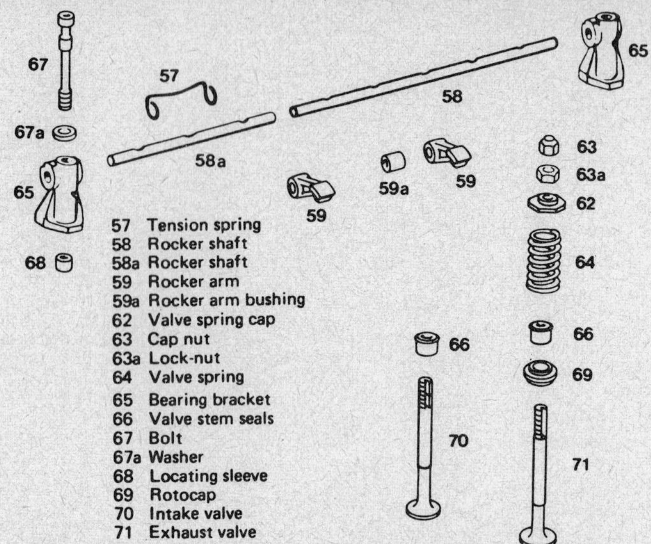

Rocker arm shaft & valve components. 616, 617 & 617 turbocharged engine

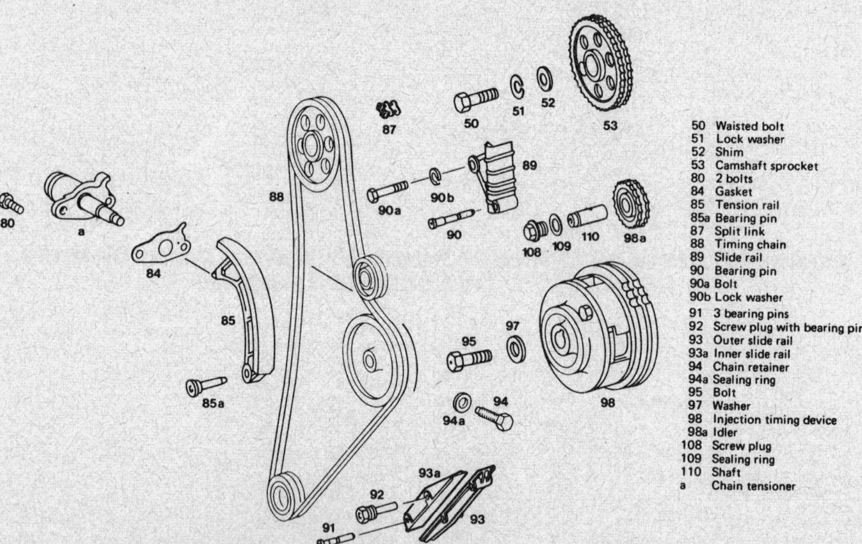

Timing chain, chain tensioner & slide rail components. 616, 617 & 167 turbocharged engine

Fig. 3 Marking camshaft sprocket and timing chain

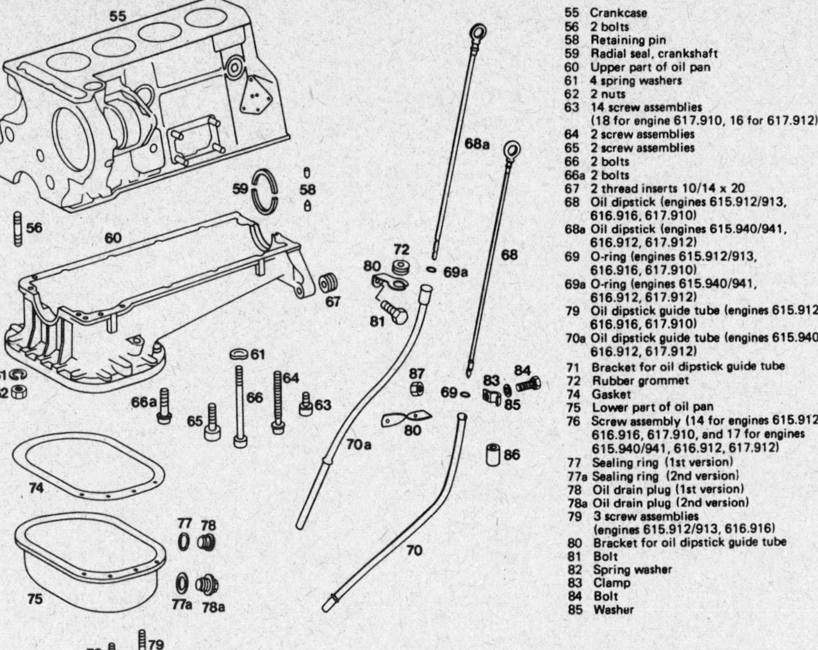

55 Crankcase
56 2 bolts
58 Retaining pin
59 Radial seal, crankshaft
60 Upper part of oil pan
61 4 spring washers
62 2 nuts
63 14 screw assemblies (18 for engine 617.910, 16 for 617.912)
64 2 screw assemblies
65 2 screw assemblies
66 2 bolts
66a 2 bolts
67 2 thread inserts 10/14 x 20
68 Oil dipstick (engines 615.912/913, 616.916, 617.910)
68a Oil dipstick (engines 615.940/941, 616.912, 617.912)
69 O-ring (engines 615.912/913, 616.916, 617.910)
69a O-ring (engines 615.940/941, 616.912, 617.912)
79 Oil dipstick guide tube (engines 615.912/913, 616.916, 617.910)
70a Oil dipstick guide tube (engines 615.940/941, 616.912, 617.912)
71 Bracket for oil dipstick guide tube
72 Rubber grommet
74 Gasket
75 Lower part of oil pan
76 Screw assembly (14 for engines 615.912/913, 616.916, 617.910, and 17 for engines 615.940/941, 616.912, 617.912)
77 Sealing ring (1st version)
77a Sealing ring (2nd version)
78 Oil drain plug (1st version)
78a Oil drain plug (2nd version)
79 3 screw assemblies (engines 615.912/913, 616.916)
80 Bracket for oil dipstick guide tube
81 Bolt
82 Spring washer
83 Clamp
84 Bolt
85 Washer

Crankcase & oil pan assembly. 616 engine

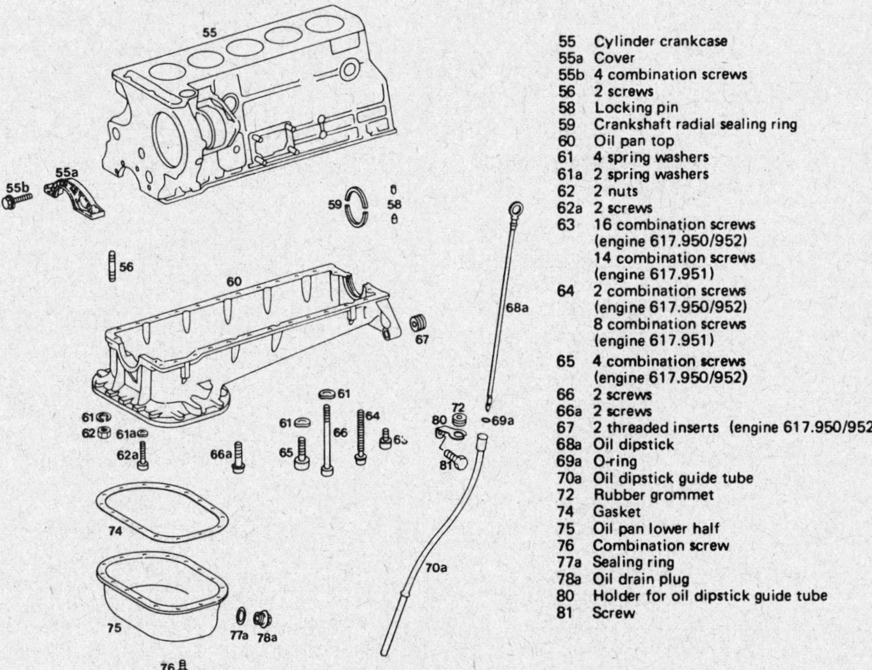

55 Cylinder crankcase
55a Cover
55b 4 combination screws
56 2 screws
58 Locking pin
59 Crankshaft radial sealing ring
60 Oil pan top
61 4 spring washers
61a 2 spring washers
62 2 nuts
62a 2 screws
63 16 combination screws (engine 617.950/952) 14 combination screws (engine 617.951)
64 2 combination screws (engine 617.950/952) 8 combination screws (engine 617.951)
65 4 combination screws (engine 617.950/952)
66 2 screws
66a 2 screws
67 2 threaded inserts (engine 617.950/952)
68a Oil dipstick
69a O-ring
70a Oil dipstick guide tube
72 Rubber grommet
74 Gasket
75 Oil pan lower half
76 Combination screw
77a Sealing ring
78a Oil drain plug
80 Holder for oil dipstick guide tube
81 Screw

Crankcase & oil pan assembly. 617 & 617 turbocharged engine

7. Using tool No. 615589650900 or equivalent, remove screw collar (50). **Firmly seat tool into screw collar grooves when removing screw collar.**
8. Using tool No. 615589650900 or equivalent, install into cylinder head and remove pre-combustion chamber (51), **Fig. 6.**
9. Remove sealing ring (52) from cylinder head.

617 Turbocharged Engine

Do not interchange pre-combustion chambers from 616 and 617 non-turbocharged engine into the 617 turbocharged engine.

1. Remove cylinder head cover.
2. Remove fuel injection lines, and disconnect fuel return lines from injection nozzles.
3. Using tool No. 001589650900 or equivalent, remove nozzle holder from cylinder head.
4. Remove glow plugs (81), **Fig. 7.**
5. Using tool No. 615589000700 or equivalent, install into threaded ring (50). Position tool sleeve into threaded ring grooves and tighten tool nut, and remove threaded ring. **Firmly seat tool into groove when removing threaded ring.**
6. Using tool No. 615589003300 or equivalent, remove pre-combustion chamber (51), **Fig. 7**, from cylinder head.
7. Remove sealing ring (52).

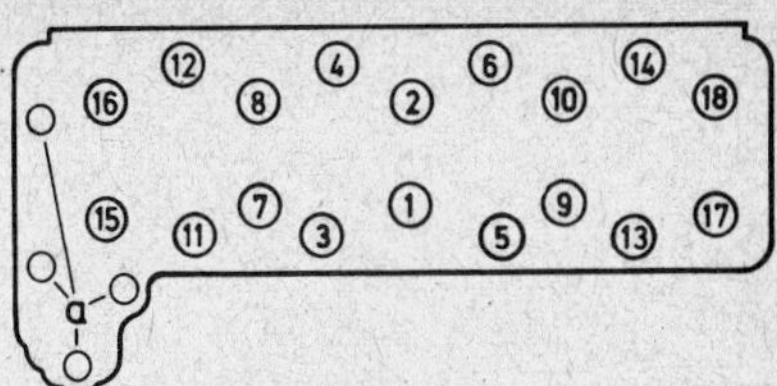

Fig. 4 Cylinder head bolt tightening sequence. 616 engine

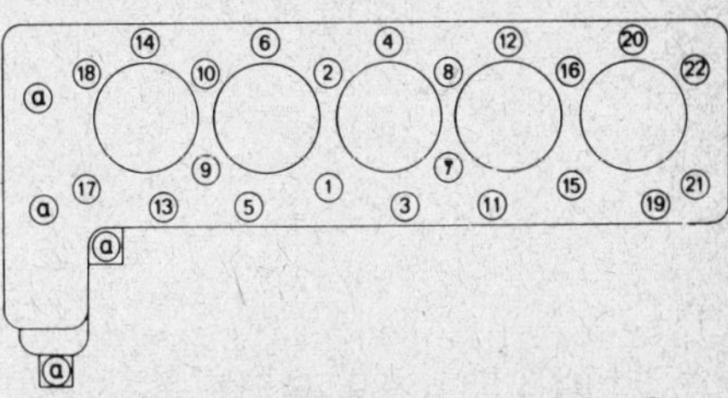

Fig. 5 Cylinder head bolt tightening sequence. 617 & 617 Turbo engine

INSTALLATION

All Engine Series

1. Reverse procedure to install, note the following:
   a. If the original pre-combustion chambers are to be installed, ensure pre-combustion chambers are in satisfactory condition. Check tips for evidence of burning. If tips are burnt or if the lower portion of the pre-combustion chamber is cracked, remove intake pipe and check for oil. If oil is present, check vacuum pump diaphragm and fuel injection pump control unit. Any malfunction with these components will be indicated by oil deposits on their vacuum hoses. Replace faulty components as necessary.
   b. Ensure sealing ring is at prescribed thickness and shape, to obtain a correct clearance of .299-.326 inch, (7.6-8.3 mm), and .307-.330 inch, (7.8-8.4 mm) between cylinder head and pre-combustion chamber. The following sealing rings are available: .075-.082 inch (1.9-2.1 mm), part No. 6150170060; .086-.094 inch (2.2-2.4 mm), part No. 6150170160; .098-.106 inch (2.5-2.7 mm), part No. 6150170260; .110-.118 inch (2.8-3.0 mm), part No. 6150170360.

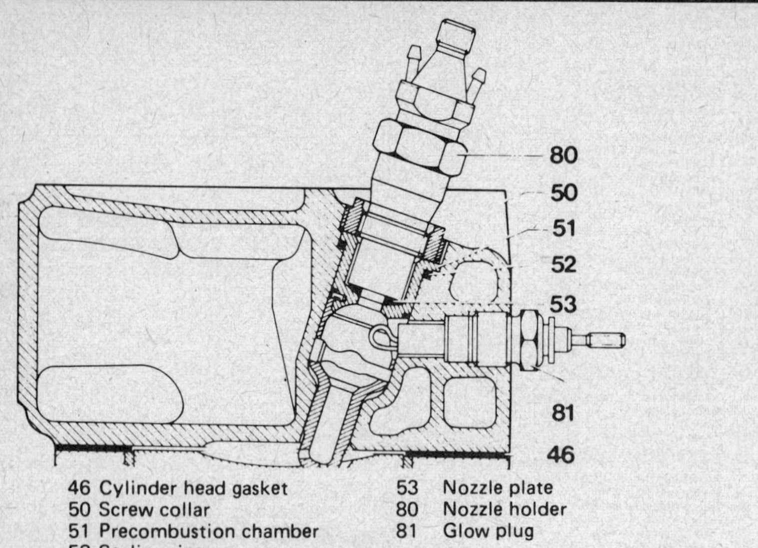

Fig. 6 Combustion chamber and related components. 616 & 617 engines

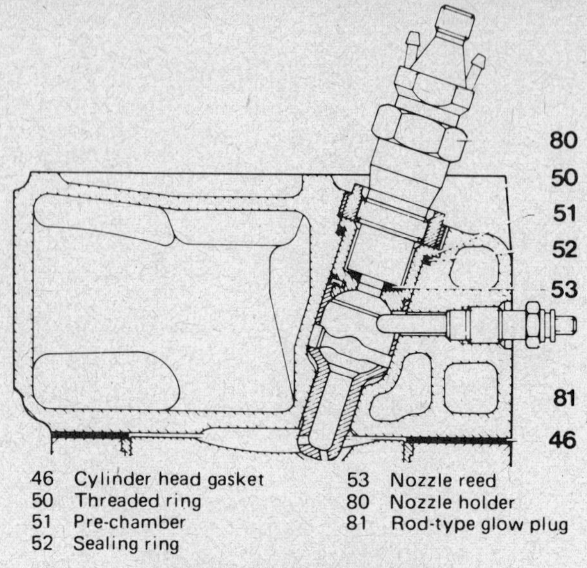

Fig. 7 Combustion chamber and related components. 617 Turbo engine

Fig. 8 Rocker arm bearing bracket bolt locations

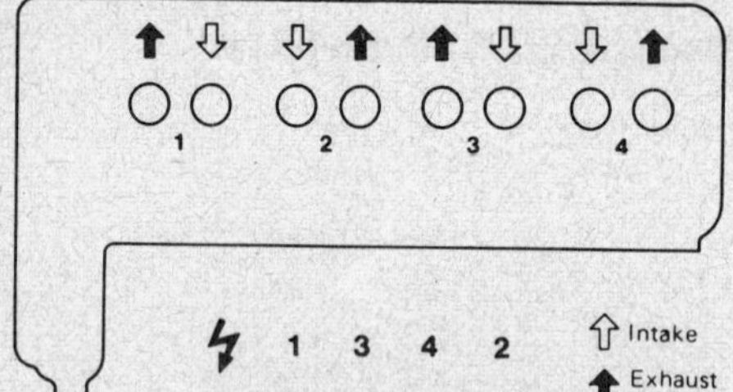

Fig. 9 Valve arrangement. 616 engine

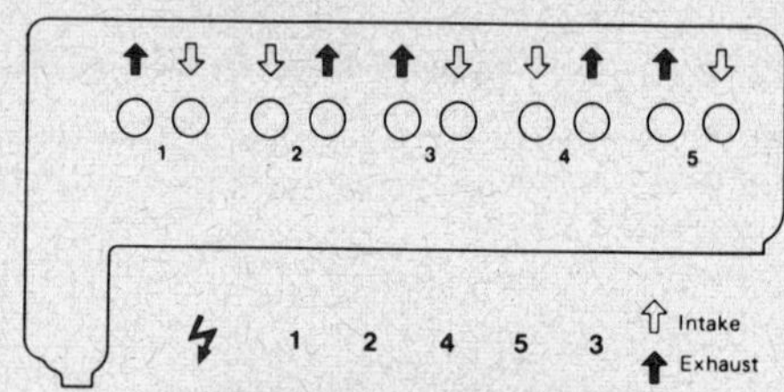

Fig. 10 Valve arrangement. 617 & 617 Turbo engines

ROCKER ARMS

REMOVAL

1. Position camshaft so rocker arms have no load on them. Use tool No. 001589650900 to rotate the engine.
2. On 616 engine, mark position of bearing brackets, rocker arms and cylinder head with paint.
3. Loosen attaching bolts of rocker arm bearing brackets, **Fig. 8.**
4. Remove rocker arms, bearing brackets and shaft. Loosen stuck bearing brackets by striking light blows with a plastic mallet.

INSTALLATION

1. Install rocker arms with bearing brackets and shaft. The rocker arm bearing brackets are positioned with the aid of hollow set pins.
2. Complete installation and check valve clearance.

VALVES

ADJUST

Check the arrangement of intake and exhaust valves, **Figs. 9 and 10.** Crank the engine using special tool No. 001589650900 or 001589462108, but do not crank the engine at the fastening bolt of the camshaft gear and do not rotate the crankshaft in reverse direction.

1. Measure valve clearance between slide surface of rocker arm and cam base circle of the camshaft, **Fig. 11.** Valve clearance is correct, if the gauge can be pulled through tightly.
2. Place holding wrench No. 615589000100 on the hexagon of the valve retainer.
3. Loosen cap nut while applying counterpressure to hex nut.
4. Adjust valve clearance to specifications by turning cap nut.
5. Upon making the adjustment lock the hex nut and recheck clearance.

TIMING CHAIN

REPLACE

1. Remove glow plugs.
2. Remove chain tensioner.
3. Cover chain housing and cut timing chain with chain separating device 116589033500.
4. Attach a new timing chain with cut link to the old timing chain.
5. Slowly rotate the engine in the direction of rotation with tool No. 001589650900 while pulling up the old timing chain until the cut link comes to rest against the uppermost point of the camshaft gear. **The timing chain must remain in mesh while the camshaft sprocket is being rotated.**
6. Disconnect the old timing chain and connect the ends of the new timing chain with a connecting link. Mount the lockwasher. **Insert new connecting link from rear so the lockwasher can be seen from the front.**
7. Rotate engine and check adjusting marks.
8. Adjust timing, if necessary.
9. Install chain tensioner.
10. Install glow plugs.

CHAIN TENSIONER

REPLACE

616 & 617 ENGINES

Two types of chain tensioners have been produced for these engines. Do not replace a chain tensioner having an O-ring with one having a flat seal, or vice versa.

1. Drain coolant.

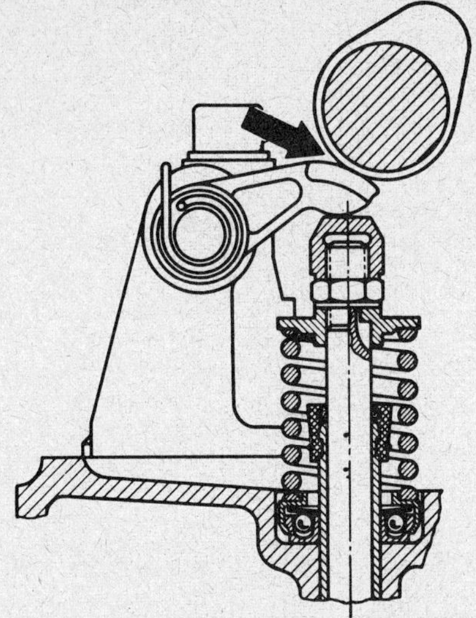

Fig. 11 Measuring valve clearance

2. Remove air A/C and mounting bracket, but do not disconnect refrigerant lines.
3. Remove thermostat housing.
4. Loosen and remove chain tensioner.
5. Replace damaged O-ring or flat seal, if necessary.
6. Place chain tensioner with pressure bolt in a downward position in engine oil. See that the level reaches above the flange.
7. Depress the pressure bolt using a press, seven to ten times slowly against the stop. As the chain tensioner is being filled, depressing it should be done slowly and uniformly and with considerable force.
8. Place chain tensioner back in housing and tighten attaching bolts and nuts uniformly.

617 TURBOCHARGED ENGINE

1. Completely drain coolant from crankcase.
2. Disconnect water hoses and remove thermostat housing.
3. Loosen chain tensioner housing plug (75), **Fig. 12. The chain tensioner housing plug is under compression spring (77) load.**
4. Remove compression spring (77).
5. Loosen chain tensioner housing and pull out.
6. Pull pressure bolt (79) out in a forward direction.
7. Thoroughly clean all parts and reverse procedure to install, note the following:
   a. Completely mount chain drive before installing chain tensioner.
   b. Install new chain tensioner seal and torque chain tensioner housing plug to 66 ft. lbs. (90 Nm).

75 Closing plug
76 Sealing ring
77 Compression spring
78 Detent spring
79 Pressure bolt
83 Chain tensioner housing

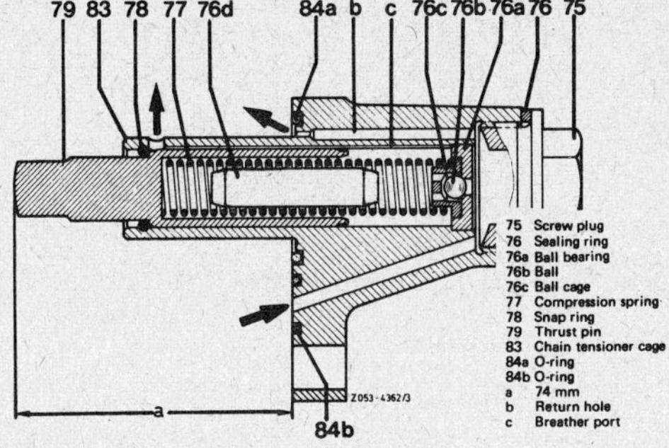

Fig. 12 Timing chain tensioner components

CAMSHAFT REPLACE

ALL ENGINE SERIES

Removal

1. Remove cylinder head cover.
2. Vehicles equipped with automatic transmissions and vacuum controlled modulating pressure, disconnect vacuum hoses from switch over valve. **Vacuum hoses and hose unions are color coded. Do not cross vacuum hoses.**
3. Vehicles equipped with longitudinal control spindles, disconnect all control rods. Remove clip and push longitudinal control spindle backward. Remove bracket and disconnect idle control cable with plastic sleeve.
4. Remove rocker arms and rocker arm brackets, **Fig. 8.**
5. Using tool No. 116589030700 or equivalent, remove bearing pin and slide rail from cylinder head.
6. Vehicles equipped with level control, remove bolts, **Fig. 1,** oil pump and position aside. Do not disconnect any oil lines.
7. Engines equipped with tension rail (A), **Fig. 2,** remove chain tensioner.
8. Engines equipped with tension rail (B), loosen thrust pin on chain tensioner.
9. Using tool No. 116589203300 or equivalent, rotate crankshaft, and position No. 1 cylinder at TDC.
10. Mark camshaft sprocket and timing chain, **Fig. 3.**
11. Using a suitable tool, remove camshaft sprocket.
12. Remove compensating shim from camshaft.
13. Using a suitable tool, remove camshaft bearing bolts, camshaft, bearings and oil line. **If camshaft bearings are stuck, use a soft faced mallet and tap bearings free.**

Installation

1. Using clean engine oil, lubricate camshaft, bearings and journals.
2. Install camshaft bearings and oil pipe onto camshaft. Note dowel pins.
3. Torque camshaft bearings bolts working outward and in steps as follows: hexagon camshaft bearing bolts torque to 74 ft. lbs. (100 Nm). Loosen remaining 14 cylinder head bolts working outward and torque them to 74 ft. lbs. (100 Nm). Twelve point cylinder head bolts step 1, 30 ft. lbs. (40 Nm); step 2, 51 ft. lbs. (70 Nm); step 3, turn bolts an additional 90°; step 4, turn bolts an additional 90°. Torque M8 bolts to 18 ft. lbs. (25 Nm).
4. Rotate camshaft by hand and check for free movement. If camshaft binds, proceed as follows:
   a. Loosen camshaft bearings individually, and rotate camshaft each time.
   b. Repeat procedure until the tight bearing is found.
   c. Using a suitable surface plate as reference, dress tight camshaft bearing at base, to compensate for amount by which camshaft is bent.
5. Install compensating shim onto camshaft sprocket journal.
6. Install camshaft sprocket, note color code.
7. Torque camshaft sprocket bolts to 59 ft. lbs. (80 Nm).
8. Install slide rail and chain tensioner.
9. Install rocker arms and brackets.
10. Vehicles equipped with level control, install oil pump. Vehicles equipped with air conditioning, install compressor.
11. Refer to "Valve, Adjust" and adjust valve clearance.
12. Install cylinder head cover.

OIL PAN

REMOVAL

1. Remove hood, air filter adapter and drain engine oil.
2. Remove fan guard and position aside.
3. Remove longitudinal regulating shaft.
4. Loosen oil dipstick guide tube bracket from power steering pump carrier.
5. Vehicles equipped with air conditioning, loosen compressor belt. Remove compressor and air-oil cooler line bracket.
6. Loosen both engine shock absorbers from crossmember.
7. Loosen exhaust pipe support from transmission.
8. Loosen engine carrier fastening bolts from engine mounts.
9. Vehicles equipped with automatic transmissions, loosen oil cooler lines.
10. Remove 4 intermediate flange nuts

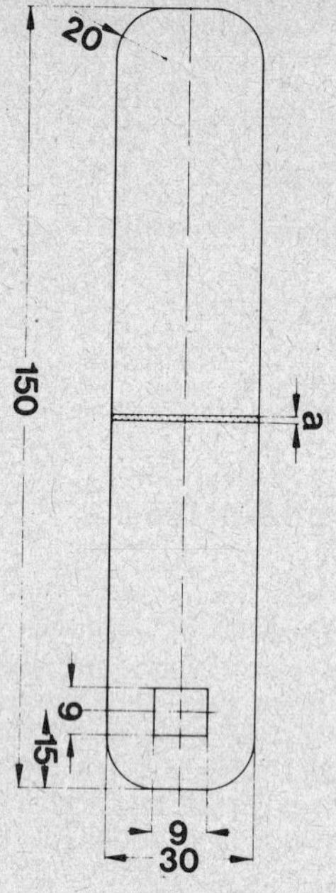

Dimension a = 1.0 mm

Fig. 13 Dimension for fabricating oil pan rear radial seal gauge

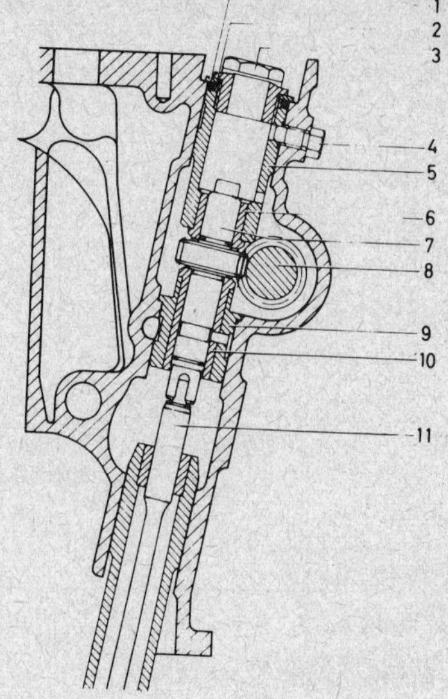

1 Rubber ring
2 Cover disc
3 Closing plug
4 Locking screw
5 Thrust piece
6 Bearing bushing
7 Helical gear
8 Intermediate gear shaft
9 Bearing body
10 Bearing bushing
11 Oil pump shaft

Fig. 14 First version oil pump drive

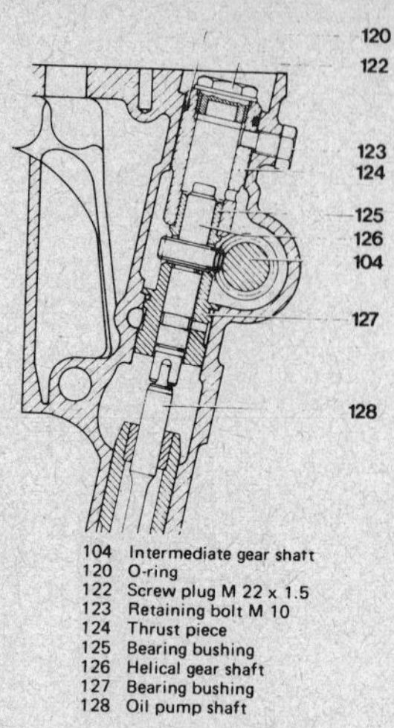

Fig. 15 Second version oil pump drive

and cover plate from intermediate flange.

11. Remove oil pan lower half. Using tool No. 117589003100 or equivalent, drive out oil dipstick guide tube. **Do not pull out oil dipstick guide tube.**
12. Remove oil pump adapter and strainer.
13. Using a suitable hoist, lift engine and remove oil pan upper half.
14. To remove oil pan, use tool No. 001589650900 or equivalent, rotate crankshaft until oil pan upper half clears connecting rods or crankshaft webs.

INSTALLATION

1. Clean surfaces on cylinder crankcase and oil pan.
2. Renew the rear radial sealing ring in the oil pan, working in the new ring securely using the handle, well-oiled, of a hammer. To obtain the required overlap, cut off the radial sealing ring about .023 inch (0.6 mm) above the parting surface. Use a gauge made to plans shown in **Fig. 13.**
3. Coat parting surface of oil pan with sealing compound and install oil pan. Torque bolts to 9.6 ft. lbs. (13 Nm).
4. Complete installation.

OIL PUMP DRIVE

There are two types of oil pump drives, first version, **Fig. 14,** and second version, **Fig. 15.** First version oil pump drives incorporate a modified locking bolt (4) so the thrust piece (5) can be easily serviced. Some first version oil pump drives incorporate a modified thrust piece. The thrust piece has thicker walls and is used in conjunction with an M10 locking bolt, previously M8. The thrust piece O-ring seal is no longer inserted beneath the cover disc. It is now incorporated into a groove in the outside diameter of the thrust piece. The cover disc on this version has been disconnected. With the exception of the O-ring, the components of either the first and second versions cannot be interchanged.

1. Remove screw plug.
2. On first version oil pump drives, remove cap and O-ring.
3. Remove retaining bolt and thrust piece. If thrust piece binds, install screw plug and turn slightly. Then using a suitable tool, remove screw plug and thrust piece.
4. Using suitable needle nose pliers, remove oil pump drive and bearing bushing.
5. Reverse procedure to install, note the following:

a. Check thrust piece. If worn, replace thrust piece.
b. Check O-ring, if worn, replace.
c. Torque locking bolts to 18-33 ft. lbs., (25-45 Nm).
d. Torque screw plug to 37 ft. lbs., (50 Nm).

REAR OIL SEAL SERVICE

REMOVAL

1. Remove engine and transmission assembly from vehicle, then separate engine from transmission.
2. Remove chain tensioner.
3. Mark camshaft gear and chain for reference and remove camshaft gear.
4. Remove oil pan.
5. Remove oil pump.
6. Remove flywheel.
7. Remove crankshaft.
8. Remove radial sealing ring from crankcase and oil pan.
9. Clean oil pan and crankcase mating surface.

INSTALLATION

1. Install new radial sealing ring into cylinder crankcase and oil pan, working seal into place with a well-oiled hammer handle.
2. To obtain required overlap, cut off the radial sealing ring in the crankcase and oil pan about .039 inch (1.0 mm) above mating surface. Fabricate gauge shown in **Fig. 13.**
3. Coat the radial sealing ring with clean engine oil.
4. Reverse procedure to assemble.
5. Remove the glow plugs and rotate the crankshaft to check for smooth operation.

FUEL PUMP

REMOVAL

1. Disconnect all fuel and electrical connections.
2. Loosen the fastening nuts.
3. Remove the fuel pump.

REPLACEMENT

1. Mount fuel pump using new gasket.
2. On engine 616, adjust the oil level in the injection pump by unscrewing the filter on the pump and adding engine oil up to the check bore.
3. Attach fuel connections.
4. Vent the injection system as described further on.
5. Check fuel pump delivery using tester 000589492100.

VENTING INJECTION SYSTEM

1. Loosen the vent plug on the fuel filter. If the fuel filter doesn't have a vent plug, loosen the hollow screw.

2. On engine 616, loosen the actuating knob of the manual delivery pump.
3. Actuate the manual delivery pump until fuel emerges that is free of bubbles at the vent plug or at the hollow screw.
4. Tighten the vent screw or hollow screw and continue pumping the manual delivery pump until the overflow valve on the injection pump opens (you will hear a buzzing noise).
5. On engine 616, tighten the actuating knob of the manual delivery pump.
6. With the engine still running, ensure connections are tight.

616 & 617 DIESEL FULL INJECTION SECTION

INDEX

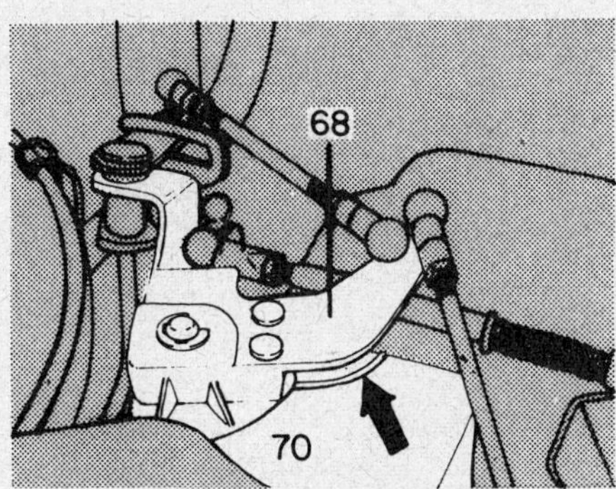

Fig. 1 Checking adjustment of throttle control linkage. 1983 616 engine

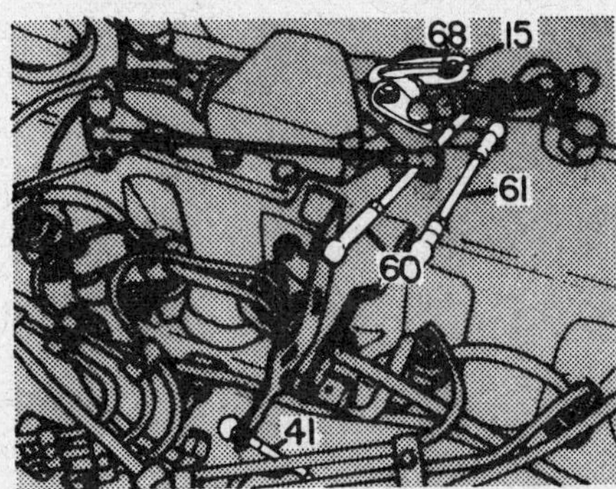

Fig. 2 Adjusting pushrod. 1983–85

Engine Series	Vehicle Series	Injection Pump Abbrev.	Max. Speed No-Load
616	123	M	4800-5200
616, 617	123	MW	4700-5200
616 & 617	123	MRSF	5000-5400
617 Turbo	116	—	4900-5200

Fig. 3 Maximum speed no load chart tensioning rail

IDLE SPEED & IDLE SPEED ADJUSTER

ADJUST

616 ENGINES

1983

1. Connect suitable tachometer and remote oil temperature gauge.
2. Run engine until oil temperature reaches 167-185°F.
3. Turn knob for idle speed adjuster on instrument panel completely to right.
4. Disconnect pushrod at angle lever.
5. Move guide lever (68), **Fig. 1,** to idle speed position. Set edge of guide lever to mark (arrow) of cap (70).
6. Check idle speed and adjust as necessary by turning idle adjusting screw. Idle should be 700-800 RPM.
7. Connect pushrod without tension. Regulating lever of injection pump should rest against idle speed stop.

617 ENGINE

1983–85

1. Connect diagnostic connector and insert suitable oil temperature gauge.
2. Run engine until oil temperature reaches 167-185°F.
3. Disconnect pushrod from bellcrank lever.
4. Check idle speed and adjust, if necessary, to 650-850 (750 midrange) RPM by loosening locknut and turning idle speed adjusting screw.
5. Adjust pushrod (60), **Fig. 2,** so that roller (16) in guide lever (68) rests against end stop without tension.
6. Adjust cruise control by disconnecting rod and pushing lever of actuating element clockwise to idle speed stop.
7. Connect connecting rod, ensuring that lever of actuating element is pushed away from idle speed stop by approximately .039 in. Adjust connecting rod as necessary.
8. Place selector lever in "D", turn on automatic climate control, and turn power steering to full lock. Engine should run smoothly. Readjust idle speed as necessary.

NO-LOAD MAXIMUM SPEED

ADJUST

1. Warm the oil to a temperature of 60-80°C. Check using oil telethermometer 116589272100.
2. Accelerate slowly using the accelerator pedal and read the tachometer. Refer to chart in **Fig. 3** for specifications.
3. If necessary, adjust speed at the throttle unit using the full stop screw. Moving the screw in reduces speed; moving the screw out increases speed.

01 DIESEL FUEL INJECTION SECTION

INDEX

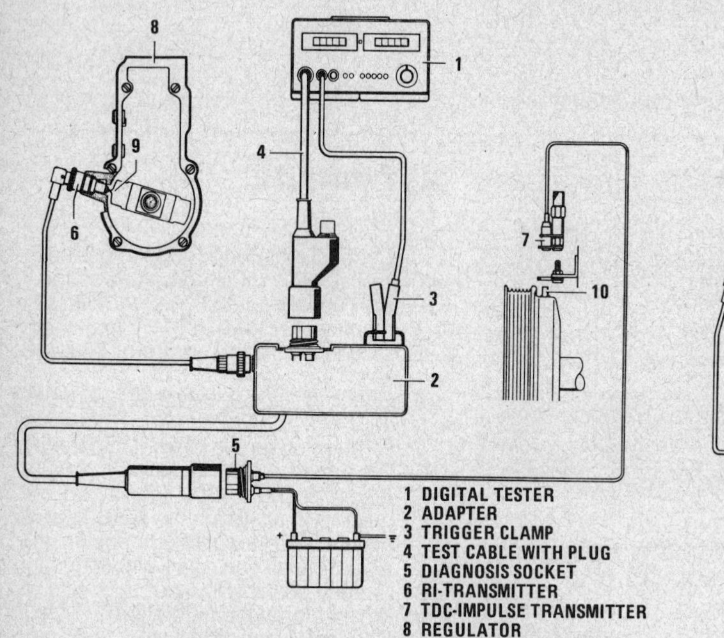

Fig. 1 Typical installation of digital tester & tester components w/adapter tool

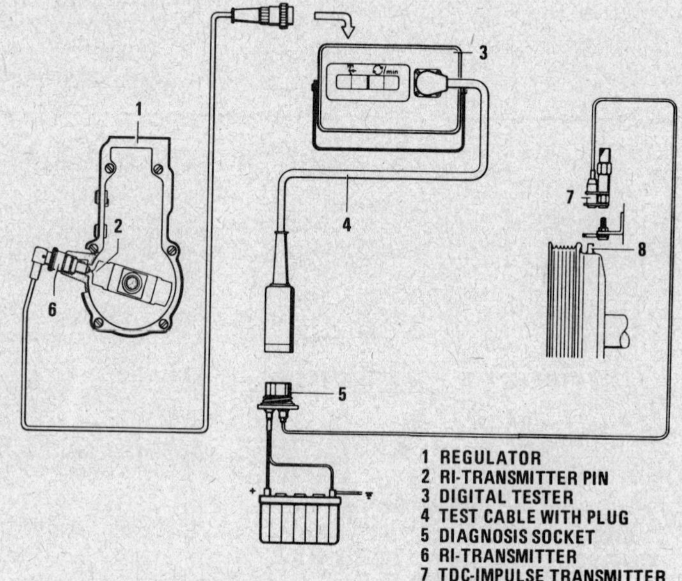

Fig. 2 Typical installation of digital tester & tester components without adapter tool

IDLE SPEED

ADJUST

1. Connect digital tester Bosch too MOT00103 or Sun tool DIT9000 and TDC impulse transmitter tool 610589042100 or equivalents.
2. Check regulator for smooth operation.
3. Start and operate engine until coolant reaches approximately 140-176 degrees F.
4. Disconnect transfer lever connecting rod.
5. Check idle speed.
6. Idle speed should be 700-800 RPM.
7. If Idle speed obtained is incorrect, turn vacuum control unit until specified idle speed is obtained.
8. Connect transfer lever connecting rod.
9. Switch on all auxiliary components and check engine for smooth operation.

INJECTION TIMING

ADJUST

HIGH PRESSURE METHOD

1. Turn crankshaft in direction of engine rotation until No. 1 cylinder is 24 degrees BTDC of compression stroke.
2. Loosen injection pump flange to support bracket attaching bolts.
3. Engage pump unit.
4. Swivel injection pump by turning adjusting screw, while watching fuel jet. **If the fuel jet changes to chain-like drops, beginning of fuel delivery (injection timing) has been attained. Nominal value obtained should be 24° BTDC.**
5. Turn adjusting screw clockwise to retard injection timing or counterclockwise to advance injection timing.
6. If the correct injection timing cannot be obtained, replace injection pump assembly.
7. Disconnect pump unit.
8. Connect all linkages that were disconnected and check regulating linkage. **When the engine is started, the injection system will automatically vent.**
9. Start and operate engine to check injection system for leaks.

POSITION PICKUP RIV METHOD

1. Rotate crankshaft until No. 1 piston is 15° ATDC.
2. Loosen fuel injection pump flange to support bracket attaching bolts.
3. Connect position indicator tool 617589662100 onto engine as per manufacturer's instructions.
4. Swivel fuel Injection pump by turning adjusting screw on injection timing unit until both lamps on position indicator light.
5. Turn adjusting screw clockwise to retard fuel injection pump timing or counterclockwise to advance fuel in-

jection pump timing. Nominal injection pump timing obtained should be 15° ATDC. **If adjustment cannot be obtained, replace fuel injection pump assembly.**

6. Tighten injection pump flange to support bracket attaching bolts.
7. Remove position indicator tool.
8. Install closing plug.
9. Install air cleaner.
10. Check control linkage for smooth operation.

RIV METHOD W/DIGITAL TESTER

1. Install TDC impulse transmitter tool No. 601589042100, R1-transmitter tool No. 617589102100, digital tester adapter tool No. 617589092100 (may or may not be used) and a suitable digital tester, onto engine as per manufacturer's instructions. **To perform this procedure, a digital tester must be used. Digital tester adapter tool No. 6175899102100 may or may not be used according to the type of tester used. Follow manufacturer's instructions carefully to avoid possible damage to injection pump, starting and/or fuel injection circuits. Refer to Fig. 1 for a typical hookup of the digital tester and tester components with the use of adapter tool. Refer to Fig. 2 for a typical hookup of the digital tester and tester components without the use of the adapter tool.**
2. Loosen fuel injection pump flange to support bracket attaching bolts.
3. Start and operate engine at 700-800 RPM.
4. Adjust R1 (indirect injection timing) by turning adjusting screw on injection timing unit.
5. Nominal value should be 15 degrees ATDC at 700-800 RPM.
6. Turn adjusting screw clockwise to retard fuel injection pump timing or counterclockwise to advance fuel injection pump timing. **If adjustment cannot be obtained, replace fuel injection pump assembly.**
7. Switch ignition switch off.
8. Disconnect tester from engine.
9. Install closing plug.
10. Install air cleaner.
11. Connect control linkage and check for smooth operation.

INJECTION PUMP

REPLACE

1. Remove radiator shield and fan.
2. Completely remove air cleaner.
3. Rotate crankshaft in direction of engine rotation until No. 1 piston is 15 degrees ATDC.
4. Disconnect belt tensioner.
5. Remove chain tensioner.
6. Disconnect and cap injection and fuel lines from injection pump.
7. Mark, then disconnect vacuum lines from idle speed vacuum control unit, vacuum control valve and stop unit.
8. Disconnect regulating linkage from adjusting lever.
9. Remove vacuum pump assembly.
10. Using a counterhold on the crankshaft, loosen central attaching bolt. **The central attaching bolt is left-hand threaded.**
11. Loosen support bracket attaching bolts.
12. Pull injection pump rearward and remove the engine.
13. Reverse procedure to install. Note the following:
    a. Ensure No. 1 piston is 15° ATDC.
    b. During installation of injection pump, rotate pump camshaft until lug of regulator is visible on the bore. Slip locking gauge inward until gauge is completely engaged. Verify engagement. **As soon as the injection pump is installed and attaching bolts tightened, remove locking gauge. When the engine is started, the fuel injection system will automatically vent.**

603 DIESEL FUEL INJECTION SECTION

INDEX

SYSTEM TEST CONDITIONS

When testing the electronic diesel system used on 603 engines, the following conditions must be adhered to:

1. Engine must be at operating temperature.
2. A/C system OFF.
3. Transmission selector lever position in P.
4. Over voltage protection fuse satisfactory.
5. Approximately 12 volts in system. Otherwise recharge battery to specification.

REQUIRED TEST EQUIPMENT

A suitable multimeter and digital tester must be used to conduct system diagnosis and testing. In addition, the following tools (tool part numbers) must be used:

1. Tool 909587002100 or equivalent.
2. Tool 603589002100 or equivalent.
3. Tool 102589046300 or equivalent.
4. Tool 201589009900 or equivalent.
5. Tool 201589132100 or equivalent.
6. Tool 903589016300 or equivalent.

Use only recommended replacement tools, if specified tool(s) are not available. Follow tool manufacturer's instructions carefully when installing test equipment to prevent tool and/or system damage.

QUICK TEST W/ON-OFF RATIO TESTER

When performing this test, the air intake hose located between the air flow sensor and the turbocharger assembly must be connected, otherwise no signal will be transmitted to the electronic diesel system (EDS) control unit for exhaust gas recirculation (EGR) and air recirculation.

1. Connect on-off ratio tester according

as shown in **Fig. 1** and refer to **Fig. 2** when testing system.
2. Press button on ratio tester marked 100% IR.
3. Start and operate engine at 1200 RPM for approximately 5 seconds.
4. To check instrument function, connect plug (a) for approximately 1 second to battery ground. Needle on tester should go to 100% and return to 0%.
5. Increase engine speed above 1200 RPM for approximately 5 seconds. If no faults are detected in the system, tester reading should be 0%. If a fault is detected in the system, tester reading should be 100%.
6. Trigger signal for system diagnosis by connecting plug (a) for approximately 1 second to battery ground. After plug (a) is removed from ground, the tester needle on the on-off ratio tester goes to 0% and starts to oscillate in regular intervals. Each oscillation has to be counted. The needle will again go to the 100% reading. One oscillation (0% to 100% to 0%). The number of oscillations indicates which electrical component is faulty.

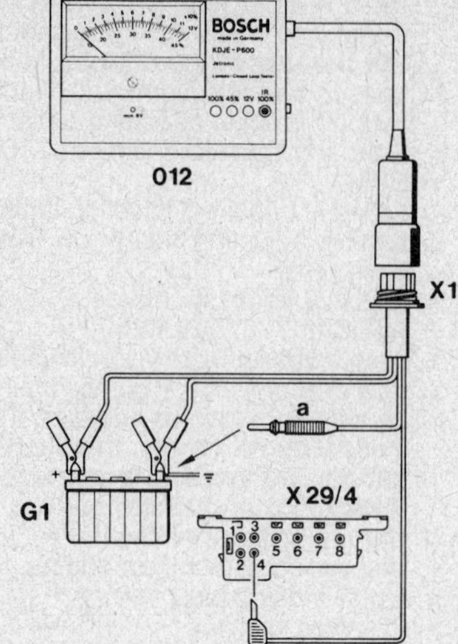

1 Connector sleeve (solder joint in harness) (X48)
2 TD - Idle speed signal
3 ATS - Exhaust test signal
4 DTS - Diagnostic test signal
G1 Battery
O12 On-off ratio tester
X11 Test cable with diagnostic socket
X29/4 Test connection (EDS)
a plug with cable to trigger signal

Fig. 1 Connecting on-off ratio tester. 603 engines

FAULT DIAGNOSIS EXPLANATION

1. With a 1x number of oscillations, the RPM sensor is faulty.
2. With a 2x number of oscillations, the fuel rack position sensor is faulty.
3. With a 3x number of oscillations, the air flow sensor is faulty.
4. With a 4x number of oscillations, the altitude correction capsule is faulty.
5. With a 5x number of oscillations, the EGR circuit is faulty. Also the following should be checked:
   a. EGR valve.
   b. Vacuum transducer.
   c. Air flow sensor.
   d. Air recirculating valve.
   e. Vacuum transducer.
6. With a 8x number of oscillations, the coolant temperature sensor is faulty.
7. With a 9x number of oscillations, the air temperature sensor is faulty.
8. With a 10x number of oscillations, the reference resistor is faulty.
9. With a 11x number of oscillations, the trimming plug (electronic idle speed control) incorrectly adjusted or faulty.

DIAGNOSIS & TESTING

1X OSCILLATIONS

1. Test RPM signal as follows:
   a. Connect multimeter to terminal 1 and 2 of test connections set multimeter to V.
   b. Start and operate engine at idle speed.
   c. Reading obtained should be 2.8 volts or more.
   d. If correct voltage is obtained, RPM signal is satisfactory.
   e. If voltage signal is incorrect, switch ignition off and disconnect electrical connector X62, **Fig. 2.**
   f. Connect multimeter and depress (ohm symbol) button and check resistance reading.
   g. Reading obtained should be 1.7-2.1 K ohms.
   h. If correct is reading obtained, RPM signal is satisfactory.
   i. If reading obtained is incorrect, replace ring gear speed sensor.
   j. Depress (V symbol) button and operate engine at idle speed. Reading obtained should be 4 volts and voltage should increase. If voltage reading is satisfactory, RPM signal is satisfactory. If voltage reading is incorrect, check ring gear speed sensor for dirt accumulation. Clean, if necessary, or repair open circuit. Check sensor mounting, replace EDS control unit if necessary.

2X OSCILLATION

1. Test fuel rack position sensor, as follows:
   a. Switch ignition off and turn safety sleeve counterclockwise.
   b. Disconnect injection pump electrical connector.
   c. Depress (ohm symbol) button on multimeter and check resistance as shown in **Fig. 3.**
   d. Reading obtained between terminals 1 and 2 should be 25 ohms. Reading obtained between terminals 1 and 3 should be 25 ohms. Reading obtained between terminals 2 and 3 should be 50 ohms. If readings obtained are correct proceed to step e. If readings obtained are incorrect, replace injection pump.
   e. Turn ignition switch to ON position (engine not operating) and depress (V equals) button on multimeter. Check voltage between terminals 1 and 2 on fuel rack position sensor plug as shown in **Fig. 4.** Reading obtained should be approximately 10 volts. If voltage obtained is correct, fuel rack position sensor is satisfactory. If voltage obtained is incorrect, repair open circuit. If no open circuit is present, replace EDS control unit.

3X OSCILLATIONS

1. Test air flow sensor circuit, as follows:
   a. With engine not operating, disconnect air flow sensor electrical connector.
   b. Depress (ohm symbol) button on multimeter and check resistance between terminals 2 and 3 of air flow sensor, **Fig. 5.**
   c. With air flow sensor plate in idle position, reading obtained should be approximately 50-200 ohms. With air flow sensor plate completely opened, reading obtained should be 560 ohms to 1.1 K ohms. If readings obtained are correct, proceed to step d. If readings obtained are incorrect, check air flow sensor plate for dirt accumulation. Replace air flow sensor, if necessary.
   d. With ignition switch turned to ON position (engine not operating), depress (V equals) button on multimeter. Check voltage between terminals 2 and 1 and 2 and 4 as shown in **Fig. 6,** on air flow sensor electrical connector. Reading obtained should be 5 volts. If reading obtained is correct, air flow sensor circuit is satisfactory. If reading obtained is incorrect, repair open circuit. If no open circuit is present, replace EDS control unit.

4X OSCILLATIONS

1. Test altitude correction capsule circuit, as follows:
   a. With steering lock in position 2 and engine not operating, disconnect altitude correction capsule electrical connector. Depress (V equals) button on multimeter. Check voltage between terminals 1 and 2 on altitude correction capsule plug, **Fig. 7.** Reading obtained should be 5 volts. If reading obtained is correct, replace altitude correction capsule. If voltage obtained is incorrect, repair open circuit. If no open circuit is present, replace EDS control unit.

5X OSCILLATIONS

1. Test EGR circuit/EGR valve, as follows:

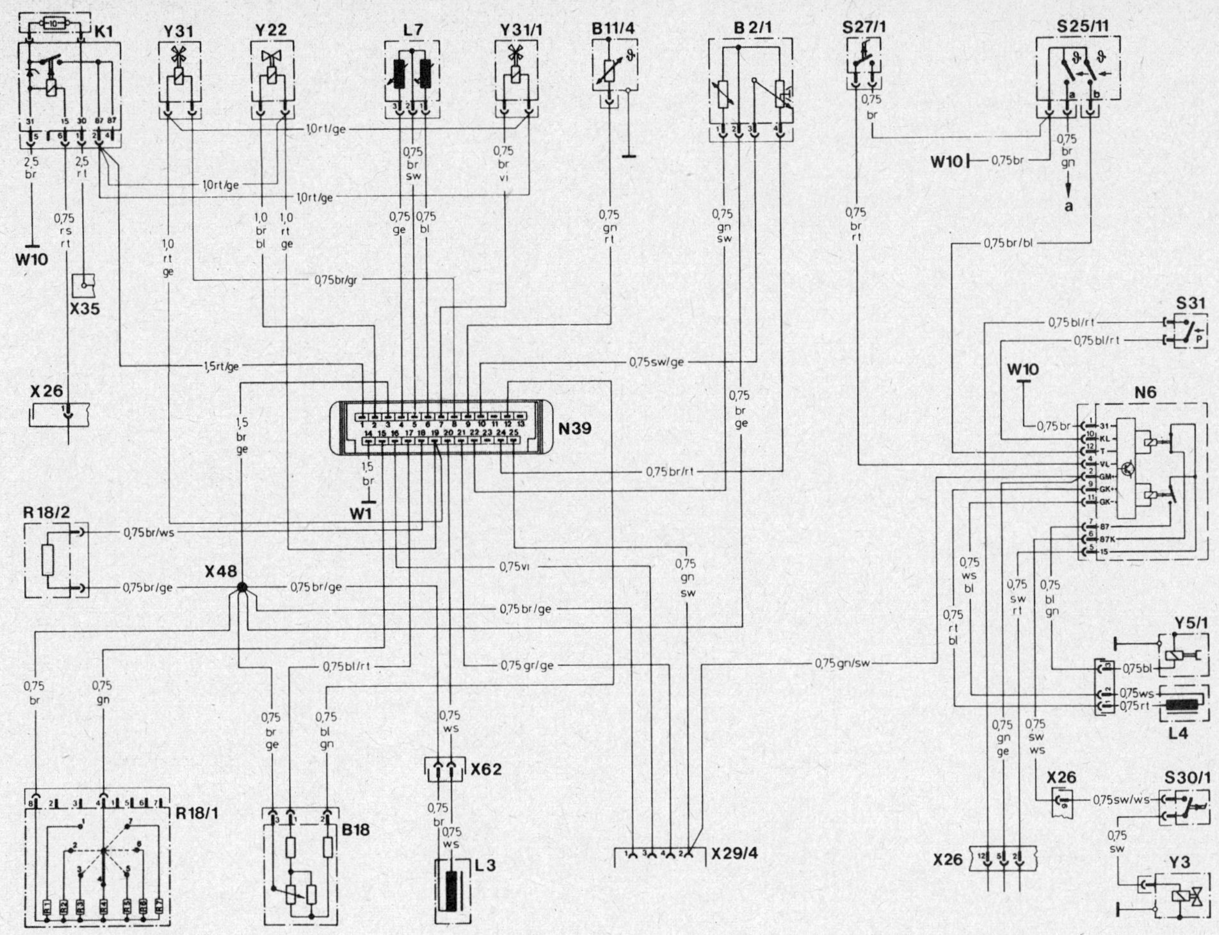

B2/1 Air flow sensor (EDS)
B11/4 Coolant temperature sensor (EDS)
B18 Altitude correction capsule
K1 Overvoltage protection relay
L3 Ring gear speed sensor
L4 A/C compressor speed sensor
L7 Fuel rack position sensor
N6 A/C compressor cut-out control unit
N39 EDS control unit
R18/1 Resistance trimming plug (ELR)
R18/2 Reference resistor (EGR)
S25/11 Coolant temperature switch 105–120°C
S27/1 A/C compressor cut-out, microswitch
S30/1 Kick-down switch
S31 Refrigerant low pressure switch

X11 Terminal block, circuit TD
X26 Connector, engine wiring harness
X29/4 Test connection, EDS (4-pole)
X35 Terminal block, circuits 30/61 (battery)
X48 Connector sleeve (solder joint in harness)
X62 Connector, ring gear speed sensor
Y3 Kick-down solenoid (automatic transmission)
Y5/1 A/C compressor clutch
Y22 Electromagnetic actuator (idle speed)
Y31 Air recirculating valve vacuum transducer
Y31/1 EGR valve, vacuum transducer
W1 Main ground (behind instrument cluster)
W10 Ground, battery

a To aux. fan relay (K9), socket 5

Fig. 2 Diesel fuel injection system (electronic diesel system) wiring circuit. 603 engines

a. With engine not operating, connect a vacuum tester to EGR valve and apply approximately 8.8 inches (225 mm Hg vacuum, 300 mbar). Disconnect vacuum line.
b. If EGR valve closes (heard or felt), EGR circuit is satisfactory. If not, remove EGR valve and apply approximately 15.3 inches (390 mm Hg vacuum, 560 mbar) with test pump to fully open the valve (this equals approximately .24 inch (6 mm) valve lift. Pull vacuum hose off EGR valve. Valve must snap back onto its seat. Replace EGR valve if it does not meet one of these test steps.

2. Connect vacuum tester with a suitable Y fitting to EGR valve. Connect multimeter with test cable between vacuum transducer and wiring harness. Depress (Ma) button on multimeter. Start engine and increase engine speed until vacuum value of approximately 7.3 inch (187 mm Hg vacuum, 250 mbar) is reached.
3. If vacuum transducer current is zero proceed to step 4. If vacuum transducer current is low, check vent line. Repair or connect line. If vacuum transducer current is high, check vacuum supply line and vacuum line between vacuum transducer and EGR valve for blockage. Check vacuum pump. If vacuum lines and pump are satisfactory, replace EGR valve vacuum transducer.
4. With engine not operating and steering lock in position 2, disconnect vacuum transducer electrical connector. Depress (V equals) button on multimeter and check voltage at 2 pin electrical connector. Voltage reading obtained should be 12 volts. If voltage reading obtained is correct, proceed to step 5. If voltage reading obtained is incorrect, repair open circuit. If no open circuit is present, replace EDS control unit.
5. Connect vacuum tester with Y fitting to EGR valve. Operate engine at 1200

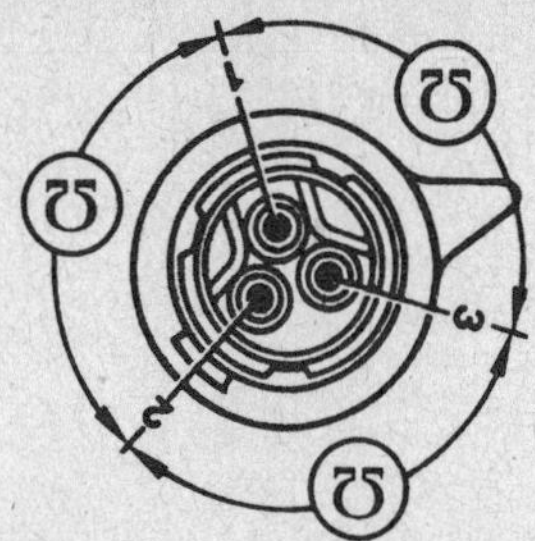

Fig. 3 Testing 2x oscillations. 603 engines

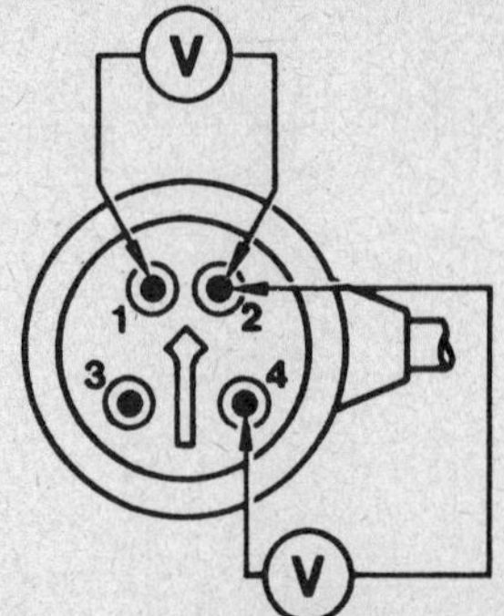

Fig. 4 Checking voltage between terminals 1 & 2, 2 & 4. 603 engines

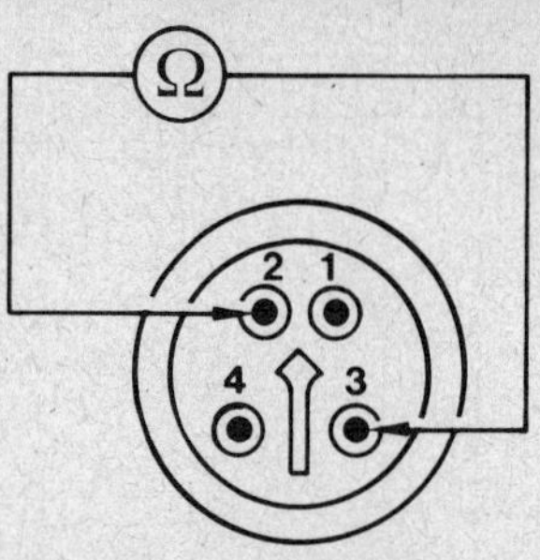

Fig. 5 Checking resistance between terminals 2 & 3. 603 engines

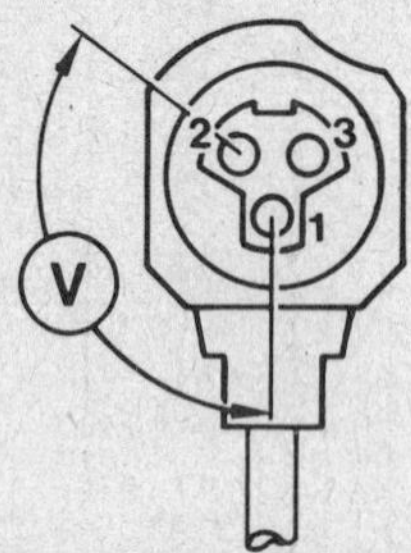

Fig. 6 Checking voltage between terminals 1 & 2 (during 3x oscillation test). 603 engines

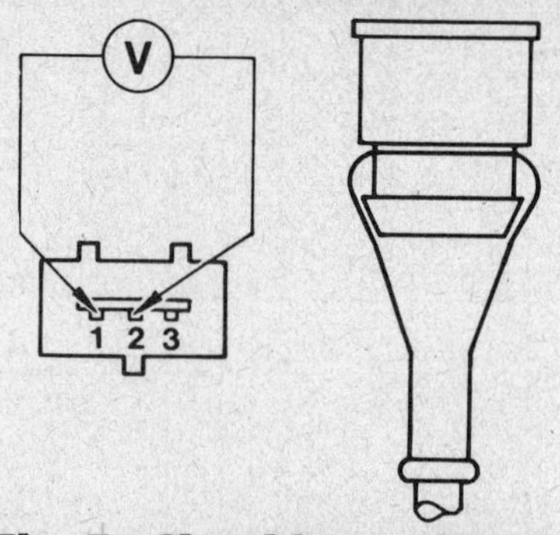

Fig. 7 Checking voltage between terminals 1 & 2 (during 4x oscillation test). 603 engines.

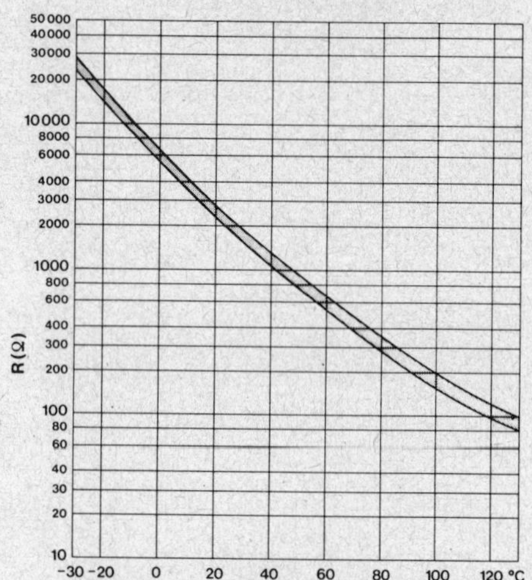

Fig. 8 Resistance & temperature chart. 603 engines

RPM and note vacuum reading. When accelerating, vacuum reading must drop. If not, replace EGR valve vacuum transducer. Check air flow sensor for proper function. If air flow sensor is satisfactory, replace EDS control unit.

6. Mechanically test air flow sensor as follows:
   a. Check air flow sensor plate for free movement.
   b. In sensor plate binds, replace air flow sensor.
7. Test air recirculation valve as follows:
   a. Connect vacuum tester to air recirculation valve.
   b. Apply approximately 15.5 inches (400 mbar) of vacuum.
   c. Vacuum drop must not exceed 1.47 inches of vacuum in 1 minute.
   d. If vacuum drop is excessive, replace air recirculation.

8X OSCILLATIONS

1. Test coolant temperature sensor, as follows:
   a. Turn engine off and check sensor resistance to ground.
   b. If zero ohms or infinity is obtained, replace coolant temperature sensor.
   c. With steering lock in 2 position, check voltage on 1 pole plug.
   d. Reading obtained should be 5 volts. If not repair open circuit. If no open circuit is present, replace EDS control unit.

9X OSCILLATIONS

1. Test air temperature sensor as follows:
   a. With engine not operating, disconnect air flow sensor electrical connector. Connect multimeter and depress (ohm symbol) button on multimeter. Check resistance between terminals 1 and 2. Check resistance according to **Fig. 8.**
   b. If resistance is not as specified, replace air flow sensor.

10X OSCILLATIONS

1. Test reference resistor as follows:
   a. With engine not operating, disconnect reference resistor from plug.
   b. Place steering lock in 2 position. Set multimeter to (V equals) and check voltage between terminals 1 and 2. Approximately 5 volts should be obtained. If resistance obtained is correct, replace reference resistor. If voltage is not obtained, repair open circuit.

11X OSCILLATIONS

1. Test trimming plug as follows:
   a. With engine off, disconnect trimming plug from socket and place steering lock in 2 position. Set multimeter to (V equals) and check voltage. Voltage obtained should be 5 volts. If voltage obtained is correct, replace trimming plug. If voltage is not as specified, repair open circuit. If no open circuit is present, Replace EDS control unit.

IDLE SPEED CONTROL TEST

1. With engine idling, remove 2-pole plug from electromagnetic actuator for 3 seconds, then connect.
2. If idle speed increases momentarily above regulated idle speed when plug is reconnected, proceed to step 3. If not, apply battery voltage to electromagnetic actuator for 3 seconds. If voltage is applied longer than 3 seconds actuator damage will result. Idle speed should increase. If not, replace electromagnetic actuator. If speed increases, operate engine at idle speed. Disconnect 2 pole plug from electromagnetic actuator and connect multimeter and depress button (V equals). Reading obtained should be 12 volts. If 12 volts is obtained, proceed to step 3. If 12 volts is not obtained, check wiring, fuse and EDS control unit. Replace EDS control unit, as necessary.
3. With engine idling, remove 2 pole electrical connector from electromagnetic actuator. Idle speed should be 570 RPM. If not adjust idle speed after loosening locknut. Refer to "Idle Speed Trimming Plug, Adjustment".

IDLE SPEED TRIMMING PLUG, ADJUSTMENT

Poor engine idle can be corrected by adjusting the idle speed trimming plug. The trimming plug positions are as follows:

1. With a trimming plug position of 1, idle speed should be 570 RPM.
2. With a trimming plug position of 2, idle speed should be 590 RPM.
3. With a trimming plug position of 3, idle speed should be 610 RPM.
4. With a trimming plug position of 4, idle speed should be 630 RPM.

5. With a trimming plug position of 5, idle speed should be 650 RPM.
6. With a trimming plug position of 6, idle speed should be 670 RPM.
7. With a trimming plug position of 7, idle speed should be 700 RPM.

CLUTCH & MANUAL TRANSMISSION SECTION

INDEX

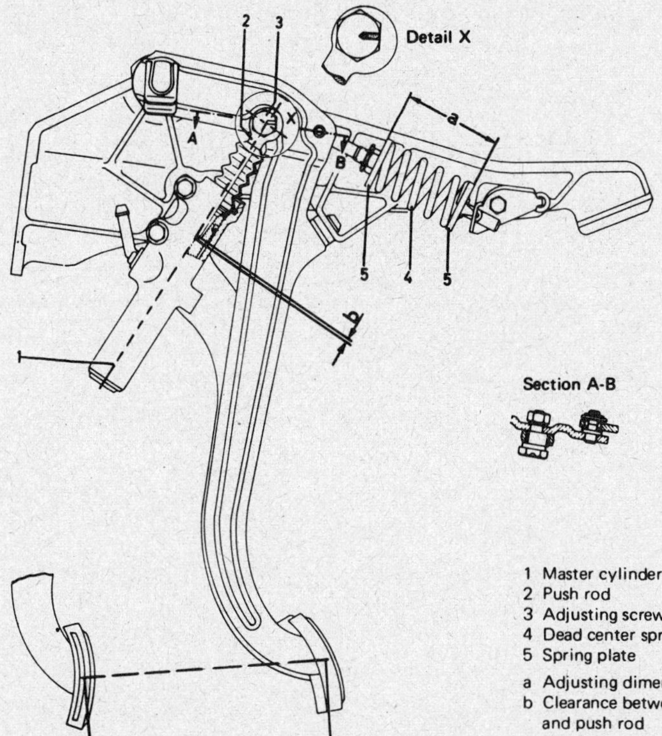

Fig. 1 Clutch adjustment. (Typical)

CLUTCH ADJUST

240D MODELS ONLY

1. Loosen adjusting screw attaching nut.
2. Turn adjusting screw so that pushrod covers the clearance path "b", **Fig. 1** to the master cylinder piston, **Fig. 2**, when the pedal is pressed. It is not possible to measure clearance between pushrod and master cylinder piston, which should be approximately .0078 inch (.2 mm). Adjustment therefore, must be made by feel.

CLUTCH REPLACE

MODELS W/G 76/18C 4 SPEED TRANSMISSION

1. Remove transmission from vehicle.
2. Loosen pressure plate attaching bolts by approximately 1 to 1½ turns each until pressure plate is free of tension. **Do not loosen, then remove each attaching bolt one at a time or clutch cup spring and/or thrust bearing damage may result.**
3. With pressure plate attaching bolts completely loosened, remove pressure and drive plates.
4. Check pressure plate and flywheel for burn cracks and scoring.
5. Replace pressure plate and refinish flywheel, if necessary.
6. Reverse procedure to install. **Handle new pressure and/or drive plates carefully. Do not drop drive plate to avoid bending (lateral runout) of plate lining. Do not allow water, dirt or grease to come into contact with flywheel, drive and pressure plate assemblies. When installing pressure plate, turn pressure plate attaching bolts one after the other 1 to 1½ turns each until a torque of 18 ft. lbs. (25 Nm) is obtained.**

TRANSMISSION REPLACE

240D MODELS

Removal

1. Disconnect battery ground cable and support transmission with a suitable jack.
2. Remove attaching screws and washers for exhaust support on the bracket plate, then turn the exhaust support downward.
3. Loosen attaching nut for the rear engine rubber mounting.
4. Loosen attaching screws for crossmember on the frame floor, then remove crossmember.
5. Disconnect the shift rods on the intermediate levers of the shift bracket.
6. Pull off speedometer (tachometer) input shaft after loosening clamp screw on the rear transmission cover.
7. Loosen bracket on the rear transmission cover and remove it together with the attaching plate for exhaust support.
8. Loosen driveshaft clamp attaching nut.
9. Disconnect driveshaft from transmission and rear axle assemblies so the two companion flanges remain on the shaft.
10. Loosen universal shaft intermediate bearing bracket.
11. Remove frame floor bracket.
12. Remove center journal from driveshaft.

13. Loosen both slave cylinder pressure line brackets.
14. Remove slave cylinder and position aside.
15. Remove starter motor and position aside.
16. Loosen transmission to intermediate flange attaching bolts. Remove the two uppermost attaching bolts last.
17. Move transmission horizontally toward the rear until the driveshaft separates from driven plate hub.
18. Remove transmission from vehicle.

Installation

1. Lightly grease centering journal and transmission input splines.
2. Engage transmission onto low 1 and introduce transmission horizontally onto clutch while rotating transmission mainshaft back and forth until the splines are aligned.
3. Install transmission attaching bolts, starting at the top. Ensure ground cable doesn't get caught.
4. Install starter and starter ground cable.
5. Install slave cylinder and plastic shim onto clutch housing.
6. Connect delivery line to slave cylinder attaching brackets.
7. Install frame floor bracket.
8. Install intermediate bearing attaching bolts. Do not tighten bolts.
9. Install driveshaft onto transmission.
10. Install plate and attaching bracket onto rear of transmission.
11. Install input shaft for tachometer (speedometer) to the rear transmission cover. Tighten clamp attaching screws.
12. Connect transmission shift rods.
13. Install crossmember.
14. Install rear engine mount onto bracket.
15. Relieve back pressure (load) on transmission and rear axle assemblies.
16. Install exhaust support.
17. Lower vehicle and move vehicle back and forth several times. Torque driveshaft clamp nut to 22-30 ft. lbs. (30-40 Nm).
18. Tighten universal shaft intermediate shaft attaching nuts.
19. Connect battery ground cable.
20. Check transmission and clutch for smooth operation.

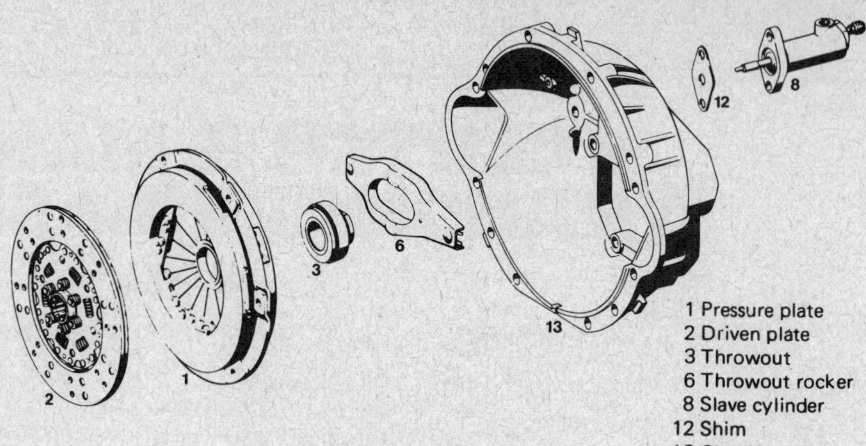

Fig. 2 Clutch components

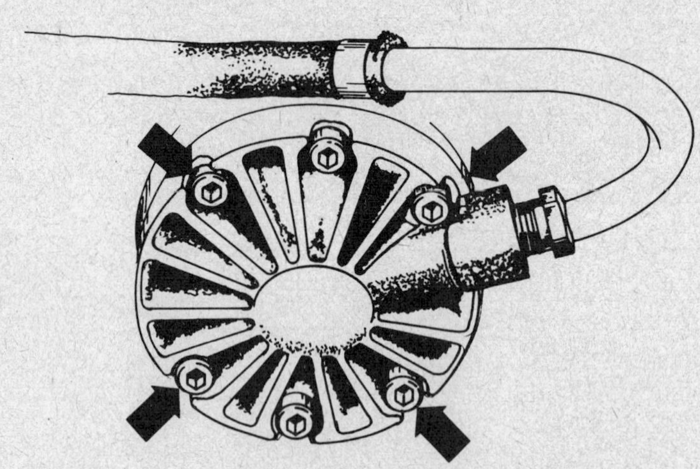

Fig. 3 Automatic level control oil pump bolt location

201 SERIES

The engine and transmission are removed as an assembly.

1. Lift hood to a 90° angle and engage left hand locking lever.
2. Disconnect battery cables and position aside. **When disconnecting battery positive cable, also remove rubber protective strip from firewall.**
3. Drain cooling system.
4. On diesel engine models, remove engine under cover, then disconnect air hose andremove air cleaner cover.
5. On all models, disconnect upper and lower coolant hoses from radiator.
6. Unfasten fan shroud and position over fan, then remove radiator.
7. On models equipped with A/C, drain refrigerant from system, then disconnect and cap refrigerant lines from compressor.
8. On models equipped with automatic level control, remove pressure oil pump by loosening bolts indicated by arrows, **Fig. 3,** then position pump aside with oil lines connected.
9. On all models, drain fluid from power steering pump tank, then disconnect hoses from power steering pump.
10. Disconnect accelerator linkage, then all electric, coolant, oil fuel and vacuum lines leading to the engine.
11. On gasoline engine models, remove screws securing test socket to holder, then disconnect TDC transmitter wire from test socket.
12. On all models, remove engine damper attaching screws and the damper.
13. Remove engine stop adjusting bolt, attaching bolts and the stop, if equipped.
14. Disconnect speedometer cable holding strap from link, then disconnect engine ground.
15. On diesel engine models equipped with tachometer, disconnect tachometer cable from bracket on oil pan.
16. On all models, disconnect propeller shaft from transmission and slide back as far as possible.
17. Disconnect exhaust pipe from exhaust manifold.
18. Remove front exhaust side support attaching nuts and bolts and swivel support downward.
19. Disconnect speedometer cable from transmission.
20. Disconnect hydraulic line between clutch slave cylinder and master cylinder.
21. Disconnect transmission shift rods from shift levers.
22. Attach suitable hoist onto engine lifting points.
23. Remove rear engine mount and carrier.
24. Remove engine carrier attaching bolts from below both front engine mounts.
25. Raise engine and transmission at approximately a 45° angle and remove assembly from vehicle.
26. Reverse procedure to install.

REAR AXLE & SUSPENSION SECTION

INDEX

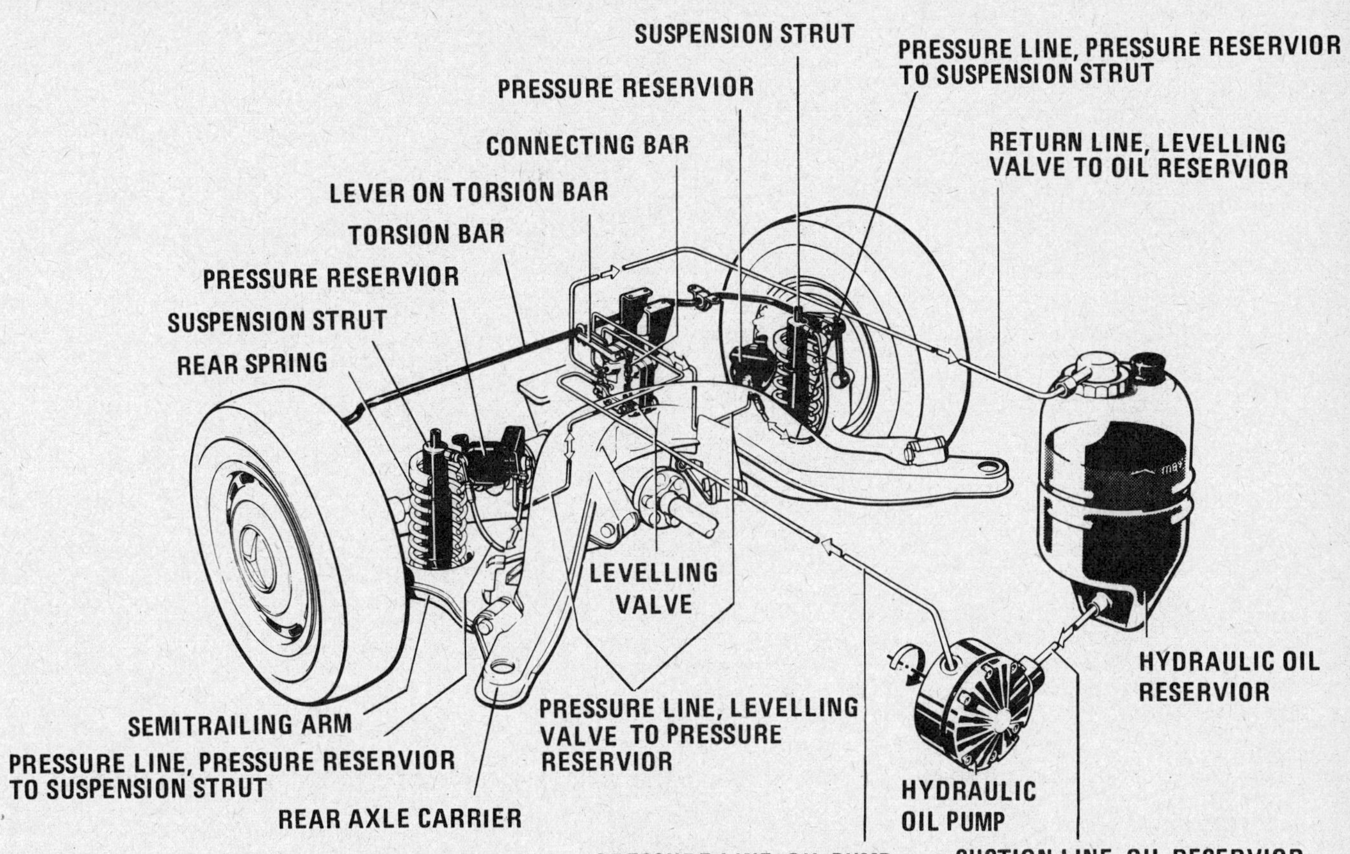

Fig. 1 Rear axle/suspension level control

REAR AXLE REPLACE

Vehicles equipped with gas pressurized shock absorbers with separating piston or with piston rod located at top of shock, ensure that when the vehicle is raised and the axle half is not under load, that the piston is not turning while the upper attaching components are released. In this condition, the deflection stop within the shock absorber rests against the operating piston and the attachment of the operating piston to the piston rod may loosen. Gas pressure within the shock absorber will then force a sudden extension of the piston rod and a loss of shock absorber oil will result.

Vehicles equipped with hydropneumatic suspension system, Fig. 1, place level adjusting switch to "S" position prior to raising the vehicle. The switch is located on the instrument panel. When lowering the vehicle after service has been completed, ensure that the vehicle is lowered only to the point where the level controllers of the system are in the "filling" position (this is particularly important when shop pits with wheel deflection boards are used). Fill the suspension system by operating the engine.

ALL SERIES

1. Disconnect battery ground cable.
2. Disconnect front exhaust pipe from exhaust manifold. Disconnect exhaust pipe and muffler assembly from attaching brackets.
3. Remove exhaust heat shield attaching bolts, then the exhaust heat shield assembly.
4. Remove shock absorbers or struts.
5. Disconnect control cables, then remove parking brake intermediate lever.
6. Disconnect and cap both brake lines.

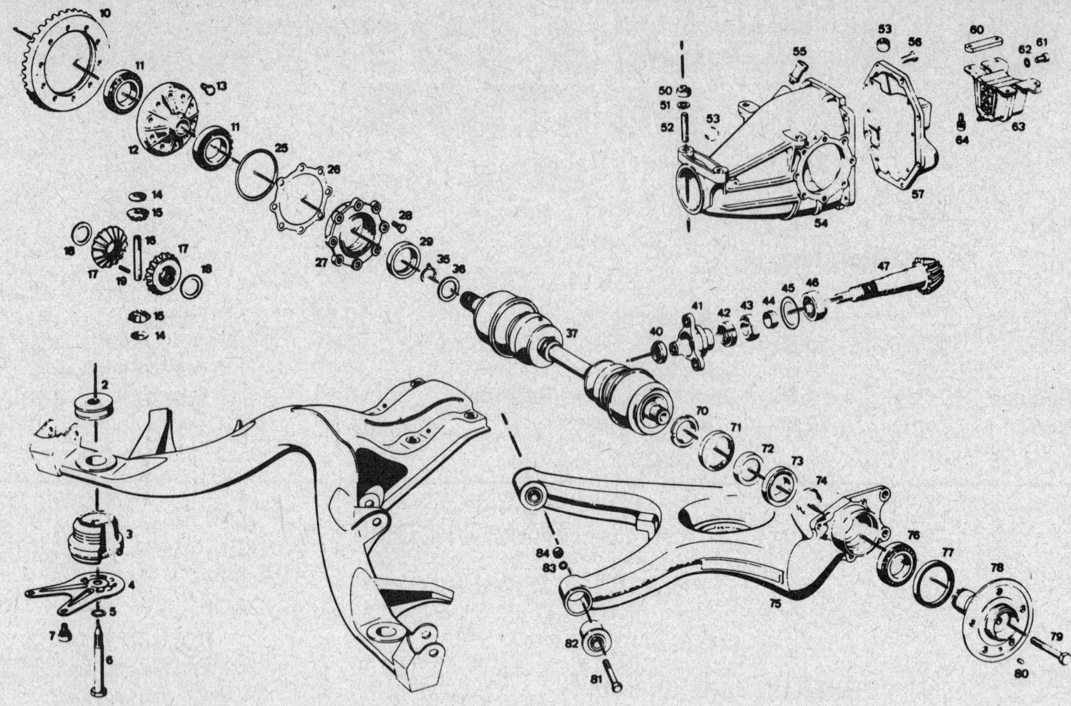

1 Rear axle carrier
2 Rubber stop
3 Rubber mounting
4 Supporting plate
5 Lock washer
6 Clamping bolt
7 Combination hex. bolt
10 Ring gear
11 Tapered roller bearing
12 Differential housing
13 Hex. bolt
14 Spherical washer
15 Differential pinion
16 Differential shaft
17 Side gear
18 Thrust washer
19 Hollow dowel pin
25 Sealing ring
26 Gasket
27 Bearing cap
28 Hex. bolt
29 Sealing ring
35 Locking ring
36 Compensating washer
37 Rear axle shaft compl.
40 Self-locking slot nut
41 Joint flange
42 Sealing ring
43 Small tapered roller bearing
44 Spacing sleeve
45 Compensating washer
46 Large tapered roller bearing
47 Drive pinion
50 Self-locking nut
51 Washer
52 Stud
53 Closing plug
54 Rear axle housing
55 Breather, compl.
56 Hex. bolt
57 End cover with oil back-up plate
60 Threaded plate
61 Hex bolt
62 Lock washer
63 Rubber mounting
64 Combination bolt
70 Slot nut
71 Sealing ring
72 Thrust ring
73 Tapered roller bearing
74 Spacing sleeve
75 Semi-trailing arm
76 Tapered roller bearing
77 Sealing ring
78 Rear axle shaft flange
79 Hex. bolt
80 Notched pin
81 Hex. bolt
82 Rubber mounting
83 Lock washer
84 Hex. nut

Fig. 2 Disassembled view of rear axle & suspension components. Exc. 201 series

7. Loosen nut, then drive shaft intermediate bearing from frame floor.
8. Loosen rear driveshaft and push forward, out of center position.
9. Remove rear springs.
10. Loosen nut and torsion bar from rear axle.
11. On vehicles equipped with anti-lock brake systems (ABS), proceed as follows:
    a. Turn ignition switch to OFF position.
    b. Loosen, then remove RPM sensor cable connector bracket and cable clamps located behind the rear seat backrest.
    c. Loosen cable-to-bracket attaching screws, then gently pull cable downward through rubber grommet in frame floor. **Do not use excessive force to pull on cable. After the cable has passed through the rubber grommet, wrap suitable tape around cable end to protect it from damage.**
12. Using a suitable jack, carefully raise axle assembly until axle contacts stop.
13. Remove front rubber bearing supporting plates from frame floor.
14. Remove rear rubber bearing from frame floor.
15. Carefully lower axle assembly. **When lowering and moving the axle assembly away from vehicle, ensure not to damage or warp brake disc cover plates.**
16. Remove rear rubber bearing from axle end cover.
17. Check front and rear rubber bearings. Replace bearings, if necessary.
18. Reverse procedure to install.

AXLE SHAFTS

REPLACE

REMOVAL

Exc. 201 Series

1. Drain fluid from axle assembly.
2. On vehicles without starting torque compensation, remove brake caliper(s) attaching pin bolts. Using a suitable piece of wire, suspend brake caliper assembly. Do not allow caliper to hang by its brake lines.
3. On vehicles equipped with starting torque compensation, disconnect and cap brake lines from caliper line holder, if necessary.

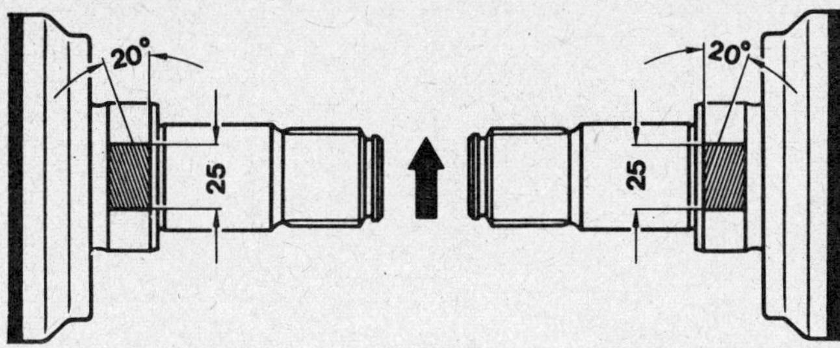

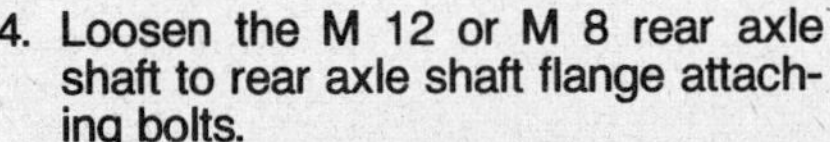
Fig. 3 Rear axle shafts. Exc. 201 series

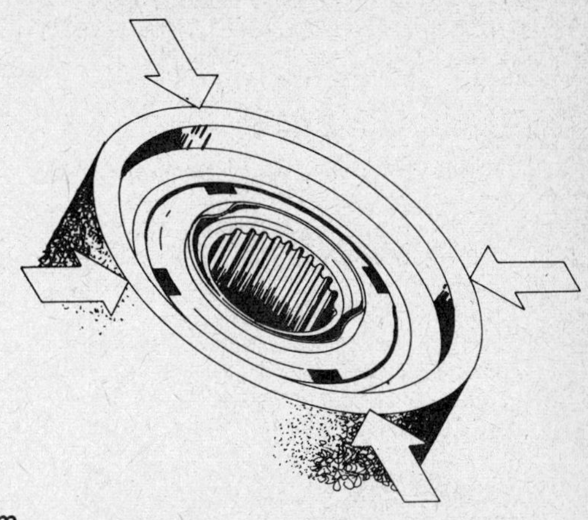
Fig. 4 Operating range of wheel carrier protective sleeve. Exc. 201 series

4. Loosen the M 12 or M 8 rear axle shaft to rear axle shaft flange attaching bolts.
5. Using a suitable puller, force rear axle shaft out of axle shaft flange. **When removing the puller, ensure to hold rear axle shaft in place. Do not allow rear axle shaft to drop, since this will damage the synchromesh joint and result in leaks. On vehicles with starting torque compensation, loosen rear axle center piece (differential and lower unit until studs are out of the rear axle carrier assembly. Gently swivel rear axle center piece (differential) to its side until rear axle shaft(s) can be removed.**
6. Support rear axle housing with a suitable jack.
7. Loosen attaching bolts from rubber bearing.
8. Wipe clean axle housing, then remove rear axle housing cover, **Fig. 2.**
9. Using suitable pliers, remove snap ring located between inner synchromesh joint and side gear assembly.
10. Pull rear axle shaft and spacer out of side gear.

201 Series

1. Loosen rear axle shaft collar nut.
2. Raise and support vehicle.
3. Secure assembly from turning, then remove attaching bolts and disconnect rear axle shaft from shaft flange.
4. Separate rear axle shaft from shaft flange by telescoping rear axle shaft in an axial direction and swiveling assembly upward.
5. Using a suitable puller, remove rear axle shaft. Push front end of shaft downward and remove from vehicle. **Ensure universal joint end cover is not loosening when removing rear axle shaft.**
6. Check synchromesh joints as well as the rubber sleeves and end cover for leaks and damage.

INSTALLATION

Exc. 201 Series

The rear axle shafts are provided with oil return threads (twists) on the contact surface of the radial sealing ring, which are different for the left and right sides. For identification, the axle shaft faces are marked with either an R or L marking. The R marking represents right side and the L marking represents left side. Do not attempt to interchange the axle shafts from side to side or serious damage will result.

1. Using 180 grit emery cloth, refinish oil return feed thread, if necessary at an angle of 20° for a length of .787-1.18 inch (20-30 mm) **Fig. 3. When installing a radial sealing ring with an alternating feed thread, refinishing of the oil feed thread is not necessary.**
2. If a new rear axle shaft is installed, place previously removed spacer ring on to inner synchromesh joint, **Fig. 2.**
3. Place complete rear axle shaft into side gear and insert a new snap ring not synchromesh joint groove. **If the axle shaft assembly cannot be inserted into the differential housing up to the contact surface, contract both joints first. Then, using a plastic head hammer, gently tap outer spider gear to knock rear axle shaft against differential housing contact surface. Do not strike stop sleeve assembly. Do not allow rear axle shaft to drop or bend sharply, since this will damage the synchromesh housing assembly.**
4. Check endplay between inner spider gear and differential housing assembly. There should be no noticeable endplay. The snap ring should just barely be able to turn in its groove. If necessary, install a thicker or thinner spacer ring.
5. Telescope rear axle shaft completely, then using puller tool 05a-05c or equivalent, insert assembly into rear axle shaft flange.
6. Rear axle shaft assemblies using M 12 bolts, torque bolts to 70 ft. lbs. (95 Nm). Rear axle shaft assemblies using the M8 bolts with clamping disc and spacing sleeve, torque bolts to 22 ft. lbs. (30 Nm). **When installing a new or reconditioned rear axle shaft with one piece protective sleeve on outer joint, check semi-trailing arm in its operating range of protective sleeve for weld residue. Remove weld beads. Check installed rear axle shaft for wiping noises. If wiping noise are heard when rotating rear axle shaft, refinish wheel carrier in operating range of protective sleeve, Fig. 4.**
7. Place suitable sealer on to end cover, and install end cover assembly. Torque end cover attaching bolts to 33 ft. lbs. (45 Nm).
8. On 107 and 123 series only, proceed as follows:
   a. Lift rear axle housing and install rubber bearing to frame floor.
   b. Torque hex head attaching bolts to 18 ft. lbs. (25 Nm) or self-locking bolts to 22 ft. lbs. (30 Nm).
9. On 126 series only, lift rear axle center piece (differential) up to frame floor and attach rubber bearing to frame floor. Torque attaching bolts to 22 ft. lbs. (30 Nm).
10. On vehicles equipped with starting torque compensation, connect brake line(s) and bleed brake system.
11. Lower and remove jack supporting rear axle housing.
12. On vehicles without starting torque compensation, install caliper onto brake disc. Install new locking plate or self-locking bolts. Torque attaching bolts to 66 ft. lbs. (90 Nm).
13. Fill rear axle housing with suitable lubricant and up to specifications.

201 Series

For installation of rear axle shafts, reverse removal procedure and proceed as follows:

1. Install new attaching bolts and collar nut, as required.
2. Protect flange-on surface between connecting flange and end cover to rear axle shaft against contamination.
3. Before installing attaching bolts, coat bolt threads with clean oil.
4. Torque attaching bolts to 51 ft.lbs. (70 Nm) and collar nut to 206-236 ft. lbs. (280-320 Nm).
5. Lock collar nut at crush flange to prevent nut from backing off.

SHOCK ABSORBER REPLACE

The rear shock absorbers simultaneously serve as a deflection stop for the rear wheels. For this reason, loosen shock absorber only with the vehicle resting on its wheels or with the semi-trailing arm properly supported. When removing gas pressurized shock absorbers with separating piston or piston rod mounted on top of shock absorber and with vehicle raised, ensure that the piston rod is turning when upper mounting components are loosened.

EXC. 201 SERIES

1. Remove rear seat and backrest assembly.
2. Remove rear wall cover attaching screws, then the cover.
3. Remove upper shock absorber mounting nut and rubber bushing.
4. Loosen lower shock absorber-to-semi-trailing arm attaching bolts.
5. Remove shock absorber by drawing shock absorber downward.
6. Reverse procedure to install.

201 SERIES

1. Remove luggage compartment lining.
2. Remove upper shock absorber mounting and bushing. **If shock absorber tube is rotating when the mounting nuts are loosened, hold tube in wheel housing. Loosen counter nut by using a suitable 11/16 (17 mm) open-end wrench.**
3. Raise and support rear of vehicle.
4. Remove spring link cover clamps and cover.
5. Remove lower shock absorber-to-spring link mounting nut.
6. Push shock absorber in a downward direction until shock clears frame floor mounting bore. Remove shock absorber from spring link and pull rearward.
7. Reverse procedure to install.

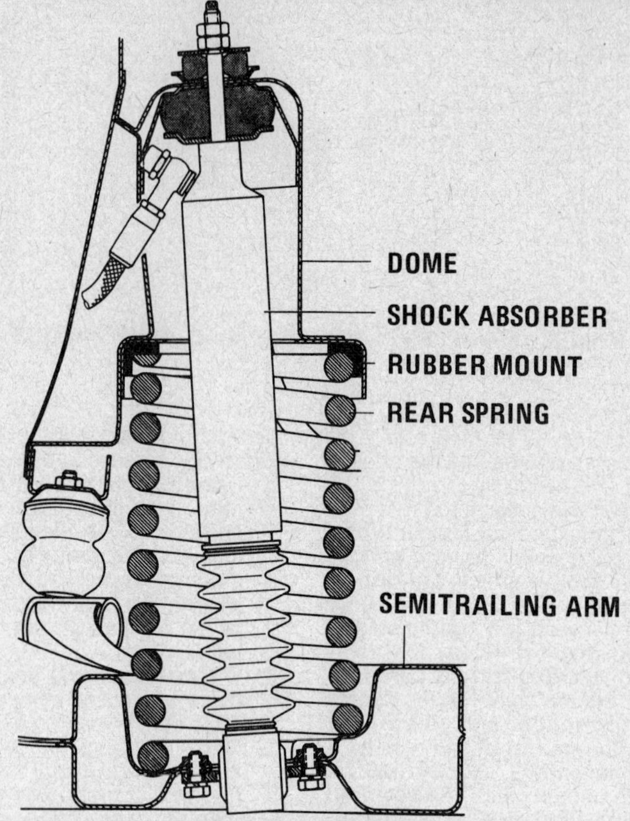

Fig. 5 Shock absorber, coil spring & related components

COIL SPRING REPLACE

EXC. 201 SERIES

1. Remove rear shock absorber or spring strut.
2. Ensure upper shock absorber mounting is released first.
3. Raise and support rear of vehicle.
4. Insert tensioner plates of spring tensioner tool parallel to each other into rear spring. Ensure at least 5 coils on spring are between tensioner plates.
5. Insert tensioner tool screw through semi-trailing arm opening.
6. Tighten screw to place tension on spring assembly.
7. Remove rear spring and rubber mount, **Fig. 5**, from vehicle.
8. Reverse procedure to install.

201 SERIES

1. Raise and support rear of vehicle.
2. Remove tire and wheel assembly.
3. Remove spring link cover clamps and cover.
4. Insert tensioner plates of spring tensioner tool offset 90° into rear spring. Ensure 5½ spring coils are between tool tensioner plates.
5. Insert tensioner tool screw through opening in spring link.
6. Turn tensioner tool screw until spring is free of load. **The webs of tensioner screw and guide sleeve must be correctly seated in the grooves of lower and upper tensioner plates.**
7. Remove lower shock absorber mounting nut.
8. Remove rear spring and rubber mount.
9. Reverse procedure to install.

TORSION BAR REPLACE

107 & 123 SERIES

1. On vehicles equipped with level control, disconnect level control rod from torsion bar lever.
2. Loosen left and right torsion bar connecting rod.
3. Loosen left and right torsion bar bearing bracket from frame floor.
4. Remove locking plates and rubber mounts from torsion bar assembly.
5. Disconnect rubber rings from rear exhaust mounting, then slightly lower exhaust pipe and support bracket assembly.
6. Remove torsion bar from vehicle.
7. Reverse procedure to install.
8. On 107 series, toque torsion bar bearing attaching bolts to 51 ft. lbs. (70 Nm) and torsion bar connecting rod ball joints to 33 ft. lbs. (45 Nm).
9. On 123 series, torque torsion bar bearing to frame floor attaching bolts as follows:
   a. Early production with spring washers to 14.7 ft. lbs. (20 Nm).
   b. Late production with micro-encapsulated attaching screws to 22 ft. lbs. (30 Nm).
   c. Torque metal torsion bar connecting rod ball joints to 33 ft. lbs. (45 Nm).
   d. Torque plastic torsion bar connecting rod ball joints to 22 ft. lbs. (30 Nm). **Do not exceed torque specifications given.**

126 SERIES

1. Move level control adjusting switch valve unit puller into "S" position. Switch is located on instrument panel.
2. Raise and support rear of vehicle.
3. Remove righthand tire and wheel assembly.
4. Remove rear exhaust system rubber mounting rings, then slightly lower rear exhaust pipe and bracket support.
5. Remove left and right wheel carrier support expanding screws.
6. Disconnect level control lever connecting rod. Using a suitable wrench, hold ball pin to remove connecting rod. **Do not pull ball pin out of ball socket.**
7. Remove left and right torsion bar bearing clip attaching bolts.
8. Remove torsion bar and torsion bar level control lever. Two different types of torsion bar ends are used. Early production torsion bar ends were used on 126 series sedan models. These torsion bar ends do not have forged ends. Starting September 1981, torsion bars with forged ends are used on 126 series sedan and coupe models. Rubber mounts for the torsion bar attachment to the frame

floor were simultaneously modified. **Ensure that contact surfaces are always absolutely clean and free of grease. When tightening, ensure rubber mount inner bushings are correctly seated. Do not tighten any attaching bolt and/or nut if a bushing if off center (not aligned with mount ends). Tighten torsion bar wheel carrier support expanding screw, only when vehicle wheels are contacting the floor. After the necessary service has been completed and with vehicle resting on floor, move level control adjusting switch valve unit puller to "N" (normal level) position. This switch is located on the instrument panel assembly. Torque torsion bar wheel carrier expanding bolt to 59 ft. lbs. (80 Nm), torsion bar bearing to frame floor attaching bolts to 51 ft. lbs. (70 Nm) and link to torsion bar attaching bolts to 7 ft. lbs. (10 Nm). Do not exceed torque specifications given.**

201 SERIES

1. Raise and support rear of vehicle.
2. Remove rear tire and wheel assembly.
3. Remove both left and right torsion bar connecting rod attaching bolts.
4. Remove torsion bar bearing to frame floor attaching bolts.
5. Remove rubber mounts.
6. Remove driveshaft intermediate bearing attaching bolts, then the bearing.
7. Remove driveshaft to rear axle flange attaching bolts, then separate driveshaft from rear axle assembly.
8. On vehicles with anti-lock brake system (ABS), loosen RPM sensor cable bracket attaching screw, then remove RPM sensor.
9. Support rear axle assembly, then remove rear axle bearing to frame floor attaching bolts.
10. Slightly lower rear axle and turn torsion bar gently to the left, then remove torsion bar.
11. Reverse procedure to install. Torque left and right torsion bar clamp attaching screws to 14.7 ft. lbs. (20 Nm). Torque rear axle front bearing attaching screws to 51 ft. lbs. (70 Nm). Torque companion flange to rear axle flange attaching bolts to 33 ft. lbs. (45 Nm). Torque intermediate lbs. (25 Nm). Torque RPM sensor to rear axle attaching screw to 6 ft. lbs. (8 Nm), if equipped. Torque left and right torsion bar connecting rod attaching bolts to 22 ft. lbs. (30 Nm).

BRAKE SECTION

INDEX

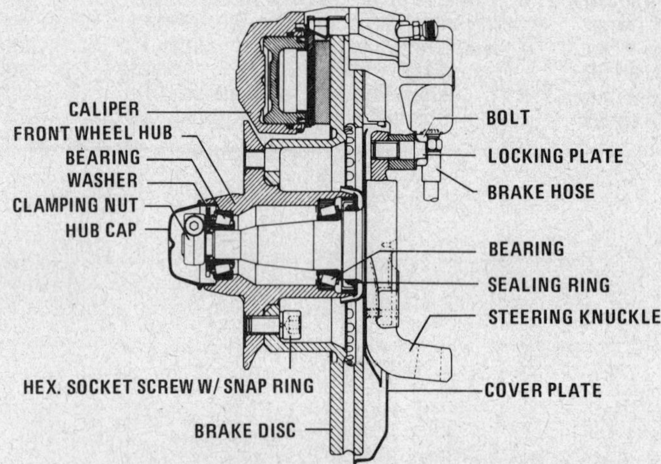

Fig. 1 Sectional view of Teves & Bendix type front brake calipers. 107 series.

FRONT DISC BRAKE SERVICE

BRAKE CALIPER, REPLACE

Removal, Exc. 201 Series

On 126 series vehicles using Girling type brake calipers, refer to 201 Series removal and installation procedures.

1. Raise and support vehicle.
2. Remove tire and wheel assembly.
3. Open brake caliper bleeder screw, then pump brake fluid out of front brake circuit.
4. Disconnect and cap brake hose from brake line.
5. On vehicles with wear indicator, pull clip sensor cables out of caliper plug connector.
6. Remove brake lining wear indicator plug connector and brake hose from caliper.
7. Cap caliper and brake hose openings.
8. Unstake locking plate, then remove caliper pin attaching bolts.
9. Remove caliper from steering knuckle.

Installation, Exc. 201 Series

When installing brake calipers, brake calipers of one axle should have the same caliper piston diameter. Only calipers of the same manufacturer should be installed on one axle side. Teves calipers with a 2.24 inch (57 mm) caliper piston diameter and 2.36 inch (60 mm) caliper piston diameter is used. Bendix and Girling type calipers with 2.36 inch (60 mm) caliper piston diameter is also used. Teves type calipers will have either a paint marking or a stamped number, indicating piston diameter which is located on the front caliper cover. 2.24 inch (57 mm) piston diameter calipers will have the number 22 painted or stamped on the caliper. 2.36 inch (60 mm) piston diameter calipers will have a stamped number 60 stamped on the caliper. Bendix type calipers will have a stamped number located to the left of the manufacturer's name. The 2.36 inch (60 mm) piston diameter caliper will be identified by the stamped number 60.

1. Using new locking plate and attaching bolts, install caliper onto steering knuckle, **Figs. 1 through 4.**
2. Torque caliper to steering knuckle attaching bolts to 84 ft. lbs. (115 Nm).
3. Insert brake hose through bracket. Ensure bracket guide bracket is not damaged.
4. Connect brake hose onto caliper.
5. On vehicles with brake lining wear indicator, connect plug connector onto caliper assembly. Insert clip sensor cable into plug connector.
6. Connect brake line onto brake hose. Ensure brake hose is not twisted.
7. Bleed brake system and check brake system for leaks.

Removal, 201 Series

1. Open caliper bleeder screw and pump fluid from front brake circuit.
2. Disconnect and cap brake hose from brake line. Cap both the hose and line.
3. Using suitable screwdrivers, lift the two holding lugs located laterally.
4. Disconnect clip sensor cable from plug connection on caliper assembly. Do not pull on the cable.
5. Disconnect brake lining wear indicator and brake hose plug connector from wheel cylinder housing. Cap wheel cylinder housing brake line.
6. Loosen brake carrier attaching bolts, then remove floating caliper from steering knuckle.

Installation, 201 Series

When installing a new floating caliper assembly, only calipers of the same manufacturer and having the same caliper piston diameter should be used on one axle side. Girling front brake calipers are used with a caliper piston diameter of 2.12 inch (54 mm).

1. Using new attaching bolts, install caliper onto steering knuckle, **Fig. 5.**
2. Torque caliper to steering knuckle attaching bolts to 84 ft. lbs. **If great force is needed to tighten attaching bolts, remove bolts and using a M12 1.5 tap, clean caliper bolt hole threads.**
3. Connect brake hose to wheel cylinder housing.

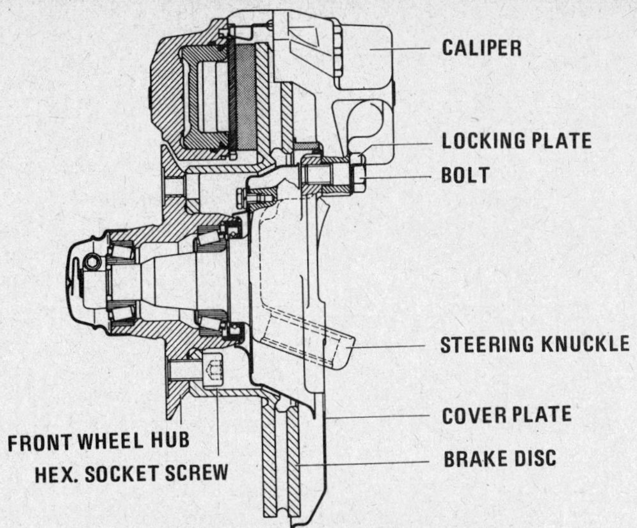

Fig. 2 Section view of Teves & Bendix type front brake calipers. 126 series

4. Install wheel cylinder plug connector.
5. Insert clip sensor cable into plug connector.
6. Connect brake line to brake hose. Ensure brake hose is not twisted.
7. Bleed front brake system and check for leaks.

BRAKE PADS, REPLACE

107 & 123 Series

Replace brake pads when the brake pad lining is down to .078 inch (2 mm) or when the pads are greasy. When the brake pads are worn to the backing plate, the caliper may also be damaged, since the lap between the sealing ring groove and the dust cap will fracture, creating caliper to leak.

1. On calipers equipped with brake lining wear indicators, pull clip sensor cables from plug connector on caliper assembly.
2. On Teves type caliper, knock holding pins from caliper assembly.
3. On Bendix and Girling type calipers, pull both locking eyes out of holding pins and remove holding pins.
4. Pull sensor from backing plate or out of brake linings. Simultaneously remove cross spring or lining holding spring. **Replace damaged sensors, as required.**
5. Using a suitable puller, pull brake pads out of caliper.
6. If brake pad wear is excessive, check caliper piston for smooth operation. If pistons are hard to move, repair or replace caliper as required. **Brake discs which are badly contaminated at the braking surface by deposits from lining (indicated by gray or blue discoloration of brake surface) must be cleaned prior to installing new break pads.**
7. Using a suitable brush, clean caliper brake pad guide.
8. Check dust cap for cracks.
9. Reverse procedure to install. **Coat brake pad lightly with lubricant at the points indicated by the arrows in Fig. 6.** Use MolyKote Paste U, Molykote Paste G Rapid, Liqui-MolyPaste 36 or Plastilube.

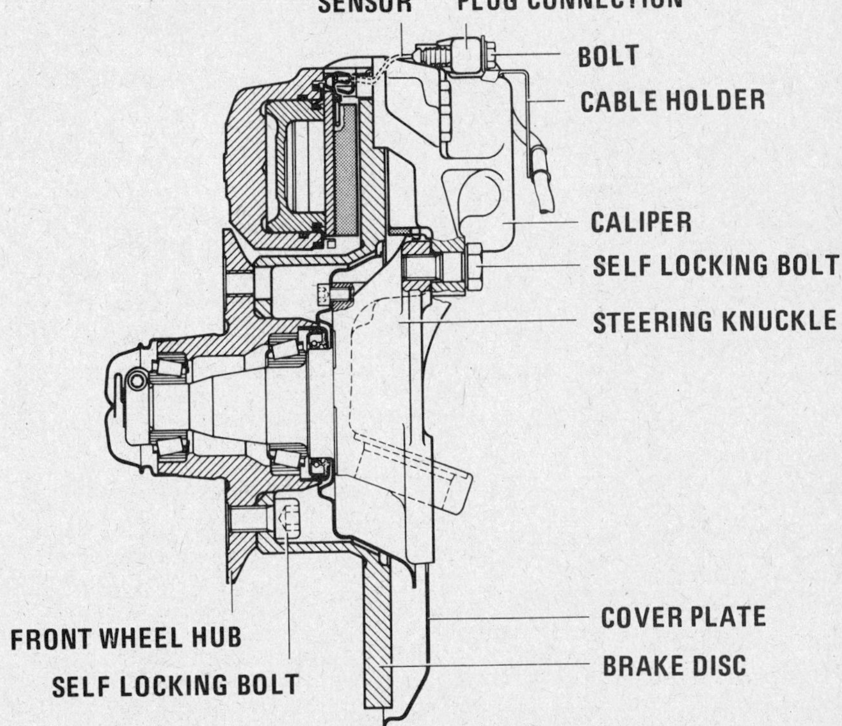

Fig. 3 Sectional view of Teves & Bendix type front brake calipers. 123 series

126 & 201 Series

1. Using a suitable screwdriver, lift the two lugs laterally on plug connector cover and open cover.
2. Loosen upper attaching bolt.
3. Fold cylinder housing downward. Suspend caliper to torsion bar using a suitable piece of wire.
4. Remove both brake pads from caliper.
5. Pull clip sensor out of lining backing plate.
6. Reverse procedure to install.

CALIPER OVERHAUL

Disassembly

When disassembling the caliper, do not separate the caliper halves. The bolts attaching the caliper halves are tightened to a specific torque by the manufacturer.

1. Remove caliper from brake disc.
2. Remove brake pads from brake caliper assembly.
3. Using a suitable screwdriver, force dust cap from caliper housing.
4. Using suitable pliers, hold one caliper piston in.
5. Using compressed air, force the other piston out from caliper. **When using compressed air, do not exceed 7 psi (.5 bars). If the caliper pistons are frozen in their bores, replace caliper as required.**

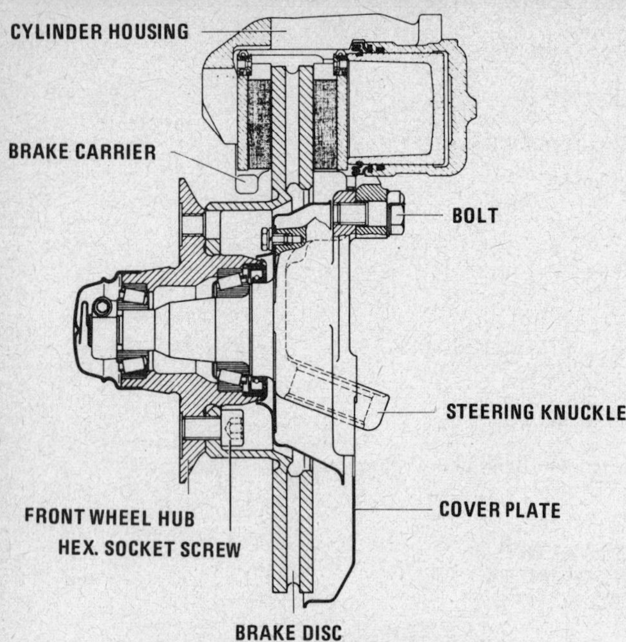

Fig. 4 Sectional view of Girling type front brake caliper. 126 series

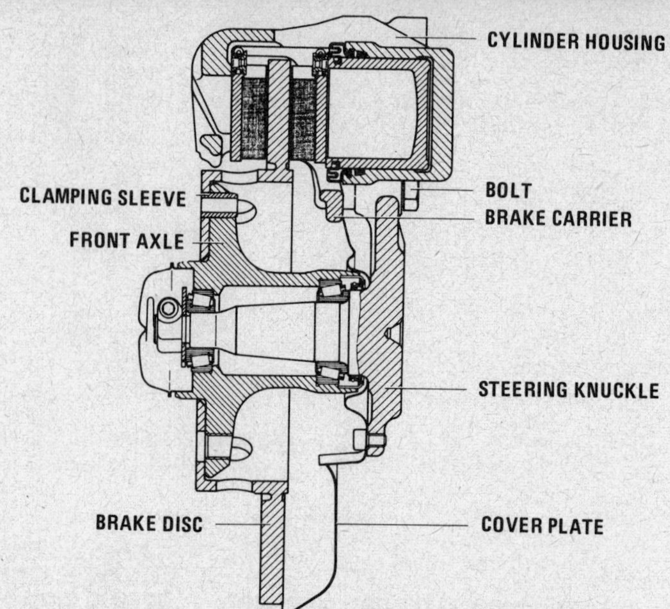

Fig. 5 Sectional view of Girling type front caliper. 102 series

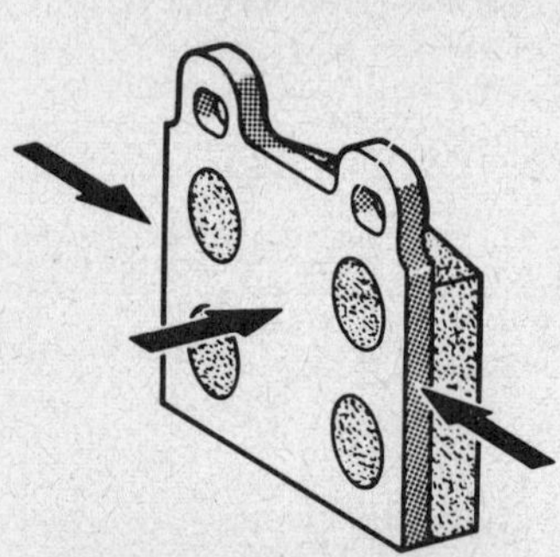

Fig. 6 Brake pad lubrication points

6. Using a suitable tool, remove caliper piston seal from caliper cylinder groove.

Inspection

1. Push heat shield away from piston.
2. Using a soft brass wire brush or a rough cleaning cloth, remove deposits from piston. Do not polish piston with emery cloth. Replace piston, if chrome surface on piston is damaged.
3. Check caliper cylinder bores for wear and/or damage. Replace complete caliper assembly if caliper bores are scored or rusted. Remove small, minor rust spots with the caliper bore with polishing cloth. Remove heavier rust spots in front of piston seal groove with fine emery paper (380 to 500 grain).

Assembly

1. Coat new piston seal slightly with clean ATE brake cylinder paste and insert seal into caliper cylinder groove. **When assembling Bendix type calipers, ensure a tight and correct seat of the pressing on seal ring.**
2. Insert piston into caliper bore, then check position of piston in caliper. **Two piston versions are used, Teves and Bendix. Ensure the correct one is installed, Fig. 7.**
3. Using suitable pliers, move piston into correct position (flush with caliper). **Install piston with elevation (marked black) on piston is pointed downward. While braking, this elevation will cause a one-sided contact of brake pads. This will reduce brake squealing.**
4. On Teves type calipers, mount dust cap onto piston, and position against caliper collar. Install discs. Install heat shield into piston with shield recess installed accurately into piston elevation. Using a suitable press, insert spacer into caliper and press heat shield into piston. **The elevation on piston should project approximately .0039 inch (.1 mm) beyond heat shield. Heat shield for the inner and outer piston are different. Do not interchange shields.**
5. On Bendix type calipers, press heat shield onto piston according to piston position. **The elevation of the piston should project approximately .0039 inch (.1 mm) beyond heat shield.**
6. Place dust cap onto piston. Using a suitable tool, mount dust cap onto caliper collar. Push piston completely back until dust cap is completely seated onto piston collar.
7. Install brake pads onto caliper.
8. Install caliper onto disc rotor.

Fig. 7 Piston identification, Bendix (left) & Teves (right)

REAR DISC BRAKE SERVICE

BRAKE CALIPER, REPLACE

Exc. 201 Series

107 series use either a Teves M38, Bendix FB38 or Girling M 10/2 type rear caliper. 123 series use either a Teves 42, Teves 38, Bendix 38 or Girling 38 type rear caliper. 126 series use either a Teves 38, Bendix 38 or Girling 38 type rear caliper. The number designations 38, 42 or 60 (located on the caliper after the manufacturer's name), indicates the caliper piston diameter. Use the same caliper (manufacturer's name and caliper piston diameter) on one axle side only. Do not interchange caliper types on one axle or uneven wear and/or braking action will occur.

1. Open caliper bleeder screw and pump brake fluid from rear brake circuit.
2. On 1st version (early production) vehicles or vehicles with starting torque

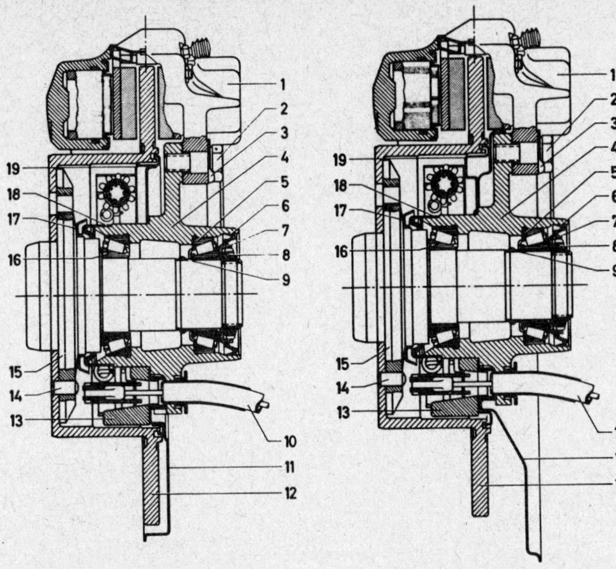

DIAGONAL SWING AXLE
EARLY PRODUCTION

DIAGONAL SWING AXLE
LATER PRODUCTION

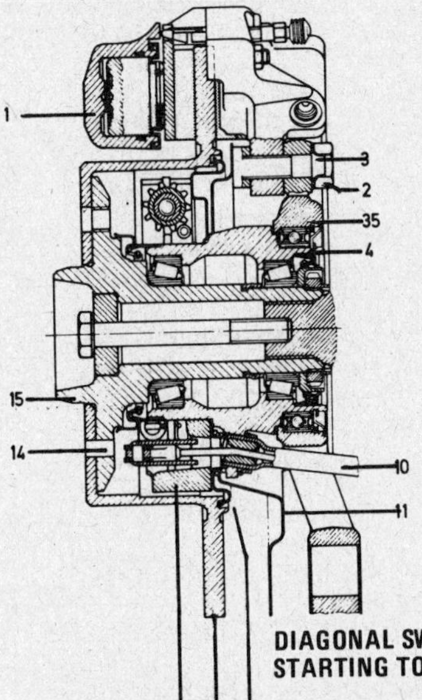

1. CALIPER
2. BOLT
3. LOCKING PLATE
4. WHEEL CARRIER
5. BEARING
6. RADIAL SEALING RING
7. SEAL RUNNING RING
8. SLOTTED NUT
9. SPACING SLEEVE
10. BRAKE CABLE CONTROL
11. COVER PLATE
12. DISC
13. BRAKE CARRIER
14. FITTED PIN
15. REAR AXLE SHAFT FLANGE
16. BEARING
17. DUST CAP
18. RADIAL SEALING RING
19. COVER RING
35. CALIPER CARRIER

DIAGONAL SWING AXLE W/
STARTING TORQUE COMPENSATION

Fig. 8 Sectional view of rear calipers (early production, later production & models w/starting torque compensation). Exc. 210 series

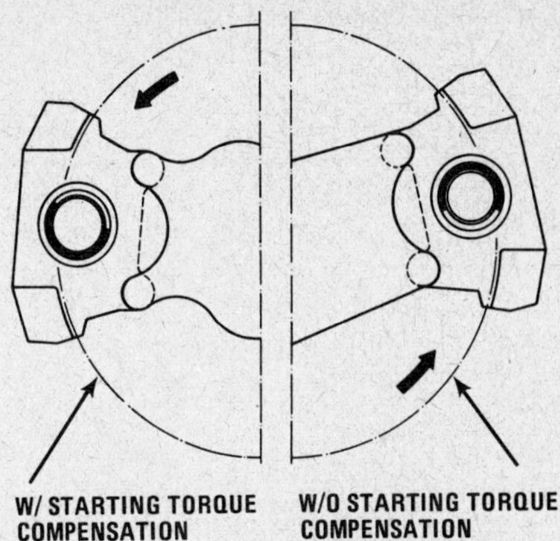

Fig. 9 Caliper location. Exc. 201 series

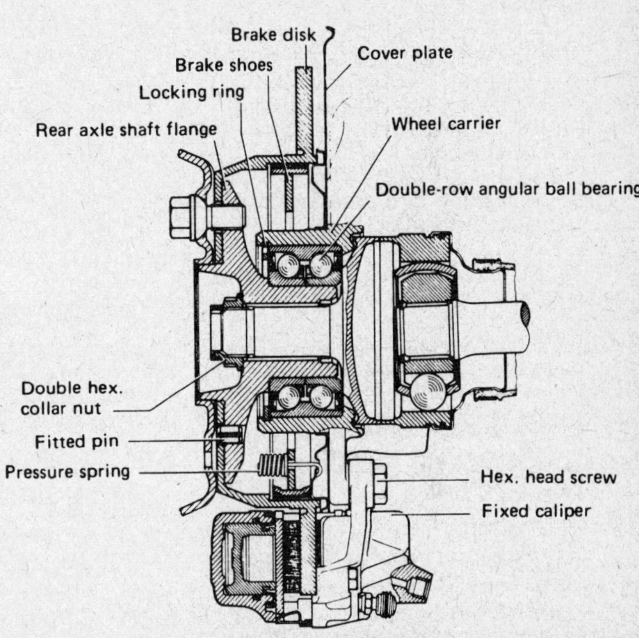

Fig. 10 Sectional view of Teves type rear caliper. 201 series

compensation, disconnect and cap brake line from caliper assembly, **Fig. 8.**

3. On 2nd version (later production) vehicles, loosen frame floor bracket brake hose from brake line. Disconnect brake line from caliper. Cap all open connections.
4. Loosen locking plate, if equipped and remove caliper attaching bolts.
5. Remove caliper attaching bolts.
6. Reverse procedure to install, noting the following:
   a. When installing a new caliper on diagonal swing axles located behind axle center, the elevation on the caliper piston must be on top, **Fig. 9.**
   b. When installing a new caliper on diagonal swing axles with starting torque compensation located in front of axle center, caliper piston elevation must be at the bottom, **Fig. 9.**
   c. When connecting brake lines and/or hoses, ensure lines and/or hoses are not twisted.
   d. After caliper is installed, check brake system for leaks.

201 Series

On 201 series, a Teves 35 type rear brake caliper is used. The number designation 35 indicates the caliper piston diameter.

1. Open caliper bleeder screw and pump brake fluid from rear brake circuit.
2. Disconnect frame floor holder brake hose from caliper assembly. Cap all open lines, **Fig. 10.**
3. Remove caliper attaching bolts, then the caliper from disc rotor.
4. Reverse procedure to install, noting the following:
   a. Calipers from different manufacturers may be installed on the rear axle, however, the calipers used must have the same caliper piston diameter.
   b. Carefully connect all brake lines and/or hoses.
   c. Check brake system for leaks.

BRAKE PADS, REPLACE

On 107 and 123 series, refer to "Front Disc Brake Service" for brake pad replacement procedures.

126 & 201 Series

Replace brake pads when the lining is down to .078 inch (2 mm) or when brake pads are greasy. When the brake pads are worn down to the lining backing plate beyond the permissible lining thickness, the caliper may be damaged since the web between the sealing ring groove and dust cap will fracture, causing the caliper to leak.

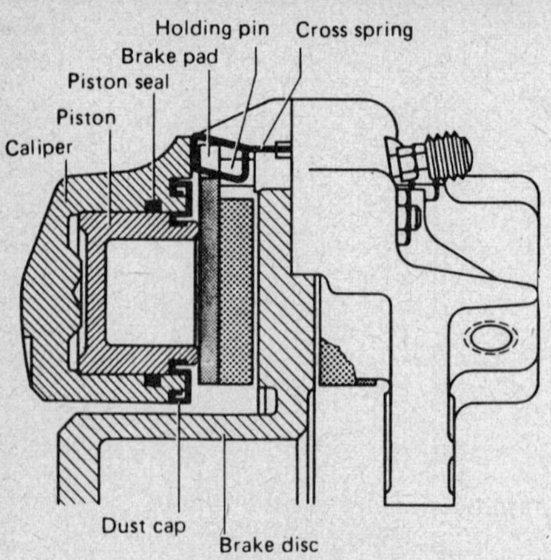

Fig. 11 Sectional view of rear caliper, piston & piston seal. Teves type rear caliper

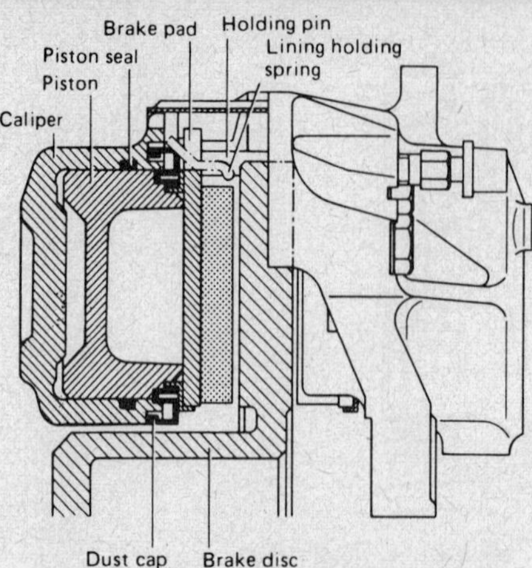

Fig. 12 Sectional view of rear caliper, piston & piston seal. Bendix type rear caliper

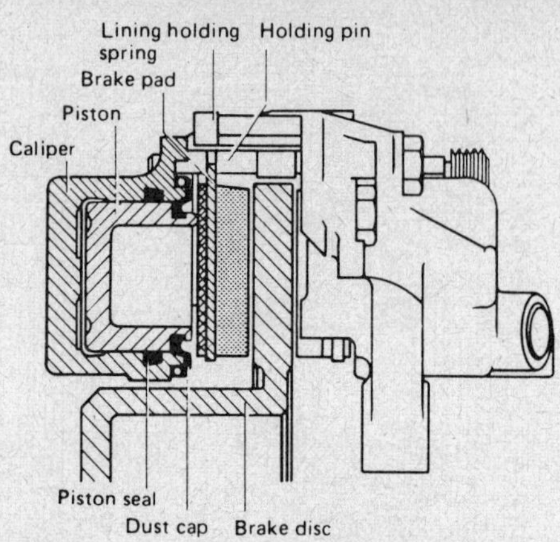

Fig. 13 Sectional view of rear caliper, piston & piston seal. Girling type rear caliper

1. On calipers with brake lining wear indicator, pull clip sensor cables from plug connectors on caliper assembly.
2. On Teves type caliper, knock holding pin from caliper by using a suitable punch and hammer.
3. On Bendix type calipers, pull both locking eyes out of the holding pins and remove holding pins.
4. Pull clip sensor out from backing plate or brake lining. Simultaneously remove cross spring or spring holding lining.
5. Using a suitable puller, remove brake pads from caliper assembly.
6. Reverse procedure to install.

CALIPER OVERHAUL

TEVES, BENDIX & GIRLING TYPE CALIPERS

Disassembly

Do not separate the two caliper halves. The attaching bolts securing the two halves are tightened to a definite torque by the manufacturer. When replacing a piston seal on a Bendix caliper, ensure that the pressed on ring is not forced off when the dust cap is removed.

1. Remove caliper from disc rotor.
2. Remove brake pads.
3. Using a suitable screwdriver, remove duct cap from caliper housing.
4. Using suitable pliers, hold one piston in the caliper. Using compressed air, force out the other caliper piston. Do not exceed 7 psi (.5 bars) to remove piston from caliper. **If piston are frozen in their bores, replace caliper assembly.**
5. Remove piston seal from cylinder bore, **Figs. 11 through 13.**

Inspection

1. On Bendix type calipers, remove heat shield from piston.
2. Remove deposits on piston with a soft brass wire brush or a rough cleaning cloth. Do not use polishing cloth or emery cloth, since this will damage the chrome-plated surface. Replace piston if surface is damaged.
3. Check caliper cylinder bores for wear. Replace caliper assembly if bores are scored or rusted. Remove small, minor rust spots in bore with polishing cloth. Remove heavier rust spots in front of piston seal groove with fine emery paper (380 to 500 grain).

Assembly

1. Coat new piston seal slightly with clean ATE brake cylinder paste and insert into caliper cylinder bore groove. **On Bendix type calipers, ensure pressed on ring is firmly and completely seated.**
2. Insert piston into caliper bore.
3. Using suitable pliers, move piston into correct position. **Insert piston with elevation (marked in black) on piston facing upward.**
4. On Teves type caliper, mount dust cap onto piston and position against caliper collar.
5. Using suitable tools, press dust cap onto caliper collar.
6. On Bendix type caliper, press heat shield onto piston according to piston position. **The elevation on piston should project approximately .0039 inch (.1 mm) beyond heat shield.**
7. Install dust cap onto piston. Mount dust cap onto caliper collar, then push piston completely backward until dust cap is seated on piston collar.
8. On Girling type calipers, mount dust cap onto piston. Push dust cap over caliper web and attach with clamping ring.
9. Install brake pads into caliper.
10. Install caliper.

MASTER CYLINDER

REPLACE

1. Drain fluid from front and rear brakes.
2. Using a suitable screwdriver, lift tangs on warning switch and disconnect electrical connector.
3. Disconnect and cap brake lines and/or hoses from master cylinder assembly.
4. On tandem master cylinders with pressure differential warning indicator, disconnect electrical connector from switch.
5. Remove master cylinder attaching bolts, then the master cylinder from vehicle.
6. Reverse procedure to install.

BRAKE BOOSTER

REPLACE

1. On vehicles with manual transmission, disconnect hose and move toward master cylinder.
2. Remove master cylinder.
3. Disconnect vacuum line from brake booster.
4. Remove instrument panel lower cover assembly.
5. Loosen brake booster pushrod on brake pedal.
6. Remove attaching nuts, then the carrier.
7. Carefully remove brake booster from vehicle.
8. Reverse procedure to install.

PARKING BRAKE

ADJUST

107 & 126 SERIES

1. Loosen each left and right shouldered bolt from rear axle.
2. Raise and support vehicle.
3. Rotate wheel until threaded hole, from which the shouldered bolt has been removed, faces forward and up at approximately a 45° angle on models with diagonal swing axle or exactly forward for models with diagonal swing axle and starting torque compensation.
4. Insert a suitable screwdriver through hole of wheel rim brake disc and rear axle shaft flange. Engage screwdriver with adjustment star and turn adjusting star until adjusting star can no longer be turned. Turn back adjusting star 2-3 turns. Turn adjusting star as follows:

a. Models with diagonal swing axle, (left side), from bottom to top.
b. Models with diagonal swing axle, (right side), from top to bottom.
c. Models with diagonal swing axle and starting torque compensation, (left side), from back to front.
d. Models with diagonal swing axle and starting torque compensation, (right side), from front to back.

123 & 201 SERIES

1. Loosen adjusting screw, ensure expanding locks are not preloaded, if equipped.
2. Loosen each left and right collar bolt at rear axle.
3. Raise and support vehicle.
4. Turn wheel until bolt hole from which the collar bolt was removed is approximately 45° in forward or upward direction on 123 series or 45° rearward upper direction on 201 models.
5. Insert a suitable screwdriver through brake disc and rear axle flange and into adjusting star. Turn adjusting star until star can no longer be turned.
6. Turn adjusting star back 2-3 teeth. Turn adjusting star as follows:
   a. Left side, from bottom to top.
   b. Right side, from top to bottom.

FRONT SUSPENSION & STEERING SECTION

INDEX

The torque values given in each procedure following are very important. Do not tighten any attaching nut or bolt without the use of a suitable torque wrench or exceed specifies torque values given.

SHOCK ABSORBER OR STRUT

REPLACE

EXCEPT 201 SERIES

The front shock absorbers also serve as a deflection stop for the front wheels. When removing, loosen shock absorber attaching nuts and bolts with vehicle wheels contacting floor or when the lower control arm is properly supported.

On gas pressurized shock absorbers with separating piston or with piston rod located on top of shock, when the vehicle is raised and the axle half is not under load, ensure piston rod is not turning while the upper attaching nut is loosened. In this condition the deflection stop within the shock absorber rests against the operating piston. The attachment of the operating piston to the piston rod may loosen. The gas pressure would then force a sudden extension of the piston rod and a loss of shock absorber fluid will result.

1. On 107 series only, remove coolant expansion tank.
2. Remove shock absorber upper attaching nuts.
3. Remove shock absorber to lower control arm attaching nuts.
4. Press shock absorber piston rod inward, then remove shock absorber from vehicle.
5. Reverse procedure to install. Torque shock absorber to lower control arm attaching nuts to 18 ft. lbs. (25 Nm).

201 SERIES

The damper struts are simultaneously serving as deflection stops for the front wheels. Loosen damper strut attaching nuts and bolts only with vehicle wheels contacting floor.

1. Raise and support front of vehicle.
2. Remove front wheel(s).
3. Install a suitable spring tensioner onto front spring. Place spring under tension until control arm is free of load. **Insert spring tensioner plates of spring tensioner offset approximately 90° into front spring. Ensure at least 7½ spring coils are engaged between spring tensioner plates. Ensure webs of tensioning screw and guide sleeve are correctly seated in the two tensioning plate grooves.**
4. While supporting control arm assembly, loosen upper strut attaching nuts as follows:
   a. Using a suitable wrench, apply a counterforce to the piston rod.
   b. Do not use an impact wrench.
   c. Do not loosen nut with axle half fully unsprung.
   d. Ensure to support control arm.
5. Loosen lower damper strut to steering knuckle attaching nuts.
6. Remove strut from vehicle.
7. Reverse procedure to install. Torque upper attaching nut to 44 ft. lbs. (60 Nm), torque lower attaching nuts to 73 ft. lbs. (100 Nm), and damper strut on steering knuckle clamp screw to 55 ft. lbs. (75 Nm).

COIL SPRING

REPLACE

On gas pressurized shock absorbers and separating pistons with the piston rod located at the top, with the vehicle raised and axle half free of load, ensure that the piston rod is not turning while loosening upper attaching nut. In this condition, the deflection stop within the shock absorber rests against the operating piston and the attachment of the operating piston to the piston rod may loosen. The gas pressure within the shock absorber may force a sudden extension of the piston rod and leaking of the shock absorber oil will result.

107 SERIES

When removing coil spring, release lower control arm. Use cradle tool 115589036300 or equivalent on to pitlift (shop lift and/or use a suitable jack). When using a pitlift, use intermediate angle piece for pitlift tool 115589026300 or equivalent. If the cradle tool is not available or if the front axle has been removed together with the coil springs, use spring tensioner BE15838 of assembly stand tool BE15798 or equivalents for tensioning the coil springs. Spindle tool 107589033110 of spring tensioner 107589033100 or equivalents may also be used.

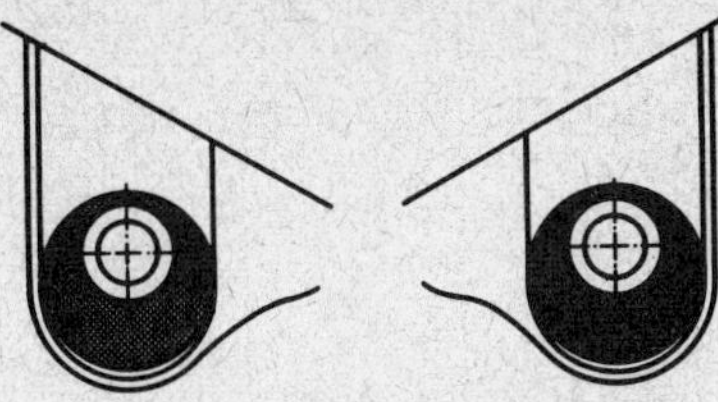

Fig. 1 Rear cam bolt position

1. Remove shock absorber and connecting linkage of torsion bar.
2. Raise and support vehicle, then remove front wheel and tire assembly.
3. Mark position of cam bolt in relation to the front axle carrier on lower control arm bearing, then loosen attaching nuts.
4. Support lower control arm with a shop pitlift or a suitable jack. Ensure tools specified previously are used.
5. Using a suitable drift and hammer, knock out cam bolt. **Do not intermix front and rear cam bolts.**
6. Carefully lower vehicle. **The cradle tool has two supporting points for the receiving bolt. When using the intermediate angle piece, in combination with a shop pitlift, secure pitlift against lateral tilting.**
7. Remove cradle, then swivel control arm forward.
8. Remove coil spring and rubber ring from vehicle.
9. Reverse procedure to install. When installing cam bolts, proceed as follows:
   a. Install cam bolts, in accordance to marks made during removal, into control arm bearings.
   b. If the position of the cam bolt has not been marked, install cam bolt in its basic position.
   c. Install rear cam bolt, as shown in **Fig. 1.**
   d. Install front cam bolt, as shown in **Fig. 2.**
   e. Torque cam bolt attaching nuts only with vehicle wheels contacting floor to 88 ft. lbs. (120 Nm).
10. Torque shock absorber lower attaching nuts to 18 ft. lbs. (25 Nm).

123 & 126 SERIES

When removing coil spring assembly, use spring tensioner tool 116589063100, spring tensioner socket tool 116589010900 and upper attaching nut socket tool 107589000900 or equivalents.

1. Remove upper shock absorber attaching nuts.
2. Raise and support vehicle, then remove front tire and wheel assembly.
3. Insert clamping plates of spring tensioner (offset by 90°) into front spring. Ensure at least 9 coils of spring are engaged between spring tensioner plate.
4. Insert tensioning screws through wheel housing dome. **The webs of the tensioning screw and guide sleeve should be correctly located in upper and lower tensioning plate grooves.**
5. Position a suitable jack under lower control arm and place spring under tension. Lift control arm while placing spring under tension load.
6. Remove front spring and rubber mount.
7. Reverse procedure to install. When installing spring, ensure water drain hole in spring retainer plate is not restricted.
8. Torque lower attaching nuts or bolts to 15 ft. lbs. (20 Nm). Tighten upper attaching nuts up to thread runout.

201 SERIES

When removing front coil springs, use spring tensioner tool 201589003100 and spring tensioner socket tool 20158901900 or equivalents.

1. Raise and support vehicle, then remove tire and wheel assembly.
2. Remove lower engine compartment lining, if equipped.
3. Insert tensioning plates of spring tensioner tool (offset by 90°) into front spring. Ensure that at least 7½ coils of spring are engaged between tensioner plates.
4. Insert tensioner screw through control arm opening. **The webs of tensioning screw and guide sleeve must be correctly seated in the two tensioning plate grooves.**
5. Place spring under tension.
6. While supporting control arm, loosen upper attaching nut. **When loosening the upper attaching nut, use a counterforce to piston rod nut. Do not use an impact wrench to loosen attaching nut. Do not loosen attaching nut with axle half fully unsprung. Ensure control arm is properly supported.**
7. Slightly lower front axle half and remove coil spring and rubber mount.
8. Reverse lower front axle half and remove coil spring and rubber mount.

TORSION BAR REPLACE

To avoid distortion of upper control arm support on torsion bar during removal, installation or when raising the vehicle, do not place jack support against frame floor. Place support against lower control arm. The rubber mounts on the torsion bar bearing may vary at the front wall to compensate body tolerances. During installation, ensure rubber mounts are returned to their original locations to avoid changes in front wheel caster. Mount and tighten torsion bar bearing on front end and support of upper control arm on torsion bar only in position in which the vehicle is ready for driving. Lubricate hex socket attaching screw on torsion bar prior to assembly.

107 SERIES

1. Loosen left and right lower control arm connecting linkage.
2. Loosen left and right torsion bar bearing holding brackets, then remove torsion bar from vehicle.

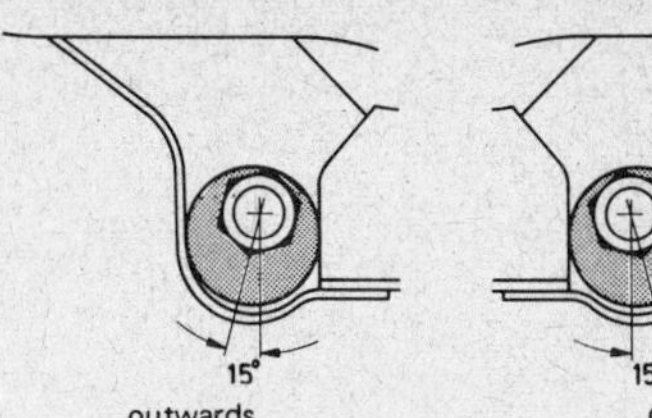

Fig. 2 Front cam bolt position

3. Reverse procedure to install. Torque torsion bar bearing attaching bolts to 14-18 ft. lbs. (20-25 Nm).

123 SERIES

1. Raise and support vehicle, place vehicle support against lower control arms.
2. Remove front wheels.
3. Loosen torsion bar upper control arm support.
4. Remove master cylinder and brake booster.
5. Disconnect coolant hoses and regulating linkage. Disconnect necessary vacuum lines and electrical connectors.
6. Loosen left and right torsion bar bearing attaching nuts from front wall, then remove bracket.
7. Remove rubber mounts from torsion bar.
8. Remove left and right front end covers.
9. Remove torsion bar from vehicle.
10. Reverse procedure to install. Torque torsion bar upper control arm support attaching bolts to 48 ft. lbs. (65 Nm). Torque torsion bar support to front wall attaching nuts to 15 ft. lbs. (20 Nm).

126 SERIES

1. Place level control adjusting switch valve unit puller to N (normal position).
2. Raise and support front of vehicle. Place vehicle support against lower control arms.
3. Remove front wheels.
4. Loosen torsion bar upper control arm support. Remove attaching screw, washer, disc washer and rubber mount from torsion bar.
5. Remove air cleaner.
6. Remove bulkhead center piece and left bulkhead side member.
7. Remove master cylinder and brake booster.
8. Remove windshield wiper motor and cover.
9. Disconnect level control connecting rod from lever. Do not pull ball pin from ball socket.
10. Remove level control bracket from front wall and pull forward together with lines attached. **Do not disconnect pressure lines. Ensure level control lever at this time is not placed in the F (filling) detent. Secure lever from moving into this position.**

11. Remove electronic RPM control unit.
12. Remove ABS (anti-lock brake system) control unit and bracket.
13. Remove battery and battery tray.
14. Drain enough coolant to allow automatic climate control regulating valve to be removed without coolant leakage.
15. Disconnect and cap coolant hoses from firewall.
16. Remove right bulkhead side member.
17. Discharge refrigerant from A/C system.
18. Disconnect and cap expansion valve lines.
19. Remove left and right brake line bracket from front wall.
20. Remove fuse panel bracket.
21. Remove lower right portion of bulkhead.
22. Remove left and right torsion bar bearing clip attaching nuts.
23. Remove left and right front end covers.
24. Using a suitable tool, push torsion bar out of control arm eye.
25. Remove torsion bar first from the right side, then after slightly turning torsion bar upward, disconnect torsion bar from the left side.
26. Reverse procedure to install, noting the following:
    a. During installation of torsion bar, install torsion bar with bend portions of torsion bar arms pointing downward.
    b. Place level control adjusting switch valve puller into N (normal level) position. If vehicle level is too low, start and operate engine until normal vehicle level (height) is obtained.
    c. Torque torsion bar upper control arm support attaching bolt to 48 ft. lbs. (65 Nm).
    d. Torque torsion bar front end support attaching nuts to 52 ft. lbs. (70 Nm).
    e. Torque torsion bar actuating level support attaching nuts to 5 ft. lbs. (7 Nm).

201 SERIES

1. Remove lower engine compartment lining, if equipped.
2. Loosen and remove left and right torsion bar bearing bracket from control arm.
3. Loosen bearings from spring leaf rockers and remove torsion bar. **The rubber torsion bar mounts do not have a slot. For this reason use rubber lubricant A0009890160 or equivalent for removal and installation.**
4. Reverse procedure to install. Torque torsion bar bearing to control arm attaching nuts to 15 ft. lbs. (20 Nm), torque torsion bar bearing to spring leaf attaching bolts and nuts to 15 ft. lbs. (20 Nm) and torsion bar spring leaf rocker to frame attaching bolts to 44 ft. lbs. (60 Nm).

FRONT WHEEL HUB REPLACE

1. Raise and support vehicle.
2. Remove front wheel(s).
3. Using a suitable puller, remove hub cap.
4. Remove radio interference suppression contact spring, if equipped.
5. Remove brake caliper from steering knuckle and suspend caliper using a suitable piece of wire. Do not disconnect brake lines.
6. Remove brake disc assembly.
7. Remove stub axle shaft clamping nut bolt clamping nut.
8. Using a suitable puller, if necessary, remove front wheel hub.
9. Reverse procedure to install. Torque caliper attaching bolts to 84 ft. lbs. (115 Nm). On 107 series, torque clamping nut attaching bolt to 15 ft. lbs. (20 Nm). On 123 and 126 series, torque clamping nut attaching bolt to 10 ft. lbs. (14 Nm). On 201 series, torque clamping nut attaching bolt to 9 ft. lbs. (12 Nm).

STEERING KNUCKLE REPLACE

EXC. 201 SERIES

1. Raise and support vehicle, then remove front wheel.
2. Loosen steering knuckle arm from steering knuckle.
3. Remove brake caliper from steering knuckle and suspend caliper on torsion. Do not place brake lines under any stress. Do not disconnect brake lines.
4. On vehicles with ABS (anti-lock brake system), remove RPM sensor from steering knuckle.
5. Remove front wheel hub.
6. Remove bracket from cover plate brake lines.
7. Using a suitable tool, remove guide joint nut and joint from steering knuckle.
8. Loosen supporting joint nut.
9. Swivel upper steering knuckle slightly outward and force supporting joint from lower control arm.
10. Remove steering knuckle.
11. Remove cover plate from steering knuckle, if necessary.
12. Reverse procedure to install, noting the following torque values:
    a. On 107 series, torque steering knuckle arm attaching bolts to 59 ft. lbs. (80 Nm). Torque guide joint attaching nut to 44 ft. lbs. (60 Nm). Torque supporting joint attaching nut to 59 ft. lbs. (80 Nm). Torque caliper attaching bolts to 84 ft. lbs. (115 Nm).
    b. On 123 and 126 series, torque guide joint attaching nut to 29 ft. lbs. (40 Nm). Torque supporting joint attaching nut to 59 ft. lbs. (80 Nm). Torque caliper attaching bolts to 84 ft. lbs. (115 Nm). Torque steering knuckle arm attaching bolt to 59 ft. lbs. (80 Nm).

201 SERIES

1. Raise and support front of vehicle.
2. Remove front wheel(s).
3. Remove brake caliper from steering knuckle and suspend using a suitable piece of wire.
4. Remove brake disc. **Do not subject brake lines to tension.**
5. Remove speed sensor from steering knuckle, if equipped.
6. Remove brake cover plate from steering knuckle.
7. Insert a suitable spring compressor onto spring. Compress spring until transverse link (control arm) is free from load.
8. Loosen steering knuckle arm to steering knuckle attaching bolts.
9. Remove shock absorber to steering knuckle attaching bolts.
10. Remove clamp joint between steering knuckle and supporting joint.
11. Remove steering knuckle from supporting joint.
12. Reverse procedure to install, noting the following torque values:
    a. Torque clamp joint between support joint and steering knuckle to 92 ft. lbs. (125 Nm).
    b. Torque steering knuckle stop to 33 ft. lbs. (45 Nm).
    c. Torque lower shock absorber to steering knuckle attaching bolts to 73 ft. lbs. (100 Nm).
    d. Torque clamping joint of shock absorber at steering knuckle to 55 ft. lbs. (75 Nm).
    e. Torque stub axle to steering knuckle attaching bolts to 84 ft. lbs. (115 Nm).
    f. Torque brake anchor plate to steering knuckle attaching bolt to 7 ft. lbs. (10 Nm).
    g. Torque steering knuckle arm attaching bolts to 59 ft. lbs. (80 Nm).
    h. Torque caliper attaching bolts to 84 ft. lbs. (115 Nm).
    i. Torque speed sensor to steering knuckle attaching bolts to 16 ft. lbs. (22 Nm).

UPPER CONTROL ARM OR TRANSVERSE LINK REPLACE

Torque upper control arm bearings, torsion bar upper control arm support and torsion bar bearings only with vehicle wheels contacting floor.

107 SERIES

1. Disconnect steering knuckle arm from steering knuckle.
2. Disconnect and cap brake hose from brake line.
3. Pull bracket from brake line.
4. Remove guide joint and supporting joint attaching nut.
5. Using a suitable tool, remove guide joint from steering knuckle.
6. Remove both upper control arm attaching nuts, then the upper control arm.
7. Reverse procedure to install. Torque supporting joint attaching nut to 59 ft.

lbs. (80 Nm). Torque guide joint attaching nut to 44 ft. lbs. (60 Nm). Torque upper control arm bearing attaching bolts to 44 ft. lbs. (60 Nm). Torque steering knuckle arm attaching bolts to 59 ft. lbs. (80 Nm).

123 & 126 SERIES

1. Raise and support front of vehicle. Place vehicle supports against lower control arm.
2. Remove front wheel(s).
3. Loosen guide joint attaching nut.
4. Using a suitable tool, remove guide joint from steering knuckle.
5. Secure steering knuckle from tilting using a suitable hook placed on the control arm.
6. Remove upper control arm support.
7. Loosen upper control arm bearing, then remove upper control arm from vehicle.
8. Reverse procedure to install. Torque upper control arm bearing attaching bolt to 59 ft. lbs. (80 Nm). Torque guide joint attaching nut to 29 ft. lbs. (40 Nm). Torque upper control arm support to torsion bar attaching bolt to 48 ft. lbs. (65 Nm).

201 SERIES

The eccentric pin on the transverse link bearing may only be tightened when the vehicle wheels are contacting floor.

1. Remove lower engine compartment lining, if equipped.
2. Raise and support vehicle.
3. Remove front wheel(s).
4. Remove torsion bar bearing from transverse link.
5. Remove front spring.
6. Mark positions of eccentric pins in relation to the frame on the transverse link bearing.
7. Remove eccentric pin attaching nuts, then the eccentric pins.
8. Lower transverse link assembly.
9. Remove clamping joint attaching bolt between steering knuckle and supporting joint.
10. Remove transverse link from steering knuckle.
11. Reverse procedure to install. Torque clamping joint attaching bolt to 92 ft. lbs. (125 Nm). Torque eccentric pin attaching nuts to 88 ft. lbs. (120 Nm). Torque transverse link torsion bar bearings attaching nuts to 15 ft. lbs. (20 Nm).

LOWER CONTROL ARM REPLACE

107 SERIES

1. Loosen lower shock absorber attaching bolts.
2. Raise and support vehicle.
3. Remove front wheel(s).
4. Disconnect steering knuckle arm from steering knuckle.
5. Disconnect and cap brake hose from brake line.
6. Disconnect bracket from brake hose.
7. Remove front spring assembly.
8. Remove attaching nuts from supporting and guide joints.
9. Using a suitable tool, remove supporting joint from steering knuckle.
10. Remove lower control arm from vehicle.
11. Reverse procedure to install, noting the following torque values:
    a. Torque guide joint attaching nut to 44 ft. lbs. (60 Nm).
    b. Torque supporting joint attaching nut to 59 ft. lbs. (80 Nm).
    c. Torque steering knuckle arm attaching nut to 59 ft. lbs. (80 Nm).
    d. Torque lower control arm cam bolts to 88 ft. lbs. (120 Nm).
    e. Torque lower shock absorber attaching nuts to 15 ft. lbs. (20 Nm).

123 & 126 SERIES

1. Remove front shock absorber.
2. Raise and support vehicle.
3. Remove front wheel(s).
4. Remove front spring.
5. Remove steering knuckle arm track rod.
6. Mark positions of eccentric bolt for frame crossmember on lower control arm bearing.
7. Remove brake support from frame floor.
8. Remove eccentric bolt from lower control arm bearing.
9. Force supporting joint from lower control arm.
10. Remove lower control arm and brake support.
11. Reverse procedure to install, noting the following torque values:
    a. Torque supporting joint nut to 59 ft. lbs. (80 Nm).
    b. Torque lower control arm bearing eccentric bolt to 132 ft. lbs. (180 Nm).
    c. Torque track rod ball joint nut ot 29 ft. lbs. (40 Nm).
    d. Torque lower shock absorber attaching nuts to 15 ft. lbs. (20 Nm).
    e. On 123 series, torque brake support to lower control arm attaching bolt to 37 ft. lbs. (50 Nm).
    f. On 126 series, torque brake support to lower control arm M10 attaching bolts to 52 ft. lbs. (70 Nm), M12 bolts to 77 ft. lbs. (105 Nm).

WHEEL BEARINGS ADJUST

1. Raise and support vehicle.
2. Remove front wheel(s).
3. Using a suitable bolts, secure brake disc to wheel hub assembly.
4. Force brake pads away from brake disc.
5. Remove hub cap.
6. Remove radio interference suppression contact spring.
7. Release internal bolt of clamping nut, and tighten clamping nut while simultaneously turning the hub until hub can only just be turned. Loosen clamping nut approximately 1/3 turn and relieve tension by striking stub axle with a plastic mallet.
8. Position a suitable dial indicator onto front hub assembly.
9. Check endplay by pulling and pushing on the flange. Turn wheel hub several times before each measurement. Endplay obtained should be .00039-.00078 inch (.01-.02 mm).

POWER STEERING GEAR REPLACE

1. Drain fluid from steering gear assembly.
2. Disconnect and fluid lines from steering gear assembly.
3. Loosen lower attaching screw from steering coupling.
4. Remove capsule nut from drag link and track rod.
5. Using a suitable puller, push ball joint track rod from pitman arm.
6. Using a suitable puller, push ball joint of drag link from pitman arm.
7. Remove self-locking nut from pitman shaft.
8. On models with V8 engine, remove rear exhaust system, then disconnect lefthand exhaust pipe from exhaust manifold.
9. Remove pitman arm from pitman shaft.
10. Remove steering shaft.
11. Remove steering gear to frame floor side member attaching bolts.
12. Remove steering gear from vehicle.
13. Reverse procedure to install. On all series except 126, torque steering gear to frame floor side member attaching bolts to 51-59 ft. lbs. (70-80 Nm). On 126 series, torque steering gear to frame floor side member bolts to 66-81 ft. lbs. (90-110 Nm). Torque steering coupling flange attaching bolts to 18 ft. lbs. (25 Nm). Torque pitman arm attaching nuts to 118-147 ft. lbs. (160-200 Nm). Torque track rod and drag link to pitman arm attaching nuts to 25 ft. lbs. (35 Nm).

WHEEL ALIGNMENT SPECIFICATIONS

INDEX

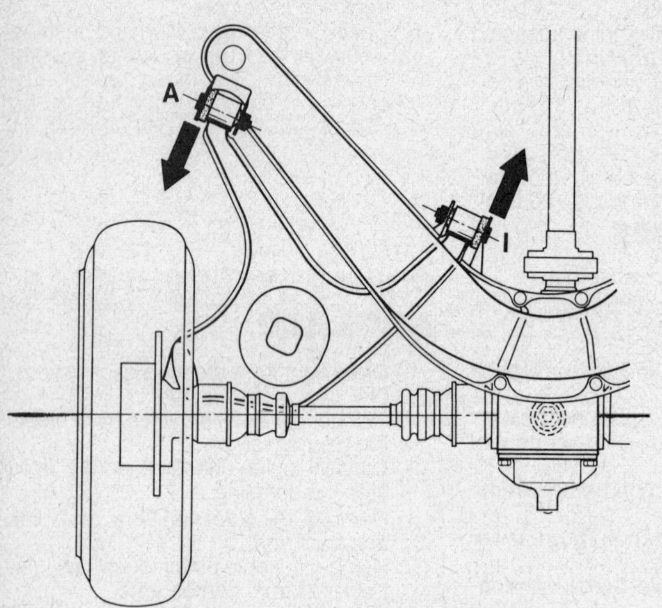

Fig. 1 Decreasing toe-in

Fig. 1 Increasing toe-in

FRONT WHEEL ALIGNMENT

FRONT CAMBER & CASTER, ADJUSTMENT

The front axle provides for combined camber and caster adjustment. Both wheel adjustments can be made together. Adjustments are made by means of eccentric bolts at the lower control arm bearing and brake support ball pin supporting joint. To adjust eccentric bolt on lower control arm bearing, loosen hex nut, then tightening hex nut while applying counter hold to eccentric bolt.

When increasing camber on eccentric bolt, caster will also increase. When decreasing camber, caster will also decrease.

To adjust supporting joint ball pin, loosen clamp and turn ball pin in supporting tube (ball pin is righthand threaded). Turning outward will increase caster, turning inward will decrease caster. When increasing caster, camber will decrease, when decreasing caster, camber will increase.

TOE-IN, ADJUSTMENT

Toe-in is the difference between the distance of the front end of the front wheels to the rear wheels measured at the rim flanges.

The elastic support of the control arms requires a higher toe-in value, which is reduced to the correct size when driving. When measuring toe-in, spread wheels apart using a suitable wheel spreading tool. This will eliminate any elasticity in steering linkage. Adjust toe-in to specifications.

REAR WHEEL ALIGNMENT

TOE-IN

Toe-in of the rear wheels results from the location of the rear axle carrier and the semi-trailing arms. Toe-in value depends within certain limits on the semi-trailing arm position of the rear axle.

Toe-in can be corrected or the nominal value can be attempted by the installation of eccentric rubber mounts in the semi-trailing arms. Semi-trailing arm eccentric rubber mount part No. 1233520765 is available to correct toe-in. To reduce toe-in, install outer rubber mount (A) with arrow pointing toward the rear as shown in **Fig. 1** and inner rubber mount (1), pointing toward the front.

To increase toe-in, install outer rubber mount (A) with arrow pointing toward the front as shown in **Fig. 2** and inner rubber mount (1), pointing toward the rear.

MERKUR (Germany)

INDEX OF SERVICE OPERATIONS

General Engine Specifications

Year	Engine Model	Fuel System	Bore Stroke Inches	Compression Ratio	Maximum HP @ RPM	Maximum Torque @ RPM	Normal Oil Pressure Psi
1985–86	4-140/2.3L	Fuel Inj.	3.780 X 3.126	8.1	176 @ 4750	219 @ 2500	40–60
1987	4-140/2.3L	Fuel Inj.	3.780 X 3.126	8.0	145 @ 4400①	180 @ 3000②	40–60

①—On models with manual transmission, 175 @ 5000.
②—On models with manual transmission, 200 @ 3000.

Alternator Specifications

Year	Model	Alternator Cold Output @ 15 Volts Amperes @ 600 RPM
1985–87	Bosch	90

Starter Motor Specifications

Year	Current Draw Under Normal Load	Current Draw Under No Load	Normal Engine Cranking Speed RPM	New Brush Length Inches	Brush Wear Limit Inches	Brush Spring Tension Oz.	Starter Relay Pull In Winding Resistance	Maximum Voltage Drop	Maximum Commutator Runout Inches
1985–87	150–250	80	180–250	.45	.25	80	3–5	.5	.005

Valve Specifications

Year	Engine	Valve Lash		Valve Angles		Valve Spring Installed Height	Valve Spring Pressure Lbs. @ In.	Stem Clearance		Stem Diameter	
		Int.	Exh.	Seat	Face			Intake	Exhaust	Intake	Exhaust
1985–87	4-140	①	①	45°	44°	1^{9-16}	75 @ 1.52	.0010–.0027	.0015–.0032	.3416–.3423	.3411–.3418

①—Collapsed tappet gap, .040–.050 inch.

Pistons, Pins, Rings, Crankshaft & Bearings

Year	Engine	Piston Clearance	Ring End Gap		Piston Pin Diameter	Rod Bearings		Main Bearings		
			Comp.	Oil		Shaft Diameter	Bearing Clearance	Shaft Diameter	Bearing Clearance	Shaft End Play
1985–87	4-140	.0030–.0038	.010–.020	.015–.055	.9118–.9124	2.0465–2.0472	.0008–.0015	2.3982–2.399	.0008–.0015	.004–.008

Engine Tightening Specifications

Year	Engine	Spark Plug Ft. Lbs.	Cylinder Head Ft. Lbs.	Intake Manifold Ft. Lbs.	Exhaust Manifold Ft. Lbs.	Rocker Cover Ft. Lbs.	Conn. Rod Cap Ft. Lbs.	Main Bearing Cap Ft. Lbs.	Flywheel To Crankshaft Ft. Lbs.	Damper or Pulley Ft. Lbs.
1985–87	4-140	7–15	①	14–21	②	5–8	③	①	56–64	100–120

①—Torque in two steps; first, 50–60 ft. lbs.; final, 80–90 ft. lbs.

②—Torque in two steps; first, 5–7 ft. lbs.; final, 16–23 ft. lbs.

③—Torque in two steps; first, 25–30 ft. lbs.; final, 30–36 ft. lbs.

Brake Specifications

Year	Model	Drum I.D.	Wheel Cyl. Bore		Disc Brake Rotor					Master Cyl. I.D.
			Rear Drum	Front Disc	Nominal Thickness	Minimum Thickness	Thickness Variation (Parallelism)	Run Out (TIR)	Finish (Micro. In.)	
1985–86	All	10	7/8	—	.95	.898	.0004	.003	—	.94
1987	All	10	7/8	—	.95	.898	.0004	.003	—	1.0

Wheel Alignment Specifications

Year	Caster Angle, Degrees		Camber Angle, Degrees				Toe-In (Inch)	
			Front		Rear			
	Limits	Desired	Limits	Desired	Limits	Desired	Front	Rear
1985–87	+1 to +3	+1 to +3	−1½ to +½	−½	①	①	1/32 to 1/8	−5/64 to 11/64

①—Camber angle varies with ride height. With ride height measured fron center of wheel to bottom of wheel opening molding, camber should be as follows: −2°50' to −½° @ 13.77–14.1 inches; −2°28' to −0°08' @ 14.1–14.5 inches; −1¾° to +½° @ 14.9–15.3 inches; −1°20' to +1° @ 15.3–15.7 inches; −1° to +1°22' @ 15.7–16.1 inches; −½° to +1¾° @ 16.1–16.5 inches. Maximum side to side variation must not exceed 1°.

Rear Axle Specifications

Year	Model	Carrier Type	Ring Gear & Pinion Backlash		Pinion Bearing Preload			Differential Bearing Preload		
			Method	Adjustment	Method	New Bearings Inch Lbs.	Used Bearings Inch Lbs.	Method	New Bearings Inch Lbs.	Used Bearings Inch Lbs.
1985–87	All	Removable	Threader Adjuster	.004–.007	Collapsible Spacer	14–18	—	Threaded Adjuster	①	—

①—Differential bearing preload is correct when .004–.007 inch backlash exists between pinion & ring gear.

Cooling System & Capacity Data

Year	Engine	Cooling Capacity Qts.	Radiator Cap Relief Pressure, Lbs.	Thermo. Opening Temp.	Fuel Tank Gals.	Engine Oil Refill Qts.①	Transmission Oil		Rear Axle Oil, Pts.
							Man. Trans. Pts.	Auto. Trans. Qts.③	
1985–87	4-140	9½	14–18	192	15	4	②	8	—

①—Add one quart with filter change.

②—On transmission with yellow paint square on left side of extension housing, fill to approximately one inch below filler plug. On transmission without yellow paint square, fill to bottom of filler hole.

③—Approximate, make final check with dipstick.

ELECTRICAL SECTION

INDEX

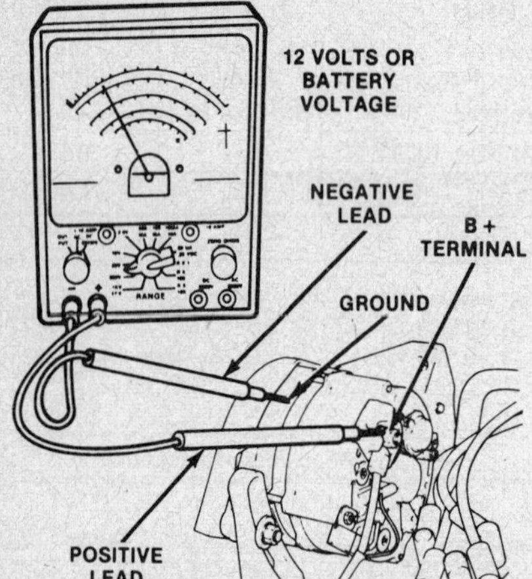

Fig. 1 Checking voltage at alternator B+ terminal

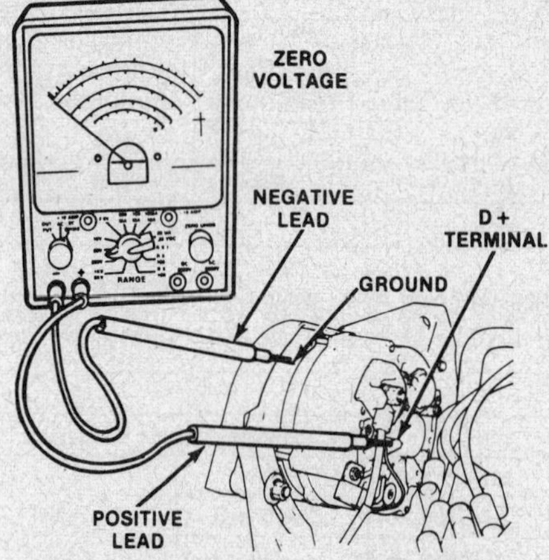

Fig. 2 Checking voltage at alternator D+ terminal

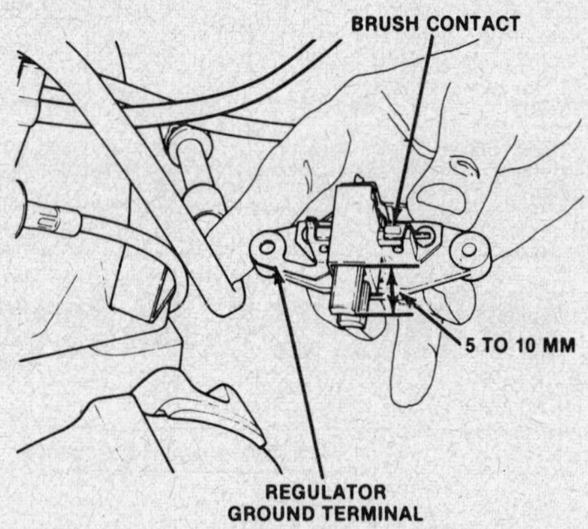

Fig. 3 Checking brush length

ALTERNATOR IN-VEHICLE TESTING

KEY OFF TEST

1. With ignition key in "OFF" position, check voltage at alternator B+ terminal, **Fig. 1.** If voltage is not approximately 12 volts, check for open in charging circuit between B+ and battery positive post.
2. Check for voltage at D+ terminal, **Fig. 2.** If voltage is present, diode(s) is shorted.

OUTPUT VOLTAGE TEST

1. With voltmeter connected as shown in **Fig. 1,** start engine and run at approximately 1500 RPM while observing output voltage.
2. Output voltage should quickly increase from the reduced start-up value as the starting load discharge is restored, then stabilize between 13.8 and 14.2 volts at approximately 77 degrees F.

DIODE TEST

1. With engine running, note output voltage at B+ terminal.
2. Turn engine off, then measure voltage at D+ terminal.
3. If D+ voltage is more than .5 volts lower than B+ voltage, field diode(s) is shorted or open.
4. If output voltage was high but diode test was satisfactory, replace regulator.
5. If D+ voltage is more than .5 volt greater than B+ voltage, output diode(s) is defective.

REGULATOR BYPASS TEST

1. If output voltage is low and diodes test satisfactorily, start engine and run at idle.
2. While watching voltage at B+ terminal, ground connecting strip between rear brush and the regulator.
3. While observing voltmeter, gradually increase engine speed.
4. If output voltage increases to 16 volts, replace regulator. If not, replace alternator. **Do not increase engine speed any more than enough to produce 16 volt output.**

EXTERNAL CIRCUIT TEST

1. If output voltage is normal but undercharge symptoms are reported, there may be excessive voltage drops in circuit between alternator and battery.
2. Start engine and run at approximately 1500 RPM, then check output voltage at B+ terminal and the battery positive post.
3. If these two readings differ by more than .2 volt, check for loose or corroded connections at the B+ circuit.
4. Check battery ground cable for voltage between negative battery post and engine ground, using voltmeter's lowest voltage range.
5. If there is a drop of more than .2 volt, check for damage or poor connection in ground cable.

EXCITATION VOLTAGE TEST

1. If voltage does not increase above battery voltage with engine running, stop engine and check for voltage at D+ terminal with key in "ON" position.
2. If battery voltage is present, the field circuit is open.
3. If voltage is between 4 volts and battery voltage, excessive resistance is present in the field coil circuit, either at

the brush holder coilspring in the alternator end frame, between the brushes and slip rings, in the field winding, in the regulator or at the regulator ground on the frame.
4. Release drive belt tension and spin rotor manually while measuring excitation voltage. If voltage fluctuates considerably but occasionally drops below 4 volts, clean or replace brushes and slip rings as necessary.

BRUSH TEST

1. If spinning rotor resulted in considerable variation of excitation voltage, disconnect battery ground cable, remove regulator and brush holder assembly and check brushes for excessive wear or damage, bad connections or sticky action.
2. Brushes should project from the brush holder approximately 5/32 to 3/8 inch (5 to 10 mm), **Fig. 3.**
3. Clean and free up brushes or replace holder and regulator assembly as necessary.
4. While brush holder assembly is out, clean and polish slip rings with crocus cloth or fine abrasive, spinning the rotor by hand with drive belt loose. Check and clean the front brush contact on the brush holder and the contact spring inside the alternator end frame. Ensure that regulator ground terminal makes good contact with alternator end frame.

FIELD TEST

1. With brush holder assembly removed, check field coil continuity and isolation with an ohmmeter.
2. Probe from slip ring to slip ring. If very low resistance is not indicated, field is partially or completely open.
3. Probe from either slip ring to alternator frame. If there is infinite ohms, field is grounded.
4. Install brush holder and regulator assembly, connect battery ground cable and repeat output voltage test.

OUTPUT CURRENT TEST

1. Disconnect battery ground cable and alternator B+ lead.
2. Connect a 100 amp ammeter between the B+ terminal and the end of the B+ lead and position B+ lead so that it cannot accidentally contact ground during test.
3. Connect voltmeter between B+ terminal and ground.
4. Connect battery ground cable and connect a carbon pile load rheostat across the battery terminals. **Ensure that carbon pile is turned to "OFF" or "NO LOAD" before connecting it.**
5. Connect tachometer, then start engine and run at idle.
6. Adjust carbon pile and engine speed until voltmeter reads 13.5 volts at idle, then note ammeter reading.
7. Repeat test at 1000 and 2000 RPM.
8. If engine speed output current at 13.5 volts is not 28-35 amps at idle, 75-85 amps at 1000 RPM and 89 amps at 2000 RPM, repair or replace alternator as necessary.

STARTER

REPLACE

REMOVAL

1. Disconnect battery ground cable, then raise and support vehicle.
2. Disconnect starter cable at starter motor terminal.
3. Remove bolt attaching heat shield to cylinder block.
4. Remove starter attaching bolts, heat shield rear support bracket, transmission to cylinder block brace and the starter.

INSTALLATION

1. Position starter, bracket, brace and heat shield.
2. Install attaching bolts, torquing to 15-20 ft. lbs.
3. Install heat shield attaching bolt.
4. Tighten starter support bracket at cylinder block, then at starter.
5. Connect starter cable, lower vehicle and connect battery ground cable.

IGNITION SWITCH

REPLACE

REMOVAL

1. Disconnect battery ground cable.
2. Remove steering column shroud.
3. Insert key in ignition switch and turn key to "ACC."
4. Using suitable tool, depress key cylinder leaf spring through access hole in lock housing, then gently jiggle key back and forth until lock barrel and key cylinder come free.
5. Remove circlip from lock barrel, being careful not to damage circlip location in lock barrel.
6. Withdraw key approximately .2 inch, then remove key barrel from cylinder.

INSTALLATION

1. Insert key fully into key barrel, then withdraw key approximately .2 inch.
2. Insert key barrel into cylinder.
3. Insert key fully and ensure that key and barrel turn freely.
4. Turn key to "ACC" position and install retaining circlip, ensuring that open jaws of clip align with keyway register of cylinder.
5. Insert cylinder assembly into housing, ensuring that cylinder is firmly seated in housing so that leaf spring fits into undercut slot in housing. Jiggle key back and forth as necessary to achieve proper alignment.
6. Check operation of lock assembly in all positions.

LIGHT SWITCH

REPLACE

1. Disconnect battery ground cable.
2. Remove retaining screws, then the upper and lower steering column shrouds.
3. Remove two screws attaching multiswitch assembly to steering column, then guide multiswitch away from steering column.
4. Disconnect multiconnector and ground wire connector, then remove multiswitch.
5. Reverse procedure to install.

STOP LIGHT SWITCH

REPLACE

REMOVAL

1. Disconnect battery ground cable.
2. Remove lower instrument panel.
3. Disconnect electrical connector at stop light switch.
4. Twist stop light switch counterclockwise and remove.

INSTALLATION

1. Insert switch into lock ring opening and push in until switch barrel touches pedal. Ensure that pedal is not removed from its stop.
2. Twist switch clockwise to lock, then reconnect electrical connector and check operation of switch.
3. Install lower instrument panel and reconnect battery ground cable.

NEUTRAL SAFETY SWITCH

REPLACE

1. Disconnect battery ground cable, then the electrical connector at switch.
2. Using only suitable socket, remove switch.
3. Remove and discard switch O-ring.
4. Reverse procedure to install, using new O-ring, and torque switch to 7-10 ft. lbs.

TURN SIGNAL SWITCH

REPLACE

When replacing turn signal switch, refer to "Light Switch, Replace" procedure.

INSTRUMENT CLUSTER

REPLACE

1. Disconnect battery ground cable.
2. Remove screw from upper steering column shroud and remove shroud.
3. Remove instrument panel illumination control and intermittent wiper control rheostats.
4. Remove four bezel retaining screws, then the bezel.
5. Remove four instrument cluster to instrument panel attaching screws and pull cluster toward steering wheel.
6. Disconnect speedometer cable, har-

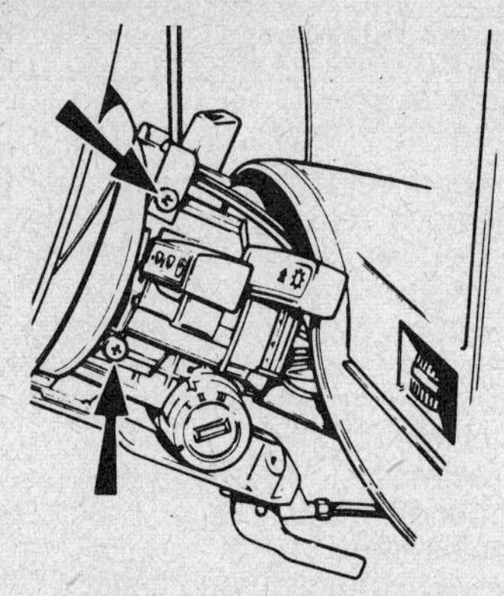
Fig. 4 Removing windshield wiper switch

ness connector, and turbo boost gauge vacuum line from rear of cluster assembly and remove cluster.
7. Reverse procedure to install.

WINDSHIELD WIPER SWITCH

REPLACE

REMOVAL

1. Disconnect battery ground cable, then remove steering column upper and lower shrouds.
2. Remove two Phillips head screws and the guide switch assembly from the steering column, **Fig. 4.**
3. Disconnect electrical connectors at switch, then remove switch.

INSTALLATION

1. Connect electrical connectors at switch.
2. Position switch on mounting bracket and retain with two Phillips head screws.
3. Install upper and lower steering column shrouds and reconnect battery ground cable.

WIPER MOTOR

REPLACE

FRONT WIPER

Removal

1. Turn wiper motor "ON," then, when blades are straight up, turn key "OFF."
2. Remove arm and blade assemblies, then disconnect battery ground cable.
3. Remove locknut from motorshaft, then remove motor arm from motor.
4. Remove three motor attaching bolts, then the motor.
5. Disconnect electrical connector at motor.

Installation

1. Connect electrical connector at motor, place motor in position and torque retaining bolts to 7-9 ft. lbs.
2. Connect wiper motor arm to shaft of windshield wiper motor, ensuring that key of motor arm is aligned to shaft, and torque locknut to 13-15 ft. lbs.
3. Connect battery ground cable.
4. Before installing arm and blade assembly on pivot shaft, cycle motor to ensure that it is in "PARK" position.

REAR WIPER

Removal

1. Unclip plastic clip from base of wiper arm, unscrew wiper arm securing nut and remove nut and washer.
2. Open liftgate and carefully pry out liftgate trim panel clips from their locations, then remove trim panel.
3. Remove three bolts attaching wiper motor bracket to liftgate, and the screw attaching ground lead, then disconnect electrical connector at motor.
4. Remove motor from liftgate, disconnecting rear washer supply hose from wiper.

Installation

1. Reconnect rear washer supply hose to wiper motor, then position motor in liftgate by pushing output shaft through grommet in liftgate outer panel and torque three attaching bolts to 4-5 ft. lbs.
2. Install wiper arm and securing nut, torquing nut to 7-9 ft. lbs.
3. Install liftgate trim panel, then check operation of system.

RADIO

REPLACE

REMOVAL

1. Disconnect battery ground cable.
2. Insert radio removing tools, T85M-19061-A or equivalents, one on either side of radio, into access holes until click is heard.
3. Apply an outward side pressure to release locking tangs and slide radio from dash.
4. Disconnect antenna, speaker, ground and power leads from radio.
5. Disengage special tool by depressing locking tangs on sides of radio while applying slight inward pressure on tool, then pull tool from access holes.
6. Remove plastic support bracket and locating plate from rear of receiver.

INSTALLATION

1. Connect power supply, speaker plugs and antenna cable to rear of receiver.
2. Install locating plate and plastic support bracket to rear of receiver and slide receiver into opening until retaining tangs lock.
3. Reconnect battery ground cable.

HEATER CORE

REPLACE

1. Disconnect battery ground cable.
2. Drain engine coolant from cooling system and remove hoses from heater core, plugging hoses and core.
3. Carefully blow air into upper of two connecting pipes to remove residual coolant.

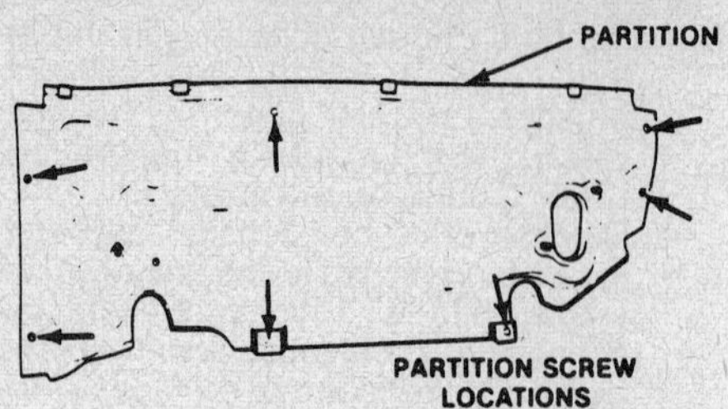

Fig. 5 Partition retaining bolt location

4. Remove cover plate and gasket from firewall.
5. Remove center console, drawing it rearward.
6. Remove side trim panel in right hand footwell.
7. Disconnect heater control lever and the leads from the glove compartment light, A/C blower switch and cigar lighter, then remove lower right hand dash panel.
8. Disconnect all duct hoses from heater housing.
9. Disconnect bowden cables from heater housing, **Fig. 4.**
10. Remove heater from firewall and draw it in until the water connectors of the heater core are clear of the firewall, then pull heater assembly to the right.
11. Remove two heater core retaining screws and slide heater core out of housing.
12. Reverse procedure to install.

BLOWER MOTOR

REPLACE

1. Disconnect both battery terminals.
2. Discharge A/C system refrigerant at service access gauge port valve.
3. Remove engine valve cover and the cowl insulator cover.
4. Pull water valve out of retaining clip and remove clip.
5. Remove two battery shield attaching screws and the shield.
6. Disconnect vacuum hose from EGR valve, then disconnect EGR valve by removing bolt attaching it to manifold and position valve out of way.
7. Remove two nuts retaining air conditioning hose plate and seal at the partition between the engine compartment and evaporator, then remove plate and seal.
8. Disconnect wiring harness from partition, pulling harness forward to disconnect tabs connecting harness to partition.
9. Remove No. 30 torx bolt retaining refrigerant lines to expansion valve, **Fig. 5.**
10. Disconnect suction and liquid lines at expansion valve.
11. Remove weather seal from upper edge of partition.
12. Remove seven retaining screws attaching partition, **Fig. 6. If screws are damaged during removal, replace with 10 mm hex head screws and washers.**

13. Remove left and right drainage valves, then the partition, by pulling partition up and out.
14. Disconnect de-icer wire at connector, then the ground wire on the evaporator.
15. Remove evaporator to firewall attaching bolts.
16. Remove cowl grille panel, then disconnect windshield wiper to windshield wiper motor arm.
17. Slide evaporator case assembly upward and forward out of engine compartment checking and replacing seal as necessary.
18. Remove three access cover attaching bolts, then pry cover open using screwdriver.
19. Remove two screws on blower scrolls to lower case and the two screws attaching the de-ice thermostat.
20. Separate evaporator case halves by removing connecting clips sealing case.
21. Remove one screw retaining blower motor to case, then the blower motor.
22. Reverse procedure to install.

ENGINE SECTION

INDEX

ENGINE REPLACE

REMOVAL

1. Disconnect battery ground cable.
2. Mark hood hinge location, disconnect ground strap near right hinge and remove hood.
3. Using vacuum pump D80P-250-A or equivalent, release pressure from EFI fuel system at fuel pressure regulator valve.
4. Remove cap from cooling system expansion tank and drain coolant.
5. Disconnect radiator upper hose from radiator, then on vehicles equipped with manual transmission, disconnect radiator air vent hose from radiator.
6. Remove radiator upper attaching bolts and disconnect cooling fan electrical connector.
7. Disconnect oil level sensor electrical connector and remove oil dipstick. **Electrical connector on dipstick only applies to 1986 models and earlier.**
8. Disconnect vacuum hose at EGR valve.
9. Disconnect fuel injector electrical connector located between upper intake manifold and oil dipstick.
10. Carefully disconnect electrical connectors at EEC-IV engine coolant temperature sensor, engine knock sensor, oil pressure sending unit, cooling fan temperature switch, throttle air bypass valve and the throttle position sensor. **When disconnecting EEC-IV system related component electrical connectors, ensure that vehicle battery ground cable is disconnected to avoid serious EEC-IV system and related component damage.**
11. Disconnect fuel line at pulse damper.
12. Using tool T82L-9500-AH or equivalent, disconnect fuel return line.
13. Disconnect throttle cable and, if equipped the transmission kickdown cable.
14. Remove accelerator cable bracket attaching screws and the bracket from the upper intake manifold, then position bracket and accelerator cable, and transmission kickdown cable if equipped, out of way.
15. Disconnect supply hose at vacuum tree located on dash panel.
16. Disconnect electrical connector at distributor TFI module.
17. Remove alternator from mounting bracket and secure out of way.
18. Remove power steering pump from mounting bracket and secure out of way.
19. Remove turbocharger air inlet tube and disconnect orange ground wire at turbocharger air inlet elbow.
20. Disconnect electrical connector at exhaust gas oxygen sensor and the vacuum hose at the turbocharger air inlet elbow.
21. Remove A/C compressor from its mounting bracket and secure out of way.
22. On vehicles equipped with automatic transmission, remove transmission dipstick tube attaching nut at turbocharger outlet flange.
23. On all vehicles, disconnect coolant supply and return hoses at heater control valve.
24. On vehicles equipped with automatic transmission, disconnect transmission oil cooling lines at radiator.
25. On all vehicles, raise and support vehicle.
26. On vehicles equipped with manual transmission, disconnect radiator refill tube at refill hose.
27. On all vehicles, disconnect radiator lower hose at radiator, then remove bolts attaching radiator to side rail and remove radiator through bottom of vehicle.
28. Remove bolt attaching chassis ground wire to A/C compressor bracket, then remove starter.
29. Remove nuts attaching catalytic converter inlet pipe to turbocharger.
30. Remove catalytic converter to converter inlet pipe flange attaching bolts and the catalytic converter support bracket bolt.
31. Remove inlet pipe.
32. On vehicles equipped with manual transmission, remove bolt attaching

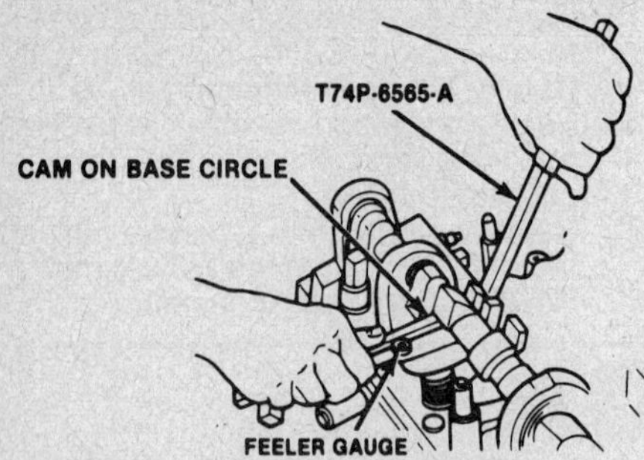

Fig. 1 Adjusting valves

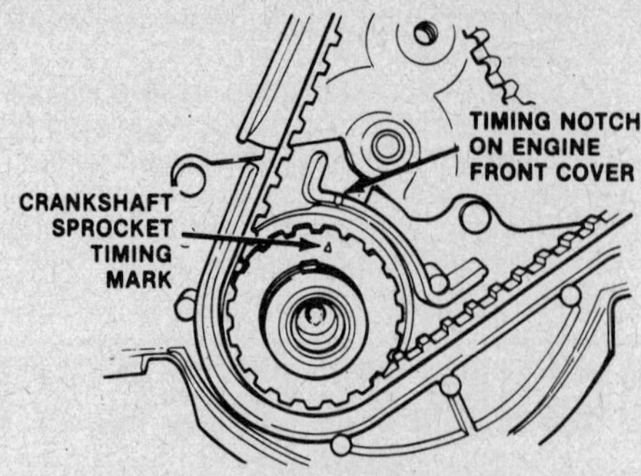

Fig. 2 Align timing marks on crankshaft sprocket & engine front cover

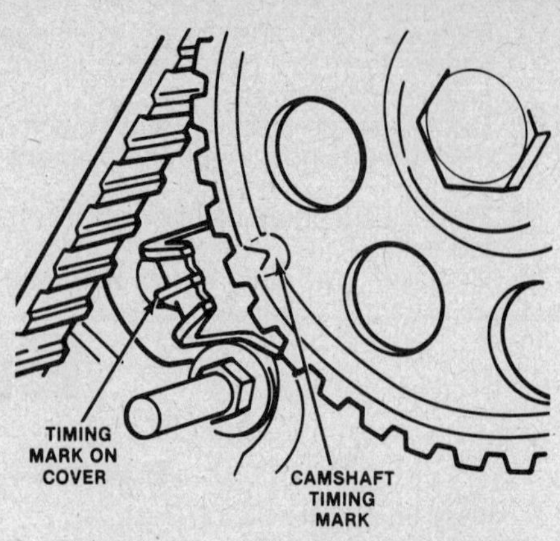

Fig. 3 Aligning timing marks on camshaft sprocket & inner timing belt cover

engine rear cover to flywheel housing.

33. On vehicles equipped with automatic transmission, remove torque converter to drive plate attaching nuts through starter opening. **To bring bolts into position, turn crankshaft with ratchet handle and socket applied to crankshaft pulley attaching bolt. Always turn crankshaft clockwise. Counterclockwise rotation may cause timing belt to jump time.**
34. On all vehicles, remove stud nuts attaching engine mounts to cross member.
35. Remove converter/flywheel housing attaching bolts. If removal of bolts at top of housing is prevented by contact with body, leave them loose and in position. If necessary, to gain access to housing to engine bolts, support transmission with suitable jack and remove nuts securing transmission mount to underbody. Remove nuts securing driveshaft center bearing support to underbody. Lower transmission and remove converter/flywheel housing to engine bolts, then raise transmission and secure transmission mount to underbody.
36. Lower vehicle.
37. Install suitable engine lifting device on engine lifting attachments.
38. Support transmission with suitable jack and raise engine until front support lower studs clear crossmember.
39. Remove bolts attaching front support brackets to engine and remove mounts and brackets as assemblies.
40. Pull engine forward to separate it from transmission, then carefully raise engine out of engine compartment.

INSTALLATION

Reverse procedure to install, noting the following:

a. Torque clutch housing to engine bolts to 53-68 ft. lbs.
b. Torque converter housing to engine bolts to 22-27 ft. lbs.
c. Torque converter to drive plate nuts to 26-28 ft. lbs.
d. Torque mount to underbody nuts to 15-20 ft. lbs.
e. Torque driveshaft center bearing support nuts to 55-60 ft. lbs.
f. Torque engine mount to front crossmember nuts to 38-47 ft. lbs.
g. After positioning inlet pipe and bracket onto converter and turbocharger, start converter to inlet pipe bolts, springs and nuts; the turbocharger to inlet pipe nuts and the converter support to transmission mount bolt.
h. Torque catalytic converter to converter inlet pipe bolts to 26-30 ft. lbs., the turbocharger to inlet pipe nuts to 26-30 ft. lbs. and the converter support to transmission mount bolt to 37-42 ft. lbs.
i. Torque starter attaching bolts to 5-8 ft. lbs. and the radiator lower attaching bolts to 5-8 ft. lbs.
j. Torque upper radiator attaching bolts to 15-18 ft. lbs.

VALVES

ADJUST

1. Remove valve cover.
2. Position camshaft so that base circle of lobe is facing cam follower of valve to be checked. To position camshaft lobes, turn crankshaft using ratchet handle and socket on crankshaft pulley attaching bolt. **Always turn crankshaft clockwise. Counterclockwise rotation may cause timing belt to jump time.**
3. Using valve spring compressor T74P-6565-A or equivalent, slowly apply pressure on lash adjuster side of cam follower until lash adjuster is completely collapsed. Holding follower in this position, measure clearance between base circle of cam and the follower using a feeler gauge, **Fig. 1.**
4. Clearance should be .0035-.0055 inch. If clearance exceeds .0055 inch, remove cam follower and inspect for damage.
5. If cam follower appears to be intact, and not excessively worn, measure valve spring assembled height.
6. If assembled height is correct, check dimensions of camshaft.
7. If camshaft dimensions are within specifications, remove, clean and test lash adjuster.

CAMSHAFT TIMING

CHECK

An access plug is provided in the cam drive belt cover so that camshaft timing can be checked without removal of the cover or any other engine components.

1. Disconnect battery ground cable.
2. Remove access plug from the cam drive belt cover.
3. Set crankshaft to TDC by aligning the TC mark on the timing belt cover with notch on the crankshaft pulley. Align timing marks by turning the crankshaft pulley attaching bolt. **Always turn the crankshaft clockwise, which is the normal direction of rotation. Reverse rotation (counterclockwise) may cause the timing belt to jump time due to the arrangement of the timing belt tensioner.**
4. Look through the access hole in the belt cover to ensure timing mark on the camshaft drive sprocket is aligned with the pointer on the inner timing belt cover assembly.
5. If the mark is not in sight, turn the crankshaft one complete revolution clockwise and check timing mark alignment.
6. If the timing marks are properly aligned, the camshaft is correctly timed to the crankshaft.
7. If the timing marks do not align, proceed with the camshaft timing adjustment procedure.

ADJUSTMENT

1. Disconnect battery ground cable.
2. Remove drive belts.
3. Remove water pump pulley.
4. Remove timing belt cover as outlined under "Timing Belt, Replace."
5. Remove crankshaft damper and pulley.

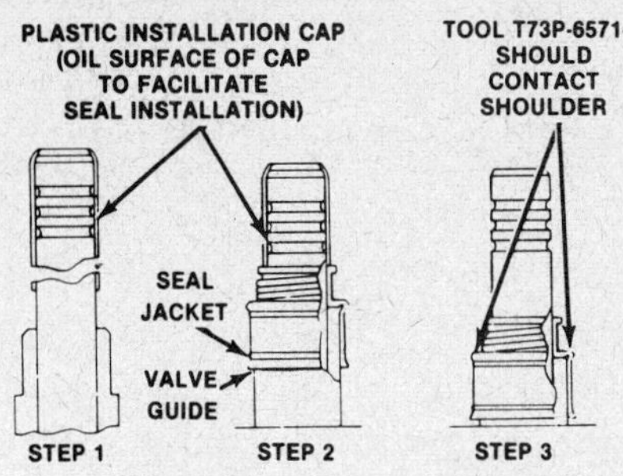

STEP #1— WITH VALVES IN HEAD, PLACE PLASTIC INSTALLATION CAP OVER END OF VALVE SYSTEM.

STEP #2— START VALVE STEM SEAL CAREFULLY OVER CAP. PUSH SEAL DOWN UNTIL JACKET TOUCHES TOP OF GUIDE.

STEP #3— REMOVE PLASTIC INSTALLATION CAP. USE INSTALLATION TOOL T73P-6571-A OR SCREWDRIVERS TO BOTTOM SEAL ON VALVE GUIDE.

Fig. 4 Installing valve springs & seals

6. Remove spark plugs, if necessary.
7. Turn crankshaft clockwise to alignment timing mark on the crankshaft sprocket with the timing mark on the engine front cover, **Fig. 2.**
8. Turn camshaft to align timing mark on the camshaft sprocket with the timing mark on the inner timing belt cover assembly, **Fig. 3.**
9. Remove distributor cap and position aside. Set distributor rotor to the number one firing position by turning the auxiliary shaft.
10. Install timing belt as outlined under "Timing Belt, Replace," and check timing mark alignment.

WATER PUMP
REPLACE

1. Disconnect battery ground cable.
2. Remove drive belts, water pump pulley and timing belt cover.
3. Loosen cap on coolant expansion tank and drain coolant from radiator.
4. Remove radiator lower hose and the heater return hose from water pump.
5. Remove water pump attaching bolts and the pump.
6. Clean gasket mating surfaces, then install new gasket, pump and attaching bolts, torquing bolts to 14-21 ft. lbs.
7. Torque water pump pulley bolts to 13-19 ft. lbs.
8. Reverse steps 1 through 4 to complete installation.

VALVE COVER
REPLACE

1. Disconnect battery ground cable.
2. Loosen clamp on PCV hose at oil separator on valve cover and disconnect hose.
3. Disconnect coolant hose that passes over rear of rocker arm cover.
4. Remove coolant pipes retaining clip screw from right front side of rocker arm cover.
5. Remove throttle body.
6. Disconnect spark plug wires at spark plugs and at rocker arm cover studs, folding wires toward distributor.
7. Remove valve cover retaining screws and studs, then the cover and gasket.
8. Reverse procedure to install, torquing studs and bolts to 5-8 ft. lbs.

HYDRAULIC LASH ADJUSTER
REPLACE

1. Disconnect battery ground cable and remove valve cover.
2. Rotate engine in normal direction of rotation until base circle of camshaft lobe of selected valve is contacting cam follower.
3. Using valve spring compressing tool T74P-6565-A or equivalent, compress valve spring until cam follower can be removed out and over the hydraulic lash adjuster.
4. Lift out hydraulic lift adjuster.
5. Repeat steps 2 through 4 as required for remaining lash adjusters.
6. Reverse procedure to install.

VALVE SPRINGS & SEALS
REPLACE

1. Disconnect battery ground cable and remove valve cover.
2. Rotate engine in direction of normal rotation until base circle of camshaft lobe of selected valve is contacting cam follower. Ensure that other valve of that cylinder is also closed.
3. Using valve spring compressor tool T74P-6565-A or equivalent, compress valve spring until cam follower can be removed out and over the hydraulic lash adjuster.
4. Install a compressed air adapter in spark plug hole with a minimum of 140 psi air pressure available, then turn on air pressure to hold that cylinder's valves against their seats. **Both valves must be closed to hold air pressure.**
5. Depress valve spring and remove locks, spring retainer, spring and seal.
6. Fasten rubber band or string to valve key groove to prevent losing valve if a valve is opened or the air pressure drops.
7. Inspect valve stems for scores, sticking, excessive or obvious stem to guide clearance and eccentricity or wobbling when rotated. If any of these conditions exist, the cylinder head must be removed for further inspection and service.
8. Apply air pressure through spark plug holes to hold valves closed. Install new valve stem seals using valve seal installer T73P-6571-A or equivalent and the plastic installation caps, **Fig. 4.**
9. Install valve springs, spring retainers and keys and remove air pressure adapter.
10. Depress valve springs and install cam followers.
11. Install valve cover and throttle body.

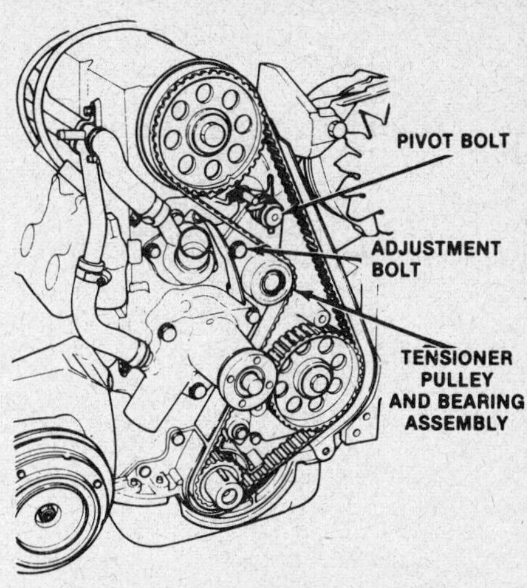

Fig. 5 Timing belt tensioner bolt location

TIMING BELT
REPLACE
REMOVAL

1. Disconnect battery ground cable.
2. Remove access plug from cam drive belt cover.
3. Set crankshaft to TDC by aligning the TDC mark on the timing belt cover with notch on crankshaft pulley. Align timing marks by turning the crankshaft pulley attaching bolt. **Always rotate crankshaft clockwise, which is the normal direction of rotation. Reverse rotation (counterclockwise) may cause the timing belt to jump time due to the arrangement of the timing belt tensioner.**
4. Look through the access hole in the belt cover to ensure timing mark on the camshaft drive sprocket is aligned with the pointer on the inner timing belt cover assembly.
5. If the mark is not in sight, turn crankshaft one complete revolution clockwise and check timing mark alignment.
6. Remove drive belts, water pump pulley, timing belt cover, and crankshaft damper and pulley.
7. Loosen timing belt tensioner adjusting bolt, **Fig. 5.**
8. Using camshaft belt tensioner tool T74P-6254-A or equivalent, pry tensioner away from timing belt.
9. While holding tensioner away from belt, secure it in released position by tightening belt tensioner adjustment bolt.
10. Remove timing belt.

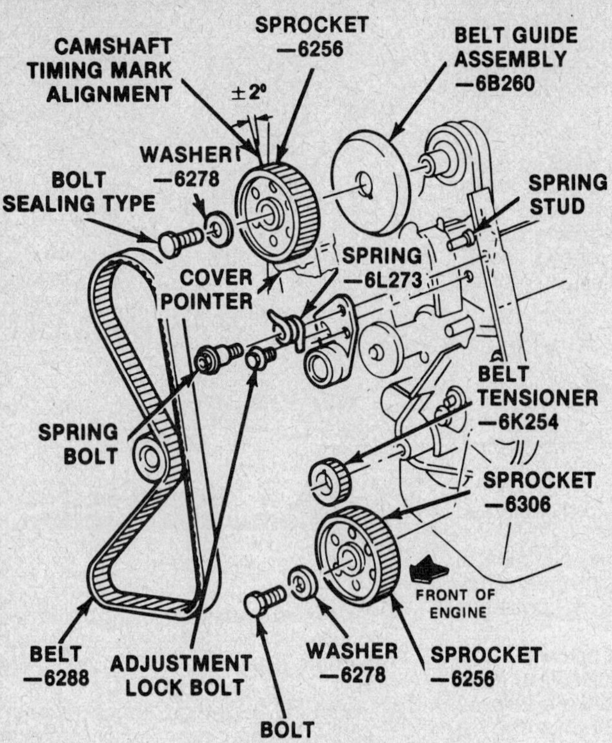

Fig. 6 Installing timing belt

Fig. 7 Installing camshaft sprocket & seal

INSTALLATION

1. Ensure that belt and sprockets are clean and not worn or damaged, and that timing marks are aligned as outlined in removal procedure.
2. Using suitable tool, move belt tensioner to no tension position, tighten the adjustment lock bolt and install the belt.
3. Loosen adjustment lock bolt and allow the tensioner to tighten the belt.
4. Torque pivot bolt to 28-40 ft. lbs. and the adjustment lock bolt to 14-21 ft. lbs., **Fig. 6.**
5. Install crankshaft damper and pulley, timing belt cover, water pump pulley and drivebelts.

CAMSHAFT SPROCKET & SEAL

REPLACE

REMOVAL

1. Disconnect battery ground cable.
2. Remove drive belts, water pump pulley, timing belt cover, crankshaft damper and pulley and timing belt.
3. Using camshaft sprocket holding/removing tool T74P-6256-B or equivalent, remove camshaft sprocket.
4. Remove camshaft sprocket belt guide.
5. Using front cover seal remover T74P-6700-B or equivalent, remove camshaft seal.

INSTALLATION

1. Ensure seal and seal surface on camshaft are clean and not damaged.
2. Lubricate camshaft seal surface and the seal lip with engine oil.
3. Install seal on front seal replacer tool T74P-6150-A or equivalent, then thread tool arbor into camshaft.
4. Turn nut on tool arbor until the seal is bottom in its bore in the camshaft front bearing tower.
5. Remove tool from camshaft.
6. Install camshaft sprocket belt guide.
7. Install camshaft sprocket, using tool T74P-6256-B or equivalent as a holding fixture, and the sprocket retaining bolt to push the sprocket onto the camshaft, **Fig. 7.**
8. Using new camshaft sprocket bolt or teflon tape when installing. Torque sprocket bolt to 50-71 ft. lbs.
9. Install timing belt as outlined under "Timing Belt, Replace," timing belt cover, crankshaft damper and pulley, water pump pulley and drive belts.

CRANKSHAFT DAMPER & PULLEY

REPLACE

1. Disconnect battery ground cable and remove drive belts.
2. Remove crankshaft damper and pulley bolt.
3. Using tool T74P-6311-A or equivalent, remove crankshaft damper and pulley.
4. Reverse procedure to install, torquing bolt to 100-120 ft. lbs.

TIMING BELT TENSIONER

REPLACE

1. Disconnect battery ground cable and remove drive belts.
2. Remove water pump pulley, timing belt cover, crankshaft damper and pulley and timing belt as outlined under "Timing Belt, Replace."
3. Remove timing belt tensioner adjustment and spring retaining bolts, then the timing belt tensioner.
4. Reverse procedure to install, installing bolts finger tight.

AUXILIARY SHAFT SPROCKET & SEAL

REPLACE

REMOVAL

1. Disconnect battery ground cable.
2. Remove drive belts, water pump pulley, timing belt cover, crankshaft damper and pulley and timing belt as outlined under "Timing Belt, Replace."
3. Using tool T74P-6256-B or equivalent, remove auxiliary shaft sprocket.
4. Using tool T74P-6700-B or equivalent, remove auxiliary shaft seal.
5. Remove auxiliary shaft cover.
6. Remove auxiliary shaft, being careful not to scratch bearings.

INSTALLATION

1. Ensure that auxiliary shaft and bearings are clean and not worn or damaged.
2. Dip auxiliary shaft in engine oil.
3. Install auxiliary shaft in bearing bores, being careful not to scratch bearings.
4. Install auxiliary shaft retaining plate.

5. Install auxiliary shaft gasket and cover without seal, torquing bolts to 6-9 ft. lbs.
6. Using suitable tool, install auxiliary shaft seal.
7. Using tool T74P-6256-B or equivalent, install auxiliary shaft sprocket. Remove center arbor, as tool is used as a holding fixture. The sprocket retaining bolt presses the sprocket onto the shaft. Torque bolt to 28-40 ft. lbs.
8. Install timing belt as outlined under "Timing Belt, Replace," crankshaft damper and pulley, timing belt cover, water pump pulley and drive belts.

CRANKSHAFT SPROCKET, FRONT COVER & SEAL

REPLACE

REMOVAL

1. Disconnect battery ground cable.
2. Remove drive belts, water pump pulley, timing belt cover, crankshaft damper and pulley and timing belt as outlined under "Timing Belt, Replace."
3. Using tool T74P-6306-A or equivalent, remove crankshaft sprocket.
4. Remove camshaft sprocket belt guide.
5. Using suitable tool, remove front cover seal.
6. Remove engine front cover.

INSTALLATION

1. Ensure that front of cylinder block and front cover are clean.
2. Position front cover gasket on cylinder block, retaining with suitable grease. **It may be necessary to trim ends of oil pan to cylinder block front seal if installing a cover without replacing oil pan gasket.**
3. Install front cover without seal in it, starting attaching bolts but leaving them loose.
4. Insert front cover aligner T74P-6019-B or equivalent into cover to align it with crankshaft, torque bolts to 6-9 ft. lbs. and remove tool.
5. Oil inner lip of cover seal and install it using suitable tool.
6. Thread tool and seal onto crankshaft, then, with outer nut, force tool and seal toward engine until seal bottoms in front cover. Remove tool.
7. Install crankshaft sprocket, timing belt as outlined under "Timing Belt, Replace," crankshaft damper and pulley, timing belt cover, water pump and drive belts.

TIMING BELT INNER COVER

REPLACE

1. Disconnect battery ground cable.
2. Remove drive belts, water pump pulley, timing belt cover, crankshaft damper and pulley, timing belt as outlined under "Timing Belt, Replace," camshaft sprocket, timing belt tensioner and auxiliary sprocket.

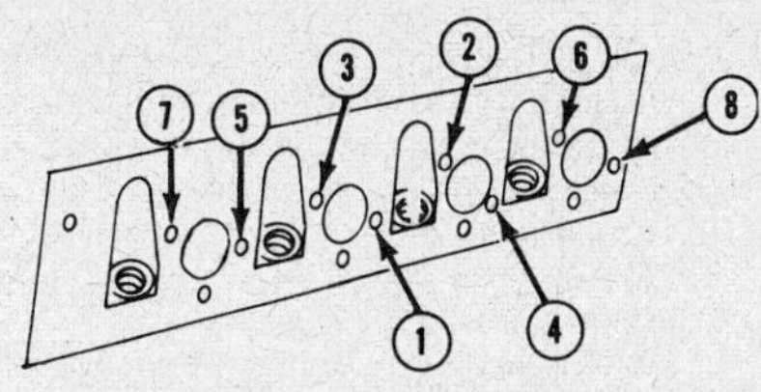

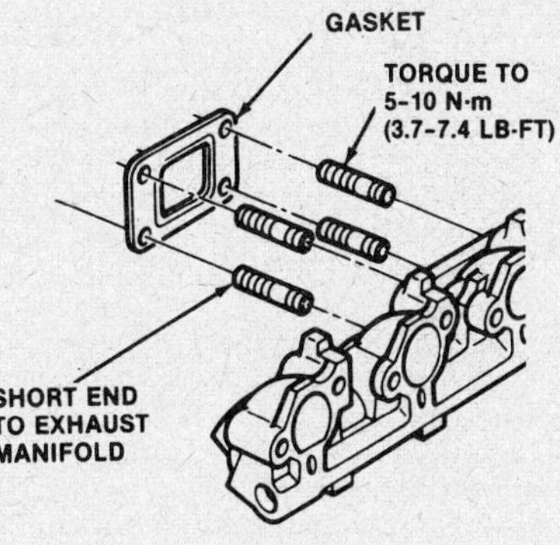

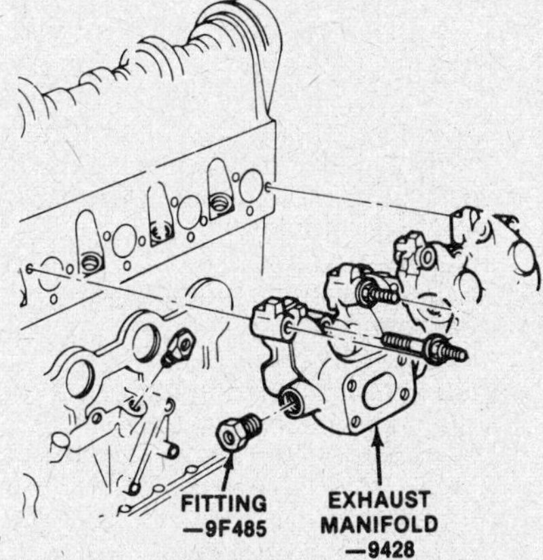

Fig. 8 Installing exhaust manifold

3. Remove attaching bolts and the timing belt inner cover.
4. Reverse procedure to install, torquing stud bolt to 14-21 ft. lbs. and the retaining bolts to 71-106 inch lbs.

EXHAUST MANIFOLD

REPLACE

REMOVAL

1. Disconnect battery ground cable.
2. Loosen cap on coolant expansion tank and drain coolant from radiator.
3. Remove heater return hose at water pump.
4. Remove screw attaching coolant pipe routing bracket to right front side of valve cover.
5. Disconnect coolant pipe to expansion tank hose at coolant pipe.
6. Disconnect turbocharger oil supply line at turbocharger.
7. Disconnect turbocharger coolant supply and return tube at the turbocharger.
8. Disconnect PCV tube at turbo air inlet adapter.
9. Remove turbo to exhaust manifold attaching nuts.
10. Remove turbo support bracket.
11. Remove exhaust manifold to cylinder head attaching bolts, then the exhaust manifold.

INSTALLATION

1. Ensure that exhaust manifold and the manifold surfaces on the cylinder head are clean.
2. Install exhaust manifold to cylinder head bolts. Torque bolts in two steps following proper torque sequence, **Fig. 8.** First, torque to 177-204 inch lbs., then to 20-30 ft. lbs.
3. Install turbocharger support bracket and the turbo to exhaust manifold nuts.
4. Connect PCV tube at turbo air inlet adapter.
5. Connect turbo coolant and oil supply lines at turbocharger.
6. Install heater pipe to coolant expansion tank hose at heater pipe.
7. Install coolant pipe retaining clip screw at valve cover.
8. Install coolant hose at water pump and refill cooling system.

UPPER INTAKE MANIFOLD

REPLACE

REMOVAL

1. Disconnect battery ground cable.
2. On vehicles equipped with automatic transmission, disconnect kickdown cable from throttle linkage.
3. On all vehicles, disconnect accelerator cable from throttle linkage.
4. Remove accelerator cable bracket attaching screws and the bracket from upper intake manifold, position bracket, accelerator cable and kickdown cable, if equipped, out of way.
5. Disconnect fuel pressure regulator vacuum hose, PCV hose and the vacuum tree supply hose at intake manifold fittings.
6. Loosen hose clamps and remove turbocharger outlet hose.
7. Remove EGR flange attaching bolts.
8. Remove nut attaching pulse damper to bracket.
9. Disconnect low oil level sensor connector and remove oil dipstick.
10. Remove oil dipstick bracket attaching screw.
11. Cut fuel injector wiring harness routing strap at pulse damper bracket as necessary.
12. Remove two pulse damper bracket attaching nuts and the bracket.
13. Remove two upper attaching screws and two lower attaching nuts connecting throttle body assembly to upper intake manifold.
14. Remove upper intake manifold attaching bolts, the manifold and gaskets.

INSTALLATION

1. Ensure both gasket surfaces on upper intake manifold and upper surface of lower intake manifold are clean.
2. Place new gasket on lower intake

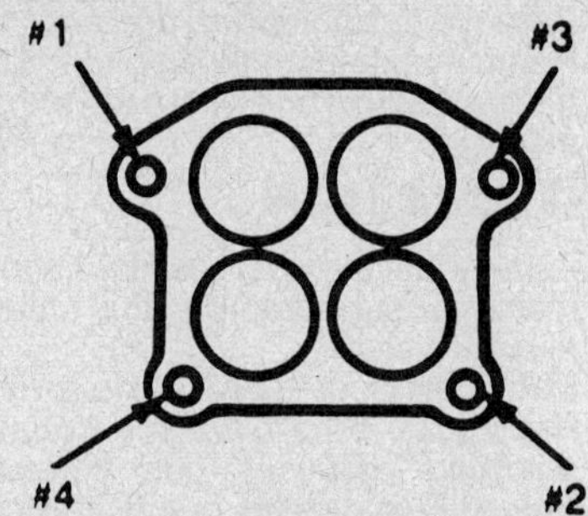

Fig. 9 Upper intake manifold bolt tightening sequence

manifold and place upper intake manifold in position, then install four attaching bolts, torquing to 15-22 ft. lbs. in proper sequence, **Fig. 9.**
3. Install two EGR flange attaching bolts, torquing to 13-19 ft. lbs.
4. Place pulse damper bracket on upper intake manifold and install attaching nuts.
5. Install new fuel injection wiring harness routing strap as necessary.
6. Install oil dipstick bracket attaching screw.
7. Install oil dipstick and connect low oil level sensor connector.
8. Place pulse damper on bracket and install attaching nut.
9. Install new gasket and the throttle body attaching screws and nuts, torquing to 11-15 ft. lbs.
10. Connect vacuum tree source hose and PCV hose to fitting on upper intake manifold.
11. Connect fuel pressure regulator vacuum hose to fuel pressure regulator and the fittings on upper intake manifold.
12. Place accelerator cable bracket against upper intake manifold and install attaching screws.
13. Connect accelerator cable.
14. Connect kickdown cable, if equipped.
15. Install turbocharger outlet hose and tighten clamp.

LOWER INTAKE MANIFOLD

REPLACE

REMOVAL

1. Disconnect battery ground cable and drain cooling system.
2. Disconnect electrical connectors at knock sensor, fan temperature sensor, fuel injection wiring harness and instrument cluster coolant temperature sender.
3. Disconnect coolant bypass line at lower intake manifold.
4. Depressurize EFI fuel system using a hand operated vacuum pump. Connect pump hose at fuel system pressure regulator and apply at least 25 inches vacuum. **Fuel supply lines will remain pressurized for some period of time after engine is shut off. System pressure must be relieved before disconnecting any fuel lines.**
5. Disconnect vacuum pump from fuel pressure regulator.
6. Disconnect fuel supply line from fuel supply manifold.
7. Disconnect fuel return line using tool T82L-950-AH or equivalent.
8. Remove nut attaching pulse damper to bracket and position pulse damper and fuel supply line out of way.
9. Remove upper intake manifold as previously described.
10. Disconnect EEC coolant temperature sensor.
11. Remove four upper and four lower attaching bolts and the lower intake manifold and gasket.
12. Remove two attaching bolts, disengage each injector and remove fuel supply manifold assembly.

INSTALLATION

1. Clean and inspect mounting surfaces of lower intake manifold and the cylinder head, ensuring that both surfaces are clean and flat.
2. Install new gasket.
3. Position lower intake manifold on cylinder head and install four upper attaching bolts finger tight.
4. Install four lower manifold bolts and torque all attaching bolts to 11-15 ft. lbs. in proper sequence, **Fig. 10.**
5. Install fuel supply manifold assembly by pressing each injector into place on lower intake manifold and installing two attaching bolts.
6. Ensure that gasket surfaces of upper and lower intake manifolds are clean.
7. Install EEC coolant temperature sensor.
8. Install upper intake manifold and two gaskets.
9. Connect fuel return line.
10. Place pulse damper on bracket and connect fuel supply line.
11. Connect coolant bypass line to lower intake manifold.
12. Connect electrical connectors at knock sensor, fan temperature sensor, fuel injection wiring harness and the instrument cluster coolant temperature sender.
13. Connect battery ground cable and refill cooling system.

FUEL SUPPLY MANIFOLD

REPLACE

REMOVAL

1. Disconnect battery ground cable.
2. On vehicles equipped with automatic transmission, disconnect kickdown cable from throttle linkage.
3. On all vehicles, disconnect accelerator cable from throttle linkage.

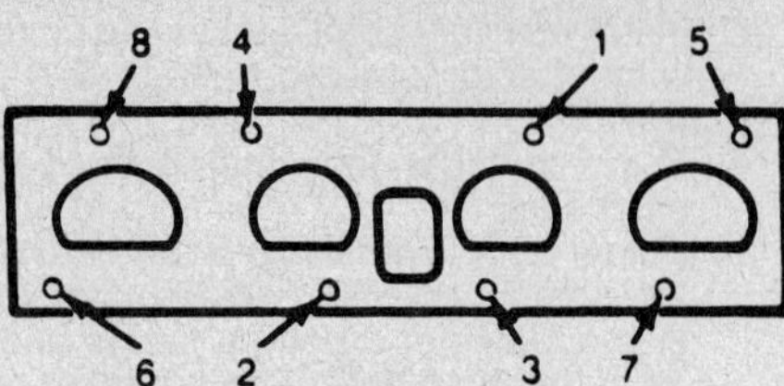

Fig. 10 Lower intake manifold bolt tightening sequence

4. Remove screws attaching accelerator cable bracket to upper intake manifold and position bracket, accelerator cable and kickdown cable, if equipped, out of way.
5. Disconnect fuel pressure regulator vacuum hose from fuel pressure regulator and the upper intake manifold fitting.
6. Disconnect PCV hose at upper intake manifold fitting.
7. Disconnect coil wire from distributor cap and position out of way.
8. Remove distributor cap attaching screws and the cap, positioning cap and attached wires out of way.
9. Depressurize EFI fuel system using a hand operated vacuum pump. Connect pump hose to fuel system pressure regulator and apply at least 25 inches vacuum.
10. Disconnect vacuum pump from fuel pressure regulator.
11. Disconnect fuel supply line from fuel supply manifold.
12. Using tool T82L-9500-AH or equivalent, disconnect fuel return line.
13. Remove nut attaching fuel pulse damper to mounting bracket.
14. Cut fuel injection wiring harness routing strap at fuel pulse damper as necessary.
15. Disconnect fuel injection wiring harness connector.
16. Disconnect electrical connector at coolant temperature sender in cylinder block.
17. Remove fuel supply manifold assembly front attaching bolt.
18. Remove fuel supply manifold assembly rear attaching bolt.
19. Remove fuel supply manifold assembly by disengaging each fuel injector from lower intake manifold, then carefully pulling whole assembly out from under upper intake manifold toward front of engine.
20. Remove three Allen head attaching screws and the fuel pressure regulator from fuel supply manifold.
21. Remove each injector from fuel supply manifold and disconnect wiring harness connector from each injector.

INSTALLATION

1. Install injectors on fuel supply manifold, then install fuel pressure regulator and three attaching screws.

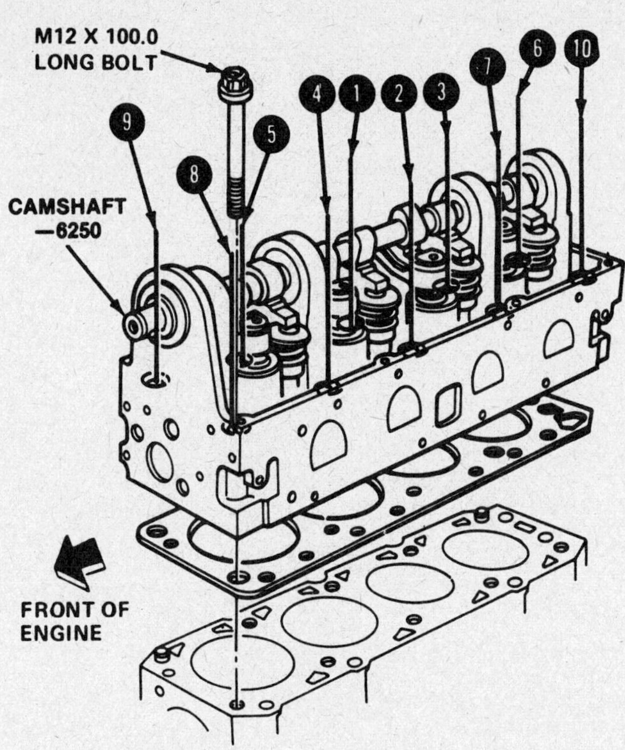

Fig. 11 Cylinder head bolt tightening sequence

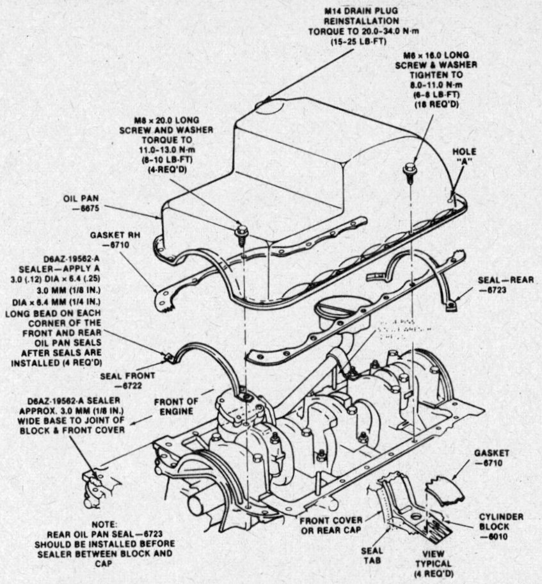

Fig. 12 Installing oil pan

2. Connect wiring harness connector to each fuel injector, then position fuel supply manifold assembly under upper intake manifold and insert each injector into its opening in lower intake manifold.
3. Install front and rear fuel supply manifold attaching bolts, torquing to 15-22 ft. lbs.
4. Connect electrical connectors at coolant temperature sender and fuel injection wiring harness.
5. Install new fuel injection wiring harness routing strap on fuel pulse damper bracket as necessary.
6. Place fuel pulse damper in mounting bracket and install attaching nut.
7. Connect fuel supply line and install retaining clip, then connect fuel return line.
8. Install distributor cap and attaching screws and connect coil wire to distributor cap.
9. Connect PCV hose and the vacuum hoses to fuel pressure regulator and upper intake manifold fittings.
10. Position accelerator cable bracket on upper intake manifold and install attaching screws.
11. Connect accelerator cable to throttle linkage.
12. On vehicles equipped with automatic transmission, connect kickdown cable to throttle linkage.
13. On all vehicles, connect battery ground cable.

CYLINDER HEAD

REPLACE

REMOVAL

1. Disconnect battery ground cable.
2. Remove drive belts, water pump pulley, timing belt cover, crankshaft damper and pulley, valve cover, timing belt, camshaft sprocket, timing belt tensioner and timing belt inner cover.
3. Remove alternator and mounting bracket to cylinder head bolts.
4. Remove exhaust manifold to cylinder head attaching bolts.
5. Remove timing belt tensioner spring stop stud from cylinder head.
6. Remove cylinder head attaching bolts and the cylinder head.

INSTALLATION

1. Ensure that cylinder head and cylinder block gasket surfaces are clean.
2. Position new cylinder head gasket on block.
3. Ensure that crankshaft sprocket and camshaft sprocket timing marks align as shown in **Figs. 2 and 3,** then lower cylinder head assembly onto cylinder block, ensuring head fits over two dowels on head surface of block.
4. Install valve cover gasket on valve cover using suitable sealant and place cover aside.
5. Oil cylinder head bolts and install in cylinder head, torquing in two steps in proper sequence, **Fig. 11.** Torque first to 50-60 ft. lbs., then to 80-90 ft. lbs.
6. Install timing belt tensioner spring stop stud into cylinder head, torquing to 14-21 ft. lbs.
7. Position exhaust manifold on cylinder head and install attaching bolts, torquing in two steps in proper sequence, **Fig. 8.** Torque first to 5-7 ft. lbs., then to 16-23 ft. lbs.
8. Install alternator bracket to cylinder head bolts.
9. Install fuel supply manifold, timing belt inner cover, auxiliary sprocket, timing belt tensioner, camshaft sprocket and seal, timing belt, crankshaft damper and pulley, timing belt cover, water pump pulley, drive belts and valve cover.

OIL PAN

REPLACE

REMOVAL

1. Disconnect battery ground cable.
2. Disconnect oil level sensor electrical connector and remove oil dipstick.
3. Install engine support tool D79P-6000-B or equivalent.
4. Raise and support vehicle, then drain engine oil.
5. Remove starter.
6. Remove pinch bolt at steering column to steering gear coupling.
7. Remove engine mount studs to crossmember attaching bolts.
8. Lower vehicle and, using support tool, raise engine as far as possible.
9. Raise vehicle, then remove steering gear to crossmember attaching bolts.
10. Disengage steering gear from steering column and pull forward, away from steering column, being careful not to bend or stretch power steering gear hoses and lines.
11. Position suitable jack under crossmember, then remove crossmember to side rail attaching bolts.

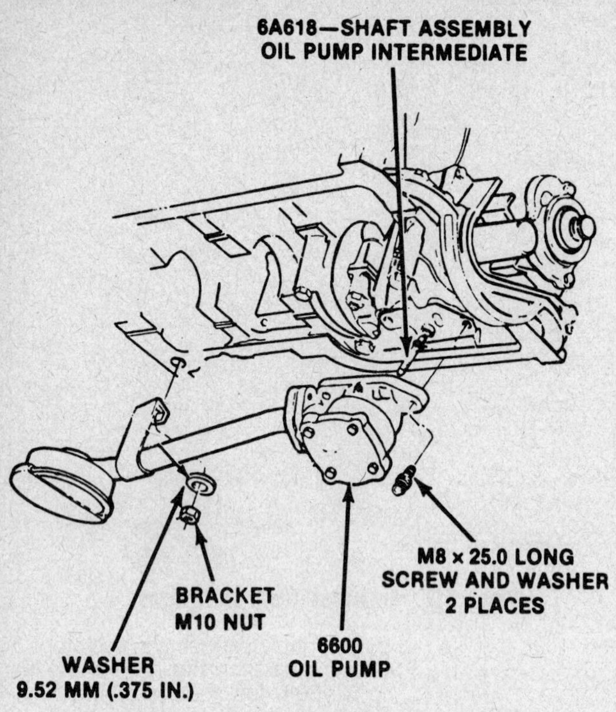

Fig. 13 Removing oil pump

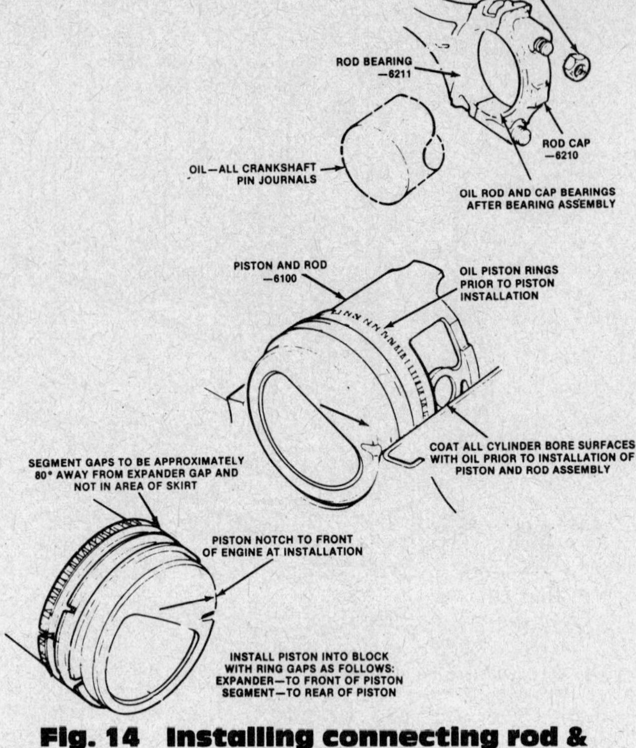

Fig. 14 Installing connecting rod & piston

12. Lower transmission jack and crossmember, then remove oil pan attaching bolts and the oil pan.

INSTALLATION

1. Clean gasket surfaces on oil pan and cylinder block.
2. Apply even coat of suitable sealant to oil pan side gaskets and allow sealant to dry past wet stage, then install on oil pan.
3. Apply 1/4 inch bead of suitable sealant along seam between cylinder block and front cover, and along seam between cylinder block and rear main bearing cap.
4. Install oil pan end seals in front cover and rear main bearing cap, **Fig. 12.**
5. Position oil pan and install attaching bolts.
6. Torque corner attaching bolts to 106-133 inch lbs. and other bolts to 80-102 inch lbs., beginning at hole "A," **Fig. 12,** and working clockwise around pan.
7. Raise crossmember into position and install crossmember to side member attaching bolts, torque bolts to 38-47 ft. lbs. and remove jack.
8. Position steering gear on crossmember and connect to steering column, then install attaching bolts and torque to 10 ft. lbs. plus additional 1/4 turn.
9. Torque steering column to gear pinch bolt to 11-15 ft. lbs.
10. Lower vehicle and remove engine support tool, then raise vehicle.
11. Install engine mount attaching nuts, torquing to 50-70 ft. lbs.
12. Install starter, then lower vehicle.
13. Fill crankcase and connect electrical connector at oil level sensor.
14. Connect battery ground cable, then start engine and check for oil leaks along edge of oil pan.

OIL PUMP REPLACE

1. Remove oil pan as previously described.
2. Remove oil pickup tube and screen support bracket nut from No. 4 main bearing cap, **Fig. 13.**
3. Remove two oil pump attaching screws and the oil pump.
4. Remove oil pump intermediate shaft.
5. Reverse procedure to install.

CONNECTING ROD & PISTON REPLACE

REMOVAL

1. Disconnect battery ground cable.
2. Remove cylinder head and oil pan as previously described.
3. Turn crankshaft until connecting rod to be removed is in down position.
4. Remove carbon from upper portion of cylinder bore. If ridge can be felt or seen at top of bore, it must be removed.
5. If necessary, install suitable ridge reamer in cylinder bore and, following tool manufacturer's instructions, remove ridge until bore is straight to top edge of cylinder.
6. Repeat steps 3 through 5 as necessary.
7. Remove connecting rod nuts, then rodcap and bearing half.
8. Using hammer handle or piece of wood or plastic, tap rod and piston upward until piston rings clear top of cylinder block.
9. Remove rod and piston assembly from top of cylinder bore.
10. Repeat steps 3 through 9 as necessary.

INSTALLATION

1. Install proper size connecting rod bearing half into connecting rod and coat it with engine oil. The installed connecting rod bearing to crankshaft clearance should be .0008-.0026 inch (0.020-0.066 mm).
2. Properly space piston ring gaps, **Fig. 14,** dip piston in suitable engine oil and install and tighten piston ring compressor tool.
3. Slide two pieces of snug fitting rubber hose over connecting rod bolts to prevent bolt to crankshaft journal contact during installation.
4. Start connecting rod/piston assembly into cylinder bore, keeping notch or arrow in piston top toward front of engine, ensuring that connecting rod number and cylinder bore numbers coincide.
5. Using hammer handle or piece of wood, tap piston/rod assembly into cylinder bore, guiding rod bolts over crankshaft journal, then remove rubber hose from bolts.
6. Insert proper size bearing half into connecting rod cap, then install cap, ensuring that number on cap and rod are on same side and that they match.
7. Install rod nuts and torque in two steps. First torque to 25-30 ft. lbs., then to 30-36 ft. lbs.

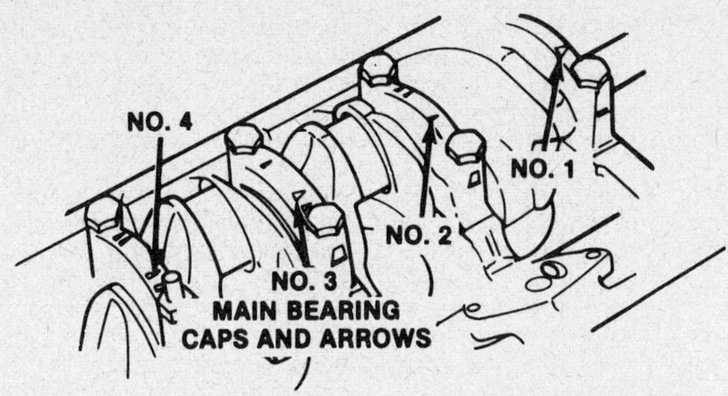

Fig. 15 Main bearing cap installation

8. Repeat steps 1 through 7 as often as necessary on remaining rod/piston assemblies.
9. Install oil pan and cylinder head.

CRANKSHAFT MAIN BEARING INSERTS

REPLACE

REMOVAL

1. Disconnect battery ground cable, then remove starter.
2. Remove oil pan and oil pump as previously described.
3. Remove main bearing cap attaching bolts. **If bearing inserts are to be replaced with engine in vehicle, leave at least two main bearing caps tight while servicing others.**
4. Remove main bearing caps and bearing inserts.
5. Using suitable tool, remove upper bearing inserts. Insert tool in crankshaft journal oil hole and turn crankshaft in normal direction of rotation to remove upper bearing half. **Always turn crankshaft clockwise. Counterclockwise rotation may cause timing belts to jump time.**
6. If bearing clearance is to be measured in vehicle using Plastigage, support crankshaft with piece of wood and jack to avoid false reading.

INSTALLATION

1. After inspecting crankshaft for knicks, scoring and wear, measure crankshaft to select proper bearing to crankshaft clearance. Clearance should be .0008-.0026 inch (0.020-0. 066 mm). Always keep two bearing caps tight while measuring others.
2. Install new bearings in caps and cylinder block, matching bearing tangs with notch in cap and block.
3. Using suitable tool, install upper bearing half.
4. Ensure that bearing caps are properly located, **Fig. 15,** torque cap bolts to 50-60 ft. lbs. After each cap is tightened, ensure that crankshaft can be rotated manually. If not, remove that bearing cap and identify source of interference.
5. Torque main bearing caps to 75-85 ft. lbs. and again check for crankshaft rotation.
6. Remove rear main bearing cap and apply a 1/8 inch bead of suitable sealant across main bearing cap to cylinder block surface. Do not apply sealant onto bearing or rear seal surface of crankshaft.
7. Install rear cap, torquing cap bolts to 75-85 ft. lbs. in two steps.
8. Install oil pump and oil pan.
9. Install starter, then connect battery ground cable.

CRANKSHAFT

REPLACE

REMOVAL

1. Remove engine, then the cylinder head, oil pan, oil pump, connecting rods and pistons and flywheel.
2. Remove main bearing caps.
3. Remove crankshaft, being careful not to damage bearing journals.

INSTALLATION

1. After cleaning, inspecting and measuring crankshaft, install proper size bearings in cylinder block and bearing caps.
2. Install crankshaft, measuring clearance with Plastigage according to manufacturer's instructions. Clearance should be .0008-.0026 inch (0.020-0.066 mm).
3. Ensure that bearing caps are properly positioned, **Fig. 15,** then torque cap bolts to 50-60 ft. lbs. After each cap is tightened, ensure that crankshaft can be rotated manually. If not, remove that bearing cap and verify source of interference.
4. Torque cap bolts to 75-85 ft. lbs.
5. Remove rear main bearing cap and apply 1/8 inch bead of suitable sealant across main bearing cap to cylinder block surface. Do not apply sealant onto bearing or rear seal surface of crankshaft.
6. Install rear cap, torquing bolts to 75-85 ft. lbs. in two steps.
7. Install connecting rods and pistons, oil pump, crankshaft rear oil seal, oil pan, flywheel and cylinder head, then the engine.

CRANKSHAFT REAR OIL SEAL

REPLACE

1. Remove transmission and flywheel.
2. Punch small hole in metal portion of rear face of seal.
3. Install sheet metal screw in punched hole.
4. Using slide hammer or roll head pry bar, remove seal.
5. Clean seal groove and seal surface of crankshaft.
6. Apply suitable engine oil to interior sealing lip of seal and to crankshaft seal surface.
7. Position seal on installer tool T82L-6701-A or equivalent.
8. Using two bolts supplied with tool, or two flywheel bolts, pull seal and tool onto crankshaft by tightening bolts alternately, then remove bolts and the tool.
9. Install flywheel and transmission.

FUEL PUMP

REPLACE

LOW PRESSURE PUMP

The low pressure pump is not serviced separately, it is replaced as an assembly with the fuel sending unit.

1. Remove fuel tank.
2. Using Lock Ring Tool D84P-9275-A or equivalent, remove sending unit/fuel pump lock ring.
3. Remove lock ring, seal ring and sending unit/fuel pump from fuel tank.
4. Reverse procedure to install. Apply a light coat of suitable grease onto new seal ring before installing.

HIGH PRESSURE PUMP

1. Depressurize EFI fuel system using a hand operated vacuum pump. Connect pump hose to fuel system pressure regulator and apply at least 25 inches vacuum. **Fuel supply lines will remain pressurized for some period of time after engine is shut off. System pressure must be relieved before disconnecting any fuel lines.**
2. Disconnect battery ground cable.
3. Raise and support vehicle, then disconnect fuel pump electrical connector.
4. Disconnect fuel lines at pump inlet and outlet fittings.
5. Remove pump bracket attaching screws and the pump.
6. Remove pump and foam insulator from mounting bracket.
7. Disconnect wiring harness at pump.
8. Reverse procedure to install.

TURBOCHARGER

The turbocharger is basically an air compressor that is connected into the air induction system to increase air flow to the engine. The turbocharger used on this vehicle is a blow-through system, the fuel injectors are mounted downstream from the turbocharger rather than upstream as they would be in a draw-through system. The energy required to compress the air is taken from the engine exhaust gases. By using pressure and heat normally discharged by the exhaust system, a turbocharged engine can increase wide-open and heavy throttle power levels while maintaining fuel economies at part load. The turbocharger converts this normally wasted energy into rotating mechanical force. The rotational force of the turbine is transferred to the compressor side of the turbocharger through the interconnecting shaft.

At operating speed, the spinning compressor wheel creates its own suction or vacuum at the air inlet elbow. This vacuum draws more air into the engine than the normal vacuum created by piston movement. This additional air pumped into the intake manifold where it is mixed with fuel supplied by electronically controlled fuel injectors. As the turbocharger pressure forces the air/fuel mixture into the cylinders, it becomes tightly packed. This heavier and denser mixture burns with increased force that boosts torque and horsepower incomparison with non-turbocharged engines of the same displacement.

The rotating assembly is supported on two pressure lubricated bearings and, because a turbocharger can operate at speeds up to 120,000 RPM, lubrication of the bearings which support the shaft is important for cooling and friction reduction.

The turbocharger bearings are lubricated with engine oil supplied through a tube routed from the turbocharger center housing to a supply fitting threaded into the oil pressure sending unit port.

A piston ring seal is used on the turbine wheel shaft end to prevent engine oil leakage into the turbine wheel housing. A carbon face seal is used on the compressor wheel shaft end to prevent engine oil leakage into the compressor wheel housing.

The engine oil drains from the turbocharger through a return hole in the center housing and returns to the engine through an oil return tube connected between the bottom of the turbocharger and the side of the engine block.

The turbocharger is also cooled by engine coolant circulating through the center housing. Coolant is routed to the turbocharger from the cylinder block, circulates through the center housing and returns to the radiator through the heater return tube.

During turbocharger boost, more and more exhaust gases are created which spin the compressor and turbine wheels at an increasing rate. This gas flow to turbine speed increase cycle could continue until a boost became great enough to damage engine. A wastegate is used to limit the amount of boost. The wastegate is located in the turbine housing and it allows exhaust gases to bypass the turbine wheel once maximum allowable boost pressure has been reached. Position of the wastegate is controlled by a diaphragm and spring actuator assembly that senses manifold pressure and correctly positions the lever and valve assembly to obtain the desired amount of bypassed exhaust gases.

The amount of pressure applied to the diaphragm is controlled by a boost control solenoid located on the right side of the engine compartment in front of the cooling system expansion tank. Hoses connect the solenoid to the pressure and vacuum sides of the turbocharger. Solenoid function is controlled by the EEC-IV electronic control assembly. When boost pressures reaches approximately 15 psi on vehicles with manual transmission, or 13 psi on vehicles with automatic transmission, the ECA will use the boost control solenoid to open the wastegate, bypassing exhaust gases away from the turbine blades.

If turbo boost rises above the safe limit, the operator is alerted to this condition through an overboost warning buzzer. The buzzer circuit is completed through a pressure sensitive switch located in the left rear corner of the engine compartment. The switch receives its signal through a hose connected to the vacuum tree, which is connected directly to the intake manifold. If pressure exceeds 18 psi, the switch contacts close and the warning buzzer sounds.

Some 1985 models may exhibit a condition where the overboost light comes on and the overboost buzzer sounds on acceleration. The activation of the overboost warning system could be cause by the turbocharger wastegate sticking shut, resulting in an overboost condition of up to 24 lbs. (boost guage may also show actual lbs. of boost). This condition can be checked and repaired by using the following procedure. **Suspect turbochargers were built prior to serial number 3827. Turbochargers built after serial number 3828 should operate satisfactorily. Serial number is located on metal tag which is similar to a carburetor identification tag.**

1. Raise and support vehicle, then install a clutch housing alignment adapter tool No. T75L-4201-A or equivalent, installed to a dial indicator with a magnetic base at the end of the actuator.
2. Set dial indicator to zero.
3. Connect a suitable gauged air pressure line to the actuator inlet port. To obtain a guaged air pressure, use a combination air pressure regulator and an air pressure dial tool No. T79P-6634-A or equivalent, connected to a source line (shop air supply).
4. Starting with zero air pressure, slowly increase air pressure until the actuator arm moves approximately .015 inch. The pressure gauge should indicate between 9.5-10.5 psi.
5. If reading is not within specification, or if no movement is measured at 10.5 psi, replace turbocharger assembly.

CLUTCH & MANUAL TRANSMISSION SECTION

INDEX

CLUTCH REPLACE

REMOVAL

Do not get grease or oil on clutch disc facing. Even a small trace of grease or oil may cause clutch grabbing or slipping. Handle disc by its edges and do not touch facings. The clutch assembly is equipped with a self adjuster which automatically adjusts cable length to maintain correct pedal height and throw out bearing preload.

1. Remove transmission as described further on.
2. If old pressure plate is to be reused, scribe alignment marks on pressure plate and flywheel for proper assembly.
3. Remove pressure plate attaching bolts, loosening bolts one turn at a time to release pressure plate spring tension evenly, then remove pressure plate and clutch disc.

INSTALLATION

1. When installing new clutch, sand friction surfaces on pressure plate and flywheel using medium-fine emory cloth or equivalent aluminum oxide paper. Sand lightly until friction surfaces are covered with fine scratch lines that run across the surface.
2. After sanding, remove all traces of grit and oil using shop towel saturated with denatured alcohol.
3. Coat crankshaft pilot bearing with small amount of suitable lubricant.
4. Position clutch disc and pressure plate on flywheel, aligning marks made during disassembly, then install clutch alignment tool T71P-7137-H or equivalent. **Ensure that clutch disc faces in proper direction. New discs are stamped "FLY WHEEL" to indicate proper installation direction. When installed correctly, damper springs will face away from flywheel.**
5. Torque pressure plate attaching bolts one turn at a time to 15-19 ft. lbs.
6. Remove clutch disc alignment tool, then install transmission.

TRANSMISSION REPLACE

1. Wedge a block of wood approximately 7 inches long under clutch pedal.
2. Disconnect battery ground cable, then raise and support vehicle.
3. Remove catalytic converter inlet pipe to turbocharger attaching nuts.
4. Remove attaching nuts at catalytic converter outlet to muffler inlet flange and the catalytic converter support bracket.
5. Remove catalytic converter and inlet pipe as an assembly.
6. Remove driveshaft, installing suitable plug in extension housing seal.
7. Remove starter, then the front stabilizer bar to body U-brackets and the body stiffener rod.
8. Position block of wood between stabilizer bar and body siderail.
9. Support transmission with suitable jack and remove bolt attaching rear mount to transmission.
10. Remove bolts attaching rear mount to body and remove mount, then loosen engine mount attaching nuts until only two or three threads are visible on end of stud.
11. Position block of wood against engine oil pan and raise front of engine with suitable stand. Raise engine until stud nuts on engine mounts contact the crossmember and, as engine tilts downward, lower jack supporting transmission.
12. Disconnect electrical connectors at back-up light switch and neutral safety switch.
13. Remove attaching bolts and raise transmission shift lever out of extension housing.
14. Remove snap ring and pull speedometer cable out of extension housing.
15. Remove clutch release lever cover, then pull rearward on clutch release cable and disengage from release lever.
16. Remove attaching screws from speedometer cable routing clips and position cable out of way on left side of vehicle.
17. Remove bolt attaching engine rear cover plate to flywheel housing.
18. Remove flywheel housing attaching bolts located at top of housing, then the four remaining flywheel housing attaching bolts.
19. Pull transmission rearward until flywheel housing contacts body.
20. Raise rear of transmission and pull rearward to clear body, then lower rear of transmission and pull rearward to remove.
21. Reverse procedure to install, noting the following:
    a. Torque flywheel housing attaching bolts to 28-38 ft. lbs.
    b. Torque engine rear cover attaching bolt to 28-38 ft. lbs.
    c. Torque engine mount stud nuts to 50-70 ft. lbs.
    d. Torque rear mount to body attaching bolts to 25-35 ft. lbs.
    e. Torque rear mount to transmission attaching bolt to 50-70 ft. lbs.
    f. Torque U-bracket and body stiffener rod attaching bolts to 33-41 ft. lbs.
    g. Torque attaching nuts to 21-30 ft. lbs. at converter outlet and 25-35 ft. lbs. at turbocharger.
22. After installation is completed, press clutch cable to floor several times to adjust clutch cable free play.

DISC BRAKES SECTION

INDEX

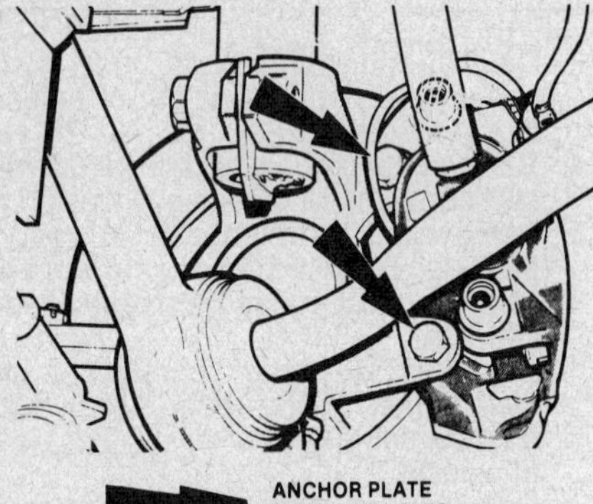

Fig. 1 Location of anchor plate attaching bolts

BRAKE PADS REPLACE

REMOVAL

1. Remove approximately $1/3$ of brake fluid from master cylinder.
2. Raise and support vehicle, then remove wheel assembly.
3. Disconnect wear sensor electrical connector at harness.
4. Remove caliper to anchor plate attaching pins and lift caliper assembly off rotor without disconnecting hydraulic hose. **Anti-rattle spring will fall off when caliper assembly is removed.**
5. Remove inboard and outboard pads.

INSTALLATION

1. Using suitable tool, push piston back into caliper bore, being careful not to damage piston boot.
2. Install inboard and outboard pads, removing backing paper from outboard pad before installation.
3. Position caliper over rotor, ensuring brake pads are properly engaged on anchor plate. **Sensor wire must be positioned between caliper and anchor before installing caliper attaching bolts. When caliper is installed, ensure that brake hose has not been kinked by rotation of caliper.**
4. Install caliper to anchor attaching pins, torquing bolts to 18-23 ft. lbs.
5. Install anti-rattle spring.
6. Connect wear sensor ensuring that O-ring is in proper position.
7. Position wear sensor electrical connector in routing clip.
8. Install wheel.
9. Pump brake pedal before moving vehicle to properly position brake pads.
10. Check master cylinder, adding fluid as necessary.

CALIPER REPLACE

1. Remove approximately $1/3$ of brake fluid from master cylinder.
2. Raise and support vehicle, then remove wheel assembly.
3. Remove caliper to anchor plate attaching pins, then slide caliper off anchor plate.
4. Loosen brake hose at caliper, rotating caliper to disconnect from hose.
5. Plug line to prevent loss of fluid or entry of dirt.
6. Reverse procedure to install, then bleed brake system.

ROTOR REPLACE

1. Raise and support vehicle, then remove wheel assembly.
2. Remove anchor plate attaching bolts, **Fig. 1.**
3. Lift caliper and anchor plate assembly off rotor and tie out of way.
4. Remove rotor retaining clip and the rotor.
5. Reverse procedure to install, torquing anchor plate to spindle carrier attaching bolts to 43-44 ft. lbs. **The hub and rotor are a matched and balanced assembly. Before removing rotor locate the paint mark or etch mark that indicates proper hub to rotor alignment. If marks are not present, mark hub and rotor for assembly alignment.**
6. If rotor has been removed without alignment marks, proceed as follows:
   a. Install rotor on hub and install wheel lug nuts.
   b. Using dial indicator with suitable holding fixture, measure rotor runout. The indicator stylus should contact the rotor approximately $7/16$ inch from the end.
   c. Rotate hub and disc assembly and record dial indicator reading.
   d. If indicator reading is .003 inch or less, this positioning of rotor may be used during assembly.

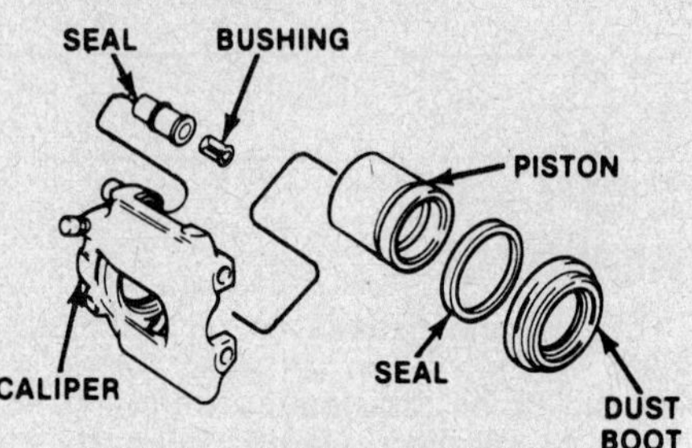

Fig. 2 Brake caliper exploded view

   e. If indicator reading is greater than .003 inch, reposition rotor on hub in 90 degree increments until lowest reading is obtained.
   f. When a reading of no more than .003 inch is obtained, mark alignment of hub and rotor.

CALIPER ANCHOR PLATE REPLACE

1. Raise and support vehicle, then remove wheel assembly.
2. Remove caliper to anchor plate attaching pins.
3. Slide caliper off rotor and tie out of way.
4. Remove caliper anchor plate attaching bolts and the caliper anchor.
5. Reverse procedure to install, torquing anchor plate attaching bolts to 43-44 ft. lbs. and the caliper to anchor plate attaching bolts to 18-23 ft. lbs.

CALIPER OVERHAUL

DISASSEMBLY

1. Remove caliper assembly and brake pads as previously described.
2. Open bleeder screw and drain fluid from caliper, then close bleeder screw.
3. Position block of wood between piston and caliper, then apply air pressure through fluid inlet port to remove piston. **Apply only enough air pressure to ease piston out of caliper.**
4. Remove dust boot from piston and discard, **Fig. 2.**
5. Remove piston seal from caliper and discard.
6. Remove caliper anchor pin bushing, then the anchor pin seal.

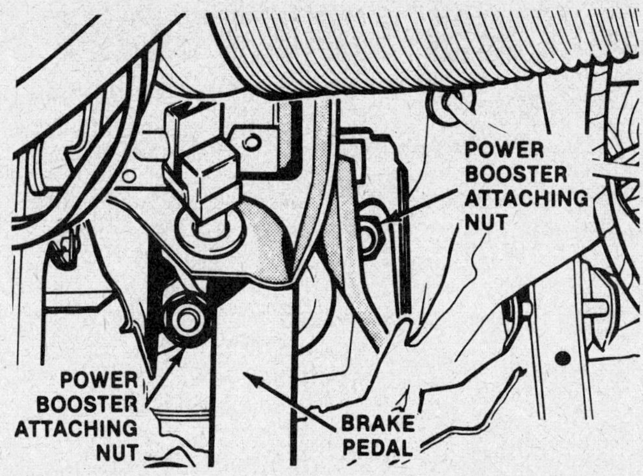

Fig. 3 Location of brake booster attaching nuts

ASSEMBLY

1. Install caliper anchor pin seal, spraying seal with silicone lubricant to aid installation.
2. Install caliper anchor pin bushing, overlapping edges of bushing slightly to fit bushing into seal. After installation, press bushing against seal to remove overlapping. When properly installed, the ends of the bushing must abut against each other.
3. Lubricate new piston seal with brake fluid and install in seal groove, ensuring that seal does not become twisted but is firmly seated in groove.
4. Position dust boot at bottom of piston and, holding dust boot on piston, pull on seal lip until seal unfolds, allowing lip seal to extend beyond bottom of piston.
5. While holding dust boot on piston, fit seal lip in caliper bore and push piston into caliper. As piston enters bore, the dust boot will refold to its original shape.

BRAKE BOOSTER REPLACE

REMOVAL

1. Depress brake pedal several times to deplete vacuum reserve in power booster.
2. Depressurize EFI fuel system using hand operated vacuum pump. Connect pump hose to fuel system pressure regulator and apply at least 25 inches vacuum.
3. Disconnect fuel inlet line at pulse damper.
4. Using tool T82L-9500-AH or equivalent, disconnect fuel return line.
5. Disconnect low oil level sensor electrical connector and remove oil dipstick.
6. Remove oil dipstick tube to pulse damper bracket attaching screw.
7. Remove pulse damper bracket to intake manifold attaching nuts, then disconnect pulse damper from fuel manifold and remove damper/bracket assembly.
8. Disconnect source hose from vacuum tree and remove vacuum tree attaching screws.
9. Disconnect low brake fluid warning electrical connector at master cylinder cap.
10. Pull vacuum check valve out of power booster.
11. Disconnect brake lines at master cylinder and plug brake tubes to prevent entry of foreign matter.
12. Remove sound deadener located under instrument panel inside passenger compartment.
13. Remove booster pushrod to brake pedal retaining clip.
14. Remove booster attaching nuts, **Fig. 3.**
15. Remove power booster, being careful not to damage any underhood painted surfaces.
16. Remove master cylinder attaching nuts and separate booster from master cylinder.

INSTALLATION

1. Install master cylinder on power booster, torquing attaching nuts to 16-20 ft. lbs.
2. Apply bead of caulking cord D6AZ-19560-A or equivalent to rear of booster where it mates to dash panel.
3. Apply light coat of suitable lubricant on bushing, install bushing on booster pushrod and position booster in vehicle.
4. Working from inside vehicle, guide booster into position.
5. Install retaining clip on booster pushrod and install booster attaching nuts.
6. Install sound deadening panel.
7. Connect brake lines at master cylinder.
8. Position vacuum tree and install attaching screw, then connect source hose to vacuum tree.
9. Install vacuum check valve in power booster and connect electrical connector at master cylinder cap.
10. Connect pulse damper to fuel rail and position bracket on intake manifold studs.
11. Install pulse damper bracket stud nuts.
12. Install oil dipstick tube bracket attaching screw, then install dipstick and connect electrical connector at low oil level sensor.
13. Connect fuel inlet line to pulse damper and the fuel supply line to fuel rail.
14. Bleed brake system.

MASTER CYLINDER REPLACE

1. Disconnect low fluid level sensor electrical connector.
2. Disconnect brake lines at master cylinder, capping lines and master cylinder ports.
3. Remove attaching nuts and the master cylinder.
4. Reverse procedure to install, torquing attaching nuts to 16-20 ft. lbs., then bleed brakes.

DRUM BRAKES SECTION

INDEX

BRAKE SHOES REPLACE

REMOVAL

1. Disconnect battery ground cable.
2. Raise and support vehicle.
3. Remove rear tire and wheel assembly.
4. Remove brake drum. Discard brake drum retaining clip.
5. Should difficulty be experienced in removal of the brake drum due to the action of the automatic self-adjuster mechanism, the self-adjuster may be released and brake drum removed, as follows:
   a. Remove wheel cylinder attaching bolts.
   b. Push wheel cylinder away from the brake backing plate to provide an access opening in the backing plate.
   c. Insert a thin-bladed screwdriver through the backing plate and rotate self-adjuster cam to the released position, **Fig. 1.**
   d. Remove brake drum.
   e. Correctly position wheel cylinder and install attaching bolts. Torque bolts to 5-7 ft. lbs.
6. Remove both brake shoe hold-down springs, **Fig. 2.** To prevent rotation during removal, hold each hold-down pin head with a suitable tool.
7. Pry lower end of the primary shoe from its position against the anchor.
8. Remove lower return spring.
9. Remove shoes and strut by passing the strut between the wheel cylinder and hub assembly.
10. Pull top of primary shoe away from the secondary shoe to disconnect strut from the secondary shoe.
11. Disconnect the parking brake cable from the secondary shoe lever.
12. Remove strut return spring from the secondary shoe.
13. Remove adjuster cam spring.
14. Pull primary shoe away from the strut while rotating the cam to the fully released position.
15. Remove the primary shoe spring.
16. Remove the primary shoe from the strut.

INSTALLATION

Before installing the brake shoes, ensure the wheel cylinder and wheel hub are tightened to specification.

1. Apply a light coating of grease supplied with the new brake shoes or high temperature grease D7AZ-

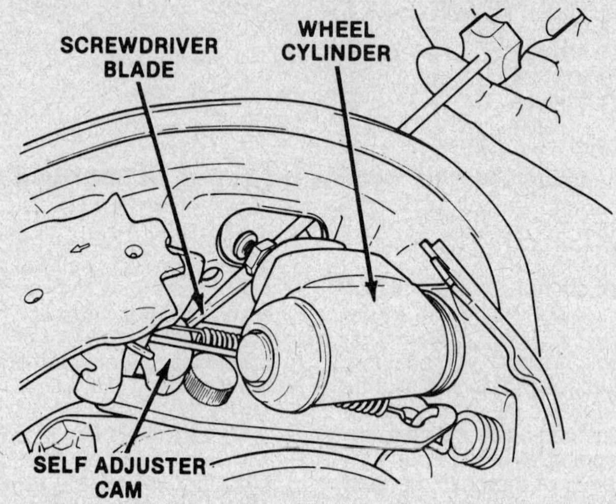

Fig. 1 Releasing self-adjuster mechanism for brake drum removal

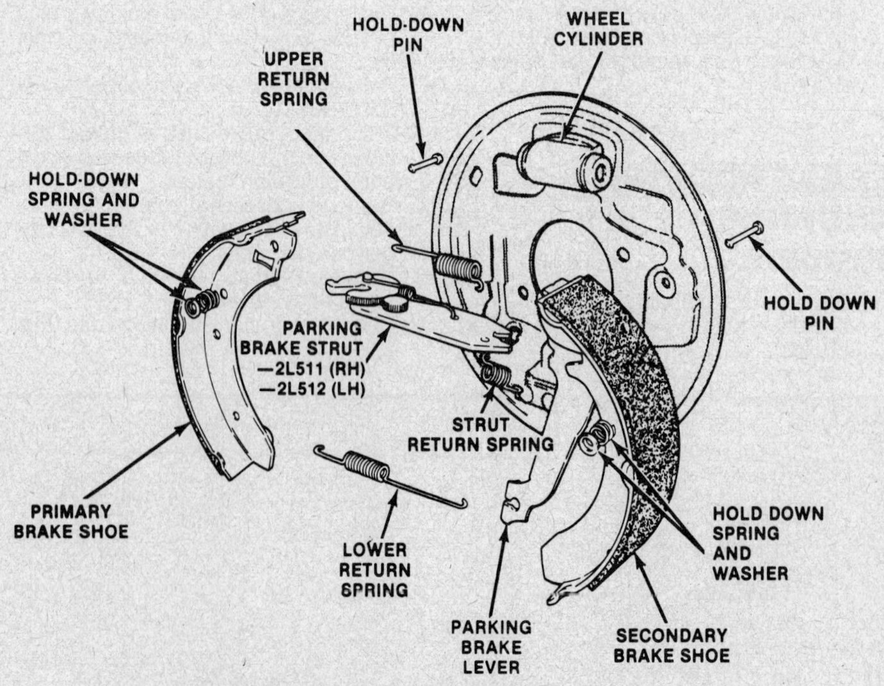

Fig. 2 Exploded view of brake drum assembly

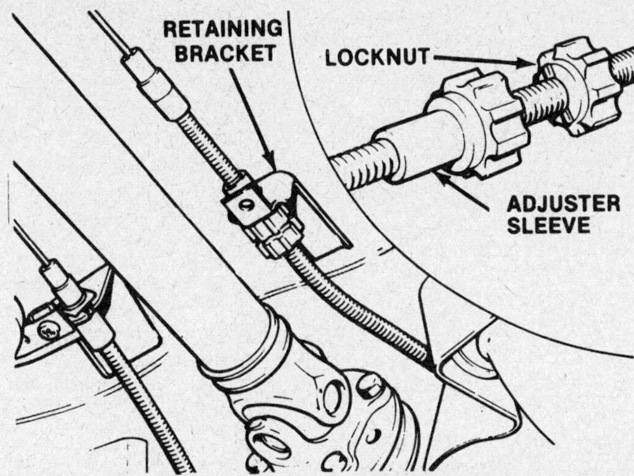

Fig. 3 Loosening parking brake cable adjustment locknut

Fig. 4 Measuring brake pedal free height

19590-A, or equivalent, to support ledges where the brake shoes contact the backing plate.

2. Connect parking brake cable to the secondary shoe lever. To connect the cable, position the cable end through the lever and grip the cable end with locking type pliers, then push lever against the spring until it can be rotated over the cable. When properly installed, the plastic washer will be between the spring and lever.
3. Position the secondary shoe and install the hold-down spring.
4. Install the strut and cam assembly on the primary shoe.
5. Rotate the cam to the fully released position.
6. Install the adjuster cam spring.
7. Install the primary shoe spring.
8. Install the strut spring in the secondary shoe and then into the strut.
9. Place the strut on the parking brake lever and move the primary shoe toward the backing plate. The strut will then "click" into place over the parking brake lever and secondary shoe web.
10. Install the lower shoe spring with the longer leg on the secondary shoe.
11. Pry the lower end of the primary shoe into position against the anchor while holding the top of the shoe against the backing plate, in contact with the cylinder piston. Ensure not to damage the cylinder boot.
12. Install the primary shoe hold-down pin, spring and washer.
13. Ensure heel of each brake shoe is located behind the anchor plate. Check each brake component for proper installation.
14. If necessary, push adjuster cam to the released position.
15. Install brake drum(s).
16. Push brake pedal hard twice to set the self-adjuster cam position. The cam will make a ratcheting sound as it resets.
17. Adjust parking brake cable as necessary.

BRAKE BOOSTER
REPLACE

Refer to Disc Brakes Section.

MASTER CYLINDER
REPLACE

Refer to Disc Brakes Section.

WHEEL CYLINDER
REPLACE

1. Disconnect battery ground cable.
2. Raise and support vehicle.
3. Remove tire and wheel assembly.
4. Remove brake drum.
5. Disconnect and cap wheel cylinder brake line.
6. Pull primary shoe away from wheel cylinder. The self-adjuster cam will rotate outward, holding the brake shoes away from the wheel cylinder assembly.
7. Remove wheel cylinder attaching bolts, wheel cylinder and O-ring.
8. Reverse procedure to install. Torque wheel cylinder attaching bolts to 5-7 ft. lbs.

BACKING PLATE
REPLACE

1. Disconnect battery ground cable.
2. Raise and support vehicle.
3. Remove tire and wheel assembly, then the brake drum.
4. Remove brake shoes.
5. Spread retaining clip and pull parking brake cable out of the backing plate.
6. Disconnect and cap wheel cylinder brake line.
7. Remove wheel flange and bearing hub. **The wheel flange attaching nuts are left and righthand threaded. The righthand threaded nuts are located on the right side of the vehicle. Never interchange left and righthand side wheel flange attaching nuts.**
8. Remove backing plate assembly.
9. Reverse procedure to install.

PARKING BRAKE
ADJUST

Parking brake stop plungers are installed in both rear backing plates. These plungers will be used to determine correct parking brake cable adjustments.

1. Ensure that parking brake hand lever is in released position.
2. Pump brake pedal to ensure brake lining self adjuster is properly set.
3. Raise and support vehicle.
4. Loosen adjuster locknut and rotate adjuster sleeve along cable casing until in and out movement can be felt at both parking brake stop plungers, **Fig. 3. Both adjuster and locknut are threaded onto cable casing. Any attempt to pry them apart will damage sleeve and or locknut. To loosen locknut, hold adjuster with suitable pliers and turn locknut counterclockwise with second pair of pliers.**
5. Tighten adjuster against retaining bracket until a slight movement is felt at each stop plunger. **When added together, the total movement of the plungers should not exceed .16 inch.**
6. Manually tighten locknut against sleeve as much as possible.
7. Tighten locknut an additional 2 "clicks" using suitable pliers.
8. Turn rear wheels manually to ensure brake linings are not dragging against drum.

BRAKE PEDAL HEIGHT MEASUREMENTS

1. With engine running, ensure that parking brake is fully released, then measure brake pedal free height and

check brake pedal travel using gauge 021-00001 or equivalent, **Fig. 4.**

2. Insert a slender sharp pointed prod through carpet and sound deadener to the dash panel metal and measure distance to center top of brake pedal pad.
3. If distance measured is not 7 1/2 inches, check brake pedal for missing, worn or damaged bushings, or loose attaching bolts, and replace as required. Also check that floor pan has not been distorted or the brake pedal bent.
4. If pedal free height is still not within specifications, check brake pedal, booster or master cylinder to ensure that correct parts are installed, replacing worn or damaged parts as necessary.

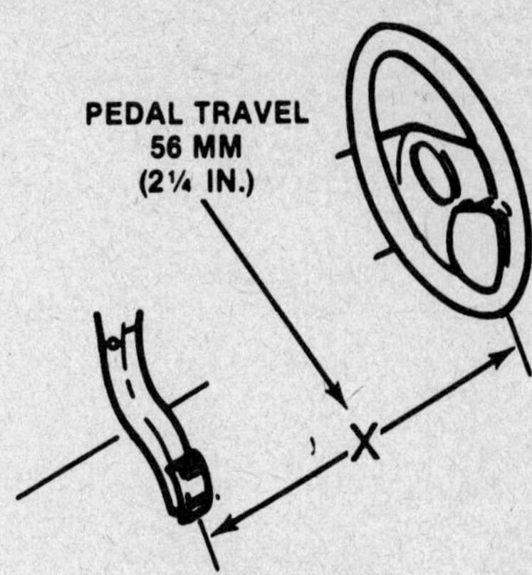

Fig. 5 Measuring brake pedal travel

BRAKE PEDAL TRAVEL MEASUREMENT

1. Ensure that parking brake is fully released and that master cylinder is filled to correct level.
2. Install brake pedal effort gauge on brake pedal pad and ensure rear brakes are fully adjusted by applying a 110 lb. load to pedal.
3. Hook a steel measuring tape to brake pedal, then measure and record distance from brake pedal free height position to reference point at 6 o'clock position on steering wheel rim, **Fig. 5.**
4. With tape still hooked to brake pedal, depress brake pedal by pressing downward on effort gauge. Apply a 25 lb. load to center of pedal and measure distance from brake pedal to fixed reference point on steering wheel rim parallel to centerline of steering column.
5. The difference between brake pedal free height and depressed pedal measurement under 25 lb. load should be 2 3/16-2 1/4 inches.
6. If pedal travel exceeds specifications, make several reverse and forward stops and, if brake pedal travel is not within specifications, make second series of stops.
7. If pedal travel is still not within specifications, remove brake drums and check brake adjusters to ensure they are functioning. Check brake linings for wear or damage, replacing parts as necessary. Adjust brake linings outside diameter to approximate inside diameter of brake drum using suitable brake adjustment gauge.
8. If all drum brake adjusters, brake drums and brake linings are functional and brake travel is not within specifications, check pedal assembly for missing or worn bushings or loose attachments.
9. If brake pedal travel still is not within specifications, bleed brakes.

REAR AXLE & SUSPENSION SECTION

INDEX

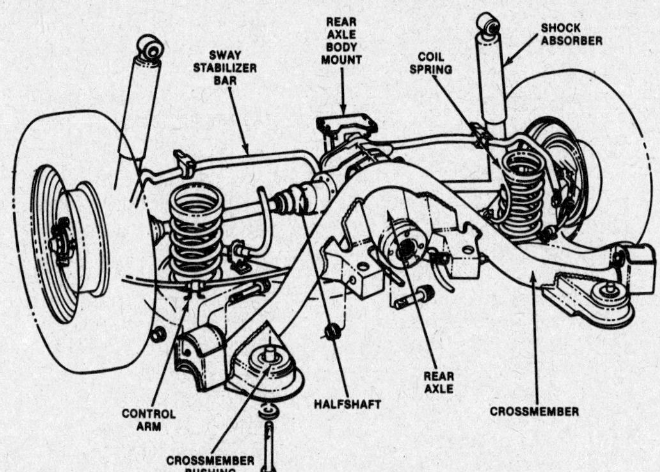

Fig. 1 Rear suspension

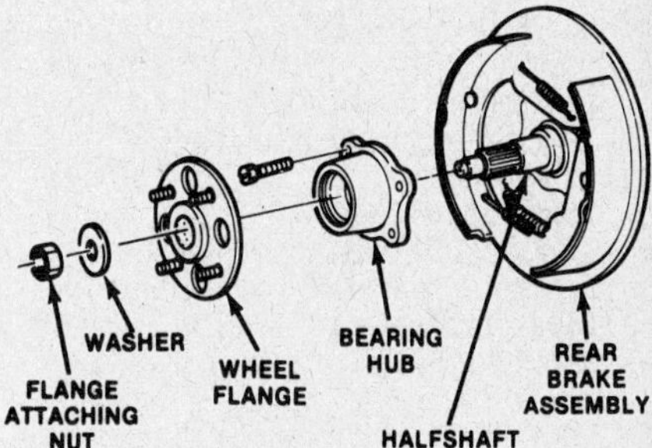

Fig. 2 Removing wheel flange

SHOCK ABSORBER REPLACE

1. Remove rear parcel shelf.
2. Remove shock absorber trim cover from rear wheel housing.
3. Raise and support rear of vehicle.
4. Position suitable jack under control arm and raise it enough to relieve coil spring tension from shock absorber.
5. Remove nut and bolt attaching upper end of shock absorber.
6. Remove cap from bottom of shock absorber.
7. Remove nut and bolt attaching lower end of shock absorber to control arm bracket.
8. Reverse procedure to install, torquing upper and lower attaching nuts to 30-37 ft. lbs., then the lower attaching bolt to 33-40 ft. lbs.

COIL SPRING REPLACE

REMOVAL

1. Raise and support vehicle with rear wheels and suspension hanging free.
2. Remove bolts attaching halfshaft to wheel stub shaft, **Fig. 1.** To prevent damage to constant velocity joints, tie halfshaft to convenient under body component.
3. Remove clip attaching rear brake hose to routing bracket on control arm.
4. Using line wrenches, disconnect brake tube from brake hose.
5. Remove cap from bottom of shock absorber.
6. Using suitable jack, raise lower control arm enough to relieve coil spring tension from shock absorber.
7. Remove lower shock absorber attaching nut and bolt.
8. Slowly and carefully lower jack until it can be removed.
9. Support axle housing using suitable jack.
10. Remove rear axle mount to body attaching bolts and disconnect axle vent tube.
11. Slowly and carefully lower jack until coil spring and its seat can be removed. Do not remove support from rear axle. Lower axle only enough to allow removal of coil spring.

INSTALLATION

1. Install spring upper seat on spring end with color code and plastic sleeve, ensuring that end of coil seats against step in spring seat and that seat tabs are positioned between first and second coil.
2. Install coil spring and seat assembly, then raise rear axle into position and install body mount attaching bolts, torquing to 14-18 ft. lbs. **The body mount bolts must be cleaned, and new Loctite applied.**
3. Remove axle support and position it under control arm, then raise jack until coil spring is compressed enough to allow installation of lower shock absorber attaching bolt.
4. Install attaching nut on shock absorber bolt, torquing nut to 30-37 ft. lbs., or bolt to 33-40 ft. lbs.
5. Remove control arm support and install shock absorber cap.
6. Position brake hose through routing bracket on control arm and connect it to brake tube.
7. Install brake hose retaining clip.
8. Position halfshaft and install attaching bolts, torquing bolts to 28-31 ft. lbs.
9. Connect axle vent hose located at top right hand corner of axle housing.
10. Ensure that stabilizer bar link is connected to control arm.
11. Bleed brake system.

CONTROL ARM & BEARING HUB REPLACE

1. Remove coil spring as previously described.

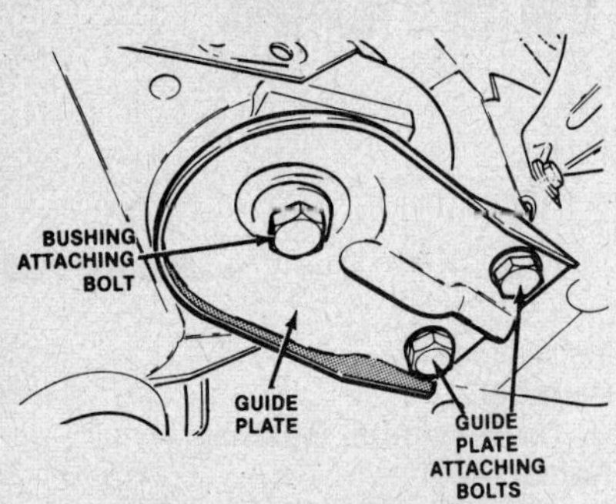

Fig. 3 Location of crossmember bushing to body attaching bolt

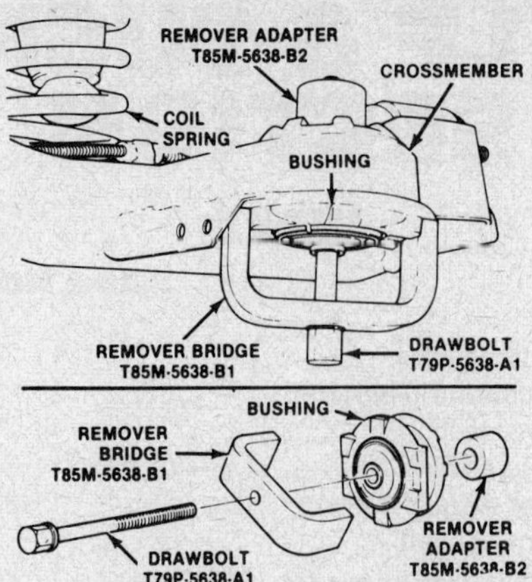

Fig. 4 Removing crossmember bushing

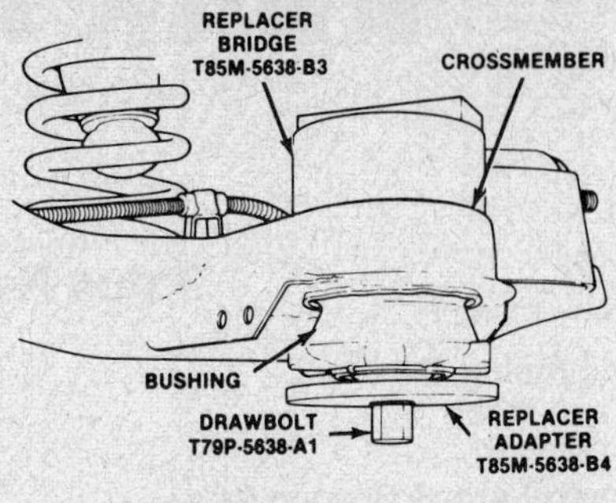

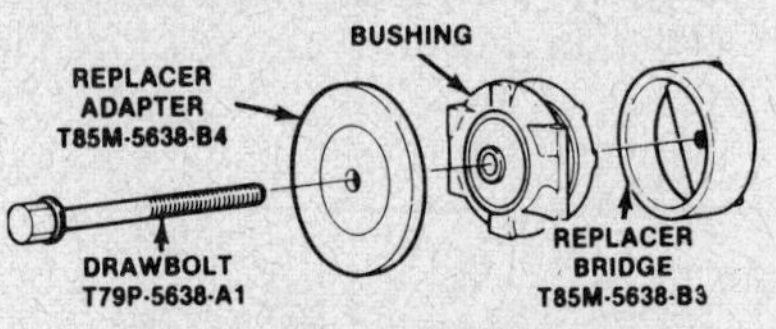

Fig. 5 Installing crossmember bushing

2. Using screwdriver, open routing clamp and disengage parking brake cable from control arm.
3. Disconnect sway stabilizer link at control arm.
4. Remove wheel flange attaching nut and washer, then wheel flange, **Fig. 2.**
5. Remove rear bearing hub and tie brake backing plate out of way.
6. Working from under vehicle, pull wheel stub shaft out of control arm.
7. Remove control arm inner and outer attaching bolts.
8. Reverse procedure to install, noting the following:
   a. When installing control arm attaching bolts, ensure bolt heads face inboard.
   b. With vehicle weight on tires, torque control arm attaching bolts to 63-74 ft. lbs.

CONTROL ARM BUSHINGS
REPLACE
REMOVAL

1. Remove control arm as previously described.
2. Using drawbolt T78P-5638-A1, receiver cup T85M-5638-A2, a 7/16 inch 20 UNF hex nut and a 7/16 inch flat washer, or equivalents, remove larger control arm bushing.
3. Using drawbolt T78P-5638-A1, receiver cup T85M-5638-A1, a 7/16 inch 20 UNF nut and a 7/16 inch flat washer, or equivalents, remove smaller control arm bushing.

INSTALLATION

1. Lubricate bushings with suitable non-petroleum lubricant.
2. Using drawbolt T78P-5638-A1, replacer cup T85M-5638-A3, a 7/16 inch 20 UNF nut and a 7/16 inch flat washer, or equivalents install new larger control arm bushing.
3. Using drawbolt T78P-5638-A1, replacer cup T78P-5638-A3, a 7/16 inch 20 UNF nut and a 7/16 inch flat washer, or equivalents, install new smaller control arm bushing.

REAR CROSSMEMBER BUSHING
REPLACE
REMOVAL

1. Raise and support vehicle with suspension and tires hanging free.
2. Position suitable jack under control arm and raise enough to support control arm against downward pressure of coil spring. **Ensure control arm is securely supported before removing bushing to body attaching bolt.**
3. Remove crossmember bushing to body attaching bolt, **Fig. 3.**
4. Remove bushing guide plate attaching bolts and the guide plate.
5. Carefully lower crossmember to provide clearance for bushing removal and installation tools.
6. Remove crossmember bushing, **Fig. 4.**

INSTALLATION

1. Lubricate replacement bushing with suitable non-petroleum lubricant.
2. Install crossmember bushing, **Fig. 5.**
3. Carefully raise crossmember into position.
4. Position bushing guide plate and install attaching bolts, torquing to 30-37 ft. lbs.
5. Install bushing to body attaching bolt and washer, torquing bolt to 59-74 ft. lbs.

REAR AXLE & SUSPENSION ASSEMBLY
REPLACE
REMOVAL

1. Remove coil springs, driveshaft and muffler and silencer assembly.
2. Loosen parking brake adjuster sleeve locknut, then thread adjuster sleeve away from body routing bracket.
3. Remove clip and clevis pin attaching parking brake cable equalizer to parking brake lever rod.
4. Disengage parking brake cable from body routing brackets.
5. Remove stabilizer bar U-brackets.
6. Position suitable jack under rear axle and secure crossmember to jack.
7. Remove crossmember bushing attaching bolt on both sides of vehicle.
8. Remove crossmember bushing guide plate attaching bolts and the guide plate on both sides of vehicle.
9. Remove bolts attaching axle mount to body, then carefully lower crossmember out of vehicle.

INSTALLATION

1. Raise crossmember into position on vehicle.
2. Install but do not tighten axle mount attaching bolts.
3. Position crossmember insulator guide plates and install attaching bolts.
4. Install crossmember bushing attaching bolts and washers, torquing guide plate attaching bolts to 30-38 ft. lbs. and the crossmember bushing attaching bolts to 59-74 ft. lbs.
5. Torque the four axle mount attaching bolts and washers to 22-26 ft. lbs.
6. Route parking brake cable through body brackets, then position parking brake equalizer and install clevis pin and retaining clip.
7. Install stabilizer bar U-brackets, torquing attaching bolts to 15-18 ft. lbs.
8. Install muffler and silencer assembly, driveshaft and coil springs.
9. Bleed rear brake system and adjust parking brake.

STABILIZER BAR
REPLACE

1. Loosen wheel lug nuts, then raise and support rear of vehicle and remove wheel.
2. Disconnect stabilizer bar links from lower control arm using screwdriver.
3. Place a piece of tape on stabilizer bar next to U-bracket and insulator for proper alignment during installation.

4. Remove U-brackets to body attaching bolts, then disengage U-brackets and remove stabilizer bar.
5. Reverse procedure to install, torquing U-brackets to body attaching bolts to 15-18 ft. lbs.

REAR AXLE
REPLACE
REMOVAL

1. Disconnect axle halfshafts from stub shaft flanges on each side of housing. Before releasing halfshafts, support them from body floor in approximately their normal position.
2. Remove driveshaft, then support rear axle housing with suitable jack and remove rear body mount attaching bolts.
3. Remove four bolts and two shims, if equipped, attaching front end of axle housing to crossmember brackets, then remove nut and through bolt attaching axle housing to crossmember.
4. Lower axle housing clear of rear suspension and remove it, then remove rear mount.

INSTALLATION

1. If axle case, axle assembly or suspension crossmember is replaced, check flange clearance as follows:
   a. Install rear mount on axle housing rear cover, torquing attaching bolts to 37-41 ft. lbs.
   b. Lift assembly into position between crossmember flanges.
   c. Install through bolt and four axle bolts to crossmember attaching bolts but do not tighten bolts.

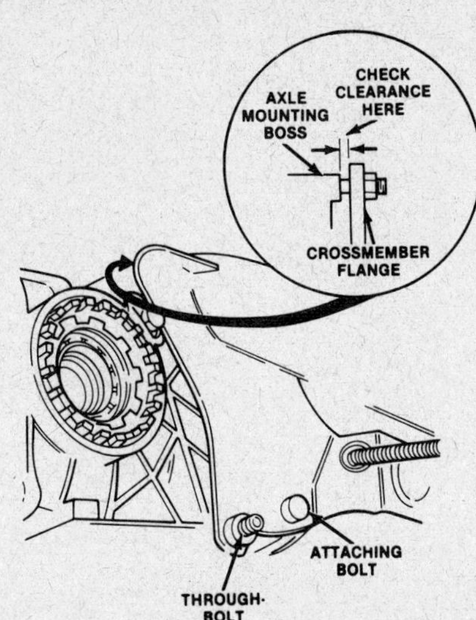

Fig. 6 Checking mounting flange clearance

   d. Position axle housing rear mount against body and secure with four bolts, torquing bolts to 14-18 ft. lbs.
   e. Torque front lower attaching bolt to 51-66 ft. lbs.
   f. Torque through bolt to 51-66 ft. lbs.
   g. Using feeler gauge, check clearance between crossmember flanges and the rear axle mounting boss, **Fig. 6.**
   h. Select appropriate shims to be installed between crossmember and axle.
2. Install shims, if required, and torque attaching bolts to 51-66 ft. lbs.
3. Install driveshaft.
4. Connect axle halfshafts to stub shaft flanges and install attaching bolts, torquing bolts to 28-31 ft. lbs.

HALFSHAFTS
REPLACE
REMOVAL

1. Ensure that transmission is in neutral and parking brake is fully released.
2. Raise and support rear of vehicle with rear wheels hanging free.
3. Remove bolts attaching halfshaft to wheel stub shaft, turning driveshaft as necessary to bring bolts into accessible position.
4. Hang halfshaft from floor of vehicle.
5. Remove bolts attaching halfshaft to rear axle stub shaft and remove halfshaft.

INSTALLATION

Halfshafts are different lengths and must be installed on the correct side of vehicle, with longer shaft being installed on right side of vehicle.

1. Pack CV joints with suitable lubricant.
2. Hang halfshaft from floor of vehicle.
3. Position halfshaft to axle stub shaft and install attaching bolts.
4. Release halfshaft from vehicle floor and position it to axle stub shaft, installing attaching bolts.
5. Torque attaching bolts to 28-31 ft. lbs.

FRONT SUSPENSION & STEERING SECTION

INDEX

CONTROL ARM AND/OR STABILIZER BAR BUSHING
REPLACE
REMOVAL

1. Remove cotter pin and attaching nut and separate control arm from spindle carrier. **With spindle carrier and control arm disconnected, the spindle carrier can easily cause damage to control arm ball joint boot.**
2. Remove pivot bolt attaching control arm to crossmember.
3. Remove stabilizer bar to control arm attaching nut, **Fig. 1.**
4. Remove front washer/plastic cover from end of stabilizer bar.
5. Remove control arm and bushings as an assembly.
6. Remove rear washer/plastic cover from end of stabilizer bar.
7. Remove bushings from control arm as necessary.

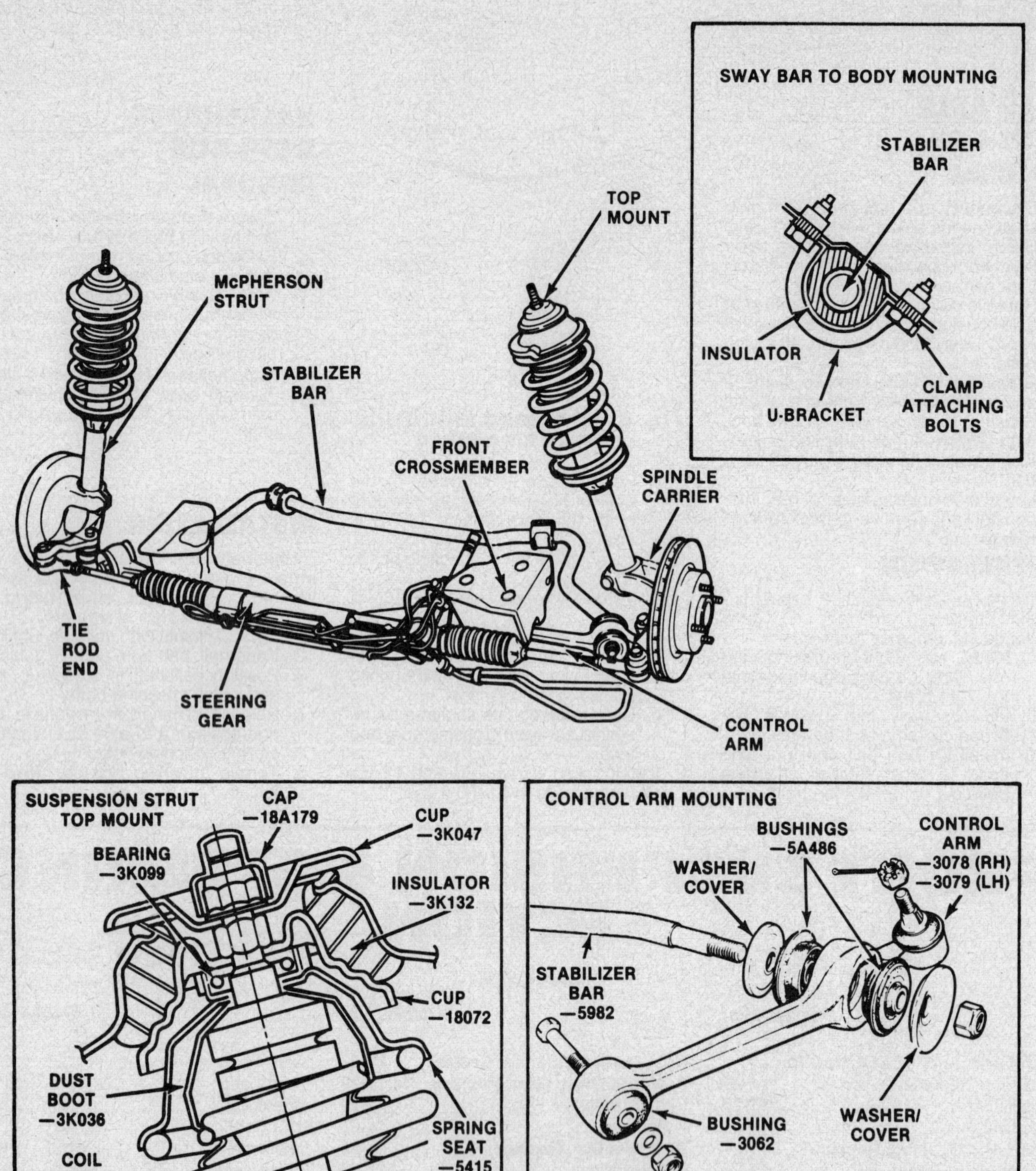
SWAY BAR TO BODY MOUNTING
STABILIZER BAR
INSULATOR
U-BRACKET
CLAMP ATTACHING BOLTS
TOP MOUNT
McPHERSON STRUT
STABILIZER BAR
FRONT CROSSMEMBER
SPINDLE CARRIER
TIE ROD END
STEERING GEAR
CONTROL ARM
SUSPENSION STRUT TOP MOUNT
CAP —18A179
CUP —3K047
BEARING —3K099
INSULATOR —3K132
CUP —18072
DUST BOOT —3K036
SPRING SEAT —5415
COIL SPRING —5310
CONTROL ARM MOUNTING
BUSHINGS —5A486
CONTROL ARM —3078 (RH) —3079 (LH)
WASHER/ COVER
STABILIZER BAR —5982
BUSHING —3062
WASHER/ COVER

Fig. 1 Front suspension

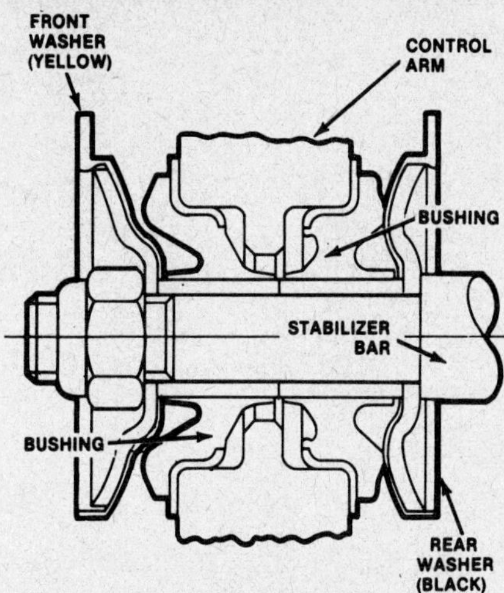

Fig. 2 Installing stabilizer bar bushings

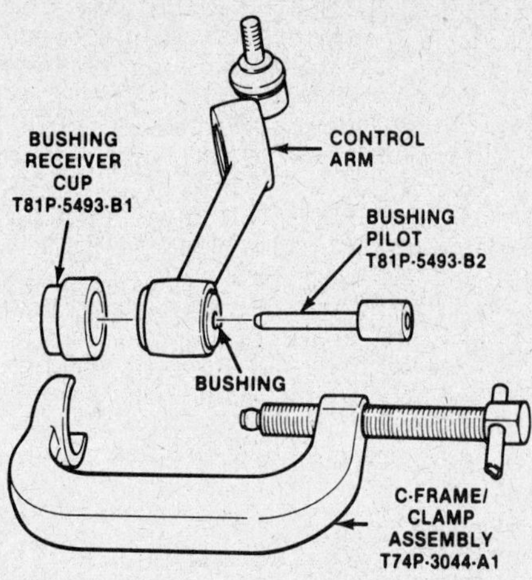

Fig. 3 Removing control arm bushings

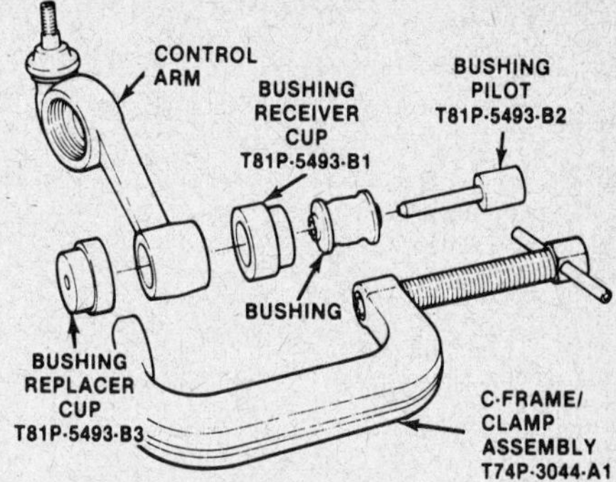

Fig. 4 Installing control arm bushings

INSTALLATION

Stabilizer bar bushings are designed to allow control arm to move backward and forward somewhat.

1. If removed, press stabilizer bar bushings into control arm.
2. Install rear washer/plastic cover on stabilizer bar. **Rear washer is black and has a shallower dish than the front washer, which is yellow. When washer is installed, ensure that plastic cover is in place between dished steel washer and the bushing and that dished side of steel washer faces away from bushing, Fig. 2.**
3. Install control arm and bushing assembly on stabilizer bar.
4. Install front washer/plastic cover on stabilizer bar, ensuring dished side of washer faces away from bushing, **Fig. 2.**
5. Install stabilizer bar attaching nut, snugging but not tightening.
6. Position control arm ball joint stud in spindle carrier and install attaching nut, torque nut to 48-63 ft. lbs. and install cotter pin. **If slots in nut do not align with cotter pin hole, tighten nut to next slot. Never loosen nut for alignment.**
7. Grip bottom of tire and pull inward until control arm enters crossmember and aligns with bolt holes, then, using drift punch to hold arm in alignment, install attaching bolt.
8. Install control arm pivot bolt, plain washer and attaching nut, snugging but not tightening attaching nut.
9. Lower vehicle.
10. With vehicle weight on tires, torque control arm pivot bolt nut to 11 ft. lbs. then additional 90 degrees, and the stabilizer bar attaching nut to 52-81 ft. lbs.

HUB, ROTOR & BEARING REPLACE

The hub and rotor are a matched and balanced assembly. Before removing rotor locate the paint mark or etch mark that indicates proper hub to rotor alignment. If marks are not present, mark hub and rotor for assembly alignment.

1. Raise and support vehicle, then remove wheel and tire assembly.
2. Remove anchor plate plate attaching bolts, then lift caliper and anchor plate assembly off rotor and tie out of way.
3. Remove rotor retaining clip, then rotor.
4. Disconnect tie rod end, control arm and stabilizer bar from spindle carrier.
5. Remove suspension strut pinch bolt, then using spindle carrier lever T85M-3206-A, or equivalent, spread spindle carrier to release from strut and remove spindle carrier.
6. Install nuts on each of the spindle wheel studs, then position spindle in a suitable vise.
7. Using a suitable drift and hammer, remove bearing plug.
8. Using a 41 mm socket, remove spindle bearing locknut. **The spindle bearing locknut will have right hand threads if spindle carrier is removed from left side of vehicle and if the spindle carrier is from the right side of vehicle, the locknut will have left hand threads.**
9. Lift spindle carrier and inner bearing off spindle shaft, then remove inner bearing and washer. If bearing is to be reused, tag it so it can be installed in its original position.
10. Install spindle carrier in vise, then using a screwdriver remove spindle seal.
11. Remove outer bearing from spindle carrier. If bearing is to be reused, tag it so it can be installed in its original position.
12. Reverse procedure to install, noting the following:
    a. Install spindle bearing locknut and torque to 229-250 ft. lbs.
    b. Torque tie rod end ball joints to 18-22 ft. lbs.
    c. Torque strut pinch bolt to 59-66 ft. lbs.
    d. Torque anchor plate to spindle carrier attaching bolts to 43-44 ft. lbs.
    e. Torque control ball joint stud in spindle carrier to 48-63 ft. lbs.
    f. Torque stabilizer bar attaching nut to 52-81 ft. lbs and control arm pivot bolt nut to 11 ft. lbs.
13. If rotor has been removed without alignment marks, proceed as follows:
    a. Install rotor on hub, then wheel lug nuts.
    b. Using a dial indicator and a suitable holding fixture, measure rotor runout. The indicator stylus should contact the rotor approximately 7/16 inch from the end.
    c. Rotate hub and disc assembly and record dial indicator reading.
    d. If indicator reading is .003 inch or less, this positioning of rotor may be used during assembly.
    e. If indicator reading is greater than .003 inch, reposition rotor on hub in 90 degree increments until lowest reading is obtained.
    f. When a reading of no more than .003 inch is obtained, mark alignment of hub and rotor.

CONTROL ARM BUSHING REPLACE

1. Remove control arm as previously described.
2. Remove control arm bushing, **Fig. 3.**
3. Coat control arm bore and outer surface of bushing with non-petroleum lubricant.
4. Install control arm bushing, **Fig. 4,** inserting bushing quickly and with a continuous motion so that bushing deforms only for a short time.
5. Install control arm as previously described.

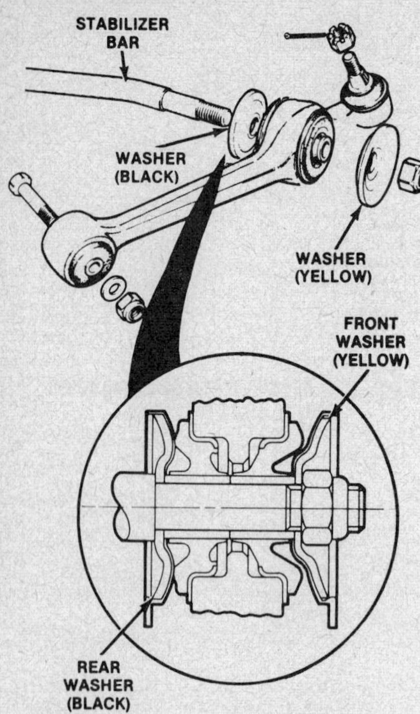

Fig. 5 Installing stabilizer bar

STABILIZER BAR
REPLACE
REMOVAL

1. Remove attaching nuts and front washers/covers from ends of stabilizer bar.
2. Remove four bolts securing two U-brackets and torque brace to body.
3. Remove one control arm pivot bolt and pull control arm out of crossmember.
4. Pull stabilizer out of lower control arms and remove from vehicle.
5. Remove rear washers/covers from stabilizer bar.
6. Remove insulators from stabilizer bar.

INSTALLATION

1. Coat inside of stabilizer bar bushings and bushing surfaces on stabilizer bar with suitable non-petroleum lubricant, then install body insulators on stabilizer bar.
2. Install rear washers/plastic covers on stabilizer bar. **Rear washer is black and has a shallower dish than front washer, which is yellow. When washer is installed, ensure plastic cover is in place between dished steel washer and the bushing and that dished side of steel washer faces away from bushing, Fig. 5.**
3. Install stabilizer bar into control arms bushings and install control arm into crossmember with pivot bolt, washer and nut, snugging but not tightening attaching nut.
4. Install U-brackets on insulators and install attaching bolts, torquing to 42-52 ft. lbs.
5. Install front washers/plastic covers on stabilizer bar. **Ensure dished side of steel washer faces away from bushing, with plastic cover in place between bushing and steel washer.**
6. Install stabilizer bar attaching nuts, snugging but not tightening.
7. Lower vehicle.
8. With vehicle weight on tires, torque stabilizer bar attaching nut to 52-81 ft. lbs. and the control arm pivot bolt nut to 11 ft. lbs. plus an additional 90 degrees.

STRUT
REPLACE
REMOVAL

If twin post hoist is used to perform this procedure, front of vehicle must be supported on safety stands to allow lowering of front post. If front post is not lowered, the lower control may contact lift and prevent removal of strut.

1. Remove wheel and raise and support vehicle.
2. Remove strut pinch bolt from spindle carrier.
3. Insert spindle carrier lever T85M-3206-A or equivalent into slot in spindle carrier and rotate it through 90 degrees to open slot.
4. Push downward on brake rotor to disengage spindle carrier from strut. **When releasing spindle carrier from strut, be careful not to damage brake hose. Place jack under control arm bushing boss to keep being pushed down too far.**
5. Remove cap from top mount attaching nut.
6. Hold piston shaft with 6 mm Allen wrench and loosen top mount attaching nut.
7. Support strut from below and remove top mount nut, retainer and strut, discarding nut.

INSTALLATION

1. Position strut through top mount insulation and install retainer and a new top mount attaching nut but do not tighten nut.
2. Position strut in spindle by pulling outward on strut and lifting spindle using brake rotor. Use spindle carrier lever or equivalent to spread spindle carrier to allow strut to center correctly. When strut enters spindle, grip rotor and pivot spindle into position. **If strut is not pulled outward to match spindle angle, it will jam as the spindle is pivoted into position.**
3. Install strut pinch bolt, torquing to 59-66 ft. lbs.
4. Ensure top of strut is centered in suspension tower and torque top mount attaching nut to 29-38 ft. lbs., holding piston shaft as necessary with 6 mm Allen wrench.
5. Install cap on top mount attaching nut and install wheel.

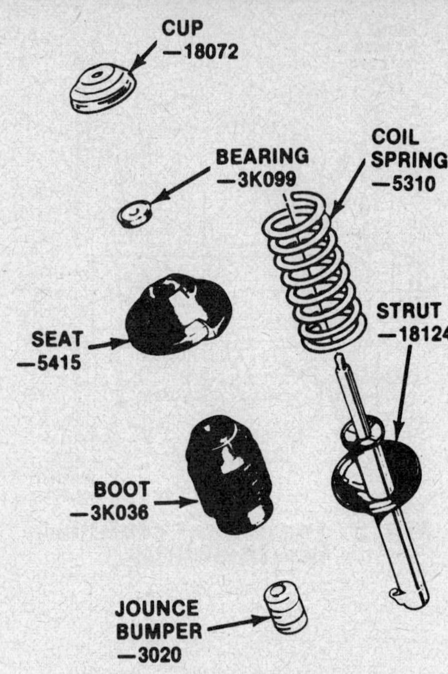

Fig. 6 Strut assembly exploded view

TOP MOUNT INSULATOR
REPLACE

1. Remove cap from top mount attaching nut.
2. Hold piston shaft with 6 mm Allen wrench and remove and discard top mount attaching nut.
3. Remove retainer from piston shaft.
4. Using pry bar, force suspension assembly downward, being careful not to stretch brake hose.
5. Remove top mount insulator.
6. Reverse procedure to install, noting the following:
   a. Ensure top of strut is centered in suspension tower before installing retainer and attaching nut.
   b. Torque new top mount attaching nut to 29-38 ft. lbs., holding piston shaft with 6 mm Allen wrench as necessary.

CROSSMEMBER
REPLACE
REMOVAL

Steering must be set straight ahead during following procedure to ensure that correct alignment is maintained.

1. Install suitable engine support fixture, then raise and support vehicle.
2. Remove pivot bolts attaching control arms to crossmember.
3. Remove control arm end from crossmember by gripping bottom of tire and pulling outward.
4. Remove pinch bolt at steering column to steering gear coupling.

5. Remove steering gear to crossmember attaching bolts and washers.
6. Disengage steering gear coupling from steering column and pull steering gear forward away from crossmember, being careful not to stretch or bend power steering gear hoses or tubes.
7. Support steering gear by tieing it out of way.
8. Remove engine mounts to crossmember attaching stud nuts.
9. Position suitable jack under crossmember and secure with safety chain.
10. Remove crossmember to side rail attaching bolts and washers.
11. Lower crossmember and remove from under vehicle.

INSTALLATION

1. Raise crossmember into position and install crossmember to side rail attaching bolts and washers.
2. Torque attaching bolts to 51-66 ft. lbs. and remove jack.
3. Position steering gear on crossmember and connect coupling to steering column, ensuring that block splines are properly mated.
4. Install steering gear attaching bolts and washers, snugging bolt to 11 ft. lbs. plus additional 90 degrees.
5. Install steering coupling pinch bolt, torquing to 18-22 ft. lbs.
6. Install engine mount attaching bolts, torquing to 38-47 ft. lbs.
7. Grip bottom of tire and pull inward until control arm enters crossmember, aligning control arm with bolt holes and install pivot bolt. Use drift punch to hold control arm in alignment while pivot bolt is installed.
8. Install pivot bolt and washer, snugging but not tightening bolt.
9. Lower vehicle.
10. With weight of vehicle on front tires, torque control arm pivot bolt to 11 ft. lbs. plus additional 90 degrees.
11. Remove engine support fixture.

STRUT SERVICE

DISASSEMBLY

1. Clamp strut spring compressor 086-00016 or equivalent in suitable vise and adjust tool to "START" position following tool manufacturer's instructions.
2. Using tool, carefully compress coil spring.
3. Hold piston shaft with 6 mm Allen wrench and remove coil spring retaining nut.
4. Release coil spring tension.
5. Remove top mount cup, bearing, upper spring seat and dust boot, **Fig. 6.**
6. Slide jounce bumper off piston shaft and remove coil spring.

ASSEMBLY

1. Install coil spring, then jounce bumper, dust boot, upper spring seat, bearing and top mount cup.
2. Compress spring using suitable tool.
3. Install coil spring retaining nut, torquing to 38-48 ft. lbs., holding piston shaft with 6 mm Allen wrench as necessary.
4. Release coil spring tension and remove strut from spring compressor.

POWER STEERING GEAR REPLACE

REMOVAL

1. Disconnect battery ground cable and turn ignition key to "ON" position.
2. Remove cotter pins and nuts attaching tie rod ends to spindle carriers.
3. Using suitable tool, separate tie rod ends from spindle carriers.
4. Remove pinch bolt from flexible coupling, rotating coupling as necessary to gain access to pinch bolt.
5. Position drain pan and disconnect power steering hoses from steering gear by removing routing clamp and the washer-head screw securing pump line plate assembly to gear housing and pulling assembly free. Plug housing port to prevent entry of foreign matter.
6. Remove steering gear mounting bolts and the gear.

INSTALLATION

1. Center steering wheel and turn ignition key to "OFF" position.
2. Center steering gear as follows:
   a. Turn steering gear input shaft clockwise to full left turn stop.
   b. Turn input shaft counterclockwise and count number of turns required to move rack from full left turn stop to full right turn stop.
   c. From right turn stop, turn input shaft clockwise exactly 1/2 the turns previously counted.
3. Position steering gear on crossmember, engaging flexible coupling with input shaft, rocking coupling as necessary to align blind splines on shaft and coupling.
4. Turn ignition key to "ON" position, then turn steering column as necessary to align blind splines on coupling and the steering shaft.
5. Connect steering gear to steering column and position on crossmember.
6. Install steering coupling pin bolt, torquing to 18-22 ft. lbs.
7. Plug pump line assembly into steering gear supply and return ports and secure line plate with washer-head screw and routing clamp.
8. Install new steering gear mounting bolts and torque to approximately 11 ft. lbs. plus additional 90 degrees.
9. Connect tie rods to spindle carriers and install castle nuts, torque nuts to 15-23 ft. lbs. and install new cotter pins. **If slots in nut do not align with cotter pin holes, tighten nut to next slot. Never loosen nut for alignment.**
10. Turn ignition key to "OFF" position.
11. Connect battery ground cable.
12. Fill power steering pump to correct level.

WHEEL ALIGNMENT SECTION

INDEX

DESCRIPTION

The angles at which suspension components operate in relation to the vehicle and wheel centerlines are calculated during vehicle design to provide maximum tire contact with the road throughout the full range of suspension travel. The checking of caster, camber and wheel toe in or out is the measurement of these suspension angles at the wheels, and the possible adjustments are performed to ensure that the tires make maximum contact with the road at all times and cause the vehicle to track in a straight line when the front wheels are centered. Proper alignment of the front and rear wheels with the vehicle chassis and each other is essential for acceptable handling and to minimize tire wear.

Prior to checking wheel alignment, ensure that tires are properly matched (same size tires on each axle set), correctly inflated and uniformly worn. Ensure that wheel bearings are properly adjusted and that suspension components are not damaged or worn. Wheel alignment should be checked with the vehicle unloaded, as any abnormal or uneven loads affect ride height which, in turn, affects suspension operating angles (wheel alignment).

Only wheel toe-in or out is adjustable on these models. Caster and camber are not adjustable. However, they should be checked as possible causes of handling or tire wear complaints. If caster and camber are not within limits suspension components should be inspected for wear and damage, and replaced as needed. If control arms, stabilizers and bushings are in good condition, check vehicle body for distortion at suspension mounting points or for collision damage.

TOE-IN & STEERING WHEEL CENTERING ADJUSTMENT

If the steering wheel is not properly centered when vehicle is driven straight ahead, mark its position with a piece of tape across the gap between steering wheel hub and steering column shroud.

If toe-in is to be adjusted, the operation can be combined with steering wheel centering. But, to avoid complications, one should be completed before starting the other. To center the steering wheel, the tie rods must be turned into one tie rod end and out of the other, in equal amounts to avoid changing the toe setting. This shifts the steering rack right or left, turning the pinion, steering column and wheel to its desired position. Center steering as follows:

1. Mark the tie rod and tie rod ends with paint or a grease pencil to indicate their original relative positions.
2. Loosen and back off the tie rod end jam nuts, then release the steering gear boot clips. Ensure boots are free on the tie rods to avoid twisting.
3. Screw tie rods into one tie rod end and out of the other, depending on which way the steering wheel is to be moved and how much. Example, if left tie rod is screwed in and right tie rod is screwed out, the steering rack moves to the left and the steering wheel movement is counterclockwise as seen from the drivers seat. For clockwise correction, the rack must be moved to the right. If the road wheels are positioned and locked in the straight ahead position during this operation, using the steering wheel tape mark as a starting point, the wheel will turn during adjustment and the centered position can be judged visually. One revolution of the tie rods will result in a steering wheel correction of approximately 19 degrees. Check marks on tie rods and tie rod ends, to ensure tie rods are turned equal amounts. Adjust toe-in as follows:
   a. Loosen jam nuts at tie rod ends and release clips at small ends of steering gear boots, ensuring boots are free on tie rods so they will not be twisted when tie rods are turned.
   b. Turn tie rods into or out of tie rod ends an equal amount on each side to keep steering wheel centered.
   c. When toe-in is within specifications, torque tie rod end jam nuts to 42-50 ft. lbs., then ensure steering gear boot ends are positioned in the reduced-diameter sections of the tie rods and install boot clips.

MITSUBISHI (Japan)

INDEX OF SERVICE OPERATIONS

General Engine Specifications

Year	Engine Displacement cu. in./cc	Fuel System	Bore & Stroke	Compression Ratio	Maximum Net H.P. @ RPM	Maximum Torque Ft. Lbs. @ RPM
1983	4-110/1800	2 Barrel	3.17 x 3.46	8.5	82 @ 5000	93 @ 3000
	4-122/2000	2 Barrel	3.35 x 3.46	8.5	90 @ 5000	107 @ 3500
	4-143/2300 ①	Fuel Inj.	3.59 x 3.54	21.0	80 @ 4200	125 @ 2500
	4-156/2600	2 Barrel	3.59 x 3.86	8.2	105 @ 5000	139 @ 2500
	4-156/2600 ②	Fuel Inj.	3.59 x 3.86	7.0	145 @ 5000	185 @ 2500
1984	4-110/1800 ②	Fuel Inj.	3.17 x 3.46	7.5	116 @ 5500	129 @ 3000
	4-122/2000	2 Barrel	3.35 x 3.46	8.5	90 @ 5000	107 @ 3500
	40143/2300 ①	Fuel Inj.	3.59 x 3.54	21.0	80 @ 4200	136 @ 2500
	4-156/2600	2 Barrel	3.59 x 3.86	8.2	108 @ 5000	142 @ 2500
	4-156/2600 ②	Fuel Inj.	3.59 x 3.86	7	145 @ 5000	185 @ 2500
1985	4-89.6/1500	2 Barrel	2.97 x 3.23	9.4	68 @ 5500	82 @ 3500
	4-97.4/1600 ②	Fuel Inj.	3.03 x 3.39	7.6	102 @ 5500	122 @ 3000
	4-109/1800 ②	Fuel Inj.	3.17 x 3.46	7.5	116 @ 5500	129 @ 3000
	4-122/2000	2 Barrel	3.35 x 3.46	8.5	88 @ 5000	108 @ 3500
	4-143/2300 ①	Fuel Inj.	3.59 x 3.54	21.0	86 @ 4200	134 @ 2000
	4-143.4/2400	Fuel Inj.	3.41 x 3.94	8.5	101 @ 5000	131 @ 2500
	4-156/2600	2 Barrel	3.59 x 3.86	8.7	106 @ 5000	142 @ 2500
	4-156/2600 ②	Fuel Inj.	3.59 x 3.86	7.0	145 @ 5000	185 @ 2500
1986	4-89.6/1500	2 Barrel	2.97 x 3.23	9.4	68 @ 5500	82 @ 3500
	4-97.4/1600 ②	Fuel Inj.	3.03 x 3.39	7.6	102 @ 5500	122 @ 3000
	4-109/1800 ②	Fuel Inj.	3.17 x 3.46	7.5	116 @ 5500	129 @ 3000
	4-122/2000	2 Barrel	3.35 x 3.46	8.5	88 @ 5000	108 @ 3500
	4-143.4/2400	Fuel Inj.	3.41 x 3.94	8.5	101 @ 4500	131 @ 2500
	4-156/2600	2 Barrel	3.59 x 3.86	8.2	106 @ 5000	142 @ 2500
	4-156/2600 ②	Fuel Inj.	3.59 x 3.86	7.0	145 @ 5000	185 @ 2500
1987	4-89.6/1500	2 Barrel	2.97 x 3.23	9.4	68 @ 5500	82 @ 3500
	4-97.4/1600 ②	Fuel Inj.	3.03 x 3.39	7.6	102 @ 5500	122 @ 3000
	4-109/1800 ②	Fuel Inj.	3.17 x 3.46	7.5	116 @ 5500	129 @ 3000
	4-122/2000	2 Barrel	3.35 x 3.46	8.5	88 @ 5000	108 @ 3500
	4-143.4/2400	Fuel Inj.	3.41 x 3.94	8.5	101 @ 4500	131 @ 2500
	4-156/2600	2 Barrel	3.59 x 3.86	8.2	106 @ 5000	142 @ 2500
	4-156/2600 ②	Fuel Inj.	3.59 x 3.86	7.0	145 @ 5000	185 @ 2500

①—Turbocharged diesel engine.
②—Turbocharged engine.

Alternator & Regulator Specifications

Year	Alternator			Regulator	
	Part No.	Rated Hot Output Amps	Output @ 14 Volts 2500 RPM Amps	Model	Constant Voltage Relay Voltage @ 68°F
1983	MD041701	45	32①	②	13.9–14.9
	MD022579	45	32①	Integral	13.9–14.9
	MD018230	65	46①	Integral	14.1–14.7
	MD025677	65	46①	Integral	14.1–14.7
1984	MD018230	65	—	Integral	13.9–14.9
	MD025677	65	45①	Integral	14.1–14.7
	MD064068	50	—	Integral	13.9–14.9
	MD074645	50	—	Integral	13.9–14.9
1985	MD064068	50	—	Integral	13.9–14.9
	MD069978	55	—	Integral	14.4–15.0
	MD074644	65	—	Integral	14.4–15.0
	MD074645	55	—	Integral	13.9–14.9
	MD074992	50	—	Integral	14.4–15.0
1986	HD063781	45	—	Integral	14.1–14.7
	MD064066	45	—	Integral	14.1–14.7
	MD064068	50	—	Integral	13.9–14.9
	MD069978	55	—	Integral	14.4–15.0
	MD074644	65	—	Integral	14.4–15.0
	MD074645	55	—	Integral	13.9–14.9
	MD074992	50	—	Integral	14.4–15.0
	MD086048	65	—	Integral	14.4–15.0
	MD091794③	65	—	Integral	13.9–14.9
	MD091794④	65	—	Integral	14.4–15.0
1987	MD108230	45	—	Integral	13.9–14.9
	MD108509	45	—	Integral	13.9–14.9
	MD110318	50	—	Integral	13.9–14.9
	—	55	—	Integral	14.4–14.6
	MD111607	60	—	Integral	14.2–15.2
	MD102085	65	—	Integral	13.9–14.9
	MD105339	65	—	Integral	13.9–14.9
	MD111151	65	—	Integral	14.2–15.2
	MD106713	75	—	Integral	13.9–14.9
	MD108305	75	—	Integral	14.2–15.2

①—Minimum.
②—Electronic voltage regulator attached to rear of alternator.
③—Cordia/Tredia.
④—Galant.

Starter Motor Specifications

Year	Part No.	Free Speed Test		
		Amps	Volts	RPM
1983–85	MD001333	60	11.5	6500
	MD050205	130	11	4000
1983–86	MD021674	60	11.5	6500
	MD027382	100	11.5	3000
	MD027401	60	11.5	6500
1984–86	MD072585	90	11.5	3300
1985–86	MD066761	60	11.5	3900
	MD081567	60	11.5	6500
1986	MD085730	60	11.5	6600
	MD085731	90	11.5	3300
1987	MD081567	60	11.5	6500
	–	60	11.5	6500
	MD100431	60	11.5	6600
	MD099667	90	11.0	3000
	MD072585	100	11.5	3000

Valve Specifications

Year	Engine	Valve Lash		Valve Angles		Valve Spring Free Height	Valve Spring Pressure Lbs. @ In.	Stem Clearance		Stem Diameter	
		Int. (hot)	Exh. (hot)	Seat	Face			Intake	Exhaust	Intake	Exhaust
1983	1800	.006 ①	.010	45	45	1.870	62 @ 1.591	.0012–.0024	.0020–.0035	.315	.315
	2000	.006 ①	.010	45	45	1.870	62 @ 1.591	.0012–.0024	.0020–.0035	.315	.315
	2300 ②	.010	.010	—	—	1.933	61 @ 1.591	.0012–.0024	.0020–.0035	.315	.315
	2600 ③	.006 ①	.010	45	45	1.870	62 @ 1.591	.0012–.0024	.0020–.0035	.315	.315
	2600 ④	.006 ①	.010	45	45	1.870	62 @ 1.591	.0012–.0024	.0020–.0035	.315	.315
1984	1800 ④	.006 ⑤	.010	45	45	1.870	62 @ 1.591	.0012–.0024	.0020–.0035	.315	.315
	2000	.006 ⑤	.010	45	45	1.870	62 @ 1.591	.0012––.0024	.0020–.0035	.315	.315
	2300 ②	.010	.010	—	—	1.933	61 @ 1.591	.0012––.0024	.0020–.0035	.315	.315
	2600 ③	.006 ⑤	.010	45	45	1.870	62 @ 1.591	.0012–.0024	.0020–.0035	.315	.315
	2600 ④	.006 ⑤	.010	45	45	1.870	62 @ 1.591	.0012–.0024	.0020–.0035	.315	.315
1985	1500 ③	.006 ⑤	.010	45	45	1.756	53 @ 1.469	.0012–.0024	.0020–.0035	.315	.315
	1600 ④	.006 ⑤	.010	45	45	1.823	62 @ 1.469	.0012–.0024	.0020–.0035	.315	.315
	1800 ④	.006 ⑤	.010	45	45	1.870	61 @ 1.591	.0012–.0024	.0020–.0035	.315	.315
	2000 ③	Hydraulic ⑤		45	45	1.960	72 @ 1.591	.0012–.0024	.0020–.0035	.315	.315
	2300 ②	.010	.010	—	—	1.933	61 @ 1.591	.0012–.0024	.0020–.0035	.315	.315
	2400 ④	Hydraulic ⑤		45	45	1.961	72 @ 1.591	.0012–.0024	.0020–.0035	.322	.315
	2600 ③	Hydraulic ⑤		45	45	1.961	72 @ 1.591	.0012–.0024	.0020–.0035	.315	.315
	2600 ④	.006 ⑤	.010	45	45	1.870	62 @ 1.591	.0012–.0024	.0020–.0035	.315	.315
1986	1500 ③	.006 ⑤	.010	45	45	1.756	53 @ 1.469	.0012–.0024	.0020–.0035	.315	.315
	1600 ④	.006 ⑤	.010	45	45	1.823	62 @ 1.469	.0012–.0024	.0020–.0035	.315	.315
	1800 ④	Hydraulic ⑤		45	45	1.870	61 @ 1.591	.0012–.0024	.0020–.0035	.315	.315
	2000 ③	Hydraulic ⑤		45	45	1.960	72 @ 1.591	.0012–.0024	.0020–.0035	.315	.315
	2400 ④	Hydraulic ⑤		45	45	1.961	72 @ 1.591	.0012–.0024	.0020–.0035	.322	.315
	2600 ③	Hydraulic ⑤		45	45	1.961	72 @ 1.591	.0012–.0024	.0020–.0035	.315	.315
	2600 ④	Hydraulic ⑤		45	45	1.961	27 @ 1.591	.0012–.0024	.0020–.0035	.315	.315

Continued

VALVE SPECIFICATIONS—Continued

Year	Engine	Valve Lash		Valve Angles		Valve Spring Free Height	Valve Spring Pressure Lbs. @ In.	Stem Clearance		Stem Diameter	
		Int. (hot)	Exh. (hot)	Seat	Face			Intake	Exhaust	Intake	Exhaust
1987	1500③	.006⑤	.010	44	45	1.756	53 @ 1.469	.0008-.0020	.0020-.0035	.260	.260
	1600④	.006⑤	.010	45	45	1.807	62 @ 1.469	.0012-.0024	.0020-.0035	.315	.315
	1800④	Hydraulic ⑤		45	45	1.870	61 @ 1.591	.0012-.0024	.0020-.0035	.315	.315
	2000③	Hydraulic ⑤		45	45	1.960	72 @ 1.591	.0012-.0024	.0020-.0035	.315	.315
	2400④	Hydraulic ⑤		45	45	1.961	72 @ 1.591	.0012-.0024	.0020-.0035	.322	.315
	2600③	Hydraulic ⑤		45	45	1.961	72 @ 1.591	.0012-.0024	.0020-.0035	.315	.315
	2600④	Hydraulic ⑤		45	45	1.961	27 @ 1.591	.0012-.0024	.0020-.0035	.315	.315

①—Jet valve lash .006 inch.
②—Turbocharged diesel engine.
③—Carbureted engine.
④—Turbocharged fuel injected engine.
⑤—Jet valve lash .010 inch.

Pistons, Pins, Rings, Crankshaft & Bearings

Year	Engine	Piston Clearance Top of Skirt	Ring end Gap		Wristpin Diameter	Rod Bearings		Main Bearings			
			Comp.	Oil		Shaft Diameter	Bearing Clearance	Shaft Diameter	Bearing Clearance	Thrust on Bear. No.	Shaft End Play
1983	1800	.0008-.0016	②	.014	—	1.772	.0008-.0020	2.244	.0008-.0020	3	.002-.007
	2000	.0008-.0016	②	.014	—	1.772	.0008-.0020	2.244	.0008-.0020	3	.002-.007
	2300④	.0016-.0024	.013	.014	—	2.087	.0008-.0024	.598	.0008-.0020	3	.0008-.0020
	2600⑤	.0008-.0016	.013	.018	—	2.087	.0008-.0024	2.362	.0008-.0020	3	.002-.007
	2600⑥	.0008-.0016	③	.022	—	2.087	.0008-.0024	2.362	.0008-.0020	3	.002-.007
1984	1800⑥	.0008-.0016	.015	.011	—	1.772	.0008-.0020	2.244	.0008-.0020	3	.002-.007
	2000	.0008-.0016	.014	.012	—	1.772	.0008-.0020	2.244	.0008-.0020	3	.002-.007
	2300④	.0016-.0024	.013	.014	—	2.087	.0008-.0024	2.598	.0008-.0020	3	.0008-.0020
	2600⑤	.0008-.0016	⑦	.018	—	2.087	.0008-.0024	2.362	.0008-.0020	3	.002-.007
	2600⑥	.0008-.0016	③	.022	—	2.087	.0008-.0024	2.362	.0008-.0020	3	.002-.007
1985	1500⑤	.0008-.0016	.008	.008	—	1.6535	.0004-.0024	1.8898	.0008-.0028	3	.002-.007
	1600⑥	.0008-.0016	⑧	.008	—	1.7717	.0004-.0024	2.2441	.0008-.0028	3	.002-.007
	1800⑥	.0008-.0016	⑨	.008	—	1.772	.0008-.0020	2.244	.0008-.0020	3	.002-.007
	2000⑤	.0008-.0016	⑧	.008	—	1.772	.0008-.0020	2.244	.0008-.0020	3	.002-.007
	2300④	.0016-.0024	.010	.010	—	2.087	.0008-.0024	2.598	.0008-.0020	3	.0008-.0020
	2400⑪	.0008-.0016	⑧	.008	—	1.772	.0008-.0020	2.244	.0008-.0020	3	.002-.007
	2600⑤	.0008-.0016	⑩	.012	—	2.087	.0008-.0024	2.362	.0008-.0020	3	.002-.007
	2600⑥	.0008-.0016	⑩	.012	—	2.087	.0008-.0024	2.362	.0008-.0020	3	.002-.007
1986	1500⑤	.0008-.0016	.008	.008	—	1.6535	.0004-.0024	1.8898	.0008-.0028	3	.002-.007
	1600⑥	.0008-.0016	⑧	.008	—	1.7717	.0004-.0024	2.2441	.0008-.0028	3	.002-.007
	1800⑥	.0008-.0016	⑨	.008	—	1.772	.0008-.0020	2.244	.0008-.0028	3	.002-.007
	2000⑤	.0008-.0016	⑧	.008	—	1.772	.0008-.0020	2.244	.0008-.0028	3	.002-.007
	2400⑪	.0008-.0016	⑧	.008	—	1.772	.0008-.0020	2.244	.0008-.0028	3	.002-.007
	2600⑤	.0008-.0016	⑩	.012	—	2.087	.0008-.0024	2.362	.0008-.0020	3	.002-.007
	2600⑥	.0008-.0016	⑩	.012	—	2.087	.0008-.0024	2.362	.0008-.0020	3	.002-.007
1987	1500⑤	.0008-.0016	.008	.008	—	1.6535	.0008-.0024	1.6535	.0008-.0028	3	.002-.007
	1600⑥	.0012-.0019	⑧	.008	—	1.7717	.0008-.0019	2.244	.0008-.0019	3	.002-.007
	1800⑥	.0008-.0016	⑨	.008	—	1.772	.0008-.0020	2.244	.0008-.0020	3	.002-.007
	2000⑤	.0004-.0012	⑧	.008	—	1.7717	.0008-.0020	2.244	.0008-.0020	3	.002-.007
	2400⑪	.0008-.0016	⑧	.008	—	1.7717	.0008-.0020	2.244	.0008-.0020	3	.002-.007
	2600⑤	.0008-.0016	⑩	.012	—	2.087	.0008-.0020	2.362	.0008-.0020	3	.002-.007
	2600⑥	.0008-.0016	⑩	.012	—	2.087	.0008-.0020	2.362	.0008-.0020	3	.002-.007

Continued

PISTONS, PINS, RINGS, CRANKSHAFT & BEARINGS—Continued

①—Fit rings in tapered bores for clearance listed in tightest portion of ring travel.
②—Top ring, .014 inch; second ring, .012 inch.
③—Top ring, .016 inch; second ring, .013 inch.
④—Turbocharged diesel engine.
⑤—Carbureted engine.
⑥—Turbocharged fuel injected engine.
⑦—Top ring, .015 inch; second ring, .0125 inch.
⑧—Top ring, .010 inch; second ring, .008 inch.
⑨—Top ring, .012 inch; second ring, .008 inch.
⑩—Top ring, .012 inch; second ring, .010 inch.
⑪—Fuel injected engine.

Engine Tightening Specifications

*Torque specifications are for clean and lightly lubricated threads only. Dry to dirty threads produce increased friction which prevents accurate measurement of tightness.

Year	Engine	Spark Plugs Ft. Lbs.	Cylinder Head Bolts Ft. Lbs.	Intake Manifold Ft. Lbs.	Exhaust Manifold Ft. Lbs.	Camshaft Bearing Caps Ft. Lbs.	Camshaft Sprocket Bolts Ft. Lbs.	Rocker Arm Nuts Ft. Lbs.	Rocker Arm Cover Ft. Lbs.	Connecting Rod Cap Bolts Ft. Lbs.	Main Bearing Cap Bolts Ft. Lbs.	Flywheel To Crankshaft Ft. Lbs.	Vibration Damper or Pulley Ft. Lbs.
1983	1800	15–21	⑦	11–14	11–14	14–15	59–72	—	4–5	33–34	37–39	94–101	11–15
	2000	15–21	⑦	11–14	11–14	14–15	59–72	—	4–5	33–34	37–39	94–101	11–15
	2300②	—	⑧	11–14	11–14	14–15	47–54	③	4–5	33–34	55–61	94–101	123–137
	2600④	15–21	⑥	11–14	11–14	14–15	7–43	—	4–5	33–34	55–61	94–101	80–94
	2600⑤	15–21	⑥	11–14	11–14	14–15	37–43	—	4–5	33–34	55–61	94–101	80–94
1984	1800⑤	15–21	⑦	11–14	11–14	14–15	59–72	—	4–5	33–34	37–39	94–101	11–15
	2000	15–21	⑦	11–14	11–14	14–15	59–72	—	4–5	33–34	37–39	94–101	11–15
	2300②	—	⑧	11–14	11–14	14–15	47–54	③	4–5	33–34	55–61	94–101	123–137
	2600④	15–21	⑥	11–14	11–14	14–15	37–43	—	4–5	33–34	55–61	94–101	80–94
	2600⑤	15–21	⑥	11–14	11–14	14–15	37–43	—	4–5	33–34	55–61	94–101	80–94
1985	1500④	15–21	①	11–14	11–14	—	47–54	15–19	1–1.5	24–25	37–39	94–101	37–43
	1600⑤	15–21	①	11–14	11–14	14–15	44–57	—	4–5	24–25	37–39	94–101	44–50
	1800⑤	—	⑦	11–14	11–14	14–15	59–72	—	4–5	33–34	37–39	94–101	11–15
	2000④	15–21	⑦	11–14	11–14	14–15	59–72	—	4–5	33–34	37–39	94–101	11–15
	2300②	—	⑧	11–14	11–14	14–15	47–54	25–28	4–5	33–34	55–61	94–101	123–137
	2400⑨	—	⑦	11–14	11–14	14–15	59–72	—	4–5	33–34	37–39	94–101	11–15
	2600④	15–21	⑥	11–14	11–14	14–15	37–43	—	4–5	33–34	55–61	94–101	80–94
	2600⑤	15–21	⑥	11–14	11–14	14–15	37–43	—	4–5	33–34	55–61	94–101	80–94
1986	1500④	15–21	①	11–14	11–14	—	47–54	15–19	1–1.5	24–25	37–39	94–101	9–10
	1600⑤	15–21	①	11–14	11–14	14–15	59–72	—	4–5	24–25	37–39	94–101	11–13
	1800⑤	—	⑦	11–14	11–14	14–15	59–72	9–13	3.7–5	37–38	37–39	94–101	15–21
	2000④	—	⑦	11–14	11–14	14–15	59–72	9–13	3.7–5	37–38	37–39	94–101	15–21
	2400⑨	—	⑦	11–14	11–14	14–15	59–72	9–13	3.7–5	37–38	37–39	94–101	15–21
	2600④	—	⑥	11–14	11–14	14–15	37–43	9–13	4–5	33–34	55–61	94–101	80–94
	2600⑤	—	⑥	11–14	11–14	14–15	37–43	9–13	4–5	33–34	55–61	94–101	80–94
1987	1500④	15–22	①	11–14	11–14	—	47–54	15–19	1–1.5	24–25	37–39	94–101	9–10
	1600⑤	15–21	①	11–14	11–14	14–15	59–72	—	4–5	24–25	37–39	94–101	11–13
	1800⑤	—	⑦	11–14	11–14	14–15	59–72	9–13	3.7–5	37–38	37–39	94–101	15–21
	2000④	15–21	⑦	11–14	11–14	14–15	59–72	9–13	3.7–5	37–38	37–39	94–101	15–21
	2400⑨	15–21	⑦	11–14	11–14	14–15	59–72	9–13	3.7–5	37–38	37–39	94–101	15–21
	2600④	15–21	⑥	11–14	11–14	14–15	37–43	9–13	4–5	33–34	55–61	94–101	80–94
	2600⑤	15–21	⑥	11–14	11–14	14–15	37–43	9–13	4–5	33–34	55–61	94–101	80–94

①—Engine cold, 51–54 ft. lbs.; engine hot, 58–61 ft. lbs.
②—Turbocharged diesel engine.
③—Rocker arm shaft bolts, 25–28 ft. lbs.
④—Carbureted engine.
⑤—Turbocharged fuel injected engine.
⑥—With engine cold, torque to 65–72 ft. lbs.; with engine hot, torque to 73–79 ft. lbs. Torque the two bolts located at front of cylinder head (forward of camshaft gear & timing chain) to 11–15 ft. lbs.
⑦—Engine cold, 65–72 ft. lbs.; engine hot, 73–79 ft. lbs.
⑧—Engine cold, 76–83 ft. lbs.; engine hot, 84–90 ft. lbs.
⑨—Fuel injected engine.

Brake Specifications

Year	Model	Drum Brake I.D.	Wheel Cylinder Bore			Master Cylinder Bore	Disc Brake Rotor				
			Front Disc	Rear Disc	Rear Drum		Nominal Thickness		Min. Thickness		Runout (T.I.R.)
							Front	Rear	Front	Rear	
1983	Cordia, Tredia	8	2.000	—	.690	.870	.510	—	.450	—	.006
	Starion	—	2.250	1.630	—	.940	—	—	.880	.650	.006
	Pickup①	9.5	2.125	—	.750	.875	.790	—	.720	—	.006
	Pickup②	10	2.125	—	.813	.875	.790	—	.720	—	.006
	Montero	10	2.120	—	.810	.870	.790	—	.720	—	.006
1984	Cordia, Tredia	8	2.120	—	.690	.870	.710	—	.650	—	.006
	Starion	—	2.250	1.630	—	.940	—	—	.880	.650	.006
	Pickup①	9.5	2.125	—	.750	.875	.790	—	.720	—	.006
	Pickup②	10	2.125	—	.813	.875	.790	—	.720	—	.006
	Montero	10	2.120	—	.810	.870	.790	—	.720	—	.006
1985	Cordia, Tredia	8	2.120	—	.690	.870	.710	—	.650	—	.006
	Galant③	8	2.120	—	.690	.940	.940	—	.650	—	.006
	Galant④	—	2.120	1.190	—	.940	.940	.400	.650	.330	.006
	Mirage⑤	7.1	2.010	—	.750	.810	.512	—	—	—	.006
	Mirage⑥	7.1	2.120	—	.750	.870	.709	—	.650	—	.006
	Montero	10	2.120	—	.810	.870	.790	—	.720	—	.006
	Pickup①	9.5	2.125	—	.750	.875	.790	—	.720	—	.006
	Pickup②	10	2.125	—	.813	.875	.790	—	.720	—	.006
	Starion	—	2.250	1.630	—	.940	—	—	.880	.650	.006
1986	Cordia, Tredia⑤	8	2.120	—	.690	.870	.710	—	.650	—	.006
	Cordia, Tredia⑥	8	2.120	—	.690	.870	.940	—	.880	—	.006
	Galant③	8	2.120	—	.690	.880	.940	—	.880	—	.006
	Galant④	—	2.120	1.190	—	.880	.940	.400	.880	.330	.006
	Mirage⑤	7.1	2.010	—	.750	.810	.512	—	.450	—	.006
	Mirage⑥	7.1	2.120	—	.750	.870	.709	—	.650	—	.006
	Montero	10	2.120	—	.810	.870	.790	—	.720	—	.006
	Pickup⑦	9.49	2.125	—	.750	.875	.790	—	.720	—	.006
	Pickup⑧	9.99	2.125	—	.813	.875	.790	—	.720	—	.006
	Starion	—	2.250	1.630	—	.940	—	—	.880	.650	.006
1987	Cordia, Tredia⑤	8	2.120	—	.690	.870	.710	—	.650	—	.006
	Cordia, Tredia⑥	8	2.120	—	.690	.870	.940	—	.880	—	.006
	Galant③	8	2.120	—	.690	.880	.940	—	.880	—	.006
	Galant④	—	2.120	1.190	—	.880	.940	.400	.880	.330	.006
	Mirage⑤	7.1	2.010	—	.750	.810	.512	—	.450	—	.006
	Mirage⑥	7.1	2.120	—	.750	.870	.709	—	.650	—	.006
	Montero	10	2.120	—	.810	.870	.790	—	.720	—	.006
	Pickup⑦	9.49	2.125	—	.750	.875	.790	—	.720	—	.006
	Pickup⑧	9.99	2.125	—	.813	.875	.790	—	.720	—	.006
	Precis	7.1	2.01	—	7.1	.810	.512	—	—	—	—
	Starion	—	2.250	1.630	—	.940	—	—	.880	.650	.006

①—Less diesel engine.
②—With diesel engine.
③—Models less 4 wheel disc brakes.
④—Models with 4 wheel disc brakes.
⑤—Models less turbo engine.
⑥—Models with turbo engine.
⑦—Models less 4 wheel drive.
⑧—Models with 4 wheel drive.

Front Wheel Alignment Specifications

Year	Model	Caster Angle, Degrees		Camber Angle, Degrees				Toe-in Inch	King Pin Inclination
				Limits		Desired			
		Limits	Desired	Left	Right	Left	Right		
1983	Cordia, Tredia	—	4/5	—	—	5/12	5/12	①	—
	Starion	—	5 1/3	—	—	0	0	②	—
	Pickup③	1½ to 3½	2½	½ to 1½	1	1	.08 to .35	8°	
	Pickup④	1 to 3	2	½ to 1½	½ to 1½	1	1	.08 to .35	8°
	Montero	2 5/16-3 5/12	2 11/12	½ to 1½	½ to 1½	1	1	.08 to .35	8°
1984	Cordia, Tredia	—	4/5	—	—	5/12	5/12	⑤	—
	Starion	—	5 1/3	—	—	0	0	②	—
	Pickup③	1½ to 3½	2½	½ to 1½	1	1	.08 to .35	8°	
	Pickup④	1 to 3	2	½ to 1½	½ to 1½	1	1	.08 to .35	8°
	Montero	2 5/16-3 5/12	2 11/12	½ to 1½	½ to 1½	1	1	.08 to .35	8°
1985	Cordia, Tredia	—	4/5	—	—	5/12	5/12	⑤	—
	Galant	1/6 to 1 1/16	½	0 to 1	0 to 1	½	½	⑤	—
	Mirage	13/60 to 1 13/60	43/60	−½ to +½	0	0	⑤	—	
	Montero	2 5/16 to 3 5/12	2 11/12	½ to 1½	½ to 1½	1	1	.08 to .35	8°
	Pickup③	1½ to 3½	2½	½ to 1½	½ to 1½	1	1	.08 to .35	8°
	Pickup④	1 to 3	2	½ to 1½	½ to 1½	1	1	.08 to .35	8°
	Starion	—	5 1/13	—	—	0	0	②	—
1986	Cordia, Tredia	3/10 to 1 3/10	4/5	−1/12 to +11/12	−1/12 to +11/12	+5/12	+5/12	⑤	—
	Galant	1/6 to 1 1/16	2/3	0 to 1	0 to 1	½	½	⑤	—
	Mirage	13/60 to 1 13/60	43/60	−½ to +½	−½ to +½	0	0	⑤	—
	Montero	2 9/20 to 3 9/20	2 19/20	½ to 1½	½ to 1½	1	1	.08 to .35	8°
	Pickup③	1½ to 3½	2½	½ to 1½	½ to 1½	1	1	.08 to .35	8°
	Pickup④	1½ to 3½	2½	1 to 3	1 to 3	2	2	.08 to .35	8°
	Starion	—	5 5/6	—	—	−½	−½	0	—
1987	Cordia, Tredia	3/10 to 1 3/10	4/5	−1/12 to +11/12	−1/12 to +11/12	+5/12	+5/12	⑤	—
	Galant	1/6 to 1 1/16	2/3	0 to 1	0 to 1	½	½	⑤	—
	Mirage ⑥	½ to 1½	1	−½ to +½	−½ to +½	0	0	⑤	—
	Mirage ⑦	1 1/16 to 2 1/16	1 2/3	−½ to +½	−½ to +½	0	0	⑤	—
	Montero	2 9/20 to 3 9/20	2 19/20	½ to 1½	½ to 1½	1	1	.08 to .35	8°
	Pickup③	1½ to 3½	2½	½ to 1½	½ to 1½	1	1	.08 to .35	8°
	Pickup④	1½ to 3½	2½	1 to 3	1 to 3	2	2	.08 to .35	8°
	Precis	½ to 1 1/6	5/6	0 to 1	0 to 1	½	½	-.08 to +.16	12 21/30°
	Starion	—	5 5/6	—	—	−½	−½	0	—

①—.06 toe-out to .06 toe-in.
②—.08 toe-out to .20 toe-in.
③—Exc. four wheel drive models.
④—Four wheel drive models.
⑤—.12 toe-out to .12 toe-in.
⑥—Models less power steering.
⑦—Models with power steering.

Rear Wheel Alignment Specifications

Year	Model	Camber Angle, Degrees		Toe-In, Inches
		Limits	Desired	
1983–85	Cordia, Tredia	−⅔ to ⅔	0	—
	Starion	−⅓ to +⅓	0	−.08 to +.08
1985	Mirage	—	−⅔	—
1986	Cordia, Tredia	—	+⅔	—
	Galant	—	0	0
	Mirage	—	−⅔	0
	Montero	—	3.1 inch	—
	Pickup	—	①	—
	Starion	—	0	−.08 to +.08
1987	Cordia, Tredia	—	+⅔	—
	Galant	—	0	0
	Mirage	—	−⅔	0
	Montero	—	0	0
	Pickup	—	0	0
	Precis	−⅙ to −1⅙	−⅔	—
	Starion	—	0	−.08 to +.08

①—Models less four wheel drive, −.24 inch; models with four wheel drive, +.16 inch.

Drive Axle Specifications

Year	Model	Carrier Type	Ring Gear & Pinion Backlash		Pinion Bearing Preload			Differential Bearing Preload	
			Method	Adjustment	Method	With Seal Inch-Lbs.	Less Seal Inch-Lbs.	Method	Adjustment
1983–84	Starion	Removable	Shims	.004–.006	Shims	9–11	6–9	Shims	⑤
	Pickup①	Removable	④	.005–.007	Shims	9–11	6–9	④	—
	Pickup②	Removable③	Shims	.005–.007	Shims	9–11	6–9	Shims	⑤
	Montero①	Removable	④	.005–.007	Shims	9–11	6–9	④	—
	Montero②	Removable③	Shims	.005–.007	Shims	9–11	6–9	Shims	⑤
1985	Montero①	Removable	④	.005–.006	Shims	9–11	6–9	④	—
	Montero②	Removable③	Shims	.005–.007	Shims	9–11	6–9	Shims	⑤
	Pickup①	Removable	④	.005–.007	Shims	9–11	6–9	④	—
	Pickup②	Removable③	Shims	.005–.007	Shims	9–11	6–9	Shims	⑤
	Starion	Removable	Shims	.004–.006	Shims	3–3.9	1.3–2.2	Shims	⑤
1986	Montero①	Removable	④	.005–.006	Shims	5.6–6.5	3.8–4.8	④	—
	Montero②	Removable③	Shims	.005–.006	Shims	3.0–3.9	1.3–2.2	Shims	⑤
	Pickup①	Removable	④	.005–.006	Shims	5.6–6 6.5	3.5–4.3	④	—
	Pickup②	Removable③	Shims	.004–.006	Shims	3.0–3.9	1.3–4.8	Shims	⑤
	Starion⑥	Removable	Shims	.004–.006	Shims	3–3.9	1.3–2.2	Shims	⑤
	Starion⑦	Removable	Shims	.005–.007	Shims	3.5–4.3	1.3–2.2	Shims	⑤

Continued

DRIVE AXLE SPECIFICATIONS—Continued

Year	Model	Carrier Type	Ring Gear & Pinion Backlash		Pinion Bearing Preload			Differential Bearing Preload	
			Method	Adjustment	Method	With Seal Inch-Lbs.	Less Seal Inch-Lbs.	Method	Adjustment
1987	Montero①	Removable	④	.005-.006	Shims	5.6-6.5	3.8-4.8	④	—
	Montero②	Removable③	Shims	.005-.006	Shims	3.0-3.9	1.3-2.2	Shims	⑤
	Pickup①	Removable	④	.005-.006	Shims	5.6-6.5	3.5-4.3	④	—
	Pickup②	Removable③	Shims	.004-.006	Shims	3.0-3.9	1.3-4.8	Shims	⑤
	Starion⑧	Removable	Shims	.004-.006	Shims	3-3.9	1.3-2.2	Shims	⑤
	Starion⑨	Removable	Shims	.005-.007	Shims	3.5-4.3	1.3-2.2	Shims	⑤

①—Rear axle.
②—Front axle.
③—Axle tubes can be removed from differential carrier.
④—Adjustment is obtained by loosening or tightening the differential side bearing adjusting nut.
⑤—Zero clearance plus .002 inch installed on both sides of differential case.
⑥—Less intercooler.
⑦—With intercooler.
⑧—Less limited slip differential.
⑨—With limited slip differential.

Cooling System & Capacity Data

Year	Engine	Model	Cooling Capacity Qts.		Radiator Cap Relief Pressure Lbs.	Thermo. Opening Temp °F	Fuel Tank Gals.	Engine Oil Refill Qts. ①	Transmission Oil			Rear Axle Oil Pints	Front Axle Oil Pints
			Less A/C	With A/C					4 Speed Pints	5 Speed Pints	Auto. Trans. Qts. ②		
1983	1800	Cordia, Tredia	7.4	7.4	13	190	13.2	4.2	4.8	4.4	6.1	—	—
	2600③	Starion	9.7	9.7	13	190	19.8	4.5	—	4.8	—	2.7	—
	2000	Pickup④	9.5	9.5	13	190	15.1	4.2	4.4	4.9	7.2	3.2	—
	2000	Pickup⑤	9.5	9.5	13	190	18	5.2	4.6	4.6	7.2	3.2	2.3
	2300⑥	Pickup④	8.5	8.5	13	180	15.1	5	—	4.9	—	3.2	—
	2300⑥	Pickup⑤	8.5	8.5	13	180	18	6.3	—	4.6	—	3.2	2.3
	2600⑦	Pickup④	9.5	9.5	13	190	15.1	5.2	4.4	4.9	7.2	3.2	—
	2600⑦	Pickup⑤	9.5	9.5	13	19-	18	6.1	4.6	4.6	7.2	3.2	2.3
	2600⑦	Montero	8.5	8.5	13	190	15.9	6.1	—	4.6	7.2	3.8	2.3
1984	1800③	Cordia, Tredia	7.4	7.4	13	190	13.2	4.2	4.9	4.9	6.1	—	—
	2000°	Cordia, Tredia	7.4	7.4	13	190	13.2	4.2	4.9	4.9	6.1	—	—
	2600③	Starion	9.7	9.7	13	190	19.8	4.5	—	4.8	7.4	2.7	—
	2000	Pickup④	9.5	9.5	13	190	15.1	4.2	4.4	4.9	7.2	3.2	—
	2000	Pickup⑤	9.5	9.5	13	190	18	5.2	4.6	4.6	7.2	3.2	2.3
	2300⑥	Pickup④	8.5	8.5	13	180	15.1	5	—	4.9	—	3.2	—
	2300⑥	Pickup⑤	8.5	8.5	13	180	18	6.3	—	4.6	—	3.2	2.3
	2600⑦	Pickup④	9.5	9.5	13	190	15.1	5.2	4.4	4.9	7.2	3.2	—
	2600⑦	Pickup⑤	9.5	9.5	13	19-	18	6.1	4.6	4.6	7.2	3.2	2.3
	2600⑦	Montero	8.5	8.5	13	190	15.9	6.1	—	4.6	7.2	3.8	2.3
1985	1500⑦	Mirage	5.3	5.3	13	190	11.9	3.2	4.4	4.4	6.1	—	—
	1600③	Mirage	5.3	5.3	13	190	11.9	3.7	4.9	4.9	6.1	—	—
	1800③	Cordia, Tredia	7.7	7.7	13	190	12.8	4.2	4.9	4.9	6.1	—	—
	2000⑦	Cordia, Tredia	7.7	7.7	13	190	12.8	4.2	4.9	4.9	6.1	—	—
	2000⑦	Pickup④	9.5	9.5	13	190	12.8	4.2	4.4	4.9	7.2	3.2	—
	2000⑦	Pickup⑤	9.5	9.5	13	190	12.8	5.2	4.6	4.6	7.2	3.2	2.3
	2300⑥	Pickup④	8.5	8.5	13	180	—	5.0	—	4.9	7.2	3.2	—
	2300⑥	Pickup⑤	8.5	8.5	13	180	—	6.3	—	4.6	7.2	3.2	2.3
	2400⑧	Galant	7.4	7.4	13	190	15.9	4.2	—	—	6.1	—	—
	2600⑦	Montero	8	8.45	13	190	15.9	6.1	—	4.6	7.2	3.8	2.3
	2600⑦	Pickup④	9.5	9.5	13	190	—	5.2	4.4	4.9	7.2	3.2	—
	2600⑦	Pickup⑤	9.5	9.5	13	190	—	6.1	4.6	4.6	7.2	3.2	2.3
	2600③	Starion	9.5	9.5	13	190	19.8	4.5	—	—	7.2	—	—

COOLING SYSTEM & CAPACITY DATA—Continued

Year	Engine	Model	Cooling Capacity Qts. Less A/C	Cooling Capacity Qts. With A/C	Radiator Cap Relief Pressure Lbs.	Thermo. Opening Temp °F	Fuel Tank Gals.	Engine Oil Refill Qts. ①	Transmission Oil 4 Speed Pints	Transmission Oil 5 Speed Pints	Transmission Oil Auto. Trans. Qts. ②	Rear Axle Oil Pints	Front Axle Oil Pints
1986	1500⑦	Mirage	5.3	5.3	13	190	11.9	3.7	4.4	4.4	6.1	—	—
	1600③	Mirage	5.3	5.3	13	190	11.9	4.5	4.9	4.9	6.1	—	—
	1800③	Cordia, Tredia	7.4	7.4	13	190	13.2	4.2	4.9	4.9	6.1	—	—
	2000⑦	Cordia, Tredia	7.4	7.4	13	190	13.2	4.2	4.9	4.9	6.1	—	—
	2000⑦	Pickup④	9.5	9.5	13	190	15.1⑨	4.2	4.4	4.9	7.2	3.2	—
	2000⑦	Pickup⑤	9.5	9.5	13	190	18	4.2	—	4.6	—	3.2	2.3
	2400⑧	Galant	7.4	7.4	13	190	15.9	4.2	—	—	6.1	—	—
	2600⑦	Montero	8.45	8.45	13	190	15.9	6.1	—	4.6	7.2	3.8	2.3
	2600⑦	Pickup④	9.5	9.5	13	190	15.1⑨	5.2	4.4	4.9	7.2	3.2	—
	2600⑦	Pickup⑤	9.5	9.5	13	190	18	5.2	—	4.6	—	3.2	2.3
	2600③	Starion	9.7	9.7	13	190	19.8	5.1	—	4.8	7.4	2.7	—
1987	1500⑦	Mirage	5.3	5.3	13	190	11.9	3.7	4.4	4.4	6.1	—	—
	1500⑦	Precis	5.3	—	13	190	10.6	3.7	2.2	—	4.2	—	—
	1600③	Mirage	5.3	5.3	13	190	11.9	4.5	4.9	4.9	6.1	—	—
	1800③	Cordia, Tredia	7.4	7.4	13	190	13.2	4.2	4.9	4.9	6.1	—	—
	2000⑦	Cordia, Tredia	7.4	7.4	13	190	13.2	4.2	4.9	4.9	6.1	—	—
	2000⑦	Pickup④	9.5	9.5	13	190	15.1⑨	4.2	4.4	4.9	7.2	3.2	—
	2000⑦	Pickup⑤	9.5	9.5	13	190	18	4.2	—	4.6	—	3.2	2.3
	2400⑧	Galant	7.4	7.4	13	190	15.9	4.2	—	—	6.1	—	—
	2600⑦	Montero	8.45	8.45	13	190	15.9	6.1	—	4.6	7.2	3.8	2.3
	2600⑦	Pickup④	9.5	9.5	13	190	15.1⑨	5.2	4.4	4.9	7.2	3.2	—
	2600⑦	Pickup⑤	9.5	9.5	13	190	18	5.2	—	4.6	—	3.2	2.3
	2600③	Starion	9.7	9.7	13	190	19.8	5.1	—	4.8	7.4	2.7	—

①—Includes filter.
②—Approximate, make final check with dipstick.
③—Turbocharged fuel injected engine.
④—Rear wheel drive.
⑤—Four wheel drive.
⑥—Turbocharged diesel engine.
⑦—Carbureted engine.
⑧—Fuel injected engine.
⑨—W/optional tank, 18 gals.

ELECTRICAL SECTION

INDEX

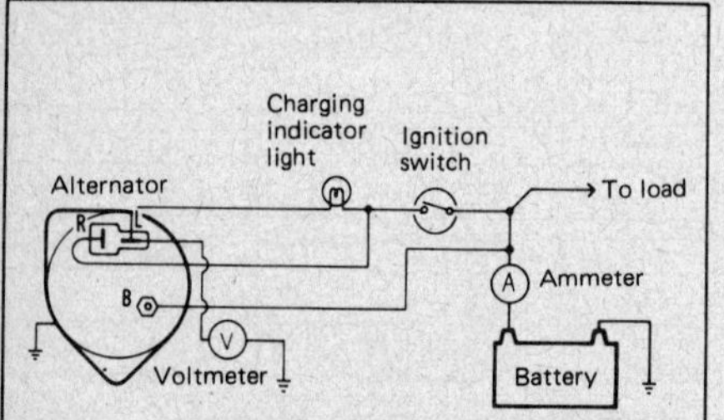

Fig. 1 Test connections for charging voltage test

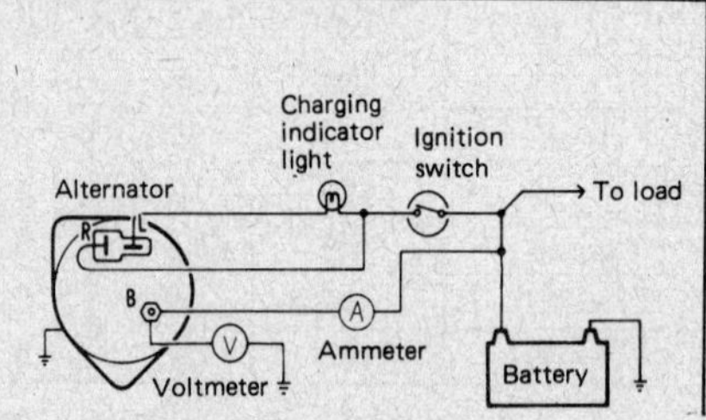

Fig. 2 Test connections for output test

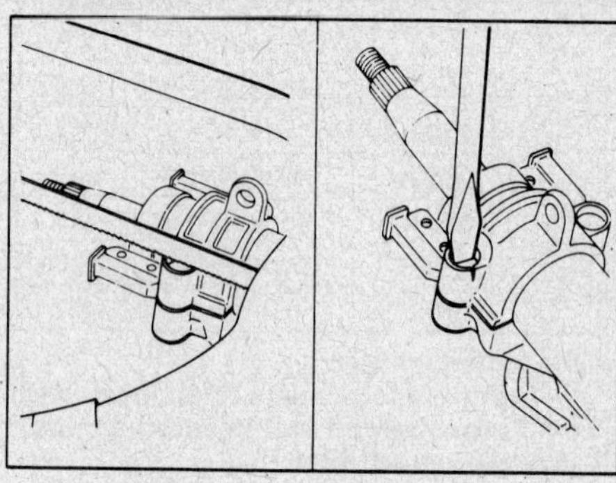

Fig. 3 Ignition lock removal

ALTERNATOR IN-VEHICLE TESTING

CHARGING VOLTAGE TEST

1. With ignition switch in the off position, disconnect battery positive cable and connect an ammeter between cable and battery positive post, **Fig. 1.**
2. Connect a voltmeter between alternator terminal L and ground and check to ensure voltage reading is zero, **Fig. 1.** If a reading or needle deflection is indicated on the voltmeter, either the alternator or alternator wiring is defective.
3. Place ignition switch in the On position and note voltmeter reading. Voltmeter should indicate a reading considerably less than battery voltage. If reading indicates battery voltage, the alternator may be defective.
4. Connect jumper cable between battery positive post and battery positive cable, then start engine. **This will prevent starting current from being applied to ammeter.**
5. Remove jumper cable connected between battery positive post and cable, then increase engine speed to 2000 to 3000 RPM and note ammeter reading. If reading is 5 amps or less, take voltage reading. If reading is above 5 amps, either continue to charge battery until reading drops to 5 amps or less or install a fully charged battery. The charging current may also be limited by installing a 1/4 ohm resistor in series with the battery.
6. Charging voltage should be as listed in the "Alternator Specification Chart."

OUTPUT TEST

1. With ignition switch in the off position, disconnect battery ground cable.
2. Disconnect wire from terminal B of alternator, then connect an ammeter between battery ground cable and alternator B terminal, **Fig. 2.**
3. Connect a voltmeter between B terminal and ground, **Fig. 2.**
4. Connect battery ground cable to battery ground post and note voltmeter reading. The voltmeter should indicate battery voltage.
5. Connect a tachometer to engine, then start engine and turn on lights.
6. Operate engine at specified speed and note ammeter reading. Refer to "Alternator Specification Chart."

STARTER REPLACE

REMOVAL

1. Disconnect battery ground cable.
2. Disconnect starter cables.
3. Remove starter mounting bolts and the starter.

INSTALLATION

1. Before mounting starter, clean the mating surfaces of starter and the engine.
2. Install starter and torque mounting bolts to 16-23 ft. lbs.
3. Connect starter cables and battery ground cable.

IGNITION LOCK REPLACE

1. Disconnect battery ground cable.
2. Remove steering column shrouds.

Fig. 4 Instrument cluster upper trim panel screw locations. Cordia

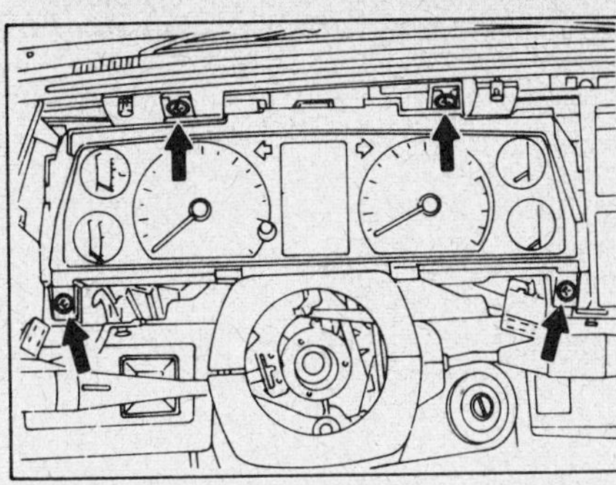

Fig. 5 Instrument cluster mounting screw locations. Cordia

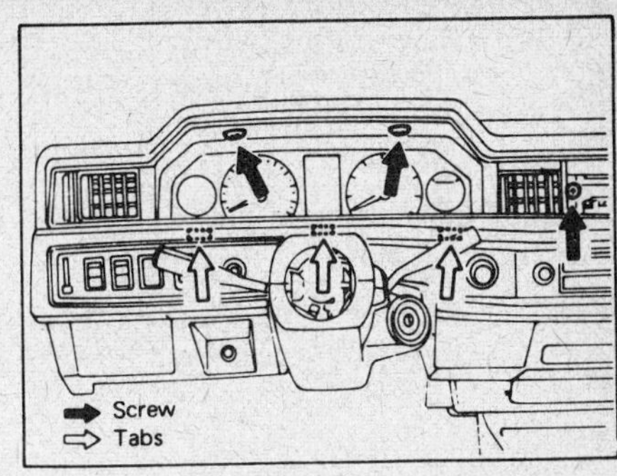

Fig. 6 Instrument cluster upper trim panel screw locations. Tredia

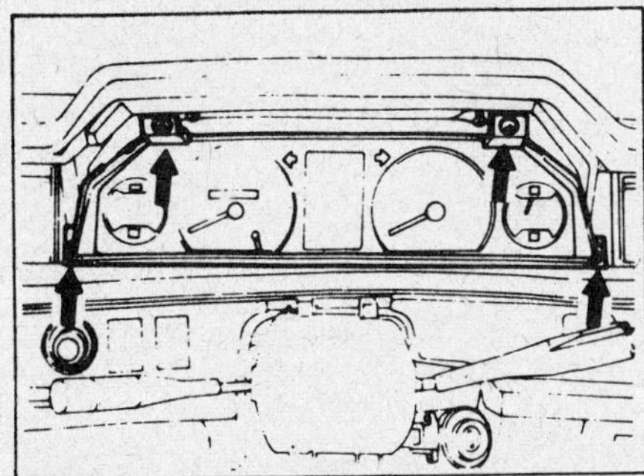

Fig. 7 Instrument cluster mounting screw locations. Tredia

Fig. 8 Instrument cluster upper trim panel screw locations. Starion

Fig. 9 Instrument cluster attaching screw and nut locations. Starion

3. Cut groove in attaching bolt head using a suitable hacksaw, then remove bolts, **Fig. 3.**
4. Remove ignition switch electrical connectors, then the lock assembly.
5. Reverse procedure to install, noting the following:
   a. Temporarily install ignition lock in alignment with column boss and check for proper switch operation.
   b. Steering lock bracket should be replaced when installing new ignition switch.
   c. Install special ignition lock attaching bolts and tighten until heads twist off.

IGNITION SWITCH REPLACE

On Cordia/Tredia models, the ignition switch is an integral part of the lock assembly. For removal procedures, refer to "Ignition Lock, Replace" procedure.

1. Disconnect battery ground cable.
2. Remove column shrouds, then the switch electrical connectors.
3. Remove switch attaching screws, then pull switch from cylinder.
4. Reverse procedure to install.

INSTRUMENT CLUSTER REPLACE

CORDIA

1. Disconnect battery ground cable.
2. Remove horn cover pad, then using suitable steering wheel puller remove steering wheel.
3. Remove instrument panel lower cover attaching screws, then remove cover.
4. Remove floor heat duct then the glove box.
5. Remove left side defroster duct and heater control cables.
6. Remove instrument cluster upper trim panel screws, **Fig. 4.**
7. Disconnect rear window wiper/washer and rear window defroster connectors.
8. Remove instrument cluster upper trim panel.
9. Disconnect speedometer cable from back of instrument cluster.
10. Remove instrument cluster mounting screws, **Fig. 5.**
11. Pull instrument cluster slightly forward to gain access to rear of cluster, then disconnect all electrical connectors.
12. Remove instrument cluster.
13. Reverse procedure to install.

TREDIA

1. Disconnect battery ground cable.
2. Remove horn cover pad, then using suitable wheel puller remove steering wheel.
3. Remove glove box, then the instrument panel under cover.
4. Remove floor heater duct, then the instrument panel lower cover.
5. Remove left side defroster duct and heater control cables.
6. Remove fuse block from instrument panel, then disconnect all instrument panel electrical connectors.
7. Remove heater control panel.
8. Remove trim panel attaching screws, then the trim panel by prying tabs from instrument cluster case, **Fig. 6.**
9. Disconnect speedometer cable from back of instrument cluster.
10. Remove instrument cluster attaching screws, **Fig. 7.**
11. Pull instrument cluster slightly forward to gain access to rear of cluster, then disconnect all electrical connectors.
12. Remove instrument cluster.
13. Reverse procedure to install.

STARION

1. Disconnect battery ground cable.
2. Remove instrument cluster upper trim panel attaching screws, **Fig. 8.**
3. Remove the panel by pulling out both edges of bottom side of upper trim panel. While holding it in position, pull upward to remove panel.
4. Disconnect cluster switch connector on both sides of upper trim panel.
5. Remove instrument cluster attaching screws and nuts, **Fig. 9.**
6. Pull cluster slightly upward and away from mounting, then disconnect speedometer cable and all wire connectors.
7. Remove cluster from dash panel.
8. Reverse procedure to install.

PICKUP

1. Disconnect battery ground cable.
2. Remove control knobs from heater fan switch, heater control and radio knobs and shaft nuts and washers.
3. Remove four instrument cluster bezel

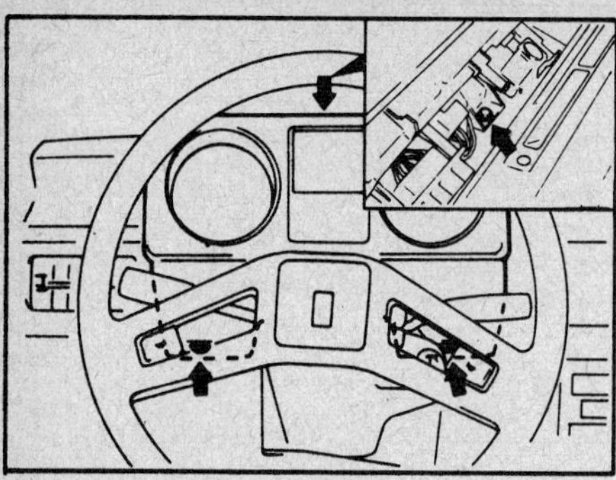

Fig. 10 Instrument cluster mounting screw locations. Montero

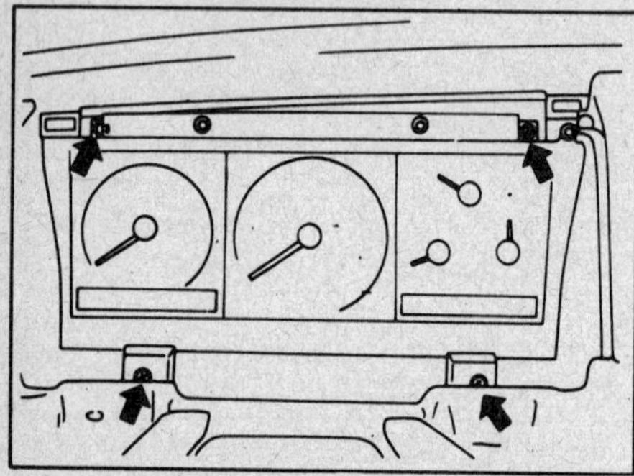

Fig. 13 Instrument cluster attaching screw locations. Mirage

attaching screws, then remove bezel.
4. Remove four instrument cluster attaching screws.
5. Disconnect speedometer cable and all wire connectors from rear of cluster, then remove cluster from instrument panel.
6. Reverse procedure to install.

MONTERO

1. Disconnect battery ground cable.
2. Remove instrument cluster upper trim cover.
3. Remove attaching screws from bottom of instrument cluster, then the attaching bolt from upper part of cluster, **Fig. 10.**
4. Disconnect speedometer cable and all electrical connectors from rear of cluster, **Fig. 11,** then remove cluster.
5. Reverse procedure to install.

MIRAGE

1. Disconnect battery ground cable, remove steering column lower cover.
2. Disconnect headlamp switch and windshield wiper switch electrical connectors.
3. Remove steering column upper cover.
4. Remove instrument cluster hood attaching screws and claws, then remove hood from instrument panel, **Fig. 12.**
5. Remove instrument cluster attaching screws, **Fig. 13,** then pull cluster slightly forward and disconnect speedometer cable and electrical connectors.

Fig. 11 Instrument cluster electrical connectors. Montero

6. Remove cluster from instrument panel.
7. Reverse procedure to install.

GALANT

1. Disconnect battery ground cable.
2. Remove left and right front pillar trims.
3. Remove defroster garnish using a suitable screwdriver in places shown in **Fig. 14.**
4. Disconnect photosensor electrical connector at center of defroster garnish.
5. Remove instrument cluster hood plugs using a suitable screwdriver.
6. Remove instrument cluster hood attaching screws, then the cluster hood.
7. Remove instrument cluster attaching screws, then pull cluster forward and disconnect all electrical connectors.
8. Remove instrument cluster from instrument panel.
9. Reverse procedure to install.

COMBINATION SWITCH REPLACE

1. Disconnect battery ground cable.
2. Remove horn pad, then the steering wheel using suitable puller.
3. Remove steering column shroud. **On vehicles equipped with tilt steering, lower steering column to facilitate shroud removal.**
4. Disconnect switch electrical connectors.
5. On Mirage models, remove switch attaching screws and unbend claws of switch.
6. On all models, remove switch from steering column.
7. Reverse procedure to install.

WING TYPE COLUMN SWITCH REPLACE

GALANT

1. Disconnect battery ground cable.
2. Remove horn pad, then the steering wheel using a suitable puller.
3. Set the tilt position of the steering shaft to the lowest position.
4. Disconnect column switch electrical connectors, then remove the cable

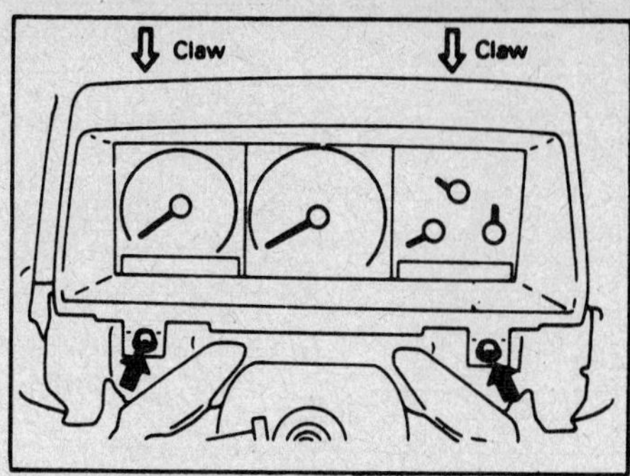

Fig. 12 Removing instrument cluster hood. Mirage

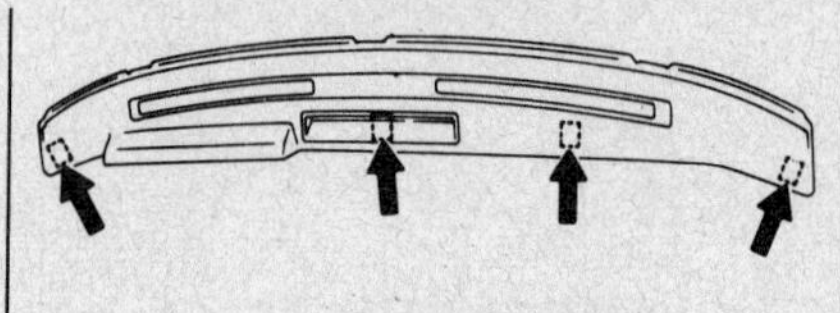

Fig. 14 Removing defroster garnish. Galant

band.
5. Remove column switch attaching screws, then the column switch from steering shaft.
6. Reverse procedure to install.

LIGHT SWITCH REPLACE

EXCEPT GALANT & MIRAGE

Refer to "Combination Switch, Replace" procedure.

GALANT

1. Remove column switch, refer to "Wing Type Column Switch, Replace" procedure.
2. Remove light switch attaching screws, then the switch.
3. Reverse procedure to install.

MIRAGE

1. Disconnect battery ground cable.
2. Remove horn pad, then the steering wheel using a suitable puller.
3. Remove steering column cover.
4. Pull light switch knob from switch.
5. Remove light switch attaching screws, then the switch from the cover.
6. Reverse procedure to install.

INHIBITOR SWITCH REPLACE

PRECIS

1. Place manual control lever in Neutral position, then remove control lever retainer and lever.
2. Disconnect electrical harness, then remove switch retaining bolts and switch assembly.
3. Reverse procedure to install, then adjust as follows:

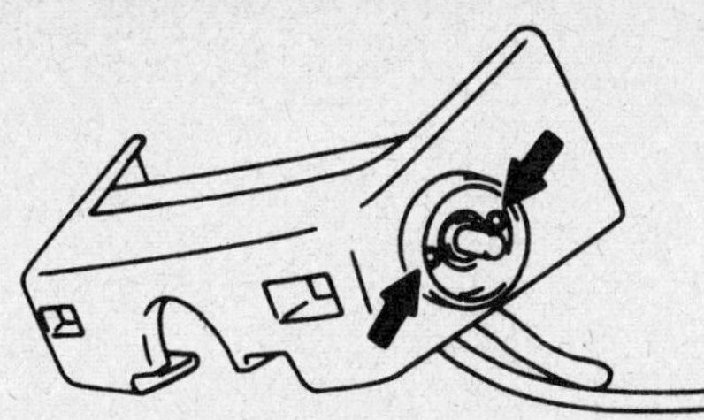

Fig. 15 Windshield wiper switch attaching screw locations. Mirage

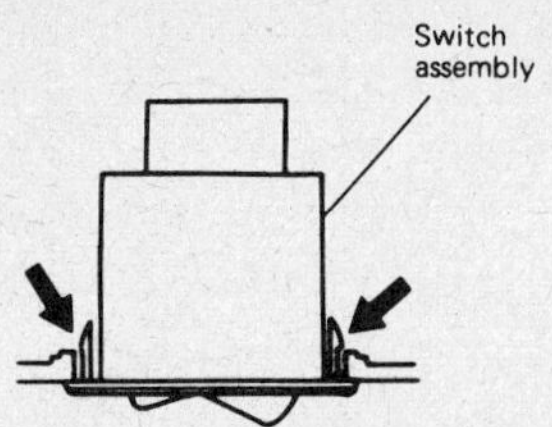

Fig. 16 Rear wiper switch. Cordia & Tredia

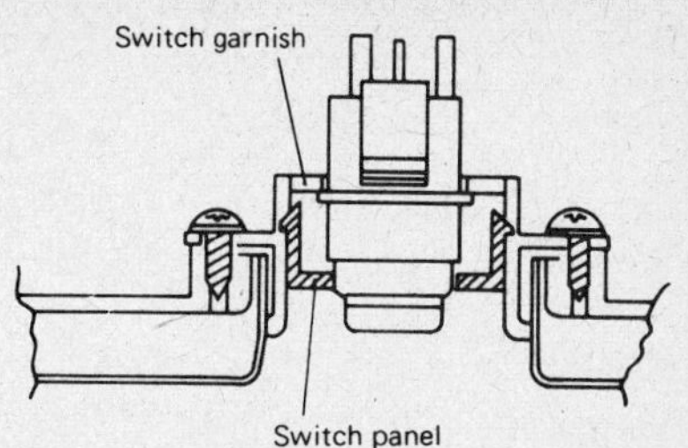

Fig. 17 Rear wiper switch. Starion

Fig. 18 Windshield wiper pivot shaft mounting nuts

a. With manual control lever in neutral position, rotate switch body until wide end of control lever overlaps switch body flange.
b. Hold switch body in position, then torque retaining bolts to 8 ft. lbs.

MALFUNCTION SWITCH

REPLACE

PRECIS

The lighting, dimmer, turn signal/hazard and wiper/washer switches are all incorporated into the malfunction switch assembly.

1. Disconnect battery ground cable.
2. Remove horn button cover, then scribe alignment marks on steering wheel and shaft to facilitate installation.
3. Remove steering wheel, using a suitable puller.
4. Remove steering column trim shroud attaching screws, then the trim shrouds.
5. Remove switch retaining screws, then disconnect switch harness connector.
6. Pull switch assembly from steering column.
7. Reverse procedure to install.

WINDSHIELD WIPER SWITCH

REPLACE

EXCEPT GALANT & MIRAGE

Refer to "Combination Switch, Replace" procedure.

GALANT

1. Remove column switch, refer to "Wing Type Column Switch, Replace" procedure.
2. Remove wiper switch attaching screws, then the wiper switch.
3. Reverse procedure to install.

MIRAGE

1. Disconnect battery ground cable.
2. Remove horn pad, then remove steering wheel using a suitable puller.
3. Remove steering column cover.
4. Pull wiper/washer knob from switch.
5. Remove wiper/washer switch attaching screws, **Fig. 15**, then remove switch from cover.
6. Reverse procedure to install.

REAR WINDOW WIPER SWITCH

REPLACE

CORDIA & TREDIA

1. Disconnect battery ground cable.
2. Remove upper instrument cluster trim panel.
3. Remove switch from trim panel by pressing tabs of switch, **Fig. 16.**
4. Reverse procedure to install.

STARION

1. Disconnect battery ground cable.
2. Remove switch panel from instrument panel.
3. Remove rear wiper and washer switch from switch garnish, **Fig. 17.**
4. Reverse procedure to install.

MONTERO

1. Disconnect battery ground cable.
2. Pry switch from instrument cluster using suitable tool.
3. Disconnect switch electrical connector, then remove switch.
4. Reverse procedure to install.

MIRAGE

Refer to "Windshield Wiper Switch, Replace" procedure.

WINDSHIELD WIPER MOTOR

REPLACE

CORDIA & TREDIA

1. Disconnect battery ground cable.
2. Remove wiper arm and panel covering wiper motor.
3. Remove pivot shaft mounting nuts and push pivot shaft inward, **Fig. 18.**

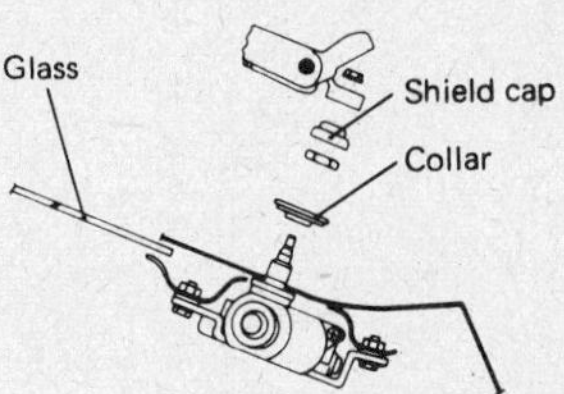

Fig. 19 Typical rear wiper motor installation

4. Remove bolts securing motor bracket to body, then remove wiper motor.
5. Reverse procedure to install.

MONTERO, PICKUP & STARION

1. Disconnect battery ground cable.
2. On Starion and Pickup, remove cover from wiper access hole located on right side front deck.
3. On all models, remove wiper arm, then the arm shaft locknut and push shaft inward.
4. Remove bolts securing motor bracket to body and remove the wiper motor assembly.
5. Reverse procedure to install.

GALANT & MIRAGE

1. Disconnect battery ground cable.
2. Remove wiper arms, then the air inlet and center garnish panels on Mirage or front deck and inlet garnish panels on Galant.
3. Remove pivot shaft attaching nuts, then push pivot shaft inward.
4. Remove wiper motor attaching bolts, then pull wiper motor slightly and disconnect motor and linkage assembly.
5. Remove wiper motor with linkage from vehicle. **Mark position of crank arm to wiper motor, if necessary to remove.**
6. Reverse procedure to install.

PRECIS

1. Disconnect battery ground cable.
2. Remove wiper arm and blade assembly.
3. Remove cowl top cover.
4. Remove linkage assembly attaching nut and washers, then remove linkage assembly.
5. Remove wiper motor attaching bolts, then the wiper motor.
6. Reverse procedure to install. Attach wiper arms as to allow stopping position of wiper blade tip to be 1.2-1.6 inch from bottom of windshield trim.

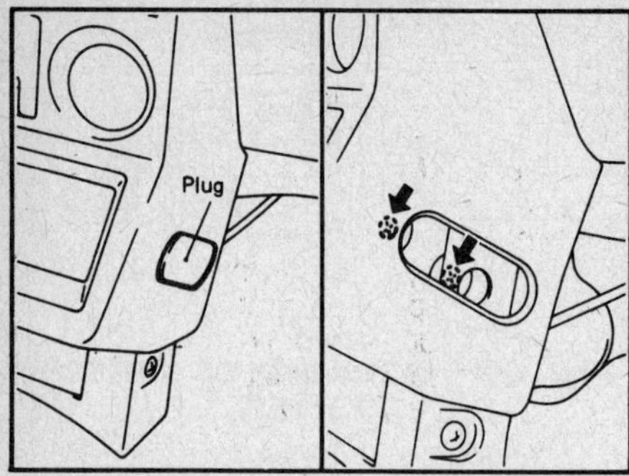

Fig. 20 Center console plug location. 1985–87 Montero

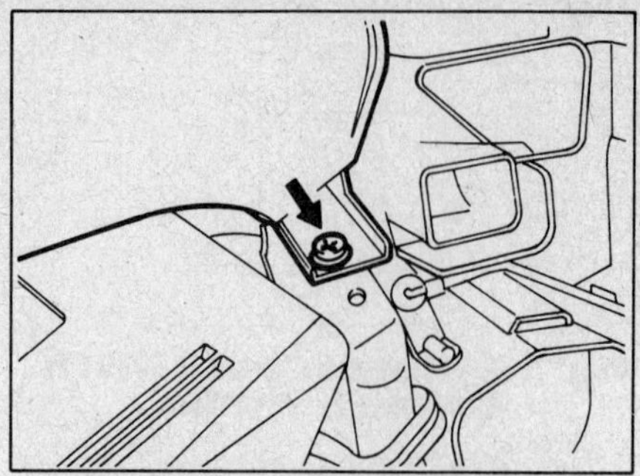

Fig. 21 Console upper attaching screw locations. Cordia & Tredia

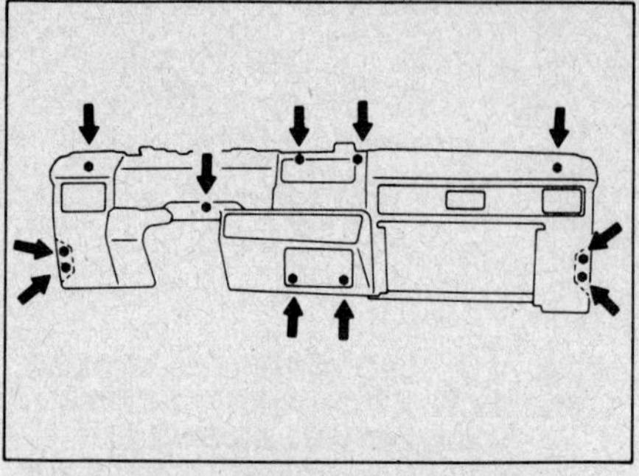

Fig. 22 Dash panel bolt & nut locations. Cordia & Tredia

REAR WINDOW WIPER MOTOR

REPLACE

EXC. PRECIS

1. Disconnect battery ground cable.
2. On Montero, remove spare wheel from back door.
3. On all models, raise wiper arm pivot cover, then remove pivot shaft locking nut.
4. Remove wiper arm and shield cap, **Fig. 19.**
5. Remove nut and collar, **Fig. 19.**
6. Remove hatch trim.
7. Remove rear wiper motor bracket mounting nuts, then remove rear wiper motor assembly from hatch.
8. Reverse procedure to install.

PRECIS

1. Disconnect battery ground cable.
2. Remove rear wiper arm assembly.
3. Remove tailgate trim.
4. Remove wiper motor assembly attaching bolts, then the wiper motor assembly.
5. Reverse procedure to install.

RADIO

REPLACE

The radio fuse box is located on the rear of the radio. If fuse is to be replaced it is necessary to remove the radio.

CORDIA & TREDIA

INSTRUMENT PANEL MOUNTED

1983–84

1. Disconnect battery ground cable.
2. On Tredia models, remove switch panel at right side of steering column.
3. Remove radio knobs and loosen attaching nuts.
4. Remove radio cover panel, then the glove box stopper and glove box.
5. Remove radio adjusting screws, then disconnect antenna lead and electrical connector from rear of radio.
6. Remove radio.
7. Reverse procedure to install.

1985–87

1. Disconnect battery ground cable.
2. Pry off radio panel using a suitable tool.
3. Remove radio attaching screws, then disconnect antenna and radio electrical connector.
4. Remove radio from instrument panel.
5. Reverse procedure to install.

CONSOLE MOUNTED

1. Disconnect battery ground cable.
2. Remove rear console attaching screws, then slide rear console backward.
3. Remove attaching screws from sides of floor console.
4. Disconnect antenna lead and electrical connectors from rear of radio.
5. Remove radio attaching screws, then the radio.
6. Reverse procedure to install.

GALANT

1. Disconnect battery ground cable.
2. Pry off lower part of radio panel using a suitable tool, then remove panel from floor console.
3. Remove radio bracket attaching screws, then disconnect antenna and radio electrical connector.
4. Remove radio from floor console.
5. Reverse procedure to install.

STARION

1. Disconnect battery ground cable.
2. Remove radio control knobs and control shaft nuts, then remove radio trim panel.
3. Remove console side covers from both sides.
4. Remove radio bracket to reinforcement attaching screws.
5. Disconnect antenna lead and feed and speaker wiring from radio, then remove radio.
6. Remove bracket attaching screws, then remove bracket from radio.
7. Reverse procedure to install.

PICKUP

1. Remove instrument cluster bezel. Refer to "Instrument Cluster, Replace."
2. Remove radio bracket attaching screws, then remove radio bracket.
3. Pull radio outward enough to gain access to rear of radio.
4. Disconnect antenna lead wire and electrical connector, then remove radio.
5. Reverse procedure to install.

MONTERO

1. Disconnect battery ground cable.
2. Remove radio control knobs and control shaft nuts, then remove radio trim panel.
3. On 1983-84 models, remove center console, then remove radio bracket attaching screws.
4. On 1985-87 models, remove plug from side of center console, then remove radio bracket attaching screws, **Fig. 20.**
5. Disconnect antenna lead and electrical connectors from rear of radio.
6. Remove radio from instrument panel.
7. Reverse procedure to install.

MIRAGE

1. Disconnect battery ground cable.
2. Remove parking brake cover, then remove ashtray from center console.
3. Remove console to floor attaching screws, then remove console.
4. Remove radio with bracket from console, then remove bracket from radio.
5. Reverse procedure to install.

HEATER CORE

REPLACE

CORDIA & TREDIA

1. Disconnect battery ground cable.
2. Move temperature control lever to Warm position.
3. Remove instrument cluster. Refer to "Instrument Cluster, Replace."
4. Remove both left and right side dash panel side covers.
5. On Cordia, remove fuse block from dash panel, then disconnect fuse block electrical connector.
6. On Tredia, remove defroster trim attaching nut, then pry off trim using suitable tool.
7. On all models, disconnect electrical connector from lower blower case.
8. Remove console upper attaching screws, **Fig. 21.**
9. Remove steering column assembly

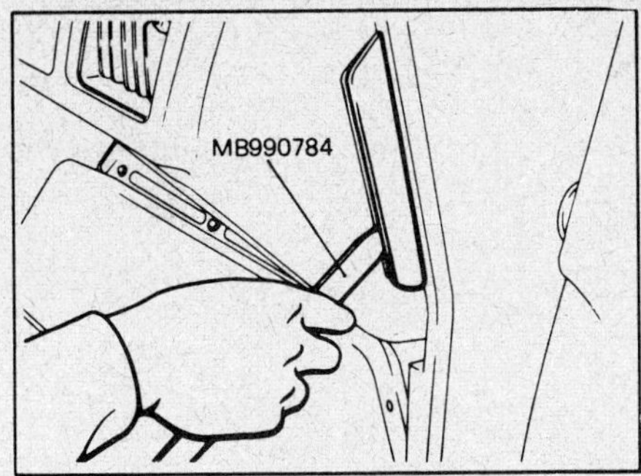

Fig. 23 Removing dash panel side cover. Starion

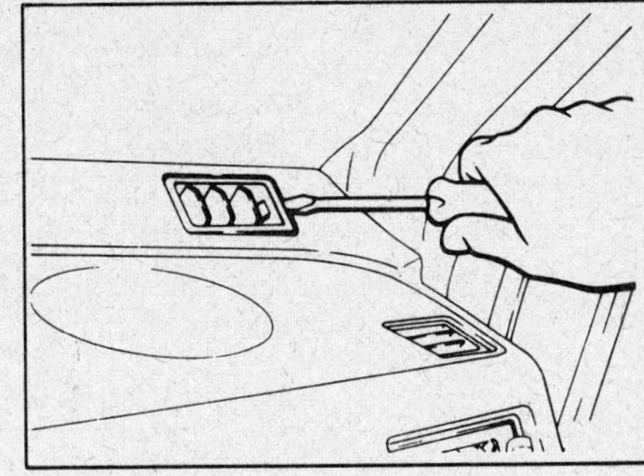

Fig. 24 Removing side defroster grille. Starion

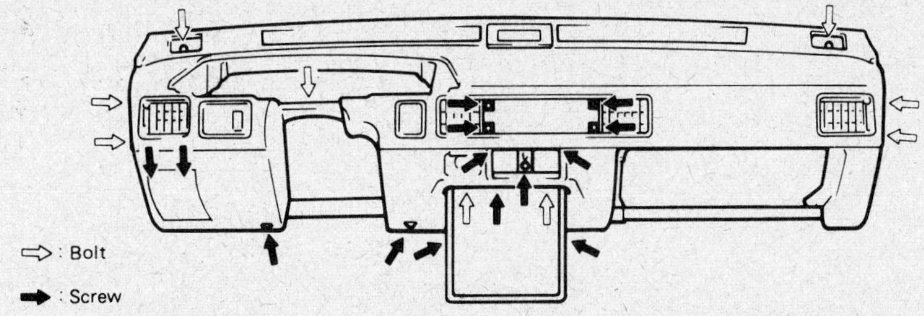

Fig. 25 Dash panel bolt and screw locations. Starion

from pedal support member.

10. Disconnect antenna lead wire from antenna.
11. Remove dash panel bolts and nuts, then remove panel, **Fig. 22.**
12. Disconnect center ventilation duct.
13. Disconnect rear heater duct A, then disconnect heater hose at heater core housing and remove housing.
14. Remove heater core from housing.
15. Reverse procedure to install.

GALANT

1. Disconnect battery ground cable.
2. Move temperature control lever to the WARM position, then drain engine coolant.
3. Remove instrument cluster, refer to "Instrument Cluster, Replace" procedure.
4. Disconnect speedometer cable at transmission end of cable.
5. Pull speedometer cable toward vehicle interior, then release lock by turning adapter to the left or right and remove adapter.
6. Remove instrument under cover attaching screws, then the under cover.
7. Remove underframe attaching screws located below steering column, then the underframe together with the heater duct.
8. Remove fuse box attaching screws, then the fuse box.
9. Remove ashtray from instrument panel, then the ashtray cover attaching screws.
10. Disconnect ashtray illumination light electrical connector, then remove ashtray cover.
11. Remove steering column cover.
12. Remove steering column lower bracket and tilt bracket attaching bolts, then lower steering column downward.
13. Remove underframe attaching bolts located on driver seat side, then the cowl side trim located on the passenger seat side.
14. Remove blower case installation bracket, then the floor console.
15. Remove heater cover, then the glove box assembly.
16. Remove heater unit to underframe attaching bolts, then the undercover.
17. Remove vacuum hose and heater control panel electrical connectors.
18. Disconnect control wire from control panel.
19. Remove underframe attaching bolts located on the passengers seat side. **A special type of bolt with a flange is used for one of the attaching bolts. Mark this bolt before removal to ensure correct location during installation.**
20. Remove instrument panel attaching nuts and bolts.
21. Disconnect instrument panel electrical connectors, then remove instrument panel.
22. Remove duct between heater unit and blower assembly.
23. Disconnect blower motor relays, automatic temperature controller and air mixing damper control motor electrical connectors.
24. Disconnect vacuum hoses, then the heater hose at heater unit.
25. Remove heater unit, then the water valve cover.
26. Disconnect water valve attaching links.
27. Remove vacuum actuator and pipe clamps.
28. Remove heater core from heater unit.
29. Reverse procedure to install.

STARION

1. Disconnect battery ground cable.
2. On 1983-84 models, move temperature control lever to the Warm position.
3. On 1985-87 models, start engine and place temperature control lever in the Max Hot position, then stop engine.
4. On all models, remove horn pad, then disconnect horn cable electrical connector.
5. Remove bolts securing steering wheel, then using a suitable puller remove steering wheel.
6. Remove column switch from steering shaft.
7. Remove instrument cluster. Refer to "Instrument Cluster, Replace."
8. Remove front and rear console.
9. Remove glove box, glove box door and ashtray.
10. Remove left and right dash panel side covers using tool MB990784 or equivalent, **Fig. 23.**
11. Remove fuse block and hood lock release handle.
12. Remove side defroster grille, **Fig. 24.**
13. Remove heater control knobs.
14. Remove heater control panel, then disconnect electrical connectors and function cables.
15. Remove bolts and screws attaching dash panel, then remove dash panel, **Fig. 24.**
16. Drain coolant from radiator, then remove heater hose from heater core housing.
17. Remove air ducts from heater core housing.
18. Remove center reinforcement and heater core housing, **Fig. 26.**
19. Remove heater core from housing.
20. Reverse procedure to install.

PICKUP

1983–86

1. Disconnect battery ground cable, then place temperature control lever in Off position and drain cooling system.
2. Remove parcel tray, center ventilation duct and grille and defroster duct, **Fig. 27.**
3. Disconnect heater hoses from heater core. Plug heater core fittings to prevent coolant spillage.
4. Disconnect wire connector from blower motor.
5. Remove upper bolts and center nuts attaching heater assembly to dash panel, then remove heater assembly.
6. Remove heater core from heater assembly.
7. Reverse procedure to install.

1987

1. Disconnect battery ground cable.
2. Place temperature control lever in extreme right position.
3. Loosen radiator drain plug and drain cooling system.
4. Remove air filter, then remove hose clamps and disconnect heater hoses from heater core.
5. Open glove box, then remove attaching screws and glove box.

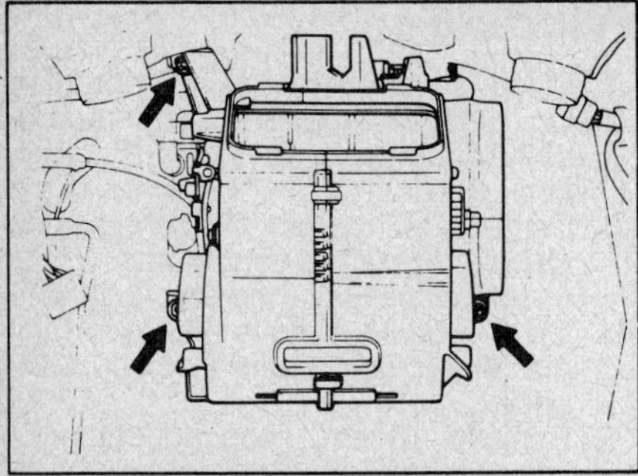

Fig. 26 Center reinforcement & heater core housing. Starion

6. On vehicles less radio, push out radio plug plate from inside glove box opening.
7. On vehicles with radio, remove radio as previously described.
8. On all models, remove heater fan switch plug, the pull out fan switch knob and control lever knobs.
9. Remove instrument cluster as previously described.
10. Remove ashtray and ashtray bracket attaching screws, then remove panel from lower left corner of cluster panel.
11. Disconnect wiring harness, then remove cluster panel.
12. Remove center console attaching screws, then disconnect wiring harness and remove console.
13. On models with tilt steering, position column in lowest position.
14. On all models, remove steering wheel, then the steering column cover.
15. Remove center air outlet attaching screws, spring washers and plain washers from outlets, then remove center air outlets, **Fig. 28.**
16. Remove instrument panel attaching screws from radio, ashtray and cluster openings, then remove instrument pad upper cover and instrument pad.
17. Remove heater duct, then the center ventilator duct.
18. Remove defroster duct, then the center reinforcement.
19. Remove heater unit and grommet, then separate heater core from heater unit.
20. Reverse procedure to install.

MONTERO

Front

1. Disconnect battery ground cable.
2. Place temperature control lever in Hot position, then drain cooling system.
3. Disconnect heater hoses from heater core, **Fig. 29.** Plug heater core fittings to prevent coolant spillage.
4. Remove steering wheel using suitable puller.
5. Remove heater control knob and heater fan switch knob, then the center console and instrument cluster. Refer to "Instrument Cluster, Replace" procedure.
6. Remove lap heater ducts and release cable bracket.
7. Remove defroster nozzle at temperature control cable side, then disconnect all control cables from control assembly.
8. Remove heater control assembly attaching screws, then pull out assembly slightly.
9. Disconnect heater fan switch electrical connector, then remove heater control assembly.
10. Remove fuse cover, then the fuse block attaching screws. Push fuse block into instrument panel.
11. Disconnect front speaker wire connectors, if equipped.
12. Remove plug from center of instrument panel, then remove both demister grilles using suitable tool.
13. Remove glove box stopper, then pull glove box rearward.
14. Disconnect heater relay from front wiring harness.
15. Remove instrument panel attaching bolts, then the instrument panel.
16. Remove center ventilator duct, defroster duct and rear heater duct.
17. Remove heater unit attaching nuts, then the heater unit.
18. Remove heater control lever arm, then the water valve cover.
19. Remove heater pipe and water valve.
20. Disconnect control arm linkage, then remove control arm.
21. Move heater core sideways and remove from heater unit. **Do not remove heater core felt when removing heater core.**
22. Reverse procedure to install.

Rear

1. Disconnect battery ground cable.
2. Drain cooling system, then disconnect heater hoses from heater assembly.
3. Disconnect heater assembly electrical connectors.
4. Remove heater assembly cover, then the heater assembly, **Fig. 30.**
5. Disconnect joint hoses, then remove water valve and piping.
6. Disconnect fan switch and blower motor electrical connectors.
7. Remove heater fan switch from water valve.
8. Remove fan and blower motor assembly from heater core, then the core attaching clips.
9. Remove heater nozzle, heater core and core cover.

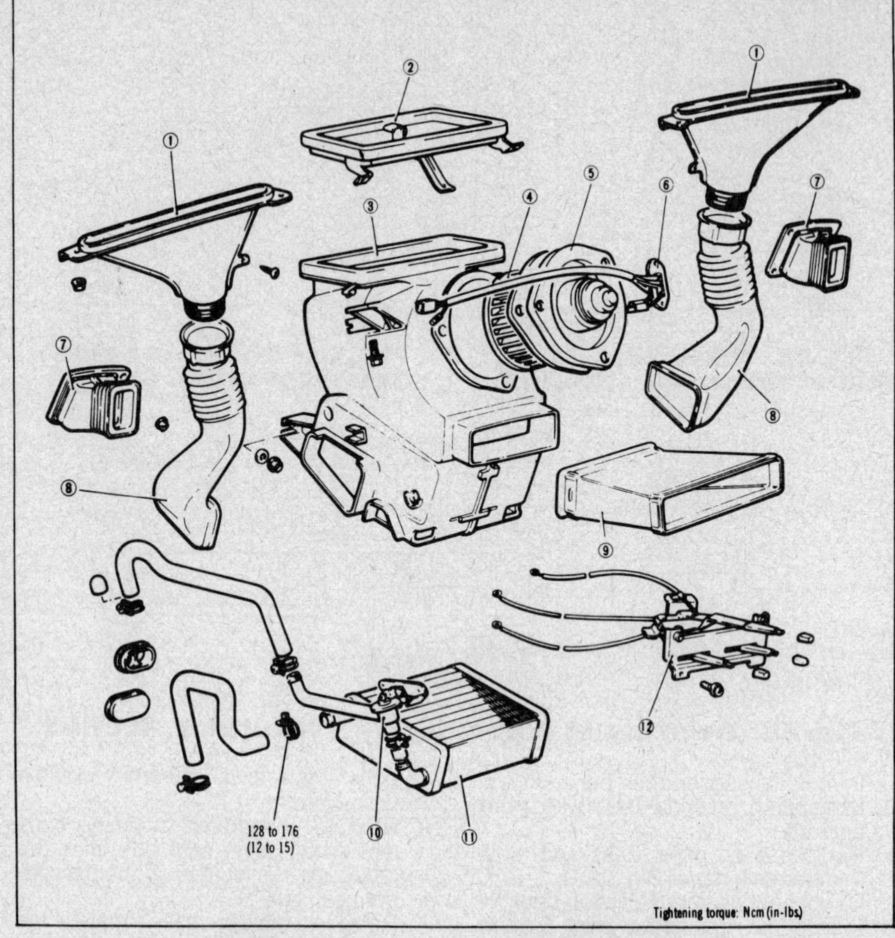

(1) Defroster nozzle
(2) Ventilator assembly
(3) Heater assembly
(4) Turbo fan
(5) Motor
(6) Heater resistor
(7) Side ventilator duct
(8) Defroster duct
(9) Center ventilator duct
(10) Water valve
(11) Heater core
(12) Heater control panel assembly

Fig. 27 Heater & ventilator exploded view. 1983–86 Pickup

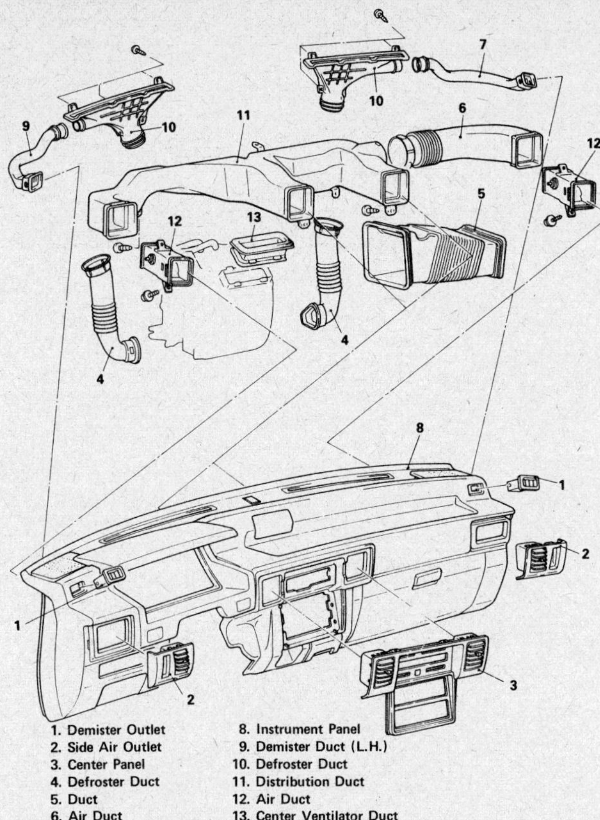

1. Demister Outlet
2. Side Air Outlet
3. Center Panel
4. Defroster Duct
5. Duct
6. Air Duct
7. Demister Duct (R.H.)
8. Instrument Panel
9. Demister Duct (L.H.)
10. Defroster Duct
11. Distribution Duct
12. Air Duct
13. Center Ventilator Duct

Fig. 28 Heater & ventilator exploded view. 1987 Pickup

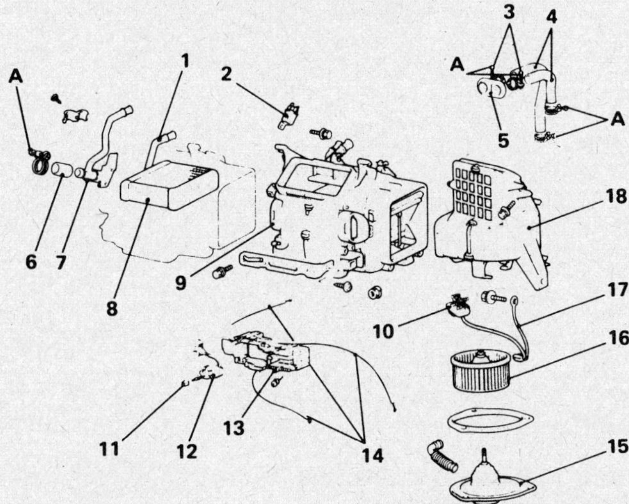

1. Heater pipe
2. Heater relay
3. Clamp
4. Water hose
5. Grommet
6. Hose
7. Water valve
8. Heater core
9. Heater case
10. Resistor
11. Heater fan switch knob
12. Heater fan switch
13. Heater control lever
14. Heater control cable
15. Blower motor
16. Fan
17. Blower motor harness
18. Blower case

	Nm	ft.lbs.
A	1.3-1.8	.9-1.3

Fig. 29 Front heater assembly exploded view. Montero

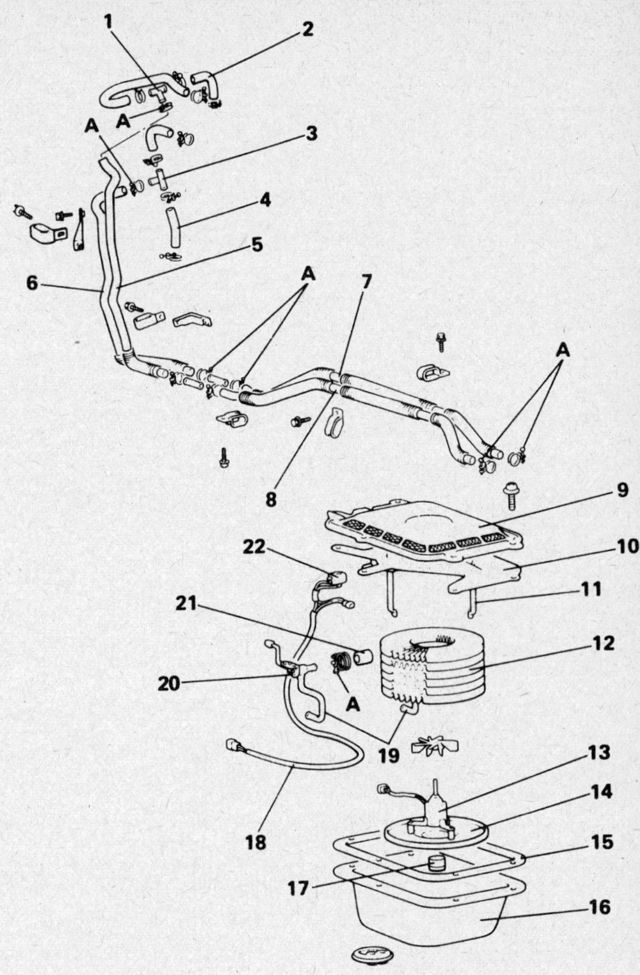

1. Joint (B)
2. Water hose (inlet side)
3. Joint (A)
4. Water hose (outlet side)
5. Water hose (C)
6. Water hose (D)
7. Water hose (B)
8. Water hose (A)
9. Cover
10. Heater nozzle
11. Clip
12. Heater core
13. Fan and motor assembly
14. Core cover
15. Secret box packing
16. Secret box
17. Rubber
18. Rear heater wiring harness
19. Piping
20. Water valve
21. Joint hose
22. Heater fan switch

	Ncm	in.lbs.
A	130-180	11-16

Fig. 30 Rear heater assembly exploded view. Montero

10. Reverse procedure to install.

MIRAGE

1. Disconnect battery ground cable.
2. Position temperature control cable in the warm position, then drain cooling system.
3. Remove horn shroud, then remove steering wheel using a suitable puller.
4. Remove glove compartment from instrument panel.
5. Remove lap heater duct assembly.
6. Remove parcel tray attaching screws, then remove parcel tray.

7. Remove steering column lower cover.
8. Disconnect headlamp and wiper switch wire connectors, then remove steering column upper cover.
9. Remove instrument panel lower cover, located below steering column.
10. Remove instrument cluster as described under "Instrument Cluster, Replace."
11. Remove steering column bracket attaching screws.
12. Remove instrument panel left hand corner panel.
13. Remove control knobs from heater control levers.
14. Using a suitable tool, pry heater control panel cover from instrument panel, then remove heater control attaching screws.
15. Remove parking brake cover and ashtray from console.
16. Remove console to floor attaching screws, then remove console.
17. Remove roof side trim attaching clips and remove trim.
18. Detach front pillar trim clips by pulling trim outward from top, then remove trim.
19. Remove door opening weather stripping.
20. Remove hooked portion of upper cowl side trim from hole in body, then remove trim by pulling downward.
21. Remove scuff plate, then remove lower side trim attaching screws and trim.
22. Remove ashtray from instrument panel.
23. Disconnect instrument panel wire connectors.
24. Pry upward on instrument panel cover using a suitable tool, **Fig. 31.**
25. Remove instrument panel attaching bolts and nuts, then remove instrument panel, **Fig. 32.**
26. Detach duct located between heater unit and blower motor assembly, **Fig. 33.**
27. Disconnect heater hose from heater unit. Cap hose and heater core fittings.
28. Remove heater unit attaching bolts, then remove heater unit, **Fig. 34.**
29. Remove hose and pipe clamps from heater unit, **Fig. 35.**
30. Remove heater core from heater unit.
31. Reverse procedure to install.

PRECIS

1. Disconnnect battery ground cable.
2. Set temperature control lever Hot position, then drain cooling system.
3. Disconnect heater hoses from heater core, then remove lower instrument panel attaching screws and the lower instrument panel.
4. Remove supplemental (upper) end of console, then disconnect electrical harness from carburetor control computer. Position computer aside.
5. Disconnect control cables from heater case.
6. On models equipped with A/C, remove heater case from vehicle.
7. On all models, remove heater case from vehicle.
8. Remove heater case cover retaining screws, then the cover.
9. Remove hoses, clamps and water

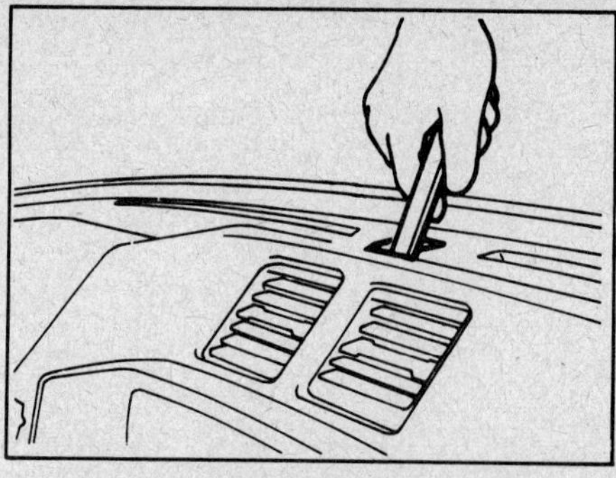

Fig. 31 Prying upward on instrument panel cover. Mirage

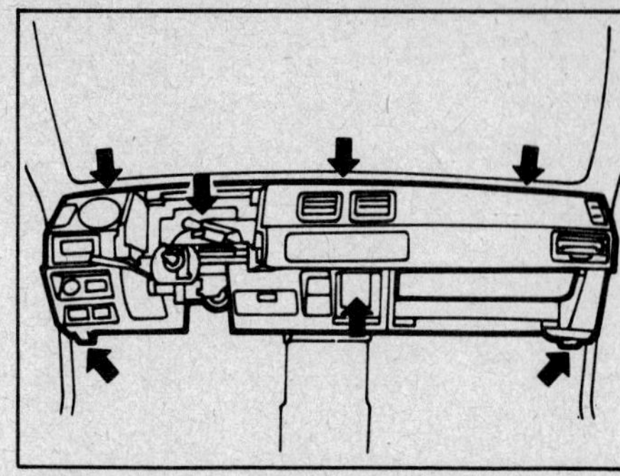

Fig. 32 Instrument panel mounting screw locations. Mirage

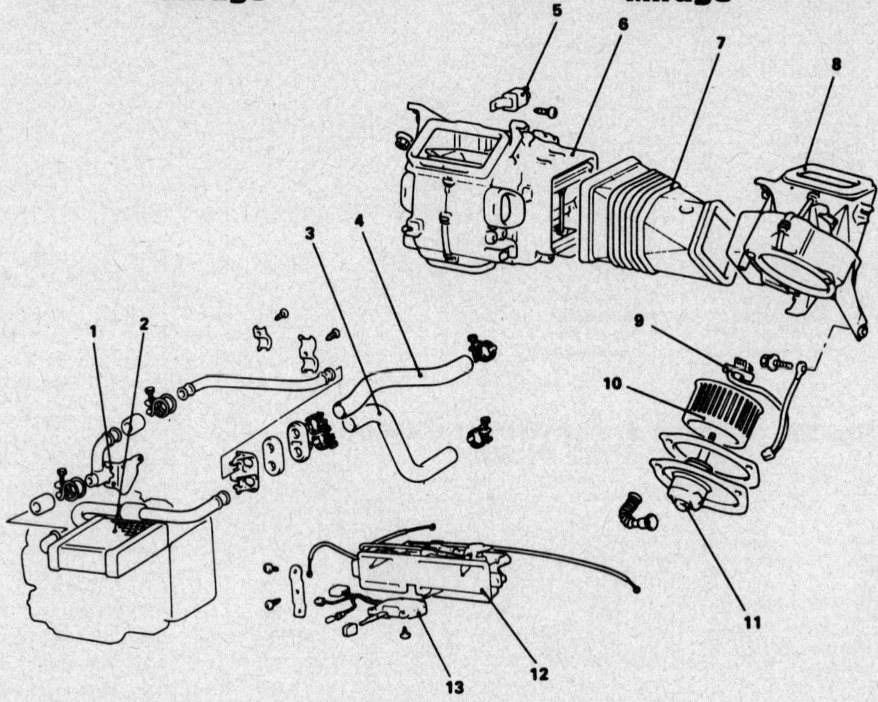

Fig. 33 Heater unit & blower motor assembly. Mirage

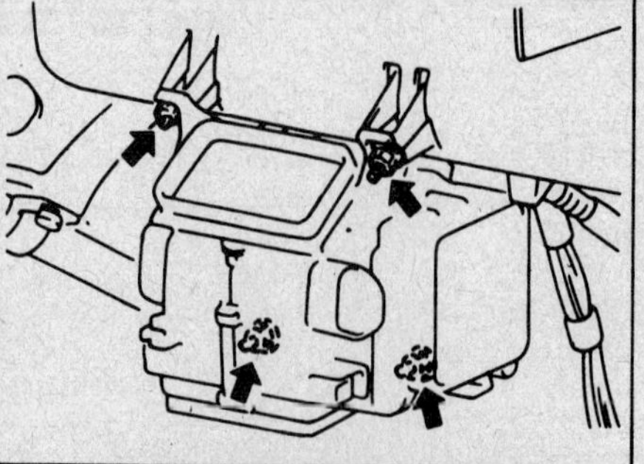

Fig. 34 Heater unit attaching screw locations. Mirage

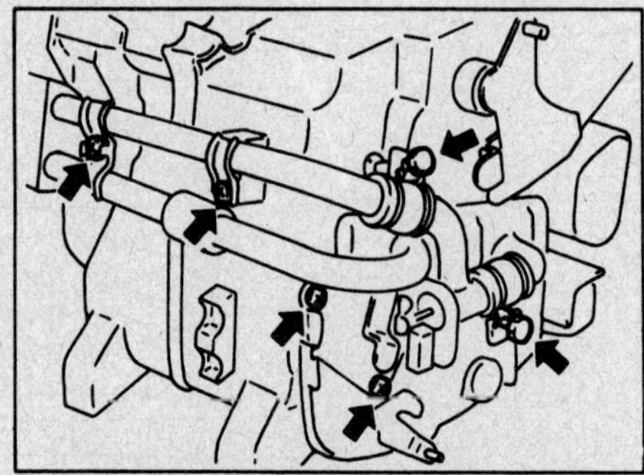

Fig. 35 Heater unit case attaching bolt locations. Mirage

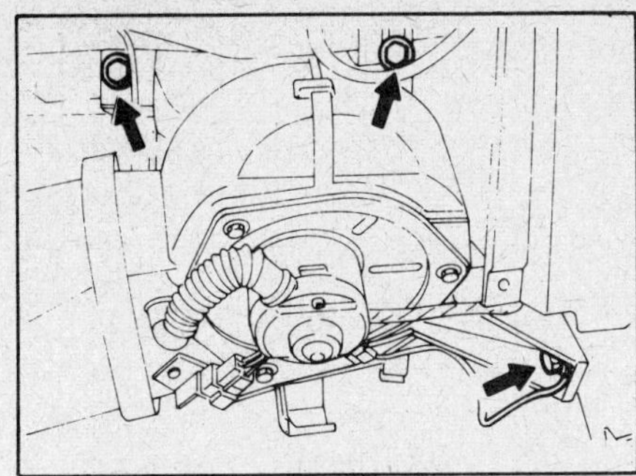

Fig. 36 Typical blower housing attaching bolt locations. Cordia, Tredia & Starion

valve from case.
10. Pulling outward, remove heater core from case.
11. Reverse procedure to install.

BLOWER MOTOR

REPLACE

CORDIA, TREDIA & STARION

1. Remove dash panel under side cover, glove box and cowl side trim.
2. Disconnect recirculation door cable from blower motor housing.
3. Disconnect blower switch connector.
4. Remove blower housing attaching bolts, **Fig. 36,** then remove housing.
5. Remove bolts attaching blower assembly to blower housing, then remove blower assembly.
6. Remove blower fan from blower motor.
7. Reverse procedure to install.

GALANT

1. Disconnect battery ground cable.
2. Remove dash panel under cover, then the glove box and passenger side underframe.
3. Remove duct between heater unit and blower assembly.
4. Remove blower assembly attaching nuts and bolts, then lower blower assembly.
5. Disconnect inside/outside air change over control vacuum hose from blower assembly.
6. Remove blower motor from blower assembly.
7. Reverse procedure to install.

PICKUP

1. Remove instrument cluster. Refer to "Instrument Cluster, Replace."
2. Disconnect blower motor electrical connector.
3. Remove bolts attaching blower assembly to heater housing.
4. Remove blower fan from blower motor.
5. Reverse procedure to install.

MONTERO

Front

1. Disconnect battery ground cable.
2. Disconnect blower motor electrical connectors, then remove lower blower motor assembly attaching bolts.
3. Remove lap heater duct.
4. Remove glove box stopper and push glove box down.
5. Remove recirculation control wire, then the remaining blower motor attaching bolts.
6. Remove blower motor assembly.

Fig. 37 Blower assembly attaching bolt locations. Mirage

7. Reverse procedure to install.

Rear

When replacing blower motor, refer to "Heater Core, Replace" procedure.

MIRAGE

1. Disconnect battery ground cable
2. Remove glove compartment from instrument panel.
3. Remove parcel tray attaching screws and parcel tray.
4. Remove blower assembly attaching screws and blower assembly, **Fig. 37.**
5. Remove blower motor to mounting attaching screws, then remove blower motor.

PRECIS

1. Disconnect battery ground cable.
2. Disconnect wire harness connector and ventilation tube at blower motor.
3. Remove blower motor to case attaching screws, then the blower motor.
4. Reverse procedure to install.

1500 & 1[illegible]

FOR SERVICE PROCEDURES ON THESE ENGINES, REFER TO DODGE • PLYMOUTH CHAPTER

1800, 2000 & 2400CC ENGINE SECTION

INDEX

ENGINE

REPLACE

CORDIA & TREDIA

1. Remove battery, then drain coolant and transaxle oil.
2. Discharge refrigerant from A/C system, if equipped.
3. Drain power steering fluid.
4. Remove radiator reservoir and washer tanks.
5. Disconnect radiator upper and lower hoses, then remove radiator.
6. Disconnect heater hoses, then remove battery tray.
7. Remove air cleaner assembly.
8. On vehicles equipped with turbocharger, remove turbocharger intake hose, then disconnect engine oil cooler hoses at engine.
9. On all models, disconnect brake booster vacuum hose.
10. On vehicles equipped with automatic transaxle, disconnect transaxle oil cooler hoses and cap hoses.
11. On vehicles equipped with a manual transaxle, disconnect clutch cable at transaxle. If equipped with automatic transaxle, disconnect control cable from transaxle.
12. Disconnect refrigerant lines from compressor, if equipped.
13. On all models, disconnect accelerator cable, right fender engine ground, speedometer cable and power steering hoses.
14. Disconnect high tension cable and lead wire from ignition coil.
15. Disconnect battery ground cable from engine.
16. Disconnect alternator wiring and oil pressure gauge unit wire connectors.
17. Remove mounting screws of vacuum control unit and solenoid valve, then disconnect connector.
18. Disconnect hoses from purge control valve, then remove the purge control valve mounting screw.
19. Disconnect fuel return hose from carburetor or injection mixer, then disconnect fuel hose from fuel filter.
20. Raise and support front of vehicle, then disconnect exhaust pipe from exhaust manifold and position aside.
21. On vehicle equipped with manual transaxle, remove shift control rod, extension and range selector control cable.
22. Disconnect left and right strut bars and stabilizer bars at lower control arms.
23. Remove No. 2 crossmember to left and right lower control arm mounting bolts.
24. Remove driveshafts from transaxle case.
25. Using a rope, carefully lower control arms and driveshafts to No. 2 crossmember.
26. Using a suitable lifting device, lift engine enough to relieve weight from engine mounts.
27. Remove left mount insulator nut and front torque link upper mounting bolt on No. 1 crossmember side.
28. Remove rear torque link insulator mounting bolt.
29. Remove nuts which attach left mount insulator to fender.
30. Remove cap from within right fender shield.
31. Remove transaxle insulator bracket mounting bolts, then remove insulator from bracket and remove bracket.
32. Remove rear roll stopper insulator bolts and left mount bracket.
33. While directing transaxle side downward, lift engine and transaxle assembly out of vehicle.
34. Reverse procedure to install.

GALANT

1. Remove battery, then drain coolant and transaxle oil.
2. Remove air cleaner, then disconnect inhibitor switch and pulse generator electrical connector.
3. Disconnect brake booster, canister and purge control valve vacuum hoses.
4. Disconnect ground wire from right wheel housing, then the front harness and engine harness electrical connector.
5. Discharge refrigerant from A/C system if equipped, then drain power steering fluid.
6. Remove compressor assembly and reserve tank assembly, if equipped with electronic controlled suspension.
7. Disconnect transaxle control cable.
8. Disconnect alternator and oil pressure gauge electrical connector.
9. Mark transaxle oil cooler lines to ensure correct position during assembly, then disconnect and cap lines.
10. Disconnect oxygen sensor and resistor electrical connector.
11. Disconnect ignition coil, engine compartment and control harness electrical connectors.
12. Disconnect water temperature switch, throttle position sensor, idle control actuator and motor position sensor electrical connectors.
13. Disconnect fuel injector electrical connectors from intake manifold.
14. Remove harness protector attaching

bolt from surge tank.

15. Disconnect accelerator cable from actuator link.
16. Disconnect fuel return hose and high pressure hose at linkage manifold. **Ensure fuel pressure has been relieved before removing fuel hoses.**
17. Disconnect upper and lower radiator hoses on engine side.
18. Disconnect heater hoses on engine side, then the speedometer cable from transaxle.
19. Disconnect and cap A/C hoses on compressor side, if equipped.
20. Disconnect power steering hoses on pump side.
21. Raise and support vehicle, then disconnect exhaust pipe from manifold and secure using suitable wire.
22. Disconnect knuckle from the lower arm ball joint using a suitable tool.
23. Disconnect tie rod from knuckle using a suitable tool, then remove driveshafts from transaxle case. Use caution not to damage driveshaft oil seal. **Cap holes of transaxle case to prevent entry of foreign material. Also replace driveshaft retainer ring whenever driveshaft is removed.**
24. Lift engine enough to relieve weight from engine mounts using a suitable lifting device.
25. Remove engine mount bracket to body attaching nut. Do not remove bolt.
26. Remove front and rear roll stopper bracket upper attaching nuts.
27. Remove cap from within right fender shield, then the transaxle mount attaching bolts.
28. Remove engine and transaxle assembly from vehicle.
29. Remove transaxle to engine attaching bolts, then separate engine from transaxle.
30. Reverse procedure to install.

PICKUP

1. Disconnect battery ground cable, then remove hood.
2. Remove air cleaner assembly.
3. Drain coolant from radiator and transmission oil from transmission.
4. Remove radiator shrouds, as needed, then disconnect radiator hoses and remove radiator.
5. Disconnect heater hoses and brake booster vacuum hose.
6. Disconnect alternator wiring harness.
7. Disconnect clutch cable from transmission.
8. Disconnect accelerator cable and fuel hoses.
9. Disconnect starter motor wiring harness.
10. Disconnect engine ground cable and coil high tension cables.
11. Disconnect water temperature gauge connector.
12. Remove power steering pump, if equipped.
13. Disconnect oil pressure switch or pressure gauge harness unit.
14. Remove radiator assembly.
15. Remove exhaust pipe from exhaust manifold pipe.

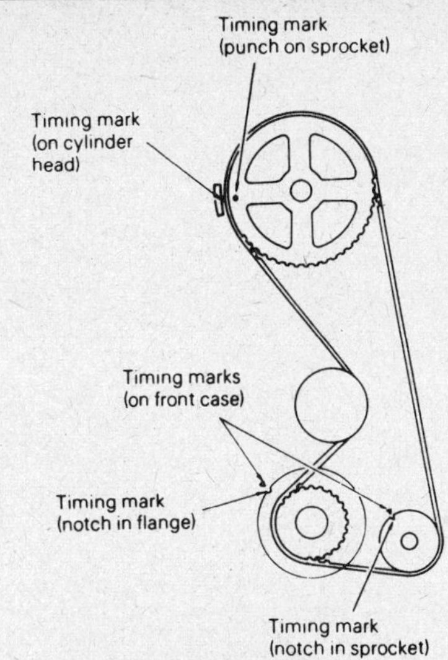

Fig. 1 Timing mark locations

16. On rear wheel drive models, remove under cover. On four wheel drive models, remove under cover, under skid plate and transfer case protector.
17. Disconnect speedometer cable from transmission.
18. Disconnect back-up switch harness. On four wheel drive models, remove four wheel drive indicator light switch harness.
19. Remove propeller shaft or shafts and gearshift lever assembly.
20. On four wheel drive models proceed as follows:
    a. Using a suitable jack support transfer case.
    b. Remove transfer case mounting bracket and support insulator.
    c. Remove plate from side frame and detach transfer case mounting bracket from transfer case.
21. Using suitable engine lifting device, remove engine and transmission assembly diagonally out of engine compartment.
22. Remove transmission attaching bolts, then remove transmission.
23. Reverse procedure to install.

ENGINE DISASSEMBLY

TIMING BELT ASSEMBLY

1. Disconnect battery ground cable, then remove hood.
2. On models with power steering, remove power steering pump pulley.
3. On all models, remove crankshaft pulley, then the cover assembly.
4. Rotate crankshaft in normal direction of rotation until No. 1 cylinder is at top dead center and camshaft and crankshaft timing marks are aligned, **Fig. 1**.
5. Remove tensioner spacer, spring, then the tensioner and spacer, **Fig. 2.**
6. Mark direction of rotation on timing belt, then remove belt.
7. Remove camshaft sprocket, then the plug on left side of cylinder block. Retain left silent shaft, using a suitable screwdriver, then remove oil pump sprocket retaining nut and sprocket.
8. Remove crankshaft sprocket, then the flange.
9. Remove tensioner "B," then mark normal direction of rotation on timing belt "B" and remove belt.
10. Remove right silent shaft sprocket and spacer, then the crankshaft "B" sprocket, key and timing belt under cover.

CAMSHAFT, ROCKER ARMS & SHAFT

1. Raise hood, then disconnect battery ground cable.
2. Remove breather hose and P.V.C. hose from rocker cover.
3. Remove oil filler cap attaching bolt, then the oil filler cap assembly, **Fig. 3.**
4. Remove rocker cover, then the gasket.
5. Rotate crankshaft in normal direction of rotation until No. 1 cylinder is at top dead center and camshaft and crankshaft timing marks are aligned.
6. On 1985 non-Turbo and all 1986-87 engines, prior to removal of rocker arm and rocker shaft assembly, install auto-lash adjuster holder tool No. MD998443-01 to ensure that the auto-lash adjuster is not allowed to fall.
7. Remove semicircular packing, then the oil seal.
8. Remove rocker arm and shaft assembly, then the auto-lash adjuster.
9. Remove camshaft.

CYLINDER HEAD

1. Disconnect battery ground cable, then drain cooling system.
2. Remove air cleaner, then disconnect control cables from throttle lever and bracket.
3. Disconnect exhaust pipe from manifold, **Fig. 4.**
4. Disconnect upper radiator hose and heater hoses as needed.
5. Disconnect spark plug wires.
6. Remove power steering pump attaching bolts and drive belt, then position pump aside.
7. Mark and disconnect necessary electrical connectors and vacuum hoses, release harness clamps, then position harness aside to prevent damage.
8. Remove timing belt upper cover, then the rocker arm cover.
9. Rotate crankshaft in normal direction of rotation until No. 1 cylinder is at top dead center and camshaft and crankshaft timing marks are aligned.
10. Place a chalk mark between timing belt and camshaft sprocket, then remove camshaft sprocket bolt, separate sprocket from camshaft, leaving belt in place on sprocket. Secure sprocket and belt on lower timing cover. Ensure sprocket does not disengage from belt and fall, and maintain tension on belt to maintain proper timing. **Do not rotate crankshaft after sprocket is removed from camshaft.**
11. Remove cylinder head attaching bolts in sequence shown, **Fig. 5.** Loosen bolts evenly in three steps, to prevent cylinder head warpage, then remove

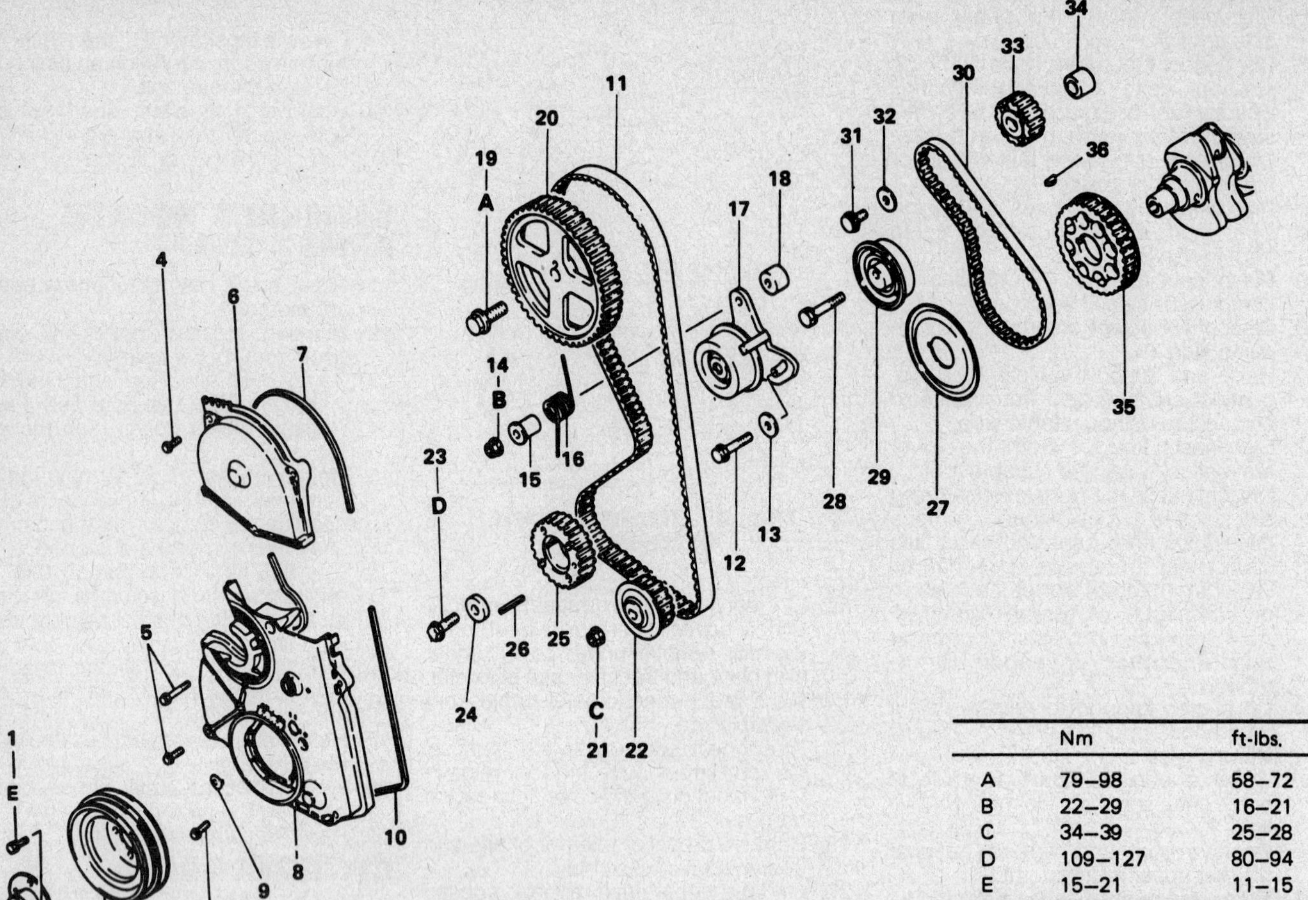

	Nm	ft-lbs.
A	79–98	58–72
B	22–29	16–21
C	34–39	25–28
D	109–127	80–94
E	15–21	11–15

1. Bolt (4)
2. Cranking adapter
3. Crankshaft pulley
4. Flange bolt (8)
5. Flange bolt (3)
6. Timing belt front upper cover
7. Gasket
8. Timing belt front lower cover
9. Access cover (2)
10. Gasket
11. Timing belt
12. Flange bolt
13. Washer
14. Flange nut
15. Spacer
16. Tensioner spring
17. Tensioner
18. Spacer
19. Flange bolt
20. Camshaft sprocket
21. Nut
22. Oil pump sprocket
23. Crankshaft sprocket bolt
24. Special washer
25. Crankshaft sprocket
26. Spring pin
27. Flange
28. Bolt
29. Tensioner "B"
30. Timing belt "B"
31. Flange bolt
32. Washer
33. Right silent shaft sprocket
34. Spacer
35. Crankshaft sprocket "B"
36. Key

Fig. 2 Exploded view of timing belt assemblies

cylinder head and gasket. Take care not to dislodge camshaft sprocket during cylinder head removal.

VALVES & SPRINGS

1. Remove cylinder head as previously described.
2. Remove jet valve assembly, using tool No. MD998310. **Make sure tool is square with respect to center of jet valve. If tool is tilted, valve stem may be bent by force of valve spring retainer.**
3. Using a suitable valve spring compressor, remove intake valve retainer lock, marking relative position of each to facilitate installation, **Fig. 6.**
4. Remove valve spring retainer, then the valve spring.
5. Remove valve spring seat, then the intake valves.
6. Remove and discard valve stem seals, then the intake valve guides and seats.
7. Using a suitable valve spring compressor, remove exhaust valve retainer lock, marking relative position of each to facilitate installation.
8. Remove valve spring retainer, then the valve spring.
9. Remove valve spring seat, then the exhaust valves.
10. Remove and discard valve stem seals, then the exhaust valve guides and seats.

SILENT SHAFT, OIL PUMP & FRONT CASE

Refer to **Fig. 7** when removing silent

1. Oil filler cap
2. Bolt (2)
3. Washer (2)
4. Oil seal (2)
5. Rocker cover
6. Rocker cover gasket
7. Semi-circular packing
8. Flange bolt (2)
9. Flange bolt (10)
10. Rocker arm and shaft assembly
   - 1 Bearing cap, rear
   - 2 Rocker arm "D" (2)
   - 3 Spring (2)
   - 4 Bearing cap, No. 4
   - 5 Rocker arm "C" (2)
   - 6 Spring (2)
   - 7 Bearing cap, No. 3
   - 8 Rocker arm "C" (2)
   - 9 Spring (2)
   - -10 Bearing cap, No. 2
   - -11 Rocker arm "C" (2)
   - -12 Spring
   - -13 Wave washer
   - -14 Nut (8)
   - -15 Adjusting screw (8)
   - -16 Rocker arm shaft, left
   - -17 Rocker arm shaft, right
   - -18 Bearing cap, front
11. Camshaft

	Nm	ft.lbs.
A	5–6.8	3.7–5.0
B	19–20	14–15
C	20–26	15–19

Fig. 3 Exploded view of camshaft, rocker arm & rocker shaft assemblies

shaft, oil pump and front case. Keep silent shaft in position by inserting a screwdriver through plug hole in left side of cylinder block and remove oil pump driven gear securing bolt.

PISTON & ROD ASSEMBLY

Refer to **Fig. 8** when removing piston and rod assembly. Keep all components, such as connecting rod caps and bearings, in proper order for installation.

CRANKSHAFT

Refer to **Fig. 9** when removing crankshaft and main bearings.

ENGINE INSPECTION & REPAIR

TIMING BELT

Check timing belt thoroughly for any damage, wear, cracks and missing teeth.

CAMSHAFT, ROCKER ARMS & SHAFT

1. Check rocker arm in the positions indicated in **Fig. 10.**
2. Check to ensure that oil holes are clear.
3. Check rocker arm shaft at rocker arm mounting positions for wear.
4. Check rocker arm shaft oil holes to ensure holes are clear.
5. Check camshaft for wear or damage and replace as necessary.

CYLINDER HEAD

Check cylinder head gasket surface for squareness, using a suitable straightedge and feeler gauge. Place a straightedge across cylinder head, then check for warpage with feeler gauge. If clearance exceeds .004 inch in any direction, replace or

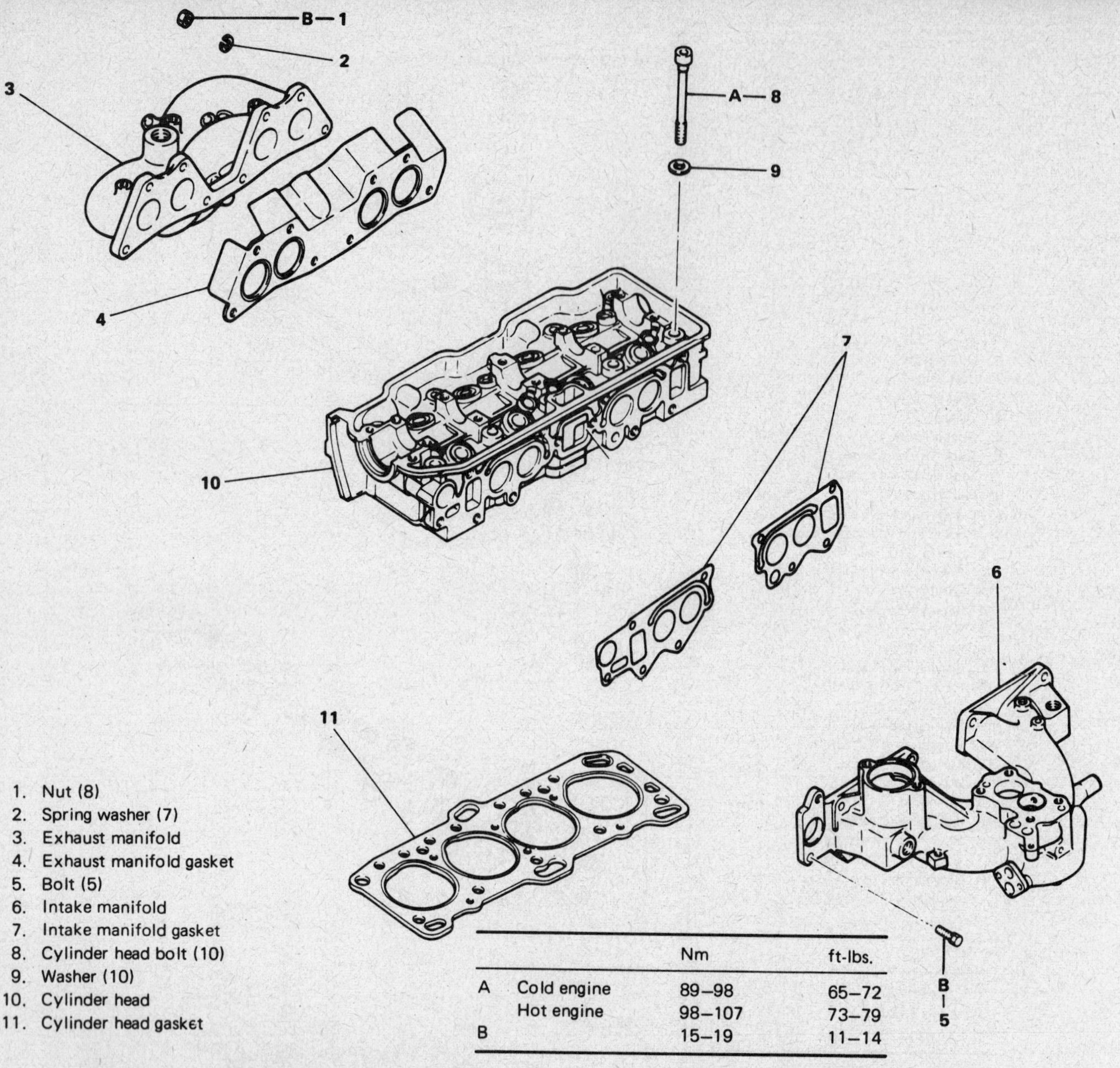

1. Nut (8)
2. Spring washer (7)
3. Exhaust manifold
4. Exhaust manifold gasket
5. Bolt (5)
6. Intake manifold
7. Intake manifold gasket
8. Cylinder head bolt (10)
9. Washer (10)
10. Cylinder head
11. Cylinder head gasket

		Nm	ft-lbs.
A	Cold engine	89–98	65–72
	Hot engine	98–107	73–79
B		15–19	11–14

Fig. 4 Exploded view of cylinder head, intake & exhaust manifolds

lightly machine cylinder head. **If machining, do not remove more than .008 inch from gasket surface.**

VALVES & SPRINGS

1. Check each valve for wear and damage or defects in valve head and stem. Replace valve if unable to repair.
2. If stem tip has been pitted, grind stem tip slightly. Also grind valve face slightly.
3. Check stem to guide clearance. If clearance is not within specification, replace valve and/or valve guide as necessary.
4. Replace valve if margin of face has decreased to less than .02 inch, **Fig. 11.**
5. If improper contact with valve seat is evident, reseat valve.
6. Check valve seat for evidence of overheating and improper contact with valve face, and replace as necessary.
7. Check free height of each valve spring, spring should measure 1.9 inches. If spring does not meet specification, replace as necessary.
8. Test spring for squareness; if it exceeds 1.5°, replace spring.

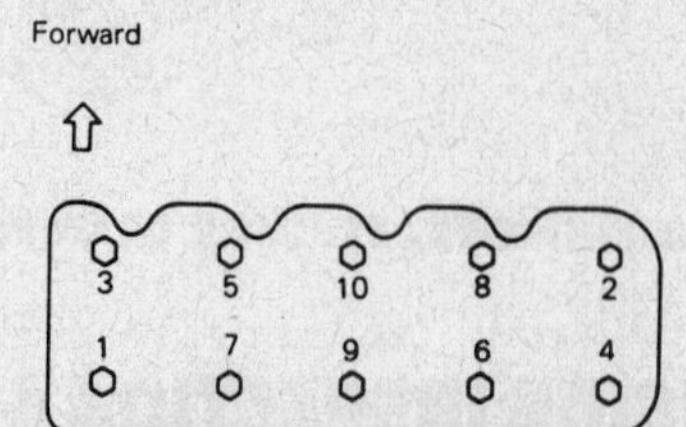

Fig. 5 Cylinder head bolt loosening sequence

SILENT SHAFT, OIL PUMP & FRONT CASE

1. Check gear contacting surface of front case and oil pump cover for step wear. If wear is evident, replace front case.
2. Check silent shaft journals for wear and damage. If excessive damage or wear is evident, check bearing. If necessary, replace silent shaft and/or bearing.

CRANKSHAFT, MAIN & ROD BEARINGS

1. Measure main bearing clearance. If clearance is not within specification, replace bearing.
2. Check crankshaft journals for damage or wear. If necessary, replace crankshaft or machine journal.

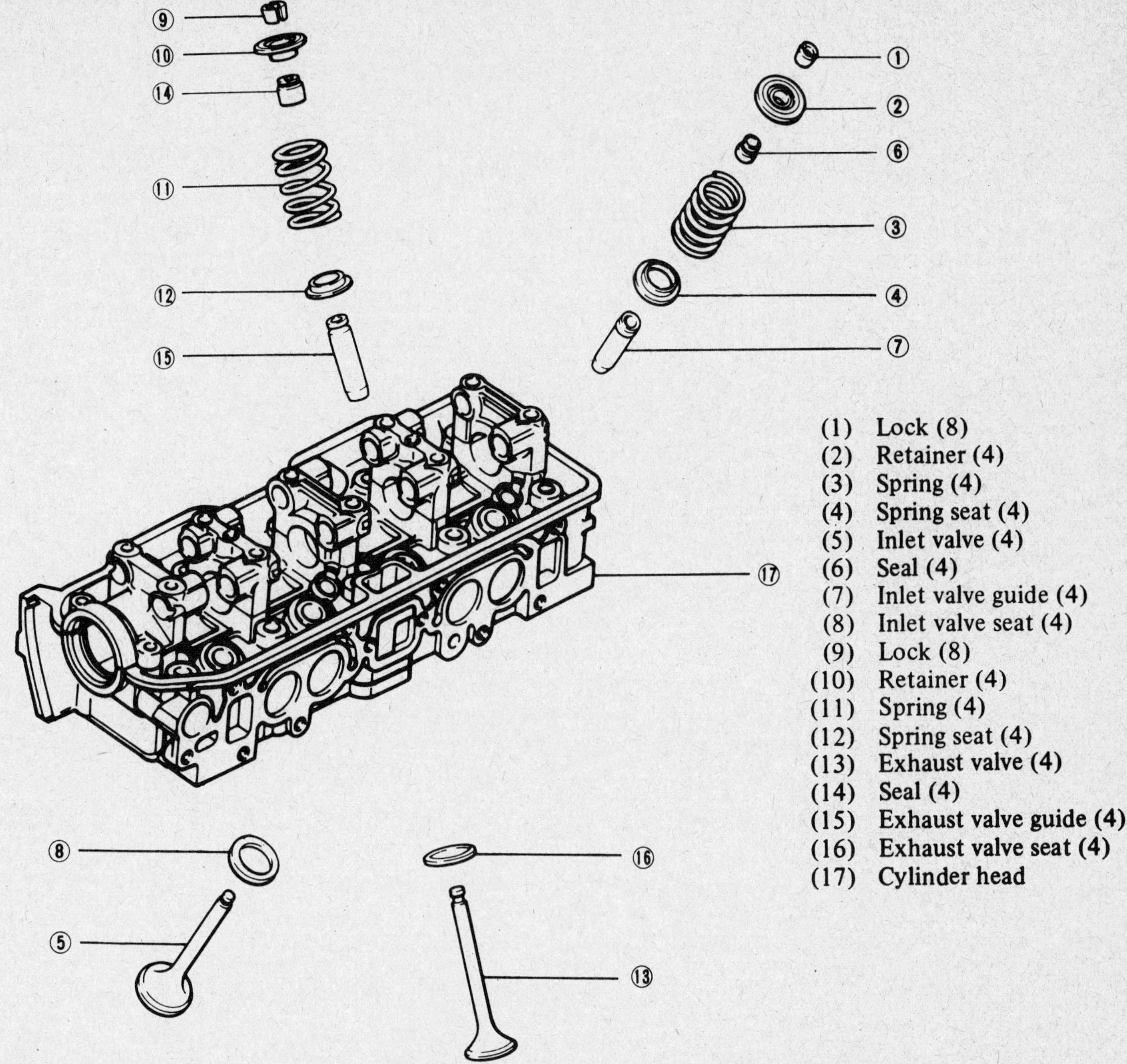

Fig. 6 Cylinder head, valves & valve springs

PISTON & ROD ASSEMBLY

The piston and rod is assembled with the indented arrow on the piston and the embossed numeral on the rod facing toward front of engine, **Fig. 12.**

PISTON, PINS & RINGS

Pistons and rings are available in standard sizes and oversizes of .010, .020, .030 and .039 inch. Oversize pins are not available.

ENGINE ASSEMBLY

CRANKSHAFT

1. Install main upper bearing on cylinder block, **Fig. 13**, and lower bearing on main bearing caps.
2. Install crankshaft and apply engine oil to journals.
3. Caps should be installed with arrows facing forward and in proper number order, **Fig. 14.**
4. Torque main bearing cap bolts to specification and check to ensure crankshaft rotates freely and has proper endplay.
5. Using crankshaft rear oil seal installer MD998376 or equivalent, install seal in case.
6. Install oil separator into case with .16 inch diameter oil hole in lowermost position.
7. Install new oil seal case gasket and oil seal case assembly.
8. Install rear plate to cylinder block.
9. On manual transmission models, install flywheel and torque bolts to specification, then check clutch mounting surface for runout.
10. On automatic transmission models, install adapter plates and drive plate, then torque bolts to specification.

PISTON & ROD ASSEMBLY

1. Position each piston ring gap as far apart as possible.
2. Ensure that each piston and rod are installed in the same cylinder bore as removed.
3. Ensure that connecting rod caps and bearings are placed on proper connecting rods, then torque bolts to specification.

SILENT SHAFTS, OIL PUMP & FRONT CASE

1. Install silent shaft in cylinder block.
2. Install oil pump drive and driven gears in front case, ensuring that the gear timing marks are aligned, **Fig. 15.**
3. Using small end of oil seal guide MD998285, install crankshaft front oil

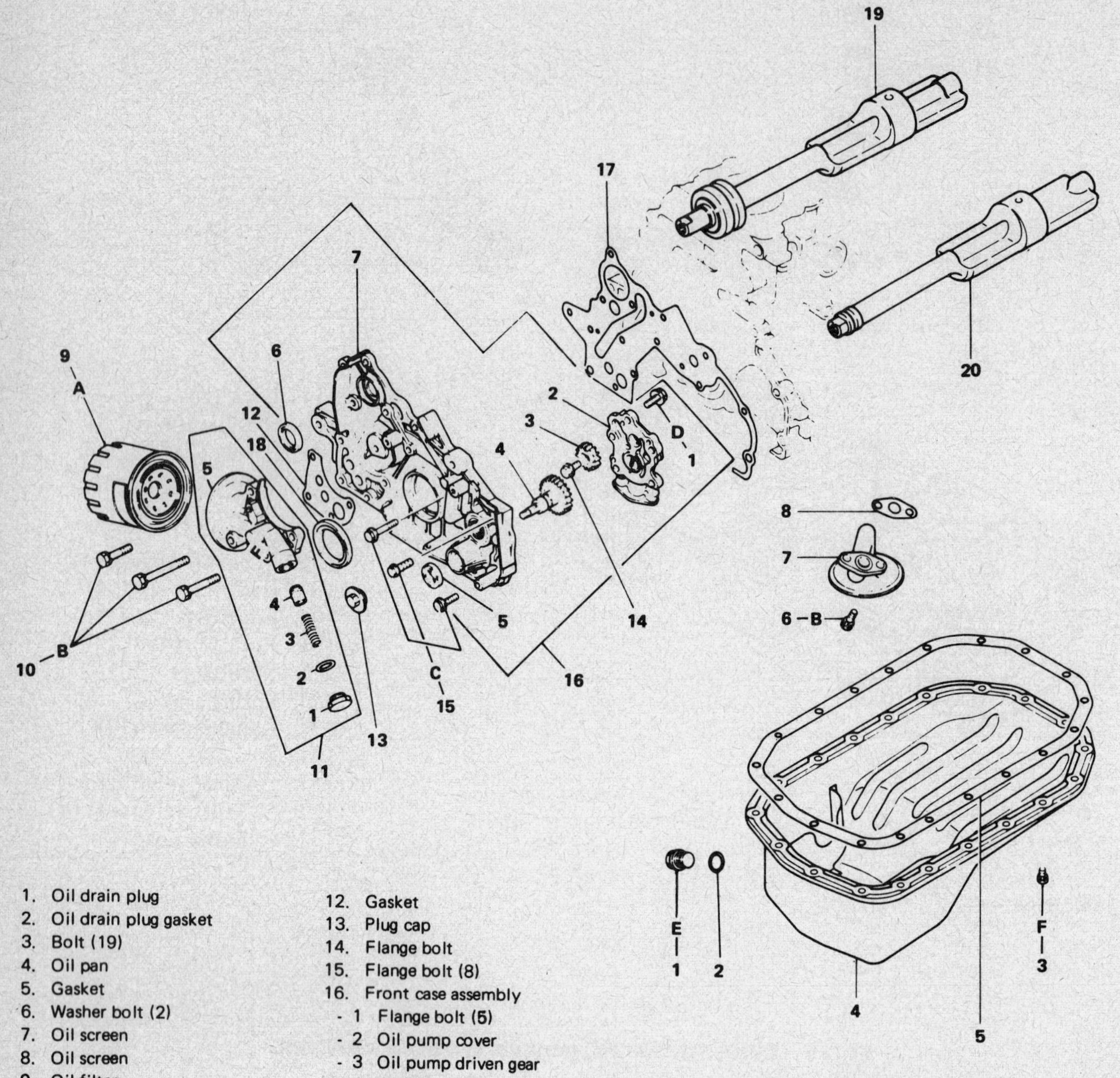

1. Oil drain plug
2. Oil drain plug gasket
3. Bolt (19)
4. Oil pan
5. Gasket
6. Washer bolt (2)
7. Oil screen
8. Oil screen
9. Oil filter
10. Bolt (4)
11. Oil filter bracket assembly
   - 1 Plug
   - 2 Gasket
   - 3 Relief spring
   - 4 Relief valve
   - 5 Oil filter bracket
12. Gasket
13. Plug cap
14. Flange bolt
15. Flange bolt (8)
16. Front case assembly
   - 1 Flange bolt (5)
   - 2 Oil pump cover
   - 3 Oil pump driven gear
   - 4 Oil pump drive gear
   - 5 Oil seal
   - 6 Oil seal
   - 7 Front case
17. Front case gasket
18. Oil seal
19. Silent shaft, right
20. Silent shaft, left

	Nm	ft-lbs.
A	11–12	8–9
B	15–21	11–15
C	20–26	15–19
D	15–17	11–13
E	59–78	44–57
F	6–7	4.5–5.5

Fig. 7 Silent shaft, oil pump & front case components

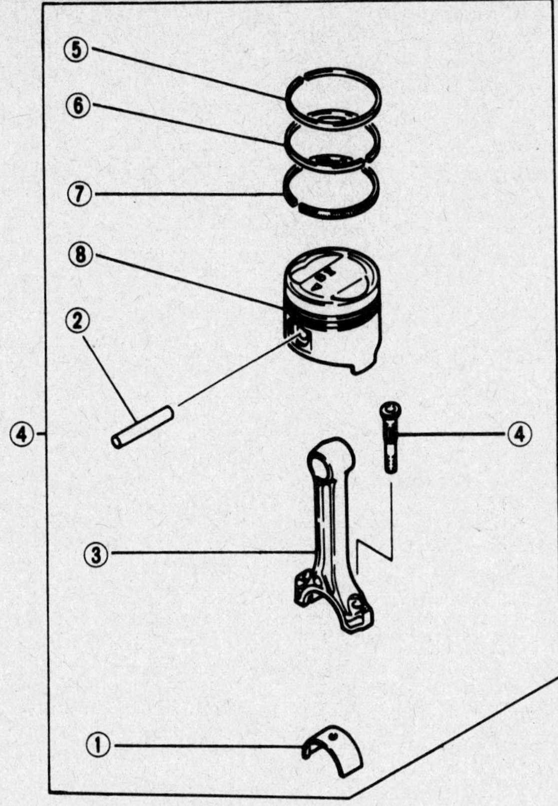

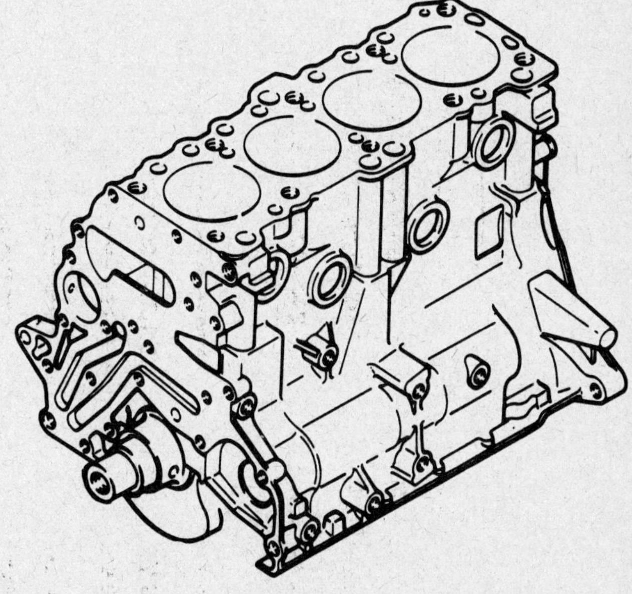

Tightening torque: Nm (ft-lbs.)

(1) Nut (8)
(2) Bearing cap (4)
(3) Bearing (4)
(4) Piston and connecting rod assembly (4)
  -(1) Bearing (4)
  -(2) Piston pin (4)
(4)-(3) Connecting rod (4)
  -(4) Bolt (8)
  -(5) No. 1 piston ring (4)
  -(6) No. 2 piston ring (4)
  -(7) Oil ring (4)
  -(8) Piston (4)

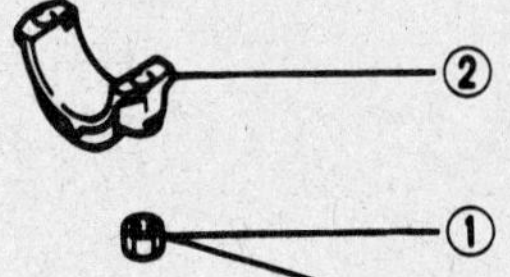

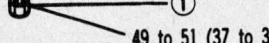

①
49 to 51 (37 to 38)

Fig. 8 Piston & rod assembly disassembly

seal, **Fig. 16. If crankshaft front oil seal is already mounted to front case, use oil seal guide for protection of oil seal.**

4. Install front case.
5. Insert a screwdriver through plug hole in left side of cylinder block to keep shaft in position, then torque bolt to 25-28 ft. lbs., **Fig. 17.**
6. Install oil filter bracket assembly and gasket, then torque front case bolts to 15-19 ft. lbs. and oil filter bracket bolts to 11-15 ft. lbs.
7. Install plug cap.
8. Install oil screen and gasket, then clean gasket surfaces of cylinder block and oil pan.
9. Install oil pan gasket using a small amount of suitable gasket sealant.
10. Install oil pan and torque bolts to 4.5-5.5 ft. lbs.

VALVES & SPRINGS

1. Reverse disassembly procedure to assemble and note the following:
   a. Apply engine oil to each valve. Insert valves into guides, using care not to damage seal.
   b. Valve spring should be installed with identification color side directed toward valve spring retainer.
   c. Using a suitable valve spring compressor, compress spring and install retainer lock.

CYLINDER HEAD

1. Clean both cylinder head and cylinder block gasket surfaces.
2. Install gasket with identification mark toward cylinder head, **Fig. 18.**
3. Install cylinder head bolts and tighten in sequence, **Fig. 19.**
4. Install intake and exhaust manifolds and gaskets.

CAMSHAFT, ROCKER ARMS & SHAFT

1. Reverse disassembly procedure to assemble and note the following:
   a. Assemble rocker arms to rocker shafts, then install on cylinder head, **Fig. 20.**

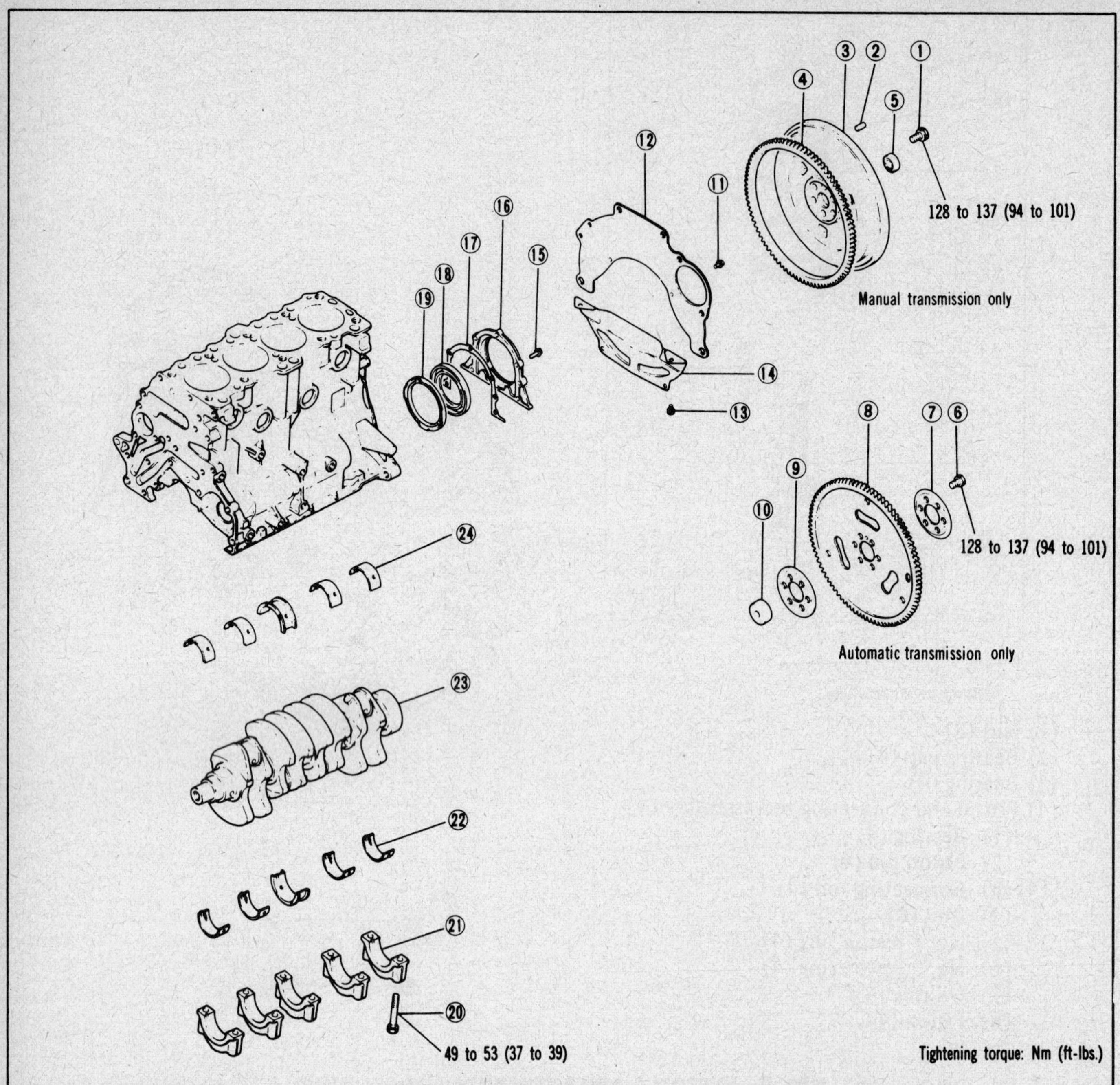

(1) Flywheel bolt (6)
(2) Dowel pin (3)
(3) Flywheel
(4) Ring gear
(5) Ball bearing
(6) Drive plate bolt (6)
(7) Adapter plate
(8) Drive plate assembly
(9) Adapter plate
(10) Crankshaft bushing
(11) Flange bolt (2)
(12) Rear plate
(13) Bolt (2)
(14) Bell housing cover
(15) Flange bolt (5)
(16) Oil seal case
(17) Gasket
(18) Rear oil seal
(19) Retainer
(20) Bearing cap bolt (10)
(21) Bearing cap (5)
(22) Crankshaft bearing (5)
(23) Crankshaft (5)
(24) Crankshaft bearing (5)

Fig. 9 Exploded view of cylinder block & crankshaft assembly

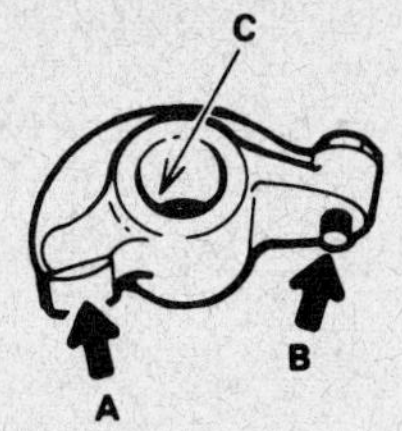

Fig. 10 Rocker arm inspection

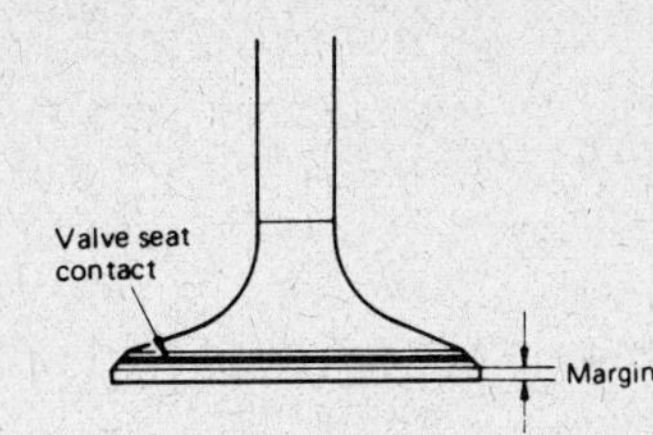

Fig. 11 Checking valve face margin

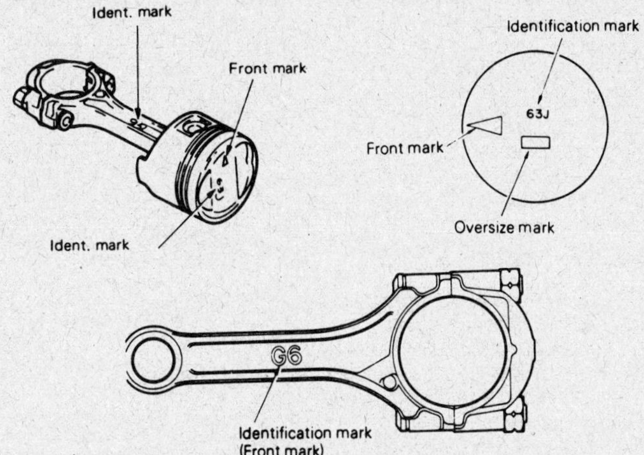

Fig. 12 Piston assembly identification marks

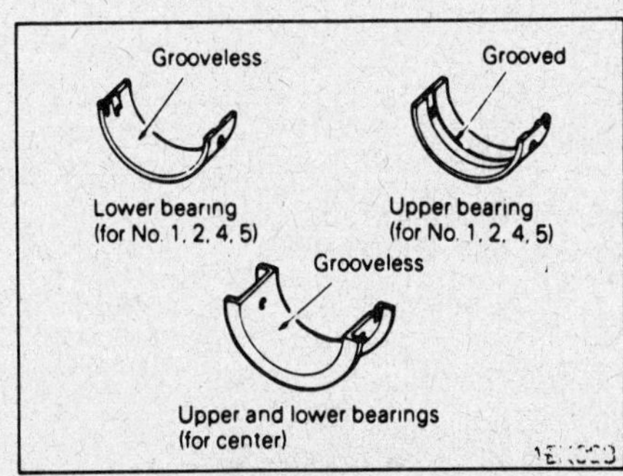

Fig. 13 Main bearing insert identification

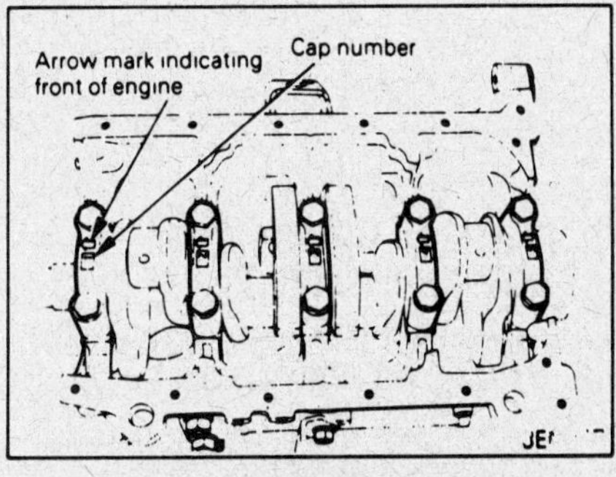

Fig. 14 Main bearing cap installation

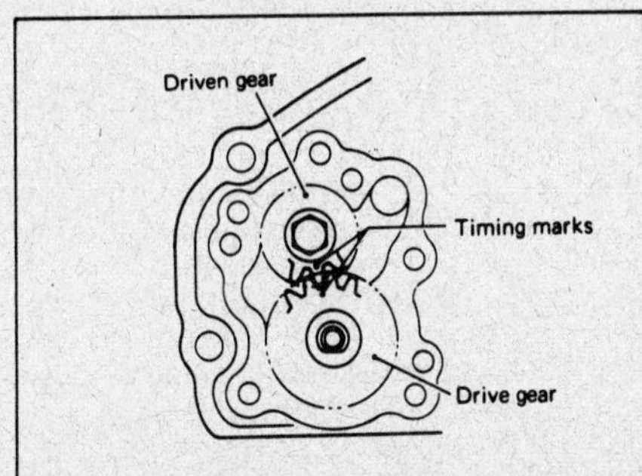

Fig. 15 Oil pump gears timing marks

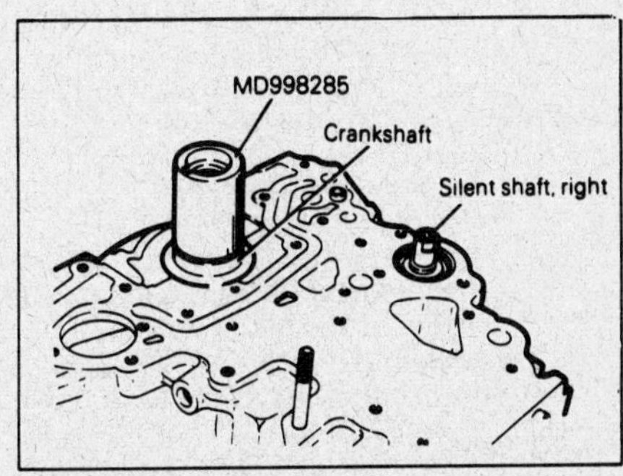

Fig. 16 Crankshaft front oil seal installation

b. Apply engine oil to inside diameter of rocker before assembly.
c. Ensure that oil hole side is down when installing rocker arm shafts into front camshaft bearing cap.
d. When valve cover is installed, use suitable gasket sealant.

TIMING BELT ASSEMBLY

1. Install right hand silent shaft sprocket and tighten attaching bolt, then install crankshaft sprocket and align timing marks of both sprockets with timing marks on engine block, **Fig. 21.**
2. Install silent shaft timing belt "B" over crankshaft and silent shaft sprockets. When installing timing belt, ensure that tension side of belt has no slack, **Fig. 21.**
3. Position right hand silent shaft pulley on shaft, with flange facing front of engine. When installing attaching bolt, position pulley so that center of pulley is to the left of the mounting bolt, **Fig. 21.**
4. Install oil pump sprocket and torque attaching nut to 25-28 ft. lbs., then align sprocket timing mark with mark on front timing case. With oil pump sprocket timing marks aligned, remove plug from left hand side of cylinder block and insert a screwdriver with a shaft diameter of .3 inch. If screwdriver can be inserted 2.4 inches or more, alignment is correct. If screwdriver can be inserted only 1 inch, rotate oil pump sprocket one revolution and realign timing marks. Then check to ensure that screwdriver can be inserted 2.4 inches or more. This check is performed to ensure that silent shaft and oil pump sprocket are properly positioned. Leave screwdriver inserted in hole until after timing belt has been installed.
5. Install timing belt tensioner spring, then install tensioner and tighten adjusting nut. The tensioner spring should be positioned so that straight end of spring is against water pump body and bent end of spring is against tensioner tang. Push on tensioner to align mounting bolt holes, then install mounting bolt.
6. Loosen tensioner mounting nut and bolt and push tensioner toward water pump as far as possible. Then tighten nut to secure tensioner in this position.
7. Check to ensure that all timing marks are aligned, **Fig. 1,** and position timing belt over crankshaft sprocket. Then install timing belt over oil pump sprocket and camshaft sprocket. When installing timing belt, ensure that tension side of belt is tight. Remove screwdriver from plug hole at left side of cylinder block and install plug.
8. Install crankshaft pulley to prevent timing belt from becoming misaligned when the crankshaft is rotated.
9. Loosen tensioner nut and bolt, then push tensioner toward adjusting nut to mesh belt and camshaft sprocket. Retighten nut and bolt.
10. Check to ensure that all timing marks

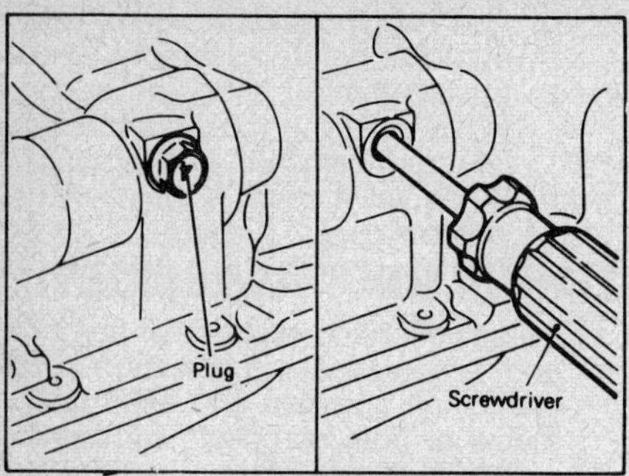

Fig. 17 Securing silent shaft

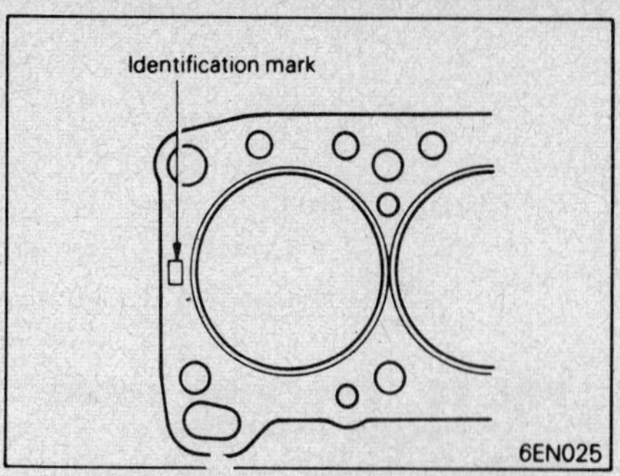

Fig. 18 Cylinder head gasket identification mark

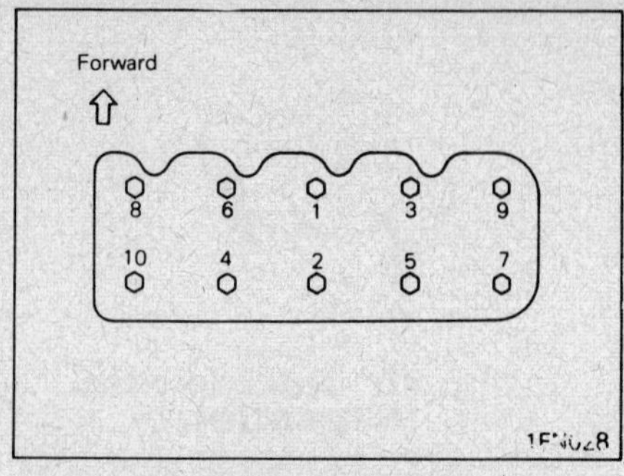

Fig. 19 Cylinder head bolt tightening sequence

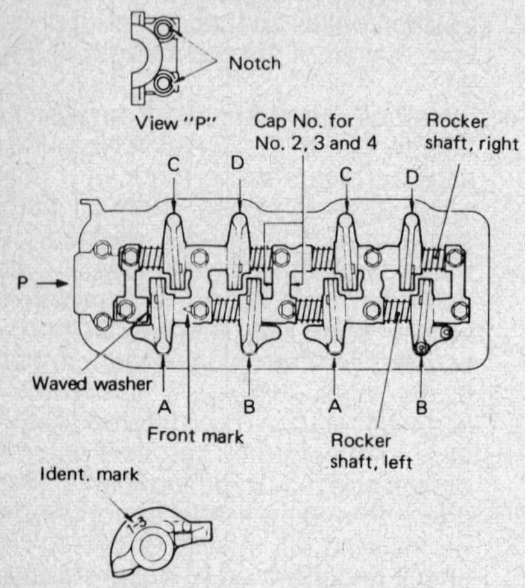

Rocker arm application			
	Ident. mark	In.	Ex.
No. 1 & 3 cyl.	1–3	A	C
No. 2 & 4 cyl.	2–4	B	D

Fig. 20 Rocker arm & shaft installation

are aligned, then rotate crankshaft one revolution in the normal direction of rotation. Crankshaft should be rotated smoothly and timing belt should not be pushed or twisted while crankshaft is being rotated. This procedure is performed to apply tension to the tension side of the timing belt.

11. Loosen tensioner bolt and nut, then tighten tensioner adjusting nut and mounting bolt. Torque bolts and nut to 16 to 21 ft. lbs. This procedure is performed to apply tension to loose side of timing belt.
12. When center of tension side of timing belt and gasket line on under cover are held between thumb and forefinger, clearance between belt and gasket should be .55 inch. If not, readjust as necessary.
13. Remove crankshaft pulley, then install timing belt lower and upper front covers.
14. Install crankshaft pulley and tighten attaching bolts to 11 to 15 ft. lbs. on 1983-85 models or 15 to 21 ft. lbs. on 1986-87 models.

JET VALVE, ADJUST

The jet valve must be adjusted before adjusting the intake valve.

Following procedure for intake and exhaust valve adjustment, position No. 1 cylinder at top dead center compression stroke. Loosen intake valve adjusting screw at least 2 turns, then loosen jet valve adjusting screw locknut. Rotate jet valve adjusting screw counterclockwise and insert specified feeler gauge blade between jet valve stem and adjusting screw. Tighten jet valve adjusting screw until it contacts the feeler gauge blade, then while holding adjusting screw in position, tighten locknut. After jet valve adjustment has been completed, adjust intake valve clearance. Continue to follow intake and exhaust valve adjustment procedure and adjust jet valves as necessary.

INTAKE & EXHAUST VALVES, ADJUST

Except 1985 Non-Turbo & All 1986–87 Engines

The jet valve must be adjusted before adjusting the intake valve.

1. With engine at operating temperature, remove rocker arm cover.
2. Disconnect high tension lead from ignition coil.
3. While observing rocker arms on No. 4 cylinder, rotate crankshaft until the exhaust valve is closing and the intake valve has just started to open with crankshaft pulley mark aligned with TDC mark on timing chain case. At this position, No. 1 cylinder is at top dead center compression stroke. Check and adjust valve clearance for both intake and exhaust valves of No. 1 cylinder, intake valve of No. 2 cylinder and exhaust valve of No. 3 cylinder.
4. Rotate crankshaft 360 degrees and check and adjust valve clearance for exhaust valve of No. 2 cylinder, intake valve of No. 3 cylinder and intake and exhaust valves of No. 4 cylinder.

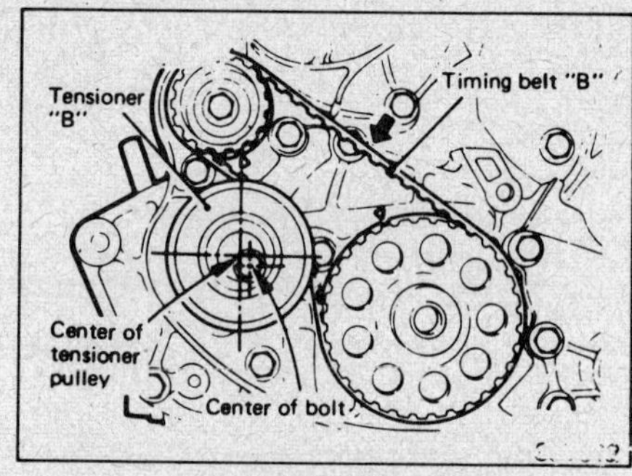

Fig. 21 Silent shaft belt tensioning pulley installation

5. After completing adjustment, install rocker arm cover and connect ignition coil high tension lead.

1985 Non-Turbo & All 1986–87 Engines

These engines use an auto-lash adjuster located in the rocker arm. No adjustments are required.

TURBOCHARGER

The turbocharger, **Fig. 22**, is an exhaust driven device which compresses the air/fuel mixture that is used to increase engine power on a demand basis, allowing a smaller, more economical engine to be used.

A turbine in the exhaust gas flow is connected through a shaft to the impeller (compressor). During normal, steady operation, the turbine does not rotate with sufficient speed to boost pressure to compress the air/fuel mixture. As speed increases, the mixture is compressed, allowing the denser mixture to enter the combustion chambers and develop more engine power during the combustion cycle.

The intake manifold pressure (boost) is controlled by a wastegate valve which is used to bypass a portion of the exhaust gasses around the turbine to a predetermined point in the cycle, limiting the boost pressure.

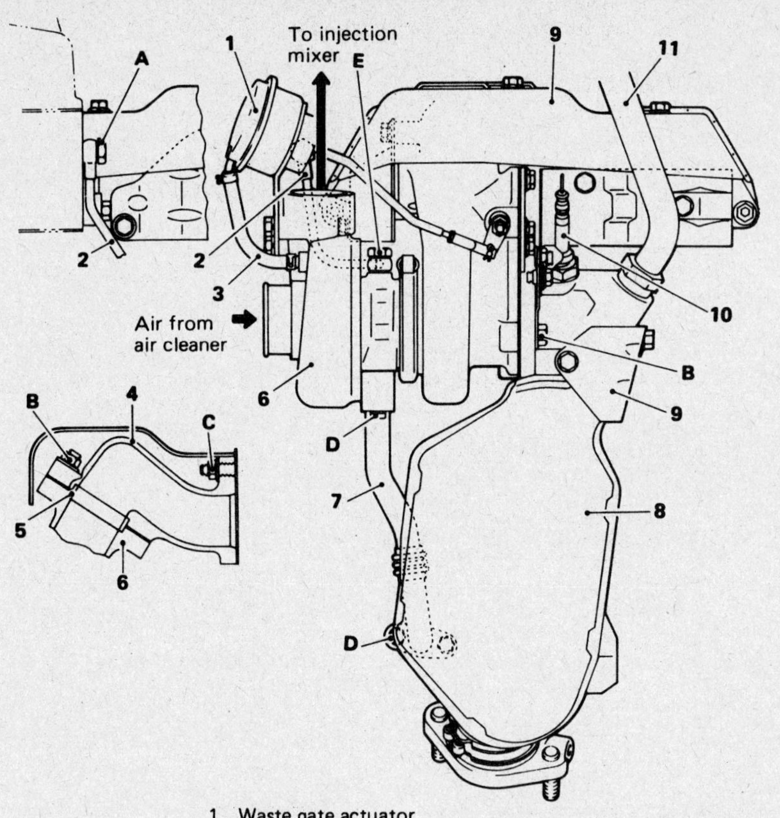

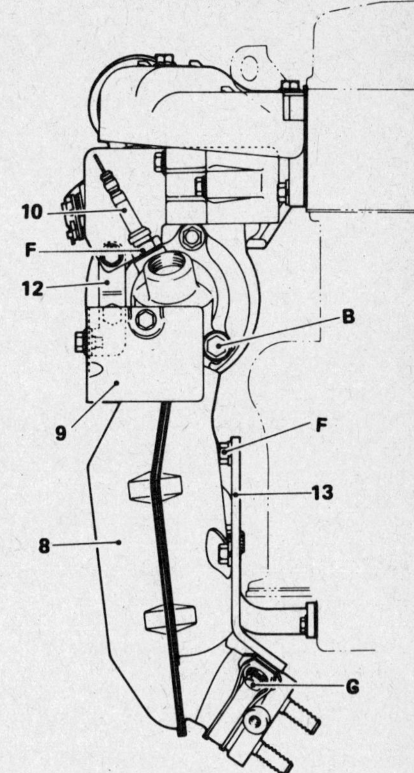

1. Waste gate actuator
2. Oil pipe
3. Hose
4. Exhaust manifold
5. Ring
6. Turbocharger
7. Oil return pipe
8. Catalytic converter
9. Heat protector
10. Oxygen sensor
11. Secondary air pipe
12. Stay
13. Convertor support bracket

	Nm	ft.lbs.
A	14–18.5	10–13.5
B	50–68	36–50
C	25–29	18–22
D	8–9.5	6–7
E	28–33	21–24.5
F	40–49	30–36
G	12–14.5	9–11

Fig. 22 Turbocharger assembly. 1984–87 1800cc engine

2600CC ENGINE SECTION

INDEX

ENGINE REPLACE

MONTERO

1983–86

1. Disconnect battery ground cable and remove hood.
2. Remove air cleaner, then disconnect heater hoses.
3. Disconnect brake booster vacuum hose, then the fuel hoses to the carburetor.
4. Disconnect accelerator cable.
5. Disconnect air temperature sensor connector, throttle position sensor connector and carburetor control wiring harness connector, if equipped.
6. Disconnect starter motor electrical connector, then remove clutch release cylinder from transmission.
7. Disconnect alternator electrical connectors, then the engine ground cable.
8. Disconnect fuel cut solenoid valve and bowl vent valve electrical connectors.
9. Disconnect coil high tension cable, then the water temperature gauge electrical connector.
10. Remove power steering pump.
11. Disconnect water temperature sensor, if equipped.
12. Disconnect vapor hose, then the purge hoses from purge control valve.
13. Disconnect oxygen sensor electrical connector, if equipped.
14. Disconnect oil pressure switch electrical connector, then remove the radiator assembly.
15. Remove front exhaust pipe, then the transfer case protector.
16. Disconnect speedometer cable, then the back-up light switch and 4 wheel drive indicator light switch electrical connectors.
17. Remove front and rear propeller shafts.
18. Remove transmission shift control lever and transfer case shift control lever.
19. Remove oil cooler hoses and tubes, if equipped with automatic transmission.
20. Remove engine mounting bolts, then using a suitable hoist, remove engine and transmission assembly from engine compartment.
21. Remove transmission to engine attaching bolts, then separate transmission from engine.
22. Reverse procedure to install.

1987

1. Disconnect battery ground cable, then mark position of hood hinges and remove hood.
2. Remove engine under cover, under skid plate, transfer case protector, cross shaft protector, then the snow protector.
3. Drain transmission fluid, then the transfer case oil.
4. Drain power steering fluid, then the A/C refrigerant.
5. Remove air filter, then disconnect accelerator cable.
6. Disconnect coolant hoses, then remove shrouds and radiator.
7. Disconnect brake booster vacuum hoses, then the heater hoses.
8. Disconnect oxygen sensor, then the control harness.
9. Disconnect battery positive cable, then the starter motor.
10. Disconnect A/C harness, then the alternator connector.
11. Disconnect water temperature gauge, switch and sensor.
12. Disconnect oil pressure gauge.
13. Disconnect power steering pressure and return hoses, then the throttle cable.
14. Disconnect fuel main and return hoses, then the A/C compressor and discharge hoses and ground strap.
15. Remove front exhaust pipe attaching nuts, then disconnect front exhaust pipe and gasket.
16. Remove control lever assembly, then the rear propeller shaft.
17. Remove front propeller shaft, then the O.D. solenoid valve connector.
18. Disconnect oil cooler feed and return tubes, then the speedometer cable.
19. Disconnect 4WD indicator lamp switch, then remove clutch release cylinder.
20. Disconnect select cross shaft, then the transmission control rod.
21. Remove insulator mounting plate attaching nuts and bolts, then the mounting plate.
22. Remove transfer mounting insulator and brackets, then the No. 2 crossmember.
23. Attach a suitable lifting device, then remove engine and transmission.
24. Remove engine to transmission attaching bolts, then separate engine from transmission.
25. Reverse procedure to install.

PICKUP

1984–86

1. Disconnect battery ground cable and remove hood.
2. Remove air cleaner assembly.
3. Drain coolant from radiator and transmission oil from transmission.
4. Disconnect heater hoses and brake booster vacuum hose.
5. Disconnect alternator wiring harness.
6. Disconnect clutch cable from transmission.
7. Disconnect accelerator cable and fuel hoses.
8. Disconnect starter motor wiring harness.
9. Disconnect engine ground cable and coil high tension cables.
10. Disconnect water temperature gauge wire connector.
11. Remove power steering pump, if equipped.
12. Disconnect oil pressure switch or pressure gauge wiring harness unit.
13. Remove radiator assembly.
14. Remove exhaust pipe from exhaust manifold.
15. On rear wheel drive models, remove engine under cover. On four wheel drive models, remove engine under cover, under skid plate and transfer case protector.
16. Disconnect speedometer cable from transmission.
17. Disconnect back-up switch harness. On four wheel drive models, also remove four wheel drive indicator light switch harness.
18. Remove propeller shaft or shafts, then the gear shift assembly.
19. On four wheel drive models, proceed

as follows:
   a. Using a suitable jack support transfer case.
   b. Remove transfer case mounting bracket and support insulator.
   c. Remove plate from side frame and detach transfer case mounting bracket from transfer case.
20. Using suitable engine lifting device, remove engine and transmission assembly diagonally out of engine compartment.
21. Remove transmission attaching bolts, then remove transmission.
22. Reverse procedure to install. Ensure that all connections, pipes and hoses are clear of engine when installing.

1987

1. Disconnect battery ground cable, then drain cooling system.
2. Mark position of hood hinges, then remove hood.
3. Remove engine under cover, then drain transmission fluid.
4. Remove air cleaner, then the radiator shrouds, as needed.
5. Disconnect radiator hoses, then remove radiator.
6. Disconnect alternator, then the starter.
7. Disconnect water temperature unit connectors, then the coil wire.
8. Disconnect battery positive cable, then the transmission harness connector.
9. Disconnect oxygen sensor connector, then the oil pressure gauge unit connector.
10. Disconnect accelerator cable, then the power steering oil pipe.
11. Disconnect air conditioner compressor pipe, then remove gear shift assembly.
12. Remove rear propeller shaft, then the No. 2 crossmember.
13. Attach a suitable lifting device, then remove engine and transmission assembly.
14. Remove engine to transmission attaching bolts, then separate engine from transmission.
15. Reverse procedure to install.

STARION

1984–86

1. Disconnect battery ground cable, then remove hood.
2. Drain coolant from radiator and transmission oil from transmission.
3. Disconnect heater hoses and brake booster vacuum hose.
4. Disconnect starter motor wiring harness.
5. Disconnect intake manifold ground cable connector.
6. Disconnect fuel hoses and coil high tension cable.
7. Remove power steering pump, then disconnect engine oil cooler.
8. Disconnect boost sensor hose and ECI unit wiring harnesses.
9. Disconnect alternator wiring harness and engine ground cable.
10. Remove radiator assembly.
11. Remove rear catalytic converter.
12. Disconnect speedometer cable from transmission.
13. Disconnect back-up light switch wiring harness.
14. Remove propeller shaft.
15. Disconnect oil pressure gauge wiring harness.
16. Remove clutch release cylinder.
17. Remove engine mounting bolts and gearshift lever assembly.
18. Using a suitable hoist, remove engine and transmission assembly from engine compartment.
19. Remove transmission to engine attaching bolts, then remove transmission from engine.
20. Reverse procedure to install.

1987

1. Drain cooling system, then the engine crankcase.
3. Remove residual fuel pressure as follows:
   a. Remove high floor panel from luggage compartment.
   b. Start engine and disconnect electrical connector from fuel tank sending unit (fuel pump connector).
   c. When engine stops from lack of fuel, turn ignition off. **Failure to release pressure prior to disconnecting fuel lines may cause fire or personal injury.**
4. Disconnect battery ground cable.
5. Drain transmission fluid, then remove engine under cover.
6. Mark position of hood hinges, then remove hood and air cleaner.
7. Remove turbocharger heat protector, then disconnect oxygen sensor harness connector.
8. Disconnect intercooler air hose connectors, then the power brake booster vacuum hose connections.
9. Disconnect heater hoses, then remove power steering oil pump V-belt.
10. Remove air conditioner compressor, then the power steering pump.
11. Remove air conditioner compressor, then disconnect exhaust system at catalytic converter.
12. Disconnect radiator hoses, then remove radiator.
13. Disconnect accelerator cable, then the fuel high pressure hose. Remove O-ring.
14. Disconnect fuel return hose connector, then the clutch tube connector.
15. Disconnect coil wire, then the speedometer cable connector.
16. Disconnect vacuum hoses, then the water temperature unit, sensor and switch harness connector.
17. Disconnect secondary air solenoid valve harness connector, then the EGR solenoid valve harness connector.
18. Disconnect injector harness connector, then the throttle position sensor harness connector.
19. Disconnect ISC servo harness connector, then the motor position sensor harness connector.
20. Disconnect distributor signal generator harness connector, then the ground connections.
21. Disconnect alternator harness connector, then the oil pressure gauge unit harness connector.
22. Disconnect starter connector, then the detonation sensor harness connector.
23. Disconnect back-up lamp switch, then the O.D. cancel solenoid.
24. Disconnect downshift solenoid harness, then the inhibitor switch harness connector.
25. Disconnect propeller shaft, then the gear shift lever.
26. Remove rear crossmember, then the engine mount attaching nuts.
27. Attach a suitable lifting device, then remove engine and transmission from vehicle.
28. Remove transmission to engine attaching bolts, then separate engine from transmission.
29. Reverse procedure to install.

CYLINDER HEAD REPLACE

MONTERO

1. Disconnect battery ground cable, then drain engine coolant.
2. Remove air filter, then disconnect accelerator cable.
3. Remove coolant hoses and shrouds as necessary, then disconnect breather hose.
4. Disconnect PCV hose, then the oxygen sensor connector.
5. Remove A/C compressor drive belt, then disconnect power steering breather pipe.
6. Mark and disconnect spark plug cables, then the coil wire.
7. Remove front exhaust pipe attaching nuts, then disconnect front exhaust pipe and remove gasket.
8. Remove rocket cover assembly, then the rocker cover gasket.
9. Rotate crankshaft in normal direction of rotation until piston of cylinder No. 1 is at TDC of compression stroke with crankshaft and camshaft timing marks aligned, **Fig. 1.**
10. Mark distributor cap and housing to facilitate installation and remove distributor.
11. Remove camshaft sprocket bolt, washer, drive gear and spacer. Pull camshaft sprocket with timing chain out from camshaft, then place sprocket on top of camshaft sprocket holder. **Do not remove belt from crankshaft sprocket. Do not rotate crankshaft or camshaft independently.**
12. Remove cylinder head attaching bolts in sequence shown, **Fig. 2,** then remove cylinder head and gasket.
13. Reverse procedure to install. Referring to bolt tightening sequence, **Fig. 3,** torque cylinder head bolts in three steps as follows:
   a. Torque all bolts except No. 11 to 69 ft. lbs. on a cold engine or 75 ft. lbs. on a hot engine.
   b. Torque cylinder head to chain case cover bolts (No. 11) to 156 inch lbs.

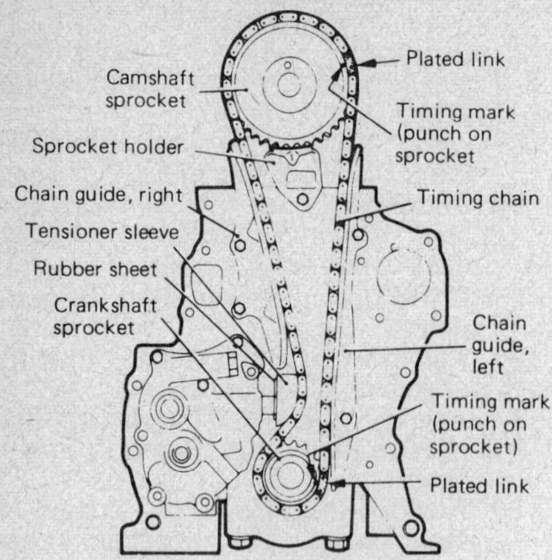

Fig. 1 Timing chain installation

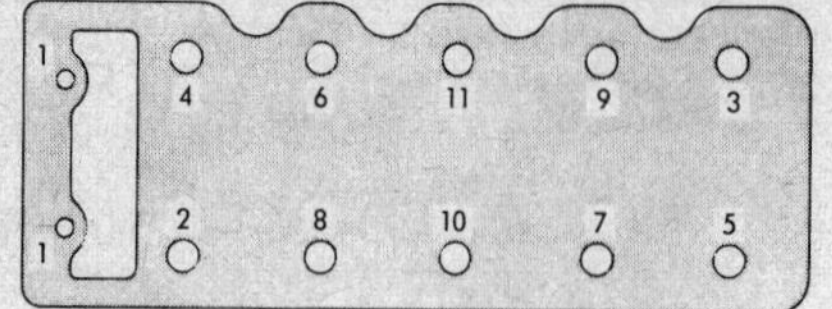

Fig. 2 Cylinder head bolt removal sequence

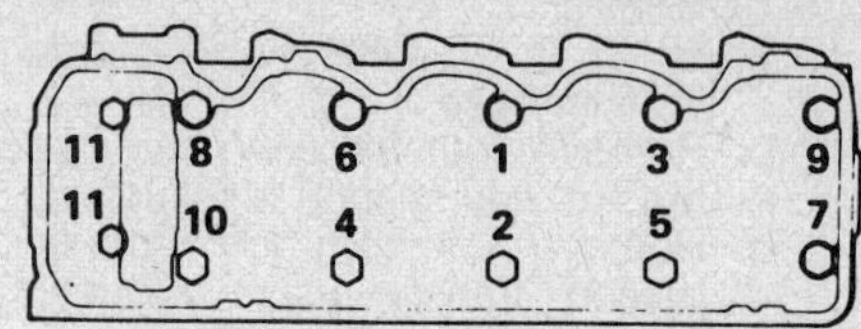

Fig. 3 Cylinder head bolt tightening sequence

PICKUP

1. Disconnect battery ground cable.
2. Drain engine coolant, then remove air cleaner and breather hoses.
3. Disconnect accelerator cable, then remove A/C compressor drive belt.
4. Rotate crankshaft in normal direction of rotation until piston of cylinder No. 1 is at TDC of compression stroke with crankshaft and camshaft timing marks aligned, **Fig. 1.**
5. Disconnect coil cable, then mark distributor cap and housing to facilitate installation and remove distributor.
6. Remove rocker cover attaching bolts, then the rocker cover.
7. Remove camshaft sprocket attaching bolt, then the cylinder head attaching bolts in sequence shown, **Fig. 2.**
8. Remove cylinder head, then the gasket.
9. Reverse procedure to install. Referring to bolt tightening sequence, **Fig. 3,** torque cylinder head bolts in three steps as follows:
   a. Torque all bolts except No. 11 to 69 ft. lbs. on a cold engine or 75 ft. lbs. on a hot engine.
   b. Torque cylinder head to chain case cover bolts (No. 11) to 156 inch lbs.

STARION

1. Drain cooling system, then the engine crankcase.
2. Remove residual fuel pressure as follows:
   a. Remove high floor panel from luggage compartment.
   b. Start engine and disconnect electrical connector from fuel tank sending unit (fuel pump connector).
   c. When engine stops from lack of fuel, turn ignition off. **Failure to release pressure prior to disconnecting fuel lines may cause fire or personal injury.**
3. Disconnect battery ground cable.
4. Remove air conditioner compressor drive belt, then the A/C receiver, condenser and compressor clutch assembly.
5. Remove brake master cylinder heat protector, then disconnect oxygen sensor harness connector.
6. Remove turbocharger heat protector, then the air cleaner.
7. On models with intercooler, remove air hoses, then the intake air temperature sensor connection.
8. On all models, coolant hoses, then the air intake pipe.
9. Remove secondary air cleaner, then the PCV valve hose.
10. Disconnect accelerator cable, then the forward cylinder head attaching bolt.
11. Remove rocker cover and gaskets, then the semicircular packing.
12. Rotate crankshaft in normal direction of rotation until piston of cylinder No. 1 is at TDC of compression stroke with crankshaft and camshaft timing marks aligned, **Fig. 1.**
13. Disconnect coil wire, then mark locations of spark plug wires and disconnect them.
14. Disconnect fuel high pressure cable connection, then the heater hoses.
15. Disconnect fuel return hose, then the power brake booster hose.
16. Disconnect heater and coolant hoses, then remove engine oil dipstick and O-ring.
17. Disconnect turbocharger oil and coolant connections, then the exhaust system at rear of catalytic converter.
18. Mark distributor cap and housing to facilitate installation, then remove distributor.
19. Disconnect vacuum hoses, then the coolant temperature sending unit, sensor and switch connector.
20. Disconnect secondary air solenoid valve harness, then the EGR solenoid valve.
21. Disconnect injector harness, then the throttle position sensor.
22. Disconnect ISC servo, then the motor position sensor.
23. Disconnect distributor signal generator, then the ground cable connection.
24. Remove camshaft sprocket to camshaft attaching bolt, then the cylinder head to timing case cover attaching bolt.
25. Remove cylinder head attaching bolts in sequence shown, **Fig. 2.**
26. Remove cylinder head, then the gasket.
27. Reverse procedure to install. Referring to bolt tightening sequence, **Fig. 3,** torque cylinder head bolts in three steps as follows:
   a. Torque all bolts except No. 11 to 69 ft. lbs. on a cold engine or 75 ft. lbs. on a hot engine.
   b. Torque cylinder head to chain case cover bolts (No. 11) to 156 inch lbs.

TIMING GEARS & OIL SEALS

TIMING CHAIN CASE COVER

1. Disconnect battery ground cable.
2. Remove alternator locking screw, then loosen jam nut and adjusting screw. Remove drive belt.
3. Remove distributor retaining nut, then remove distributor from cylinder head and position aside.
4. Remove front and rear A/C compressor to bracket attaching screws, then remove A/C compressor and position aside.
5. Remove power steering pump pivot and lock screws, then remove drive belt.
6. Remove power steering pump mounting screw and nut, then position power steering pump aside.
7. Remove power steering pump bracket to engine attaching screws, then remove bracket.
8. Raise vehicle and remove right inner splash shield.
9. Drain crankcase, then remove crankshaft drive pulley.
10. Lower vehicle and position a suitable jack under engine.
11. Remove engine mount to frame side rail through bolt, then remove engine oil dipstick.
12. Remove air cleaner assembly.
13. Disconnect battery ground cable, then the spark plug wires.
14. Disconnect vacuum hoses from cylinder head cover.
15. Remove cylinder head cover screws, then the cylinder head cover.
16. Remove oil pan attaching screws, then remove oil pan.
17. Remove timing indicator plate from timing chain case cover.
18. Remove engine mounting plate from timing chain case cover.
19. Remove cylinder head cover as previously described.
20. Remove two front cylinder head screws. **Do not disturb any other cylinder head bolts.**
21. Remove remaining chain case cover to engine block retaining screws, **Fig. 4.**

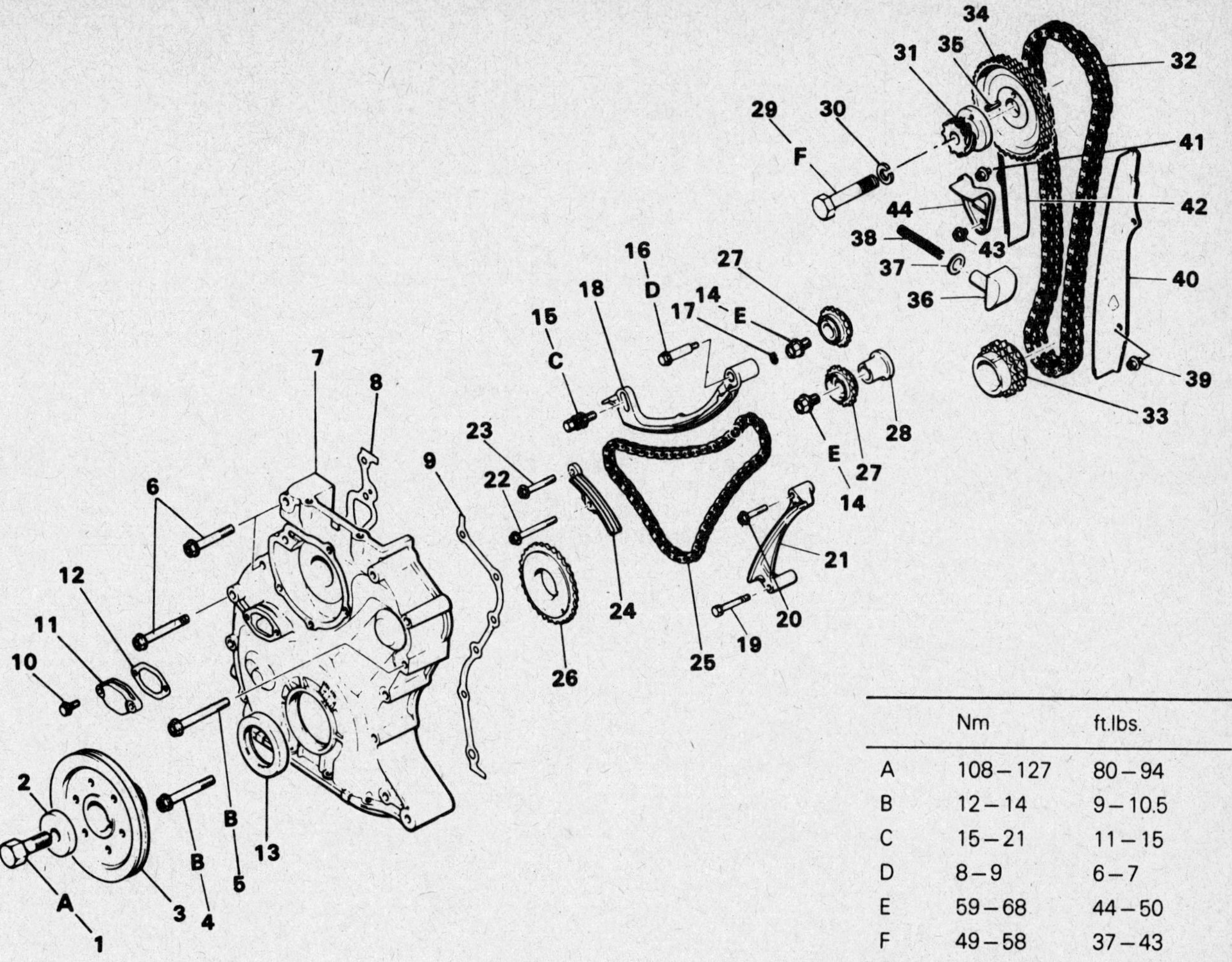

	Nm	ft.lbs.
A	108–127	80–94
B	12–14	9–10.5
C	15–21	11–15
D	8–9	6–7
E	59–68	44–50
F	49–58	37–43

1. Crankshaft pulley bolt
2. Special washer
3. Pulley
4. Flange bolt (8)
5. Flange bolt
6. Flange bolt (2)
7. Timing chain case
8. Chain case gasket (R)
9. Chain case gasket (L)
10. Flange bolt (2)
11. Cover
12. Gasket
13. Oil seal
14. Flange bolt (2)
15. Special bolt "B"
16. Special bolt "A"
17. Spring washer
18. Chain guide "B"
19. Flange bolt
20. Flange bolt
21. Chain guide "A"
22. Flange bolt
23. Flange bolt
24. Chain guide "C"
25. Chain "B"
26. Crankshaft sprocket "B"
27. Sprocket "B" (2)
28. Spacer
29. Bolt w/washer
30. Plain washer
31. Distributor gear
32. Timing chain
33. Crankshaft sprocket
34. Camshaft sprocket
35. Spring pin
36. Tensioner
37. Rubber washer
38. Spring
39. Flange bolt
40. Tension side chain guide
41. Flange bolt (2)
42. Loose side chain guide
43. Flange bolt (2)
44. Sprocket holder

Fig. 4 Timing chain assembly

TIMING CHAIN, REMOVAL

1. Remove crankshaft pulley attaching bolt, then the washer and crankshaft pulley, **Fig. 4.**
2. Remove timing chain case attaching bolts, then the timing chain case and gasket.
3. Remove chain guide access hole cover, then the gasket.
4. Remove oil seal, then chain guides B, A and C.
5. Remove chain B, then crankshaft sprocket B.
6. Remove oil pump sprocket, then the left silent shaft sprocket with spacer.
7. Remove tension sleeve, rubber sheet, then the tensioner spring.
8. Remove distributor drive gear, then the spring pin.
9. Remove camshaft sprocket, then the timing chain and crankshaft sprocket.
10. Remove chain guides, then the sprocket holder.

SILENT SHAFT DRIVE CHAIN

1. Remove chain case cover as previously described.
2. Remove sprocket screws, then the

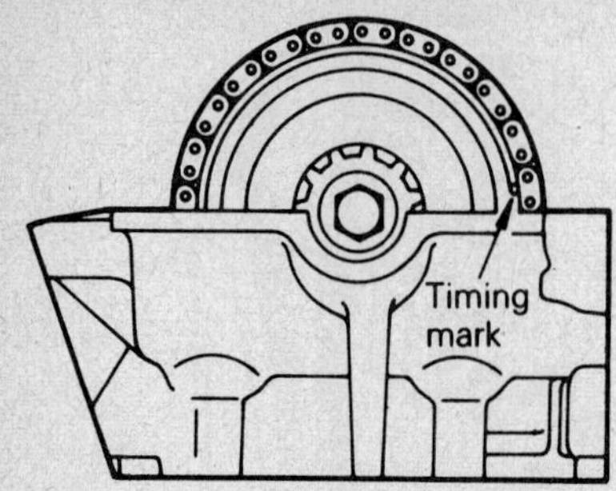

Fig. 5 Camshaft timing mark alignment

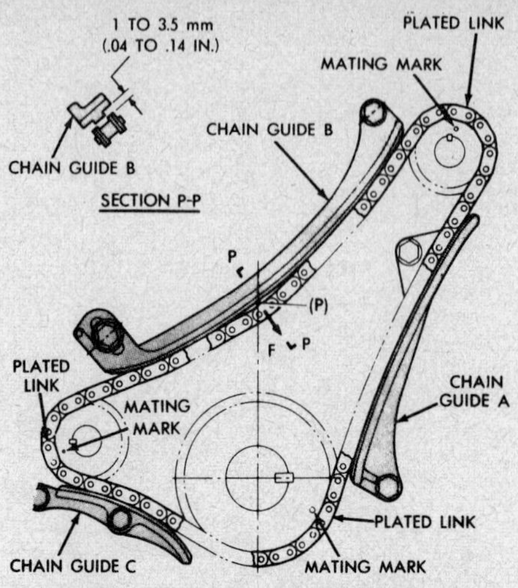

Fig. 6 Silent shaft chain adjustment & installation

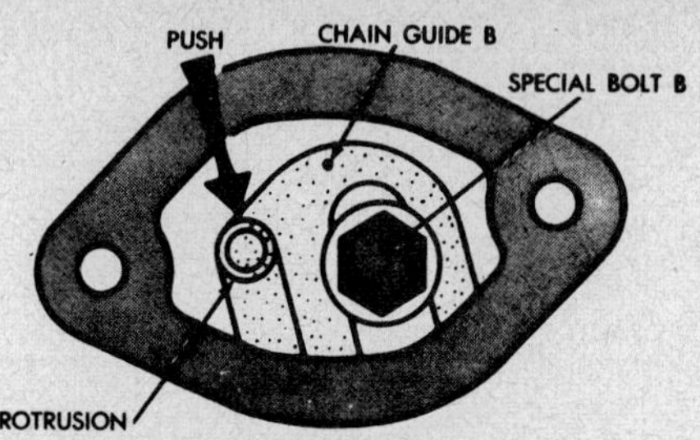

Fig. 7 Silent shaft chain adjustment with engine installed

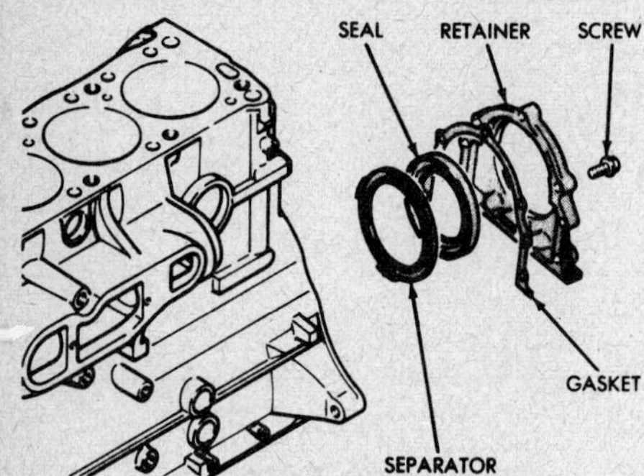

Fig. 8 Rear oil seal removal

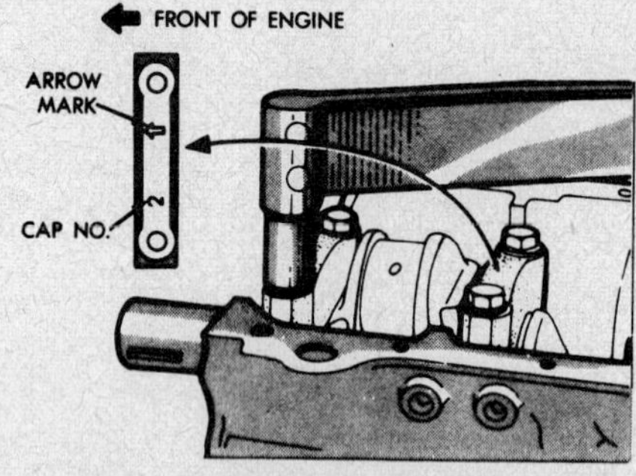

Fig. 9 Main bearing cap installation

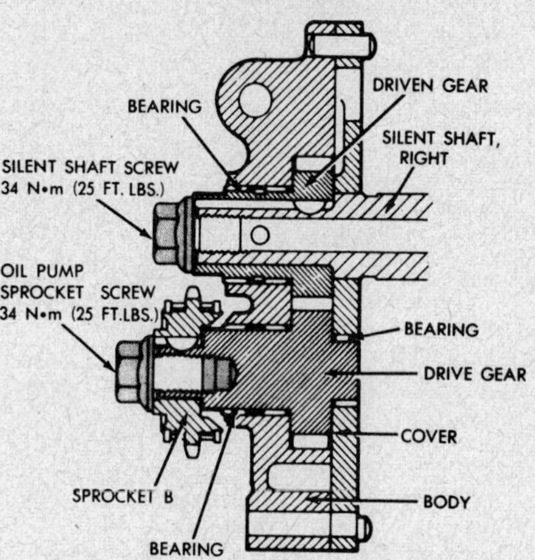

Fig. 10 Oil pump & silent shaft removal

drive chain, crankshaft sprocket and silent shaft sprocket, **Fig. 4.**

CAMSHAFT DRIVE CHAIN

1. Remove chain case cover as previously described.
2. Remove camshaft sprocket holder, then the left and right timing chain guides, **Fig. 4.**
3. Depress tensioner to remove drive chain.
4. Remove crankshaft and camshaft sprockets.

CAMSHAFT INSTALLATION

1. With camshaft bearing caps installed, rotate camshaft until timing marks are aligned as shown, **Fig. 5.**

TIMING CHAIN INSTALLATION

1. Install sprocket holder, then left and right chain guides, **Fig. 4.**
2. Rotate crankshaft in normal direction of rotation until piston of cylinder No. 1 is at TDC of compression stroke with crankshaft and camshaft sprocket timing marks aligned, **Fig. 1.**
3. Install tensioner spring assembly onto oil pump body, **Fig. 6.**
4. Install timing chain on camshaft sprocket and crankshaft sprocket. Ensure timing marks are aligned, **Fig. 5.** Timing marks on sprockets are punch marks on the teeth while timing marks on chain are plated links.
5. Align crankshaft sprocket to the crankshaft keyway and slide into place. Align camshaft sprocket dowel hole to camshaft dowel hole.
6. Install dowel pin, then the distributor drive gear. Install sprocket screw onto camshaft and torque to 40 ft. lbs.

SILENT SHAFT CHAIN INSTALLATION & ADJUSTMENT

1. Install silent shaft chain drive pulley onto crankshaft.
2. Install silent shaft chain onto oil pump sprocket and silent shaft sprocket.
3. Ensure timing marks are aligned. Timing marks on the sprockets are punch marks on the teeth, while timing marks on the chain are plated links.
4. Align crankshaft sprocket plated link with punch mark on sprocket.
5. Position chain on crankshaft sprocket, then install oil pump sprocket and silent shaft sprockets on their respective shafts.
6. Install oil pump and silent shaft sprocket screws and torque to 25 ft. lbs.
7. Install three chain guides. Snugly tighten retaining bolts.
8. Refer to **Fig. 6** and adjust silent shaft chain tension as follows:
   a. Tighten chain guide "A" mounting screws.
   b. Tighten chain guide "B" mounting screws.
   c. Shake oil pump and silent shaft sprockets to collect slack at point "P."
   d. Adjust position of chain guide "B" so that when the chain is pulled in direction of arrow "F," clearance between chain guide "B" and chain links will be .04-.14 inch. Tighten chain guide "B" mounting screws.
9. Install new gasket on chain case, coat gasket with suitable sealant, then install chain case to block and torque attaching screws to 10 ft. lbs.

TENSION ADJUSTMENT WITH ENGINE INSTALLED

1. Remove cover over access hole in chain case cover, **Fig. 7.**
2. Loosen bolt "B," **Fig. 7.**
3. Apply pressure by hand on boss indicated in **Fig. 7,** then torque bolt "B" to 8 ft. lbs.

CRANKSHAFT, BEARINGS & SILENT SHAFT

REAR OIL SEAL, REPLACE

1. Remove screws attaching crankshaft rear oil seal retainer, then the retainer, **Fig. 8.**
2. Remove separator from retainer, then the oil seal.
3. Install new seal into retainer, then the separator. Ensure oil hole is positioned at separator bottom.

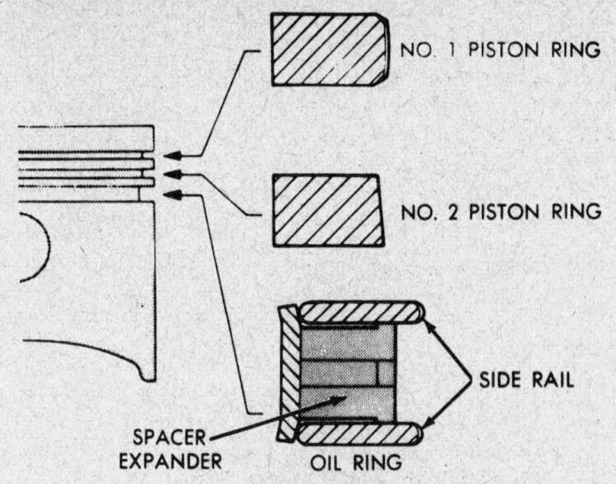

Fig. 11 Piston ring installation

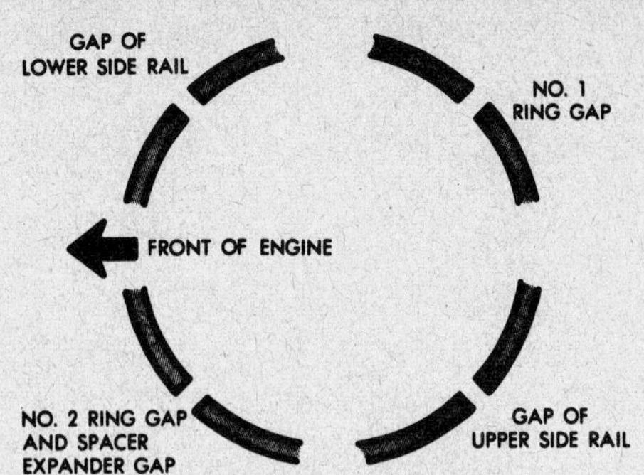

Fig. 12 Piston ring end gap alignment

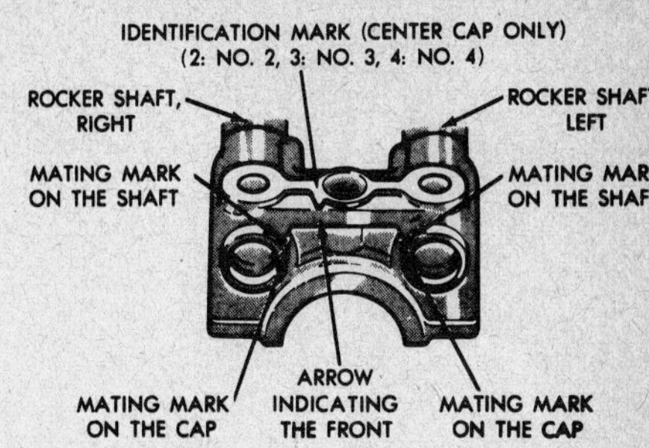

Fig. 13 Camshaft bearing cap installation

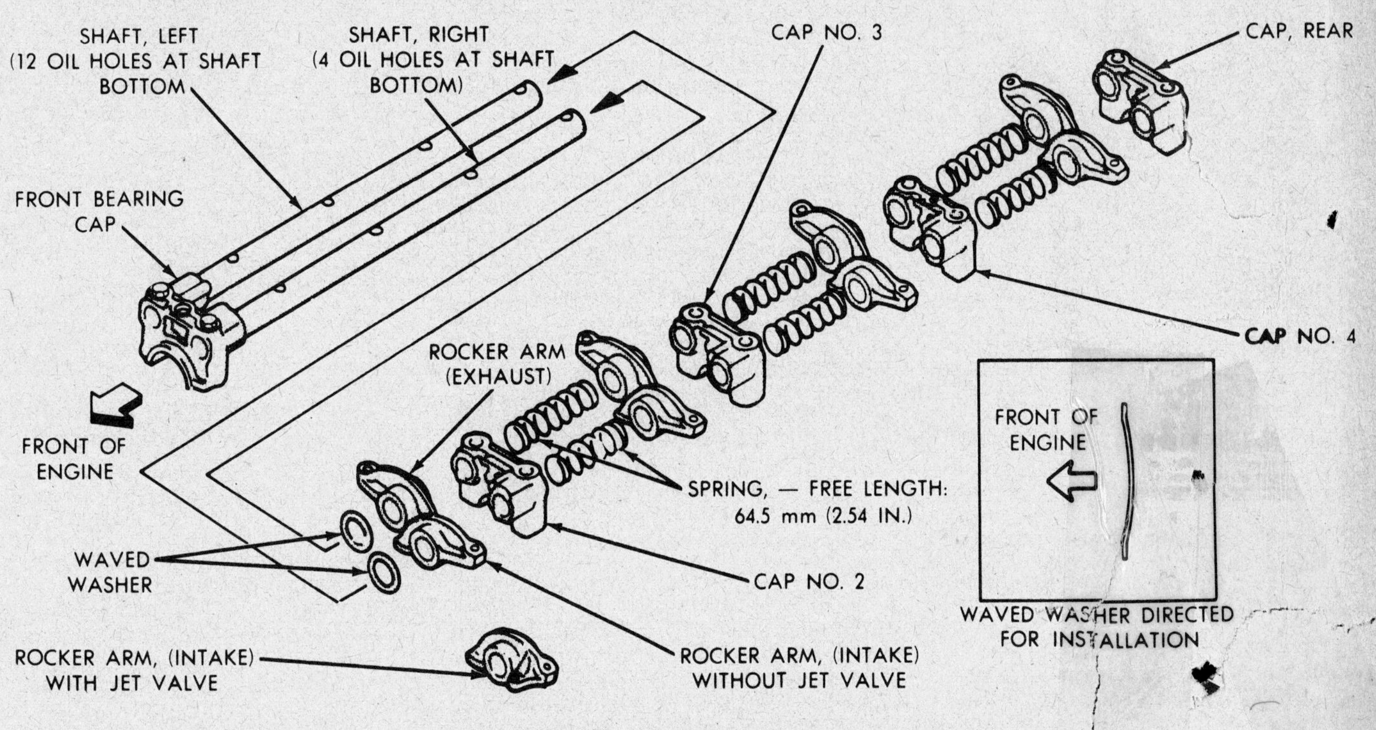

Fig. 14 Rocker arm shaft assembly

MAIN BEARING CAPS

1. Install main bearing caps in sequence and ensure arrows on caps are pointed in direction of timing chain, **Fig. 9.**

OIL PUMP & SILENT SHAFT

1. Refer to **Fig. 10** and remove silent shaft screw, then the silent shaft.
2. Remove oil pump to cylinder block screw, then the oil pump.

PISTONS & RODS

Refer to **Fig. 11** for correct piston ring installation and note the following side clearances:

1. No. 1 ring: .002-.004 inch.
2. No. 2ring: .001-.002 inch.

INSTALLING PISTON RING SIDE RAIL

1. Place one end of side rail between piston ring groove and spacer expander.
2. Hold end of ring firmly and press downward on portion to be installed until side rail is in position. Do not use a piston ring expander.
3. Install upper side rail first, then the lower side rail.

PISTON RING END GAP LOCATION

1. Position piston ring end gaps as shown, **Fig. 12.**
2. Position oil ring expander gap at least 45° from side rail gaps but not on piston pin center line or in thrust direction.

CYLINDER HEAD & VALVE ASSEMBLY

CAMSHAFT BEARING CAP

1. Align camshaft bearing caps with arrows pointing toward timing chain, **Fig. 13.** Install caps in numerical order.

ROCKER ARM SHAFT ASSEMBLY

1. Refer to **Fig. 14** and install bolts into front bearing caps.
2. Install wave washers, rocker arms, bearing caps and springs in order shown, **Fig. 14.**
3. Place rocker shaft assembly into position, then rotate camshaft until dowel pin hole is at vertical centerline, **Fig. 5.**
4. Tighten camshaft bearing cap bolts in the following order:
   a. No. 3 cap bolts to 85 inch lbs.
   b. No. 2 cap bolts to 85 inch lbs.
   c. No. 4 cap bolts to 85 inch lbs.
   d. Front cap bolts to 85 inch lbs.
   e. Rear cap bolts to 85 inch lbs.
5. Repeat steps 4a through 4e, increasing torque to 175 inch lbs.

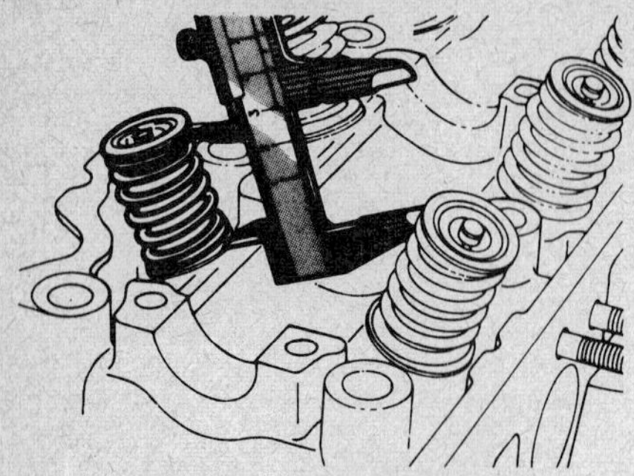

Fig. 15 Measuring installed valve spring height

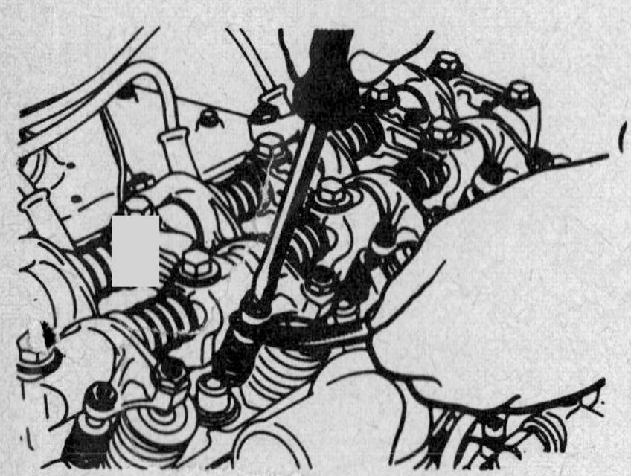

Fig. 17 Jet valve clearance adjustment

INSTALLED VALVE SPRING HEIGHT

1. Measure installed height of valve spring between spring seat and spring retainer, **Fig. 15**. Installed height should be 1.590 inch. If height is greater than 1.629 inch, replace spring.

VALVE CLEARANCE ADJUSTMENT

1985 non-turbo and all 1986-87 engines use an auto-lash adjuster located in the rocker arm. No adjustments are required.

1. Check torque on cylinder head bolts before performing valve adjustments.
2. With engine at operating temperature, position piston at TDC on compression stroke.
3. Loosen valve adjuster locknut, then adjust valve clearance by rotating adjusting screw while measuring with a feeler gauge, **Fig. 16**.
4. Valve clearance should be as follows: Intake — .006 inch.; Exhaust — .010 inch.
5. Tighten locknut securely while holding adjusting screw with screwdriver.

JET VALVE SERVICE

1. Install jet valve assembly into cylinder head.
2. Using suitable socket, torque jet valve to 168 inch lbs. **Ensure that socket wrench is not tilted with respect to centerline of jet valve as damage to the valve stem may result. Check torque on cylinder head bolts before performing jet valve adjustments.**
3. With engine at operating temperature, position piston at TDC of compression stroke.
4. Loosen jet valve adjuster locknut, **Fig. 17.**
5. Proper valve clearance is obtained by rotating adjusting screw while measuring clearance with feeler gauge.
6. Valve clearance should be .006 inch on 1983 models or .010 inch on 1984-87 models.
7. Tighten locknut securely while holding adjusting screw with screwdriver.

INTAKE MANIFOLD, REPLACE

Montero

1. Disconnect battery ground cable, then drain engine coolant.
2. Remove carburetor assembly, then the gasket.
3. Disconnect engine coolant hoses, then the heater hoses.
4. Disconnect vacuum hoses from manifold, then the brake booster vacuum hose.
5. On models with A/C, disconnect water temperature switch connector.
6. On all models, disconnect water temperature sensor, then the water temperature gauge unit.
7. Disconnect thermo switch.
8. Remove intake manifold attaching bolts, then the intake manifold and gasket.
9. Reverse procedure to install. Refer to specifications for intake manifold attaching bolt torque.

Pickup

1. Disconnect battery ground cable, then drain engine coolant.
2. Remove carburetor assembly with gasket, then the coolant outlet fitting, gasket and thermostat.
3. Remove purge control valve hose, then disconnect and remove heater hoses.
4. Remove brake booster vacuum hose, then the manifold coolant hose.
5. Remove vacuum connector hose.
6. Remove intake manifold attaching bolts, then the intake manifold and gasket.
7. Reverse procedure to install. Refer to specifications for intake manifold attaching bolt torque.

Starion

1. Disconnect battery ground cable and drain coolant system.
2. Remove residual fuel pressure as follows:
   a. Remove high floor panel from luggage compartment.
   b. Start engine and disconnect electrical connector from fuel tank sending unit (fuel pump connector).
   c. When engine stops from lack of fuel, turn ignition off. **Failure to release pressure prior to disconnecting fuel lines may cause fire or personal injury.**

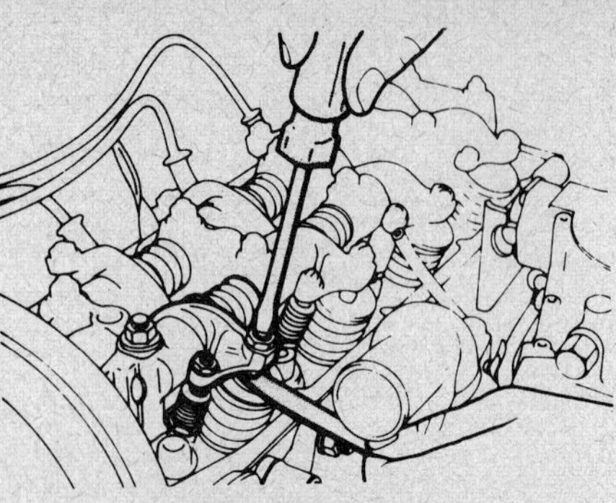

Fig. 16 Valve clearance adjustment

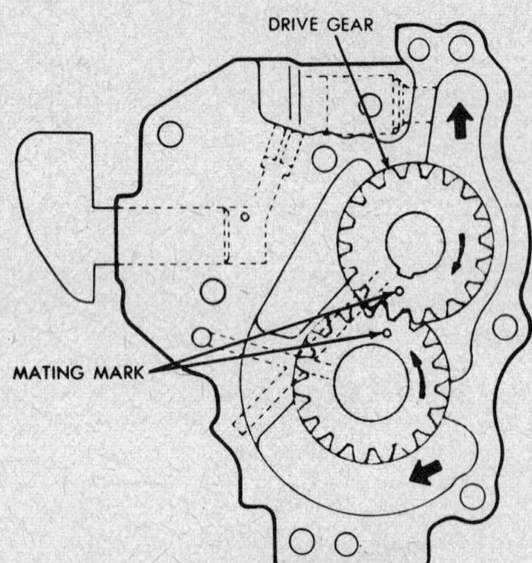

Fig. 18 Oil pump gear alignment

3. Remove water outlet fitting, then the gasket and thermostat.
4. Remove secondary air cleaner assembly, then the secondary air pipe.
5. Remove oil dipstick assembly, then the A/C compressor and clutch assembly.
6. Remove compressor bracket, then the heater hoses.
7. Remove manifold fitting at brake booster, then disconnect brake booster vacuum hose.
8. Remove water trap, then the manifold coolant hose.
9. Disconnect accelerator cable with clamp, then disconnect manifold electrical connectors.
10. Disconnect engine coolant temperature sensor, then the hose nipple.
11. Remove intake manifold attaching bolts, then the intake manifold and gasket.
12. Reverse procedure to install. Refer to specifications for intake manifold attaching bolt torque.

WATER PUMP REPLACE

1. Disconnect battery ground cable.
2. Drain cooling system.
3. Disconnect radiator hose, bypass hose, and heater hose from water pump.

1. Oil pipe joint
2. Gasket
3. Turbocharger assembly
4. Oil pipe
5. Hose clamp (2)
6. Oil hose
7. Oil return pipe
8. Gasket
9. Ring
10. Gasket
11. Gasket
12. Catalytic converter
13. Heat protector stay
14. Heat protector

	Nm	ft.lbs.
A	22–26	16.5–19.5
B	49–68	37–50
C	8–9.5	6–7
D	16–23	12–17

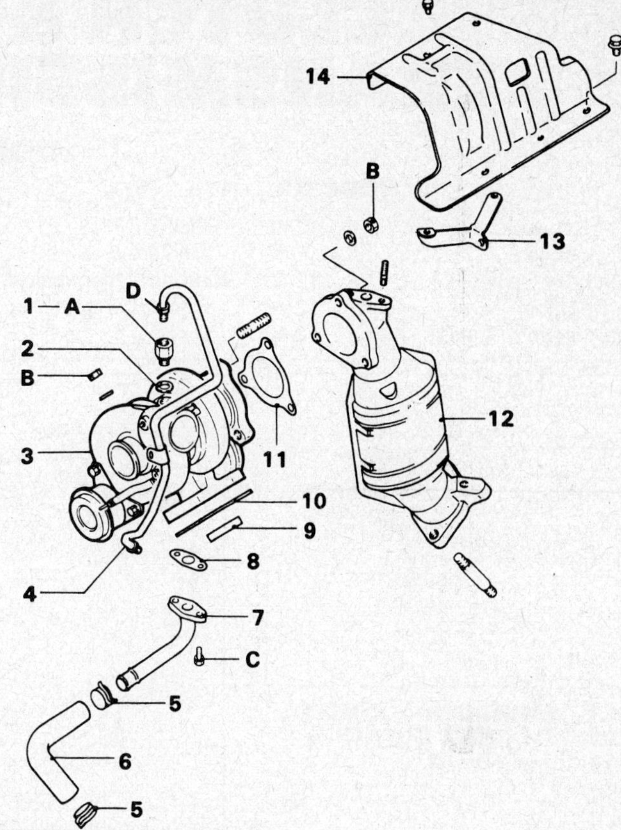

Fig. 19 Turbocharger assembly

4. Remove drive pulley shield.
5. Remove locking screw and pivot screws.
6. Remove drive belt and remove water pump from engine.
7. Reverse procedure to install.

ENGINE LUBRICATION SYSTEM

OIL PUMP CLEARANCES

Refer to **Fig. 10** and measure the following clearances:

1. Drive gear to body–.0043-.0059 inch (.11-.15 mm).
2. Driven gear to bearing–.008-.0020 inch (.02-.05 mm).
3. Driven gear endplay–.0024-.0047 inch (.06-.12 mm).
4. Drive gear endplay–.0016-.0028 inch (.04-.07 mm).
5. Drive gear to body clearance–.0043-.0059 inch (.11-.15 mm).
6. Drive gear to bearing–.0008-.0020 inch (.02-.05 mm).
7. Relief valve spring length–1.850 inch (47 mm).
8. Relief valve spring load–9.5 lbs. at 1.575 inch (40 mm).

Refer to **Fig. 18**, and align mating marks of drive and driven gears, then prime pump with clean oil and install onto engine.

TURBOCHARGER

The turbocharger, **Fig. 19**, is an exhaust driven device which compresses the air/fuel mixture that is used to increase engine power on a demand basis, allowing a smaller, more economical engine to be used.

A turbine in the exhaust gas flow is connected through a shaft to the impeller (compressor). During normal, steady operation, the turbine does not rotate with sufficient speed to boost pressure to compress the air/fuel mixture. As speed increases, the mixture is compressed, allowing the denser mixture to enter the combustion chambers and develop more engine power during the combustion cycle.

The intake manifold pressure (boost) is controlled by a wastegate valve which is used to bypass a portion of the exhaust gasses around the turbine at a predetermined point in the cycle, limiting the boost pressure.

DIESEL ENGINE SECTION

FOR SERVICE PROCEDURES ON DIESEL ENGINES, DIESEL FUEL INJECTION SYSTEMS & DIESEL GLOW PLUG SYSTEMS, REFER TO THE DODGE • PLYMOUTH DIESEL ENGINE SECTION.

CLUTCH & MANUAL TRANSMISSION SECTION

INDEX

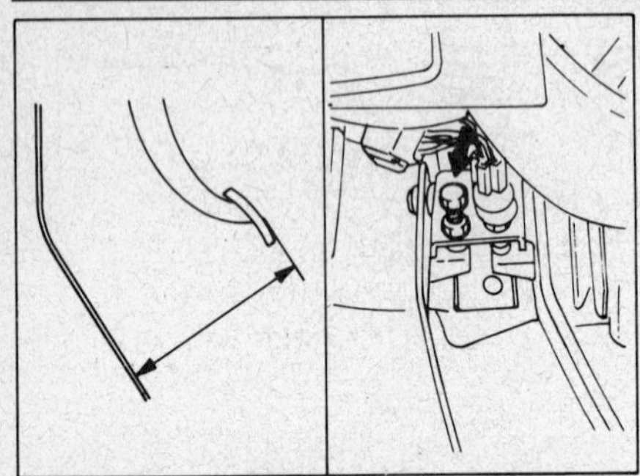

Fig. 1 Measuring clutch pedal height. Cordia & Tredia

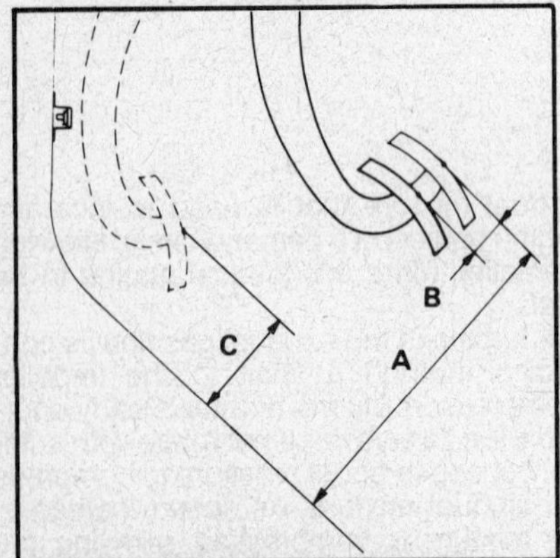

Fig. 4 Measuring clutch pedal height, freeplay & floorboard clearance. Cordia, Tredia, Montero & Mirage

CLUTCH PEDAL ADJUST

CABLE OPERATED

CORDIA & TREDIA

1. Measure clutch pedal height as shown, **Fig. 1.**
2. If height is not 6.9-7.1 inches, turn clutch pedal height adjusting bolt until height is correct.
3. Measure clutch pedal freeplay by depressing pedal by hand.
4. If freeplay is not .8-1.2 inches on 1983 models or .6-.8 inch on 1984-87 models, adjust as follows:
   a. Turn outer cable adjusting nut at floor pan and adjust clutch cable freeplay to zero-.04 inch.
   b. After adjustment, depress clutch pedal several times, then check that clutch pedal freeplay is within specifications.

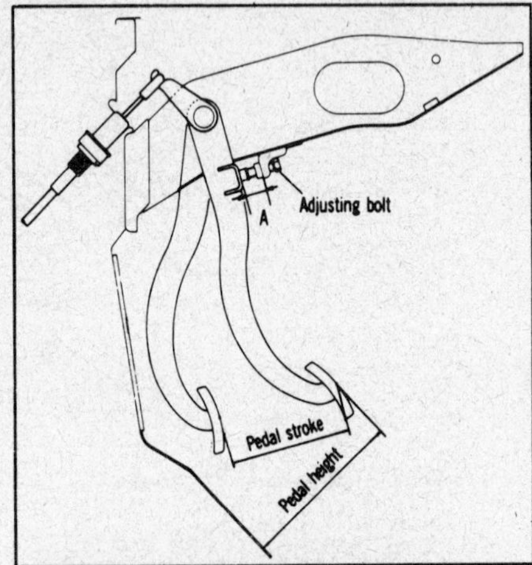

Fig. 2 Adjusting clutch pedal height. Gasoline engine Pickup

1983–86 GASOLINE ENGINE PICKUP

1. Adjust pedal height to specifications by turning adjusting bolt and check pedal stroke and dimension "A," **Fig. 2.** Dimension "A" 4-122 engine .9 inch. 4-156 engine .8 inch. Pedal height 4-122 engine 6.5 inch. 4-156 engine 6.9 inch. Pedal stroke 4-122 engine 5.5 inch. 4-156 engine 5.9 inch. **Insufficient pedal stroke will result in insufficient clutch release.**
2. Draw outer cable slightly to engine compartment side and set clearance between adjusting wheel and insulator, **Fig. 3.**
3. Ensure that pedal freeplay is .8-1.4 inch.

1987 PICKUP

1. Measure clutch pedal height as shown, **Fig. 2.** Clutch pedal height should be 6.5-6.7 inches. If clutch pedal height is not as specified, rotate pedal stopper until specified dimension is obtained.
2. Measure clutch pedal freeplay by lightly depressing on clutch pedal until light resistance is felt. Clutch pedal freeplay should be .8-1.4 inches. If clutch pedal freeplay is not as specified, pull clutch cable lightly at toe board, then rotate adjusting nut until adjusting nut to insulator clearance clearance, **Fig. 3**, is .12-.16 inch.
3. Check clutch pedal height and freeplay after making adjustments.
4. Measure distance between face of clutch pedal and floor board, with clutch pedal depressed. Distance should be 2.4 inch or more.

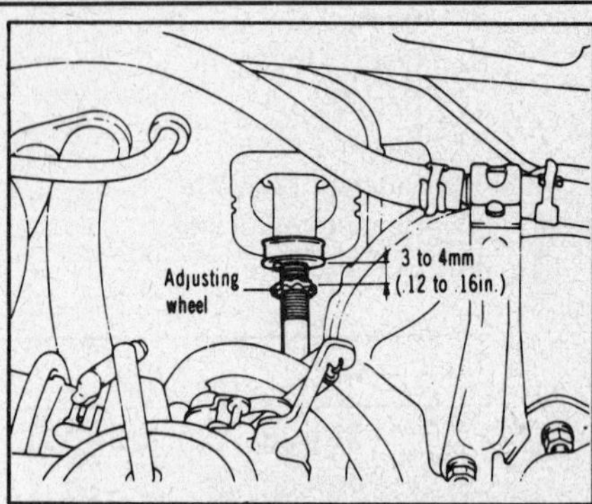

Fig. 3 Adjusting clutch pedal freeplay. Gasoline engine Pickup

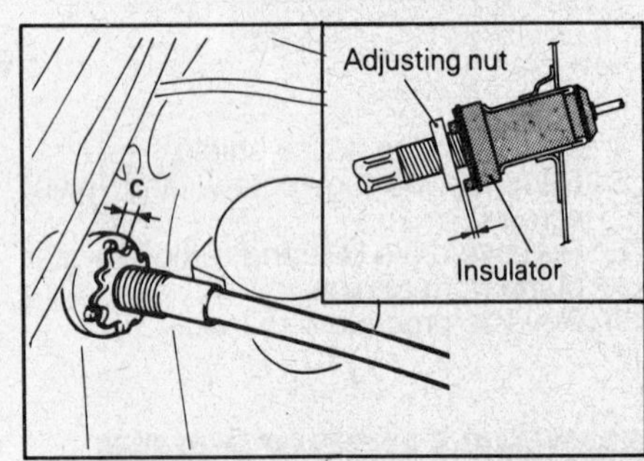

Fig. 5 Adjusting clutch pedal freeplay. Mirage

MIRAGE

1. Measure distance between upper surface of floor board and top of clutch pedal. Pedal height should be 6.2-6.4 inch.
2. If clutch pedal height is not as specified in step 1, check pedal stopper of pedal support member for deterioration. Repair as required.
3. Measure clutch pedal freeplay "B", **Fig. 4.** Freeplay should be .8-1.2 inch.
4. If freeplay is not as specified in step 3,

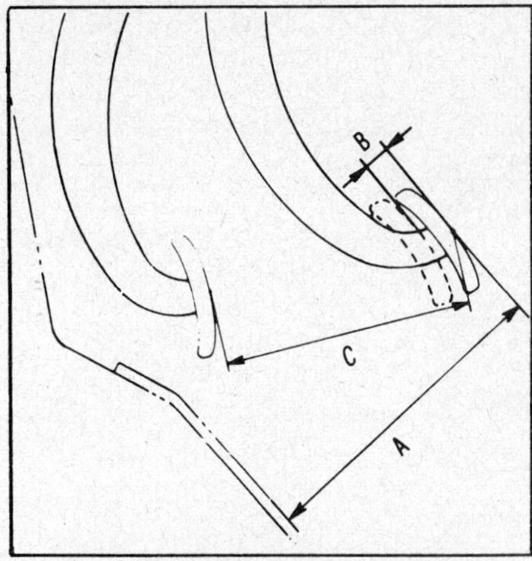

Fig. 6 Measuring clutch pedal height, freeplay & stroke. Diesel engine Pickup

turn outer cable adjusting nut at the bulkhead in engine compartment and adjust clutch cable freeplay "C" to .20-.25 inch, **Fig. 5.**

5. After adjusting pedal freeplay, depress clutch pedal several times, then with pedal fully depressed check clutch pedal to floor board clearance. Clearance should be 3.1 inch or more.
6. If clutch pedal clearance is not as specified in step 5, clutch assembly is defective. Repair clutch assembly as required.

HYDRAULICALLY OPERATED

DIESEL ENGINE PICKUP

1. Measure clutch pedal height (A), **Fig. 6.** Clutch pedal height should be 6.9 inches.
2. If height is not within specifications, adjust as follows:
   a. Back off adjusting bolt slightly, then loosen jam nut on operating rod.
   b. Turn pushrod to adjust pedal height to specified value.
   c. Tighten jam nut to lock yoke to rod, then set adjusting bolt so that it does not depress the pedal lever.
3. After above adjustment is completed, check clutch pedal freeplay (B) and clutch pedal stroke (C), **Fig. 6.** Clutch pedal freeplay should be .4-.5 inch and pedal stroke should be 5.9 inches.
4. If clutch pedal freeplay and stroke are not as specified, check for air in hydraulic system or defective clutch assembly.

STARION

1983–84

1. Measure clutch pedal height (A) and clutch pedal freeplay (B), **Fig. 7.** Clutch pedal height should be 7.5-7.7 inches for 1983 models or 7.0-7.2 inches for 1984 models. Freeplay should be .2-.4 inch.
2. If clutch pedal height is not within specifications, adjust as follows:

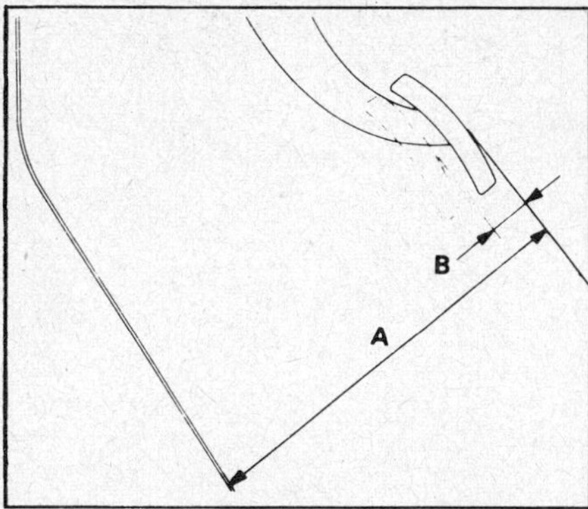

Fig. 7 Measuring clutch pedal height & freeplay. Starion

   a. Back off on pedal stopper bolt until it does not contact pedal arm.
   b. Loosen pushrod locknut and adjust pedal height to specifications by turning pushrod.
   c. Turn pedal stopper bolt until it contacts pedal arm, then tighten locknut.

1985–87

1. Measure clutch pedal height and clevis pin play at pedal pad upper surface. Clutch pedal height should be 7.4-7.6 inches and clutch pedal clevis pin play should be .04-.10 inch on 1985-86 models or .04-.12 inch on 1987 models.
2. If clutch pedal height and play are not as specified in step 1, adjust as follows:
   a. Adjust pedal height by turning clutch switch and secure with locknut.
   b. Adjust clutch pedal clevis pin play by turning pushrod and secure with locknut.
3. Measure total clutch pedal freeplay "B", **Fig. 7,** and distance between pedal and upper surface and floor board with clutch pedal fully depressed. Total freeplay should be .2-.5 inch and distance between pedal pad upper surface and floor board should be 1.4 inch.
4. If measurements are not as specified in step 3, check for defective master cylinder or clutch assembly or for air in hydraulic system.

CORDIA, TREDIA & MONTERO

1. Measure clutch pedal height (A) and clutch pedal freeplay (B), **Fig. 4.** Clutch pedal height should be 6.9-7.1 inches on Cordia and Tredia or 7.3-7.5 inches on Montero. Clutch pedal freeplay should be .04-.12 inch.
2. If clutch pedal height and freeplay are not within specifications, adjust as follows:
   a. Back off pedal stopper bolt until it does not contact pedal arm, **Fig. 8.**
   b. Loosen pushrod locknut, then adjust pedal height to specified value by turning the pushrod, **Fig. 8.**
   c. Turn pedal stopper bolt until it comes into contact with pedal arm,

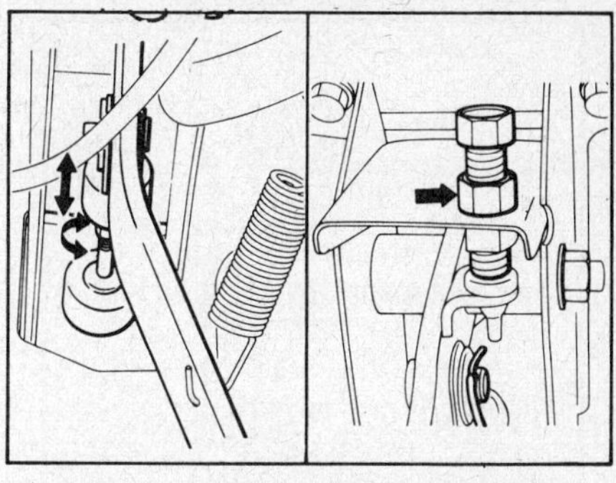

Fig. 8 Adjusting clutch pedal height & freeplay. Cordia, Tredia & Montero

then tighten the locknut.

3. After above adjustment is completed, depress clutch pedal and check the clutch pedal to floorboard clearance (C), **Fig. 4.** Pedal to floorboard clearance should be 2.2 inches or more on Cordia and Tredia or 1.4 inches or more on Montero.
4. If clutch pedal to floorboard clearance is less than specified value, check for air in hydraulic system or defective clutch assembly.

CLUTCH REPLACE

CORDIA, MIRAGE & TREDIA

1. Remove transmission as described under "Transmission, Replace."
2. Insert tool MD998126 or equivalent into center hole to prevent dropping of clutch disc, then diagonally loosen bolts that hold clutch cover assembly to remove clutch cover assembly. **Do not clean clutch disc or release bearing with cleaning solvent.**
3. Remove snap ring, clevis pin and release cylinder assembly if equipped.
4. Remove return clip, then the release bearing.
5. Remove spring pins from clutch release fork and shaft using a suitable punch.
6. Install release shaft and packings, then the return spring and release fork.
7. Align lock pin holes of shift arm and control shaft and, using tool MD998245 or equivalent, drive in two new spring pins.
8. When installing spring pins ensure that spring pin slot direction is at right angles to center line of control shaft.
9. Remove grease from clutch facing by wiping with clean cloth.
10. Apply small amount of grease to clutch disc spline and input shaft spline.
11. Using tool MD998126 or equivalent, install clutch disc and clutch cover assembly to flywheel. When installing clutch disc, make certain that surface with manufacturer's stamped mark is on pressure plate side.

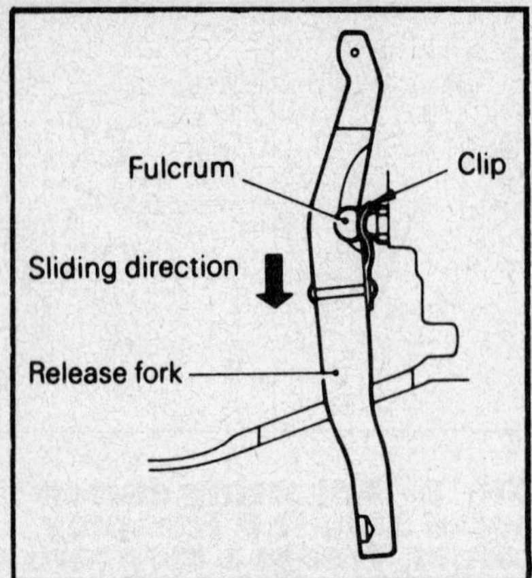

Fig. 9 Disengaging release fork

	Nm	ft.lbs.	O.D. x Length mm (in.)	Bolt indentification
A	43–55	31–40	(7) 10 x 40 (1.6)	(7) A x B
B	43–55	31–40	(7) 10 x 65 (2.6)	
C	22–32	16–23	(7) 10 x 55 (2.2)	A
D	30–34	22–25	(10) 10 x 60 (2.4)	
E	10–12	7–9	(7) 8 x 14 (0.6)	B
F	15–22	11–16	(7) 8 x 20 (0.8)	

Fig. 10 Engine to transaxle attaching bolts torque values. Cordia, Mirage & Tredia

PICKUP

1. Remove transmission as described under "Transmission, Replace."
2. Insert suitable tool into center hole to prevent dropping clutch disc, then diagonally loosen bolts holding clutch cover assembly and remove assembly.
3. Remove clutch disc and tool.
4. Remove two return clips on transmission side and remove release bearing.
5. On vehicles with gasoline engines, remove shift arm spring pin and control lever shaft assembly with 3/16 inch punch, then remove clutch shift arm, two felt packings and two return springs.
6. On vehicles equipped with diesel engines, remove release lever, then remove boot from transmission case. When removing release lever, slide release lever in direction of arrow, **Fig. 9,** to disengage fulcrum from clip.
7. On vehicles equipped with gasoline engines, apply grease to inside surface of bushing and oil seal lips and apply engine oil to two felt packings.
8. On vehicles equipped with gasoline engines, insert clutch control lever and shaft assembly into transmission case from left, then install clutch shift arm, two felt packings, and two return springs onto shaft.
9. On vehicles equipped with gasoline engines, align lock pinholes on shift arm and control shaft, then drive in two spring pins, ensuring that the spring pin slot direction is at right angles to control shaft.
10. On vehicles equipped with diesel engines, install release lever to fulcrum, then install release fork boot to transmission case.
11. Apply ample amount of rubber grease to outer surface of piston and piston cup and insert them in release cylinder, then install pushrod and rubber boot.
12. Install release cylinder assembly to transmission case.
13. Fill groove of bearing inside diameter with grease.
14. Install release bearing to transmission front bearing retainer, then install return clips.
15. Rub grease in clutch disc spline and transmission main gear spline.
16. Using suitable tool, install clutch disc and clutch cover assembly on flywheel. When installing clutch disc, make certain that surface with manufacturer's stamped mark is on pressure plate side.
17. Install transmission.

MONTERO & STARION

1. Insert tool MB998127 or equivalent in center hole to prevent dropping of clutch disc.
2. Diagonally loosen bolts that hold clutch cover assembly and remove assembly.
3. Slide release fork in direction of arrow, **Fig. 9,** to disengage fulcrum from clip.
4. Pack release fork fulcrum hole and release cylinder pushrod hole with grease.
5. Pack grease in groove on release bearing inside diameter.
6. Clean clutch facing and pressure plate with clean cloth.
7. Lightly grease clutch disc spline and main drive gear spline of transmission.
8. Using tool MB998127 or equivalent, install clutch disc and clutch cover assembly on flywheel. When installing clutch disc, make certain that surface with manufacturer's stamped mark is on pressure plate side.

MANUAL TRANSMISSION REPLACE

CORDIA & TREDIA

1. Remove battery and battery tray.
2. Remove reservoir tank and windshield washer tank.
3. Remove air cleaner case.
4. Remove clutch cable, speedometer cable, and back-up lamp harness from transaxle.
5. Disconnect wiring at starter.
6. Remove 5 upper engine to transaxle attaching bolts.
7. Remove starter.
8. Raise and support vehicle.
9. Remove wheels from vehicle, then drain transaxle oil.
10. Remove extension, shift control rod, and range selector control cable from under engine compartment.
11. Remove stabilizer and strut bars from lower arm.
12. Remove right and left driveshafts.
13. Using suitable jack, support lower part of transaxle.
14. Remove bellhousing cover.
15. Remove lower engine to transaxle attaching bolts.
16. Remove transaxle mount insulator bolt, then remove blanking cover from inside right fender shield.
17. Remove transaxle insulator bracket attaching bolts and remove bracket if equipped.
18. Remove transaxle mount bracket.
19. Slide transaxle to right, then lower assembly to remove.
20. Reverse procedure to install, noting the following:
    a. Bolts should be torqued to: transaxle mounting bracket bolt 22-30 ft. lbs., 814 mm bellhousing cover to transaxle attaching bolts 7-9 ft. lbs., 820 mm bellhousing cover to transaxle attaching bolts 11-16 ft. lbs., extension to transaxle bolt 43-51 ft. lbs., starter mounting bolt to 16-23 ft. lbs., back-up lamp switch 22 ft. lbs., and engine to transaxle attaching bolts as shown, **Fig. 10.**

b. Refill transaxle with suitable oil and torque fill plug to 22-25 ft. lbs.
c. Adjust clutch cable.
d. Adjust gear shift lever and range selector lever.

MIRAGE

1985–86

1. Remove battery and battery tray.
2. On models equipped with turbocharger, remove air cleaner case.
3. On models equipped with five speed transaxle, disconnect select control valve electrical connector.
4. On models equipped with turbocharger, remove actuator attaching bolts and actuator to shaft coupling pin, then the actuator assembly.
5. On all models, remove speedometer cable and clutch control cable.
6. Disconnect back-up lamp and starter motor electrical connectors.
7. Remove upper transaxle to engine attaching bolts.
8. Remove starter, then raise and support vehicle.
9. Remove under cover, then drain transaxle fluid.
10. Remove extension rod and shift rod from under the engine compartment.
11. Remove stabilizer bar from lower arm, then the lower arm at the body side.
12. Remove left and right driveshafts and position aside.
13. Support lower part of transaxle using a suitable jack. Use caution not to damage oil pan.
14. Remove bellhousing cover, then the remaining transaxle to engine attaching bolts.
15. Remove transaxle mount insulator bolt, then the blind cover from inside right fender shield.
16. Remove transaxle bracket assembly, then the transaxle mount bracket.
17. Slide transaxle to the right, then lower assembly to remove.
18. Reverse procedure to install, noting the following:
    a. Bolts should be torqued to: transaxle mounting bracket bolt, 22-30 ft. lbs.; 814 mm bellhousing cover to transaxle attaching bolts 7-9 ft. lbs.; 820 mm bellhousing cover to transaxle attaching bolts 11-16 ft, lbs.; extension to transaxle bolt, 43-51 ft. lbs.; starter attaching bolt, 16-23 ft. lbs.; back-up lamp switch, 22 ft. lbs. and engine to transaxle attaching bolts as shown, **Fig. 10.**
    b. Refill transaxle with suitable oil and torque fill plug to 22-25 ft. lbs.
    c. Adjust clutch cable.
    d. Adjust gear shift lever and range selector lever.

1987

1. Drain transaxle fluid and clutch fluid into suitable containers.
2. Remove under cover.
3. On models equipped with turbocharged engine, remove air cleaner assembly.
4. On all models, remove battery and battery tray.
5. Disconnect clutch cable or tube, as equipped, from transaxle case.
6. Disconnect shift and select cables from transaxle case.
7. Disconnect back-up light switch electrical connector, speedometer cable and ground cable from transaxle case.
8. Disconnect starter motor wiring harness, then remove starter motor attaching bolts and the starter motor.
9. Disconnect stabilizer bar from lower control arm.
10. Remove front driveshafts as follows:
    a. Loosen ball joint stud nut, then break ball joint loose from steering knuckle using a suitable tool.
    b. Loosen tie rod end stud nut, then disconnect tie rod end from steering knuckle using a suitable tool.
    c. On models equipped with driveshaft center bearing, remove bearing snap ring. Lightly tap tripod joint outer race to remove driveshaft from transaxle, then remove center bearing. **Do not insert pry bar between transaxle case and driveshaft. Do not remove driveshaft from Birfield joint side.**
    d. On models less driveshaft center bearing, insert suitable pry bar between transaxle case and driveshaft, then pry driveshaft from transaxle. **Do not pull on driveshaft and do not insert pry bar deep enough to damage oil seal.**
    e. On all models, secure driveshaft to body.
11. Remove bellhousing cover attaching bolts and the cover.
12. Support transaxle assembly with a suitable jack.
13. Remove transaxle mounting strut, then the mounting bracket bolt caps, bolts and the brackets.
14. Carefully lower transaxle assembly from vehicle.
15. Reverse procedure to install, noting the following torques: tie rod end stud nut, 11-25 ft. lbs.; ball joint stud nut, 42-52 ft. lbs.; transaxle mounting bracket-to-transaxle attaching bolts, 65-80 ft. lbs.; transaxle mounting bracket-to-body attaching bolts, 22-29 ft. lbs.; bellhousing cover attaching bolts, 7-9 ft. lbs.; starter motor attaching bolts, 20-25 ft. lbs.; filler and drain plugs, 22-25 ft. lbs.; transaxle-to-engine attaching bolts, 32-39 ft. lbs.; transaxle mounting strut-to-transaxle attaching bolts, 43-51 ft. lbs.; transaxle mounting strut-to-bracket attaching bolts, 33-43 ft. lbs.

PICKUP

1. Disconnect battery ground cable.
2. Remove air cleaner and starter motor.
3. Remove two upper transmission mounting bolts from bellhousing.
4. On models equipped with a console box, remove lock screws and lift up console box.
5. On models not equipped with a console box, remove backbone carpet.
6. On all models, remove attaching screws and lift out dust cover retaining plate.
7. Turn up dust cover and remove control housing attaching bolts from extension housing, then remove control lever assembly.
8. Raise and support vehicle, then drain transmission oil.
9. Remove propeller shafts and disconnect speedometer cable.
10. Disconnect back-up light switch harness and, on 4 wheel drive models, the 4 wheel drive indicator light switch harness.
11. Disconnect front exhaust pipe.
12. On models with gasoline engine, disconnect clutch cable from clutch control lever.
13. On models with diesel engine, remove clutch release cylinder.
14. On all models, support rear of engine with suitable jack.
15. On models with 4 wheel drive, disconnect plate and remove transfer case mounting bracket.
16. On all models, using suitable jack, support transmission and remove No. 2 crossmember. **Transmission supporting area should be as wide as possible.**
17. Remove bellhousing cover, then the remaining transmission mounting bolts.
18. Withdraw transmission from engine, being careful not to twist front end of main drive gear.
19. Lower jack and remove transmission from under vehicle.
20. Reverse procedure to install, noting the following:
    a. On 1983-86 models, torque bolts as follows on rear wheel drive models: transmission mounting bolts, 31-40 ft. lbs.; transmission to insulator nut, 15-17 ft. lbs.; and starter motor mounting nuts, 16-23 ft. lbs.
    b. On 1983-86 models, torque bolts as follows on 4 wheel drive models: transmission mounting bolts, 31-40 ft. lbs.; transmission to rear insulator, 14-18 ft. lbs.; starter motor mounting bolts, 16-23 ft. lbs.; frame to plate bolts, 14-18 ft. lbs.; transfer case support insulator to transfer case mounting bracket bolts, 14-18 ft. lbs.; and transfer case mounting bracket to transfer case bolts, 14-18 ft. lbs.
    c. On 1987 rear wheel drive models, torque 10 x 40 mm and 10 x 65 transmission mounting bolts to 31-40 ft. lbs., 8 x 25 mm and 8 x 55 mm transmission mounting bolts to 15-20 ft. lbs. and 10 x 60 mm mounting bolts to 16-23 ft. lbs.
    d. On 1987 4 wheel drive models, torque torque 10 x 40 mm transmission mounting bolts to 31-40 ft. lbs., 8 x 25 mm and 8 x 55 mm and 10 x 65 mm transmission mounting bolts to 15-20 ft. lbs. and 10 x 60 mm mounting bolts to 16-23 ft. lbs.
    e. When installing control lever assembly on rear wheel drive models, place gearshift lever in 2nd

speed position on 4 speed transmission, or in 1st speed position on 5 speed transmission.

f. When installing gearshift lever assembly on 4 wheel drive models, set transmission gearshift lever to Neutral position and transfer case gearshift lever to "4H" position.

g. Ensure bellhousing cover is not bent.

h. Install dust cover onto tunnel hole, then install retaining plate with attaching screws.

i. Adjust clutch and fill transmission to specifications with suitable fluid.

STARION

1. Disconnect battery ground cable.
2. Raise and support vehicle, then drain transmission oil.
3. Remove propeller shaft.
4. Disconnect speedometer cable and back-up light switch wiring harness.
5. Remove clutch release cylinder, bellhousing cover, and starter motor.
6. Using suitable jack, support transmission.
7. Remove transmission to engine attaching bolts.
8. Remove engine support bracket, insulator assembly, and ground cable.
9. Place gearshift lever in neutral position and remove gearshift lever assembly. **Place a piece of cloth on rear of cylinder head to prevent damage to firewall.**
10. Lower jack and remove transmission from under vehicle.
11. Reverse procedure to install, torquing bolts as follows: starter motor mounting bolts, 16-23 ft. lbs.; engine to transmission mounting bolts, 31-40 ft. lbs.; drain plug, 44 ft. lbs.; oil filler plug, 22-25 ft. lbs.; back-up light switch, 22 ft. lbs.; under cover attaching bolts, 6-7 ft. lbs.; and speedometer sleeve clamp bolt, 7.5-9 ft. lbs.

MONTERO

1. Disconnect battery ground cable.
2. Place transmission gearshift lever in Neutral position and the transfer gear shift lever in high range position.
3. Remove transmission gearshift lever and transfer gearshift lever.
4. Raise and support vehicle.
5. Remove transfer case protector.
6. Drain transmission and transfer case fluid into a suitable container.
7. Remove front and rear propeller shafts.
8. Disconnect speedometer cable, back-up lamp switch electrical connector and 4 wheel drive indicator light electrical connector from transmission case.
9. Remove clutch release cylinder from transmission.
10. Remove bellhousing cover, then the starter motor from transmission.
11. Remove rear engine mount from No. 2 crossmember.
12. Support transmission and transfer case using a suitable jack, then remove the No. 2 crossmember.
13. Remove transfer bracket attaching bolts, then the transmission-to-engine attaching bolts.
14. Disconnect transmission assembly by pulling it toward rear of vehicle.
15. Lower transmission jack and remove transmission from under vehicle.
16. Reverse procedure to install, noting the following:
    a. Torque fasteners to the following specifications: starter motor attaching bolts, 16-23 ft. lbs.; engine-to-transmission attaching bolts, 31-40 ft. lbs. **On 1987 models, torque 10 x 40 mm and 10 x 65 mm bolts to 31-40 ft. lbs., 8 x 25 mm and 8 x 55 mm bolts to 15-20 ft. lbs. and 10 x 60 mm bolts to 20-25 ft. lbs.**; bellhousing attaching bolts, 6-7 ft. lbs.; transmiss ion drain plug, 43 ft. lbs.; transfer case drain plug, 22-25 ft. lbs.
    b. Refill transmission and transfer case with suitable lubricant.

DISC BRAKES SECTION

INDEX

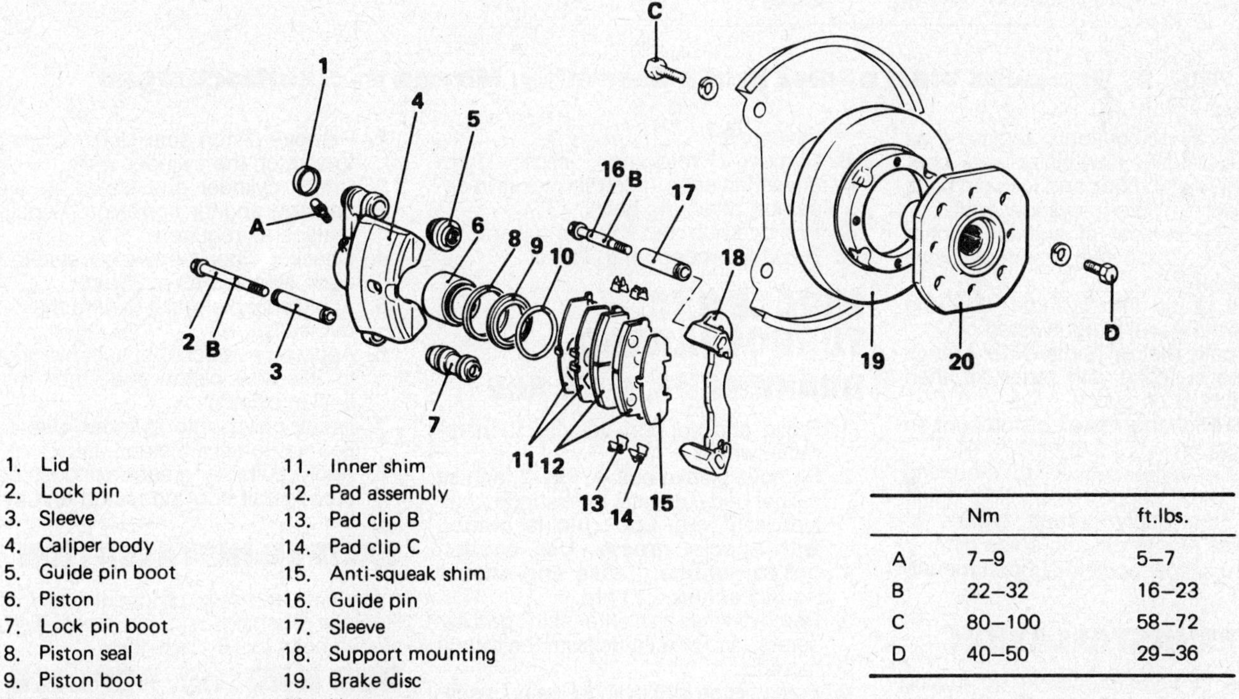

	Nm	ft.lbs.
A	7–9	5–7
B	22–32	16–23
C	80–100	58–72
D	40–50	29–36

Fig. 1 Exploded view of disc brake assembly. Cordia, Tredia & Turbocharged Mirage

CORDIA, TREDIA & TURBOCHARGED MIRAGE

BRAKE PADS, REPLACE

1. Raise and support vehicle.
2. Remove wheel.
3. Remove lock pin, **Fig. 1,** and lift caliper body upward, then support caliper with wire. **Lock pin is coated with special grease. Be careful not to remove grease and ensure that no dirt adheres to pin.**
4. Remove inner shim(s), anti-squeak shim, and pad assembly from support mounting.
5. Remove pad clips "B" and "C".
6. Press piston into cylinder.
7. Install pad clip "B", pad clip "C", pad assembly, inner shim(s), and anti-squeak shim onto support mounting.
8. Lower caliper body and install lower lock pin, torquing to 16-23 ft. lbs.
9. Install wheel.

CALIPER REMOVAL

1. Raise and support vehicle.
2. Remove front wheel and tire assembly.
3. Loosen brake line to brake hose connection at strut.
4. Remove strut brake hose clips, then remove brake hoses.
5. Remove front brake assembly.
6. Remove to caliper to steering knuckle retaining bolts.
7. Remove caliper body from brake assembly.

CALIPER SERVICE

1. Remove boot ring.
2. Place rag in front of piston, then remove piston and dust boot by applying compressed air through brake hose fitting hole. Keep fingers clear of front of piston.
3. Remove piston seal, being careful not to scratch cylinder walls.
4. Clean piston surfaces and cylinder walls with brake fluid.
5. Remove sleeve and boot from caliper body.

1. Sleeve bolt B
2. Sleeve
3. Caliper
4. Bushing
5. Sleeve bolt A
6. Pin boot
7. Piston
8. Piston seal
9. Dust boot
10. Inner shim
11. Pad assembly
12. Pad liner
13. Outer shim
14. Torque member
15. Brake disc
16. Hub

	Nm	ft.lbs.
A	80–100	58–72
B	22–32	16–23
C	7–9	5–7
D	50–60	36–43

Fig. 2 Exploded view of disc brake assembly. Mirage exc. turbocharged

6. Inspect all components, replacing as necessary. Use new piston seal, boot ring, guide pin boot, and lock pin boot.
7. Apply brake fluid to cylinder walls.
8. Apply even coat of suitable rubber grease to piston seal, then install seal in cylinder.
9. Install piston into cylinder, ensuring that piston seal is not twisted.
10. Lubricate piston boots with orange grease supplied with repair kit, then install boot on piston.
11. Using boot ring, mount piston boot on cylinder.
12. Apply suitable sealant to mounting threads of support mounting guide pin, then apply orange grease to sleeves of lock pin and guide pin.
13. Mount caliper body to support mounting.

CALIPER INSTALLATION

Reverse removal procedure to install, then bleed brake system.

HUB & ROTOR, REPLACE

1. Remove hub dust cap, then loosen driveshaft nut.
2. Raise and support front of vehicle. Remove wheel and tire assembly, then the under cover.
3. Remove cotter pin, then the wheel bearing nut and washer.
4. Disconnect caliper assembly from knuckle, then tie and suspend brake line from strut.
5. Disconnect lower control arm ball joint from knuckle, using tool No. MB991113, or equivalent. **Loosen but do not remove attaching nut.**
6. Remove tie rod end cotter pin, then disconnect tie rod end from knuckle, using tool No. MB991113, or equivalent. **Loosen but do not remove attaching nut.**
7. Remove stabilizer bar, then the driveshaft.
8. Remove retaining clips from driveshaft ends, then remove strut assembly attaching bolts.
9. Remove hub and knuckle assembly.
10. Reverse procedure to install

MIRAGE EXC. TURBOCHARGED

BRAKE PADS, REPLACE

1. Raise and support vehicle, then remove wheel.
2. Remove sleeve bolt, A, **Fig. 2,** and lift caliper body upward, then support caliper with wire. **Lock pin is coated with special grease. Use caution not to remove grease and ensure no dirt adheres to pin.**
3. Remove inner and outer shim, pad assembly and pad liners from the torque member.
4. Press piston into cylinder using a suitable tool.
5. Install pad liners, pad assemblies and inner and outer shim onto the torque member.
6. Lower caliper body into position, then install sleeve bolt A. Torque bolt to 16-23 ft. lbs.
7. Install wheel.

CALIPER REMOVAL

1. Raise and support vehicle, then remove wheel.
2. Disconnect and cap brake hose.
3. Remove sleeve bolts, sleeves, boot pins and bushings, then the caliper body from torque member.

CALIPER SERVICE

1. Place rag in front of piston, then remove piston and dust boot by applying compressed air through brake hose fitting hole. Keep fingers clear of front of piston.
2. Remove piston seal. Use caution not to scratch the cylinder walls.
3. Check cylinder and piston for wear, damage and/or corrosion. Repair or replace as required.
4. Check caliper body and sleeve for wear. Replace as required.
5. Apply suitable brake fluid to the cylinder walls.
6. Apply an even coat of suitable grease to the new piston seal, then install seal in cylinder.
7. Install piston into cylinder. Use caution not to twist piston seal.
8. Apply suitable grease to dust boot, then install boot on piston and cylinder.

CALIPER INSTALLATION

Reverse removal procedure to install. Replace bushing and pin boot. Torque sleeve bolts to 16-23 ft. lbs.

HUB & ROTOR, REPLACE

1. Remove hub dust cap, then loosen driveshaft nut.
2. Raise and support front of vehicle. Remove wheel and tire assembly, then the under cover.
3. Remove cotter pin, then the wheel bearing nut and washer.
4. Disconnect caliper assembly from knuckle, then tie and suspend brake line from strut.
5. Disconnect lower control arm ball joint from knuckle, using tool No. MB991113, or equivalent. **Loosen but do not remove attaching nut.**
6. Remove tie rod end cotter pin, then disconnect tie rod end from knuckle, using tool No. MB991113, or equivalent. **Loosen but do not remove attaching nut.**
7. Remove stabilizer bar, then the driveshaft.
8. Remove retaining clips from driveshaft ends, then remove strut as-

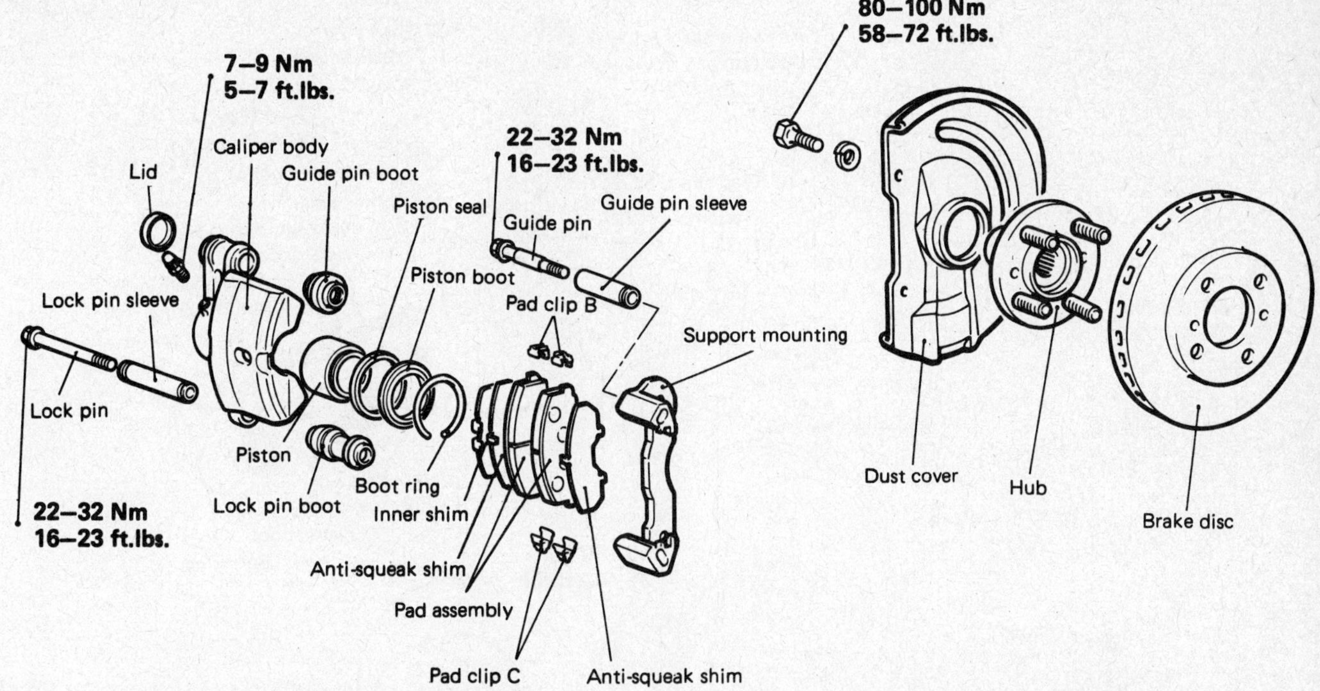

Fig. 3 Exploded view of typical front disc brake assembly. Galant

sembly attaching bolts.

9. Remove hub and knuckle assembly.
10. Reverse procedure to install

GALANT

FRONT BRAKES

Brake Pad, Replace

1. Raise and support vehicle, then remove wheel.
2. Remove lower lock pin, **Fig. 3,** and lift caliper body upward, then support caliper with wire. **Lock pin is coated with special grease. Use caution not to remove grease and ensure no dirt adheres to pin.**
3. Remove inner shim, anti-squeak shim and pad assemblies from support mounting.
4. Remove pad clips B and C.
5. Press piston into cylinder using a suitable tool.
6. Install pad clip B and C, pad assemblies, inner shim and anti-squeak shim onto the support mounting.
7. Apply a coating of suitable grease to the pad and anti-squeak shim contact surface and to the anti-squeak shim and inner shim contact surface.
8. Lower caliper body into position, then install lower lock pin. Torque bolt to 16-23 ft. lbs.
9. Install wheel.

Caliper Removal

1. Raise and support vehicle, then remove front wheels.
2. Remove strut brake hose clips, then the brake hoses.
3. Remove lock pins, then the caliper assembly.

Caliper Service

1. Remove boot ring.
2. Place rag in front of piston, then remove piston and dust boot by applying compressed air through brake hose fitting hole. Keep fingers clear of front of piston.
3. Remove piston seal. Use caution not to scratch the cylinder walls.
4. Remove sleeve and boot from caliper body.
5. Check cylinder and piston for wear, damage and/or corrosion. Repair or replace as required.
6. Check caliper body and sleeve for wear. Replace as required.
7. Apply suitable brake fluid to the cylinder walls.
8. Apply an even coat of suitable grease to the new piston seal, then install seal in cylinder.
9. Install piston into cylinder. Use caution not to twist piston seal.
10. Apply suitable grease to dust boot, then install boot on piston.
11. Attach piston boot onto cylinder with the boot ring.
12. Apply suitable grease to sliding parts of caliper body and sleeves, guide pin and lock pin boot.

Caliper Installation

Reverse removal procedure to install. Replace pin boots. Torque sleeve bolts to 16-23 ft. lbs.

Hub & Rotor, Replace

1. Raise and support vehicle, then remove front wheels.
2. Disconnect brake caliper assembly and support using suitable wire.
3. Disconnect lower control arm ball joint from knuckle using a suitable tool.
4. Remove stabilizer bar from lower control arm.
5. Disconnect tie rod end from knuckle using a suitable tool.
6. Remove drive shaft from hub.
7. Remove hub and knuckle as an assembly from strut assembly.
8. Reverse procedure to install.

REAR BRAKES

Brake Pads, Replace

1. Raise and support vehicle, then remove wheel.
2. Remove parking brake cable.
3. Remove lower lock pin, **Fig. 4**, and lift caliper body upward, then support caliper with wire. **Lock pin is coated with special grease. Use caution not to remove grease and ensure no dirt adheres to pin.**
4. Remove outer shim and pad assembly from caliper support.
5. Remove pad clips B and C.
6. Press piston into cylinder using a suitable tool. Ensure stopper grooves in rear of piston are in the vertical position.
7. Install pad clips, then the pad and shim as an assembly onto the caliper support. Pins on back side of brake pad must be placed in grooves of piston.
8. Lower caliper body into position, then install lower lock pin. Torque bolt to 16-23 ft. lbs.
9. Install wheel.

Rotor, Replace

1. Raise and support vehicle, then remove rear wheels.

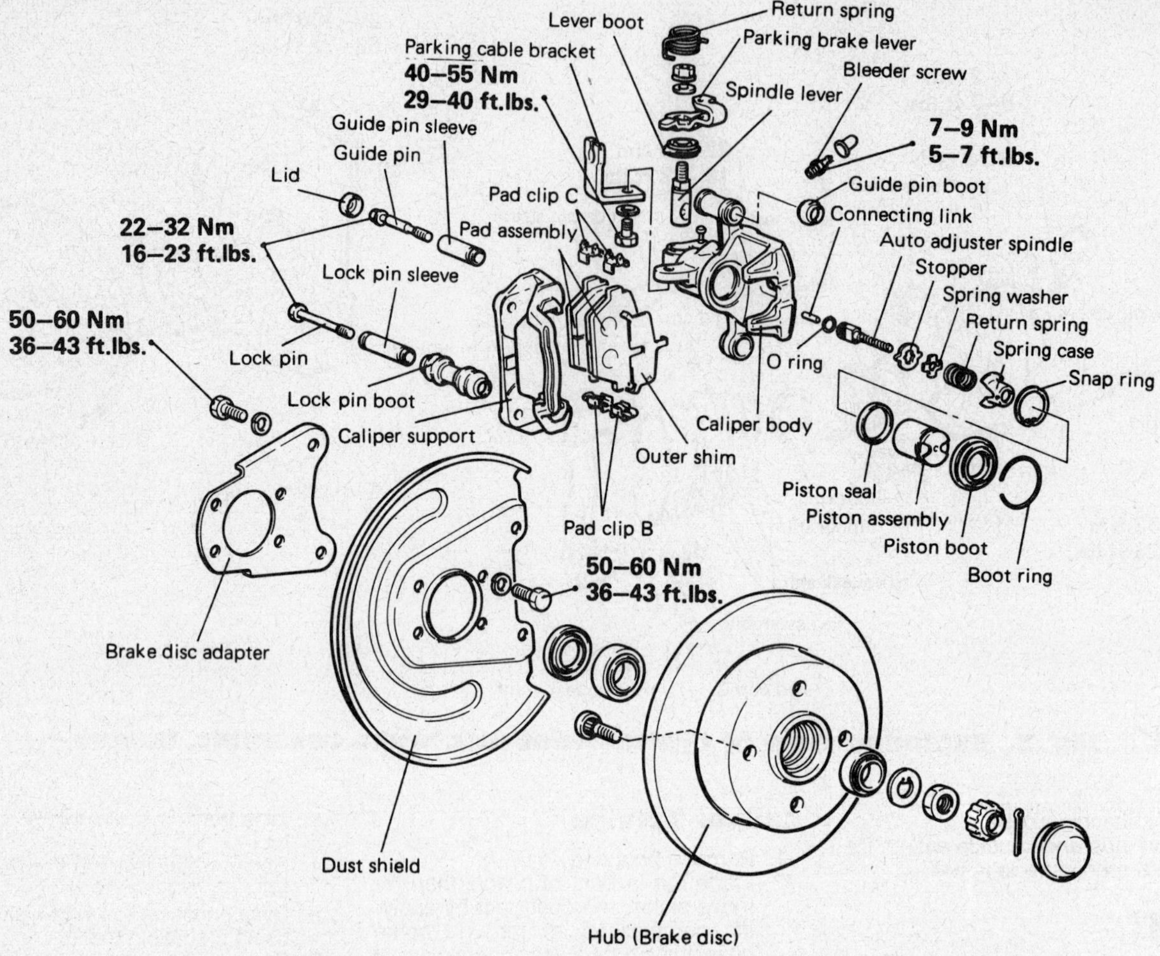

Fig. 4 Exploded view of rear disc brake assembly. Galant

2. Remove hub cap, then the cotter pin and cap.
3. Remove wheel bearing nut, then the washer and outer wheel bearing inner race.
4. Disconnect and suspend brake tube, using a suitable wire.
5. Disconnect parking brake cable from caliper assembly.
6. Remove lock pins from caliper assembly, then the caliper assembly to adapter attaching bolts and caliper assembly.
7. Remove rotor assembly.
8. Reverse procedure to install.

Caliper Removal

1. Raise and support vehicle, then remove rear wheels.
2. Disconnect parking brake cable from caliper assembly.
3. Disconnect brake hoses and brake tubes.
4. Remove lock pins from caliper assembly.
5. Remove caliper assembly to adapter attaching bolts.
6. Remove caliper assembly.

Caliper Service

1. Remove boot ring from caliper body, then the piston boot.
2. Twist piston out of caliper body using suitable tool.
3. Press spring case into caliper body using a .75 inch diameter steel pipe, then remove snap ring from caliper body using a suitable tool.
4. Remove spring case, return spring, washer and stopper from caliper body.
5. Pull auto-adjuster spindle out of caliper body and remove connecting link at the same time.
6. Remove O-ring from auto-adjuster spindle. Use caution not to scratch cylinder walls.
7. Remove piston seal from caliper body.
8. Disconnect return spring, then remove parking brake lever attaching nut.
9. Pull parking brake lever and spindle lever out of caliper body, then remove lever boot.
10. Pull sleeve, boot and lid out of the caliper body.
11. Remove guide pin and sleeve from caliper support.
12. Check connecting link and spindle for wear or damage. Replace as required.
13. Check caliper body, spindle lever shaft and piston for cracks or rust. Repair or replace as required.
14. Apply suitable grease to new piston seal and cylinder walls, then install piston seal into cylinder.
15. Apply suitable grease to bearing, spindle lever shaft, boot lever, connecting link, auto-adjuster spindle and caliper body.
16. Align hole in bearing with hole in connecting link.
17. Press dust boot into caliper body, then install shaft with groove facing hole in bearing.
18. Install connecting link from cylinder side.
19. Install O-ring on auto-adjuster spindle, then coat it with suitable brake fluid.
20. Install auto-adjuster spindle, then the stopper, spring washer, spring and spring case into caliper body.
21. Press in spring case using a suitable .75 inch diameter pipe, then install snap ring in caliper body and remove pipe. **Install snap ring in caliper body with opening facing bleeder.**
22. Twist piston in cylinder using a suitable tool.
23. Apply suitable grease to piston boot mounting grooves in caliper body and piston, then install piston boot and boot ring.
24. Install guide pin and sleeve into caliper support.
25. Apply suitable grease to sliding part of sleeve, caliper body, boot mounting groove and lid mounting.
26. Press in lid until edges are in contact

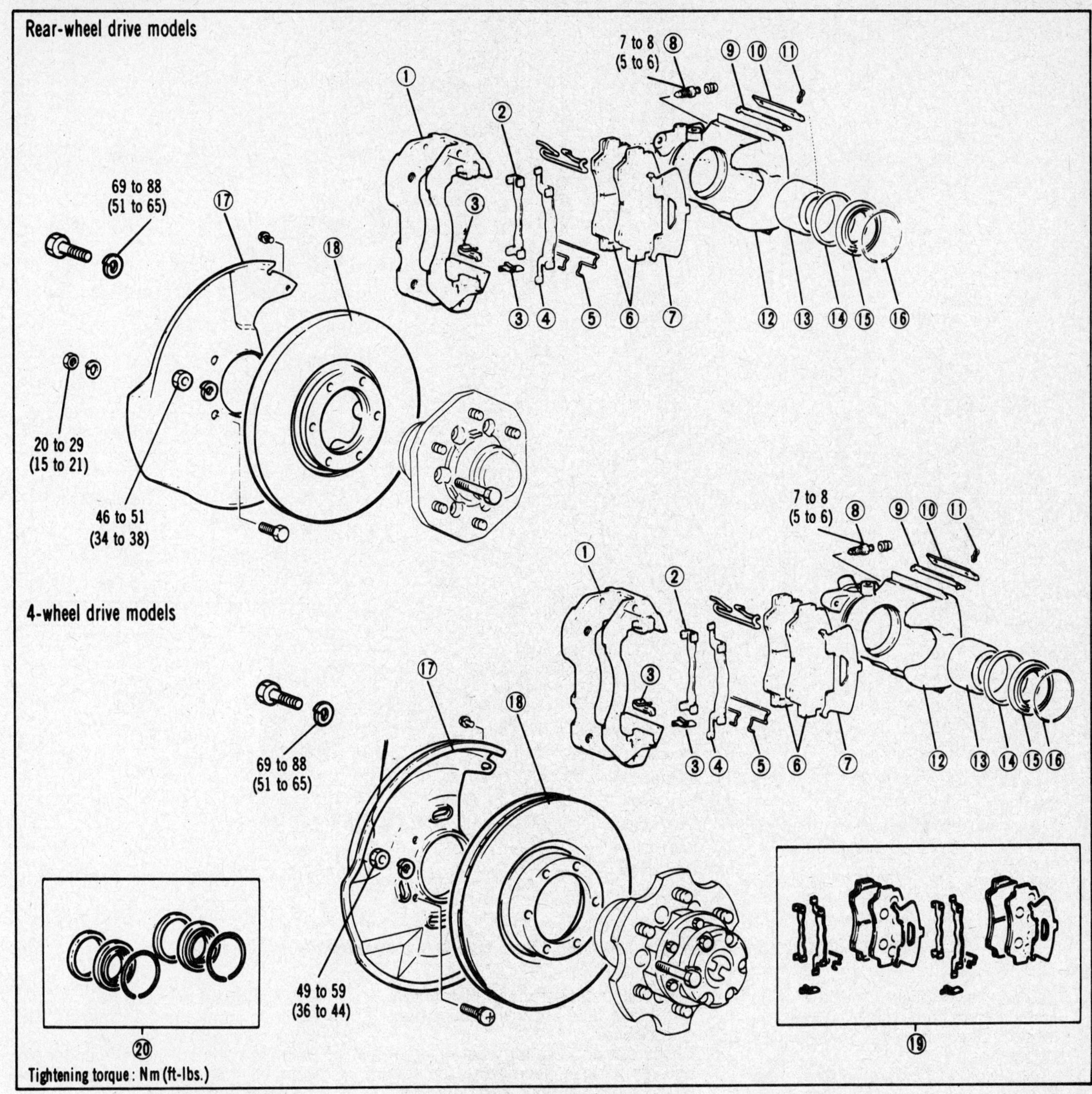

(1) Caliper support
(2) Pad clip (inner)
(3) Pad clip B
(4) Pad clip (outer)
(5) Anti-rattle spring
(6) Brake pad
(7) Anti-squeak shim
(8) Bleeder screw
(9) Pad support plate
(10) Stopper plug
(11) Spigot pin
(12) Caliper body
(13) Piston
(14) Piston seal
(15) Dust boot
(16) Boot ring
(17) Dust cover
(18) Brake disc
(19) Pad repair kit
(20) Seal and boot repair kit

Fig. 5 Exploded view of disc brake assembly. Montero & Pickup

with caliper body.

27. Attach caliper support to caliper assembly.

Caliper Installation

Reverse removal procedure to install.

MONTERO & PICKUP

BRAKE PADS, REPLACE

1. Raise and support vehicle, then remove front wheel.
2. Remove spigot pin and pull out stopper plug, **Fig. 5.**
3. Remove pad support plates, then repeatedly pull caliper assembly diagonally upward and downward to remove it. Position caliper out of way

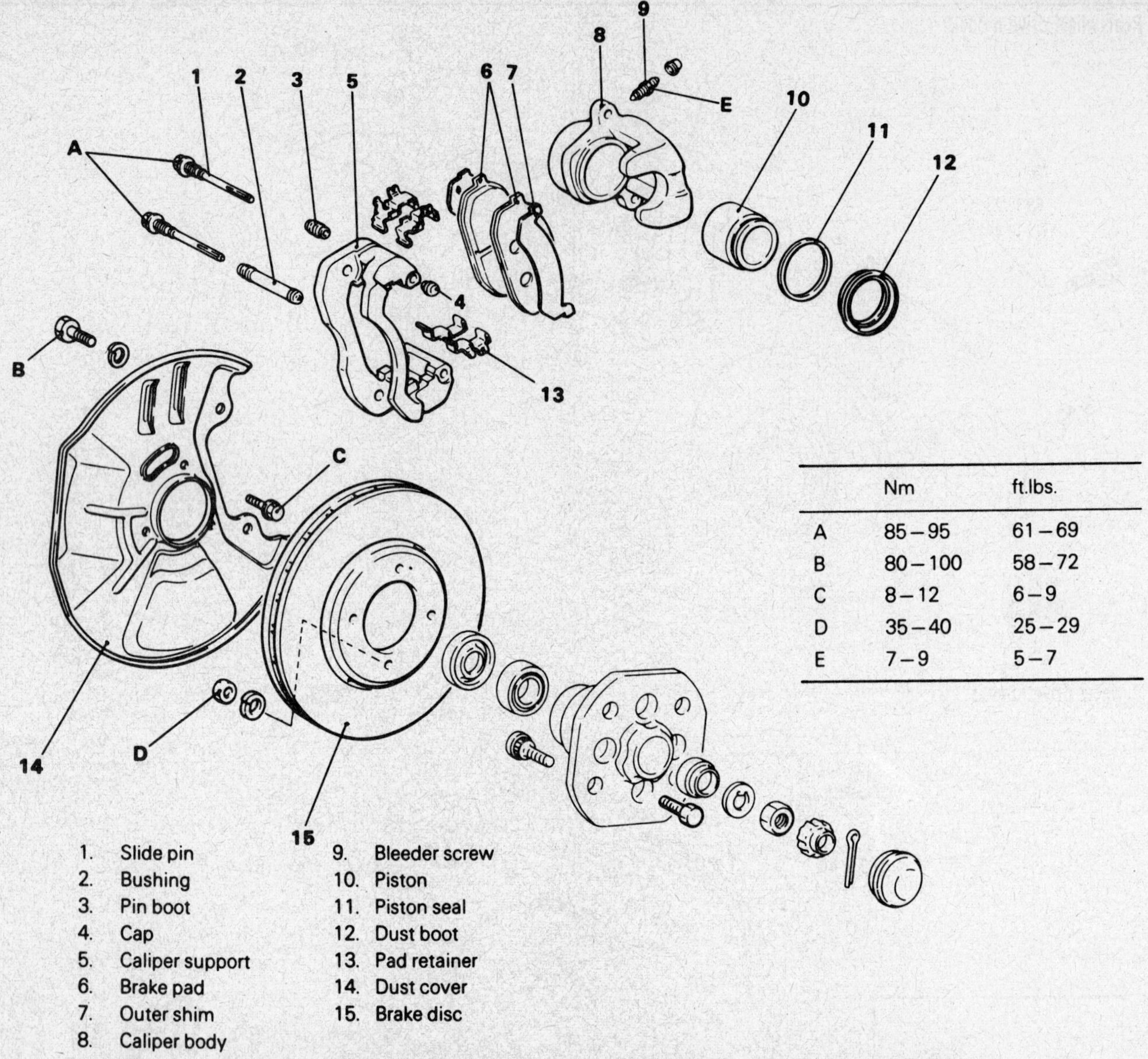

	Nm	ft.lbs.
A	85–95	61–69
B	80–100	58–72
C	8–12	6–9
D	35–40	25–29
E	7–9	5–7

1. Slide pin
2. Bushing
3. Pin boot
4. Cap
5. Caliper support
6. Brake pad
7. Outer shim
8. Caliper body
9. Bleeder screw
10. Piston
11. Piston seal
12. Dust boot
13. Pad retainer
14. Dust cover
15. Brake disc

Fig. 6 Exploded view of front disc brake assembly. Starion

and support with wire.
4. Remove pad from caliper support.
5. Inspect all components, replacing as necessary.
6. Clean exposed part of piston, then compress piston.
7. Reverse procedure to install, ensuring that pad clip "B" inner pad clip, and outer pad clip are properly installed.

CALIPER REMOVAL

1. Raise and support vehicle, then remove front wheel.
2. Disconnect brake hose.
3. Separate caliper body from caliper support.

CALIPER SERVICE

1. Remove dust boot.
2. Cover inner side of caliper with rag, then slowly inject compressed air through brake hose fitting to push out piston.
3. Remove piston seal, being careful not to damage cylinder.
4. Clean all metal parts and piston seal with brake fluid and clean dust boot with alcohol.
5. Check components for wear or damage, replacing as necessary. Use new piston seal, dust boot, and boot ring.
6. Apply rubber grease supplied with repair kit to piston seal, fit seal into cylinder groove, and install piston by hand, being careful not to twist seal.
7. Apply orange grease supplied with repair kit to dust boot attaching groove in caliper, then install dust boot.
8. Install brake pad.
9. Apply Plastilube 2 or equivalent brake grease to stopper plug and pad support plate sliding surface, then install caliper and spigot pin.

CALIPER INSTALLATION

Reverse removal procedure to install, torquing brake hose fitting to 10-12 ft. lbs., then bleed brake system.

HUB & ROTOR, REPLACE

1. Disconnect battery ground cable.
2. Raise and support vehicle.
3. Remove front brake assembly and suspend assembly with wire.
4. Remove hub cap, then the cotter pin.
5. Remove slotted nut and washer, then the outer bearing.
6. Remove front hub and rotor assembly.
7. Reverse procedure to install.

STARION

FRONT BRAKES

Brake Pads, Replace

1. Raise and support vehicle, then remove front wheel.
2. Remove lower caliper slide pin, **Fig. 6.** Slide pin is coated with special grease. Do not remove this grease or get dirt on pin.
3. Lift caliper up and support with wire.
4. Using tool MB990520 or equivalent, push piston into caliper.
5. Install pad retainer.
6. Install pad and shim to caliper support

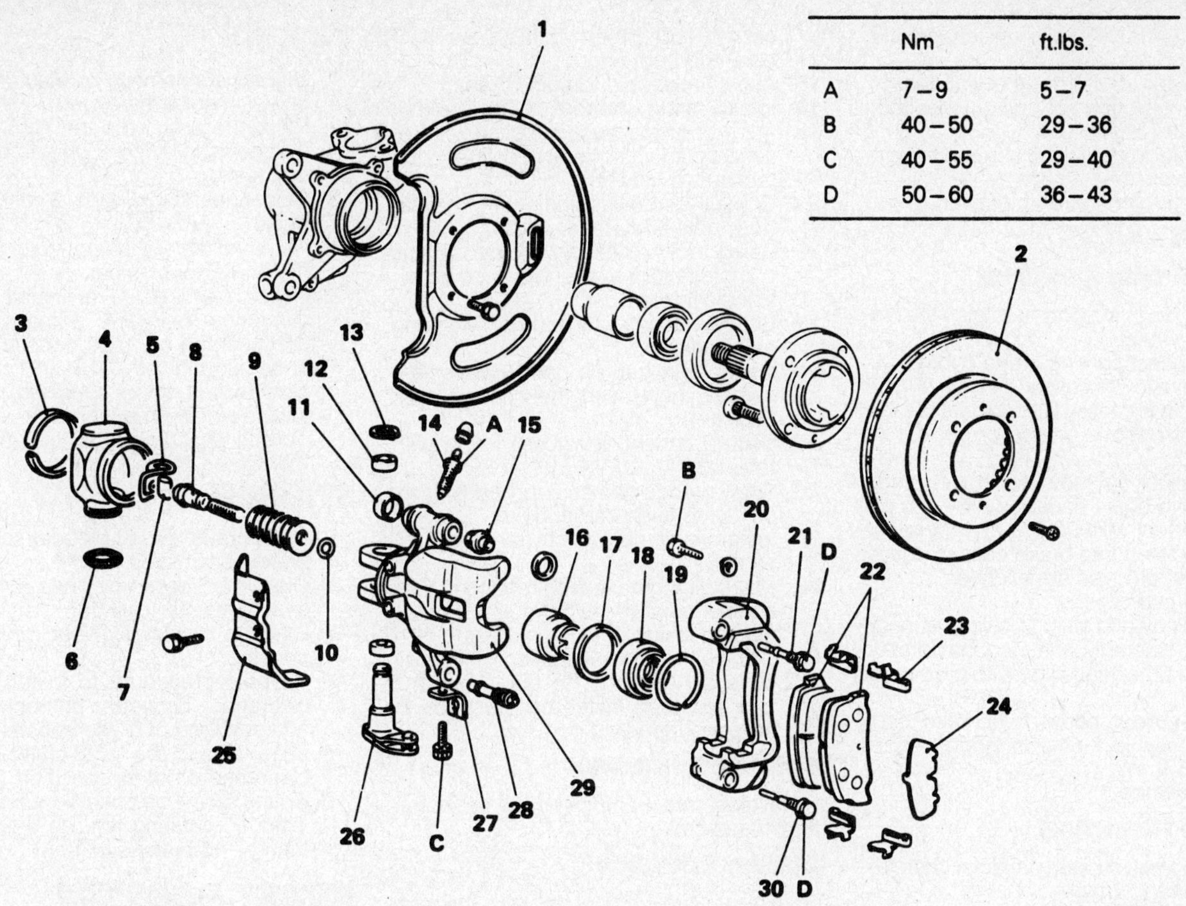

	Nm	ft.lbs.
A	7–9	5–7
B	40–50	29–36
C	40–55	29–40
D	50–60	36–43

1. Dust cover
2. Brake disc
3. Cap ring
4. Lever cap
5. Return spring
6. Garter spring
7. Connecting link
8. Spindle
9. Spring washer
10. Spindle seal
11. Lid
12. Bearing
13. Retaining ring
14. Bleeder screw
15. Guide pin boot
16. Piston assembly
17. Piston seal
18. Piston boot
19. Boot ring
20. Caliper support
21. Guide pin
22. Brake pad
23. Pad clip
24. Outer shim
25. Dust cover
26. Parking lever assembly
27. Parking cable bracket
28. Lock pin boot
29. Caliper body
30. Lock pin

Fig. 7 Exploded view of rear disc brake assembly. Starion

as an assembly.

7. Slide caliper body over brake pads and install slide pin, torquing to 61-69 ft. lbs.
8. Install wheel.

Caliper Removal

1. Raise and support vehicle, then remove wheel.
2. Disconnect brake hose at wheel house and strut assembly.
3. Remove front brake assembly.
4. Remove brake pads, then separate caliper body from caliper support.

Caliper Service

1. Using slide pin, push out bushing from caliper support.
2. Remove cap and pin boot from caliper support.
3. Place rag in front of piston and remove piston and dust boot by slowly applying compressed air through brake hose fitting hole.
4. Using screwdriver, remove piston seal, being careful not to damage cylinder bore.
5. Clean caliper bore with brake fluid.
6. Inspect all components, replacing as necessary.
7. Insert new piston seal into cylinder. New piston seal is coated with special grease. Do not wipe off this grease.
8. Apply pink grease supplied with repair kit to lip of cylinder.
9. Apply brake fluid to external surface of piston.
10. Install new dust boot on piston.
11. Fit end of dust boot into caliper body groove and insert piston into cylinder head by hand. Ensure that end of dust boot is fitted into piston groove.
12. Apply pink grease supplied with repair kit to contact surface of slide pin, seat surface of cap for caliper support, and inside surface of pin boot.
13. Mount cap and pin boot to caliper support.
14. Apply pink grease supplied with repair kit to inside surface of bushing.
15. Apply adhesive supplied with repair kit to lip of slide pin bushing and insert bushing into caliper support using slide pin.
16. Apply brake fluid to screw part of slide pin.
17. Using pink grease supplied with repair kit, apply thin coat to slide pin, then install caliper body to caliper support.

Caliper Installation

Reverse removal procedure to install, then bleed brake system.

Front Hub & Rotor, Replace

1. Disconnect battery ground cable.
2. Raise and support vehicle.

3. Remove front brake assembly and suspend assembly with wire.
4. Remove hub cap, then the cotter pin.
5. Remove slotted nut and washer, then the outer bearing.
6. Remove front hub and rotor assembly.
7. Reverse procedure to install.

REAR BRAKES

Brake Pads, Replace

1. Raise and support vehicle, the remove wheel.
2. Disconnect parking brake cable.
3. Remove lower caliper lock pin, **Fig. 7.** Lock pin is coated with special grease. Do not remove grease or get dirt on pin.
4. Lift caliper up and support with wire.
5. Remove brake pads.
6. Using tool MB990652 or equivalent, push piston into brake caliper, ensuring that grooves are aligned.
7. Install pad clips.
8. Install pad and shim to caliper support as an assembly, ensuring that pins on rear of brake pad align with grooves in piston.
9. Slide caliper body over brake pads and install lock pins, torquing them to 36-45 ft. lbs.
10. Install wheel.

Caliper Removal

1. Raise and support vehicle, then remove rear wheel.
2. Disconnect brake hose.
3. Disconnect parking brake cable from rear brake assembly.
4. Remove rear brake assembly.
5. Remove brake pads, then separate caliper body from caliper support.

Caliper Service

1. Remove cap ring and garter spring from lever cap.
2. Remove lever cap from caliper groove.
3. Remove retaining ring and pull out parking lever assembly.
4. Remove spindle by unscrewing it.
5. Remove boot ring.
6. Push piston out of caliper body.
7. Remove piston seal, being careful not to damage caliper bore.
8. Using tool MB990665 or equivalent, press out bearings.
9. Remove guide pin boot and lock pin boot from caliper body.
10. Clean caliper bore with brake fluid.
11. Inspect all components, replacing as necessary.
12. Apply orange repair grease supplied with repair kit to bearing.
13. Using tool MB990665 or equivalent, press in bearing until it is flush with caliper body.
14. Insert new piston seal into caliper body.
15. Apply brake fluid to piston seal and inside surface of cylinder.
16. Insert piston assembly into cylinder by hand, being careful not to damage piston.
17. Apply orange grease supplied with repair kit to dust boot fitting groove in caliper body, then install new dust boot and boot ring.
18. Apply brake fluid to spindle seal.
19. Install spring washers onto spindle.
20. Apply orange grease supplied with repair kit contact surface of caliper body and spring washer.
21. Carefully screw spindle into caliper body until it rotates freely.
22. Using tool MB990666 or equivalent, compress spring washers, then screw spindle into caliper.
23. Set connecting link and return spring on spindle.
24. Install lever cap on parking lever assembly, then insert them into caliper body.
25. Secure parking lever assembly with retaining ring.
26. Apply orange grease supplied with repair kit to lever cap and lip.
27. Install lever cap to caliper body assembly.
28. Using pink grease with repair kit, coat contact point of caliper support guide pin and inside of lock pin boot.
29. Using pink grease supplied with repair kit, apply thin coat to guide pin and lock pin, then install caliper body to caliper support.

Caliper Support

Reverse removal procedure to install, then bleed brake system.

Rotor, Replace

1. Raise and support vehicle, then remove rear wheels.
2. Remove hub cap, then the cotter pin and cap.
3. Remove wheel bearing nut, then the washer and outer wheel bearing inner race.
4. Disconnect and suspend brake tube, using a suitable wire.
5. Disconnect parking brake cable from caliper assembly.
6. Remove lock pins from caliper assembly, then the caliper assembly to adapter attaching bolts and caliper assembly.
7. Remove rotor assembly.
8. Reverse procedure to install.

MASTER CYLINDER REPLACE

CORDIA, GALANT, MIRAGE, MONTERO & TREDIA

1. Disconnect harness connector of fluid lever sensor.
2. Disconnect brake lines at master cylinder.
3. Remove master cylinder from brake booster.
4. Reverse procedure to install. Check clearance between primary piston and pushrod of brake booster. Clearance should be .016-.031 inch. If clearance is not as specified, turn adjusting screw on pushrod as required. Torque attaching nuts to 6-9 ft. lbs., then bleed brake system.

PICKUP

1. Disconnect harness connector of fluid lever sensor, if equipped.
2. Disconnect brake tube from master cylinder and slowly depress pedal to drain fluid.
3. Disconnect brake lines at master cylinder.
4. Remove two retaining nuts and remove master cylinder.
5. Reverse procedure to install. Check clearance between primary piston and pushrod of brake booster. Clearance should be .016-.031 inch. If clearance is not as specified, turn adjusting screw on pushrod as required. Torque attaching nuts to 6-8 ft. lbs., then bleed brake system.

STARION

1. Drain brake fluid at bleeder screws of brake assemblies.
2. Disconnect reservoir lines and brake lines at master cylinder.
3. Remove master cylinder from brake booster.
4. Reverse procedure to install. Check clearance between primary piston and push rod of brake booster. Clearance should be .028-.043 inch. If clearance is not as specified, turn adjusting screw on pushrod as required. Torque attaching nuts to 6-9 ft. lbs., then bleed brake system.

BRAKE BOOSTER REPLACE

CORDIA, GALANT, MONTERO, STARION & TREDIA

1. Remove master cylinder as previously described.
2. Disconnect vacuum hose from power brake.
3. Remove pin connecting power brake rod with pedal.
4. Remove booster attaching nuts and remove booster.
5. Reverse procedure to install.

PICKUP & MIRAGE

1. Remove master cylinder as previously described.
2. Disconnect vacuum hose from power brake.
3. Remove pin connecting power brake rod with pedal.
4. Remove booster attaching nuts and remove booster.
5. Reverse procedure to install.

PARKING BRAKE ADJUSTMENT

GALANT

1. Pull parking brake lever with a force of approximately 45 lbs. and count number of clicks. Lever stroke should be 5-7 clicks.
2. If parking brake lever stroke is not within specifications, proceed as follows:

a. Remove center console, then loosen adjusting nut on end of cable rod to free parking brake cable.
b. With engine idling, depress brake pedal several times and confirm that the pedal stroke stops changing. **If pedal stroke stops changing, it indicates that automatic adjusting mechanism is functioning properly to adjust clearance between pads and disc to correct value.**
c. Ensure parking lever on caliper side is in contact with the stopper.
d. Turn adjusting nut to adjust parking brake lever stroke to specified range. **If number of brake lever notches engaged are less than specified value, cable has been pulled excessively and failure of the automatic adjuster mechanism may result.**
e. After adjusting lever stroke, raise and support rear of vehicle. With parking brake lever released, turn rear wheels to ensure rear brakes are not dragging.
f. Ensure parking brake lever on caliper side is in contact with the stopper.

STARION

1. Pull parking brake lever and check that lever stroke is 4-5 notches.
2. If stroke if incorrect, adjust by removing center console and turning adjusting nut.

DRUM BRAKE SECTION

INDEX

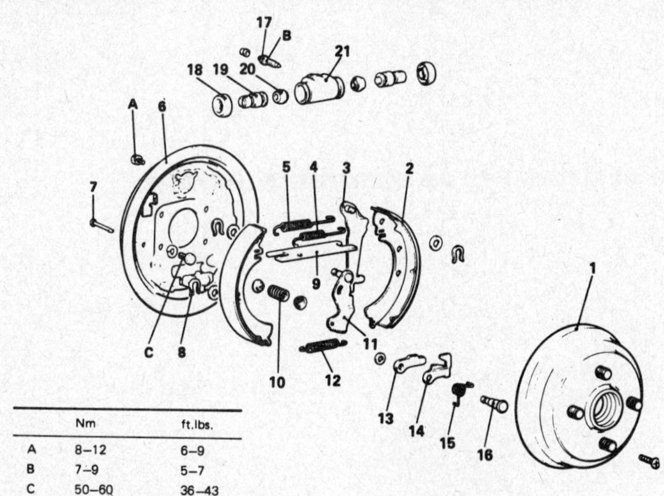

	Nm	ft.lbs.
A	8–12	6–9
B	7–9	5–7
C	50–60	36–43

1. Brake drum
2. Shoe lining assembly
3. Parking brake lever
4. Shoe-to-strut spring
5. Shoe-to-shoe spring
6. Backing plate
7. Shoe hold-down pin
8. Retainer
9. Strut
10. Shoe hold-down spring
11. Adjuster lever
12. Shoe retainer spring
13. Latch
14. Stopper
15. Auto adjuster latch spring
16. Pin
17. Bleeder screw
18. Wheel cylinder boot
19. Wheel cylinder piston
20. Piston cup
21. Wheel cylinder body

Fig. 1 Exploded view of drum brake assembly. Cordia, Galant & Tredia

DRUM BRAKE SERVICE

For drum brake service procedures, refer to **Figs. 1 through 5.**

SERVICE BRAKE ADJUSTMENT

Rear brakes should be adjusted after rear brake service or before adjusting parking brake. These brakes have self-adjusting shoe mechanisms that ensure correct brake lining-to-drum clearances at all times. The automatic self-adjusting mechanism operates whenever the parking brake lever is applied on all models except the Duo-servo type. On Duo-servo type, the self-adjusting mechanism operates when the brakes are applied as the truck is moving rearward.

PARKING BRAKE ADJUSTMENT

CORDIA, MONTERO & TREDIA

1. Pull parking brake lever with force of approximately 45 lbs. Lever stroke should be 5-7 notches on Cordia and Tredia or 4-6 notches on Montero.
2. If lever stroke is not within specifications, pull parking brake lever repeatedly to adjust shoe clearance, then adjust parking brake lever stroke by turning cable adjusting nut.
3. Raise and support rear of vehicle and, with parking brake lever released, turn rear wheels to ensure that rear brakes are not dragging.

GALANT

1. Pull parking brake lever with a force of approximately 45 lbs. and count number of clicks. Lever stroke should be 5-7 clicks.
2. If parking brake lever stroke is not within specifications, proceed as follows:
   a. Remove center console, then loosen adjusting nut to end of cable rod to free parking brake cable.
   b. With engine idling, depress brake pedal several times and confirm that the pedal stroke stops changing. **If pedal stroke stops changing, it indicates that automatic adjusting mechanism is functioning properly to adjust clearance between drum and shoe assembly to correct value.**
   c. Turn adjusting nut to adjust parking brake lever stroke to specified range. **If number of brake lever notches engaged is less than specified value, cable has been pulled excessively and failure of the automatic adjuster mechanism may result.**
   d. After adjusting lever stroke, raise and support rear of vehicle. With parking brake lever released, turn rear wheels to ensure rear brakes are not dragging.

MIRAGE

1. Pull parking brake lever with a force of approximately 45 lbs. and count number of clicks. Lever stroke should be 5-7 clicks.
2. If parking brake lever stroke is not within specifications, proceed as fol-

1. Bleeder screw
2. Wheel cylinder boot
3. Wheel cylinder piston
4. Piston cup
5. Wheel cylinder body
6. Backing plate
7. Shoe hold-down pin
8. Spring
9. Adjuster
10. Automatic adjuster lever
11. Shoe assembly
12. Shoe hold-down spring
13. Shoe retainer spring
14. Shoe-to-shoe spring
15. Clip spring
16. Brake drum

	Nm	ft.lbs.
A	8–12	6–9
B	7–9	5–7
C	50–60	36–43

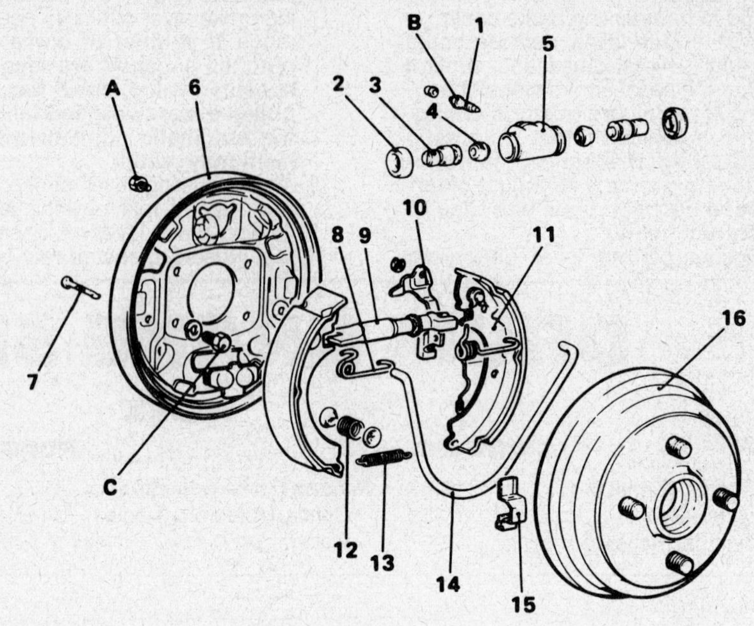

Fig. 2 Exploded view of drum brake assembly. Mirage

1. Bleeder screw
2. Wheel cylinder boot
3. Wheel cylinder piston
4. Piston cup
5. Wheel cylinder body
6. Shoe hold-down pin
7. Backing plate
8. Shoe and lining assembly
9. Shoe return spring
10. Brake shoe adjuster
11. Shoe and lever assembly
12. Adjusting spring
13. Shoe hold-down spring
14. Shoe retainer spring
15. Brake drum

	Nm	ft. lbs.
A	7-9	5-7
B	18-21	13-15
C	50-60	36-43

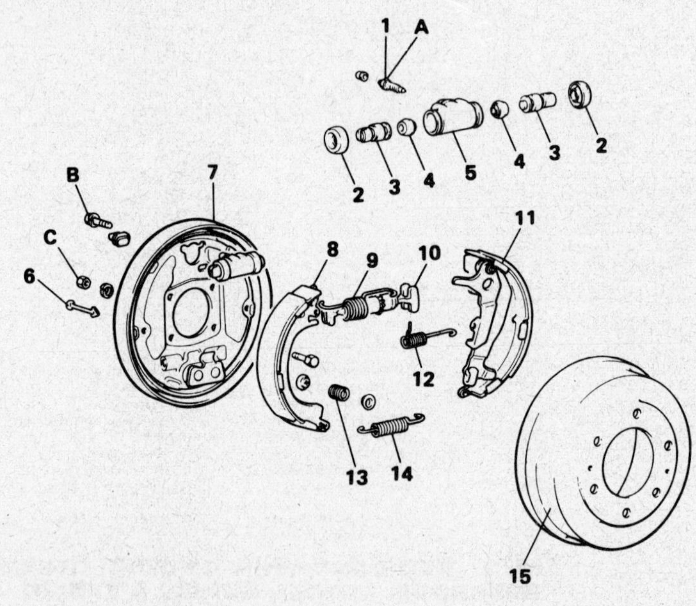

Fig. 3 Exploded view of drum brake assembly. Montero

lows:

a. Remove center console, then with parking brake lever released, loosen cable adjuster locknut.
b. After slacking off parking brake cable locknut, tighten cable adjuster locknut to take up slack in cable. **Excessive pulling of cable may result in failure of the automatic adjuster mechanism.**
c. Pull parking brake lever repeatedly while depressing brake pedal until no more clicks are heard from the automatic adjuster mechanism.
d. Adjust parking brake lever to the specified stroke, then secure with locknut.
e. After adjusting lever stroke, raise and support rear of vehicle. With parking brake lever released, turn rear wheels to ensure rear brakes are not dragging.

PICKUP

1. Adjust rear brake shoe clearance.
2. On rear wheel drive models, adjust turnbuckle so that lever stroke is 16-17 notches with pulling force of 66

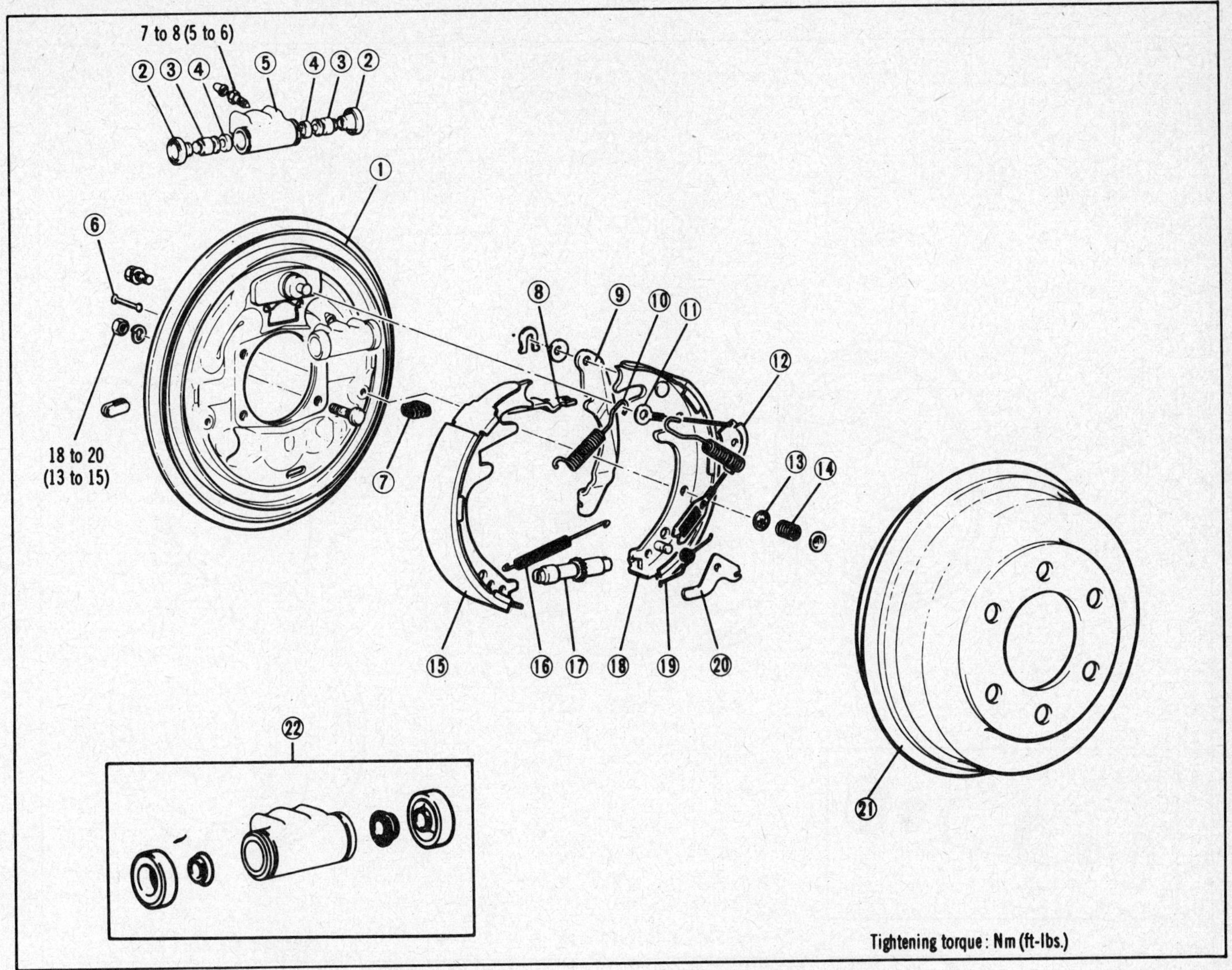

(1) Backing plate
(2) Wheel cylinder boot
(3) Wheel cylinder piston
(4) Wheel cylinder piston cup
(5) Wheel cylinder body
(6) Shoe hold-down pin
(7) Anti-rattle spring
(8) Parking brake strut
(9) Parking brake lever
(10) Shoe return spring
(11) Adjusting cable
(12) Cable guide
(13) Shoe hold-down cup
(14) Shoe hold-down spring
(15) Primary shoe assembly
(16) Adjusting spring
(17) Adjuster assembly
(18) Secondary shoe assembly
(19) Adjuster spring
(20) Autoadjuster lever
(21) Brake drum
(22) Wheel cylinder repair kit

Fig. 4 Exploded view of Duo-Servo drum brake assembly. Pickup

lbs.

3. On 4 wheel drive models, turn adjusting nut to obtain lever stroke as described in step 2.
4. Ensure that rear parking brake cable is not taut.
5. On rear wheel drive models, ensure that balancer is almost parallel with center line of truck.
6. On 4 wheel drive models, ensure that joint and equalizer are at right angles to each other.
7. If, after above adjustments, stroke is not 16-17 notches, rear brake automatic adjusters are malfunctioning. Correct as necessary.

BRAKE BOOSTER & MASTER CYLINDER

REPLACE

Refer to "Disc Brakes Section" for brake booster and master cylinder replacement procedures.

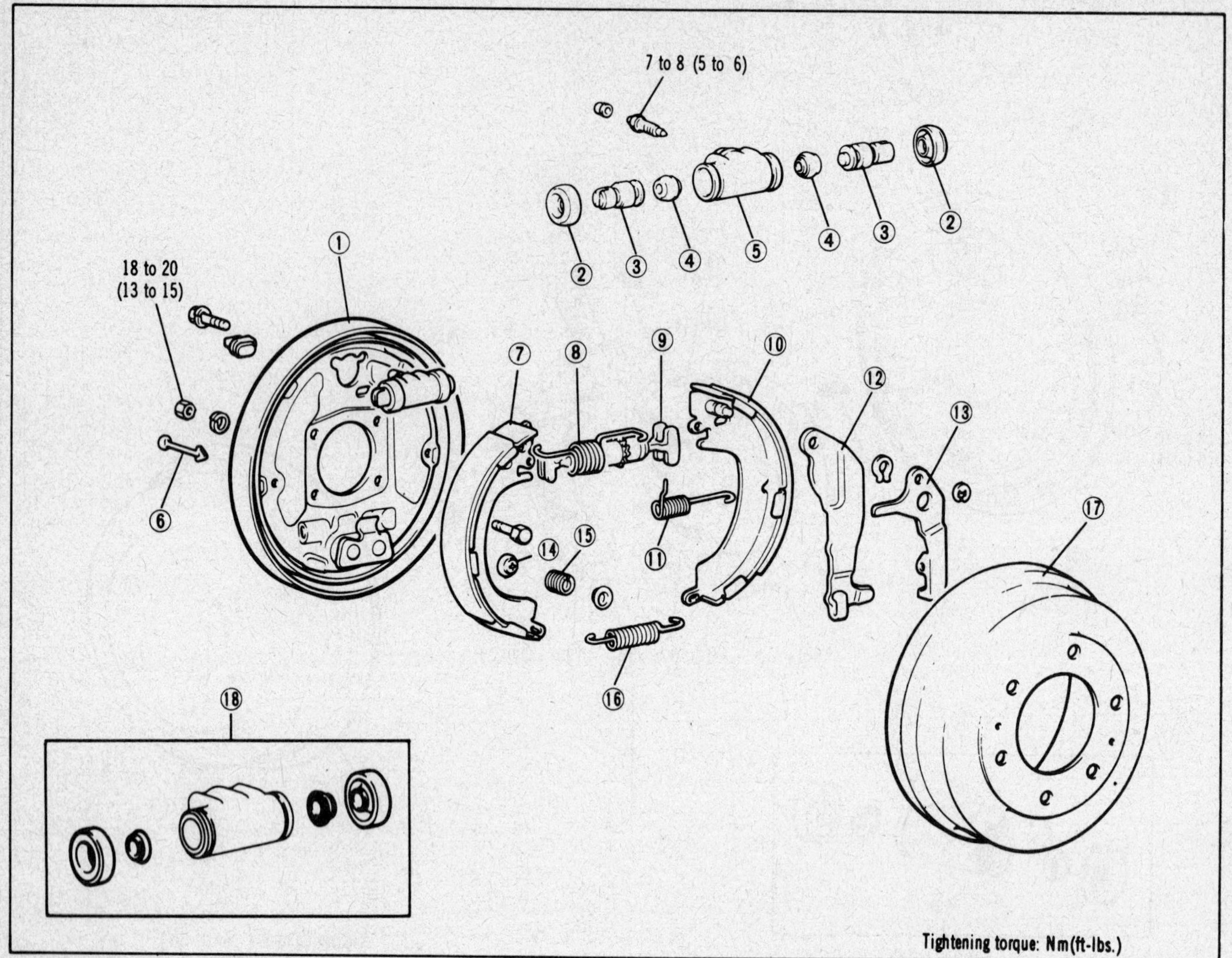

(1) Backing plate
(2) Wheel cylinder boot
(3) Wheel cylinder piston
(4) Wheel cylinder piston cup
(5) Wheel cylinder body
(6) Shoe hold-down pin
(7) Shoe and lining assembly
(8) Shoe return spring
(9) Brake shoe adjuster
(10) Shoe and lever assembly
(11) Adjusting spring
(12) Parking brake lever
(13) Autoadjuster lever
(14) Shoe hold-down cup
(15) Shoe hold-down spring
(16) Shoe retaining spring
(17) Brake drum
(18) Wheel cylinder repair kit

Fig. 5 Exploded view of Leading-Trailing drum brake assembly. Pickup

REAR AXLE & SUSPENSION SECTION

INDEX

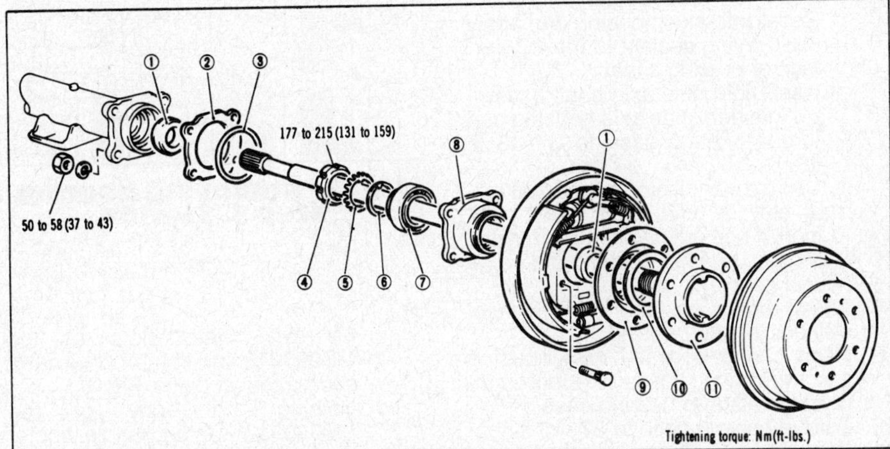

(1) Oil seal
(2) Shim
(3) O Ring
(4) Lock nut
(5) Lock washer
(6) Washer
(7) Wheel bearing
(8) Bearing case
(9) Dust cover
(10) Packing
(11) Axle shaft

Fig. 1 Exploded view of axle shaft. Montero & Pickup

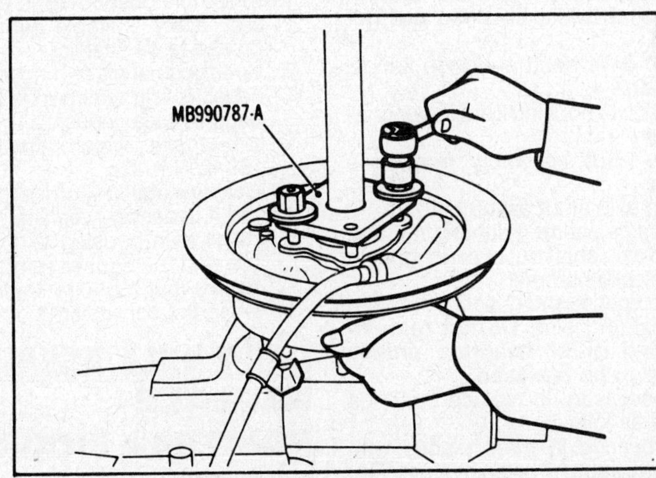

Fig. 2 Removing wheel bearing. Montero & Pickup

REAR AXLE SHAFT REPLACE

MONTERO & PICKUP

Removal

1. Raise and support rear of vehicle, then remove rear wheel and brake drum and disconnect brake hose at wheel cylinder.
2. Disconnect bearing case from axle housing end, **Fig. 1.**
3. Remove brake backing plate, if equipped, bearing case, and axle shaft as an assembly, using tools MB990211 and MB990241 or equivalents to remove axle shaft if necessary.
4. Remove O-ring and wheel bearing preload shims, retaining shims for assembly.
5. Using tools MB990211 and MB990212 or equivalents, remove oil seal.
6. Remove wheel bearing by first removing lock washer and then, using tool MB990785 or equivalent, removing locknut.
7. Remove lock washer and washer, then reinsert locknut on axle shaft approximately three turns.
8. Install tool MB990787 or equivalent as shown, **Fig. 2,** installing nuts and washers diagonally.
9. Remove wheel bearing by turning nuts evenly.
10. Using hammer and drift, remove bearing outer race from bearing case.
11. Remove oil seal from bearing case.
12. Check all components for wear or damage and check axle shaft for runout.

Installation

1. After applying suitable grease to outer surface of wheel bearing outer race and lip of new oil seal, then drive them into bearing case using tool Nos. MB990935, MB990937, and MB990938 on 1983-86 models or tool Nos. MB990938-01 and MB990937-01 on 1987 models or equivalents.

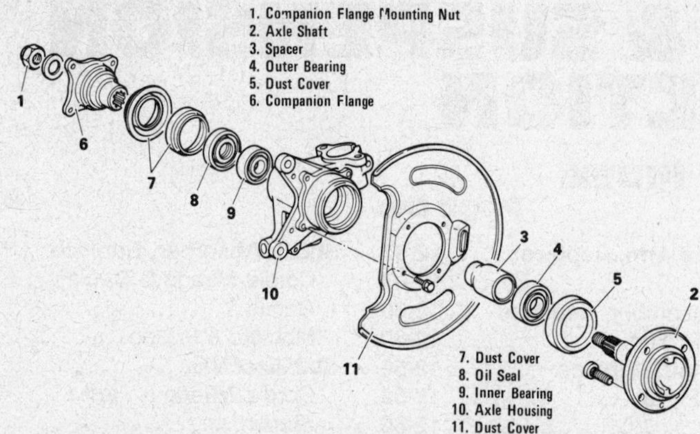

Fig. 3 Exploded view of axle shaft. Starion

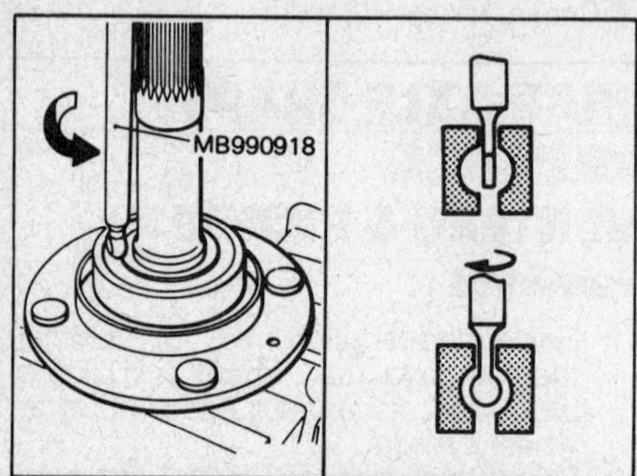

Fig. 5 Removing bearing step 2. Starion

2. Slide bearing case and wheel bearing over axle shaft and lubricate wheel bearing rollers, then install wheel bearing inner race with tool MB990799 or equivalent.
3. Install washer, lock washer, and locknut, torquing locknut to 131-159 ft. lbs. with tool MB990785 or equivalent.
4. Bend tab on lock washer into groove on locknut, tightening nut as necessary to align tab and groove.
5. Lubricate lip of new oil seal, then using tools MB990930 on 1983-86 models or MB990932 on 1987 models and MB990938 or equivalents, drive oil seal into axle housing.
6. Adjust axial play of rear axle shaft as follows:
   a. Remove any old sealer or rust from mating surfaces of bearing case and axle housing.
   b. Insert a .04 inch shim and O-ring into left side of axle housing and apply semi-drying sealer to mating surface of bearing case.
   c. Insert left side axle shaft assembly into left side of axle housing and torque bearing case to 37-43 ft. lbs.
   d. Insert right side axle shaft assembly into right side axle housing without using shim or O-ring, then torque bearing case to 4 ft. lbs. Measure gap between bearing case and axle housing.
   e. Loosen nut and separate right side axle shaft assembly from axle housing.
   f. Using a shim with thickness equal to that of measured gap and a shim with thickness of .0020-.0079 inch, insert shims and O-ring into axle housing and apply semi-drying sealant to mating surface of bearing case.
   g. Insert right side axle shaft assembly into right side axle housing and torque bearing case to 37-43 ft. lbs.
   h. Using dial indicator, check that axial play of axle shaft is.002-.008 inch. If not, adjust shim thickness.
7. Lubricate bearing case and axle housing end.
8. Attach brake assembly with wheel cylinder to axle housing.
9. Insert O-ring between axle housing end and bearing case and apply semi-drying sealant to bearing case.
10. Torque bearing case to 37-43 ft. lbs.
11. Connect brake line to wheel cylinder and install rear brake drum and wheel.

STARION

Removal

1. Disconnect parking brake cable from rear brake caliper assembly.
2. Remove caliper assembly, caliper support, and brake disc. **Using a suitable wire, support caliper assembly so that brake lines do not get twisted.**
3. Remove drive shaft and axle flange, **Figs. 3 and 4.**
4. Remove axle housing from lower control arm.
5. Remove strut assembly from axle housing.
6. Remove axle shaft assembly.
7. Loosen axle flange mounting nut and then tap axle shaft out of axle housing with a plastic hammer.
8. Remove spacer and dust covers from inside axle housing. **Do not remove inner and outer bearings unless they are to be replaced.**
9. If it is necessary to replace bearings proceed as follows:
   a. Cut bearing in three places with tool MB990918 or equivalent, **Fig. 4.**
   b. Insert claws of tool MB990918 into the three cuts in bearing and turn claw 90°, **Fig. 5.**

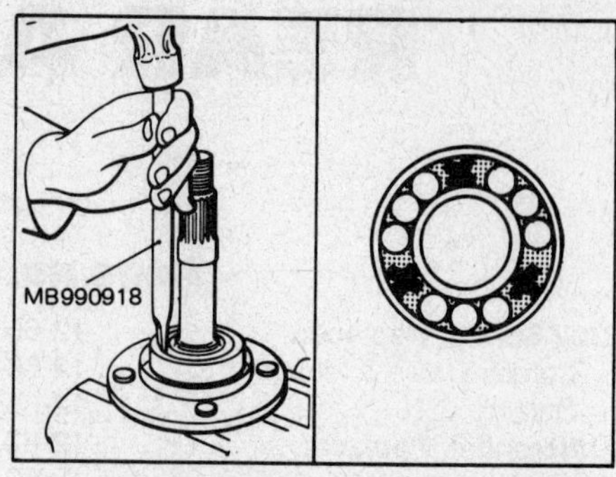

Fig. 4 Removing bearing, step 1. Starion

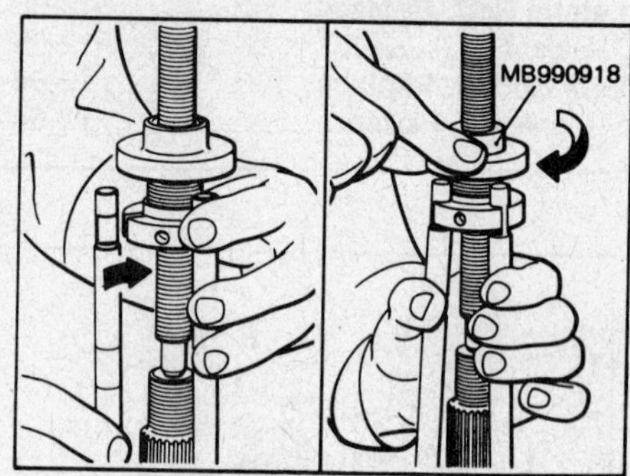

Fig. 6 Removing bearing step 3. Starion

   c. Fit claws into slots of tool MB990918 and tighten claw nut to secure tool in place, **Fig. 6.**
   d. Holding the body of tool MB990918 with its handle, tighten center bolt to remove outer bearing.
   e. Using a suitable drift drive inner bearing and oil seal from axle housing.
10. Remove axle housing, then, if equipped, the dust cover.

Installation

1. Assemble dust cover to axle housing and apply suitable wheel bearing grease to oil seal lip.
2. Insert axle shaft and spacer into axle housing, and attach axle flange.
3. Secure axle housing in vise and torque axle flange attaching nut to 188-217 ft. lbs.
4. Measure starting torque of axle shaft and if necessary replace spacer.
5. Install axle housing to lower control arm and the strut assembly.
6. Assure that the axle shaft endplay is within the service limit.

REAR AXLE ASSEMBLY REPLACE

MONTERO & PICKUP

1983-86

1. Loosen rear wheel lug nuts, then jack up rear of vehicle with jack placed under differential.

Normal Suspension   Electronic Controlled Suspension

1. Cap
2. Washer
3. Upper bushing (A)
4. Bracket assembly
5. Collar
6. Spring pad
7. Upper bushing (B)
8. Cup assembly
9. Bump rubber
10. Dust cover
11. Coil spring
12. Shock absorber assembly
13. Joint
14. Connect
15. O ring
16. Dust cover
17. Snap ring
18. Actuator
19. Adapter
20. Joint assembly
21. Actuator bracket
22. Insulator assembly
23. Sub tank
24. Lower spring pad
25. Arm bushing
26. Torsion axle and arm assembly
27. Lateral rod bushing
28. Lateral rod

	Nm	ft. lbs.
A	25-35	18-25
B	20-25	14-18
C	100-120	72-87
D	45-55	33-40

NOTE
*marks: To be tightened with vehicle lowered to the ground.

Fig. 7 Rear suspension assembly. Galant

2. Remove rear wheels and support vehicle on axle stands placed forward of rear spring front bracket, with jack still applying slight upward pressure on axle assembly.
3. Make mating marks on rear propeller shaft flange yoke and companion flange of differential case to facilitate installation, then remove propeller shaft. Remove adjusting nuts, then disconnect parking brake cables.
4. Loosen joint between brake hose and brake line and pull out stops to disconnect brake hose.
5. Disconnect rear cable of parking brake at balancer.
6. Remove shock absorbers.
7. Remove spring U-bolts, then remove spring seats.
8. Remove spring shackle pin nuts, then remove shackle plate, being careful not to drop axle housing from jack.
9. Remove axle housing by slowly lowering jack.
10. Reverse procedure to install. Align match marks when installing propeller shaft. Install spring support so that distance between hole on load sensing proportioning valve lever and spring support hole is 6.77-6.93 inch, then bleed rear brake system.

1987

1. Loosen rear wheel lug nuts, then jack up rear of vehicle with jack placed under differential.
2. Remove rear wheels and support vehicle on axle stands placed forward of rear spring front bracket, with jack still applying slight upward pressure on axle assembly.
3. Remove propeller shaft, then remove adjusting nuts and disconnect parking brake cables.
4. Loosen joint between brake hose and brake line and pull out stops to disconnect brake hose.
5. Disconnect rear cable of parking brake at balancer.
6. On 4WD models, disconnect breather hose.

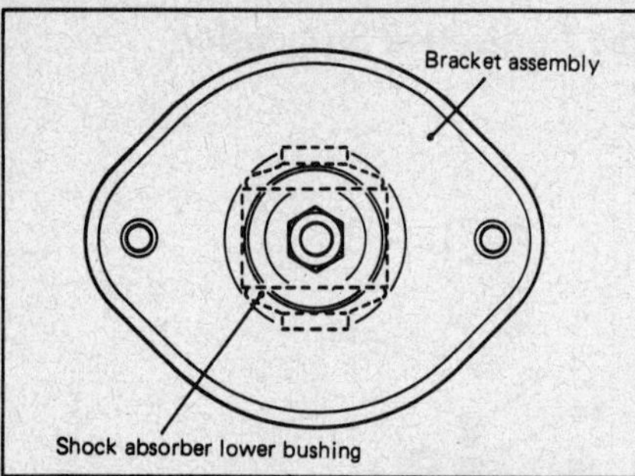

Fig. 8 Bracket assembly installation. Galant less electronically controlled suspension

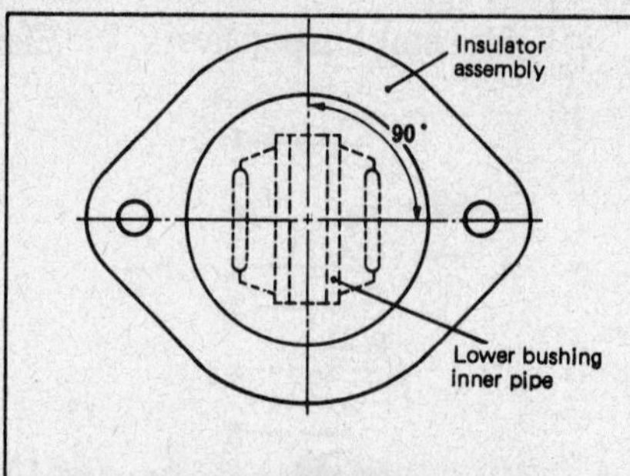

Fig. 9 Bracket assembly installation. Galant w/electronically controlled suspension

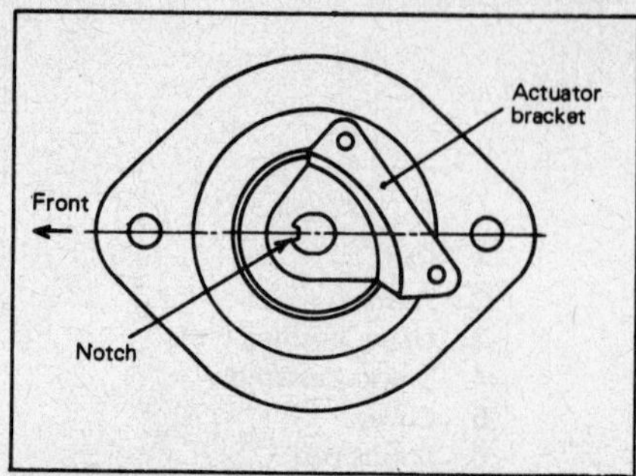

Fig. 10 Aligning piston rod. Galant w/electronically controlled suspension

7. On all models, disconnect shock absorbers at lower end.
8. Remove spring U-bolts, then remove spring seats.
9. Remove spring shackle pin nuts, then remove shackle plate, being careful not to drop axle housing from jack.
10. Remove axle housing by slowly lowering jack.
11. Reverse procedure to install, then bleed rear brake system.

DIFFERENTIAL REPLACE

STARION

1. Drain gear oil.
2. Remove driveshafts from differential carrier assembly.
3. Remove torque tube.
4. Remove nuts connecting rear support insulator to crossmember and nuts connecting rear support to rear support insulator.
5. Raise differential with jack and disconnect differential from rear support insulators, then remove differential.
6. Reverse procedure to install.

MONTERO

1. Drain gear oil.
2. Disconnect parking brake cables, then remove heat protectors.
3. Raise and support vehicle, then remove wheel and tire assembly.
4. Remove brake drum, then the axle shaft assembly as previously described.
5. Disconnect rear propeller shaft from differential assembly.
6. Remove differential carrier.
7. Reverse procedure to install.

PICKUP

1. Drain gear oil.
2. Remove parking brake cable adjusting nuts, then disconnect parking brake cables.
3. Raise and support vehicle, then remove wheel and tire assembly.
4. Remove brake drum, then the axle shaft assembly as previously described.
5. Disconnect rear propeller shaft from differential assembly.
6. Remove differential carrier.
7. Reverse procedure to install.

SHOCK ABSORBER REPLACE

CORDIA, MIRAGE & TREDIA

1. Raise rear of vehicle and position jack stands under frame side rails.
2. Position suitable jack under suspension arm to keep it raised.
3. Remove wheel and tire assembly, then remove upper and lower shock absorber mounting bolts and remove shock absorber.
4. Reverse procedure to install, torquing upper and lower mounting bolts to 47-58 ft. lbs.

GALANT

Exc. Electronically Controlled Suspension

1. Raise and support vehicle, then remove rear wheels.
2. Position suitable jack under torsion axle and arm assembly, **Fig. 7.**
3. Remove trunk compartment front trim.
4. Remove shock absorber cap, then the shock absorber attaching nuts.
5. Remove shock absorber assembly from torsion axle and arm assembly.
6. Compress coil spring using suitable tool, then while holding piston rod, remove piston rod attaching nut.
7. Remove washer, upper bushing (A), bracket, spring pad, upper bushing (B), collar, cup, dust cover, rubber bumper and coil spring from shock absorber.
8. Inspect rubber parts and coil springs for cracks, damage or deterioration. Replace as required. **If coil spring replacement is necessary, be sure to use spring having the correct identification marks.**
9. Fully compress coil spring using suitable tool, then install spring into shock absorber.
10. Install dust cover on cup assembly.
11. Extend piston rod as far as possible, then install rubber bumper, cup assembly, collar, upper bushing (B), spring pad, bracket assembly, upper bushing (A) and washer.
12. Position bracket assembly as shown, **Fig. 8**, then torque piston rod attaching nut to 14-18 ft. lbs. and remove spring compressor.
13. Install shock absorber assembly in torsion axle and arm assembly. Torque attaching bolts to 58-72 ft. lbs.
14. Install cap, then the shock absorber attaching nuts. Torque nuts to 18-25 ft. lbs.
15. Install trunk compartment front trim, then remove jack from torsion axle and arm assembly.
16. Install rear wheels.

Electronically Controlled Suspension

1. Remove rear seat.
2. Remove dust cover, **Fig. 7,** then disconnect and cap air tube from shock absorber. Use caution not to bend air tube.
3. Remove actuator from actuator bracket.
4. Remove adapter and snap ring, then the joint assembly from piston rod.
5. Remove O-ring and actuator bracket from piston rod.
6. Raise and support vehicle, then remove rear wheels.
7. Remove shock absorber assembly from torsion axle and arm assembly.
8. Remove shock absorber attaching nuts, then the shock absorber assembly from wheel housing. Use caution not to damage piston rod.
9. Check shock absorber assembly for air leaks as follows:
   a. Install joint assembly to shock absorber assembly and secure with snap ring.
   b. Using vehicles air compressor for air supply, disconnect white air tube from solenoid valve, then connect tool No. MB991075 or equivalent and inject 71 psi of air.
   c. Submerse shock absorber assembly into a water tank and check for air leakage.
   d. If air leakage is present, check sub-tank, O-ring and shock absorber assembly in that order. Repair as required.
10. Remove insulator attaching nut, then the insulator assembly, sub-tank, coil spring and lower spring pad.
11. Remove O-ring from sub-tank.
12. Check rubber parts, sub-tank and coil

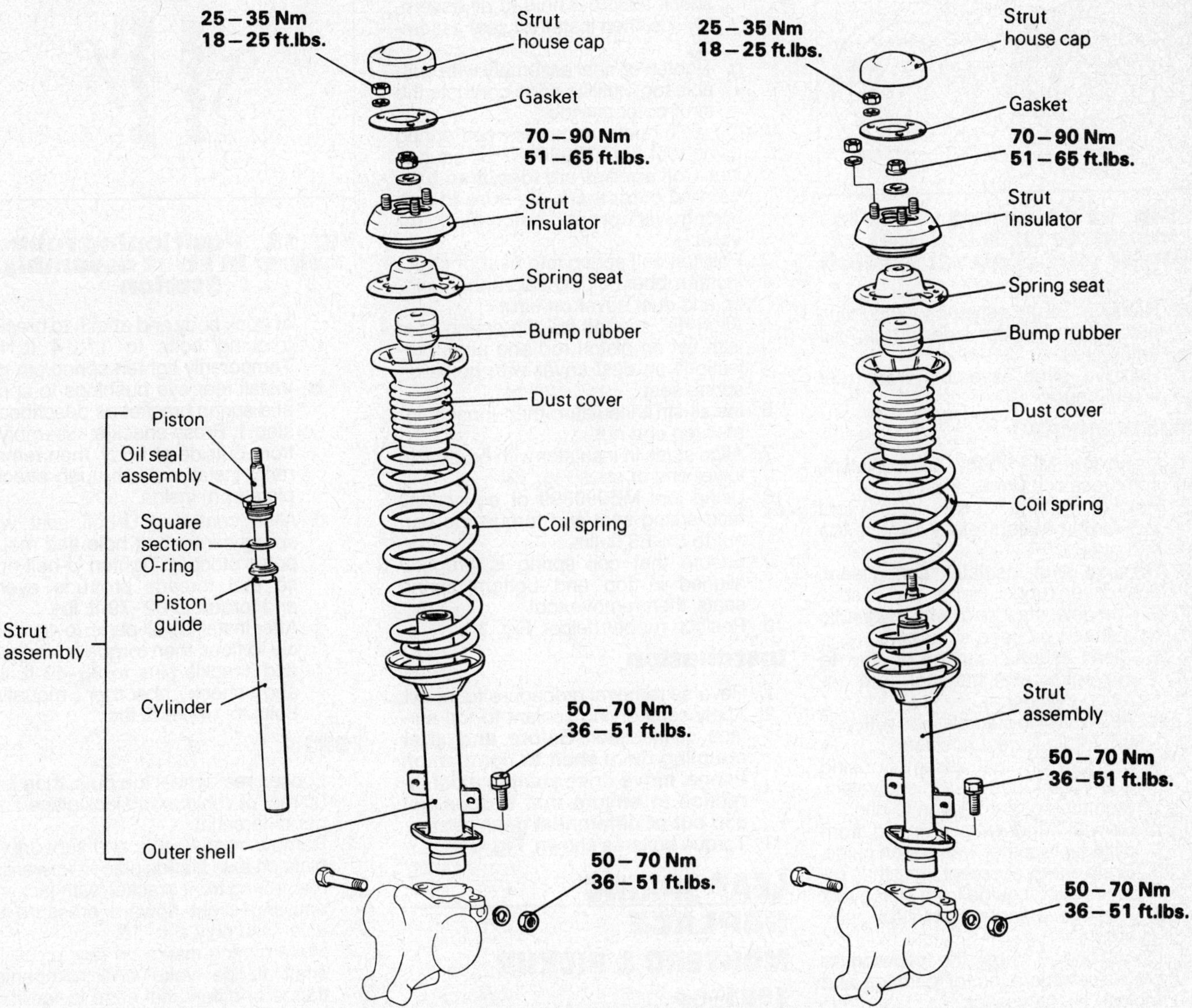

Fig. 11 Disassembling strut. Starion

spring for damage, deterioration, deformation or cracks. Repair as required.

13. Install lower spring pad and coil spring on shock absorber. **When replacing coil spring, note that the left and right identification marks are different.**
14. Coat O-ring with suitable grease, then install O-ring in sub-tank.
15. Install sub-tank, then the insulator assembly while temporarily tightening nut so installation angle of insulator assembly and lower bushing inner pipe is as shown, **Fig. 9.**
16. Recheck shock absorber assembly for air leaks, refer to step 9.
17. Install shock absorber assembly, then lower vehicle as slow as possible to prevent damaging or deforming diaphragm.
18. Position piston rod notch as shown, **Fig. 10,** then hold end of piston rod using a suitable wrench and torque insulator assembly attaching nuts to 18-25 ft. lbs.
19. Install actuator bracket and torque to 33-40 ft. lbs.
20. Install O-ring on piston rod, then the joint assembly and secure with snap ring.
21. Install adapter and actuator, then connect air tubes.
22. Start engine and check for air leaks, then install dust cover.

MONTERO & PICKUP

1. Raise rear of vehicle and position jack stands under frame side sills.
2. Remove wheel and tire assembly, then disconnect shock absorbers at upper and lower mountings and remove from vehicle.
3. Reverse procedure to install, torquing shock absorber attaching nuts to 14-18 ft. lbs.

STRUT ASSEMBLY REPLACE

STARION

Removal

1. Remove rear suspension assembly as described under "Rear Suspension Assembly, Replace."
2. Disconnect rear brake hose at strut assembly.
3. Separate drive shaft from companion flange.
4. Remove strut assembly to axle housing attaching bolts.
5. Separate strut assembly from axle housing by pushing axle housing downward while opening coupling on housing.

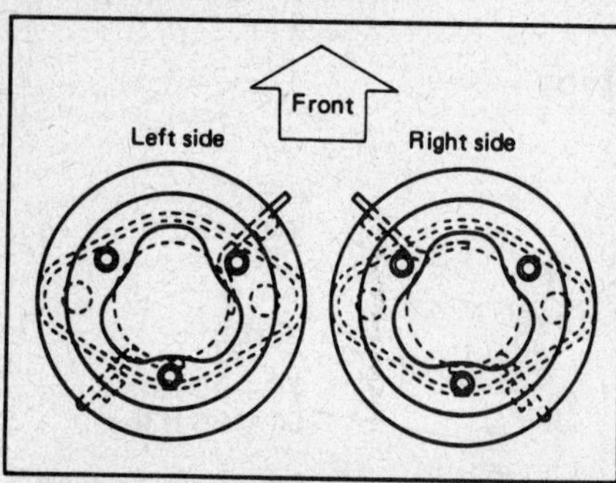

Fig. 12 Aligning studs in insulator with bracket at lower end of strut. Starion

6. Remove strut assembly mounting nuts, located under side trim in rear hatch area.
7. Remove strut assembly from rear wheel house.

Disassembly

1. Using tool MB990987 or equivalent, compress coil spring, **Fig. 11.**
2. Holding spring seat with tool MB990899 or equivalent, remove top end nut.
3. Remove strut insulator, spring seat, dust cover, rubber helper and seat.
4. On models equipped with hydraulic type shock, proceed as follows:
   a. Clean external surface of strut to prevent foreign material from entering cylinder.
   b. Place strut in suitable vise with piston rod in lowest position.
   c. Remove oil seal assembly using tool MB990899-01 or equivalent, then the square section O-ring.
   d. Slowly withdraw piston rod from cylinder together with piston guide.
   e. Drain shock absorber fluid, then remove piston guide from piston rod.
   f. Remove cylinder from strut outer shell.
5. On all models, check the following for cracks, deterioration, or damage and replace as necessary:
   a. Strut insulator.
   b. Spring seat.
   c. Rubber helper and seat.
   d. Dust cover.
   e. Coil spring.
   f. Strut housing.
6. Check strut assembly for oil leakage.
7. Check strut position rod for bends or wear.

Assembly

1. On models equipped with hydraulic type shock, proceed as follows:
   a. Apply suitable shock absorber fluid to cylinder, piston and each sliding surface.
   b. Slowly insert piston rod into cylinder, then install cylinder and piston assembly in outer shell.
   c. Move piston rod slowly up and down while pouring shock absorber fluid into cylinder.
   d. With flange part of piston guide facing upward, install piston guide onto piston rod until it contacts edge of cylinder.
   e. Install new square section O-ring into piston guide.
   f. Cover piston rod end and apply shock absorber fluid to oil assembly lips, then install oil seal assembly.
   g. Tighten oil seal assembly with suitable tool until its edge contacts the strut outer cylinder.
2. On all models, compress coil spring using tool No. MB990987 or equivalent. **Coil springs are identified by a painted color mark. Be sure to use spring with proper color mark for vehicle.**
3. Position coil spring into seat of strut.
4. Install rubber helper seat, rubber helper, and dust cover on strut.
5. Align "D" shaped hole in spring seat with flat on piston rod and align projections on dust cover with holes on spring seat.
6. Install strut insulator, then loosely install top end nut.
7. Align studs in insulator with bracket at lower end of strut, **Fig. 12.**
8. Using tool MB990899 or equivalent, hold spring seat and torque top end nut to 51-65 ft. lbs.
9. Ensure that coil spring is properly aligned in top and bottom spring seats, then remove tool.
10. Position rubber helper, **Fig. 13.**

Installation

1. Reverse removal procedure to install.
2. Apply semi-drying sealant to top surface of insulator. **Before and after coupling drive shaft to companion flange, move drive shaft in axial direction to ensure that it does not slip out of differential gear carrier.**
3. Torque bolts as shown, **Fig. 11.**

LEAF SPRING REPLACE

MONTERO & PICKUP

1983–86

1. Loosen wheel lug nuts, then raise rear of vehicle with suitable jack placed under center of rear axle.
2. Support side frames on jack stands, remove wheel, and slowly lower jack.
3. Remove parking brake cable clamp from leaf spring, then drain fluid at bleeder screw and disconnect brake lines.
4. Disconnect shock absorber upper and lower attaching bolts and disengage upper end.
5. Loosen U-bolt nuts and jack up rear axle housing until axle housing clears U-bolt seat, then remove U-bolt seat.
6. Remove spring pin at front end of spring assembly and spring shackle at rear end, then remove spring assembly, **Fig. 14**
7. Reverse procedure to install, noting the following:
   a. Install spring front eye bushings from both sides of eye with bushing flanges facing outside. Insert spring pin assembly from outside of truck body and attach to bracket, torquing bolts to 11-14 ft. lbs. Temporarily tighten spring pin nut.
   b. Install rear eye bushings to spring and spring bracket as described in step 1. Press shackle assembly in from outside of body, then temporarily install nuts through shackle plate from inside.
   c. Align center of U-bolt seat with spring center bolt hole and mount bump stopper. Tighten U-bolt nuts so that threads protrude evenly and torque to 62-79 ft. lbs.
   d. After installing all parts, lower vehicle to floor, then torque spring pins and shackle pins to 33-43 ft. lbs. and shock absorber mounting bolts to 14-18 ft. lbs.

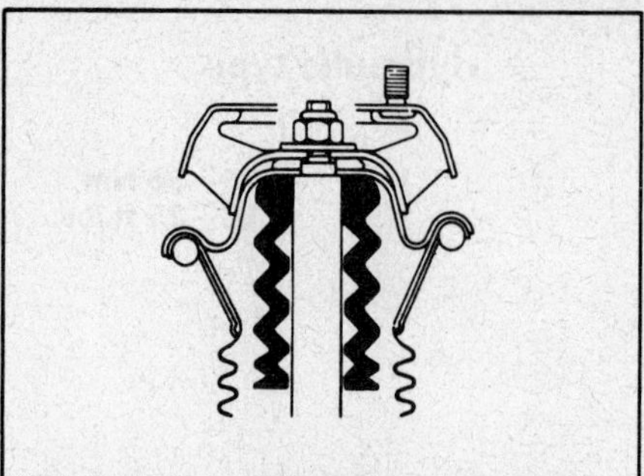

Fig. 13 Positioning rubber helper in strut assembly. Starion

1987

1. Loosen rear wheel lug nuts, then jack up rear of vehicle with jack placed under differential.
2. Remove rear wheels and support vehicle on axle stands placed forward of rear spring front bracket, with jack still applying slight upward pressure on axle assembly, **Fig. 15.**
3. Make mating marks on rear propeller shaft flange yoke and companion flange of differential case to facilitate installation, then remove propeller shaft. Remove adjusting nuts, then disconnect parking brake cables.
4. Loosen joint between brake hose and brake line and pull out stops to disconnect brake hose.
5. Disconnect rear cable of parking brake at balancer.
6. On 4WD models, disconnect breather hose.
7. On all models, disconnect shock absorbers at lower end.
8. Remove spring U-bolts, then remove spring seats.
9. Remove spring shackle pin nuts, then remove shackle plate, being careful not to drop axle housing from jack.
10. Remove axle housing by slowly lowering jack.
11. Reverse procedure to install. Align match marks when installing propeller shaft. Install spring support so that distance between hole on load sensing proportioning valve lever and spring support hole is 6.77-6.93 inch, then bleed rear brake system.

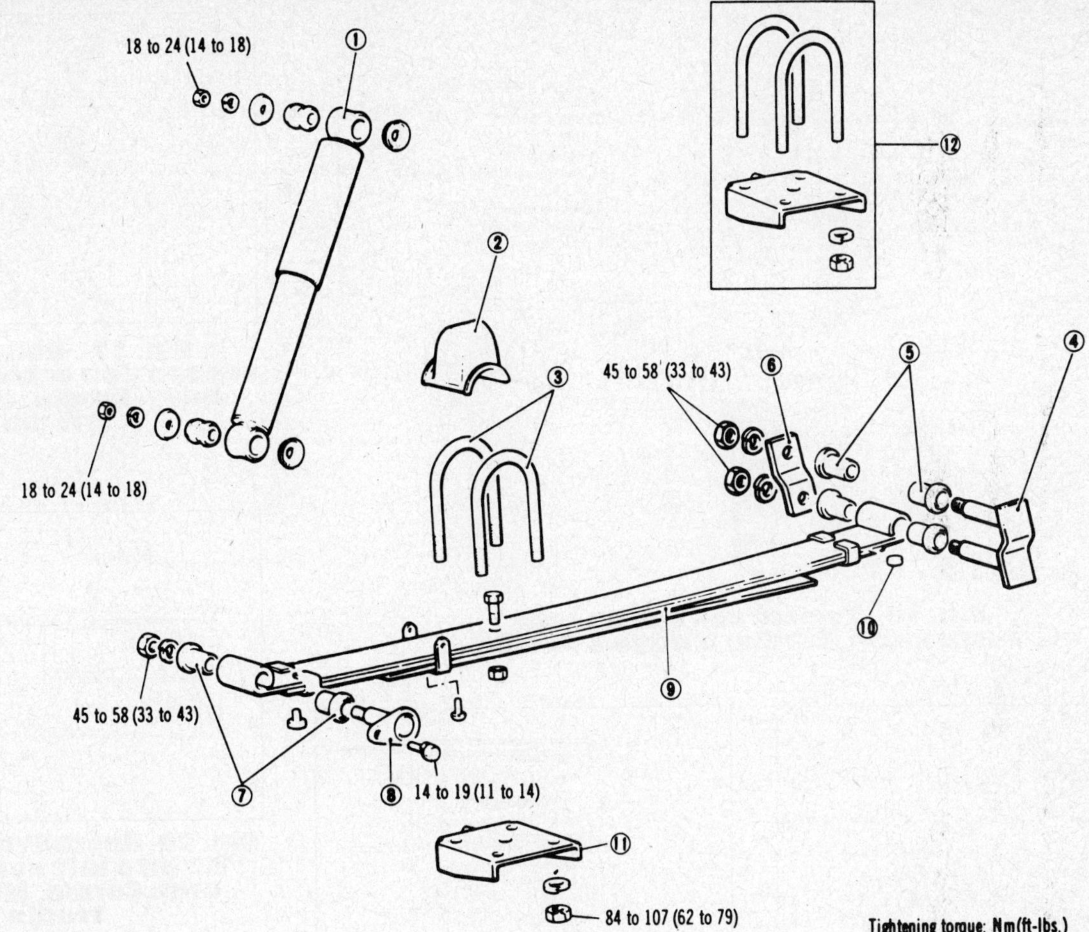

(1) Shock absorber
(2) Bump stop
(3) Spring U-bolt
(4) Spring shackle assembly
(5) Rear eye bushing
(6) Shackle plate
(7) Front eye bushing
(8) Spring pin assembly
(9) Leaf spring assembly
(10) Silencer
(11) U-bolt seat
(12) U-bolt repair kit

Fig. 14 Replacing leaf spring. 1983–86 Montero & Pickup

1. Suspension arm (R.H.)
2. Dust cover
3. Clamp
4. Bushing A
5. Bushing B
6. Rubber stopper
7. Suspension arm (L.H.)
8. Fixture
9. Rubber bushing
10. Washer
11. Spring upper seat
12. Coil spring
13. Spring lower seat
14. Shock absorber
15. Bump stopper
16. Stabilizer bar (vehicles with a turbocharger)

	Nm	ft.lbs.
A	65–80	47–58
B	70–90	51–65
C	80–100	58–72
D	18–25	13–18

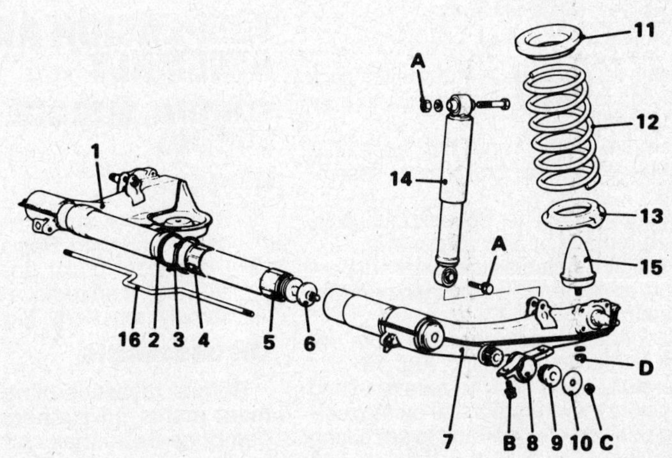

Fig. 15 Replacing leaf spring. 1987 Montero & Pickup

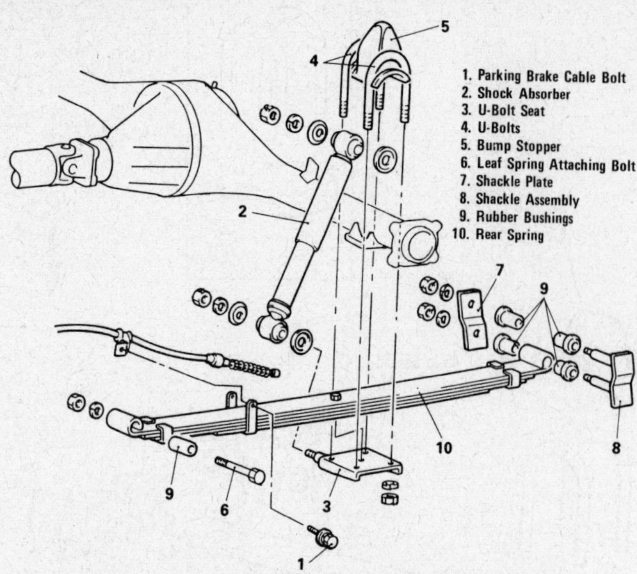

Fig. 16 Typical coil spring rear suspension. Cordia, Mirage & Tredia

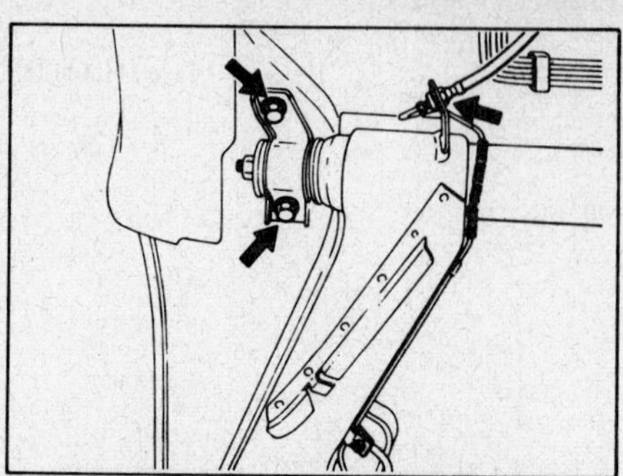

Fig. 17 Removing suspension assembly from body. Cordia, Mirage & Tredia

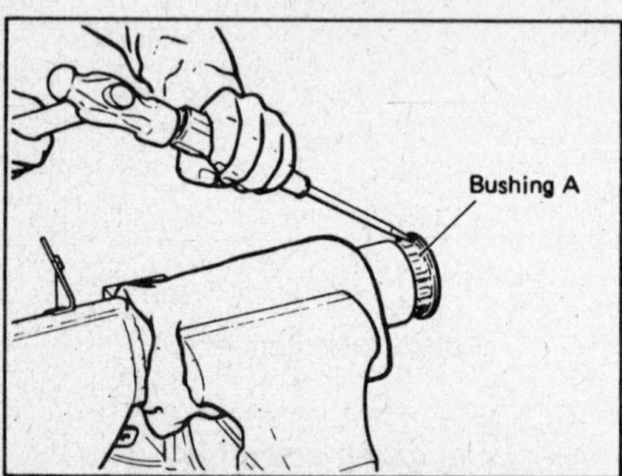

Fig. 18 Removing bushing "A" from left suspension arm. Cordia, Mirage & Tredia

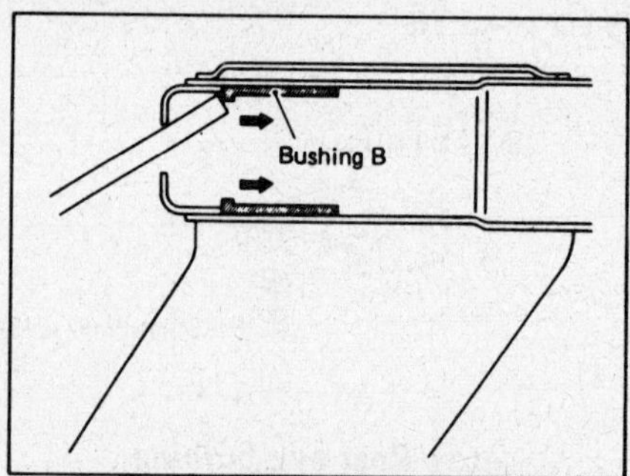

Fig. 19 Removing bushing "B" from left suspension arm. Cordia, Mirage & Tredia

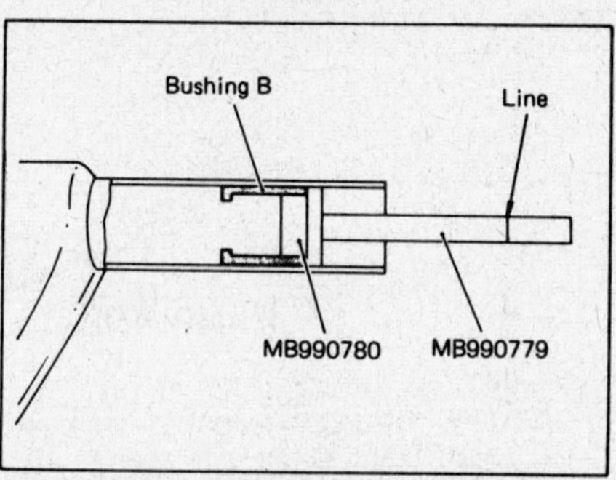

Fig. 20 Installing bushing "B" into left suspension arm. Cordia, Mirage & Tredia

COIL SPRING REPLACE

CORDIA, TREDIA & MIRAGE

1. Raise rear of vehicle and position jack stands under frame side rails to support body.
2. Remove wheel and tire assembly, then remove rear brake drum assembly.
3. Disconnect muffler from exhaust pipe, then remove muffler assembly.
4. Position a suitable jack under suspension arm, then raise suspension arm slightly.
5. Disconnect shock absorber from upper and lower mounting, **Fig. 16.**
6. Carefully lower jack to relieve spring tension, then remove coil spring, noting position of upper and lower spring seats.
7. Reverse procedure to install. After completing installation, bleed brake system and adjust rear wheel bearings.

GALANT

Refer to "Shock Absorber, Replace" procedure.

SUSPENSION ARM ASSEMBLY

CORDIA, MIRAGE & TREDIA

Removal

1. Remove coil spring as described under "Coil Spring, Replace."
2. Disconnect brake hoses at suspension arm, then remove suspension assembly from body, **Fig. 17.**

Disassemble

Before disassembling, place alignment marks on suspension arms and components so they can be assembled in the same position. On models equipped with stabilizer bar, make alignment marks on stabilizer bar and stabilizer bracket.

1. Remove nuts on both ends of suspension arm, then remove fixtures and rubber bushings.
2. Remove dust cover clamp and slide dust cover to right, being careful not to damage it.
3. Separate suspension arm into right and left arms.
4. Using screwdriver, remove bushing "A" from lefthand suspension arm, **Fig. 18.**
5. Using suitable drift, drive bushing "B" from lefthand suspension arm, **Fig. 19.**
6. Inspect all components for wear or damage, replacing as necessary.

Assemble

1. Apply suitable grease to inside of left suspension arm and on outer edge of right suspension arm. If dust cover was replaced, push new dust cover up to stopper positioned on right arm before applying grease.
2. Install rubber stopper on right suspension arm.
3. Apply suitable grease to inner edges of bushings "A" and "B".
4. Using tools MB990779 and MB990780 or equivalents, press fit bushing "B" into left suspension arm until bushing reaches bottom of suspension arm, **Fig. 20.**
5. Using tool MB990780 or equivalent, install bushing "A" on left suspension arm, **Fig. 21.**
6. Wrap tape on threads of right suspension arm to prevent grease from get-

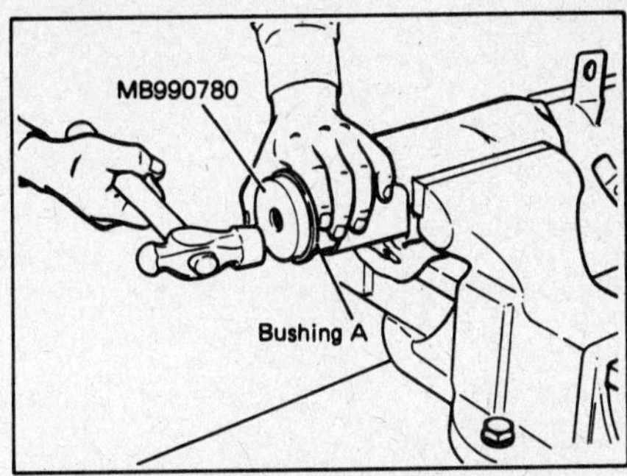

Fig. 21 Installing bushing "A" into left suspension arm. Cordia, Mirage & Tredia

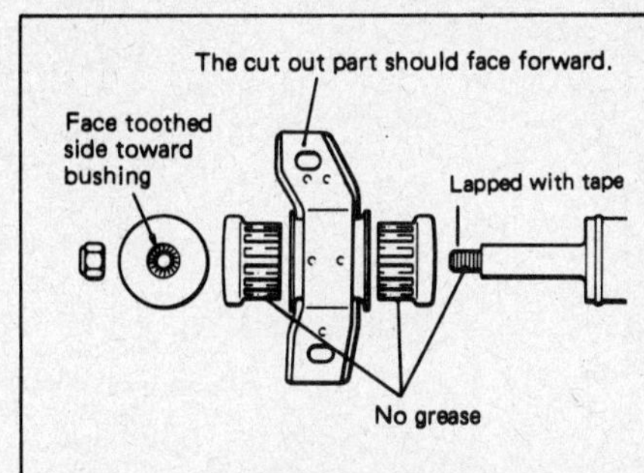

Fig. 22 Proper mounting of washers & fixtures. Cordia & Tredia

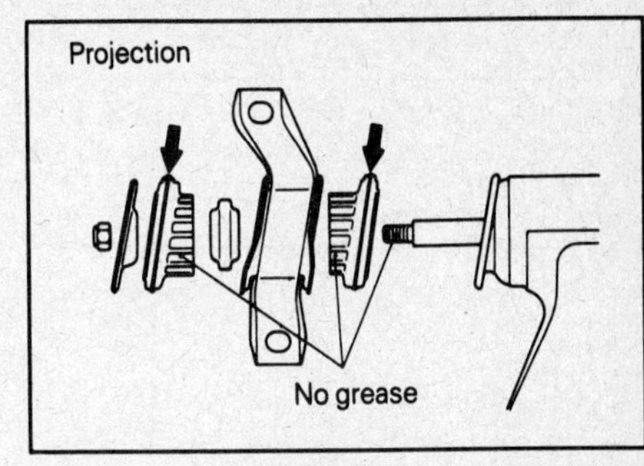

Fig. 23 Proper mounting of washers & fixtures. Mirage

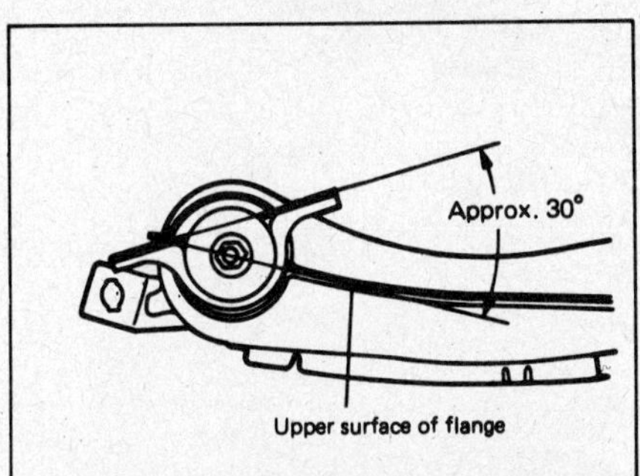

Fig. 24 Correct installation angle. Cordia & Tredia

ting on them and fit right and left suspension arms together, wiping away any grease that comes out.

7. After fitting suspension arms together, mount rubber bushings, fittings, and washers, **Figs. 22 and 23.**
8. After aligning suspension arm and components according to alignment marks, torque nut to 58-72 ft. lbs.
9. On Cordia and Tredia, ensure that fixture is installed in correct angle, **Fig. 24.**
10. On all models, pack suitable grease in dust cover and lip, then secure with new clamp.

Installation

Reverse removal procedure to install, paying attention to different shapes of upper and lower spring seats. Ensure that proper coil spring is being installed by painted identification mark on spring.

REAR SUSPENSION REPLACE

GALANT

1. Raise and support vehicle, then remove rear wheels.
2. Disconnect parking brake cable from rear brake assembly and from the torsion axle and arm assembly, **Fig. 7.**
3. Remove brake hose bracket from torsion axle and arm assembly.
4. Remove rear brake assembly and secure out of way.
5. Support torsion axle and arm assembly with a suitable jack.

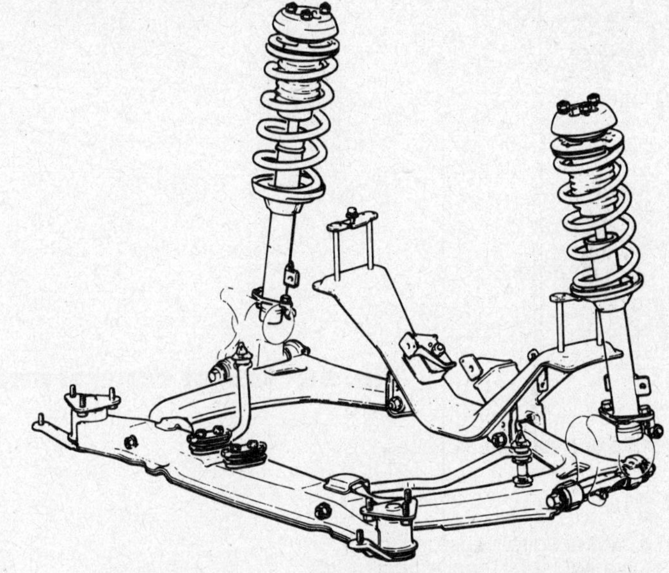

Fig. 25 Rear suspension assembly. Starion

6. On models equipped with electronically controlled suspension, disconnect height sensor rod from lateral rod.
7. On all models, remove lateral rod from body, refer to "Lateral Rod, Replace" procedure.
8. Remove torsion axle and arm assembly from body, then disconnect top of shock absorber.
9. Lower jack and remove rear suspension assembly from body.
10. Reverse procedure to install.

STARION

1. Raise vehicle and support with jackstands at specified locations. Jack stands must be extended at least 24 inch.
2. Use wire to secure strut assembly to crossmember, **Fig. 25.**
3. Support rear suspension assembly with suitable wooden beam and floor jack.
4. Disconnect propeller shaft from torque tube.
5. Remove center exhaust pipe and muffler.
6. Disconnect parking brake cable from rear disc brake and lower control arm.
7. Disconnect brake hose at rear floor.
8. Disconnect strut assembly mounting bolts located under side trim in rear hatch area.
9. Remove crossmember mounting nuts.
10. Remove front supporting mounting nuts and bolts.
11. Lower jack slowly. Assistance may be necessary to stabilize assembly as it is being lowered.
12. Reverse procedure to install.

LOWER CONTROL ARM REPLACE

STARION

Removal

1. Disconnect parking brake cable from lower control arm, **Fig. 26.**
2. Disconnect stabilizer bar.
3. Remove nuts and bolts connecting lower control arm to axle housing.
4. Remove nut and bolt connecting lower control arm to front support.
5. Remove nut and bolt connecting lower control arm to crossmember.
6. Remove lower control arm from vehicle.
7. Check condition of control arm, bush-

	Nm	ft.lbs.
A	130 – 150	94 – 108
B	70 – 80	51 – 58
C	15 – 20	11 – 14

1. Bushing A
2. Bushing B
3. Lower control arm
4. Bushing C
5. Locking pin

Fig. 26 Lower control arm. Starion

ings, and bolts and replace as necessary.

Installation

1. Apply a thin coat of suitable grease to cut out section of shaft connecting lower control to axle housing, making certain not to get any grease on bushings.
2. Insert shaft with mark on its head facing downward.
3. Install remaining nuts and bolts into lower control arm assembly as shown, **Fig. 26.**
4. When installing lower control arm to crossmember, alignment mark on crossmember with reference line on plate.
5. Check rear wheel alignment.

STABILIZER BAR REPLACE

CORDIA, MIRAGE & TREDIA

Refer to **Fig. 16** for stabilizer bar replacement procedure.

STARION

1. Remove bolt and bushings from both ends of stabilizer bar.
2. Remove stabilizer bar to front support attaching brackets.
3. Remove center exhaust pipe rubber O-rings from hanger.
4. Remove stabilizer bar.
5. Inspect stabilizer bar, bushings, and bolts and replace as necessary.
6. Reverse procedure to install, as shown in **Fig. 27.**

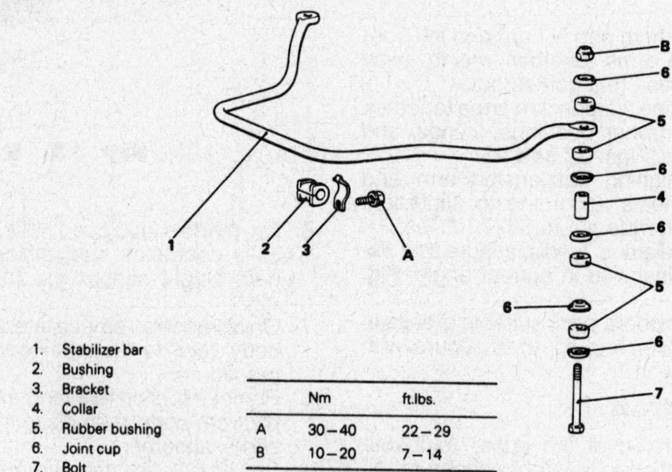

1. Stabilizer bar
2. Bushing
3. Bracket
4. Collar
5. Rubber bushing
6. Joint cup
7. Bolt

	Nm	ft.lbs.
A	30 – 40	22 – 29
B	10 – 20	7 – 14

Fig. 27 Stabilizer bar. Starion

LATERAL ROD REPLACE

GALANT

1. Raise and support vehicle, then remove rear wheels.
2. On models equipped with electronically controlled suspension, disconnect height sensor rod from lateral rod.
3. On all models, remove lateral rod attaching nuts and bolts, then the lateral rod.
4. Reverse procedure to install. Torque lateral rod attaching nuts and bolts to 58-72 ft. lbs.

FRONT SUSPENSION, DRIVE AXLE & STEERING SECTION

INDEX

Vehicles without a turbocharger

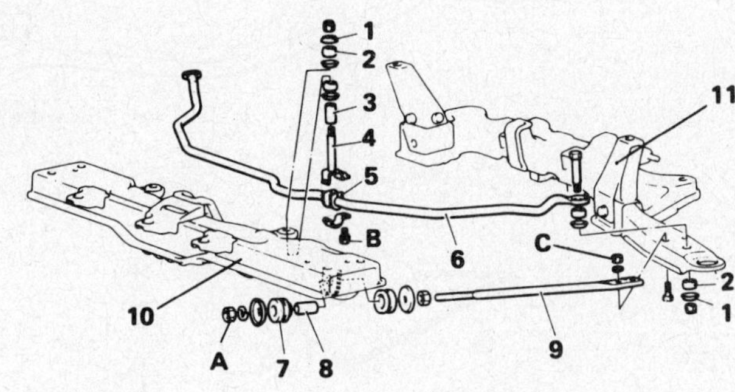

1. Joint cup
2. Stabilizer rubber
3. Collar
4. Bracket
5. Bushing
6. Stabilizer bar
7. Strut bar bushing
8. Collar
9. Strut bar
10. No. 1 crossmember
11. No. 2 crossmember

Vehicles with a turbocharger

	Nm	ft. lbs.
A	135–160	98–115
B	10–13	7–9
C	60–70	43–50

Fig. 1 Exploded view of stabilizer & strut bar assemblies. Cordia & Tredia

LOWER CONTROL ARM REPLACE

CORDIA & TREDIA

1. Disconnect stabilizer bar and strut bar from lower arm, **Fig. 1.**
2. Loosen ball joint stud nut and disconnect ball joint, using tool MB990778 or equivalent, from knuckle.
3. Remove lower arm from No. 2 crossmember, **Fig. 2.**
4. Inspect lower arm, bushings, and dust cover, replacing as necessary.
5. Check ball joint starting torque, which should be 78.1 inch lbs.
6. Install lower arm to crossmember, ensuring that it does not become twisted, and torque bolt to 87-108 ft. lbs.
7. Loosely install strut and stabilizer bars.
8. Tighten all parts while there is no load on vehicles. Torque ball joint nut to 43-52 ft. lbs.

1983–86 STARION

1. Disconnect stabilizer and strut bars from lower control arm, **Fig. 3.**
2. Disconnect tie rod from knuckle arm.
3. Disconnect MacPherson strut from knuckle arm.
4. Remove lower control arm assembly and knuckle arm from crossmember, **Fig. 4.**
5. Inspect lower arm, bushings, ball joint dust cover and bolts, replacing as necessary.
6. Check ball joint starting torque, which should be 43-69 ft. lbs.
7. Apply semi-drying sealant to flange of knuckle arm, then install knuckle arm to MacPherson strut.
8. Tighten lower control arm shaft and strut bar with vehicle lowered to ground. Torque shaft nut to 58-69 ft. lbs., strut bar nut beneath lower arm to 7-14 ft. lbs., and strut bar nut on top of lower arm to 43-51 ft. lbs.

LOWER CONTROL ARM & BALL JOINT REPLACE

1987 STARION

1. Remove cotter pin, then disconnect tie rod end assembly from knuckle arm, **Fig. 5,** using tool No. MB990778-01 or equivalent.
2. Disconnect strut assembly, then the strut bar.

3. Remove stabilizer bar self locking nut from, then disconnect stabilizer bar.
4. Disconnect lower control arm.
5. Remove self locking nut from ball joint, then disconnect ball joint from knuckle arm.
6. Remove ball joint attaching bolts, then the ball joint.
7. Remove lower control arm shaft bushings.
8. Reverse procedure to install. Refer to **Fig. 5** for torque specifications.

GALANT

1. Raise and support vehicle, then remove front wheels.
2. Disconnect stabilizer bar from lower control arm, **Fig. 6.**
3. On models equipped with electronically controlled suspension, disconnect rod of height sensor from lower control arm if right side control arm is to be removed.
4. On all models, loosen ball joint stud nut, then disconnect ball joint from knuckle using a suitable tool.
5. Remove lower control arm from crossmember.
6. Inspect control arm and bushings, replacing as necessary.
7. Check ball joint starting torque. Starting torque should be 17-78 inch lbs. Replace ball joint as required.
8. Check ball joint dust cover for cracks and damage. If necessary, remove defective dust cover and replace with new cover using tool No. MB990800 or equivalent.
9. Reverse procedure to install. Refer to **Fig. 6** for torque specifications.

MIRAGE

1. Raise and support vehicle, then remove under cover from under body.
2. Disconnect stabilizer bar from lower control arm, **Fig. 7.**
3. Disconnect lower control arm ball joint from knuckle using a suitable tool.
4. Remove bushing support bracket attaching bolts, then the bushing support bracket.
5. Loosen lower control arm shaft nut, then remove lower control arm shaft attaching bolts.
6. Remove lower control arm assembly from vehicle.
7. Inspect control arm and bushings, replacing as necessary.
8. Check ball joint starting torque. Starting torque should be 22-87 inch lbs. Replace lower control arm and ball joint assembly if starting torque is not as specified.
9. Check ball joint dust cover for cracks and damage. If necessary, remove defective dust cover and replace with new cover using tool No. MB990800 or equivalent.
10. Reverse procedure to install. Refer to **Fig. 7** for torque specifications.

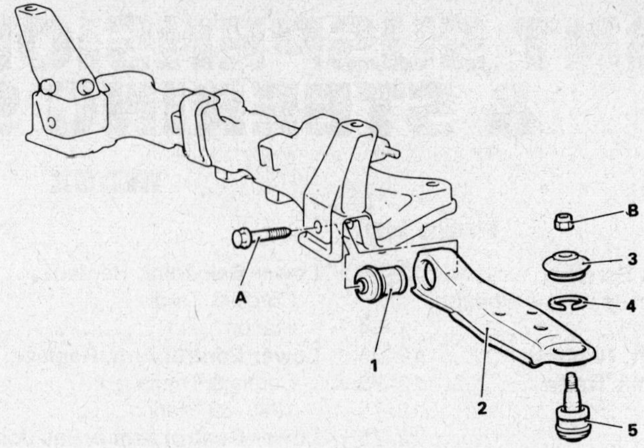

1. Lower arm bushing
2. Lower arm
3. Dust cover
4. Snap ring
5. Ball joint
6. No. 2 crossmember

	Nm	ft. lbs.
A	120–150	87–108
B	60–72	43–52

Fig. 2 Exploded view of lower control arm assembly. Cordia & Tredia

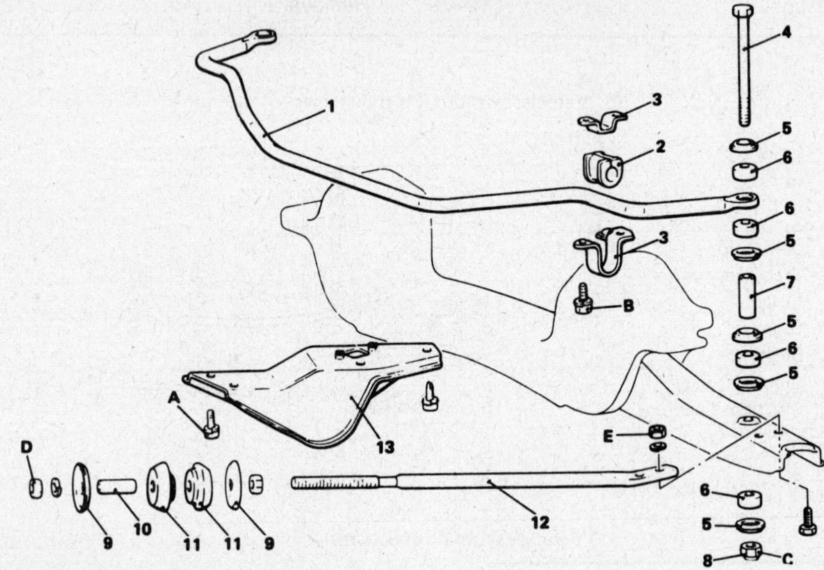

1. Stabilizer bar
2. Stabilizer bar bushing
3. Stabilizer bar bracket
4. Bolt
5. Joint cup
6. Rubber bushing
7. Collar
8. Self-locking nut
9. Washer
10. Strut bar collar
11. Strut bar bushing
12. Strut bar
13. Strut bar bracket

	Nm	ft.lbs.
A	35–45	25–33
B	8–12	6–9
C	10–20	7–14
D	75–85	54–61
E	60–70	43–51

Fig. 3 Exploded view of stabilizer & strut bar assemblies. Starion

LOWER BALL JOINT REPLACE

CORDIA & TREDIA

1. Remove ball joint stud nut.
2. Using tool MB990778 or equivalent, disconnect ball joint from knuckle.
3. Remove ball joint dust cover.
4. Using suitable pliers, remove snap ring from ball joint.
5. Using tools MB990800 and MB991005, or equivalents, press out ball joint.
6. Reverse procedure to install, noting

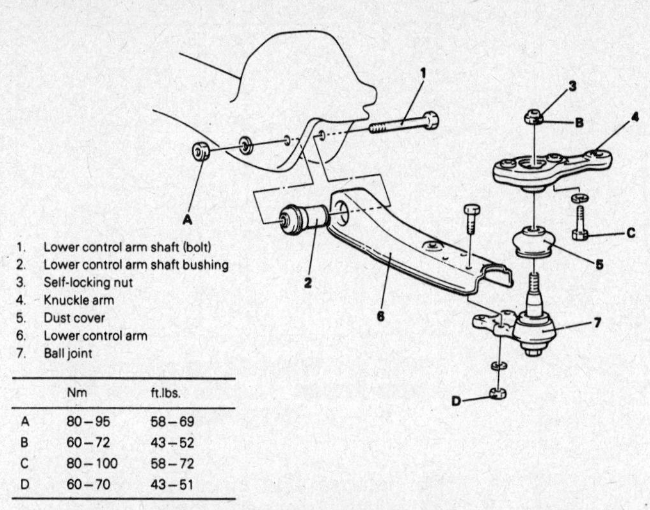

	Nm	ft.lbs.
A	80–95	58–69
B	60–72	43–52
C	80–100	58–72
D	60–70	43–51

Fig. 4 Exploded view of lower control arm assembly. 1983–86 Starion

the following:

a. If snap ring does not fit tightly in groove, replace with new one.
b. Apply suitable grease to lip and inside dust cover.
c. Use tool MB990800 or equivalent to drive in dust cover until it contacts snap ring.

1. Cotter Pin
2. Tie Rod End
3. Strut Assembly
4. Strut Bar
5. Stabilizer Bar Attaching Nut
6. Stabilizer Bar
7. Lower Control Arm
8. Self Locking Nut
9. Knuckle Arm
10. Ball Joint
11. Lower Arm Shaft Bushing

35–45 Nm 25–33 ft.lbs.
60–72 Nm 43–52 ft.lbs.
80–95 Nm 58–69 ft.lbs.
60–70 Nm 43–51 ft.lbs.
80–100 Nm 58–72 ft.lbs.
60–70 Nm 43–51 ft.lbs.

Fig. 5 Exploded view of lower control arm assembly. 1987 Starion

STARION

1. Disconnect stabilizer bar and strut bar from lower control arm.
2. Disconnect tie rod from knuckle arm.
3. Disconnect MacPherson strut from knuckle arm.
4. Remove lower control arm assembly and knuckle arm from crossmember.
5. Using tool MB990635 or equivalent, remove knuckle arm from lower control arm ball joint.
6. Remove ball joint attaching bolts and remove ball joint.
7. Reverse procedure to install.

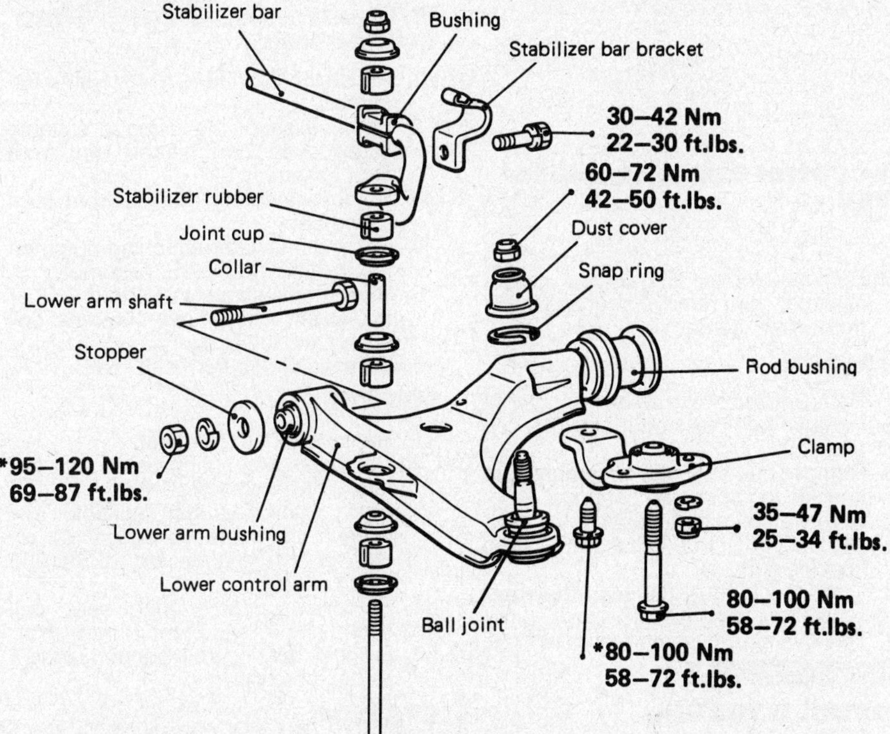

Fig. 6 Exploded view of lower control arm & stabilizer bar. Galant

MacPHERSON STRUT SERVICE

REMOVAL

CORDIA & TREDIA

1. Detach brake hose from strut assembly.
2. Disconnect strut assembly from knuckle arm.
3. Remove strut insulator to strut house panel mounting nuts.
4. Remove strut assembly from wheel house.

GALANT

Less Electronically Controlled Suspension

1. Raise and support vehicle, then remove front wheel.
2. Remove brake hose bracket from strut assembly.
3. Disconnect strut assembly from knuckle arm.
4. Remove dust cover from strut assembly.
5. Hold piston rod with a suitable hex wrench, then remove strut assembly attaching nut using tool No. MB991038 or equivalent.
6. Remove stopper and stopper rubber insulator, then remove strut assembly from wheel house.

W/Electronically Controlled Suspension

1. Raise and support vehicle, then remove front wheel.

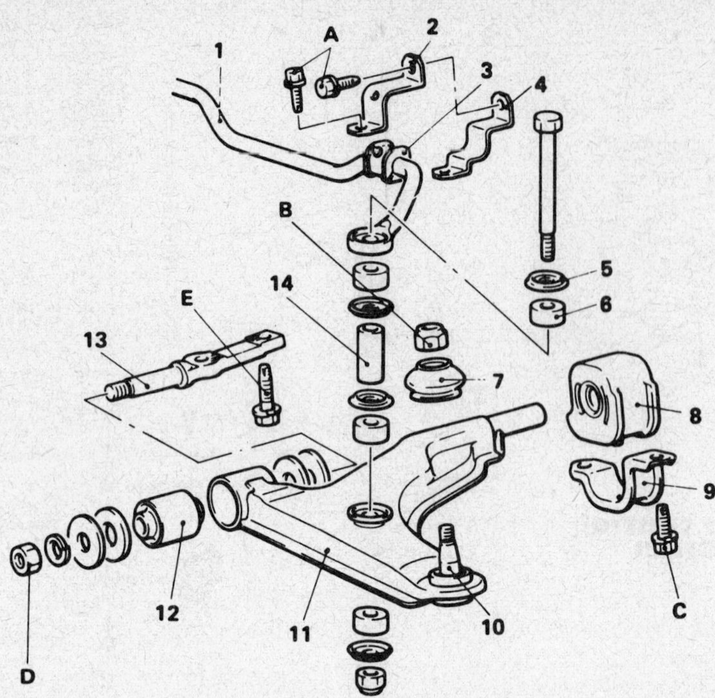

1. Stabilizer bar
2. Upper fixture
3. Stabilizer bushing
4. Lower fixture
5. Joint cup
6. Stabilizer rubber
7. Dust cover
8. Lower arm bushing (B)
9. Bushing support bracket
10. Ball joint assembly
11. Lower arm
12. Lower arm bushing
13. Lower arm shaft
14. Collar

	Nm	ft.lbs.
A	17–26	12–19
B	60–72	43–52
C	60–80	43–58
D	95–120	69–87
E	160–190	116–137

Fig. 7 Exploded view of lower control arm & stabilizer bar. Mirage

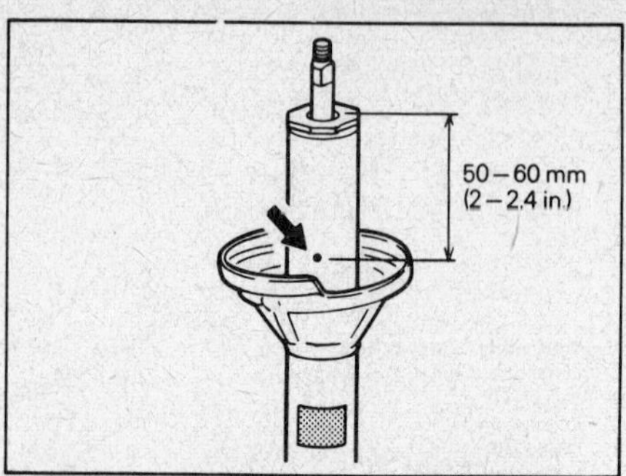

Fig. 8 Bleeding nitrogen gas from shock absorber. Starion

2. Remove brake hose bracket from strut assembly.
3. Disconnect height sensor rod from lower control arm.
4. Disconnect strut assembly from knuckle arm, then support knuckle assembly with a suitable piece of wire.
5. Disconnect and cap air tube from strut assembly joint, then remove dust cover. Use caution not to bend air tube.
6. Remove strut assembly attaching nuts, then remove strut assembly from wheel house.

MIRAGE

1. Remove brake hose bracket attaching bolt, then the brake hose bracket.
2. Disconnect strut assembly from knuckle arm.
3. Remove dust cover from strut assembly.
4. Hold piston rod with a suitable hex wrench, then remove strut assembly attaching nut using tool No. MB991036 or equivalent.
5. Remove stopper and stopper rubber insulator, then remove strut assembly from wheel house.

STARION

1. Remove disc brake caliper assembly.
2. Remove hub cap, cotter pin, lock cap and nut.
3. Remove hub and rotor assembly from knuckle together with bearings.
4. Remove brake dust cover.
5. Disconnect strut assembly from knuckle arm.
6. Disconnect strut insulator to wheel house mounting nuts.
7. Remove strut assembly from vehicle.

DISASSEMBLY

CORDIA & TREDIA

1. Using tool MB990987 or equivalent, compress coil spring.
2. Pry up insulator cap from insulator.
3. Using tool MB990775 or equivalent, hold spring seat and remove top end nut.
4. Remove strut insulator, spring seat, spring upper pad, bumper rubber, coil spring, and spring lower pad from strut.

GALANT

Less Electronically Controlled Suspension

1. Compress coil spring using tool No. MB990987 or equivalent.
2. Hold piston rod with suitable hex wrench, then remove piston rod attaching nut using tool No. MB991036 or equivalent.
3. Remove rubber insulator, support, spring seat, spring pad, rubber bumper, dust cover and coil spring from strut.
4. Remove bearing from support using a suitable brass rod.

W/Electronically Controlled Suspension

1. Attach tool No. MB991043 to strut assembly.
2. Remove snap ring using a suitable screwdriver, then the air joint from strut assembly.
3. Remove actuator bracket from strut assembly.
4. Remove insulator attaching nut, then the insulator from strut assembly.
5. Slowly loosen tool No. MB9901043 or equivalent and remove sub-tank, coil spring and lower spring pad.
6. Remove O-ring from sub-tank.

MIRAGE

1. Remove rubber insulator.
2. Compress coil spring using tool No. MB990987 or equivalent.
3. Hold piston rod with suitable hex wrench, then remove piston rod attaching nut using tool No. MB991036 or equivalent.
4. Remove support, spring seat, coil spring and rubber bumper from strut.
5. Remove bearing from support using a suitable brass rod.

STARION

1. Using tool MB990987 or equivalent, compress coil spring.
2. Remove insulator cap from insulator.
3. Using tool MB990564 or equivalent, hold spring seat and remove top end nut.

4. Remove insulator, spring seat, rubber helper, dust cover, coil spring and rubber helper seat from strut.
5. On models equipped with hydraulic type shock absorber, proceed as follows:
   a. Clean external surface of strut to prevent entry of foreign material into the cylinder.
   b. Place strut assembly in vise, allowing piston rod to bottom. **When placing strut in vise, close vise on knuckle part, not the outer shell.**
   c. Remove oil seal assembly using a suitable tool.
   d. Pry square section O-ring from cylinder, then slowly remove piston rod from cylinder together with piston guide. Use caution not to damage piston rod.
   e. Drain shock absorber fluid.
   f. Remove piston guide from piston rod, then the cylinder from strut outer shell.
6. On models equipped with gas damper type shocks, proceed as follows if shock absorber replacement is required:
   a. Drill .16 inch or less diameter hole as shown, **Fig. 8,** to bleed nitrogen gas.
   b. Using tool MB990564 or equivalent, remove ring nut.
   c. Remove shock absorber assembly from strut.

INSPECTION

Check all strut assembly components for wear or damage and replace as necessary.

ASSEMBLY

Coil springs have color marks to indicate coil spring identification and load classification. This identification mark indicates applicable vehicle model equipped with that particular coil spring. When replacing coil spring, be sure to use spring having appropriate identification mark.

CORDIA & TREDIA

1. Mount spring lower pad on strut.
2. Using tool MB990987 or equivalent, fully compress spring and install onto strut.
3. Extend piston rod as far as possible, then install bumper rubber and spring upper pad.
4. Mount spring upper seat onto piston rod, then align "D" shaped hole with notch in rod.
5. Using tool MB990775 or equivalent, hold spring seat and torque strut insulator to 43-50 ft. lbs.
6. After aligning both ends of spring with grooves in spring seat, loosen tool MB990987.
7. Apply suitable grease to strut insulator bearing, being careful not to get any grease on rubber part of insulator.

GALANT

Less Electronically Controlled Suspension

1. With support facing black retainer side of bearing, press bearing into support using suitable tool.
2. Compress spring using tool No. MB990987 or equivalent, then install spring into strut.
3. Extend piston rod as far as possible, then install dust cover, rubber bumper and spring pad.
4. Install spring upper seat onto piston rod and align D-shaped hole with notch in rod.
5. Install support on piston rod, then torque nut to 40-50 ft. lbs. using suitable tool.
6. Align both ends of coil spring with grooves in spring seat, then slowly loosen spring compressor. Ensure spring seat does not become twisted. **The upper and lower spring seats can be easily aligned by inserting a .4 inch diameter rod into holes in the seats.**
7. Install rubber insulator on strut assembly.

W/Electronically Controlled Suspension

1. Apply a coating of suitable grease to sub-tank O-ring, then install O-ring in sub-tank.
2. Install strut assembly lower spring pad, coil spring and sub-tank into tool No. MB991043 or equivalent. **Ensure larger outer diameter of coil spring is facing downward.**
3. Compress coil spring while aligning notched portion of piston rod to fit the D shape of sub-tank. Ensure lower edge of coil spring, spring pad and sub-tank are properly aligned.
4. Install insulator on strut assembly, then the insulator attaching nut. Torque nut to 58-72 ft. lbs.
5. Remove tool No. MB991043 or equivalent and apply a coating of suitable grease to the insulator bearing channel.
6. Align notch of piston rod with D shape of actuator bracket.
7. Install actuator bracket to strut assembly, then the actuator bracket attaching nut. Torque nut to 29-43 ft. lbs.
8. Apply a coating of suitable grease to piston rod O-ring, then install O-ring on piston rod.
9. Install air joint on strut assembly, then using suitable pliers to pull piston rod upward, attach snap ring to piston rod.
10. Ensure joint turns smoothly, then check strut assembly for air leaks as follows:
    a. Disconnect white air tube (for HARD/SOFT mode switching) of front solenoid valve from reserve tank.
    b. Using air pressure gauge No. MB991075 or equivalent and adapter A, connect white air tube to air tube at shut off valve side of gauge.
    c. Using adapter D of air pressure gauge, connect air tube on other end of pressure gauge to joint of strut assembly. **To prevent moisture from getting into strut assembly, use air which has passed through reserve tank.**
    d. Disconnect air compressor electrical connector and apply battery voltage to operate air compressor.
    e. Submerse strut assembly into water tank and check for air leakage at an air pressure of about 71 psi.
    f. If air leakage is found, check sub-tank O-ring, sub-tank and strut assembly in that order. Repair as required.
    g. Align adapter with notch in piston rod, then attach actuator.
    h. Exchange adapter D, connected to strut side, with adapter B and connect to joint part of actuator.
    i. Apply air at a pressure of 100 psi from joint part of actuator, then check to ensure that there is no air leakage and system changes over to HARD mode.
    j. If air leak is found, repair as required.

MIRAGE

1. With support facing black retainer side of bearing, press bearing into support using suitable tool.
2. Compress spring using tool No. MB990987 or equivalent, then install spring into strut.
3. Extend piston rod as far as possible, then install rubber bumper.
4. Install spring upper seat onto piston rod.
5. Install support on piston rod, then torque nut to 25-36 ft. lbs. using suitable tool.
6. Align both ends of coil spring with grooves in spring seat, then slowly loosen spring compressor. Ensure spring seat does not become twisted.
7. Install rubber insulator on strut assembly.

STARION

1. On models equipped with hydraulic type shock absorber, proceed as follows:
   a. Install cylinder and piston assembly into strut outer shell.
   b. Gradually pour shock absorber fluid into the cylinder while slowly moving piston up and down.
   c. With flange of piston guide facing upward, install piston guide into piston rod until it contacts cylinder end.
   d. Install new square section O-ring in piston guide.
   e. Apply shock absorber fluid to oil seal assembly lips, then cover piston rod end and install oil seal assembly.
   f. Tighten oil seal assembly with a suitable tool, until seal edge contacts strut outer cylinder.
2. On models equipped with gas damper type shocks, proceed as follows if shock absorber was removed:
   a. Install new shock absorber assem-

bly into strut.
   b. Torque ring nut to 101-108 ft. lbs. using tool MB990564 or equivalent.
   c. Attach label furnished with new shock absorber over drilled hole in strut to prevent entry of water.
3. On all models, fully compress coil spring using tool MB990987 or equivalent.
4. Using suitable drying adhesive, bond spring seat to rubber helper.
5. Install rubber helper seat, coil spring, dust cover, rubber helper, and spring seat onto strut.
6. Align "D" shaped hole in spring seat with flat on piston rod and align projections on dust cover with holes in spring seat.
7. Install strut insulator, hold spring seat with tool MB990564 or equivalent, and torque top end nut to 43-57 ft. lbs.
8. After ensuring that coil spring is properly aligned in top and bottom spring seats, remove tool MB990987.
9. Pack grease in strut insulator, being careful not to get any on rubber parts, and install cap.

INSTALLATION

CORDOA & TREDIA

Reverse removal procedure to install, torquing strut to wheel house nuts to 18-25 ft. lbs. and strut to knuckle nuts to 54-65 ft. lbs.

GALANT

Reverse removal procedure to install. On models equipped with electronically controlled suspension, torque strut to wheel house attaching nuts to 18-25 ft. lbs., strut to knuckle attaching nuts to 65-75 ft. lbs. and air tube attaching nuts to 6-7 ft. lbs. On models less electronically controlled suspension, torque strut to wheel housing attaching nut to 36-43 ft. lbs. and strut to knuckle attaching nuts to 65-76 ft. lbs.

MIRAGE

Reverse removal procedure to install, torquing strut to wheel housing attaching nut to 25-36 ft. lbs. and strut to knuckle attaching nuts to 54-65 ft. lbs.

STARION

Reverse removal procedure to install, torquing strut to wheel house nuts to 18-25 ft. lbs.

STABILIZER BAR

REPLACE

GALANT

1. Raise and support vehicle, then remove front wheels.
2. Disconnect stabilizer bar from lower control arm.
3. Remove stabilizer bar bracket attaching bolt, then the stabilizer bracket and bushing.
4. Remove stabilizer bar from crossmember.
5. Reverse procedure to install, noting the following:
   a. Face marked part of stabilizer bar downward, then attach stabilizer bracket so end of mark is aligned with end of bushing.
   b. Torque stabilizer bar bracket attaching bolts to 22-30 ft. lbs.
   c. When installing ends of stabilizer bar to control arm, tighten self locking attaching nut so that distance from base of nut to end of bolt is .63-70 inch.

MIRAGE

1. Raise and support vehicle.
2. Remove under cover attaching bolt, then the under cover.
3. Remove stabilizer bar to lower control arm attaching bolt and nut.
4. Remove joint cup, bushing and collar.
5. Remove fixture attaching bolts, then the upper and lower fixtures from stabilizer bar.
6. Remove stabilizer bar from vehicle.
7. Reverse procedure to install, noting the following:
   a. Torque fixture attaching bolts to 12-19 ft. lbs.
   b. When installing ends of stabilizer bar to control arm, tighten self locking attaching nut so that distance from base of nut to end of bolt is .83-.91 inch.

MONTERO & PICKUP WITH 4 WHEEL DRIVE

1. Remove stabilizer bar from lower arm and stabilizer link assembly.
2. Inspect stabilizer bar, bushings, and stabilizer link assembly, and repair or replace as necessary.
3. Install stabilizer bar, noting the following:
   a. When installing stabilizer link assembly to No. 1 crossmember, tighten self locking nut so that distance from base of nut to top of stud is .63-.71 inch on 1983-84 models or .24-.31 inch on 1985-87 models.
   b. When installing ends of stabilizer bar to lower arms, tighten self locking nuts so that distance from base of nut to end of bolt is .63-.71 inch on 1983-84 models or .24-.31 inch on 1985-87 models.
   c. Torque stabilizer bracket attaching nuts to 6-8 ft. lbs.

STABILIZER & STRUT BAR

REPLACE

CORDIA & TREDIA

1. Raise and support vehicle.
2. Disconnect stabilizer bar from lower arms and No. 1 crossmember and remove bar.
3. Disconnect strut bar at lower arm and No. 1 crossmember and remove bar.
4. Inspect stabilizer bar, strut bar and all bushings, replacing as necessary.
5. If strut bar nut has been loosened or removed, reset nut so that distance between outer edge of nut and end of strut bar is 3.07 inch
6. Install strut bar, torquing strut bar to lower control arm bolt to 43-50 ft. lbs. and strut bar to crossmember nut to 101-115 ft. lbs.
7. Install stabilizer bar and tighten stabilizer bar mounting nuts so that distance between nut and end of bolt is .31-.39 inch
8. Torque stabilizer bar bracket bolts to 7-9 ft. lbs.

PICKUP LESS 4 WHEEL DRIVE

1. Disconnect strut bar at lower control arm.
2. Disconnect strut bar at strut bar bracket and slide bar out.
3. Disconnect stabilizer bar at stabilizer bracket and at stabilizer links and remove bar.
4. Inspect stabilizer bar, strut bar, and bushings, replacing as necessary.
5. Reverse procedure to install, noting the following:
   a. Left hand strut bar is marked with "L".
   b. Strut bar bushings for front side and rear side are different. Bushing with convex surface is installed on front side.
   c. When installing strut bar to strut bar bracket, distance between face of innermost nut and end of strut bar should be 3.8 inch on 1983-84 models or 2.9 inch on 1985-87 models. Torque top end nut to 55-61 ft. lbs. after vehicle is lowered to ground. Check caster adjustment and correct as necessary, then adjust distance between nut face and bar end as necessary.
   d. When installing stabilizer bar to links, tighten first nut so that distance between top of nut and end of bolt is .87-.94 inch
   e. Torque stabilizer bracket attaching bolts to 6-8 ft. lbs.

STARION

1. Disconnect strut bar at lower control arm.
2. Disconnect strut bar at strut bar bracket and remove bar.
3. Disconnect stabilizer bar at lower control arm and stabilizer bar bracket, then remove stabilizer bar.
4. Inspect stabilizer bar, strut bar, and bushings, replacing as necessary.
5. Reverse procedure to install, noting the following:
   a. Tighten nuts for stabilizer bar links so that distance between face of nuts and end of bolts is .59-.67 inch
   b. Strut bars are marked with "L" or white mark for left side and "R" or no mark for right side.
   c. Tighten nut on strut bar so that distance between front surface of nut and end of bar is 3.19 inch on models with intercooler or 3.29 inch on models less intercooler.
   d. Be sure to install strut bar bushings correctly, as front and rear bushings are different.
   e. After lowering vehicle to ground,

torque top end nut to 54-61 ft. lbs., then check caster.

FRONT DRIVESHAFT REPLACE

CORDIA, GALANT & TREDIA

1. Remove dust cover and driveshaft nut.
2. Raise and support vehicle.
3. Drain transmission oil.
4. Disconnect lower arm ball joint from knuckle, then remove stabilizer and strut bars from lower arm.
5. Insert suitable pry bar between transmission case and driveshaft, then pry driveshaft from transmission. **Do not pull on driveshaft and do not insert pry bar deep enough to damage oil seal.**
6. Using tool MB990241 or equivalent, remove driveshaft from hub.
7. Reverse procedure to install, noting the following:
   a. Ensure that driveshaft washer is correctly installed.
   b. Lower vehicle to ground, then attach and adjust driveshaft nut, torquing to 144-188 ft. lbs.
   c. If cotter pin holes do not line up, tighten bolt without exceeding torque of 188 ft. lbs. until holes line up.
   d. Install cotter pin.

MIRAGE

1. Raise and support vehicle, then remove front wheels.
2. Remove cotter pin, wheel bearing nut and washer.
3. Disconnect lower control arm ball joint from knuckle using tool MB991113 or equivalent.
4. Disconnect tie rod end from knuckle using tool MB991113 or equivalent.
5. Disconnect center bearing snap ring, if equipped.
6. On models without center bearing, proceed as follows:
   a. Insert suitable pry bar between transaxle case and driveshaft, then pry driveshaft from transaxle. **Do not pull on driveshaft or insert pry bar deep enough to damage oil seal.**
   b. Force driveshaft from hub using tool MB990241-01 or equivalent, then remove circlip from driveshaft.
7. On models with center bearing, proceed as follows:
   a. Remove drive shaft from transaxle by lightly tapping driveshaft outer race with a plastic hammer. **Do not pull on driveshaft or insert pry bar between transaxle case and driveshaft.**
   b. Force driveshaft out of hub by lightly tapping driveshaft end with plastic hammer.
   c. Remove center bearing bracket attaching bolts, then the center bearing bracket and spacers.
8. Reverse procedure to install, noting the following:
   a. On models with center bearing, press in driveshaft until center bearing comes in contact with center bearing bracket, then install snap ring into center bearing bracket.
   b. On all models, lower vehicle to ground, then attach and adjust driveshaft nut. Torque nut to 144-188 ft. lbs.
   c. If cotter pin hole does not line up, tighten bolt without exceeding torque of 188 ft. lbs. until hole lines up.

MONTERO

1. Raise and support vehicle.
2. Remove wheel.
3. Remove caliper assembly without disconnecting brake hose and support caliper out of way so as not to strain brake hose.
4. Remove freewheeling hub cover assembly and remove snap ring from driveshaft.
5. Remove knuckle and front hub assembly as an assembly.
6. Pull left driveshaft out of differential carrier assembly with damaging oil seal.
7. Remove right driveshaft to differential carrier inner shaft attaching bolts, then pull driveshaft from differential assembly.
8. Reverse procedure to install, noting the following:
   a. Install left driveshaft into front differential carrier using a plastic hammer.
   b. Torque right driveshaft to inner shaft attaching bolts to 36-43 ft. lbs.
   c. Adjust driveshaft endplay to .008-.020 inch by installing spacers between driveshaft circlip and hub.

PICKUP WITH 4 WHEEL DRIVE

1. Raise and support vehicle.
2. Remove wheel.
3. Remove caliper assembly without disconnecting brake hose and support caliper out of way so as not to strain brake hose.
4. Remove free wheeling hub cover assembly and remove snap ring from driveshaft.
5. Remove knuckle and front hub assembly as an assembly.
6. Pull left driveshaft out of differential carrier assembly without damaging oil seal.
7. Using suitable jack, raise lower arm.
8. Remove upper mounting nuts from right shock absorber, then remove shock absorber from arm post of side frame. **Do not lower jack while disconnecting shock absorber or while it is disconnected. Do not remove jack until upper part of shock absorber has been reconnected to arm post of side frame.**
9. Detach right driveshaft from inner shaft assembly and remove right driveshaft.
10. Using tools MB990211 and MB990906 or equivalents, pull inner shaft out of differential carrier without damaging oil seal.
11. Using screwdriver, remove dust seal from housing tube assembly.
12. Reverse procedure to install, noting the following:
    a. Torque upper knuckle to ball joint bolts to 44-65 ft. lbs., lower knuckle at ball joints to 87-130 ft. lbs., and freewheeling hub assembly bolts to 8-10 ft. lbs.
    b. Apply suitable grease to lip of dust seal and, using tools MB990938 and MB990985 or equivalents, drive dust seal into housing tube end.
    c. Using tools MB990211 and MB990906 or equivalents, drive inner shaft assembly into differential carrier assembly without damaging oil seal.
    d. Replace circlip which is attached to Birfield joint (B.J.) side spline with new one.
    e. Install right driveshaft to inner shaft assembly and torque bolts to 37-43 ft. lbs.
    f. Attach shock absorber to arm post of side frame by installing double nuts. Install first nut so that distance between base of nut and end of strut is .81 inch, then torque second nut to 9-13 ft. lbs.
    g. Using plastic mallet, drive left driveshaft into differential carrier assembly without damaging oil seal.
    h. Replace circlip which is attached to B.J. side spline with new one.
    i. Mount knuckle and front hub assembly, then adjust driveshaft axial play as necessary.

FRONT DRIVESHAFT SERVICE

CORDIA, GALANT & TREDIA

DISASSEMBLE

1. Remove double offset joint (D.O.J.) boot band, **Fig. 9.**
2. Remove D.O.J. boot from D.O.J. outer race.
3. Using screwdriver, remove circlip.
4. Remove D.O.J. outer race and wipe off grease.
5. Remove snap ring, then remove D.O.J. inner race, cage, and balls as an assembly and clean this assembly. If balls drop out of cage, press them back in with inner race.
6. Wipe grease off spline portion.
7. Remove Birfield joint (B.J.) boot band.
8. Remove D.O.J. boot and B.J. boot. If boots can be reused, wrap vinyl tape around driveshaft spline so that boots are not damaged as they are removed.
9. Wipe grease off B.J. Do not disassemble B.J.
10. Inspect all components and replace as necessary.

ASSEMBLE

1. Wrap vinyl tape around driveshaft spline, then install B.J. and D.O.J. boots in that order.
2. Fill inside of B.J. and B.J. boot with suitable grease.
3. Place B.J. boot over B.J., then use new B.J. boot band and small boot band to secure boot.
4. Using grease supplied with repair kit, lubricate D.O.J. cage, balls and inner race.
5. Install D.O.J. cage, balls and inner race onto driveshaft, then fit snap ring securely into groove on driveshaft.
6. Using grease supplied with repair kit, lubricate D.O.J. outer race and fit driveshaft into D.O.J. outer race, then apply more grease to D.O.J. outer race.
7. Install new circlip on driveshaft.
8. Set new boot bands to specified distance, **Fig. 10,** then tighten bands securely.
9. Wipe excess grease from lips of D.O.J. and B.J. boots.
10. Install new circlip onto D.O.J. outer race.

1. Circlip (small)
2. D.O.J. outer race
3. Circlip
4. Snap ring
5. D.O.J. inner race
6. D.O.J. cage
7. Ball
8. D.O.J. boot
9. D.O.J. boot band
10. Boot band (small)
11. B.J. boot band
12. B.J. boot
13. B.J. assembly

NOTE
B.J. – Birfield joint
D.O.J. – Double offset joint

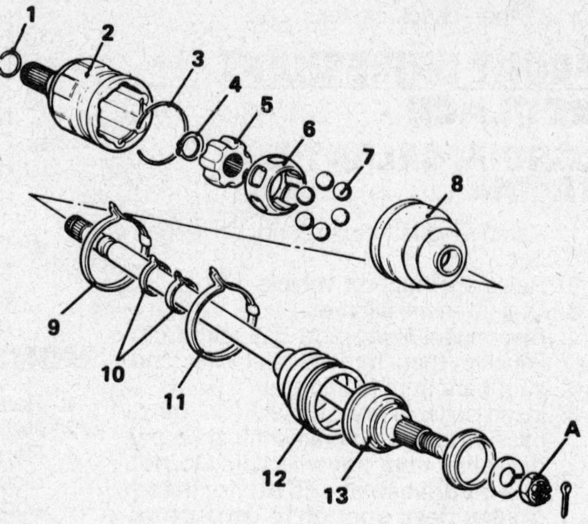

	Nm	ft. lbs.
A	200–260	144–188

Fig. 9 Exploded view of front driveshaft. Cordia, Galant & Tredia

Year	Left Side	Right Side
1983	2.83-3.23 inches	2.95-3.35 inches
1984①	3.15-3.55 inches	3.30-3.70 inches
1984②	3.15-3.55 inches	3.50-3.90 inches
1985①	3.23-3.47 inches	3.42-3.66 inches
1985②	3.23-3.47 inches	3.23-3.47 inches
1986①	3.42-3.66 inches	3.42-3.66 inches
1986②	3.42-3.66 inches	3.23-3.47 inches
1987①	3.42-3.66 inches	3.42-3.66 inches
1987②	3.42-3.66 inches	3.23-3.47 inches

①—Without fuel injection.
②—With fuel injection.

Fig. 10 Boot length specification chart. Cordia, Galant & Tredia

MIRAGE

DOUBLE OFFSET/BIRFIELD JOINT TYPE DRIVESHAFT LESS CENTER BEARING

1. Remove double offset joint (D.O.J.) boot band, **Fig. 11.**
2. Wrap suitable tape around driveshaft spline, then remove D.O.J. boot from outer race.
3. Remove outer race circlip, then place alignment marks on D.O.J. outer race and D.O.J. cage.
4. Remove D.O.J. outer race from shaft.
5. Remove D.O.J. cage assembly snap ring, then the D.O.J. inner race, cage and balls. Use caution not to drop balls.
6. Remove dynamic damper band, then the dynamic damper.
7. Remove birfield joint (B.J.) boot band, then the B.J. boot.
8. Remove dust cover and circlip from B.J. and shaft assembly. Do not disassemble B.J. as it is serviced as an assembly.
9. Reverse procedure to assemble, noting the following:
   a. To install dynamic damper, keep B.J. and shaft in a straight line, then attach dynamic damper with dynamic damper band as shown in **Fig. 12.** Distance between dynamic damper and out board joint should be 16.9-17.2 inches.
   b. Apply suitable grease to D.O.J. cage, balls and D.O.J. inner race.
   c. Fill D.O.J. outer race with suitable grease, fit driveshaft into D.O.J. outer race, then apply more grease into the D.O.J. outer race.
   d. When installing D.O.J. boot bands, ensure distance between center of bands is 3.1 inches for L.H. shaft on models equipped with 1.5L engine or 3.3. inches on all others.

DOUBLE OFFSET/BIRFIELD JOINT TYPE DRIVESHAFT WITH CENTER BEARING

1. Remove double offset joint (D.O.J.) boot band, **Fig. 11.**
2. Wrap suitable tape around driveshaft spline, then remove D.O.J. boot from outer race.
3. Remove outer race circlip, then place alignment marks on D.O.J. outer race and D.O.J. cage.
4. Remove D.O.J. outer race and shaft assembly.
5. Remove D.O.J. cage assembly snap ring, then the D.O.J. inner race, cage and balls. Use caution not to drop balls.
6. Remove birfield joint (B.J.) boot band, then the B.J. boot.
7. Remove B.J. and shaft assembly. Do not disassemble B.J. as it is serviced as an assembly
8. Remove sleeve and dust cover using a suitable press.
9. Partially grind one part of bearing retainer and dust cover until retainer thickness becomes .04-.06 inch, then remove bearing retainer and dust cover using a chisel. **Use caution not to damage driveshaft.**
10. Remove center bearing using a suitable press, then the snap ring, dust cover and center bearing bracket.
11. Reverse procedure to assemble, noting the following:
   a. After installing dust cover and snap ring onto D.O.J. outer race, press fit bearing onto D.O.J. outer race using a suitable tool.
   b. Install new dust cover and bearing retainer on D.O.J. outer race so ground surface of bearing retainer faces bearing.
   c. Install sleeve and dust cover until it contacts stepped portion of driveshaft using a suitable press.
   d. Fill inside of B.J. and B.J. boot with suitable grease.
   e. Apply suitable grease to D.O.J. cage, balls and D.O.J. inner race.
   f. Fill D.O.J. outer race with suitable grease, fit driveshaft into D.O.J. outer race, then apply more grease into the D.O.J. outer race.

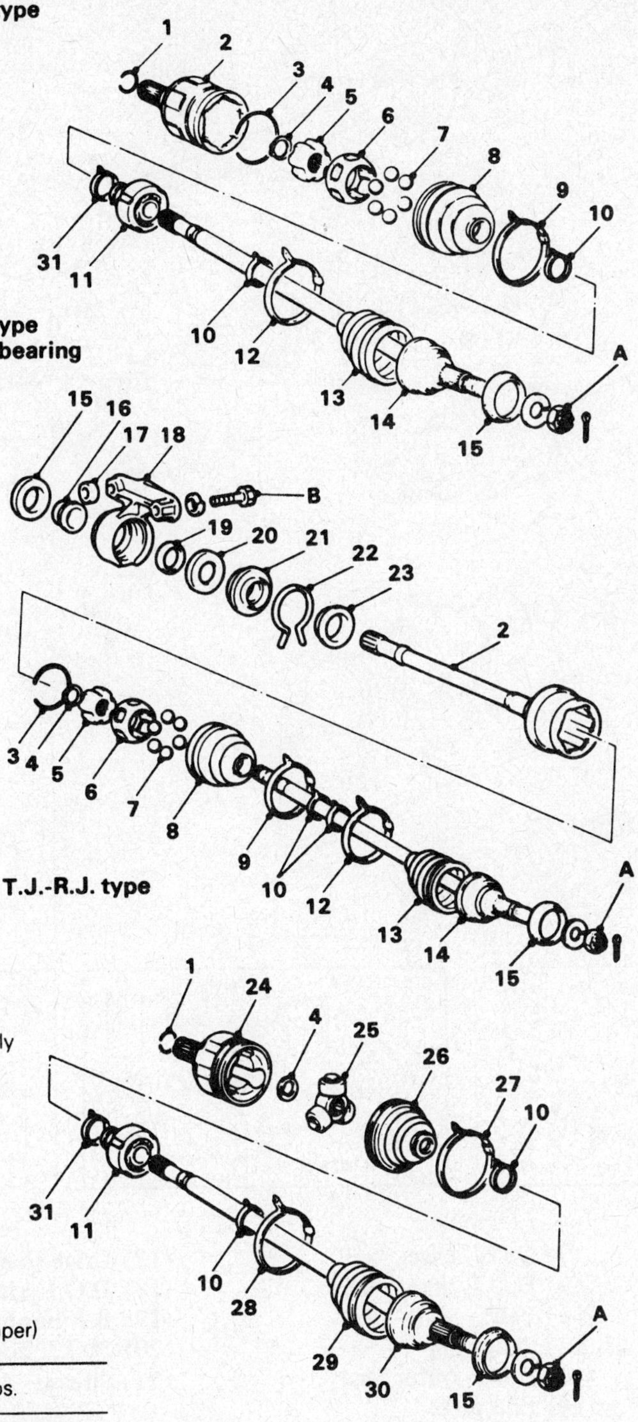

D.O.J.-B.J. type

D.O.J.-B.J. type with center bearing

T.J.-R.J. type

1. Circlip (small)
2. D.O.J. outer race
3. Circlip
4. Snap ring
5. D.O.J. inner race
6. D.O.J. cage
7. Ball
8. D.O.J. boot
9. D.O.J. boot band
10. Boot band (small)
11. Dynamic damper
12. B.J. boot band
13. B.J. boot
14. B.J. assembly
15. Dust cover
16. Sleeve
17. Spacer
18. Center bearing bracket
19. Bearing retainer
20. Dust cover
21. Center bearing assembly
22. Snap ring
23. Dust cover
24. T.J. case
25. Spider assembly
26. T.J. boot
27. T.J. boot band
28. R.J. boot band
29. R.J. boot
30. R.J. assembly
31. Band (for dynamic damper)

	Nm	ft.lbs.
A	200–260	144–188
B	35–40	25–29

Fig. 11 Exploded view of front driveshaft. Mirage

g. When installing D.O.J. boot bands, ensure distance between center of bands is 3.1 inches for L.H. shaft on models equipped with 1.5L engine or 3.3 inches on all others.

TRIPOD/RZEPPA JOINT TYPE DRIVESHAFT

1. Remove tripod joint (T.J.) boot band, **Fig. 11.**
2. Wrap suitable tape around driveshaft spline, then remove T.J. boot.

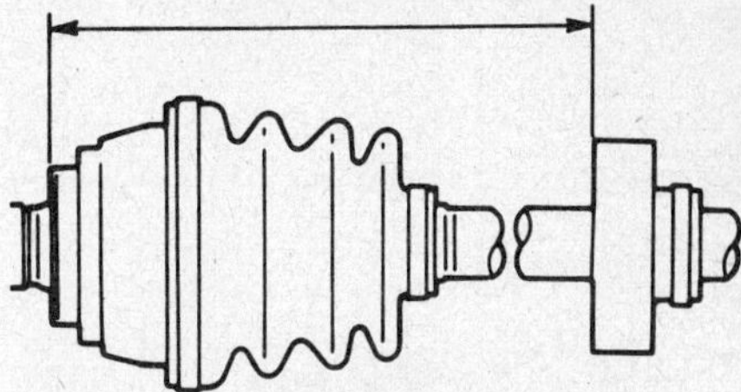

Fig. 12 Dynamic damper installation

3. Place alignment marks on T.J. case and spider assembly, then remove T.J. case.
4. Remove spider assembly snap ring, then the spider assembly. **Do not disassemble spider assembly as it is serviced as an assembly.**
5. Remove dynamic damper band, then the dynamic damper.
6. Remove Rzeppa joint (R.J.) boot band, then the R.J. boot.
7. Remove R.J. and shaft assembly. **R.J. is non-serviceable and should be replaced as an assembly.**
8. Remove dust cover and circlip.
9. Reverse procedure to assemble, noting the following:
   a. Fill inside of R.J. and R.J. boot with suitable grease.
   b. To install dynamic damper, keep R.J. and shaft in a straight line, then attach dynamic damper with dynamic damper band as shown in **Fig. 12.** Distance between dynamic damper and out board joint should be 16.9-17.2 inches.
   c. Apply suitable grease to space between spider journal and roller spider assembly.
   d. Fill T.J. case with suitable grease, fit driveshaft into T.J. case, then apply more grease into the T.J. case.
   e. When installing T.J. boot bands, ensure distance between center of bands is 3.1 inches for L.H. shaft and 3.3 inches for R.H. shaft.

MONTERO & PICKUP WITH 4 WHEEL DRIVE

DISASSEMBLE

Driveshaft

1. Using screwdriver, remove boot bands, **Fig. 13.**
2. Using screwdriver, remove circlip from D.O.J. outer race.
3. Remove driveshaft from D.O.J. outer race and wipe away grease.
4. Using screwdriver, remove balls from D.O.J. cage.
5. Remove D.O.J. cage from D.O.J. inner race in direction of B.J. by turning D.O.J. cage 30° from position at which balls were removed.
6. Using suitable pliers, remove snap ring from driveshaft, then remove D.O.J. inner race from driveshaft.
7. Remove circlip from driveshaft.
8. Remove D.O.J. and B.J. boots from driveshaft. Wrap vinyl tape around spline on D.O.J. side of driveshaft so that boots are not damaged when they are removed.

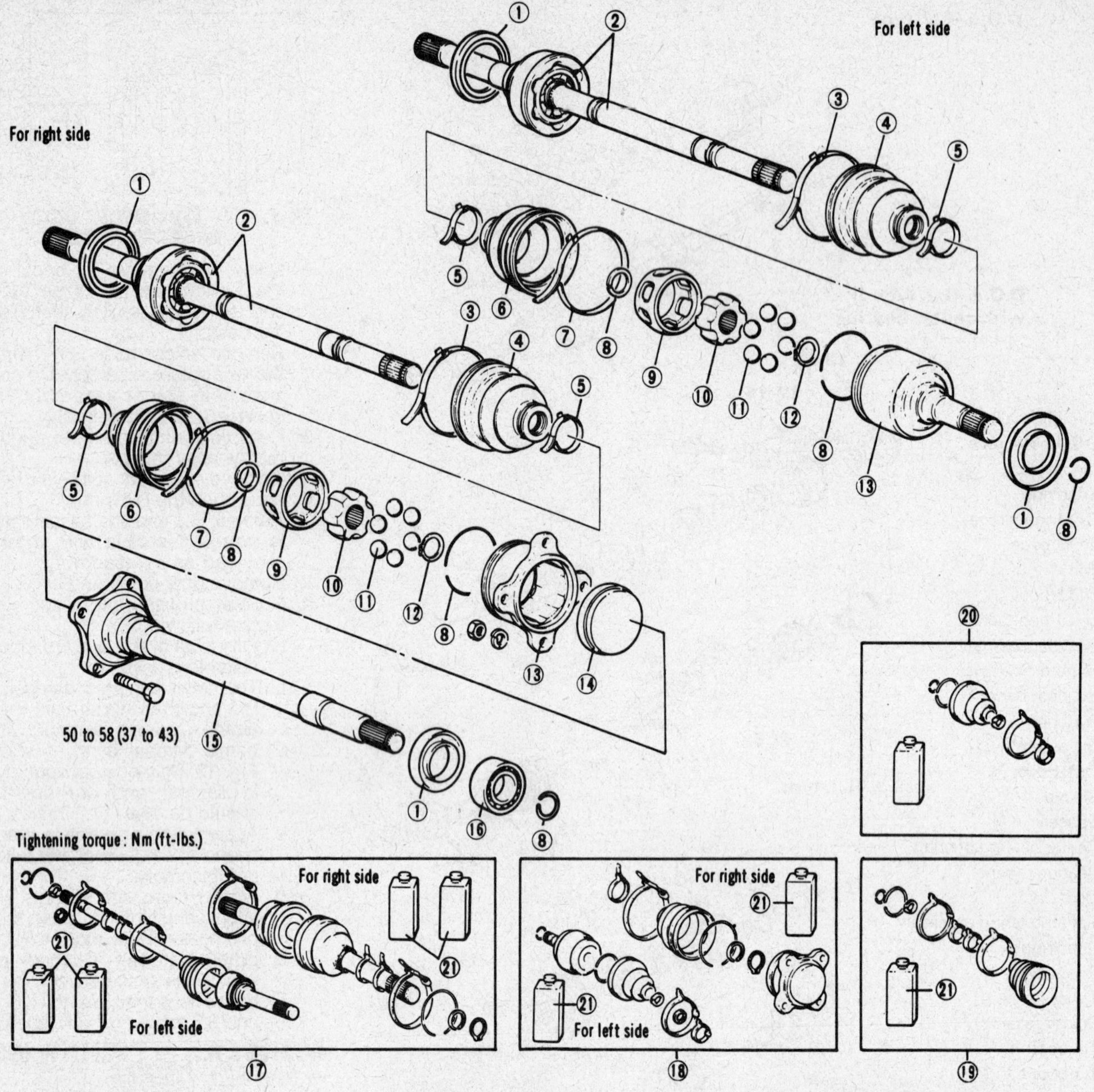

(1) Dust cover
(2) Drive shaft and B.J.
(3) Boot band (A)
(4) B.J. boot
(5) Boot band (C)
(6) D.O.J. boot
(7) Boot band (B)
(8) Circlip
(9) D.O.J. cage
(10) D.O.J. inner race
(11) Ball
(12) Snap ring
(13) D.O.J. outer race
(14) End plate
(15) Inner shaft
(16) Bearing
(17) Drive shaft and B.J. kit
(18) D.O.J. kit
(19) B.J. boot kit
(20) D.O.J. boot kit
(21) Grease

Abbreviation:
D.O.J. – Double offset joint
B.J. – Birfield joint

Fig. 13 Exploded view of front driveshaft. Montero & Pickup with 4 wheel drive

9. Using a screwdriver, remove dust cover.
10. Inspect all parts and replace as necessary. **Do not disassemble B.J.**

Inner Shaft

1. Using hammer, bend down outer circumference of dust cover.
2. Set tool MB990560 as shown, then tighten nuts until portion "A" contacts bearing outer race, **Fig. 14**, and press bearing from shaft.
3. Using screwdriver, remove dust cover.
4. Inspect all parts and replace as necessary.

ASSEMBLE

Inner Shaft

1. Using pipe with outside diameter of 2.95 inch and metal thickness of .16 inch, press dust cover onto inner shaft.
2. Using tool MB990560 or equivalent, press bearing onto shaft.

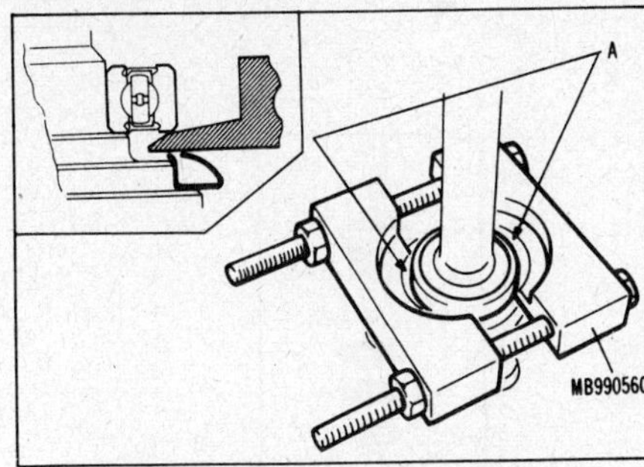

Fig. 14 Pressing bearing from inner shaft

Driveshaft

1. Using pipe with outside diameter of 2.71 inch and metal thickness of .09 inch, press dust cover onto B.J. side.
2. Using pipe with outside diameter of 2.24 inch and metal thickness of .24 inch, press dust cover onto D.O.J. side.
3. Wrap vinyl tape around driveshaft splines to prevent damage to boots.
4. Using grease supplied with repair kit, lubricate driveshaft.
5. Install B.J. boot, new boot bands, and D.O.J. boot on driveshaft and B.J. in that order. **B.J. and D.O.J. boots are of different size and shape and must be installed correctly.**
6. Install D.O.J. cage, small diameter side first, onto driveshaft, then install circlip on driveshaft.
7. Install D.O.J. inner race onto driveshaft and secure with snap ring.
8. Using grease supplied with repair kit, lubricate D.O.J. inner race and D.O.J. cage, then fit balls into cage.
9. Using grease supplied with repair kit, apply 1.8-2.8 oz. to D.O.J. outer race and install on driveshaft.
10. Apply an additional 1.8-2.5 oz. of above grease to D.O.J. outer race and install circlip.
11. Using grease supplied with repair kit, lubricate B.J. side, then install B.J. boot.
12. Ensure that distance of 3.1 inch exists between boot bands, then tighten them securely.

FRONT WHEEL DRIVE HUB & KNUCKLE

CORDIA & TREDIA

Replace

1. Raise and support vehicle and remove front wheels.
2. Remove brake caliper and wire aside.
3. Disconnect lower arm ball joint from knuckle.
4. Remove stabilizer and strut bars from lower control arm.
5. Disconnect tie rod end from knuckle.
6. Remove driveshaft from hub.
7. Remove hub and knuckle as an assembly from strut assembly.
8. Inspect hub, spline, oil seal, brake disc, steering knuckle and bearing, replacing as necessary.
9. Reverse procedure to install.

Service

1. Using tools MB990998 and MB991001 or equivalents, remove hub from knuckle.
2. Secure knuckle in vise, then remove brake disc from hub.
3. Using tools MB990339, MB990370 and MB990781 or equivalents, remove outer bearing inner race from hub.
4. Using screwdriver, remove oil seal from knuckle.
5. Drive bearing outer race from knuckle. **If either outer or inner race needs replacement, they must be replaced as a set.**
6. Ensure that identification marks on bearing and hub are correct. Do not use bearing or hub without identification marks.
7. Apply suitable grease to outside surface of bearing outer race.
8. Using tools MB990933, MB990938 and MB990776 or equivalents, install bearing outer race into knuckle. Replace knuckle if press fitting force required is less than 4400 lbs.
9. Install disc to hub and torque to 36-43 ft. lbs.
10. Apply suitable grease to bearings and inside surface of hub.
11. Place outside bearing inner race into knuckle.
12. Using tools MB990934 and MB990938 or equivalents, drive hub side oil seal into knuckle.
13. Apply suitable grease to lip of oil seal surfaces that contact hub.
14. Insert inner bearing into knuckle.
15. Using tool MB990998 or equivalent, torque hub to knuckle nut to 144-188 ft. lbs.
16. Rotate hub to seat bearing.
17. Measure total preload, which should be 18.2 inch lbs. or less for 1983 models or 11.3 inch lbs. or less for 1984-87 models. If total preload is zero inch lbs., measure hub axial play, which should be .004 inch or less.
18. If total preload and hub axial play are not within specifications, repeat service procedure.
19. Remove tool MB990998.
20. Apply suitable grease to bearing and inside of knuckle.
21. Using tool MB990934 and MB990938 or equivalents, drive driveshaft side oil seal into knuckle until it contacts bearing outer race.
22. Apply suitable grease to lip of oil seal.

GALANT

Replace

1. Raise and support vehicle, then remove front wheels.
2. Disconnect brake caliper assembly and support using suitable wire.
3. Disconnect lower control arm ball joint from knuckle using a suitable tool.
4. Remove stabilizer bar from lower control arm.
5. Disconnect tie rod end from knuckle using a suitable tool.
6. Remove drive shaft from hub.

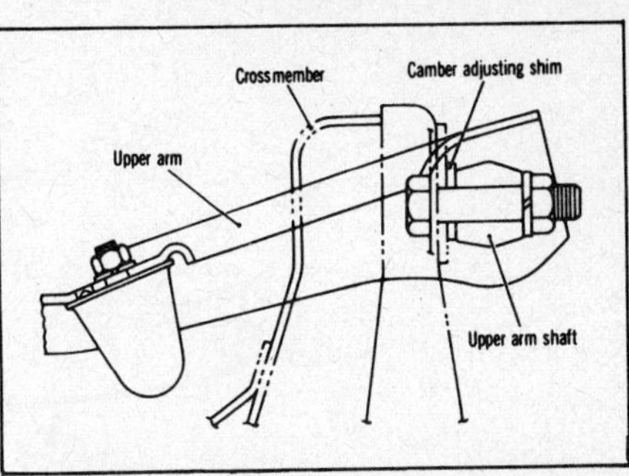

Fig. 15 Installing upper arm to crossmember bolts. Pickup less 4 wheel drive

7. Remove hub and knuckle as an assembly from strut assembly.
8. Reverse procedure to install.

Service

1. Attach tools MB990998-01 and MB991056 or equivalent to knuckle and hub, then secure knuckle in vise.
2. Remove hub from knuckle by tightening nut of tool.
3. Remove outside bearing inner race from hub using tool MB990810-01 or equivalent.
4. Remove hub side oil seal from hub.
5. Remove brake disc from hub.
6. Remove driveshaft side oil seal from knuckle.
7. Remove snap ring from knuckle, then the wheel bearing using a suitable tool.
8. Pack wheel bearing with suitable grease.
9. Apply a thin coating of grease to knuckle and bearing contact surfaces.
10. With inside wheel bearing inner race removed, press in bearing using a suitable tool.
11. Install wheel bearing inner race to wheel bearing, then attach snap ring.
12. Drive hub side oil seal into knuckle using a suitable tool until it is flush with knuckle end surface.
13. Apply grease to lip of oil seal and surfaces of oil seal which contact hub.
14. Mount hub onto knuckle using tool MB990998-01 or equivalent. Torque nut of tool to 145-187 ft. lbs.
15. Rotate hub to seat bearing, then check hub turning torque. Turning torque should be 16 inch lbs. or less.
16. Mount knuckle in vise, then check hub endplay using a suitable dial gauge. Endplay should be .008 inch.
17. If turning torque and hub endplay are not as specified, hub and/or knuckle may have been installed incorrectly. Repeat service procedures.
18. Apply grease to bearing and inside of knuckle, then drive driveshaft side oil seal into knuckle until it contacts snap ring.
19. Apply grease to lip of oil seal.

MIRAGE

Replace

1. Raise and support vehicle, then remove front wheels.
2. Remove cotter pin, wheel bearing nut and washer.

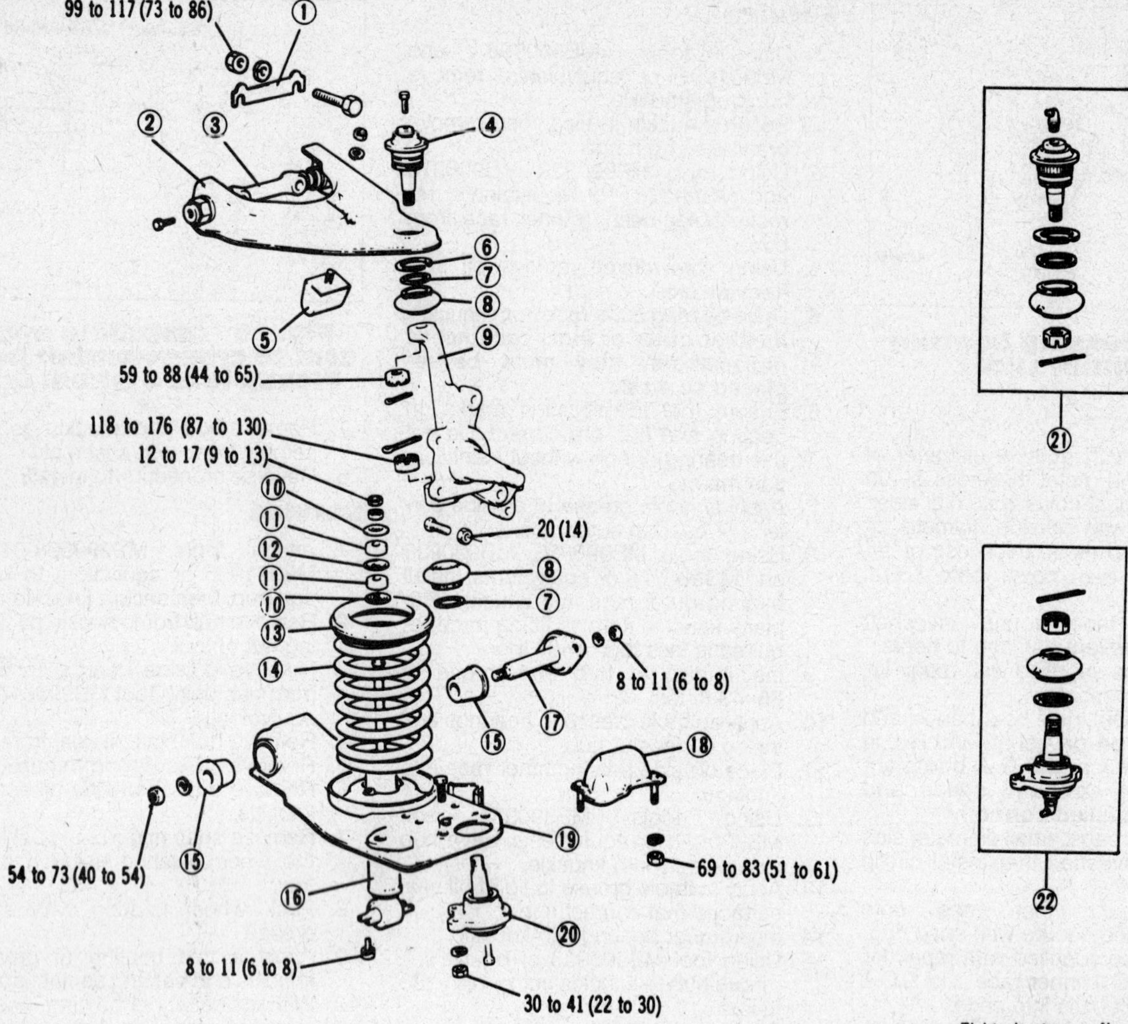

Tightening torque: Nm (ft-lbs.)

(1) Camber adjusting shim
(2) Upper arm
(3) Upper arm shaft
(4) Upper ball joint
(5) Rebound stop
(6) Snap ring
(7) Ring
(8) Dust cover
(9) Knuckle
(10) Joint cup (A)
(11) Bushing
(12) Joint cup (B)
(13) Spring seat
(14) Coil spring
(15) Lower arm bushing
(16) Shock absorber
(17) Lower arm shaft
(18) Bump stop
(19) Lower arm
(20) Lower ball joint
(21) Upper ball joint kit
(22) Lower ball joint kit

Fig. 16 Exploded view of front suspension. Pickup less 4 wheel drive

3. Disconnect brake caliper assembly and support using suitable wire.
4. Disconnect lower control arm ball joint from knuckle using a suitable tool.
5. Disconnect tie rod end from knuckle using a suitable tool.
6. Remove drive shaft from hub, then the circlip.
7. Remove hub and knuckle as an assembly from strut assembly.
8. Reverse procedure to install.

Service

1. Attach tools MB990998-01 and MB991056 or equivalent to knuckle and hub, then secure knuckle in vise.
2. Remove hub from knuckle by tightening nut of tool.
3. Remove dust cover, then the hub and disc assembly attaching bolts and nuts.
4. Remove brake disc, then the inner oil seal.
5. Remove inner bearing inner race, then the outer bearing inner race using suitable tools.
6. Remove outer oil seal, then the outer and inner bearing outer race using a suitable punch. **If either outer or inner race needs replacement, they should be replaced as a set.**
7. Install outer and inner bearing outer race using a suitable tool.
8. Pack outer and inner bearing inner race with suitable grease, then install bearings.
9. Drive outer oil seal into knuckle using a suitable tool until it is flush with knuckle end surface.
10. Apply suitable grease to lip and side lip of oil seal.
11. Install brake disc, then the hub and disc assembly attaching bolts and nuts. Torque nuts to 36-43 ft. lbs.
12. Install dust cover, then the inner bearing into knuckle.
13. Rotate hub to seat bearing, then check hub turning torque. Turning torque should be 11.3 inch lbs. or less.
14. Mount knuckle in vise, then check hub

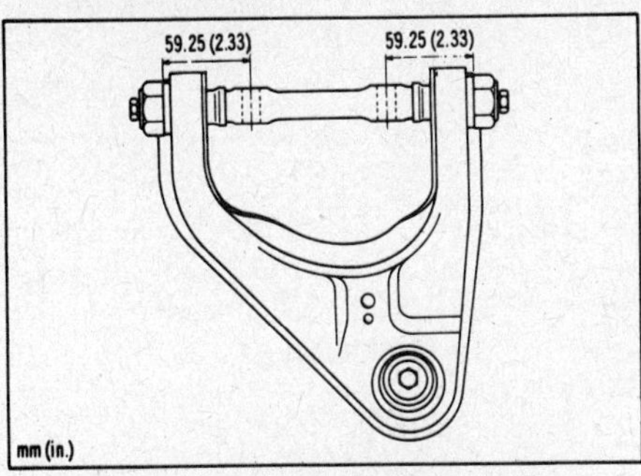

Fig. 17 Adjusting upper arm shaft to caster specifications. Pickup less 4 wheel drive

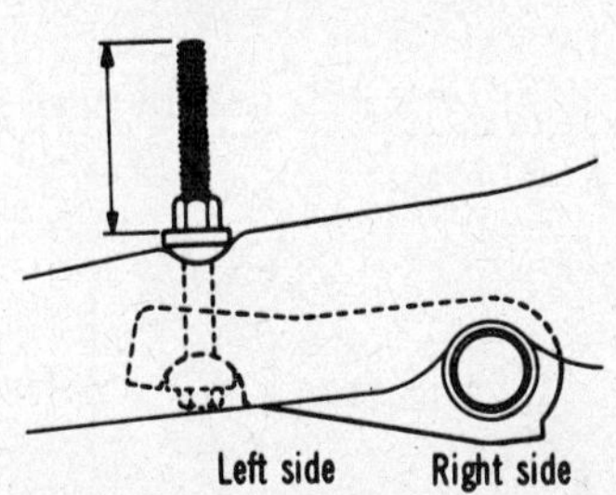

Fig. 20 Tightening torsion bar adjusting nut. Montero & Pickup with 4 wheel drive

endplay using a suitable dial gauge. Endplay should be .008 inch.

15. If turning torque and hub endplay are not as specified, hub and/or knuckle may have been installed incorrectly. Repeat service procedures.
16. Install inner oil seal using suitable tool until it projects from knuckle to a height of .10 inch, then apply grease to lip of seal.

MONTERO & PICKUP FRONT SUSPENSION SERVICE

PICKUP LESS 4 WHEEL DRIVE

Replace

1. Raise and support vehicle.
2. Remove front wheel, caliper assembly, and front hub assembly.
3. Loosen adjusting nut at tip of strut bar, then disconnect stabilizer and strut bars from lower control arm.
4. Remove shock absorber.
5. Using tool MB990792 or equivalent, compress coil spring.
6. Remove cotter pin and slotted nut from upper and lower ball joint studs.
7. Using tool MB990635 or equivalent, loosen connection between ball joint and knuckle, tapping knuckle with plastic mallet. **After disconnecting upper ball joint from knuckle, disconnect lower ball joint from knuckle. Slotted nut should be temporarily tightened to upper ball joint.**

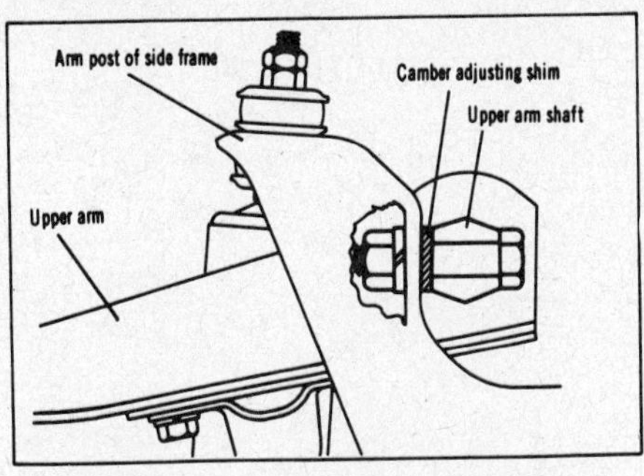

Fig. 18 Installing upper arm to crossmember bolts

8. Loosen tool MB990792, remove coil spring, and disconnect knuckle from ball joint.
9. Remove lower arm shaft and lower arm.
10. Remove bolts connecting upper arm shaft to crossmember, then remove upper arm as an assembly. Retain camber adjusting shims.
11. Reverse procedure to install, noting the following:
    a. Install camber adjusting shims between upper arm shaft and crossmember. Install bolts connecting upper arm shaft to crossmember in direction shown, **Fig. 15,** then torque bolts to 73-86 ft. lbs.
    b. Install lower arm shaft to crossmember, leaving nut to lower arm shaft loose. After completion of front suspension installation and with vehicle lowered to ground, torque nut to 6-8 ft. lbs.
    c. When installing front spring, insert spring seat between coil spring upper end and crossmember, and place other end in groove of lower arm.
    d. Coil springs have identification marks inscribed. Ensure that springs are paired and that they are proper springs for vehicle.
    e. Using tool MB990792 or equivalent, compress springs until lower arm is brought to level position.
    f. Assemble knuckle with upper and lower ball joints, then torque upper knuckle to ball joint bolt to 44-65 ft. lbs. and lower knuckle to ball joint bolt to 87-130 ft. lbs.
    g. Install shock absorber and torque shock absorber to crossmember nut to 9-13 ft. lbs. and shock absorber to lower arm nuts to 6-8 ft. lbs.
    h. Install strut bar to lower arm and torque nuts to 51-61 ft. lbs.
    i. When installing ends of stabilizer bar, tighten first nut so that distance between face of nut and end of bolt is .87-.94 inch, then torque second nut to 19-25 ft. lbs.
    j. Install front hub and caliper assemblies, then install wheel.
    k. Lower vehicle to ground, then torque lower arm shaft flange to crossmember to 6-8 ft. lbs. and lower arm shaft tightening nut to 40-54 ft. lbs.

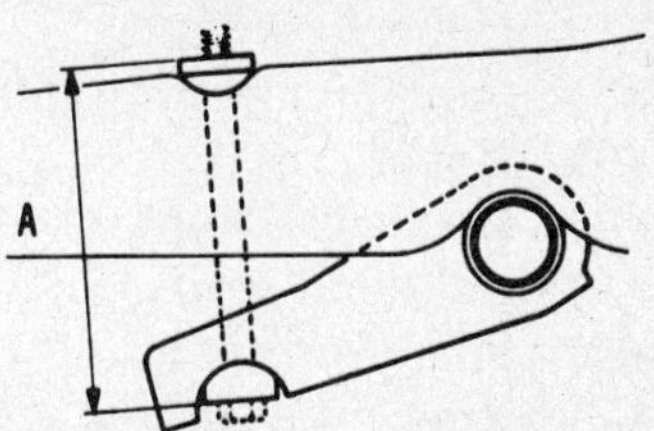

Fig. 19 Assembling torsion bar & anchor arm. Montero & Pickup with 4 wheel drive

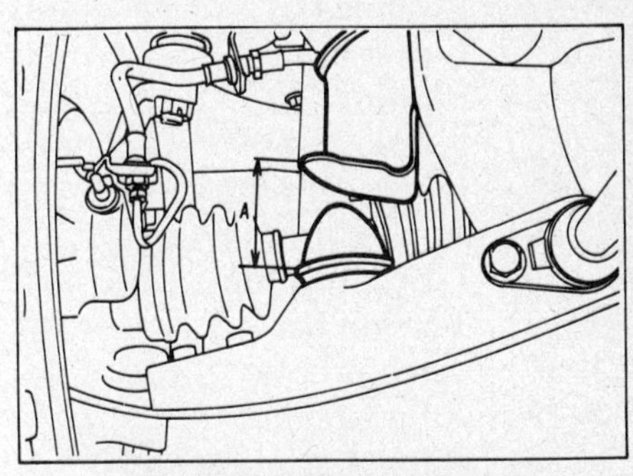

Fig. 21 Measuring distance between bump stop & bump stop bracket

Service

1. Remove rebound stop, **Fig. 16.**
2. Remove ring and dust cover from upper ball joint, then remove snap ring.
3. Using tools MB990799 and MB990800 or equivalents, remove upper ball joint.
4. Remove ring and dust cover from lower ball joint, then remove lower ball joint from lower arm.
5. Inspect all components and replace as necessary.
6. Line up upper ball joint to upper arm mating marks and, using tools MB990799 and MB990800 or equivalents, press ball joint into upper arm. Replace upper arm or ball joint is standard ball joint installation pressure is not obtained. Initial pressure should be 1550 lbs. and final pressure should be 11000 lbs.
7. Insert snap ring into groove in ball joint case. If snap ring is not tightly fitted, install new snap ring.
8. Install dust cover and ring and fit to groove of ball joint.
9. Turn upper arm shaft to obtain specified dimension, **Fig. 17.**
10. Assemble lower ball joint to lower arm and torque bolts to 22-30 ft. lbs.
11. Install dust cover with embossed portion facing front of vehicle, then install ring into groove of ball joint case.

MONTERO & PICKUP WITH 4 WHEEL DRIVE

Replace

1. Raise and support vehicle.
2. Detach dust covers from anchor arm assembly and anchor arm.
3. Scribe alignment mark on torsion bar to line up with mark on anchor arm.

(1) Upper arm shaft
(2) Camber adjusting shim
(3) Upper arm
(4) Upper ball joint
(5) Rebound stop
(6) Snap ring
(7) Ring
(8) Dust cover
(9) Joint cup (A)
(10) Bushing
(11) Shock absorber
(12) Bushing (B)
(13) Lower arm
(14) Bushing (A)
(15) Bump stop
(16) Lower arm shaft
(17) Anchor arm (B)
(18) Lower ball joint
(19) Torsion bar
(20) Anchor bolt
(21) Adjusting nut
(22) Anchor arm assembly
(23) Oil seal
(24) Spacer
(25) Needle bearing
(26) Knuckle

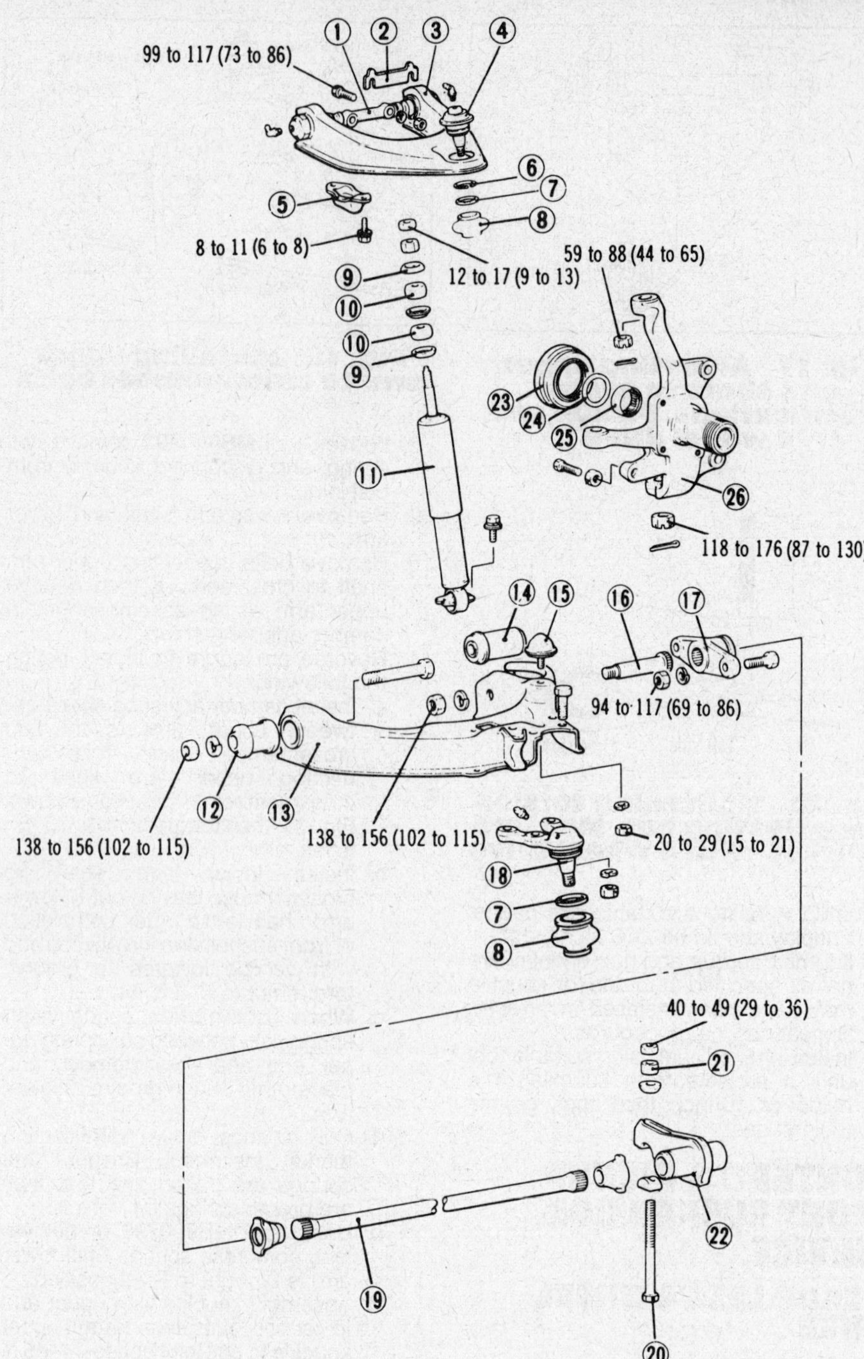

Tightening torque: Nm (ft-lbs.)

Fig. 22 Exploded view of front suspension. Montero & Pickup with 4 wheel drive

4. Loosen adjusting nut and remove torsion bar from anchor arm. It may be necessary to remove anchor arm assembly to remove torsion bar.
5. Detach stabilizer bar from lower arm.
6. Remove shock absorber.
7. Remove cotter pin and slotted nut from tie rod end and upper and lower ball joint studs.
8. Using tool MB990635 or equlvalent, disconnect tie rod from knuckle.
9. Using tools MB990635 and MB990809 or equivalents, loosen connection between ball joint and knuckle, tapping knuckle with plastic mallet.
10. After upper ball joint has been removed from knuckle, disconnect lower ball joint. Slotted nut should be temporarily tightened to upper ball joint. **When knuckle is removed, be careful not to damage Birfield joint boots.**
11. Disconnect knuckle from ball joint.
12. Remove bolts connecting upper arm shaft to arm post of side frame, then remove upper arm assembly, retaining camber adjusting shims.
13. Remove lower arm assembly.
14. Reverse procedure to install, noting the following:
    a. Install camber adjusting shims between upper arm shaft and arm post of side frame, then install bolt connecting upper arm shaft to arm post of side frame as shown, **Fig. 18,** and torque to 73-86 ft. lbs.
    b. Assemble lower arm to bracket of side frame. Do not tighten at this time.
    c. Assemble knuckle to upper and lower ball joints, then torque upper knuckle to ball joint to 44-65 ft. lbs. and lower knuckle to ball joint to 87-130 ft. lbs.
    d. Attach shock absorber to arm post of side frame with double nuts. Tighten first nut so that distance

1. Oil seal
2. Inner bearing
3. Brake disc
4. Front hub
5. Outer bearing
6. Lock nut
7. Lock washer
8. Spacer
9. Snap ring
10. Automatic free-wheeling hub assembly
11. Manual free-wheeling hub assembly

	Nm	ft.lbs.
A	50-60	36-43

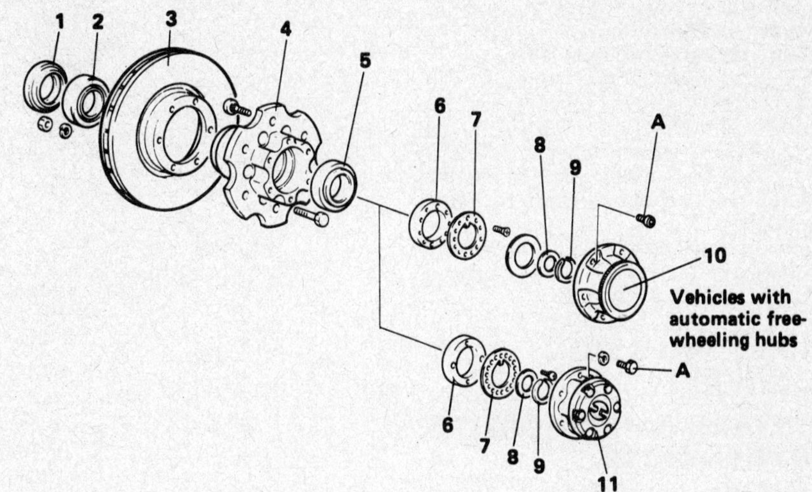

Fig. 23 Exploded view of front axle hub

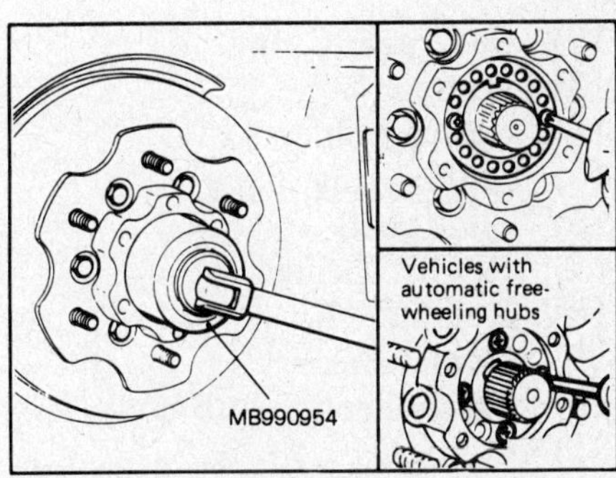

Fig. 24 Removing spindle nut

between bottom of nut and end of strut is .81 inch, then torque second nut to 9-13 ft. lbs. Torque shock absorber to lower arm attaching nuts to 6-8 ft. lbs.

e. Apply suitable grease to torsion bar serrations, serrations of anchor arms, inside of dust boot, and anchor bolt thread.
f. Left and right torsion bars are marked for identification.
g. Face end of torsion bar with identification mark forward and align mark on anchor arm with mating mark on torsion bar when torsion bar is inserted in anchor arm. If installing new torsion bar, align serration painted white with mark on anchor arm.
h. When torsion bar and anchor arm are assembled, and rebound stop is in contact with side frame, dimension "A," **Fig. 19,** should be 5.52-5.82 inch for left side and 5.32-5.62 inch for right side on Pickup or 5.43-5.73 inches for left side and 5.04-5.35 inches for right side on Montero.
i. Tighten adjusting nut so that dimension, **Fig. 20,** is 2.8 inches for left side and 2.7 inches for right side on Pickup with 4-122 engine; 3.0 inches for left side and 2.7 inches for right side on Pickup with 4-156 engine; 3.2 inches for left side and 3.1 inches for right side on Pickup with diesel engine; or 2.1 7 inches for left side and 2.68 inches for right side on Montero.
j. Install stabilizer bar to lower arm so that distance between bottom of nut and end of bolt is .63-.71 inch
k. Install front hub and caliper assemblies.
l. Check driveshaft play in axial direction.
m. Install wheel.
n. With vehicle lowered to ground, torque lower arm to bracket of side frame to 102-115 ft. lbs.
o. Measure distance "A," **Fig. 21,** and if not 2.8 inch on 1983-86 models or 3.1 inch on 1987 models, tighten adjusting nut of anchor bolt to obtain correct distance. When tightening adjusting nuts, ensure that anchor bolt protrusion does not exceed 3.5 inch on left side or 3.3 inch on right side.
p. Torque anchor bolt jam nut to 29-36 ft. lbs.

Service

1. Remove knuckle oil seal and take out spacer, **Fig. 22.**
2. Drive out needle bearing by tapping needles uniformly.
3. Remove rebound stop.
4. Remove ring, dust cover, and snap ring from upper ball joint.
5. Using tools MB990799 and MB990800 or equivalents, remove upper ball joint.
6. Remove lower ball joint from lower arm.
7. Remove ring and dust cover from lower ball joint.
8. Using tools MB990883 and MB990957 or equivalents, remove bushing "B" from lower arm.
9. Using tool MB990958 or equivalent, remove bushing "A" from front suspension crossmember bracket. When removing left hand bushing, detach differential carrier.
10. Inspect all components, replacing as necessary.
11. Apply suitable grease to roller surface of needle bearing.
12. Using tool MB990956 or equivalent, press in needle bearing until it is flush with knuckle end face.
13. Install spacer into knuckle with smaller inside diameter side toward needle bearing.
14. Using tool MB990985 or equivalent, press in oil seal.
15. Pack suitable grease inside oil seal and on lip.
16. Line up mating marks on upper ball joint with that on upper arm.
17. Using tools MB990799 and MB990800 or equivalents, press ball joint into upper arm.
18. Insert snap ring into groove in ball joint case. If snap ring is loose, replace it.
19. Install dust cover and ring and fit to groove of ball joint.

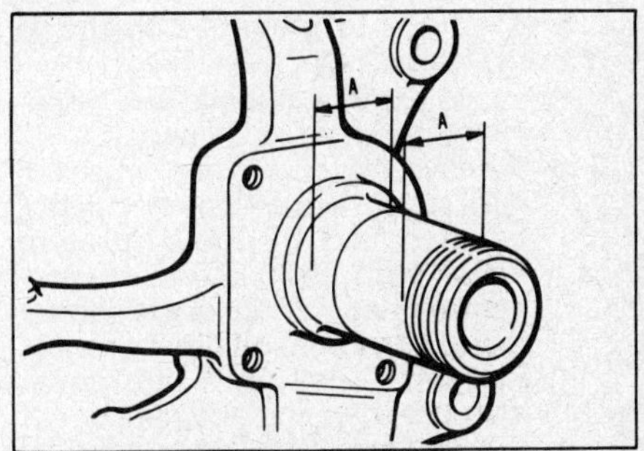

Fig. 25 Checking spindle for wear

20. Assemble ball joint to lower arm and torque bolts to 87-130 ft. lbs.
21. Install dust cover with embossed portion facing forward, then install ring into groove of ball joint case.
22. Coat bushing "B" and lower arm with soap solution, then press bushing into lower arm, using tools MB990883 and MB990957 or equivalents. Press in bushing so that both ends of bushing protrude from lower arm by same amount.
23. Using tool MB990958 or equivalent, press in busing "A" with collar of bushing facing forward.

FRONT AXLE HUB SERVICE

MONTERO & PICKUP WITH 4 WHEEL DRIVE

REMOVAL

1. Remove wheel and tire assembly, then remove brake caliper assembly with brake hose connected. **Suspend caliper assembly from frame using a wire hook to prevent damage to brake hose.**
2. On models with automatic free wheeling hubs, proceed as follows:
   a. Remove automatic free wheeling hub cover. **When cover cannot be loosened by hand, protect cover with shop towel to prevent damage, then loosen cover using a suitable oil filter wrench.**
   b. Remove O-ring from hub cover, then the snap ring and spacer.
   c. Remove automatic free wheeling hub using tool MD998360 or equivalent, **Fig. 23.**
3. On models with manual free wheeling hubs, proceed as follows:
   a. Place hub in Free position, then remove free wheeling hub cover.
   b. Remove snap ring attaching free wheeling hub body to driveshaft.
   c. Remove free wheeling hub to front hub attaching bolts, then the free wheeling hub assembly, **Fig. 23.**
4. On all models, remove lock washer, then the hub locknut using tool No. MB990954, **Fig. 24.**
5. Pull front hub with brake disc from knuckle, using care not to drop outer wheel bearing inner race.
6. Remove grease from inside front hub, then using a suitable drift, drive bearing races from hub.
7. Place alignment marks on brake disc and hub, then separate hub and disc as necessary.
8. Inspect all components for wear and damage. Measure spindle bearing seating area diameter, **Fig. 25.** Diameter should be 1.7805 to 1.7812 inch.

DISASSEMBLY

1983-86 Automatic Free Wheeling Hub

1. Remove housing C-ring using a screwdriver, **Fig. 26.**
2. Remove brake (B) and (A) and brake spring, then the housing snap ring.

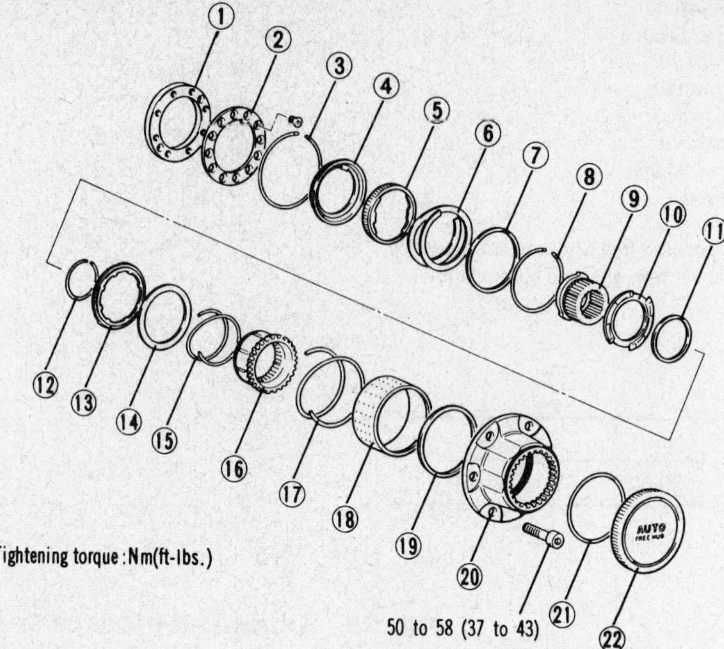

(1) Lock nut
(2) Lock washer
(3) Housing C ring
(4) Brake (B)
(5) Brake (A)
(6) Brake spring
(7) Housing snap ring
(8) Retainer (B) C ring
(9) Drive gear
(10) Retainer (A)
(11) Drive gear snap ring
(12) Slide gear C ring
(13) Cam
(14) Spring holder
(15) Shift spring
(16) Slide gear
(17) Return spring
(18) Retainer (B)
(19) Thrust washer
(20) Free wheeling hub body
(21) O-ring
(22) Free wheeling hub cover

Fig. 26 Automatic free wheeling hub components. 1983-86 models

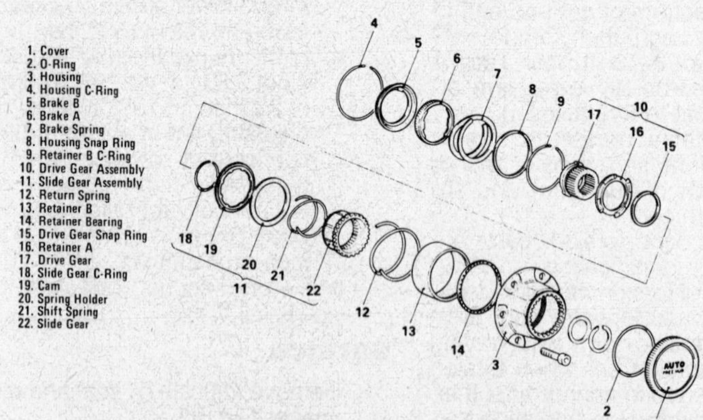

Fig. 27 Automatic free wheeling hub components. 1987 models

3. Push in drive gear using press MB990811-01 or equivalent, then remove retainer. **Ensure pressing force does not exceed 441 lbs.**
4. Slowly reduce pressure of press until return spring fully relaxes. Use caution retainer (A) is not caught by retainer (B) when reducing pressure of press.
5. Remove retainer (B), return spring, slide gear assembly and drive gear assembly from body.
6. Push in cam, then remove slide gear C-ring while spring is compressed.

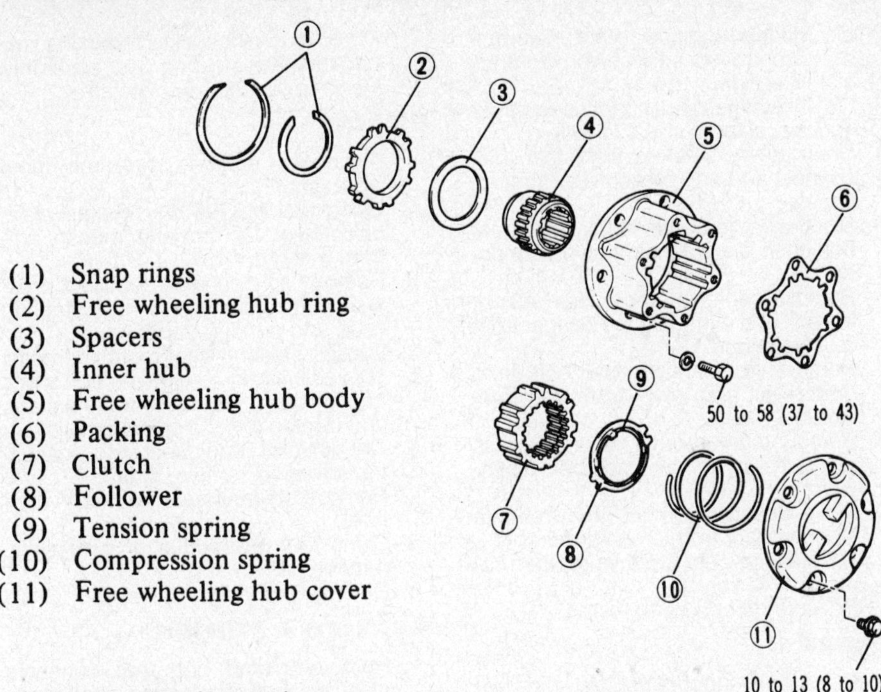

Fig. 28 Manual free wheeling hub components

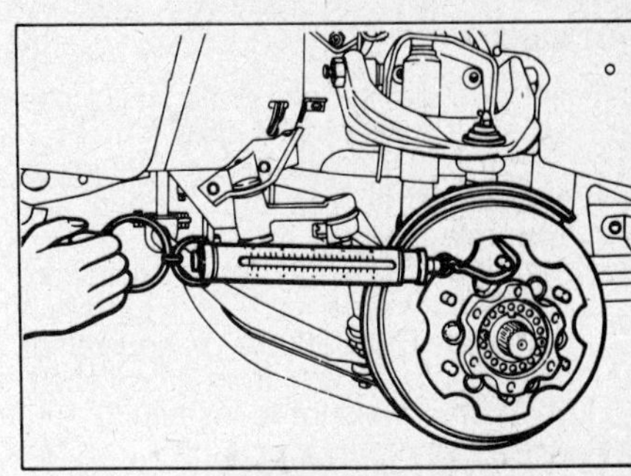

Fig. 29 Checking front hub assembly bearing adjustment

1987 Automatic Free Wheeling Hub

1. Remove cover, then the O-ring, **Fig. 27.**
2. Remove housing, then depress brake B, and remove C-ring.
3. Remove brakes B and A, then the brake spring.
4. Remove housing snap ring, then using tool No. MB990811-01, depress drive gear and remove retainer (B) C-ring.
5. Using tool No. MB990811-01 and a suitable press, remove drive gear, slide gear and return spring.
6. Remove retainer B, then the retainer bearing.
7. Remove drive gear snap ring, using a suitable tool, then discard.
8. Remove retainer A, then the drive gear.
9. Depress cam, then remove slide gear C ring.
10. Remove cam, then the spring holder, shift spring and slide gear.

Manual Free Wheeling Hub

1. Remove snap ring and inner hub from free wheeling hub body using a suitable screwdriver, **Fig. 28.**
2. Remove snap ring from inner hub with snap ring pliers.

ASSEMBLY

1983–87 Automatic Free Wheeling Hub

Reverse disassembly procedure to assemble, noting the following:

1. Apply suitable grease to mounting surfaces of all components.
2. Pack groove in brake (B), groove around outside of retainer (B) and both sides of bearing with suitable grease.
3. Install return spring with smaller coil diameter side toward spring seat.

Manual Free Wheeling Hub

Reverse disassembly procedure to assemble, noting the following:

1. Apply suitable grease to outer surface of free wheeling hub ring, inner hub and clutch and inside of free wheeling hub body.

INSTALLATION

1. Apply grease to wheel bearing outer races, then using a suitable drift, drive outer races into front hub.
2. Pack inner and outer bearings with suitable grease. Apply grease to oil seal lip.
3. Evenly coat inner wall of front hub with grease.
4. Position inner bearing and oil seal on hub, then install oil seal using tool No. MB990985 or equivalent.
5. If removed, install brake disc on front hub, **Fig. 23,** tightening attaching bolts alternately and evenly to 36-44 ft. lbs. After assembling, check brake disc runout. Brake disc runout should not exceed .006 inch.
6. Carefully install front hub on steering knuckle spindle.
7. Install outer bearing on spindle, then install and torque spindle nut to 94-145 ft. lbs. Loosen spindle nut and retighten to 18 ft. lbs., then back-off and install lock washer. **If hole in lock washer is not aligned with hole in spindle nut, then nut may be loosened up to an additional 20° to obtain proper alignment.**
8. Measure force required to rotate front hub, using a suitable spring scale, **Fig. 29.** The force required to rotate front hub assembly should be between .9-3.1 lbs. on Pickup or .9-4.1 lbs. on Montero. If not within specifications, readjust bearings as described in step 7.
9. Apply grease to inner surface of free wheeling hub body assembly.
10. Apply semi-dry sealant to front hub surface to which the free wheeling hub body assembly is attached.
11. Install free wheeling hub body assembly on front hub, then torque attaching bolts to 36-43 ft. lbs.
12. Install free wheeling hub cover. Torque attaching screws to 7-10 ft. lbs., if equipped with manual free wheeling hubs.
13. Install brake caliper assembly.

STEERING GEAR REPLACE

MANUAL STEERING

Cordia & Tredia

1. Raise and support front of vehicle, then remove wheels.
2. Disconnect joint assembly from steering gear.
3. Using tool No. MB990635 or equivalent, disconnect tie rod from knuckle.
4. Remove sub-member from No. 2 crossmember.
5. Remove steering gear from No. 2 crossmember.
6. Pull steering gear out from right side of vehicle.
7. Reverse procedure to install.

Mirage

1. Raise and support from of vehicle, then remove wheel and tire assembly.
2. Remove shaft assembly and gear box attaching bolt.
3. Remove tie rod end ball joint from knuckle, using a suitable tool.
4. Remove dust cover band.
5. Remove gear housing clamp attaching bolts, then the gear housing clamps.
6. Remove gear housing mounting rubber, then the steering gear assembly.
7. Reverse procedure to install.

Pickup

1. Remove clamp bolt connecting steering shaft and steering gear.
2. Using tool MB990635 or equivalent, disconnect tie rod and pitman arm from relay rod.
3. Remove steering gear downward from body frame.
4. Using tool MB990809 or equivalent, remove pitman arm from cross shaft.
5. Reverse procedure to install.

POWER STEERING

Cordia & Tredia

1. Raise and support front of vehicle.
2. Using tool MB990635 or equivalent, disconnect tie rod from knuckle.
3. Drain power steering fluid.
4. Disconnect pressure and return hoses at steering gear.
5. Disconnect joint assembly from steering gear.
6. Disconnect fuel hose from bottom of fuel filter and plug hose.
7. Remove fuel line installation clips as necessary to free fuel line.
8. Remove rear roll stopper stay on engine.
9. Remove sub-member from No. 2 crossmember.
10. Remove steering gear from No. 2 crossmember.
11. Pull steering gear out from right.
12. Reverse procedure to install.

Galant

1. Raise and support front of vehicle, then remove front wheels.
2. On models equipped with electronically controlled suspension, remove stabilizer bar.
3. On all models, disconnect tie rod from knuckle, using a suitable tool.
4. Drain power steering fluid, then disconnect and cap pressure and return hoses.
5. Disconnect joint assembly from gear box, then the solenoid valve connector.
6. Remove center member rear attaching bolt and exhaust pipe hanger from crossmember.
7. Remove front roll stopper bolt, then disconnect and lower front end front exhaust pipe.
8. Remove stay at left side, then press rear side of center member downward.
9. Move rack to the right, then remove steering gear from crossmember.
10. Tilt steering gear downward, then remove from vehicle.
11. Reverse procedure to install.

Mirage

1. Raise and support vehicle, then remove front wheels.
2. Disconnect return hose and drain power steering fluid.
3. Remove shaft assembly and gear box attaching bolt.
4. Remove tie rod end ball joint from knuckle, using a suitable tool.
5. Remove power steering feed hose, then the dust cover band.
6. Remove gear housing clamp attaching bolts, then the gear housing clamps.
7. Remove gear housing mounting rubber, then the steering gear assembly.
8. Reverse procedure to install.

Pickup

1. Disconnect steering shaft from input worm shaft.
2. Using tool MB990635 or equivalent, disconnect tie rod and pitman arm from relay rod.
3. Remove air cleaner, disconnect pressure and return hoses from steering gear, and remove under cover.
4. Loosen steering gear mounting bolts.
5. On vehicles equipped with automatic transmission, remove throttle linkage and throttle linkage splash shield.
6. On vehicles equipped with manual transmission, remove starter.
7. Remove steering gear from below vehicle.
8. Using tool MB990809 or equivalent, remove pitman arm.
9. Reverse procedure to install.

Montero & Starion

1. Remove clamp bolt that connects steering shaft to steering gear mainshaft.
2. Using tools MB990716 and MB990717 or equivalents, disconnect pressure and return hoses from steering gear.
3. Using MB990635 or equivalent, disconnect pitman arm from relay rod.
4. Remove steering gear.
5. Using tool MB990915 or equivalent, remove pitman arm from steering gear.
6. Reverse procedure to install.

WHEEL ALIGNMENT SECTION

INDEX

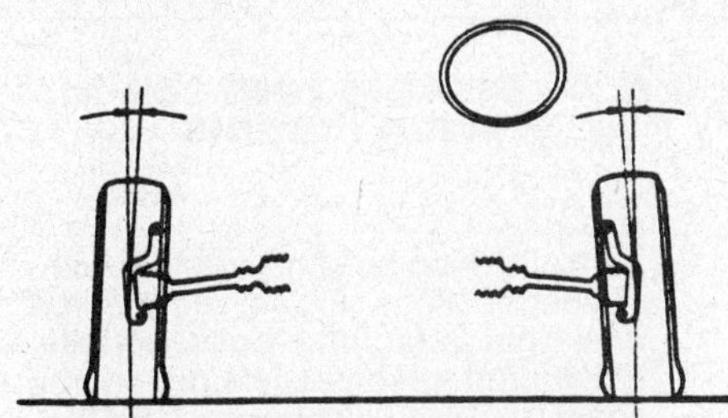

Fig. 1 Camber setting

PRELIMINARY CHECK

1. Ensure tires are inflated to correct pressure, then check for uneven wear.
2. Check front wheel bearings, suspension arm, and ball joints for damage and replace components as necessary, to eliminate improper alignment due to faulty components.
3. Check steering gear for damage and adjust as necessary.
4. Check shocks for damage and replace as necessary.
5. Rock vehicle backward and forward and bounce it upward and downward to settle vehicle prior to alignment.
6. Ensure vehicle is unloaded and on a suitable alignment rack according manufacturers' instructions. **When measuring equipment is attached directly to outer end of driveshaft and front wheels are on turntables, apply brake to prevent improper vehicle movement.**

CAMBER SETTING

DESCRIPTION

Camber refers to the angle at which a wheel leans in or out, **Fig. 1.** Positive camber is when the wheel leans outward and negative camber is when the wheel leans inward.

FRONT ADJUSTMENT

Cordia, Galant, Mirage, Starion & Tredia

Camber on these vehicles is preset to specifications and cannot be adjusted. If camber is out of specification, bent or damaged components must be replaced.

Pickup Less 4 Wheel Drive

1. Hold upper arm shaft to crossmember bolt and remove nut from engine compartment side.
2. Adjust number of shims between upper arm shaft and crossmember. A total of approximately .16 in. of shim thickness is normally required for standard camber. A .039 in. adjustment of shim thickness provides approximately 13 minutes adjustment of camber.

Montero & Pickup With 4 Wheel Drive

Adjust camber by adjusting number of shims between upper arm shaft and arm post of side frame. A .039 in. adjustment of shim thickness provides approximately 13 minutes adjustment of camber.

REAR ADJUSTMENT

Camber on these vehicles is preset to specifications and cannot be adjusted. If camber is out of specification, bent or damaged components must be replaced.

CASTER SETTING

DESCRIPTION

Caster angle refers to the angle at which the wheel center deviates from vertical when viewed from the side, **Fig. 2.**

ADJUSTMENT

Cordia, Starion & Tredia

Generally, caster on these vehicles requires no adjustment, although it is slightly adjustable by means of threaded end of strut bar.

Galant & Mirage

Caster is preset to specifications and cannot be adjusted. If caster is out of specification, bent or damaged components must be replaced.

Montero & Pickup

Adjustment of caster on these vehicles is made by turning the eccentrics on upper arm shaft. A half turn of upper arm shaft will cause .049 in. fore or aft movement of upper arm shaft, resulting in approximately 16 minutes adjustment of caster.

TOE SETTING

DESCRIPTION

As viewed from above, the wheels must be set so that distances A and B, **Fig. 3,** measured at wheel rims and at axle height, are different at a given value. If distance A is smaller than distance B, the setting is known as toe-in. If distance A is greater than distance B, the setting is known as toe-out. The toe setting is given in inches (mm) and refers to the difference between A and B. If distances A and B are the same, the toe setting is 0.

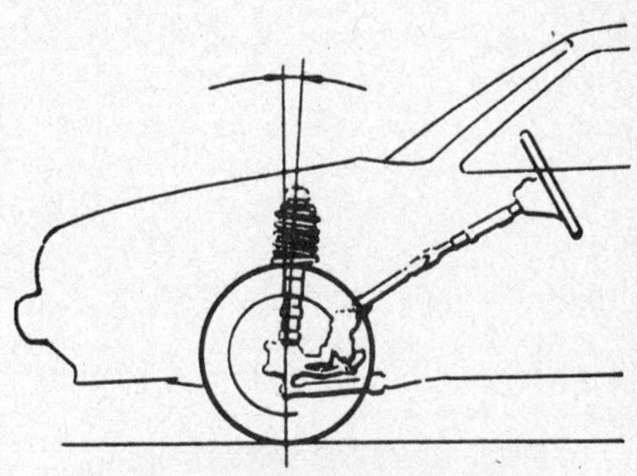

Fig. 2 Caster setting

FRONT TOE-IN, ADJUST

Cordia, Galant, Mirage & Tredia

1. Adjust toe-in by undoing clips and turning left and right tie rod turnbuckles by same amount in opposite directions.
2. To increase toe-out, turn left turnbuckle toward front of vehicle and right turnbuckle toward rear of vehicle. To increase toe-in, turn turnbuckles in other direction. Toe-in is adjusted .24 in. on all except Mirage or .48 in. on Mirage for each half turn of left and right tie rods.
3. After adjusting toe-in, check that steering wheel turning angle is within specifications.

Pickup Less 4 Wheel Drive

1. Adjust toe-in by turning left tie rod turnbuckle. Toe-in is increased by turning tie rod toward front of vehicle or decreased by turning tie rod toward rear of vehicle. One complete turn of turnbuckle changes toe-in adjustment by approximately .3 in.
2. After adjusting toe-in, check difference in length of left and right tie rods. If difference is greater than .2 in., remove right tie rod and adjust length until difference is reduced to .2 in. or less. "L" stamped on outer surface of tie rod indicates lefthand thread.

Montero & Pickup With 4 Wheel Drive

1. Adjust toe-in by turning left and right tie rod turnbuckles equal amounts in opposite directions.
2. Toe-in on left wheel is reduced by turning tie rod toward front of vehicle or increased by turning tie rod toward rear of vehicle. Toe-in on right wheel is reduced by turning tie rod toward rear of vehicle or increased by turning

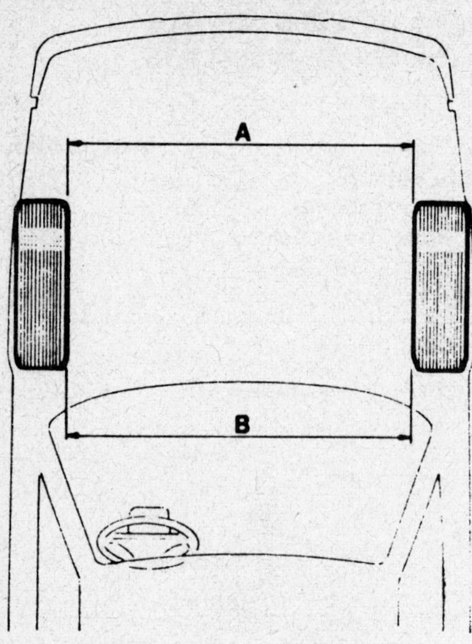

Fig. 3 Toe setting

tie rod toward front of vehicle. A half turn of turnbuckles changes toe-in approximately .3 in.

Starion

1. Measure difference in length between left and right tie rods. If difference is greater than .2 in., remove right tie rod from knuckle and adjust its length until difference is .2 in. or less.
2. Adjust toe-in by turning left tie rod turnbuckle. Toe-in is reduced when turnbuckle is turned toward front of vehicle or increased when turnbuckle is turned toward rear of vehicle. One complete turn of tie rod changes toe-in approximately .29 in. on 1983-84 models or .59 in. on 1985-87 models.

REAR TOE-IN, ADJUST

Starion

1. Loosen lower control arm to crossmember locknut while holding attaching bolt.

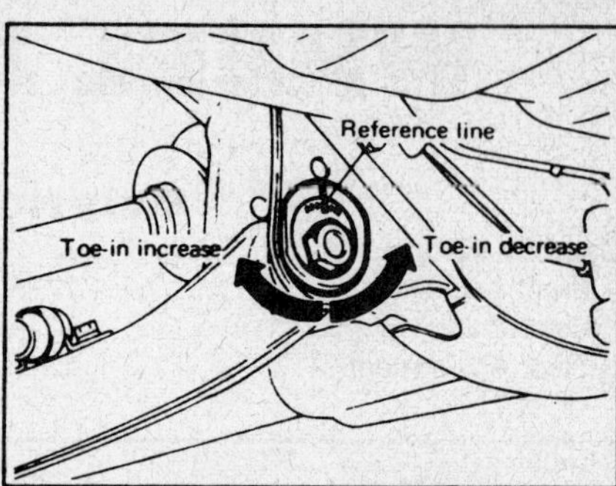

Fig. 4 Setting rear toe-in. Starion models

2. Turn attaching bolt until toe-in is within specifications, **Fig. 4. Rotate left and right attaching bolts equally. Movement of one division on the scale per side will change total toe-in approximately .08 inch.**
3. Torque locknut to 94-108 ft. lbs.

NISSAN/DATSUN (Japan)

INDEX OF SERVICE OPERATIONS

General Engine Specifications

Year	Engine Model	Fuel System	Displacement CID/Liters	Bore & Stroke Inches (mm)	Compression Ratio	Maximum HP @ RPM	Maximum Torque @ RPM	Normal Oil Pressure PSI
1983	CA20	2 Bore	120.4/2.0L	—	8.5	88 @ 5200	112 @ 2800	57
	CD17	Fuel Inj.	—	—	—	—	—	—
	E15	2 Bore	90.8/1.5L	2.99 x 3.23 (76 x 82)	9.4	69 @ 5200	92 @ 3200	57
	E16	2 Bore	97.5/1.6L	—	9.4	69 @ 5200	92 @ 3200	57
	L24E	Fuel Inj.	146/2.4L	3.268 x 2.902 (83 x 73.7)	8.9	120 @ 5200	134 @ 2800	—
	L28E	Fuel Inj.	168/2.8L	3.386 x 3.110 (86 x 79)	8.3	145 @ 5200	156 @ 4000	—
	L28ET	Fuel Inj.	168/2.8L	3.386 x 3.110 (86 x 79)	7.4	180 @ 5600	202 @ 2800	—
	LD28	Fuel Inj.	170/2.8L	3.327 x 3.270 (84.5 x 83)	22.7	80 @ 4600	120 @ 2400	—
	SD22	Fuel Inj.	132/2.2L	3.27 x 3.94 (83 x 100)	21.6	61 @ 4000	102 @ 1800	—
	Z22	2 Bore	133.4/2.2L	3.43 x 3.62 (87 x 92)	8.5	88 @ 5200	112 @ 2800	—
	Z22E	Fuel Inj.	133.4/2.2L	3.43 x 3.62 (87 x 92)	8.5	102 @ 2800	129 @ 2800	—
1984	CA18ET	Fuel Inj.	110.4/1.8L	3.27 x 3.29 (83 x 83.6)	8.0	120 @ 5200	134 @ 3200	71
	CA20E	Fuel Inj.	120.4/2.0L	3.33 x 3.47 (84.5 x 88)	8.5	③	④	57
	CD17	Fuel Inj.	102.5/1.7L	3.15 x 3.29 (80 x 83.6)	21.9	55 @ 2800	75 @ 2800	—
	E16S	2 Bore	97.5/1.6L	2.99 x 3.47 (76 x 88)	9.4	69 @ 5200	92 @ 3200	57
	L24E	Fuel Inj.	146/2.4L	3.27 x 2.90 (83 x 73.7)	8.9	120 @ 5200	134 @ 2800	—
	SD25	Fuel Inj.	151.8/2.5L	3.50 x 3.94 (89 x 100)	21.4	—	—	—
	VG30E	Fuel Inj.	180.6/2.9L	3.43 x 3.27 (87 x 83)	9.0	160 @ 5200	173 @ 4000	57
	VG30ET	Fuel Inj.	180.6/2.9L	3.43 x 3.27 (87 x 83)	7.8	200 @ 5200	227 @ 3600	57
	Z20	2 Bore	119.1/1.9L	3.50 x 3.78 (85 x 86)	9.4	—	—	—
	Z24	2 Bore	145.8/2.4L	3.35 x 3.39 (89 x 96)	8.3	—	—	—
1985	CA18ET	Fuel Inj.	110.4/1.8L	3.27 x 3.29 (83 x 83.6)	8.0	120 @ 5200	134 @ 3200	71
	CA20E	Fuel Inj.	120.4/2.0L	3.33 x 3.47 (84.5 x 88)	8.5	⑤	⑥	57
	CD17	Fuel Inj.	102.5/1.7L	3.5 x 3.29 (80 x 83.6)	21.9	55 @ 2800	75 @ 2800	—
	E16S	2 Bore	97.5/1.6L	2.99 x 3.47 (76 x 88)	9.4	69 @ 5200	92 @ 3200	57
	SD25	Fuel Inj.	151.8/2.5L	3.50 x 3.94 (89 x 100)	⑧	—	—	—
	VG30E	Fuel Inj.	180.6/2.9L	3.43 x 3.2 (87 x 83)	9.0	①	②	57
	VG30ET	Fuel Inj.	180.6/2.9L	3.43 x 3.27 (87 x 83)	7.8	200 @ 5200	227 @ 3600	57
	Z20	2 Bore	119.1/1.9L	3.50 x 3.78 (85 x 86)	9.4	—	—	—
	Z24	2 Bore	145.8/2.4L	3.35 x 3.39 (89 x 96)	8.3	—	—	—
1986	CA18ET	Fuel Inj.	110.4/1.8L	3.27 x 3.29 (83 x 83.6)	8.0	120 @ 5200	134 @ 3200	71
	CA18ET ⑦	Fuel Inj.	110.4/1.8L	3.27 x 3.30 (83 x 83.6)	8.0	—	—	57
	CA20E	Fuel Inj.	120.4/2.0L	3.33 x 3.47 (84.5 x 88)	8.5	⑤	⑥	57
	CA20E ⑦	Fuel Inj.	120.5/2.0L	3.33 x 3.47 (84.5 x 88)	8.5	—	—	57
	CD17	Fuel Inj.	102.5/1.7L	3.15 x 3.29 (80 x 83.6)	21.9	—	—	—
	E16S	2 Bore	97.5/1.6L	2.99 x 3.47 (76 x 88)	9.4	69 @ 5200	92 @ 3200	57
	SD25	Fuel Inj.	151.8/2.5L	3.50 x 3.94 (89 x 100)	⑧	—	—	—
	VG30E	Fuel Inj.	180.6/2.9L	3.43 x 3.27 (87 x 83)	9.0	①	②	57
	VG30ET	Fuel Inj.	180.6/2.9L	3.43 x 3.27 (87 x 83)	7.8	200 @ 5200	227 @ 3600	57
	Z20	2 Bore	119.1/1.9L	3.35 x 3.39 (85 x 86)	9.4	—	—	—
	Z24	2 Bore	145.8/2.4L	3.50 x 3.78 (89 x 96)	8.3	—	—	—
	Z24i	Fuel Inj.	145.8/2.4L	3.50 x 3.78 (89 x 96)	8.3	—	—	—
1987	CA16DE	Fuel Inj.	97.5/1.6L	3.07 x 3.29 (78 x 83.6)	10.0	113 @ 6400	99 @ 4800	85
	CA20E	Fuel Inj.	120.5/2.0L	3.33 x 3.47 (84.5 x 88)	8.5	⑧	⑨	57
	E16i	Fuel Inj.	97.5/1.6L	2.99 x 3.47 (76 x 88)	9.4	⑩	⑪	57
	E16S	2 Bore	97.5/1.6L	2.99 x 3.47 (76 x 88)	9.4	70 @ 5000	92 @ 2800	57
	VG30E	Fuel Inj.	180.6/3.0L	3.43 x 3.27 (87 x 83)	9.0	⑫	⑬	57
	VG30ET	Fuel Inj.	180.6/3.0L	3.43 x 3.27 (87 x 83)	7.8	200 @ 5200	227 @ 3600	57
	VG30i ⑭	Fuel Inj.	180.6/3.0L	3.43 x 3.27 (87 x 83)	9.0	—	—	61
	Z24i ⑭	Fuel Inj.	145.8/2.4L	3.50 x 3.78 (89 x 96)	8.3	—	—	57

Continued

GENERAL ENGINE SPECIFICATIONS—Continued

—Not Available.
①—Maxima, 152 @ 5200; 300ZX, 160 @ 5200.
②—Maxima, 167 @ 3600; 300ZX, 173 @ 4000.
③—Stanza, 97 @ 5200; 200SX, 114 @ 3200.
④—Exc. Calif., 21.4; Calif., 21.9
⑤—Stanza, 97 @ 5200; 200SX, 102 @ 5200.
⑥—Stanza, 114 @ 3200; 200SX, 116 @ 3200.
⑦—Mid year model change.
⑧—Stanza, 97 @ 5200; 200SX, 102 @ 5200.
⑨—Stanza exc. Wagon, 114 @ 2800; Stanza Wagon, 114 @ 3200; 200SX, 116 @ 3200.
⑩—Pulsar, 70 @ 5000.
⑪—Pulsar, 94 @ 2800.
⑫—Maxima, 152 @ 5200; 200SX & 300ZX, 160 @ 5200.
⑬—Maxima, 167 @ 3600; 200SX & 300ZX, 174 @ 4000.
⑭—Includes 1986 mid year introduction.

Valve Specifications

Year	Engine	Valve Lash		Valve Angles		Valve Spring Installed Height	Valve Spring Pressure Lbs. @ In.	Stem Clearance		Stem Diameter	
		Int.	Exh.	Seat	Face			Intake	Exhaust	Intake	Exhaust
1983	CA20	.012H	.012H	45	45.5	①	—	.0008-.0021	.0016-.0028	.2742-.2748	.2734-.2740
	CD17	.010H	.018H	45.5	—	⑤	—	.0008-.0021	.0016-.0029	.2742-.2748	.2734-.2740
	E15, E16	.011H	.011H	45.5	—	1.54	—	.0008-.0020	.0018-.0030	.2744-.2750	.2734-.2740
	L24E	.010H	.012H	45.5	—	①	—	.0008-.0021	.0016-.0029	.3136-.3142	.3128-.3134
	L28E, ET	.010H	.012H	45.5	—	①	—	.0008-.0021	.0016-.0029	.3136-.3142	.3128-.3134
	LD28	.010H	.012H	45.5	—	1.57	—	.0008-.0021	.0016-.0029	.3136-.3142	.3128-.3134
	SD22	.014H	.014H	45.25	—	1.54	135 @ 1.20	.0006-.0018	.0016-.0028	.3138-.3144	.3128-.3134
	Z22, Z22E	.012H	.012H	45.5	—	①	④	.0008-.0021	.0016-.0029	.3136-.3142	.3128-.3134
1984	CA18ET, CA20E	.012H	.012H	45	45.5	①	⑥	.0008-.0021	.0016-.0029	.2742-.2748	.2734-.2740
	CD17	.010H	.018H	45	45.5	⑤	—	.0008-.0020	.0016-.0028	.2742-.2748	.2734-.2740
	E16S	.011H	.011H	45	45.5	1.54	—	.0008-.0020	.0018-.0030	.2744-.2750	.2734-.2740
	L24E	.010H	.012H	45	45.5	①	—	.0008-.0021	.0016-.0029	.3136-.3142	.3128-.3134
	SD25	.014H	.014H	45	45.25	1.56	148 @ 1.22	.0006-.0018	.0016-.0028	.3138-.3144	.3128-.3134
	VG30E, ET	Hydraulic		45	45.5	①	⑦	.0008-.0021	.0016-.0029	.2742-.2748	.3128-.3134
	Z20, Z24	.012H	.012H	45	45.5	①	④	.0008-.0021	.0016-.0029	.3136-.3142	.3128-.3134
1985	CA18ET, CA20E	.012H	.012H	45	45.5	①	⑥	.0008-.0021	.0016-.0029	.2742-.2748	.2734-.2740
	CD17	.010H	.018H	45	45.5	⑤	—	.0008-.0020	0016-.0028	.2742-.2748	.2734-.2740
	E16S	.011H	.011H	45	45.5	1.54	—	.0008-.0020	.0018-.0030	.2744-.2750	.2734-.2740
	SD25	.014H	.014H	45	45.25	1.56	148 @ 1.22	.0006-.0018	.0016-.0028	.3138-.3144	.3128-.3144
	VG30E, VG30ET	Hydraulic		45	45.5	—	⑧	.0008-.0021	.0016-.0029	.2742-.2748	.3136-.3138
	Z20, Z24	.012H	.012H	45	45.5	①	④	.0008-.0021	.0016-.0029	.3136-.3142	.3128-.3134
1986	CA18ET, CA20E ②	.012H	.012H	45	45.5	①	⑥	.0008-.0021	.0016-.0029	.2742-.2748	.2734-.2740
	CD17	.010H	.018H	45	45.5	⑤	—	.0008-.0020	.0016-.0028	.2742-.2748	.2734-.2740
	E16S	.011H	.011H	45	45.5	1.54	—	.0008-.0020	.0018-.0030	.2744-.2750	.2734-.2740
	SD25	.014H	.014H	45	45.25	1.56	148 @ 1.22	.0006-.0018	.0016-.0028	.3138-.3144	.3128-.3134
	VG30E, VG30ET	Hydraulic		45	45.5	①	⑧	.0008-.0021	.0016-.0029	.2742-.2748	.3136-.3138
	Z20, Z24, Z24i	.012H	.012H	45	45.5	①	④	.0008-.0021	.0016-.0029	.3136-.3142	.3128-.3134
1987	CA16DE	Hydraulic		45	45.5	—	121 @ 1.05	.0008-.0021	.0016-.0029	.2348-.2354	.2341-.2346
	CA20E	③	③	45	45.5	⑨	⑩	.0008-.0021	.0016-.0029	.2742-.2748	.2734-.2740
	E16i, E16S	.011H	.011H	45	45.5	1.54	—	.0008-.0020	.0018-.0030	.2744-.2750	.2734-.2740
	VG30E, VG30ET	Hydraulic		45	45.5	①	⑧	.0008-.0021	.0016-.0029	.2742-.2748	.3136-.3138
	VG30i ②	Hydraulic		45	45.5	—	⑧	.0008-.0021	.0012-.0018	.2742-.2748	.3136-.3138
	Z24i	.012H	.012H	45	45.5	①	—	.0008-.0021	.0016-.0029	.3136-.3142	.3128-.3134

①—Inner, 1.38; outer, 1.57.
②—Includes 1986 mid year introduction.
③—Stanza exc. Wagon & 200SX, hydraulic; Stanza Wagon, .012H.
④—Inner, 57 @ .98; outer, 115 @ 1.18.
⑤—Inner, 1.42; outer, 1.56.
⑥—Inner, 57 @ .98; outer, 108 @ 1.16.
⑦—Inner, 56 @ .96; outer, 117 @ 1.18.
⑧—Inner, 57 @ .98; outer, 117 @ 1.18.
⑨—Stanza Wagon: inner, 138; outer, 1.57.
⑩—Stanza Wagon: inner, 57 @ .98; outer, 108 @ 1.16.

Pistons, Pins & Rings

Year	Engine	Piston Clearance	Ring End Gap		Wristpin Diameter
			Comp.	Oil	
1983	CA20	.0010-.0018	②	.0118	.7873
	CD17	.0020-.0028	.0079	.0118	.9448
	E15, E16	.0009-.0017	④	.0118	.7479
	L24E	.0010-.0018	②	.0118	.7873
	L28E, ET	.0010-.0018	⑧	.0120	.8266
	LD28	.0020-.0028	⑦	.0118	.9842
	SD22	.0016-.0043	⑨	.0059	1.0234
	Z22	.0006-.0034	②	.0018	.8266
	Z22E	.0010-.0018	②	.0018	.8266
1984	CA18E, CA20E	.0010-.0018	①	.0079	.7873
	CD17	.0020-.0028	.0079	.0118	.9448
	E16S	.0009-.0017	④	.0118	.7479
	L24E	.0010-.0018	②	.0118	.7873
	SD25	.0031-.0041	⑨	.0059	1.0234
	VG30E, ET	.0010-.0018	⑭	.0079	.8266
	Z20, Z24	.0010-.0018	②	.0118	.8266
1985	CA18ET, CA20E	.0010-.0018	①	.0079	.7873
	CD17	.0020-.0028	.0079	.0118	.9448
	E16S	.0009-.0017	④	.0118	.7479
	SD25	.0031-.0041	⑨	.0059	1.0234
	VG30E, ET	.0010-.0018	⑭	.0079	.8266
	Z20, Z24	.0010-.0018	②	.0118	.8266
1986	CA18ET, CA20E ③	.0010-.0018	①	.0079	.7873
	CD17	.0020-.0028	.079	.0118	.9448
	E16S	.0009-.0017	④	.0118	.7479
	SD25	.0031-.0041	⑨	.0059	1.0234
	VG30E, VG30ET	.0010-.0018	⑭	.0079	.8266
	Z20, Z24, Z24i	.0010-.0018	②	.0118	.8266
1987	CA16DE	.0006-.0014	⑤	.0079	.7872
	CA20E ⑪	.0010-.0018	②	.0079	.7873
	CA20E ⑩	.0010-.0018	⑫	⑥	.7873
	CA20E ⑱	.0010-.0018	②	.0059	.7873
	E16i ⑲	.0009-.0017	⑰	.0079	.7479
	E16i, E16S ⑯	.0009-.0017	④	.0118	.7479
	VG30E,ET	.0010-.0018	⑭	.0079	.8266
	VG30i ③	.0010-.0018	⑭	.0079	.8266
	Z24i ③	.0010-.0018	⑮	.0079	.8266

① —Top ring: except CA18ET engine with No. 3, 4 or 5 piston grade, .0098; CA18ET engine with No. 3, 4 or 5 piston grade, 1984 .0075, 1985-86 .0110. Second ring, .0059.

② —Top ring, .0098; second ring, .0059.

③ —Includes 1986 mid year introduction.

④ —Top ring, .0079; second ring, .0059.

⑤ —Top ring, .0087; second ring, .0075.

⑥ —Grade 1, .0079; grade 2, .0091; grade 3, .0102; grade 4, .0114; grade 5, .0130.

⑦ —Top ring with mark, .0055; top ring without mark, .0079; second ring, .0079.

⑧ —L28E top ring, .0098; L28ET top ring, .0075; second ring, .0059.

⑨ —Top ring, .0118; second ring, .0079.

⑩ —Stanza exc. Wagon.

⑪ —Stanza Wagon

⑫ —Grade 1, .0098; grade 2, .0110; grade 3, .0122, grade 4, .0134; grade 5, .0150.

⑬ —Exc. MPG, nos. 1 and 5, .0012-.0030; nos. 2, 3 and 4, .0012-.0036; MPG, nos. 1, 3 and 5, .0019-.0030; nos. 2 and 4, .0012-.0036.

⑭ —Top ring, .0083; second ring, .0071.

⑮ —Top ring, .0110; second ring, .0098.

⑯ —Sentra.

⑰ —Top ring: type 1, .0055; type 2, .0079; second ring; type 1, .0110; type 2, .0059.

⑱ —200SX.

⑲ —Pulsar.

Crankshaft & Bearings

Year	Engine	Rod Bearings		Main Bearings		Shaft End Play
		Shaft Diameter	Bearing Clearance	Shaft Diameter	Bearing Clearance	
1983	CA20	1.7701–1.7706	.0008–.0024	2.0847–2.0852	.0016–.0024	.002–.007
	CD17	1.7701–1.7706	.0009–.0026	2.0847–2.0852	.0015–.0026	.002–.007
	E15, E16	1.5730–1.5738	.0012–.0024	1.9663–1.9671	④	.002–.007
	L24E	1.7701–1.7706	.0009–.0026	2.1631–2.1636	.0008–.0026	.002–.007
	L28E, ET	1.9670–1.9675	.0009–.0026	2.1631–2.1636	.0008–.0026	.002–.007
	LD28	1.7701–1.7706	.0008–.0024	2.1631–2.1636	.0008–.0024	.002–.007
	SD22	2.0832–2.0837	.0014–.0034	2.7916–2.7921	.0014–.0037	.0024–.0055
	Z22	1.9670–1.9675	.0010–.0022	2.1631–2.1636	.0008–.0024	.002–.007
	Z22E	1.9670–1.9675	.0005–.0021	2.3599–2.3604	.0008–.0024	.002–.007
1984	CA18E, CA20E	1.7701–1.7706	.0008–.0024	2.0847–2.0852	.0016–.0024	.002–.007
	CD17	1.7701–1.7706	.0009–.0026	2.0847–2.0852	.0015–.0026	.002–.007
	E16S	1.5730–1.5738	.0012–.0024	1.9663–1.9671	④	.002–.007
	L24E	1.7701–1.7706	.0009–.0026	2.1631–2.1636	.0008–.0026	.002–.007
	SD25	2.0832–2.0837	.0014–.0032	2.7916–2.7921	.0014–.0034	.0024–.0055
	VG30E, ET	1.9670–1.9675	.0004–.0020	⑤	.0010–.0022	.002–.007
	Z20, Z24	1.9670–1.9675	.0005–.0021	2.1631–2.1636	.0008–.0024	.002–.007
1985	CA18ET, CA20E	1.7701–1.7706	.0008–.0024	2.0847–2.0852	.0016–.0024	.002–.007
	CD17	1.7701–1.7706	.0009–.0026	2.0847–2.0852	.0015–.0026	.002–.007
	E16S	1.5730–1.5738	.0004–.0017	1.9663–1.9671	⑥	.002–.007
	SD25	2.0832–2.0837	.0014–.0034	2.7916–2.7921	.0014–.0037	.0024–.0055
	VG30E, ET	1.9670–1.9675	.0004–.0020	⑤	.0011–.0022	.002–.007
	Z20, Z24	1.9670–1.9675	.0005–.0021	2.1631–2.1636	.0008–.0024	.002–.007
1986	CA18ET, CA20E ①	1.7701–1.7706	.0008–.0024	2.0847–2.0852	.0016–.0024	.002–.007
	CD17	1.7701–1.7706	.0009–.0026	2.0847–2.0852	.0015–.0026	.002–.007
	E16S	1.5730–1.5738	.0004–.0017	1.9663–1.9671	⑥	.002–.007
	SD25	2.0832–2.0837	.0014–.0034	2.7916–2.7921	.0014–.0036	.0024–.0055
	VG30E, VG30ET	1.9670–1.9675	.0004–.0020	⑤	.0011–.0022	.002–.0067
	Z20, Z24, Z24i	1.9670–1.9675	.0005–.0021	2.3599–2.3604	.0008–.0024	.002–.007
1987	CA16DE	1.7698–1.7706	.0007–.0018	2.0847–2.0856	.0008–.0019	.002–.007
	CA20E ③	1.7701–1.7706	.0008–.0024	2.0847–2.0852	.0016–.0024	.002–.007
	CA20E ②	1.7701–1.7706	.0004–.0017	2.0847–2.0852	.0008–.0019	.002–.007
	CA20E ⑦	1.7701–1.7706	.0008–.0024	2.0847–2.0852	.0016–.0024	.002–.007
	E16i ⑧	1.5733–1.5738	.0004–.0017	1.9661–1.9671	⑥	.002–.007
	E16i, E16S ⑨	1.5730–1.5738	.0004–.0017	1.9661–1.9671	⑥	.002–.007
	VG30E,ET	1.9670–1.9675	.0004–.0020	⑤	.0011–.0022	.002–.007
	VG30i ①	1.9670–1.9675	.0004–.0020	⑤	.0011–.0022	.002–.007
	Z24i ①	1.9670–1.9675	.0005–.0021	2.3599–2.3604	⑩	.002–.007

①—Includes 1986 mid year introduction.
②—Stanza exc. Wagon.
③—Stanza Wagon
④—Exc. MPG, nos. 1 and 5, .0012–.0030; nos. 2, 3 and 4, .0012–.0036; MPG, nos. 1, 3 and 5, .0019–.0030; nos. 2 and 4, .0012–.0036.
⑤—Grade No. 0, 2.4790–2.4793; Grade No. 1, 2.4787–2.4790; Grade No. 2, 2.4784–2.4787.
⑥—Nos. 1, 3 and 5, .0012–.0022; nos. 2 and 4, .0012–.0036.
⑦—200SX.
⑧—Pulsar.
⑨—Sentra.
⑩—Nos. 1 & 5, .0008–.0024; Nos, 2, 3 & 4, .0008–.0030.

Engine Tightening Specifications

***Torque specifications listed are in Ft. Lbs. and are for clean and lightly lubricated threads only. Dry or dirty threads produce increased friction which prevents accurate measurement of tightness.**

Year	Engine	Spark Plugs	Cylinder Bolts Head	Manifold Nuts or Bolts	Rocker Shaft Bracket Bolts	Camshaft Sprocket Bolt(s)	Oil Pan Bolts	Connecting Rod Cap Bolts	Main Bearing Cap Bolts	Flywheel to Crankshaft	Vibration Damper or Pulley
1983	CA20	13	62	15	15	39	4.4	25	37	76	94
	CD17	13⑦	⑨	15	—	72	4.4	25	37	76	94
	E15, E16	13	⑥	14	14	5	3.2	25	40	61	96
	L24E	13	62	④	—	101	5.7	37	37	101	109
	L28E, ET	13	62	④	—	101	5.7	37	37	101	109
	LD28	16⑦	91	⑧	—	102	5.4	37	55	109	109
	SD22	—	⑤	12	16	35	8	40	125	35	228
	Z22	13	62	14	15	102	4.4	37	37	109	102
	Z22E	13	62	14	15	102	5.7	37	37	109	109
1984	CA18ET, CA20E	18	⑯	18	15	62	4.4	25	37	76	94
	CD17	13⑦	⑨	15	—	72	4.4	25	37	76	94
	E16S	18	53	14	14	8	3.6	25	40	62	96
	L24E	13	⑯	④	—	101	5.8	25	37	101	109
	SD25	—	⑩	⑯	16	35	6.2	51	125	116	228
	VG30E, ET	18	⑯	①	15	62	4.4	37	71	76	94
	Z20, Z24	13	⑯	14	15	102	4.4	37	37	109	102
1985	CA18ET, CA20E	18	⑯	18	15	62	4.4	25	37	76	94
	CD17	13⑦	⑨	15	—	72	4.4	25	37	76	94
	E16S	18	⑯	14	14	8	3.6	25	40	62	96
	SD25	—	⑩	12	16	35	6.2	51	125	116	228
	VG30E, ET	18	⑯	①	15	62	4.4	37	71	76	94
	Z20, Z24	18	⑯	14	15	102	4.4	37	37	109	102
1986	CA18ET, CA20E②	18	⑯	18	15	62	4.4	25	37	76	94
	CD17	13⑦	⑨	15	—	72	4.4	25	37	76	94
	E16S	18	⑯	14	14	8	3.6	25	40	62	87
	SD25	13⑦	⑩	12	16	35	6.2	51	125	116	228
	VG30E, VG30ET	18	⑯	①	15	62	4.4	37	71	76	94
	Z20, Z24, Z24i	18	⑯	14	15	102	4.4	37	37	109	109
1987	CA16DE	18	⑯	③	—	12	5.4	⑧	36	⑯	108
	CA20E	18	⑯	18	14	61	4.4	25	36	76	94
	E16i⑪	18	⑯	③	—	12	5.4	⑧	36	65	108
	E16i,E16S⑫	18	⑯	14	14	8	5.3	25	40	61	87
	VG30E⑬	18	⑯	14	14	61	4.4	36	71	76	94
	VG30E, ET⑭	18	⑯	⑮	14	61	4.4	36	71	76	94
	VG30i②	18	⑯	14	14	61	4.4	36	71	76	94
	Z24i②	18	⑯	14	14	102	4.4	36	36	108	102

①—Intake manifold, 19; exhaust manifold, 15.

②—Includes 1986 mid year introduction.

③—Intake manifold, 16; exhaust manifold, 31.

④—Size 8M bolts, 14.5; Size 10M bolts, 29; Size M8 nuts, 11.

⑤—Main bolts, 98, sub bolts, 42.

⑥—Torque in two steps: first to 29–33 ft. lbs.; then to 51–54 ft. lbs.

⑦—Glow plugs.

⑧—Torque in two steps: first to 10–12 ft. lbs.; then to 30–33 ft. lbs.

⑨—Torque in two steps: first to 43–51 ft. lbs.; then to 72–80 ft. lbs.

⑩—Main bolt, 87–94 ft. lbs.; sub bolt, 33–40 ft. lbs.

⑪—Pulsar.

⑫—Sentra.

⑬—Maxima & 200SX.

⑭—300ZX.

⑮—Intake manifold: torque nut in two steps; first step, 2.2–3.6 ft. lbs., then torque to 17–20 ft. lbs.; torque bolt in two steps; first step, 2.2–3.6 ft. lbs., then torque to 12–14 ft. lbs. Exhaust manifold, 13–16 ft. lbs. Refer to text.

Alternator & Regulator Specifications

	Alternator			Regulator
Year	Model	Rated Hot Output Amps.	Hot Output Amps. @ 2500 RPM	Regulated Voltage
1983	LR150-98B	50	40	14.5–15
	LR150-125B	50	42	14.5–15
	LR150-133E	50	42	14.5–15
	LR150-402	50	42	14.5–15
	LR160-78	60	50	14.5–15
	LR160-78B	60	50	14.5–15
	LR160-82B	60	50	14.5–15
	LR160-97B	50	42	14.5–15
	LR160-97C	60	52	14.5–15
1984	A2T48195	70	50	14.1–14.7
	LR150-98B	50	40	14.4–15
	LR150-125B	50	42	14.4–15
	LR150-177	50	40	14.4–15
	LR150-402	50	42	14.4–15
	LR160-78B	60	50	14.4–15
	LR160-82B	60	50	14.4–15
	LR160-104	60	50	14.4–15.1
	LR160-121	60	50	14.4–15
	LR160-401	60	50	14.4–15
	LR170-701B	70	50	14.4–15
	LR170-706	70	50	14.4–15
1985	A2T48195	70	50	14.1–14.7
	LR150-98B	50	40	14.4–15
	LR150-125B	50	42	14.4–15
	LR150-177	50	40	14.4–15
	LR150-194B	50	40	14.4–15
	LR150-197B	50	40	14.4–15
	LR150-402	50	42	14.4–15
	LR150-403	50	42	14.4–15
	LR160-78B	60	50	14.5–15
	LR160-104	60	50	14.5–15.1
	LR160-140B	60	50	14.4–15
	LR160-401	60	50	14.4–15
	LR170-701B	70	50	14.4–15
	LR170-702B	70	50	14.4–15
	LR170-706	70	50	14.4–15
1986	A2T48195	70	50	14.1–14.7
	LR150-98B	50	40	14.4–15.0
	LR150-177	50	40	14.4–15.0
	LR150-194B	50	40	14.4–15.0
	LR150-197B	50	40	14.4–15.0
	LR150-402	50	42	14.4–15.0
	LR150-403	50	42	14.4–15.0
	LR160-78B	60	50	14.4–15.0
	LR160-104	60	50	14.4–15.1
	LR160-121	60	50	14.4–15.0
	LR160-140B	60	50	14.4–15.0
	LR170-14	70	50	14.4–15.0

Continued

ALTERNATOR & REGULATOR SPECIFICATIONS—Continued

Year	Alternator			Regulator
	Model	Rated Hot Output Amps.	Hot Output Amps. @ 2500 RPM	Regulated Voltage
	LR170-18	70	50	14.4–15.0
	LR170-701B	70	50	14.4–15.0
	LR170-706	70	50	14.4–15.0
	LR190-704	90	65	14.1–14.7
1986½	LR150-194B	50	40	14.4–15.0
	LR150-197B	50	40	14.4–15.0
	LR160-151	60	48	14.4–15.0
	LR170-717	70	50	14.1–14.7
1987	A2T46395	70	50	14.1–14.7
	A2T48195	70	50	14.1–14.7
	A2T48292	70	50	14.1–14.7
	A2T48298	70	50	14.1–14.7
	A5T41592②	60	50	14.1–14.7
	A5T41592①	70	50	14.1–14.7
	LR150-194B	50	40	14.4–15.0
	LR150-197B	50	40	14.4–15.0
	LR160-151	60	48	14.4–15.0
	LR160-715	60	48	14.1–14.7
	LR170-18	70	50	14.4–15.0
	LR170-22	70	50	14.1–14.7
	LR170-716	70	50	14.1–14.7
	LR170-717	70	50	14.1–14.7
	LR190-704	90	65	14.1–14.7

①—Pulsar. ②—Sentra.

Starter Motor Specifications

Year	Engine	Starter Number	Brush Spring Tension Oz.	Free Speed Test		
				Amps.①	Volts	RPM②
1983	CA20	S114-320A	71	60	12	7000
	CA20⑦	S114-322	63	100	12	3900
	CD17	S144-357	71	100	12	3900
	E15, E16④	S114-317	71	60	12	7000
	E15, E16③	S114-315	71	60	12	7000
	E15, E16⑧	S114-316	71	60	12	7000
	L24E	S114-254D	63	100	12	3900
	L28E, ET	S114-254D	63	100	12	3900
	LD28	S13-65	106	140	12	3900
	SD22	S13-45B	126	150	12	3500
	Z22③	S114-229F	57	60	12	6000
	Z22④	S114-295	57	60	12	7000
	Z22E③	S114-348	71	60	12	7000
	Z22E④	S114-295	71	60	12	6000
1984	CA18ET, CA20E	S114-320A	71	60	12	7000
	CA18ET, CA20E⑦	S114-322	63	100	12	3900
	CD17	S114-357A	63	100	12	3900
	E16S③	S114-316	71	60	12	7000
	E16S④	S114-345A	71	60	12	2000
	L24E	S114-254D	63	100	12	3900

Continued

STARTER MOTOR SPECIFICATIONS—Continued

Year	Engine	Starter Number	Brush Spring Tension Oz.	Free Speed Test		
				Amps. ①	Volts	RPM ②
	SD25	S13-45B	126	150	12	3500
	VG30E, ET	S114-374B	63	100	12	3900
	Z20, Z24③	S114-348	71	60	12	7000
	Z20, Z24④	S114-295	71	60	12	6000
1985	CA18ET, CA20E	S114-320A	71	60	12	7000
	CA18ET, CA20E⑦	S114-322	63	100	12	3900
	CD17	S114-357A	63	100	12	3900
	E16S③	S114-316	71	60	12	7000
	E16S④	S114-345A	71	60	12	2000
	E16S⑤	S114-318A	71	60	12	2000
	SD25	S13-45B	126	150	12	3500
	VG30ET, ET⑥	S114-374B	63	100	12	3900
	VG30E⑨	S114-430A	69	100	12	3000
	Z20, Z24③ ⑩	S114-426	71	60	12	7000
	Z20, Z24③ ⑪	S114-348	71	60	12	7000
	Z20, Z24④ ⑩	S114-427	71	60	12	6000
	Z20, Z24④ ⑪	S114-295	71	60	12	6000
1986	CA18ET, CA20E⑫	S114-320A	63	100	12	3900
	CA18ET, CA20E⑫ ⑬	S114-322A	63	100	12	3900
	CA20E⑭	S114-393	63	100	12	3900
	CD17, E16S③ ⑮	S114-440	63	100	12	3900
	CD17, E16S④ ⑯	S114-441A	71	70	12	1800
	E16S④ ⑰	M3T26685	70	70	12	1800
	SD25	S13-45B	126	150	12	3500
	VG30E③ ⑨	S114-430A	69	100	12	3000
	VG30E④ ⑨	S114-439	70	100	12	3000
	VG30E, VG30ET⑥	S114-374B	63	100	12	3900
	VG30E, VG30ET⑥	S114-403B	63	100	12	3900
	Z20, Z24, Z24i④ ⑪	S114-295	71	60	12	6000
	Z20, Z24, Z24i③ ⑪	S114-348	71	60	12	7000
	Z20, Z24, Z24i③ ⑩	S114-426	71	60	12	7000
	Z20, Z24, Z24i④ ⑩	S114-427	71	60	12	6000
1986½	CA18ET,CA20E⑫	S114-320A	63	100	12	3900
	CA18ET,CA20E⑫	S114-322A	63	100	12	3900
	VG30i	S114-503	72	90	12	2650
	Z24i④ ⑪ ⑱	S114-295	72	60	12	6000
	Z24i⑪ ⑲	S114-304	64	100	12	3900
	Z24i③ ⑪ ⑱	S114-348	72	60	12	7000
	Z24i③ ⑩ ⑱	S114-426	72	60	12	7000
	Z24i④ ⑩ ⑱	S114-427	72	60	12	6000
	Z24i⑩ ⑲	S114-446	64	100	12	3900
1987	CA16DE	M1T71681	68	75	12	3000
	CA20E⑭ ⑱	S114-393	64	100	12	3900
	CA20E⑭ ⑲	M1T71081	75	12	3000	
	CA20E⑬	M2T53781	67	100	12	2750
	CA20E⑫	S114-322A	64	100	12	3900
	E16i,E16S③ ⑯	S114-440	64	100	12	3900
	E16i,E16S④ ⑯	S114-441A	71	70	12	1800
	E16i,E16S④ ⑯	M3T26685	69	70	12	1800
	E16i③ ⑰	M2T53881	68	100	12	2900
	E16i④ ⑰	M3T26685	69	70	12	1800

Continued

STARTER MOTOR SPECIFICATIONS—Continued

Year	Engine	Starter Number	Brush Spring Tension Oz.	Free Speed Test		
				Amps.①	Volts	RPM②
	VG30E③⑨	S114-430A	58	100	12	3000
	VG30E④⑨	S114-439	68	100	12	3000
	VG30E⑫	S114-403B	64	100	12	3900
	VG30E,ET⑥	S114-457	64	100	12	3900
	VG30i	S114-503A	69	90	12	2650
	Z24i③⑩⑳	S114-605	69	69	12	7000
	Z24i④⑧⑩⑳	S114-606A	69	100	12	6000
	Z24i⑦⑩⑳	S114-454	64	100	12	3900
	Z24i③⑪⑳	S114-607	69	100	12	7000
	Z24i④⑧⑪⑳	S114-608A	69	100	12	6000
	Z24i⑦⑪⑳	S114-453	64	100	12	3900
	Z24i③⑩⑱㉑	S114-605	69	60	12	7000
	Z24i④⑩⑱㉑	S114-606	69	100	12	6000
	Z24i⑩⑲㉑	S114-454	64	100	12	3900
	Z24i③⑪⑱㉑	S114-607	69	100	12	7000
	Z24i④⑪⑱㉑	S114-608	69	100	12	6000
	Z24i⑪⑲㉑	S114-453	64	100	12	3900

①—Maximum.
②—Minimum.
③—Manual trans.
④—Auto. trans.
⑤—Optional on Calif. models with auto. trans.
⑥—300ZX.
⑦—Used on man. trans. & auto. trans. with optional equipment.
⑧—Used on man. trans. with optional equipment.
⑨—Maxima.
⑩—Exc. Calif.
⑪—Calif.
⑫—200SX.
⑬—Stanza exc. Wagon.
⑭—Stanza Wagon.
⑮—Pulsar & Sentra.
⑯—Sentra.
⑰—Pulsar.
⑱—2 wheel drive.
⑲—4 wheel drive.
⑳—Van.
㉑—Pathfinder & Pickup.

Brake Specifications

Year	Model	Brake Drum Inside Diameter	Wheel Cylinder Bore Diameter		Master Cylinder Bore Diameter	Disc Brake Rotor Specifications			
			Disc Brake	Rear Drum Brake		Nominal Thickness	Minimum Refinish Thickness	Thickness Variation Parallelism	Lateral Run-out (T.I.R.)
1983	200SX	④	⑧	—	7/8	⑰	㉑	.0012	.0024⑨
	280ZX	④	—	—	15/16	⑮	⑯	.0012	.0028
	Maxima	9.0	①	7/8	7/8	⑲	㉒	.0012	.0028
	Pulsar	7.01	1.894	11/16	⑦	—	.394	.0012	.0028
	Sentra	⑩	⑪	11/16	⑫	⑬	⑭	.0012	.0028
	Stanza	8.0	2.012	11/16	13/16	.710	.630	.0012	.0028
	Pickup	10.0	2.125	5/8	7/8	.492	.413	.0028	.0059
1984	200SX	9.0	⑧	7/8	15/16	—	㉒	—	.0028
	300ZX	④	⑤	—	15/16	—	㉔	—	.0028
	Maxima	9.0	①	7/8	7/8	⑲	㉒	—	.0028
	Pulsar	7.09	1.894	11/16	⑦	—	.394	—	.0028
	Sentra	⑩	⑪	11/16	⑫	⑬	㉗	—	.0028
	Stanza	8.0	2.012	11/16	13/16	.710	.630	—	.0028
	Pickup	㉘	2.386	㉙	15/16	.866	.787	.012	.0028
1985	200SX	④	⑧	—	15/16	—	㉒	—	.0028
	300ZX	④	⑤	—	15/16	—	㉔	—	.0028
	Maxima	④	⑤	—	1.0	—	㉔	—	.0028
	Pulsar	8.05	1.894	11/16	⑦	—	.394	—	.0028
	Sentra	8.0	⑪	11/16	㉛	⑬	㉗	.0012	.0028
	Stanza	8.0	2.012	11/16	13/16	.710	.630	—	.0028
	Pickup	㉘	2.386	㉙	15/16	.866	.787	.0008	.0028
1986	200SX	④	⑧	—	15/16	—	㉒	—	.0028
	300ZX	④	⑤	—	15/16	—	㉔	—	.0028
	Maxima	④	㉕	—	1.0	—	㉔	—	.0028
	Pulsar	8.0	1.894	11/16	⑦	—	.433	—	.0028
	Sentra	8.0	⑪	11/16	㉛	—	㉖	—	.0028
	Stanza㉓	8.0	2.012	11/16	13/16	.710	.630	—	.0028
	Stanza㉜	9.0	2.386	3/4	15/16	—	.787	—	.0028
	Stanza㉝	10.24	2.386	11/16	1.0	—	.787	—	.0028
	Pickup	㉘	2.386	㉙	15/16	.866	.787	.0008	.0028
1986½	200SX	④	①	—	15/16	—	㉒	—	.0028
	Pickup	②	③	⑥	⑱	—	⑳	—	.0028
1987	200SX	④	㉚	—	15/16	—	㉞	—	.0028
	300ZX	④	㉟	—	15/16	—	㊱	—	.0028
	Maxima	④	㉕	—	1.0	—	㉔	—	.0028
	Pathfinder	10.0	1.685	11/16	15/16	—	.945	—	.0028
	Pickup	②	③	⑥	⑱	—	⑳	—	.0028
	Pulsar	8.0	1.894	5/8	㊲	—	㊳	—	.0028
	Sentra㉓㉜	8.0	1.894	5/8	⑦	—	㊴	—	.0028
	Sentra㉝	9.0	1.894	11/16	㊵	—	.630	—	.0028
	Stanza㉓	10.24	2.386	11/16	1.0	—	.787	—	.0028
	Stanza㉜	9.0	2.386	3/4	15/16	—	.787	—	.0028
	Stanza㉝	9.0	2.386	3/4	1.0	—	.787	—	.0028
	Van	10.24	1.685	13/16	1.0	—	.945	—	.0028

①—Front, 2.126"; rear, 1.500".

②—Z24i engine w/2 WD & VG30i engine w/2 WD exc. heavy duty & Cab & Chassis, 10.24"; heavy duty models w/VG30i engine & 2 WD, 10.00"; Cab & Chassis models w/VG30i engine & 2 WD, 8.66".

③—Z24i engine w/2 WD, 2.386"; exc. Z24i engine w/2 WD, 1.685" each.

④—Equipped with four wheel disc brakes.

⑤—Front, 2.386"; rear, 1.685".

⑥—2 WD models exc. heavy duty & Cab & Chassis w/VG30i engine, 15/16"; Heavy duty & Cab & Chassis models w/VG30i engine & 2 WD & all w/4 WD, 11/16".

⑦—Large, 15/16"; small, 3/4".

Continued

BRAKE SPECIFICATIONS—Continued

(8)—Front, 2.125"; rear, 1.500".
(9)—Rear, .0028.
(10)—LT18A, 7.09; LT20A, 8.0.
(11)—CL18B, 1.894; AD20V, 2.012.
(12)—CL18B and LT18A: small, 3/4; large, 15/16. AD20V and LT20A: small, 15/16; large, 1.0.
(13)—CL18B, N/A; AD20V, .710.
(14)—CL18B, .390; AD20V, .630.
(15)—Front, .787"; rear, .378".
(16)—Front, .709"; rear, .339".
(17)—Front, .492"; rear, .378".
(18)—All 4 WD, 2 WD STD model w/Z24i engine & heavy duty & Cab & Chassis models w/VG30i engine, 15/16"; 2 WD w/Z24i engine exc. STD model & 2 WD w/VG30i engine exc. heavy duty & Cab & Chassis models, 1.0".
(19)—Front, .709"; rear, .378".
(20)—2 WD w/Z24i engine, .787"; exc. 2 WD w/Z24i engine, .945".
(21)—Front, .413"; rear, .354".
(22)—Front, .630"; rear, .354".
(23)—Exc. Wagon.
(24)—Front, .787"; rear, .354".
(25)—Front, 2.386"; rear, 1.503".
(26)—AD20V, .630". CL18B, .433".
(27)—CL18B, .394"; AD20V, .630".
(28)—Dual rear wheels, 8.66"; except dual rear wheels, 10".
(29)—2 WD, 11/16"; 4 WD, 5/8".
(30)—Front: CA20E engine, 2.126"; VG30E engine", 2.386. Rear: CA20E engine, 1.503"; VG30E engine, 1.685".
(31)—CL18B and LT20A: small, 3/4; large, 15/16. AD20V and LT20V: small, 13/16; large, 1.0.
(32)—Wagon exc. 4 WD.
(33)—4 WD Wagon.
(34)—CA20E engine: front, .630"; rear, .354". VG30E engine: front, .787"; rear, .354".
(35)—Front: VG30E engine, 2.386"; VG30ET engine, 1.685". Rear, 1.685".
(36)—Front: VG30E engine, .787"; VG30ET engine, .945". Rear, .709".
(37)—CA16DE engine: large, 1.0"; small, 13/16". E16i engine: large, 15/16"; small, 3/4".
(38)—CA16DE engine, .630"; E16i engine, .394".
(39)—Exc. Wagon, .394"; Wagon, .630".
(40)—Large, 1.0"; small, 13/16".

Front Wheel Alignment Specifications

Year	Model	Caster Angle, Degrees		Camber Angle, Degrees		Toe-in Inch	King Pin Inclination
		Limits	Desired	Limits	Desired		
1983	200SX	+1 3/4 to +3 1/4	+2 1/2	−2/3 to +5/6	+1/12	0 to .08	+8 1/6
	280ZX	+4 1/6 to +5 2/3	+4 11/12	−7/12 to +11/12	+1/6	.04 to .12	+9 1/6
	Maxima	+2 11/12 to +4 5/12	+3 2/3	−1/3 to +1 1/6	+5/12	−.04 to +.04	+12 1/6
	Pulsar	+3/4 to + 2 1/4	+1 1/2	−7/12 to +1 1/12	+1/4	0 to .08	+12 11/12
	Sentra	+3/4 to +2 1/4	+1 1/2	−7/12 to +1 1/12	+1/4	.12 to .20	+12 11/12
	Stanza	+2/3 to +2 1/6	+1 5/12	−3/4 to +3/4	0	0 to .08	+14 5/12
	Pick-up	(10)	(5)	0 to +1	+1/2	.20 to .28	(9)
1984	200SX	+2 3/4 to +4 1/4	+3 1/2	−1/4 to +1 1/12	+5/6	−.02 to +.06	+12 5/12
	300ZX	+5 5/6 to +7 1/3	+6 7/12	−7/12 to +11/12	+1/3	.04 to .12	+13
	Maxima	+2 11/12 to +4 5/12	+3 2/3	−1/3 to +1 1/6	+5/12	−.04 to +.04	+12 1/6
	Pulsar	+3/4 to + 2 1/4	+1 1/2	−5/12 to +1 1/12	+1/3	.12 to .20	+12 11/12
	Sentra	+3/4 to + 2 1/4	+1 1/2	−5/12 to +1 1/12	+1/3	.12 to .20	+12 11/12
	Stanza	+2/3 to +2 1/6	+1 5/12	−3/4 to +3/4	0	0 to .08	+14 5/12
	Pick-up (1)	+1 1/6 to +2 1/6	+1 2/3	0 to +1	+1/2	(3)	+9
	Pick-up (2)	+11/12 to +1 11/12	+1 5/12	+1/6 to +1 1/6	+2/3	.08 to .28	+8
1985	200SX	+2 3/4 to +4 1/4	+3 1/2	−5/12 to +1 1/12	+1/3	−.02 to +.06	+12 5/12
	300ZX	+5 5/6 to +7 1/3	+6 7/12	−7/12 to +11/12	+1/3	.04 to .12	+13
	Maxima	+1 1/4 to +2 3/4	+2	−5/12 to +1 1/12	+1/3	.04 to .12	+14 1/2
	Pulsar	+3/4 to +2 1/4	+1 1/2	−5/12 to +1 1/12	+1/3	.12 to .20	+12 11/12
	Sentra	+3/4 to +2 1/4	+1 1/2	−5/12 to +1 1/12	+1/3	.12 to .20	+12 11/12
	Stanza	+2/3 to +2 1/6	+1 5/12	−5/12 to +1 1/12	0	0 to .08	+14 5/12
	Pick-up (1)	+5/6 to +1 5/6	+1 1/3	0 to +1	+1/2	(3)	+9
	Pick-up (2)	+11/12 to +1 11/12	+1 5/12	+1/6 to +1 1/6	+2/3	.04 to .12	+8
1986	200SX	+2 3/4 to +4 1/4	+3 1/2	−5/12 to +1 1/12	+1/3	−.02 to +.06	+12 3/4
	300ZX	+5 5/6 to +7 1/3	+6 7/12	−7/12 to +11/12	+1/6	+.04 to +.12	+13
	Maxima	+1 1/4 to +2 3/4	+2	−5/12 to +1 1/12	+1/3	+.04 to +.12	+14 1/2
	Pulsar	+3/4 to +2 1/4	+1 1/2	−5/12 to +1 1/12	+1/3	+.12 to +.20	+12 11/12
	Sentra	+3/4 to +2 1/4	+1 1/2	5/12 to +1 1/12	+1/3	+.12 to +.20	+12 11/12
	Stanza (11)	+2/3 to + 2 1/6	+1 5/12	−5/12 to +1 1/12	+1/3	0 to +.08	+14 5/12
	Stanza (12)	+3/4 to + 2 1/4	+1 1/2	−1/4 to +1 1/4	+1/2	+.059 to + .138	+12
	Stanza (13)	+7/12 to + 2 1/12	+1 1/3	−8/15 to +1 1/30	+1/2	−.016 to +.063	+11 43/60
	Pickup (1)	+5/6 to +1 5/6	+1 1/3	0 to +1	+1/2	(3)	+9

Continued

FRONT WHEEL ALIGNMENT SPECIFICATIONS—Continued

Year	Model	Caster Angle, Degrees		Camber Angle, Degrees		Toe-in Inch	King Pin Inclination
		Limits	Desired	Limits	Desired		
	Pickup②	+11/12 to +1 11/12	+1 5/12	+1/6 to +1 1/6	+2/3	+.04 to +.12	+8
1986½	200SX	+2 3/4 to +4 1/4	+3 1/2	−5/12 to +1 1/12	+1/3	−.02 to +.059	+12 5/12
	Pickup①	−2/15 to +13/15	+1/2	−1/12 to +11/12	+1/2	④	+9 1/12
	Pickup②	+4/5 to +1 4/5	+1 3/10	+1/6 to +1 1/6	+2/3	⑥	+8 1/10
1987	200SX	+2 3/4 to +4 1/4	+3 1/2	−5/12 to +1 1/12	+1/3	−.02 to +.059	+12 5/12
	300ZX	+5 5/6 to +7 1/3	+6 7/12	−7/12 to +11/12	+3/4	+.04 to +.12	+13 2/3
	Maxima	+1 1/4 to +2 3/4	+2	−5/12 to +1 1/12	+3/4	+.04 to +.12	+14 7/12
	Pathfinder	+4/5 to +1 4/5	+1 3/10	+1/6 to +1 1/6	+2/3	+.04 to +.12	+8 1/10
	Pickup①	−2/15 to +13/15	+1/2	−1/12 to +11/12	+1/2	④	+9 1/12
	Pickup②	+4/5 to +1 4/5	+1 3/10	+1/6 to +1 1/6	+2/3	⑥	+8 1/10
	Pulsar	+1 1/6 to +2 2/3	+1 11/12	−1 1/40E° to +1/4	+3/4	−.04 to +.04	+14 11/24
	Sentra⑦	+1 1/4 to +2 3/4	+2	−1 1/12 to +5/12	+3/4	−.04 to +.04	+14 1/3
	Sentra⑧	+1 1/12 to +2 7/12	+1 5/6	−11/12 to +7/12	+3/4	−.04 to +.04	+14
	Sentra⑬	+1/6 to +1 2/3	+11/12	−5/6 to +2/3	+3/4	+.02 to +.059	+13 7/12
	Stanza⑪	+1 1/4 to +2 3/4	+2	−5/12 to +1 1/12	+1 3/40	+.04 to +.12	+14 7/12
	Stanza⑫	+3/4 to +2 1/4	+1 1/2	−1/4 to +1 1/4	+3/4	+.059 to +.138	+12
	Stanza⑬	+7/12 to +2 1/12	+1 1/3	−7/15 to +1 1/30	+3/4	−.016 to +.063	+11 7/10
	Van	+1 to +2	+1 1/2	−1/4 to +3/4	+1/2	−.04 to +.04	+9 1/2

①—2WD models.
②—4WD models.
③—Radial tires, .08–.16; bias tires, .20–.28.
④—Radial tires, .08–.16; bias tires, .16–.24.
⑤—2WD, +1 1/3; 4WD, +1 5/6.
⑥—Radial tires, .12–.20, bias tires, .16–.24.
⑦—Coupe.
⑧—Exc. Coupe & 4WD Wagon.
⑨—2WD, +9; 4WD, +11.
⑩—2WD, +5/6 to +1 5/6; 4WD, +1 1/6 to +2 1/6.
⑪—Exc. Wagon.
⑫—Wagon exc. 4WD.
⑬—4WD Wagon.

Rear Wheel Alignment Specifications

Model	Year	Camber, Degrees		Toe-In	
		Limits	Desired	Per Wheel Inch	Total Degrees
200SX	1983–87	−1 1/4 to +1/4	+3/4	−.08 to 0	−1/5 to 0
300ZX	1984	−1 11/12 to −5/12	−1 1/6	−.08 to +.08	−1/5 to +1/5
	1985–87	−1 11/12 to −5/12	−1 1/6	−.059 to +.098	−2/15 to +7/30
Maxima Sedan	1985–86	−1/2 to +1	+3/4	−.24 to −.08	−8/15 to −1/6
	1987	−1 1/6 to +1/3	+3/4	+.08 to +.24	+1/5 to +37/60
Maxima Wagon	1985–86	−1/3 to +1 1/6	+3/4	−.28 to −.12	−19/30 to −4/15
	1987	−1 1/6 to +1/3	+3/4	+.08 to +.24	+1/5 to +37/60
Pulsar	1985–86	−1 3/4 to −1/4	−3/4	−.256 to +.256	−21/30 to +21/30
	1987	−2 to −1/2	−1 1/4	−.059 to +.098	−3/20 to +1/4
Sentra Coupe	1985–86	−1 3/4 to −1/4	−3/4	−.266 to +.256	−21/30 to +21/30
	1987	−1 11/12 to −5/12	−1/5	+.04 to +.20	+1/10 to +31/60
Sentra Exc. Coupe & 4WD Wagon	1985–86	−1 3/4 to −1/4	−3/4	−.266 to +.256	−21/30 to +21/30
	1987	−1 3/4 to −1/4	−3/4	+.04 to +.20	+1/10 to +31/60
Sentra 4WD Wagon	1987	−11/12 to +7/12	−5/12	+.08 to +.24	+1/5 to +37/60
Stanza Exc. Wagon	1985–86	0 to 1 1/2	+3/4	−.276 to +.236	−21/30 to +3/5
	1987	−1 1/6 to +1/3	−1/6	0 to +.16	+1/5 to +37/60
Stanza 4WD Wagon	1986–87	0 to +1 1/2	+3/4	−.16 to 0	−11/30 to 0

Rear Axle Specifications

Year	Model	Carrier Type	Ring Gear & Pinion Backlash		Pinion Bearing Preload		Differential Bearing Preload	
			Method	Adjustment	Method	Torque Reading In./Lbs.	Method	Adjustment
1983	280ZX	Integral	Shim	⑮	Shim	⑱	Shim	—
	200SX	Removable	Shim	.006–.008	Collapsible Spacer	⑥	Shim	—
	Maxima	⑧	Shim	⑭	②	③	Shim	—
	Pick-up	④	Shim	⑦	⑩	⑰	Shim	⑫ ⑲
1984	300ZX	Integral	Shim	.005–.007	Adjusting Spacer & Washer	㉕	Shim	—
	200SX	⑳	Shim	⑨	⑪	⑬	Shim	—
	Maxima	⑧	Shim	⑭	②	③	Shim	—
	Pickup	㉑	Shim	㉒	㉓	㉔	Shim	—
1985	300ZX	Integral	Shim	.005–.007	Adjusting Spacer & Washer	㉕	Shim	—
	200SX	Integral	Shim	.005–.007	Adjusting Spacer & Washer	⑱	Shim	—
	Pickup	㉑	Shim	㉒	㉓	㉔	Shim	—
1986	200SX	Integral	Shim	.005–.007	Adjusting Spacer & Washer	⑱	Shim	—
	300ZX	Integral	Shim	.005–.007	Adjusting Spacer & Washer	㉕	Shim	—
	Stanza ㉗	Integral	Shim	.005–.007	Adjusting Spacer & Washer	㉖	Shim	—
	Pickup	㉑	Shim	㉒	㉓	㉔	Shim	—
1986½	200SX	Integral	Shim	.005–.007	Adjusting Spacer & Washer	⑱	Shim	—
	Pickup	①	⑤	⑯	㉘	㉙	⑤	—
1987	200SX	Integral	Shim	.005–.007	Adjusting Spacer & Washer	⑱	Shim	—
	300ZX	Integral	Shim	.005–.007	Adjusting Spacer & Washer	㉕	Shim	—
	Pathfinder	Shim	⑤	⑯	㉚	㉙	Shim	—
	Pickup	①	⑤	⑯	㉘	㉙	⑤	—
	Sentra ㉗	Integral	Shim	.004–.008	Adjusting Spacer & Washer	㉛	Shim	—
	Stanza ㉗	Integral	Shim	.005–.007	Adjusting Spacer & Washer	㉖	Shim	—
	Van	Integral	Shim	.005–.007	Collapsible Spacer	㉜	Shim	—

① —4WD w/Z24i engine, integral; exc. 4WD w/Z24i engine, removable.

② —Differential carrier model R180, adjusting spacer and washer; model H190-ML, collapsible spacer.

③ —Differential carrier model R180 with seal installed, 7.8–14.8; with seal removed, 8.7–11.3; model H190-ML with seal installed, 9.5–13.9; with seal removed, 6.1–13.0.

④ —2WD, removable; 4WD, front, integral; rear, removable.

⑤ —With VG30i engine, threaded adjuster; with Z24i engine, shim.

⑥ —With seal installed, 9.5–13.9; with seal removed, 6.1–13.0.

⑦ —Differential carrier model R180, .005–.007; models H190-ML, H190-A, .006–.008.

⑧ —Sedan and hardtop, integral type; wagon, removable type.

⑨ —Differential carrier model H-190-ML, .006–.008; model R200, .005–.007.

⑩ —Differential carrier model R180, solid spacer and washer; models H190-ML, H190-A, collapsible spacer.

⑪ —Differential carrier model H-190-ML, collapsible spacer; model R200, adjusting spacer and washer.

⑫ —Measured with spring scale off of ring gear bolt.

⑬ —Differential carrier model H190-ML with seal installed, 9.5–13.9. Model R200 with seal removed, 8.7–11.3; with seal installed, 10.0–15.2.

⑭ —Differential carrier model R180, .004–.008; model H190-ML, .006–.008.

⑮ —Differential carrier model R180, .004–.008; model R200, .005–.007.

⑯ —VG30i engine, .006–.008; Z24i engine, .005–.007

⑰ —Differential carrier model R180 with seal installed, 7.8–14.8; with seal removed, 8.7–11.3. Models H190-ML, H190-A with seal installed, 9.5–13.9; with seal removed, 6.1–13.0.

⑱ —Differential carrier model R180 with seal installed, 7.8–14.8; with seal removed, 8.7–11.3 Model R200 with seal installed, 10.0–15.2; with seal removed, 8.7–11.3.

⑲ —Differential carrier model R180, 4.0–6.6; models H190-ML, H190-A, 3.7–6.2.

⑳ —Turbocharged, integral; non-turbocharged, removable.

㉑ —2WD with single rear wheels, removable; 2WD with dual rear wheels and 4WD, integral.

㉒ —Differential carrier models R180 and C200, .005–.007; models H190A and H190-ML, .006–.008.

㉓ —Differential carrier model R180, solid spacer and washer; models C200, H190A and H190-ML, collapsible spacer.

㉔ —Differential carrier models R180, 7.8–14.8; models H190A and H190-ML, 9.5–13.9; model C200, 9.5–14.8. All with seal installed.

㉕ —With seal removed, 8.7–11.3; with seal installed, 10.0–15.2.

㉖ —With seal removed, 8.7–11.3; with seal installed, 7.8–14.8.

㉗ —4WD Wagon.

㉘ —VG30i engine, Adjusting Spacer & Washer; Z24i engine, Collapsible Spacer.

㉙ —With seal installed: VG30i engine, 4.3–8.7; Z24i engine w/2WD, 9.5–13.9; Z24i engine w/4WD, 9.5–14.8.

㉚ —VG30i engine, removable; Z24i engine, integral.

㉛ —With seal installed, 6.5–13.5.

㉜ —With seal installed, 9.5–14.8.

Cooling System & Capacity Data

Year	Model	Cooling Cap. Qts.	Radiator, Cap Relief Pressure Lbs.	Thermo. Opening Temp.	Fuel Tank Gals.	Engine Oil Refill Qts. (3)	Transmission Oil: Manual Trans. Pt.	Transmission Oil: Auto. Trans. Qts. (34)	Rear Axle Oil Pints
1983	200SX	10	13	180	(19)	4 1/2	4 1/4	5 7/8	2 1/8
	280ZX	(17)	13	180	21 1/8	(30)	(31)	5 7/8	(14)
	Maxima	(5)	13	180	(26)	(6)	4 1/4	7 3/8	2 1/8
	Pulsar	(32)	13	180	13 1/4	4 1/8	5 3/4	6 3/8	—
	Sentra	(29)	13	180	13 1/4	4 1/8	(1)	6 3/8	—
	Stanza	(33)	13	180	14 1/4	4 1/8	5 3/4	6 3/8	—
	Pickup	(27)	13	180	(16) (24)	(35)	(2)	5 7/8	(25)
1984	200SX	9 1/8	13	180	14	4	4 1/4	7 3/8	(4)
	300ZX	(7)	14	170	19	4 1/4	4	7 3/8	2 3/4
	Maxima	11 5/8	13	180	(26)	5 1/4	4 1/4	7 3/8	2 1/8
	Pulsar	(29)	13	180	13 1/4	3 7/8	5 3/4	6 3/8	—
	Sentra	(29) (38)	13	180	(39)	(40)	(1)	6 3/8	—
	Stanza	(33)	13	180	14 1/4	4 1/8	5 3/4	6 3/8	—
	Pickup	(9)	13	180	(16) (24)	(36)	4 1/4	5 7/8	(25) (37)
1985	200SX	9 1/8	13	180	14	3 7/8	4 1/2	7 3/8	(4)
	300ZX	(7)	14	170	19	4 1/4	4	7 3/8	2 3/4
	Maxima	9 3/4	14	170	15 7/8	4 1/2	10	7 3/8	—
	Pulsar	(29)	13	180	13 1/4	3 3/8	5 3/4	6 3/8	—
	Sentra	(29) (38)	13	(10)	(39)	(41)	(1)	6 3/8	—
	Stanza	(33)	13	180	14 1/4	3 5/8	5 3/4	6 3/8	—
	Pickup	(9)	13	180	(16) (24)	(42)	4 1/2	5 7/8	(25) (37)
1986	200SX	9 1/8	13	180	14	3 7/8	4 1/2	7 3/8	(4)
	300ZX	(7)	14	170	19	4 1/4	4	7 3/8	2 3/4
	Maxima	9 3/4	13	170	15 7/8	4 1/2	10	7 3/8	—
	Pulsar	(29)	13	180	13 1/4	3 3/8	5 3/4	6 3/8	—
	Sentra	(29) (38)	13	(10)	(39)	(41)	(1)	6 3/8	—
	Stanza (13)	(33)	13	180	14 1/4	3 3/4	5 3/4	6 3/8	—
	Stanza (8)	7 1/8	13	180	15 7/8	3 3/4	10	(15)	2 1/8 (43)
	Pickup	(9)	13	180	(16) (24)	(42)	4 1/2	5 7/8	(25) (37)
1986 1/2	200SX	9 1/8	13	180	14	3 7/8	4 1/4	7 3/8	(4)
	Pickup	(11)	13	190	(12)	(18)	(20)	7 3/8	(21)
1987	200SX	(22)	13	180	14	(23)	4 1/4	7 3/8	(4)
	300ZX	(7)	13	170	19	4 1/4	4 1/4	7 3/8	2 3/4
	Maxima	9 3/4	13	170	15 7/8	4 1/2	5	7 3/4	—
	Pathfinder	(11)	13	(28)	15 7/8	(18)	(20)	7 7/8	(21)
	Pickup	(11)	13	(28)	15 7/8	(18)	(20)	(44)	(21)
	Pulsar	(45)	13	180	13 1/4	(46)	5 3/4	6 5/8	—
	Sentra	(47)	13	180	13 3/4	3 3/8	5 3/4	5 1/2	—
	Sentra (43)	4 7/8	13	182	12 3/8	3 3/8	5 3/4	—	2 1/8
	Stanza (13)	7 3/4	—	190	15 7/8	3 3/4	10	7 1/4	—
	Stanza (8)	7 1/8	13	180	(48)	3 3/4	10	7 1/4	2 1/8 (43)
	Van	9 5/8	13	190	17 1/8	4 3/8	4 1/4	7 3/8	2 3/4

Continued

COOLING SYSTEM & CAPACITY DATA—Continued

①—4 speed, 4 7/8 pts.; 5 speed, 5 3/4 pts.
②—4 speed, 3 5/8 pts.; 5 speed, 4 1/4 pts.
③—Includes filter.
④—Differential carrier R200, 2 3/4 pts.; H190 or R180, 2 1/8 pts.
⑤—Gasoline engine, 11 5/8 qts.; diesel engine, 11 qts.
⑥—Gasoline engine, 5 1/4 qts.; diesel engine, 6 1/2 qts.
⑦—Turbocharged, 11 5/8 qts.; non-turbocharged, 11 1/8 qts.
⑧—Wagon model.
⑨—Gasoline engine with manual trans., 10 3/4 pts.; with auto. trans., 10 qts. Diesel Engine, 11 1/8 qts.
⑩—Gasoline engine, 180; diesel engine, 190.
⑪—VG30i engine, 10 1/2 qts.; Z24i engine, 8 5/8 qts.
⑫—Heavy duty & King Cab models w/VG30i engine, 21 1/8 gal.; exc. heavy duty & King Cab models w/VG30i engine, 15 7/8 gal.
⑬—Exc. Wagon.
⑭—Differential carrier R-200, 2 3/4 pts.; R180, 2 1/8 pts.
⑮—2WD, 6 7/8 qts.; 4WD, 7 1/4 qts.
⑯—Standard wheelbase, 13 1/4 gals.; long wheelbase, 16 7/8 gals.
⑰—With reservoir, 11 1/8 pts.; without reservoir, 10 1/4 qts.
⑱—2WD: VG30i engine, 4 1/4 qts.; Z24i engine, 4 qts. 4WD: VG30i engine, 3 5/8 qts.; Z24i engine, 4 1/2 qts.
⑲—Hardtop, 14 gals.; hatchback, 15 7/8 gals.
⑳—2WD: FS5W71C trans., 4 1/4 pts.; FS5R30A trans., 5 1/8 pts. 4WD: FS5W71C trans., 8 1/2 pts.; FS5R30A trans., 7 5/8 pts.
㉑—Model H190A, 3 1/8 pts.; model C200, 2 3/4 pts.; model H233B, 5 7/8 pts. 4WD front units: model R180A, 2 3/4 pts.; model R200A, 3 1/8 pts.
㉒—CA20E engine, 9 1/8 qts.; VG30E engine, 9 5/8 qts.
㉓—CA20E engine, 3 7/8 qts.; VG30E engine, 4 1/2 qts.
㉔—Standard wheelbase 4WD, 15 7/8 gals.; long wheelbase 4WD 19 7/8 gals.
㉕—Rear axle, 2 5/8 pts.; front axle (4WD), 2 1/8 pts.
㉖—Exc. wagon, 16 3/8 gals.; wagon, 15 7/8 gals.
㉗—Gasoline engine with manual trans., 10 3/4 pts.; with auto. trans., 10 5/8 qts. Diesel engine, 10 1/2 qts.
㉘—VG30i engine, 155°F.; Z24i engine, 180°F.
㉙—Gasoline engine: Manual trans., 5 qts.; auto. trans., 5 5/8 qts.
㉚—Turbocharged, 5 1/2 qts.; non-turbocharged, 4 3/4 qts.
㉛—Model FS5W71B, 4 1/4 pts.; model FS5R90A, 4 pts.
㉜—Manual trans., 5 3/4 qts.; auto. trans., 6 3/8 qts.
㉝—Manual trans., 7 1/8 qts.; auto. trans., 7 1/2 qts.
㉞—Approximate, make final check with dipstick.
㉟—Gasoline engine: 2WD, 4 5/8 qts.; 4WD, 4 1/2 qts. Diesel engine, 5 1/2 qts.
㊱—Gasoline engine: 2WD, 4 3/8 qts.; 4WD, 4 1/2 qts. Diesel engine, 5 3/8 qts.
㊲—Dual wheel models, 2 3/4 pts.
㊳—Diesel engine, 7 3/8 qts.
㊴—Gasoline engine, 13 1/4 gals.; diesel engine, 10 5/8 gals.
㊵—Gasoline engine, 5 7/8 qts.; diesel engine, 4 3/8 qts.
㊶—Gasoline engine, 3 3/8 qts.; diesel engine, 4 1/4 qts.
㊷—Gasoline engine: 2WD, 3 7/8 qts.; 4WD, 4 1/4 qts. Diesel engine, 5 5/8 qts.
㊸—4WD models.
㊹—L3N71B trans., 7 7/8 qts.; exc. L3N71B trans., 7 3/8 qts.
㊺—Auto. trans., 5 1/2 qts.; man. trans.: CA16DE engine, 5 7/8 qts.; E16i engine, 4 7/8 qts.
㊻—CA16DE engine, 3 3/4 qts.; E16i engine, 3 3/8 qts.
㊼—Man. trans., 4 7/8 qts.; auto. trans., 5 1/2 qts.
㊽—2WD, 15 7/8 gal.; 4WD, 13 1/4 gal.

ELECTRICAL SECTION

INDEX

ALTERNATOR TESTING

1. Turn ignition switch to on position and note charge lamp.
2. If lamp lights proceed to step 7. If lamp does not light proceed to next step.
3. Disconnect two wire connectors labeled S and L, then using a jumper wire connect L terminal to a suitable ground.
4. If charge lamp lights proceed to next step. If lamp does not light the bulb in the instrument cluster is defective. **Steps 5 and 6 do not apply to 300ZX and Pulsar models equipped with Mitsubishi alternator. On these models, if charge lamp lights, the internal regulator or some other internal component is defective and the alternator must be removed for bench testing.**
5. Reconnect two wire connectors, then insert a short stiff length of wire through the access hole at back of alternator until it contacts outer brush. Ground other end of wire to alternator case which will actually ground the F terminal internally, **Fig. 1. On diesel models, except 1983-86 Sentra and 1984-86 Pickup, to ground F terminal, contact tip of brush with a screwdriver, then ground screwdriver to alternator case. On 1983-86 Sentra diesel and 1984-86 Pickup models, remove vacuum pump, then using a suitable length of wire, make contact with brush and ground opposite end of wire to alternator case.**
6. If charge lamp remains lit, the internal regulator is defective and will require disassembly of the alternator for repair. If lamp goes out, some other internal component is defective therefore alternator must be removed for bench testing.

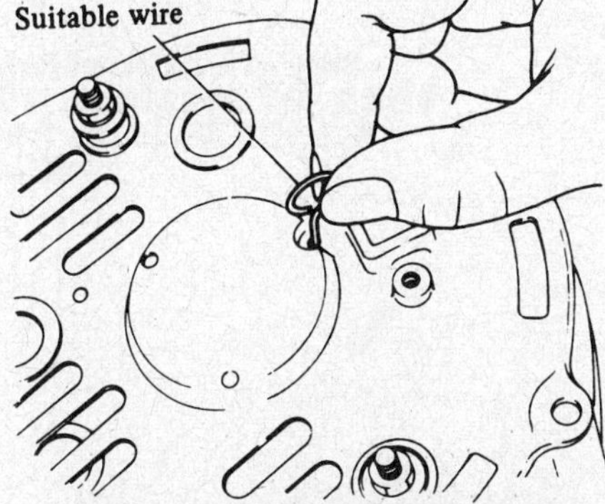

Fig. 1 Grounding field circuit to test alternator output

7. With engine idling if charge lamp is lit, a defective internal component exists in the alternator and requires removal for bench testing. If the charge lamp is not lit, proceed to next step.
8. With engine speed at 1500 RPM and headlights on, if charge lamp is not lit proceed to next step. If lamp is lit dimly, let engine idle and measure voltage across B and L terminals. If voltage is more than .5 volts a defective internal component exists in the alternator and requires removal for bench testing. **If voltage is less than .5 volts, alternator if considered to be in satisfactory condition.**
9. With engine at 1500 RPM measure voltage at B terminal, making sure S terminal is properly connected.
10. If voltage reading is above 15.5 volts, the internal regulator is faulty and requires removal of alternator for replacement. If voltage reading is between 13 and 15 volts proceed to next step.
11. With engine idling and headlights on, if charge lamp is lit a defective internal component exists in the alternator and requires removal for bench testing. If charge lamp is not lit, alternator is considered to be in satisfactory condition.

STARTER
REPLACE

1. Disconnect battery ground cable.
2. Disconnect starter wiring from starter.
3. Remove starter retaining bolts and the starter.
4. Reverse procedure to install.

IGNITION SWITCH
REPLACE

1. Remove the four upper and lower shell cover retaining screws, then the shell covers.
2. Disconnect electrical connectors from switch.
3. Remove switch retaining screw from steering lock, **Fig. 2.**
4. Remove switch.
5. Reverse procedure to install.

IGNITION LOCK
REPLACE

The ignition lock is retained by two shear type screws, **Fig. 3.** It is necessary to drill out these screws to remove ignition lock from steering tube. When installing,

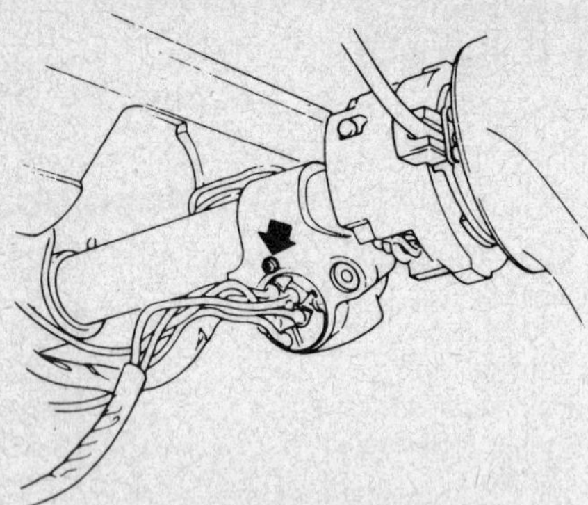

Fig. 2 Ignition switch replacement

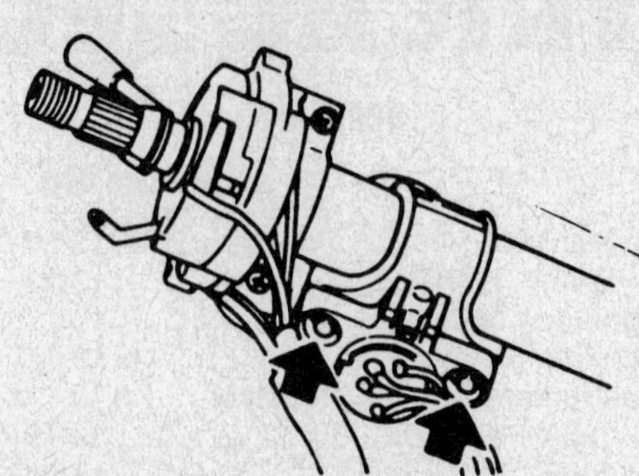

Fig. 3 Ignition lock replacement

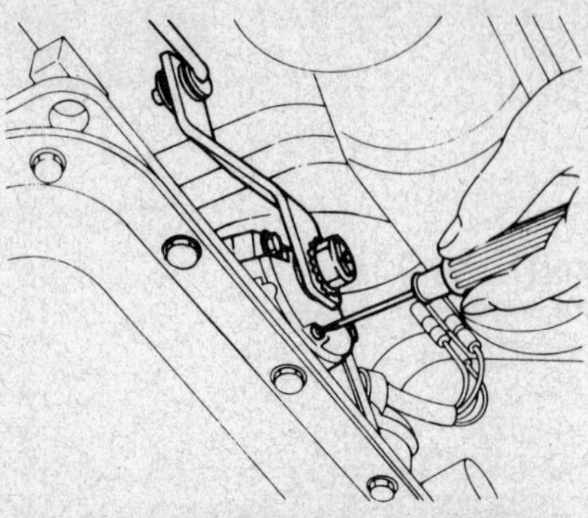

Fig. 4 Adjusting inhibitor switch. 200SX, 280ZX, 300ZX, Pathfinder, Pickup, Van & 1982–84 Maxima

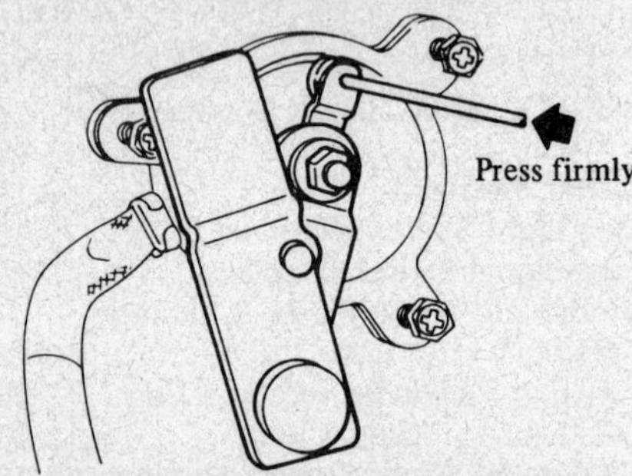

Fig. 5 Adjusting inhibitor switch. 1983–85 Stanza exc. Wagon, Sentra & Pulsar

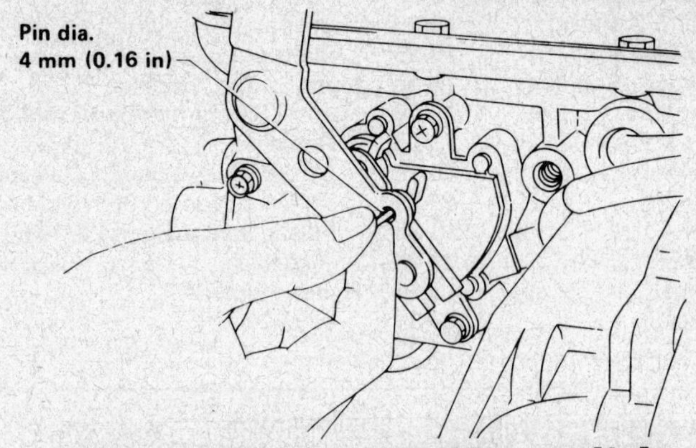

Fig. 6 Adjusting inhibitor switch. 1985–87 Maxima, 1986–87 Stanza Wagon & 1987 Pulsar, Sentra & Stanza exc. Wagon

ensure that the shear type screws are used.

NEUTRAL SAFETY (INHIBITOR) SWITCH

ADJUST

200SX, 280ZX, 300ZX, PATHFINDER, PICKUP, VAN & 1983–84 MAXIMA

1. Place manual valve in Neutral (vertical position).
2. Remove adjustment cover screw, **Fig. 4.**
3. Loosen switch attaching screws.
4. Using suitable alignment pin, move switch until pin falls into hole in rotor.
5. Tighten attaching bolts, then check switch for continuity, replacing as necessary.

PULSAR, SENTRA, STANZA & 1985–87 MAXIMA

1. Loosen inhibitor switch attaching screws, **Figs. 5 through 7.**
2. Set selector lever manual shaft at Neutral position.
3. Insert suitable pin into adjustment holes in both inhibitor switch and switch lever as near vertical as possible, then tighten screws.
4. Check switch for continuity, replacing as necessary.

STOP LIGHT SWITCH

REPLACE

The stop light switch is located on the

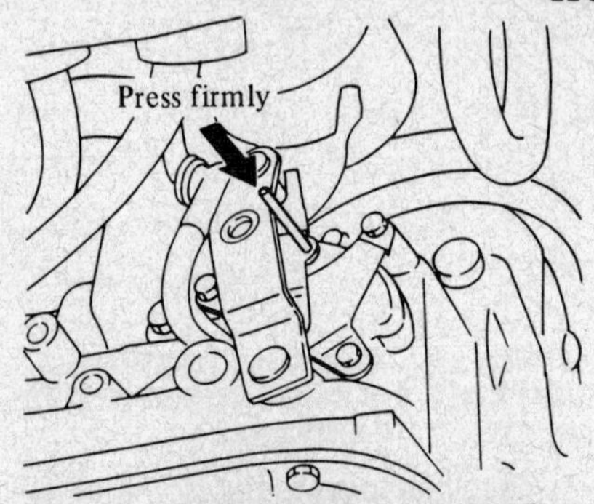

Fig. 7 Adjusting inhibitor switch. 1986 Pulsar, Sentra & Stanza Wagon

brake pedal support.

1. Disconnect the switch electrical connectors.
2. Loosen switch retaining locknut and remove switch.
3. Reverse procedure to install.

LIGHT SWITCH

REPLACE

Refer to "Combination Switch, Replace". It is not necessary to remove combination switch base to replace light switch.

TURN SIGNAL SWITCH

REPLACE

Refer to "Combination Switch, Replace".

COMBINATION SWITCH

REPLACE

1. Disconnect battery ground cable.
2. Remove horn cover and steering wheel.
3. Remove steering column shell covers.
4. Disconnect switch electrical connections.
5. Remove retaining screw and switch.
6. Reverse procedure to install.

WINDSHIELD WIPER SWITCH

REPLACE

Refer to the "Combination Switch, Replace" procedure for wiper switch replacement. It is not necessary to remove combination switch base to remove windshield wiper switch.

REAR WIPER SWITCH

REPLACE

280ZX & MAXIMA

1. Disconnect battery ground cable.
2. On 810 models, remove cluster lid as outlined under "Instrument Cluster, Replace".
3. Disconnect electrical connector from switch.

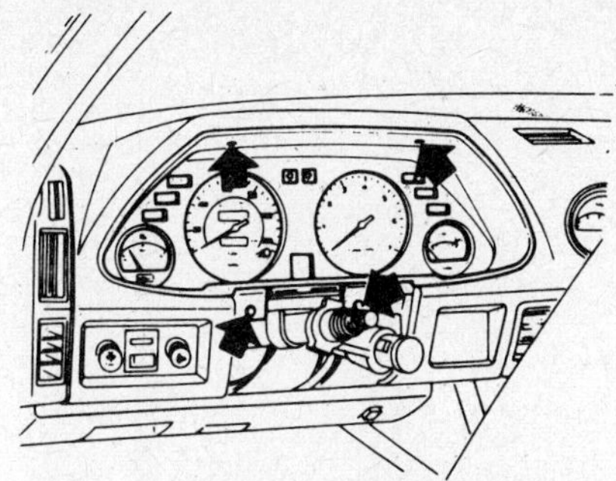

Fig. 8 Cluster retaining screws. 280ZX

4. Remove switch knob by depressing and twisting.
5. Remove switch retaining nut and switch.
6. Reverse procedure to install.

200SX

1. Disconnect battery ground cable.
2. Disconnect electrical connector from switch.
3. Remove switch retaining screw and switch.
4. Reverse procedure to install.

300ZX, PULSAR, SENTRA, STANZA & VAN

1. Disconnect battery ground cable.
2. Reach under instrument panel and disconnect multi-pin connector from rear of switch.
3. Depress two switch retaining clips and push switch out of panel.
4. Reverse procedure to install.

INSTRUMENT CLUSTER REPLACE

1983–87 200SX

1. Disconnect battery ground cable.
2. Remove steering column cover and steering wheel.
3. Remove lower left instrument panel cover.
4. Remove cluster lid retaining screws and remove cluster lid.
5. Disconnect speedometer cable by pushing connector cap and turning counterclockwise. Remove cluster retaining screws.
6. Disconnect electrical connections and remove cluster.
7. Reverse procedure to install.

1983–87 MAXIMA

1. Disconnect battery ground cable.
2. Remove steering wheel, shell cover, and combination switch.
3. Remove screws securing cluster lid "A" and remove cluster lid.
4. Disconnect electrical connectors and speedometer cable from instrument cluster.
5. On 1985-87 Maxima models, remove lower cluster lid attaching screws and the lid.
6. On all models, remove instrument cluster attaching screws and the cluster.

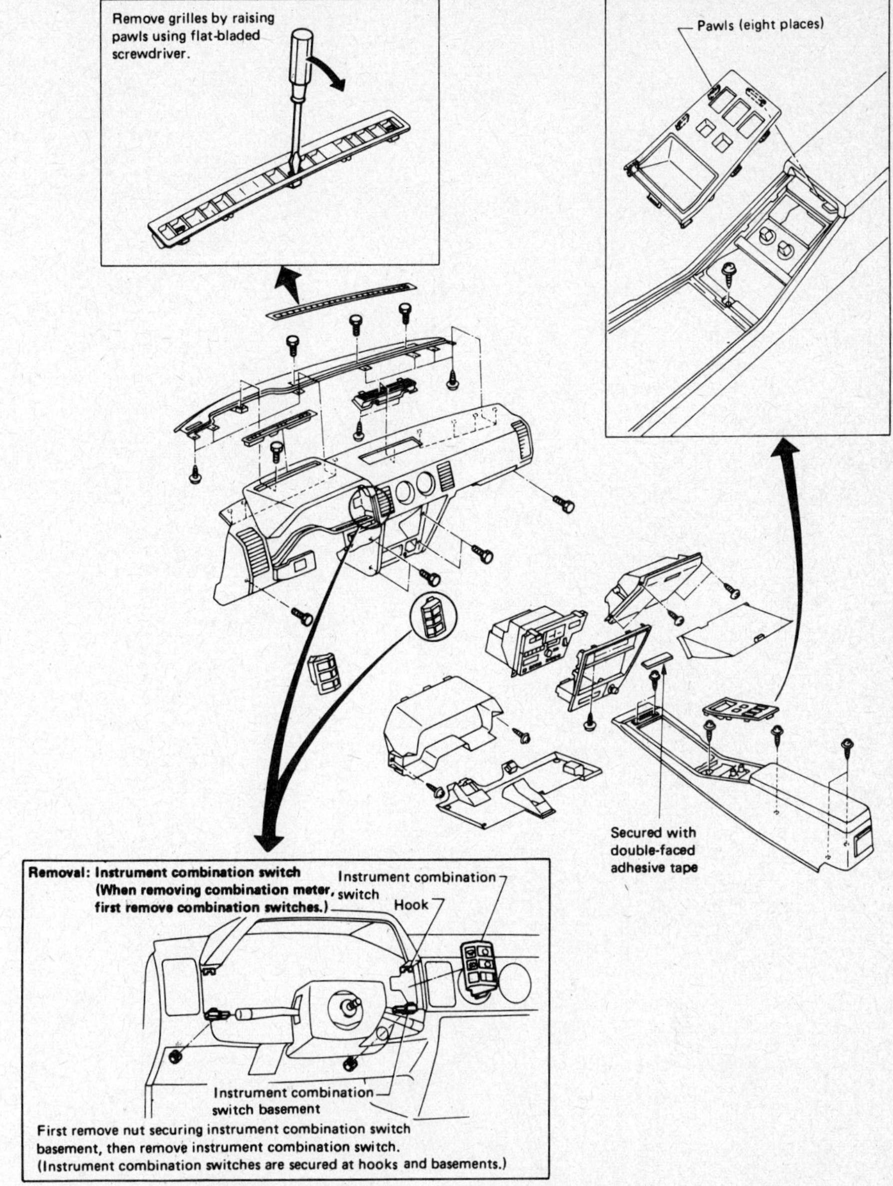

Fig. 9 Instrument panel exploded view. 300ZX

7. Reverse procedure to install.

280ZX

1. Disconnect battery ground cable.
2. Remove steering wheel and steering column cover.
3. Remove lower left instrument panel cover.
4. Disconnect speedometer cable at intermediate connection.
5. Disconnect electrical connections and remove combination switch.
6. Remove cluster retaining screws and carefully pull out instrument cluster, **Fig. 8.**
7. Disconnect electrical connections and remove instrument cluster.
8. To install, reverse procedure.

300ZX

1. Disconnect battery ground cable.
2. Disconnect electrical connectors from combination switch, **Fig. 9.**
3. Remove combination switch attaching screws and the switch.
4. Remove instrument cluster attaching screws and carefully pull cluster back to provide access to electrical connectors.
5. Disconnect electrical connectors from cluster and remove cluster from vehicle.
6. Reverse procedure to install.

PULSAR

1. Disconnect battery ground cable.
2. Remove steering column covers.
3. Remove instrument cluster lid "A" attaching screws, then the cluster lid, **Figs. 10 and 11.**
4. Remove instrument cluster attaching screws, then pull the cluster back just far enough to provide access to electrical connectors and speedometer cable.
5. Disconnect speedometer cable and

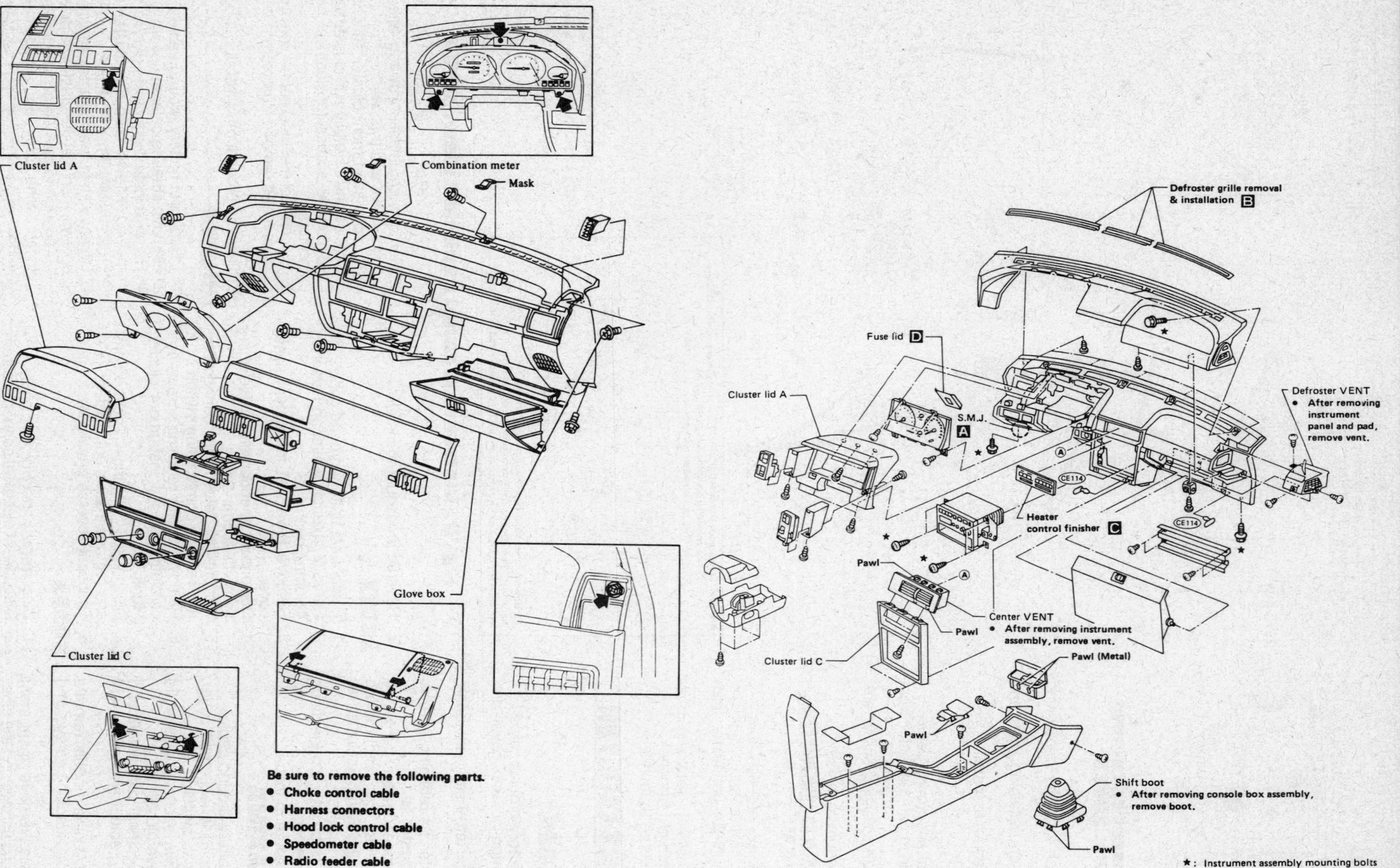

Fig. 10 Instrument panel exploded view. 1983–86 Pulsar

Fig. 11 Instrument panel exploded view. 1987 Pulsar

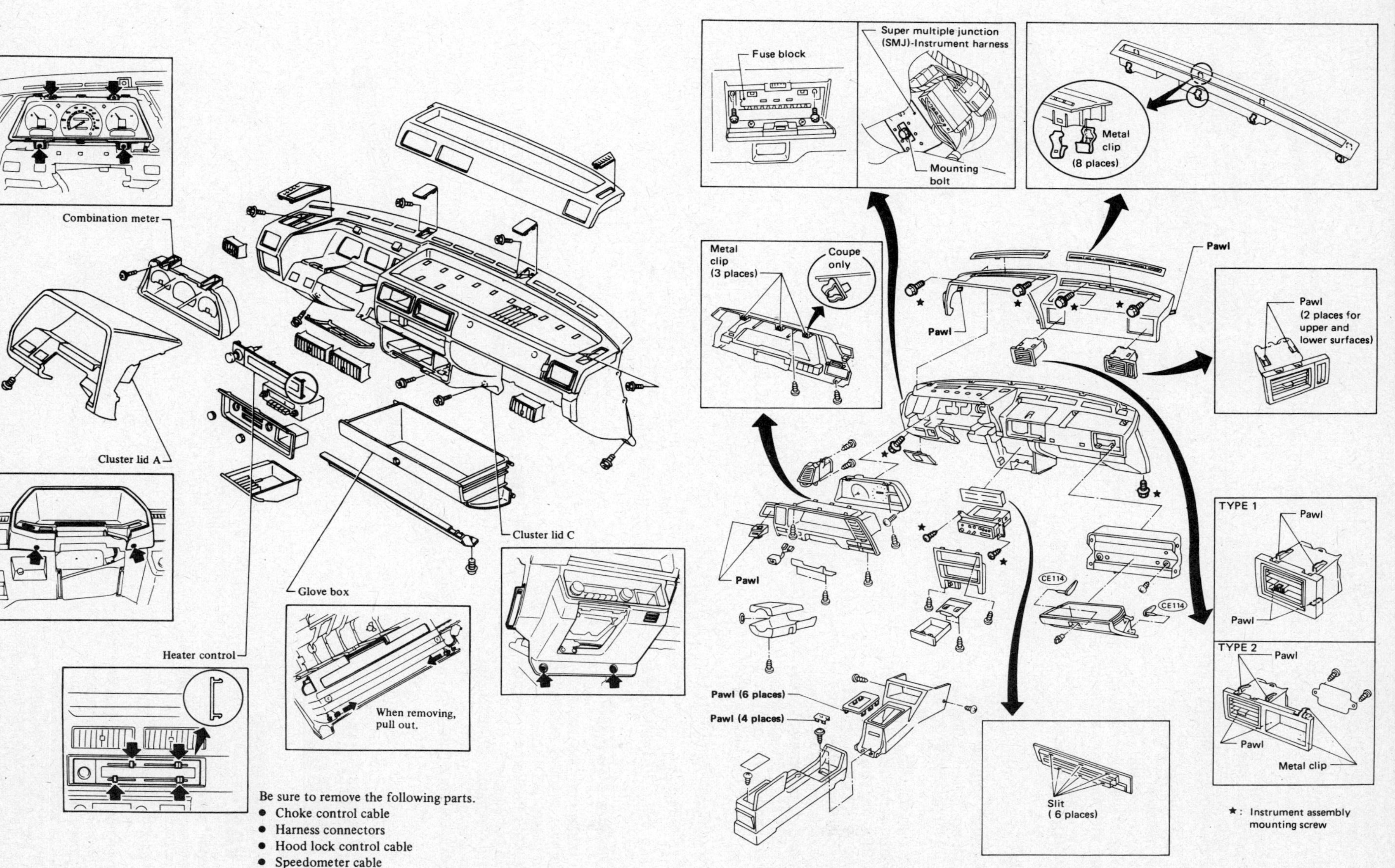

Fig. 12 Exploded view of instrument panel. 1983–86 Sentra

Fig. 13 Exploded view of instrument panel. 1987 Sentra

electrical connectors from instrument cluster, then remove the cluster from vehicle.
6. Reverse procedure to install.

SENTRA

1. Disconnect battery ground cable.
2. Remove steering column covers.
3. Remove screws securing cluster lid "A", then remove the cluster lid, **Fig. 12 and 13.**
4. Disconnect electrical connectors from combination meter.
5. Disconnect speedometer cable.
6. Remove combination meter retaining screws, then the combination meter, **Fig. 16.**
7. Reverse procedure to install.

STANZA

Exc. Wagon

1. Disconnect battery ground cable.
2. Loosen steering tilt adjusting lever and lower steering column as far as possible.
3. Remove steering column cover.
4. Remove instrument cluster lid attaching screws, then the cluster lid.
5. Remove instrument cluster attaching screws, then pull the cluster back just enough to provide access to electrical connectors and speedometer cable.
6. Disconnect electrical connectors and speedometer cable from instrument cluster, then remove the cluster from vehicle.
7. Reverse procedure to install.

Wagon

Refer to **Fig. 14** for instrument cluster removal on these models.

PATHFINDER & PICKUP

1. Disconnect battery ground cable.
2. Remove screws holding cluster lid and remove cluster lid.
3. Remove cluster retaining screws and carefully pull out cluster.
4. Disconnect electrical connections and remove cluster.
5. To install, reverse procedure.

WINDSHIELD WIPER MOTOR & LINKAGE REPLACE

ALL EXC. PATHFINDER, PICKUP & VAN

1. Remove wiper arms by raising the arms off the glass and removing locknut.
2. Disconnect electrical connector from motor.
3. Remove top grille retaining screws and top grille, where possible, to gain access to wiper linkage.
4. Remove wiper motor mounting bolts.
5. Pull motor away from firewall if necessary to gain access. Disconnect motor shaft from linkage taking care not to bend linkage.

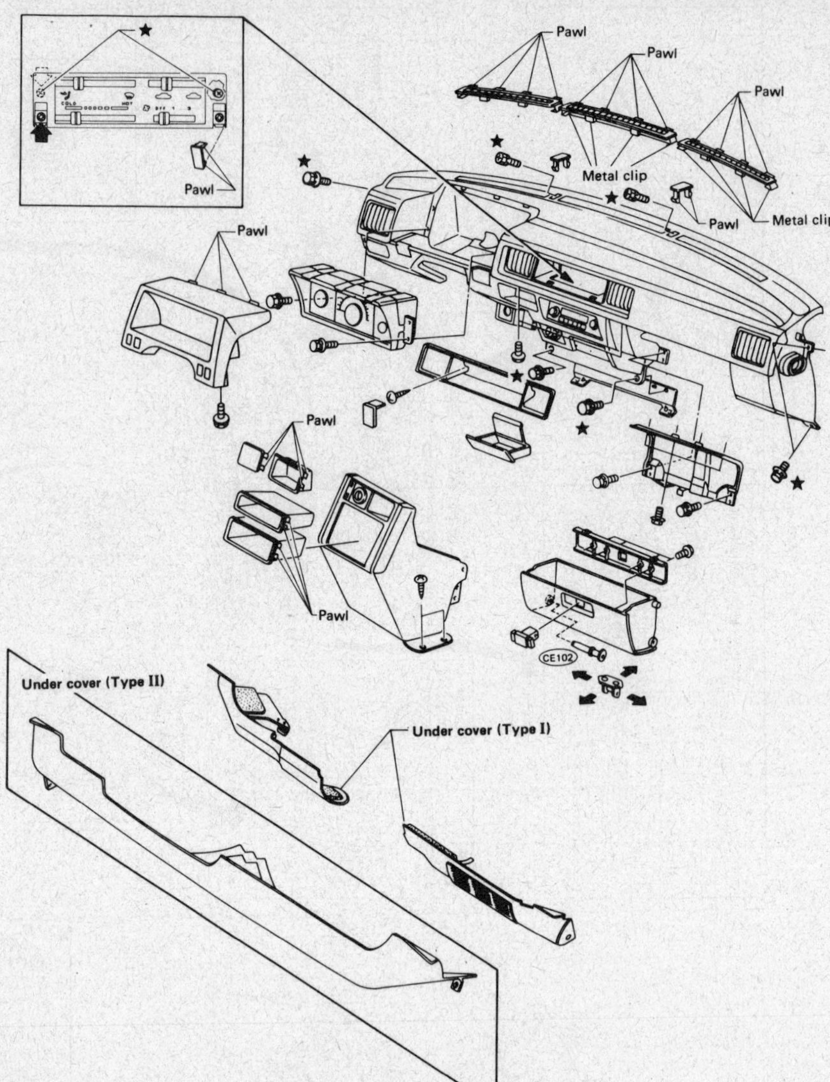

Fig. 14 Instrument panel exploded view. 1986–87 Stanza wagon

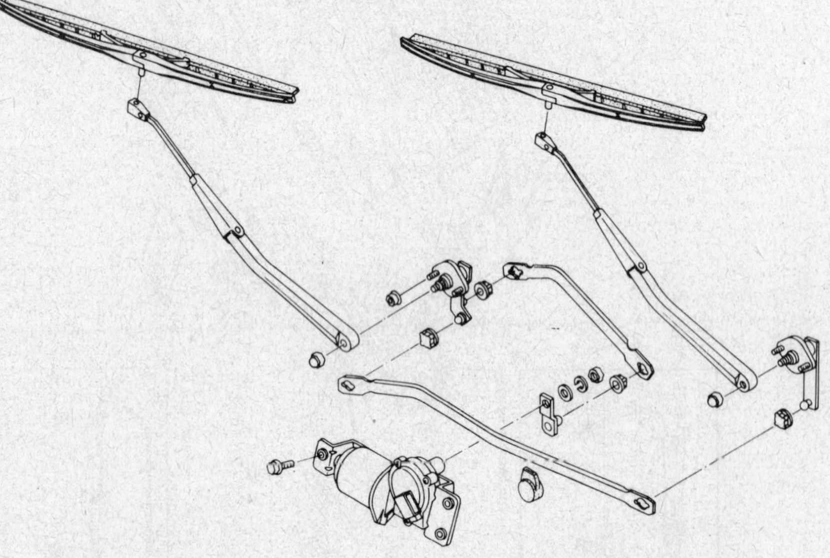

Fig. 15 Windshield wiper system (typical)

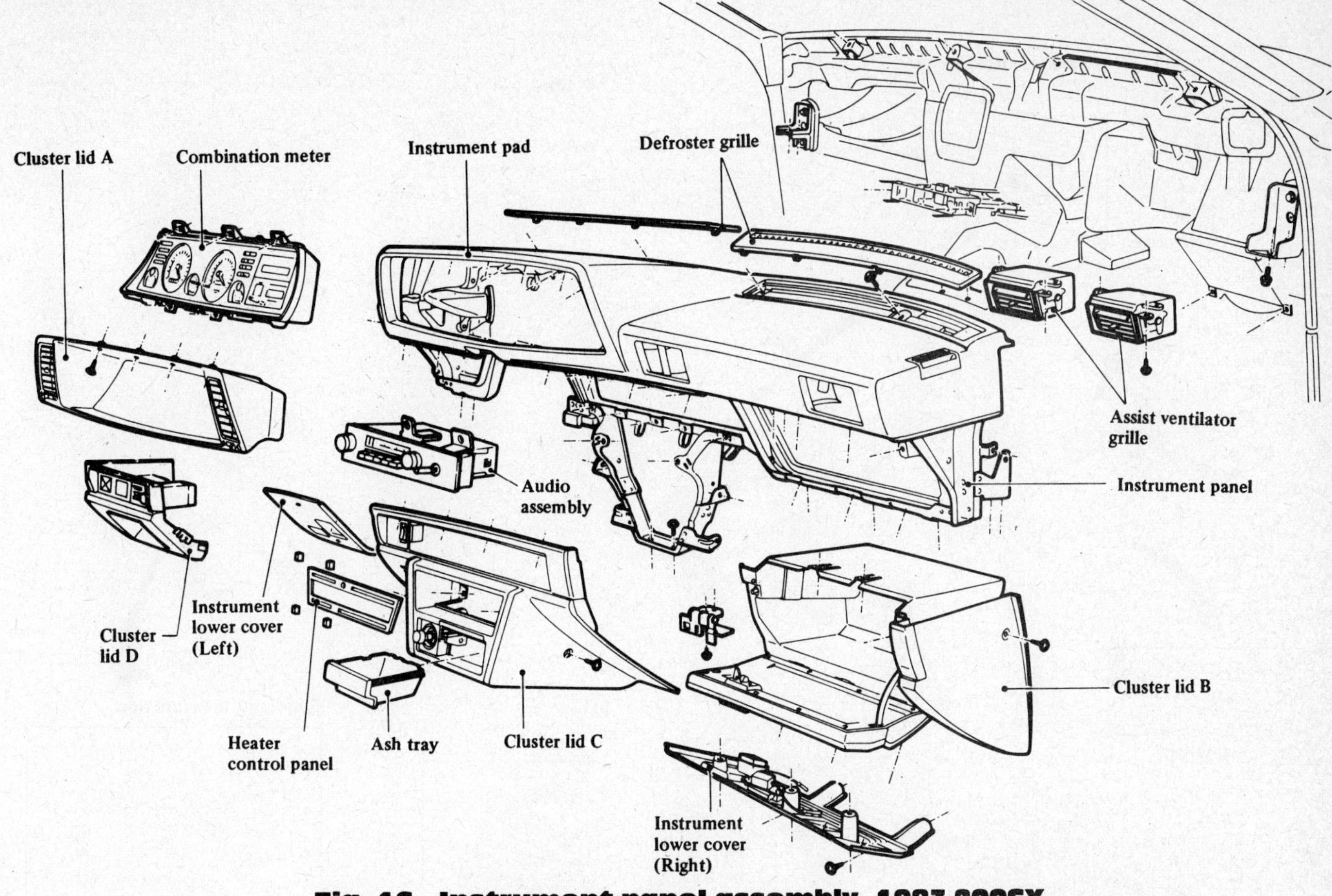

Fig. 16 Instrument panel assembly. 1983 200SX

6. Remove wiper motor.
7. Remove flange nuts or screws holding pivot to top cowl panel and remove linkage. To install, reverse procedure, See **Fig. 15** for typical installation.

PATHFINDER, PICKUP & VAN

1. Remove wiper arms.
2. Remove cowl top grille.
3. Remove stop ring connecting wiper motor arm to connecting rod.
4. Disconnect wiper motor electrical connector from beneath instrument panel.
5. Remove wiper motor retaining bolts and the wiper motor.
6. Remove flange nuts retaining pivot to cowl top.
7. Remove wiper motor linkage.
8. Reverse procedure to install.

REAR WIPER MOTOR

REPLACE

1. Disconnect battery ground cable.
2. To remove, raise rear wiper arm off glass and remove retaining nut.
3. Remove tailgate inner trim panel, if necessary, and disconnect electrical connection at motor.
4. Remove wiper motor retaining bolts.
5. Remove wiper motor.
6. To install, reverse procedure.

RADIO

REPLACE

1983 200SX

1. Disconnect battery ground cable.
2. Remove screws securing cluster lid C to instrument panel and then remove cluster lid C, **Fig. 16.**
3. Remove radio knobs and stem nuts, then the radio bracket, if equipped.
4. Disconnect electrical connectors from radio and remove radio.
5. Reverse procedure to install.

1984–87 200SX

1. Disconnect battery ground cable.
2. Refer to **Fig. 17** for remainder of replacement procedure.

MAXIMA

1. Disconnect battery ground cable.
2. Remove cluster lid as outlined under "Instrument Cluster, Replace" procedure for Maxima models. On 1983-87 models, remove lower right trim panel.
3. Remove radio bracket to instrument panel attaching screw.
4. Disconnect electrical leads from radio.
5. Remove radio from vehicle.
6. Reverse procedure to install.

280ZX

1. Disconnect battery ground cable.
2. Remove lower instrument cover and instrument console.
3. Remove knobs, dials, stem nuts, and escutcheons from radio.
4. Remove screws retaining radio in console.
5. Disconnect electrical connectors, then remove radio.
6. Reverse procedure to install.

300ZX

1. Disconnect battery ground cable.
2. Remove radio knobs and trim panel.
3. Remove radio attaching bolts, then disconnect electrical connectors and remove radio from vehicle, **Fig. 9.**
4. Reverse procedure to install.

PULSAR & SENTRA

1. Disconnect battery ground cable.
2. Remove ashtray with bracket.
3. Remove radio attaching bolts, then the radio control knobs and trim panel.
4. Disconnect electrical connectors from radio, then remove radio from vehicle.
5. Reverse procedure to install.

STANZA

Exc. Wagon

1. Disconnect battery ground cable.
2. Remove lower center cluster lid from instrument panel.
3. Remove radio attaching screws, then disconnect electrical connectors from radio and remove unit from vehicle.

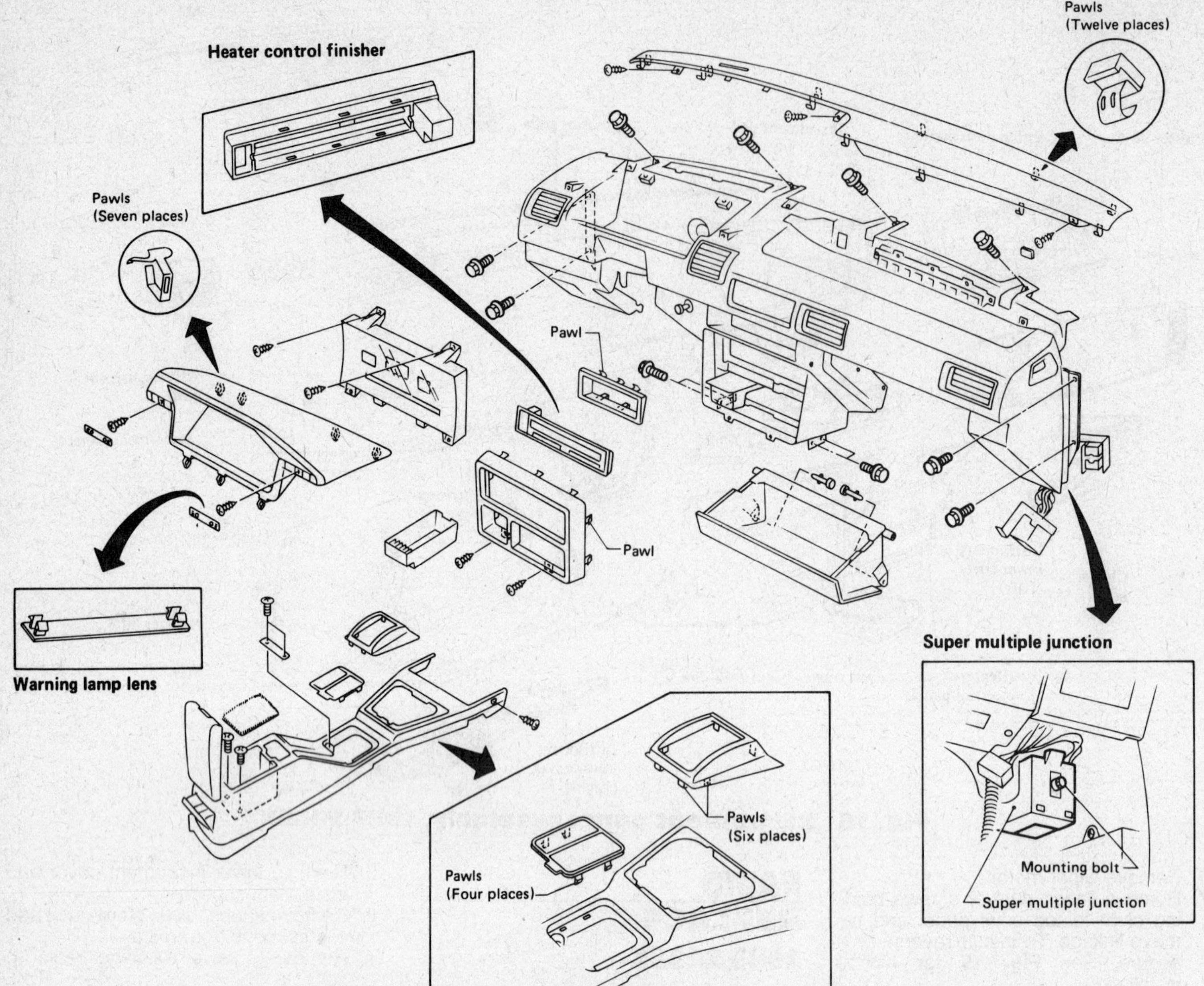

Fig. 17 Instrument panel exploded view. 1984–87 200SX

4. Reverse procedure to install.

Wagon

Refer to **Fig. 14** for radio replacement on these models.

PATHFINDER & PICKUP

1. Disconnect battery ground cable.
2. Remove ash tray and heater/air conditioner control panel.
3. Remove plug in lower dash panel, then the radio retaining screws from underneath unit.
4. Pull radio outward, then disconnect electrical connectors and antenna lead.
5. Reverse procedure to install.

VAN

1. Disconnect battery ground cable.
2. Remove radio knobs and ashtray.
3. Remove radio cover lid attaching screws and lid.
4. Remove radio attaching screws and pull radio forward, then disconnect electrical connectors and antenna lead.
5. Reverse procedure to install.

BLOWER MOTOR REPLACE

1983–84 MAXIMA

1. Disconnect battery ground cable.
2. Remove screws securing RH lower dash and glove box panels and remove panels.
3. Disconnect wiring harness connector and control cable at air intake housing.
4. Remove screws securing air intake housing and remove housing assembly.
5. Remove screws securing blower motor to housing and remove motor.
6. Reverse procedure to install, then adjust control cable.

1985–87 MAXIMA

Refer to **Fig. 18** for blower motor replacement on these models.

1983 200SX

1. Disconnect battery ground cable.
2. Remove screws securing RH lower dash panel and glove box assembly, and remove panels.
3. Disconnect wiring harness connector and control cable at air intake housing.
4. Remove 3 bolts securing air intake housing and remove housing assembly, **Fig. 18.**
5. Remove 3 screws securing blower motor to housing, disconnect vent hose, and remove blower motor.
6. Reverse procedure to install, and adjust air intake door control cable.

1984–87 200SX

Refer to **Fig. 20** for blower motor replacement on these models.

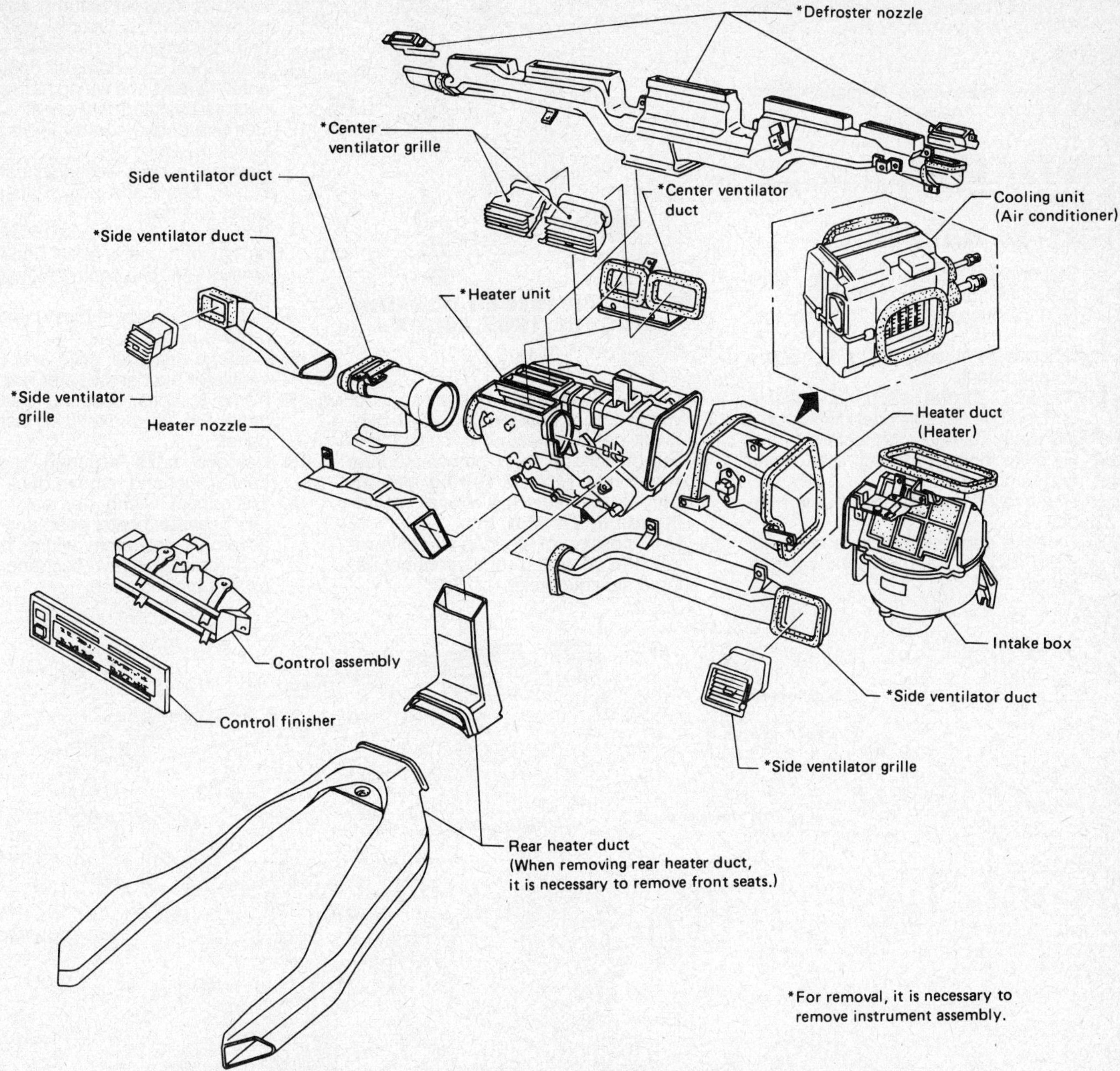

Fig. 18 Heater system exploded view. 1985–87 Maxima

280ZX

1. Disconnect battery ground cable.
2. Remove RH lower dash panel and floor nozzle.
3. Remove RH defroster hose, if needed, and disconnect wiring harness connector to blower motor.
4. Remove screws securing blower motor and remove motor and fan assembly.
5. Reverse procedure to install.

300ZX

Refer to **Fig. 21** for blower motor replacement on these models.

1983–86 PULSAR & SENTRA

1. Disconnect battery ground cable.
2. Remove lower blower housing, then disconnect electrical connector from blower motor.
3. Remove blower motor attaching screws, then the blower motor.
4. Reverse procedure to install.

1987 PULSAR & SENTRA

Refer to "Heater Core, Replace" when replacing blower motor.

STANZA

Exc. Wagon

1. Disconnect battery ground cable.
2. Remove clips securing blower motor cover and pull cover away from motor.
3. Disconnect motor vent tube and wiring harness connector to motor.
4. Remove nuts securing blower motor to housing, push down on blower cover and remove blower motor from engine compartment, **Fig. 22.**

Wagon

Refer to **Fig. 23** for blower motor replacement on these models.

1983–87 PICKUP & 1987 PATHFINDER

1. Disconnect battery ground cable.
2. Remove screws securing package tray and remove tray.
3. On models without A/C, remove duct to heater case.
4. Disconnect control cable and wiring harness connectors to air intake housing.
5. Remove 2 nuts securing air intake housing and remove housing assembly, **Fig. 24.**
6. Remove screws securing blower motor to housing and remove motor and fan assembly.

7. Reverse procedure to install, then adjust air intake control cable.

VAN

Refer to "Heater Core, Replace" under "Van".

HEATER CORE
REPLACE
1983–84 MAXIMA

1. Disconnect battery ground cable, place temperature control lever in HOT position, and drain cooling system.
2. Disconnect heater hoses in engine compartment.
3. Remove screws securing console and remove console after disconnecting wiring harness connectors.
4. Remove bolts securing front seats and remove seats.
5. Remove left and right lower dash panels.
6. Remove door sill moldings and seat belts as needed, then remove front carpet.

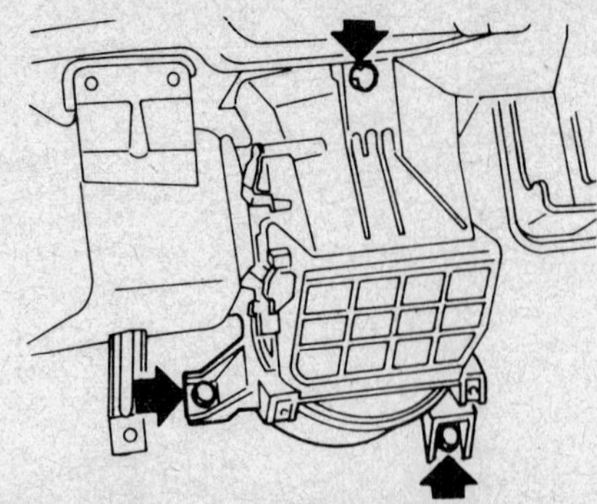

Fig. 19 Air intake housing removal. 1983 200SX

7. Remove fuse block and disconnect wiring harness connectors to junction block, noting position for reassembly.
8. Pull off horn pad and remove steering wheel retaining nut. **During assembly, torque steering wheel retaining nut to 27-38 ft. lbs.**
9. Mark position of steering wheel in relation to shaft and remove wheel using a suitable puller.
10. Remove steering column cover and screws securing combination switch, then disconnect and remove switch.
11. Disconnect speedometer cable, radio antenna lead, and wiring harness connectors to instrument panel.
12. Remove choke control knob and retainer.
13. Remove screws securing instrument cluster bezel and pad, then remove bezel and pad.
14. Pull off A/C-heater control knobs, remove control face plate, and remove screws securing control to instrument panel.
15. Remove screws securing radio and remove radio.
16. Remove defroster grille and LH side ventilator duct and heater nozzle.
17. Remove bolts securing instrument panel, **Fig. 25**, and remove instrument panel.
18. Remove bolts securing rear seat heater duct and remove duct.
19. Disconnect wiring harness connectors between heater case and control assembly and main wiring harness, and remove screw securing heater control ground strap.

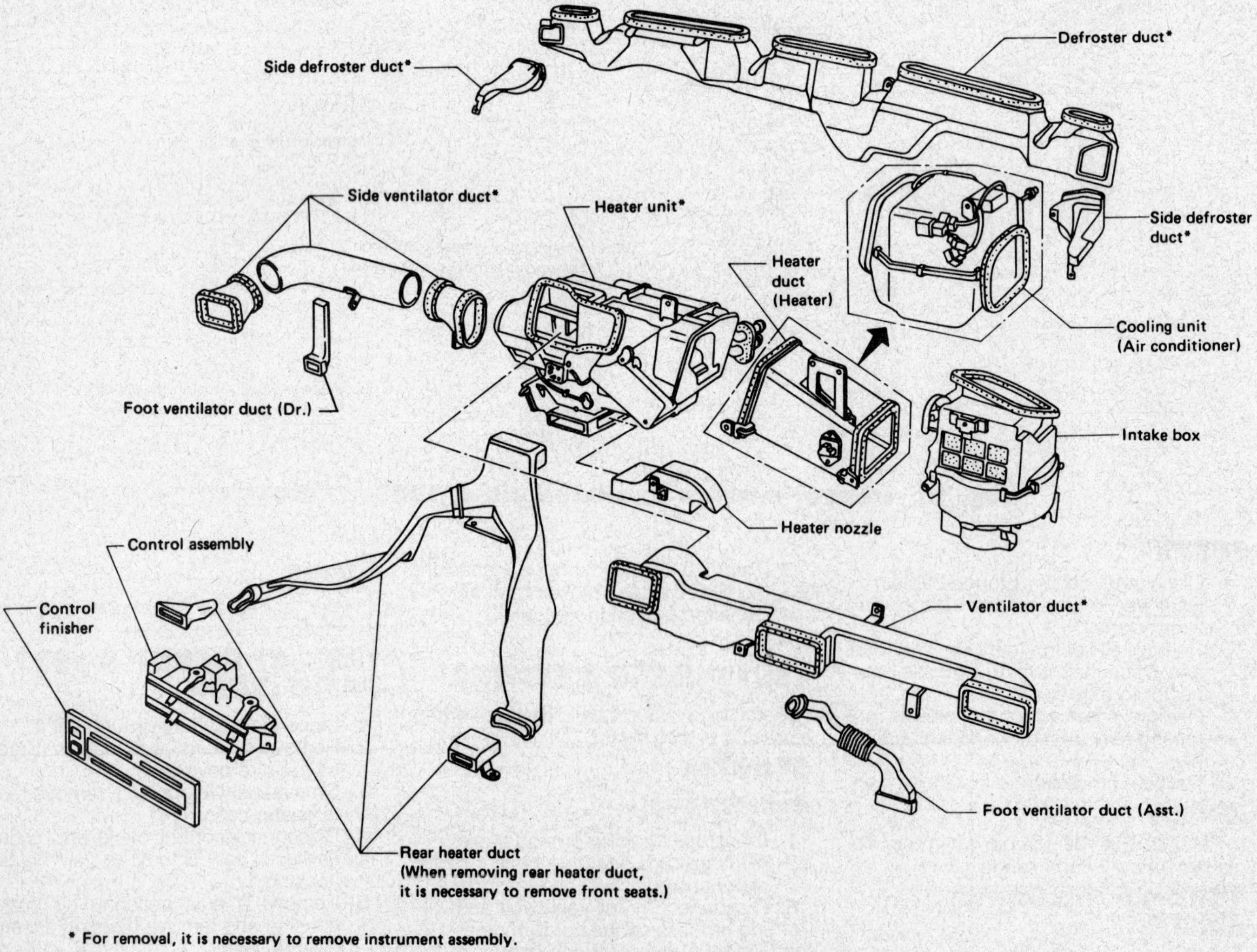

* For removal, it is necessary to remove instrument assembly.

Fig. 20 Heater system exploded view. 1984–87 200SX

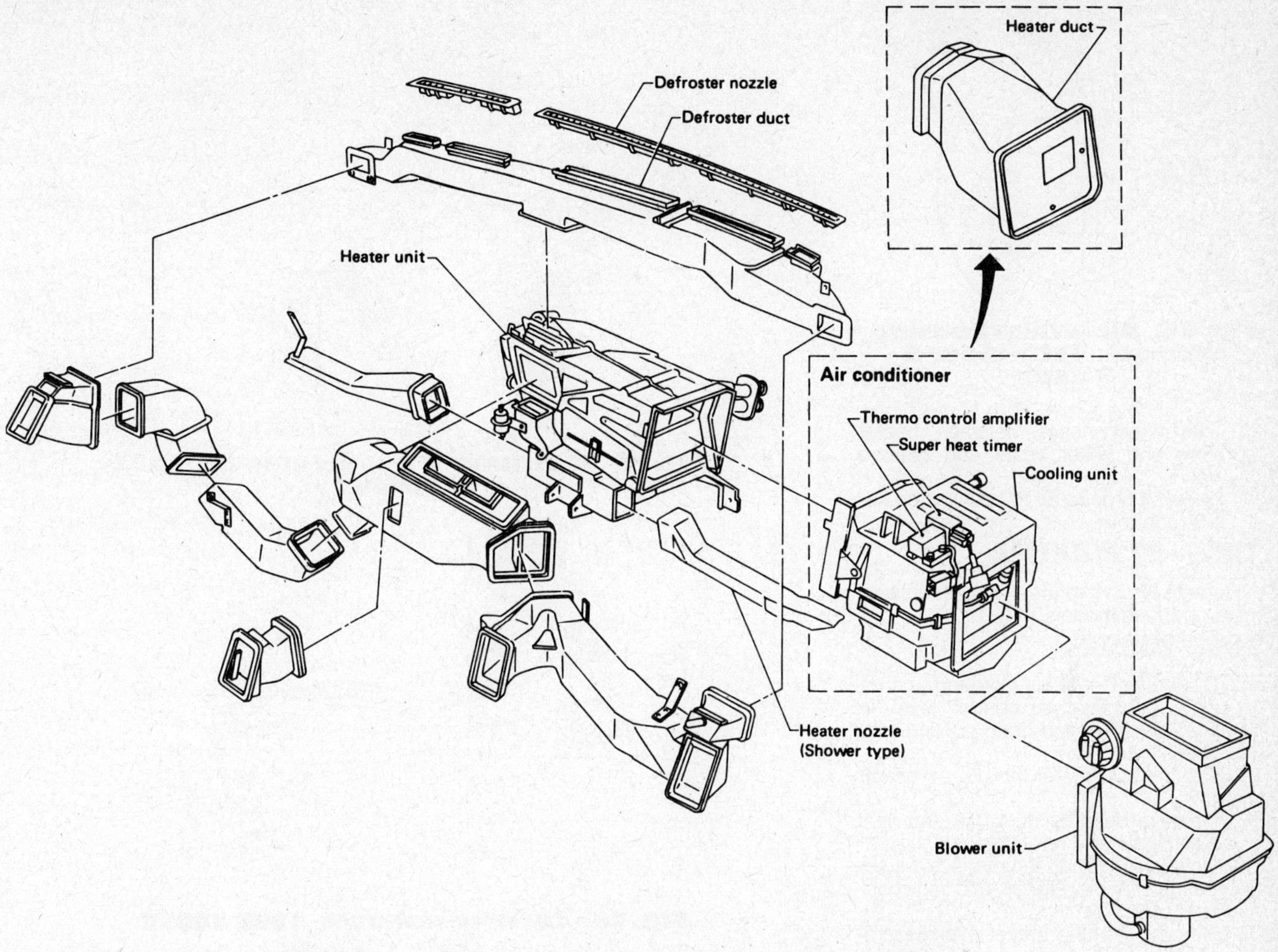

Fig. 21 Heater system exploded view. 300ZX

20. Disconnect control cable at air intake housing, remove bolts securing heater case, and remove heater case and control assembly.
21. Disconnect control cables at heater case, remove clips securing control, and remove control.
22. Disconnect control linkage to water valve, remove bolts securing valve and heater core, and remove valve and core as an assembly.

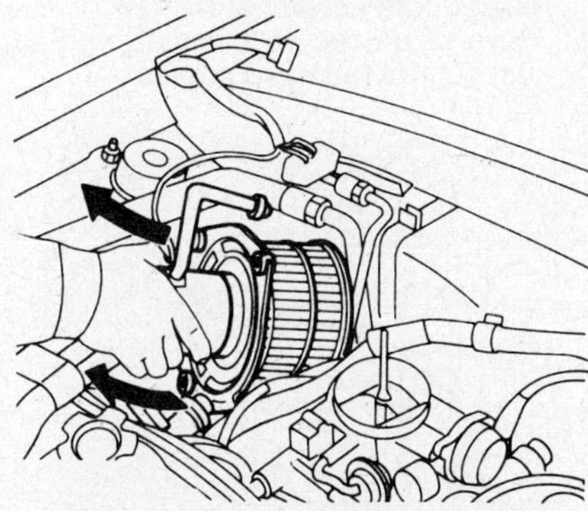

Fig. 22 Blower motor removal. Stanza exc. wagon.

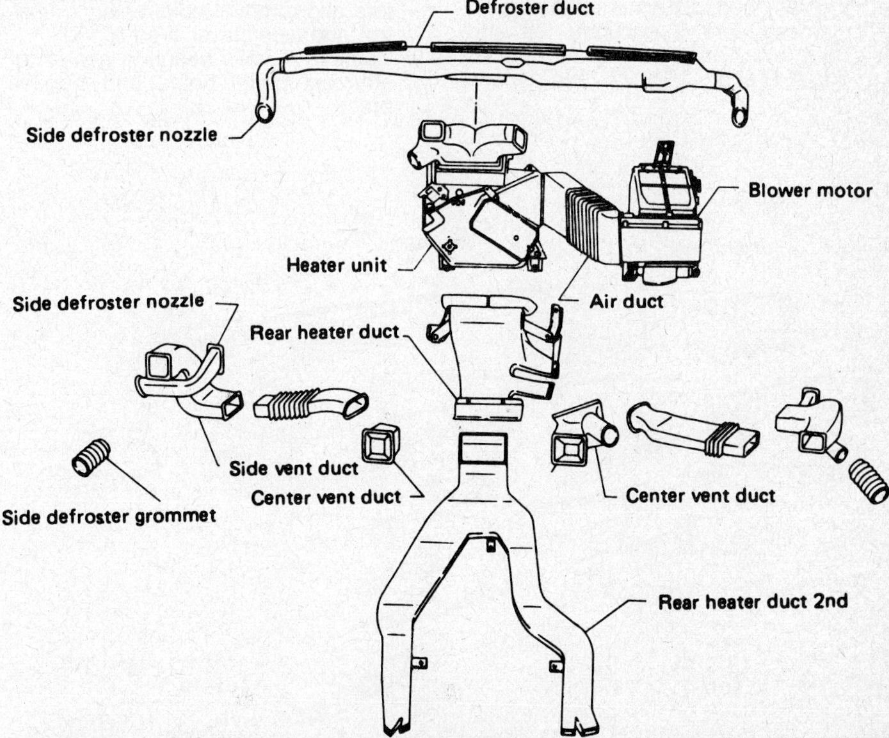

Fig. 23 Heater system exploded view. 1986–87 Stanza wagon

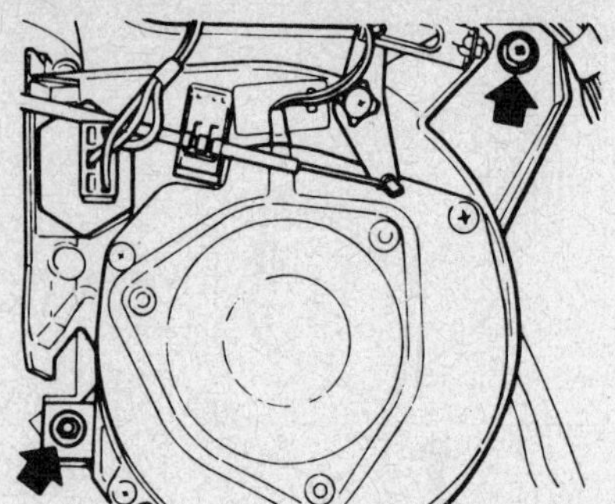

Fig. 24 Air intake housing removal. Pathfinder & Pickup

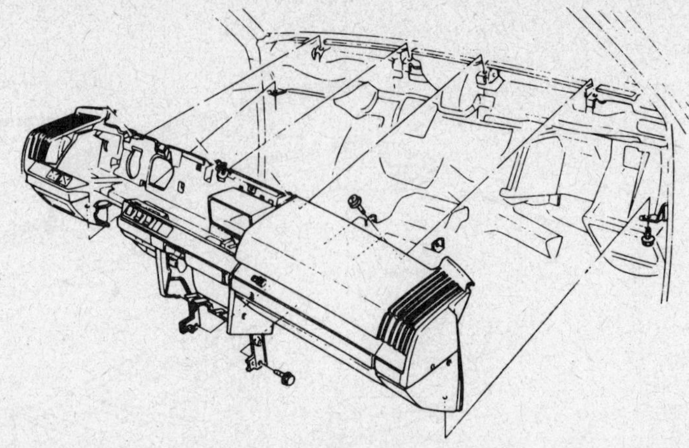

Fig. 25 Instrument panel removal. 1983 Maxima

23. Disconnect hoses between heater core and water valve and remove valve.
24. Reverse procedure to install, then adjust controls.

1985–87 MAXIMA

Refer to **Fig. 18** for heater core replacement on these models.

1983 200SX

1. Disconnect battery ground cable, place temperature control lever in HOT position, and drain cooling system.
2. Disconnect heater hoses at heater unit.
3. Remove bolts securing left and right front seats and remove seats.
4. Untie shifter boot, remove screws securing console, **Fig. 26**, and slide console back.
5. Remove parking brake lever assembly, then remove console.
6. Remove seat belts and door sill moldings as needed, then remove carpet.
7. Remove screws securing left and right lower dash panels and cluster lids A, B and C, **Fig. 27**, then remove panels.

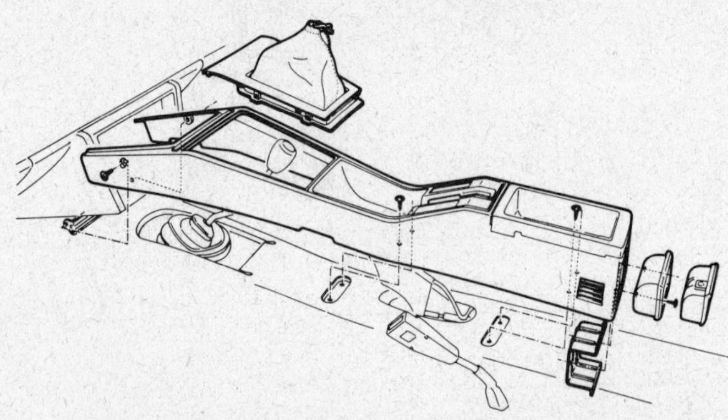

Fig. 26 Console removal. 1983 200SX

8. Disconnect wiring harness connectors and remove radio, balance control, and tape player, if equipped.
9. Remove 6 bolts securing center instrument panel brace and remove brace.
10. Remove 5 bolts securing rear seat air duct and remove duct.
11. Remove screws securing LH side ventilator and center ventilator, and remove vents.
12. Remove left and right lower air guides from heater case.
13. Disconnect wiring harness connectors to heater case and control.
14. Remove 2 remaining bolts securing heater case and remove case and control as an assembly.
15. Disconnect linkage, remove retaining screws, and remove water valve and heater core assembly.
16. Reverse procedure to install, and adjust control rods and cables.

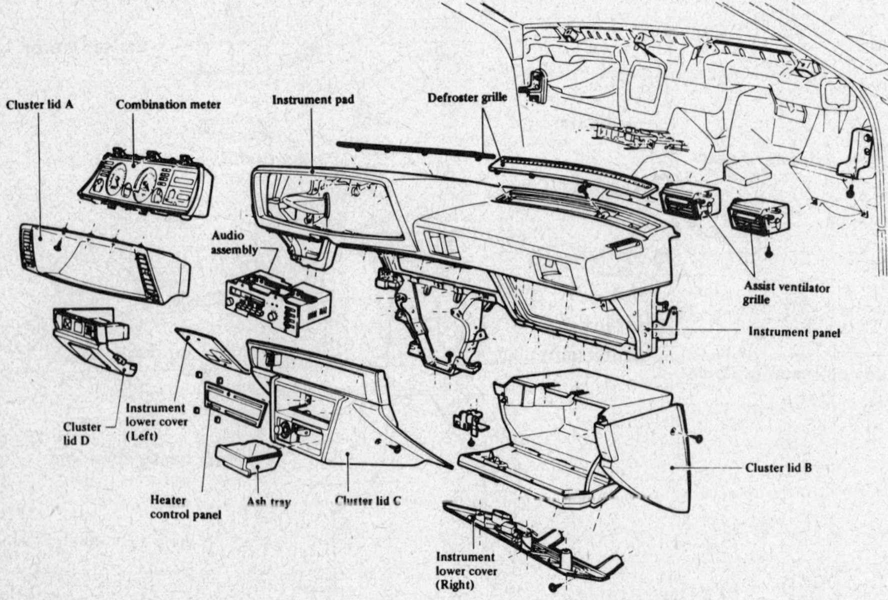

Fig. 27 Exploded view of instrument panel. 1983 200SX

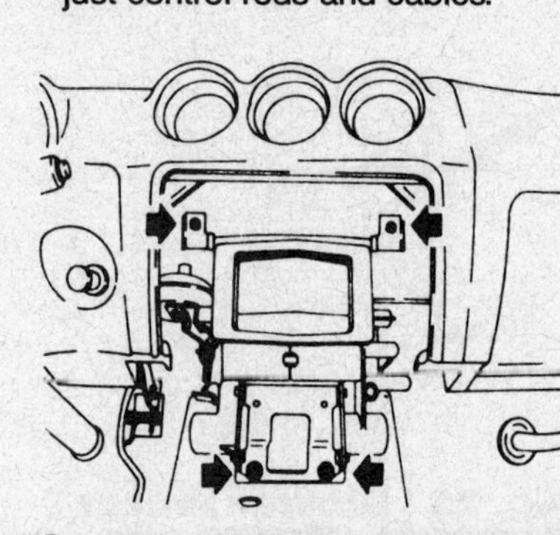

Fig. 28 Heater assembly removal. 280ZX

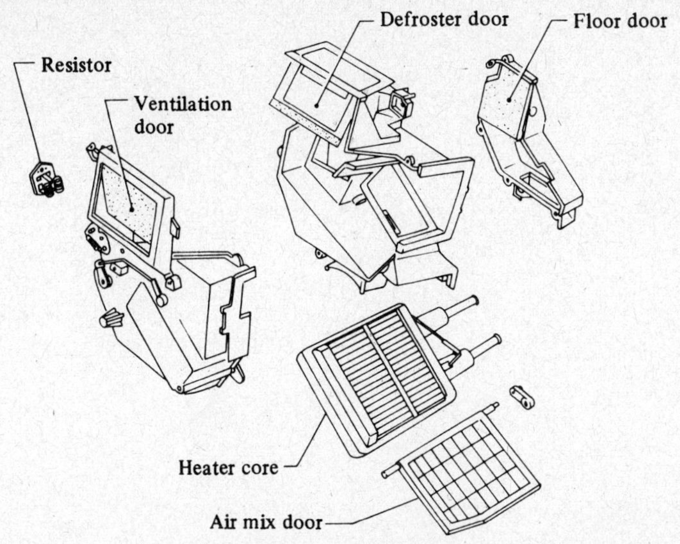

Fig. 29 Exploded view of heater. 1983–86 Pulsar & Sentra

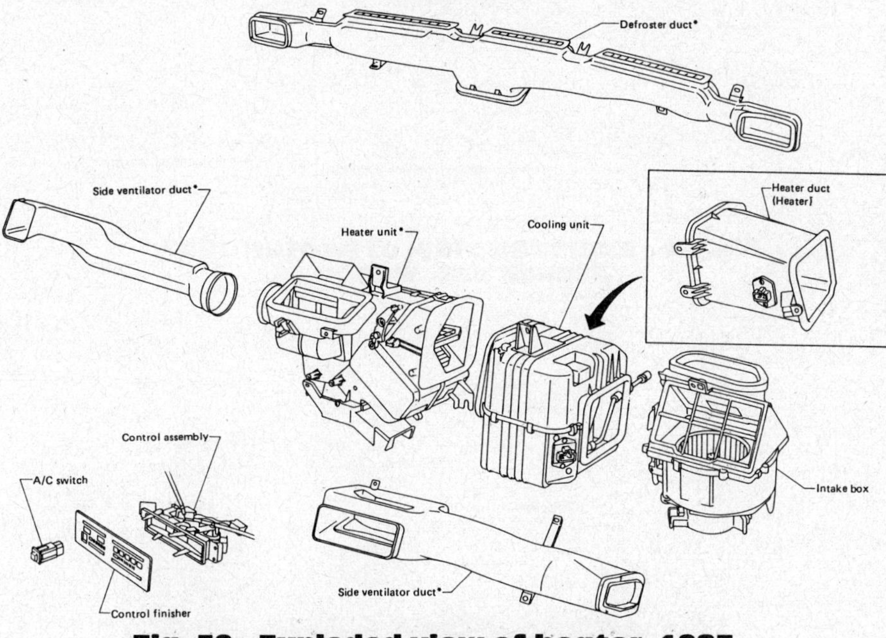

Fig. 30 Exploded view of heater. 1987 Pulsar shown, 1987 Sentra similar

1984–87 200SX

Refer to **Fig. 20** for heater core replacement on these models.

280ZX

1. Disconnect battery ground cable, place temperature control lever in HOT position, drain cooling system.
2. On models with A/C, discharge A/C system, disconnect refrigerant lines to evaporator, then plug lines and open fittings.
3. Remove A/C-heater control as follows:
   a. Remove left and right lower dash panels, floor nozzles and side defroster ducts.
   b. Remove left and right instrument console bracket covers, remove bolts securing console and lower console.
   c. Disconnect wiring harness connectors and remove instrument console.
   d. Remove screws securing center vent housing and remove housing and center duct.
   e. Disconnect control cables and rod at heater case, and disconnect wiring harness connectors to control.
   f. On models with A/C, mark and disconnect vacuum hoses at vacuum selector or remove vacuum selector from control.
   g. Remove screws securing control and remove control assembly.
4. Remove screws securing glove box and remove glove box.
5. Disconnect control cable or vacuum lines at air intake door control, and disconnect wiring harness connector to blower motor.
6. Remove bolts securing air intake and blower housing and remove housing assembly.
7. On models with A/C, remove evaporator case.
8. Disconnect heater hoses at water valve inlet and heater core outlet, taking care not to drip coolant in passenger compartment.
9. Remove bolts securing heater case, **Fig. 28**, and remove heater assembly.
10. Remove screws securing water control valve, disconnect hose at heater core, and remove valve and hose.

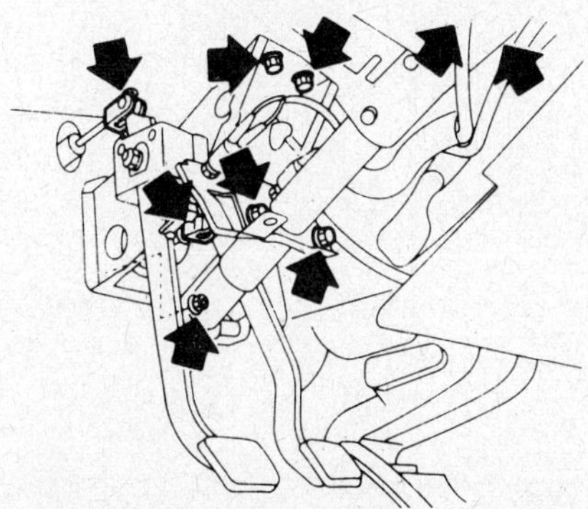

Fig. 31 Pedal & steering column bracket removal. Stanza exc. wagon.

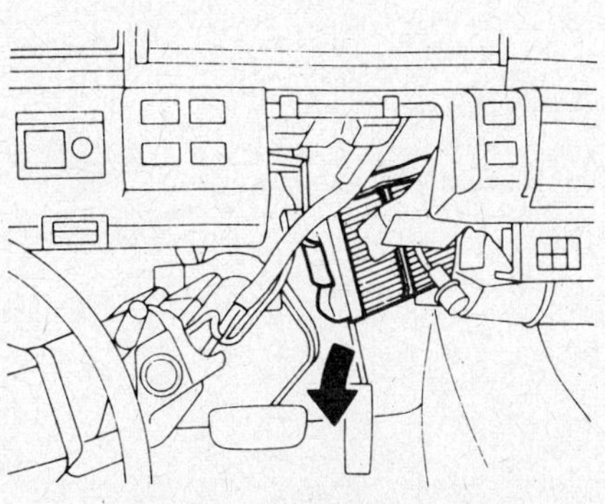

Fig. 32 Heater core removal. Stanza exc. wagon

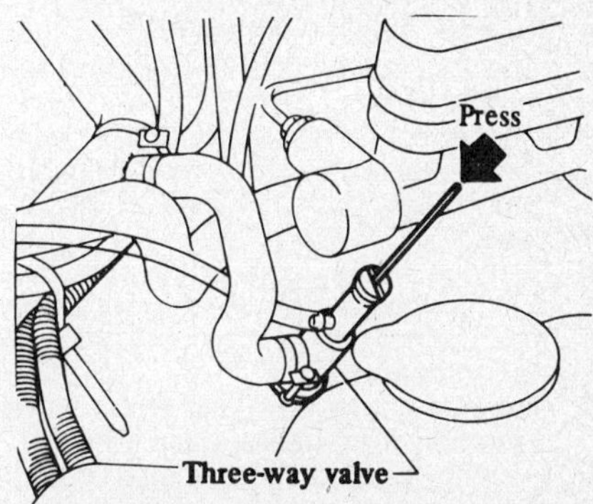

Fig. 33 Bleeding heater system at 3-way valve. Stanza exc. wagon

11. Remove clips securing heater case, separate case, and remove heater core.
12. Reverse procedure to install.

300ZX

Refer to **Fig. 21** for heater core replacement on these models.

PULSAR & SENTRA

1983–86

1. Disconnect battery ground cable, place temperature control in HOT position, and drain cooling system.
2. Disconnect heater hoses at fire wall connections, taking care not to damage heater tubes.
3. Remove instrument panel assembly, **Figs. 10 and 12.**
4. Remove A/C-heater control as follows:
   a. Remove lower dash panels.
   b. Disconnect control cables at heater case and disconnect wiring harness connectors to control.
   c. Pull off control knobs, pull control face plate away from dash, and remove face plate after disconnecting wiring harness connector to lighter.
   d. Remove screws securing control to instrument panel and remove control assembly.
5. Remove 4 bolts securing heater case and remove heater assembly.
6. Separate heater case, **Fig. 29** and remove core.
7. Reverse procedure to install.

1987

1. Disconnect battery ground cable.
2. Disconnect heater hose at firewall connections of heater core.
3. Remove instrument panel, **Figs. 11 and 13.**
4. Refer to **Fig. 30** to complete removal of heater core.
5. Reverse procedure to install.

STANZA

EXC. WAGON

1983–86

1. Disconnect battery ground cable.
2. Remove bolts securing pedal and steering column brackets, **Fig. 31**, disconnect brake and clutch control rods, and move pedal and column assembly to left.
3. Disconnect air mix door control cable and water valve rod, then remove control link from LH side of heater case.
4. Remove heater core cover and disconnect hoses from heater core, taking care not to drip coolant in passenger compartment.
5. Remove heater core and water valve assembly from heater case, **Fig. 32.**
6. Reverse procedure to install, noting the following:
   a. Make sure that steering column is properly aligned and that brake and clutch pedal free play are within specifications.

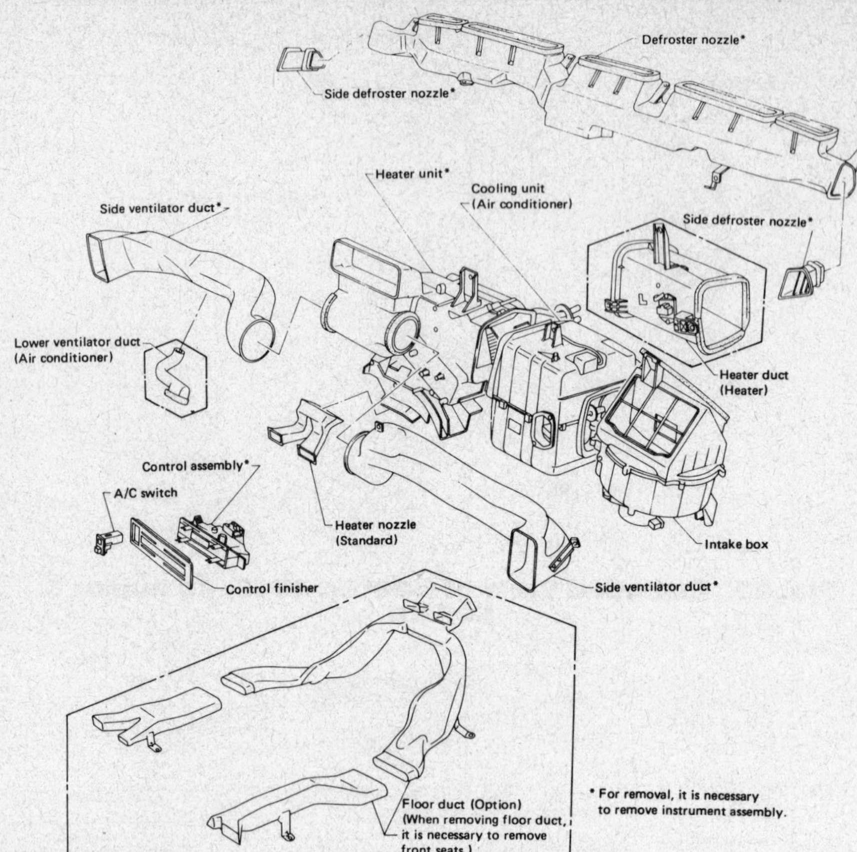

Fig. 34 Exploded view of heater. 1987 Stanza exc. Wagon

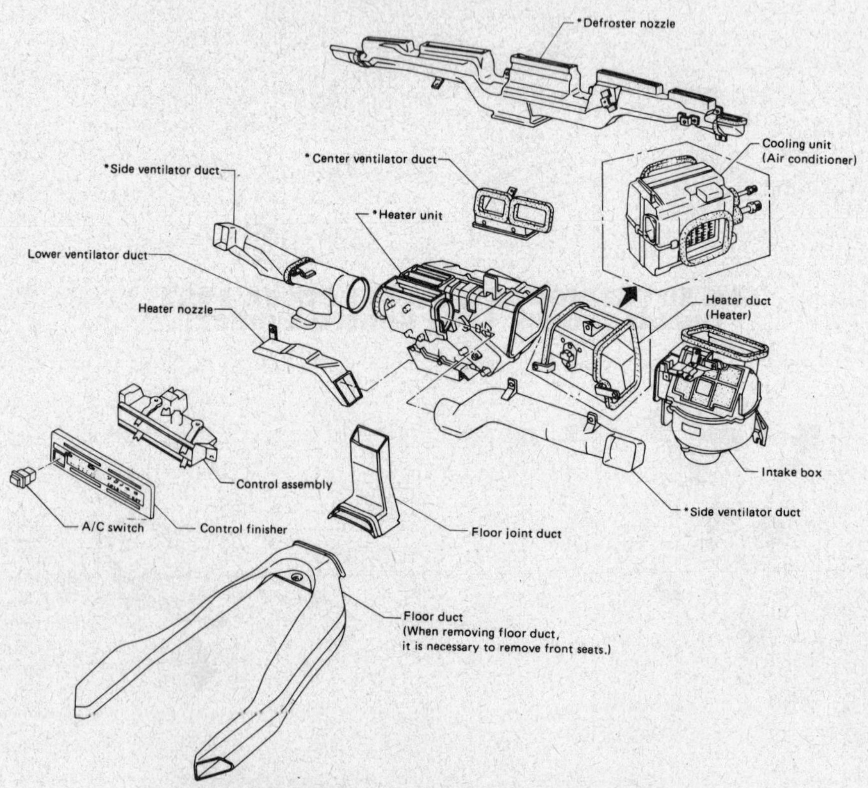

Fig. 35 Exploded view of heater. 1986½–87 Pickup & 1987 Pathfinder

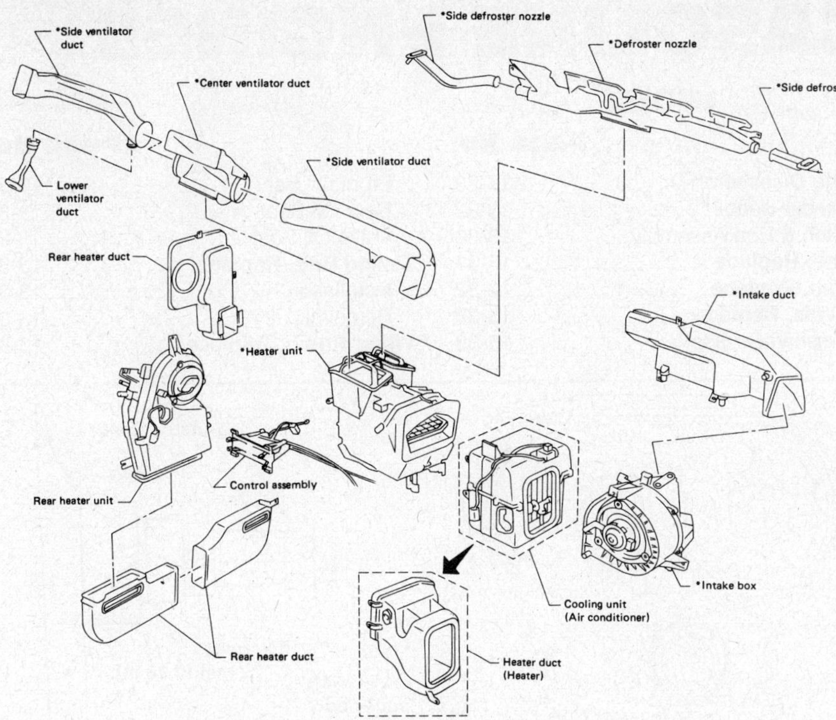

Fig. 36 Exploded view of front heater assembly. Van

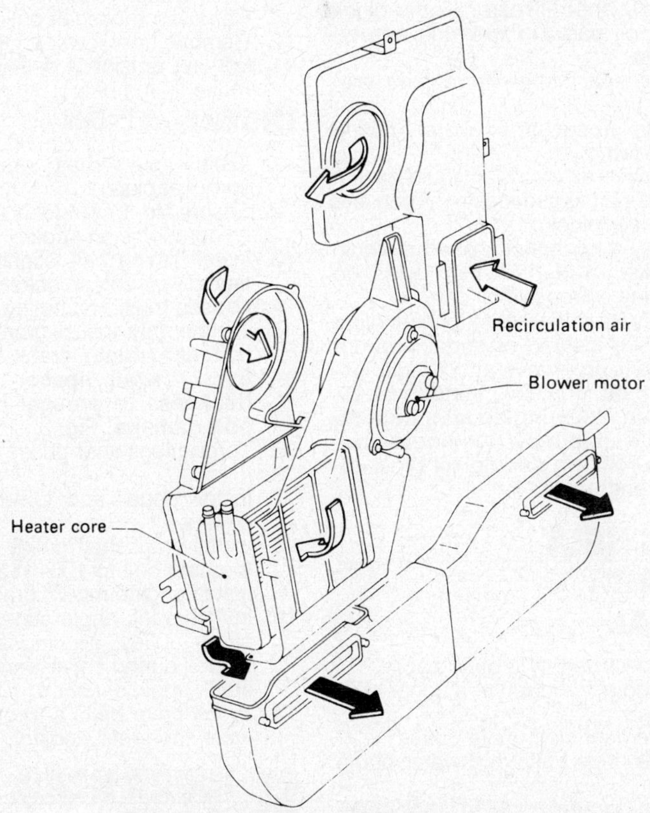

Fig. 37 Exploded view of rear heater assembly. Van

b. Adjust mix door cable and water valve rod.
c. Remove radiator cap and add coolant to system.
d. Insert pin into bleeder hole in 3-way valve, **Fig. 33.**
e. Force pin into valve to bleed heater system while maintaining coolant level, then remove pin. **Do not start engine while bleeder valve is open.**

1987

Refer to **Fig. 34** for heater core replacement on these models.

WAGON

Refer to **Fig. 23** for heater core replacement on these models.

PATHFINDER & PICKUP

1983–86

1. Disconnect battery ground cable and drain cooling system.
2. On models with A/C, disconnect heater hoses in engine compartment.
3. Remove screws securing console and remove console.
4. Remove steering column shroud and package, if equipped.
5. Disconnect speedometer cable, antenna lead and wiring harness connectors to instrument panel.
6. Remove 3 bolts securing instrument panel at base of windshield, remove bolt securing panel bracket above parking brake handle, and remove bolt inside glove box.
7. Remove 2 bolts securing instrument panel at each end, then remove instrument panel assembly.
8. On models without A/C:
   a. Remove duct to bower housing and disconnect control cable at air intake door.
   b. Disconnect heater hoses at heater unit, taking care not to drip coolant in passenger compartment.
9. On models with A/C, remove air intake housing as outlined in "Blower Motor, Replace," and remove bolts securing evaporator case.
10. Remove bolts securing heater case and remove case and control as an assembly.
11. Set temperature control lever in COLD position, disconnect control cables, and remove control assembly.
12. Disconnect control rod at water valve and heater hoses at heater core.
13. Remove screws securing water valve and remove valve and hoses.
14. Remove clips securing heater case, separate case and remove heater core.
15. Reverse procedure to install, then adjust controls.

1986½–1987 PICKUP & 1987 PATHFINDER

Refer to **Fig. 35** for heater core replacement on these models.

VAN

Refer to **Figs. 36 and 37** for heater core replacement on these models.

CA1 DE GASOLINE ENGINES

INDEX

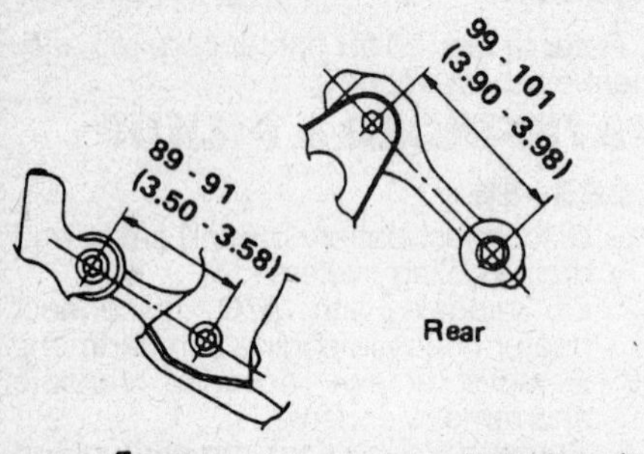

Fig. 1 Adjusting buffer rod bolts

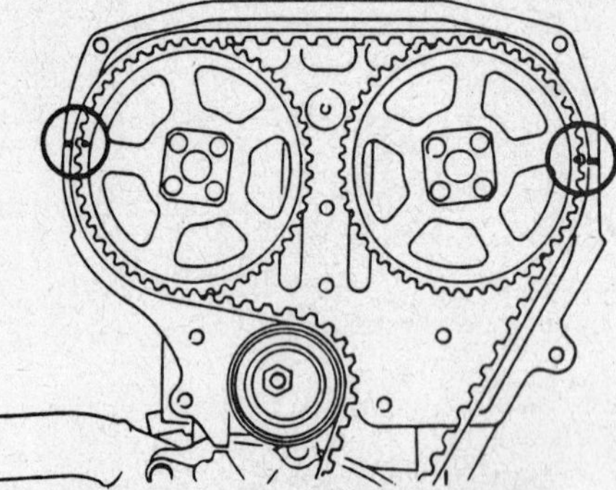

Fig. 2 Aligning timing marks on crank pulley sprockets

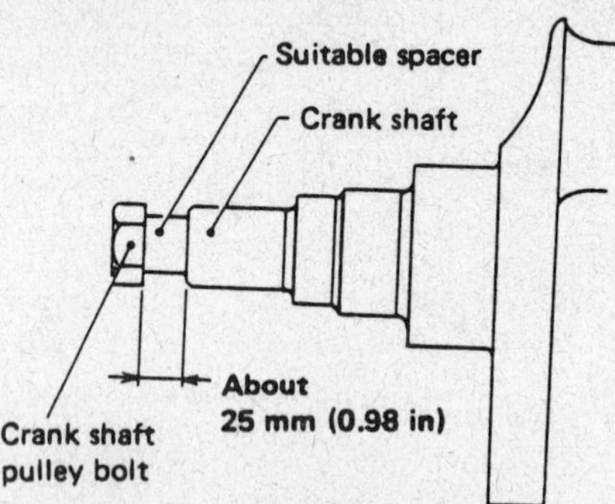

Fig. 3 Temporarily installing crankshaft pulley bolt

ENGINE

REPLACE

1. Disconnect battery ground cable.
2. Drain coolant and remove drive belts.
3. Raise and support vehicle.
4. Remove front tires and the under covers.
5. Remove brake caliper assembly, leaving brake hose connected.
6. Disconnect traverse link and tie rod ball joints on both sides.
7. Remove knuckle to strut bolts on both sides.
8. Remove both driveshafts, being careful not to damage grease seal on transaxle side.
9. Remove transaxle support rod bolt.
10. Remove center crossmember and the front exhaust pipe.
11. Disconnect front buffer rod.
12. On models with manual transaxle, disconnect rear buffer rod.
13. On all models, remove air cleaner and disconnect wires, harness, pipes and hoses.
14. Raise engine slightly and disconnect or remove all engine mountings.
15. Reverse procedure to install. On Pulsar models, adjust the length between buffer rod bolts, **Fig. 1.**

OIL PAN

REPLACE

1. Raise and support vehicle and drain engine oil.
2. Remove splash cover and under cover from right side.
3. Remove center crossmember.
4. Remove front exhaust pipe.
5. Remove front buffer rod and buffer rod bracket.
6. Remove engine gussets.
7. Remove oil pan as follows:
   a. Insert seal cutter KV10111100 or equivalent between cylinder block and oil pan. **Do not use screwdriver.**
   b. Slide seal cutter by tapping with hammer.
8. Reverse procedure to install, noting the following:
   a. Remove all traces of liquid gasket from mating surfaces of oil pan and cylinder block.
   b. Apply a continuous bead of liquid gasket, .138-.177 inch wide, to mating surface of oil pan.
   c. Apply liquid gasket to inner sealing surface instead of surface where there is no groove at bolt hole. **Attach oil pan to cylinder block within five minutes after coating and wait at least 30 minutes before refilling engine oil or starting engine.**

TIMING BELT

REPLACE

REMOVAL

1. Disconnect battery ground cable.
2. Drain coolant and remove upper radiator hose.
3. Remove right side under cover.
4. Remove drive belts and water pump pulley.
5. Scribe alignment mark on crank angle sensor and timing belt cover, then remove crank angle sensor.
6. Support engine with suitable jack and remove engine mount bracket.
7. Remove front upper timing belt cover, then align timing marks on crank pulley sprockets, **Fig. 2.**
8. Remove side cover from inside right-hand wheel house.
9. Remove crankshaft pulley.
10. Remove front lower timing belt cover.
11. Loosen tensioner pulley nut and remove timing belt.

INSTALLATION

1. Install crankshaft sprocket with sprocket plate.
2. Ensure No. 1 cylinder is set at TDC on its compression stroke.
3. Install timing belt, aligning marks on timing belt and sprockets.
4. Loosen tensioner pulley nut.
5. Temporarily install crankshaft pulley bolt and rotate crankshaft two full turns. **Install spacer of suitable thickness to prevent crank pulley bolt damage, Fig. 3.**
6. Torque tensioner pulley nut to 16-22 ft. lbs.
7. Install upper and lower timing belt covers.
8. Install crankshaft pulley with washer, torquing bolt to 105-112 ft. lbs.
9. Install engine mount bracket.
10. Install crank angle sensor and water pump pulley, aligning scribe marks made during disassembly. Torque crank angle sensor to 5.1-5.8 ft. lbs.
11. Install drive belts and upper radiator hose, then refill coolant.

CYLINDER HEAD

REPLACE

REMOVAL

1. Remove timing belt as previously described.

Loosening order

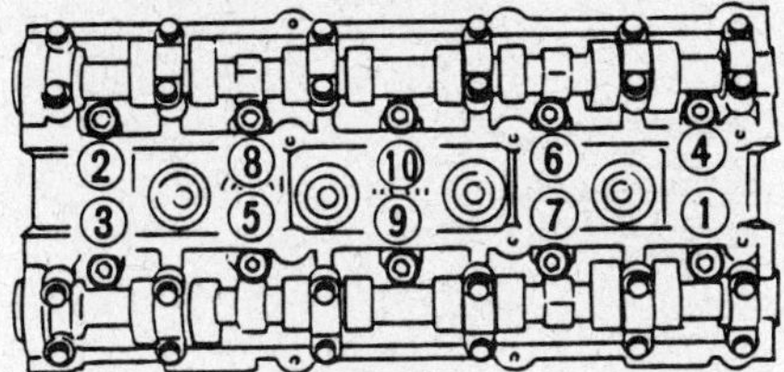

Fig. 4 Cylinder head bolt loosening sequence

Loosening order

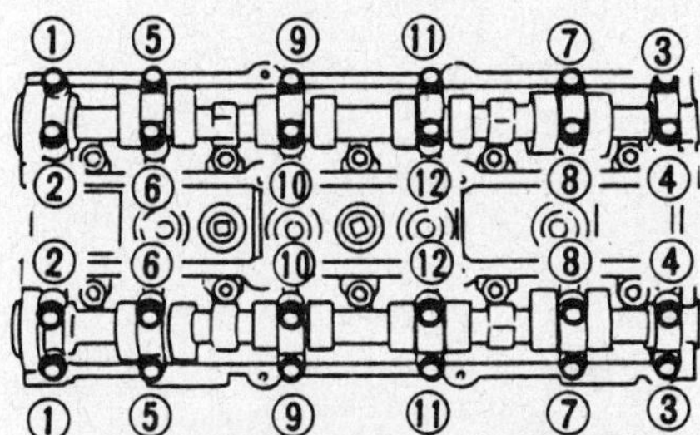

Fig. 7 Camshaft bracket bolt loosening sequence

2. Remove breather separator.
3. Loosen cylinder head bolts in sequence, **Fig. 4.**
4. Remove cylinder head.

INSTALLATION

1. Install cylinder head with new gasket. **Do not rotate crankshaft and camshaft separately.**
2. Apply engine oil to threaded portion and seat surface of bolts and tighten cylinder head bolts with washers, in sequence, **Fig. 5,** as follows:
   a. Torque all bolts to 22 ft. lbs.
   b. Torque all bolts to 76 ft. lbs.
   c. Loosen all bolts completely.
   d. Torque all bolts to 22 ft. lbs.
   e. Torque all bolts to 76 ft. lbs. or, if angle wrench is available, tighten bolts 85-90° clockwise.
3. Ensure No. 1 cylinder is set at TDC on its compression stroke.
4. Install timing belt and adjust belt tension as previously described.
5. Install remaining parts in reverse order of removal.

OIL SEALS

REPLACE

CAMSHAFT OIL SEAL

1. Set No. 1 piston at TDC on its compression stroke.
2. Remove crank angle sensor, front cover, timing belt, camshaft sprockets and rear dust cover.
3. Using suitable puller, remove camshaft oil seal, being careful not to scratch camshaft.
4. Apply engine oil to lip of new seal and drive into place.
5. Install removed parts in reverse order of removal.

Tightening order

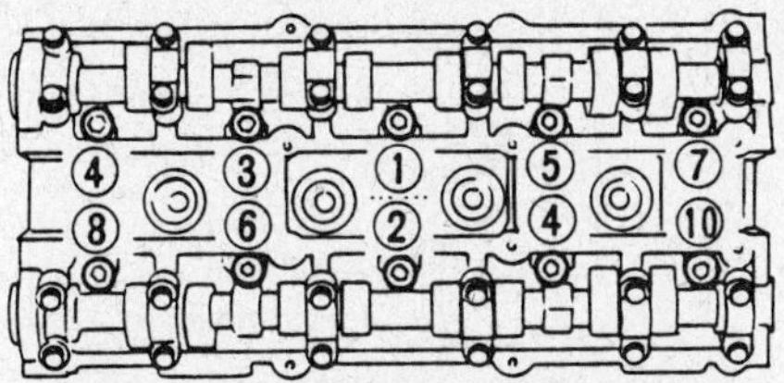

Fig. 5 Cylinder head bolt tightening sequence

FRONT OIL SEAL

1. Set No. 1 piston at TDC on its compression stroke.
2. Remove timing belt and crankshaft sprocket.
3. Remove front oil seal.
4. Apply engine oil to lip of new oil seal and install in position.
5. Install timing belt and crankshaft sprocket.

REAR OIL SEAL

1. Remove transaxle and flywheel.
2. Remove rear oil seal from retainer.
3. Apply engine oil to lip of new seal and install in position.
4. Install transaxle and flywheel.

VALVE OIL SEAL

1. Set piston of cylinder to be serviced at TDC on its compression stroke.
2. Remove throttle chamber and rocker covers.
3. Remove camshafts and valve lifters.
4. Remove spark plug.
5. Install air hose adapter into spark plug bore of cylinder to be serviced and apply 71 psi of compressed air to hold valves in place.
6. Remove valve springs and valve oil seals.
7. Apply engine oil to valve oil seal and drive into place.
8. Assemble valve mechanism, camshafts and timing belt.
9. Install remaining parts in reverse order of removal.

ENGINE DISASSEMBLY

1. Remove engine outer components.
2. Place engine on suitable work stand.
3. Drain coolant and engine oil.
4. Remove timing belt as previously described.
5. Remove water pump.
6. Remove oil pan and oil pump as previously described.
7. Remove cylinder head as previously described.
8. Remove pistons.
9. Remove bearing caps and crankshaft, loosening attaching nuts in sequence, **Fig. 6.**

PISTON & ROD ASSEMBLY

1. Remove piston rings with ring expander.
2. When disassembling piston and connecting rod, heat piston to 140-158°F or use piston pin press stand at room temperature.

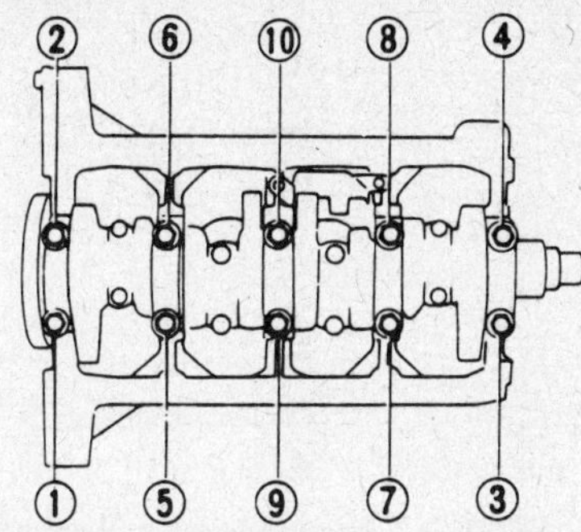

Loosen in numerical order.

Fig. 6 Main bearing cap nut loosening sequence

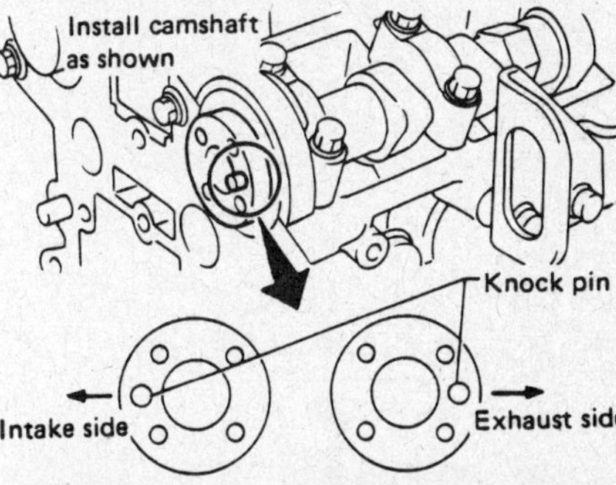

Fig. 8 Installing camshaft

CYLINDER HEAD

1. Remove camshaft sprockets.
2. Remove tensioner pulley and rear cover.
3. Remove camshaft bracket, loosening bolts gradually, in sequence, **Fig. 7,** in two or three steps.
4. Remove front oil seals, then the camshafts.
5. Remove hydraulic valve lifters, noting the following:
   a. Do not place hydraulic valve lifters upside down.
   b. Do not disassemble hydraulic valve lifter.
   c. Tag valve lifters so as not to mix them up.
6. Using suitable tools, disassemble valve mechanism.
7. Using suitable puller, remove valve oil seal.

ENGINE ASSEMBLY

CYLINDER HEAD

1. Install valve component parts, noting the following:
   a. Always use new valve oil seal.
   b. Install valve spring with its narrow pitch side (painted side) toward cylinder head side.
2. Install camshafts, **Fig. 8. Exhaust side camshaft has spline for crank angle sensor.**
3. Install camshaft brackets. **Camshaft bracket number and direction are stamped on camshaft bracket.**
4. Apply engine oil to lip of new camshaft oil seal and install seal in place.
5. Torque camshaft bracket bolts, in se-

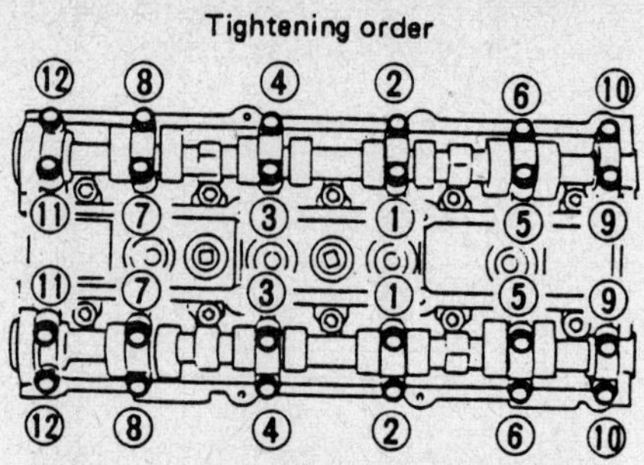

Fig. 9 Camshaft bracket bolt tightening sequence

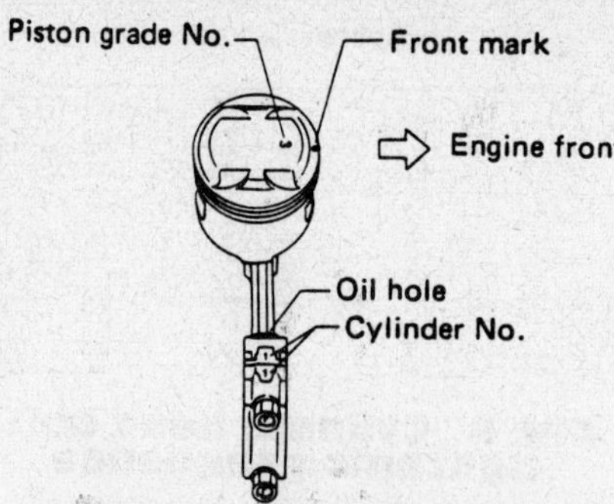

Fig. 10 Piston & rod assembly

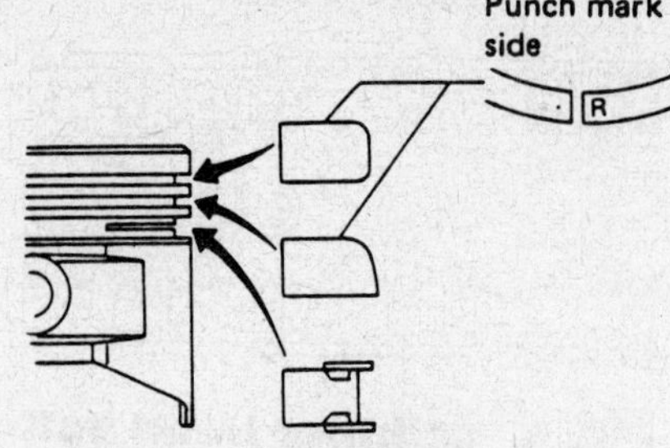

Fig. 11 Installing piston rings

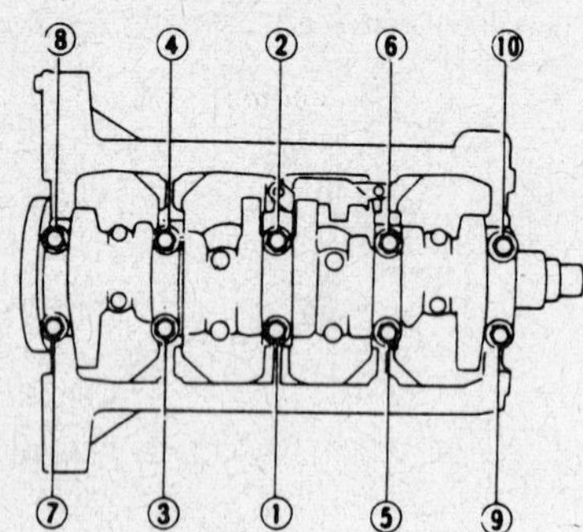

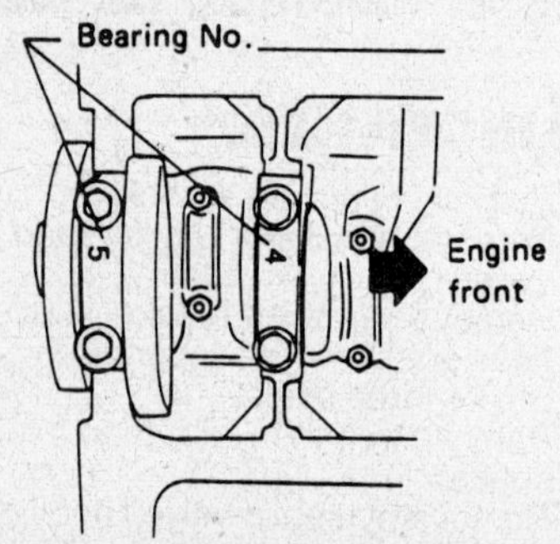

Fig. 12 Main bearing cap bolt tightening sequence

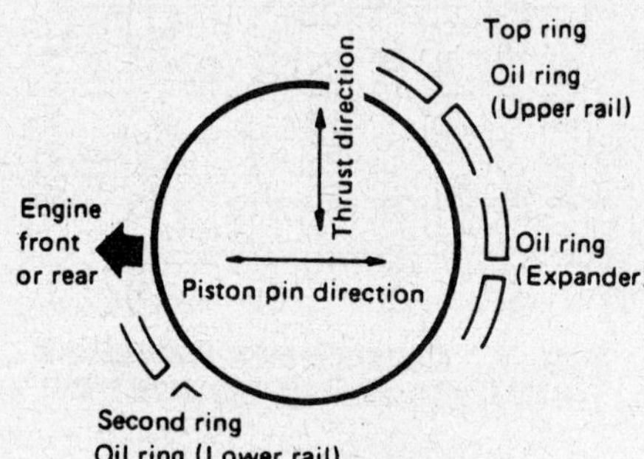

Fig. 13 Ring end gap positioning

quence, **Fig. 9**, in two or three steps to 6.5-8.7 ft. lbs.

6. Install rear timing cover, torquing attaching bolts to 5.1-5.8 ft. lbs.
7. Install timing belt tensioner, torquing tensioner attaching nut to 16-22 ft. lbs.
8. Install camshaft sprockets, torquing attaching bolts to 10-14 ft. lbs. **Counterhold camshaft while tightening bolts.**
9. Adjust timing belt tension as described under "Timing Belt, Replace."
10. Install remaining parts in reverse order of removal.

PISTON & ROD ASSEMBLY

1. Numbers stamped on connecting rod and cap correspond to each cylinder, **Fig. 10.** Care should be taken to avoid mismatching, including bearing and connecting rod direction.
2. When pressing piston pin in connecting rod, apply engine oil to pin and small end of connecting rod.
3. After assembling, ensure piston swings smoothly.
4. Install piston rings, **Fig. 11.**

ENGINE ASSEMBLY

1. Set main bearings in proper position on cylinder block, noting the following:
   a. If crankshaft, cylinder block, or main bearing is reused, it is necessary to measure main bearing clearance.
   b. Upper bearings have oil groove.
2. Apply engine oil to main bearing surfaces on both sides of cylinder block and cap.
3. Install crankshaft and main bearing caps, noting the following:
   a. Arrange parts so that indicated number on bearing cap is in a row from front of engine, **Fig. 12.**
   b. Before tightening bearing cap bolts, place bearing cap in proper position by shifting crankshaft in axial direction.
   c. Tighten bearing cap bolts gradually in two or three steps in sequence.
   d. After tightening bearing cap bolts, ensure crankshaft turns smoothly.
4. Ensure crankshaft end play, measured at center bearing, is .002-.007 inch.
5. Install connecting rod bearings in the connecting rods and connecting rod caps, noting the following:
   a. Install bearings so that oil hole in connecting rod aligns with oil hole of bearing.
   b. Ensure ring end gaps are properly positioned, **Fig. 13.**
6. Install pistons with connecting rods, noting the following:
   a. Be careful not to scratch cylinder wall with connecting rod.
   b. Apply engine oil to cylinder wall, piston and bearing.
   c. Arrange so that front mark on piston head faces toward front of engine.
7. Install connecting rod bearing caps, noting the following:
   a. Torque connecting rod bearing nut to 10-12 ft. lbs.
   b. Torque nut to 30-33 ft. lbs. or, if angle wrench is available, tighten nut 60-65° clockwise.
8. Ensure connecting rod side clearance is .0079-.0138 inch.

WATER PUMP REPLACE

1. Disconnect battery ground cable.
2. Loosen water pump pulley attaching bolts.
3. Remove drive belts, then the water pump pulley.
4. Remove water pump attaching bolts and the water pump.
5. Reverse procedure to install, using new gasket.

CA18ET, CA20 & CA20E GASOLINE ENGINES

INDEX

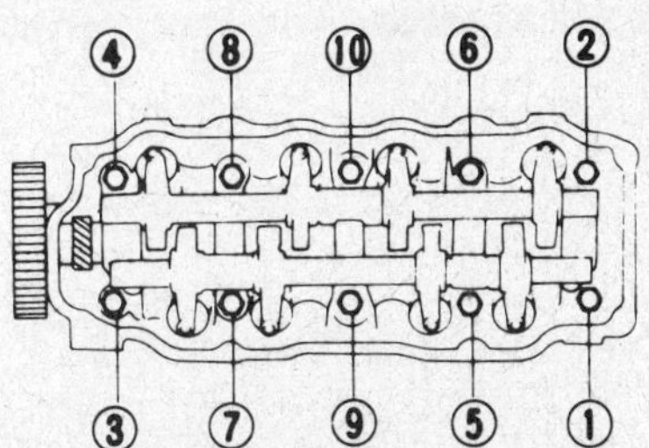

Fig. 1 Cylinder head bolt loosening sequence

1983–85 STANZA

ENGINE, REPLACE

1. On models equipped with CA20E engine, release fuel system pressure as follows:
   a. Start engine, then disconnect fuel pump electrical connector, located under assist seat.
   b. After engine stalls, crank engine 2 or 3 times.
   c. Turn ignition switch Off, then reconnect fuel pump electrical connector.
2. On all models, disconnect battery cables, then remove radiator reservoir tank, battery and battery support bracket.
3. Scribe hood hinge locations and remove hood.
4. Remove air cleaner and fresh air duct. **Plug air horn of carburetor to prevent contamination.**
5. Remove undercover, then drain engine coolant.
6. Remove radiator with fan.
7. On models equipped with power steering, remove power steering pump.
8. On models equipped with A/C, remove A/C compressor and idler pulley. **Do not discharge refrigerant from A/C system.**
9. Disconnect exhaust pipe from exhaust manifold.
10. On manual transaxle models, disconnect control rod link support rod from transaxle.
11. On automatic transaxle models, disconnect control wire from transaxle.
12. Disconnect clutch wire, then remove speedometer cable with pinion from transaxle.
13. Disconnect accelerator linkage, then remove EGR valve with bracket.
14. Disconnect all electrical connectors and vacuum hoses necessary for engine removal.
15. Disconnect fuel lines from fuel pump.
16. On 1983 models, remove lower ball joint, then drain gear oil.
17. Disconnect both driveshafts from transaxle.
18. Attach suitable engine lifting equipment to engine.
19. Disconnect engine mounting insulators and buffer rod, then lift engine from vehicle and separate from transaxle.
20. Reverse procedure to install.

ENGINE DISASSEMBLY

1. Separate engine from transaxle, then remove clutch assembly using tool KV30101000, or equivalent.
2. If equipped, remove A/C compressor bracket and/or power steering pump bracket and pump idler pulley.
3. Remove air induction pipes on carbureted engines, then the exhaust manifold with cover and hot air duct.
4. Completely drain engine coolant and oil into suitable containers, then mount engine to a suitable work stand.
5. Remove drive belts, then the engine front cover.
6. Remove water pump pulley and crankshaft pulley.
7. Remove vacuum tube assembly for distributor and fuel vapor canister.
8. Remove alternator adjusting bar.
9. Remove distributor cap with high tension cables, then the distributor and spark plugs.
10. Remove intake manifold support, then the alternator.
11. Remove oil filter and oil pressure switch.
12. Remove carburetor and insulator if equipped, then the PCV valve hose.
13. Remove intake manifold assembly.
14. Remove oil pan and oil strainer, then the valve rocker cover.
15. Remove timing belt tensioner, then the camshaft sprocket and timing belt.
16. Remove cylinder head. Loosen bolts in sequence, **Fig. 1. When removing cylinder head with engine installed in vehicle, rotate crankshaft until No. 1 piston is at TDC of compression stroke.**
17. Remove oil pump and water pump assemblies.
18. Remove connecting rod caps and bearings. Push piston/connecting rod assemblies out toward cylinder head surface. **Numbers are stamped on connecting rods and caps corresponding to each cylinder. Care should be taken to keep all parts, including bearings in correct order.**
19. Remove flywheel and end plate.
20. Remove main bearing caps and bearings. Loosen bolts in sequence, beginning with the outer bolts.
21. Remove rear oil seal retainer, then the crankshaft and bearings.
22. Remove baffle plate from cylinder block.

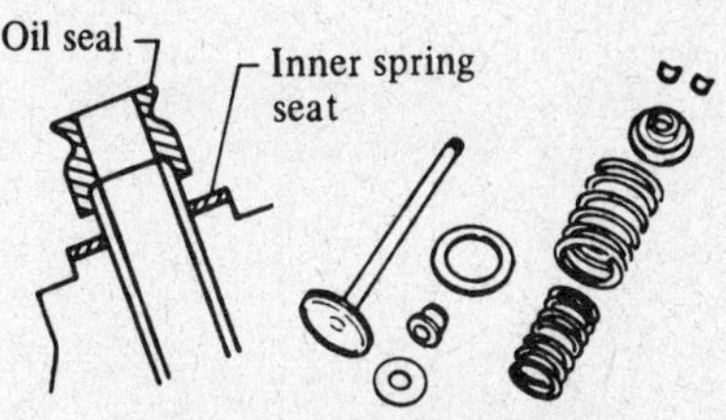

Fig. 2 Valve & valve components

Piston & Rod Disassembly

1. Remove piston rings with a ring remover.
2. Press out piston pin. **Keep disassembled parts in order.**

Cylinder Head Disassembly

1. Remove rocker shaft assembly. Loosen bolts in sequence beginning with the outer bolts.
2. Remove camshaft, then the valves and valve components.

ENGINE ASSEMBLY

Cylinder Head Assembly

1. Install valves and valve components in order shown, **Fig. 2.** Apply clean en-

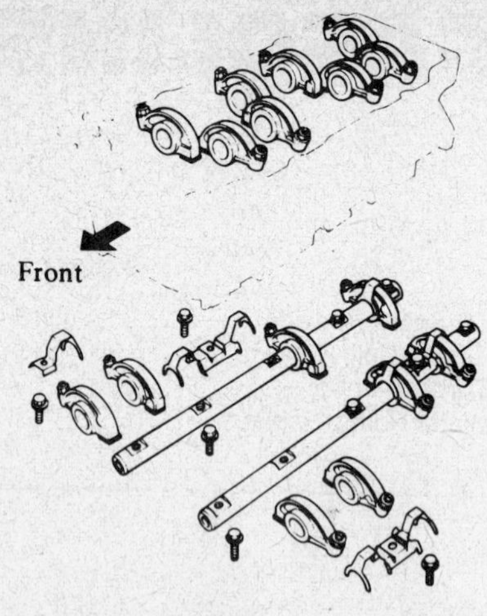

Fig. 3 Rocker shaft assembly

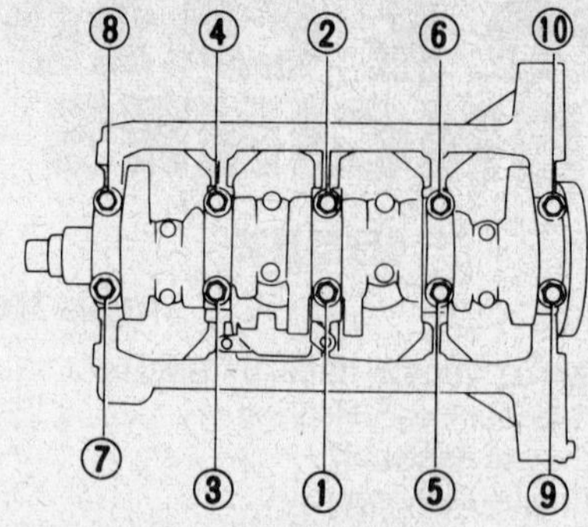

Fig. 4 Main bearing cap bolt tightening sequence. 1983–84

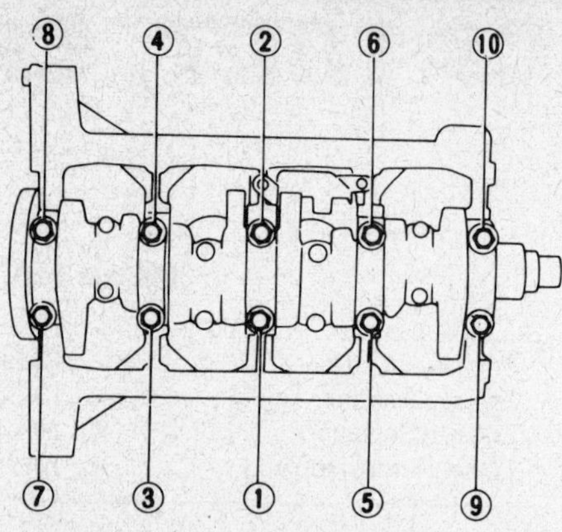

Fig. 5 Main bearing cap bolt tightening sequence. 1985–87

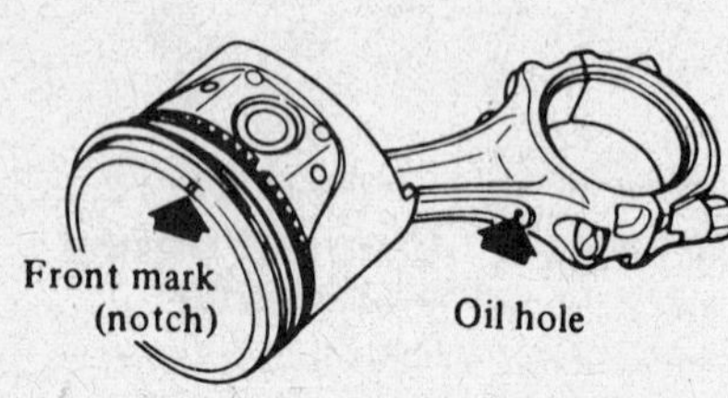

Fig. 6 Piston & connecting rod assembly

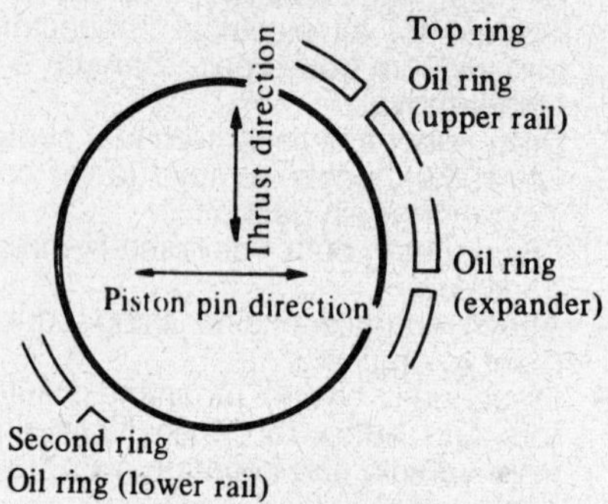

Fig. 7 Piston ring installation

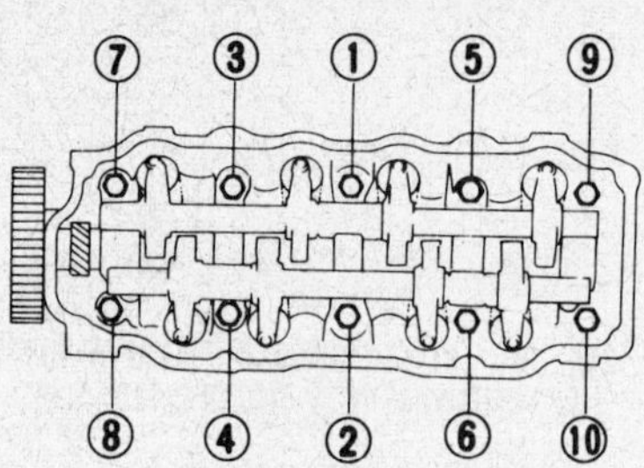

Fig. 8 Cylinder head bolt tightening sequence

gine oil to valve stem and lip of valve oil seal. **Install valve spring with narrow pitch (painted) side toward cylinder head side.**

2. Install camshaft so that the dowel pin at front end is at 12 o'clock position on vehicles less camshaft locate plate.
3. Assemble, then install rocker shaft assembly, **Fig. 3.** Note the following:
   a. Intake rocker shaft is identified by a slit on front surface.
   b. Assemble both shafts so that punched marks on front surface are on top.
   c. Torque bolts to specifications. Tighten bolts in two or three steps, beginning with center bolts and working outward.
4. Rotate camshaft until No. 1 piston is at TDC of compression stroke.
5. Install fuel pump cam. Torque retaining bolt to 58-65 ft. lbs.
6. Install cylinder head rear cover. Torque attaching bolts to 4.3-7.2 ft. lbs.

Piston & Rod Assembly

1. Assemble pistons, piston pins and connecting rods of designated cylinders. Note the following:
   a. Apply clean engine oil to piston and small end of connecting rod before pressing pin into rod.
   b. Assemble so that oil hole in connecting rod big end points toward right side of cylinder block.
2. Install piston rings. Ensure that identification marks on rings face upward.

Engine Assembly

1. Install baffle plate into crankcase.
2. Install upper main bearings into cylinder block. Note that the No. 3 bearing is the only one of the flanged type. **Upper and lower bearings are not interchangeable. Upper bearings can be identified as those having an oil groove.**
3. Apply clean engine oil to main bearing surfaces on both sides of cylinder block and cap.
4. Install crankshaft, then the lower main bearings and caps. Torque bolts to specifications in two or three steps in sequence shown, **Fig. 4 and 5.** Ensure that crankshaft turns smoothly.
5. Measure crankshaft end play and make sure it is within specifications.
6. Apply clean engine oil to lip of rear oil seal and mating shaft and coat inner surface of seal with grease. Install seal in retainer, then install the retainer to cylinder block.
7. Install rear end plate and flywheel. Torque retaining bolts to specifications.
8. Install lubricated piston and rod assemblies into corresponding cylinders. Assemble so that front mark on piston head, **Fig. 6**, faces front of engine. **Set piston rings as shown in Fig. 7.**
9. Install connecting rod bearing caps and torque cap nuts to specifications. Ensure that cylinder numbers face in same direction.
10. Install cylinder head as follows:
    a. Thoroughly clean cylinder block and head mating surface. Do not apply sealant to mating surface.
    b. Install camshaft sprocket and torque retaining bolt to specifications.
    c. Ensure there is sufficient clearance between valves and pistons. Loosen rocker arm adjusting screws to draw valves in, if necessary.
    d. Install cylinder head assembly with new gasket. Torque bolts in sequence, **Fig. 8,** to 22 ft. lbs.
    e. Retorque all bolts in sequence to 58 ft. lbs., then completely loosen all bolts.
    f. Torque bolts to 22 ft. lbs., then to 54-61 ft. lbs. in sequence. If an angle wrench is available, instead of torquing bolts to 54-61 ft. lbs., turn bolt No. 8 83-88°, and other bolts to 75-80 degrees, in clockwise direction.
11. Install oil pump and torque attaching bolts to 9-12 ft. lbs.
12. Install water pump and torque attaching bolts to 12-14 ft. lbs. on 1983 models, or 9-12 ft. lbs. on 1984-85 models.
13. Install timing belt tensioner. Do not tighten bolts at this time.
14. Install timing belt plate and crankshaft sprocket. Ensure timing marks on sprocket face forward.
15. Install timing belt on camshaft and crankshaft sprockets with timing marks aligned, **Fig. 9.**
16. Torque belt tensioner attaching bolts

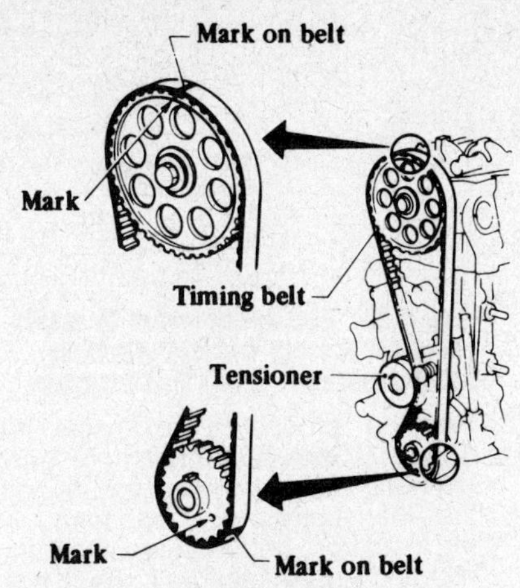

Fig. 9 Timing belt installation

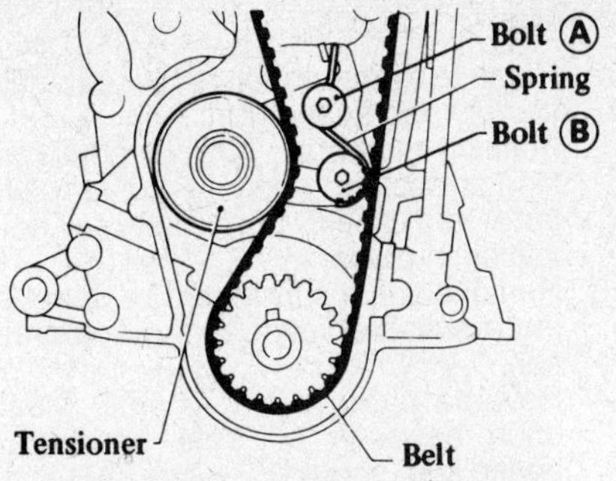

Fig. 10 Timing belt tensioner adjustment

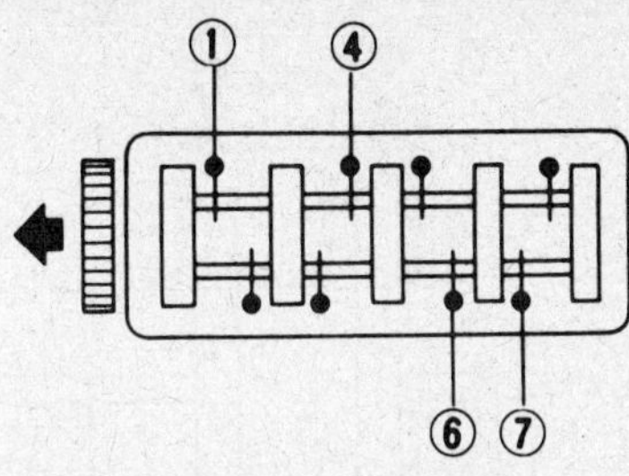

Fig. 11 Valve clearance adjustment

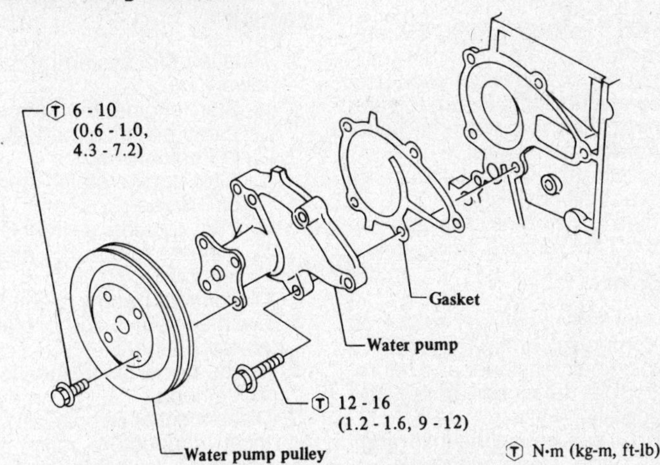

Fig. 13 Replacing water pump

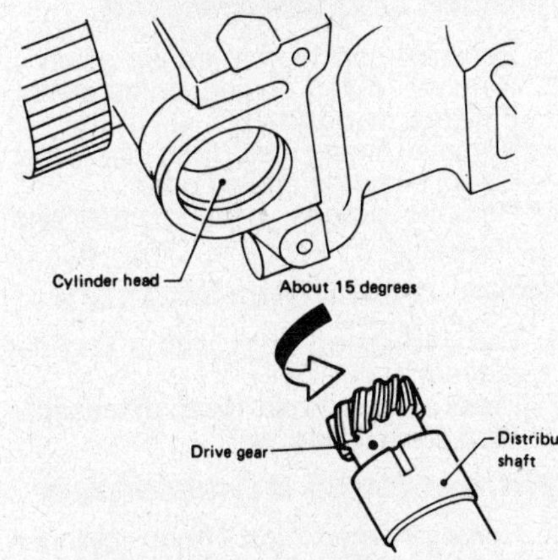

Fig. 12 Distributor installation

to 13-16 ft. lbs. **Set belt tensioner spring by first hooking one end on bolt "B" side, Fig. 10, then hooking opposite end on tensioner bracket pawl. Tighten bolt "B", then bolt "A" and belt tension will automatically be set to specifications.**

17. Install front cover oil seal.
18. Install lower front cover with new gaskets. Torque attaching bolts to 2.2-3.6 ft. lbs.
19. Install vibration damper with backing plate. Torque retaining bolt to specifications.
20. Install crankshaft pulley and torque retaining bolts to 9-10 ft. lbs.
21. Temporarily adjust valve clearance as follows:
    a. Rotate crankshaft until high point of No. 1 cam lobe is at the 6 o'clock position.
    b. Adjust valves 1, 4, 6 and 7, **Fig. 11.**
    c. Insert feeler gauge between tip of valve stem and rocker arm screw and adjust valve clearance to the following specifications: exhaust valves, .009 inch; intake valves, .008 inch.
    d. Rotate crankshaft until high point of No. 1 cam lobe is at the 12 o'clock position, then adjust remaining valves.
22. Install valve rocker cover with new gasket. Torque attaching bolts to .7-2.2 ft. lbs. in a crisscross pattern.
23. Install upper front cover with new gasket and torque attaching bolts to 2.2-3.6 ft. lbs.
24. Install oil strainer and oil pan with new gasket. Apply suitable sealant to oil pan mating surface and torque attaching bolts to specifications in a crisscross pattern.
25. Install engine outer parts in reverse order of removal. Refer to steps 1 thru 13 under "Engine Disassembly." Install distributor as positioned in **Fig. 12.**

WATER PUMP, REPLACE

Refer to **Fig. 13** for water pump replacement procedure on these models.

1984–87 200SX, 1986–87 STANZA

CYLINDER HEAD, REPLACE

Removal

1. On models equipped with CA18ET engine, remove air intake pipe.
2. On all models, remove timing belt as described under "Timing Belt, Replace."
3. Remove camshaft pulley.
4. Remove cylinder head and manifolds as an assembly. Loosen cylinder head attaching bolts in several steps in sequence, **Fig. 1.**

Installation

1. Position No. 1 cylinder at TDC of compression stroke by setting crankshaft key at 11 o'clock position and camshaft knock pin at 12 o'clock position.
2. Install cylinder head with new gasket. Torque bolts in sequence, **Fig. 8,** to 22 ft. lbs. Retorque all bolts in sequence to 58 ft. lbs., then loosen all bolts completely. Again, torque bolts to 22 ft. lbs. and finally to 54-61 ft. lbs. in sequence. If angle wrench is available, make final torque of bolt 8 83 to 88° and other bolts 75 to 80° clockwise.
3. Install camshaft pulley, then the timing belt and air intake pipe, if equipped.

TIMING BELT, REPLACE

Removal

1. On 200SX models equipped with CA20E engine, remove air intake duct.
2. On Stanza Sedan and Hatchback, raise and support front of vehicle, then remove right front wheel, dust cover and under cover.
3. On Stanza wagon models, remove distributor, power steering pump, front right side dust cover and front engine support stay.
4. On 200SX models, remove cooling fan and radiator shroud.
5. On all models, remove alternator drive belt, power steering pump drive belt and A/C compressor drive belt as equipped.

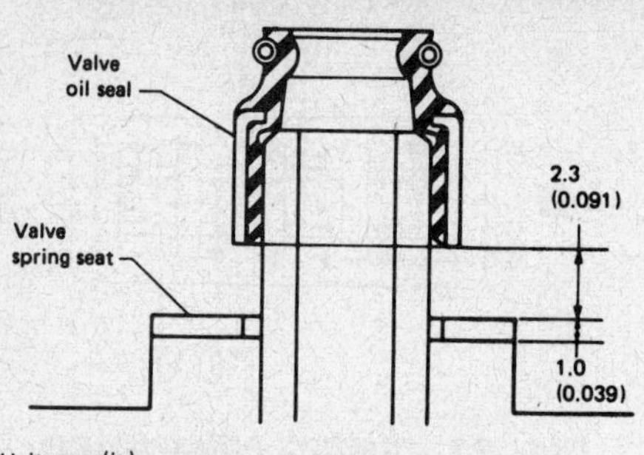

Fig. 14 Valve oil seal installation

6. Position No. 1 cylinder at TDC of compression stroke.
7. On Stanza Sedan and Hatchback, use a suitable engine lifting fixture to support engine, then remove right hand engine mount and bracket.
8. On all models, remove front upper and lower timing belt covers.
9. Loosen timing belt tensioner and return spring, then remove timing belt.

Installation

1. Ensure that No. 1 cylinder is set at TDC of compression stroke.
2. Install timing belt tensioner and return spring. Ensure tensioner pulley rotates smoothly.
3. Install timing belt, noting the following:
   a. Ensure belt is clean and dry.
   b. Align white reference lines on belt with punch mark on camshaft pulleys and crankshaft pulley.
   c. Ensure arrow on timing belt points toward front covers.
4. Tighten belt tensioner, then set tensioner spring as follows:
   a. Hook one end of spring on bolt "B" side, **Fig. 10**, and opposite end on tensioner bracket pawl.
   b. Rotate crankshaft two complete revolutions clockwise.
   c. Tighten bolt "B," then bolt "A," **Fig. 10**, to automatically set belt tension to specifications.

OIL SEALS, REPLACE

Camshaft Oil Seal

1. Remove timing belt as described under "Timing Belt, Replace."
2. Remove camshaft oil seal using a suitable drift and soft faced hammer.
3. Reverse procedure to install. Apply clean engine oil to seal prior to installation.

Crankshaft Front Oil Seal

1. Remove oil pump assembly, then pry front oil seal out of bore.
2. Apply clean engine oil to seal, then install seal and oil pump.

Crankshaft Rear Oil Seal

1. Remove flywheel and rear oil seal retainer.
2. Remove seal from retainer using suitable pliers.
3. Reverse procedure to install. Apply clean engine oil to seal prior to installation.

Valve Oil Seal

1. Remove rocker cover, rocker shaft assembly and spark plug.
2. Position piston at TDC of compression stroke and apply 71 psi air pressure into spark plug hole to hold valves in place.
3. Remove valve spring and oil seal using a suitable valve spring compressor.
4. Reverse procedure to install. Clearance between oil seal and valve spring seat should measure .091 inch, **Fig. 14**.

ENGINE, REPLACE

200SX

1. Release fuel system pressure as follows:
   a. Start engine, then disconnect fuel pump electrical connector, located in trunk tool box.
   b. After engine stalls, crank engine 2 or 3 times.
   c. Turn ignition switch Off, then reconnect fuel pump electrical connector.
2. Disconnect battery ground cable.
3. Drain engine oil and coolant into suitable containers.
4. Scribe hood hinge locations and remove hood.
5. Disconnect or remove all hoses, electrical connectors and accessories necessary for engine removal.
6. On models equipped with manual transmission, remove shift lever.
7. On models equipped with automatic transmission, disconnect shift rod from manual shaft.
8. On all models, disconnect exhaust pipe from exhaust manifold.
9. Mark relationship between propeller shaft and rear axle companion flange and remove propeller shaft.
10. Attach suitable lifting equipment to engine.
11. Remove engine mounting bolts, then lift engine and transmission as an assembly from vehicle.
12. Reverse procedure to install.

Stanza

1. Release fuel system pressure as follows:
   a. Disconnect fuel pump relay located above fuse block.
   b. Start engine.
   c. After engine stalls, crank engine 2 or 3 times.
   d. Turn ignition switch Off, then reconnect fuel pump relay.
2. Disconnect battery ground cable.
3. Scribe hood hinge locations and remove hood.
4. Disconnect or remove all hoses, electrical connectors, accessories, cables and linkages necessary for engine removal.
5. Disconnect both driveshafts from transaxle.
6. Attach suitable lifting equipment to engine.
7. Remove engine mounting bolts, then lift engine and transaxle as an assembly from vehicle.

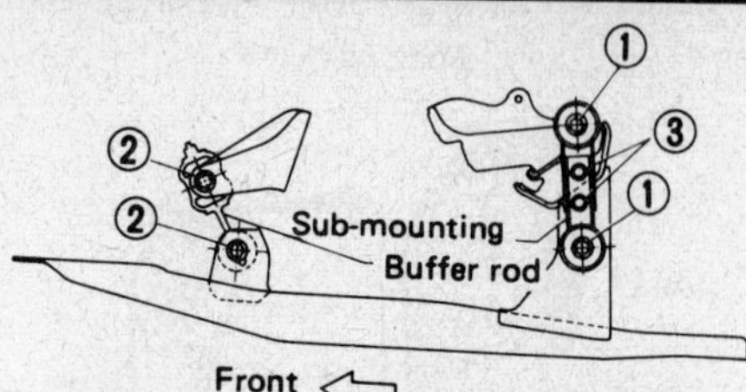

Fig. 15 Buffer rod & sub mounting tightening sequence. 1987 Stanza

8. Reverse procedure to install. On 1986-87 Stanza, tighten right hand, left hand and rear engine mount bolts first, then apply engine load to mounting insulators before tightening buffer rod and sub-mounting. Torque bolts in numerical order, **Fig. 15**, when tightening buffer rod and sub-mounting.

ENGINE DISASSEMBLY

1. Separate engine from transmission.
2. Remove outer engine components, **Figs. 16 through 19.**
3. Remove timing belt, then the water pump, oil pump and oil pan.
4. Remove pistons, bearing caps and crankshaft.

Piston & Rod Disassembly

1. Remove piston rings with a ring remover.
2. Press out piston pin. **Keep disassembled parts in order.**

Cylinder Head Disassembly

1. Remove manifolds from cylinder head.
2. Loosen rocker arm adjusting screws fully, then remove rocker shaft assembly. Loosen attaching bolts in two or three steps.
3. Remove camshaft and camshaft oil seal.
4. Remove valves and valve components using a suitable valve compressor tool.

ENGINE ASSEMBLY

Cylinder Head Assembly

1. Install valves and valve components in order shown, **Fig. 2.** Apply clean engine oil to valve stem and lip of valve oil seal.

Piston & Rod Assembly

1. Assemble pistons, piston pins and connecting rods of designated cylinders. Apply clean engine oil to piston and small end of connecting rod before pressing pin into rod.
2. Install piston rings. Ensure identification marks on rings face upward. **Install outer valve spring with narrow pitch side toward cylinder head.**
3. Install camshaft and camshaft oil seal. Apply clean engine oil to seal prior to installation.
4. Install rocker shaft assembly.

Engine Assembly

1. Install main bearings in proper position on cylinder block. **The No. 3**

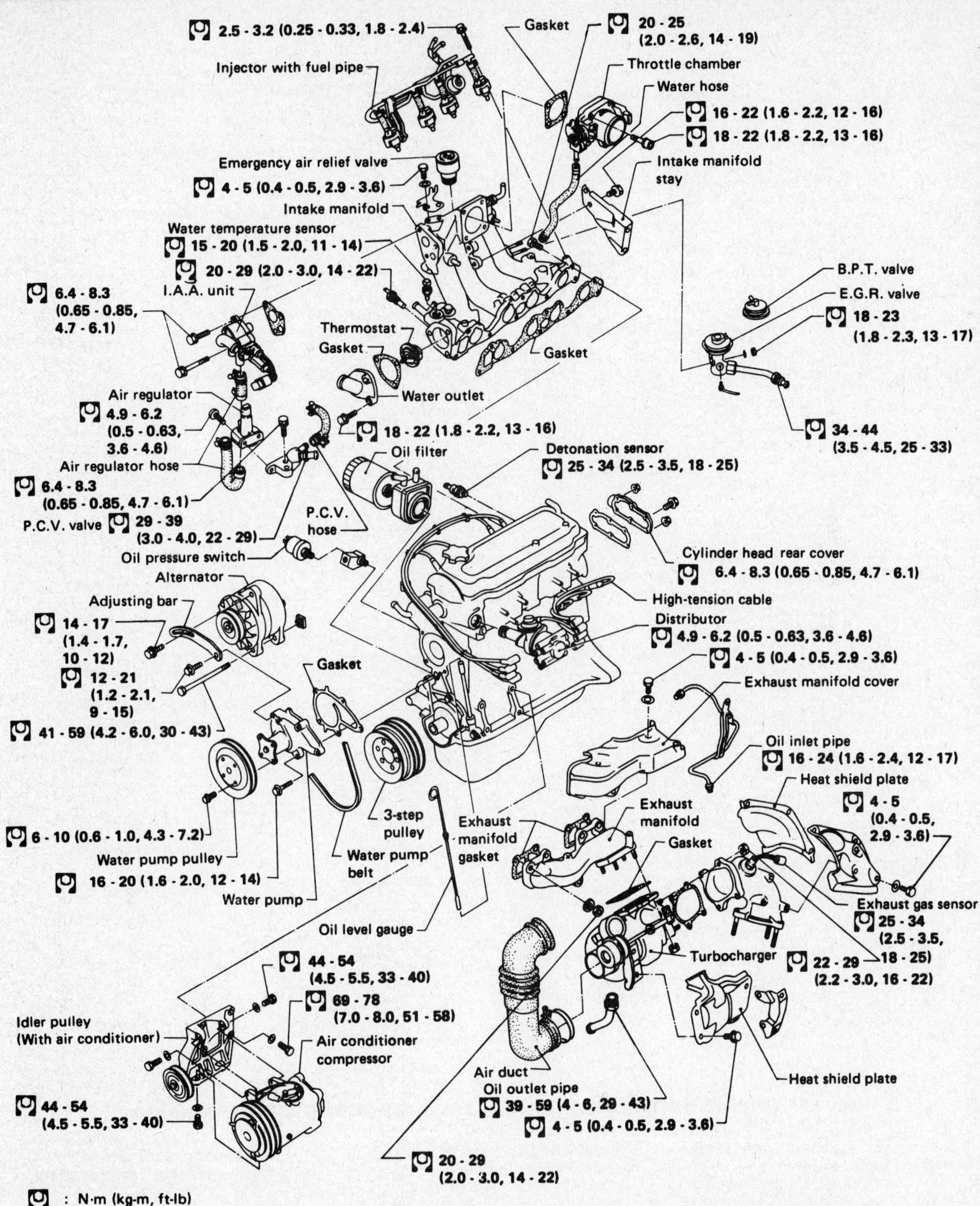
2.5 - 3.2 (0.25 - 0.33, 1.8 - 2.4)
Gasket
20 - 25
(2.0 - 2.6, 14 - 19)
Injector with fuel pipe
Throttle chamber
Water hose
16 - 22 (1.6 - 2.2, 12 - 16)
18 - 22 (1.8 - 2.2, 13 - 16)
Emergency air relief valve
4 - 5 (0.4 - 0.5, 2.9 - 3.6)
Intake manifold
stay
Intake manifold
Water temperature sensor
15 - 20 (1.5 - 2.0, 11 - 14)
20 - 29 (2.0 - 3.0, 14 - 22)
B.P.T. valve
E.G.R. valve
6.4 - 8.3
(0.65 - 0.85,
4.7 - 6.1)
I.A.A. unit
18 - 23
(1.8 - 2.3, 13 - 17)
Thermostat
Gasket
Gasket
Air regulator
Water outlet
4.9 - 6.2
(0.5 - 0.63,
3.6 - 4.6)
18 - 22 (1.8 - 2.2, 13 - 16)
34 - 44
(3.5 - 4.5, 25 - 33)
Oil filter
Detonation sensor
25 - 34 (2.5 - 3.5, 18 - 25)
Air regulator hose
6.4 - 8.3
(0.65 - 0.85, 4.7 - 6.1)
P.C.V. valve
29 - 39
(3.0 - 4.0, 22 - 29)
P.C.V.
hose
Oil pressure switch
Cylinder head rear cover
6.4 - 8.3 (0.65 - 0.85, 4.7 - 6.1)
Alternator
Adjusting bar
High-tension cable
Distributor
4.9 - 6.2 (0.5 - 0.63, 3.6 - 4.6)
14 - 17
(1.4 - 1.7,
10 - 12)
4 - 5 (0.4 - 0.5, 2.9 - 3.6)
Gasket
Exhaust manifold cover
12 - 21
(1.2 - 2.1,
9 - 15)
41 - 59 (4.2 - 6.0, 30 - 43)
Oil inlet pipe
16 - 24 (1.6 - 2.4, 12 - 17)
Heat shield plate
4 - 5
(0.4 - 0.5,
2.9 - 3.6)
Exhaust
manifold
3-step
pulley
Exhaust
manifold
gasket
Gasket
6 - 10 (0.6 - 1.0, 4.3 - 7.2)
Water pump pulley
Water pump
belt
16 - 20 (1.6 - 2.0, 12 - 14)
Water pump
Exhaust gas sensor
25 - 34
(2.5 - 3.5,
18 - 25)
Oil level gauge
Turbocharger
22 - 29
(2.2 - 3.0, 16 - 22)
44 - 54
(4.5 - 5.5, 33 - 40)
69 - 78
(7.0 - 8.0, 51 - 58)
Idler pulley
(With air conditioner)
Air conditioner
compressor
Air duct
Heat shield plate
Oil outlet pipe
39 - 59 (4 - 6, 29 - 43)
44 - 54
(4.5 - 5.5, 33 - 40)
4 - 5 (0.4 - 0.5, 2.9 - 3.6)
20 - 29
(2.0 - 3.0, 14 - 22)
: N·m (kg-m, ft-lb)

Fig. 16 Engine outer components. 1984–86 200SX w/CA18ET engine

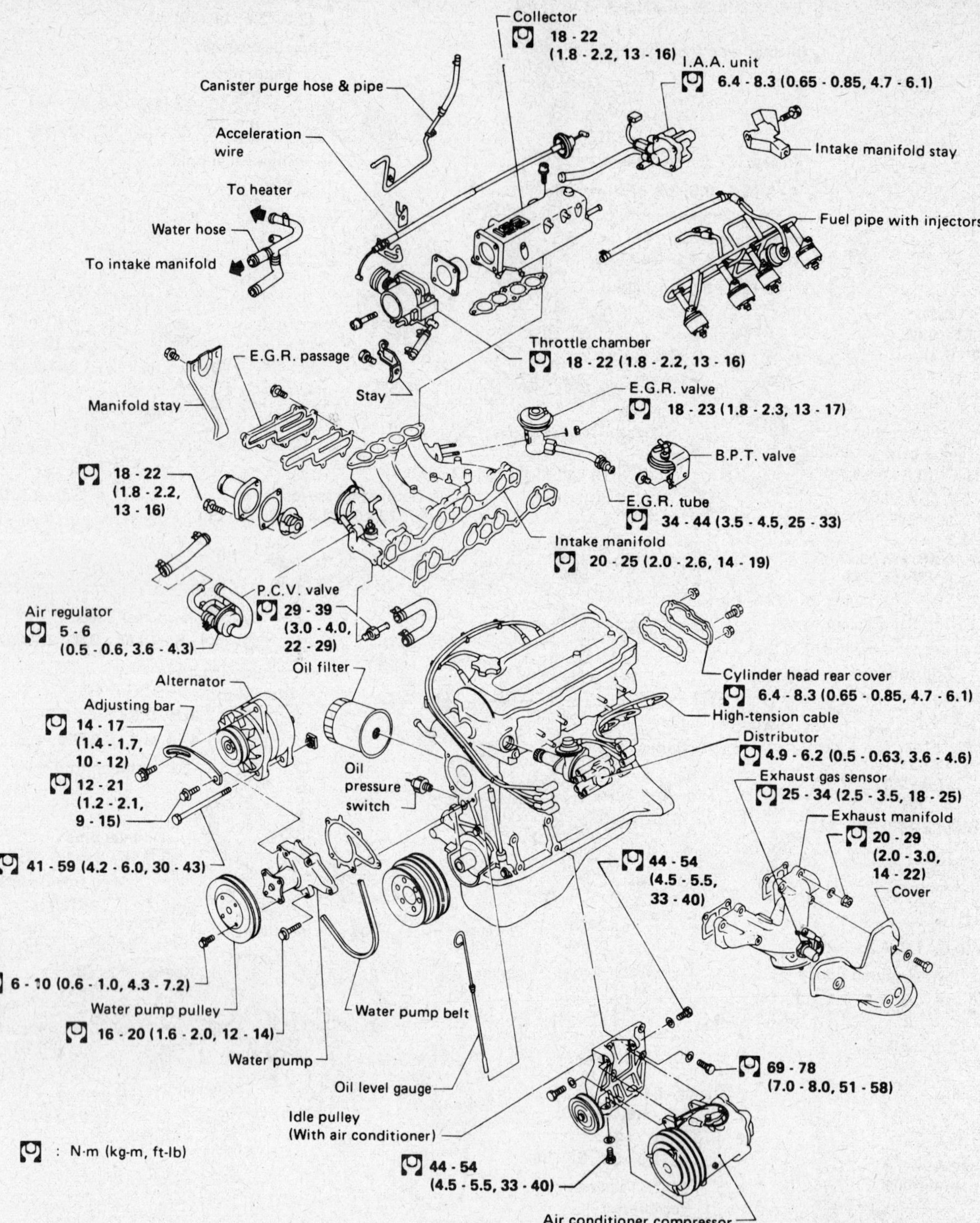

Fig. 17 Engine outer components. 1984–87 200SX w/CA20E engine

bearing is the only one of the flanged type.

2. Apply clean engine oil to main bearing surfaces on both sides of cylinder block and caps.
3. Install crankshaft, then the lower main bearings and caps. Torque bolts to specifications in two or three steps in sequence shown, **Fig. 5.** Ensure crankshaft turns smoothly.
4. Measure crankshaft end play and ensure it is within specifications.
5. Install lubricated piston and rod assemblies into corresponding cylinders. Assemble so that front mark on piston head, **Fig. 6,** faces front of engine. **Set piston rings as shown in Fig. 7.**
6. Install connecting rod bearing caps and torque cap nuts to specifications. Ensure cylinder numbers face in same direction.
7. Install engine outer components, **Figs. 16 through 19.** Install distributor as positioned in **Fig. 12.**

WATER PUMP, REPLACE

Refer to **Fig. 13** for water pump replacement procedure on these models.

TURBOCHARGER

The turbocharger is installed on the exhaust manifold. It utilizes exhaust gas energy to drive the turbine wheel which drives the compressor turbine through a

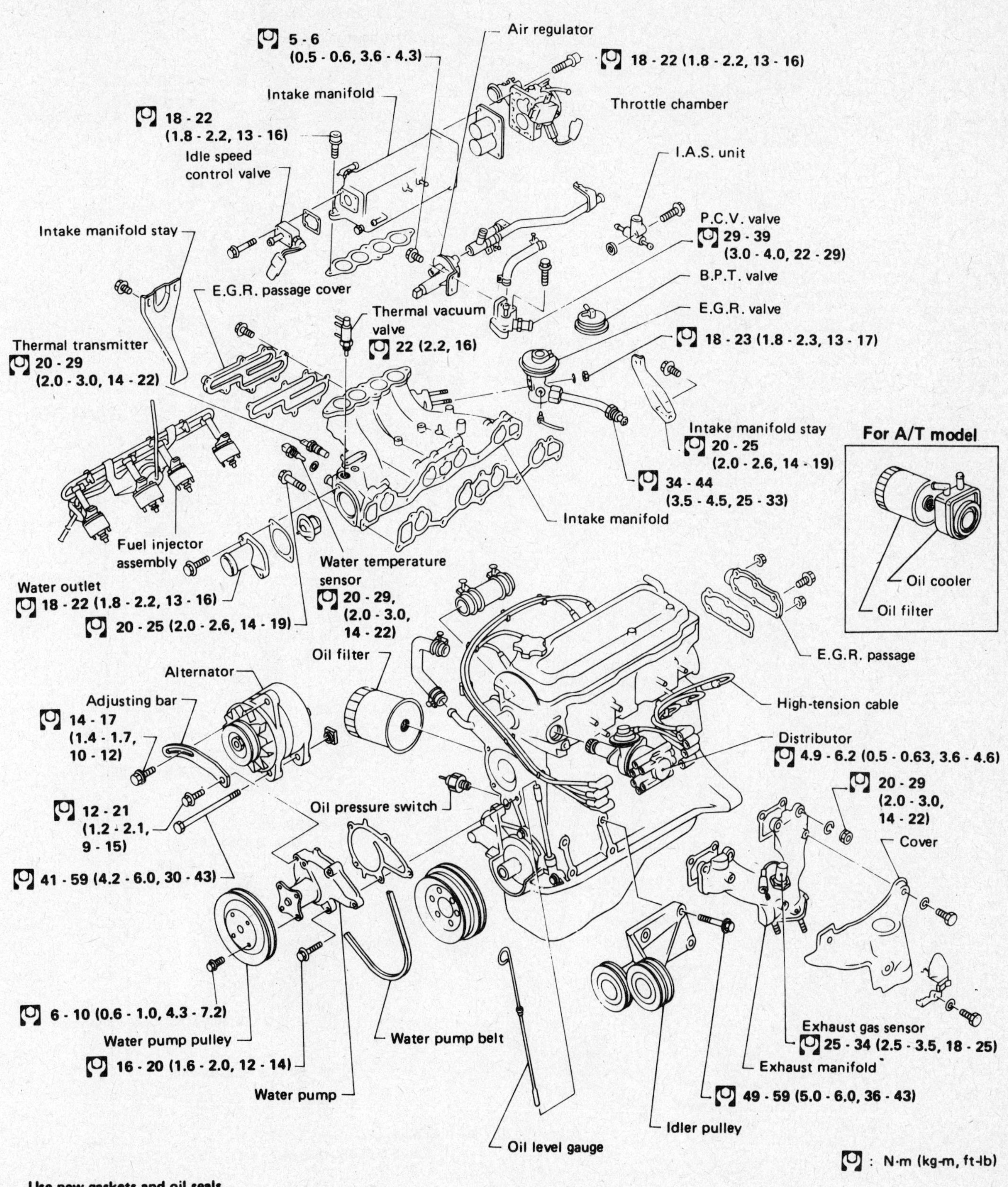

Fig. 18 Engine outer components. 1986–87 Stanza Wagon

common shaft. The compressor provides compressed air to the engine, increasing efficiency. This increased efficiency improves engine output and torque while maintaining fuel economy.

Maximum charging pressure is 12.80-14.37 inches Hg. At 15.35 inches Hg, pressure is relieved by an emergency relief valve.

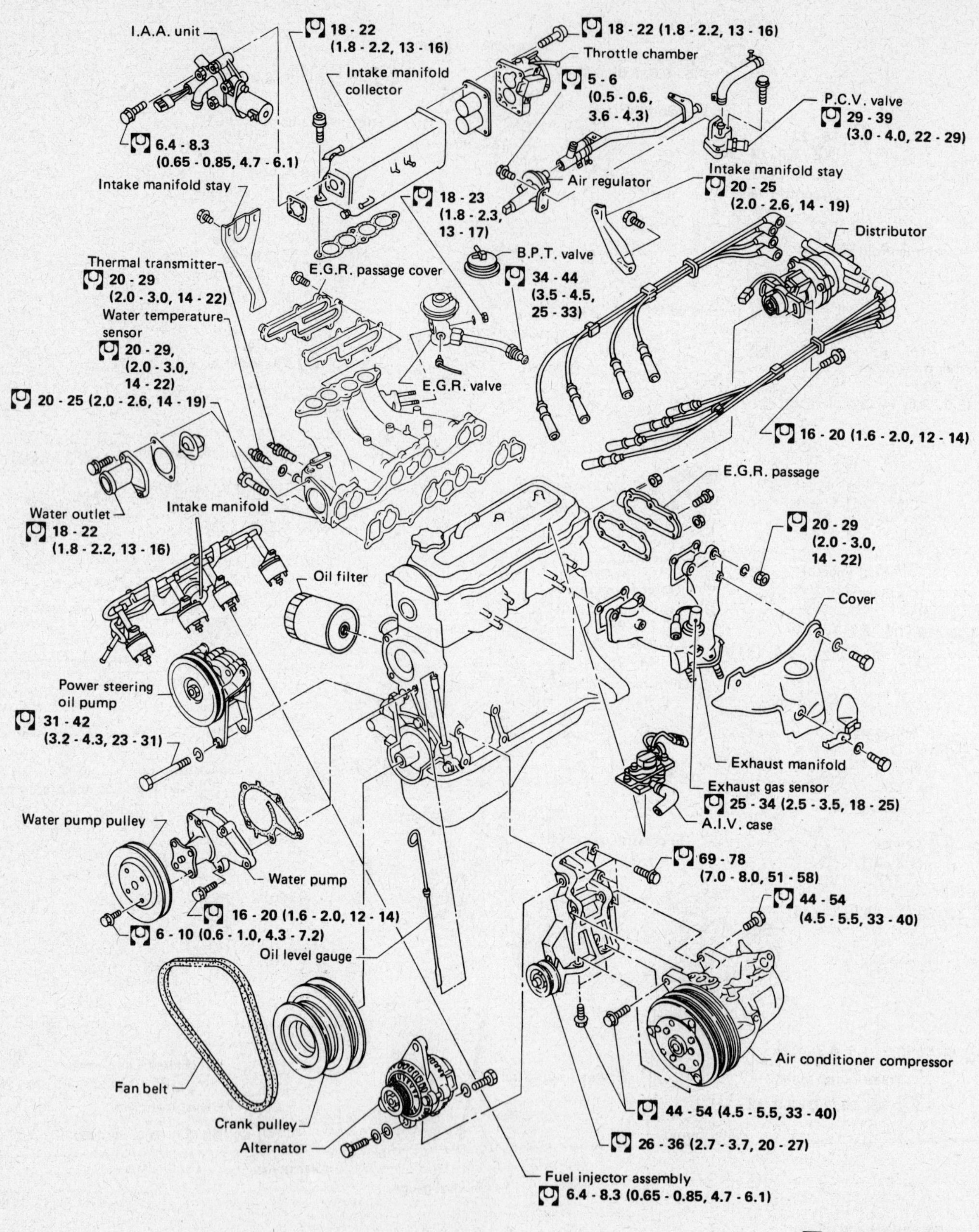
I.A.A. unit
18 - 22
(1.8 - 2.2, 13 - 16)
Intake manifold collector
18 - 22 (1.8 - 2.2, 13 - 16)
Throttle chamber
5 - 6
(0.5 - 0.6,
3.6 - 4.3)
P.C.V. valve
29 - 39
(3.0 - 4.0, 22 - 29)
6.4 - 8.3
(0.65 - 0.85, 4.7 - 6.1)
Air regulator
Intake manifold stay
20 - 25
(2.0 - 2.6, 14 - 19)
Intake manifold stay
18 - 23
(1.8 - 2.3,
13 - 17)
Distributor
B.P.T. valve
Thermal transmitter
20 - 29
(2.0 - 3.0, 14 - 22)
E.G.R. passage cover
34 - 44
(3.5 - 4.5,
25 - 33)
Water temperature sensor
20 - 29,
(2.0 - 3.0,
14 - 22)
E.G.R. valve
20 - 25 (2.0 - 2.6, 14 - 19)
16 - 20 (1.6 - 2.0, 12 - 14)
E.G.R. passage
Water outlet
Intake manifold
18 - 22
(1.8 - 2.2, 13 - 16)
20 - 29
(2.0 - 3.0,
14 - 22)
Oil filter
Cover
Power steering oil pump
31 - 42
(3.2 - 4.3, 23 - 31)
Exhaust manifold
Exhaust gas sensor
25 - 34 (2.5 - 3.5, 18 - 25)
Water pump pulley
A.I.V. case
69 - 78
(7.0 - 8.0, 51 - 58)
Water pump
44 - 54
(4.5 - 5.5, 33 - 40)
16 - 20 (1.6 - 2.0, 12 - 14)
6 - 10 (0.6 - 1.0, 4.3 - 7.2)
Oil level gauge
Air conditioner compressor
Fan belt
44 - 54 (4.5 - 5.5, 33 - 40)
Crank pulley
Alternator
26 - 36 (2.7 - 3.7, 20 - 27)
Fuel injector assembly
6.4 - 8.3 (0.65 - 0.85, 4.7 - 6.1)
: N·m (kg-m, ft-lb)

Fig. 19 Engine outer components. 1986–87 Stanza

E15, E16, E16i & E16S GASOLINE ENGINES

INDEX

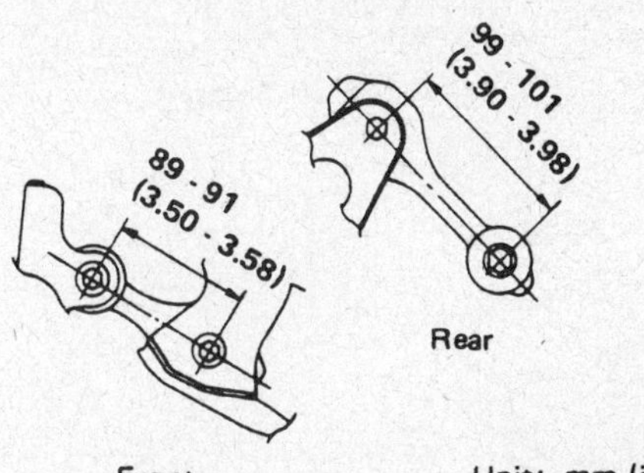

Fig. 1 Adjusting buffer rod bolts. 1987 Pulsar

ENGINE

REPLACE

1983–86 PULSAR & SENTRA

1. Disconnect battery cables, then remove battery, with support bracket, from vehicle.
2. Scribe hood hinge locations and remove hood.
3. Remove air cleaner.
4. Drain engine coolant, then remove radiator with cooling fan.
5. On models equipped with power steering, remove power steering pump.
6. On models equipped with A/C, remove A/C compressor and idler pulley. **Do not discharge refrigerant from A/C system.**
7. On all models, disconnect exhaust pipe from exhaust manifold.
8. On manual transaxle models, disconnect control rod link support rod from transaxle.
9. On automatic transaxle models, disconnect control wire from the transaxle.
10. On Sentra and Pulsar models, remove lower ball joint, then drain gear oil. Loosen strut head bolts and disconnect both drive shafts from transaxle.
11. On all models, disconnect clutch wire, then remove speedometer cable with pinion from transaxle.
12. Disconnect all electrical connectors and vacuum hoses necessary for engine removal.
13. Disconnect fuel lines from fuel pump.
14. Attach suitable engine lifting equipment to engine.
15. Disconnect engine mounting insulators, then lift engine from vehicle and separate from transaxle.
16. Reverse procedure to install.

1987 PULSAR & SENTRA

1. Disconnect battery ground cable.
2. Drain coolant and remove drive belts.
3. Raise and support vehicle.
4. Remove front tires and the under covers.
5. Remove brake caliper assembly, leaving brake hose connected.
6. Disconnect transverse link and tierod ball joints on both sides.
7. Remove knuckle to strut bolts on both sides.
8. Remove both driveshafts, being careful not to damage grease seal on transaxle side.
9. Remove transaxle support rod bolt.
10. Remove center crossmember and the front exhaust pipe.
11. Disconnect front buffer rod.
12. On Pulsar with manual transaxle, disconnect rear buffer rod.
13. On all models, remove air cleaner and disconnect wires, harness, pipes and hoses.
14. Raise engine slightly and disconnect or remove all engine mountings.
15. Reverse procedure to install. On Pulsar models, adjust the length between buffer rod bolts, **Fig. 1.**

ENGINE DISASSEMBLY

1983–86 PULSAR & STANZA

1. Remove transaxle assembly with starter motor.
2. Remove clutch assembly, then mount engine to a suitable work stand.
3. Drain engine oil and coolant into a suitable container.
4. Remove distributor with high tension cable.
5. Remove air induction pipe bracket and EGR tube at EGR valve side.
6. Remove EGR and air induction pipes from exhaust manifold.
7. Remove exhaust manifold cover, then the manifold.

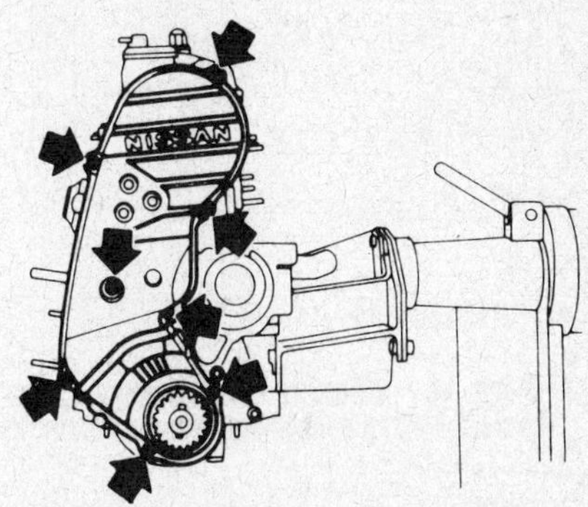

Fig. 2 Timing belt cover removal

8. If equipped, remove A/C compressor bracket and/or power steering pump bracket.
9. Remove intake manifold with carburetor.
10. Loosen water pump pulley bolts, then remove alternator, alternator bracket and drive belt.
11. Remove oil filter, oil pump with gasket and the fuel pump with spacer.
12. Remove oil pan, gasket, seal, oil strainer and thermostat housing.
13. Remove flywheel or drive plate, then the rear plate.
14. Remove water pump and crankshaft pulleys, then the water pump assembly with gasket.
15. Remove upper and lower timing belt covers, **Fig. 2,** then the timing belt tensioner pulley and timing belt. **Place a rotating direction mark on timing belt for assembly reference.**
16. Remove jack shaft pulley, then the crankshaft sprocket with spacer.
17. Remove spark plugs, valve rocker cover and cylinder head bolts, then remove cylinder head. Remove cylinder head bolts in sequence, **Fig. 3,** in two or three steps.
18. Remove cylinder block front cover, then the jack shaft locating plate and jack shaft.
19. Remove connecting rod caps and bearings. Push piston and connecting rod assemblies out toward cylinder head surface. **Numbers are stamped on connecting rods and caps corresponding to each cylinder. Care should be taken to keep all parts,**

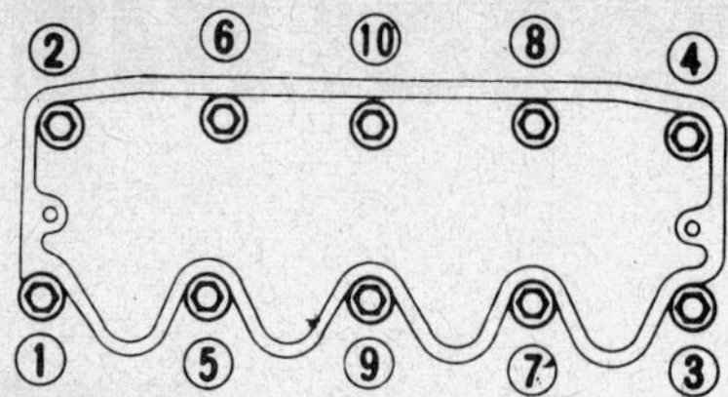

Fig. 3 Cylinder head bolt loosening sequence

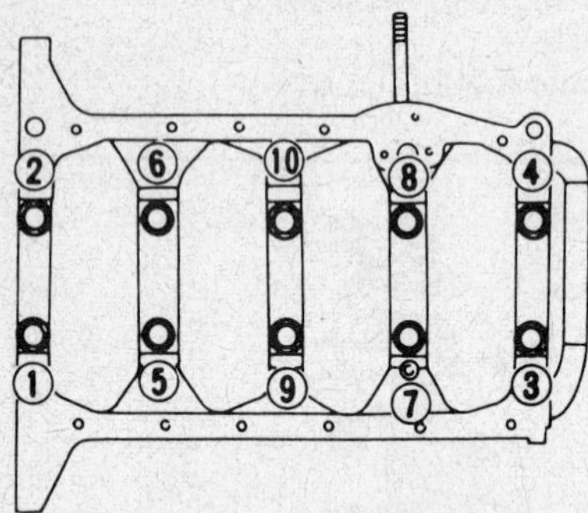

Fig. 4 Main bearing cap bolt loosening sequence

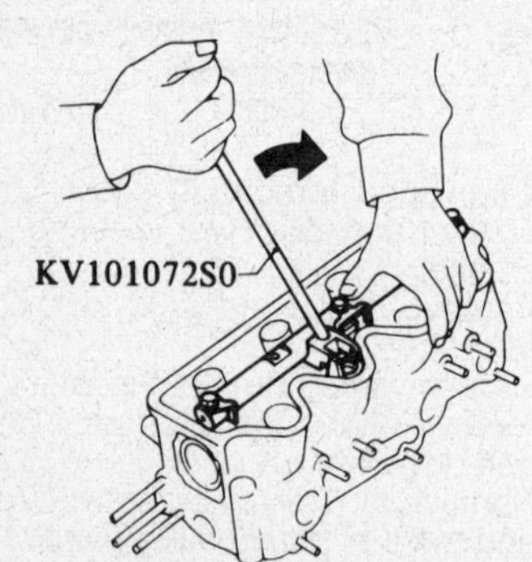

Fig. 6 Valve removal. 1983–86

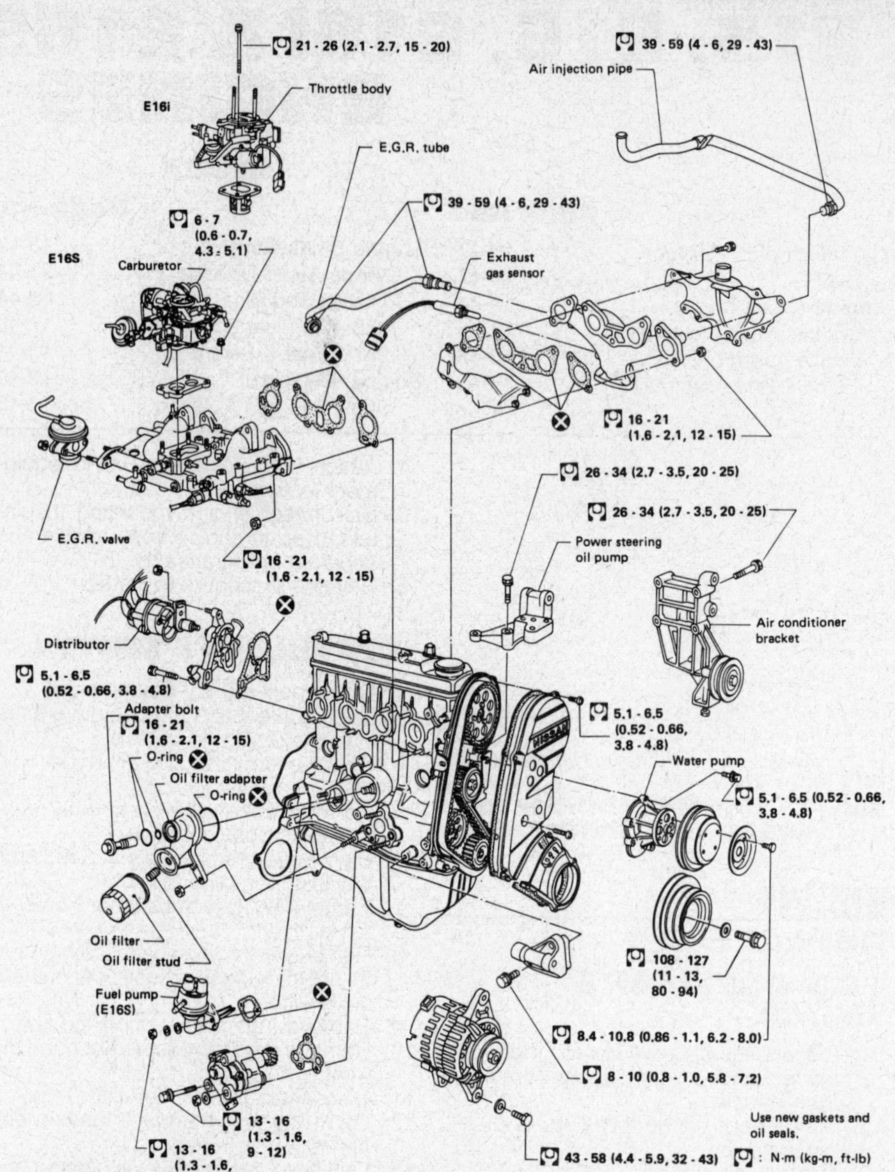

Fig. 5 Engine outer components. 1987 E16i & E16S engines

including bearings, in correct order.

20. Remove crankshaft oil seal retainer, then the main bearing caps with bearing. Loosen bolts in sequence, **Fig. 4.**
21. Remove crankshaft and bearings.

1987 PULSAR & SENTRA

1. Remove external components from engine, **Fig. 5,** then mount engine on suitable work stand.
2. Remove timing belt as described under "Timing Belt, Replace."
3. Drain coolant and engine oil.
4. Remove water pump as described under "Water Pump, Replace."
5. Remove oil pan and strainer as described under "Oil Pan, Replace."
6. Remove cylinder head as described under "Cylinder Head, Replace."
7. Remove pistons.
8. Remove bearing caps and crankshaft, loosening main bearing cap bolts in sequence, **Fig. 4.**

PISTON & ROD DISASSEMBLY

1. Remove piston rings with a ring remover.
2. Press out piston pin. **Keep disassembled parts in order.**

CYLINDER HEAD DISASSEMBLY

1983–86

1. Remove camshaft sprocket, then the cylinder head cover.
2. On 1984-86 models, remove bolt stopper from Nos. 1 and 5 rocker shaft attaching bolts.
3. Remove rocker shaft assembly, then the camshaft.
4. Temporarily install rocker shaft and remove valves and valve components, **Fig. 6.**
5. Remove valve oil seals, **Fig. 7.**
6. Remove rocker shaft from cylinder head, then remove springs and retainers from rocker shaft assembly, **Fig. 8.**

1987

1. Remove rocker shaft with rocker arms, loosening bolts in two or three stages. Keep rocker shaft components in correct order.
2. Remove camshaft from front side.
3. Using suitable tool, remove valve component parts.

ENGINE ASSEMBLY

CYLINDER HEAD ASSEMBLY

1983–86

1. Install valve oil seal, **Fig. 9.**
2. Apply clean engine oil to valve stem and lip of valve seal, then install valve

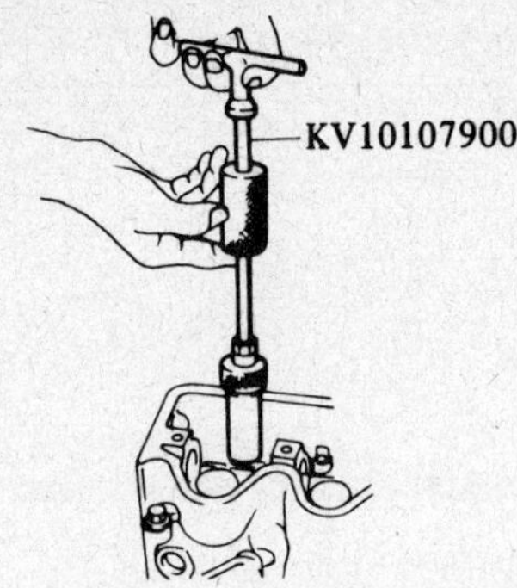

Fig. 7 Valve oil seal removal. 1983–86

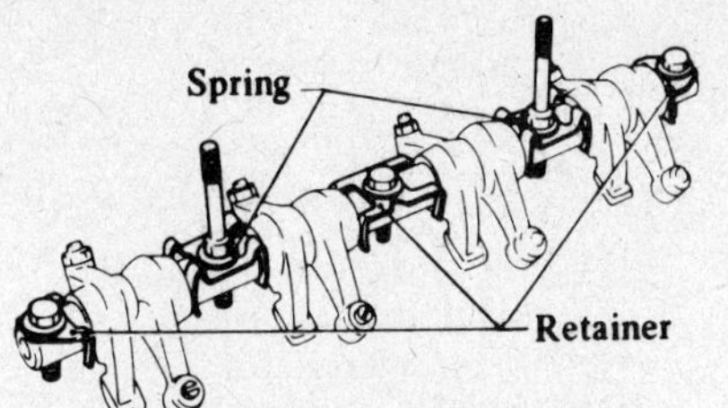

Fig. 8 Rocker shaft assembly

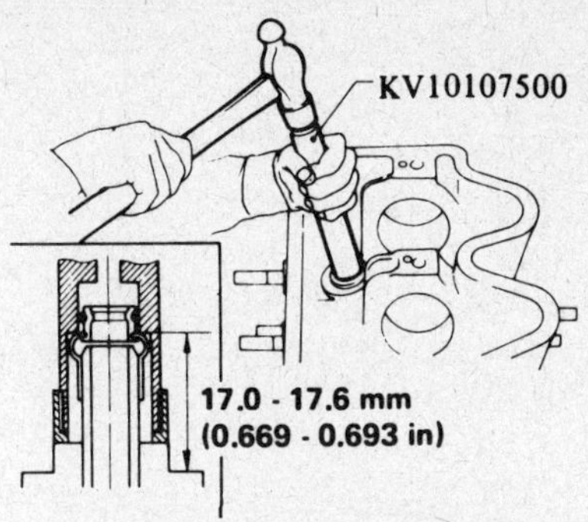

Fig. 9 Valve oil seal installation. 1983–86

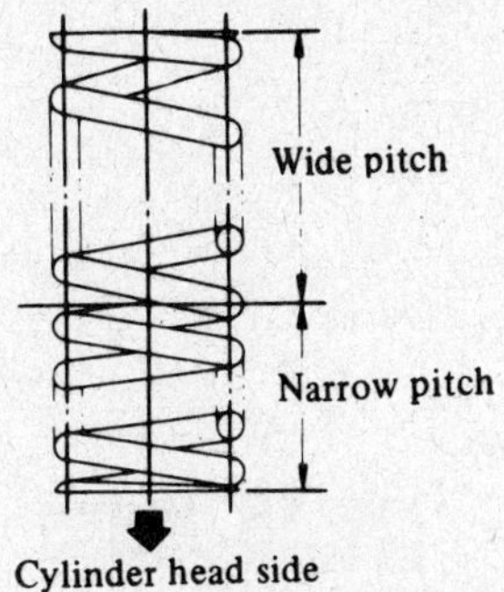

Fig. 10 Valve spring installation

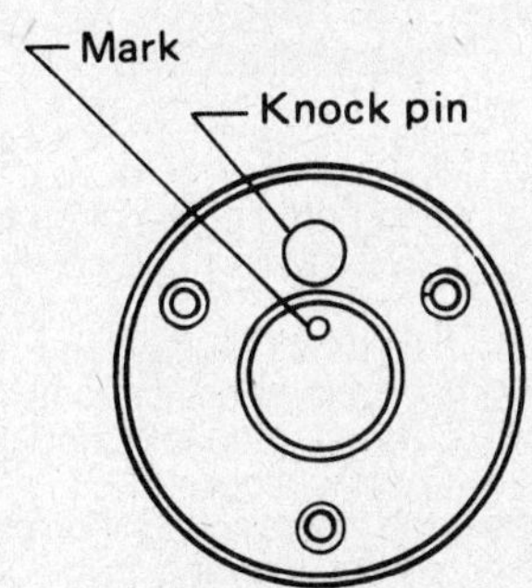

Fig. 11 Aligning camshaft knock pin

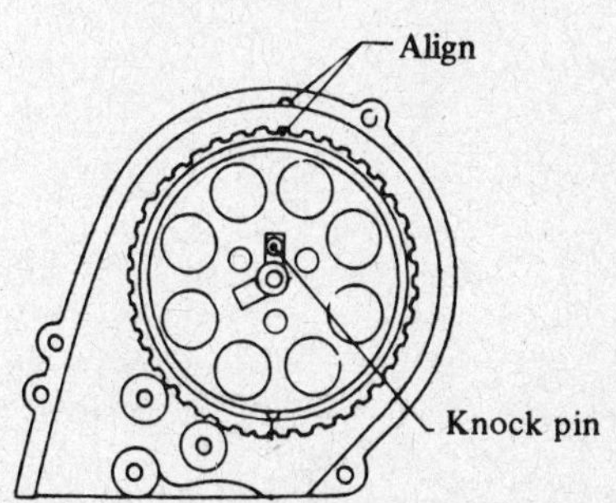

Fig. 12 Camshaft sprocket timing mark alignment

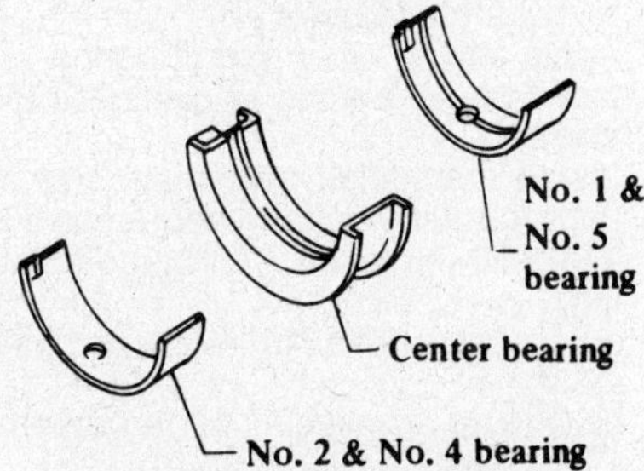

Fig. 13 Main bearing identification

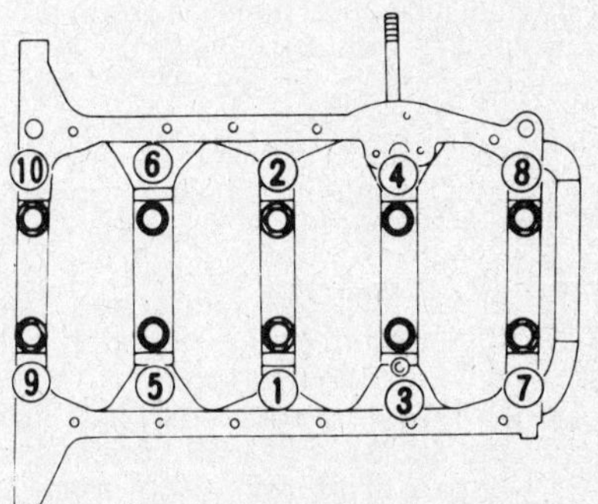

Fig. 14 Main bearing cap bolt tightening sequence

and valve components. **Install valve spring with narrow pitch side toward cylinder head side, Fig. 10.**

3. Apply clean engine oil to camshaft and bearing interior, then install camshaft.
4. Assemble, then install rocker shaft assembly. Note the following:
   a. Apply clean engine oil to camshaft and bearing interior.
   b. Install rocker shaft so that oil hole in shaft faces downward.
   c. Ensure that cutout in center retainer of rocker shaft faces exhaust manifold.
   d. On 1984-86 models, install new bolt stoppers on Nos. 1 and 5 rocker shaft attaching bolts.
5. Install cylinder head cover, then the camshaft sprocket.

1987

1. Install valve component parts, noting the following:
   a. Always use new valve oil seal.
   b. Before installing valve oil seal, install valve spring seat.
   c. Install valve spring with narrow pitch side toward cylinder head side, **Fig. 10.**
2. Install camshaft and upper front cover in cylinder head with new camshaft oil seal.
3. Set knock pin upper side, **Fig. 11.**
4. Install camshaft sprocket, aligning camshaft sprocket mark with upper front cover mark, **Fig. 12.**
5. Align crankshaft sprocket mark with lower front cover mark.
6. Install intake manifold, torquing attaching bolts to 12-15 ft. lbs.

PISTON & ROD ASSEMBLY

1. Assemble pistons, piston pins and connecting rods of designated cylinders. Note the following:
   a. Apply clean engine oil to piston pin and small end of connecting rod before pressing pin into rod.
   b. Assemble piston to rod so that oil hole on connecting rod points toward right side of cylinder block.
2. Install piston rings. Ensure that identification marks on rings face upward.

ENGINE ASSEMBLY

1983–86

1. Install upper main bearings in proper position in cylinder block, **Fig 13. Apply clean engine oil to main bearing surfaces on both sides of cylinder block and cap.**
2. Install crankshaft, then the lower main bearings and caps. Torque bolts to specifications in sequence shown, **Fig. 14.**
3. Measure crankshaft end play and make sure it is within specifications.
4. Apply clean engine oil to the rear oil seal and mating shaft, then install the oil seal into retainer and install assembly to cylinder block. **The lip of the oil seal must face to the outside of the crankshaft.**
5. Install piston and rod assemblies into corresponding cylinders. Assemble so that front mark on piston head, **Fig. 15,** faces front of engine. **Set piston rings as shown in Fig. 16.**
6. Install connecting rod caps and torque cap nuts to specifications. Make sure that cylinder numbers face in same direction.
7. Install rear plate, then the flywheel or drive plate. Torque retaining bolts to specifications.
8. Carefully install jack shaft, then the jack shaft locating plate.
9. Install water pump with a new gasket.
10. Install oil slinger, then the cylinder block cover with oil seal collar.

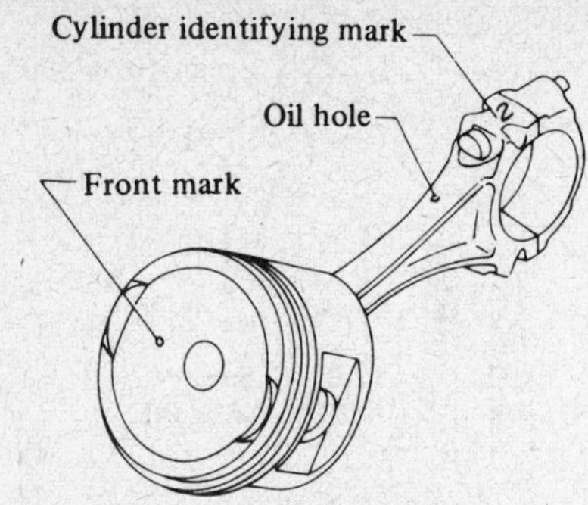

Fig. 15 Piston & connecting rod assembly

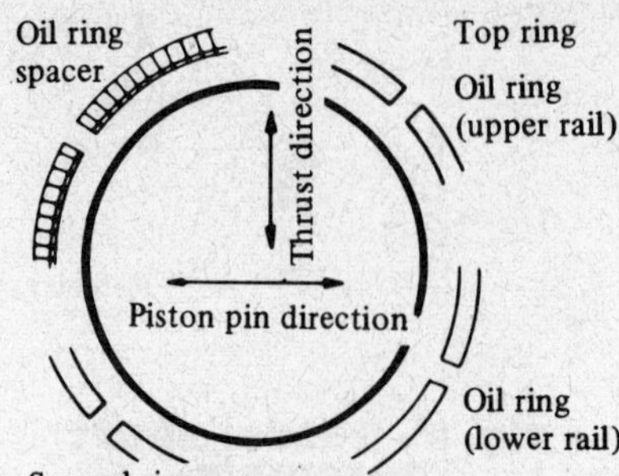

Fig. 16 Piston ring installation

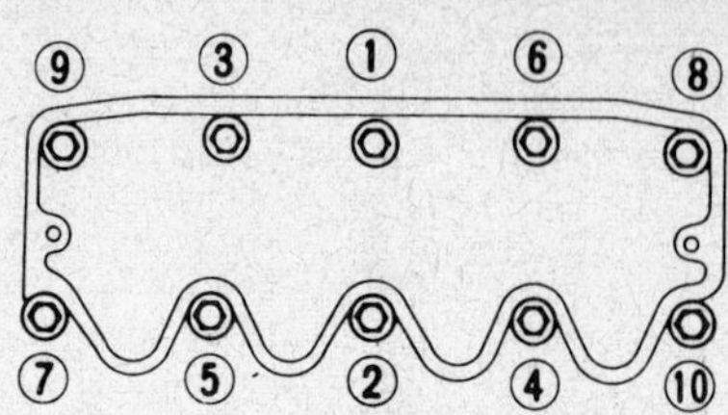

Fig. 17 Cylinder head bolt tightening sequence

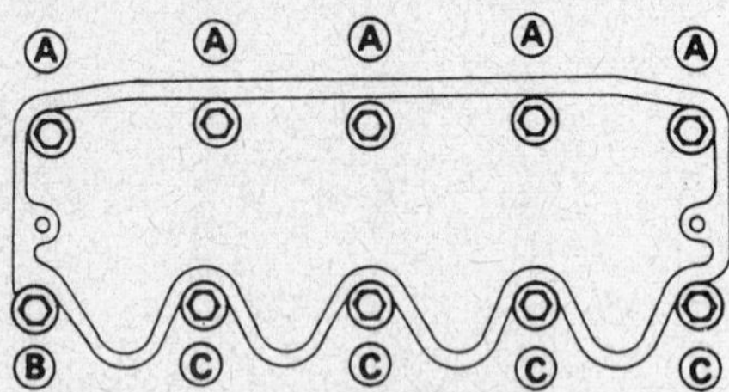

Fig. 18 Cylinder head bolt identification

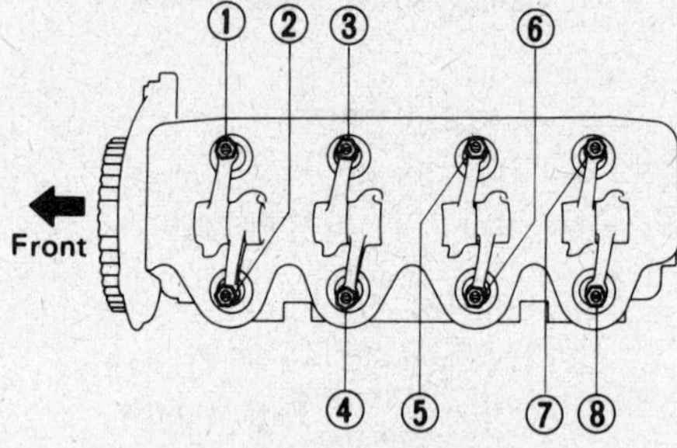

Fig. 19 Valve identification

11. Install jack shaft pulley. Torque pulley retaining bolt to 4.3-5.8 ft. lbs. on 1983 models, or 6.5-8.7 ft. lbs. on 1984-86 models.
12. Install crankshaft sprocket, then temporarily install the tensioner pulley.
13. Install cylinder head assembly as follows:
    a. Clean cylinder block and head mating surface. Do not apply sealant to mating surface.
    b. Rotate crankshaft until No. 1 cylinder is at TDC of compression stroke. This will align mark on crankshaft sprocket with mark on cylinder block cover.
    c. Align mark on camshaft sprocket with mark on cylinder head cover, **Fig. 12.**
    d. Install cylinder head assembly with new gasket. Torque bolts in sequence, **Fig. 17,** to 22 ft. lbs.
    e. Retorque all cylinder head bolts in sequence to 51 ft. lbs., then loosen all bolts completely.
    f. Torque bolts to 22 ft. lbs., then to 51-54 ft lbs. in sequence.
14. Install spark plugs and torque to specifications.
15. Install timing belt as follows:
    a. Ensure that timing marks are aligned, then rotate tensioner clockwise approximately 70 to 80° and temporarily tighten locknut.
    b. Position timing belt on sprocket, then loosen tensioner locknut so that tensioner pushes on belt.
    c. Rotate camshaft sprocket clockwise approximately 20°, then torque tensioner lock nut to 12-15 ft. lbs. while preventing tensioner from turning.
16. Install water pump pulley, then the upper and lower timing belt covers with spacer.
17. Install crankshaft pulley and torque retaining bolt to specifications.
18. Install exhaust manifold and torque nuts to specifications.
19. If equipped, install A/C compressor and/or power steering pump brackets.
20. Install oil pump with new gasket. Torque attaching bolts and nuts to 6.7-8.7 ft. lbs. on 1983 models, 6.5-10.1 ft. lbs. on 1984 models, or 5.8-7.2 ft. lbs. on 1985 models.
21. Install fuel pump with insulator. Torque attaching nuts to 6.7-8.7 ft. lbs.
22. Install oil filter, then the alternator bracket and alternator.
23. Install intake manifold with carburetor. Torque nuts to specifications.
24. Install thermostat housing with distributor. Torque thermostat housing attaching bolt to 2.7-3.7 ft. lbs. on 1983 models, or 2.9-4.3 ft. lbs. on 1984-86 models.
25. Install clutch assembly using tool No. KV30100900 on 1983 models, or KV30101000 on 1984-86 models. Torque retaining bolt to 5.1-7.2 ft. lbs. on 1983-84 models, or 16-22 ft. lbs on 1985-86 models.

1987

1. Assemble pistons, noting the following:
    a. Numbers are stamped on connecting rod and cap corresponding to each cylinder, **Fig. 15.**
    b. Arrange so that front mark on piston head faces toward front of engine.
    c. When pressing piston pin in connecting rod, apply engine oil to pin and small end of connecting rod.
    d. After assembling, ensure piston swings smoothly.
    e. Set piston rings as shown, **Fig. 16.** Install so that stamped mark on ring faces upward and apply engine oil to sliding parts.
2. Set main bearings in proper position on cylinder block, noting the following:
    a. Only center bearing (No. 3 bearing) is flanged, **Fig. 13.**
    b. Nos. 2 and 4 bearings and Nos, 1 and 5 bearings are the same.
    c. Upper and lower bearings are not interchangeable as upper bearings have oil grooves.
3. Apply engine oil to main bearing surfaces on both sides of cylinder block and cap.
4. Install crankshaft and main bearing caps, torquing bolts, in sequence, **Fig. 14,** to 36-43 ft. lbs., noting the following:
    a. Torque bolts in two or three stages.
    b. Ensure crankshaft turns smoothly by hand.
5. Ensure crankshaft endplay, measured at center bearing, is .002-.007 inch.
6. Using suitable tool, install pistons in respective cylinders, noting the following:
    a. Be careful not to scratch cylinder wall with connecting rod.
    b. Apply engine oil to cylinder wall, piston and bearing.
    c. Arrange so that front mark on piston head faces toward front of engine.
7. Install connecting rod bearing caps, torquing nuts to 23-27 ft. lbs.
8. Measure connecting rod side clearance. If clearance is not .0039-.0146 inch, replace connecting rod and/or crankshaft as necessary.
9. Install cylinder head. Refer to "Cylinder Head, Replace."
10. Install oil pan. Refer to "Oil Pan, Replace."
11. Install water pump. Refer to "Water Pump, Replace."
12. Install timing belt. Refer to "Timing Belt, Replace."
13. Install external components on engine, **Fig. 5.**

OIL PAN

REPLACE

1987

1. Raise and support vehicle and drain engine oil.
2. Remove splash cover and under cover from right side.
3. Remove center crossmember.
4. Remove front exhaust pipe.
5. Remove front buffer rod and buffer rod bracket.
6. Remove engine gussets.
7. Remove oil pan as follows:
   a. Insert seal cutter KV10111100 or equivalent between cylinder block and oil pan. **Do not use screwdriver.**
   b. Slide seal cutter by tapping with hammer.
8. Reverse procedure to install, noting the following:
   a. Remove all traces of liquid gasket from mating surfaces of oil pan and cylinder block.
   b. Apply a continuous bead of liquid gasket, .138-.177 inch wide, to mating surface of oil pan.
   c. Apply liquid gasket to inner sealing surface instead of surface where there is no groove at bolt hole. **Attach oil pan to cylinder block within five minutes after coating and wait at least 30 minutes before refilling engine oil or starting engine.**

TIMING BELT

REPLACE

1987

Removal

1. Disconnect battery ground cable.
2. Remove splash cover and under cover from right side of vehicle.
3. Remove drive belts.
4. Set No. 1 cylinder at top dead center (TDC) on its compression stroke.
5. Remove water pump and crankshaft pulleys.
6. Support engine with suitable jack and remove right side engine mounting bracket.
7. Remove upper and lower dust covers, **Fig. 2.**
8. Loosen timing belt tensioner locknut and rotate tensioner clockwise, then tighten tensioner locknut. **Mark rotating direction mark on timing belt.**
9. Remove timing belt. **After removing timing belt, do not rotate crankshaft and camshaft separately.**
10. Remove belt tensioner and return spring.

Installation

1. Ensure No. 1 cylinder is set at TDC on its compression stroke and that marks on camshaft sprocket and upper front cover and marks on crankshaft sprocket and lower front cover are properly aligned.
2. Temporarily install tensioner and return spring.
3. Rotate tensioner clockwise approximately 70-80° and temporarily tighten locknut.
4. Set timing belt, noting the following:
   a. Ensure timing belt and sprockets are clean and free of oil or water.
   b. Do not bend timing belt tightly.
   c. Install timing belt with rotating direction mark facing engine rotation direction.
   d. Ensure timing belt is not loose around jack shaft and camshaft sprockets.
5. Loosen tensioner locknut so that tensioner pulley pushes on timing belt.
6. With all spark plugs removed, turn camshaft sprocket approximately 20° (2 cogs) clockwise.
7. Torque tensioner locknut to 12-15 ft. lbs. while counterholding tensioner.
8. Install crank sprocket plate and upper and lower dust covers.

CYLINDER HEAD

REPLACE

1987

Removal

1. Remove timing belt as previously described.
2. Remove camshaft sprocket and front cover.
3. Remove exhaust manifold, air cleaner, rocker cover and distributor.
4. Remove cylinder head with intake manifold, noting the following:
   a. Bolts should be loosened in two or three stages.
   b. Head warpage or cracking may result from removing in incorrect order, **Fig. 3.**
5. Remove intake manifold from cylinder head.

Installation

1. Install cylinder head with new gasket, noting the following:
   a. Be sure to install washers between cylinder head and bolts.
   b. There are three kinds of cylinder head bolts of varying lengths, **Fig. 18.** Bolts A are 3.74 inches (95 mm), bolt B is 4.33 inches (110 mm) and bolts C are 3.15 inch (80 mm).
2. Apply oil to threaded portion and seat surface of cylinder head bolts and tighten cylinder head bolts as follows, **Fig. 17.**
   a. Torque all bolts to 22 ft. lbs.
   b. Torque all bolts to 51 ft. lbs.
   c. Loosen all bolts completely.
   d. Torque all bolts to 22 ft. lbs.
   e. Torque all bolts to 51-54 ft. lbs. or, if angle wrench is available, turn bolts A, **Fig. 18,** 45° clockwise, bolt B 55° clockwise and bolts C 40° clockwise.
3. Install timing belt and adjust belt tension.
4. Install rocker shaft with rocker arms, noting the following:
   a. Apply engine oil to rocker shaft and interior of rocker arm.
   b. Ensure punched mark on rocker shaft faces toward front side and oil holes in rocker shaft face downward.
   c. Ensure cutout in center retainer of rocker shaft faces toward exhaust manifold side.
5. Tighten rocker shaft bolts, noting the following:
   a. Ensure valve clearance adjusting screws are fully loosened.
   b. Tighten bolts gradually, in two or three steps, from center outward.
6. Install new bolt stopper on Nos. 1 and 5 bolts.
7. Adjust valve clearance as follows:
   a. Set No. 1 cylinder in TDC on its compression stroke and adjust valve clearance 1, 2, 3 and 6, **Fig. 19.**
   b. Set No. 4 cylinder in TDC on its compression stroke and adjust valve clearance 4, 5, 7 and 8.
8. Install exhaust manifold.
9. Install distributor.
10. Install rocker cover, dust covers, water pump and crankshaft pulleys and the drive belts.

WATER PUMP

REPLACE

1. Disconnect battery ground cable and drain cooling system.
2. Remove power steering drive belt and the power steering oil pump.
3. Remove alternator drive belt.
4. Loosen alternator attaching bolts and push alternator toward engine.
5. Remove water pump pulley, then the water pump and gasket.
6. Reverse procedure to install, using new gasket.

L24E, L28E & L28ET GASOLINE ENGINES

INDEX

ENGINE REPLACE

280 ZX

Perform the following to relieve pressure in fuel system:

1. On non-turbocharged models:
   a. Start engine and remove fuel pump relay-2 while engine is running.
   b. After engine stalls, crank engine momentarily.
   c. Turn ignition switch to off position and reinstall relay.
2. On turbocharged models:
   a. Start engine.
   b. Open rear door and pull back center tonneau cover.
   c. Disconnect wiring harness connector to fuel pump with engine running.
   d. After engine stalls, crank engine momentarily.
   e. Turn ignition switch to off position and reconnect fuel pump harness connector.
3. Disconnect battery ground cable.
4. Remove splash pan.
5. Drain engine coolant and oil pan.
6. Scribe hood hinge locations and remove hood.
7. Disconnect upper and lower radiator hoses.
8. Remove radiator shrouds.
9. On models equipped with automatic transmission, disconnect oil cooler lines.
10. Remove reservoir tank from radiator and remove radiator.
11. On models with power steering, remove pump drive belt, remove power steering pump, and position aside.
12. On air conditioned models, remove drive belt, dismount compressor and move aside. **Never discharge gas from compressor while work is being performed.**
13. Disconnect or remove the following:
    a. Wiring harness connectors at alternator.
    b. Wiring harness connector at oil pressure switch.
    c. Wiring harness connector and battery cable at starter.

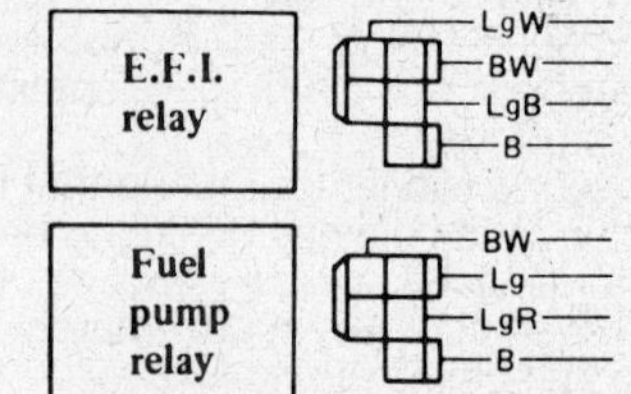

Both of the above relays are green, but can be distinguished by the color of harness.

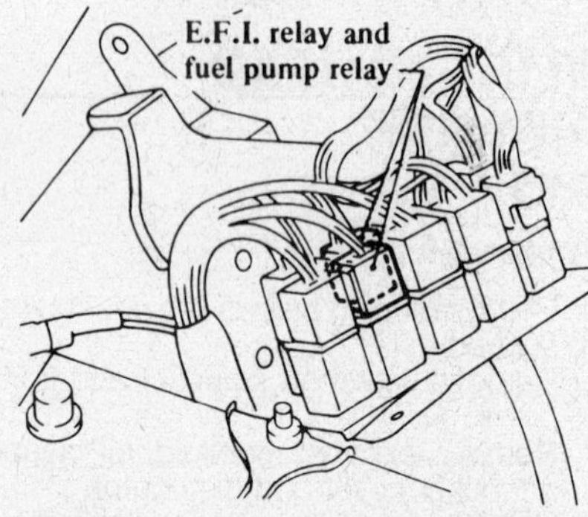

Fig. 1 Fuel pump relay location. 1983 Maxima

    d. Wiring harness connector at auxiliary fan.
    e. Heater hoses.
    f. Fuel and canister hoses.
    g. Wiring harness connector to distributor.
    h. E.F.I. harness connector.
    i. V.C.M. from bracket on turbocharged models.
    j. Wiring harness connectors at thermal transmitter and water temperature sending switch or cylinder head temperature sensor.
    k. High tension coil wire.
    l. F.I.C.D. and A.S.C.D. vacuum hoses.
    m. Brake booster vacuum hose at intake manifold.
    n. Accelerator cable and torsion shaft.
    o. Air flow meter ducting.
    p. Engine oil cooler hoses at oil filter bracket, if equipped.
14. Disconnect speedometer cable at extension housing.
15. Disconnect wiring harness connectors at all transmission mounted switches.
16. On manual transmission models, remove clutch operating cylinder from transmission housing and remove shift lever.
17. On automatic transmission models, disconnect range selector rod at transmission.
18. Remove heat shield beside master cylinder and disconnect front exhaust pipe.
19. Mark relationship of propeller shaft to differential carrier companion flange and remove propeller shaft. Plug hole in transmission housing to prevent oil loss.
20. Support transmission with suitable jack and remove transmission crossmember.
21. Attach suitable lifting equipment to engine.
22. Remove nuts and bolts from front engine mounts.
23. Remove engine and transmission from vehicle as an assembly.
24. Reverse procedure to install.

MAXIMA

1. Relieve fuel system pressure. Remove relay bracket, then start engine and disconnect fuel pump relay electrical connector, **Fig. 1.** After engine stalls, crank engine momentarily, then turn ignition switch to the Off position and reconnect fuel pump relay. If engine will not start, disconnect fuel pump relay and crank engine for approximately five seconds, then turn ignition switch off.
2. Disconnect battery ground cable.
3. Remove hood.
4. Drain cooling system and oil pan.
5. Remove air cleaner ducts.
6. Disconnect radiator upper and lower hoses.
7. Remove air cleaner and air flow meter assembly.
8. Disconnect carbon canister hoses.
9. Remove radiator and shroud.
10. On models equipped with automatic transmission:
    a. Remove splash board.
    b. Disconnect oil cooler lines from radiator.

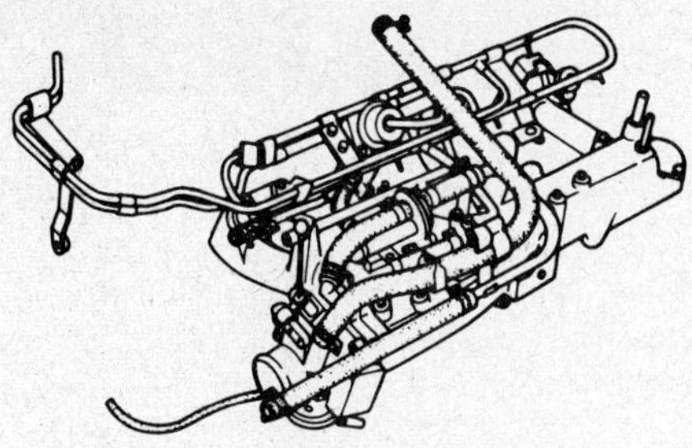

Fig. 2 Intake manifold & fuel injection assembly (Typical)

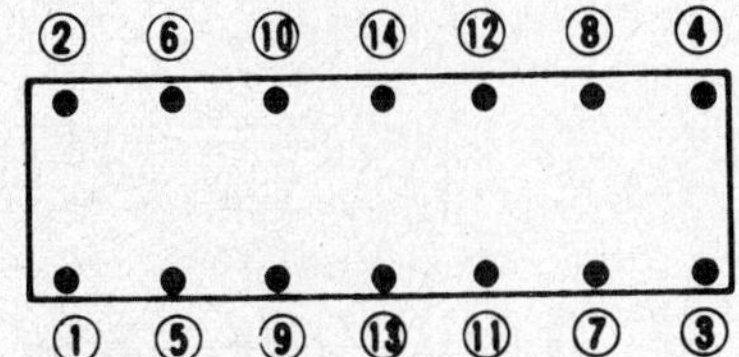

Fig. 5 Cylinder head bolt loosening sequence

c. Disconnect vacuum hose.

11. On models equipped with A/C and power steering:
    a. Remove power steering pump and bracket.
    b. Remove A/C compressor and bracket.
12. Disconnect accelerator cable from car.
13. Disconnect the following cables and hoses: engine ground cable, starter motor wiring, EGR solenoid wire, fuel injector wiring, throttle valve switch wiring, BCDD wiring, high tension wire between ignition coil and distributor, wire to block terminal distributor harness, wire to thermostat housing, vacuum cutting solenoid wiring, cold start valve wiring, air regulator wiring, fuel hoses, heater hoses, Master-Vac vacuum hose, alternator wiring, oil pressure switch wiring, back-up lamp switch wiring, neutral switch wiring, top switch wiring, inhibitor switch housing and downshift solenoid wiring.
14. Disconnect speedometer cable.
15. If equipped with manual transmission, remove C-ring and shift lever pin from transmission striking rod, then the shift lever.
16. If equipped with automatic transmission disconnect range lever.
17. On all models, disconnect exhaust pipe from exhaust manifold.
18. Remove exhaust pipe bracket from rear mounting insulator.
19. Remove propeller shaft center bearing bracket and the propeller shaft.
20. Support transmission with a suitable jack.
21. Remove bolts securing rear engine crossmember to body.
22. Attach suitable engine lifting equipment to engine and raise engine slightly.
23. Remove front engine mount bolts.

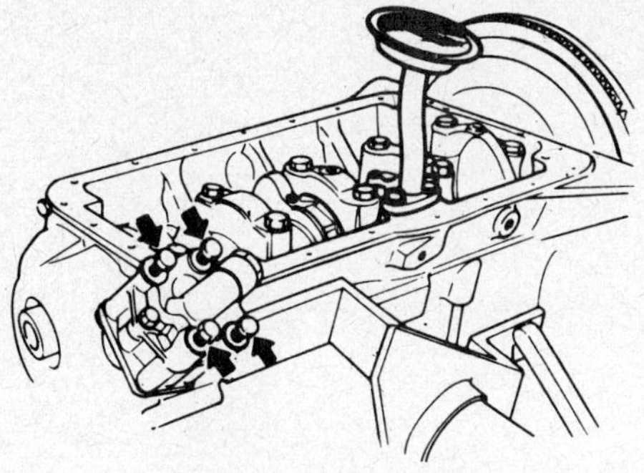

Fig. 3 Oil pump replacement

24. Remove engine and transmission assembly from vehicle.
25. Reverse procedure to install.

ENGINE DISASSEMBLY

1. Remove starter motor.
2. Separate transmission from engine:
    a. On automatic transmission models, remove converter dust cover and remove bolts securing torque converter to drive plate.
    b. Remove bolts securing transmission and remove transmission.
3. Remove clutch assembly from flywheel.
4. Remove auxiliary cooling fan and duct, where equipped.
5. Remove alternator and alternator bracket.
6. Remove R.H. engine mount.
7. Remove oil filter and bracket (L28ET) and remove oil pressure switch.
8. Completely drain engine oil and coolant into a suitable container, by removing drain plugs.
9. Disconnect and remove following components:
    a. Distributor cap and high tension cables.
    b. Distributor assembly.
    c. Hoses connected to engine.
10. Remove fan, fan coupling and fan pulley.
11. Remove alternator adjusting bar and pulley bracket with idler pulley for power steering if so equipped.
12. Remove intake manifold as an assembly with fuel pipes and air regulator.
    a. Disconnect hose between throttle chamber and rocker cover at rocker cover.
    b. Disconnect pipe between heater housing and water inlet at water inlet.
    c. Remove bolt securing water pipe and fuel pipe to cylinder head.
    d. Remove tube connecting heater housing to thermostat housing.
    e. Remove bolts securing intake manifold to cylinder head and remove intake manifold assembly, **Fig. 2.**
    f. Remove P.C.V. hose, sub heat shield plate, and E.G.R. tube if so equipped.
13. Remove crankshaft pulley, using suitable puller.

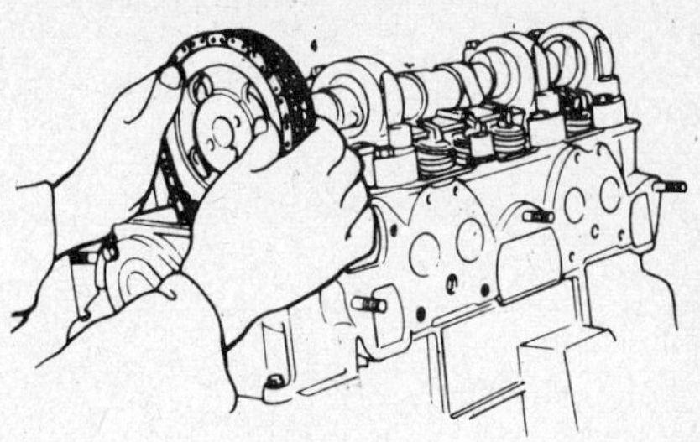

Fig. 4 Camshaft sprocket removal

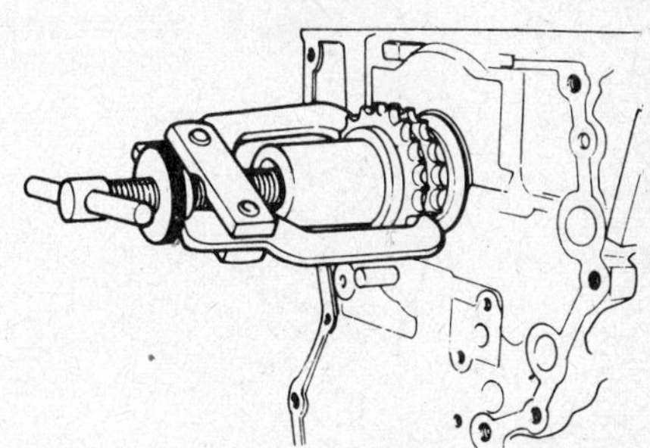

Fig. 6 Crankshaft sprocket removal

14. Remove turbocharger assembly (L28ET) with exhaust outlet.
15. Remove exhaust manifold.
16. Remove thermostat housing and water pump.
17. On L28ET remove air conditioner idler pulley bracket and compressor bracket with crank angle sensor.
18. Remove air conditioning compressor bracket where equipped.
19. Remove L.H. engine mount.
20. Remove water inlet and water pipes.
21. Remove spark plugs and oil gauge.
22. Remove oil pump and oil pump drive spindle, **Fig. 3.**
23. Remove oil pan and oil strainer.
24. Remove rocker cover.
25. Lock camshaft and remove camshaft bolt.
26. Remove camshaft sprocket, **Fig. 4,** and slowly lower timing chain. **Before removing camshaft sprocket be sure to mark position of camshaft dowel pin in camshaft sprocket. This step is extremely important to insure proper installation of timing chain during assembly.**
27. Remove bolts securing cylinder head to front cover and loosen cylinder head bolts in sequence, **Fig. 5,** and remove cylinder head.
28. Remove front cover, timing chain, chain tensioner and guides, oil thrower, oil pump drive gear and crankshaft sprocket, **Fig. 6.**
29. Lock crankshaft and remove flywheel or drive plate.
30. Remove connecting rod bearing caps and bearings. Push piston/connecting rod assemblies out toward cylinder head surface. **Numbers are stamped on connecting rods and caps corresponding to each cylinder. Care should be taken to keep all parts, including bearings, in correct order.**

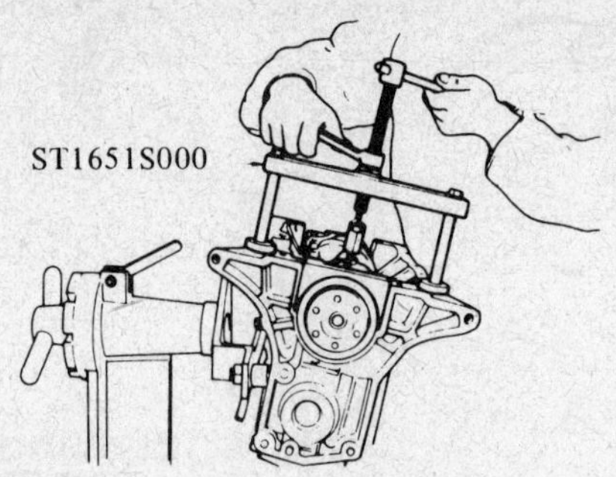

Fig. 7 Rear main bearing cap removal

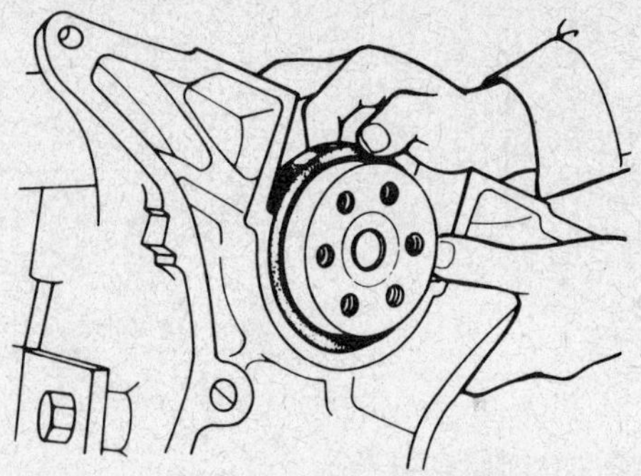

Fig. 8 Rear oil seal removal

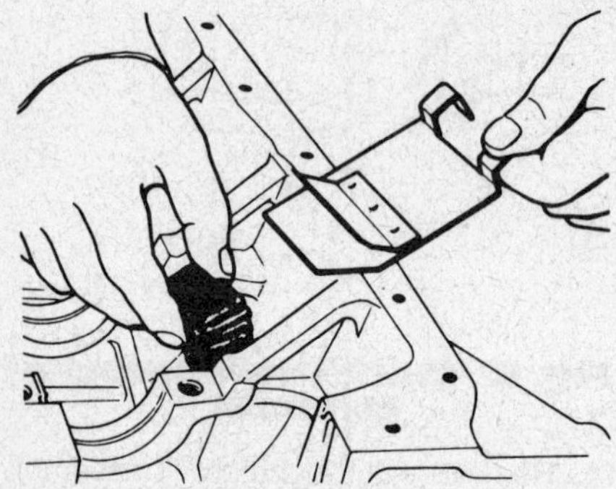

Fig. 9 Baffle plate & steel net replacement

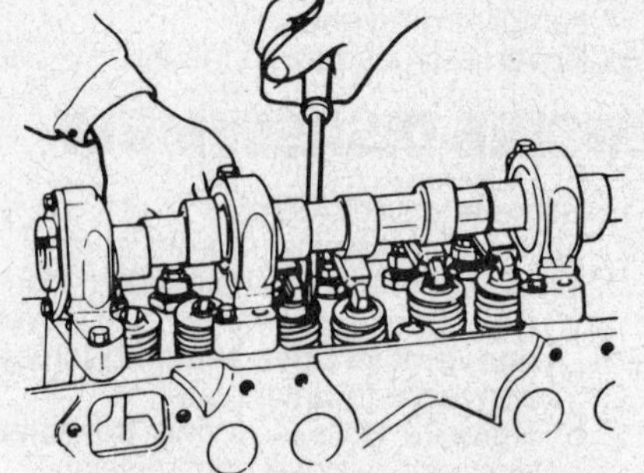

Fig. 10 Rocker arm assembly removal

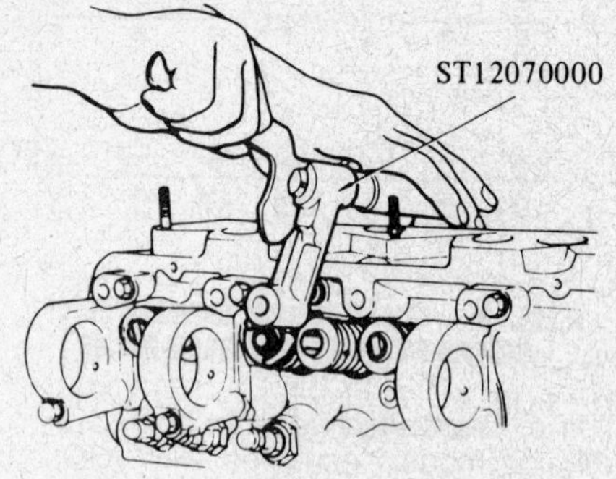

Fig. 11 Valve removal

31. Loosen main bearing cap bolts in three stages working from the outside toward the center cap. Remove main bearing caps and lower bearings, keeping them in correct order. Use tool, **Fig. 7,** to remove center and rear main caps.
32. Remove rear main seal, **Fig. 8,** and remove crankshaft.
33. Remove upper main bearings, keeping them in correct order.
34. Remove baffle plate and steel net from cylinder block, **Fig. 9.**

PISTON & ROD DISASSEMBLY

1. Remove piston rings with a ring remover.
2. Press piston pin.

CYLINDER HEAD DISASSEMBLY

1. Remove valve rocker springs. Loosen valve rocker pivot locknut and remove rocker arm by pressing valve spring downward, **Fig. 10.**
2. Remove locating plate, and the camshaft. Be careful not to damage camshaft bearings and cam lobes.
3. Remove valves,**Figs. 11 and 12.**

ENGINE ASSEMBLY

CYLINDER HEAD ASSEMBLY

1. Valve assembly and valve spring:
   a. Place valve spring seat in position and install valve guide with oil seal, **Fig. 11.**
   b. Assemble valve as follows: valve, inner and outer valve springs, spring retainer, valve collet and valve rocker guide, **Fig. 12.**
2. Valve rocker pivot assembly:
   a. Screw valve rocker pivots joined with locknuts into pivot bushing.
3. Camshaft assembly:
   a. Install locating plate and carefully install camshaft in cylinder head. Do not damage the bearing inside. Oblong groove of locating plate must be directed toward front side of engine.
4. Install camshaft sprocket in position marked during disassembly, install fuel pump cam where equipped, and torque bolt to specifications, **Fig. 13.**
5. Install rocker arms by pressing valve springs down with a screwdriver, **Fig. 10.**
6. Install valve rocker springs.
7. Rotate camshaft so both valves for 1 cylinder are closed.

PISTON & ROD ASSEMBLY

1. Assemble pistons, piston pins and connecting rods on the designated cylinder. Assemble so that oil jet of connecting rod big end is directed toward right side of cylinder block. Be sure to install piston in cylinders with notch mark of piston head toward front of engine, **Fig. 14.**
2. Install piston rings. Install top and second rings in right position, with marked side up, **Fig. 15.**
3. Install bearings on connecting rod and connecting rod cap.

ENGINE ASSEMBLY

1. Set main bearings at the proper porting of cylinder block.
2. Install baffle plate and cylinder block net.
3. Apply engine oil to main bearing surfaces on both sides of cylinder block and cap and then install crankshaft.
4. Install main bearing cap and torque bolts to specifications, in sequence, **Fig. 16.**
5. Make sure that crankshaft has proper end play.
6. Install side oil seals into rear main bearing cap, **Fig. 17.** Prior to installing, apply sealant to seals.
7. Install rear oil seal, **Fig. 18.**
8. Install rear end plate.
9. Install flywheel securely, and tighten bolts to specified torque.
10. Insert pistons in corresponding cylinder. Install so that notch mark on piston head faces to front of engine, **Fig. 14.**
11. Install and torque connecting rod caps.
12. Rotate crankshaft until No. 1 piston is at top dead center.
13. Make sure that both valves on No. 1 cylinder are closed, and that camshaft sprocket is correctly indexed. Install cylinder head. **Do not rotate crankshaft and camshaft independently after cylinder head installation, or valves will contact pistons.**
14. Install crankshaft sprocket, oil pump drive gear, and oil thrower.
15. Install timing chain by aligning mating marks on timing chain with the correct

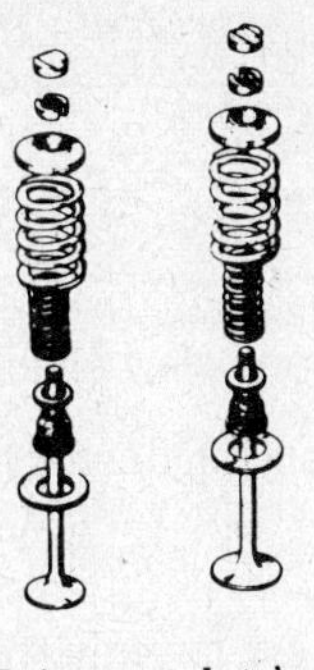

Fig. 12 Valve components

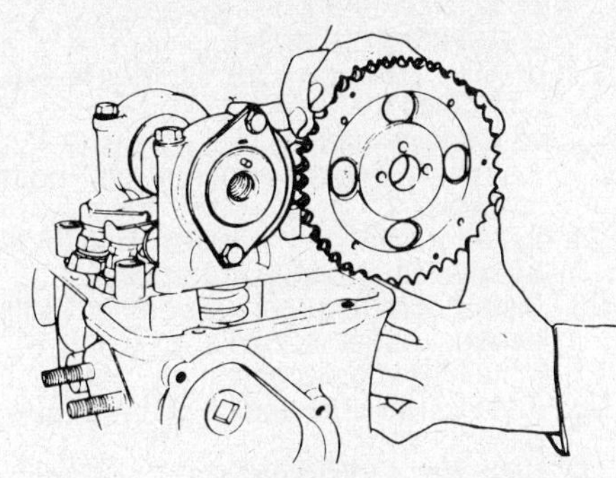

Fig. 13 Camshaft sprocket installation

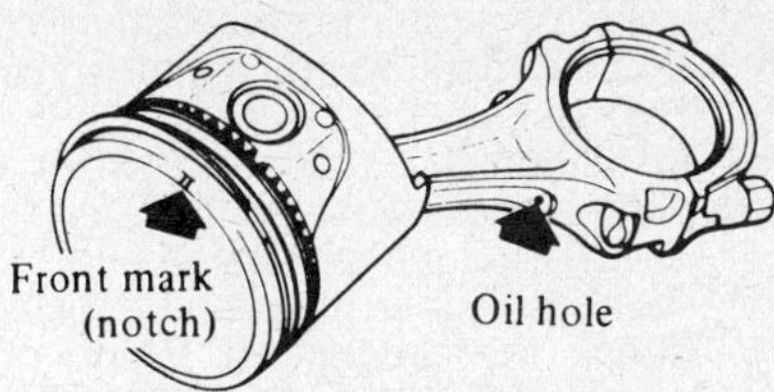

Fig. 14 Piston & rod assembly

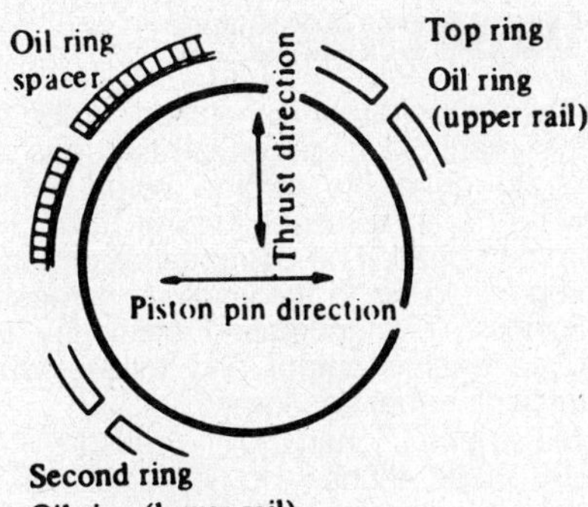

Fig. 15 Piston ring installation

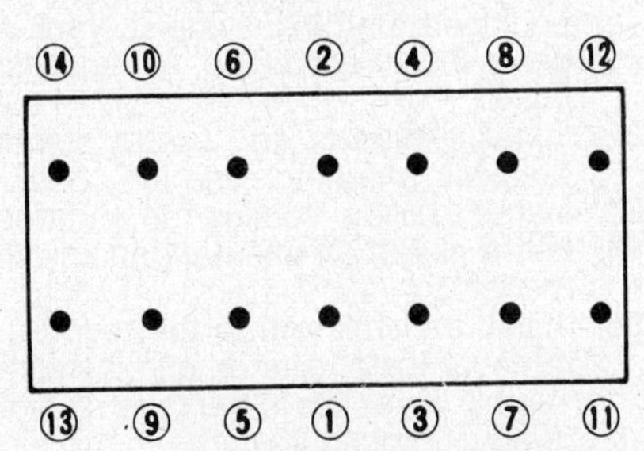

Fig. 16 Main bearing cap & cylinder head bolt tightening sequence

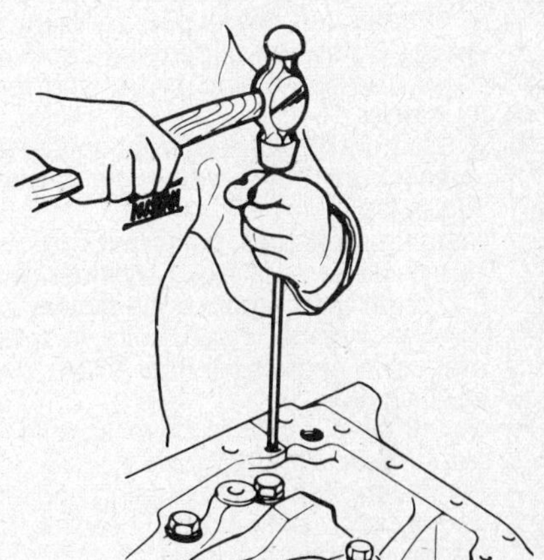

Fig. 17 Side oil seal installation

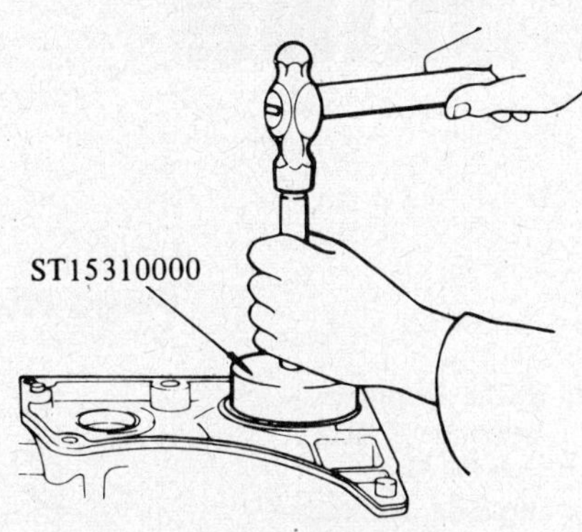

Fig. 18 Rear oil seal installation

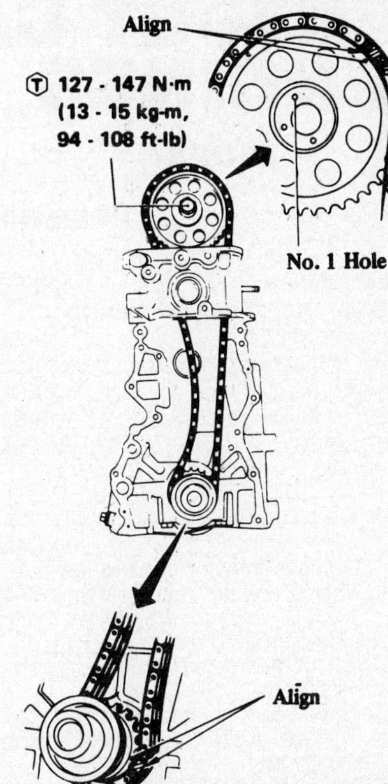

Fig. 19 Timing chain installation (Typical)

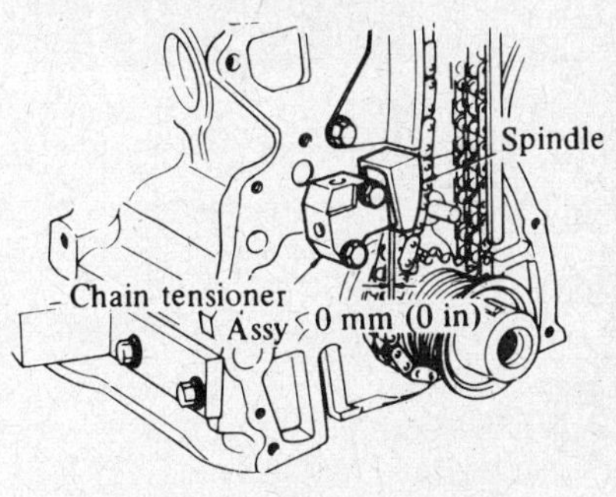

Fig. 20 Timing chain tensioner installation

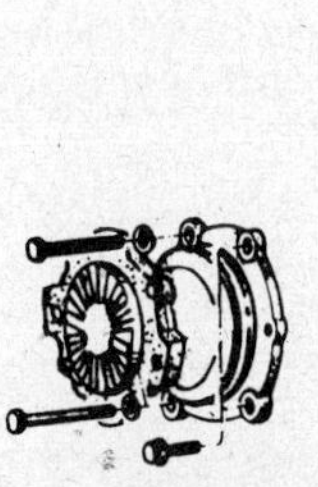

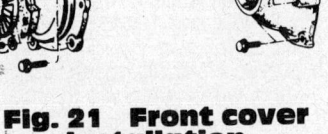

Fig. 21 Front cover installation

Fig. 22 Oil pump installation

index mark on the camshaft sprocket and the mark on crankshaft sprocket, **Fig. 19.**

16. Install chain guide and chain tensioner and adjust so that tensioner spindle is flush with guide, **Fig. 20.**
17. After tensioner has been installed, check the amount of timing chain stretch. If timing chain is stretched excessively:
    a. Remove tensioner, timing chain, and camshaft sprocket.
    b. Advance camshaft sprocket to next dowel position and complete installation of camshaft sprocket.
    c. If camshaft dowel pin is already in No. 3 position of camshaft sprocket, replace timing chain and tensioner.
18. Press new oil seal into front cover and install front cover with new gasket, **Fig. 21.**
19. Install crankshaft pulley and water pump. Make sure No. 1 cylinder is at T.D.C. on the compression stroke.
20. Torque cylinder head bolts in three stages in sequence, **Fig. 16,** to final specification.
21. Install oil pump and drive spindle in front cover, **Fig. 22.**
22. Install fan pulley, fan coupling and fan.
23. Install idler pulley and bracket for power steering if equipped.
24. Install engine right side parts:
    a. Spark plugs.
    b. Oil filter and bracket (L28ET).
    c. Oil pressure switch.
    d. Oil passage for turbocharger (L28ET).
    e. Oil level gauge.
    f. Install engine mounts on both sides.
25. Install intake and exhaust manifolds by reversing removal procedure.
26. Install turbocharger assembly with exhaust outlet (L28ET).
27. Install thermostat assembly.
28. Install oil strainer and oil pan with new gasket.
29. With No. 1 piston at T.D.C. of compression stroke, install distributor as outlined under "Distributor, Replace."
30. Install distributor cap and connect high tension cables.
31. Install air conditioning brackets where equipped. On L28ET adjust crank angle sensor according to specifications.
32. Install alternator and power steering brackets, alternator, and fan belts.
33. Install auxiliary cooling fan and duct.
34. Install clutch on manual transmission models.
35. Install transmission in the reverse of removal, install starter, and install assembly in vehicle in the reverse of the removal procedure.
36. After installation, fill engine oil and coolant to specified levels and make all necessary adjustments.

WATER PUMP REPLACE

1. Disconnect battery ground cable and drain cooling system.
2. Remove radiator shroud.
3. Loosen fan pulley attaching nuts and the fan belt.
4. Loosen alternator attaching bolts and push alternator toward engine.
5. Loosen power steering oil pump drive belt.
6. Remove fan, fan coupling and fan pulley as an assembly.
7. Remove water pump and gasket.
8. Reverse procedure to install, using new gasket.

TURBOCHARGER

The turbocharger is installed on the exhaust manifold. It utilizes exhaust gas energy to drive the turbine wheel which drives the compressor turbine through a common shaft. The compressor provides compressed air to the engine, increasing efficiency. This increased efficiency improves engine output and torque while maintaining fuel economy.

Maximum charging pressure is 12.60-14.96 inches Hg. At 14.96-15.75 inches Hg, pressure is relieved by an emergency relief valve.

VG30E & VG30ET GASOLINE ENGINES

INDEX

TIMING BELT REPLACE

REMOVAL

1. On 200SX and 300ZX models, remove radiator shroud, fan and pulleys.
2. On all models, remove engine under cover(s) and drain cooling system.
3. On 1986-87 Maxima, proceed as follows:
    a. Raise and support front of vehicle.
    b. Remove front righthand wheel and engine side cover.
    c. Remove injector cooling fan duct, engine coolant reservoir tank and A.S.C.D. actuator from right hand side of engine compartment.
4. On all models, remove radiator hoses and fan belts.
5. Remove spark plugs and position No. 1 cylinder at TDC of compression stroke.
6. Remove idler bracket of compressor drive belt and crankshaft pulley.
7. Remove front upper and lower timing belt covers, **Fig. 1.**
8. Loosen timing belt tensioner and return spring and remove timing belt.

After removing timing belt, do not rotate crankshaft and camshaft separately.

INSTALLATION

1. Ensure that No. 1 cylinder is at TDC of compression stroke, **Fig. 2.**
2. On 200SX and 1986-87 300ZX, proceed as follows:
    a. Disconnect all hoses, connectors and wires attached to intake collector and rocker covers.
    b. Remove compressor from compressor bracket and secure out of way.

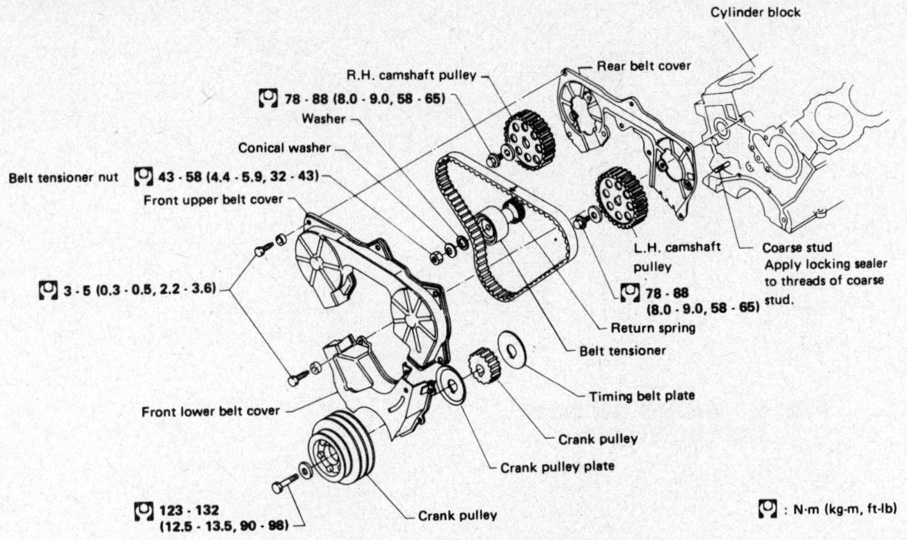

Fig. 1 Timing belt replacement

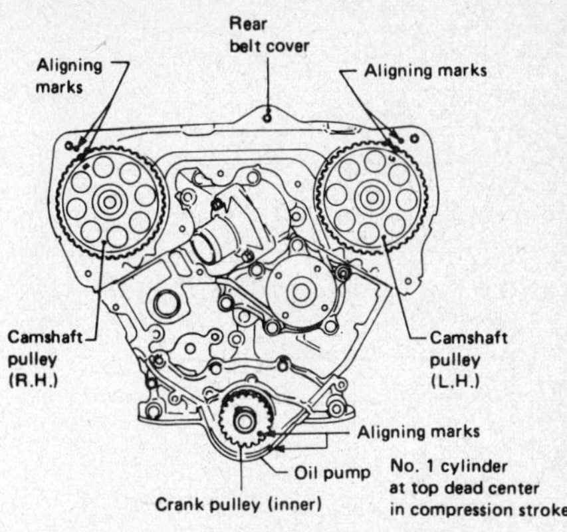

Fig. 2 Timing marks

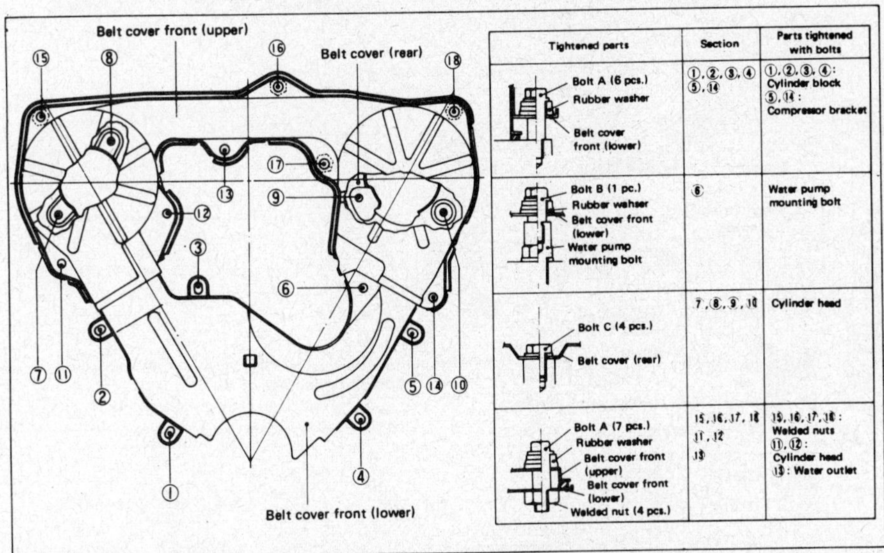

Tightened parts	Section	Parts tightened with bolts
Bolt A (6 pcs.), Rubber washer, Belt cover front (lower)	①, ②, ③, ④ ⑤, ⑭	①, ②, ③, ④: Cylinder block ⑤, ⑭: Compressor bracket
Bolt B (1 pc.), Rubber wehser, Belt cover front (lower), Water pump mounting bolt	⑥	Water pump mounting bolt
Bolt C (4 pcs.), Belt cover (rear)	⑦, ⑧, ⑨, ⑩	Cylinder head
Bolt A (7 pcs.), Rubber washer, Belt cover front (upper), Belt cover front (lower), Welded nut (4 pcs.)	⑮, ⑯, ⑰, ⑱ ⑪, ⑫ ⑬	⑮, ⑯, ⑰, ⑱: Welded nuts ⑪, ⑫: Cylinder head ⑬: Water outlet

Fig. 3 Timing belt cover installation

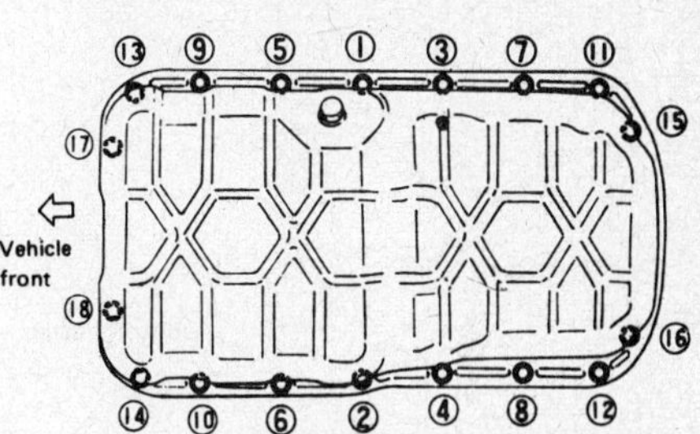

Fig. 4 Oil pan sealant application

c. Remove collector cover and intake collector.
3. On all models, remove both rocker covers and loosen all rocker shaft attaching bolts.
4. Install tensioner and return spring.
5. Using hexagon wrench, turn tensioner clockwise and temporarily tighten tension locknut.
6. Install timing belt, noting the following:
   a. Ensure belt is clean and dry.
   b. Align white reference line on belt with punch mark on camshaft pulleys and crankshaft pulley.
   c. Ensure arrow on timing belt points toward front covers.
7. Loosen tensioner locknut.
8. Rotate tensioner several times in each direction using a suitable Allen wrench, ensuring last turn of wrench is in clockwise direction, then torque tensioner locknut to 32-43 ft. lbs.
9. Torque rocker shaft attaching bolts to 13-16 ft. lbs. in 2 or 3 steps.
10. Install lower and upper timing belt covers, **Fig. 3**.
11. Install rocker covers and, if equipped, intake collector and intake manifold.
12. Connect hoses, connectors and wires.
13. Install compressor if removed.
14. Install crankshaft pulley and idler bracket of compressor drive belt, torquing pulley bolt to specifications.
15. Install radiator hoses, drive belts and spark plugs.
16. On 200SX and 300ZX models, install fan and radiator shroud.
17. On all models, fill cooling system, run engine and check for leaks.

OIL PAN & OIL PUMP REPLACE

1984–87 300ZX

1. Raise and support vehicle.
2. Remove front stabilizer bar attaching nuts and bolts from crossmember.
3. Remove steering column shaft from gear housing.
4. Remove tension rod-to-transverse link attaching nuts.
5. Raise and support engine.
6. Remove rear plate cover from transmission case.
7. Remove oil pan attaching nuts.
8. Remove crossmember attaching bolts, then the strut mounting insulator attaching nuts.
9. Unfasten power steering tubes and refrigerant lines from crossmember, then lower crossmember and remove oil pan from rear side.
10. Remove strainer from oil pump and cylinder head, then lower oil pump assembly from vehicle.
11. Reverse procedure to install. Apply suitable sealant to designated areas, **Fig. 4.** Torque oil pan attaching nuts in sequence, **Fig. 5**, to specifications.

1985–87 MAXIMA

1. Scribe hood hinge locations and remove hood.
2. Lift engine slightly and support in place.
3. Remove engine lower covers.
4. Remove engine mount bolts and nuts.
5. Remove center crossmember assembly.
6. Remove front exhaust pipe attaching nuts.
7. Remove oil pan attaching nuts and the oil pan.
8. Remove strainer from oil pump and cylinder head, then lower oil pump assembly from vehicle.

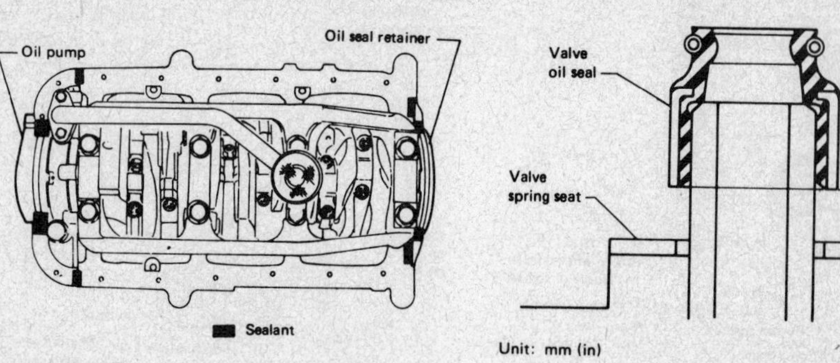

Fig. 5 Oil pan attaching nut torque sequence

Fig. 6 Valve oil seal installation

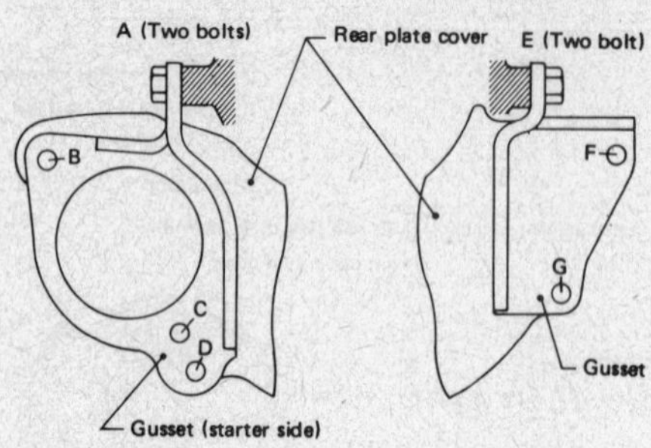

Tightening order

1st	2nd	3rd	4th	5th	6th
A*1	D*2	A*2	F*2 and G*2	E*2	A*2 and E*2

*1: Tighten temporarily.
*2: Tighten completely.

Fig. 7 Engine gusset torque sequence. 1984–87 300ZX & 1987 200SX

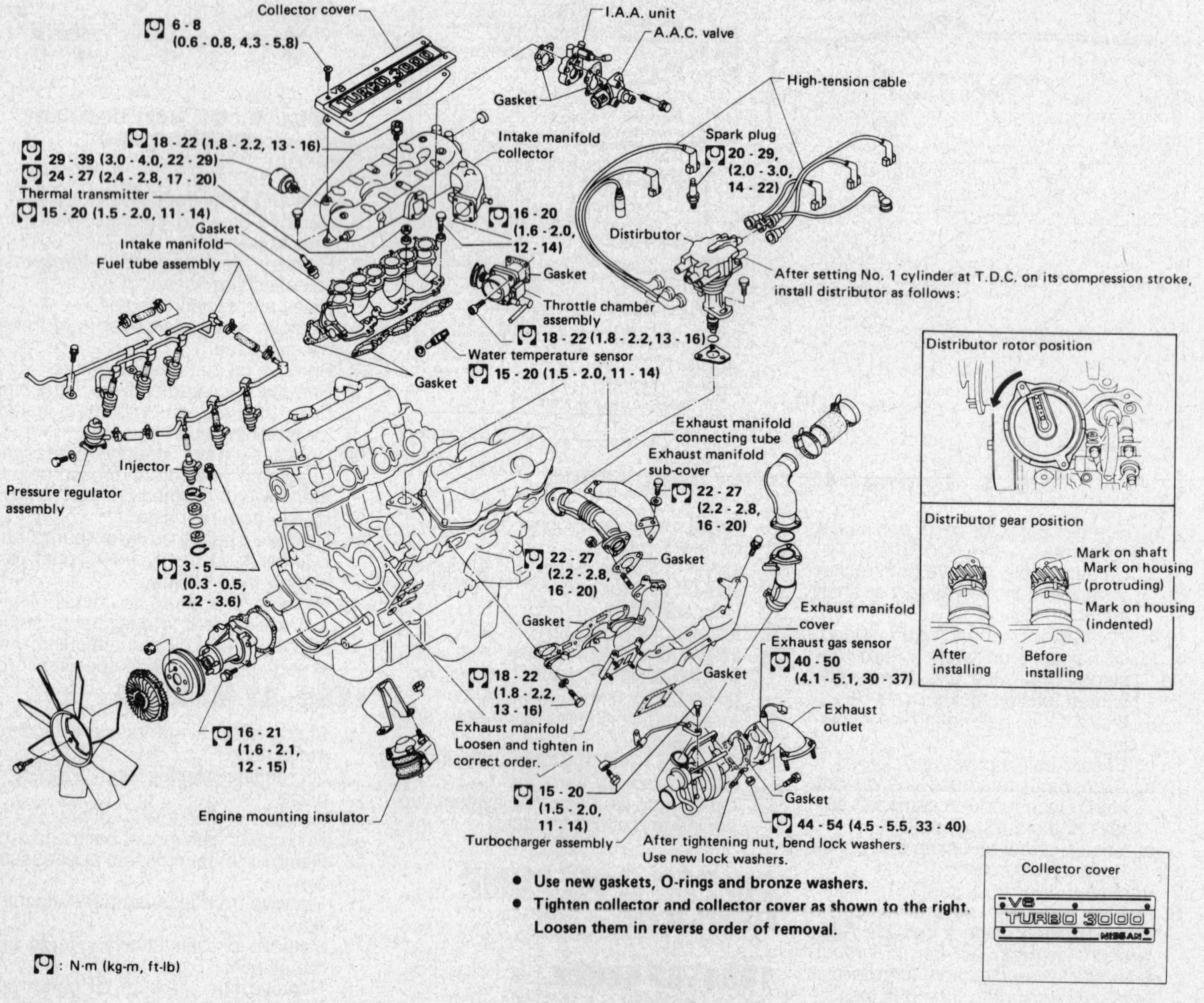

- Use new gaskets, O-rings and bronze washers.
- Tighten collector and collector cover as shown to the right. Loosen them in reverse order of removal.

: N·m (kg-m, ft-lb)

Fig. 8 External engine components (typical)

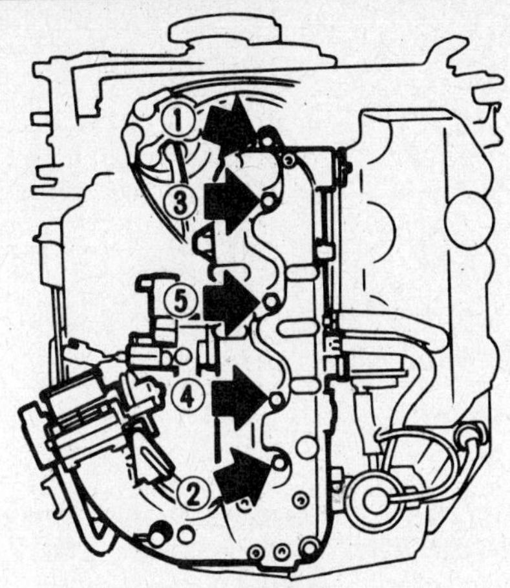

Loosen in numerical order and tighten in reverse order of removal.

Fig. 9 Intake manifold collector bolt loosening sequence. 300ZX & Maxima

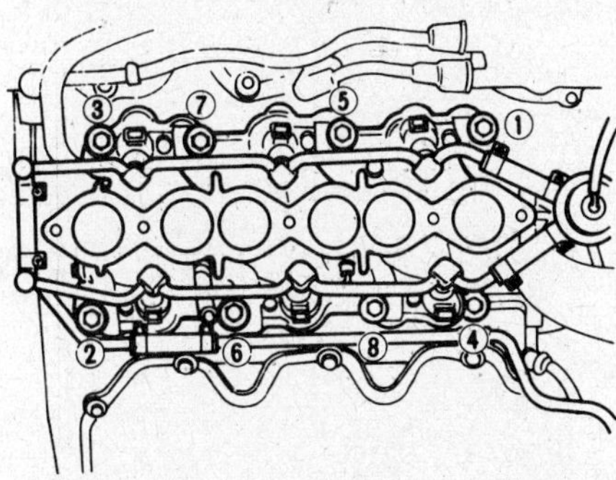

Fig. 12 Intake manifold bolt loosening sequence. 1984–86 300ZX

9. Reverse procedure to install. Apply suitable sealant to designated areas, **Fig. 4.** Torque oil pan attaching nuts in sequence, **Fig. 5**, to specifications.

1987 200SX

1. Raise and support vehicle and drain engine oil.
2. Lower suspension crossmember, to obtain sufficient clearance under oil pan, as follows:
   a. Remove power steering gear bracket from suspension crossmember.
   b. Remove front stabilizer bar to transverse link attaching nuts and bolts.
   c. Remove tension rod to transverse link attaching nuts.
   d. Remove front engine mount attaching nuts.
   e. Raise and support engine.
   f. Remove oil pan attaching nuts.
   g. Remove suspension crossmember attaching bolts.
   h. Remove screws attaching power steering oil tubes to suspension crossmember.
   i. Lower suspension crossmember.
3. Remove oil pan by pulling forward.
4. Remove oil pump assembly.
5. Reverse procedure to install. Apply suitable sealant to designated areas, **Fig. 4.** Torque oil pan attaching nuts in sequence, **Fig. 5,** to specifications.

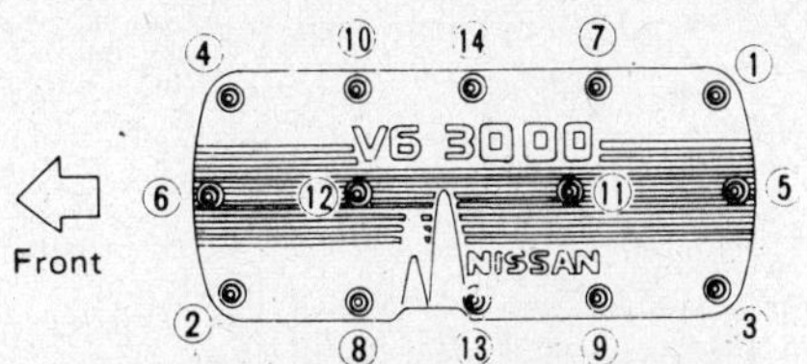

Fig. 10 Intake manifold collector cover bolt loosening sequence. 200SX

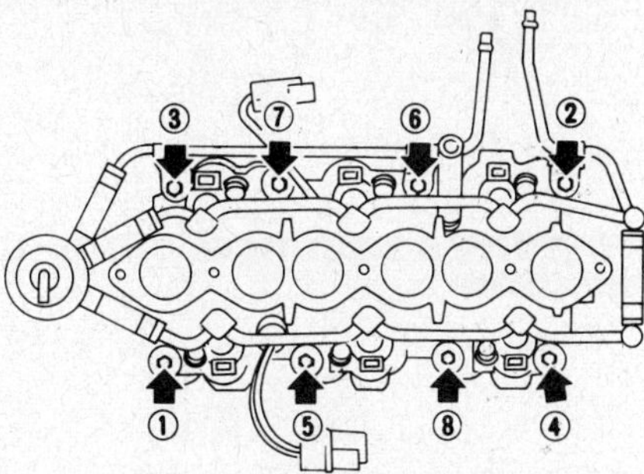

Fig. 13 Intake manifold bolt loosening sequence. 1985–87 Maxima

OIL SEALS

REPLACE

CAMSHAFT OIL SEAL

1. Remove timing belt as described under "Timing Belt, Replace".
2. Remove camshaft sprockets, then the camshaft oil seal.
3. Reverse procedure to install. Apply clean engine oil to seal prior to installation.

VALVE OIL SEAL

1. Remove components necessary for valve cover removal.
2. Remove valve cover, then the rocker shaft assembly and valve lifters with valve guide.
3. Remove valve springs, retainer and collets using a suitable valve spring compressor.
4. Remove valve oil seal using suitable pliers.
5. Reverse procedure to install. Apply clean engine oil to seal prior to installation. Clearance between oil seal and valve spring seat should measure .091 inch, **Fig. 6.**

ENGINE

REPLACE

On 1985-87 Maxima models, the engine and transaxle must be removed as an assembly.

1984–87 300ZX, 1985–87 MAXIMA & 1987 200SX

1. Release fuel system pressure as follows:
   a. Start engine, then disconnect fuel pump electrical connector, located under luggage floor mat.
   b. After engine stalls, crank engine 2 or 3 times.
   c. Turn ignition switch off, then reconnect fuel pump electrical connector.
2. Disconnect battery ground cable.
3. Disconnect or remove all hoses, linkages, electrical connectors and accessories necessary for engine removal.
4. Attach suitable lifting equipment to engine and, on 200SX and 300ZX models, support transmission with a suitable jack.
5. Remove engine mounting bolts.
6. On 300ZX models, remove right side exhaust manifold and exhaust connecting tube, then separate engine from transmission and lift engine assembly from vehicle.
7. On Maxima models, carefully lift engine and transaxle assembly from vehicle, then separate transaxle from engine.
8. On all models reverse procedure to install. On 200SX and 300ZX models, torque engine gussets in 6 steps, **Fig. 7.**

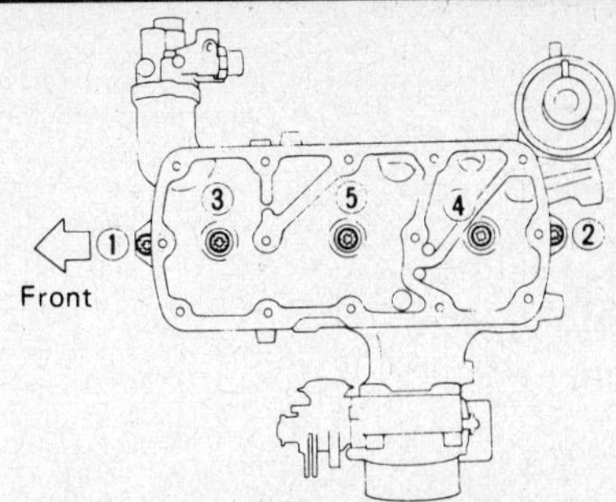

Fig. 11 Intake manifold collector bolt loosening sequence. 200SX

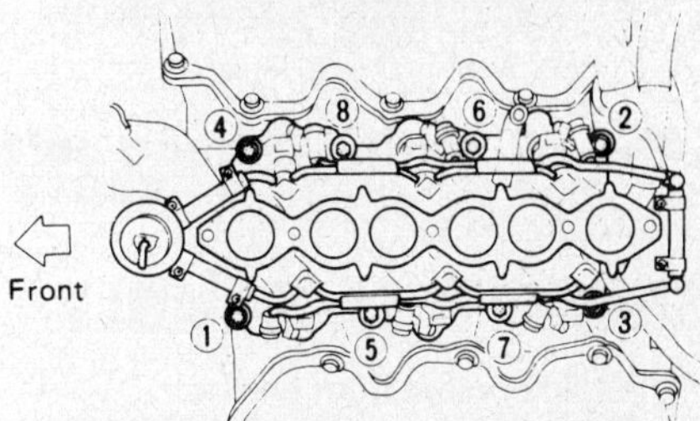

Fig. 14 Intake manifold bolt loosening sequence. 1987 200SX & 300ZX

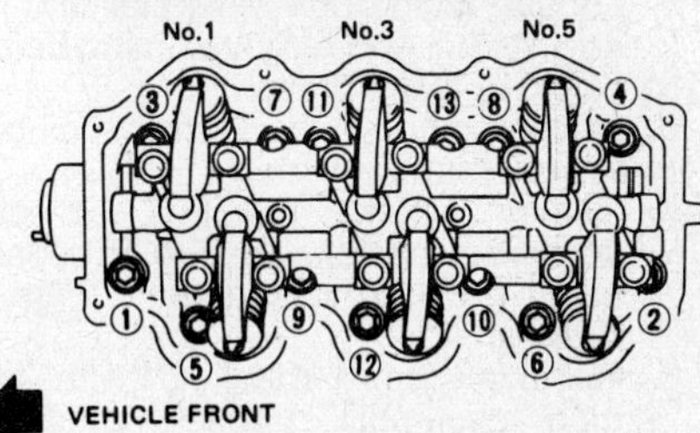

Fig. 15 Cylinder head bolt loosening sequence. 1984–85

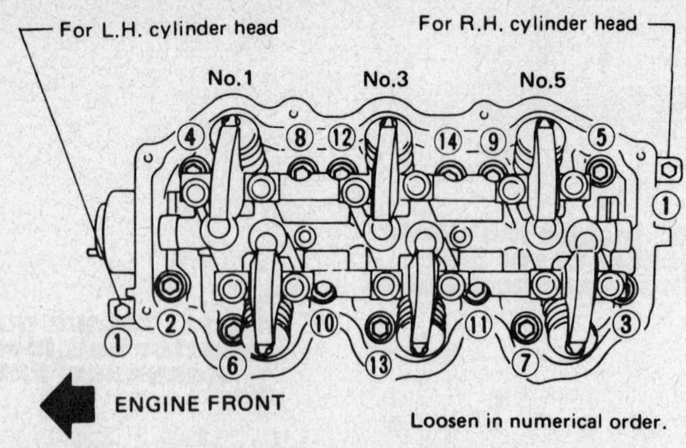

Fig. 16 Cylinder head bolt loosening sequence. 1986–87 300ZX & Maxima

Fig. 17 Cylinder head bolt loosening sequence. 1987 200SX

ENGINE DISASSEMBLY

1. Drain coolant from engine.
2. Position No. 1 cylinder at TDC of compression stroke.
3. Remove upper and lower timing belt covers, **Fig. 1.**
4. Loosen timing belt tensioner and return spring, and remove timing belt.
5. Remove water pump.
6. Drain engine oil, then remove oil pan and oil pump.
7. Remove intake manifold collector cover and the collector, **Fig. 8.** Loosen attaching bolts in sequence, **Figs. 9 through 11.**
8. Remove intake manifold with fuel tube assembly. Loosen attaching bolts in sequence, **Figs. 12 through 14.**
9. Remove power steering pump bracket, then the exhaust manifold covers.
10. Disconnect exhaust manifold connecting tube, then remove camshaft sprockets and rear timing cover attaching bolts.
11. Remove cylinder head attaching bolts, then the cylinder heads with exhaust manifolds attached. Loosen attaching bolts in sequence, **Figs. 15 through 17.**
12. Remove connecting rod caps and bearings, then the piston and connecting rod assemblies.
13. Remove main bearing cap and crankshaft, **Fig. 18.** Loosen attaching bolts in sequence, **Fig. 19.**

PISTON & ROD DISASSEMBLY

1. Remove piston rings with a ring remover.
2. Press out piston pin. **Keep disassembled parts in order.**

CYLINDER HEAD DISASSEMBLY

1. Remove exhaust manifolds, then the rocker shafts with rocker arms. Loosen exhaust manifold attaching bolts in sequence, **Figs. 20 through 22,** in 2 or 3 steps.
2. Remove hydraulic valve lifters and lifter guide, **Fig. 23,** noting the following:

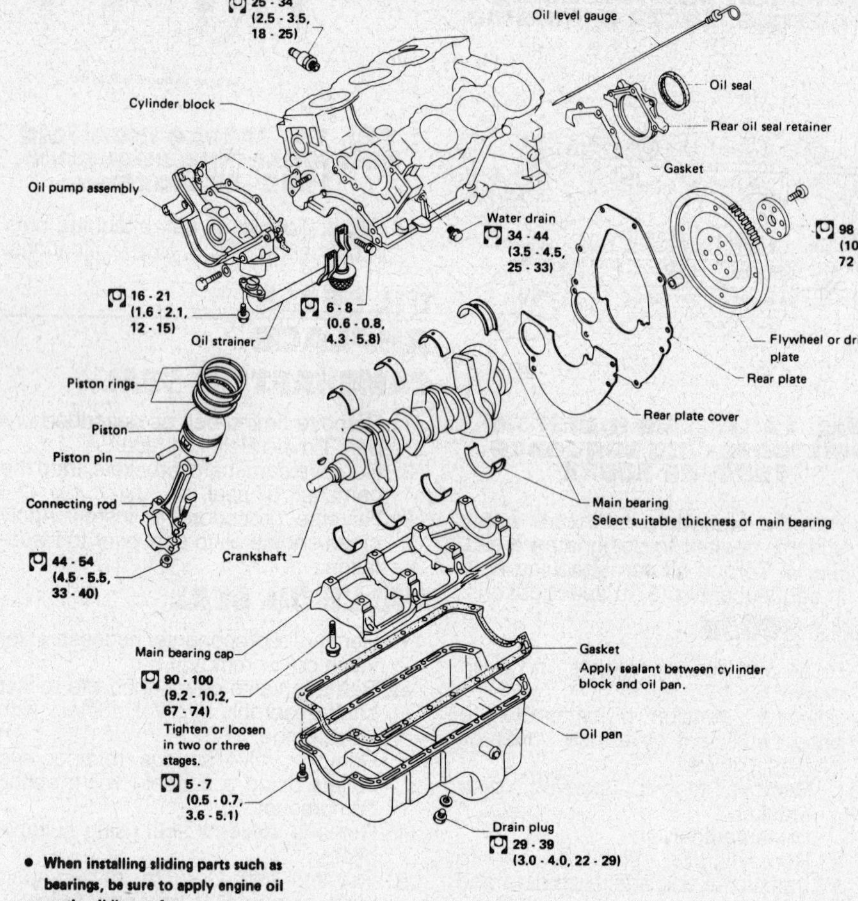

Fig. 18 Cylinder block, crankshaft & piston exploded view.

a. Secure lifters with safety wire to prevent them from falling out of guide, **Fig. 24.**
b. Do not invert lifters to prevent air from entering them.
c. Valve lifters are serviced as an assembly only and must not be disassembled.
d. Mark lifters so they may be reinstalled in their original positions.

3. Remove camshaft and camshaft oil seal.
4. Remove valves and valve components using a suitable valve spring compressor.

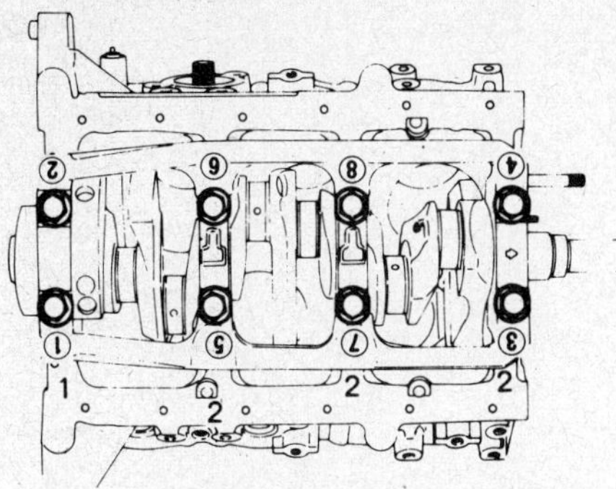

Fig. 19 Main bearing cap bolt loosening sequence

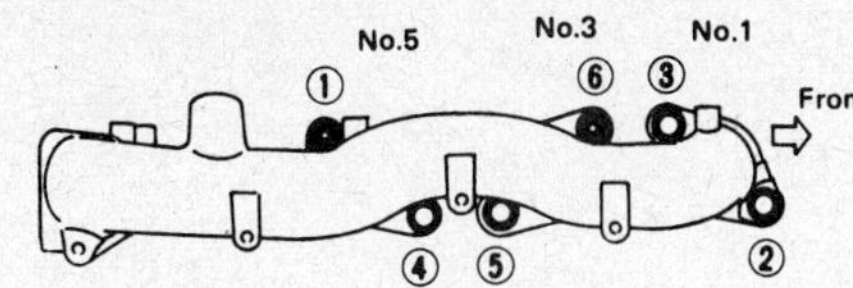

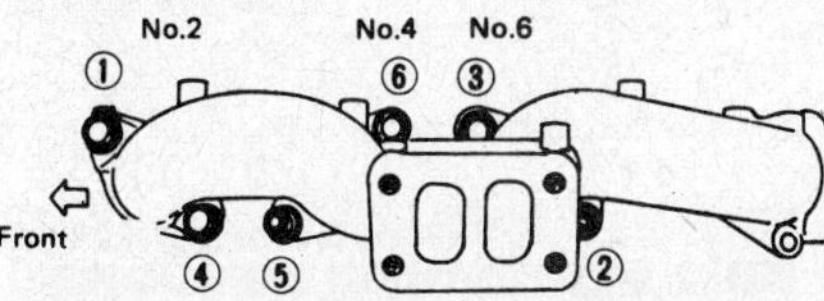

Fig. 20 Exhaust manifold bolt loosening sequence. 1984–87 300ZX & 1984–86 Maxima.

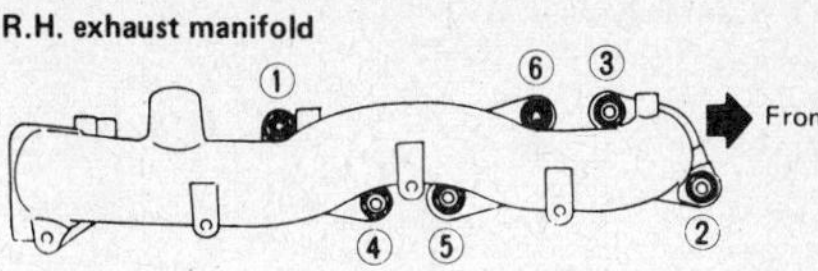

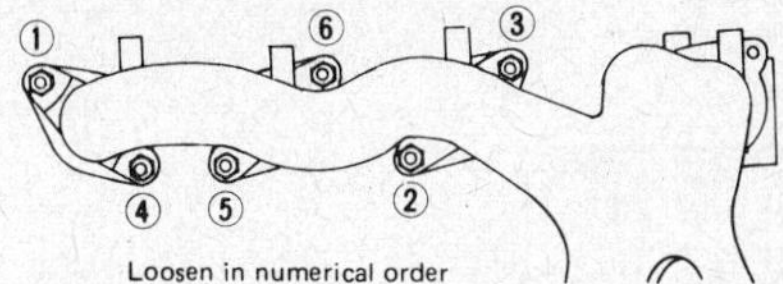

Fig. 21 Exhaust manifold bolt loosening sequence. 1987 Maxima

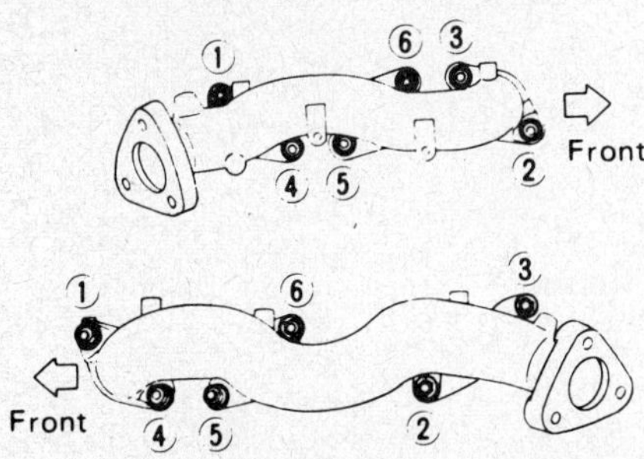

Fig. 22 Exhaust manifold bolt loosening sequence. 1987 200SX

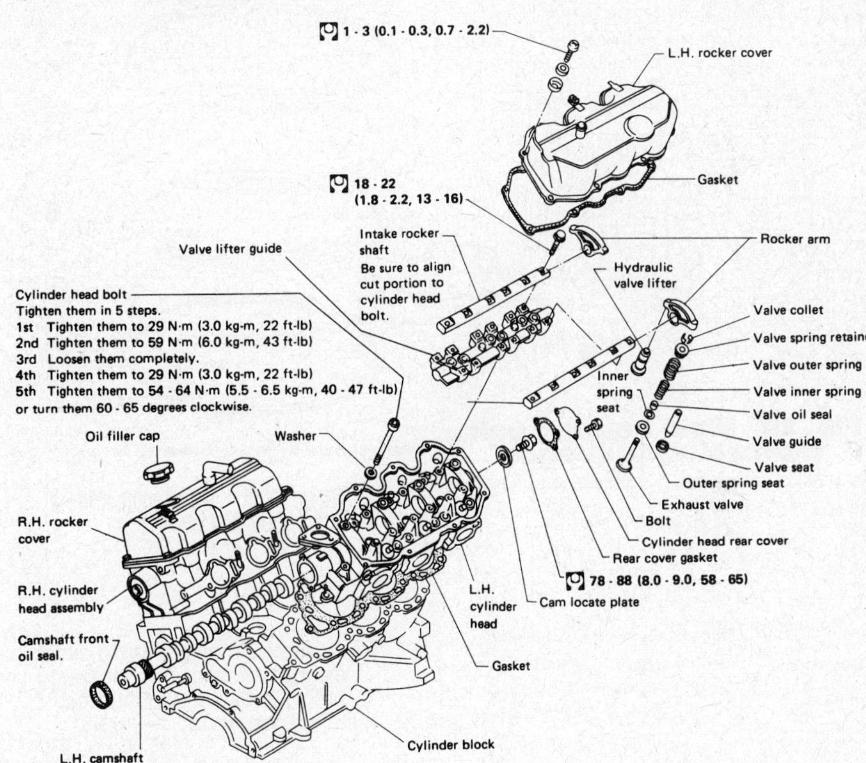

- When installing sliding parts such as bearings, be sure to apply engine oil on the sliding surfaces.
- Use new gaskets and oil seals.

: N·m (kg-m, ft-lb)

Fig. 23 Cylinder head exploded view

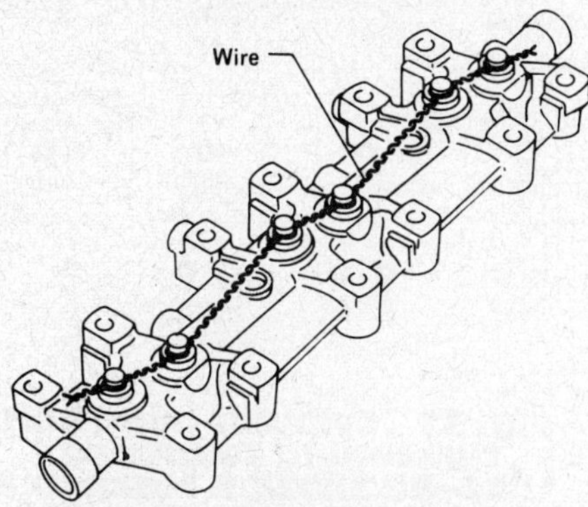

Fig. 24 Securing valve lifters to valve guide

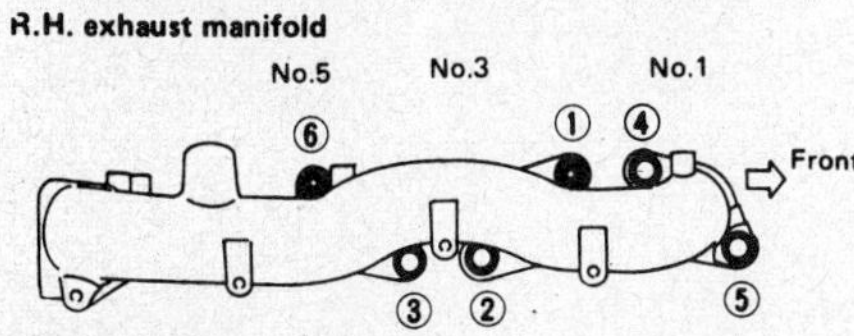

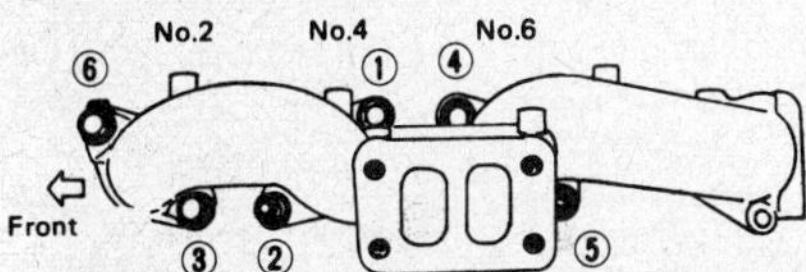

Fig. 25 Exhaust manifold bolt tightening sequence. 1984–87 300ZX & 1984–86 Maxima

ENGINE ASSEMBLY

CYLINDER HEAD ASSEMBLY

1. Install valves and valve components. Install outer valve springs with narrow pitch side towards cylinder head.
2. Install camshaft, then the camshaft oil seal. Apply clean engine oil to seal prior to installation.
3. Install hydraulic valve lifters and lifter guide.
4. Install rocker shaft assemblies, then the exhaust manifolds. Torque manifold attaching bolts to specifications in sequence, **Figs. 25 through 27.**

PISTON & ROD ASSEMBLY

1. Assemble pistons, piston pins and connecting rods of designated cylinders, noting the following:
   a. Ensure stamped numbers on connecting rod and cap correspond to each cylinder.

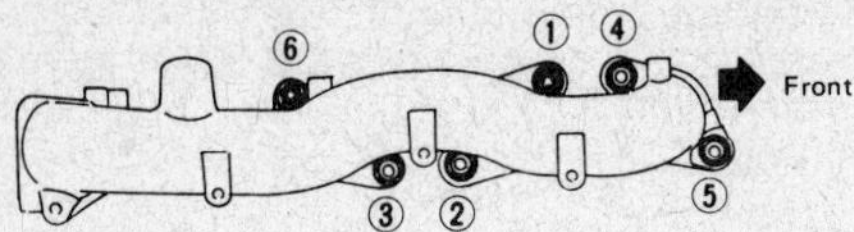

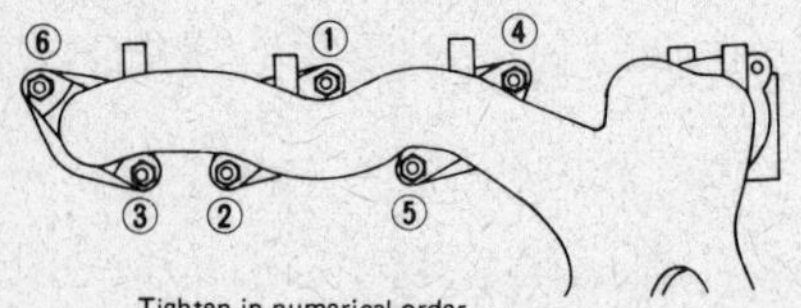

Fig. 26 Exhaust manifold bolt tightening sequence. 1987 Maxima

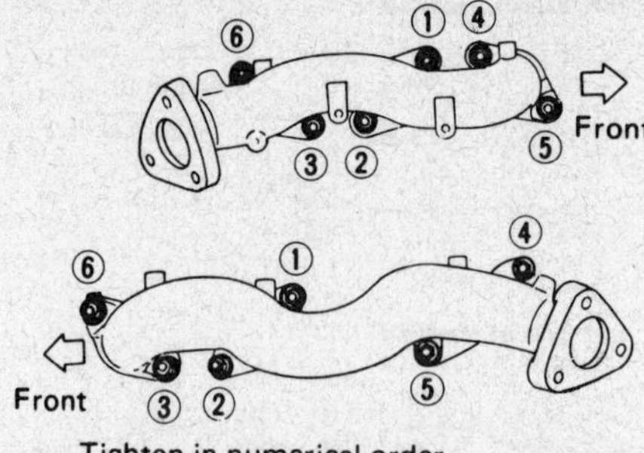

Fig. 27 Exhaust manifold bolt tightening sequence. 1987 200SX

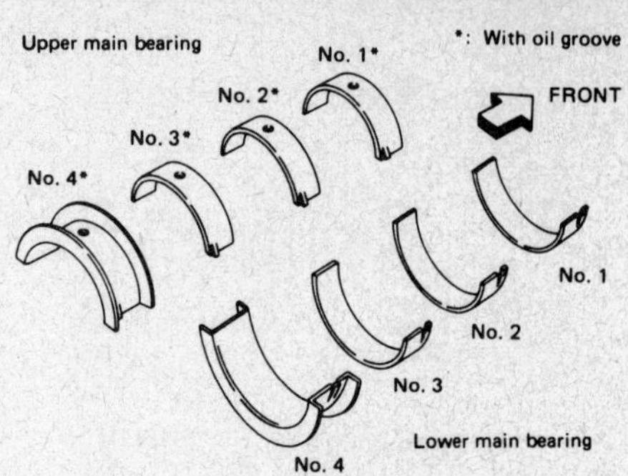

Fig. 28 Main bearing identification

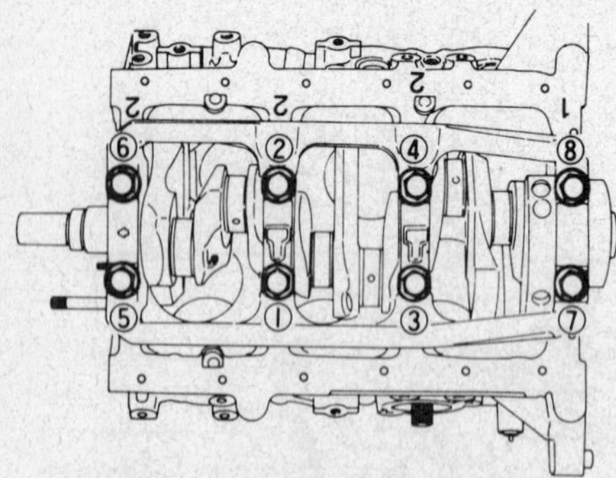

Fig. 29 Main bearing bolt tightening sequence

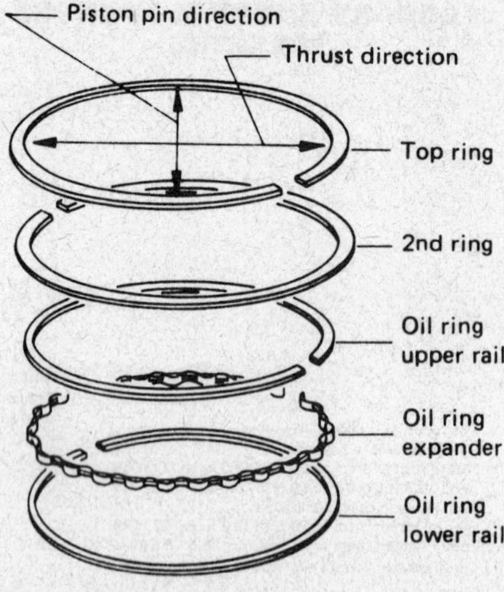

Fig. 30 Piston ring positioning

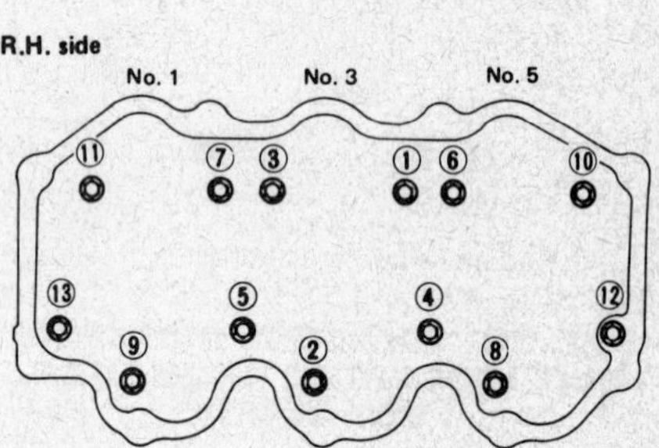

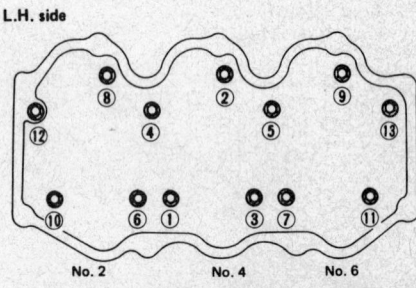

Fig. 31 Cylinder head bolt tightening sequence. 1984–86 300ZX & Maxima & 1987 200SX

- Tightening order

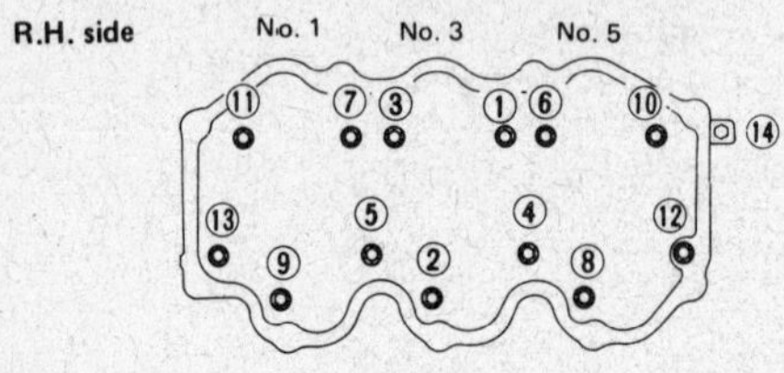

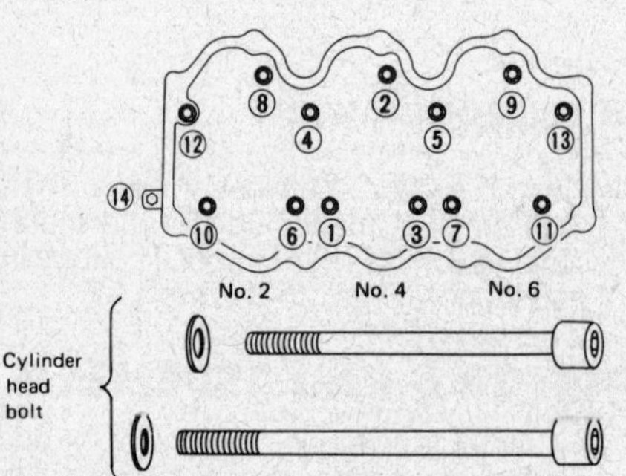

Fig. 32 Cylinder head bolt tightening sequence. 1987 300ZX & Maxima

b. Apply clean engine oil to piston pin and small end of connecting rod before pressing pin into rod.
2. Install piston rings.

ENGINE ASSEMBLY

1. Install main bearings, **Fig. 28,** crankshaft and bearing cap. Torque attaching screws to specifications in sequence, **Fig. 29,** in 2 or 3 steps.
2. Install piston assemblies with rings properly positioned, **Fig. 30.**
3. Reverse remainder of "Engine Disassembly" procedure to complete assembly, noting the following:
   a. Torque cylinder head attaching bolts in sequence, **Figs. 31 and 32,** to specifications as illustrated in **Fig. 23.**
   b. Torque intake manifold attaching bolts in sequence, **Fig. 33,** to specifications in 2 or 3 steps.

TURBOCHARGER

The turbocharger is installed on the ex-

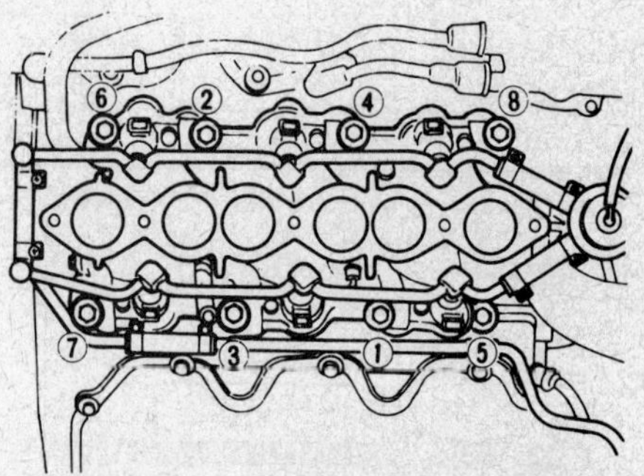

Fig. 33 Intake manifold bolt tightening sequence

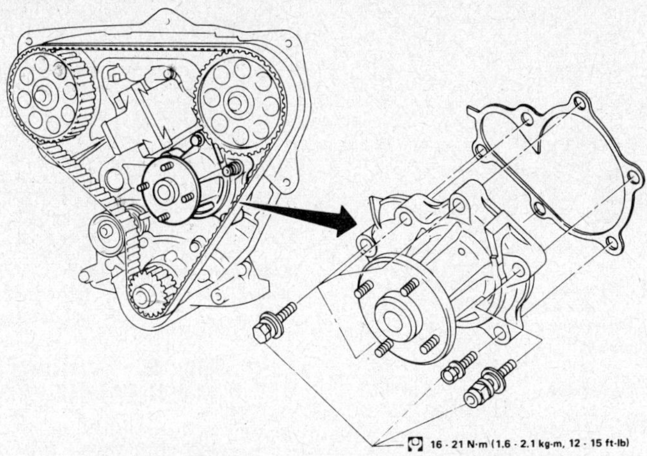

Fig. 34 Replacing water pump

haust manifold. It utilizes exhaust gas energy to drive the turbine wheel which drives the compressor turbine through a common shaft. The compressor provides compressed air to the engine, increasing efficiency. This increased efficiency improves engine output and torque while maintaining fuel economy.

Maximum charge pressure is 12.60-14.96 inches Hg. At 14.96-15.75 (1985, 16.34-18.70) inches Hg, pressure is relieved by an emergency relief valve.

WATER PUMP

REPLACE

1. Disconnect battery ground cable and drain coolant from right side drain cocks on cylinder block and radiator.
2. Refer to **Fig. 34** to complete water pump replacement procedure.

VG30i GASOLINE ENGINES

INDEX

ENGINE

REPLACE

1. Disconnect battery ground cable.
2. Raise and support vehicle.
3. Drain engine oil and coolant.
4. Remove radiator with shroud and cooling fan.
5. Remove under cover.
6. Remove A/C compressor and power steering pump.
7. On 4 x 4 models, remove starter motor.
8. On 2 x 4 models, disconnect electrical connectors at starter motor.
9. On all models, disconnect exhaust manifold from front exhaust pipe.
10. Remove front exhaust pipe.
11. On 4 x 4 models, disconnect front propeller shaft from front differential car rier.
12. Remove bolts securing front driveshafts.
13. Remove front differential carrier attaching bolts and the carrier.
14. Remove differential front mounting bolts.
15. Remove transmission to rear engine mounting bracket nuts.
16. Remove front engine mounting bolts.
17. Raise and support engine.
18. Remove front differential carrier.
19. on 2 x 4 models, disconnect rear propeller shaft from transmission.
20. Remove transmission to rear engine mounting bracket bolts.
21. Remove transmission crossmember.
22. On 4 x 4 models, remove engine to transmission attaching bolts.
23. On 2 x 4 models, remove front engine mounting bolts.
24. On all models, carefully withdraw engine.
25. Reverse procedure to install.

OIL PAN

REPLACE

1. Disconnect battery ground cable.
2. Raise and support vehicle.
3. Remove under cover.
4. Drain engine oil.
5. On 2 x 4 models, remove stabilizer bracket bolts.
6. On 4 x 4 models, proceed as follows:
   a. Disconnect front propeller shaft at front differential carrier.
   b. Remove front driveshaft attaching bolts.
   c. Remove front differential carrier member bolts.
   d. Support front differential carrier with suitable jack and remove attaching bolts.
   e. Remove front differential carrier bleeder hose.
7. On 2 x 4 models, remove front suspension crossmember.
8. On 4 x 4 models, proceed as follows:
   a. Remove differential front mounting bolts.
   b. Remove front differential carrier.
   c. Remove front differential carrier mounting bracket.
9. On all models, remove idler arm.
10. Remove starter motor.
11. On 4 x 4 models, proceed as follows:
    a. Remove transmission to rear engine mounting bracket attaching nuts.
    b. Remove engine mounting bolts or nuts.
12. On all models, remove engine gussets.
13. On 4 x 4 models, raise engine and disconnect exhaust pipe as necessary.
14. On all models, remove oil pan attaching bolts and the oil pan.
15. Reverse procedure to install.

TIMING BELT

REPLACE

REMOVAL

1. Disconnect battery ground cable.
2. Remove radiator shroud, fan and pulleys.
3. Drain coolant from radiator and remove water pump hose, being careful not to spill coolant on drive belts.
4. Remove all spark plugs.
5. Remove drive belts.
6. Remove rocker cover and rocker shaft assembly.
7. Set No. 1 cylinder at TDC on its compression stroke and set crankshaft

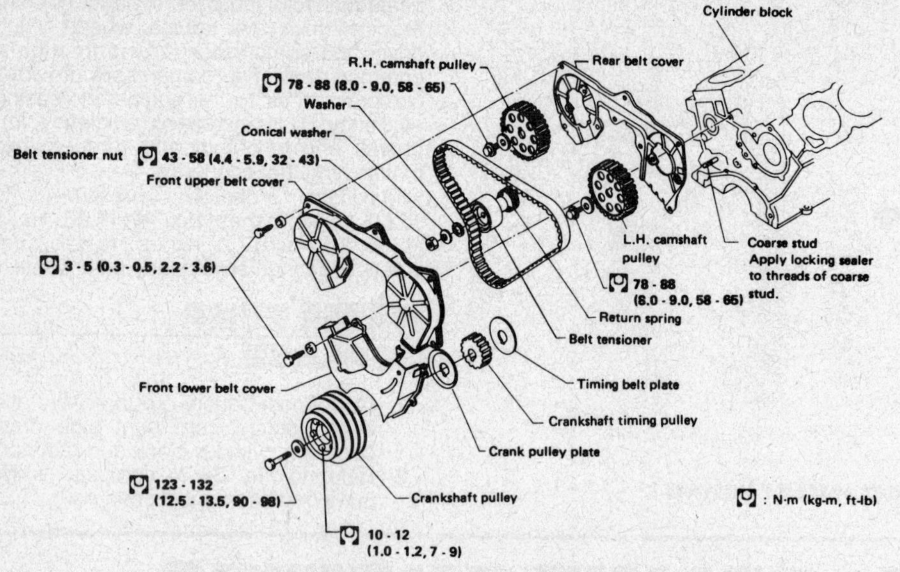

Fig. 1 Exploded view of timing belt

Fig. 2 Timing belt alignment marks

pulley at TDC.

8. Remove front upper and lower belt covers, **Fig. 1.**
9. Loosen timing belt tensioner and return spring, then remove timing belt. **After removing timing belt, do not rotate crankshaft and camshaft separately.**

INSTALLATION

1. Ensure No. 1 cylinder is set at TDC on its compression stroke. **Aligning marks on pulleys should be matched to marks on engine, Fig. 2.**
2. Remove both rocker covers and loosen all rocker shaft securing bolts. **Loosen all rocker shaft securing bolts thoroughly so that timing belt tension can be correctly adjusted.**
3. Install tensioner and return spring.
4. Turn tensioner fully clockwise with hexagon wrench and temporarily tighten lock nut.
5. Set timing belt, noting the following:
   a. Ensure timing belt and pulleys are clean and free from oil or water. Do not bend.
   b. Align white marks on timing belt with punch mark on camshaft pulleys and crankshaft pulley.
   c. Ensure arrow on timing belt points toward front belt covers.
   d. Ensure timing belt has 133 teeth and that there are 40 teeth between left and right camshaft pulleys and 43 teeth between left camshaft pulley and crankshaft timing pulley.
6. Loosen tensioner lock nut while counterholding tensioner.
7. Slowly turn tensioner clockwise and counterclockwise two or three turns, then torque tensioner lock nut to 32-43 ft. lbs.
8. Torque rocker shaft attaching bolts to 13-16 ft. lbs. in two or three stages, ensuring camshaft lobe is at position where lobe is not lifted.
9. Install upper and lower timing belt covers, **Fig. 3.**

CYLINDER HEAD

REPLACE

REMOVAL

1. Disconnect battery ground cable.
2. Remove timing belt as previously described.

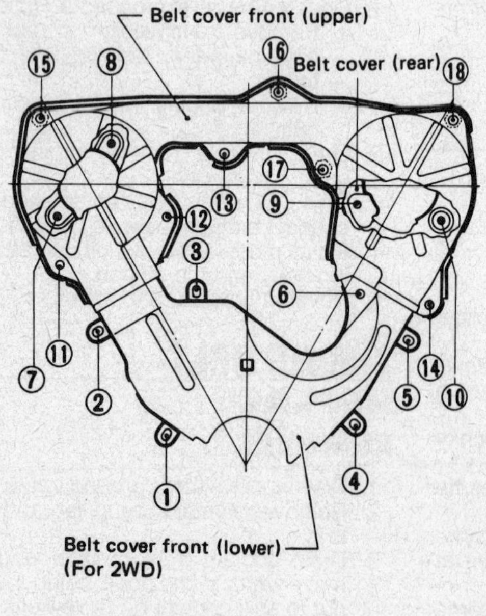

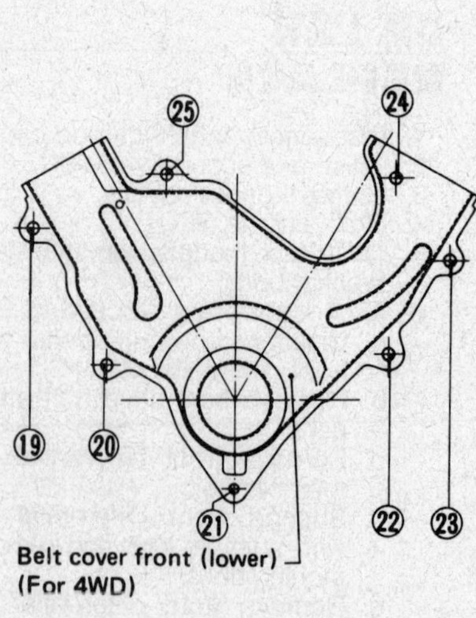

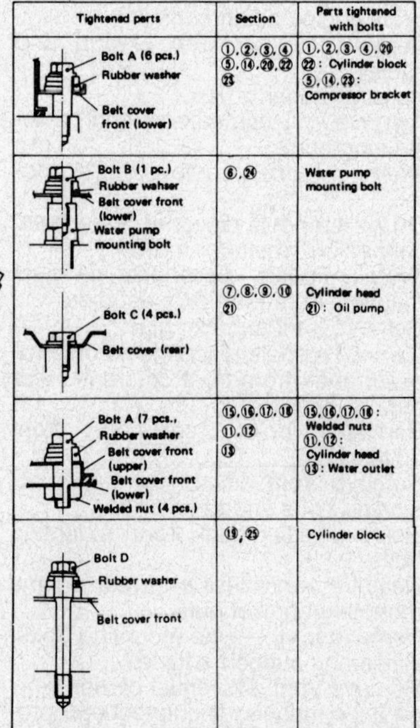

Tightened parts	Section	Parts tightened with bolts
Bolt A (6 pcs.), Rubber washer, Belt cover front (lower)	①, ②, ③, ④, ⑤, ⑭, ⑳, ㉒, ㉓	①, ②, ③, ④, ⑳, ㉒: Cylinder block; ⑤, ⑭, ㉓: Compressor bracket
Bolt B (1 pc.), Rubber wahser, Belt cover front (lower), Water pump mounting bolt	⑥, ㉔	Water pump mounting bolt
Bolt C (4 pcs.), Belt cover (rear)	⑦, ⑧, ⑨, ⑩, ㉑	Cylinder head; ㉑: Oil pump
Bolt A (7 pcs., Rubber washer, Belt cover front (upper), Belt cover front (lower), Welded nut (4 pcs.)	⑮, ⑯, ⑰, ⑱, ⑪, ⑫, ⑬	⑮, ⑯, ⑰, ⑱: Welded nuts; ⑪, ⑫: Cylinder head; ⑬: Water outlet
Bolt D, Rubber washer, Belt cover front	⑲, ㉕	Cylinder block

Fig. 3 Installing timing belt covers

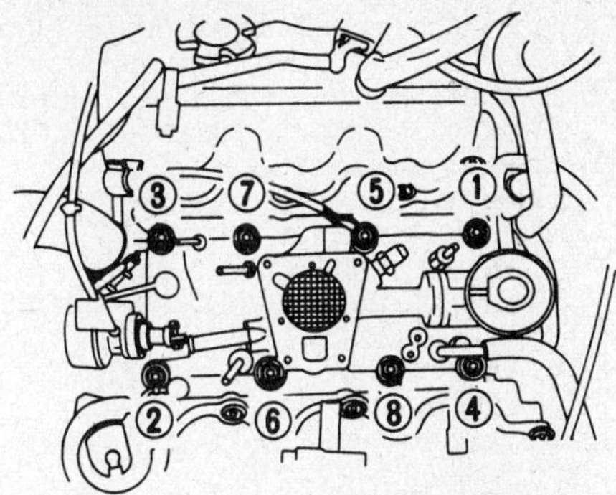

Fig. 4 Intake manifold bolt loosening sequence

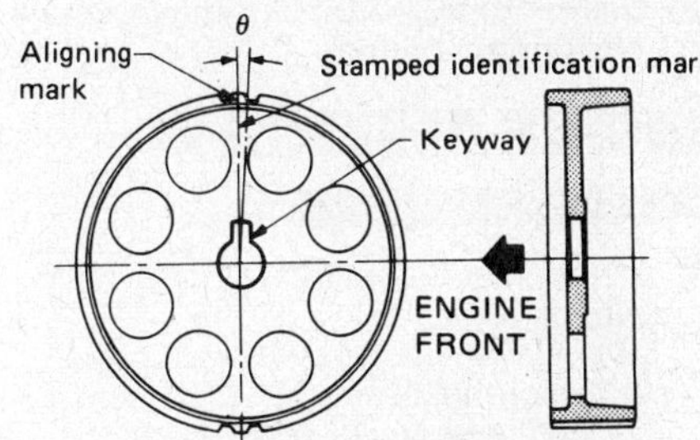

Fig. 7 Camshaft pulley identification

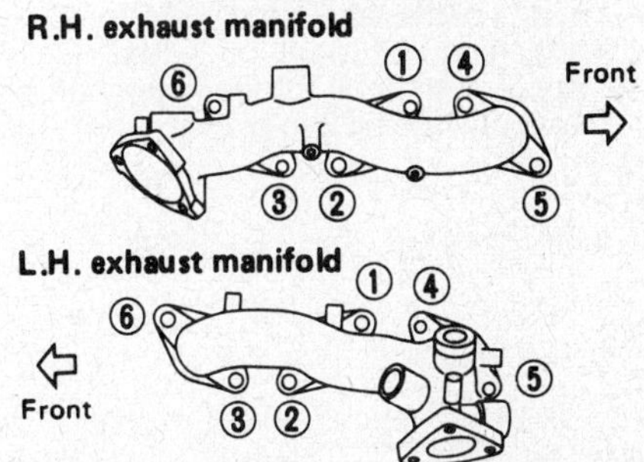

Fig. 9 Exhaust manifold bolt tightening sequence

3. Remove air cleaner and the intake manifold with injection body, loosening intake manifold attaching bolts in sequence, **Fig. 4.**
4. Remove power steering pump bracket.
5. Remove camshaft pulleys and the rear timing cover attaching bolts.
6. Remove compressor and rocker covers.
7. Remove cylinder head with exhaust manifold, loosening attaching bolts in sequence, **Fig. 5.**

INSTALLATION

1. Install cylinder head with new gasket.
2. Apply oil to threaded portion and seat surface of bolts and tighten cylinder head bolts with washers, in sequence, **Fig. 6,** as follows. **Bolt Nos. 4, 5, 12 and 13 are 127 mm long and all others are 106 mm long.**
   a. Torque all bolts to 22 ft. lbs.
   b. Torque all bolts to 43 ft. lbs.
   c. Loosen all bolts completely.
   d. Torque all bolts to 22 ft. lbs.

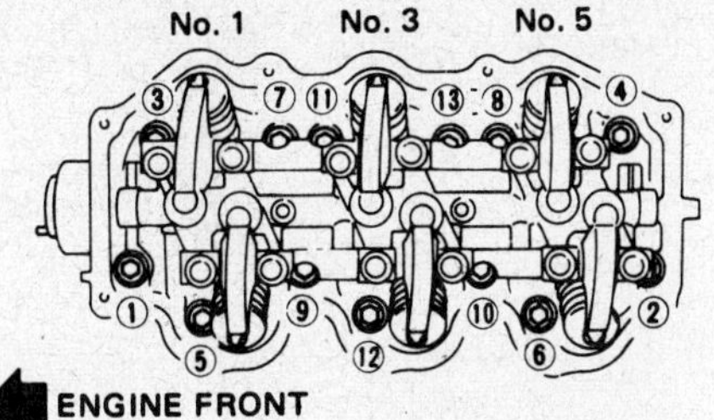

Fig. 5 Cylinder head bolt loosening sequence

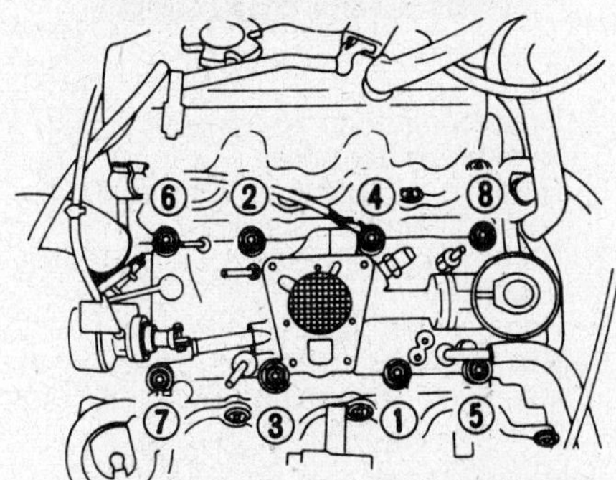

Fig. 8 Intake nut & bolt tightening sequence

   e. Torque all bolts to 40-47 ft. lbs. or, if angle wrench is available, turn all bolts 60-65° clockwise.
3. Install rear belt cover.
4. Install camshaft, locate plate, rear cover and camshaft pulley. Torque camshaft pulley attaching bolt to 58-65 ft. lbs. while counterholding pulley and torque locate plate bolt to 58-65 ft. lbs. **Do not intermix camshaft pulleys. Right hand pulley has R3 stamped on it and the aligning mark is 53 minutes off center, Fig. 7, while left hand pulley has L3 stamped on it and the aligning mark is −3° 27 minutes off center.**
5. Ensure No. 1 cylinder is set at TDC on its compression stroke. Crankshaft timing pulley mark should be aligned with mark on oil pump housing and camshaft pulley mark should be aligned with mark on left cover.
6. Install timing belt and adjust belt tension, then install front upper and lower belt covers. Refer to "Timing Belt, Replace."
7. Install valve lifters and lifter guide. Assemble valve lifters to their original positions and secure with wire.
8. Install rocker shafts with rocker arms and tighten rocker shaft attaching bolts. Torque bolts to 13-16 ft. lbs. gradually in two or three stages, working outward from center position.
9. Install rocker cover, ensuring rocker cover bolts, washers and trays are free from oil.
10. Install intake manifold, tightening attaching nuts and bolts in sequence, **Fig. 8**, as follows:
    a. Torque nuts to 2.2-3.6 ft. lbs.
    b. Torque nuts to 17-20 ft. lbs.
    c. Torque bolts to 2.2-3.6 ft. lbs.

R.H. side

L.H. side

Cylinder head bolt

Fig. 6 Cylinder head bolt tightening sequence

Distributor gear position

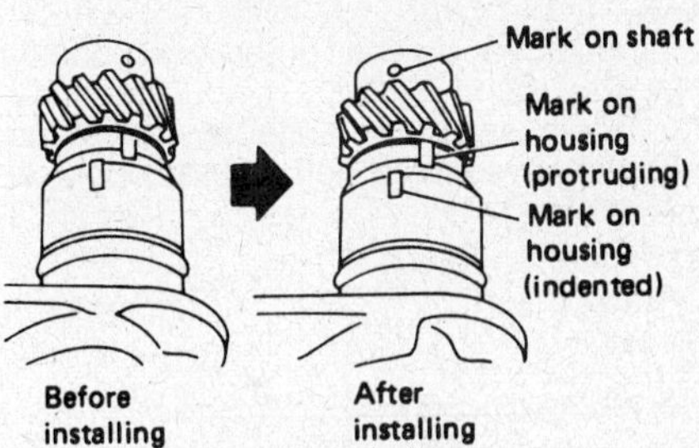

Fig. 10 Setting distributor gear position

    d. Torque bolts to 12-14 ft. lbs.
11. Install exhaust manifolds and connecting tube, torquing attaching bolts in sequence, **Fig. 9,** to 13-16 ft. lbs.
12. Set distributor gear position, **Fig. 10,** ensuring No. 1 piston is at TDC on its compression stroke.
13. Install distributor to cylinder head.

OIL SEALS REPLACE

CAMSHAFT OIL SEAL

1. Remove timing belt as previously described.
2. Remove camshaft pulleys.
3. Remove camshaft oil seal, being careful not to scratch camshaft.
4. Apply engine oil to new camshaft oil seal and drive it into place.
5. Install camshaft pulleys.
6. Install timing belt as previously described.

CRANKSHAFT FRONT OIL SEAL

1. Remove oil pump assembly, then the oil seal.

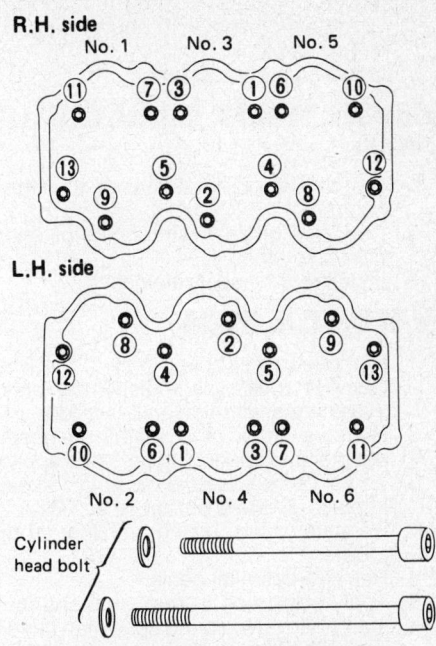

2. Coat new oil seal with engine oil and drive into place.
3. Install oil pump assembly.

CRANKSHAFT REAR OIL SEAL

1. Remove rear oil seal retainer, then the seal.
2. Coat new oil seal with engine oil and drive into place.
3. Install rear oil seal retainer.

VALVE OIL SEAL

1. Remove rocker cover.
2. Remove rocker shaft assembly and valve lifters with valve lifter guide.
3. Remove spark plug, install air hose adapter into spark plug hole and apply 71 psi compressed air to hold valves in place. **Ensure piston is at TDC.**
4. Remove valve spring, retainer and collets.
5. Remove valve oil seals.
6. Apply engine oil to new seal and install inner valve spring seat, then drive seal into place.
7. Ensure seal is properly installed, **Fig. 11.**

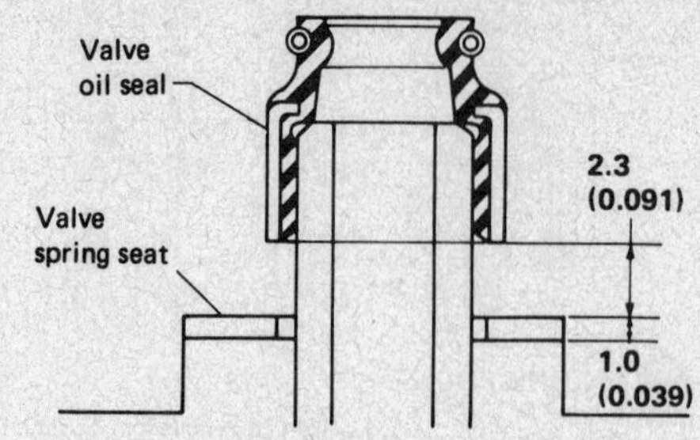

Fig. 11 Valve oil seal installed position

ENGINE DISASSEMBLY

1. Remove engine outer components, **Fig. 12.**
2. Place engine on suitable work stand.
3. Remove timing belt as previously described.
4. Drain coolant and engine oil.
5. Remove water pump.
6. Remove oil pan, as previously described, and the oil pump.
7. Remove cylinder heads as previously described.
8. Remove pistons.
9. Remove bearing caps and crankshaft, loosening attaching bolts in sequence, **Fig. 13.**

PISTON & ROD ASSEMBLY

1. Using suitable tool, remove piston rings.
2. Using suitable tool, drive out pin.

CYLINDER HEAD

1. Remove exhaust manifolds, loosening attaching bolts in sequence, **Fig. 14**
2. Remove rocker shafts with rocker arms, loosening attaching bolts in two or three stages.
3. Remove hydraulic valve lifters and lifter guide, noting the following:
   a. Hold hydraulic valve lifters with wire so that they do not drop from lifter guide.
   b. Do not place hydraulic lifters upside down.
   c. Do not disassemble hydraulic valve lifter.
   d. Attach identifying tags to valve lifters.
4. Remove camshaft end plate.
5. Remove camshaft from front side.
6. Using suitable tool, remove valve component parts.

ENGINE ASSEMBLY

CYLINDER HEAD

1. Install valve component parts, noting the following:
   a. Always use new valve oil seals.
   b. Before installing valve oil seal, install inner valve spring seat.
   c. Install outer valve spring with its narrow pitch side toward cylinder head side.
2. Install camshaft.
3. Install camshaft locate plate, torquing attaching bolt to 58-65 ft. lbs.
4. Apply engine oil to new camshaft oil seal and install it in place.

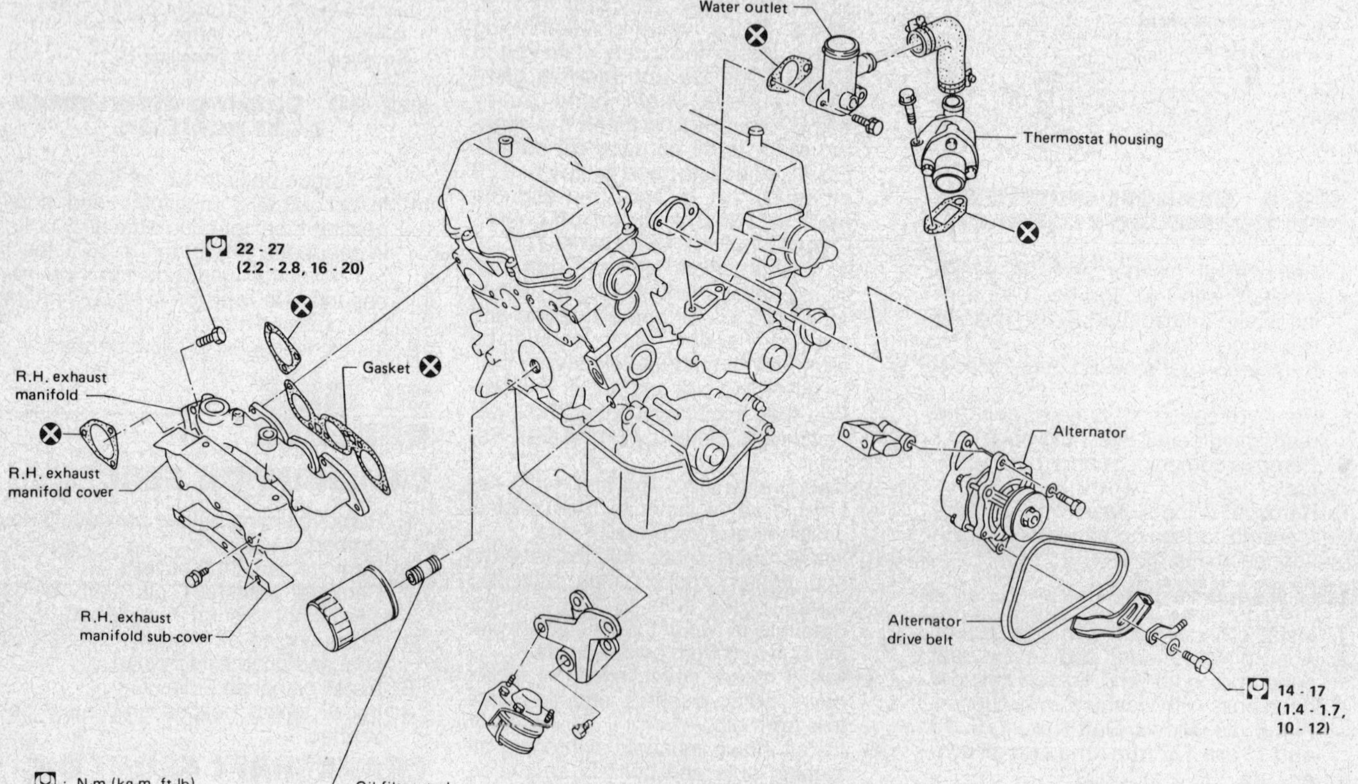

Fig. 12 Engine outer components (Part 1 of 2)

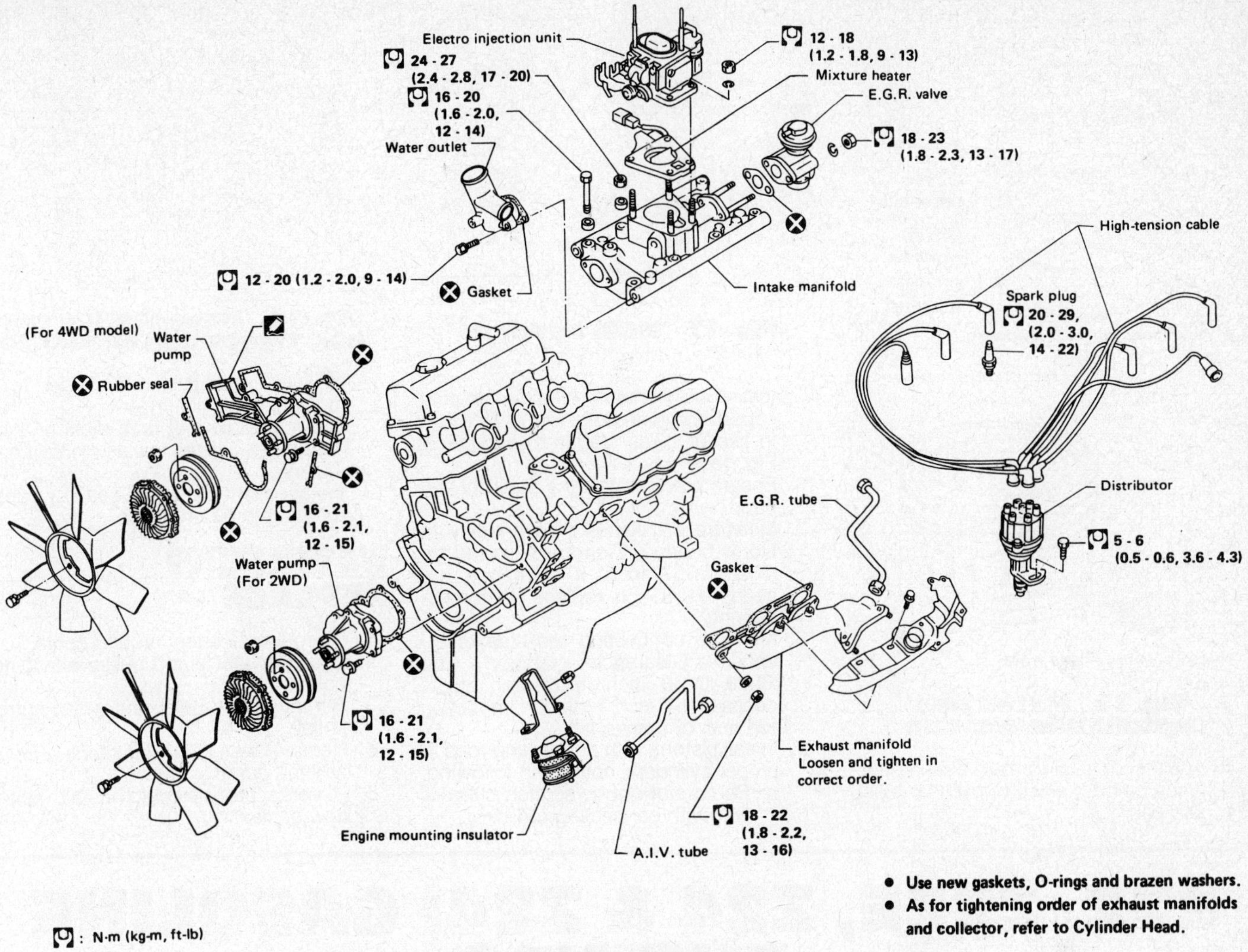

Electro injection unit
24 - 27 (2.4 - 2.8, 17 - 20)
16 - 20 (1.6 - 2.0, 12 - 14)
Water outlet
12 - 18 (1.2 - 1.8, 9 - 13)
Mixture heater
E.G.R. valve
18 - 23 (1.8 - 2.3, 13 - 17)
High-tension cable
12 - 20 (1.2 - 2.0, 9 - 14)
Gasket
Intake manifold
Spark plug
20 - 29, (2.0 - 3.0, 14 - 22)
(For 4WD model)
Water pump
Rubber seal
16 - 21 (1.6 - 2.1, 12 - 15)
Distributor
E.G.R. tube
5 - 6 (0.5 - 0.6, 3.6 - 4.3)
Water pump (For 2WD)
Gasket
16 - 21 (1.6 - 2.1, 12 - 15)
Exhaust manifold
Loosen and tighten in correct order.
18 - 22 (1.8 - 2.2, 13 - 16)
Engine mounting insulator
A.I.V. tube
: N·m (kg-m, ft-lb)

- Use new gaskets, O-rings and brazen washers.
- As for tightening order of exhaust manifolds and collector, refer to Cylinder Head.

Fig. 12 Engine outer components (Part 2 of 2)

3
7
5
1
4
8
6
2

Loosen in numerical order.

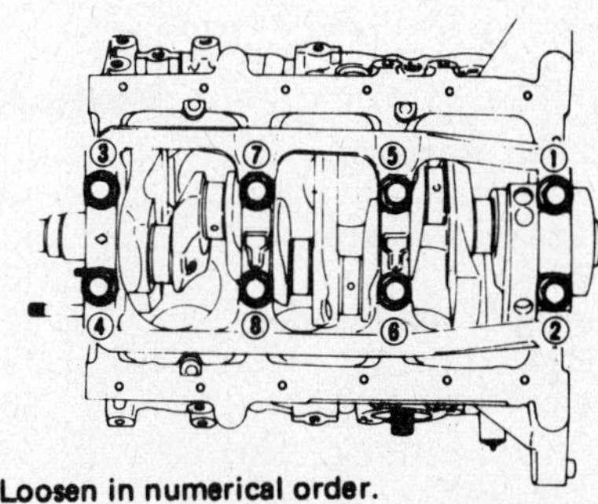

Fig. 13 Main bearing caps bolt loosening sequence

R.H. exhaust manifold
Front
1
6
3
4
5
2
L.H. exhaust manifold
Front

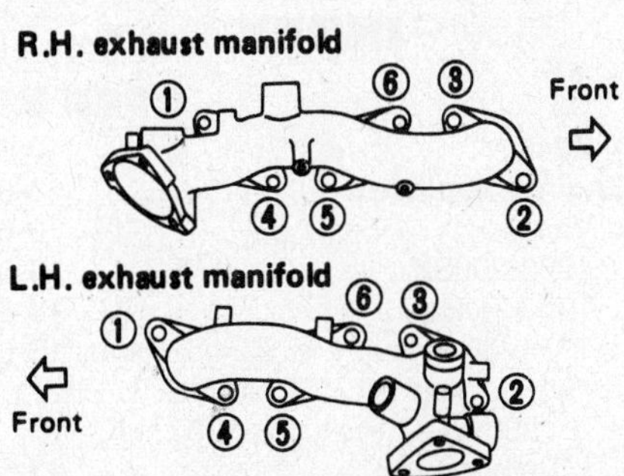

Fig. 14 Exhaust manifold bolt loosening sequence

Oil hole
Cylinder No.
Piston grade
Piston front mark
Engine front

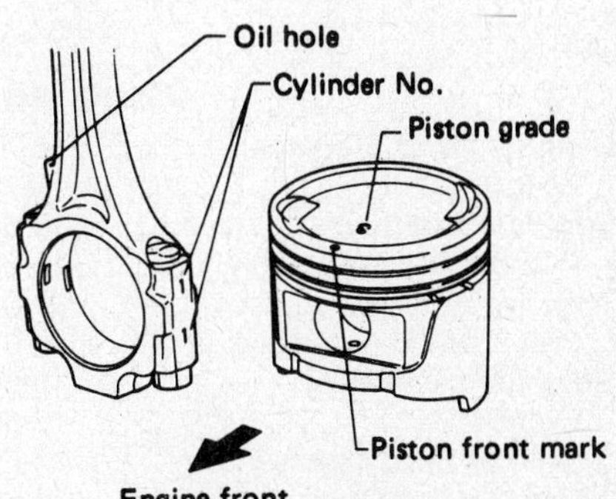

Fig. 15 Piston & connecting rod identifying marks

PISTON & ROD ASSEMBLY

1. Numbers are stamped on connecting rod and cap corresponding to each piston, **Fig. 15.** Do not intermix parts.
2. When pressing piston pin into connecting rod, apply engine oil to pin and small end of connecting rod.
3. After assembling, ensure piston swings freely.

ENGINE ASSEMBLY

1. Install piston assembly, setting piston rings as shown, **Fig. 16.**
2. Set main bearings in proper position on cylinder block, **Fig. 17. If cylinder block, crankshaft or main bearing is reused, main bearing clearance must be measured. Upper bearings have oil groove.**
3. If crankshaft, cylinder block and main bearing are replaced, thickness of main bearings must be selected as follows:
   a. Grade No. of each cylinder block main journal is punched on respective cylinder block.
   b. Grade No. of each crankshaft main journal is punched on respective crankshaft.
   c. Select main bearing whose thickness grade is equal to sum of thickness grades of crankshaft journal and main journal.

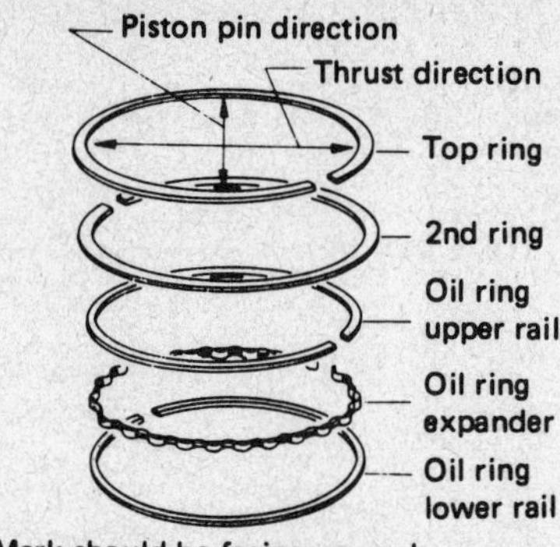

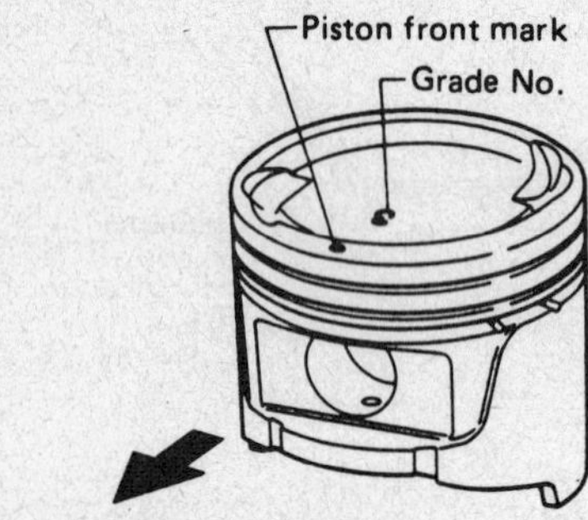

Fig. 16 Piston ring installation position

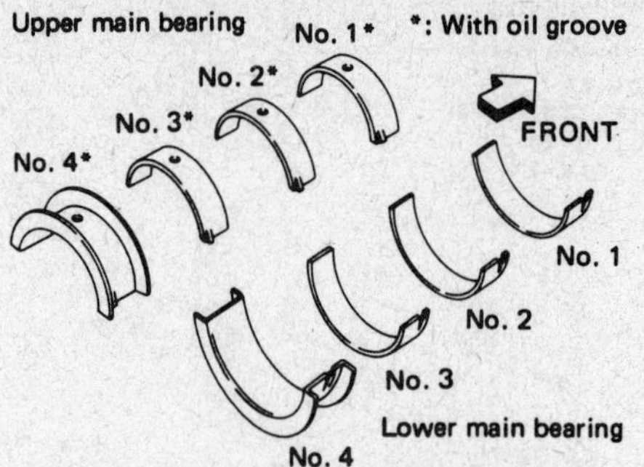

Fig. 17 Main bearings

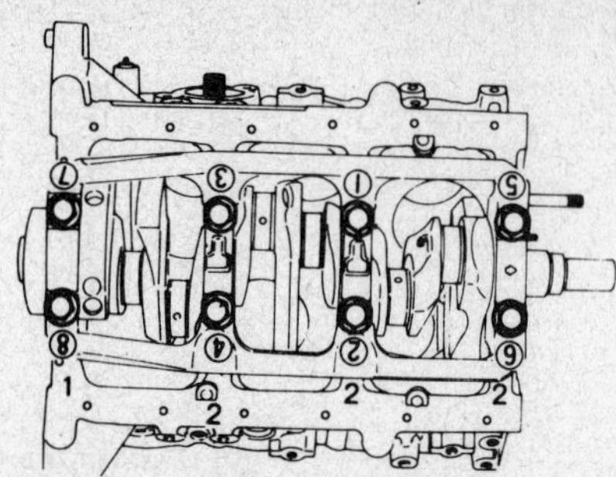

Fig. 18 Main bearing cap bolt tightening sequence

4. Apply engine oil to main bearing surfaces on both sides of cylinder block and cap.
5. Install crankshaft and main bearing caps, retorquing bolts to 67-74 ft. lbs. in two or three stages in sequence, **Fig. 18.**
6. Ensure crankshaft turns smoothly by hand.
7. Measure crankshaft free endplay at No. 4 bearing. Clearance should be .0020-.0067 inch. If clearance exceeds .0118 inch, replace No. 4 main bearing.
8. Measure connecting rod side clearance. Clearance should be .0079-.0138 inch. If clearance exceeds .0157 inch, replace connecting rod and/or crankshaft.
9. Install pistons with connecting rods in proper cylinders, noting the following:
   a. Be careful not to scratch cylinder wall with connecting rod.
   b. Apply engine oil to cylinder wall, piston and bearing.
   c. Arrange so that front mark on piston head faces toward front of engine.
10. Install connecting rod bearing caps, torquing to 33-40 ft. lbs.

WATER PUMP
REPLACE

1. Disconnect battery ground cable.
2. Loosen water pump pulley attaching bolts.
3. Remove drive belts and water pump pulley.
4. Remove water pump attaching bolts and the pump.
5. Reverse procedure to install, using new gasket.

Z22, Z22E, Z24 & Z24i GASOLINE ENGINES

INDEX

ENGINE
REPLACE
1983 200SX

1. To reduce fuel pressure, perform the following:
   a. Start engine.
   b. Disconnect wiring harness connector at fuel pump relay while engine is running.
   c. After engine stalls, crank engine momentarily.
   d. Turn ignition switch to off position and reconnect fuel pump relay wiring harness connector.
2. Disconnect battery ground cable.
3. Drain engine coolant and engine oil into a suitable container.
4. Scribe hood hinge locations and remove hood.
5. Disconnect or remove all wires, hoses and accessories indicated by arrows, **Fig. 1.**
6. On models equipped with air conditioning, remove compressor drive belt and remove compressor and position aside. **Never discharge gas from air conditioning system while work is being performed.**
7. On models equipped with power steering, remove pump drive belt and remove pump and position aside.
8. On manual transmission models, remove shift lever. On automatic transmission models, disconnect shift rod at manual shaft.
9. Remove radiator and radiator shroud. On automatic transmission models,

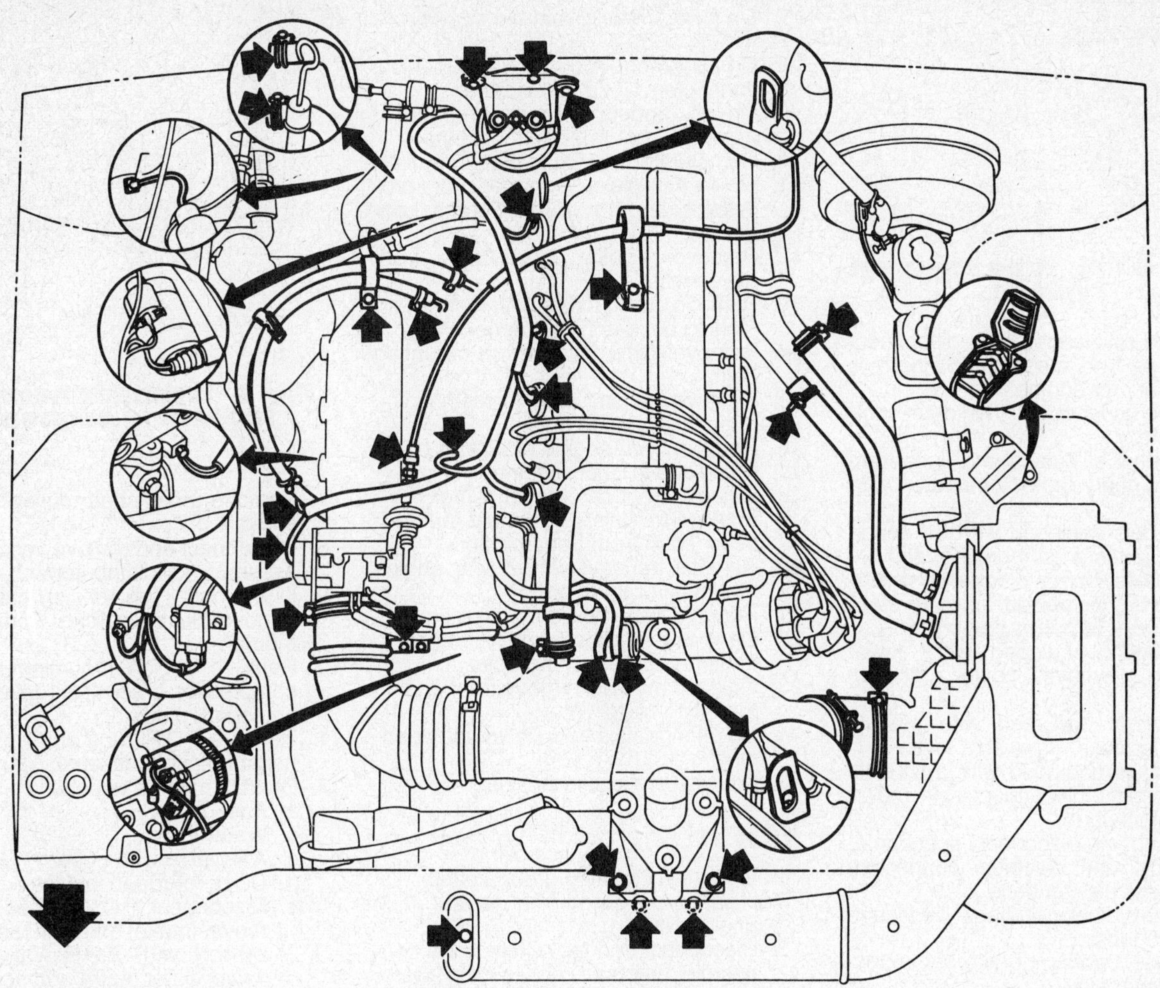

Fig. 1 Underhood accessory removal

disconnect cooling lines at radiator and transmission and plug ports in transmission.

10. Disconnect speedometer cable at transmission.
11. On automatic transmission models, disconnect wiring harness connectors at downshift solenoid and inhibitor switch and disconnect vacuum hose at modulator.
12. On manual transmission models, remove clutch operating cylinder from transmission housing, and position aside.
13. Disconnect exhaust pipe from exhaust manifold and front hanger.
14. Mark relationship between propeller shaft and rear axle companion flange and remove propeller shaft. Plug opening in transmission extension housing to prevent fluid loss.
15. Attach suitable lifting equipment to engine.
16. Remove transmission crossmember.
17. Remove front engine mounting bolts.
18. Remove engine and transmission as an assembly from vehicle.
19. Reverse procedure to install.

1983 PICKUP

1. Disconnect battery ground cable, then drain cooling system.
2. Scribe hood hinge locations, then remove hood.
3. Remove air cleaner, then disconnect all wires and hoses necessary for engine removal.
4. On models equipped with air conditioning, remove compressor and position aside. **Never discharge refrigerant from air conditioning system while work is being performed.**
5. On manual transmission models, remove shift lever. On automatic transmission models, disconnect shift rod at manual shaft.
6. Disconnect radiator hoses, then remove radiator with shroud from vehicle. **On automatic transmission models, disconnect oil cooler lines.**
7. On 4 x 2 models, disconnect speedometer cable.
8. On all models, disconnect all electrical connectors at transmission case.
9. Disconnect parking brake cable at brake lever side.
10. On 4 x 4 models, remove both propeller shafts. Plug opening in rear extension h ousing to prevent oil loss.
11. On 4 x 4 models, remove rear differential attaching bolts, then the front carri er mounting bolt.
12. On automatic transmission models, disconnect vacuum hose and oil cooler lines.
13. On 4 x 2 models, mark relationship between propeller shaft and rear axle compan ion flange and remove propeller shaft. Plug opening in rear extension housing to prevent oil loss.
14. On manual transmission models, remove clutch operating cylinder from transmission housing, and position aside.
15. Disconnect exhaust pipe from exhaust manifold.
16. Attach suitable lifting equipment to engine, then raise engine slightly to relieve weight from front and rear mount insulators.
17. On 4 x 4 models, remove differential rear mounting member.
18. On all models, remove rear engine mount attaching bolts, then the front engine mounting bolts.
19. Remove engine and transmission as an assembly from vehicle.
20. Reverse procedure to install.

1984–86 PICKUP EXC. Z24I ENGINE

1. Disconnect battery ground cable.
2. Scribe hood hinge locations and remove hood.

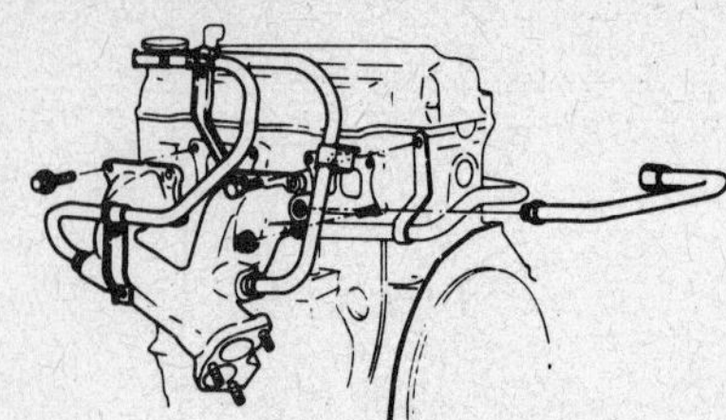

Fig. 2 E.G.R. tube removal (Typical)

3. Remove air cleaner, then disconnect all hoses and electrical connectors necessary for engine removal.
4. Remove under cover, then drain cooling system.
5. Disconnect all hoses and lines from radiator, then remove radiator with shroud.
6. On models equipped with air conditioning, unfasten compressor and position aside. **Never discharge refrigerant from air conditioning system while work is being performed.**
7. On models equipped with power steering, remove power steering pump.
8. On models equipped with manual transmission, remove shift lever.
9. On models equipped with automatic transmission, disconnect shift rod at manual shaft.
10. On all models, disconnect speedometer cable and electrical connectors from transmission case.
11. Remove clutch operating cylinder and exhaust tube.
12. Disconnect parking brake cable from brake lever side.
13. Mark relationship between propeller shaft and rear axle companion flange and remove propeller shaft. Plug opening in rear extension housing to prevent leakage.
14. On 4 x 4 models, remove front propeller shaft.
15. On all models, attach suitable engine lifting equipment and lift engine to relieve weight from mounts.
16. On 4 x 4 models, support front differential carrier with a suitable jack. Rem ove differential mounting bolts and support member, then carefully lower differential from vehicle.
17. On all models, remove rear engine mounting support-to-body attaching bolts and the front engine mounting bolts.
18. Remove engine and transmission as an assembly from vehicle.
19. Reverse procedure to install.

1986 PICKUP W/Z24i ENGINE, 1986½–1987 PICKUP & 1987 PATHFINDER

1. Disconnect battery ground cable.
2. Raise and support vehicle.
3. Drain engine oil and coolant.
4. Remove radiator with shroud and cooling fan.
5. Remove under cover.
6. Remove A/C compressor and power steering pump.
7. On 4 x 4 models, remove starter motor.
8. On 2 x 4 models, disconnect electrical connectors at starter motor.
9. On all models, disconnect exhaust manifold from front exhaust pipe.
10. Remove front exhaust pipe.
11. On 4 x 4 models, disconnect front propeller shaft from front differential car rier.
12. Remove bolts securing front driveshafts.
13. Remove front differential carrier attaching bolts and the carrier.
14. Remove differential front mounting bolts.
15. Remove transmission to rear engine mounting bracket nuts.
16. Remove front engine mounting bolts.
17. Raise and support engine.
18. Remove front differential carrier.
19. on 2 x 4 models, disconnect rear propeller shaft from transmission.
20. Remove transmission to rear engine mounting bracket bolts.
21. Remove transmission crossmember.
22. On 4 x 4 models, remove engine to transmission attaching bolts.
23. On 2 x 4 models, remove front engine mounting bolts.
24. On all models, carefully withdraw engine.
25. Reverse procedure to install.

VAN

1. Disconnect battery ground cable.
2. Raise and support vehicle and drain engine oil.
3. Disconnect and tag all electrical connectors, vacuum hoses and water hoses that would interfere with engine removal.
4. Support engine with suitable jack and remove center crossmember.
5. Remove engine to transmission attaching bolts.
6. Remove engine to mount attaching bolts.
7. Support transmission with suitable jack and carefully lower engine from vehicle.

ENGINE DISASSEMBLY

EXC. Z24I

1. Remove starter motor.
2. Separate engine from transmission:
   a. On automatic transmission models, remove converter dust cover and remove bolts securing torque converter to drive plate.
   b. Remove bolts securing transmission to engine and remove transmission.
   c. On manual transmission models, remove clutch assembly from flywheel.
3. Remove intake manifold stays (Z22E), alternator and alternator bracket.
4. Remove oil filter and oil pressure switch.
5. Completely drain engine oil and coolant by removing plugs from block.
6. Remove accessories and brackets from front of engine.

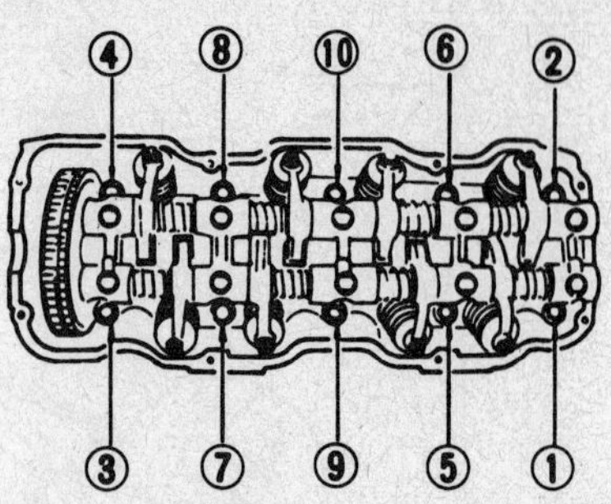

Fig. 3 Cylinder head bolt loosening sequence

7. Remove crankshaft pulley using a suitable puller.
8. Disconnect and remove vacuum tube assembly for distributor and canister.
9. Disconnect high tension cables and remove distributor cap. Remove distributor.
10. Remove engine mounting brackets, compressor bracket, oil level gauge, and spark plugs.
11. Remove E.G.R. tube and remove exhaust manifold assembly, **Fig. 2.**
12. On Z22 models remove:
    a. Fuel pump.
    b. Water inlet.
    c. A.B. valve with hose.
    d. Carburetor and insulator.
    e. Disconnect P.C.V. hoses and remove intake manifold as an assembly with E.G.R. valve, P.C.V. valve, water outlet, and accelerator cable bracket.
13. On and Z22E models remove:
    a. Cylinder block to P.C.V. valve hose.
    b. Power steering pump bracket and throttle chamber stay.
    c. Remove intake manifold as an assembly including water inlet, water pipes, water outlet, vacuum tubes, E.G.R. valve, and EFI assembly.
14. On Z24 models, remove:
    a. Power steering pump brackets and engine mounting bracket.
    b. Water inlet.
    c. A.B. valve with hose.
    d. Carburetor and insulator.
    e. Intake manifold as an assembly with E.G.R. valve, P.C.V. valve, water inlet and accelerator cable bracket.
15. Remove oil pump and drive spindle.
16. Remove oil pan and strainer.
17. Remove rocker cover.
18. Mark camshaft dowel pin position and remove camshaft sprocket.
19. Loosen cylinder head bolts in correct sequence, **Fig. 3,** remove bolts securing cylinder head to front cover, and remove cylinder head.
20. Remove front cover, timing chain tensioner and chain guide, and timing chain. Refer to **Fig. 4.**
21. Remove oil thrower and oil pump drive gear, **Fig. 4.** Remove crankshaft gear using a suitable puller.
22. Remove connecting rod caps and bearings, and push connecting

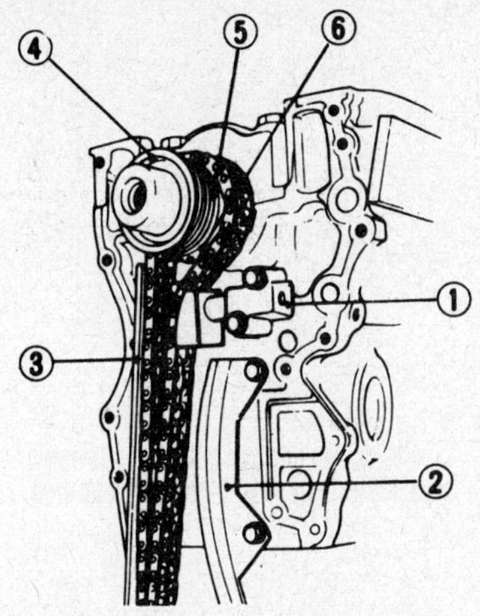

1 Chain tensioner
2 Slack side chain guide
3 Tension side chain guide
4 Oil thrower
5 Oil pump drive gear
6 Crankshaft sprocket

Fig. 4 Engine front side component removal

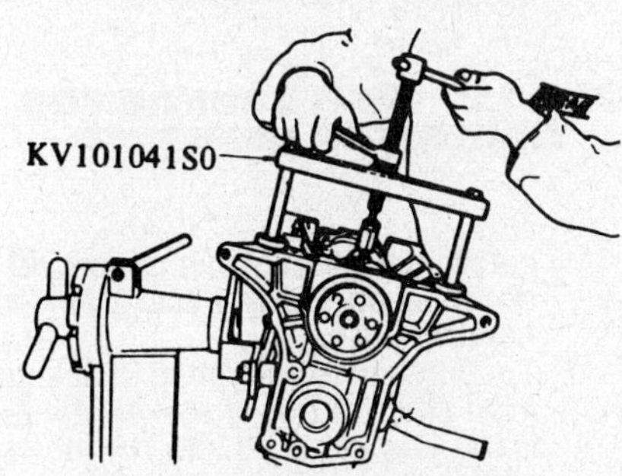

Fig. 5 Rear main bearing cap removal

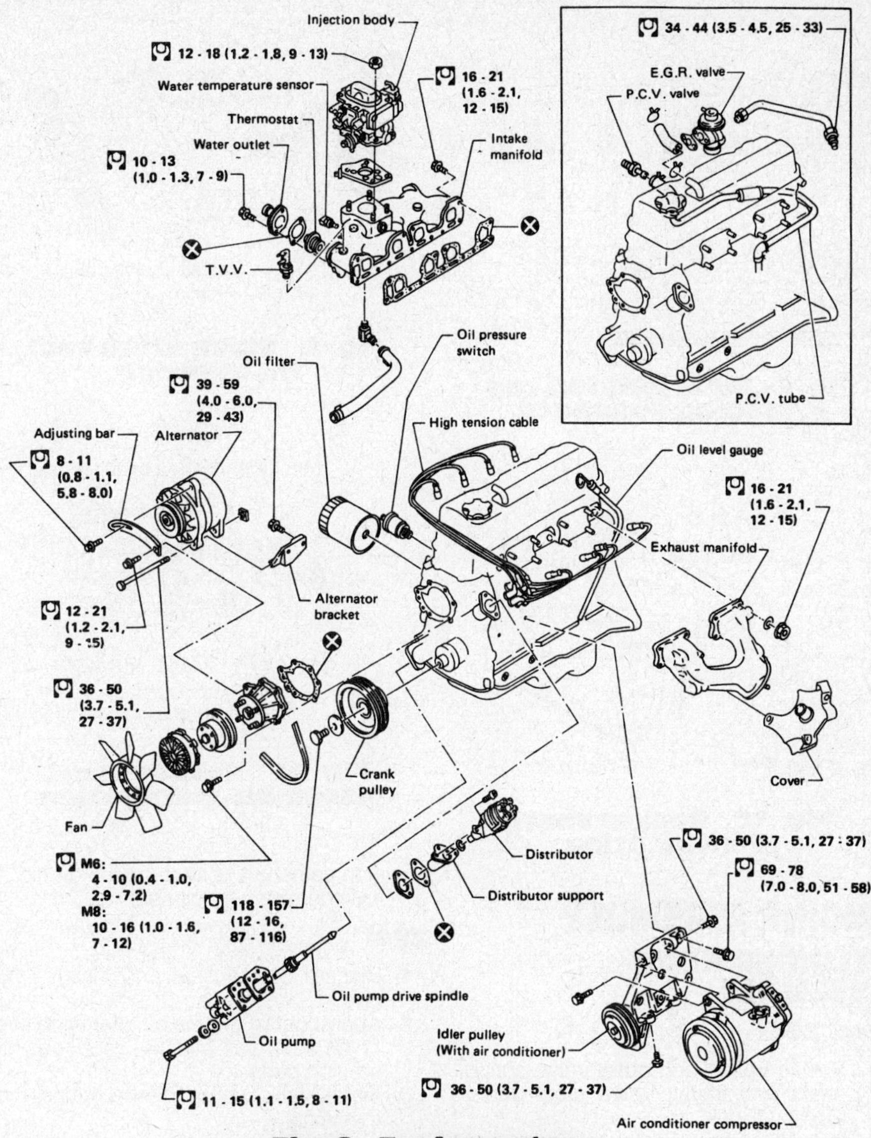

Fig. 6 Engine outer components. Pathfinder & Pickup w/Z24i engine shown, Van similar

rod/piston combinations out towards cylinder head surface. **Numbers are stamped on the connecting rods and caps corresponding to each cylinder. Care should be taken to keep all parts, including bearings in correct order.**

23. Remove flywheel or drive plate and engine end plate.
24. Loosen main bearing cap bolts working from the outside toward the center main cap.
25. Remove main bearing caps with lower bearings. Refer to **Fig. 5**, to remove center and rear main bearing cap.
26. Remove rear oil seal, crankshaft, and upper bearings. Keep all bearings and main caps in correct order.
27. Remove baffle plate and steel net from engine block.

Z24i

1. Remove engine outer components., **Fig. 6.**
2. Place engine on suitable work stand.
3. Drain coolant and engine oil.
4. Remove water pump. Refer to "Water Pump, Replace."
5. Remove oil pan and oil pump. Refer to "Oil Pump, Replace."
6. Remove cylinder heads. Refer to "Cylinder Heads, Replace."
7. Remove pistons.
8. Remove bearing caps and crankshaft, loosening bolts in sequence, **Fig. 7.**

PISTON & ROD DISASSEMBLY

1. Remove piston rings with a piston ring expander.
2. Press out piston pins.

CYLINDER HEAD DISASSEMBLY

Exc. Z24i

1. Remove rocker shaft assembly together with securing bolts, observing the following:
   a. Do not remove bolts at No. 1 and No. 5 brackets or rocker shaft brackets and rocker arms will spring out.
   b. Loosen rocker shaft bolts in sequence, working from the outside toward the center.
2. Remove camshaft.
3. Remove valves, valve springs, and related components using a suitable valve spring compressor.

Z24i

1. Remove intake manifold with injection body and exhaust manifold.
2. Remove rocker shaft assembly together with securing bolts, noting the following:
   a. Do not remove bolts at Nos. 1 and 5 brackets.
   b. Evenly loosen bolts from outside in sequence.
3. Remove camshaft.
4. Using suitable tool, remove valves, valve springs and related parts.

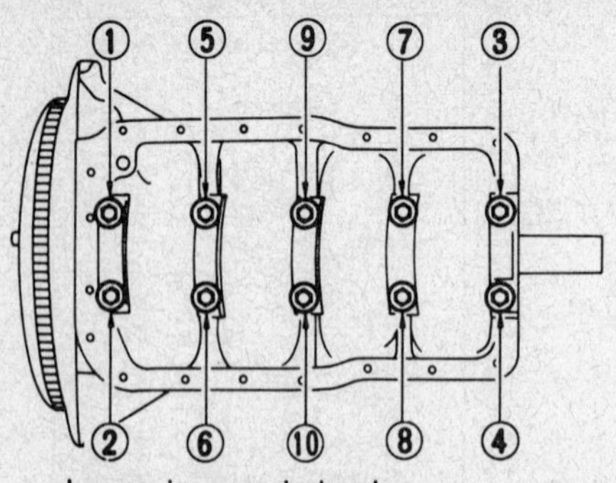

Fig. 7 Main bearing cap loosening sequence

Fig. 8 Valve stem seal installation

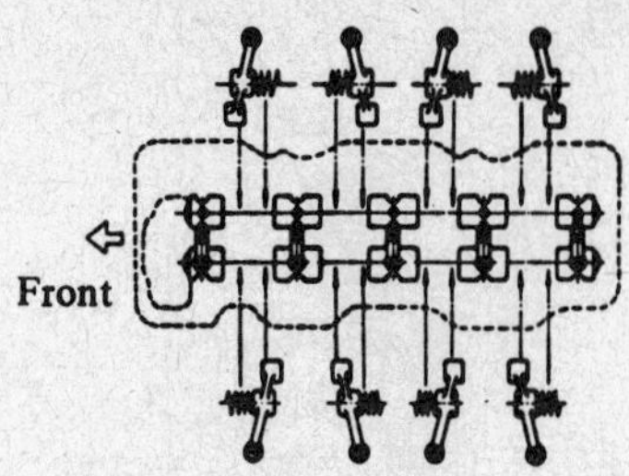

Fig. 9 Rocker arm assembly sequence

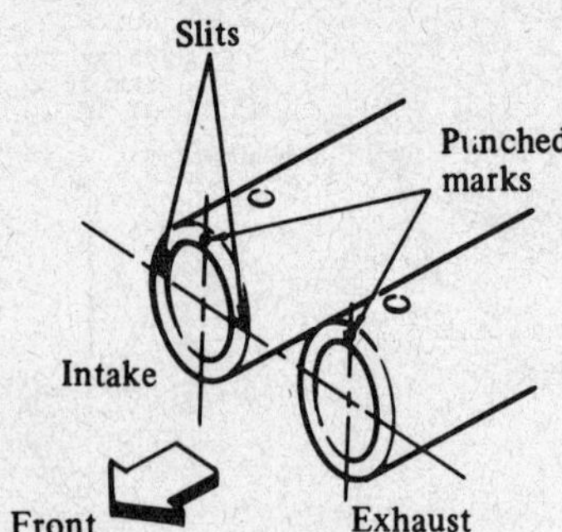

Fig. 10 Rocker shaft identification

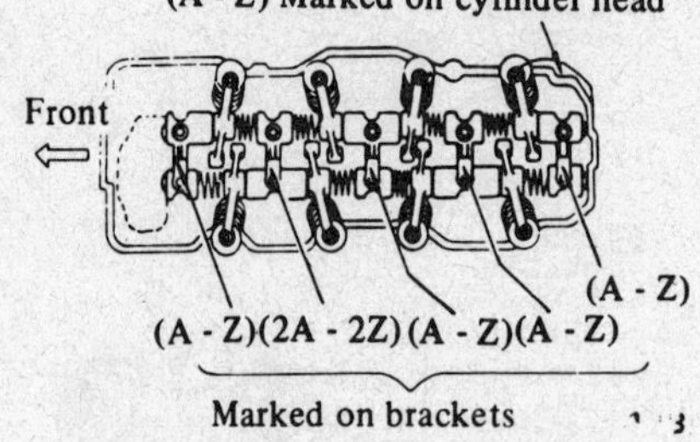

Fig. 11 Rocker shaft assembly installation

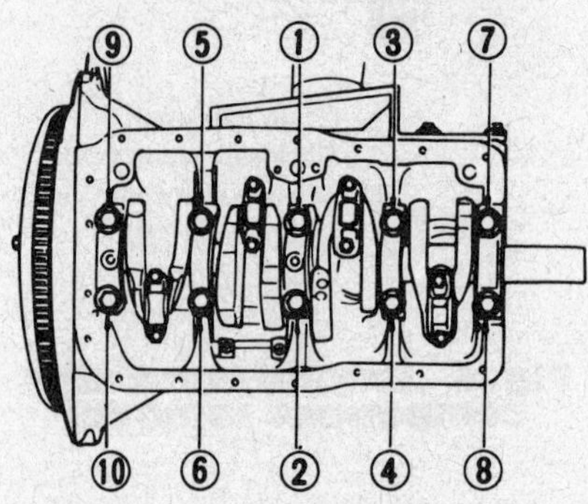

Fig. 12 Main bearing cap tightening sequence

ENGINE ASSEMBLY

CYLINDER HEAD ASSEMBLY

Exc. Z24i

1. Position inner and outer valve spring seats and install valve stem seals, **Fig. 8.**
2. Install valves, springs, retainers, and locking collets using valve spring compressor. **Painted end of valve spring must face toward cylinder head surface.**
3. Assemble rocker shaft assembly, **Fig. 9,** observing the following:
   a. Intake rocker shaft, **Fig. 10,** has slots on front surface for identification.
   b. Both rocker shafts should be assembled so that punch marks on front surface face up.
   c. Rocker arms with identification mark No. 1 are for cylinders 1 and 3. Rocker arms with identification mark No. 2 are for cylinders 2 and 4.
   d. Install rocker shaft brackets as marked, **Fig. 11.**
   e. Install retaining bolts in brackets No. 1 and No. 5 to hold assembly during installation.
5. Install camshaft into cylinder head with dowel pin in front pointing up.
6. Mount rocker shaft assembly on cylinder head and tighten retaining bolts to specifications in sequence working from the outside toward the center.
7. After assembling cylinder head, position camshaft so that valves on No. 1 cylinder are fully closed.

Z24I

1. Discard old oil seal and install new one.
2. Apply coat of engine oil to sealing lips of oil seal and frictional surfaces of moving parts.
3. Install valve components, noting the following:
   a. Before installing valve oil seal, install inner valve spring seat.
   b. Install outer valve spring with its narrow pitch side toward cylinder head side.
4. Install rocker shaft bracket, valve rocker and spring on valve rocker shaft, noting the following:
   a. Intake rocker shaft has identification mark (slit on front surface), but exhaust rocker shaft does not, **Fig. 10.**
   b. Rocker shafts should be assembled so that punched marks on front surfaces face up.
   c. On Pathfinder and Pickup, Nos. 1 and 3 cylinder's intake and exhaust valve rockers are same parts and provide identification mark "1" and Nos. 2 and 4 cylinder's intake and exhaust valve rockers are same parts and provide identification mark "2".
   d. On Van, Nos. 2 and 4 cylinder's intake and exhaust valve rockers are same parts and provide identification mark "2-4".
   e. Be careful not to miss original position of rocker shaft brackets. On Pathfinder and Pickup, alphabetical identification marks are provided on each bracket and cylinder head, **Fig. 11.**
   f. To prevent rocker shaft brackets from slipping out of rocker shafts, insert bracket bolts into bolt holes of Nos. 1 and 5 rocker shaft bracket.
5. Mount camshaft onto cylinder head, placing knock pin at front end to top position. **Apply engine oil to camshaft when mounting onto cylinder head.**
6. Mount valve rocker shaft assembly on cylinder head by accommodating to knock pin of head, then torque to 11-18 ft. lbs., noting the following:
   a. Tighten bolts gradually, in two or three steps, working outwardly from center bracket.
   b. When tightening bolts, provide adequate clearance under cylinder head.

PISTON & ROD ASSEMBLY

Exc. Z24i

1. Assemble pistons, pins and connecting rods of designated cylinder by pressing pins into the connecting rod. **Oil hole in connecting rod big end should face right side of engine, while the notch on piston crown should face front of engine.**
2. Install piston rings with piston ring expander. Stamped mark on piston ring should face up. Second ring has a larger tapered surface than top ring and oil scrapers are identical.

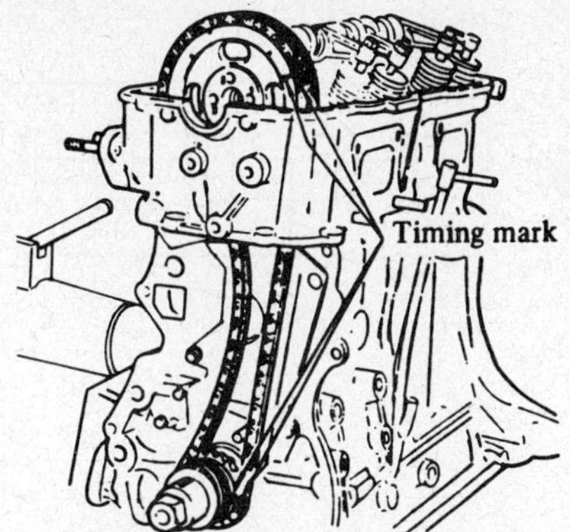

Fig. 13 Timing chain installation. Exc. Z24i

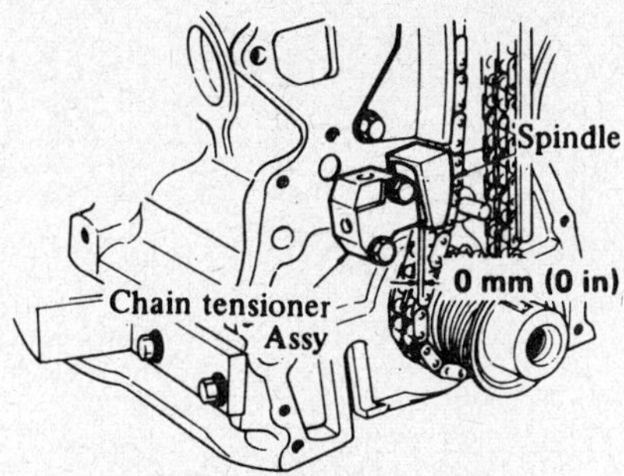

Fig. 14 Timing chain tensioner installation

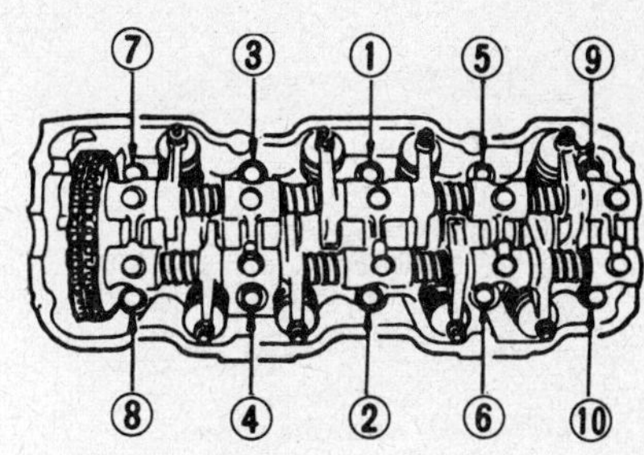

Fig. 15 Cylinder head bolt tightening sequence

Z24I

1. Assemble pistons, pins and connecting rods of designated cylinder by pressing pins into connecting rod. Numbers are stamped on connecting rod and cap corresponding to each cylinder. When pressing piston pin into connecting rod, apply engine oil to pin and small end of connecting rod. After assembly, ensure piston swings smoothly.
2. Install piston rings so that stamped mark on ring faces upward. Top ring is barrel face type. Second ring is undercut type. Apply engine oil to sliding parts. Arrange so that front mark on piston head faces to front of engine.

ENGINE ASSEMBLY

Exc. Z24I

1. Install baffle plate and steel net into engine block.
2. Place upper main bearings into engine block, observing the following:
   a. Upper main bearings contain an oil groove.
   b. No. 3 main bearing is the thrust bearing.
   c. No. 1 and No. 5 bearings are the same type, and No. 2 and No. 4 bearings are the same type.
3. Install crankshaft into engine and install lower main bearings into bearing caps.
4. Install bearing caps observing the following:
   a. Apply sealer to both sides of rear main cap and each corner of block.
   b. Install bearing caps with arrows pointing toward front of engine.
   c. Tighten to specified torque in sequence, **Fig. 12.**
   d. Make sure crankshaft rotates smoothly and endplay is within specification.
6. Apply sealer to side oil seals and install seals in rear bearing cap, **Fig. 12.**
7. Lubricate rear oil seal, then install with lip facing out using a seal driver.
8. Install rear end plate and flywheel, then torque flywheel bolts to specifications.
9. Install piston and connecting rod assemblies into engine noting the following.
   a. Using piston ring compressor install them into corresponding cylinders with mark on piston facing forwards.
   b. Apply engine oil to all sliding parts.
   c. Install corresponding connecting rod caps and torque to specifications.
   d. Check connecting rod to crankshaft endplay.
10. Thoroughly clean cylinder block and cylinder head mating surfaces.
11. Turn crankshaft until No. 1 piston is at TDC on compression stroke.
12. When installing cylinder head be sure clearance exists between valves and piston heads. If necessary loosen valve adjustments to draw in valves.
13. Temporarily tighten 2 center head bolts slightly. **Do not rotate camshaft or crankshaft independently when performing the proceeding steps.**
14. Install crankshaft sprocket with timing mark facing front of engine.
15. Install oil pump drive gear so that large chamfered inner side faces rearward.
16. Install timing chain guides.
17. Set timing chain on camshaft and crankshaft sprockets aligning matching marks on chain with marks on sprockets, **Fig. 13,** and install camshaft sprocket with dowel pin in position marked during removal. Torque sprocket bolt to specification.
18. Install timing chain tensioner assembly and adjust protrusion of tensioner to 0 inch, **Fig. 14. After tensioner has been installed, check amount of timing chain stretch. If timing chain is excessively stretched, remove tensioner and timing chain, remove camshaft sprocket and advance it to the next dowel pin position. Repeat installation procedure outlined above. If dowel pin is already in position No. 3 of camshaft sprocket, replace timing chain and tensioner assembly.**
19. Install oil seal in front cover using seal driver, then place front cover gaskets on engine and apply sealer to coolant passages.
20. Install front cover making sure that correct length bolts are used.
21. Apply lithium grease to front seal lip.
22. Torque front cover bolts to specifications.
23. Install crankshaft pulley and torque bolt to specifications.
24. Torque head bolts to specifications in sequence, **Fig. 15.**
25. Adjust valve clearance to specifications.
26. Install valve rocker cover.
27. Install oil strainer, then install oil pan.
28. Install oil pump and distributor driving spindle in front cover.
29. Partially thread intake manifold bolts and nut with washers into lower and center positions on cylinder head, **Fig. 16.**
30. Install intake manifold and related components in reverse order of removal.
31. With No. 1 piston T.D.C. of the compression stroke, install distributor.
32. Install remaining components in reverse order of removal and install assembly in vehicle.
33. Fill engine oil and coolant to specified levels and make necessary adjustments.

Z24I

1. Set main bearings in proper position on cylinder block, noting the following:
   a. If crankshaft, cylinder block or main bearing is reused, it is necessary to measure main bearing clearance.
   b. Only No. 3 bearing is flanged.
   c. Bearing Nos. 2 an 4 are same type.
   d. Bearing Nos. 1 and 5 are same type.
   e. Upper and lower bearings are not interchangeable because upper bearings have oil groove.
   f. On Pathfinder and Pickup, if crankshaft, cylinder block and main bearing are all replaced, It is necessary to select main bearings of proper thickness. If grade number of No. 1, 3 and 5 cylinder block main journal, stamped on cylinder block, is 0 select grade A bearing. If grade No. is 1, select grade B bearing. Use grade B bearing for Nos. 2 and 4 main journals.
2. Apply engine oil to main bearing surfaces on both sides of cylinder block and cap.

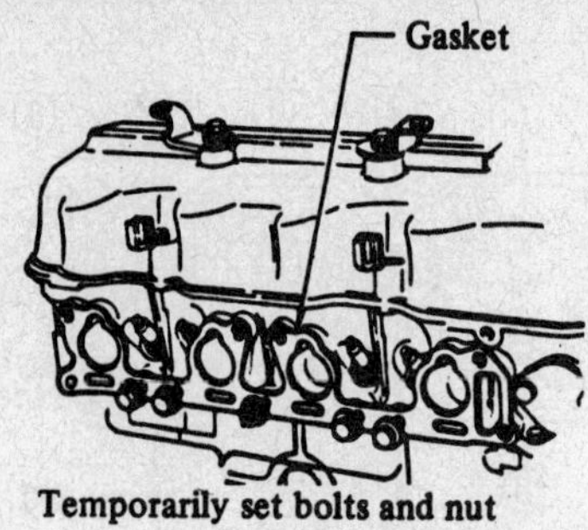

Fig. 16 Intake manifold installation

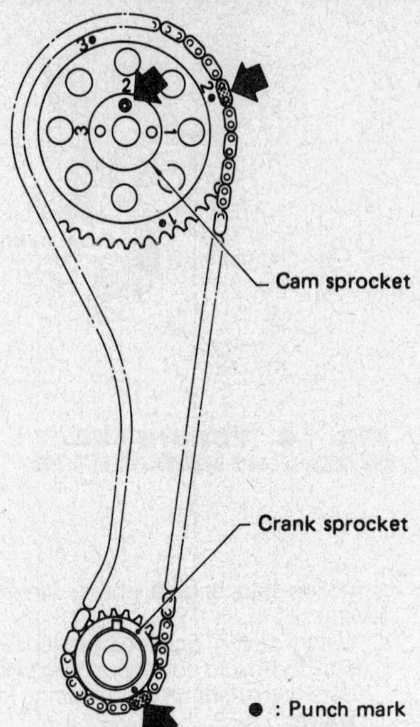

Fig. 17 Timing chain installation. Z24i

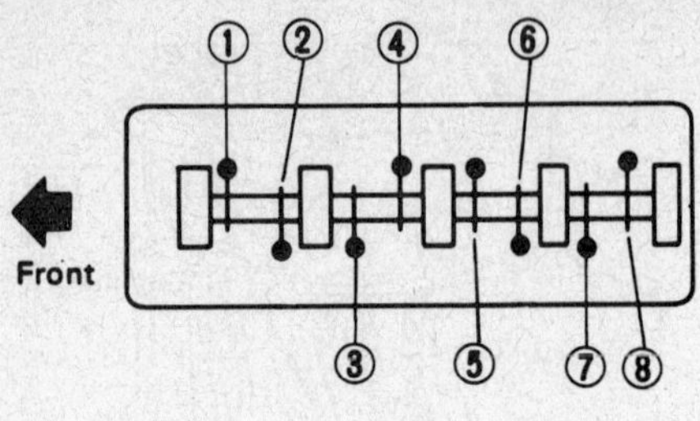

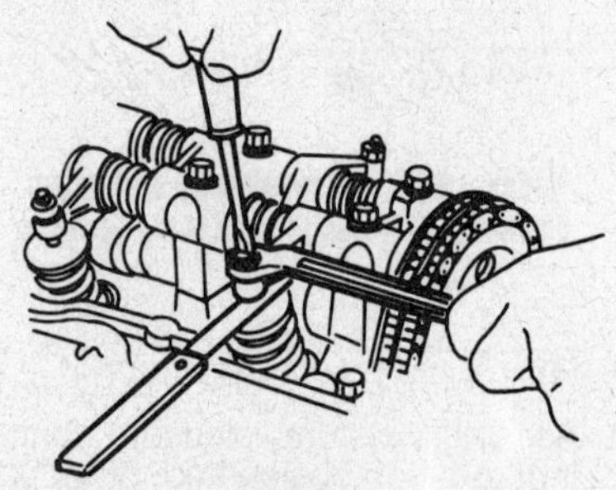

Fig. 18 Adjusting valves. Z24i

3. Install crankshaft and main bearing caps, torquing bolts to 33-40 ft. lbs. in two or three steps in sequence, **Fig. 12,** then ensure crankshaft turns smoothly by hand.
4. Ensure crankshaft end play, measured at center bearing, is .002-.007 inch.
5. Measure connecting rod side clearance. If clearance is not .0079-.0118 inch, replace connecting rod and/or crankshaft.
6. Using suitable tool, install pistons with connecting rods, noting the following:
   a. Be careful not to scratch cylinder wall with connecting rod.
   b. Apply engine oil to cylinder wall, piston and bearing.
   c. Arrange so that front mark on piston head faces to front of engine.
7. Install connecting rod bearing caps, torquing nuts to 33-40 ft. lbs.

OIL PAN REPLACE

Z24I

Pathfinder & Pickup

1. Disconnect battery ground cable.
2. Raise and support vehicle.
3. Remove under cover.
4. Drain engine oil.
5. On 4 x 4 models, remove front differential carrier member attaching bolts.
6. Remove front differential carrier attaching bolts and support differential with suitable jack.
7. On 4 x 2 models, remove front suspension crossmember.
8. On 4 x 4 models, Remove transmission to rear engine mounting bracket nuts.
9. Remove engine mounting bolts or nuts.
10. Raise and support engine and disconnect front exhaust pipe as necessary.
11. On all models, remove oil pan attaching bolts and the oil pan.
12. Reverse procedure to install.

Van

1. Disconnect battery ground cable.
2. Raise and support vehicle.
3. Drain engine oil.
4. Remove oil pan attaching bolts.
5. Insert seal cutter KV10111100 or equivalent between cylinder block and oil pan and slide by tapping with hammer.
6. Remove oil pan.
7. reverse procedure to install, noting the following:
   a. Remove all traces of liquid gasket from mating surfaces of oil pan and cylinder block.
   b. Apply continuous bead of liquid gasket, .138-.177 inch wide, to mating surface of oil pan.
   c. Apply liquid gasket to inner sealing surface instead of surface where there is no groove at bolt hole.
   d. Attach oil pan to cylinder block within five minutes after coating.
   e. Wait at least 30 minutes before refilling engine oil or starting engine.

TIMING CHAIN REPLACE

Z24I

Removal

1. Disconnect battery ground cable.
2. Drain coolant from radiator, being careful not to spill coolant on drive belts.
3. Remove radiator.
4. Remove cooling fan.
5. Remove drive belts.
6. Set No. 1 cylinder at top dead center (TDC) on its compression stroke.
7. Remove power steering pump, idler pulley and power steering brackets.
8. Remove compressor idler and crankshaft pulleys.
9. Remove oil pump with pump drive spindle.
10. Remove rocker cover.
11. Remove oil pan as previously described.
12. Remove front cover, being careful not to damage oil pan or cylinder head gaskets.
13. Remove chain tensioner, being careful that spring does not fall into oil pan.
14. Remove chain guides, timing chain and sprocket. **After removing timing chain, do not rotate crankshaft and camshaft separately.**
15. Remove oil thrower, oil pump drive gear and crankshaft sprocket.

Installation

1. Ensure No. 1 cylinder is at TDC of its compression stroke.
2. Install crankshaft sprocket, oil pump drive gear and oil thrower, noting the following:
   a. Ensure mating marks of crankshaft sprocket face engine front.
   b. Install oil pump drive gear so that large chamfered inner faces rearward.
3. Install camshaft sprocket and timing chain, noting the following:
   a. Set timing chain by aligning its mating marks with those of crankshaft sprocket and camshaft sprocket, **Fig. 17.**
   b. Camshaft sprocket should be installed by fitting knock pin of camshaft into its No. 2 hole, **Fig. 17,** and No. 2 timing mark must also be used.
4. Torque camshaft sprocket bolt to 87-116 ft. lbs.
5. Install chain guide and chain guide tensioner, noting the following:
   a. Torque bolt to 4.3-7.2 ft. lbs.
   b. When installing chain guide, move chain guide in direction that gives strain to chain.
   c. Adjust protrusion of chain tensioner spindle to 0 mm with slack side of chain guide, **Fig. 14.**
6. Apply sealant to upper and lower portions of front cover.

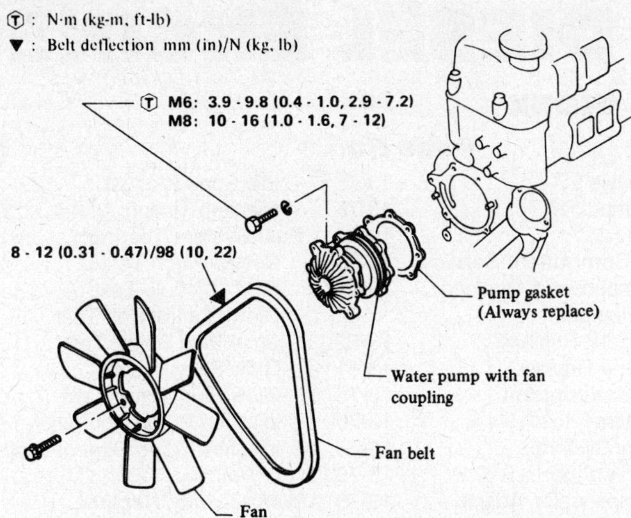

Fig. 19 Replacing water pump

7. Apply lithium grease to sealing lip of crankshaft oil seal.
8. Install front cover, torquing M8 bolts to 7-12 ft. lbs. and M6 bolts to 2.9-7.2 ft. lbs.
9. Apply suitable sealant to sealing point of cylinder head and install rubber plug.
10. Install oil pan, torquing attaching bolts to 3.6-5.1 ft. lbs.
11. Install crankshaft pulley, torquing bolt to 87-116 ft. lbs.
12. Install oil pump and distributor driving spindle in front cover, noting the following:
    a. Torque attaching bolts to 8-11 ft. lbs.
    b. Assemble oil pump and driving spindle, aligning driving spindle face with oil pump hole.
13. Ensure No. 1 cylinder is set at TDC of its compression stroke and that distributor rotor is set at No. 1 cylinder spark position.
14. Slowly rotate crankshaft to ensure pistons do not interfere with valves. **Do not rotate crankshaft quickly or with force.**
15. Install, rocker cover, compressor idler pulley, power steering pump, idler pulley, power steering brackets, fan, pulley, drive belts and remaining parts.

CYLINDER HEAD

REPLACE

Z24i

Removal

1. Disconnect battery ground cable.
2. Drain coolant, being careful not to spill coolant on drive belts.
3. Remove power steering pump drive belt, power steering pump, idler pulley and power steering brackets.
4. Disconnect front exhaust pipe from exhaust manifold.
5. Remove rocker cover.
6. Set No. 1 cylinder at TDC of its compression stroke.
7. Loosen camshaft sprocket bolt and support timing chain by placing wooden block in center of chain.
8. Remove camshaft sprocket.
9. Loosen cylinder head bolts in sequence, **Fig. 3.**
10. Remove cylinder head to front cover attaching bolts.
11. Remove cylinder head together with intake and exhaust manifolds.

Installation

1. Install cylinder head with new gasket and torque bolts, in sequence, **Fig. 15,** as follows:
    a. Torque all bolts to 22 ft. lbs.
    b. Torque all bolts to 58 ft. lbs.
    c. Loosen all bolts completely.
    d. Torque all bolts to 22 ft. lbs.
    e. Torque all bolts to 54-61 ft. lbs. or, if angle wrench is available, turn all bolts 90-95° clockwise.
2. Ensure that No. 1 cylinder is at TDC on its compression stroke.
3. Ensure that front knock pin is positioned at upper surface of camshaft.
4. Set chain on camshaft sprocket by aligning each mating mark, then install camshaft sprocket on camshaft, torquing bolt to 87-116 ft. lbs. **Camshaft sprocket should be installed by fitting knock pin of camshaft into its No. 2 hole. No. 2 timing mark must also be used.**
5. Apply suitable sealant to sealing point of cylinder head and install rubber plug.
6. Adjust valve clearance as follows:
    a. Set No. 1 cylinder to TDC on its compression stroke and adjust valve clearance Nos. 1, 2, 4 and 6 **Fig. 18.**
    b. Rotate crankshaft one turn so that No. 4 cylinder is at TDC on its compression stroke and adjust valve clearance Nos. 3, 5, 7 and 8.
7. Install rocker cover, power steering pump, idler pulley, power steering brackets and power steering drive belt.
8. Connect exhaust pipe at exhaust manifold.

OIL SEALS

REPLACE

Z24i

Crankshaft Front Oil Seal

1. Remove cooling fan, radiator shroud and crankshaft pulley.
2. Remove oil seal, being careful not to damage surface of crankshaft.
3. Apply engine oil to new seal and drive into place with suitable tool.
4. Install crankshaft pulley, cooling fan and radiator shroud.

Crankshaft Rear Oil Seal

1. Remove transmission and flywheel.
2. Remove oil seal, being careful not to damage surface of crankshaft.
3. Apply engine oil to new seal and drive into position.
4. Install transmission.

Valve Oil Seal

1. Remove rocker cover.
2. Remove rocker arm and rocker shaft assembly.
3. Remove all spark plugs.
4. Install air hose adapter into spark plug hole and apply 71 psi air pressure to hold valves in place. **When performing this operation, piston should be at TDC.**
5. Remove valve spring and valve oil seal.
6. Apply engine oil to valve oil seal and install it in place. **Before installing valve oil seal, install inner valve spring seat.**
7. Install parts in reverse order of removal.

WATER PUMP

REPLACE

Refer to **Fig. 19** for water pump replacement procedure on these models.

SD22 & SD25 DIESEL ENGINES

INDEX

ENGINE REPLACE

1983–86 DIESEL PICKUP

1. Disconnect battery ground cable.
2. Drain engine coolant.
3. Scribe location of hood hinges on hood to aid reinstallation, and remove hood.
4. Remove air cleaner duct and duct hose.
5. Remove wire and hose connections indicated by arrows in **Figs. 1 and 2.**
6. Remove radiator and radiator shroud.
7. On models equipped with air conditioning, remove compressor and position aside. **Never discharge refrigerant from air conditioning system when work is being performed.**
8. On 1984-86 models equipped with power steering, remove power steering pump and reservoir tank.
9. On all models, remove transmission control linkage as described under "Transmission, Replace."
10. Disconnect speedometer cable and electrical connectors from transmission.
11. Disconnect parking brake cables at cable clamps.
12. Mark propeller shaft to insure proper installation, and remove propeller shaft. **Plug hole in extension housing to prevent oil loss.**
13. Remove clutch operating cylinder and exhaust pipe.
14. Attach lifting equipment to engine slingers, **Fig. 1,** and raise engine slightly to take weight off front and rear engine mounts.
15. Remove bolts securing rear engine mount to transmission and body.
16. Remove front engine mount bolts.
17. Turn steering wheel all the way to right or left and raise engine with transmission and remove as a unit from vehicle.
18. To install, reverse procedure.

ENGINE DISASSEMBLY

1. Separate engine and transmission and remove clutch cover and disc.
2. Drain engine oil and coolant into suitable containers.
3. Remove accessories and mounting brackets.
4. Remove engine mounts.
5. Remove intake manifold with venturi and air duct.
6. Remove exhaust manifold and engine sling.
7. Remove front engine components: fan, temp-coupling, fan pulley, alternator adjusting bar, crank pulley, thermostat housing, and water pump.
8. Remove timing cover and using a suitable puller, remove timer assembly, **Fig. 3.**
9. Remove front cover and vacuum tube assembly.
10. Disconnect fuel pipes from injectors and injection pump assembly and remove fuel pipes.
11. Remove spill tube, injectors and injector washers. Plug injector nozzle holes to prevent entry of dirt.
12. Remove oil filter, oil cooler, and oil filter bracket.
13. Remove injection pump and diesel pump controller assemblies.
14. Disconnect and remove glow plug harness and oil cooler hose.
15. Remove rocker cover and rocker shaft assembly.
16. Remove pushrods and keep them in correct order.
17. Remove cylinder head bolts in proper sequence, **Fig. 4,** and remove cylinder head.
18. To remove oil pump:
    a. Remove spindle support and drive spindle, **Fig. 5.**
    b. Invert engine and remove oil pan. Then remove oil pump.
19. Straighten lock tabs and remove flywheel.
20. Remove camshaft locking plate, bring crankshaft to upper side, **Fig. 6,** and remove camshaft.
21. Remove valve lifters and keep in correct order.
22. Remove crankshaft gear using a suitable puller, then remove front plate.
23. Remove oil jet bolts and oil jets, **Fig. 7.**
24. Remove connecting rod caps and bearings.
25. Using a suitable drift, drive connecting rod/piston combinations out through cylinder head side taking care not to damage assemblies or crankshaft.
26. Remove main bearing caps with bearings using tool, **Fig. 8,** to remove rear cap.
27. Remove crankshaft and bearings. Keep bearings and caps in order.
28. Remove oil seal from crankshaft and rear bearing cap.

PISTON & ROD DISASSEMBLY

1. Remove piston rings with piston rings expander.
2. Remove piston pin retainer, immerse piston in oil of 176°F. and push out piston pin.

CYLINDER HEAD DISASSEMBLY

1. Remove glow plugs.
2. Remove valves, springs and related components using a suitable spring compressor, keeping all components in correct order.
3. Remove valve stem seals from valve guide bosses.

ROCKER SHAFT DISASSEMBLY

1. Remove cotter pin, washer, and outer spring, **Fig. 9.**
2. Remove valve rockers, inner springs, and rocker shaft brackets, making sure to keep all components in correct order. If rocker shaft brackets are difficult to remove, immerse rocker shaft assembly in oil of 158°F. for a few minutes and remove brackets.
3. To assemble rocker shaft, reverse disassembly procedure.

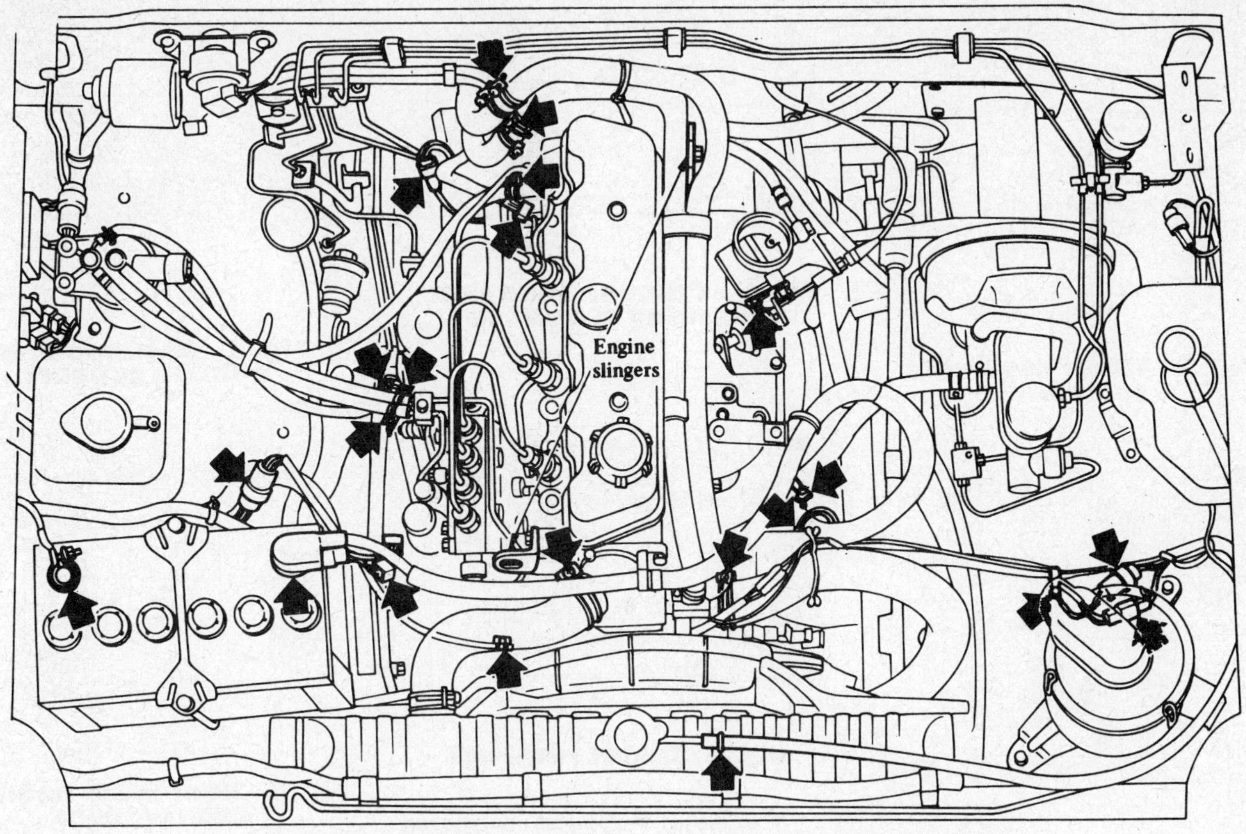

Fig. 1 Underhood accessory removal. SD22 engine

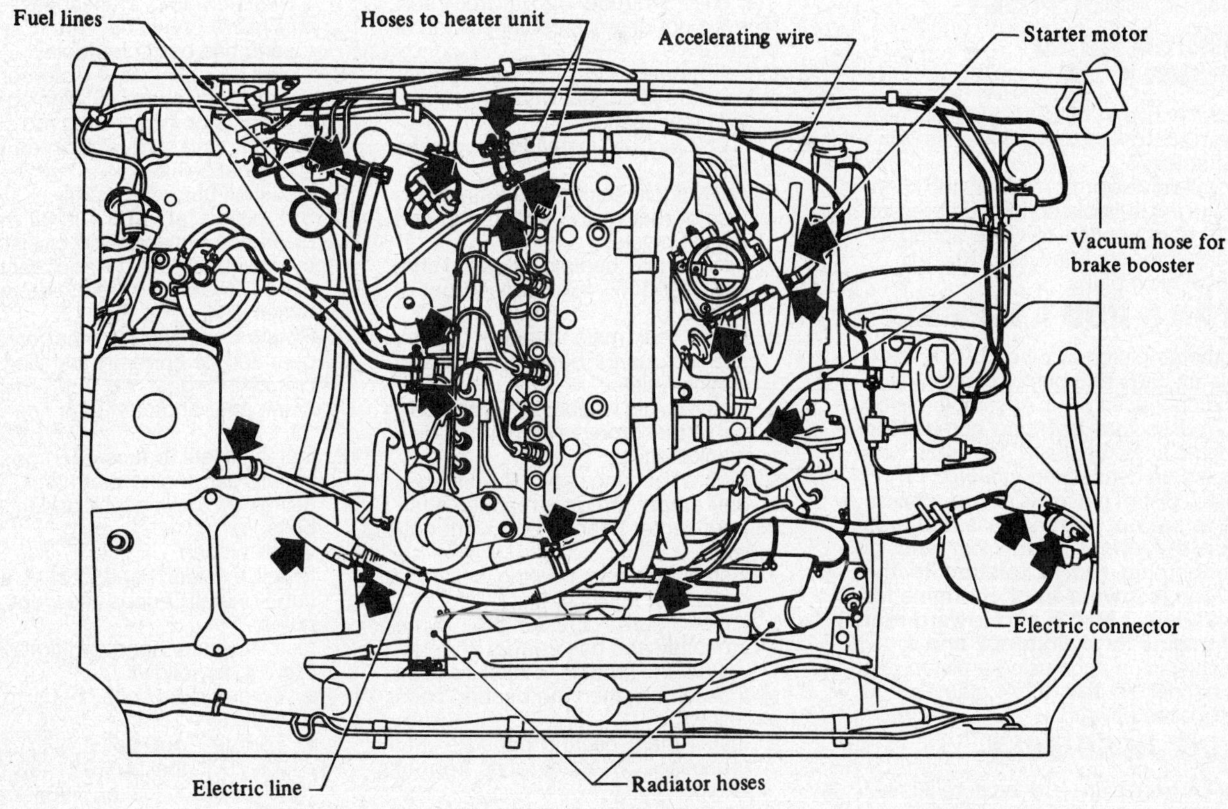

Fig. 2 Underhood accessory removal. SD25 engine

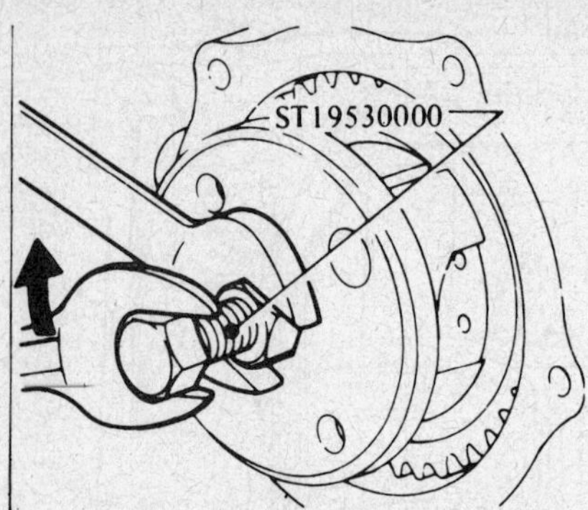

Fig. 3 Timer assembly removal

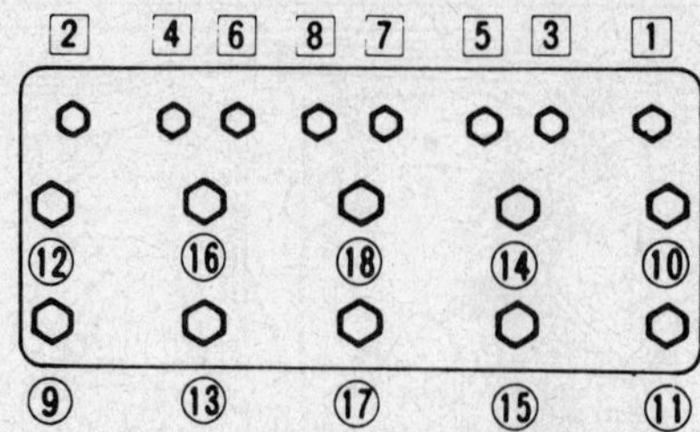

Fig. 4 Cylinder head bolt loosening sequence

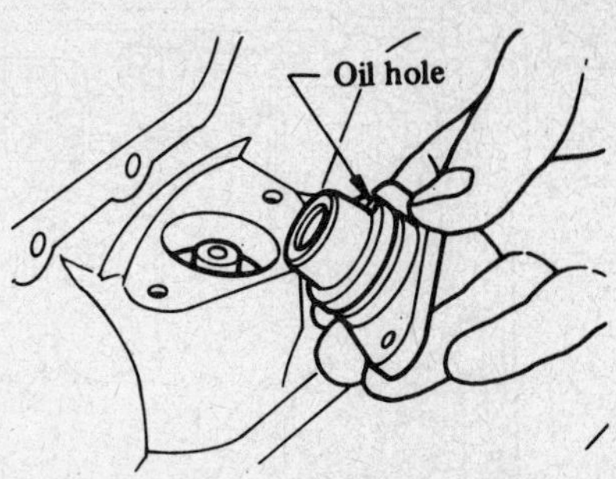

Fig. 5 Oil pump drive spindle support

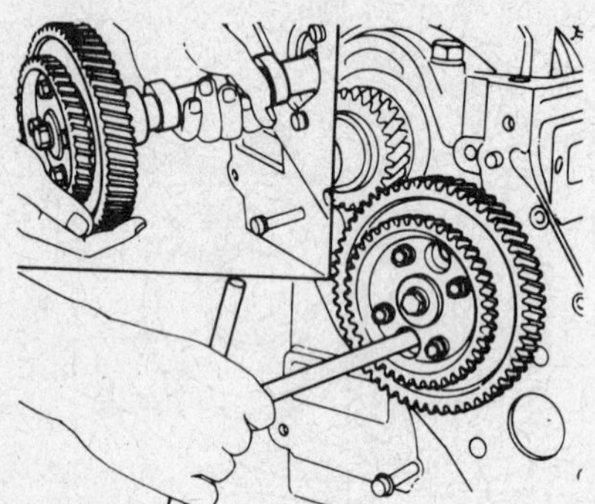

Fig. 6 Camshaft removal

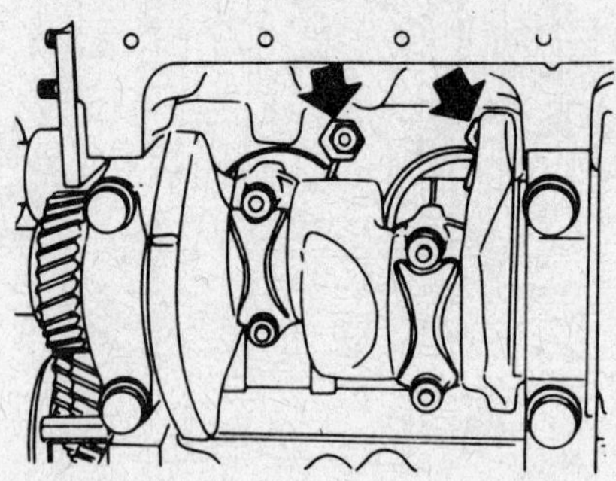

Fig. 7 Oil jet removal

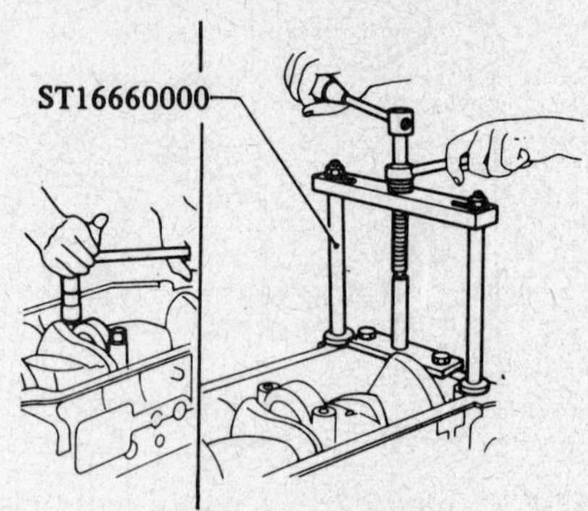

Fig. 8 Rear main bearing cap removal

ENGINE ASSEMBLY

CYLINDER HEAD ASSEMBLY

1. Install valve in head and install valve stem seal over valve guide boss using suitable tool.
2. Install valve spring, retainer, and keepers using suitable spring compressor, with narrow pitch of valve spring towards cylinder head, **Fig. 10.**
3. Install glow plugs.

PISTON & ROD ASSEMBLY

1. Immerse piston in oil of 176°F. for a few minutes and push pin into piston and connecting rod. Assemble piston to rod so that leaf type combustion chamber is opposite the matching marks on connecting rod, **Fig. 11.**
2. Install piston pin locks. **If rod assemblies are not marked, assemble so that the offset of the big end of connecting rod in relation to the piston is toward front of engine for cylinders 1 and 3, and toward rear of engine for cylinders 2 and 4.**
3. Install piston rings using a piston ring expander so that mark stamped on ring faces upward.

ENGINE ASSEMBLY

1. Install front plate, making sure it is not warped.
2. Install valve lifters and camshaft.
3. Install oil grooved halves of main bearings into proper position in engine block and install ungrooved halves in corresponding main bearing caps.
4. On 1983 models, install rear oil seals in engine block and rear main cap so that ends protrude .020 in from surface. Do not depress center portion of oil seal.
5. On all models, coat crankshaft contact portion of oil seal with grease and install crankshaft.
6. On 1983 models, install bearing caps as follows:
   a. Apply liquid sealant to contact surface of rear main bearing cap and engine block.
   b. Install main bearing caps so that embossed "F" mark faces front of engine.
   c. Install rear main bearing cap by aligning marks between cap and engine block.
   d. Install thrust washer at center journal so that grooves on bearing face crankshaft.
   e. Tighten bearing cap bolts in stages until proper torque is reached. Start from center bearing and work outward.
   f. Install new rear bearing cap side seals with liquid sealer.
   g. Make sure crankshaft turns smoothly and has correct endplay.
7. On 1984-86 models, install rear oil seal assembly, then the bearing caps as follows:
   a. Install main bearing caps so that embossed "F" mark faces front of engine.
   b. Tighten bearing cap bolts in stages until proper torque is reached. Start from center bearing and move outward.
   c. Install thrust washer at 4th journal from front so that oil groove on washer faces crankshaft.
   d. Ensure crankshaft turns smoothly and has correct endplay.
8. On all models install piston connecting rod assemblies by aligning matching marks on connecting rod and cap, **Fig. 11,** and torque rod cap nuts to specification.
9. Install oil pump assembly.
10. Set piston at T.D.C. and measure clearance between top of piston and cylinder block at front and rear of each piston. Maximum readings are between .016-.012, **Fig. 12.**
11. Rotate crankshaft so that crankshaft gear can be correctly installed. Install crankshaft gear so that marks on crank gear and cam gear line up, **Fig. 13.**
12. Install oil jets to face each gear.
13. Install rear engine plate and flywheel using new locking tabs under flywheel bolts.
14. Install oil pan.
15. Install cylinder head gasket and securely install O-rings into water and oil holes.
16. Install cylinder head and tighten bolts, **Fig. 14,** as follows:
    a. Torque main bolts (1-10) to 43-58 ft. lbs.
    b. Torque sub-bolts (11-18) to 22-29 ft. lbs. on 1981-83 models or 14-22 ft. lbs. on 1984-86 models.
    c. Torque main bolts to 87-108 ft. lbs. on 1983 models or 87-94 ft. lbs. on 1984-86 models.

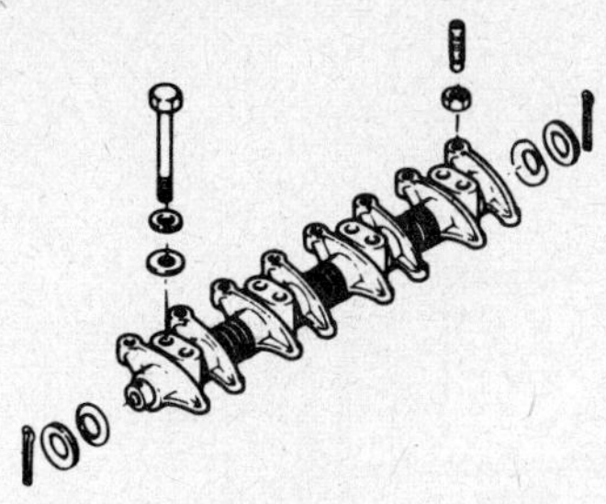
Fig. 9 Rocker shaft assembly

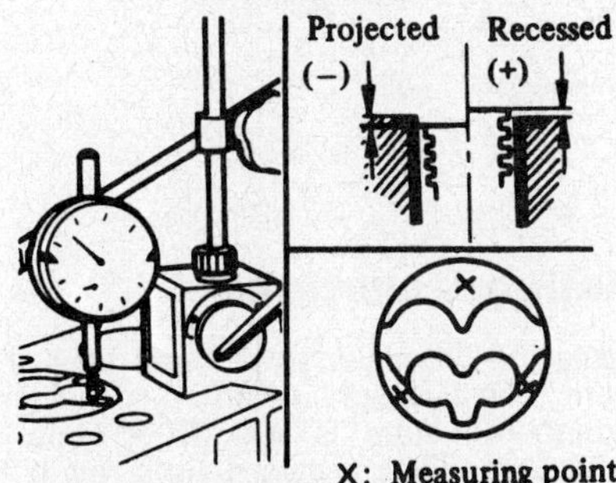

Fig. 12 Piston deck height measurement

d. Torque sub-bolts to 36-47 ft. lbs. on 1983 models or 33-40 ft. lbs. on 1984-–86 models.

17. Install push rods and rocker shaft assembly.
18. Install front cover with new oil seal.
19. Install front pulley. Prevent crankshaft from turning and torque pulley retainer to 217-239 ft. lbs.
20. Install water pump and thermostat housing.
21. Align grooves on camshaft, oil pump drive gear, and oil pump drive shaft, and install oil pump spindle, **Fig. 5.**
22. Connect oil cooler hose to cylinder head and install glow plug harness.
23. Set No. 1 piston at T.D.C. and install injection pump.
24. Install injectors using new washers.
25. Install spill tube and injector pipe assembly.
26. Install oil cooler, oil filter bracket, and oil pipe and gradually tighten them.
27. Install vacuum tube assembly.
28. Install diesel pump controller and connect rod to injection pump lever. Make sure there is play in pump lever.
29. Adjust valves as outlined to specification.
30. Install breather assembly, intake, and exhaust manifolds.
31. Install alternator bracket and alternator, alternator adjusting bar, fan pulley, temp-coupling, fan, and fan belt.
32. Install engine mounts and engine accessories.
33. Install clutch disc and cover using suitable alignment tool.
34. Couple transmission to engine and install assembly.
35. After installation: fill engine oil and coolant to proper levels, bleed fuel system, adjust drive belt, injection timing, and idle speed. After engine has been warmed-up, remove rocker cover, retorque cylinder head, and readjust valve clearances.

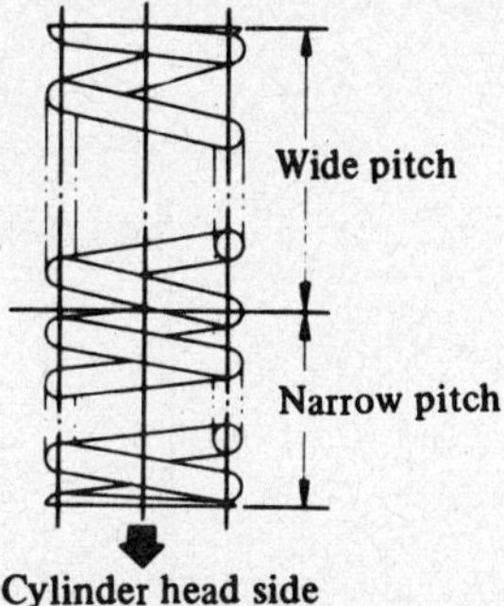

Fig. 10 Valve spring installation

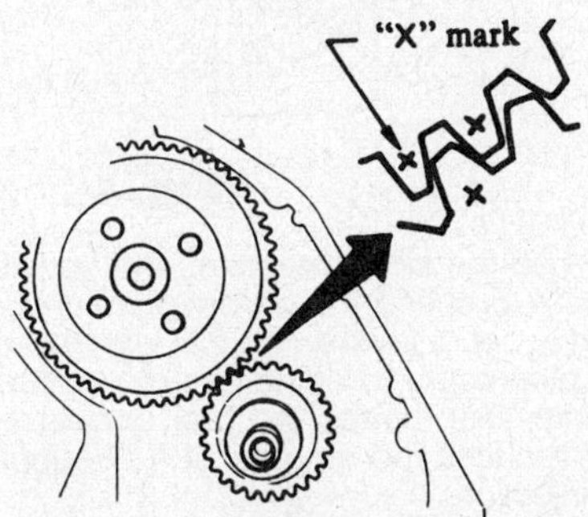

Fig. 13 Crankshaft gear installation

FUEL SYSTEM DESCRIPTION

Through the action of a governor and timer, the diesel fuel system feeds highly pressurized fuel in the required amount, at the correct time to the combustion chamber depending upon engine operating conditions.

FUEL DELIVERY SYSTEM

Fuel is pumped from the fuel tank, **Fig. 15,** by a feed pump located on the injection pump assembly to the fuel filter. The fuel filter maintains a constant volume of fuel and returns excess fuel to the tank through an overflow valve on top of the filter. Fuel passes through the filter into the injection pump plunger which pressurizes a metered amount of fuel into the delivery valve. Fuel is injected into the combustion chamber through the nozzle under constant injection starting pressure.

CONTROL SYSTEM

The diesel pump control system is provided to control excess fuel when starting, cut fuel when stopping the engine, and control engine speed under normal driving conditions. The governor, which is coupled to the injection pump maintains the fixed engine speed when the fuel injection rack is held at a fixed position, maintains idle speed, and provides maximum engine speed control. Fuel enrichment for starting and fuel shut off when shutting off the engine are controlled by diesel pump controller assembly, D.P.C. module, and ignition switch.

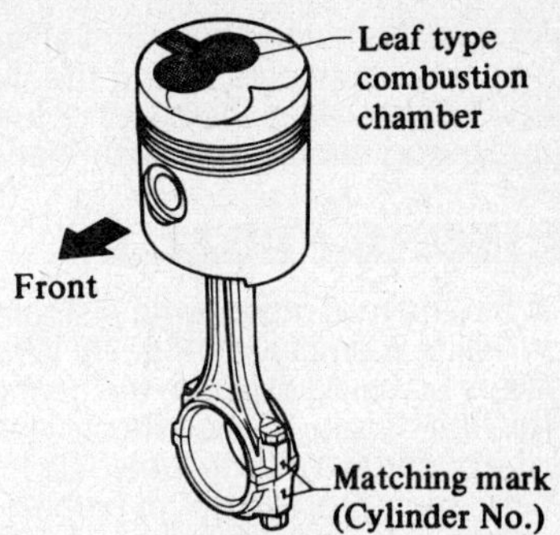

Fig. 11 Piston & rod assembly

Fig. 14 Cylinder head tightening sequence

FUEL SYSTEM COMPONENTS

INJECTION PUMP

The fuel injection pump, **Fig. 16,** delivers pressurized fuel under the correct injection timing, and controls the amount of fuel delivered according to engine load conditions. The pump is an inline type pump with one plunger per cylinder.

The pump consists of plunger barrels and plungers. The plungers are driven by a camshaft, reciprocate within the plunger barrels, and deliver fuel under high pressure. The quantity of fuel injected is changed by the control rack. The control rack moves corresponding to a vacuum signal created by the movement of the accelerator pedal. The control rack turns the plungers, changing their effective stroke, **Fig. 17,** changing the amount of fuel delivered.

The position in which the inlet port is fully closed by the plunger is called the beginning of injection. As the slanted cut on the plunger connects with the fuel inlet port and fuel flows from the vertical hold in the plunger, pressure in the barrel is released. This is called the end of injection, **Fig. 18.**

DELIVERY VALVE

After the plunger completes fuel delivery, the delivery valve prevents reverse flow of fuel from the injection tube. The sucking action of the delivery valve piston controls residual pressure in the injection tube. This improves the spray of fuel without allowing dribbling or secondary injection.

INJECTION NOZZLE

A throttle type nozzle with a single injection orifice is employed, **Fig. 19.** When fuel delivery pressure exceeds the spring force within the nozzle, the needle valve pushes up the pushrod allowing fuel to be injected. When spring pressure overcomes fuel pressure, injection stops.

GOVERNOR & CONTROLLER SYSTEM

The armature, **Fig. 20**, begins to rotate when it receives a signal from the control unit. This turns the crankpin which engages and rotates the Geneva gear. When the Geneva gear contacts any of the three terminals within the housing, the armature stops rotating and holds the injection pump control lever in position.

With the ignition switch in the start position, the control lever is moved to the "excess fuel" position to make starting easier, **Fig. 21.**

With ignition switch in on position after the engine has started, the injection pump control lever is shifted to the "normal driving" position. The high vacuum created by a closed throttle plate at idle is applied to the governor chamber, **Fig. 22.** The governor spring is compressed causing the diaphragm to contact idling spring. The diaphragm becomes stationary when the pressure between the vacuum and the governor spring equalize maintaining the proper fuel delivery for idling operation.

Under normal driving conditions, as the throttle plate is moved, vacuum is reduced, and the governor spring pressure overcomes the vacuum. Depending on operating conditions the diaphragm will stabilize at different positions to allow the correct fuel delivery by varying the position of the injection pump control rack, **Fig. 17.**

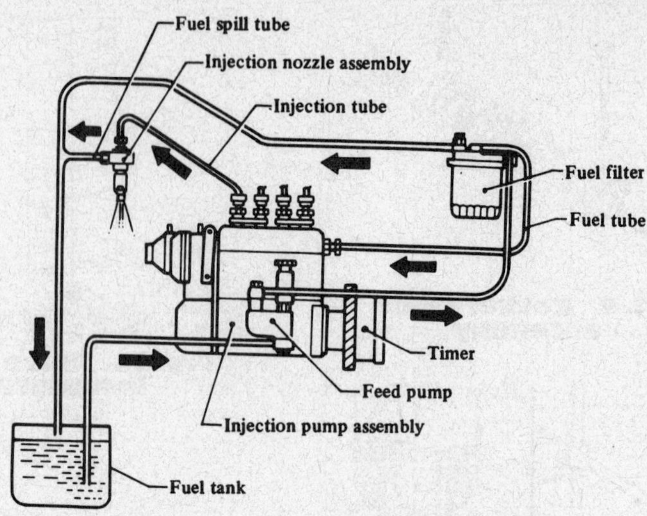

Fig. 15 Fuel delivery system

When the engine reaches the specified maximum speed, the governor weights operate a set of levers, **Fig. 22,** which cause the diaphragm to compress the governor spring. This moves the fuel control rack and reduces the amount of fuel supplied for injection.

When ignition switch is in off position, the fuel control lever is moved to the fuel "shut off" position, **Fig. 23,** shutting off fuel supply and stopping the engine.

ALTITUDE COMPENSATOR

The altitude compensator, **Fig. 24,** responds to atmospheric pressure. The rod attached to the bellows operates the injection pump control lever reducing the amount of fuel as the bellows expands.

TIMER

The timer automatically changes the fuel injection timing depending on engine RPM. As engine RPM increases, the flyweights expand on the holder pin due to centrifugal force. The curved surface contacts the timer flange pin and acts as a cam. The flyweights compress the timer spring from state "B," **Fig. 25,** to state "C" while expanding outward. As a result, the flyweight holder pin changes its position with respect to the timer flange pin, altering the timing by an angle "A."

FUEL SYSTEM SERVICE

FUEL SYSTEM BLEEDING

Air should be bled from the fuel system whenever it is opened or repaired.

1. Remove cap that covers priming pump, 2, and loosen air vent screw, 1, **Fig. 26.**
2. Turn priming pump counterclockwise to engage.
3. Operate priming pump up and down observing air vent until no further air is observed.
4. Tighten air vent screw, push and turn pump clockwise, and install priming pump cap.

INJECTION TIMING, ADJUST

1. Check marks on pump and engine front cover, and move pump, if necessary, to align marks.
2. Turn crank pulley in direction of engine rotation and align first mark on

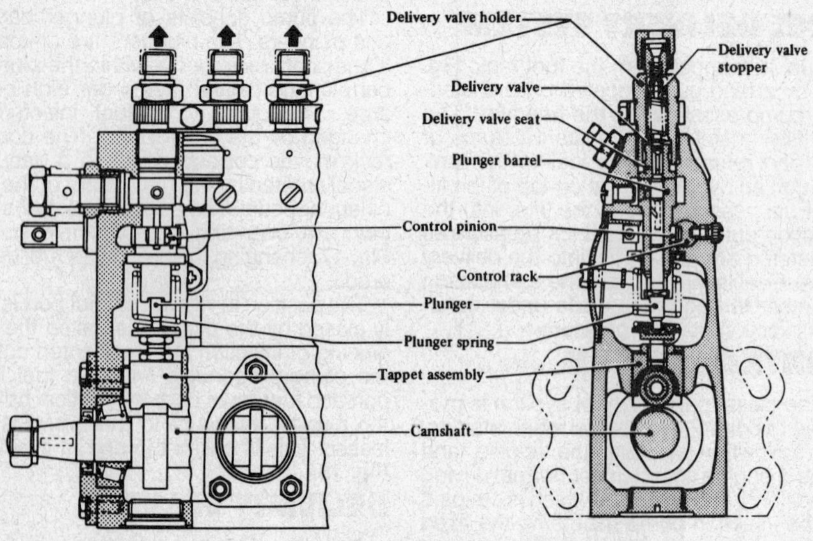

Fig. 16 Fuel injection pump

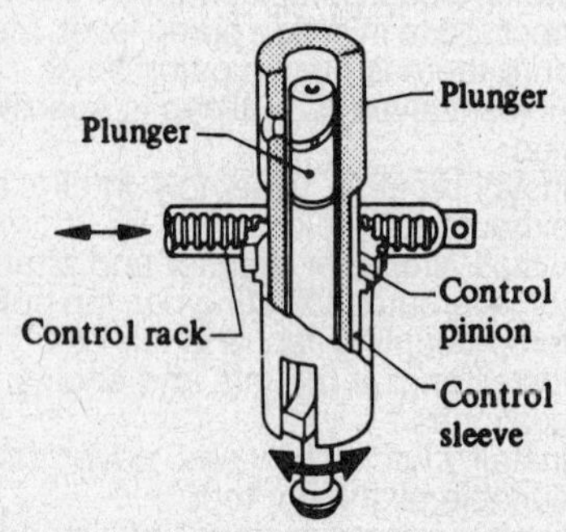

Fig. 17 Fuel injection plunger & control rack

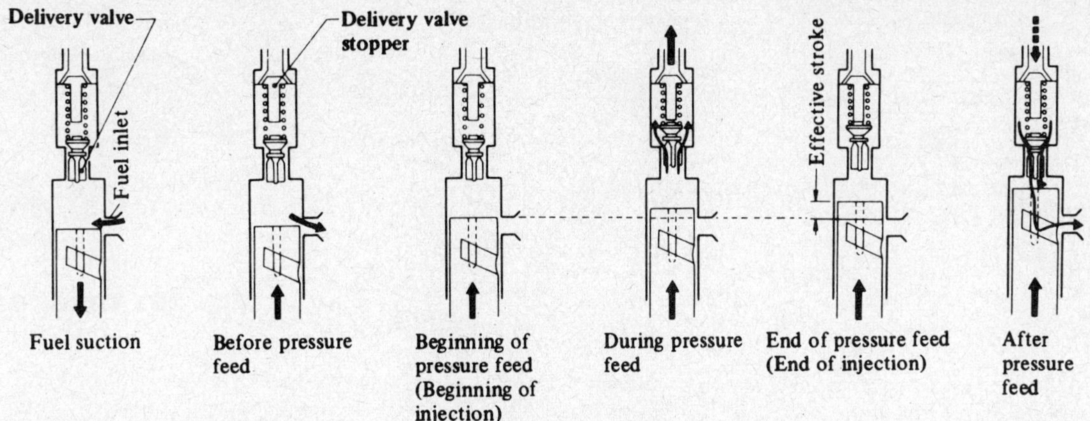

Fig. 18 Diesel fuel injection cycle

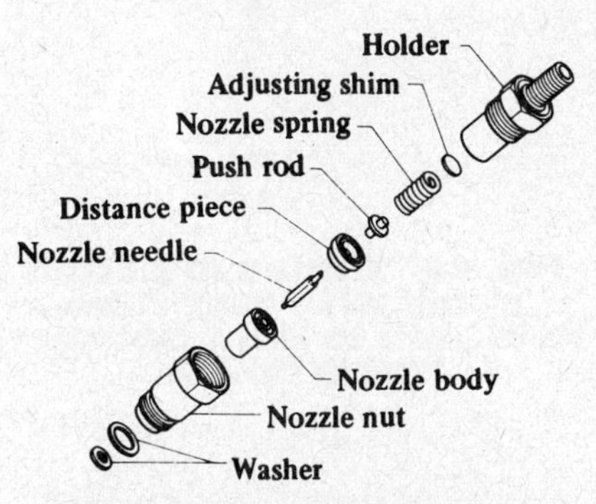

Fig. 19 Fuel injection nozzle assembly

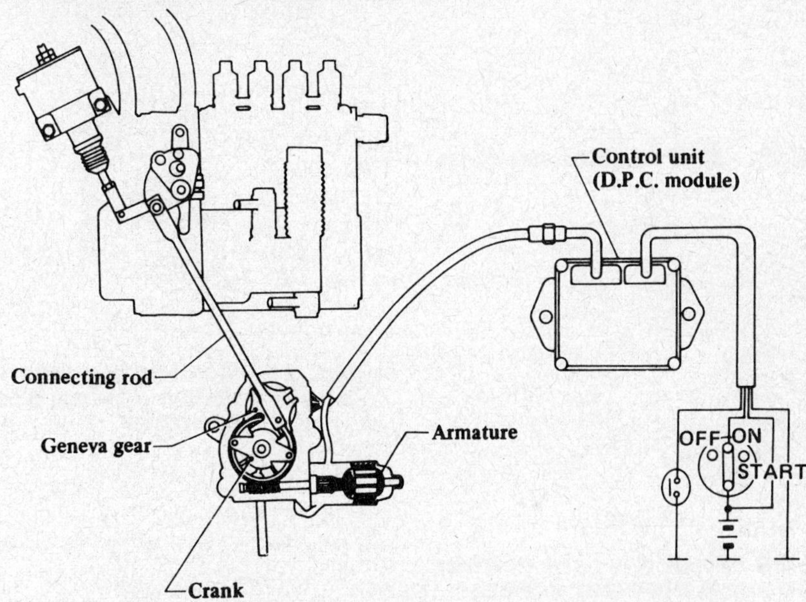

Fig. 20 Injection pump control assembly

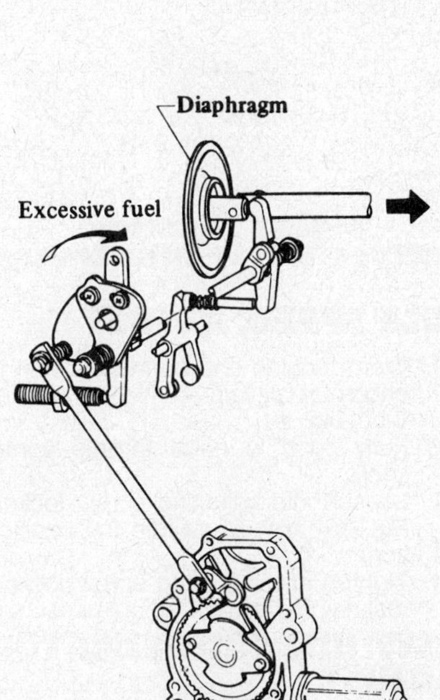

Fig. 21 Engine starting enrichment

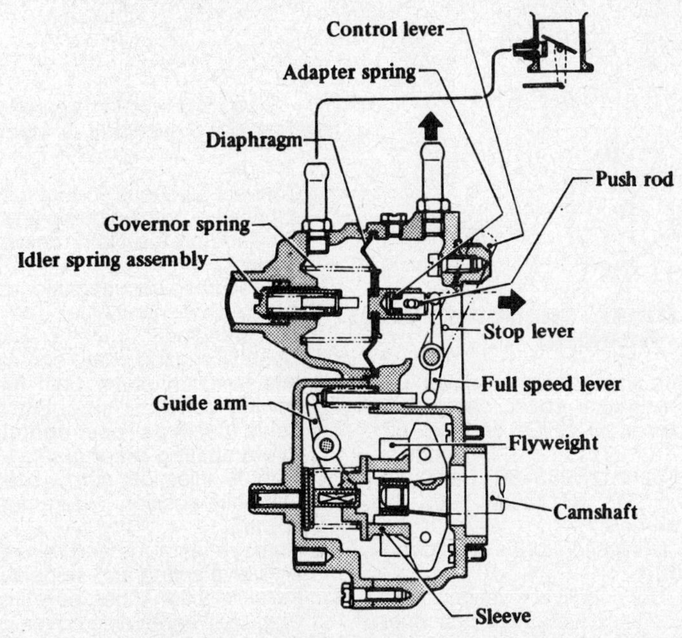

Fig. 22 Governor assembly

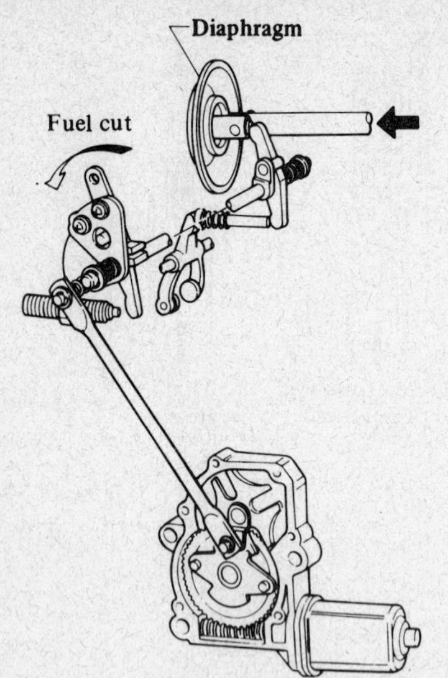

Fig. 23 Fuel cut operation

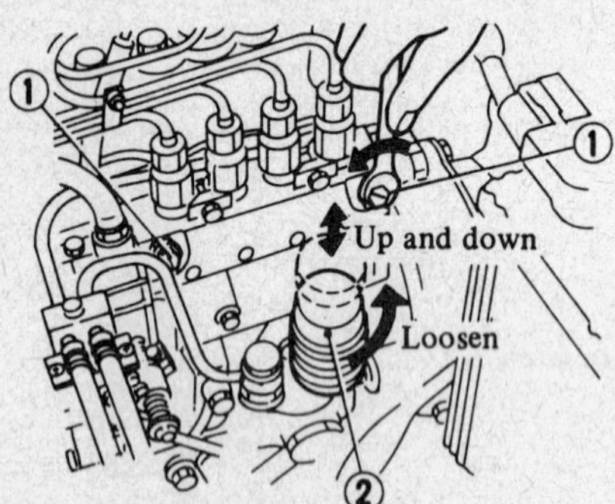

Fig. 26 Fuel system primer pump & bleeder screw

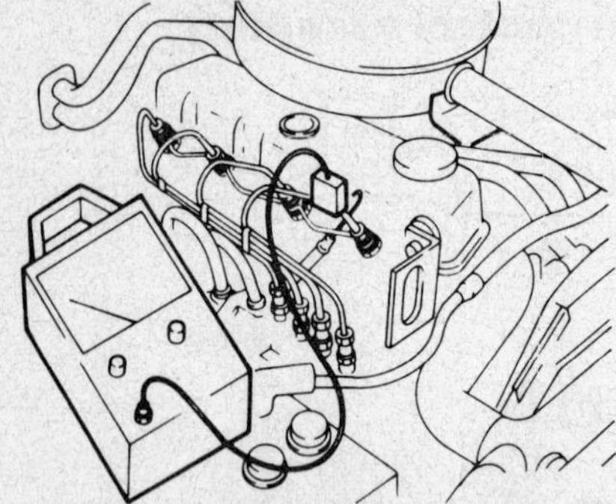
Fig. 29 Diesel tachometer hook-up

pulley with timing mark on cover, remove timing gear cover, check that No. 1 piston is 20° BTDC on 1981-83 models, 18° BTDC on 1984 models, 15° BTDC on 1985-86 California models, or 16° BTDC on 1985-86 Federal models.

3. Remove all injection tubes and governor hoses.
4. Remove No. 1 delivery valve holder and pull out delivery valve stopper and spring, **Fig. 27.**
5. Install delivery valve holder without stopper and spring.

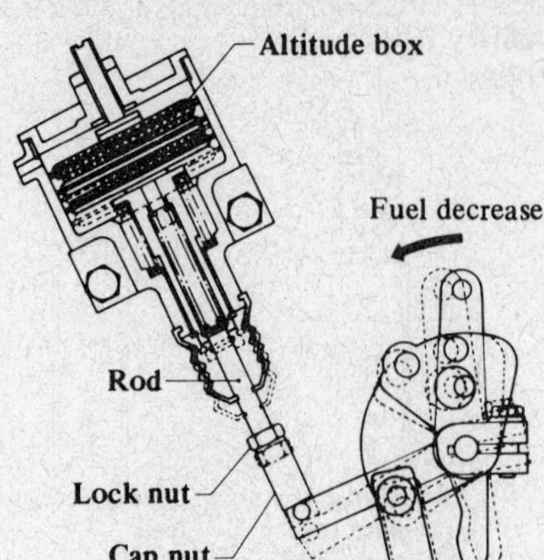

Fig. 24 Altitude compensator assembly

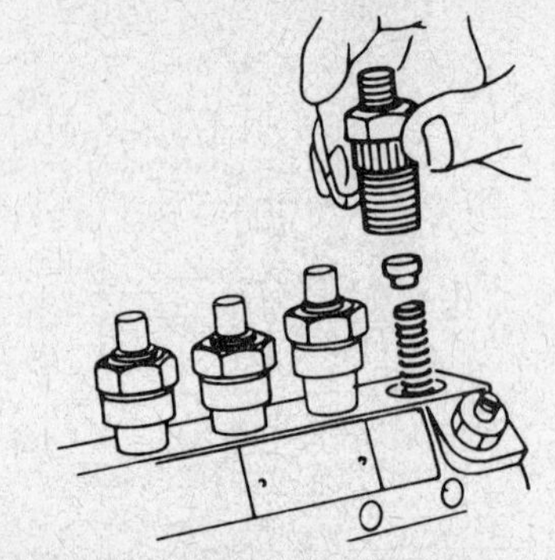
Fig. 27 Removing No. 1 delivery valve spring and stopper

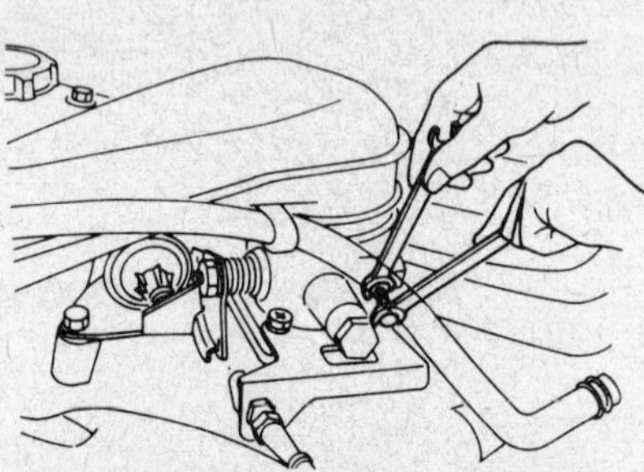
Fig. 30 Idle speed adjusting screw & locknut

6. Connect fuel hose so that fuel can be supplied to priming pump and install a test tube on the No. 1 delivery valve holder.
7. Loosen bolts securing injection pump and push assembly all the way towards engine.
8. Operate priming pump and slowly rotate injection pump until fuel stops flowing from test tube, **Fig. 28. Receive fuel in a proper container and avoid spilling on engine.**
9. Tighten injection pump bolts to fix pump in position where fuel stops flowing.
10. Remove test tube and reinstall delivery valve spring and stopper.
11. Install injection tubes, new timing cover gasket, and timing cover.
12. Connect governor hoses and fuel hoses in proper position and bleed fuel system.

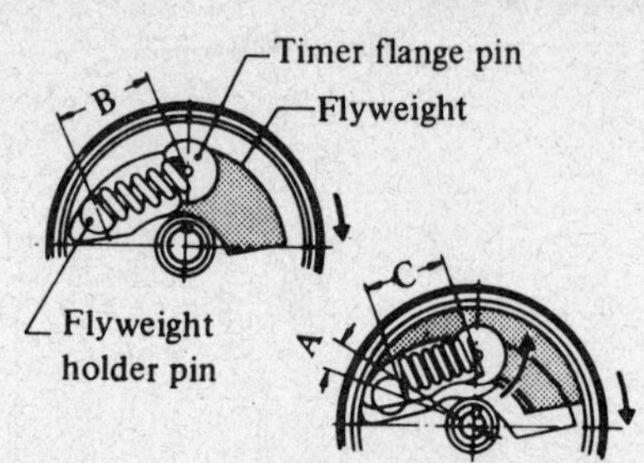

Fig. 25 Timer assembly

Fig. 28 Timing injection pump with test tube attached to No. 1 delivery valve holder

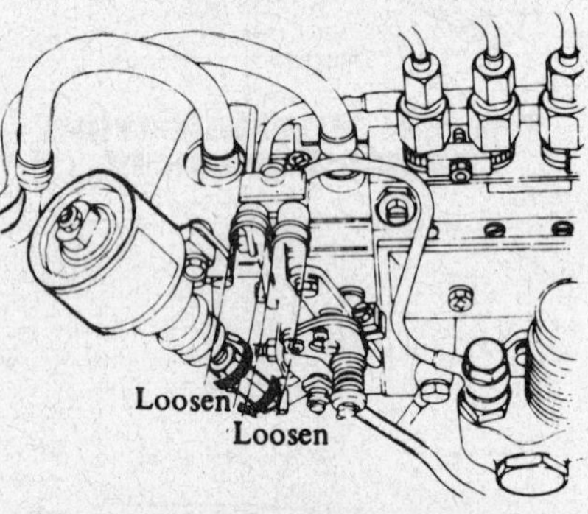

Fig. 31 Altitude compensator adjustment

IDLE SPEED, ADJUST

1. Warm engine and connect diesel tachometer pickup to No. 1 injection tube, **Fig. 29.**
2. Fully push in hand throttle control knob.
3. Loosen idle adjusting screw locknut, **Fig. 30**, and adjust idle to specification.
4. Tighten idle adjusting screw locknut, maintaining correct adjustment.

ALTITUDE COMPENSATOR, ADJUST

Perform this adjustment with injection lever in the free position.

1. Disconnect diesel pump controller rod.
2. Loosen altitude compensator locknut and cap nut, **Fig. 31.** Turn cap nut until it just contacts injection lever, then temporarily tighten locknut.
3. Loosen cap nut according to vehicle operating altitude. Refer to **Fig. 32** for specifications.

Approximate altitude m (ft)	0 (0)	120 (394)	700 (2,297)	1,300 (4,265)	2,000 (6,562)	2,700 (8,859)	3,400 (11,155)
Amount of loosening of cap nut (No. of revolutions of cap nut)	0	0.1~0.3	0.4~0.8	0.9~1.3	1.4~1.8	1.9~2.3	2.4~2.6

Fig. 32 Altitude compensator adjustment chart

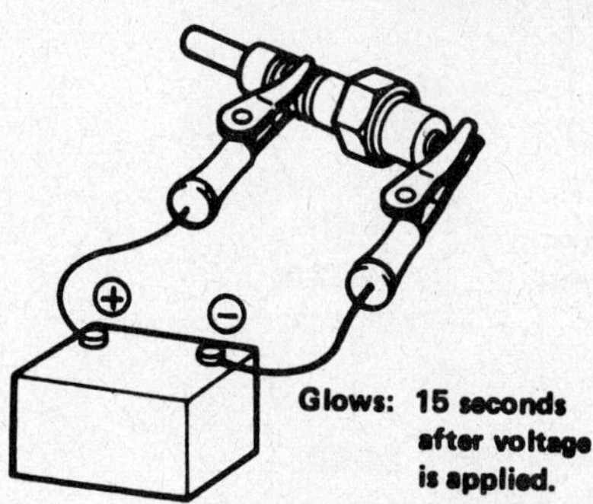

Fig. 34 Glow plug test connections

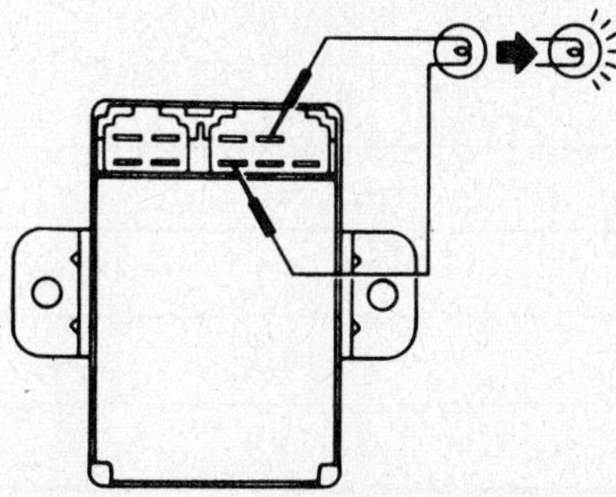

Fig. 36 Glow plug timer test connections. SD22 engine

4. Tighten locknut and install diesel pump controller rod. **Make sure that nut contacts injection pump lever. If not, loosen nut and readjust.**

FUEL SYSTEM TESTING

COMPRESSION TEST

1. Warm up engine and remove injection nozzles as outlined in this section.
2. Install compression gauge and adapter in cylinder head,**Fig. 33**, making sure bleeder screw is closed. **Diesel engine compression must be tested with a suitable gauge. A gasoline engine compression tester is not suitable for the higher pressures generated by a diesel engine.**
3. Crank engine and observe readings. Pressures should be 356-427 psi with no more than 43 psi difference between cylinders.
4. Remove compression gauge assembly and loosen bleeder screw. Reinstall fuel injection tubes and bleed fuel system.

GLOW PLUGS, TEST

1. Remove glow plugs and apply battery voltage to plug as shown in **Fig. 34**.

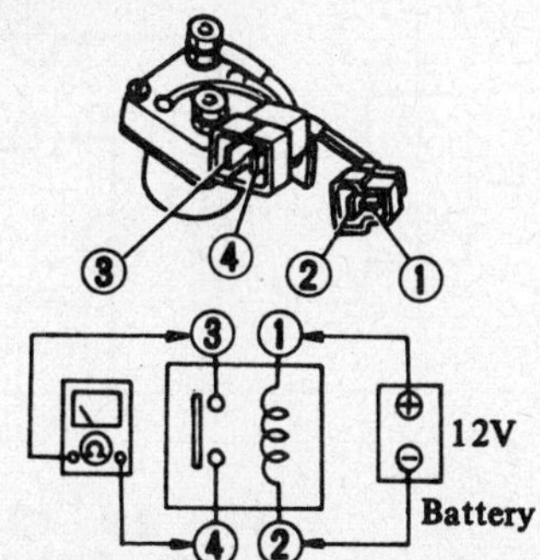

Fig. 35 Glow plug relay test connections. SD22 engine

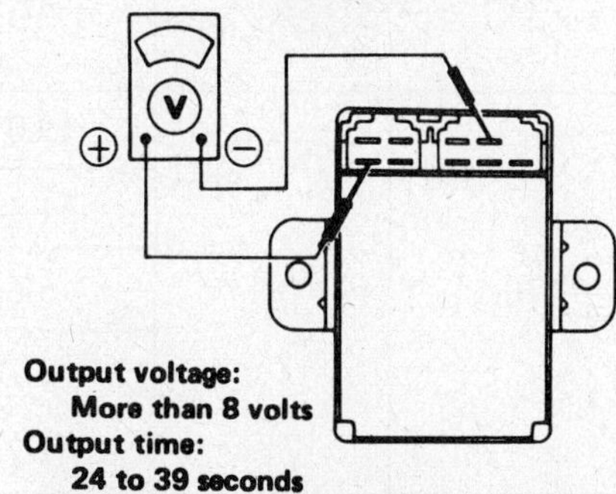

Fig. 37 Glow plug timer voltage test connections. SD22 engine

Plug should glow after about 15 seconds. If not, replace glow plug. Do not continue to apply voltage to glow plugs after they start glowing.

GLOW PLUG RELAY, TEST

1983

1. Remove glow plug relay and apply voltage to terminals as shown in **Fig. 35.**
2. Connect test lamp between terminals 1 and 2, lamp should light.
3. Connect test lamp between terminals 3 and 4, lamp should light.
4. Disconnect battery voltage from terminals 1 and 2 and connect test lamp between terminals 3 and 4, lamp should not light.

GLOW PLUG TIMER, TEST

1983

1. Turn ignition switch to On position, indicator lamp should light.
2. If lamp does not light, connect test lamp between terminals, **Fig. 36,** lamp should light. If test lamp does not light, glow plug timer is defective.
3. If test lamp lights, connect voltmeter as shown in **Fig. 37.** Meter should read 8 volts.
4. Check length of time required to preheat glow plugs. If output voltage above corresponds to preheating time, **Fig. 38,** system is normal.

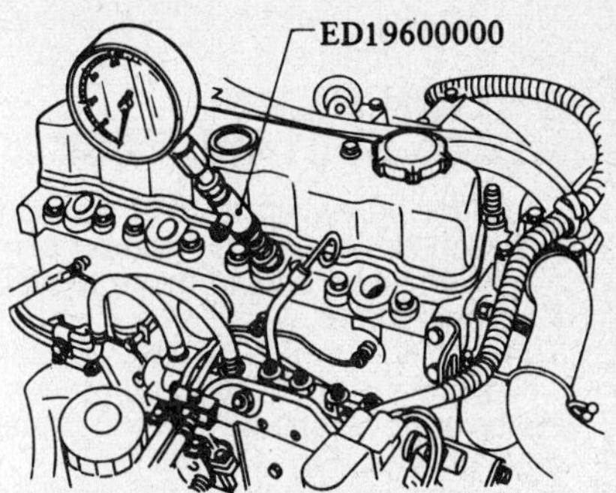

Fig. 33 Compression gauge in injector nozzle hole

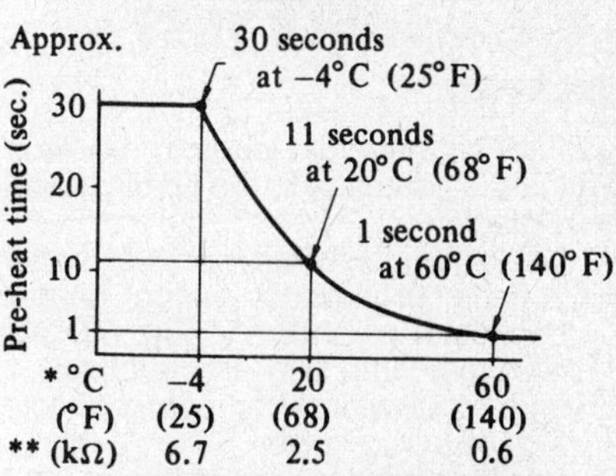

Fig. 38 Glow plug timer preheat specification chart. SD22 engine

5. Disconnect wiring harness connector at starter "S" terminal. Test after-glow, by measuring voltage produced and length of time required to produce output voltage, **Fig. 37,** when key is returned from start to on position.

GLOW CONTROL UNIT TEST

1984

1. Connect lead wires to control unit as shown in **Fig. 39.**
2. Connect resistors indicated in **Figs. 40 through 42,** to terminal 2 and ensure lamp goes out in specified time.

1985–86

1. Connect test lamp to glow control unit as shown in **Fig. 43.**
2. Turn ignition on and ensure test lamp remains lit 2-7 seconds. **If the ignition switch is off only a short time, the test lamp will not remain lit as long. To avoid erroneous results, leave ignition switch off for at least one minute before turning switch.**
3. Connect test lamp to glow control unit as shown in **Fig. 44.**
4. Disconnect "S" terminal lead from starter motor and note length of time test lamp remains lit. Lamp should remain lit 20-50 seconds with coolant temperature below 68°F, approximately 20 seconds with coolant temperature 68-122°F and should not light with coolant temperature above 122°F.
5. Connect test lamp to flow control unit as shown in **Fig. 45.**

6. Turn ignition switch on and ensure test lamp remains lit .5-7 seconds.

INJECTION PUMP CONTROL SYSTEM, TEST

1. Turn ignition switch to start position, while observing injection pump control lever. Lever should move to start position, **Fig. 46.**
2. Turn ignition switch to On position while observing injection pump control lever. Lever should move to center drive position, **Fig. 47.**
3. Turn ignition switch to Off position while observing injection pump control lever. Lever should move to off position, **Fig. 48.**

D.P.C. MODULE TEST

1983–84

Do not connect test leads to the wrong terminals, as damage to the D.P.C. module could result.

1. Using jumper wires, connect battery voltage to module wiring harness connector as shown in **Fig. 49.** Connect test lamp between terminals 13 and 14 of wiring harness connector, **Fig. 49.**
2. Connect jumper wire between terminals 12 and 10 and between terminals 12 and 8. Test lamp should light for approximately 15 seconds.
3. Connect jumper wire between terminals 12 and 11 and between terminals 12 and 9. Test lamp should not light.
4. Using jumper wires, connect positive battery terminal to terminals 2, 3, and 6, **Fig. 49.** Connect battery negative terminal to terminals 4 and 5. Connect jumper wire between terminals 12 and 9 and between 12 and 8, lamp should go out after 15 seconds.
5. Connect jumper wires between terminals 12 and 11 and between 12 and 10. Test lamp should not light.
6. Connect jumper wire between terminals 12 and 9 and disconnect positive lead from terminal 3. Test lamp should go out in 10 seconds.
7. Leave positive lead disconnected from terminal 3, connect jumper wire between terminals 12 and 10 and between terminals 12 and 8. Test lamp should go out after 15 seconds.
8. Connect jumper wire between terminals 12 and 11 and between terminals 12 and 9. Test lamp should not light.
9. Disconnect negative lead from terminal 4. Connect jumper wire between terminals 12 and 11 and between 12 and 8. Test lamp should go out after 15 seconds.
10. Connect jumper wire between terminals 12 and 10 and between 12 and 9. Test lamp should not light.
11. D.P.C. module should be replaced if it fails any of the above tests.

1985–86

1. With ignition switch off, disconnect electrical connector from starter motor "S" terminal.
2. Connect test lamp between terminals M+ and M of injection pump control unit, **Fig. 50.**

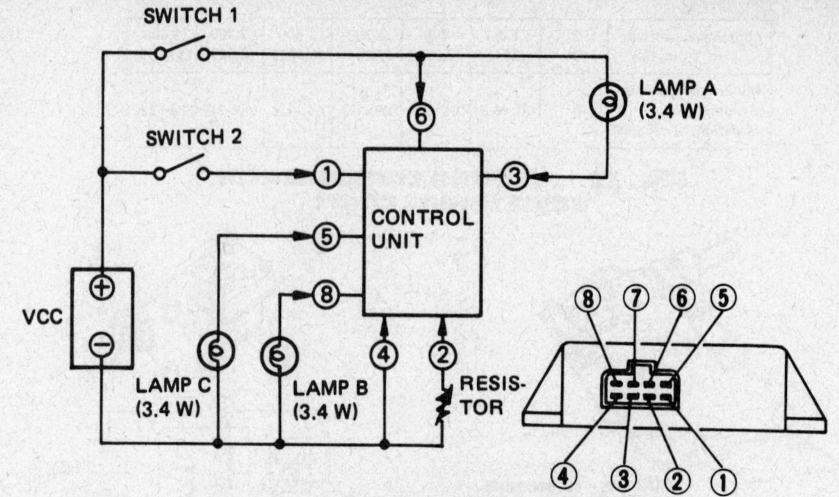

Fig. 39 Glow control unit test connections. 1984

Vcc [V]	Switch 1	Resistor [kΩ]	Time in which lamp goes out (Seconds) Lamp A
10.5	ON	19.0	5 - 7
		11.5	4.5 - 6.3
		5.6	3.5 - 5.1
		3.7	2.9 - 4.3
		1.2	0.6 - 1.9

Fig. 40 Glow control unit glow lamp test specifications. 1984

Vcc [V]	Switch 1	Switch 2	Resistor [kΩ]	Time in which lamp goes out (Seconds) Lamp B
10.5	ON	OFF	30	5.3 - 6.7
	ON	ON	20	5.5 - 7.5

Fig. 41 Glow control unit pre-glow test specifications. 1984

Vcc [V]	Switch 1	Switch 2	Resistor [kΩ]	Time in which lamp goes out (Seconds) Lamp C
12.0	ON	ON first, then OFF	19.0	38 - 55
			11.5	33 - 49
			5.6	25 - 39
			3.7	20 - 31
			1.2	15 - 25

Fig. 42 Glow control unit after-glow test specifications. 1984

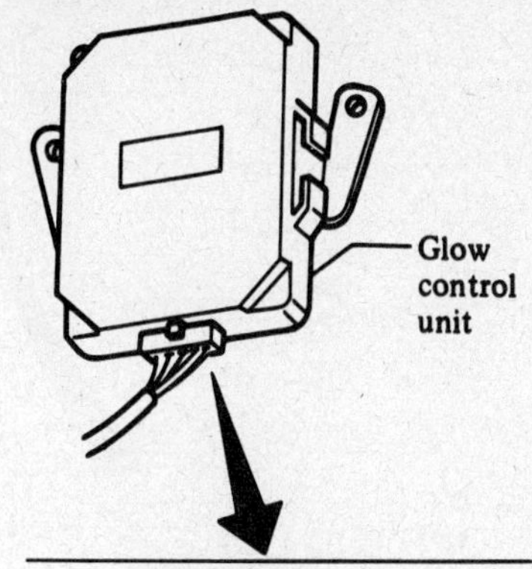

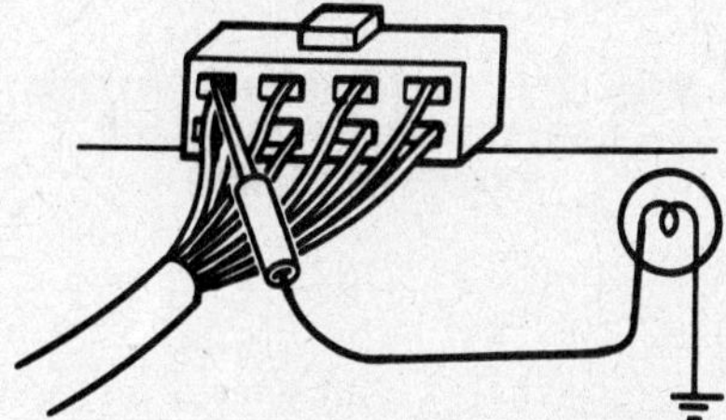

Fig. 43 Glow control unit pre-glow control test connections. 1985–86

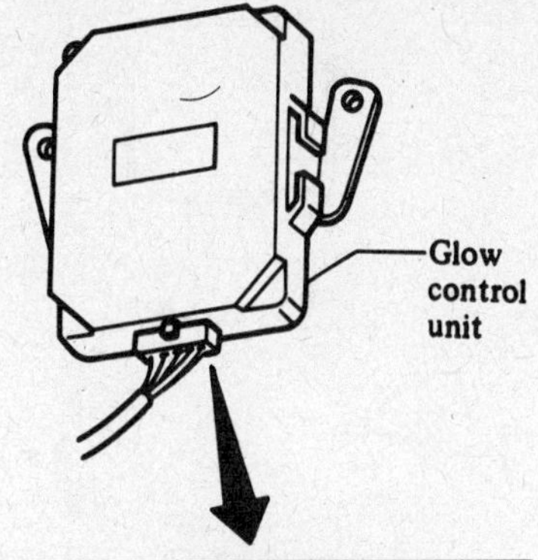

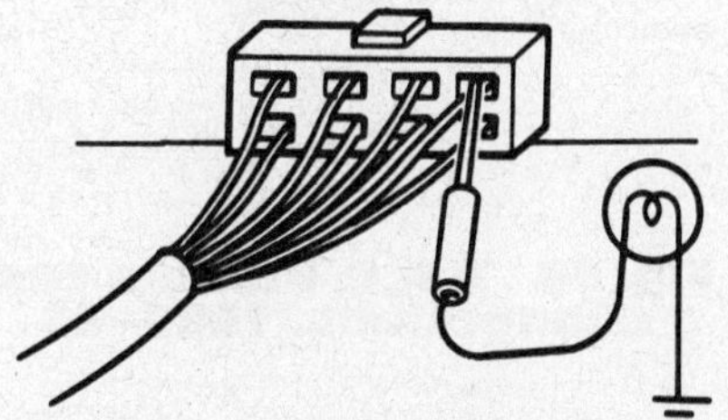

Fig. 44 Glow control unit after-glow control test connections. 1985–86

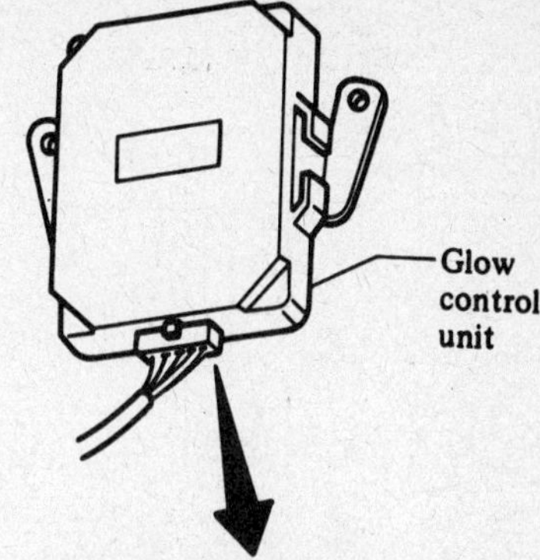

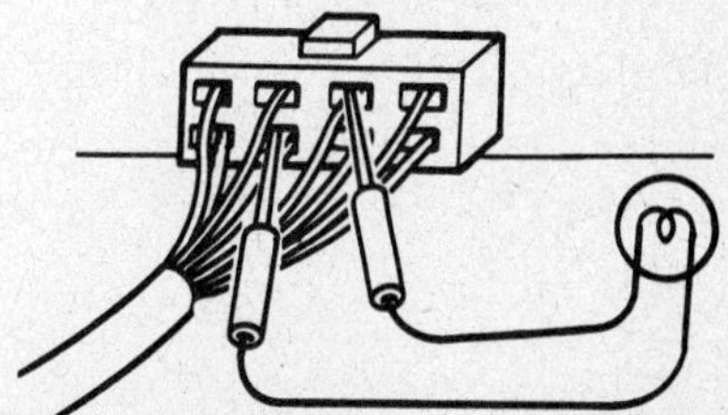

Fig. 45 Glow control unit glow indicator control test connections. 1985–86

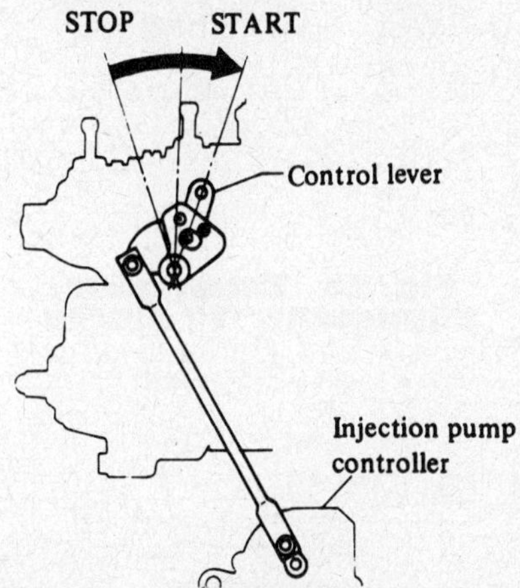

Fig. 46 Control lever start position

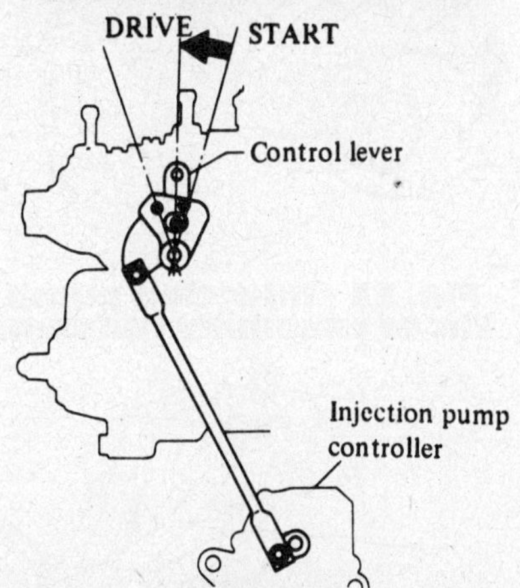

Fig. 47 Control lever stop position

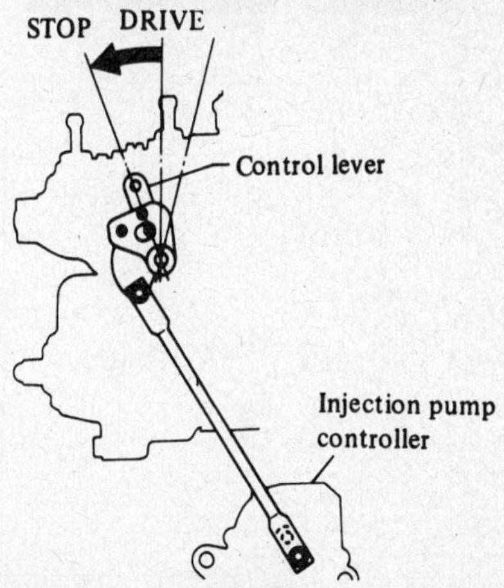

Fig. 48 Control lever stop position

3. Disconnect electrical connector from oil pressure switch.
4. Connect jumper wire between terminals S and C, **Fig. 50.** Test lamp should light for 10-20 seconds.
5. Reconnect jumper wire between terminals D and C, **Fig. 50.** Turn ignition switch on and ensure test lamp lights for 10-20 seconds.
6. Turn ignition switch off, then ground oil pressure switch electrical connector.
7. Reconnect jumper wire between terminals D and C, **Fig. 50.** Turn ignition switch to start position and ensure test lamp lights for 10-20 seconds.
8. Turn ignition switch off. With oil pressure switch still grounded, reconnect jumper wire between terminals S and C, **Fig. 50.** Turn ignition switch on and ensure test lamp lights for 10-20 seconds.

INJECTION PUMP CONTROLLER, TEST

1. Disconnect wiring harness connector at injection pump controller, and using jumper wires, connect battery positive terminal to terminal 13, **Fig. 51,** and negative battery terminal to terminal 14 on wiring harness connector, **Fig. 51.** Injection pump controller motor should run.
2. Using jumper wires, connect battery and jumper wire as shown in **Fig. 52.**
3. Connect jumper wire between battery positive terminal and terminal 9. Injection pump lever should move to start position, **Fig. 46.**
4. Connect jumper wire between battery positive terminal and terminal 10. Injection pump lever should move to stop position, **Fig. 47.**
5. Connect jumper wire between battery positive terminal and terminal 11. Injection pump lever should move to drive position, **Fig. 48.**
6. If injection pump controller does not operate according to tests, controller is defective.

FUEL SYSTEM COMPONENT SERVICE

INJECTION PUMP, REPLACE

1. Remove temp-coupling and fan, drain cooling system, and remove radiator.
2. Remove injection tube assembly. Plug delivery holders and injection nozzles to prevent entrance of dirt.
3. Disconnect governor hose, fuel hoses, diesel pump controller rod, and remove oil feed pipe bolt.
4. Remove timing gear cover and timing gear round nut.
5. Remove timing assembly, using a suitable puller, **Fig. 53.**
6. Remove bolts securing injection pump assembly, and remove assembly from vehicle.

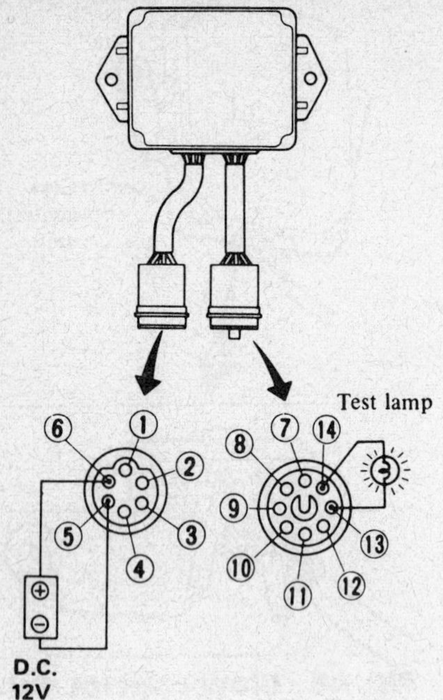

Fig. 49 D.P.C. module test connections. 1983–84

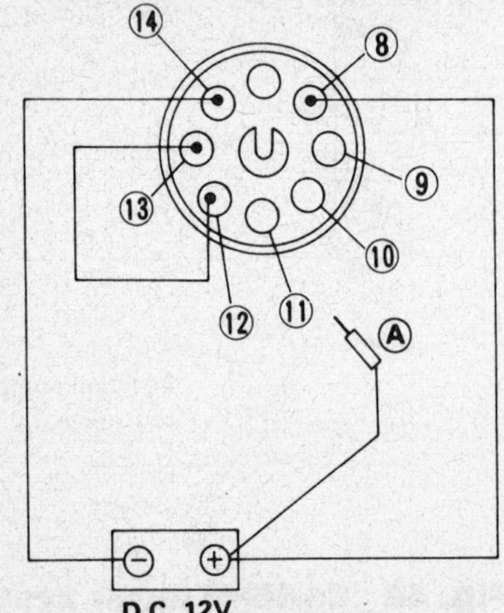

Fig. 52 Injection pump controller function test connections

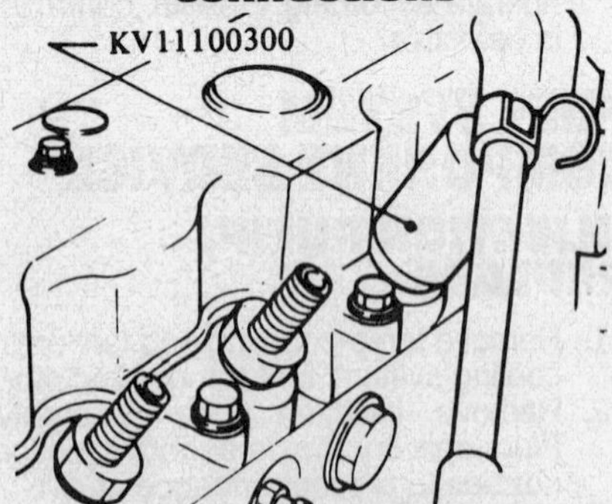

Fig. 55 Fuel injection nozzle removal

7. To install, set No. 1 piston at T.D.C. by aligning second mark on crank pulley with mark on front cover.
8. Temporarily install injection pump in position.
9. Install injection pump drive gear so that drive gear and idler gear teeth

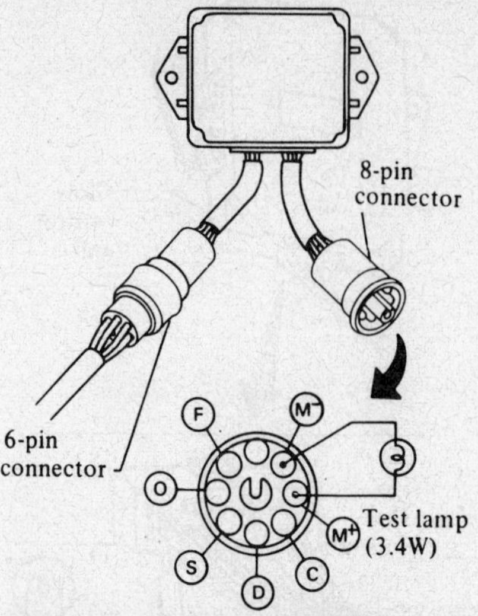

Fig. 50 D.P.C. module test connections. 1985–86

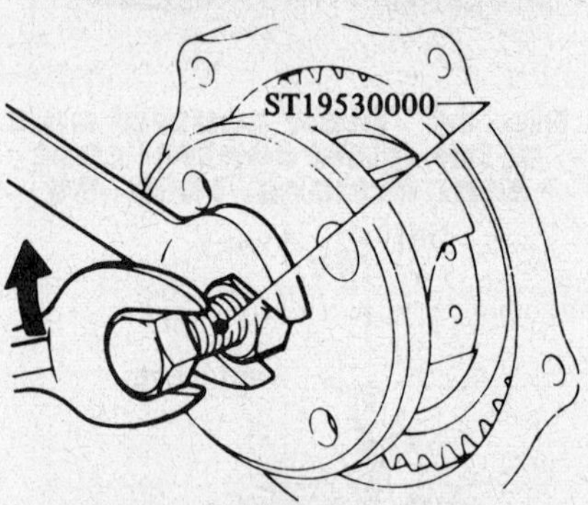

Fig. 53 Injection pump timer assembly removal

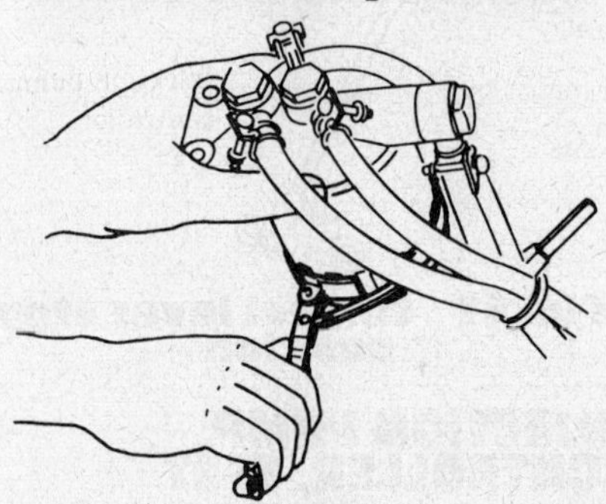

Fig. 56 Fuel filter removal

mesh at "Y" marks, Fig. 54.

10. Secure timing assembly with lock washer and round nut and torque nut to 43-51 ft. lbs.
11. Adjust injection pump timing as outlined in this section.
12. Bleed fuel system, as outlined, after setting injection timing and reassembling injector pipes.
13. Reinstall radiator, fan and temp-coupling, and fill cooling system to capacity.

INJECTION NOZZLE, REPLACE

1. Remove injection tube and spill tube assemblies.
2. Remove injection nozzles with suitable tool, Fig. 55.

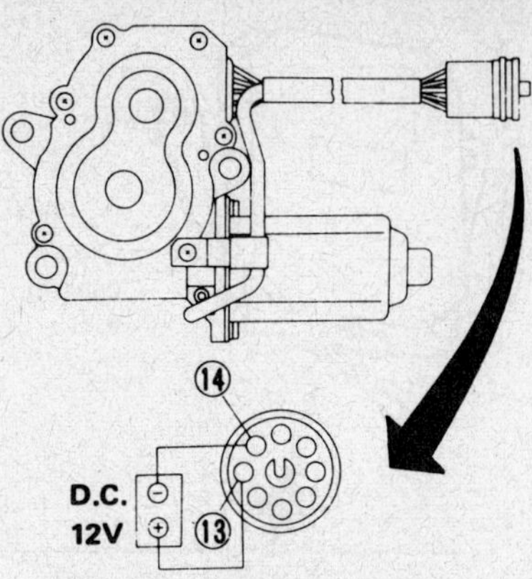

Fig. 51 Injection pump controller run test connections

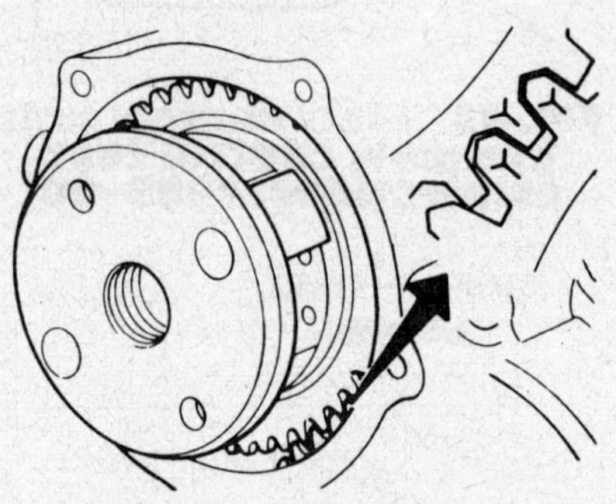

Fig. 54 Timer gear alignment "Y" marks

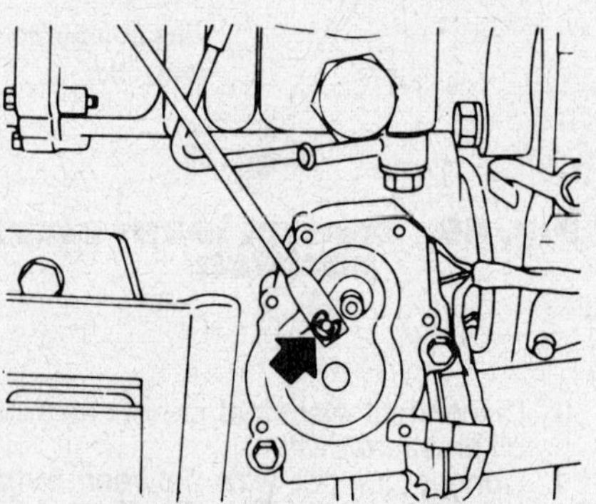

Fig. 57 Altitude compensator removal

3. Install in the reverse order and bleed fuel system as outlined in this section.

FUEL FILTER, REPLACE

1. Remove bolts securing fuel filter bracket and position to gain access to filter.
2. Remove fuel filter from fuel filter bracket, Fig. 56.
3. Install new filter on bracket and tighten by hand.
4. Remount fuel filter bracket and bleed fuel system as outlined in this section.

ALTITUDE COMPENSATOR, REPLACE

1. Remove altitude compensator attaching screws, then remove compensator from bracket, **Fig. 57.**
2. Disconnect vacuum hose and remove bracket from injection pump.
3. Reverse procedure to install.

WATER PUMP
REPLACE

1. Disconnect battery ground cable and drain coolant.
2. Remove radiator fan shroud.
3. Loosen fan pulley attaching nuts.
4. Loosen fan belt, then loosen alternator attaching bolts and push alternator toward engine.
5. Remove fan pulley with temp-coupling and the fan.
6. Disconnect coolant hose on thermostat housing side.
7. Remove water pump attaching bolts and the pump.
8. Reverse procedure to install, using new gasket.

CD17 DIESEL ENGINES

INDEX

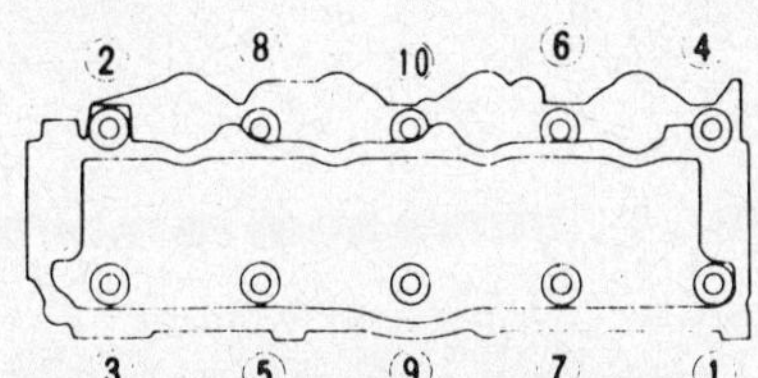

Fig. 1 Cylinder head bolt loosening sequence

ENGINE
REPLACE
1983–86 SENTRA

1. Disconnect battery cables, then remove battery, with support bracket, from vehicle.
2. Scribe hood hinge locations and remove hood.
3. Remove air cleaner.
4. Drain engine coolant, then remove radiator with cooling fan.
5. On models equipped with power steering, remove power steering pump.
6. On models equipped with air conditioning, remove compressor and idler pulley. **Do not discharge refrigerant from air conditioning system when work is being performed.**
7. Disconnect exhaust pipe from exhaust manifold.
8. On manual transaxle models, disconnect control rod link support rod from transaxle.
9. On automatic transaxle models, disconnect control wire from transaxle.
10. Remove lower ball joint, then drain gear oil.
11. Loosen strut head bolts and disconnect both drive shafts from transaxle.
12. Disconnect clutch wire, then remove speedometer cable with pinion from transaxle.
13. Disconnect accelerator cable and all electrical connectors and vacuum hoses necessary for engine removal.
14. Disconnect fuel lines from fuel pump.
15. Attach suitable lifting equipment to engine.
16. Disconnect engine mounting insulators, then remove engine and transaxle, as an assembly, from vehicle.
17. Reverse procedure to install.

CYLINDER HEAD
REPLACE
REMOVAL

1. Disconnect battery ground cable.
2. Drain coolant and disconnect water hose.
3. Set No. 1 cylinder at TDC on its compression stroke.
4. Remove valve timing belt on camshaft pulley side and remove injection timing belt as described under "Timing Belt, Replace," noting the following:
   a. Ensure timing belt is free from oil and water and do not bend belt.
   b. Timing belt removed from camshaft pulley should not be rotated from removed position.
5. Loosen injection pump pulley nut and remove pulley.
6. Remove rear cover.
7. Remove all injection tubes.
8. Remove cylinder head, loosening attaching bolts in sequence, **Fig. 1.**

INSTALLATION

Install cylinder head in reverse order of removal, noting the following:

1. Install cylinder head with new gasket, torquing bolts first to 43-51 ft. lbs., then to 72-80 ft. lbs., in sequence described under "Engine Assembly."
2. Install valve timing belt and injection pump timing belt as described under "Timing Belt, Replace."

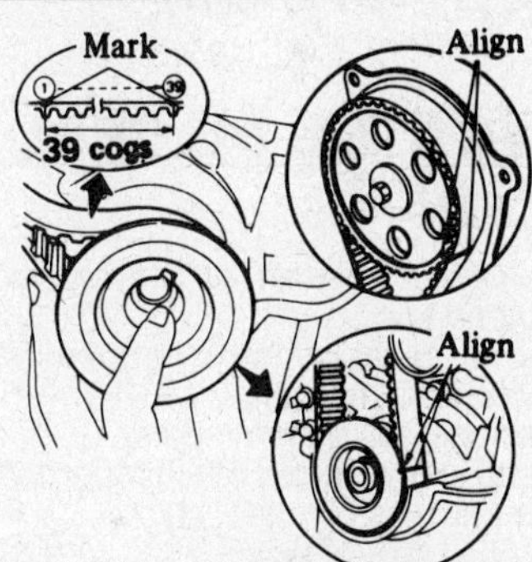

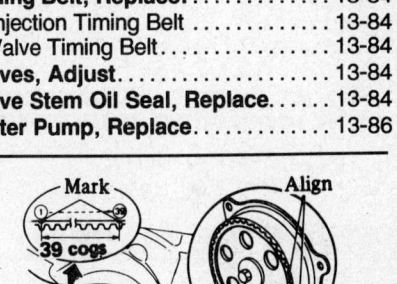

Fig. 2 Installing valve timing belt

CAMSHAFT & CAMSHAFT OIL SEAL
REPLACE

1. Disconnect battery ground cable.
2. Remove timing belts as described under "Timing Belt, Replace."
3. Remove front and rear camshaft pulleys. **When removing front back cover, loosen tensioner to remove bolt at back of tensioner.**
4. Remove cam bracket caps, then the camshaft and oil seals. **It is not necessary to remove camshaft to just replace oil seals.**
5. Install new oil seals.
6. Install front and rear back covers and the camshaft pulley. **Turn tensioner counterclockwise after installing front back cover.** Torque front back cover attaching bolts to 4.6-6.1 ft. lbs., rear back cover attaching bolts to 2.7-3.7 ft. lbs and the camshaft pulley mounting bolts to 68-75 ft. lbs.
7. Install cylinder head as previously described.
8. Install timing belts as described under "Timing Belt, Replace."

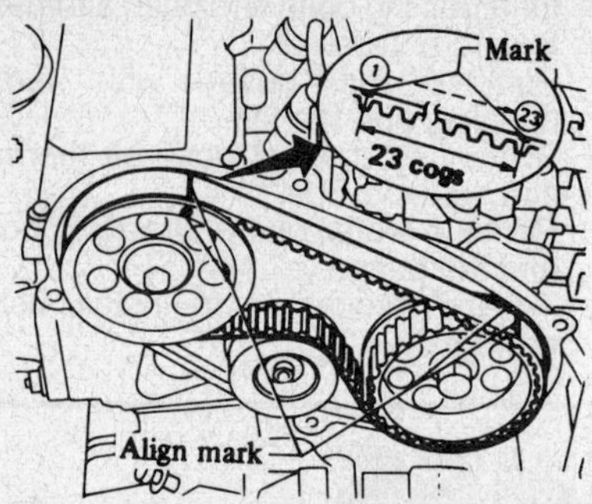

ig. 3 Installing injection timing belt

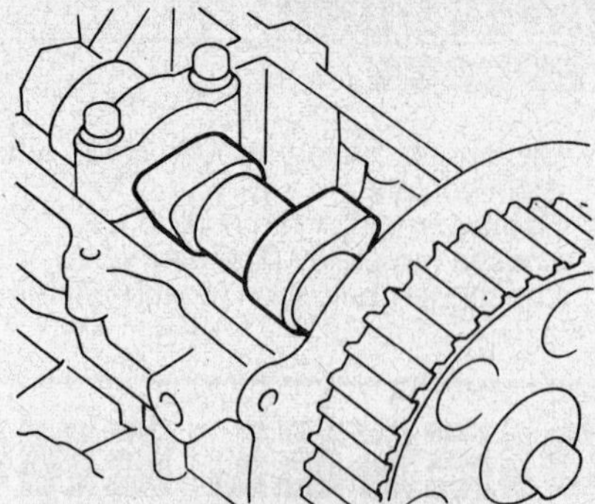

Fig. 4 Positioning No. 1 cam

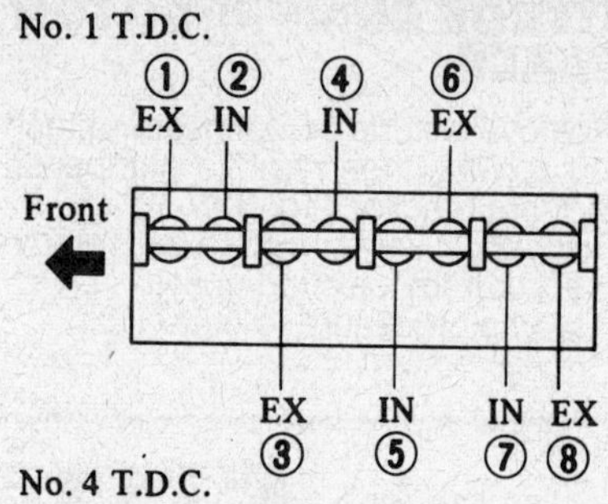

Fig. 5 Adjusting valve clearance

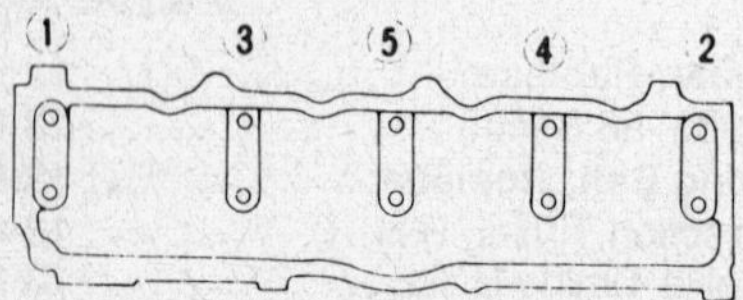

Fig. 6 Camshaft bracket nut loosening sequence

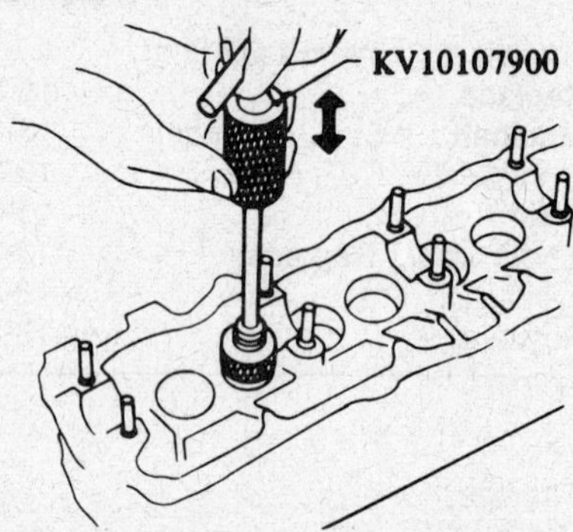

Fig. 7 Valve seal removal

VALVE STEM OIL SEAL

R PLACE

1. Remove camshaft as previously described.
2. Using suitable tool, remove valve spring retainer parts.
3. Replace valve stem seals.
4. Install valve spring retainer parts, then the camshaft.

CRANKSHAFT OIL SEAL

R PLACE

FRONT SEAL

1. Remove valve timing belt as described under "Timing Belt, Replace."
2. Remove oil seal.
3. Install new oil seal, coating sealing lip, oil seal periphery and mating shaft with engine oil.
4. Install valve timing belt as described under "Timing Belt, Replace."

R AR OIL SEAL

1. Remove transmission.
2. Remove flywheel, then the oil seal.
3. Install new oil seal, coating sealing lip, oil seal periphery and mating shaft with engine oil.
4. Install flywheel, torquing attaching bolt to 72-80 ft. lbs.
5. Install transmission.

TI--ING BELT

R PLACE

VALVE TIMING BELT

1. Disconnect battery ground cable.
2. Raise and support engine, then remove right side engine mount.
3. Set No. 1 cylinder at TDC on its compression stroke.
4. Remove alternator and compressor drive belt.
5. Remove crank damper pulley.
6. Remove timing belt as follows:
   a. Loosen tensioner pulley and set it to free position.
   b. Remove idler pulley.
   c. Remove crankshaft pulley with timing belt.
7. Install timing belt as follows:
   a. Clean all parts that contact timing belt.
   b. Ensure timing belt is clean and free from oil or dust.
   c. When installing crank pulley plate, ensure proper direction.
8. Place a mark at 39th cog on timing belt as necessary, **Fig. 2.**
9. Align each mark and install crankshaft pulley with timing belt.
10. Install idler pulley.
11. Loosen tensioner bolt and turn crankshaft two times in its normal rotating direction.
12. Tighten tensioner while counterholding it.

INJECTION TIMING BELT

1. Disconnect battery ground cable.
2. Remove air cleaner housing with air duct.
3. Set No. 1 cylinder at TDC on its compression stroke.
4. Set tensioner to free position, then remove timing belt.
5. Install timing belt as follows:
   a. Clean all parts that contact timing belt.
   b. Ensure timing belt is clean and free from oil or dust.
   c. Place mark at 23rd cog on timing belt, if necessary, **Fig. 3.**
   d. Align each mark.
   e. Loosen tensioner and turn crankshaft two times in normal rotating direction.
   f. Tighten tensioner while counterholding it.

VALVES

ADJUST

1. Warm up engine until it reaches operating temperature.
2. Set No. 1 or No. 4 cylinder at TDC on its compression stroke, ensuring cam of camshaft is in position shown, **Fig. 4.**
3. Adjust valve clearance as shown, **Fig. 5,** to .008-.012 inch (intake) or .016-.020 (exhaust), as follows:
   a. Measure clearance between cam and valve lifter.
   b. If clearance is not within specifications, adjust by changing lifter plate. **Lifter plate cannot be replaced at TDC. Lifter plate replacement is performed after each is set at approximately 1/4 turn (90°) over TDC. Tool Kv11102600 or equivalent can only be inserted on nozzle side.**
   c. Set cutout portion of lifter forward to manifold side for lifting up plate.
   d. Install adjusting shim with identification number facing down.

ENGINE DISASSEMBLY

1. Separate engine and transaxle.
2. Drain engine oil and coolant into suitable containers.
3. Remove engine front and rear side components.
4. Position No. 1 piston at TDC of compression stroke.
5. Loosen valve timing belt tensioner and set it to the "free" position. Remove idler pulley, then the crankshaft sprocket and valve timing belt.
6. Set injection timing belt tensioner to the "free" position and remove the belt.
7. Remove injection pump pulley, then the injection pump.
8. Remove oil pan and oil pump, then the rocker cover.
9. Remove cylinder head. Loosen bolts in several steps in sequence, **Fig.1.**

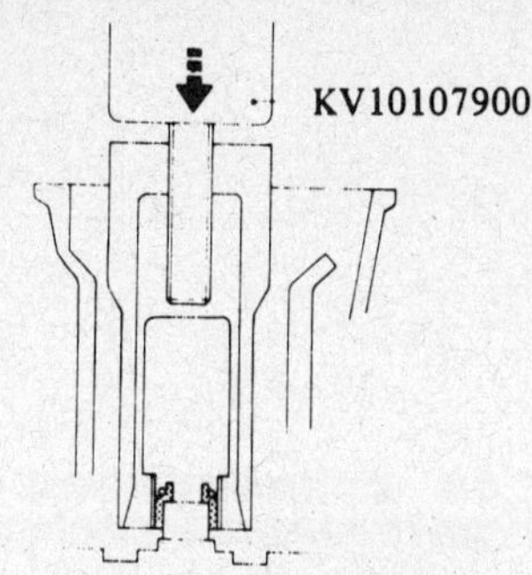

Fig. 8 Valve seal installation

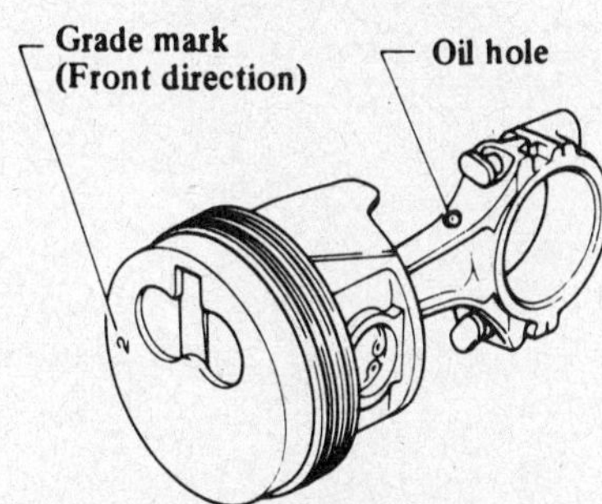

Fig. 11 Piston & rod assembly

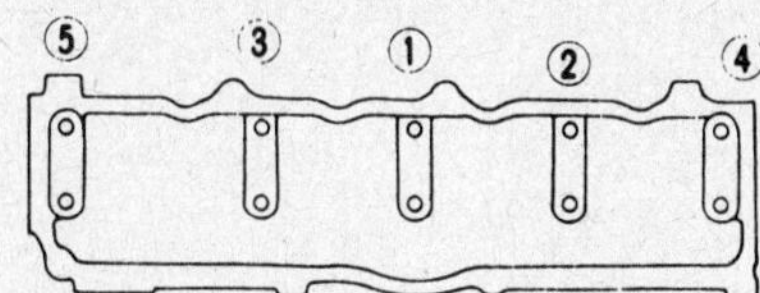

Fig. 9 Camshaft bracket nut tightening sequence

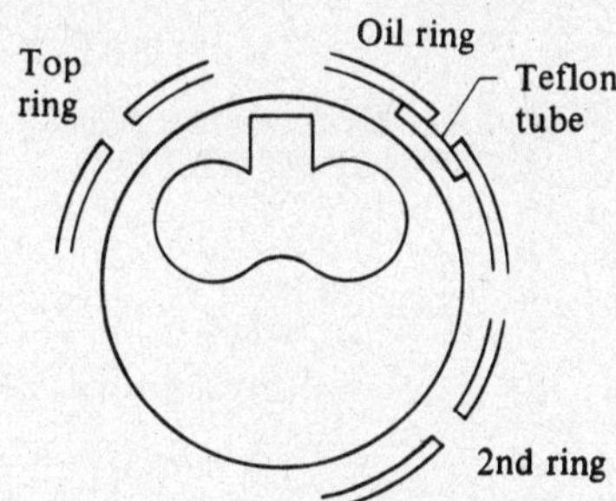

Fig. 12 Piston ring installation

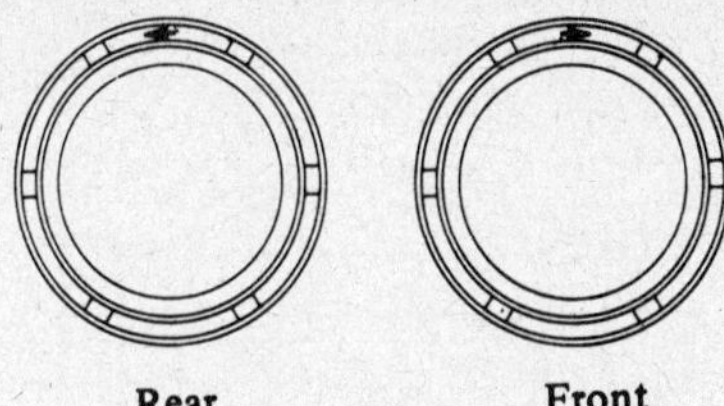

Fig. 10 Camshaft seal installation

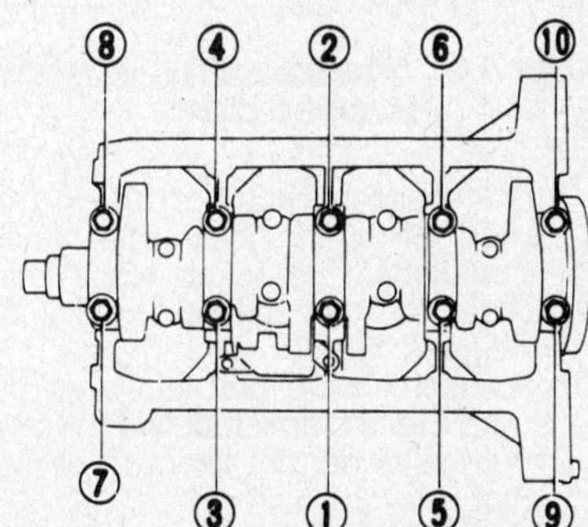

Fig. 13 Main bearing cap bolt tightening sequence

10. Remove connecting rod caps and bearings, then push piston/connecting rod assemblies out towards the cylinder head side.
11. Remove main bearing caps and bearings, then the rear oil seal with retainer.
12. Remove crankshaft.

PISTON & ROD DISASSEMBLY

1. Remove piston rings with a ring expander.
2. Heat piston to approximately 140-158°F and tap out piston pin using a suitable drift.

CYLINDER HEAD DISASSEMBLY

1. Remove intake and exhaust manifolds.
2. Remove both camshaft sprockets, then the camshaft bracket cap nuts. Loosen nuts in sequence, **Fig. 6.**
3. Remove camshaft and oil seals.
4. Remove valve lifters and lifter plates.
5. Remove valves, springs and related components using a suitable spring compressor. Keep all parts in order.
6. Remove valve seals, **Fig. 7.**

ENGINE ASSEMBLY

CYLINDER HEAD ASSEMBLY

1. Install valve seals until contact is made with valve guide, **Fig. 8.**
2. Install valves and related components.
3. Install valve lifters and lifter plates. Install plate so that mark faces valve lifter side.
4. Install camshaft and measure valve clearance. Cold valve clearance should be .0071 inch at intake valves and .0160 inch at exhaust valves. Replace valve lifter plates as necessary to bring valve clearances to specifications.
5. Install camshaft bracket. Torque nuts to 13-16 ft. lbs. in sequence, **Fig. 9.**
6. Lubricate new camshaft seals with clean engine oil, then install the seals, **Fig. 10.**
7. Install camshaft sprockets, then the intake and exhaust manifolds.

PISTON & ROD ASSEMBLY

1. Heat piston to approximately 140-158°F, then push piston pin into piston. Assemble piston to rod so that oil hole in connecting rod is parallel to the valve relief, **Figs. 11 and 12.**
2. Install piston pin snap rings.
3. Install piston rings so that stamped mark on top of rings faces upward. Align teflon tube with ring gap.

ENGINE ASSEMBLY

1. Install upper main bearing into cylinder block. **The upper bearings can be identified as those having an oil hole and groove.**
2. Install crankshaft, then the main bearings and caps. Torque cap bolt to specifications in sequence, **Fig. 13.**
3. Install new seal into rear oil seal retainer, then install the retainer. Ensure that crankshaft rotates smoothly and check crankshaft for correct endplay.
4. With piston rings properly positioned, **Fig. 12,** install piston/connecting rod assemblies into corresponding cylinders. Make sure that number stamped on piston head faces forward.
5. Install connecting rod caps and torque nuts to specifications.
6. Determine proper cylinder head gasket as follows:
   a. Thoroughly clean cylinder block mating surface.
   b. Using suitable straightedge, measure piston projection at two points on each cylinder, **Fig. 14.**
   c. If average value of all piston projections is less than .0205 inch, select a gasket with a thickness of .0453 inch (identified by one cutout).
   d. If average value of all piston projections is .0205-.0224 inch, select a gasket with a thickness of .0472 inch (identified by two cutouts).
   e. If average value of all piston projections is more than .0224 inch, select a gasket with a thickness of .0492 inch (identified by three cutouts). **If any one measurement is more than .0020 inch greater than the average of all projection measurements, use a gasket which is one grade thicker.**
7. Install cylinder head assembly, noting the following:
   a. Ensure cylinder No. 1 is at TDC, **Fig. 15.**
   b. Ensure No. 1 cam of camshaft is in position shown, **Fig. 4.**
   c. Torque cylinder head bolts in sequence, **Fig. 16,** in two steps: first to 43-51 ft. lbs., then to 72-80 ft. lbs.
8. Install rocker cover, water pump, front camshaft sprocket, oil pump, oil pan and crankshaft sprocket plate, with cupped side towards crankshaft.
9. Install valve timing belt as follows:

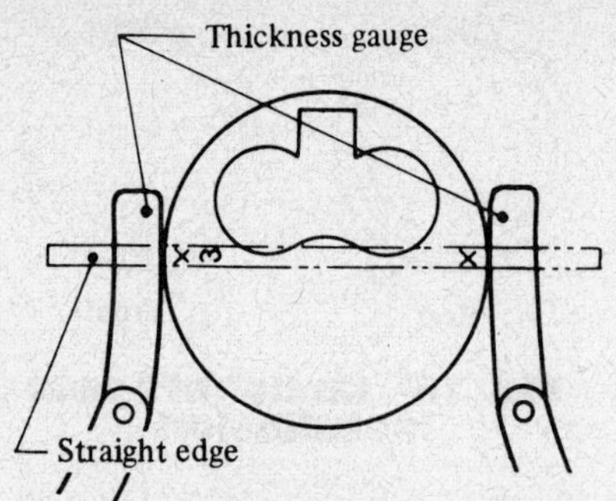

Fig. 14 Measuring piston projection

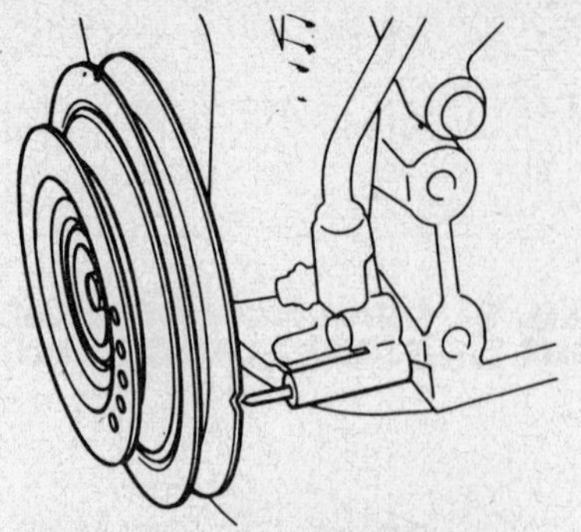
Fig. 15 Ensuring No. 1 cylinder is at TDC

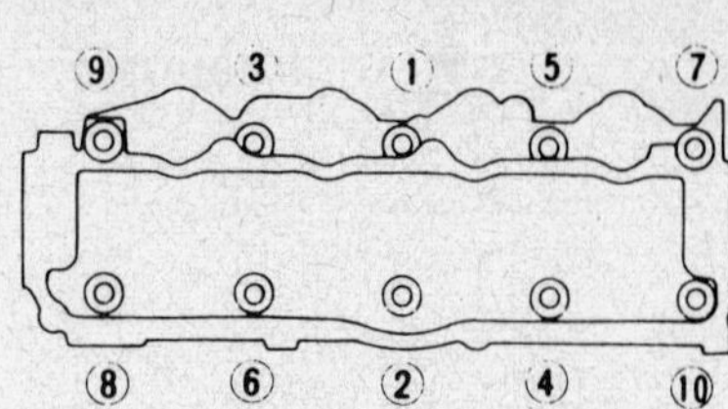

Fig. 16 Cylinder head bolt tightening sequence

a. If necessary, put a mark on 39th cog of timing belt, then install crankshaft sprocket with timing belt so that timing marks are aligned, **Fig. 2.**
b. Loosen timing belt tensioner bolt and rotate crankshaft two full revolutions in normal direction of rotation.
c. Tighten tensioner bolt while holding it from rotation.

10. Install timing belt cover. Torque cover attaching bolts to 2.2-3.6 ft. lbs.
11. Install crankshaft pulley and torque retaining bolt to specifications.
12. Install water pipe, then the injection pump bracket support.
13. Install rear camshaft sprocket and torque retaining bolt to specifications.
14. Install injection nozzles, glow plugs and glow plug connecting plate. Torque injection nozzles to 43-51 ft. lbs.
15. Install injection pump and pump bracket and adjust injection timing.
16. Install injection pump sprocket.
17. Install injection timing belt as follows:
    a. If necessary, put a mark on 23rd cog of timing belt, then install belt with timing marks aligned, **Fig. 3.**
    b. Loosen timing belt tensioner and rotate crankshaft two full revolutions in normal direction of rotation.
    c. Tighten tensioner bolt while holding it from rotation.
18. Install remaining front and rear engine components.

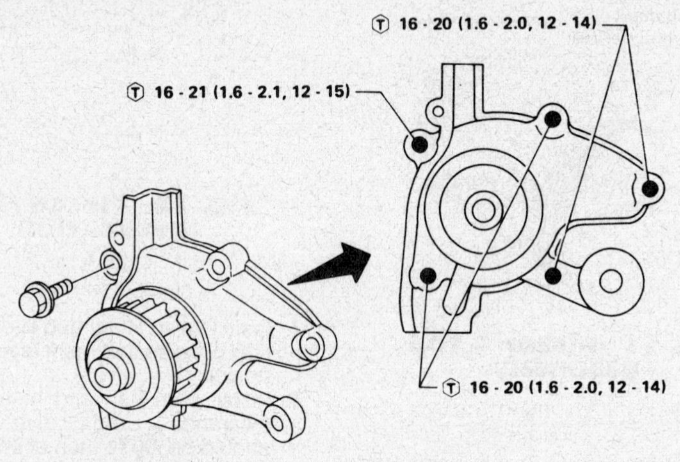

Fig. 17 Replacing water pump. 1983 shown, others similar

WATER PUMP REPLACE

Refer to **Fig. 17** for water pump replacement procedure for these models.

LD28 DIESEL ENGINES

INDEX

ENGINE REPLACE

1983 MAXIMA

1. Disconnect battery cable, then remove battery from vehicle.
2. Scribe hood hinge locations, then remove hood.
3. Remove air duct, then drain cooling system.
4. Disconnect wire and hose connections indicated by arrows in **Fig. 1.**
5. Remove radiator and radiator shroud. **On automatic transmission models, disconnect oil cooler hoses.**
6. On models equipped with air conditioning, remove compressor and position aside. **Never discharge refrigerant from air conditioning system when work is being performed.**
7. On models equipped with power steering, remove power steering pump and position aside.
8. Remove transmission control linkage, then disconnect speedometer cable.
9. On automatic transmission models, disconnect downshift solenoid and inhibitor switch electrical connectors.

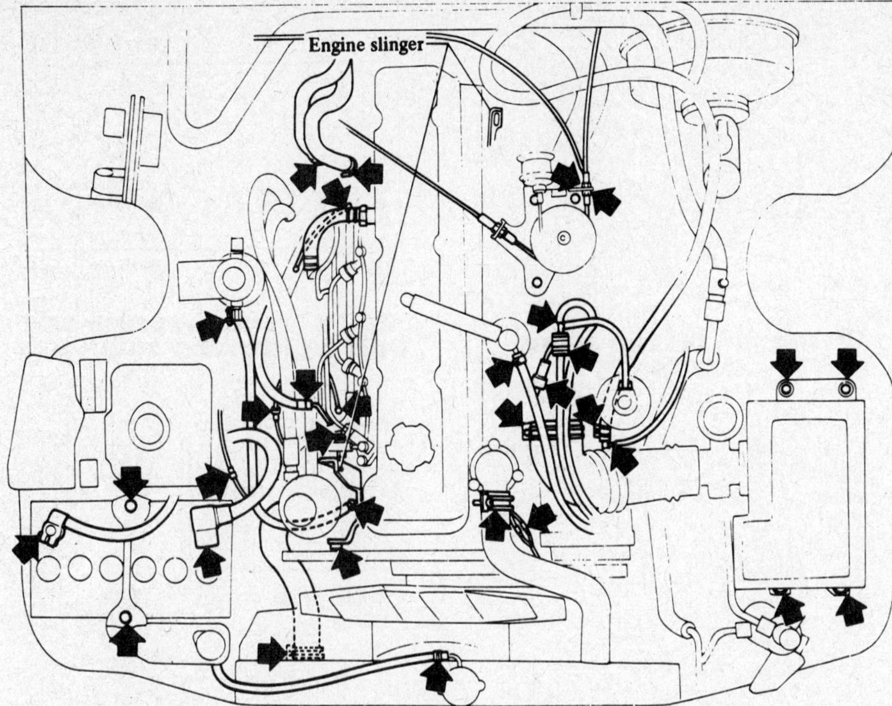

Fig. 1 Underhood accessory removal

② ⑥ ⑩ ⑭ ⑫ ⑧ ④

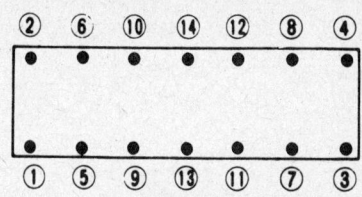

① ⑤ ⑨ ⑬ ⑪ ⑦ ③

Fig. 2 Cylinder head bolt loosening sequence

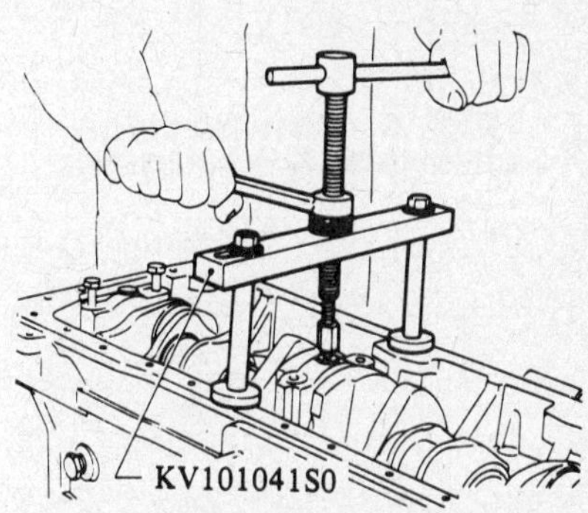

Fig. 3 Center & rear main bearing cap removal

10. On manual transmission models, remove clutch operating cylinder and position aside.
11. Disconnect exhaust pipe from manifold.
12. Mark propeller shaft for assembly reference, then remove propeller shaft. **Plug hole in extension housing to prevent oil loss.**
13. Attach lifting equipment to engine slingers, **Fig. 1,** and raise engine slightly to take weight off front and rear engine mounts.
14. Remove engine mounting damper, then the front engine mount bolts.
15. Remove bolt securing rear engine mount to transmission and body.
16. Remove engine and transmission as an assembly from vehicle.
17. Reverse procedure to install.

ENGINE DISASSEMBLY

1. Remove starter motor, then separate engine and transmission.
2. Remove engine mounting bracket, alternator, fan belt and alternator bracket.
3. Remove EGR valve and vacuum hose.
4. Drain engine oil and coolant into suitable containers.
5. Remove the following front engine components: fan, fan coupling, fan pulley, alternator adjusting bar, crankshaft pulley, pulley bracket with idler pulley, if equipped, and timing chain cover.
6. Remove the following left side engine components: thermostat housing and lower bypass inlet with hose, intake, exhaust manifold and engine slinger, oil feed pipe and oil return line from oil pan.
7. Remove the following right side engine components: spill tube, fuel return line, injection tubes at nozzle side, injection nozzles, nozzle washers, oil cooler with coolant hoses and oil filter, heater tube with hose, water inlet, oil level dipstick, engine mounting bracket, engine slinger and oil pump. If equipped, remove power steering pump bracket.
8. Remove oil pan and oil strainer.
9. Remove timing chain tensioner shaft and set spring, then the tensioner pulley.
10. Remove injection pump drive belt and gear, then remove the injection pump assembly with injection lines.
11. Remove water pump, then the rocker cover.
12. Remove camshaft sprocket attaching bolt, then the sprocket.
13. Loosen cylinder head attaching bolts in sequence, **Fig. 2,** in several steps, then remove the bolts and cylinder head.
14. Remove injection pump drive gear bolt, then remove the gear using a suitable puller.
15. Remove cylinder block front cover, then the timing chain, chain tensioner and chain guides.
16. Remove oil slinger, oil pump drive gear and crankshaft sprocket.
17. Remove drive plate, or flywheel and rear plate.
18. Remove connecting rod caps and bearings.
19. Remove connecting rod/piston combinations out through cylinder head side. Use care not to damage assemblies or crankshaft.
20. Remove main bearing caps and bearings. Remove center and rear caps using tool, **Fig 3. Loosen cap bolts in several steps, in sequence, beginning with the outer bolts.**
21. Remove rear oil seal, then the crankshaft.
22. Remove main bearing from side of block.

PISTON & ROD DISASSEMBLY

1. Remove top and second piston rings with a piston ring expander. Remove oil ring by hand.
2. Heat piston to approximately 140-158°F and tap piston pin out using a suitable drift.

CYLINDER HEAD DISASSEMBLY

1. Remove glow plug connecting plate and glow plugs.
2. Remove valve rocker spring, then loosen valve rocker pivot locknut and position cam nose at the upper position.
3. Depress valve springs and remove rocker arms.
4. Remove camshaft.
5. Remove valves, valve springs and related components. Keep disassembled parts in order. **Do not remove rocker pivot bushings or camshaft bearing from cylinder head.**
6. If necessary, combustion chambers may be driven out of cylinder head. When installing new combustion chambers, chill combustion chambers in dry ice for approximately 5-10 minutes prior to installation. Align knock pin on combustion chamber with notch in cylinder head and gently tap into place, **Fig. 4.**

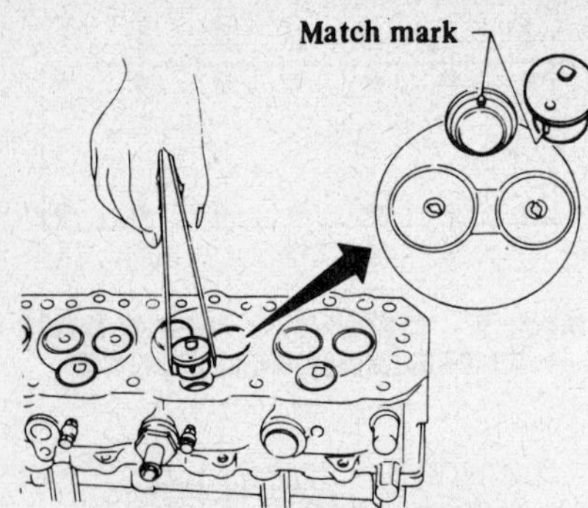

Fig. 4 Combustion chamber installation

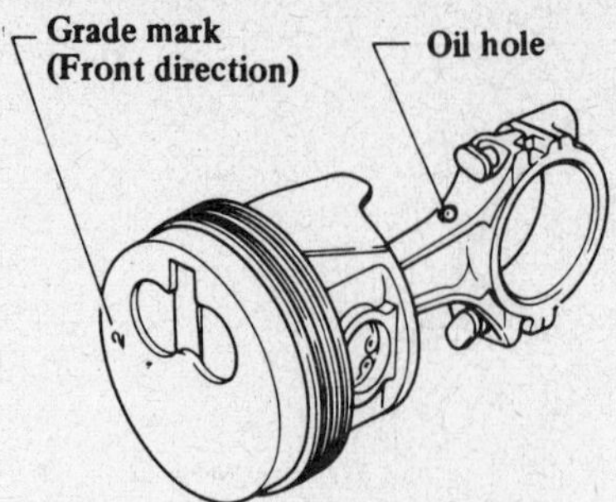

Fig. 5 Piston & rod assembly

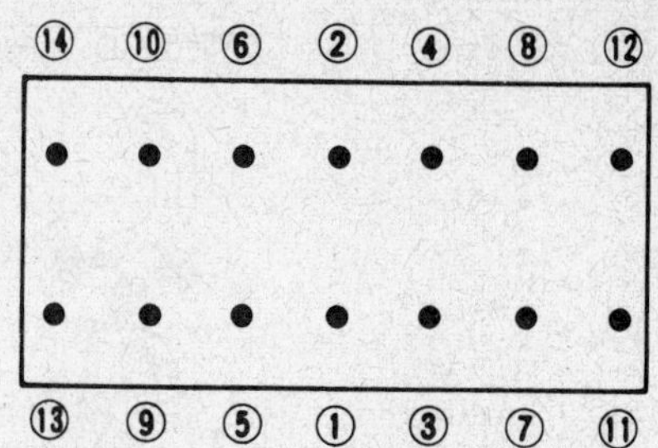

Fig. 6 Main bearing cap bolt tightening sequence

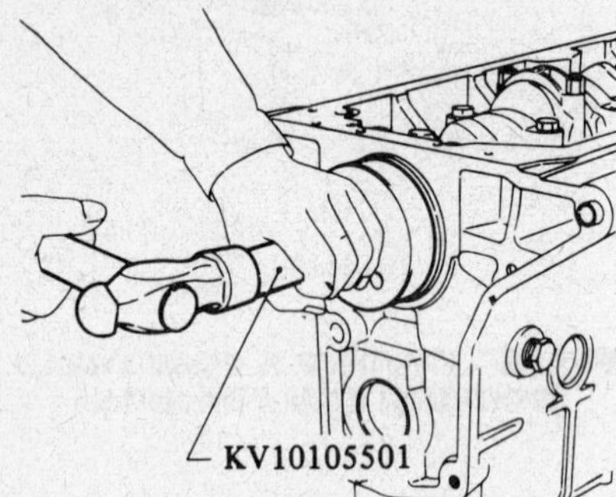

Fig. 7 Rear oil seal installation

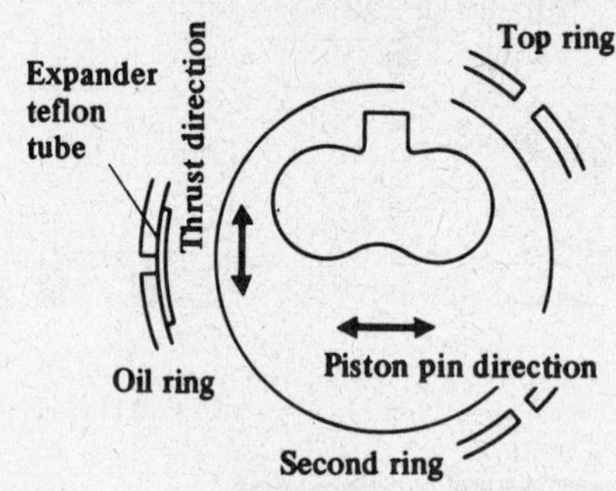

Fig. 8 Positioning rings on piston

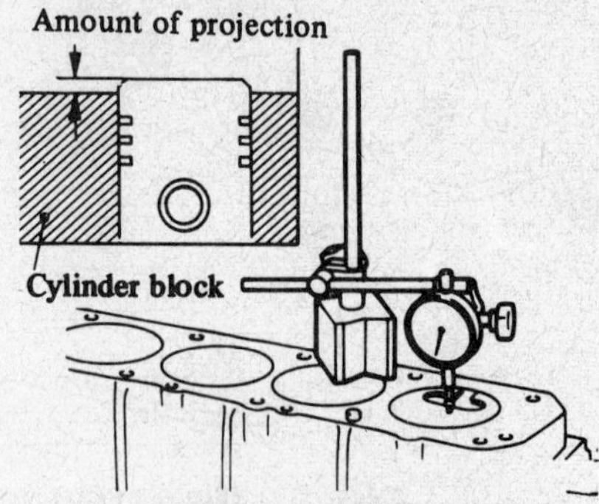

Fig. 9 Measuring piston projection

ENGINE ASSEMBLY

CYLINDER HEAD ASSEMBLY

1. Apply clean engine oil to valve stem and lip of valve oil seal.
2. Position valve spring seat and valve oil seal over valve guide.
3. Install valve, valve spring, spring retainer and collet.
4. Install valve rocker pivots with locknuts into pivot bushings.
5. Install valve rocker spring retainer.
6. Install camshaft and thrust plate. Torque thrust plate attaching bolts to 4.3-7.2 ft. lbs. **The oblong groove on thrust plate must face front of engine.**
7. Install valve rocker guides, then depress valve springs with a screwdriver and install the rocker arms.
8. Install valve rocker springs, then the glow plugs and glow plug connecting plate. Torque glow plugs to 14-18 ft. lbs. and glow plug connecting plate attaching bolts to .7-1.1 ft. lbs.

PISTON & ROD ASSEMBLY

1. Heat piston to approximately 140-158°F, the push piston pin into piston. Assemble piston to rod so that oil jet of connecting rod big end is directed toward right side of cylinder block, **Fig. 5.**
2. Install piston rings so that stamped mark on top of rings faces upward. Align teflon tube with ring gap. **When bore grade stamped near cylinder block bore is "1" or "2", use top and second rings which have no marks. When bore grade is "3", "4" or "5", use top and second rings stamped "S".**

ENGINE ASSEMBLY

1. Install upper main bearings in cylinder block. **Upper bearing can be identified as those having an oil hole and groove. Only the center bearing is of the flanged type.**
2. Apply clean engine oil to main bearing surfaces on both sides of cylinder block and cap, then install the crankshaft.
3. Install bearing caps as follows:
   a. Apply suitable sealant to each side of rear main bearing cap and each corner of cylinder block.
   b. Install main bearing caps so that arrow mark on cap faces toward front of engine.
   c. Torque cap bolts to specifications in several steps in sequence, **Fig. 6.**
   d. Make sure crankshaft turns smoothly and has correct endplay.
4. Apply suitable sealant to side oil seals, then install seals into main bearing cap.
5. Apply clean engine oil to rear oil seal and seal mating surface, then install the seal, **Fig. 7. Install seal so that lip of dust seal faces outward.**
6. Install lubricated piston/connecting rod assemblies into corresponding cylinders so that mark on piston head faces front of engine. Position piston rings as shown in **Fig. 8.**
7. Install connecting rod caps and torque nuts to specifications.
8. Install rear plate and flywheel, or drive plate. Torque attaching bolts to specifications.
9. If pistons are being replaced, determine proper cylinder head gasket as follows:
   a. Thoroughly clean cylinder block mating surface.
   b. Position dial indicator on cylinder block, **Fig. 9,** and zero the indicator.
   c. Measure piston projection at three points on each cylinder, **Fig. 10,** and note maximum projection.
   d. If piston projection is less than .0192 inch, use a gasket with a thickness of .0441 inch (identified by one cut-out).
   e. If piston projection is .0192-.0226 inch, use a gasket with a thickness of .0470 inch (identified by two cut-outs).
   f. If piston projection is more than .0226 inch, use gasket with a thickness of .0504 inch (identified by three cut-outs). **If pistons are not being replaced, select gasket of the same thickness as that removed.**
10. Install cylinder head as follows:
    a. Thoroughly clean cylinder head and block mating surface. Do not use sealant on mating surface.
    b. Rotate crankshaft until No. 1 piston is at TDC of compression stroke.
    c. Ensure that there is sufficient clearance between valves and pistons. Loosen rocker arm adjusting

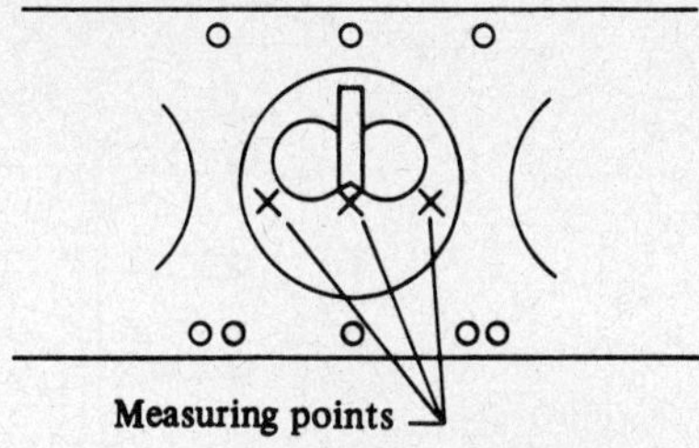

Fig. 10 Piston projection measuring points

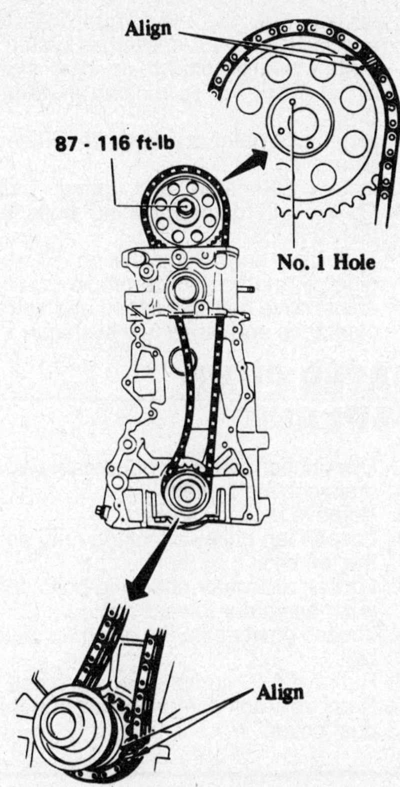

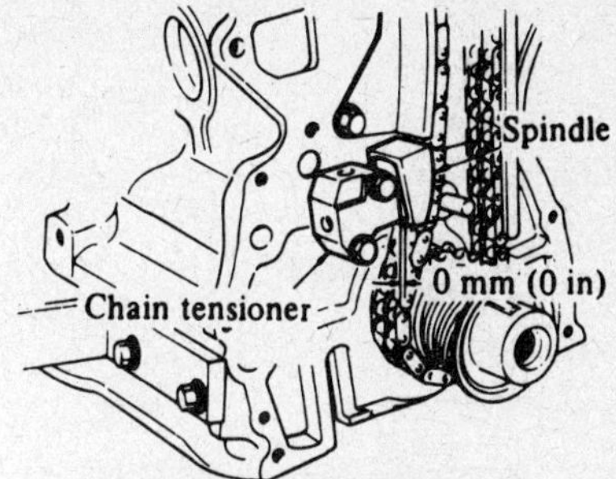

Fig. 11 Timing chain installation

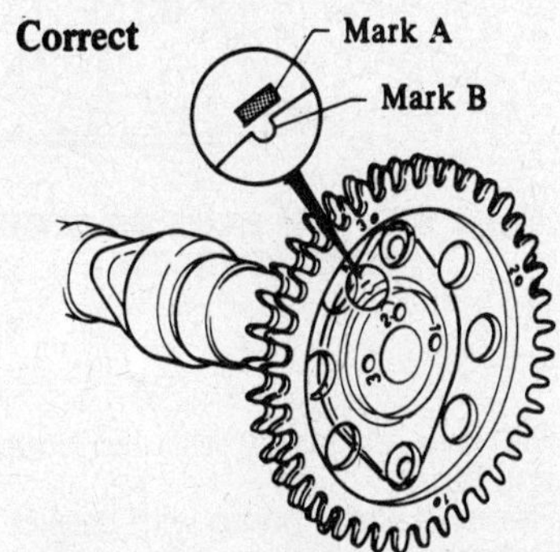

Fig. 12 Timing chain tensioner adjustment

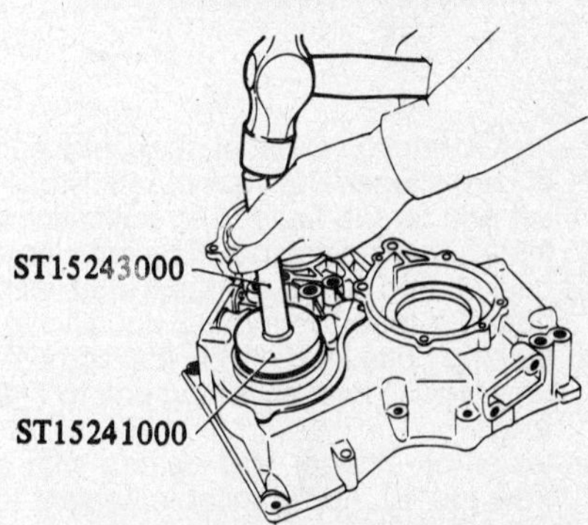

Fig. 14 Front cover seal installation

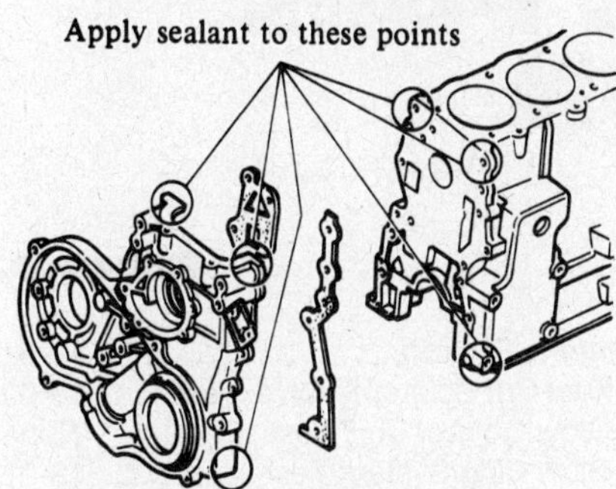

Fig. 15 Front cover sealant application

Fig. 13 Camshaft sprocket & locating plate alignment marks

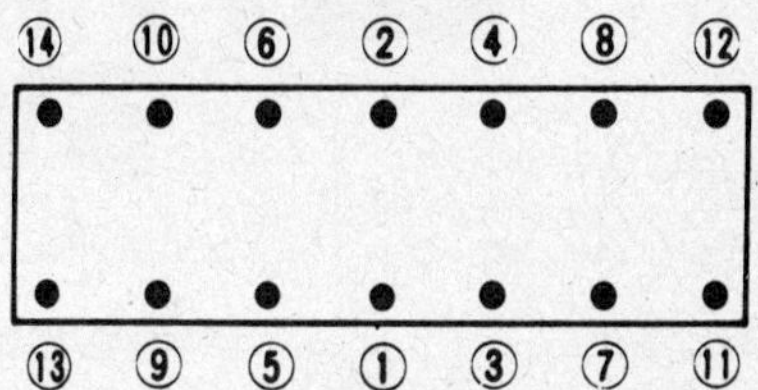

Fig. 16 Cylinder head bolt tightening sequence

screws to draw valves in, if necessary.

d. Install cylinder head with new gasket. Tighten only the two center bolts at this time. Final tightening will be accomplished further on in this procedure.

11. Install crankshaft sprocket, oil pump drive gear and oil slinger. Ensure that alignment marks on crankshaft sprocket face forward and chamfered inner side of oil pump drive gear faces rearward.
12. Install timing chain with timing marks in alignment, **Fig. 11.**
13. Insert camshaft dowel pin into No. 1 hole in camshaft sprocket, then install sprocket retaining bolt and torque to specifications.
14. Install timing chain guide and tensioner. Adjust protrusion of tensioner to 0 inch, **Fig. 12.** Torque tensioner retaining bolt to 4.3-7.2 ft. lbs.
15. Check position of marks on camshaft locating plate and sprocket. Marks should line up as shown in **Fig. 13.** If not, change position of dowel hole in sprocket, then reinstall the sprocket and recheck marks. **No. 2 mark on camshaft sprocket should be aligned with mark on timing chain and the sprocket should be installed with knock pin through No. 2 hole. If both marks on locating plate and camshaft sprocket are displaced to the left side, use No. 3 hole in sprocket and adjust. If, after adjustment, the mark is still on left side, the timing chain must be replaced.**
16. Install new seal in cylinder block front cover, **Fig. 14,** so that dust seal lip faces outward.
17. Apply suitable sealant to front cover, **Fig. 15,** and coat oil seal with clean engine oil.
18. Install front cover with new gasket.
19. Temporarily tighten front cover-to-cylinder block attaching bolts and measure height difference between cylinder block upper face and front cover upper face. The difference in height must be less than .0059 inch.
20. Torque cylinder head attaching bolts to specifications in several steps in sequence, **Fig. 16.**
21. Torque front cover attaching bolts to 6.5-8.7 ft. lbs. (M8 bolts); 2.9-3.6 ft. lbs. (M6 bolts).
22. Install injection pump, pump drive gear, pump drive crankshaft pulley, tensioner pulley and drive belt. Note the following torques: injection pump attaching nuts, 12-15 ft. lbs.; bracket attaching bolts, 22-26 ft. lbs.; drive gear retaining nut, 43-51 ft. lbs.; tensioner shaft and spring set pin, 22-30 ft. lbs.
23. Install water pump, then the crankshaft pulley.
24. Install timing chain cover and torque attaching bolts to 2.9-3.6 ft. lbs.
25. Install fan pulley, fan coupling, fan and, if equipped, the power steering pump idler pulley.
26. Install injection nozzle assemblies with new washers, **Fig. 17.** Torque nozzles to 12-15 ft. lbs.
27. Install fuel injection lines and torque flare nuts to 16-18 ft. lbs.
28. Install spill tube with new washers and torque attaching bolts to 11-13 ft. lbs.
29. Install fuel return hose, then the oil cooler with coolant hoses and oil filter.
30. Install oil lever dipstick, then the engine mounting brackets. Torque bracket bolts to 22-29 ft. lbs.
31. Install oil feed pipe and torque attaching bolt to 14-18 ft. lbs.

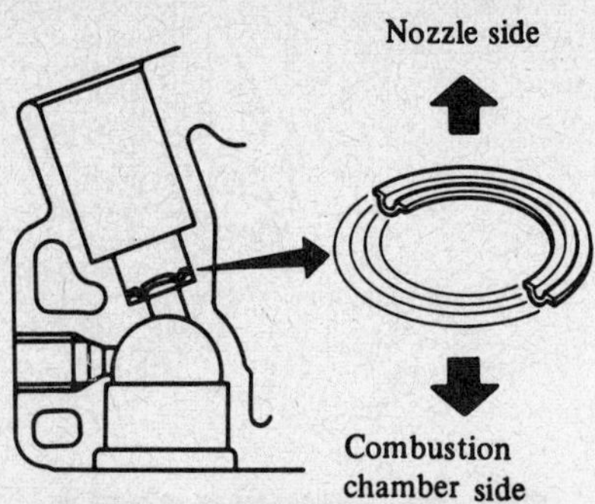

Fig. 17 Injection nozzle washer installation

32. Install intake, exhaust manifold and engine slinger. Use new manifold gasket and torque bolts to specifications.
33. Install thermostat housing with new gasket and lower bypass inlet with hose. Torque thermostat housing attaching bolts to 12-15 ft. lbs. and bottom bypass inlet attaching bolt to 7-9 ft. lbs.
34. Install oil strainer and oil pan with a new gasket. Apply suitable sealant to oil pan, **Fig. 18,** and torque bolts to specifications in a crisscross pattern. **Install reinforcement on rear side of oil pan prior to oil pan installation.**
35. Install alternator bracket with oil feed pipe.
36. Install alternator and drive belt. Torque alternator retaining bolts to 22-29 ft. lbs.
37. Following engine installation, fill engine oil and coolant to proper levels, adjust drive belt, idle speed and valve clearance and bleed fuel system.

WATER PUMP REPLACE

1. Disconnect battery ground cable and drain cooling system.
2. Remove radiator shroud.
3. Loosen fan pulley attaching nuts and the fan belt.
4. Loosen alternator attaching bolts and push alternator toward engine.
5. Loosen power steering oil pump drive belt.
6. Remove A/C compressor drive belt.
7. Remove crank damper pulley and the dust cover.

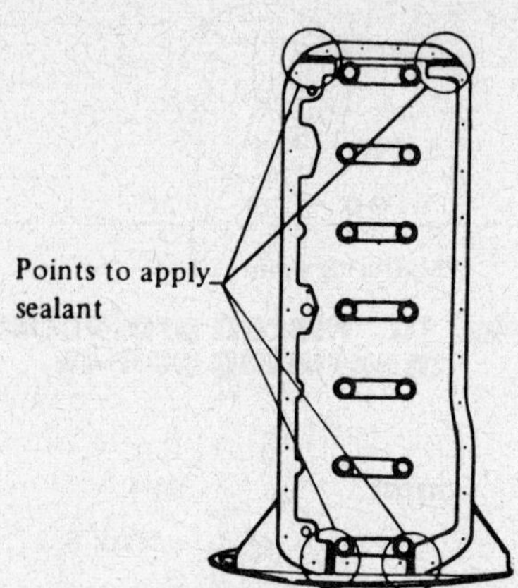

Fig. 18 Oil pan sealant application

8. Remove fan pulley with fan coupling and fan.
9. Remove water pump with gasket.
10. Reverse procedure to install, using new gasket.

CD17 & LD28 DIESEL FUEL SYSTEM SECTION

INDEX

SYSTEM SERVICE

FUEL SYSTEM BLEEDING

Air should be bled from the fuel system whenever the system is opened or repaired.

Maxima

1. Loosen priming pump vent screw, **Fig. 1,** and operate priming pump until fuel overflows at vent screw.
2. Tighten vent screw, then disconnect fuel return hose and attach suitable hose to overflow connector. Position container beneath hose.
3. Operate priming pump until fuel flows from hose, then remove hose and reinstall fuel return hose.

Sentra

1. Loosen priming pump vent screw, **Fig. 2,** and operate priming pump until fuel overflows at vent screw.

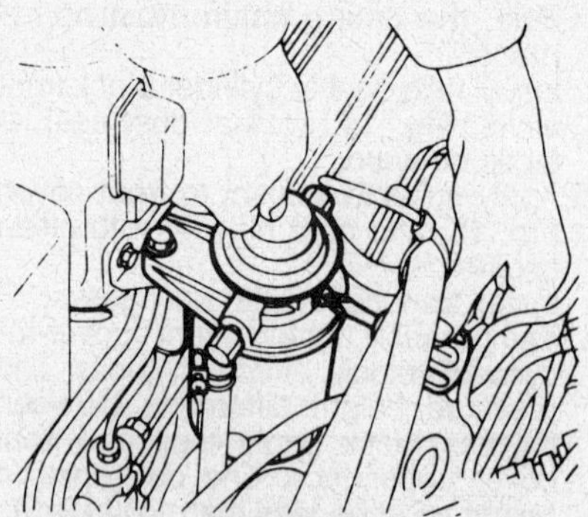

Fig. 1 Fuel system primer pump & bleeder screw. Maxima

2. Tighten vent screw, then disconnect fuel return hose at fuel line side.
3. Operate priming pump until fuel flows from disconnected fuel hose, then reconnect the hose. If engine will not start, loosen injection lines at nozzles and crank engine until fuel overflows from the lines, then retighten flare nuts.

INJECTION TIMING, ADJUST

Maxima

1. Remove under cover, then drain enough coolant to bring coolant level below cold start device. Disconnect water hoses from cold start device.
2. If equipped, remove power steering pump.
3. Rotate crankshaft until No. 1 cylinder is at TDC of compression stroke. Ensure that grooves in drive plate and rear plate are aligned with each other.
4. Disconnect fuel lines at injection nozzles.
5. turn cold start device control linkage and insert a block, approximately .59 inch thick between piston and linkage,

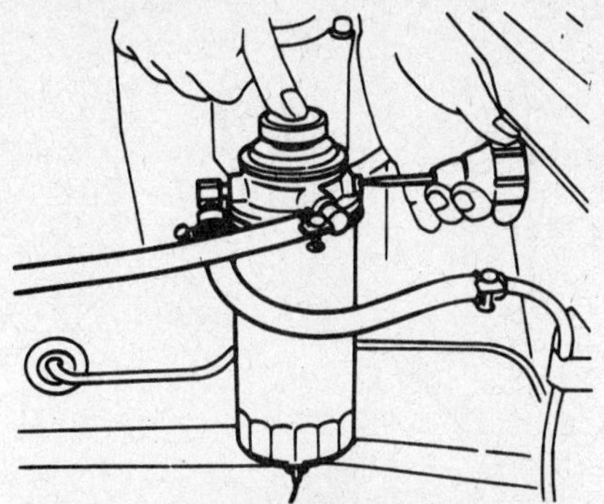
Fig. 2 Fuel system primer pump & bleeder screw. Sentra

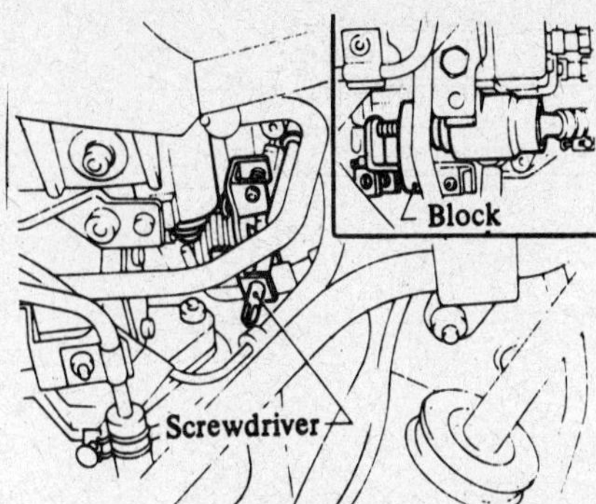

Fig. 3 Cold start device. Maxima

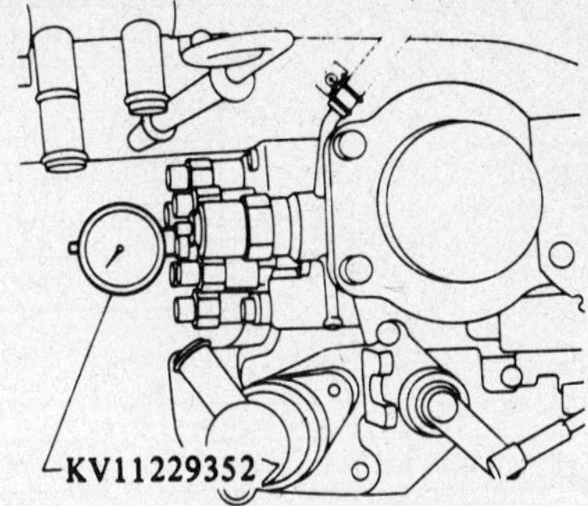

Fig. 4 Measuring injection pump plunger lift

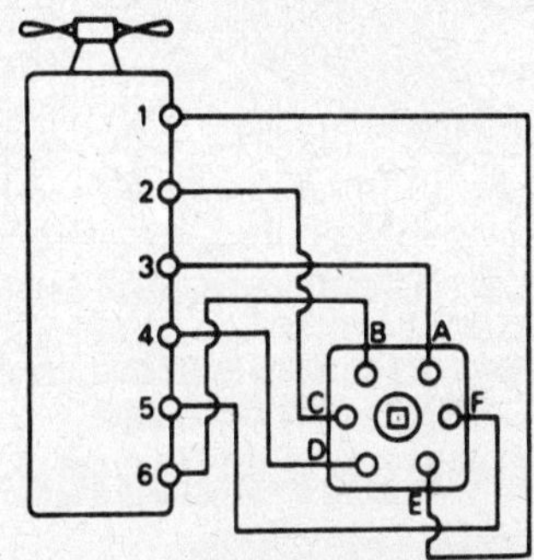

Fig. 5 Injection line installation. Maxima

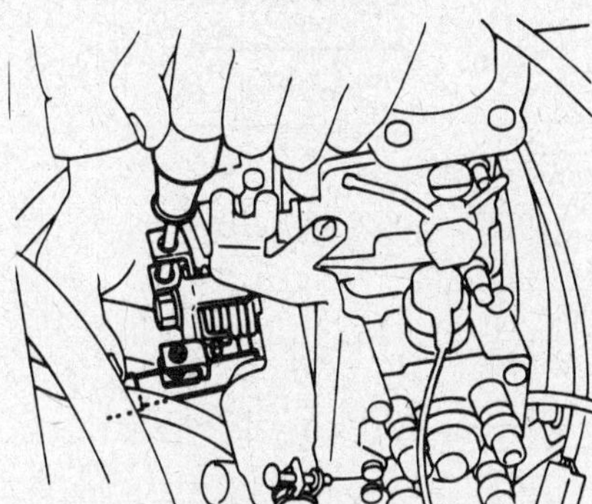
Fig. 6 Cold start device. Sentra

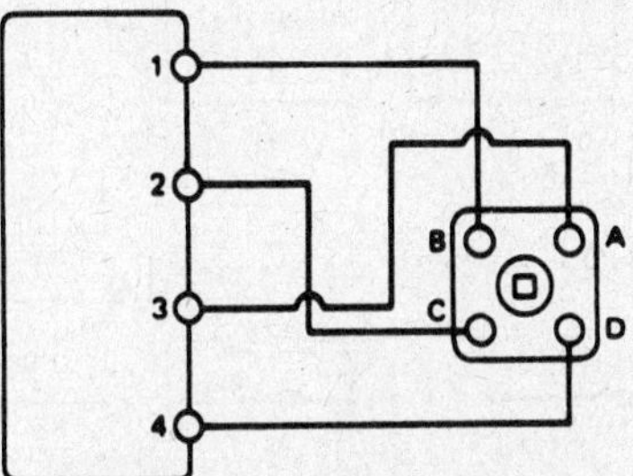

Fig. 7 Injection line installation. Sentra

Fig. 3.

6. On all models, remove plug bolt from rear side of injection pump and install dial indicator, **Fig. 4.**
7. Loosen injection pump attaching nuts and bracket bolt.
8. Rotate crankshaft 15-20°F. counterclockwise, then zero the dial indicator.
9. On all models, rotate crankshaft clockwise until No. 1 cylinder is at TDC of compression stroke and note dial indicator reading. Measurement should be within the following specifications: low alt., .0327-.0351 inch; high alt., .0346-.0370 inch.
10. If reading is below specifications, rotate injection pump body counterclockwise until it is within specifications.
11. If reading exceeds specifications, rotate injection pump body clockwise until it is within specifications.
12. Torque pump attaching nuts to 7-15 ft. lbs. and the bracket bolt to 22-26 ft. lbs.
13. Remove dial indicator and reinstall plug bolt with new washer. Torque plug bolt to 10-14 ft. lbs.
14. Reset cold start device in its original position, then reconnect injection lines. **Install injection lines, Fig. 5,** in the following sequence: 4, 2, 6, 1, 5, 3.
15. Install power steering pump and reconnect water hoses to cold start device.
16. Replenish cooling system and install under cover.

Sentra

1. Rotate crankshaft until No. 1 cylinder is at TDC of compression stroke. Make sure that indicator and mark on vibration damper are aligned.
2. Disconnect fuel lines at injection nozzles.
3. Turn cold start device clockwise and insert a block, approximately .59 inch thick, between piston and linkage, **Fig. 6.**
4. Remove plug bolt from rear of injection pump and install dial indicator, **Fig. 4.**
5. Loosen injection pump attaching nuts and bracket bolt.
6. Rotate crankshaft 15-20° counterclockwise, then zero the dial indicator.
7. Rotate crankshaft clockwise until No. 1 cylinder is at TDC of compression stroke and note dial indicator reading. Measurement should be within the following specifications: 1983 man. trans. low alt. and auto. trans. high alt., and all 1984-86, .0358-.0382 inch; 1983 auto. trans. low alt., .0334-.0358 inch; 1983 man. trans. high alt., .0382-.0406 inch.
8. If reading exceeds specifications, rotate injection pump clockwise until it is within specifications.
9. If reading is below specifications, rotate injection pump counterclockwise until it is within specifications.
10. Torque injection pump attaching nuts to 9-13 ft. lbs. and the bracket bolt to 36-43 ft. lbs.
11. Remove dial indicator and reinstall plug bolt with new washer. Torque plug bolt to 10-14 ft. lbs.
12. Reset cold start device in its original position, then reconnect injection lines. **Install injection lines, Fig. 7,** in the following sequence: 4, 3, 2, 1.

IDLE SPEED, ADJUST

1. Warm engine and connect diesel tachometer pickup to No. 1 injection tube.
2. Run engine at approximately 2000 RPM for two minutes, then at idle for one minute and check idle speed.
3. Adjust idle speed as follows:
   a. Stop engine, then loosen idle adjusting screw locknut.
   b. Start engine and turn idle adjusting screw to bring idle speed within specifications, then stop engine and tighten locknut.

SYSTEM TESTING

GLOW PLUG SYSTEM, TEST

Refer to **Fig. 8** for diagnosis of the glow plug system.

GLOW CONTROL UNIT, TEST

1983–86

1. Connect suitable test lamp to blue wire (Sentra), or blue/yellow wire (Maxima), at glow plug control unit, **Fig. 9.**
2. Turn ignition switch on and note length of time test lamp remains lit. On 1983-84 models, if coolant temperature is below 122°F and glow plug terminal voltage is 8 volts, test lamp should light for 12 seconds (Sentra),

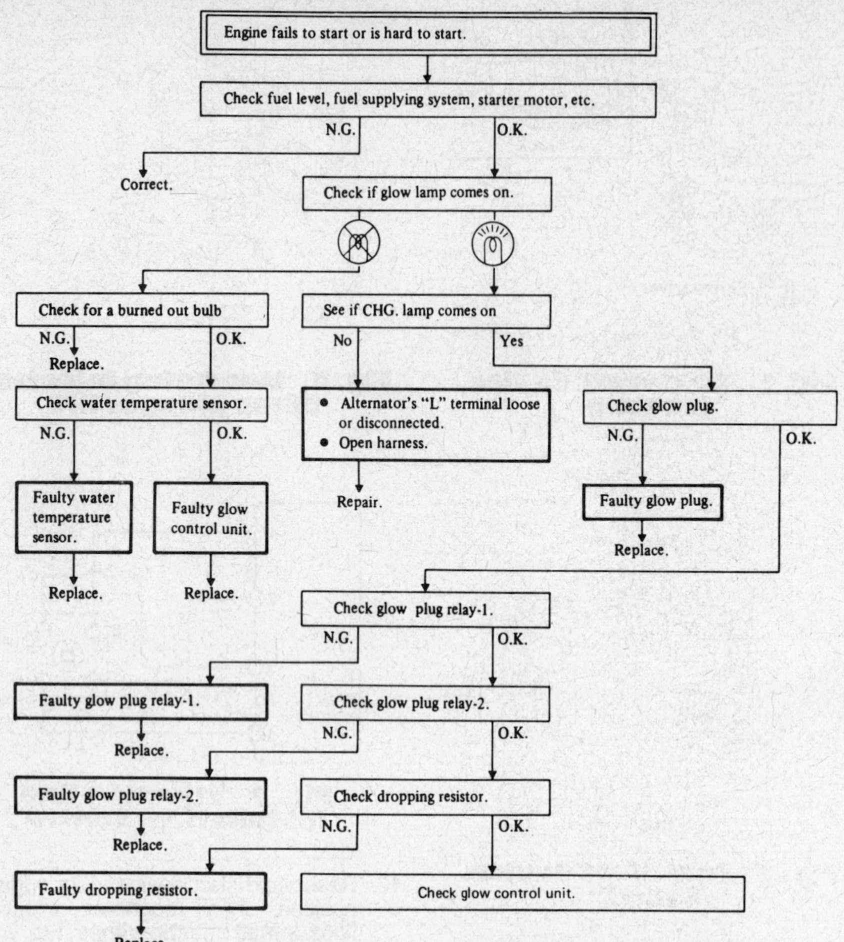

Fig. 8 Glow plug system diagnostic chart. 1983 Maxima & 1983–86 Sentra

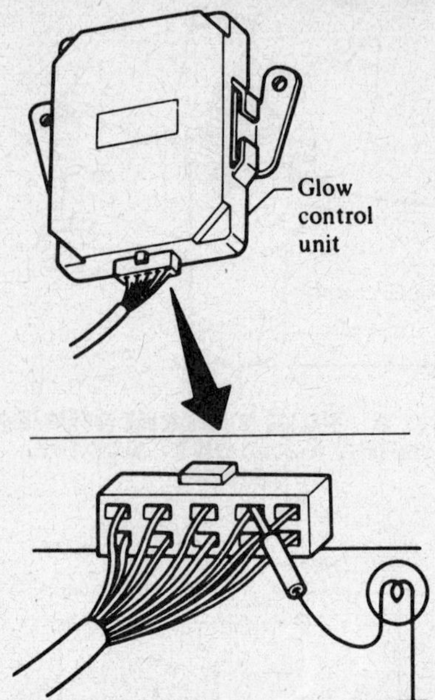

Fig. 9 Glow control unit test connections (pre-glow operation). 1983 Maxima & 1983–86 Sentra

or 13 seconds (Maxima). On 1985-86 models, if coolant temperature is below 122°F, test lamp should light for 4-13 seconds. On 1983-84 models, if coolant temperature is below 122°F and glow plug terminal voltage is 10.5 volts, test lamp should light for 6 seconds. On all models, if coolant temperature is above 122°F, test lamp should not light. **On 1983-84 models, if engine is restarted within 60 seconds (Sentra) or 80 seconds (Maxima), of shutdown, the test lamp should remain lit for less than 6 seconds. On 1985 models, ensure ignition switch is off for at least 5 minutes before turning on to avoid erroneous test results.**

3. On 1983-84 models, connect suitable test lamp to black/white wire (Sentra), or blue/red wire (Maxima), at glow control unit, **Fig. 10.**
4. On 1985-86 models, connect test lamp between black/white and white wires.
5. On all models, turn ignition switch on and note length of time test lamp remains lit. On 1985-86 models, if coolant temperature is below 13°F, test lamp should remain lit approximately 31 seconds. On all models, if coolant temperature is approximately 68°F, test lamp should remain lit for 11 seconds (Sentra), or 17 seconds (Maxima). If coolant temperature is approximately 86-122°F, (Sentra), or 104°F (Maxima), test lamp should remain lit for 5 seconds (Sentra), or 9 seconds (Maxima). If coolant temperature is above 122°F, test lamp should not light. **With ignition switch in Start position, test lamp should remain lit continuously.**

FUEL CUT SOLENOID VALVE, TEST

Sentra

If a clicking noise is heard when ignition switch is turned on, the fuel cut solenoid valve may be faulty. Perform the following test to verify condition of valve.

1. Remove valve from vehicle and connect suitable jumper wires between valve and battery, **Fig. 11.**
2. With battery voltage applied to valve, the valve plunger should move. If not, the plunger may be restricted by an accumulation of dirt. Clean or replace valve as necessary.
3. If valve operates satisfactorily, check condition of starting system.

COMPONENT SERVICE

INJECTION PUMP, REPLACE

Maxima

1. Disconnect battery ground cable and remove air cleaner duct.
2. Remove under cover, then drain cooling system.
3. Remove radiator shroud and all drive belts.
4. If equipped, remove power steering pump.
5. Disconnect the following: accelerator cable, overflow hose at spill tube side, fuel cut solenoid electrical connector, fuel return line, potentiometer connector, injection timing control solenoid valve wire, cold start device water hoses at 4 way connector and vacuum modulator hoses on automatic transmission models.
6. Remove timing belt cover.
7. Loosen belt tensioner assembly and set in the "free" position, then retighten.
8. Remove injection pump timing belt, then the pump drive gear.
9. Disconnect fuel lines at injection nozzles.
10. Remove injection pump attaching nuts and bracket bolt, then the pump assembly with injection lines.
11. To install, set No. 1 cylinder at TDC of compression stroke by aligning in rear plate and flywheel.
12. Temporarily install injection pump in position.
13. Install injection pump drive gear, then the timing belt. Ensure that timing marks on belt align with marks on injection pump drive gear as well as those on crankshaft sprocket. **If timing marks on belt are not clear enough to permit proper align-**

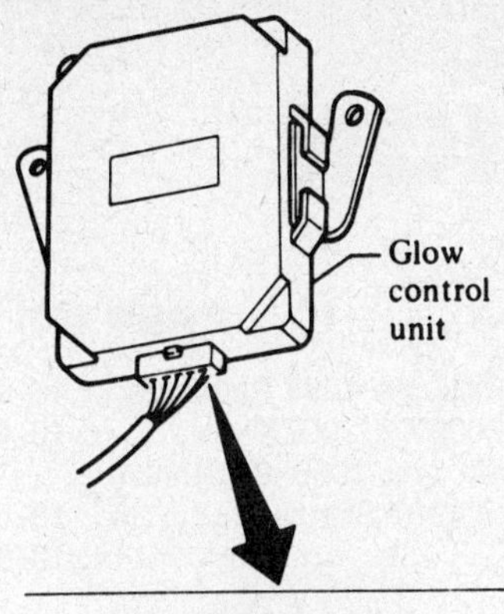

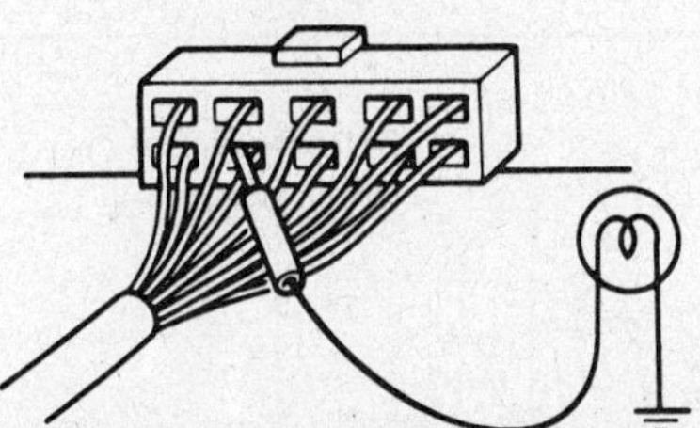

Fig. 10 Glow control unit test connections (After-glow operation). 1983 Maxima & 1983–84 Sentra

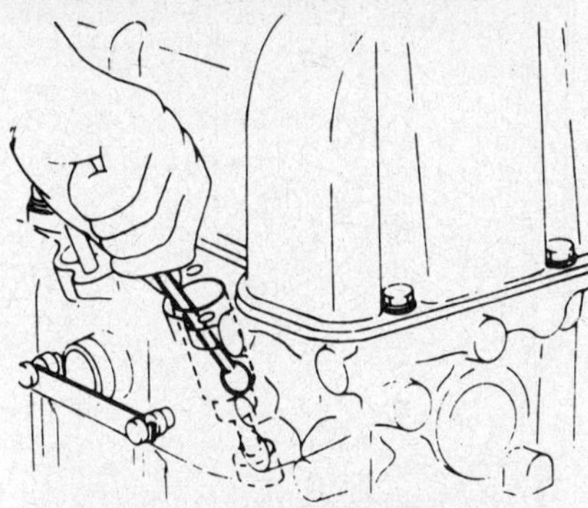

Fig. 12 Fuel injection nozzle removal. Maxima

ment, position marks on crankshaft sprocket and pump drive gear so that there are 20 cogs of the timing belt between these two marks.

14. Loosen spring set pin and tensioner to automatically set belt tension.
15. Rotate crankshaft clockwise two complete revolutions, then adjust injection timing as described under "Injection Timing, Adjust."
16. Reinstall and connect components in the reverse order of steps 1 thru 6, then refill cooling system and bleed fuel system.

Sentra

1. Disconnect battery ground cable, then drain cooling system.
2. Disconnect the following: accelerator cable, overflow hose at spill tube side, fuel cut solenoid connector, fuel return line, potentiometer, engine speed sensor connectors and cold start device water hoses.
3. Remove air cleaner housing with air duct, then rotate crankshaft until No. 1 cylinder is at TDC of compression stroke.
4. Remove rear timing belt cover, then set belt tensioner to the "free" position and remove the timing belt.
5. Remove injection pump drive gear.
6. Disconnect fuel lines at injection nozzles.
7. Remove injection pump attaching nuts and bracket bolt, then the pump assembly with injection lines.
8. To install, set No. 1 cylinder at TDC of compression stroke by aligning indicator and mark on vibration damper.
9. Temporarily install injection pump in position, then install the pump drive gear.
10. If necessary, put a mark on 23rd cog of timing belt, then install belt with timing marks aligned.
11. Loosen timing belt tensioner and rotate crankshaft two revolutions in normal direction of rotation, then tighten tensioner bolt.
12. Adjust injection timing as described under "Injection Timing, Adjust."
13. Install rear timing belt cover and the air cleaner housing with air duct.
14. Reconnect components in the reverse order of steps 1 and 2, then refill cooling system and bleed fuel system.

INJECTION NOZZLE, REPLACE

Maxima

1. Disconnect injection lines at nozzle and spill tube assembly.
2. Remove injection nozzles using suitable tool, **Fig. 12.**
3. Reverse procedure to install, using a new gasket. **Install gasket with grooved side toward nozzle.**

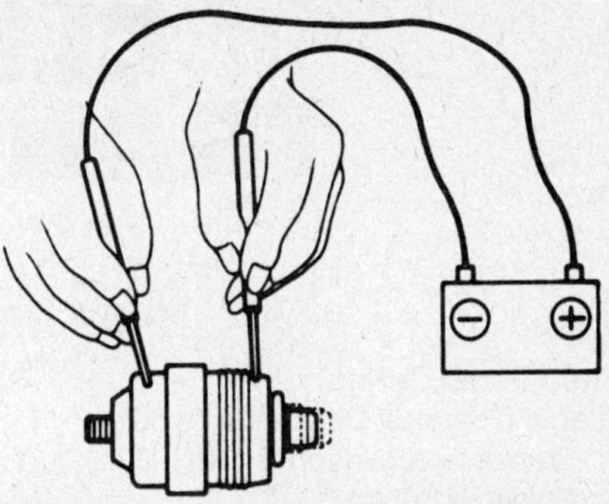

Fig. 11 Fuel cut solenoid valve test connections. Sentra

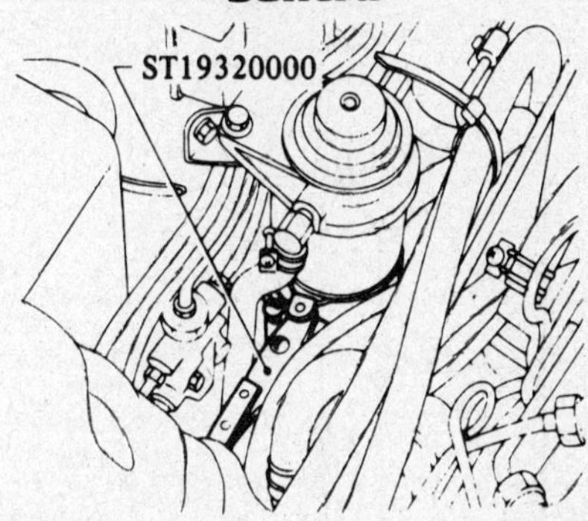

Fig. 13 Fuel filter removal

Sentra

1. Disconnect injection lines at nozzle and loosen at injection pump.
2. Remove spill tube assembly, then the injection nozzles.
3. Reverse procedure to install, using a new gasket. **Install gasket with grooved side toward nozzle.**

FUEL FILTER, REPLACE

1. Remove fuel filter sensor and drain fuel from filter.
2. Remove filter using suitable tool, **Fig. 13.**
3. Reverse procedure to install. Install filter hand tight only.

CLUTCH & MANUAL TRANSMISSION SECTION

INDEX

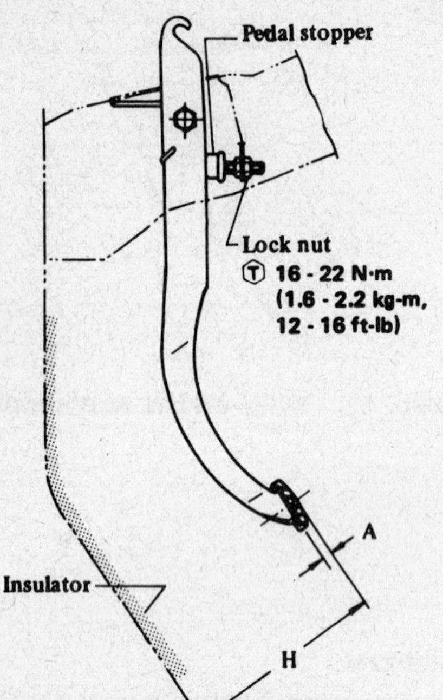

Fig. 1 Clutch pedal free travel & height adjustment. 1983–86 Stanza

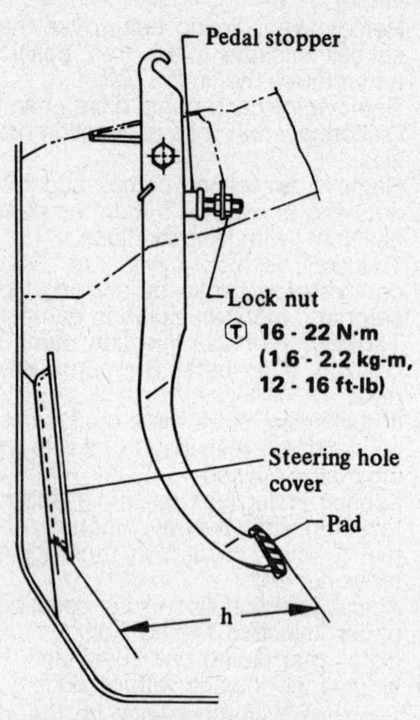

Fig. 2 Clutch pedal free travel & height adjustment. 1983–84 Pulsar & Sentra

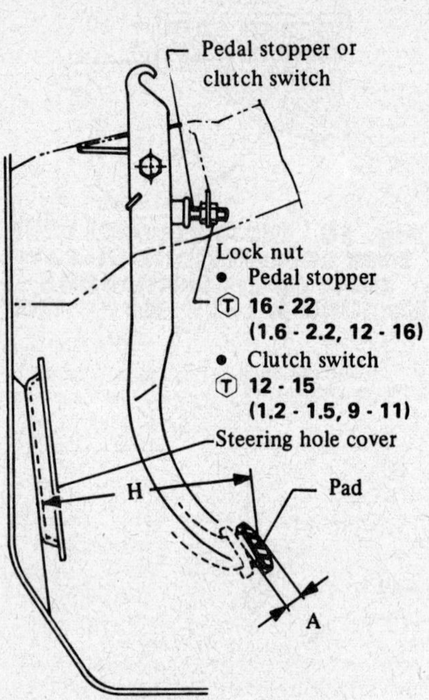

Fig. 3 Clutch pedal free travel & height adjustment. 1985–86 Pulsar & Sentra

CLUTCH PEDAL

ADJUST

CABLE OPERATED CLUTCH 1983–86 STANZA EXC. STANZA WAGON & 1983–87 PULSAR & SENTRA

1. Adjust clutch pedal height so that dimension H, **Figs. 1 through 4,** is within specifications, **Fig. 5.**
2. Adjust withdrawal lever play, dimension B, **Figs. 6 through 8,** with the adjuster or locknuts, to specifications, **Fig. 2.**
3. Measure clutch pedal freeplay as shown in **Figs. 1 through 4,** dimension A. Freeplay should be as shown, **Fig. 2.**
4. After the above adjustments have been completed, cycle clutch pedal several times to ensure that clutch linkage operates smoothly without binding.

Model	Year	Clutch Pedal Adjustment: Pedal Height In. (mm)	Withdrawal Lever Play In. (mm)	Pedal Freeplay In. (mm)
Pulsar	1983–84	7.64–8.03 (194–204)	.08–.16 (2–4)	.43–.83 (11–21)
	1985	8.23–8.43 (209–214)	.098–.138 (2.5–3.5)	.492–.689 (12.5–17.5)
	1986	7.76–8.15 (197–207)	.098–.138 (2.5–3.5)	.492–.689 (12.5–17.5)
	1987	6.38–6.77 (162–172)	.098–.138 (2.5–3.5)	.492–.689 (12.5–17.5)
Sentra	1983–84	7.64–8.03 (194–204)	.08–.16 (2–4)	.43–.83 (11–21)
	1985	8.23–8.43 (209–214)	.098–.138 (2.5–3.5)	.492–.689 (12.5–17.5)
	1986	7.76–8.15 (197–207)	.098–.138 (2.5–3.5)	.492–.689 (12.5–17.5)
	1987	6.38–6.77 (162–172)	.098–.138 (2.5–3.5)	.492–.689 (12.5–17.5)
Stanza	1983–84	5.85–6.24 (148.5–158.5)	.08–.12 (2–3)	.43–.63 (11–16)
	1985–86	6.02–6.42 (153–163)	.098–.138 (2.5–3.5)	.47–.67 (12–17)

Fig. 5 Clutch pedal height, withdrawal lever play & freeplay & specifications. 1983–86 Stanza Exc. Stanza Wagon & 1983–87 Pulsar & Sentra

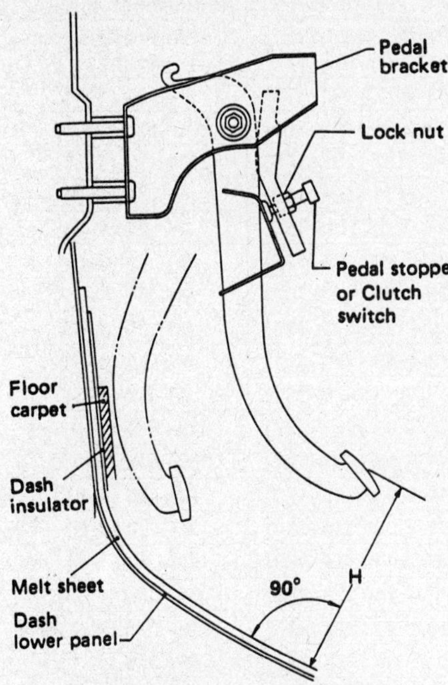

Fig. 4 Clutch pedal free travel & height adjustment. 1987 Pulsar & Sentra

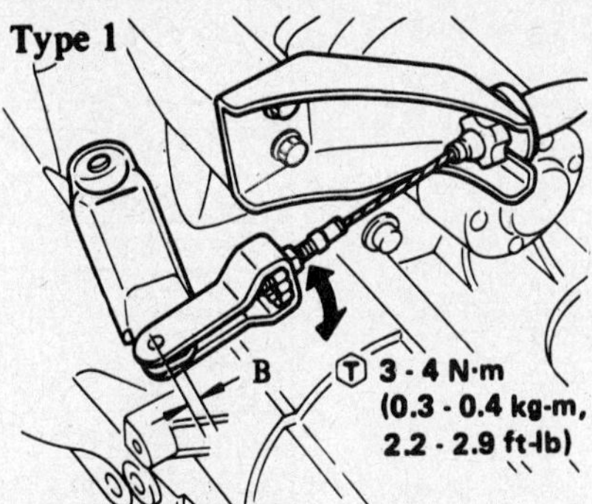

Fig. 6 Withdrawal lever adjustment. Type 1 exc. Stanza

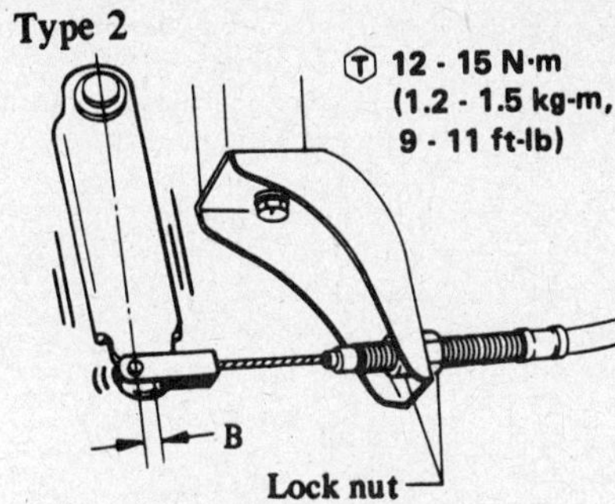

Fig. 7 Withdrawal lever adjustment. Type 2 exc. Stanza

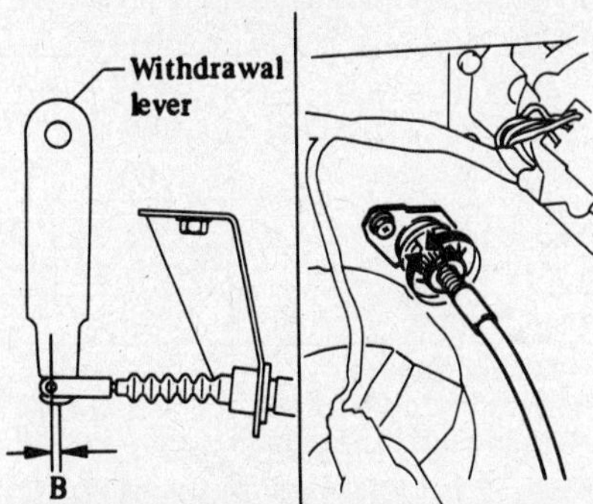

Fig. 8 Withdrawal lever adjustment. Stanza

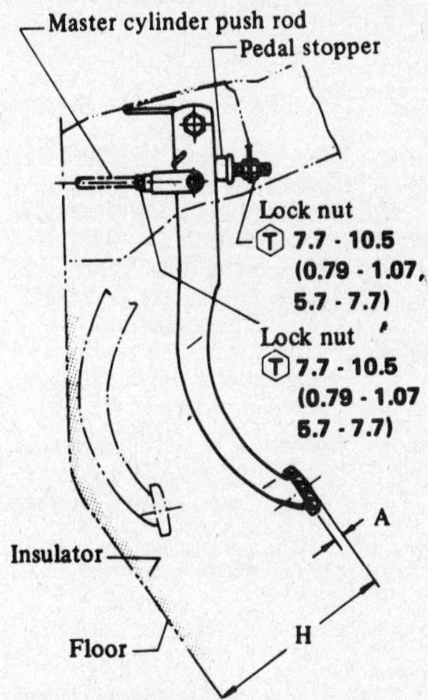

Fig. 9 Clutch pedal free travel & height adjustment. Hydraulic operated clutch. Exc. 1984–87 200SX & 300ZX, 1986–87 Stanza Wagon, 1986½–87 Pickup & 1987 Pathfinder, Stanza & Van

HYDRAULIC OPERATED CLUTCH

The clutch hydraulic system must be bled whenever a clutch line has been disconnected or when air has entered the system. The bleed valve is located on the clutch operating cylinder.

CLUTCH PEDAL HEIGHT & FREEPLAY, ADJUST

1983–86 Pickup, 1983–87 200SX & Maxima, 1984–87 300ZX & 1986–87 Stanza Wagon

1. Measure clutch pedal height from floor panel to center of clutch pedal, **Figs. 9 and 10,** dimension H. Clutch pedal height should be as specified in **Fig. 11.** Adjust clutch pedal height by adjusting the pedal stopper. After completing adjustment, tighten locknut.
2. Measure clutch pedal freeplay as shown in **Figs. 9 and 10,** dimension A. Clutch pedal freeplay should be as specified in **Fig. 11.** Adjust clutch pedal freeplay by rotating the clutch master cylinder inward or outward until the specified freeplay is obtained. After completing freeplay adjustment, tighten locknut. Clutch pedal freeplay is the sum of play between the clevis pin and clevis pin hole and play between the piston and piston rod.
3. After the above adjustments have been completed, cycle clutch pedal several times to ensure that clutch linkage operates smoothly without binding.

1983 280ZX

1. Check to ensure that adjusting rod length is 6.1 in. (155mm), **Fig. 12.** If adjusting rod length must be adjusted, loosen locknut at each end of adjuster, then rotate adjuster until the specified length is obtained. Tighten locknuts after adjustment has been completed.
2. Loosen clutch pedal stop or clutch switch and clutch pedal push rod locknut. Rotate clutch pushrod until distance between floor panel and center of clutch pedal is 8.03 in. (204mm), **Fig. 9** dimension H, then tighten locknut. **When adjusting clutch pedal height, ensure that clutch pedal does not contact pedal stop or clutch switch.**
3. Adjust clutch pedal stop or clutch switch so that distance between floor panel and clutch pedal is 7.91 in. (201mm), **Fig. 9** dimension H, then tighten lock nut.
4. After completing the clutch pedal height adjustment, check clutch pedal freeplay, **Fig. 9** dimension A. Clutch pedal freeplay should be .04 to .20 in. (1 to 5mm).
5. Check initial effort to depress clutch pedal. The initial effort to depress the clutch pedal should be 3.5 to 4.2 lbs. (15.7 to 18.6 N). If not within limits, check adjusting length, refer to step 1.
6. After completing adjustments, cycle clutch pedal several times to ensure that clutch linkage operates smoothly without binding.

1986½–87 Pickup & 1987 Pathfinder

1. Adjust clutch pedal height, dimension "H" in **Fig. 13,** to specifications, **Fig. 11,** using the pedal stopper or clutch switch.
2. Adjust clutch pedal freeplay, dimension "A" in **Fig. 13,** to specifications, **Fig. 11,** using the pushrod.
3. Adjust dimension "C," **Fig. 14,** to .012-.039 inch with clutch pedal fully depressed.

1987 Stanza

1. Adjust clutch pedal height "H," **Fig. 10,** to 6.73-7.13 inches (171-181 mm) by turning clutch switch or pedal stopper, then torque clutch switch

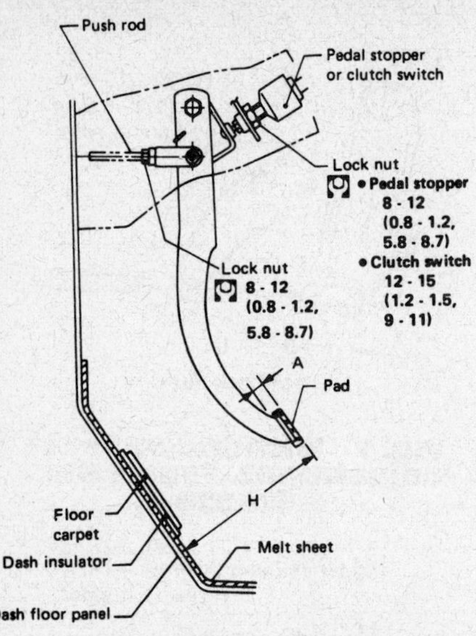

Fig. 10 Clutch pedal free travel & height adjustment. Hydraulic operated clutch. 1984–87 200SX & 300ZX, 1986–87 Stanza Wagon & 1987 Stanza

Adjusting rod length "L":
155 mm (6.10 in)

Lock nut
Ⓣ 7.8 - 10.8 N·m
(0.8 - 1.1 kg-m, 5.8 - 8.0 ft-lb)

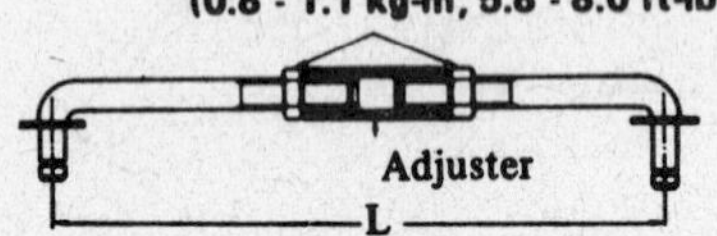

Fig. 12 Adjusting rod length adjustment. 1983 280ZX

locknut to 9-11 ft. lbs. or pedal stopper locknut to 14-19 ft. lbs.

2. Adjust pedal freeplay "A," **Fig. 10,** to .04-.12 inch (1-3 mm) by turning pushrod, then torque pushrod locknut to 5.8-8 ft. lbs.
3. Adjust clearance "C," **Fig. 14,** between pedal stopper rubber and threaded end of clutch interlock switch to .039-.079 inch (1-2 mm) while depressing clutch pedal fully.

1987 Van

1. Adjust clutch pedal height, dimension "H" in **Fig. 15,** to 6.97-7.25 inches using clutch switch and A.S.C.D. switch.
2. Adjust clutch pedal freeplay, dimension "A" in **Fig. 15,** to .039-.118 inch using pushrod.
3. Adjust dimension "C," **Fig. 16,** to .012-.039 inch with clutch pedal fully depressed.

CLUTCH REPLACE

1. Remove transmission as outlined elsewhere in this section.
2. Insert a dummy shaft into the clutch disc hub.
3. Loosen clutch cover attaching bolts alternately.
4. Remove clutch disc and cover assembly.
5. Remove release bearing.
6. Reverse procedure to install.

Model	Year	Clutch Pedal Adjustment: Pedal Height In. (mm)	Clutch Pedal Adjustment: Pedal Freeplay In. (mm)
200SX	1983	6.38–6.77 (162–172)	.04–.20 (1–5)
	1984–85	7.60–7.99 (193–203)	.04–.06 (1–1.5)
	1986–87⑤	7.44–7.83 (189–199)	.04–.12 (1–3)
	1987⑥	7.72–8.11 (196–206)	.04–.12 (1–3)
300ZX	1984–87	7.68–8.07 (195–205	.04–.12 (1–3)
Maxima	1983②	6.09–7.28 (175–185)	.04–.20 (1–5)
	1983–84③	6.69–7.09 (170–180)	.04–.20 (1–5)
	1984②	6.89–7.28 (175–185)	.04–.20 (1–5)
	1985	6.73–7.13 (171–181)	.04–.20 (1–5)
	1986–87	6.73–7.13 (171–181)	.04–.12 (1–3)
Pathfinder	1987⑦	8.94–9.33 (227–237)	.039–.059 (1–1.5)
	1987⑧	9.29–9.69 (236–246)	.039–.059 (1–1.5)
Pickup	1983④	6.54–6.93 (166–176)	.04–.20 (1–5)
	1983①	6.84–7.24 (174–184)	.04–.20 (1–5)
	1984–85	7.05–7.44 (179–189)	.04–.20 (1–5)
	1986	7.05–7.44 (179–189)	.04–.06 (1–1.5)
	1986½–87⑦	8.94–9.33 (227–237)	.039–.059 (1–1.5)
	1986½–87⑧	9.29–9.69 (236–246)	.039–.059 (1–1.5)
Stanza Wagon	1986–87	9.29–9.69 (236–246)	.04–.12 (1–3)

①—Diesel engine.
②—With clutch damper.
③—Less clutch damper.
④—Gasoline engine.
⑤—CA18ET & CA20E engines.
⑥—VG30E engine.
⑦—VG30i engine.
⑧—Z24i engine.

Fig. 11 Clutch pedal height & freeplay specifications. 200SX, 300ZX, Maxima, Pathfinder, Pickup & Stanza Wagon

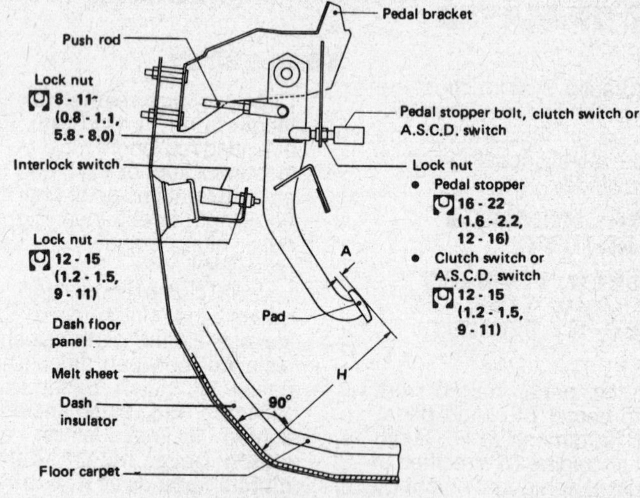

Fig. 13 Clutch pedal free travel & height adjustment. 1986½–87 Pickup & 1987 Pathfinder

TRANSMISSION REPLACE

1983–84 MAXIMA

1. Disconnect battery ground cable.
2. Remove accelerator linkage.
3. Raise and support vehicle.
4. Disconnect front exhaust pipe.
5. Disconnect back-up switch wiring.
6. Disconnect speedometer cable from extension housing.
7. Remove propeller shaft. **Install plug at rear extension housing opening to prevent fluid spillage.**
8. Remove clutch operating cylinder.
9. Support engine with suitable jack.
10. Support transmission with suitable jack.
11. Remove console box.
12. Place selector lever in Neutral, then

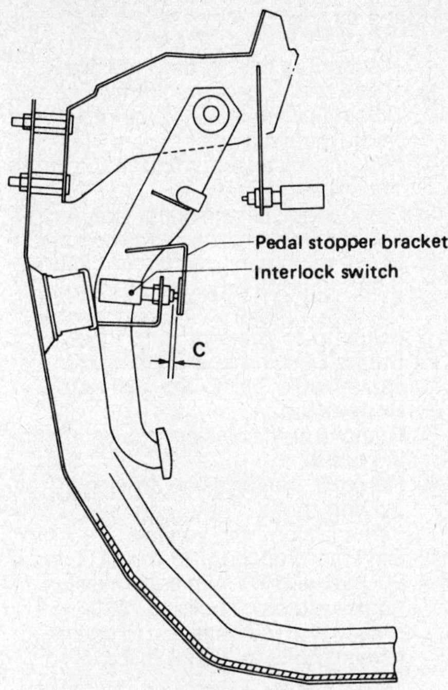

Fig. 14 Clutch interlock switch adjustment. 1986½–1987 Pickup & 1987 Pathfinder & Stanza

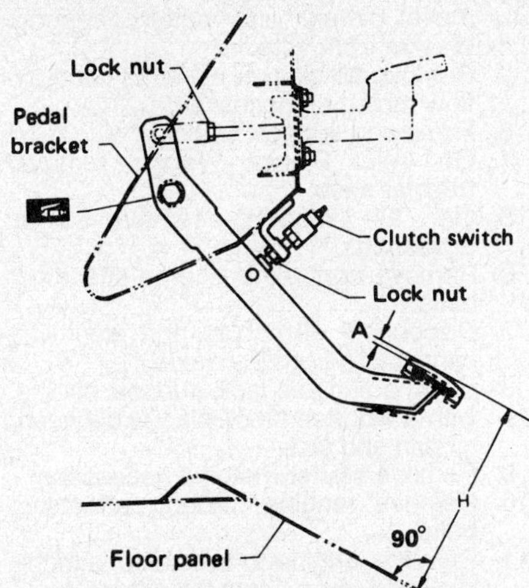

Fig. 15 Clutch pedal free travel & height adjustment. 1987 Van

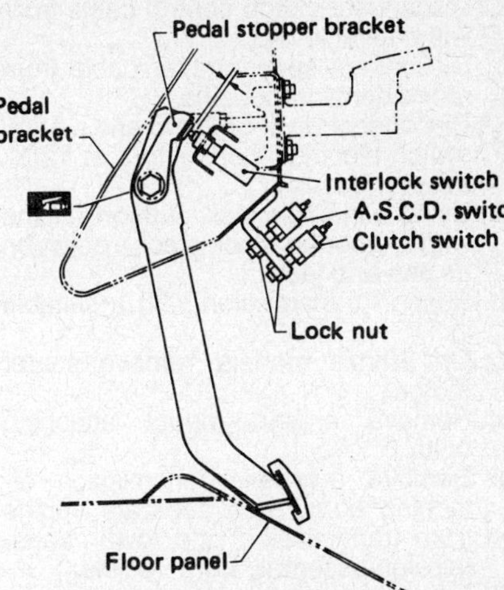

Fig. 16 Clutch interlock switch adjustment. 1987 Van

remove E-ring and selector lever.

13. Remove rear engine mount attaching nuts, crossmember mounting nuts, and exhaust mounting bracket attaching nut.
14. Remove bolts attaching transmission to engine and gusset.
15. Slide transmission rearward and lower from vehicle.
16. Reverse procedure to install.

1983–87 PICKUP & 1987 PATHFINDER

1. Disconnect battery ground cable.
2. On 1983-84 models, disconnect accelerator wire.
3. On all models, raise and support vehicle.
4. On 1985-87 models, disconnect parking brake cable.
5. On vehicles equipped with 4 wheel drive, remove primary propeller shaft.
6. On 2 wheel drive vehicles, remove propeller shaft.
7. On vehicles equipped with 4 wheel drive, remove front propeller shaft.
8. On vehicles equipped with 4 wheel drive, remove front differential carrier crossmember.
9. Disconnect front exhaust pipe.
10. Disconnect wiring of back-up lamp and neutral, top, and overdrive switches as equipped.
11. On 2 wheel drive vehicles, disconnect speedometer cable.
12. Remove clutch operating cylinder.
13. Remove starter motor.
14. Support transmission with suitable jack.
15. Remove console box.
16. Place selector lever in Neutral, then remove F-ring and selector lever.
17. Remove rear engine mount attaching nuts, then remove crossmember.
18. Remove transmission to engine attaching bolts.
19. Slide transmission rearward and lower from vehicle.
20. Reverse procedure to install.

1983–87 200SX & 300ZX

1. Disconnect battery ground cable.
2. Remove accelerator linkage.
3. Raise and support vehicle.
4. On 200SX models, disconnect front exhaust pipe.
5. On 300ZX models, remove front exhaust pipe, catalytic converter and exhaust manifold connecting tube.
6. On all models, disconnect electrical connectors from transmission case.
7. Disconnect speedometer cable from extension housing.
8. Remove propeller shaft. **Install a plug in extension housing rear opening to prevent fluid spillage.**
9. Remove clutch operating cylinder from clutch housing.
10. Using a suitable jack support engine with a wooden block placed between oil pan and jack. **Do not place jack under oil pan drain plug.**
11. Remove console.
12. Place transmission control lever in Neutral, then remove E-ring and control lever.
13. Remove rear engine mount and crossmember attaching bolts.
14. Remove starting motor.
15. Remove bolts attaching transmission to engine, then move transmission rearward and lower from vehicle.
16. Reverse procedure to install.

1983 280ZX

1. Disconnect battery ground cable.
2. Disconnect accelerator linkage.
3. Remove center console.
4. Place shift lever in "Neutral" position.
5. Remove C-ring and shift lever pin from transmission striking rod, then the shift lever.
6. Raise and support vehicle.
7. Disconnect exhaust pipe from exhaust manifold.
8. Remove exhaust pipe bracket from extension housing.
9. Disconnect back-up lamp switch and neutral switch wiring.
10. Remove clutch operating cylinder from transmission case.
11. Disconnect speedometer cable from extension housing.
12. Remove insulator attaching bolts and position insulator on exhaust pipe.
13. Remove propeller shaft.
14. Support engine with a suitable jack.
15. Support transmission with a suitable jack.
16. Remove nut attaching mounting member to rear mounting insulator. Remove mounting member attaching bolts, then the mounting member.
17. Remove starter motor.
18. Remove engine to transmission bolts.
19. Lower and remove transmission from vehicle.
20. Reverse procedure to install.

1983–86 STANZA & 1983–87 PULSAR & SENTRA

1. Disconnect battery cables, then remove battery and battery support bracket from vehicle.
2. Remove radiator reservoir tank, then drain transmission fluid.
3. Raise and support vehicle and remove driveshafts. **When disconnecting driveshafts, use care not to damage oil seals. After disconnecting the driveshafts, insert a suitable bar so that the side gears will not rotate and fall into the differential case.**
4. Remove wheel house protector, then disconnect control and support rods from transmission.
5. On Pulsar NX and Sentra models, remove engine gusset securing bolt and engine mounting.
6. On Stanza models, remove exhaust pipe attaching bolt and nuts, then the engine gusset attaching bolts and transmission protector.

7. Disconnect clutch control cable from withdrawal lever.
8. Disconnect speedometer cable from rear extension housing.
9. Disconnect back-up lamp and neutral switch electrical connectors at transmission case.
10. Using a suitable jack, support engine with a wooden block placed between oil pan and jack.
11. Support transmission with a suitable jack.
12. On Stanza models, remove starter motor.
13. Remove engine mount attaching bolts.
14. Remove engine-to-transmission attaching bolts, then separate engine from transmission and lower transmission assembly from vehicle.
15. Reverse procedure to install.

1985-87 MAXIMA, 1986-87 STANZA WAGON & 1987 STANZA

1. Disconnect battery cables, then remove battery and battery support bracket from vehicle.
2. Remove air cleaner assembly and air flow meter, as necessary.
3. Raise and support vehicle.
4. On 4WD Stanza Wagon, remove transfer case.
5. On all models, remove both driveshafts.
6. Remove front exhaust pipe attaching bolts.
7. Disconnect all cables and electrical connectors from transaxle.
8. Using a suitable jack, support engine with a wooden block placed between oil pan and jack.
9. Remove starter motor, if necessary.
10. Remove engine mount attaching bolts.
11. Remove engine-to-transaxle attaching bolts, then separate engine from transaxle and lower transaxle assembly from vehicle.
12. Reverse procedure to install.

1987 VAN

1. Disconnect battery ground cable.
2. Raise and support vehicle.
3. Disconnect exhaust pipe from exhaust manifold.
4. Disconnect speedometer cable from transmission case.
5. Disconnect all electrical connectors and cables from transmission case.
6. Draw alignment marks on flanges, then separate propeller shaft from final drive. **Plug rear of extension housing to prevent fluid loss.**
7. Support engine and transmission using suitable jacks. **Do not support under oil pan.**
8. Remove transmission mount attaching bolts.
9. Remove transmission to engine attaching bolts, then carefully lower transmission from vehicle.
10. Reverse procedure to install. Torque 60 mm and 65 mm transmission to engine attaching bolts to 29-36 ft. lbs. and 40 mm transmission to engine attaching bolts to 22-29 ft. lbs.

DISC BRAKES SECTION

INDEX

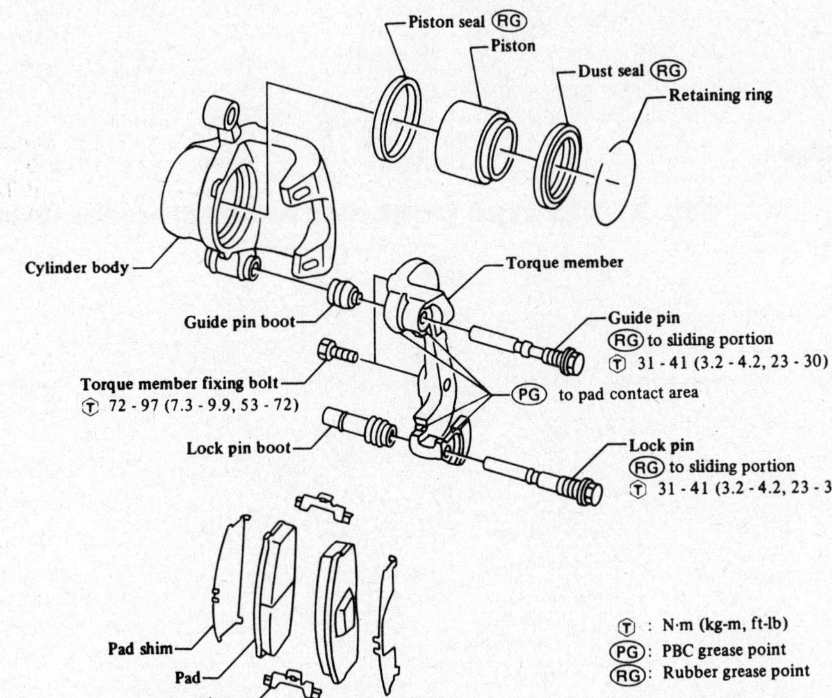

Fig. 1 AD20V type front disc brake disassembled

FRONT DISC BRAKE SERVICE

AD20V & AD22V TYPE

Brake Pad, Replace

1. Raise and support front of vehicle and remove wheel.
2. Remove guide pin, **Figs. 1 and 2,** and pivot caliper body upwards.
3. Remove pad retainers, then the pads.
4. Reverse procedure to install. Install inner pad, then pull cylinder body out and install outer pad.

Caliper, Replace

1. Raise and support front of vehicle and remove wheel.
2. Disconnect brake hose from brake tube.
3. Remove caliper attaching bolts, then the caliper assembly from vehicle.
4. Reverse procedure to install.

Caliper, Overhaul

1. Separate cylinder body and torque member, **Figs. 1 and 2.**
2. Remove brake hose, then press out piston with dust seal and retainer ring.
3. Remove piston seal, guide pin, lock pin, guide pin boot and lock pin boot.
4. Reverse procedure to assemble.

N22 TYPE

Brake Pad, Replace

1. Raise and support front of vehicle and remove wheel.
2. Remove clip, then the pad pins securing anti-squeal springs, **Fig. 3.**
3. Remove brake shoes from caliper.
4. Reverse procedure to install. Push piston into caliper, then install shoes.

Caliper, Replace

1. Remove brake shoes as outlined previously.
2. Disconnect brake line from caliper.
3. Remove caliper attachments, **Fig. 3.**
4. Remove caliper from vehicle.
5. Reverse procedure to install.

Caliper Overhaul

1. Remove gripper pin attaching nuts.
2. Separate yoke and caliper body.
3. Remove yoke holder from piston.
4. Remove retaining rings and dust seals from both pistons, **Fig. 3.**
5. To remove pistons, apply compressed air to fluid port.
6. Remove piston seals.
7. Remove gripper, if necessary.
8. Reverse procedure to assemble.

AD18B, AD18V & CL18B TYPE

Brake Pad, Replace

1. Raise and support front of vehicle and remove wheel.
2. Remove lock pin, **Figs. 4, 5 and 6,** and pivot caliper body upwards.
3. Remove pad retainers, then the pads.
4. Reverse procedure to install. Install inner pad, then pull cylinder body out and install outer pad.

Caliper, Replace

1. Raise and support front of vehicle and remove wheel.
2. Disconnect brake hose from brake tube.
3. Remove caliper attaching bolts, then the caliper assembly from vehicle.
4. Reverse procedure to install.

Caliper Overhaul

1. Separate cylinder body and torque member, **Figs. 4, 5 and 6.**
2. Remove brake hose, then press out piston with dust seal and retainer ring.
3. Remove piston seal, guide pin and lock pin from torque member.
4. Reverse procedure to assemble.

CL22V & CL28V TYPE

Brake Pad, Replace

1. Raise and support front of vehicle and remove wheel.
2. Remove lower pin bolt, **Fig. 7,** and pivot caliper body upwards.
3. Remove pad retainers, inner and outer shims, and detach brake pads from torque member.
4. Install new inner pad and pivot caliper downward.

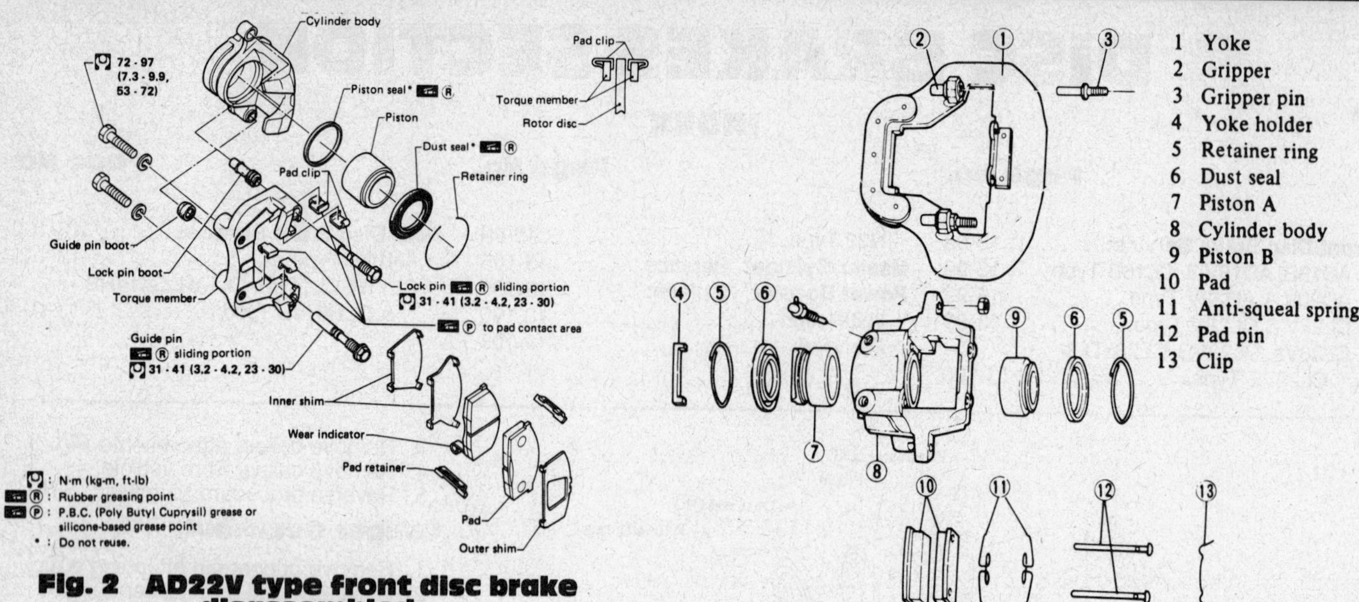

Fig. 2 AD22V type front disc brake disassembled

Fig. 3 N22 type front disc brake disassembled

5. Compress piston by inserting bar through caliper opening and prying against torque member.
6. Pivot caliper upwards, install outer pad and inner and outer shims, and install pad retainers.
7. Position caliper body and install lower pin bolt.

Caliper, Replace

1. Raise and support front of vehicle and remove wheel.
2. Disconnect brake hose from brake tube.
3. Remove caliper as an assembly from spindle.
4. To install, reverse procedure.

Caliper Overhaul

1. Remove pin bolts and separate cylinder body from torque member, **Fig. 7.**
2. Remove pad retainers, shims and brake pads.
3. Feed compressed air gradually into caliper port and force out pistons with dust seals.
4. Remove piston seals, sub pins, main pins and dust seals, **Fig. 7.**
5. To assemble, reverse procedure.

CL28VA, CL28VB, CL28VD & CL28VE TYPE

Brake Pad, Replace

1. Raise and support front of vehicle and remove wheel.
2. Remove brake hose lock spring and lower pin bolt, **Figs. 8, 9 and 10,** then pivot caliper body upwards.
3. Remove pad retainers, inner and outer shims and the pads.
4. Install new inner pad and pivot caliper downward.
5. Compress piston(s) by inserting bar through caliper opening and prying against torque member.
6. Pivot caliper upwards, then install outer pad, inner and outer shims and pad retainers.
7. Position caliper body and install lower pin.

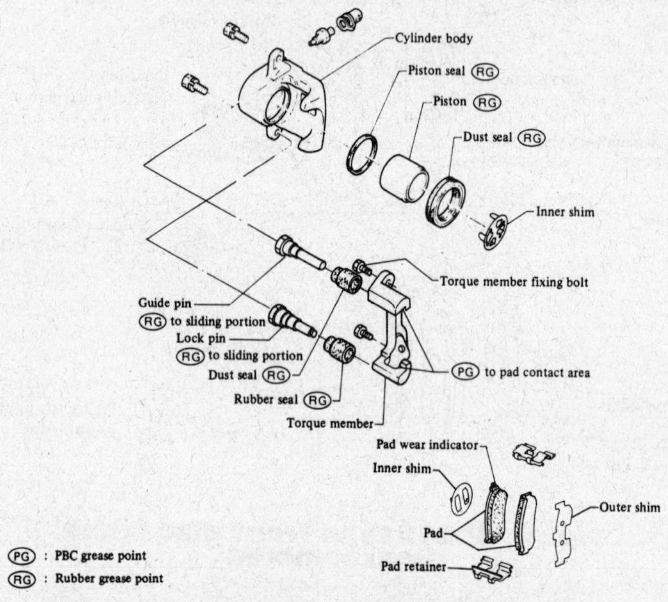

Fig. 4 CL18B type front disc brake disassembled

Caliper, Replace

1. Raise and support front of vehicle and remove wheel.
2. Disconnect brake hose from brake tube.
3. Remove caliper assembly from spindle.
4. Reverse procedure to install.

Caliper Overhaul

1. Remove pin bolts and separate cylinder body from torque member, **Figs. 8, 9 and 10.**
2. Remove dust cover, then gradually feed air pressure into caliper port to force piston(s) out.
3. Remove piston seal(s), pads and pad retainers.
4. Reverse procedure to assemble.

REAR DISC BRAKE SERVICE

AN12H TYPE

Brake Pad, Replace

1. Raise and support rear of vehicle and remove wheels.
2. Remove clip pad retainer pins, and anti-squeal springs, **Fig. 11.**
3. Remove pads from caliper assembly.
4. To install new pads, bring piston and yoke into position by turning outer piston clockwise until it retracts into caliper body, **Fig. 12.**
5. Move yoke with lever until clearance to install inner and outer pads are equal.
6. Install pads, making sure tab on back of pad is aligned with groove in piston.

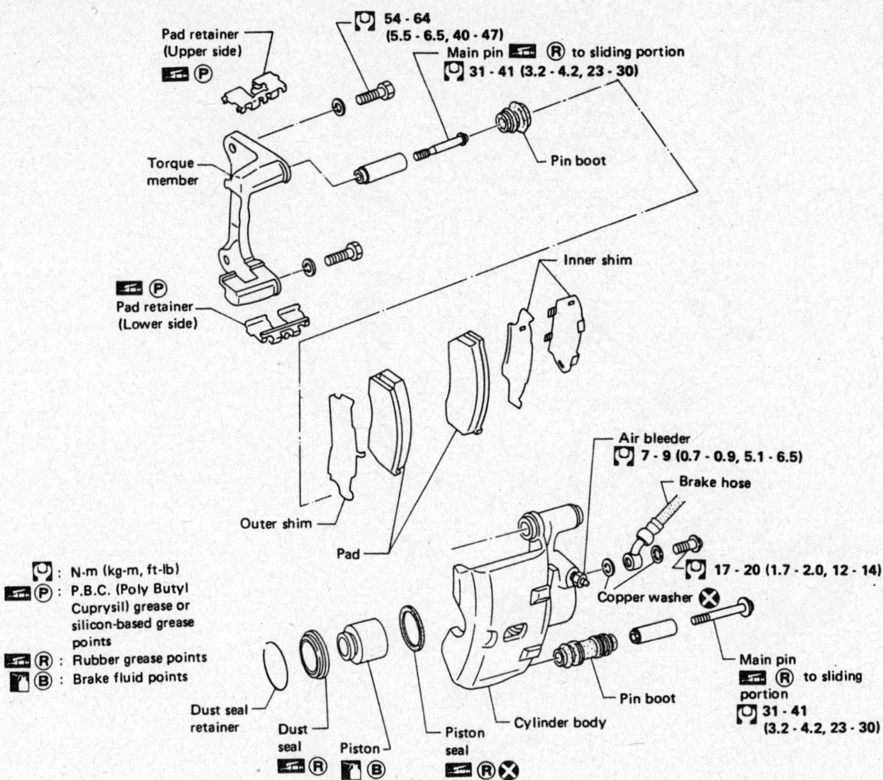

Fig. 5 AD18B type front disc brake disassembled

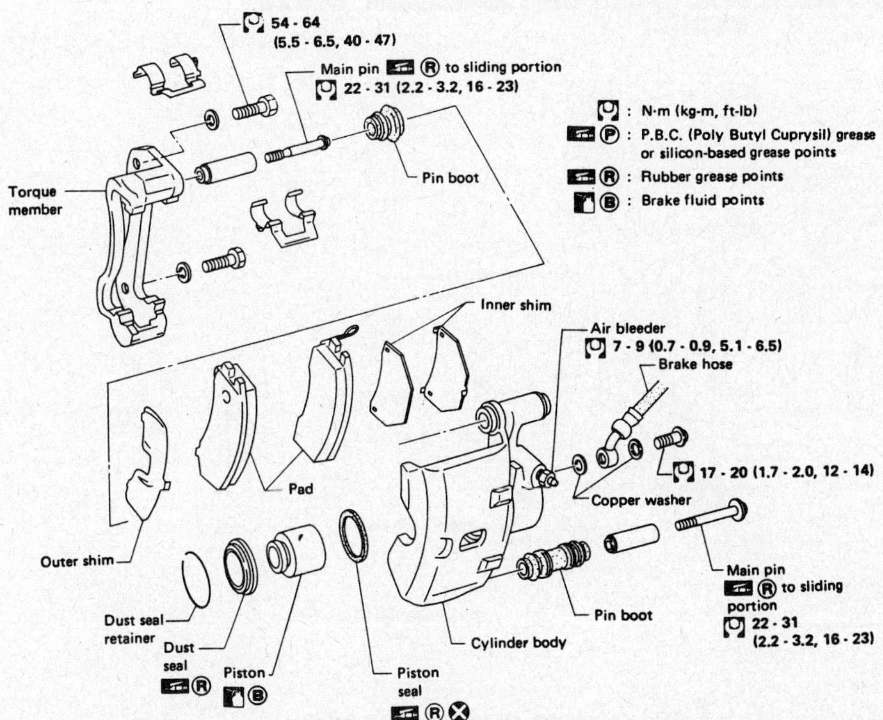

Fig. 6 AD18V type front disc brake disassembled

7. Install anti-squeal springs, pad retainer pins, and clip.

Caliper, Replace

1. Disconnect brake tube and hand brake cable from caliper assembly.
2. Remove caliper mounting bolts and remove caliper.
3. To install, reverse procedure.

Caliper Overhaul

1. Remove brake pads as outlined under "Brake Pad, Replace."
2. Stand yoke on work bench and push cylinder body down to separate from yoke.
3. Remove retaining rings and dust seals from bend of both pistons, **Fig. 11.**
4. Push in on outer piston to drive out piston assembly.
5. Remove piston seals from housing, remove yoke spring from yoke, and separate inner and outer pistons by turning outer piston counterclockwise.
6. Disassemble outer piston as follows:
   a. Remove snap ring B, **Fig. 11.**
   b. Disassemble adjusting nut, ball bearing, spacers, and wave washers.
7. Disassemble inner piston as follows:
   a. Remove snap ring A, **Fig. 11** and remove spring cover, spring, and spring seat.
   b. Remove snap ring C, **Fig. 11,** and remove key plate, push rod, and strut.
   c. Hold hand brake lever in a vise and remove return spring and nut.
   d. Remove hand brake lever, dust seal, and cam.
8. To assemble, reverse disassembly.

CL11H, CL11HB, CL14H, CL14HB & CL14HVB TYPE

Brake Pad, Replace

1. Raise and support rear of vehicle and remove wheel.
2. Disconnect parking brake cable and remove spring retainer, if necessary.
3. Remove pin bolts, **Figs. 13 and 14.**
4. Remove pad springs, pads and pad shim.
5. Reverse procedure to install. Turn piston clockwise to retract it into cylinder body.

Caliper, Replace

1. Disconnect parking brake cable and brake hose.
2. Remove caliper attaching bolts, then the caliper from vehicle.
3. Reverse procedure to install.

Caliper, Overhaul

1. Remove outer spring retainer, if equipped.
2. Remove pin bolts, then separate cylinder body and torque member.
3. Remove piston by rotating it counterclockwise with suitable pliers.
4. Remove ring, adjusting nut, ball bearing, wave washer, spacers and cup from piston, as required.
5. Pry ring A, **Figs. 13 and 14,** off of cyl-

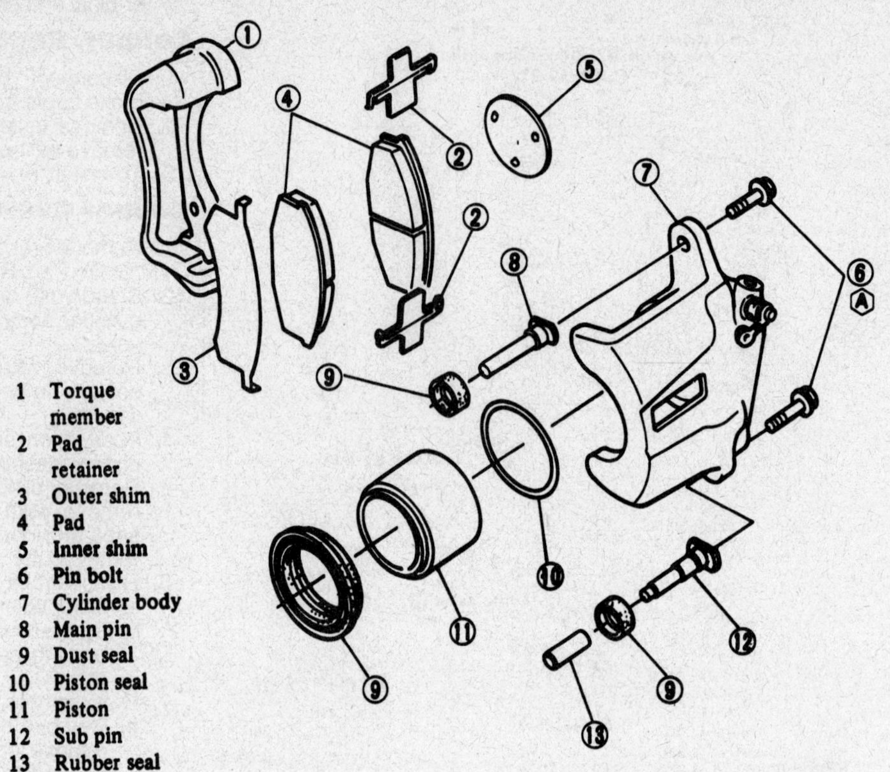

Tightening torque N·m (kg-m, ft-lb)

Ⓐ : 22 - 31 (2.2 - 3.2, 16 - 23)

Fig. 7 CL28V type front disc brake disassembled, CL22V similar

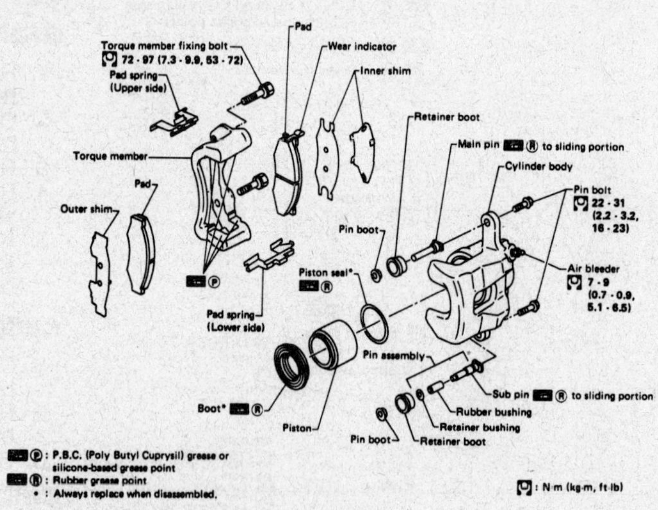

Fig. 8 CL28VB type front disc brake disassembled, CL28VA similar

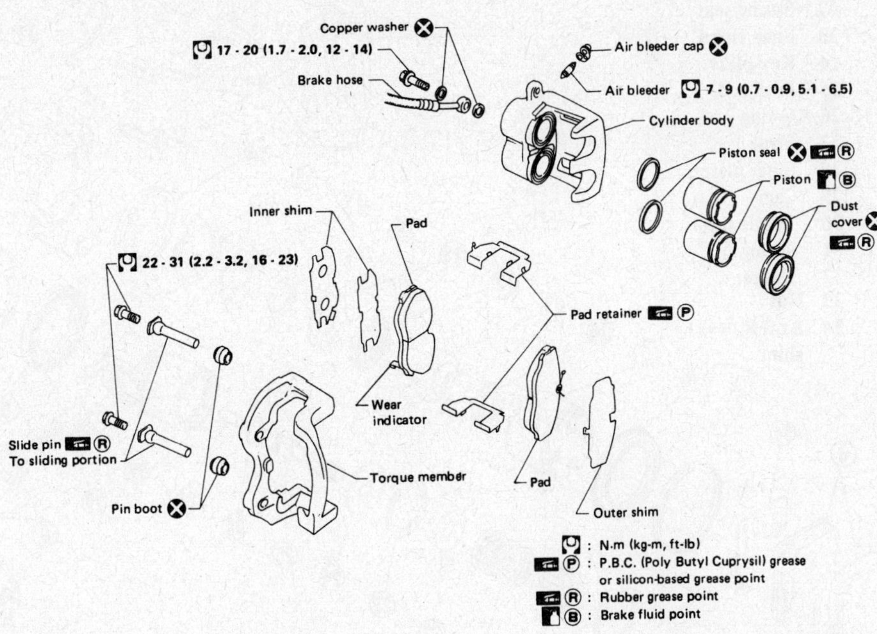

Fig. 9 CL28VE type front disc brake disassembled

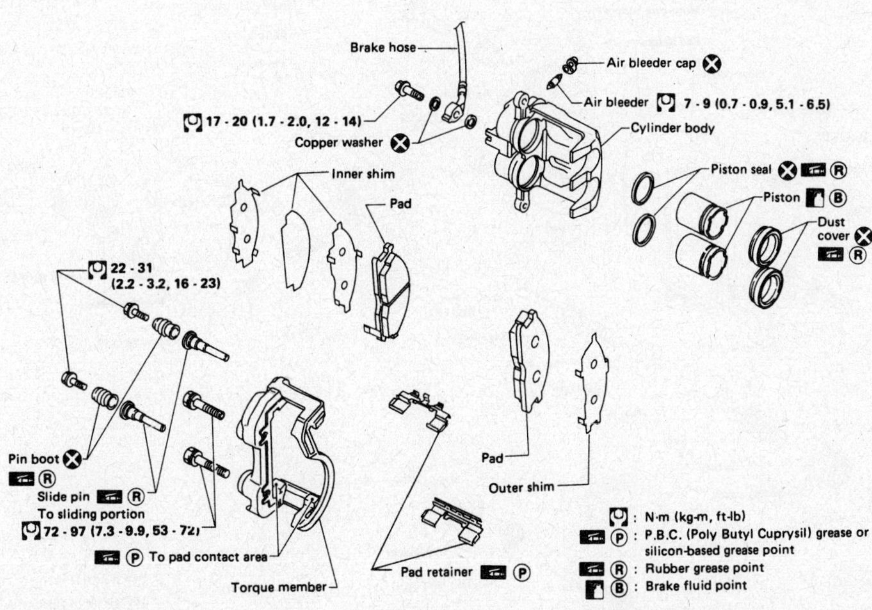

Fig. 10 CL28VD type front disc brake disassembled

1 Yoke
2 Yoke spring
3 Clip
4 Pad pin
5 Anti-squeal spring
6 Pad
7 Retaining ring
8 Dust seal
9 Outer piston
10 Oil seal
11 Adjusting nut
12 Bearing
13 Spacer
14 Wave washer
15 Snap ring B
16 Piston seal
17 Cylinder body
18 Retainer
19 Snap ring A
20 Spring cover
21 Spring
22 Spring seat
23 Snap ring C
24 Key plate
25 Push rod
26 O-ring
27 Strut
28 Inner piston
29 Cam
30 Toggle lever
31 Spring
32 Washer
33 Nut
34 Anti-squeal shim

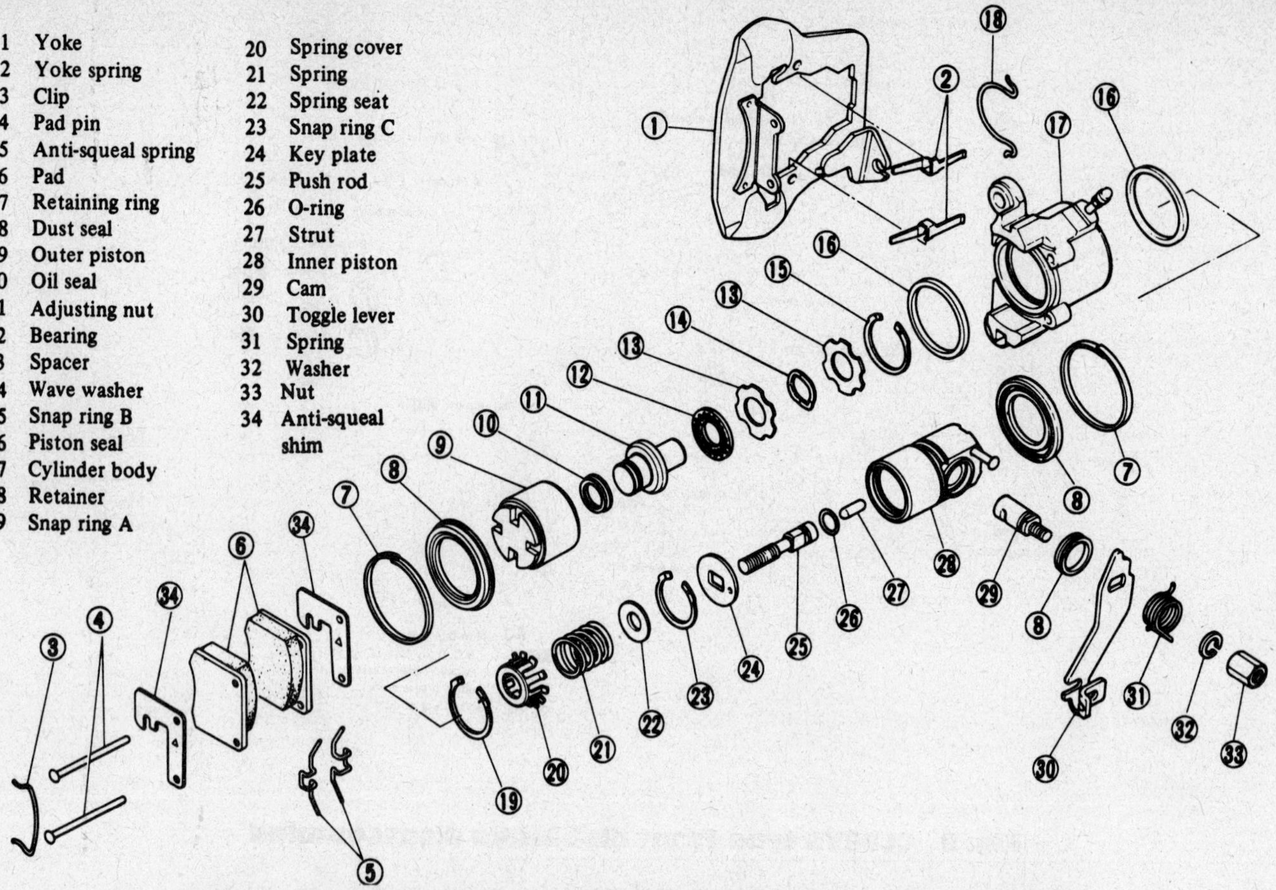

Fig. 11 AN12H type rear disc brake disassembled (Typical)

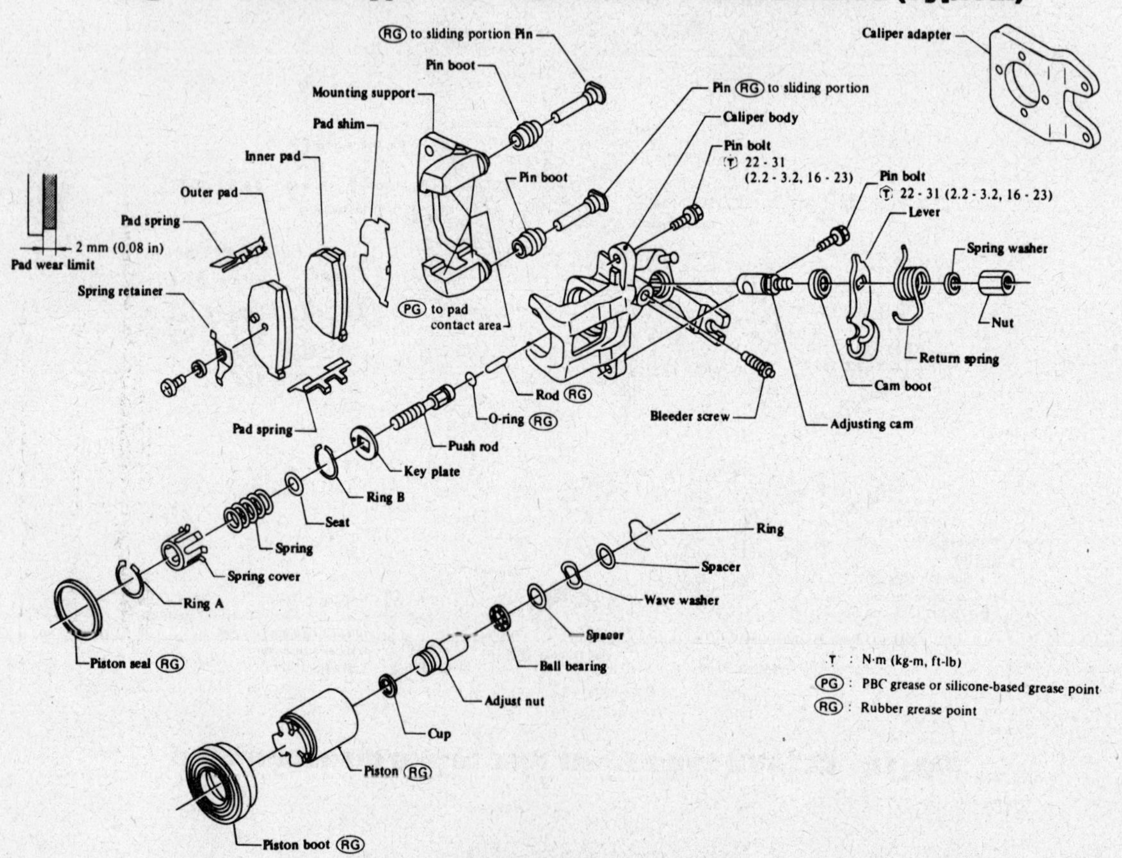

Fig. 13 CL11H, CL11HB, CL14H & CL14HB type rear disc brake disassembled

inder body, then remove spring cover, spring and seat.

6. Pry ring B off of cylinder body, then remove key plate, push rod and rod.
7. Remove O-ring from push rod, then pry piston seal out of cylinder body.
8. Remove return spring, nut, spring washer and lever, then adjusting cam and cam boot.
9. Remove pins and pin boots.
10. Reverse procedure to assemble.

MASTER CYLINDER

REPLACE

1. Disconnect brake lines from master cylinder. Plug lines and master cylinder ports.
2. Remove master cylinder retaining nuts and the master cylinder.
3. Reverse procedure to install.

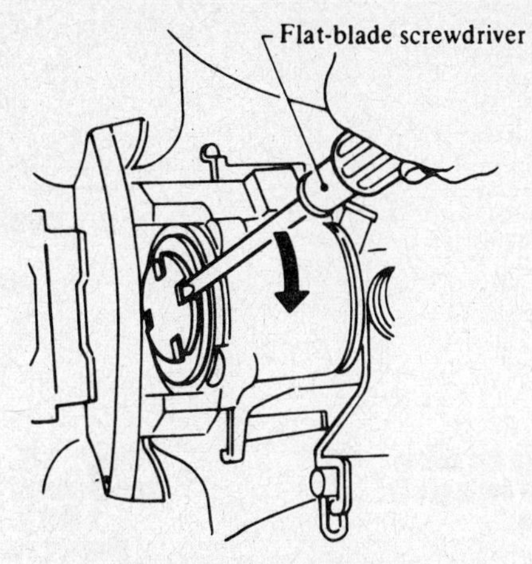

Fig. 12 Piston adjustment during rear brake pad replacement

POWER BOOSTER

REPLACE

REMOVAL

1. Remove master cylinder as previously described.
2. Disconnect brake booster at brake pedal.
3. Disconnect check valve hose at power booster.
4. Disconnect vacuum hose(s), if equipped.
5. Remove booster attaching bolts and/or nuts and the booster.

INSTALLATION

1983 280ZX & Pickup

1. Adjust output rod length A, **Figs. 15 and 16,** to specifications, **Fig. 17.** If required adjustment exceeds .02 inch on Pickup models, replace booster.

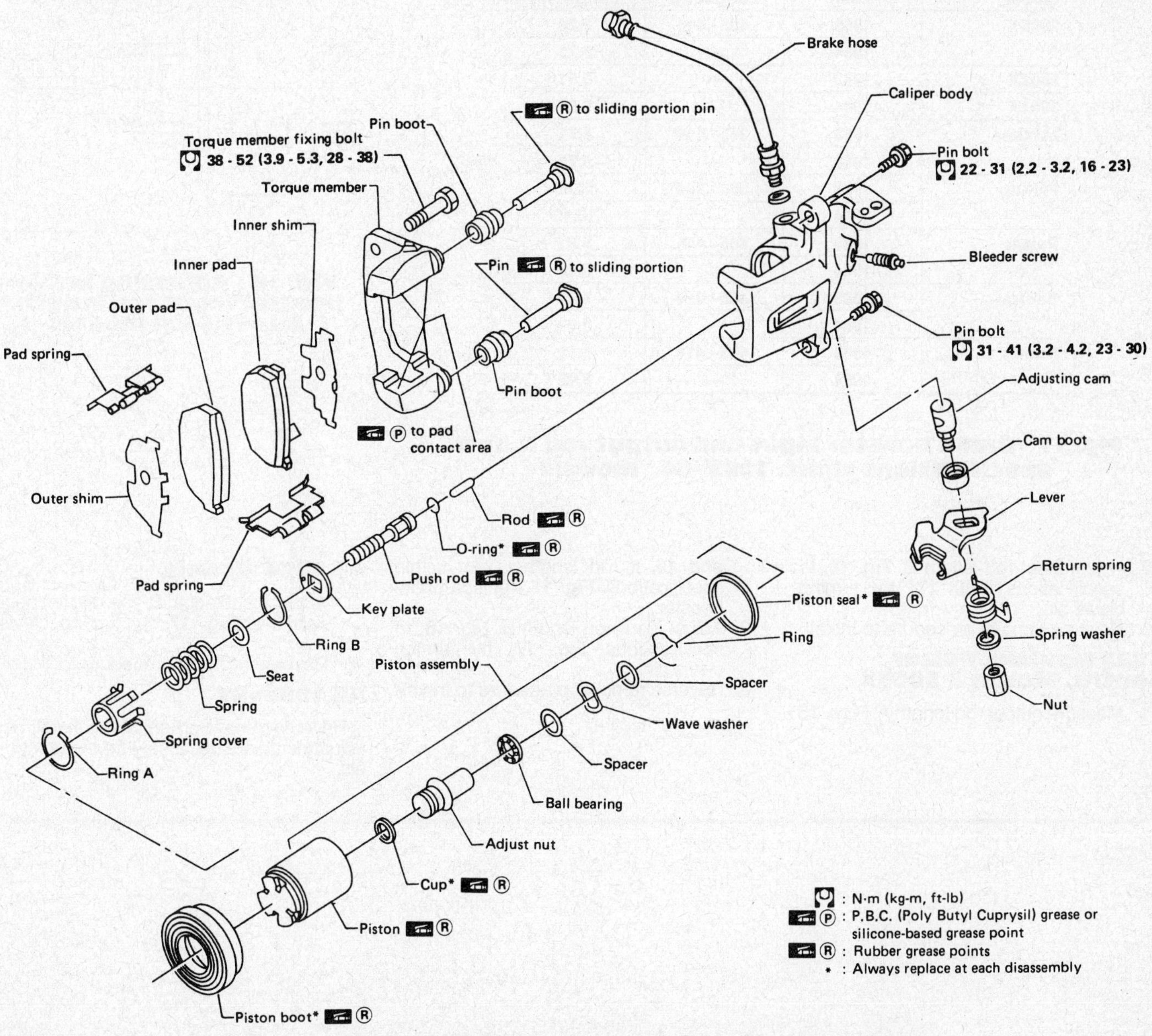

Brake hose
Caliper body
(R) to sliding portion pin
Pin boot
Torque member fixing bolt
38 - 52 (3.9 - 5.3, 28 - 38)
Pin bolt
22 - 31 (2.2 - 3.2, 16 - 23)
Torque member
Inner shim
Bleeder screw
Inner pad
Pin (R) to sliding portion
Outer pad
Pin bolt
31 - 41 (3.2 - 4.2, 23 - 30)
Pad spring
Pin boot
Adjusting cam
(P) to pad contact area
Cam boot
Outer shim
Lever
Rod (R)
O-ring* (R)
Push rod (R)
Return spring
Pad spring
Key plate
Piston seal* (R)
Ring B
Ring
Spring washer
Seat
Piston assembly
Spacer
Nut
Spring
Wave washer
Spring cover
Spacer
Ring A
Ball bearing
Adjust nut
Cup* (R)
Piston (R)
Piston boot* (R)

: N·m (kg-m, ft-lb)
(P) : P.B.C. (Poly Butyl Cuprysil) grease or silicone-based grease point
(R) : Rubber grease points
* : Always replace at each disassembly

Fig. 14 CL14HVB type rear disc brake disassembled

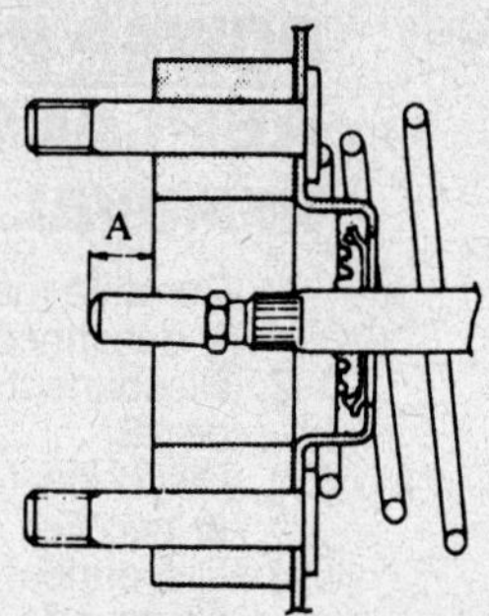

Fig. 15 Measuring brake booster output rod length. 1983 Pickup

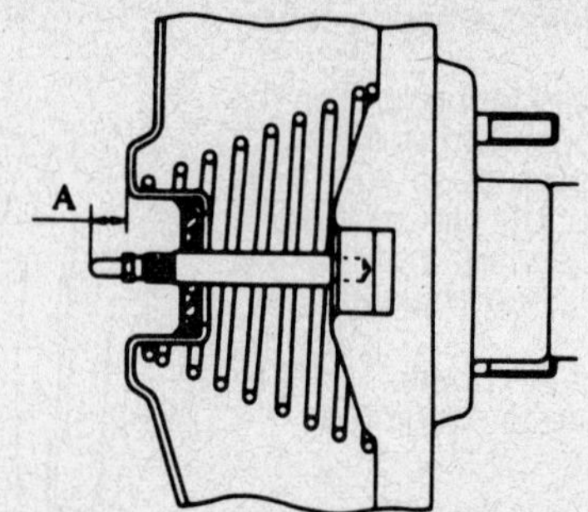

Fig. 16 Measuring brake booster output rod length. 1983 Maxima, Pulsar, Sentra, Stanza, 200SX & 280ZX & All 1985–86 models

Model	Year	Output Rod Length In.	Input Rod Length In.
200SX	1983	.405–.414	5.24
	1984	—	5.71
280ZX	1983	—	5.51
300ZX	1984	—	5.51
Maxima	1983	.365–.414	5.71
	1984	—	5.71
Pickup	1983	.384–.394	10.83
	1984	—	10.10
Pulsar	1983	.405–.414	5.91
	1984	—	5.91
Sentra	1983	.405–.414	5.91
	1984	—	5.91
Stanza	1983	.405–.414	5.12
	1984	—	5.12

Fig. 17 Brake booster input and output rod length specifications chart. 1983–84 models

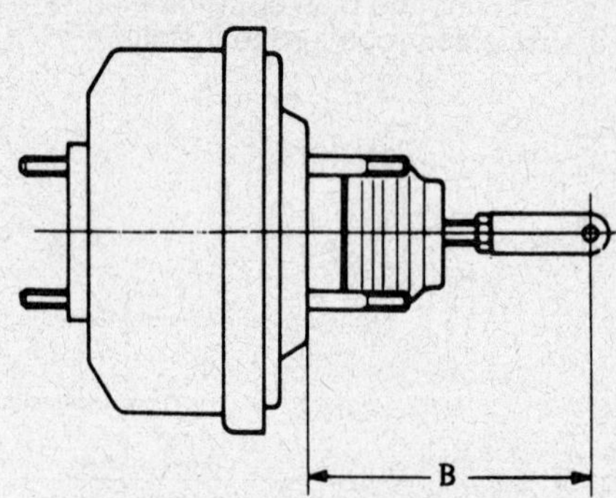

Fig. 18 Adjusting brake booster input rod length. All 1983–84 models

2. Adjust input rod length B, **Fig. 18,** to specifications, **Fig. 17,** by turning clevis pin.
3. Reverse remove procedure to install.

1983 Maxima, Pulsar, Sentra, Stanza & 200SX

1. Measure output rod length A, **Figs. 15 and 16.** If rod length is not within specifications, **Fig. 17,** replace brake booster.
2. Adjust input rod length B, **Fig. 18,** to specifications, **Fig. 17,** by turning clevis pin.
3. Reverse removal procedure to install.

All 1984 Models

1. Adjust input length B, **Fig. 18,** to specifications, **Fig. 17,** by turning clevis pin.
2. Reverse removal procedure to install.

All 1985–87

Reverse remove procedure to install. No adjustments are necessary on these models.

DRUM BRAKES SECTION

INDEX

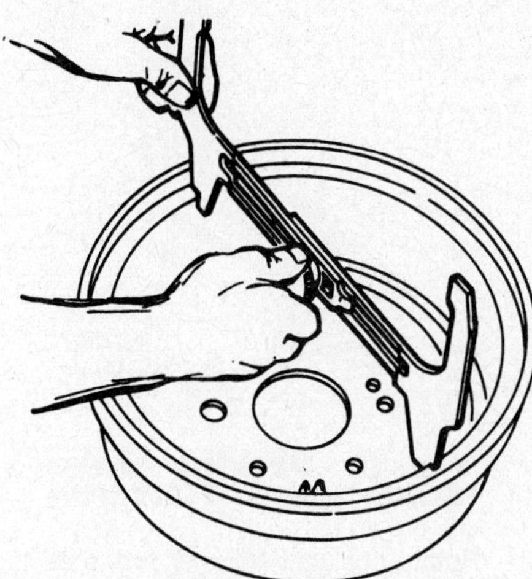

Fig. 1 Measuring brake drum inside diameter

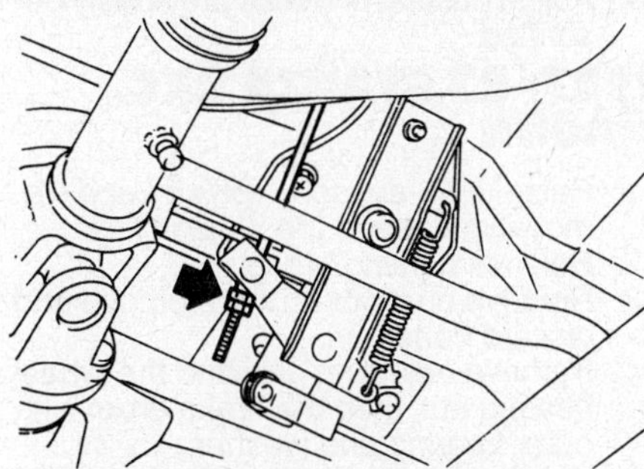

Fig. 4 Parking brake adjustment. 1986–87 Stanza 4WD Wagon

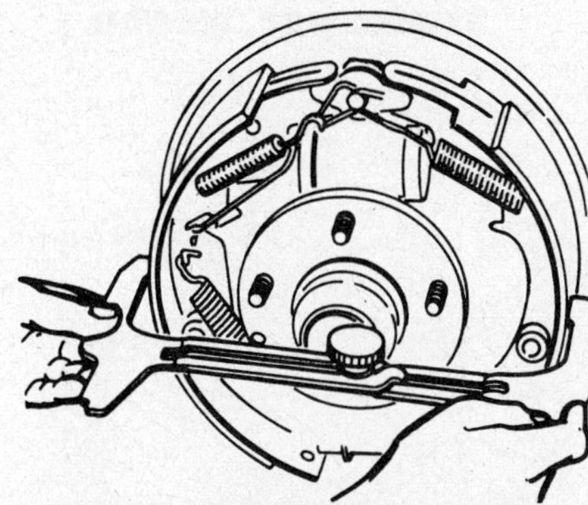

Fig. 2 Adjusting brake shoes to brake drum inside diameter

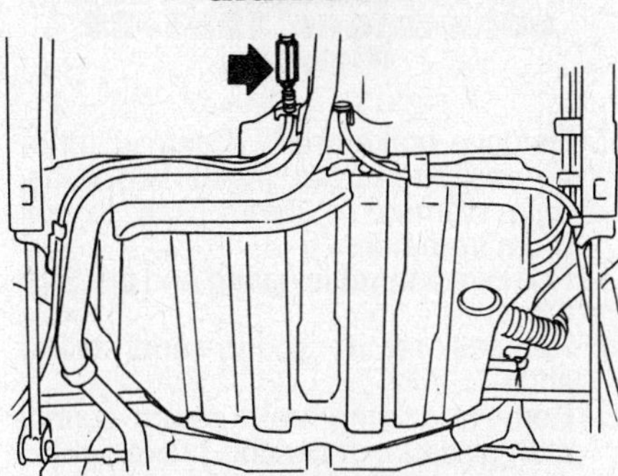

Fig. 5 Parking brake adjustment. 1985–86 Maxima

Fig. 3 Parking brake adjustment. 1983 200SX, 1983–84 Maxima, 1986–87 Stanza 2WD Wagon, 1986½–87 Pickup & 1987 Pathfinder

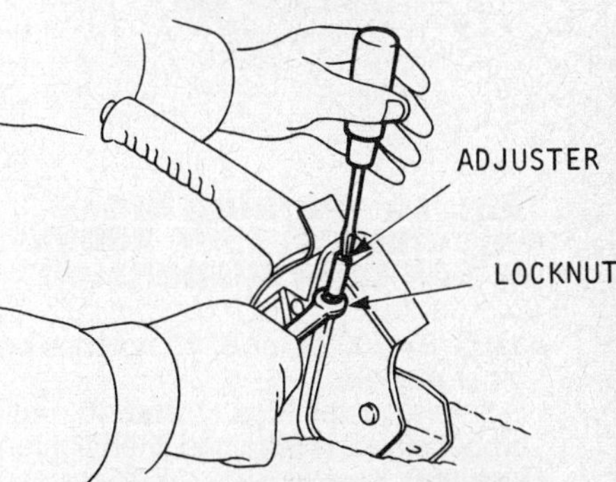

Fig. 6 Parking brake adjustment. 1987 Maxima, Pulsar, Sentra & Stanza exc. Wagon

BRAKE ADJUSTMENTS

280ZX and 300ZX models, 1983 and 1985-87 200SX models and some 1983-87 Maxima models are equipped with four wheel disc brakes, therefore, no adjustments are necessary on these models.

Models equipped with drum brakes have self-adjusting shoe mechanisms that ensure correct lining-to-drum clearance through actuation of the parking brake. Although the brakes are self-adjusting, an initial adjustment is necessary after the brake shoes have been replaced.

To perform adjustment, measure brake drum inside diameter using a suitable brake drum-to-shoe gauge, Fig. 1. Adjust brake shoes to dimension obtained on outside of gauge, Fig. 2.

PARKING BRAKE ADJUST

1983 200SX, 1983–87 MAXIMA & 1986–87 STANZA WAGON

1. Pull parking brake lever with a force of 44 lbs. and ensure lever travels 7-9 notches on 1983 Maxima, 11-17 notches on 1986-87 2WD Stanza Wagon, 8-9 notches on 1986-87 4WD Stanza Wagon, 11-13 notches on 1987 Maxima, or 7-8 notches on other models.
2. Rotate adjuster, **Figs. 3, 4, 5 and 6** until proper stroke is obtained, then tighten lock nut.

SENTRA, PULSAR & STANZA EXC. WAGON

1. Pull parking brake lever with a force of 44 lbs. and ensure lever travels 6-7 notches on 1983-86 Sentra and Pulsar, 7-8 notches on 1983-86 Stanza, 7-11 notches on 1987 Pulsar or 11-13 notches on 1987 Sentra and Stanza.
2. Rotate adjuster, **Figs. 6, 7 and 8** until proper stroke is obtained, then tighten lock nut.

280ZX

1. Pull parking brake lever with a force of 44 lbs. and ensure lever travels 4-6 notches.
2. Rotate adjusting nut, **Fig. 9,** until proper stroke is obtained, then tighten lock nut.

1984–87 200SX & 300ZX

1. Pull parking brake lever with a force of 44 lbs. and ensure lever travels exactly 8 notches on 1984 200SX models with drum brakes, 7-8 notches on

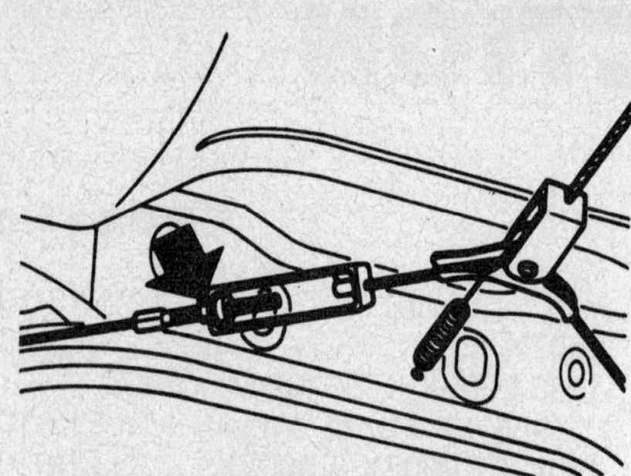

Fig. 7 Parking brake adjustment. 1983–86 Sentra & Pulsar (300ZX & 1984–87 200SX w/independent suspension similar)

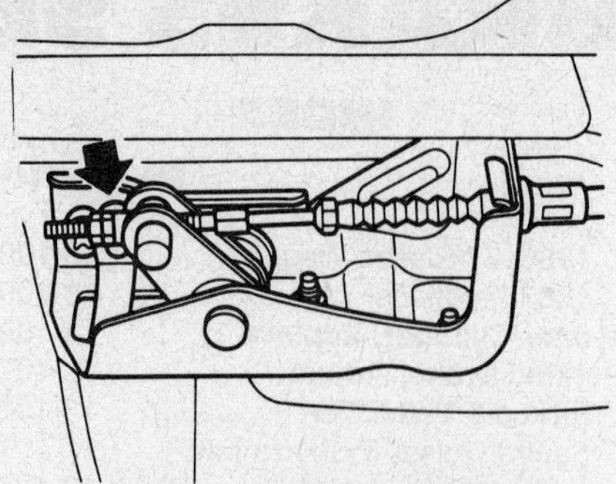

Fig. 8 Parking brake adjustment. 1983–86 Stanza exc. Wagon

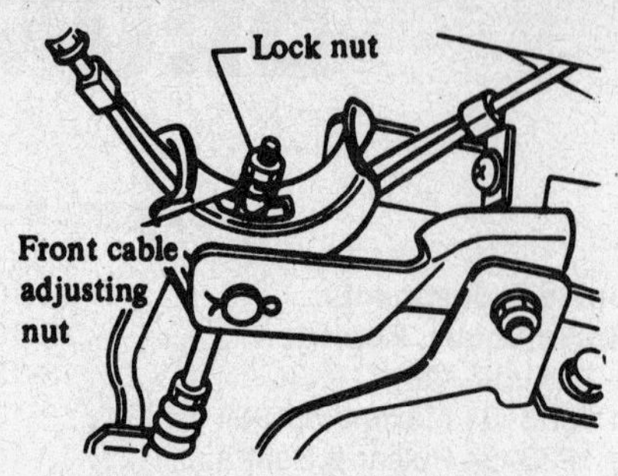

Fig. 9 Parking brake adjustment. 280ZX

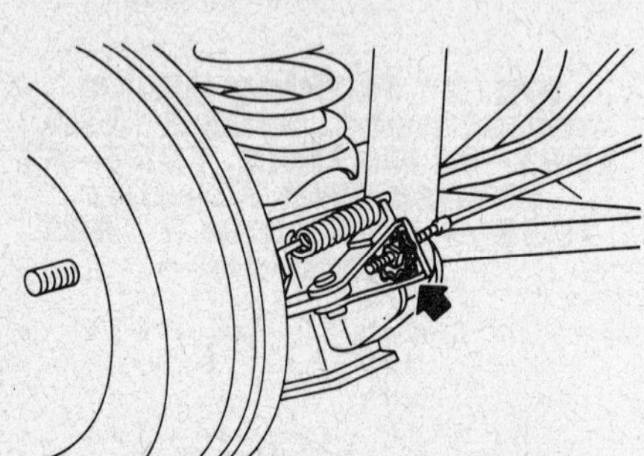

Fig. 10 Parking brake adjustment. 1984 200SX w/link type suspension

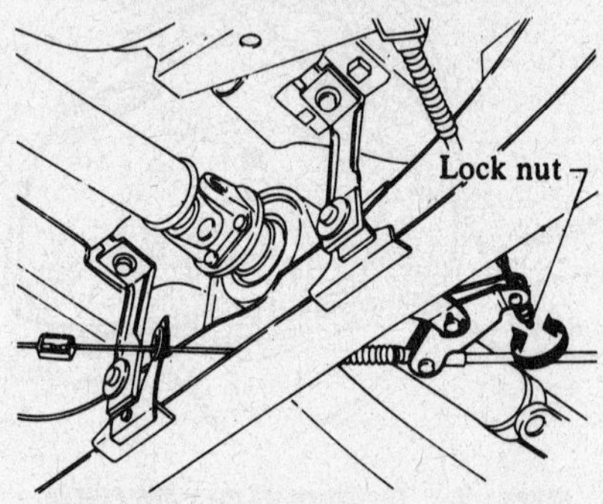

Fig. 11 Parking brake adjustment. 1983–86 Pickup

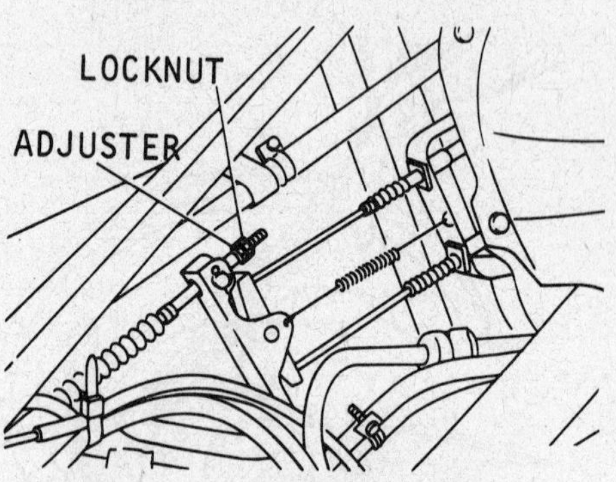

Fig. 12 Parking brake adjustment. 1987 Van

1985-87 200SX, or 8-10 notches on other models.

2. Rotate adjuster, **Figs. 7 and 10,** until proper stroke is obtained, then tighten lock nut.

PICKUP & PATHFINDER

1. Pull parking brake lever with a force of 44 lbs. and ensure lever travels 6-10 notches on 1983 Pickup, 13-16 notches on 1984-86 Pickup, 10-12 notches on 1986½-87 Pickup less 4WD, 9-11 notches on 1986½-87 Pickup w/4WD or 7-9 notches on 1987 Pathfinder.
2. Rotate adjuster, **Figs. 3 and 11,** until proper stroke is obtained, then tighten locknut.

VAN

1. Pull parking brake lever with a force of 44 lbs. and ensure lever travels 5-7 notches.
2. Loosen locknut, then rotate adjuster nut, **Fig. 12,** until proper stroke is obtained.
3. Tighten locknut.

BRAKE SHOES REPLACE

1983–84 MAXIMA & 1984 200SX

1. Raise and support vehicle and remove wheel and tire assemblies.
2. Remove brake drum. If drum cannot be easily removed, install two bolts, 8mm diameter, 1.25mm pitch, to pull drum from hub.
3. Remove anti-rattle spring and pin, **Fig. 13.**
4. Remove return spring and brake shoe.
5. Remove parking brake return spring, then disconnect parking brake cable.
6. Remove adjuster assembly.
7. Apply suitable lubricant to lubricating points, **Fig. 13.**
8. Reverse procedure to install.
9. Adjust brakes by operating hand brake lever several times.

1983–84 PULSAR & SENTRA

1. Raise and support vehicle and remove wheel and tire assemblies.
2. Release parking brake.
3. Remove dust cover, then remove and discard cotter pin.
4. Remove adjusting cap and the wheel bearing nut, then the brake drum with outer bearing and washer.
5. Remove anti-rattle spring and pin, **Fig. 14.**
6. Remove retainer, then the return spring and brake shoes.
7. Remove rear cable adjusting nut.
8. Remove adjuster assembly.
9. Remove toggle lever spring and clip, then separate toggle lever and shoe.
10. Apply suitable lubricant to lubricating points, **Fig. 14.**
11. Rotate nut until adjuster rod is at its shortest point.
12. Reverse procedure to install.
13. Adjust brakes by operating parking brake several times.
14. Adjust parking brake as previously described.

1983–87 STANZA EXC. WAGON

1. Raise and support vehicle and remove wheel and tire assemblies.
2. Release parking brake.
3. Remove dust cover, then remove and discard cotter pin.
4. Remove adjusting cap and the wheel bearing nut, then the brake drum with outer bearing and washer.
5. Remove anti-rattle spring and pin, **Figs. 15 and 16.**
6. Remove return springs and brake shoes.
7. Remove clevis pin and disconnect parking brake cable.
8. Remove adjuster assembly.
9. Apply suitable lubricant to lubricating points, **Figs. 15 and 16.**
10. Rotate nut until adjuster rod is at its shortest length.
11. Reverse procedure to install.
12. Adjust brakes by applying hand brake several times.
13. Adjust parking brake as previously described.

PICKUP & VAN

1983 Pickup

1. Raise and support vehicle and remove wheel and tire assemblies.
2. Remove drum. If drum is difficult to re-

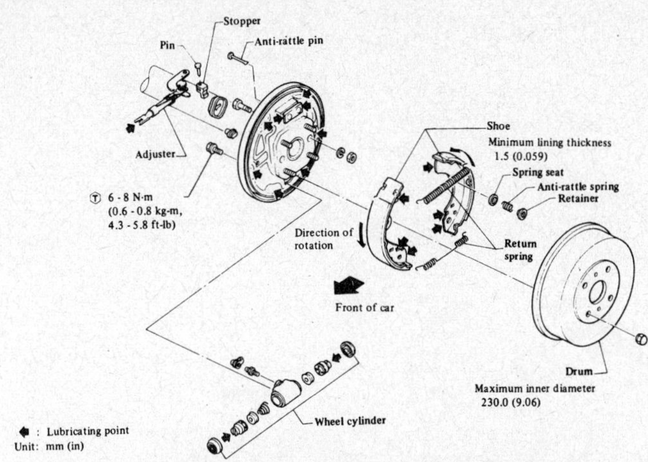

Fig. 13 Exploded view of drum brakes. 1983–84 Maxima (1984 200SX similar)

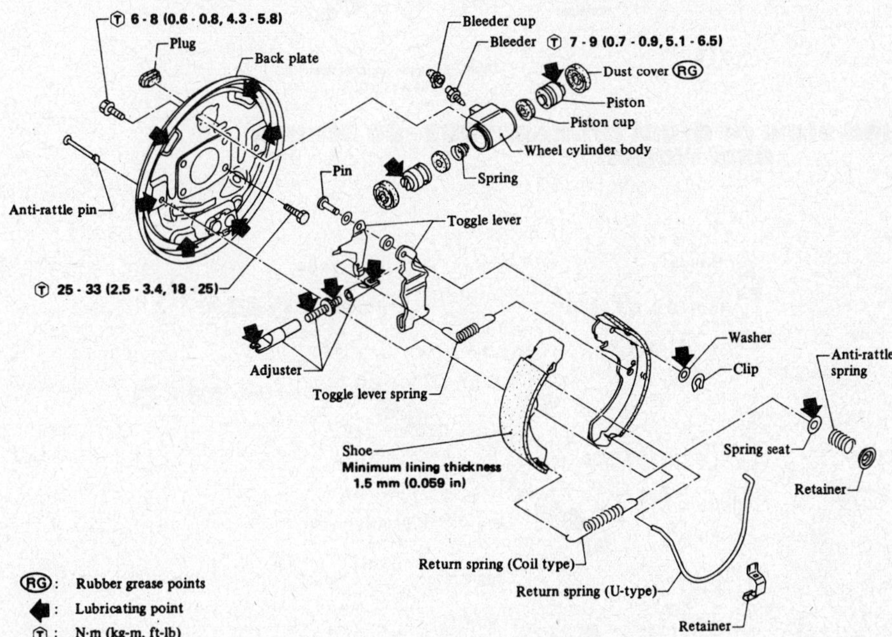

Fig. 14 Exploded view of drum brakes. 1983–84 Pulsar & Sentra

move, screw in bolt to pull drum out.

3. Remove anti-rattle spring and pin, **Fig. 17.**
4. Remove two lower return springs, open brake shoes outward and remove upper return spring, then remove extension link.
5. Remove shoe assemblies.
6. Separate secondary shoe from toggle lever by removing pin.
7. If necessary, remove rubber boot, adjuster shim, lock plate and adjuster springs, then the adjuster assembly.
8. Reverse procedure to install, noting the following:
   a. Apply suitable lubricant to adjuster housing bore, adjuster wheel and adjuster screw.
   b. Apply suitable lubricant to sliding surfaces of backing plate, adjuster and return spring.
   c. Apply suitable lubricant to brake shoe installing grooves of adjuster and wheel assembly, extension link installing grooves, lower surface of spring seat and contact surfaces between brake disc and brake shoe assembly.
9. Adjust brakes as previously described.

All 1984–86 Pickup & 1986½–87 2WD Pickup Heavy Duty & Cab & Chassis Models

1. Raise and support vehicle and remove wheel and tire assemblies.
2. Remove brake drum. If drum is difficult to remove, screw in bolt to pull drum out.
3. Remove anti-rattle spring and pin, **Fig. 18.**
4. Remove lower return spring, open brake shoes outward and remove two upper return springs, then remove extension link.
5. Remove shoe assemblies.
6. Separate secondary shoe from toggle lever by removing pin.
7. Apply suitable lubricant to lubricating points, **Fig. 18.**
8. Reverse procedure to install.

1987 Van & 1986½–87 2WD Pickup Exc. Heavy Duty, Cab & Chassis Models

When replacing rear brake shoes, refer to **Fig. 16.**

1986½–1987 4WD Pickup

When replacing rear brake shoes, refer to **Fig. 19.**

1985–87 PULSAR & SENTRA

1. Raise and support vehicle and remove wheel and tire assemblies.
2. Release parking brake.
3. Remove dust cap, then remove and discard cotter pin.
4. Take out adjusting cap and wheel bearing nut.
5. Remove brake drum with outer bearing and washer.
6. Remove parking brake rear cable.
7. Remove anti-rattle spring and pin, **Fig. 20.**
8. Remove retainer, then the return springs and brake shoes.
9. Separate equalizer and rear cable.
10. Remove adjuster assembly.
11. Remove toggle lever spring and clip, then separate toggle lever and shoe.
12. Apply suitable lubricant to lubricating points,**Fig. 20.**
13. Reverse procedure to install.
14. Adjust brakes by apply parking brake several times.
15. Adjust parking brake.

1986–87 STANZA WAGON

When replacing rear brake shoes, refer to **Fig. 21.**

1987 PATHFINDER

When replacing rear brake shoes, refer to **Fig. 22.**

MASTER CYLINDER REPLACE

Refer to "Disc Brakes Section" for "Master Cylinder, Replace" procedure.

POWER BOOSTER REPLACE

Refer to "Disc Brakes Section" for "Power Booster, Replace" procedure.

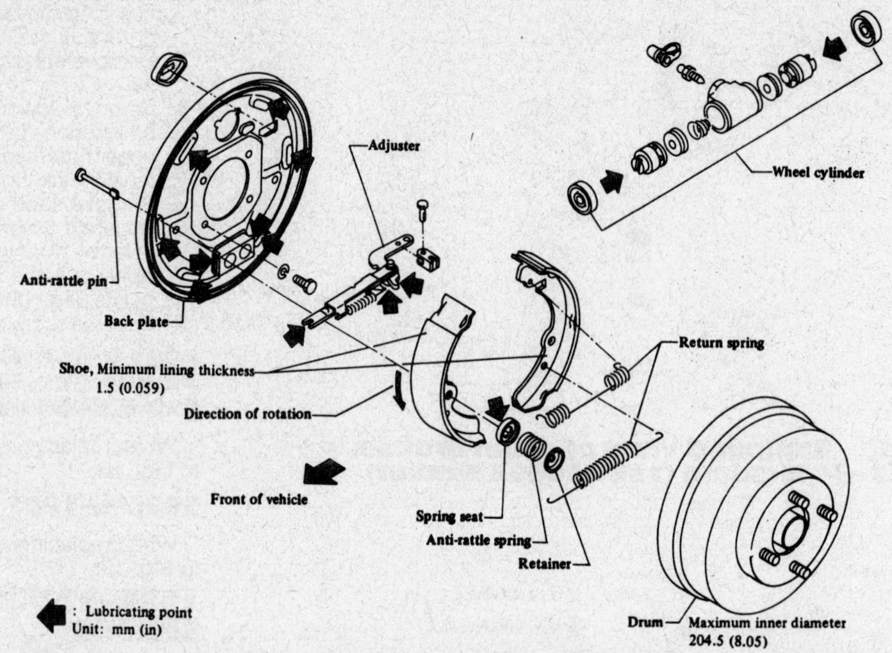

Fig. 15 Exploded view of drum brakes. 1983–86 Stanza exc. Wagon

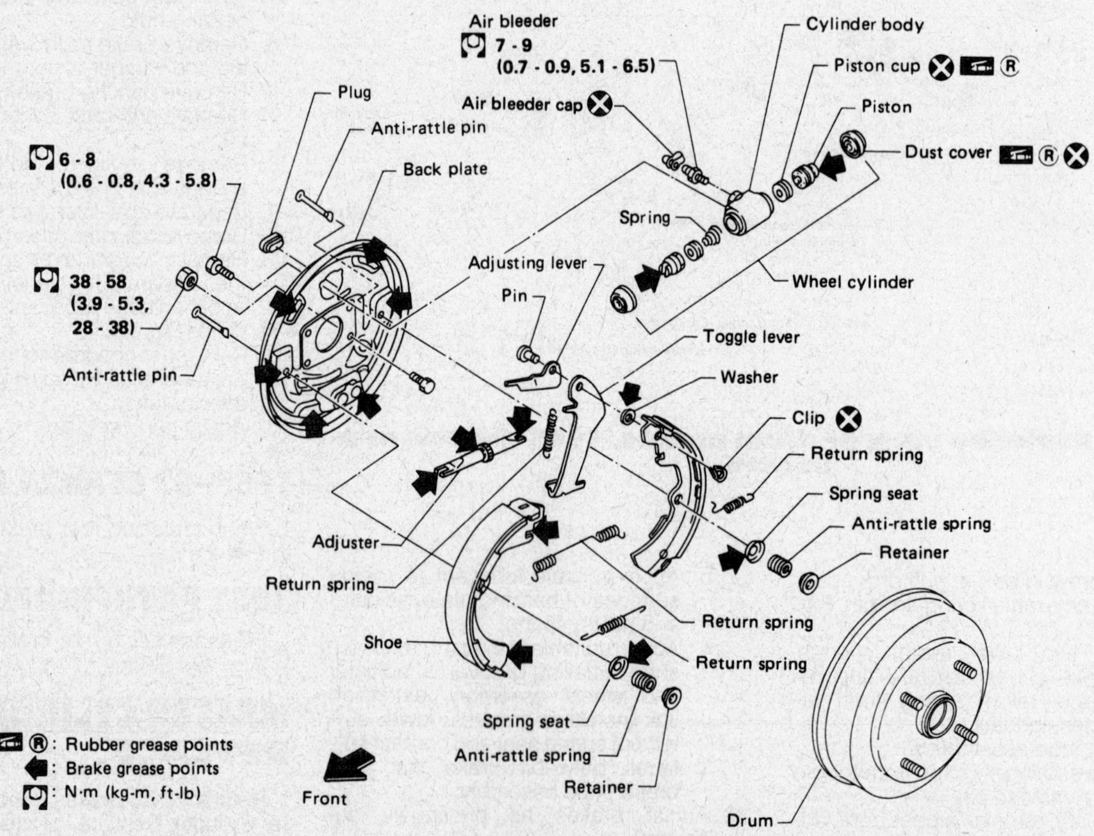

Fig. 16 Exploded view of drum brakes. 1987 Van & Stanza exc. Wagon & 1986½–87 2WD Pickup Exc. Heavy Duty, Cab & Chassis Models

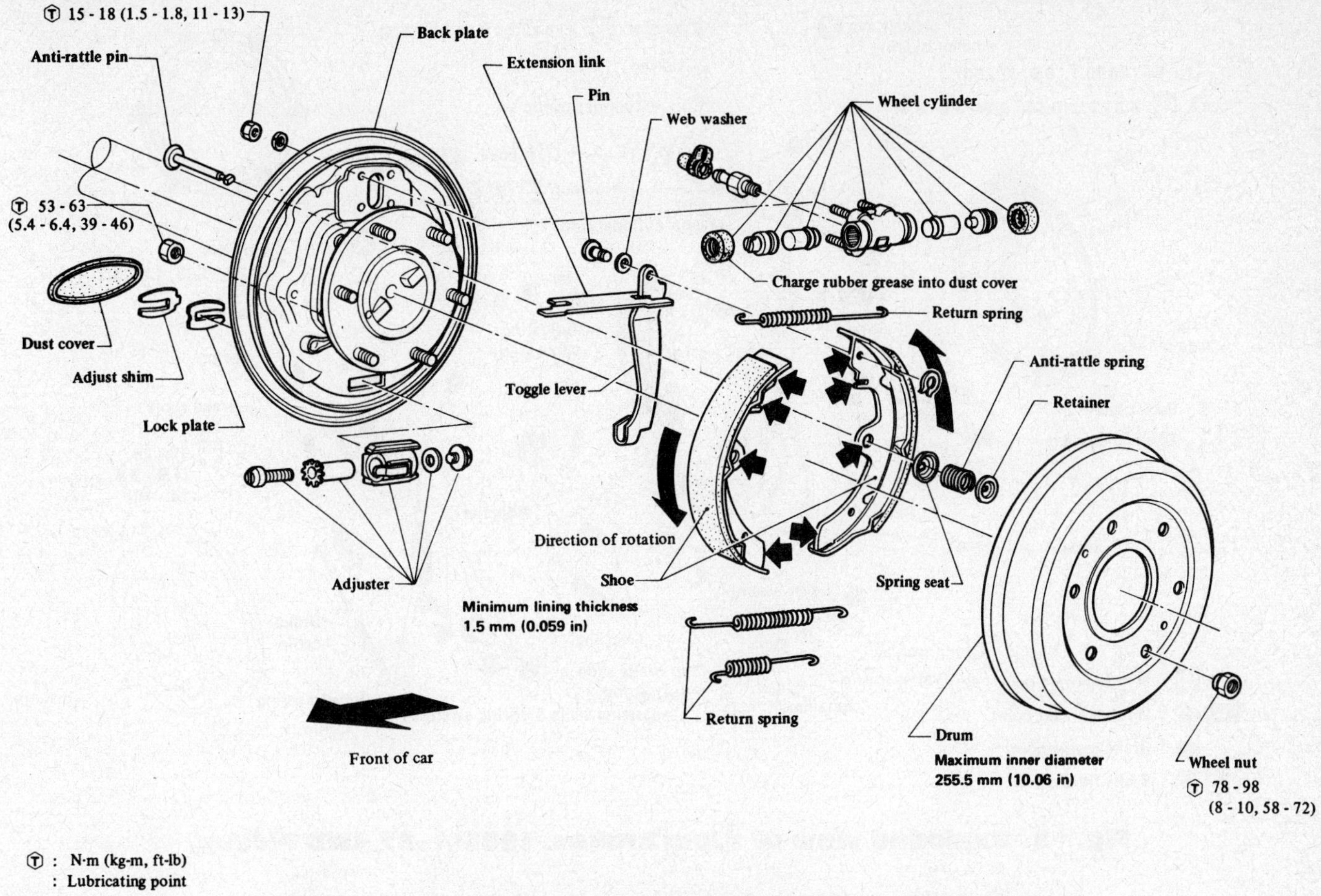

Ⓣ 15 - 18 (1.5 - 1.8, 11 - 13)
Back plate
Anti-rattle pin
Extension link
Pin
Web washer
Wheel cylinder
Ⓣ 53 - 63
(5.4 - 6.4, 39 - 46)
Charge rubber grease into dust cover
Return spring
Dust cover
Adjust shim
Anti-rattle spring
Toggle lever
Retainer
Lock plate
Direction of rotation
Adjuster
Shoe
Spring seat
Minimum lining thickness
1.5 mm (0.059 in)
Return spring
Drum
Front of car
Maximum inner diameter
255.5 mm (10.06 in)
Wheel nut
Ⓣ 78 - 98
(8 - 10, 58 - 72)

Ⓣ : N·m (kg-m, ft-lb)
: Lubricating point

Fig. 17 Exploded view of drum brakes. 1983 Pickup

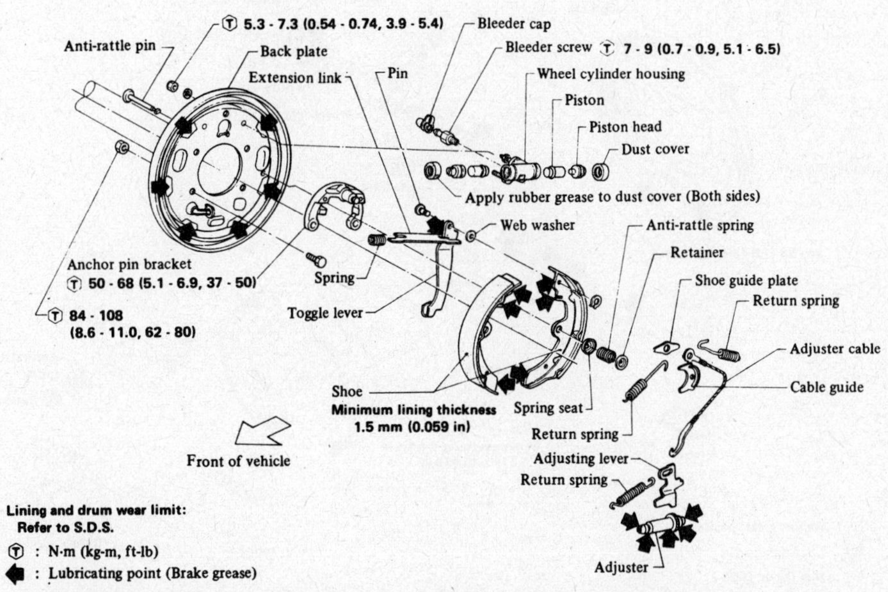

Fig. 18 Exploded view of drum brakes. All 1984–86 Pickup & 1986½–87 2WD Pickup Heavy Duty & Cab & Chassis Models

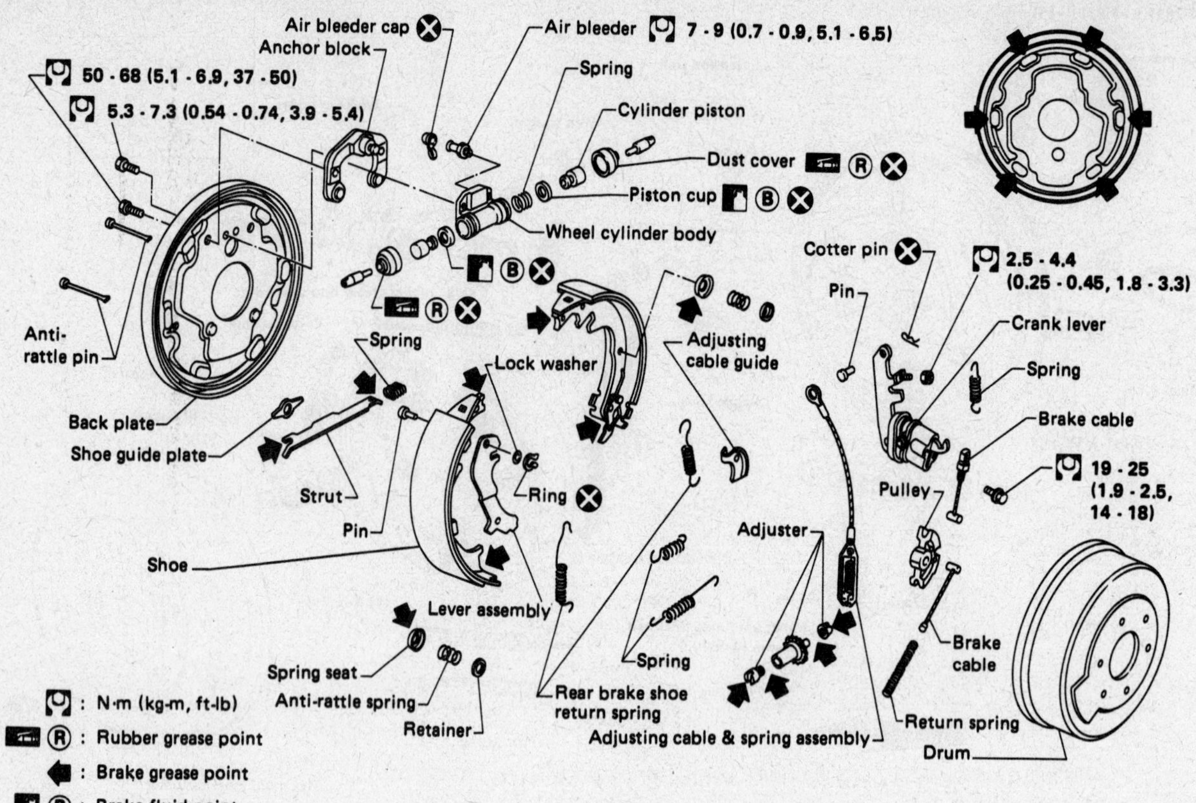

Fig. 19 Exploded view of drum brakes. 1986½–87 4WD Pickup

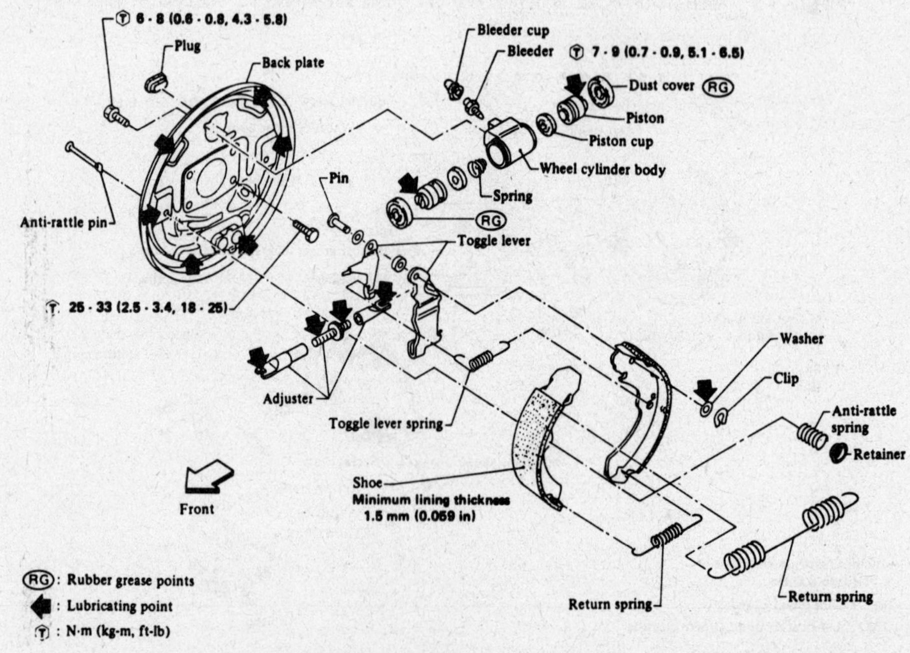

Fig. 20 Exploded view of drum brakes. 1985–87 Pulsar & Sentra

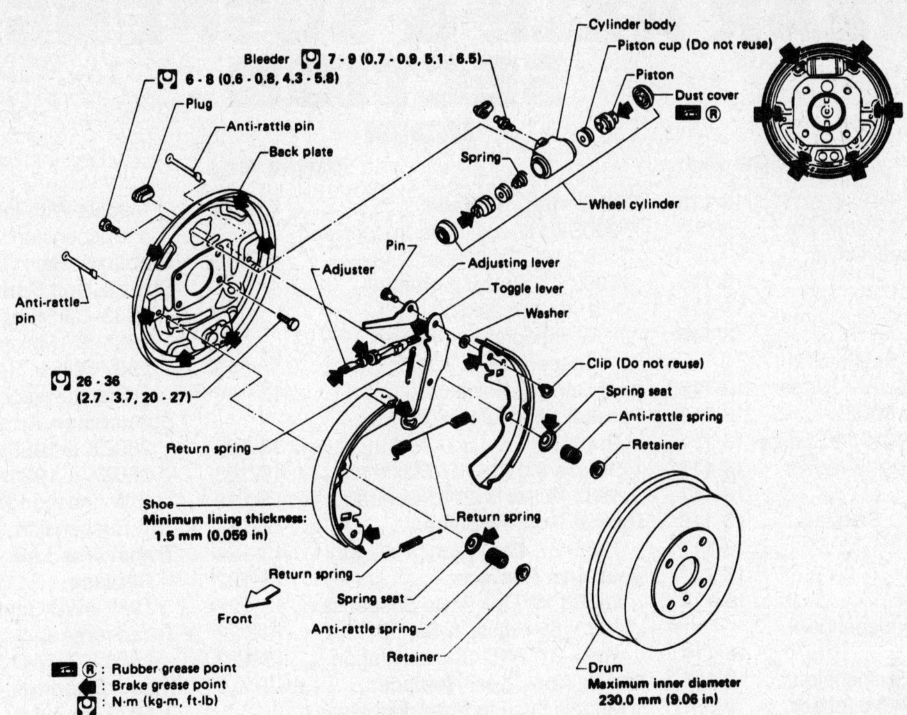
Cylinder body
Piston cup (Do not reuse)
Bleeder 7 - 9 (0.7 - 0.9, 5.1 - 6.5)
6 - 8 (0.6 - 0.8, 4.3 - 5.8)
Piston
Dust cover
Plug
Anti-rattle pin
Back plate
Spring
Wheel cylinder
Pin
Adjusting lever
Adjuster
Toggle lever
Washer
Anti-rattle pin
26 - 36 (2.7 - 3.7, 20 - 27)
Clip (Do not reuse)
Spring seat
Anti-rattle spring
Retainer
Return spring
Shoe
Minimum lining thickness: 1.5 mm (0.059 in)
Return spring
Return spring
Spring seat
Front
Anti-rattle spring
Retainer
Drum
Maximum inner diameter 230.0 mm (9.06 in)
Ⓡ : Rubber grease point
: Brake grease point
: N·m (kg-m, ft-lb)

Fig. 21 Exploded view of drum brakes. 1986–87 Stanza Wagon

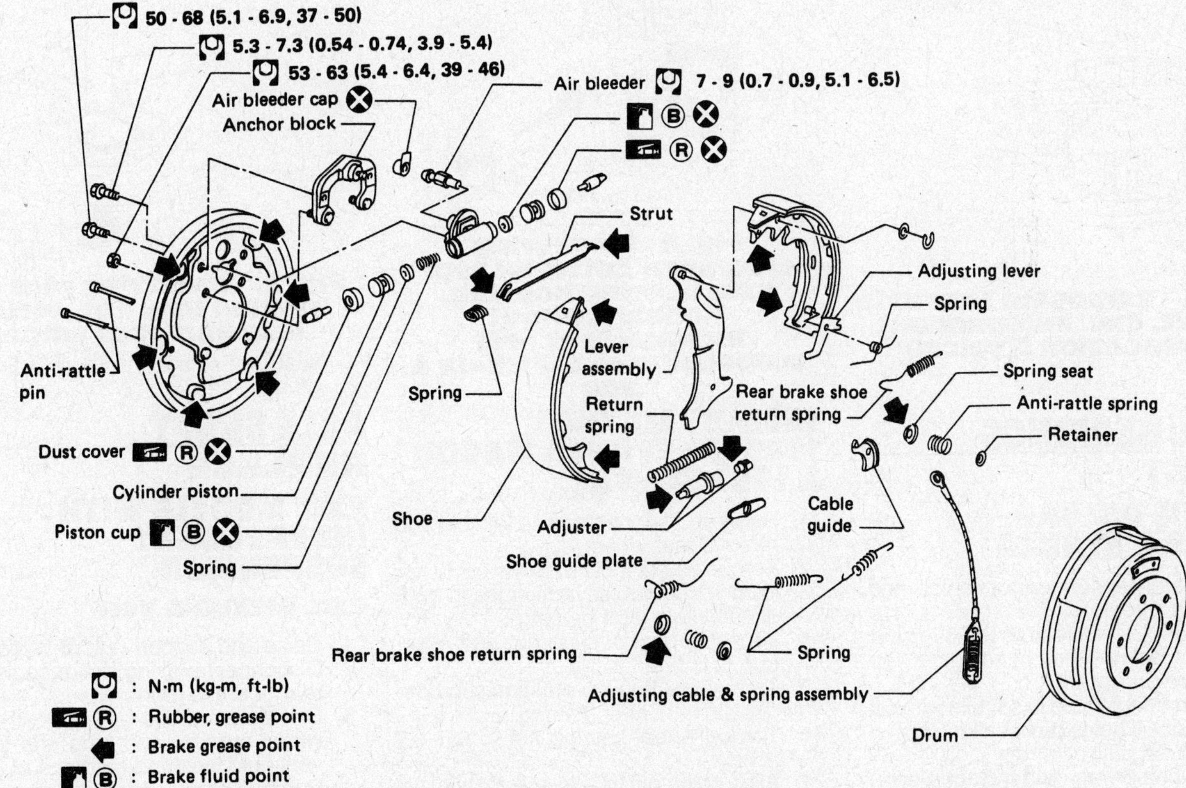
50 - 68 (5.1 - 6.9, 37 - 50)
5.3 - 7.3 (0.54 - 0.74, 3.9 - 5.4)
53 - 63 (5.4 - 6.4, 39 - 46)
Air bleeder cap
Anchor block
Air bleeder 7 - 9 (0.7 - 0.9, 5.1 - 6.5)
Strut
Adjusting lever
Spring
Anti-rattle pin
Lever assembly
Spring
Return spring
Rear brake shoe return spring
Spring seat
Anti-rattle spring
Retainer
Dust cover Ⓡ
Cylinder piston
Piston cup Ⓑ
Spring
Shoe
Adjuster
Cable guide
Shoe guide plate
Rear brake shoe return spring
Spring
Adjusting cable & spring assembly
Drum
: N·m (kg-m, ft-lb)
Ⓡ : Rubber, grease point
: Brake grease point
Ⓑ : Brake fluid point

Fig. 22 Exploded view of drum brakes. 1987 Pathfinder

REAR AXLE & SUSPENSION SECTION

INDEX

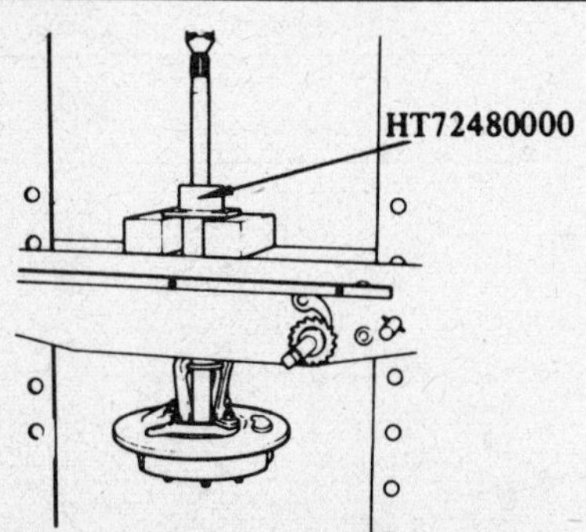

Fig. 1 Removing rear axle shaft. Exc. independent suspension (Typical)

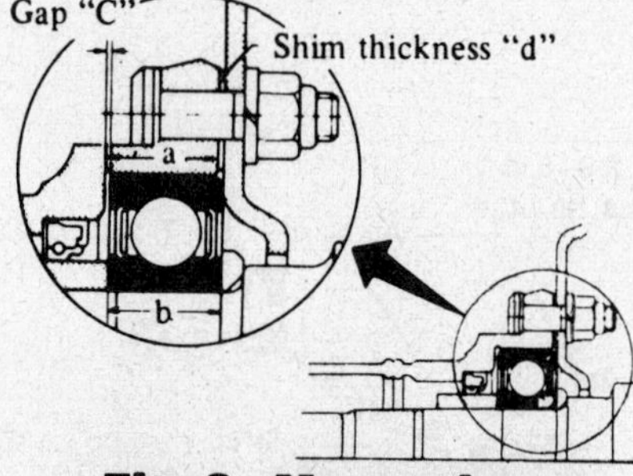

Fig. 2 Measuring clearance between rear axle bearing housing. Models without independent rear suspension exc. Pick-up & Van

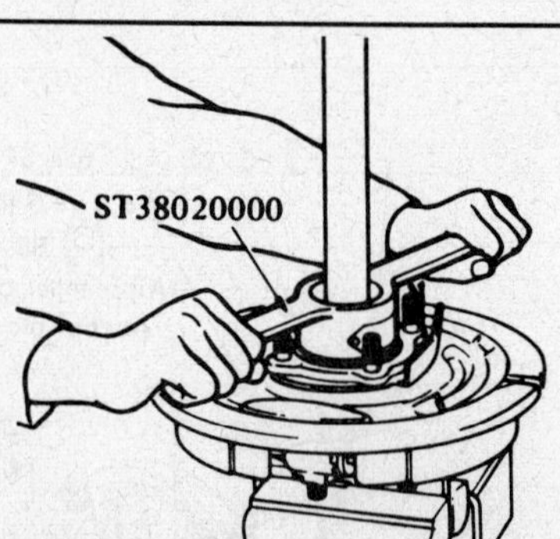

Fig. 3 Removing rear axle bearing lock nut. Pick-up less dual rear wheels

WHEEL BEARINGS

ADJUST

1983–86 PULSAR, SENTRA & STANZA

1. Raise and support rear of vehicle and remove wheel.
2. Torque wheel locknut to 29-33 ft. lbs.
3. Loosen locknut, then hand tighten the nut, using a socket.
4. Align cotter pin hole in spindle with slit in locknut. If holes do not align, tighten locknut slightly.
5. Measuring wheel bearing torque required to start rotation. Using a spring scale hooked on a hub bolt, starting torque should be as follows:
   a. With new grease seal, 3.1 lbs. maximum.
   b. With used grease seal, 1.5 lbs. maximum.

1985–87 MAXIMA, 1986–87 STANZA WAGON & 1987 STANZA

1. Raise and support rear of vehicle and remove rear wheel.
2. Torque wheel locknut to 18-25 ft. lbs.
3. Turn wheel hub several times in both directions to seat bearing.
4. Loosen wheel bearing nut and retorque to 6.5-8.7 ft. lbs.
5. Turn wheel hub several times in both directions to seat bearing.
6. Torque wheel bearing nut to 6.5-8.7 ft. lbs.
7. Align cotter pin hole in spindle with slit in lock nut. If holes do not align, tighten lock nut slightly.
5. Measuring wheel bearing torque required to start rotation. Using a spring scale hooked on a hub bolt, measure starting torque. Starting torque should be 3.1 lbs. maximum with new grease seal or 2.4 lbs. maximum with used grease seal.

AXLE SHAFT

REPLACE

EXC. MODELS WITH INDEPENDENT SUSPENSION

Exc. Pickup & Van

1. Raise and support rear of vehicle.
2. Disconnect parking brake cable from rear of brake drum.
3. Disconnect brake hydraulic line from wheel cylinder and plug end to prevent fluid loss and entrance of dirt.
4. Remove brake drum, or disc brake caliper.
5. Remove nuts retaining brake support plate to axle.
6. With a suitable puller, pull axle shaft and brake support plate from axle assembly.
7. Replace oil seal in axle tube.

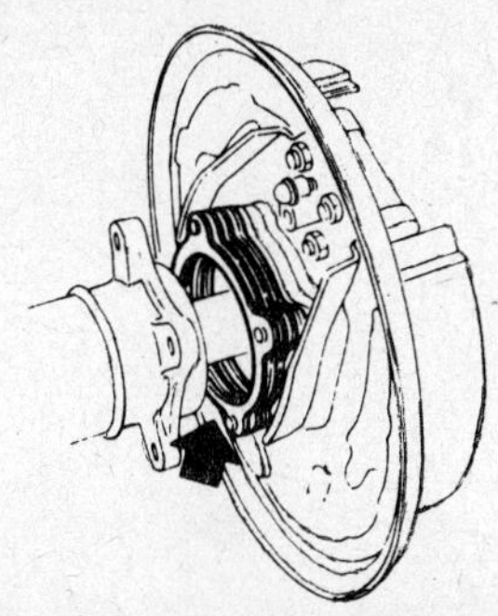

Fig. 4 Rear axle bearing installation. Pick-up less dual rear wheels

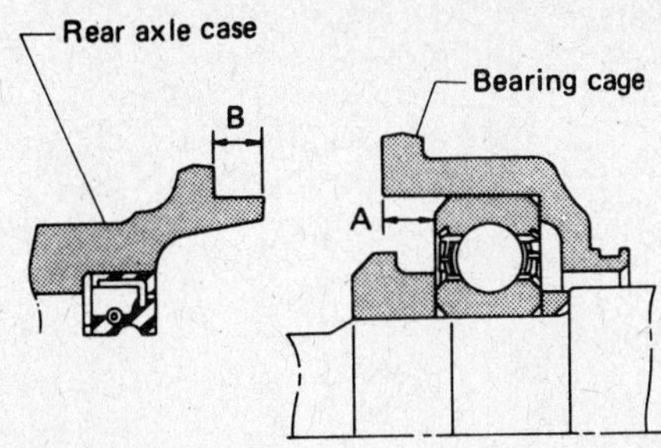

Fig. 5 Rear axle end play adjustment shims. Pick-up less dual rear wheels

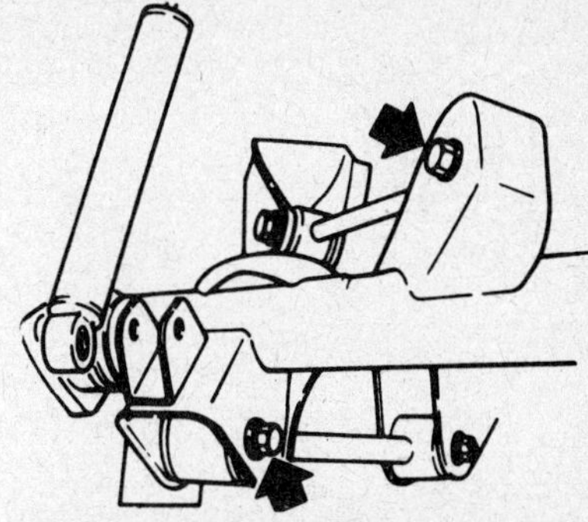

Fig. 6 Upper & lower link connections. Models with link type rear suspension

8. Cut a notch in bearing collar with a chisel.
9. Press bearing from axle shaft, **Fig. 1.**
10. Install bearing onto axle shaft by reversing procedure using new seal and bearing collar.
11. Insert axle assembly into axle housing taking care not to damage housing seal.
12. Adjust gap C, **Fig. 2,** between wheel bearing and axle tube end to .004 in. maximum by selecting shims.
13. Complete installation of axle assembly by reversing removal procedure. Measure axle shaft end play and make sure end play is within specification in "Rear Axle Specification" section.

Pickup Less Dual Rear Wheels

1. Raise and support rear of vehicle and remove rear wheel.
2. Disconnect parking brake cable and brake hydraulic line. Plug end of hydraulic line to prevent fluid loss and entrance of dirt.
3. Remove nuts securing backing plate to axle housing and remove brake drum.
4. With a suitable puller, pull axle and backing plate assembly away from axle housing.
5. Replace oil seal in axle tube.
6. Support axle assembly in a vise, **Fig. 3,** and bend lock washer away from bearing locknut.
7. Remove bearing lock nut using proper tool, **Fig. 3.**
8. Remove wheel bearing, bearing cage and backing plate from axle using tool as shown in **Fig. 1.**
9. Replace oil seal in bearing cage.
10. Place bearing cage and backing plate assembly and bearing spacer on axle shaft. Install bearing cone using a brass drift.
11. Adjust axle end play to specification in "Rear Axle Specification" chart by applying case end shims, **Fig. 4.**
12. To install axle, reverse removal procedure.

Pickup w/Dual Rear Wheels

1. Raise and support rear of vehicle and remove rear wheels.
2. Disconnect parking brake cable and brake hydraulic line. Plug end of hydraulic line to prevent fluid loss and contamination.
3. Remove backing plate-to-axle housing attaching nuts, then the brake drum.
4. Slide axle shaft out of axle housing.
5. Unfasten lock washer from rear wheel bearing nut.
6. Remove rear wheel bearing nut, inner bearing outer race, grease seal and outer bearing outer race. Discard grease seal.
7. Reverse procedure to install. Adjust axle end play to specifications in "Rear Axle Specifications" chart.

Van

1. Raise and support vehicle.
2. Disconnect parking brake cable and brake line at wheel.
3. Remove tire and wheel assembly and the brake drum.
4. Remove axle shaft retaining nuts.
5. Using suitable tools, pull out axle shaft.
6. Remove oil seal.
7. Using suitable tool, cut bearing collar, being careful not to damage axle.
8. Using suitable tools, pull off wheel bearing and collar.
9. Install bearing spacer with chamfer side facing axle shaft flange.
10. Using suitable press, press in new bearing and collar, ensuring oil or grease does not come into contact with surface of axle shaft, bearing and collar.
11. Using suitable tool, drive in new oil seal, then coat sealing lip with multipurpose grease.
12. Insert axle shaft with backing plate, bearing and bearing collar with tool ST27840000 or equivalent.
13. Using depth gauge, measure distances A and B, **Fig. 5,** to determine proper thickness of shim. Shim thickness should be (B − A) to (B − A + .1 mm).
14. Measure end play of axle shaft. If axial end play is not 0-.004 inch, reselect rear axle case end shims. **While adjusting axle end play, be careful not to damage oil seal.**

WITH INDEPENDENT SUSPENSION

280ZX, 300ZX, 1983–84 Maxima, & 1984–87 200SX

1. Raise and support rear of vehicle and remove rear wheels.
2. Disconnect parking brake cable and brake hydraulic line. Plug brake hydraulic line to prevent fluid loss and entrance of dirt.
3. Remove brake caliper and rotor as outlined under "Caliper, Replace" in "Disc Brake Section."
4. Disconnect driveshaft from axle shaft.
5. Remove wheel bearing locknut.
6. Remove axle shaft with suitable puller.
7. Remove companion flange, grease seal, and inner bearing.
8. Remove outer bearing from axle shaft, using suitable puller.
9. To install, reverse procedure.

AXLE REPLACE

EXC. 200SX, 300ZX, PATHFINDER, VAN & FRONT WHEEL DRIVE MODELS

1. Raise and support rear of vehicle.
2. Disconnect propeller shaft from differential companion flange.
3. Remove propeller shaft from vehicle.
4. Disconnect parking brake cable from turnbuckle.
5. Disconnect brake pipe at body side.
6. Disconnect shock absorbers at lower mountings.
7. Lower jack under differential case and remove U-bolts from springs.
8. Move axle assembly rearward and lower from vehicle. When removing the assembly, tilt the assembly to pass under the springs.
9. Reverse procedure to install.

1983 200SX

1. Raise and support rear of vehicle. Place support stands solidly under body member on both sides.
2. Remove stabilizer bar.
3. Support center of differential with floor jack and remove rear wheels.
4. Disconnect propeller shaft at differential companion flange and remove propeller shaft from vehicle.
5. Disconnect parking brake cable and disconnect brake hydraulic hose at body. Plug both open ends of brake hydraulic system to prevent fluid loss and entrance of dirt.

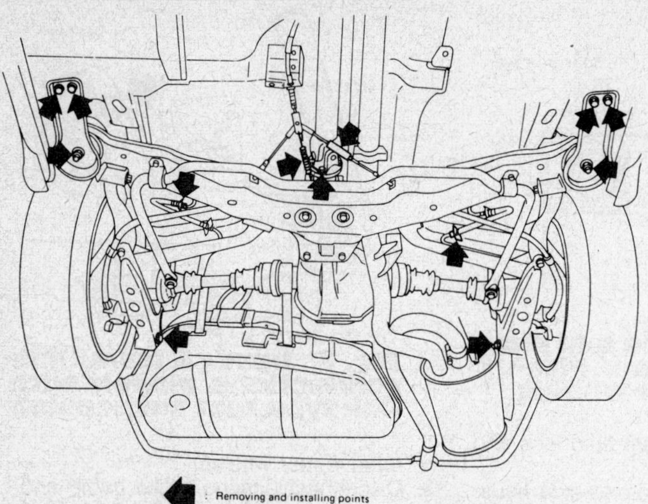

Fig. 7 Rear axle replacement. 1984–87 200SX w/independent suspension

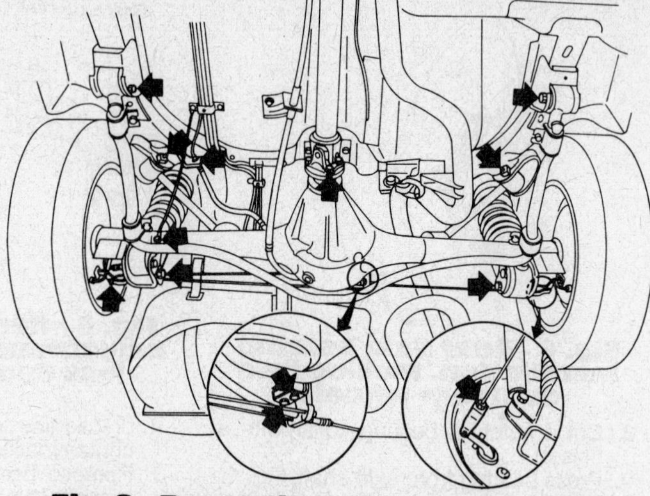
Fig. 8 Rear axle replacement. 1984 200SX less independent suspension

6. Disconnect shock absorbers at lower mounts.
7. Lower floor jack slowly and remove coil springs once they are fully extended.
8. Raise floor jack to original position.
9. Remove bolts securing upper and lower links to axle housing, **Fig. 6.**
10. Lower floor jack slowly and remove axle assembly towards rear of car.

1983–86 STANZA

1. Raise and support rear of vehicle and remove wheel.
2. Disconnect hydraulic brake line.
3. Remove exhaust pipe mounting bracket, if working on left side.
4. Disconnect parking brake cable.
5. Remove radius rod and parallel link bracket.
6. Support lower end of rear strut with a suitable jack.
7. Remove rear strut attaching nuts, then lower axle assembly from vehicle.
8. Reverse procedure to install.

1983–86 PULSAR & SENTRA & 1986–87 2WD STANZA WAGON

Refer to "Rear Arm, Replace" for procedure.

1984–87 200SX & 300ZX

Refer to **Figs. 7 through 9** for replacement.

1985–87 MAXIMA & 1987 STANZA

Refer to "Strut & Coil Spring, Replace" for procedure.

1987 PULSAR & 2WD SENTRA

Refer to **Fig. 10** for replacement, noting the following:

1. When raising and supporting vehicle, do not jack up at parallel links.

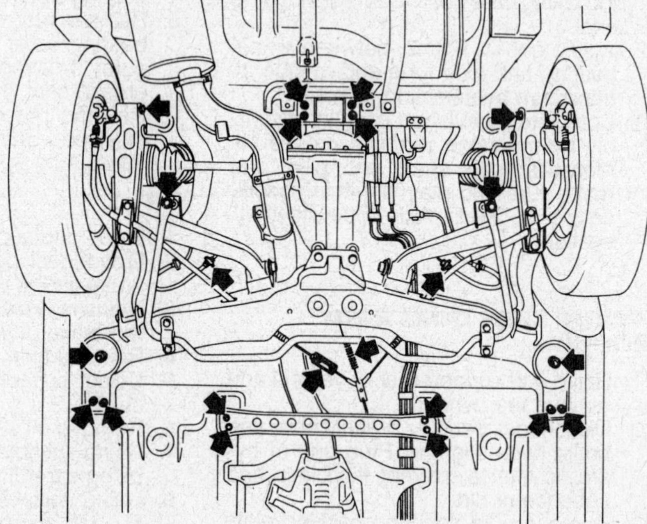

Fig. 9 Rear axle replacement. 1984–87 300ZX

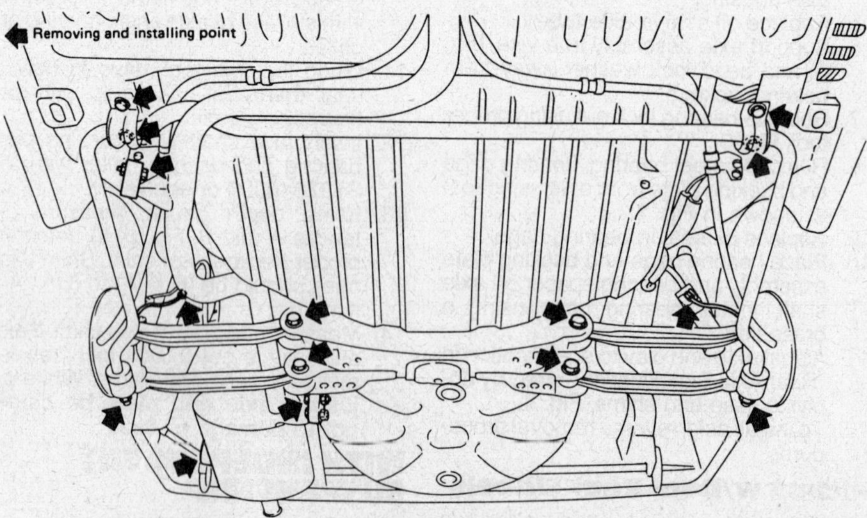

Fig. 10 Rear axle replacement. 1987 Pulsar & 2WD Sentra

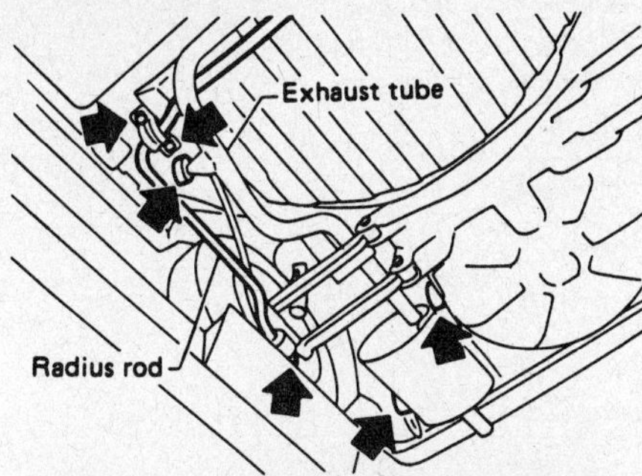

Fig. 11 Removing exhaust pipe & radius rod. 1987 Pulsar & 2WD Sentra

2. Disconnect brake hydraulic line and parking brake cable at equalizer.
3. Remove exhaust pipe attaching bolts, **Fig. 11**, then radius rod attaching bolts and pull out radius rod, pushing exhaust pipe downward.
4. Remove shock absorber upper attaching bolts.

1986–87 4WD STANZA WAGON

Refer to **Fig. 12** for replacement, noting the following:

1. Disconnect brake hydraulic line and parking brake cable.
2. Remove radius rod.
3. Remove rear exhaust pipe attaching bolts and nuts.
4. Remove propeller shaft.

1987 4WD SENTRA

Refer to **Fig. 13** for replacement, noting the following:

1. When raising and supporting vehicle, do not jack up at transverse links.
2. Disconnect brake hydraulic line and parking brake cable at equalizer.
3. Remove exhaust pipe and muffler attaching bolts.
4. Remove upper shock absorber attaching bolts.

1987 PATHFINDER

1. Raise and support vehicle.
2. Disconnect brake hydraulic line and parking brake cable.
3. Support axle with suitable jack.
4. Disconnect stabilizer rod, upper and lower links and the panhard rod from body.
5. Disconnect propeller shaft.
6. Remove upper shock absorber attaching nuts.
7. Reverse procedure to install. When tightening rubber parts, vehicle should be in unloaded condition with tires on ground.

1987 VAN

Refer to **Fig. 14** for replacement, noting the following:

1. Disconnect brake hydraulic line and parking brake cable.
2. Remove stabilizer bar.
3. Remove upper shock absorber attaching nuts from under third seat.
4. Disconnect propeller shaft.
5. When tightening rubber parts, vehicle should be in unloaded condition with tires on ground.

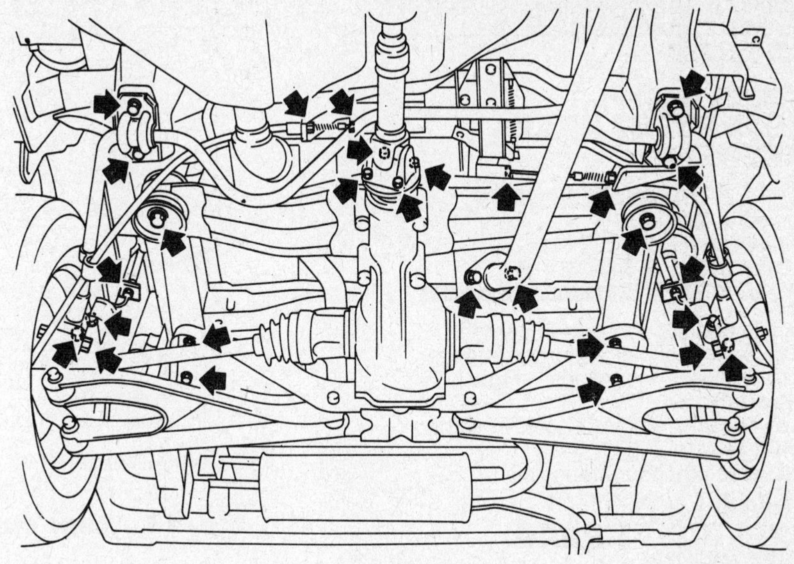

Fig. 12 Rear axle replacement. 1986–87 4WD Stanza Wagon

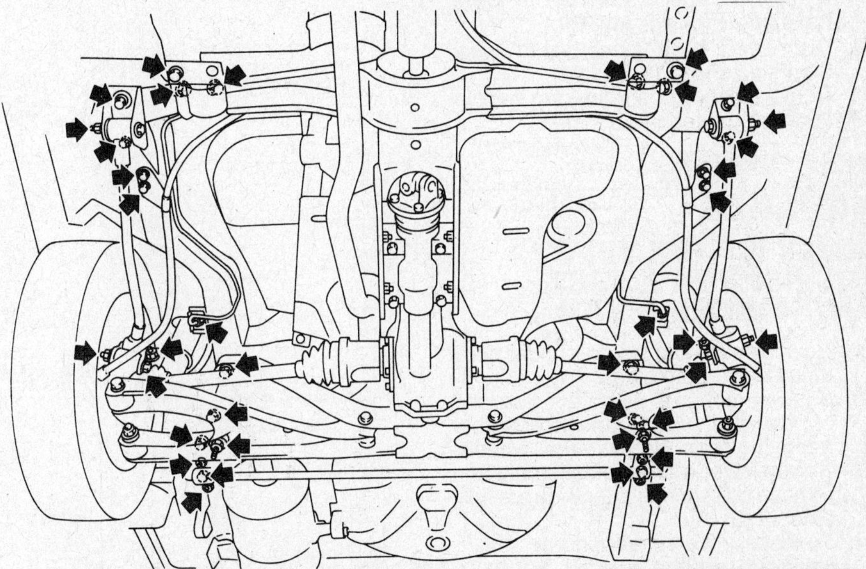

Fig. 13 Rear axle replacement. 1987 4WD Sentra

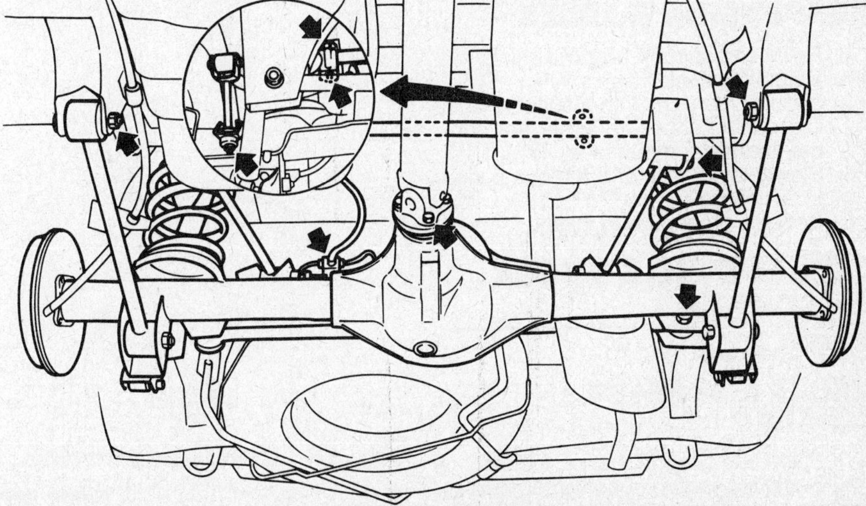

Fig. 14 Rear axle replacement. 1987 Van

SHOCK ABSORBER

REPLACE

MODELS WITH INDEPENDENT REAR SUSPENSION

1983–86 Pulsar & Sentra, 1984–87 200SX w/Independent Rear Suspension & 300ZX & 1986–87 2WD Stanza Wagon

1. Raise and support rear of vehicle.
2. Disconnect shock absorber at upper and lower mountings, **Figs. 15 through 18.**
3. Lower jack remove shock absorber from vehicle.
4. Reverse procedure to install.

MODELS LESS INDEPENDENT REAR SUSPENSION

1. Raise and support rear of vehicle at rear axle.
2. Disconnect shock absorber at lower mounting, **Figs. 19 and 20.**
3. Disconnect shock absorber at upper mounting, **Figs. 19 and 20.**
4. Remove shock absorber from vehicle.
5. Reverse procedure to install.

COIL SPRING

REPLACE

200SX W/LINK TYPE SUSPENSION & 1987 PATHFINDER & VAN

1. Raise vehicle and support under body member on both sides.
2. Support rear axle with floor jack and remove both lower shock absorber mounting bolts. Remove rear wheels.
3. Slowly lower rear axle assembly and remove coil springs after they are fully extended.
4. To install, reverse procedure.

1983–86 PULSAR & SENTRA, 1984–87 200SX W/INDEPENDENT REAR SUSPENSION & 300ZX

1. Raise and support rear of vehicle.
2. Remove wheel.
3. Support rear arm with a suitable jack.
4. Disconnect shock absorber from upper and lower mountings.
5. Slowly lower jack and remove spring from vehicle.
6. Reverse procedure to install.

COIL SPRING & SHOCK ABSORBER

REPLACE

280ZX & 1983–84 MAXIMA

1. Raise and support rear of vehicle.
2. Remove shock upper attachments from inside rear of vehicle, **Figs. 21 and 22**

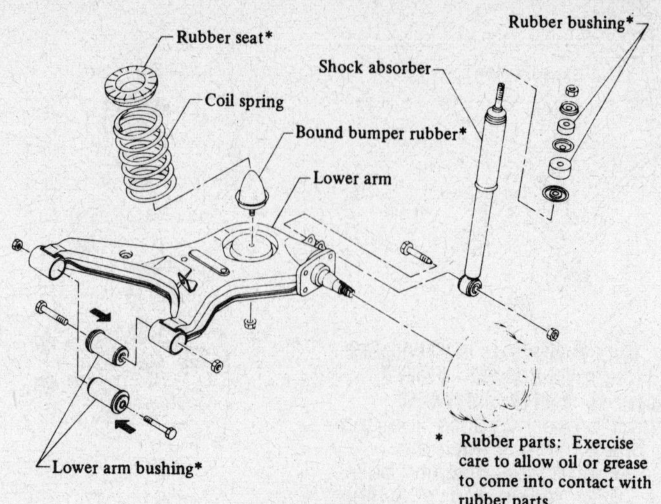

Fig. 15 Rear suspension. 1983–86 Pulsar & Sentra

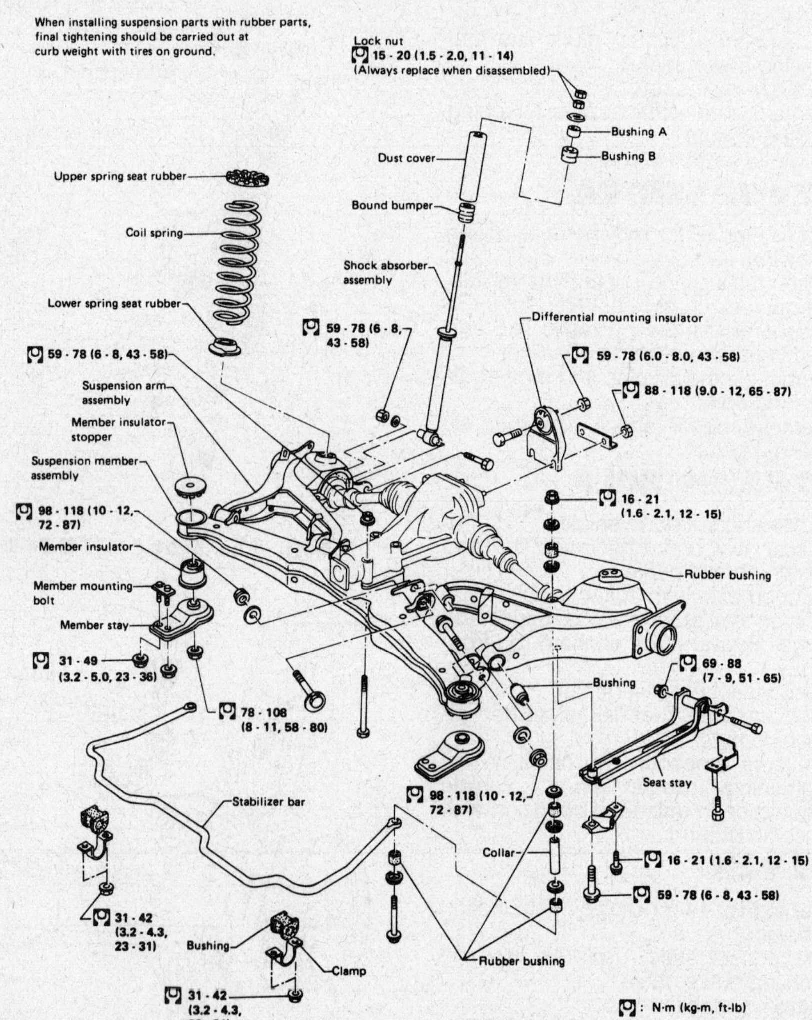

Fig. 16 Rear suspension. 1984–87 200SX w/independent rear suspension

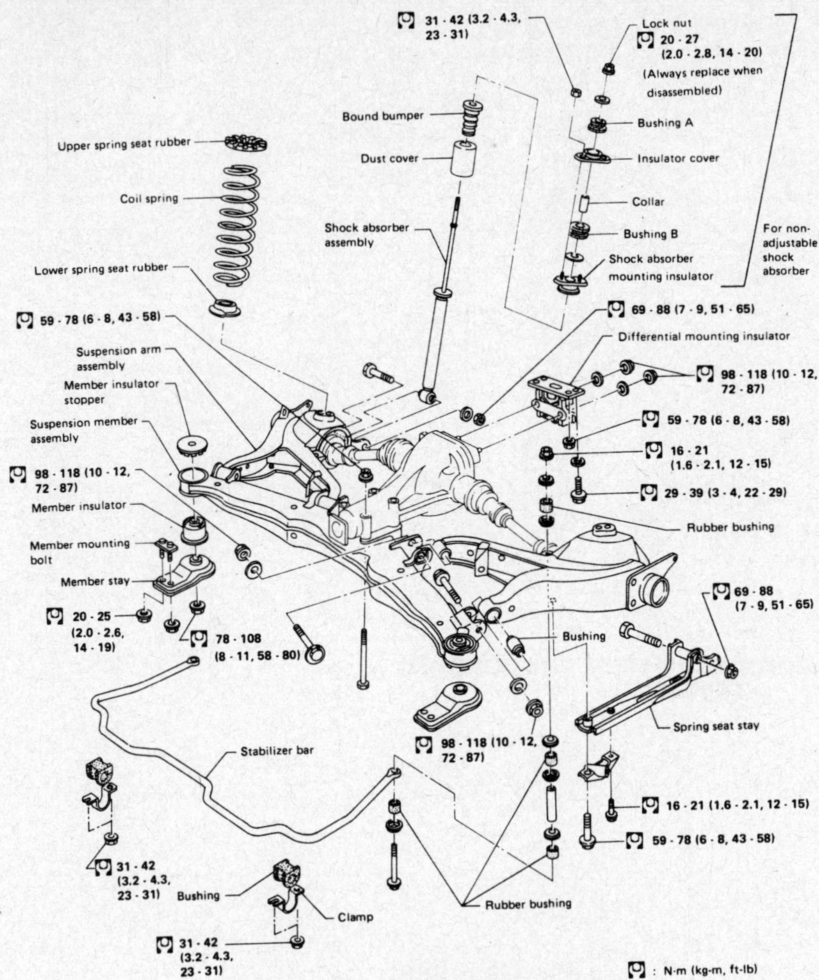

Fig. 17 Rear suspension. 300ZX

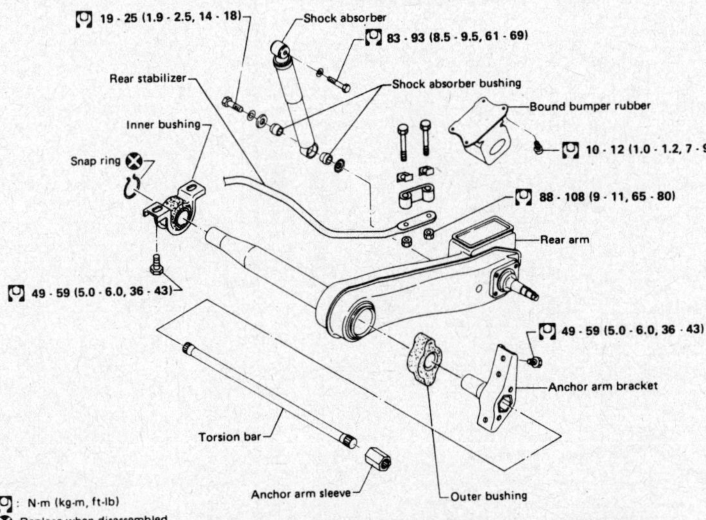

Fig. 18 Rear suspension. 1986–87 2WD Stanza Wagon

3. Disconnect shock absorber from lower mounting, **Figs. 21 and 22.**
4. Remove shock absorber and coil spring assembly from vehicle, **Figs. 21 and 22.**
5. Reverse procedure to install.

STRUT & COIL SPRING REPLACE

1983–86 STANZA

1. Raise and support rear of vehicle and remove wheel. **Do not support vehicle at the parallel links or radius rod.**
2. Disconnect brake line and parking brake cable.
3. If necessary, remove wheel bearing and brake assembly.
4. Disconnect parallel links and radius rod from lower end of strut, **Fig. 23.**
5. Support strut with a suitable jack, then remove strut attachments at upper mounting and remove strut from vehicle.
6. Reverse procedure to install.

1985–87 MAXIMA & 1987 STANZA

1. Raise and support rear of vehicle and remove wheel and tire assemblies.
2. Remove both brake assemblies, leaving brake lines attached.
3. Remove parallel link, radius rod, stabilizer bar and stabilizer bar bracket attaching bolts, **Fig. 24.**
4. Remove rear seat and parcel shelf assembly.
5. Remove right hand strut attaching nuts from top end, then lower strut from vehicle.
6. Disconnect exhaust pipe clamps installed after flexible hose.
7. Remove front radius rod attaching bolt, then the stabilizer bar connecting rod bracket and suspension crossmember attaching nuts.
8. Remove left hand strut attaching nuts from top end, then lower strut from vehicle.

1987 PULSAR, SENTRA & 4WD STANZA WAGON

1. Raise and support vehicle.
2. Disconnect brake line and parking brake cable.
3. Remove upper and lower strut attaching bolts and nuts, **Figs. 25 through 27.**
4. Reverse procedure to install.

LEAF SPRING REPLACE

1. Raise and support rear of vehicle at chassis. Support rear axle to relieve tension from spring.
2. Disconnect shock absorber at lower mounting and remove U" bolts and spring plates.
3. On 4WD pick-up models, remove one or two parking brake rear cable clamps on side of leaf springs.

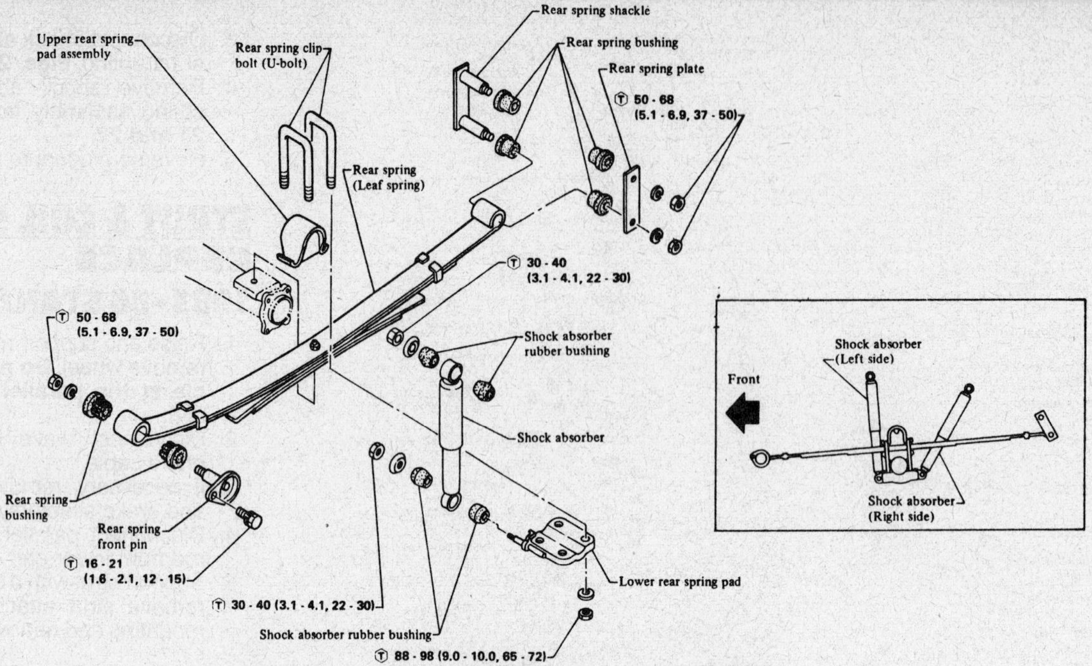

Fig. 19 Leaf spring rear suspension (Typical)

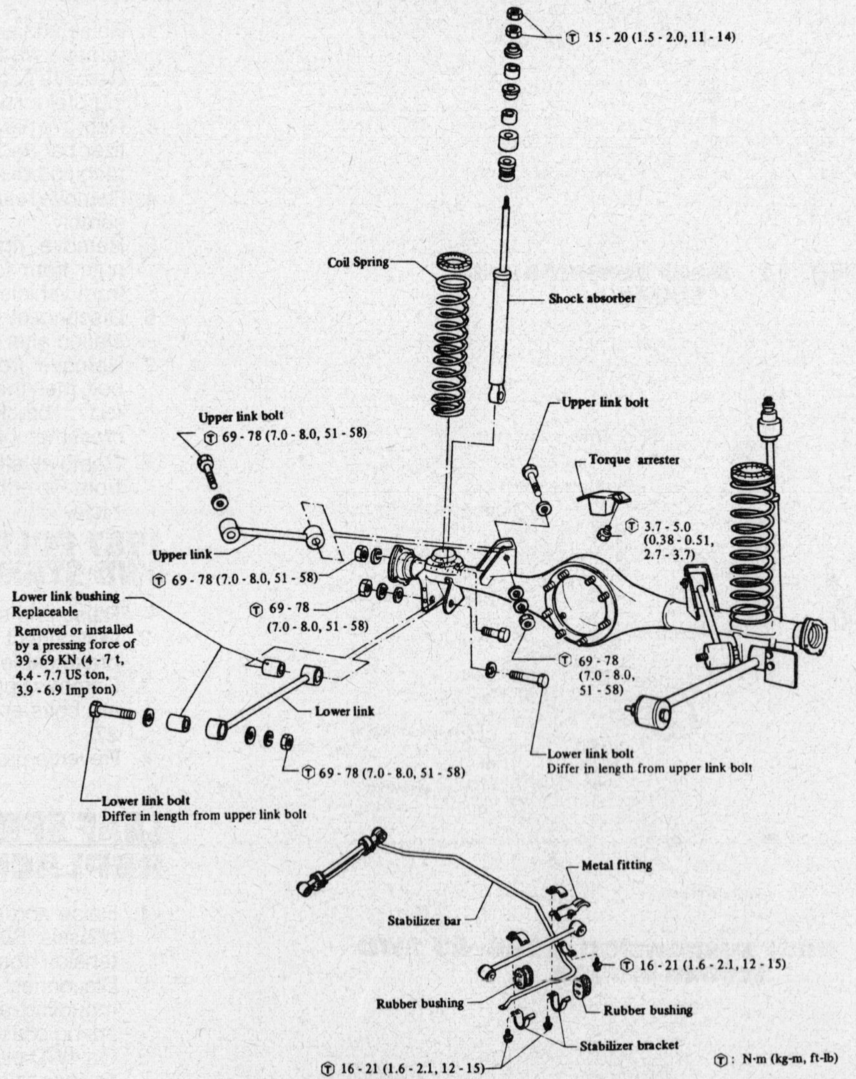

Fig. 20 Link type rear suspension (Typical)

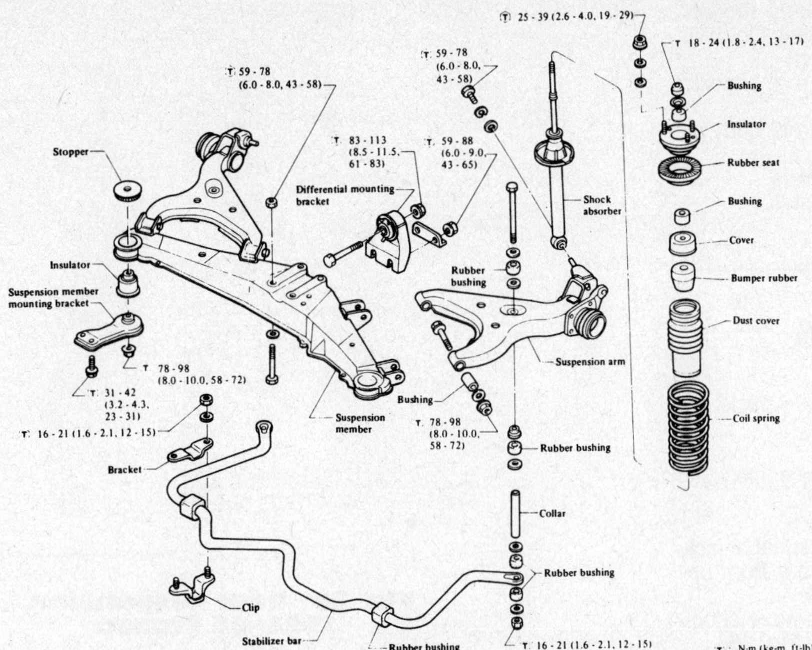

Fig. 21 Rear suspension 1983–84 Maxima

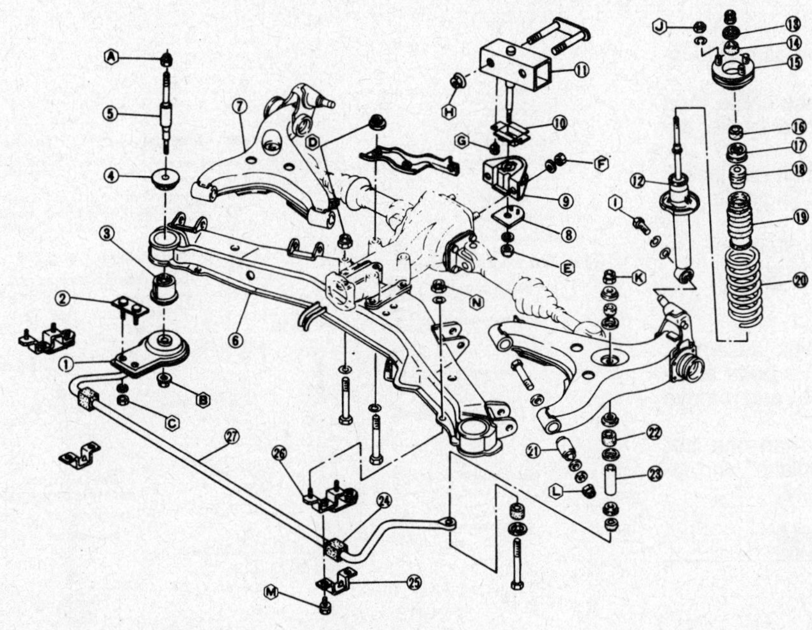

1 Suspension member mounting stay
2 Suspension member mounting bolt
3 Member mounting insulator
4 Member mounting upper stopper
5 Suspension mounting bolt
6 Suspension member assembly
7 Suspension arm assembly
8 Differential mounting plate
9 Differential mounting insulator
10 Differential mounting adapter plate
11 Differential mounting bracket
12 Shock absorber assembly
13 Special washer
14 Shock absorber mounting bushing A
15 Shock absorber mounting insulator
16 Shock absorber mounting bushing B
17 Bound bumper cover
18 Bound bumper
19 Dust cover
20 Coil spring
21 Suspension arm bushing
22 Stabilizer bushing
23 Stabilizer collar
24 Stabilizer mounting bushing
25 Stabilizer mounting clip
26 Stabilizer mounting bracket
27 Rear stabilizer

Tightening torque N·m (kg-m, ft-lb)

Ⓐ : 118 - 157 (12 - 16, 87 - 116)
Ⓑ : 78 - 98 (8 - 10, 58 - 72)
Ⓒ : 20 - 25 (2.0 - 2.6, 14 - 19)
Ⓓ : 59 - 78 (6 - 8, 43 - 58)
Ⓔ : 118 - 147 (12 - 15, 87 - 108)
Ⓕ : R200 Diff.:
88 - 118 (9 - 12, 65 - 87)
R180 Diff.:
59 - 78 (6 - 8, 43 - 58)
Ⓖ : 31 - 42 (3.2 - 4.3, 23 - 31)
Ⓗ : 59 - 78 (6 - 8, 43 - 58)
Ⓘ : 59 - 78 (6 - 8, 43 - 58)
Ⓙ : 29 - 39 (3 - 4, 22 - 29)
Ⓚ : 16 - 21 (1.6 - 2.1, 12 - 15)
Ⓛ : 78 - 98 (8 - 10, 58 - 72)
Ⓜ : 16 - 21 (1.6 - 2.1, 12 - 15)
Ⓝ : 16 - 21 (1.6 - 2.1, 12 - 15)

Fig. 22 Rear suspension. 280ZX

4. On all except 4WD pick-up models, raise jack under differential. On 4WD pick-up models, lower jack.
5. Disconnect spring from rear shackle, **Fig. 19.**
6. Disconnect spring from front body attachment.
7. Remove spring from vehicle.
8. Reverse procedure to install.

REAR ARM
REPLACE

1983–86 PULSAR & SENTRA

1. Raise and support rear of vehicle.
2. Remove wheel.
3. Disconnect brake tube.
4. Disconnect parking brake cable.
5. Remove brake drum.
6. Remove brake assembly.
7. Support rear arm with a suitable jack.
8. Disconnect shock absorber from upper and lower mountings.
9. Slowly lower jack and remove shock absorber and coil spring, **Fig. 15.**
10. Remove rear arm attaching bolts and the rear arm from vehicle.
11. Reverse procedure to install.

1986–87 2WD STANZA WAGON

1. Remove shock absorber as previously described.
2. Disconnect parking brake cable, then remove brake drum and brake assembly.
3. Support rear arm with suitable jack.
4. Remove rear arm attaching bolts and the rear arm, **Fig. 18.**
5. Reverse procedure to install.

200SX W/LINK TYPE SUSPENSION

1. When removing one link assembly, (upper or lower) remove bolts at either end of link assembly, and remove link.
2. When removing more than one link, refer to "Rear Axle, Replace" and remove rear axle assembly.

SUSPENSION ARM
REPLACE

280ZX & 1983–84 MAXIMA

1. Raise and support rear of vehicle and remove wheels.
2. Disconnect brake tube from brake hose and caliper and remove brake tube.
3. Disconnect brake cable and remove cable from suspension arm.
4. Remove stabilizer bolt, 280ZX models.
5. Remove rear axle and driveshaft, refer to "Rear Axle, Replace."
6. Disconnect shock absorber at lower end.
7. Remove pins securing suspension arm to crossmember and remove suspension arm, **Figs. 21 and 22.**

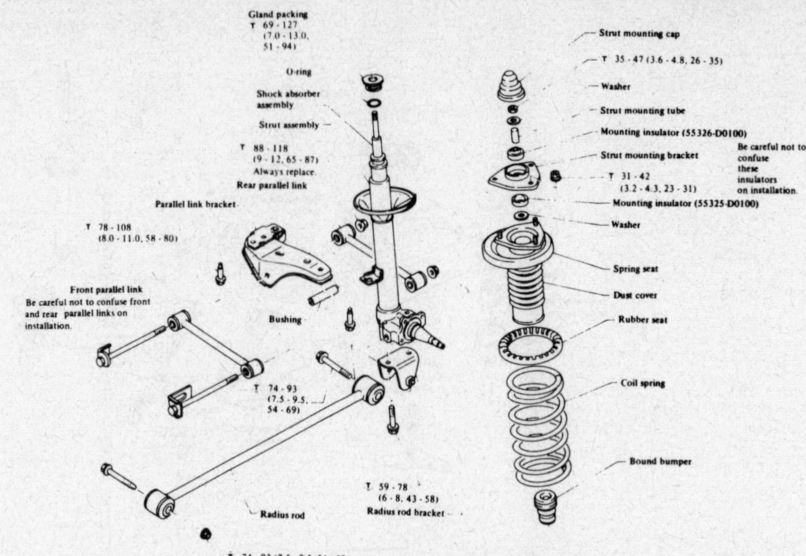

Fig. 23 Rear suspension. 1983–86 Stanza

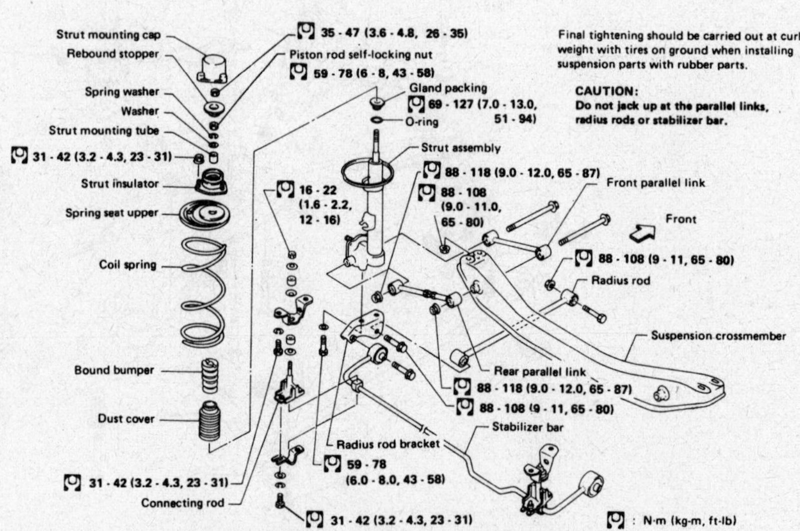

Fig. 24 Rear suspension. 1985–87 Maxima & 1987 Stanza

300ZX & 1984–87 200SX W/INDEPENDENT REAR SUSPENSION

1. Remove axle shaft as described under "Axle Shaft, Replace," in the "Rear Axle & Suspension Section."
2. Remove stabilizer bar attaching bolt.
3. Disconnect shock absorber from lower mounting, **Figs. 16 and 17**
4. Scribe alignment marks on suspension arm pin and arm, then remove suspension arm pin and the arm.
5. Reverse procedure to install, then adjust rear wheel alignment as described in "Wheel Alignment Section."

STABILIZER BAR
REPLACE

1. Raise and support vehicle.
2. Remove muffler.
3. Disconnect stabilizer bar from side member and remove stabilizer bar.
4. Reverse procedure to install.

CAUTION:
Do not jack up at the parallel links.

When installing each rubber part, final tightening must be carried out under unladen condition* with tires on ground.

- Fuel, radiator coolant and engine oil full. Spare tire, jack, hand tools and mats in designated positions.

62 - 72 (6.3 - 7.3, 46 - 53)
25 - 29 (2.5 - 3.0, 18 - 22)
Strut mounting insulator
Upper spring seat
Spring rubber seat (Upper)
Coil spring
Spring rubber seat (Lower)
Dust cover
Strut assembly (Non-disassembly type)
98 - 118 (10.0 - 12.0, 72 - 87)
98 - 118 (10.0 - 12.0, 72 - 87)
Front
98 - 118 (10.0 - 12.0, 72 - 87)
Toe adjusting pin
98 - 118 (10.0 - 12.0, 72 - 87)
Parallel link
64 - 83 (6.5 - 8.5, 47 - 61)
Collar
Rubber bush
Radius rod
: N·m (kg-m, ft-lb)
88 - 108 (9.0 - 11.0, 65 - 80)

Fig. 25 Rear suspension. 1987 Pulsar & 2WD Sentra

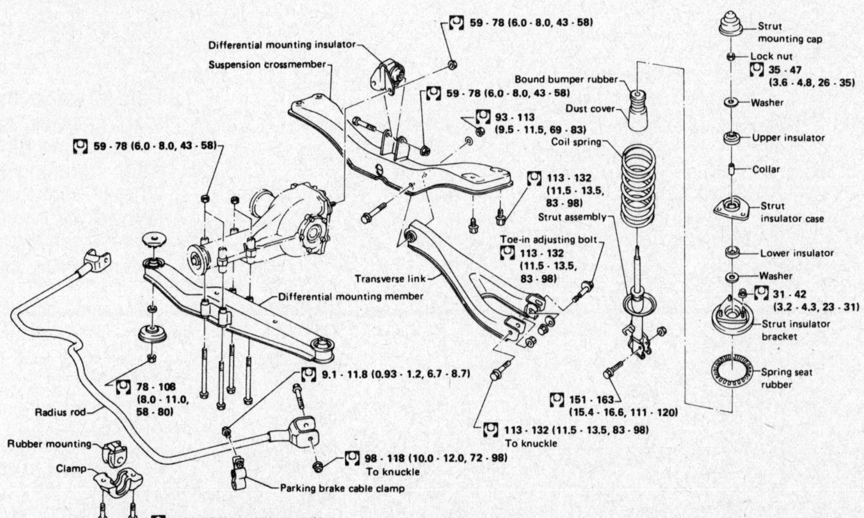

Fig. 26 Rear suspension. 1986–87 4WD Stanza Wagon

PARALLEL LINK & RADIUS ROD

REPLACE

STANZA & 1985–87 MAXIMA

1. Raise and support rear of vehicle and remove wheel. **Do not support vehicle at the parallel links or radius rod.**
2. Remove parallel link or radius rod attaching bolts, then the link or rod, **Figs. 23 and 24. If removing front parallel link, remove exhaust pipe mounting bracket (LH side only), parking brake cable support bracket and the parallel link bracket, if necessary.**
3. Reverse procedure to install, using new parallel link nuts.

1987 PULSAR & 2WD SENTRA

When replacing parallel link and.or radius rod, refer to "Axle, Replace," noting the following:

1. Before removing parallel link attaching bolts, scribe alignment marks on toe adjusting pin and frame.
2. When installing parallel link, install ones with green mark in front and ones with blue mark in rear.
3. When installing radius rod rubber bushings and/or clamps, ensure proper direction.

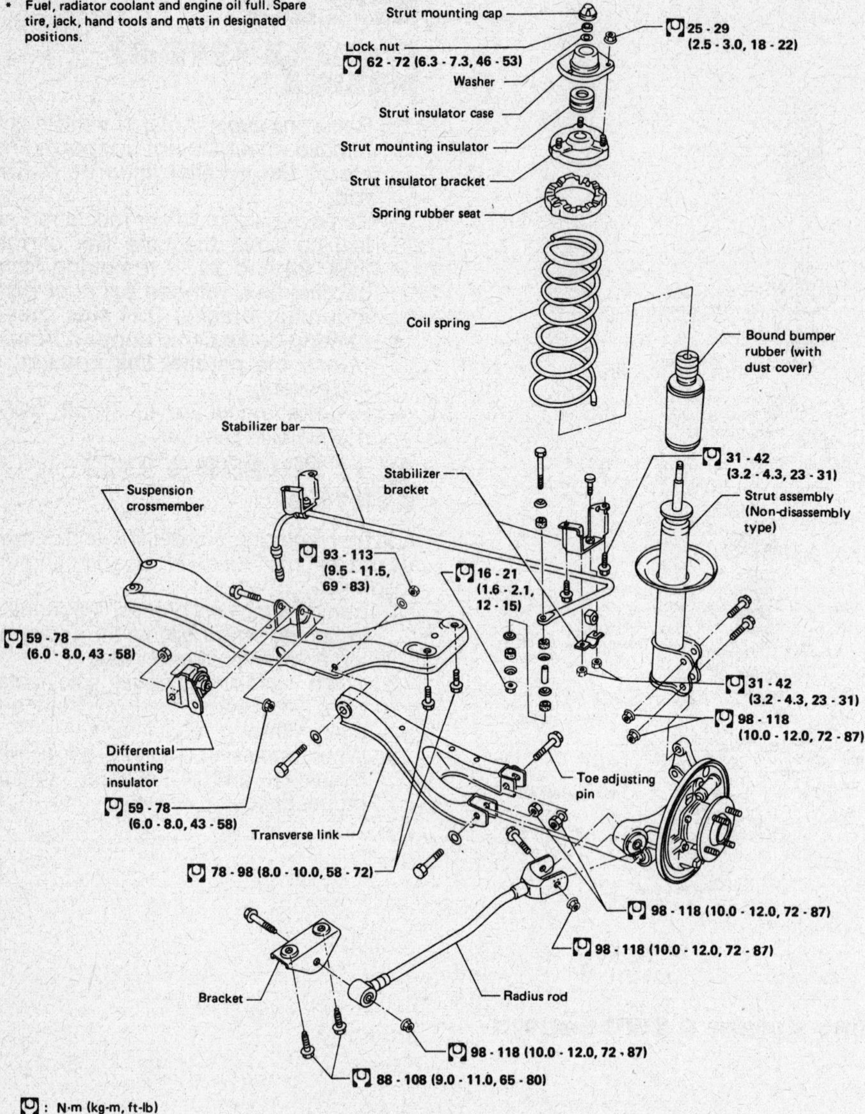

Fig. 27 Rear suspension. 1987 4WD Sentra

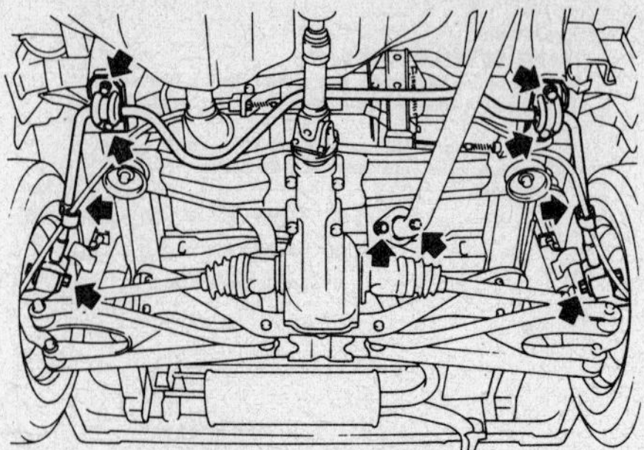

Fig. 28 Radius rod attaching bolt locations. 1986–87 4WD Stanza Wagon

TRANSVERSE LINK
REPLACE
1986–87 4WD STANZA WAGON

1. Raise and support vehicle.
2. Scribe alignment marks on toe-in adjusting bolt and transverse link.
3. Remove transverse link attaching bolts and the link.
4. Reverse procedure to install, then adjust wheel alignment.

RADIUS ROD
REPLACE
1986–87 4WD STANZA WAGON

1. Raise and support vehicle.
2. Remove exhaust pipe attaching nuts and the parking brake cable clamps.
3. Remove radius rod attaching bolts, **Fig. 28**, then the radius rod.
4. Reverse procedure to install.

TRANSVERSE LINK & RADIUS ROD
REPLACE
1987 4WD SENTRA

When replacing transverse link and/or radius rod, refer to **Fig. 27** and note the following:

1. Before removing transverse link attaching bolts, scribe alignment mark on adjusting pin.
2. After installing transverse link, adjust wheel alignment as described in "Wheel Alignment Section."
3. When installing radius rod bracket, ensure arrow points forward.

FRONT SUSPENSION & STEERING SECTION

NOTE: On 1983-87 Pickup and 1987 Pathfinder equipped with four wheel drive, refer to "Pickup & Pathfinder Front Drive Axle Section" when performing service procedures on front drive axle.

INDEX

WHEEL BEARINGS

ADJUST

1. Raise and support front of vehicle.
2. Remove brake pads.
3. While rotating disc, torque wheel bearing lock nut to 18-22 ft. lbs on all except Pickup models. On Pickup, torque to 25-29 ft. lbs.
4. Loosen lock nut approximately 60 degrees on all except Pickup models. On Pickup, loosen 45 degrees. Install adjusting cap and align groove of nut with hole in spindle. If alignment cannot be obtained, change position of adjusting cap. Also, if alignment cannot be obtained, loosen lock nut slightly, but not more than 15 degrees.
5. Install brake pads.

SHOCK ABSORBER

REPLACE

PATHFINDER, PICKUP & VAN MODELS

1. Raise and support vehicle.
2. Remove wheel.
3. Disconnect shock absorber from upper mounting.
4. Disconnect shock absorber from lower mounting.
5. Remove shock absorber from vehicle.
6. Reverse procedure to install.

UPPER LINK & BALL JOINT

REPLACE

PATHFINDER & PICKUP MODELS

1. Raise and support front of vehicle and remove wheel.
2. Remove shock absorber upper attaching bolt, if necessary.
3. Using suitable jack, raise lower link and remove ball joint tightening nut.
4. Press ball joint out of knuckle spindle, then remove the upper link spindle.
5. Remove ball joint attaching nuts, then the ball joint, **Fig. 1.**
6. Remove nuts and washers from both ends of upper link spindle, then press spindle and bushings out of link.
7. Reverse procedure to install.

1987 VAN MODELS

1. Raise and support front of vehicle and remove wheel.
2. Raise lower link using suitable jack, then remove ball joint attaching nuts and ball joint, **Fig. 2.**
3. Remove upper link spindle attaching bolts, then the upper link.
4. Remove nuts and washers from both ends of upper link spindle, then press spindle and bushings out of link.
5. Reverse procedure to install.

LOWER LINK & BALL JOINT

REPLACE

PATHFINDER & PICKUP MODELS

1. Raise and support front of vehicle and remove wheel.
2. On 2WD Pickup, proceed as follows:
   a. Remove torsion bar spring anchor bolt.
   b. Remove dust cover and snap ring from anchor arm.
   c. Slide anchor arm rearward, then remove torsion bar spring and torque arm.
3. On 4WD Pickup and Pathfinder, remove torque arm attaching nuts, then the torsion bar spring with torque arm.
4. On all models, remove lower shock absorber attaching bolt.

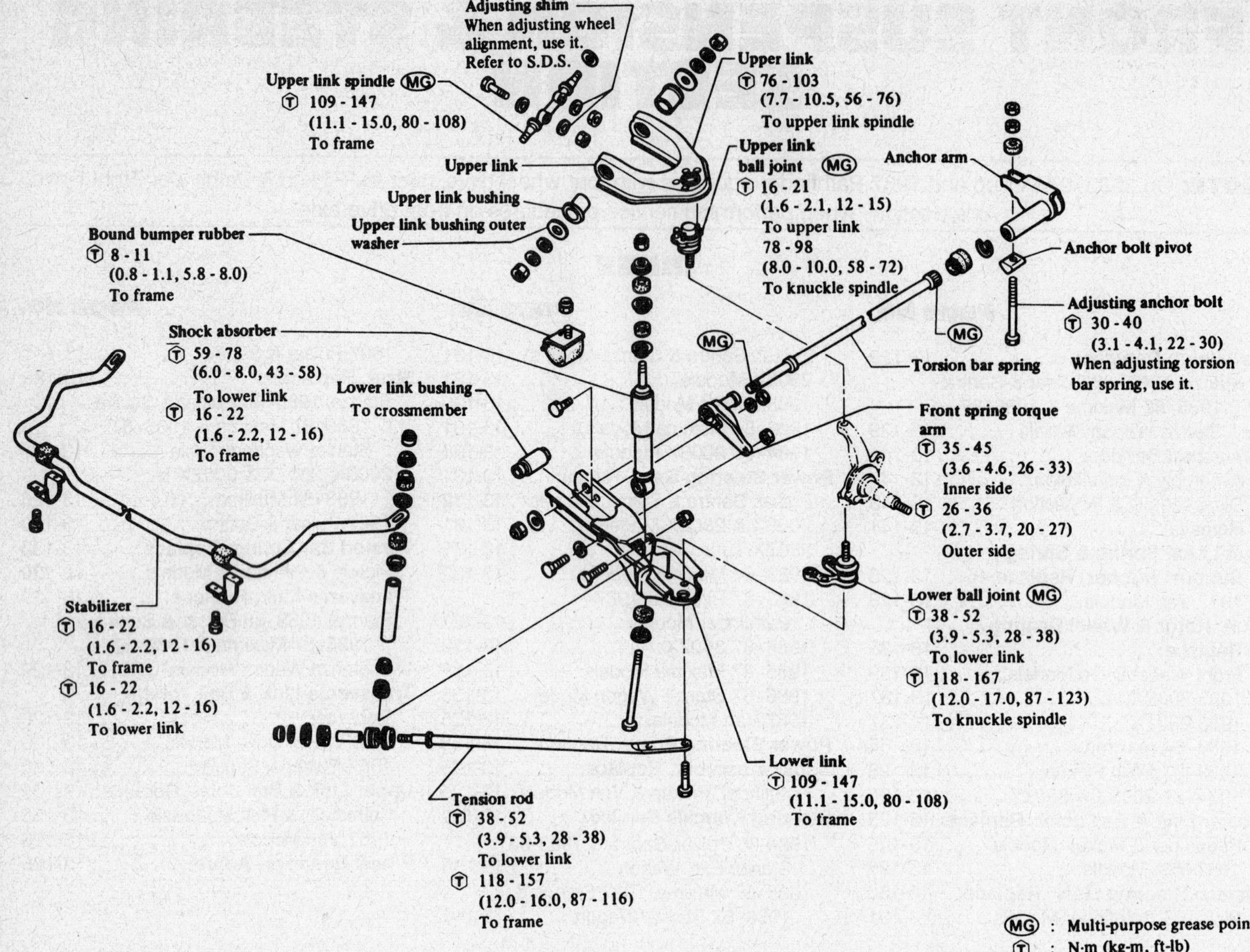

Fig. 1 Front suspension. 1986 2WD Pickup shown, other Pickups similar

5. Remove ball joint from knuckle spindle or lower link.
6. Disconnect stabilizer connecting rod and tension or compression rod from lower link.
7. Press bushing out of lower link.
8. Reverse procedure to install.

1987 VAN MODELS

1. Raise and support front of vehicle and remove wheel.
2. Separate knuckle spindle from lower ball joint using a suitable tool.
3. Remove stabilizer bar brackets from lower links and swing stabilizer bar down away from lower links.
4. Support lower link with suitable jack, then remove shock absorber lower attaching nut.
5. Remove compression rod, then the leaf spring to spring support rubber attaching nuts.
6. Lower jack until no tension is present on spring.
7. Move lower link downward, then jack up end of leaf spring.
8. Remove lower link pin to suspension member attaching nut.
9. Remove lower link and ball joint assembly.
10. Reverse procedure to install.

FRONT LEAF SPRING & SPRING SUPPORT RUBBER

REPLACE

1987 VAN MODELS

1. Remove one side of lower link, refer to "Lower Link & Ball Joint, Replace" procedure.
2. Take out leaf spring toward removed lower link side.

STRUT

REPLACE

200SX, 280ZX & 300ZX & 1983–84 MAXIMA MODELS

1. Raise and support front of vehicle and remove wheel.
2. Loosen brake tube and remove brake hose locking spring. Remove plate and brake hose from strut bracket.
3. Remove caliper.
4. On models equipped with adjustable shocks, disconnect shock electrical connectors.
5. Remove strut to steering knuckle attaching bolts.
6. Disconnect knuckle arm from bottom of strut.
7. Support strut with a suitable jack.
8. Remove upper strut attachments.
9. Slowly lower jack and remove strut from vehicle.
10. Reverse procedure to install. Torque upper strut attaching bolts to 25 ft. lbs. and strut to lower knuckle arm attaching bolts to 53–72 ft. lbs.

STANZA, 1983–86 PULSAR & SENTRA, 1985–87 MAXIMA & 1986–87 STANZA WAGON MODELS

1. Raise and support front of vehicle and remove wheel.

- When removing each suspension part, check wheel alignment and adjust if necessary.
- When installing a bushing, do not allow it to project beyond the surface area of the washer.
- Do not allow the bushings and washers to come in contact with grease, oil soapy water, etc.

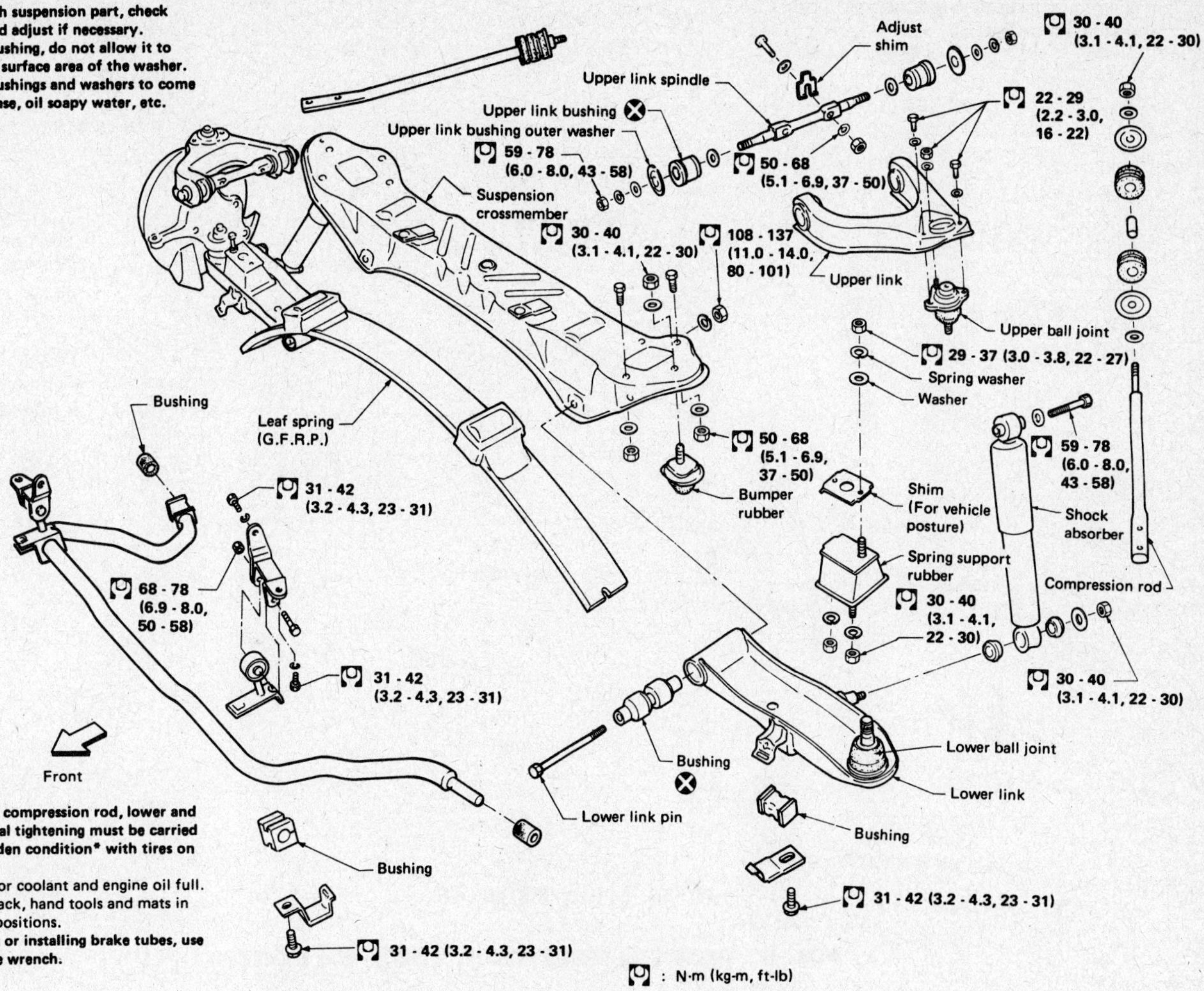

Adjust shim
30 - 40 (3.1 - 4.1, 22 - 30)
Upper link spindle
22 - 29 (2.2 - 3.0, 16 - 22)
Upper link bushing
Upper link bushing outer washer
59 - 78 (6.0 - 8.0, 43 - 58)
50 - 68 (5.1 - 6.9, 37 - 50)
Suspension crossmember
30 - 40 (3.1 - 4.1, 22 - 30)
108 - 137 (11.0 - 14.0, 80 - 101)
Upper link
Upper ball joint
29 - 37 (3.0 - 3.8, 22 - 27)
Spring washer
Washer
Bushing
Leaf spring (G.F.R.P.)
50 - 68 (5.1 - 6.9, 37 - 50)
Bumper rubber
59 - 78 (6.0 - 8.0, 43 - 58)
Shim (For vehicle posture)
Shock absorber
31 - 42 (3.2 - 4.3, 23 - 31)
Spring support rubber
Compression rod
68 - 78 (6.9 - 8.0, 50 - 58)
30 - 40 (3.1 - 4.1, 22 - 30)
31 - 42 (3.2 - 4.3, 23 - 31)
30 - 40 (3.1 - 4.1, 22 - 30)
Front
Bushing
Lower ball joint
Lower link
Lower link pin
Bushing
Bushing
31 - 42 (3.2 - 4.3, 23 - 31)
31 - 42 (3.2 - 4.3, 23 - 31)
: N·m (kg-m, ft-lb)

- When installing compression rod, lower and upper links, final tightening must be carried out under unladen condition* with tires on the ground.
  - * Fuel, radiator coolant and engine oil full. Spare tire, jack, hand tools and mats in designated positions.
- When removing or installing brake tubes, use flare nut torque wrench.

Fig. 2 Front suspension. 1987 Van

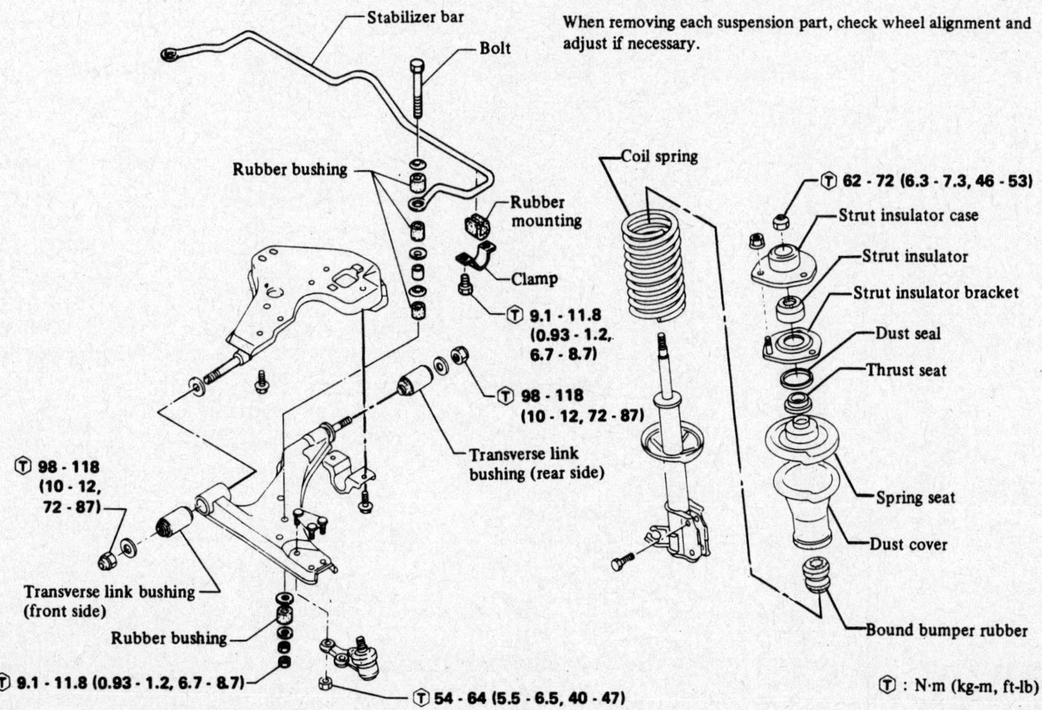

Fig. 3 Front suspension. 1983–86 Pulsar, 1985–86 Sentra & 1986–87 Stanza Wagon less 4WD

When removing each suspension part, check wheel alignment and adjust if necessary.

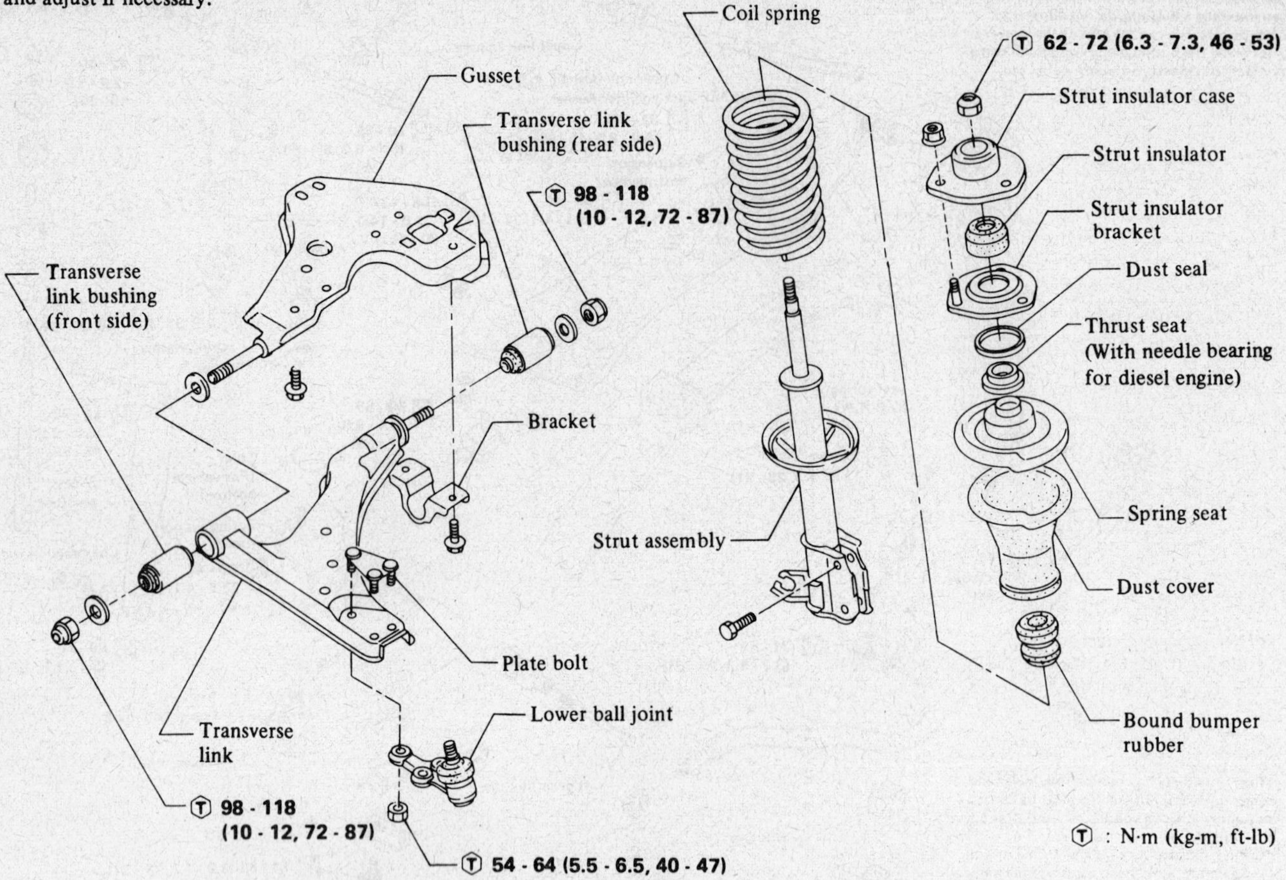

Coil spring
Ⓣ 62 - 72 (6.3 - 7.3, 46 - 53)
Strut insulator case
Gusset
Transverse link bushing (rear side)
Strut insulator
Ⓣ 98 - 118 (10 - 12, 72 - 87)
Strut insulator bracket
Transverse link bushing (front side)
Dust seal
Thrust seat (With needle bearing for diesel engine)
Bracket
Spring seat
Strut assembly
Dust cover
Plate bolt
Lower ball joint
Bound bumper rubber
Transverse link
Ⓣ 98 - 118 (10 - 12, 72 - 87)
Ⓣ : N·m (kg-m, ft-lb)
Ⓣ 54 - 64 (5.5 - 6.5, 40 - 47)

Fig. 4 Front suspension. 1983–84 Sentra

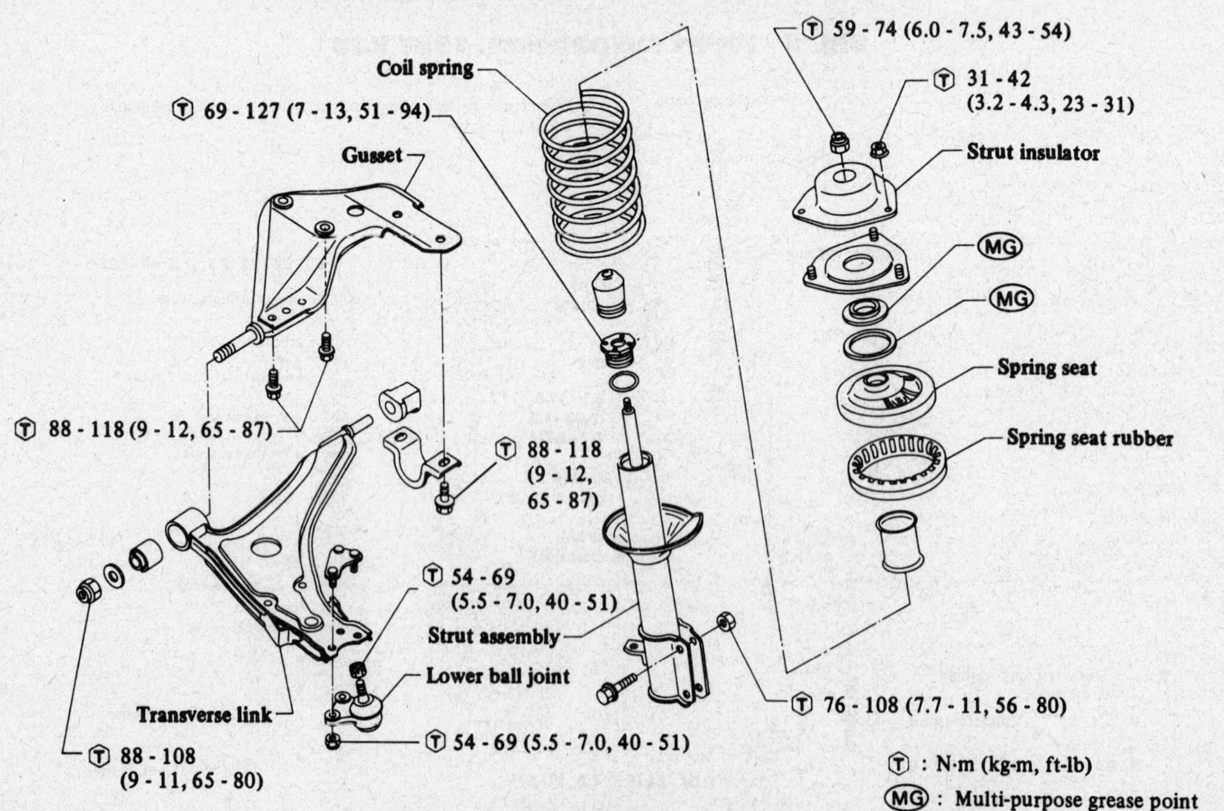

Fig. 5 Front suspension. 1983–86 Stanza exc. Wagon

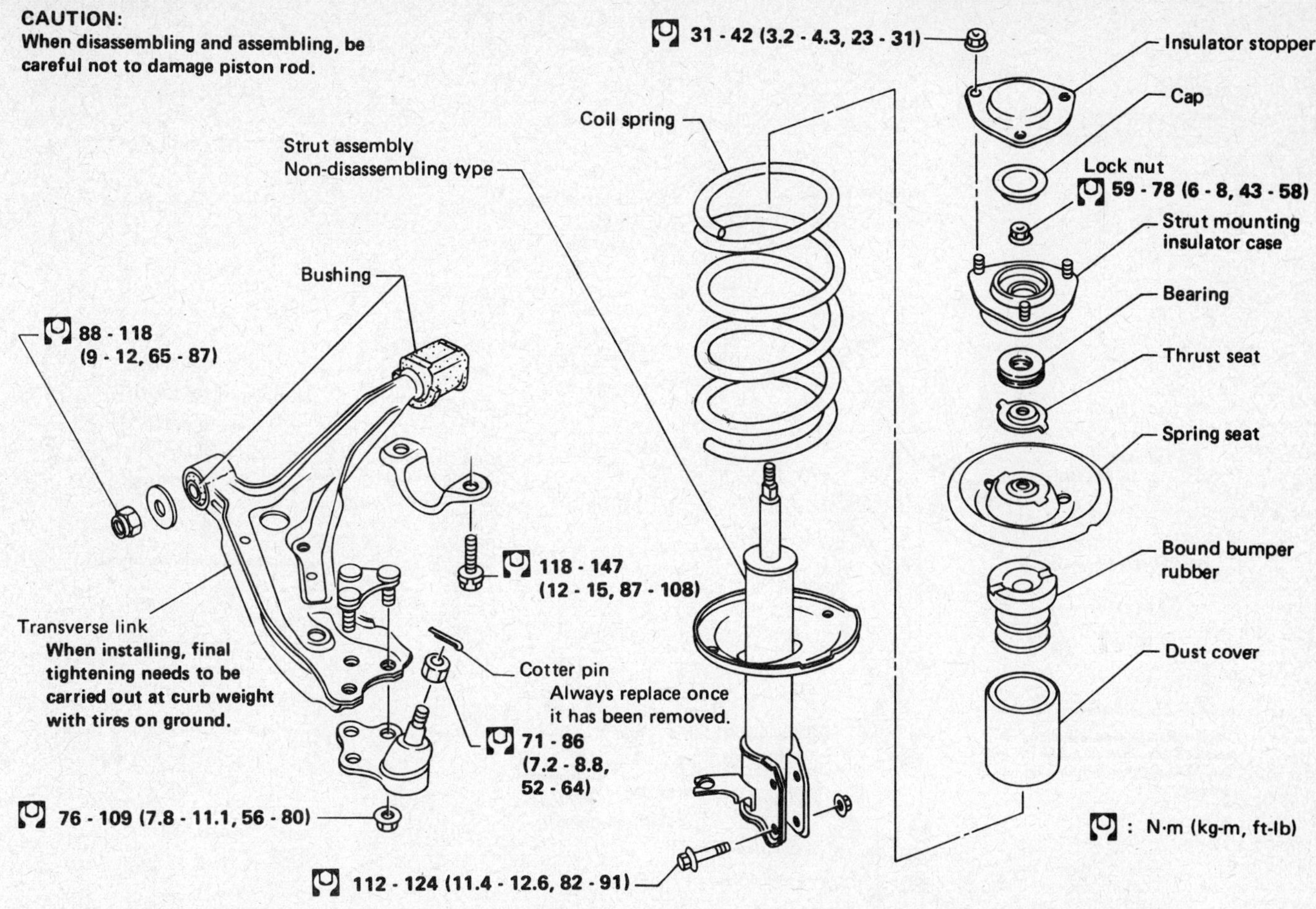

Fig. 6 Front suspension. 1985–87 Maxima & 1987 Stanza exc. Wagon

2. Disconnect brake line from strut.
3. Support transverse link with a suitable jack.
4. Remove strut to steering knuckle attaching bolts, then separate strut from knuckle, **Figs. 3 through 7**
5. On Maxima and Stanza models, loosen, but do not remove, the piston rod lock nut.
6. On all models, remove strut attaching nuts, then the strut assembly from vehicle.
7. Reverse procedure to install.

1987 PULSAR & SENTRA MODELS

Refer to **Fig. 8** for strut replacement, noting the following:

1. Place alignment marks on strut lower bracket and camber adjusting pin.
2. Do not remove piston rod locknut with strut assembly installed on vehicle.

TRANSVERSE LINK

REPLACE

STANZA, 1983–86 PULSAR & SENTRA, 1985–87 MAXIMA & 1986–87 STANZA WAGON MODELS

1. Raise and support front of vehicle and remove wheel.
2. Remove stabilizer bar, as required.
3. On all models, except Maxima, remove ball joint.
4. Remove transverse link attaching bolts, then the transverse link and gusset.
5. Reverse procedure to install. On 1986-87 4WD Stanza wagon models, tighten transverse link gusset attaching bolts in proper sequence, **Figs. 9 and 10.**

BALL JOINT

REPLACE

STANZA, 1983–86 PULSAR & SENTRA, 1985–87 MAXIMA & 1986–87 STANZA WAGON MODELS

1. Remove driveshaft as described under "Drive Shaft Service."
2. Remove ball joint using suitable tool.
3. Reverse procedure to install.

TRANSVERSE LINK & BALL JOINT

REPLACE

REAR WHEEL DRIVE MODELS

1. Raise and support vehicle and remove wheels.

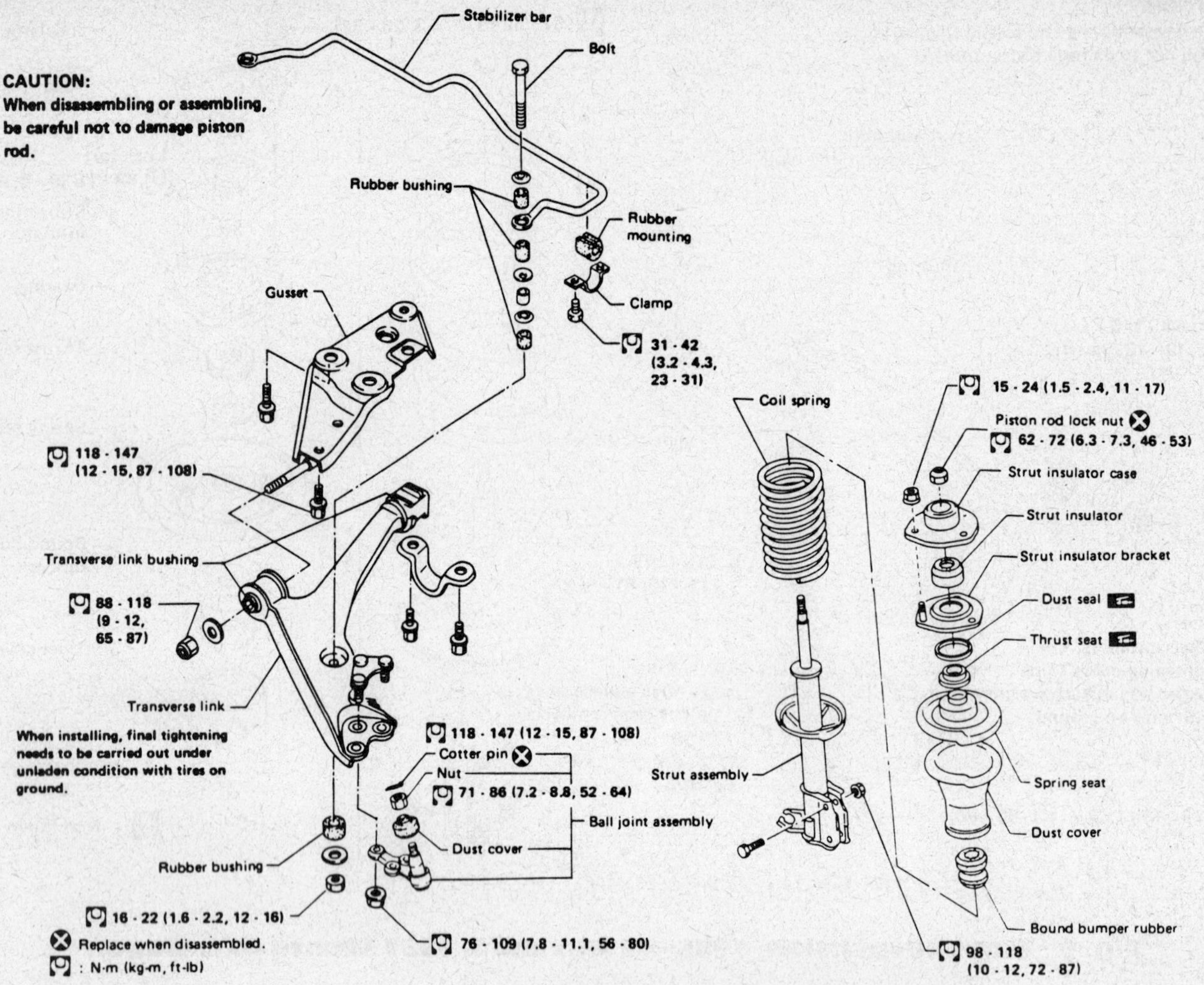

Fig. 7 Front suspension. 1986–87 Stanza Wagon w/4WD

2. Disconnect side rod stud from steering knuckle.
3. Remove steering knuckle attaching bolts and disconnect knuckle arm from bottom of strut.
4. Remove compression or tension rod and stabilizer bar.
5. Loosen transverse link mounting bar and separate link from crossmember.
6. Remove transverse link with ball joint and knuckle arm.
7. Place transverse link in a vise and remove bolt securing ball joint to transverse arm and the ball joint from the arm.
8. Reverse procedure to install.

1987 PULSAR & SENTRA MODELS

1. Remove wheel bearing locknut.
2. Remove tie rod ball joint.
2. Remove strut lower bracket attaching nuts and bolts.
3. Separate driveshaft from knuckle by tapping driveshaft end with a suitable hammer. **Use caution not to damage driveshaft boots.**
4. Separate lower ball joint stud from knuckle using a suitable tool.
5. Remove stabilizer bar attaching bolt from transverse link and ball joint assembly.
6. Remove transverse link bracket attaching bolts, then the transverse link bracket.
7. Remove remaining transverse link assembly attaching bolt, then the transverse link and ball joint assembly.
8. Reverse procedure to install.

TORSION BAR SPRING

REPLACE

PICKUP & PATHFINDER MODELS

1. Raise and support vehicle.
2. Remove wheel.
3. Remove torsion bar nuts.
4. Remove dust cover, then disconnect snap ring from anchor arm.
5. On 2WD models, pull anchor arm rearward, then remove torsion bar spring rearward. Remove torque arm.
6. On 4WD models, remove torque arm attaching nuts, then pull torsion bar spring forward and remove with torque arm.
7. Reverse procedure to install.

MANUAL STEERING GEAR

REPLACE

1983 200SX MODELS

1. Disconnect exhaust pipe from exhaust manifold, if necessary.
2. Remove bolt securing exhaust pipe to transmission mounting insulator.
3. Remove bolt securing worm shaft to rubber coupling.
4. Remove nut securing pitman arm to sector shaft, then the pitman arm.
5. Remove steering gear attaching bolts and the steering gear from vehicle.
6. Reverse procedure to install.

1984–86 200SX MODELS

1. Remove tie rod ball studs from knuckle arms using tool No. HT72520000 or equivalent.
2. Disconnect steering column lower joint.
3. Refer to **Fig. 11** for remainder of removal procedure.
4. Reverse procedure to install.

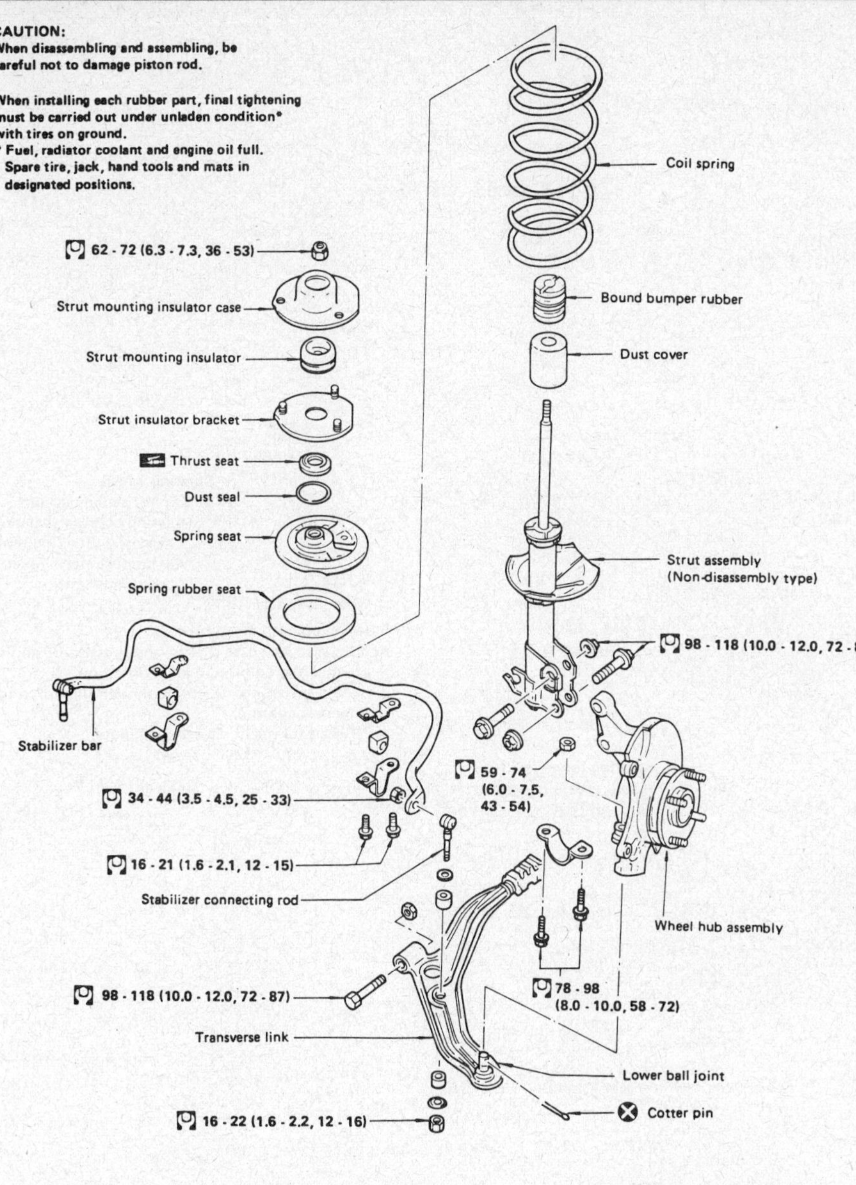

Fig. 8 Front suspension. 1987 Pulsar & Sentra

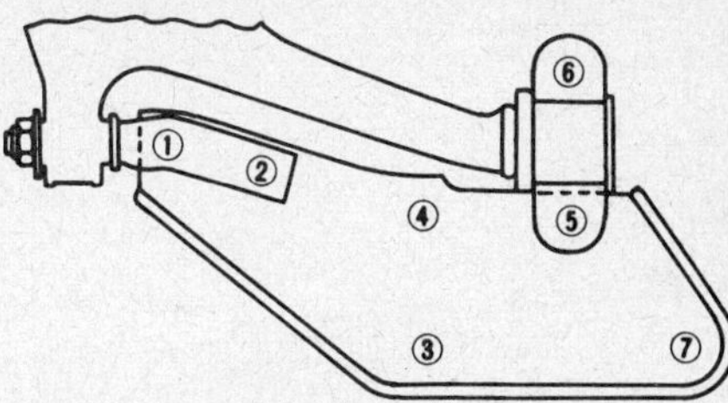

Fig. 9 Left side transverse link gusset attaching bolt tightening sequence. 1986–87 Stanza wagon w/4WD

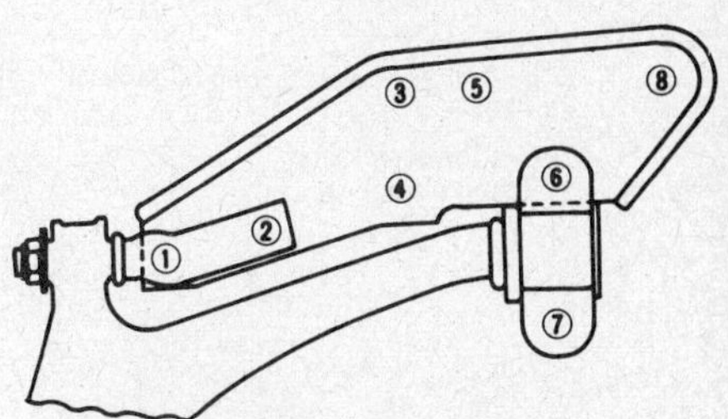

Fig. 10 Right side transverse link gusset attaching bolt tightening sequence. 1986–87 Stanza wagon w/4WD

280ZX MODELS

1. Raise and support front of vehicle and remove wheels.
2. Disconnect lower joint from steering column at rubber coupling.
3. Loosen bolt securing lower joint assembly to pinion, then the lower joint assembly.
4. Remove splash board.
5. Disconnect side rod studs from steering knuckles.
6. Remove gear housing to crossmember bolts and the gear assembly from vehicle.
7. Reverse procedure to install.

1983–84 MAXIMA MODELS

1. Raise and support front of vehicle and remove wheels.
2. Disconnect side rod studs from steering knuckle.
3. Loosen bolts securing steering gear to crossmember and loosen bolt securing lower shaft to rubber coupling.
4. Remove bolt securing lower joint to steering gear pinion, and remove lower joint from pinion.
5. Remove bolts securing steering gear to crossmember and remove steering gear.
6. To install, reverse procedure.

PULSAR, SENTRA & STANZA MODELS

1. Raise and support front of vehicle and remove wheels.
2. Disconnect tie rod from steering knuckle.
3. Loosen steering gear attaching bolts, then remove bolt securing lower joint to steering gear pinion and remove lower joint from pinion.
4. Remove steering gear housing-to-body attaching bolts, then the steering gear and linkage assembly from vehicle.
5. Reverse procedure to install.

PICKUP & PATHFINDER MODELS

Refer to **Fig. 12** for manual steering gear replacement procedure on these models.

POWER STEERING GEAR REPLACE

200SX & 280ZX MODELS

For steering gear replacement procedure on 1984-87 200SX models, refer to **Fig. 11.**

1. Remove air cleaner.
2. Remove bolt securing universal joint to worm shaft.
3. Disconnect hoses from power steering gear. Cap hoses and ports.
4. Remove nut securing pitman arm to sector shaft, then the pitman arm from sector shaft.
5. Remove steering attaching bolts and the steering gear from vehicle.
6. Reverse procedure to install.

280ZX TURBO MODELS

1. Raise and support front of vehicle and remove wheels.
2. Remove bolts securing power steering hose clamps to crossmember.
3. Disconnect power steering hoses at steering gear and drain gear into a suitable container. Plug hose ends and ports in steering gear.
4. Disconnect side rod studs from steering knuckles.
5. Loosen bolt securing lower shaft to rubber coupling.

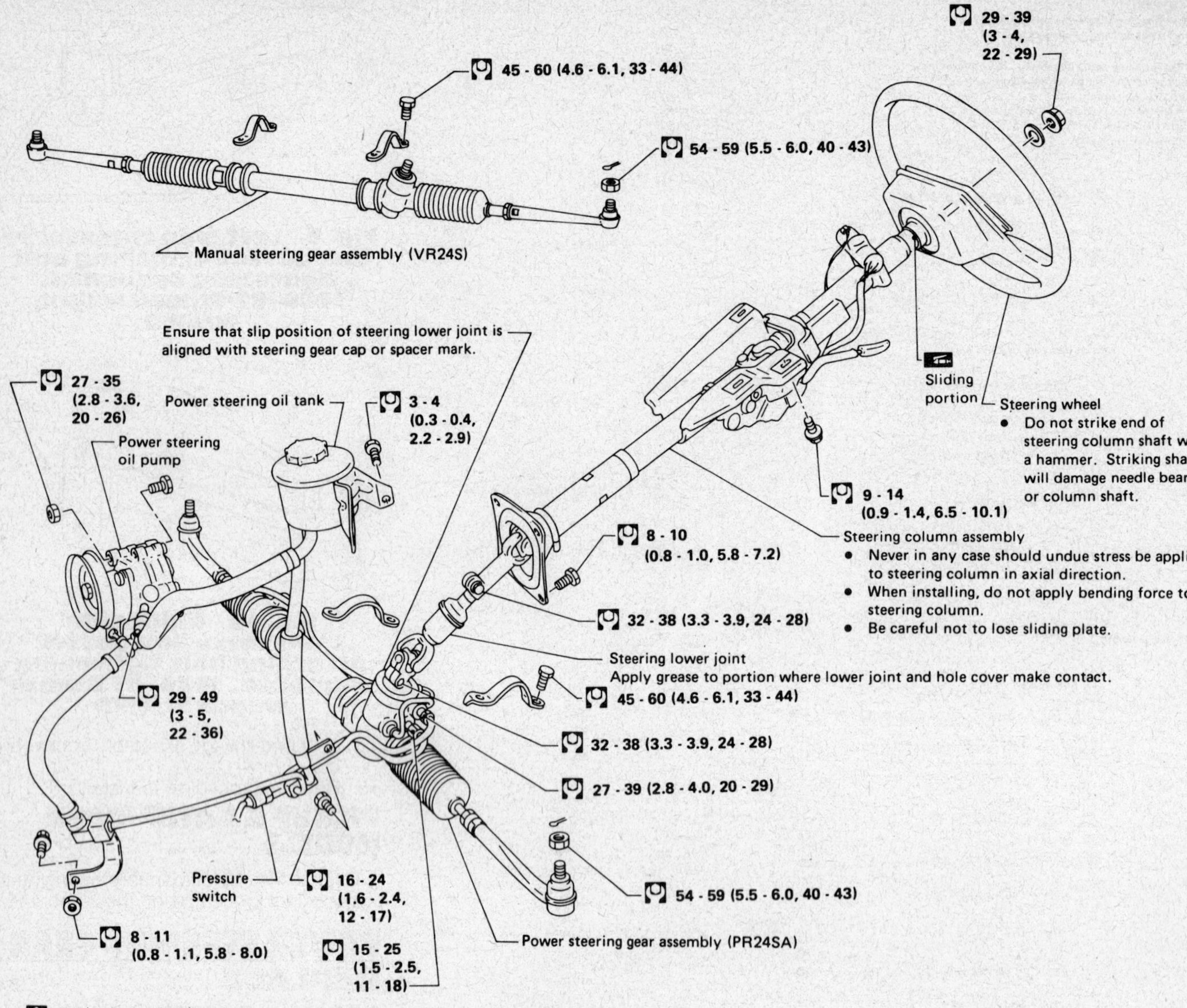
29 - 39 (3 - 4, 22 - 29)
45 - 60 (4.6 - 6.1, 33 - 44)
54 - 59 (5.5 - 6.0, 40 - 43)
Manual steering gear assembly (VR24S)
Ensure that slip position of steering lower joint is aligned with steering gear cap or spacer mark.
27 - 35 (2.8 - 3.6, 20 - 26)
Power steering oil tank
3 - 4 (0.3 - 0.4, 2.2 - 2.9)
Power steering oil pump
Sliding portion
Steering wheel
• Do not strike end of steering column shaft with a hammer. Striking shaft will damage needle bearing or column shaft.
9 - 14 (0.9 - 1.4, 6.5 - 10.1)
8 - 10 (0.8 - 1.0, 5.8 - 7.2)
Steering column assembly
• Never in any case should undue stress be applied to steering column in axial direction.
• When installing, do not apply bending force to steering column.
• Be careful not to lose sliding plate.
32 - 38 (3.3 - 3.9, 24 - 28)
Steering lower joint
Apply grease to portion where lower joint and hole cover make contact.
45 - 60 (4.6 - 6.1, 33 - 44)
29 - 49 (3 - 5, 22 - 36)
32 - 38 (3.3 - 3.9, 24 - 28)
27 - 39 (2.8 - 4.0, 20 - 29)
Pressure switch
16 - 24 (1.6 - 2.4, 12 - 17)
54 - 59 (5.5 - 6.0, 40 - 43)
8 - 11 (0.8 - 1.1, 5.8 - 8.0)
15 - 25 (1.5 - 2.5, 11 - 18)
Power steering gear assembly (PR24SA)
: N·m (kg-m, ft-lb)

Fig. 11 Steering gear replacement. 1984–87 200SX

6. Remove bolt securing lower joint to pinion shaft and remove lower joint from pinion.
7. Remove nuts securing engine mount insulators to crossmember.
8. Refer to "Engine, Replace," remove hood and attach suitable lifting device to engine.
9. Raise engine to release pressure on crossmember and support crossmember with a floor jack.
10. Loosen steering gear mounting bolts and remove bolts securing crossmember to body, **Fig. 13.**
11. Lower floor jack supporting crossmember slowly, remove bolts securing steering gear to crossmember, and remove steering gear and linkage from vehicle.
12. To install, reverse procedure.

1984–87 300ZX MODELS

Refer to **Fig. 14** for power steering gear replacement procedure on these models.

1983–84 MAXIMA MODELS

1. Raise and support front of vehicle and remove wheels.
2. Remove bolt securing power steering hose clamp to steering gear mounting bracket.
3. Disconnect power steering hoses at steering gear and drain into a suitable container. Plug hose ends and ports in steering gear.
4. Disconnect side rod studs at steering knuckles.
5. Loosen bolt securing lower shaft to rubber coupling.
6. Remove bolt securing lower joint to pinion shaft and remove joint from pinion.
7. Remove bolts securing steering gear to crossmember and remove steering gear and linkage from vehicle.
8. To install, reverse procedure.

PULSAR, SENTRA & STANZA MODELS

1. Raise and support front of vehicle and remove wheels.
2. Disconnect power steering hose clamp, then the hose at steering gear and drain fluid into a suitable container.
3. Disconnect side rod studs from steering knuckles.
4. On Pulsar and Sentra models, support transaxle with a suitable jack, then remove exhaust pipe and rear engine mounts, if necessary.
5. On all models, remove bolt securing lower joint to steering gear pinion and remove lower joint from pinion.
6. Remove steering gear attaching bolts and, on 1983-86 Stanza models, the cylinder tubes.
7. Remove steering gear and linkage assembly from vehicle.
8. Reverse procedure to install.

Worm shaft to rubber coupling
Ⓣ 39 - 49 (4.0 - 5.0, 29 - 36)
Align the groove in worm shaft with the bolt hole in rubber coupling flange yoke, and press coupling bolt through the undercut section of worm shaft.
Ⓣ: N·m (kg-m, ft-lb)
Undercut section
Sector shaft to idler arm
Ⓣ 127 - 147 (13 - 15, 94 - 108)
• Remove gear arm
ST29020001
• Install gear arm
Align four grooves of gear arm serrations with four projections of sector shaft serrations, and install and tighten lock washer and nut.
Gear housing to frame
Ⓣ 84 - 96 (8.6 - 9.8, 62 - 71)

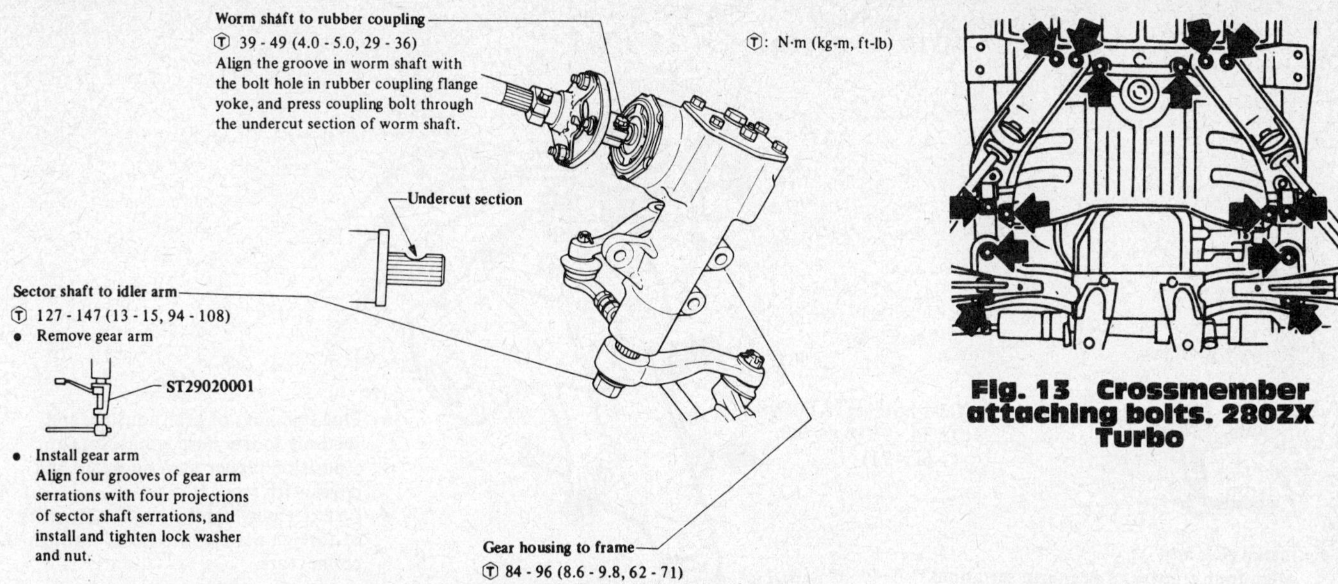

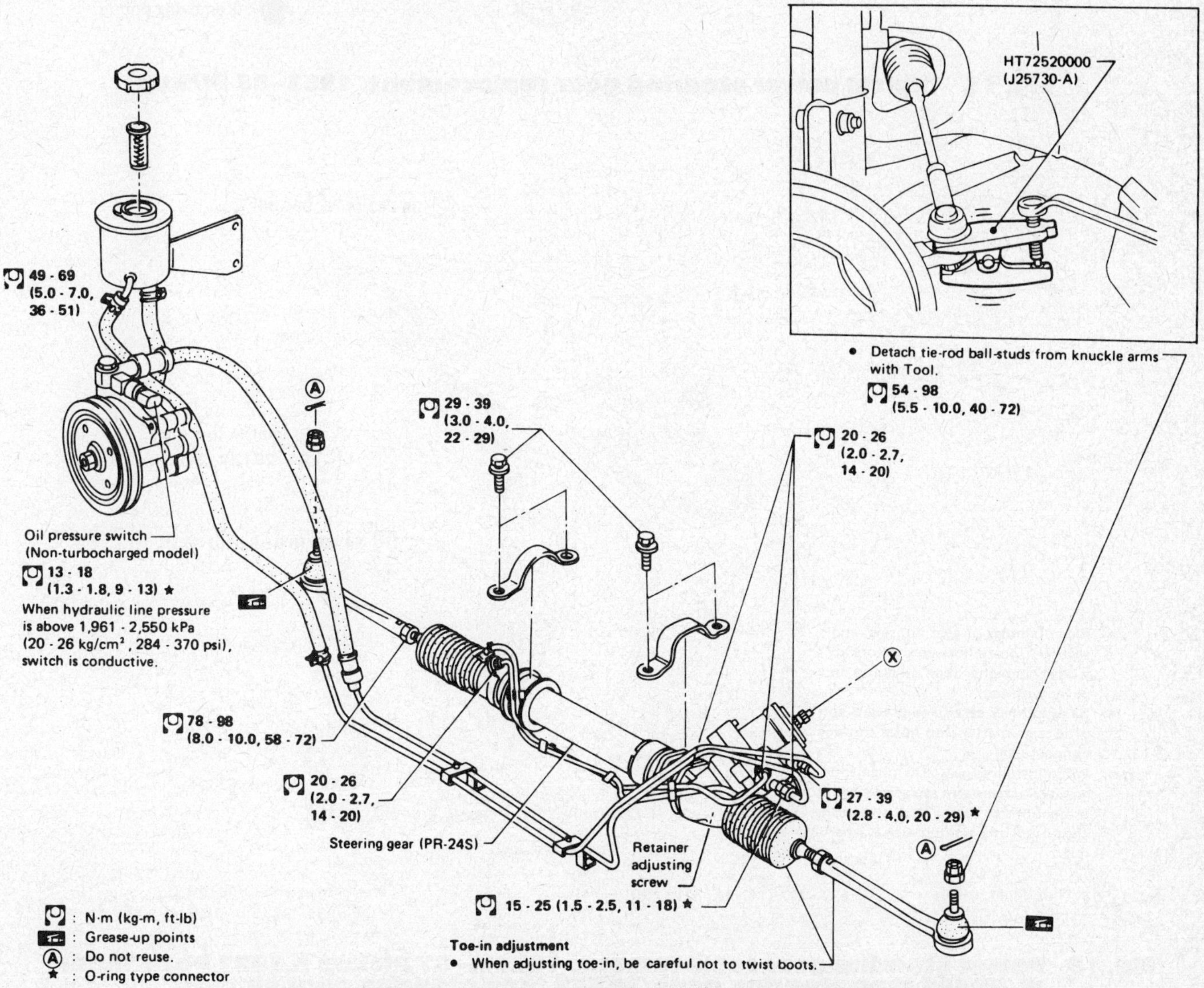

Fig. 12 Typical manual steering gear replacement. Pickup & Pathfinder

Fig. 13 Crossmember attaching bolts. 280ZX Turbo

HT72520000
(J25730-A)
• Detach tie-rod ball-studs from knuckle arms with Tool.
54 - 98
(5.5 - 10.0, 40 - 72)
49 - 69
(5.0 - 7.0,
36 - 51)
Ⓐ
29 - 39
(3.0 - 4.0,
22 - 29)
20 - 26
(2.0 - 2.7,
14 - 20)
Oil pressure switch
(Non-turbocharged model)
13 - 18
(1.3 - 1.8, 9 - 13) ★
When hydraulic line pressure is above 1,961 - 2,550 kPa (20 - 26 kg/cm², 284 - 370 psi), switch is conductive.
Ⓧ
78 - 98
(8.0 - 10.0, 58 - 72)
20 - 26
(2.0 - 2.7,
14 - 20)
27 - 39
(2.8 - 4.0, 20 - 29) ★
Steering gear (PR-24S)
Retainer
adjusting
screw
Ⓐ
15 - 25 (1.5 - 2.5, 11 - 18) ★
: N·m (kg-m, ft-lb)
: Grease-up points
Ⓐ : Do not reuse.
★ : O-ring type connector
Toe-in adjustment
• When adjusting toe-in, be careful not to twist boots.

Fig. 14 Power steering gear replacement. 1984–87 300ZX

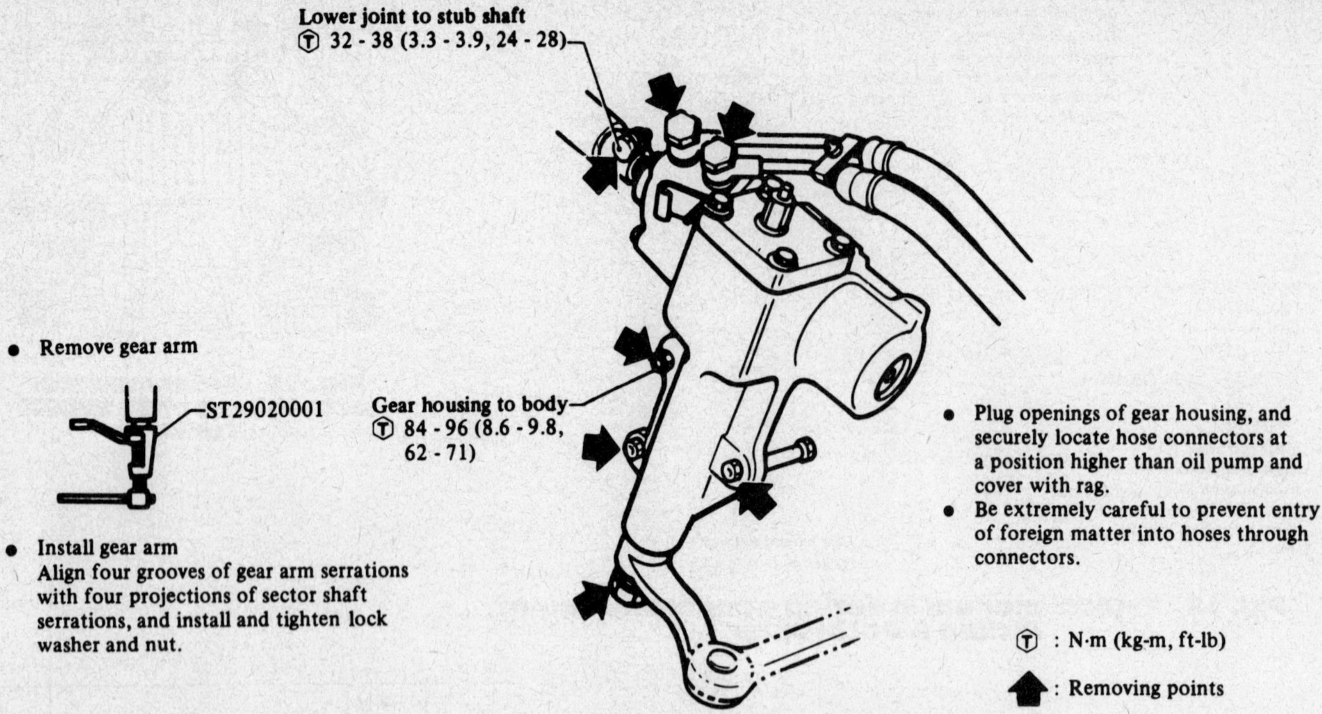
Lower joint to stub shaft
Ⓣ 32 - 38 (3.3 - 3.9, 24 - 28)
• Remove gear arm
ST29020001
Gear housing to body
Ⓣ 84 - 96 (8.6 - 9.8, 62 - 71)
• Install gear arm
Align four grooves of gear arm serrations with four projections of sector shaft serrations, and install and tighten lock washer and nut.
• Plug openings of gear housing, and securely locate hose connectors at a position higher than oil pump and cover with rag.
• Be extremely careful to prevent entry of foreign matter into hoses through connectors.
Ⓣ : N·m (kg-m, ft-lb)
: Removing points

Fig. 15 Typical power steering gear replacement. 1983–86 Pickup

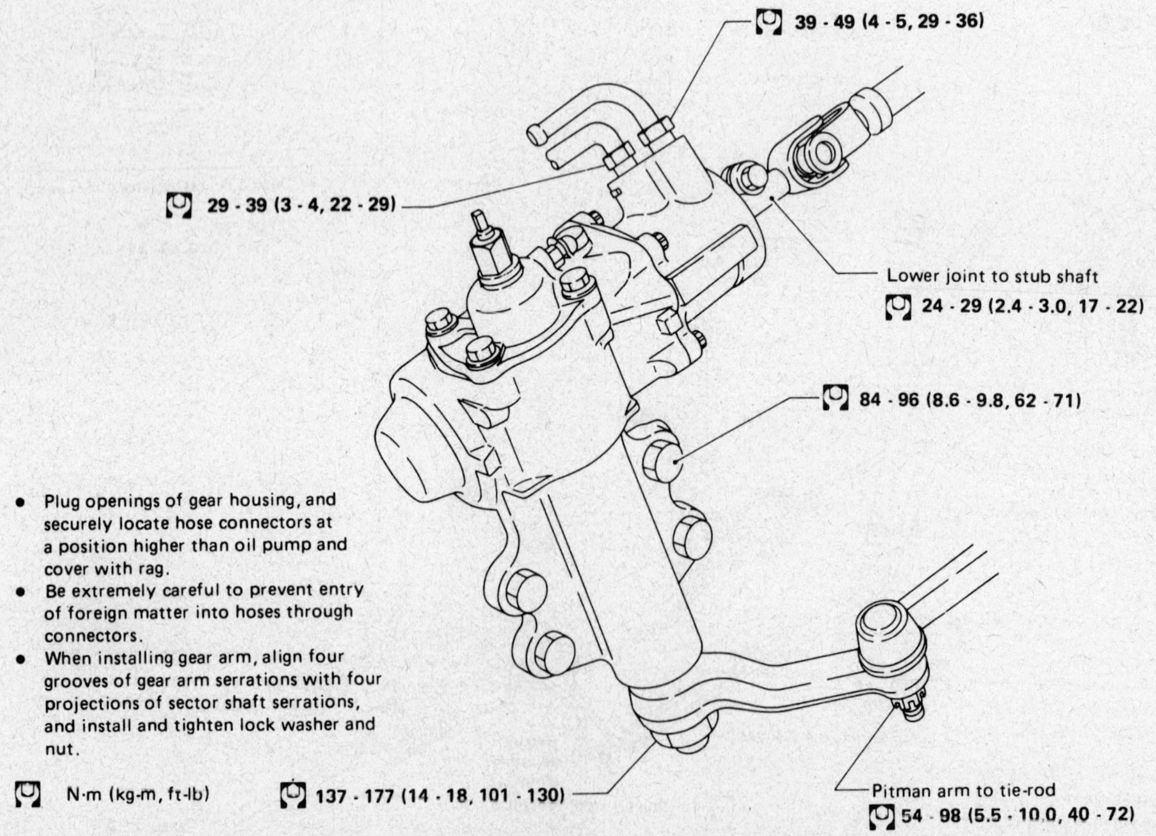
39 - 49 (4 - 5, 29 - 36)
29 - 39 (3 - 4, 22 - 29)
Lower joint to stub shaft
24 - 29 (2.4 - 3.0, 17 - 22)
84 - 96 (8.6 - 9.8, 62 - 71)
• Plug openings of gear housing, and securely locate hose connectors at a position higher than oil pump and cover with rag.
• Be extremely careful to prevent entry of foreign matter into hoses through connectors.
• When installing gear arm, align four grooves of gear arm serrations with four projections of sector shaft serrations, and install and tighten lock washer and nut.
N·m (kg-m, ft-lb)
137 - 177 (14 - 18, 101 - 130)
Pitman arm to tie-rod
54 - 98 (5.5 - 10.0, 40 - 72)

Fig. 16 Power steering gear replacement. 1886½–87 Pickup & 1987 Pathfinder w/PB48S type steering gear (PB56S type steering gear similar)

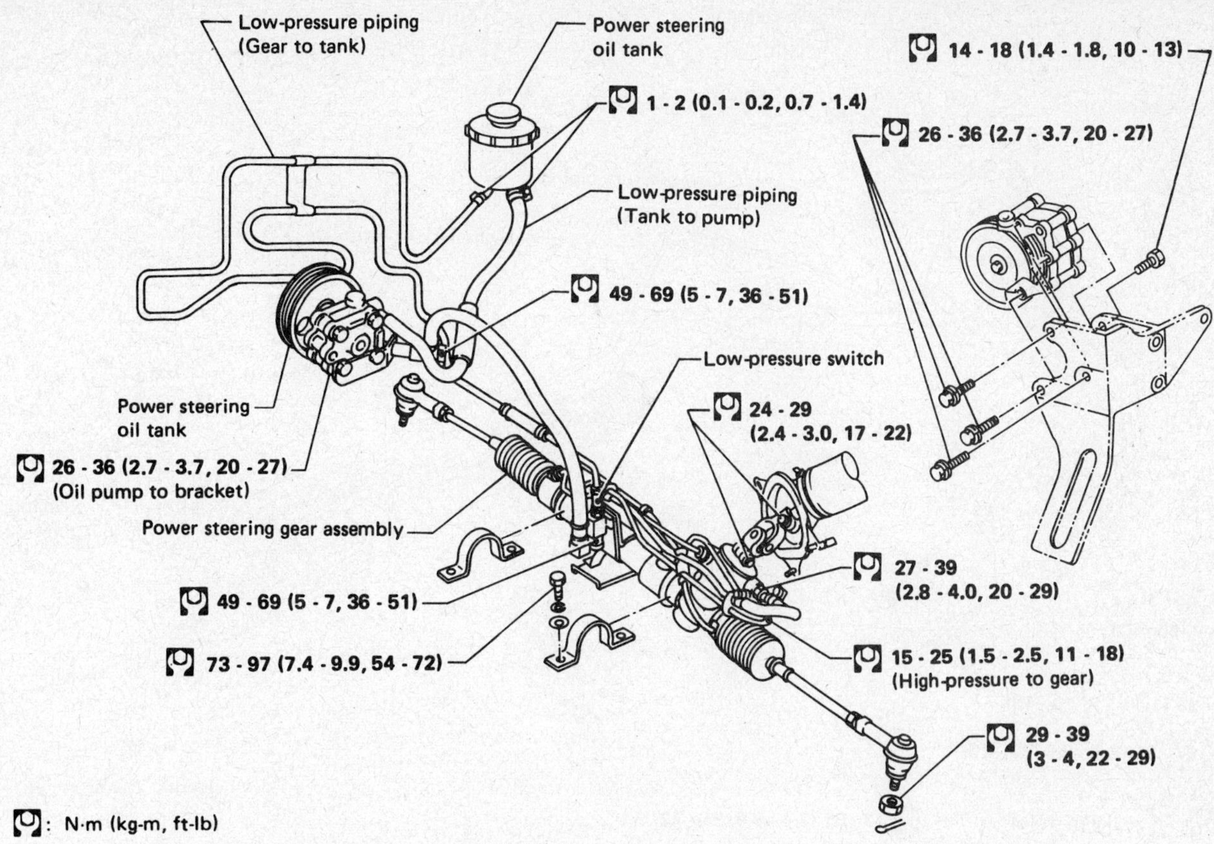

Fig. 17 Power steering gear replacement. 1985–87 Maxima

1983–87 PICKUP & PATHFINDER MODELS

Refer to **Figs. 15 and 16** for power steering gear replacement procedure on these models.

1985–87 MAXIMA MODELS

Refer to **Fig. 17** for power steering gear replacement procedure on these models, noting the following:

1. Detach tie rod ball studs from steering knuckle arms using suitable tool.
2. Remove exhaust pipe attaching nut and manual transaxle control linkage or automatic transaxle control cable.

1986–87 STANZA WAGON MODELS

Refer to **Fig. 18** for power steering gear replacement procedure on these models, noting the following:

1. Detach tie rod ball studs from steering knuckle arms using suitable tool.
2. Remove charcoal canister, exhaust pipe attaching nut and manual transaxle control linkage or automatic transaxle control cable.

1987 VAN MODELS

Refer to **Fig. 19** for power steering gear replacement procedure.

POWER STEERING PUMP REPLACE

1. Remove air cleaner duct at air cleaner on 200SX models, as required.
2. Loosen idler pulley lock nut, turn adjusting nut counterclockwise, and remove power steering pump drive belt. **On some air conditioned models, remove air conditioning compressor drive belt.**
3. Loosen power steering hoses at pump and remove bolts securing power steering pump to brackets.
4. Raise pump and disconnect power steering hoses. Catch fluid in a suitable container, plug hose ends and ports in power steering pump, and remove pump from vehicle.
5. Reinstall power steering pump by reversing procedure and bleed system as follows:

   a. Raise and support front of vehicle.
   b. Run engine for 3-5 seconds, stop engine, check and fill power steering pump reservoir as needed.
   c. Quickly turn steering wheel all the way to right and left 10 times.
   d. Start engine and idle for 3-5 second. Stop engine, check and fill power steering pump reservoir as needed.
   e. With steering wheel all the way to the right, open bleeder screw, to expel air and tighten bleeder screw.
   f. Repeat procedure until all air has been bled from system.
   g. If air cannot be bled completely after repeated attempts, repeat step e with engine running.

HUB ROTOR & WHEEL BEARING REPLACE

1983–84 MAXIMA

Removal

1. Block rear wheels, then raise and support front of vehicle.
2. Remove tire and wheel assembly.
3. Remove caliper assembly.
4. Remove hub cap, **Fig. 20.**
5. Remove cotter pin, adjusting cap and wheel bearing nut.
6. Remove wheel hub and rotor.
7. Separate outside (outboard) wheel bearing inner race and washer.
8. Separate brake rotor and hub.
9. Remove inside (inboard) wheel bearing outer race, grease seal and outer race assembly. **Do not drop wheel bearing or bearing damage will result.**

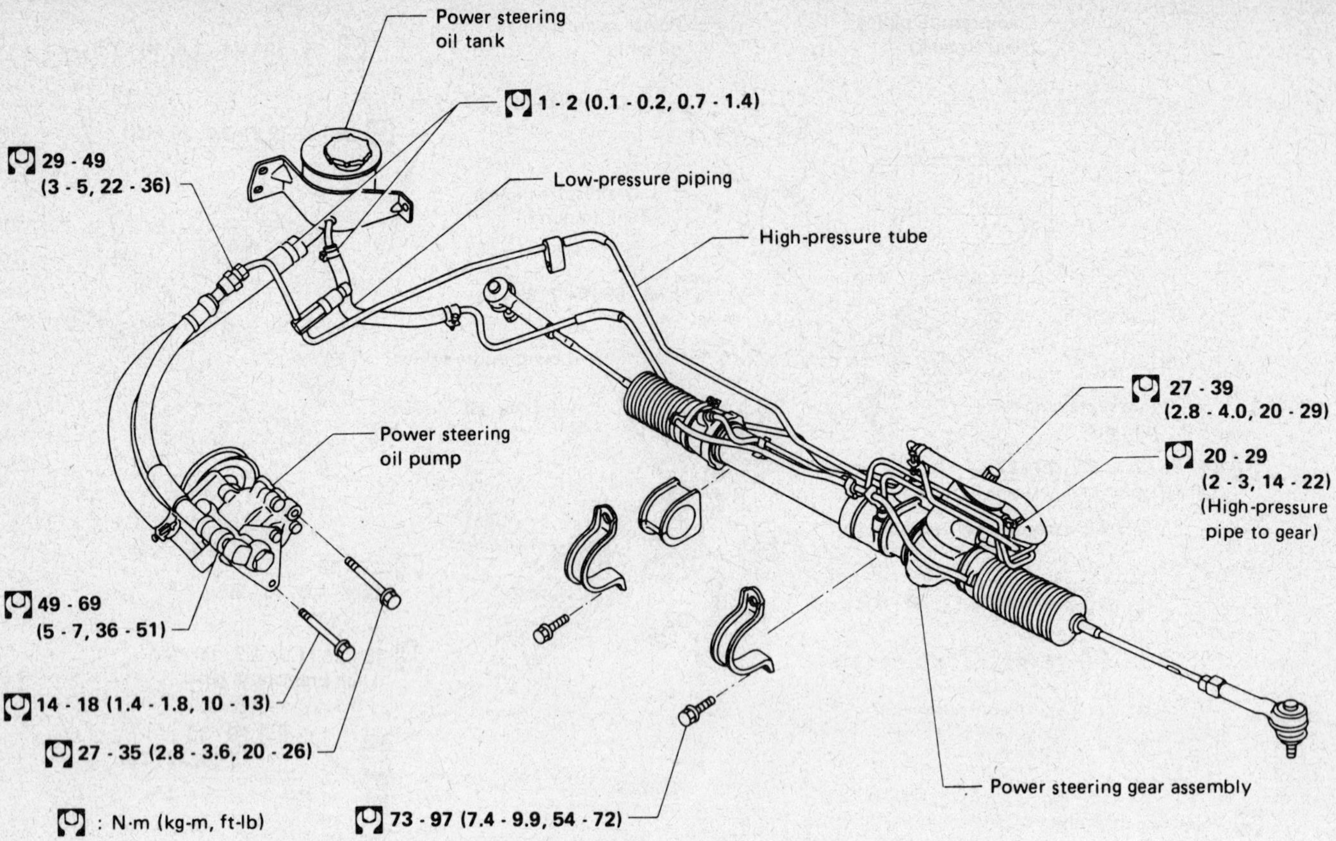

Power steering oil tank
1 - 2 (0.1 - 0.2, 0.7 - 1.4)
29 - 49 (3 - 5, 22 - 36)
Low-pressure piping
High-pressure tube
27 - 39 (2.8 - 4.0, 20 - 29)
20 - 29 (2 - 3, 14 - 22) (High-pressure pipe to gear)
Power steering oil pump
49 - 69 (5 - 7, 36 - 51)
14 - 18 (1.4 - 1.8, 10 - 13)
27 - 35 (2.8 - 3.6, 20 - 26)
Power steering gear assembly
: N·m (kg-m, ft-lb)
73 - 97 (7.4 - 9.9, 54 - 72)

Fig. 18 Power steering gear replacement. 1986–87 Stanza wagon

Steering column lower shaft
39 - 49 (4.0 - 5.0, 29 - 36)
24 - 29 (2.4 - 3.0, 17 - 22)
29 - 39 (3.0 - 4.0, 22 - 29)
137 - 177 (14 - 18, 101 - 130)
84 - 108 (8.6 - 11.0, 62 - 80)
: N·m (kg-m, ft-lb)

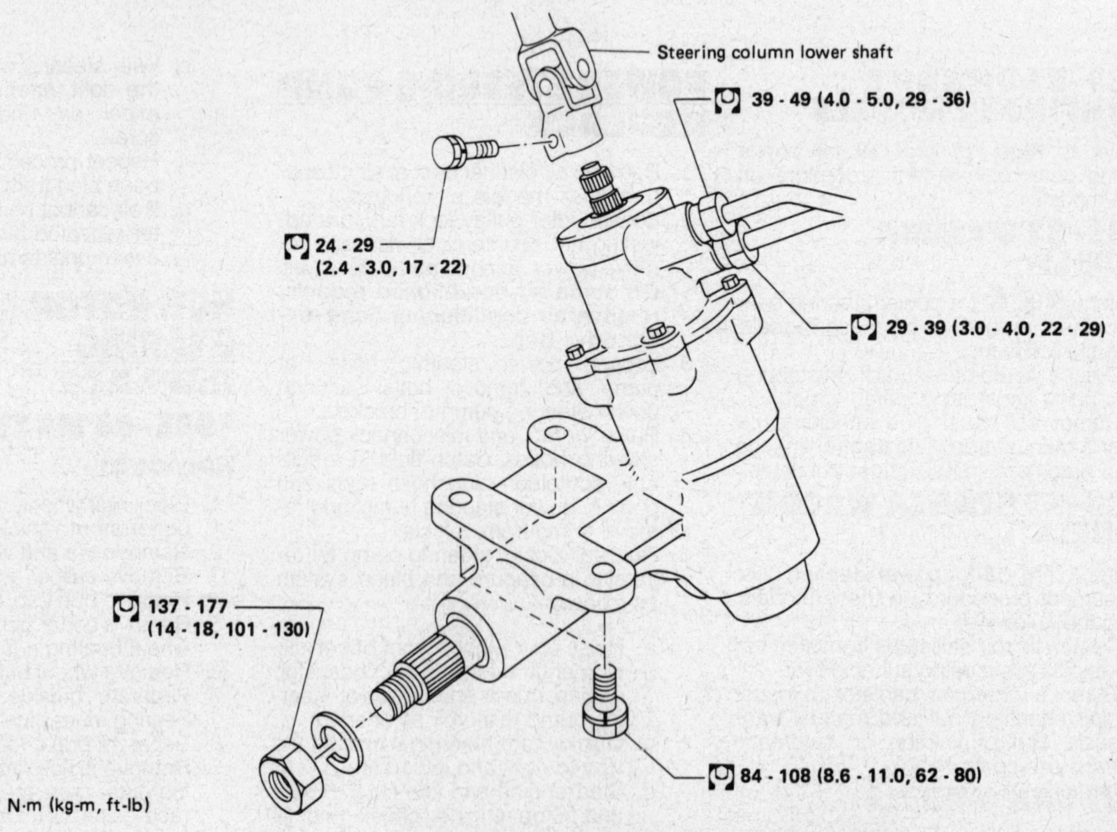

Fig. 19 Power steering gear replacement. 1987 Van

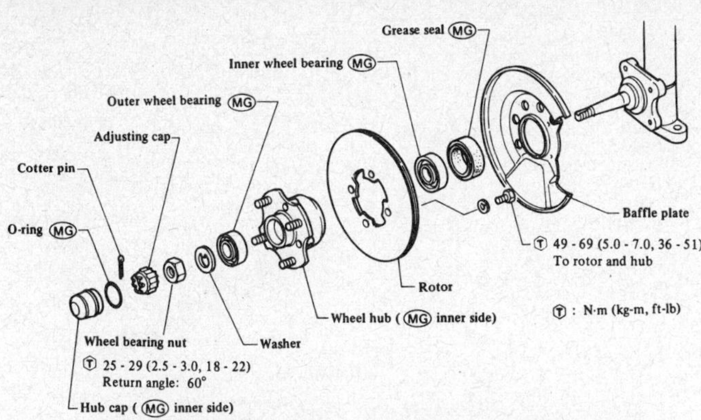

Fig. 20 Exploded view of wheel hub assembly. 1983–84 Maxima

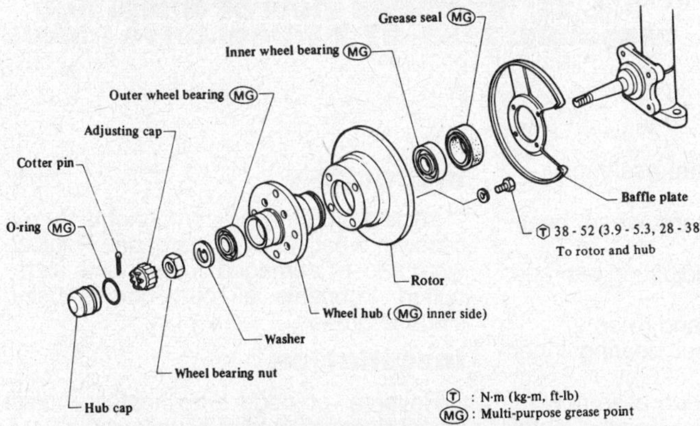

Fig. 22 Exploded view of wheel hub assembly. 1983 200SX

Inspection

Inspect all removed components for excessive wear and/or damage. Replace worn and/or damaged components as required.

Installation

1. Using a suitable tool, install bearing outer race into hub assembly.
2. Using suitable grease, pack hub cap and lubricate new O-ring.
3. Coat bearings with suitable grease.
4. Place inner bearing into hub, then install a new grease seal. Coat seal lips with suitable grease.
5. Install rotor onto hub assembly.
6. Lubricate threaded portion of spindle and bearing washer, using suitable grease.
7. Install hub assembly onto spindle. Install washer and wheel bearing nut.
8. Install hub cap, O-ring and caliper assembly.

1983 280ZX

Removal

1. Block rear wheels, then raise and support vehicle.
2. Remove wheel and tire assembly.
3. Remove caliper.
4. Remove hub cap, **Fig. 21.**
5. Remove cotter pin, adjusting cap and wheel bearing lock nut.
6. Remove wheel hub and rotor from spindle.
7. Remove outer bearing inner race and washer.

1 Hub cap
2 O-ring
3 Adjusting cap
4 Wheel bearing nut
5 Wheel bearing washer
6 Outer wheel bearing
7 Wheel hub
8 Disc brake rotor
9 Inner wheel bearing
10 Grease seal
11 Stopper bolt cap
12 Stopper bolt
13 Knuckle arm
14 Dust cover
15 Lower ball joint

Tightening torque N·m (kg-m, ft-lb)

(A) : 25 - 29 (2.5 - 3.0, 18 - 22)
(B) : 54 - 74 (5.5 - 7.5, 40 - 54)
(C) : 96 - 120 (9.8 - 12.2, 71 - 88)
(D) : 72 - 97 (7.3 - 9.9, 53 - 72)
(E) : 44 - 54 (4.5 - 5.5, 33 - 40)
(F) : 44 - 54 (4.5 - 5.5, 33 - 40)

Fig. 21 Exploded view of wheel hub assembly. 1983 280SX

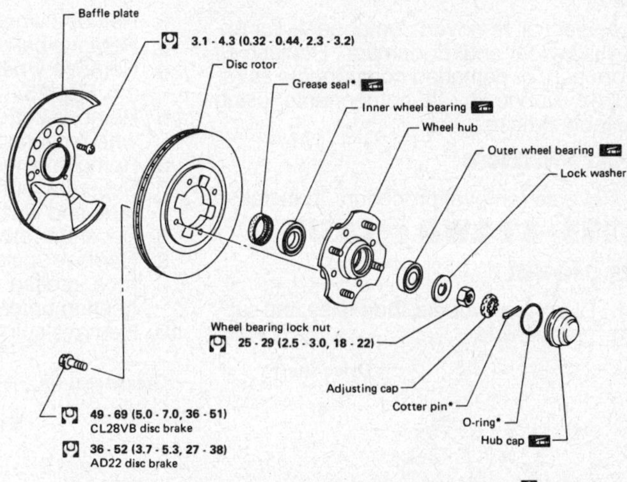

Fig. 23 Exploded view of wheel hub assembly. 1984–87 200SX

8. Remove rotor from wheel hub assembly.
9. Remove inner bearing race.

Inspection

Inspect all removed components for excessive wear and/or damage. Replace worn and/or damaged components as required.

Installation

Reverse removal procedure to install. Lubricate all components with suitable grease before installation.

1983 200SX

Removal

1. Block rear wheels, then raise and support vehicle.
2. Remove tire and wheel assembly.
3. Remove hub cap, **Fig. 22.**
4. Remove cotter pin, adjusting cap and wheel bearing nut.
5. Remove wheel hub disc and rotor.
6. Separate outer wheel bearing inner race from washer.
7. Separate rotor from hub assembly.
8. Remove grease seal, inner wheel bearing inner race, outer and inner wheel bearing outer races.

Inspection

Inspect all removed components for excessive wear and/or damage. Replace worn and/or damaged components as required.

Installation

Reverse removal procedure to install. Lubricate all components using suitable grease.

1984–87 200SX & 300ZX

Removal

1. Block rear wheels, then raise and support vehicle.
2. Remove wheel and tire assembly.
3. Remove caliper.
4. Remove wheel hub, rotor and wheel bearing from spindle, **Figs. 23 and 24.**
5. Using a suitable tool, remove bearing outer race, if necessary, from hub assembly.

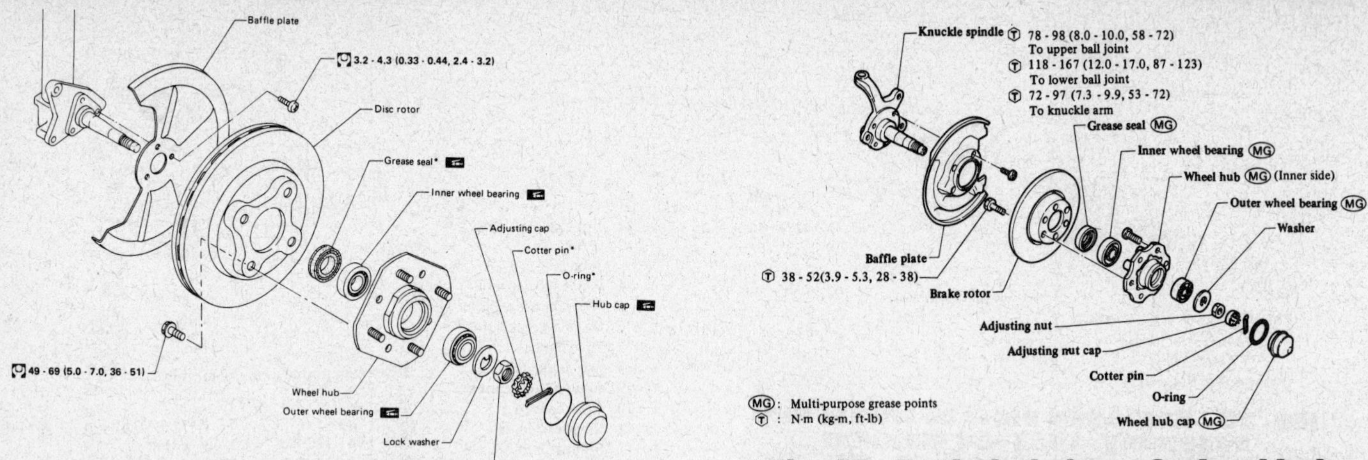

Fig. 24 Exploded view of wheel hub assembly. 1984–87 300ZX

Fig. 25 Exploded view of wheel hub assembly. 1983–87 2-Wheel Drive Pickup

Inspection

Inspect all removed components for excessive wear and/or damage. Replace all worn and/or damaged components as required. Lubricate all components using suitable grease.

Installation

Reverse removal procedure to install.

1983–87 2WD PICKUP

Removal

1. Block rear wheels, then raise and support vehicle.
2. Remove wheel and tire assembly.
3. Remove caliper.
4. Remove wheel hub and wheel bearing, **Fig. 25.**
5. Remove cotter pin, adjusting cap and wheel bearing nut.
6. Remove wheel hub and rotor.
7. Separate outer wheel bearing inner race and washer.
8. Separate rotor from hub assembly.
9. Remove inside wheel bearing outer race, grease seal and outside wheel bearing outer race.
10. Remove spindle and arm.

Inspection

Inspect all removed components for excessive wear and/or damage. Replace worn and/or damaged components as required. Lubricate all components using suitable grease.

Installation

Reverse procedure to install. Adjust wheel bearing preload as follows:

1. Tighten wheel bearing lock nut to 25-29 ft. lbs.
2. Turn wheel hub several times in both

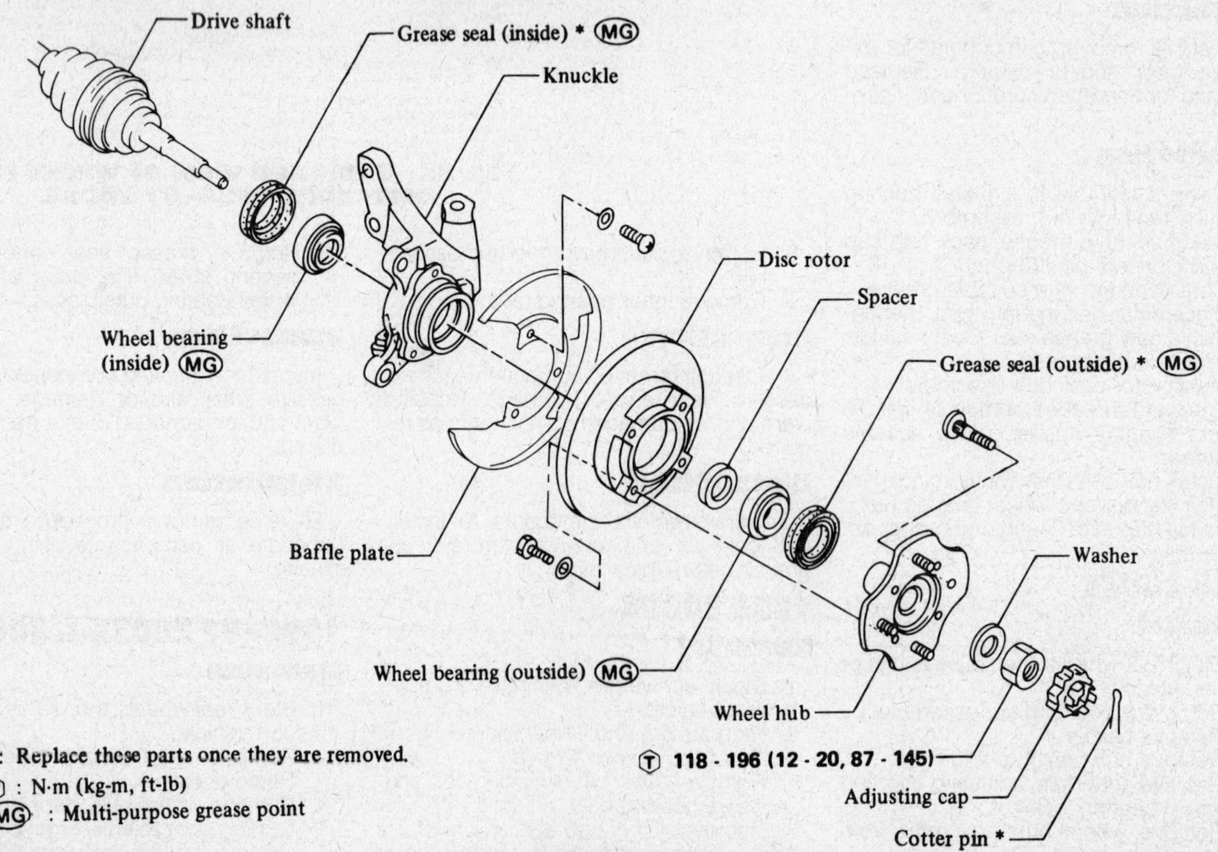

Fig. 26 Exploded view of wheel hub & steering knuckle assembly. 1983–86 Pulsar & Sentra

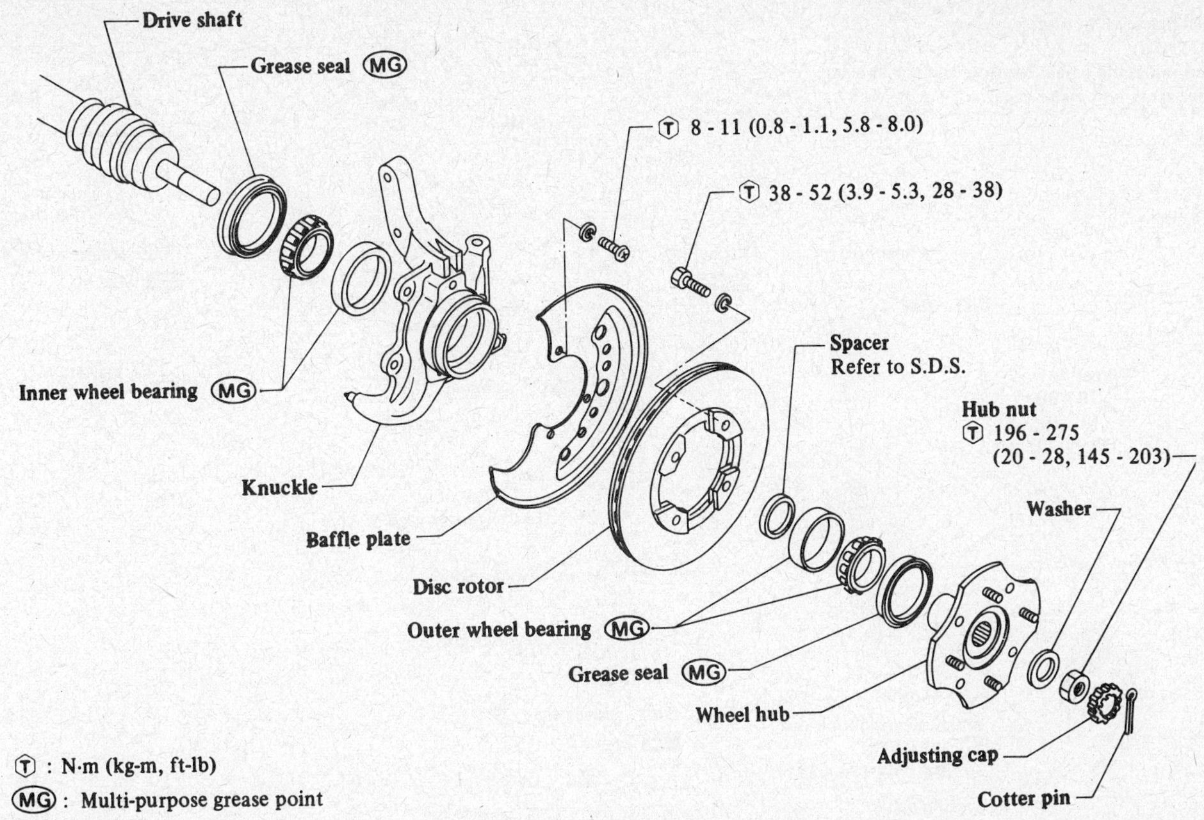

Fig. 27 Exploded view of wheel hub & steering knuckle assembly. 1983–86 Stanza

directions to seat wheel bearing correctly.

3. Again tighten tighten bearing lock nut to 25-29 ft. lbs.
4. Turn back wheel bearing lock nut 45°.
5. Install adjusting cap and a new cotter pin. Align cotter pin slot by loosening nut approximately 15° or less. **Do not exceed 15°.**
6. Measure wheel bearing preload and axial end play. Axial end play should be 0 inch (as measured at the wheel hub bolt). With a new grease installed, preload obtained should be 2.2-6.4 lbs. With a used grease seal installed, preload obtained should be 2.2-5.3 lbs.
7. Repeat steps 1 through 6 until correct bearing preload is obtained.

FRONT WHEEL DRIVE MODELS

Refer to "Steering Knuckle Service" for procedures.

STEERING KNUCKLE SERVICE

1983-86 PULSAR, SENTRA & 1983–86 STANZA EXC. WAGON

Removal

1. Raise and support vehicle and remove wheel.
2. Disconnect and plug brake line, then remove brake caliper assembly.
3. Remove cotter pin, then loosen hub, **Figs. 26 and 27,** nut while preventing hub from turning.
4. Disconnect side rod ball stud.
5. Disconnect lower ball joint from transverse link.
6. Drain transaxle fluid into suitable container, then disconnect drive shaft from transaxle. Insert suitable rod into transaxle to prevent side gear from falling off. **On some models, remove transaxle oil seal, if equipped.**
7. Remove attaching bolts, then the wheel hub, steering knuckle and drive shaft as an assembly.
8. Remove hub nut, then separate drive shaft and wheel hub.
9. Remove ball joint from steering knuckle using suitable puller.
10. Separate wheel hub and knuckle using suitable tool.

Disassembly & Inspection

1. Remove wheel hub-to-rotor attaching bolts and separate hub from rotor.
2. Remove outer wheel bearing.
3. Remove inner grease seal and wheel bearing outer race from steering knuckle.
4. Clean wheel bearing with suitable solvent and dry with moisture-free compressed air.
5. Inspect wheel bearing for wear or damage and replace as necessary.
6. Inspect wheel hub and steering knuckle for cracks by magnetic particle or dye penetrant test method. Replace components(s) if any cracks are evident.

Assemble & Install

Pack seal with suitable grease, then to assemble and install steering knuckle on Pulsar, Sentra and 1983-86 Stanza models, proceed as follows:

1. Lubricate wheel bearings with suitable grease, then install bearing outer races to each side of knuckle.
2. Install inside bearing inner race and grease seal, then the outside grease seal and bearing using a suitable drift.
3. Determine proper spacer to be used as follows:
   a. If steering knuckle is not being replaced, replace spacer with one having same mark as old one, or reinstall old spacer, if serviceable.
   b. If knuckle is being replaced, measure distance between outer races of bearings and subtract the following amount from this measurement: Stanza, .0209 inch; Pulsar and Sentra, .0063 inch. This indicates spacer to be used. Refer to chart, **Fig. 29,** to determine correlation between spacer thickness and mark on spacer.
4. Install spacer, then the wheel hub to disc rotor.
5. Insert drive shaft into knuckle, then clamp drive shaft into a vise and install knuckle with bearings, spacer and hub nut. Torque hub nut to 87-145 ft. lbs. (Stanza, 145-203 ft. lbs.).
6. Ensure that wheel hub spins freely in both directions, then measure bearing preload at wheel hub bolt, using a suitable spring scale. Preload should

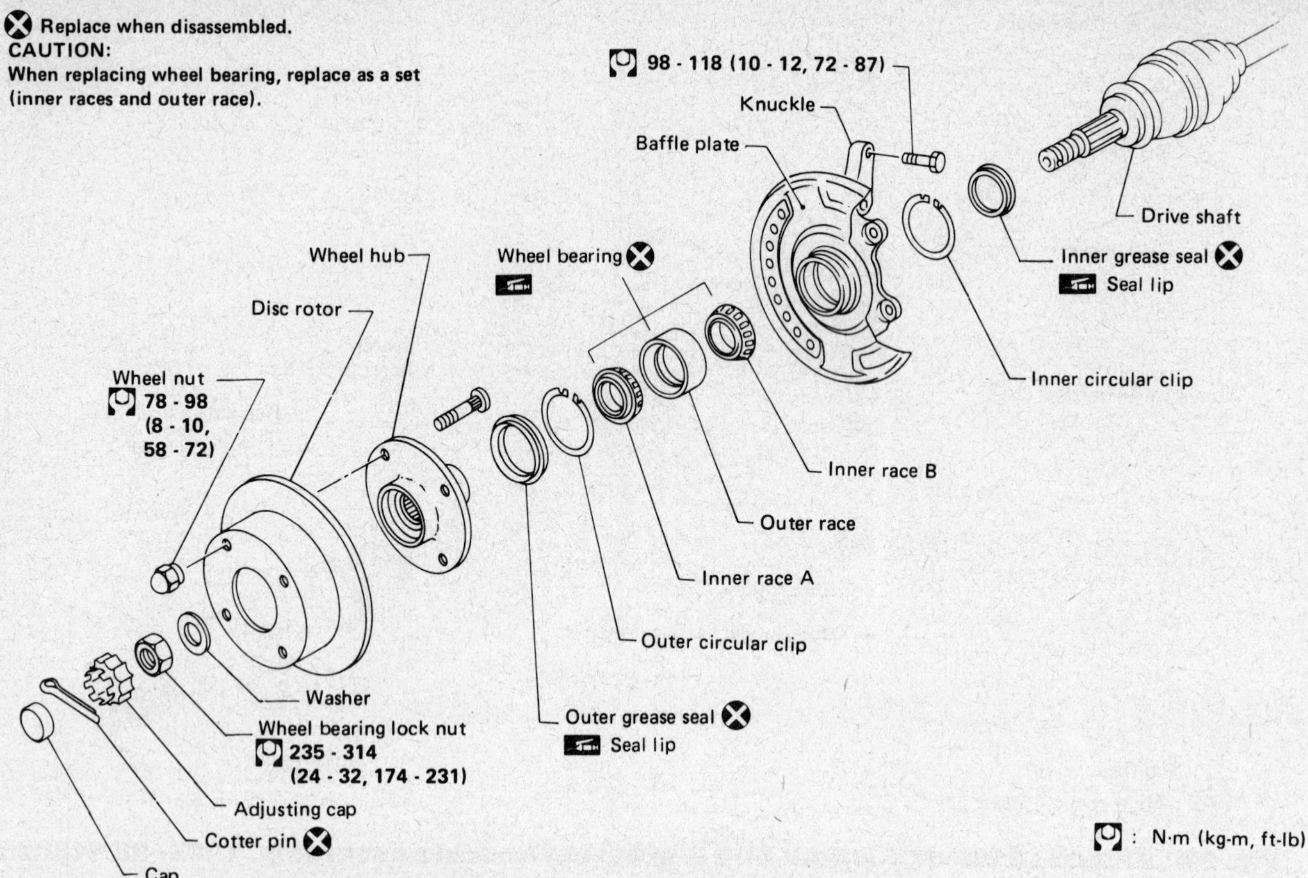

Fig. 28 Exploded view of wheel hub & steering knuckle assembly. 1985–87 Maxima, 1987 Stanza & 1986–87 Stanza wagon

measure 3.1-10.8 lbs. If not, replace spacer to bring preload within specifications.

7. Install the assembly in reverse order of removal as outlined previously.

1985–87 MAXIMA, 1987 STANZA & 1986–87 STANZA WAGON

Removal

To remove steering knuckle, proceed as follows:

1. Raise and support vehicle and remove wheel.
2. Unfasten brake caliper assembly, leaving brake line attached.
3. Separate driveshaft from steering knuckle, tapping as necessary.
4. Disconnect tie-rod from ball joint, then remove lower ball joint attaching nuts.
5. Remove steering knuckle-to-strut attaching bolts.
6. Remove wheel hub and steering knuckle, **Fig. 28**, as an assembly.
7. Separate wheel hub and steering knuckle using a suitable tool.

Assembly & Install

1. Install outer circlip into groove in steering knuckle, then press bearing outer race into knuckle.
2. Lubricate inner and outer bearing races with suitable grease.
3. Install inner circlip into groove in knuckle.

Spacer thickness	
Mark	H mm (in)
05	7.381 - 7.440 (0.2906 - 0.2929)
06	7.441 - 7.500 (0.2930 - 0.2953)
07	7.501 - 7.560 (0.2953 - 0.2976)
08	7.561 - 7.620 (0.2977 - 0.3000)
09	7.621 - 7.680 (0.3000 - 0.3024)
10	7.681 - 7.740 (0.3024 - 0.3047)
11	7.741 - 7.800 (0.3048 - 0.3071)
12	7.801 - 7.860 (0.3071 - 0.3094)
13	7.861 - 7.920 (0.3095 - 0.3118)
14	7.921 - 7.980 (0.3118 - 0.3142)
15	7.981 - 8.040 (0.3142 - 0.3165)
16	8.041 - 8.100 (0.3166 - 0.3189)
17	8.101 - 8.160 (0.3189 - 0.3213)
18	8.161 - 8.220 (0.3213 - 0.3236)
19	8.221 - 8.280 (0.3237 - 0.3260)
20	8.281 - 8.340 (0.3260 - 0.3283)
21	8.341 - 8.400 (0.3284 - 0.3307)
22	8.401 - 8.460 (0.3307 - 0.3331)

Fig. 29 Hub spacer thickness chart

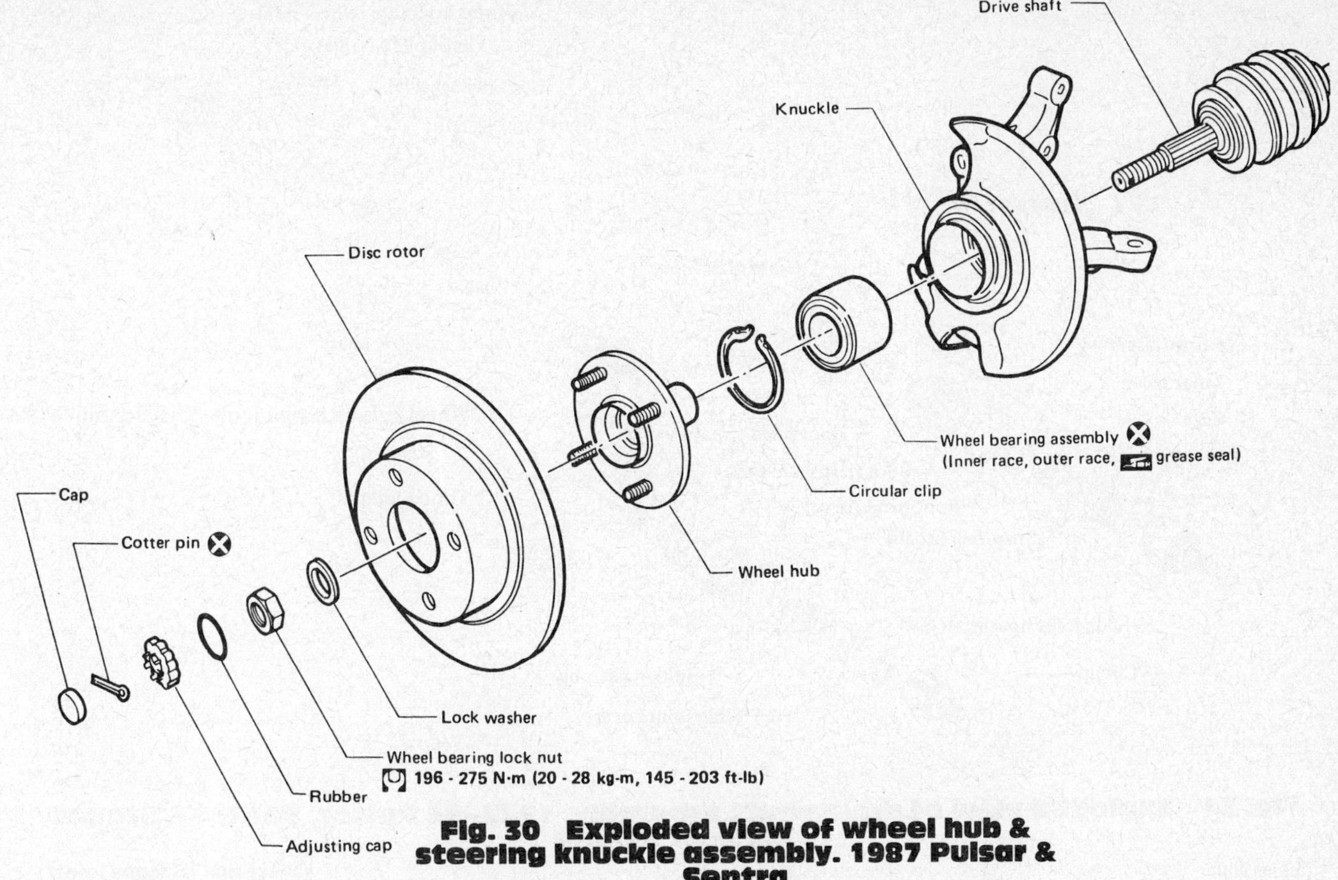

Fig. 30 Exploded view of wheel hub & steering knuckle assembly. 1987 Pulsar & Sentra

4. Install bearing inner races, then the outer grease seal.
5. Press hub into steering knuckle.
6. If driveshaft has not been removed from transaxle, adjust bearing preload as follows:
   a. Apply 5.5 tons pressure to bearing with a suitable press.
   b. Spin knuckle several times in each direction, then measure bearing preload using a suitable spring scale.
   c. Preload should measure .9-4.2 lbs. on 1985 models, .9-4.0 lbs. on 1986 models or .4-4.0 lbs on 1987 models. If reading is not within specifications, the wheel bearing must be replaced.
7. If driveshaft has been removed from transaxle, adjust bearing preload as follows:
   a. Position drive shaft in hub and torque wheel bearing locknut to 174-231 ft. lbs.
   b. Spin wheel hub several times in each direction, then measure preload using a suitable spring scale.
   c. Preload should measure 2.4-10.1 lbs. on 1985 models, 2.2-9.9 lbs. on 1986 models or 1.1-10.1 lbs. on 1987 models. If reading is not within specifications, the wheel bearing must be replaced.
   d. Remove wheel bearing nut, then slide driveshaft out of hub.
8. Install inner grease seal into knuckle.
9. Install the assembly in reverse order of removal as outlined previously.

1987 PULSAR & SENTRA

Removal

1. Raise and support vehicle.
2. Remove wheel and tire assembly.
3. Remove wheel bearing lock nut while depressing brake pedal, **Fig. 30.**
4. Remove caliper.
5. Using tool HT72520000 or equivalent, remove tie rod ball joint.
6. Separate drive shaft from knuckle.
7. Support arm assembly, then remove adjusting pin bolts.
8. Using tool HT72520000 or equivalent, remove lower ball joint attaching nut.
9. Separate knuckle from lower ball joint stud, using a suitable tool.
10. Remove steering knuckle.

Disassembly

1. Remove outer hub inner race from knuckle.
2. Remove outside inner race from wheel hub.
3. Remove inner race from wheel bearing.
4. Remove snap ring.
5. Install inner race (inside) of removed wheel bearing, then remove wheel bearing assembly from knuckle.

Inspection

Inspect removed components for excessive wear and/or damage. Replace worn or damaged components as required.

Assembly

1. Press new wheel bearing assembly into knuckle working from outside of knuckle.
2. Install snap ring.
3. Coat seal lip with suitable grease.
4. Press hub into knuckle. **Do not exceed 3.3 tons.**
5. Check bearing preload as follows:
   a. Place press load onto wheel hub shaft (approximately 5 tons).
   b. Spin knuckle several times in both directions.
   c. Ensure wheels bearings operate smoothly.

Installation

Reverse removal procedure to install.

DRIVESHAFT SERVICE

REMOVAL

Pulsar, Sentra, Stanza, 1985–87 Maxima & Stanza Wagon

Refer to "Steering Knuckle Service" section for drive shaft replacement procedure on these models.

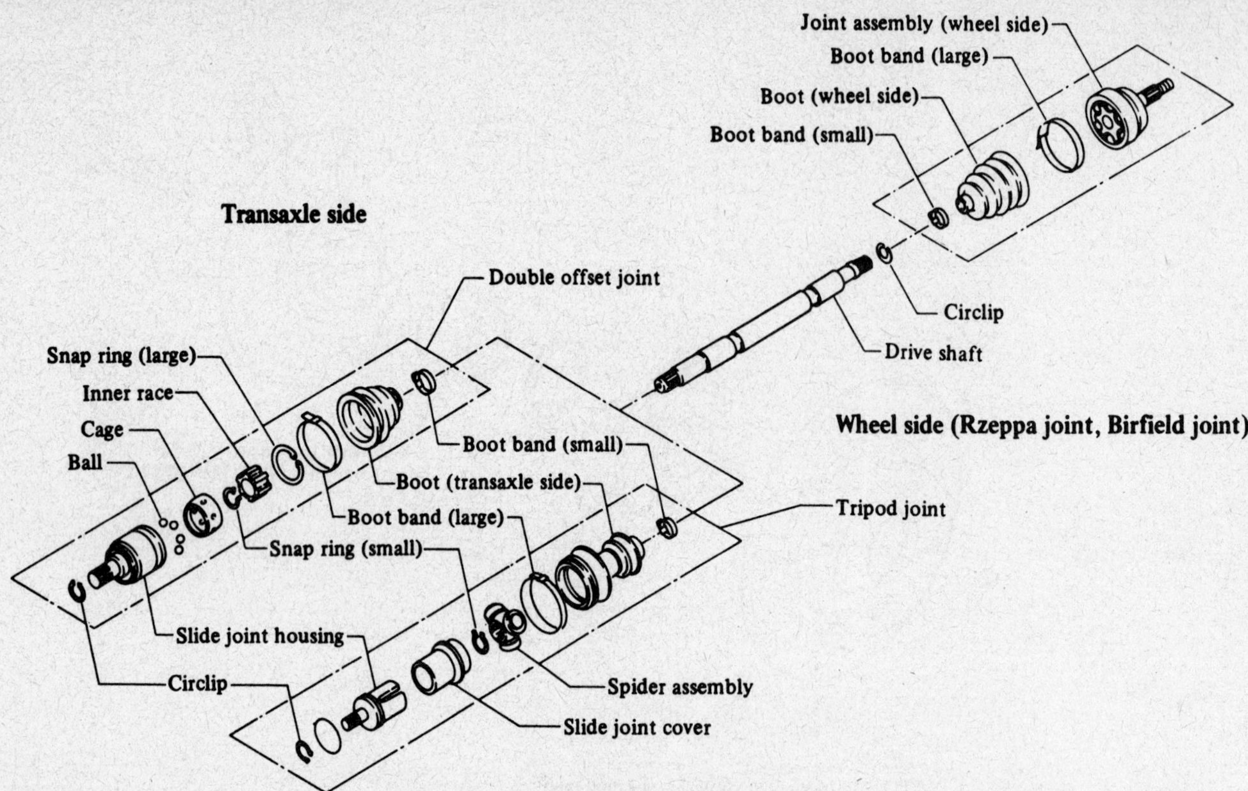

Fig. 31 Exploded view of drive shaft assembly. 1983–84 Pulsar, Sentra & Stanza, 1985–87 similar

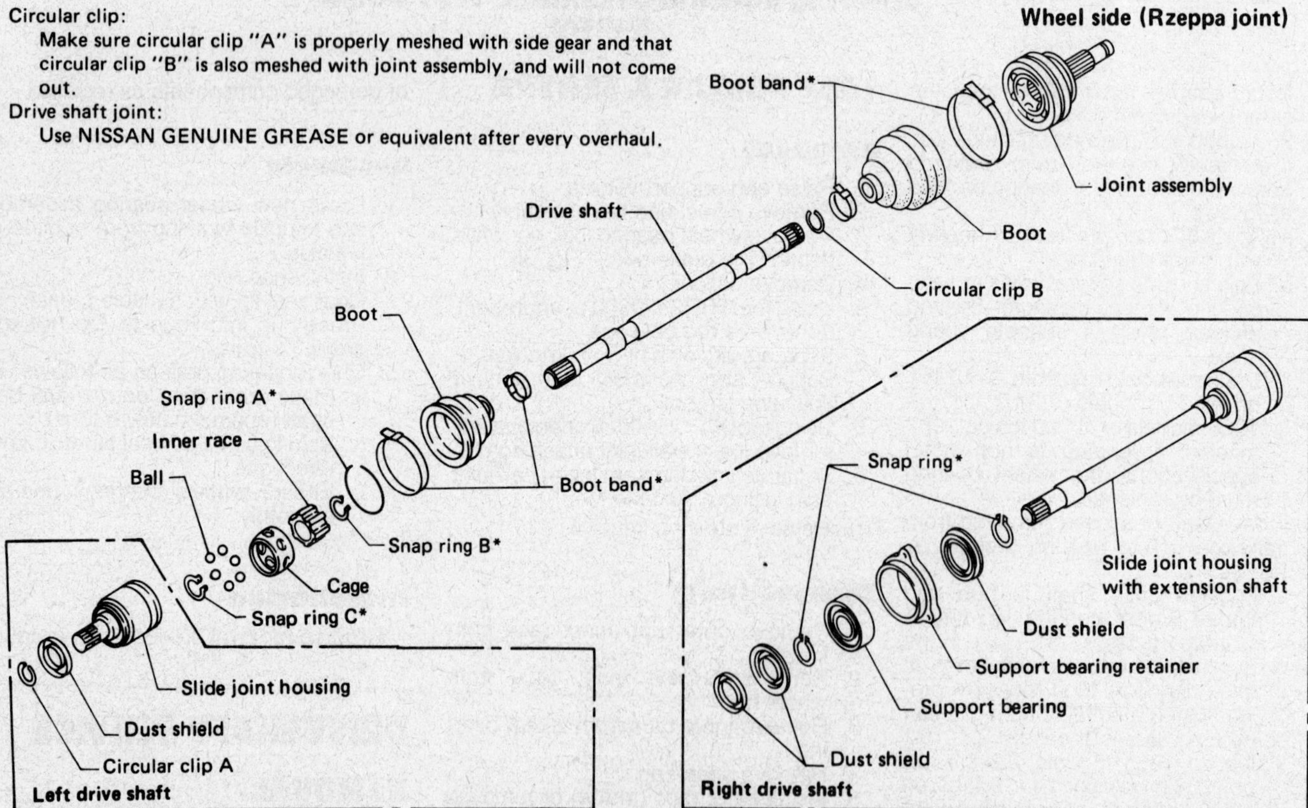

Fig. 32 Exploded view of driveshaft assembly. 1985–87 Maxima

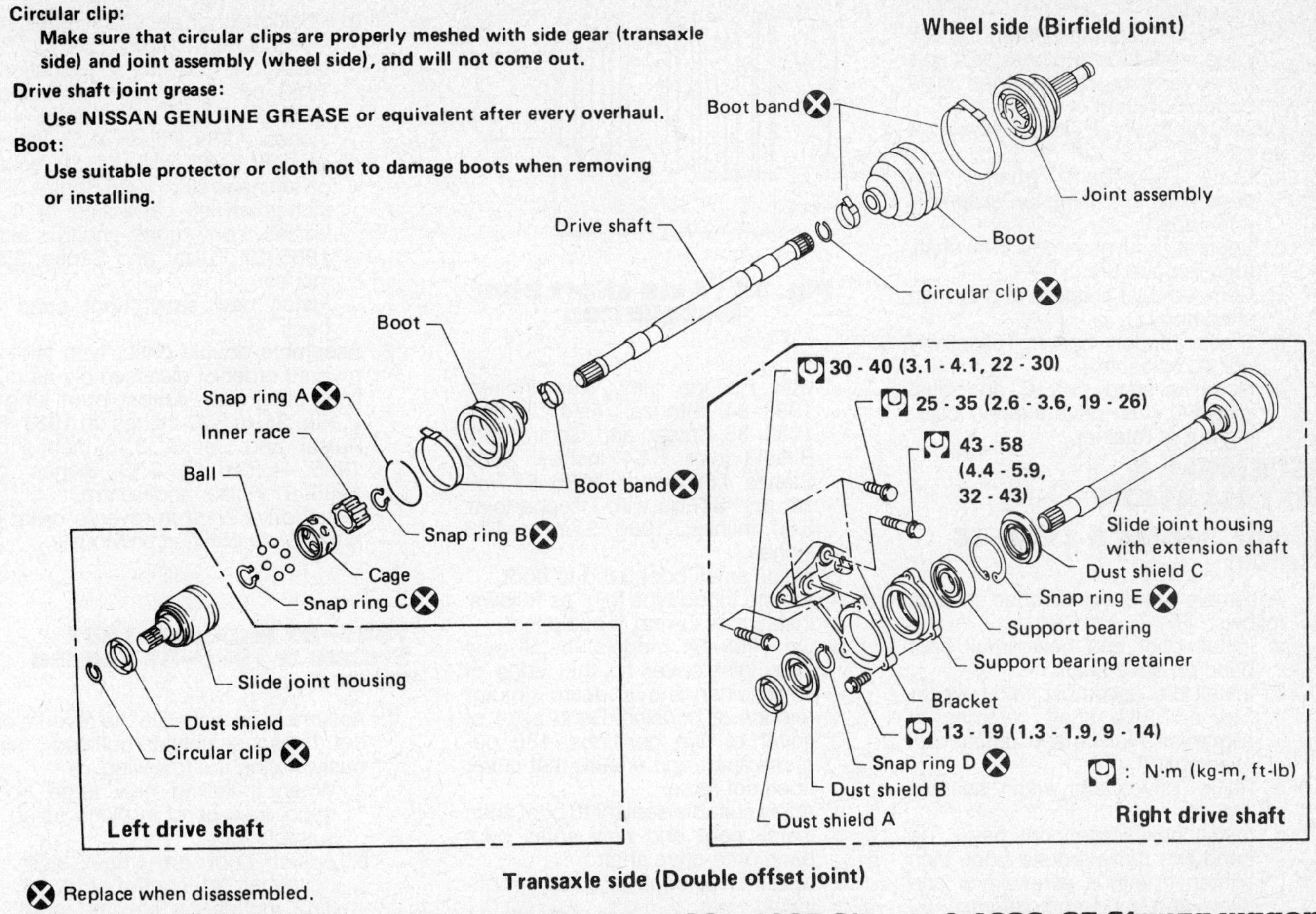

Circular clip:
Make sure that circular clips are properly meshed with side gear (transaxle side) and joint assembly (wheel side), and will not come out.

Drive shaft joint grease:
Use NISSAN GENUINE GREASE or equivalent after every overhaul.

Boot:
Use suitable protector or cloth not to damage boots when removing or installing.

Fig. 33 Exploded view of driveshaft assembly. 1987 Stanza & 1986–87 Stanza wagon

DISASSEMBLY & INSPECTION

Pulsar, Sentra & 1983–86 Stanza Exc. Wagon

1. Disassemble tripod type joint as follows:
   a. Install drive shaft in suitable soft-jawed vise.
   b. Remove and discard boot bands, **Fig. 31.**
   c. Separate slide joint housing with cover, and the drive shaft with spider assembly. Scribe an alignment mark for assembly reference.
   d. Remove and discard snap ring, then press spider assembly off of shaft.
   e. On 1983-84 models, remove boot, the cut edge of slide joint cover and remove and discard the cover. Remove and discard O-ring.
   f. On 1985-87 models, remove and discard boot bands. Scribe alignment marks on joint assembly and shaft, then remove joint assembly and boot.
2. Disassemble double offset type joint as follows:
   a. Install drive shaft in suitable soft-jawed vise.
   b. Remove and discard boot bands, **Fig. 31.**
   c. Remove snap ring, then the slide joint housing.
   d. Clean grease off of bearing cage and drive out balls, then rotate cage approximately 180 degrees and remove from inner race.
   e. Remove and discard small snap ring, then tap inner race off of shaft and remove boot.
3. Remove and discard boot bands from wheel side of shaft.
4. Scribe alignment mark on drive shaft and joint assembly, then remove the joint assembly and boot.
5. Clean all components with suitable solvent and dry with compressed air.
6. Inspect drive shaft and replace it if twisted or cracked.
7. Inspect wheel side joint assembly for wear or damage and replace as necessary.
8. On tripod type joint, check spider assembly and slide joint housing for wear or damage and replace as necessary.
9. On double offset type joint, check all components for wear, damage or excessive play and replace as necessary.

1985–87 Maxima

1. Disassemble transaxle side of driveshaft as follows:
   a. Install driveshaft in a suitable soft-jawed vise.
   b. Remove and discard boot bands, **Fig. 32.**
   c. Draw alignment marks on slide joint housing and inner race for assembly reference.
   d. Remove snap ring C, then the ball cage, inner race and balls as a unit.
   e. Remove snap ring B, then slide boot off of shaft.
2. Disassemble wheel side of driveshaft as follows:
   a. Draw alignment marks on driveshaft and joint for assembly reference.
   b. Separate joint assembly from shaft, then remove boot.
   c. Remove dust shield, then the snap ring.
   d. Press support bearing assembly out of shaft.
   e. Press support bearing out of shaft.

1987 Stanza & 1986–87 Stanza Wagon

1. Disassemble transaxle side of driveshaft as follows:
   a. Install driveshaft in a suitable soft-jawed vise.
   b. Remove and discard boot bands, **Fig. 33.**
   c. Draw alignment marks on slide joint housing and inner race for assembly reference.
   d. Remove snap ring A, then pull out slide joint housing.
   e. Draw alignment marks on inner race and driveshaft for assembly

reference.

f. Remove snap ring C, then the ball cage, inner race and balls as a unit.

g. Remove snap ring B, then slide boot off of shaft.

2. Disassemble wheel side of driveshaft as follows:
   a. Draw alignment marks on driveshaft and joint for assembly reference.
   b. Separate joint assembly from shaft, then remove boot.
   c. Remove dust shield A and B, then snap ring D.
   d. Press support bearing assembly out of driveshaft.
   e. Remove snap ring E and dust shield C, then drive support bearing out of retainer.

ASSEMBLY & INSTALLATION

Pulsar, Sentra & 1983–86 Stanza

1. Assemble wheel side of drive shaft as follows:
   a. Install boot and new small boot band on drive shaft.
   b. Install joint assembly, with new circlip, on drive shaft, referring to alignment mark made during disassembly.
   c. Pack driveshaft with suitable grease.
   d. Install new large boot band. Tie band two turns around boot, then tighten it with a screwdriver and pliers and bend approximately 90 degrees. Lock band in place with a punch, leaving length the same as its width, then bend band back over itself.
   e. Position boot so that it does not swell or deform when length L, **Fig. 34**, meets the following specifications: 1983-85 Pulsar and Sentra

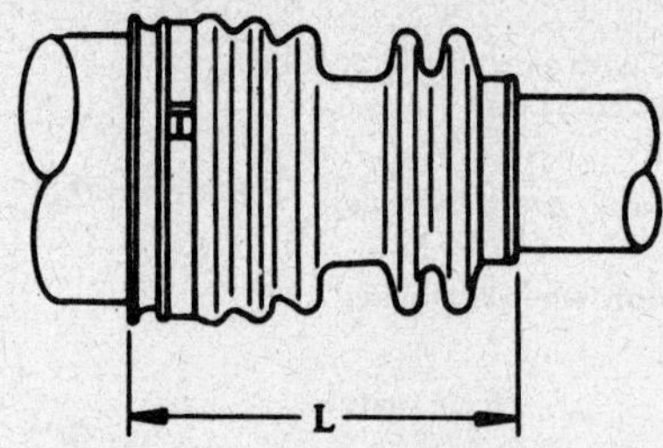

Fig. 34 Axle shaft boot installation

with Rzeppa joint, 3.94 inches; 1983-84 Stanza, 4.74 inches; 1983-85 Pulsar and Sentra with Birfield joint, 3.54 inches; 1985 Stanza, 4.69 inches; 1986-87 Pulsar and Sentra with Rzeppa joint, 3.60 inches; 1986 Stanza, 4.70 inches.
   f. Install small boot band to boot.
2. Assemble tripod type joint as follows:
   a. Install new O-ring, if equipped.
   b. On 1983-84 models, install new slide joint cover so that edge of cover extends over entire circumference of housing. Bend edge of cover at two positions, 180 degrees apart and ensure that cover does not rattle.
   c. Apply suitable sealant to boot, then install boot and new small boot band onto drive shaft.
   d. Install drive shaft in suitable soft-jawed vise.
   e. Install spider assembly, referring to alignment mark made during disassembly.
   f. Install new snap ring so that rounded surface faces spider assembly.
   g. Pack spider assembly with suitable grease, then install new large boot band.
   h. Position boot so that it does not swell when length L, **Fig. 34,** meets the following specifications: 1983-86 Stanza, 4.45 inches; 1983-84 Pulsar and Sentra, 4.41 inches; 1985 Pulsar, 4.33 inches on right hand side, or 3.82 inches on left hand side; 1985 Sentra, 3.78 inches on left hand side, or 4.35 inches on right hand side; 1986-87 Pulsar and Sentra, 3.80 inches.
   i. Install new small boot band to boot.
3. Assemble double offset type joint in reverse order of disassembly as outlined previously. **Adjust boot length L, Fig. 34**, to 3.31 inches on 1983-84 Pulsar and Sentra, 3.35 inches on 1985 Pulsar or 3.33 inches on 1986-87 Pulsar and Sentra.
4. Install drive shaft in reverse order of removal as outlined previously.

1985–87 Maxima, 1987 Stanza & 1986–87 Stanza Wagon

1. Assemble driveshaft in the reverse order of disassembly as outlined previously, noting the following:
   a. When installing new large boot band, lock band in place using a suitable tool.
   b. Adjust boot on wheel side of driveshaft so length L, **Fig. 34,** is 3.82 inches on Maxima or 3.96 inches on 2WD Stanza wagon , or 3.78-3.86 inches on 4WD Stanza wagon.
   c. Adjust boot on transaxle side of driveshaft so length L, **Fig. 31,** is 3.86 inches on Maxima and 2WD Stanza wagon, or 3.82-3.90 inches on 4WD Stanza wagon.

PATHFINDER & PICKUP FRONT DRIVE AXLE SECTION

INDEX

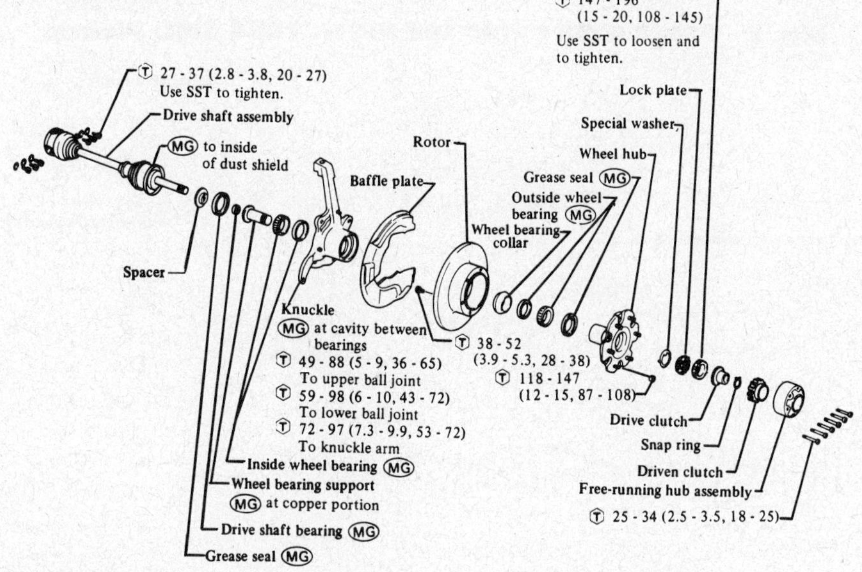

Fig. 1 Front axle exploded view. 1983 4WD Pickup

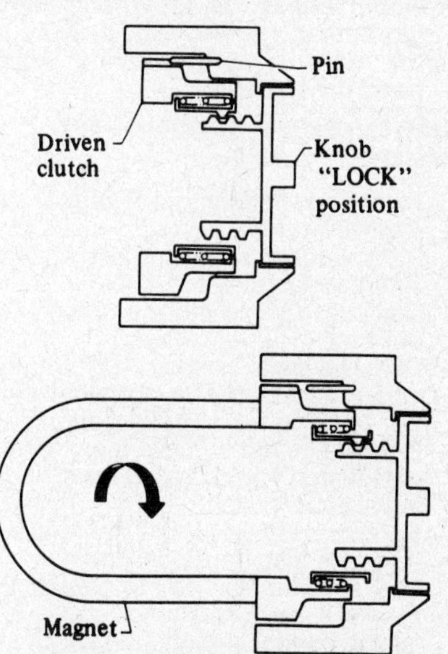

Fig. 2 Driven clutch removal. 1983 4WD Pickup

LOCKING HUB SERVICE

1983 PICKUP

1. Raise and support front of vehicle and remove wheel.
2. Remove locking hub attaching bolts, then the hub, **Fig. 1.**
3. To disassemble hub, set hub in the locked position, then remove driven clutch by turning it clockwise. When removing driven clutch, draw lock pin, **Fig. 2**, out with a magnet.
4. To assemble hub, set knob in the free position, then install driven clutch. Screw clutch on hand tight only until it can no longer be turned, then back it off until it aligns with bolt hole.
5. Install hub and torque attaching bolts to 18-25 ft. lbs.

1984 PICKUP

1. Raise and support front of vehicle and remove wheel.
2. Remove locking hub attaching bolts, then the hub, **Fig. 3.**
3. Reverse procedure to install.

1985-86 PICKUP

1. Raise and support front of vehicle.
2. Support axle case with a suitable jack and remove wheel and tire assembly.
3. Remove locking hub attaching bolts and the hub, **Fig. 4.**
4. On models with manual hub, remove snap ring and drive clutch, then the second snap ring, lock washer and wheel bearing locknut, **Fig. 4.**
5. On models with automatic hub, proceed as follows:
   a. Remove washers and snap ring, **Fig. 5.**
   b. Remove large snap ring, lock washer and wheel bearing locknut.
6. Reverse procedure to assemble and install. On automatic hub, ensure brake A and B set does not measure less than .539 inch thick, **Fig. 6.**

PATHFINDER & 1986½–87 PICKUP

1. Place locking hub in free position, raise and support front of vehicle, and remove wheel.
2. Remove bolts securing locking hub housing, then the housing assembly, **Fig. 7.**
3. On models with manual locking hub, remove snap ring from drive axle, then withdraw drive clutch from hub.
4. On models with automatic locking hub, proceed as follows:
   a. Remove snap ring from drive axle, then withdraw washer A, washer B and brake B from hub, **Fig. 5.**
   b. Remove brake A from housing, assemble brakes A and B together as shown in **Fig. 6,** then measure thickness of assembly. If assembly thickness is less than .606 inch (15.4mm), brakes should be replaced.
   c. Reassemble housing using new O-ring.
5. On all models, reverse procedure to install, using new snap rings and

torque locking hub mounting bolts to 18-25 ft. lbs.

DRIVESHAFT SERVICE

REMOVAL

1983-86 Pickup

1. Raise and support front of vehicle and remove wheel.
2. Remove locking hub assembly as outlined.
3. On 1983 models, remove stabilizer bar lower link attaching bolt.
4. On 1984-86 models, remove lower ball joint attaching nuts and shock absorber lower mounting bolt.
5. On all models, remove bolts securing driveshaft to differential carrier, then the driveshaft assembly from vehicle. Do not remove boots. **Turn steering wheel fully to the left when removing lefthand driveshaft, or fully to the right when removing righthand driveshaft.**

Pathfinder & 1986½-87 Pickup

1. Raise and support front of vehicle and remove wheel.
2. Remove bolts securing drive shaft to differential carrier.
3. Remove locking hub assembly as outlined.
4. Remove brake caliper bolts and secure caliper aside. **Do not allow caliper to hang from brake hose.**
5. Remove tie rod end nut, then disconnect tie rod from steering knuckle using suitable puller.
6. Support lower link with suitable jack to relieve spring tension, then remove nuts securing ball joint to lower link.
7. Remove bolts securing upper ball joint to control arm and the shock absorber lower mounting bolt.
8. Remove hub, steering knuckle and drive shaft as an assembly.
9. Secure knuckle in vise, then separate drive shaft from knuckle by tapping on end of shaft. **Do not strike end of shaft directly. Place block of wood over end of shaft to prevent damage.**

DISASSEMBLY

1. Install driveshaft in suitable soft-jawed vise.
2. Remove plug, then the plug seal, **Figs. 8 and 9.**
3. Remove and discard boot bands.
4. Move boot and the slide joint housing toward wheel side of driveshaft and scribe an alignment mark on the spider assembly and shaft.
5. Remove spider assembly from shaft, using suitable press.
6. Remove boot and boot bands.
7. On 1983 models, remove boot bands and boot from wheel side of driveshaft.
8. On 1984-87 models, disassemble wheel side of drive shaft as follows:
   a. Remove and discard boot bands.
   b. Scribe an alignment mark on driveshaft and joint assembly for assembly reference.

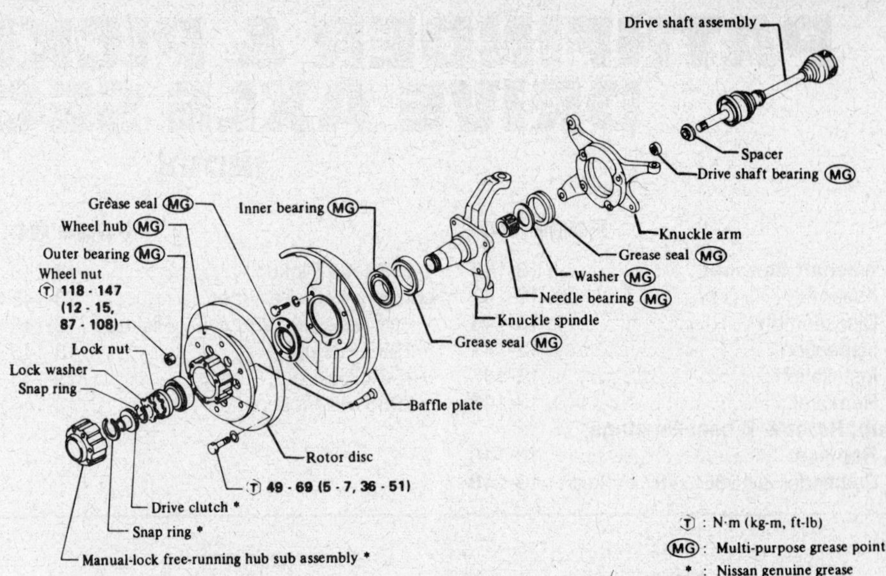

Fig. 3 Front axle exploded view. 1984 4WD Pickup

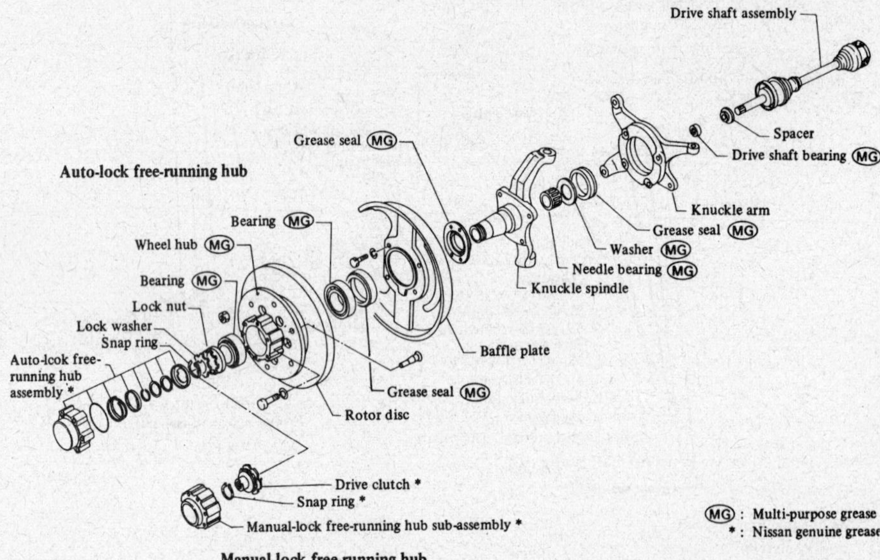

Fig. 4 Front axle exploded view. 1985-86 4WD Pickup

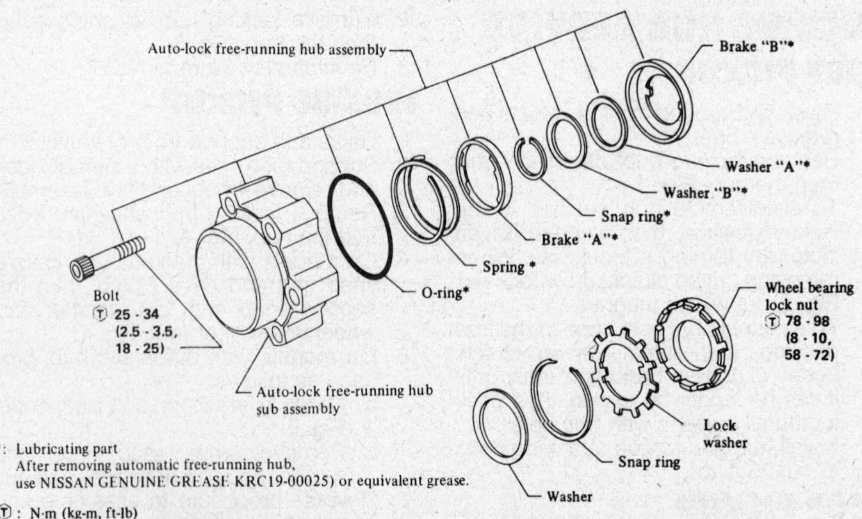

Fig. 5 Exploded view of automatic locking hub assembly. 1985-87 4WD Pick-Up

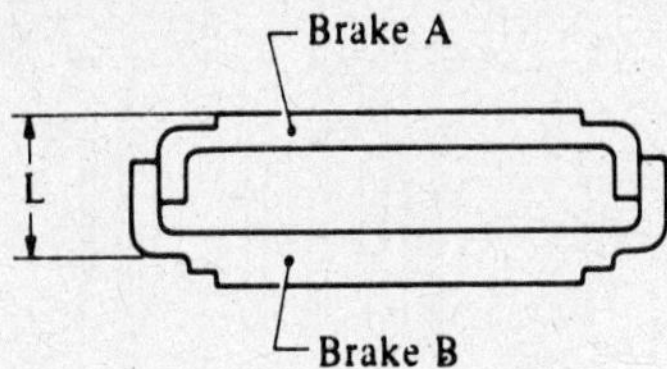

Wear limit L:
More than 13.7 mm (0.539 in)

Fig. 6 Typical brake set thickness measurement. Models w/automatic locking hub

c. Remove joint assembly and boot from driveshaft, **Fig. 8.**

INSPECTION

1. Clean all components in suitable solvent and dry with compressed air.
2. Inspect all components for wear or damage and replace parts as necessary.

ASSEMBLY

1. On 1984-87 models, assemble wheel side of driveshaft as follows:
   a. Install boot and new small boot band onto driveshaft.
   b. Install joint assembly with new circlip and gently tap into position. Ensure reference marks made during disassembly are aligned.
2. On all models, pack joints with suitable grease, then install boot and new large boot band on wheel side of shaft. Adjust boot length L, **Fig. 10**, to 4.65 inches on 1983 models, 3.82 inches on 1984-86 models or 3.78-3.86 inches on 1986½-87 models.
3. Install boot, new boot bands and slide joint housing onto driveshaft.
4. Install driveshaft in suitable soft-jawed vise.
5. Install spider assembly, referring to alignment mark made during disassembly.
6. Caulk serrations of drive shaft equally at three places, then pack spider assembly with suitable grease. **Do not caulk areas which were previously caulked. Make sure that each caulking is applied to two serrations and is at least .04 inch wide.**
7. Install new large boot band, then the plug seal and plug.
8. Caulk plug at three places using dummy bolts.
9. Adjust boot length L, **Fig. 11,** to 4.06 inches, on 1983-84 models, 3.58 inches on 1985-86 carbureted models, 3.98 inches on 1986 fuel injected models or 4.02-4.09 inches on 1986½-87 models.

INSTALLATION

1. Apply suitable grease to copper portion of wheel bearing support.
2. Install spacer on driveshaft with concave side facing shaft.
3. Reverse removal procedure to install shaft, then check endplay using suitable dial indicator.

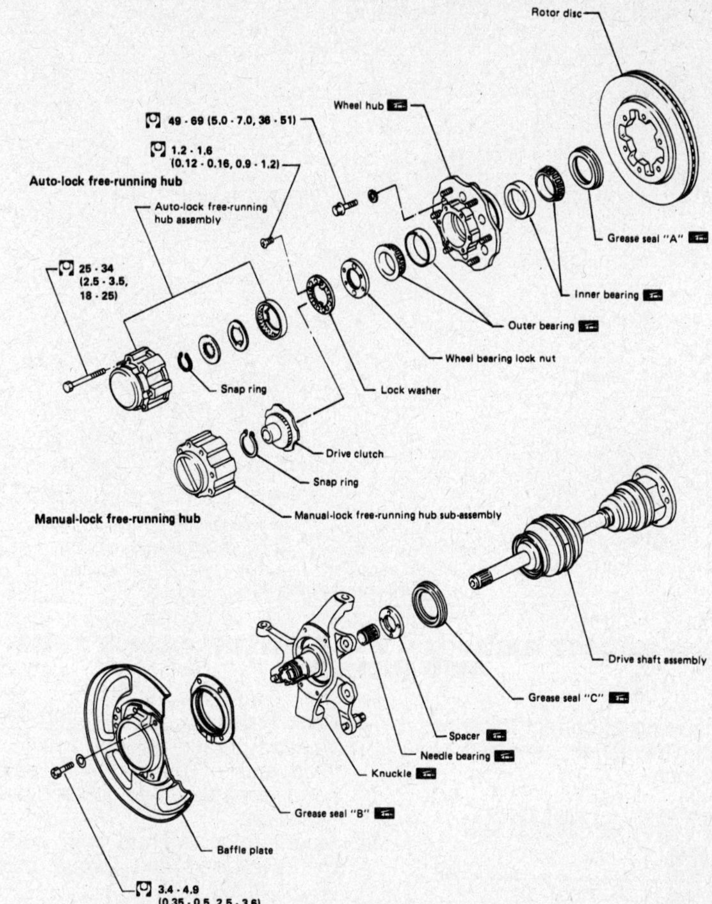

Fig. 7 Front axle exploded view. Pathfinder & 1986½ 4WD Pickup

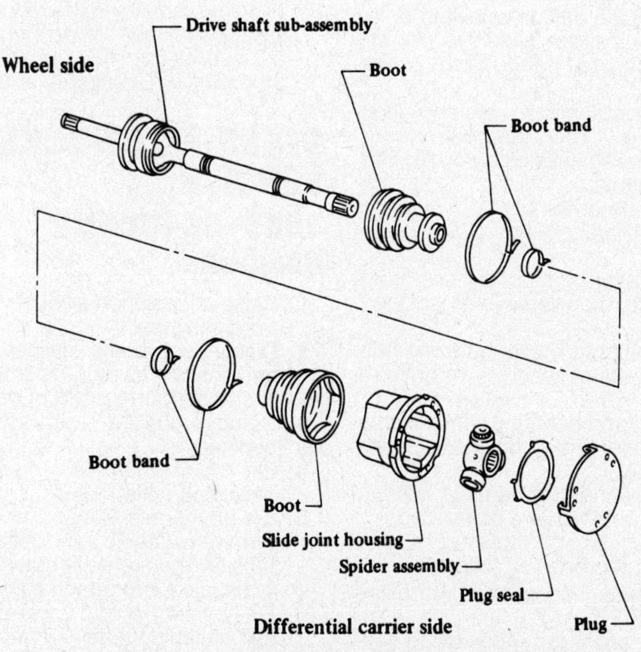

Fig. 8 Drive shaft exploded view. 1983 4WD Pickup

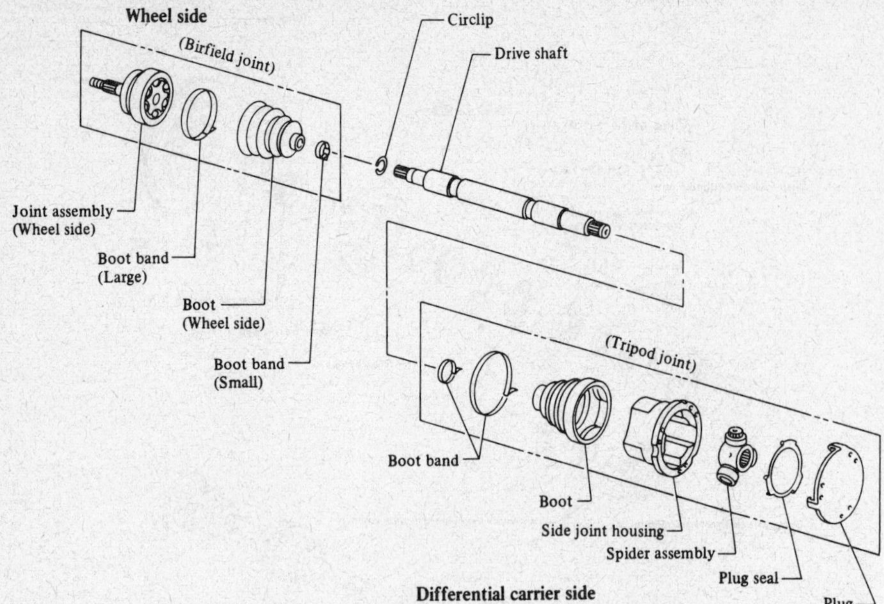

Fig. 9 Drive shaft exploded view. Pathfinder & 1984–87 4WD Pickup

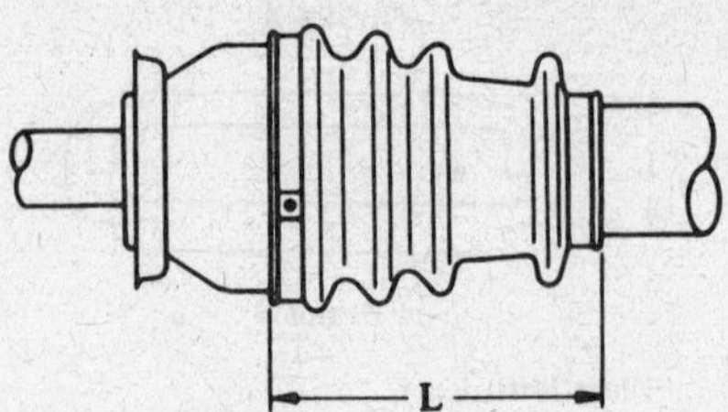

Fig. 10 Drive shaft outer boot installation. Pathfinder & 4WD Pickup

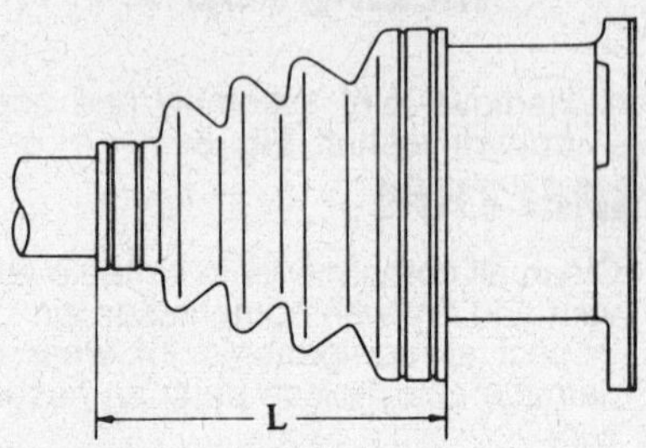

Length "L": 103 mm (4.06 in)

Fig. 11 Drive shaft inner boot installation. Pathfinder &4WD Pickup

4. Select snap ring of correct thickness to adjust driveshaft endplay to .004-.012 inch.

HUB, ROTOR & WHEEL BEARINGS

REPLACE

1983–86 PICKUP

Refer to "Steering Knuckle Service" for replacement procedures.

PATHFINDER & 1986½–87 PICKUP

1. Remove locking hub as outlined.
2. Remove brake caliper retaining bolts and secure caliper aside. **Do not allow caliper to hang from brake hose.**
3. Remove retaining screw and lock washer, **Fig. 7, then remove bearing lock nut using wrench KV40105400 or equivalent.**
4. Remove hub assembly from steering knuckle, taking care not to drop outer bearing.
5. Remove outer bearing, pry seal from rear of hub, then remove inner bearing.
6. Scribe matching marks between hub and rotor, then separate rotor from hub.
7. Clean hub and bearings with suitable solvent and blow dry with compressed air.
8. Inspect bearings for damage scoring and wear, and replace as needed.
9. If bearings are to be replaced, replace bearing outer races as follows:
   a. Drive outer races from hub using suitable drift.
   b. Install new outer races using suitable driver, ensuring races are fully seated in hub. Replace hub if bearing outer races are loose in hub.
10. Pack bearings with suitable grease, working grease through rollers from wide end of bearing with palm of hand. Keep bearings covered until installation.
11. Mount rotor on hub with matching marks aligned and torque bolts to 36-51 ft. lbs.
12. Pack center of hub with suitable grease, then install inner bearing in hub.
13. Coat seal lip with grease, then install seal in rear of hub using suitable driver.
14. Install hub assembly and adjust wheel bearing preload as outlined under "Wheel Bearings, Adjust."
15. Reverse remaining procedure to complete installation. When installing locking hub, select snap ring that will provide .004-.012 endplay at drive axle.

STEERING KNUCKLE SERVICE

1983–86 PICKUP

REMOVAL

1. Raise and support front of vehicle and remove wheel.
2. Disconnect brake caliper assembly and position aside. Do not allow brake line to support weight of caliper.
3. Remove locking hub assembly as outlined.
4. On 1984-86 models, disconnect tie rod using suitable tool.
5. On all models, support lower control arm with suitable jack to relieve spring tension, then remove steering knuckle to knuckle arm attaching bolt.
6. Remove upper and lower ball joint-to-link attaching nuts.
7. Separate steering knuckle from upper and lower links, then remove knuckle and hub assembly from vehicle.

DISASSEMBLY & INSPECTION

1983

1. Remove lock washer, then front wheel lock nut from shaft.
2. Remove lock washer and special washer, **Fig. 1.**
3. Remove and discard inside grease seal.
4. Remove wheel bearing support from hub.
5. Separate hub from steering knuckle using suitable slide hammer.
6. Remove wheel bearing collar.
7. Remove inside wheel bearing using suitable drift.
8. Scribe matching marks between hub and rotor, then separate rotor from hub.
9. Tap hub assembly on a wooden block to shift the position of outside bearing.
10. Remove outside wheel bearing from hub using press and suitable bearing separators, then remove and discard grease seal.
10. Remove driveshaft bearing from wheel bearing support using suitable drift.
11. Clean bearing with suitable solvent and dry with compressed air.
12. Inspect components for wear or damage and replace as necessary. Check wheel hub and steering knuckle for cracks by magnetic particle or penetrating dye test method.

1984–86

1. Remove snap ring, lock washer and front wheel locknut, **Figs. 3 and 4.**
2. Separate hub from steering knuckle.
3. Scribe matching marks between hub and rotor, then separate rotor from hub.

4. Remove and discard inner grease seal from back plate.
5. Remove inner wheel bearing using a suitable drift.
6. Clean bearing with suitable solvent and dry with compressed air.
7. Inspect components for wear or damage and replace as necessary. Check wheel hub and steering knuckle for cracks by magnetic particle or penetrating dye test method.

ASSEMBLY & INSTALLATION

Assemble wheel hub and steering knuckle in reverse order of disassembly. During assembly and installation, note the following:

1. Install rotor aligning matching marks, then torque bolts to 28-38 ft. lbs. on 1983 models or 36-51 ft. lbs. on 1984-86 models.
2. On 1983 models, select wheel bearing collar as follows:
   a. Install wheel bearing collar which was originally used, or one with the same marking.
   b. Install inside bearing using press and a suitable drift.
   c. Install special washer and a new lock washer.
   d. Install locknut and torque to 108-145 ft. lbs.
   e. Rotate hub several times in both directions to seat bearing, then measure wheel bearing preload, using suitable spring scale, at a wheel hub bolt.
   f. Bearing preload should measure 2.2-9.5 lbs. If not, replace wheel bearing collar as necessary to bring preload within specifications.
3. Install wheel hub and steering knuckle in reverse order of removal.
4. Adjust wheel bearing preload as outlined under "Wheel Bearings, Adjust."
5. When installing locking hub, select snap ring which will provide .004-.012 inch end play at drive axle.

PATHFINDER & 1986½–87 PICKUP

1. Remove hub assembly as outlined.
2. Separate drive shaft from knuckle by tapping on end of shaft. **Do not strike end of shaft directly. Place block of wood over end of shaft to prevent damage.**
3. Remove tie rod nut, then separate tie rod from knuckle using suitable puller.
4. Loosen but do not remove nuts securing upper and lower ball joints to steering knuckle.
5. Release upper and lower ball joints from knuckle using suitable puller. **Do not remove ball joint retaining nuts until lower link is supported with jack.**
6. Support lower link with jack to relieve spring tension, remove ball joint nuts, then remove spindle.
7. Inspect drive axle needle bearing for damage, scoring and wear. If replacement is necessary, proceed as follows;
   a. Remove bearing using drift or suitable puller.
   b. Install replacement bearing using driver with the same outer diameter as bearing. When installing needle bearing, ensure seal surface faces out.
8. Reverse remaining procedure to complete installation. Torque lower ball joint nut to 87-141 ft. lbs., upper ball joint nut to 58-108 ft. lbs. and tie rod nut to 40-72 ft. lbs.

WHEEL BEARINGS ADJUST

Prior to adjusting wheel bearing preload, ensure that bearings are in satisfactory condition and properly lubricated. Apply suitable grease to threaded portion of spindle and the contact surface of the outer bearing to ensure proper adjustment.

1983 PICKUP

1. Raise and support front of vehicle, then remove wheel, locking hub assembly and the brake pads.
2. Measure hub rotating torque at wheel hub bolt with suitable spring scale.
3. Rotating torque should be 2.2-9.5 lbs.
4. If preload is not within specifications, refer to "Steering Knuckle Service" for bearing collar selection and bearing adjustment procedure.

PATHFINDER & 1984–87 PICKUP

1. Raise and support front of vehicle, then remove wheel and locking hub assembly.
2. Remove caliper retaining bolts and secure caliper aside. **Do not allow caliper to hang from brake hose.**
3. Torque wheel bearing lock nut to 58-72 ft. lbs., then rotate hub several revolutions in both directions to seat bearings.
4. Loosen wheel bearing nut until torque on nut is zero and bearing axial play is zero.
5. Torque bearing locknut to .4-1.1 ft. lbs., then rotate hub several revolutions to seat bearings, then retorque lock nut to .4-1.1 ft. lbs.
6. Connect spring scale to wheel stud, measure hub starting torque through 90° of rotation and record measurement as A.
7. Install lock washer and retaining screw, if equipped, tightening bearing lock nut up to an additional 30° to align washer and nut.
8. Rotate hub several turns in each direction to seat bearings, then connect spring scale to wheel stud, measure hub starting torque through 90° of rotation and record measurement as B.
9. Calculate wheel bearing preload by subtracting measurement A from measurement B. If remainder is not 1.59-4.72 lbs., repeat steps 3-8 until correct preload is obtained.
10. If bearings do not operate smoothly, or if preload cannot be properly adjusted as outlined, remove hub and inspect bearings.

WHEEL ALIGNMENT SECTION

INDEX

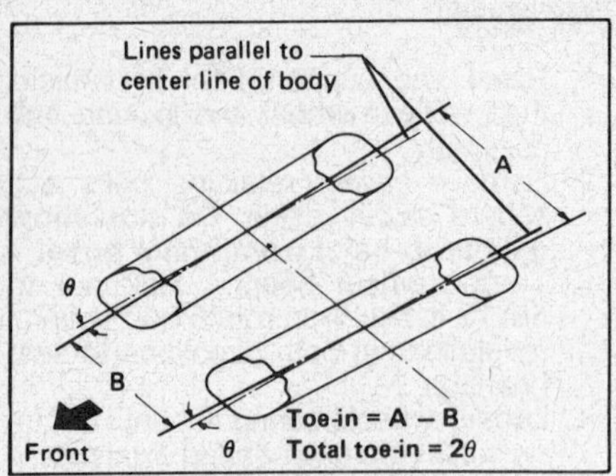

Fig. 1 Typical toe-in measurement

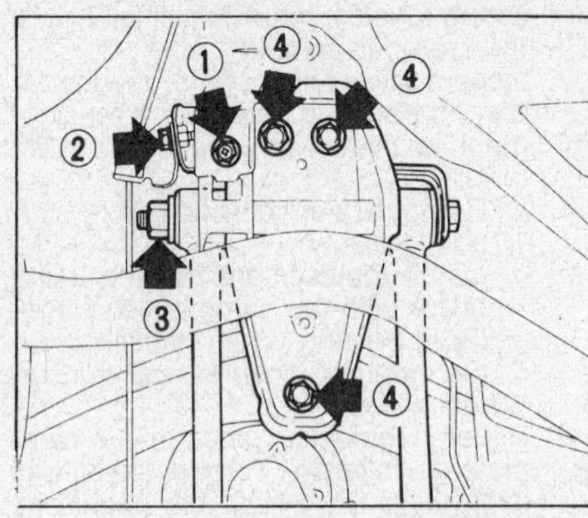

1 Exhaust tube mounting bracket (Left side only)
2 Parking brake cable supporting bracket
3 Parallel link
4 Parallel link bracket

Fig. 2 Rear toe-in adjustment. 1983–86 Stanza Exc. 1986 Stanza Wagon

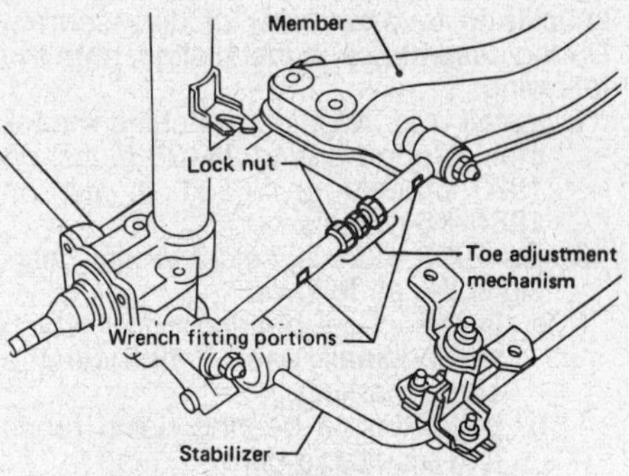

Fig. 3 Rear toe-in adjustment. 1985–87 Maxima & 1987 Stanza Exc. Wagon

PRELIMINARY CHECK

Prior to checking and adjusting wheel alignment angles, perform the following checks:

1. Check tire pressures and adjust as needed.
2. Ensure tires are of the proper size and that tires are properly matched.
3. Ensure wheel bearings (front and rear) are properly adjusted.
4. Check steering gear adjustment and ensure that steering gear is properly secured to frame.
5. Inspect steering linkage and suspension components for damage and wear, and repair or replace components as needed.
6. Measure vehicle ride height with vehicle unloaded, and ensure springs are not collapsed.
7. Place unladen vehicle on suitable alignment rack following manufacturer's instructions, then jounce vehicle several times to settle suspension.
8. Check and correct rear wheel camber and toe first, if applicable, then check and correct front suspension angles in in the following order: caster and kingpin inclination, camber, toe setting and turning angle (toe-out on turns).

INSPECTION & ADJUSTMENTS

REAR WHEELS

The proper alignment of the rear suspension and wheels is essential for proper handling and to providing a reference for front wheel alignment. Always ensure that rear wheel alignment is within specifications prior to checking and adjusting front wheel alignment.

CAMBER

On models with independent rear suspension, rear wheel camber must be within specifications for proper vehicle handling and to prevent uneven tire wear. Rear camber cannot be adjusted. If rear camber is not within specifications, check for damaged or worn suspension components and deformed sheet metal, and repair as needed.

TOE-IN

On models with independent rear suspension, rear toe is the measurement of the rear wheels in relation to the vehicle centerline, **Fig. 1.** The leading edge of each rear wheel should toe-in slightly toward the vehicle centerline to ensure proper vehicle tracking. Rear toe should be inspected using suitable alignment gauges, following manufacturer's instructions. When checking or adjusting rear toe, always ensure that the amount that the left and right wheels toe-in is as nearly equal as possible.

Models W/Independent Rear Suspension Exc. Stanza, 1984—87 200SX & 300ZX, 1985–87 Maxima & 1987 Pulsar & Sentra

Rear toe is not adjustable on these models. If toe-in is not within specifications, check for damaged or worn suspension components and deformed sheet metal, and repair as needed.

1983–86 Stanza Exc. 1986 Stanza Wagon

On these models, rear toe-in is adjusted by varying the position of the parallel link bracket, **Fig. 2.**

1. Measure total toe-in and toe-in for each wheel following manufacturer's instructions.
2. Reposition parallel link brackets to obtain specified toe-in.
3. If toe-in is not within specifications and both brackets have been removed, adjust as follows:
   a. Set rear wheels on turning radius gauge.
   b. Temporarily secure parallel link bracket (on one side) with fixing bolt, **Fig. 2.**
   c. Turn rear wheels left and right, then tighten bracket bolt with wheel at 0 or straight ahead position.
   d. Position remaining bracket to obtain specified toe-in, then tighten bracket bolts.
   e. Torque bracket bolts to 43-58 ft. lbs., than ensure toe-in is still within specifications.

1985–87 Maxima & 1987 Stanza Exc. Wagon

Rear toe-in is adjusted by varying the length of the rear parallel links, **Fig. 3.**

1. Measure total toe-in and toe-in for each wheel following equipment manufacturer's instructions.
2. Loosen lock nuts and adjust parallel link length to obtain specified toe-in, noting the following:
   a. Adjust left and right rear parallel links to the same length A, **Fig. 4.**
   b. Standard length is 1.949 inches for 1985-86 Maxima or 1.97-2.17

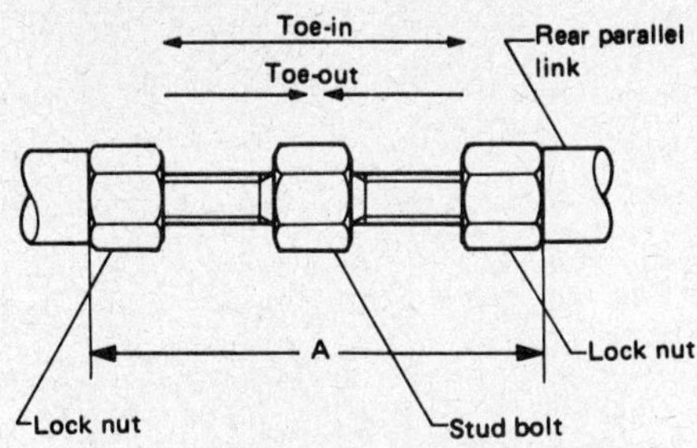

Fig. 4 Measuring parallel link length. 1985–87 Maxima & 1987 Stanza Exc. Wagon

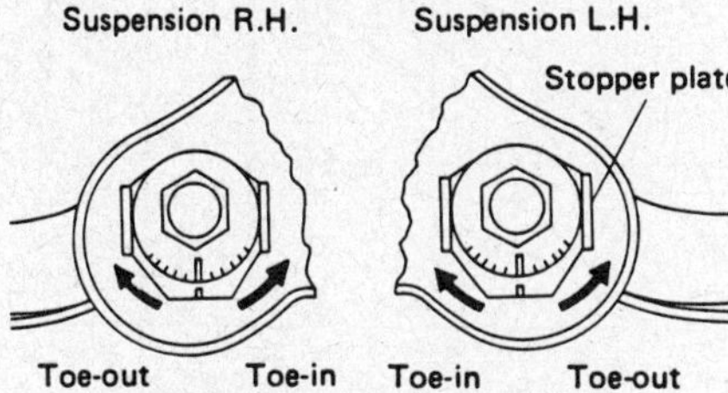

Fig. 7 Rear toe-in adjustment. 1987 Pulsar & Sentra

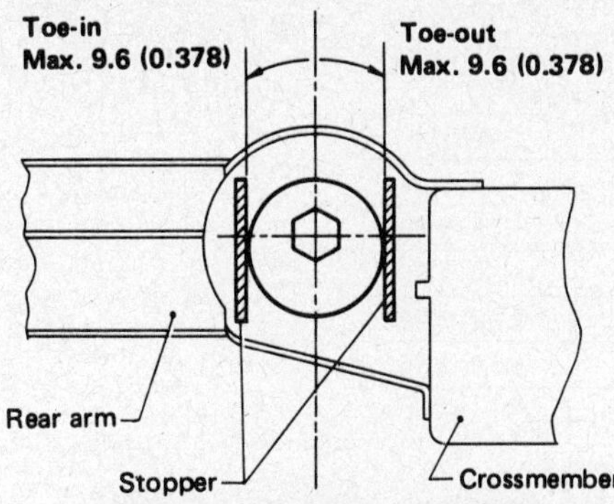

Fig. 5 Rear toe-in adjustment. 1984–87 200SX & 300ZX

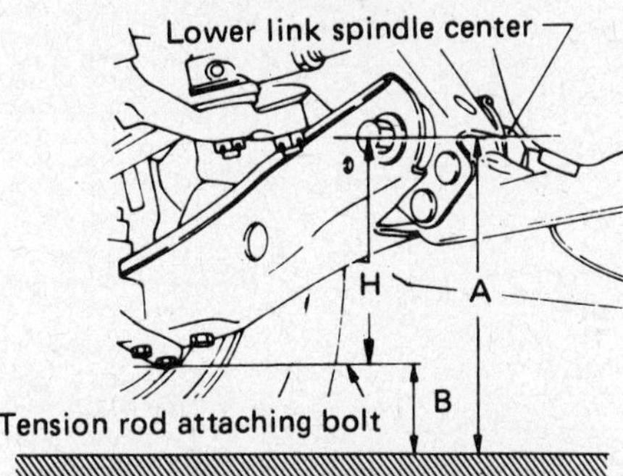

Fig. 8 Front suspension height measurement. Pickup & Pathfinder exc. 1984–87 models w/4 wheel drive.

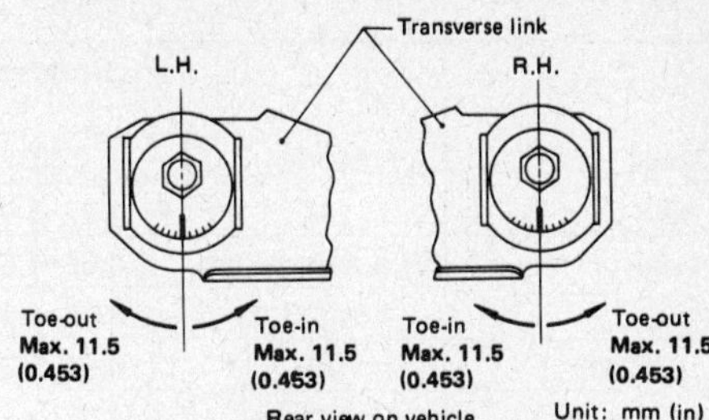

Fig. 6 Rear toe-in adjustment. 1986–87 Stanza Wagon, 1987 Sentra w/4 Wheel Drive similar

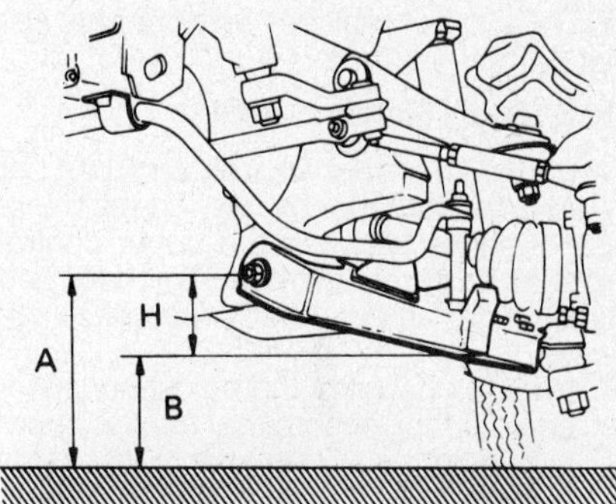

Fig. 9 Front suspension height measurement. Pathfinder & 1984–87 Pickup w/4 wheel drive

inches for 1987 Maxima and Stanza. If toe-in cannot be properly adjusted with links at equal length, and at or near specified standard length, check rear suspension for damage and wear, and repair as needed.

3. After adjustment, hold link with suitable wrench to prevent bushing from twisting, then torque lock nuts to 58-72 ft. lbs.

1984–87 200SX & 300ZX

Rear toe-in is adjusted by rotating the cam bolts which secure the inner rear control arm bushings, **Fig. 5.**

1. Measure total toe-in and toe-in for each wheel following equipment manufacturer's instructions.
2. Scribe matching mark between cam and control arm, then loosen nut securing inner control arm bushing bolt.
3. Rotate cam bolt, as needed, to bring toe-in within specifications. **Always set the right and left cam bolts in the same position.**
4. When toe-in is within specifications, hold position of cam bolt and torque nut to 72-87 ft. lbs.
5. Ensure toe-in is still within specifications.

1986–87 Stanza Wagon & 1987 Sentra 4 Wheel Drive

Rear toe-in is adjusted by rotating the cam bolts which secure the transverse link to the axle carrier, **Fig. 6.**

1. Measure total toe-in and toe-in for each wheel following equipment manufacturer's instructions.
2. Scribe matching mark between cam and control arm, then loosen nut securing cam bolt.
3. Rotate cam bolt as needed, **Fig. 6,** to bring toe-in within specifications. Ensure that total toe-in is within specifications and divided equally between left and right wheels.
4. Hold position of cam and torque nut to 83–98 ft. lbs.
5. Ensure toe-in is still within specifications.

1987 Pulsar & Sentra

Rear toe-in is adjusted by rotating the cam bolts which secure the rear parallel link to the crossmember.

1. Measure total toe-in and toe-in for each wheel following equipment manufacturer's instructions.
2. Scribe matching mark between cam and parallel link, then loosen nut securing cam bolt.
3. Rotate cam bolt(s) as needed, **Fig. 7,** to obtain specified toe-in. On graduation on scale varies toe-in approximately .08 inch. Ensure that total toe-in is within specifications and divided equally between left and right wheels.
4. Hold position of cam bolt(s) and torque retaining nuts to 72-87 ft. lbs.
5. Ensure toe-in is still within specifications.

FRONT WHEELS

Correct front wheel alignment is necessary to provide proper handling and to prevent uneven tire wear. To ensure correct alignment, angles should be checked, and if necessary corrected, in the following sequence: caster and kingpin inclination, camber, toe-setting, and the turning angle and toe-out on turns. Front wheel alignment should only be checked after ensuring that the rear wheels are properly aligned in relation to the vehicle centerline, as most equipment uses the rear wheels as reference for correct front wheel alignment. Front wheel alignment should be checked with the vehicle unladen, at normal ride height, and following equipment manufacturer's instructions.

CASTER & KINGPIN INCLINATION

Kingpin inclination is a function of the steering knuckle design and cannot be adjusted. Caster, the alignment angle which provides the self-centering steering effect, is only adjustable on truck models which do not use strut-type front suspensions. If caster or kingpin angle are not within specifications on models with strut-type front suspension, check suspension components and sheet metal for damage, distortion and excessive wear, and repair as needed. For caster adjustment On Pathfinder, Pickup and Van, refer to camber adjustment, as the caster and camber are both adjusted by inserting shims between the upper control arm spindle and the crossmember.

CAMBER

Exc. Pathfinder, Pickup & 1987 Pulsar & Sentra

Camber cannot be adjusted on these models. If camber is not within specifica-

Year	Model	Suspension Height "H" (Inches)	
		2WD	4WD
1983	All	4.88–5.08	5.28–5.47
1984	Exc. King Cab	4.65–4.80	1.73–1.89
	King Cab	4.45–4.61	1.54–1.69
1985–86	All	5.04–5.20	2.09–2.24
1987	All①	4.37–4.53	1.73–1.89

①—Includes 1986 mid-year introduction.

Fig. 10 Suspension height specifications. Pickup & Pathfinder

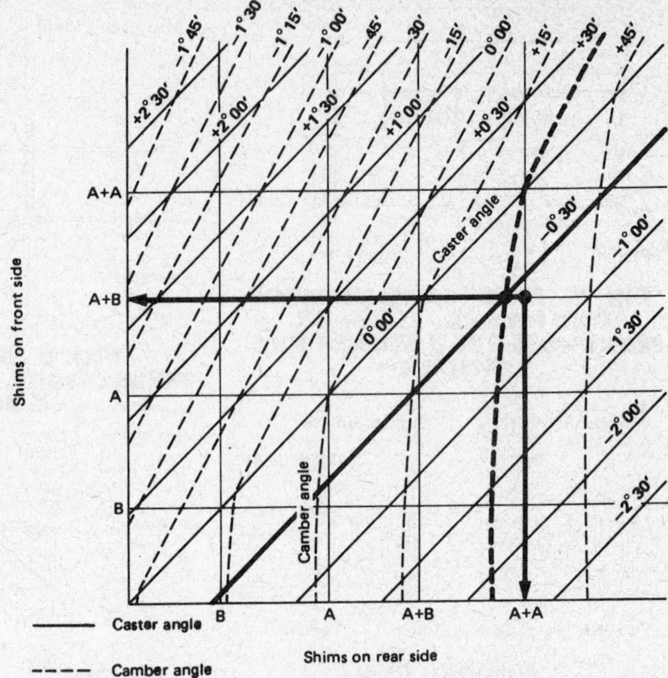

Fig. 11 Caster & camber adjusting shim selection. Van

tions, inspect suspension and sheet metal for damage, distortion and excessive wear, and repair or replace components as needed.

Pickup & Pathfinder

On these models, caster and camber are adjusted together by varying the thickness of shims between the upper control arm shaft and crossmember. To check and adjust caster and camber, proceed as follows:

1. Prior to checking and adjusting caster and camber, ensure that front suspension height is within specifications as follows:
   a. Measure suspension height of suspension arm pivot (A) and height of tension rod attaching bolt or steering stopper bracket (B), **Figs. 8 and 9.**
   b. Subtract measurement (B) from measurement (A) to determine suspension height (H), **Figs. 8 and9,** and compare remainder to specifications shown in chart, **Fig. 10.**
   c. If unladen vehicle height is not within specifications, jounce vehicle several times to settle suspension. If height is still not within specifications, check suspension and repair or replace component as needed before continuing with alignment procedure.
2. Check caster and camber and refer to wheel alignment specifications.
3. If caster and or camber are not within specifications, place suitable jack under lower control arm, raise arm to remove tension from upper control arm and loosen nuts securing upper control arm to crossmember.
4. Replace shims between upper control arm shaft and crossmember, noting the following:
   a. Do not use more than 3 shims at any one position, and ensure that shim thickness does not exceed .236 inch (6mm) on 1983-84 all and 1985-86 2WD models, or .315 inch (8mm) on 1985-86 4WD models and all 1987 models.
   b. When installing shims with a right angle tab at the top, ensure tab faces control arm shaft, insert shim from bracket side and only use one shim of this type at any one position.
   c. To adjust caster, vary thickness of shims between front and rear positions. When thickness of front shim is increased, caster decreases. When increasing shim thickness at the rear position, caster increases. When performing adjustment, ensure that difference in shim thickness between front and rear positions does not exceed .079 inch (2mm). **Camber angle is affected by varying shim thickness to perform caster adjustment. Always adjust caster angle first, then reduce or increase shim thickness equally at front and rear positions to adjust camber.**
   d. To adjust camber, add shims of equal thickness to both front and rear positions to move camber toward a more positive value, or decrease shim thickness equally at front and rear positions to move camber toward a more negative value.
5. Tighten upper control arm nuts and ensure caster and camber are still within specifications.

Van

On these models, caster and camber are adjusted together by varying the thickness of shims between the upper control arm shaft and crossmember. To check and adjust caster and camber, proceed as follows:

1. Check caster and camber and refer to wheel alignment specifications.
2. If caster and or camber are not within specifications, place suitable jack under lower control arm, raise arm to remove tension from upper control arm and loosen nuts securing upper control arm to crossmember.
3. Replace shims between upper control arm shaft and crossmember, noting the following:
   a. Do not install more than 2 shims at any one position.
   b. When installing shims with a right angle tab at the top, ensure tab faces control arm shaft, insert shim from bracket side and only use one shim of this type at any one position.
   c. Determine necessary shims by referring to **Fig. 11.** Note that shim A = .102 inch (2.6mm) and shim B = .47 inch (1.2mm).
4. Tighten upper control arm nuts and ensure caster and camber are still within specifications.

1987 Pulsar & Sentra

Camber is adjusted by rotating the eccentric strut mounting pin, **Fig. 12.** The pin is factory installed with the flat portion facing down. If camber is not within specifications, the pin must removed and reinstalled with the flat portion facing up.

1. Check camber following equipment manufacturer's instructions.
2. If camber is not within specifications, remove adjusting pin as outlined in strut replacement procedures, then install pin with flat side facing up and leave nut loose to allow adjustment.
3. Turn adjusting pin as needed to bring camber within specifications. One graduation of the adjusting pin changes camber by approximately 1/4°.
4. When camber is within specifications, hold adjusting pin and torque nut to 72-87 ft. lbs., then ensure camber is still within specifications.

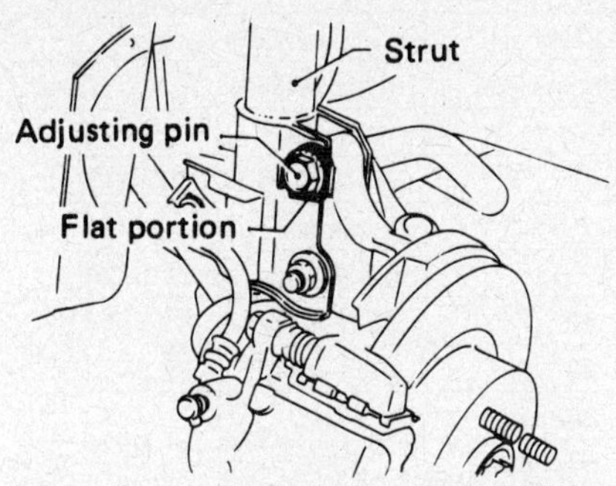

Fig. 12 Camber adjusting pin. 1987 Pulsar & Sentra

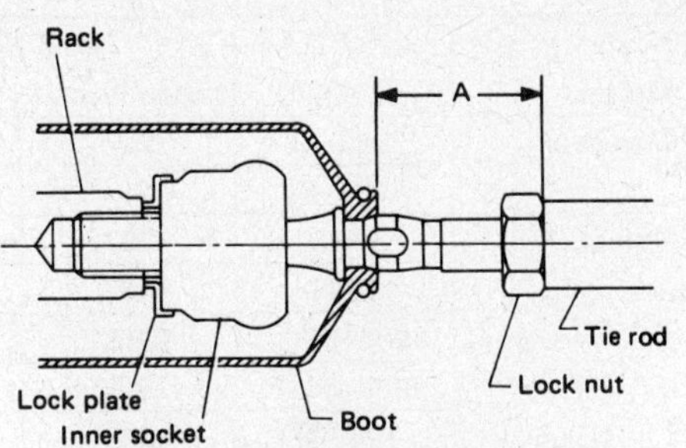

Fig. 13 Typical tie rod length measurement. 280ZX, 300ZX, 1983–84 Maxima & 1983–87 200SX

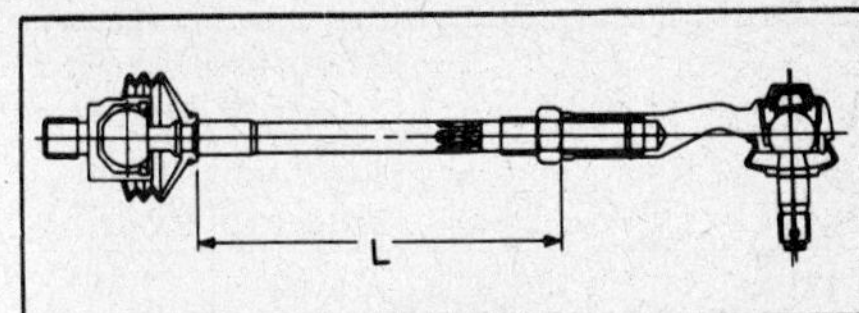

Fig. 14 Typical tie rod length measurement. Pulsar, Sentra & 1985–87 Stanza

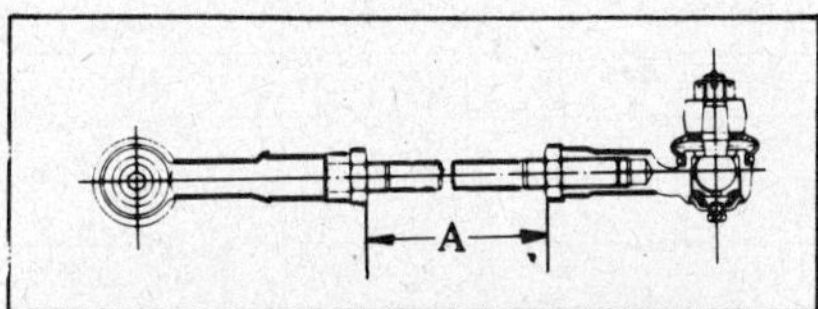

Fig. 15 Tie rod length measurement. 1983 2000SX

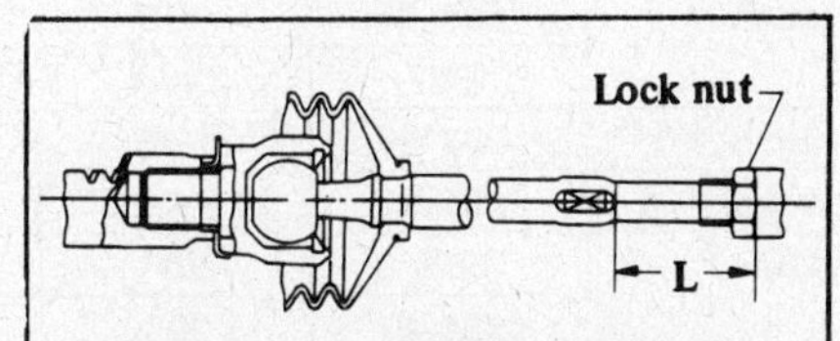

Fig. 16 Tie rod length measurement. 1983–84 Stanza

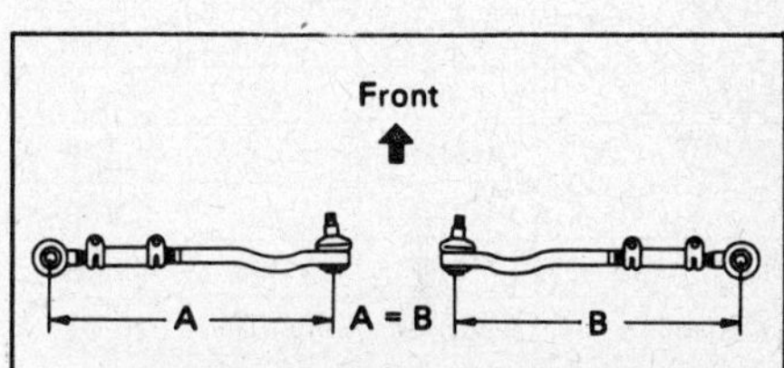

Fig. 17 Typical tie rod length measurement. Pathfinder, Pickup & Van

TOE SETTING

The toe setting is the measurement of the wheels in relation to the vehicle centerline, **Fig. 1.** The leading edge of each wheel should toe-in or toe-out slightly in relation to the vehicle centerline to ensure proper vehicle tracking. Toe should be inspected using suitable alignment gauges, following manufacturer's instructions. When checking or adjusting toe, always ensure that the setting of the left and right wheels is as nearly equal as possible.

Toe is adjusted by loosening the tie rod lock nuts or adjusting sleeve bolts and equally altering the length of the tie rods. After toe has been adjusted to specifications, the lengths of the left and right tie rods, **Figs. 13-17,** should be nearly equal and close to the length specified in **Fig. 18.** If tie rod lengths are incorrect, tie rods should be disassembled and adjusted to specifications, and the toe setting should be readjusted before checking steering angles. Incorrect tie rod length will adversely affect steering angles and toe-out on turns.

STEERING ANGLE

When a vehicle negotiates a turn, the inner wheel must turn at a sharper angle than the outer wheel, and the outer wheel must travel farther than the inner wheel. Vehicle steering geometry is calculated to allow for these variations, causing the outer wheel to to-out by a calibrated amount. This toe-out on turns is also referred to as steering angle and on these models, is generally checked at two positions. The first position is at a reference point on the inner wheel travel while the second position of measurement is at full steering lock. To check steering angles, proceed as follows:

1. Place unladen vehicle on suitable alignment rack and ensure that kingpin angle, caster, camber and toe settings are within specifications.
2. Turn wheels from straight-ahead position until the inner wheel is at the position specified for "Toe-Out On Turns" shown in **Fig. 19.** If the outer wheel reference angle is incorrect, check for damaged or improperly adjusted tie rods. Perform check in both left and right directions.
3. On models less rack and pinion steering, proceed as follows:
   a. Rotate steering to full lock in each direction.
   b. Adjust inner wheel "Turning Angle" to value specified in **Fig. 19,** by adjusting position of steering stop.
   c. With inner wheel adjusted to specifications, outer wheel turning angle should be as specified in **Fig. 19.** If outer wheel turning angle is incorrect, repair or replace steering linkage as needed.
4. On models with rack and pinion steering, proceed as follows:
   a. Turn steering to full lock and measure inner and outer wheel turning angles.
   b. If "Turning Angles" at full lock are not within specifications, **Fig. 19,** check for damaged steering linkage or improperly adjusted tie rods.
   c. If steering linkage and tie rods are satisfactory, check for improper rack or rack piston stroke and repair steering gear as needed.

Model	Year	Standard Tie Rod Length Inches	
		Manual Steering	Power Steering
Maxima	1983–84	1.42	1.68
	1985	—	6.00
	1986	—	6.79
	1987	—	7.02
Pulsar, Sentra	1983–87	6.93	6.93
Stanza①	1983–84	1.677	1.677
	1985	6.92	6.92
	1986	7.10	7.10
	1987	—	7.05
Stanza②	1986	—	6.95
Stanza② ③	1987	—	6.95
Stanza② ④	1987	—	6.88
200SX	1983	2.795	2.795
	1984–87	1.429	1.689
280ZX	1983	1.161	1.38
300ZX	1984	—	1.476
	1985–87	—	1.689
Pathfinder	1987	11.06	11.06
Pickup③	1983–86	13.07	13.07
	1987⑤	13.54	13.54
Pickup④	1983	10.83	10.83
	1984–86	11.54	11.54
	1987⑤	11.06	11.06
Van	1987	—	12.83

①—Exc. Wagon.
②—Wagon.
③—2 Wheel drive.
④—4 wheel drive.
⑤—Includes 1986 mid-year introduction.

Fig. 18 Tie rod length specifications

Model	Year	Toe-Out On Turns		Turning Angle①	
		Inner Wheel	Outer Wheel	Inner Wheel	Outer Wheel
Maxima	1983–84	20°	18⅔°	36–40°	30–34°
	1985–87	22⅓°	20°	34–38°⑨	27–31°⑨
Pulsar	1983	20°	17.5°	40–44°	31–35°
	1984	20°	17.5°	40.5–43.5°	31.5–34.5°
	1985–86②	22.5°	20°	40.5–43.5°	31.5–34.5°
	1985–86③	22.5°	20°	37.5–40.5°	29.5–32.5°
	1987④	21⅗°	20°	37-40°	32.5°
	1987⑤	22⅖°	20°	36-39°	30°
Sentra⑭	1983	20°	17.5°	⑥	⑥
	1984	20°	17.5°	40.5–43.5°	31.5–34.5
	1985②	22.5°	20°	40.5–43.5°	31.5–34.5°
	1985③	22.5°	20°	37.5–40.5°	29.5–32.5°
	1986	22.5°	20°	⑦	⑦
	1987	21⅗°	20°	⑧	⑧
Sentra⑮	1987	22⅕°	20°	37.5-40.5°⑨	31°⑨
Stanza⑫	1983–86	20°	18.5°	36–40°	30–34
	1987	22⅓°	20°	38-42°	29-33°
Stanza⑬ ⑭	1986–87	20–23°	20°	⑯	⑯
Stanza⑬ ⑮	1986–87	21.5–24.5°	20°	⑰	⑰
200SX	1983	20°	18.7	⑩	⑩
	1984–87	20°	18⅔°	36–39°⑨	30–33°⑨
280ZX	1983	20°	⑪	32–36°	24.5–28.5°
300ZX	1984–87	22.5°	20°	35–39°⑨	27–31°⑨
Pathfinder	1987	22°	20°	⑱	⑱
Pickup⑭	1983–84	20°	18°	34–36°	30–32°
	1985–86	20°	18°	34–36°	31–33°
	1987⑲	22°	20°	36–38°	33–35°
Pickup⑮	1983	18.5°	18°	29–33°	27–29°
	1984–86	20°	18°	31–33°	29–31°
	1987⑲	22°	20°	⑱	⑱
Van	1987	20°	19°	32.5–35.5°	28–31°

①—At full lock.
②—Exc. auto. trans. w/manual steering
③—Auto. trans. w/manual steering
④—E16i engine.
⑤—CA16DE engine.
⑥—E15 engine: Inner wheel, 40–44°; Outer wheel, 31–35°. CD17 engine w/auto. trans.: Inner wheel, 33–37°; outer wheel, 27–31°. CD17 engine w/manual trans.: Inner wheel, 37–41°; outer wheel, 29–33°.
⑦—E16 engine exc. auto. trans w/manual steering: Inner wheel, 40.5–43.5°; outer wheel, 31.5–34.5°. E16 engine w/auto. trans. & manual steering, and CD17 engine all: Inner wheel, 37.5–40.5°; outer wheel, 29.5–32.5°.
⑧—Exc. Coupe SE w/power steering & models W/CD17 engine: Inner wheel, 37–40°; outer wheel, 32.5°. Coupe SE w/power steering & Models w/CD17 engine: Inner wheel, 39.5–42.5°; outer wheel, 34°.
⑨—Models w/power steering: With engine idling & turning force of 22–33 lbs. applied to rim of steering wheel.
⑩—Manual steering: Inner wheel, 32–35°; outer wheel, 27–29°. Power steering: Inner wheel, 34–36°; outer wheel, 28–30°
⑪—Manual Steering, 18.1°; power steering, 18.7°.
⑫—Exc. Wagon.
⑬—Wagon.
⑭—2 wheel drive.
⑮—4 wheel drive.
⑯—Auto. trans.: Inner wheel, 31.5–34.5°; outer wheel, 26.5–29.5°. Manual trans.: Inner wheel, 33–36°; outer wheel, 27.5–30.5°.
⑰—Auto. trans.; Inner wheel, 35.5–37.5°; outer wheel, 26.5–29.5°. Manual trans.: 35.5–38.5°l; outer wheel, 27–30°.
⑱—Exc. 31 10.5 R15 tires: Inner wheel, 33–35°; outer wheel, 31–33°. 31 10.5 R15 tires: Inner wheel, 27–29°; outer wheel 25–27°.
⑲—Includes 1986 mid-year introduction.

Fig. 19 Turning angle specifications

PEUGEOT (France)

INDEX OF SERVICE OPERATIONS

General Engine Specifications

Year	Engine CID①/cc	Carb. Type	Bore & Stroke Inches (mm)	Comp. Ratio	Horsepower @ RPM	Torque Lbs. Ft. @ RPM	Normal Oil Pressure Lbs.
1983	4-120/1971②	Fuel Inj.⑨	3.465 x 3.189 (88 x 81)	8.35	97 @ 5000	116 @ 3500	47.8–48
	4-140/2304③	Fuel Inj.⑤	3.70 x 3.267 (94 x 93)	21	80 @ 4150	135 @ 2000	38–52
	4-140/2304④	Fuel Inj.⑤	3.70 x 3.267 (94 x 83)	23	71 @ 4500	99 @ 2500	38–52
1984	4-120/1971②	Fuel Inj.	3.465 x 3.189 (88 x 81)	8.35	97 @ 5000	116 @ 3500	—
	4-140/2304③ ⑥	Fuel Inj.	3.70 x 3.267 (94 x 93)	21	80 @ 4150	133.4 @ 2000	—
	4-140/2304④	Fuel Inj.	3.70 x 3.267 (94 x 93)	23	71 @ 4500	99 @ 2500	—
	4-140/2304③ ⑦	Fuel Inj.	3.70 x 3.267 (94 x 93)	21	80 @ 4150	135.6 @ 2000	—
1985	4-120/1971②	Fuel Inj.	3.465 x 3.189 (88 x 81)	8.3	97 @ 5000	116 @ 3500	—
	4-134/2156⑧	Fuel Inj.	3.61 x 3.21 (91.7 x 81.6)	7	142 @ 5600	163 @ 3800	—
	4-152/2.5L③	Fuel Inj.	—	21	95 @ 4150	133.4 @ 2000	—
1986	4-120/1971②	Fuel Inj.	3.465 x 3.189 (88 x 81)	8.3	97 @ 5000	116 @ 3500	—
	4-134/2156⑧	Fuel Inj.	3.61 x 3.21 (91.7 x 81.6)	7	150 @ 5000	181 @ 2750	—
	4-152/2.5L③	Fuel Inj.	—	21	95 @ 4150	152 @ 2000	—
1987	4-134/2156②	Fuel Inj.	3.61 x 3.21 (91.7 x 81.6)	8.8	120 @ 5000	131 @ 3500	—
	4-134/2156⑧	Fuel Inj.	3.61 x 3.21 (91.7 x 81.6)	7.5	150 @ 5000	180 @ 2750	—
	4-152/2.5L③	Fuel Inj.	—	21	95 @ 4150	133 @ 2000	—
	V6-170/2.8L	Fuel Inj.	—	9.5	145 @ 5000	173 @ 3750	—

—Not Available.
①—Cubic inch displacement.
②—Gasoline.
③—Turbocharged diesel.
④—Diesel.
⑤—Bosch mechanical.
⑥—604 models.
⑦—505 models.
⑧—Turbocharged gasoline engine.
⑨—Bosch K-Jetronic.

Alternator & Regulator Specifications

Alternator					Regulator
			Output @ 14 Volts		
Model No.	Rated Output Watts	Field Current 12 Volts @ 80°F	3500 RPM Amps.	5000 RPM Amps.	Model
A13R120	750	—	48	—	8364
A13R144	750	—	45	—	8731
A13R152	750	—	45	—	AYB21
A13R171	750	—	45	—	AYB2119
A13R178	750	—	45	—	72711302
A13R184	750	—	—	40	—
A13R185	750	—	45	—	—

—Not Available.

Rear Axle Specifications

		Ring Gear & Pinion Backlash		Pinion Bearing Preload			Differential Bearing Preload	
Model	Carrier Type	Method	Adjustment	Method	With Seal Inch-Lbs.	Less Seal Inch-Lbs.	Method	Adjustment
504	Integral	Shims	0.007–0.0098	Shims	—	—	Shims	—
604	Integral	Shims	0.0059–0.010	Shims	—	—	Shims	—
505	Integral	Shims	0.0059–0.0103	Shims	—	—	Shims	—

—Not Available.

Starting Motor Applications

Engine	Model No.
4-120/1971cc	G189
	D8E76
	D8E96
	D8E122
	D8E124
4-134/2156cc	—
4-140/2304cc Diesel	G109
	D11E109
	D11E142
	D11E159
4-140/2304cc Turbo Diesel	G207
	D11E126
	D11E156
	D001362045
	JF12V2KW
4-152/2.5L Diesel	—
V6-170/2.8L	—

—Not Available.

Pistons, Pins, Rings, Crankshaft & Bearings

Engine	Nominal Piston Clearance	Ring End Gap ① Comp.	Ring End Gap ① Oil	Wrist Pin Diameter	Rod Bearings Shaft Diameter	Rod Bearings Bearing Clearance	Main Bearings Shaft Diameter	Main Bearings Bearing Clearance	Main Bearings Thrust on Bear. No.	Main Bearings Shaft Endplay
4-120/1971cc	.0023	②	.010	.905	1.9678—1.9685	③	④	③	5	.0031-.0079
4-134/2156cc	.0023	—	—	—	⑤	—	2.242-2.2428	—	3	.0035-.0106
4-140/2304cc ⑥	.0051	.014	.006	1.181	2.165-2.166	.0015-.0036	2.362-2.363	③	3	.0031-.0079
4-140/2304cc ⑦	.0051	⑧	.006	1.181	2.165-2.166	.0015-.0036	2.362-2.363	③	3	.0031-.0079
4-152/2.5L ⑦	—	—	—	—	—	—	—	—	—	—
V6-170/2.8L	—	—	—	—	—	—	—	—	—	—

—Not Available.
①—Minimum.
②—Top, 0.008 inch; second, .015 inch.
③—Refer to text.
④—Rear journal, 2.1616-2.1646; int. rear journal, 2.2102-2.2112; center journal, 2.2509-2.2515; int. front journal, 2.3050-2.3060; front journal, 2.3386-2.3392.
⑤—Red, 2.0456-2.0459; blue, 2.0453-2.0456.
⑥—Diesel.
⑦—Turbocharged diesel.
⑧—Top, 0.010 inch; second, 0.008 inch.

Valve Specifications

Year	Model	Valve Lash Int.	Valve Lash Exh.	Valve Angles Seat	Valve Angles Face	Valve Spring Installed Height	Valve Spring Pressure Lbs. @ In.	Stem Clearance Intake	Stem Clearance Exhaust	Stem Diameter Intake	Stem Diameter Exhaust
1983–84	4-140/2304cc ①	.010	.010	③	③	④	⑤	.0014	.0018	.3339–.3344	.3331–.3337
	4-140/2304cc ②	.006	.010	45	45	④	⑤	.0014	.0018	.3339–.3344	.3331–.3337
1983–86	4-120/1971cc	.004C	.010C	③	③	⑥	—	.0008–.0014	.0008–.0014	.3149	.3165
1985–87	4-134	.008	.012	44	45	⑦	10.8 @ 1.46	—	—	.3539	.3530
	4-152/2.5L ②	—	—	—	—	—	—	—	—	—	—
1987	V6-170/2.8L	—	—	—	—	—	—	—	—	—	—

—Not Available.
①—Diesel.
②—Turbo Diesel.
③—Intake, 30°; exhaust 45°.
④—Inner: installed height, 1.22 inches; free length, 1.614 inches. Outer: installed height, 1.377 inches; free length, 1.755 inches.
⑤—Inner: 16.8 lbs. @ 1.22 inches; 34.8 lbs. @ .866 inch. Outer: 48.5 lbs. @ 1.377 inches; 101.4 lbs. @ 1.023 inches.
⑥—Free length: inner, 1.55 inches; outer, 1.73 inches.
⑦—Free length, 2.059 inches.

Wheel Alignment Specifications

Model	Caster Angle, Degrees Limits	Caster Angle, Degrees Desired	Camber Angle, Degrees Limits Left	Camber Angle, Degrees Limits Right	Camber Angle, Degrees Desired Left	Camber Angle, Degrees Desired Right	Toe-In Inch	Toe-out on Turns Degrees Outer Wheel	Toe-out on Turns Degrees Inner Wheel
504	+2.2 to +3.2	+2.7	+.1 to +1.1	+.1 to +1.1	+.6	+.6	0.12	19.4	20.7
604	+3 to +4	+3.5	−.25 to +1.25	−.25 to +1.25	+.5	+.5	0.118	—	—
505	+3 to +4	+3.5	−.05 to +1.45	−.05 to +1.45	+.7	+.7	0.16	—	—

—Not Available.

Gasoline Engine Tightening Specifications

*Torque specifications are for clean and lightly lubricated threads only. Dry or dirty threads produce increased friction which prevents accurate measurement of tightness.

Year	Engine	Spark Plugs Ft. Lbs.	Cylinder Head Bolts Ft. Lbs.	Intake Manifold Ft. Lbs.	Exhaust Manifold Ft. Lbs.	Camshaft Bearing Caps Ft. Lbs.	Camshaft Sprocket Bolts Ft. Lbs.	Rocker Arm Nuts Ft. Lbs.	Rocker Arm Cover Ft. Lbs.	Connecting Rod Cap Bolts Ft. Lbs.	Main Bearing Cap Bolts Ft. Lbs.	Flywheel To Crankshaft Ft. Lbs.	Vibration Damper or Pulley Ft. Lbs.
1980–86	4-120/1971cc	22	①	—	—	—	16	11	—	29	55	49	123.5
1985–87	4-134	22	①	11	15	—	11	—	3.6	47	80	58	98
1987	V6-170/2.8L	—	—	—	—	—	—	—	—	—	—	—	—

—Not Available.
①—Refer to text.

Diesel Engine Tightening Specifications

*Torque specifications are for clean and lightly lubricated threads only. Dry or dirty threads produce increased friction which prevents accurate measurement of tightness.

Year	Engine	Preheating Plugs Ft. Lbs.	Cylinder Head Bolts Ft. Lbs.	Injector Holder to Cyl. Head Ft. Lbs.	Injector Cap Nut to Holder Ft. Lbs.	Injection Pump Ft. Lbs.	Rocker Arm Nuts Ft. Lbs.	Connecting Rod Cap Bolts Ft. Lbs.	Main Bearing Cap Bolts Ft. Lbs.	Flywheel To Crankshaft Ft. Lbs.	Vibration Damper or Pulley Ft. Lbs.
1983–84	4-140/2304cc②	—	①	—	—	—	③	41.3	79.75	55.8	39.88④
	4-140/2304cc⑥	16.3	①	65.1	43.4	14.5	⑤	43	79.6	56	39④
1985–87	4-152/2.5L	—	—	—	—	—	—	—	—	—	—

—Not Available.
①—Refer to text.
②—Exc. turbocharged diesel
③—Intermediate bearings, 34.44 ft. lbs.; end bearings, 14.5 ft. lbs.
④—Plus 60° angular tightening.
⑤—Rocker shaft bearing nuts, 28.9 ft. lbs.; rocker shaft end bearing bolts, 19.9 ft. lbs.
⑥—Turbocharged diesel.

Brake Specifications

			Wheel Cylinder Bore			Master Cylinder Bore		Disc Brake Rotor				
								Nominal Thickness		Min. Thickness		
Year	Model	Drum Brake I.D.	Front Disc	Rear Disc	Rear Drum	Manual	Power	Front	Rear	Front	Rear	Runout (T.I.R.)
1983–84	604	—	—	—	—	—	—	—	—	—	—	—
1983–86	505	—	—	—	—	—	—	.502	.472	.423	.413	.0028

—Not Available.

Cooling System & Capacity Data

		Cooling Capacity Qts.						Transmission Oil			
Year	Engine or Model	Less A/C	With A/C	Radiator Cap Relief Pressure Lbs.	Thermo. Opening Temp. °F	Fuel Tank Gals.	Engine Oil Refill Qts.	4 Speed Pints	5 Speed Pints	Auto. Trans. Qts. ①	Rear Axle Oil Pints
1983–84	505 Sedan	7.7	7.7	14.5	—	18	4.2	—	3.4	5.4	3.2
	505 Diesel Sedan	10.6	10.6	14.5	—	17.4	5.3	2.42	—	5.4	3.3
	504 Diesel Wagon	10.6	10.6	14.5	—	15.8	5.25	2.5	—	5.5°	3.4
1983–84	505 Turbo Diesel	10.6	10.6	14.5	—	18	5.7	—	3.28	—	3.28
1983–84	604 Turbo Diesel	10.6	10.6	14.5	—	18	5.7	—	3.28	—	3.28
1985–86	505 Sedan	10	10	—	—	18	4.2	3.1	3.9	②	—
	505 Turbo Sedan	10	10	—	—	18	5.3	3.1	3.9	②	—
	505 Turbo Diesel Wagon	10.6	10.6	②	—	18	5.3	3.1	3.9	②	—

—Not Available.
①—Capacity approximate, make final check with dipstick.
②—Drain & refill, 1.7 qts.; overhaul, 5.5 qts.

ELECTRICAL SECTION

INDEX

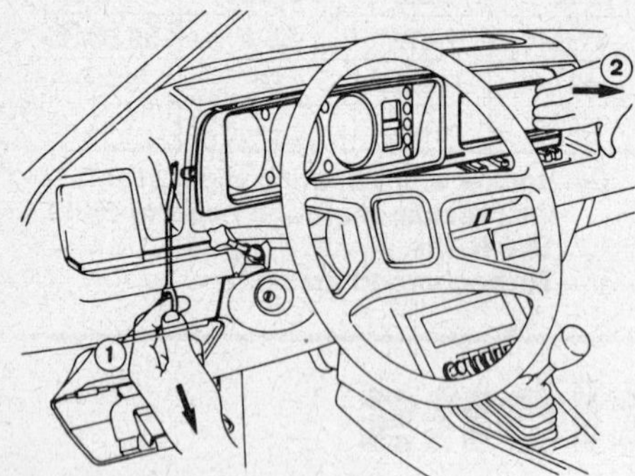

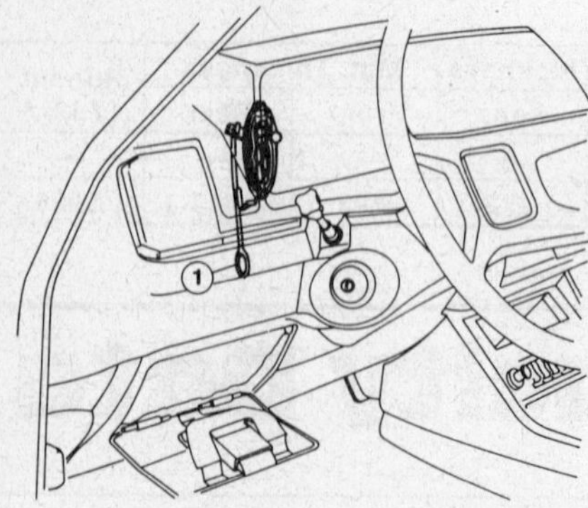

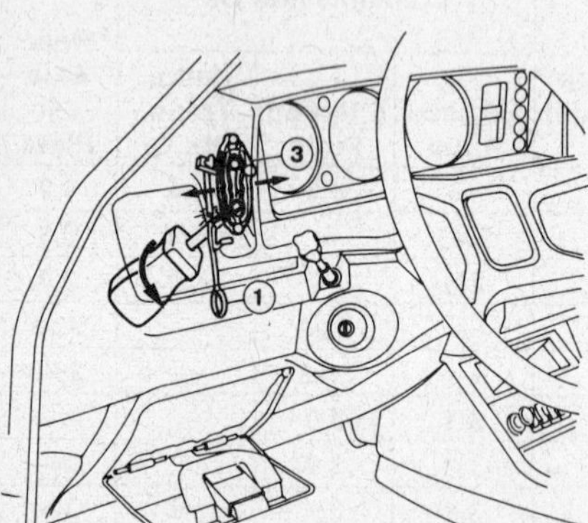

Fig. 1 Instrument cluster removal. 604 models

STARTER
REPLACE

1. Disconnect battery ground cable.
2. Disconnect starter wiring from starter.
3. Remove starter retaining bolts and starter.
4. Reverse procedure to install.

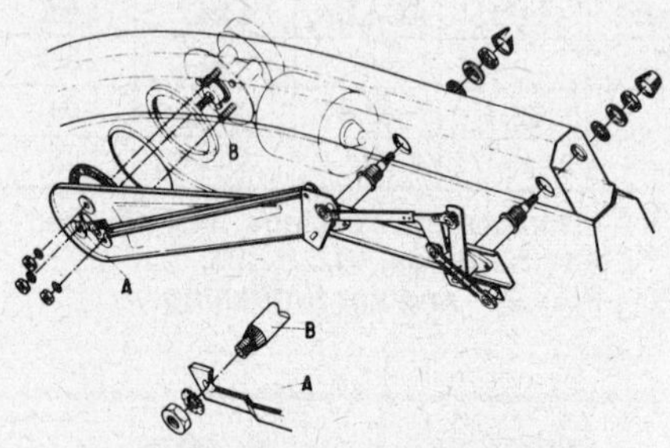

Fig. 2 Wiper motor & linkage. 604 models

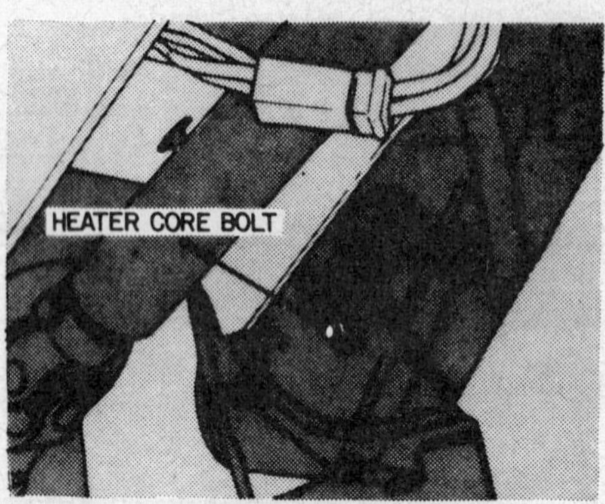

Fig. 4 Removing heater core securing bolt. 505 models

STOP LIGHT SWITCH
REPLACE

1. Disconnect switch electrical connectors.
2. Loosen switch retaining locknut and remove switch.
3. Reverse procedure to install.

INSTRUMENT CLUSTER
REPLACE
604

1. Disconnect battery.
2. Disconnect speedometer cable.
3. Unclip left side of panel by pulling release (1), **Fig. 1. If pulling on release (1) does not free panel, it is possible to push directly on the release pin by opening up guide (3), Fig. 1.**
4. Remove panel by unclipping right side (2), **Fig. 1.**
5. Disconnect leads.

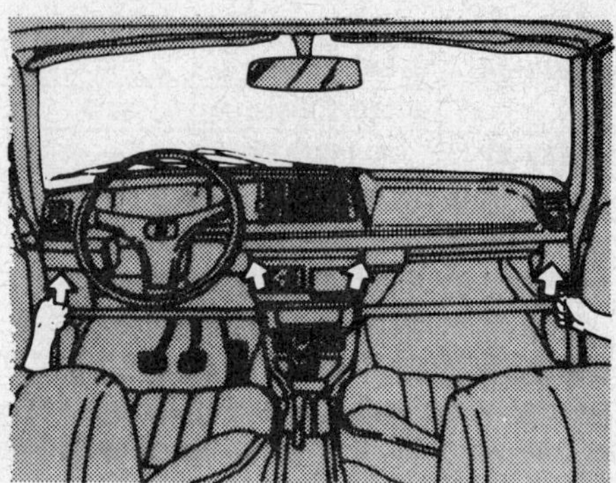

Fig. 3 Removing dashboard. 604 models

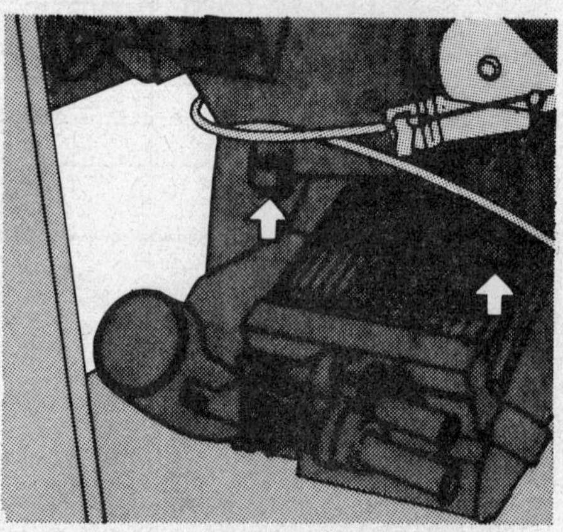

Fig. 5 Removing heater core. 604 models

6. Reverse procedure to install ensuring that speedometer drive cable clicks into position.

WINDSHIELD WIPER MOTOR & LINKAGE
REPLACE
604

1. Disconnect battery.
2. Remove cowl grille.
3. Disconnect wiring.
4. Refer to "Instrument Cluster, Replace" procedure to remove the instrument panel.
5. Remove drive spindle nut, **Fig. 2,** and remove the three nuts securing wiper motor.
6. Remove motor.
7. Remove wiper arms.
8. Remove plastic cap over center screw securing heater control panel.

9. Remove heater/ventilation control trim panel.
10. Remove 6 glove compartment retaining screws and the glove compartment assembly.
11. Disconnect glove compartment and map lights.
12. Remove steering column cover.
13. Remove left side lower trim panel.
14. Remove nuts securing dashboard, **Fig. 3.**
15. Disconnect heater control cable, rocker switches and instrument panel lights.
16. Remove dashboard.
17. Refer to **Fig. 2,** and remove wiper linkage.
18. Reverse procedure to install.

HEATER CORE

REPLACE

505

1. Drain cooling system.
2. Remove glove compartment.
3. Remove steering column cover and lower dashboard trim panel.
4. Disconnect heater valve cable.
5. Clamp shut and disconnect heater hoses.
6. Remove heater core securing bolt, **Fig. 4** and heater core.
7. Reverse procedure to install. When filling cooling system, open heater valve by setting control lever to red dot.

604

1. Drain cooling system.
2. Remove glove compartment from under dashboard.
3. Remove screws from water valve control and heater air door.
4. Pull back carpeting and remove air duct to rear seats on right side.
5. Remove clips and heater core, **Fig. 5.**
6. Reverse procedure to install taking care that rubber seals are positioned properly.

BLOWER

REPLACE

505

Less A/C

1. Unclip front right side brake line from firewall.
2. Remove heater sound proofing.
3. Compress corrugated section of duct and carefully free end from blower housing. **Duct is clipped to firewall and is not to be removed.**
4. Disconnect blower wiring.
5. Remove clips from circumference of blower scroll housing.
6. Remove blower.
7. Reverse procedure to install.

With A/C

1. Unclip sound proofing shield along top edge.
2. Remove the following on appropriate vehicles:
   a. Auxiliary air device on fuel injection engines.
   b. Coolant expansion tank on diesel engines.
3. Remove nipple on upper right corner of shield and first clip along lower edge.
4. Loosen clips and remove blower to evaporator duct.
5. Remove 7 clips from circumference of blower scroll housing.
6. Disconnect electrical lead and remove blower motor assembly.
7. Reverse procedure to install.

4-120/1971cc GASOLINE ENGINE SECTION

INDEX

ENGINE

REPLACE

504

1. On models with automatic transmissions, drain transmission fluid. On all models, remove battery and tray, hood, radiator, ignition coil, starter and windshield washer reservoir.
2. Disconnect heater hoses, fuel line, carburetor controls, Master-Vac vacuum line, and wiring. On models with automatic transmissions, remove air filter and bracket.
3. Remove steering rack attaching bolts and lower steering rack (turn steering wheel towards left).
4. Disconnect exhaust pipe from exhaust manifold. Remove flywheel guard plates and clutch housing bolts.
5. Position hoisting apparatus on engine and raise until loaded.
6. Remove engine mount bolts from crossmember. **Left side brake line must be up against crossmember.**
7. Raise engine until transmission contacts tunnel.
8. Support transmission. On models with automatic transmission, remove four bolts holding torque converter to flywheel. **Engine must not be removed with torque converter attached. Converter must remain attached to transmission.**
9. On all models, separate engine from transmission and lift out.
10. Reverse procedure to install. On automatic transmission models, torque converter bolts should be torqued to 16 ft. lbs.

505

1. Remove hood, battery and fan shroud.
2. Drain radiator. Disconnect hoses and temperature sender wires. Remove lower radiator mounting bolts.
3. Disconnect rubber duct hose from mixture regulator. Remove throttle plate housing and hoses.
4. Disconnect fuel supply and return hoses, cold start injector hose and PCV hose.
5. Remove injectors, mixture regulator and air filter.
6. Unbolt air conditioning compressor and disconnect freon hose clamp from alternator bracket. Secure compressor aside.
7. Disconnect accelerator cable and engine electrical harness. Disconnect harness from engine TDC sensor diagnostic plug and separate high tension lead connectors. Disconnect evaporative canister hoses.
8. Disconnect heater hose, power steering fluid reservoir, Lambda sensor wire and air injection hose to catalytic converter.
9. Disconnect vacuum switch hoses and wires.
10. Remove starter, upper bellhousing bolts, and disconnect engine mounts.
11. Disconnect power steering pump and exhaust header pipe.
12. Remove bellhousing inspection plates. On automatic transmission models, position torque converter support plate so as not to alter TDC sensor adjustment. Mark TDC sensor

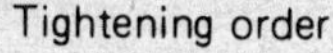

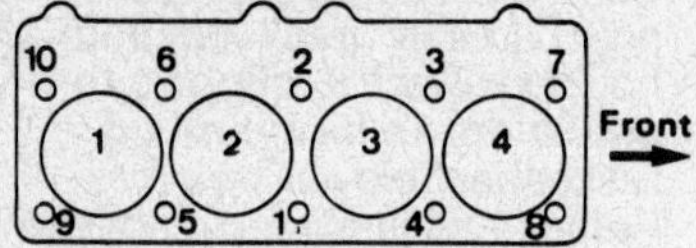

Fig. 1 Cylinder head torque sequence

Place exhaust valve in the fully open position	To adjust: Intake	Exhaust
⊗ 1	● 3	⊗ 4
⊗ 3	● 4	⊗ 2
⊗ 4	● 2	⊗ 1
⊗ 2	● 1	⊗ 3

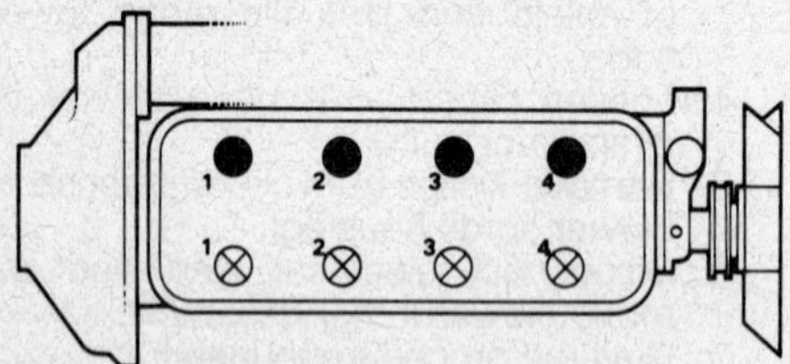

Reminder: Firing order: 1 - 3 - 4 - 2.
Number 1 cylinder located flywheel side.

Fig. 2 Valve adjusting sequence

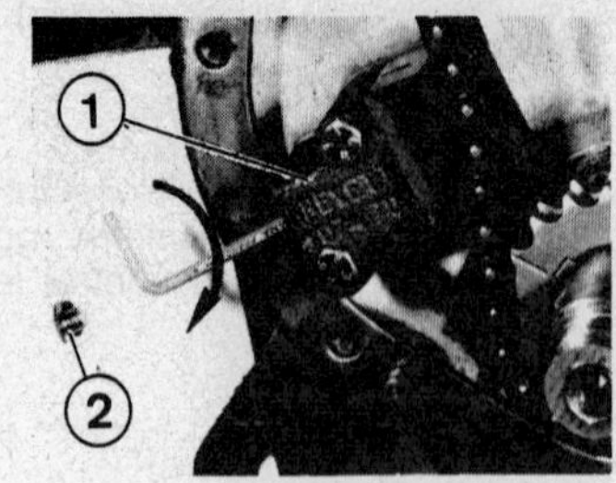

Fig. 3 Releasing chain tension

notch in relation to support plate. Remove converter bolts and retain torque converter in housing.

13. On all models, unbolt and move condenser and receiver dryer assembly towards left leaving hoses attached.
14. Install lifting equipment on engine and support transmission. Remove engine.
15. Reverse procedure to install. Note the following: On automatic transmission models, lubricate torque converter centering nipple with Calysol grease F 3015 or equivalent. Position TDC sensor notch and align reference marks. Coat torque converter bolts with suitable thread locking compound and torque to 21.75 ft. lbs. On manual transmission models, lubricate main shaft splines and pilot bushing with Molykote 321 or equivalent. Torque engine mount bolts to 21.75 ft. lbs. and bellhousing bolts to 39.88 ft. lbs. Adjust new TDC sensor to bring the three nipples in contact. Adjust gap between used sensor and flywheel to .007 inch (1.7 mm).

CYLINDER HEAD
REPLACE

Removal

Cylinder head must be removed only when engine is cold to avoid risk of distortion.

1. Drain coolant from block and remove air filter, intake manifold, PCV pipe, upper radiator hose, water pump drive belt, distributor cap, spark plugs and valve cover.
2. Disconnect leads and hoses as necessary. Remove spark plug tube seals and cups.
3. Disconnect exhaust pipe from manifold. Remove outermost cylinder head bolts on exhaust side and fit suitable cylinder head guides.
4. Remove rocker shaft assembly and push rods.
5. Remove head guide from front bolt hole and pivot head to separate from the block and cylinder liners.
6. Remove cylinder head and gasket and cylinder head guide. Lock liners with two retaining screws.

Installation

1. Clean face of block including threaded holes in block. Do not scrape carbon off pistons as damage to liners may result.
2. Clean face of cylinder head, head bolts and pushrods.
3. Check surface of cylinder head. Distortion must not exceed 0.002 inch (0.05 mm). Cylinder head may be milled 0.020 (0.5 mm).
4. Install gasket with word "DESSUS" facing up.
5. Install pushrods and rocker shaft assembly. Smear bolt threads with tallow, fit flat washers, and screw bolts down lightly. Bolts should turn freely.
6. Pretorque head in sequence shown in **Fig. 1,** to 36 ft. lbs. (5 m-kg).
7. Torque rocker shaft support nuts to 11 ft. lbs. (1.5 m-kg).
8. Loosen No. 1 bolt completely and torque to 14.47 ft. lbs. (2 m-kg). Then tighten additional 1/4 turn. Follow this procedure for remaining head bolts in sequence shown in **Fig. 1.**

VALVES
ADJUST

Adjust valves as shown in **Fig. 2** with engine cold.

TIMING COVER
REPLACE

1. Remove radiator and fan belt.
2. Remove spark plugs.
3. Remove crankshaft pulley nut. With manual transmission, apply handbrake and engage 4th gear. With automatic transmission, remove bellhousing access plates and lock flywheel.
4. Remove timing cover.
5. Reverse procedure to install.

TIMING CHAIN
REPLACE

1. Refer to "Timing Cover, Replace" procedure to remove timing cover.
2. Release chain tensioner. Two types are used, Renold and Sedis. On XM, XM7 and XN1 engines with Renold tensioner (1), **Fig. 3** top left view, remove plug (2), insert a 3 mm Allen wrench and turn clockwise to release. On KF6, KF5 and XN2 engines use pad retaining tool 0.0137, **Fig. 3** lower left view. On engines with Sedis tensioner (3), **Fig. 3** top right view, place ratchet (a) in position shown.
3. Remove tensioner, plate, and filter, **Fig. 3,** lower right view.
4. Remove in following order: camshaft sprocket, timing chain, crankshaft sprocket, Woodruff key.
5. Without altering position of crankshaft, install Woodruff key and crank-

Fig. 4 Positioning camshaft

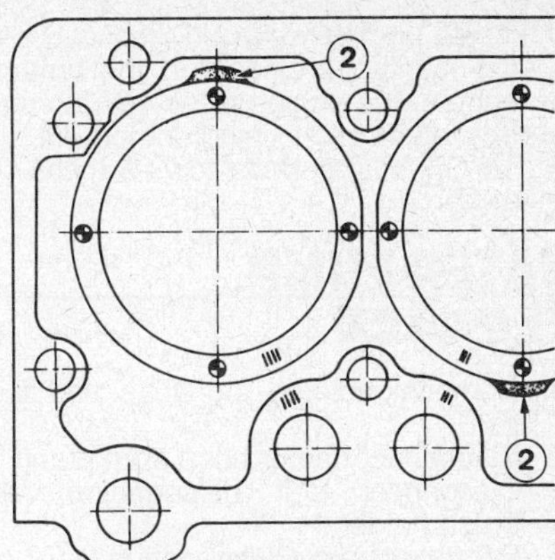

Fig. 5 Liner tab positioning

shaft sprocket.

6. Position camshaft, then crankshaft as shown in **Fig. 4.**
7. Install chain on camshaft sprocket, then assembly on crankshaft sprocket as shown in **Fig. 4. Reference marks on sprockets must be in line with axes of crankshaft and camshaft. Camshaft sprocket mark up and crankshaft sprocket mark down.**
8. Place new tab washer on camshaft sprocket and torque bolts to 16.3 ft. lbs. (2.25 m-kg). Bend tab washer up around bolt heads.
9. Insert filter and install tensioner. On Renold tensioners, load tensioner by turning Allen key clockwise. Fit new tab washer on plug and install plug. Bend tab up around plug head. On KF6, KF5 and XN2 engines with Renold tensioner, install retaining tool, load tensioner and fit plug and tab washer before installing tensioner on block. Remove tool when tensioner is installed. On Sedis tensioner, load tensioner by turning screw clockwise. **Do not assist tensioner action.**

CAMSHAFT
REPLACE

1. Refer to "Cylinder Head, Replace" procedure to remove cylinder head.
2. Remove cam followers noting their locations.
3. Remove distributor, support and driveshaft.
4. Refer to "Timing Cover, Replace" procedure to remove timing cover.
5. Refer to "Timing Chains, Replace" procedure to remove timing chain.
6. Remove camshaft thrust plate and remove camshaft.
7. Reverse procedure to install.

PISTON, ROD & LINER ASSEMBLY

Pistons and liners are available only as matched sets. Pistons may be removed from connecting rods by removing piston pin circlips and piston pins. Assemble piston and connecting rod so arrow and AV mark point forward and oil thrower hole on connecting rod is facing away from camshaft. If necessary, heat pistons in boiling water to ease piston pin installation. Install oil scraper with gaps .79-1.97 inch (20-50 mm) from center of piston pin hole. Install remaining rings with gaps about 120° from pin centerline. Marks on piston ring must face top of piston.

When installing piston and liner assemblies, do not mix assemblies and make sure there are no burr marks on face of engine block. Insert liners without pistons and base gaskets into block with flats on liners 1-2 and 3-4 facing. Using dial indicator, measure protrusion above block face at four points on each liner. Maximum difference between two diametrically opposed points cannot exceed 0.003 inch (0.07 mm). A base gasket must be selected for each liner which will give a protrusion (including gasket) of 0.003-0.006 inch (0.07-0.14 mm) at the highest point, with the preferred setting as close as possible to 0.006 inch. Gaskets are available in four thicknesses as indicated by notches in reference tab: no notch, 0.0028-0.0041 inch (0.070-0.105 mm); one notch, 0.0033-0.0047 inch (0.085-0.120 mm); two notches, 0.0041-0.0055 inch (0.105-0.140 mm); three notches, 0.0051-0.0065 inch (0.130-0.165 mm). Place selected gasket on liner and engage the inner tabs in the grooves. Install liners in engine block with tabs positioned as shown in **Fig. 5.** Using tool 8.0128, **Fig. 6,** press liners down. Check protrusion at (A), (B), (C) and (D), **Fig. 6.** Protrusion should not exceed 0.006 inch (0.14 mm) and the difference between the four checking points must not exceed 0.003 inch (0.07 mm). The difference in protrusion height of the liner must not exceed 0.0016 inch (0.04 mm).

ROD BEARING SIZING

To ensure proper bearing clearance, bearing shell thickness must be 0.0713-0.0716 inch (1.812-1.818 mm). Oversize shells for reground crankshafts are 0.0772-0.0775 inch (1.962-1.968 mm) thick.

MAIN BEARING SIZING

To ensure proper bearing clearance, main bearing shells must be 0.0426-0.0743 inch (1.082-1.888 mm) thick. Oversize shells for reground crankshafts are 0.0800-0.0802 inch (2.032-2.038 mm) thick.

CRANKSHAFT REAR OIL SEAL
REPLACE

1. Remove transmission, clutch, flywheel and oil pan.
2. Remove rear bearing cap and carefully remove packing from groove.
3. Work new packing into cylinder block and bearing cap.
4. Make sure packing is correctly located in groove without being crushed.
5. Cut packing off perfectly flush with mating surface, no frayed material should project.
6. Place new lateral seals (3) on bearing cap and hold in place with tool 8.0110 W.
7. Lubricated shim plates and tighten by hand. Engage assembly into block at angle.
8. Position cap correctly and install bolts. Remove tool. Torque bolts to 55 ft.lbs., (7.5m-kg). Make sure that cap is bearing on block.
9. Cut off lateral seals at 0.020 inch (0.5 mm) from block.
10. Install flywheel and torque bolts to 49 ft. lbs. (6.75 m-kg). Torque clutch bolt to 11 ft. lbs. (1.5 m-kg).

OIL PUMP
REPLACE

1. Remove oil pan.
2. Remove oil pump.
3. Install centering pins on block and new O-ring on pump.
4. Install pump and torque bolts to 7.25 ft. lbs. (1 m-kg).

5. Install oil pan with new gasket. Coat the four bolts closest to the bottom edge of the engine block with normal holding thread-locking compound.
6. Torque oil pan bolts. to 7.25 ft. lbs. (1 m-kg).

WATER PUMP
REPLACE

1. Remove radiator, top hose and fan belt.
2. Disconnect heater hose from pump.
3. Disconnect self disengaging fan brush holder.
4. Remove pump. Clean mating faces of pump and head.
5. Reverse procedure to install.

FUEL PUMP
REPLACE
504

1. Disconnect inlet and outlet lines at fuel pump.
2. Unfasten and remove fuel pump.
3. Reverse procedure to install.

505

The electric fuel pump is located under the car behind the left rear footwell, ahead of the rear suspension crossmember.

1. Clamp and disconnect fuel lines.
2. Remove nuts holding pump/ accumulator assembly in position.
3. Remove fuel pump and fuel accumulator as an assembly.
4. Reverse procedure to install.

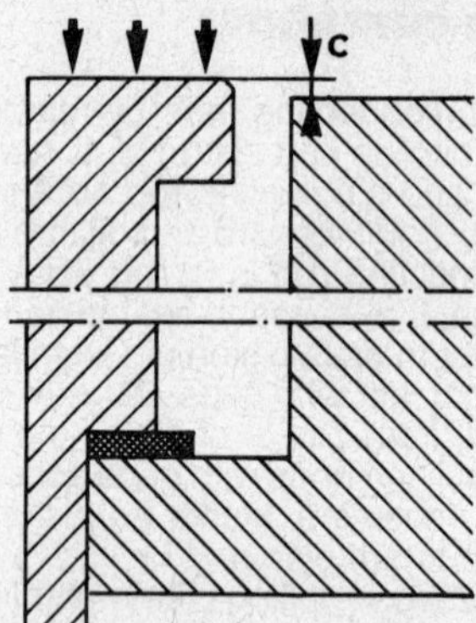

Fig. 6 Depressing cylinder liners

4-134 GASOLINE ENGINE SECTION

INDEX

ENGINE DISASSEMBLY

1. On models equipped with A/C, remove compressor mount.
2. On all models, remove turbocharger and turbocharger ducting pipes.
3. Mount engine onto suitable engine stand. **Do not rest engine on oil pan because of possible damage to oil pump.**
4. Remove starter, distributor, spark plug wiring harness and alternator.
5. Remove intake manifold, power steering pump, motor mounts, coolant inlet housing, oil filter, dipstick and accessory drive belts.
6. Remove clutch and pressure plate. Use tool No. 35327 or equivalent to hold flywheel.
7. Remove water pump, then the crankshaft pulley.
8. Remove valve cover, then the upper part of timing chain cover.
9. Remove oil level sending unit, oil pan, flywheel plate, and flywheel.
10. Remove power steering pump bracket, then the lower part of timing chain cover.
11. Remove oil pump and oil pump drive chain.
12. Unload timing chain tensioner, as follows:
    a. On Brampton tensioner (a) **Fig. 1** remove bolt (10), then release tension using a suitable Allen wrench (11).
    b. On Winklofer tensioner (A), **Fig. 1,** push in shaft (12) using suitable tool, then rotate tool to the right.
13. Remove chain tensioner, both fixed pads, camshaft pinion, and timing chain.
14. Remove crankshaft pinion, using a suitable puller.
15. Remove cylinder head bolts, then the head, using "L" handles, tool No. J35339 or equivalent.
16. Remove connecting rod bearing caps. **Mark position of bearing caps and connecting rods to facilitate installation. Place mark on side closest to oil filter.**
17. Remove piston and rod assemblies, then the main bearing caps and crankshaft.
18. Remove cylinder head rear inspection plate (1), **Fig. 2,** then camshaft retaining clamp (2).

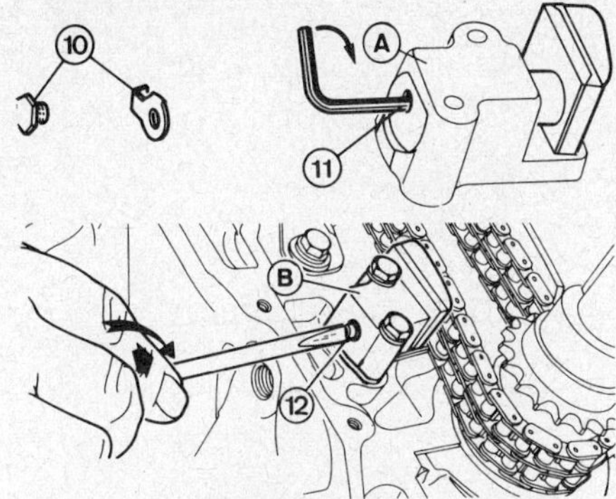

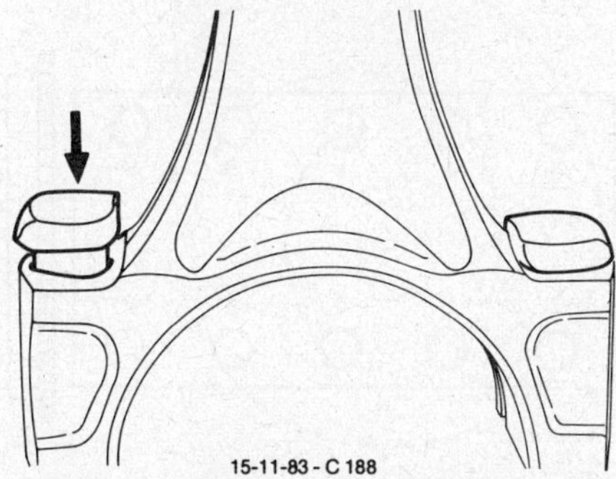

Fig. 1 Unloading timing chain tensioner

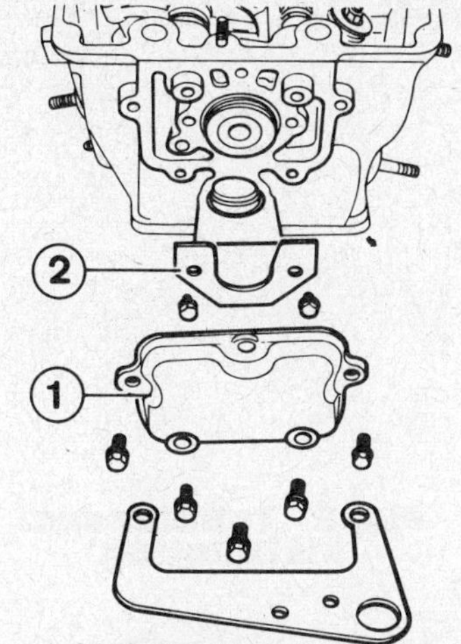

Fig. 2 Camshaft retaining clamp

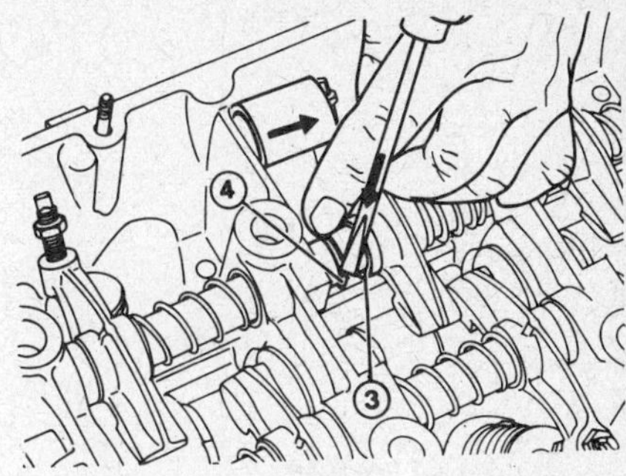

Fig. 3 Removing circlips

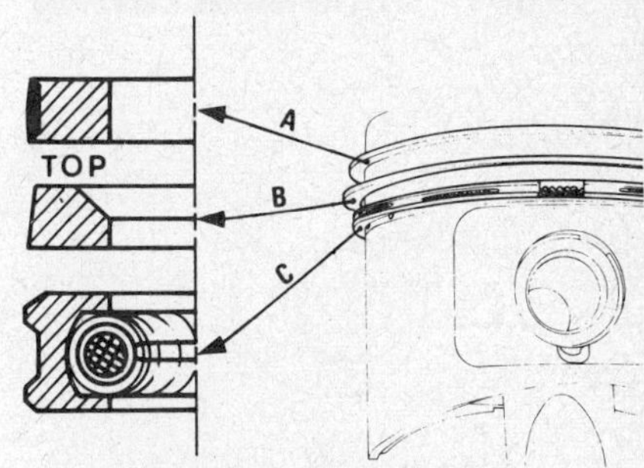

Fig. 6 Piston ring positioning

15-11-83 - C 188

Fig. 4 Rod bolt positioning

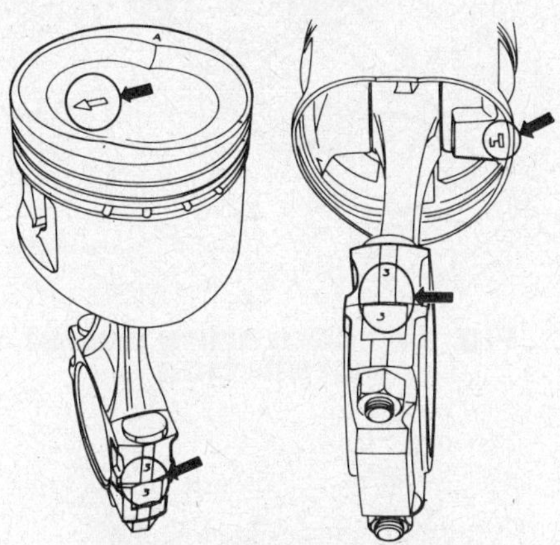

Fig. 5 Piston & rod identification marks

19. Loosen rocker arm adjusting screws, then push spacer (3), **Fig. 3**, to one side and remove circlips (4) for each rocker arm.
20. Remove rocker arm shafts from cylinder head, then the rocker arms, springs and spacers from cylinder head.
21. Pull camshaft from cylinder head.
22. Remove valve springs and valves, then the valve stem seals, using tool No. J28612 or equivalent.

PISTON & ROD ASSEMBLY OVERHAUL

1. Remove circlips and drive out piston pins, using drift tool No. J35336 or equivalent.
2. Replace rod bolts if necessary. Ensure bolt heads are properly positioned, **Fig. 4.**
3. Assemble piston and rod maintaining relationship shown, **Fig. 5. When properly assembled, numbered surface of rod will be on oil filter side of engine. The arrow located on top of piston will point toward timing chain and/or casting graph, located on piston pin boss, will be on flywheel side.**
4. Heat pistons in boiling water. Insert lubricated piston pin into hot piston, then install two new circlips.
5. Install piston rings and stagger gaps 120 degrees apart. On ring B, **Fig. 6,** reference top should face up.

ENGINE ASSEMBLY

During assembly procedures, apply a suitable lubricant to mating surfaces of components.

1. Install lower spring cups, then valve stem seals. Assemble springs, washers, keepers and valves in reverse order of removal.
2. Insert camshaft into cylinder head. **Ensure lubricating holes on rockers and rocker arm shafts align.**
3. Install rocker shafts, rocker arms, springs and spacers in cylinder head.
4. Install rocker arm shaft and camshaft retaining plate.
5. Install cylinder head rear inspection plate and gasket.
6. Install circlips on rocker arm shafts.
7. Place a drop of non-hardening cement into grooves of rear main seal carrier and cylinder block.
8. Insert rope seals into their grooves, using tool No. J35222 or equivalent. **Do not alter or modify length or shape of rope seal.**
9. Select main bearing inserts from three types available as follows:
   a. Type A, used on block side of Nos. 1, 3 and 5 main bearings is smooth and incorporates an oil hole.
   b. Type B, used on the cap side of main bearings 1, 3 and 5, is smooth but does not incorporate an oil hole.
   c. Type C, is used on main bearings 2 and 4 on cap and block side and incorporates a groove an oil hole.
10. Install half thrust washers on either side of center main, with grooves facing crankshaft.
11. Install crankshaft.
12. Install main bearing caps, then torque to specifications.
13. Check endplay with tool No. J35331 or equivalent. Endplay should measure .004-.011 inch (.090-.270 mm). Adjust endplay to specifications by inserting thrust washers of different thicknesses.
14. Apply a suitable silicone compound to lateral grooves (1) and contact faces of rope seal carrier (2), **Fig. 7.**
15. Install rope seal carrier.
16. Insert a tubular seal into each groove (1), **Fig. 8,** using tool No. J35326 or equivalent.
17. Install flywheel and flywheel plate. Apply a suitable locking compound to threads of bolts, then torque to specifications. Retain flywheel, using tool No. J35317 or equivalent, then ensure crankshaft rotates freely when tool is removed.
18. Install piston and rod assemblies using suitable compressor. **Reference on rod (a) must point toward oil filter side of engine, Fig. 9. Machined face of nuts (A) must ride against rod caps. Torque nuts to specifications.**
19. Position crankshaft with pistons 1 and 4 at TDC and lock in this position using flywheel locking pawl.
20. Position camshaft over valves of No. 1 cylinder in such a way that both

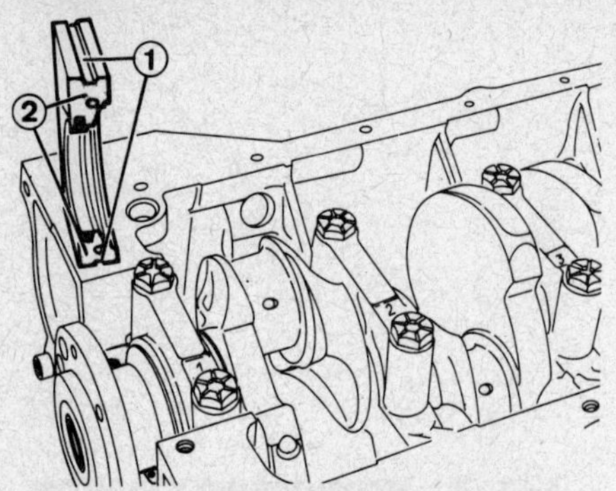

Fig. 7 Rope seal carrier

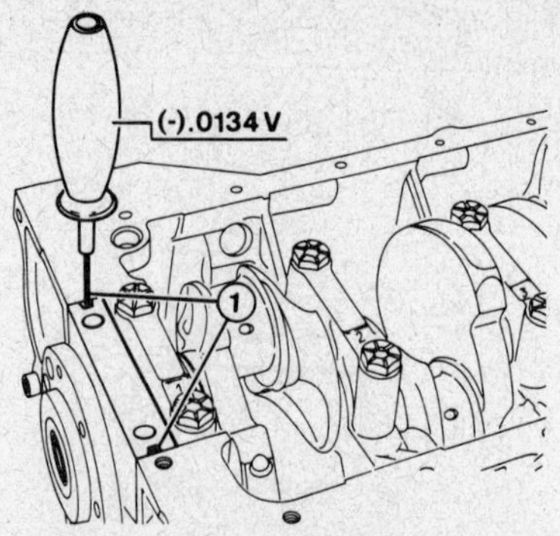

Fig. 8 Tubular seal installation

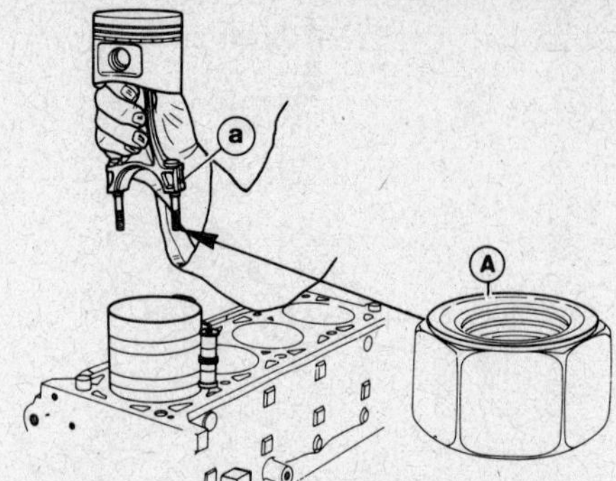

Fig. 9 Piston installation

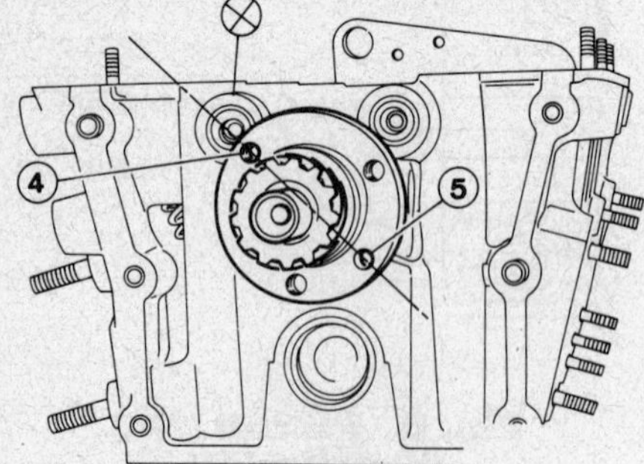

Fig. 10 Positioning camshaft

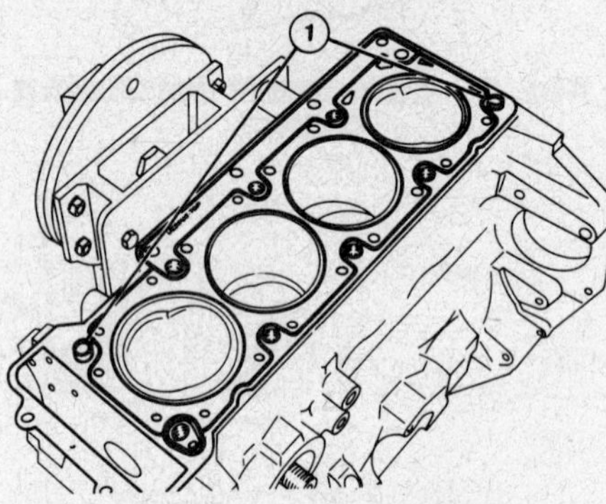

Fig. 11 Centering dowel installation

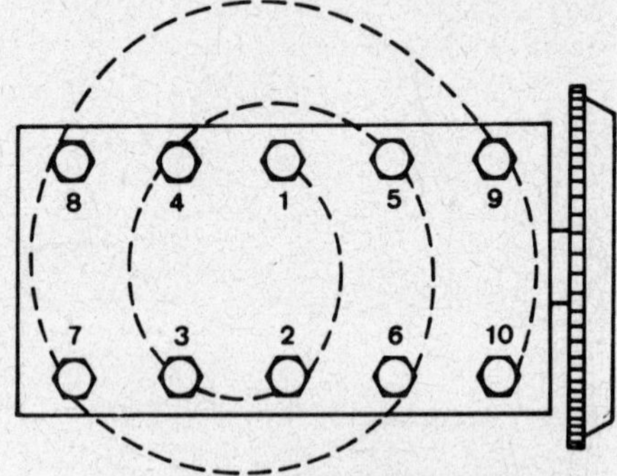

Fig. 12 Cylinder head torquing sequence

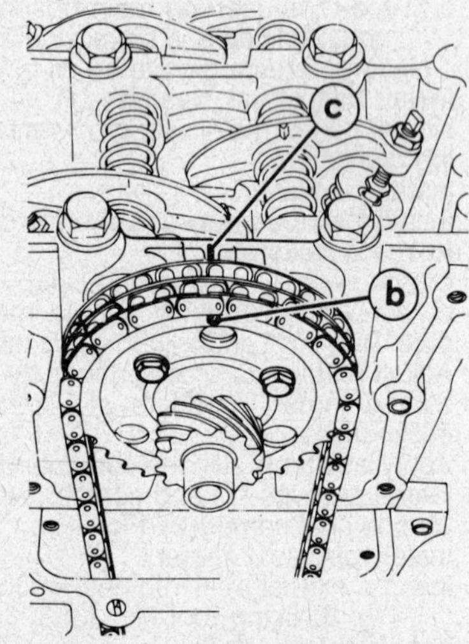

Fig. 13 Timing chain installation

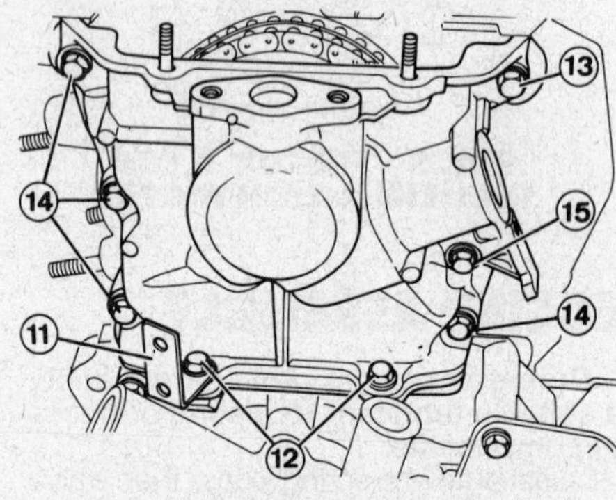

Fig. 14 Upper timing chain cover installation

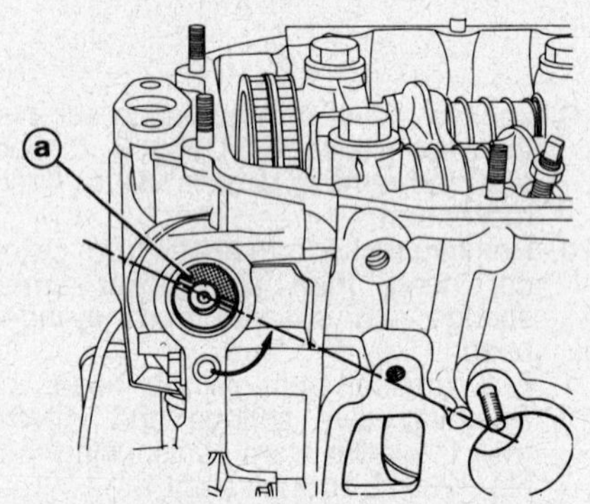

Fig. 15 Distributor drive shaft installation

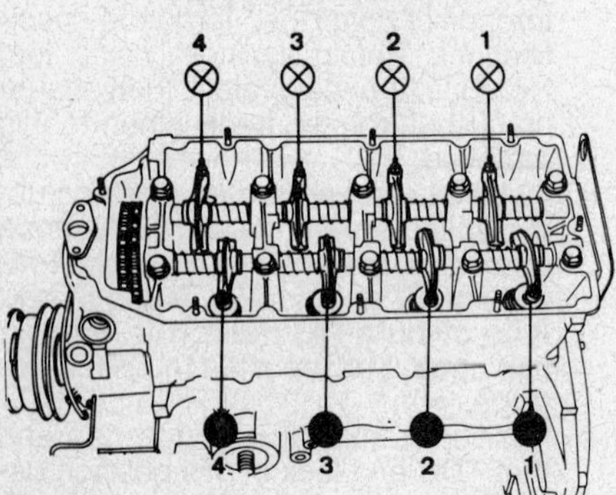

Fig. 16 Valve positions

Adjust the Valves:

● Intake : 0.20mm (0.008")

⊗ Exhaust: 0.30mm (0.012")

Two methods may be used

Valve Fully Open	Adjust	Valves Rocking	Adjust
⊗ 1	3 ● ⊗ 4	1 ● ⊗ 1	4 ● ⊗ 4
⊗ 3	4 ● ⊗ 2	3 ● ⊗ 3	2 ● ⊗ 2
⊗ 4	2 ● ⊗ 1	4 ● ⊗ 4	1 ● ⊗ 1
⊗ 2	1 ● ⊗ 3	2 ● ⊗ 2	3 ● ⊗ 3

Fig. 17 Valve adjusting sequence

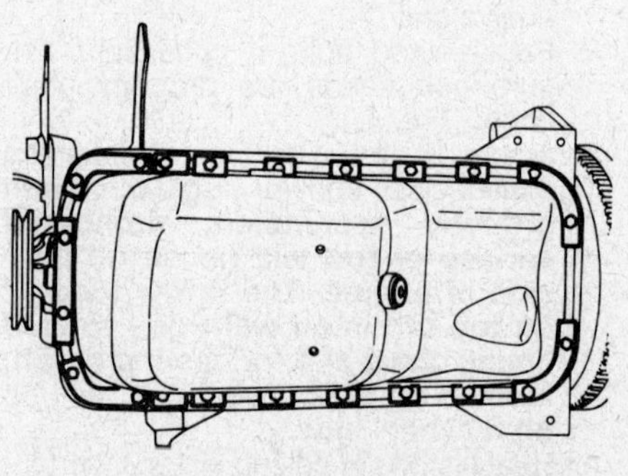

Fig. 18 Oil pan reinforcing plates

valves are closed. Align threaded hole (4) of camshaft sprocket, **Fig. 10** and smooth hole (5) with exhaust rocker shaft center line.

21. Install two centering dowels (1), **Fig. 11.** Place dry head gasket on engine block with marking DESSUS-TOP facing up.
22. Install cylinder head, then apply a suitable lubricant to head bolts. insert attaching bolts and washers, then torque to specifications in sequence shown in **Fig. 12,** first torque to 37 ft. lbs. (84 Nm), then to 61 ft. lbs. (84 Nm).
23. Position Woodruff key in crankshaft, then install pinion with double row of teeth toward block.
24. Place camshaft pinion, with insert facing camshaft flange, on camshaft. Position punch mark "b" on pinion, **Fig. 13,** in line with reference on cylinder head. Remove pinion and reinstall with timing chain in place.
25. Install chain guide pads. Use adjustable pad to remove slack in timing chain.
26. Recheck alignment of references "b" and "c", **Fig. 13.**
27. Install timing chain tensioner as follows:
    a. On Brampton tensioner release pad by turning a 3 mm Allen wrench counterclockwise. Install lock plate and bolt, then bend lock plate.
    b. On Winklofer tensioner, insert support plate under tensioner, then insert and tighten attaching bolt. Unload tensioner, using a suitable screwdriver, by turning it counterclockwise.
28. Install oil pump centering dowels. Position oil pump with chain installed, then torque bolts to 14 ft. lbs. (20 Nm).
29. Apply a suitable lubricant to new seal, then install in timing chain housing cover.
30. Place spacer and key on end of crankshaft, then place timing chain centering dowels into block.
31. Apply a suitable grease to gaskets, then a thin coat of silicone sealant to top face of timing chain cover. Install timing chain cover.
32. Install water pump, power steering pump and alternator bracket.
33. Apply a suitable silicone sealing compound to top surface of protruding head gasket.
34. Apply a suitable grease to timing chain cover upper half gasket, then ensure timing chain cover upper half centering dowels are in place. Install timing chain upper half and new gasket. Tighten bolts in numerical order, **Fig. 14,** beginning with No. 12. Remember to install fan brush wire support (11).
35. Install distributor driveshaft with No. 4 cylinder in TDC position of compression stroke. Insert shaft with thin side "a," **Fig. 15,** of drive gear toward cylinder head. When seated, slot should be positioned as shown. Remove flywheel locking pawl.
36. Adjust valves, **Fig. 16,** as shown in **Fig. 17.**
37. Install valve cover, then the ignition wire supports.
38. Install oil pan, positioning reinforcing plates as shown, **Fig. 18.**
39. Lock flywheel, then install clutch plate and pressure plate, using suitable centering tool. Torque bolts to 18 ft. lbs. (24 Nm).
40. Install oil level sender, then torque to 14 ft. lbs. (20 Nm).
41. Install crankshaft pulley, then torque to 97 ft. lbs. (132 Nm).
42. Remove flywheel locking pawl.
43. Install front lifting bracket.
44. Install intake manifold, power steering pump, motor mounts, coolant inlet housing, oil filter and dipstick.
45. Install starter, distributor, spark plug wiring harness, alternator and accessory drive belts.
46. Install turbocharger, then the turbocharger ducting pipes.
47. Install A/C compressor mount.

DIESEL ENGINE SECTION

INDEX

ENGINE
REPLACE

504

1. Remove hood, battery and tray, expansion tank and air cleaner.
2. Disconnect intake pipe on vacuum pump.
3. Remove upper and lower radiator mounts.
4. Disconnect fan cut-out switch. Remove fan and radiator.
5. Disconnect injection pump controls and fuel inlet and return lines.
6. Remove heater return hose.
7. Disconnect starter, oil pressure switch, preheating circuit and thermistor.
8. Remove starter.
9. Disconnect alternator and exhaust pipe.
10. Remove nut from RH engine support block.
11. Remove clutch housing access plates.
12. Remove upper clutch housing bolt and remove nut from LH engine support block.
13. Remove bolt holding exhaust pipe bracket to transmission. Remove RH clutch housing cover plate.
14. Using engine hoist fixture 8.0102 X or equivalent, raise engine until transmission contacts top of tunnel.
15. Using support 8.0125 or equivalent, support transmission.
16. Remove the two lower clutch housing bolts and remove engine.
17. Reverse procedure to install. Torque the three clutch housing bolts to 43.5 ft. lbs. (6 m-kg).

505

1. Drain cooling system and disconnect battery.
2. Remove battery and tray.
3. On models with automatic transmission, remove grille. On all models, remove air filter, coolant overflow bottle and radiator expansion tank.
4. Disconnect hoses, control cables and wire harnesses.
5. Disconnect power steering hoses from pump and secure to prevent drainage of fluid.
6. On models with automatic transmission, disconnect transmission oil cooler lines.
7. On all models, remove radiator.
8. Remove fan and fan belt, starter and bellhousing access plates.
9. On air conditioned models, protect condenser with a piece of sheet metal or plywood. Unbolt AC compressor from engine leaving freon lines connected and hang it from inner fender. Route freon hoses to back of engine.
10. On all models, remove sound proofing

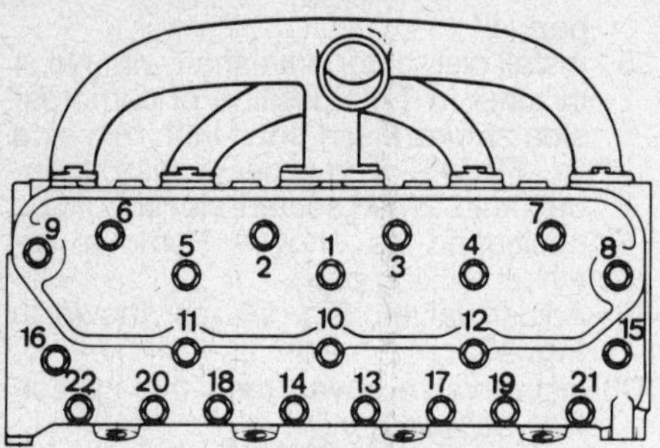

Fig. 1 Cylinder head torque sequence. XD2 engines

panel clips on cowl and remove degassing tank bracket.

11. Disconnect exhaust pipe from exhaust manifold and disconnect intermediate exhaust muffler bracket.
12. On air conditioned models, lower the compressor cut-out switch from crossmember.
13. On all models, remove bolts and lower front crossmember. Retain crossmember with two M12 150 bolts about 70 to 100 mm long.
14. On models with automatic transmission, remove the 4 torque converter bolts. Move torque converter back from flywheel.
15. On all models, loosen the 3 engine/bellhousing bolts slightly. Remove top bolt.
16. Remove the 4 engine mount bolts on crossmember.
17. Using tool 8.0102 X or equivalent, lift engine until transmission contacts tunnel.
18. Using tool 8.0125 or equivalent, support transmission.
19. If necessary, disconnect power steering return hose going to distribution valve.
20. Remove the 2 lower bellhousing bolts and remove engine.
21. Reverse procedure to install. Torque bell housing bolts to 43 ft. lbs. (6 m-kg) and torque converter bolts to 16.31 ft. lbs. (2.25 m-kg).

CYLINDER HEAD
REPLACE
504

Engine must be cold before cylinder head is removed.

1. Drain cooling system.
2. Remove air filter, expansion hoses, water hoses and vacuum pump inlet pipe.
3. Remove vacuum pump and belt.
4. Remove water pump belt and idler pulley.
5. Disconnect air conditioner pipe, rocker shaft lubricating union and exhaust pipe flange.
6. Disconnect injection pipes, remove return piping and disconnect wiring.
7. Remove rocker cover, rocker shaft assembly and pushrods.
8. Remove injector holders, cylinder head bolts, noting length and location, and cylinder head.
9. Remove head gasket and hold liners in place with bolts 8.0110 F.
10. On XD2/XD2 engines, select a head gasket according to amount of piston protrusion. If protrusion is no greater than .033 inch (.84 mm), use a gasket .062 inch (1.58 mm) thick (compressed thickness .058 inch, 1.48 mm). If protrusion is greater than .033 inch (.84 mm), use a gasket that is .067 inch (1.70 mm) thick (compressed thickness .063 inch, 1.60 mm).
11. Position cylinder head gasket. On XD2, XD2P engines, torque cylinder head in sequence, **Fig. 1.** Pretorque to 33 ft. lbs. (4.5 m-kg), then torque to 47 ft. lbs. (6.5 m-kg). Loosen each bolt 1/4 turn and retorque to 47 ft. lbs.
12. Install injector holders, using new seals, with injector shield and wave washers, as necessary.
13. Install pushrods and rocker shaft assembly.
14. Insert a .0039 inch (.10 mm) thick shim between the sides of the two end bearings and inlet rockers 1 and 4. Torque intermediate blocks to 36 ft. lbs. (5 m-kg), end blocks to 14 ft. lbs. (2 m-kg). Remove shims and check rockers for free movement.
15. Adjust valve clearance .004 inch (.10 mm) greater than specification.
16. Reinstall ancillary equipment and connect hoses.
17. Retorque cylinder head at 30 and 600 miles.

505 & 604

1. Drain cooling system, disconnect battery, and disconnect exhaust pipe from manifold.
2. Remove battery, air filter, radiator overflow bottle, vacuum pump, and fuel injection pipes.
3. Disconnect water hoses at water pump.
4. Disconnect electrical connections.
5. Disconnect heater hose and rocker shaft oil feed line at cylinder head.
6. Remove valve cover, rocker shaft assembly and pushrods.
7. Loosen cylinder head bolts according to sequence in **Fig. 1.**
8. Remove cylinder head.
9. Select head gasket according to piston projection above deck. If projection is no greater than .033 inch (.84 mm) on XD2 and XD2C engines, or .031 inch (.079 mm) on XD2S engines use a gasket with a thickness of .062 inch (1.58 mm). If projection is greater than .033 inch (.84 mm), on XD2 and XD2C engines or .031 inch (.079 mm) on XD2S engines use a gasket with thickness of .067 inch (1.70 mm).
10. Install gasket dry with oblong flame ring side facing cylinder head plane.
11. Install cylinder head. Torque in sequence, **Fig. 1.** On XD2 and XD2C engines, pretorque to 21.75 ft. lbs. (3 m-kg), then torque to 47.13 ft. lbs. (6.5 m-kg). Then loosen each bolt 1/4 turn and retorque to 47.13 ft. lbs. On XD2S engines, pretorque to 21.75 ft. lbs., then to 50.75 ft. lbs. (7 m-kg). Loosen each

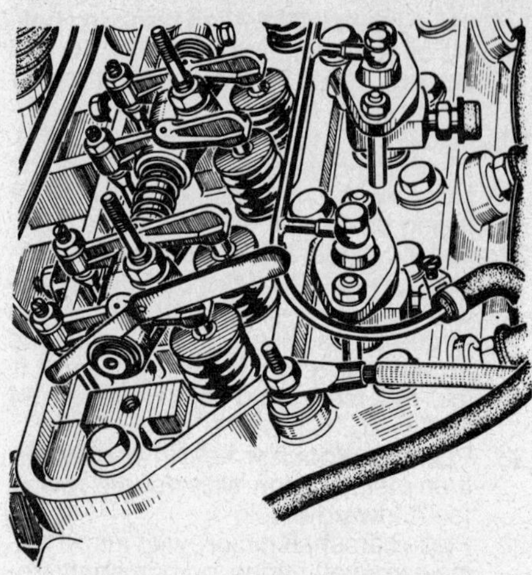

Fig. 2 Rocker arm play

bolt 1/4 turn and retorque to 50.75 ft. lbs.

12. Install pushrods, rocker shaft assembly and oil feed union with its seal.
13. Tighten rocker shaft bearing blocks progressively, allowing .004 inch (.10 mm) play at the two end rocker arms, **Fig. 2.** Torque intermediate support nuts to 34 ft. lbs. (4.7 m-kg). Torque end support bolts to 14.5 ft. lbs. (2 m-kg).
14. Adjust valves and install valve cover.
15. Reinstall heater hose and rocker shaft oil feed pipe.
16. Reinstall hoses, pipes and manifolds.
17. Reinstall water pump belt, vacuum pump, fuel injection pipes, air filter, radiator overflow bottle and battery.

VALVES
ADJUST

Adjust valves as shown in **Fig. 3.**

TIMING COVER
REPLACE

1. Remove radiator.
2. Remove belt-driven accessories as necessary.
3. Remove crankshaft pulley.
4. Remove timing cover.
5. Reverse procedure to install.

TIMING CHAINS
REPLACE

1. Refer to "Timing Cover, Replace" to remove timing cover.
2. Release chain tensioner, **Fig. 4.**
3. Loosen eccentric rod gear fastening nut (3), **Fig. 4,** and move pinion to position where chain has the most slack.
4. As shown in **Fig. 4,** remove injection pump sprocket (1) and chain. Remove pump pinion hub and bearing.
5. Remove rod gear (2) with its eccentric.
6. Remove guide shoe and chain (4), if necessary.
7. Remove chain tensioner (6).
8. Reverse procedure to install. Position chain and sprockets as shown in **Fig.**

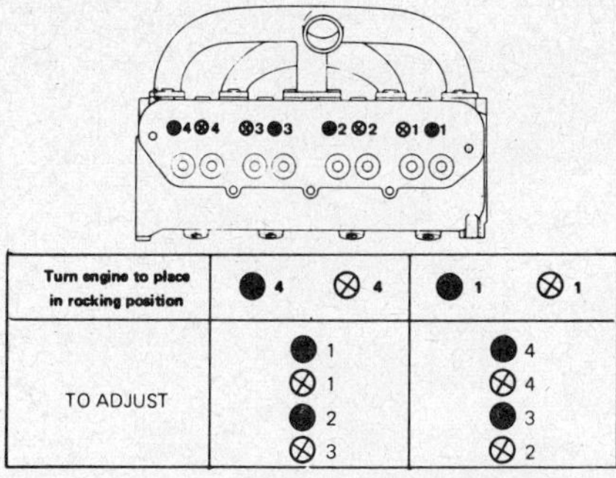

Turn engine to place in rocking position	● 4	⊗ 4	● 1	⊗ 1
TO ADJUST	● 1 ⊗ 1 ● 2 ⊗ 3		● 4 ⊗ 4 ● 3 ⊗ 2	

Fig. 3 Valve adjusting sequence. Diesel engines

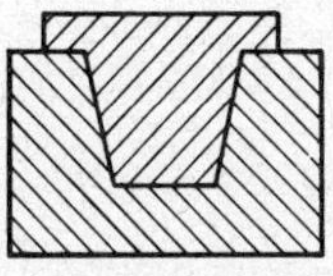
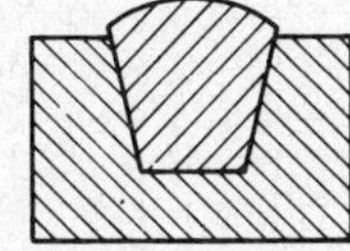

Wrong fitting Correct fitting

Fig. 6 Fitting rope seal

5. Adjust chain tension by turning idler sprocket eccentric so that play between tensioner pad and its support is from .020-.039 inch (.5-1.0 mm). Torque eccentric nut to 36 ft. lbs. (5 m-kg) and load tensioner by turning Allen key to the right.

CAMSHAFT

REPLACE

1. Refer to "Timing Chain, Replace" procedure to remove timing chain.
2. Remove rocker shaft assembly, tappet inspection cover, pushrods and tappets.
3. Remove camshaft (8), **Fig. 4.**
4. Camshaft sprocket or gear is pressed on. Install sprocket or gear by heating in oil. Install front thrust plate, then shaft key, and finally sprocket or gear. Make sure there is .002-.006 inch (.05-.15 mm) clearance between sprocket or gear hub and shaft flange.
5. Install camshaft, valve train components, timing chain and cover.

PISTON & ROD ASSEMBLY

Install pistons in block so swirl chamber is towards injector side of engine, away

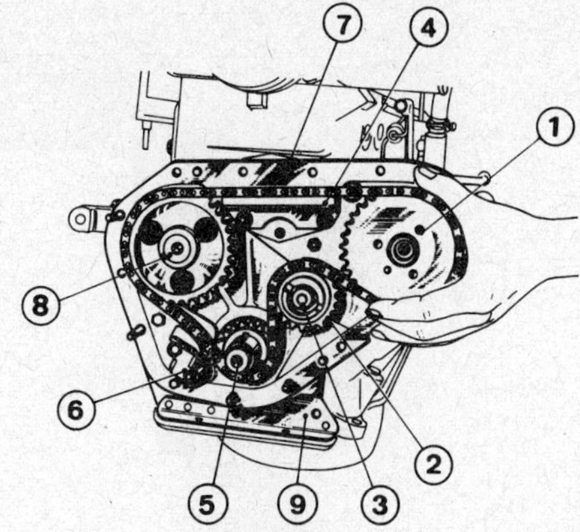

Fig. 4 Timing chain and sprockets

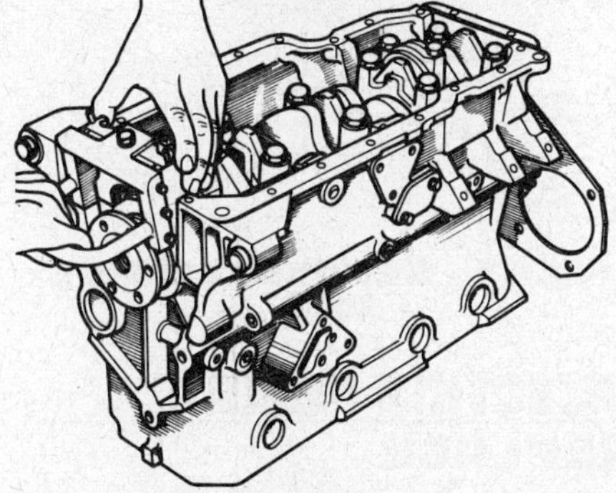

Fig. 7 Installing rear main cap

from oil pump side. Swirl chamber and reference mark on connecting rod must be on same side.

PISTON PINS

Piston pins are retained by circlips. Oil pins before installing.

PISTONS & RINGS

On engines with removable liners, pistons, rings and liners come as a matched set. Remove pistons from liners and clean thoroughly. Check that piston rings move freely in their grooves. Position gaps 120° from each other and install pistons using suitable compressor. Liner projection above cylinder block deck should be .0012-.0028 inch (.03-.07 mm).

ROD BEARING SIZING

XD2 & XD2C ENGINES

To ensure proper bearing clearance, bearing shell thickness must be 0.0715-0.0717 inch (1.816-1.822 mm). Big end bearings are available in three thicknesses for regrinding crankshaft up to three times: 1) 0.0774-0.0776 inch (1.966-1.972 mm), 2) 0.0813-0.0816 inch (2.066-2.072 mm), 3) 0.0872-0.0875 inch (2.216-2.222 mm).

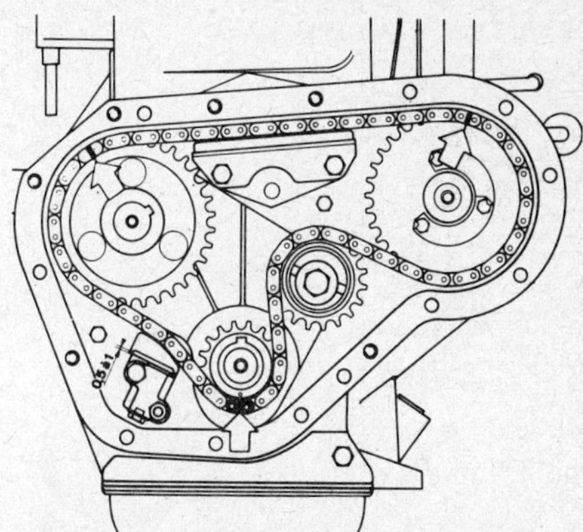

Fig. 5 Positioning timing chain and sprockets for assembly

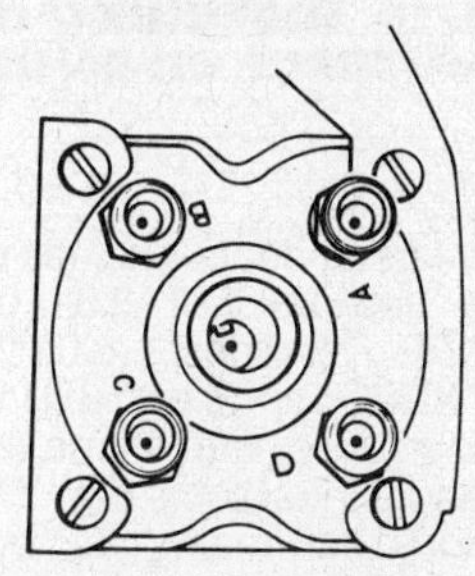

Fig. 8 Aligning pump piston timing groove

XD2S ENGINES

To ensure proper bearing clearance, bearing shell thickness must be 0.0721-0.0724 inch (1.832-1.838 mm). Big end bearings are available in three thicknesses for regrinding crankshaft up to three times: 1) 0.0780-0.0783 inch (1.982-1.988 mm), 2) 0.0820-0.0822 inch (2.082-2.088 mm), 3) 0.0879-0.0881 inch (2.232-2.238 mm).

MAIN BEARING SIZING

XD2, XD2C & XD2S ENGINES

To ensure proper main bearing clearance, the bearing shell must be 0.0720-0.0722 inch (1.829-1.835 mm) thick. Bearing shells are available for regrinding crankshafts up to three times: 1) 0.0779-0.0781 inch (1.979-1.985 mm), 2) 0.0819-0.0821 inch (2.079-2.085 mm), 3) 0.0878-0.0880 inch (2.229-2.235 mm).

CRANKSHAFT REAR OIL SEAL

REPLACE

1. Remove transmission, clutch, flywheel and oil pan.
2. Remove rear main cap and remove rope seal from grooves in block and cap.
3. Install new rope seal in block using tool 8.0110 A, **Fig. 6.** Make sure packing is correctly located in its groove without being crushed. Cut off packing flush with mating surface.

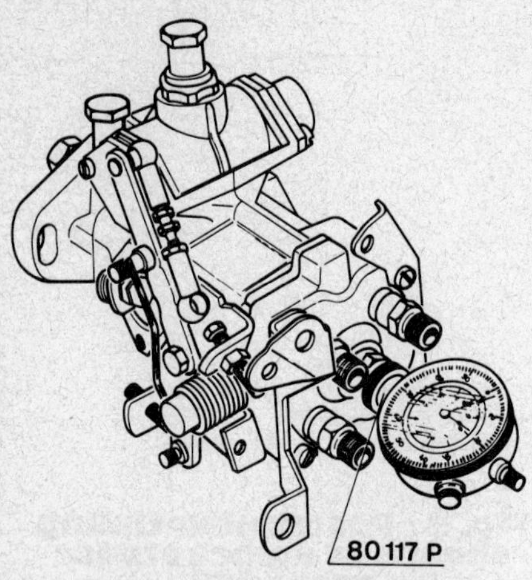

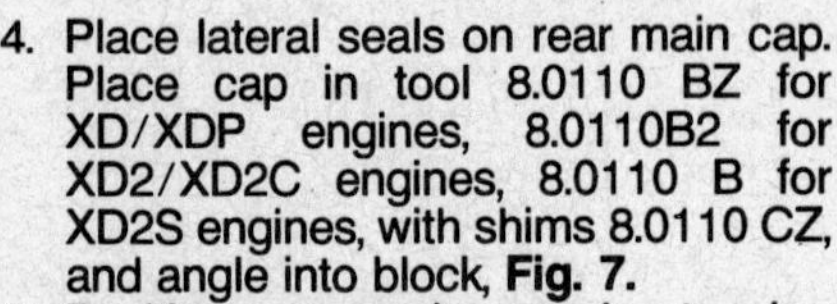

Fig. 9 Installing dial indicator on pump

Fig. 10 Roto-Diesel injection pump

4. Place lateral seals on rear main cap. Place cap in tool 8.0110 BZ for XD/XDP engines, 8.0110B2 for XD2/XD2C engines, 8.0110 B for XD2S engines, with shims 8.0110 CZ, and angle into block, **Fig. 7.**
5. Position rear main cap by tapping lightly with hammer.
6. Torque cap bolts to 72.5 ft. lbs. (10 m-kg).
7. Trim lateral seals so they protrude by .020 inch (.5 mm) from lower crankcase mating surface.
8. Reinstall oil pan, flywheel, clutch and transmission.

OIL PUMP
REPLACE

1. Remove oil pan.
2. Remove the acorn nut and tapered locating screw at the side of block.
3. Remove endplay cap nut and remove oil pump.
4. Install pump into seat and position with tapered hole in body aligned with threaded hole in block.
5. Install tapered screw and torque to 16.31 ft. lbs. (2.25 m-kg).
6. Install acorn nut with new copper gasket and torque to 21.75 ft. lbs. (3 m-kg).
7. Install endplay cap nut without shim and tighten lightly.
8. Using feeler gauge, measure gap between cap nut bearing face and block through slot.
9. Install a shim with a thickness .002-.004 inch (.05-.10 mm) greater than the feeler gauge reading to obtain the correct oil pump shaft endplay. Torque cap nut to 65.25 ft. lbs. (9 m-kg).
10. Install oil pan.

WATER PUMP
REPLACE

Refer to "Water Pump, Replace" procedure in Gasoline Engine Section.

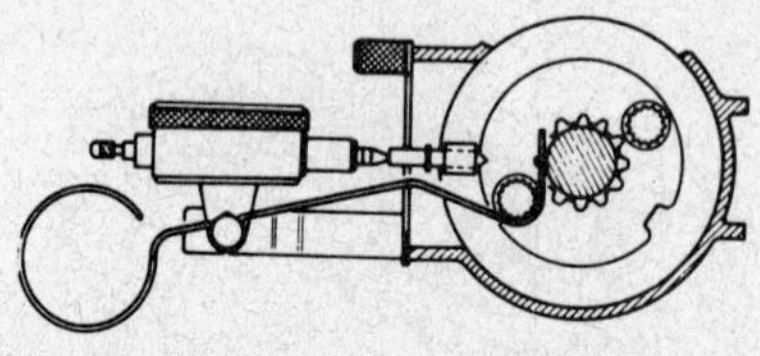

Fig. 11 Backlash take-up tool

INJECTION PUMP
REPLACE

504 WITH BOSCH EP/VAC PUMP

Removal

1. Disconnect battery and turn ignition switch on.
2. Disconnect stop, fast idle and accelerator controls from injection pump.
3. Disconnect the injector return line and fuel inlet and outlet couplings from injection pump.
4. Remove injector pipe assembly and leave couplings on pump and injector holder.
5. Plug or cap all couplings.
6. Remove pump rear support from engine block.
7. On engines with timing chains, remove the two screws holding pump to bearing support (ignition advance adjusting screw) using key 8.0117 D. On engines with timing gears, remove bolt and two screws securing pump intermediate flange to timing gear housing. Remove pump by moving it backwards while turning it towards engine to disengage gear.

Installation & Adjusting

1. Bring No. 1 cylinder to the Exhaust Opening Lead point. Depress No. 4 exhaust valve spring with tool No. 8.0105 Y. Slide No. 4 rocker toward rear. **Do not pull pushrod up.**
2. Bring No. 1 cylinder valves to position where rockers are free to rock.
3. Remove valve keepers and retainers and spring from No. 4 exhaust valve.
4. Make sure valve moves freely and let it rest on piston.
5. Remove plug connector bar and No. 3 and 4 cylinder plugs.
6. Using the front rocker cover mounting stud, mount the G1 support from kit 8.0504 Z. Then mount dial indicator 8.1504 with plunger resting on valve.
7. Calibrate dial indicator at TDC.
8. Rotate crankshaft in opposite direction of normal rotation until dial indicator needle shows piston is .157 inch (4 mm) into bore.
9. Rotate crankshaft in normal direction to obtain a No. 4 piston setting corresponding to value of pump setting: EP/VA CR 173, 0.0201 inch (0.51 mm) before TDC.
10. Remove deferred injection accumulator from injection pump.
11. Rotate drive shaft to bring pump piston timing groove in line with discharge connection B, **Fig. 8.**
12. Install dial indicator support 8.0117 F. Install dial indicator with plunger extension, **Fig. 9.**
13. Place new seal on pump and insert pump, with dial indicator attached, into timing housing.
14. Adjust pump lift with slotted holes. Pump lift should be .026 inch (.65 mm). Tighten flange screws.
15. Check TDC engine setting at dial indicator on No. 4 exhaust valve. Rotate crankshaft backwards until "engine" dial indicator shows piston is .276 inch (7 mm) into bore. During last revolution, "pump" dial indicator should be stabilized in pump BDC range.
16. Rotate crankshaft in normal direction and make sure that position of piston and pump lift correspond. Pump lift should be .026 inch (.65 mm) and piston position before TDC should be .020 inch (.51 mm).
17. Bring piston to TDC position and remove dial indicators.
18. Install delayed injection accumulator. Install new seals and torque to 36 ft. lbs. (5 m-kg).

19. Install valve spring, retainer and valve keeper on No. 4 exhaust valve.
20. Turn crankshaft backwards until piston No. 1 is at Exhaust Opening Lead point.
21. Reposition the rocker on No. 4 exhaust valve.
22. Secure pump rear mounting bracket to engine block.
23. Check valve clearances.
24. Install injector pipe assembly and connect fuel inlet and outlet couplings and injector return line to injector pump.
25. Connect stop cable allowing adequate clearance to lock control in stop position.
26. Connect accelerator cable and fast idle cable.

504 EXC. BOSCH EP/VAC PUMP

To remove pump refer to steps 1-7 of "504 with Bosch EP/VAC pump" removal procedure. For installation and adjusting follow steps 1-7 of "504 with Bosch EP/VAC pump Installation & Adjusting" procedure. Then proceed with the following steps.

1. Turn crankshaft backwards until dial indicator shows piston is .267 inch (7 mm) into bore in order to take up slack.
2. Turn crankshaft in normal direction to obtain piston setting before TDC corresponding to pump setting: XD88, .131 inch (3.34 mm); XD90, .193 inch (4.91 mm); XD2, .179 inch (4.54 mm).
3. Injection pump should be equipped with intermediate flange, Allen head screws should be centered in slotted holes. Drive sprocket or gear should be torqued to 14.5 ft. lbs. (2 m-kg).
4. Remove access plate (1), **Fig. 10,** and bring coupling sleeve grove (2) in alignment with setting finger guide (3).
5. Attach the following adjustment tools: dial indicator 8.0117 F, angle support bracket 8.0117 G, finger extension 8.0117 H, setting hook 8.0117 J or R, knurled head screws (two) 8.0117 K, dial indicator attachment screws 8.0117 L.
6. Turn pump drive in normal direction of rotation until setting grove is aligned with finger extension.
7. Inward travel of finger extension should be maximum as indicated by dial indicator pointer.
8. Position pump with new gasket and adjusting tool, tilted towards engine.
9. Insert pump and tighten intermediate flange-to-timing gear housing attaching screws.
10. Loosen pump from intermediate flange and rotate pump outward. Install backlash take-up hook, **Fig. 11.**
11. Rotate pump until inward travel of plunger is at maximum as indicated by dial indicator.
12. Tighten pump and install rear support.
13. Place No. 4 cylinder at TDC.
14. Turn crankshaft in reverse until dial indicator pointer shows piston is .276 inch, (7 mm) into bore.
15. Turn crankshaft in normal direction of rotation until pump dial indicator indicates maximum entry.
16. In this position engine mounted dial indicator should indicate position of No. 4 as .131 inch (3.34 mm) for XD88; .193 inch (4.91 mm) for XD90; .179 inch (4.54 mm) for XD2. Adjust if necessary.
17. Turn crankshaft so No. 4 piston is at TDC and remove dial indicator, supports and adjusting feeler.
18. Install valve spring, spring retainer and keepers.
19. Rotate crankshaft backwards until cylinder No. 1 reaches No. 1 Exhaust Opening Lead point.
20. Replace rocker and secure injection pump access plate.

505 & 604

Removal

1. Remove battery.
2. On pump, disconnect supply and return lines, control cables, fuel shut-off valve wire, and on XD2C engine, load sensor harness.
3. Remove injector pipes.
4. Remove two front mounting bolts and pump's rear support.
5. Remove pump and cap all openings.

Installation & Adjustment

1. Remove valve cover.
2. Turn crankshaft so rockers of No. 1 cylinder are free to rock, then turn crankshaft back about 90°.
3. Compress No. 4 exhaust valve spring and slide rocker arm over.
4. Turn crankshaft back so that No. 1 rockers are free to rock.
5. Remove valve keepers, retainer and spring from No. 4 exhaust valve. **Valve's stem length will prevent it from dropping into cylinder.**
6. Install dial indicator on No. 4 exhaust valve stem.
7. Bring No. 4 cylinder to TDC and zero dial indicator.
8. Turn crankshaft backwards until piston is .276 inch (7 mm) down into bore.
9. Pump must be completely clean. Clean hydraulic head and remove inspection plug.
10. Turn pump shaft to bring double tooth on pinion in line with double groove in drive sprocket hub.
11. Coat new gasket with grease and position on pump flange.
12. Install pump onto engine and install mounting bolts without tightening them.
13. Rotate pump body away from engine (full retard).
14. Install dial indicator 8.0117 F with extension 8.0117 T, support 8.0117 P and reducer 8.0117 S.
15. Turn engine and locate BDC and TDC points on pump's dial indicator. At BDC, dial indicator should have slight preload.
16. Zero the pump's dial indicator at BDC.
17. Turn engine so piston No. 4 is at TDC on compression stroke. Check zero point of engine dial indicator.
18. Turn engine backwards 90°, then recheck pump dial indicator.
19. Turn engine in normal direction and bring piston No. 4 to .0531 (1.35 mm) below TDC on XD2 engines; .0382 inch (.97 mm) below TDC on XD2C engines; .0157 inch (.40 mm) on Federal XD2S engines; .0201 inch (.51 mm) on XD2S Calif. engines beginning in 1984.
20. Rotate pump towards engine (advance) until dial indicator shows pump lift of .0197 inch (.50 mm).
21. Tighten front and rear pump mounting bolts.
22. Check timing by turning engine 2 turns in normal direction then back 1/4 turn. Slowly turn engine in normal direction until pump dial indicator shows a lift of .0197 inch (.50 mm). No. 4 piston should be at position indicated in step 19.
23. Install inspection plug with new gasket.
24. Install valve spring, valve keepers and retainer of No. 4 exhaust valve.
25. Install valve cover, pipes, hoses and controls.

CLUTCH & MANUAL TRANSMISSION SECTION

INDEX

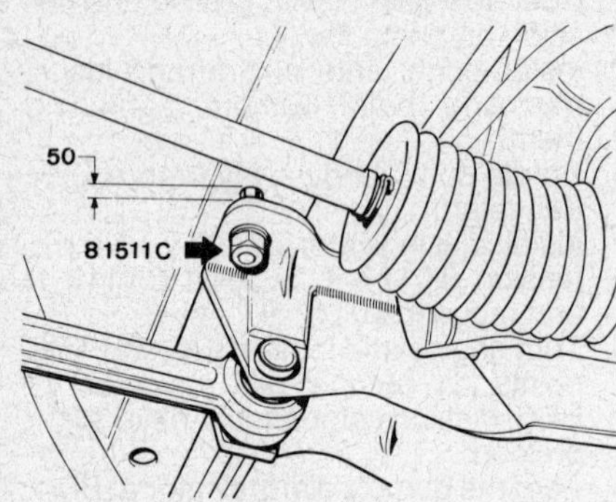

Fig. 1 Lowering front crossmember. 505 models

CLUTCH

REPLACE

504

1. Refer to "Engine, Replace" procedure to remove engine.
2. Mark pressure plate in relation to flywheel.
3. Unscrew six bolts using 6 mm Allen wrench and remove pressure plate and clutch.
4. Position disc with flexible hub towards transmission.
5. Install pressure plate aligned with marks made during removal.
6. Torque bolts to 11 ft. lbs. (1.5 m-kg).
7. Reinstall engine.

505

1. Refer to "Manual Transmission, Replace" procedure and remove transmission.
2. Mark orientation of pressure plate on flywheel.
3. Using 6 mm Allen wrench, remove 6 pressure plate bolts.
4. Remove clutch pressure plate and disc.
5. Reverse procedure to install. Torque pressure plate bolts to 10.88 ft. lbs.

MANUAL TRANSMISSION

REPLACE

504

1. Disconnect battery.
2. Drain transmission.
3. Remove ignition coil, radiator upper mounting, and the two lower radiator mounting bolts on front crossmember.
4. Remove starter without disconnecting cable.
5. Remove bellhousing plate.
6. Remove air cleaner to avoid damage.
7. Disconnect exhaust pipe from manifold.
8. Remove front muffler mount.
9. Turn steering wheel clockwise. Disengage front pipe and let pipe rest on rear crossmember.
10. Remove heat shield and support transmission.
11. Using Facom extension J236/ET8 or equivalent, remove three of the four bolts connecting torque tube to transmission. Loosen but do not remove fourth screw.
12. Remove both Allen bolts holding differential to rear suspension crossmember.
13. Separate torque tube from gearbox by about .8 inch (20 mm) and insert propeller shaft holding plate 8.0403 S.
14. Using two M10 150 bolts secure plate to lower part of tube.
15. Remove propeller shaft from transmission.
16. Disconnect clutch slave cylinder from bellhousing leaving pipe attached.
17. Remove counter lever with rods.
18. Disconnect back-up light switch, ground wire on transmission and speedometer cable.
19. Remove deflector clamp bolt and steering gear housing bolts.
20. Lower steering gear housing without disconnecting tie rod ends.
21. Remove bellhousing access plates.
22. Remove the three Allen bolts that secure transmission to engine.
23. Attach suitable engine hoist to engine.
24. Rotate engine on mounts as far as possible to disengage transmission under tunnel.
25. Remove transmission by rotating 1/4 turn counterclockwise to allow starter motor to clear tunnel.
26. Remove clutch thrust ball bearing.
27. Reverse procedure to install, noting the following torques: engine to bellhousing bolts, 40 ft. lbs. (5.5 m-kg); torque tube to transmission bolts, 43.5 ft. lbs. (6 m-kg); transmission drain plug, 20 ft. lbs. (2.75 m-kg); radiator to front crossmember, 7.2 ft. lbs. (1 m-kg); differential to crossmember, 27 ft. lbs. (3.75 m-kg); starter motor, 14.5 ft. lbs. (2 m-kg).

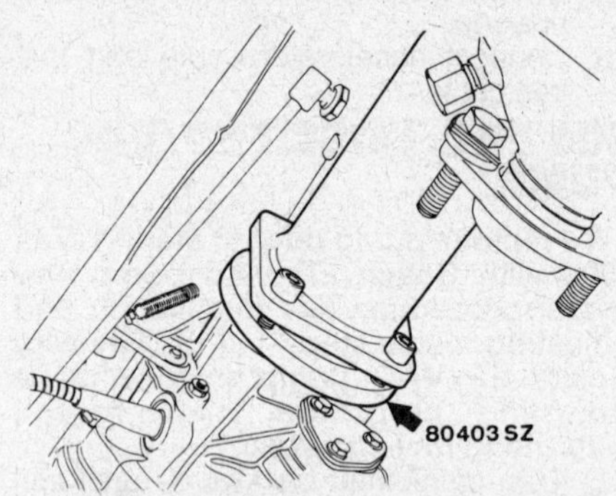

Fig. 2 Installing spacer 8.0403 SZ. 505 models

505

1. Disconnect battery and remove fan shroud.
2. Raise and support vehicle.
3. Remove front exhaust pipe and disconnect wire from Lambda sensor.
4. Remove catalytic converter heat shield and air injection hose.
5. Remove front seat track floor brace from under vehicle.
6. Remove rear tail pipe brackets and differential mounting bolts.
7. Mark position of steering shaft coupling and disconnect.
8. Replace one bolt at each end of front crossmember with bolt 8.1511 C and thread.
9. Remove remaining crossmember bolts and lower crossmember about 2 inches (50 mm) by alternately loosening the 2 long bolts 8.1511 C, **Fig. 1.**
10. Place suitable jack under transmission and remove torque tube bolts.
11. Separate torque tube from transmission by about .8 inch (20 mm) and insert plate 8.0403 SZ, **Fig. 2.** Disengage transmission output shaft.
12. Remove front mount of gear selector rod. Disconnect shifting link rod, selector link rod, back-up light switch wire and speedometer cable.
13. Remove inspection plates from bellhousing.
14. Remove clutch slave cylinder circlip and flexible hose bracket.
15. Lower jack to tilt transmission as far as possible. Support engine at front with suitable engine hoist using hooks 8.0102 G for diesel engines and hooks 8.0102 G and E for gasoline engines.

16. Remove bellhousing and starter bolts.
17. Pull back, turn, and lower transmission from vehicle.
18. Reverse procedure to install.

604

1. Remove hood, air mixer casing and air filter.
2. Drain transmission and cooling system.
3. Remove upper radiator struts and battery.
4. Disconnect radiator hoses.
5. Disconnect engine ground strap, temperature switch lead, power brake vacuum hose and fuel pump hoses.
6. Disconnect carburetor linkages and ignition coil leads.
7. Disconnect heater hoses and starter and alternator wiring.
8. Disconnect front exhaust pipes from manifolds.
9. Remove engine mount bolts.
10. Remove muffler front mount, exhaust pipe center mount and exhaust heat shield.
11. Remove bellhousing lower cover plate. Remove starter and alternator wiring retaining clip.
12. Remove power steering pump mounting bolts and belt. Raise engine with suitable hoist until transmission clears transmission tunnel by about 1/2 inch. Hang power steering pump aside without disconnecting hoses.
13. Working inside vehicle, push back front seats and remove front seat track bolts nearest tunnel.
14. Working under vehicle, screw threaded rods 8.1511 B into seat track mounting nuts. Place two flat washers and nuts on exposed ends of studs inside vehicle and tighten, to prevent breaking welded seat track nuts from floorpan.
15. Install propeller tube support bracket 8.1511 A on studs and tighten slightly.
16. Remove bolt front steering shaft coupling upper flange.
17. Replace on bolt at each end of front crossmember with long bolt 8.1511 C.
18. Remove 2 remaining crossmember bolts and lower crossmember about 1 inch by alternately loosening long bolts.
19. Remove clutch slave cylinder circlip and push cylinder back about 1 inch. Remove plunger and free slave cylinder and position aside.
20. Disconnect back up light switch wires, shift linkage and speedometer cable.
21. Remove bolts securing propeller shaft tube to transmission.
22. Separate transmission and propeller shaft tube by about 1 inch and insert retaining plate 8.0403 SZ. Install two M10 1.50 bolts 20 mm long.
23. Tilt engine/transmission assembly toward rear and remove from vehicle.
24. Separate engine and transmission.
25. Reverse procedure to install.

DISC BRAKES SECTION

INDEX

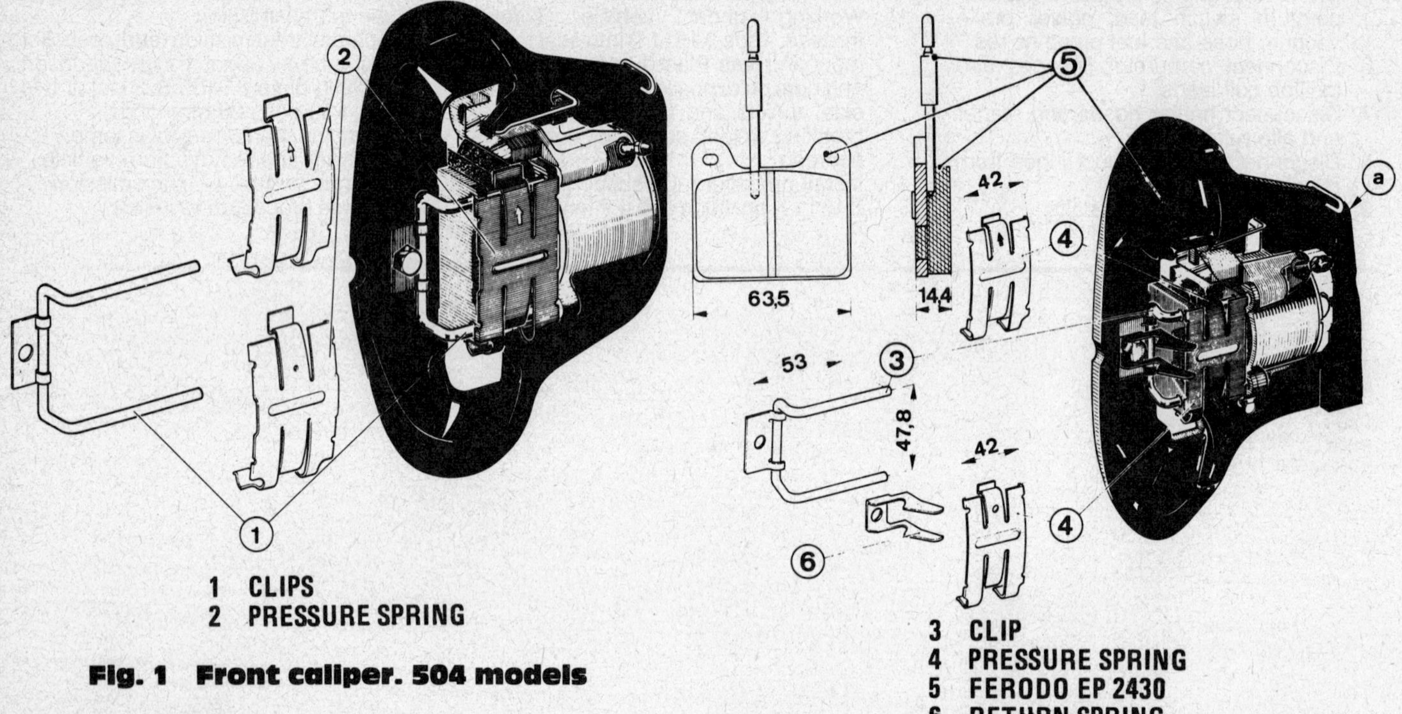

Fig. 1 Front caliper. 504 models

Fig. 2 MK I rear caliper (rounded at a). 504 models

BRAKE PADS REPLACE

504 MODELS

Front Pads

1. Raise and support front of vehicle, then remove wheel and tire assembly.
2. Drain a portion of brake fluid from master cylinder reservoir.
3. Remove clips and pressure spring, then the pads, **Fig. 1.**
4. Return piston to its original position.
5. Clean all components and ensure caliper slides freely.
6. Reverse procedure to install.

Rear Pads

1. Raise and support rear of vehicle, then remove wheel and tire assembly.
2. Drain a portion of brake fluid from master cylinder reservoir.
3. Remove clips, pressure spring and return spring, if equipped, then the rear pads, **Figs. 2 and 3.**
4. Rotate piston 1/8 turn, **Fig. 4,** then return to its original position.
5. Clean all components and ensure caliper slides freely.
6. Reverse procedure to install.

505 MODELS

Front Pads w/DBA Series IV Calipers

1. Raise and support front of vehicle, then remove wheel and tire assembly.
2. Drain a portion of brake fluid from master cylinder reservoir.
3. Turn steering wheel fully to one side.
4. Disconnect brake warning light electrical connector.
5. Remove clip and pad retaining key.
6. Push cylinder towards disc by levering against shock absorber body, then remove outer pad.
7. Push caliper in and remove inner pad.
8. Clean all components and ensure caliper slides freely.
9. Reverse procedure to install.

Front Pads w/Teves Calipers

1. Raise and support front of vehicle, then remove wheel and tire assembly.
2. Drain a portion of brake fluid from master cylinder reservoir.
3. Remove retaining clip, pad pins and retaining springs.
4. Disconnect brake warning light electrical connector.
5. Push cylinder towards disc, then lift caliper and remove inner pad.
6. Push caliper outward and remove outer pad.
7. Clean all components and ensure caliper slides freely.
8. Reverse procedure to install.

Rear Pads

1. Raise and support rear of vehicle, then remove wheel and tire assembly.
2. Disconnect brake warning light electrical connector.
3. Remove safety clip and retaining spring, then disconnect both ends of damping spring.
4. Remove pad retaining fork, then the spring and pads.
5. Rotate piston 1/8 turn, **Fig. 4,** then return to its original position.
6. Clean all components and ensure caliper slides freely.
7. Reverse procedure to install.

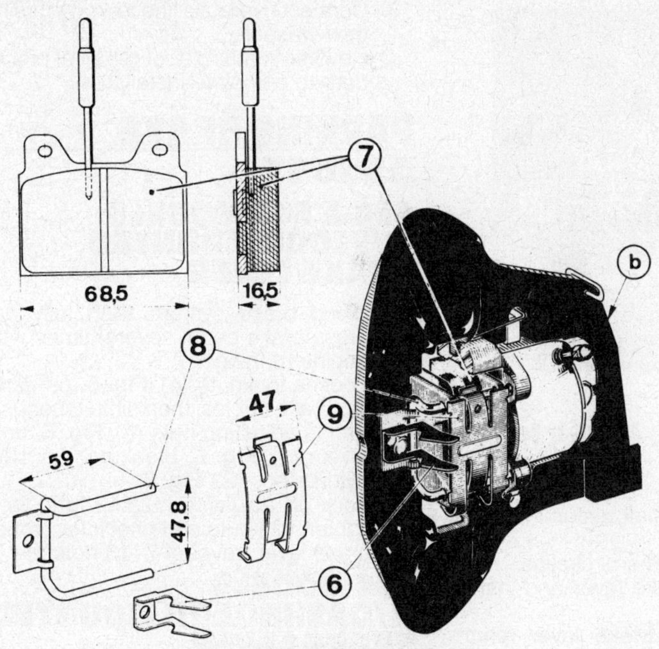

6 RETURN SPRING
7 PADS
8 CLIPS
9 PRESSURE SPRING

Fig. 3 MK III rear caliper (chamfered at b). 504 models

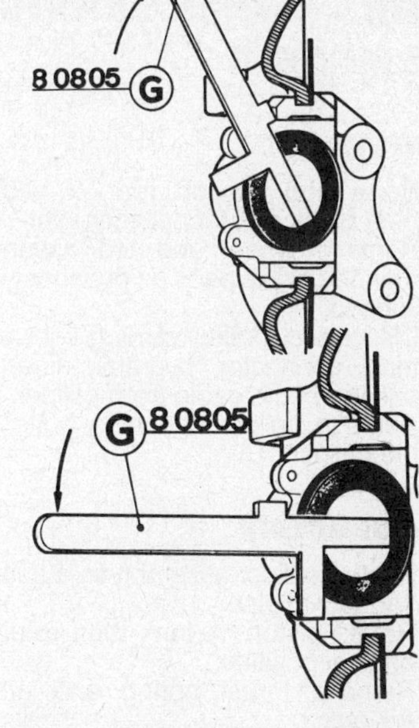

Fig. 4 Rotating piston

Fig. 5 Parking brake cable adjusters

604 MODELS

Front Pads

1. Raise and support front of vehicle, then remove wheel and tire assembly.
2. Drain a portion of brake fluid from master cylinder reservoir.
3. Remove pad wear indicator wire.
4. Drive out retaining pins, then remove spring.
5. Push caliper back and remove inner pad.
6. Pull caliper back and remove outer pad.
7. Clean all components and ensure caliper slides freely.
8. Reverse procedure to install.

Rear Pads

1. Raise and support rear of vehicle, then remove wheel and tire assembly.
2. Drain a portion of brake fluid from master cylinder reservoir.
3. Remove return spring, retaining clips and brake pads.
4. Rotate piston 1/8 turn, **Fig. 4**, then return to its original position.
5. Clean all components and ensure caliper slides freely.
6. Reverse procedure to install.

FRONT CALIPER SERVICE

504 MODELS

Removal

1. Raise and support front of vehicle, then block master cylinder inlet.
2. Remove wheel and tire assembly, then the brake pads as previously described.
3. Disconnect brake warning light electrical connector and hydraulic line from caliper.
4. Remove caliper attaching bolts and the caliper.

Disassembly

1. Secure caliper assembly in a suitable soft-jawed vise.
2. Slide piston forward, then remove thrust spring and adapter.
3. Remove retaining circlips and piston boots, then the piston from caliper.
4. Remove nylon spacer and seals from caliper body.

Assembly

1. Lightly lubricate and install new seals into caliper.
2. Lubricate piston, then install with nylon spacer.
3. Install piston boots and circlips.
4. Install adapter using two .008 inch (.20 mm) shims.
5. Install thrust spring.

Installation

1. Apply suitable locking compound to caliper bolt threads.
2. Install caliper using new lockwashers on bolts and torque to 50 ft. lbs.
3. Connect hydraulic line to caliper using new washers.
4. Reverse remainder of removal procedure to complete installation.

REAR CALIPER SERVICE

504 MODELS

Removal

1. Raise and support rear of vehicle, then block master cylinder inlet.
2. Remove wheel and tire assembly, then the brake pads as previously described.
3. Disconnect brake warning light electrical connector, hydraulic line and parking brake cable from caliper.
4. Remove caliper attaching bolts and the caliper.

Disassembly

1. Secure caliper assembly in a suitable soft-jawed vise.
2. Rotate piston 1/8 turn, then return to original position.
3. Remove thrust spring and caliper adapter.
4. Remove snap ring, then the parking brake lever return spring.
5. Raise parking brake lever and remove nylon spacer.
6. Remove retaining circlips and piston boots, then the piston.
7. Remove seals from caliper body.

Assembly

1. Lightly lubricate and install new seals into caliper.

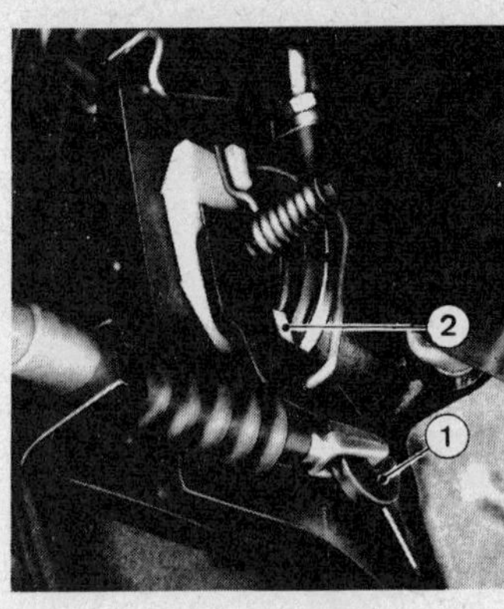

Fig. 6 Parking brake lever

2. Lubricate, then install, piston into caliper.
3. Install piston boots and circlips.
4. Raise parking brake lever and install nylon spacer.
5. Connect parking brake lever return spring, then install new snap ring or spring anchors, as equipped.
6. Install adapter using two .008 inch (.20 mm) shims.
7. Install thrust spring.

Installation

1. Apply suitable locking compound to caliper bolt threads.
2. Install caliper using new lockwashers on bolts and torque to 31 ft. lbs.
3. Connect hydraulic line to caliper using new washers.
4. Reverse remainder of removal procedure to complete installation.

PARKING BRAKE

ADJUST

504 & 505 MODELS W/FLOOR MOUNTED BRAKE LEVER

1. Bleed brake system, then fully depress brake pedal several times with engine running.
2. Loosen locknuts (4), **Fig. 5,** on parking brake cables, then simultaneously turn in adjusting nuts (5), **Fig. 5,** until levers (1), **Fig. 6,** break contact with nylon stops (2), **Fig. 6.**
3. Back off adjusting nuts 1/2 turn, then tighten locknuts and check for proper brake lever travel of 7-13 notches.

504 MODELS W/DASHBOARD MOUNTED BRAKE LEVER

1. Bleed brake system, then fully depress brake pedal several times with engine running.
2. Loosen equalizer arm locknut and adjusting nut.
3. Tighten adjusting nut to provide .039-.059 inch (1-1.5 mm) freeplay of the spring washer.
4. Tighten locknut while holding adjusting nut in position.

DRUM BRAKES SECTION

INDEX

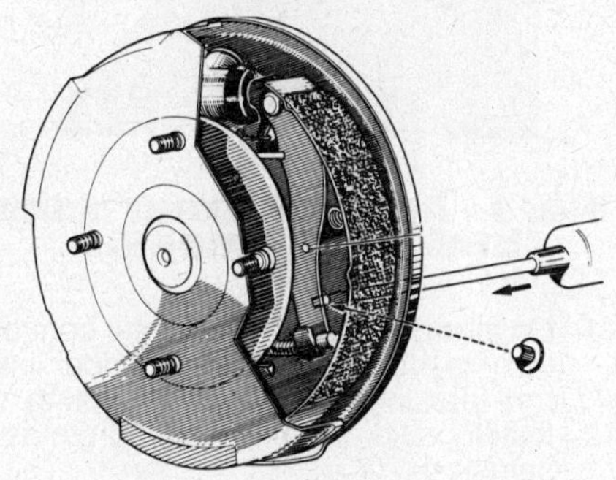

Fig. 1 Releasing brake shoes.

GIRLING BRAKE SERVICE

REMOVAL

1. Raise and support rear of vehicle, then remove wheel and tire assembly.
2. Loosen parking brake cable locknuts, then remove adjusting nuts.
3. Remove plug from drum, **Fig. 1**, then insert a screwdriver through back plate and move parking brake lever outward to release brake shoes.
4. Reinstall plug, then remove drum.
5. Remove lower return spring using a suitable tool, **Fig. 2.**
6. Release upper return spring, then position a suitable clamp on brake cylinder and move shoes outward as far as possible.
7. Remove adjusting lever with spring, spacer cup and pushrod.
8. Remove hold-down springs, then the leading and trailing shoes.
9. Disconnect parking brake cable from lever, then remove return spring.

INSPECTION

1. Clean drum and back plate with suitable solvent.
2. Check for proper sealing of the pistons.
3. Inspect rubber boots for wear or damage.
4. Check drum for excessive wear and grind if necessary.
5. Replace any damaged or excessively worn components.

INSTALLATION

1. Lightly lubricate brake shoe pressure pads on back plate.
2. Install leading shoe with hold-down spring.
3. Insert end of lower return spring through hole in leading shoe.
4. Attach parking brake cable to lever.
5. Connect short end of upper return spring, then install trailing shoe.
6. Attach lower return spring to trailing shoe using a suitable tool, **Fig. 2.**
7. Position automatic adjuster nut .197 inch (5 mm) from stop on yoke, then install pushrod, **Fig. 3.**
8. Connect upper return spring to leading shoe.
9. Install spacer cup, then the adjustment lever with spring. **Ensure lower arm of spring passes behind the anchor.**
10. Install brake drum, wheel and tire assembly.
11. Check master cylinder fluid level and replenish as necessary.
12. Check brake pedal for proper feel and return.
13. Lower vehicle and road test.

DBA TYPE 1 BRAKE SERVICE

REMOVAL

1. Raise and support rear of vehicle, then remove wheel and tire assembly.
2. Loosen parking brake cable locknuts, then remove adjusting nuts.
3. Remove plug from drum, **Fig. 1**, then insert a screwdriver through backplate and move parking brake lever outward to release brake shoes.
4. Reinstall plug, then remove drum.
5. Remove lower shoe return spring using a suitable tool, **Fig. 4.**
6. Ensure automatic adjuster lever link clearance measures .035-.043 inch (.9-1.1 mm).
7. Remove upper return spring, then position a suitable clamp on brake cylinder.
8. Remove and discard hold-down spring from leading shoe, then swing adjusting lever towards hub and move leading shoe outward.
9. Disconnect link rod from leading shoe, then remove the shoe.
10. Disconnect parking brake cable from lever, then remove and discard hold-down spring from trailing shoe.
11. Remove trailing shoe and link rod.

INSPECTION

1. Clean drum and back plate with suitable solvent.

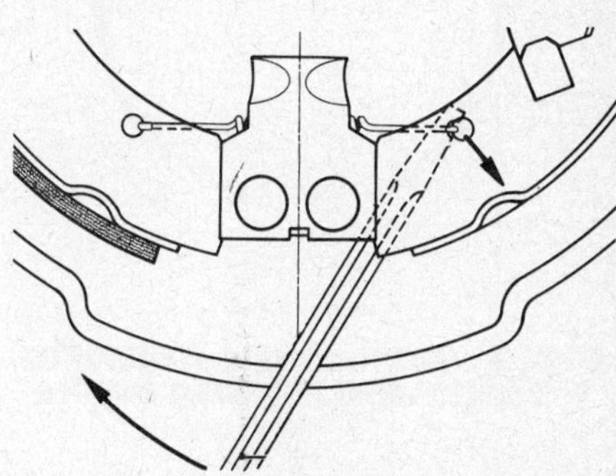

Fig. 2 Lower return spring. Girling & DBA type 2 brakes

2. Check for proper sealing of the pistons.
3. Inspect rubber boots for wear or damage.
4. Check drum for excessive wear and grind if necessary.
5. Replace any damaged or excessively worn components.

INSTALLATION

1. Lightly lubricate brake shoe pressure pads on backplate.
2. Transfer serviceable components to replacement brake shoes.
3. Attach parking brake cable to lever.
4. Install trailing shoe with new hold-down spring.
5. Swing adjusting lever towards hub, then connect link rod to lever. Lower pawl and push lever downward.
6. Install leading shoe with new hold-down spring.
7. Install lower and upper return springs and secure to brake shoes.
8. Install brake drum, wheel and tire assembly.
9. Actuate brake pedal several times to set the automatic adjuster.
10. Check master cylinder fluid level and replenish as necessary.
11. Check brake pedal for proper feel and return.
12. Lower vehicle and road test.

DBA TYPE 2 BRAKE SERVICE

REMOVAL

1. Raise and support rear of vehicle, then remove wheel and tire assembly.

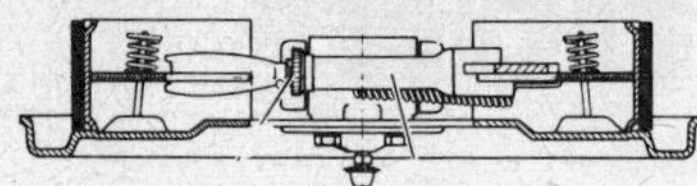

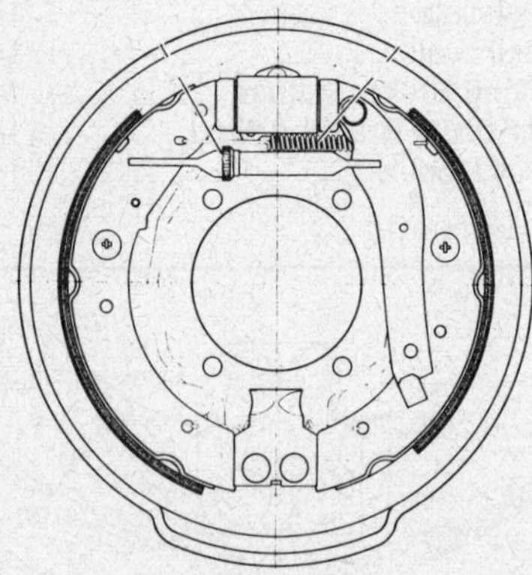

Fig. 3 Automatic adjuster installation. Girling brake

2. Loosen parking brake cable locknuts, then remove adjusting nuts.
3. Remove plug from drum, **Fig. 1**, then insert a screwdriver through backplate and move parking brake lever outward to release brake shoes.
4. Reinstall plug, then remove drum.
5. On sedan models, remove lower return spring using a suitable tool, **Fig. 2.**
6. On all models, remove upper return spring, then position a suitable clamp on brake cylinder.
7. Remove hold-down springs, then the leading shoe.
8. Disconnect parking brake cable from lever, then remove trailing shoe with link rod.
9. Remove parking brake lever, automatic adjuster and pivoted control lever from brake shoes.

INSPECTION

1. Clean drum and back plate with suitable solvent.
2. Check for proper sealing of the pistons.
3. Inspect rubber boots for wear or damage.

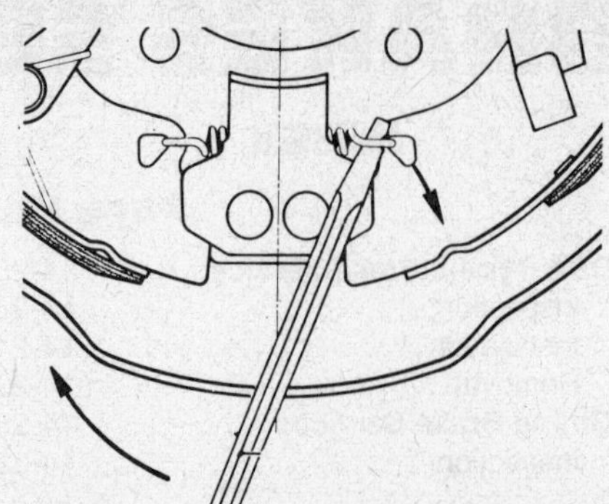

Fig. 4 Lower return spring. Girling & DBA type 1 brake

4. Check drum for excessive wear and grind if necessary.
5. Check that automatic adjuster assembly bolt turns freely.
6. Ensure automatic adjuster nut faces slight resistance when turned clockwise and much greater resistance when turned counterclockwise.
7. Replace any damaged or excessively worn components.

INSTALLATION

1. Lightly lubricate brake shoe pressure pads on back plate.
2. Cover automatic adjuster bolt threads with a protective sleeve, .670 inch (17 mm) long on sedan models, or .945 inch (24 mm) long on wagon models.
3. Insert adjuster bolt into pawl, then slide ratchet guide into pawl groove.
4. Install automatic adjuster control lever to adjuster lever, then secure return spring to adjuster.
5. Attach automatic adjuster assembly to leading brake shoe using a new locking ring.
6. Attach parking brake lever to trailing brake shoe.
7. Attach hooked end of link rod to parking brake lever, then lock assembly by sliding support spring under yoke plate and inserting tab in hole in lever.
8. Connect parking brake cable to lever, then install trailing shoe to backplate.
9. On sedan models, install leading shoe, then the lower return spring.
10. On wagon models, assemble shoes with lower return spring, then install the leading shoe.

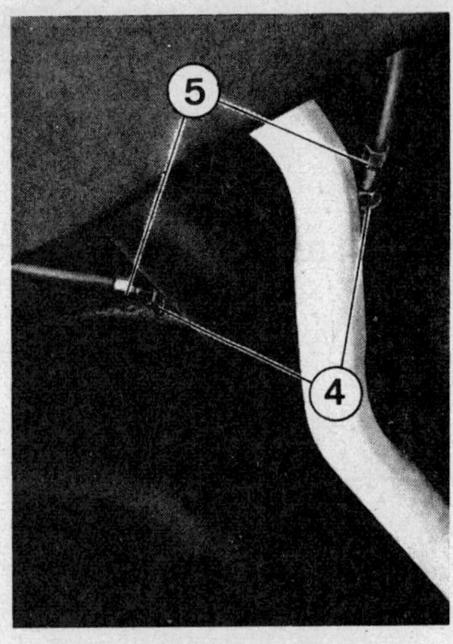

Fig. 5 Adjusting rear drum brakes. 504 models

11. On all models, ensure adjuster control lever is properly positioned under link rod, then install upper return spring.
12. Install brake drum, wheel and tire assembly.
13. Actuate brake pedal several times to set the automatic adjuster.
14. Check master cylinder fluid level and replenish as necessary.
15. Check brake pedal for proper feel and return.
16. Lower vehicle and road test.

REAR DRUM BRAKE ADJUST

504 MODELS

1. Raise and support rear of vehicle.
2. Rotate wheel in normal direction of rotation and turn each adjuster down (1), **Fig. 5**, until wheel locks.
3. Turn adjuster up (2), **Fig. 5**, until wheel just turns freely in normal direction of rotation.

PARKING BRAKE ADJUST

1. Raise and support rear of vehicle.
2. Loosen locknut, then turn adjusting screw as necessary to provide brake lever travel of 4-7 notches.
3. Tighten locknut and ensure wheels turn freely by hand.

REAR AXLE & SUSPENSION SECTION

INDEX

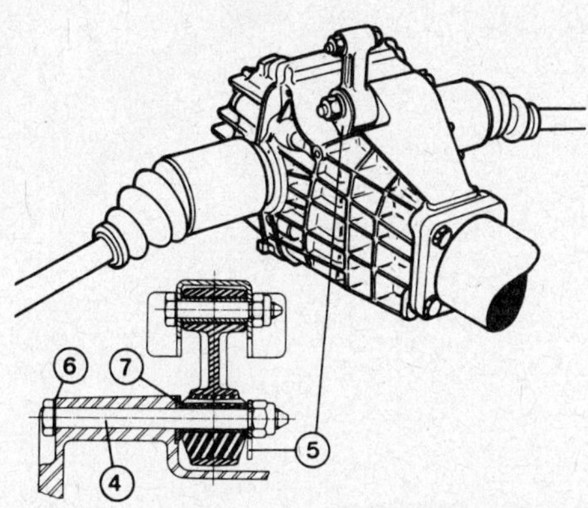

Fig. 1 Differential support

HUB, ROTOR & WHEEL BEARINGS REPLACE

505

1. Raise and support rear of vehicle and remove wheel.
2. Disconnect brake hose from suspension arm and remove stub axle.
3. Remove brake caliper and secure aside.
4. Remove 4 bolts securing stub axle carrier to suspension arm.
5. Remove hub, rotor, stub axle and drive axle as an assembly, taking care not to stress CV joints.
6. Press stub axle from hub using suitable bearing separators.
7. Remove hub from stub axle carrier using press or suitable puller.
8. Mark position of rotor, remove bolts and separate hub from rotor.
9. On models with second design hub, remove bearing inner race from hub using suitable puller, then remove seal.
10. On all models, reverse procedure to install, noting the following:
    a. On models with second design hub, position inner race in stub axle carrier, then press new seal into carrier until seal is fully seated against shoulder of carrier.
    b. On all models, assemble rotor on hub aligning matching marks, apply suitable thread locking compound, then evenly torque retaining bolts to 27 ft. lbs. in crossing pattern.
    c. Secure drive axle assembly in vise, mount hub assembly on stub axle and install new retaining nut, torque nut to 43.5 ft. lbs, then stake nut to stub axle.
    d. Torque stub axle carrier bolts to 36 ft. lbs. and caliper mounting bolts to 31 ft. lbs.

REAR AXLE ASSEMBLY REPLACE

504 & 505

Removal of differential requires removal of left hand drive shaft.

1. Raise rear of car and support under rear arms.
2. Remove left rear wheel.
3. Remove brake pad anti-squeal spring, retaining fork and brake pads.
4. Disconnect brake hose retaining clip on rear arm.
5. Remove brake caliper bolts and remove brake caliper. Hang caliper from body.
6. Remove screws holding disc to hub. Mark position of screw on disc.
7. Remove disc.
8. Remove Allen screw holding hub carrier to rear arm.
9. Remove hub carrier drive shaft assembly.
10. Remove thrust plate and bolts.
11. Drain differential.
12. Remove brake compensator lever pivot from body.
13. Remove the four nuts securing torque tube to differential.
14. Remove the two Allen screws holding differential to suspension crossmember.
15. Disengage differential by pulling towards rear and then towards left.
16. Reverse procedure to install, noting the following torques: torque tube to differential, 43.5 ft. lbs. (6 m-kg); differential to crossmember, 27.1 ft. lbs. (3.75 m-kg); hub carrier to rear arm, 29 ft. lbs. (4 m-kg).

604

Removal of differential requires removal of left hand drive shaft.

1. Raise vehicle and place stands under rear suspension arms. Remove rear wheel.
2. Remove brake line retaining clip and caliper bolts.
3. Unclip hand brake cable.
4. Remove brake caliper and hang aside.
5. Remove stub axle securing bolts and remove driveshaft assembly.
6. Place stands under rear crossmember supports.
7. Unlock and remove crossmember securing nuts.
8. Remove plastic plugs and screw in guide dowels 8.0906 or equivalent and leave pins in place.
9. Disconnect rear muffler mount and remove heat shield.
10. Remove differential securing bolts.
11. Place stands under rear of car.
12. Lower rear crossmember until pins come against body.
13. Remove the four nuts holding torque tube to differential.
14. Remove differential towards rear making sure that propeller shaft remains in place.
15. Reverse procedure to install, noting the following torques: torque tube to differential, 43 ft. lbs. (6 m-kg); crossmember to body, 47 ft. lbs. (6.5 m-kg); differential, 27 ft. lbs. (3.75 m-

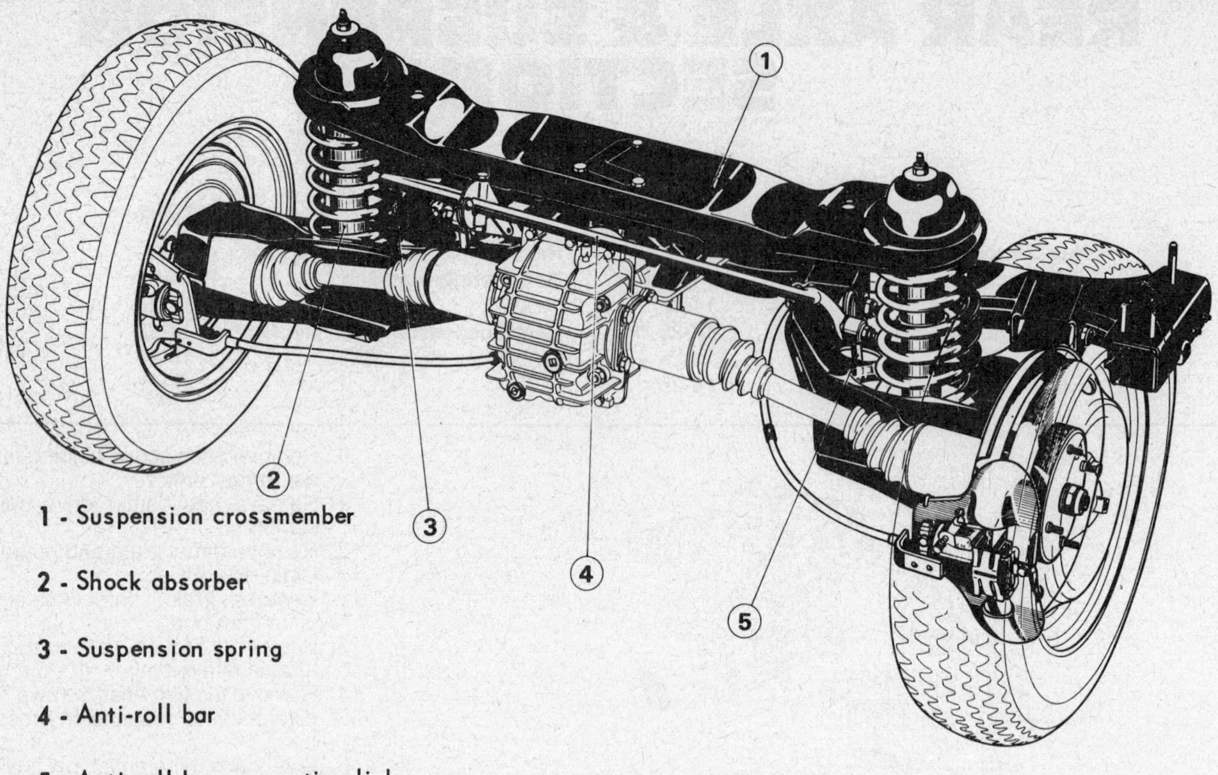

Fig. 2 Rear suspension. Typical

kg); stub axle to suspension arm, 29 ft. lbs. (4 m-kg); caliper bolts, 36 ft. lbs. (5 m-kg); wheel nuts, 61 ft. lbs. (8.5 m-kg).

REAR SHOCK ABSORBER REPLACE

1. Working inside trunk, remove locknut while holding shock rod.
2. Remove upper steel cup and rubber bushing.
3. Working under car, remove lower shock pivot from rear suspension arm.
4. Remove shock absorber down through suspension arm.
5. When installing shock absorber, replace rubber washers, upper metal cup, and locknut.
6. Fully extend shock absorber rod.
7. Install in following order: thrust cup, rod protector, center cup, rubber washer and nylon spacer.
8. Under vehicle, position shock absorber placing rod in hole on crossmember.
9. Install lower shock pivot with new lockwasher. Install nut without tightening.
10. Working inside trunk, place upper rubber bush, steel cup and locknut on shock rod.
11. Torque upper locknut to 9 ft. lbs.(1.25 m-kg) and lower pivot nut to 33 ft. lbs. (4.5 m-kg).

REAR SPRING REPLACE

505

1. Raise and support vehicle.
2. Remove rear nut on exhaust pipe support, and rear stabilizer bearing clamps.
3. Disconnect muffler heat shield.
4. On rear crossmember, remove the four bolts and place limiter casing aside.
5. On models with 106 engine, remove the two bolts from axle side supports. On models with 829 engine, remove pin (4), **Fig. 1.** Take care not to lose plate (5), washers (6) and (7).
6. On all models, place torque tube on rear crossmember and loosen rear suspension arm pins.
7. Place suitable jack under right hand crossmember side support.
8. Remove rear seat cushion and remove front nut securing crossmember.
9. Lift sheet metal locking plate and remove plastic plug.
10. Screw in pilot guide 8.0906 K1 and tighten with pin K2. Leave pin in place to retain crossmember.
11. Remove the two rear crossmember securing nuts and lower crossmember until pin contacts vehicle floor.
12. Repeat steps 7-11 on left side. Support rear suspension arms.
13. Remove wheels and rear shock absorbers.
14. Raise vehicle or lower rear arms until springs are freed. Remove springs and rubber cups.
15. Reverse procedure to install springs, noting the following torques: crossmember securing nuts, 47 ft. lbs. (6.5 m-kg); on models with 106 engine, side support bolts, 14 ft. lbs. (3.75 m-kg); on models with 829 engine, locknut (6), **Fig. 1,** 8 ft. lbs. (9.5 m-kg); limiter casing bolts, 9.4 ft. lbs. (1.3 m-kg); suspension arm hinge pins, 47 ft. lbs. (6.9 m-kg); shock absorber pivot nut, 32 ft. lbs. (4.5 m-kg); stabilizer clamps, 14 ft. lbs. (3.75 m-kg).

REAR SUSPENSION ARM REPLACE

504

1. Raise and support vehicle.
2. Disconnect exhaust pipe and let rest on rear crossmember. Support at front.

3. Remove heat shield.
4. Remove Allen bolts holding differential housing. Rest torque tube on rear crossmember.
5. Refer to steps 7-12 of "Rear Spring, Replace" procedure for 505 models.
6. Separate differential from torque tube, then move differential to the rear.
7. Remove four Allen bolts holding torque tube to transmission.
8. Separate tube from transmission by 20 mm (.787 inch) and insert propeller shaft holding plate 8.0403S between them. Use two Allen screws M10150 to retain plate to tube lower part.
9. Lower exhaust pipe down at front and separate propeller shaft from transmission.
10. Bring propeller shaft/torque tube assembly forward and remove.
11. Support both rear suspension arms with suitable jack. Raise arms to take load off shock absorber.
12. Remove shock absorber (2), **Fig. 2.**
13. Disconnect brake hose from lug on rear arm by loosening nut on hose.
14. Unclip parking brake cable from rear arm.
15. Disconnect stabilizer link (5), **Fig. 2,** from arm.
16. Unscrew rear arm pivot nuts.
17. Lower jack carefully until spring is free. Remove spring.
18. Remove rear arm pivots and remove rear arm.
19. Reverse procedure to install, noting the following torques: shock absorber upper nut, 9 ft. lbs. (1.25 m-kg); stabilizer bar link, 9 ft. lbs. (1.25 m-kg); lower shock absorber pivot, 33 ft. lbs. (4.5 m-kg); rear arm pivots, 47 ft. lbs. (6.5 m-kg).

604

1. Remove fastening retaining brake hose to rear arm.
2. Remove brake pads and handbrake cable.
3. Remove caliper without disconnecting brake lines.
4. Remove half shaft without loosening center nut.
5. Support suspension arms and remove shock absorbers.
6. Disconnect stabilizer link and suspension pivot nuts.
7. Carefully lower arms until springs are free.
8. Remove spring.
9. Support arm in horizontal position.
10. Knock out innermost pin with bronze hammer and replace with pin 8.0906J.
11. Using tool 8.0909Z, press out pin. Do not press pin out completely.
12. Remove tool 8.0909Z and knock pin out.
13. Remove suspension arm.
14. Reverse procedure to install, noting the following torques: stabilizer link, 9 ft. lbs. (1.25 m-kg); half shaft assembly to suspension arm, 36 ft. lbs. (5 m-kg); brake caliper bolts, 30 ft. lbs. (4.25 m-kg); shock absorber lower pivot, 47 ft. lbs. (6.5 m-kg); suspension pivot nuts, 39 ft. lbs. (5.5 m-kg).

FRONT SUSPENSION & STEERING SECTION

INDEX

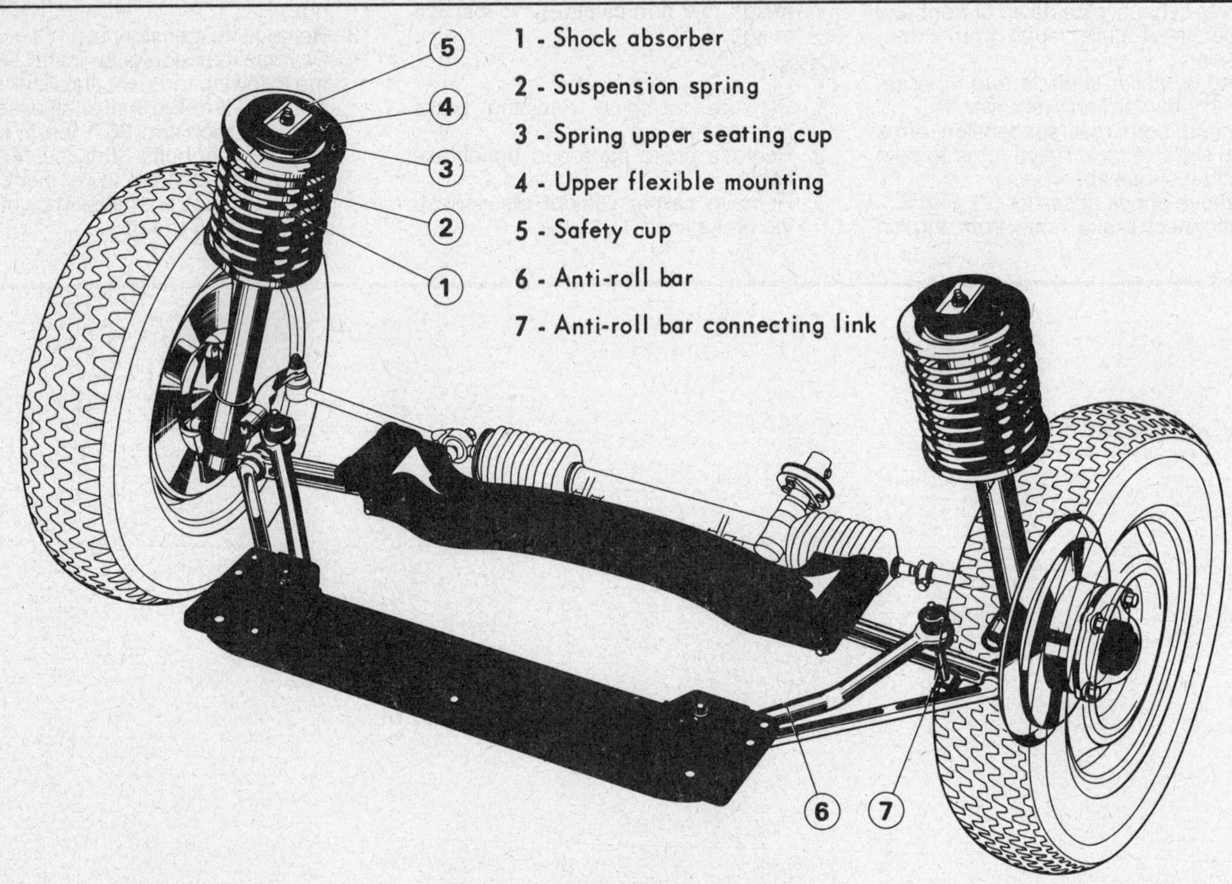

Fig. 1 Front suspension. Typical

WHEEL BEARINGS ADJUST

ANGLE CONTACT BALL BEARINGS

1. Raise and support front of vehicle.
2. Remove wheel.
3. Remove hub dust cap and nut.
4. Install new nut and pretorque to 22 ft. lbs. (3 m-kg).
5. Loosen nut and torque to 7.2 ft. lbs. (1 m-kg).
6. Lock nut in the two grooves provided.

TAPER ROLLER BEARINGS

1. Raise and support front of vehicle.
2. Remove wheel.
3. Remove hub dust cap and nut.
4. Install new nut.
5. While rotating hub torque nut to 29 ft. lbs. (4 m-kg).
6. Loosen axle nut then retorque to 7.23 ft. lbs. (1 m-kg).

HUB, ROTOR & WHEEL BEARINGS REPLACE

505

1. Raise and support front of vehicle and remove wheel.
2. Remove brake caliper leaving hose connected and secure caliper aside. **Do not allow caliper to hang from brake hose.**
3. Remove hub cap and nut, then remove hub assembly, taking care not to drop outer bearing.
4. If inner bearing is seized on spindle, remove bearing using suitable puller.
5. Mark position of rotor, remove bolts, then separate rotor from hub.
6. Clean and inspect bearings and replace as needed.
7. Pack bearings with suitable grease, working grease through rollers from wide end of bearing with palm of hand. Keep bearings covered until installation.
8. Assemble hub and rotor aligning matching marks, apply suitable thread locking compound to threads, then torque bolts to 27 ft. lbs.
9. Install bearings in hub, then press new seal into rear of hub.
10. Install hub assembly, adjust wheel bearings as outlined, then reverse remaining procedure to complete installation.

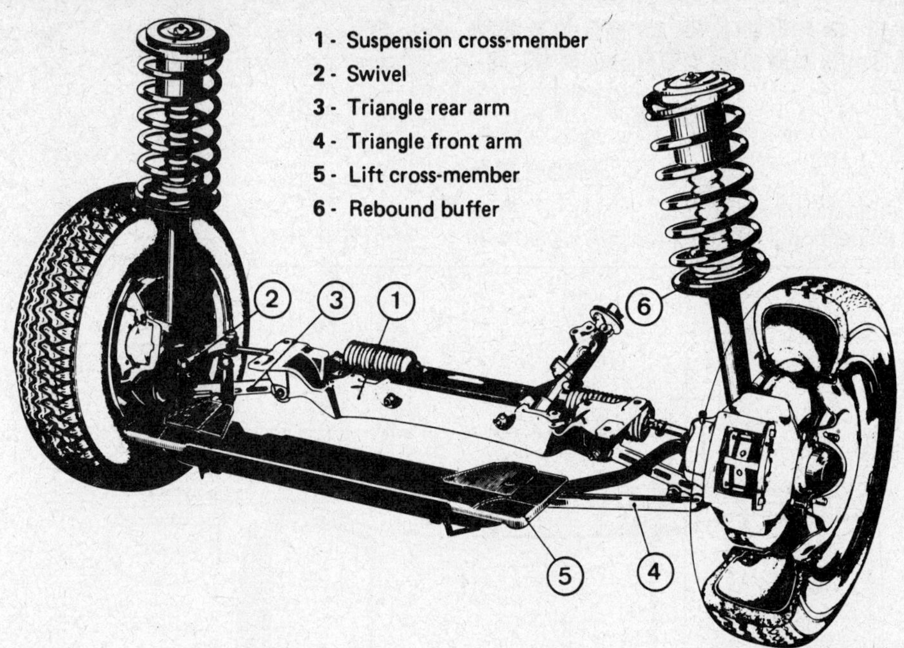

Fig. 2 Front suspension with power steering. Typical

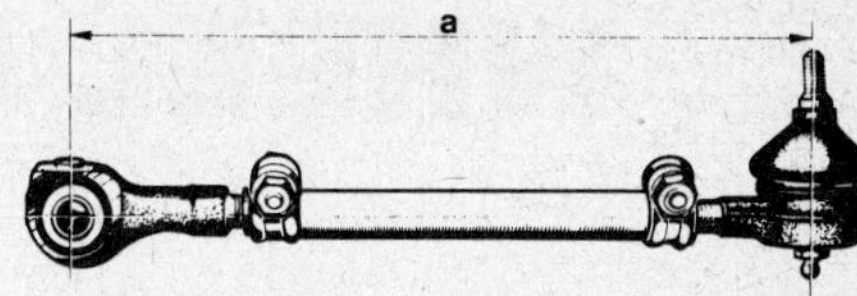

Fig. 3 Righthand steering link. 504 & 604 models

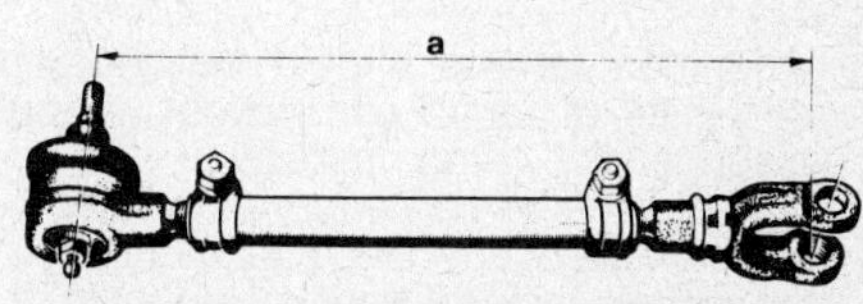

Fig. 4 Lefthand steering link. 504 & 604 models

MacPHERSON STRUT REPLACE

1. Raise and support vehicle.
2. Remove wheel.
3. Remove brake caliper and hand aside without disconnecting brake lines.
4. Remove tie rod ball joint.
5. Disconnect stabilizer bar link (7), **Fig. 1.**
6. Remove pivot from transverse control arm (3), **Fig. 2,** by tapping until splined part is disengaged.
7. Remove nut securing front arm (4), **Fig. 2,** to transverse control arm.
8. Place suitable jack under wheel hub.
9. Remove the three bolts holding MacPherson strut to strut tower.
10. Lower jack while guiding strut and remove strut.
11. Reverse procedure to install, noting the following torques: MacPherson strut to strut tower, 7.2 ft. lbs. (1 m-kg); tie rod end, 33 ft. lbs. (4.5 m-kg); brake caliper bolts, 51 ft. lbs. (7 m-kg); wheel nuts, 43.5 ft. lbs. (6 m-kg). With vehicle resting on suspension, torque the following to 33 ft. lbs. (4.5 m-kg): transverse control arm pivot, stabilizer bar link and nut securing front arm to control arm.

STEERING GEAR REPLACE

MANUAL STEERING

1. Raise and support vehicle.
2. Disconnect tie rod ends.
3. Remove steering shaft collar bolt.
4. Remove two bolts securing steering gear to crossmember.
5. Insert 6 mm punch in shaft collar bolt hole and disengage steering shaft.
6. Remove steering gear.
7. Reverse procedure to install.

POWER STEERING

1. Raise and support vehicle.
2. Disconnect battery.
3. Drain hydraulic system by removing filler cap and disconnecting high pressure hose.
4. Disconnect low pressure hose.
5. On 604 models only, support engine, disconnect engine mounts.
6. On all models, disconnect steering shaft coupling.
7. On 604 models, lower crossmember about 1 1/2 inches.
8. On all models, remove safety spring clips and steering gear bolts.
9. Disconnect tie rod ends.
10. Remove nut securing steering arm to front crossmember and remove steering gear towards rear.
11. Reverse procedure to install. On 504 and 604 models steering links length should be adjusted to get approximate wheel alignment. Dimension (a) in **Figs. 3 and 4** should be 10.97 inch (278.6 mm) on 504 models, and 11.73 inch (298 mm) on 604 models.

W EEL ALIGNM NT SECTION

INDEX

INSPECTION

Alignment angles should be checked with vehicle at normal curb weight, without passengers or cargo. Inspection and adjustments should be performed on equipment capable of checking alignment of the front wheels with the rear wheels, **Fig. 1.** Prior to checking alignment angles, ensure that the steering gear is centered. As the steering lock on power steering models is limited by the power assisted ram travel, the steering lock does not include a positive stop. On models equipped with power steering, place steering ram in center of its travel as follows:

1. Place vehicle on alignment rack with front wheels resting on turntables, then unlock turntables.
2. Start engine and run at idle speed.
3. Move steering through full lock to the right and hold it as far as it will travel, then measure the amount that the ram piston projects from the steering gear and record measurement.
4. Move steering through full lock to the left and hold it as far as it will travel, then measure the amount that the piston rod projects from the steering gear and record measurement.
5. To center the steering gear, move steering until piston rod projection is 1/2 the sum of the measurements obtained in steps 3 and 4, then stop engine. (Add the measurements obtained in steps 3 and 4, then divide the sum by 2).

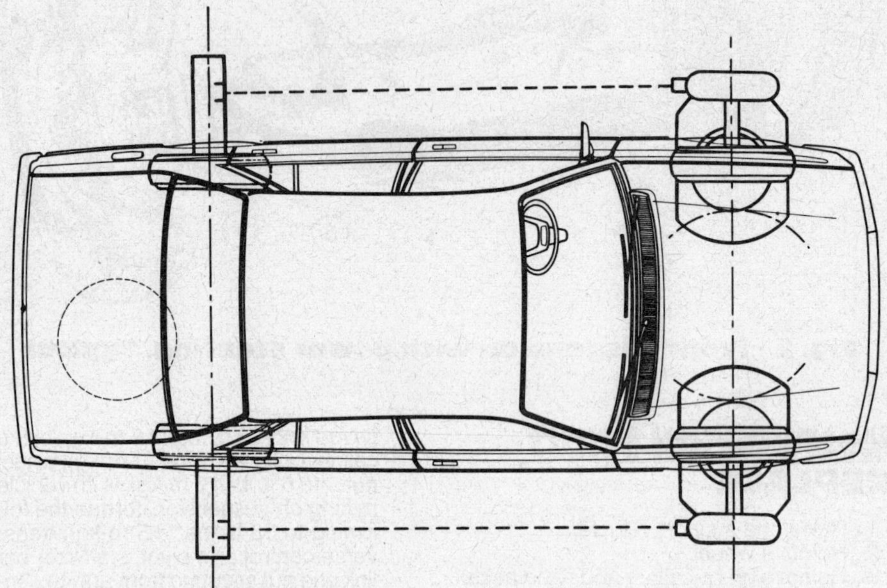

Fig. 1 Checking alignment of front wheels

ADJUSTMENTS

Caster and camber are not adjustable. If these values are not within specifications, check for damaged, deformed or worn suspension components, or damaged under body, and repair as needed. To adjust the toe setting, proceed as follows:

1. Loosen tie rod clamp nuts.
2. Turn both tie rods at the same time to obtain specified toe-in.
3. Torque clamp nuts to 7.23 ft. lbs. (1 m-kg), then return tie rod ball joints to the horizontal position.
4. After performing adjustment, check position of steering wheel.
5. If wheel is not centered with front wheels in straight-ahead position, reposition steering wheel on shaft as needed.

(Germany)

INDEX OF SERVICE OPERATIONS

General Engine Specifications

Year	Engine	Carburetor	Bore Stroke Inch (mm)	Compression Ratio	Maximum HP @ RPM	Maximum Torque @ RPM	Normal Oil Pressure
1983	4-151/2500cc	Fuel Inj.	3.94 x 3.11 (100 x 78.9)	9.5	143@ 5500	137 @ 3000	58④
	6-182.7/2994cc	Fuel Inj.	3.74 x 2.77 (95 x 70.4)	9.3	172 @ 5500	175 @ 4200	57④
	8-285/4600cc	Fuel Inj.	3.82 x 3.11 (97 x 78.9)	9.3	234 @ 5500	263 @ 4000	72②
1984	4-151/2500cc	Fuel Inj.	3.94 x 3.11 (100 x 78.9)	9.5	143@ 5500	137 @ 3000	58①
	6-193.2/3200cc	Fuel Inj.	—	9.5	200 @ 5900	185 @ 4800	—
	8-285/4600cc	Fuel Inj.	3.82 x 3.11 (97 x 78.9)	9.3	234 @ 5250	263 @ 4000	72②
1985	4-151/2500cc	Fuel Inj.	3.94 x 3.11 (100 x 78.9)	9.5	143@ 5500	137 @ 3000	58①
	4-151/2500cc③	Fuel Inj.	3.94 x 3.11 (100 x 78.9)	8.0	220 @ 5800	243 @ 3500	58①
	6-193.2/3200cc	Fuel Inj.	—	9.5	207 @ 5900	185 @ 4800	—
	8-302/5000cc	Fuel Inj.	—	10.0	288 @ 5750	302 @ 2700	—
1986	4-151/2500cc	Fuel Inj.	3.94 x 3.11 (100 x 78.9)	9.7	143 @ 5500	137 @ 3000	58①
	4-151/2500cc③	Fuel Inj.	3.94 x 3.11 (100 x 78.9)	8.0	217 @ 5800	243 @ 3500	58①
	6-193.2/3200cc	Fuel Inj.	—	9.5	200 @ 5900	185 @ 4800	—
	6-201.3/3300cc③	Fuel Inj.	—	7.0	282 @ 5900	278 @ 4800	—
	8-302.5/5000cc	Fuel Inj.	—	10.0	288 @ 5750	302 @ 2700	—
1987	4-151/2500cc	Fuel Inj.	3.94 x 3.11 (100 x 78.9)	9.7	147 @ 5800	140 @ 3000	—
	6-193.2/3200cc	Fuel Inj.	3.74 x 2.92 (95 x 74.4)	9.5	214 @ 5900	195 @ 4800	—
	6-201.3/3300cc③	Fuel Inj.	—	7.0	282 @ 4000	278 @ 4000	—
	8-302.5/5000cc	Fuel Inj.	3.93 x 3.106 (100 x 78.9)	10.1	316 @ 6000	317 @ 3000	—

①—176°F (80°C) @ 5000 RPM.
②—176–212°F (88–100°C) @ 5000 RPM.
③—Turbocharged.
④—195°F (90°C) @ 5000 RPM.

Alternator & Regulator Specifications

Ident. No.	Current Rating		Voltage Regulator	
	Amperes	Volts	Ident. No.	Voltage @ 75°F
0120469503	75	14	0192052006	13.7–14.5
0120469502	75	14	0192052006	13.7–14.5
91160312002	—	14	—	13.5–14.5
91160312004	—	14	91160391301	13.5–14.5
92860311303	90	14	—	13.5–14.5
92860311400	90	14	91160391301	13.5–14.5

Starting Motor Specifications

Year	Model/ Engine	Ident. No.	Brush Spring Tension Ounces	No Load Test			Torque Test		
				Amperes	Volts	R.P.M.	Amperes	Volts	Torque Lbs.
1983	924/2.0	1311122	40.5–45.8	30–50	11.5	5500–7500	350–450	8.5	13.02
	924/2.0②	1208221	40.5–47.6	35–55	11.5	6000–8000	320–410	8.5	9.04
	924/2.0①②	1311134	40.5–45.8	30–50	11.5	5500–7500	350–450	8.5	13.02
	911/3.0	1312100	28–31	55–85	11.5	8500–10500	650–730	6	13.74
	928/4.5	1312102	28.2–31.7	55–85	11.5	8500–10500	650–730	6	13.74

①—Heavy duty.
②—Turbocharged.

Valve Specifications

Year	Model/Engine	Valve Lash		Valve Angles		Valve Spring Installed Height	Valve Spring Pressure Lbs. @ In.	Stem Clearance		Stem Diameter, Standard	
		Int.	Exh.	Seat	Face			Intake	Exhaust	Intake	Exhaust
1983	944/4-151	③	③	45	45	②	—	.031	.031	.3531	.3524
	911SC/6-183	.0039	.0039	45	45	1.358	①	.0039	.0039	.3531	.3524
	928S/8-285	③	③	45	45	②	—	—	—	.3531	.3524
1984	944/4-151	③	③	45	45	②	—	.031	.031	.3531	.3524
	911 Carrera/6-193.2	—	—	—	—	—	—	—	—	—	—
	928S/8-285	③	③	45	45	②	—	—	—	.3531	.3524
1985	944/4-151	③	③	45	45	④	—	.031	.031	.3531	.3524
	944 Turbo/4-151	③	③	45	45	④	—	.031	.031	.3531	.3524
	911 Carrera/6-193.2	—	—	—	—	—	—	—	—	—	—
	928S/8-302	③	③	45	45	⑤	—	—	—	.2744	.2732
1986–87	944/4-151	③	③	45	45	1.614–1.634	—	.031	.031	.3531	.3524
	924S/4-151	③	③	45	45	1.614–1.634	—	.031	.031	—	—
	944 Turbo/4-151	③	③	45	45	1.614–1.634	—	.031	.031	.3531	.3524
	911 Carrera/6-193.2	—	—	—	—	—	—	—	—	—	—
	911 Turbo/6-201.3	—	—	—	—	—	—	—	—	—	—
	928S/8-302.5	③	③	45	45	⑤	—	—	—	.2744	.2732

①—Intake 176.4 lbs. @ 1.2 inch; exhaust 165.3 lbs. @ 1.24 inch.
②—Intake 1.614–1.634 inch; exhaust 1.575–1.594 inch.
③—Hydraulic cam followers, zero lash.
④—Intake 1.614–1.634 inch; exhaust, early models 1.575–1.594 inch, late models 1.614–1.634 inch.
⑤—Intake 1.677–1.697 inch; exhaust, 1.638–1.657 inch.

Engine Tightening Specifications

Torque specifications are for clean and lightly lubricated threads only. Dry or dirty threads produce increased friction which prevents accurate measurement of tightness.

Year	Model/Engine	Spark Plugs Ft. Lbs.	Cylinder Head Bolts Ft. Lbs.	Intake Manifold Ft. Lbs.	Exhaust Manifold Ft. Lbs.	Rocker Arm Shaft Camshaft Bracket Ft. Lbs.	Rocker Arm or Camshaft Cover Ft. Lbs.	Connecting Rod Cap Bolts Ft. Lbs.	Main Bearing Cap Bolts Ft. Lbs.	Flywheel to Crankshaft Ft. Lbs.	Vibration Damper or Pulley Ft. Lbs.
1983	944/4-151	20	⑥	—	—	③	14	⑤	②	66	151
	911SC/6-183	20	24	—	—	—	—	36.2	—	65	—
	928S/8-285	20	①	—	—	—	14	⑤	④	65	213
1984	944/4-151	20	⑥	—	—	③	14	⑤	②	66	151
	911 Carrera/6-193.2	—	—	—	—	—	—	—	—	—	—
	928S/8-285	20	①	—	—	—	14	⑤	④	65	213
1985	944/4-151	20	⑥	—	—	③	14	⑤	②	66	151
	944 Turbo/4-151	20	⑥	—	—	③	14	⑤	②	66	151
	911 Carrera/6-193.2	—	—	—	—	—	—	—	—	—	—
	928S/8-302	20	①	—	—	—	14	54	④	65	213
1986–87	944/4-151	20	⑥	—	—	③	14	⑤	②	66	151
	924S/4-151	20	⑥	—	—	③	14	⑤	④	66	151
	944 Turbo/4-151	20	⑥	—	—	③	14	⑤	②	66	151
	911 Carrera/6-193.2	—	—	—	—	—	—	—	—	—	—
	911 Turbo/6-201.3	—	—	—	—	—	—	—	—	—	—
	928S/302.5	20	①	—	—	—	14	54	④	65	213

Continued

ENGINE TIGHTENING SPECIFICATIONS—Continued

①—Grayish black colored bolts, torque in proper sequence in three steps to 14, 36 and 65 ft. lbs. Yellowish gold colored bolts, torque in proper sequence in three steps to 14 ft. lbs., plus an additional ½ turn in 90° increments.

②—Torque in proper sequence, M12 1.5 nuts in three steps; 14, 29 and 54 ft.lbs., and M10 nuts in two steps; 14 and 36 ft. lbs.

③—Hex socket bolt, 32 ft. lbs.; polygon socket bolt, 47 ft. lbs.

④—Torque in proper sequence. Engines with no "X" next to crankcase number: M12 1.5 nuts in three steps - 14, 29 and 43-46.6 ft. lbs., and M10 nuts in two steps 14 and 29-32.6 ft. lbs. Engines with "X" next to crankcase number: M12 1.5 nuts in three steps - 14, 29 and 54-57.6 ft. lbs. and M10 nuts in two steps - 14 and 36-39.6 ft. lbs.

⑤—With smooth bearing surface, 42-45 ft. lbs.; with ribbed bearing surface, 55-59 ft. lbs.

⑥—Torque in proper sequence to 14, 36 and 66 ft. lbs.

Pistons, Rings & Pins Specifications

Year	Model/Engine	Piston Clearance	Ring End Gap, ① Inch		Piston Pin Diameter Inch
			Comp.	Oil	
1983	944/2500	.0003-.00125	.0079-.0177	.01496-.0551	.9449
	911/3000	③	.004	④	.866
	928S/4600	.0009-.0019	.0078-.0157	.0157-.0551	.94492
1984	944/2500	.0003-.00125	.0079-.0177	.01496-.0551	.9449
	911/3200	—	—	—	—
	928S/4600	.0009-.0019	.0078-.0157	.0157-.0551	.9449
1985	944/2500	.0003-.00125	.0079-.0177	.01496-.0551	.9449
	944/2500②	.0003-.00125	.0079-.0177	.01496-.0551	.9449
	911/3200	—	—	—	—
	928S/5000	.0009-.0019	.0078-.0157	.0157-.0551	.9449
1986-87	944/2500	.0003-.00125	.0079-.0177	.01496-.0551	.9449
	924S	.0003-.00125	.0079-.0177	.01496-.0551	.9449
	944/2500②	.0003-.00125	.0079-.00125	.01496-.0551	.9449
	911/3200	—	—	—	—
	911/3300②	—	—	—	—
	928S/5000	.0009-.0019	.0078-.0157	.0157-.0551	.9449

①—Fit rings in tapered bore for clearance in tightest portion of ring travel.

②—Turbo.

③—Mahle type, .00098-.0016 inch; KS type, .00090-.0017 inch.

④—Standard type, .00098-.0018 inch, LS Schmidt type, .0014-.0023 inch; LS Mahle type, .0011-.0020 inch.

Crankshaft & Bearing Specifications

Year	Model/Engine	Rod Bearings, Inch		Main Bearings, Inch		Thrust on Bearing No.	Crankshaft End Play Inch
		Shaft Diameter	Bearing Clearance	Shaft Diameter	Bearing Clearance		
1983	944/2500	2.046–2.0468	.00133–.0036	2.7548–2.7555	.00078–.00385	1	.0043–.0123
	911/3000	2.085–2.086	—	①	③	1	.004–.007
	928S/4600	.046–2.0468	.0008–.00275	2.7548–2.7555	.0008–.0385	3	.0043–.0123
1984	944/2500	2.046–2.0468	.00133–.0036	2.7548–2.7555	.00078–.00385	1	.0043–.0123
	911/3200	—	—	—	—	—	—
	928S/4600	2.046–2.0468	.0008–.00275	2.7548–2.7555	.0008–.0385	3	.0043–.0123
1985	944/2500	2.046–2.0468	.00133–.0036	2.7548–2.7555	.0008–.0385	1	.0043–.0123
	944/2500②	2.046–2.0468	.00133–.0036	2.7548–2.7555	.0008–.0385	1	.0043–.0123
	911/3200	—	—	—	—	—	—
	928S/5000	2.046–2.0468	.0008–.00275	2.7548–2.7555	.0008–.0385	3	.0043–.0123
1986–87	944/2500	2.046–2.0468	.00133–.0036	2.7548–2.7555	.0008–.0385	1	.0043–.0123
	924S	2.046–2.0468	.00133–.0036	2.7548–2.7555	.0008–.0385	1	.0043–.0123
	944/2500②	2.046–2.0468	.00133–.0036	2.7548–2.7555	.0008–.0385	1	.0043–.0123
	911/3200	—	—	—	—	—	—
	911/3300②	—	—	—	—	—	—
	928S/5000	2.046–2.0468	.0008–.00275	2.7548–2.7555	.0008–.0385	3	.0043–.0123

①—No. 8 bearing shaft diameter, 1.2196–1.22019 inch; all others, 2.3610–2.3618 inch.
②—Turbo.
③—No. 8 bearing clearance, .0018–.004 inch; all others, .003–.0028 inch.

Front Wheel Alignment Specifications

Model	Caster Angle, Degrees		Camber Angle, Degrees		Toe Angle Degrees	Steering Axis	Track Differential Angle @ 20°	Front Axle Height Inch
	Limits	Desired	Limits	Desired				
911	5°50' to 6°20'	+6°5'	+20' to +40'	①	+10' to +20'	10°55'	0° to 30'	3.89 ± .196②
928	3° to 4°	3°30'	−40' to −20'	−30'	+10 to +20'	—	−1°20' to −40'	6.69-8.27③
944	2°15' to 3°	2°30'	−35' to −5'	−20'	+5' to +15'	—	−1°20' to −40'	—
944②	2°30' to 3°	2°30'	−35' to −5'	−20'	+5' to +15'	—	−1°20' to −40'	—

①—Max. camber difference, left to right 10'.
②—Wheel center above torsion bar center.
③—Wheel ground surface to measuring surface on crossmember.

Rear Wheel Alignment Specifications

Model	Camber Angle, Degrees Limits	Camber Angle, Degrees Desired	Toe-In, Degrees	Rear Axle Height
911	−10' to +10'	0°	0° to +20'	1.26 to 1.65 in.①
928	−50' to −30'	−40'	5' to 15'	6.4173 to 7.2047 in.③
944	−1°20' to −40'	−1°	−5' to +5'②	④

①—Height adjustment measured from center of wheel to center of rear torsion bar.
②—Per wheel.
③—Height adjustment measured from wheel ground surface to measuring surface on crossmember.
④—Distance from measuring point on level ground to upper edge of bumper must be 19.7637–21.3385 inches.

Brake Specifications

Year	Model	Rear Drum I.D.	Wheel Cyl. Bore Front Disc	Wheel Cyl. Bore Rear Drum	Nominal Thickness Front	Nominal Thickness Rear	Minimum Thickness Front	Minimum Thickness Rear	Thickness Variation (Parallelism) Front	Thickness Variation (Parallelism) Rear	Run Out (TIR) Front	Run Out (TIR) Rear	Finish (microinch) Front	Finish (microinch) Rear	Master Cylinder I.D.
1983	911	—	—	—	.807	.787	.752	.732	.0007	.0007	.0039	.0039	.0023	.0023	.8125
1983–87	928	—	—	—	②	.787	①	.756	.00079	.00079	.0039	.0039	.00023	.00023	.9374
1983–87	944	—	—	—	.807	.787	.752	.756	.00079	.00079	.0039	.0039	.00023	.00023	.9374

(Columns "Nominal Thickness" through "Finish (microinch)" are under the heading "Disc Brake Rotor".)

①—Floating frame .7559 inch; floating caliper 1.2283 inch.
②—Floating frame less grooved disc, .7874 inch; floating frame with grooved disc .8071 inch; floating caliper 1.2598 inch.

Cooling System & Capacity Data

Year	Model	Cooling Capacity, Qts. With A/C	Cooling Capacity, Qts. Less A/C	Radiator Cap Relief Pressure With A/C	Radiator Cap Relief Pressure Less A/C	Thermo. Opening Temp. F°	Fuel Tank Gals.	Engine Oil Refill Qts.	Transmission Oil Pts. Manual	Transmission Oil Pts. Auto.	Final Drive Oil Pts.
1983	911SC	—	—	—	—	—	21.1	13.7④	—	5.2①	—
1983	928S	16.9	16.9	—	—	—	22.7	7.9④	8	③	②
1983	944	8.2	8.2	—	—	177.5–184.5	17.4	5.8④	5.4	③	2.1
1984	944	9	9	—	—	177.5–184.5	16.4	5.3④	4	6.9④	2.2
1984–85	911 Carrera	—	—	—	—	—	21	13.7④	—	—	—
1984–87	928S	16	16	13–16	13–16	178–185	22.7	7.9④	8	③	—
1985	944	9	9	—	—	177.5–184.5	16.4	5.3④	4	6.9④	2.2
1985	944 Turbo	9	9	—	—	177.5–184.5	16.4	5.3④	4	6.9④	2.2
1986–87	911 Carrera	—	—	—	—	—	22.5	13.7④	—	—	—
1986–87	911 Turbo	—	—	—	—	—	22.5	13.7④	—	—	—
1986–87	944	9	9	—	—	177.5–184.5	21	6.3④	4	6.9④	2.2
1986–87	944 Turbo	9	9	—	—	177.5–184.5	21	6.9④	4	6.9④	2.2

①—Transmission with differential.
②—Automatic transmission only.
③—Refill, 5.8 qts.
④—Total capacity.

ELECTRICAL SECTION

INDEX

ALTERNATOR IN-VEHICLE TESTS

911

1. Connect suitable alternator test equipment as per manufacturer's instructions.
2. Turn off all electrical accessories, then start engine and run at 3000 RPM.
3. Adjust load to maximum ammeter reading while maintaining voltage of at least 12 volts.
4. If ammeter reading is more than 16 amps below alternator rating, replace regulator and retest.
5. If ammeter reading is still too low, replace alternator.

STARTER REPLACE

1. Disconnect battery ground cable.
2. Disconnect battery and alternator wiring, if equipped.
3. Disconnect ignition lead.
4. Remove starter attaching bolts, then the starter.
5. Reverse procedure to install.

IGNITION SWITCH REPLACE

911

1. Disconnect battery ground cable.
2. Remove ignition switch cover.
3. Drill out shear bolts and remove retaining screw.
4. Pull switch down far enough to allow removal of electrical connectors.
5. Remove ignition/starter switch retaining screws, then the switch.
6. Reverse procedure to install, tightening shear bolts until heads break off.

928

1. Disconnect battery ground cable.
2. Remove steering column switch cover.
3. Remove steering column switch attaching bolt.
4. Disconnect switch electrical connector(s), then remove switch.
5. Reverse procedure to install.

HEADLIGHT SWITCH REPLACE

924S & 944

1. Press retainers on top and bottom of switch together.
2. Remove switch through back of dash.
3. Disconnect switch wiring.
4. Reverse procedure to install.

928

1. Remove switch knob.
2. Compress retaining springs.
3. Remove switch through front of instrument panel.

STOPLIGHT SWITCH REPLACE

911

1. Disconnect flat electrical connector.
2. Remove retaining screws and remove switch.
3. Reverse procedure to install.

928

1983

1. Disconnect electrical connections from brake switch.
2. Remove switch from master cylinder.
3. Reverse procedure to install.

1984–87

1. Disconnect electrical connectors at switch.
2. Remove mounting nuts attaching switch to bracket adjacent to brake pedal.
3. Remove stop light switch.
4. Reverse procedure to install.

924S & 944

1. Disconnect electrical connectors at switch.
2. Remove mounting nuts attaching switch to bracket adjacent to brake pedal.
3. Remove stop light switch.
4. Reverse procedure to install.

NEUTRAL SAFETY SWITCH REPLACE

928

1. Place transmission lever in neutral position.
2. Disconnect electrical connections.
3. Remove operating lever retaining bolt.
4. Remove switch mounting bolts.
5. Install switch and mounting bolts.
6. Install operating lever on shaft.
7. Install lugs of driving dog into switch.
8. Install retaining bolt.
9. Install electrical connection.
10. Place transmission lever in neutral position.
11. Loosen adjusting nut.
12. Install 4 mm pin from US8030 tool set through drive dog into locating hole in case.
13. Tighten adjusting screw and remove locating pin.

928S

1. Disconnect selector lever cable at transmission.
2. Remove range selector lever retaining bolt and disconnect lever at transmission.
3. Unlock neutral safety and back-up light switch electrical connector by turning white plastic ring clockwise.
4. Carefully pry off plug with two screwdrivers.
5. Remove two switch mounting screws and the switch.
6. Install switch but do not tighten mounting screws.

7. Install range selector lever that lug on switch engages and move range selector lever to "N" position.
8. Install range selector lever retaining bolt, torquing to 7 ft. lbs.
9. Insert 4 mm drill bit through lug into locating bore in switch housing.
10. Torque switch attaching screws to 7 ft. lbs., then remove drill bit.
11. Press on electrical connector and turn white plastic ring counterclockwise to lock.
12. Attach selector lever cable on selector range lever.

TURN SIGNAL, HEADLIGHT DIMMER & HORN SWITCH

REPLACE

928

1. Disconnect battery ground cable.
2. Remove steering wheel.
3. Remove cover under steering column switch.
4. Remove steering column mounting bolts.
5. Remove instrument cover mounting screws.
6. Remove instrument cover and disconnect electrical connections.
7. Remove instrument column switch.
8. Reverse procedure to install.

924S & 944

1. Disconnect battery ground cable.
2. Manually pull off steering wheel cover.
3. Remove steering column cover mounting screws.
4. Remove steering column switch attaching screws and the steering column cover.
5. Disconnect electrical connector at switch.
6. Disconnect electrical connector for cruise control switch.
7. Reverse procedure to install.

INSTRUMENT CLUSTER

REPLACE

911

Electrical connections are accessible from luggage compartment.

1. Disconnect battery ground cable.
2. Disconnect electrical connections from instrument to be removed.
3. On models with mechanical speedometer, remove flex shaft knurled nut.
4. Remove knurled instrument retaining nuts and retaining clamp.
5. Remove instrument from passenger compartment.
6. Reverse procedure to install.

1983–84 & EARLY 1985 944

1. Disconnect battery ground cable.
2. Reach behind instrument panel and push tachometer and combination instrument from cluster.
3. Reach through tachometer and combination instrument openings and push speedometer from cluster.
4. Reverse procedure to install. **Do not apply pressure to glass when installing.**

928

1. Disconnect battery ground cable.
2. Remove steering wheel.
3. Remove steering column switch.
4. Remove instrument cover mounting screws.
5. Remove rear window wiper and defogger switch.
6. Disconnect electrical connections.
7. Lift and tilt instrument cluster to rear.
8. Remove mounting bolt and remove cluster.
9. Reverse procedure to install.

924S, LATE 1985 & 1986–87 944

1. Disconnect battery ground cable.
2. Manually remove steering wheel cover.
3. Remove steering wheel.
4. Remove eight instrument cover attaching screws and the cover.
5. Remove four instrument cluster attaching screws.
6. Pull cluster out far enough to gain access to electrical connectors.
7. Unlock and disconnect electrical connectors at cluster.
8. Remove cluster from vehicle.
9. Reverse procedure to install.

WINDSHIELD WIPER SWITCH

REPLACE

928

Refer to "Turn Signal, Headlight Dimmer & Horn Switch, Replace" procedure.

WINDSHIELD WIPER MOTOR & TRANSMISSION

REPLACE

911

1. Disconnect battery ground cable.
2. Remove luggage compartment cover from rear of compartment.
3. Remove wiper arms.
4. Remove rubber discs located below wiper arms, then the retaining hex nuts.
5. Remove wiper motor with linkage downward and disconnect electrical connector.
6. Remove wiper motor from linkage.
7. Reverse procedure to install.

1983–84 & EARLY 1985 944

1. Disconnect battery ground cable.
2. Remove cover from wiper motor.
3. Disconnect wiper linkage.
4. Disconnect electrical connections.
5. Remove motor retaining bolts.
6. Remove frame mounting bolt and lift frame slightly.
7. Remove motor. **Install electrical connections and turn on ignition before securing linkage. Position arms in off position and install linkage.**

928S

1. Disconnect battery ground cable.
2. Remove fresh air chamber seal, then pull cover off.
3. Remove wiper arms and wiper arm bases.
4. Disconnect electrical connection in fresh air chamber.
5. Remove wiper assembly by pulling toward right side.
6. Disconnect wiper motor from wiper assembly.
7. Reverse procedure to install.

924S, LATE 1985 & 1986–87 944

1. Disconnect battery ground cable.
2. Remove windshield wiper arms.
3. Pull off rubber seal with cover from above and loosen cement of cover below windshield.
4. Disconnect wiper motor electrical connector.
5. Remove wiper assembly attaching screws and the assembly.
6. Reverse procedure to install.

HEATER CORE

REPLACE

928

1. If equipped with AC, discharge system refrigerant.
2. On vehicles equipped with electric seat operation, run seat back to rearmost position.
3. Disconnect battery ground cable from body.
4. Remove steering wheel impact pad and disconnect horn leads. Mark relation of steering wheel to shaft (paint mark), remove retaining nut, and remove steering wheel.
5. Remove covers below instrument cowl (pod) and steering column switch.
6. Loosen steering column switch mounting screw.
7. Remove instrument cowl (pod) mounting screws. Lift cowl, disconnect harness plugs at steering column switch, and remove switch.
8. Remove five switches mounted in cowl by removing knobs, then pressing in on spring clips to release switches from cowl. Disconnect harness plugs from switches. Mark for installation.
9. Disconnect harness plugs to printed circuit and mark for installation.
10. Lift cowl off and remove.
11. Remove heater A/C control as follows:
    a. Remove accelerator pedal kick plate, then remove carpet panel retaining screws at console sides. Remove carpet panels and insulation sheets.
    b. Remove parcel tray and glove box assembly.
    c. Remove gearshift knob and boot.
    d. Remove center vent control knob.

then carefully pry out center vent assembly. **Center vent must be removed without turning or twisting housing, as mounting pins may be broken off.**

e. Remove console mounting screws at instrument panel and tunnel.
f. Remove radio mounting nut at bracket (disregard for plug in type).
g. Remove harness leads at hazard switch, ashtray lamp, radio, clock, seat belt lamp, heater/fresh air control switch, central warning panel, blower switch, power window, and electric sunroof controls.
h. Disengage spring clips at control switch and disconnect vacuum line adapter.
i. Disconnect heater flap control cable at heater-A/C unit. Carefully draw cable from between instrument panel and heater-A/C unit.
j. Lift off console assembly to gain access to rear of control assembly. Remove control assembly.

12. Remove bracket for radio and speed control, then place to right side.
13. Remove three retaining screws at instrument panel, then remove steering protection tube.
14. Remove left and right side instrument panel mounting screws. Disconnect side ventilation.
15. Disconnect vacuum line clips. Disconnect yellow and green vacuum lines from actuators at footwell flap and defroster flap.
16. Remove instrument panel.
17. Remove duct hoses from side ventilators to A/C-heater unit.
18. Remove four screws and remove defroster vents.
19. Open vehicle hood. Remove blower cover at right cowl.
20. Remove two clamping screws at rubber connection between blower and A/C-heater unit. Disconnect harness leads at temperature switch.
21. Disconnect wiper linkage at wiper motor to provide clearance.
22. Disconnect harness plugs at resistor block/safety switch. Disconnect violet vacuum line at shut-off flap actuator.
23. Disconnect refrigerant lines at expansion valve, and plug open connections.
24. Disconnect heater hoses at heater core.
25. Remove upper and lower mounting nuts at A/C-heater unit. Disconnect drain hose, then lift out unit from mounting.
26. Remove heater core from heater A/C housing.
27. Reverse procedure to install.

924S & 944

1. Disconnect battery ground cable.
2. Remove splash guard and drain cooling system.
3. Remove steering wheel, if necessary, and steering column switch.
4. Remove instrument cluster frame.
5. Remove radio.
6. Remove A/C knee guard or shelf, if equipped.
7. Remove control switch and blower knobs, then remove frame from heater control assembly.
8. Remove instrument cluster assembly.
9. Disconnect control switch electrical connector. Disengage and pull out blower switch and disconnect electrical connector.
10. Disconnect electrical connectors from center console, then remove center console.
11. Remove radio speaker cover and speakers. Remove instrument panel center.
12. Remove left and right A pillar covers.
13. Remove instrument panel from the left and right sides.
14. Remove instrument panel from heater control housing, then disconnect air hoses and pull out instrument panel.
15. Remove pulse transmitter plug holder and position aside.
16. Disconnect heater valve control cable and remove heater valve.
17. Press out plastic button on blower cover, then disconnect seal on body and remove cover.
18. Remove flap duct (box) assembly.
19. Disconnect electrical connector, then remove blower assembly attaching bolts.
20. Remove blower.
21. Remove inside holder above heater core case.
22. Coat heater hoses in engine compartment with soapy water, then remove heater core case with heater hoses.
23. Separate case halves and remove heater core.
24. Reverse procedure to install, noting the following:
    a. Check position of cables between control switch and defroster flap as well as heater valve.
    b. Connect heater hoses before installing heater core case.
    c. Lubricate double grommet and heater hoses with soapy water and slide heater hoses in while installing heater core case assembly.
    d. Place cover into fresh air chamber before tightening heater core case attaching screws.
    e. Lengthen seal uniformly before installing onto cover assembly.
    f. Temporarily place strip of plastic sheeting on seal in rear of cover while installing cover assembly.

BLOWER MOTOR REPLACE

928

1. Disconnect battery ground cable.
2. Mark position of hood and remove.
3. Remove right windshield wiper arm.
4. Remove blower cover and mounting bolts from left and right fenders.
5. Open rubber connector between blower and heater/air conditioner. **Do not remove rubber connector from heater/air conditioner.**
6. Disconnect blower electrical connections.
7. Remove blower mounting bolts as follows:
    a. Open flap of intake housing by moving control lever to "air conditioner."
    b. Using a suitable screwdriver, remove mounting screw through open flap.
    c. Remove screw on outside and inside of blower housing.
8. Close main shut-off flap and lift apron outer section.
9. Remove blower.
10. Reverse procedure to install.

924S & 944

1. Disconnect battery ground cable.
2. Remove splash guard and drain coolant.
3. Remove steering wheel and steering column switch.
4. Remove instrument cluster frame.
5. Remove radio housing.
6. Remove A/C knee guard or shelf, if equipped.
7. Remove radio.
8. Remove control switch and blower knobs, then the heater control assembly frame.
9. Remove instrument cluster.
10. Disconnect electrical connector from control switch and remove switch.
11. Disconnect electrical connectors from center console, then remove center console.
12. Remove radio speaker mask and speakers, then the instrument panel center.
13. Remove left and right A pillar covers.
14. Remove instrument panel from left and right sides.
15. Remove instrument panel from heater housing assembly.
16. Disconnect air hoses and remove instrument panel.
17. Remove pulse transmitter plug holder and position aside.
18. Disconnect heater valve control cable and remove heater valve.
19. Press out plastic button on blower cover, then disconnect seal on body and remove cover.
20. Remove flap housing (box) assembly.
21. Disconnect electrical connector, remove blower assembly attaching bolts, then the blower motor.
22. Reverse procedure to install.

4 CYLINDER ENGINE SECTION

INDEX

HYDRAULIC ENGINE MOUNTS REPLACE

REMOVAL

1. Disconnect battery ground cable.
2. Suspend engine from front transport bracket using tool VW10-222 or equivalent and hold firmly in installed position. **It may be necessary to disconnect air flow sensor electrical connector and/or vent hose at air cleaner to gain access to transport bracket.**
3. Raise and support vehicle.
4. Remove splash guard.
5. Disconnect stabilizer mounts at control arms and the stabilizer suspension at side members and remove stabilizer.
6. Remove right engine mount shield attaching nut from front axle crossmember.
7. Remove hydraulic engine mount attaching nut from front axle crossmember.
8. On vehicles equipped with power steering, proceed as follows:
   a. On 1983 models, disconnect brake pad wear indicator wire and remove clip from bolt.
   b. On all models, disconnect power steering return line at side member.
9. On all models, disconnect universal joint at steering gear, hydraulic engine mount at engine brackets and front axle crossmember at side members. Mark relationship of universal joint to steering gear for proper assembly. Do not loosen control arm mounting bolts.
10. Pull down front axle crossmember far enough to allow removal of engine mount and disconnect driveshaft universal joint at steering gear.
11. Disengage top of engine mount from front axle crossmember.
12. Remove mount toward front of vehicle, turning mount 180° as necessary to facilitate removal.

INSTALLATION

1. Insert mount so that twist is positioned on stop at rear on right hand side and press top of mount into front axle crossmember.
2. Push correctly positioned driveshaft universal joint onto steering gear pinion.
3. Install front axle crossmember, raise crossmember with suitable lifting device to facilitate insertion of bolts, center crossmember and torque mounting bolts to 62 ft. lbs.
4. install but do not tighten mount attaching nuts and bolts.
5. Remove tool VW10-222, then connect air flow sensor electrical connector and the air cleaner vent hose.
6. Using new self locking nuts, torque to 22 ft. lbs. in order; hydraulic engine mount to front axle crossmember, hydraulic engine mount to engine brackets, universal joint to steering gear.
7. On vehicles equipped with power steering, secure return line and, if applicable, the brake pad wear indicator wire on side member.
8. Install right engine mount shield, stabilizer and splash guard, torquing stabilizer to body and control arms attaching bolts to 17 ft. lbs.

ENGINE REPLACE

924S & 944 W/MANUAL TRANSMISSION

1. Disconnect battery ground cable.
2. Raise and support vehicle.
3. Disconnect positive battery cable and push through splash wall together with rubber grommet.
4. Disconnect two engine wiring harness plugs and remove wire clamps.
5. Disconnect wire plugs from control unit located by steering column.
6. Push wires and plugs through splash wall, then disconnect sensor wire bracket from intake pipe.
7. Disconnect throttle operating cable.
8. Disconnect and remove vacuum hose from brake booster.
9. Remove distributor cap, distributor rotor, and dust cap.
10. Disconnect ground wire at splash wall.
11. Clamp fuel return line and disconnect fuel feed line.
12. Disconnect fuel return line.
13. Attach tool VW 10-222 or equivalent to front transport bracket of engine and secure engine in installed position.
14. Open heater regulating valve and remove cap from expansion tank.
15. Remove splash shield.
16. Remove exhaust assembly by unscrewing flange, exhaust manifold and exhaust pipe connections, and suspension points.
17. Disconnect oxygen sensor plug and wire in metal lug on firewall.
18. Disconnect electrical connections of starter, then remove starter mounting bolts and the starter.
19. Remove clutch line clamp located on engine.
20. Disconnect clutch slave cylinder from clutch housing, leaving lines connected.
21. Disconnect stabilizer at body and control arms and remove stabilizer.
22. Remove right engine mount shield from front axle crossmember.
23. Unscrew universal joint on steering gear, tie rods on steering arms, upper hydraulic engine mount on engine braces, left and right control arms on front axle crossmember, and remove front axle crossmember with steering from underneath vehicle.
24. On vehicles with air conditioning, proceed as follows:
   a. Unscrew poly-rib belt tensioner and remove belt.
   b. Remove compressor from mount, leaving hoses attached, and suspend compressor from spring strut.
25. Drain coolant through drain plug bore in radiator.
26. Remove coolant hose from bottom of radiator.

27. Remove upper central tube attaching bolts.
28. Lower vehicle.
29. Remove coolant hose from heater valve, heater coolant return hose, and coolant feed hoses from expansion tank.
30. Remove A/C fast idle hose and the charcoal venting hose.
31. Disconnect vacuum lines at vent valve and thermo valve.
32. Remove upper radiator hose and radiator vent hose.
33. Disconnect electrical connectors of temperature switch and both cooling fans.
34. Remove upper radiator brackets and lift out radiator with cooling fans.
35. Attach tool US 1105 or equivalent to engine with shorter end toward rear of engine.
36. Lift engine slightly and remove tool VW 10-222.
37. Remove lower central tube mounting bolts.
38. Lower engine, pull forward, and remove from underneath vehicle.
39. Reverse procedure to install.

944 TURBO W/MANUAL TRANSMISSION

1. Disconnect battery ground cable.
2. Raise and support vehicle.
3. Remove both tire and wheel assemblies.
4. Disconnect ground lead from battery and body.
5. Disconnect battery positive cable, separate cable harness and push both cables with rubber grommet through firewall.
6. Label, then disconnect all electrical connectors and vacuum lines from engine.
7. Loosen fuel return hose clamp and disconnect hose.
8. Disconnect fuel feed hose.
9. Disconnect cable from cruise control motor.
10. Remove upper air cleaner assembly.
11. Remove both charging/air guide pipes.
12. Remove lower air cleaner assembly and air flow sensor.
13. Loosen, then remove distributor cover.
14. Remove oil filter and supply reservoir.
15. Disconnect throttle operating cable.
16. Remove coolant expansion tank cap.
17. Remove front and lower trim panel and engine splash guard.
18. Loosen coolant drain plug. Disconnect alternator vent hose.
19. Disconnect coolant line from radiator.
20. Disconnect oil cooler from body.
21. Disconnect cooling fan electrical connectors.
22. Remove cooling fan.
23. Loosen coolant hoses on coolant pipe (crossmember) and remove crossmember.
24. Disconnect coolant and vent hose from radiator.
25. Disconnect temperature switch electrical connector from radiator.
26. Disconnect turbocharger to expansion tank cooling line.
27. Disconnect tank discharging valve suction line from intake air cowl.
28. Remove coolant (water) pump and bracket assembly from body.
29. Remove radiator holder and radiator assembly.
30. Attach support tool 10-222A or equivalent to front transport bracket and secure in installed position.
31. Loosen drive belt tensioner on A/C compressor and remove drive belt.
32. Loosen A/C compressor attaching bolts and position compressor aside. Do not disconnect refrigerant lines.
33. Remove stabilizer bar attaching bolts, then the stabilizer bar.
34. Disconnect left and right tie rods.
35. Disconnect and cap cooler lines and steering gear lines.
36. Loosen power steering pump attaching bolts and allow to hang down on steering gear assembly.
37. Loosen left and right control arms on front axle crossmember and rear mount. Pull assembly out from the front. Do not loosen console attaching bolts.
38. Remove exhaust assembly together with catalytic converter. Loosen bolts on flange between turbocharger and exhaust pipe as well as flange on bypass valve.
39. Loosen hose clamp, exhaust flange and bypass valve holder. Remove bypass valve. Loosen bracket on transaxle from bottom and push backward.
40. Loosen upper transaxle/clutch housing attaching bolts.
41. Disconnect heater coolant hoses from cylinder head and above exhaust manifold.
42. Loosen wire strap on firewall. Disconnect two pin and multi-pin electrical connectors. Remove diagnosis electrical connector downward.
43. Connect tool 3033 or equivalent, onto engine transport bracket as follow:
    a. With tool in position 3 (pulley), the threaded rod is below the suspension unit.
    b. With tool in position 11 (flywheel), the threaded rod is above the suspension fixture.
44. Using a suitable hoist, slightly tighten suspension fixture on engine and remove tool 10-222A.
45. Remove lower transaxle/clutch housing attaching bolts.
46. Pull engine forward, press rubber sleeve out of separating wall toward engine compartment and carefully remove wire harness.
47. Separate engine from central tube or central shaft (driveshaft), then lower engine.
48. Reverse procedure to install.

CYLINDER HEAD REPLACE

1. Disconnect battery ground cable.
2. Remove cap from expansion tank.
3. Remove splash guard.
4. Drain coolant through coolant drain plug on radiator.
5. Remove drive belt, then the drive belt cover.
6. Turn engine to TDC of cylinder No. 1.
7. Remove distributor cap, distributor rotor, and dust cover.
8. Remove distributor cap mount.
9. Slacken belt tension and pull camshaft belt off of camshaft sprocket.
10. Loosen two mounting bolts on rear drive belt cover.
11. Disconnect fuel lines.
12. Remove plastic cover from fuel collection tube, pull off wire plugs on fuel injectors, and position wiring harness out of way.
13. Unscrew aluminum plugs, coolant line, and bolts with attached washers, then remove camshaft housing from cylinder head. **Ensure that hydraulic valve tappets do not fall out and are not mixed up.**
14. Remove air cleaner assembly.
15. Remove intake brace attaching bolt.
16. Remove intake distributor by dismantling holder on oil dipstick tube, hose on brake booster, hose on intake distributor, retaining clamp on accelerator cable, and mounting bolts of intake distributor/cylinder head.
17. Remove bolts from flange connecting catalytic converter and exhaust manifold.
18. Remove hose clamp from heater regulating valve and the two screws on neck of cooling circuit.
19. Remove cylinder head attaching bolts in a criss-cross fashion from outside to inside, then remove cylinder head.
20. Reverse procedure to install, noting the following:
    a. Coat threads of cylinder head bolts with light film of engine oil.
    b. Torque bolts in sequence, **Fig. 1**, to 14, 38 and 65 ft. lbs. **When torquing cylinder head bolts, never lubricate bolts. Only lightly coat stud threads with clean engine oil. The washers must not turn when torquing.**
    c. Wait 30 minutes, then unscrew bolts 1/2 turn and torque to 61 ft. lbs. in sequence, **Fig. 1. Washers must not turn when torquing cylinder head bolts.**
    d. Torque camshaft housing socket head bolts to 14 ft. lbs. and aluminum plugs to 29 ft. lbs.

VALVE ARRANGEMENT

Front to rear . . . . E-I-E-I-E-I-E-I

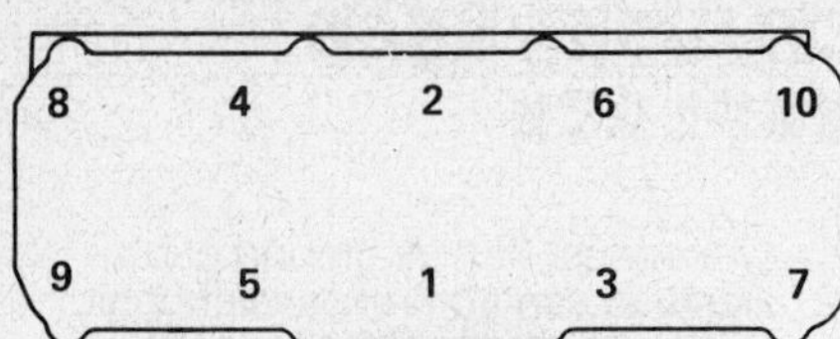

Fig. 1 Cylinder head tightening sequence. 1986–87 924S & 944

VALVE LIFT SPECIFICATIONS

Vehicle	Year	Intake	Exhaust
944	1983-87	.315 inch	.315 inch

VALVE TIMING

INTAKE OPENS AFTER TDC

Year	Model	Degrees
1983-87	944	1

VALVE GUIDES

924S & 944

1. Clean and inspect cylinder head. Cylinder heads whose valve seats or sealing surfaces can no longer be machined are not suitable for replacement of valve guides.
2. Using spot facer, grind off enough of valve guides protruding from camshaft end so that guides are flush with cylinder head. **Be careful not to damage guide collar for spring retainers.**
3. Place cylinder head on tool 9220 or equivalent.
4. Using tool 9224 or equivalent, loosen valve guides from camshaft end by tapping lightly, then press out rest of guides using suitable press.
5. Measure bores in cylinder head with an internal gauge.
6. Using replacement valve guide part No. 92810432852, grind until outside diameter is .0024-.0031 inch greater than bore measurement.
7. Coat valve guides with talcum powder and install by tapping lightly, then, using tool 9221 or equivalent, align valve guides and press into cylinder head against stop from camshaft side. **If suitable equipment is available, cool valve guides in liquid oxygen and press into cylinder head heated to 374°F. Cylinder head should not be heated to 374°F. for longer than 90 minutes.**
8. Using broach, ream out valve guides to .3543-.3549 inch.

CAMSHAFT REPLACE

924S & 944

1. Disassemble balance shaft drive, **Fig. 2**, noting the following:
   a. Handle balance shaft drive belt with care, do not twist or turn. Store separately.
   b. When removing upper balance shaft drive gear attaching bolt, hold gear with tool 9200 or equivalent.
2. Disassemble camshaft drive, **Fig. 2**, noting the following:
   a. When removing camshaft sprocket attaching bolt, hold dog with tool 9205 or equivalent.
3. Disassemble camshaft housing, **Fig. 3**, noting the following:
   a. Store valve tappets in order with oil bores facing up.
4. Assemble camshaft housing, noting the following:
   a. Cylinder No. 1 must be at TDC and camshaft sprocket must be aligned with mark when installing camshaft housing.
   b. Never crank engine when camshaft belt is loose or removed.
   c. Apply suitable locking compound to distributor rotor attaching bolt and connector attaching bolt when installing.
   d. Ensure that distributor dust cap is correctly positioned.
   e. When installing camshaft sprocket attaching bolt, hold dog with tool 9205 or equivalent and torque bolt to 48 ft. lbs. Use only polygon head bolts when assembling.
   f. Install camshaft sprocket with mark aligned.
   g. Lubricate sealing lip of new front shaft seal and install seal using tool 9202 or equivalent. Install new camshaft bearing cap gasket.
   h. Lubricate and install new camshaft bearing cap O-ring.
   i. Torque valve cover attaching bolts to 14 ft. lbs.
   j. Lubricate camshaft bearings with suitable lubricant.
   k. Install new valve cover gasket with "TOP" mark facing up.
   l. Install new gasket for rear camshaft housing cover.
5. Assemble camshaft drive, installing camshaft drive belt as follows:
   a. Turn engine crankshaft to TDC for cylinder No. 1. TDC marks on flywheel and cast clutch housing must be aligned.
   b. Align mark on camshaft sprocket with mark on rear drive belt cover.
   c. Place belt on crankshaft sprocket, tension roller, water pump pulley, and camshaft sprocket, in that order, slightly preloading belt by hand each time.
   d. Turn tensioner counterclockwise to tighten belt, then torque attaching nut to 32 ft. lbs.
   e. Turn engine two revolutions clockwise and align TDC mark on camshaft sprocket with cast mark in mount for distributor cap.
   f. Turn crankshaft clockwise approximately 10°, then check drive belt tension and correct as necessary.
6. Assemble balance shaft drive.
7. On 1983 models, install balance shaft upper drive gear as follows:
   a. Ensure that woodruff key groove of balance shaft faces up, then install drive gear with groove code "O" toward woodruff key.

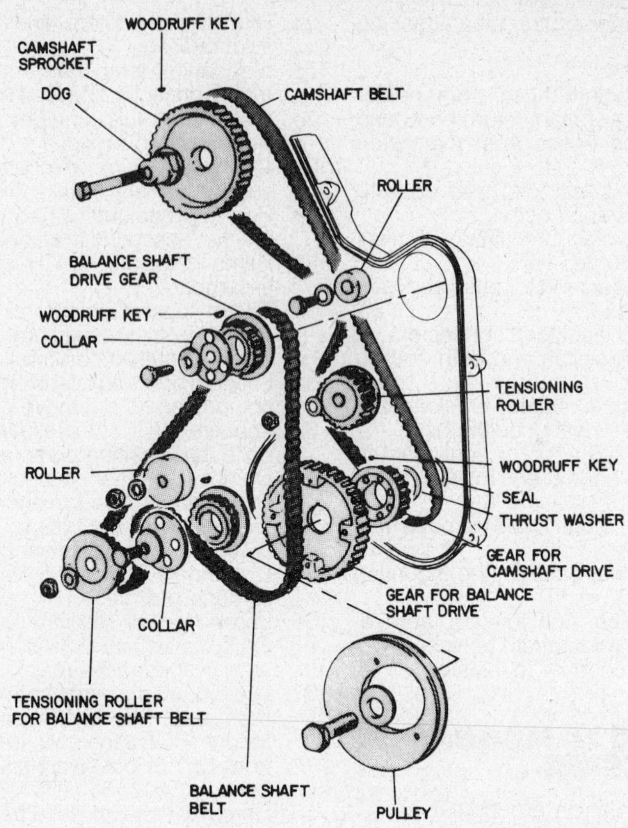

Fig. 2 Balance shaft drive & camshaft drive exploded view. 1986–87 924S & 944

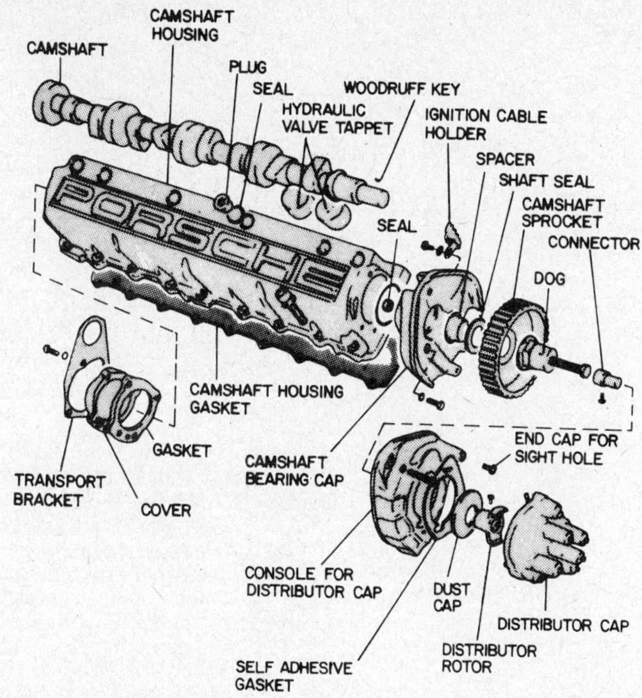

Fig. 3 Camshaft housing exploded view. 1986–87 924S & 944

b. Install bolt, washer and collar, aligning collar so that codes "O" and "U" can be seen in large bores.

8. On 1983 models, install balance shaft lower drive gear as follows:
   a. Ensure that woodruff key groove of balance shaft faces up, then install drive gear with groove code "U" facing woodruff key.
   b. Using tool 9200 or equivalent, tighten bolt.
9. On 1984-87 models, install balance shaft upper drive gear as follows:
   a. Ensure that woodruff key groove of balance shaft faces up and insert woodruff key.
   b. Apply thin coat of Optimoly HT or equivalent on drive gear bearing surface.
   c. Install drive gear with groove code "O" toward woodruff key.
   d. Install collar with locating tab inserted into unmarked groove of drive gear so that code "O" is visible in large bore of collar.
   e. Coat threads of bolt with suitable locking compound and install bolt and washer.
   f. Using tool 9200 or equivalent, torque bolt to 33 ft. lbs.
10. On 1984-87 models, install balance shaft lower drive gear as follows:
   a. Ensure that woodruff key of balance shaft faces up and insert woodruff key.
   b. Apply thin coat of Optimoly HT or equivalent on drive gear bearing surface.
   c. Install drive gear with groove code "O" opposite woodruff key.
   d. Install collar with its locating tab inserted into groove "O" of drive gear so that "O" is visible in square opening of collar.
   e. Coat threads of bolt with suitable locking compound and install bolt and washer.
   f. Using tool 9200 or equivalent, torque bolt to 33 ft. lbs.
11. Install balance shaft drive belt as follows:
   a. Turn crankshaft clockwise until TDC mark on camshaft sprocket is aligned with mark cast on distributor cap mount.
   b. Ensure that TDC marks on flywheel and cast clutch housing are aligned.
   c. Rotate both balance shafts until marks of balance shaft sprockets align with marks on rear drive belt cover.
   d. Install drive belt with color coded tooth facing out. Do not twist belt.
12. Adjust balance shaft portion of drive belt as follows:
   a. Loosen idler pulley so pulley does not contact drive belt.
   b. Turn crankshaft clockwise until TDC mark on camshaft sprocket aligns with cast marking on distributor cap mount.
   c. With engine in this position, TDC marks on flywheel and cast clutch housing must also be aligned properly.
   d. Alignment marks on sprockets should be aligned with marks of rear drive belt cover.
   e. Install tool P9201 or equivalent. Pull out lock pin on tool and push out gauge pin opposite the lock pin completely.
   f. Zero the telltale needle.
   g. Slide tool onto belt. Push in gauge needle until lock pin engages (audible click).
   h. Note reading obtained from dial gauge of tool. **Always zero the telltale needle on gauge tool after the lock pin has engaged (turned counterclockwise) to eliminate incorrect gauge readings.**
   i. Reading obtained should be 2.4-3. To adjust, turn tensioner clockwise to tighten or counterclockwise to loosen. After adjustment tighten attaching nut.
   j. After adjusting tension, adjust idler pulley. Using tool 9207 or a .0196 inch (.5 mm) feeler gauge, ensure a clearance of .0196 inch (.5 mm) between drive belt and pulley when upper portion of drive belt is preloaded approximately 0-.039 inch (0-1 mm). With correct clearance obtained, tighten idler pulley attaching nut. If correct clearance cannot be obtained, turn idler pulley 180° and repeat adjustment. After adjustment tighten nut.
13. Adjust camshaft portion of drive belt as follows:
   a. Turn crankshaft clockwise slowly until TDC mark on camshaft sprocket is aligned with cast marking in distributor cap console.
   b. Ensure TDC mark on flywheel and cast boss on clutch housing are also aligned.
   c. Turn engine counterclockwise (approximately 10° on crankshaft which is equal to approximately 1.5 teeth toward mark on the camshaft sprocket).
   d. Install tool 9201 or equivalent. Pull out lock pin on tool and push test pin opposite lock pin completely. Align drag needle with gauge needle.
   e. Slide tool onto drive belt. Press test point slowly until lock pin engages and note reading obtained. **Always align drag needle and gauge needle after engagement of the lock pin to eliminate incorrect display.**
   f. Reading obtained for a new belt should be 3.7-4.3. Reading obtained for a used belt should be 2.4-3. **Sliding shoes must have complete contact on drive belt surface. The tool must not be turned or moved on the belt while checking.**
   g. Turn tensioner roller counterclockwise while tightening or clockwise while loosening.
   h. Tighten mounting nuts.
   i. Rotate crankshaft clockwise two complete turns and align TDC mark on camshaft sprocket with cast mark on distributor cap console, then turn crankshaft counterclockwise approximately 10° on crankshaft from this position. Check drive belt tension, adjust if necessary.

PISTON & ROD ASSEMBLY

Code numbers on connecting rod upper

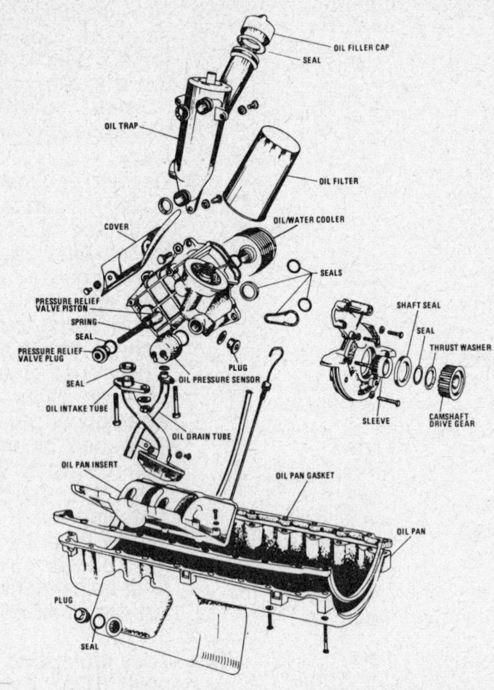

Fig. 4 Exploded view of lubricating system. 1986–87 924S & 944

Fig. 5 Exploded view of oil pump. 1986–87 924S & 944

and lower sections must be mounted together and all face one side. Piston must be installed so that rounded edges of valve reliefs face in forward direction.

PISTONS, PINS & RINGS

The cylinder codes are stamped on the engine block and piston codes are stamped on the piston crowns. Piston oversizes are available in 3.9559 inch (100.48 mm), 3.9563 inch (100.49 mm), 3.9567 inch (100.5 mm), 3.9756 inch (100.98 mm), 3.9560 inch (100.99 mm), and 3.9764 inch (101 mm). When installing rings, offset 120°.

OIL PAN
REPLACE
924S & 944

1. Drain crankcase and remove dipstick.
2. Disconnect battery ground cable.
3. Remove oil pan attaching bolts.
4. To loosen pan, strike gently with a soft faced hammer.
5. Disconnect steering at crossmember, if necessary.
6. Remove crossmember and loosen left engine mount bolts, if necessary.
7. Remove pan.
8. Reverse procedure to install.

LUBRICATING SYSTEM SERVICE
924S & 944

1. When removing lubricating system components, refer to **Fig. 4,** noting the following:
   a. When removing oil pan, be careful not to damage oil intake pipe.
   b. When removing oil trap, intake distributor must be removed.
2. When disassembling oil pump, **Fig. 5,** on late 1985 and all 1986 models, use suitable tools to remove housing insert.
3. When assembling oil pump, note the following:
   a. Install new shaft seal. Apply suitable lubricant to seal lip and install seal together with toothed sleeve and drive in using tool 10-203 or equivalent.
   b. Torque countersunk screws to 6 ft. lbs.
   c. Apply suitable sealant on outside diameter of housing insert.
   d. Lubricate inner and outer rotors with suitable oil and ensure punch mark on outer rotor faces out.
   e. Apply suitable sealant to face end of oil pump housing.
4. When installing lubricating system components, note the following:
   a. When installing oil dipstick guide tube, use suitable sealant.
   b. When installing new drain plug, use new seal ring and torque plug to 36 ft. lbs.
   c. Coat threads of oil pan insert attaching bolts with suitable locking compound.
   d. Before installing oil pan insert, open tabs and clean inside.
   e. Coat oil drain pipe attaching bolt with suitable locking compound.
   f. Torque oil intake pipe attaching bolts to 36 ft. lbs.
   g. When installing camshaft drive gear, ensure belt collar faces balance shaft drive gear.
   h. Replace housing plug seal and torque plug to 25 ft. lbs.
   i. Replace oil pressure sensor O-ring seal and torque sensor to 25 ft. lbs.
   j. Replace pressure relief valve plug seal and torque plug to 33 ft. lbs.
   k. Check pressure relief valve piston for wear or signs of seizure, replacing as necessary.
   l. When installing oil/water cooler, pre-assemble in housing and install together with crankcase upper section.
5. When installing oil pan, torque bolts in three steps in proper sequence, **Fig. 6.** Install bolts finger tight, torque to 3 ft. lbs. and torque to 6 ft. lbs.
6. When installing oil pump on late 1985 and all 1986-87 models, note the following:
   a. Align oil pump body surface with upper crankcase section before tightening mounting bolts.
   b. Apply toothed sleeve on sealing lip and seal simultaneously and drive in using tool 10-203 or equivalent.
   c. Coat both sides of gasket in area of corners with sealant before installing oil pan gasket. **New oil pump for late 1985 and all 1986-87 models cannot be installed in older engines.**

BALANCE SHAFT DRIVE
REPLACE
924S & 944

1. Disassemble balance shaft drive as described under "Camshaft, Replace."
2. Disassemble camshaft drive as described under "Camshaft, Replace."
3. When removing and installing balance shaft drive, refer to **Fig. 7.**
4. When installing balance shaft housing, proceed as follows:
   a. Tighten all hexagon head bolts and hexagon nuts finger tight.
   b. Install bearing housing with new lightly oiled O-ring without tightening attaching nuts.
   c. Torque bolts in sequence, **Fig. 8.** Torque M6 bolts to 6 ft. lbs. Torque M8 stud nuts in two steps to 11 and 22 ft. lbs. Torque M8 bolts in two steps to 11 and 14 ft. lbs. Check movement of balance shaft between each tightening step.

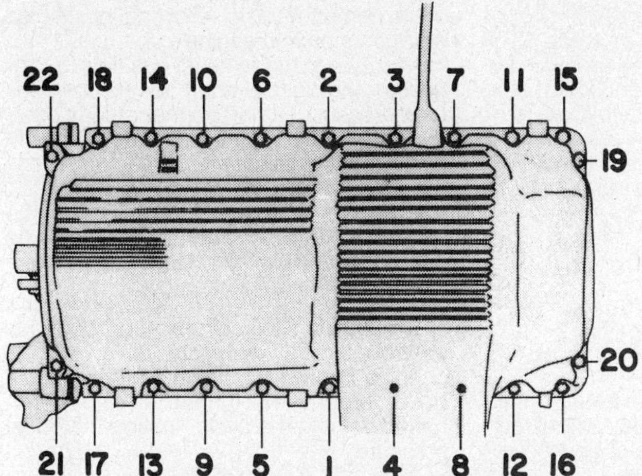

Fig. 6 Oil pan bolt tightening sequence. 1986–87 924S & 944

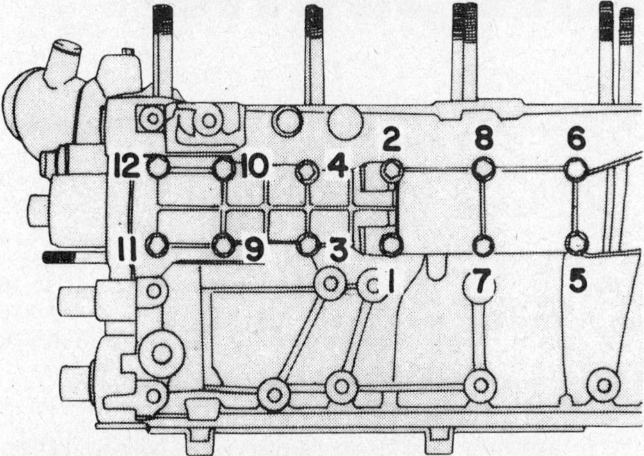

Fig. 8 Balance shaft housing cover attaching bolt tightening sequence. 1986–87 924S & 944

5. Refer to "Camshaft, Replace" for assembling camshaft drive, assembling balance shaft drive, installing balance shaft drive gears, and installing and adjusting balance shaft drive belt.

COMPENSATING SHAFT DRIVE

REPLACE

924S & 944

Balance shaft drive used on earlier models was replaced in mid-1985 by a compensating shaft drive, Fig. 9. For all operations concerning compensating shaft other than those mentioned, follow operations as described for balance shaft.

1. Crankcase upper and lower sections and bearing bridges of compensating shaft are matched and must be installed as set with code numbers matching exactly.
2. When bearing bridges are correctly installed, codes of both bridges should be readable from front.
3. Right side bearing bridges are stamped with a 1 and the left side with a 2.

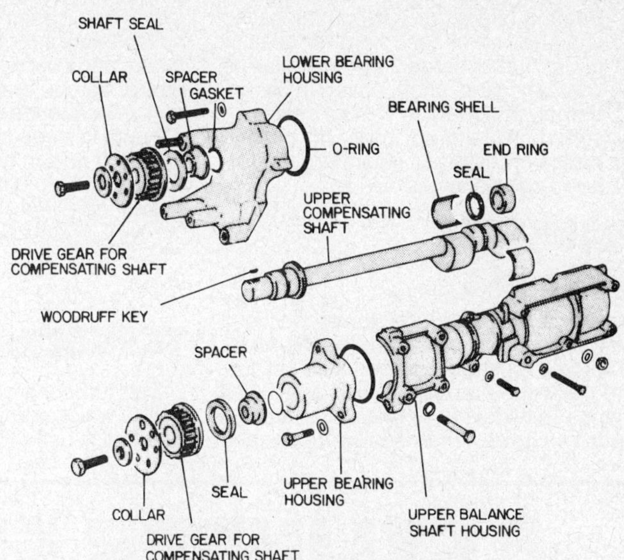

Fig. 7 Balance shaft drive components exploded view. 1986–87 924S & 944

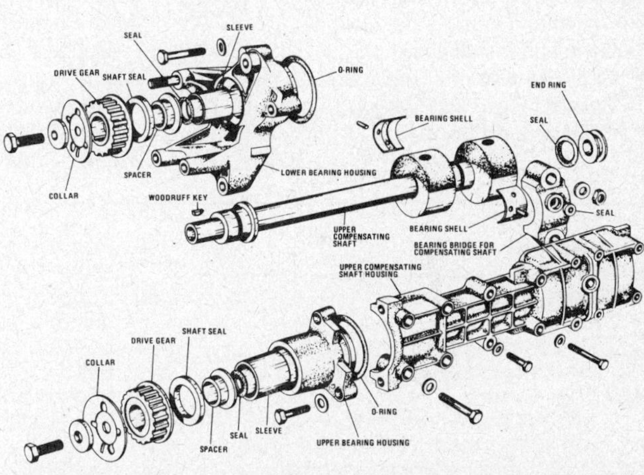

Fig. 9 Exploded view of compensating shaft. 1986–87 924S & 944

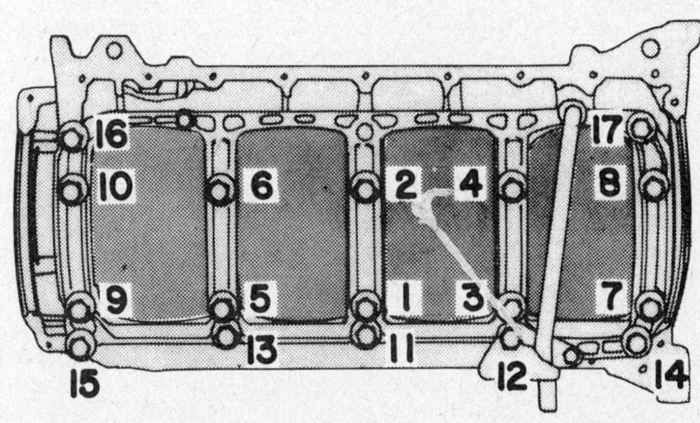

Fig. 10 Crankcase halves attaching bolts tightening sequence. 1986–87 924S & 944

4. Bearing bridge for left compensating shaft has an oil feed bore for oil supply to turbocharger. When installing compensating shaft cover, it is extremely important to ensure seal is inserted in take-up bore of bearing bridge on naturally aspirated and turbocharged engines.

CRANKCASE

924S & 944

Crankcase upper and lower sections and balance shaft cover are machined together and must be replaced as a set. Ensure that code numbers match and install balance shaft covers so that codes are visible from above. When sealing upper and lower crankcase halves, apply thin coat of suitable locking compound in areas of oil intake and sealing surface in areas of flywheel. Torque crankcase connecting stud nuts in sequence, **Fig. 10**, as follows; M12 1.5 nuts in three steps to 14, 29 and 54 ft. lbs., M10 nuts in two steps to 14 and 36 ft. lbs., M6 nuts to 6 ft. lbs., and M8 nuts to 14 ft. lbs.

TURBOCHARGER

The turbocharger is an exhaust driven device which compresses the air/fuel mixture that is used to increase engine power on a demand basis, allowing a smaller, more economical engine to be used.

A turbine in the exhaust gas flow is connected through a shaft to the impeller (compressor). During normal, steady operation, the turbine does not rotate with sufficient speed to boost pressure to compress the air/fuel mixture. As speed increases, the mixture is compressed, allowing the denser mixture to enter the combustion chambers and develop more engine power during the combustion cycle.

The intake manifold pressure (boost) is controlled by a wastegate valve which is used to bypass a portion of the exhaust gases around the turbine at a predetermined point in the cycle, limiting the boost pressure.

6 CYLINDER ENGINE SECTION

INDEX

ENGINE

REPLACE

1. Raise and support vehicle.
2. Disconnect battery ground cable.
3. Loosen A/C compressor bracket attaching bolts and position aside. **Do not disconnect refrigerant lines.**
4. Remove air cleaner assembly.
5. Label for identification, then disconnect all electrical connectors, vacuum lines and coolant hoses from engine.
6. Disconnect and cap fuel lines, as necessary.
7. Remove rear end cover attaching bolts, then the cover.
8. Pull seal off of retaining edge on body and push forward over selector rod.
9. Raise vehicle and drain engine oil. Disconnect oil hose or oil line on engine and pan.
10. Remove rear stabilizer bar.
11. Disconnect ground strap on body.
12. Disconnect electrical connectors and cables from starter motor.
13. Loosen clutch cable retainer.
14. Remove clutch release lever and spring.
15. Remove positioning lever and spring.
16. Remove release lever from release lever shaft.
17. Remove driveshaft from differential flange.
18. Suspend left driveshaft from vehicle using a suitable piece of wire.
19. Remove rear cowl panel attaching screws, then the rear cowl panel.
20. Support transaxle assembly with a suitable jack.
21. Loosen transaxle carrier attaching bolts.
22. Loosen engine carrier attaching bolts.
23. Lower support jack slightly, then disconnect electrical connector from shock absorber crossmember as well as plug on air flow sensor.
24. Lower jack with engine/transaxle carefully and roll out toward rear of vehicle. **If vehicle has to be moved after removal of engine/transaxle assembly, suspend driveshafts from vehicle in a horizontal position.**
25. Reverse procedure to install.

ENGINE DISASSEMBLY

When disassembling the engine or when removing components from the engine, never use a lead pencil to place alignment marks on cylinder head assemblies or use a sharp tool to pry off engine components as damage may result. Keep disassembled components in order and on a clean workbench to facilitate assembly.

1. Install engine in suitable working fixture.
2. Remove air filter cover and filter.
3. Remove air injection pump with filter, bracket and hoses, if equipped.
4. Remove EGR valve, connecting pipe and bracket from air distribution/filter housing, if equipped.
5. Disconnect injection system electrical connectors and position connectors clear of intake pipes.
6. Remove throttle control rod and return spring from throttle housing.
7. Remove auxiliary air regulator and auxiliary air valve from right side of engine.
8. Remove all hose clamps and tie wraps.
9. Remove nuts attaching intake manifold and carefully lift manifold off together with air distribution/filter housing fuel distributor, fuel lines and injectors.
10. Mark distributor cap, housing and rotor alignment for assembly, then remove distributor cap, ignition wires and ignition coil.
11. Remove distributor from engine.
12. Disconnect air ducts connecting air blower outlets and heat exchanger inlets and remove together with cover shrouds.
13. Remove all retaining screws for cooling air ducts and cover shrouds.
14. Loosen two screws of band strap on alternator/blower housing.
15. Pull blower housing rearward and remove air guide from alternator.
16. Disconnect electrical connectors at alternator and remove alternator with blower housing and fan.

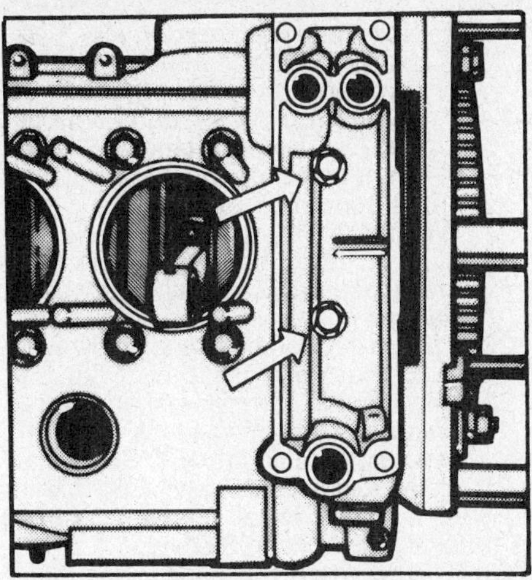

Fig. 1 Bearing No. 1 cap nuts location. 911 models

17. Remove upper air guide with wiring harness.
18. Remove rear engine mount crossmember from engine mount.
19. Remove muffler flange attaching bolts and nuts.
20. Loosen muffler straps at rear center mount and remove muffler.
21. Remove engine mount attaching bolts.
22. Remove heat exchangers, removing thermal reactors, catalytic converter, EGR filter with lines and air injection lines as equipped.
23. On vehicles equipped with air conditioning, remove compressor bracket from right chain housing cover.
24. Disconnect camshaft oil supply lines, then remove both chain housing covers.
25. Remove chain tensioner attaching nuts and pull tensioner out with idler pulley.
26. Using tool P9191 or equivalent, remove camshaft sprocket attaching nuts.
27. Using tool P212 or equivalent, withdraw aligning dowels from chain housing.
28. Remove chain guides from chain housing. **Ensure that pistons do not collide with valves when rotating crankshaft or camshafts.**
29. Remove sprocket wheels and wheel flanges.
30. Remove woodruff keys from camshafts.
31. Remove three sealing flange retaining bolts and push out flange with suitable tool.
32. Remove nuts attaching chain housings to crankcase.
33. Remove stud bolts, then the chain guides, from inside of crankcase.
34. Remove oil cooler attaching nuts and the oil cooler.
35. Remove oil pressure relief valve and safety valve.
36. Remove intermediate shaft cover, then the intake and exhaust valve covers.
37. To remove cylinder heads individually, proceed as follows: **When reusing original parts, mark relationship for assembly in original position. The design of the engine allows individual cylinder heads to be removed. Do not place marks of any kind on cylinder head such as lead pencil marks or use a screwdriver to pry off cylinder head or serious engine damage will result. If no work is to be performed on either the cylinder heads or camshaft housings, the entire cylinder head bank can be removed as an assembly.**
    a. Disconnect battery ground cable.
    b. Remove cover plates and heat exchanger only from the side from which it is desired to remove the cylinder head.
    c. Remove rear engine support and exhaust muffler assembly.
    d. Carefully remove camshaft drive only from desired side.
    e. Loosen camshaft housing attaching nuts, then remove spring washers and lift off camshaft housing. **There are three (3) .315 inch (3 8 mm) internal hexagon attaching nuts on the camshaft housing.**
    f. Loosen cylinder head attaching nuts and lift cylinder head from engine.
38. To remove camshaft housing and cylinder heads as an assembly, proceed as follows:
    a. Loosen evenly, then remove cylinder head attaching nuts.
    b. Remove cylinder heads with camshaft housing, then cooling air shrouds and cylinders.
39. Remove piston pin retaining clips and drive out piston pin with suitable tool.
40. Remove engine crankcase breather cover, oil pressure sensor, thermostat and oil drain cover with screen.
41. Remove M8 nuts and washers attaching crankcase halves together.
42. Using suitable tools, remove flywheel.
43. Remove nuts from studs at bearing No. 1, **Fig. 1**, then the nuts inside the oil cooler flange on right crankcase half. **Crankcase must be turned so left crankcase half faces upward and right crankcase half can support crankshaft and intermediate shaft.**
44. Remove nut on stud inside left chain housing, **Fig. 2.**
45. Remove attaching bolts, then separate crankcase halves.
46. Remove crankshaft and mount in tool P209a or equivalent. Label connecting rods according to cylinder, then remove connecting rods.
47. Remove oil pump attaching nuts, then remove oil pump, connecting shaft, intermediate shaft and chains as an assembly.

ENGINE ASSEMBLY

Engine is assembled in reverse order of disassembly, following instructions given for different assembly groups.

FLYWHEEL INSTALLATION

1. Ensure that contact surfaces of crankshaft and flywheel are clean.
2. Install and torque flywheel attaching bolts to 65 ft. lbs.

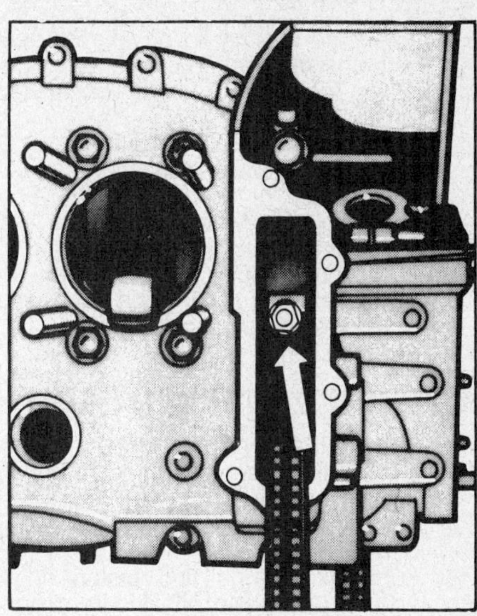

Fig. 2 Removing nut in left chain housing. 911 models

DRIVESHAFT PILOT BEARING, REPLACE

Replace driveshaft pilot bearing with flywheel installed on vehicle.

1. Remove driveshaft pilot bearing attaching bolts.
2. Coat threads of attaching screws with suitable locking compound and torque to 7 ft. lbs.

MAIN BEARING NO. 1 OIL SEAL, REPLACE

1. Remove flywheel as previously described.
2. Using screwdriver, pry out oil seal at cutout in left crankcase half.
3. Clean seal contact surface of crankshaft.
4. Coat outer surface of new oil seal with suitable sealing compound.
5. Lubricate sealing lip of new oil seal.
6. Using suitable tools, drive in oil seal until flush with crankcase.
7. Install flywheel as previously described.

MAIN BEARING NO. 8 OIL SEAL, REPLACE

Crankshaft oil seal can be replaced without removing engine from vehicle.

1. Remove drive belt pulley as follows:
    a. Using tool P208b or equivalent, remove cooling fan pulley attaching nut.
    b. Loosen A/C compressor and remove drive belt.
    c. Loosen and remove drive belt pulley attaching bolt, then remove pulley.
2. Pry out oil seal at cutout in crankshaft bearing No. 8.
3. Clean oil seal contact surface on crankshaft.
4. Coat outer sealing surface of new oil seal with suitable sealant.

5. Lubricate sealing lip of new oil seal and position seal on crankshaft.
6. Using tool P216 or equivalent, install oil seal.
7. Install drive belt pulley as follows:
   a. Clean pulley to crankshaft contact surfaces.
   b. Install pulley on crankshaft and align with locating pin.
   c. Torque single groove pulley attaching bolt to 58 ft. lbs., or double groove pulley attaching bolt to 122 ft. lbs.

CYLINDER INSTALLATION

1. Ensure that mating surfaces at the joints with the crankshaft and cylinder head are clean.
2. Install new gaskets at base of cylinders.
3. Lubricate pistons and piston rings with clean engine oil. Ensure piston rings are installed with "TOP" marking facing upward.
4. Stagger piston ring gaps opposite each other (approximately 90° apart) with oil scraper ring gap to the top.
5. Using tool US1008a or equivalent, compress piston rings.
6. Apply light coat of clean engine oil to cylinder bore and install cylinder. Ensure studs protruding from crankcase do not contact cylinder cooling fins. **The installed height of the cylinder is divided into two categories. Only cylinders of the same height and bearing the same mark stamped on the lower flange should be installed in the same bank. The mark consists of an equilateral triangle containing a number denoting cylinder height. Do not interchange cylinders.**
7. Install air deflector plates.
8. Install cylinder heads.

PISTON INSTALLATION

1. Ensure that connecting rod tolerances are within specifications.
2. Clean piston, removing any heavy oil discoloration on piston crown and in ring grooves, being careful not to damage surfaces. **An uneven blue mark or one sided traces of carbon deposits on piston body at a right angle to piston axis may be caused by a bent connecting rod.**
3. Ensure piston rings are in good condition and that ring gaps and groove clearances are within specifications.
4. Measure piston. Dimensional groups are marked on crowns of pistons.
5. Using tool VW121b or equivalent, install piston rings with "TOP" mark facing upward.
6. Install piston pin circlip on one side of piston, then insert piston pin from opposite side of piston.
7. Install piston on connecting rod so that larger valve pocket machined on piston faces intake side.
8. Install second circlip so that opening in circlip faces either piston crown or in opposite direction.
9. Install cylinders.

ASSEMBLING CRANKCASE HALVES

1. Clean gasket sealing surfaces of crankcase halves.
2. Bolt together crankcase halves and measure bearing housings in crankcase. Bore diameter should be 2.55095-2.5598 inches.
3. Recondition main bearing bores as necessary.
4. Clean out all oil passages and blow clear using compressed air. An annular groove is cut around main bearing No. 7 through bolt on left hand crankcase half sealing surface. Keep groove free of dirt or sealing compound.
5. Place intermediate shaft with connecting shaft and oil pump in crankcase without drive chain.
6. Turn intermediate shaft by hand and ensure that intermediate shaft, connecting shaft and oil pump turn and mesh smoothly. If any out-of-roundness is visible, gear teeth in mesh must be altered until all parts rotate freely.
7. Remove intermediate shaft with connecting shaft, but do not separate gear wheels.
8. Place drive chains on intermediate shaft chain wheels.
9. Insert sealing ring in oil passage between right hand crankcase half and oil pump housing.
10. Install intermediate shaft with oil pump into right hand crankcase half with new tab washers and nuts, then torque nuts to 18 ft. lbs. and bend up tab washers.
11. Place main bearing shells for bearings 2 through 7 in position in both crankcase halves.
12. Place shells for main bearing No. 1 in position in both crankcase halves.
13. Install crankshaft with bearing No. 8 into right crankcase half.
14. Coat shaft sealing ring at outer extremity with suitable sealant and install flush with exterior of crankcase half.
15. Position and tighten retaining clips for connecting rod and chain.
16. Position sealing rings between oil pump and left hand crankcase half and the sealing ring linking oil passage between two halves of crankcase.
17. Apply thin coat of suitable sealant to mating surface of crankcase.
18. Install tools P221 and P222 or equivalents in right crankcase half.
19. Install left hand crankcase half.
20. Assemble through bolts as follows:
    a. Install double chamfer washer in bore so that smoother surface faces crankshaft.
    b. Push on O-ring.
    c. Push through bolt into position from right hand half of crankcase.
    d. Place O-ring on end of through bolt.
    e. Install second double chamfer washer so that smoother surface faces crankshaft.
    f. Install cap nut. **Bearing No. 1 has studs for attachment rather than through bolts. The studs are inserted into the left hand side below oil cooler flange. Sealing rings and nuts must be installed as described in step 20.**
21. When attaching main bearing No. 7 to stud in chain housing of left hand crankcase half, use standard washer and nut.
22. Torque through bolts and studs evenly across crankcase to 25 ft. lbs.
23. Use No. 8 spring washers on all crankcase retaining studs, replacing nuts and torquing to 16-18 ft. lbs.
24. Using tools P236 and US1006 or equivalents, install flywheel, torquing attaching bolts to 65 ft. lbs.
25. Ensure that crankshaft turns freely and that chains and connecting rods do not jam.
26. Install pistons, ensuring that flat spot of piston faces intake valve.
27. Cover crankcase openings, then install piston pin retaining circlips so that open end of circlip faces either crankshaft or piston top.
28. Using tool US1008a or equivalent, compress piston rings.
29. Install new cylinder base gasket on cylinder and carefully push cylinder onto piston until cylinder covers all piston rings.
30. Remove tool and push cylinder into its base in crankcase until it seats on sealing surface.
31. Secure cylinder in position by placing spacer bushings onto two diagonally opposed studs and tightening nuts.
32. Install remaining cylinders.

CYLINDER HEAD INSTALLATION

Reverse removal step 37 to install cylinder head, noting the following:

1. Before installing cylinder head assembly, ensure head and block surfaces are clean and in good condition.
2. Install a new cylinder head gasket.
3. Threads of cylinder head attaching nuts must be lubricated with "Moly" grease part No. 999 917 728 00 or equivalent to ensure correct attaching nut torque.
4. Insert washers .413 .826 .118 inch (10.5 21 3 mm) and tighten hexagon nuts. **Tighten cylinder head attaching nuts only lightly to allow movement of cylinder head to properly align camshaft housing.**
5. The mating surface on which the camshaft housing rests is also a sealing surface. No gasket is provided, but the cylinder head face should be coated with suitable sealing compound.
6. Assemble camshaft housing and oil return pipes. Place spring washers and nuts in correct position but do not tighten.
7. Torque cylinder head attaching nuts evenly to 21-24 ft. lbs.

VALVES, REPLACE

1. Remove cylinder head as previously described.

2. Using tool US1020 or equivalent, compress valve spring.
3. Remove split valve keepers and valve spring retainer.
4. Remove valve springs and spring seat.
5. Remove burrs from valve cotter seats as necessary.
6. Remove valves.
7. Remove valve stem seal and valve spring height adjustment shims.
8. Recondition cylinder head and/or valves as necessary.
9. Check valve springs with standard spring tester. When replacing valve spring, inner and outer spring must be replaced as a set.
10. Check installed length of valve spring as follows:
    a. Install tool P10c or equivalent with respective spring retainer and both valve keepers.
    b. Determine indicated value. Installed length of intake valve should be 1.346-1.370 inch. Installed length of exhaust valve should be 1.346-1.370 inch.
    c. If installed length of valve is not within specifications, adjust with correct number of shims. Thickness of shim is .0197 inch.
11. Replace valve stem seals on both intake and exhaust valve guides.
12. Install valve springs. Outer spring is progressively wound and the closely wound coils should be at cylinder head side. **It is not necessary to check installed length of inner springs.**
13. Test valve seating.

CAMSHAFT HOUSING INSTALLATION

The camshaft housing is designed to be fitted to either cylinder block. Press fit cover plate accordingly.

1. Clean sealing surfaces of cylinder heads.
2. Ensure cylinder head studs in cylinder head are firmly seated.
3. Apply very thin coat of suitable sealant on mating surface of camshaft housing.
4. Install oil return tubes into crankcase.
5. Place camshaft housing on cylinder head and oil return tubes. **Cylinder heads may have to be moved slightly to align with camshaft housing.**
6. Place nuts and spring washers on camshaft housing securing studs and loosely tighten.
7. Evenly torque cylinder head nuts to 24 ft. lbs.
8. Install camshaft in camshaft housing.
9. Torque camshaft housing nuts progressively across cylinder heads to 18 ft. lbs. **When tightening camshaft housing, check camshaft for binding in its bearings. If camshaft binds, loosen camshaft housing and retighten in a different order until stresses are relieved and camshaft turns freely.**
10. Install chain guides in crankcase, inserting retaining stud bolts and chain guides at same time.

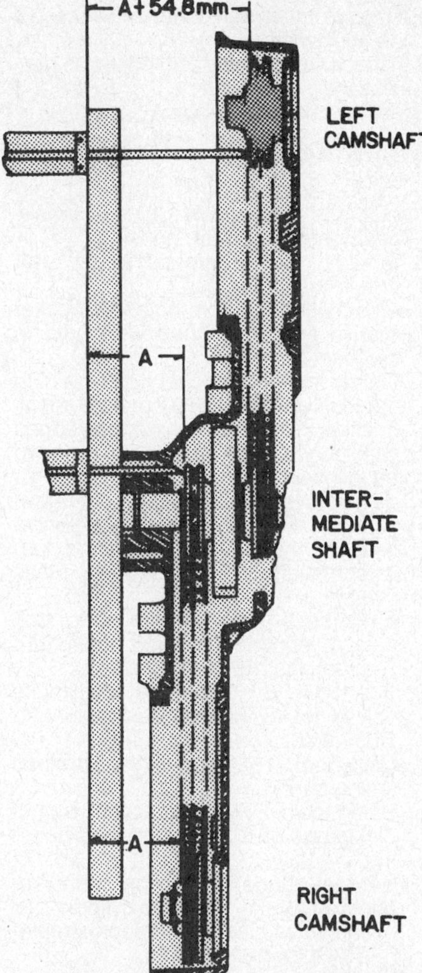

Fig. 3 Aligning camshaft sprockets. 911 models

11. Check for proper positioning of chain guide in groove of stud bolt and torque to 18 ft. lbs. **Chain guides are installed with longer portion of guide pointing toward nearest gear. Lower right chain guide is brown plastic and remaining five chain guides are black plastic.**
12. Install chain housing gaskets on crankcase.
13. Install chain housings and torque housing retaining nuts to 18 ft. lbs.
14. Install remaining chain guides on their respective supports.

ROCKER ARMS INSTALLATION

1. Install rockers on shafts. **End rocker arm shafts must always be replaced so that the heads of the Allen head screw securing them face toward cylinders 2 and 5.**
2. Insert rocker shaft until feeler gauge can be passed between camshaft housing and the rocker into the groove formed on the rocker shaft.
3. Push rocker shaft further in direction of assembly until feeler gauge is held firmly in position then remove feeler gauge.
4. Push rocker arm shaft in an additional .059 inch and torque to 13 ft. lbs.

CAMSHAFT INSTALLATION

1. Install camshaft and ensure that it turns freely.
2. Lubricate rotating surfaces with suitable lubricant.
3. Install new sealing ring and O-ring and tighten three attaching screws.
4. Install thrust washer, replacing as necessary.
5. Install spacing washers to same thickness as removed, then install key.
6. Install camshaft sprocket flange.
7. Install camshaft sprockets. Camshaft sprockets are axially offset but are interchangeable. Mount camshaft sprocket on left bank so that deeper recess is visible. Mount camshaft sprocket on right bank so that shallow recess faces back.
8. Torque camshaft sprocket attaching nut to 108 ft. lbs., or attaching bolt to 86 ft. lbs.
9. Align camshaft sprockets in relation to drive sprockets as follows:
    a. Push intermediate shaft and camshaft toward flywheel to seat shafts against bearing thrust flanks.
    b. Using straightedge and depth gauge, measure through the hole below the intermediate shaft against front flank of drive sprocket.
    c. Rest straightedge against crankcase in line with camshaft end and measure from near side of straightedge to front flank of drive sprocket.
    d. If measurement obtained in steps b and c differ by more than .01 inch, add or remove spacers between camshaft sprocket flange and thrust plate as necessary.
    e. Push camshaft of cylinders 1 through 3 forward to rest against flank and repeat steps b and c. When checking alignment of camshaft sprocket for cylinders 1 through 3, add 2.157 to distance "A," **Fig. 3.**
    f. Adjust camshaft sprocket for cylinders 4 through 6 so that distance "A," **Fig. 3,** is the same for both sprockets.
10. Install rocker arms, adjust valve timing and adjust valve clearance.

VALVES, ADJUST

When adjusting valve clearances, the valves should be checked in the normal firing order, 1-6-2-4-3-5. The piston of the appropriate cylinder must be at TDC (both intake and exhaust valves closed). TDC markings for each cylinder are located on the belt pulley assembly. Beginning with the No. 1 cylinder, the crankshaft and belt pulley should be turned to the right (normal direction of engine rotation), until both the intake and exhaust valves are closed and the cylinder TDC marking (Z1) on the belt pulley coincides with the mark on the crankcase. To adjust the valves, proceed as follows:

1. Remove valve covers and gaskets, if necessary.
2. Rotate engine until piston of cylinder to be checked is at TDC of compression stroke (in firing order).
3. Using a suitable feeler gauge, check valve clearance.
4. Loosen adjusting screw hexagon nut.
5. Adjust clearance by turning adjusting screw using a suitable screwdriver while holding nut secure. With engine cold, intake and exhaust valve clearance should be .0039 inch (.1 mm).
6. Hold adjusting screw and check to ensure clearance has not changed.
7. Rotate crankshaft in direction of engine rotation until next mark is reached (120°). In this position, check valve clearances for No. 6 cylinder.
8. Turn crankshaft another 120° until piston of No. 2 cylinder is at TDC and check valve clearances.
9. Repeat this procedure until all the valves have been checked.

CHAIN TENSIONERS, REPLACE

Chain tensioners can be replaced without removing engine if muffler and engine rear shrouding are removed.

1. Turn crankshaft to bring No. 1 piston to TDC.
2. Remove chain housing cover.
3. Remove chain tensioner retaining nut and take out tensioner.
4. When installing new chain tensioner, proceed as follows. **Use only chain tensioner, part No. 93010505300, with spacer, part No. 93010551300.**
   a. Push tensioner assembly on shaft of sprocket wheel carrier until half of plunger shaft head is covered by the tensioner arm.
   b. Turn lock ring until hold down clamp can be removed.
   c. Push chain tensioner fully on sprocket wheel carrier and secure.
5. When installing reconditioned chain tensioner, proceed as follows:
   a. Compress tensioner assembly in suitable vise.
   b. Slowly tighten vise until plunger is depressed, then hold piston in depressed position with tool P214 or equivalent.
   c. Install tensioner and remove tool.
6. Torque chain tensioner retaining nut to 18 ft. lbs.
7. Check valve timing and adjust as necessary.
8. Install chain housing cover.

VALVE TIMING, ADJUST

1. Turn crankshaft until mark "Z1" on pulley is aligned with joint of crankcase or stripe on fan housing.
2. Position both camshafts so that punch marks face up.
3. Insert locating pin in hole in sprocket that is exactly aligned with hole in sprocket flange.
4. Lightly tighten sprocket bolts, holding sprocket with tool 9191 or equivalent.
5. If either camshaft is not positioned with punch mark facing up, proceed as follows:
   a. Remove locating pin from camshaft which is correctly positioned.
   b. Using tool 9191 or equivalent, turn camshaft until punch mark faces up.
   c. Remove sprocket mounting bolt and locating pin and again turn crankshaft to mark "Z1."
6. Adjust valve clearance of intake valves for cylinders No. 1 and 4 to .0039 inch.
7. Using tool 9182 or equivalent, preload timing chains.
8. Using tool P207 or equivalent, mount dial gauge on stud of camshaft housing.
9. Set dial gauge to zero on spring retainer of intake valve for cylinder No. 1 with valve closed and approximately .394 inch preload.
10. Slowly turn crankshaft clockwise and observe dial indicator. Turn crankshaft until dial indicator reads .061 inch.
11. Remove left sprocket mounting bolt, then, using tool P212 or equivalent, pull out locating spring.
12. Turn crankshaft until mark "Z1" on pulley is exactly aligned with joint of crankcase or stripe on fan housing.
13. Install locating pin and tighten bolt finger tight.
14. Turn crankshaft 720° and check gauge reading. Reading should be .0551-.0669 inch.
15. Using tool P9191 or equivalent, hold camshaft and torque bolt to 86 ft. lbs.
16. Set cylinder No. 4 to TDC, then perform steps 8 through 15 on cylinder No. 4.

SPLIT TIMING CHAIN INSTALLATION

Split timing chains can be replaced without removing and disassembling engine. When replacing both chains, they must be replaced one after the other as chains run in opposite directions.

1. Remove spark plugs, then turn crankshaft to mark "Z1" of cylinder No. 1.
2. Remove chain tensioner, sprocket wheel with support, and camshaft gear.
3. Grind open both pins of one link of old chain, protecting engine from grinding dust.
4. Attach new chain with chain lock to end of old chain.
5. Using suitable tool, move camshaft approximately 45° outward.
6. Slowly turn crankshaft in direction of normal engine rotation while keeping chain tensioned.
7. Turn engine until connecting link can be inserted at other end of new chain.
8. Remove old chain and close new chain with connecting link. Insert connecting link from front with shims, then install spring lock with closed end pointing in direction of rotation.
9. Install camshaft gear, sprocket wheel and chain tensioner.
10. Check valve timing and adjust as necessary.

TURBOCHARGER

The turbocharger is an exhaust driven device which compresses the air/fuel mixture that is used to increase engine power on a demand basis, allowing a smaller, more economical engine to be used.

A turbine in the exhaust gas flow is connected through a shaft to the impeller (compressor). During normal, steady operation, the turbine does not rotate with sufficient speed to boost pressure to compress the air/fuel mixture. As the speed increases, the mixture is compressed allowing the denser mixture to enter the combustion chambers and develop more engine power during the combustion cycle.

V8 ENGINE SECTION

INDEX

ENGINE REPLACE

1983–84

1. Disconnect battery ground cable in spare tire well.
2. Remove engine compartment cross brace. **Vehicle must not be raised when brace is removed.**
3. Position suitable vehicle hoist, but do not raise vehicle.
4. Disconnect windshield washer hoses and engine compartment wiring.
5. Disconnect top of engine hood supports.
6. Remove engine hood bolts and hood.
7. Remove cap from coolant expansion tank.
8. Remove air intake hoses and air cleaner assembly.
9. Raise and support vehicle.
10. Position piece of wood between central tube and rear tunnel brace.
11. Remove engine splash shield.
12. Remove drain plug from bottom of radiator and drain coolant.
13. Remove drain plug from left and right side of crankcase and drain coolant.
14. Drain engine oil.
15. Remove lower body brace from underside of vehicle.
16. Remove exhaust pipes from exhaust manifolds.
17. Remove heat shields from left and right sides.
18. Disconnect body ground cable.
19. Install oil drain plug.
20. Install coolant drain plugs.
21. Remove clutch slave cylinder at clutch housing with hydraulic line connected.
22. Remove mounting strap for hydraulic line to slave cylinder.
23. Disconnect starter wiring.
24. Remove clutch housing cover and starter.
25. Press release lever downward to disconnect lever at ball pin.
26. Remove starter wiring clamps along steering crossmember.
27. Remove socket head bolts and slide clamping sleeve at driveshaft.
28. Remove release bearing mounting bolts and push sleeve toward clutch.
29. Remove left and right engine shock absorbers from control arms.
30. Remove left and right engine shock absorbers along with engine mounts.
31. On vehicles with A/C, proceed as follows:
    a. Disconnect temperature switch wiring at radiator.
    b. Disconnect compressor electrical connector on right drive belt cover.
    c. Remove compressor from bracket, leave hoses connected.
32. Remove air pump filter housing.
33. Disconnect alternator cooling hose.
34. Remove lower fan shroud from radiator.
35. Disconnect coolant hoses from radiator.
36. Disconnect lower oil hose at radiator.
37. Position suitable jack under oil pan.
38. Position suitable wood block on lifting pad and raise engine slightly.
39. Remove one engine mount.
40. Lower engine onto front crossmember.
41. Remove second engine mount.
42. Lower vehicle and disconnect vent hose at T-adapter for radiator and thermostat housing.
43. Disconnect coolant hoses at thermostat housing.
44. Disconnect upper oil hose at radiator.
45. Using Allen head adapter, remove upper radiator mounting bolts and radiator.
46. Loosen hose clamp and remove hose between heater valve and neck.
47. Disconnect B + wire above ignition control unit.
48. Disconnect sensor wire between distributor and ignition control unit.
49. Disconnect engine wiring harness electrical connector.
50. Remove control unit.
51. Remove ignition coil and position aside.
52. Disconnect fuel feed and return lines below intake runners.
53. Disconnect hydraulic line at power steering pump.
54. Disconnect oil hoses at supply tank of power steering pump.
55. Drain oil and remove tank.
56. Disconnect brake booster vacuum hose at manifold.
57. Remove throttle cable retaining screws, cable, and holder.
58. On vehicles with A/C, cover condenser with a suitable piece of plywood to prevent damage.
59. Install adapter 9137 or a suitable lifting device on engine.
60. Raise engine slightly.
61. Remove upper engine block/clutch housing mounting bolts.
62. Pull engine forward carefully and remove short driveshaft with guide tube.
63. Remove engine.
64. Reverse procedure to install.

1985–87

1. Disconnect battery ground cable.
2. Remove cross strut.
3. Disconnect windshield washer and heated spray jet hoses and the engine compartment light electrical connector.
4. Disconnect gas pressure prop lock at bottom and remove hood.
5. Remove air cleaner assembly with intake hoses.
6. Remove coolant expansion tank cap and the radiator upper air guide section.
7. Raise and support vehicle.
8. Remove engine splash guard and drain coolant from radiator.
9. Remove water drain plugs on both sides of upper crankcase section.
10. Drain oil from crankcase.
11. Disconnect exhaust pipes and secondary air injection lines at exhaust manifolds.
12. Disconnect engine to body ground wire at engine.
13. Install radiator drain plug, torquing to 13-17 inch lbs.
14. Remove radiator lower air guide section from radiator.
15. Disconnect ventilation hose at alternator.
16. Disconnect electrical connectors at starter.
17. Disconnect starter wiring clamps on steering crossmember and pull forward toward alternator.
18. Remove clutch housing cover.
19. Remove drive plate attaching bolts, loosen clamping sleeve bolt and push drive plate back on central shaft. **Pins**

for TDC sensor must face down when removing engine.

20. Remove bolts attaching transaxle mounts.
21. Disconnect automatic transaxle vacuum hose at cylinder head and remove clamp.
22. Remove clutch housing mounting bolts at engine block and push transaxle rearward approximately .197-.236 inch (5-6 mm).
23. Lower vehicle.
24. Disconnect electrical connector at A/C compressor, remove compressor attaching bolts and position compressor out of way with hoses still attached.
25. Remove air pump filter housing.
26. Detach radiator to governor housing coolant hoses at housing.
27. Disconnect engine and automatic transaxle cooling lines at radiator.
28. Disconnect temperature switch electrical connector at radiator.
29. Disconnect vent hose at top left of radiator, then remove radiator attaching bolts and remove radiator from above.
30. Disconnect coolant feed hose on coolant pipe at front right, then disconnect adjacent multiple pin plug and the B+ terminal wire.
31. Remove engine to coolant expansion tank vent hose.
32. Remove hose between heater valve and engine connector.
33. Disconnect fuel feed line.
34. Remove TDC sensor.
35. Disconnect fuel return line.
36. Disconnect ignition lead wires on both sides of distributor cap, then detach both ignition coils and position out of way.
37. Disconnect ground wire at body in front of right ignition coil.
38. Detach flushing valve from holder, the charging valve carbon canister hose and the EZF control unit vacuum hose.
39. Detach vacuum hose at brake booster.
40. Disconnect throttle, cruise control and automatic transaxle cables, then remove retainers and clamp on console and position cables out of way.
41. Disconnect hoses at power steering supply tank, drain oil, loosen hose clamp on tank and remove tank.
42. Remove central electric board cover and disconnect plugs for sensor heating and ignition control units and the oxygen sensor.
43. Disconnect multiple pin plugs at EZF and LH control units and the multiple pin plug on right side of central electric board.
44. Push rubber cover out of holder in central electric board and into engine compartment.
45. Raise and support vehicle.
46. Remove attaching bolts for left and right engine mounts.
47. Lower vehicle.
48. Attach suitable lifting equipment to engine lifting eyes and tension slightly.
49. Place wooden block between central tube and crossmember.

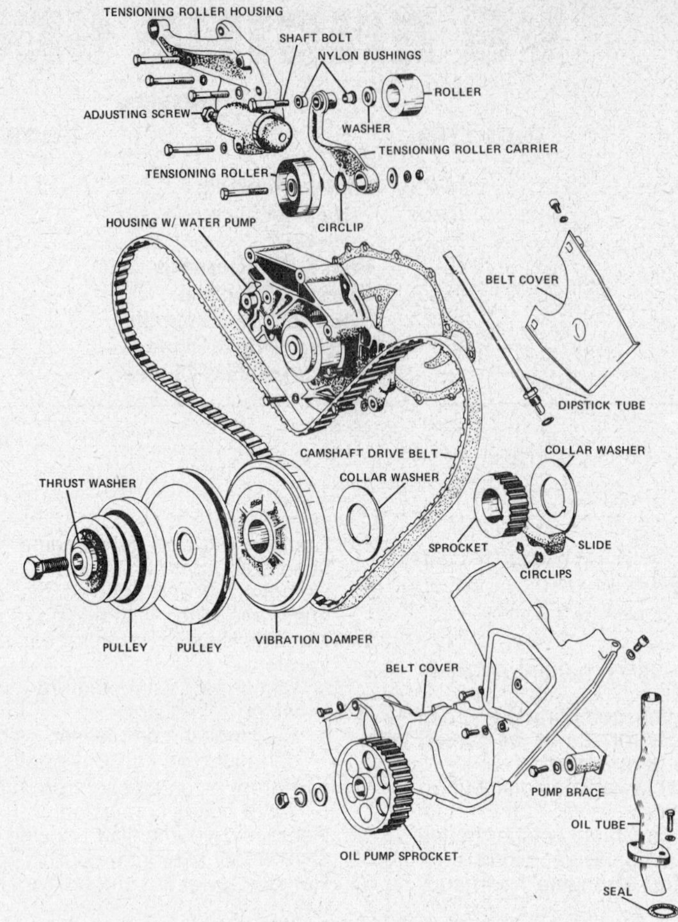

Fig. 1 Exploded view of timing belt assembly. 928 models

50. Tilt engine forward and lift slightly at same time, ensuring engine block and clutch housing have been completely disconnected.
51. Mark installed position of and remove power steering pump pressure hose.
52. Lift engine out of vehicle, ensuring that central electric wire harness does not snag.
53. Reverse procedure to install, noting the following:
    a. Push back transaxle and place wooden block between central tube and crossmember.
    b. Install power steering pump pressure hose in marked position before installing engine.
    c. Ensure central electric wire harness is properly routed.
    d. After lowering engine into hydraulic mounts, remove lifting equipment.
    e. Lift clutch housing and transaxle slightly with suitable jack to move engine into installed position.

VALVE TIMING

INTAKE OPENS AFTER TDC

Engine	Year	Degrees
4664cc	1983-87	11

VALVE GUIDES

1. Using suitable tool, machine off protruding valve guides from camshaft side until guides are flush with cylinder head.
2. Place cylinder head on tool 9220 or equivalent.
3. Loosen valve guides from camshaft end with short blows from hammer on tool 9224 or equivalent and press out remainder of guides toward combustion side.
4. Coat valve guides with tallow, insert with light knock and align and press into cylinder head against stop from camshaft side. Press fit for valve guides is .0024-.0031 inch (.06-.08 mm). **Valve seat inserts must be machined after replacing valve guides. On 1987 928S 4 models, intake valve head diameter is changed from 1.377 inch (35 mm) to 1.456 inch (37 mm). Exhaust valve head diameter is changed from 1.259 inch (32 mm) to 1.338 inch (34 mm). Valve springs and installed distances correspond with those of the 1986 928S. The bearing surface on the cylinder head, however, is machined .078 inch (2 mm) deeper, which is compensat-**

Fig. 2 Aligning right cam sprocket w/indicator. 928 models

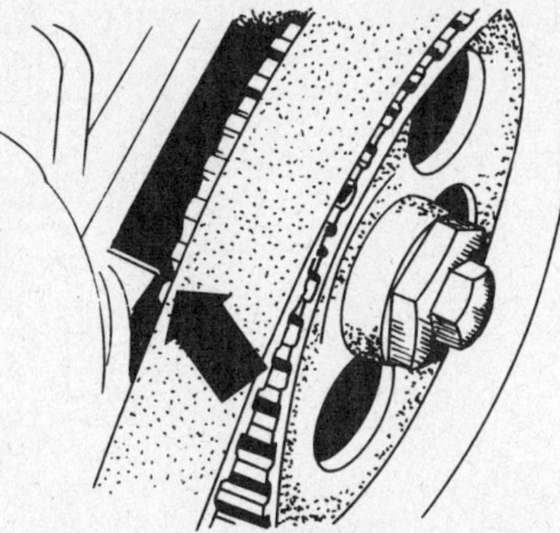

Fig. 3 Aligning left cam sprocket w/indicator. 928 models

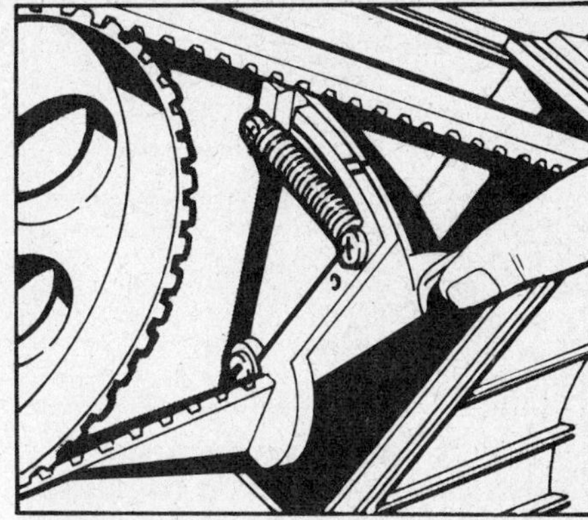

Fig. 4 Checking camshaft belt tension. 928 models

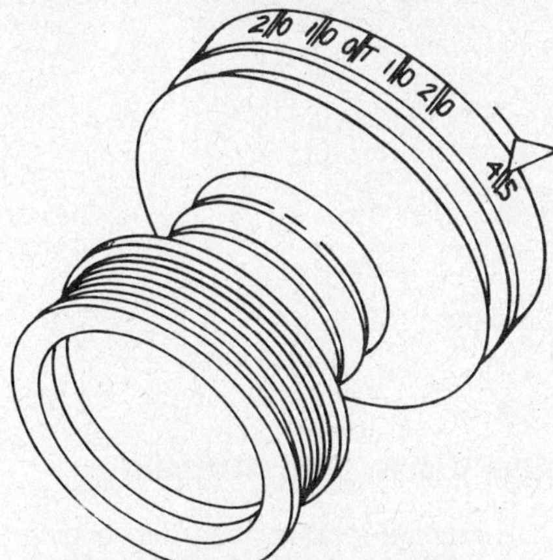

Fig. 5 Aligning 45° BTDC mark. 928 models

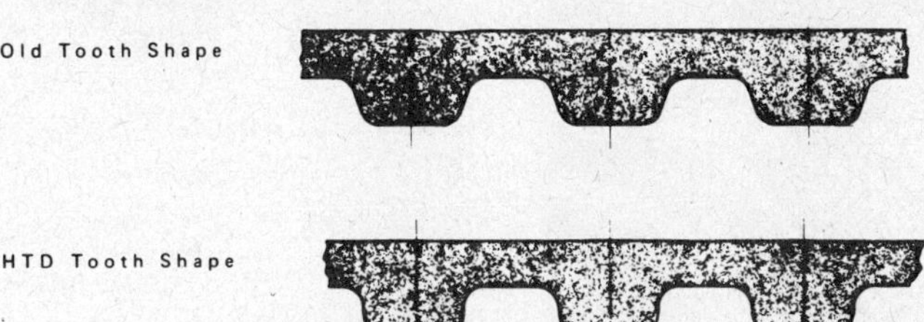

Fig. 6 Timing belt identification. 928 models

ed for by the use of .078 inch (2 mm) thicker stepped washers.

TIMING BELT REPLACE

1983–84

1. When removing timing belt, refer to **Fig. 1.**
2. Line up TDC mark on vibration damper with red indicator on cover by turning crankshaft clockwise. **Vibration damper must be removed again for installation of timing belt.**
3. Turn both camshafts until notches in both camshaft sprockets are aligned with marks cast on camshaft bearing caps, **Figs. 2 and 3.**
4. Install timing belt, always preloaded by hand, in the following order:
   a. On crankshaft sprocket.
   b. On oil pump sprocket.
   c. Over left camshaft sprocket.
   d. On bottom of water pump sprocket.
   e. On right camshaft sprocket.
   f. Over timing belt tensioner roller.
5. If teeth of hand tightened timing belt do not match sprocket pitch, carefully turn camshaft sprocket counterclockwise until teeth match. **Turn camshaft sprocket only enough to allow teeth meshing.**
6. Tighten timing belt to specifications using tool 9131 or equivalent, **Fig. 4.**
7. Turn engine clockwise 720° to align red indicator and TDC mark.
8. Check position of marks.
9. Retighten timing belt.
10. Turn engine clockwise 720° to align red indicator and TDC mark.

1985–87

1. Disconnect battery ground cable.
2. Remove air cleaner intake hoses.
3. Remove drive belts from alternator, power steering pump, air pump and A/C compressor.
4. Disconnect cables for throttle, cruise control and automatic transaxle, then remove retainers and the clamp on console and position cables out of way.
5. Remove fan console from engine.
6. Disconnect right and left side ignition leads at distributor cap, then remove cap and position out of way.
7. Remove both distributor rotors, then disconnect electrical connectors at A/C compressor and the timing belt tightness indicator.
8. Remove right hand upper timing belt cover.
9. Detach power steering pump and position out of way.
10. Remove clutch slave cylinder; remove clamp from clutch hose holder and remove pushrod, letting cylinder hang by connected hose. **Never operate clutch pedal after removing slave cylinder.**
11. Align mark for 45° before TDC (cylinder No. 1) on vibration damper with red needle, **Fig. 5,** by turning crankshaft clockwise. **Camshafts may be turned without damaging valves after aligning 45° mark.**
12. Lock crankshaft by installing tool 9161/1 or equivalent, securing tool with slave cylinder mounting bolts.
13. Remove crankshaft pulley mounting bolt, then both pulleys, vibration damper and the collar.
14. Remove oil dipstick guide tube.
15. Remove alternator together with console.
16. Remove left upper and center timing belt covers.
17. Loosen timing belt with timing belt tensioner.
18. Remove tensioning roller console.
19. Remove timing belt from right hand side over cylinders 1-4 camshaft sprocket, water pump sprocket, cylinders 5-8 camshaft sprocket, oil pump sprocket and crankshaft sprocket.
20. Reverse procedure to install, noting the following:
    a. Install timing belt in reverse order of that described in step 19.
    b. Turn engine in direction of rotation to TDC (cylinder No. 1), then turn camshafts to mark and hold camshafts firmly in position.
    c. Adjust timing belt.

TIMING BELT ADJUST

1983–84

Beginning with 1983 models, the shape of teeth on the timing belt was changed to high torque drive (HTD), Fig. 6. New HTD timing belts can be used on older engines if sprockets with new tooth shape are installed. Sprockets with difference tooth shapes should never be mixed.

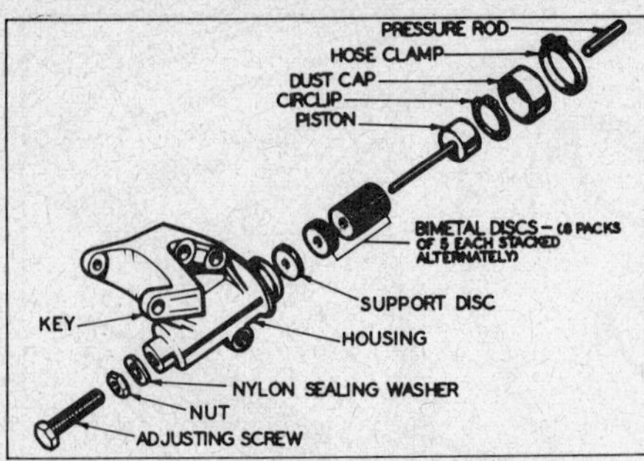

Fig. 7 Belt tensioner exploded view. 928 models

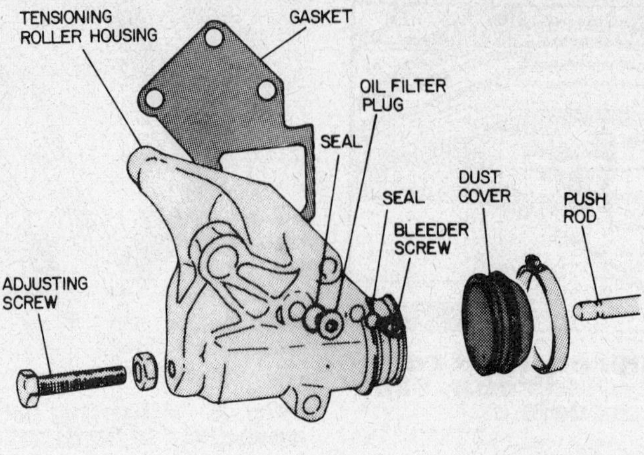

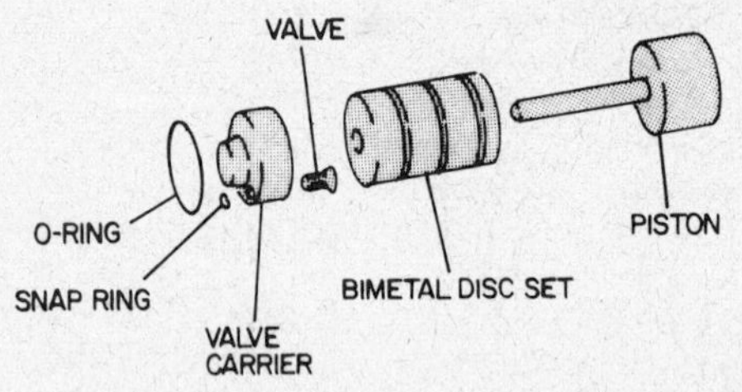

Fig. 8 Belt tensioner exploded view. 928 models

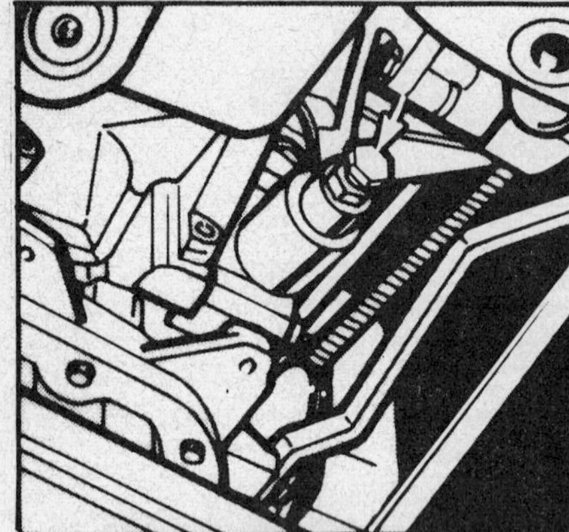

Fig. 9 Adjusting screw location. 928 models

Models Less HTD Timing Belt

1. Remove upper section of timing belt covers on both sides.
2. Turn engine in direction of rotation to TDC (cylinder No. 1) and check whether marks on vibration damper, and camshaft sprockets, **Figs. 2 and 3,** are properly aligned.
3. Turn engine 720° until TDC mark is again reached, checking timing belt for wear and/or damage.
4. Using tool 9131 or equivalent, check timing belt tightness between tension roller and camshaft sprocket on relaxed section of belt **Fig. 4. Tension is correct when marks on tool are aligned. Adjust at hydraulic tensioner, Figs. 7 and 8.**
5. To adjust tensioner, proceed as follows:
   a. Loosen adjusting screw locknut and turn adjusting screw until timing belt tightness is correct. Adjusting screw is located on bottom of engine at front right hand side, **Fig. 9. Tightening screw tightens belt and loosening screw loosens belt.**
   b. Tighten locknut, then turn engine 720° and recheck tightness of belt.

Models With HTD Timing Belt

1. Remove air guide hoses.
2. Remove air guide upper section from above.
3. Remove timing belt upper covers on both sides.
4. Turn engine in direction of rotation to TDC (cylinder No. 1) and check whether marks on vibration dampor, and camshaft sprockets, **Figs. 2 and 3,** are properly aligned.
5. Turn engine 720° until TDC mark is again reached, checking timing belt for wear and/or damage.
6. Prepare tool 9201, or equivalent, for checking by pulling out lock pin and fully sliding out gage pin opposite lock pin, then align maximum indicator with gage indicator.
7. Slide tool on relaxed section of drive belt with sliding shoes on smooth surface and rollers in tooth gap.
8. Slowly press down on tool case until gage button resting on air pump bracket engages.
9. Turning counterclockwise, align maximum indicator with gage indicator.
10. Note reading while keeping tool horizontal to timing belt, ensuring tool does not contact plastic cover. **Sliding shoes must rest on belt with their complete surface. Tool must not be turned or moved on belt while checking.**
11. Pull out lock pin to disengage gage button. Repeat test two or three times.
12. If adjusting value is not 4.5 scale units, adjust as follows:
    a. Loosen adjusting screw locknut and turn adjusting screw until timing belt tightness is correct. Adjusting screw is located on bottom of engine at front right hand side, **Fig. 9. Tightening screw tightens belt and loosening screw loosens belt.**
    b. Tighten locknut, then turn engine 720° and recheck tightness of belt.

1985–87

1. Remove air guide hoses.
2. Remove upper air guide section from above.
3. Remove distributor caps and the upper right hand timing belt cover.
4. Detach upper left hand timing belt cover and push forward.
5. Turn engine in direction of rotation to TDC (cylinder No. 1), ensuring marks on camshaft and flange bearings are aligned.
6. Turn engine 720° until TDC mark is reached again, then continue turning while checking timing belt for wear and/or damage.
7. Prepare tool 9201, or equivalent, for checking by pulling out lock pin and moving testing pin opposite lock pin to starting position, then place drag needle on gage needle.
8. Slide tool on relaxed section of drive belt with sliding shoes on smooth surface and rollers in tooth gap.
9. Slowly press down on tool case until gage button resting on air pump bracket engages.
10. Read test value while keeping tool horizontal to timing belt, ensuring tool does not rest on plastic cover. **Sliding shoes must rest on belt with their complete surface. Tool must not be turned or moved on belt while checking. The drag needle must always be placed on the gage needle after the lock pin has been engaged to eliminate faulty gauge readings. Turn counterclockwise.**
11. Pull out lock pin to disengage gage tip. Repeat test two or three times.

	Piston Dia. KS	Cylinder Bore Dia.	Tolerance Group Code
Standard	3.7385 inches (94.960mm)	3.7387 inches (94.964mm)	0
	3.7389 inches (94.970mm)	3.7391 inches (94.974mm)	1
	3.7393 inches (94.980mm)	3.7395 inches (94.984mm)	2
1st Oversize	3.7582 inches (95.460mm)	3.7584 inches (95.464mm)	0 KD 1
	3.7586 inches (95.470mm)	3.7588 inches (95.474mm)	1 KD 1
	3.7590 inches (95.480mm)	3.7592 inches (95.484mm)	2 KD 1
2nd Oversize	3.7779 inches (95.960mm)	3.7781 inches (95.964mm)	0 KD 2
	3.7783 inches (95.970mm)	3.7785 inches (95.974mm)	1 KD 2
	3.7787 inches (95.980mm)	3.7789 inches (95.984mm)	2 KD 2

Fig. 10 Piston dimension chart. 928 models

Fig. 12 Piston installation position. 928 models

	Piston Dia. KS	Cylinder Bore Dia.	Tolerance Group Code
Standard	3.8179 inches (96.975mm)	3.8189 inches (97.00mm)	0
	3.8183 inches (96.985mm)	3.8192 inches (97.01mm)	1
	3.8187 inches (96.995mm)	3.8197 inches (97.02mm)	2
1st Oversize	3.8376 inches (97.475mm)	3.8386 inches (97.50mm)	0 KD 1
	3.8380 inches (97.485mm)	3.8390 inches (97.51mm)	1 KD 1
	3.8384 inches (97.495mm)	3.8394 inches (97.52mm)	2 KD 1
2nd Oversize	3.8573 inches (97.975mm)	3.8583 inches (90.00mm)	0 KD 2
	3.8577 inches (97.985mm)	3.8587 inches (98.01mm)	1 KD 2
	3.8581 inches (97.995mm)	3.8590 inches (98.02mm)	2 KD 2

Fig. 11 Piston dimension chart. 928 models

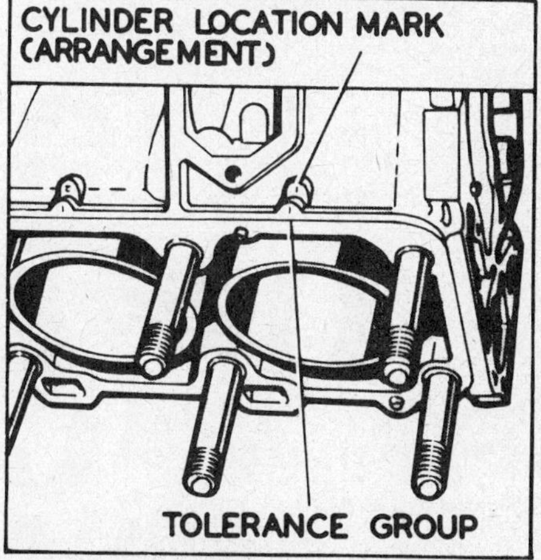

Fig. 13 Cylinder location & tolerance group mark. 928 models

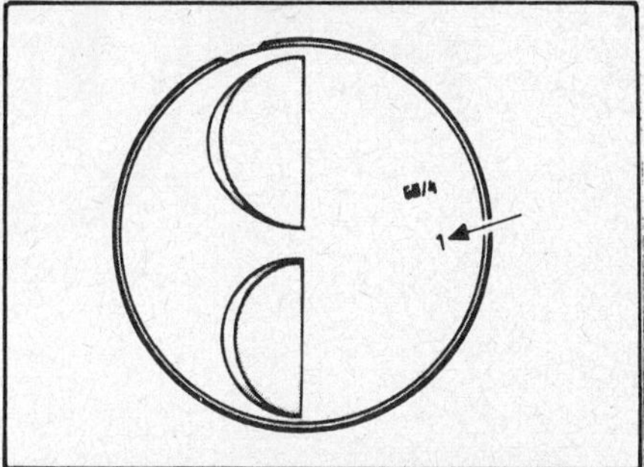

Fig. 14 Piston tolerance group mark. 928 models

12. If adjusting value is not 4.7-5.3, adjust as follows:
    a. Loosen adjusting screw locknut and turn adjusting screw until timing belt tightness is correct. Adjusting screw is located on bottom of engine at front right hand side, **Fig. 9. Tightening screw tightens belt and loosening screw loosens belt.**
    b. Tighten locknut, then turn engine 720° and recheck tightness of belt.

PISTONS, PINS & RINGS

Refer to **Figs. 10 and 11** for piston standard and oversize. Different tolerance groups can be used in the same engine.

PISTON & ROD ASSEMBLY

Install pistons to rods so that valve reliefs face outboard, **Fig. 12.** Install pistons into cylinders of same tolerance group, **Figs. 13 and 14.**

Pistons and piston pins are paired according to weight. Pistons are weighed with piston pins, piston rings and circlips. Piston pins must always remain in corresponding pistons and must not be interchanged within a set of pistons for one engine. If pistons and pins are interchanged, they must be rearranged by checking total weight. Weight of each piston assembly should be 25.3454-25.6278 ounces. **Different tolerance groups could be used in the same engine.**

MAIN & ROD BEARINGS

Narrow side of connecting rod and cap face adjacent connecting rod. Wide side faces crankshaft counterweight, **Figs. 15 and 16.** Torque crankshaft lower section attaching bolts in sequence shown in **Fig. 17.**

REAR CRANKSHAFT OIL SEAL

Refer to **Fig. 15** for service. Align and install seal using tool 9126 or equivalent.

OIL PUMP

REPLACE

1. Hold oil pump drive sprocket using tool 9157 or suitable fixture.
2. Remove oil pump mounting bolts and pump.
3. Reverse procedure to install.

CAMSHAFT

REPLACE

1983–84

1. Disconnect battery ground cable.
2. Remove timing belt as previously described.
3. Remove camshaft housing.
4. Remove shaft seal, spacer, O-ring, distributor gear and spacer.
5. Remove flange bearings.
6. Remove camshaft from housing.
7. Reverse procedure to install, noting the following:
    a. Install new seals and O-ring.
    b. Ensure spacer is correctly positioned.
    c. When installing washer for camshaft sprocket attaching bolt, ensure flat surface faces sprocket.
    d. Torque camshaft sprocket attaching bolt in 47 ft. lbs. while holding hexagon washer.
    e. Install new camshaft housing gasket, ensuring "TOP" mark faces up.
    f. Torque camshaft housing attaching bolts to 14 ft. lbs.
    g. Lightly lubricate camshaft housing plugs and install by hand. If alumi-

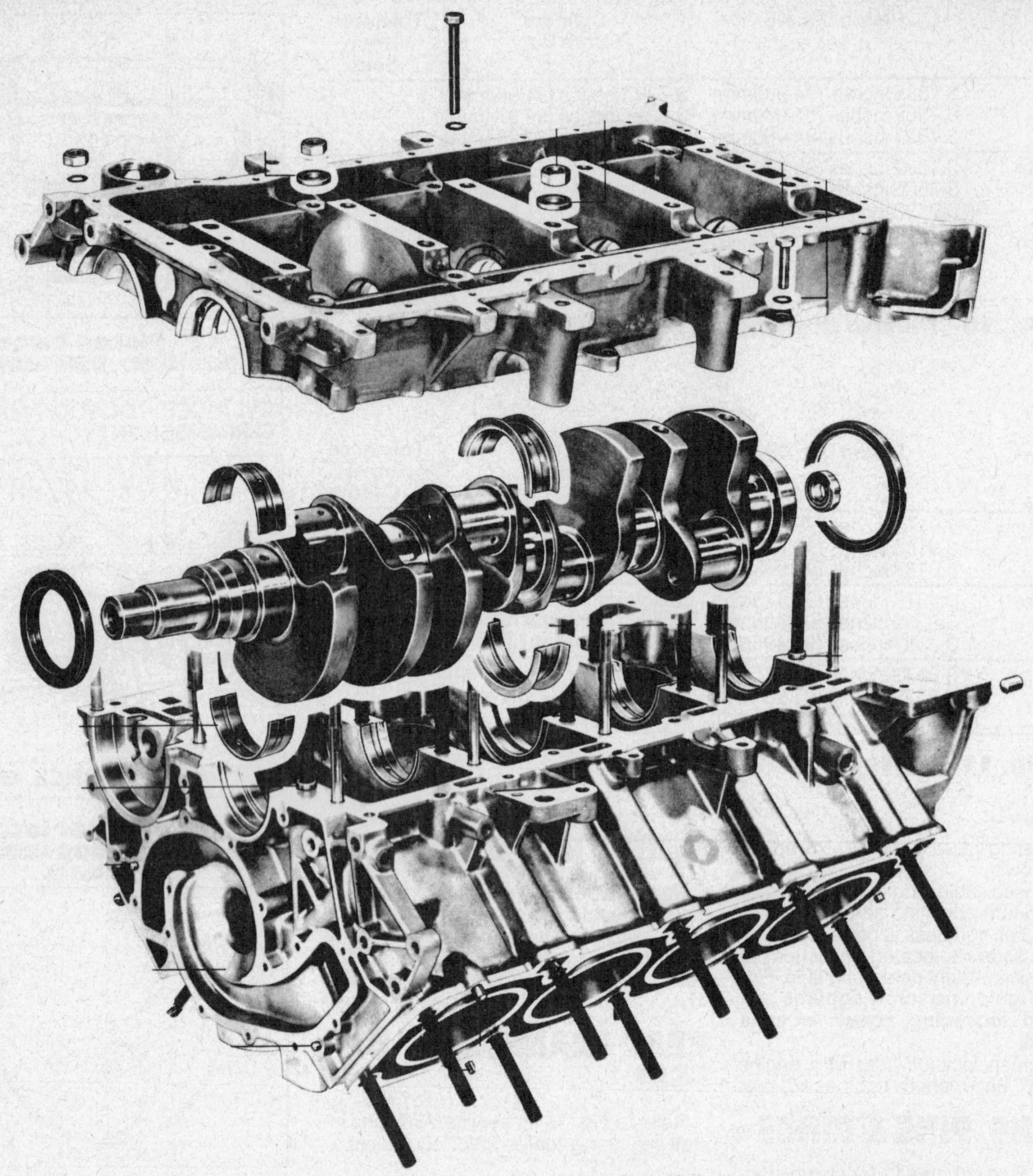

Fig. 15 Crankcase & crankshaft exploded view. 928 models

num plugs are used, torque to 29 ft. lbs.

1985–87

1. Disconnect battery ground cable.
2. Remove crossmember.
3. Remove air cleaner assembly with intake hoses.
4. Remove intake air distributor.
5. Remove distributor cap, distributor rotor, timing belt upper section and the cylinder head cover.
6. Turn crankshaft clockwise to align 45° before TDC mark (cylinder No. 1) on vibration damper with cast boss of center timing belt cover. **At 45° mark, camshafts can be turned without damaging valves.**
7. Loosen timing belt with tensioner and remove belt from camshaft sprocket.
8. Remove camshaft attaching bolt, then the sprocket, drive hub and woodruff key from exhaust camshaft.
9. Remove rear timing belt cover.
10. Set marks on camshafts to face up by turning exhaust camshaft with suitable tool.
11. Remove timing chain tensioner. Tensioner piston has spring force. Compress piston for removal and hold together with suitable piece of wire after removing.
12. Secure camshafts in bearings using tool 9226 or equivalent and remove bearing bridges and caps.
13. Release tool uniformly and remove camshafts together with timing chain.
14. Place camshafts in timing chain so that marks on camshafts or cast bosses are aligned with marked chain links, then lubricate bearing surfaces with oil and carefully place timing chain in bearings.
15. Mount camshafts on cylinder head using tool 9226 or equivalent.
16. Install bearing bridges and bearing caps, torquing to 7 ft. lbs. **Bearing bridges and caps are machined together with cylinder head and must always be installed in correct position. Ensure that codes and pairing numbers match.**
17. Coat sealing surfaces of front and rear double bearing bridges with suitable

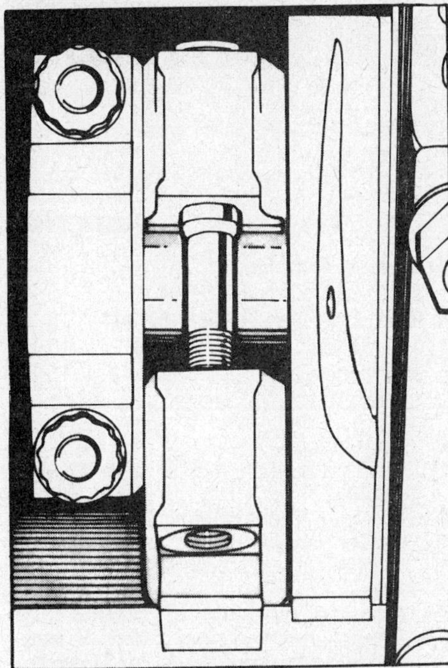

Fig. 16 Connecting rod & cap installation. 928 models

locking compound.

18. Recheck camshaft position using gage from tool 9226, or equivalent.
19. Using tools 9233 and 9234, or equivalents, drive seal on to drive end of camshaft. Lubricate sealing lip before installing.
20. Reverse remainder of removal procedure to complete installation, then adjust camshafts as follows:
    a. Turn engine in operating direction to TDC (cylinder No. 1) and ensure both distributor rotors face left, marks on camshaft sprockets and flange bearings are aligned, and marks on camshafts face exhaust side.
    b. Mount dial gage with holder VW387 or equivalent on cylinder head. Set dial gage on hydraulic lifter of cylinder No. 1 intake valve to 0 with 5 mm preload.
    c. Set dial gage on hydraulic lifter of cylinder No. 6 intake valve and zero indicator. Dial gage must be aligned perpendicular to intake valve.
    d. Turn crankshaft further from TDC while observing dial gage. Turn until a value of 1-3 mm lift is obtained and ensure mark for 20° after TDC (cylinder No. 6) is aligned with pointer on timing belt cover. If alignment is not correct, proceed to step e.
    e. Install three M5 15 screws in camshaft sprockets to prevent sprockets or camshafts from turning.
    f. Turn crankshaft in operating direction until dial gage shows 1-3 mm lift.
    g. Remove camshaft attaching bolts while counter holding then remove M5 screws.
    h. Turn crankshaft to 20° after TDC (cylinder No. 6).
    i. Install camshaft sprockets, first installing three M5 15 screws, then torquing attaching bolts (M10) to 47 ft. lbs.
    j. Turn crankshaft 720°, then recheck adjustment. Reading should be 1-3 mm at 20° after TDC for cylinder No. 6. Repeat adjusting procedures as necessary.
    k. Remove M5 15 screws.

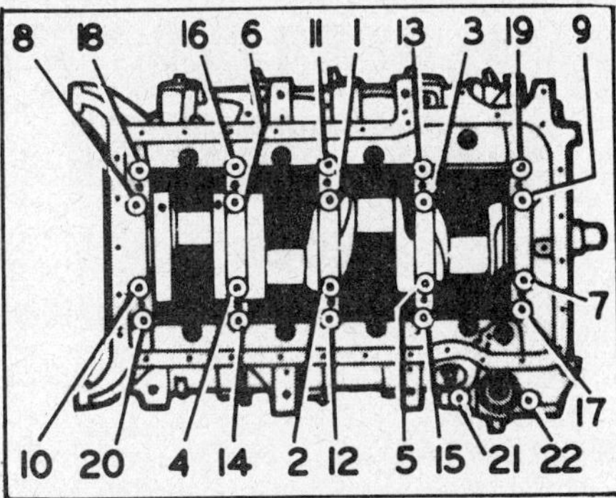

Fig. 17 Crankshaft tightening sequence. 928 models

CYLINDER HEAD

1983–84

Cylinder head can be removed with engine installed in vehicle.

1. Disconnect battery ground cable.
2. Remove timing belt as previously described.
3. Remove camshaft housing.
4. Remove cylinder head attaching nuts, loosening in reverse order of tightening sequence, **Fig. 18.**
5. When installing cylinder head gasket, ensure "TOP" mark faces up and arrow faces front of engine.

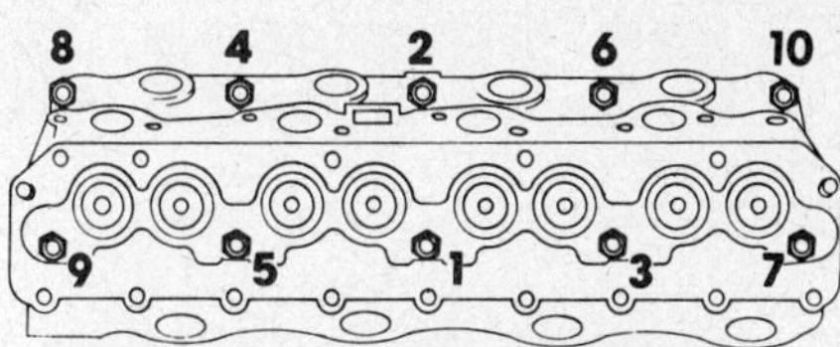

Fig. 18 Cylinder head tightening sequence. 1983–84 928 models

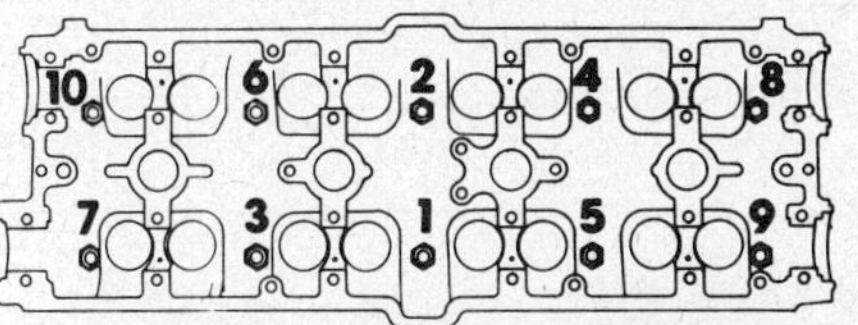

Fig.19 Cylinder head tightening sequence. 1985–87 928 models

6. Apply light coat of oil to cylinder head studs.
7. Torque cylinder head nuts to specifications in proper sequence, **Fig. 18.**
8. When tightening cylinder head nuts, ensure washers do not turn.
9. When installing camshaft housing gasket, ensure "TOP" mark faces up and camshaft oil bore is clear.
10. When installing camshaft housing, torque attaching bolts to 14 ft. lbs.
11. Lightly lubricate camshaft housing plugs and install by hand. If aluminum plugs are used, torque to 29 ft. lbs. and install new seals.
12. Install and adjust timing belt as previously described.

1985–87

Cylinder head cannot be replaced unless engine is removed from vehicle.

1. Remove timing chain and camshafts as previously described.
2. Remove cylinder head attaching bolts in reverse order of tightening sequence, **Fig. 19,** then the cylinder head.
3. Reverse procedure to install noting the following:
    a. Apply light coat of oil to cylinder head studs.
    b. Install new cylinder head gasket, ensuring "TOP" mark faces up and arrow faces front.
    c. Torque cylinder head bolts to specifications in proper sequence, **Fig. 19.**

CLUTCH & MANUAL TRANSAXLE SECTION

INDEX

CLUTCH
ADJUST
911

Since clutch play cannot be measured accurately at the pedal because of the auxiliary spring, clutch play is measured at the transaxle adjusting lever.

1. Disconnect the clutch cable or loosen completely at the holder.
2. Using a feeler gauge, adjust the clutch play to .047 inch (1.2 mm), and lock the adjusting screw.
3. Reconnect the clutch cable.
4. Tighten the clutch cable until clutch play is .045 inch (1.0 mm).

924S, 928, & 944

The release mechanism is a hydraulic, automatic adjustment type. To ensure correct clutch operation, there must be approximately 3 mm of freeplay at the pedal edge.

To check for clutch disc wear limit, remove the plastic inspection plug at the clutch slave cylinder. The wear limit has been reached when the front edge of the release lever just appears in the inspection hole.

CLUTCH
REPLACE
911

1. Remove engine/transaxle assembly from vehicle.
2. Separate engine from transaxle.
3. Loosen clutch attaching bolts alternately and diagonally a little at a time until spring tension is relieved.
4. Remove clutch assembly.
5. Reverse procedure to install.

928

1. Disconnect battery ground cable.
2. Remove lower body brace, if equipped.
3. Loosen clutch slave cylinder attaching bolts.
4. Remove clutch hose bracket.
5. Remove cylinder with line connected.
6. Remove clutch housing cover and starter.
7. Remove catalytic converter.
8. Remove coupling attaching bolts, then push coupling backward on drive shaft. On models equipped with long coupling assembling, remove plug from central tube (torque tube) and remove rear bolt.
9. Remove guide tube attaching bolts, then slide guide tube toward flywheel.
10. Mark position of pressure plate, intermediate plate and flywheel in relation to each other for installation. On models equipped with dowel pin centered clutches, drive pins in direction of pressure plate far enough so they are beyond the centering bore on flywheel.
11. Loosen clutch attaching bolts 1 to 1 1/2 turns until spring tension is relieved from pressure plate. Disconnect release lever from ball stud.
12. Remove clutch assembly from vehicle.
13. Reverse procedure to install.

924S & 944

1. Disconnect battery ground cable.
2. Disconnect ground strap from clutch housing.
3. Disconnect electrical connectors, then remove reference mark sensor and speed sensors.
4. Remove starter harness bracket from clutch assembly.
5. Disconnect exhaust assembly enough to allow clutch removal.
6. Remove heat shield from catalytic converter.
7. Remove splash guard, if equipped.
8. Loosen central tube (torque tube) to rear exhaust pipe bracket attaching bolts.
9. Remove or push back dust cover.
10. Remove shift lever knob retainer.
11. Remove snap ring from shift lever.
12. Pull off selector rod and washer on shift lever bolt.
13. Mark position, then remove shift lever.
14. Press down on insulation and push selector rod forward in cavity.
15. Loosen two uppermost attaching bolts from clutch housing.
16. Remove end cap from central tube (torque tube). Push back protective tube for selector rod far enough, that it is outside of the central tube housing.
17. Remove clamping sleeve attaching bolts.
18. Disconnect joint shafts from transaxle. Do not allow joint shafts to hang.
19. Disconnect back-up light electrical connector.
20. Using a suitable jack lift transmission slightly.
21. Remove transaxle suspension bolts.
22. Lower transaxle with central tube until central tube rests on rear axle cross tube.
23. Remove transaxle to central tube flange attaching bolts. Remove transaxle downward.
24. Remove starter.
25. Pull back on selector rod.
26. Move back central tube far enough until central tube housing rests on transaxle carrier. If central tube cannot be moved out of clutch housing without applying force, secure engine from moving using a suitable hoist and tool VW 10-222 or equivalent.
27. Remove clutch housing guard and right support, if equipped.
28. Remove engine mount nuts and push engine slightly to the right. Remove lower clutch housing attaching bolts.
29. Move out guard and clutch housing with release lever.
30. Remove clutch assembly.
31. Reverse procedure to install.

SHIFT LEVER
ADJUST
911

1. Remove access cover from shift rod tunnel in front of rear seats.
2. Loosen shift rod clamp, then turn shift rod for selector shaft to the right in neutral position.
3. Move shift lever in neutral to the point where lower part of shift lever is positioned vertically and touching left stop.
4. Lightly tighten shift rod clamp.
5. Ensure that travel is equal in gears 1 through 4 and that 5th and reverse gears can be easily engaged, adjusting as necessary.
6. Torque clamp nut to 18 ft. lbs.
7. Shift into 5th gear, then, with dust boot at shift rod coupling pushed back, ensure that rotational play is evident at selector shaft.

924S & 944

1. Place shift lever in neutral.
2. Adjust shift lever to an inclination of 85° by moving shift lever console.

TRANSAXLE

REPLACE

911

Refer to "Engine, Replace" under 4 Cylinder Engine Section for transaxle replacement procedure since the engine and transaxle are removed as an assembly.

1983–84 & EARLY 1985 944

1. Remove catalytic converter together with muffler.
2. Push back dust boot and remove lock wire from shift linkage bolt and remove linkage bolt.
3. Fold back dust boot and inner cover on shift lever.
4. Remove clamp from shift lever knob and remove knob.
5. Remove shift lever circlip and pull off shift rod and spring washer from shift lever pin.
6. Turn shift lever 180°.
7. Press down insulation sheet and push shift lever forward into cavity.
8. Remove plug from central tube housing and push back shift rod protective tube far enough so that it is outside of central tube housing.
9. Insert a large screwdriver through opening in tube housing and open tab on protective tube.
10. Remove coupling screws through openings and move coupling toward transaxle.
11. Remove axle shafts at transaxle and suspend shafts from car with wire to prevent damage.
12. Disconnect wires from back-up light switch.
13. Position a suitable transaxle jack under transaxle with adapter tools US618 and 618/1 or equivalents and move transaxle weight from mounts.
14. Remove transaxle central tube housing flange bolts and transaxle suspension rubber/metal bolts.
15. Lower transaxle and central tube and rest on axle cross tube. Remove transaxle.
16. Reverse procedure to install using the following torque values: oil filler plug in final drive housing 18 ft. lbs. (25 Nm), selector shaft to final drive housing 5 ft. lbs. (6-10 Nm), back-up light switch to final drive housing 22 ft. lbs. (30 Nm), central tube flange to clutch housing 42 ft. lbs. (30 Nm), guide sleeve to clutch housing 10 ft. lbs. (16 Nm), transaxle mount to transaxle 30 ft. lbs. (42 Nm), transaxle mount to rear axle crosstube 30 ft. lbs. (42 Nm), central tube to front transaxle cover 61 ft. lbs. (85 Nm), shift rod to inner shift rod/transaxle 13 ft. lbs. (18 Nm), guide bracket to central floor pan section 6.5 ft. lbs. (9 Nm), and ball socket to guide tube 17 ft. lbs. (23 Nm).

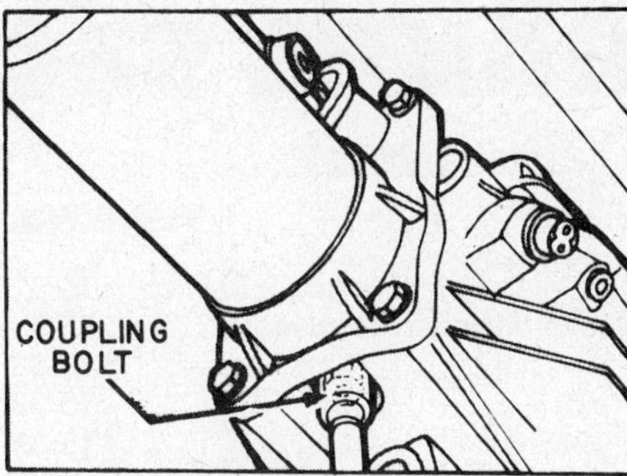

Fig. 1 Removing coupling bolt

924S, LATE 1985 & 1986–87 944

1. Disconnect battery ground cable.
2. Remove rear muffler.
3. Disconnect driveshafts at transaxle and suspend from vehicle horizontally.
4. Disconnect electrical connectors at back-up light switch and speedometer drive.
5. Push back dust cover on shift rod and remove lock wire from bolt, then remove bolt.
6. Carefully press shift knob leather cover out of center console and push up.
7. Remove shift lever knob mounting clamp and the knob.
8. Remove circlip from shift lever.
9. Turn shift lever 180°, press down on insulation sheet and push shift rod forward into produced cavity by approximately 12 inches (300 mm).
10. Working through assembly openings, remove clamping sleeve screws, then push clamping sleeve toward transaxle.
11. Press in retainer with large screwdriver and push protective tube back through large opening in case far enough to clear central pipe housing.
12. Place wooden block between cross tube and central pipe to hold transaxle and central pipe in installed position.
13. Place suitable jack under transaxle and attach securely.
14. Remove transaxle suspension mounting bolts.
15. Remove transaxle to central pipe housing attaching bolts.
16. Remove transaxle toward rear of vehicle.
17. Reverse procedure to install, noting the following:
    a. If shift rod protective tube retainers are excessively worn, replace tube.
    b. Place shift rod protective tube in transaxle, torquing bolts as follows: M10 60, 31 ft. lbs.; M12 75 and M12 80, 62 ft. lbs.
    c. Push shift rod protective tube forward until retainer engages in transaxle case.
    d. Mount shift rod on intermediate lever and lock clamping bolt with steel wire.
    e. On models with double point transaxle suspension, torque bolts as follows: transaxle mount to body, 34 ft. lbs.; mount to bracket and bracket transaxle, 18 ft. lbs.
    f. On models with single point transaxle suspension torque bolts as follows: transaxle carrier to body, 34 ft. lbs.; transaxle mount to carrier, bracket to transaxle mount and bracket to transaxle, 17 ft. lbs.

928

1. Raise and support vehicle. Loosen rear wheel lug nuts.
2. Remove battery. Remove nuts securing rear springs struts in trunk.
3. Shift transaxle into 5th gear.
4. Remove rubber plug from transaxle inspection hole and disconnect coupling, Fig. 1. **To position coupling for bolt removal, hold one wheel and turn the other.**
5. Shift transaxle into neutral, remove rear wheels then disconnect and suspend brake calipers.
6. From catalytic converter rearward remove exhaust system.
7. Remove heat shields and battery box.
8. Disconnect wiring from back-up light switch and speedometer transmitter, then remove wiring from clips.
9. Pull back shift boot, remove Allen head setscrew from coupling and shift rod from main rod.
10. Disconnect axles from transaxle and support in a horizontal position.
11. Disconnect stabilizer bar from lower control arms.
12. Secure transaxle housing to stabilizer bar with wire.
13. Remove crossmember to transaxle bolts and the two crossmember to frame bolts located near transaxle mounts.
14. Place a transaxle jack under crossmember. Mark crossmember to body location, then remove remaining bolts.
15. Tilt rear axle assembly carefully; make sure spring struts and control arms do not twist. **Support rear axle in a tilted position to keep weight off lower control arm link pins.**
16. Position transaxle jack under transaxle. Disconnect central tube and remove transaxle from stabilizer bar. Move transaxle back to one side, then lower from vehicle.
17. Reverse procedure to install.

DISC BRAKES SECTION

INDEX

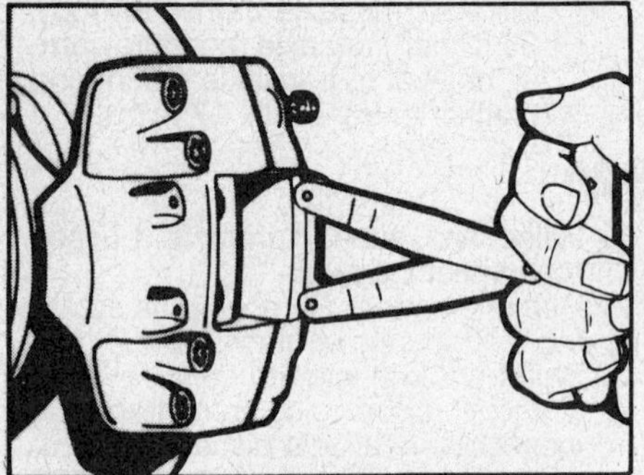

Fig. 1 Removing brake pads

Fig. 2 Positioning caliper pistons

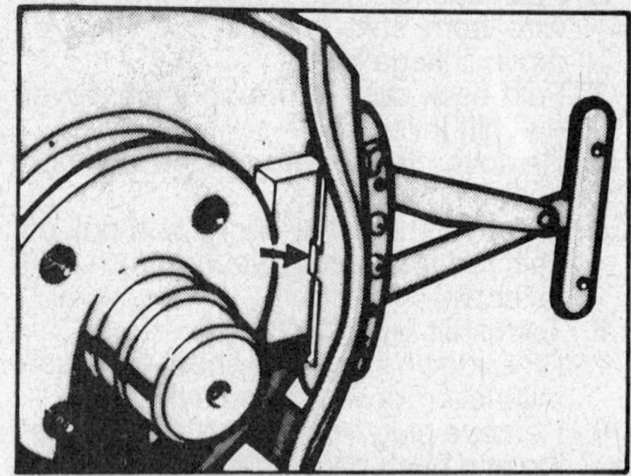

Fig. 3 Removing outboard brake pads

FRONT DISC BRAKE SERVICE

BRAKE PADS, REPLACE

911

1. Raise and support vehicle.
2. Using a pair of suitable pliers, remove brake pad pin retainers.
3. Drive pad retaining pins out with a suitable drift and hammer.
4. For pads that are still serviceable, mark their original positions so that they may be reinstalled in original position.
5. Remove the pads using tool P86, **Fig. 1.**
6. Position pistons back in caliper using tool P83, **Fig. 2. Brake fluid will be forced back into the reservoir. To prevent overflowing, siphon some fluid from reservoir.**
7. Clean brake pad contact surface in their slots in the caliper. **Do not use mineral solvents or sharp edged tools.**
8. Check dust boots and clamping rings for damage and replace hard or porous boots.
9. Clean brake discs with fine emery cloth.
10. Install new brake pads in caliper slots together with retaining pins, springs, and pin retainers. **Depress brake pedal several times before moving vehicle to properly position caliper pistons.**
11. Check brake fluid level.

911 Turbo

If brake pads are going to be reused, mark pads for installation. Do not interchange pads from inboard to outboard or from left to right wheel assemblies.

1. Disconnect battery ground cable.
2. Raise and support vehicle.
3. Remove wheel and tire assembly.
4. Using suitable pliers, pull out warning contact (wear indicator) from brake pad plate. **Replace wear indicators, if lead core is ground through. The wear indicator is still usable, if only the plastic portion of the indicator has signs of grinding.**
5. Using tool 1966-2 or equivalent, remove brake pads.
6. Reverse procedure to install.

924S & 944

If brake pads are serviceable, pads must be marked for installation in original position.

1. Raise and support vehicle, then remove wheel and tire assembly.
2. Remove retaining pin spring locks, if equipped.
3. Drive out brake paid retaining pins with suitable hammer and drift.
4. Pull brake pad wear indicator warning contact out of pad plate, if equipped.
5. Remove inboard brake pad with tool P86 or equivalent, **Fig. 1.**
6. Using a suitable screwdriver, pry floating frame to full outboard position and remove outboard brake pad. **Outboard brake pad is guided by a tab on the floating caliper frame, Fig. 3.**
7. Replace oil contaminated, cracked or loose pads.
8. Press caliper pistons back into position. **Ensure brake fluid reservoir does not overflow during step 8 by siphoning off any excess.**
9. Clean pad seats and sliding surfaces in caliper. **Do not use cleaning fluids containing mineral oils.**
10. Check that caliper piston is positioned at 20°, if necessary adjust with special pliers. **When using a piston gauge, hold gauge at bottom guide surface of front caliper and top of rear brake caliper, Fig. 4.**
11. Install outboard brake pad and press floating caliper frame toward brake disc so pin engages in groove of pad backplate.
12. Install inboard brake pad.
13. Install retaining pins and cross spring.
14. Press brake pad wear indicator warning contact into inner pad backplate, if equipped.
15. Install retaining pin spring locks, if equipped. **Before moving vehicle, depress brake pedal several times to properly position caliper piston.**

944 Turbo

If brake pads are going to be reused, mark pads for installation. Do not interchange brake pads from outboard to inboard or from one wheel to other.

1. Disconnect battery ground cable.
2. Raise and support vehicle.
3. Remove tire and wheel assembly.
4. Compress, then remove cross spring.
5. Disconnect wear indicator electrical connector, then pull indicator from brake pad backing plate.
6. Using a suitable tool, remove brake pads from caliper(s).

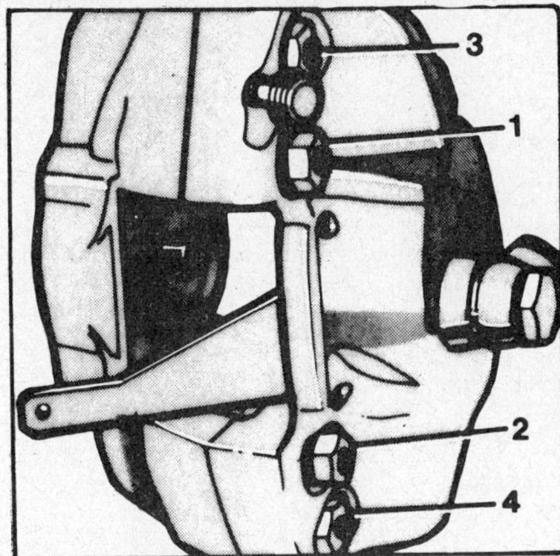

Fig. 4 Brake piston position gauge

7. Replace worn and/or cracked brake pads, as necessary. **Always replace all four brake pads on one axle side. Do not replace only one brake pad.**
8. Using a suitable tool, push brake pad into position. **In order to prevent brake fluid reservoir from overflowing. Siphon some brake fluid from reservoir.**
9. Clean brake pad bearing and sliding surfaces in brake calipers with methylated spirits and a suitable brush. Never use solvents containing mineral oils, or sharp edged metal tools. Brake pad recess play should be .015-.023 inch (.4-.6 mm).
10. Check position of larger brake pistons in front fixed calipers. The edges of the shoulder on the piston must be parallel to the sliding surfaces of the brake lining. The shoulder (offset surface) must face the brake disc inlet.

928

1. Raise and support vehicle, then remove wheel and tire assembly.
2. Pull wear sensor warning contact out of inner pad plate.
3. Apply pressure in center of housing retaining spring until it disengages from housing bores and remove spring outward without applying force.
4. Remove dirt on guide pins between holder and housing.
5. Pull plugs out of guide sleeve, then remove guide pins.
6. Pull housing toward outside of vehicle to depress piston slightly, then remove housing and pull inboard brake pad out of piston.
7. Position housing out of way and suspend from vehicle body with wire.
8. Remove outboard brake pad from holder.
9. Using suitable tool, bottom piston in housing.
10. Clean pad gliding surfaces in housing and holder. Do not use mineral solvents or sharp edged tools.
11. Check 20° piston position and adjust with special pliers as necessary.

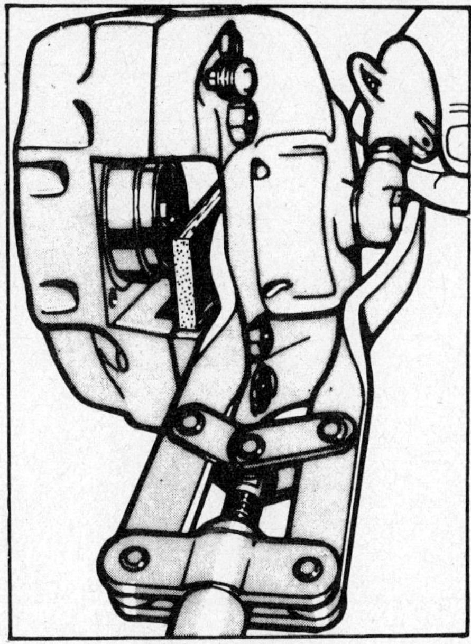

Fig. 5 Brake caliper piston removal

12. Push brake pad with riveted retaining clip into piston and place other pad on outside of holder's guiding surface on brake disc.
13. Place housing over brake disc and brake pad and install guide pins.
14. Insert plugs in guide sleeves.
15. Insert housing retaining spring, ensuring it engages in housing bore.
16. Insert warning contact.
17. Depress brake pedal several times to position piston and pads.
18. Add brake fluid to master cylinder as necessary.

FRONT CALIPER, REPLACE & SERVICE

911

1. Raise and support vehicle.
2. Remove wheels and brake pads.
3. Disconnect brake hydraulic line. **Using a suitable device, depress and hold brake pedal to restrict flow of brake fluid from reservoir.**
4. Remove caliper retaining bolts, caliper, and metal shield.
5. Loosen bleeder valve and carefully blow hydraulic fluid out of caliper. **The recommended air pressure for fluid removal is 14 psi.**
6. Position the caliper in a soft jaw vise and remove the clamping ring and dust boot.
7. Depress one caliper piston with tool P83 and position a wood block approximately 1/3 inches thick between the tool arm and the piston being removed, **Fig. 5**. Apply pressure. **Start with 29 psi, and raise the pressure as necessary. Keep fingers clear of caliper slot. Repair cylinders one at a time since pressure cannot be built up with one removed.**
8. Remove piston seal with a plastic pin to prevent damage to cylinder bore groove.

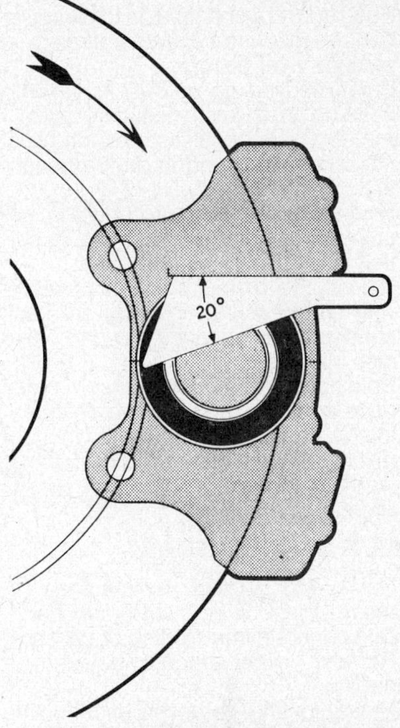

Fig. 6 Aligning piston in caliper cylinder

9. Clean parts in alcohol. **Disassemble calipers only if the O-rings which seal the fluid passages between both caliper halves are defective and leak.**
10. Check cylinder bore, piston, and slot surfaces for damage.
11. Coat cylinder bore, piston, and piston seal with ATE brake paste.
12. Install piston seal into cylinder bore groove.
13. Position piston into caliper cylinder using aligning tool P84, **Fig. 6.**
14. Remove brake cylinder paste from piston ridge and install dust covers.
15. Install caliper and bleed brake hydraulic system.

928

1. Raise and support vehicle, then remove wheel and tire assembly.
2. Disconnect hydraulic line and the wear indicator warning contact.
3. Remove housing attaching bolts and the housing assembly.
4. Remove housing retaining spring, **Fig. 7.**
5. Pull plugs out of guides and remove guide pins.
6. Remove housing, then take outboard brake pad out of holder and pull inboard brake pad out of piston.
7. Support piston firmly on piece of wood and press piston halfway out of housing with compressed air, take sealing lip of dust cover out of piston groove, then press piston fully out of housing.
8. Remove seal with a plastic needle.
9. Apply a very thin coat of brake cylinder paste on cylinder bore, piston and seal.

10. Push dust cover on inside of piston far enough that large diameter sealing lip extends over piston.
11. Press sealing lip of dust cover into housing groove with piston in approximately correct position, ensuring seal fits properly around its entire periphery.
12. Press piston slowly into housing, ensuring small diameter sealing lip settles in groove of piston.
13. Adjust 20° piston position precisely with piston pliers, ensuring set back surface of piston faces down to brake disc inlet side.
14. Bolt holder to housing, insert brake pads and housing retaining springs.
15. Install housing assembly, then connect hydraulic line and wear sensor warning contact.
16. Bleed brake system.

924S & 944 MODELS

1. Raise and support vehicle then remove wheel on side to be serviced.
2. Disconnect hydraulic line at caliper.
3. Remove caliper attaching bolt and the caliper.
4. Press floating frame off of mounting frame.
5. Remove spring guide, if equipped, then run mounting frame out of floating frame.
6. Drive brake cylinder off of floating frame with a plastic hammer applied alternately to both sides using a wooden liner in floating frame to avoid damage.
7. Press piston out of cylinder with compressed air, supporting piston firmly on block of wood.
8. Remove seal using a plastic rod.
9. Apply a very thin seal of brake cylinder paste to cylinder bore, piston and seal.
10. Press piston into cylinder in approximately correct position (20° chamfer).
11. Drive brake cylinder with spring guide on to floating frame with a soft mandrel applied alternately to both sides.
12. Insert mounting frame, being careful not to damage slides, if equipped.
13. Accurately adjust piston to the 20° position with suitable piston turning pliers.
14. Install caliper, torquing attaching bolt to 61 ft. lbs.
15. Connect hydraulic lines at caliper.
16. Install wheel and bleed brake system.

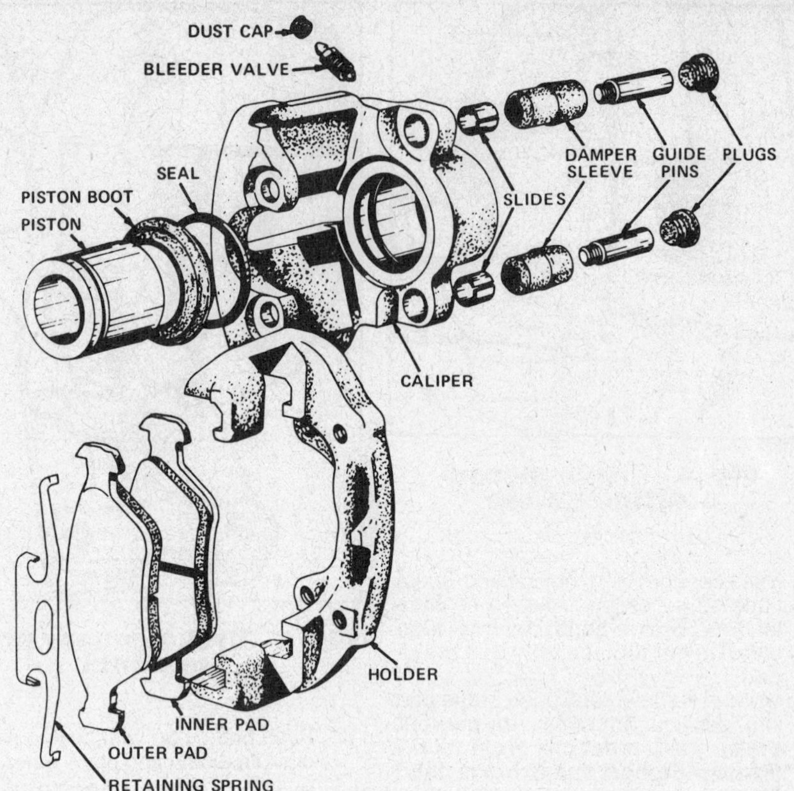

Fig. 7 Exploded view of floating brake caliper

REAR DISC BRAKE SERVICE

911, 924S, 928, & 944

Refer to "Front Disc Brake Service" for these models.

PARKING BRAKE ADJUST

911

1. Raise and support vehicle.
2. Remove rear wheels.
3. Release brake cable tension at adjusting nuts behind disc splash shield.
4. Insert screwdriver into adjustment opening in rear brake disc assembly.
5. Rotate parking brake adjustment sprocket so that disc can no longer be rotated by hand.
6. Repeat step 5 on opposite side.
7. Adjust cable tension until slack is removed by rotating adjustment nuts behind brake disc splash shield.
8. Remove tunnel cover and parking brake lever boot and check position of cable equalizer.
9. Position the equalizer in the two inspection holes when lever is pulled up.
10. To adjust the position of equalizer, rotate the adjustment nuts behind splash shield.
11. After equalizer has been properly positioned, lock adjustment nuts.
12. Back off adjustment sprockets inside each brake drum 4-5 teeth, so that disc rotates freely. **The parking brake should be set when the lever is pulled up 4 clicks.**

928

Adjust parking brake if lever can be pulled beyond 8 clicks with average force and no braking effect is noted.

1. Raise and support vehicle.
2. Remove rear wheels.
3. Release parking brake and press pads into rear caliper until disc rotates freely.
4. Remove brake lever boot and rotate adjusting nut on lever/cable connector until cable is tension free.
5. Insert screwdriver into adjustment hole in rear brake disc and rotate adjuster until it stops.
6. Rotate adjuster back until wheel turns freely.
7. Pull up parking brake lever two teeth, and rotate adjustment nut under boot until wheels can be rotated by hand.
8. Release parking brake lever and check that wheels rotate freely.
9. Tighten adjuster locknut.

924S & 944

1. Raise and support vehicle and remove rear wheels.
2. Release parking brake and press back disc brake pads on rear wheels until brake disc can be turned easily.
3. Loosen adjusting nut on clamp enough to relieve cable tension.
4. Insert screwdriver into hole in disc and turn adjusting device until wheel cannot be turned.
5. Turn adjusting device back until wheel can be turned freely.
6. Pull up parking brake lever two teeth and turn adjusting nut until wheels can still be turned by hand.
7. Ensure that wheels cannot be turned by hand at fourth tooth.
8. Release parking brake lever and ensure that both wheels turn freely.
9. Lock adjusting nut.
10. Install wheels and lower vehicle.

MASTER CYLINDER REPLACE

911

1. Remove operating rod lock pin.
2. Remove master cylinder mounting bolt located inside on luggage compartment floor plate.
3. Drain brake fluid reservoir with suitable siphon.
4. Disconnect stop light switches, vacuum hose clamp, and brake lines.
5. Remove upper bolt from booster body and booster base retaining nuts.
6. Reverse procedure to install.

928

1. Remove intake hoses and upper section of air cleaner assembly.
2. Drain both chambers of master cylinder by pumping out brake fluid via bleeder valves of front or rear brake calipers.
3. Disconnect vacuum hose with check valve at brake booster.
4. Disconnect vacuum line on branch, electrical connector for warning device, and hose for clutch control.
5. Remove brake fluid tank and disconnect electrical connectors for stop light switches.
6. Disconnect brake lines.
7. Remove master cylinder attaching bolts and the master cylinder.
8. Reverse procedure to install, noting the following:
   a. Replace O-ring between master cylinder and brake booster.
   b. Install master cylinder and connect brake lines.
   c. Press brake fluid tank into sealing plugs in master cylinder.
   d. Fill brake fluid tank with suitable fluid and bleed brake/clutch system.

924S & 944

1. Place rags underneath master cylinder and on left wheel housing.
2. Pull brake fluid tank out of master cylinder and catch escaping brake fluid.
3. Place tank with connected clutch hose on wheel house.
4. Disconnect brake lines at master cylinder.
5. Remove master cylinder attaching nuts and the master cylinder.
6. Reverse procedure to install, noting the following:
   a. Install new seal between master cylinder and brake booster and new plugs in the brake fluid tank.
   b. Bleed brakes and clutch.

BRAKE BOOSTER REPLACE

911

1. Remove brake booster operating rod lock pin.
2. Remove master cylinder attaching bolt from luggage compartment floor plate.
3. Drain brake fluid reservoir.
4. Disconnect electrical connectors for stop light switch, then disconnect vacuum hose at brake booster and the brake lines at master cylinder.
5. Remove brake booster brace upper attaching bolt and the booster base attaching nuts, then remove master cylinder and booster as an assembly. **Brace and operating rod do not have to be disconnected at pedal assembly to remove brake booster.**
6. Reverse procedure to install, noting the following:
   a. Clevis for operating rod must be installed so that clevis clip can be installed from above. **Operating rod must be attached when brake pedal is at its rest position without any force applied to operating lever. The play set at the factory must not be changed.**
   b. Torque booster base nuts and the master cylinder bolt to 18 ft. lbs.
   c. Torque support to rod bolt to 25 ft. lbs.
   d. Pull brake pedal back to stop.
   e. Loosen nuts on operating rod, then adjust rod until lock pin for operating lever can be installed without tension.
   f. Tighten nuts on operating rod, then bleed brake system.
   g. Check operating rod play at brake pedal by manual operation with engine off. Play must be at least .4 inch (10 mm).

928

1. Remove master cylinder as previously described.
2. On 1983 models, remove brake pressure regulator on wheel house.
3. On all models, depress, brake pedal and clamp master cylinder pushrod.
4. Adjust connector to limit amount of protrusion of brake pushrod from booster, then again depress brake pedal and adjust clamp.
5. Remove connector.
6. Remove cover and the booster attaching bolts.
7. If applicable, remove brake line for right front wheel from holder on cross wall and carefully push toward engine, then route hose for clutch master cylinder and electric wires out of way.
8. Remove booster, removing lower section of air cleaner as necessary to facilitate removal.
9. If necessary, replace gasket between booster and firewall. Use 2 mm thick gasket for ten inch booster and a 4 mm or two 2 mm gaskets for nine inch booster.
10. Install booster, ensuring caps fit properly above control housing.
11. Install brake pressure regulator and the master cylinder, replacing seal between booster and master cylinder.
12. Mount brake pushrod and connector on brake pedal.
13. Pull back brake pedal arm to stop, then loosen locknut on pushrod and adjust pushrod until play of at least .4 inch (10 mm) is obtained.
14. Tighten locknut on pushrod and, on 1984-87 models, connect position of stop light switch by turning mounting nuts until there is a distance of .197 inch (5 mm) between switch and pedal arm when pedal is on stop.
15. Bleed brake/clutch system.

924S & 944

1. Remove master cylinder as previously described.
2. Disconnect vacuum line at brake booster and remove oil dipstick.
3. Uniformly pry off fuel line holding clip on mounting bolt adjacent to adapter.
4. Remove pushrod lock pin at brake pedal.
5. Disconnect throttle cable at accelerator pedal, then pull down insulation sheet in footwell.
6. Remove brake booster/adapter assembly mounting nuts, then remove brake booster from above at engine compartment end.
7. Screw swivel joint on brake pushrod and adjust so that distance between circumference of larger lip and center of hole of pushrod mounting is 7.28-7.36 inches (185-187 mm).
8. Attach brake booster to adapter in correct position.
9. Install booster in vehicle, guiding in and mounting pushrod swivel joint on brake pedal.
10. Adjust stop light switch as necessary by turning mounting bolts so that distance between switch and brake pedal is .197 inch (5 mm) with pedal in neutral position.
11. Mount fuel line retaining clips.
12. Install master cylinder, using new seal between master cylinder and booster and new plugs for brake fluid reservoir.
13. Bleed brakes and clutch.

REAR SUSPENSION & AXLE SHAFTS SECTION

INDEX

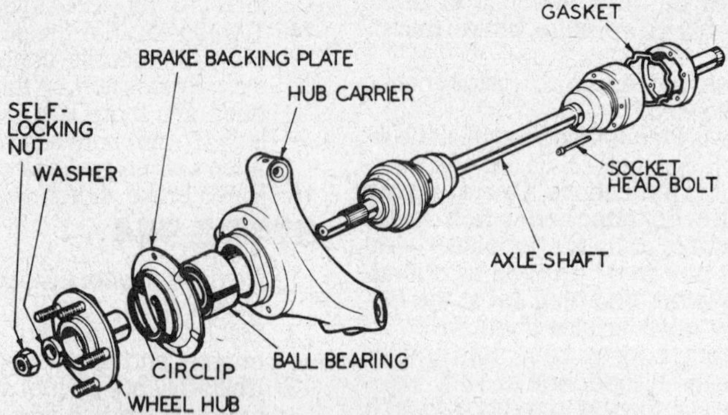

Fig. 1 Hub carrier & axle shaft

Fig. 2 Removing rear wheel hub. 911 models

LOWER CONTROL ARM REPLACE

928

1. Raise and support vehicle.
2. Remove axle shaft with stub axle, **Fig. 1.**
3. Remove brake caliper.
4. Remove brake disc retaining screws and disc.
5. Remove parking brake shoes and spreader lever.
6. Remove parking brake cable from guide in hub assembly.
7. Remove hub assembly.
8. Remove lower diagonal control arm after removing eccentric bolts and stabilizer bar link bolt, **Fig. 1.**
9. Reverse procedure to install. **Check axle alignment.**

TRAILING ARM SERVICE

911

1. Raise and support vehicle, then remove rear wheels.
2. Depress brake pedal slightly and hold in position.
3. Remove brake line between fixed caliper and brake hose.
4. Remove brake hose clip from rear axle semi-trailing arm, then disconnect brake hose.
5. Loosen brake caliper attaching bolts and remove caliper.
6. Loosen countersunk head bolts on brake disc and remove disc.
7. Support trailing arm with suitable jack and remove shock absorber attaching bolt.
8. Remove cotter pin from castellated nut and remove nut.
9. Remove half shaft to joint flange attaching bolts, strike with flat chisel near flange gasket to separate half shaft from joint flange, and remove half shaft.
10. Drive out axle shaft toward center of vehicle.
11. Using tool No. P297a or equivalent, drive out rear wheel hub, **Fig. 2.**
12. Remove cotter pin and castellated nut from brake cable end and pull brake cable out toward center of vehicle.
13. Unscrew hexagon nut attaching shield plate.
14. Remove four brake carrier plate attaching nuts and remove brake carrier plate and shield plate.
15. Disconnect hand brake cable guide.
16. Remove attaching bolts and nuts and eccentric bolts of rear axle semi-trailing arm flange.
17. Remove semi-trailing arm pivot bearing attaching nut, then pull out bolt.
18. Press ball bearing out with suitable press.
19. Press in new ball bearing with suitable press, applying pressure to bearing outer race.
20. Install new self locking nut on M14 bolt on trailing arm and torque to 43.2 ft. lbs. while lifting arm until lower edge is level with upper edge of spring plate.
21. Torque spring plate retaining bolts to 68.4 ft. lbs. and the camber and toe-in adjustment cams to 43.2 ft. lbs.
22. Torque hexagon bolts for parking brake support plate and shield plate to 18 ft. lbs.
23. Tighten hand brake cable castellated nut until cotter pin hole and slot are aligned, then install new cotter pin. **Ensure that expander clip is positioned correctly.**
24. Using tool No. P298b or equivalent and driveshaft, pull rear wheel hub into radial ball thrust bearing. **Do not use impact wrench to pull wheel hub into bearings.**
25. Ensure that joint shaft flange surface is smooth and free of grease, then install new gasket and torque M10 Allen screws to 60 ft. lbs. and M8 Allen head screws to 30.2 ft. lbs.
26. Torque driveshaft castellated nut to 216-252 ft. lbs. and install new cotter pin.
27. Torque shock absorber attaching bolts to 90.4 ft. lbs.

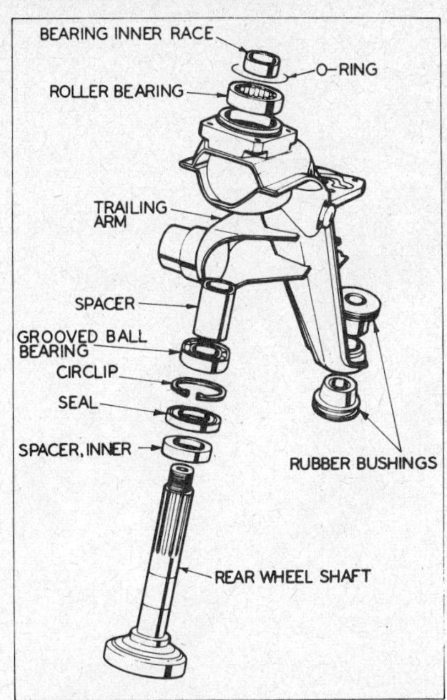

Fig. 3 Exploded view of trailing arm. 944 models less aluminum trailing arm

28. Install brake caliper with new spring washers and torque attaching bolts to 43.2 ft. lbs.
29. Bleed brakes and check for leaks.
30. Check hand brake setting, adjusting as necessary.
31. Adjust toe-in and camber.

924S & 944 MODELS

Exc. Aluminum Trailing Arm

1. Remove constant velocity joint at stub axle mounting flange, **Fig. 3.**
2. Mark location of torsion plate on trailing arm flange with a suitable scribe.
3. Remove brake line.
4. Remove shock absorber attaching bolt.
5. Remove torsion plate. **Use caution during this operation, plate is under extreme tension.**
6. Press out rear wheel shaft.
7. Using a suitable screwdriver, remove seal.
8. Press grooved ball bearings and axle stub in control arm.
9. Drive roller bearing outer race in using tool VW415A or equivalent. **Flange edge of bearing outer race must face outside of vehicle.**
10. Press roller bearing inner race and spacer into control arm using tool VW454 or equivalent and a castellated nut, **Fig. 4.**

Aluminum Trailing Arm

1. Raise and support vehicle.
2. Remove rear wheel, then the self locking nut on driveshaft, **Fig. 5.**
3. Disconnect parking brake cable at parking brake lever.
4. Lift trailing arm slightly with suitable jack, then disconnect vibration damper at trailing arm.
5. Remove axle shaft attaching bolts at transmission and remove complete driveshaft. **When working on left side, push up transmission end of shaft in direction of intermediate shift lever on transmission to remove.**
6. Disconnect brake hose at trailing arm by removing spring lock and unscrewing brake pipe. Plug brake hose or hold brake pedal in slightly depressed position with suitable tool.
7. Remove brake pad wear indicator wiring from holder.
8. Remove brake pad wear indicator wiring plug from its holder and disconnect.
9. Remove brake caliper and the disc.
10. Using tool P297a or equivalent, drive out rear wheel hub.
11. Remove parking brake shoes and spreader arm, then pull parking brake cable out of trailing arm.
12. Mark position of, then remove trailing arm.
13. Take off brake guard and remove circlip for angular ball bearing.
14. Heat trailing arm to 250-300°F. and, using suitable tools, press out angular ball bearing.
15. If necessary, remove rubber mounts and the bearing inner race.
16. Using suitable tools, set up and align trailing arm.
17. Remove trailing arm from press and heat to 250-300°F., then insert angular ball bearing and press in slightly on aligned bases.
18. If removed, press in new rubber mounts against stops.
19. Install circlip and press in wheel hub.
20. Install trailing arm. Torque trailing arm to rear axle strut locknuts to 66 ft. lbs. (camber eccentric) and 76 ft. lbs. and the trailing arm to cross tube locknuts to 45 ft. lbs. **Insert driveshaft before mounting vibration damper on trailing arm on left side.**
21. Adjust parking brake, bleed brakes and check wheel alignment.

SHOCK ABSORBER
REPLACE

911

1. With vehicle standing on ground, remove shock attaching nut from shock in engine compartment.
2. Raise and support vehicle.
3. Remove shock attaching bolt and nut from trailing arm.
4. Reverse procedure to install, noting the following:
   a. Install shock absorber in shock tower and torque attaching nut to 18.1 ft. lbs.
   b. Tension trailing arm and extend shock absorber to install attaching nut and bolt, torquing to 90 ft. lbs.

928

1. Remove three self-locking nuts from spring strut in luggage compartment.
2. Raise and support vehicle, then remove wheel.

Fig. 4 Installing axle stub shaft

3. Remove front nut on pivot pin of lower control arm, counter holding and counter locking rear nut with a M14 1.5 nut then remove pivot.
4. Disconnect stabilizer bar link at control arm.
5. Disassemble and assemble spring strut as shown, **Fig. 6,** noting the following:
   a. Tension coil spring using tool No. VW540 or equivalent, then remove self locking nuts and take out mounting plate with support.
   b. Relax coil spring by loosening clamping pins alternately.
6. Reverse procedure to install, noting the following:
   a. Torque spring strut self locking nuts to 33 ft. lbs.
   b. Using suitable compound make a new permanently elastic seal on mounting plate 300 mm long and circular in shape.
   c. Ensure that lower shock absorber is in proper installed position.

SPRING STRUT
REPLACE

928

1. Remove the three spring strut locknuts in luggage compartment.
2. Raise vehicle and support.
3. Remove wheel.
4. Remove front nut from pivot pin of lower control arm, **Fig. 7. Counterlock and counter hold the rear nut with a separate M14 1.5 nut.**
5. Remove stabilizer bar link at control arm.
6. Position strut assembly in vise and install a suitable spring compressor.
7. Remove locknuts and mounting plate with support, **Fig. 6.**
8. Slowly relieve coil spring tension.
9. Check shock absorber for leaks.
10. Reverse procedure to install.

TORSION BAR
REPLACE

911

Refer to "Lower Control Arm, Replace" and "Torsion Bar, Adjust" procedures.

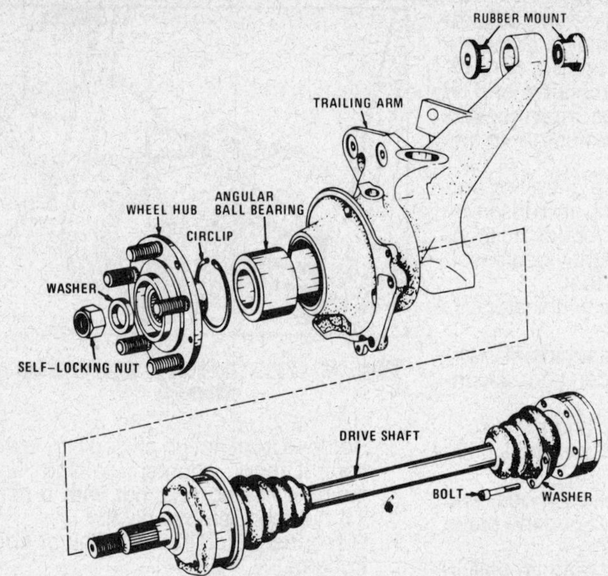

Fig. 5 Exploded view of trailing arm. 1986–87 924S & 944 w/aluminum trailing arm

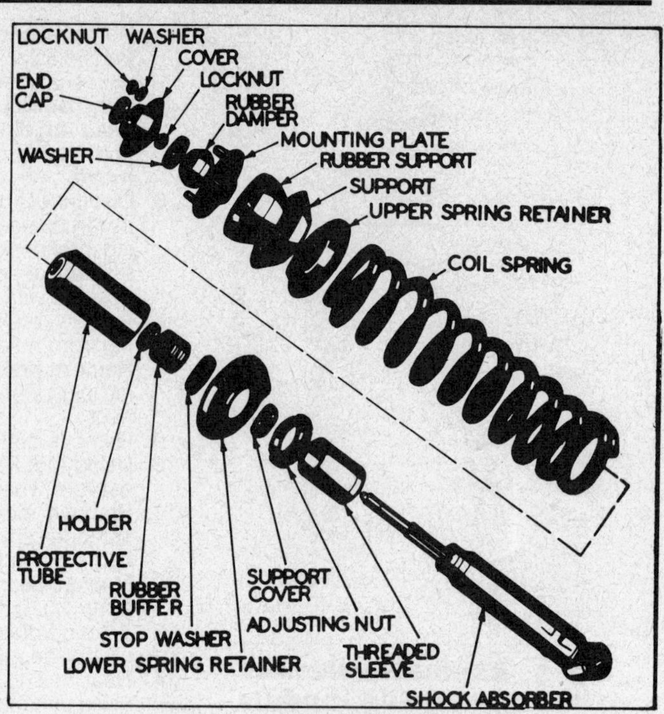

Fig. 6 Spring strut. 928 models

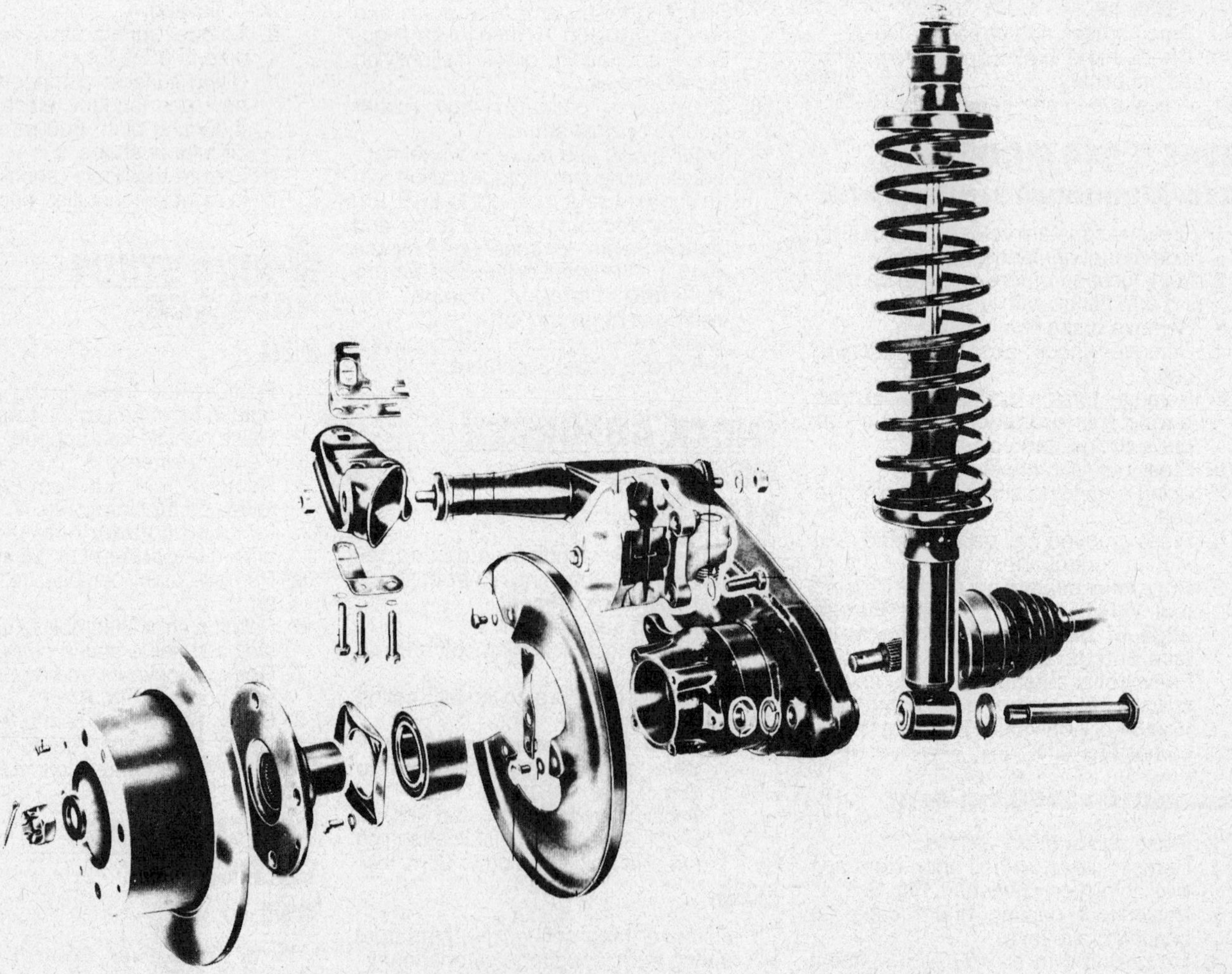

Fig. 7 Rear suspension exploded view. 928 models

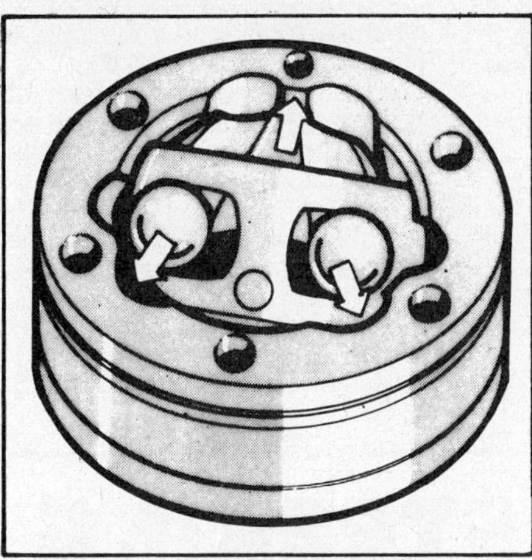

Fig. 8 Removing hub

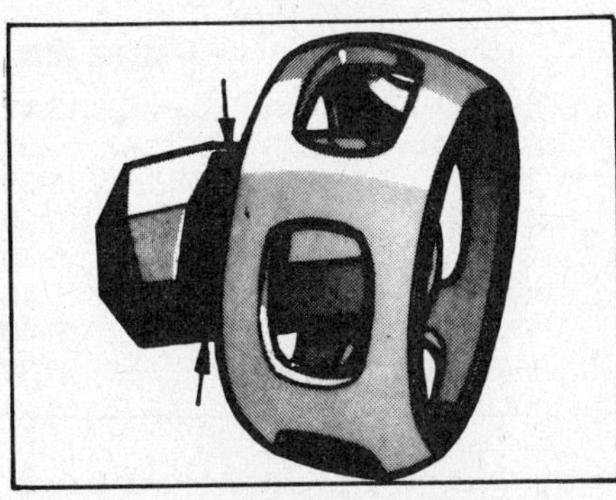

Fig. 10 Removing ball hub from cage

1. Raise and support vehicle.
2. Support radius arm with tool P289.
3. Remove lower shock absorber retaining bolt.
4. Remove control arm retaining and eccentric bolts.
5. Remove radius arm cover retaining bolts.
6. Remove single spacer.
7. Pry radius arm cover with two large screwdrivers.
8. Remove radius arm tool P289.
9. Remove body plug and the radius arm and torsion bar. **Do not mar torsion bar protective paint.**
10. Reverse procedure to install. Refer to "Torsion Bar, Adjust".

AXLE SHAFT

REPLACE

911

1. Raise and support vehicle.
2. Remove cotter pin from hub castle nut.
3. Remove castle nut with tools P42a, P36b, P44a, and P296.
4. Remove Allen bolts from axle flanges.
5. Remove axle shaft.
6. Reverse procedure to install. Torque axle shaft nuts to 31 ft. lbs. and half shaft castle nut to 217-253 ft. lbs.

928

Axle Shaft Bolted On Both Sides

1. Raise and support vehicle, then remove left rear wheel and tire assembly.
2. Remove socket head bolts from drive flanges.
3. Remove right hand axle shaft inward.
4. Remove left hand axle shaft outward.
5. Reverse procedure to install, ensuring flange surfaces are free of grease, and torque socket head bolts to 60 ft. lbs.

Axle Shaft Welded On One Side

1. Raise and support vehicle.
2. Remove socket head bolts on transmission end.
3. Remove wheel cover to gain access, then remove self locking nuts on wheel end.
4. Remove both axle shafts toward inside, lowering rear of left side exhaust assembly as necessary.
5. Run axle shafts into wheel hub on wheel end.
6. Ensure axle shaft flanges are free of grease and install socket head bolts, torquing to 60 ft. lbs.
7. Torque self locking nuts to 333 ft. lbs.

AXLE SHAFT SERVICE

928

1. Clamp axle shaft in suitable vise.
2. Remove clamp and push dust boot with sealing flange toward inside of axle shaft.
3. Remove circlip.
4. Using suitable tools, press off constant velocity joint.
5. Swing out ball hub and ball cage from joint and press out in direction of arrow, **Fig. 8. Ball hubs and joints are matched. Do not mix.**
6. Tilt ball hub out of ball cage through ball grove, **Fig. 9.**
7. Check joint, ball hub, ball cage and balls for pitting. Replace joint if there is excessive radial play in joint.
8. Place ball hub in ball cage, then press balls into cage, **Fig. 10.**
9. Install hub with cage and balls pointing up, ensuring after swinging in hub into joint that one wide ball groove on joint is together on one side with a narrow groove of hub. **Groove of ball hub and running around periphery of outside diameter on joint must face end of axle shaft.**
10. Swing in ball hub with cage by swinging out hub from cage far enough so that balls are at same distance as grooves, **Fig. 11.**
11. Push hub with balls into joint.
12. Check operation of joint. CV joint has been properly assembled if ball hub can be pushed back and forth by hand over entire range of travel.

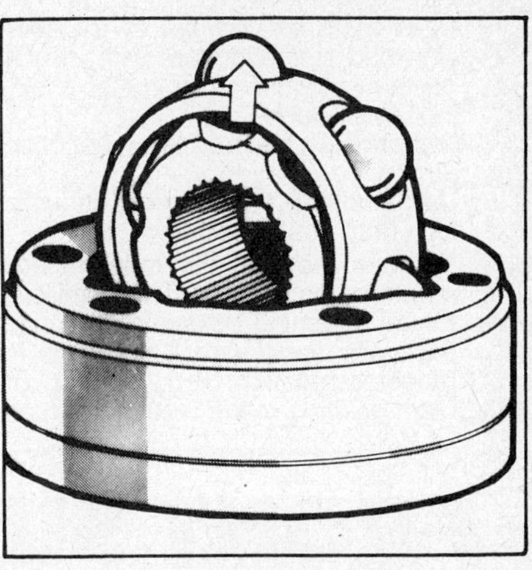

Fig. 9 Removing ball cage & hub

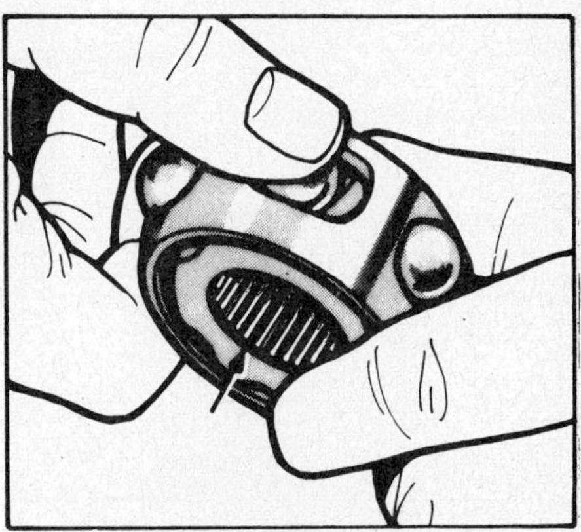

Fig. 11 Ball bearing installation

13. Seal large diameter and of new dust boot with suitable adhesive.
14. Using suitable tool, squeeze new clamp between machined shoulders of sealing flange.
15. Replace gasket on flange cover.
16. Push dust boot with sealing flange onto shaft.
17. Pack CV joint from each side with approximately 40 grams of grease supplied in repair kit.
18. Press CV joint onto shaft and install new circlip.
19. Position dust boot correctly, then install clamp.

REAR AXLE ASSEMBLY

REPLACE

928

1. Remove upper strut retainer attaching nuts from inside luggage compartment.
2. Raise and support vehicle, then remove rear wheel and tire assemblies.
3. Disconnect parking brake cable at connector and pull back out of guide.
4. Remove brake calipers and suspend from body with wire, leaving brake hoses connected.
5. Remove exhaust system components as necessary.

6. Disconnect axle shafts at transmission and suspend from wire in horizontal position on rear axle crossmember.
7. Disconnect stabilizer at lower control arm.
8. Using suitable tool, support transmission from stabilizer bar.
9. Remove two rear axle crossmember mounting bolts and the transmission mount attaching bolts. Note quantity, thickness and location of shims for proper installation.
10. Mark position of toe adjusting eccentric bolts, then remove bolts from rear axle crossmember.
11. Place suitable jack under rear axle crossmember, then mark position of crossmember and remove remaining four attaching bolts.
12. Carefully lower rear axle, being sure not to twist spring struts, control arms or rear axle crossmember.
13. Reverse procedure to install, noting the following:
    a. Check spring strut seal, repairing as necessary.
    b. Position rear axle, then install mounting bolts and align axle to original position as marked.
    c. Torque crossmember to body attaching bolts to 33 ft. lbs., toe adjusting bolt locknut to 87 ft. lbs., brake caliper attaching bolts to 61 ft. lbs., axle shaft to flange attaching bolts to 59 ft. lbs. and the upper strut retainer attaching nuts to 42 ft. lbs.
    d. Align transmission suspension and torque transmission mount to crossmember attaching bolts to 61 ft. lbs.

FRONT SUSPENSION & STEERING SECTION

INDEX

WHEEL BEARINGS ADJUST

1. Raise and support vehicle.
2. Remove wheels and axle hub cap.
3. Loosen adjustment nut retaining bolt.
4. While rotating the hub by hand, tighten the adjustment nut slightly.
5. Loosen adjusting nut until thrust washer can just be moved using finger pressure on a screwdriver. **Do not support the screwdriver against the hub for use as a lever.**
6. Torque the Allen head adjusting nut retainer bolt to 11 ft. lbs.

LOWER CONTROL ARM REPLACE

911

1. Raise and support vehicle and remove front wheel.
2. Remove torsion bar adjusting screw and the adjusting arm.
3. Remove ball joint retaining bolt nut and drive out double wedge bolt.
4. Pull ball joint out of strut by pressing control arm downward.
5. Remove hexagon bolts from front transverse control arm bearing and remove protective cap.
6. Remove transverse control arm to subframe attaching bolt and pull control arm toward front.
7. Clamp control arm in suitable vise and remove keeper from slotted locking plate, then remove ball joint nut using tool P280b or equivalent. **When removing bolt transverse control arms, the subframe retaining bolts must be installed hand tight to hold subframe firmly in position.**
8. Reverse procedure to install, noting the following:
    a. Torque ball joint slotted nut to 108 ft. lbs. and keep from turning by bending over peg of keeper plate.
    b. Apply light coat of lithium base grease to entire surface of torsion bar and push torsion bar into wishbone. Do not force out the end cap from the wishbone.
    c. Install transverse control arm with torsion bar into subframe. **Torsion bars are preloaded during production. Never interchange torsion bars. Torsion bars are marked on end with "L" for left side or "R" for right side.**
    d. Torque hexagon bolt for front control arm bearing and protection bracket to 34 ft. lbs.
    e. Torque hexagon bolt for rear control arm bearing and subframe to 65 ft. lbs.
    f. Coat double wedge bolt with suitable grease before installing.
    g. Ensure that double wedge is installed so that attaching nut points forward in direction of travel and that notch on face of double wedge bolt and wedge contour point toward wheel stub axle.
    h. Ensure that double wedge bolt is properly seated by tapping bolt before torquing nut to 15.8 ft. lbs.
    i. Slide OWA seal onto torsion bar on rear of subframe.
    j. Using suitable pry bar, push transverse control arm down as far as attached shock absorber strut allows, then slide torsion bar adjusting lever onto torsion bar splines, leaving as little clearance as possible at the lever adjusting point.
    k. Coat threads of adjusting screw with MoS_2 grease or equivalent and lightly tighten screw in place.
    l. Adjust front end height and check wheel alignment.

924S & 944

1. Raise and support vehicle.
2. Remove wheels and ball joint bolt, **Fig. 1.**
3. Remove two metal/rubber rear bushing bolts.
4. Remove bushing clamp and bushing.
5. Remove front metal/rubber bushing bolt.
6. Remove control arm.
7. Reverse procedure to install.

928

1. Raise and support vehicle.
2. Remove wheels and disconnect tie rod from steering knuckle, **Fig. 2.**
3. Remove wheel alignment eccentric locknuts and eccentrics.
4. Remove control arm bracket retaining bolts and bracket.
5. Remove tie down bracket retaining bolts and bracket.
6. Reverse procedure to install.

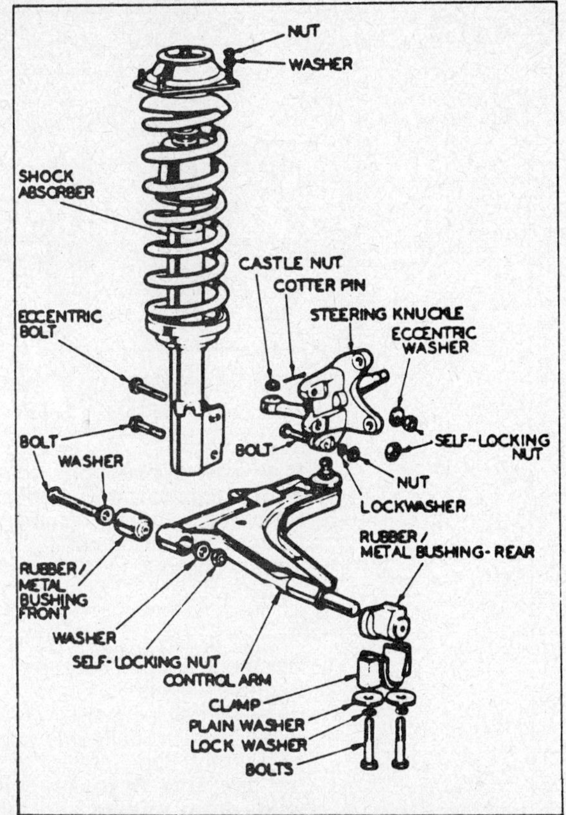

Fig. 1 Front suspension exploded view. 1986–87 924S & 944 models

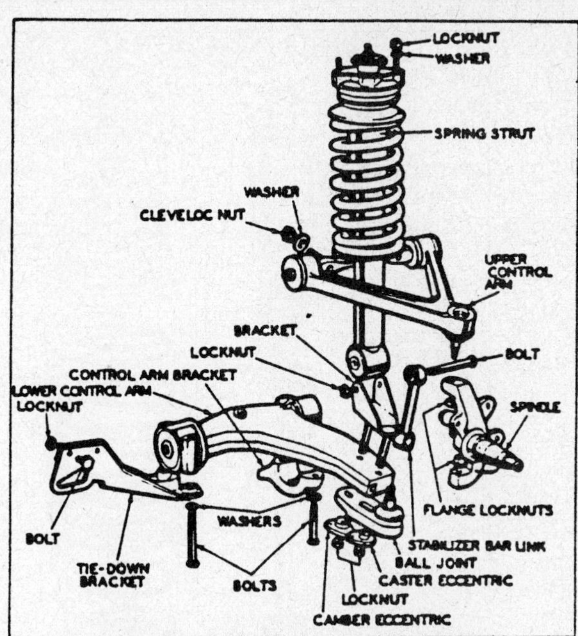

Fig. 2 Front suspension exploded view. 928 models

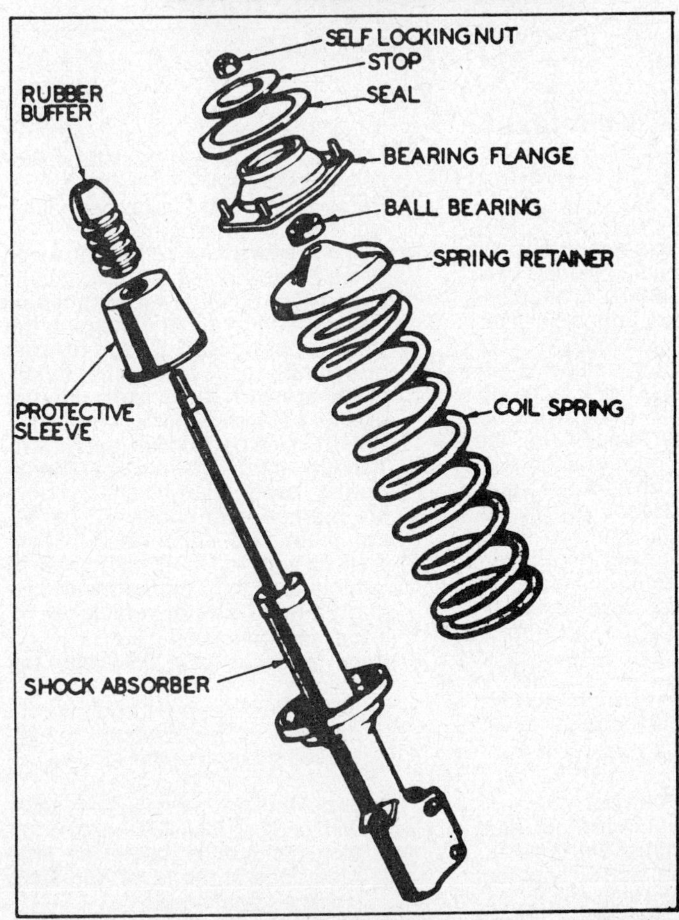

Fig. 3 Strut exploded view. 1986–87 924S & 944 models

STRUT REPLACE

911

1. Raise and support vehicle.
2. Remove wheels and disconnect brake line at hose support bracket.
3. Depress pedal with a suitable device to prevent brake fluid from leaking from reservoir.
4. Remove caliper retaining bolts and complete caliper.
5. Remove grease cap from wheel hub.
6. Loosen bearing adjustment nut and remove brake disc and bearing.
7. Remove disc guard plate.
8. Position aside carpet in luggage compartment covering shock towers.
9. Remove cotter pins and castle nuts from tie rods and ball joints.
10. Remove ball joint from strut using a suitable puller.
11. Remove nut from the top of strut in front luggage compartment.
12. Remove strut and install in vise.
13. Reverse procedure to install.

924S & 944

1. Raise and support vehicle.
2. Remove wheels and disconnect brake line at hose support bracket.
3. Support lower control arm and steering knuckle with suitable jack stand.
4. Remove strut retaining and eccentric bolts and strut from steering knuckle.
5. Remove three bearing flange bolts and the shock assembly, **Fig. 3.**
6. Position strut assembly in a suitable spring compressor.
7. Compress spring and remove the strut locknut, stop and flange.
8. Release spring tension and remove the coil spring.

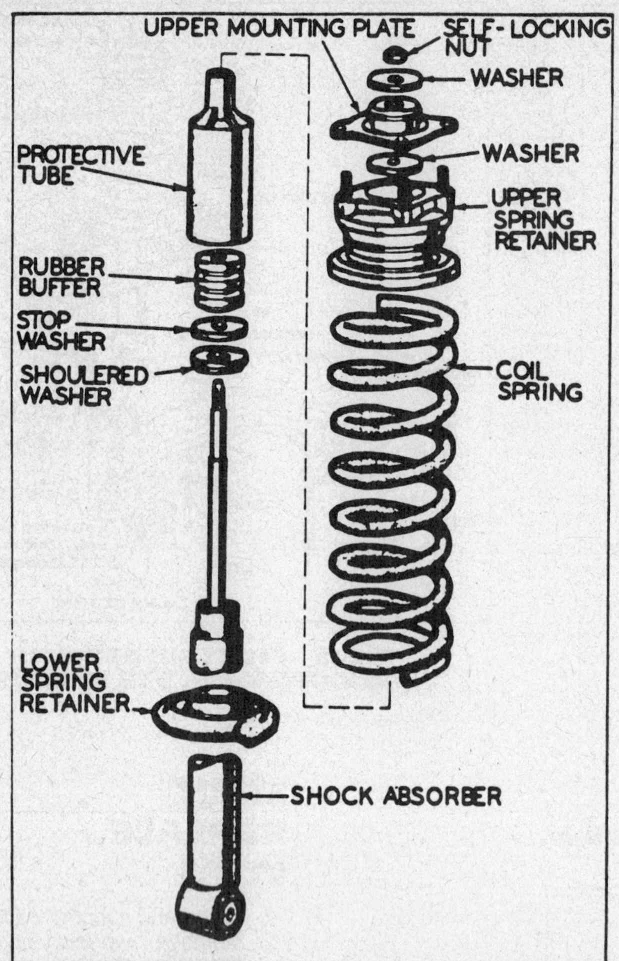

Fig. 4 Exploded view of strut. 928 non-adjustable strut shown, adjustable strut similar

9. Remove components from piston rod.
10. Reverse procedure to install. **Install coil spring in strut unit with straight cut end of spring down.**

928

1. Remove three locknuts from shock tower mount in engine compartment, **Fig. 4.**
2. Raise and support vehicle.
3. Remove wheel and flange locknut.
4. Press off upper ball joint.
5. Remove upper control arm locknuts in engine compartment.
6. Remove strut mounting bolt.
7. Support lower control arm to prevent damage to brake hose.
8. Compress coil spring with a suitable spring compressor and remove strut locknut.
9. Remove washer and upper mounting plate.
10. Carefully remove the tension from coil spring.
11. Remove upper spring retainer, coil spring, and piston rod components.
12. Mark lower spring retainer position for reassembly. Replace struts with major leaks. There are three spring tolerance groups for non-adjustable struts and Boge adjustable struts. Groups are identified by the number of stripes; green for non-adjustable struts, blue for Boge adjustable struts to chassis No. 92A0810714 on 928 models or to chassis No. 92A0820127 on 928S models, and white for Boge adjustable struts from chassis No. 92A0820128 for 928S models. One stripe is assigned to the 1,433-1,477 lb. group, two stripes to the 1,478-1,521 lb. group, and three stripes to the 1,522-1,565 lb. group. Springs with three white stripes, installed in some vehicles, are no longer available; replace with springs with two white stripes. Bilstein struts are identified by a green and white stripe and are available in only one type. Always replace springs in pairs.

BALL JOINT
REPLACE

911

1. Raise and support vehicle.
2. Remove wheel and drive out stud with a suitable hammer and drift.
3. Remove cotter pin and, using tool P280b, the four point nut.
4. Coat stud with multi-purpose grease and insert into position. **Check that retaining nut is in front as seen from driving direction and notch in stud points toward wheel spindle.**

Fig. 5 Centering steering gear

5. Seat stud with light hammer prior to tightening retaining nut.
6. Torque locknut to 15.9 ft. lbs. (2.2 mkp.).

928

1. Raise and support vehicle.
2. Remove wheels.
3. Press off ball joints using VW 267 a.
4. When installing ball joints, apply pressure on the upper control arm with a pry bar. **This is to keep the ball studs from turning and facilitates flange nut installation.**

TORSION BAR
REPLACE

911

1. Raise and support vehicle.
2. Remove wheels and torsion bar adjustment screw.
3. Remove seal and torsion bar adjusting lever from torsion bar.
4. Remove forward rubber mount cover.
5. Using a suitable punch, drive torsion bar forward out of lower control arm. **Use caution to avoid damaging the torsion bar splines. Check for rust or damage to the torsion bar finish. Coat torsion bar with lithium grease before installing.**
6. Install torsion bar in lower control arm. **Torsion bars are under tension during production. Torsion bars are marked with either "L" or "R" on their end face. Install bars marked with "L" in left hand side of vehicle and bars marked with "R" in right hand side of vehicle.**
7. Install seal on torsion bar.
8. Install adjusting lever on torsion bar as follows:
   a. Using a pry bar, pull the lower control arm as far down as the attached shock absorber strut will allow.
   b. Slide torsion bar adjusting lever with end cap installed onto the torsion bar splines. **Leave as little clearance at the lever adjusting point as possible.**
   c. Coat adjusting screw threads with MoS_2 grease and lightly tighten screw.

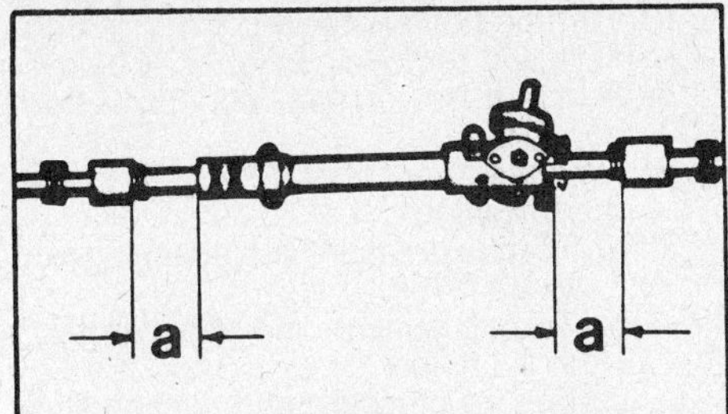

Fig. 6 Installing tie rod ends

9. Check that end cap is properly seated in control arm.
10. Install rubber mount cover bracket. Torque the retaining bolts to 34 ft. lbs.
11. Adjust front end height and check wheel alignment.

MANUAL STEERING GEAR

REPLACE

911

1. Raise and support vehicle.
2. Remove wheels and separate steering shaft at universal joint.
3. Remove castle nuts from tie rod ends.
4. Remove tie rods with a suitable puller.
5. Remove front axle stone shield.
6. Loosen steering gear to auxiliary carrier bolts.
7. Remove torsion bar adjustment screws.
8. Remove torsion bar adjustment levers and seals.
9. Remove lower control arm and auxiliary carrier bolts.
10. Remove carrier and steering gear with tie rods.
11. Reverse procedure to install.

924S & 944

1. Raise and support vehicle.
2. Remove wheels and press off tie rods with tool VW 266 H or an equivalent.
3. Remove steering gear universal joint bolt.
4. Remove steering rack retaining bolts.
5. Remove rack.
6. Center steering gear with tool 9116, Fig. 5. **There are two types of steering tie rods. The new design is machined for a distance of .511 inch (13 mm) on the joint for the rubber stop ring. The old design was machined for a .236 inch (6 mm) distance. Only the new version is available for replacement.**
7. Screw tie rods on evenly. Measure from the ridge on the rubber stop ring to steering housing, **Fig. 6.** Distance "a" should equal 2.55 inches ± .0196 inch (65 mm ± 5 mm).
8. Torque tie rod locknuts to 31-41 ft. lbs. (43-57 Nm).
9. Torque rack to crossmember bolts to 14-17 ft. lbs. (20-24 Nm).
10. Torque tie rod to steering knuckle bolts to 22-36 ft. lbs. (30-50 Nm).
11. To adjust rack proceed as follows:
    a. Tighten adjusting screw until it just touches the thrust washer, **Fig. 7.**
    b. Hold adjusting screw with a suitable wrench, and rotate locknut with a second wrench.

POWER STEERING GEAR

REPLACE

928

1. Using a suitable siphon drain hydraulic fluid from reservoir.
2. Using a suitable puller, remove tie rods.
3. Remove hose retaining clamp near starter motor.
4. Remove stabilizer bar mounting bolts and allow bar to hang free.
5. Disconnect pressure and return line at steering gear.
6. Remove five reinforcement plate retaining bolts from the engine crossmember.
7. Loosen but do not remove the four steering gear locknuts.
8. Remove universal joint intermediate shaft bolt and disconnect steering intermediate shaft.
9. Remove four steering gear mounting nuts and lower steering gear from vehicle.
10. Reverse procedure to install. Add hydraulic fluid and bleed steering system.

924S & 944

1. Raise and support vehicle.
2. Remove stabilizer by disconnecting stabilizer mounts on control arms and stabilizer suspension on side members.
3. Disconnect ground wire on front axle crossmember.
4. Using tool No. 9183 or equivalent and torque wrench, loosen but do not remove tie rods at steering rack, then run rack out of steering gear case on disconnecting side only as far as necessary.
5. Disconnect pressure line on power steering pump, catching hydraulic fluid draining out of pump or tank and power steering gear. Position pressure line connection lower than steering and turn steering wheel from stop to stop several times.
6. Remove bolt on universal joint, then loosen but do not remove four steering gear attaching bolts until shaft can be removed from steering pinion. **Unscrew pressure line clamp on steering gear to gain access to left lower attaching bolt.**
7. Press out tie rods (ball joints) with suitable puller.
8. Disconnect return line at steering gear.
9. Remove four steering gear attaching bolts and remove steering gear toward front of vehicle.
10. If installing new steering gear, mount rubber inserts and clamps in correct position before installing steering gear in vehicle. To facilitate mounting of

Fig. 7 Steering rack adjustment

rubber inserts and clamps, use suitable lubricant that will not deteriorate rubber parts.
11. Connect pressure line to steering gear, torquing to 14 ft. lbs.
12. Coat ends of fully extended rack with suitable grease.
13. With steering wheel and steering gear in centered position, slide shaft onto steering gear in correct position. **Steering gear attaching bolts should be screwed in only lightly to facilitate installation.**
14. Attach steering gear, torquing attaching bolts to 17 ft. lbs. and the shaft mounting bolt to 22 ft. lbs.
15. Install tie rods on rack, if removed, torquing to 61 ft. lbs., then bend down collar on opening of rack to lock, being careful not to damage surface of rack.
16. After completing installation, fill system with suitable fluid, bleed steering system, check for leaks, and test operation.
17. Adjust toe, if necessary.

POWER STEERING PUMP

REPLACE

928

1. Disconnect battery ground cable.
2. Disconnect intake hose at left side of air cleaner.
3. Remove fluid from power steering pump reservoir.
4. Raise and support vehicle.
5. Remove splash shield.
6. Slightly loosen attaching bolts at front of power steering pump.
7. Remove attaching bolt at rear of power steering pump.
8. Remove power steering drive belt.
9. Remove left upper section of timing belt cover.
10. Disconnect pressure hose at power steering pump.
11. Loosen clamp, then disconnect suction hose at power steering pump.
12. Remove attaching bolts at front of power steering pump, then remove pump and bracket as an assembly.
13. Reverse procedure to install, noting the following:

a. Position pump by tightening front attaching bolts, then insert but do not tighten rear attaching bolt.
b. When installing replacement pressure hose, ensure protective ring rests on spring strut mount.
c. When installing original pressure hose fitted with asbestos sleeve, leave not more than 25 mm between inner wheel well and hose.
d. Torque suction hose attaching bolt to 43 ft. lbs.
e. Adjust power steering and alternator drive belts and bleed steering system.

924S & 944 MODELS

1. Disconnect battery ground cable, then remove splash shield.
2. Disconnect pressure line at power steering pump.
3. Loosen clamp, then disconnect suction hose at power steering pump.
4. Disconnect connecting rod at power steering pump, then loosen nut at other end and swing rod downward.
5. Remove power steering pump attaching nut and bolt and remove power steering drive belt.
6. Turn up power steering pump in console and remove spacer from below.
7. Remove power steering pump from console.
8. Reverse procedure to install noting the following:
   a. Torque pressure line attaching bolt to 22 ft. lbs.
   b. Torque suction line attaching bolt to 33 ft. lbs.
   c. Ensure pressure and suction lines are correctly routed to prevent rubbing.
   d. Bleed steering system.

WHEEL ALIGNMENT SECTION

INDEX

FRONT WHEEL ALIGNMENT

Accurate front axle height adjustment is critical to toe-in, camber, and caster adjustments. Ensure tire pressures are at their specified values, fuel tank is full, spare tire is in place, and a weight approximately the same as the driver, positioned on the driver's seat.

AXLE HEIGHT, ADJUST

911

1. Depress front of vehicle several times and allow to rebound to proper height.
2. Measure distance between level floor or ramp to center of wheel hub (dimension a).
3. Value "a" minus 4.25 inches should equal value "b." **Value "b" equals the distance between the torsion bar center and the level surface on which the vehicle is positioned.**
4. Remove torsion bar dust cover at adjusting lever. Use torsion bar centering mark as a reference mark.
5. Loosen or tighten torsion bar adjusting bolt until value "b" is obtained at the torsion bar center.
6. Depress front of vehicle and allow to rebound to proper height. Recheck vehicle height. **The allowable difference in height between left and right sides of the vehicle is .2 inch (5 mm).**

928 Less Adjustable Spring Struts

1. Measure distance from floor to milled surface of lower control arm mount, **Fig. 1.** Distance should be 6.6929-7.4803 inches (170-190 mm) with a maximum left to right difference of .3937 inch (10 mm).
2. Slight adjustment can be made by the installation of spacers underneath the lower spring retainer. Each spacer will increase axle height approximately .3937 inch (10 mm). Never use more than two spacers per spring strut.
3. If axle height cannot be adjusted to specifications with spacers, front springs must be replaced. Springs which have approximately 45 lbs. more spring force for the same test strength will increase front axle height by approximately .1969-.5906 inch (5-15 mm).

928 W/Adjustable Spring Struts

1. Measure distance from floor to milled surface of lower control arm mount, **Fig. 1.** Distance should be 6.6929-7.4803 inches (170-190 mm) with a maximum left to right difference of .3937 inch (10 mm).
2. To adjust axle height, turn adjusting nuts at bottom of spring on strut. With vehicle resting on ground, turn wheels against lock accordingly to gain access to adjusting nuts. Turn nuts clockwise to increase height or counterclockwise to decrease height. **The adjusting range for lowering the vehicle is limited by a stop for the adjusting nut on vehicles with Bilstein spring struts. On vehicles with Boge spring struts, the lowest position has been reached when the adjusting nut turns easily.**

CAMBER & CASTER, ADJUST

911

1. Pull front luggage compartment carpeting away from shock towers.
2. Remove sealing compound from pressure plates and movable dish ring.
3. Mark position of single and double hole plates and screws.
4. Position shock absorber strut supporting bearing to adjust caster or camber.
5. Torque bolts to 33.8 ft. lbs. and seal plates with a suitable sealing compound.

924S & 944

1. Adjust camber by turning eccentric bolt on lower strut mounting.
2. On models w/steel control arms, adjust caster by moving rear of suspension control arm from side to side.
3. On models w/aluminum control arms, adjust caster by loosening self locking nuts and turning caster eccentric until caster is within specifications, **Fig. 2,** then torque nuts to 62 ft. lbs.

928

On vehicles w/aluminum joint carriers, adjust caster and camber by rotating two eccentrics on lower control arm, **Fig. 3.**

Caster and camber on vehicles w/steel joint carrier is adjusted in same way, but location of caster and camber eccentrics are opposite those shown in **Fig. 3.**

On vehicles w/aluminum joint carrier, always turn caster eccentric from small caster in direction of large caster. When caster is excessive, first turn the eccentric back completely and then adjust to correct value. If specified caster cannot be obtained, opposite side may be corrected to a value of up to 4°30'.

Fig. 1 Front suspension height check point. 928 models

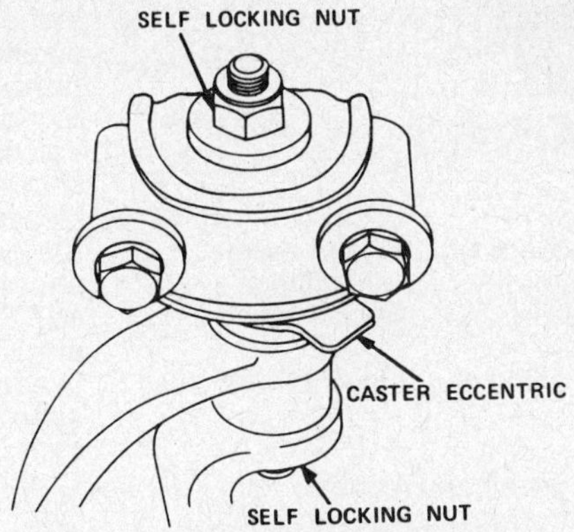

Fig. 2 Adjusting front caster. 1986–87 924S & 944 models W/aluminum control arms

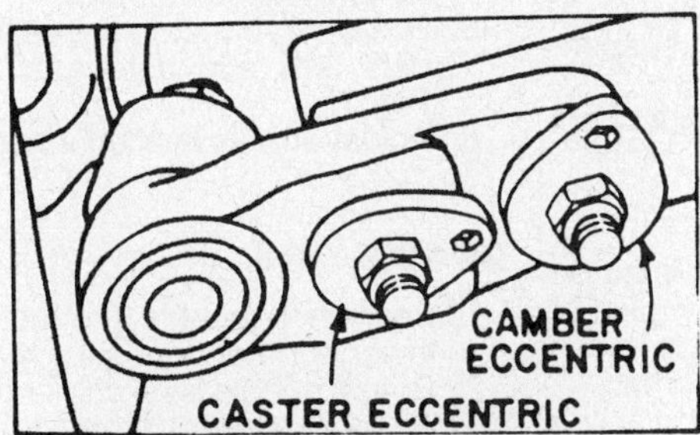

Fig. 3 Front caster & camber adjustment eccentrics. 928 models w/aluminum joint carriers

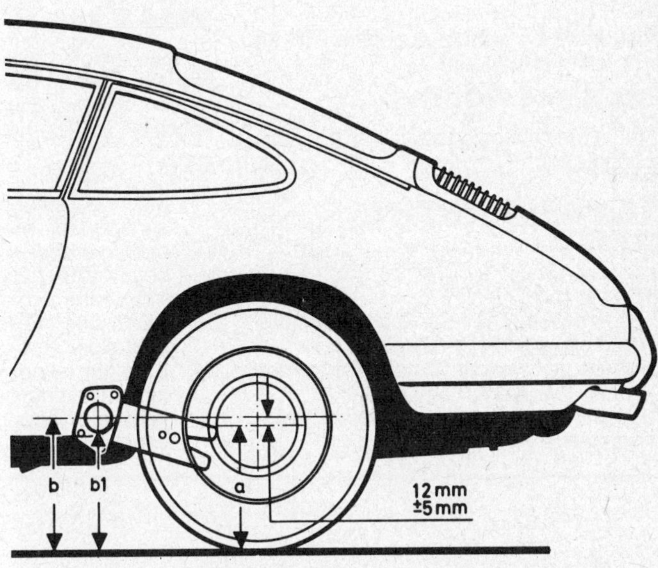

Fig. 4 Rear axle height adjustment

Fig. 5 Rear axle height measurement

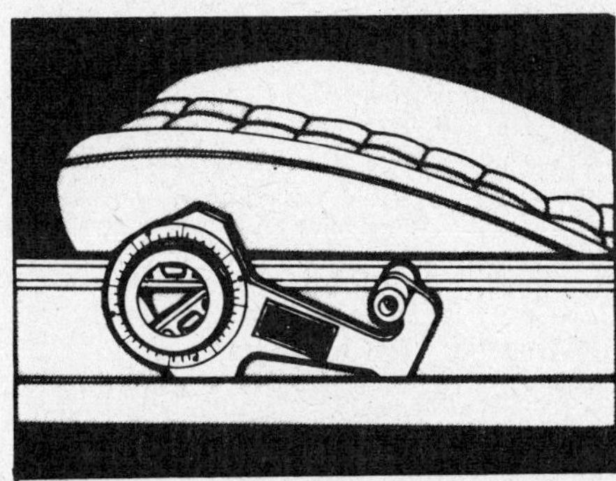

Fig. 6 Door sill protractor position

Fig. 7 Torsion plate or radius arm protractor position

REAR WHEEL ALIGNMENT

CAMBER, ADJUST

911

1. Loosen retaining bolt nuts and eccentric bolt nuts at the rear axle flange.
2. Rotate tracking and camber eccentrics to adjust.
3. Tighten eccentric and retaining nuts.

928

Camber adjustments are made by rotating the inner control arm bushing eccentric bolt.

924S & 944

Camber adjustment is made by loosening joint between spring strut and trailing arm, then turning camber eccentric.

TOE, ADJUST

928

Adjust toe by turning eccentric bolt on front control arm mount.

924S & 944 MODELS

Adjust toe by moving trailing arm in slots of spring strut.

REAR AXLE HEIGHT, ADJUST

911

1. Depress rear of vehicle several times and allow body to rebound.
2. Measure vertical distance between rear wheel center and level section of alignment ramp or level floor (distance a), **Fig. 4.**
3. Value of "a" plus .4724 inch (12 mm) equals value "b". **The value "b" cannot be measured since the torsion bar is off center.**
4. Value "b" less bushing cover radius (1/2 diameter) equals value "b1".
5. Measure height of vehicle (value "b1"), **Fig. 4. The actual value "b1" should not differ from the calculated "b1" by more than .1968 inch (5 mm). The height difference between right and left sides of the vehicle should be no more than .3145 inch (8 mm).** For example: value "a", 12.40inches (315 mm) + .47inch (12 mm) = 12.87inches (327 mm) − bushing cover radius, 1.18 inches (30 mm) = 11.69 inches (297 mm) = "b1" or vehicle height.
6. If proper suspension height cannot be achieved, proceed as follows:
   a. Check adjustment of front suspension and correct if necessary.
   b. Check rear torsion bar adjustment and correct if necessary.

924S & 944

Rear vehicle height can be adjusted on two piece spring plate, without removal of torsion bars. If spring plate angle is as specified, vehicle height will be correct.

928

1. Measure distance from wheel ground surface to measuring surface on crossmember, **Fig. 5.** Height should be 6.4173-7.2047 inches (163-183 mm) with a maximum difference of .3937 inch (10 mm) between left and right side.
2. If height is not within specifications, turn adjusting nut clockwise to raise vehicle or counterclockwise to lower vehicle.

TORSION BAR, ADJUST

If the torsion bar is reset by one spline at its inner end, a 9° change is obtained. If the radius arm is reset by one spline at the outer end of the torsion bar, a change of 8 3/20° is obtained. This arrangement allows a change of 5/6° if the torsion bar and radius arm are positioned towards each other.

911

1. Install torsion bar into transverse tube.
2. Install radius arm onto outer end of splines.
3. Position a bubble protractor on the lower edge of the door sill, **Fig. 6.**
4. Adjust so that the bubble is in the center of the glass tube.
5. Position protractor on free hanging radius arm and note arm inclination; **Fig. 7.**
6. Adjust arm inclination if necessary.

924S & 944

1. Position a bubble protractor on the lower edge of door sill, **Fig. 6.**
2. Rotate bubble level carrier on VW 261 or an equivalent protractor to specified torsion plate angle.
3. With torsion plate cover removed, position protractor on torsion plate, **Fig. 7. Lift the plate enough to remove play from splines.**
4. According to angle measurement at door sill, if front of vehicle is lower than rear, add door sill measurement to torsion plate value. If rear of vehicle is lower than front, subtract door sill measurement from torsion plate value.

RENAULT (France)

INDEX OF SERVICE OPERATIONS

G neral Engin Specifications

Year	Engine	Carburetor	Bore x Stroke	Compression Ratio	Maximum Brake HP @ RPM	Maximum Torque Ft. Lbs. @ RPM	Normal Oil Pressure Pounds
1983	4-85/1397cc ①	2 Barrel	2.99 x 3.03 (76 x 77mm)	8.8	—	75 @ 2000	50
	4-100/1647cc ②	Fuel Inj.	3.110 x 3.307 (79 x 84mm)	8.6	81.3 @ 5500	86.3 @ 2500	58
1983–85	4-95/1565cc ③	Fuel Inj.	3.03 x 3.3 (77 x 84mm)	8.0	107 @ 5500	120 @ 2500	58
1983–87	4-85/1397cc ④	Fuel Inj.	2.99 x 3.03 (76 x 77mm)	9.0	56 @ 4200	75 @ 2500	52
1984–86	4-132/2165cc ⑤	Fuel Inj.	3.46 x 3.50 (88 x 89mm)	8.7	91 @ 4000	123 @ 2500	⑧
1985–87	4-105/1721cc ④	Fuel Inj.	3.19 x 3.29 (81 x 83.5mm)	9.5	77.5 @ 5000	96 @ 3000	⑦
1987	4-120/1965cc ⑥	Fuel Inj.	3.228 x 3.661 (82 x 93)	9.5	95 @ 5250	114 @ 2750	⑦

①—Le Car.
②—18i/Fuego.
③—Fuego Turbo.
④—Alliance/Encore.
⑤—18i Wagon (Sportwagon).
⑥—GTA.
⑦—28 psi @ 1000 RPM; 51 psi @ 3000 RPM.
⑧—10 psi at idle; 50 psi @ 4000 RPM.

Alternator & Regulator Specifications

Year	Alternator				Regulator	
	Model	Rated Output Amps.	Output @ 14 Volts: 1250 RPM ① Amps.	Output @ 14 Volts: 3000 RPM ① Amps.	Model	Voltage @ 125°F
1983	A13R154	50	10	45 ②	AYB218	13.4–14.4
	A13R243	—	—	—	Integral	13.5–15
	9AR2659/T	—	—	—	Integral	13.5–15
1983–86	A14N51	75	12	61	Integral	13.5–15
1983–87	A13N12	50	10	43	Integral	13.5–15
	A13N116	60	19 ③	53	Integral	13.5–15
	A14N99	75	26 ③	61	Integral	13.5–15
	516025	50	10	43	Integral	13.5–15
	516030	70	20	61	Integral	13.5–15

①—Alternator RPM.
①—At 3500 RPM.
③—At 1500 RPM.

Starting Motor Specifications

Year	Model	Output (Watts)	Torque Test: Amp.	Torque Test: Torque, Ft. Lbs.
1983	D8E121	900	400	9
	D10E79	950	600	14
1983–87	D9E39	—	460	6
	D9E39	—	460	6
	D9E52	—	420	10
	D10E921	—	—	—
	534019	—	350	7
	534031	—	340	8
1986–87	DW14	—	①	—

①—No load test: 75 amps draw (maximum) @ 11.5 volts. Cold cranking test w/battery @ 12.5 volts: 120 amps @ 9.6 volts (minimum).

Valve Specifications

Year	Engine	Valve Lash Int.	Valve Lash Exh.	Valve Angles Seat	Valve Angles Face	Valve Spring Pressures Lbs. @ In.	Stem Diameter Intake	Stem Diameter Exhaust
1983	4-85/1397cc ①	.006C	.008C	45	45	80 @ 1.0	.276	.276
	4-100/1647cc	.008C	.010C	45	45	②	.315	.315
1983–85	4-95/1565cc	.008C	.010C	45	45	③	.315	.315
1983–87	4-85/1397cc ④	.006C	.008C	⑤	⑤	81 @ .984	.315	.315
1984–86	4-132	.004C	.008C	③	④	—	.315	.315
1985–87	4-105/1721cc	.008C	.015C	⑤	⑤	66.9 @ 1.39	.314	.314
1987	4-120/1965cc	.008	.015	⑤	⑤	66.9 @ 1.39	.314	.314

①—Le Car.
②—18i, 158 lbs. @ 1.173 inches; Fuego, 116.89 lbs. @ 1.20 inches.
③—Outer spring, 116.89 @ 1.201; inner spring, 35.97 @ .965.
④—Alliance/Encore.
⑤—Intake, 60°; exhaust, 45°.

Piston, Pins, Rings, Crankshaft & Bearings

Year	Engine	Piston Clearance	Cylinder Liner Protrusion ①	Ring End Gap	Wrist Pin Diameter	Rod Bearings Shaft Diameter	Rod Bearings Bearing Clearance	Main Bearings Shaft Diameter	Main Bearings Bearing Clearance	Thrust On Bear. No.	Shaft End Play
1983	4-85/1397cc ②	—	.001-.004	③	.790	1.732	.001-.0026	2.158	.0004-.0014	3	.0039-.009
	4-100/1647cc	—	.004-.007	③	.828	1.890	—	2.158	—	3	.002-.009
1983—85	4-95/1565cc	.0019-.0020	.004-.007	③	.828	1.890	—	2.157	—	3	.002-.009
1983-87	4-85/1397cc ④	—	.001-.004	③	.787	1.73	—	2.16	—	3	.0039-.009
1984-86	4-132/2165cc	—	.003-.006	③	.905	2.215	—	2.476	—	3	.005-.011
1985-87	4-105/1721cc	.0009-.0018	—	③	.826	1.889	—	2.157	—	2	.002-.009
1987	4-120/1965cc	.0009-.0018	—	③	.826	1.889	—	2.157	—	2	.002-.009

—Not Available.
①—Protrusion without O-ring seal.
②—Le Car.
③—Ring gap preset.
④—Alliance/Encore.

Engine Tightening Specifications

*Torque specifications are for clean and lightly lubricated threads only. Dry or dirty threads produce increased friction which prevents accurate measurement of tightness.

Engine	Spark Plugs	Cylinder Head Bolts Ft. Lbs.	Connecting Rod Cap Bolts Ft. Lbs.	Main Bearing Cap Bolts Ft. Lbs.	Intake Manifold Ft. Lbs.	Exhaust Manifold Ft. Lbs.	Camshaft Sprocket Ft. Lbs.	Flywheel to Crankshaft Ft. Lbs.	Vibration Damper or Pulley Ft. Lbs.
4-85/1397cc ①	21	40	30	45	10	10	20	35	81
4-85/1397cc ②	21	42	31③	44	12	12	21	③④	81
4-95/1565cc	—	57-61	33③	48	—	—	—	③④	67
4-100/1647cc	—	57-61	33	48	—	—	—	④	67
4-105/1721cc	21	⑤	35③	47	12	12	⑥	39③	70
4-120/1965cc	21	⑤	35③	47	12	12	⑥	39③	70
4-132/2165cc	21	⑤	46③	69	—	—	37	44③	96

Continued

ENGINE TIGHTENING SPECIFICATIONS—Continued

—Not available.
①—LeCar.
②—Alliance/Encore.
③—On 1985–87 models, do not reuse (torque) original connecting rod or flywheel attaching bolts. Use new bolts.
④—Manual transmission, 37 ft. lbs.; Automatic transmission, 50 ft. lbs.
⑤—Refer to text for procedure.
⑥—Camshaft sprocket bolt, 39 ft. lbs. Camshaft bearing caps: 6 mm bolts, 7 ft. lbs.; 8 mm bolts, 15 ft. lbs.

Brake Specifications

Year	Model	Drum Brake I.D.	Wheel Cylinder Bore		Master Cylinder Bore	Disc Brake Rotor	
			Front Disc	Rear Drum		Nominal Thickness	Minimum Thickness
1983	5/Le Car	7.096	1.772	.866	.811	.394	.354
	18i	8.996	1.890	.866	.748	.472	.354
	Fuego	8.996	1.890	.866	.748	①	②
Alliance	8.000	1.890	.813	.827	.472	.433	
1984–86	Fuego & Sportwagon	8.996	1.890	.866	.748	.788	.709
1984–87	Alliance, Encore	8.000	1.890	.813	.827	.472	.433
1987	GTA	8.000	1.890	.813	.827	.787	.758

—Not available.
①—4-95/1565cc engine, .788 inch; 4-100/1647cc engine, .472 inch.
②—4-95/1565cc engine, .709 inch; 4-100/1647cc engine, .433 inch.

Wheel Alignment Specifications

Year	Model	Caster Angle, Degrees		Camber Angle, Degrees				Toe-Out Inch
				Limits		Desired		
		Limits	Desired	Left	Right	Left	Right	
1983	Le Car	①	①	0 to +1	0 to +1	+1/2	+1/2	0 to 5/64
1983–86	18i, Sportwagon②	①	①	−1/2 to +1/2	−1/2 to +1/2	0	0	0 to .08
	18i, Sportwagon③	—	—	—	—	+1/2	+1/2	④
1983–86	Fuego②	①	①	−1/2 to +1/2	−1/2 to +1/2	0	0	0 to .08
	Fuego③	—	—	—	—	+1/2	+1/2	④
1983–87	Alliance, Encore②	+1/2 to +2	+1 1/4	−3/16 to +5/16	−3/16 to +5/16	+1/16	+1/16	⑤
	Alliance, Encore③	—	—	−1 to −1/2	−1 to −1/2	−3/4	−3/4	⑥
1987	GTA②	+1/2 to +2	+1 1/4	−1 5/8 to −1 1/8	−1 5/8 to −1 1/8	−1 3/8	−1 3/8	⑤
	GTA③	—	—	−1 1/2 to −1 1/4	−1 1/2 to −1 1/4	—	—	⑦

①—Refer to caster & ride height adjustments in "Wheel Alignment Section."
②—Front.
③—Rear.
④—Zero to .059 inch toe-out.
⑤—Zero to 1/8 inch toe-out.
⑥—Zero ±1/2°.
⑦—1/4° to 1/2° toe-in.

Cooling System & Capacity Data

Year	Model or Engine	Cooling Capacity Qts. Less A/C	Cooling Capacity Qts. With A/C	Radiator Cap Relief Pressure Lbs.	Thermo. Opening Temp.	Fuel Tank Gals.	Engine Oil Refill Qts. ①	Transmission Oil 4 Speed Qts.	Transmission Oil 5 Speed Qts.	Transmission Oil Auto. Trans. Qts.
1983	Le Car	6.5	6.5	12	182	10	3.5	2	—	—
	Fuego	7⅓	7⅓	②	187	15	4.5	—	2.1	③
	18i	6.6	6.6	②	187	④	4.5	2.1	2.1	③
	Alliance	4.4	4.8	14	188	12.5	3.50	3.4	3.6	⑤
1984	Alliance, Encore	4.4	4.8	14	188	4.0	3.4	3.6	⑤	
1984—85	Fuego ⑥	7⅓	7⅓	②	187	15	4.5	—	2.1	—
1984-86	Fuego & Sportwagon ⑦	6.8	6.8	—	187	15	5.8	—	2.1	⑧
1985-87	Alliance, Encore	7.0	7.0	14	188	12.5	⑨	3.4	3.6	3.7⑤
1987	GTA	7.0	7.0	—	—	12.5	5.0	—	3.6	—

—Not Available.
①—Includes filter.
②—Measured at overflow reservoir. Vehicles equipped with plastic valve: white, 12 psi; brown, 17 psi; Vehicles equipped with metal valve: as indicated on valve.
③—Drain & refill, 2.6 qts.; total capacity, 5.3 qts.
④—Exc. station wagon, 14 gals.; Station wagon, 15 gals.
⑤—Drain & refill, 2.5 qts.; total capacity, 4.5 quarts.
⑥—Turbo.
⑦—Exc. Fuego Turbo.
⑧—Drain & refill, 2.6 qts.; total capacity, 6.4 qts.
⑨—4-85/1397cc engine, 4 qts. 4-105/1721cc engine: 1985-86, 5.5 qts.; 1987, 5.0 qts.

ELECTRICAL SECTION

INDEX

ALTERNATOR IN-CAR TESTING

Disconnect battery and alternator before arc welding on vehicle.

ALLIANCE, ENCORE, FUEGO & GTA

1. Connect voltmeter across battery terminals and read battery voltage.
2. Start engine and raise engine speed until voltmeter needle stabilizes. Voltage reading should be 12.5-15 volts within 10 minutes.
3. Return engine to idle and turn on all accessories.
4. Gradually increase engine speed until voltage reading stabilizes. Voltage reading should be 12.5-15 volts within 10 minutes.
5. If voltage readings are within specifications, charging system is satisfactory. If readings are consistently below 12.5 volts, inspect charging system and repair as needed. If reading is consistently above 15 volts, check for defective regulator.

LE CAR, 18i & SPORTWAGON

The alternator can be checked on the vehicle using a voltmeter. Connect a voltmeter across the battery (+) and (−) terminals.

1. At idle, the voltmeter should read approximately 14 volts.
2. On acceleration at 2,000 RPM, the voltmeter should read approximately 15 volts at no load.
3. At 2,000 RPM, turn on the headlights, heater, rear window defogger, and windshield wipers. The voltmeter should read approximately 13 to 14 volts.

ALTERNATOR TROUBLESHOOTING

The alternator warning lamp should light as soon as the ignition is switched on, and the lamp should go out soon after the engine starts. However, if there is a fault in the charging system the warning lamp should remain on while the engine is running.

1. If indicator does not light momentarily when ignition switch is turned on:
   a. Check that voltage regulator electrical connector is properly seated.
   b. Check alternator ground. Resistance between alternator frame and negative battery post should be less than 2 ohms.
   c. Check that bulb is not blown by grounding .25 in. "L" terminal on connector. Bulb should illuminate.
2. If indicator comes on while engine is running:
   a. Check alternator belt for breakage or incorrect tension.
   b. Check for broken charging lead.
   c. Check for internal damage to alternator.
   d. Check for malfunctioning regulator.
3. If charging voltage is consistently below 13.5 volts but the indicator functions normally, check the following:
   a. Defective diodes. Diode should have continuity with current applied in one direction and no continuity with current applied in opposite direction.
   b. Open stator windings.
   c. Excessive carbon on slip rings.
   d. Worn or sticking brushes.
   e. Poor electrical connections.
   f. Defective battery.

STARTER REPLACE

ALLIANCE & ENCORE

4-85/1397cc ENGINE

1. Disconnect battery ground cable, then disconnect wiring from solenoid.
2. Remove bracket at rear of starter, the three starter mounting bolts and the starter, noting position of locating dowel.
3. Reverse procedure to install, ensuring that locating dowel is centered in hole of appropriate mounting bolt. **The three mounting bolts must be tightened before tightening bracket.**

4-105/1721cc & 4-120/1965cc ENGINES

1984–85

1. Disconnect battery ground cable, then raise and support vehicle.
2. Remove right driveshaft, then disconnect exhaust pipe from manifold.
3. Remove 3 starter mounting bolts, starter bracket at brush end of motor and the starter, noting installation position of locating dowel.
4. Reverse procedure to install, ensuring that locating dowel is centered in hole of appropriate mounting bolt. **The three mounting bolts must be tightened before tightening bracket.**

1986–87 (Bosch Starter)

1. Disconnect battery ground cable and disconnect wiring at starter solenoid.
2. Remove 3 starter mounting bolts and the starter motor, noting installation position of locating dowel.
3. Reverse procedure to install, ensuring that locating dowel is centered in hole of appropriate mounting bolt.

FUEGO

1. Disconnect battery ground cable.
2. Disconnect starter wiring.
3. Remove catalytic converter heat shield, catalytic converter, and starter heat shield.
4. Loosen rear support bracket bolt and retain motor mount spacer.
5. Remove three starter mounting bolts, then remove starter.
6. Reverse procedure to install, tightening three starter mounting bolts before installing starter rear mounting bracket.

LE CAR

1. Disconnect battery ground cable.

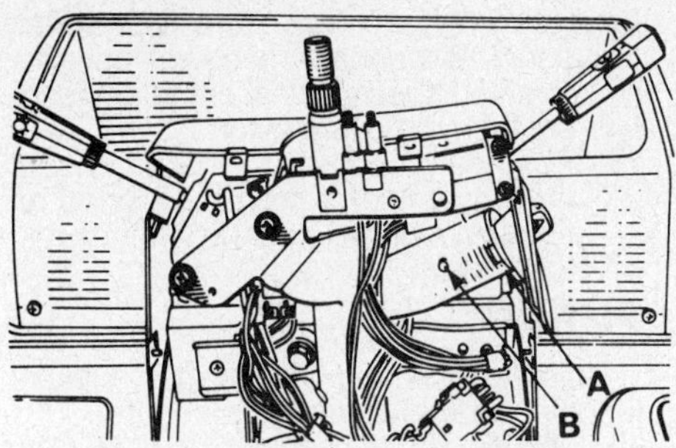

Fig. 1 Typical ignition switch removal. Alliance, Encore & GTA

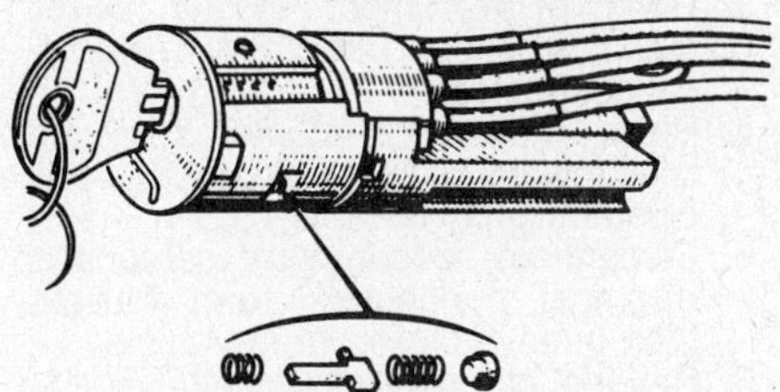

Fig. 3 Ignition switch tumbler removal (Typical)

2. Remove air cleaner and carburetor air cleaner air intake.
3. Clamp and disconnect the carburetor heating hoses. Remove the carburetor linkage.
4. Disconnect exhaust pipe and remove intake/exhaust manifold.
5. Disconnect positive battery cable from the starter, then the solenoid feed wire.
6. Remove starter bolts. Remove upper bolt with a suitable tool.
7. Remove starter.
8. Reverse procedure to install.
9. Check the coolant level and bleed the cooling system.

18i & SPORTWAGON

1. Disconnect battery ground cable and remove catalytic converter shield.
2. Remove catalytic converter and starter heat shield.
3. Disconnect starter motor electrical connectors.
4. Disconnect coolant hoses as necessary, then remove upper left bolt and loosen upper right bolt of motor mount.
5. Loosen starter rear support bolt, then remove starter retaining bolts and the starter.
6. Reverse procedure to install. Tighten starter retaining bolts before tightening starter bracket retaining bolt.

IGNITION SWITCH REPLACE

ALLIANCE, ENCORE & GTA

1. Disconnect battery ground cable.
2. Remove steering column upper and lower housing covers.
3. Disconnect wire connector from switch.
4. Turn key to "OFF" on 1983 vehicles, or to position between "ACC" and "ON" on 1984-87 vehicles, and remove key.
5. Remove attaching screw (A), **Fig. 1**, then, using suitable tool, push in retaining pin (B) and remove switch by pushing from rear. Retaining pin is located on upper side on 1983-85 models and on lower side on 1986-87 models.
6. Reverse procedure to install.

FUEGO

1. Disconnect battery ground cable.
2. Remove steering wheel and two half housings around steering column.
3. Disconnect ignition switch junction block.
4. Position key at stop between "ACC" and "ON".
5. Unscrew attaching screw (A), **Fig. 2**, then, using suitable tool, push in retaining pin, then remove switch by pushing from rear.
6. Reverse procedure to install.

LE CAR, 18i & SPORTWAGON

1. Disconnect battery ground cable.
2. On 18i and Sportwagon, remove steering wheel.
3. Remove the combination lighting-direction indicator switch shell. On Le Car, remove bottom half only.
4. On all models, remove wiring junction plug.
5. Turn key to (G) "garage" position and remove key.
6. Remove retaining screw.
7. Push in retaining pin with a punch and push the switch out from behind.
8. Insert key and turn the key to the (S) "stop" position.
9. Remove key to free locking tumbler, **Fig. 3.**
10. Remove two screws on the rear of the switch.
11. Pull the switch apart.
12. Reverse procedure to install.

LIGHT SWITCH REPLACE

ALLIANCE, ENCORE & GTA

The lighting, turn signal, and windshield wiper switch is removed as an assembly.

1. Disconnect battery ground cable.
2. Remove steering column upper and lower housing covers.
3. Disconnect connectors.
4. Remove switch attaching screws, then remove switch.
5. Reverse procedure to install.

FUEGO

1. Disconnect battery ground cable.
2. Remove steering wheel and steering column housing halves.
3. Remove attaching bolt and screws.
4. Disconnect junction blocks.
5. Remove assembly by pulling upward.
6. Remove light switch from assembly by using round rod .15 in. in diameter and piece of tubing .315 in. in diameter to push out connecting pin, **Fig. 4.**

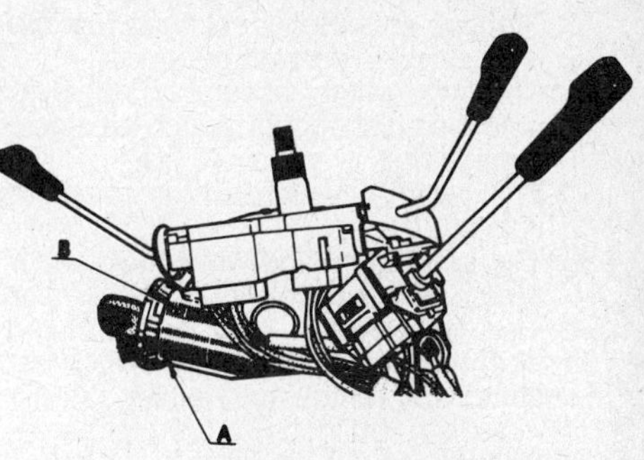

Fig. 2 Ignition switch removal. Fuego

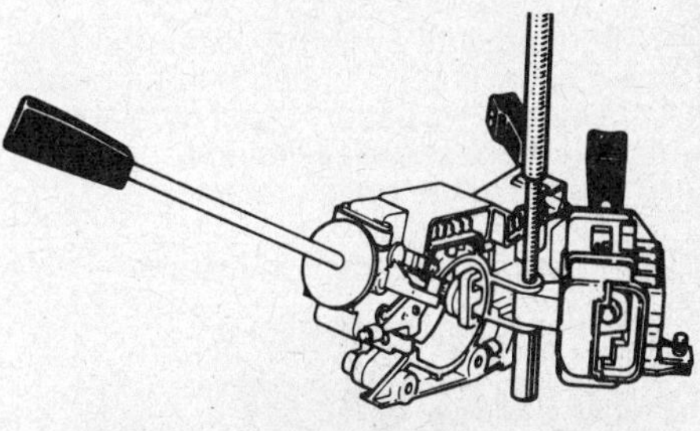

Fig. 4 Separating turn signal & wiper switch from light switch. Fuego, 18i & Sportwagon

7. Reverse procedure to install.

LE CAR

EXC. MODELS W/COMBINATION SWITCH

Hi-Low Beam Switch

1. Disconnect battery ground cable.
2. Remove under dash panel cover screws and the cover.
3. Remove switch retaining screws.
4. Disconnect wiring plugs and remove switch.
5. Reverse procedure to install.

On-Off Switch

1. Disconnect battery ground cable.
2. Remove under dashboard lower panel containing the switch.
3. Remove switch knob by turning to the left.
4. Remove switch retaining nut with suitable tool.
5. Remove switch from the under dash panel.
6. Reverse procedure to install.

MODELS W/COMBINATION SWITCH

1. Disconnect battery ground cable.
2. Remove instrument panel housing screws.
3. Remove switch bottom shell, then the switch attaching screws.
4. Disconnect junction blocks, then remove switch.
5. Reverse procedure to install.

18i & SPORTWAGON

The lighting, turn signal and windshield wiper switch is removed as an assembly.

1. Disconnect battery ground cable.
2. Remove steering wheel, then remove both steering column supports.
3. Remove switch assembly retaining bolt, then disconnect switch electrical connectors.
4. Pull switch upward and remove from vehicle.
5. The turn signal and windshield wiper switch are serviced as an assembly. The light switch may be removed from the turn signal/wiper switch assembly by removing retaining pin using a rod .150 inch (3.8 mm) in diameter to press out pin, **Fig. 4.**

STOP LIGHT SWITCH
REPLACE

The stop light switch is located on the brake pedal linkage under the dashboard.
1. Disconnect battery ground cable.
2. Disconnect switch wiring.
3. Remove the switch retainer.
4. Remove the switch.
5. Reverse procedure to install.

BACK-UP LAMP & NEUTRAL SAFETY SWITCH
REPLACE
MANUAL TRANSMISSION
Back-Up Lamp Switch

The switch is located to the lower right of the transmission shift rail.
1. Disconnect battery ground cable.
2. Raise vehicle.
3. Disconnect switch wiring and remove switch.
4. Reinstall switch with a new copper O-ring. Reconnect the wiring.
5. Check the transmission lubricant level.
6. Lower vehicle and reconnect battery.

AUTOMATIC TRANSMISSION

The back-up and neutral safety switches are combined in a multifunction switch located on the transmission. The switch is cam driven by the gear shift linkage. To replace the switch, raise and support vehicle, disconnect switch electrical connectors, then remove switch.

TURN SIGNAL SWITCH
REPLACE

On all models except Le Car with separate switches, the lighting, turn signal and wiper switching functions are included in a combination switch. On these models, refer to "Light Switch, Replace" for replacement of turn signal switch. On Le Car models with separate switches use the following procedure for turn signal switch replacement.
1. Disconnect battery ground cable.
2. Remove bottom half of the combination lighting-turn signal switch shell.
3. Remove switch retaining screws.

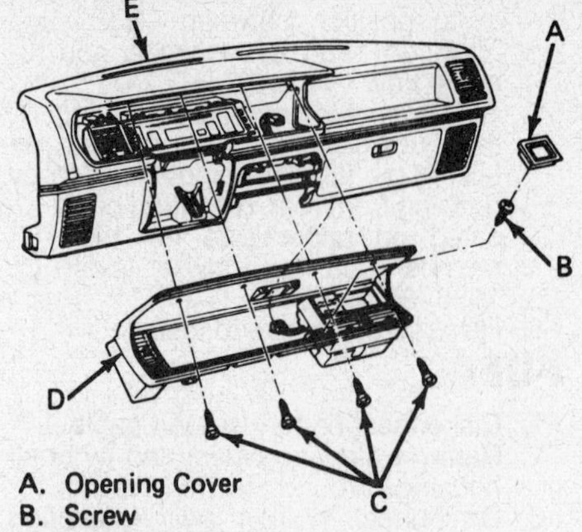

A. Opening Cover
B. Screw
C. Screw
D. Cluster Bezel
E. Instrument Panel

Fig. 5 Instrument cluster bezel removal. 1986–87 Alliance Encore & GTA

4. Disconnect wiring connectors.
5. Remove switch.
6. Reverse procedure to install.

INSTRUMENT CLUSTER
REPLACE
ALLIANCE, ENCORE & GTA
1983–85

1. Disconnect battery ground cable.
2. Remove screw from each lower corner of cluster bezel, press in on sides of bezel to disengage retaining clips and remove bezel.
3. Release 2 clips at top of cluster and remove 3 cluster retaining screws.
4. Pull cluster away from instrument panel, disconnect electrical connector and speedometer cable, then remove cluster.
5. Reverse procedure to install.

1986–87

1. Disconnect battery ground cable, then remove steering wheel as follows:
   a. Remove steering wheel cover.
   b. Scribe index mark between steering wheel and shaft, then loosen but do not remove steering wheel retaining nut.
   c. Grasp steering wheel and give it a quick pull to disengage wheel from shaft. **Do not tap against steering shaft to release wheel as the steering column will be damaged.**
   d. Remove retaining nut and the steering wheel.
2. Remove small cover A from lower right side of cluster to gain access to lower bezel retaining screw B, **Fig. 5.**
3. Remove cluster bezel retaining screws B and C, disconnect electrical connectors as needed, then remove the bezel.
4. On models with analog cluster, remove cluster retaining screws. On models with digital cluster, press down and release 2 retainers at top of cluster.
5. Pull cluster away from instrument panel, disconnect electrical connectors and speedometer cable as needed, then remove cluster.
6. Reverse procedure to install. Ensure steering wheel is properly aligned on shaft and torque steering wheel nut to 33 ft. lbs.

FUEGO

Refer to "18i and Sportwagon, Deluxe Models" for replacement procedure.

LE CAR

1. Disconnect battery ground cable.
2. Remove steering column shroud, then carefully lower steering column.
3. Remove instrument cluster bezel, then disconnect control switch electrical connectors.
4. Press instrument cluster retaining clips toward center of cluster and pull cluster slightly forward.
5. Disconnect speedometer cable and electrical connectors from cluster, then remove cluster from vehicle.
6. Reverse procedure to install.

18i & SPORTWAGON
Custom Models

1. Disconnect battery ground cable and remove steering wheel.
2. Remove both lower steering column covers, then remove two panel to dash attaching screws, **Fig. 6.**
3. Disconnect speedometer cable and instrument panel electrical connectors.
4. Tilt instrument panel forward, then using screwdriver, pry upper part of instrument panel outward while pressing lower part inward and remove instrument panel from vehicle.
5. Reverse procedure to install. Tilt instrument panel forward until it can be attached to pins located in instrument cluster opening.

Deluxe Models

1. Disconnect battery ground cable, then remove instrument panel covers (1), **Fig. 7.**
2. Remove screws (A), then remove bezel (3) from switch panel (4).
3. Disconnect electrical connectors from switches, then remove switch panel (4).
4. Press instrument cluster retaining clips toward center of cluster and pull cluster slightly forward. Disconnect speedometer cable and instrument panel electrical connectors, then remove instrument panel.
5. Reverse procedure to install.

WINDSHIELD WIPER SWITCH
REPLACE

On all models except Le Car with separate switches, the lighting, turn signal and wiper switching functions are included in a combination switch. On these models, refer to "Light Switch, Replace" for replacement of front wiper switch. On Le Car mod-

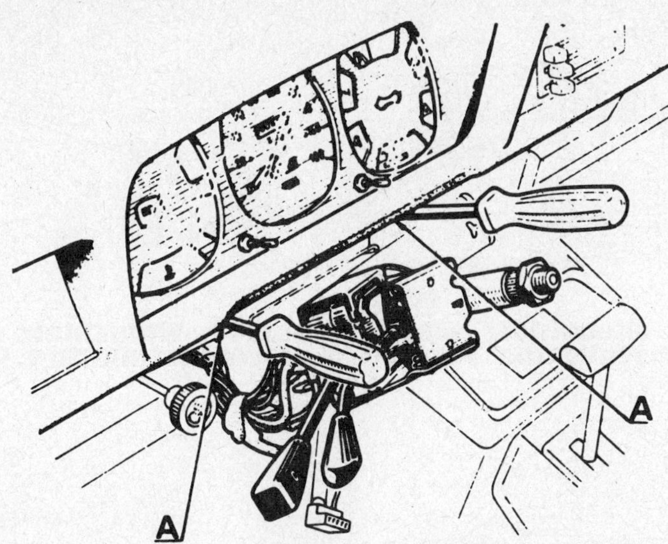

Fig. 6 Instrument cluster removal. 18i & Sportwagon Custom models

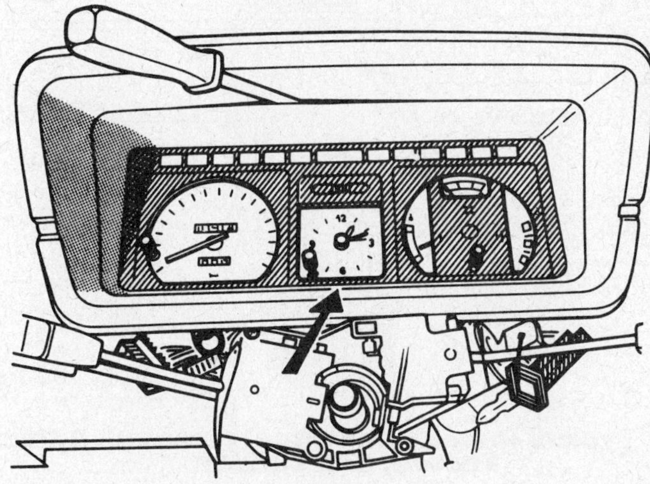

Fig. 7 Instrument cluster removal. 18i & Sportwagon Deluxe models, Fuego similar

Fig. 8 Plenum cover panel removal. Alliance, Encore & GTA

els with separate switches use the following procedure for front wiper switch replacement.

1. Disconnect battery ground cable.
2. Pry up the switch from the bottom using a small screwdriver and pull out of the dashboard.
3. Remove the wiring plug.
4. Reverse procedure to install.

WINDSHIELD WIPER MOTOR

REPLACE

ALLIANCE, ENCORE & GTA

1. Disconnect battery ground cable.
2. Remove wiper arms, outside spindle bearing nuts, junction block, and plate attaching bolts.
3. On vehicles equipped with A/C, reposition evaporator to provide clearance as follows:
   a. Remove ignition coil.
   b. Remove four bolts securing plenum cover panel, **Fig. 8.**
   c. Remove heater/air distribution housing assembly as outlined under "Heater Core, Replace."
   d. Remove four bolts securing evaporator housing and position housing out of way. Two upper bolts securing evaporator housing are accessible from inside passenger compartment, under the left side of the instrument panel.
4. Remove windshield wiper assembly.
5. Remove crank nut (A), **Fig. 9.**
6. Remove three motor retaining bolts, (B), then remove motor.
7. Reverse procedure to install, noting the following:
   a. When installing motor, ensure that arm (C) and crank (D) are aligned when motor is in park position, **Fig. 9.**
   b. Ensure that defroster ducts are correctly aligned before installing instrumental panel.
   c. Install wiper assembly junction block after assembly is in position.
   d. Ensure that motor is in park position before installing wiper arms.

FUEGO

1. Disconnect battery ground cable.
2. Remove wiper arms, outer attaching bolts, junction block, ground wire, and plate attaching bolt.
3. Push inward to free two spindles, then pull assembly to left to remove assembly.
4. Unscrew drive link attaching nut (2), **Fig. 10.**
5. Remove three motor attaching bolts, (1), then remove motor.
6. Reverse steps 4 and 5 to install motor, ensuring that drive links (A) and (B) are in line with motor in park position.
7. Position windshield wiper assembly from left until two spindles can be seen through two holes in cowl panel.
8. Push assembly up through holes and install two attaching nuts.
9. Tighten plate bolt.
10. Connect ground wire and junction block.

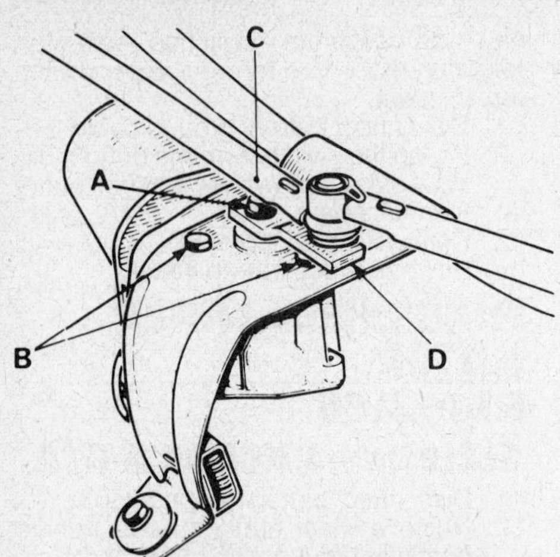

Fig. 9 Windshield Wiper motor installation. Alliance, Encore & GTA

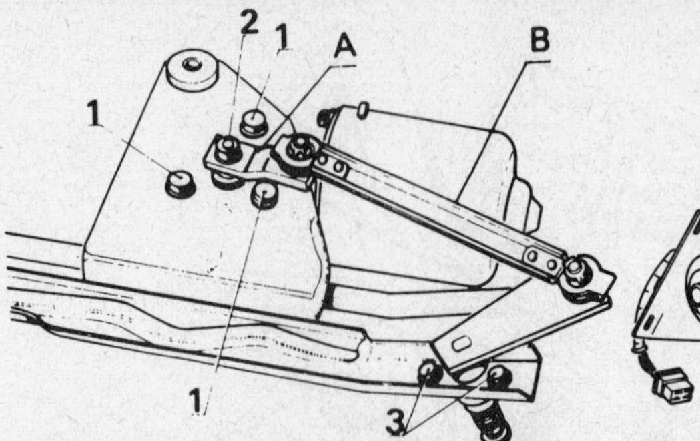

Fig. 10 Windshield wiper motor installation. Fuego

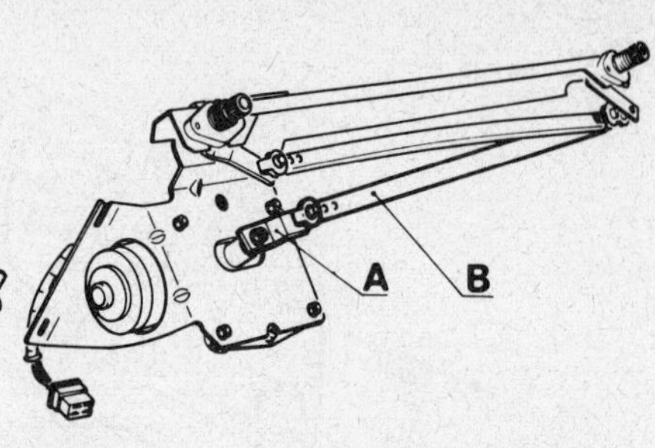

Fig. 11 Windshield wiper motor installation. Le Car

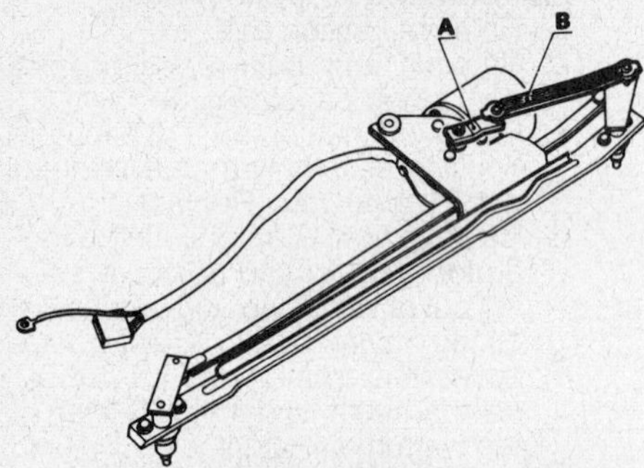

Fig. 12 Windshield wiper motor installation. 18i & Sportwagon

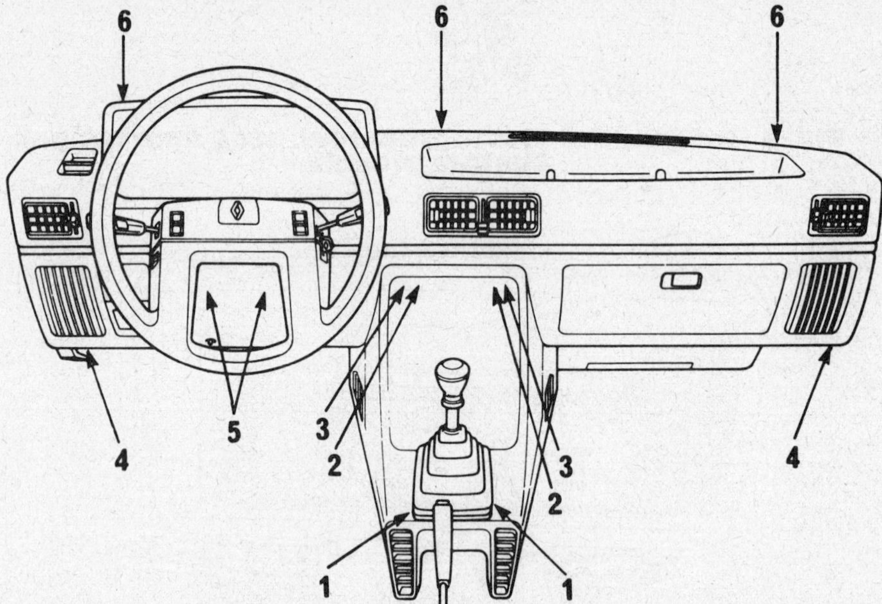

Fig. 13 Typical instrument panel removal. Alliance & Encore, GTA similar

11. Install wiper arms, ensuring that drive links (A) and (B) are aligned.

LE CAR

1. Disconnect battery ground cable.
2. Remove the wiper arms by lifting the base of the arm and removing the retaining nut.
3. Remove large nuts securing the arm pivots to the cowl.
4. Disconnect the wiring at the plug.
5. Remove bolts securing motor mounting bracket.
6. Lower the motor and bracket assembly and remove along with linkage by pulling out sideways.
7. Remove driving arm nut from motor shaft.
8. Remove motor mounting screws and the motor from the assembly.
9. Reverse procedure to install. Driving arm (A) and linkage (B) must be exactly in line for reassembly with the motor in the park position, **Fig. 11**.

18i & SPORTWAGON

1. Disconnect battery ground cable.
2. Remove wiper arms by lifting base of arm and removing locknut.
3. Remove nuts securing arm pivots to cowl.
4. Disconnect wiper motor electrical connector and ground wire, then remove mounting plate retaining bolts.
5. Press motor assembly inward to free spindles, then position wiper linkage to the right as viewed from front of vehicle.
6. Remove wiper linkage assembly.
7. Remove motor drive link retaining nut.
8. Remove motor retaining screws, then the wiper motor.
9. Reverse procedure to install. Check to ensure that all drive links are aligned, **Fig. 12**, and that motor is in Park position prior to installation.

RADIO

REPLACE

ALLIANCE, ENCORE & GTA

1983–85

1. Disconnect battery ground cable.
2. Pry up 2 hole plugs from lower rear of radio trim plate, then remove 4 retaining screws, 2 from under hole plugs and 2 from top of trim plate.
3. On manually tuned radios, remove knobs and shaft nuts.
4. On all models, pull out on bottom of trim plate while pushing down at the top, remove trim plate and position aside.
5. Remove 2 screws from bottom of radio and pull radio away from instrument panel.
6. Disconnect antenna lead and electrical connectors, then remove radio.
7. Reverse procedure to install.

1986–87

1. Disconnect battery ground cable.
2. Remove small covers from each side of heater control to gain access to trim plate retaining screws. Covers snap into place.
3. Remove 4 screws securing trim plate and position trim plate aside.
4. Remove screws securing radio, disconnect antenna lead and electrical connectors, as equipped, then remove radio. Radio and equalizer, if equipped, must be removed together to gain access to patch cable between units.
5. Reverse procedure to install.

LE CAR

1. Disconnect battery ground cable.
2. Remove two Phillips screws at bottom of radio console.

3. Remove radio knobs and the radio shaft securing nuts.
4. Pull out the bottom of the radio console, reach in behind the console and pull out the radio.
5. Reverse procedure to install.

BLOWER MOTOR REPLACE

ALLIANCE, ENCORE & GTA

1. Disconnect battery ground cable.
2. On 1983-84 models, remove ignition coil.
3. On all models, remove plenum panel seal (3), plenum cover attaching screws (1) and the cover panel, **Fig. 8.**
4. Remove 3 blower housing nuts.
5. Disconnect electrical connectors from motor and blower resistor.
6. Lift blower motor and housing assembly from vehicle.
7. Reverse procedure to install.

LE CAR

1. Disconnect battery ground cable and motor wiring.
2. Remove air flap lever control cable and cable sleeve.
3. Unclip bleed hose and accelerator cable from blower motor housing.
4. Remove two housing attaching bolts located on the fender well and next to the carburetor. Lift out the blower housing assembly.
5. Separate the two halves of the housing after removing the securing clips.
6. Remove the two clips on the air intake side and then remove the flap support panel.
7. Remove the 3 motor mount screws on the top of the housing and remove the motor. Retain the rubber anti-vibration washers.
8. Pull off the fan blade locking sleeve and separate the fan from the motor. Do not pry the locking sleeve off from the bottom.
9. Reverse procedure to install. Be sure to reinstall the rubber anti-vibration washers.

18i, FUEGO & SPORTWAGON

Less A/C

1. Disconnect battery ground cable and drain cooling system.
2. Disconnect heater hoses at blower motor housing.
3. Disconnect blower motor and windshield wiper motor electrical connectors.
4. Disconnect retaining clip at airflow door cable sleeve, then disconnect cable at door.
5. Working in engine compartment, remove screws securing blower motor housing to firewall.

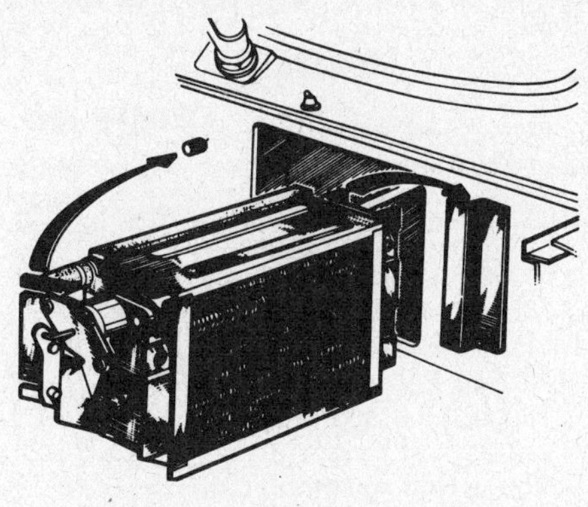

Fig. 14 Heater core removal. Le Car

6. Working from under dashboard, remove two nuts securing heater-ventilator assembly to firewall.
7. Remove blower motor housing and heater ventilator duct assembly as a unit from vehicle.
8. To separate blower motor from blower motor housing and heater-ventilator duct assembly, remove seal, then remove clips on assembly housing.
9. Remove center bolt from heater-ventilator assembly, then separate shells of housing.
10. Remove blower motor and blower wheel assembly from housing. **The blower motor and blower wheels are serviced as a unit only.**
11. Reverse procedure to install. Check to ensure that blower motor and blower wheels are centered properly in blower motor housing.

With A/C

1. Disconnect battery ground cable.
2. Remove both console side panels, then remove two lower console mounting bolts.
3. Disconnect blower motor electrical connectors.
4. Remove blower motor mounting bolts, then raise center console and remove blower motor.
5. Reverse procedure to install.

HEATER CORE REPLACE

ALLIANCE, ENCORE & GTA

1. Disconnect battery ground cable.
2. Remove instrument panel as follows:
   a. Remove steering wheel cover, mark installation position of steering wheel in relation to shaft, then loosen but do not remove steering wheel retaining nut.
   b. Grasp steering wheel and give it a quick pull to disengage wheel from shaft, then remove nut and steering wheel. **Do not tap against steering shaft to release wheel as the steering column will be damaged.**
   c. Remove upper and lower steering column covers, instrument cluster, console tray and console switches.
   d. Remove gearshift lever boot, then release clips at positions (1) and (2), **Fig. 13**, and lift out console.
   e. Remove instrument panel screws (3), (4) and (5).
   f. Remove nut securing ground wire to steering column.
   g. Lift instrument panel up to clear defroster duct and release clips (6), **Fig. 13**, disconnect necessary electrical connectors and remove instrument panel.
3. Remove blower motor assembly attaching screws, then disconnect junction block.
4. Clamp heater core hoses with suitable clamps, then disconnect hoses at firewall.
5. Remove heater housing assembly by pulling it out to the right.
6. Bend out 4 lock tabs securing heater core and remove core from housing.
7. Reverse procedure to install.

LE CAR

1. Remove blower motor and housing assembly.
2. Clamp off the heater hoses leading to the heater core. Remove the bottom heater hose, the heater valve and the bleeder hose. Use Renault clamp Mot. 453 or suitable tool.
3. Remove the heater core mounting bolts and remove the heater core, **Fig. 14.**
4. Reverse procedure to install.
5. Check the operation of the heater valve control cable. Adjust the cable so that there is a slight clearance at lever when the heater valve is completely closed.
6. Install the motor housing assembly.
7. Adjust the air flap control lever so that there is a slight clearance at lever 2 when the air flap is completely closed.
8. Start the engine and bleed the cooling system through the heater core bleed screw.

18i, FUEGO & SPORTWAGON

1. Remove blower motor housing assembly as described under "Blower Motor, Replace," then separate housing as outlined.
2. Disconnect drain hose from heater core, then remove heater core from housing assembly.
3. Reverse procedure to install.

ENGINE SECTION

INDEX

ENGINE REPLACE

ALLIANCE, ENCORE & GTA

4-85/1397cc Engines

1. Disconnect battery cable and drain cooling system.
2. Disconnect washer hoses, mark position of bolts securing hinges to hood, support hood and remove bolts, then lift hood from vehicle.
3. Remove air intake assembly and radiator, and disconnect wiring from starter motor.
4. Mark and disconnect necessary vacuum hoses, electrical connectors, heater hoses, fuel pipes and throttle cables, noting position for installation.
5. Drain engine oil.
6. Disconnect exhaust pipe from manifold and remove support rod between engine and transaxle.
7. Remove flywheel cover and the torque converter to drive plate bolts, if equipped.
8. Remove water pump/alternator belt, crankshaft pulley, and hub.
9. Support engine cradle with jack and suitable block, **Fig. 1**, then remove cradle bolts.
10. On air conditioning equipped vehicles, remove compressor belt, pulley and compressor mounting bolts, and secure compressor aside.
11. Disconnect clutch cable at fork end.
12. Remove TDC sensor.
13. Remove 5 bolts connecting engine to transaxle.

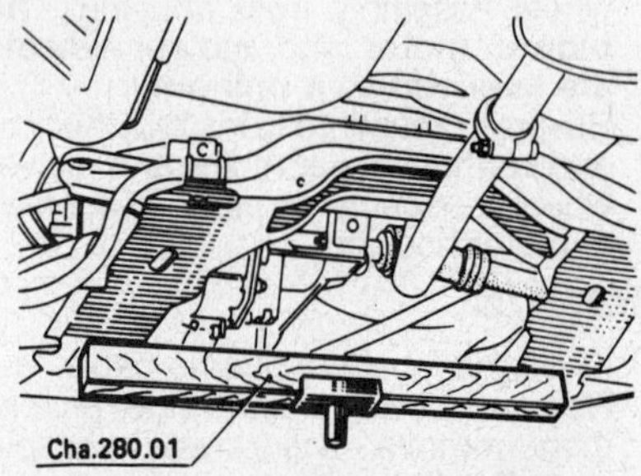

Fig. 1 Engine cradle support. Alliance & Encore w/4-85/1397cc engine

14. Position suitable jack under right hand mounting pad to support transaxle and prevent it from tilting.
15. Install suitable lifting equipment and lift engine from engine compartment as follows:
    a. On models less cruise control, move fuel pipe and bracket and attach suitable adapters to exhaust manifold.
    b. On models with cruise control, remove cruise control cable and ignition coil cable brackets, and install suitable adapters in place of brackets.
    c. Connect lift to adapters, raise engine and separate engine from transaxle.
    d. Ensure all necessary components are disconnected, then remove engine from vehicle.
16. Reverse procedure to install, and fill cooling system as outlined.

4-105/1721cc & 4-120/1965cc Engines

Engine and transaxle are removed as an assembly on these models.

1. Disconnect cables from battery and remove battery.
2. Disconnect washer hoses, mark position of bolts securing hinges to hood, support hood and remove bolts, then lift hood from vehicle.
3. Remove block drain plug from right side of engine and drain coolant, then drain engine oil.
4. On models with A/C, isolate compressor by turning service valves to the fully clockwise (front seated) position, then disconnect hoses and electrical connector from compressor. **Plug hoses and open fittings on compressor.**
5. On all models, remove air cleaner assembly and disconnect accelerator, throttle and cruise control cables, as equipped.
6. Remove gas cap from tank filler neck, then disconnect fuel lines. **1985-87 models are equipped with a fuel tank vent check valve. Gas cap must be removed to release pressure prior to disconnecting fuel lines.**
7. Disconnect radiator hoses and remove radiator.
8. Mark and disconnect necessary electrical connectors and vacuum hoses from engine and transaxle.
9. Disconnect heater hoses, brake booster hose, clutch cable and transaxle cooler lines, as equipped.
10. Disconnect gear selector rod at transaxle lever (manual) or transaxle piv-

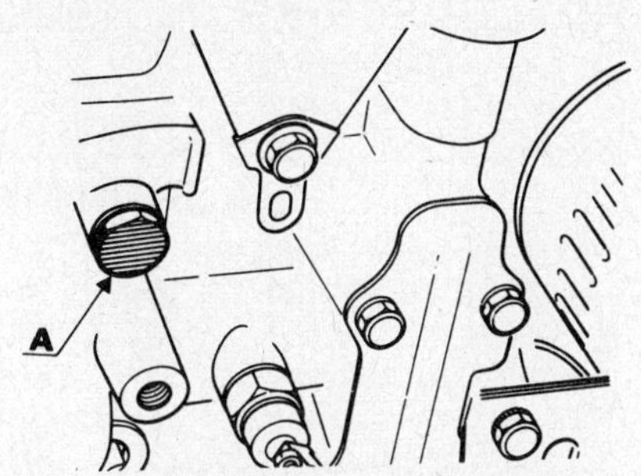

Fig. 2 Cylinder block drain plug. Fuego, 18i & Sportwagon

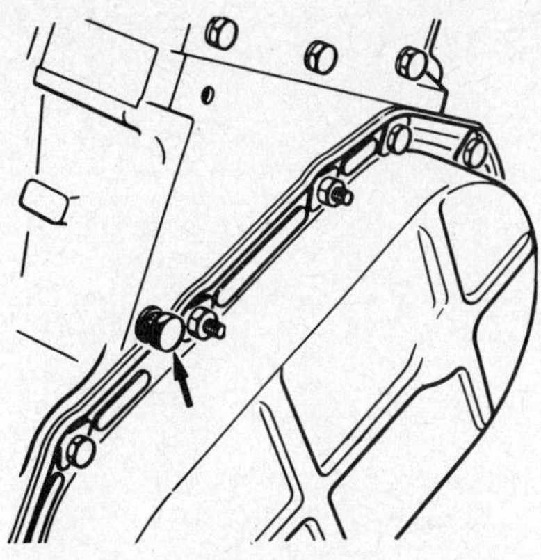

Fig. 3 Block drain plug. Le Car

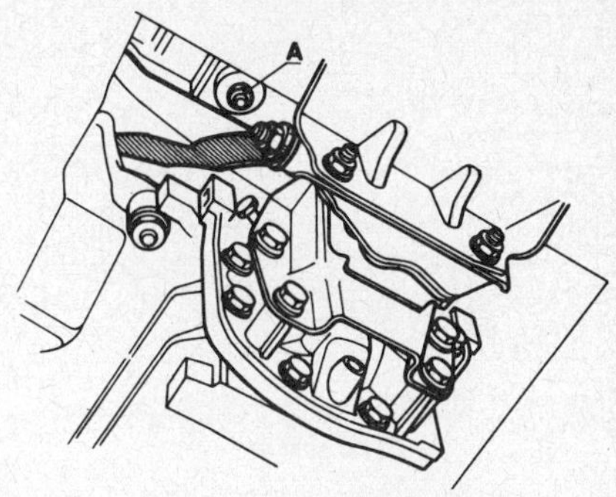

Fig. 4 Radiator attachments. Le Car

ot lever (automatic).

11. Raise and support vehicle and remove front wheels, brake calipers and driveshafts.
12. Disconnect wiring from starter motor and disconnect ground straps from engine and transaxle. Engine ground is attached to block directly under manifolds.
13. Disconnect hoses from power steering pump and plug hoses and pump fittings.
14. Remove speedometer cable from transaxle.
15. Remove nuts and bolts securing front and rear transaxle mounts to subframe.
16. Connect suitable lifting equipment, raise engine and ensure all necessary components have been disconnected, then remove engine and transaxle from vehicle as an assembly.
17. Install engine/transaxle assembly, align mounts, and torque fasteners to 25 ft. lbs.
18. Reverse remaining procedure to complete installation, then fill cooling system as outlined.

FUEGO & SPORTWAGON

1. Disconnect battery cables.
2. Drain cooling system at lower radiator hose and cylinder block drain plug (A), **Fig. 2.**
3. Drain engine oil and air conditioning system as necessary.
4. Remove radiator grille and upper crossmember of grille.
5. Remove radiator and cooling fan(s).
6. On air conditioning equipped vehicles, disconnect hoses from and remove radiator condenser and remove cooling fan.
7. Remove exhaust heat shields and catalytic converter.
8. Remove air intake hose.
9. Remove clutch cable and bracket.
10. Remove starter to transmission bolts.
11. Disconnect electrical connectors.
12. Disconnect power steering pump and hoses as an assembly and position out of way.
13. On air conditioning equipped vehicles, disconnect refrigerant lines between cooling system and compressor and cooling system and condenser.
14. Note location of and disconnect heater hoses, vacuum hoses, and emission control hoses.
15. Disconnect accelerator cable.
16. On automatic transmission equipped vehicles, disconnect governor cable.
17. Disconnect fuel lines. Cap lines to prevent fuel tank from draining.
18. On speed control equipped vehicles, disconnect control cable.
19. Remove engine to transmission bolts.
20. Remove electronic ignition module.
21. Remove sensor on clutch or converter housing.
22. Remove flywheel or converter shield.
23. Remove drive plate to converter attaching bolts.
24. Install suitable lifting tool and raise engine until transmission touches steering crossmember, then secure transmission in this position.
25. Pull engine forward to disengage clutch shaft or converter hub and remove engine. **On automatic transmission equipped vehicles, be careful not to pull out converter while disengaging engine.**
26. After disengaging engine, install tool B.Vi.465 or equivalent to prevent movement of converter.
27. Reverse procedure to install.

LE CAR

The engine is removed with the transaxle attached and removed from above. The use of Renault lifting tool, Mot. 498 or a chain pull with support of the engine and transaxle is recommended.

1. Raise vehicle and support the front end on jack stands.
2. Disconnect and remove battery.
3. Drain the cooling system from the radiator and the drain plug next to the timing gear cover, **Fig. 3.**
4. Drain transaxle oil and engine oil.
5. Remove hood, grille, two inner fender support braces and air filter.
6. Mark and disconnect the water hoses, vacuum hoses, wires and control cables.
7. Remove windshield washer bottle and position aside.
8. Remove splash pan under transaxle.
9. Remove air filter support.
10. Disconnect exhaust pipe from exhaust manifold.
11. Remove nuts holding the radiator, **Fig. 4,** and the radiator cooling fan assembly.
12. Remove steering column flex coupling bolts. Do not lose the rubber bushing.
13. Remove front wheels and brake calipers. Do not disconnect the brake lines.
14. Disconnect tie rods at rack end.
15. Disconnect upper ball joints using Renault tool T. Av. 476 or equivalent, tilt the spindles down and pull the axles out of the transaxle.
16. Remove two bolts securing the steering rack and the rack. **If the steering rack is not being changed, mark the right and left hand shims so that the correct steering rack height can be obtained after reassembly, Fig. 5.**
17. Remove air pump filter, air pump and pump bracket. If the vehicle is equipped with the notched type air pump drive belt, discard the belt. A new belt is mandatory for reassembly.
18. Remove two top bolts on bellhousing.
19. Position the Renault Mot. 498 lifting hook and use two 1 3/8" (35 mm) long bolts to bolt the lifting hook to the transaxle bolt holes. The long bolts are used to distribute the load over a sufficient number of threads, **Fig. 6.**
20. Remove engine mounts from the bottom of engine.
21. Remove right side reinforcement mounting bolts.
22. Remove bolts holding the shift rod support, **Fig. 7.** Pull shift rod downward from the shift linkage.
23. Loosen clutch adjusting nuts and remove clutch cable from release fork. Using a screwdriver, push back the cable sleeve retainer and push out the cable assembly from the support bracket.
24. Attach the chain fall to the lifting device to support the engine.
25. Remove the transaxle front mount.
26. Make sure the axle shaft ends are clear of the transaxle.
27. Remove the engine and transaxle assembly.
28. Reverse procedure to install, noting the following:
    a. Install a new air pump drive belt if vehicle is equipped with a notched type belt.
    b. Refill and bleed cooling system as outlined.

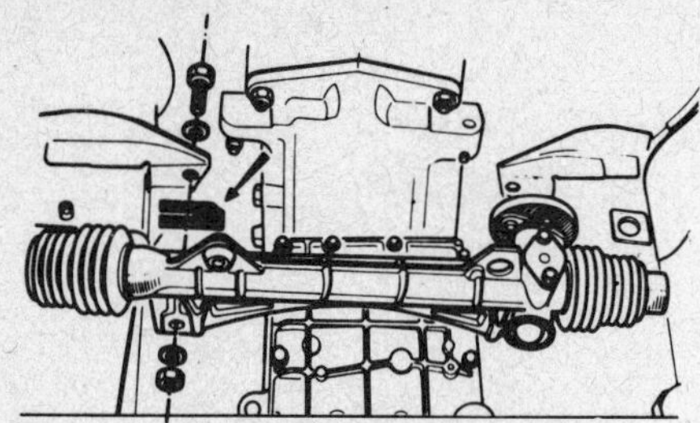

Fig. 5 Steering rack shims. Le Car

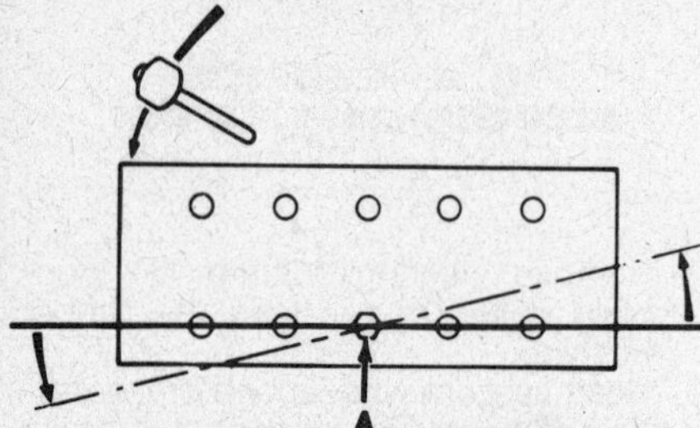

Fig. 8 Typical cylinder head removal. 4-85/1397cc, 4-95/1565cc & 4-100/1647cc engines

18i

1. Disconnect battery ground cable and drain cooling system.
2. Remove engine under cover, parking lamps and radiator grille.
3. Remove grille upper crossmember, radiator and cooling fan.
4. On vehicles equipped with air conditioning, remove cooling fans, then disconnect condenser from radiator and position on bumper leaving all lines attached.
5. Remove battery, starter motor and exhaust heat shields.
6. Remove catalytic converter and air intake hose.
7. Disconnect clutch cable from bracket, then remove bracket on vehicles equipped with manual transmission.
8. Disconnect alternator electrical connectors, then remove alternator.
9. On vehicles equipped with power steering, remove power steering pump and position aside with hoses attached.
10. On vehicles equipped with air conditioning, remove compressor from bracket and position aside with all lines attached.
11. Disconnect all heater hoses, vacuum hoses and emission control system hoses and mark location for reference during reassembly.
12. On vehicles equipped with automatic transmission, disconnect governor cable from engine. On vehicles equipped with manual transmission, disconnect accelerator linkage at engine.
13. On vehicles equipped with speed control, disconnect speed control cable.
14. Disconnect fuel lines from engine and plug all openings to prevent fuel from leaking.

Fig. 6 Installing engine lifting device. Le Car

15. Remove all cylinder head sending units.
16. Remove upper engine to transmission bolts, engine to flywheel protective shield, lower engine to transmission bolts and engine side attaching bolts.
17. On vehicles equipped with automatic transmission, remove converter shield and converter to drive plate bolts.
18. Install suitable engine lifting device to engine, then raise engine until transmission contacts steering crossmember. Secure transmission in this position.
19. Position engine towards front of vehicle to disengage transmission input shaft from engine, then remove engine from vehicle. Check to ensure that torque converter remains with transmission during engine removal.
20. Reverse procedure to install. In order to align distributor timing mark located on converter, painted mark on converter must face part of driving plate blade with sharp edges. Also, new drive plate to converter attaching bolts must be used.

CYLINDER HEAD REPLACE

ALLIANCE, ENCORE & GTA

4-85/1397cc ENGINES

1. Disconnect battery ground cable and drain cooling system, then remove block drain plugs and drain remaining coolant.
2. Remove air cleaner, drive belts and any additional accessories attached to cylinder head.
3. Disconnect exhaust pipe from manifold.
4. Mark installation position, then disconnect necessary hoses, electrical connectors and control cables from cylinder head.
5. Remove distributor cap and spark plug wires as an assembly.
6. Mark position of distributor rotor and distributor position, disconnect electrical connectors and remove hold-down clamp, then remove distributor. **Do not rotate crankshaft after distributor has been removed.**

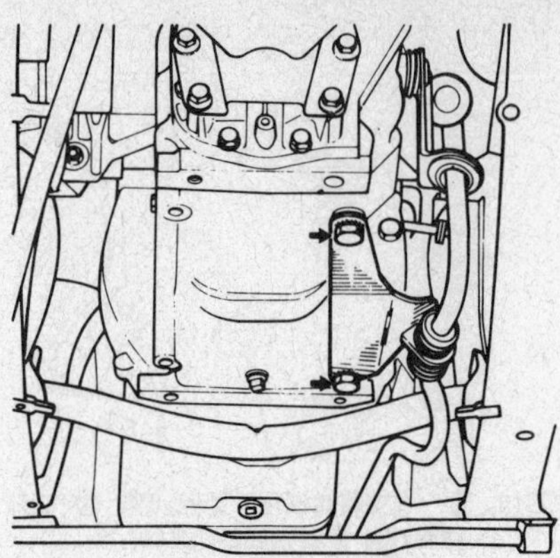

Fig. 7 Shift rod support bolts. Le Car

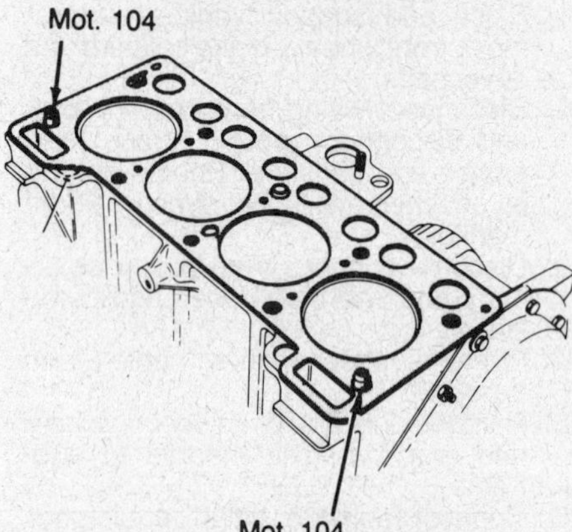

Fig. 9 Cylinder head guide stud installation. 4-85/1397cc engines

7. Remove rocker arm cover, back-off rocker arm adjusting screws, then remove pushrods.
8. Remove all cylinder head retaining bolts except bolt A, **Fig. 8.** Loosen bolt A approximately 1/2 turn. **Because cylinder head gasket seals to the head, block and cylinder liners, the cylinder head cannot be initially lifted off block, as the liners will be moved and the seal between the liners and cylinder block will be broken.**
9. Using a wooden block and a hammer or a plastic hammer, break the cylinder head loose from the cylinder liners by tapping on the ends of the head, **Fig. 8**, then remove the bolt and the cylinder head. **Do not remove center head bolt until cylinder head is completely detached from gasket and cylinder block.**
10. Secure cylinder liners in block with fixture Mot. 521-01 or equivalent. **Do not rotate crankshaft with head removed unless liners are secured in block, as liners will move and the seals will be broken.**
11. Clean gasket material from sealing surfaces using suitable gasket removal solution. **Do not scratch or mar sealing surfaces.**
12. Ensure that all foreign material is removed from oil passages, and remove any oil remaining in head bolt holes

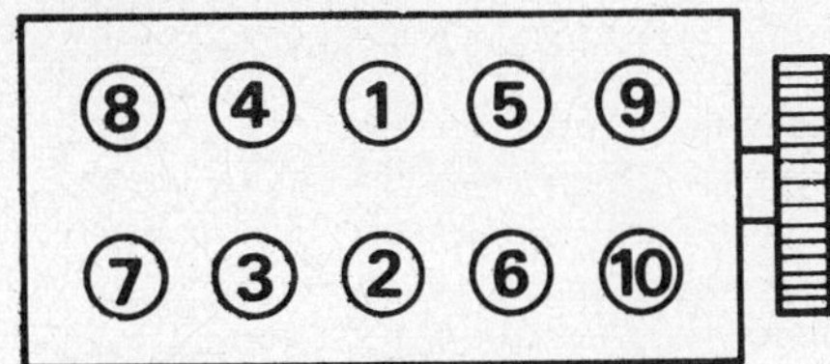

Fig. 10 Cylinder head tightening sequence

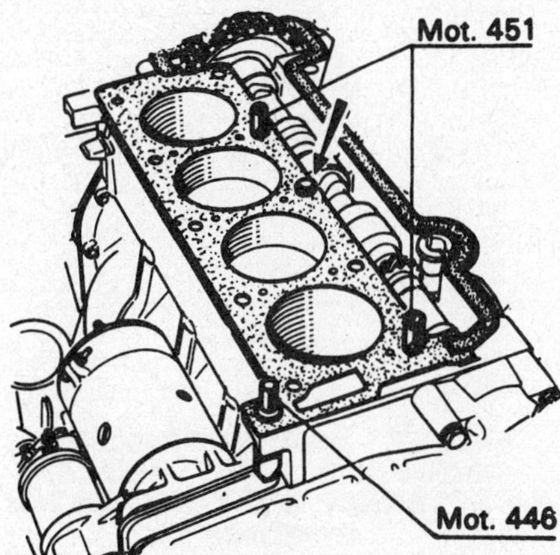

Fig. 12 Cylinder head positioning tool installation. 4-95/1565cc & 4-100/1647cc engines

with syringe to allow proper torquing of head bolts.
13. Remove cylinder liner retaining fixture, then install cylinder head guide studs and new head gasket as shown in **Fig. 9.**
14. Install cylinder head and several head bolts, remove guide pins, then install remaining head bolts.
15. Tighten all head bolts hand tight, ensuring bolts tighten smoothly, then torque bolts to specifications in sequence shown in **Fig. 10.**
16. Reverse remaining procedure to complete installation, noting the following:
    a. If single, notched type drive belt is used, new belt must be installed.
    b. Refill and bleed cooling system as outlined.
    c. Adjust rocker arm clearances to specifications.
    d. Run engine for approximately 20 minutes, stop engine and allow to cool for 2 1/2 hours.
    e. Remove rocker cover and retorque head bolts to specifications in sequence shown in **Fig. 10.**
    f. Loosen each head bolt 1/2 turn, then retorque bolts to specifications in proper sequence, **Fig. 10.**
    g. Recheck rocker arm clearances.

4-105/1721cc & 4-120/1965cc ENGINES

1. Drain coolant from radiator, then remove engine block drain plug from right side of engine.
2. Remove air cleaner assembly, timing belt cover attaching bolts and timing belt cover.
3. Rotate crankshaft until cylinder No. 1 is at TDC compression stroke, then align camshaft timing marks. **If cover plate behind camshaft sprocket does not have a timing mark, scribe a reference mark in-line with camshaft alignment mark.**
4. Loosen accessory drive belt tensioner, then remove drive belt. Loosen timing belt tensioner and remove timing belt.
5. On 1987 models, remove timing belt tensioner.
6. Remove secondary ignition cables, then the valve cover.
7. Remove cylinder head retaining bolts, then using a suitable block of wood, pry off cylinder head. **Lift cylinder head only. Do not attempt to rotate, as it is positioned by dowel pins.**
8. Remove cylinder head with manifolds attached.
9. After cylinder head removal, ensure head bolt threads are clean and the bolts thread easily in and out of cylinder block.
10. Ensure camshaft and crankshaft timing marks are properly aligned, then install cylinder head gasket and cylinder head on cylinder block. Lubricate bolt threads and underside of bolt heads with clean engine oil and install head bolts.
11. Tighten cylinder head bolts as follows:
    a. Torque to 22 ft. lbs. following sequence shown in **Fig. 10.**
    b. Torque to 52 ft. lbs. following sequence shown in **Fig. 10.**
    c. Wait at least 3 minutes, then completely loosen all bolts.
    d. Torque to 15 ft. lbs. following sequence shown in **Fig. 10.**
    e. Attach angular wrench Mot. 591.03(M) or equivalent to torque wrench and tighten head bolts an additional 121-125 degrees.
12. Reverse remaining steps to complete installation, noting the following:
    a. Ensure valve timing is correct and install timing belt as outlined under "Timing Belt, Replace."
    b. Refill and bleed cooling system as outlined.

FUEGO, 18i & SPORTWAGON

EXC. 4-132/2165cc ENGINE

Removal

1. Disconnect battery ground cable and drain cooling system, then remove cylinder block drain plug (A), **Fig. 2.**
2. Remove radiator grille and grille upper crossmember, heat shields, water pump belt, air intake hose, and diagnostic socket.
3. Mark installation position, then disconnect vacuum hoses, electrical connectors and control cables.
4. Disconnect heater hoses at water pump.

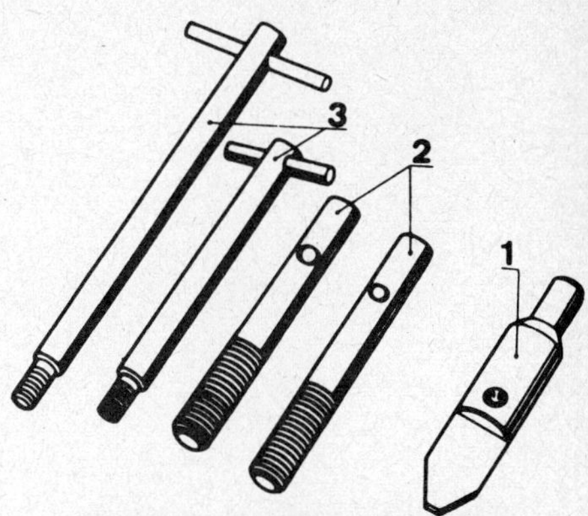

Fig. 11 Cylinder head positioning tools. 4-95/1565cc & 4-100/1647cc engines

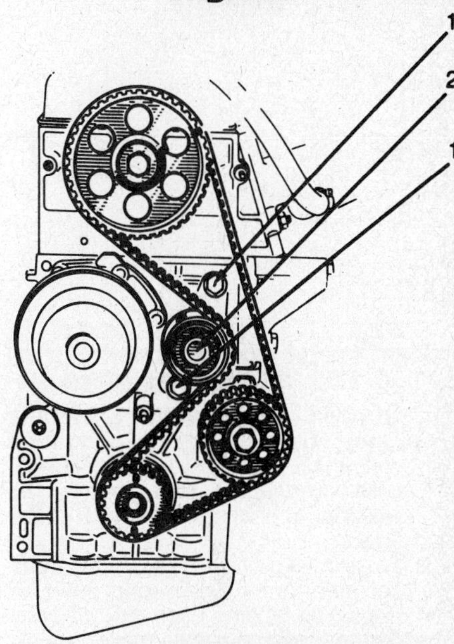

Fig. 13 Loosening timing belt tensioner. 4-132/2165cc engine

5. Disconnect and plug fuel lines.
6. Remove distributor cap and wires, mark position of rotor and distributor body, then remove distributor. **Do not rotate crankshaft with distributor removed.**
7. Disconnect exhaust pipe and remove catalytic converter. On 18i sedan models, remove exhaust manifold
8. On turbo engine, remove connecting hose between turbo and air cooler, and disconnect oil lines and EGR hose.
9. Remove rocker cover, loosen rocker arm adjusting screws and remove pushrods, arranging them in correct sequence.
10. Loosen cylinder head bolts and remove six inner bolts.
11. Remove rubber washers and cups in spark plug recesses.
12. Install rubber band or string around four remaining cylinder head bolts to secure rocker arm assemblies, then remove rocker arm assemblies and cylinder head bolts together. **Do not**

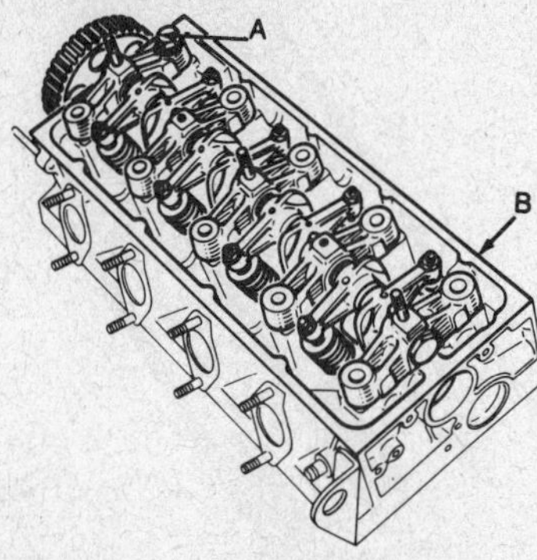

Fig. 14 Cylinder head removal. 4-132/2165cc engine

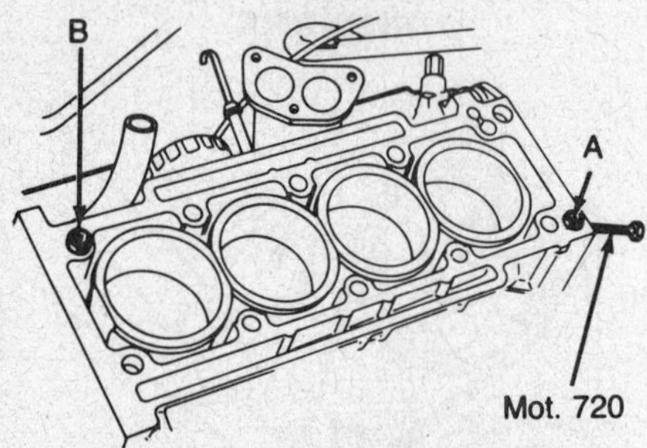

Fig. 15 Cylinder head alignment tool installation. 4-132/2165cc engine

lift cylinder head from cylinder block. The cylinder head gaskets will stick to the cylinder head, block and liners and destroy the water tight seal at the bottom of the liners.

13. To remove cylinder head, rotate cylinder head around centering dowel A, **Fig. 8,** by tapping each side of cylinder head with a plastic mallet.
14. Raise cylinder head slightly and remove lifters.
15. Remove cylinder head and lifter chamber seal. Install liner clamp Mot. 521-01 or equivalent onto cylinder block. **Do not rotate engine until cylinder liners are clamped. If liners are moved, liner seals may break and cause water leaks after assembly.**
16. Clean head gasket and block surfaces with suitable gasket remover. **Do not use any sharp edged tools for cleaning.**

Installation

Cylinder head positioning is very important. The alignment of the distributor driveshaft gear depends on this operation. Renault positioning tools Mot. 446 (1) and Mot. 451 (2), Fig. 11, or suitable equivalents must be used.

1. Ensure all foreign material is removed from oil passages and remove oil or water from cylinder head bolt holes to allow bolts to be properly tightened.
2. Ensure that centering dowel of cylinder head and distributor drive pinion are properly positioned in cylinder block.
3. Remove liner clamp and position cylinder head gasket on block. Once gasket is installed it should not be moved. If gasket is moved, do not reuse it.
4. Install Mot. 451 studs, **Fig. 12,** tightening studs until ball contacts cylinder head gasket and holds gasket in place on cylinder block.
5. Install rubber lifter chamber gasket. Ensure gasket fits into the slots of the head gasket and into the positioning holes in the block.
6. Install positioning tool MOT. 446 in the hole in front of the cylinder block, **Fig. 12.**
7. Install the lifters into their correct order in the cylinder head. Tap them lightly to secure into cylinder head.
8. Assemble rocker shaft assemblies to cylinder head. Check to ensure that rocker arm support holes align with centering dowels.
9. Check to ensure distributor drive gear is properly positioned, then install cylinder head onto block and hand tighten 4 end head bolts securing rocker arm assemblies.
10. Remove locating studs with stud remover (3), **Fig. 11.**
11. Lubricate cylinder head bolts and washers with engine oil, then torque bolts in sequence shown in **Fig. 10** to 57-61 ft. lbs.
12. Remove tool Mot. 446, then install pushrods.
13. Tap lightly on each rocker arm adjusting screw to ensure that lifter is completely up against cam lobe, then adjust rocker arm clearance.
14. Ensure that positioning tabs on valve cover are all inside cylinder head and that gasket is resting properly on cylinder head, then tighten valve cover bolts.
15. Reverse remaining steps to complete installation, then fill and bleed cooling system as outlined.
16. Run engine until cooling fan goes on, shut engine off and allow it to cool for at least 2½ hours, then retighten cylinder head as follows:
    a. Unscrew bolt No. 1 one half turn and torque to 57-61 ft. lbs.
    b. Repeat above step for each bolt in sequence.
    c. Adjust rocker arms.

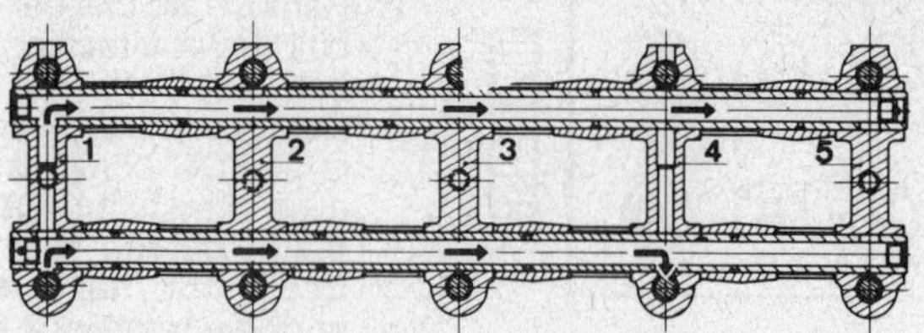

Fig. 16 Hemi-head rocker shaft oil hole positions

4-132/2165cc ENGINE

Removal

1. Remove accessory drive belts from engine, then the accessories.
2. Drain radiator coolant, then remove engine drain plugs and drain remaining coolant. Install drain plugs.

Exhaust valve to be set wide open	Intake valve to be adjusted	Exhaust valve to be adjusted
1	3	4
3	4	2
4	2	1
2	1	3

Fig. 17 Valve adjusting sequence. 4-85/1397cc, 4-95/1565cc & 4-100/1647cc engines

3. Remove vibration damper, then the intake and exhaust manifolds and brackets.
4. Remove timing belt cover, align timing marks, loosen timing belt tensioner bolts 1 and 2, **Fig. 13,** then remove timing belt. Refer to "Timing Belt, Replace" for complete removal and installation procedure.
5. Remove valve cover, then while holding camshaft sprocket with tool Mot. 855 or suitable strap wrench, remove camshaft sprocket retaining bolt and sprocket.
6. Remove all cylinder head bolts except for bolt marked (A), **Fig. 14. Do not lift cylinder head from cylinder block. The cylinder head gaskets will stick to the cylinder head, block and liners and destroy the water tight seal at the bottom of the liners.**
7. Loosen bolt (A), then using a suitable block of wood placed at point B, **Fig. 14,** pivot cylinder head on bolt (A), by tapping block of wood with hammer.
8. Remove remaining head bolt and the cylinder head, then install cylinder liner clamps, Mot. 588, on cylinder head to retain cylinder liners. **Do not rotate engine until cylinder liners are clamped. If liners are moved, liner seals may break and cause water leaks after assembly.**
9. Clean head gasket and block surfaces with suitable gasket remover. **Do not use any sharp edged tools for cleaning.**
10. Ensure all foreign material is removed from oil passages and remove oil or water from cylinder head bolt holes to allow bolts to be properly tightened.

Installation

1. Install cylinder head locating tool Mot.

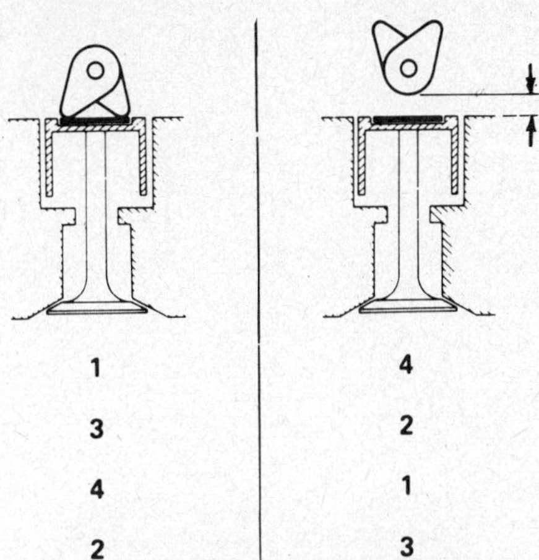

Fig. 18 Valve adjustment check. 4-105/1721cc & 4-120/1965cc engines engine

720, then remove the cylinder liner clamps.
2. Install cylinder head gasket.
3. Use tool Mot. 720 at (A) and the dowel (B) for cylinder head alignment, **Fig. 15.**
4. Ensure camshaft and crankshaft timing marks are properly aligned, then install cylinder head and hand tighten cylinder head bolts.
5. Tighten cylinder head bolts as follows:
   a. Torque to 37 ft. lbs. following sequence shown in **Fig. 10.**
   b. Torque to 59 ft. lbs. following sequence shown in **Fig. 10.**
   c. Loosen head bolts 1/2 turn, then torque to 68 ft. lbs. following sequence shown in **Fig. 10.**
6. Remove tool Mot. 720.
7. Reverse remaining steps to complete installation, noting the following:
   a. Install and tension timing belt as outlined under "Timing Belt, Replace."
   b. Refill and bleed cooling system as outlined.

LE CAR

Refer to procedure for Alliance and Encore 4-85/1397cc engines.

ROCKER ARM SHAFT SERVICE

The rocker arm shaft is not serviceable except for disassembly. Remove the clips on the end of the shaft for disassembly of the rocker arm shaft from the wedge head engines. To disassemble the rocker shaft from the hemi-head engines, remove the roll pins on the end of each shaft. The hemi-head rocker shafts supports 1 and 4 have lubrication holes, and supports 2, 3 and 5 have no lubrication holes, **Fig. 16.**

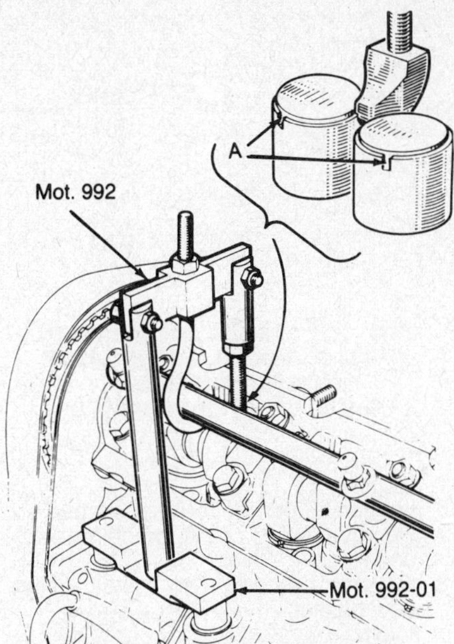

Fig. 19 Tappet pad replacement. 4-1051721cc & 4-120/1965cc engine

VALVES

ADJUST

4-85/1397cc, 4-95/1565cc & 4-100/1647cc ENGINES

1. Connect a remote control starter switch between the starter solenoid and the battery.
2. Disconnect the coil ignition lead.
3. Crank over engine until the exhaust valve on cylinder 1 is fully open. (Cylinder 1 is next to the flywheel.) Adjust the intake valve on cylinder No. 3 and the exhaust valve on cylinder No. 4.
4. Repeat step 3 to adjust the remaining valves, refer to **Fig. 17** for sequence.

4-105/1721cc & 4-120/1965cc ENGINES

1. Rotate crankshaft to position camshaft in such a way that intake valve for cylinder No. 1 has just closed and the exhaust valve for cylinder No. 1 is about to open, **Fig. 18,** (cylinder No. 1 is next to flexplate/flywheel assembly).
2. Measure and record camshaft-to-tappet clearance for cylinder No. 4.
3. Continue positioning camshaft as outlined in left column of **Fig. 18.** Then check camshaft-to-tappet clearance as indicated in right column of **Fig. 18.**
4. Compare measurements to valve specifications. If clearances are excessive, the tappet pad should be changed. Tappet pads are available in sizes of 3.25 to 4.25 mm (0.1279 to 0.1673) in increments of 0.05 mm and 4.30 mm, 4.40 mm and 4.50 mm (0.1692 inch, 0.1732 inch and 0.1771 inch).

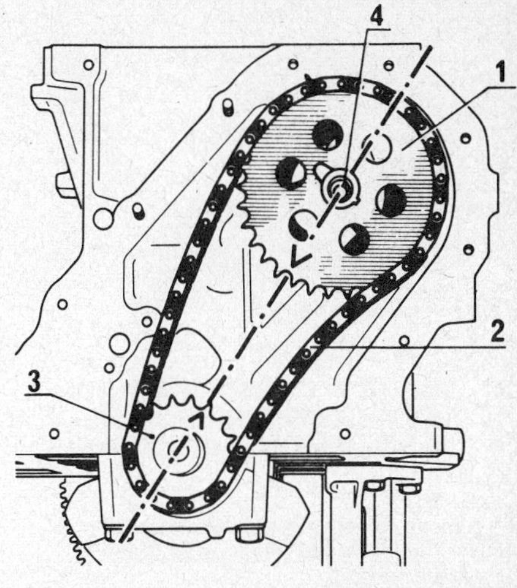

Fig. 20 Aligning timing marks. 4-85/1397cc engine

5. Using tools Mot. 992 and 992-01, remove tappet pad, **Fig. 19.**
6. When installing tappet pad, locate slots (A), **Fig. 19,** at right angles to camshaft. Insert pad so size marking faces the tappet.

4-132/2165cc ENGINE

1. Rotate crankshaft clockwise until camshaft sprocket TDC mark is aligned with timing belt cover front window. **Ensure piston is at TDC. Piston No. 1 is located at the flywheel/flexplate side of cylinder head.**
2. Continue to rotate crankshaft clockwise (viewed from front of engine) until camshaft sprocket first mark B, is aligned with the index mark in the timing belt cover rear window.
3. With first mark aligned as outlined in step 2, adjust cylinder No. 2 intake valve and cylinder No. 4 exhaust valve.
4. Continue to rotate crankshaft clockwise (viewed from front of engine) until camshaft sprocket second mark is aligned with the index mark in the timing belt cover rear window.
5. With mark aligned as outlined above, adjust cylinder No. 1 intake valve and cylinder No. 2 exhaust valve.
6. Continue to rotate crankshaft clockwise (viewed from front of engine) until camshaft sprocket third mark is aligned with the index mark in the timing belt cover rear window.
7. With mark aligned as outlined above, adjust cylinder No. 3 intake valve and cylinder No. 1 exhaust valve.
8. Continue to rotate crankshaft clockwise (viewed from front of engine) until camshaft fourth mark is aligned with the index mark in the timing belt cover rear window.
9. With mark aligned as outlined above, adjust cylinder No. 4 intake valve and cylinder No. 3 exhaust valve.

Fig. 21 Timing chain tensioner removal. 4-85/1397cc engines

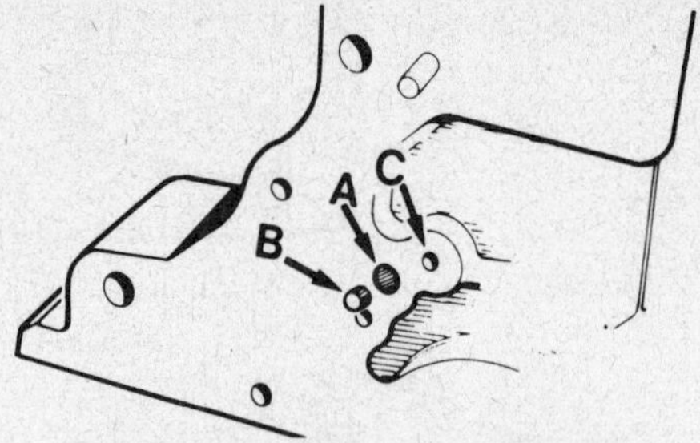

Fig. 22 Main oil gallery plug & chain tensioner locating dowel. 4-85/1397cc engine

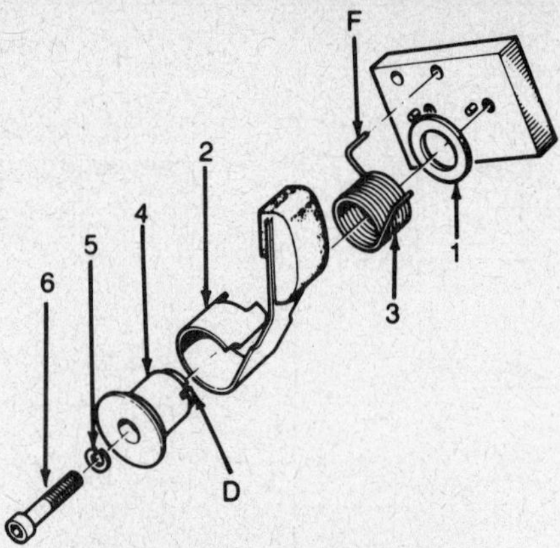

Fig. 23 Timing chain tensioner assembly. 4-85/1397cc engines

TIMING CHAIN COVER REPLACE

4-85/1397cc ENGINE

Exc. Le Car

1. Disconnect battery ground cable.
2. Remove support rod and spacer, drain engine oil and remove oil pan.
3. Remove accessory drive belts and the water pump pulley and hub.
4. On vehicles equipped with A/C, place suitable jack under engine cradle and remove the two bolts on right hand side, then lower jack until pulley clears side member.
5. On all models, remove crankshaft pulley and timing case cover.
6. Reverse procedure to install, noting the following:
   a. Using Permatex Form-A-Gasket 6 or equivalent, apply a bead of approximately 1/4 inch diameter along sealing surfaces of oil pan and timing cover, applying a double bead at four corners of oil pan.
   b. Using Permatex Form-A-Gasket 6 or equivalent, apply a bead on the outside of the No. 1 main bearing cap, adjacent to flange.
   c. Ensure that timing cover is properly positioned on locating dowels.
   d. Use tool Mot. 964 or equivalent to install pulley oil seal.
   e. On vehicles equipped with A/C, torque 10 mm cradle bolts to 30 ft. lbs. and 12 mm cradle bolts to 70 ft. lbs.

Le Car

1. Remove engine from vehicle.
2. Remove bolts securing timing cover and the cover.
3. Replace cover using new cork gasket and new neoprene oil pan gasket section.

4-95/1565cc & 4-100/1647cc ENGINES

1. Remove engine from vehicle.
2. Drain oil.
3. Remove cylinder head as previously described.
4. Install sleeve holder Mot. 521-01 or equivalent.
5. Remove crankshaft pulley, using flywheel locking tool Mot. 582 or equivalent.
6. Loosen oil pan bolts, if necessary.
7. Remove timing cover attaching bolts and remove cover.
8. Reverse procedure to install, using new gasket.

TIMING BELT COVER REPLACE

4-105/1721cc & 4-120/1965cc ENGINES

1. Remove timing belt cover attaching screws.
2. Remove timing belt cover.
3. Reverse procedure to install.

4-132/2165cc ENGINE

1. Remove accessory drive belts.
2. Remove crankshaft pulley.
3. Remove intake and exhaust manifolds.
4. Remove timing belt cover attaching screws, then the cover.
5. Reverse procedure to install.

TIMING CHAIN REPLACE

4-85/1397cc ENGINE

Removal

1. Remove timing cover, then rotate crankshaft until timing marks are aligned as shown in **Fig. 20.**
2. Tilt chain tensioner over as far as possible and install retaining tool Mot. 761 or equivalent, **Fig. 21,** then remove chain tensioner and retaining tool as an assembly. Use assembly plate from Mot. 761 to disconnect tensioner from retaining tool for inspection.
3. Remove camshaft sprocket retaining bolt.
4. Remove camshaft sprocket and timing chain using suitable puller to release sprocket from camshaft.
5. Install bolt in nose of crankshaft, then remove crankshaft sprocket using suitable puller.

Installation

1. Install crankshaft sprocket using suitable driver, ensuring timing mark faces out.
2. Install camshaft sprocket with timing chain, aligning timing marks as shown, **Fig. 20.**
3. Torque camshaft sprocket retaining bolt to 22 ft. lbs.
4. Ensure that main oil gallery plug (A), **Fig. 22,** is in position, then insert locating dowel (B) for chain tensioner.
5. Assemble chain tensioner onto assembly plate in numerical order shown in **Fig. 23,** then install holding tool Mot. 761, rotating tensioner as far as possible to the right.
6. Remove tensioner and holder assembly from support plate, then mount on engine block ensuring dowel (B) engages slot (D) in tensioner shaft and free end of spring (F) is in hole (C) in block, **Figs. 22 and 23.**
8. Tighten tensioner bolt, then remove holding fixture.
9. Install timing cover as outlined.

4-95/1565cc & 4-100/1647cc ENGINES

Removal

1. Remove timing chain cover.
2. Remove the chain tensioner and the chain guide shoes.
3. Loosen the camshaft securing bolts.
4. Place a bolt, with a small centering hole drilled in the center of the bolt head, in the end of the crankshaft. Remove the crankshaft pulley key.
5. Remove crankshaft sprocket with timing chain using a suitable puller, holding camshaft in place while pulling, then remove the timing chain and sprocket.

Installation

1. Place chain over camshaft sprocket and align mark on sprocket with center of crankshaft and center of camshaft, **Fig. 24.**
2. Place key on crankshaft.
3. Position crankshaft sprocket on chain with timing mark facing outward, align marks as shown, **Fig. 25,** then install crankshaft sprocket using suitable driver.
4. Install and tighten two camshaft clamp bolts, ensuring that camshaft sprocket is properly seated.

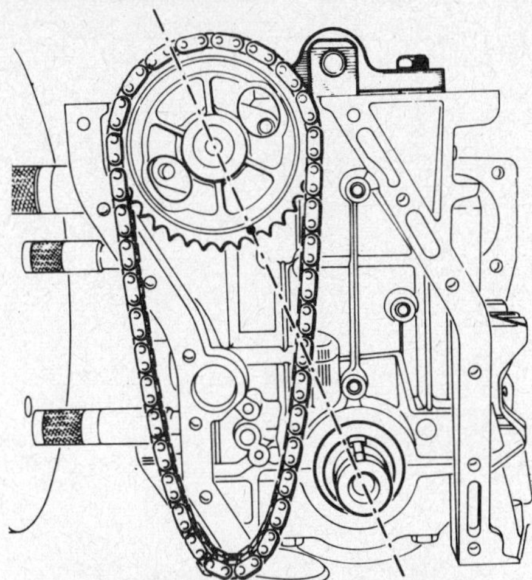

Fig. 24 Timing chain installation. 4-95/1565cc & 4-100/1647cc engines

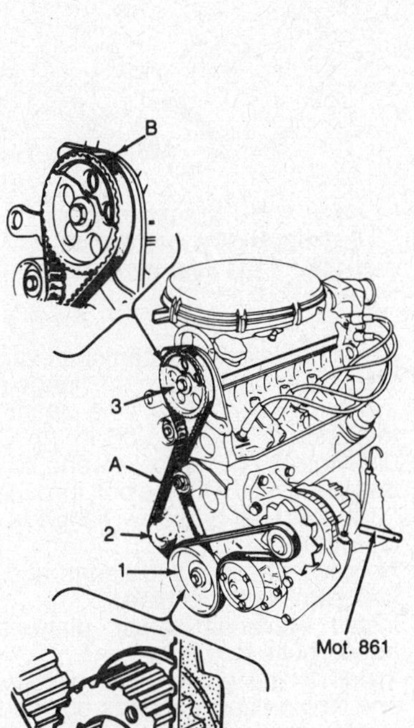

Fig. 27 Timing belt installation. 4-105/1721cc & 4-120/1965cc engines

5. Install chain tensioner with its filter and thrust plate, then tighten two bolts.
6. Install chain play limiting pads.
7. Stretch timing chain and position play limiting pads so that there is approximately .020 inch clearance between chain and pads.
8. Install crankshaft pulley key.
9. Install timing cover centering dowels on cylinder block.
10. Install timing cover, using new gaskets.

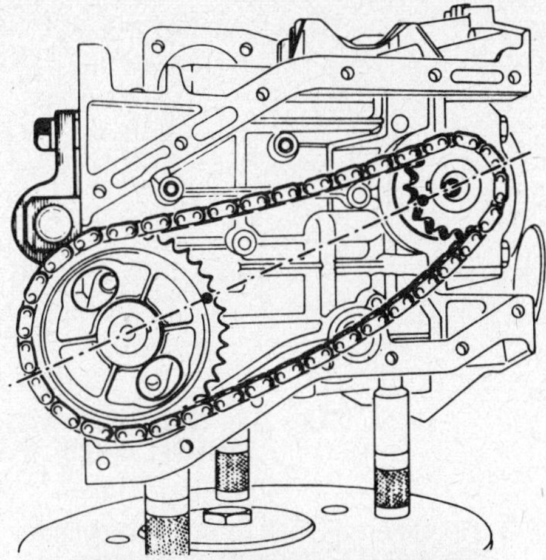

Fig. 25 Aligning valve timing marks. 4-95/1565cc & 4-100/1647cc engines

TIMING BELT REPLACE

4-105/1721cc & 4-120/1965cc ENGINES

Removal

1. Remove accessory drive belts and timing belt cover.
2. Rotate crankshaft until No. 1 cylinder is at TDC of compression stroke, ensure camshaft is positioned as shown in **Fig. 26,** then insert TDC lock pin Mot. 861 or equivalent through opening in side of block, **Fig. 27,** and ensure tool engages slot in crankshaft. **If there is no reference mark on camshaft sprocket rear cover plate, scribe a matching mark in line with timing mark on sprocket.**
3. Loosen timing belt tensioner, then remove timing belt. **Do not rotate crankshaft or camshaft with timing belt removed.**

Installation

1. Ensure TDC tool Mot. 861 is properly seated in and align camshaft sprocket timing mark with mark on rear cover plate, **Fig. 26.**
2. Position timing belt over crankshaft sprocket (1) first, then intermediate shaft sprocket (2), and then camshaft sprocket (3), **Fig. 27.**
3. Position timing belt arrow (A), indicating direction of rotation between intermediate shaft sprocket and idler pulley, **Fig. 27.**
4. Align timing belt marks with timing mark on camshaft sprocket (B) and crankshaft sprocket (B), **Fig. 27. Intermediate shaft sprocket does not have a timing mark.**
5. Adjust initial belt tension as follows:
   a. On 4-105/1721cc engines, loosen tensioner pulley locknut, then turn tensioner pulley nut counterclockwise until timing belt is taut. Hold tensioner pulley nut from turning and tighten the locknut.
   b. On 4-120/1965cc engines, pry tensioner inward toward belt until belt is taut, then tighten tensioner pulley locknut.
6. Remove TDC tool Mot. 861 from crankcase, then rotate crankshaft clockwise, 2 complete revolutions, then reinstall TDC tool Mot. 861 through crankcase into crankshaft.
7. Ensure camshaft sprocket timing mark is aligned with mark on rear cover plate, **Fig. 26.**
8. There should be 66 timing belt teeth (cogs) between camshaft sprocket timing mark (C) and crankshaft sprocket timing mark (B), **Fig. 27.**
9. Remove TDC tool Mot. 861 and install plug in cylinder block.
10. Check timing belt tension as follows:
    a. Check timing belt deflection between intermediate shaft sprocket and idler pulley.

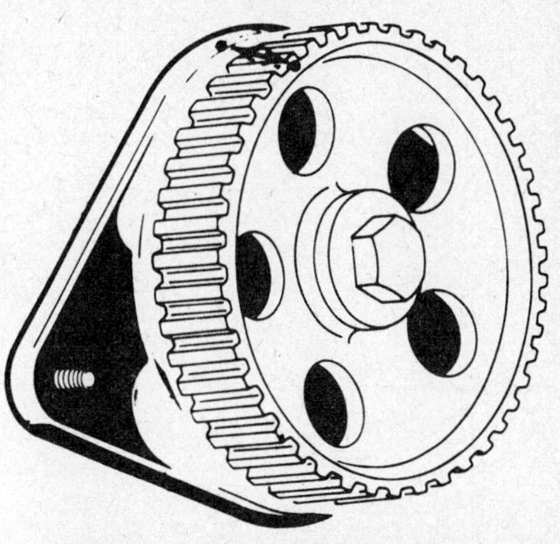

Fig. 26 Camshaft sprocket alignment. 4-105/1721cc & 4-120/1965cc engines

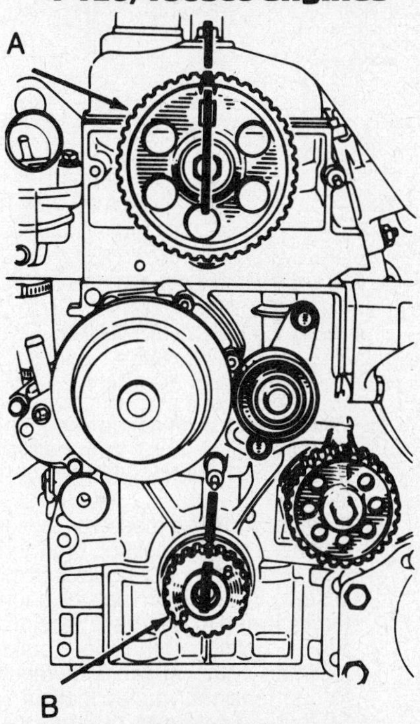

Fig. 28 Aligning camshaft & crankshaft sprockets. 4-132/2165cc engine

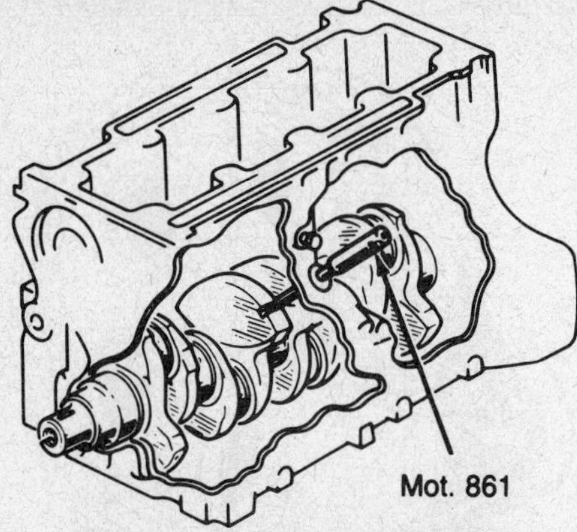

Fig. 29 Installing TDC locking tool Mot. 861. 4-132/2165cc engine

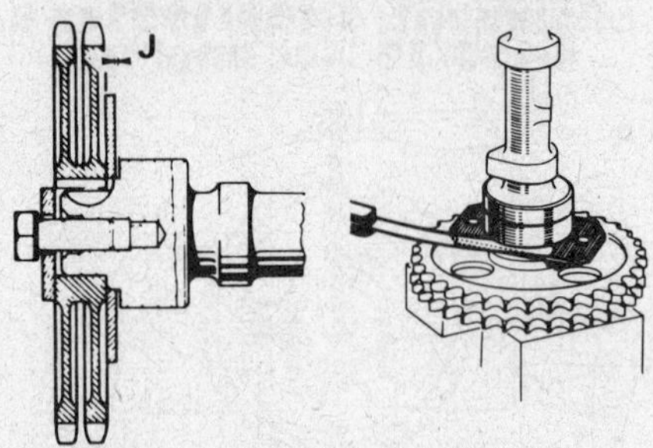

Fig. 30 Checking camshaft flange clearance. 4-85/1397cc engine

b. With belt cold, deflection should be 7.5 mm (0.295 inch). With belt hot deflection should be 5.5 mm (0.216 inch).
c. If deflection is excessive, loosen tensioner pulley locknut, then turn tensioner pulley nut counterclockwise to increase tension or counterclockwise to decrease tension.
d. While holding tensioner pulley locknut with suitable wrench, torque tensioner pulley locknut to 30 ft. lbs. **Tensioner pulley locknut must be torqued to 30 ft. lbs. to prevent loosening of timing belt, which may cause engine damage.**

11. Install timing belt cover and drive belts.

4-132/2165cc ENGINE

Removal

1. Remove accessory drive belts and accessories.
2. Remove vibration damper using suitable puller.
3. Remove intake and exhaust manifolds and brackets.
4. Remove timing belt cover, loosen tensioner bolt (1) and tensioner (2), **Fig. 13,** then remove timing belt.

Installation

1. Align camshaft sprocket (A) timing mark with cylinder head static timing mark, **Fig. 28.**
2. Rotate crankshaft to position cylinder No. 1 at TDC compression stroke, **Fig. 28.** Remove crankcase plug, then install TDC tool Mot. 861 through crankcase hole and into crankshaft TDC hole, **Fig. 29. Do not use TDC tool Mot. 861 to restrain crankshaft from turning while removing or installing bolts.**
3. Install timing belt on sprockets, ensuring belt is tight between crankshaft and idler shaft sprockets, and between idler shaft and camshaft sprockets.
4. Position timing belt cover over sprockets and ensure camshaft timing mark is aligned with index mark on cover.
5. To adjust belt tension, proceed as follows:
   a. Remove TDC tool Mot. 861 from crankshaft and install crankcase plug.
   b. Rotate crankshaft clockwise 2 complete revolutions. **Do not rotate crankshaft counterclockwise.**
   c. Remove timing belt cover, then loosen belt tensioner bolts 1/4 turn.
   d. The belt tensioner will automatically adjust to the proper tension.
   e. Torque bottom tensioner attaching bolt to 18 ft. lbs., then the top bolt to 18 ft. lbs.
   f. Check timing belt deflection between camshaft sprocket and intermediate shaft. Deflection should be 5.5-7.0 mm (0.216-0.276 inch).
6. Install timing belt cover.

CAMSHAFT REPLACE

4-85/1397cc ENGINES

1. Remove the engine and cylinder head. **Be sure to clamp the cylinder liners down with a suitable tool to prevent accidental breakage of liners base seals.**
2. Remove the valve lifters. Remove the distributor and drive gear.
3. Remove the timing chain cover, the timing chain, the camshaft sprocket and camshaft retaining flange, and the rear drive pulley if equipped.
4. Pull the camshaft out from the timing chain end of the engine, then remove camshaft seal.

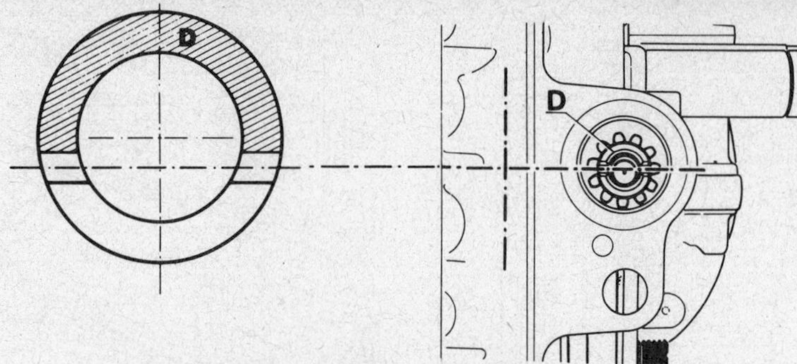

Fig. 31 Positioning distributor drive gear. 4-85/1397cc engine

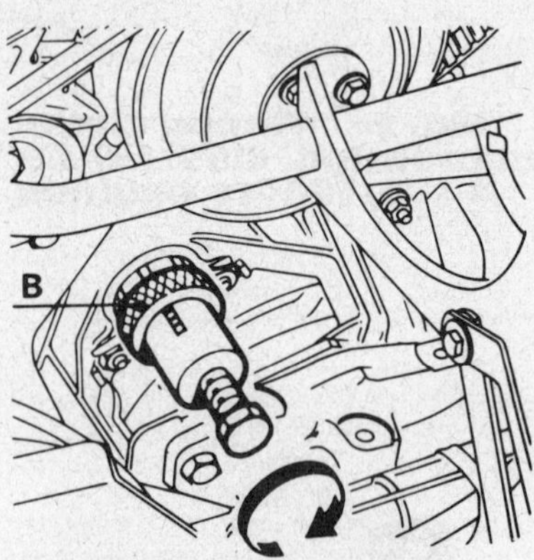

Fig. 32 Removing camshaft oil seal. 4-85/1397cc engine

5. Before installation of camshaft, check the clearance between the flange and the camshaft, **Fig. 30.** The clearance tolerance is .002 to .005 in. (0.05 to 0.12 mm). The sprocket should be bolted in place with the bolt torqued to 20 ft. lbs. Use of a new flange is required.
6. Remove sprocket and flange and install camshaft in engine.
7. Install camshaft thrust plate and torque bolts to 6 ft. lbs.
8. Install timing chain, chain tensioner and timing chain cover as outlined.
9. Install camshaft rear seal using suitable driver, then install pullet, if equipped.
10. Reverse remaining procedure to complete installation and note the following:
    a. Turn the engine to bring the No. 1 cylinder to firing position (No. 1 cylinder is at the flywheel end of the engine).
    b. Insert distributor drive gear using a bolt (12 mm diameter-175 pitch). Install with the largest offset (D) facing the clutch and the slot at right angles to the camshaft, **Fig. 31.**

Camshaft Oil Seal, Replace

The camshaft oil seal can be replaced without the engine or the camshaft being removed. Changing the seal requires removal of the air filter and support bracket, the air pump and support bracket, and the

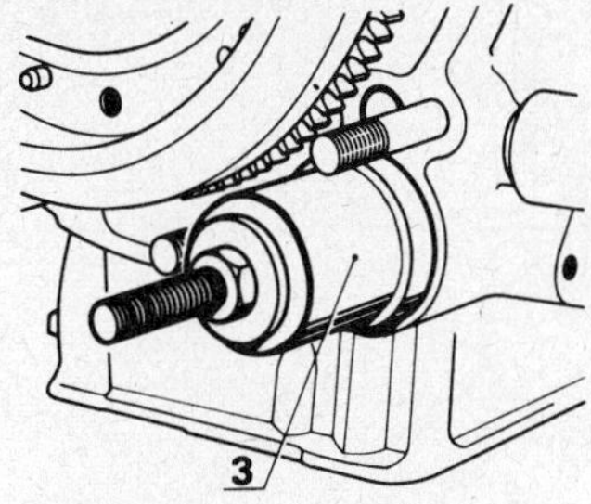

Fig. 33 Installing camshaft oil seal. 4-85/1397cc engine

camshaft drive pulley, as equipped. The use of Renault Tool Mot. 500-01 is required.

1. Remove the components listed above. Cover the opening in the bell-housing with a rag.
2. Put the Mot. 500-01 extracting tool in position and push it in all the way until the lip of the oil seal slips over the shoulder of the tool. Push sleeve (B) fully in, **Fig. 32.**
3. Extract the seal by tightening the screw on the tool.
4. Lubricate new oil seal, position the sleeve on the end of the camshaft and push the seal onto the sleeve.
5. Press the seal into position with the inserting tool until the seal just touches the block.
6. Using a threaded rod and nut or bolt, together with a washer, draw the tool and seal onto the camshaft until the tool just touches the block, **Fig. 33.**
7. Install the camshaft drive pulley. Install a new water pump/air pump drive belt and tighten the air pump.

4-105/1721cc & 4-120/1965cc ENGINES

1. Remove timing belt. Refer to "Timing Belt, Replace" for procedure.
2. Remove distributor cap, rotor and distributor housing. **Rotor is secured to distributor shaft with Loctite. Rotor must be broken to remove from distributor shaft.**
3. Remove valve cover, thermostat housing and thermostat.
4. Using sprocket retaining tool Mot. 855 or suitable strap wrench to hold camshaft sprocket, remove sprocket attaching bolt, then the sprocket.
5. Remove camshaft sprocket key, cover plate attaching bolts and the cover plate.
6. Remove spark plugs, then camshaft bearing cap bolts. **Camshaft bearing caps are numbered 1 through 5 from flywheel/flexplate side of cylinder head. Mark bearing caps accordingly for assembly reference.**
7. Remove bearing caps and camshaft.
8. Coat camshaft with suitable assembly lubricant, then position camshaft on cylinder head.
9. Apply Permatex 6 Br. or other suitable sealer to camshaft bearing caps to provide a good seal at the cylinder head and install caps in their original location.

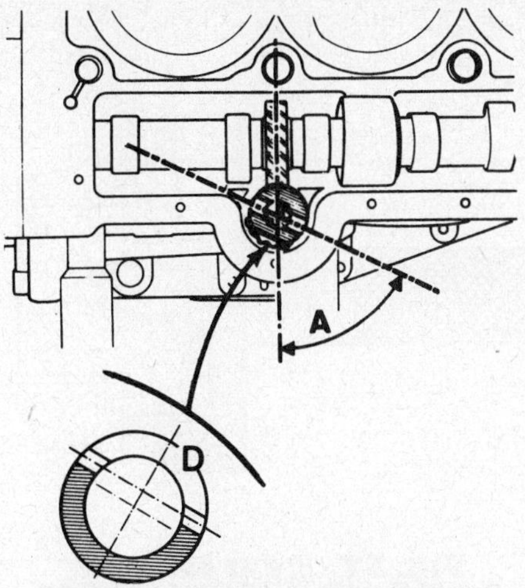

Fig. 34 Distributor drive gear installation. 4-95/1565cc & 4-100/1647cc engines

10. Apply a small amount of Loctite 242 or equivalent to cap bolt threads, then install bolts and torque to 88 inch lbs.
11. Install camshaft front seal using tool Mot. 988-01.
12. Install camshaft rear seal using tool Mot. 1010.
13. Install cover plate, attaching bolts and camshaft key.
14. Install camshaft sprocket and attaching bolt. Torque bolt to 37 ft. lbs.
15. Install thermostat and housing, distributor housing, rotor and cap.
16. Install timing belt. Refer to "Timing Belt, Replace" for procedure.
17. Install valve cover.

4-95/1565cc & 4-100/1647cc ENGINES

1. Remove engine and cylinder head as described previously.
2. Remove distributor, distributor drive gear and valve lifters.
3. Remove timing chain cover and timing chain as described previously.
4. Remove camshaft from engine.
5. To install camshaft, lubricate camshaft bearings with engine oil, then carefully install camshaft.
6. Install timing chain and sprockets as described previously.
7. Install camshaft/distributor drive gear with smallest offset (D) facing towards camshaft, **Fig. 34.** Check to ensure that angle (A) of 53° is formed by drive gear slot and line drawn perpendicular to camshaft.
8. Fill camshaft oil gallery with oil, install camshaft bearing cover plate if removed.
9. Install lifters, then install cylinder head as described previously. Install distributor.
10. Install engine in vehicle.

4-132/2165cc ENGINE

1. Remove cylinder head. Refer to "Cylinder Head, Replace" for procedure.
2. Remove rocker arm assembly. **Keep all rocker arm components in order they were removed from cylinder head for assembly reference.**

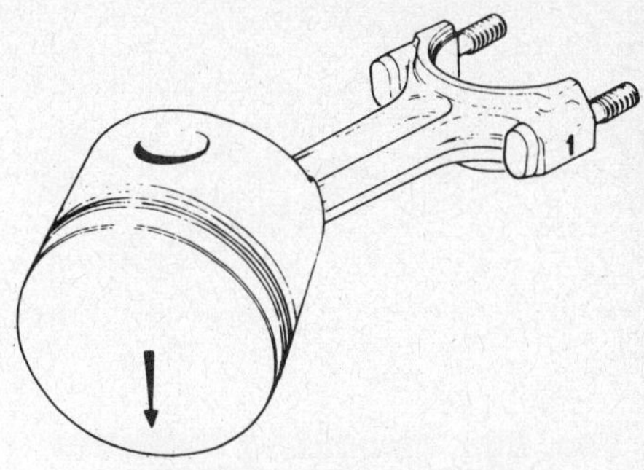

Fig.35 Piston & rod identification marks

3. Remove camshaft front oil seal using a small pry tool. **Use caution not to damage camshaft oil seal contact surface.**
4. Remove camshaft.
5. Position replacement camshaft in cylinder head. **Coat camshaft with suitable assembly lubricant prior to installation**
6. Install rocker arm assembly.
7. Install camshaft seal using tool Mot. 791-01.
8. Install cylinder head.

PISTON, ROD & LINER SERVICE

EXC. 4-105/1721cc & 4-120/1965cc ENGINES

The pistons and liners are serviceable without removing the engine from the vehicle. Pistons and liners are available in standard size only and are matched sets. **Do not mix the pistons or liners during assembly.**

To remove the piston assemblies, remove the head and oil pan. Check the rods for numbering. If necessary, mark sides of the rods facing away from the camshaft. No. 1 cylinder is located next to the engine flywheel/flexplate.

Using a press to press the piston pin, mount the pistons to the rods with the arrow on the piston facing toward the flywheel and the mark on the connecting rod, made during disassembly, facing away from the camshaft, **Fig. 35.**

Liner protrusion must be checked prior to the final assembly of the piston and liners in the block. The liners must protrude slightly above the block to insure proper sealing by the head gasket and the head. All engine blocks are fitted with O-rings for sealing. Liner protrusion cannot be changed in blocks fitted with O-rings. However, the protrusion should be checked to ensure proper cylinder and head sealing.

Checking Liner Protrusion

1. Install liners in block without O-ring seal.
2. Install dial indicator in gauge block Mot. 251.01 and tighten screw clamp, **Fig. 36.**
3. Place thrust plate Mot. 252.01 across each cylinder liner, **Fig. 36,** and measure liner protrusion above block with dial indicator.

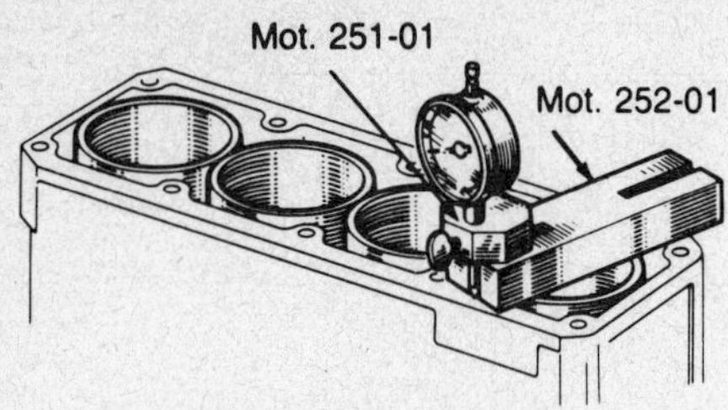

Fig. 36 Checking cylinder liner protrusion

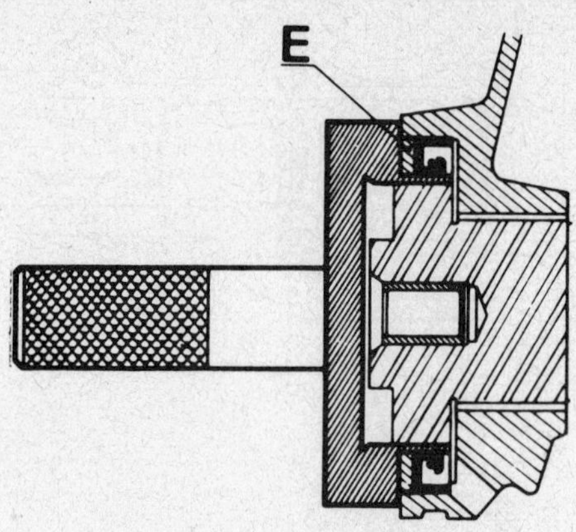

Fig. 37 Rear oil seal installation. 4-85/1397cc engines

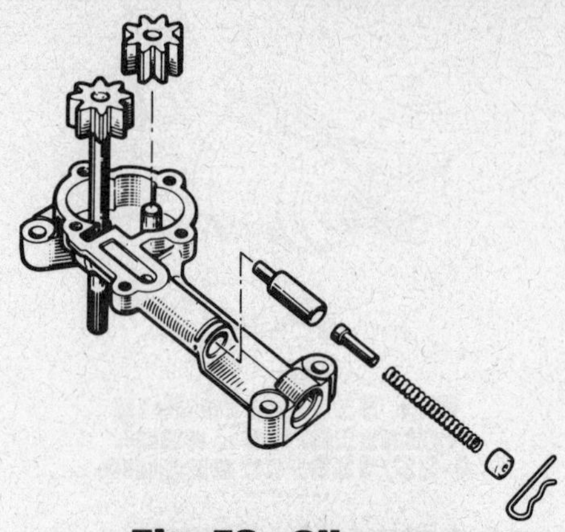

Fig. 38 Oil pump disassembled. 4-105/1721cc & 4-120/1965cc engines

4. If liner protrusion is not within specifications, measure protrusion of replacement liner to determine whether liner or cylinder block is defective, and replace components as needed.
5. When protrusion of all liners is within specifications, arrange liners so that the difference in protrusion between adjacent liners does not exceed .002 inch (.04 mm), and so that the protrusions are stepped down from the No. 1 cylinder to the No. 4 cylinder.
6. After the liner protrusion has been checked, remove the liners from the block and assemble the piston, rod and liner assemblies as outlined.

Piston & Liner Assembly

1. Install new O-ring seal onto each liner, ensuring O-ring is not twisted.
2. Assemble pistons, rods, piston rings and bearing inserts, noting matching marks and installation position.
3. Lubricate the pistons and rings with engine oil.
4. Compress rings with suitable tool and insert piston and connecting rod assemblies through bottom of liner, ensuring machined sides of the connecting rod bearing end are parallel with the flat edge on the top of the liner.
5. Lubricate connecting rod journals and bearing inserts in connecting rod and cap, then install the piston liner assemblies into the block. Ensure O-ring is not twisted. Mount as follows:
   a. Number 1 piston at the flywheel/flexplate end.
   b. Number on the connecting rod facing away from the camshaft.
   c. Arrow on piston must face towards the flywheel/flexplate.

PISTON & ROD ASSEMBLY

4-105/1721cc & 4-120/1965cc ENGINES

These engines use cylinder blocks with integral non-replaceable liners.

The piston tops are marked with an arrow and/or a "V." The marks must point towards the flywheel/flexplate after installation.

To install rods-to-pistons, install rods so end cap locating dowels are on opposite side of piston identification arrow and/or "V."

REAR OIL SEAL

REPLACE

4-85/1397cc, 4-95/1565cc & 4-100/1647cc ENGINES

1. Remove the transmission, clutch and flywheel/flexplate.
2. Remove the old oil seal. Be careful not to damage any machined surfaces.
3. To install the new seal the use of Renault tool Mot. 259-01 is recommended. Mount the new seal on the tool. Be careful when mounting the seal. The lip of the seal is extremely delicate.
4. Lubricate the outside of the seal. Position the tool on the end of the crankshaft and lightly tap the seal into position until the tool touches the block.
5. If the seal is being mounted on a used crankshaft, mount the seal as above and then remove the tool, mount the spacer (E) and push the seal in further until the tool touches the block, **Fig. 37.** This operation will mount the seal approximately 1/8 inch deeper into the block.
6. Reinstall all related components.

4-105/1721cc, 4-120/1965cc & 4-132/2165cc ENGINES

1. Remove transmission, clutch/torque converter and flywheel/flexplate.
2. Remove old oil seal. Be careful not to damage any machined surfaces.
3. Lubricate replacement seal.
4. On 4-105/1721cc and 4-120/1965cc engines, install new seal using tool Mot. 991. The tool is designed to position new seal to compensate for sealing surface wear.
5. On 4-132/2165cc engines, install new seal using tool Mot. 788. If sealing surface is worn, a .06 inch (1.5 mm) washer should be placed between seal and tool to position seal further inward on crankshaft.

OIL PAN

REPLACE

ALLIANCE, ENCORE & GTA

1. Raise and support vehicle.
2. Drain engine oil.
3. Remove support rod and spacer.
4. Remove oil pan.
5. Reverse procedure to install, using new gasket.

FUEGO

1. Raise and support vehicle.
2. Drain engine oil.
3. Remove oil pan.
4. Reverse procedure to install, using new gasket.

LE CAR

1. Drain the engine oil.
2. Remove the transaxle belly pan, loosen and lower the stabilizer bar and remove the two bolts securing the gear shift control rod. Remove the right reinforcement bracket. Remove the clutch cover.
3. Loosen the transaxle front support and jack up the transaxle as high as possible.
4. Remove the oil pan by tilting it down toward the back of the vehicle. If necessary turn the crankshaft so the counterweights are horizontal.
5. Remove the gaskets and clean the gasket surfaces.
6. Install new rubber gaskets on the front and rear main bearings. Use gasket cement if necessary.
7. Position new cork gaskets on the block. Make sure these gaskets overlap the ends of the bearing gaskets. Use gasket cement if necessary.
8. Install the oil pan. Be careful not to scrape the brake lines or disturb the gaskets.
9. Reinstall all other related components.
10. Fill the engine with oil.

18i & SPORTWAGON

1. Raise and support vehicle.
2. Drain engine oil, then remove flywheel

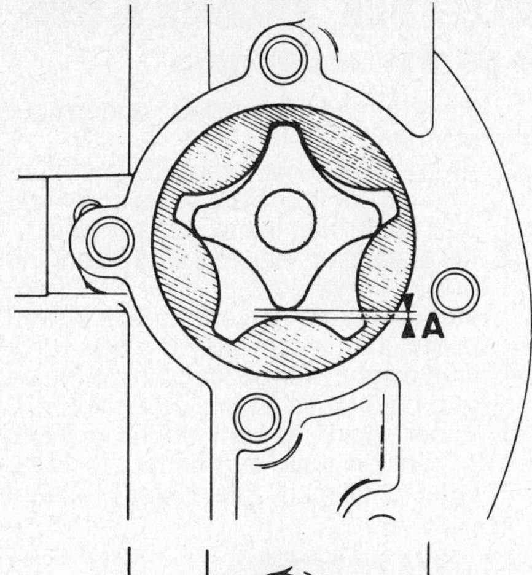

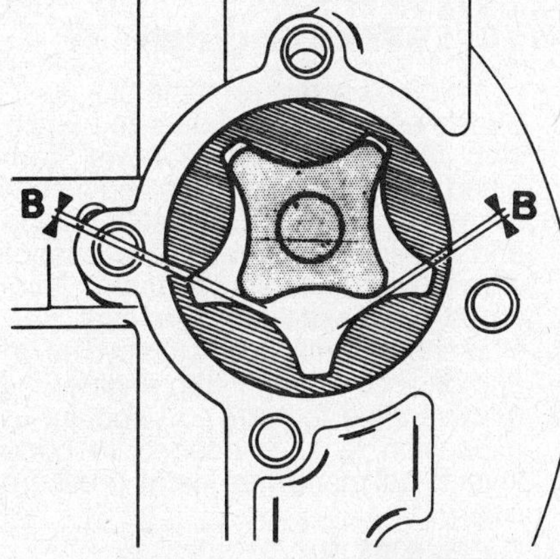

Fig. 39 Oil pump clearances. 4-95/1565cc & 4-100/1647cc engines

under cover.
3. Remove oil pan retaining bolts and the oil pan.
4. Clean cylinder block oil pan mounting surface and oil pan to block mating surface of old gasket material.
5. Install oil pan, then install flywheel under cover.
6. Refill engine with oil, then lower vehicle to ground.

OIL PUMP SERVICE

ALLIANCE, ENCORE & GTA

4-85/1397cc Engine

1. Raise and support vehicle.
2. Drain engine oil.
3. Remove oil pan.
4. Remove gasket and seals and clean mating surfaces.
5. Remove three oil pump attaching bolts and remove pump.
6. Remove four pump cover bolts, being careful to prevent ball seat, ball, and pressure relief spring from flying out.
7. Remove driven gear, driving gear, and shaft.
8. Clean and inspect all parts.
9. If clearance between pump body and gears is greater than .079 in., replace gears.
10. Reassemble pump, then reverse steps 1 through 5 to install.

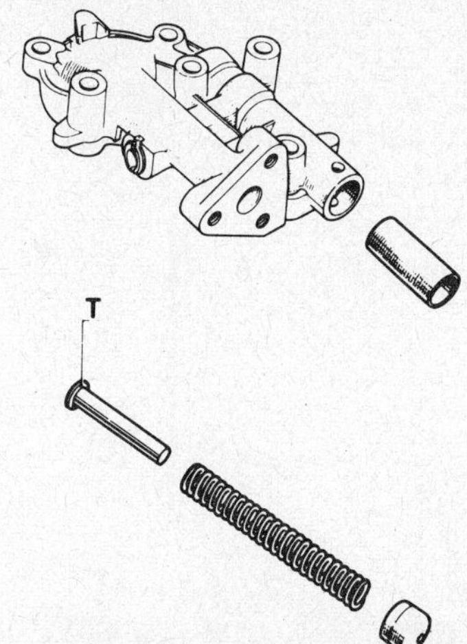

Fig. 40 Oil pump pressure relief valve, spring & guide installation. 4- 95/1565cc & 4-100/1647cc engines

4-105/1721cc & 4-120/1965cc Engines

1. Remove oil pan, then the oil pump.
2. Remove oil pump cover, pressure relief spring and spring retaining pin, **Fig. 38.**
3. Measure gear-to-housing clearance. Minimum clearance is .0039 inch (.1 mm). Maximum clearance is .0094 inch.
4. Measure gear-to-cover clearance. Minimum clearance is .00078 inch (.02 mm). Maximum clearance is .0033 inch (.085 mm).
5. Replace worn components as necessary. Install removed parts.
6. Install pump on cylinder block. Install bolts and torque to 15-18 ft. lbs.
7. Install oil pan using new gasket.

FUEGO, 18i & SPORTWAGON

4-95/1565cc & 4-100/1647cc Engines

1. Raise and support vehicle.
2. Drain engine oil.
3. Remove flywheel protective cover, if necessary.
4. Remove oil pan.
5. Remove gasket and clean contact surface.
6. Remove oil pump and two rotors.
7. Check clearances of A and B of rotors, **Fig. 39.**
   a. .002"-.011" (.04 mm-.29 mm)
   b. .001"-.006" (.02 mm-.14 mm)

If clearances exceed specifications, replace rotors. Inner rotor is supplied with driving shaft.

8. Reverse procedure to install, using new gasket. **When installing pressure relief valve, ensure head of spring guide (T), Fig. 40, is inserted into piston first.**
9. The following must be performed on turbo engines before starting engine:
   a. Disconnect three prong connector at electronic module.
   b. Disconnect hose leading to turbo charger and fill with oil.

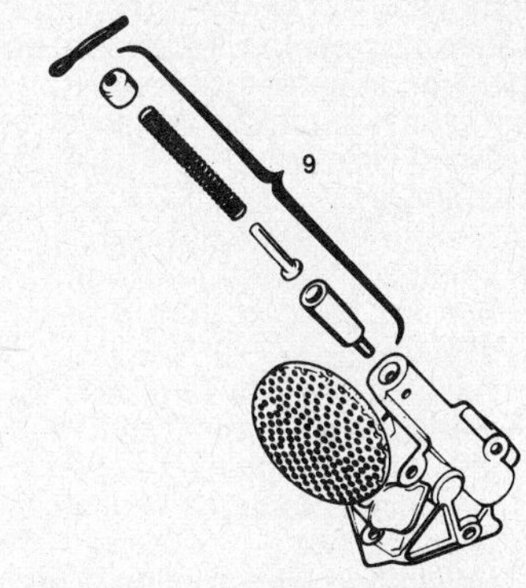

Fig. 41 Oil pump pressure relief valve removal. 4-132/2165cc engine engine

   c. Activate starter until oil flows from oil line to turbo charger.
   d. Reconnect oil hose to turbo charger and reconnect connector to module.
   e. Run engine at idle to reestablish oil flow to turbo charger.

4-132/2165cc Engine

1. Drain engine oil, then remove oil pan.
2. Remove oil pump.
3. Remove oil pump pressure relief valve (6) from pump housing, **Fig. 41.**
4. Remove oil pump housing cover.
5. Measure gear-to-housing clearance. Minimum clearance is .002 inch (.05 mm). Maximum clearance is .005 inch (.12 mm).
6. Measure gear-to-cover clearance. Minimum clearance is .001 inch. Maximum clearance is .004 inch (.10 mm).
7. Replace any worn parts, then reassemble.
8. Install oil pump. Torque bolts to 30-33 ft. lbs.
9. Install oil pan using new gasket.

LE CAR

1. Remove the oil pan.
2. Remove the bolts securing the pump to the block and remove the pump.
3. Remove screws securing pick-up/cover assembly to pump body and separate cover, **Fig. 42.**
4. If the clearance between the gears and the pump body exceeds .008 inch (0.2 mm) replace the pump.
5. Reverse procedure to install.

WATER PUMP REPLACE

ALLIANCE, ENCORE & GTA

1983–84

1. Disconnect battery ground cable.
2. Drain cooling system at cylinder block draincock and either radiator draincock or lower radiator hose.

3. Disconnect hoses from water pump.
4. Remove water pump belt and alternator bracket.
5. Remove water pump attaching bolts, then remove pump, tapping as necessary with suitable hammer.
6. Clean gasket mating surfaces.
7. Reverse procedure to install, noting the following:
   a. Ensure thermostat ball check valve is installed in upward direction so air can vent when filling system.
   b. Adjust drive belt to obtain 1.4-1.7 inches deflection when 90-115 lbs. force is applied to the run between the crankshaft pulley and alternator.
   c. Refill and bleed cooling system as outlined.

1985–87

1. Disconnect battery ground cable and remove splash shield.
2. Remove pressure cap from expansion tank, drain cooling system and remove block drain plugs.
3. Raise and support vehicle, then remove right front wheel and inner fender panel.
4. Loosen adjusting nuts on drive belt tension rod, alternator adjuster bolt and alternator pivot bolt, then move alternator downward and remove serpentine drive belt.
5. Remove water pump mounting bolts, then remove pump and pulley assembly through fender panel opening.
6. Remove pulley from pump.
7. Install pulley on replacement pump and tighten bolts hand tight.
8. Position gasket on pump, install pump assembly through fender opening and tighten retaining bolts.
9. Install drive belt over pump pulley and tighten pulley bolts.
10. Reverse remaining procedure to complete installation, noting the following:
    a. Adjust drive belt tension to 140-160 lbs. for model less A/C. On models with A/C, tension new belt to 180-200 lbs. or used belt to 140-160 lbs.
    b. Refill and bleed cooling system as outlined.

FUEGO

1. Disconnect battery ground cable.
2. Drain cooling system.
3. Remove upper grille crossmember and remove grille.
4. Remove radiator and cooling fan(s).
5. On air conditioning equipped vehicles, remove condenser.
6. Remove water pump belt.
7. Remove all water pump attaching bolts except centermost bolt, which should be loosened completely and left in pump, then remove pump.
8. Reverse procedure to install. Refill and bleed cooling system as outlined.

LE CAR

1. Disconnect battery ground cable.
2. Drain the cooling system.
3. Loosen alternator, remove the drive pulley on the water pump and the alternator belt.
4. Loosen air pump and remove the air pump drive belt. If a notched type belt is used, this belt should be discarded and replaced with a new belt.
5. Disconnect radiator and heater hoses. Remove the temperature switch.
6. Loosen bolts securing the pump to the head, lightly tap the pump with a hard rubber hammer and remove the pump.
7. Clean the gasket surfaces. **The pump must be mounted with the gasket dry. The gasket surfaces must be clean and dry, free of any oil or dirt.**
8. Reverse procedure to install.
9. A new notched type belt is required for reassembly.
10. Reconnect battery, then refill and bleed cooling system as outlined.

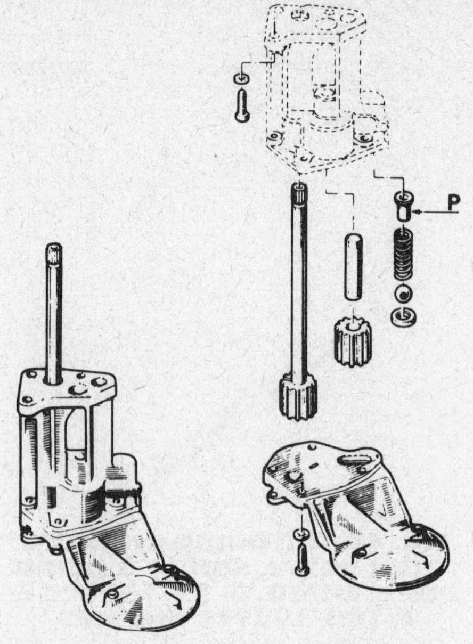

Fig. 42 Oil pump assembly. 4-85/1397cc engine

18i & SPORTWAGON

1. Disconnect battery ground cable.
2. Drain cooling system.
3. Remove upper grille crossmember, then remove grille.
4. Remove radiator and cooling fan.
5. Remove water pump drive belt.
6. Remove water pump to engine bolts, then remove water pump.
7. Reverse procedure to install. Refill and bleed cooling system as outlined.

COOLING SYSTEM SERVICE

Whenever the cooling system is opened, either due to a malfunction or during component service, the system must be refilled and purged of all air to ensure proper engine cooling. Refer to the following procedures when filling the cooling system.

ALLIANCE, ENCORE & GTA

4-85/1397cc Engine

1. Remove cap from radiator and expansion tank.
2. Slowly add coolant mixture to expansion tank until coolant flows from radiator neck, then install radiator cap.
3. Fill expansion tank to top, start engine and observe coolant level in expansion tank. Add coolant to tank if level drops, then install pressure cap.
4. Run engine until cooling fan cycles on and off 3 times, then stop engine.
5. Allow engine to cool, add coolant to expansion tank, as needed, to bring level to full mark, then install pressure cap.

4-105/1721cc & 4-120/1965cc Engines

1. Open bleed screw on radiator.
2. Slowly add coolant mixture to expansion tank until coolant flows from bleed screw, then tighten bleed screw.
3. Fill expansion tank to top, start engine and observe coolant level in expansion tank. Add coolant to tank if level drops, then install pressure cap.
4. Run engine until cooling fan cycles on and off 3 times, then stop engine.
5. Allow engine to cool, add coolant to expansion tank, as needed, to bring level to full mark, then install pressure cap.

FUEGO 18i & SPORTWAGON

1. Ensure all drain plugs are securely tightened, then open bleed screws on heater return hose and upper radiator hose.
2. Move heater control lever to the full heat position.
3. Remove expansion tank from mounting and secure as high as possible.
4. Slowly fill radiator with coolant mixture until no more can be added, then install pressure cap.
5. Continue filling system through expansion tank and close bleed screws as soon as coolant mixture begins to run out.
6. Ensure level in expansion tank is approximately 1 1/2 inches from bottom, start engine and run until thermostat opens.
7. Open bleed screws, then close screws as soon as coolant flows without bubbles.
8. Stop engine, return expansion tank to proper position and allow engine to cool completely.
9. Check level in expansion tank, and ensure coolant level is 3/4-1 1/2 inches from bottom of tank.

LE CAR

1. Ensure all drain plugs are securely tightened, then open bleed screws. Bleed screws are located on special hose from at heater core and on hose between water outlet and carburetor base.
2. Move heater control lever to the full heat position.

3. Remove expansion tank from mounting and secure as high as possible.
4. Slowly fill radiator with coolant mixture until no more can be added, then install pressure cap.
5. Continue filling system through expansion tank and close bleed screws as soon as coolant mixture begins to run out.
6. Ensure level in expansion tank is approximately $2\frac{3}{4}$ inches above "MAX" mark, start engine and run until thermostat opens.
7. Open bleed screws, then close screws as soon as coolant flows without bubbles.
8. Stop engine, return expansion tank to proper position and allow engine to cool completely.
9. Check level in expansion tank, and ensure coolant level is between maximum and minimum markings on tank.

FUEL PUMP

REPLACE

ALLIANCE, ENCORE & GTA

1. Disconnect battery ground cable.
2. Remove filler cap and drain fuel from fuel tank.
3. Disconnect pump/gauge sending unit electrical connector which is located adjacent to spare tire well in trunk on 1983 models or under the trunk ahead of the right wheel on 1984-87 models.
4. Position suitable jack beneath fuel tank.
5. Separate filler tube from fuel tank.
6. Remove fuel tank retaining bolts, then gradually lower fuel tank with jack.
7. Disconnect fuel supply, return, and vent hoses.
8. Turn fuel gauge sending unit retainer ring with a screwdriver and remove retainer ring.
9. Separate fuel pump from sending unit.
10. Reverse procedure to install.

FUEGO

1. Disconnect battery ground cable.
2. Raise and support vehicle.
3. Disconnect electrical leads from pump which is located next to right rear side rail.
4. Clamp fuel lines with suitable clamps.
5. Remove clamps and screw, then the pump.
6. Reverse procedure to install.

LE CAR

1. Remove distributor cap.
2. Remove fuel lines at the pump, label lines for proper positioning after pump replacement.
3. Remove the securing bolts and remove the pump.
4. Reverse procedure to install. Be sure to use a new gasket.

18i & SPORTWAGON

1. Disconnect battery ground cable.
2. Raise the vehicle to allow for access to the fuel pump located above the right rear axle.
3. Disconnect fuel lines and remove the pump.
4. Reverse procedure to install.

CLUTCH & MANUAL TRANSAXLE SECTION

INDEX

CLUTCH FREE TRAVEL

ADJUST

ALLIANCE, ENCORE & GTA

Clutch pedal free travel is maintained by a self adjusting release mechanism. The pedal return spring exerts constant pressure on release quadrant, maintaining tension on the release cable and holding the release bearing in constant contact with the pressure plate diaphragm.

When the clutch pedal is depressed, the notched cam engages teeth on the release quadrant, preventing the quadrant from pivoting and therefore pulling the clutch release cable. When the clutch pedal is released, the quadrant and cam "ratchet", allowing spring tension to remove slack from the release cable.

LE CAR

1. Loosen locknut (1), **Fig. 1,** then turn adjusting nut (2) in or out to obtain clearance of 1/8 inch to 5/32 inch (3-4 mm) at end of lever.
2. After adjustment is made, tighten locknut and recheck clearance.

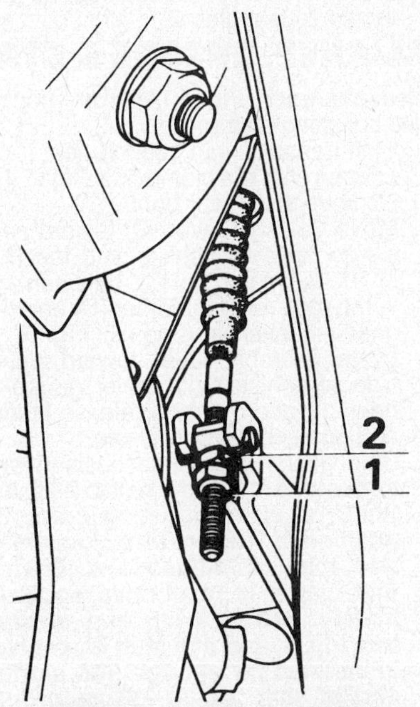

Fig. 1 Clutch pedal adjustment. Le Car

FUEGO, 18i & SPORTWAGON

1. Disconnect return spring from clutch pedal.
2. Hold release bearing against pressure plate diaphragm by pulling lever (L) in direction A as shown in **Fig. 2.**
3. Turn nut (E) in or out to obtain freeplay of 3/32 inch (2.5 mm) at point J.
4. After adjustment is made, tighten locknut and recheck clearance.

CLUTCH

REPLACE

1. Remove transaxle, and on Alliance, Encore and GTA models, remove clutch housing.
2. Evenly loosen pressure plate bolts, a few turns at a time, while supporting clutch assembly.
3. Remove pressure plate and disc.
4. Remove any dirt or grease from flywheel.
5. Position disc on flywheel with damper flange toward transaxle, then mount pressure plate on flywheel and hand tighten bolts.

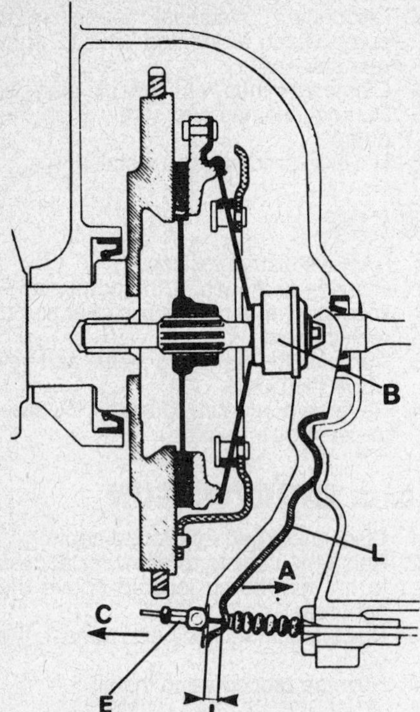

Fig. 2 Clutch pedal adjustment. Renault 18i, Fuego & Sportwagon

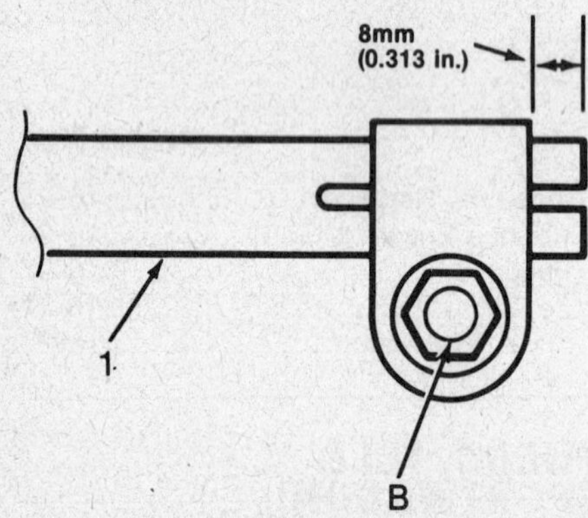

Fig. 5 Positioning shift rod clamp. Alliance, Encore & GTA

6. Visually center disc or align disc with suitable pilot.
7. Evenly tighten pressure plate bolts until pressure plate is flush against flywheel, then torque bolts to 16.5 ft. lbs. on 4-85/1397cc engines or 23 ft. lbs. for all other engines
8. Using suitable lubricant, lightly lubricate diaphragm to release bearing contact surface.

GEARSHIFT LINKAGE

ADJUST

LE CAR

1. Check that clearance (A), **Fig. 3,** is 3/16-9/32 inch (5-7 mm) with end of lever contacting plate.

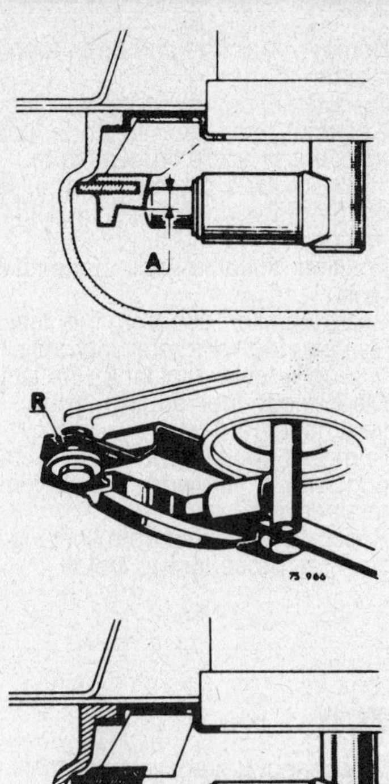

Fig. 3 Gearshift linkage adjustment. Le Car

2. To adjust, place washers between stop plate and floor panel (R), **Fig. 3.**
3. On Renault 5 (Le Car) models, recheck adjustment, place gearshift lever in third gear position, then check clearance (J), **Fig. 3.** Clearance should be 1/8 inch (3 mm).
4. Place gearshift lever in fourth gear position. Clearance (J) should be zero.
5. If proper clearances cannot be obtained, repeat step 2.

ALLIANCE, ENCORE & GTA

Prevent lever, Fig. 4 (A), from moving while adjusting shift rod.

1. Shift transaxle into second gear.
2. Loosen shift rod clamp bolt, **Fig. 5** (B).
3. Remove shift lever boot.
4. Move gearshift lever (C) toward passenger side of vehicle and insert a .0197 in. feeler gauge between reverse stop release holder (D) and the gearshift lever housing (E), **Fig. 6.**
5. Move gearshift lever toward driver side of vehicle until feeler gauge is held in place between release holder and gearshift lever housing.
6. Hold gearshift lever in position and torque shift rod clamp bolt to 20 ft. lbs. **Shift rod clamp must be correctly positioned to prevent loosening and loss of adjustment. Ensure that clamp is positioned approximately .313 in. from end of shift rod, Fig. 5, and that shift lever pivot is inserted far enough into slotted end of shift rod to assure proper clamping action on pivot.**
7. Install gearshift lever boot, then shift transaxle through all gears to ensure proper operation and gear engagement.

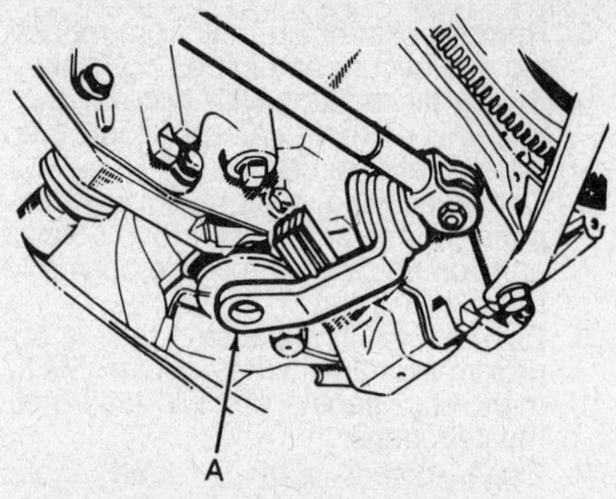

Fig. 4 Shift rod lever location. Alliance, Encore & GTA

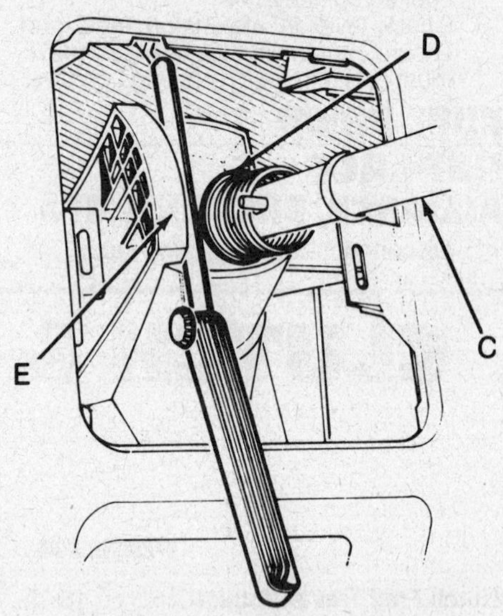

Fig. 6 Gearshift linkage adjustment. Alliance, Encore & GTA

FUEGO, 18i & SPORTWAGON

1. Loosen yoke retaining nut, then position gearshift lever at transaxle in third-fourth gear position.
2. Install .079 inch shim (2 mm) on four speed transaxles or .394 inch shim (10 mm) on five speed transaxles between end piece (Q) and housing surface (F), **Fig. 7.**
3. Tighten yoke retaining nut, then remove shim.

TRANSAXLE

REPLACE

ALLIANCE, ENCORE & GTA

1. Disconnect battery ground cable and remove air cleaner.
2. Raise and support vehicle.
3. Remove filler and drain plugs and drain transaxle.
4. Remove front wheels and disconnect driveshafts.

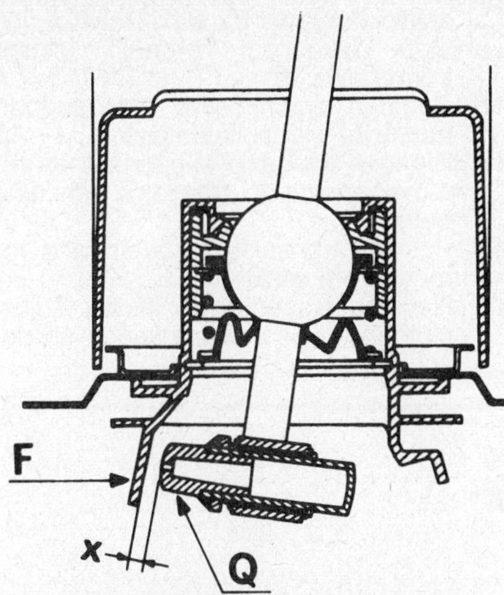

Fig. 7 Gearshift linkage adjustment. 18i & Sportwagon

5. Disconnect gearshift lever linkage and engine/transaxle support rod.
6. Remove clutch shield and mounting pad nuts.
7. Disconnect back-up lamp switch electrical connector and remove TDC sensor.
8. Disconnect clutch cable, speedometer cable, and ground wire.
9. Remove radiator and position out of way without disconnecting hoses.
10. Using suitable lifting device, raise engine slightly to free rear mounts.
11. Attach another suitable lifting device to clutch cable bracket and bolt A on transaxle, **Fig. 8.**
12. Remove starter motor mounting bolts.
13. Remove transaxle retaining bolts, then separate transaxle from engine and lift free of chassis. On 5-speed transaxle, slide 5th speed casing between sidemembers.
14. Raise engine and slide transaxle into clutch splines.
15. Install transaxle retaining nuts, then remove lifting device from transaxle.
16. Install starter motor mounting bolts.
17. Lower engine onto mounting pads and install nuts, torquing them to 26 ft. lbs.
18. Install radiator and clutch shield.
19. Connect clutch cable, speedometer cable, and ground wire. Secure speedometer cable with clip.
20. Connect back-up lamp switch electrical connector and install TDC sensor.
21. Install air filter.
22. Connect gearshift lever linkage and engine/transaxle support.
23. Connect driveshafts.
24. Install front wheels and torque lugs to 55 ft. lbs.
25. Remove transaxle breather plug, fill transaxle, and install breather plug.

FUEGO

1. Disconnect battery ground cable.
2. Remove three starter attaching bolts.
3. Disconnect clutch cable from fork and remove housing stop.
4. Place T.Av. 509-01 support spacers or equivalent between lower shock absorber attaching pins and lower suspension arm shafts.
5. Loosen lug nuts on front wheels.
6. Raise and support vehicle, ensuring that spacers remain in place.
7. Remove front wheels.
8. Remove brake calipers.
9. Using pin drift B.Vi. 31-01 or equivalent, punch out drive shaft roll pins on side gear shafts.
10. Remove steering tie rod ball joint nut.
11. Using ball joint puller T.Av. 476 or equivalent as necessary, loosen steering ball joint cone.
12. Disengage drive shaft from side gear shaft by tilting stub axle carrier.
13. Proceed in same manner for other side.
14. Disconnect speedometer cable, gearshift linkage, and electrical connectors for back-up lights and emission control switches.
15. Remove clutch cover.
16. Install suitable jack under transaxle, then remove transaxle mounts.
17. Remove engine to transaxle attaching bolts.
18. Pull transaxle toward rear of vehicle, being careful not to catch it on pressure plate.
19. Using suitable lubricant, lightly lubricate clutch splines.
20. Engage transaxle, being careful not to catch clutch mechanism.
21. Mount engine and transaxle, then attach transaxle mounts.
22. Remove jack.
23. Install clutch cover, ensuring it is clear of TDC sensor, if equipped.
24. Reconnect speedometer cable, gearshift lever, and electrical connectors for back-up lights and emission control switches.
25. Using suitable lubricant, lightly lubricate differential side gear splines.
26. Position drive shaft next to side gear.
27. Engage drive shaft in side gear by tilting stub axle carrier. Use elbow pin drift B.Vi. 31-01 or equivalent to line up holes, if necessary.
28. Engage stub axle carrier in upper suspension ball joint.
29. Using suitable tool, lock cone and torque nut to 48 ft. lbs.
30. Engage steering tie rod ball joint, then, using suitable tool, lock cone and torque nut to 29 ft. lbs.
31. Install front brake calipers.
32. Proceed in same manner for other side.
33. Install front wheels and lower vehicle to ground, then torque lug nuts to 59 ft. lbs.
34. Remove spacers.
35. Connect clutch cable to fork.
36. Place starter in housing, then pull support bracket into line and tighten bolt.
37. Tighten starter bolts and reconnect wires.
38. Adjust gearshift lever and clutch clearance.
39. Connect battery ground cable.

LE CAR

1. Disconnect battery and remove transaxle ground cable.

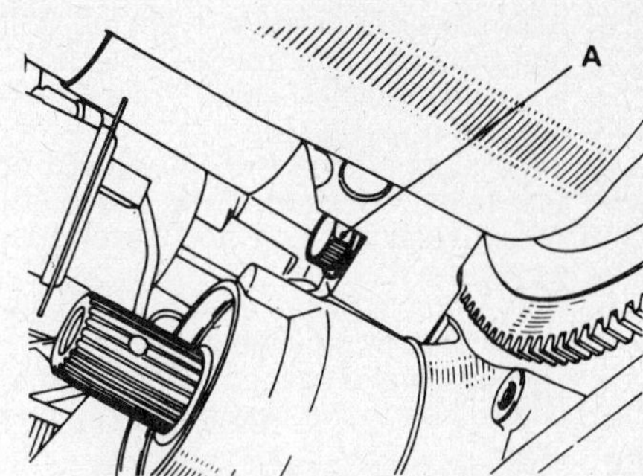

Fig. 8 Lifting device attaching point on transaxle. Alliance, Encore & GTA

2. Disconnect speedometer cable, then remove air cleaner and support bracket.
3. Remove water pump drive belt. If this belt is a notched type belt, discard belt. A new belt is required for reinstallation.
4. Remove camshaft pulley, air pump and mounting bracket. Check for any spacers below air pump bracket and retain these for replacement of bracket.
5. Remove two upper bolts on starter. Use of Renault tool No. Ele. 565 is recommended.
6. Remove clutch housing mounting bolts which are on engine. The use of Renault tool No. Mot. 253 is recommended to remove lower left nut of clutch housing.
7. Remove brake calipers without removing brake hoses. Caution: Do not allow calipers to hang under their own weight and stretch brake hoses.
8. Disconnect tie rods at stub axle carriers.
9. Disconnect upper ball joint stub axle carriers.
10. Remove axles from transaxle by tilting stub axle carriers down. **Do not damage transaxle side seals when removing drive shafts.**
11. Remove two bolts securing shift linkage support. Pull shift linkage rod down and away from transaxle.
12. Disconnect clutch cable at lever. Push against cable sleeve retainer with a screwdriver to free it from supporting tab.
13. Remove tubular crossmember.
14. Support front of transaxle with a jack.
15. Remove front mount and bracket.
16. Remove starter by removing lower mounting bolt. Leave starter sitting next to engine. Do not remove from vehicle.
17. Remove side reinforcement mounting bolts and clutch cover.
18. Remove transaxle.
19. Reverse procedure to install.
20. Lightly coat splines on input shaft and drive shaft splines with white grease before installation. **Make sure end of drive shaft is fully seated in differential side gears.**

18i & SPORTWAGON

1. Disconnect battery ground cable.
2. Remove starter motor, then loosen

rear stabilizer bracket retaining bolt and position stabilizer bracket aside.
3. Disconnect clutch cable at fork, then remove housing stop.
4. Install support spacers T.Av. 50901 or equivalent between lower shock absorber retaining bolt and lower suspension arm.
5. Raise and support vehicle, then remove both front wheels.
6. Remove brake calipers and attach to chassis so that calipers do not hang by brake hoses.
7. Remove driveshaft roll pins at transaxle side of driveshaft.
8. Remove tie rod ends from stub axle carriers and disconnect upper ball joint.
9. Tilt stub axle carriers downward and pull axles from transaxle.
10. Disconnect speedometer cable and all electrical connectors from transaxle.
11. Loosen Allen screw securing gearshift linkage to transaxle shift lever, then disconnect gearshift linkage from transaxle.
12. Remove clutch cover, then support transaxle with suitable jack.
13. Remove transaxle supports, then remove engine to transaxle retaining bolts.
14. Position transaxle rearward and remove from vehicle.
15. Reverse procedure to install. Adjust clutch and gearshift linkages as described previously.

DISC BRAKES

INDEX

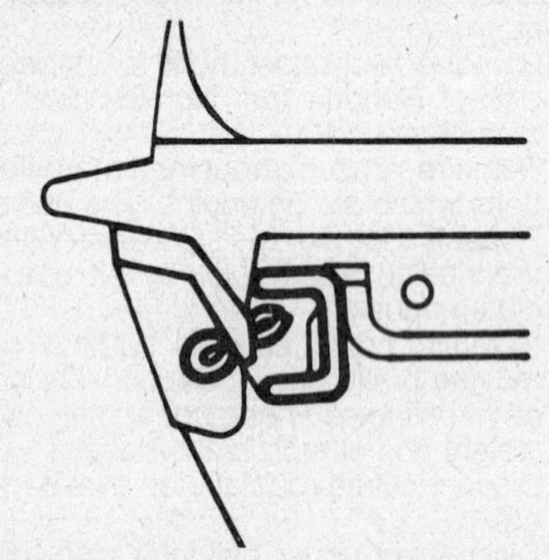

Fig. 1 Caliper spring clip & retaining key installation. Le Car

FRONT BRAKE PADS REPLACE

Disc brake pads must be changed in complete axle sets. Do not mix pads of different makes or grades.

ALLIANCE, ENCORE & GTA

1. Drain approximately 2/3 of brake fluid from master cylinder reservoir. Do not drain fluid completely.
2. Loosen wheel lug nuts, raise and support front of vehicle, and remove front wheels.
3. Using suitable tool, depress caliper piston to bottom of caliper bore.
4. Remove caliper mounting pins, then remove caliper.
5. Place caliper out of way so that brake hose does not support weight of caliper.
6. Hold anti-rattle clip against caliper anchor plate and remove outer pad.
7. Remove inner pad and anti-rattle clip.
8. Inspect caliper and repair if any signs of leakage are evident.
9. Clean anchor plate to caliper contact surfaces, then lubricate with suitable lubricant.
10. Install anti-rattle clip on trailing end of anchor plate with split end of clip facing rotor.
11. Hold back on clip and install inner and outer brake pads.
12. Reverse procedure to install, torquing caliper mounting pins to 25-27 ft. lbs.

LE CAR

1. Remove four spring clips, then remove two caliper keys.
2. Remove caliper from support plate. Place caliper on one of suspension components. Do not let it hang and stretch brake hose.
3. Remove pads and anti-rattle springs on caliper holder.
4. Pull dust cover back and inspect caliper for leaking brake fluid. If necessary, rebuild caliper.
5. Push piston back into caliper using a large C-clamp or suitable tool.
6. Install two new anti-rattle springs on each backing plate, with shortest inside.
7. Install new brake pads. Place into position so that metal button on pad backing plate is at top when pad is in position.
8. Place caliper into position so that both wire springs are compressed.
9. Install one key at bottom of caliper. Install second key at the top. If necessary, pry caliper down slightly so key can be slipped in.
10. Install new spring clips to retain keys.
11. When installed properly, large wire spring should be behind caliper, and keys between caliper and caliper support, **Fig. 1.**
12. Press brake pedal several times to seat pistons against pads, then refill master cylinder.

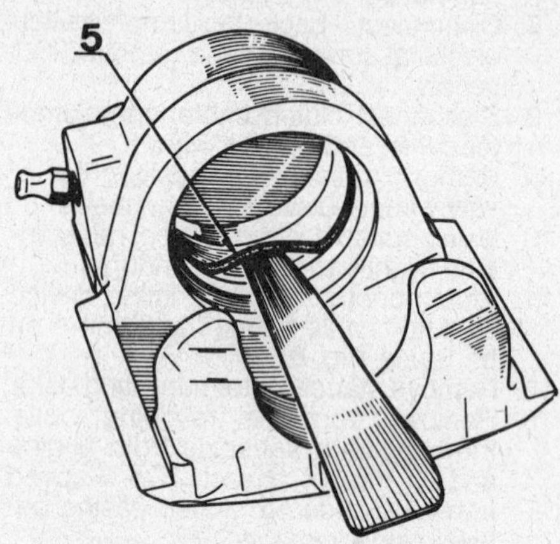

Fig. 2 Typical piston seal removal

FUEGO, 18i & SPORTWAGON

1. Raise and support vehicle and remove front wheels.
2. Disconnect wear warning electrical connector at caliper.
3. Remove clip and retaining key from caliper.
4. Carefully pry between disc and pad with suitable tool to force caliper piston into its bore.
5. Remove brake pads.
6. Check condition of caliper dust cap and bellows that protect caliper sliding bushings and replace if necessary. Clean end of caliper piston and bushings with brake fluid prior to installing replacement parts. Lubricate new parts with brake fluid.
7. Install anti-squeal springs on new disc pads and install pads into caliper.
8. Install retaining key and clip and connect wear warning electrical connector.

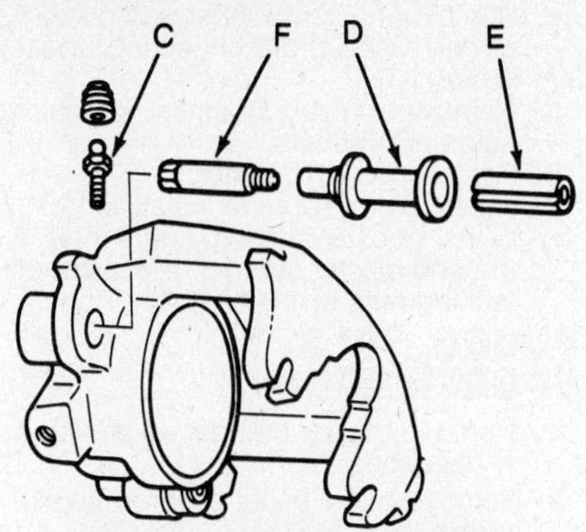

Fig. 3 Brake caliper mounting sleeves & bushings. Alliance, Encore & GTA

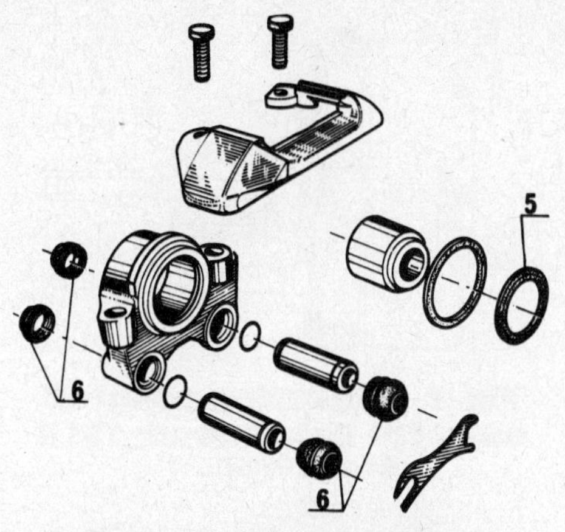

Fig. 4 Brake caliper exploded view. Fuego, 18i & Sportwagon

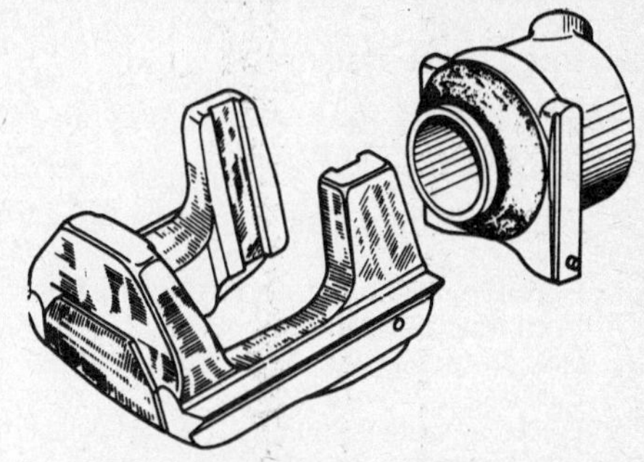

Fig. 5 Two piece caliper assembly. Le Car

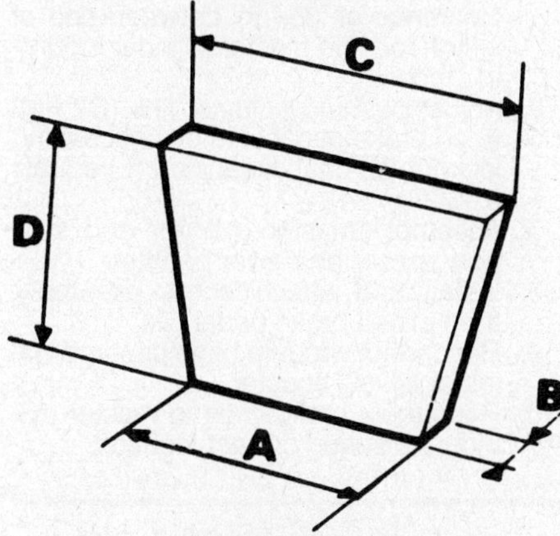

Fig. 6 Wedge dimensions for two-piece caliper disassembly

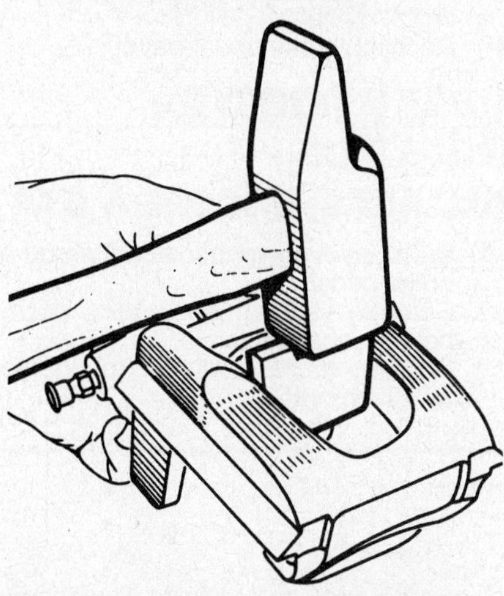

Fig. 7 Spreading cast iron bracket. Two-piece caliper

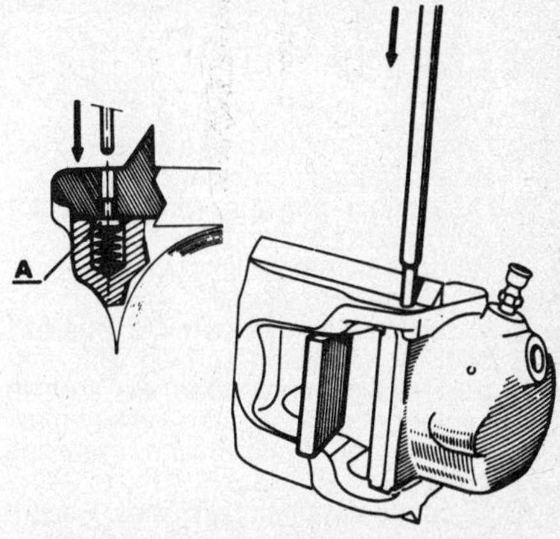

Fig. 8 Removing cylinder stop peg. Two-piece caliper

CALIPER SERVICE

ALLIANCE ENCORE & GTA

1. Remove caliper and disconnect brake hose, then clean outside of caliper with brake cleaning solvent.
2. Place block of wood inside caliper, then force piston from caliper using compressed air. **Do not place fingers between piston and caliper.**
3. Remove dust boot with screwdriver, then remove piston seal with a suitable tool with rounded edges, **Fig. 2. Take care not to mar caliper bore.**
4. Remove bleeder screw (C), plastic sleeves (D) and rubber bushings (E) from caliper, **Fig. 3.**
5. Clean caliper and piston using a suitable disc brake cleaner. Inspect piston and caliper bore for scratches or scores. Replace if necessary.
6. Lubricate a new piston seal with clean brake fluid, position seal into caliper groove and press firmly into place.
7. Install new dust boot on piston, sliding metal portion of seal over open end of piston, then pulling seal rearward until lip seats in piston groove. When dust boot is seated, push metal retainer upward until retainer is flush with rim at open end of piston and snap seal fold into place.
8. Lubricate piston and caliper bore with clean brake fluid. Press piston into caliper, taking care not to pinch or roll over piston seal.
9. Press piston to bottom of caliper, then seat dust boot in caliper with suitable driver.
10. Install bleeder screw (C), new plastic sleeves (E) and new rubber bushings (F), **Fig. 3.**
11. Fill the caliper with brake fluid through the hole for the brake hose, then tighten bleeder screw.
12. Install the brake hose with a new copper washer.
13. Reinstall the caliper, then bleed brake system.

FUEGO, 18i & SPORTWAGON

1. Remove caliper from vehicle.
2. Remove rubber dust cap (5), **Fig. 4.**
3. Remove piston using compressed air using caution not to damage piston or cause personal injury.
4. Disassemble remaining parts of caliper as shown in **Fig. 5.**
5. Lubricate all parts prior to assembly with suitable grease, then assemble caliper as shown in **Fig. 4.**

LE CAR

Le Car models are equipped with two piece calipers, **Fig. 5.** The cylinder with piston can be replaced separately from caliper bracket.

Disassembly

1. Fabricate a wedge as shown in **Fig. 6.** Wedge dimensions should be as follows: A 2 1/32 inches (51.5 mm), B 5/16 inch (8 mm), C 2 7/32 inches (56 mm), D 1 3/8 inches (35 mm).
2. Spread legs of cast iron bracket a small amount using the wedge, **Fig. 7.**
3. Using a pin punch, press cylinder stop peg (A) and remove cylinder, **Fig. 8.** Do not remove wedge.
4. Install new cylinder, press in peg and spring assembly and slide into position. Be sure to locate peg into hole in bracket. Remove wedge.
5. Install caliper assembly.

MASTER CYLINDER REPLACE

ALLIANCE, ENCORE & GTA

1. Disconnect brake lines at master cylinder.
2. Remove master cylinder to power booster attaching nuts, then remove master cylinder.
3. Reverse procedure to install, torquing attaching nuts to 11-19 ft. lbs. and line fittings to 116 in. lbs.

4. Fill master cylinder reservoir to maximum level.
5. Bleed brake system.

FUEGO, 18i & SPORTWAGON

1. Drain fluid from master cylinder reservoir.
2. Remove reservoir and rubber rings from master cylinder.
3. Disconnect brake lines from master cylinder.
4. Remove nuts securing master cylinder to brake booster, then remove master cylinder.
5. Reverse procedure to install. Check that brake pedal pushrod protrudes .354 inch (9 mm) from opening at master cylinder side of brake booster.

LE CAR

1. Drain brake fluid reservoir.
2. Disconnect metal brake lines. Do not loosen fittings in master cylinder.
3. Disconnect pressure drop indicator wire and brake pedal pushrod.
4. Remove two mounting bolts, then remove master cylinder.
5. Install master cylinder into position, seal the mounting surface with suitable sealing compound. Be sure to center brake pedal push rod into master cylinder. Secure with mounting bolts.
6. Reconnect metal brake lines. Reconnect pressure drop indicator wire.

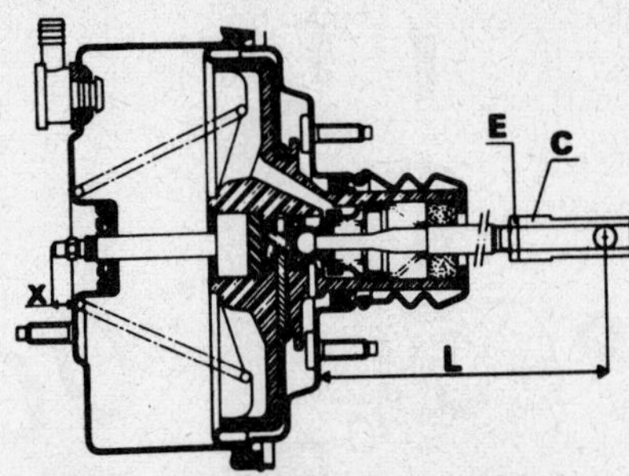

Fig. 9 Adjusting pushrod adjuster link. Fuego, 18i & Sportwagon

7. Adjust rear brakes.
8. Adjust brake pedal push rod so that brake pedal has 13/64 in. (5 mm) of travel.
9. Bleed brake lines and the rear brake pressure distribution valve bypass circuit.
10. Recheck brake pedal travel.

BRAKE BOOSTER REPLACE

ALLIANCE, ENCORE & GTA

1. Disconnect power booster pushrod at brake pedal.
2. Remove vacuum hose from power booster check valve.
3. Remove master cylinder to booster attaching nuts.
4. Remove master cylinder and position aside without disconnecting brake lines.
5. Remove power booster attaching nuts and washers.
6. Remove power booster.
7. Reverse procedure to install, torquing power booster attaching nuts to 18 ft. lbs. and master cylinder to booster attaching nuts to 11-19 ft. lbs.

FUEGO, 18i & SPORTWAGON

1. Remove master cylinder as previously described.
2. Remove brake pedal pushrod adjusting pin.
3. Remove brake booster attaching nuts.
4. Remove brake booster, retaining support spacer.
5. Adjust master cylinder clearance by adjusting piston rod nut to obtain a clearance of .354 in. between end of piston rod and master cylinder mounting face.
6. Adjust pushrod adjuster link (C), **Fig. 9,** on brake pedal side by unscrewing locknut (E) until dimension (L) equals 5.063 in.
7. Assemble master cylinder and support spacer on power booster.
8. Install and attach entire assembly, then install brake pedal pin.
9. Reconnect vacuum hose pushrod adjuster link to booster.
10. Reconnect brake lines to master cylinder, ensuring correct location.

DRUM BRAKES SECTIO

INDEX

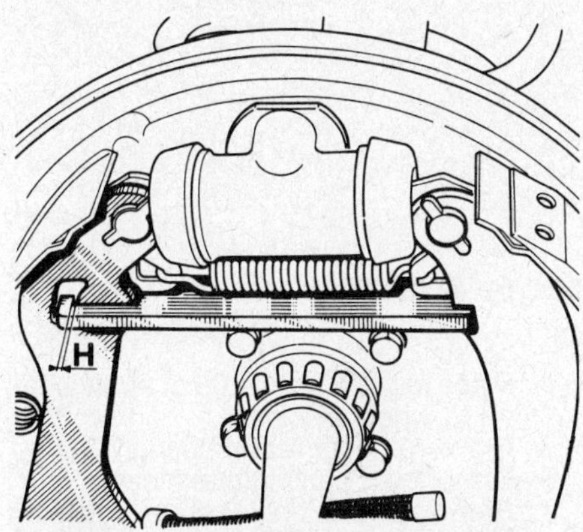

Fig. 1 Rear brake drum adjustment. Fuego, 18i & Sportwagon

REAR DRUM BRAKE
ADJUST
ALLIANCE, ENCORE & GTA

1. Ensure parking brake is fully released, then raise and support rear of vehicle.
2. Remove access plug from backing plate.
3. Turn star wheel on adjuster until adjuster screw is tight, then mark position of star wheel.
4. Hold adjuster lever off star wheel with suitable tool, then back star wheel off (loosen) 1 complete revolution.
5. Repeat procedure for opposite side.

LE CAR

1. Adjust brakes using a suitable open end wrench.
2. Adjust leading shoe first by turning adjustment lug in an arc towards floor to tighten shoe and upwards to retract shoe.
3. Rotate wheel while adjusting.
4. Adjust secondary shoe in the same manner, then check parking brake adjustment.

FUEGO, 18I & SPORTWAGON

1. Check dimension H, **Fig. 1** for clearance of .039 inch (1mm) between link and primary brake shoe. Parking brake lever must be contacting brake shoe when performing measurement.
2. If measurement is not as specified, replace link tension spring and brake shoe return springs.

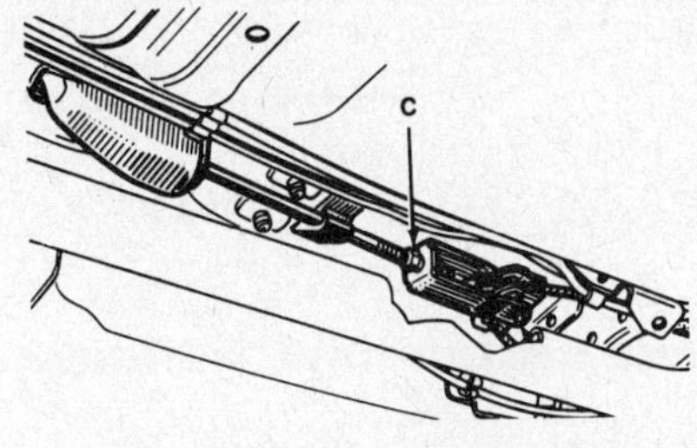

Fig. 2 Parking brake adjuster. Alliance, Encore & GTA

PARKING BRAKE
ADJUST
ALLIANCE, ENCORE & GTA

It is necessary that parking brake be adjusted as described below in order for the self adjusting mechanism to work properly. Parking brake should only be adjusted if brake shoes, parking brake cable or parking brake lever is being replaced.

1. Release hand brake.
2. Raise and support rear of vehicle, then remove heat shield covering secondary parking brake cable and shift linkage.
3. Loosen locknut (C), **Fig. 2.**
4. Turn primary rod nut until shoes lightly contact drum.
5. Slightly loosen nut so wheels turn freely.
6. Tighten locknut (C).
7. Operate parking brake to ensure that there is parking brake lever travel of 7 to 8 notches.

LE CAR

1. Adjust rear brakes.
2. Loosen locknut 2 on parking brake adjustment rod. Tighten or loosen nut (1) to obtain parking brake lever travel of 6 notches, **Fig. 3.**
3. Tighten locknut (2) and recheck parking brake lever travel.

FUEGO, 18I & SPORTWAGON

1. Raise and support vehicle and release parking brake.
2. Adjust locknut (2), **Fig. 3,** until secondary parking brake cable can be deflected 3/4 inch (20 mm) at its midpoint.
3. After adjustment, check for parking brake lever travel of 12 notches.

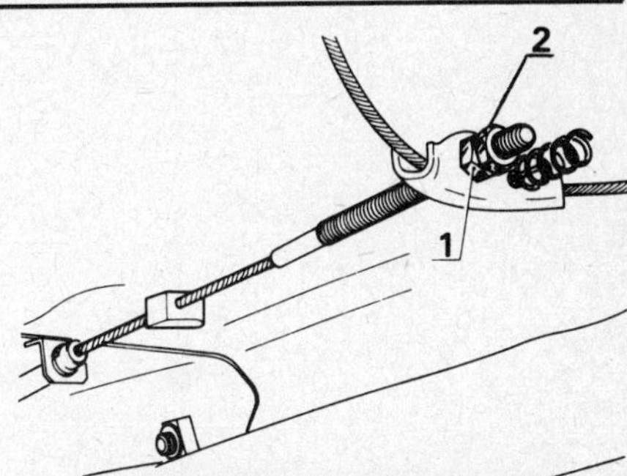

Fig. 3 Parking brake adjustment. Exc. Alliance, Encore & GTA

MASTER CYLINDER
REPLACE

Refer to Disc Brakes Section.

BRAKE BOOSTER
REPLACE

Refer to Disc Brakes Section.

BRAKE DRUM
REPLACE
ALLIANCE, ENCORE & GTA

1. Disconnect battery ground cable.
2. Raise and support vehicle.
3. Remove tire and wheel assembly.
4. Loosen parking brake secondary cable.
5. Remove stub axle grease cup, hub nut and washer.
6. Remove drum assembly. If brake drum is difficult to remove, retract the brake shoes. Remove access plug located at rear of support plate. Using a suitable tool, loosen automatic adjuster lever and back off adjuster screw.
7. Reverse procedure to install.

FUEGO, 18I & SPORTWAGON

1. Disconnect battery ground cable.
2. Raise and support vehicle.
3. Remove rear tire and wheel assembly.
4. Loosen parking brake and parking brake secondary cables to allow parking brake lever to be freed.

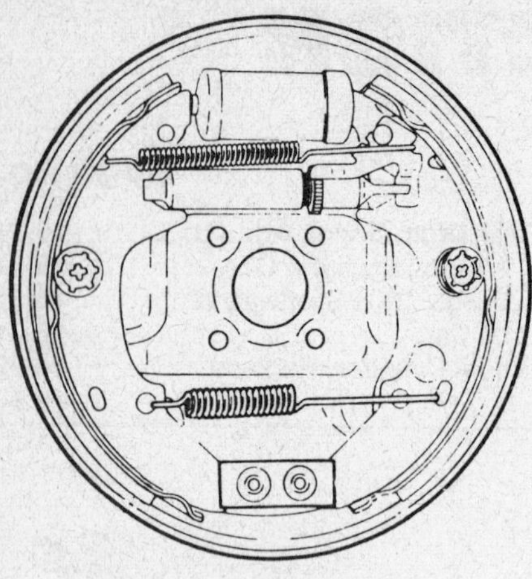
TYPE I
(1983-1985)

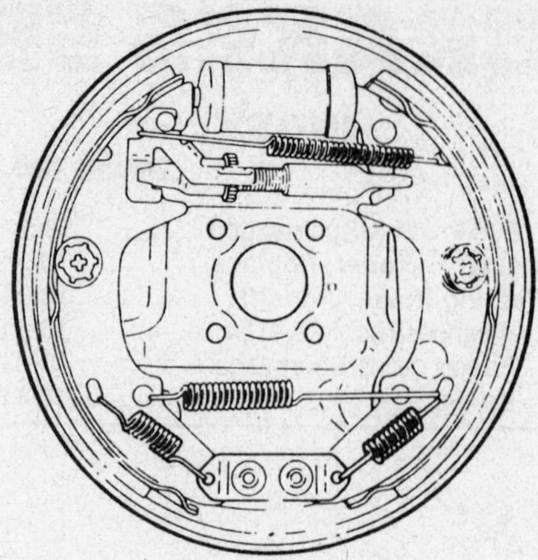
TYPE II
(Early 1986)

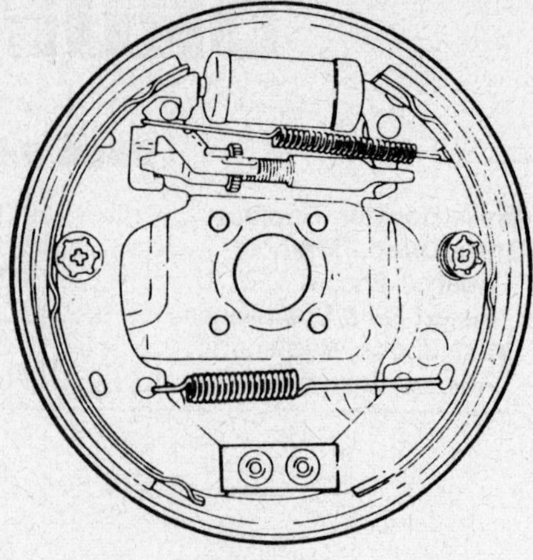
TYPE III

Fig. 4 Rear brake assemblies. Alliance, Encore & GTA

5. Remove backing plate dust plug as follows:
   a. Place a suitable screwdriver against parking brake lever and push peg from brake shoe assembly.
   b. After freeing the peg, loosen lever by pushing lever rearward.
6. Remove grease cap from drum.
7. Remove cotter pin and locknut.
8. Remove drum hub nut and washer assembly.
9. Remove drum assembly.
10. Reverse procedure to install.

BRAKE SHOES
REPLACE
ALLIANCE, ENCORE & GTA

Three different rear brake shoes are used, **Fig. 4**, referred to as Type I, Type II and Type III. Brake shoes and wheel cylinders are common to all three types. However, backing plates, springs, adjusters and mounting hardware are different. When servicing these assemblies, **do not** install two different type assemblies on the same axle.

Type I

1. Disconnect battery ground cable.
2. Raise and support vehicle.
3. Remove brake drum.
4. Place tool clamp Fre. 05 or equivalent, onto wheel cylinder.
5. Remove two brake shoe hold down springs and retaining pins.
6. Remove return springs, adjuster and brake shoes from backing plate, noting position for installation. **Do not bend adjuster lever during removal.**
7. Remove retracting springs from upper and lower shoe attaching points.
8. Remove parking brake cable from parking brake lever.
9. Remove parking brake lever from trailing shoe as follows:
   a. Remove horseshoe retaining clip and spring washer.
   b. Slide lever off parking brake lever pin on trailing shoe assembly.
10. Reverse procedure to install.

Type II & Type III

1. Raise and support rear of vehicle, then remove wheel and brake drum.
2. Loosen parking brake cables.
3. Install suitable clamp on wheel cylinder.
4. Remove pull down springs from between lower hole on shoe and backing plate (Type II only), then remove adjuster spring and lever, return spring and the adjuster screw assembly.
5. Remove hold down springs and pins, then the leading brake shoe.
6. Remove trailing shoe and parking brake lever from backing plate, then disconnect cable from parking brake lever.
7. Pry open clip securing parking brake lever, then remove spring washer and lever from trailing shoe.
8. Clean backing plate and lubricate contact surfaces with suitable brake grease, then reverse procedure to install brake assembly.

FUEGO 18i & SPORTWAGON

1. Disconnect battery ground cable.
2. Raise and support vehicle.
3. Remove brake drum.
4. Place tool clamp Fre. 05 or equivalent, on to wheel cylinder.
5. Remove upper return spring.
6. Disconnect parking brake cable.
7. Remove two brake shoe retaining springs.
8. Tilt toothed lever as far as possible toward axle shaft assembly.
9. Carefully separate brake shoes from wheel cylinder.
10. Pull primary brake shoe link outward from primary brake shoe assembly.
11. Move toothed section back to its initial position.
12. Tilt primary brake shoe 90 degrees.
13. Using a suitable screwdriver, remove lower spring.
14. Loosen, then remove primary brake shoe.
15. Remove secondary brake shoe.
16. Reverse procedure to install.

WHEEL CYLINDER
REPLACE

1. Disconnect battery ground cable.
2. Raise and support vehicle.
3. Remove tire and wheel assembly.
4. Remove drum and brake shoes.
5. Disconnect brake line from wheel cylinder.
6. Remove wheel cylinder attaching bolts, then the wheel cylinder. **Prevent brake fluid from contacting the brake linings. Contaminated linings must be replaced.**
7. Reverse procedure to install.

REAR AXLE & SUSPENSION SECTION

INDEX

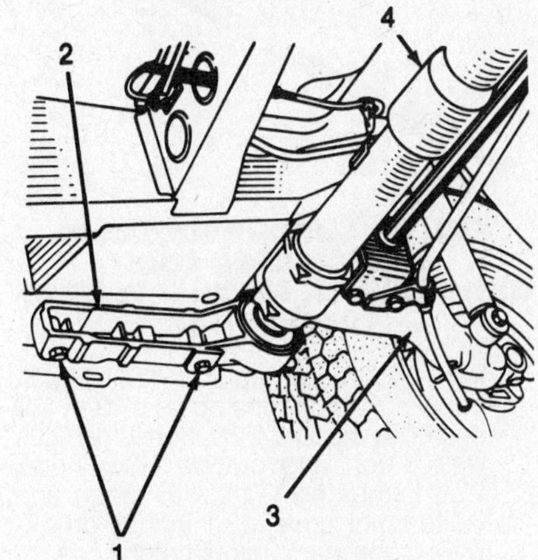

Fig. 1 Axle tube & suspension arm removal. Alliance, Encore & GTA

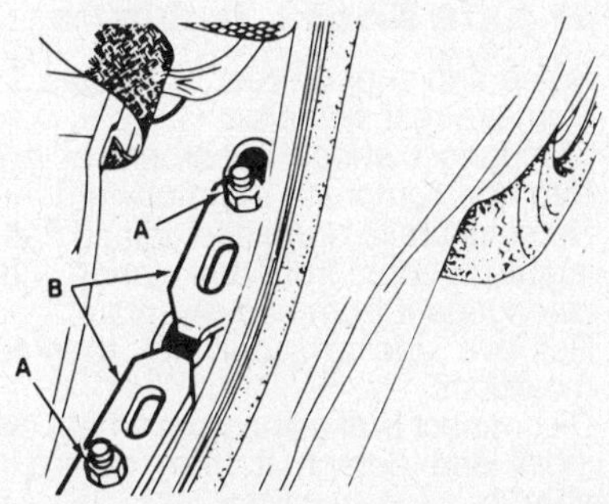

Fig. 2 Suspension arm nut plate removal. Alliance, Encore & GTA

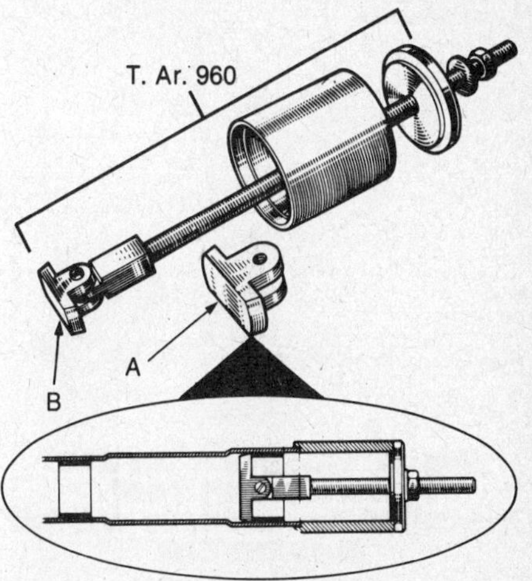

Fig. 3 Axle tube bushing removal. Alliance, Encore & GTA

REAR AXLE & SUSPENSION ARM SERVICE

ALLIANCE, ENCORE & GTA

Axle Tube & Suspension Arms, Replace

The suspension arm and tube are serviced as an assembly. Do not try to separate them.

1. Raise and support rear of vehicle and remove wheels.
2. Disconnect brake hose from axle lines and plug open fittings.
3. Disconnect shock absorbers, stabilizer bar and parking brake cable, and remove exhaust pipe heat shield.
4. Remove brake drum, backing plate, and brake shoes.
5. Remove bracket bolts (1), **Fig. 1**, then remove torsion bar and axle bracket (2) using suitable slide hammer.
6. Remove suspension arm (3) and axle tube (4) as an assembly, **Fig. 1.**
7. Inspect axle tube bushings and axle bracket nut plates, and replace as needed.
8. Reverse procedure to install, noting the following:
   a. Lubricate suspension arm tube bushings and bushing surfaces of inner tube with suitable lubricant.
   b. Torque axle bracket nuts to 59 ft. lbs., stabilizer mounts to 37 ft. lbs., then lower vehicle and torque shock absorber lower nut to 59 ft. lbs.
   c. Adjust underbody height as outlined in "Wheel Alignment Section."
   d. Bleed brakes as needed and adjust parking brake cable.

Axle Bracket Nut Plates, Replace

1. Remove rear axle tube and suspension arm assembly as outlined.
2. Remove rear seat cushion.
3. Remove trim panel beside seat cushion.
4. Remove bracket bolts (a), **Fig. 2,** from inside of vehicle.
5. Pry up damaged nut plate and install replacement.

Axle Tube Bushing, Replace

1. Remove driver's side axle tube and suspension arm and clamp assembly in suitable vise.
2. Remove large diameter outer bushing using puller adapter A, then remove smaller diameter bushing with adapter B, **Fig. 3.**
3. Inspect bushing seats, retainers and contact surfaces in each tube, and replace axle tube assembly if damaged or excessively worn.
4. Fabricate installer from length of steel tube or pipe 2 inches in diameter, start small bushing into tube by hand, then press bushing in to a depth of 7±.078 inches (178 mm±2 mm).
5. Fabricate installer from length steel tube or pipe 2.44 inches in diameter, start large bushing into tube by hand, then press bushing in to a depth of .590±.078 inch (15 mm±2 mm).
6. Install new axle tube seal.
7. Lubricate bushings with Molykote 33 medium or equivalent, then assemble axle tubes, pressing them together as far as possible by hand.
8. Reverse remaining procedure to complete installation.

FUEGO 18i & SPORTWAGON

Rear Axle Assembly, Replace

1. Raise and support rear of vehicle.
2. Remove wheels.
3. Remove shock absorber lower mountings and compress shock absorbers upward.

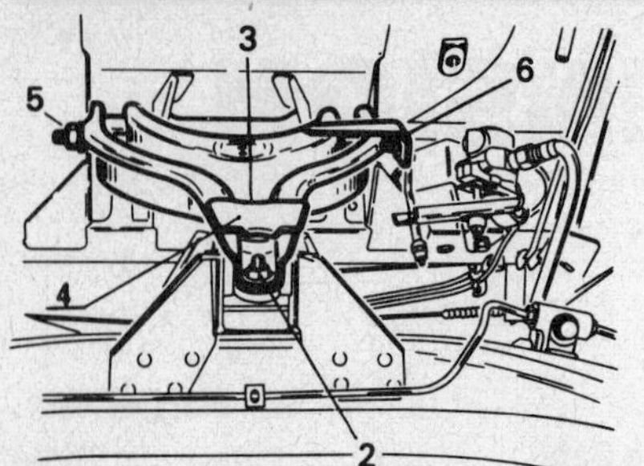

Fig. 4 Center arm removal. Fuego, 18i & Sportwagon

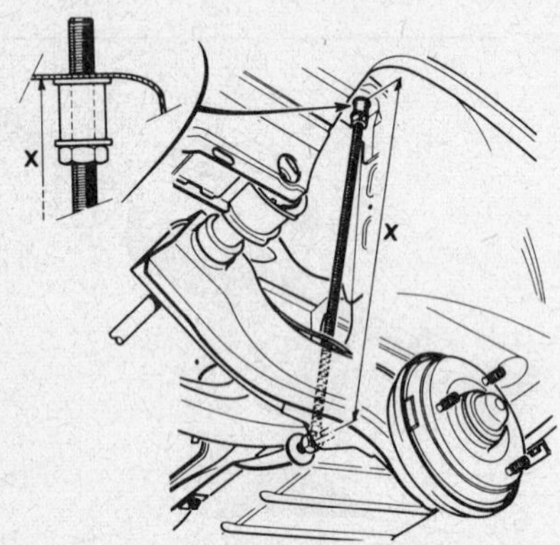

Fig. 6 Suspension arm positioning tool installation. Models w/rear torsion bar

4. Remove flexible brake lines from limiter.
5. Pull rear axle downward and remove springs.
6. Remove two side arm nuts on chassis side, then remove two bolts.
7. Disconnect parking brake cables at adjuster and remove them from retaining bracket.
8. Place suitable jack under rear axle shaft.
9. Disconnect brake limiter valve.
10. Remove two center arm bolts.
11. Remove rear axle assembly.
12. Reverse procedure to install. Torque center arm bolts to 59 ft. lbs., side arm bolts to 26-30 ft. lbs., and wheel lug nuts to 59 ft. lbs.
13. Bleed rear brake circuit.
14. Check adjustment of brake limiter valve and parking brake.

Center Arm, Replace

1. Raise and support vehicle.
2. Disconnect brake limiter control rod.
3. Unscrew nuts (2) and (3) of clamp (4), **Fig. 4.**
4. Unscrew nuts (5) and (6) on left and right bolts.
5. Remove clamp and two bolts.
6. Remove center arm.
7. Using suitable lubricant, lubricate two bolts.
8. Position arm on chassis, then insert bolts.
9. Install nuts (5) and (6) and hand tighten.
10. Install rubber bushing clamp (4) and slowly screw nuts (2) and (3) on alternately to avoid pinching rubber bushing.
11. With rear suspension properly aligned, torque bolt nuts to 51-67 ft. lbs. and center bushing clamp nuts to 9-13 ft. lbs.
12. Check adjustment of limiter valve.

Side Arms, Replace

1. Raise and support vehicle.
2. Disconnect two parking brake cables.
3. Remove side arm attaching nuts, then drive out bolts.
4. Remove side arms/stabilizer bar assembly.
5. Reverse procedure to install, torquing bolts on chassis side to 22-30 ft. lbs. and bolts on rear axle shaft to 22-38 ft. lbs.

Rear Axle Shaft, Replace

1. Raise and support rear of vehicle.
2. Remove rear wheels.
3. Disconnect shock absorbers at bottom and compress them upward.
4. Remove brake drum and detach parking brake cable from brake shoe, then disengage it from backing plate.
5. Remove side arm bolt nut, then remove bolt.
6. Disconnect brake line from wheel cylinder and detach it from rear axle shaft.
7. Remove brake lines.
8. Swing rear axle shaft downward.
9. Remove spring.
10. Repeat steps 4 through 9 for other side.
11. Place suitable jack under rear axle shaft.
12. Remove center bushing clamp.
13. Remove rear axle shaft.
14. Remove inner bearings, deflectors, drum backing plates, and center arm rubber bushing.
15. Reverse procedure to install. Torque center arm bushing bolt to 26-34 ft. lbs., drum backing plate bolts to 22-30 ft. lbs., side arm bolts to 22-38 ft. lbs., shock absorber lower nuts to 18-26 ft. lbs., and wheel lug nuts to 59 ft. lbs.
16. Bleed rear brake circuit.
17. Check adjustment of brake limiter valve and parking brake.

REAR TORSION BAR REPLACE

ALLIANCE, ENCORE & GTA

1. Raise and support vehicle with wheels hanging free.
2. Remove sway bar.
3. Remove wheel and shock absorber on side being serviced.
4. Using impact tool Emb. 880 or suitable slide hammer, extract torsion bar from axle tube.
5. Fabricate suspension arm positioning tool as shown in **Fig. 5.**
6. Install fabricated tool in place of shock absorber.

A - 14 mm (0.551 in.) dia.
B - 12 mm (0.472 in.) dia.
C - 12 mm (0.472 in.) dia. threaded rod - length 660 mm (25.9 in.)
D - 12 mm (0.472 in.) bore washers
E - 20 mm (0.787 in.) dia. spacer with 12.5 mm (0.492 in.) dia. hole - length 60 mm (2.362 in.)
F - weld

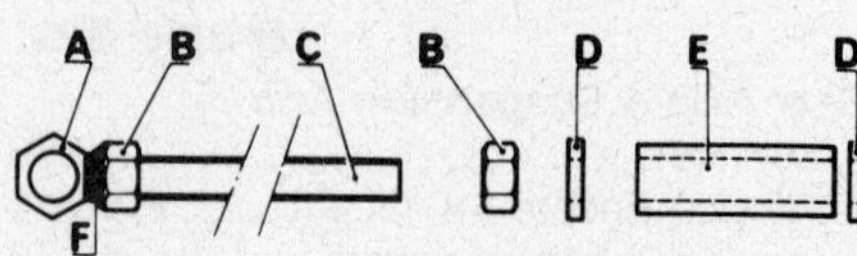

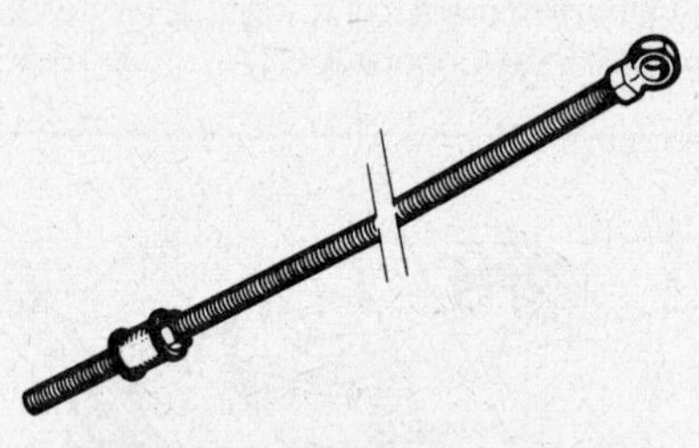

Fig. 5 Suspension arm positioning tool dimensions. Models w/rear torsion bar

7. Turn nut until length of tool (X), **Fig. 6,** equals 24.04 inches on all except GS and GTA models, 22.9 inches on GTA with green and orange color code, 22.6 inches on GTA with green and white color code, 23.1 inches on GS with green and yellow color code, or 22.8 inches on GS with white and orange color code. **Color code consists of 2 paint marks on top of the suspension arm.**
8. Coat torsion bar splines with suitable lubricant and install it in bearing and arm, feeling for position in which it will slide into both easily. **Do not interchange torsion bars, and ensure bar is installed properly in axle tube.** Left and right torsion bars are identified by diamond shaped symbols on the splined end of the bar. Left torsion bars have 2 marks, while right torsion bars have 3 marks. In addition, the number of splines on each end of the bar is different. There are 24 splines at the arm end of the torsion bar and 25 splines at the anchorage end.
9. Remove fabricated tool, then install shock absorber and sway bar.
10. Install wheel and lower vehicle, then check and adjust underbody height as outlined in "Wheel Alignment Section."

LE CAR

1. Fabricate suspension arm positioning tool, **Fig. 5.**
2. Raise and support vehicle at frame side rails.
3. Mark relationship of torsion bar to torsion bar retaining housing for reference during installation.
4. Remove shock absorber. Assemble torsion bar removal tool and install in place of shock absorber, **Fig. 6.**

5. Tighten nut A of tool until suspension travel is under tension, then remove torsion bar. **Prior to installing torsion bars, adjust nut A of tool until dimension X, Fig. 6 is 23 1/4 inches (590 mm) for right hand side and 23 5/8 (600 mm) for left hand side.**
6. Lubricate splines and install torsion bar in reverse order of removal, ensuring that torsion bar removal tool is set to specifications previously described. Align torsion bar with mark made on torsion bar retaining housing prior to removal. Loosen housing retaining bolts as necessary to align torsion bar with housing.

REAR SPRING REPLACE

FUEGO, 18i & SPORTWAGON

1. Raise and support rear of vehicle, then remove wheels.
2. Disconnect brake hose retaining clip from axle housing.
3. Remove shock absorber lower retaining bolt, then compress shock absorber upward.
4. Remove rear coil spring.
5. Reverse procedure to install. Check to ensure that coil spring ends contact cup stops.

SHOCK ABSORBER REPLACE

ALLIANCE, ENCORE & GTA

1. With vehicle on level surface, remove upper attaching nut from inside trunk.
2. Raise and support vehicle, then remove lower attaching nut.
3. Remove shock absorber.
4. Reverse procedure to install, coating lower mounting pin with suitable lubricant, and torque upper mount to 18 ft. lbs. and lower mount to 59 ft. lbs.

FUEGO & LE CAR

1. Remove shock absorber upper nuts from inside of trunk.
2. Raise vehicle and remove lower nuts.
3. Remove shock absorber.
4. Reverse procedure to install. Attach upper mount first.
5. Lower vehicle and tighten bolts when vehicle is in normal ground position.

18i & SPORTWAGON

1. From inside trunk, remove gas tank shield.
2. Remove upper shock absorber retaining bolt.
3. Raise and support vehicle and remove rear wheels.

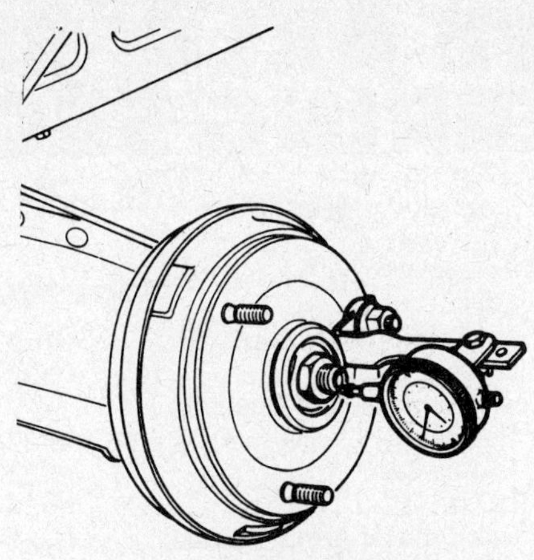

Fig. 7 Rear wheel bearing endplay check

4. Remove lower shock absorber retaining nut, then compress shock absorber upward.
5. Remove brake hose retaining clip from axle housing.
6. Lower axle housing and remove shock absorber and spring as an assembly.
7. Reverse procedure to install.

REAR WHEEL BEARING ADJUST

EXC. ALLIANCE, ENCORE & GTA

1. Raise and support vehicle, then remove rear wheels.
2. Remove grease cap, cotter pin and locknut plate, then loosen axle nut.
3. torque axle nut to 25 ft. lbs. (3 Nm).
4. Loosen nut 1/8 turn on Le Car or 1/6 turn on Fuego, 18i and Sport wagon.
5. Install dial indicator onto drum to measure end play, **Fig. 7.**
6. Adjust axle nut to obtain .001-.002 inch (.01-.05 mm) end play on Le Car, orzero-.001 inch (0-.03 mm) on Renault 18i, Sportwagon and Fuego.
7. Install lock nut plate and cotter pin. Place small amount of grease in grease cap and install into position.

REAR STABILIZER BAR REPLACE

ALLIANCE, ENCORE & GTA

1. Raise and support vehicle with wheels hanging free.
2. Remove two sway bar attaching bolts on either side and retain nuts.
3. Remove sway bar.
4. Reverse procedure to install.

FUEGO 18i & SPORTWAGON

Refer to "Side Arms, Replace."

REAR HUB & BEARINGS REPLACE

ALLIANCE, ENCORE & GTA

1. Release parking brake, raise and support vehicle, then remove wheel.
2. Loosen handbrake secondary cable.
3. Remove grease cap, stub axle nut and washer.
4. Remove brake drum and hub assembly using slide hammer and suitable adapter. If brake drums are difficult to remove, retract brake shoes by removing access cover at rear of support plate, unseat automatic adjuster lever, and back off adjuster screw.
5. Remove bearing snap ring and bearing from drum.
6. Reverse procedure to install, torquing locking nut to 118 ft. lbs. and wheel lug nuts to 55 ft. lbs.

EXC. ALLIANCE, ENCORE & GTA

1. Remove grease cover with a suitable tool.
2. Remove cotter pin, locknut plate, axle nut and washer. Remove outer wheel bearing.
3. Pull brake drum or disc off stub axle. On vehicles with self-adjusting rear brakes, release brake adjustment by pushing a pin punch through access hole in backing plate.
4. Remove inner bearing with a suitable puller.
5. Place locating sleeve over stub axle. Assemble two split half-shells into position over bearing. The half-shells can be placed over bearing. The half-shells can be placed over bearing two ways so that bearing only can be pulled or so bearing and thrust washer can be pulled. Place sleeve over half-shells.
6. Pull off bearing assembly with suitable puller.
7. Remove bearing inner seal.
8. Clean bearings and repack with suitable wheel bearing grease.
9. Reinstall bearing seal, thrust washer and inner bearing. Reinstall drum or disc outer bearing, thrust washer and stub axle nut.
10. Adjust rear wheel bearings as described under "Rear Wheel Bearings, Adjust".
11. Install locknut plate and cotter pin. Place a small amount of grease in grease cup and install into position.

FRONT DRIVE AXLE, SUSPENSION & STEERING SECTION

INDEX

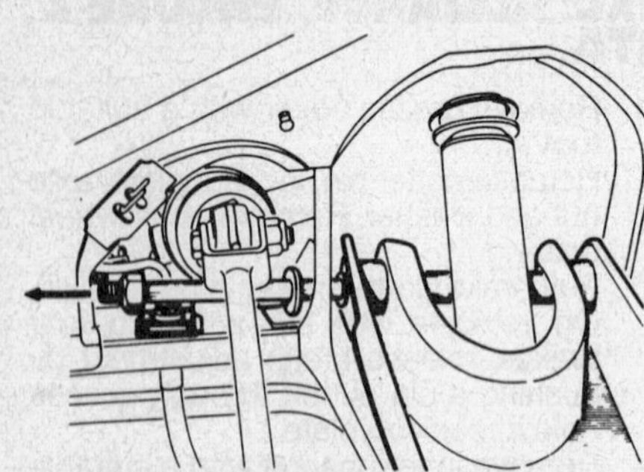

Fig. 1 Upper control arm installation. Le Car

UPPER CONTROL ARM REPLACE

LE CAR

1. Remove the radiator expansion bottle on the right side and the ignition coil on the left side of the vehicle.
2. Raise vehicle and let wheels hang.
3. Disconnect upper ball joint.
4. Screw on and tighten a locknut (1) on the front end of the suspension arm hinge pin, **Fig. 1.**
5. Hold the locknut assembly and remove the nut on the other end of the suspension arm hinge pin.
6. Remove the locknut hinge pin assembly by pulling out the front of the vehicle.
7. Remove the suspension arm.
8. Reverse procedure to install. Lubricate the hinge pin with suitable grease.
9. Screw the front hinge pin nut onto the end of the shaft's threads. After installation, install the nut on the end of the hinge pin which is located in the engine compartment.

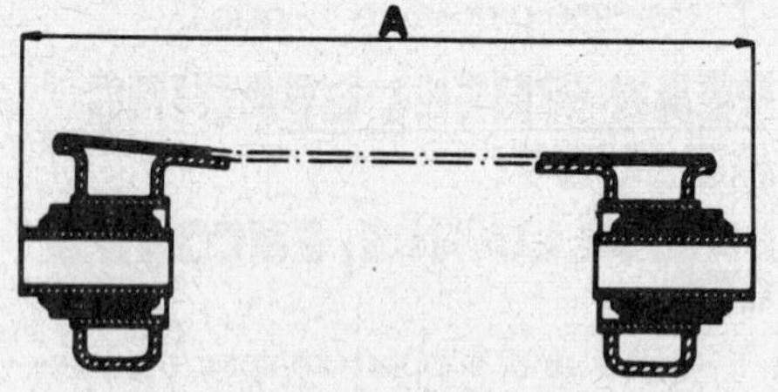

Fig. 2 Upper control arm bushing installation. Le Car

10. Lower the vehicle so that the wheels are in normal position on the ground.
11. Tighten the hinge pin nuts.

FUEGO, 18i & SPORTWAGON

1. Raise and support vehicle, then remove front wheels.
2. Loosen shock absorber lower locknut, then disconnect caster link from control arm.
3. Disconnect upper ball joint and remove control arm to chassis retaining bolt.
4. Raise control arm and disconnect shock absorber tube.
5. Remove control arm from vehicle.
6. To install, position control arm in chassis and connect shock absorber tube.
7. Connect upper ball joint to spindle, but do not tighten nut.
8. Install upper control arm to chassis bolt and shock absorber tube bolt but do not tighten.
9. Connect caster link, but do not tighten retaining bolt.
10. Tighten upper ball joint retaining nut.
11. Install wheels, then lower vehicle to floor.
12. Tighten upper control arm to chassis bolt, shock absorber tube bolt and caster link nut.

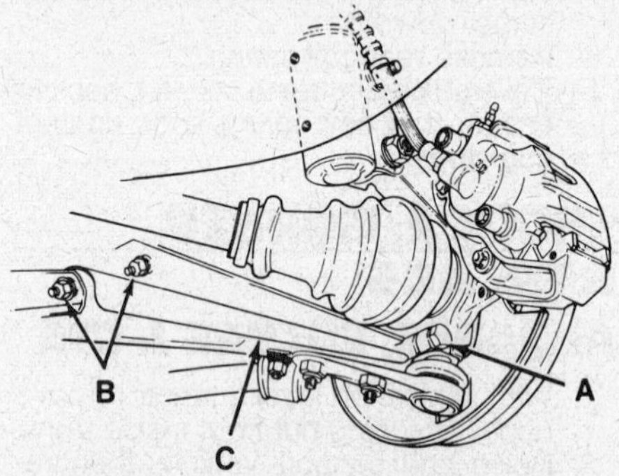

Fig. 3 Lower control arm installation. Alliance, Encore & GTA

UPPER CONTROL ARM BUSHING REPLACE

LE CAR

Bushings must be replaced one at a time so that they are properly spaced in relation to the center line of the suspension arm.

1. Press out one of the worn bushings. Use a tube which has an outside diameter of 1 in., and another which has an inside diameter of 1¼ in. to aid in bushing removal.
2. Install one new bushing. Keep dimension (A), **Fig. 2,** 6 11/16 in. (170.4 mm).
3. Remove and install the second bushing in the same procedure as the first.

FUEGO, 18i & SPORTWAGON

1. Remove upper control arm as described previously.
2. Press out old bushing using tube with

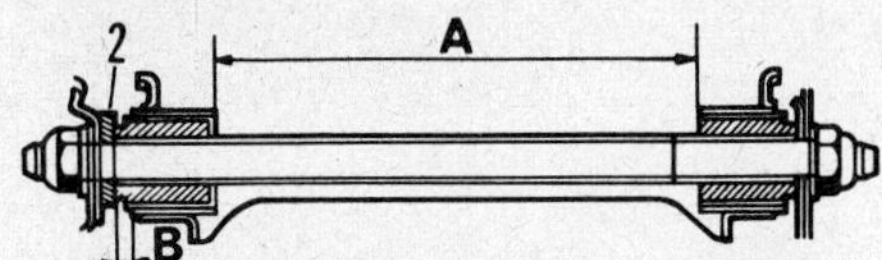

Fig. 4 Caster shim and control arm bushing installation. Fuego, 18i & Sportwagon

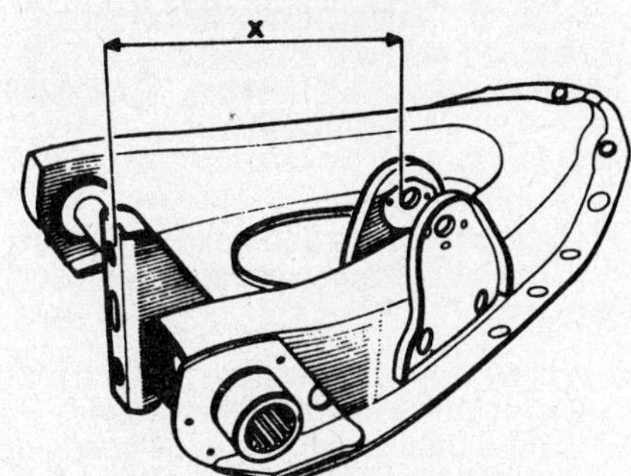

Fig. 6 Positioning hinge pin tube. Le Car

diameter of 1.024 inch (26 mm).

3. Install new bushing until it is centered in arm.

LOWER CONTROL ARM REPLACE

ALLIANCE, ENCORE & GTA

1. Remove sway bar.
2. Raise and support side of vehicle to be serviced.
3. Remove wheel.
4. Remove lower ball joint pinch bolt and nut (A), then the pivot bolts (B), **Fig. 3.**
5. Disengage ball joint stem from steering knuckle and remove control arm assembly.
6. Position control arm on frame brackets, then install but do not tighten pivot bolts.
7. Position washer over ball joint stud, insert stud into steering knuckle, then install pinch bolt and nut.
8. Install sway bar, but do not fully tighten mountings.
9. Install wheel and lower vehicle.
10. Move vehicle back and forth several times to seat suspension components, then torque control arm pivot bolts to 59 ft. lbs., pinch to 40 ft. lbs., sway bar to sill bolts to 21 ft. lbs., and sway bar mount nuts to 55 ft. lbs.

FUEGO, 18i & SPORTWAGON

1. Raise and support vehicle, then remove front wheels.
2. Loosen lower ball joint nut until it contacts drive shaft constant velocity joint.
3. Continue backing off ball joint nut until ball joint is free of spindle. Because lower ball joint nut is used to press out ball joint from spindle, nut must be replaced with a new one.
4. Remove bolt securing control arm to frame, then remove control arm.

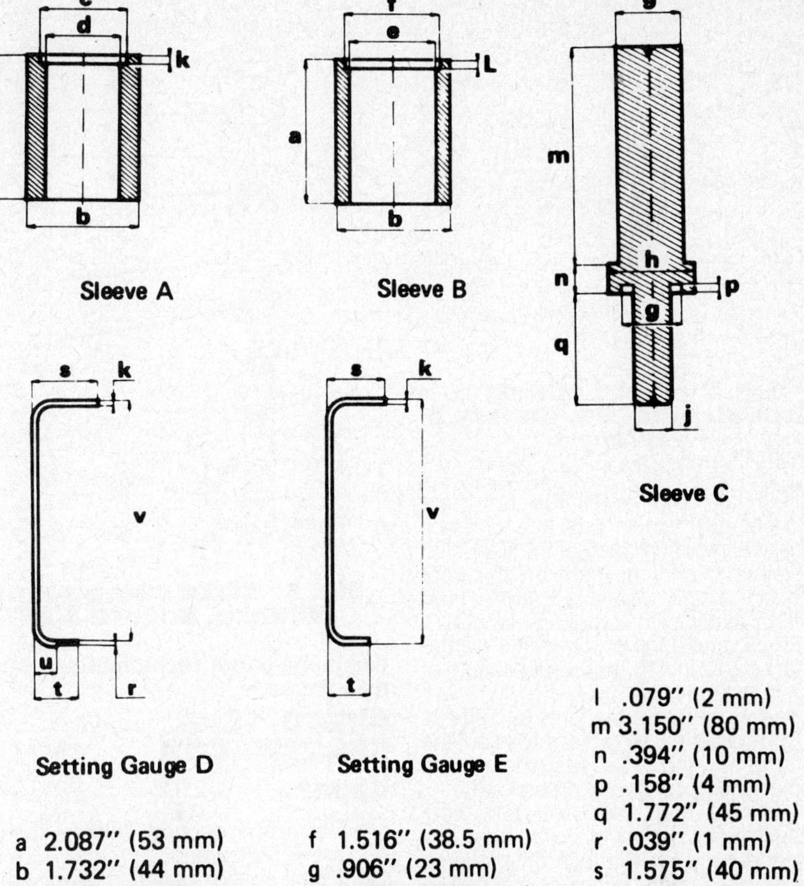

a 2.087" (53 mm)
b 1.732" (44 mm)
c 1.358" (34.5 mm)
d 1.102" (28 mm)
e 1.378" (35 mm)
f 1.516" (38.5 mm)
g .906" (23 mm)
h 1.280" (32.5 mm)
j .547" (13.9 mm)
k .118" (3 mm)
l .079" (2 mm)
m 3.150" (80 mm)
n .394" (10 mm)
p .158" (4 mm)
q 1.772" (45 mm)
r .039" (1 mm)
s 1.575" (40 mm)
t 1.260" (32 mm)
u 1.063" (27 mm)
v 5.906" (150 mm)

Fig. 5 Lower control arm bushing replacement tools. Le Car

5. Reverse procedure to install. Check to ensure that caster adjusting shim is installed as shown in **Fig. 4.** Shim (2) must be installed at front bushing on vehicles with manual steering or rear bushing on vehicles with power steering. Do not tighten control arm to chassis bolts until vehicle has been lowered to floor.

LE CAR

1. Raise the vehicle and remove the torsion bar.
2. Remove the stub axle nut. Break loose the stub axle shaft end from the wheel hub.
3. Remove the anti-sway bar from the side of the vehicle being worked on. Loosen and remove the shock absorber lower mounting pin.
4. Remove the steering tie rod ball joint and remove the lower suspension arm ball joint.
5. Push in the axle to free the bottom ball joint from the stub axle carrier. Do not remove the drive shaft.
6. Turn the suspension assembly to the right or to the left and remove the lower suspension arm.
7. Reverse procedure to install.
8. Be sure to replace the caster adjustment shims between the suspension arm and the frame.
9. Tighten all bolts and nuts on the anti-sway bar, shock absorber lower mount and the lower suspension, with the front wheel in the normal "Road" position.
10. Check the front axle alignment.

LOWER CONTROL ARM BUSHING REPLACE

LE CAR

The bushings must be replaced one at a time so that they are properly spaced in relation to the center line of the suspension arm.

All parts removed during this operation must be replaced with new parts.

1. Fabricate the tools shown in **Fig. 5.**
2. Using a press and a .512 inch (13 mm) shaft push the hinge pin tube out of the lower suspension arm. The suspension arm must not receive any press load.
3. Using a splined portion of the torsion bar and sleeve (A) press out toe rear bushing.

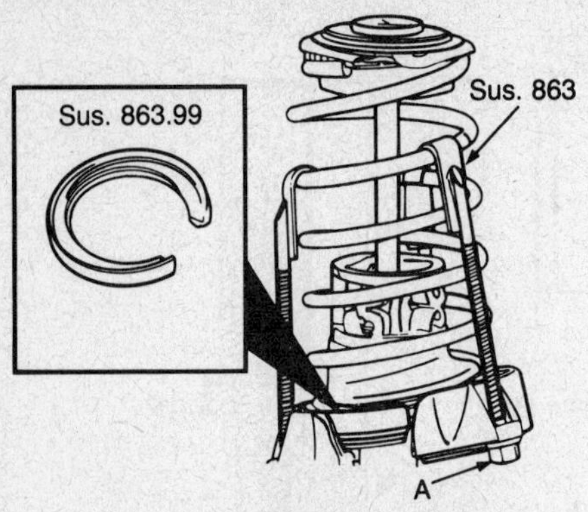

Fig. 7 Front spring removal. Alliance, Encore & GTA

4. Lubricate and install the new rear bushing. Press in until the distance between bottom face of the flange on sleeve C and the face on the front bushing inner sleeve is 5.906 in. (150 mm). Install with centering mandrel C, **Fig. 5,** and a thrust rod with a diameter of .512 in. (13 mm) and a length of 7 in. (180 mm).
5. Use a centering mandrel (C), sleeve (B) and the thrust rod, to press out the front bushing. The suspension arm must not receive any press load.
6. Lubricate and install the new front bushing. Press in place so that distance between the face on the inner sleeves on both bushings is 5.906 in. (150 mm).
7. Lubricate and reinstall the hinge pin tube with its bracket and spacer.
8. Line up the bracket in relation to the edge of the shock absorber mounting pin hole, **Fig. 6.** Measure and adjust dimension, "X," to 6½ in. (165 mm).
9. Install hinge pin, use sleeve B, **Fig. 5,** with an old bushing to prevent distortion of the hinge pin tube during installation. **When installed properly, the hinge pin tube should not have any endplay.**

EXC. LE CAR

1. Remove lower control arm.
2. Press one bushing out, using suitable press and spacer. **Bushings must be replaced one at a time so they are properly spaced in relation to the center line of the suspension arm.**
3. Lubricate and install new bushing. Install so that distance between bushings is 5.77-5.81 inches for Alliance, Encore and GTA, or 7.126 for Fuego, 18i and Sportwagon.
4. Install second bushing following same procedure as for the first.

BALL JOINT REPLACE

ALLIANCE, ENCORE & GTA

The suspension arm and ball joints are not serviced separately. If ball joint replacement is necessary, ball joint and suspension arm must be replaced as an assembly. **Use of aftermarket replacement ball joints is not recommended by the manufacturer.**

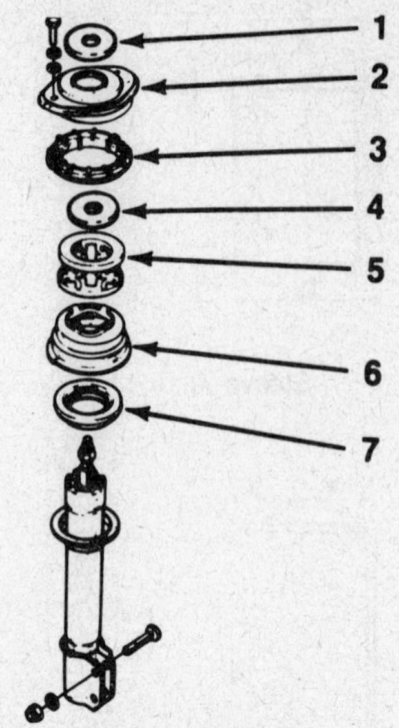

Fig. 8 Strut components. Alliance, Encore & GTA

FUEGO, 18i & SPORTWAGON

Upper

1. Raise and support vehicle, then remove front wheel.
2. Install spacer between lower control arm pivot bolt and shock absorber lower mount. This will keep spring compressed.
3. Disconnect upper ball joint from spindle.
4. Remove caster link nut and ball joint retaining bolts from upper arm, then remove ball joint.
5. Reverse procedure to install.

Lower

1. Remove lower control arm from vehicle as described previously.
2. Remove heads of rivets securing ball joint to lower arm, then punch out rivets.
3. Install new ball joint using nuts and bolts supplied with replacement joint. **Install bolts with bolt heads on ball joint bellows side of control arm.**
4. Install lower control arm.

LE CAR

Upper

1. Raise the vehicle or place the side being worked on on jack stands.
2. Remove the ball joint securing nut and disconnect the ball stud from steering knuckle.
3. Remove the ball joint securing rivets and the ball joint.
4. Install the new ball joint into position on the suspension arm, and place the shim which is supplied with the kit on top of the suspension arm.
5. Secure the ball joint with the nuts and bolts supplied. Place the bolt head on the dust cover side.
6. Install the ball joint into position on the stub axle carrier.
7. Tighten all nuts and bolts.
8. Check the front axle alignment.

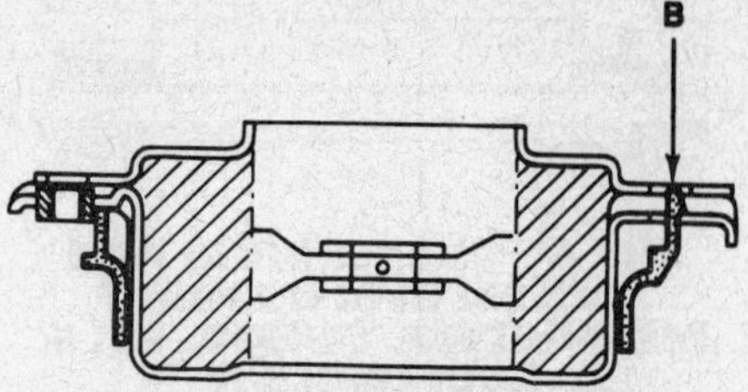

Fig. 9 Aligning locating peg of strut cushion with lower cup. Alliance, Encore & GTA

Lower

1. Raise side of the vehicle and place on jack stands. Remove the wheel.
2. Chisel off the ball joint rivet heads on the ball joint side.
3. Remove the ball joint securing nut and the ball joint. **Do not pull on the driveshaft.**
4. Install the new ball joint into the stub axle carrier; hold in place with securing nut. Do not fully tighten securing nut.
5. Raise the lower suspension arm and locate the ball joint into position.
6. Install the securing bolts with the heads of the bolts on the dust cover side.
7. Tighten all nuts and bolts.
8. Check the front axle alignment.

FRONT STABILIZER BAR REPLACE

ALLIANCE, ENCORE & GTA

1. Raise and support vehicle.
2. Disconnect front exhaust pipe.
3. Remove gear shift linkage.
4. Remove cradle bushings and bushing on bottom of suspension arms, then remove sway bar.
5. Reverse procedure to install, torquing front sway bar clamp nuts to 17 ft. lbs.

SHOCK ABSORBER REPLACE

ALLIANCE, ENCORE & GTA

1. Raise and support side of vehicle to be serviced.
2. Remove wheel.
3. Remove bottom shock absorber mounting nuts and bolts, then the two top mounting bolts.
4. Remove assembly by pressing lower control arm down so that it will not contact driveshaft boot.
5. Clamp bottom of shock absorber in suitable vise.
6. Install adapter Sus. 863.99 in base of spring compressor, just below spring mount, install compressor on spring, then tighten nuts (A) gradually and evenly, **Fig.7 .**
7. Remove nut on top of shock absorber piston rod.

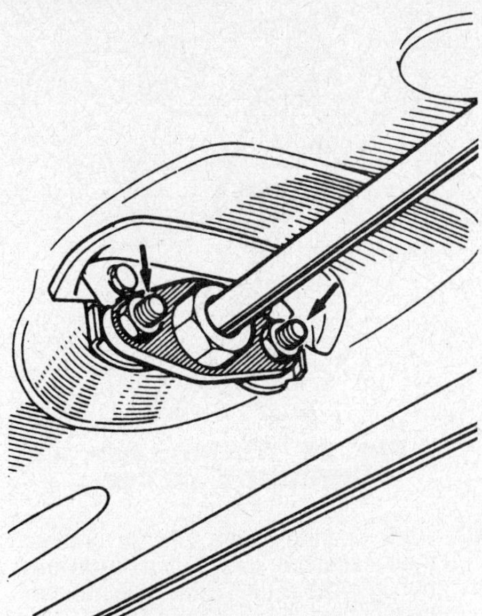

Fig. 10 Removing front torsion bar bearing mounting bolts. Le Car

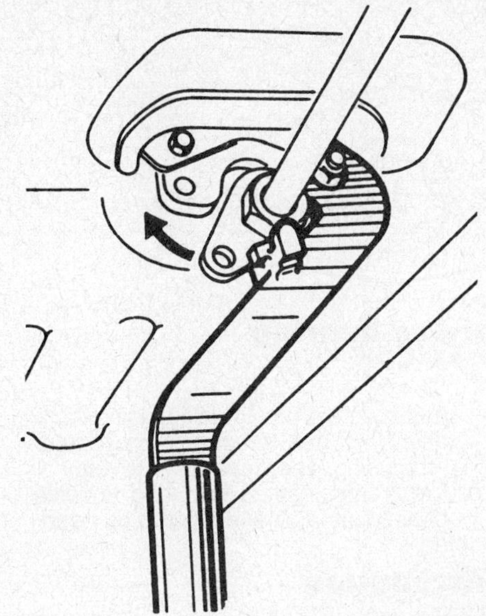

Fig. 11 Releasing torsion bar tension. Le Car

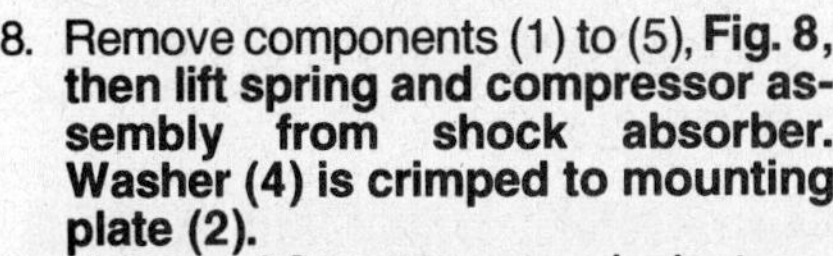

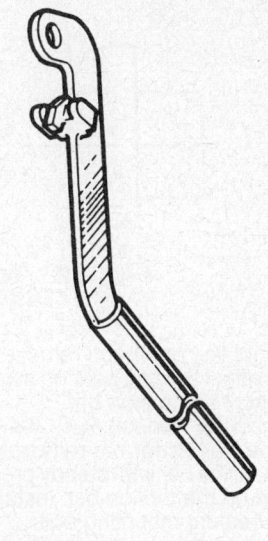

8. Remove components (1) to (5), **Fig. 8**, **then lift spring and compressor assembly from shock absorber. Washer (4) is crimped to mounting plate (2).**
9. Using tool Sus. 594 or equivalent, secure rod of tool in vise and install spring together with its bottom cup and tool Sus. 863 over tool Sus. 594.
10. Compress spring with tools Sus. 594 and Sus. 594-02 or equivalents to remove tool Sus. 863.
11. Slowly release spring until it reaches its free length and remove spring.
12. Install spring bottom cup and spring over rod of tool Sus. 594 or equivalent.
13. Using tools Sus. 594 and Sus. 594-02 or equivalents, compress spring until sixth coil can be held by tool Sus. 863 or equivalent, then remove tools Sus. 594 and Sus. 594-02.
14. Secure body of new shock absorber in vise, then install components (7), (6) and (5), **Fig. 8**, shock absorber.
15. Install spring, with tool Sus. 863, ensuring that end of bottom coil rests against stop in bottom cup.
16. Install washer (4) and component (2) with its plastic spring thrust cup, noting locating peg (B), **Fig. 9.**
17. Install washer and nut, then remove tool Sus. 863 and torque piston rod nut to 44 ft. lbs.
18. Install spring and shock absorber assembly on vehicle by pressing lower suspension arm down so that shock absorber does not contact driveshaft boot.
19. Install two shock absorber top mounting bolts and torque to 17 ft. lbs.
20. Install two bottom mounting bolts and nuts with nuts toward front of vehicle and torque nuts to 55 ft. lbs.
21. Install wheel and lower vehicle.

LE CAR

1. Raise front of vehicle and place on jack stands. Position jack stands on the frame members.
2. Raise lower control arm with suitable jack to counter the tension of the torsion bar and the anti-sway bar.
3. Remove the nuts on top of the shock absorber. Disconnect the anti-sway bar where it attaches to the shock absorber lower bolt and where it attaches to the frame behind the shock absorber.
4. Remove the nut on the shock absorber bottom pin and remove the pin.
5. Remove the shock absorber.
6. Reverse procedure to install, noting the following:
   a. Lubricate the lower shock absorber pin with suitable grease.
   b. Install shock absorber and hand tighten all nuts.
   c. Lower vehicle and tighten all nuts with the wheels on the ground.

FUEGO, 18i & SPORTWAGON

1. Raise and support vehicle, then remove front wheels.
2. Position suitable jack under lower ball joint and raise suspension until vehicle is lifted from vehicle support on that side.
3. Compress coil spring using suitable spring compressor, then lower suspension until spring is freed from upper spring cup.
4. Loosen stabilizer bar link to lower shock absorber mounting bolt, then disconnect upper end of shock absorber.
5. Disconnect lower end of shock absorber by holding locknut and rotating shock absorber until spring, compressor tool and shock absorber can be removed as an assembly.
6. Reverse procedure to install.

FRONT TORSION BAR REPLACE

LE CAR

1. Raise vehicle on a lift and allow the wheels to hang free.
2. At the suspension end of the torsion bar, mark the torsion bar and the suspension arm with paint or chalk to show where the torsion bar is located in the suspension arm. Mark the other end of the torsion bar and the end bearing to show the location of the end bearing to the torsion bar.
3. Loosen the two bearing mounting bolts, **Fig. 10.**
4. Remove outer nut and washer from the bearing.
5. Install Renault tool Sus. 704 over the outer bolt referred to in the above step and secure with the nut.
6. Insert a 3 to 4 foot pipe on the end of the Sus. 704 wrench. Pull up on the bar slightly and remove the inner bearing bolt, **Fig. 11.** Lower the tool and allow the torsion bar to unwind.
7. Remove the tool, the bearing outer bolt and the torsion bar.
8. Assemble the end bearing to the torsion bar with side A towards the top and offset B towards the front of the vehicle, **Fig. 12. The rubber sleeve is closer to one end of the torsion bar and should be installed toward the front of the vehicle.**
9. With the end bearing assembled correctly to the torsion bar, push the bearing over the splines and onto the bar.
10. Using the outer bolt only, attach the bearing and hand tighten the nut. Align the bearing as shown **Fig. 13,** with the dimension Y = $2\frac{11}{16}'' \pm \frac{5}{64}$ (68 mm ±2 mm).
11. Insert the torsion bar into the lower suspension arm and the end bearing. The marks made during disassembly

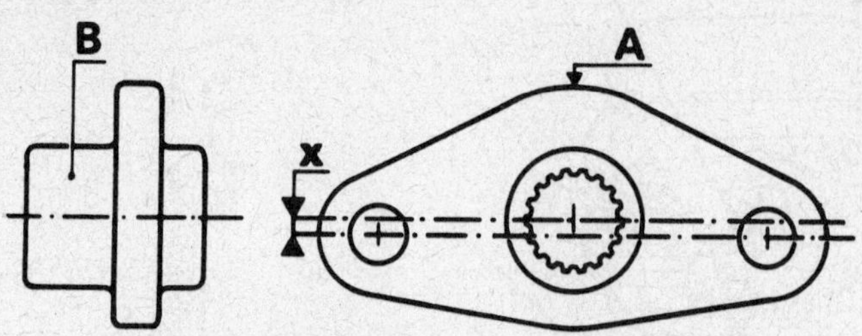

Fig. 12 Torsion bar end bearing installation. Le Car

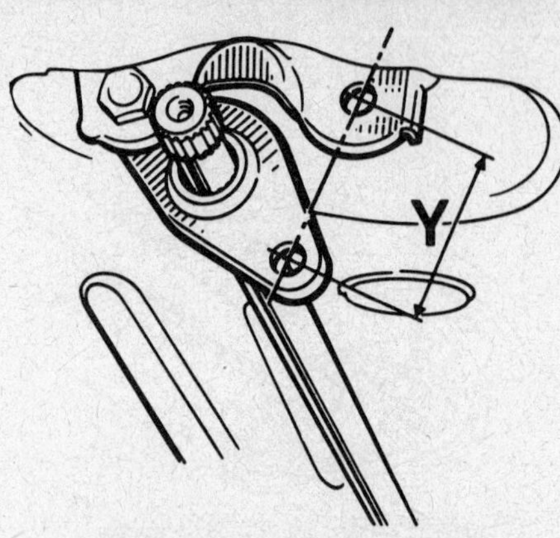

Fig. 13 Torsion bar alignment. Le Car

should line up. If not, remove the bar and offset the end bearing slightly and reinstall the torsion bar.

12. Attach the Renault Sus. 704 tool the same way as for bar removal.
13. Pull up the bar with steady pressure to wind up the torsion bar. Install the inner bearing mounting bolt.
14. Remove the tool and tighten both bolts to 90 ft. lbs. (12 N-m).
15. Lower the vehicle and drive for 1/2 mile to settle the suspension.
16. Check and adjust ride height as outlined in "Wheel Alignment Section."

FRONT SPRING
REPLACE
EXC. LE CAR

Follow procedure given in "Shock Absorber, Replace."

FRONT HUB, ROTOR & WHEEL BEARINGS
REPLACE
ALLIANCE, ENCORE & GTA
Removal

1. Raise and support front of vehicle, allowing wheels to hang free, then remove wheel.
2. Remove caliper and secure aside, taking care not to stretch brake hose.
3. Hold hub with suitable bar, then remove nut from end of drive axle.
4. Remove machine screws or stamped nuts, if equipped, then remove brake rotor from hub.
5. Remove hub assembly with slide type puller, ensuring puller is installed directly in line with centerline of hub. **Use of any type puller which attaches to the outer rim of the hub and is offset from centerline may damage hub and/or bearings.**
6. Remove bearing sleeve from hub using suitable puller.
7. Remove bolts securing strut to steering knuckle and remove ball joint pinch bolt.
8. Press drive axle inward and remove steering knuckle, then secure axle to prevent it from falling. **Do not allow axle to slip out of transaxle, and do not stress CV joints.**
9. Remove bearing snap ring from steering knuckle, drive bearing inner race and rollers from knuckle using suitable drift, then remove bearing outer race using inner race as a driver.
10. Clean and inspect hub and knuckle bearing surface, and replace as needed.

Installation

1. Press new bearing into knuckle using 2.5 inch diameter spacer, ensuring bearing is seated in knuckle. **Apply press force to bearing outer race only. Bearing will be damaged if force is applied to inner race.**
2. Install bearing snap ring in steering knuckle and press new bearing sleeve onto hub.
3. Lubricate bearing seal lips, then install hub in steering knuckle.
4. Guide drive axle through steering knuckle and hub, mount knuckle on ball joint, then install pinch bolt and strut retaining bolts and torque strut bolts to 55 ft. lbs. and pinch bolt to 40 ft. lbs.
5. Reverse remaining procedure to complete installation, and torque drive axle nut to 154 ft. lbs.

FUEGO, 18i & SPORTWAGON

1. Remove hub cap, then loosen but do not remove drive axle nut.
2. Install spacer T.Av. 509.01 or equivalent between shock mounting on upper control arm and lower control arm shaft to unload suspension, raise and support vehicle, and remove wheel.
3. Remove brake pads, then the caliper mounting bolts, and secure caliper aside taking care not to stretch brake hose.
4. Remove bolts securing rotor to hub, then the rotor.
5. Remove drive axle nut, position suitable block behind hub, then remove hub by threading 2 wheel bolts through hub, 180° apart, and pressing against block. Tighten bolts gradually and evenly to ensure hub is pressed off straight.
6. Remove outer bearing from hub using suitable puller.
7. Remove 6 torx bolts securing bearing retainer to steering knuckle, the bearing and inner race.
8. Slide bearing over stub axle, seat bearing in knuckle and torque retaining bolts to 11 ft. lbs.
9. Press bearing race onto hub using 1.575 inch diameter spacer.
10. Pack bearings with suitable grease, then install hub over stub axle, driving hub into place until drive axle nut can be installed.
11. Hold hub with suitable bar and torque drive axle nut to 185 ft. lbs, then reverse remaining procedure to complete installation.

STEERING KNUCKLE
REPLACE
ALLIANCE, ENCORE & GTA

Refer to "Front Hub, Rotor and Wheel Bearings, Replace."

FUEGO, 18i & SPORTWAGON

1. Remove hub cap, then loosen but do not remove drive axle nut.
2. Raise vehicle, support lower control arms and remove wheel.
3. Remove brake pads, then the caliper mounting bolts, and secure caliper aside taking care not to stretch brake hose.
4. Remove drive axle nut, bolts securing rotor to hub, then the rotor.
5. Remove 6 wheel bearing retaining nuts through opening in hub, then remove hub and bearing as an assembly.
6. Disconnect tie rod and the upper and lower ball joints, then remove steering knuckle.
7. Reverse procedure to install.

FRONT DRIVE AXLE
REPLACE
ALLIANCE, ENCORE & GTA

1. Raise and support side of vehicle to be serviced.
2. Remove wheel.
3. Remove caliper assembly and position out of way without straining brake hose.
4. Remove nut and disconnect tie rod from steering knuckle using suitable puller.
5. Remove bolts securing strut to steering knuckle.
6. Hold hub with suitable bar, then remove stub axle nut.

7. If removing left side, proceed as follows:
   a. Drain oil from transaxle.
   b. Remove three shaft mounting bolts, then slide shaft and boot out of transaxle. **Use extreme caution to ensure that the three rollers on the constant velocity shaft are not dislodged. After removing shaft, tape constant velocity joint to prevent components from falling apart.**
   c. Slide drive axle out of hub and remove from vehicle.
8. If removing right side, proceed as follows;
   a. Drive out roll pin securing inner CV joint to transaxle side gear using drift B.Vi. 31-01 or equivalent.
   b. Tilt steering knuckle outward, then slide drive axle out of hub, then the transaxle.
9. Reverse procedure to install, torquing shock absorber bottom mounting nuts to 40 ft. lbs., transaxle bellows bolts to 18 ft. lbs., steering arm ball joint nut to 25 ft. lbs., brake caliper bolts to 26 ft. lbs., drive shaft hub nut to 154 ft. lbs., and wheel lug nuts to 55 ft. lbs.

FUEGO

1. Compress front half-axle and place spacer T.Av. 509-01 or equivalent between lower arm pivot shaft and shock absorber bottom pillar shaft.
2. Raise and support side of vehicle to be serviced and remove wheel.
3. Using tool Rou. 604-01 or equivalent remove stub axle nut.
4. Loosen but do not remove upper ball joint nut and steering arm ball joint nut.
5. Using tool T.Av. 476 or equivalent, loosen ball joint cones.
6. Remove brake caliper assembly without disconnecting lines.
7. Remove ball joint nuts and tilt stub axle carrier to disengage driveshaft.
8. Using drift pin B.Vi. 31-01 or equivalent, drive out roll pins from coupling on transmission housing side.
9. Remove driveshaft.
10. Reverse procedure to install, torquing upper ball joint nut to 48 ft. lbs., steering arm ball joint to 30 ft. lbs., stub axle nut to 185 ft. lbs., and wheel lug nuts to 59 ft. lbs.

LE CAR, 18i & SPORTWAGON

1. Raise vehicle and let the wheels hang free. On 18i & Sportwagon install Renault spacer bar T.Av. 509 or suitable spacer between the lower hinge pin and the lower mount of the shock absorber. Position as far forward as possible against the upper arm so that it will not interfere with removal of the drive axle.
2. On 18i & Sportwagon, remove the roll pins at the transmission end of the drive axle with a drift.
3. Loosen but do not remove the tie rod and the upper ball joint on the stub axle carrier.
4. Remove the stub axle nut and washer.
5. Using suitable tool, press in the end of the drive axle to break loose from the stub axle carrier.
6. Remove the brake caliper and place in a secure place so that it does not hang by the brake hose.
7. Remove the upper ball joint and the tie rod end from the stub axle carrier.
8. Tilt the stub axle carrier outward and back and pull the end of the axle out of the stub axle carrier.
9. Pull the axle out of the transmission.
10. Lubricate the splines and insert the drive axle into the transmission. On 18i & Sportwagon, be sure to line up the roll pin holes and install the roll pins. Seal the ends of the roll pins with suitable sealer.
11. Position the outer end of the drive axle into the stub axle carrier.
12. Reposition the stub axle carrier and pull the driveshaft through the hub. Reconnect the upper ball joint and the tie rod end.
13. Install the stub axle washer and a new stub axle nut. Torque to: Model 5 (Le Car) — 90 ft. lbs. (12 N-m) Model 18i and Sportwagon — 185 ft. lbs. (25 N-m).
14. Reinstall brake caliper.
15. Lower the vehicle and remove the upper suspension arm spacer on Renault 18i and Sportwagon vehicles.

STEERING GEAR REPLACE

ALLIANCE, ENCORE & GTA

1. Raise and support front of vehicle.
2. Remove steering arm ball joint nuts.
3. Using tool T.Av. 476 or equivalent, remove ball joint assembly.
4. Remove universal joint bolt.
5. Note position of steering wheel, universal joint, and steering rack and pinion in relation to each other. Mark position of steering rack and pinion.
6. Remove two steering rack and pinion mounting bolts.
7. Remove steering rack and pinion complete with arms.
8. Reverse procedure to install, torquing steering ball joint nut to 26 ft. lbs., and steering rack and pinion mounting bolts to 40 ft. lbs.

FUEGO

1. If equipped with power steering, clamp each hose on oil reservoir.
2. If equipped with power steering, disconnect pipes on rotating valve from reservoir and high pressure pump.
3. Raise and support front of vehicle.
4. Remove tie rod end nuts.
5. Remove steering universal joint key bolt and disconnect universal joint, marking its position in relation to splines of steering pinion.
6. Remove four rack housing bolts on crossmember.
7. Remove entire steering rack assembly through hole on cowl side.
8. Reverse procedure to install, torquing ball joint assembly nut to 30 ft. lbs. and tie rod locknut to 26 ft. lbs.

LE CAR 18i & SPORTWAGON

1. Remove the battery and the battery tray.
2. Disconnect the steering shaft at the flex coupling. Retain the rubber spacer.
3. Disconnect the tie rods at the rack end.
4. On vehicles equipped with power steering, disconnect power steering hoses at steering gear and plug openings to prevent entry of dirt.
5. Remove the rack mounting bolts, mark and remove the shims. If equipped with eccentric cams, do not move the cams. Remove the rack.
6. Reverse procedure to install. Be sure to install the adjustment shims in correct position marked during removal.

POWER STEERING VALVE REPLACE

FUEGO, 18i & SPORTWAGON

1. Remove battery and battery support.
2. Remove plastic clips securing metal shield to firewall, then remove shields.
3. Position power steering valve dust boot rearward toward firewall.
4. Remove steering column instrument panel support.
5. Disconnect steering column from power steering valve, then remove steering column.
6. Loosen power steering valve adjusting nut, then remove valve retaining bolts and the valve.
7. Reverse procedure to install. To adjust valve, torque adjusting nut to 8 ft. lbs. (1 Nm), then back off nut 1/4 turn. Secure adjusting nut by bending locknut tabs downward.

WHEEL ALIGNMENT SECTION

INDEX

PRELIMINARY CHECK

1. Road test vehicle noting any abnormal steering or handling characteristics.
2. Ensure tires are the proper type, correctly inflated and that tires on each axle are the same size.
3. Inspect ball joints, suspension arms, bushings and tie rods, and repair or replace any component that is damaged or excessively worn.
4. Ensure wheel runout is not excessive, and that wheel bearings are properly adjusted.
5. Check underbody height (ride height) and correct as needed. If ride height is not within specified ranges, check for excessive or uneven vehicle loading, weak springs and damaged suspension components.
6. Jounce vehicle several times to settle suspension.
7. Place vehicle on suitable alignment rack following manufacturer's instructions.
8. Center steering gear as follows:
   a. Turn steering wheel to full left turn position, then place reference mark on steering wheel rim.
   b. Turn steering wheel to full right turn position, counting number of turns necessary.
   c. Turn wheel back to the left, one-half the number of turns counted in previous step, then secure steering wheel in this position. **If steering wheel is not straight with steering gear centered, remove wheel and align as needed. If front wheels are not in straight ahead position adjust tie rods to obtain correct toe, as needed, prior to performing other checks.**
9. Check and correct alignment angles in the following sequence: Rear toe and camber, caster, front camber and front toe.
10. Correct any angle that is not within specifications. If no adjustment is possible, check for damaged or worn suspension components and/or damaged or distorted chassis and correct as needed.

RIDE HEIGHT ADJUSTMENT

ALLIANCE, ENCORE & GTA

Only the rear ride height can be adjusted on these vehicles. If front ride height cannot be brought within specifications by adjusting rear height, check for damaged or worn suspension components and replace as needed.

1. Adjust tire pressures to 35 psi, ensure vehicle is unloaded and that fuel tank is full. **Tank must be full to obtain accurate ride height measurement.**
2. Place unloaded vehicle on flat surface.
3. Measure distance between top center of each wheelwell and the floor, along the centerline of the wheel.
4. Distances should be as shown in chart, **Fig. 1,** and left to right side variation should not exceed .315 inch (8 mm).
5. If ride height is not within specifications, adjust as follows:
   a. Raise and support vehicle and remove torsion bar as outlined in "Rear Suspension Section."
   b. Install fabricated suspension arm positioning tool in place of shock absorber, and adjust length of tool to 24.04 inches on all except GS and GTA models, 22.9 inches on GTA with green and orange color code, 22.6 inches on GTA with green and white color code, 23.1 inches on GS with green and yellow color code, or 22.8 inches on GS with white and orange color code. **Color code consists of 2 paint marks on top of the suspension arm.**
   c. Reinstall torsion bar, then the shock absorber and recheck and record ride height.
   d. If ride height is still not not within specifications, remove torsion bar and reinstall suspension positioning tool in place of shock absorber.
   e. Increase or decrease length of positioning tool in 3 mm increments to adjust ride height. To increase rear ride height by .12 inch, increase length of tool by 3 mm. To decrease rear ride height by .12 inch, decrease length of tool by 3 mm.
   f. Install torsion bar, then remove positioning tool and install shock absorber and check adjustment.
   g. Repeat procedure, as needed, until ride height is within specifications.
6. Check headlight aim and adjust as necessary.

	FRONT	REAR
Encore 3-Door	635 to 648 mm (25.0 to 25.51 in.)	630 to 643 mm (24.80 to 25.32 in.)
Encore 5-Door	635 to 648 mm (25.0 to 25.51 in.)	515 to 528 mm (20.28 to 20.79 in.)
Alliance 4-Door	635 to 648 mm (25.0 to 25.51 in.)	515 to 528 mm (20.28 to 20.79 in.)
Alliance 2-Door	635 to 648 mm (25.0 to 25.51 in.)	604 to 617 mm (23.78 to 24.29 in.)
Convertible	635 to 648 mm (25.0 to 25.51 in.)	604 to 617 mm (23.78 to 24.29 in.)
GTA	615 to 628 mm (24.21 to 24.72 in.)	594 to 607 mm (23.39 to 23.90 in.)

Fig. 1 Ride height specifications. Alliance, Encore & GTA

FUEGO 18I & SPORTWAGON

Ride height on these vehicles is not adjustable. Front and rear ride height must be measured in order to calculate the angle of the floor pan, which is used to determine the correct caster angle. Measure ride height and determine floor pan angle as follows:

1. Place unloaded vehicle on flat surface.
2. Measure and record front ride height (H2) between front side rail and ground at centerline of front wheels, **Fig. 2.**
3. Measure and record rear ride height (H5) between side arm bolt and ground, **Figs. 2 and 3.**
4. Calculate the difference between the measurements and record difference to determine correct caster angle.

LE CAR

Ride height and road clearance are de-

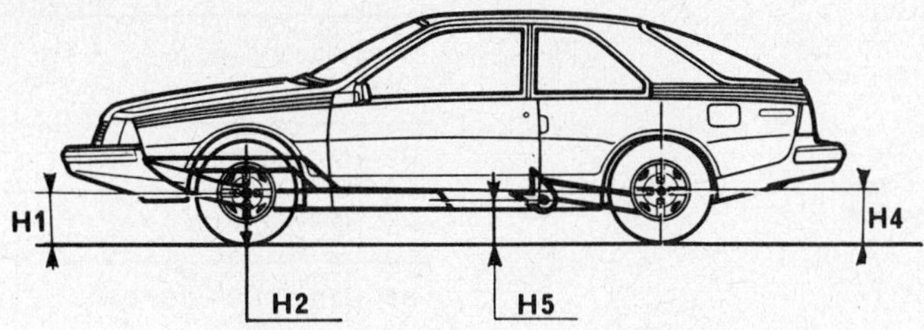

Fig. 1 Ride height measurements. Fuego, 18i & Sportwagon

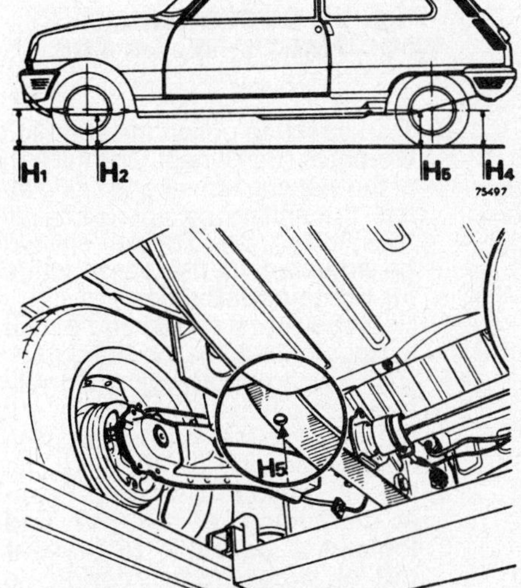

Fig. 4 Ride height measurements. Le Car

termined by measuring the height of the wheel center from the ground minus the height of the frame side member from the ground, and the correct caster angle is determined by subtracting the front ride height from the rear ride height. In order to calculate the correct caster angle, both front and rear ride height must be within specifications.

Ride height is adjusted by increasing or decreasing torsion bar preload. To check and adjust ride height, proceed as follows:

1. Place unloaded vehicle on flat surface.
2. Measure and record heights H1 and H4 from wheel centerlines to the ground, **Fig. 4.**
3. Measure and record heights H2 and H5 from frame side members to ground. Measure H2 from level area of frame, and measure H5 from punched hole, **Fig. 4.**
4. Calculate the difference between H1 and H2 for both right and left sides and record remainders. Difference should be 1⅞-2⅝ inches (48-68 mm), and the maximum variation between right and left sides must not exceed ⅜ inch (10 mm).
5. Calculate the difference between H4 and H5 for both right and left sides and record remainders. Difference should be −7/16-−1/16 inch (−11-−1 mm), and the maximum variation between right and left sides must not exceed ⅜ inch (10 mm).
6. If ride height is not within specifications, adjust torsion bar tension by rotating adjusting cam at end of torsion bar. If correct height cannot be obtained within range of adjusting cam, remove cam housing cover and lower torsion bar as outlined in applicable "Torsion Bar, Replace" procedure, then offset adjusting lever one spline on the end of the torsion bar.
7. When ride height is within specifications, measure and record frame member heights (H2 and H5) for use in determining correct caster angle.

CASTER ADJUSTMENT

ALLIANCE, ENCORE & GTA

Check caster angle with vehicle unloaded and ride height within specifications. Caster angle should be +/12° to +2° and maximum variation between right and left side settings should not exceed ¾°.

Caster angle is not adjustable. The most common causes for incorrect caster angle are damaged suspension arm or side sill, damaged front end sheet metal particularly in strut tower area, and damaged steering knuckle or strut. **If caster angle is incorrect, loosen top strut mounting nut and rotate strut shaft. If caster angle changes, strut shaft is bent.**

FUEGO, 18i & SPORTWAGON

Caster angle on these vehicles is dependent on the angle of the vehicle floor in relation to the ground. To determine correct caster angle, measure front and rear ride height as outlined, calculate and record the difference between measurements and check and adjust caster as follows:

1. Check caster angle with vehicle unloaded and compare to specifications, **Fig. 5.**
2. If caster is not within specifications, remove bolt securing strut rod to upper control arm and adjust rod length to alter setting. One full turn of rod will alter caster angle by ¼°.
3. Reconnect strut rod, and recheck caster angle, repeating adjustment until caster is within specifications shown in **Fig. 5,** ensuring that maximum variation between right and left side settings does not exceed 1°.
4. When caster angle is within specifications, tighten strut rod locknut and torque mounting bolt to 59 ft. lbs.

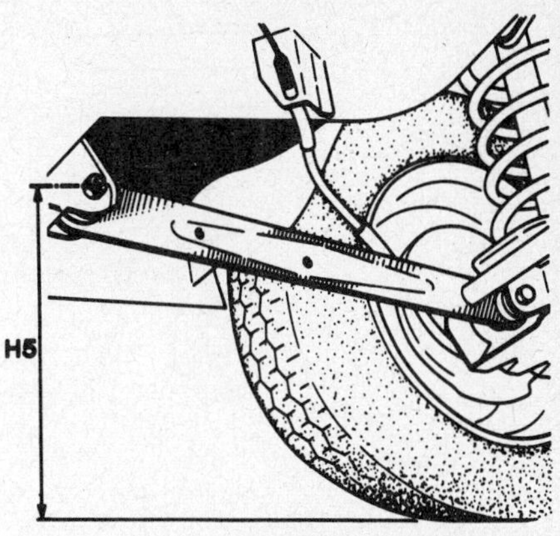

Fig. 3 Measuring rear suspension height. Fuego, 18i & Sportwagon

Vehicle Floor Position H5 – H2 Inches	Caster Angle ±½°
H5 – H2 = 20mm	3°30'
H5 – H2 = 35mm	3°
H5 – H2 = 55mm	2°30'
H5 – H2 = 70mm	2D

Fig. 5 Caster angle specifications. Fuego, 18i & Sportwagon

LE CAR

Caster is adjusted by adding shims (1) to the lower suspension arm, **Fig. 6.**

1. Measure and record front and rear ride height for both left and right sides as outlined. **If ride height is not within specifications , adjust as needed prior to checking caster angle.**
2. Subtract front ride height from rear ride height and refer to **Fig. 7** to calculate correct caster angle.
3. Check caster angle following equipment manufacturer's instructions. Caster angle should be as shown in **Fig. 7,** and maximum variation between left and right side settings should not exceed 1°.
4. If caster angle is incorrect, loosen the two lower suspension arm bushing mounting bolts.
5. Add a shim to increase the caster and remove to decrease.
6. One shim changes the caster approximately 1°. Do not use more than two adjusting shims on each side of the vehicle.

CAMBER ADJUSTMENT

FRONT

Measure camber angle with vehicle unloaded following equipment manufacturer's instructions. Camber should be as shown in "Wheel Alignment Specifications," and the maximum variation between left and right side settings should not exceed ¾° for Alliance, Encore and GTA, or 1° for all other models.

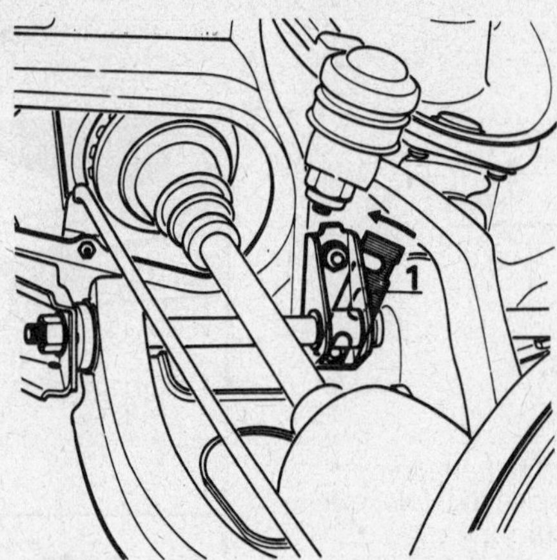

Fig. 6 Caster adjustment. Renault 5 (Le Car)

Vehicle floor position	Castor angle value
H5–H2 = 1 9/16" (40 mm)	12°30′
H5–H2 = 2 3/8" (60 mm)	12°
H5–H2 = 3 1/8" (80 mm)	11°30′
H5–H2 = 3 15/16" (100 mm)	11°
H5–H2 = 4 3/4" (120 mm)	10°30′
H5–H2 = 5 1/2" (140 mm)	10°

Fig. 7 Caster angle specifications. Le Car

Camber angle is not adjustable. The most common causes for incorrect camber angle are bent wheels, worn suspension arm bushings, damaged suspension arm, side sill or sheet metal, particularly in strut tower ares, and damaged steering knuckle or strut. **If camber angle is incorrect, loosen top strut mounting nut and rotate strut shaft. If camber angle changes, strut shaft is bent.**

REAR

Rear camber angle should be checked with vehicle unloaded and ride height adjusted to specifications as outlined, and after rear toe setting and equalization of toe over the two rear wheels has been brought within specifications. Camber angle should be as shown in "Wheel Alignment Specifications," and maximum variation between left and right side settings should not exceed 1°.

Rear camber is not adjustable. If settings are not within specifications, check for damaged, distorted, or worn suspension components and damaged sheet metal, and correct as needed.

TOE-OUT ADJUSTMENT

FRONT

1. Ensure that steering gear is centered as outlined in "Preliminary Checks," and that steering wheel is in the straight ahead position.
2. Using a suitable tool, lock steering wheel in the straight ahead position.
3. Measure total toe-out and distribution over two wheels, either in relation to the rear wheel assembly or in relation to the body sill.
4. If toe-out setting is not within specifications, adjust as follows:
   a. Hold tie rod on flat with suitable adjusting wrench and loosen tie rod end locknut.
   b. Turn tie rod to obtain the specified toe-out at each wheel. One full turn of the steering arm or end fitting alters toe setting by approximately .125 inch (3 mm). **Toe out should be adjusted to the same value for right and left sides.**
   c. Hold position of tie rod and torque locknut to 26 ft. lbs. on Fuego, LeCar, 18i and Sportwagon. On Alliance, Encore and GTA, torque lock nut to 30 ft. lbs. on models with manual steering or 40 ft. lbs. on models with power steering. **Proper tightening of tie rod end locknut is essential to prevent dirt or water from entering tie rod.**

REAR

Rear toe should be checked with vehicle unloaded and ride height adjusted to specifications as outlined. Total toe should be within specifications, and toe for left and right wheels should be equal.

Rear toe is not adjustable. If settings are not within specifications, check for damaged, distorted, or worn suspension components and damaged sheet metal, and correct as needed.

SAAB (Sweden)

INDEX OF SERVICE OPERATIONS

General Engine Specifications

Year	Engine	Fuel System	Bore x Stroke In. (mm)	Comp. Ratio	Maximum Brake H.P. @ RPM	Maximum Torque Ft. Lbs. @ RPM	Normal Oil Pressure psi
1983–84	4-121/1985cc ①	Fuel Inj.	3.54 x 3.07 (90 x 78)	9.25	110 @ 5250	119 @ 3500	43
	4-121/1985cc ②	Fuel Inj.	3.54 x 3.07 (90 x 78)	③	135 @ 4800	160 @ 3500	43
1985–86	4-121/1985cc ①	Fuel Inj.	3.54 x 3.07 (90 x 78)	9.25	110 @ 5250	119 @ 3500	43
	4-121/1985cc ④	Fuel Inj.	3.54 x 3.07 (90 x 78)	8.5	135 @ 4800	160 @ 3500	43
	4-121/1985cc ⑤	Fuel Inj.	3.54 x 3.07 (90 x 78)	9.0	160 @ 5500	188 @ 3000	43
1986	4-121/1985cc ⑥	Fuel Inj.	3.54 x 3.07 (90 x 78)	9.2	110 @ 5250	119 @ 3500	—
	4-121/1985cc ⑦	Fuel Inj.	3.54 x 3.07 (90 x 78)	9.0	160 @ 5500	188 @ 3000	—
	4-121/1985cc ⑧	Fuel Inj.	3.54 x 3.07 (90 x 78)	9.0	160 @ 5500	188 @ 3000	—
1987	4-121/1985cc ⑥	Fuel Inj.	3.54 x 3.07 (90 x 78)	9.2	110 @ 5250	119 @ 3500	—
	4-121/1985cc ⑧	Fuel Inj.	3.54 x 3.07 (90 x 78)	10.1	125 @ 5500	123 @ 3000	—
	4-121/1985cc ⑨	Fuel Inj.	3.54 x 3.07 (90 x 78)	10.1	125 @ 5500	123 @ 3000	—
	4-121/1985cc ②	Fuel Inj.	3.54 x 3.07 (90 x 78)	9.0	160 @ 5500	188 @ 3000	—
	4-121/1985cc ⑦	Fuel Inj.	3.54 x 3.07 (90 x 78)	9.0	165 @ 5500	195 @ 3000	—

①—Except turbocharged models.
②—Turbocharged models.
③—Except APC, 7.2; w/APC, 8.5.
④—Turbocharged APC engine.
⑤—Turbocharged 16 engine.
⑥—900 sedan model.
⑦—900 Turbo 3-door model.
⑧—Saab 9000.
⑨—900S, 16 valve non-turbocharged engines.

Alternator & Regulator Specifications

Year	Alternator					Regulator
		Rated Hot Output		Output @ 14 Volts		
	Model	Amps.	Volts	Amps. @ RPM ① ②	Amps. @ RPM ①	
1983–87	Bosch K1-14V 55A 20	55	14	36 @ 2000	55 @ 6000	Integral
	Bosch K1-14V 65A 21	65	14	44 @ 2100	65 @ 6000	Integral
	Bosch K1-14V 70A 20	70	14	46 @ 2000	70 @ 6000	Integral
	Bosch N1-14V 80A 19	80	14	54 @ 1900	80 @ 6000	Integral
	Motorola 70A	70	14	36.5 @ 1800	72 @ 8000	Integral
	Bosch K1-14V 70A 20	70	14	46 @ 2000	70 @ 6000	Integral
	Bosch N1-14V 80A 19	80	14	54 @ 2000	80 @ 6000	Integral
	Bosch K1-14V 70A 20	70	14	46 @ 2000	70 @ 6000	Integral

①—Alternator RPM.
②—"In Car Test" specifications.

Starting Motor Specifications

Year	Model	Starter Number	Brush Spring Tension Oz.	No Load Test			Load Test		
				Amps	Volts	RPM	Amps	Volts	RPM
1983–84	900	0 001 311 108	41–46	32–55	11.5	6500–8500	205–235	9	1000–1300
1985–87	900 & 9000	0 001 108 012	—	70	12	3000 ①	315	9	1700 ①

①—Minimum.

Valve Specifications

Year	Engine Model	Valve Lash		Valve Angles		Valve Spring Installed Height	Valve Spring Pressure Lbs. @ In.	Stem Clearance		Stem Diameter	
		Int.	Exh.	Seat	Face			Intake	Exhaust	Intake	Exhaust
1983–84	2.0 litre⑥	.009	.017①	45	44.5	1.555	176 @ 1.16	.01968	.01968	.3134–.3140	.3132–.3142
1985	2.0 litre② ⑥	.009	.017①	45	44.5	1.555	176 @ 1.16	.01968	.01968	.3134–.3140	.3132–.3142
	2.0 litre③ ⑥	.009	.019	45	44.5	1.457	139 @ 1.12	.01968	.01968	.3134–.3140	.3132–.3142
1986	2.0 litre③ ⑤	④	④	45	44.5	1.457	139 @ 1.12	.01968	.01968	.2740–.2746	.2738–.2798
1987	2.0 litre③ ⑥	.009	.019	45	44.5	1.457	139 @ 1.12	.01968	.01968	.3134–.3140	.3132–.3142
1987	2.0 litre③ ⑤	④	④	45	44.5	1.457	139 @ 1.12	.01968	.01968	.2740–.2746	.2738–.2798

①—Turbo, .019.
②—Exc. turbo 16 engine.
③—Turbo 16 engine.
④—Non-adjustable.
⑤—9000 model.
⑥—900 model.

Pistons, Pins, Rings, Crankshaft & Bearings

Year	Engine Model	Piston Clearance	Ring End Gap		Wrist Pin Diameter	Rod Bearings		Main Bearings			
			Comp.	Oil		Shaft Diameter	Bearing Clearance	Shaft Diameter	Bearing Clearance	Thrust on Bear. No.	Shaft End Play
1983–87	2.0 litre② ⑦	③	①	.0149	.9448	2.0465—2.0472	.0010–.0024	2872–2.2835	.00078–.0024	3	.003–.011
	2.0 litre④ ⑦	.0009–.0020	①	.0149	.9448	2.0465–2.0472	.0010–.0024	2.2872–2.2835	.00078–.0024	3	.003–.011
1986–87	2.0 litre⑤ ⑥	.0008–.0020	①	.0149	.9448	2.0465–2.0472	.0010–.0024	2.2827–2.2835	.0008–.0024	3	.003–.011

①—Upper ring, .013–.021 in.; lower ring, .0118–.0177 in.
②—Non-turbocharged engines and turbo 16 engine.
③—W/Mahle pistons, .0006–.0013 in.; w/Schmidt pistons, .0006–.0019 in.
④—Turbocharged engines.
⑤—Turbo 16 engine.
⑥—9000 model.
⑦—900 model.
⑧—99 model.

Engine Tightening Specifications

*Torque specifications are for clean and lightly lubricated threads only. Dry or dirty threads produce increased friction which prevents accurate measurement of tightness.

Year	Model	Spark Plugs Ft. Lbs.	Cylinder Head Bolts Ft. Lbs.	Intake Manifold Ft. Lbs.	Exhaust Manifold Ft. Lbs.	Camshaft Bearing Cap Ft. Lbs.	Rocker Arm Cover Ft. Lbs.	Connecting Rod Cap Bolts Ft. Lbs.	Main Bearing Cap Bolts Ft. Lbs.	Flywheel To Crankshaft Ft. Lbs.	Vibration Damper or Pulley Ft. L bs.
1983–87	900	20	①	13	③	④	②	40	81	44	140
1986–87	9000	20	⑤	13.5	19	11	3.7	40	81	44	140

①—Bolts with 17 mm head, 69 ft. lbs.; bolts with 15 mm head, 65 ft. lbs. Refer to text.
②—1983–87, 3.6 ft. lbs.; turbo 16 engine, 11 ft. lbs.
③—Turbo, 18 ft. lbs.; non-turbo, 15 ft. lbs.
④—Exc. turbo 16 engine, 13 ft. lbs.; turbo 16 engine, 11 ft. lbs.
⑤—Torque all bolts to 66 ft. lbs., then tighten each bolt an additional 90°.

Brake Specifications

Year	Model	Caliper Bore Diameter		Master Cylinder Bore Diameter	Disc Brake Rotor					
					Nominal Thickness		Minimum Thickness		Run Out (TIR)	
		Front	Rear		Front	Rear	Front	Rear	Front	Rear
1983–87	900	2.126	1.181	7/8	.500	.413	.461	.374	.004	.004
1986–87	9000	—	—	7/8	.866	.354	.787	.295	.003	.003

Cooling System & Capacity Data

Year	Model	Cooling System Capacity Qts.	Rad. Cap Relief Pressure Lbs.	Thermostat Opening Temp. Deg. F.	Fuel Tank Capacity Gals.	Engine Oil Refill Qts. ①	Transaxle Capacity Pints			
							Manual		Automatic	
							4 Speed	5 Speed	Trans.	Final Drive
1983–87	900	10.5	12.9–17.1	④	16.6	3.7②	5.2	6.4	17	③
1986–87	9000	10.5	13–17	192	18	②	—	5.1	—	—

①—Includes oil for filter change.
②—With turbocharger, 4.3 qts.; turbo 16 engine, 14.7 qts.
③—Trans. type BW-35, 2.6 pts.; trans. type BW-37, 3.0 pts.
④—1981–82, 192°F; 1983–85, 180°F.

Wheel Alignment Specifications

Year	Model	Caster Angle, Degrees		Camber Angle, Degrees				Toe-In, Inches		Toe-Out On Turns, Degrees	
				Front		Rear					
		Limits	Desired	Limits	Desired	Limits	Desired	Front	Rear	Inner Wheel	Outer Wheel
1983–87	900	①	②	0 to +1	+1/2	−3/4 to −1/4	−1/2	.04 to .12	.04 to .12③	20 1/4 to 21 1/4	20
1986–87	9000	+1.15 to +2.15	+1.65	−.65 to 1.15	−.65	0 to −.50	−.25	+.02 to +.10 ③	+.04 to +.20 ③	20 1/2 to 21 1/2	20

①—Exc. power steering, +1/2°–+1 1/2°; power steering, +1 1/2°–+2 1/2°.
②—Exc. power steering, +1°; power steering, +2°.
③—Per side.

ELECTRICAL SECTION

INDEX

ALTERNATOR IN-VEHICLE TESTING

1. Connect a suitable volt/amp tester to electrical system following manufacturers' instructions. **Alternator output voltage should be checked between the battery positive post and the alternator ground.**
2. Connect a suitable tachometer to engine, start engine and run until it reaches normal operating temperature.
3. Apply current load to alternator and set engine to run at following speeds. Engine RPM specifications are approximate speeds calculated to obtain the alternator RPM specified for testing.
   a. 55 amp alternator, 900 RPM.
   b. 65 amp alternator, 950 RPM.
   c. 70 amp Motorola, 800 RPM.
   d. 1983 70 amp Bosch, 975 RPM.
   e. 1984-87 70 amp Bosch, 850 RPM.
   f. 80 amp alternator, 800 RPM.
4. Alternator should deliver specified output, at the rated voltage, as listed in "Alternator Specifications."
5. If output is not within specifications, check drivebelt, feed and ground circuits, and repair as needed.
6. If wiring and drive belt are satisfactory, but output is not within specifications, alternator must be repaired or replaced.

STARTER REPLACE

MODEL 900, EXC. TURBO

1. Disconnect battery ground cable and starter motor cables.
2. Remove flywheel cover and the transmission dipstick on cars with manual transmissions.
3. Remove starter motor heat shield and rear starter motor mount, **Fig. 1.**
4. Remove front starter motor mounting bolts.
5. Position motor so that it will clear recess and remove from engine compartment.
6. Reverse procedure to install.

MODEL 900 TURBO

1. Disconnect battery ground cable and starter motor wires.
2. Remove turbocharger suction pipe, preheater hose and flywheel cover.
3. Remove dipstick on vehicles with manual transmissions.
4. Remove brace between turbocharger and transmission.
5. Loosen oil return pipe on turbocharger to allow it to be positioned outward.
6. Remove starter motor heat shield and rear motor mounting, **Fig. 1.**
7. Remove front motor mounting bolts.
8. Tilt motor downward slightly and lift out forward while carefully bending turbocharger return pipe out of the way.
9. Reverse procedure to install. Install a new gasket between oil return pipe and connecting flange on turbocharger.

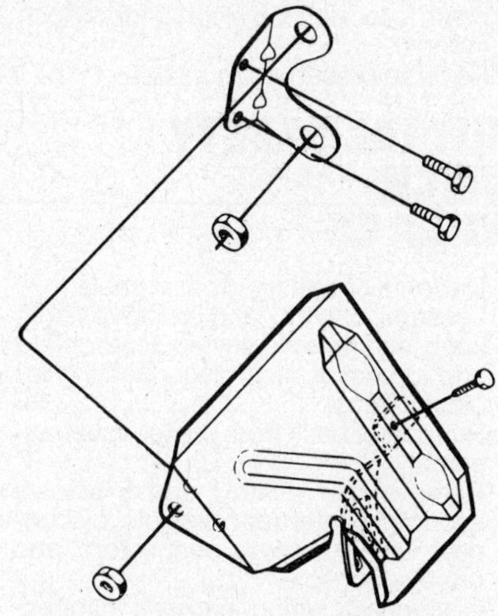

Fig. 1 Starter heat shield & rear brace assembly. Model 900

MODEL 9000

1. Disconnect battery ground cable.
2. Disconnect starter motor electrical connectors.
3. Loosen starter motor bracket bar upper attaching bolt. Do not remove bolt.
4. Remove both starter motor to engine block attaching bolts.
5. Remove starter motor from vehicle.
6. Reverse procedure to install.

IGNITION SWITCH & LOCK CYLINDER REPLACE

MODEL 900

1. Disconnect battery ground cable.
2. Disconnect wiring harness connector to driver's seat heating element, if equipped, and remove seat.
3. Place automatic transmission in park or manual transmission in reverse and remove ignition key.
4. On automatic transmission models, remove shift indicator plate and top cover after disconnecting indicator lamp; on manual transmission models, remove shifter boot and top cover.
5. Pull carpet away from shifter cover.
6. Remove center rear console as follows:
   a. Move seats to rear and apply handbrake.
   b. Remove rear ashtray and 5 console retaining screws.
   c. Disconnect wiring harness connectors and remove console, then remove heater duct.
7. If lock cylinder is to be replaced on manual transmission models, remove tapered pin from joint between gear lever and selector rod, and disconnect selector rod.
8. Disconnect wiring harness connectors to ignition switch, noting position for reassembly.
9. Disconnect wiring harness connectors to back-up lamp and neutral safety switches, if equipped.
10. Remove bolts securing gear lever housing using tool 891237 on all except Model 900 with manual transmission. On 900 manual transmission models, use tool 8790370.
11. Replace ignition switch as follows:
    a. Raise housing slightly, twist to expose cover plate screws, and remove plate.
    b. Remove ignition switch retaining screws and switch.
    c. Rotate switch to align mark (2) with arrow (3), **Fig. 2.**
    d. Ensure that key is in lock (L) position and install switch with locating stud (1), **Fig. 2**, in slot on gear lever housing.
12. Replace lock cylinder with key as fol-

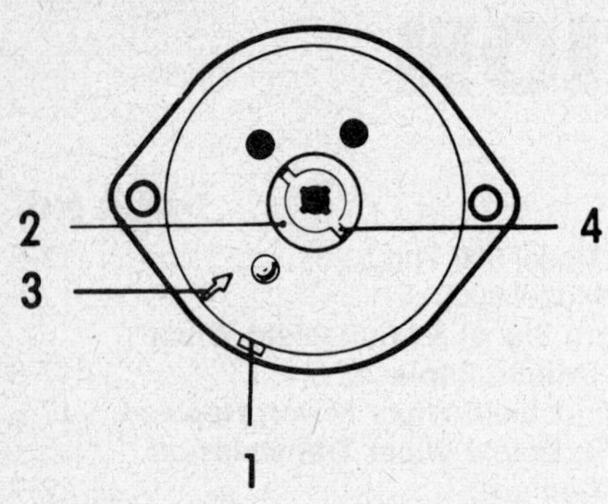

Fig. 2 Ignition & starter switch contact alignment

lows:

a. On automatic transmission models, loosen bottom cover screws, remove cable bracket clip, and remove gear lever housing.
b. On manual transmission models, remove gear lever housing assembly.
c. Turn ignition key half way between Lock (L) and garage (G) positions.
d. Depress lock cylinder retaining pin, **Fig. 3**, with a suitable pick, and pull cylinder from housing.
e. Install lock with key turned as in step c., ensuring that cylinder is aligned with drive gear.

13. Replace lock cylinder with key missing as follows:
    a. Drill out plug covering hole for lock cylinder retaining pin on LH side of gear lever housing.
    b. Using a suitable punch, drive lock retaining pin in approximately .008 inch, **Fig. 4**, and remove lock cylinder. **Lock cylinder must be replaced after forcing retaining pin.**
    c. Install new lock cylinder as in step 13.
14. Reverse procedure to install components and adjust transmission linkage as needed.

MODEL 9000

1. Disconnect battery ground cable.
2. Remove steering wheel.
3. Remove wiper/washer and turn signal switch covers.
4. Remove upper section of instrument panel.
5. Remove air ducts both in and above the steering column.
6. Cut off clip securing wiring harness and flexible ducts to the steering column.
7. Disconnect wiper/washer and turn signal electrical connectors. Disconnect horn switch and ignition switch leads.
8. Remove upper joint pinch bolt. Loosen remaining bolt and withdraw universal joint from steering column shaft splines.
9. Remove steering wheel adjustment as follows:
    a. Using a hammer and drift, tap out tubular dowel.
    b. Remove nut and washer.
    c. Withdraw shaft from clamp.
    d. Lift off upper section of the steering wheel adjustment assembly.
10. Remove three attaching screws, then lift off turn signal switch.
11. Remove rubber bushing from housing, then the upper section of the steering column.
12. Remove washer and steering column bearing.
13. Loosen attaching screws, then remove ignition switch.
14. Turn ignition switch key to position 1, press in locking tab and withdraw lock cylinder.
15. Reverse procedure to install.

NEUTRAL SAFETY SWITCH REPLACE

1. Disconnect battery ground cable.
2. Loosen locknut and remove shift knob, and remove shift indicator plate and top cover after disconnecting indicator lamp.
3. Pull carpet back from shifter cover assembly.
4. Remove rear ashtray and 5 screws securing center rear console, disconnect wiring harness connectors, and remove console.
5. Disconnect wiring harness connectors to switch assembly, remove screws securing switch to shifter assembly, and remove switch.
6. Place transmission selector in neutral and install switch with screws finger tight.
7. Rotate switch until line on switch is aligned with lever, and secure switch.
8. Reconnect wiring harness connectors and reverse procedure to install remaining components.

TURN SIGNAL & WINDSHIELD WIPER SWITCH REPLACE

Switches for direction indicator lights and the wiper/washer system are fitted in a panel mounted on the steering wheel bearing support. The panel can be removed after the cover beneath the support is removed.

INSTRUMENT CLUSTER REPLACE

MODEL 900

1. Disconnect battery ground cable.
2. On models with standard steering wheel and models with EMS trim, remove screws securing wheel pad and the pad, after disconnecting horn contact.

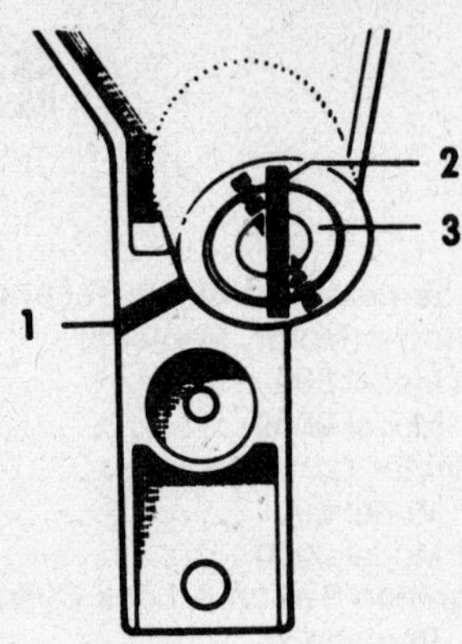

Fig. 3 Ignition lock cylinder removal with key

3. On models with sport type steering wheel, carefully pry center emblem from wheel pad.
4. Remove nut and washer securing steering wheel, then the wheel, using a suitable puller.
5. Remove 4 screws securing lower edge of instrument cluster bezel, noting position of each screw for reassembly.
6. Tilt bezel forward, disconnect electrical connectors and vacuum hoses, if equipped, then remove bezel.
7. Remove left speaker/defroster grill, then disconnect electrical connectors and speedometer cable from cluster.
8. Remove instrument cluster retaining screws and the cluster.
9. Reverse procedure to install. **Cluster bezel retaining screws are of different lengths and are, not interchangeable. The bezel will be damaged if screws are installed improperly.**

MODEL 9000

1. Disconnect battery ground cable.
2. Remove both speaker grilles on either side of instrument panel.
3. Remove instrument panel attaching screws, then panel.
4. Remove duct.
5. Disconnect vacuum hose from turbo pressure gauge, speedometer cable, and all connectors from instrument cluster.
6. Remove instrument cluster attaching screw, then instrument cluster.
7. Reverse procedure to install.

WINDSHIELD WIPER MOTOR REPLACE

The wiper assembly is an integral unit mounted on the bulkhead in the engine compartment. Two rectangular openings in the bulkhead accommodate the wiper spindles.

Fig. 4 Ignition lock cylinder removal with key missing

These openings are sealed with rubber grommets. Power from the motor is transferred to the spindles by means of a cable and linkage. The wiper arms are fitted in splines and retained by means of a nut, **Fig. 5.**

1. Lift wiper arm away from windshield, lift cover and remove nut and wiper arm.
2. Remove rubber grommet.
3. Remove wiper motor bolts and motor assembly.
4. Reverse procedure to install.

WINDSHIELD WIPER TRANSMISSION REPLACE

MODEL 9000

1. Disconnect battery ground cable.
2. Remove wiper arms by lifting covers and removing attaching nuts.
3. Remove rubber grommets from spindles.
4. Remove four bulkhead panel bolts from underneath hood.
5. Lift out bulkhead for access to wiper transmission.
6. Reverse procedure to install.

RADIO REPLACE

MODEL 900

1. Disconnect the battery ground cable.
2. Remove the speakers from behind the defroster grilles located on top of instrument panel.
3. If installed, remove speakers from rear package shelf.
4. Remove radio knobs and face plate retaining nuts and washers.
5. Remove face plate and radio. Remove rear radio support bracket if installed.
6. Remove antenna cable and electrical connections.
7. Reverse procedure to install.

BLOWER MOTOR REPLACE

MODEL 900

1. Disconnect battery ground cable.
2. Remove steering wheel and cluster bezel retaining screws as outlined under "Instrument Cluster, Replace."
3. Tilt panel rearward and disconnect electrical connections and hose connections at vacuum distributor.
4. Remove panel, then the two speaker/defroster grilles.
5. Remove the upper instrument panel retaining screws at base of windshield and under glovebox and remove panel.
6. Disconnect fan motor electrical connectors.
7. Remove right-hand defroster valve housing retaining screws.
8. Remove fan motor retaining screws and fan motor.
9. Reverse procedure to install.

MODEL 9000

Less A/C

1. Disconnect battery ground cable.
2. Remove cover from wiper motor.
3. Remove fresh air filter.
4. Remove all connectors from fan motor.
5. Disconnect temperature control cable.
6. Release clips from either side of fan housing and rotate to remove.
7. Separate the fan housing by removing screw in middle of housing.
8. Remove attaching screws, then lift out motor and impeller as an assembly.
9. Reverse procedure to install.

With A/C

1. Disconnect battery ground cable.
2. Remove hood and wiper arms.
3. Remove wiper motor and evaporator covers.
4. On models with automatic climate control, disconnect fan control unit electrical connector.
5. Remove bulkhead panel.
6. Remove plastic drainage molding under windshield molding.
7. Remove electronic ignition control unit attaching screws and position aside.
8. Remove wiper assembly.
9. Drain a few quarts of coolant, then disconnect heater hoses from heater core.
10. Remove throttle dashpot.
11. Remove cruise control vacuum pump attaching screws and position aside.
12. Remove evaporator body attaching screws and clips securing refrigerant lines.
13. Disconnect temperature control cable.
14. Pull out evaporator and release clips securing fan housing, rotate housing to remove.
15. Separate fan housing by removing screw in middle of housing.
16. Remove attaching screws, then lift out motor and impeller as an assembly.
17. Reverse procedure to install.

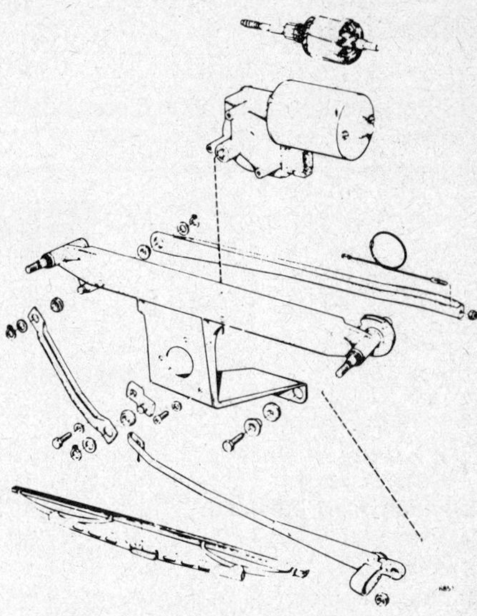

Fig. 5 Windshield wiper assembly exploded view. Model 900

HEATER CORE REPLACE

MODEL 900

The heater core and water valve are removed as a unit.

1. Remove cover under switches on steering column.
2. Remove front center console, if equipped, and remove lower section of instrument panel.
3. Remove air diffuser retaining screws.
4. Remove left-hand defroster/speaker grille.
5. Remove control rod from between water valve and control knob by sliding the rod forward until released from knob.
6. Pull rod back to separate from water valve. **Plastic joint at control knob is accessible from underneath once switches below heater controls have been pressed backwards.**
7. Remove lower section of heater housing.
8. Partially drain cooling system, disconnect heater hoses in engine compartment, and plug open fittings on core and water valve.
9. Disconnect brake pedal return spring and depress pedal.
10. Remove heater core and water valve to the rear and downwards past brake pedal.
11. Separate water valve and capillary tube, if equipped, from heater core.
12. Reverse procedure to install, using a new gasket between water valve and heater core.

MODEL 9000

1. Perform steps 1 through 8 on models less A/C or steps 1 through 15 on models with A/C of "Blower Motor, Replace," Model 9000, then proceed to step 2.
2. Drain coolant.
3. Release clips, then disconnect heater hoses from heater core.
4. Before installing new heater core, check condition of hose connectors and replace O-rings, if necessary.
5. Reverse procedure to install.

ENGINE SECTION

INDEX

ENGINE REPLACE

MODEL 900

Exc. Turbo 16 Engine

On these vehicles, the engine and transmission must be removed as a complete unit.

1. Disconnect battery ground cable and drain coolant.
2. Disconnect windshield washer hose and hood hinge links and remove hood.
3. Disconnect and/or remove following components, **Fig. 1**, noting position for reassembly:
   a. Upper radiator hose.
   b. Engine ground straps.
   c. Wiring harness connectors to distributor and coil, and high tension lead at distributor.
   d. Disconnect hoses and remove preheater valve.
   e. Vacuum hoses to vacuum tank, crankcase ventilation, and brake booster.
   f. Hydraulic line to clutch slave cylinder. **Plug line and open fitting on slave cylinder.**
   g. Main harness connector at rear of engine.
   h. Wiring harness connectors at alternator and oil pressure switch.
   i. Heater and expansion tank hoses.
   j. Lower radiator hose.
   k. Throttle cable at housing and bracket.
   l. Wiring harness connector to oxygen sensor.
   m. Fuel lines to engine. **Thoroughly clean area around lines to prevent contamination, then plug lines and open fittings to prevent fuel spillage.**
   n. Oil cooler lines. **Plug lines and open fittings.**
   o. Remove power steering pump and set aside.
   p. Wiring harness connectors to APC solenoid.
   q. Remove APC solenoid.
   r. Wiring harness connector to knock sensor, if equipped.
   s. If equipped with A/C, remove compressor mounting bolts, secure compressor in right hand wheel housing, disconnect A/C wiring harness connectors, and remove auxiliary fan.
4. Remove clamps and boots from inner driveshafts.
5. Place spacer tool 8393209 between upper control arm underside and car body. Insert tool from wheel housing side, and ensure that tool is properly installed to unload suspension when vehicle is raised.
6. Raise and support front of vehicle.
7. Separate lower steering knuckle from lower control arm. Pull out and support on control arm outer end.
8. On manual transmission models, position gear lever in Neutral. Remove nut and tap out taper pin in gear shift rod joint. Separate joint from gear shift rod.
9. On automatic transmission models:
   a. Remove retaining screw for gear selector cable at transmission.
   b. Withdraw cable with gear selector rod in its extreme forward position.
   c. Slide back spring loaded sleeve on gear shift rod and unhook end of cable.
10. Remove exhaust pipe from engine.
11. Remove speedometer cable from transmission.
12. Remove rear engine mounting bolts.
13. Loosen front engine mounting nut to allow mount to be lifted out of bracket.
14. Install lifting yoke and raise engine slightly. Move engine to free universal joints. Remove engine from vehicle.
15. On cars with power steering, disconnect two hydraulic lines at servo pump and plug exposed openings.
16. Reverse procedure to install.

Turbo 16 Engine

1. Scribe hood hinge locations and remove hood.
2. Install tool No. 8393209 or equivalent under upper control arm on right hand side.
3. Disconnect battery positive cable.
4. Drain cooling system.
5. Loosen lug nuts on right hand front wheel.
6. Raise front of vehicle and support with jack stands under forward jacking points.
7. Shift transmission to Reverse.
8. Remove tapered pin from gear shift rod joint.
9. Disconnect speedometer cable, then remove exhaust pipe-to-clamp bracket attaching bolt from transmission.
10. Loosen boot bands on inner universal joints and slide boots away.
11. Remove right front wheel and tire assembly.
12. Separate ball joint from lower control arm.
13. Separate universal joint and position steering knuckle aside.
14. Disconnect battery positive cable from body clips.
15. Disconnect ground cable from transmission.
16. Disconnect starter motor leads.
17. Disconnect exhaust pipe from exhaust manifold.

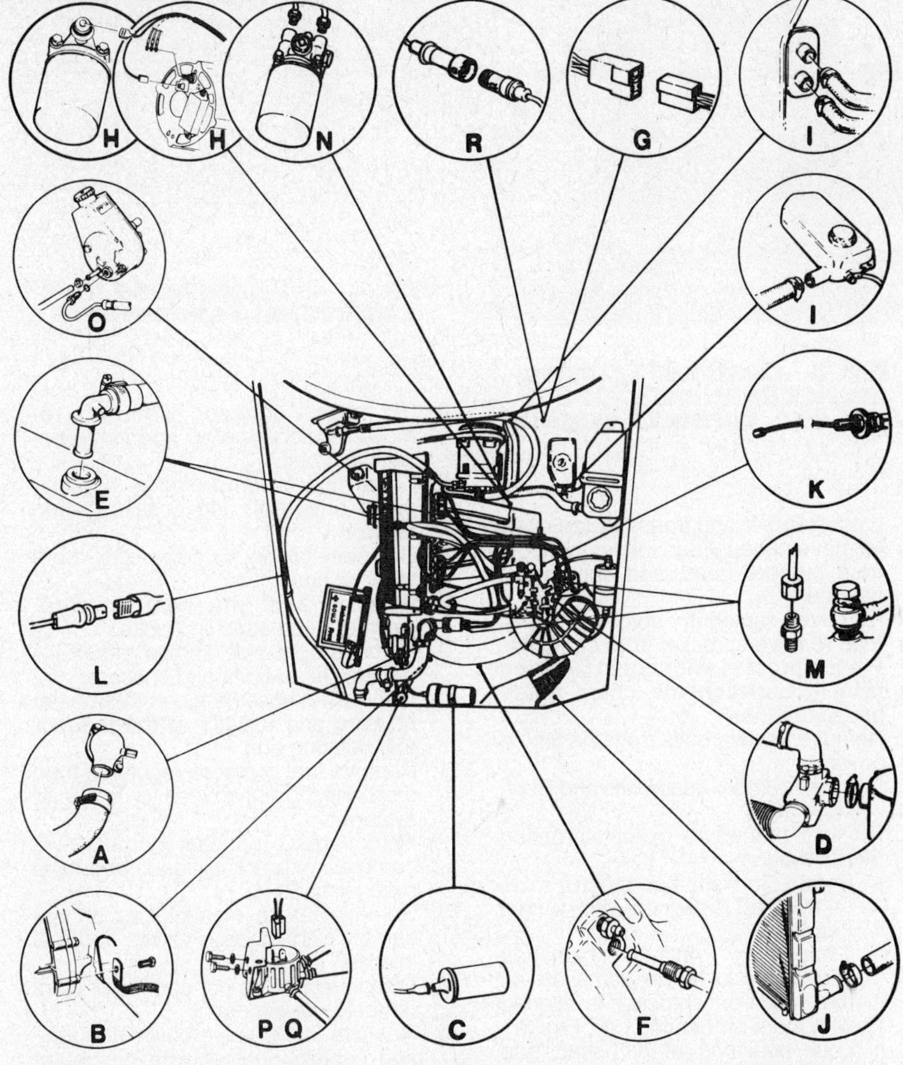

Fig. 1 Engine removal. Model 900 exc. turbo 16 engine

18. Disconnect and plug pressure line from power steering pump.
19. On models equipped with A/C, remove A/C compressor drive belt.
20. On all models, disconnect coolant hoses from heat exchanger valve, expansion tank, thermostat housing and bottom of radiator.
21. Disconnect the following electrical connectors from components on left hand side of engine:
    a. Air mass meter.
    b. Throttle switch.
    c. A.I.C. actuator.
    d. Injection valves.
    e. Thermostatic switch.
    f. Ground connectors at forward lifting lug.
22. Disconnect the following electrical connectors from components on right hand side of engine:
    a. A/C compressor, if equipped.
    b. Alternator and regulator.
    c. Blue wire at oil pressure switch.
    d. A.I.C. actuator.
    e. Yellow/white wire at temperature sensor.
    f. Gray wire at knock sensor.
23. Disconnect electrical connector from clip on fuel injection manifold, from rear of engine and from coolant hose between engine and coolant overflow tank.
24. Remove harness from engine compartment and position aside.
25. Remove alternator drive belt, then unfasten alternator and position aside.
26. Disconnect brake servo hose from intake manifold, then unfasten throttle cable.
27. On models equipped with A/C, unfasten A/C compressor and position aside.
28. On all models, disconnect fuel lines from front of fuel injection manifold and fuel pressure regulator.
29. Remove ignition coil, then disconnect turbo pressure line from turbocharger and induction air cooler/throttle housing.
30. Remove auxiliary fan.
31. Remove turbocharger air mass meter together with suction pipe.
32. Disconnect vacuum hoses from solenoid valve and the crankcase ventilation from suction pipe.
33. Disconnect electrical connector from hall switch and coil in distributor.
34. Unfasten hall switch cable from clips on clutch cover.
35. Disconnect solenoid valve hoses from turbocharger and charging pressure regulator.
36. Disconnect and plug hydraulic line from slave cylinder.
37. Remove engine mounting bolts.
38. Attach suitable lifting equipment to engine and raise engine until left hand inner universal joint can be disconnected.
39. Continue to raise engine and disconnect oil cooler hoses and power steering pump hose, then remove engine from vehicle.
40. Reverse procedure to install.

MODEL 9000

1. Raise and support front of vehicle.
2. Drain coolant.
3. Remove battery.
4. Disconnect hoses, then remove expansion tank.
5. Disconnect coolant hoses from pump upper outlet.
6. Loosen drive belt and A/C compressor attaching bolts, then position compressor aside. **Do not disconnect refrigerant lines.**
7. Remove turbocharger pressure pipe located between turbocharger unit and intercooler assembly.
8. Label, cap, then disconnect all electrical connectors, vacuum lines and fuel lines from engine assembly.
9. Loosen flange joint from between exhaust pipe and exhaust manifold. Push exhaust pipe to one side and remove front rubber hangers.
10. Disconnect upper and lower radiator hoses.
11. Remove lower radiator fan attaching bolt.
12. Disconnect speedometer cable from transmission.
13. Engage transmission into fourth gear, then separate rubber joint from gear selector linkage.
14. Remove universal joint inboard boot clips, then slide boots from joint assembly.
15. Remove battery tray.
16. Remove fan.
17. Remove air intake duct.
18. Remove air cleaner.
19. Disconnect relief valve hose from turbocharger pressure pipe, then remove pipe assembly.
20. Disconnect Hall transducer, ground strap from transmission and electrical connector from back-up light switch.
21. Disconnect throttle cable from linkage.
22. Using a suitable clamp, pinch clutch slave cylinder line, then disconnect hydraulic line from clutch slave cylinder.
23. Remove front wheels.
24. Loosen, then remove engine stay bracket.
25. Remove steering servo reservoir.
26. Disconnect and cap large-bore hose and delivery hose from steering servo pump.

Fig. 2 Flywheel timing mark alignment

27. Disconnect fuel return hose from pressure regulator.
28. Remove rear engine mount nuts. Loosen front engine mount nuts a few turns.
29. Attach suitable engine lifting equipment onto engine lifting eyes.
30. Lift engine sufficiently to provide access, then disconnect vacuum hoses from intake manifold. Remove coolant hose located between heat exchanger and water pump pipe.
31. Loosen fuel pipe to fuel injection manifold coupling.
32. Remove remaining engine mount attaching nuts and bolts.
33. Lift engine and transmission assembly from vehicle.
34. Reverse procedure to install.

CYLINDER HEAD REPLACE

MODEL 900

Exc. Turbo 16 Engine

1. Disconnect battery ground cable.
2. Drain coolant and remove upper radiator hose.
3. Remove crankcase ventilation hoses from valve cover.
4. Disconnect wires from distributor and temperature transmitter.
5. Remove warm-up regulator and auxiliary air valve from cylinder head.
6. Rotate crankshaft until flywheel (0) mark is aligned with line on clutch cover and mark on camshaft sprocket is aligned with mark on bearing cap.
7. Remove valve cover retaining bolts and cover. **Design of distributor driving dog allows the valve cover to be removed only when cylinder 1 or 4 is at TDC.**
8. Install a jack under transmission case. Remove stay between right engine mount and cylinder head and rotate it to one side.
9. Jack the engine up slightly and support it on a piece of wood between the crossmember and transmission case.

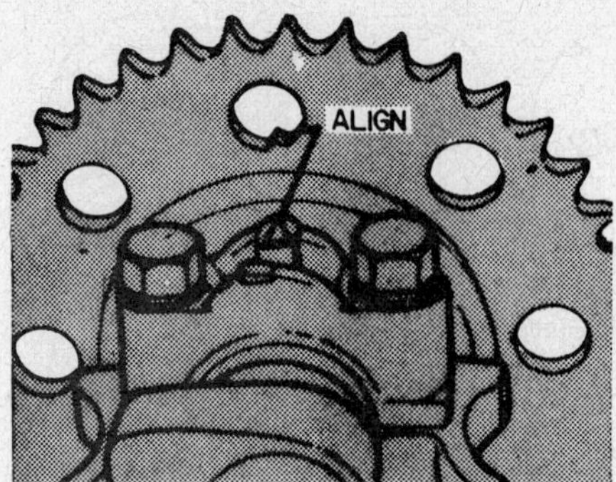

Fig. 3 Camshaft timing mark alignment. Model 900, exc. turbo 16 engine

10. Remove exhaust and intake manifold from cylinder head, and support as needed.
11. Remove camshaft sprocket bolts, then remove sprocket from camshaft. **Place sprocket with chain hanging from it between the chain guide and tensioner.**
12. Remove the two bolts from the timing cover.
13. Remove cylinder head bolts and lift off cylinder head.
14. Reverse procedure to install, noting the following:
    a. Rotate crankshaft so that (0) mark on flywheel is aligned with pointer, **Fig. 2.**
    b. Temporarily install camshaft sprocket and rotate camshaft so that mark on sprocket is aligned with mark on bearing cap, **Fig. 3.**
    c. Lock positions of camshaft and crankshaft. **Do not allow either shaft to rotate until timing chain is properly installed. If engine rotates with shafts not synchronized, engine will be damaged.**
    d. Position timing chain on camshaft sprocket, place chain between guide and tensioner, and install cylinder head.
    e. Torque cylinder head bolts in sequence shown, **Fig. 4**, first torquing bolts to 43 ft. lb., then to specifications.
    f. Warm engine to operating temperature, then allow to cool for 30 minutes.
    g. Back off each head bolt 1/2 turn, retorque to specifications in sequence shown, **Fig. 4**, then tighten each bolt an additional 1/4 turn in sequence.

Turbo 16 Engine

1. Scribe hood hinge locations and remove hood.
2. Disconnect battery cables and remove battery from engine compartment.
3. Drain engine coolant from radiator and block.
4. Remove exhaust manifold and turbocharger unit.

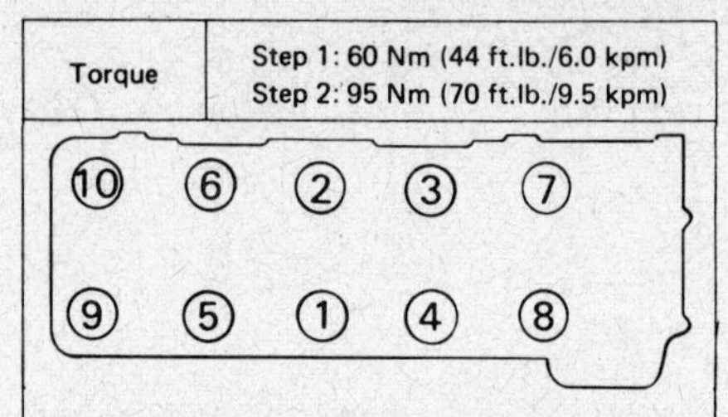

Fig. 4 Cylinder head bolt tightening sequence

5. On models equipped with A/C, remove tensioner pulley and compressor drive belt.
6. On all models, remove power steering pump drive belt and position pump aside.
7. Unfasten wiring harness clips from cylinder head.
8. Remove 2 engine front cover-to-cylinder head attaching bolts.
9. Remove right side engine mount-to-cylinder head bolts and spacers.
10. Disconnect hose between thermostat housing and radiator at the thermostat housing end.
11. Remove fuel pressure regulator, then disconnect ground wires for left hand system.
12. Remove A.I.C. actuator, then the A/C compressor bracket, if equipped, from cylinder head.
13. Remove intake manifold as an assembly with injection valves and fuel injection manifold.
14. Disconnect electrical connector from temperature sender.
15. Remove lid on valve cover and ignition cables together with distributor cap.
16. Remove valve cover. Disconnect crankcase ventilation hose and remove rubber plug halves from cylinder head.
17. On models equipped with A/C, unfasten A/C compressor and position aside.
18. On all models, align flywheel (0) mark with line on clutch cover and notches on camshaft with marks on bearing cap, then remove chain tensioner, camshaft sprockets and timing chain.
19. Raise engine to lift cylinder head off engine mounts, then remove cylinder head attaching bolts and the cylinder head.
20. Reverse procedure to install:
    a. Rotate crankshaft so that (0) mark on flywheel is aligned with timing mark on end plate.
    b. Align notches on camshaft with marks on bearing.
    c. Install camshaft sprocket for exhaust valve camshaft first. Ensure chain between camshaft and crankshaft sprockets is tight, then install camshaft sprocket for inlet valve camshaft.
    d. Adjust chain tension with camshaft sprocket center bolts not fully tightened. Tighten tensioner bolt, then

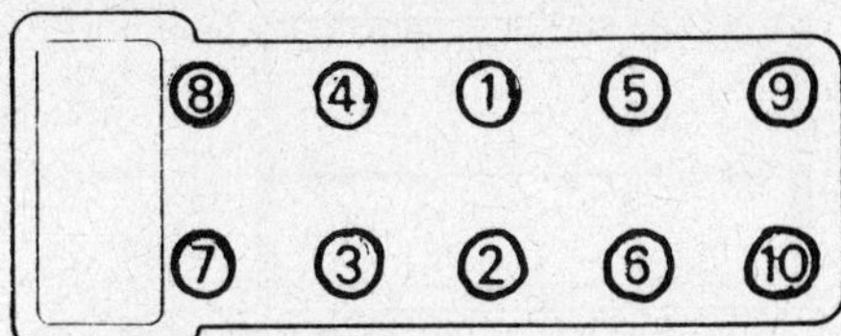

Fig. 5 Cylinder head bolt tightening sequence. Model 9000

release tensioner by pressing pivoting guide firmly against it. Depress pivoting guide to verify proper tensioner operation, then rotate engine two complete turns. Ensure crankshaft and camshafts are still properly aligned, then torque sprocket bolts to specifications.

e. When installing cylinder head, remember to install the 2 bolts on underside of head.

MODEL 9000

1. Raise and support front of vehicle.
2. Remove right-hand wheel.
3. Remove front wheel liner assembly.
4. Drain coolant from engine.
5. Disconnect battery ground cable.
6. Remove expansion tank.
7. Loosen A/C compressor drive belt, then disconnect electrical connectors and position compressor aside. **Do not disconnect refrigerant lines.**
8. Loosen front exhaust pipe flange, then disconnect rubber hangers.
9. Remove turbocharger bracket bar, then the oil return line.
10. Disconnect inter-cooler hose from turbocharger assembly.
11. Disconnect oil supply line from turbocharger assembly.
12. Label, disconnect and cap all vacuum lines, fuel lines, oil lines and electrical connectors from cylinder head and distributor assembly.
13. Disconnect coolant lines and hoses from cylinder head.
14. Remove exhaust manifold and turbocharger assembly.
15. Remove engine stay bracket.
16. Remove engine stay bracket from cylinder head.
17. Remove intake manifold from cylinder head.
18. Disconnect breather hose from camshaft cover.
19. Remove spark plug inspection plates.
20. Remove camshaft cover attaching bolts, then the camshaft cover.
21. Turn crankshaft in normal direction of rotation until zero (0) mark on crankshaft and engine block align and camshaft timing marks are also aligned properly.
22. With crankshaft and camshaft timing marks properly aligned, remove camshaft sprockets and timing chain tensioner.
23. Remove the two cylinder head bolts adjacent to the timing case cover. Bolts are accessible from below.
24. Remove the ten, Torx-type cylinder head attaching bolts.
25. Install a suitable guide pin in the drilled hole in the top right hand corner of the cylinder head. Ensure timing chain is positioned correctly, so that the pivoting chain guide will not obstruct the cylinder head and carefully lift cylinder head from engine block.
26. Reverse procedure to install. When installing cylinder head and torquing cylinder head bolts, proceed as follows:
    a. First step, torque cylinder head bolts in sequence shown in **Fig. 5** to 44 ft. lbs.
    b. Second step, torque cylinder head bolts in sequence to 66 ft. lbs.
    c. Third step, start and operate engine until normal operating temperature is reached, then allow engine to cool for approximately 30 minutes.
    d. Fourth step, loosen cylinder head bolts, then torque each cylinder head bolt in sequence to 66 ft. lbs.
    e. Fifth step, turn all cylinder head bolts in sequence an additional 90°.
    f. Torque camshaft cover attaching bolts to 16 ft. lbs.
    g. Torque intake manifold attaching bolts to 16 ft. lbs.

INTAKE MANIFOLD, THROTTLE BODY & INJECTION MANIFOLD

REPLACE

MODEL 9000

1. Disconnect battery positive cable.
2. Drain coolant from engine.
3. Disconnect throttle cable.
4. Disconnect pre-heater hose from throttle body.
5. Remove oil filler pipe from intake manifold.
6. Disconnect hoses from signal converter and distributor assembly.
7. Disconnect hose and tee piece from brake servo outlet from intake manifold.
8. Disconnect fuel pressure regulator and pressure transmitter tee hoses.
9. Relieve fuel system pressure by loosening banjo coupling on fuel filter. Hold a suitable cloth or shop towel round the coupling while doing this to soak up the escaping fuel.
10. Disconnect fuel hose from fuel injection manifold. Do not allow fuel to drip onto the starter motor assembly.
11. Disconnect fuel return line from fuel pressure regulator outlet.
12. Disconnect turbocharger pressure pipe from the throttle body.
13. Disconnect throttle switch, auxiliary air valve, temperature sensor (NTC resistor) and injection valve electrical connectors.
14. Loosen intake manifold to throttle body attaching bracket bar bolts.
15. Disconnect breather hose from camshaft cover.
16. Loosen intake manifold attaching bolts, then lift intake manifold assembly from engine.
17. Reverse procedure to install.

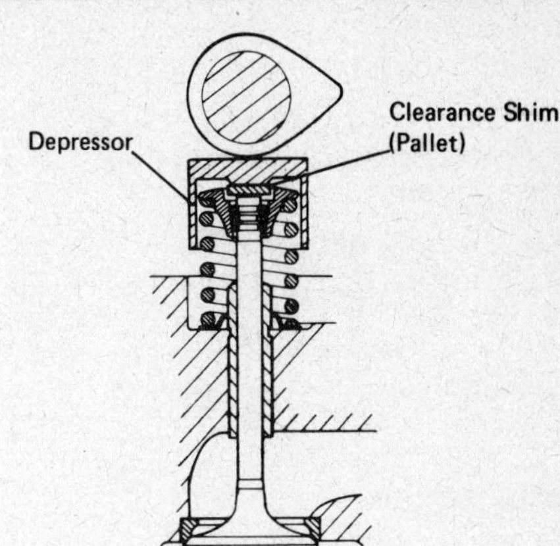

Fig. 6 Cross sectional view of valve depressor & adjusting pallet

VALVES

ADJUST

MODEL 9000

Exc. Turbo 16 Engine

1. Remove valve cover and rotate engine until highpoint of cam lobe of valve to be checked is facing upward. One other lobe will also be facing upward.
2. Check clearance between camshaft and depressor using suitable feeler gauges. If clearance is not within 0.003 inch of specification on non-turbo engines, or within 0.002 inch on turbocharged engines, install fixture No. 8391450 and dial indicator No. 7840622 over valve.
3. Fixture must be mounted and screwed on so that its claws grip valve depressor (follower).
4. Mount indicator so that its contact tip rests on cam tip and zero indicator.
5. Now lift depressor and note reading.
6. Remove camshaft, depressor and pallet, **Fig. 6**. Measure pallet thickness in fixture No. 8391633 with indicator from step 2 installed.
7. Calculate new pallet as follows: reading from step 5, 0.004 inch + reading from step 6, .009 inch = total distance, 0.103 inch. Total distance − specified inlet clear, 0.009 inch = required pallet thickness, 0.984 inch.
8. Repeat procedure on all valves not found within limits.

Turbo 16 Engine

Hydraulic valve lifters are used on this engine and no adjustment is required.

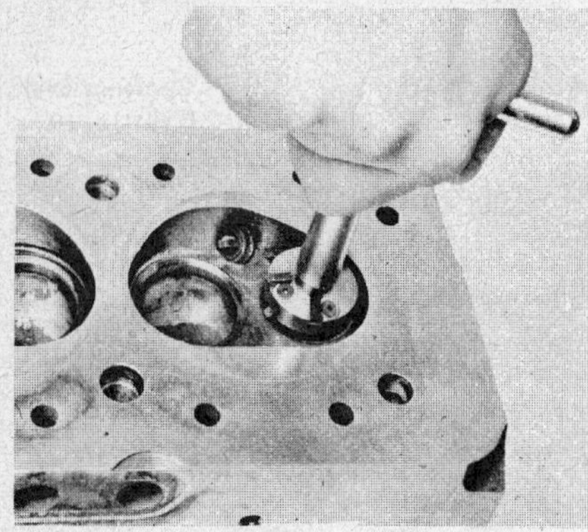

Fig. 7 Milling valve seats

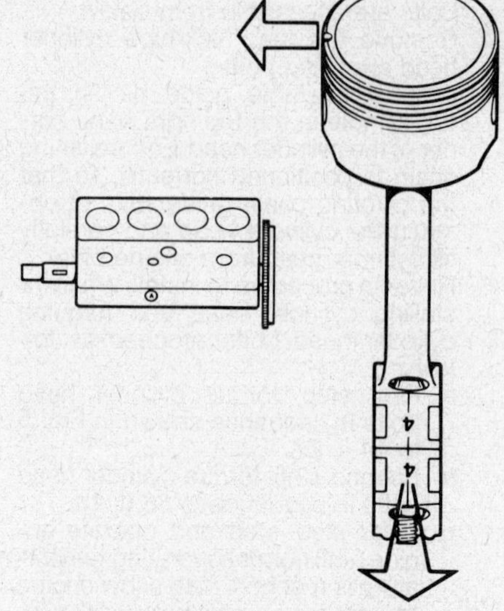

Fig. 8 Piston & connecting rod installation

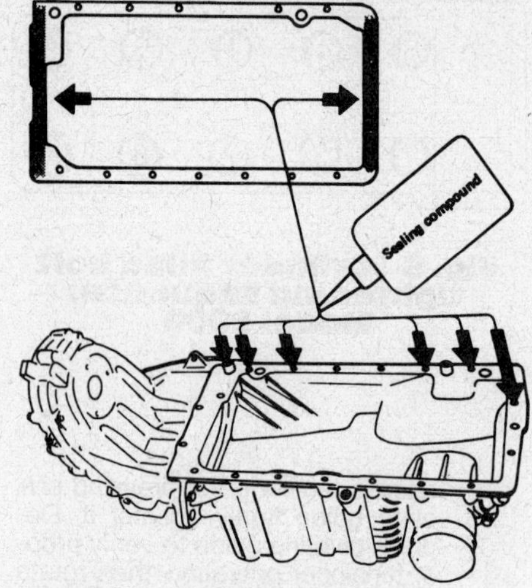

Fig. 9 Sealing areas for engine & transmission assembly

VALVE GUIDES
REPLACE

EXC. TURBO 16 ENGINE

Before removing valve guide, flush cylinder head with hot water. Remove guide from camshaft side using tool 8392631. To install, flush cylinder head with hot water. Press in guide with tool 8392631. Insert centering drift from underside of head and press in guide from above using drift. **In final stage of installation, guide tool moves to one side and guide can be installed in position.**

TURBO 16 ENGINE

Before removing valve guide, flush cylinder head with hot water. Remove guide using tool No. 8393811 with spacer No. 8393829 and nut No. 8393845. Install guide from top after flushing cylinder head with hot water and cooling guide with cold water. Install guide using tool No. 8393811 with stop No. 8393837, centering sleeve No. 8390379 and nut No. 8393845. Center tool in valve seat and draw guide into position using tool.

VALVE SEATS

EXC. TURBO 16 ENGINE

Machine valve seats as needed using a 45° milling cutter, **Fig. 7.** After cutting, use marking dye to check width of each valve seat. Exhaust valve seats should be reduced from the bottom only, using a 75° cutter, with the contact area extending to the periphery of the valve face and measuring approximately 0.060 inch. Intake valve seats should be narrowed using a 75° cutter from the bottom and an 11° cutter from the top, to produce a contact area of approximately 0.060 inch which lies in the middle of the machined valve face.

TURBO 16 ENGINE

Machine valve seats as necessary using a 60 milling cutter. Width of intake valve seat should measure 1-1.5 mm and width of exhaust valve seat should measure 1.25-1.75 mm.

TIMING CHAIN
REPLACE

EXC. TURBO 16 ENGINE

1. Remove distributor cap. Rotate engine until (0) mark on flywheel is aligned with pointer, **Fig. 2**, and distributor rotor is aligned with mark on housing, then disconnect battery ground cable.
2. Remove valve cover and cam sprocket from camshaft. Allow the chain to remain on the sprocket.
3. Remove crankshaft pulley and oil pump.
4. Remove the pulley and water pump.
5. Remove timing cover bolts and cover.
6. Remove timing chain and chain sprocket.
7. Remove chain tensioner assembly. **Do not rotate camshaft or crankshaft with timing chain removed.**
8. Temporary install camshaft sprocket, and ensure that timing marks are aligned, **Fig. 3.**
9. Ensure that crankshaft timing marks are aligned as in step 1 and install camshaft sprocket and timing chain on crankshaft, suspending assembly between chain tensioner and guide.
10. Apply sealer to mating surfaces and install cover, pulling up on chain and sprocket assembly. Trim excess gasket from mating surface.
11. Insert hook 8393357 through chain opening and pull up on tensioner to relieve tension.
12. Install sprocket on camshaft, rotating sprocket in chain to align timing marks.
13. Secure camshaft sprocket and release chain tensioner. Ensure that all timing marks are properly aligned, then reverse procedure to install remaining components.

TURBO 16 ENGINE

Refer to "Cylinder Head, Replace" procedure to replace timing chain.

CAMSHAFT
REPLACE

EXC. TURBO 16 ENGINE

1. Rotate engine until (0) mark on flywheel is aligned with pointer, **Fig. 2**, and remove camshaft cover.
2. If needed, rotate engine 360° to alignment on camshaft or sprocket with mark on bearing cap, **Fig. 3.**
3. Remove camshaft sprocket retaining bolts, separate sprocket from and hang sprocket on chain over chain guide.
4. Remove camshaft bearing caps, noting position for reassembly, and remove camshaft.
5. Reverse procedure to install.

TURBO 16 ENGINE

1. With cylinder head removed from vehicle, remove distributor.
2. Remove oil pipe, then the camshaft bearing caps and camshafts.
3. Reverse procedure to install.

PISTONS & RINGS

The type pistons used varies with the engine compression ratio. Either Mahle or Karl Schmidt pistons may be fitted to the engine, but pistons of different makes should not be installed in the same engine as an imbalance condition may be created.

Pistons and rings are available in standard, 0.020 inch (0.5 mm) oversize and 0.040 inch (1 mm) oversize. Standard size pistons are supplied in 3 different size classes, and all pistons and cylinder bores should be measured prior to installation. Pistons should be measured at right angles to the piston pin hole at a point 0.63 inch (16 mm) above lower edge of skirt for

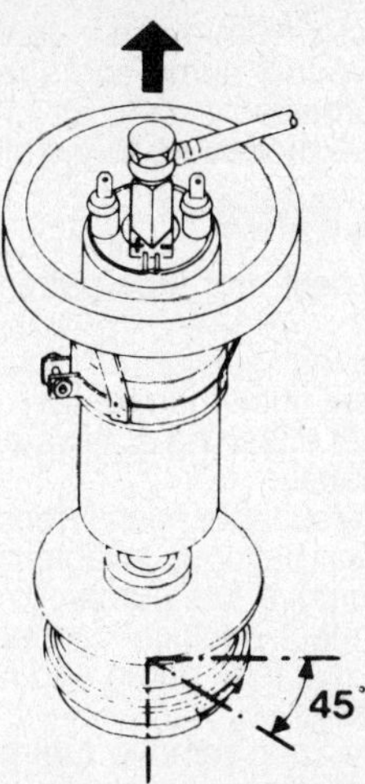

Fig. 10 Fuel pump installation. Exc. 1984–87 second design

Mahle pistons, or 1.03 inch (26 mm) above edge of skirt for Schmidt pistons.

Measure piston installation clearance using a suitable spring gauge and feeler gauges 1/2 inch wide. Clearance should be measured with piston installed in a lightly oiled bore, without rings, at right angle to piston pin bore. When indication on spring gauge used to pull feeler gauge between piston and bore is 1.8–2.6 lbs., piston clearance is equal to the thickness of the feeler gauge used.

Piston ring gap should be measured in the finished bore, using suitable feeler gauges. Push each ring into bore using an inverted piston to properly position rings. New rings fitted to a worn cylinder bore should be checked at the bottom of the piston travel, as the cylinder will be narrowest at this point.

Install piston and rod assemblies with "FRONT" mark or notch pointing toward timing cover, **Fig. 8**. Piston and rod should be assembled so that reference stampings on connecting rod, **Fig. 8**, face exhaust side of engine. Use a piston ring installation tool to position the lower compression ring with the side marked "top" uppermost. Rotate compression rings so that gaps in alternate rings are 180° in relation to each other, positioned over the ends of the piston pins. Make sure that the ring gaps of the top and bottom rings in the three piece scraper ring are staggered.

MAIN & ROD BEARINGS

Rod and main bearings are available in standard size and under sizes of .010 in. (.25 mm), .020 in. (.5 mm), .030 in. (.75 mm) and .040 in. (1 mm).

REAR OIL SEAL

REPLACE

MODEL 900

1. Remove clutch and flywheel.
2. Using a suitable screwdriver, pry old oil seal.
3. Before installing, lubricate lip of new seal with engine oil, then install seal using tool No. 8392540.
4. Seat seal in place, using a mallet and suitable drift.

FRONT OIL SEAL

REPLACE

MODEL 9000

1. Raise and support front of vehicle.
2. Remove front fender inner liner.
3. Loosen accessory attaching bolts, then remove drive belts.
4. Using tool 8393993 or equivalent, secure crankshaft from turning, then remove crankshaft pulley attaching bolt.
5. Remove crankshaft pulley.
6. Using a suitable screwdriver, break out old front seal from crankshaft.
7. Using tool 8393349 or equivalent, install new front seal onto crankshaft.
8. Install crankshaft pulley. Torque pulley attaching bolt to 134 ft. lbs.
9. Install drive belts, tighten attaching bolts, install fender liner and wheel and lower vehicle.

OIL PAN

REPLACE

Engine oil pan is an integral part of engine case. To remove pan, remove engine and transmission assembly as outlined in "Engine, Replace."

AUTOMATIC TRANSMISSION

1. Drain engine oil, remove flywheel cover and starter, and support assembly in an upright level position.
2. Disconnect throttle downshift cable at throttle housing.
3. Remove bolts securing engine to transmission, and remove 4 bolts securing flywheel (flex plate) to torque converter.
4. Turn flex plate so that bolt holes are aligned with vertical and horizontal axes of engine.
5. Lift engine from transmission, taking care not to disturb torque converter.
6. Install torque converter support tool No. 8790255.
7. Reverse procedure to install, applying a suitable sealer to bolts and areas shown by arrows, **Fig. 9.**

MANUAL TRANSMISSION

1. Drain engine oil, remove clutch cover and starter motor, and support assembly in an upright level position.
2. Remove clutch shaft as outlined in "Clutch, Replace."
3. Remove clutch slave cylinder.
4. Remove bolts securing engine to transmission and lift engine from transmission, removing release bearing guide sleeve as assemblies are separated.
5. Reverse procedure to install, using a suitable sealer on areas shown by arrows, **Fig. 9.**

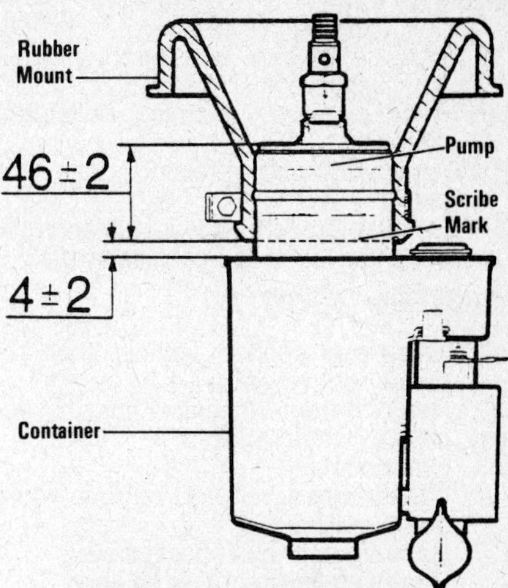

Fig. 11 Fuel pump installation. 1984–87 second design

OIL PUMP

REPLACE

MODEL 900

1. Clean pump area.
2. Remove crankshaft pulley retaining bolt. **Retain crankshaft by installing locking device, tool No. 8392987 on flywheel ring gear.**
3. Remove pump retaining bolts, then remove pump.
4. Reverse procedure to install, noting the following:
   a. Apply a suitable lubricant to gear wheels.
   b. Install ring gear with mark on face visible.
   c. Install new sealing ring in pump body groove, then install dowel.
   d. To facilitate positioning gear on driving plate, pull pump gear slightly outward.
   e. Ensure oil pump is primed with oil prior to installation.

MODEL 9000

1. Raise and support front of vehicle.
2. Remove front fender inner liner and right-hand side wheel.
3. Remove drive belts.
4. Secure crankshaft from turning, then remove crankshaft pulley attaching bolt.
5. Remove oil pump cover attaching bolts, then the oil pump.
6. To install, proceed as follows:
   a. Ensure pump O-ring is not damaged.
   b. Install oil pump and tighten attaching bolt.
   c. Install crankshaft pulley and drive belts.
   d. Install fender inner liner and wheel.
   e. Lower vehicle.

WATER PUMP

REPLACE

MODEL 900

1. Disconnect battery ground cable and

drain cooling system.
2. Release tension and remove water pump drive belt.
3. Remove pulley retaining bolts and pulley.
4. Remove pump retaining bolts and pump.
5. Reverse procedure to install and refill cooling system to specifications.

MODEL 9000

1. Raise and support vehicle, then remove right wheel.
2. Remove front wheelwell liner for access to water pump.
3. Drain coolant.
4. Loosen drive belt and remove water pump pulley.
5. Remove belt tensioner pulley.
6. Remove clips securing oil lines.
7. Remove clip securing water pipe to block.
8. Disconnect hoses from pump and remove pump attaching bolts, then the pump.
9. Reverse procedure to install.

FUEL PUMP

REPLACE

The fuel system on models with fuel injection is under constant pressure. Exercise caution when disconnecting fuel lines to release pressure slowly and prevent fuel from spraying.

MODEL 900

Exc. Turbo 16 Engine

1. Disconnect battery ground cable.
2. Remove rear floor panel in luggage compartment and round panel from above fuel pump.
3. Disconnect body harness connector and fuel lines from pump, using an open end wrench to support pump when loosening fuel line nuts.
4. Loosen pump mounting bracket using a jointed screw driver. **The mounting screw is accessible through the small hole next to the pump installation opening.**
5. On 1983-87 models with early design pump, remove pump assembly from tank.
6. On 1984-87 models with late design pump, lift pump from tank, disconnect electrical connections and return hose, withdraw pump assembly, then remove rubber mount from pump and pump from container.
7. On models with early design pump, position pump on mount so that distance between base of strainer and upper edge of mount is 9.3 inches (236 mm). On models with late design pump, proceed to step 10.
8. Ensure that fuel return line is connected to splash guard holder in bottom of tank.
9. Install pump assembly as follows:
   a. Tilt positive electrical connection toward left of vehicle.
   b. Tilt strainer inlet rearward and to the right, **Fig. 10.**
   c. Install pump in tank and reverse remaining procedure to complete installation.
10. On 1984-87 models with late design pump, scribe a line 1.181 inches (46 mm) from end of pump, **Fig. 11.**
11. Press rubber mount onto scribed line, then secure with clamp.
12. Install pump in container so that clearance between mount and container is 11.0.16 inch (4 mm), **Fig. 11.**
13. Position pump in tank opening with electrical connection tilted to the left, connect return hose and electrical connector to pump and lower assembly into tank. **Ensure that pump strainer inlet faces straight to the rear.**
14. Tighten clamp securing rubber mount to body and connect body harness connector and fuel lines to pump.

Turbo 16 Engine

1. Disconnect battery ground cable.
2. Remove panel at rear of luggage compartment floor.
3. Lift fuel pump cover, then disconnect electrical connectors from fuel pump, feed pump and fuel flow transmitter and remove the cover.
4. Disconnect fuel line from pump, then remove clamp around pump sealing collar.
5. Lift out fuel pump and container.
6. Disconnect return fuel line from container and the feed pump electrical connector from gland in tank.
7. Remove fuel pump and strainer from fuel container.
8. Reverse procedure to install.

MODEL 9000

1. Disconnect and tape battery positive cable.
2. Lift up rear section of luggage compartment floor, then remove two floor-to-panel attaching screws and lift out floor panel.
3. Using a suitable Allen wrench, loosen the two bayonet attaching screws, then remove fuel pump cover.
4. Disconnect electrical connectors from fuel pump, feed pump and fuel gauge transmitter.
5. Loosen, then remove fuel pipe banjo coupling. Retain washers.
6. Remove fuel pump rubber collar clip.
7. Remove fuel pump and suction reservoir.
8. Reverse procedure to install.

TURBOCHARGER

A turbocharger is used on some models to induce a greater mass of air on the engine's intake stroke, which increases combustion efficiency and enables the engine to develop greater horsepower and torque.

Turbocharged engines can achieve a level of performance comparable to that developed by larger displacement engines yet still retain better fuel economy, smaller engine size and weight advantages.

The turbocharger turbine wheel, which is driven by the exhaust gasses, is used to drive the compressor wheel. The exhaust gases flow through the turbine wheel blades causing the turbine wheel to rotate.

The turbine wheel and the compressor impeller are mounted on a common shaft and rotate at the same speed. The impeller is mounted inside the induction system and provides better charging of the combustion chamber.

The turbocharger is designed to operate at low engine speeds and provides a higher torque within the speed range existing under normal driving conditions.

Turbocharger boost is controlled by a waste-gate to protect the engine from over-boost conditions.

CLUTCH & MANUAL TRANSMISSION SECTION

INDEX

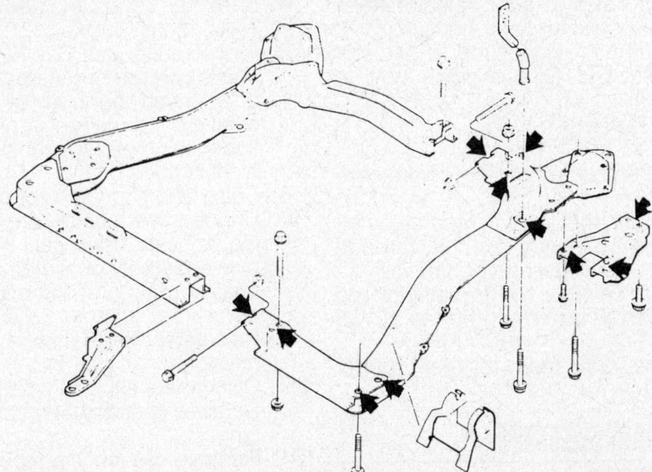

Fig. 1 Subframe mounting bolts. Model 9000

CLUTCH PEDAL ADJUST

No adjustment is necessary since clutch adjustment is automatic. The sliding lock ring on the slave cylinder moves along the piston to compensate for clutch disc wear.

CLUTCH INSPECTION

An inspection opening has been included in the clutch housing to check clutch wear.

1. Remove plug from inspection opening in clutch cover.
2. Depress and release clutch pedal and ensure that release bearing is in contact with pressure plate fingers.
3. Measure clearance between front edge of plastic sleeve and edge of release bearing.
4. Clearance should be .08-.35 inch. If clearance is less than .08 inch, clutch should be replaced.

CLUTCH REPLACE

MODEL 900

1. Disconnect battery ground cable.
2. Remove bolts securing clutch housing and remove housing.
3. With clutch pedal depressed (clutch released), insert spacer 8390023 between pressure plate diaphragm spring and housing. **If clutch cannot be released in normal manner, use tool No. 8393175 or equivalent to depress diaphragm spring.**
4. Remove lock ring, seal cap, and plastic propeller from clutch shaft at gear housing.
5. Remove clutch shaft, using a suitable lever, tool No. 8393175.
6. Remove 3 bolts securing slave cylinder bolts securing pressure plate to flywheel.
7. Remove clutch disc, pressure plate, and release mechanism as an assembly, then separate components. **It is not necessary to disconnect hydraulic hose to slave cylinder.**
8. Check condition of clutch shaft seal in gear housing, and replace as needed.
9. Position new clutch disc, pressure plate, and release mechanism on flywheel, ensuring that hardened face of release bearing faces flywheel, and install 2 pressure plate retaining bolts finger tight.
10. Insert clutch shaft, ensuring that shaft engages clutch disc and pilot bearing.
11. Using a suitable hammer, drive clutch shaft into place, ensuring that lock ring engages groove in gear housing.
12. Reverse procedure to complete installation, noting the following:
    a. Depress clutch pedal to remove spacer tool from pressure plate. **Do not depress pedal farther than necessary to remove spacer. Slave cylinder seal may be forced out of position, causing fluid leakage.**
    b. Depress clutch pedal and position plastic sleeve against release bearing.

MODEL 9000

1983–85 Models

1. Disconnect battery cables and remove battery.
2. Raise and support front of vehicle.
3. Remove or disconnect the following:
    a. All air cleaner ducts and air cleaner body.
    b. Battery tray, fuel filter, and fuse block.
    c. Air mass meter and turbocharger pressure pipe.
    d. Left hand motor mount.
    e. Speedometer cable.
4. Separate selector rod joint.
5. Install engine lifting beam tool no. 8393977 or equivalent.
6. Remove left wheel and inner fender liner.
7. Separate suspension arm from ball joint.
8. Remove roll bar link from suspension arm, then the suspension arm.
9. Loosen bracket bar from intake manifold to starter, then remove starter motor.
10. Remove all bolts from subframe shown with arrows in **Fig. 1.**
11. Remove transaxle attaching bolts, then the transaxle.
12. Remove pressure plate attaching bolts, then the clutch disc and pressure plate.
13. Position new disc and plate loosely, then install an old input shaft to align the disc. Tighten bolts to 10.4 -19.4 ft. lbs.
14. Reverse procedure to install, noting the following:
    a. Torque ball joint nut to 15-20 ft. lbs.
    b. Torque all subframe bolts to 32-42 ft. lbs.
    c. Torque transaxle to engine attaching bolts to 40-70 ft. lbs.
    d. Tighten engine mount bolt to 52 ft. lbs.

1986–87 Models

1. Disconnect battery cables, then remove battery.
2. Remove washer fluid reservoir, then disconnect positive lead from terminal block.
3. Remove fuel filter, terminal block, then the battery shelf.

4. Disconnect electrical connector from air mass meter, then remove meter.
5. Remove air cleaner intake duct, then disconnect hall transmitter lead from distributor.
6. Remove cover and filter element from air cleaner, then the air cleaner body.
7. Remove turbo pressure pipe, then disconnect battery ground lead and back-up lamp switch from gear box.
8. Attach a clamp to hose in slave cylinder pressure line, the tighten clamp securely to break pressure line between pipe and hose. Remove oil supply pipe clamp.
9. Disconnect left hand engine mount, then connect engine to lifting device, tool No. 8393977, or equivalent.
10. Remove left front wheel and wing insert panel, then separate suspension arm from ball joint.
11. Disconnect speedometer cable, then carefully remove cable as not to allow it to fall into transmission.
12. Separate selector rod joint halves, then remove clip from dust cover on intermediate drive shaft.
13. Disconnect intake manifold brace, then remove starter motor attaching bolts and starter.
14. Remove engine to transmission attaching bolts, except bolt positioned at top flange between engine and transmission. Insert locating dowels in holes, using tool No. 8392128.
15. Loosen two subframe pivot mountings, then remove four attaching bolts.
16. Remove attaching bolts and screws from subframe attaching point, then remove wheel arch bracket lower attaching point attaching bolts, allowing subframe to hang from anti-roll bar.
17. Remove rubber gaiter to U-joint retaining clip, then remove driveshaft and install protective covers on open ends of gaiter and driver cup.
18. Attach lifting sling to transmission, then remove last attaching bolt. Withdraw transmission, and allow to hang from sling.
19. Install flywheel lock, tool No. 8692987 to top of locating dowel, then lift off clutch assembly and remove driven plate.
20. Reverse procedure to install, noting the following:
    a. Torque pressure plate attaching bolts to 10-19 ft. lbs.
    b. Torque ball joint nut to 15-20 ft. lbs.
    c. Torque all subframe bolts to 32-42 ft. lbs.
    d. Torque transaxle to engine attaching bolts to 40-74 ft. lbs.
    e. Tighten engine mount bolt to 52 ft. lbs.

SHIFT LINKAGE

ADJUST

MODEL 900

W/Tapered Pin Gearshift Rod Joint

1. Place gear shift lever in Reverse, then turn ignition key to locked position.
2. Gear shift rod free play should be .12-.16 inch (3-4 mm).
3. Adjust free play by positioning gear lever housing forward or backward until freeplay is within specification. Use tool 8790370 or equivalent to remove gear lever housing attaching bolts.

W/Clamped Gearshift Rod Joint

1. Pry out and lift rubber boot from console.
2. Loosen pinch bolt at selector rod joint.
3. Lock gear selector lever in reverse by inserting a .157 inch (4 mm) drill bit through holes in gear selector lever and gear selector lever housing.
4. Connect the selector rod to selector rod joint and tighten pinch bolt to 22-25 ft. lbs.

MODEL 9000

1. Pry out and lift rubber boot from console.
2. Place gear shift lever in reverse by inserting a .16 inch (4 mm) drill through fixing holes in gear lever housing.
3. Connect selector rod to selector rod joint, then torque pinch bolt to 22-25 ft. lbs.
4. Remove drill, then reinstall rubber boot.

TRANSMISSION

REPLACE

900 MODELS

Exc. Turbo 16 Engine

1. Disconnect battery ground cable, then drain coolant into suitable container.
2. Disconnect windshield washer hose and hood hinge links, then remove hood.
3. Disconnect and/or remove the following components:
    a. Upper radiator hose.
    b. Engine ground straps.
    c. Wiring harness connectors to distributor and ignition coil and distributor high tension lead.
    d. Disconnect hoses, then remove pre-heater valve.
    e. Hoses to vacuum pump, crankcase ventilation system and brake booster.
    f. Hydraulic hose to clutch slave cylinder. **Plug hose and cylinder openings to prevent entry of dirt.**
    g. Main harness connector at rear of engine.
    h. Wiring harness connectors at alternator and oil pressure switch.
    i. Heater and expansion tank hoses.
    j. Lower radiator hose.
    k. Throttle cable at housing and bracket.
    l. Wiring harness connector to oxygen sensor.
    m. Fuel lines to engine. **Prior to removal, clean area surrounding fuel lines to prevent contamination. After fuel line removal, plug openings to prevent fuel spillage.**
    n. Oil cooler hoses. **Plug hoses and open fittings.**
    o. Remove power steering pump and set aside.
    p. Wiring harness connectors to APC solenoid, if equipped.
    q. Remove APC solenoid, if equipped.
    r. Wiring harness connector to knock sensor, if equipped.
    s. If equipped with A/C, remove compressor mounting bolts, secure compressor in right hand wheel housing, disconnect A/C wiring harness connectors and remove auxiliary fan.
4. Remove clamps and boots from inner ends of driveshafts.
5. Place spacer tool 83 93 209 between upper control arm underside and car body. Insert tool from wheel housing side and ensure tool is properly positioned to unload suspension when vehicle is raised.
6. Raise and support front of vehicle.
7. Unbolt lower control arm from steering knuckle, then pull knuckle and axle assembly outwards and support against outer end of the lower control arm.
8. Disconnect shift linkage from transmission.
9. Disconnect exhaust pipe from engine.
10. Remove speedometer cable from engine.
11. Remove rear engine mounting bolts.
12. Loosen front engine mounting nut enough to allow mount to be lifted out of bracket.
13. On models equipped with power steering, disconnect hydraulic hoses at servo pump and plug exposed openings.
14. Install suitable lifting device on engine and raise engine/transmission assembly slightly. Move engine/transmission assembly from side to side to free universal joints, then remove assembly.
15. Remove engine/transmission assembly from chassis. Place protective covers on universal joints and boots to prevent entry of dirt.
16. Separation of the engine/transmission assembly is not necessary to overhaul the transmission. If the transmission is to be overhauled while attached to the engine, the flywheel and starter must be removed. If transmission separation is desired, use the following procedure:
    a. Clean engine/transmission assembly.
    b. Drain engine oil, then remove ring gear cover.
    c. Using slide hammer No. 83 90 270 and joint 87 90 529, remove clutch shaft.
    d. Remove slave cylinder attaching bolts, then engine-to-transmission attaching bolts.
    e. Carefully separate transmission from engine. **Do not force attempt to force engine and transmission apart without first ensuring all bolts have been removed.**
17. Reverse procedure to install.

W/Turbo 16 Engine

1. Scribe hood hinge reference marks, then remove hood.
2. Install tool 83 93 209 or equivalent under upper control arm on right hand side.
3. Disconnect battery ground cable, then positive cable.
4. Drain cooling system into suitable container.
5. Loosen lug nuts on right front wheel, then raise and support front of vehicle.
6. Disconnect shift linkage from transmission.
7. Disconnect speedometer cable, then remove exhaust pipe-to-clamp bracket attaching bolt from transmission.
8. Loosen boot clamps on inner ends of drive axles, and slide boots outwards.
9. Remove right front wheel and tire assembly.
10. Separate ball joint from lower control arm.
11. Separate universal joint and position steering knuckle aside.
12. Disconnect battery positive cable from body clips.
13. Disconnect ground cable from transmission.
14. Disconnect starter motor wiring.
15. Disconnect exhaust pipe from exhaust manifold.
16. Disconnect and plug pressure line from power steering pump.
17. On models equipped with A/C, remove A/C compressor drive belt.
18. On all models, disconnect coolant hoses from heat exchanger valve, expansion tank, thermostat housing and bottom of radiator.
19. Disconnect the following electrical connectors from components on left hand side of engine:
    a. Air mass meter.
    b. Throttle switch.
    c. A.I.C. actuator.
    d. Injection valves.
    e. Thermostatic switch.
    f. Ground connections at forward lift-ing lug.
20. Disconnect the following electrical connectors from components on right hand side of engine:
    a. A/C compressor, if equipped.
    b. Alternator and regulator.
    c. Blue wire at oil pressure switch.
    d. A.I.C. actuator.
    e. Yellow/white wire at temperature sensor.
    f. Gray wire at knock sensor.
21. Disconnect electrical connector from clip on fuel injection manifold, from rear of engine and from coolant hose between engine and coolant overflow tank.
22. Remove harness from engine compartment and position aside.
23. Remove alternator drive belt, then remove alternator and position aside.
24. Disconnect brake servo hose from intake manifold, then disconnect throttle cable.
25. On models equipped with A/C, remove compressor and position aside.
26. On all models, disconnect fuel lines from front of fuel injection manifold and fuel pressure regulator.
27. Remove ignition coil, then disconnect turbo pressure line from turbocharger and induction air cooler/throttle housing.
28. Remove auxiliary fan.
29. Remove turbocharger air mass meter together with suction pipe.
30. Disconnect vacuum hoses from solenoid valve and the crankcase ventilation system from suction pipe.
31. Disconnect electrical connector from hall switch and coil in distributor.
32. Unfasten hall switch cable from clips on clutch cover.
33. Disconnect solenoid valve hoses from turbocharger and charging pressure regulator.
34. Disconnect and plug hydraulic hose from clutch slave cylinder.
35. Remove engine mounting bolts.
36. Attach suitable lifting device to engine/transmission assembly, then raise assembly until left hand inner universal joint can be disconnected.
37. Continue to raise engine/transmission assembly and disconnect oil cooler hoses and power steering pump hose.
38. Remove engine/transmission assembly from chassis. Place protective covers on universal joints and boots to prevent entry of dirt.
39. Separation of the engine/transmission assembly is not necessary to overhaul the transmission. If the transmission is to be overhauled while attached to the engine, the flywheel and starter must be removed. If transmission separation is desired, use the following procedure:
    a. Clean engine/transmission assembly.
    b. Drain engine oil, then remove ring gear cover.
    c. Using slide hammer No. 83 90 270 and joint 87 90 529, remove clutch shaft.
    d. Remove slave cylinder attaching bolts, then engine-to-transmission attaching bolts.
    e. Carefully separate transmission from engine. **Do not attempt to force engine and transmission apart without first ensuring all bolts have been removed.**
40. Reverse procedure to install.

MODEL 9000

1. Raise and support front of vehicle.
2. Disconnect battery cables, then remove battery.
3. Remove air intake duct.
4. Remove windshield washer fluid reservoir, then disconnect positive leads from terminal block and battery tray.
5. Remove fuel filter, terminal block and battery tray.
6. Disconnect electrical connector from air mass meter, then remove air mass meter. Carefully handle air mass meter.
7. Remove air cleaner intake duct.
8. Disconnect Hall transmitter electrical connector from distributor.
9. Remove cover and filter element from air cleaner.
10. Remove air cleaner housing.
11. Remove turbocharger pressure pipe.
12. Disconnect back-up light switch electrical connector.
13. Pinch slave cylinder pressure line, then remove oil pressure pipe.
14. Remove lefthand engine mount.
15. Attach engine lift tool 8393977 or equivalent, onto engine lifting eyes.
16. Ensure lifting tool is properly seated on fender liner.
17. Remove left front wheel and inner fender liner.
18. Separate suspension arm from ball joint.
19. Disconnect speedometer cable from transaxle.
20. Separate the two halves of selector rod joint. Remove clip from dust cover on intermediate drive shaft.
21. Loosen intake manifold bracket bar.
22. Remove starter motor from transaxle.
23. Remove all except the one top bolt located between the engine and transaxle assembly.
24. Install locating dowels 8392128 or equivalents, into attaching bolt holes.
25. Loosen the two sub-frame pivot mountings and remove the four attaching bolts.
26. Loosen front and rear mounting brackets.
27. Remove the four attaching bolts located on the back of the sub-frame.
28. Remove bolts attaching lower wheel-arch attachment point and allow the sub-frame to hang from the anti-roll bar.
29. Loosen anti-roll bar top attaching bolt.
30. Loosen anti-roll bar link from suspension arm, then remove suspension arm.
31. Loosen, then slide universal joint boot away from joint. Remove clip, then withdraw drive shaft.
32. Attach a suitable lifting sling onto transaxle and remove the remaining attaching bolt. Withdraw transaxle and lower it to the ground.
33. Reverse procedure to install.

DISC BRAKES SECTION

INDEX

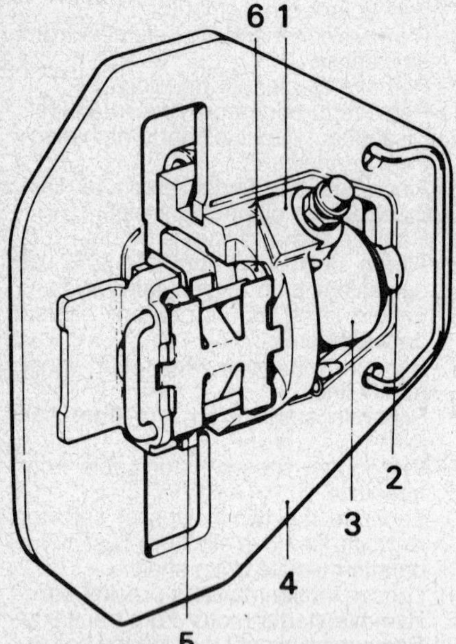

1. Cylinder housing
2. Piston (indirect)
3. Piston (direct)
4. Yoke
5. Brake pad (outer)
6. Brake pad (inner)

Fig. 1 Disc brake caliper. Girling type

BRAKE PADS
REPLACE

1. Raise vehicle and remove wheel.
2. Rotate disc so recess in disc aligns with pads.
3. Remove damper spring, pin retaining clip, and U-pin on Girling type caliper, **Fig. 1,** or retaining pins, and spring on ATE type caliper, **Fig. 2.** On 9000 models, remove lower guide pin bolt and pivot caliper upwards, **Fig. 3.**
4. Remove pads either by hand or with extractor No. 8995771.
5. On Girling type calipers, lubricate sliding surfaces of caliper yoke.
6. Loosen bleeder valve and press caliper pistons back into bore as follows:
   a. On front caliper, rotate piston clockwise using tool 8996043 until edge of piston is in line with hole for pad retaining pin, then close bleeder valve.
   b. On rear caliper, push piston into bore using handle of tool 8996043, then close bleeder valve.
7. Reverse procedure to install brake pads, noting the following:
   a. Pump brake pedal until brakes just begin to operate.
   b. If front pads are replaced, lift hand brake lever 5 notches and pump brake pedal until hand brake will hold with lever raised 7-8 notches, then check adjustment. **Do not move vehicle until brakes are operating properly.**

CALIPER
REPLACE

1. Remove brake pads as outlined previously.
2. On 900 models, disconnect brake cable from front caliper.
3. On 9000 models, disconnect brake cable from rear caliper.
4. On all modles, disconnect hydraulic hose to caliper and plug hose and open fitting.
5. Remove 2 bolts securing caliper to steering knuckle or axle and remove caliper.
6. Reverse procedure to install, bleed system, and adjust hand brake as needed.

CALIPER OVERHAUL
GIRLING TYPE

Front and rear calipers are the same except for the parking brake mechanism incorporated in the front caliper.

1. Remove caliper, clean housing, and mount in vise.
2. Remove return spring from hand brake lever, remove yoke from housing, then remove yoke spring and hand brake lever, **Fig. 4.**

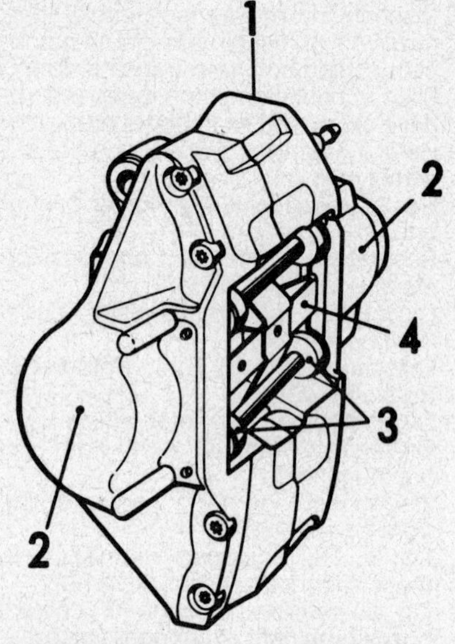

1. Cylinder housing
2. Piston
3. Brake pad
4. Retaining spring

Fig. 2 Disc brake caliper. ATE type

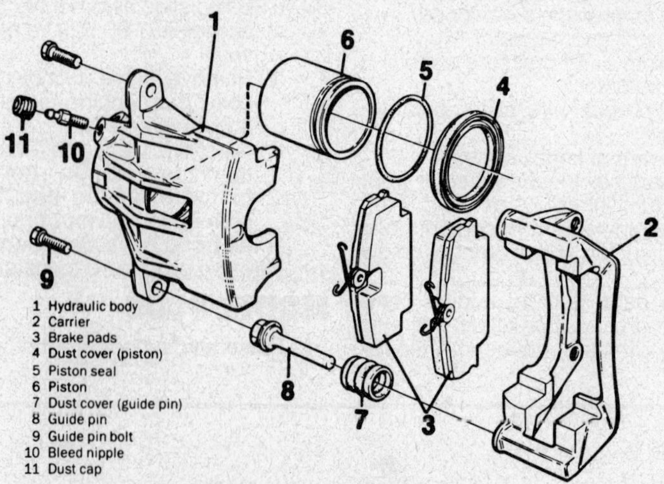

Fig. 3 Front brake caliper exploded view, Model 9000, Girling type

1. Dust cover holder
2. Dust cover
3. Piston (direct)
4. Push rod
5. Brake housing
6. Piston seal
7. Guide clip
8. Bleeder nipple
9. O-ring
10. Piston (indirect acting)
11. Yoke spring
12. Spring (handbrake lever)
13. Handbrake lever
14. Yoke
15. Pad retaining pin
16. Lock clip
17. Brake pad
18. Spring
19. Damper spring
20. Retainer (two O-rings)

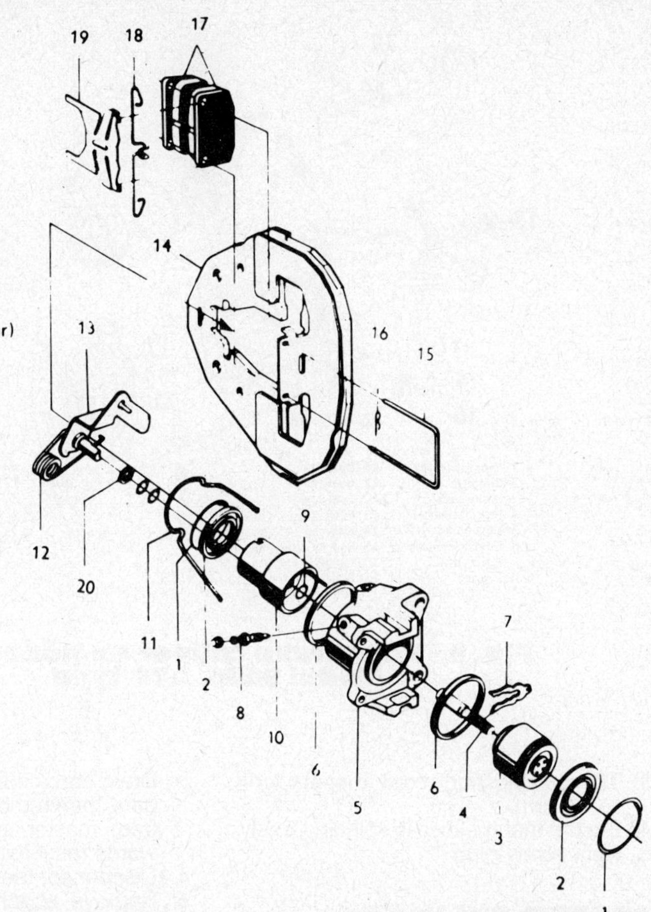

Fig. 4 Disc brake caliper exploded view. Girling type

3. Remove dust cover retaining ring and dust cover, then force indirect piston out using compressed air.
4. Remove direct piston by applying hand pressure to pushrod.
5. Remove O-rings and seals from pistons and caliper bores, and remove 2 O-ring retainers from hand brake lever opening.
6. Wash parts in solvent, rinse with clean brake fluid and blow dry with compressed air. **Do not wash indirect piston in solvent or brake fluid, as lubrication will be washed out. Wipe piston clean for inspection, and if found defective, replace as an assembly.**
7. Inspect components and replace as needed.

1 Hydraulic body
2 Carrier
3 Brake pads
4 Pad retainer
5 Dust cover
6 Dust cover retainer
7 Piston seal
8 Piston
9 Bleed nipple
10 Dust cap
11 Guide pin
12 Dust cover
13 Bush
14 Dust cap
15 Plug for adjusting screw
16 Handbrake lever
17 Stop pin
18 Return spring

Fig. 6 Disc brake caliper exploded view. ATE type

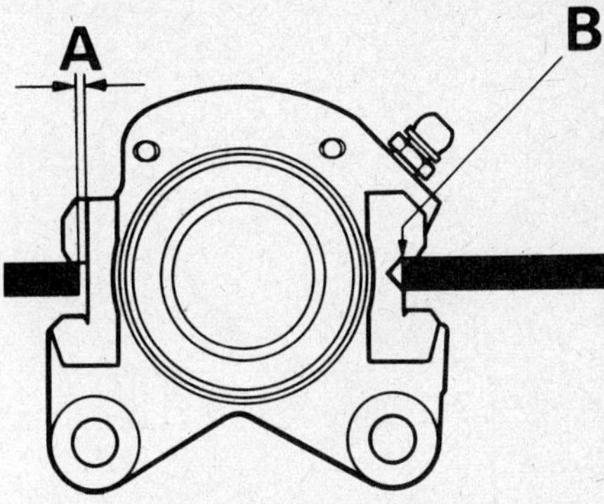

A = 0.006–0.012 in. (0.15–0.30 mm)
B = No clearance
S 7178

Fig. 5 Housing to yoke clearance check. Girling caliper

8. Install new O-rings lightly lubricated with clean brake fluid.
9. Mount brake housing in vise. Lubricate piston bore with clean brake fluid, and hand brake lever opening with suitable grease.
10. Fit anchor plate on pushrod, insert rod in indirect piston, and ensure that recess in anchor plate fits over piston pin.
11. Lubricate indirect piston with clean brake fluid and insert piston in housing so that recess for yoke is aligned with groove in housing.
12. Lubricate direct piston with clean brake fluid, insert piston into housing, and screw piston onto pushrod.
13. Install both pistons so that groove for dust boot is even with housing, then install new dust boots and retaining rings.
14. Install yoke spring and hand brake lever on yoke and install yoke, lifting hand brake lever to engage shaft with hole in indirect piston and ensuring that yoke fits into groove in piston.
15. Install hand brake lever return spring and check clearance between yoke and brake housing, **Fig. 5.**

ATE TYPE

1. Remove caliper and clean housing, **Fig. 6.**
2. Remove dust boot from each piston, then force out pistons using compressed air.

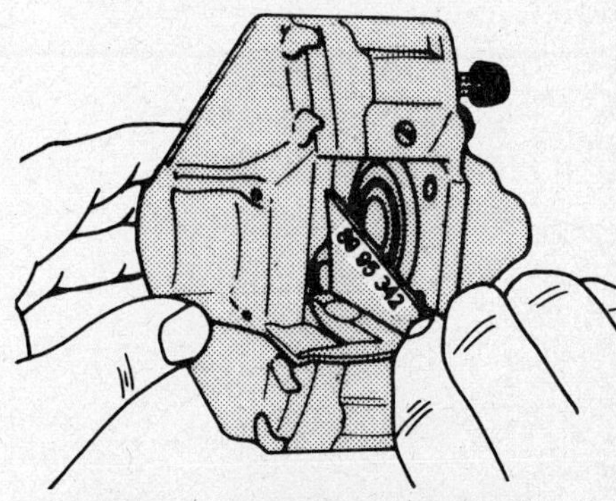

Fig. 7 Caliper piston alignment. ATE type caliper

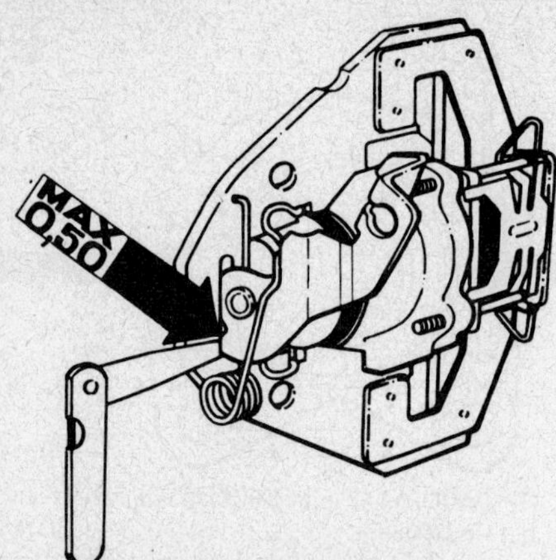

Fig. 8 Hand brake adjustment clearance

3. Remove piston seals from grooves in cylinder walls, taking care not to mar cylinder. **Do not separate caliper housing.**
4. Wash parts in solvent, rinse with clean brake fluid, and blow dry with compressed air.
5. Replace any components found defective, lightly lubricate cylinder bores and pistons with clean brake fluid, install new seals, and insert pistons into bores.
6. Install new dust boots over pistons, and seat pistons in bores.
7. Rotate pistons into position with tool No. 8995367, checking that notch on piston is properly aligned with tool No. 8995342, **Fig. 7.**

PARKING BRAKE

ADJUST

MODEL 900

1. Adjust by turning nut at hand brake lever, after applying several times to make sure cable is stretched.
2. Check for proper adjustment by making sure the clearance between yoke and lever at housing is 0.019 inches (.5 mm) as in **Fig. 8.**

MODEL 9000

1. Release hand brake.
2. Remove screw plug from adjusting screw on back side of rear caliper, **Fig. 9.**

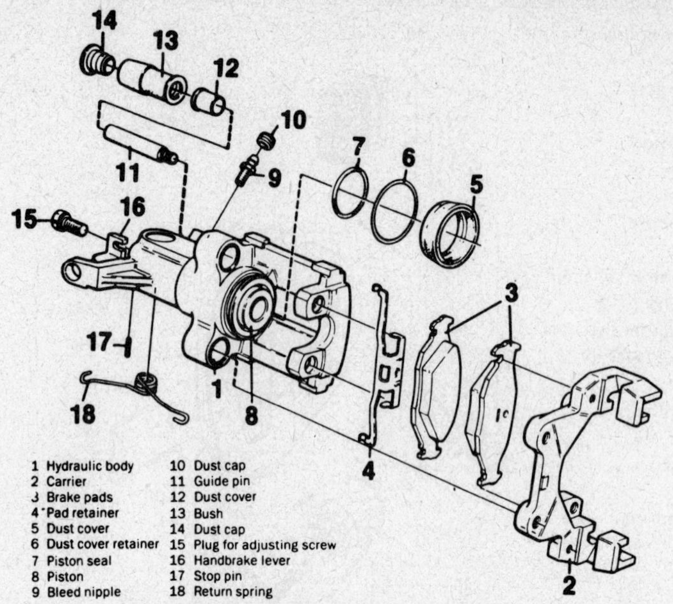

Fig. 9 Rear brake caliper exploded view Model 9000, ATE type

3. Tighten adjusting screw, then back off 1/4-1/2 turn.
4. Ensure that the disc is spinning freely.
5. Refit screw plug.

MASTER CYLINDER

REPLACE

MODEL 900

1. Disconnect hydraulic lines from cylinder.
2. Temporarily plug these lines to avoid loss of fluid.
3. Disconnect brake/warning switch connector, if equipped.
4. Remove the two nuts connecting cylinder to servo, then the master cylinder.
5. Reverse procedure to install.

MODEL 9000

1. Disconnect battery cables and remove battery.
2. Disconnect fuel filter mounting and move to one side.
3. Drain brake fluid from both front calipers, then remove lines with adapters from master cylinder and move towards reservoir.
4. Disconnect the brake lines.
5. Remove attaching nuts and master cylinder.
6. Reverse procedure to install.

POWER BRAKE BOOSTER

REPLACE

MODEL 9000

1. Remove master cylinder as outlined previously.
2. Remove vacuum hose from booster.
3. Remove trim panel for access to brake pedal mounting.
4. Remove retaining clip and pin from linkage between pedal and pushrod to booster.
5. Remove four bolts securing booster to pedal mounting, remove booster.
6. Reverse procedure to install.

REAR AXLE & SUSPENSION SECTION

INDEX

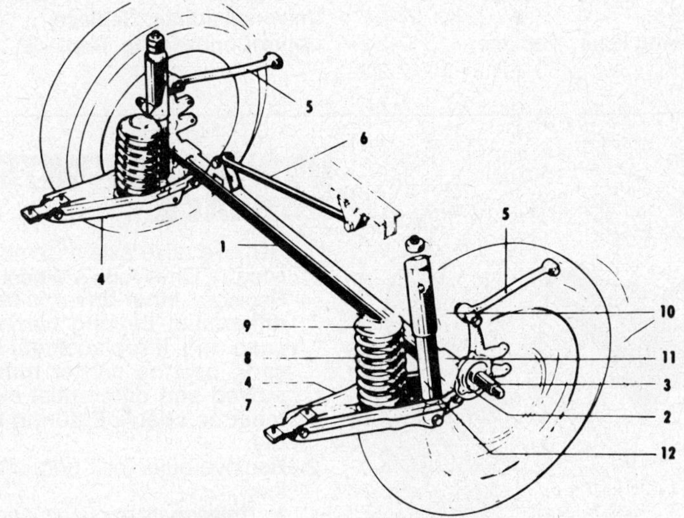

1. Rear axle
2. End piece
3. Stub axle
4. Spring links
5. Rear links
6. Cross bar
7. Spring seat
8. Coil spring
9. Spring insulator
10. Rubber buffer
11. Stop
12. Shock absorber

Fig. 1 Typical rear suspension assembly

COIL SPRING REPLACE

1. Apply hand brake and remove rear hub cap.
2. Raise vehicle and support.
3. Remove wheel and position a jack under spring link, **Fig. 1.**
4. Support spring link with a jack and remove lower end of shock absorber.
5. Position a jack stand of suitable height under rear axle to prevent brake line damage.
6. Lower spring link so that spring can be removed together with upper spring support.
7. Reverse procedure to install.

REAR AXLE HUBS, BEARINGS & SEALS REPLACE

MODEL 900

1. Raise rear of vehicle and support at frame.
2. Remove wheel, caliper and disc.
3. Remove dust cap, locking device nut and washer.
4. Remove hub assembly, using a suitable puller if needed. **Hub, bearing, and seals are an integral unit and must be serviced as an assembly.**
5. Remove seal from hub, using a suitable tool.
6. Remove both inner races and drive out the outer races with a brass drift inserted into the three milled recesses in hub.
7. Press in new outer races using drift or equivalent.
8. Fill the inner bearing space with chassis grease and install inner races.
9. Seat new seal using tools from step 7.
10. Reverse procedure to assemble.
11. Torque locknut to 36 ft. lbs. Loosen nut completely, then retorque 1.4-2.9 ft. lbs.

MODEL 9000

1. Raise and support vehicle, remove wheels.
2. Remove caliper and brake disc.
3. Remove dust cap, locking nut and thrust washer.
4. Pull off hub.
5. Reverse procedure to install.
6. Torque locking nut to 195-208 ft. lbs., secure locknut by hitting the flange with a suitable drift.

SHOCK ABSORBER REPLACE

EXC. EMS & TURBO

1. Raise vehicle and remove wheel.
2. Remove shock mounting hardware at both ends, **Fig. 1.**
3. Remove shock absorber from vehicle.
4. Reverse procedure to install.

EMS & TURBO MODELS

1. Raise and support vehicle at rear jacking point.
2. Position an additional jack stand under rear axle to prevent it from dropping and stretching brake lines.
3. Position a jack at rear of spring link.
4. Remove shock absorber nuts, **Fig. 1.**
5. Remove bolts in spring link mounting on rear axle.
6. Using jack, lower spring link so that shock absorber can be removed.
7. Reverse procedure to install.

FRONT DRIVE AXLE, SUSPENSION & STEERING SECTION

INDEX

DRIVE AXLE, HUB & WHEEL BEARINGS

REPLACE

MODEL 900

1. Position tool 8393209 under upper A-frame.
2. Loosen wheel nuts and raise and support vehicle.
3. Rotate brake disc so that recess in edge of disc lines up with brake pads.
4. Remove brake caliper and hang it to one side so that brake hose and pipe are not damaged.
5. Remove brake disc from hub.
6. Use tool 8995409 to remove the tie rod end from control arm.
7. Remove upper and lower ball joints in their respective A-frame. Pull vertical link and hub off driveshaft and A-frames.
8. Use tools 7841067, 8996456 and 8996449 to press off hub. Pull inner bearing race off hub using universal puller. If there are no recesses for puller, chisel off race.
9. Remove circlips from vertical link and press out bearing using tool Nos. 8390114, 8996456 and 8996449.
10. To assemble, lubricate bearing recess in steering knuckle housing with Molycote Paste G.
11. Use tools 8390114 and 8996464 to press in bearing up to circlip.
12. Fit outer circlip.
13. Use tool Nos. 8390114 and 8996464 to press hub into bearing.
14. Lubricate driveshaft splines with Molycote Paste G, install driveshaft into hub.
15. Replace steering knuckle housing by reinstalling the ball joints to upper and lower A-frames.
16. Install hub nut, brake disc, brake caliper and brake pads.
17. Install tie rod to control arm.
18. Install wheel, lower car and torque hub nut and wheel nuts. Lock hub by punching flange into stub axle groove.
19. Install hub cap and remove tool 8393209 from below upper A-frame.

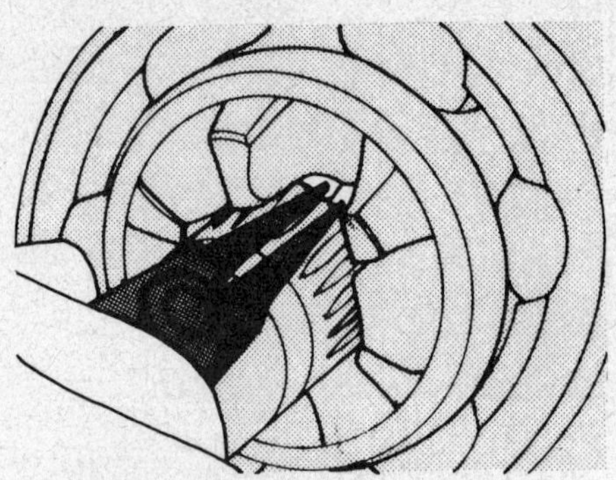

Fig. 1 Universal joint removal

MODEL 9000

Wheel Bearings

1. Loosen center nut and wheel attaching bolts.
2. Raise and support front of vehicle.
3. Remove caliper and brake disc from hub assembly.
4. Gently push in on drive shaft, then remove four hub-to-steering spindle attaching bolts.
5. Remove hub and backing plate. **Wheel bearings are an integral part of the hub assembly. If the wheel bearings are defective, hub assembly must be replaced.**
6. Reverse procedure to install. Ensure slot in hub faces upward. Torque center nut to 195-208 ft. lbs.

Driveshafts

1. Remove dust cap and loosen locking nut.
2. Raise and support vehicle and remove wheels.
3. Remove wheelwell liners.
4. Remove strut-to-steering member attaching bolts. Disconnect brake line from strut.
5. Remove clamp securing inboard dust boot, then separate the two halves of the joint.
6. Loosen center nut, then remove driveshaft.
7. Reverse procedure to install.

UNIVERSAL JOINTS

REPLACE

1. Remove drive axle assembly as outlined in "Drive Axle & Wheel Bearings, Replace." **Inner driver is retained in differential bearing carrier with a snap ring. If replacement is necessary, bearing carrier must be removed and differential clearances must be checked during reassembly.**
2. Remove outer joint from shaft as follows:
   a. Release clamp securing boot to outer joint and slide boot toward center of shaft.
   b. Open retaining clip, **Fig. 1,** and remove joint from end of shaft.
3. Rubber boots can be removed, if necessary, by sliding off outer end of shaft.
4. To remove inner joint spider assembly, remove retaining clip and press spider from shaft, using a suitable spacer. **The intermediate shaft uses a tapered shoulder as an inner stop for the spider, replacing the lock ring previously used. Only the conforming type spider can be fitted to the tapered shaft. However, this type spider assembly can be fitted to early type shaft previously used, Fig. 2.**
5. Reverse procedure to install, pack joints and needle bearings with grease, and install rubber boots.
6. Clean inner driver and pack with grease. Reverse procedure to install axle assembly.

UPPER CONTROL ARM

REPLACE

1. If left hand control arm is to be replaced, remove engine and transmission assembly as outlined under "Engine, Replace" in "Engine Section."
2. Remove top shock absorber nut, raise and support vehicle, and remove wheel and shock absorber, **Fig. 3.**
3. Compress coil spring using tool No. 8995839 or equivalent.
4. Remove bolts securing upper ball joint to control arm and support steer-

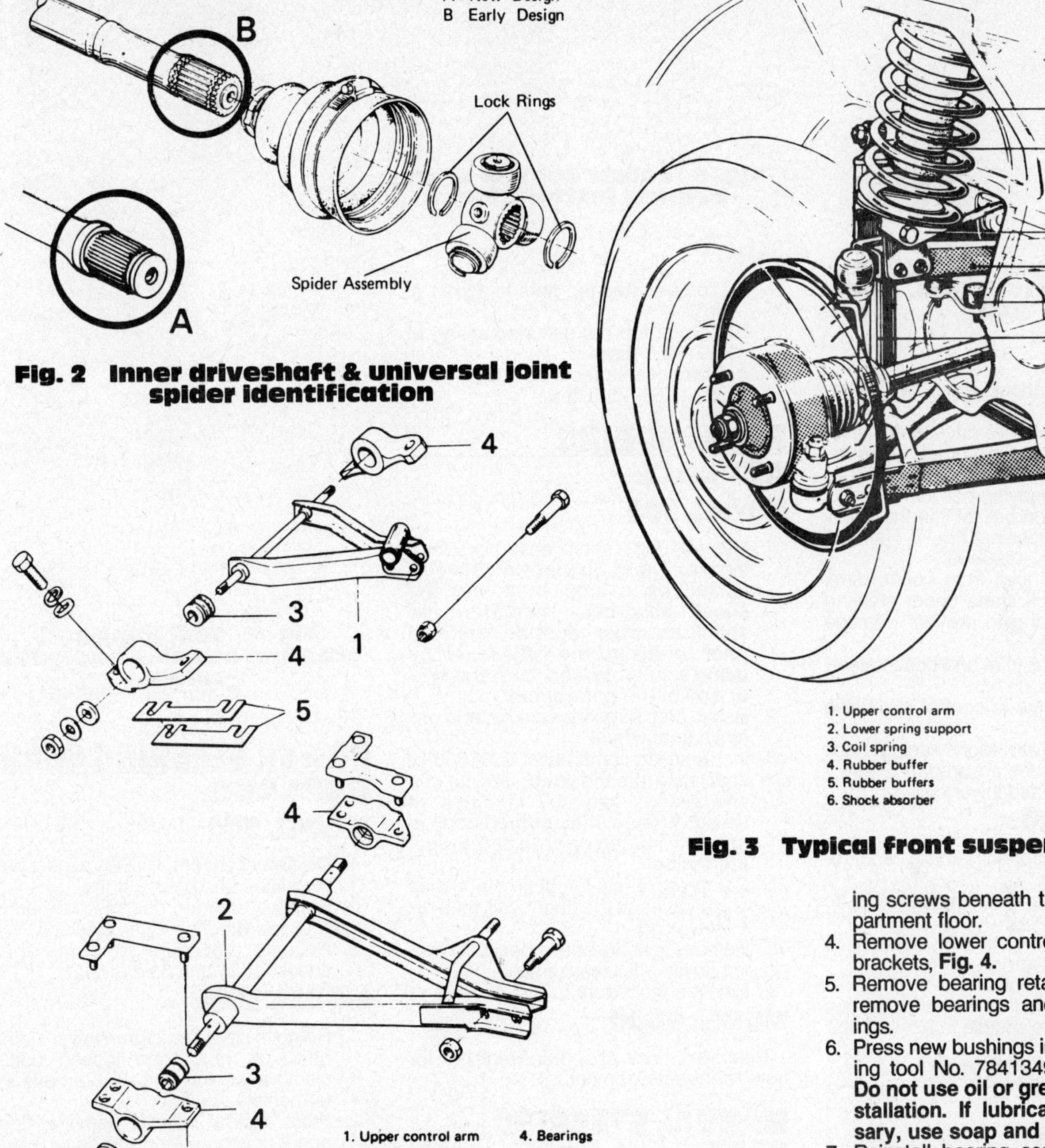

Fig. 2 Inner driveshaft & universal joint spider identification

Fig. 3 Typical front suspension

Fig. 4 Exploded view of control arm assemblies

ing knuckle.

5. Remove bolts securing control arm bearings, **Fig. 4,** then the control arm and spring.
6. Remove nuts securing bearings to control arm and remove bearings and rubber bushings.
7. Press new bushings into bearings using tool No. 7841331 or equivalent. **Do not use oil or grease to ease installation. If lubrication is necessary, use a soap and water solution.**
8. Reinstall bearing assemblies, torquing nuts to 54-66 ft. lbs. and noting proper angle between control arm and bearing, **Fig. 5.**
9. Reverse procedure to install control arm, road test vehicle, then check alignment.

LOWER CONTROL ARM
REPLACE

1. Raise vehicle, remove wheel and disconnect lower end of shock.
2. Disconnect lower ball joint from control arm.
3. Disconnect lower control arm attaching screws beneath the engine compartment floor.
4. Remove lower control arm with the brackets, **Fig. 4.**
5. Remove bearing retaining nuts and remove bearings and rubber bushings.
6. Press new bushings into bearings using tool No. 7841349 or equivalent. **Do not use oil or grease to ease installation. If lubrication is necessary, use soap and water solution.**
7. Reinstall bearing assemblies, torquing nuts to 70-77 ft. lbs. and noting proper angle between control arm and bearing, **Fig. 6.**
8. Reverse procedure to install control arm, road test vehicle, then check alignment.

BALL JOINTS
REPLACE
MODEL 900

1. Raise and support vehicle.
2. Clean ball joint and surrounding area.
3. Remove brake caliper and position aside. **Maximum travel of control arm is limited by shock absorber. Remove weight from travel stop before loosening shock absorber.**
4. Position jack under outer end of lower control arm and raise slightly. Re-

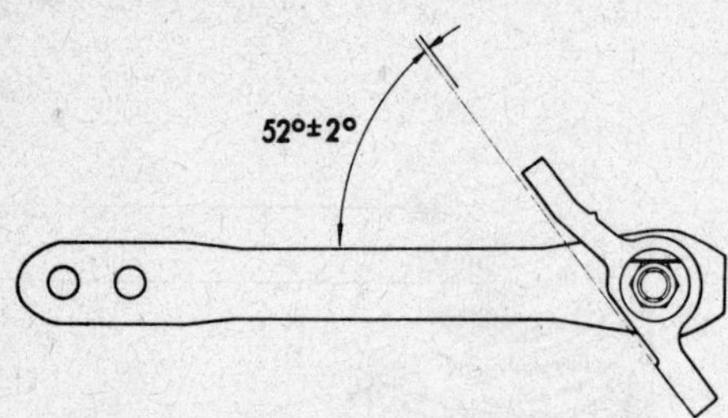

Fig. 5 Upper control arm bearing installation. Model 900

move lower shock absorber mounting.

5. Lower jack so that driveshaft meets body flush at grommet aperture. Leave jack in position to provide support when removing ball joint.
6. Remove nut on ball joint in the steering knuckle housing, **Fig. 7.** Remove bolt using tool 8995409.
7. Separate ball joint from control arm. Position a jack stand under steering knuckle housing to prevent damage to brake hose.
8. Install new ball joint and bolt in steering knuckle housing.
9. Install ball joints to control arm using new locknuts.
10. Raise control arm slightly using a jack and install shock absorber.
11. Install wheel and lower car.

MODEL 9000

1. Raise and support vehicle, and remove wheels.
2. Remove bolts attaching ball joint to spindle.
3. Remove bolts attaching ball joint to lower control arm.
4. Remove ball joint.
5. Reverse procedure to install, torque ball joint nut to spindle to 32-41 ft. lbs.

SHOCK ABSORBER REPLACE

MODEL 900

1. Raise and support vehicle, using suitable jack stands.
2. Disconnect shock absorber at upper and lower mountings, **Fig. 3.**
3. Remove shock absorber from vehicle.
4. Reverse procedure to install.

MODEL 9000

1. Raise and support vehicle.
2. Remove brake line from strut.
3. Remove bolts attaching strut to spindle.
4. Remove three bolts attaching top of strut, then the strut.
5. Using a suitable tool, compress spring.
6. Remove top nut, then the spring and boots.
7. Remove shock.
8. Reverse procedure to install, noting the following:

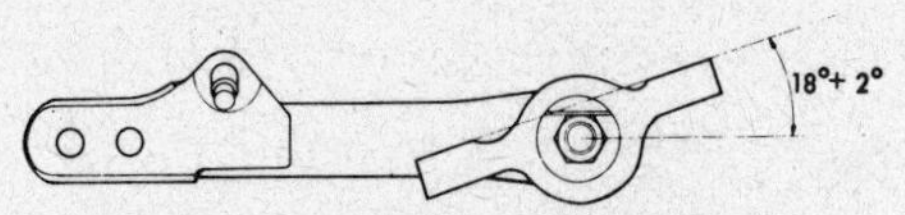

Fig. 6 Lower control arm bearing installation

a. Torque three top nuts to 16-21 ft. lbs.
b. Torque top nut securing spring to 49-59 ft. lbs.
c. Torque bolts securing strut to spindle to 56-75 ft. lbs.

FRONT SPRING REPLACE

MODEL 900

1. Remove upper shock absorber retaining nuts, Fig. 3. **Suspension travel is limited by a stop built into the shock absorber. Therefore, the shock absorber must be removed prior to raising the vehicle, or by using a suitable jack to lift the outer end of the control arm.**
2. Raise and support vehicle and remove front wheel.
3. Install spring compressor 8995839 or equivalent on the lower spring cup and second free coil from top of spring. **Ensure that compressor is properly seated prior to compressing spring.**
4. Compress spring to obtain 1½ inches of clearance at the upper coil, then remove spring.
5. Remove spacers and upper cone, noting position for reassembly.
6. Reverse procedure to install.

MODEL 9000

Refer to "Shock Absorber, Replace" for front spring replacement.

MANUAL STEERING GEAR REPLACE

MODEL 900

1. Remove clamp bolt where joint of steering column shaft is connected to steering gear.
2. Raise vehicle and support vehicle.
3. Remove front wheels and tie rod end nuts.
4. Separate tie rod ends from steering arms using tool No. 8995409.
5. From under vehicle, remove the two steering gear bolts.
6. Separate steering column joint from steering gear, position steering gear to side and remove by guiding it diagonally downwards through opening in engine compartment floor. **Use caution to avoid damaging rubber bellows on edges of lower body work.**

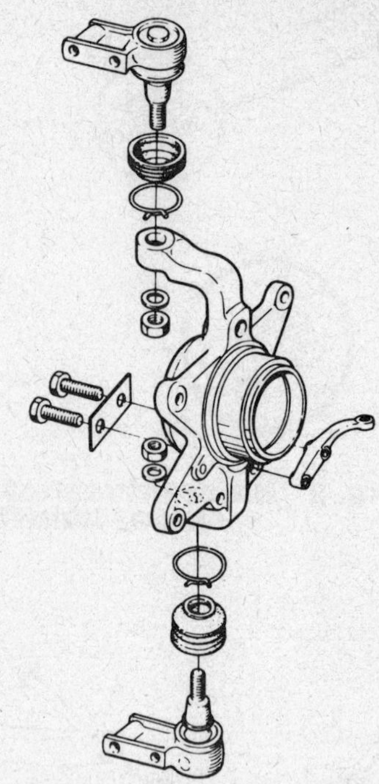

Fig. 7 Ball joint and steering knuckle exploded view

POWER STEERING GEAR REPLACE

MODEL 900

1. Disconnect hydraulic lines at gear and plug lines and open fittings.
2. Remove steering gear as outlined in "Manual Steering Gear, Replace."
3. Reverse procedure to install, then check toe-in and fluid level.

MODEL 9000

1. Remove steering column lower clamp attaching bolt, then loosen upper clamp attaching bolt, and remove intermediate shaft.
2. From inside vehicle, remove floor panel covering, then the cover plate, gasket, seal and plastic bushing.
3. Raise and support front of vehicle, then remove wheel assemblies.
4. Remove left hand fender rear under cover.
5. Remove track rod ends from track arms, using tool No. 8995409.
6. Clean surfaces of hydraulic line connectors at pump reservoir, then drain reservoir fluid.
7. Disconnect servo pump hoses, then the reservoir return hose. **Cap all line and reservoir openings to prevent entry of foreign material.**
8. Remove rack and pinion gear attaching bolts, then the vertical brace between engine and body subframe.
9. Remove steering gear through left-hand wheelwell, using care not to damage brake components, gear unit or surrounding components.
10. Reverse procedure to install.

POWER STEERING PUMP REPLACE

1. Disconnect battery ground cable.
2. Disconnect return line at pump and drain fluid into a suitable container.
3. Remove pump as follows:
   a. Loosen pivot and adjusting bolts and remove drive belt.
   b. Remove pivot bolt and bolt securing adjusting bracket to engine, disconnect and plug pressure line, and remove pump and brackets. **Hold hex fitting on pump with second wrench when disconnecting pressure line.**
4. Remove pump pulley with puller No. 8996423 or equivalent.
5. Remove bolts securing brackets to pump and remove brackets.
6. Reverse procedure to install, noting the following:
   a. Press pulley onto pump shaft using tool 8996415. Shaft should be flush with hub. On 9000 models, ensure distance from pump backing plate to front pulley is 4.23 inch.
   b. Adjust drive belt tension to specifications.
   c. Fill reservoir, bleed system by turning steering wheel from lock to lock, then refill system to full mark on dipstick.

WHEEL ALIGNMENT

INDEX

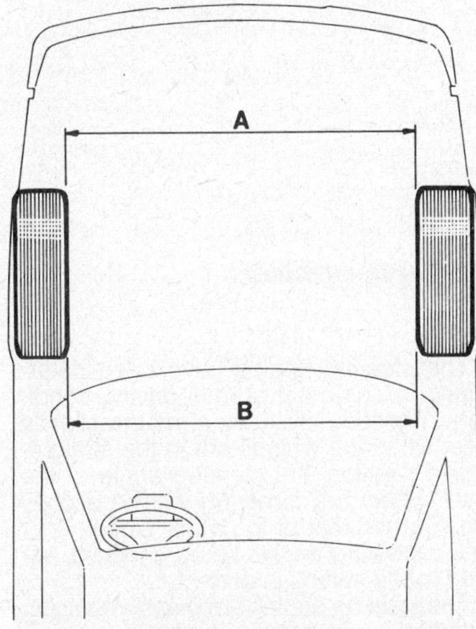

Fig. 1 Positioning vehicle for toe setting

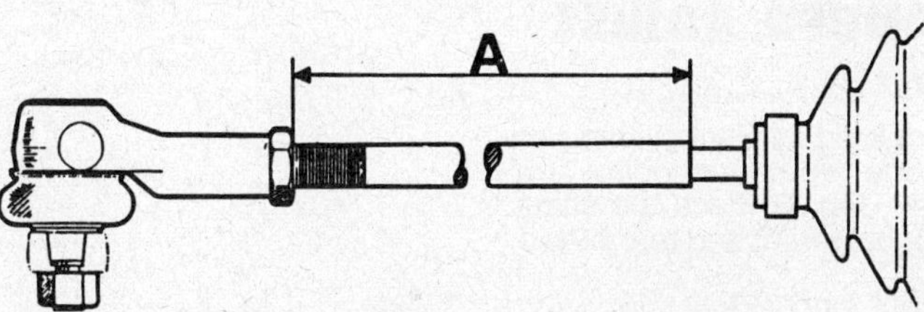

Fig. 2 Measuring toe-in

PRELIMINARY CHECK

1. Ensure tires are inflated to correct pressure, and check for uneven wear.
2. Check front wheel bearings, suspension arm bearing, ball joints and track rods for damage and replace components as necessary, to eliminate improper alignment due to faulty components.
3. Check rack and pinion steering gear and adjust as necessary.
4. Check shocks for damage and replace as necessary.
5. Rock vehicle backward and forward and bounce it upward and downward to settle vehicle prior to alignment.
6. Ensure vehicle is unloaded and on a suitable alignment rack following manufacturers' instructions. **When measuring equipment is attached directly to outer end of driveshaft and front wheels are on turntables, apply brake to prevent improper vehicle movement.**

TOE SETTING

DESCRIPTION

As viewed from above, the wheels must be set so that distances A and B, **Fig. 1**, measured at wheel rims and at axle height, are different at a given value. If distance A is smaller than distance B, the setting is known as toe-in. If Distance A is greater than distance B, the setting is known as toe-out. The toe setting is given in inches (mm) and refers to the difference between A and B. If distances A and B are the same, the toe setting is 0.

TOE-IN, ADJUST

Front

1. Roll vehicle straight forward on level floor and stop without using brakes.
2. Take a reading at dimension "A," **Fig. 1**, using a suitable toe-in gauge between the front wheel rims level with axle. Mark measurement parts with chalk.
3. Roll vehicle forward until chalk marks are level with, but behind, axles and take reading of B, **Fig. 1.** Any necessary adjustment is made by altering length of tie rod.
4. Remove rubber bellows to track rod retaining clip.
5. Push rubber bellows towards steering gear housing to expose groove in which bellows seals.
6. Measure distance A, **Fig. 2.** Distance A should not exceed 3.94 (100 mm) on 900 models or 5.51 inches (140 mm) on 9000 models.
7. Perform steps 4 through 6 on opposite side of vehicle, then compare measurements calculated at each side of vehicle. Difference between measurements must not exceed .079 inch (2 mm).
8. If necessary to adjust, loosen nut on outer end of tie rod, then rotate tie rod until distance A, is as specified.

Rear

Toe-in setting is not adjustable. If setting is not within specified limits, defective components must be replaced.

CAMBER SETTING

DESCRIPTION

Caster refers to the angle at which a wheel leans in or out as shown, **Fig. 3.** Positive camber is when the wheel leans outward and negative camber is when the wheel leans inward.

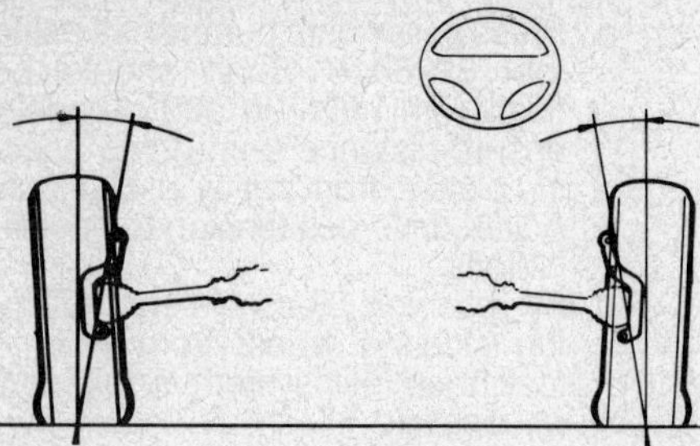

Fig. 3 Measuring camber

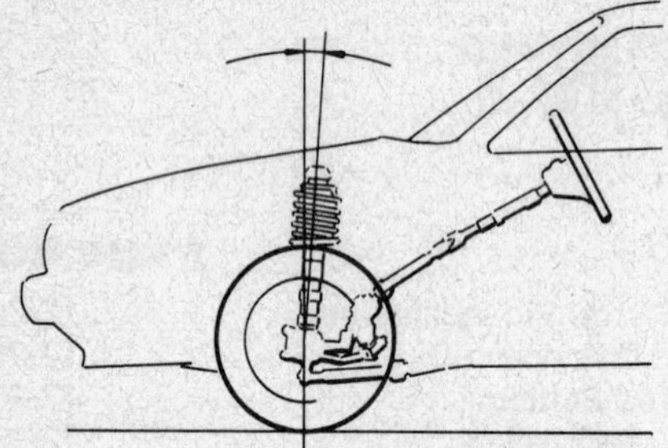

Fig. 5 Measuring caster

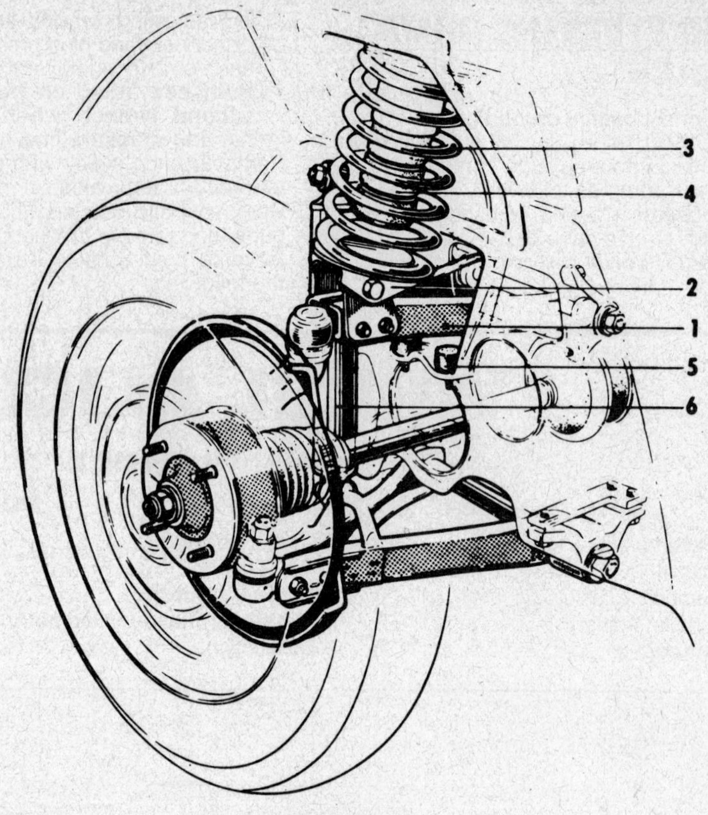

1. Upper control arm
2. Lower spring support
3. Coil spring
4. Rubber buffer
5. Rubber buffers
6. Shock absorber

Fig. 4 Typical front suspension

FRONT CAMBER, ADJUST

Model 900

Camber is adjusted by placing shims or spacers under the two upper control arm bearing brackets, **Fig. 4.** Place the same thickness under both front and rear bracket.

Model 9000

Camber cannot be adjusted. If setting is not within specified limits, defective components must be replaced.

REAR CAMBER, ADJUST

Camber cannot be adjusted. If setting is not within specified limits, defective components must be replaced.

CASTER SETTING

DESCRIPTION

Caster angle refers to the angle at which the swivel pin (king pin) deviates from vertical when viewed from the side, **Fig. 5.**

CASTER, ADJUST

Model 900

To increase the caster, transfer shims from front upper control arm bracket to rear upper control arm bracket, **Fig. 4.** To decrease the caster, transfer shims from back to front.

Model 9000

Caster cannot be adjusted. If setting is not within specified limits, defective components must be replaced.

SWIVEL-PIN INCLINATION

DESCRIPTION

The inclination of the swivel pin cannot be adjusted, since the angle is determined by the steering swivel member. If the swivel pin inclination is incorrect, but camber is satisfactory, a faulty steering swivel member is indicated and replacement is necessary.

ROAD WHEEL STEERING GEOMETRY

DESCRIPTION

The steering angles that will allow perfect rolling of the wheels on cornering vary slightly according to the speed at which the vehicle is travelling and the sharpness of the corner, because of suspension movement and tire deflection.

The steering angles have been determined to suit most normal driving conditions. Because the track arms are slightly inset when the wheels are in the straight-ahead position, the steering angle of the inner wheel on cornering will be slightly greater than that of the outer wheel. Prior to the steering angles being checked, ensure to toe setting is correct.

The steering angles are measured using standard graduated turntables together with optical measuring equipment. The turntables should be positioned as close to the swivel axes of the wheels as possible.

Rotate steering wheel to the left, until the right wheel (outer wheel) shows a deflection of 20°. If steering angle is correct, the inner wheel should show a deflection of $21^{\circ} \pm_{1-2}^{\circ}$. Repeat measurement with wheels rotated in opposite direction. If measurements are incorrect, one or both track arms are defective. Do not bend defective track arms to compensate for incorrect measurements, they must be replaced.

SPECTRUM (Japan)

INDEX OF SERVICE OPERATIONS

General Engine Specifications

Year	Engine CID ①/Liters	Carb. Type	Bores & Stroke Inches (mm)	Comp. Ratio	Horsepower @ RPM	Torque Lbs. Ft. @ RPM	Normal Oil Pressure Lbs.
1985–87	4-90/1.5L	2 Barrel	3.03 x 3.11 (77 x 79)	9.6	70 @ 5400	87 @ 3400	64

①—Cubic inch displacement.

Alternator & Regulator Specifications

Year	Alternator					Regulator			
				Output @ 13.5 Volts			Constant Voltage Relay		
	Model No.	Rated Hot Output Amps.	Field Current 12 Volts @ 80°F	2500 RPM Amps.	5000 RPM Amps.	Model	Air Gap In.	Point Gap In.	Voltage @ 68°F
1985–86	①	30	—	—	48	Integral	—	—	14.2–14.8
	②	60	—	—	62	Integral	—	—	14.2–14.8
1987	①	50	—	—	48	Integral	—	—	14.2–14.8

①—Man. trans. ②—Models with A/C.

Starting Motor Specifications

Year	Engine	Model No.	Rotation	Brush Spring Tension Lbs.	No Load Test			Torque Test		
					Amperes (Max.)	Volts	RPM (Min.)	Amperes (Max.)	Volts	Torque Ft. Lbs. (Min.)
1985–87	4-90/1.5L	①	CW	—	50	11	5000	260	9.5	3.6
	4-90/1.5L	②	CW	—	50	11	5000	270	9.5	5.0

①—Man. trans. ②—Auto. trans.

Valve Specifications

Year	Engine	Valve Lash		Valve Angles		Valve Spring Installed Height	Valve Spring Pressure Lbs. @ In.	Stem Clearance		Stem Diameter	
		Int.	Exh.	Seat	Face			Intake	Exhaust	Intake	Exhaust
1985–86	4-90/1.5L	.006C	.010C	—	45°	—	—	.0009–.0022	.0012–.0025	.2738–.2747	.2737–.2744
1987	4-90/1.5L	.006C	.010C	—	45°	—	—	.0009–.0020	.00118–.00248	0.274–0.275	0.274–0.2744

Pistons, Pins, Rings, Crankshaft & Bearings

Year	Engine	Piston Clearance	Ring End Gap①		Wrist pin Diameter	Rod Bearings		Main Bearings			Shaft End Play
			Comp.	Oil		Shaft Diameter	Bearing Clearance	Shaft Diameter	Bearing Clearance	Thrust on Bearing No.	
1985–86	4-90/1.5L	.0011–.0019	.010	.004	.7086	1.5720–1.5726	.0010–.0023	1.8865–1.8873	.0008–.0020	—	—
1987	4-90/1.5L	.0011–.0019	.010	.004	.7085–.7088	1.572–1.5726	②	1.8865–1.8873	.0008–.0019	—	—

①—Minimum.
②—Type 1, Color Blue: .0009–.0021; Type 2, Black: .0010–.0022; Type 3, Brown; .0011–.0023.

Engine Tightening Specifications

*Torque specifications are for clean and lightly lubricated threads only. Dry or dirty threads produce increase friction which prevents accurate measurement of tightness.

Year	Engine	Spark Plugs Ft. Lbs.	Cylinder Head Bolts Ft. Lbs.	Intake Manifold Ft. Lbs.	Exhaust Manifold Ft. Lbs.	Camshaft Sprocket Bolts Ft. Lbs.	Rocker Shaft Nuts Ft. Lbs.	Rocker Arm Cover Ft. Lbs.	Connecting Rod Cap Bolts Ft. Lbs.	Main Bearing Cap Bolts Ft. Lbs.	Flywheel to Crankshaft Ft. Lbs.	Vibration Damper or Pulley Ft. Lbs.
1985–86	4-90/1.5L	14.7	58	17	17	7	16	7	25	68	22	109
1987	4-90/1.5L	13.7	58	17.4	17.4	7.2	16	7.2	25	65	21.7	108.5

Brake Specifications

Year	Model	Drum Brake I.D.	Wheel Cylinder Bore		Master Cylinder Bore	Disc Brake Rotor Specifications		
			Front Disc	Rear Drum	Power	Nominal Thickness	Minimum Thickness	Runout (T.I.R.)
1985–87	All	7.09	2.13	.690	.810	.433	.378	.006

Wheel Alignment Specifications

Year	Model	Caster Angle Degrees		Camber Angle Degrees				Toe-In Inch	Kingpin Inclination
				Limits		Desired			
		Limits	Desired	Left	Right	Left	Right		
1985–86	All	$+1\frac{3}{4}$ to $+2\frac{3}{4}$	$+1\frac{1}{4}$	$-\frac{5}{12}$ to $+1\frac{1}{12}$	$-\frac{5}{12}$ to $+1\frac{1}{12}$	$+\frac{1}{3}$	$+\frac{1}{3}$	−.08 to +.08	$11\frac{5}{6}$°
1987	All	$+1\frac{3}{4}$ to $+2\frac{3}{4}$	$+1\frac{1}{4}$	$-\frac{1}{3}$ to $+1\frac{1}{3}$ ① ②	$-\frac{1}{3}$ to $+1\frac{1}{3}$ ① ②	+1 ① ③	+1 ① ③	−.08 to +.08 ① ④	$11\frac{5}{6}$°

①—Front Wheels.
②—Rear Wheels, $+\frac{3}{4}$ to $-\frac{1}{4}$.
③—Rear Wheels, $+\frac{1}{2}$.
④—Rear Wheels, 0 to +.19.

Cooling System & Capacity Data

Year	Model	Cooling Capacity Qts.		Radiator Cap Relief Pressure Lbs.	Thermo Opening Temp. °F	Fuel Tank Gals.	Engine Oil Refill Qts. ①	Transmission Oil			Drive Axle Oil Pints
		Auto. Trans.	Man. Trans.					4 Speed Pints	5 Speed Pints	Auto Trans. Qts. ②	
1985–86	All	6.7	6.7	15	180	11	3.4	—	5.6	6.3	—
1987	All	6.8	6.8	15	180	11	4.0	—	5.8	6.1	—

①—Includes filter.
②—Approximate; make final check with dipstick.

L CT ICAL S CTIO

INDEX

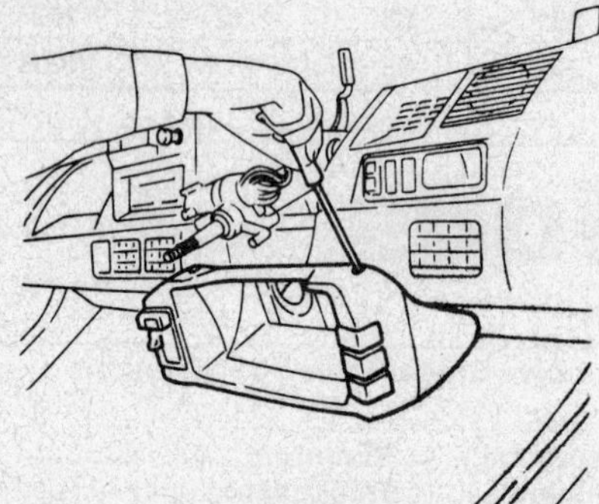

Fig. 1 Instrument cluster bezel removal

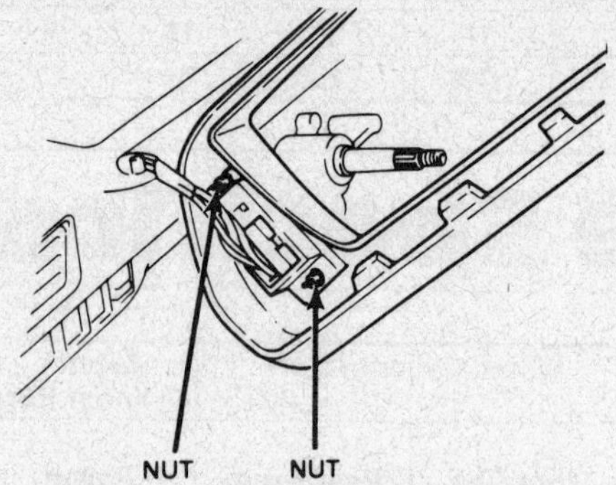

Fig. 2 Headlamp switch replacement

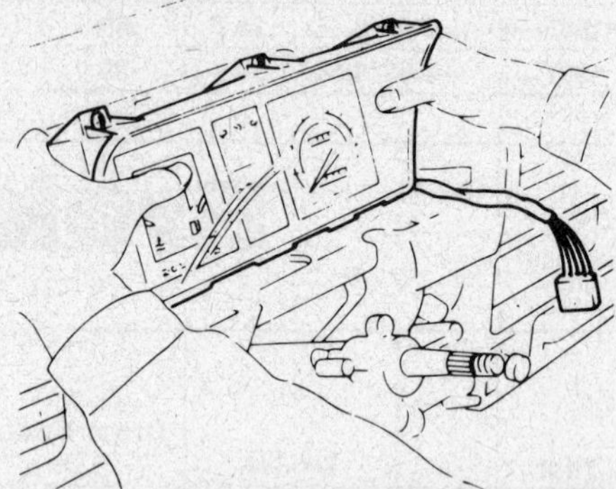

Fig. 3 Instrument cluster replacement

ALTERNATOR TESTING

1. Turn headlamp hi-beams on and switch heater blower to its highest position.
2. Start engine and run at 2000 RPM.
3. If alternator output current exceeds 32, the alternator is functioning properly.

REGULATOR TESTING

1. Connect voltmeter and ammeter to charging circuit.
2. Turn ignition switch to On position and ensure charge lamp lights.
3. Start engine and ensure charge lamp goes out.
4. Start engine and run at 2000 RPM.
5. Ensure proper battery voltage is indicated when output current is approximately 10 amps.

STARTER
REPLACE

1. Disconnect battery ground cable.
2. Disconnect magnetic switch lead wire and battery cable from starter motor.
3. Remove starter motor attaching bolts and the starter.
4. Reverse procedure to install.

TURN SIGNAL/DIMMER SWITCH
REPLACE

1. Disconnect battery ground cable.
2. Remove horn shroud.
3. Remove steering wheel assembly.
4. Remove steering cowl attaching screws, then steering cowl.
5. Disconnect combination switch and starter switch electrical connectors.
6. Remove combination switch attaching screws, then combination switch.
7. Reverse procedure to install.

IGNITION SWITCH
REPLACE

1. Disconnect battery ground cable.
2. Remove steering wheel and cowl.
3. Remove combination switch.
4. Disconnect electrical connector from ignition switch.
5. Remove ignition switch attaching screws and the switch.
6. Reverse procedure to install.

HEADLAMP SWITCH
REPLACE

1. Disconnect battery ground cable.
2. Remove instrument cluster bezel attaching screws and the bezel, **Fig. 1.**
3. Disconnect electrical connectors from headlamp switch and windshield wiper switch.
4. Remove 2 nuts from rear of headlamp switch, then remove the switch from cluster bezel, **Fig. 2.**
5. Reverse procedure to install.

INSTRUMENT CLUSTER
REPLACE

1. Disconnect battery ground cable.
2. Remove instrument cluster bezel attaching screws and the bezel, **Fig. 1.**
3. Disconnect electrical connectors from headlamp switch and wiper switch.
4. Remove instrument cluster attaching screws and the cluster, **Fig. 3.**
5. Reverse procedure to install.

WIPER SWITCH
REPLACE
FRONT

1. Disconnect battery ground cable.
2. Remove instrument cluster bezel attaching screws and pull bezel out.
3. Disconnect electrical connectors from headlamp switch and wiper switch.
4. Remove bezel inside attaching nuts and bracket, then push switch out of bezel, **Fig. 4.**
5. Reverse procedure to install.

REAR

1. Disconnect battery ground cable.
2. Pry switch panel open with a screwdriver and pull switch out.
3. Disconnect electrical connector, then remove switch, **Fig. 5.**
4. Reverse procedure to install.

WIPER MOTOR & TRANSMISSION
REPLACE
FRONT

1. Disconnect battery ground cable.
2. Remove wiper arm locknuts and the wiper arms.
3. Remove cowl cover, then the wiper motor cover.
4. Disconnect electrical connector from wiper motor.
5. Separate wiper drive arm from wiper link.

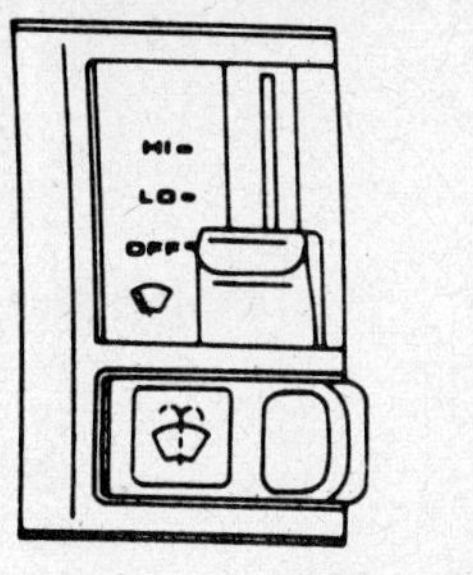

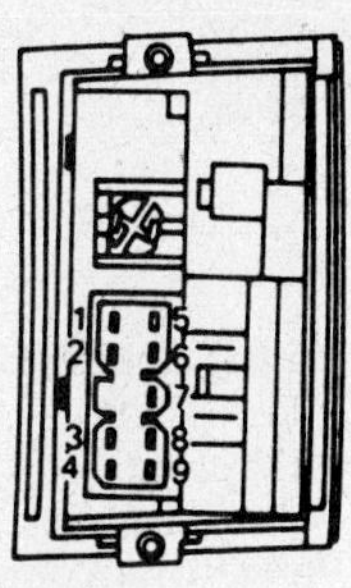

Fig. 4 Front wiper switch replacement

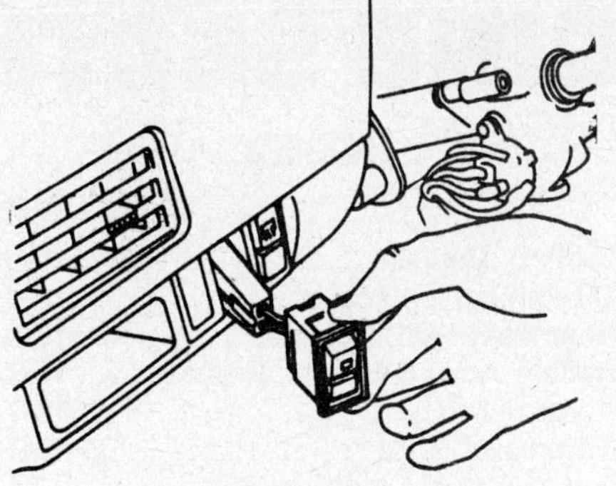

Fig. 5 Rear wiper switch replacement

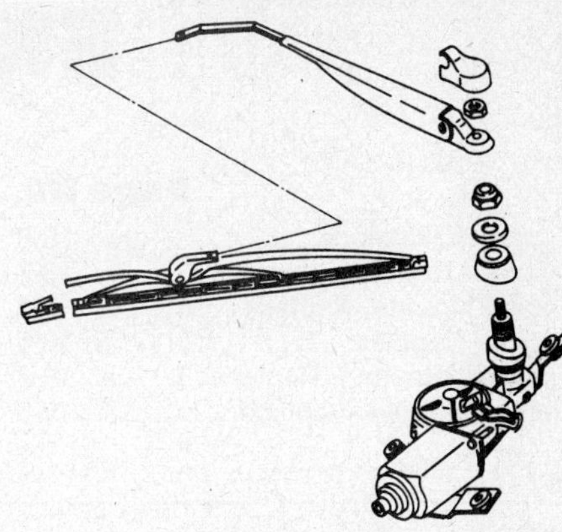

Fig. 7 Rear wiper motor assembly

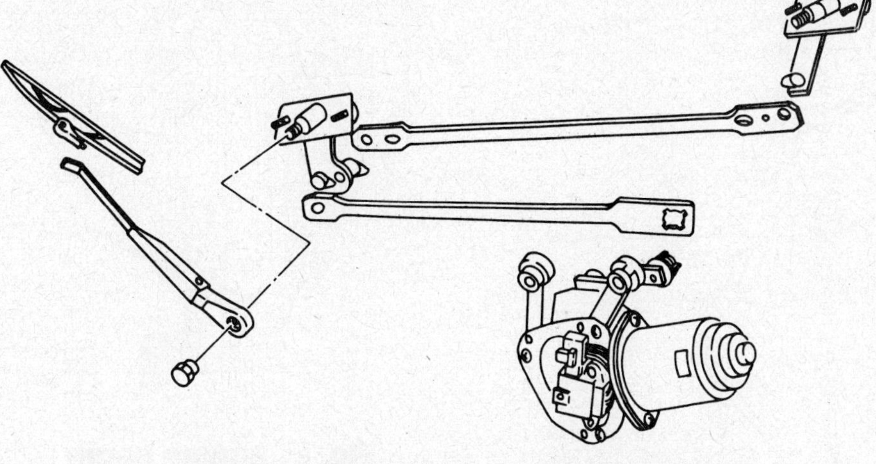

Fig. 6 Front wiper motor assembly

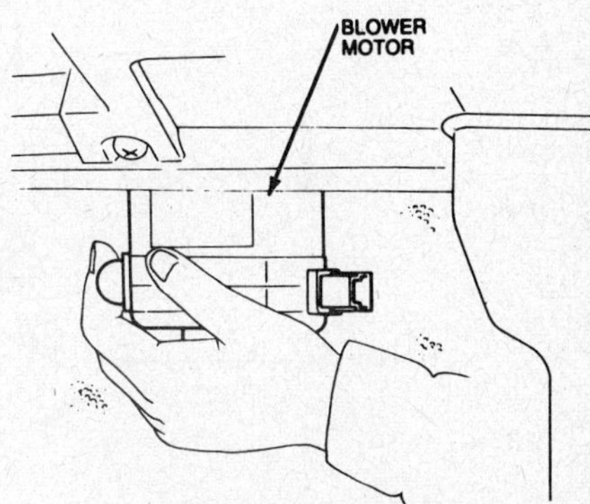

Fig. 8 Blower motor replacement

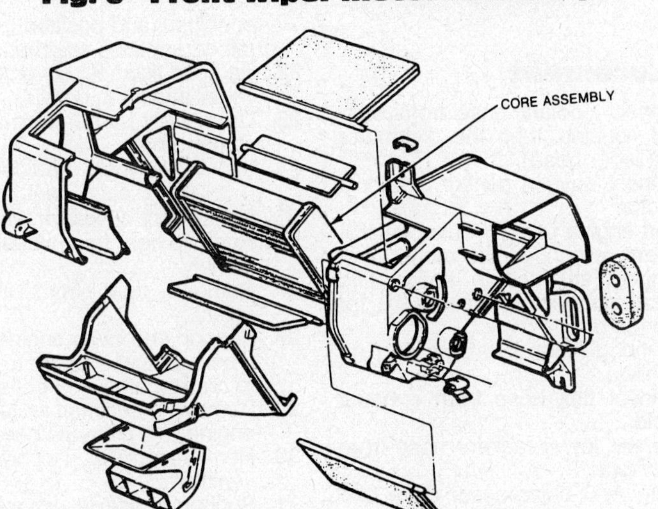

Fig. 9 Heater core assembly

6. Disconnect wiper link from wiper motor arm.
7. Remove wiper motor attaching bolt, then the wiper and link, **Fig. 6.**
8. Reverse procedure to install.

REAR

1. Disconnect batttery ground cable.
2. Remove trim pad assembly.
3. Remove wiper arm assembly.
4. Remove wiper motor fasteners, then disconnect electrical connector and remove motor, **Fig. 7.**
5. Reverse procedure to install.

BLOWER MOTOR REPLACE

1. Disconnect battery ground cable.
2. Disconnect blower motor electrical connector from motor case.
3. On models equipped with A/C, disconnect rubber hose from case.
4. On all models, rotate blower motor counterclockwise and remove from case, **Fig. 8.**
5. Reverse procedure to install.

HEATER CORE REPLACE

1. Disconnect battery ground cable.
2. Disconnect heater hoses from core. **When disconnecting heater hoses at core tube connection, take care not to use excessive force, or damage to core may result.**
3. Remove 6 retaining clips, then the lower part of heater case.
4. Carefully pry open lower part of heater case and remove heater core, **Fig. 9.**
5. Reverse procedure to install.

ENGINE SECTION

INDEX

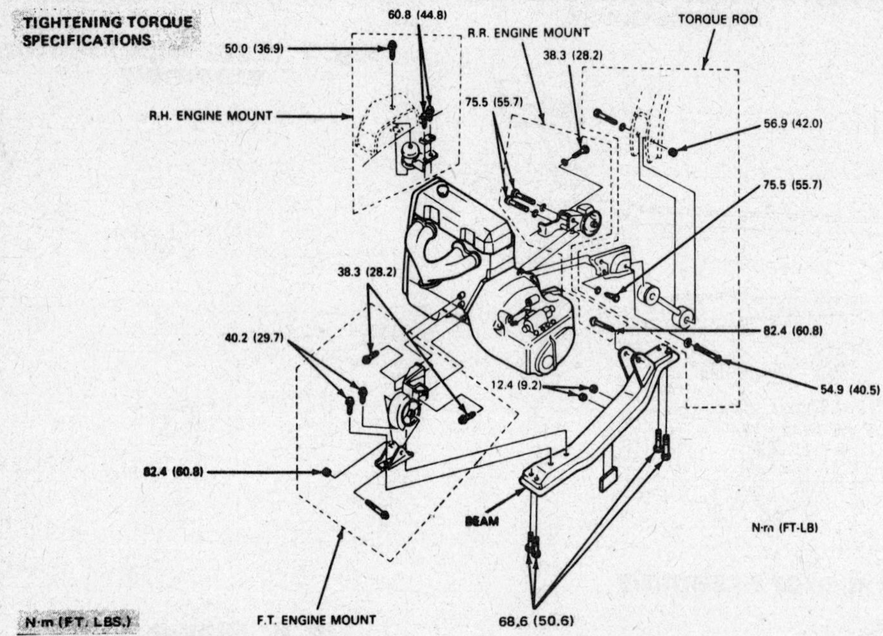

Fig. 1 Engine mount replacement

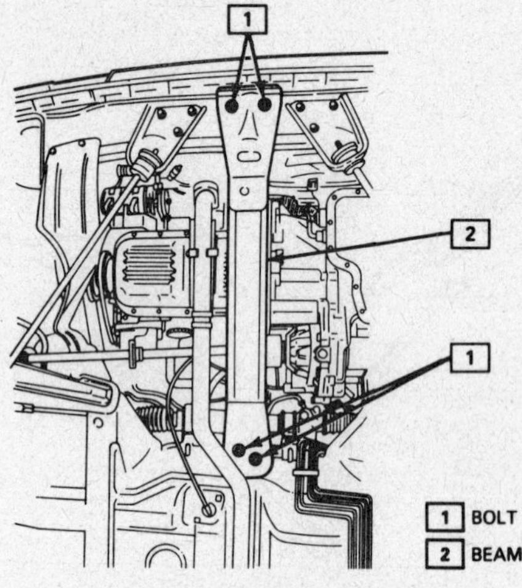

Fig. 2 Engine beam removal

ENGINE MOUNTS
REPLACE

1. Disconnect battery ground cable.
2. Support engine using a suitable jack.
3. Remove two bolts and plate from right side of engine.
4. Remove right side mount attaching bolt and the mount, **Fig. 1.**
5. Remove engine side bolt, body side nut and bolt the torque rod, **Fig. 1.**
6. Remove through bolts and nuts from front and rear engine mounts.
7. Remove 4 beam attaching bolts and the beam, **Fig. 2.**
8. Remove front and rear engine mounts.
9. Reverse procedure to install.

ENGINE
REPLACE

1. Disconnect battery ground cable.
2. Drain cooling system, then remove air cleaner.
3. Disconnect throttle cable from carburetor.
4. Disconnect heater hose from intake manifold, then the thermostat housing from cylinder head.
5. Disconnect coolant hose from thermostat housing, then the distributor from cylinder head.
6. Disconnect oxygen sensor electrical connector.
7. Support engine using a suitable jack, then remove right engine mount.
8. Disconnect all vacuum hoses and electrical connectors necessary for engine removal.
9. Scribe hood hinge locations and remove hood.
10. Disconnect flex hose from exhaust manifold.
11. Disconnect lower radiator hose from engine block.
12. Remove A/C compressor drive belt and power steering pump drive belt, as equipped.
13. Disconnect fuel lines from fuel pump.
14. Disconnect electrical connectors under carburetor.
15. Remove upper starter attaching bolt.
16. Raise and support vehicle.
17. Drain crankcase and remove oil filter.
18. Disconnect oil temperature switch electrical connector.
19. Disconnect exhaust pipe bracket from cylinder block.
20. Disconnect exhaust pipe from exhaust manifold.
21. Unfasten A/C compressor, if equipped, and position aside, leaving refrigerant lines attached.
22. Remove flywheel cover and the converter attaching bolts.
23. Disconnect starter wire and remove starter motor.
24. Install flywheel holder tool No. J-35271 or equivalent.
25. Disconnect alternator wires.
26. Remove right front wheel and tire assembly.
27. Remove right front inner splash shield.
28. Support and lower engine by lowering crossmember enough to gain access to crankshaft pulley bolts.
29. Remove crankshaft pulley, then raise engine and crossmember.
30. Remove engine support, then lower vehicle.
31. Support transaxle with a suitable jack, then remove engine to transaxle bolts and the engine from vehicle.
32. Reverse procedure to install.

INTAKE MANIFOLD
REPLACE

1. Disconnect battery ground cable, then drain cooling system.
2. Remove alternator adjusting plate bolt.
3. Disconnect all hoses and electrical connectors from air cleaner, then remove air cleaner assembly.

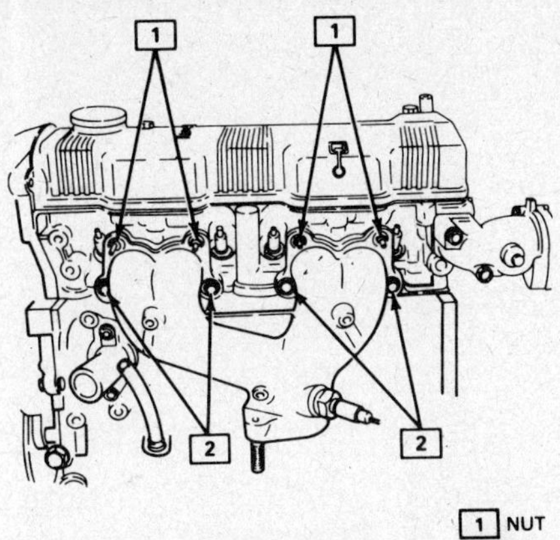

Fig. 3 Exhaust manifold replacement

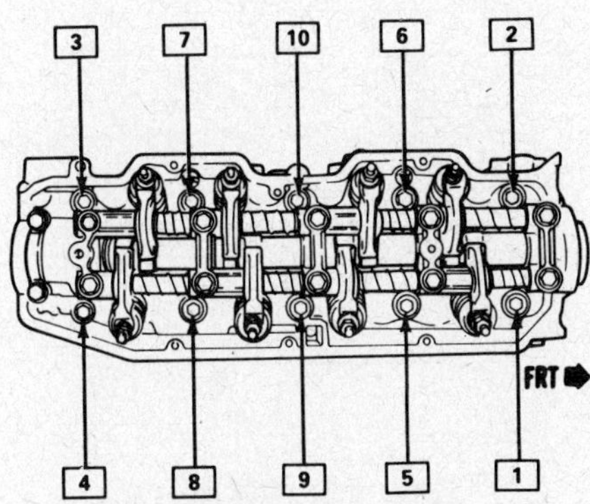

Fig. 4 Cylinder head bolt loosening sequence

4. Disconnect all hoses, electrical connectors and cables from carburetor, then remove carburetor assembly.
5. Disconnect all coolant and vacuum hoses and electrical connectors from intake manifold.
6. Remove intake manifold, attaching bolts and the intake manifold.
7. Reverse procedure to install.

EXHAUST MANIFOLD

REPLACE

1. Disconnect battery ground cable.
2. Disconnect oxygen sensor electrical connector.
3. Disconnect TCA flex hose, then remove hot air cover.
4. Raise and support vehicle.
5. Disconnect exhaust pipe from exhaust manifold, then lower vehicle.
6. Remove exhaust manifold attaching nuts and bolts, then the exhaust manifold, **Fig. 3.**
7. Reverse procedure to install, noting the following:
   a. Using a straightedge and feeler gauge, check cylinder head surface for warpage.
   b. Exhaust manifold must be replaced if warpage exceeds .0157 inch (0.4 mm).

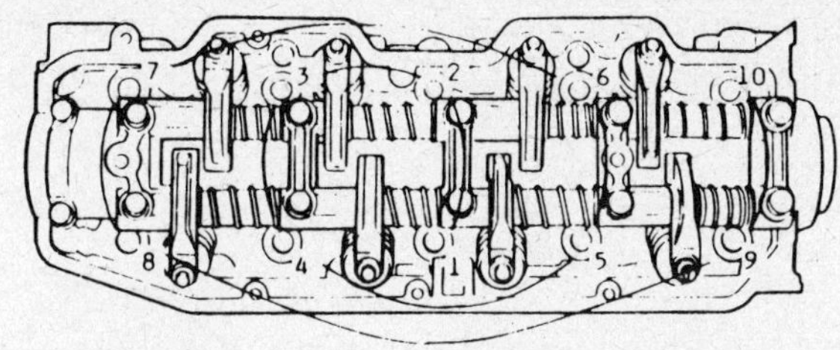

Fig. 5 Cylinder head bolt tightening sequence

CYLINDER HEAD

REPLACE

1. Disconnect battery ground cable.
2. Drain cooling system, then remove air cleaner assembly.
3. Disconnect flex hose from exhaust manifold.
4. Disconnect electrical connector from oxygen sensor.
5. Disconnect exhaust pipe bracket from block, then the exhaust pipe from manifold.
6. Disconnect spark plug wires from plugs.
7. Disconnect thermostat housing and distributor from cylinder head.
8. Disconnect vacuum advance hoses, then the fuel lines from fuel pump.
9. Disconnect ground cable from intake manifold.
10. Disconnect necessary hoses and the throttle cable from carburetor.
11. Disconnect vacuum switching valve electrical connector.
12. Disconnect heater hoses from intake manifold.
13. Remove power steering pump drive belt, if equipped.
14. Support engine using a suitable jack.
15. Remove right side engine mount and bracket from front cover.
16. Remove A/C compressor drive belt, if equipped.
17. Remove alternator drive belt, then align timing marks and remove front cover.
18. Loosen tension pulley, then remove timing belt.
19. Remove alternator bracket bolt from intake manifold.
20. On models equipped with power steering, remove power steering pump through bolt from pump bracket, then the pump mounting bracket from block.
21. On all models, disconnect carburetor fuel line from fuel pump, then remove the pump.
22. Disconnect coolant hoses from intake manifold.
23. Remove cylinder head attaching bolts in sequence, **Fig. 4.**
24. Remove cylinder head.
25. Reverse procedure to install. Torque head attaching bolts to specifications in sequence, **Fig. 5.**

VALVE ARRANGEMENT

FRONT TO REAR

All....................... I-E-E-I-I-E-E-I

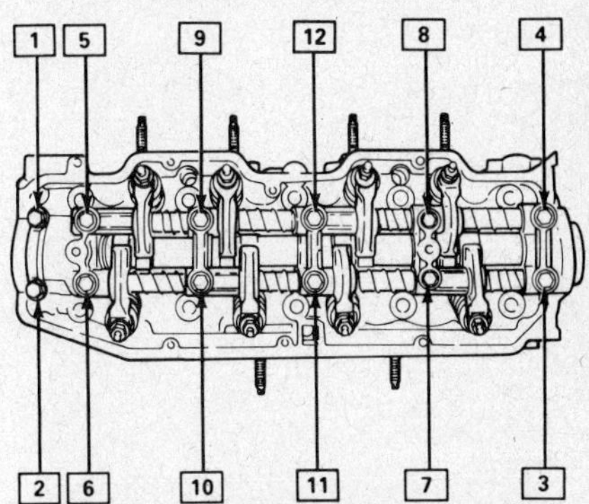

Fig. 6 Rocker arm shaft removal & installation sequence

VALVES

ADJUST

1. Turn crankshaft in normal direction of rotation until No. 1 or No. 4 piston is at TDC of compression stroke.
2. Measure valve clearance between rocker arm and valve stem and adjust to specifications.
3. Rotate crankshaft one complete turn and adjust clearances of remaining valves.

ROCKER ARMS & SHAFTS

REPLACE

REMOVAL

1. Disconnect battery ground cable.
2. Disconnect CPV hoses and unclip spark plug wires from valve cover.
3. Disconnect ground wire from valve cover.
4. Remove right side engine mounting rubber.
5. Support engine with a suitable jack.
6. Remove bolts and plate from side of engine.
7. Remove bracket from front cover.
8. Remove 4 front cover attaching bolts.
9. Remove valve cover attaching bolts.
10. Loosen front cover, then remove valve cover.
11. Remove rocker arm bracket bolts in sequence, **Fig. 6.**
12. Remove rocker arm shaft and rocker arms.

INSTALLATION

1. Lightly lubricate rocker arms and shafts with clean engine oil.

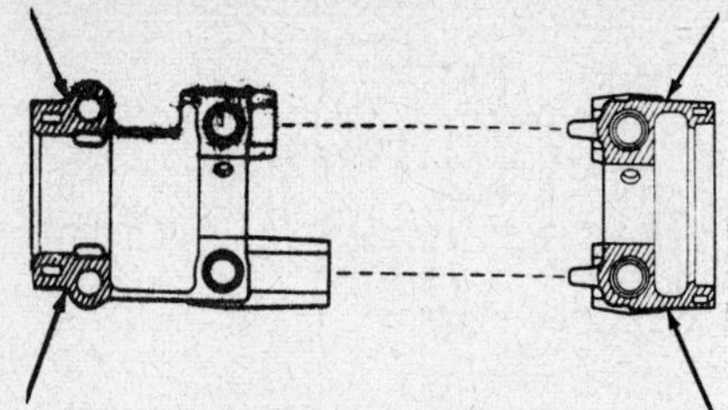

Fig. 7 Applying sealant to rocker brackets

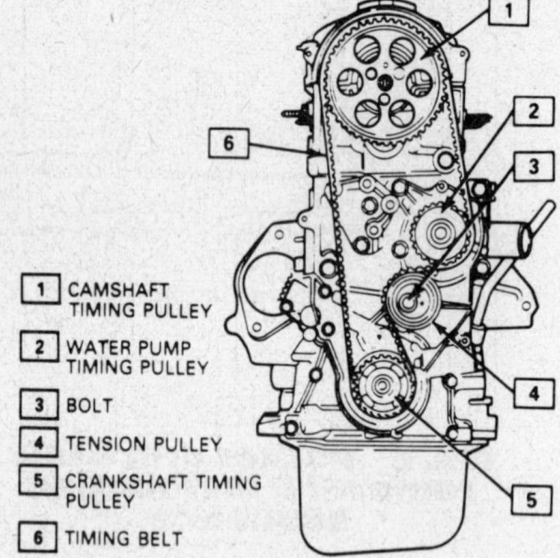

Fig. 10 Timing belt installation

2. Install rocker shafts with identification marks to the front of engine.
3. Remove residual oil from contact surfaces of Nos. 1 and 5 rocker brackets on cylinder head.
4. Apply suitable sealant to contact surfaces of Nos. 1 and 5 rocker brackets, **Fig. 7.**
5. Install rocker assembly, tightening rocker arm bolts to specifications in sequence, **Fig. 6.**

TIMING BELT REPLACE

REMOVAL

1. Remove engine as described under "Engine, Replace".
2. Remove accessory drive belts, then the engine mounting bracket from front cover.
3. Rotate crankshaft to position No. 4 piston at TDC of compression stroke.
4. Remove starter motor, then install flywheel holder tool No. J-35271 or equivalent.
5. Remove crankshaft bolt, then the boss and crank pulley.
6. Remove front cover, then loosen tension pulley fixing bolt.
7. Loosen timing belt tension using a hex wrench in the tension pulley hole.
8. Remove timing belt.

INSTALLATION

1. Install crankshaft timing pulley, ensuring woodruff key is properly positioned, **Fig. 8.**

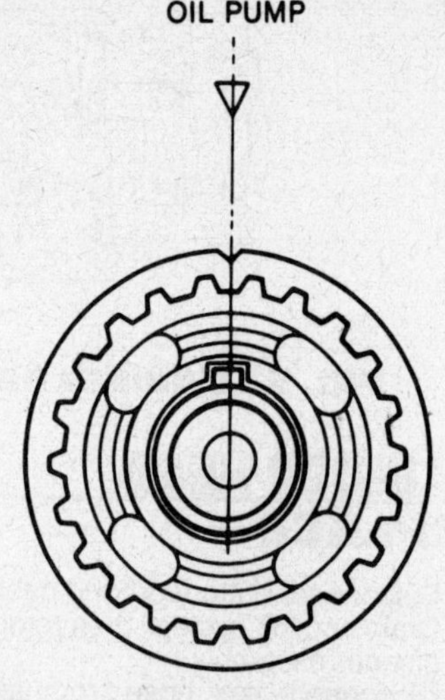

Fig. 8 Crankshaft pulley alignment

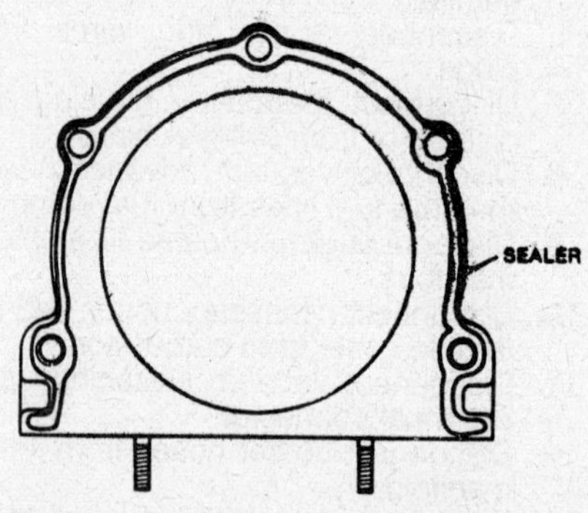

Fig. 11 Applying sealant to rear seal retainer

2. Position pulley on crankshaft, aligning pulley timing groove with mark on oil pump, **Fig. 8.**
3. Ensure camshaft pulley timing mark is aligned with upper surface of cylinder head and dowel pin is in up position, **Fig. 9.**
4. Position timing belt arrow mark in direction of engine rotation and install belt over pulleys, **Fig. 10,** in the following order: crankshaft, camshaft, water pump, tension.
5. Loosen tension pulley bolt. Insert a hex wrench into tension pulley hole, then temporarily tighten bolt while holding pulley stationary.
6. Turn crankshaft two complete revolutions and align crankshaft timing pulley groove with mark on oil pump.
7. Loosen tension pulley bolt, then apply tension to belt and torque bolt to 37 ft. lbs., while holding pulley stationary.
8. Turn crankshaft back approximately 50° and set crankshaft at that position.
9. Check belt tension using suitable tension gauge. Tension should measure 33.1-41.9 lbs.
10. Check valve clearances as previously described.

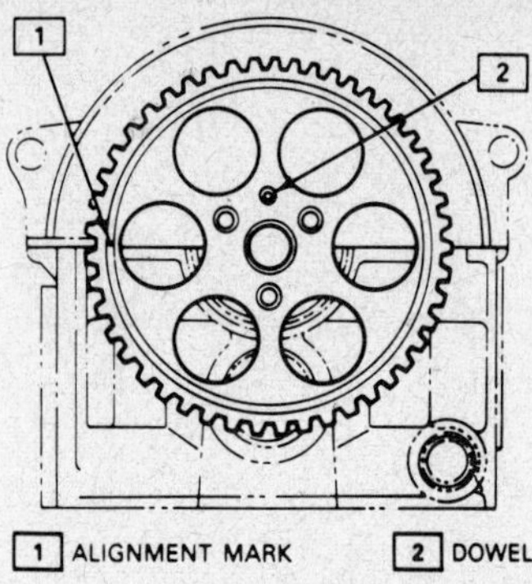

Fig. 9 Camshaft pulley alignment

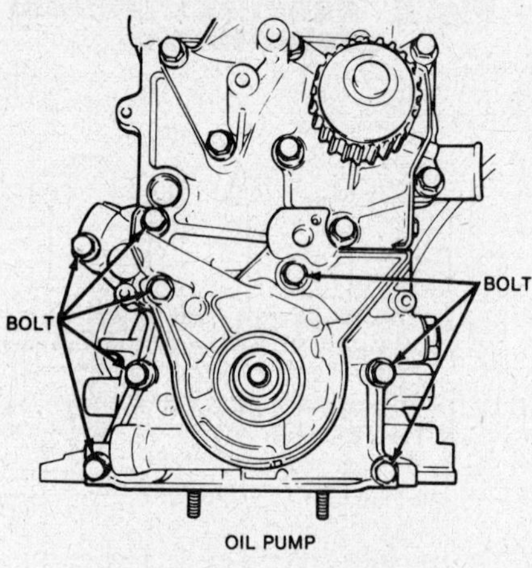

Fig. 12 Oil pump replacement

11. Apply suitable sealant to cylinder head mating surface and four points of each arched area of Nos. 1 and 5 rocker brackets.
12. Install valve cover and torque bolts to 7 ft. lbs.
13. Install timing cover and torque bolts to 7.2 ft. lbs.
14. Install crankshaft pulley and torque bolt to 108.5 ft. lbs.
15. Install starter and torque bolts to 36.9 ft. lbs.
16. Install engine mount bracket and torque bolts to 17.3 ft. lbs.
17. Install engine.

CAMSHAFT REPLACE

1. Disconnect battery ground cable.
2. Align mark on crankshaft pulley with "0" mark on front cover.
3. Remove valve cover, then loosen camshaft pulley bolts.
4. Loosen timing belt tensioner, then remove timing belt.
5. Remove rocker arm shafts as previously described.
6. Remove camshaft pulley, then the distributor and camshaft.
7. Reverse procedure to install. Ensure dowel pin is in up position when installing camshaft.

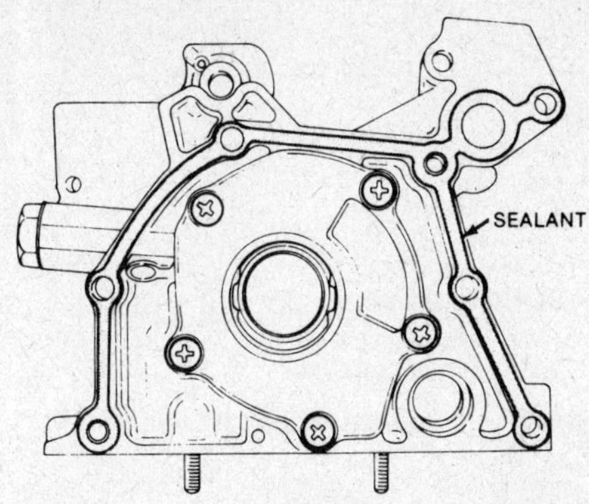

Fig. 13 Applying sealant to oil pump mating surface

REAR MAIN SEAL
REPLACE

1. Remove transaxle as described elsewhere in this chapter.
2. Disconnect exhaust pipe bracket.
3. Remove oil pan as described under "Oil Pan, Replace."
4. Remove rear retainer, then the rear main oil seal.
5. Clean retainer mating surface and apply suitable sealant as shown, **Fig. 11.**
6. Apply clean engine oil to seal lip, then install retainer and the seal using tool No. J-35264 or equivalent.

OIL PAN
REPLACE

1. Disconnect battery ground cable.
2. Raise and support vehicle.
3. Drain engine oil, then disconnect exhaust pipe bracket from block.
4. Disconnect exhaust pipe from exhaust manifold.
5. Disconnect right hand tension rod under bumper.
6. Remove oil pan attaching bolts and the oil pan.
7. Reverse procedure to install. Ensure pan and cylinder case mating surfaces are clean prior to mounting pan.

OIL PUMP
REPLACE

1. Remove engine assembly as previously described.
2. Drain crankcase, then remove alternator drive belt.
3. Remove starter motor, then install flywheel holder tool No. J-35271 or equivalent.
4. Remove crankshaft pulley and boss.
5. Remove front cover, then the timing belt.
6. Remove crankshaft timing pulley and tension pulley.
7. Remove oil pan attaching bolts and the oil pan.
8. Remove oil strainer attaching bolt and the strainer.
9. Remove oil attaching bolts and the oil pump, **Fig. 12.**
10. Reverse procedure to install. Apply suitable sealant to oil pump mating surface, **Fig. 13.**

WATER PUMP
REPLACE

1. Drain cooling system.

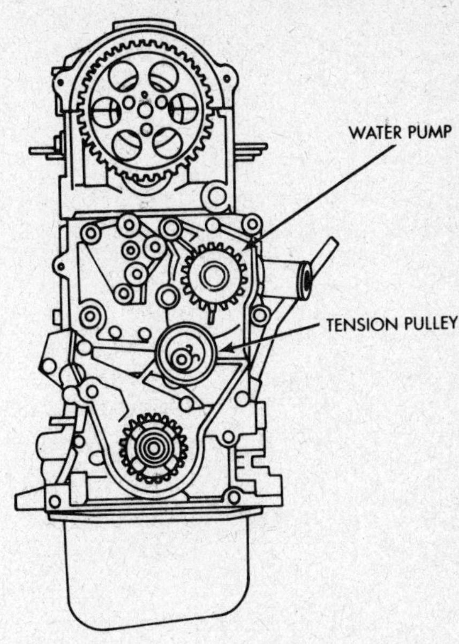

Fig. 14 Water pump replacement

2. Remove power steering pump drive belt.
3. Remove timing belt as previously described.
4. Remove tension pulley and tension spring.
5. Remove water pump attaching bolts and the water pump, **Fig. 14.**
6. Reverse procedure to install. Torque bolts to 17. 4 ft. lbs.

CLUTCH & MANUAL TRANSAXLE SECTION

INDEX

Page No.

CLUTCH PEDAL
ADJUST

1. Disconnect battery ground cable.
2. Loosen clutch cable adjusting nut, **Fig. 1,** then pull cable rearward until it turns freely.
3. Turn adjusting nut as needed to adjust cable length. Release cable when pedal free play is within specifications, **Fig. 2.**
4. Tighten locknut securely.

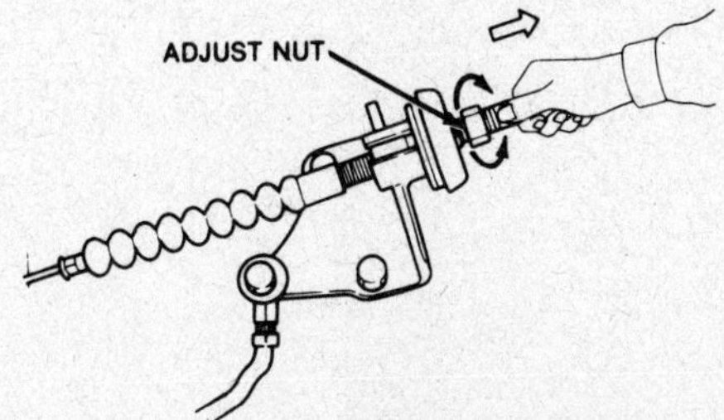

Fig. 1 Clutch cable adjustment

CLUTCH
REPLACE

1. Remove transaxle as described under "Transaxle, Replace."
2. Install tool No. J-35282 or equivalent into pilot bearing to support clutch.
3. Mark clutch cover and flywheel, if not already done, for assembly reference.
4. Loosen clutch cover-to-flywheel attaching bolts evenly, one at a time, until spring pressure is relieved.

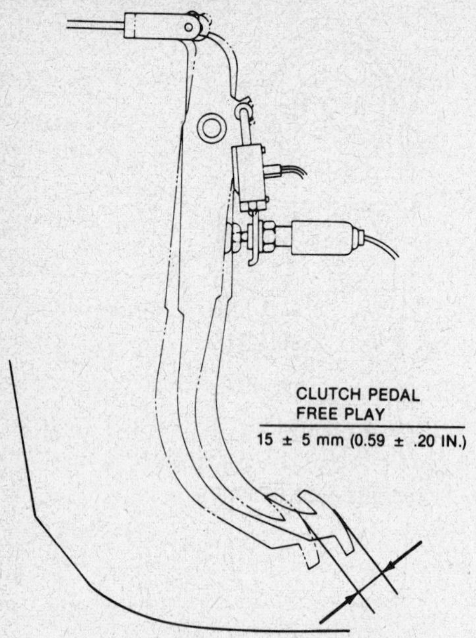

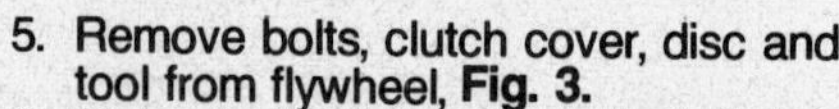

Fig. 2 Clutch pedal free travel measurement

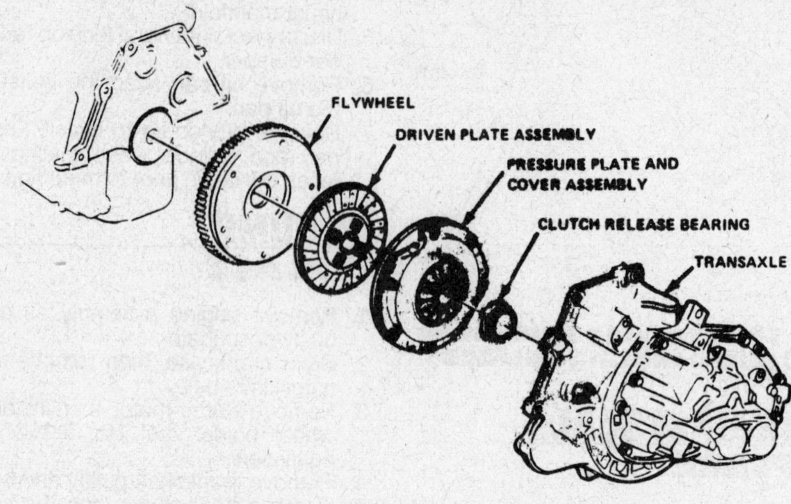

Fig. 3 Exploded view of clutch assembly

5. Remove bolts, clutch cover, disc and tool from flywheel, **Fig. 3.**
6. Reverse procedure to install. Lubricate input shaft splines and release bearing with suitable grease during installation.

TRANSAXLE
REPLACE

1. Disconnect battery ground cable.
2. Drain transaxle oil.
3. Disconnect ground cable and electrical connectors from transaxle.
4. Disconnect speedometer cable and clutch cable from transaxle.
5. Disconnect shift and select cables from transaxle.
6. Remove air cleaner heat tube.
7. Remove upper engine-to-transaxle attaching bolts.
8. Raise and support vehicle.
9. Remove left front wheel and tire assembly.
10. Remove splash shield.
11. Disconnect left tie rod from steering knuckle.
12. Remove left tension rod.
13. Disconnect drive axles from transaxle, using care to avoid damaging oil seals.
14. Remove dust cover from clutch housing.
15. Support transaxle using a suitable jack.
16. Remove remaining transaxle-to-engine attaching bolts.
17. Slide transaxle assembly toward driver's side, away from engine. Carefully lower jack while guiding right shaft out of transaxle and remove assembly from vehicle.
18. Reverse procedure to install, noting the following:
    a. When installing transaxle, guide right axle shaft into its bore as assembly is raised.
    b. Torque transaxle-to-engine attaching bolts to 55 ft. lbs.
    c. Torque left tension rod attaching bolts to 80 ft. lbs.

DISC BRAKES SECTION

INDEX

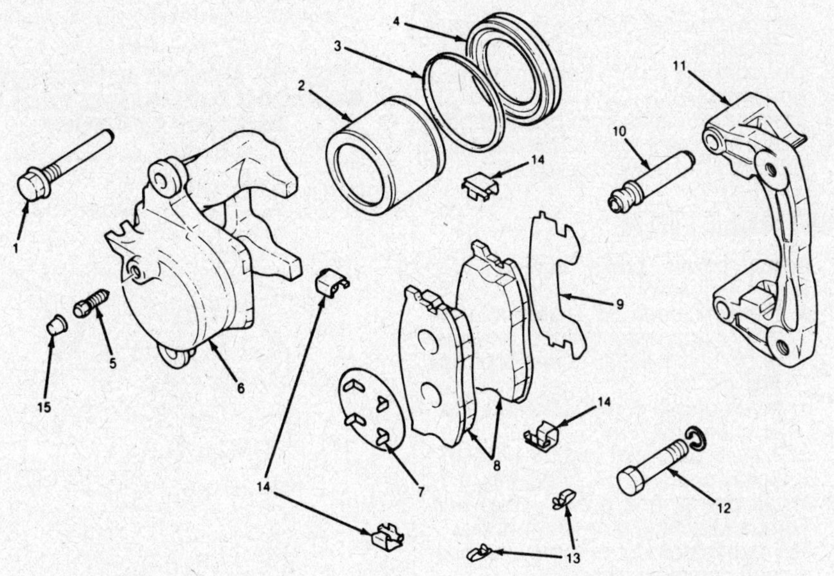

1. SLIDE PIN BOLT
2. PISTON
3. PISTON SEAL
4. PISTON BOOT
5. BLEEDER SCREW
6. CALIPER BODY
7. INNER SHIM
8. PADS
9. OUTER SHIM
10. SLIDE PIN BOOT
11. BRACKET
12. BOLT
13. WEAR INDICATOR
14. RETAINER
15. CAP

Fig. 1 Exploded view of disc brake caliper assembly

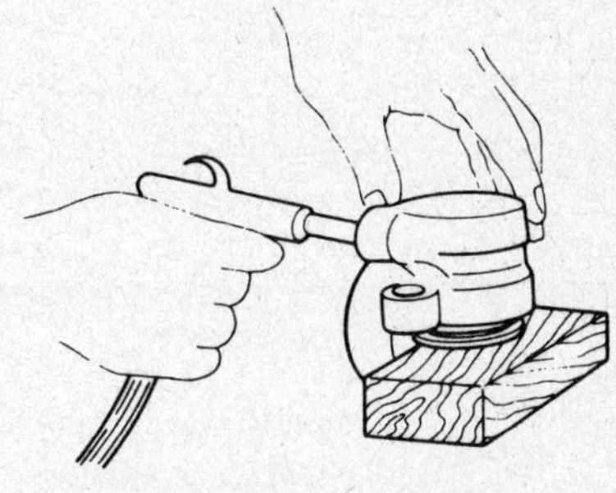

CAUTION: Do not place fingers in front of the piston in an attempt to catch or protect it when applying compressed air. This could result in serious injury.

NOTICE: Use just enough air to ease the piston out of the bore. If the piston is blown out, even with padding provided, it may be damaged.

Fig. 2 Removing caliper piston

BRAKE PADS REPLACE

1. Remove approximately 2/3 of brake fluid from master cylinder.
2. Raise and support vehicle.
3. Mark relationship between front wheel and axle, then remove wheel and tire assembly.
4. Remove 2 caliper slide pins from bracket.
5. Unfasten caliper and support with a length of wire, leaving hydraulic lines connected.
6. Remove brake pads, shims, wear indicators and retainers, **Fig. 1.**
7. Reverse procedure to install.

CALIPER SERVICE

REMOVAL

1. Remove approximately 2/3 of brake fluid from master cylinder.
2. Raise and support vehicle.
3. Mark relationship between front wheel and axle, then remove wheel and tire assembly.
4. Disconnect and cap flexible hose from caliper.
5. Remove caliper slide pins and the caliper.
6. Remove pad assembly.
7. Remove bracket attaching bolts and the bracket.
8. Remove slide pin boot from bracket.

DISASSEMBLY

1. Insert a block of wood into caliper and remove piston with compressed air, **Fig. 2.**
2. Remove boot from piston.
3. Remove piston seal from caliper.

ASSEMBLY

1. Clean all components with suitable solvent. Use dry, filtered compressed air to dry components and blow out all passages in caliper body and bleeder valve.
2. Apply suitable grease to piston seal and cylinder wall, then install the seal.
3. Apply suitable grease to sliding portion of piston and install the dust boot.
4. Insert edge of dust boot into boot groove, then slowly force piston fully into cylinder.

INSTALLATION

1. Apply suitable grease to inner face of slide pin boot.
2. Install slide pin boot to bracket.
3. Install bracket and torque attaching bolts to 40.5 ft. lbs.
4. Install pad assembly, ensuring wear indicator and retainer are properly attached to pad.
5. Install caliper assembly to bracket. Torque attaching bolts to 36 ft. lbs.
6. Attach flexible hose to caliper and torque fitting to 13.4 ft. lbs.
7. Install wheel and tire assembly, then lower vehicle.
8. Fill master cylinder to proper level and bleed brakes.

BRAKE PEDAL HEIGHT ADJUST

1. Ensure pedal is fully returned by pedal return spring, then measure brake pedal height, **Fig. 3.**
2. If measurement does not meet specification, perform adjustment as follows:

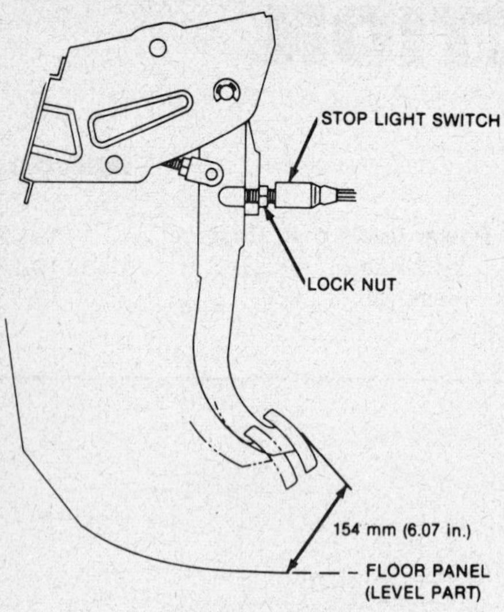

Fig. 3 Brake pedal height adjustment

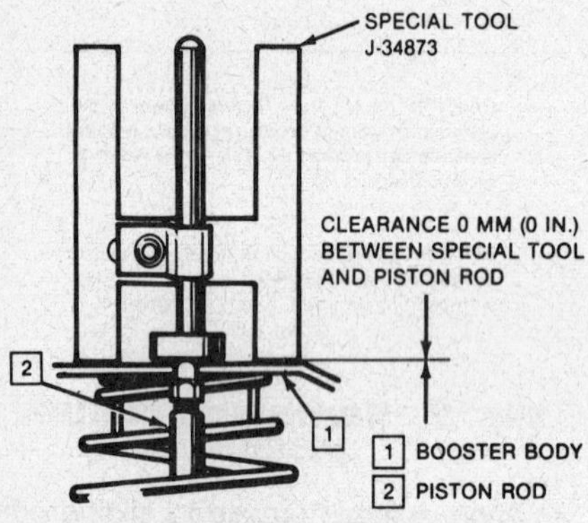

Fig. 5 Power brake unit pushrod adjusting tool on power brake unit

a. Loosen stop light switch and the locknut on pushrod.
b. Adjust push rod until brake pedal extends approximately 6.07 inches from floorboard.
c. Position tip of stop lamp switch to rest lightly on pedal arm rubber stop.
d. Carefully rotate stop lamp switch until free play between pedal arm and push rod is eliminated from brake pedal.
e. Tighten locknut.

POWER BRAKE UNIT REPLACE

REMOVAL

1. Remove master cylinder as previously described.
2. Disconnect vacuum hose from vacuum servo.
3. Disconnect clevis from brake pedal.
4. Remove power brake unit attaching nuts and the power brake unit.

INSTALLATION

1. Adjust power brake unit pushrod length as follows:
   a. Position pushrod gauge No. J-34873 on master cylinder and lower pin until it lightly contacts piston, **Fig. 4.**
   b. Invert gauge and position on power brake unit, **Fig. 5.**
   c. Adjust pushrod length until rod lightly contacts pin head, **Fig. 6.**
2. Install gasket and power brake unit. Torque attaching nuts to 14 ft. lbs.
3. Reverse remainder of removal procedure to complete installation.

MASTER CYLINDER REPLACE

1. Clean area around reservoir and brake lines at master cylinder.
2. Remove brake fluid from master cylinder.
3. Disconnect and cap the 4 brake lines from master cylinder.
4. Disconnect brake level warning switch electrical connector.

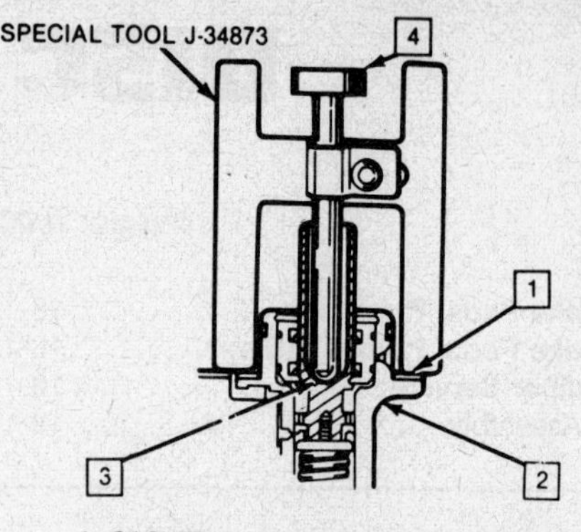

Fig. 4 Power brake unit pushrod adjusting tool on master cylinder

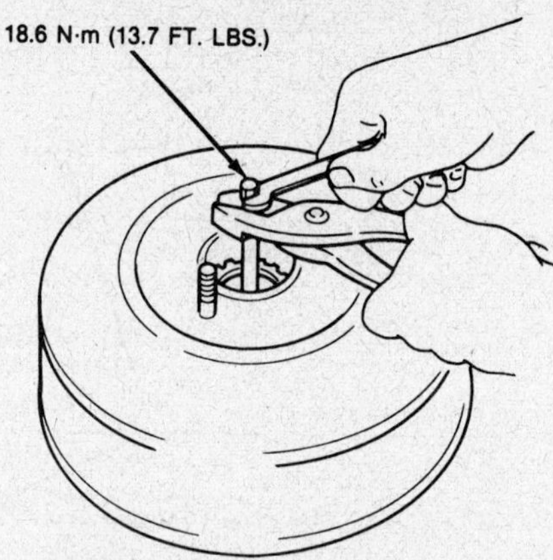

Fig. 6 Power brake unit pushrod final adjustment

5. Remove 2 master cylinder attaching nuts and the master cylinder.
6. Reverse procedure to install, noting the following:
   a. Adjust power brake unit pushrod length prior to installing master cylinder. Refer to "Power Brake Unit, Replace."

DRUM BRAKES SECTION

INDEX

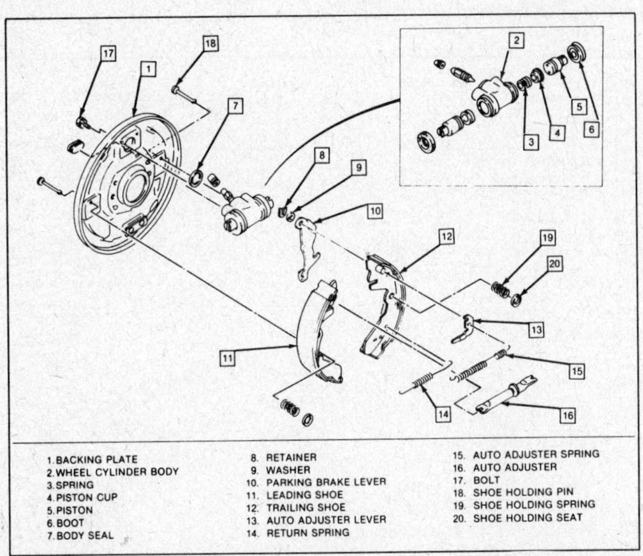

Fig. 1 Exploded view of rear drum brake assembly

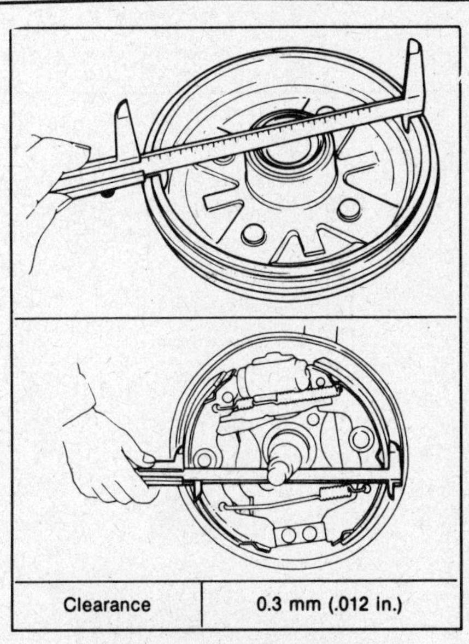

Fig. 2 Drum brake adjustment

BRAKE SHOES
REPLACE

1. Raise and support rear of vehicle.
2. Remove wheels and brake drums.
3. Remove return spring and auto adjuster spring.
4. Remove leading shoe hold-down spring and pin, **Fig. 1.**
5. Remove leading shoe and auto adjuster.
6. Remove trailing shoe hold-down spring and pin, then shoe.
7. Remove parking brake cable and lever.
8. Apply suitable grease to the supports on the backing plate where the shoes contact.
9. Reverse procedure to install. Take care not to damage wheel cylinder boots.

MASTER CYLINDER
REPLACE

Refer to Disc Brakes Section.

POWER BRAKE UNIT
REPLACE

Refer to Disc Brakes Section.

DRUM BRAKES
ADJUST

1. Measure brake drum inside diameter and brake shoe diameter, **Fig. 2.**
2. Ensure clearance between diameters is as specified. **Fig. 2.**

PARKING BRAKE
ADJUST

Parking brake stroke should measure 7-9 notches with approximately 14 lbs. pressure applied. Lever stroke is automatically adjusted when rear brakes are adjusted. If stroke is not within specifications after adjusting rear brakes, it may be adjusted by rotating the turnbuckle.

BRAKE PEDAL HEIGHT
ADJUST

Refer to Disc Brakes Section.

REAR AXLE & SUSPENSION SECTION

INDEX

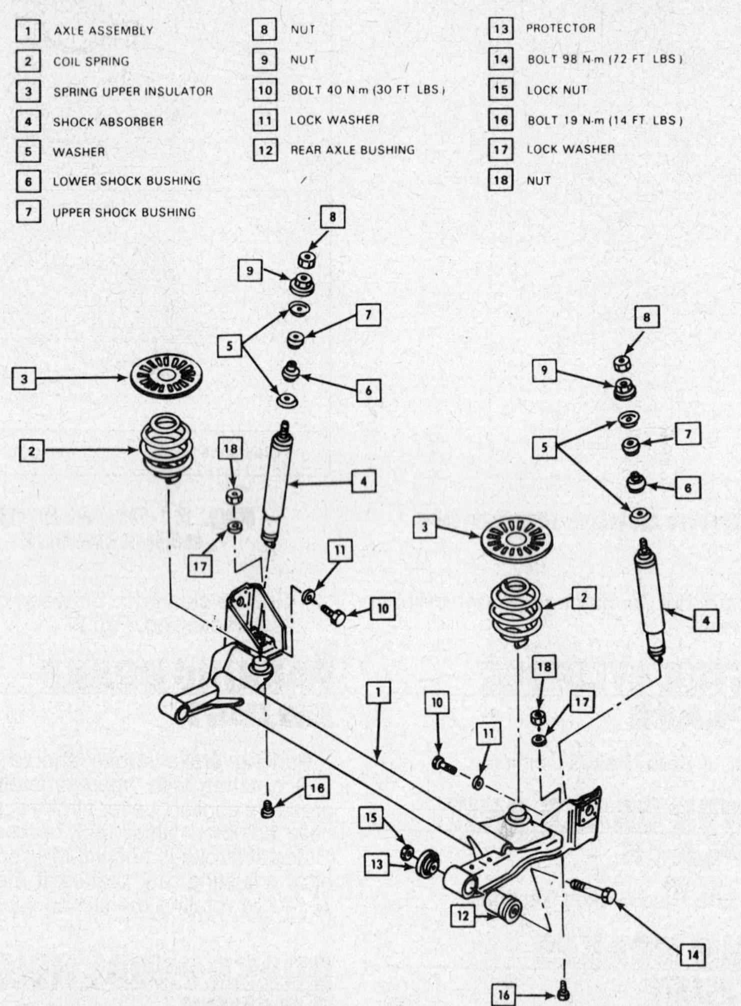

Fig. 1 Exploded view of rear axle & suspension assembly

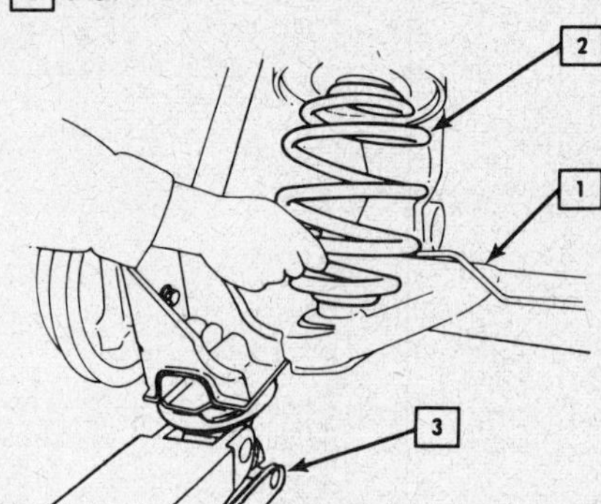

Fig. 2 Coil spring removal

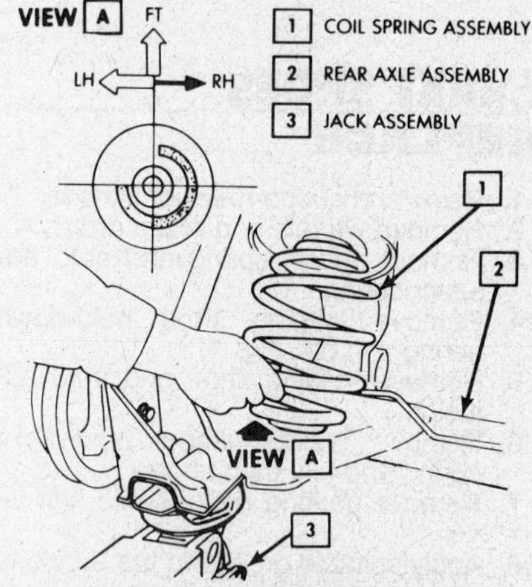

Fig. 3 Coil spring installation

DESCRIPTION

The semi-independent suspension, **Fig. 1**, consists of an axle with trailing arms and twisting cross beam, two coil springs, shock absorbers, upper spring insulators and spring compression bumpers. The axle assembly is attached to the underbody through rubber bushings located at the front end of rear axle. The rear axle brackets are integral with the underbody side rails. The two coil springs support the weight of the vehicle in the rear. Each spring is retained between a seat in the underbody and a seat welded to the top of the rear axle. A rubber cushion isolates the coil spring upper end from the underbody seat.

REAR AXLE & COIL SPRINGS

REPLACE

1. Raise and support rear of vehicle.
2. Remove both rear wheel and tire assemblies.
3. Remove brake line, retaining clip and flexible hose from center of axle.
4. Remove tension spring, then disconnect parking brake cable and cable joint.
5. Support lower side of axle with a suitable jack.
6. Remove lower shock absorber bolt and disconnect shock from axle, **Fig. 1.**
7. Lower jack supporting axle and remove coil spring, **Fig. 2.**
8. Remove axle-to-body attaching bolts, then lower rear axle assembly from vehicle.
9. Reverse procedure to install, noting the following:
   a. When installing coil springs, the thinner end of spring must be attached at upper end and the bottom of spring must be positioned

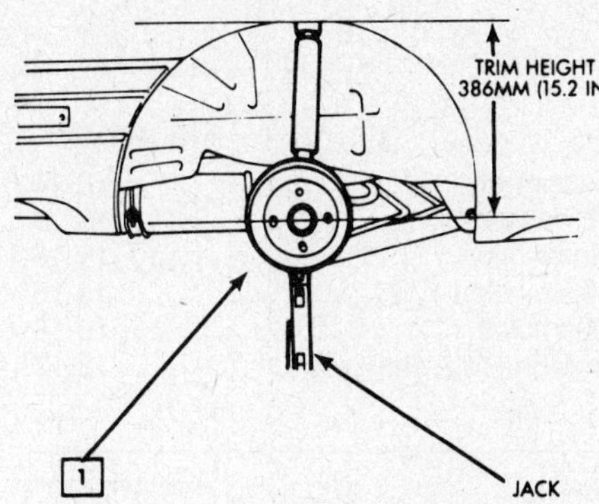

Fig. 4 Setting rear trim height

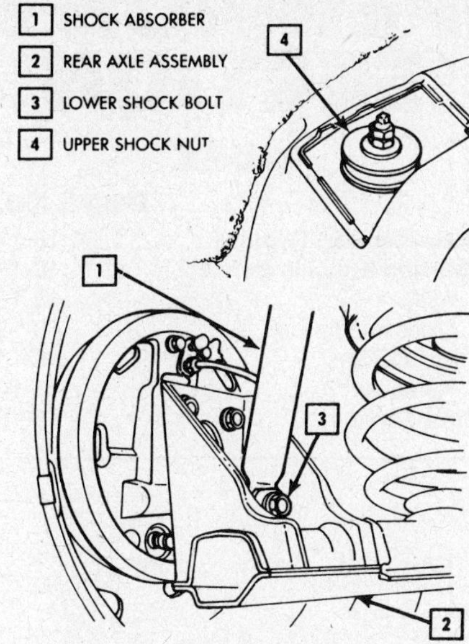

Fig. 5 Shock absorber replacement

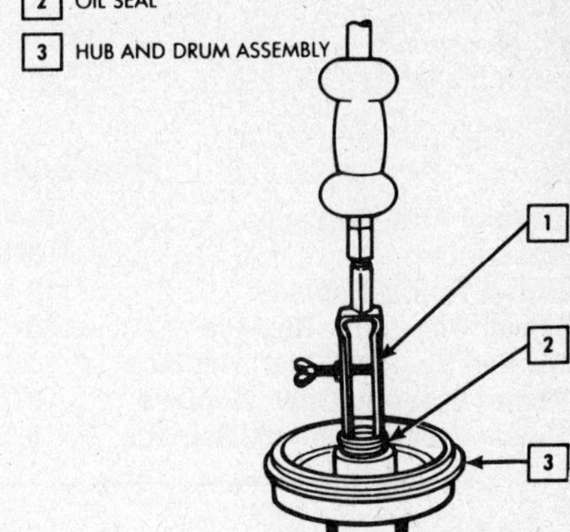

Fig. 6 Axle seal removal

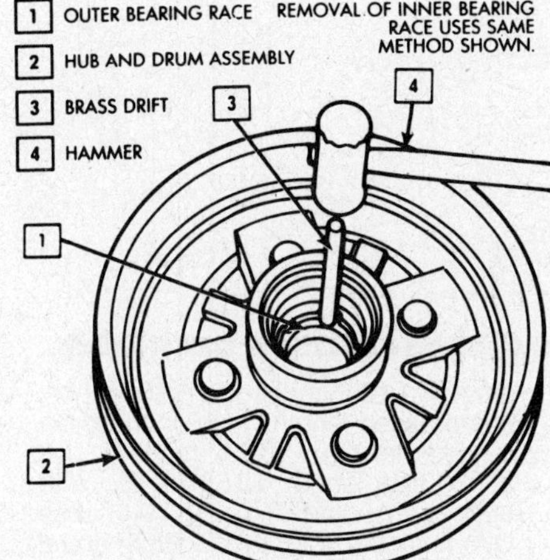

Fig. 7 Bearing race removal

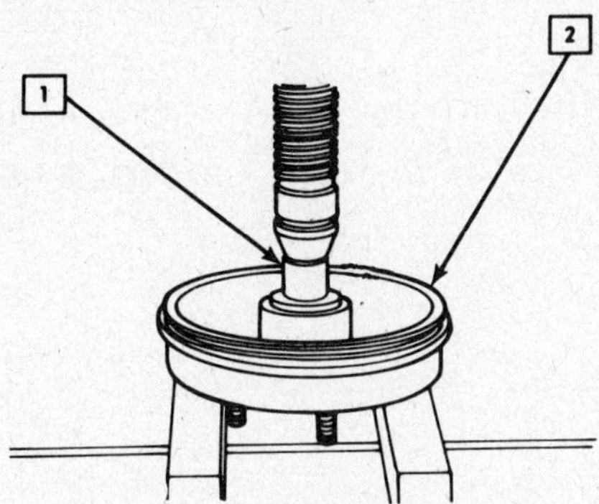

Fig. 8 Bearing race installation

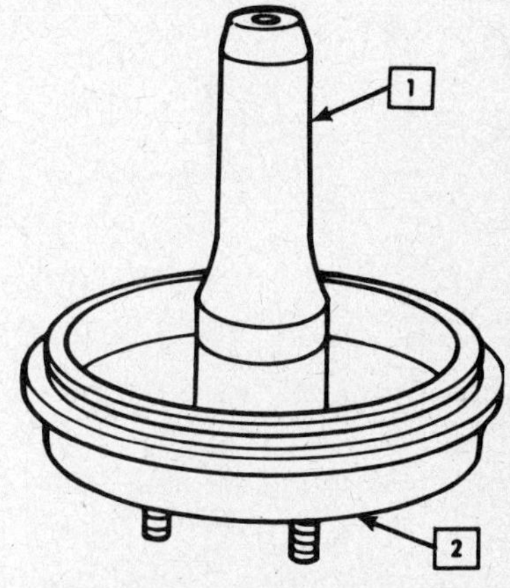

Fig. 9 Axle seal installation

as shown, **Fig. 3.**

b. Rear trim height, **Fig. 4,** must be set to 15 inches prior to tightening rear axle bolts.

SHOCK ABSORBER

REPLACE

1. On hatchback models, remove trim cover from upper shock nut.
2. On all models, remove upper shock nut.
3. Remove lower shock absorber bolt, **Fig. 5,** then the shock absorber.
4. Reverse procedure to install.

REAR HUB & WHEEL BEARINGS

REPLACE

1. Raise and support rear of vehicle.
2. Remove wheel and tire assembly.
3. Remove hub cap, cotter pin and nut and washer, then the hub and brake drum assembly.
4. Remove outer bearing from hub by hand.
5. Remove oil seal from hub using tool No. J-26941 or equivalent, **Fig. 6.**
6. Remove inner bearing from hub by hand.
7. Tap inner bearing outer race and outer bearing outer race out of hub, **Fig. 7.**
8. Install inner and outer bearing races using tool J-35307-1 and J-35307-2 respectively, **Fig. 8.**
9. Install new oil seal in inner side of hub using tool No. J-35305 or equivalent, **Fig. 9.**
10. Pack bearings using suitable grease.
11. Reverse procedure to install, and adjust wheel bearings as follows:
    a. Tighten hub nut to 22 ft. lbs.
    b. Loosen hub nut, then tighten finger tight.
    c. Install retainer, then cotter pin.

FRONT SUSPENSION & STEERING SECTION

INDEX

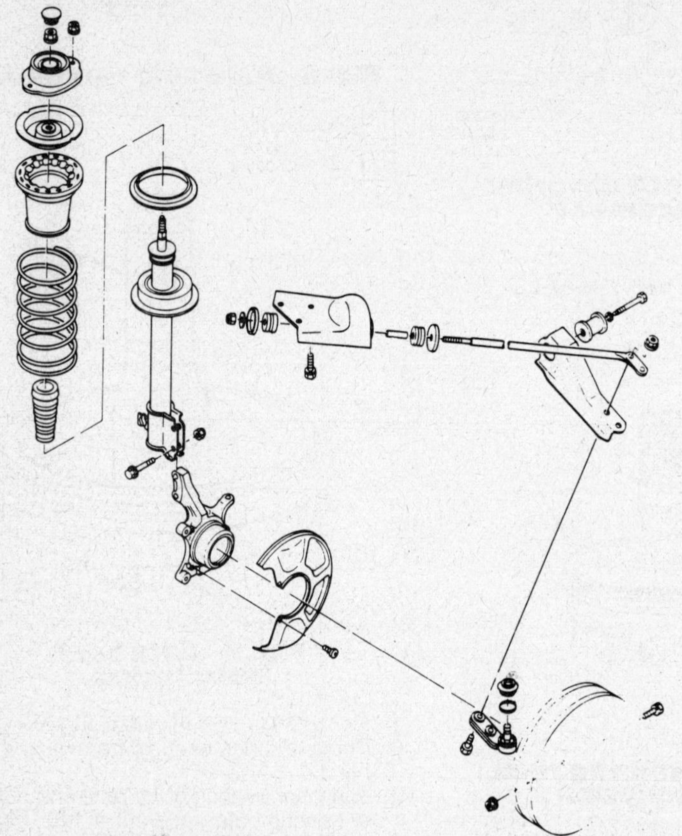

Fig. 1 Exploded view of front suspension assembly

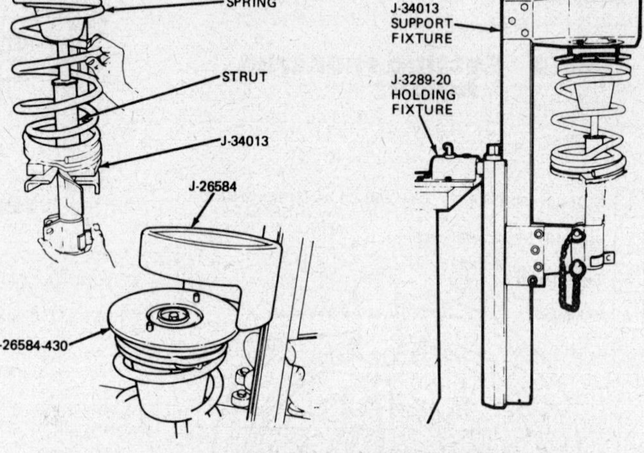

Fig. 2 Strut disassembly & assembly

DESCRIPTION

The front suspension, **Fig. 1,** is of the MacPherson strut, independent type. A strut support anchors the upper end of the strut to the body. The lower end of the strut is connected to the upper end of the steering knuckle. The lower end of the steering knuckle is attached to the ball joint, which is mounted to the suspension control arm.

STRUT SERVICE

REMOVAL

1. Remove both strut-to-body attaching nuts.
2. Raise and support front of vehicle.
3. Remove wheel and tire assembly.
4. Remove brake hose clip from strut, then disconnect hose from caliper.
5. Pull brake hose back through opening in strut bracket, then cap hose and open port in caliper to prevent contamination.
6. Remove both strut-to-knuckle attaching nuts and bolts, then the strut assembly, **Fig. 1.**

DISASSEMBLY

1. Secure strut spring compressor in a vise or suitable holding fixture.
2. Install strut into compressing tool, **Fig. 2,** and compress spring just enough to release spring tension.
3. Remove nut from strut shaft, then release spring and disassemble strut, **Fig. 3.**

INSPECTION

1. Ensure the following items meet specified measurements: piston diameter, 1.18 inch; stroke, 5.75 inches; compressed length, 14.65 inches; extended length, 20.39 inches; coil spring free length, 13.50 inches with auto. trans. and A/C, 13.70 inches with auto. trans. less A/C and manual trans. with A/C.
2. Check shock for oil leaks and defective operation.
3. Check coil spring for wear, cracks or distortion.
4. Check upper strut mounting for abnormal noise, binding or defective turning, or any other defects.

ASSEMBLY

1. Assemble strut in compressor tool, **Fig. 3,** ensuring "IN" marking on inside of spring upper seat faces inside of vehicle.
2. Compress spring just enough to allow installation of shaft nut.
3. Install shaft nut and tighten until shaft begins to rotate.
4. Release spring compressing tool, then torque shaft nut to 43 ft. lbs.

INSTALLATION

1. Install strut-to-knuckle attaching bolts and torque to 80 ft. lbs.
2. Route flex hose back through strut bracket opening. Connect fitting to caliper and torque to 13 ft. lbs.
3. Install wheel and tire assembly.
4. Lower vehicle to a height where upper mount can be aligned with holes in body, then install and torque nuts to 41 ft. lbs.

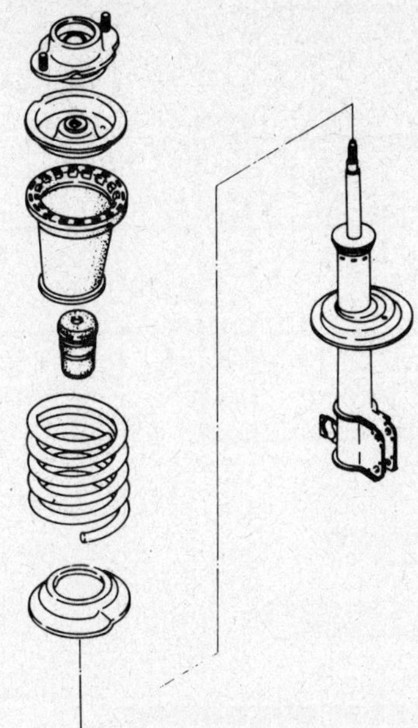

Fig. 3 Exploded view of strut assembly

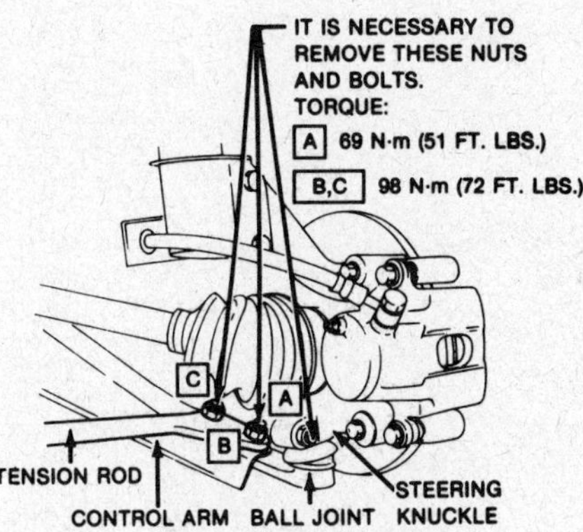

Fig. 6 Ball joint replacement

5. Lower vehicle to ground and tighten wheel nuts.

CONTROL ARM REPLACE

1. Raise and support front of vehicle.
2. Remove lower control arm-to-tension rod attaching nuts and bolts.
3. Remove control arm-to-body attaching bolt and nut.
4. Remove control arm, **Fig. 1.**
5. Reverse procedure to install, noting the following:
   a. Replace self-locking nuts when installing arm.
   b. When attaching control arm to body, first jack up lower part of arm to 15.18 inches, **Fig. 4,** then torque attaching bolts to specifications, **Fig. 5.**

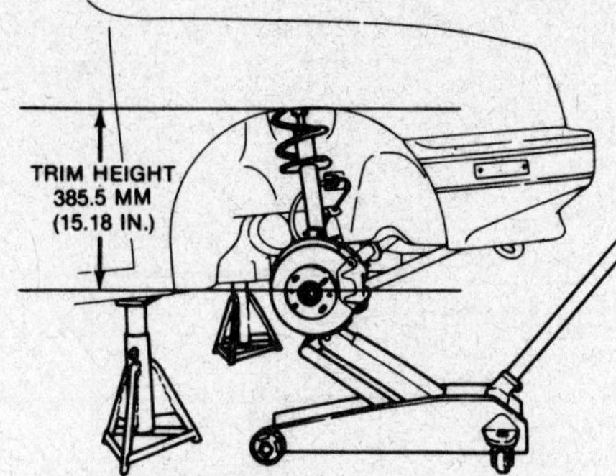

Fig. 4 Setting vehicle trim height

LOWER BALL JOINT REPLACE

1. Raise and support front of vehicle.
2. Remove wheel and tire assembly.
3. Remove 2 nuts and bolts attaching ball joint, tension rod and control arm.
4. Remove ball joint-to-knuckle pinch bolt, then the ball joint, **Fig. 6.**
5. Reverse procedure to install. Torque knuckle-to-ball joint nut to 51 ft. lbs. and ball joint, tension rod and control arm attaching nuts to 72 ft. lbs.

TENSION ROD REPLACE

1. Raise and support front of vehicle.
2. Remove stabilizer bar-to-tension rod bracket and insulator attaching nuts and bolts, if equipped.
3. Remove tension rod-to-body attaching nut and washer.
4. Remove tension rod-to-control arm attaching nuts and bolts and the tension rod, **Fig. 7.**
5. Reverse procedure to install, using new self-locking nut. Torque tension rod-to-body nut to 72 ft. lbs. and tension rod-to-control arm bolts to 80 ft. lbs.

STABILIZER BAR REPLACE

1. Raise and support front of vehicle.
2. Remove 4 stabilizer bar bracket and insulator attaching nuts and bolts, then the stabilizer bar, **Fig. 7.**
3. Reverse procedure to install, noting the following:
   a. Align stabilizer bar front side insulator as shown, **Fig. 8.**
   b. Torque stabilizer bar attaching bolts to 6 ft. lbs.

HUB & ROTOR REPLACE

1. Raise and support front of vehicle.
2. Loosen wheel lug nuts, then remove wheel and tire assembly.
3. Remove caliper to knuckle attaching bolts, then position caliper aside.
4. Trmove cotter pin, castle nut and washer, then remove rotor, **Fig. 9.**
5. Using tools J-34866 and J-2619-01, remove hub, **Fig. 10.**
6. Reverse procedure to install, noting the following:
   a. Replace all bearings, seals and self locking nuts.
   b. Torque caliper to knuckle attaching bolts to 41 ft. lbs.
   c. Torque axle to hub castle nut to 137 ft. lbs.
   d. Torque wheel lug nuts to 65 ft. lbs.

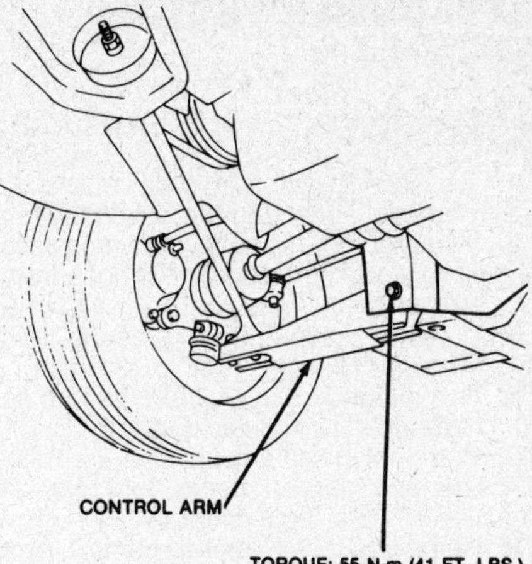

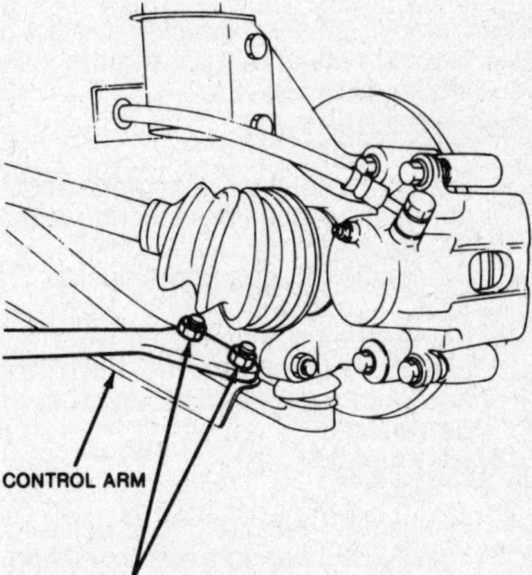

Fig. 5 Control arm installation

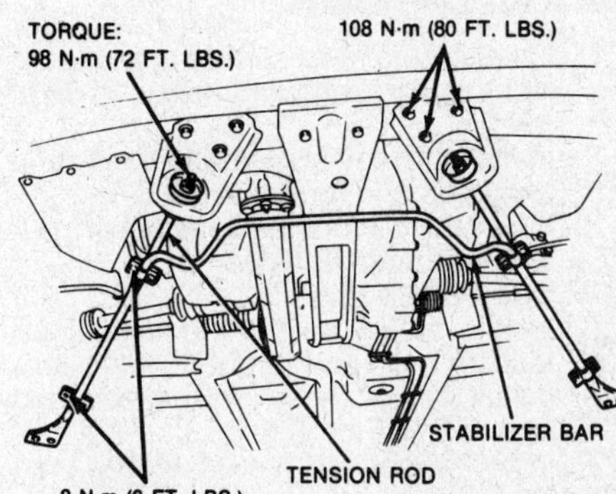

Fig. 7 Tension rod & stabilizer bar replacement

STEERING KNUCKLE SERVICE

REMOVAL

1. Raise and support front of vehicle.
2. Remove wheel and tire assembly.
3. Remove brake hose retaining clip from strut, then disconnect hose from caliper.
4. Unfasten caliper from steering and support caliper.
5. Remove rotor, **Fig. 9**, then the hub as mentioned previously, **Fig. 10.**
6. Remove splash shield.
7. Remove tie rod using tool No. J-21687-02 or equivalent.
8. Remove 2 ball joint-to-control arm and tension rod attaching nuts and bolts.
9. Remove steering knuckle-to-strut attaching nuts and bolts and the steering knuckle, **Fig. 11.**

DISASSEMBLY

1. Remove inner seal, snap rings and inner bearing race from steering knuckle, **Fig. 9.**
2. Press hub bearing from knuckle, **Fig. 12.**
3. Press outer bearing race from hub, **Fig. 13. The hub bearing, both inner and outer seals and races must not be reused.**

ASSEMBLY

1. Install outer snap ring to knuckle.
2. Install hub bearing assembly using a suitable press.
3. Install inner snap ring, then the inner and outer seals using tool J-35303 or equivalent.
4. Install outer race using tool No. J-3502 or equivalent.

INSTALLATION

1. Install ball joint-to-control arm attaching nuts and bolts and torque to 80 ft. lbs.
2. Install strut-to-knuckle attaching nuts and bolts and torque to 80 ft. lbs.
3. Install tie rod-to-knuckle attaching nut and torque to 42 ft. lbs.
4. Install brake rotor.
5. Install brake caliper-to-knuckle attaching bolts and torque to 41 ft. lbs.
6. Install brake hose to caliper and torque fitting to 13 ft. lbs.
7. Install wheel and tire assembly, then lower vehicle.
8. Apply suitable grease to axle shaft threads and nut, then install axle-to-hub attaching nut, washer and cotter pin. Torque nut to 137 ft. lbs.
9. Tighten wheel nuts, then bleed brake system.

MANUAL STEERING GEAR

REPLACE

1. Remove intermediate shaft cover.
2. Loosen upper pinch bolt, then remove lower pinch bolt from pinion shaft.
3. Raise and support front of vehicle.

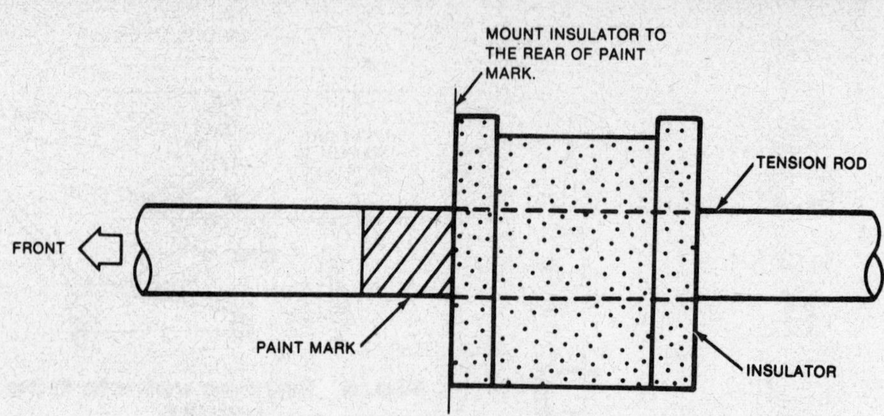

Fig. 8 Stabilizer bar insulator alignment

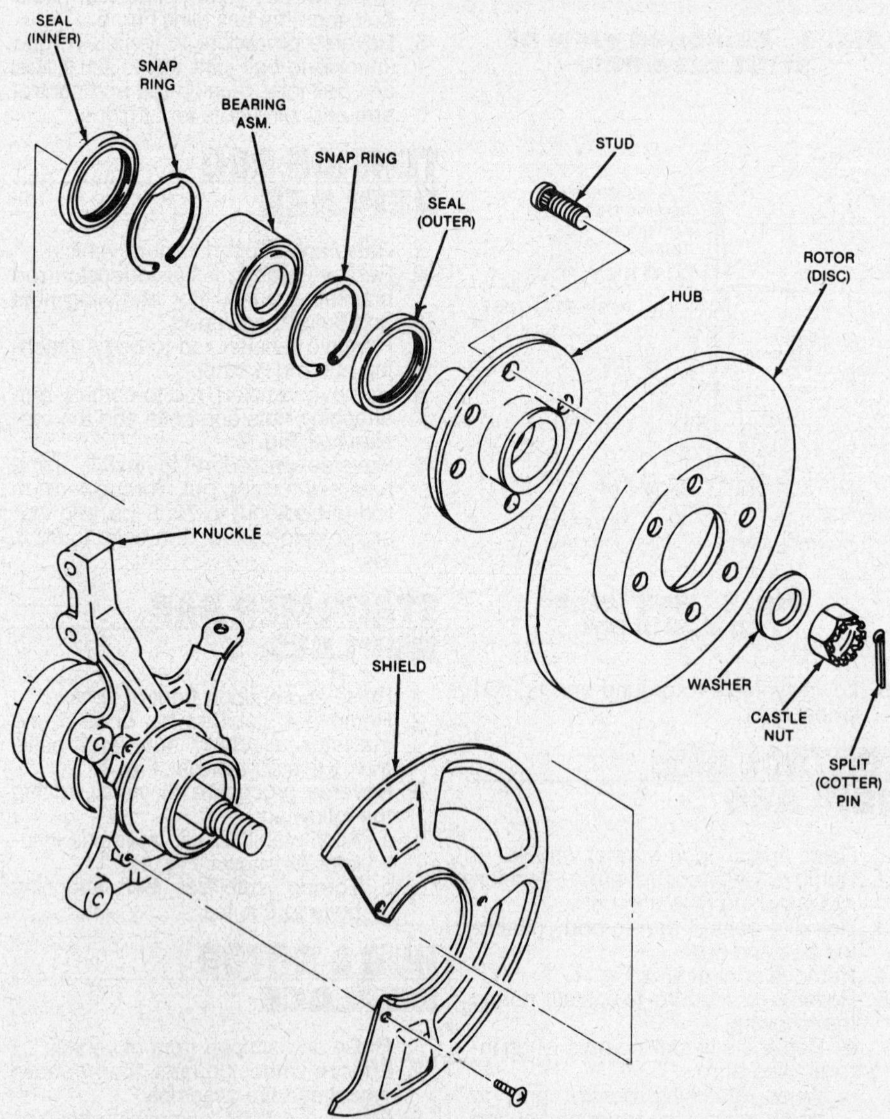

Fig. 9 Exploded view of steering knuckle & hub assembly

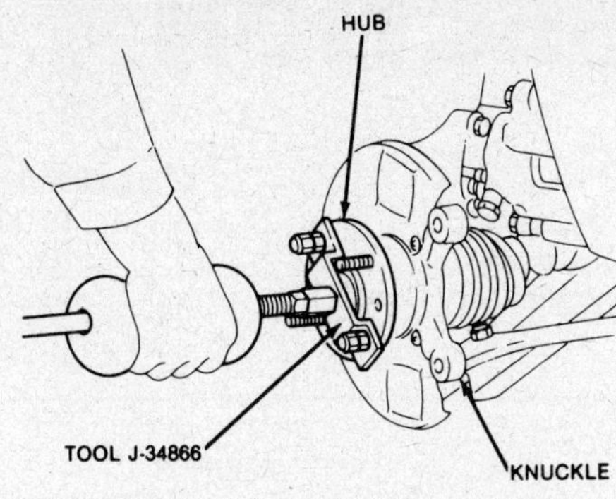

Fig. 10 Hub removal

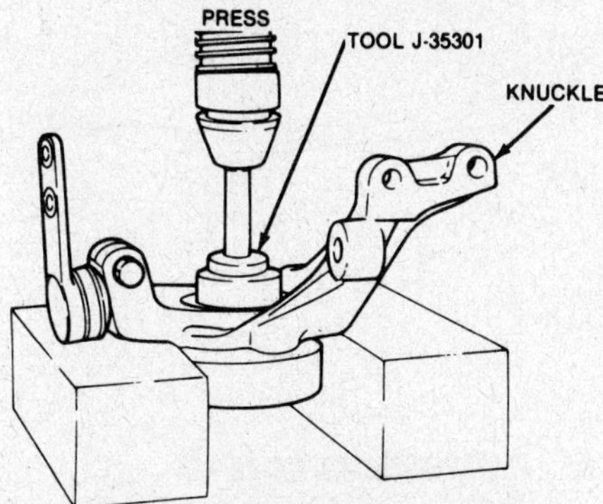

Fig. 12 Hub bearing removal

4. Remove both front wheel and tire assemblies.
5. Disconnect both tie rod ends from steering knuckles using tool No. J-21687-02 or equivalent.
6. Remove steering gear-to-body mounting nuts.
7. Remove band from left boot, then slide boot off steering gear.
8. Straighten lock washer between inner tie rod and rack, then separate tie rod from rack.
9. Reverse procedure to install.

POWER STEERING GEAR REPLACE

1. Remove intermediate steering shaft protector.
2. Loosen upper and remove lower intermediate shaft pinch bolts.
3. Position suitable container below gear.
4. Clean area around pressure and return hoses at gear valve.
5. Raise and support front of vehicle.
6. Remove both front wheel and tire assemblies.
7. Disconnect both tie rod ends from steering knuckles.
8. Remove steering gear-to-dash mounting nuts.
9. Cut plastic retaining straps from power steering pipes and hose.
10. Disconnect inner boot band from right rack boot.
11. Pull boot back to provide access to inner tie rod.
12. Straighten lock washer between inner tie rod and rack, then separate tie rod from rack.
13. Reverse procedure to install.

POWER STEERING PUMP REPLACE

1. Position suitable container below pump.
2. Remove pressure hose clamp.
3. Disconnect pressure and return hoses from pump.
4. Remove adjusting bolt, pivot bolt and drive belt.
5. Remove pump and pump bracket.
6. Remove pulley from pump.

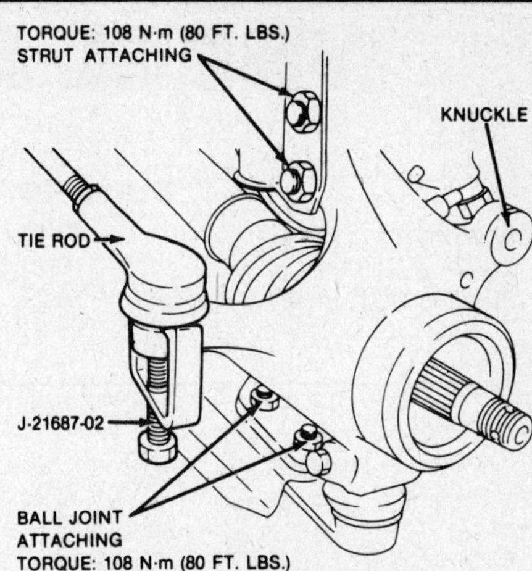

Fig. 11 Steering knuckle removal

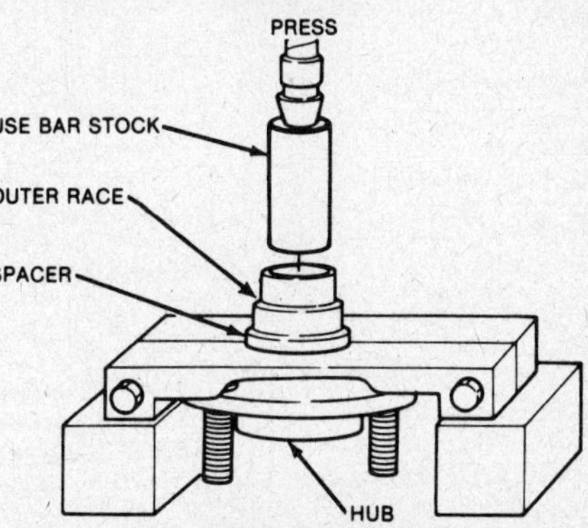

Fig. 13 Outer bearing race removal

7. Reverse procedure to install, noting the following:
   a. Torque pressure hose fitting to 20 ft. lbs.
   b. Using a suitable belt tension gauge, adjust drive belt to 70 to 110 in. lbs.

WHEEL ALIGNMENT SECTION

INDEX

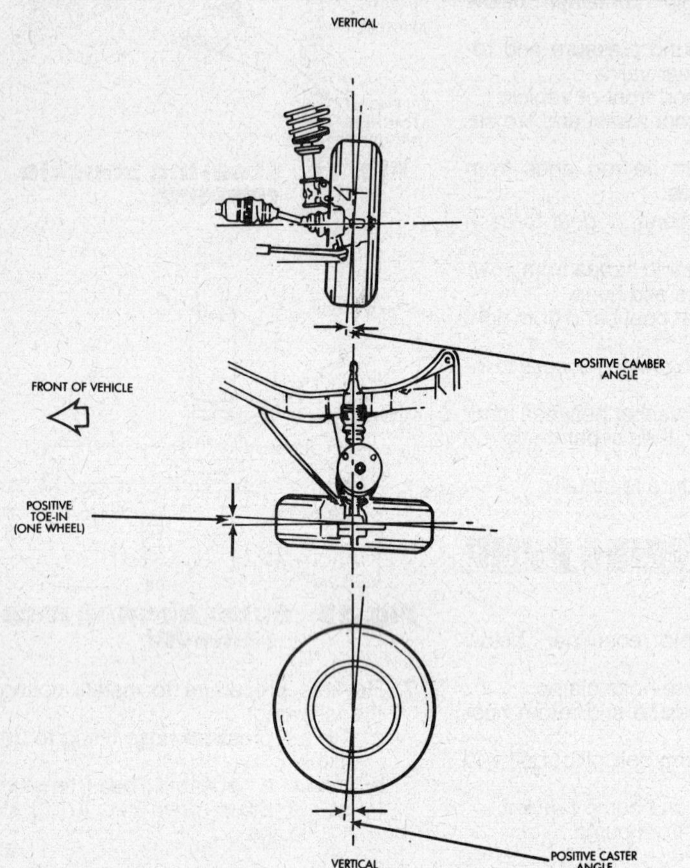

Fig. 1 Suspension geometry

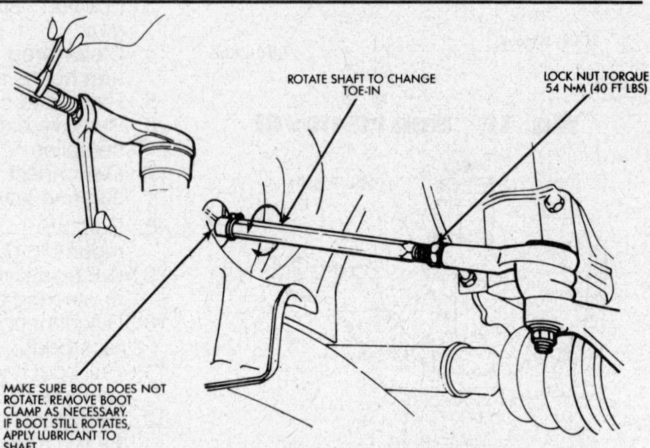

Fig. 2 Adjusting toe-in

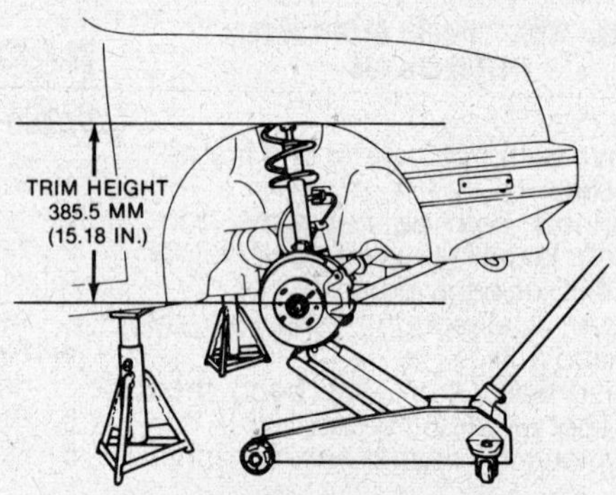

Fig. 3 Adjusting front trim height

DESCRIPTION

Wheel alignment is the angular relationship between the wheels, suspension attaching parts and ground. The angle of the knuckle away from the vertical, pointing in or out of wheels, tilt of the wheels from vertical (when viewed from front of vehicle) and tilt of suspension members from vertical (when viewed from side of vehicle), all of these are involved in proper alignment, **Fig. 1.**

CASTER

Caster is tilting of the front steering axis either forward or backward from the vertical (when viewed from side of vehicle). A backward tilt is positive (+) and a forward tilt is negitive (−). On short and long arm type suspensions you cannot see a caster angle without using a special instrument, but if you look straight down from the top of the upper control arm to the ground you would find that ball joints do not line up (fore and aft) when a caster angle other than 0° is present.

CAMBER

Camber is the tilting of front and rear wheels from the vertical when viewed from front of vehicle. When wheels tilt outward at top, camber is positive (+). When wheels tilt inward, camber is negative (−). Amount of tilt is measured in degrees from the vertical and this is camber angle.

TOE-IN

Toe is the turning in or out of wheels. The actual amount of toe is normally .078 inch (2 mm). The purpose of toe is to ensure parallel rolling of wheels. **Excessive toe-in or toe-out may increase tire wear.** Toe also serves to offset small deflections of the suspension which occurs when vehicle is moving.

PRELIMINARY CHECK

Steering and vibration problems are not always the result of alignment. An additional problem to be checked is tire lead due to worn or improperly manufactured tires. "Lead" is the deviation of the vehicle from a straight path on a level road without hand pressure on the steering wheel.

To insure correct alignment readings and alignment specifications, the following checks and inspections should be made.

1. Check tire for proper inflation and thread wear.
2. Check for loose ball joints and tie rod ends. If excessive looseness is noted, replace defective parts before adjusting toe.
3. Check for wheel and tire assembly runout.
4. Check trim heights. If not within specifications, correct before adjusting toe.
5. Check for loose control arms.
6. Check for loose or missing stabilizer bar components.

7. Consideration must be given to excess loads, such as tool boxes, etc. If excess load is normally carried in vehicle, it should remain during alignment checks.

ADJUSTMENTS

CASTER & CAMBER

Caster and camber angles are pre-set and cannot be adjusted. If caster and/or camber are out of specifications, the cause must be found. If worn or damaged suspension components are the cause, they should be replaced. If problem is body related, the body should be repaired as needed.

TOE-IN

Toe-in is adjusted by altering tie rod length. To perform adjustment, loosen small end boot clamps and slide from the boot. Loosen right and left tie rod end locknuts, then turn both tie rods, **Fig. 2,** the same amount to bring toe-in within specifications. Ensure right and left tie rods are equal in length, then tighten locknuts. When adjustment is complete, ensure boots are not twisted.

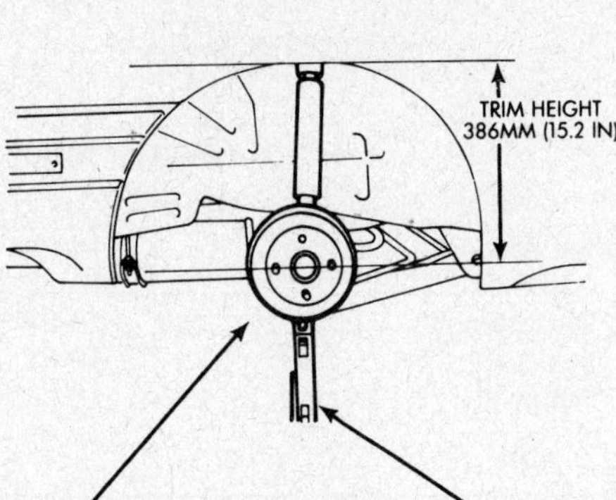

Fig. 4 Adjusting rear trim height

STEERING ANGLE

When a tie rod or tie rod end is replaced, check toe and steering angle using suitable turning radius gauges. If steering angle is not 37 2/3° inside and 32 1/2° outside, check right and left tie rods for equal length. **If tie rod length is changed to correct steering angle, reinspect toe-in.**

TRIM HEIGHT

Front

1. Loosen wheel lug nuts.
2. Raise and support vehicle using suitable jack stands.
3. Remove wheel and tire assemblies.
4. Loosen control arm to body, then tension rod attaching bolts.
5. Using a suitable jack, jack up the lower part of control arm to 15.18 inches (385.5 mm), **Fig. 3,** tighten control arm to body attaching bolts to 41 ft. lbs and tension rod bolts to 80 ft. lbs.

Rear

1. Loosen wheel lug nuts.
2. Raise and support vehicle using suitable jack stands.
3. Remove wheel and tire assemblies.
4. Loosen rear axle attaching bolts.
5. Using a suitable jack, jack up lower part of rear axle and set rear trim height to 15.2 inches (386 mm), **Fig. 4,** then tighten rear axle bolts to 72 ft. lbs.

DRIVE AXLE SECTION

INDEX

Page No.

DRIVE AXLE SERVICE

REMOVAL

1. Remove wheel cover, cotter pin and driveshaft nut, then loosen wheel nuts.
2. Raise and support vehicle.
3. Remove front wheel and tire assembly.
4. Drain transaxle oil.
5. Detach snap ring installed on spline of inboard joint using a large screwdriver.
6. Remove knuckle and hub assembly as described in the "Front Suspension & Steering Section."
7. Unfasten inboard joint from differential side gear and outboard joint from steering knuckle, then remove drive axle assembly.

DISASSEMBLY

Double Offset Joint

1. Secure axle assembly, **Fig. 1,** in a suitable soft-jawed vise.
2. Remove boot band from differential side joint, **Fig. 2.**
3. Move boot slightly and remove circular clip, **Fig. 3.**
4. Separate case from shaft and remove 6 balls with a suitable screwdriver, **Fig. 4.**
5. Turn ball guide on an angle and move it to center shaft side.
6. Remove snap ring from shaft, **Fig. 5,** then slide out ball guide and retainer.
7. Remove boot from shaft.

Birfield Joint

The Birfield joint must be serviced as an assembly only. However, the boot may be removed in the same manner as described for the Double Offset type joint.

Tripod Joint

1. Secure axle assembly, **Fig. 1,** in a suitable soft-jawed vise.
2. Using a screwdriver, remove boot band from differential side joint.
3. Mark alignment marks on both housing and shaft, then remove housing from shaft, **Fig. 6.**
4. Remove snap ring from shaft, then mark alignment marks on both shaft and tripod, **Fig. 7.**

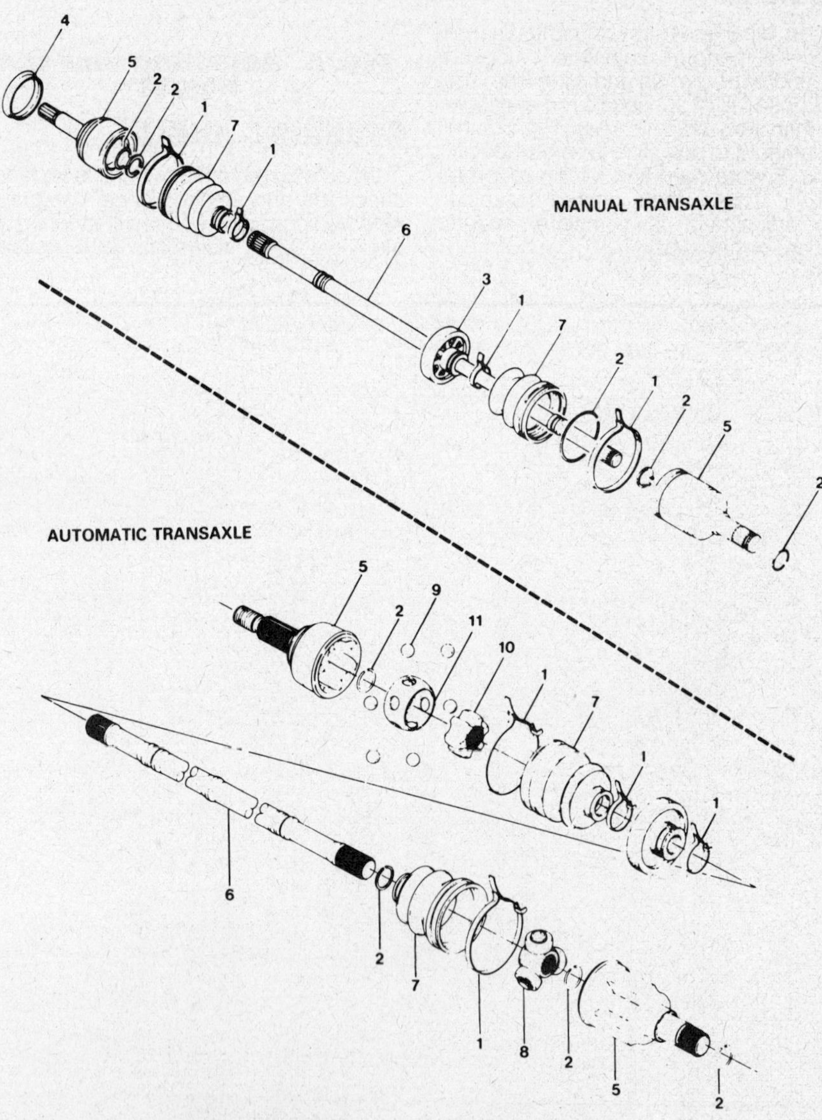

1. BAND, BOOT SEAL
2. RING, SNAP
3. DAMPER, DYNAMIC
4. SEAL, DUST
5. HOUSING
6. SHAFT, CENTER
7. BOOT, SEAL
8. TRIPOD
9. BALLS
10. INNER RACE (BALL RETAINER)
11. CAGE (BALL GUIDE)

Fig. 1 Exploded view of drive axle assembly

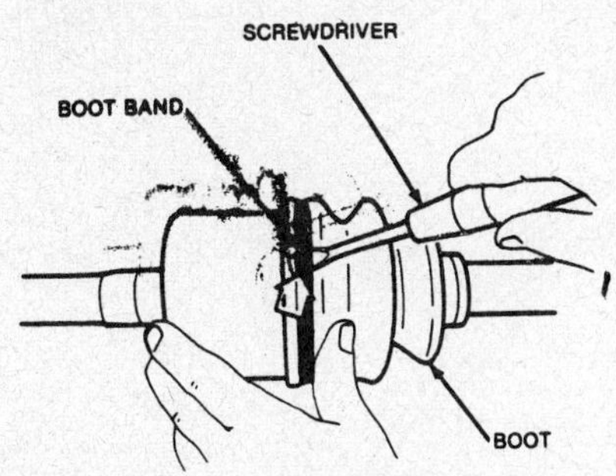

Fig. 2 Boot band removal

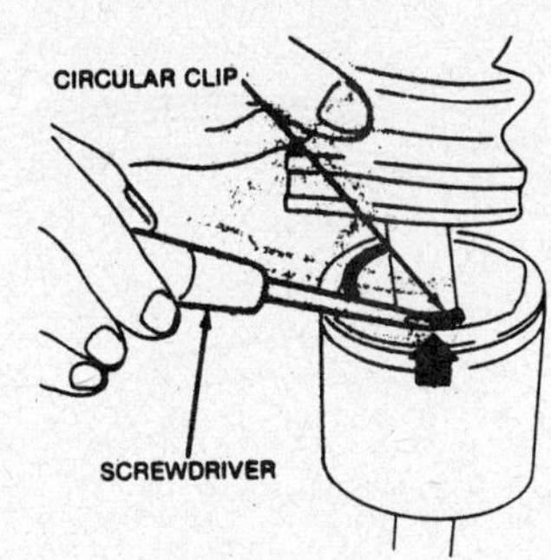

Fig. 3 Circular clip removal

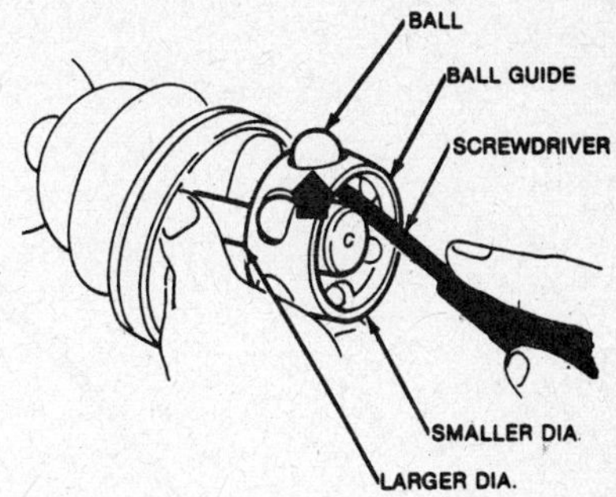

Fig. 4 Bearing removal

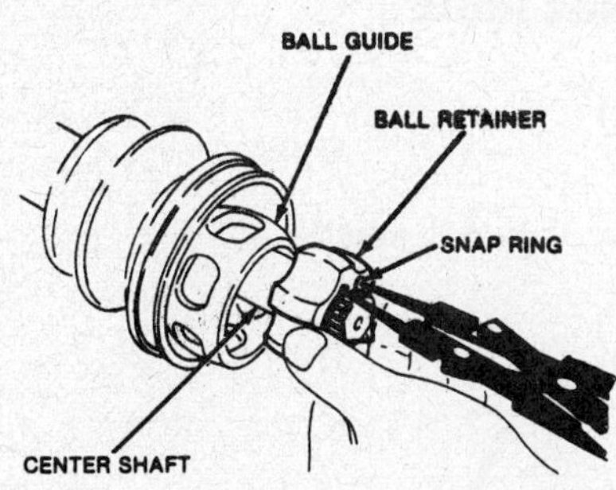

Fig. 5 Snap ring removal

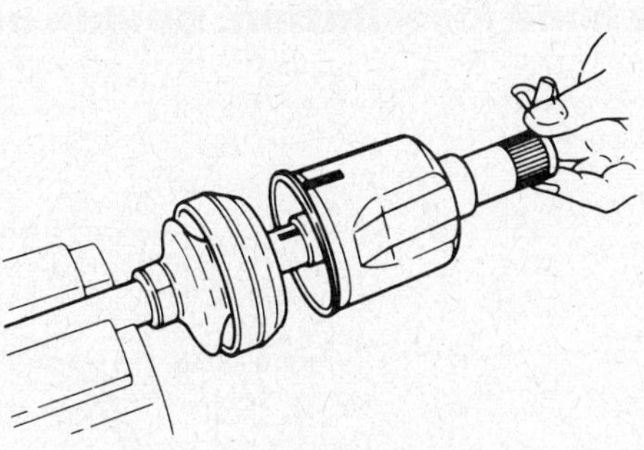

Fig. 6 Removing housing from shaft

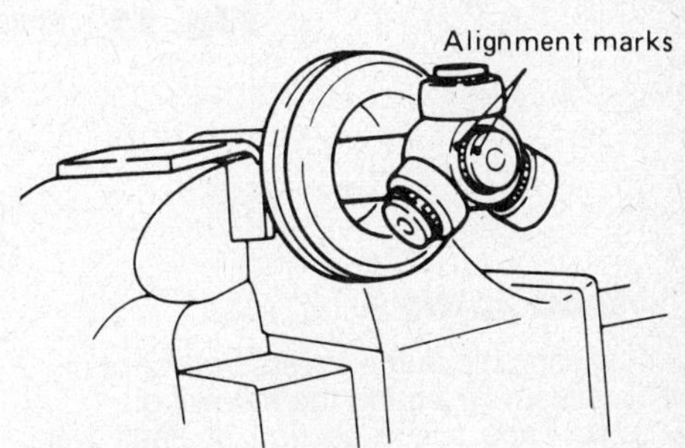

Fig. 7 Tripod removal

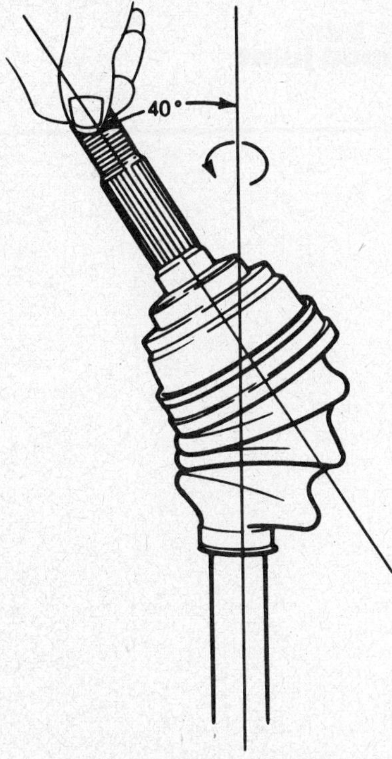

Fig. 8 Birfield joint inspection

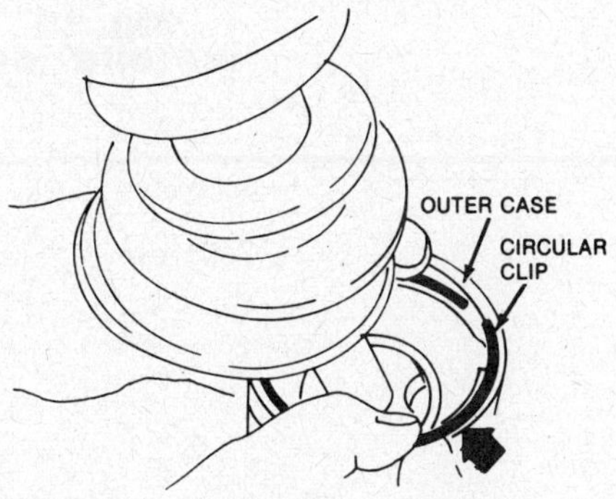

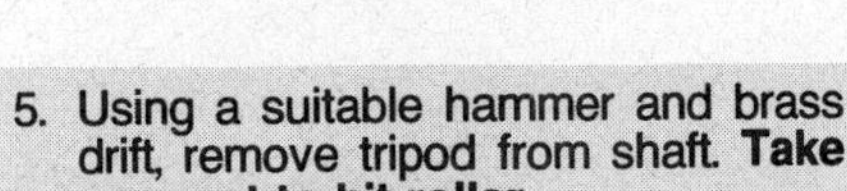

Fig. 9 Circular clip installation

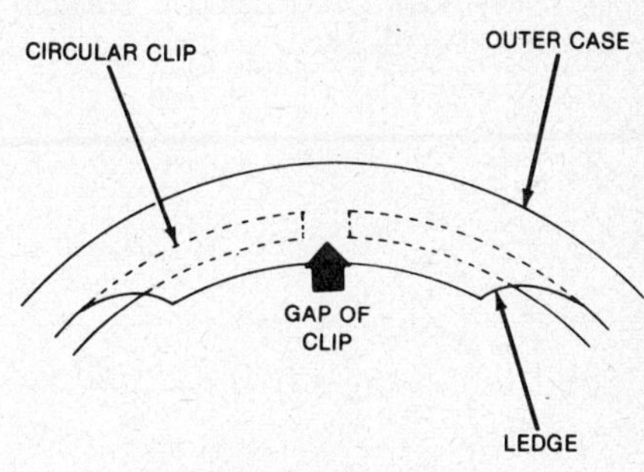

Fig. 10 Circulat clip alignment

5. Using a suitable hammer and brass drift, remove tripod from shaft. **Take care not to hit roller.**
6. Remove boot from shaft, and if necessary, dynamic damper.

INSPECTION

1. Visually inspect all components and replace those showing signs of damage or excessive wear.
2. Check Birfield joint by bending joint approximately 40° and rotating the shaft to ensure smooth and normal rotation, **Fig. 8.**

ASSEMBLY

Double Offset Joint

1. Assemble in the reverse order of disassembly, noting the following:
   a. Use care to avoid damaging boot when installing boot on shaft.
   b. Install and align circular clip as shown, **Figs. 9 and 10.**
   c. To install boot band, first insert a screwdriver into end of boot, then install band as shown, **Fig. 11.** Ensure band end clip is securely tightened around the band and boot is not twisted.

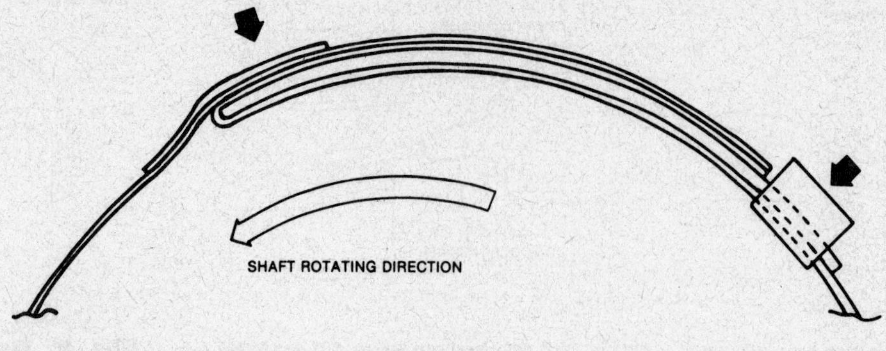

Fig. 11 Boot band installation. Double offset joint

Tripod Joint

1. Assemble in the reverse order of disassembly, noting the following:
   a. Tape spline section of shaft with tape to prevent damage to boot when installing.
   b. Install tripod onto shaft with shorter spline positioned on the outer side.
   c. Ensure all alignment marks align before assembling.
   d. Wind boot band twice, **Fig. 12**, then tighten band using pliers. Finally, lock band using a suitable punch, **Fig. 12**.

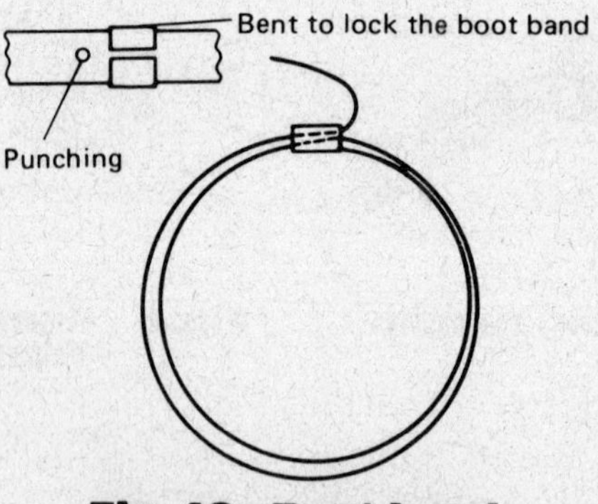

Fig. 12 Boot band installation. Tripod joint

SPRINT (Japan)

INDEX OF SERVICE OPERATIONS

General Engine Specifications

Year	Engine CID/cc	Carb.	Bore & Stroke Inch (mm)	Comp. Ratio	Maximum Brake HP @ RPM	Maximum Torque Lbs. Ft @ RPM	Normal Oil Pressure psi @ 3000 RPM
1985–87	3-60.6/993	2 Barrel	2.91 x 3.03 (74 x 77)	9.5	48 @ 5100	57 @ 3200	42.7-54
1987 ①	3-60.6/993	Fuel Inj.	2.91 x 3.03 (74 x 77)	8.3	70 @ 5500	107 @ 3500	42.7-54

①—Turbocharged.

Alternator & Regulator Specifications

Year	Model	Current Rating		Voltage Regulator	
		Amps	Volts	Voltage	RPM
1985–87	—	45	—	—	—

Starter General Specifications

Trans.	Volt	Output kw	Direction of Rotation	Brush Length Inch	No. of Pinion Teeth	Max. Solenoid Operating Voltage
Man.	12	.8	CW	.63	8	8
Auto.	12	1.0	CW	.53	9	8

Starter Current Draw Specifications

Trans.	No Load			Load				Locked Rotor		
	Max. Amps.	Volts	Min. RPM	Max. Amps.	Volts	Torque Ft. Lbs.	Min. RPM	Max. Amps.	Volts	Torque Ft. Lbs.
Man.	50	11	5000	270	9.5	5.06	1200	600	7.7	9.4
Auto.	90	11.5	3000	230	8	4.7	1180	300	2.5	5.06

Valve Specifications

Year	Valve Lash		Valve Angles		Valve Spring Installed Height	Valve Spring Pressure Lbs. @ In.	Stem Clearance		Stem Diameter	
	Int.	Exh.	Seat	Face			Intake	Exhaust	Intake	Exhaust
1985–87	.006	.008	45°	45°	—	①	.0008–.0019	.0014–.0025	.2742–.2748	.2737–.2742

①—54.7–64.3 lbs. per inch; no less than 50.2 lbs. per inch.

Pistons, Pins, Rings, Crankshaft & Bearings

Year	Piston Clearance	Ring End Gap: Comp.	Ring End Gap: Oil	Wrist Pin Diameter	Rod Bearings: Shaft Diameter	Rod Bearings: Bearing Clearance	Main Bearings: Shaft Diameter	Main Bearings: Bearing Clearance	Main Bearings: Thrust On Bearing No.	Shaft End Play
1985–87	.0008–.0015	.0079–.0137	.0079–.0275	—	1.6529–1.6535	.0012–.0019	1.7710–1.7716	.0008–.0015	3	.0044–.0122

Engine Tightening Specifications

Year	Spark Plug Ft. Lbs.	Cylinder Head Bolts Ft. Lbs.	Intake Manifold Ft. Lbs.	Exhaust Manifold Ft. Lbs.	Rocker Arm Shaft Bracket Ft. Lbs.	Rocker Arm Cover Ft. Lbs.	Connecting Rod Cap Bolts Ft. Lbs.	Main Bearing Cap Bolts Ft. Lbs.	Flywheel to Crankshaft Ft. Lbs.	Vibration Damper or Pulley Ft. Lbs.
1985–87	—	46–50.5	14–20	14–20	—	—	24–26	36–41	41–47	—

Brake Specifications

Year	Brake Drum Inside Diameter	Wheel Cylinder Bore Diameter: Front Disc	Wheel Cylinder Bore Diameter: Rear Drum	Master Cylinder Bore Diameter	Disc Brake Rotor: Nominal Thickness	Disc Brake Rotor: Minimum Thickness	Runout (T.I.R.)
1985–87	7.09	2.01	.69	.75	.394	.315	.0028

Wheel Alignment Specifications

Year	Caster Angle, Degrees: Limits	Caster Angle, Degrees: Desired	Camber Angles, Degrees: Limits	Camber Angles, Degrees: Desired	Toe-Out Inch
1985–87	—	3°10'	—	1°	0–.157

Cooling System & Capacity Data

Year	Cooling System Capacity Qts.	Radiator Cap Relief Pressure psi	Thermostat Open Temp. °F	Fuel Tank Gals.	Engine Oil Qts.	Transmission: Man. Trans.	Transmission: Auto. Trans. Refill
1985–87	4.54	12.8	190	8.3	3.7	2.3	3.7

ELECTRICAL SECTIO

INDEX

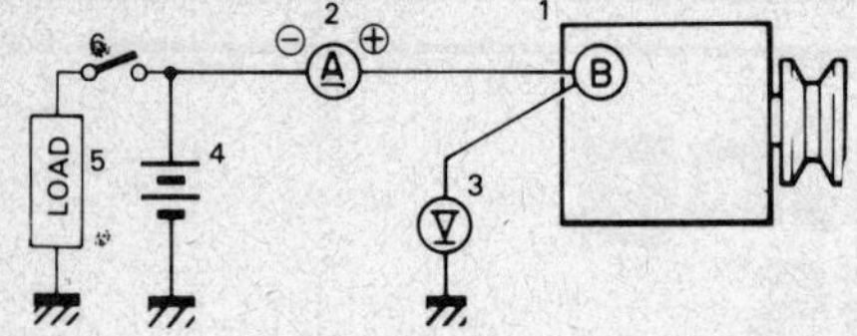

1. GENERATOR
2. AMP METER
3. VOLT METER
4. BATTERY
5. LOAD
6. SWITCH

Fig. 1 Alternator test connections

ALTERNATOR TESTING

When testing alternator, observe the following:

1. Do not reverse polarities of IG and L terminals.
2. Do not short IG and L terminals. Always connect these terminals through a lamp.
3. Do not connect any load between L and E terminals.

UNDERCHARGED BATTERY

1. Check that undercharged condition has not been caused by accessories left on for extended periods.
2. Check drive belt for proper tension.
3. Inspect wiring for defects. Check that all connections are clean and tight, including slip connectors at alternator and bulkhead. Also check battery cable connections at battery, starter and ignition ground cable.
4. Connect voltmeter and ammeter as shown in **Fig. 1.** Connect voltmeter between alternator B terminal and ground. Connect ammeter between alternator B terminal and battery positive terminal.
5. Perform no-load check as follows:
   a. Increase engine speed from idle to 2000 RPM and read meters. Note that voltage readings will vary with regulator case temperature.
   b. If voltage is higher than 14.2-14.8 volts @ 77 degrees F., replace IC regulator.
   c. If voltage is below specification, check IC regulator and alternator by measuring voltage at B terminal while grounding F terminal. If voltage is above specification, replace IC regulator. If voltage is below specification, test alternator.
6. Perform load check as follows:
   a. Run engine at 2000 RPM and switch on headlights and heater blower motor. Check that current is at least 20 amps, if less, alternator is defective.

OVERCHARGED BATTERY

If an obvious overcharging condition exists such as spewing of electrolyte, proceed to unit repair section and check field windings for grounds and shorts. If defective, replace rotor and test regulator with suitable tester.

STARTER

REPLACE

1. Disconnect battery ground cable.
2. Disconnect solenoid lead and battery cable from starter terminals.
3. Remove 2 starter mounting bolts, then starter.
4. Reverse procedure to install.

IGNITION & MULTI-FUNCTION SWITCH

REPLACE

1. Disconnect battery ground cable.
2. Remove steering joint cover.
3. Remove steering wheel pad.
4. Using suitable puller, remove steering wheel.
5. Remove steering column lower cover, **Fig. 2.**
6. Disconnect main switch and turn signal/dimmer switch connectors.
7. Remove turn signal/dimmer switch, **Fig. 2.**
8. Remove ignition switch screws, then switch, **Fig. 3.**
9. Reverse procedure to install. Position ignition switch so recess is mated with tab on bracket, **Fig. 4.**

HEADLAMP & WIPER/WASHER SWITCH

REPLACE

1. Disconnect battery ground cable.
2. Remove steering column trim panel.
3. Lower steering column.
4. Remove instrument cluster bezel screws and pull bezel out.
5. Remove headlamp switch from bezel.
6. Remove cluster to instrument panel attaching screws.
7. Pull cluster rearward to reach and disconnect headlamp and/or wiper/washer switch connector.
8. Remove headlamp and/or wiper/washer switch.

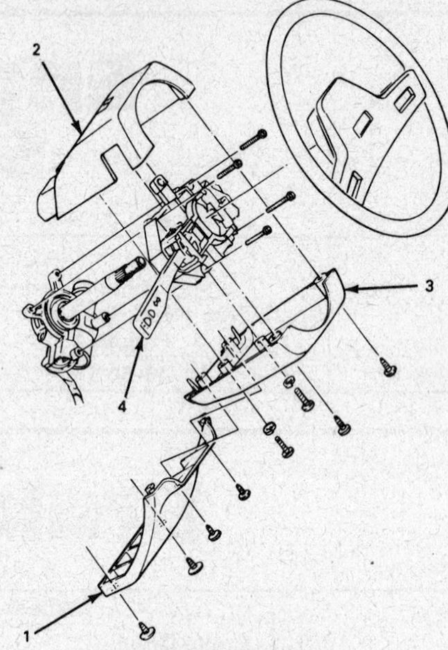

1. STEERING JOINT COVER
2. UPPER COLUMN COVER
3. LOWER COLUMN COVER
4. TURN SIG./DIMMER SWITCH

Fig. 2 Turn signal/dimmer switch removal

INSTRUMENT CLUSTER

REPLACE

1. Disconnect battery ground cable.
2. Remove steering column trim panel.
3. Lower steering column.
4. Remove instrument panel cluster bezel screws and bezel, **Figs. 5 and 6.**
5. Remove 2 switches from bezel.
6. Remove cluster screws and cluster.
7. Remove lens.
8. Reverse procedure to install.

INSTRUMENT CLUSTER PRINTED CIRCUIT

REPLACE

1. Disconnect battery ground cable.
2. Disconnect speedometer cable at transmission.
3. Remove steering column trim panel.
4. Lower steering column.
5. Remove steering column trim cover.

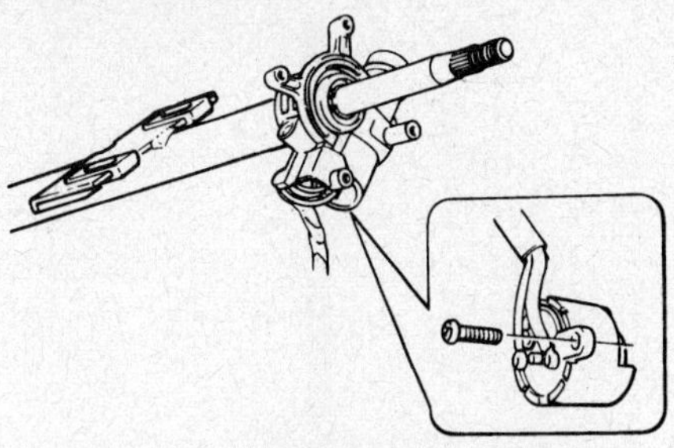

Fig. 3 Ignition switch removal

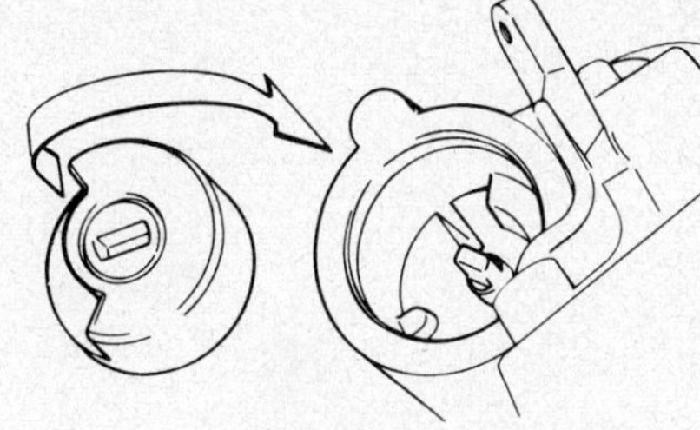

Fig. 4 Ignition switch installation

6. Remove switch from bezel, allow bezel and other switch to hang.
7. Remove cluster screws and remove cluster.
8. Disconnect electrical connector and speedometer cable.
9. Remove cluster lens.
10. Remove speedometer head assembly. Remove clock and tachometer, if necessary.
11. Remove all bulbs.
12. Remove seat belt buzzer.
13. Remove coolant temperature gauge and fuel gauge.
14. Remove seat belt buzzer timer.
15. Remove printed circuit.
16. Reverse procedure to install.

WINDSHIELD WIPER MOTOR

REPLACE

Refer to **Fig. 7** for wiper motor and linkage service.

BLOWER MOTOR

REPLACE

1. Disconnect defroster hose on driver's side, **Fig. 8.**
2. Disconnect blower motor lead wire.
3. Remove 3 blower motor mounting screws and blower motor, **Fig. 9.**
4. Reverse procedure to install.

HEATER CORE

REPLACE

1. Drain cooling system.
2. Disconnect water hoses from heater core.
3. Remove glove box compartment.
4. Disconnect defroster hoses from heater housing, **Fig. 8.**
5. Disconnect connectors from blower motor and heater resistor.
6. Disconnect 3 control cables from heater case side levers.
7. Pull out center vent louvre.
8. Disconnect right and left side vent ducts from center vent duct.
9. Remove center vent duct.
10. Remove ashtray upper plate.
11. Remove instrument member stay.
12. Remove 2 heater assembly mounting nuts.
13. Loosen heater case top side mounting bolts from glove box side.
14. Remove heater control assembly.
15. Remove retaining clips from heater case halves, **Fig. 9.**
16. Remove heater core from housing.

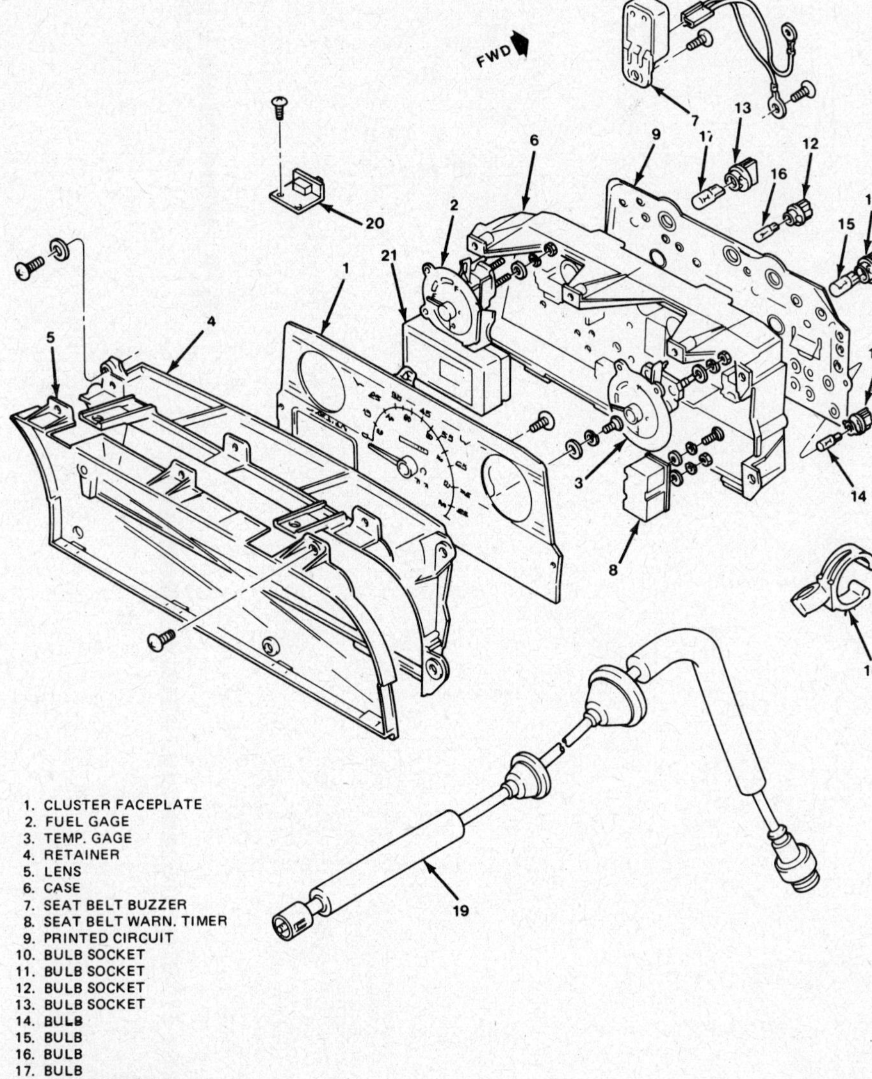

1. CLUSTER FACEPLATE
2. FUEL GAGE
3. TEMP. GAGE
4. RETAINER
5. LENS
6. CASE
7. SEAT BELT BUZZER
8. SEAT BELT WARN. TIMER
9. PRINTED CIRCUIT
10. BULB SOCKET
11. BULB SOCKET
12. BULB SOCKET
13. BULB SOCKET
14. BULB
15. BULB
16. BULB
17. BULB
18. SPEEDO CABLE CLAMP
19. SPEEDO CABLE ASSY
20. CANCEL SWITCH
21. CLOCK (IF EQUIPPED)
22. TACHOMETER (IF EQUIPPED)

Fig. 5 Instrument cluster assembly. Less tachometer

RADIO

REPLACE

1. Disconnect battery ground cable.
2. Remove ashtray and radio knobs.
3. Remove ashtray assembly.
4. Remove radio face plate.
5. Remove radio mounting nuts.
6. Disconnect electrical connector and antenna cable.
7. Remove radio.
8. Reverse procedure to install.

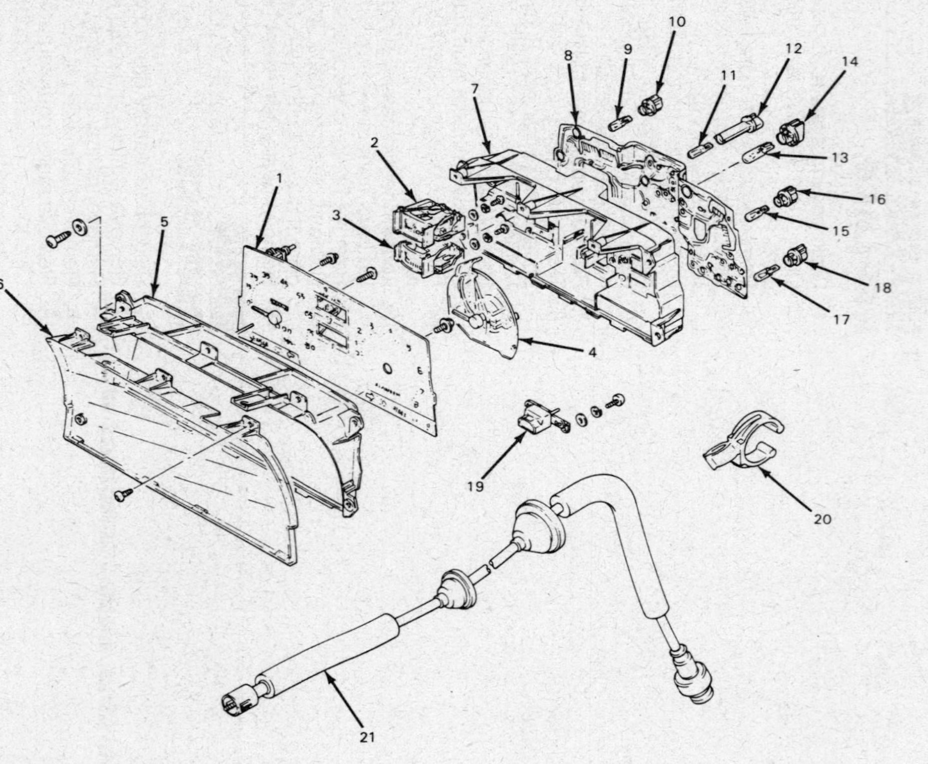

Fig. 6 Instrument cluster assembly. With tachometer

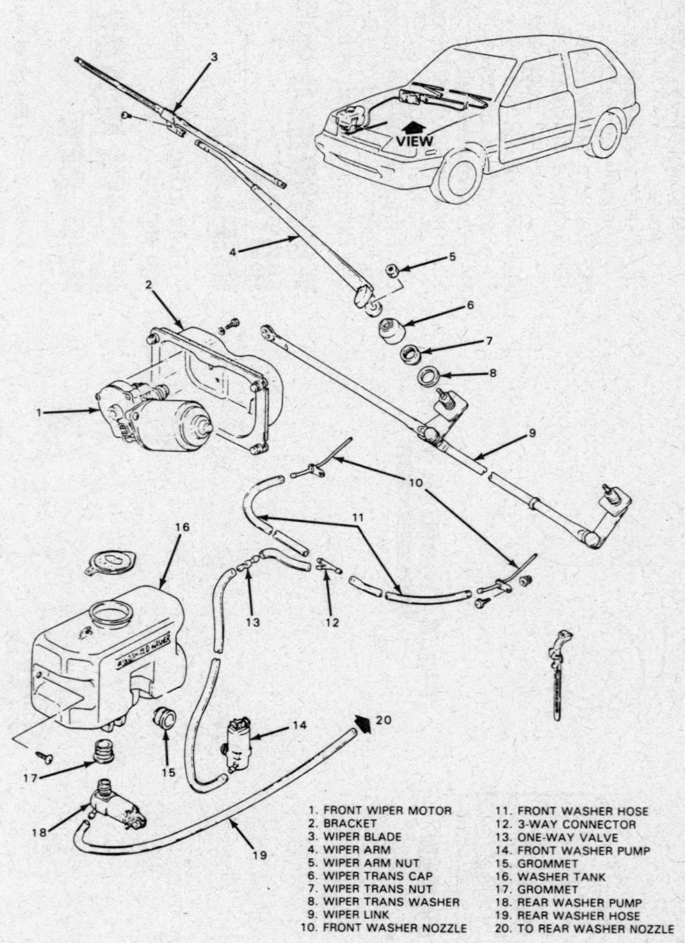

Fig. 7 Windshield wiper/washer motor & linkage assembly

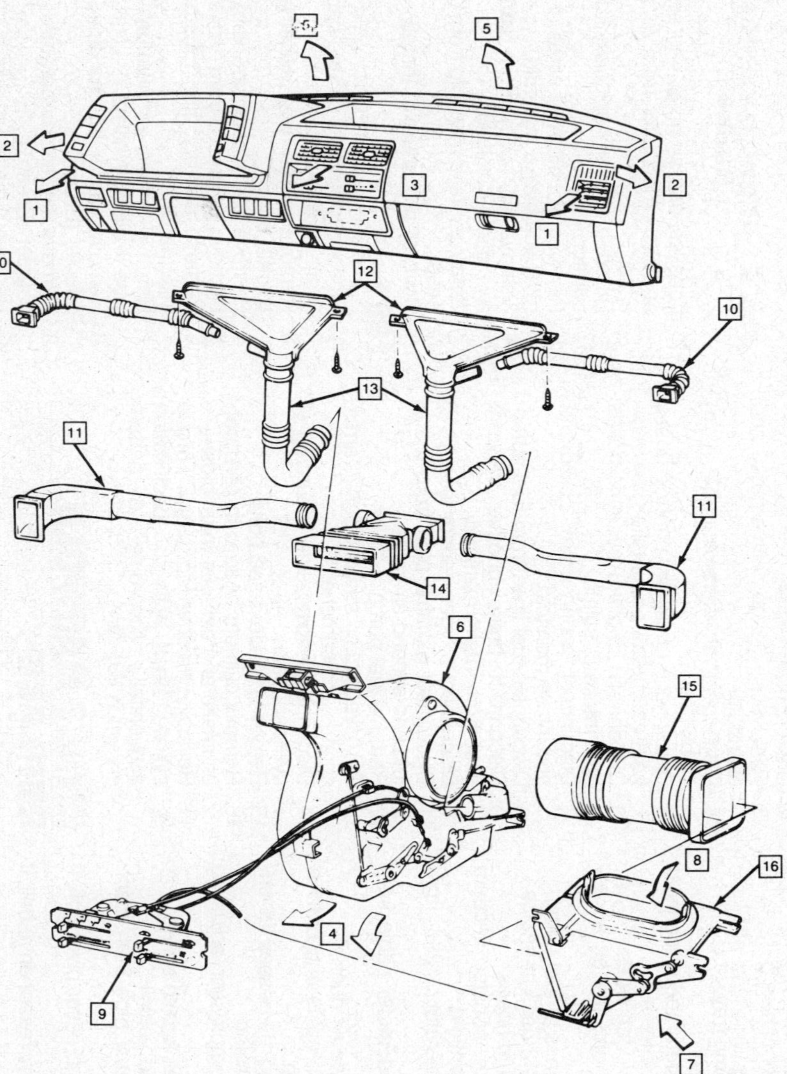
1. SIDE VENT OUTLET
2. SIDE DEFROSTER OUTLET
3. CENTER VENT OUTLET
4. FLOOR OUTLET
5. FRONT DEFROSTER OUTLET
6. BLOWER MOTOR
7. INSIDE AIR
8. OUTSIDE AIR
9. CONTROL LEVER
10. DEFROSTER HOSE
11. SIDE VENT DUCT
12. DEFROSTER NOZZLE
13. DEFROSTER HOSE
14. CENTER VENT DUCT
15. AIR DUCT
16. AIR DAMPER

Fig. 8 Heater & defroster assembly

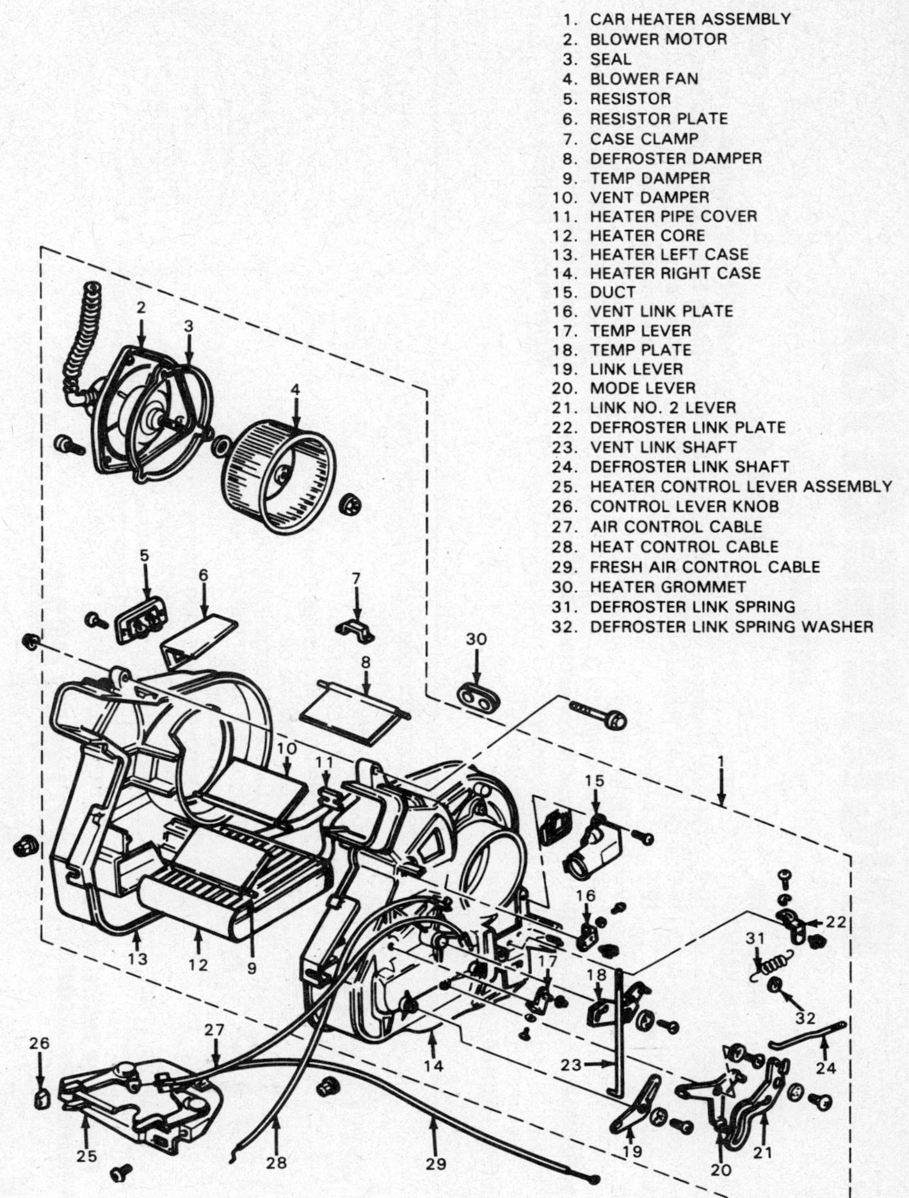
1. CAR HEATER ASSEMBLY
2. BLOWER MOTOR
3. SEAL
4. BLOWER FAN
5. RESISTOR
6. RESISTOR PLATE
7. CASE CLAMP
8. DEFROSTER DAMPER
9. TEMP DAMPER
10. VENT DAMPER
11. HEATER PIPE COVER
12. HEATER CORE
13. HEATER LEFT CASE
14. HEATER RIGHT CASE
15. DUCT
16. VENT LINK PLATE
17. TEMP LEVER
18. TEMP PLATE
19. LINK LEVER
20. MODE LEVER
21. LINK NO. 2 LEVER
22. DEFROSTER LINK PLATE
23. VENT LINK SHAFT
24. DEFROSTER LINK SHAFT
25. HEATER CONTROL LEVER ASSEMBLY
26. CONTROL LEVER KNOB
27. AIR CONTROL CABLE
28. HEAT CONTROL CABLE
29. FRESH AIR CONTROL CABLE
30. HEATER GROMMET
31. DEFROSTER LINK SPRING
32. DEFROSTER LINK SPRING WASHER

Fig. 9 Heater core case assembly

ENGINE SECTION

INDEX

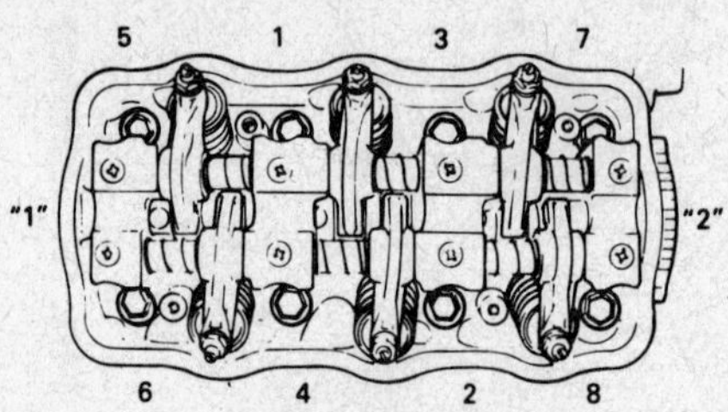

Fig. 1 Cylinder head bolt tightening sequence

ENGINE REPLACE

1. Disconnect battery cables.
2. Remove hood.
3. Remove battery and tray.
4. Remove air cleaner.
5. Drain cooling system and disconnect radiator hoses at engine.
6. Disconnect cooling fan wires.
7. Remove radiator and fan as an assembly.
8. Disconnect fuel lines at fuel pump.
9. Disconnect heater hoses at engine.
10. Disconnect vacuum hoses.
11. Disconnect brake booster vacuum hose at intake manifold.
12. Disconnect accelerator cable from carburetor.
13. Disconnect speedometer cable from transmission.
14. Disconnect outside air duct.
15. Disconnect clutch cable and bracket from transmission.
16. Disconnect wiring harnesses at engine and transmission.
17. Remove A/C compressor adjusting bolt, if equipped.
18. Remove drive belt splash shield.
19. Raise and support vehicle.
20. Disconnect exhaust pipe from manifold.
21. Loosen A/C compressor pivot bolt, if equipped.
22. Remove A/C compressor drive belt, if equipped.
23. Remove A/C compressor bracket from engine, if equipped.
24. Disconnect gearshift control shaft from transmission.
25. Disconnect gearshift extension rod from transmission.
26. Disconnect ball joints.
27. Drain transaxle.
28. Remove drive axles from transaxle.
29. Drain engine oil.
30. Disconnect engine torque rods.
31. Remove transmission mount nut.
32. Lower vehicle.
33. Remove engine side mount.
34. Remove engine mount nuts.
35. Using suitable hoist, remove engine and transaxle as an assembly.
36. Reverse procedure to install.

CYLINDER HEAD REPLACE

1. Disconnect battery ground cable.
2. Drain cooling system.
3. Remove air cleaner, valve cover and distributor.
4. Disconnect accelerator cable from carburetor.
5. Disconnect emission control hoses from carburetor and intake manifold.
6. Disconnect cooling system hoses from intake manifold.
7. Disconnect wiring from carburetor and intake manifold.
8. Disconnect fuel lines from fuel pump.
9. Disconnect brake booster vacuum hose from intake manifold.
10. Disconnect oxygen sensor lead.
11. Disconnect exhaust pipe from manifold and second air valve.
12. Remove fuel pump.
13. Remove rocker shafts, rocker arms, springs and camshaft.
14. Disconnect engine side mounting at cylinder head.
15. Remove cylinder head bolts.
16. Remove cylinder head with carburetor, intake and exhaust manifolds.
17. Reverse procedure to install. Torque cylinder head bolts to specification sequentially according to pattern shown in **Fig. 1.**

INTAKE MANIFOLD REPLACE

1985–86

1. Disconnect battery ground cable.
2. Drain coolant.
3. Disconnect warm air hose, cool air hose, second air hose, vacuum hose and EGR modulator from air cleaner case.
4. Remove accelerator cable from carburetor.
5. Remove electric lead wires at carburetor and intake manifold.
6. Remove all hoses from carburetor and intake manifold.
7. Remove intake manifold from cylinder head.
8. Reverse procedure to install.

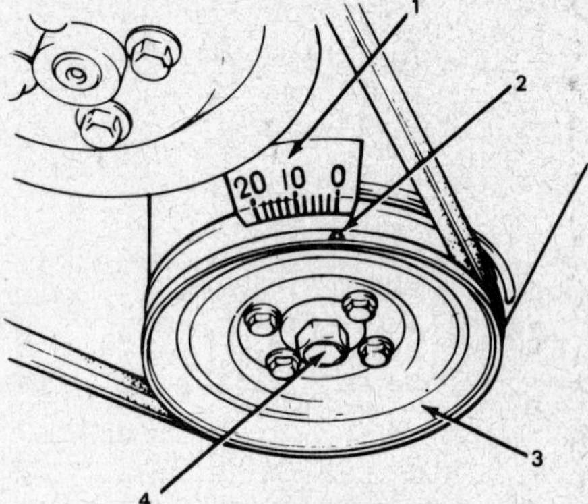

Fig. 2 Aligning crankshaft pulley

1987

1. Disconnect battery ground cable.
2. Drain cooling system.
3. Remove surge tank together with throttle body.
4. Remove fuel injector couplers.
5. Remove fuel hoses from delivery pipe.
6. Remove delivery pipe together with injectors.
7. Remove water temperature gauge wire (Yellow/White).
8. Remove starter injector time switch coupler (Brown).
9. Remove water temperature sensor coupler (Green).
10. Remove radiator fan switch coupler.
11. Remove water hoses.
12. Remove EGR valve vacuum hoses.
13. Remove intake manifold.
14. Reverse procedure to install.

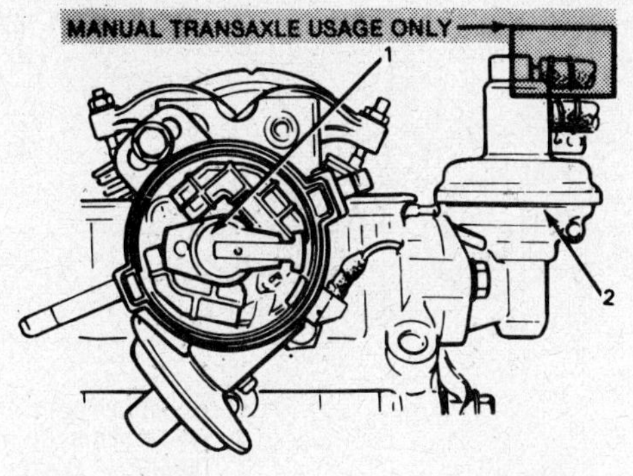

Fig. 3 Distributor rotor at TDC position

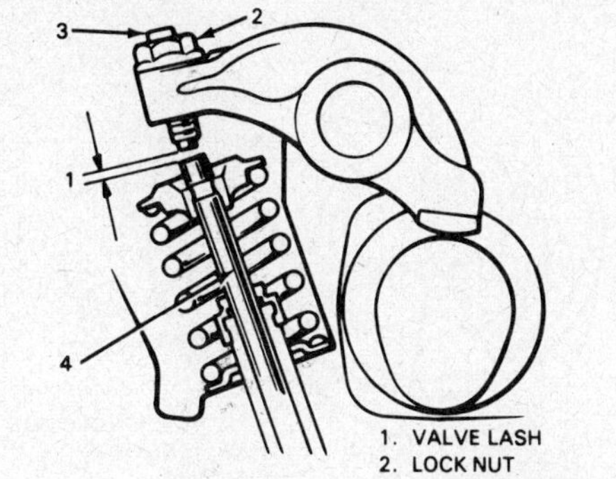

1. VALVE LASH
2. LOCK NUT
3. ADJUSTING SCREW
4. VALVE STEM

Fig. 4 Adjusting valve lash

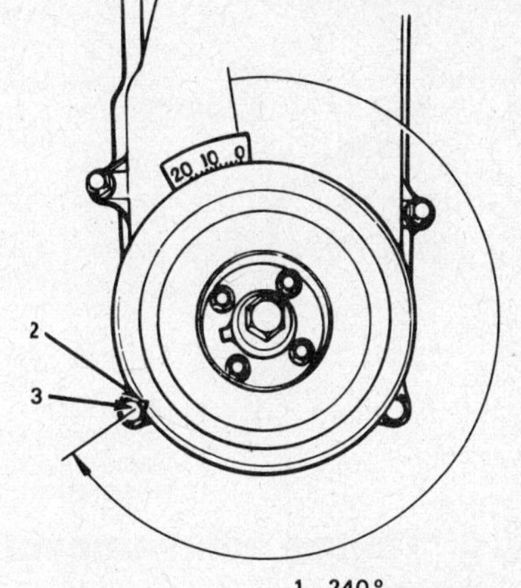

Fig. 5 Crankshaft pulley alignment w/left side timing belt cover bolt

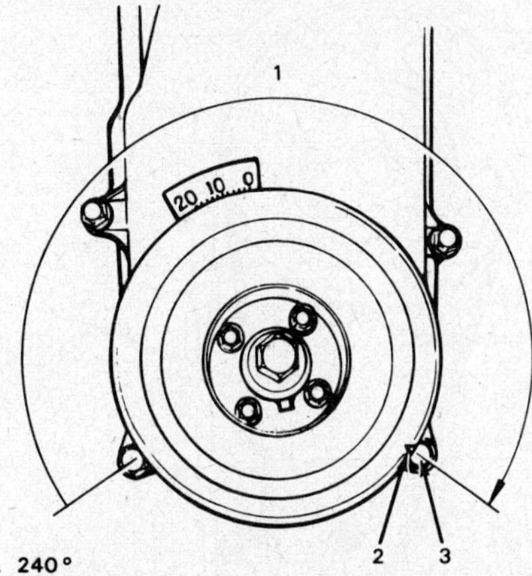

Fig. 6 Crankshaft pulley alignment w/right side timing belt cover bolt

1. OUTSIDE COVER
2. OUTSIDE COVER SEAL
3. INSIDE COVER
4. INSIDE COVER SEAL
5. SEAL
6. TIMING BELT
7. CAMSHAFT TIMING PULLEY
8. PIN
9. PULLEY BOLT
10. TENSIONER
11. TENSIONER BOLT
12. TENSIONER PLATE
13. WASHER
14. TENSIONER STUD
15. TENSIONER SPRING
16. SPRING DAMPER
17. SPRING SCREW

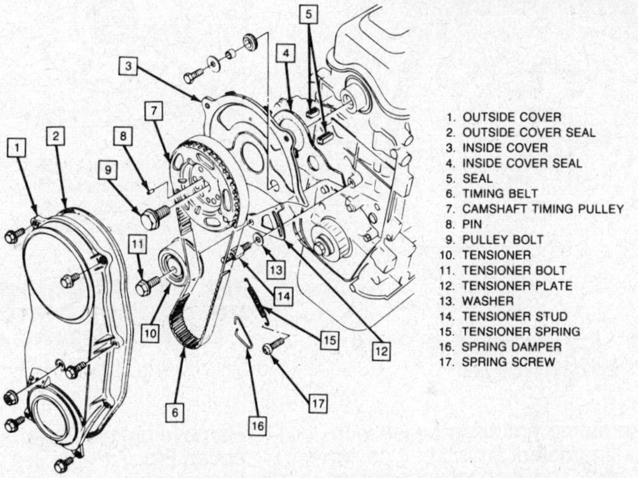

Fig. 7 Timing belt and cover assembly

EXHAUST MANIFOLD
REPLACE
1985–86

1. Disconnect battery ground cable.
2. Raise and support vehicle.
3. Remove exhaust pipe at manifold.
4. Remove lower heat shield bolt.
5. Remove air pipe at manifold.
6. Remove air conditioning belt.
7. Lower vehicle and remove air compressor lower adjusting brace.
8. Remove spark plug wires.
9. Remove oxygen sensor wire from sensor and block.
10. Remove exhaust manifold hot air shroud.
11. Remove exhaust manifold.
12. Reverse procedure to install.

1987

1. Remove turbocharger.
2. Remove exhaust manifold.

TURBOCHARGER
REPLACE

1. Disconnect battery ground cable.
2. Drain cooling system.
3. Remove hood.
4. Remove front grill.
5. Remove intercooler.
6. Remove radiator hoses.
7. Remove radiator fan motor coupler.
8. Remove front upper member.
9. Remove A/C condenser.
10. Remove radiator.
11. Remove front bumper from damper flange.
12. Remove exhaust pipe bolts.
13. Remove compressor.
14. Remove turbocharger cover.
15. Unclamp oxygen sensor wire.
16. Remover turbocharger side cover.
17. Remove lower exhaust pipe support bracket bolt.
18. Remove upper exhaust pipe together with lower exhaust pipe.
19. Remove air outlet pipe.
20. Remove air inlet hose clamp bolt on cylinder head.
21. Remove air inlet pipe.
22. Remove oil pipe from cylinder block.
23. Remove oil drain hose.
24. Remove water pipe cylinder head clamp bolt.
25. Remove water hoses.
26. Remove turbocharger.
27. Reverse procedure to install.

VALVES
ADJUST

1. Remove air cleaner and cylinder head cover.
2. Turn crankshaft clockwise and align timing notch on crankshaft pulley with 0 mark on timing tab, **Fig. 2.**
3. Remove distributor cap. Engine is at TDC when distributor rotor is positioned as shown in **Fig. 3.** If engine is not at TDC, turn crankshaft 360 degrees so timing notch is at 0 mark again.
4. Using feeler gauge, measure No. 1 cylinder intake and exhaust valve clearances at 1 in **Fig. 4.**
5. Adjust valve lash, if necessary, by turning adjusting screw after loosening locknut, **Fig. 4.** After adjustment, tighten locknut to specified torque.
6. After checking No. 1 cylinder, turn crankshaft 240 degrees clockwise

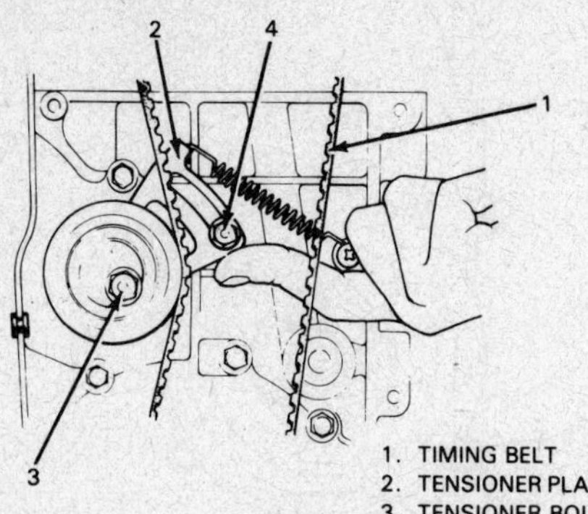

Fig. 8 Timing belt removal

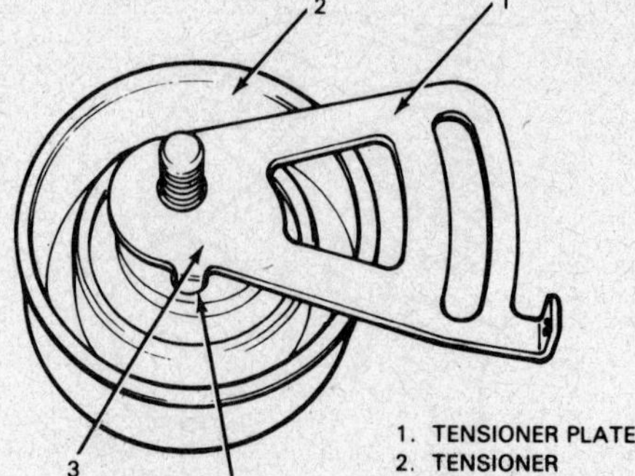

Fig. 9 Tensioner assembly

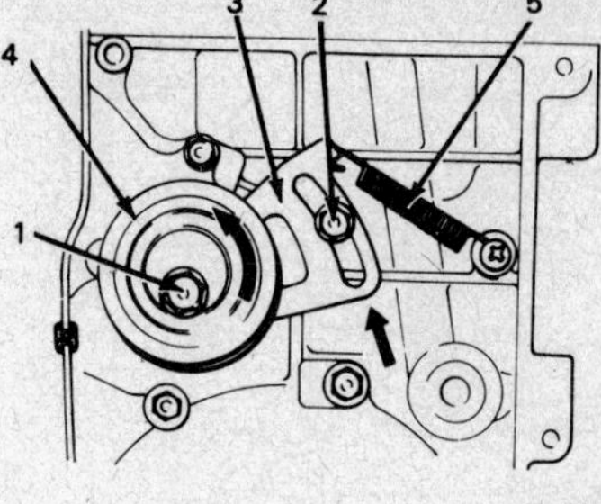

Fig. 10 Checking tensioner plate movement

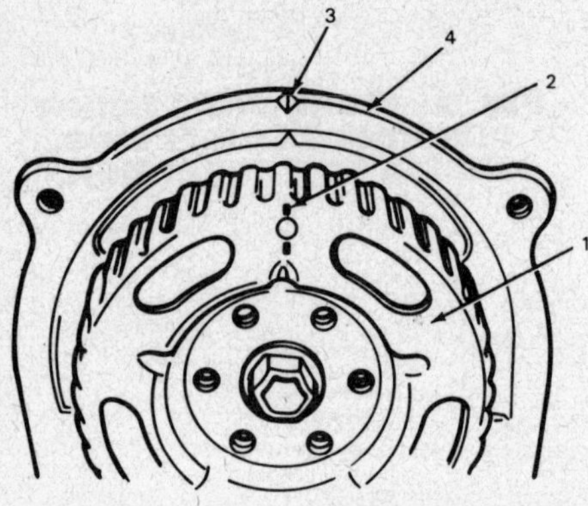

Fig. 11 Camshaft pulley alignment

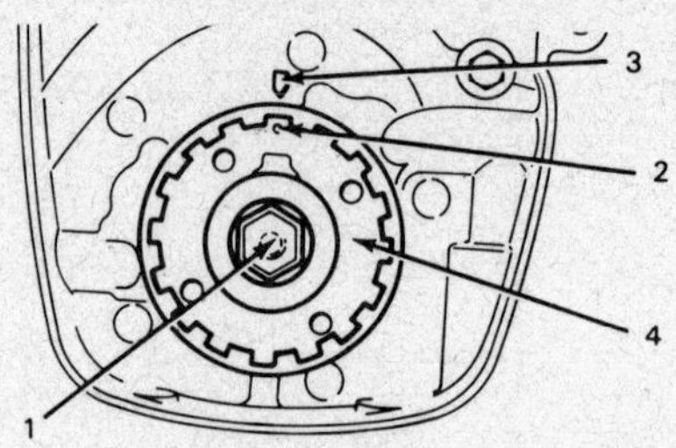

Fig. 12 Aligning timing belt pulley punch mark with oil pump arrow

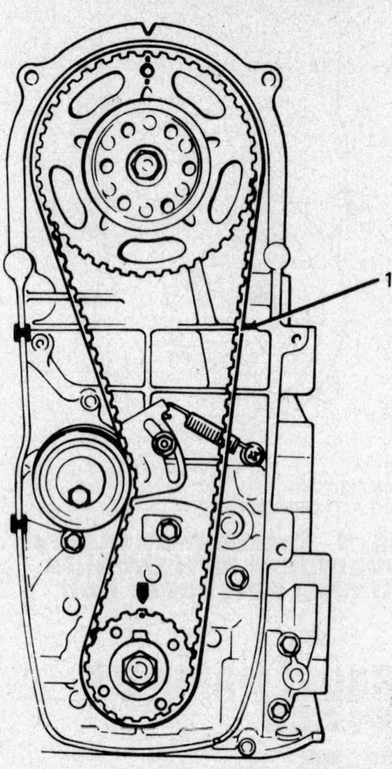

Fig. 13 Timing belt installation

and align timing notch on pulley with left mounting bolt of timing belt cover, **Fig. 5.** Check and, if necessary, adjust intake and exhaust valves of No. 3 cylinder.

7. Rotate crankshaft 240 degrees clockwise from left mounting bolt, and align timing notch with right mounting bolt as shown in **Fig. 6.** Then, check and, if necessary, adjust intake and exhaust valves of No. 2 cylinder.
8. After checking and adjusting valves, install distributor cap, cylinder head cover and air cleaner.

TIMING BELT & COVER REPLACE

REMOVAL

1. Disconnect battery ground cable.
2. Loosen water pump pulley bolts.
3. Remove A/C compressor adjusting bolt, if equipped.
4. Loosen alternator adjusting bolt.
5. Raise and support vehicle.
6. Remove drive belt splash shield.
7. Remove plug in right fender well.
8. Remove A/C compressor drive belt, if equipped.
9. Remove alternator belt.
10. Remove crankshaft pulley and water pump pulley.
11. Remove bolts at bottom of timing belt cover, **Fig. 7.**
12. Lower vehicle.
13. Remove bolts at top of timing belt cover and cover.
14. Remove cylinder head cover.
15. Loosen rocker arm adjusting screws.
16. Remove distributor cap.
17. Loosen tensioner bolt and stud, and remove belt as shown in **Fig. 8.**
18. Remove tensioner, tensioner plate and tensioner spring.

INSPECTION

1. Check timing belt for wear or cracks. Replace as necessary.
2. Check tensioner for smooth rotation.

INSTALLATION

1. Install tensioner plate to tensioner. Insert lug of tensioner plate into hole of tensioner, **Fig. 9.**
2. Install tensioner, tensioner plate and spring. Hand tighten tensioner bolt and stud only. Check that plate movement is in direction shown in **Fig. 10.** If no movement occurs between plate and tensioner, remove tensioner and plate and re-insert plate lug into tensioner hole.
3. Turn camshaft pulley clockwise and align timing mark on camshaft pulley with V mark on inside belt cover, **Fig. 11.**
4. Using 17 mm wrench, turn crankshaft clockwise and align punch mark on timing belt pulley with arrow mark on oil pump, **Fig. 12.**
5. With all 4 marks aligned, install timing belt on sprockets so that drive side of belt is free of any slack and so tensioner plate is positioned as shown in **Fig. 13.**
6. To ensure timing belt is free of slack, turn crankshaft one rotation clockwise after installing belt. After removing slack, first torque tensioner stud, and then tensioner bolt to 17-21 ft. lbs.
7. Install timing belt outer cover.
8. Install crankshaft pulley and torque 4 bolts to 7-9 ft. lbs.
9. Refer to "Valves, Adjust" procedure and adjust intake and exhaust valves.

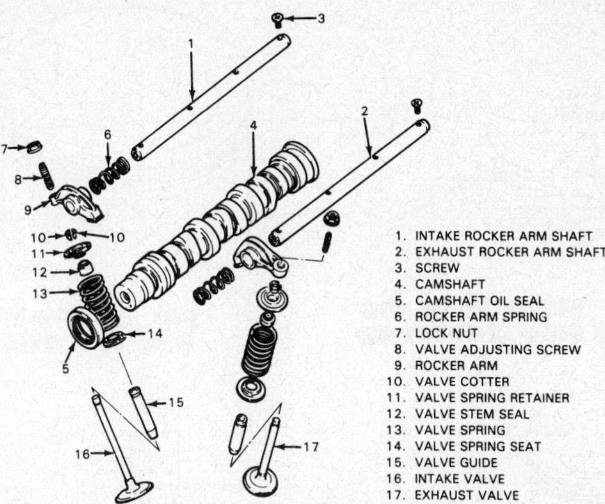

Fig. 14 Exploded view of valve train assembly

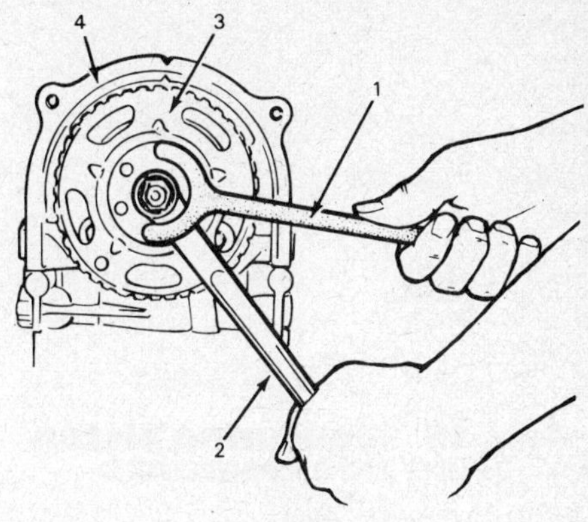

Fig. 15 Timing belt sprocket removal

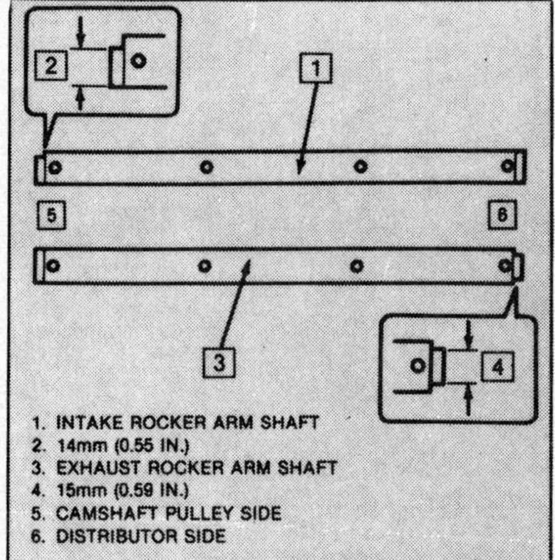

Fig. 16 Rocker arm shaft identification

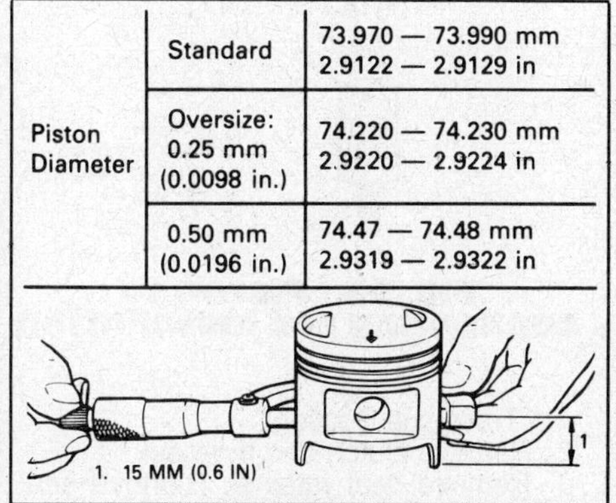

Piston Diameter	Standard	73.970 — 73.990 mm 2.9122 — 2.9129 in
	Oversize: 0.25 mm (0.0098 in.)	74.220 — 74.230 mm 2.9220 — 2.9224 in
	0.50 mm (0.0196 in.)	74.47 — 74.48 mm 2.9319 — 2.9322 in

Fig. 17 Measuring piston diameter

Cylinder Bore Dia. Limit	74.15 mm 2.9193 in
Taper and Out-of-Round Limit	0.10 mm 0.0039 in

1. 50 MM (1.96 IN)
2. 95 MM (3.74 IN)

Fig. 18 Measuring piston bore diameter

10. Install water pump pulley and drive belt.
11. Install cylinder head cover and air cleaner.
12. Connect battery ground cable.

CAMSHAFT & ROCKER ARMS

REPLACE

1. Disconnect battery ground cable.
2. Remove air cleaner and cylinder head cover.
3. Remove distributor and case from cylinder head.
4. Loosen all valve adjusting screw locknuts and turn adjusting screws completely back to allow rocker arms to move freely.
5. Remove rocker arm shaft screws and rocker arm shafts. Then, remove rocker arms and springs, **Fig. 14.**
6. Remove fuel pump and pushrod from cylinder head.
7. Refer to "Timing Belt & Cover, Replace" procedure to remove crankshaft pulley and timing belt outer cover.
8. Using tool J-34836, remove timing belt sprocket and timing belt inner cover, **Fig. 15.**
9. Remove camshaft from cylinder head.
10. Reverse procedure to install. Torque camshaft sprocket to 41-46 ft. lbs. Refer to **Fig. 16** for rocker shaft identification.

PISTON & CONNECTING ROD SERVICE

INSPECTION

1. Inspect piston for cracks or other damage. Replace as necessary.
2. Measure piston diameter at a height of .59 inches (15 mm) from piston skirt end in perpendicular direction to piston pin, **Fig. 17.**
3. Measure cylinder bore diameter, **Fig. 18,** and piston diameter to determine piston clearance. Piston clearance should be .0008-.0015 inch. If clearance is excessive, rebore cylinder and install oversize piston. All cylinders must be overbored to same size to ensure balance.
4. With piston grooves clean, dry and free of carbon, insert piston ring into groove, and measure clearance between ring and ring land with feeler gauge, **Fig. 19.** If clearance is out of specification, replace piston.
5. Piston pin should fit into piston bore with easy finger push at normal room temperature. Check piston pin and piston pin bore for wear or damage. If badly worn or damaged, replace pin or piston as necessary.
6. Install connecting rod on its journal and check that side clearance does not exceed .0137 inch, **Fig. 20.** If so, replace connecting rod.

ASSEMBLY

Two sizes of pistons are available as standard size spare parts to ensure proper piston-to-cylinder clearance. When installing standard piston, match piston to its bore as follows:

a. Each piston has number 1 or 2 stamped on top, **Fig. 21,** to indicate its outside diameter.
b. The engine block is stamped as shown in **Fig. 22,** to indicate size of piston in each bore.

Assemble pistons, rings and rods as fol-

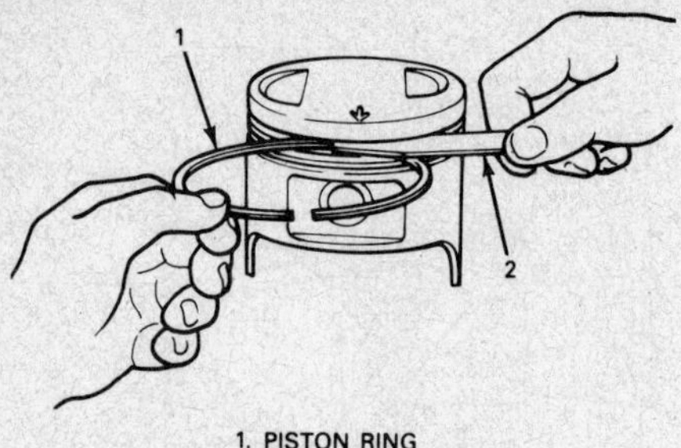

Fig. 19 Measuring piston ring side clearance

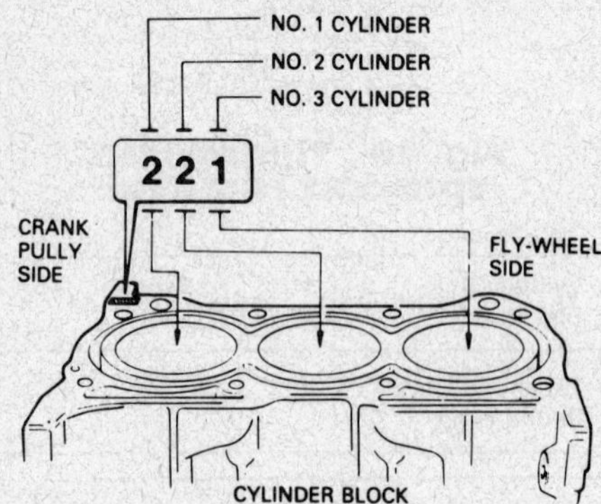

Fig. 22 Engine block stamping

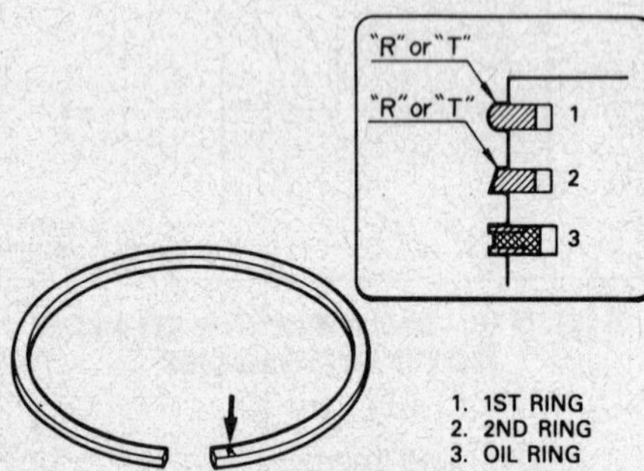

Fig. 25 Piston ring installation

lows:

1. Apply engine oil to piston pin bores in piston and rod and fit connecting rod to piston as shown in **Fig. 23.**
2. Place piston on tool J-34838 so arrow mark on piston head faces up. Press piston pin into piston and connecting rod, **Fig. 24.**
3. Install piston rings so marked side of each ring faces top of piston, **Fig. 25.** Note shape of rings 1 and 2.
4. Install oil ring spacer first, then 2 rails.
5. Align ring end gaps as shown in **Fig. 26.** Pistons and connecting rod assemblies must be installed in block so arrows on pistons face front (pulley end) of engine.

REAR OIL SEAL
REPLACE

1. Remove transaxle as described in "Transaxle Section."
2. Remove clutch and flywheel.
3. Remove seal retainer. Remove seal from retainer.
4. Reverse procedure to install.

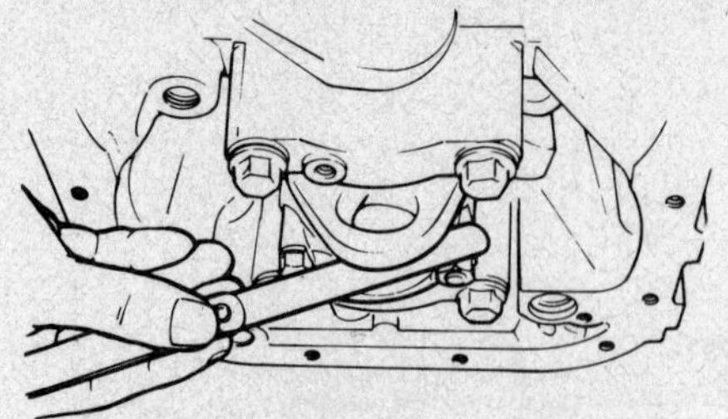

Fig. 20 Measuring rod bearing side clearance

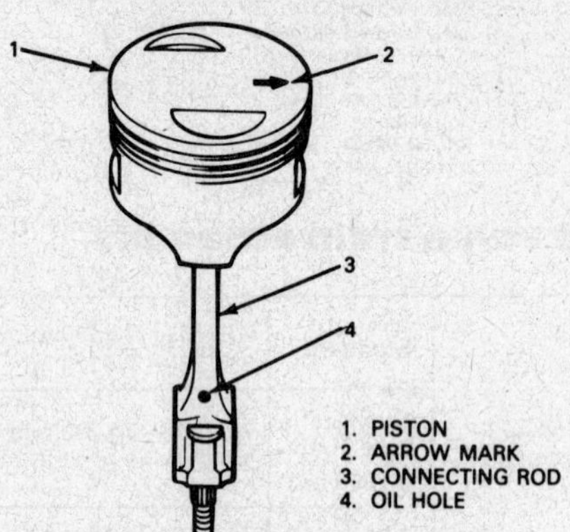

Fig. 23 Piston to connecting rod installation

OIL PAN
REPLACE

1. Disconnect battery ground cable.
2. Raise and support vehicle.
3. Drain oil pan.
4. Remove flywheel dust cover.
5. Disconnect exhaust pipe at manifold.
6. Remove oil pan bolts and pan, **Fig. 27.**
7. Remove oil pump screen.
8. Reverse procedure to install. Apply continuous bead of silicon type sealer to oil pan flange inside bolt holes. Starting at center and working outwards, torque oil pan bolts to 7-9 ft. lbs. Torque drain plug to 22-29 ft. lbs.

OIL PUMP
REPLACE
REMOVAL

1. Refer to "Timing Belt, Replace" procedure to remove timing belt.
2. Refer to "Oil Pan, Replace" procedure to remove oil pan.
3. Remove crankshaft timing belt sprocket.
4. Remove alternator mounting bracket.
5. Remove A/C compressor mounting bracket, if so equipped.
6. Remove alternator adjusting bolt and upper cover bolt.
7. Remove oil pump bolts and pump, **Fig. 28.**

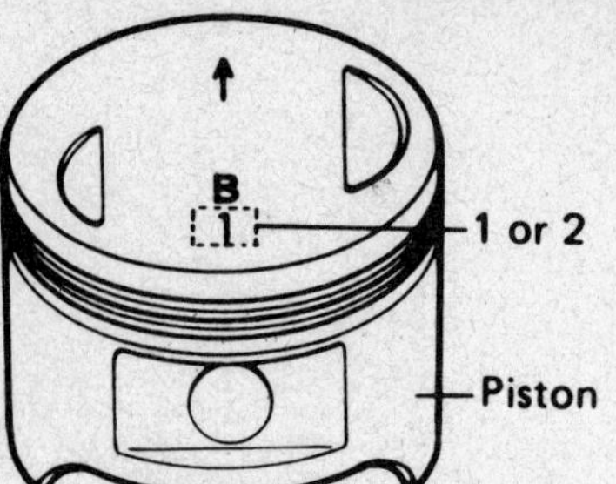

Fig. 21 Piston identification

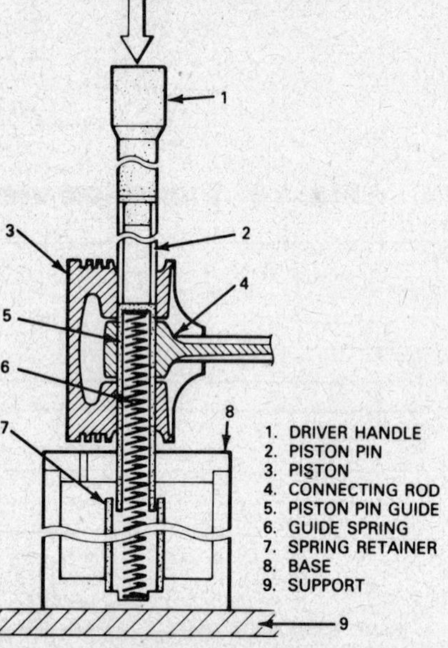

Fig. 24 Piston pin installation

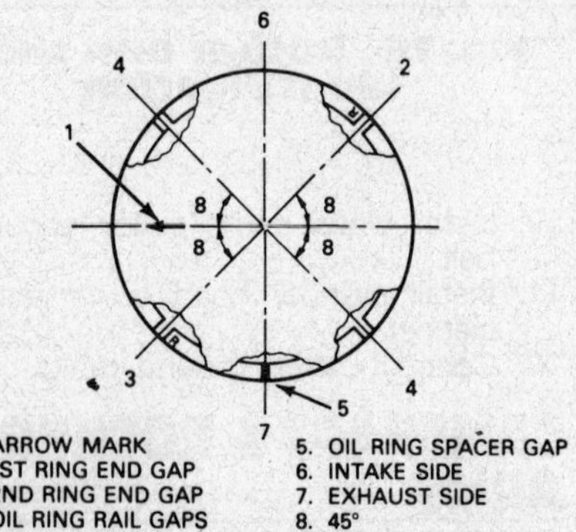

Fig. 26 Ring end gap alignment

INSPECTION

1. Remove dipstick tube from oil pump.
2. Remove gear plate screws and gear plate.
3. Remove outer and inner gear.
4. Inspect oil seal lip for damage and replace as necessary.
5. Inspect outer and inner gears, gear plate, and oil pump case for excessive

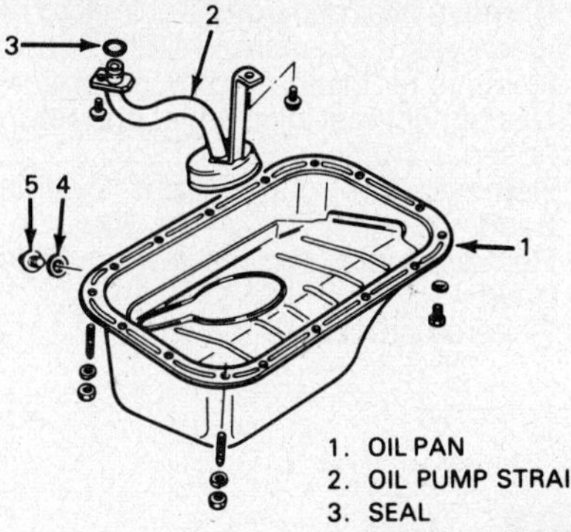

Fig. 27 Oil pan removal

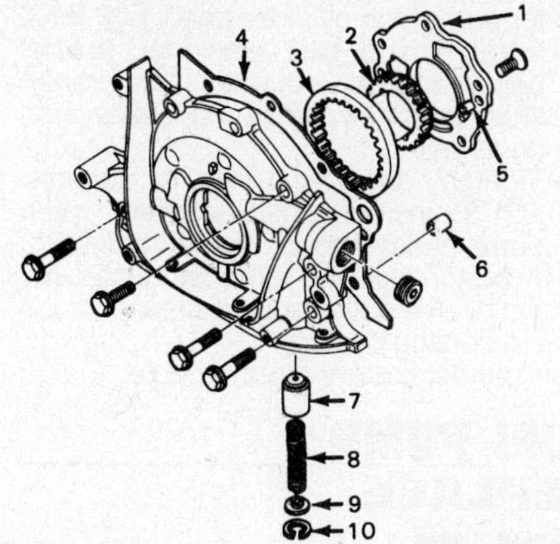

Fig. 28 Oil pump removal

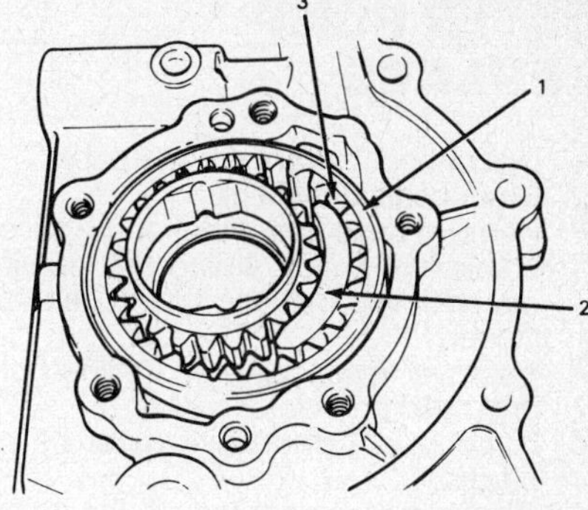

Fig. 29 Checking oil pump gear radial clearance

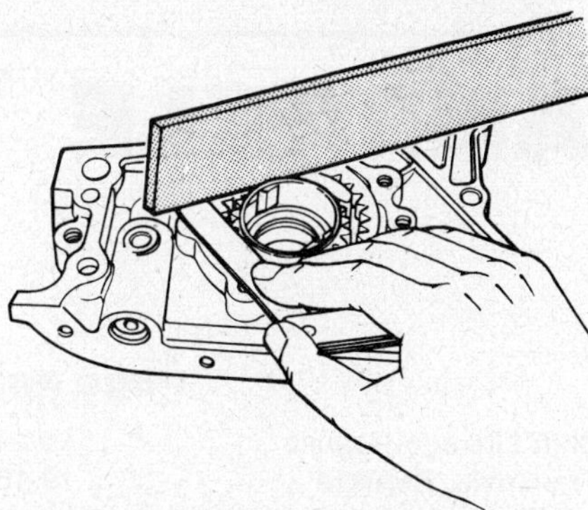

Fig. 30 Checking oil pump gear side clearance

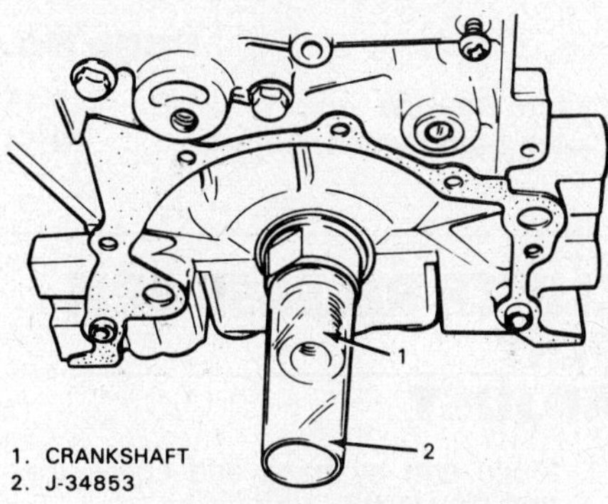

Fig. 31 Tool J-34853 installation

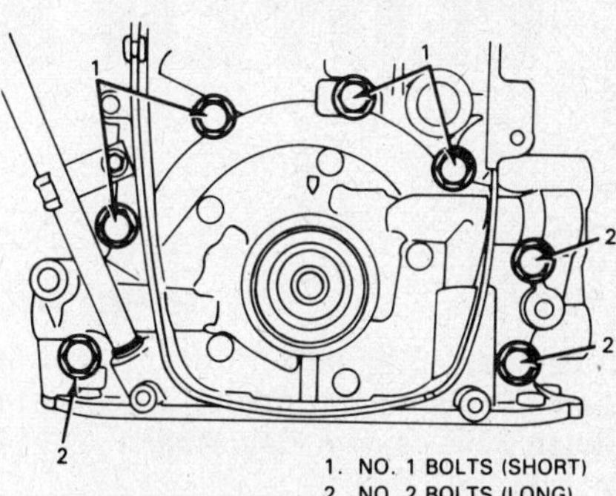

Fig. 32 Oil pump bolt location

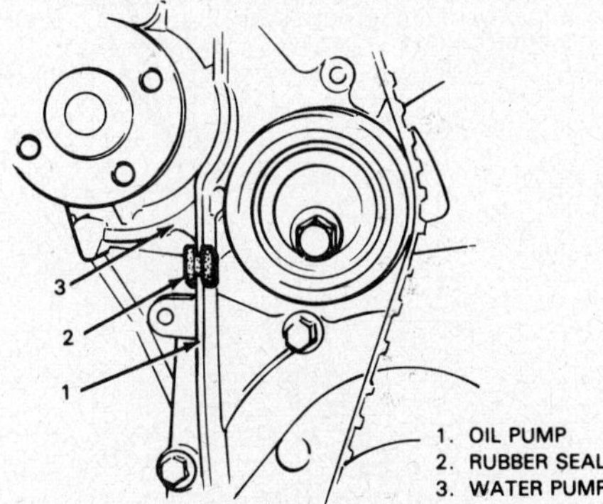

Fig. 33 Rubber seal installation

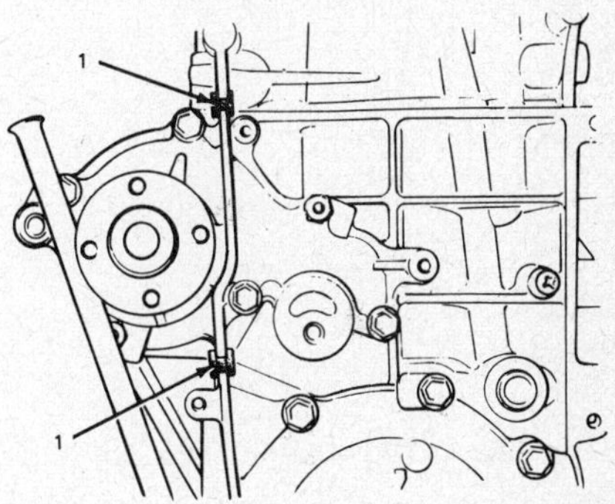

Fig. 34 Installing rubber seals

wear or damage.

6. Using feeler gauge, check radial clearance between outer gear and crescent, **Fig. 29.** If clearance exceeds .0122 inch, replace outer gear.
7. Using straightedge and feeler gauge, measure side clearance which should not exceed .0059 inch, **Fig. 30.**
8. Wash, clean and dry all oil pump parts.
9. Apply light coat of engine oil to inner and outer gears, oil seal lip portion, and inside surfaces of oil pump case and plate.
10. Install outer and inner gears in pump case.
11. Install gear plate and tighten screws securely. Check that gears turn smoothly by hand.
12. Install O-ring in pump case, then dipstick tube.

ASSEMBLY

1. Install oil pump pins and gasket on engine block.
2. Install tool J-34853 (oil seal guide) onto crankshaft to prevent damage to oil seal lip, **Fig. 31.** Apply engine oil to special tool.
3. Install oil pump onto crankshaft and engine block. Note location of mounting bolts, **Fig. 32.**
4. After installing oil pump, check that oil seal lip is not twisted, then remove tool.
5. Install rubber seal between oil pump and water pump, **Fig. 33.**
6. If necessary, trim edges of oil pump seal flush with oil pan mating surface.
7. Install timing belt guide, key and crankshaft timing sprocket. Note that timing belt guide must be installed so that curved side faces oil pump.
8. Torque crankshaft timing sprocket bolt to 47-54 ft. lbs.
9. Install timing belt and tensioner components.
10. Adjust intake and exhaust valves.
11. Adjust water pump tension.
12. Fill crankcase.
13. Connect battery ground cable.
14. Run engine to check that oil pressure is correct.

WATER PUMP
REPLACE

1. Disconnect battery ground cable.
2. Drain cooling system.
3. Remove drive belt, water pump pulley, crankshaft pulley, timing belt outside cover, timing belt and timing belt tensioner.
4. Remove water pump mounting bolts and nuts, and water pump.
5. If pump is defective, it must be replaced.
6. Place new water pump gasket on engine block.
7. Install water pump on engine block.
8. Install rubber seals between water pump and oil pump, and between water pump and cylinder head, **Fig. 34.**
9. Install timing belt tensioner, timing belt, timing belt outside cover, crankshaft pulley, water pump pulley and drive belt.
10. Tighten drive belt so it deflects .25-.35 inch on span between water pump pulley and crankshaft pulley.
11. Adjust intake and exhaust valves. Install valve cover and air cleaner.
12. Fill cooling system.
13. Connect battery ground cable.

FUEL PUMP
REPLACE
1985–86

1. Disconnect battery ground cable.
2. Remove filler cap from fuel tank to release vapor pressure. Reinstall cap.
3. Remove air cleaner from carburetor.
4. Disconnect fuel inlet, outlet and return hoses from fuel pump.
5. Remove fuel pump from cylinder head.
6. Remove fuel pump rod from cylinder head.
7. Reverse procedure to install.

1987

1. An electric fuel pump is installed in the fuel tank, ON/OFF operation is controlled by the ECM.

CLUTCH & MANUAL TRANSAXLE SECTION

INDEX

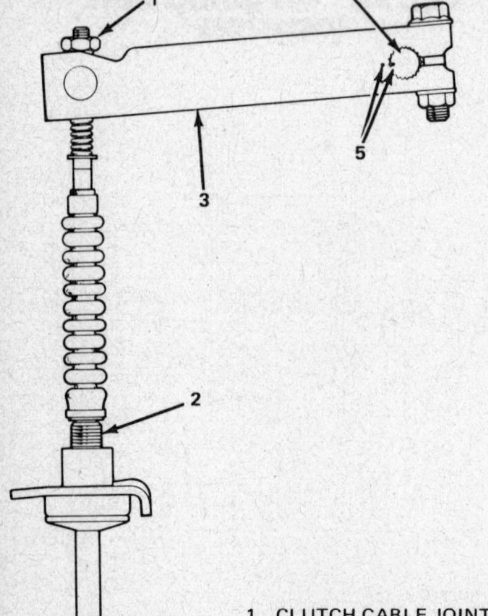

Fig. 1 Clutch cable adjustment

CLUTCH PEDAL HEIGHT
ADJUST

Using clutch pedal stop bolt, adjust height of clutch pedal so it is even with brake pedal.

CLUTCH RELEASE ARM PLAY
ADJUST

1. Move arm by hand and check that arm play is .08-.16 inch.
2. If play is out of specification, loosen or tighten clutch cable joint nut as necessary, **Fig. 1.**

CLUTCH START SWITCH
ADJUST

1. Apply parking brake firmly and place shift lever in Neutral position.
2. Disconnect wiring from switch.
3. Loosen locknut and screw switch out.
4. Depress clutch pedal completely to floor. Allow pedal to come up .4-1.1 inch from floor.
5. Connect ohmmeter to switch. Slowly screw switch in until it is on. Hold switch in this position, and tighten locknut to 8-11 ft. lbs.
6. Connect wiring to switch.

SHIFT LINKAGE, ADJUST

1. Loosen gear shift control housing nuts and guide plate bolts.
2. Adjust guide plate by moving it forwards or backwards until shift lever is positioned in middle of guide plate and at a right angle, **Fig. 2.**
3. When guide plate is positioned properly, tighten guide plate bolts and housing nuts.

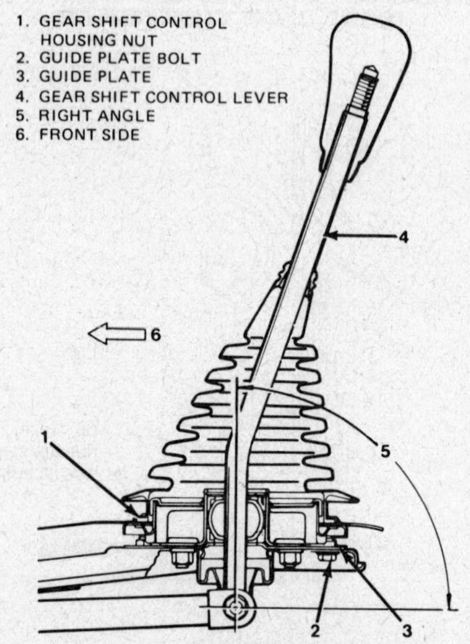

Fig. 2 Shift linkage adjustment

CLUTCH CABLE
REPLACE

1. Disconnect battery ground cable at battery.
2. Remove clutch cable joint nut, and disconnect cable from release arm.
3. Remove clutch cable bracket bolts and bracket.
4. Remove cable retaining bolts at clutch pedal.

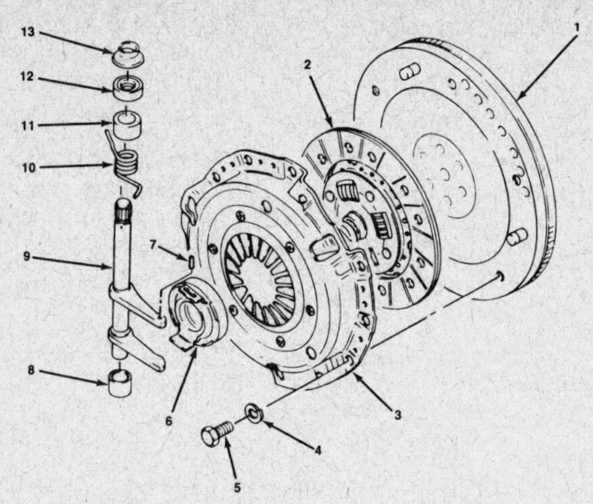

1. FLYWHEEL
2. DISC
3. CLUTCH COVER
4. LOCK WASHER
5. BOLT
6. RELEASE BEARING
7. RELEASE FORK PIN
8. NO. 2 BUSHING
9. RELEASE SHAFT
10. RETURN SPRING
11. NO. 1 BUSHING
12. SHAFT SEAL
13. SHAFT COVER

Fig. 3 Clutch assembly

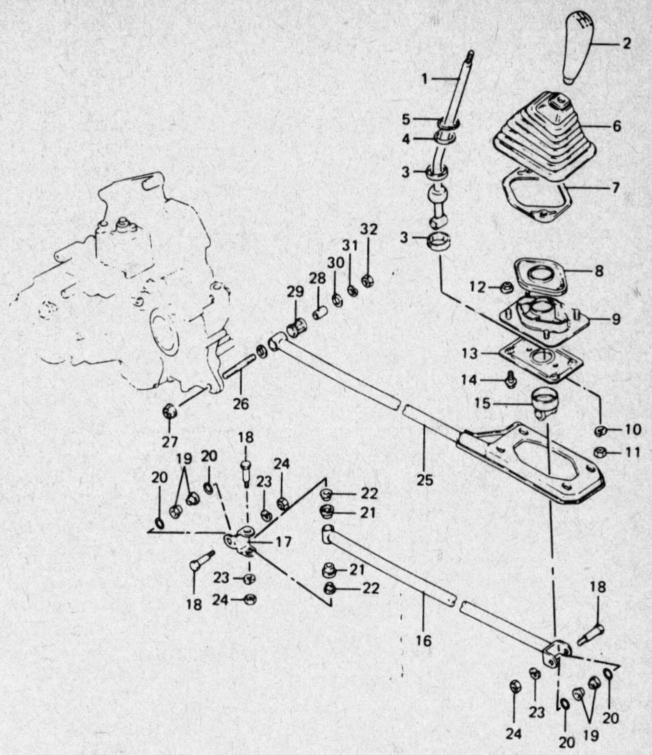

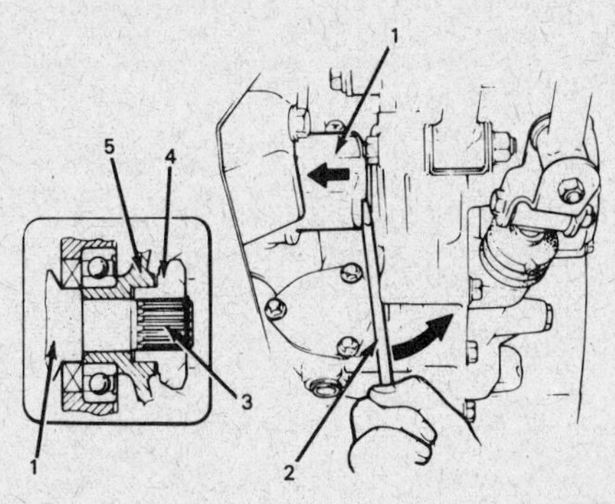

1. INBOARD JOINT OF DRIVE AXLE
2. PRY BAR
3. SNAP RING
4. DIFF. SIDE GEAR
5. DIFF. CARRIER

Fig. 5 Disengaging snap rings

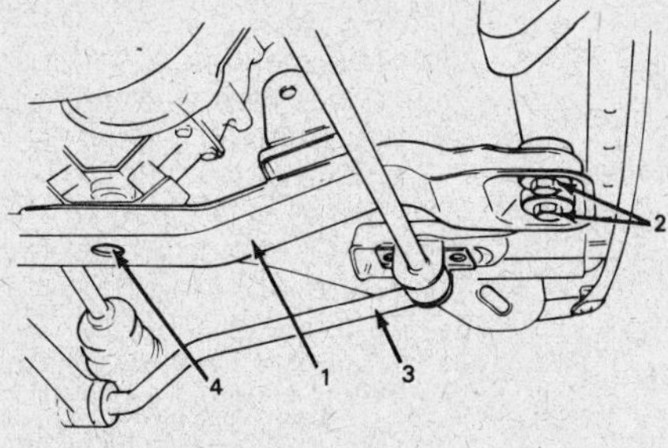

1. MOUNTING MEMBER
2. MOUNTING MEMBER BOLTS 50 – 60 N·m (37-43 FT. LBS.)
3. STABILIZER BAR
4. TRANSAXLE MOUNT NUT 40 – 50 N·m (29-36 FT. LBS.)

Fig. 6 Mounting member removal

1. GEAR SHIFT CONT. LEVER
2. KNOB
3. LEVER SEAT
4. LEVER SHIM
5. LEVER RING
6. BOOT
7. BOOT COVER
8. HOUSING DUST COVER
9. GEAR SHIFT CONT. HOUSING
10. LOCK WASHER
11. NUT
12. HOUSING NUT
13. GUIDE PLATE
14. GUIDE PLATE BOLT
15. REAR BOOT
16. GEAR SHIFT CONT. SHAFT
17. GEAR SHIFT CONT. JOINT
18. CONT. SHAFT BOLT
19. BUSHING
20. BUSHING SEAL
21. OUTER BUSHING
22. INNER BUSHING
23. LOCK WASHER
24. SHAFT BOLT NUT
25. EXTENSION ROD
26. ROD STUD
27. STUD NUT
28. SPACER
29. BUSHING
30. WASHER
31. LOCK WASHER
32. ROD NUT

Fig. 4 Shift linkage components

5. Remove clutch cable from vehicle.
6. Reverse procedure to install. Refer to "Clutch Pedal Height, Adjust" procedure to adjust cable.

CLUTCH REPLACE

1. Refer to "Transaxle, Replace" procedure to remove transaxle.
2. Install tool J-34860 into pilot bearing to support clutch assembly during removal.
3. Check for X mark or white painted letter on clutch cover and corresponding mark stamped on flywheel. If no markings are found, mark flywheel and clutch cover for assembly purposes.
4. Loosen clutch cover to flywheel mounting bolts 1 turn at a time until spring pressure is released, **Fig. 3.** Remove bolts, clutch cover, clutch disc, and tool J-34860 from flywheel.
5. Reverse procedure to install.

TRANSAXLE
REPLACE

1. Disconnect battery ground cable.
2. Disconnect negative cable at transaxle.
3. Remove air cleaner and heat pipe.
4. Disconnect clutch cable from clutch release lever.
5. Remove starter motor from transaxle.
6. Disconnect speedometer cable at transaxle.
7. Disconnect wiring from transaxle.
8. Disconnect front and rear torque rods from transaxle.
9. Raise and support vehicle.
10. Drain transaxle lubricant.
11. Disconnect exhaust pipe from manifold and from first exhaust pipe hanger.
12. Remove clutch housing lower plate.
13. Disconnect gearshift linkage and extension rod from transaxle, **Fig. 4.**
14. Remove left front wheel.
15. Disconnect snap rings on RH and LH drive axles from differential side gears, **Fig. 5.** Pry inboard joint out to disengage snap ring fitted on spline.
16. Disconnect stabilizer bar mounting bolts and ball stud bolt on left side. Disconnect ball stud from steering knuckle by pushing down on stabilizer bar.
17. Pull inboard joint of left drive axle out of transaxle.
18. Remove front torque rod.
19. Using suitable jack, support transaxle securely for removal.
20. Remove mounting member bolts from body and transaxle, **Fig. 6.**
21. Remove engine to transaxle mounting bolts and nuts.
22. Slide transaxle to left to disengage from engine, then lower from vehicle.
23. Reverse procedure to install, noting the following:
    a. Guide right drive axle into transaxle as it is raised into vehicle.
    b. Push RH and LH drive axles into differential side gears until snap rings on axle engage side gears.

REAR AXLE & SUSPENSION SECTION

INDEX

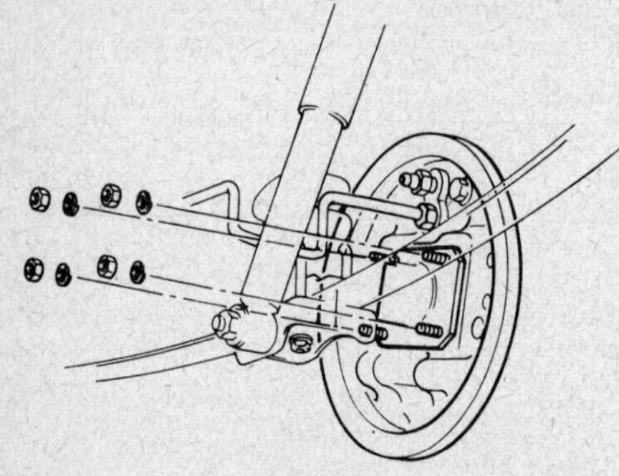

Fig. 1 Removing backing plate to axle attaching nuts

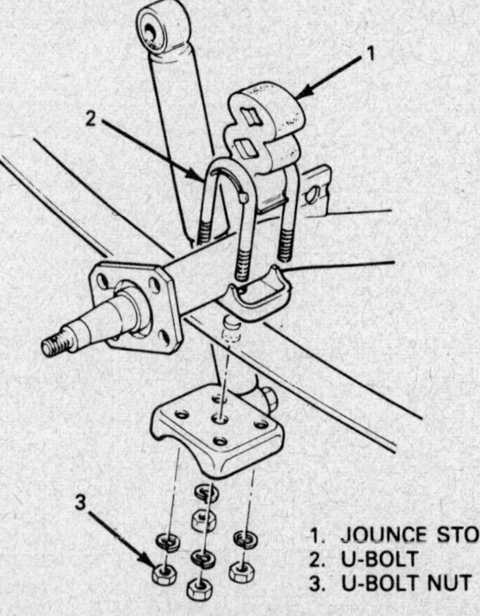

Fig. 2 Axle attachment parts removal

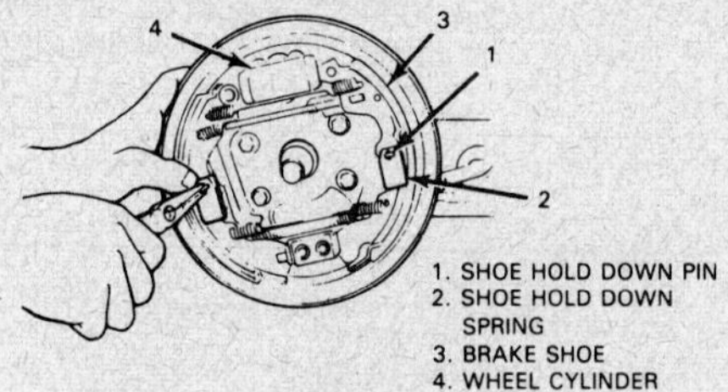

Fig. 3 Brake shoe hold down spring removal

REAR AXLE
REPLACE
1985–86

1. Raise and support vehicle.
2. Remove rear brake drums.
3. Disconnect brake hoses from lines.
4. Disconnect brake hoses and retainers from axle brackets.
5. Plug brake hoses to prevent loss of brake fluid.
6. Remove backing plate to axle nuts, **Fig. 1.**
7. Remove U-bolt nuts, U-bolts and jounce stop, **Fig. 2.**
8. Remove rear axle.
9. Reverse procedure to install. Note that alignment pin in leaf spring must engage in hole in axle bracket, **Fig. 2.** Tighten U-bolt nuts so equal amounts of threaded area are exposed.

1987

1. Raise and support vehicle.
2. Remove rear brake drums.
3. Disconnect brake hoses from lines.
4. Disconnect brake hoses and retainers from trailing arm.
5. Plug brake hoses to prevent loss of brake fluid.
6. Remove brake shoe hold down spring by turning shoe hold down pin as shown in **Fig. 3.**
7. Disconnect parking brake cable from parking brake shoe lever and remove brake shoes. Remove cable from back plate.
8. Remove brake back plate from rear axle.
9. Support center of axle with suitable jack.
10. Remove lateral rod body side bolt **Fig. 4.**
11. Remove shock absorber lower mounting bolt.
12. Lower rear axle slowly, until tension of suspension spring is relieved. Remove spring.
13. Remove trailing arm front side bolt and lower rear axle.
14. Remove trailing arm bushing with suitable tool.
15. Reverse procedure to install. **When press fitting bushing into trailing arm, direct its slit side toward front and rear.**
16. Refer to **Fig. 5** for torque specifications. •

SHOCK ABSORBER
REPLACE

1. Raise and support vehicle.
2. Remove shock absorber lower mounting bolt and lock washer.
3. Remove upper mounting locknut and absorber nut.
4. Remove shock absorber.
5. Reverse procedure to install.

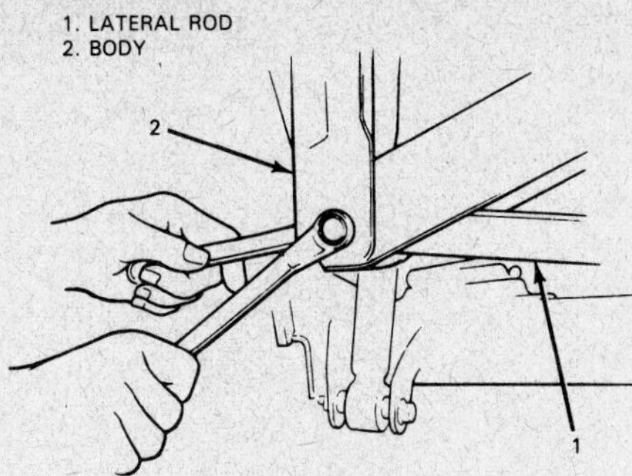

Fig. 4 Lateral rod body side bolt location

RECOMMENDED TORQUE SPECIFICATIONS

Fastening parts	Tightening torque		
	N·m	kg-m	lb-ft
Shock absorber upper lock nut	18 – 28	1.8 – 2.8	13.5 – 20.0
Shock absorber upper nut	18 – 28	1.8 – 2.8	13.5 – 20.0
Shock absorber lower bolt	45 – 70	4.5 – 7.0	32.5 – 50.5
Lateral rod nut	45 – 70	4.5 – 7.0	32.5 – 50.5
Lateral rod bolt	45 – 70	4.5 – 7.0	32.5 – 50.5
Rear axle castle nut	80 – 120	8.0 – 12.0	58.0 – 86.5
Rear brake back plate bolt	18 – 28	1.8 – 2.8	13.5 – 20.0
Brake pipe flare nut	14 – 18	1.4 – 1.8	10.5 – 13.0
Rear wheel nut	40 – 70	4.0 – 7.0	29.0 – 50.5
Trailing arm front side nut	70 – 90	7.0 – 9.0	50.5 – 65.0

Fig. 5 Rear axle torque specifications

REAR SPRING REPLACE

To replace coil springs on 1987 models, refer to "Rear Axle, Replace." To replace leaf springs on 1983-86 models, proceed as follows:

1. Raise and support vehicle.
2. Support axle and remove U-bolt nuts, **Fig. 2.**
3. Remove shackle nuts and front pivot nut.
4. Remove front leaf spring pivot bolt and disengage leaf spring from shackle pin.
5. Reverse procedure to install. Lubricate leaf spring bushings with silicone grease. Tighten U-bolt nuts so equal amounts of threaded area are exposed.

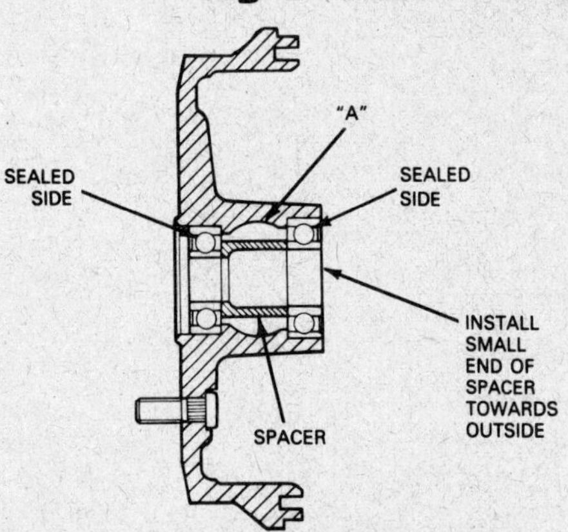

Fig. 6 Wheel bearing installation

WHEEL BEARING REPLACE

1. Raise and support vehicle.
2. Remove brake drum.
3. Using drift, drive bearings out of brake drum.
4. Using bearing installer J-34482 or equivalent, install bearings with stamped side outwards. Refer to **Fig. 6** for spacer positioning.
5. Install brake drum.
6. Lower vehicle.

FRONT SUSPENSION & STEERING SECTION

INDEX

MacPHERSON STRUT REPLACE

1. Raise and support vehicle allowing front suspension to hang free.
2. Remove front wheel.
3. Remove E-clip from brake hose and disengage hose from strut bracket, **Fig. 1.**
4. Support lower control arm and knuckle assembly and remove strut to knuckle bolts.
5. Remove upper strut mount nuts and remove strut from vehicle.
6. Reverse procedure to install.

MacPHERSON STRUT SERVICE

1. Mount strut in suitable spring compressor.
2. Compress spring to about 1/2 its height. Do not bottom spring.
3. Remove nut from strut shaft and remove components, **Fig. 2.**
4. Reverse procedure to assemble. Compress spring so strut shaft protrudes through cap by about 1 inch. Torque nut to 29 ft. lbs.

STABILIZER BAR REPLACE

1. Raise and support vehicle.
2. Remove both front wheels.
3. Remove stabilizer bar bracket bolts, **Fig. 3.**
4. Remove nuts from stabilizer bar ends and disconnect stabilizer bar ends from suspension control arms.
5. Reverse procedure to install. Refer to **Fig. 4** for proper orientation of stabilizer bar.

WHEEL HUB & BEARING REPLACE

1. Raise and support vehicle and remove front wheel.
2. Remove cotter pin and driveshaft castle nut.
3. Remove caliper bolts and caliper. Hang caliper aside.
4. Refer to **Fig. 5,** and measure dimension A for assembly reference. Pull hub out of knuckle.
5. Disconnect tie rod end from knuckle with tool J-21687-02 or equivalent.
6. Remove strut to knuckle bolts and then ball joint stud pinch bolt, **Fig. 6.**
7. Remove knuckle.
8. Using suitable drift, remove outer, then inner bearing from knuckle.
9. Apply suitable grease to balls and oil seal lips of wheel bearings. Fill area A, **Fig. 7,** with grease.
10. Install wheel bearings using bearing installer J-34856 or equivalent.
11. Install wheel bearing seal 5, **Fig. 7,** using tool J-34881 or equivalent.
12. Install spacer on hub with bevel side first, **Fig. 8.**
13. Check that wheel bearing spacer bore is aligned with bearing bores. If not, move spacer until aligned.
14. Using plastic hammer, tap hub lightly into knuckle, taking care that hub does not cock.

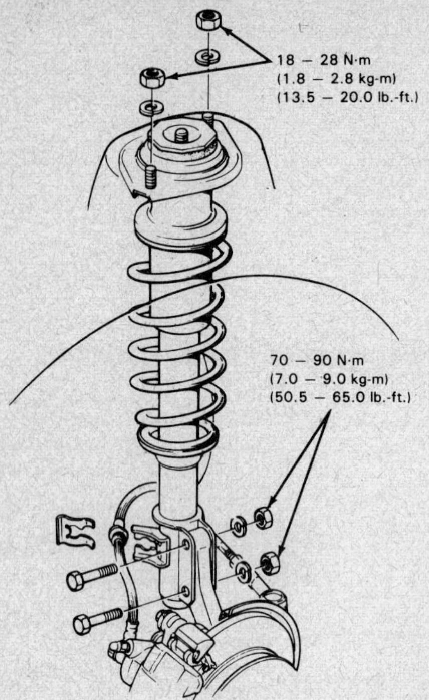

Fig. 1 Removing MacPherson strut

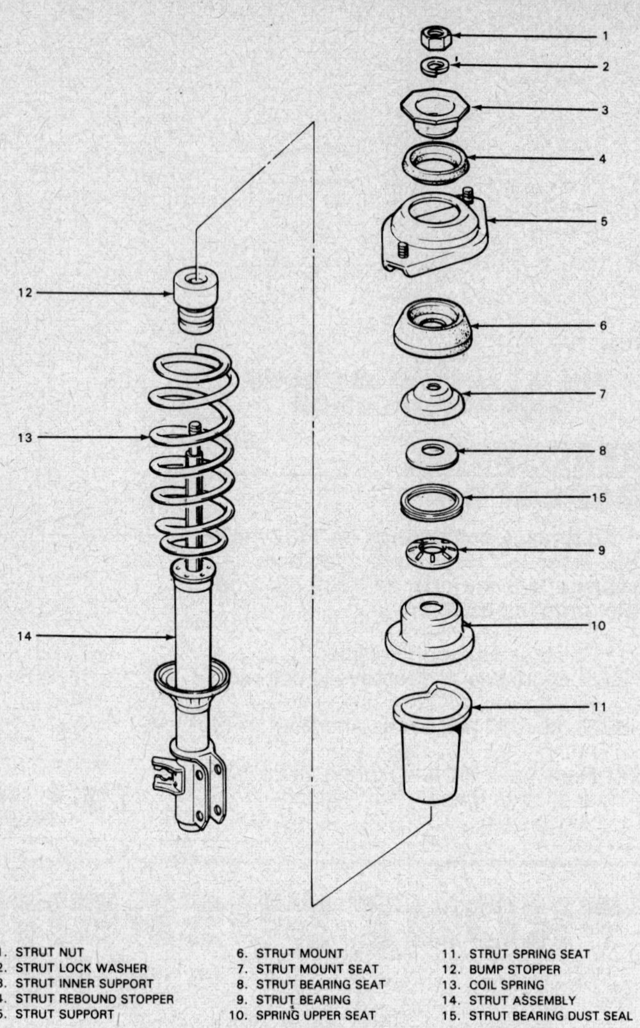

Fig. 2 MacPherson strut assembly exploded view

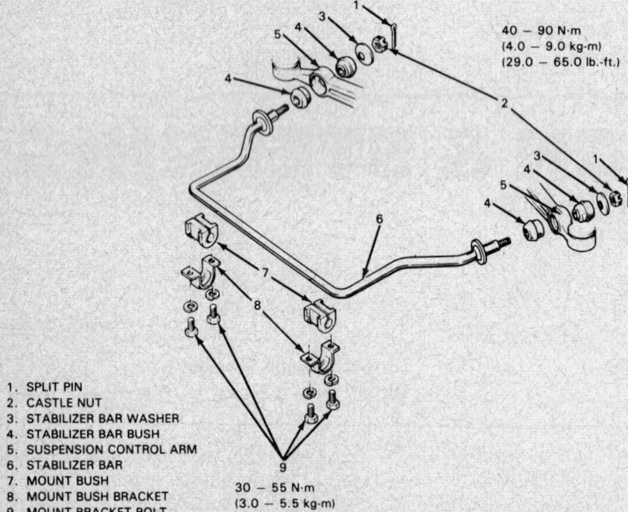

Fig. 3 Stabilizer bar and bushings

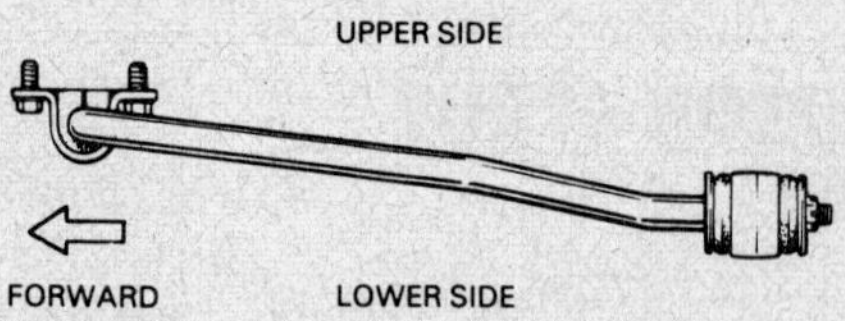

Fig. 4 Correct installation of stabilizer bar

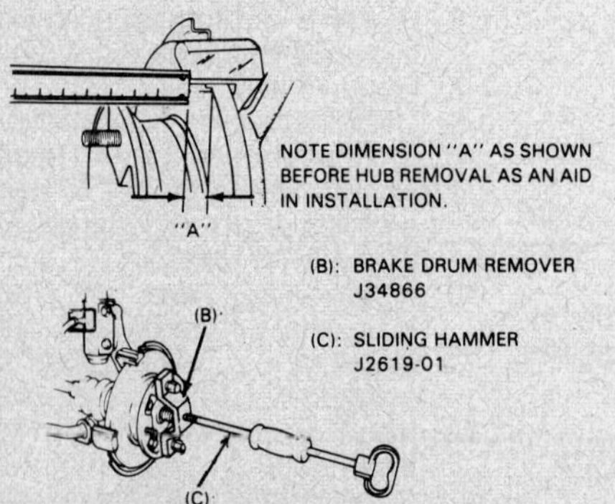

Fig. 5 Checking dimension "A" to assure proper installation of hub

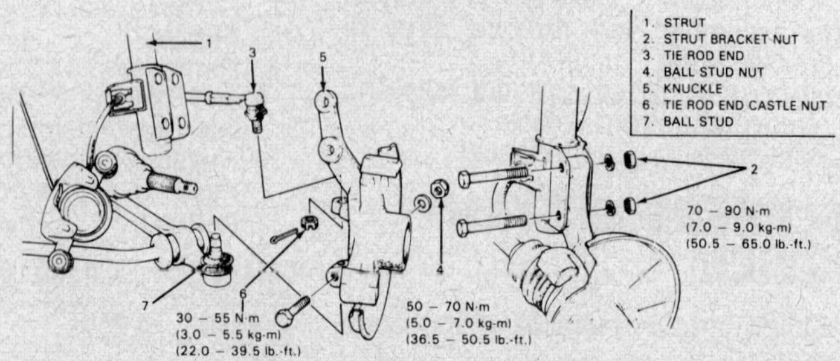

Fig. 6 Removing steering knuckle

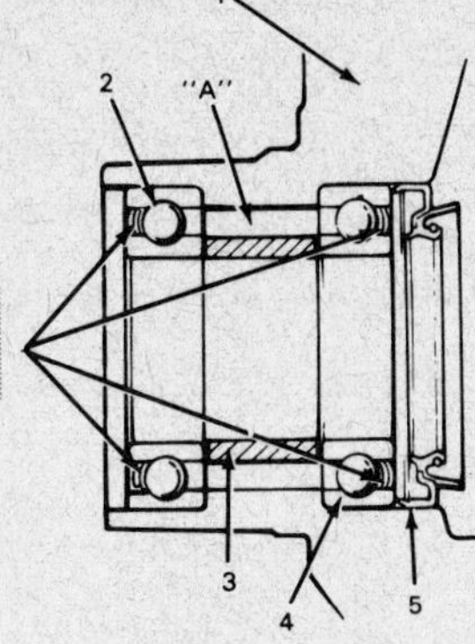

Fig. 7 Steering knuckle hub bearings and seal

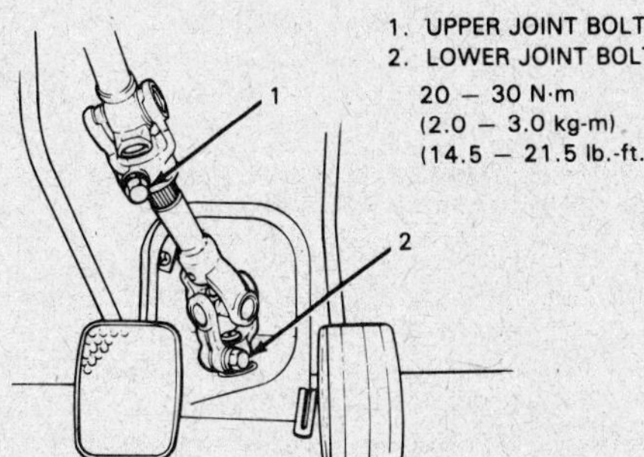

Fig. 10 Steering shaft upper and lower joint bolts

15. Using installing tool J-34856 or J-7079-2 or equivalent, drive hub until dimension A, noted in step 4, is obtained.
16. Install brake pad and caliper.
17. Torque caliper bolts to 17.5-26 ft. lbs.
18. Torque drive shaft castle nut to 108.5-195 ft. lbs.
19. Install cotter pin.
20. Install wheel and lower vehicle.

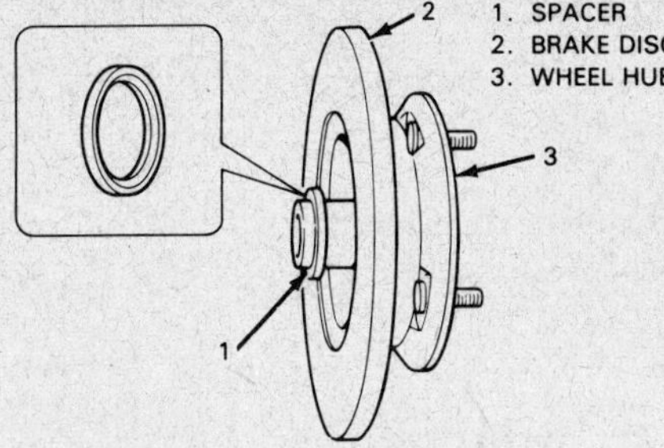

Fig. 8 Installing spacer on wheel hub

LOWER CONTROL ARM REPLACE

1. Raise and support vehicle.
2. Remove stabilizer bar cotter pin, castle nut, washer and bushing, **Fig. 9.**
3. Remove stabilizer bar bracket bolts on same side as control arm to be removed.
4. Remove ball joint stud bolt 2, **Fig. 9.**
5. Remove control arm bolt 5, **Fig. 9,** and control arm.
6. Reverse procedure to install.

STEERING GEAR REPLACE

1. Slide driver's seat back.
2. Pull off front part of floor mat on driver's side. Remove steering shaft joint cover.
3. Loosen steering shaft upper joint bolt without removing, **Fig. 10.**
4. Remove steering shaft lower joint bolt and disconnect lower joint from pinion.
5. Raise and support vehicle.
6. Remove front wheels.
7. Remove cotter pins and castle nuts from tie rod ends.

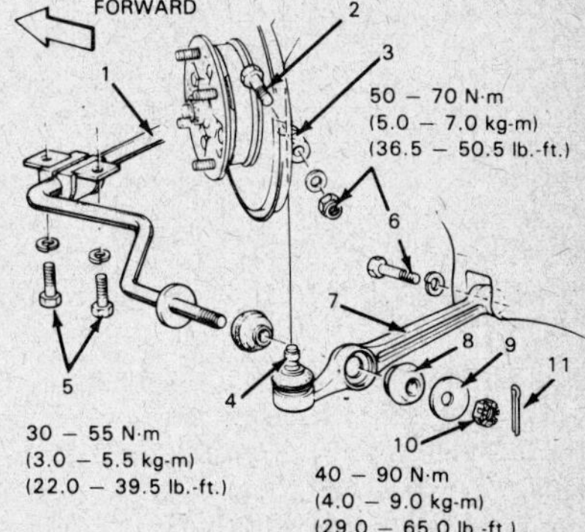

Fig. 9 Removing lower control arm

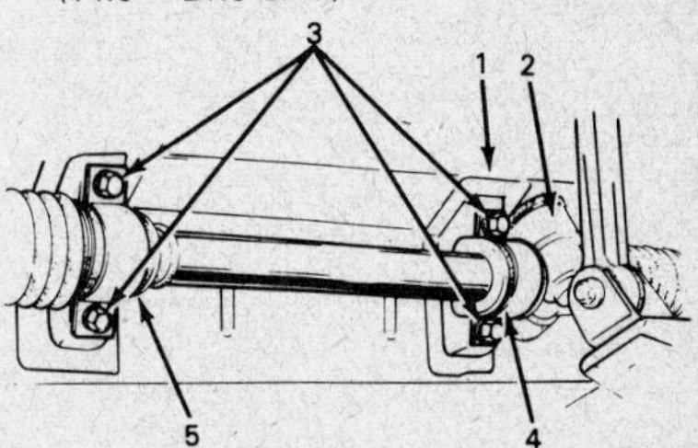

Fig. 11 Steering gear attaching bolts and brackets

8. Using tie rod end remover J-21687-02 or equivalent, disconnect tie rods from knuckles.
9. Remove steering gear housing mounting bolts, brackets and steering gear, **Fig. 11.**
10. Reverse procedure to install.

WHEEL ALIGNMENT SECTION

INDEX

CAMBER & CASTER ADJUSTMENT

1. Position vehicle on suitable alignment fixture following manufacturer's instructions and check caster and camber angles. Refer to **Fig. 1** for specifications. Bumper should be bounced three times before inspection, to prevent incorrect reading.
2. Camber and caster cannot be adjusted. Should either be found out of specification, locate the cause first.
3. If improper alignment is caused by damaged, worn or loose suspension parts, they should be replaced. If vehicle body or chassis is damaged, it should be repaired.

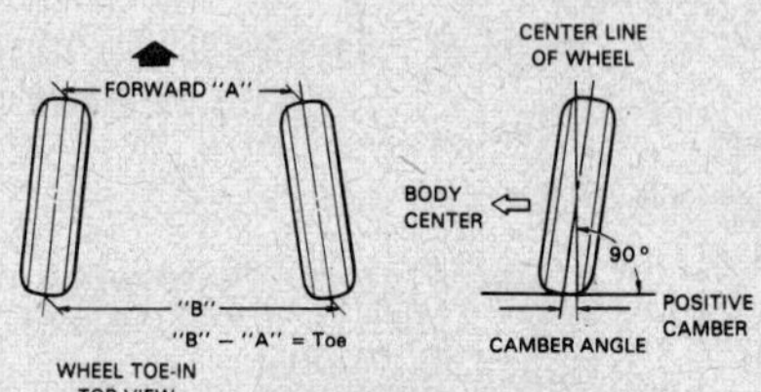

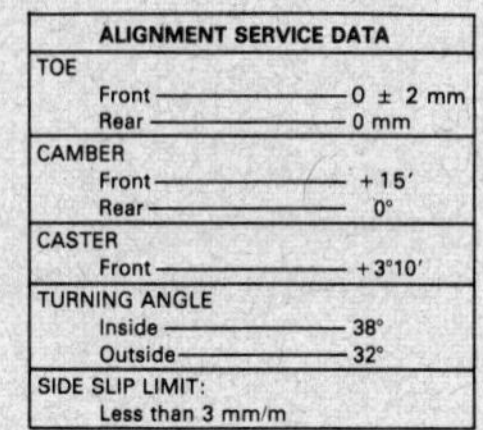

ALIGNMENT SERVICE DATA	
TOE	
Front	0 ± 2 mm
Rear	0 mm
CAMBER	
Front	+15′
Rear	0°
CASTER	
Front	+3°10′
TURNING ANGLE	
Inside	38°
Outside	32°
SIDE SLIP LIMIT:	
Less than 3 mm/m	

Fig. 1 Wheel alignment specifications

TOE ADJUSTMENT

1. Loosen right and left tie rod end locknuts.
2. Turn right and left tie rods by the same amount to align toe to specification. **Right and left tie rods should become equal in length.**
3. After adjustment, tighten locknuts to a torque of 25.5-39.5 ft. lbs. and ensure rack boots are not twisted.

STEERING ANGLE

1. When a tie rod or tie rod end is replaced, check toe and steering angle with turning radius gages. If steering angle is not correct, check right and left tie rods for equal length.

DRIVE AXLE SECTION

INDEX

DRIVE AXLE

REPLACE

1. Remove wheel center cap.
2. Remove cotter pin, then drive shaft nut.
3. Loosen wheel lug nuts.
4. Raise and support vehicle.
5. Remove front wheel.
6. Drain transaxle fluid.
7. Using suitable lever, pry inboard drive shaft joint from differential side gear to disengage snap ring on shaft spline, **Fig. 1.**
8. Remove 2 stabilizer bar mount bracket bolts and ball joint stud bolt. Pull down on stabilizer bar to disconnect ball joint stud from steering knuckle, **Fig. 2.**
9. Disconnect inboard joint from differential side gear, then outboard joint from steering knuckle. Remove drive shaft.
10. Reverse procedure to install. Torque drive shaft nut to 108.5-195 ft. lbs.

1. SNAP RING
2. INBOARD SIDE JOINT (CONSTANT VELOCITY TRIPOD JOINT)
3. SNAP RING
4. INBOARD SIDE BOOT BAND
5. INBOARD SIDE BOOT
6. BOOT BAND
7. DRIVE AXLE
8. BOOT BAND
9. OUTBOARD SIDE BOOT
10. OUTBOARD SIDE BOOT BAND
11. OUTBOARD SIDE JOINT (CONSTANT VELOCITY BALL JOINT)
12. FRONT WHEEL BEARING SEAL
13. INNER BEARING
14. SPACER
15. OUTER BEARING
16. OUTER SPACER
17. FRONT WHEEL HUB
18. WASHER
19. DRIVE SHAFT NUT
20. PIN

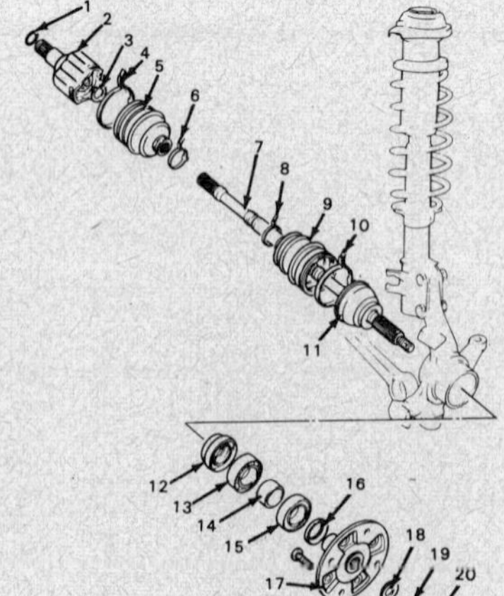

Fig. 1 Exploded view of front driving axle

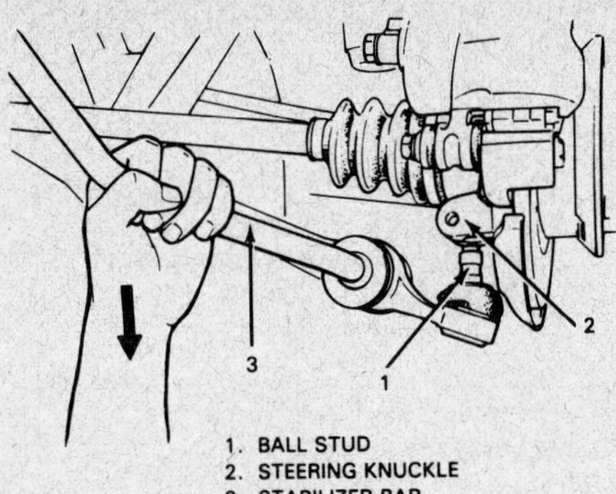

Fig. 2 Removing ball joint stud from steering knuckle

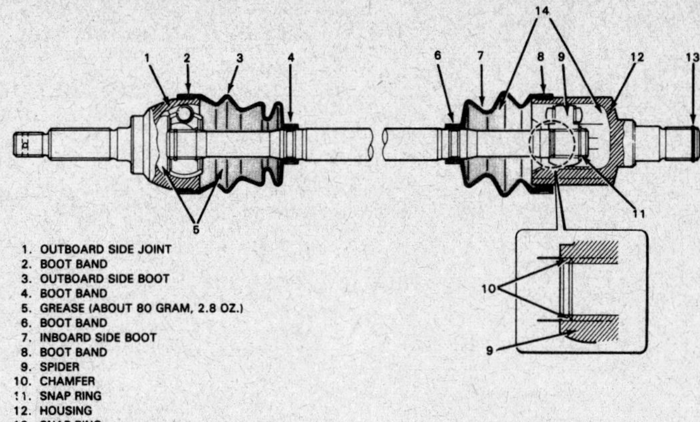

Fig. 3 Drive axle assembly

DISASSEMBLY

1. Remove boot band from inboard joint, **Fig. 1.**
2. Remove housing from inboard joint.
3. Remove snap ring, then spider from shaft.
4. Remove inside and outside boots from shaft. **Do not disassemble outboard joint. If joint is defective, it must be replaced as an assembly. Do not disassemble inboard joint spider as it is serviced as an assembly.**

INSPECTION

1. Check boots for tears or deterioration. Replace as necessary.
2. Check circlip, snap ring and boot bands for breakage or deformation. Replace as required.

CLEANING

1. Wash disassembled parts (except boots and spider) in degreaser.
2. Clean boots with rag. Do not use gasoline or kerosene, etc.
3. Clean spider with clean towel. To prevent spider needle bearings from becoming degreased, do not wash spider in degreaser.

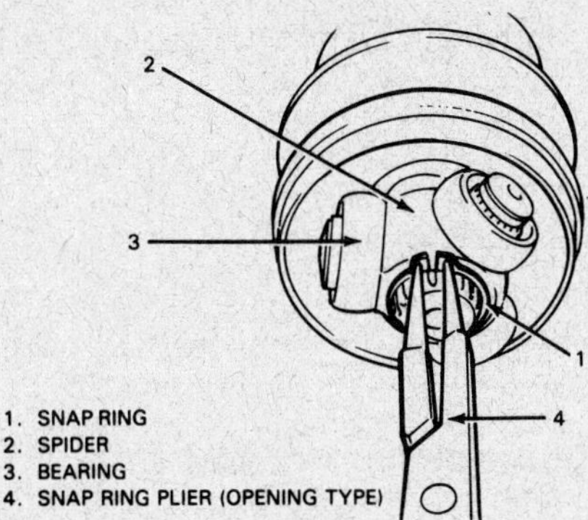

Fig. 4 Installing axle snap ring

ASSEMBLY

1. Liberally apply black grease included in outboard boot kit to outboard joint.
2. Install outboard boot on shaft. Fill inside of boot with about 2.8 oz. of joint grease, **Fig. 3.**
3. Install inboard boot on shaft.
4. Rally apply yellow joint grease included in inboard boot kit to inboard joint.
5. Install inboard spider on drive shaft with chamfered side toward outboard joint as shown in **Fig. 3.**
6. Install snap ring in shaft groove, **Fig. 4.**
7. Fill inside of inboard boot with about 4.5 oz. of joint grease and install housing, **Fig. 3.** Attach boot to housing with boot band.
8. Check boots for distortion and correct as necessary.

DISC BRAKES SECTION

INDEX

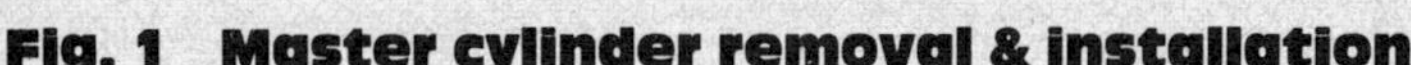

Fig. 1 Master cylinder removal & installation

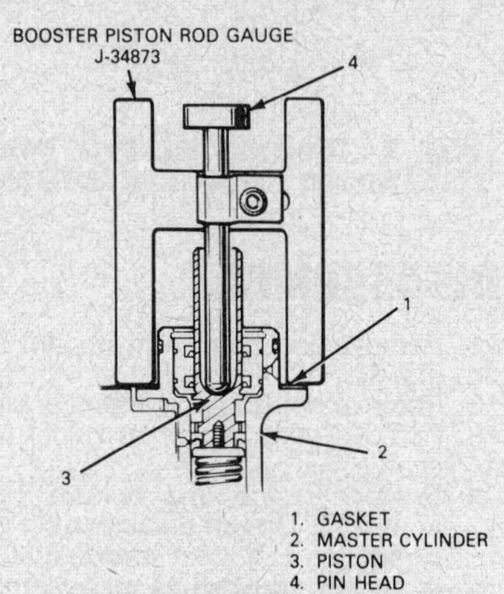

Fig. 2 Tool J-34873 installation

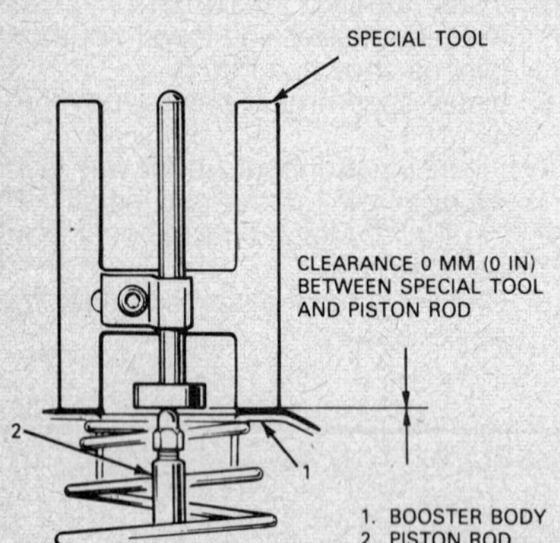

Fig. 3 Adjusting clearance between tool and piston rod

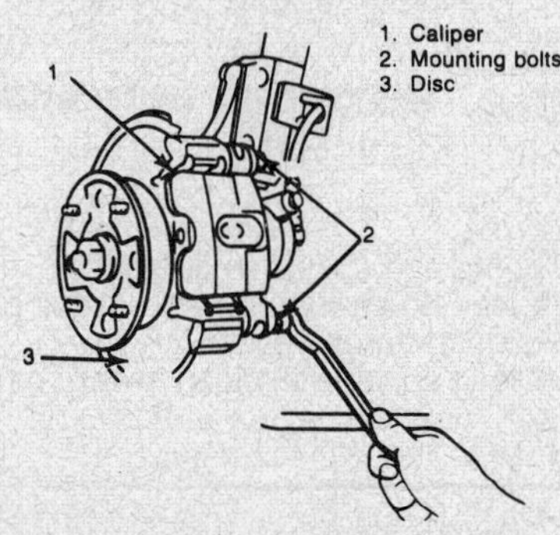

Fig. 4 Removing caliper mounting bolts

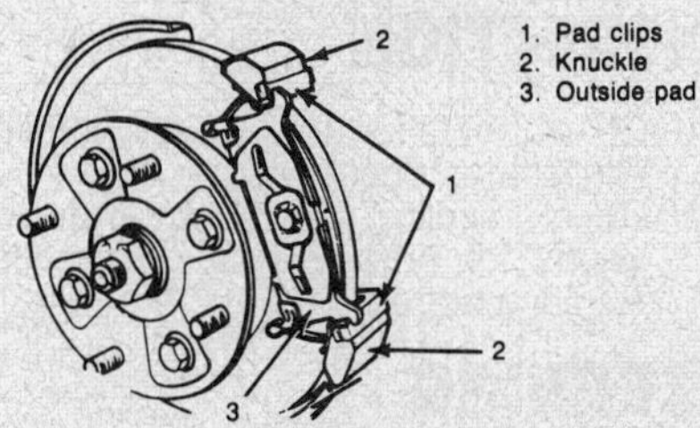

Fig. 5 Installing outside pad

MASTER CYLINDER REPLACE

1. Clean any dirt from around reservoir cap. Remove cap and remove brake fluid.
2. Disconnect 2 brake lines at master cylinder, taking care that brake fluid does not spill on painted surfaces, **Fig. 1.**
3. Remove mounting nuts and washers, and master cylinder.
4. Adjust clearance of booster piston rod to master cylinder piston as follows:
   a. Push piston rod several times to make sure reaction disc is in place.
   b. Measure with gasket in place on master cylinder and booster at atmospheric pressure.
   c. Set measuring tool J-34873 on master cylinder and push pin until it contacts piston, **Fig. 2.**
   d. Turn tool upside down and place on booster, **Fig. 3.** Adjust booster piston rod length until rod end contacts pin head.
5. Install master cylinder on studs. Install mounting nuts.
6. Connect hydraulic lines.
7. Fill reservoir with brake fluid.

FRONT PADS REPLACE

1. Raise and support vehicle and remove wheel.
2. Remove caliper mounting bolts, **Fig. 4.**
3. Remove caliper from knuckle, taking care not to drop inside pad. Hang caliper aside.
4. Remove outside pad.
5. Install caliper and inside pad to knuckle, **Fig. 5.**
6. Install caliper and inside pad to knuckle, **Fig. 6.** Position outer springs over caliper as shown.
7. Torque caliper bolts to 17.5-26 ft. lbs.
8. Install front wheel.
9. Lower vehicle and perform brake test.

CALIPER SERVICE

1. Raise and support vehicle.
2. Disconnect brake hose from caliper.
3. Remove caliper mounting bolts.
4. Remove caliper from knuckle.
5. Clean caliper with brake fluid.
6. Remove cylinder boot set ring and boot from cylinder groove, **Fig. 7.**
7. Using compressed air, remove brake cylinder. Keep fingers away from piston.
8. Remove piston seal, taking care not to damage cylinder bore.

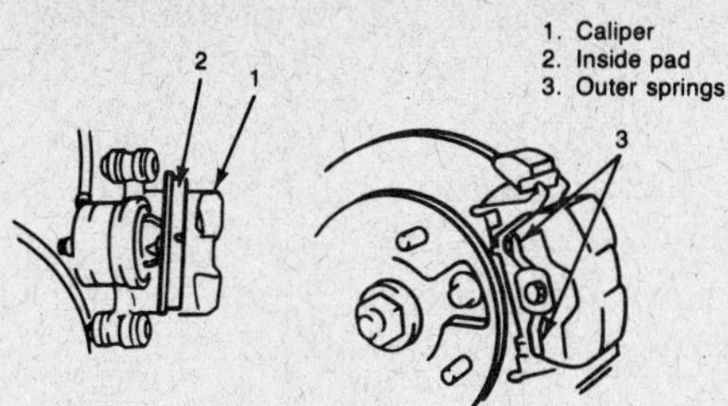

Fig. 6 Installing inside pad & caliper

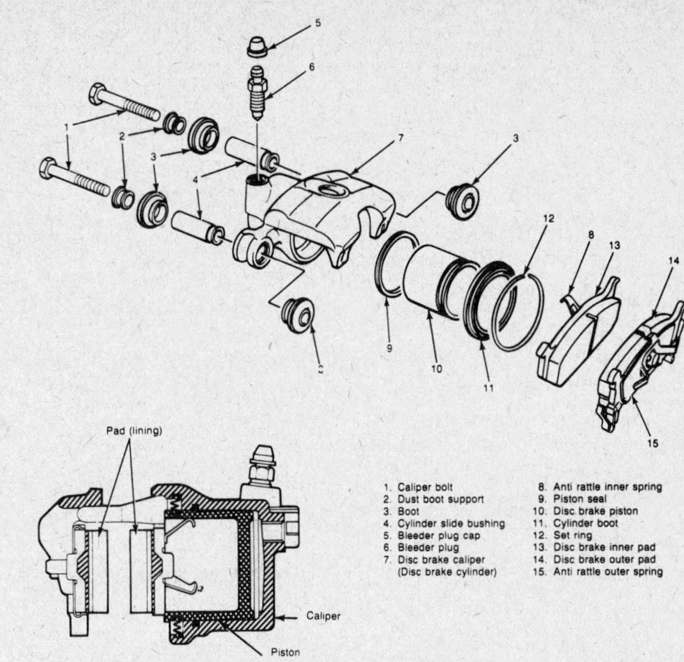

Fig. 7 Disassembled view of brake caliper

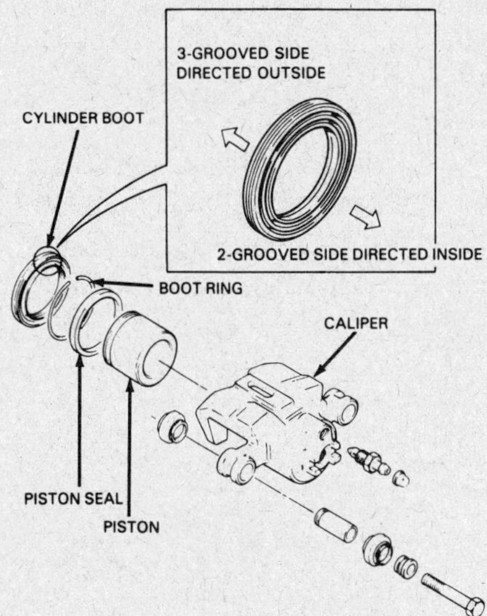

Fig. 8 Installing caliper boot

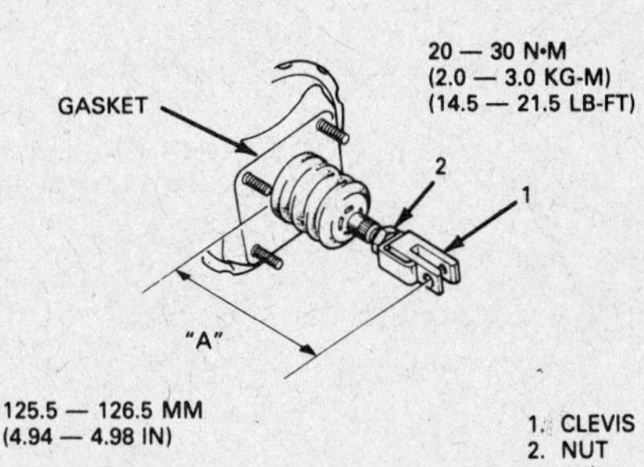

Fig. 9 Checking master cylinder pushrod length

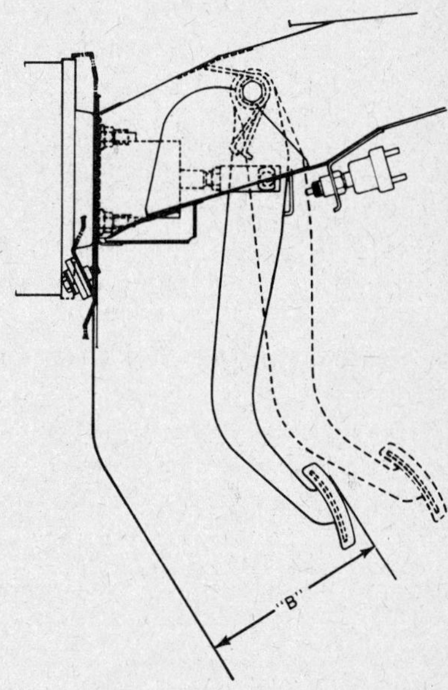

Fig. 10 Checking brake pedal travel

9. Install new piston seal in cylinder.
10. Install new boot on piston so side with 2 grooves faces in toward cylinder and side with 3 grooves faces out, **Fig. 8.**
11. Install piston in caliper so it projects about .4 inch to ease installation. Install boot set ring.
12. Check that caliper slide bushings are lubricated with rubber grease. Check that slide bushing in each carrier hole can be moved smoothly in each direction.
13. Install caliper and inside pad on knuckle.
14. Tighten caliper bolts.
15. Connect brake hose.
16. Install wheel.
17. Lower vehicle and test brakes.

BRAKE PEDAL HEIGHT

ADJUST

1. Brake pedal should normally be at same height as clutch pedal. Check that distance between brake booster mounting surface (with gasket) and pushrod clevis pin hole is 4.94-4.98 inches, **Fig. 9.**

BRAKE PEDAL TRAVEL CHECK

1. With engine off, pump brake pedal several times to exhaust all vacuum from booster.
2. Apply about 66 lb. load to brake pedal and measure pedal arm to fire wall clearance B, **Fig. 10.** Clearance must not be less than 3.35 inches.
3. Possible causes for a low pedal are:
   a. Worn rear brake shoes.
   b. Brake lines need bleeding.
   c. Booster pushrod out of alignment.
   d. Rear brake shoe adjusters malfunctioning.

POWER BRAKE BOOSTER

REPLACE

1. Remove master cylinder from booster as described in "Master Cylinder, Replace".
2. Disconnect pushrod clevis from brake pedal arm, **Fig. 11.**
3. Remove vacuum hose from booster.
4. Remove booster attaching nuts, then booster.
5. Refer to "Master Cylinder, Replace" for adjustment procedure of the booster piston rod to master cylinder piston.
6. Reverse procedure to install.

STOP LIGHT SWITCH

ADJUST

Pull up brake pedal and adjust switch position so that clearance between end of thread and brake pedal contact plate A is .02-.04 inch, **Fig. 12.** Tighten locknut.

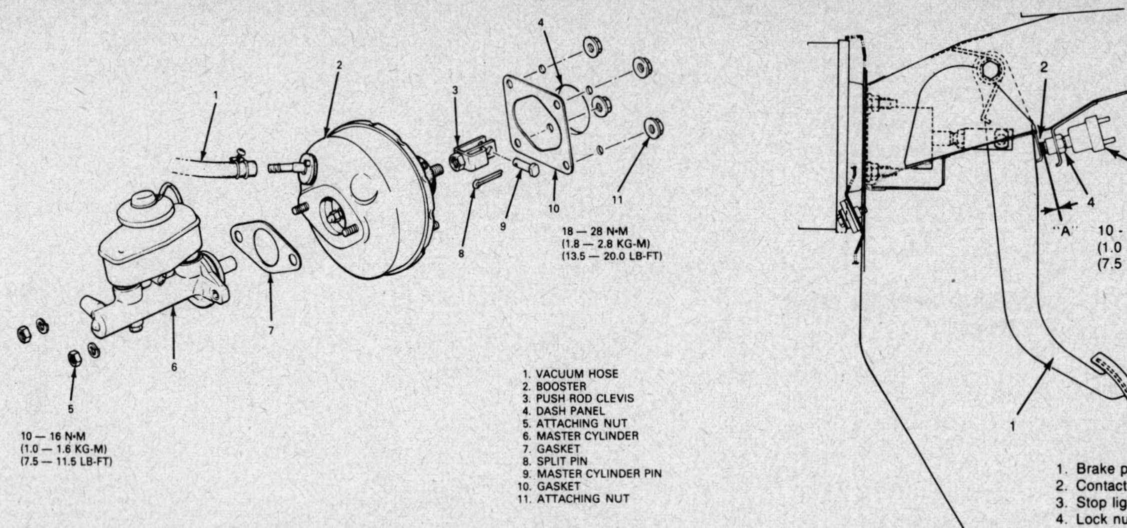

Fig. 11 Disassembled view of master cylinder and power brake

Fig. 12 Adjusting stop light switch adjustment

DRUM BRAKES SECTION

INDEX

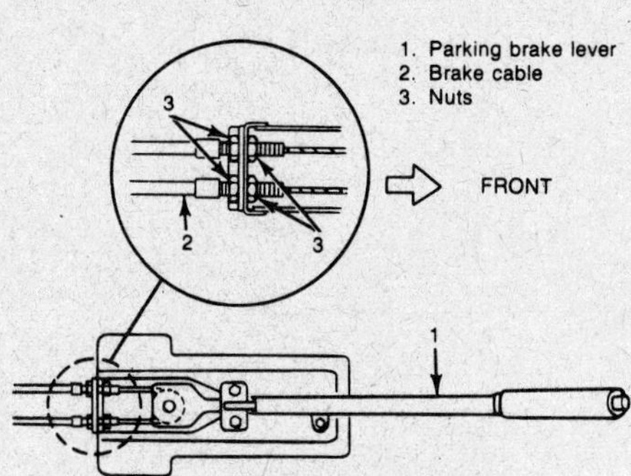

Fig. 1 Parking brake adjustment

MASTER CYLINDER REPLACE

Refer to Disc Brakes Section.

POWER BRAKE BOOSTER REPLACE

Refer to Disc Brakes Section.

DRUM BRAKES ADJUST

Adjustment is accomplished automatically by applying brake pedal 3-5 times with about 66 lbs. of pressure.

PARKING BRAKE ADJUST

Parking brake lever should be adjusted so lever comes up 3-8 notches with 44 lbs. of pull applied.

Adjust travel by loosening adjustment nuts, **Fig. 1.**

BRAKE PEDAL HEIGHT ADJUST

Refer to Disc Brakes Section.

STOP LIGHT SWITCH ADJUST

Refer to Disc Brakes Section.

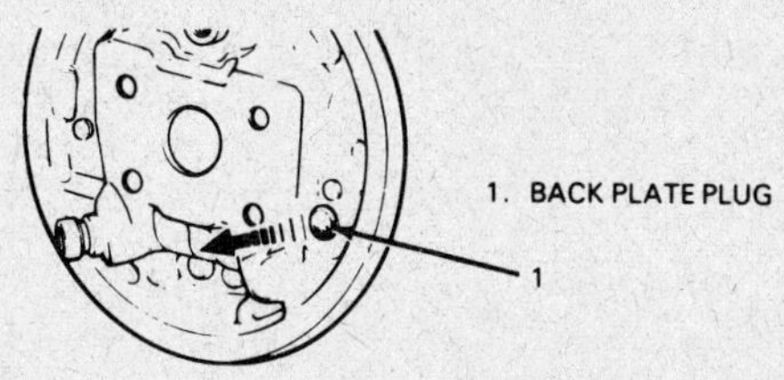

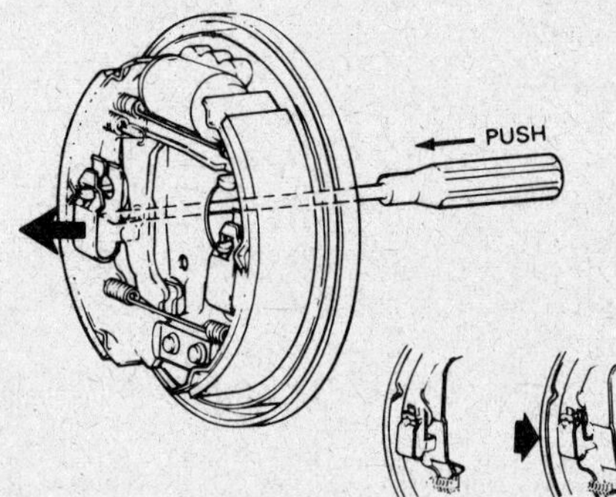

Fig. 2 Removing backing plate plug

BRAKE PEDAL TRAVEL CHECK

Refer to Disc Brakes Section.

DRUM BRAKE SERVICE

1. Raise and support vehicle.
2. Remove spindle cap by hammering lightly at 3 points around cap.
3. Remove cotter pin, castle nut and washer.
4. Loosen parking brake cable adjusting nuts.
5. Remove backing plate plug, **Fig. 2.**
6. Insert screwdriver into plug hole and push in direction shown. This pushes hold down spring up and releases parking brake shoe lever from hold down spring, resulting in added clearance between shoe and drum.
7. Using slide hammer J-2619-01 and brake drum remover J-34866, pull off brake drum.
8. Remove brake shoe hold down springs by turning shoe hold down springs, **Fig. 3.**
9. Disconnect parking brake cable from parking brake shoe lever and remove brake shoes.

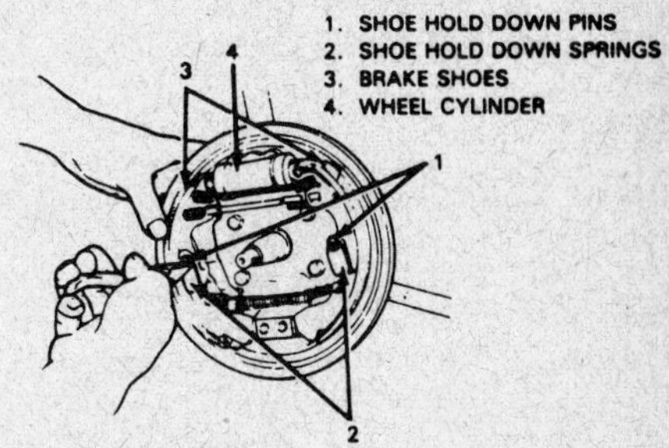

Fig. 3 Removing brake lining hold down springs

10. Remove spring 1 in **Fig. 4,** pull primary shoe in direction of arrow and disengage strut 4 and return spring 2.
11. Disconnect return spring 3 from shoe.
12. Disconnect parking brake shoe lever from shoe.
13. Remove bleeder screw from wheel cylinder.
14. Slightly loosen brake line flare nut.
15. Remove wheel cylinder mounting bolts. Disconnect brake line from wheel cylinder and put bleeder cap plug onto brake line to prevent brake fluid spillage.
16. Install new gasket on wheel cylinder. Remove bleed cap plug from brake line and connect line to wheel cylinder. Do not final tighten.
17. Torque wheel cylinder mounting bolts to 7.5-9 ft. lbs.
18. Torque brake line flare nut to 10.5-13 ft. lbs.
19. Install bleeder cap plug on bleeder.
20. Assemble brake shoes, levers and springs as shown in **Fig. 5.**
21. Push shoe hold down springs down into place. Turn hold down pins to engage springs.
22. To minimize dimension "A-A," **Fig. 6,** push strut towards backplate while pushing out on shoe as shown.
23. Position tab of spring clip behind parking lever.
24. Install brake drum and torque castle nut to 58-86.5 ft. lbs. Install cotter pin.
25. Install spindle cap.
26. Install wheel.
27. Depress brake pedal several times to obtain proper drum to shoe clearance and adjust parking brake.
28. Check that brake drum does not drag.
29. Lower vehicle and test brake operation.

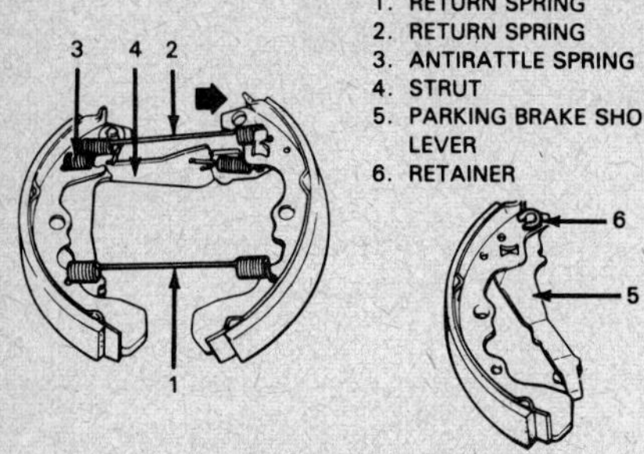

Fig. 4 Brake shoe return spring identification

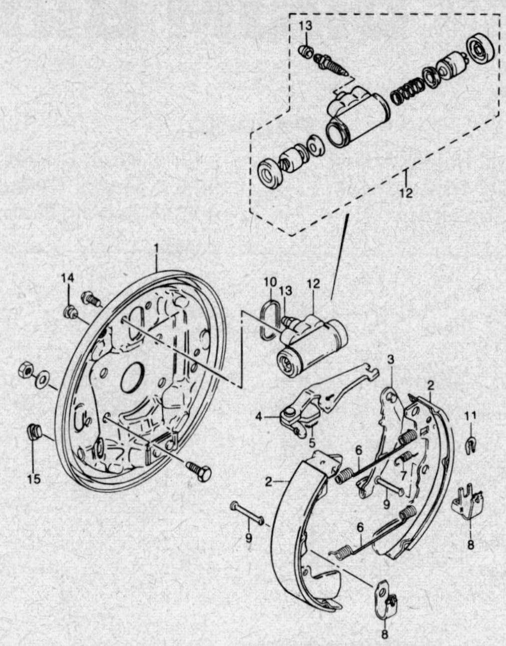

1. Brake back plate
2. Brake shoe
3. Parking brake shoe lever
4. Brake strut
5. Quadrant spring
6. Shoe return spring
7. Antirattle spring
8. Shoe hold down spring
9. Shoe hold down pin
10. Packing
11. Parking level retainer
12. Wheel cylinder
13. Bleeder plug cap
14. Rubber plug
15. Rubber plug

Fig. 5 Assembling rear brake unit

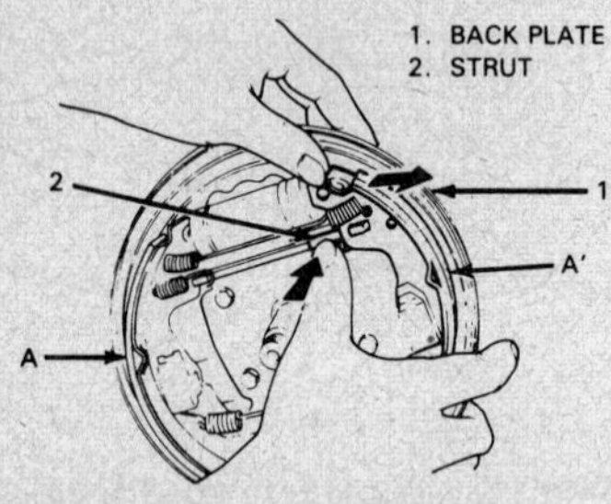

Fig. 6 Brake lining installation

SUBARU (Japan)

INDEX OF SERVICE OPERATIONS

General Engine Specifications

Year	Engine	Carburetor	Bore Stroke Inch (mm)	Compression Ratio	Max. H.P. @ RPM	Max. Torque @ RPM	Normal Oil Pressure
1983	4-97/1600cc	2 Bbl.	3.62 x 2.36 (92 x 60)	9.0	69 @ 4800	86 @ 2800	36–57
	4-109/1800cc	③	3.62 x 2.64 (92 x 67)	8.7	73 @ 4400	94 @ 2400	50–57
1984	4-97/1600cc	2 Bbl.	3.62 x 2.36 (92 x 60)	9.0	69 @ 4800	86 @ 2800	36–57
	4-109/1800cc ②	③	3.62 x 2.64 (92 x 67)	8.7	73 @ 4400	94 @ 2400	50–57
	4-109/1800cc ⑥	Fuel Inj.	3.62 x 2.64 (92 x 67)	7.7	95 @ 4800	123 @ 2000	50–57
1985	4-97/1600cc	2 Bbl.	3.62 x 2.36 (92 x 60)	9.0	69 @ 4800	86 @ 2800	36–57
	4-109/1800cc ① ②	2 Bbl.	3.62 x 2.64 (92 x 67)	8.7	73 @ 4400	94 @ 2400	57–64
	4-109/1800cc ②	2 Bbl.	3.62 x 2.64 (92 x 67)	9.0	82 @ 4800	101 @ 2800	57–64
	4-109/1800cc ① ②	Fuel Inj.	3.62 x 2.64 (92 x 67)	9.0	94 @ 5200	101 @ 2800	57–64
	4-109/1800cc ⑥	Fuel Inj.	3.62 x 2.64 (92 x 67)	7.7	111 @ 4800	134 @ 2800	57–64
1986	4-97/1600cc	2 Bbl.	3.62 x 2.36 (92 x 60)	⑩	69 @ 4800	86 @ 2800	36–57
	4-109/1800cc	2 Bbl.	3.62 x 2.64 (92 x 67)	9.0	⑪	⑫	57–64
	4-109/1800cc ⑤	Fuel Inj.	3.62 x 2.64 (92 x 67)	9.5	90 @ 5600	101 @ 2800	57–64
	4-109/1800cc ④ ⑥	Fuel Inj.	3.62 x 2.64 (92 x 67)	7.7	110 @ 4800	134 @ 2800	57–64
	4-109/1800cc ② ⑥	Fuel Inj.	3.62 x 2.64 (92 x 67)	9.0	82 @ 4800	137 @ 2800	57–64
1987	3-73/1200cc	2 Bbl.	3.62 x 3.27 (78 x 83)	9.1	66 @ 5200	70 @ 3600	—
	4-97/1600cc	2 Bbl.	3.62 x 2.36 (92 x 60)	9.0	69 @ 4800	86 @ 2800	36–57
	4-109/1800cc	2 Bbl.	3.62 x 2.64 (92 x 67)	⑩	⑦	⑧	57–64
	4-109/1800cc ⑧	Fuel Inj.	3.62 x 2.64 (92 x 67)	9.5	90 @ 5200	101 @ 2800	57–64
	4-109/1800cc ④ ⑥	Fuel Inj.	3.62 x 2.64 (92 x 67)	7.7	⑨	134 @ 2800	57–64
	4-109/1800cc ② ⑥	Fuel Inj.	3.62 x 2.64 (92 x 67)	9.0	94 @ 5200	101 @ 2800	57–64

①—4-wheel drive GL models.
②—Exc. Turbocharged.
③—Sedan DL & Hatchback DL, 68 @ 4800; except Sedan DL & Hatchback DL, 67 @ 5200.
④—Turbocharged.
⑤—With SPFI (Single Point Fuel Injection).
⑥—With MPFI (Multi Point Fuel Injection).
⑦—Brat & Hatchback, 73 @ 4400; exc. Brat & Hatchback, 84 @ 5200.
⑧—Brat & Hatchback, 94 @ 2400; exc. Brat & Hatchback, 101 @ 3200.
⑨—XT Coupe, 110 @ 4800; exc. XT Coupe, 115 @ 5200.
⑩—Brat & Hatchback, 8.7; exc. Brat & Hatchback, 9.0.
⑪—Brat & Hatchback, 73 @ 4400; exc. Brat & Hatchback, 82 @ 4800.
⑫—Brat & Hatchback, 94 @ 2400; exc. Brat & Hatchback, 101 @ 2800.

Alternator & Regulator Specifications

Year	Ident. No.	Current Rating		Field Current		Voltage Regulator ②	
		Amps. ①	Volts	Amps.	Volts	Ident. No.	Voltage 68°F
1983–85	LR155-15C	55	14–15	—	12	TRIZ-56	14.5
1984	LR155-23	55	12	—	—	TR1Z-56	—
	LR155-24	55	12	—	—	TR1Z-56	—
1985–87	LR160-137	60	12	—	—	TR1Z-56	14.2–14.8
	LR160-138	60	12	—	—	TR1Z-56	14.2–14.8
	LR165-704	65	12	—	—	TR1Z-219	14.2–14.8

①—@ 5000 RPM.
②—Integral.

Starter Motor Specifications

Year	Ident. No.	Brush Spring Tension Ounces	No Load Test			Torque Test		
			Amperes	Volts	RPM	Amperes	Volts	Ft. Lbs.
1983	28000-6520 ①	37.0–47.6	50	11	5000	600	7.7	9
1983–84	28000-8570 ①	37.0–47.6	90	11.5	4100	400	2.4	8
	28000-8580 ①	37.0–47.6	90	11.5	3000	300	2.5	5
1983–85	28000-9810 ①	—	50	11	5000	600	7.7	9
1985–87	028000-8581 ①	—	90	11.5	3000	230	8	4.7
	028000-9800 ①	—	90	11	4000	370	8	10
	M1T70381 ②	—	90	11	3000	280	8	6.3
	M1T74081 ②	—	90	11	2900	370	8	10

①—Nippondenso.
②—Mitsubishi.

Valve Specifications

Year	Engine	Valve Lash		Valve Angles		Valve Spring Installed Height	Valve Spring Pressure Lbs. @ In.	Stem Clearance		Stem Diameter	
		Int.	Exh.	Seat	Face			Intake	Exhaust	Intake	Exhaust
1983–87	4-97/1600cc	.010	.014	45	45	①	②	.0014–.0026	.0016–.0028	.3130–.3136	.3128–.3134
1983–84	4-109/1800cc	③	③	45	45	①	④	.0014–.0026	.0016–.0028	.3130–.3136	.3128–.3134
1985–87	4-109/1800cc	⑤	⑤	—	—	⑥	⑦	.0014–.0026	.0016–.0028	.2736–.2742	.2734–.2740
1987	3-73/1200cc	—	—	—	—	—	—	—	—	—	—

①—Outer spring, 1.555 inches; inner spring, 1.476 inches.
②—Outer spring, 112.5–127.9 lbs. @ 1.201 inches; inner spring, 41.7–48.3 lbs. @ 1.122 inches.
③—Except auto. trans. models, intake .010C, exhaust .014C; auto. trans. models are equipped with zero lash hydraulic lifters.
④—On man. trans. models, see note ③. On auto. trans. models, outer spring, 116.6–134.7 lbs. @ 1.260 inches; inner spring, 45.2–51.8 lbs. @ 1.181 inches.
⑤—Valves maintained at zero lash by hydraulic adjusters.
⑥—Exc. GL 4-5: Inner spring, 1.516 inch; outer spring, 1.634 inch. GL 4-5, 1.634 inch.
⑦—Exc. GL 4-5: Inner spring, 51.8 lbs. @ 1.122 inch; Outer spring, 115. 5 lbs. @ 1.240 inch. GL 4-5, 118.2 lbs. @ 1.299 inch.

Pistons, Pins, Rings, Crankshaft & Bearings

Year	Engine	Piston Clearance	Ring End Gap		Piston-pin Diameter	Rod Bearings		Main Bearings			Shaft Endplay
			Comp.	Oil		Shaft Diameter	Bearing Clearance	Shaft Diameter	Bearing Clearance	Thrust on Bear. No.	
1983–85	All	.0004–.0016	.0079	①	.8265–.8268	1.7715–1.7720	.0008–.0028	②	③	2	.0004–.0037
1986	4-97/1600cc	.0004–.0016	.0079	.0079	.8265–.8268	1.7715–1.7720	.0008–.0028	②	③	2	.0004–.0037
	4-109/1800cc	.0004–.0016	.0079	.012	.8265–.8268	1.7715–1.7720	.0004–.0021	2.1636–2.1642	④	2	.0004–.0037
1987	3-73/1200cc	—	—	—	—	—	—	—	—	—	—
	4-97/1600cc	.0004–.0016	.0079	.0079	.8265–.8268	1.7715–1.7720	.0008–.0028	②	③	2	.0004–.0037
	4-109/1800cc	—	—	—	—	—	—	—	—	—	—

①—Exc. 1985 4-109/1800cc, .0079 inch; 1985 4-109/1800cc, .012 inch.
②—4-97/1600cc, front & rear, 1.9668–1.9673 inches; center, 1.9673–1.9678 inches. 4-109/1800cc front, center & rear, 2.1636–2.1642 inches.
③—4-97/1600cc front & rear, .0004–.0014 inch; center, .0004–.0012 inch. 4-109/1800cc front & rear, .0004–.0012 inch; center, .0004–.0010 inch.
④—Front & rear .0001–.0014; center, .0003–.0001.

Engine Tightening Specifications

Year	Engine	Spark Plugs Ft. Lbs.	Cylinder Head Bolts Ft. Lbs.	Intake Manifold Ft. Lbs.	Exhaust Manifold Ft. Lbs.	Rocker Arm Shaft Or Camshaft Bracket	Rocker Arm or Camshaft Cover	Connecting Rod Cap Nuts	Crankcase Halves	Flywheel to Crankshaft	Vibration Damper or Pulley
1983–84	All	13–17	①	13–16	19–22	37–43	2.2–2.9	29–31	②	③	47–54
1985–86	All	13–17	①	13–16	19–22	12.7–14.8	3.3–4.0	29–31	②	51–55	66–79
1987	Exc. 3-73/1200cc	13–17	①	13–16	19–22	12.7–14.8	3.3–4.0	29–31	②	51–55	66–79
	3-73/1200cc	—	—	—	—	—	—	—	—	—	—

①—Step 1, 22 ft. lbs.; Step 2, 43 ft. lbs.; Step 3, 47 ft. lbs.
②—6 mm bolts, 3.3–4 ft. lbs.; 8 mm bolts, 17–20 ft. lbs.; 10 mm bolts, 29–35 ft. lbs.
③—Flywheel, 30–33 ft. lbs.; flex plate, 36–39 ft. lbs.

Front Wheel Alignment Specifications

Year	Model	Caster Angle, Degrees		Camber Angle, Degrees		Toe-In Inch
		Limits	Desired	Limits	Desired	
1983–84	All②	−1 1/6 to 1/3	−5/12	3/4 to 2 1/4	1 1/2	.0 to .08
	Station Wagon	−5/6 to 2/3	−1/2	1 to 2 1/2	1 3/4	.0 to .08
	Hatchback③	−1 1/4 to 1/4	−1/2	1 2/ to 3 1/6	2 5/6	.16 to .24④
	Station Wagon③	−1 5/12 to 1/12	−2/3	1 2/3 to 3 1/6	2 5/6	.16 to .24④
1985	Sedan① ⑤	+1 3/4 to +3 1/4	+2 1/2	0 to +1 1/2	+3/4	−.04 to +.20
	Sedan③ ⑤	+1 1/12 to +2 7/12	+1 5/6	+11/12 to +2 5/12	+1 3/4	−.04 to +.20
	Sedan⑥	+1 5/12 to +2 11/12	2 1/6	+5/12 to +1 11/12	+1 1/6	−.04 to +.20
	Station Wagon①	+1 1/3 to +2 5/6	+2 1/12	+1/4 to +1 3/4	+1	−.04 to +.20
	Station Wagon③	+5/6 to +2 1/3	1 7/12	+11/12 to +2 5/12	+1 3/4	−.04 to +.20
	XT Coupe①	+3 1/3 to +4 5/6	4 1/12	−3/4 to +3/4	0	0
	XT Coupe③ ⑥	+2 3/4 to +4 1/6	+3 5/12	−1/12 to +1 5/12	+2/3	.08
1986	Sedan① ⑤	+1 3/4 to +3 1/4	+2 1/2	−3/4 to +3/4	0	.08
	Sedan③ ⑤	+1 1/2 to +2 7/12	+1 5/6	+5/6 to +2 5/12	+1 2/3	.08
	Sedan⑥	+1 7/12 to +2 11/12	+2 1/6	−7/12 to +1 11/12	+1 1/6	.08
	Station Wagon①	+1/2 to +2 5/6	+2 1/12	−1/4 to +1 3/4	+1	.08
	Station Wagon③	+5/6 to +2 2/6	+1 5/12	+1 to 2 1/2	+1 3/4	.08
	XT Coupe①	+3 1/2 to +4 5/6	+4 1/12	−3/4 to +3/4	0	0
	XT Coupe③	+2 5/6 to +4 1/6	+3 5/12	−11/12 to +1 5/12	+2/3	.08
1987	Justy	—	—	—	—	—
	Sedan① ⑤	+1 3/4 to +3 1/4	+2 1/2	−3/4 to +3/4	0	.08
	Sedan③ ⑤	+1 1/2 to +2 7/12	+1 5/6	+5/6 to +2 5/12	+1 2/3	.08
	Sedan⑥	+1 7/12 to +2 11/12	+2 1/6	−7/12 to +1 11/12	+1 1/6	.08
	Station Wagon①	+1/2 to +2 5/6	+2 1/12	−1/4 to +1 3/4	+1	.08
	Station Wagon③	+5/6 to +2 2/6	+1 5/12	+1 to 2 1/2	+1 3/4	.08
	XT Coupe①	+3 1/2 to +4 5/6	+4 1/12	−3/4 to +3/4	0	0
	XT Coupe③	+2 5/6 to +4 1/6	+3 5/12	−11/12 to +1 5/12	+2/3	.08

①—Except 4 wheel drive.
②—Except Hatchback 4 wheel drive, Station Wagon, and Station Wagon 4 wheel drive.
③—4 wheel drive.
④—Toe-out.
⑤—Conventional suspension.
⑥—Pneumatic suspension.

Rear Wheel Alignment Specifications

Year	Model	Camber Angle, Degrees		Toe-In Inch
		Limits	Desired	
1983–84	Exc. 4 wheel drive Station Wagon	−3/4 to 3/4	1	−.12 to .12
	4 wheel drive Station Wagon	−5/12 to 1 1/12	3/4	−.12 to .12
1985	Exc. XT Coupe	−3/4 to +3/4	0	−.12 to +.12
	XT Coupe	−1/2 to +1/2	0	−.12 to +.12
1986	Exc. XT Coupe	−3/4 to +3/4	0	−.12 to +.12
	XT Coupe	0	0	−.12 to +.12
1987	Exc. Justy & XT Coupe	−3/4 to +3/4	0	−.12 to +.12
	Justy	—	—	—
	XT Coupe	0	0	−.12 to +.12

Brake Specifications

Year	Model	Front Brake Drum I.D.	Rear Brake Drum I.D.	Wheel Cylinder Bore		Master Cylinder		Disc Brake Rotor	
				Front Disc	Rear Drum	Hydraulic Cylinder	Power Booster	Nominal Thickness	Minimum Thickness
1983–84	All	7.24①	7.09	2 1/8	④	13/16	②⑤	.709	.610
1985–86	All⑥	7.56①②	7.09	2.1248	⑧	⑨	8.07②	7.09	.630
	All⑦	7.56①②	7.48①②	2.1248	⑩	⑨	8.07②	⑪	③
1987	Exc. Justy⑥	7.56①②	7.09	2.1248	⑧	⑨	8.07②	7.09	.630
	Exc. Justy⑦	7.56①②	7.48①②	2.1248	⑩	⑨	8.07②	⑪	③
	Justy	—	—	—	—	—	—	—	—

①—Disc brake diameter.
②—Effective diameter.
③—Front, .630 inch; rear, .335 inch.
④—Except Station Wagon and 4 wheel drive, 5/8; Station Wagon, 11/16; 4 wheel drive, 3/4.
⑤—Except Station Wagon and 4 wheel drive, 6 in.; Station Wagon and 4 wheel drive, 7 in.
⑥—Exc. turbocharged models.
⑦—Turbocharged models.
⑧—Exc. Station Wagon, 11/16 inch; Station Wagon, 3/4 inch.
⑨—Small cylinder, 13/16 inch; large cylinder, 1 inch.
⑩—Rear disc brake. Exc. Station Wagon, 1.1902 inch; Station Wagon, 1.3370 inch.
⑪—Front, .709 inch; rear, .390 inch.

Cooling System & Capacity Data

Year	Model	Cooling Capacity Qts.		Radiator Cap Relief Pressure Lbs.	Thermo. Opening Temp.	Fuel Tank Gals.	Engine Oil Refill Qts.	Transmission Oil			Axle Oil Pints
		With Heater	With A/C					4 Speed Pints	5 Speed Pints	Auto. Trans. Qts.	
1983–84	All	③	③	13	190	⑥	⑤	⑦	5.8	5.9–6.3	⑦
1985	Exc. XT Coupe	③	③	13	190	15.9	⑤	5.4	①	②	④
	XT Coupe	5.8	5.8	13	195	15.9	4.2	—	①	②	④
1986	All	③	③	13	190	15.9	⑤	—	①	②	④

①—Exc. 4 wheel drive & XT Turbo, 5.4 pts.; 4 wheel drive & XT Turbo, 7.0 pts.
②—Exc. 4 wheel drive, 6.3–6.8 qts.; 4 wheel drive 7.2–7.6 qts.
③—4-97/1600cc, 5.6; 4-109/1800cc, 5.8.
④—4 wheel drive rear differential, 1.7; differential gear oil, auto. trans., 2.6.
⑤—4-97/1600cc, 3.7; 4-109/1800cc, 4.2.
⑥—4 wheel drive Hatchback, 11.9; Hatchback except 4 wheel drive, 13.2; all 4 wheel drive except Hatchback, 14.5; Sedan, Hardtop and Station Wagon except 4 wheel drive, 15.8.
⑦—Exc. 4 wheel drive, 5.8; 4 wheel drive, 6.4.

ELECTRICAL SECTION

INDEX

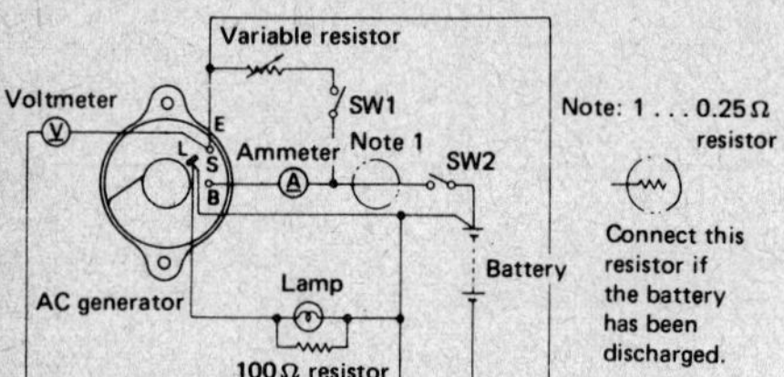

Fig.1 Circuit for testing alternator voltage & current output. Exc. XT Coupe

ALTERNATOR TESTING

Mount alternator securely in a suitable test stand prior to testing. Ensure test stand battery is fully charged before conducting any alternator tests.

1. Make the appropriate test connections shown in **Figs. 1 and 2** to test alternator output speed.
2. Open switch SW1 and close switch SW2, then operate alternator test stand.
3. Slowly increase alternator speed while observing alternator output voltage.
4. Output should be 13.5 volts at 1150 RPM on XT Coupe, or 13.5 volts at 900 RPM on all other models.
5. Continue raising alternator speed while observing voltmeter. Voltage should remain within specified regulated range at 6000 RPM for XT Coupe or 6000 RPM for all other models.
6. Check current output with test connections as shown in **Figs. 1 and 2**. Close switches 1 and 2, then set variable resistor at minimum value.
7. Increase alternator speed, using variable resistor to maintain voltage at 13.5 volts.
8. Amperage should be within 10% of specified output at an alternator speed of 6000 RPM for XT Coupe or 5000 RPM for all other models.

STARTER
REPLACE

1. Disconnect battery ground cable.
2. Disconnect battery cable and solenoid wiring at starter.
3. Remove starter retaining bolts and then the starter from bellhousing.

IGNITION SWITCH
REPLACE

1. Remove steering wheel, then the mast jacket plastic cover held by four screws to expose the switch mounting.
2. Drill two rounded bolt heads then remove bolts with an easy-out.
3. Remove two bolts with conventional hex heads.
4. Pull out switch with clamps.
5. Refit new switch with clamp. If clamp bolts are same as original equipment, tow will have a double-head. The top portion permits tightening with a wrench, and when the necessary torque is reached, the top portion can be snapped off, leaving only the tamper-resistant lower head.

LIGHT SWITCH
REPLACE

For switch replacement procedures on XT Coupe, refer to "Control Wing Switches, Replace."

1. Remove steering column retaining screws, then pull steering column down.
2. Remove combination meter visor retaining screws and meter visor.
3. Disconnect electrical connection at switch.
4. Remove knob and nut.
5. Remove switch.
6. Reverse procedure to install.

STOP LIGHT SWITCH
REPLACE

Switch is located on bracket under dashboard, near top of brake pedal.

1. Remove locknut on pedal side of bracket.
2. Push switch through bracket and remove wiring connector.
3. Reverse procedure to install.

Fig.2 Circuit for testing alternator voltage & current output. XT Coupe

NEUTRAL SAFETY SWITCH
REPLACE

1. Disconnect the battery ground cable.
2. Remove hand brake cover and center console.
3. Disconnect indicator light and neutral safety switch electrical connections.
4. Remove selector lever assembly retaining screws and lever assembly.
5. Remove safety switch retaining screws and switch from the selector lever assembly.

CONTROL WING SWITCHES
REPLACE
XT COUPE

1. Disconnect battery ground cable and remove combination switch as outlined.
2. Release control wing harness retaining straps and disconnect electrical connectors.
3. Remove 4 screws securing control wing to steering column, then the control wing assembly.
4. Remove retaining screws, then separate front and rear housing sections of control wing assembly, **Fig. 3.**
5. Remove individual switch knobs by inserting probe to release pawl, **Fig. 4**, then pulling knob from switch.

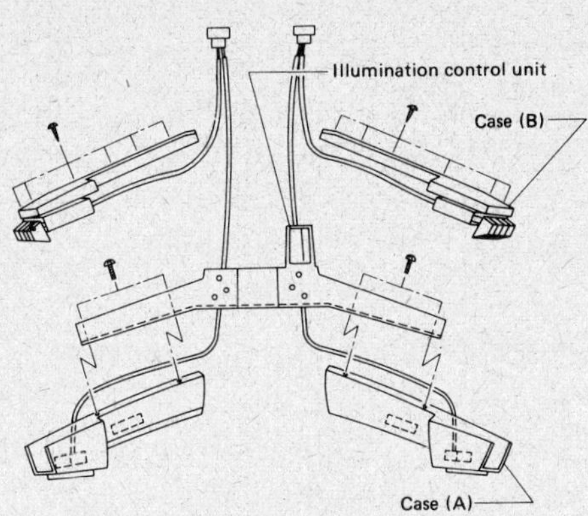

Fig. 3 Control wing disassembly. XT Coupe

6. Install knobs by holding finger at rear of switch and pressing knob on with thumb. **Care must be taken not to damage switch or brushes when removing and installing control knobs.**
7. Reverse procedure to install, ensuring wiring harnesses are properly aligned and secured.

TURN SIGNAL SWITCH REPLACE

Refer to "Combination Switch, Replace" for removal procedure.

COMBINATION SWITCH REPLACE

1. Disconnect battery ground cable and remove steering wheel trim pad.
2. Mark installation position of steering wheel, remove retaining nut, then remove steering wheel using suitable puller.
3. Remove screws securing lower steering column cover and the cover.
4. Remove steering column upper mounting screws and pull down on column as needed, then remove upper column cover.
5. Release switch harness retaining straps and remove combination switch mounting screws.
6. Disconnect electrical connectors and remove combination switch assembly.
7. Reverse procedure to install.

WINDSHIELD WIPER SWITCH REPLACE

1983–84

1. Disconnect battery ground cable and remove lower steering column cover and column bracket retaining bolts.
2. Remove instrument cluster bezel retaining screws and the bezel.
3. Pry off switch knob taking care not to damage knob or panel, then remove switch retaining nut.
4. Pull down on steering column just enough to gain access to switch, then withdraw switch from rear of panel.
5. Disconnect electrical connector and remove wiper/washer switch.
6. Reverse procedure to install.

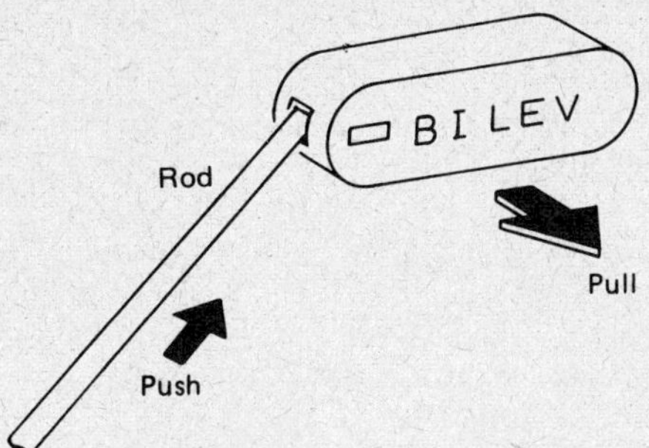

Fig. 4 Control switch knob removal. XT Coupe

1985–87

Exc. XT Coupe

1. Pry off all control buttons and knobs from switch panel to right of cluster, taking care not to damage knobs or panel.
2. Remove screws securing switch panel and withdraw switch assembly from instrument panel.
3. Disconnect electrical connectors and remove switch panel assembly.
4. Remove wiper switch.
5. Reverse procedure to install.

XT Coupe

Refer to "Control Wing Switches, Replace."

WINDSHIELD WIPER MOTOR REPLACE

EXC. XT COUPE

Front

1. Disconnect battery ground cable and motor electrical connections.
2. Remove wiper arm retaining nuts and wiper arms.
3. Open engine hood and remove the four plastic cowl retaining clips. Later models have retaining screws.
4. Remove the cowl and the four wiper link retaining nuts.
5. Remove the windshield washer tank.
6. Remove the three wiper motor retaining bolts.
7. Remove the wiper motor and link assembly.
8. Reverse procedure to install.

Rear

1. Remove back door inner trim.
2. Remove the wiper arm from the shaft.
3. Disconnect the wiper motor electrical connections.
4. Remove wiper motor retaining bolts and motor.
5. Reverse procedure to install.

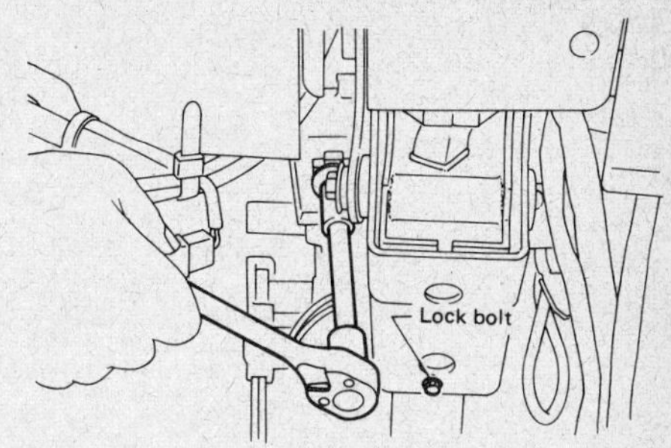

Fig. 5 Tilt wheel locking installation

XT COUPE

1. Disconnect battery ground cable, remove plugs securing cowl cover and pull back cover.
2. Disconnect wiper motor electrical connector.
3. Remove wiper motor mounting bolts.
4. Remove fasteners securing transmission, disconnect transmission and remove wiper motor.
5. Reverse procedure to install. Torque transmission mounting bolts to 4.7-6.9 ft. lbs., transmission to motor mounting nut to 16-22 ft. lbs., and wiper motor retaining bolts to 3.3-5.4 ft. lbs.

WINDSHIELD WIPER TRANSMISSION REPLACE

1. Refer to the "Wiper Motor, Replace" section and remove the wiper motor assembly.
2. Remove wiper link from motor. **Use a suitable washer to depress the four plastic retaining claws.**
3. Remove the motor to transmission retaining screws.
4. Separate the yoke from the transmission.
5. Hold the brush and remove the rotor. **Use caution to avoid the loss of the balls installed at each end of the rotor.**
6. Reverse procedure to assemble.

RADIO REPLACE

1983–84

1. Remove the center console.
2. Disconnect wiring harness and antenna line.
3. Pull off tuning and volume control knobs from radio.
4. Remove radio retaining nuts.
5. Remove radio mounting bolt and radio.
6. Reverse procedure to install.

1985–87

Exc. XT Coupe

1. Disconnect battery ground cable and disconnect center instrument panel trim plate.

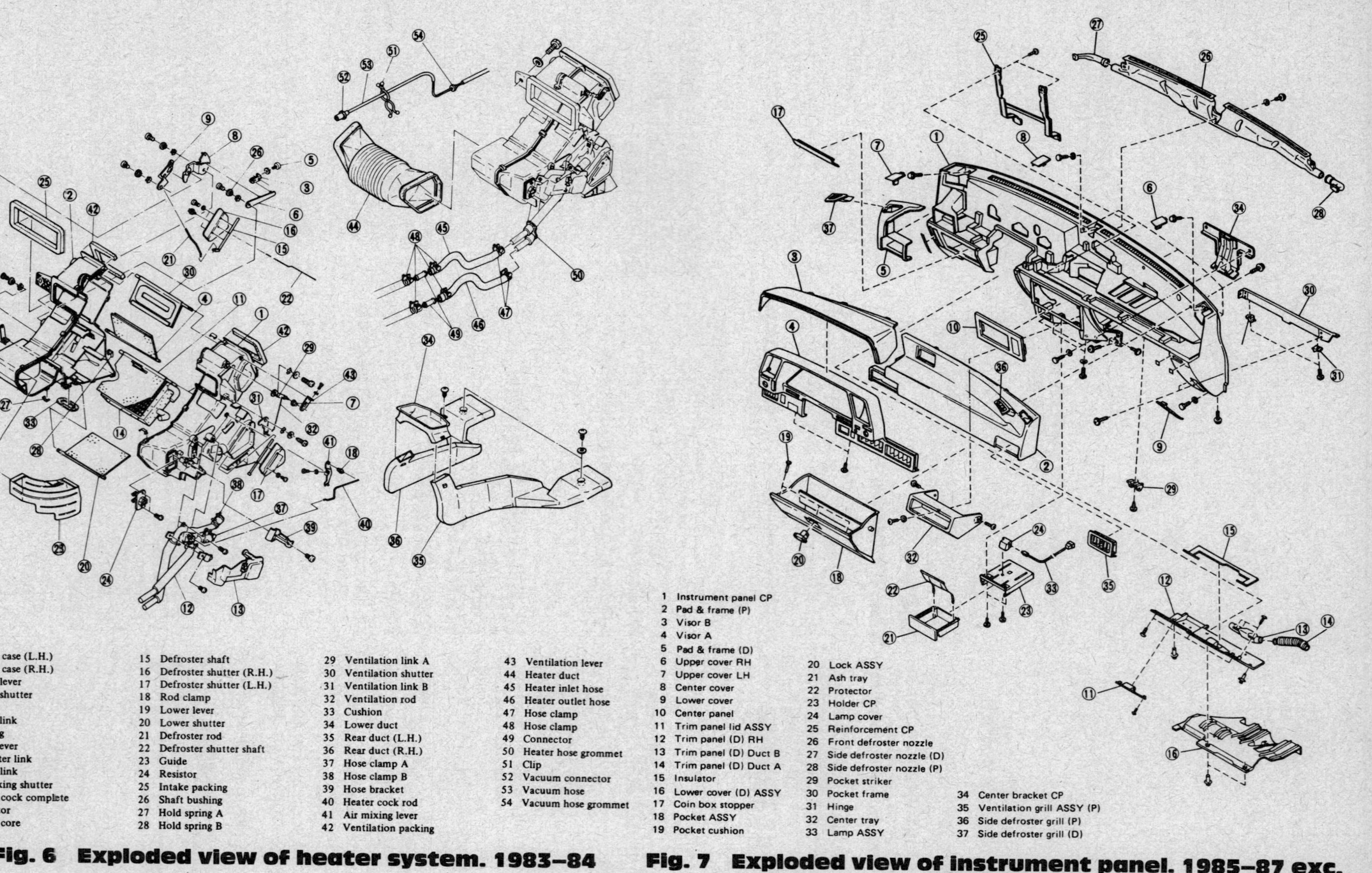

1 Heater case (L.H.)
2 Heater case (R.H.)
3 Upper lever
4 Upper shutter
5 Screw
6 Upper link
7 Bushing
8 Mode lever
9 Defroster link
10 Lower link
11 Air mixing shutter
12 Heater cock complete
13 Protector
14 Heater core
15 Defroster shaft
16 Defroster shutter (R.H.)
17 Defroster shutter (L.H.)
18 Rod clamp
19 Lower lever
20 Lower shutter
21 Defroster rod
22 Defroster shutter shaft
23 Guide
24 Resistor
25 Intake packing
26 Shaft bushing
27 Hold spring A
28 Hold spring B
29 Ventilation link A
30 Ventilation shutter
31 Ventilation link B
32 Ventilation rod
33 Cushion
34 Lower duct
35 Rear duct (L.H.)
36 Rear duct (R.H.)
37 Hose clamp A
38 Hose clamp B
39 Hose bracket
40 Heater cock rod
41 Air mixing lever
42 Ventilation packing
43 Ventilation lever
44 Heater duct
45 Heater inlet hose
46 Heater outlet hose
47 Hose clamp
48 Hose clamp
49 Connector
50 Heater hose grommet
51 Clip
52 Vacuum connector
53 Vacuum hose
54 Vacuum hose grommet

Fig. 6 Exploded view of heater system. 1983–84

1 Instrument panel CP
2 Pad & frame (P)
3 Visor B
4 Visor A
5 Pad & frame (D)
6 Upper cover RH
7 Upper cover LH
8 Center cover
9 Lower cover
10 Center panel
11 Trim panel lid ASSY
12 Trim panel (D) RH
13 Trim panel (D) Duct B
14 Trim panel (D) Duct A
15 Insulator
16 Lower cover (D) ASSY
17 Coin box stopper
18 Pocket ASSY
19 Pocket cushion
20 Lock ASSY
21 Ash tray
22 Protector
23 Holder CP
24 Lamp cover
25 Reinforcement CP
26 Front defroster nozzle
27 Side defroster nozzle (D)
28 Side defroster nozzle (P)
29 Pocket striker
30 Pocket frame
31 Hinge
32 Center tray
33 Lamp ASSY
34 Center bracket CP
35 Ventilation grill ASSY (P)
36 Side defroster grill (P)
37 Side defroster grill (D)

Fig. 7 Exploded view of instrument panel. 1985–87 exc. XT Coupe

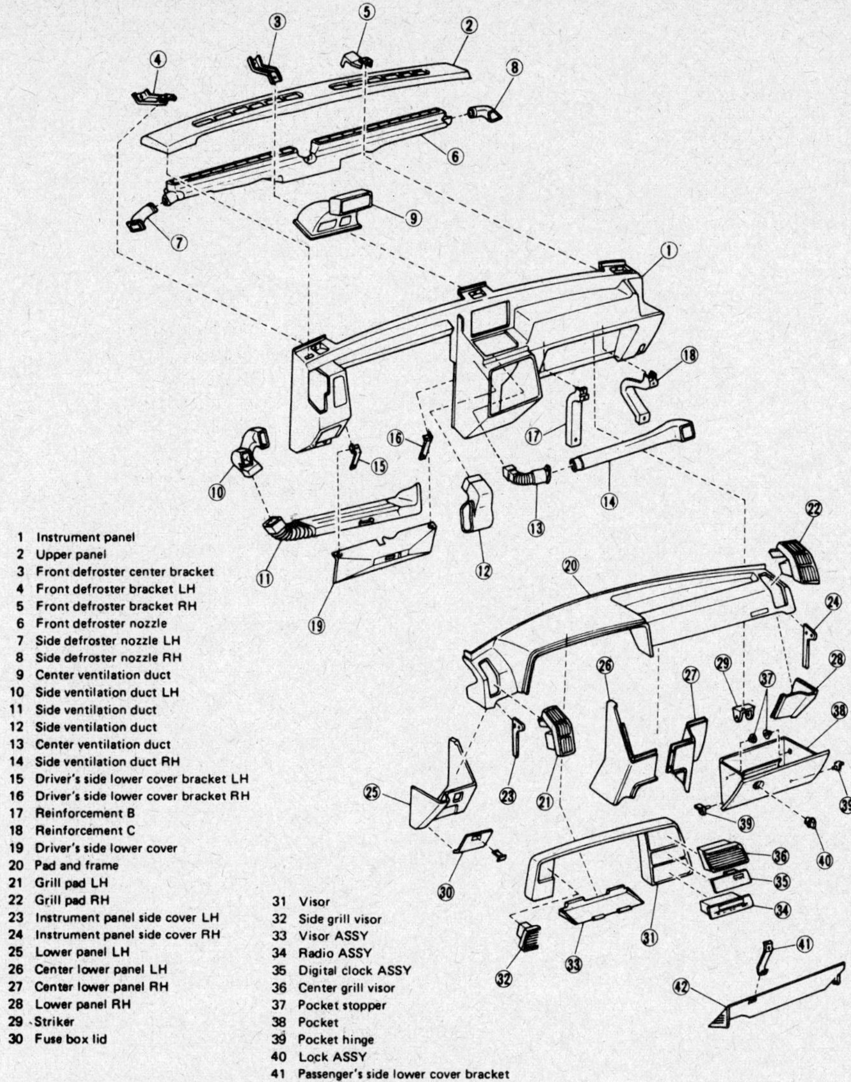

Fig. 8 Exploded view of instrument panel. 1985–87 XT Coupe

2. Remove radio mounting screws.
3. Disconnect electrical connectors and antenna lead, then remove radio.
4. Reverse procedure to install.

XT Coupe

1. Disconnect battery ground cable and remove clock.
2. Remove radio bracket retaining screws and withdraw radio.
3. Disconnect electrical connectors and antenna lead, then remove radio and bracket assembly.
4. Reverse procedure to install.

INSTRUMENT CLUSTER REPLACE

1983–84

1. Disconnect the battery ground cable.
2. Remove the steering column retaining bolts and pull it down.
3. Remove the instrument cover retaining screws.
4. Disconnect all cluster electrical connections.
5. On GL and GLF models, remove the center ventilator control lever.
6. On Hatchback 4 wheel drive GL and Station Wagon 4 wheel drive GL models, remove the center ventilator control lever and passing lamp switch.
7. On all models, remove the instrument cluster retaining screws.
8. Pull the instrument cluster slightly out of the dash.
9. Disconnect the speedometer cable and cluster electrical connections.
10. Remove the instrument cluster from the dash.
11. Reverse procedure to install.

1985–87

Exc. XT Coupe

1. Disconnect battery ground cable and remove knobs from wiper switch and upper and lower switches on right side switch panel.
2. Remove screws securing instrument cluster bezel and switch panel, disconnect electrical connectors, then remove panel and bezel.
3. Remove cluster retaining screws and pull cluster away from instrument panel.
4. Disconnect electrical connectors and speedometer cable, taking care not to damage speed sensor assembly, then remove cluster.
5. Reverse procedure to install.

XT Coupe

1. Disconnect battery ground cable, then disconnect and remove steering shaft universal joint.
2. Remove left lower instrument panel cover and duct below steering column.
3. Disconnect electrical connectors to ignition and combination switches, wing switch assembly and the instrument cluster, then remove screws securing harness brackets to steering column.
4. Remove meter cable.
5. Pull knob to "pop-up" steering column, remove tilt control cable, then push down on steering wheel and lock mechanism.
6. Install 8 mm 16 mm bolt to secure column, **Fig. 5.**
7. Remove steering column mounting bolts from under instrument panel.
8. Pull column assembly from mounting at toe board, then remove steering column and instrument cluster assembly.
9. Remove instrument cluster from column.
10. Reverse procedure to install.

HEATER CORE REPLACE

1983–84

1. Disconnect battery ground cable.
2. Drain coolant from radiator using drain plug.
3. Disconnect both heater inlet and outlet hoses from the heater unit, **Fig. 6.**
4. Using a suitable screwdriver, remove the heater hose grommet from the inside firewall.
5. Remove the six radio housing or console retaining screws and the unit with which the model is equipped.
6. Remove the instrument panel and package tray.
7. Remove the large duct between the blower assembly and the heater unit.
8. Remove the left and right defroster nozzles.
9. Remove the two upper heater unit retaining bolts.
10. Lift the heater unit up approximately .39 inches and remove from installed position.
11. Remove the heater core fitting assembly cover.
12. Disconnect the rod from the plastic clamp.
13. Remove both the inlet and outlet hose clamps. **Twist the cotter pin counterclockwise to remove the outlet hose clamp.**
14. To remove the heater core fitting assembly, remove the retaining screws and pull the assembly up and forward.

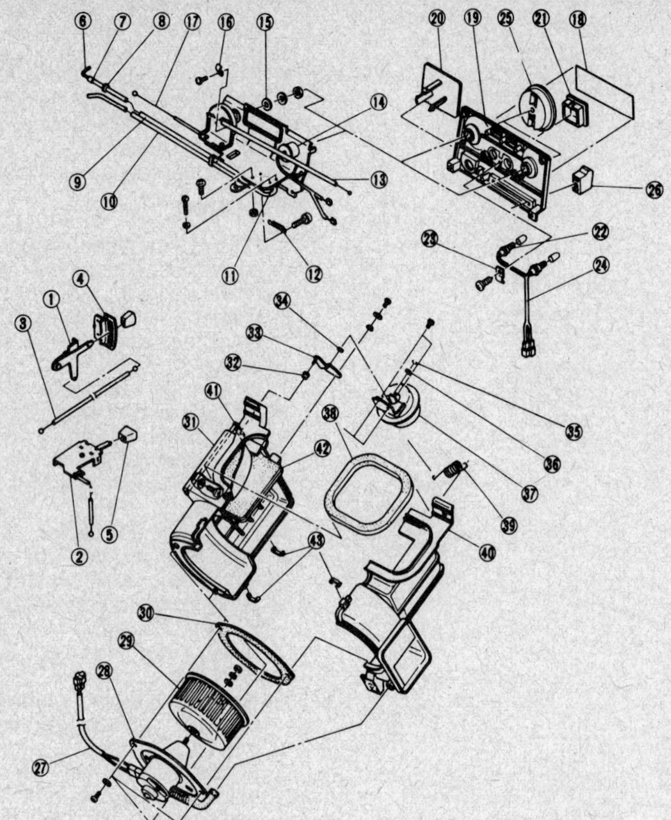

1	Fresh air ventilation lever (Standard type)	15	Bushing	30	Packing
2	Fresh air ventilation lever (Multi type)	16	Cable clamp	31	Blower case (R.H.)
3	Ventilation cable	17	Mode control cable	32	Bushing
4	Ventilation grille	18	Plate	33	Intake shutter lever
5	Ventilation knob	19	Panel	34	Spacer
6	Vacuum pipe	20	Cigarette lighter cap	35	Clip
7	Vacuum hose	21	Rear defogger switch	36	Bushing
8	Check valve	22	Bulbs	37	Actuator
9	Vacuum hose	23	Cord clamp	38	Packing
10	Vacuum hose	24	Cord assembly	39	Intake shutter return spring
11	Vacuum switch	25	Fan and temperature control knobs	40	Blower case (L.H.)
12	Spring	26	Mode lever knob	41	Intake shutter shaft
13	Temperature control cable	27	Harness	42	Intake shutter
14	Fan switch	28	Motor assembly	43	Springs
		29	Blower		

Fig. 9 Exploded view of blower motor & housing. 1983–84

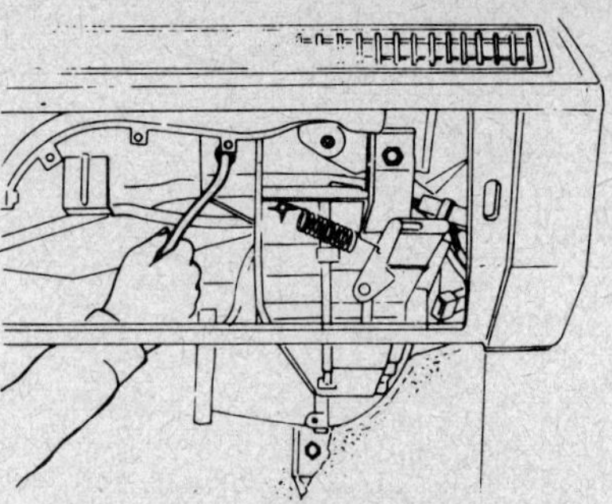

Fig. 10 Blower motor retaining bolts location. 1983–84

15. Disconnect the defroster flap control rod.
16. Remove the twelve heater case retaining clips and separate the halves.
17. Remove the heater core.
18. Reverse procedure to install.

1985–87

1. Disconnect battery ground cable.
2. Disconnect inlet and outlet heater hoses in engine compartment.
3. Drain as much coolant as possible from heater unit and plug disconnected hoses.
4. Disconnect heater control cable and vacuum hose from heater unit joint.
5. On all exc. XT coupe, remove instrument panel as follows:
   a. Remove trim panel D from driver's side, **Fig. 7.**
   b. Remove tapping screws from lower side of instrument panel in three places.
   c. Remove clip from steering column shaft while lowering cover, if equipped.
   d. Disconnect ventilation duct combined with trim panel from heater.
   e. Remove fuse box attaching bolts and the fuse box.
   f. Disconnect fresh air ventilation cable on driver's side by removing cable from clamp on rear left side of instrument panel and disconnecting cable from fresh air ventilation lever rod.
   g. Disconnect heater control cable by removing cable from clamp on left side of heater unit and disconnecting cable from select lever rod.
   h. Disconnect vacuum hoses.
   i. Disconnect instrument and body harness connectors on driver's side.
   j. Remove steering wheel and disconnect steering column from vehicle body.
   k. Disconnect speedometer cable from rear side of combination meter.
   l. Remove center tray attaching screws and the tray.
   m. Remove console box.
   n. Remove trim panel on passenger side by removing resin clips from lower end of instrument panel in two places, removing resin clip on pillar side and detaching trim panel from heater side.
   o. Remove glove box pocket by remove screws holding hinges to lower end of pocket and detaching lock from striker.
   p. Disconnect blower motor vacuum hose from upper rear side of pocket frame.
   q. Disconnect electrical connectors on passenger side.
   r. Remove instrument panel covers.
   s. Remove instrument panel attaching bolts.
   t. Disconnect radio antenna lead from rear side of instrument panel.
   u. Carefully remove lower instrument panel.
6. On XT Coupe, remove instrument panel as follows:
   a. Remove lower cover on driver's side, **Fig. 8.**
   b. Remove side ventilation duct.
   c. Open fuse box lid, remove attaching screws and detach fuse box from instrument panel.
   d. Remove lower cover on passenger side.
   e. Remove instrument panel upper cover by prying with suitable screwdriver at both ends and in middle.
   f. Remove console box.
   g. Remove steering shaft assembly, combination meter and control wiring as a unit.
   h. Disconnect all electrical connectors from instrument panel.
   i. Remove instrument panel attaching bolts and the instrument panel.
7. Remove heater unit.
8. Remove heater core from heater unit.
9. Reverse procedure to install, noting the following:
   a. Fitting length of heater hose to pipe is .79-.98 inch.
   b. On all except XT Coupe models, fitting length of vacuum hose must exceed .31 inch.
   c. Torque heater unit attaching bolts to 4.0-6.9 ft. lbs.

BLOWER MOTOR REPLACE

1983–84

1. Disconnect battery ground cable.
2. Remove blower cover and package tray, **Fig. 9.**
3. Remove glove box from dash.
4. Remove the large duct between the heater and blower assemblies.
5. Set the actuator lever to the CIRC position and disconnect the vacuum hose from the servo. **If the lever is not set to the CIRC position it will be difficult to remove the vacuum hose.**
6. Disconnect the blower motor electrical connections.
7. Remove the servo retaining screws and clip.
8. Remove the servo from the blower assembly.
9. Remove the blower retaining nuts and bolts and blower, **Fig. 10.**
10. Reverse procedure to install.

1985–87

1. Disconnect battery ground cable.
2. Remove passenger side trim panel.
3. Remove glove compartment pocket.
4. Remove pocket frame.
5. On models less A/C, remove heater duct.
6. On models with A/C, separate evaporator from blower assembly.
7. On all models, disconnect blower vacuum hose from instrument panel vacuum hose.
8. Disconnect blower motor and resistor electrical connectors.
9. Remove blower attaching bolts and nuts.
10. Remove ventilation duct bracket and the blower motor assembly.
11. Reverse procedure to install, noting the following:
    a. On all except XT Coupe models, fitting length of vacuum hose must exceed .31 inch.
    b. Torque blower attaching nuts and bolts to 4.0-6.9 ft. lbs.

ENGINE SECTION

INDEX

ENGINE REPLACE

1983–84

1. Remove spare tire and disconnect battery ground cables. **On fuel injected models, relieve fuel system pressure before disconnecting ground cables as follows:**
    a. Raise and support vehicle, then disconnect fuel pump electrical connector.
    b. Lower vehicle and start engine.
    c. After engine stops, crank engine for approximately five seconds, then turn ignition switch to the OFF position.
    d. Raise and support vehicle, then connect fuel pump electrical connector.
    e. Lower vehicle.
2. Disconnect necessary vacuum hoses and ducts noting installation position, then remove air cleaner and air flow sensor assemblies, as equipped.
3. Remove spare tire bracket, then disconnect and plug fuel lines to engine.
4. On automatic transmission models, disconnect diaphragm vacuum hose from intake manifold.
5. On all models, disconnect two multiple wire connectors, then the distributor high tension cable, alternator electrical connectors, vacuum switch hose and starter electrical connectors.
6. Remove accelerator cable adjusting nut and disconnect cable.
7. On manual transmission models, remove clutch return spring.
8. On models equipped with hill-holder, disconnect the pressure hold valve at bracket.
9. On all models, remove the pitching stopper, **Fig. 1.**

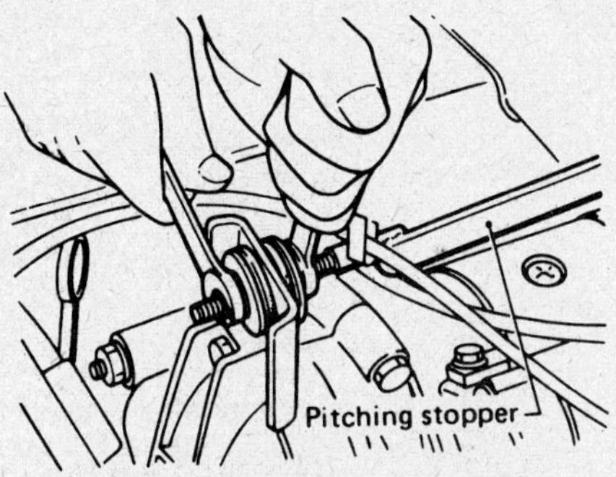

Fig. 1 Engine pitching stopper removal

10. On automatic transmission models, remove four torque converter to drive plate retaining bolts through the timing hole. **Use caution to avoid dropping bolts into housing during removal.**
11. On all models, loosen two upper bolts and two lower nuts retaining engine to transmission. **Do not remove starter from housing.**
12. Remove two upper engine to transmission retaining bolts.
13. Remove splash shield located below radiator fan.
14. Drain coolant and disconnect both inlet and outlet radiator hoses.
15. Disconnect thermoswitch and fan motor electrical connections.
16. Disconnect and plug transmission cooling lines, if equipped, then remove radiator mounting bolts and the radiator.
17. On models equipped with A/C, remove compressor as follows:
    a. Discharge A/C system, disconnect refrigerant lines from compressor, then plug open lines and fittings.
    b. Disconnect electrical connector from compressor clutch and remove pulser.
    c. Remove alternator, front drive belt and the upper compressor bracket.
    d. Remove cooling fan and clutch assembly, rear drive belt and the idler pulley assembly.
    e. Remove compressor and lower bracket as an assembly.
18. On vehicles equipped with power steering, remove oil pump assembly and bracket as follows:
    a. Remove idler pulley cap. **Cover the idler cap with a soft cloth to prevent damage.**
    b. Loosen pulley lock bolt.
    c. Loosen adjustment bolt and remove oil pump belt.
    d. Remove oil pump retaining bolts and position pump aside. **Position pump carefully to avoid damage to hoses or loss of oil.**
    e. Remove pump bracket.
19. On all models, disconnect heater inlet and outlet hose.
20. Raise and support front of vehicle.
21. Remove hot air intake hose and stove from exhaust pipe.
22. If equipped, remove oxygen sensor electrical connector.
23. Remove exhaust manifold assembly retaining bolts and manifold assembly.
24. On automatic transmission models, loosen the IEM bracket retaining bolts approximately .4 inches.
25. On manual transmission models, remove the IEM bracket retaining bolt securing the bracket to the exhaust assembly. Secure the exhaust manifold assembly to a crossmember with wire.
26. On all models, remove front engine mount nuts.

27. Remove the two lower engine to transmission retaining nuts.
28. Support transmission with suitable jack, then lower vehicle and remove engine using suitable lifting device.
29. Reverse procedure to install, noting the following:
    a. When installing the pitching stopper, tighten nut securely at vehicle body side, then tighten the rear nut on the engine side so there is a clearance of .03-.05 inch on manual transmission models or .07-.09 inch on automatic transmission models between the rubber cushion and the washer. Torque the front nut to 10 ft. lbs. while restraining the rear nut from turning.
    b. Torque the following fasteners: engine mount nuts to 14-25 ft. lbs. (2-3.4 kg-m), front exhaust pipe to engine bolts to 19-22 ft. lbs. (2.6-3 kg-m), front exhaust pipe to rear exhaust pipe to 31-38 ft. lbs. (4.3-5.3 kg-m), front exhaust pipe to bracket bolt to 6.5-9.4 ft. lbs. (.9-1.3 kg-m), pitching stopper nut to 2.2-6.5 ft. lbs. (.3-.9 kg-m), radiator mounting bolts to 7-13 ft. lbs. (1-1.8 kg-m), and if equipped, torque converter to drive-plate bolts to 17-20 ft. lbs. (2.3-2.7 kg-m).

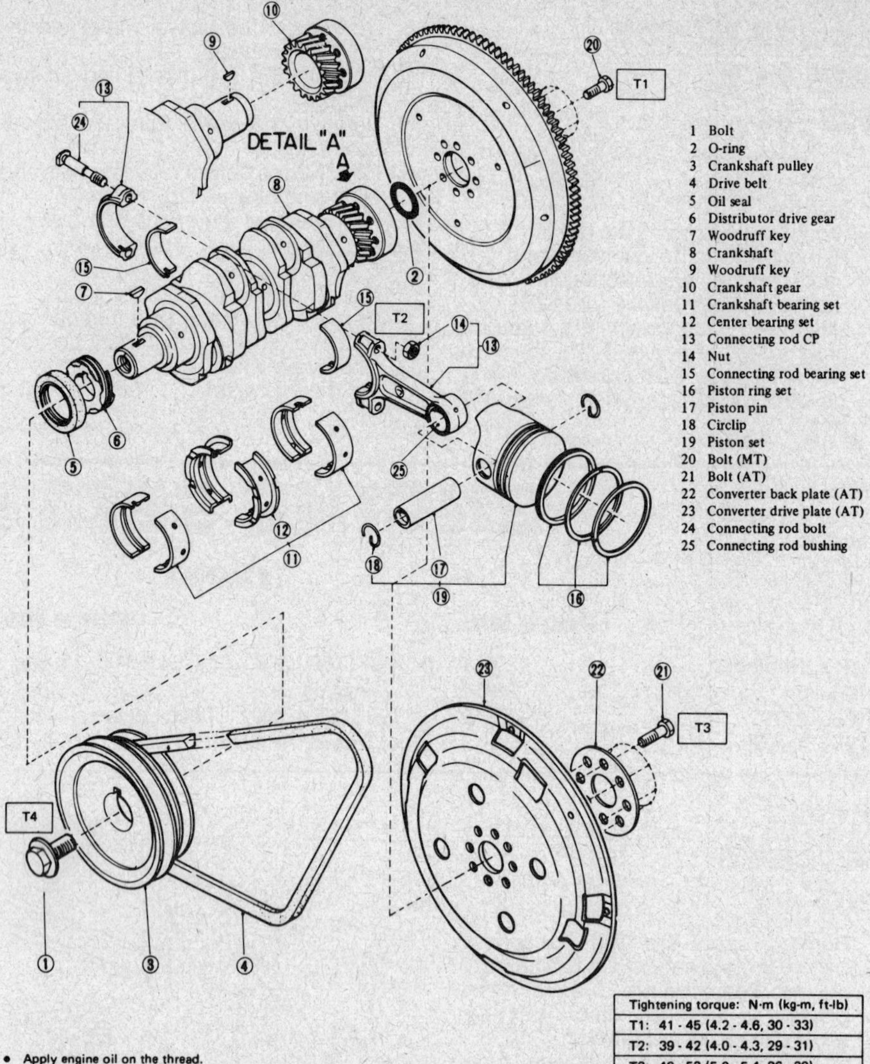

Fig. 2 Crankshaft, flywheel & converter drive plate assembly. 4-97/1600cc & 1983–84 4-109/1800cc engines

1985–87

1. Remove spare tire from engine compartment.
2. On models equipped with multi-point fuel injection, relieve fuel system pressure as follows:
    a. Raise and support vehicle.
    b. Disconnect fuel pump electrical connector, then lower vehicle.
    c. Start engine. After engine stalls, crank for approximately five seconds, then turn ignition off.
    d. Reconnect fuel pump electrical connector.
3. On all models, disconnect battery ground cable from battery and engine.
4. Remove spare support clamp and the support.
5. On models equipped with carbureted engine, disconnect vacuum hoses from charcoal canister, then remove air cleaner assembly.
6. On models equipped with fuel injected engine, disconnect vacuum hoses from charcoal canister, then remove upper air cleaner case and filter and disconnect electrical connector.
7. On all models, disconnect fuel delivery, return and evaporation hoses.
8. On models equipped with automatic transmission, disconnect diaphragm vacuum hose.
9. On all models, disconnect wire harness connectors between engine and body.
10. Disconnect accelerator cable from carburetor or throttle body.
11. On models equipped with manual transmission, remove release lever spring, then disconnect hill holder cable, if equipped.
12. On all models, remove pitching stopper rod, **Fig. 1.**
13. On models equipped with turbocharged engine, proceed as follows:
    a. Remove transmission heat shield, then the turbocharger side heat shield.
    b. Raise and support vehicle.
    c. Loosen front exhaust pipe connection, then lower vehicle and remove heat shield cover from center exhaust pipe.
    d. Disconnect center exhaust pipe from turbocharger.
    e. Raise and support vehicle.
    f. Disconnect center exhaust pipe from rear exhaust pipe, then unfasten and remove center exhaust pipe and lower vehicle.
14. On models equipped with automatic transmission, remove timing hole plug, then the four torque converter-to-drive plate attaching bolts.
15. On all models, drain cooling system, then disconnect radiator hoses and remove radiator from vehicle.
16. Disconnect heater hoses from engine.
17. Unfasten power steering pump, if equipped, and position aside.
18. Raise and support vehicle.
19. On models equipped with non-turbocharged engine, proceed as follows:
    a. Disconnect front exhaust pipe from engine. **Leave one nut installed to temporarily hold exhaust pipe.**
    b. Disconnect front exhaust pipe from rear exhaust pipe.
    c. Unfasten and remove front exhaust pipe.
20. On all models, remove engine mount.
21. Remove lower engine-to-transmission attaching nuts, the lower vehicle.
22. Support engine using suitable lifting equipment.
23. Remove upper engine-to-transmission attaching bolts and nuts.
24. Support transmission with a suitable jack, then raise engine and transmission slightly.
25. On models equipped with manual transmission, move engine back until

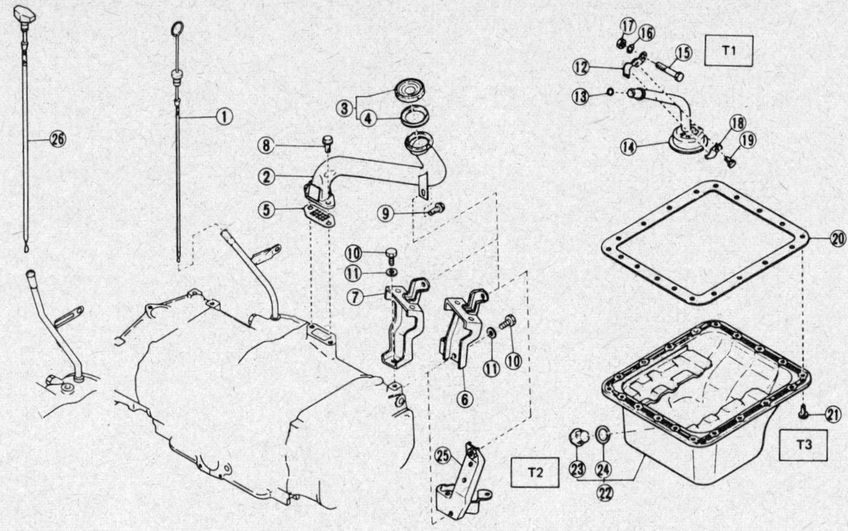

Tightening torque: N·m (kg-m, ft-lb)
T1: 23 - 26 (2.3 - 2.7, 17 - 20)
T2: 22 - 27 (2.2 - 2.8, 16 - 20)
T3: 4.4 - 5.4 (0.45 - 0.55, 3.3 - 4.0)

1 Oil level gauge
2 Oil filler duct
3 Oil filler cap CP
4 Gasket
5 Air breather duct gasket
6 Oil filler duct stay (SUBARU 1800)
7 Oil filler duct stay (SUBARU 1600)
8 Bolt and washer
9 Bolt and washer
10 Bolt
11 Spring washer
12 Oil strainer stay
13 O-ring
14 Oil strainer
15 Bolt
16 Spring washer
17 Nut
18 Oil strainer stay 2
19 Bolt & washer
20 Oil pan gasket
21 Bolt & washer
22 Oil pan CP
23 Plug
24 Gasket
25 Oil filler duct stay (TURBO)
26 Oil level gauge (TURBO)

Fig. 3 Oil pan, oil filter duct & fittings. 4-97/1600cc & 1983–84 4-109/1800cc engines

mainshaft clears clutch cover.

26. On all models, carefully lift engine and remove from vehicle.
27. Reverse procedure to install, noting the following torques: engine-to-transmission nuts and bolts, 34-40 ft. lbs.; torque converter bolts, 17-20 ft. lbs.; power steering pump bolts, 22-36 ft. lbs.; power steering pump pulley bolt, 31-46 ft. lbs.; front engine mount nuts, 17-27 ft. lbs.; center exhaust pipe-to-turbocharger and transmission bolts, 18-25 ft. lbs.; center exhaust pipe-to-rear exhaust pipe bolts, 9-17 ft. lbs.; front exhaust pipe-to-cylinder head bolts, 19-22 ft. lbs.; front exhaust pipe-to-bracket bolts, 18-25 ft. lbs.; radiator attaching bolts, 7-13 ft. lbs.; pitching stopper rod-to-body bolts, 27-49 ft. lbs.; pitching stopper-to-engine or transmission, 33-40 ft. lbs.

ENGINE SERVICE

4-97/1600cc & 1983–84 4-109/1800cc ENGINES

Disassembly

1. On carbureted engines, proceed as follows:
   a. Remove carburetor protector, if equipped, mount engine in suitable stands, drain coolant and engine oil, then reinstall drain plugs.
   b. Disconnect high tension leads from spark plugs and ignition coil, then separate leads from retaining clips.
   c. Disconnect vacuum and PCV hoses, then remove distributor and hold down plate.
   d. On models less A/C, loosen water pump pulley nut, then remove alternator mounting bolts and the alternator, along with air cleaner and plug wire brackets.
   e. Remove silencers, Air Switching Valve (ASV) and ASV pipes, as equipped, then the EGR cover.
   f. Remove battery cable, ASV and power steering pump brackets, as equipped, then the EGR pipe.
   g. Disconnect and remove crankcase ventilation and coolant hoses, noting position for assembly.
   h. Disconnect engine harness electrical connectors noting position for installation, then remove harness.
   i. Remove intake manifold retaining nuts and washers, then the manifold.
2. On fuel injected and turbocharged engines, proceed as follows:
   a. Remove air intake duct.
   b. On turbocharged models, disconnect coolant hoses from turbocharger, then remove turbocharger and front exhaust pipe.
   c. On all models, mount engine in suitable stands, drain coolant and engine oil, then reinstall drain plugs.
   d. Disconnect high tension leads from spark plugs and ignition coil, and remove leads from support bracket.
   e. Remove PCV and distributor vacuum hoses, wiring harness clips and ground terminal fastener, disconnect connectors and remove wiring harness.
   f. Remove hold down bolts and the distributor.
   g. On models less A/C, loosen water pump pulley nut, then remove alternator and drive belt.
   h. Disconnect electrical connector from oil pressure switch and air bleed hose from intake manifold.
   i. Remove EGR pipe clamps, EGR cover and the EGR pipe.
   j. Remove intake manifold assembly.
3. Remove power steering pump and alternator brackets.
4. On turbocharged models, remove knock sensor.
5. Remove fuel injectors, if equipped.
6. On all models, remove oil filler pipe, water pipes and air bleed hoses. **On 4 wheel drive vehicles, remove the stiffener.**
7. Remove crankshaft pulley bolt, **Fig. 2. To prevent crank from turning, insert a screwdriver through the timing hole.**
8. Remove crankshaft pulley by tapping it lightly with a suitable soft-faced hammer.
9. Remove oil pump and filter assembly.
10. Remove water pump and heater hose assemblies.
11. On manual transmission models, remove clutch cover, disc and flywheel, **Fig. 2.**
12. On automatic transmission models, remove drive and back plate.
13. On all models, invert engine and remove oil pan, oil pan gasket, and transmission cover, **Fig. 3.**
14. Remove oil level gauge bracket and pitching stopper bracket.
15. Remove flywheel housing.
16. Remove the valve rocker covers and gaskets, **Fig. 4.**
17. Remove valve rocker locknuts and adjusting screws.
18. Remove rocker assemblies and pushrods, **Fig. 5. If pushrods are to be reused, keep them in order. They should be reinstalled in their original positions.**
19. Remove cylinder head nuts in sequence shown in **Fig. 6.**
20. Remove cylinder heads and gaskets, **Fig. 7.**
21. Remove oil strainer retaining bolt and

nut. **Never attempt to remove strainer unless necessary.**

22. To remove piston pin circlip on rear side of No. 3 and 4 piston proceed as follows:
    a. Install crankshaft pulley bolt. Using a suitable wrench rotate crankshaft.
    b. Rotate piston to BDC.
    c. Insert long needle nose pliers through the rear service hole to reach the pin circlip.
23. Remove No. 3 and 4 piston pins using piston pin remover 399094300 through rear service holes.
24. Remove crankcase plugs from case using an Allen wrench 14 mm wide across the flats.
25. Remove No. 1 and 2 piston pin circlips and pins in the same manner as previously described. **Use the front service holes for these cylinders.**
26. Straighten camshaft retaining bolt lockwashers and remove bolts.
27. Install valve lifter clips 899804100 to prevent lifters from dropping. **On models equipped with hydraulic lifters, tilt crankcase and remove lifters.**
28. Pull camshaft rearward so that it does not interfere with crankcase removal.
29. Separate the crankcase halves by removing the retaining nuts and bolts with cylinder No. 1 and 3 facing upward, **Fig. 8.**
30. Remove front oil seal, O-ring, and back-up ring.
31. Remove crankshaft, connecting rods, distributor gear and crankshaft gear as a unit.
32. Remove camshaft and camshaft gear and plate as an assembly.
33. Remove valve lifters and keep them in order. They should be reinstalled in their original positions.
34. Remove pistons from the crankcase. **Keep the piston pins together with their respective pistons and make marks on the pistons in order to return them to their original positions.**
35. Remove crankshaft bearings. **If the bearings are to be used again, mark them in order to return them to their original positions.**
36. Remove oil pressure switch or plug and remove engine stands from the case halves.

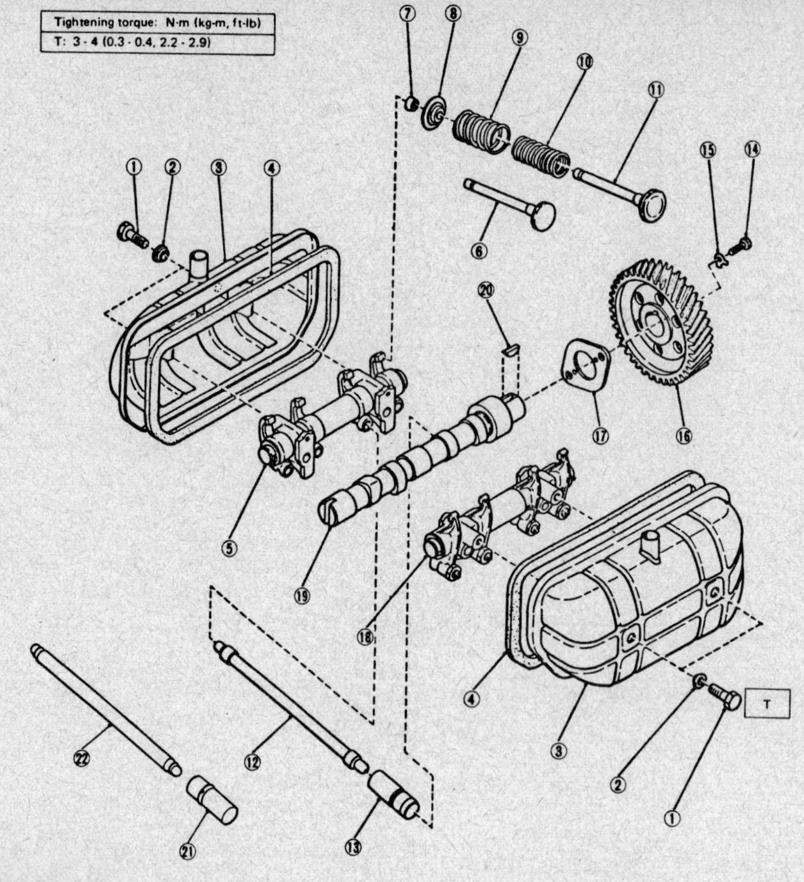

1 Bolt
2 Valve rocker cover seal washer
3 Valve rocker cover
4 Valve rocker cover gasket
5 Valve rocker ASSY (R.H.)
6 Exhaust valve
7 Valve spring retainer key
8 Valve spring retainer
9 Valve spring
10 Valve spring 2
11 Intake valve
12 Valve push rod
13 Valve lifter
14 Bolt
15 Lock washer
16 Camshaft gear
17 Camshaft plate
18 Valve rocker ASSY
19 Camshaft
20 Woodruff key
21 Hydraulic valve lifter
22 Push rod (for hydraulic valve lifter)

Fig. 4 Valve train components. 4-97/1600cc & 1983–84 4-109/1800cc engines

Assembly

1. Install engine stands onto each crankcase half.
2. Apply sealant to oil pressure switch threads and torque switch to 16-20 ft. lbs.
3. Check that oil passages are clear using compressed air.
4. Install crankshaft bearings into crankcase.
5. Install valve lifters into lifter holes in case. **Apply engine oil to lifters prior to installation.**
6. Install camshaft and crankshaft into the No. 2 and 4 cylinder crankcase half. **Apply engine oil to the crankshaft and camshaft bearings prior to installation.**
7. Install the O-ring and back-up ring into the No. 2 and 4 cylinder crankcase half.
8. Align crankshaft and camshaft gears, **Fig. 9.**
9. Apply liquid sealant to the mating surfaces of crankcase halves.
10. Install valve lifter clips 899804100 between the valve lifters in the No. 1 and 3 cylinders crankcase to prevent lifters from dropping off.
11. Position crankcase halves together and torque retaining bolts and nuts to 29-35 ft. lbs. for 10 mm thread sizes, 17-20 ft. lbs. for 8 mm thread sizes, and 3.3-4.0 ft. lbs. for 6 mm thread sizes. Follow sequence in **Fig. 10. Check that O-ring is installed correctly. On 4 wheel drive vehicles, install stiffener temporarily.**
12. Install camshaft plate onto crankcase with two lockwashers and bolts. Bend lockwashers to secure bolts.
13. To install pistons, proceed as follows:
    a. Apply oil to piston's circumference and cylinder walls.
    b. With cylinders No. 2 and 4 facing downward, rotate crankshaft until No. 2 connecting rod is positioned at BDC.
    c. Install No. 2 piston using tool 398744300 and a suitable soft faced hammer.
14. Install piston pin and circlip through front service hole after aligning the service hole, piston pin hole, and connecting rod small end using tool 399284300, **Fig. 11.**
15. Install circlip using long needle nosed pliers.
16. Install No. 4 piston, piston pin, and circlip into cylinder in same manner as described previously. **The service hole for cylinder No. 4 is on the flywheel housing side.**
17. Position crankcase so that cylinders No. 1 and 3 face downward. Install pistons for these cylinders in same manner as described previously.
18. Rotate crankshaft to check that piston pins are correctly installed.
19. Apply liquid gasket to the crankcase plugs. Install aluminum gasket and torque the plugs to 46-56 ft. lbs.
20. If strainer was removed, reinstall with new O-ring.

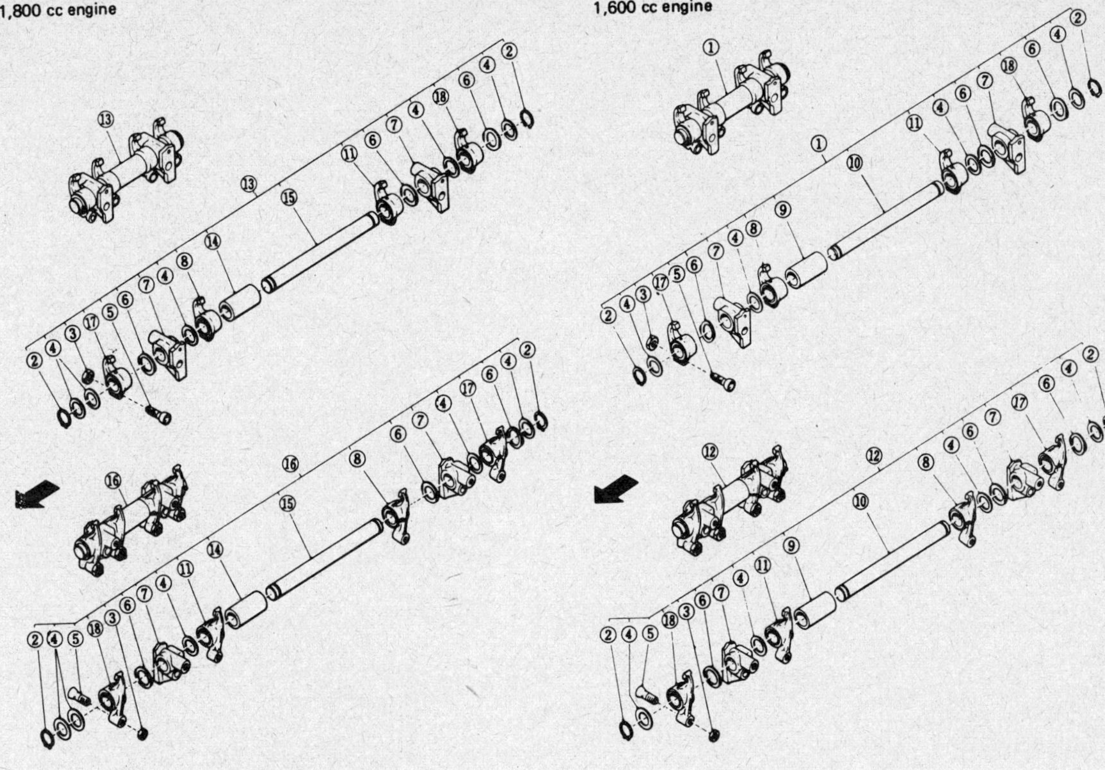

1	Valve rocker assembly (R.H.)	10	Valve rocker shaft
2	Snap ring	11	Valve rocker arm CP. 2
3	Nut	12	Valve rocker assembly (L.H.)
4	Washer	13	Valve rocker assembly (R.H.)
5	Valve rocker screw	14	Rocker shaft spacer
6	Rocker shaft spring washer	15	Valve rocker shaft
7	Rocker shaft supporter	16	Valve rocker assembly
8	Valve rocker arm CP	17	Valve rocker arm
9	Rocker shaft spacer	18	Valve rocker arm 2

Fig. 5 Valve rocker assembly. 4-97/1600cc & 1983–84 4-109/1800cc engines

21. Install oil strainer stay and torque retaining bolt to 17-20 ft. lbs.
22. Clean mating surfaces of cylinder head and crankcase. Apply head gasket sealant to both sides of new cylinder head gasket.
23. Install No. 2 and 4 cylinder head and align pushrods with valve lifters, **Fig. 12.**
24. Install valve rocker.
25. Apply oil to cylinder head stud and bolt threads and torque them in correct sequence in three steps, **Fig. 13.** The first torque step is 22 ft. lbs. The second step is 43 ft. lbs. The final step is 47 ft. lbs. Use wrench 499987006 to torque nuts No. 1 and 9.
26. Torque 6 mm bolts to 6.5-8.0 ft. lbs., after seven nuts and two bolts in sequence to their final specified torque.
27. Install No. 1 and 3 cylinder head using the same procedure as described previously.
28. If rear oil seal has been removed, press it back into the flywheel housing. **Apply oil to circumference prior to installation.**
29. Apply sealant to flywheel housing mating surfaces and torque retaining bolts to 14-20 ft. lbs.

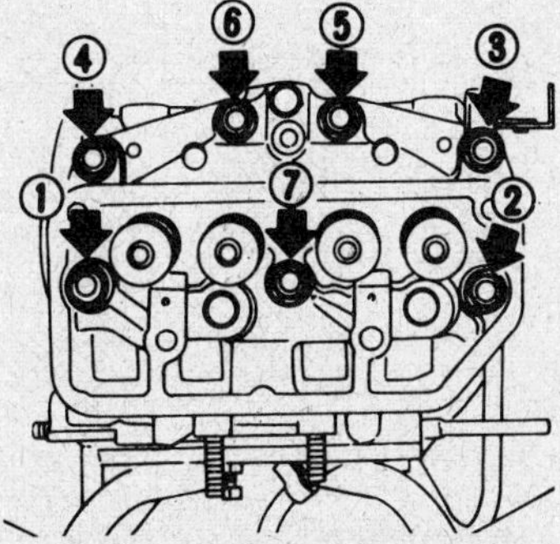

Fig. 6 Cylinder head loosening sequence. 4-97/1600cc & 1983–84 4-109/1800cc engines

30. Remove valve lifter retaining clips prior to installing oil pan.
31. Install crankcase oil pan, pan gasket, and transmission cover. Torque retaining bolts to 3.3-4.0 ft. lbs.
32. Install pitching stopper bracket and crankcase rear hanger to flywheel housing. **On 4 wheel drive vehicles, install fuel pipe stay and pitching stopper bracket to the flywheel housing.**
33. Apply sealant to flywheel or converter drive plate with back plate retaining bolt threads.
34. On manual transmission models, torque the flywheel retaining bolts to 30-33 ft. lbs.
35. On automatic transmission models, torque the drive plate to 36-39 ft. lbs. **The flywheel can only be installed in one position because retaining bolt holes are not positioned at equal intervals. When installing the back plate, align the mark on the back plate and the hole in the drive plate. Apply grease to the crankshaft needle bearing.**
36. On all models, position tool 399740100 into clutch disc and cover. Install disc and cover using tool to align disc and crankshaft. Position tool into crankshaft needle bearing and then remove the tool. **Position clutch cover so that "0" mark on flywheel and clutch cover are at least 120° apart.**
37. Install water pump, heater pipe and hoses as an assembly.
38. Install oil filter onto oil pump assembly.

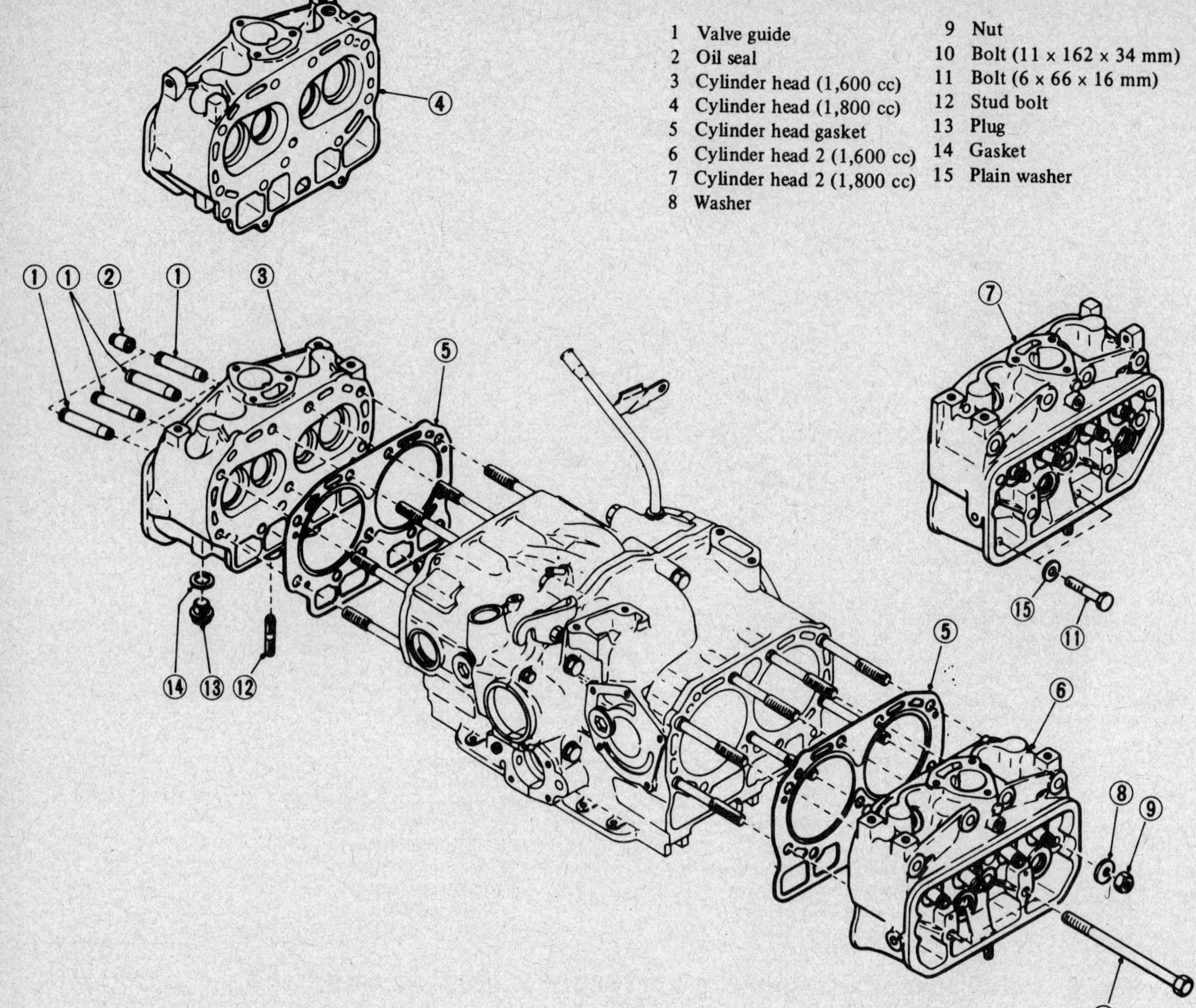

Fig. 7 Cylinder head assembly. 4-97/1600cc & 1983–84 4-109/1800cc engines

39. Install oil pump assembly O-ring and gasket between crankcase and pump assembly.
40. Install pump assembly and torque retaining bolts to 15.9-20.3 ft. lbs.
41. Install front oil seal using tool 499067000 and a suitable soft faced hammer.
42. Install front crankshaft pulley and torque retaining bolt to 47-54 ft. lbs. **To prevent the crankshaft from rotating during tightening, insert a suitable screwdriver into the timing hole and into a hole in either the flywheel or drive plate.**
43. Install oil filler duct, stay and gasket onto crankcase. **On 4 wheel drive models, install the oil filler duct, stiffener, and gasket on the crankcase.**
44. Tighten alternator bracket retaining bolts until spring washer is slightly deformed. Back off retaining bolts, then torque to 9-14 ft. lbs.
45. To adjust valve clearances, proceed as follows:
    a. Position piston into cylinder to be checked at TDC on compression stroke.
    b. Insert feeler gauge between valve stem and rocker arm to measure clearance.
    c. Loosen locknuts and rotate adjustment screw to obtain specified valve clearance. **Adjust the clearances when the engine is cold. If the adjustment is made during the first service interval, retorque the cylinder head retaining nuts and bolts prior to adjustment.**
46. Install valve rocker covers, gaskets, and seal washers. Torque retaining bolts to 2.2-2.9 ft. lbs.
47. Torque spark plugs to specified torque value.
48. To install intake manifold proceed as follows:
    a. Install intake manifold assembly, intake manifold gasket, air cleaner bracket, fuel hose bracket, and EGR pipe.
    b. Connect water bypass hoses, oil pressure switch or gauge electrical connections, and PCV hose to the rocker cover. **Check that the electronic control unit ground is connected to left rear bolt.**
49. Install EGR pipes into cylinder heads.
50. Reverse remaining procedure to complete installation.

1985–87 4-109/1800cc ENGINE

Disassembly

1. Perform steps 1 through 9 as outlined for "4-97/1600cc & 1983-84 4-109/1800cc Engines."
2. Remove water pump pulley and pulley cover.
3. Remove dipstick and dipstick tube, **Fig. 14.**
4. Remove timing belt cover plate (Turbo models), then the left and right

Thread size	Torque
10 mm	39 - 47 N·m (4.0 - 4.8 kg-m, 29 - 35 ft-lb)
8 mm	23 - 26 N·m (2.3 - 2.7 kg-m, 17 - 20 ft-lb)
6 mm	4.4 - 5.4 N·m (0.45 - 0.55 kg-m, 3.3 - 4.0 ft-lb)

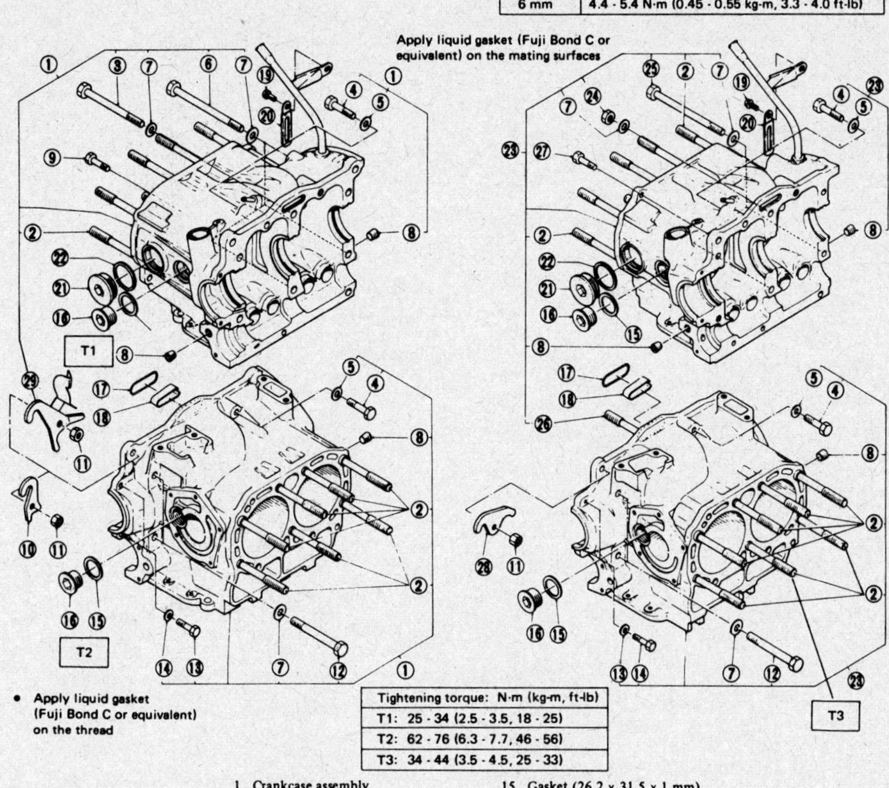

Tightening torque: N·m (kg-m, ft-lb)
T1: 25 - 34 (2.5 - 3.5, 18 - 25)
T2: 62 - 76 (6.3 - 7.7, 46 - 56)
T3: 34 - 44 (3.5 - 4.5, 25 - 33)

1 Crankcase assembly
2 Stud bolt
3 Bolt (10 x 108 x 28 mm)
4 Bolt
5 Washer
6 Bolt (10 x 145 x 28 mm)
7 Washer (10.5 x 18 x 2 mm)
8 Main gallery plug
9 Bolt
10 Crankcase front hanger (Hitachi carburetor)
11 Nut
12 Bolt (10 x 70 x 28 mm)
13 Bolt
14 Washer
15 Gasket (26.2 x 31.5 x 1 mm)
16 Crankcase plug
17 Crankcase O-ring
18 Back up ring
19 Bolt & washer (6 x 13 x 13 mm)
20 Clip
21 Crankcase plug
22 Gasket (36.2 x 44 x 1 mm)
23 Crankcase assembly
24 Nut (10 x 8 mm)
25 Bolt (10 x 135 x 28 mm)
26 Stud bolt (10 x 120 x 26 mm)
27 Bolt
28 Crankcase front hanger
29 Crankcase front hanger (C-W carburetor)

Fig. 8 Crankcase assembly. 4-97/1600cc & 1983–84 4-109/1800cc engines

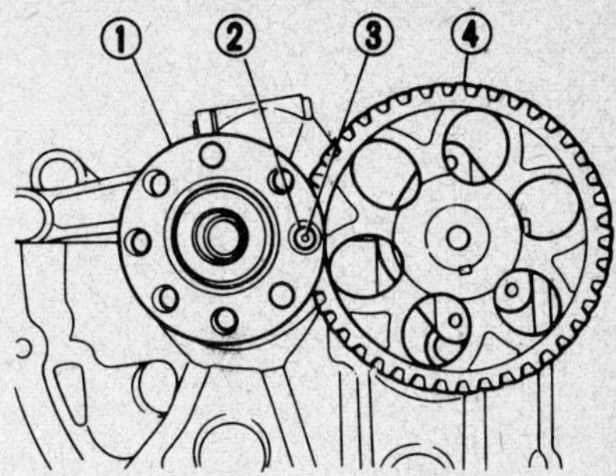

1 Crankshaft gear
2 Large chamfer
3 Punch
4 Camshaft gear

Fig. 9 Aligning camshaft & crankshaft gears. 4-97/1600cc & 1983–84 4-109/1800cc engines

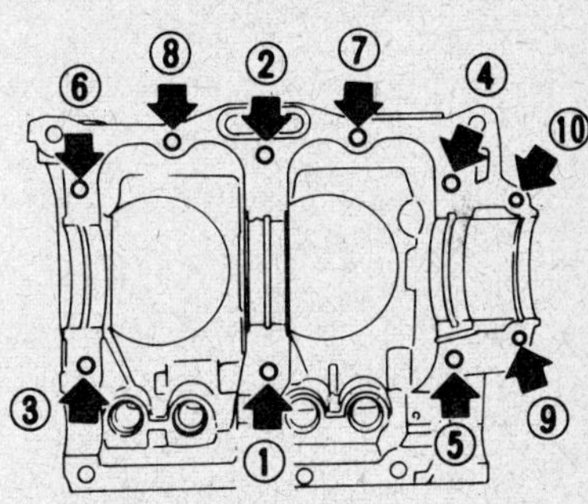

Fig. 10 Crankcase bolt tightening sequence

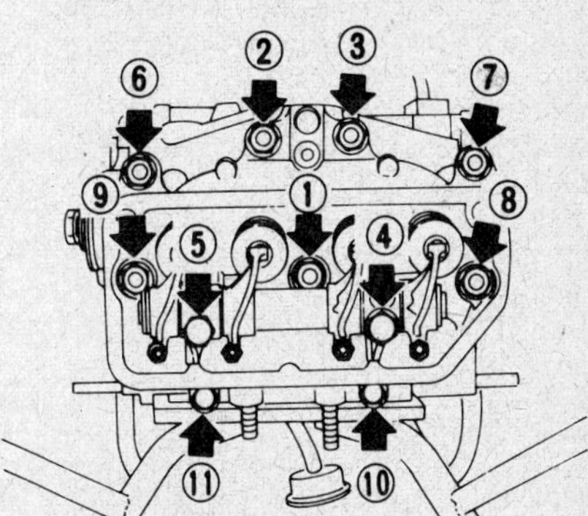

Fig. 13 Cylinder head tightening sequence. 4-97/1600cc & 1983–84 4-109/1800cc engines

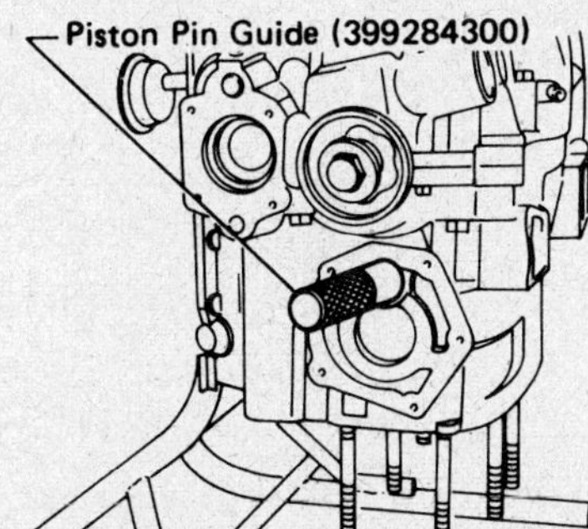

Fig. 11 Service hole location & piston pin guide tool

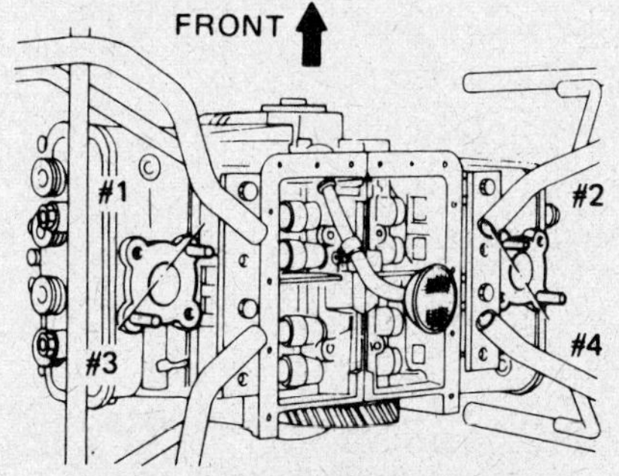

Fig. 12 Cylinder head installation position. 4-97/1600cc & 4-109/1800cc engines

front timing belt covers, **Fig. 15.**

5. Loosen bolts securing timing belt tensioner to No. 1 cylinder, rotate tensioner to fully released position, then retighten bolts, **Fig. 16.**
6. Mark rotational direction, then remove timing belt.
7. Loosen bolts securing tensioner 2 to No. 2 cylinder, rotate tensioner to fully relaxed position using wrench 499007000 or equivalent, then retighten bolts.
8. Remove first crankshaft sprocket.
9. Mark rotational direction of remaining belt, then remove belt and second crankshaft sprocket.
10. Remove both belt tensioner assemblies along with tensioner springs.
11. Secure camshaft sprockets with suitable wrench, then remove sprocket retaining bolts and the sprockets.
12. Remove remaining timing belt covers.
13. Remove water pump, hose and pipe as an assembly.
14. Align oil pump sprocket notch with retaining bolt, then remove bolts and pump rotor assembly from cylinder block.
15. Remove clutch assembly and flywheel or automatic transmission flex plate, as equipped, then the flywheel housing.
16. Remove spark plugs, camshaft cov-

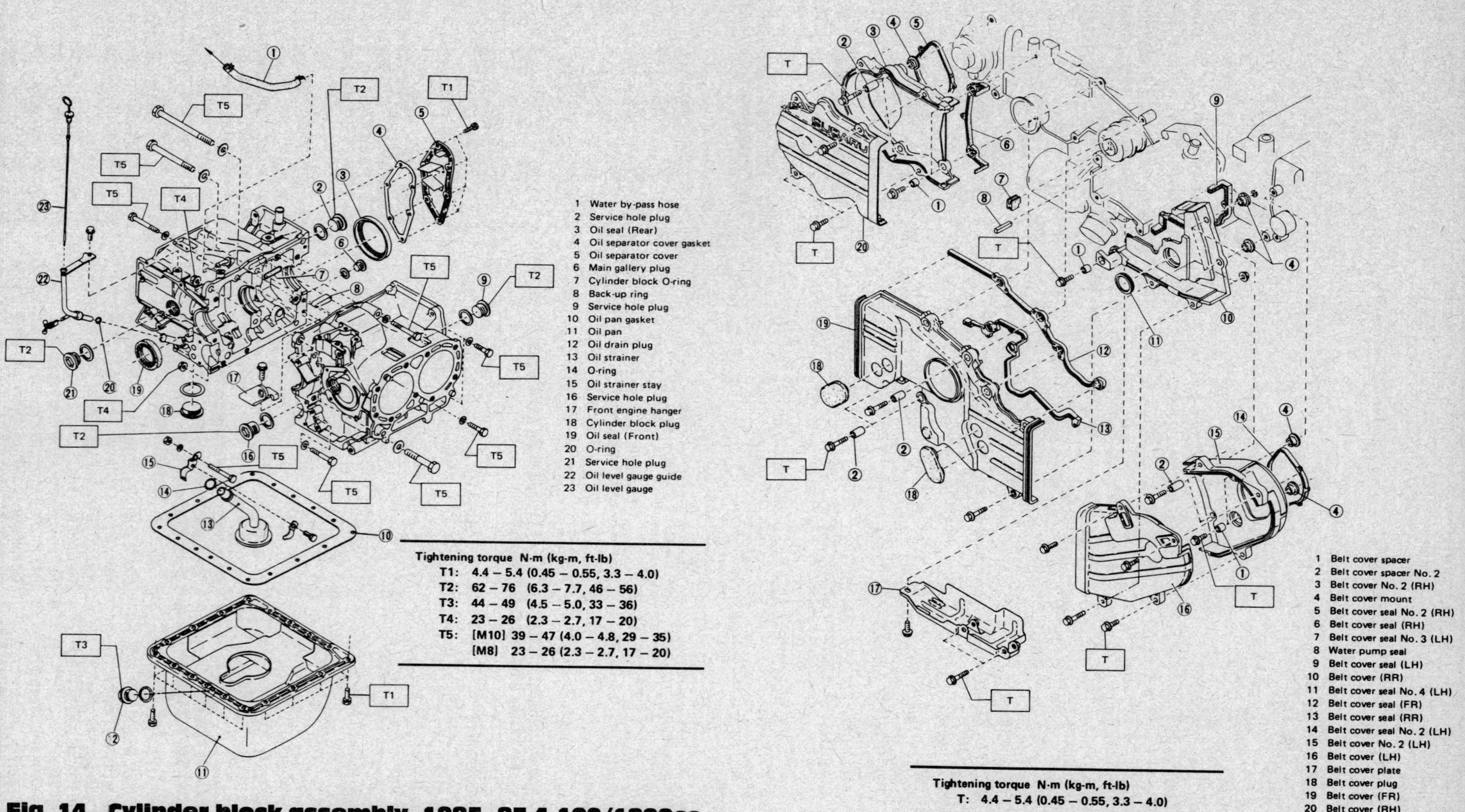

1 Water by-pass hose
2 Service hole plug
3 Oil seal (Rear)
4 Oil separator cover gasket
5 Oil separator cover
6 Main gallery plug
7 Cylinder block O-ring
8 Back-up ring
9 Service hole plug
10 Oil pan gasket
11 Oil pan
12 Oil drain plug
13 Oil strainer
14 O-ring
15 Oil strainer stay
16 Service hole plug
17 Front engine hanger
18 Cylinder block plug
19 Oil seal (Front)
20 O-ring
21 Service hole plug
22 Oil level gauge guide
23 Oil level gauge

Tightening torque N·m (kg-m, ft-lb)

T1: 4.4 – 5.4 (0.45 – 0.55, 3.3 – 4.0)
T2: 62 – 76 (6.3 – 7.7, 46 – 56)
T3: 44 – 49 (4.5 – 5.0, 33 – 36)
T4: 23 – 26 (2.3 – 2.7, 17 – 20)
T5: [M10] 39 – 47 (4.0 – 4.8, 29 – 35)
[M8] 23 – 26 (2.3 – 2.7, 17 – 20)

Fig. 14 Cylinder block assembly. 1985–87 4-109/1800cc engine

1 Belt cover spacer
2 Belt cover spacer No. 2
3 Belt cover No. 2 (RH)
4 Belt cover mount
5 Belt cover seal No. 2 (RH)
6 Belt cover seal (RH)
7 Belt cover seal No. 3 (LH)
8 Water pump seal
9 Belt cover seal (LH)
10 Belt cover (RR)
11 Belt cover seal No. 4 (LH)
12 Belt cover seal (FR)
13 Belt cover seal (RR)
14 Belt cover seal No. 2 (LH)
15 Belt cover No. 2 (LH)
16 Belt cover (LH)
17 Belt cover plate
18 Belt cover plug
19 Belt cover (FR)
20 Belt cover (RH)

Tightening torque N·m (kg-m, ft-lb)

T: 4.4 – 5.4 (0.45 – 0.55, 3.3 – 4.0)

Fig. 15 Timing belt cover assembly. 1985–87 4-109/1800cc engine

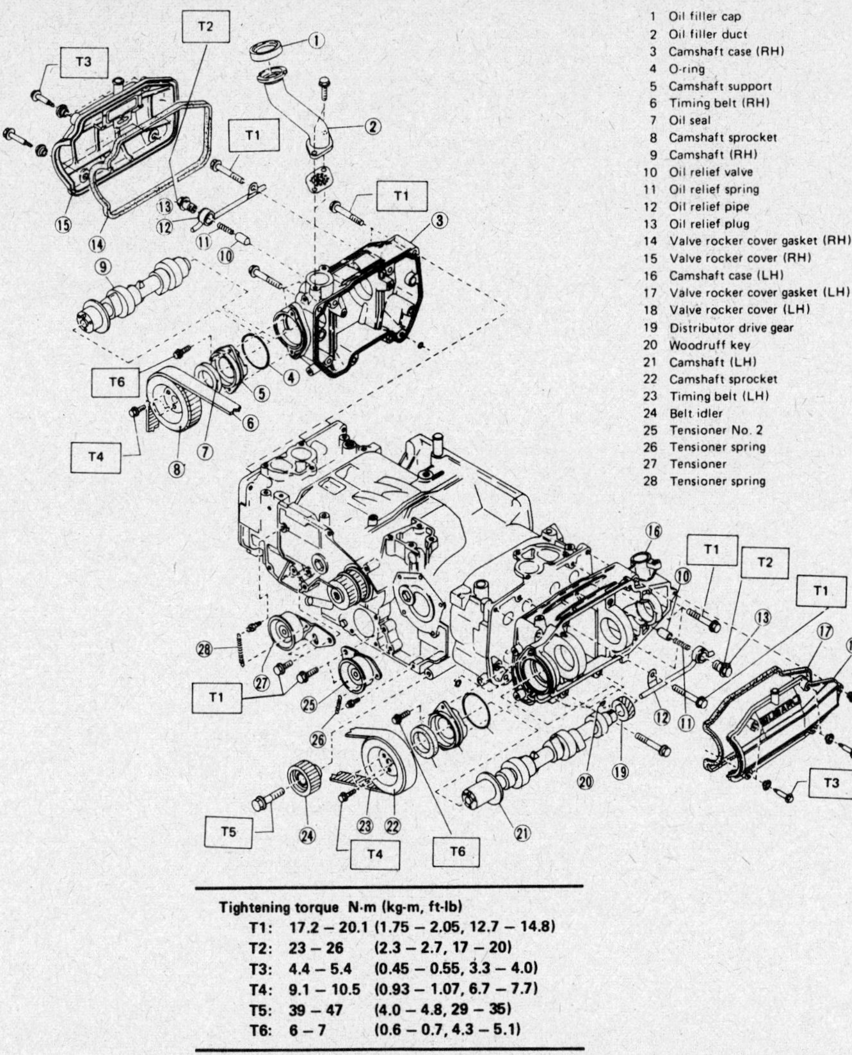

Tightening torque N·m (kg-m, ft-lb)

T1:	17.2 – 20.1	(1.75 – 2.05, 12.7 – 14.8)
T2:	23 – 26	(2.3 – 2.7, 17 – 20)
T3:	4.4 – 5.4	(0.45 – 0.55, 3.3 – 4.0)
T4:	9.1 – 10.5	(0.93 – 1.07, 6.7 – 7.7)
T5:	39 – 47	(4.0 – 4.8, 29 – 35)
T6:	6 – 7	(0.6 – 0.7, 4.3 – 5.1)

Fig. 16 Camshaft & belt drive installation. 1985–87 4-109/1800cc engine

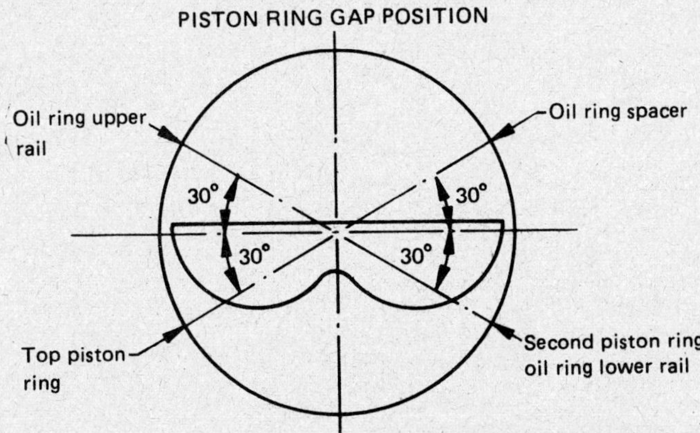

Fig. 17 Piston ring installation. 1985–87 4-109/1800cc engine

ers and cover gaskets.

17. Evenly loosen bolts securing camshaft cases, then remove case, camshaft support and camshaft assemblies.
18. Remove rocker arms and hydraulic lifters, keeping components in proper order for assembly. **Do not store lifters on their sides; keep them upright.**
19. On turbocharged models, remove turbocharger cooling pipe, union and gasket from cylinder head.
20. Remove cylinder head retaining bolts and the cylinder heads.
21. Remove service access plugs from cylinder block, then rotate crankshaft to bring Nos. 1 and 2 pistons to BDC.
22. Remove piston pin retainers through service openings, then withdraw piston pins using suitable remover.
23. Rotate crankshaft to position Nos. 3 and 4 pistons at BDC, then remove piston pin retainers and piston pins.
24. Remove all cylinder block retaining bolts except 10 mm bolt under center crankshaft journal, and loosen the 10 mm bolt until it can be turned by hand.
25. Position cylinder block assembly with cylinders No. 3 and 4 facing up, then separate left and right halves of block, **Fig. 14.**
26. Remove coolant passage O-ring and back-up ring from LH cylinder block, and front and rear oil seals from crankshaft.
27. Remove crankshaft and connecting rod assembly.
28. Mark and remove pistons from cylinder block halves, and mate pistons with respective pins. **Keep all components in order to ensure proper assembly. Components that are to be reused should be installed in original position.**
29. Remove main bearings from crankcase halves.
30. Remove oil relief plug, oil relief pipe and spring and the oil relief valve from camshaft case.

Assembly

Ensure all components are clean and free from foreign material, and that oil passages are clear. Coat all friction surfaces with oil or suitable assembly lubricant, and coat seal lips with grease prior to assembly. Replace all gaskets, seals and damaged fasteners during assembly. Components that are to be reused should be installed in original position.

1. Seat bearings in connecting rods and rod caps, then install connecting rods on crankshaft noting the following:
   a. Ensure connecting rod and cap matching marks are aligned, and install connecting rod assemblies with crescent shaped mark facing forward.
   b. Lubricate connecting rod bolt threads and ensure bolts are properly seated in cap and that caps are fully seated against connecting rods.
   c. Evenly tighten connecting rod nuts until specified torque value is obtained.
2. Install piston rings, staggering ring and oil expander gaps as shown in **Fig. 17. Install compression rings with "N" or "R" mark facing up.**
3. Install pin retainer in each piston as shown in **Fig. 18.**
4. Install new valve guide oil seals, valves, springs and retainers, noting the following:
   a. Coat valve stems with oil prior to installation and take care not to damage seal lips when inserting valves.
   b. Install valve springs with close-coiled end toward cylinder head.
   c. After releasing spring tension

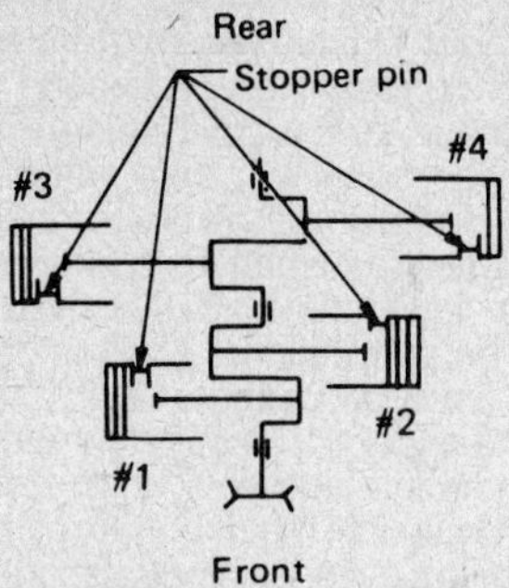

Fig. 18 Piston pin retainer installation. 1985–87 4-109/1800cc engine

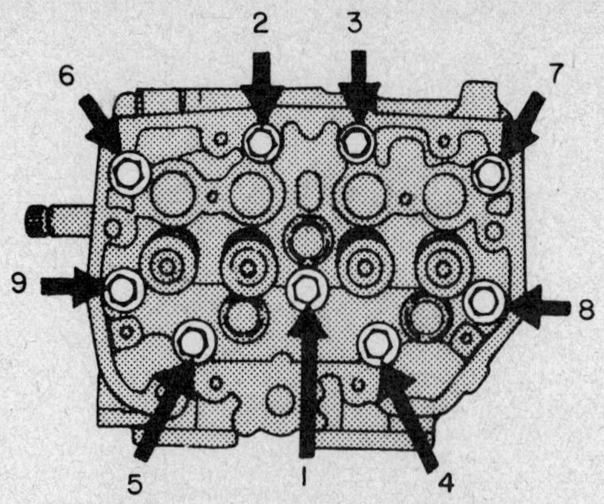

Fig. 19 Cylinder head bolt tightening sequence. 1985–87 4-109/1800cc engine

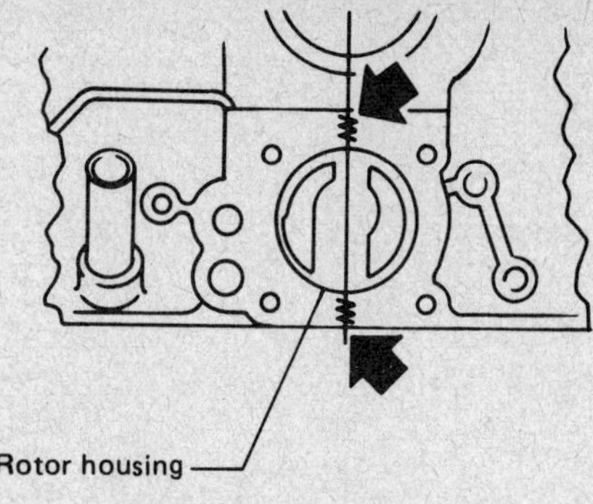

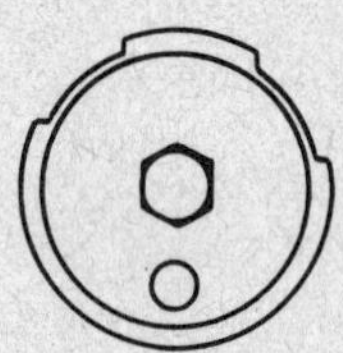

Fig. 20 Oil pump installation. 1985–87 4-109/1800cc engine

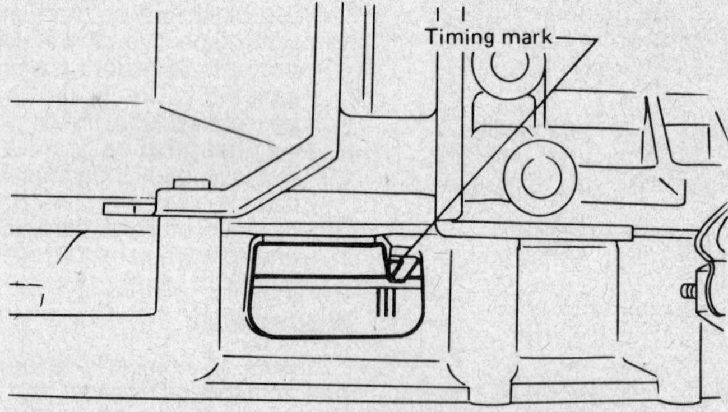

Fig. 21 Flywheel timing mark alignment. 1985–87 4-109/1800cc engine

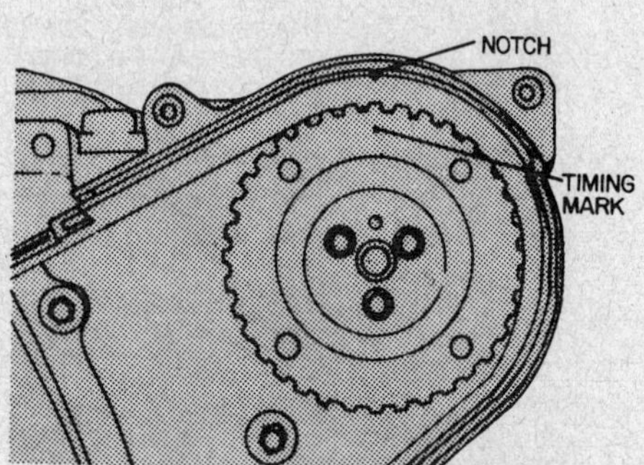

Fig. 22 Camshaft timing mark alignment. 1985–87 4-109/1800cc engine

against valve key, tap valve stem with suitable mallet to ensure keys are seated in retainer and valve stem grooves.

5. Press new seals into camshaft support plates and install new O-rings.
6. Install oil pressure relief valve, spring, pipe and plug, and torque plug to 17-20 ft. lbs.
7. Install woodruff key and press on distributor drive gear, if removed, securing camshaft in suitable holder. **When pressing on distributor drive gear, do not support camshaft on end, as shaft may be distorted.**
8. Insert camshafts into cases, install support plate, seal and O-ring assemblies, **Fig. 15,** then torque support plate bolts to 6.7-7.7 ft. lbs.
9. Mount cylinder block halves on stands 498027000 or equivalent, installing bolts marked "R" into cylinder 1 and 3 section and bolts marked "L" into cylinder 2 and 4 section.
10. Seat main bearings into cylinder block webs, ensuring that tangs are properly engaged and that oil holes are properly aligned.
11. Install coolant passage O-ring and support ring in groove in LH cylinder block.
12. Install crankshaft assembly into LH cylinder block.
13. Apply liquid gasket compound Three-bond 1215 or equivalent to cylinder block mating surfaces, then align connecting rods and install RH cylinder block assembly, ensuring that O-ring remains in place.
14. Tighten cylinder block bolts evenly, then lay block down and torque 8 mm bolts to 17-20 ft. lbs. and 10 mm bolts to 29-35 ft. lbs. in sequence shown in **Fig. 10.**
15. Position cylinder block with cylinders 3 and 4 facing downward and rotate crankshaft until Nos. 1 and 2 connecting rods are at BDC. **Take care not to mar cylinder walls when positioning connecting rods.**
16. Coat pistons and cylinder walls with assembly lubricant, install pistons No. 1 and 2, align pin bores in pistons and connecting rods using pin guide 399284300 or equivalent, **Fig. 11,** piston pins and retainers.
17. Invert cylinder block assembly, rotate crankshaft to position Nos. 3 and 4 connecting rods, then install Nos. 3 and 4 pistons, pins and retainers as outlined previously.
18. Apply Fuji-bond C sealer or equivalent to service access plugs, install new aluminum sealing gaskets and access plugs, and torque plugs to 46-56 ft. lbs.
19. Install new cylinder head gaskets and the cylinder heads, dip head bolts in oil and install all bolts hand tight.
20. Torque cylinder head bolts to specifications in 3 steps, following sequence shown in **Fig. 19.**
21. On turbocharged models, install turbocharger coolant pipe and union along with new gasket, and torque bolts securing pipe to cylinder head to 15.6-17.7 ft. lbs.
22. On all models, secure oil strainer to cylinder block with new retaining clips.
23. Install oil pan and clutch housing cover with gasket positioned in between, and torque retaining bolts to 4 ft. lbs.
24. Press rear crankshaft seal into cylinder block using driver 499587000 or equivalent, then install flywheel housing and torque bolts to 25-30 ft. lbs.
25. Install pitch stopper bracket on cylin-

	Belt tension	Torque to cam sprocket
When both timing belt and head gasket are new	147 – 245 N (15 – 25 kg, 33 – 55 lb)	24 – 25 N·m (2.4 – 2.6 kg-m, 17 – 19 ft-lb)
Other than the above	108 – 206 N (11 – 21 kg, 24 – 46 lb)	14 – 16 N·m (1.4 – 1.6 kg-m, 10 – 12 ft-lb)

Fig. 23 Timing belt tension specifications. 1985–87 4-109/1800cc engine

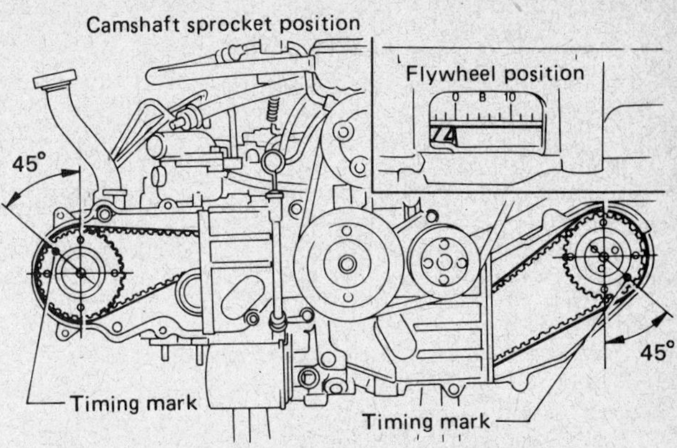

Fig. 24 Timing mark alignment for distributor installation. 1985–87 4-109/1800cc engine

der block and mount clip No. 3 on bracket.

26. On turbocharged models, install oil separator cover and new gasket on RH cylinder block and torque bolts to 4 ft. lbs.
27. Install flywheel or auto. trans. flex plate and reinforcement and torque bolts to specifications.
28. On manual trans. models, install clutch and pressure plate assembly, ensuring that "0" markings on flywheel and pressure plate are spaced 180 degrees apart, insert suitable alignment tool and evenly torque pressure plate bolts to 12 ft. lbs.
29. On all models, press seal into water pump, then install water pump along with new gasket.
30. Ensure excess sealer is removed from oil pump rotor housing in cylinder block, then install oil pump as follows:
    a. Apply small amount of Three-bond 1215 sealer or equivalent to split line in housing as shown by arrows in **Fig. 20.**
    b. Liberally coat housing with oil, then install outer rotor into housing in direction shown in **Fig. 20.**
    c. Position oil pump pulley as shown in **Fig. 20,** then install pulley and front housing and ensure pulley rotates smoothly.
    d. Install pressure switch or pressure gauge on oil pump, ensure gauge lead is properly routed along side of Nos. 1 and 3 cylinders and torque to 16-20 ft. lbs.
31. Install belt cover seal LH No. 3 on cylinder block, **Fig. 15.**
32. Press new front crankshaft seal into block using suitable driver.
33. Insert hydraulic lifters into proper bores, coat rocker arms with grease to aid retention, then mount rocker arms over lifters and valve stems.
34. Rotate crankshaft until timing mark on flywheel is aligned with pointer on housing and orient each camshaft pin so that pin faces up when assembly is installed on engine.
35. Install O-ring, if used and apply Three-bond sealer 1215 or equivalent to camshaft housing sealing groove.
36. Install camshaft and housing assemblies, then evenly torque retaining bolts to 12.7-14.8 ft. lbs.
37. Install camshaft cover gaskets and covers, then evenly torque retaining bolts to 3.1-4.1 ft. lbs.
38. Install belt cover LH seal, belt cover No. 4 LH seal and belt cover mount on cover RR, then mount assembly on cylinder block ensuring that spacers are properly positioned, **Fig. 15,** and torque bolts to 4 ft. lbs.
39. Install belt cover No. 2 LH seal and mount on belt cover No. 2 LH, then mount assembly on cylinder block and camshaft housing, **Fig. 15,** and torque bolts to 4 ft. lbs.
40. Install belt cover RH seal, No. 2 RH seal and mount on belt cover No. 2 RH, then mount assembly on cylinder head and camshaft cover, **Fig. 15,** and torque bolts to 4 ft. lbs.
41. Install camshaft sprockets and retaining bolts, hold position of sprocket with suitable wrench, then evenly torque retaining bolts to 7-8 ft. lbs. in several steps.
42. Install tensioner, **Fig. 16,** as follows:
    a. Connect tensioner spring to tensioner and mount assembly on RH cylinder block, temporarily hand tightening bolts.
    b. Connect tensioner spring to mounting stud, tighten inner tensioner mounting bolt, then loosen bolt 1/2 turn.
    c. Push tensioner down to stop, then tighten inner tensioner mounting bolt to secure position.
43. Install tensioner No. 2, **Fig. 16,** as follows:
    a. Connect tensioner spring to tensioner and mount assembly on LH cylinder block, temporarily hand tightening bolts.
    b. Connect tensioner spring to mounting stud, tighten upper tensioner mounting bolt, then loosen bolt 1/2 turn.
    c. Raise tensioner to stop using suitable lever, then tighten lower tensioner mounting bolt to secure position.
44. Install belt idler on cylinder block taking care not to damage seal, and torque bolts to 29-35 ft. lbs.
45. Install timing belt No. 2, **Fig. 16,** as follows:
    a. Install sprocket No. 2 on crankshaft.
    b. Ensure center mark on flywheel is aligned with housing pointer, **Fig. 21,** and that timing mark on camshaft sprocket is aligned with notch in belt cover, **Fig. 22.**
    c. Route timing belt No. 2 over crankshaft sprocket, oil pump sprocket, belt idler and camshaft sprocket in order, noting belt rotation direction and avoiding downward slackening of belt.
    d. Loosen lower mounting bolt on tensioner No. 2, 1/2 turn, and press in on belt to ensure smooth movement of belt tensioner.
    e. Apply torque shown in **Fig. 23** to camshaft sprocket in counterclockwise direction using belt tension wrench 499437000.
    f. While holding tension on camshaft sprocket, temporarily tighten tensioner No. 2 mounting bolts to secure position. **Applying torque to camshaft sprocket sets belt tension to specifications. Care must be taken not to apply excessive force to sprocket, as excessive tension will reduce belt life.**
    g. Torque tensioner No. 2 mounting bolts to 13-15 ft. lbs., tightening lower mounting bolt first.
    h. Ensure camshaft and flywheel timing marks are still properly aligned, **Figs. 21 and 22.**
46. Install remaining timing belt as follows:
    a. Rotate crankshaft 1 revolution in clockwise direction from position where No. 2 belt was installed, realigning center flywheel timing mark with pointer, **Fig. 21.**
    b. Install sprocket on crankshaft and align timing mark on camshaft sprocket with notch in belt cover.
    c. Install timing belt over crankshaft and camshaft sprockets, noting direction of rotation and avoiding slack on upper run of belt.
    d. Loosen inner bolt securing tensioner No. 1, 1/2 turn, pushing on belt to ensure smooth movement of tensioner.
    e. Apply torque shown in **Fig. 23** to camshaft sprocket in counter-

clockwise direction, using belt tension wrench 499437000.
   f. While holding tension on sprocket, temporarily tighten tensioner mounting bolts to secure position.
   g. Torque tensioner bolts to 13-15 ft. lbs., tightening outer bolt first.
   h. Ensure sprocket and flywheel timing marks are still aligned.
47. Install seals and plug on belt cover FR, **Fig. 15,** then mount belt cover on cylinder block.
48. Install crankshaft pulley and torque bolt to specifications.
49. Install water pump pulley and cover and temporarily tighten bolts.
50. Reverse remaining procedure to complete assembly, and install distributor as follows:
   a. Rotate crankshaft until No. 1 piston is at TDC on compression stroke with timing marks aligned as shown in **Fig. 24.**
   b. Align matching marks on distributor drive gear and housing to position distributor in firing position for No. 1 cylinder.
   c. Insert distributor and ensure rotor contact points toward No. 1 cylinder contact in cap.

FUEL PUMP

REPLACE

CARBURETED ENGINE

1. Disconnect fuel pump electrical connectors.
2. Remove fuel pump bracket with fuel pump from suspension bracket reinforcement.
3. Remove pump from bracket, then disconnect fuel delivery hoses from fuel pump.

FUEL INJECTED ENGINE

1. Relieve fuel system pressure as follows:
   a. Disconnect fuel pump electrical connector.
   b. Crank engine for approximately 5 seconds. If engine starts, let engine run until it stops.
2. Raise and support vehicle.
3. Clamp portion of hose connecting pipe and pump, to prevent fuel from flowing out.
4. Loosen hose clamp, then disconnect hose.
5. Remove pump bracket attaching bolts, then remove pump together with pump damper.

TURBOCHARGER

The turbocharger is an exhaust driven device which compresses the air charge being delivered to the engine through the intake system. The turbocharger increases engine power on a demand basis. Exhaust gases flow through a turbine which is connected through a shaft to the impeller wheel (compressor). During normal operation, the turbine does not rotate fast enough to boost air pressure. As turbine speed increases, the air is compressed allowing a denser mixture to enter the combustion chambers in turn developing more engine power during the combustion process. Intake manifold pressure (boost pressure) is controlled by a wastegate valve which is used to bypass a portion of the exhaust gasses around the turbine wheel at a predetermined point in the cycle, limiting boost pressure.

CLUTCH & MANUAL TRANSMISSION SECTION

INDEX

HILL HOLDER

ADJUST

For Hill holder adjustments, refer to Disc Brakes Section.

CLUTCH PEDAL

ADJUST

1. Remove clutch fork return spring.
2. Turn adjusting nut to obtain an endplay of .08-.12 inch (2-3 mm) on 2 wheel drive non-turbo models and .12-.16 inch (3-4 mm) on 4 wheel drive and 2 wheel drive models with turbo, at fork end, **Fig. 1. When performing adjustment, use care not to twist clutch cable.**
3. Check to ensure clutch release lever full stroke measures 1.004-1.063 inch (25.5-27.0 mm) on 1985-87 4 wheel drive models and 1986-87 2 wheel drive turbo models, or .67-.71 inch (17-18 mm) on all other models.

CLUTCH

REPLACE

1. Remove transmission as described under "Transmission, Replace."
2. Remove six attaching bolts from pressure plate, then remove pressure plate and clutch disc.
3. When installing, apply light coat of grease to transmission main driveshaft spline.
4. Install clutch disc guide into clutch disc. Then install on flywheel by inserting end of guide into needle bearing.
5. Install pressure plate and to torque attaching bolts to 12 ft. lbs. (1.6 kg-m). **Clutch pressure plate should be installed so there is a gap of 120° or more between "O" marks on flywheel and pressure plate, to insure best balance.**
6. Remove clutch disc guide and reinstall transmission.

TRANSMISSION

REPLACE

1983–84 MODELS

1. Open hood, then remove spare tire and support.
2. Disconnect battery ground cable.
3. Disconnect clutch cable return spring and clutch cable at release fork, then remove rubber boot.
4. Disconnect speedometer from transmission.
5. Disconnect wiring from back-up light switch, vehicle body ground cable and starter motor harness.
6. Remove starter motor and battery cable and position on bulkhead.
7. Remove upper bolts attaching transmission to engine, then loosen lower transmission to engine attaching nuts.
8. Loosen nut which retains pitching stopper to transmission side approximately 10 mm and tighten nut on en-

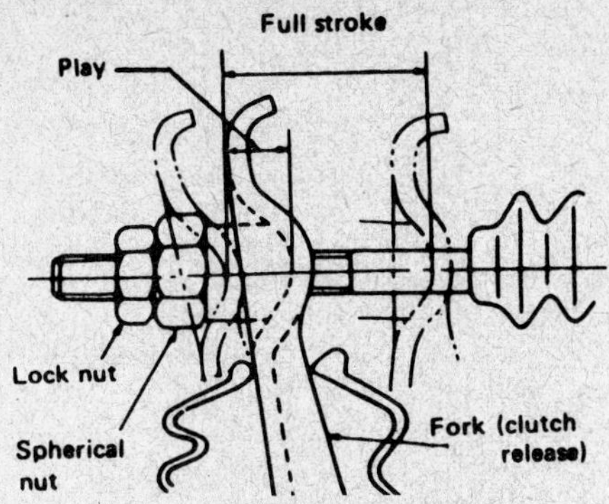

Fig. 1 Clutch pedal adjustments

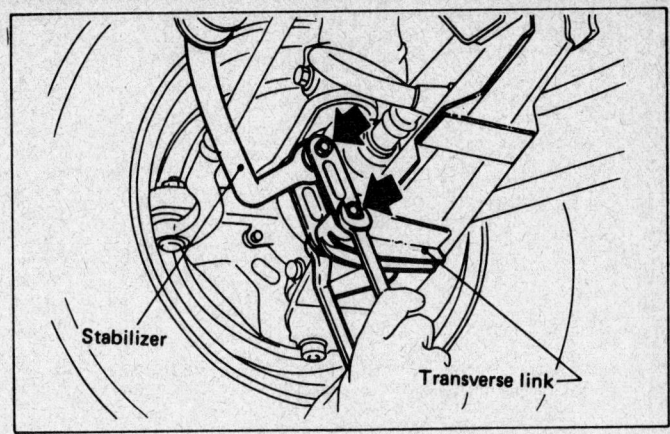

Stabilizer
Transverse link

Fig. 2 Stabilizer bar removal

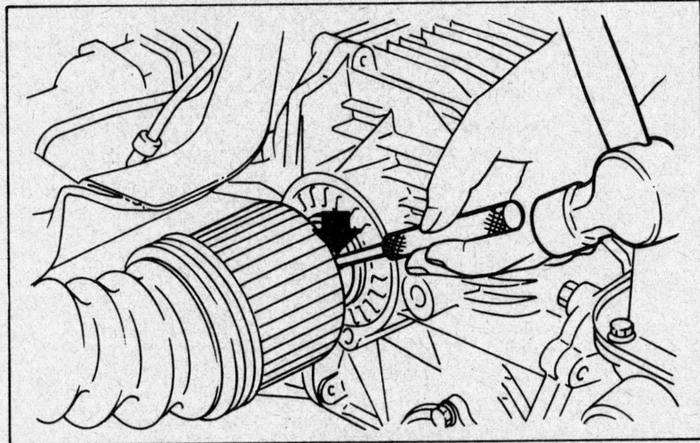

Fig. 3 Spring pin removal

gine side by an equal amount. Slightly tilt engine rearward to facilitate transmission removal. **Do not tighten engine pitching stopper nut more than 10 mm.**

9. On 4 wheel drive dual range models:
   a. Separate the range selector from gear shift lever by removing hand brake tray and cover. Place the range selector in 4 wheel drive position and remove rod cover.
   b. Remove nut from rod connecting range and gear shift lever.
10. Raise front of vehicle and position safety stands at jack pads located in front of side sills.
11. Remove oxygen sensor and front exhaust pipe from vehicle.
12. On 4 wheel drive models, remove transmission cover, then remove bolts that attach propeller to differential flange. **When removing propeller shaft, use care not to damage oil seal. Also, cap open end of driveshaft to prevent oil spillage.**
13. On models less 4 wheel drive, remove exhaust cover, then remove bolts attaching gearshift mechanism to transmission.
14. On models with 4 wheel drive, remove bolts attaching 4 wheel drive selector system and gear shift mechanism to transmission.
15. Remove stabilizer bar, then remove bolts that attach left and right transverse links to front crossmember and lower transverse links.
16. Drive left and right spring pins from axle shaft. Spring pins should be discarded and new spring pins installed during assembly.
17. Push wheels outward to separate axle shaft from driveshaft.
18. Remove clamp on left hand side of parking brake cable to facilitate removal of center crossmember.
19. Remove nuts attaching left and right transmission mount insulators.
20. Support transmission using a suitable jack, then remove crossmember.
21. Remove two bolts attaching transmission to engine and move transmission away from engine just enough for mainshaft to clear engine, then carefully lower transmission from vehicle.
22. Reverse procedure to install.

1985–87 MODELS

1. Open hood, then remove spare tire and support.
2. Disconnect battery ground cable.
3. Remove hill-holder cable, locknut and clips, if equipped.
4. Remove clutch cable, return spring, locknut, adjusting nut and clips.
5. On carbureted models, remove air duct.
6. Disconnect speedometer cable from transmission.
7. Disconnect wiring from transmission and starter, then remove starter.
8. On models equipped with turbocharger, proceed as follows:
   a. Remove heat shield cover from transmission side and turbocharger side.
   b. Remove center exhaust pipe heat shields.
   c. Raise and support vehicle, then remove center exhaust pipe. Lower vehicle.
9. Remove engine-to-transmission mounting nut and bolt from right side.
10. On models less turbocharger, raise and support vehicle, then disconnect front exhaust pipe from engine by removing all nuts except one.
11. Disconnect front exhaust pipe from rear exhaust pipe.
12. On 4 wheel drive models, disconnect rear exhaust pipe from muffler.
13. On models less turbocharger, disconnect front exhaust pipe from hanger bracket, then remove nut remaining from step 10.
14. On all models, remove rigid crossmember.
15. On 4 wheel drive models, remove propeller shaft. **Plug opening at rear extension to prevent oil from flowing out.**
16. On all models, remove gear shift system as follows:
   a. Remove spring.
   b. Disconnect rod from transmission.
   c. Disconnect stay from transmission.
17. Loosen nut and bolt on lower side of plate, **Fig. 2,** then remove stabilizer from transverse link.
18. Remove bolt attaching transverse link to front crossmember on each side.
19. Remove hand brake cable bracket from transverse link, nut and bolt, then lower transverse link.
20. Using a suitable drift and hammer, remove spring pin and separate axle shaft from drive shaft on each side, **Fig. 3.**
21. Remove engine-to-transmission attaching nuts, then position a suitable transmission jack under transmission.
22. Remove rear rubber cushion attaching nuts, then rear and rigid crossmembers.
23. Remove transmission. **Move transmission jack toward rear until mainshaft is withdrawn from clutch cover.**
24. Reverse procedure to install.

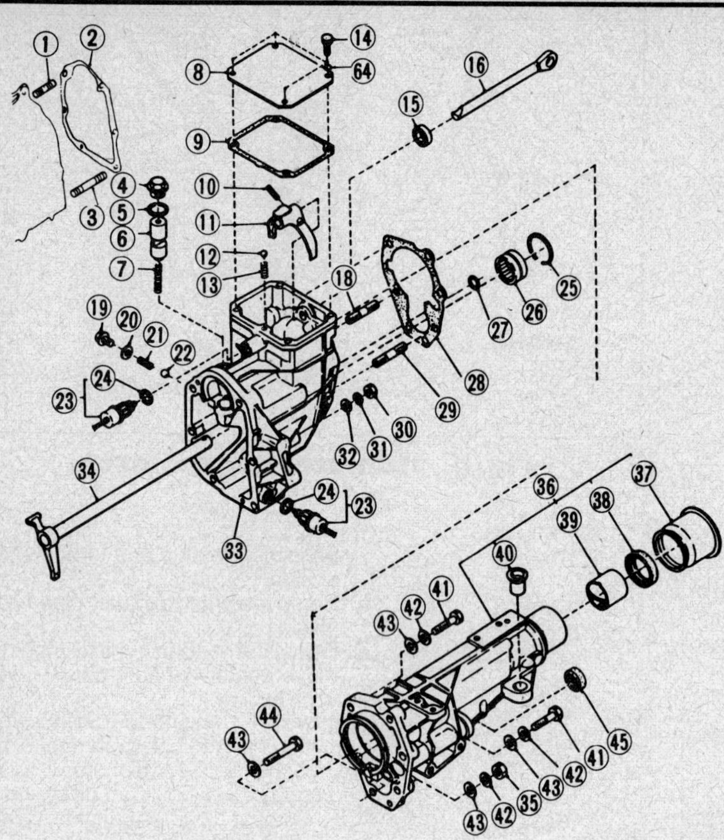

1 Stud bolt (8 x 48 x 20 mm)
2 Transmission gasket
3 Stud bolt (8 x 76 x 20 mm)
4 Plug (22 x 8 mm)
5 Gasket
6 Reverse accent shaft
7 Reverse return spring
8 Transfer case cover
9 Transfer cover gasket
10 Straight pin (5 x 22 mm)
11 Transfer shifter fork
12 Ball (6.350 mm)
13 Shifter fork rail spring
14 Bolt
15 Oil seal
16 Transfer shifter rail
17 Transfer driven gear
18 Stud bolt
19 Filler
20 Aluminum gasket
21 Reverse accent spring
22 7.144 ball
23 Back-up lamp switch ass'y
24 Aluminum gasket
25 Snap ring (inner 45)
26 Needle bearing
27 "O" ring
28 Transfer rear gasket
29 Stud bolt
30 Nut
32 Spring washer
32 Washer
33 Transfer case
34 Shifter arm cp.
35 Nut (10 x 8 mm)
36 Extension cp.
37 Extension dust cover
38 Oil seal
39 Bushing
40 Change rod bushing
41 Bolt
42 Spring washer
43 Washer
44 Bolt
45 Oil seal

Fig. 4 Exploded view of transfer & extension case

TRANSFER & EXTENSION CASE REPLACE

4 WHEEL DRIVE MODELS

Removal

1. Remove transmission from vehicle. Refer to "Transmission, Replace" for procedure.
2. Disconnect return springs from release bearing holder.
3. Remove transfer case cover and gasket, **Fig. 4.**
4. Remove straight pin (522 mm) with punch, then transfer shifter rail and fork, ball (6.35 mm) and shifter fork rail spring.
5. Remove extension case assembly and transfer case rear gasket.
6. Secure transmission mainshaft, then remove locknut and transfer drive gear from drive pinion. **Before turning locknut, be sure to release staked part of nut. Also, shift gear to "1st" position to prevent shaft from turning.**
7. Remove transfer case assembly with gasket and shim. Retain shim for reinstallation.

Installation

1. Install transfer case assembly with new gasket and shim onto main transmission unit, then torque nuts to 20 ft. lbs. (2.7 kg-m). **Transfer drive gear should be installed before tightening nuts.**
2. Secure transmission mainshaft, then install and torque lock washer and nut to 58 ft. lbs. (8 kg-m). After tightening locknut, stake it to prevent turning.
3. Install extension assembly with new transfer case rear gasket, then torque bolts to 27.5 ft. lbs. (3.8 kg-m). **When installing, transfer drive and driven gears should engage each other.**
4. Install transfer shifter fork, rail spring and ball (6.35 mm), then shifter rail into transfer case.
5. Install straight pin into shifter fork, then transfer case cover and new gasket. Torque bolts to 14 ft. lbs. (2 kg-m).
6. Adjust neutral position as follows:
   a. Insert a suitable bar through shifter arm hole and shift into 3rd gear position. The shifter arm should turn lightly toward 1st/2nd gear side but heavily toward reverse. Make adjustment so reverse side heavy stroke becomes same as 1st/2nd side light stroke.
   b. To adjust, remove plug on transfer case and change thickness of aluminum gasket.
7. Fill internal groove of clutch release bearing holder with grease, then install clutch release fork and bearing holder and secure with return springs.
8. Install transmission.

DISC BRAKES SECTION

INDEX

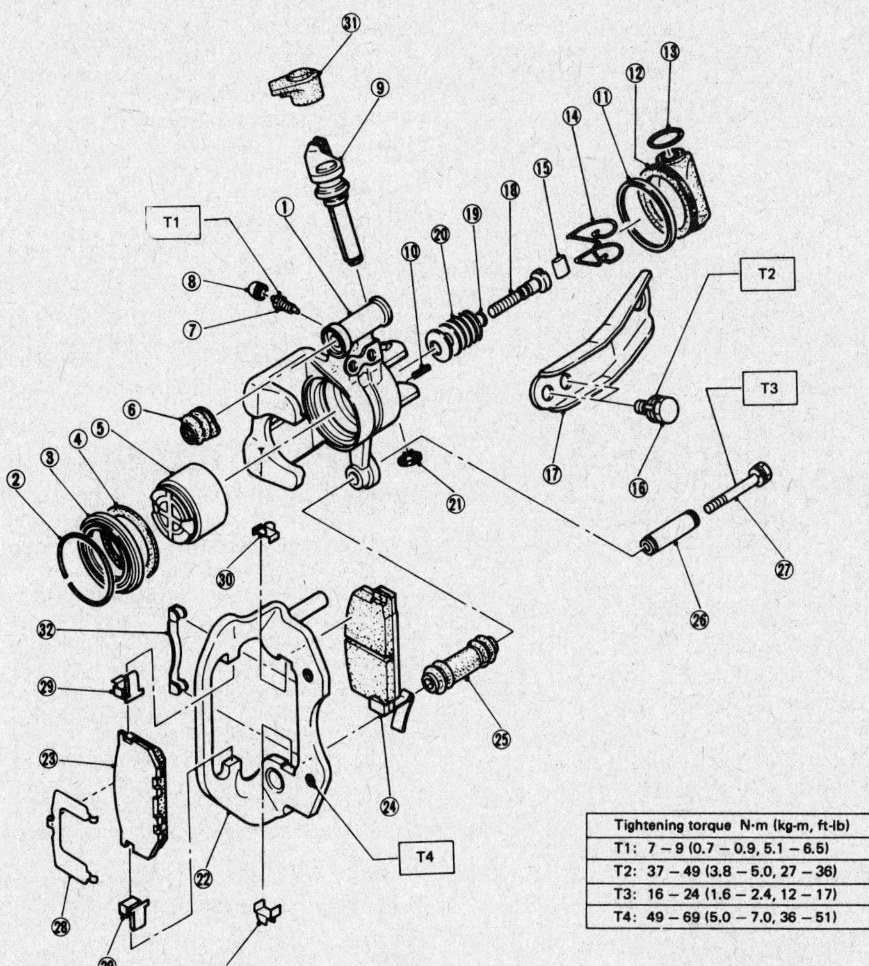

Tightening torque N·m (kg-m, ft-lb)
T1: 7 – 9 (0.7 – 0.9, 5.1 – 6.5)
T2: 37 – 49 (3.8 – 5.0, 27 – 36)
T3: 16 – 24 (1.6 – 2.4, 12 – 17)
T4: 49 – 69 (5.0 – 7.0, 36 – 51)

1 Caliper body
2 Boot ring
3 Piston boot
4 Piston seal
5 Piston
6 Guide pin boot
7 Air bleeder screw
8 Air bleeder cap
9 Lever & spindle
10 Spring pin
11 Cap ring
12 Lever cap
13 Garter spring
14 Return spring
15 Connecting link
16 Bolt ASSY
17 Bracket
18 Spindle
19 O-ring
20 Cone spring
21 Snap ring
22 Support
23 Outer pad
24 Inner pad
25 Lock pin boot
26 Sleeve
27 Lock pin
28 Shim
29 Outer pad clip
30 Inner pad clip
31 Lever cap (upper)
32 Inner pad clip

Fig. 1 Exploded view of front caliper assembly. 1983–84

BRAKE PADS

REPLACE

FRONT

1. Raise front of vehicle and remove wheels.
2. Remove outer parking brake cable clip, then disconnect cable.
3. Remove bolt connecting support with caliper body, then loosen lock pin and pull out, **Figs. 1 and 2. Do not pull out lock pin until loosened to position shown in Fig. 3.**
4. Turn caliper body on guide pin and remove pads from support. Remove caliper.
5. Install new brake pads in support.
6. Using suitable tool, slowly rotate caliper piston into caliper bore. When piston is fully seated, rotate piston so notch in piston face is aligned with tab on brake pad backing plate.
7. Reverse procedure to install. Torque lock pin to 33-54 ft. lbs. (4.5-7.5 kg-m.).

REAR

1. Raise and support rear of vehicle and remove wheels.
2. Remove lower caliper retaining bolt, then pivot caliper assembly upward.
3. Remove brake pads and springs from caliper support bracket, noting position of springs for installation, **Fig. 4.**
4. Compress piston into caliper body using suitable clamp. **Loosen bleeder screw prior to compressing piston, and ensure bleed screw is securely tightened once piston has been compressed into caliper body.**
5. Install springs and brake pads into caliper support bracket.
6. Rotate caliper down over brake pads, install lower bolt and torque both caliper retaining bolts to 16-23 ft. lbs. **Depress brake pedal several times to press brake pads against rotor. If pedal stroke is excessive, check and bleed hydraulic system as needed.**

CALIPER

REPLACE

FRONT

1. Remove union bolt and disconnect brake hose from caliper assembly.
2. Remove brake pads as described under "Brake Pads, Replace."

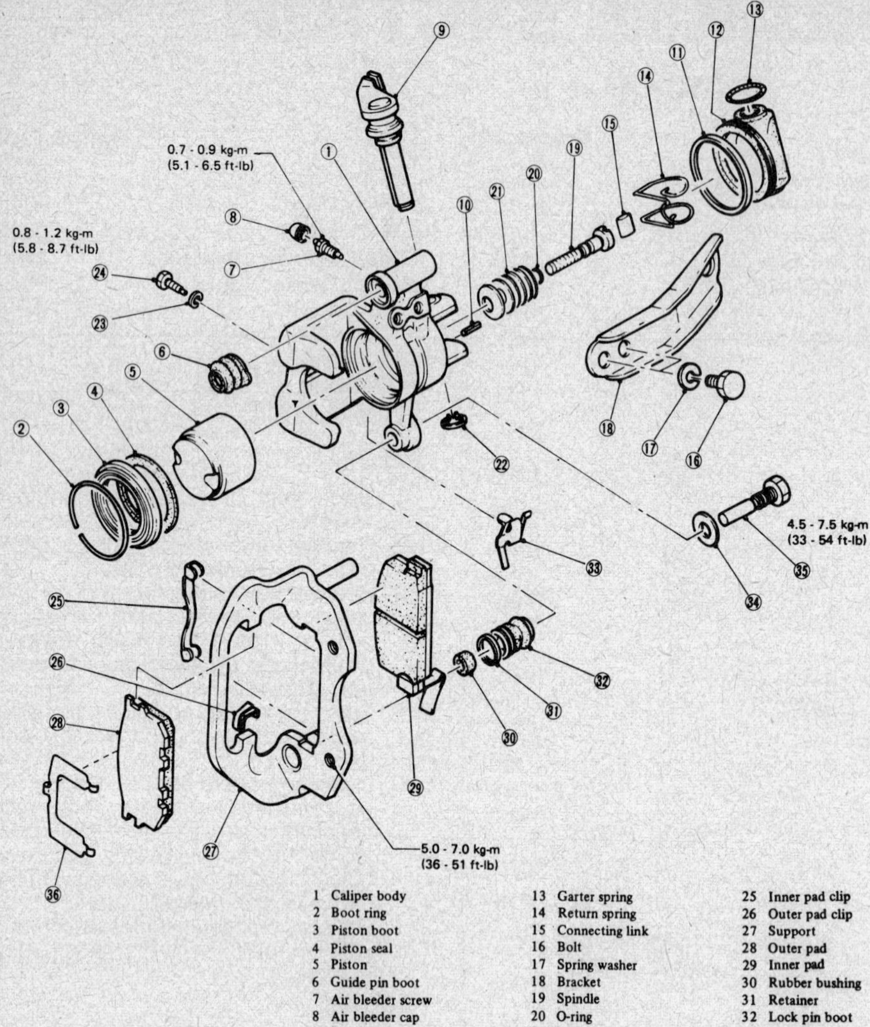

Fig. 2 Exploded view of front caliper assembly. 1985–87

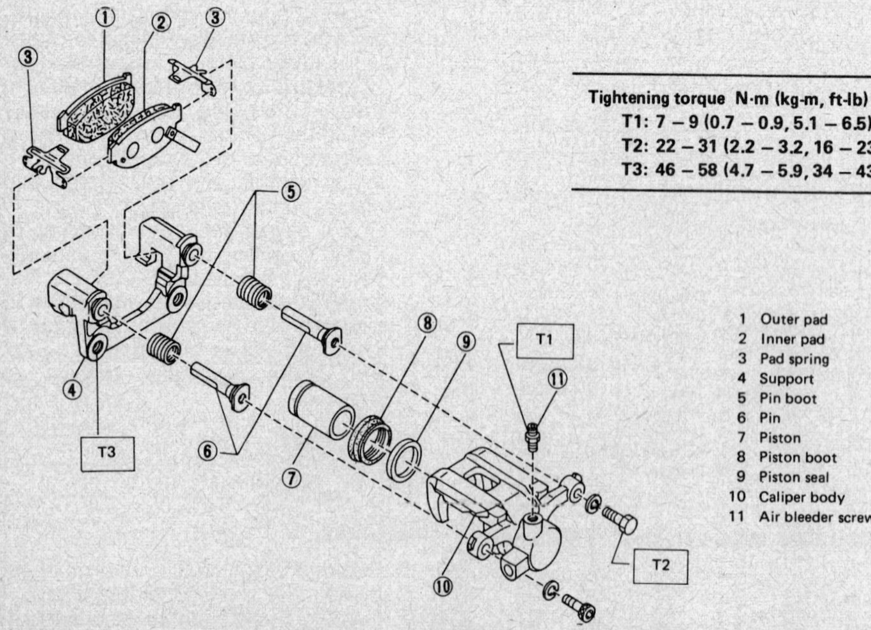

Fig. 4 Exploded view of rear brake caliper assembly

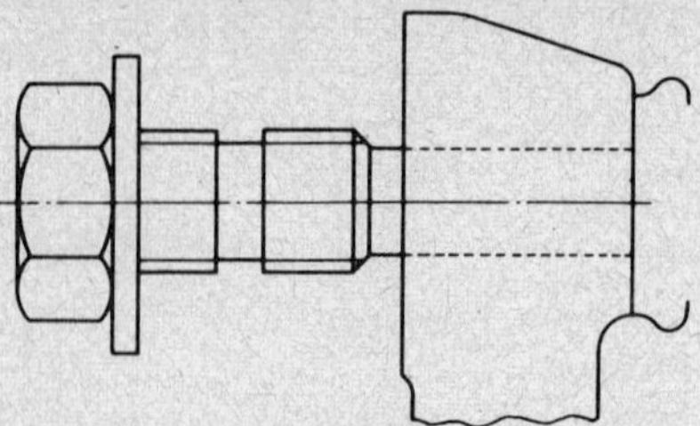

Fig. 3 Positioning front caliper stop bolt for removal

3. Remove caliper assembly by pulling from support, **Figs. 1 and 2.**
4. Reverse procedure to install. Torque union bolt to 11-15 ft. lbs. (1.5-2 kg-m) and, if removed, support bolt to 36-51 ft. lbs. (5-7 kg-m). Also bleed brakes after installation.

REAR

1. Raise and support rear of vehicle and remove wheels.
2. Disconnect brake hose from caliper body and plug hose.
3. Remove bolts securing caliper support bracket to trailing arm, then the caliper and support assembly, **Fig. 4.**
4. Reverse procedure to install, torquing support bolts to 34-43 ft. lbs., then bleed brakes as needed.

CALIPER OVERHAUL

FRONT

1. Remove caliper as outlined under "Caliper, Replace."
2. Remove sleeve, then lock pin boot, **Figs. 1 and 2.**
3. Using a suitable screwdriver, remove boot ring and piston boot.
4. Using compressed air and a block of wood in caliper body, draw out piston from caliper body.
5. Using a suitable screwdriver, remove piston seal taking care not to damage inner wall of cylinder.
6. Remove guide pin boot from caliper body.
7. Remove retainer and lever cap, then retaining spring from lever and spindle.
8. Using puller 925471000 or equivalent, compress spring washer to eliminate load applied to lever and spindle, then pull out lever and spindle.
9. Remove puller, then connecting link and return spring.
10. Reverse procedure to install. Refer to **Figs. 1 and 2** for torque specifications.

REAR

1. Remove caliper as outlined under "Caliper, Replace."
2. Remove bolts securing caliper support to caliper body, then separate caliper support from caliper body.
3. Remove pads and pad springs.
4. Using compressed air and a block of wood in caliper body, remove piston from caliper body.

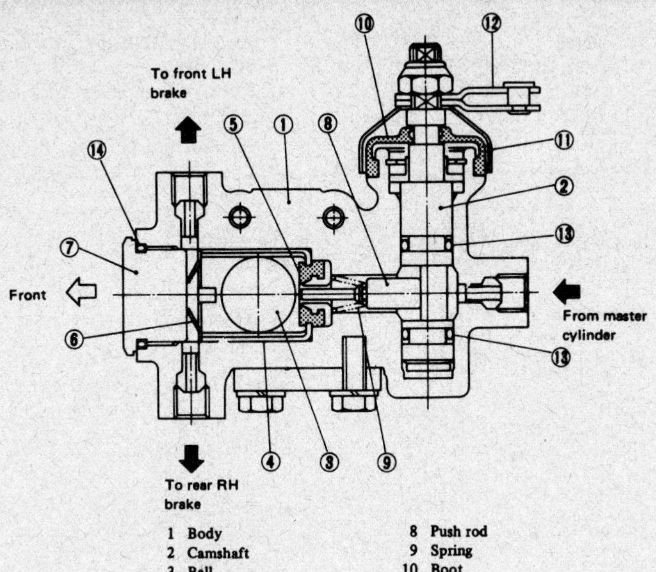

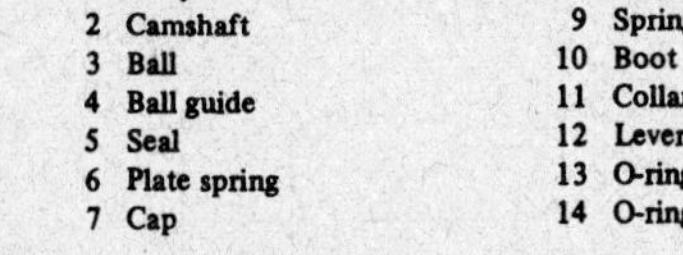

Fig. 5 Hill holder (PHV) valve

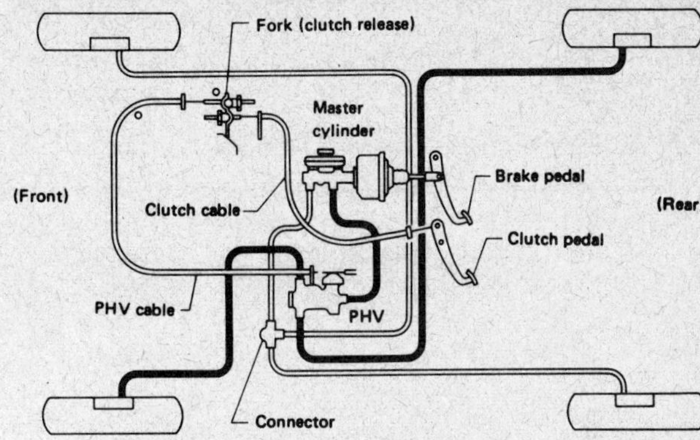

Fig. 6 Hill holder installation

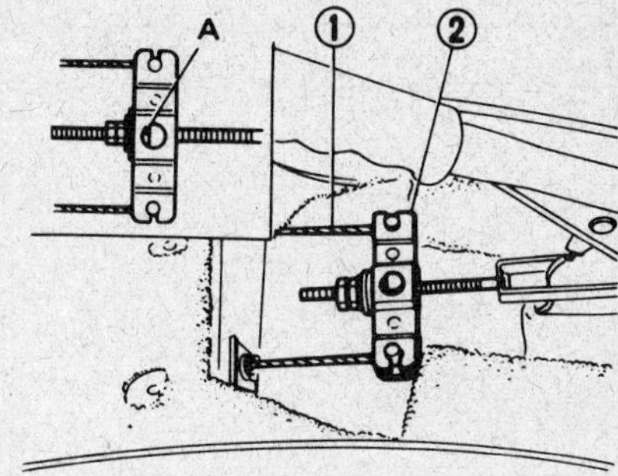

1 Cable
2 Equalizer

Fig. 9 Parking brake adjustment

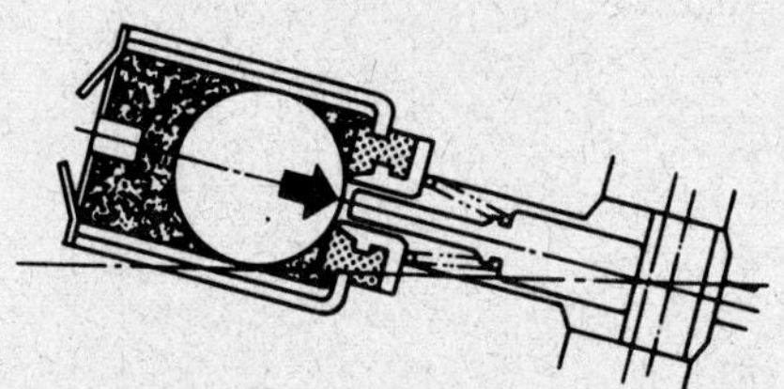

Fig. 7 Hill holder activated

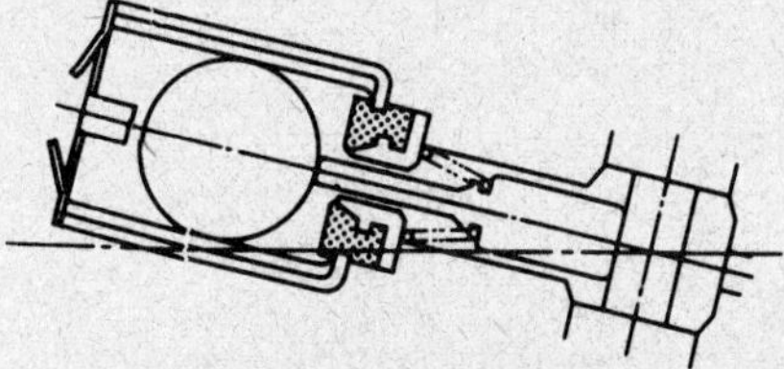

Fig. 8 Hill holder deactivated

5. Using a suitable screwdriver, remove piston boot and seal.
6. Remove pins and boots from support.
7. Reverse procedure to install. Refer to **Fig. 4** for torque specifications.

HILL HOLDER

The Hill holder is essentially a Pressure Hold Valve (PHV), **Fig. 5,** built into one brake circuit, that maintains hydraulic pressure in the brake circuit when the vehicle is facing uphill and the clutch pedal depressed, **Fig. 6.**

The PHV lever, **Fig. 5,** is connected through a linkage to the clutch pedal and control a camshaft which provides the motion to the PHV driveshaft. The PHV driveshaft controls the clearance between the PHV inertia controlled ball and seal.

When the clutch pedal is depressed, the PHV driveshaft is pulled into the seal, allowing the ball free movement. If the vehicle is facing uphill, inertia will cause the ball to roll onto the seal, **Fig. 7,** thereby holding hydraulic pressure. When the clutch is released, **Fig. 8,** the driveshaft is forced into the ball chamber, unsealing the ball and releasing hydraulic pressure.

REMOVAL

1. Drain primary side of master cylinder.
2. Remove cable adjusting nut and clamp from clutch release bearing fork, then disconnect cable from engine bracket.
3. Remove cable from PHV.
4. Separate connector bracket from PHV, then remove brake lines using a suitable flare wrench.
5. Remove PHV bracket securing bolts from frame, then remove PHV. **Do not allow any dirt to enter PHV.**

INSPECTION

1. Inspect PHV cable boots and outer casing for damage, replace as necessary.
2. Inspect PHV cable inner core for corrosion and wear, replace as necessary.
3. Inspect PHV return spring for damage or corrosion.
4. Tilt PHV assembly and listen for ball rolling to ensure free operation.
5. Operate lever to ensure smooth operation. **Do not attempt to disassemble PHV. If unit is defective, it should be replaced.**

INSTALLATION

To install, reverse removal procedure, noting the following:

1. Apply lubricant to hooked portion of return spring, cable end of lever and cable end at clutch release bearing fork.
2. Bleed brakes after installation.

ADJUSTMENT

After replacing PHV cable or clutch cable, operate clutch pedal approximately 30 times to seat new parts prior to making any adjustments.

1. Ensure clutch is adjusted properly. Refer to "Clutch and Manual Transmission Section."
2. Road test vehicle to determine Hill holder performance on an uphill road of 3° inclination or more. If Hill holder is released late (engine tends to stall), loosen adjustment nut gradually, until smooth starting is obtained. If Hill holder releases early (vehicle rolls down incline), tighten adjustment nut until Hill holder releases late (engine tends to stall), then loosen adjustment nut gradually, until smooth starting is obtained.
3. Torque adjustment nut to 1.81-3.26 ft. lbs.

MASTER CYLINDER REPLACE

1. Disconnect brake tubes from master cylinder and plug ends.
2. Remove two or three nuts retaining master cylinder and pull off studs.
3. Reverse procedure to install.

PARKING BRAKE

ADJUST

1. Pull the parking brake lever, three to five times.
2. Rotate the equalizer cable adjustment nut until play at "A" in **Fig. 9** is set at 0-.02 inch (0-.5 mm). Lock adjustment nut. **The brake lever mechanism should click six to seven times when a force of 55 lbs. is exerted on the lever.**

DRUM BRAKES SECTION

INDEX

Page No.

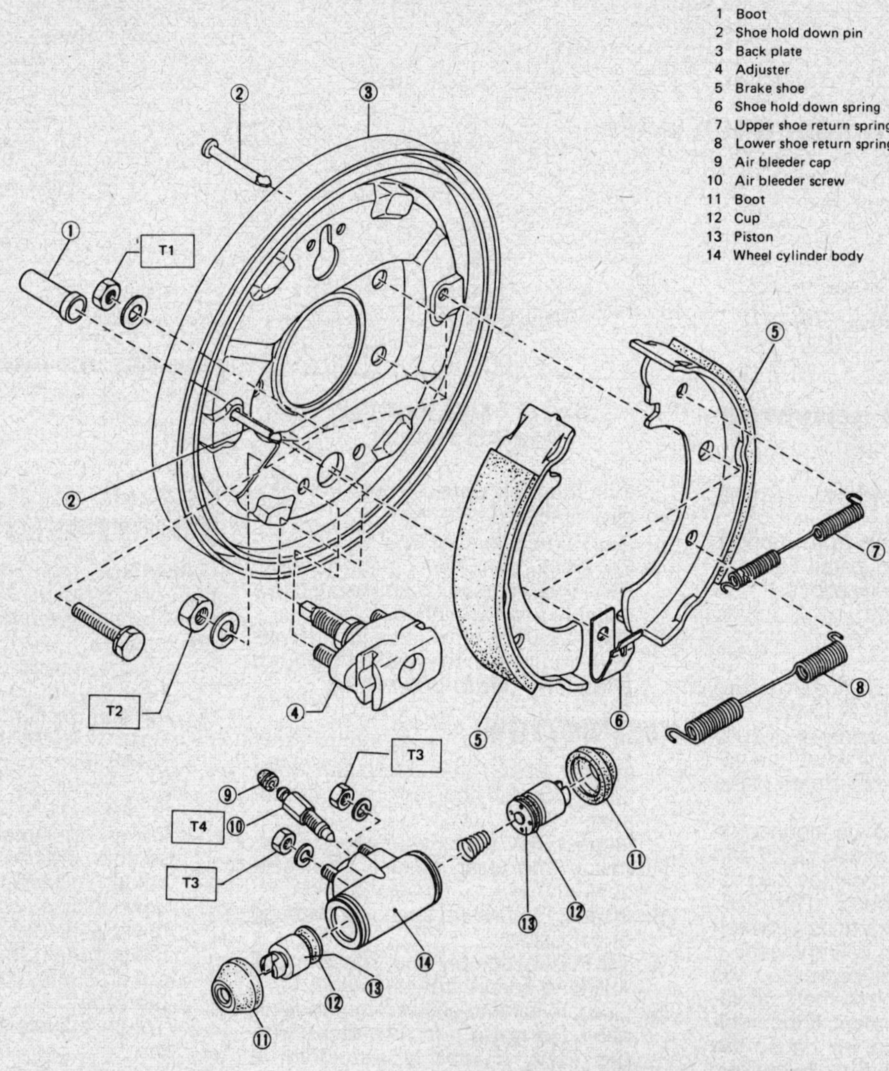

Fig. 1 Exploded view of drum brake assembly. Exc. 4 wheel drive models

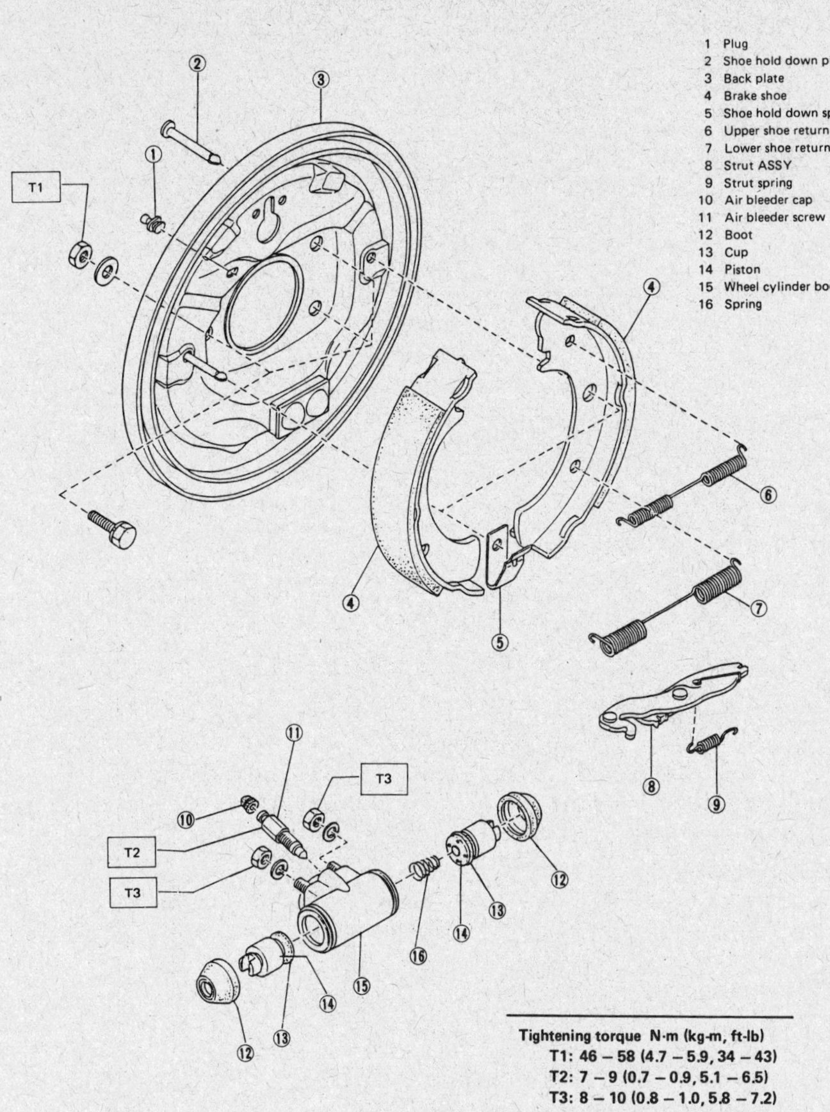

Fig. 2 Exploded view of drum brake assembly. 4 wheel drive models

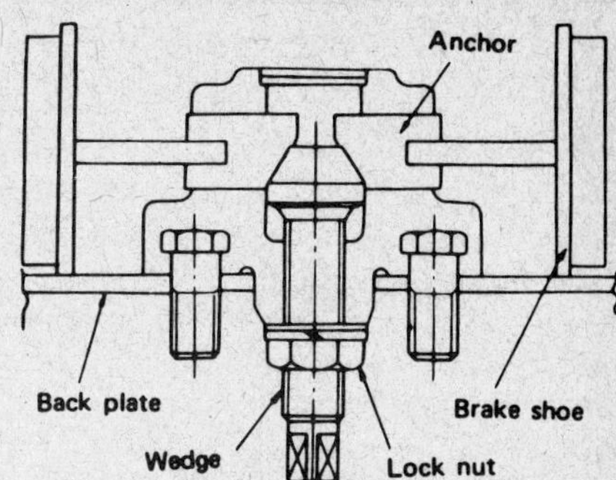

Fig. 3 Brake adjustment mechanism

BRAKE SHOES

REPLACE

1. Loosen wheel nuts, raise and support rear of vehicle, then remove wheel assembly.
2. Remove brake drum.
3. Disconnect brake line from back plate.
4. Using suitable pliers, remove shoe hold down springs, **Figs. 1 and 2.**
5. Remove shoes.
6. Reverse procedure to install. Refer to **Figs. 1 and 2** for torque specifications.

MASTER CYLINDER

Refer to "Disc Brakes Section" for procedure.

DRUM BRAKE ADJUSTMENTS

To adjust rear drum brake, loosen locknut of wedge adjuster and tighten wedge adjuster until wheel can no longer be rotated, then back off adjuster 180° to provide a clearance of .004-.006 inch between brake shoe and drum and retighten adjuster locknut, **Fig. 3.**

PARKING BRAKE

ADJUST

Refer to "Disc Brakes Section" for procedure.

DRIVE AXLE SECTION

INDEX

FRONT AXLE SHAFT REPLACE

1. Raise front of vehicle and support with safety stands, then remove wheels.
2. Remove parking brake cable bracket from transverse link, **Figs. 1 and 2.**
3. Remove and discard axle-to-driveshaft spring pin.
4. Remove disc brake assembly.
5. Disconnect tie rod, transverse link and damper strut.
6. Remove axle shaft with housing from differential.
7. Remove axle shaft from housing using suitable tool. **Check axle housing bearing for wear or damage and replace oil seals, Fig. 3.**
8. Reverse procedure to install. Torque axle nut to 145 ft. lbs. (20 kg-m), transverse link bolt to 22-29 ft. lbs. (3-4 kg-m), damper strut bolt to 22-29 ft. lbs. (3-4 kg-m), tie rod nut to 18-22 ft. lbs. (2.5-3 kg-m), disc brake assembly bolt to 36-51 ft. lbs. (5-7 kg-m), and disc brake cover bolt to 4.3-10 ft. lbs. (.6-1.4 kg-m).

FRONT AXLE SHAFT SERVICE

The following abbreviations are used in this section, D.O.J. for double offset joint and C.V.J. for constant velocity joint.

DISASSEMBLY

1. Refer to "Front Axle Shaft, Replace" procedure and remove axle from vehicle.
2. Straighten bent claw of large end of boot on D.O.J. side of axle shaft, then loosen boot band.
3. Remove boot band on small end of D.O.J. side in same manner, then slide boot away from joint.
4. Remove round circlip at neck of outer race on D.O.J. side with screwdriver.
5. Remove outer race on D.O.J. side from shaft assembly.
6. Remove balls and move cage to boot side, then turn cage by 1/2 pitch to track groove of inner race and remove snap ring, inner race, cage and boot. **The C.V.J. is not to be disassembled.**

INSPECTION

1. Check D.O.J. and C.V.J. for seizure, corrosion, damage, or excessive wear.
2. Check shaft for bending, twisting, damage and wear.
3. Check boot for wear, warping and cracking.

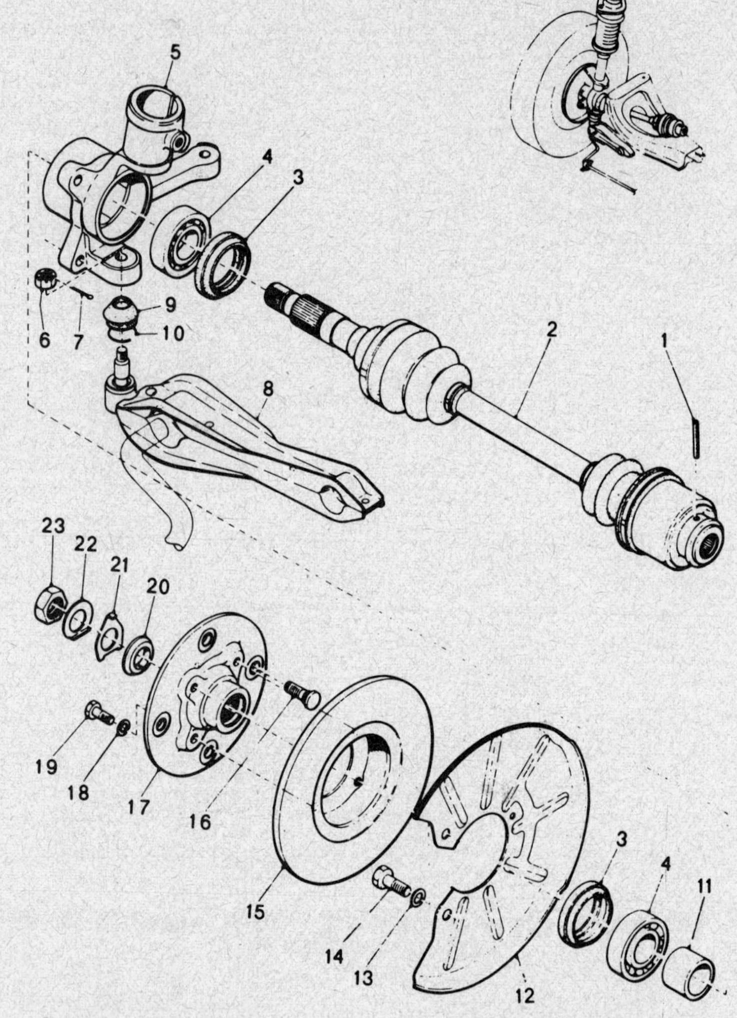

1. Spring pin
2. Axle shaft
3. Oil seal
4. Bearing
5. Housing
6. Castle nut
7. Cotter pin
8. Transverse link
9. Dust seal (Ball joint)
10. Circlip
11. Spacer
12. Disc cover
13. Spring washer
14. Bolt
15. Disc
16. Hub bolt
17. Disc hub
18. Spring washer
19. Bolt
20. Center piece
21. Lock washer
22. Lock plate
23. Nut

Fig. 1 Exploded view of front drive axle. 1983–84

ASSEMBLY

1. Install boot on C.V.J. side and fill with 2-2.5 oz. of special constant velocity joint grease Molylex No. 2 or equivalent.
2. Position boot from D.O.J. side at cen-

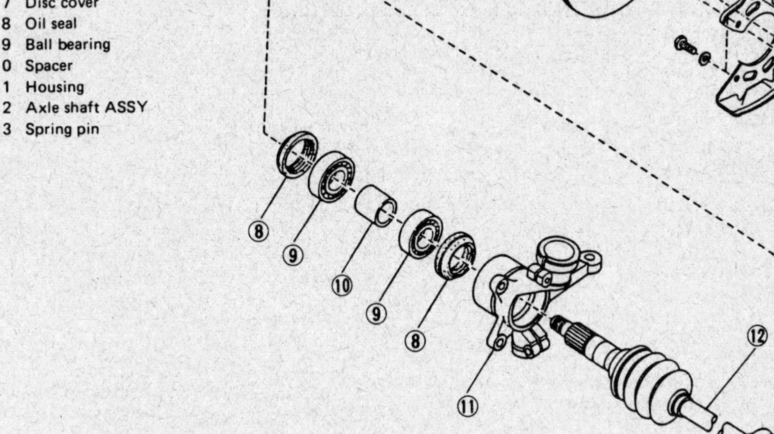

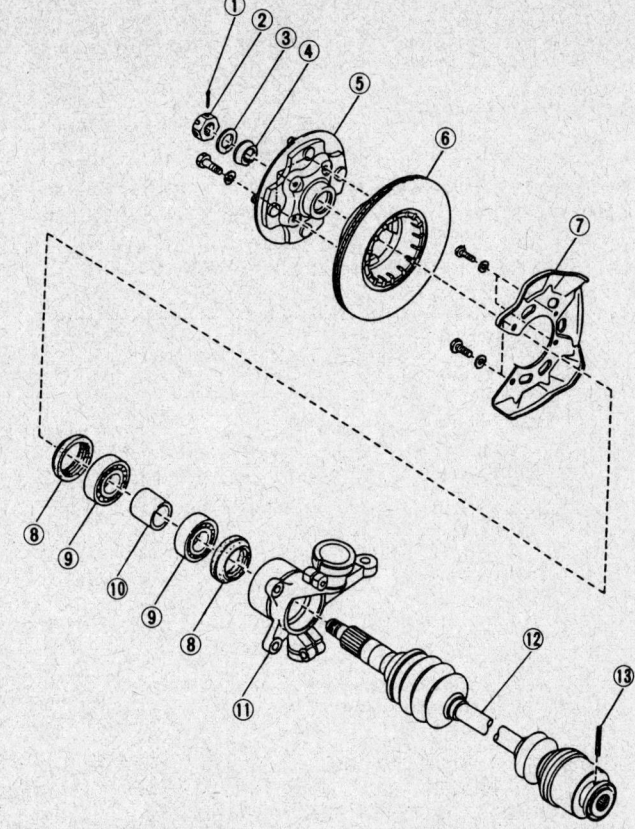

Fig. 2 Exploded view of front drive axle. 1985–87

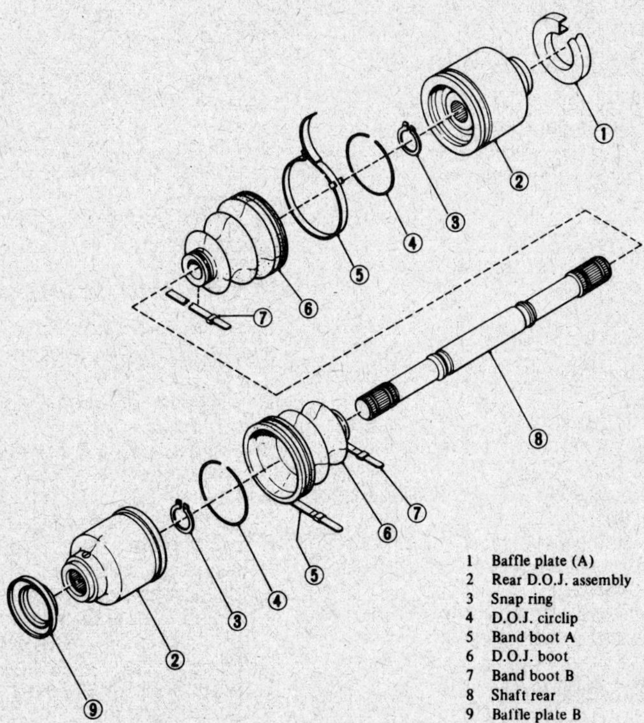

Fig. 4 Exploded view of rear drive axle

ter of shaft, then insert cage of D.O.J. with recess facing outward.

3. Install inner race of D.O.J. onto shaft and secure with snap ring.
4. Install cage, which was previously positioned, with protruding part aligned with track on inner race and then turn by 1/2 pitch. Apply .75-1 oz. of special grease to cage pocket and insert 6 balls into cage pocket, then fill interior of outer race with .75-1 oz. of special grease.

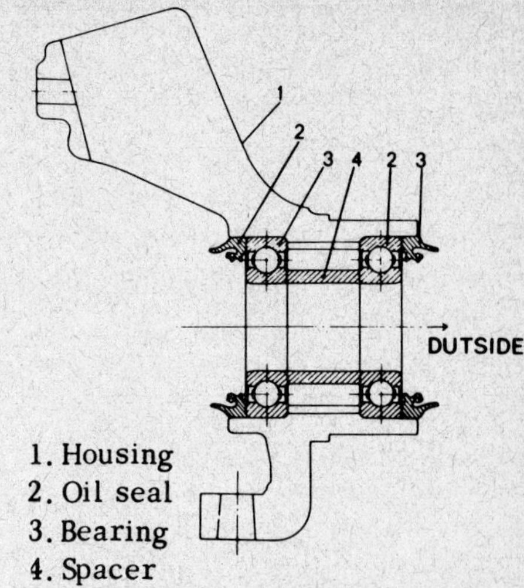

Fig. 3 Bearing & seal installation

5. Align outer race track and ball positions, then fit outer race to inner race and cage.
6. Install circlip into groove on outer race of D.O.J., then pull shaft to ensure circlip is seated in groove.
7. Apply .75-1 oz. of grease to interior of D.O.J. and shaft area, then fill boot with .75-1 oz. of grease and install. **When installing boot, position outer race of D.O.J. at center of its travel.**
8. Install new boot bands using suitable tool and tighten until it cannot be moved by hand. **While tightening band, be sure there is enough air within boot.**
9. Tap on clip of band with suitable punch at end of tightening tool and cut off excess band at about .4 inch (10 mm) from clip, then bend band over clip.
10. Fill C.V.J. boot and C.V.J. with special grease and install in same manner as D.O.J. boot.

REAR AXLE SHAFT REPLACE

1. Remove bolts from upper shock absorber attaching body.
2. Raise rear of vehicle and support with safety stands, then remove wheels.
3. Drive out spring pins at both ends of drive axle, **Fig. 4.**
4. Remove outer D.O.J. (double offset joint) from rear axle spindle by pushing inner D.O.J. fully toward rear differential and pushing brake drum downward. Then remove inner end of drive axle.
5. Reverse procedure to install. Torque shock absorber upper bolts to 65-94 ft. lbs. (9-13 kg-m).

REAR AXLE SHAFT SERVICE

Refer to "Front Axle Shaft Service" for disassembly and assembly procedures of the double offset joints of axle shaft, **Fig. 4.**

REAR SUSPENSION SECTION

INDEX

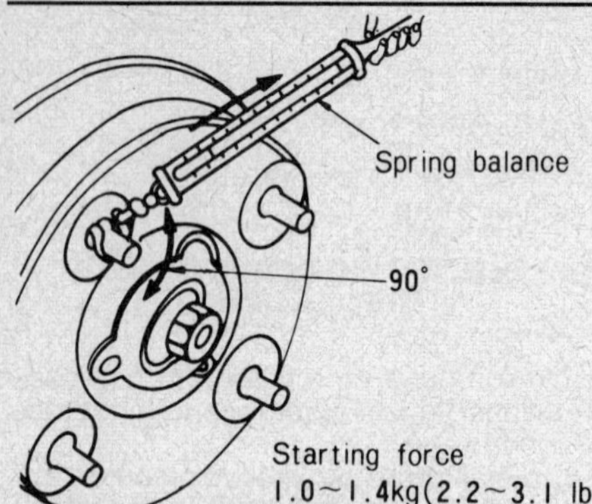

Fig. 1 Checking rear wheel bearing adjustment

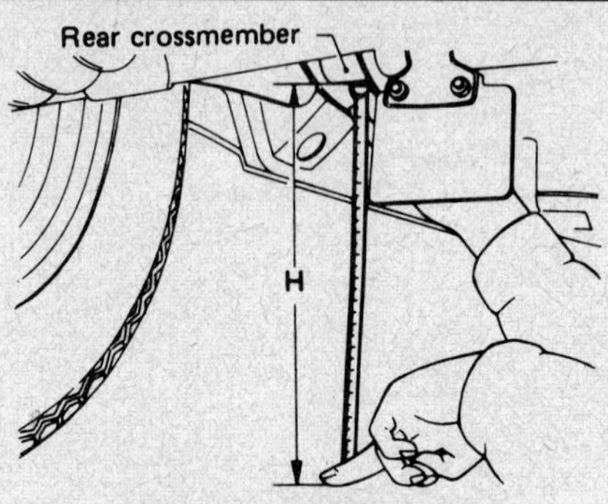

Fig. 2 Measuring dimension H

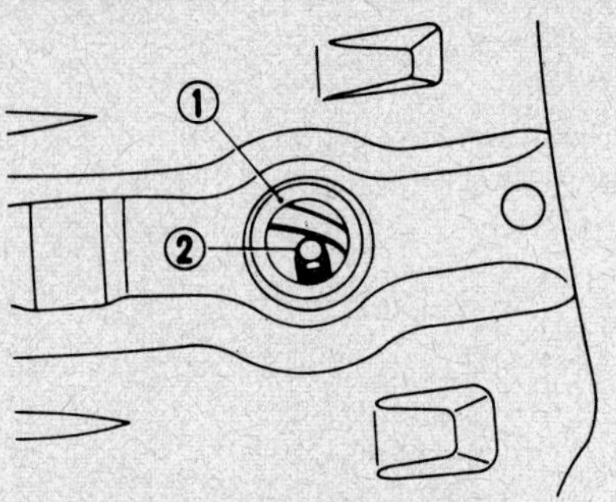

Fig. 3 4 wheel drive vehicle rear height adjustment. 1983–84

REAR WHEEL BEARING ADJUST

EXC. 4 WHEEL DRIVE MODELS

1. Tighten axle nut to approximately 36 ft. lbs. (5 kg-m).
2. Loosen nut 1/8 to 1/10 turn. Using a suitable spring scale measure starting force, **Fig. 1.** Starting force should be 1.9-3.2 lbs.
3. Bend lock plate to locknut in position, then install bearing cap and gasket.

GROUND CLEARANCE ADJUST

4 WHEEL DRIVE MODELS

1983–84

1. Measure crossmember height from ground, **Fig. 2.**
2. Rotate bolt in service hole provided in vehicle floor, **Fig. 3. Clockwise rotation increases vehicle height. Counterclockwise decreases vehicle height.**

1985–87

Conventional Suspension

1. Measure clearance between lowest point of rear crossmember and ground, **Fig. 2.**
2. If clearance is less than 9.65-10.83 inches for sedan models or 10.24-11.42 inches for wagon models, remove rear coil spring/shock absorber assemblies.
3. Compress coil springs using suitable tool, until lower spring seat can be rotated.
4. Position spring seat on shock absorber to alter ground clearance. **Ground clearance is increased by .59 inch for each adjustment notch on spring seat.**
5. Reinstall spring/shock absorber assembly and recheck ground clearance.

Pneumatic Suspension

If ride height is incorrect on these models, check for leaking air pipe or tank fittings, leaking or defective solenoid valves, defective height sensors or defective control unit.

HUB & ROTOR REPLACE

EXC. 4 WHEEL DRIVE

1. Apply parking brake and loosen wheel lug nuts.
2. Raise and support rear of vehicle.
3. Remove wheel and tire assembly.
4. Flatten lock washer and loosen axle nut, then remove lock washer and lock plate.
5. On models equipped with disc brakes, unfasten caliper assembly and position aside.
6. On all models, remove hub and drum or hub and rotor assembly.
7. Reverse procedure to install.

4 WHEEL DRIVE

1. Apply parking brake.
2. Remove wheel cap and cotter pin, then loosen castle nut and lug nuts.
3. Raise and support vehicle.
4. Remove wheel and tire assembly.
5. On models equipped with disc brakes, unfasten caliper assembly and position aside, leaving brake line attached.
6. On all models, remove castle nut, then the hub and drum or hub and rotor assembly.
7. Reverse procedure to install.

SHOCK ABSORBER REPLACE

1983–84

1. Raise and support rear of vehicle, placing suitable support under control arm.
2. Remove upper and lower mounting bolts and the shock absorber, **Figs. 4 and 5.**
3. Reverse procedure to install.

1985–87

Conventional Suspension

1. Raise and support rear of vehicle, ensuring that rear suspension is unloaded.
2. Remove 2 upper shock absorber mounting bolts.
3. Remove lower mounting bolt and the coil spring/shock absorber assembly.
4. Mount assembly in suitable spring compressor ensuring that projections on compressor are seated on inner diameter of spring.
5. Compress spring until tension is relieved from spring seats, then remove rod connecting nuts, **Figs. 6 and 7.**
6. Remove body mounting bracket, plate and upper spring seat as an assembly.
7. Slowly release spring tension, then remove coil spring from shock absorber body.
8. Remove helper assembly from shock absorber.
9. Reverse procedure to install, noting the following:
   a. Mount coil spring with flat face toward lower spring seat.
   b. Ensure body mounting bracket is

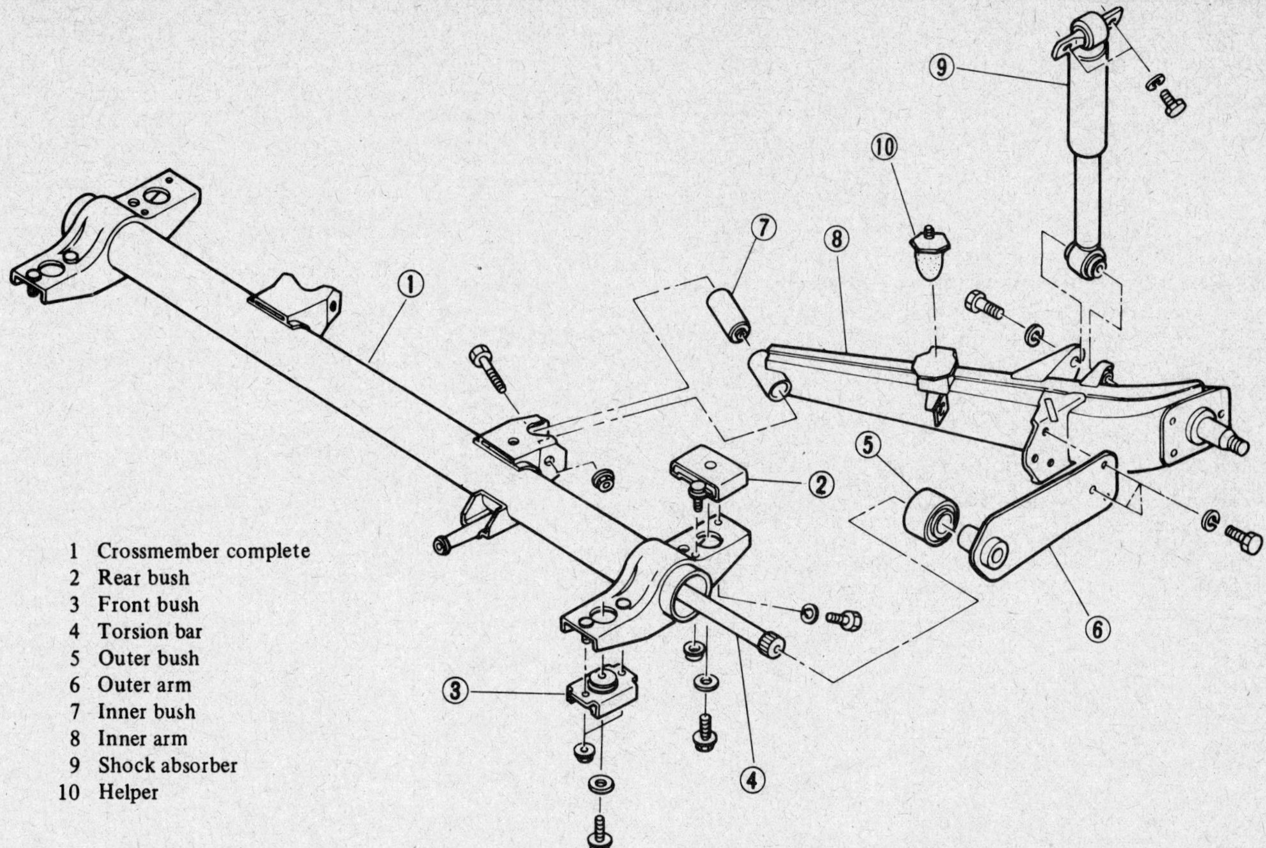

Fig. 4 Rear suspension exploded view. 1983–84 less 4 wheel drive

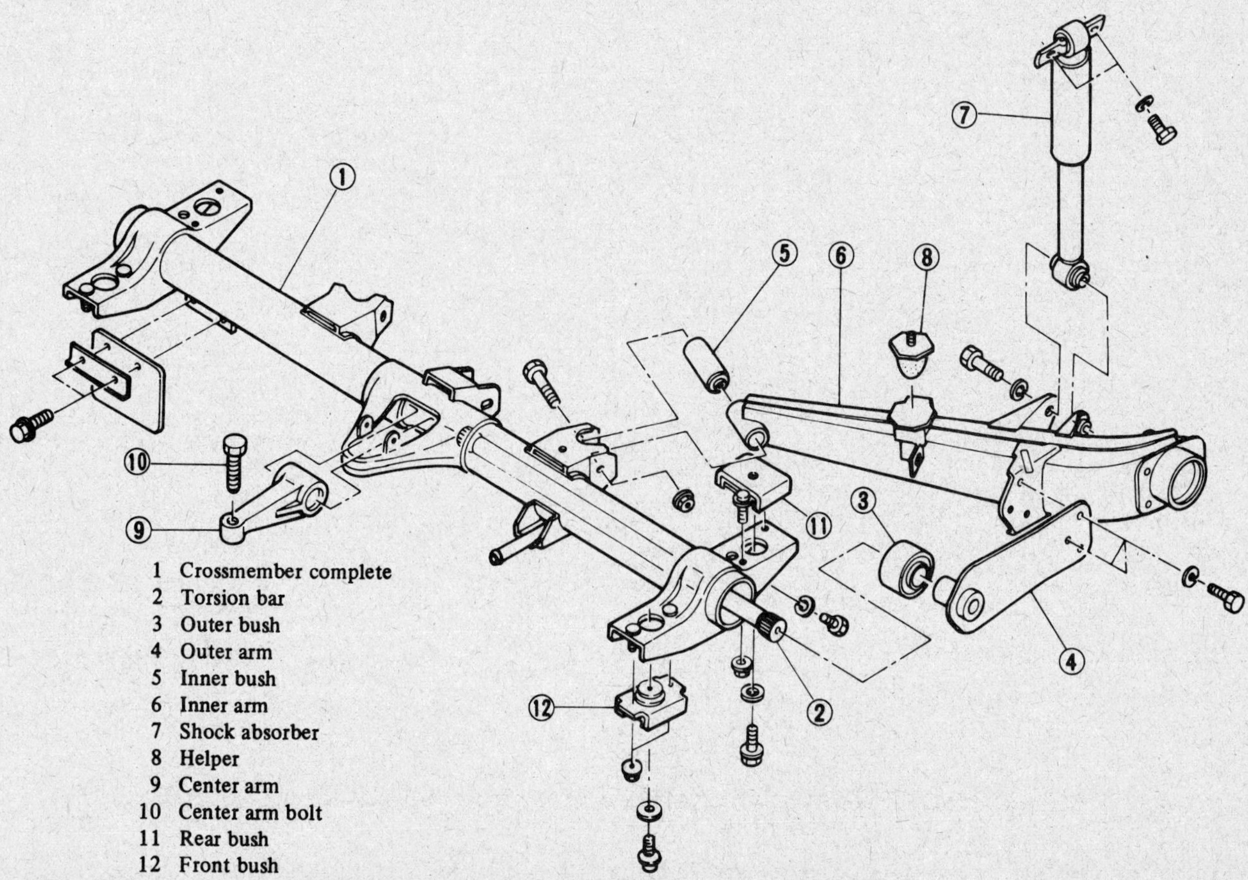

Fig. 5 Rear suspension exploded view. 1983–84 w/4 wheel drive

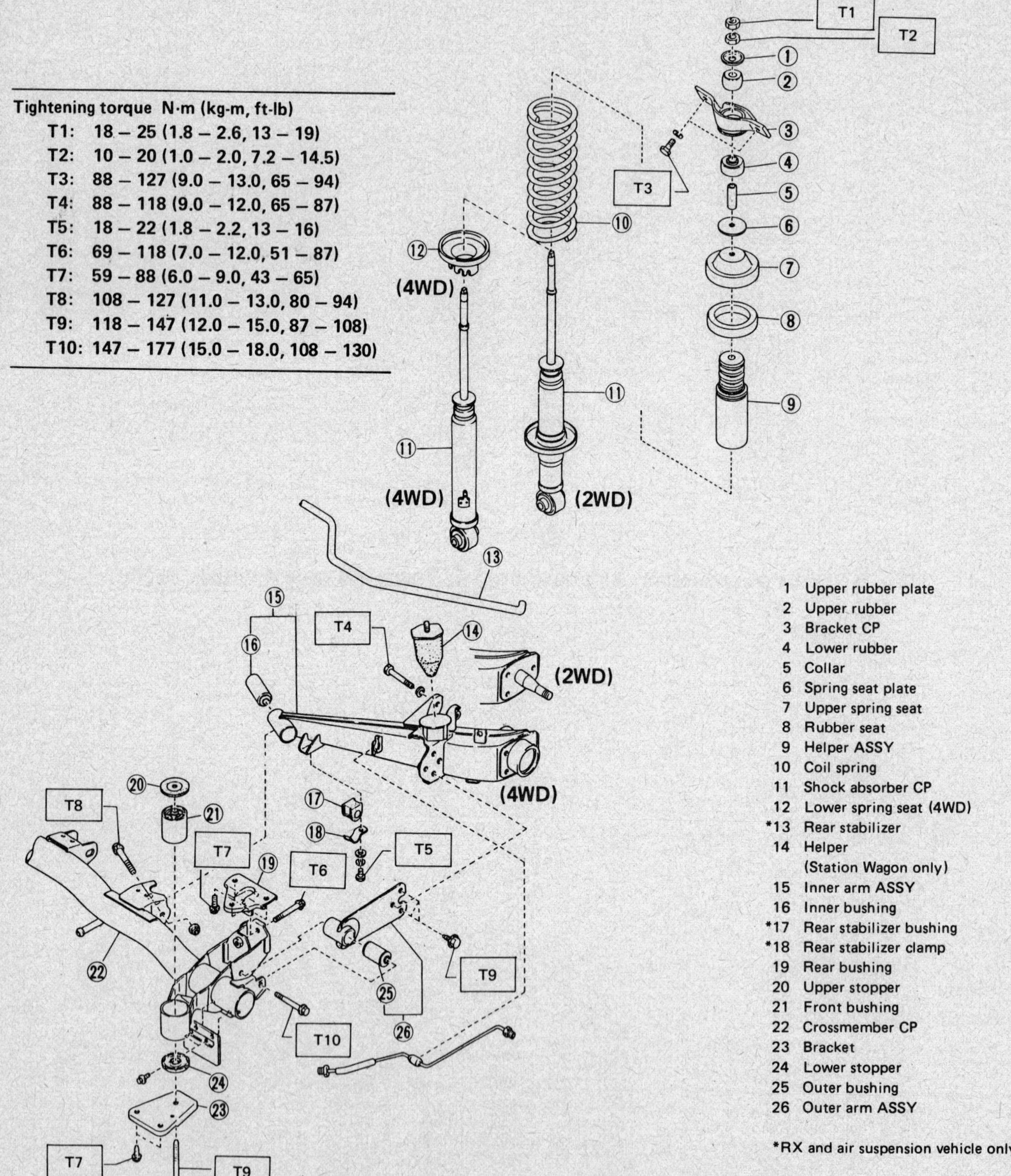
Tightening torque N·m (kg-m, ft-lb)
T1: 18 – 25 (1.8 – 2.6, 13 – 19)
T2: 10 – 20 (1.0 – 2.0, 7.2 – 14.5)
T3: 88 – 127 (9.0 – 13.0, 65 – 94)
T4: 88 – 118 (9.0 – 12.0, 65 – 87)
T5: 18 – 22 (1.8 – 2.2, 13 – 16)
T6: 69 – 118 (7.0 – 12.0, 51 – 87)
T7: 59 – 88 (6.0 – 9.0, 43 – 65)
T8: 108 – 127 (11.0 – 13.0, 80 – 94)
T9: 118 – 147 (12.0 – 15.0, 87 – 108)
T10: 147 – 177 (15.0 – 18.0, 108 – 130)
(4WD)
(2WD)
1 Upper rubber plate
2 Upper rubber
3 Bracket CP
4 Lower rubber
5 Collar
6 Spring seat plate
7 Upper spring seat
8 Rubber seat
9 Helper ASSY
10 Coil spring
11 Shock absorber CP
12 Lower spring seat (4WD)
*13 Rear stabilizer
14 Helper (Station Wagon only)
15 Inner arm ASSY
16 Inner bushing
*17 Rear stabilizer bushing
*18 Rear stabilizer clamp
19 Rear bushing
20 Upper stopper
21 Front bushing
22 Crossmember CP
23 Bracket
24 Lower stopper
25 Outer bushing
26 Outer arm ASSY
*RX and air suspension vehicle only

Fig. 6 Conventional rear suspension assembly exploded view. 1986–87

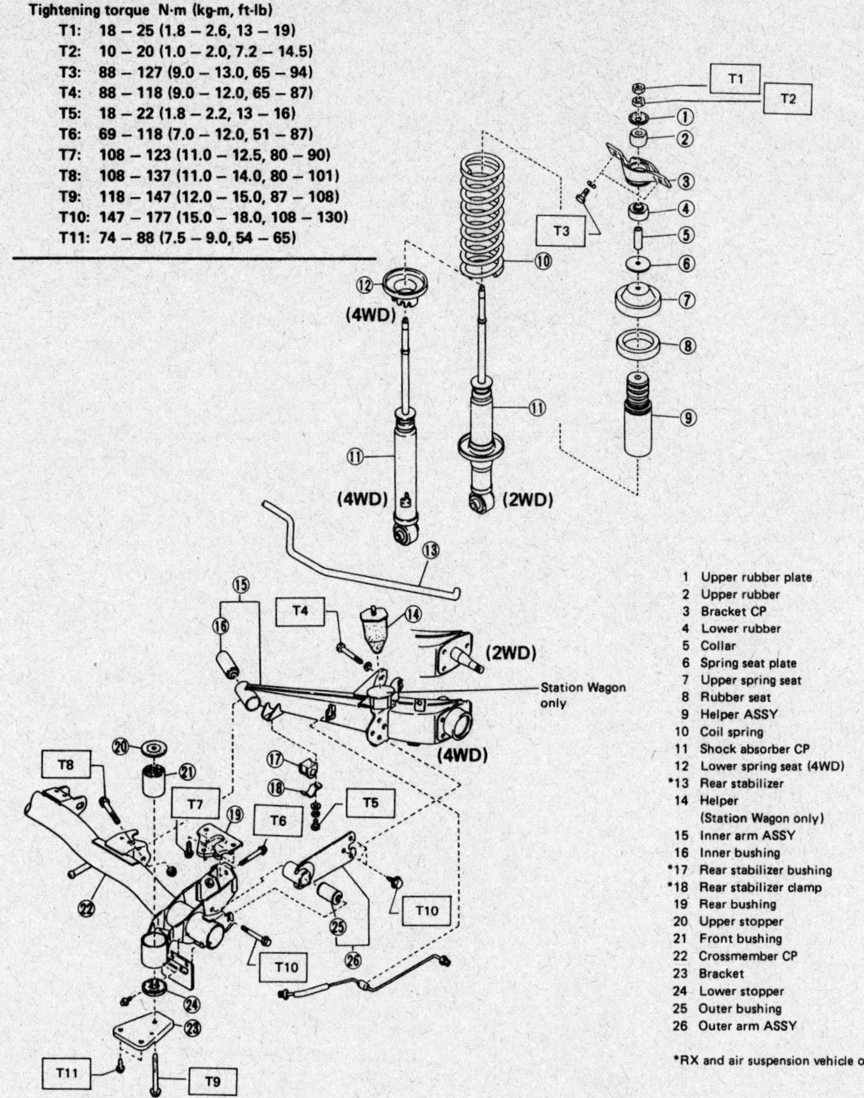

Fig. 7 Conventional rear suspension assembly exploded view. 1985

properly aligned and that rubber seat does not extrude from spring seat.

c. Ensure upper end of spring is fully seated in upper seat.
d. Torque all fasteners to specifications, **Figs. 6 and 7.**

Pneumatic Suspension

1. Disconnect battery ground cable, raise and support vehicle ensuring that rear suspension is unloaded, then remove wheels.
2. Remove rear apron protector, **Fig. 8.**
3. Pry up lock sleeve using suitable tool and disconnect air line.
4. Remove solenoid valve from air spring body.
5. Withdraw height sensor harness from access hole in body, then disconnect electrical connector.
6. Remove upper and lower mounting bolts and the air spring assembly.
7. Reverse procedure to install, using new O-rings when connecting air line and ensuring that air lines and wiring harnesses are properly aligned.
8. Torque upper mounting bolts to 65-94 ft. lbs. and lower bolt to 65-87 ft. lbs.

REAR SUSPENSION REPLACE

1983–84

1. Remove the two upper shock absorber retaining bolts. **Lift vehicle slightly and use an extension to facilitate upper shock absorber bolts removal.**
2. Loosen wheel nuts but do not remove wheels.
3. Raise and support vehicle on suitable rigid rack.
4. Remove wheels.
5. Disconnect rear drive system of 4 wheel drive vehicles as follows:
   a. Using a suitable drift, drive out driveshaft spring pins, **Fig. 9.**
   b. Remove outer driveshaft D.O.J. from rear axle spindle by pushing inside of D.O.J. toward rear differential and pushing rear brake drum downward, **Fig. 10. D.O.J. designates double offset joint.**
   c. Remove inner end of driveshaft.
   d. Perform same procedure as previously described on opposite driveshaft.
   e. Remove the four propeller shaft to rear differential retaining bolts. **When propeller shaft is removed from transmission, oil will flow from transmission. Prepare a suitable cap to insert into the transmission opening and a container to catch the escaping oil.**
   f. Set container at rear end of transmission, and slowly remove propeller shaft.
   g. Insert cap into transmission opening.
   h. Support rear differential with suitable jack. **Remove differential and installation bracket as an assembly from body.**
   i. Remove the differential bracket to body locking retaining nuts.
   j. Position a suitable transmission jack under the differential.
   k. Remove the four differential to body retaining bolts and remove differential.
6. On all models less 4 wheel drive, remove the exhaust manifold and exhaust pipe retaining bolts, and then the muffler and exhaust pipe.
7. On models with 4 wheel drive, remove the exhaust pipe and muffler assembly separately.
8. On all models, remove the exhaust covers.
9. Disconnect brake hose and pipe at inner arm side bracket by loosening flare nut.
10. Perform the same procedure on the opposite side.
11. Position a suitable jack at rear crossmember center.
12. Support crossmember and remove the four crossmember retaining bolts.
13. Lower jack and remove crossmember from vehicle.
14. On all models less 4 wheel drive, remove floating bushing flange nut at crossmember bracket, **Fig. 11.**
15. Remove lower shock absorber retaining nut and shock absorber.
16. Loosen outer bushing lock bolt.
17. Remove inner to outer arm retaining bolts.
18. Remove outer arm and torsion bar.
19. Remove torsion bar from outer arm.
20. Remove inner arm to crossmember retaining bolt and nut.
21. Reverse procedure to assemble and install.

1985–87

Conventional Suspension

1. Perform steps 1 through 10 outlined for 1983-84 models, referring to **Figs.**

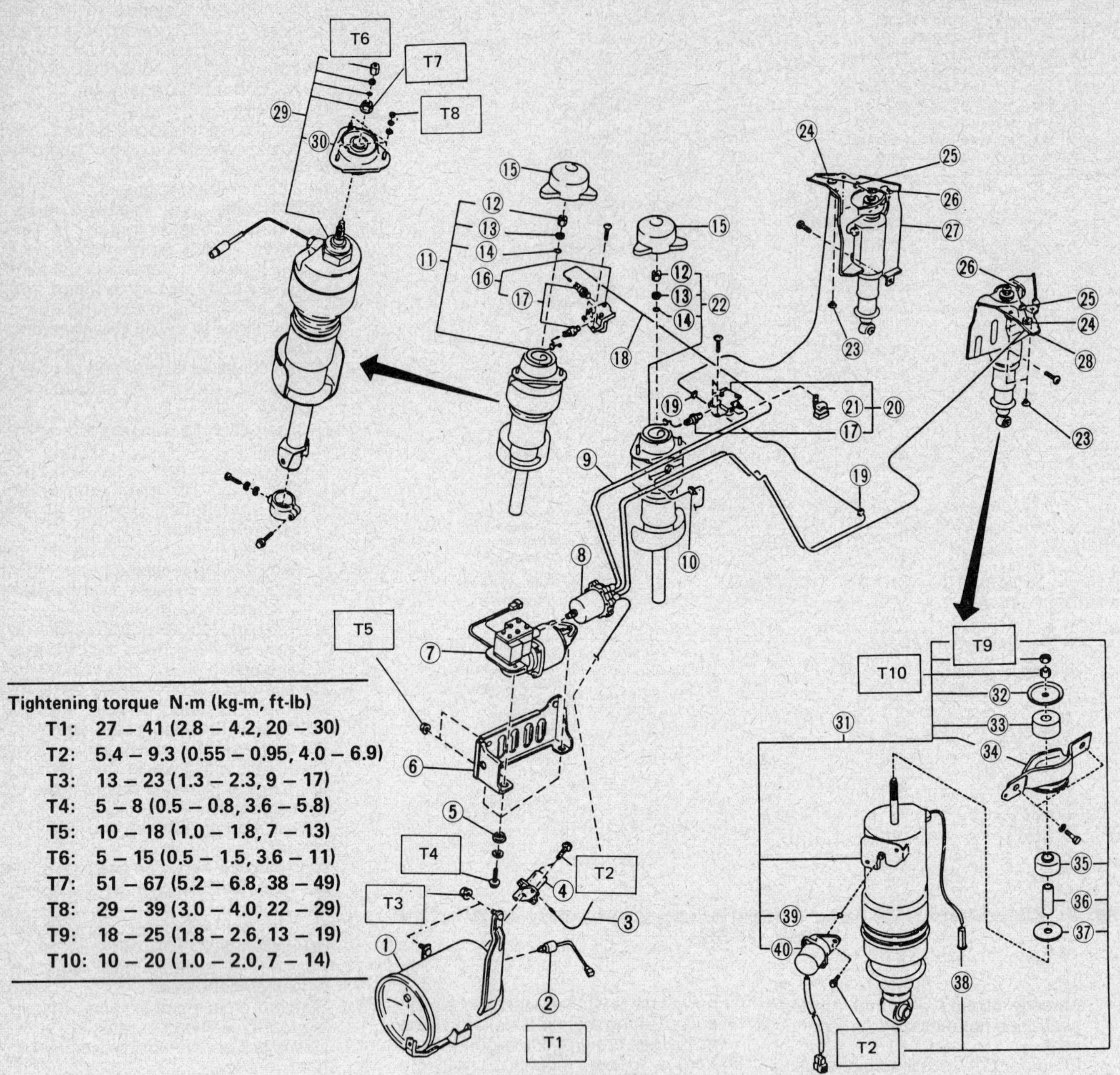

1 Air tank CP
2 Pressure switch
3 Pipe
4 Solenoid valve ASSY
5 Insulator
6 Compressor bracket
7 Compressor
8 Drier
9 Pipe
10 Clip
11 Pipe kit (F. sus. RH)
12 Cap
13 Bush
14 O-ring
15 Strut mount cap
16 Solenoid valve ASSY (RH)
17 Air joint ASSY
18 Pipe
19 Holder
20 Solenoid valve ASSY (LH)
21 Relay ASSY
22 Pipe kit (F. sus. LH)
23 Protector clip
24 Grommet
25 Clip
26 Clip
27 Protector (RH)
28 Protector (LH)
29 Front air suspension ASSY (LH or RH)
30 Strut mount
31 Rear air suspension ASSY (LH or RH)
32 Upper rubber plate
33 Upper rubber
34 Bracket CP (LH or RH)
35 Lower rubber
36 Collar
37 Upper plate
38 Connector
39 O-ring
40 Solenoid valve ASSY

Fig. 8 Pneumatic suspension system components

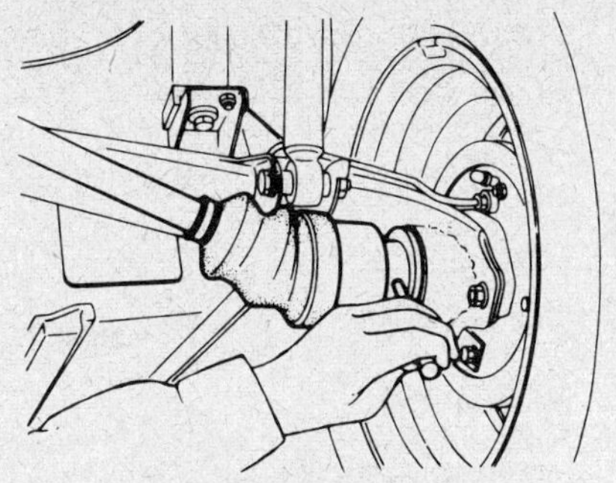

Fig. 9 Driveshaft spring pin removal

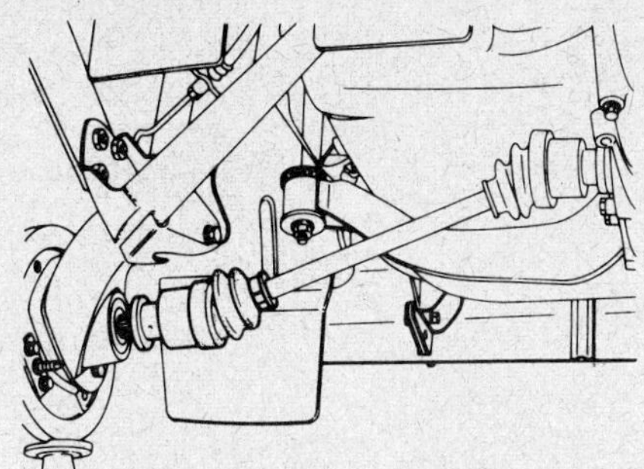

Fig. 10 Removing outer double offset joints

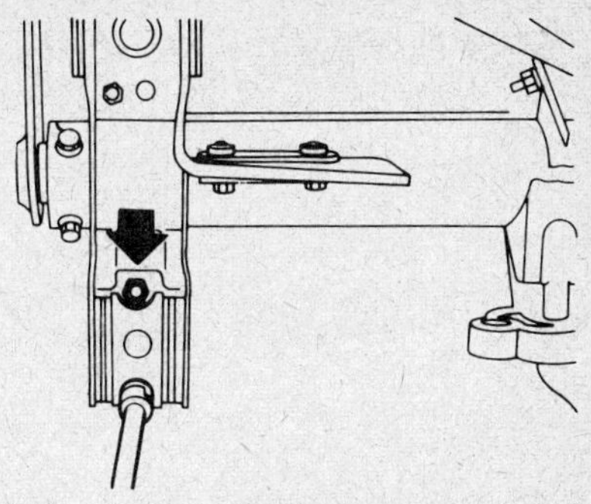

Fig. 11 Bushing removal. 1983–84

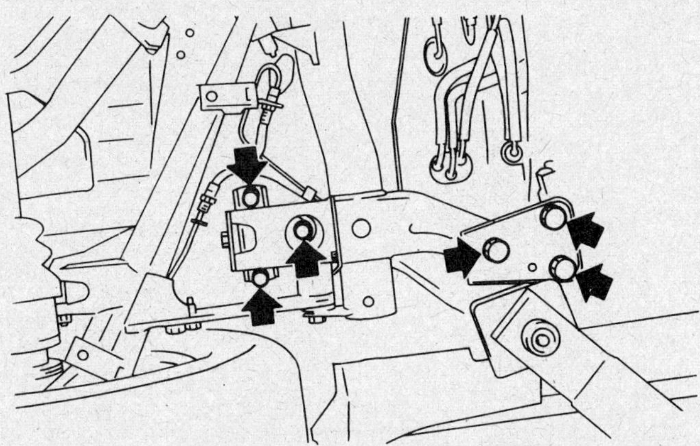

Fig. 12 Rear suspension crossmember mounting bolts. 1985–87

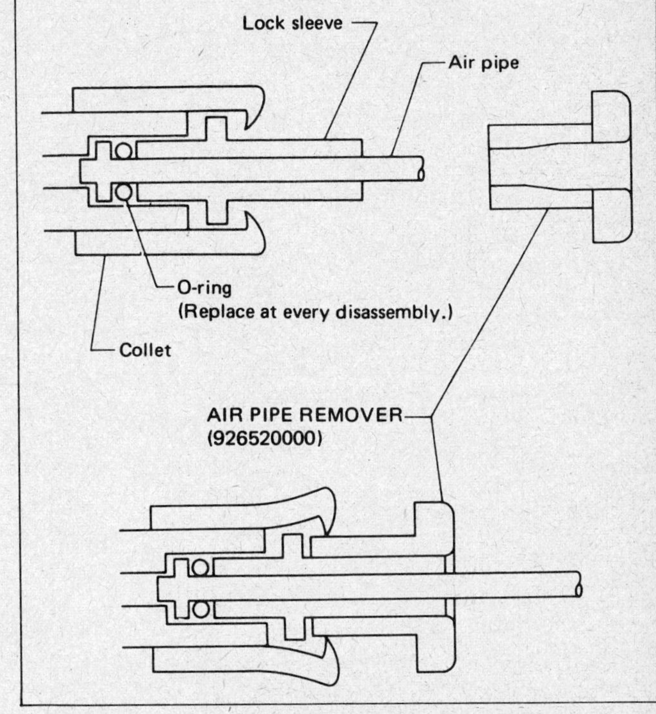

Fig. 13 Air line removal & installation. Models w/pneumatic suspension system

6 and 7 for component identification.

2. Position suitable jack under center of rear crossmember.
3. Remove retaining bolts, **Fig. 12**, from both ends of crossmember.
4. Slowly lower jack and withdraw suspension assembly from under vehicle.
5. Reverse procedure to install, torquing all fasteners to specifications shown in **Figs. 6 and 7.**

Pneumatic Suspension

Removal and installation procedures for models with pneumatic suspension are basically similar to those for models with conventional suspension. When removing pneumatic suspension assembly or individual components, refer to **Figs. 6, 7 and 8** for component identification, and observe the following precautions:

1. Before disassembling suspension components, ensure ignition switch is off, and disconnect battery ground cable.
2. Disconnect air lines using suitable tool, **Fig. 13,** and take care not to damage fittings or O-ring sealing surfaces.
3. Ensure air pressure is discharged before removing air spring mounting fasteners.
4. Always use new O-rings, lightly lubricated with multi-purpose grease, when connecting air lines or fittings.
5. During installation, ensure wiring harnesses and air lines are properly aligned and secured in brackets and retaining straps.
6. When installing components of the pneumatic suspension system, torque fasteners to values shown in **Fig. 8.**

FRONT SUSPENSION & STEERING SECTION

INDEX

HUB & ROTOR REPLACE

1. Apply parking brake, then loosen wheel lug nuts.
2. Remove grease cap and cotter pin, then loosen axle castle nut.
3. Raise and support front of vehicle.
4. Remove wheel and tire assembly.
5. Unfasten caliper and position aside, leaving brake line attached.
6. Remove caliper mounting bracket.
7. Remove axle castle nut and washer, then the hub and rotor assembly.
8. Reverse procedure to install.

STABILIZER REPLACE

1983–84

1. Raise and support front of vehicle, then remove wheel and tire assembly.
2. Remove the bolt at the bracket connecting one end of the stabilizer to the leading rod, **Figs. 1 and 2.**
3. Remove the bracket to rear crossmember retaining bolt.
4. Remove bracket and bushing from stabilizer.
5. Disconnect stabilizer from leading rod and rear crossmember.
6. Reverse procedure to install.

1985–87

1. Raise and support front of vehicle and remove wheels.
2. Remove bolts securing stabilizer shaft bracket to left and right transverse links, then disconnect brackets.
3. Remove bolts securing stabilizer bushing brackets to front crossmember and the brackets.
4. Remove crossmember jack-up plate retaining bolts, plate and the stabilizer shaft assembly, **Fig. 3.**
5. Transfer end brackets to replacement shaft and ensure crossmember bushing is positioned in bent portion of shaft.
6. Reverse procedure to install, torquing all fasteners to specifications shown in **Fig. 3** with vehicle at normal ride height.

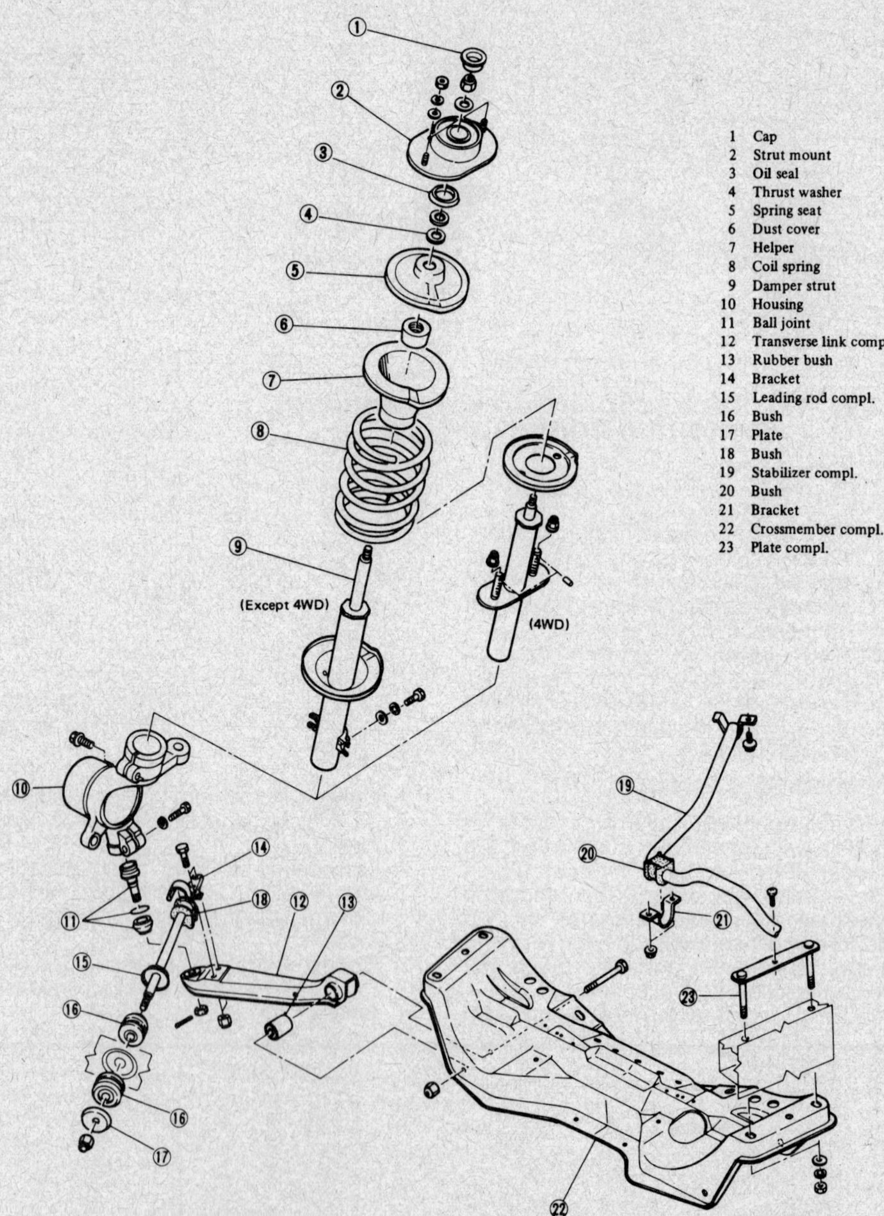

Fig. 1 Exploded view of front suspension. 1983–84

SUSPENSION STRUT REPLACE

CONVENTIONAL SUSPENSION

1. Disconnect battery ground cable.
2. Raise and support front of vehicle then remove wheel and tire assembly.
3. Release parking brake and disconnect brake hose from brake pipe at apron bracket inside wheelwell.
4. Remove brake hose at caliper body.
5. Plug brake line to avoid loss of fluid.
6. Remove brake hose from strut bracket by removing brake hose clip.
7. Remove bolts securing strut and strut bracket to axle housing, **Figs. 1 and 3.**
8. Carefully remove the strut from housing with housing positioned downward.
9. Remove strut to shock tower retaining bolts.
10. Remove strut assembly from vehicle.
11. Position strut assembly in tool No. 925651000.
12. Position the tool hook in the upper end of coil spring.
13. Install tool No. 925651000 on the strut upper retaining bolts.
14. Remove locknut from strut rod using suitable 17 mm box wrench.
15. Pull strut mount of rod.
16. Remove thrust washer, oil seal, and thrust bearing washer.
17. Remove the upper spring retainer from the rod.
18. Carefully release spring tension and remove tool.
19. Remove oil seal assembly using tool No. 925390000.
20. To disassemble strut assembly, proceed as follows:
    a. Compress strut to minimum length to prevent piston rod damage.
    b. Pull piston rod out slightly, packing should be released from strut tube.
    c. Pull out piston rod and rod guide.
    d. Slowly remove inner cylinder.
    e. Pour oil out of strut tube.
    f. Slowly insert piston rod into inner cylinder liner.
    g. Slowly insert inner cylinder with piston rod into strut tube.
    h. Pour 205cc of oil into strut tube on all models except 4 wheel drive.
    i. Pour 220cc of oil into 4 wheel drive model shock tubes.
    j. Position packing on rod guide.
    k. Install rod guide assembly into inner cylinder. **Use caution to avoid damage to packing from strut rod threads.**
    l. Install oil seal assembly on piston rod using tool 925380000.
    m. Apply grease to the oil seal lips.
21. Reinstall oil seal assembly.
22. Reverse procedure to assemble and install.

PNEUMATIC SUSPENSION

Strut replacement procedures on these models are similar to those for conventional suspension. However, service on air spring strut assemblies is limited to replacement of the upper mount and replacement of the entire strut assembly. To service air spring strut assemblies, proceed as follows:

1. Disconnect battery ground cable and remove cap from top of strut, **Fig. 4.**
2. Disconnect air line from top of strut, then remove mud guard.
3. Release vehicle height sensor lead from clip and disconnect electrical connector.
4. Raise and support vehicle and remove strut assembly as outlined for models with conventional suspension.
5. Ensure all air has been discharged from air spring chamber, then remove strut mount retaining nut while holding strut shaft with spanner wrench 926510000 or equivalent. **Strut rod must be properly secured with spanner wrench to prevent damaging diaphragm.**
6. Transfer mount to replacement stud and torque retaining nut to 38-49 ft. lbs. while holding strut shaft with spanner wrench.
7. Install strut assembly as outlined for models with conventional suspension.
8. Secure height sensor lead in clip at a point 8.27 inches from strut and reconnect electrical connector.
9. Connect air line using new O-ring seal, lightly lubricated with multipurpose grease, and torque fitting to 3.6-10.8 ft. lbs.
10. Reverse remaining procedure to complete installation.

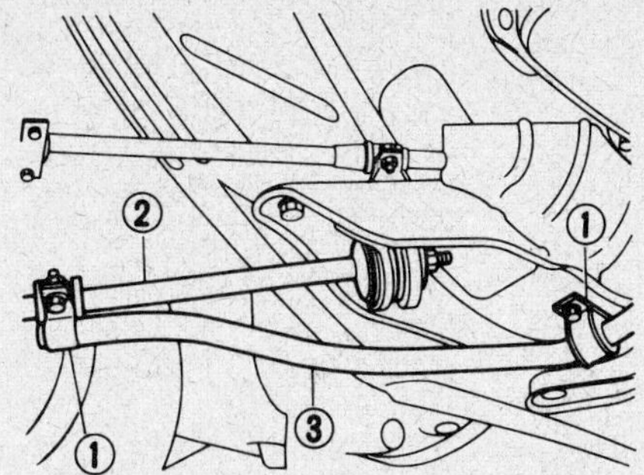

1 Bracket
2 Leading rod
3 Stabilizer

Fig. 2 Stabilizer removal. 1983-84

BALL JOINT REPLACE

1. Raise and support front of vehicle, then remove wheel and tire assembly.
2. Remove cotter pin and castle nut from ball stud, **Fig. 5,** and disconnect ball stud from transverse link.
3. Remove ball joint to housing retaining bolt.
4. Remove ball joint from housing.
5. Reverse procedure to install. **Torque castle nut to 29 ft. lbs. and ball joint to housing retaining bolts to 28-37 ft. lbs.**

CROSSMEMBER REPLACE

1. Disconnect battery ground cable.
2. Remove spare tire and raise and support front of vehicle, then remove wheel and tire assembly.
3. Remove air cleaner assembly and pitching stopper rod. **Install a dust cover over carburetor to prevent entry of foreign material.**
4. Remove parking brake cable bracket from transverse link.
5. Remove ball stud cotter pin and castle nut and disconnect tie rod from housing knuckle arm.
6. Remove front exhaust pipe.
7. Remove nut from transverse link bushing and disconnect link from crossmember.
8. Remove engine mount to crossmember retaining link.
9. Remove torque rod to pinion shaft retaining bolts.
10. Raise engine .39 inches (10 mm) using a suitable chain hoist or jack.
11. Position a suitable jack under the crossmember.
12. Remove crossmember to body retaining nuts and carefully lower crossmember from vehicle.
13. Reverse procedure to install. Torque transverse link bushing to crossmember retaining bolts to 40-47 ft. lbs. Torque tie rod end to housing to 43-51 ft. lbs. on 1983 models, or 18-22 ft. lbs. on 1984-87 models. Torque engine mount to crossmember 14-24 ft. lbs., steering pinion shaft to steering torque rod 10-14 ft. lbs., and crossmember to body to 40-47 ft. lbs.

MANUAL STEERING GEAR REPLACE

1983-84

1. Disconnect battery ground cable.
2. Raise and support front of vehicle and remove wheel and tire assembly.
3. Remove tie rod end castle nut cotter pin and loosen castle nut.
4. Remove tie rod end using suitable puller. **Apply penetrating oil to tie rod end to facilitate removal.**
5. Remove rubber coupling retaining nuts and disconnect pinion with steering gearbox from rubber coupling.
6. Remove exhaust air stove.
7. Remove exhaust manifold to engine retaining nuts and disconnect exhaust manifold.
8. Remove boot protector.
9. Remove steering gearbox to crossmember retaining bolts.
10. Pull steering gearbox down until pinion flange is out of crossmember. **Rotate gearbox and pull toward left to remove. Use caution to avoid damage to steering gearbox boots.**

1985-87

1. Disconnect battery ground cable,

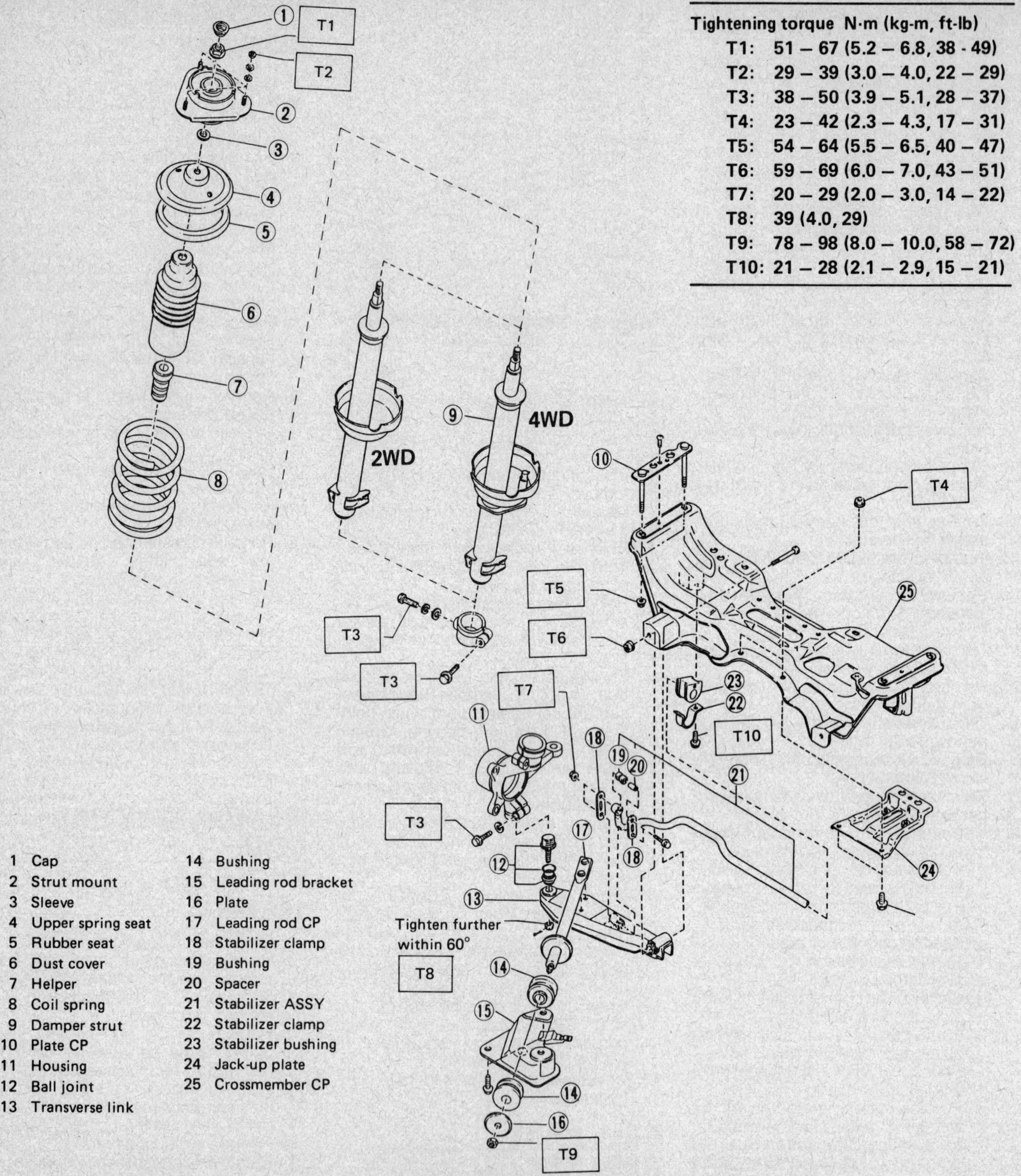

Fig. 3 Exploded view of conventional front suspension. 1985–87

raise and support vehicle, and remove front wheels.

2. Remove cotter pins from tie rod end castle nuts and the nuts, then disconnect tie rod ends from steering knuckles.
3. Remove pinch bolt securing steering shaft universal joint to steering gear.
4. Disconnect exhaust pipe from manifold and lower pipe.
5. Remove 4 steering gear mounting bolts and withdraw steering gear toward pinion side.
6. When shaft disengages torque rod universal joint, rotate steering gear toward rear and remove from vehicle.
7. Reverse procedure to install, torquing steering gear clamp bolts to 35-52 ft. lbs. and universal joint pinch bolt to 15-20 ft. lbs.

POWER STEERING GEAR REPLACE

1983–84

1. Disconnect the battery ground cable.
2. Raise and support vehicle on suitable jackstands and remove front wheels.
3. Remove tie rod end castle nut cotter

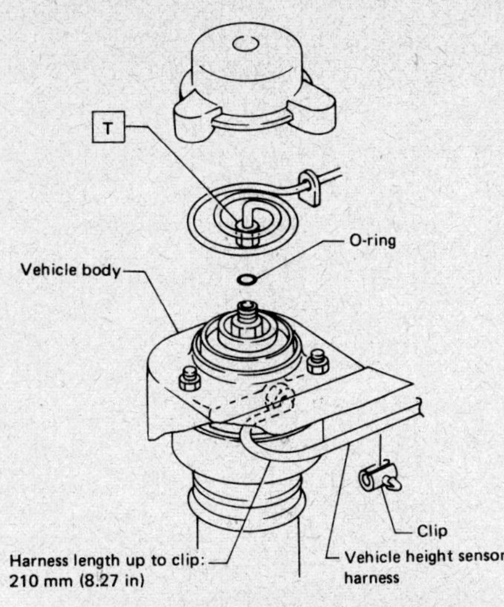

Fig. 4 Typical air spring installation

pin and loosen castle nut.

4. Remove tie rod end from knuckle arm using a suitable puller. **Apply penetrating oil to tie rod end to facilitate removal.**
5. Remove skid plate to gain access to steering gear.
6. Remove exhaust air stove.
7. Disconnect oxygen sensor and remove exhaust manifold to engine retaining nuts.
8. Remove boot protector.
9. Remove flare nuts from center of power steering gearbox.
10. Drain fluid by rotating steering wheel clockwise and counterclockwise. **It will facilitate power steering fluid removal to install vinyl pipes to gearbox to direct fluid into suitable container.**
11. Remove bolts on bottom and top sides of universal joint assembly.
12. Remove control valve flare nuts above crossmember. **Remove flare nut with 14 mm width across flat with tools 925670000 and 925680000.**
13. Remove piping and gearbox to crossmember retaining bolts.
14. Remove power steering piping.
15. Remove gear box to crossmember retaining bolts and power steering gear box and clamp.

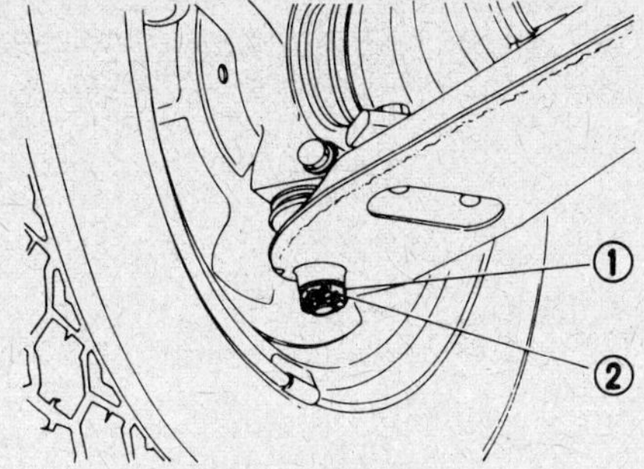

1 Castle nut
2 Cotter pin

Fig. 5 Ball joint removal

16. Reverse procedure to install. Torque gearbox to crossmember retaining bolts to 33-40 ft. lbs. Torque pipe A and B to 11.59-14.49 ft. lbs., pipe C to 18.1-25.4 ft. lbs. and pipe D to 28.9-32.6 ft. lbs., **Fig. 6.** Torque the exhaust manifold to engine nuts to 18.8-21.7 ft. lbs., exhaust pipe nuts and bolts to 31.2-38.4 ft. lbs. and hanger bolt to 18.1-25.4 ft. lbs. Torque the nuts at the yoke to 15.9-18.8 ft. lbs. Torque the tie rod end castle nut to 18-22 ft. lbs.

1985–87

Removal

1. Disconnect battery ground cable, remove spare tire (exc. XT Coupe), and on turbocharged models, remove spare tire support.
2. Disconnect electrical connector to thermo sensor, raise and support vehicle, and remove front wheels.
3. Remove front exhaust pipe assembly.
4. Remove cotter pins securing tie rod castle nuts and the castle nuts, then disconnect tie rods from steering knuckles using suitable puller.
5. Remove jack-up plate and stabilizer bushing clamp from crossmember.
6. Disconnect fluid lines at center of steering gear, connect suitable extension tubing and discharge fluid by turning steering wheel from lock to lock.
7. Remove upper and lower bolts securing universal joint to steering gear and intermediate shaft, scribe matching marks between shaft, universal joint and steering gear, then disconnect joint from steering gear.
8. Disconnect fluid lines from upper side of steering gear control valve housing.
9. Disconnect fluid lines from lower side of steering gear control valve housing, disconnecting upper line first.
10. Remove bolts securing steering gear clamps, then remove steering gear from crossmember.

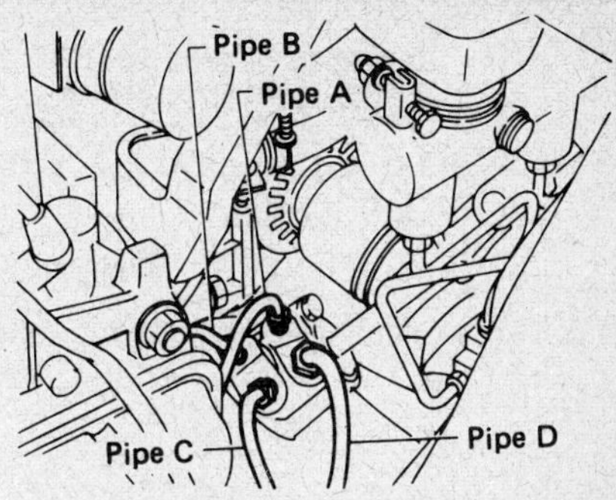

Fig. 6 Power steering fluid pipe locations

Installation

1. Position steering gear on crossmember, install clamps and retaining bolts and torque bolts to 35-52 ft. lbs.
2. Connect fluid lines to lower port of valve housing and to center ports on gear, connecting upper pipe first, and torque fittings to 7-12 ft. lbs.
3. Connect fluid lines to upper ports in valve housing, connecting lower pipe first, and torque fittings to 7-14 ft. lbs.
4. Install steering shaft joint as follows:
   a. Align bolt hole on long end of yoke with notch in steering shaft and push joint onto shaft.
   b. Align bolt hole in short end of yoke with notch in steering gear pinion shaft and engager yoke with pinion shaft.
   c. Ensure matching marks made during assembly are aligned, install universal yoke retaining bolts, ensuring that both bolts are properly engaged in shaft notches and torque bolts to 16-19 ft. lbs.
5. Reverse remaining procedure to complete installation.

WHEEL ALIGNMENT SECTION

INDEX

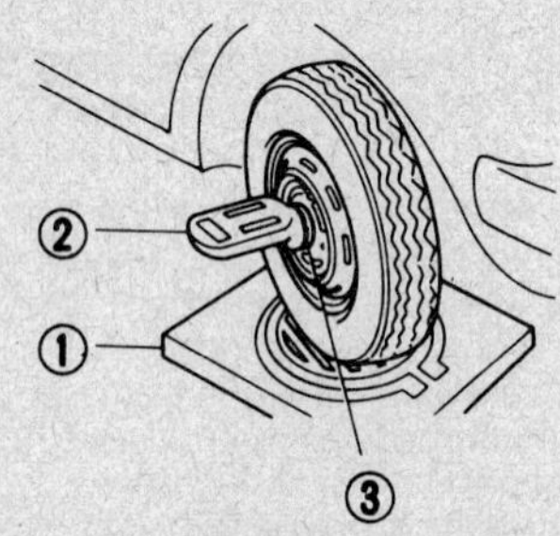

Fig. 1 Caster & camber measurement

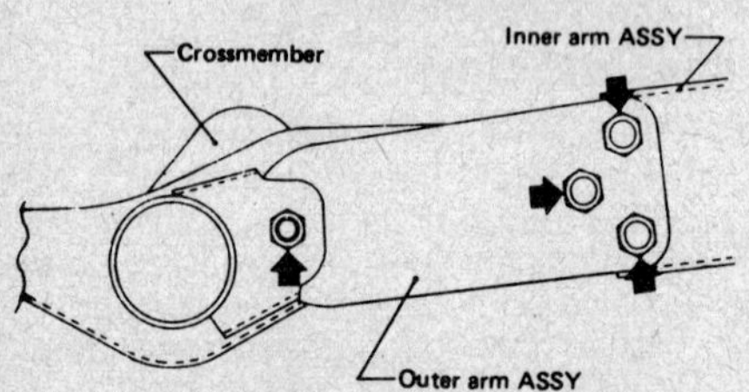

Fig. 3 Changing relative angle between inner & outer arms

CASTER INSPECTION

Caster angles are not adjustable, however, the following procedure may be used to ensure caster is within specifications. **Ensure tires are properly inflated prior to checking caster angles.**

1. Raise front of vehicle and position turning radius gauges under front wheels, then lower vehicle.
2. Install suitable adapter and gauge into center of wheel and measure caster angle, **Fig. 1.**
3. If caster is not within specifications, inspect suspension components for damage and repair as necessary, then recheck.

CAMBER INSPECTION & ADJUSTMENT

Ensure tires are properly inflated prior to checking or adjusting camber angles.

FRONT

Front camber angles are not adjustable, however, the following procedure may be used to ensure camber is within specifications.

1. Raise front of vehicle and position turning radius gauges under front wheels, then lower vehicle.
2. Install suitable adapter and gauge into center of wheel and measure camber angle, **Fig. 1.**
3. If camber is not within specifications, inspect suspension components for damage and repair as necessary, then recheck.

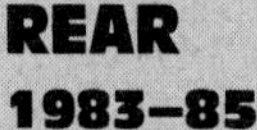

REAR

1983–85

Rear camber angle cannot be adjusted. If camber is not within specifications, inspect suspension components for damage and replace as necessary.

1986–87

Rear camber angle can be adjusted using the following procedure:

1. Raise and support rear of vehicle, then remove wheel and tire assembly.
2. Remove lower end of shock absorber to inner arm attaching bolt, then loosen outer arm mounting bolts, **Fig. 2.**
3. If camber angle is excessive in positive direction, use a suitable piece of wood as a lever and change angle as necessary so that angle formed by inner arm and outer arm centerlines increases, **Fig. 3.**
4. If camber angle is excessive in negative direction, use a suitable piece of wood as a lever and change angle as necessary so that angle formed by inner arm and outer arm centerlines decreases, **Fig. 3.**
5. Install shock absorber and tighten loosened bolts.

TOE INSPECTION & ADJUSTMENT

Ensure tires are properly inflated prior to checking or adjusting toe.

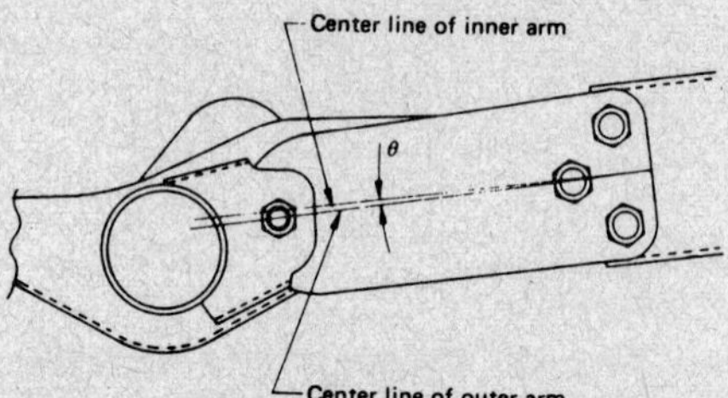

Fig. 2 Outer arm mounting bolts

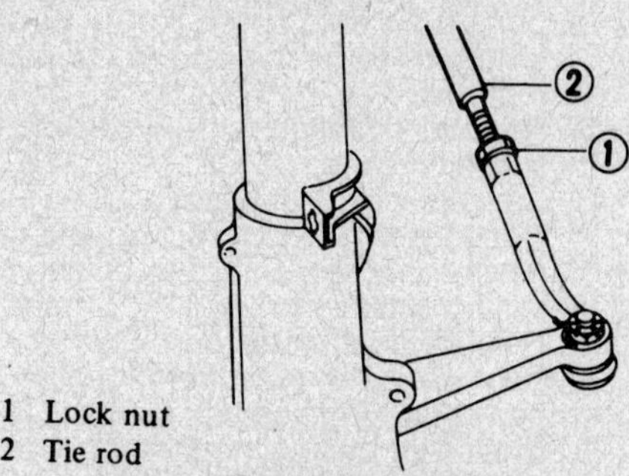

Fig. 4 Front toe-in adjustment

FRONT

The following procedure may be used to correct toe-in, if out of specifications.

1. Loosen both left and right tie rod locknuts, **Fig. 4.**
2. Turn both tie rods an equal amount until toe-in is within specifications.

REAR

1983–85

Toe cannot be adjusted. If toe is outside specifications, inspect suspension components for damage and replace as necessary.

1986–87

The following procedure may be used to correct toe, if out of specifications.

1. Raise and support rear of vehicle, then remove rear wheel and tire assembly.
2. Loosen outer arm mounting bolts, **Fig. 2.**
3. If toe-in is excessive, tighten outer arm mounting bolts while pushing end of spindle towards rear of vehicle.
4. If toe-out is excessive, tighten outer arm mounting bolts while pulling end of spindle toward front of vehicle.
5. Tighten outer arm attaching mounting bolt.

SUZUKI SAMURAI (Japan)

INDEX OF SERVICE OPERATIONS

General Engine Specifications

Year	Engine CID/ Liters	Carburetor	Bore & Stroke Inch (mm)	Compression Ratio	Maximum Brake HP @ RPM	Maximum Torque Ft. Lbs. @ RPM	Normal Oil Pressure psi @ 3000 RPM
1986–87	4-80.8/1.3L	2 Barrel	2.91 x 3.03 (74 x 77)	8.9	—	—	42.7–59.7

Alternator & Regulator Specifications

Year	Model	Current Rating		Voltage Regulator	
		Amps	Volts	Voltage	RPM
1986–87	—	45	—	14.2–14.8	—

Starter Motor Specifications

Year	Volt	Output kw	Direction of Rotation	Brush Length Inch	No. of Pinion Teeth	Brush Spring Tension Lbs.
1986–87	12	.9	CW	.67	8	3.53

Valve Specifications

Year	Valve Lash①		Valve Angles		Valve Spring Installed Height	Valve Spring Pressure Lbs. @ In.	Stem Clearance		Stem Diameter	
	Int.	Exh.	Seat	Face			Intake	Exhaust	Intake	Exhaust
1986–87	.0051–.0067②	.0063–.0079②	45°	—	—	③	.0008–.0019	.0014–.0025	.2742–.2748	.2737–.2742

①—When coolant temp. is 59–77°F.

②—When coolant temp. is 140–154°F; Int., .009–.011 inch and Exh., .0102–.0118 inch.

③—54.7–64.3 lbs. per inch; no less than 50.2 lbs. per inch.

Pistons, Pins, Rings, Crankshaft & Bearings

Year	Piston Clearance	Ring End Gap Comp.	Ring End Gap Oil	Wrist Pin Diameter	Rod Bearings Shaft Diameter	Rod Bearings Bearing Clearance	Main Bearings Shaft Dia.	Main Bearings Bearing Clearance	Main Bearings Thrust On Bearing No.	Shaft Endplay
1986–87	.0008–.0015	.0079–.0137 ①	.0079–.0275	.6691–.6693	1.6529–1.6535	.0012–.0019	1.7710–1.7716	.0008–.0016	3	.0044–.0122

①—Top ring, .0079–.0129 inch.

Engine Tightening Specifications

Year	Spark Plug Ft. Lbs.	Cylinder Head Bolts Ft. Lbs.	Intake Manifold Ft. Lbs.	Exhaust Manifold Ft. Lbs.	Rocker Arm Shaft Bracket Ft. Lbs.	Rocker Arm Cover Ft. Lbs.	Connecting Rod Cap Bolts Ft. Lbs.	Main Bearing Cap Bolts Ft. Lbs.	Flywheel to Crankshaft Ft. Lbs.	Vibration Damper or Pulley Ft. Lbs.
1986–87	14.5–21.5	46–50.5	13.5–20	13.5–20	—	3–3.5	24–26.5	36.5–41	41.5–47	—

Brake Specifications

Year	Brake Drum Inside Diameter	Wheel Cylinder Bore Diameter Front Disc	Wheel Cylinder Bore Diameter Rear Drum	Master Cylinder Bore Diameter	Disc Brake Rotor Nominal Thickness	Disc Brake Rotor Minimum Thickness	Runout (T.I.R.)
1986–87	8.66	—	—	—	.394	.334	—

Wheel Alignment Specifications

Year	Caster Angle, Degrees Limits	Caster Angle, Degrees Desired	Camber Angles, Degrees Limits	Camber Angles, Degrees Desired	Toe-In Inch	Kingpin Inclination
1986–87	—	3½°	—	1°	.08–.24	9°

Cooling System & Capacity Data

Year	Cooling System Capacity Qts.	Radiator Cap Relief Pressure psi	Thermostat Open Temp. °F	Fuel Tank Gals.	Engine Oil Qts.	Transmission	
						Man. Trans. Pts.	Auto. Trans. Refill Qts.
1986–87	5.3	12.8	①	10.6	3.7	2.7	—

①—Thermostat marked "A," 179° F and thermostat marked "B," 190° F.

ELECTRICAL SECTION

INDEX

ALTERNATOR TESTING

When testing alternator, note the following:

1. Do not reverse polarities of IG and L terminals.
2. Do not short IG and L terminals. Always connect these terminals through a lamp.
3. Do not connect any load between L & E terminals.

UNDERCHARGED BATTERY

1. Ensure that undercharged condition has not been caused by accessories left on for extended periods.
2. Check drive belt for proper tension.
3. Inspect wiring for defects. Ensure that all connections are clean and tight, including slip connectors at alternator and bulkhead. Also, check battery cable connections at battery, starter and ignition ground cable.
4. Connect a suitable voltmeter and ammeter as shown in **Fig. 1.** Connect voltmeter between alternator B terminal and ground. Connect ammeter between alternator B terminal and battery positive terminal.
5. Perform no-load check as follows:
   a. Increase engine speed from idle to 2000 RPM and note readings. Voltage readings will vary with regulator case temperature.
   b. If voltage is higher than 14.2-14.8 volts at 77 degrees F, replace IC regulator.
   c. If voltage is below specification, check IC regulator and alternator by measuring voltage at B terminal while grounding F terminal. If voltage is above specification, replace IC regulator. If voltage is below specification, test alternator.
6. Perform load check as follows:
   a. Run engine at 2000 RPM and switch on headlights and heater blower motor. Ensure that current is at least 20 amps, if less, alternator is defective.

OVERCHARGED BATTERY

If an overcharging condition exists, such as spewing of electrolyte, check field windings for grounds and shorts. If defective, replace rotor and test regulator using a suitable tester.

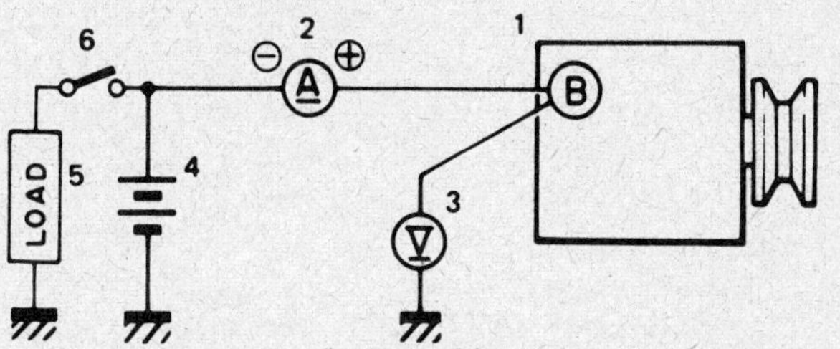

Fig. 1 Alternator test connections

STARTER REPLACE

1. Disconnect battery ground cable.
2. Disconnect solenoid electrical connector and battery cable from starter terminals.
3. Remove two starter motor attaching bolts, then starter.
4. Reverse procedure to install.

IGNITION SWITCH REPLACE

1. Disconnect battery ground cable.
2. Remove two screws and four nuts securing steering column upper and lower trim panels.
3. Cut shear bolts securing ignition switch, then disconnect electrical connector and remove switch and lock assembly. **It may be necessary to remove column to gain access to ignition switch.**
4. Reverse procedure to install noting the following:
   a. Tighten ignition switch shear bolts, until head of each bolt breaks off.

HEADLAMP & WIPER WASHER SWITCH REPLACE

1. Disconnect battery ground cable.
2. Remove steering wheel pad.
3. Using a suitable puller, remove steering wheel.
4. Remove combination switch attaching bolts, disconnect electrical connectors, then combination switch.
5. Reverse procedure to install.

TURN SIGNAL SWITCH REPLACE

Refer to "Headlamp & Wiper Washer Switch, Replace" for removal procedure.

INSTRUMENT CLUSTER REPLACE

1. Disconnect battery ground cable.
2. Remove steering wheel trim panels.
3. Lower steering column.
4. Remove instrument panel cluster bezel attaching screws and bezel, **Fig. 2.**
5. Disconnect speedometer cable and wire harness electrical connector, then remove instrument cluster.
6. Reverse procedure to install.

BLOWER MOTOR REPLACE

1. Disconnect battery ground cable, then drain cooling system.
2. Disconnect heater inlet and outlet hoses from heater unit pipes.
3. Remove instrument panel assembly as follows:
   a. Remove horn pad, then steering wheel using a suitable puller.
   b. Remove radio case stay screws and pull out radio case with radio and cigarette lighter, then disconnect radio and cigarette lighter electrical connectors.
   c. Remove ashtray, then ashtray plate attaching screws.
   d. Disconnect front hood opening cable from lock assembly.
   e. Loosen glove compartment stay screw and hood opening cable locknut from backside of glove compartment cover.

[Combination meter without tachometer]

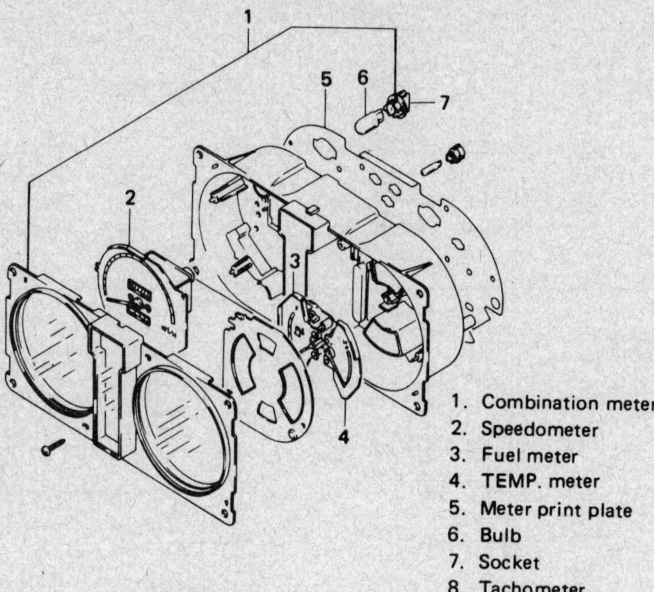

[Combination meter with tachometer]

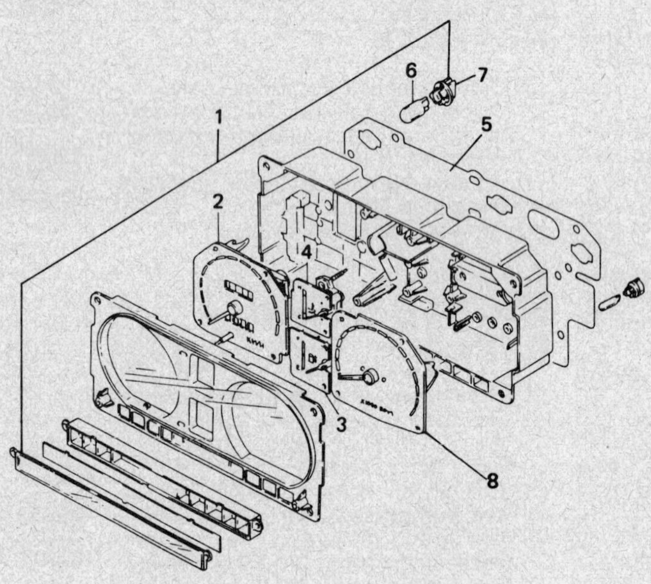

Fig. 2 Instrument cluster removal

f. Disconnect electrical connectors and control cables from heater control panel, **Fig. 3.**
g. Pull out heater control knobs and plate, then loosen heater lever case screws.
h. Disconnect electrical connectors from speedometer and instrument panel.
i. Disconnect speedometer cable.
j. Release wire harness clamps installed to instrument panel.
k. Loosen screws securing instrument panel, then remove instrument panel.

4. Loosening front door stopper screws, then remove steering column holder. Disconnect blower motor and resistor electrical connectors. Loosen heater case securing nut from inside engine compartment, then remove heater assembly.
7. Remove blower motor, **Fig. 3.**
8. Reverse procedure to install.

HEATER CORE REPLACE

Repeat procedure for "Blower Motor, Replace" then refer to **Fig. 3** for heater core removal.

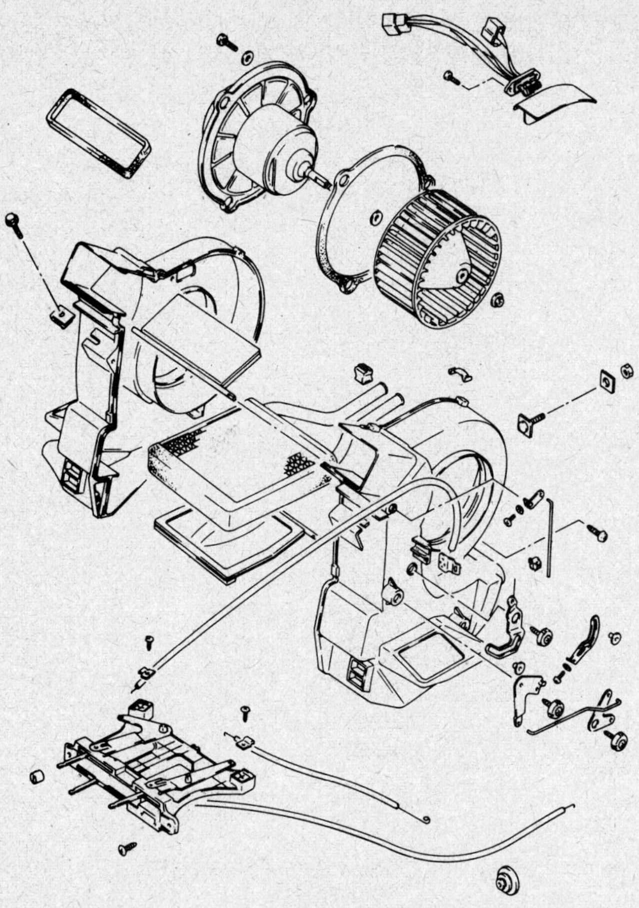

Fig. 3 Heater assembly exploded view

RADIO

REPLACE

1. Disconnect battery ground cable.
2. Remove radio knobs, then radio mounting nuts.
3. Disconnect radio electrical connector and antenna cable.
4. Remove radio.
5. Reverse procedure to install.

ENGINE SECTION

INDEX

ENGINE
REPLACE

1. Disconnect battery cables.
2. Disconnect electrical connectors from starter.
3. Disconnect electrical connectors from alternator.
4. Disconnect water temperature gauge and thermal switch electrical connectors from intake manifold, then the ground wire.
5. Disconnect carburetor fuel cut solenoid valve, vent solenoid valve and mixture control solenoid valve, then the TWSV (Three Way Solenoid Valve) and VSV (Vacuum Switching Valve).
6. Remove breather hoses from air cleaner case.
7. Remove air intake case from carburetor body, then air inlet hose.
8. Disconnect accelerator cable from carburetor.
9. Disconnect vacuum hoses from Thermostatically Controlled Air Cleaner (TCAC) and canister from intake manifold.
10. Remove fuel tank filler cap to release fuel pressure, then disconnect fuel feed and return hoses from fuel pump.
11. Disconnect electrical connector from oil pressure sending unit and oxygen sensor.
12. Disconnect electrical connectors from transmission.
13. Disconnect electrical connector from distributor, then remove high tension cable from ignition coil.
14. Drain cooling system and disconnect radiator hoses from engine.
15. Remove fan shroud and cooling fan, then the radiator.
16. Disconnect brake booster vacuum hose from pipe.
17. Disconnect electrical connector from distributor gear case.
18. Remove bolts attaching gear shift lever boot and slide boot upward.
19. Slide inner gear shift lever dust boot upwards, then remove gear shift lever attaching bolts and remove gear shift lever.
20. Raise and support vehicle.
21. Disconnect exhaust pipe from manifold.
22. Disconnect clutch cable from engine mounting bracket and clutch release lever.
23. Drain transmission oil.

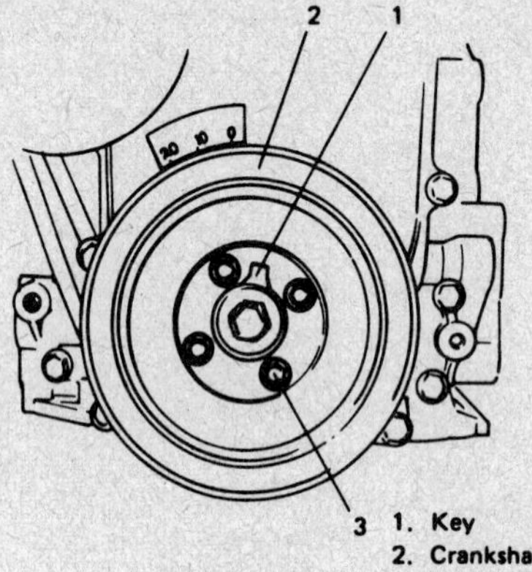

Fig. 1 Crankshaft pulley removal

24. Disconnect propeller shafts from transmission and transfer case.
25. Install a suitable engine lifting device to prevent engine from dropping.
26. Remove catalytic converter bracket mounting bolts.
27. Remove transmission crossmember attaching bolts, then crossmember.
28. Lower vehicle, then remove bolts securing engine mounts.
29. Remove engine and transmission as an assembly. **Before removing engine, ensure that all hoses, cables and electrical connectors are disconnected.**
30. Remove clutch lower plate and separate transmission from engine.
31. Reverse procedure to install.

TIMING BELT
REPLACE

1. Disconnect battery ground cable.
2. Loosen fan drive belt and remove bolts securing radiator fan shroud and cooling fan, then remove shroud and fan.
3. Remove water pump belt and pump pulley.
4. Remove crankshaft pulley attaching bolts and the pulley, **Fig. 1.** It is not necessary to remove crankshaft pulley center bolt.
5. Remove timing belt cover attaching bolts, then timing belt cover.
6. Loosen tensioner nut and bolt, **Fig. 2,** and remove timing belt.
7. Remove valve cover, then loosen all valve adjusting screws all the way to allow free rotation of camshaft.
8. Rotate camshaft pulley clockwise and align timing mark on camshaft pulley with "V" mark on belt inside cover as shown in **Fig. 3.**
9. Rotate crankshaft clockwise using a 17 mm wrench on crankshaft timing belt pulley bolt, **Fig. 4,** and align punch mark on timing belt pulley with arrow mark on oil pump as shown in **Fig. 4.**
10. With all timing marks aligned, install timing belt so that drive side of belt is free from any slack with tensioner plate pushed up by finger, **Fig. 2. When installing timing belt, match arrow on timing belt with rotating direction of crankshaft.**
11. Rotate crankshaft two complete revolutions to allow belt to be free of any slack, then tighten tensioner stud to 7-8.5 ft. lbs. and tensioner bolt to 17.5-21.5 ft. lbs., **Fig. 5.**
12. Install timing belt cover and tighten bolts to 7-8.5 ft. lbs.
13. Install water pump belt and pulley.
14. Install crankshaft pulley bolts, **Fig. 1,** and torque bolts to 7.5-9.0 ft. lbs.
15. Refer to "Valves, Adjust" and adjust valve clearance.

VALVES
ADJUST

1. Remove air cleaner assembly, then valve cover.
2. Rotate crankshaft to position cam lobe and rocker arm as shown in **Fig. 6.**
3. Using a suitable feeler gauge measure clearance at gap (A). Clearance should be as noted in **Fig. 6.**
4. If clearance is not as specified, adjust by turning adjusting screw until correct clearance is obtained, **Fig. 6.**
5. After adjustment, torque screw locknut to 11-13.5 ft. lbs.
6. Install valve cover and torque bolts to 3-3.5 ft. lbs.
7. Install air cleaner assembly.

ENGINE DISASSEMBLY

1. Drain engine oil.
2. Using Flywheel Holder 09924-17810, or equivalent, remove clutch cover attaching bolts, then clutch cover and disc.

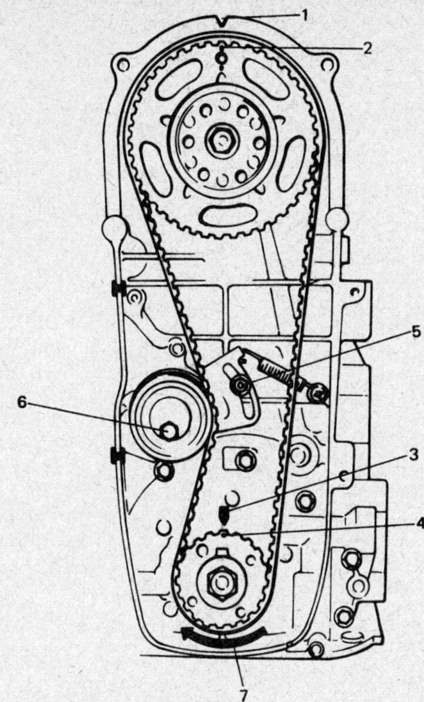

1. "V" mark
2. Timing mark
3. Arrow mark
4. Punch mark
5. Tensioner nut
6. Tensioner bolt
7. Turning direction

Fig. 2 Timing belt installation & removal

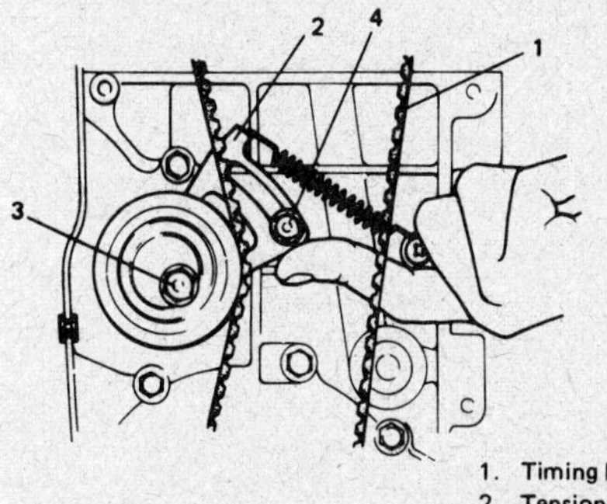

1. Timing belt
2. Tensioner plate
3. Tensioner bolt
4. Tensioner stud

Fig. 7 Timing belt removal

3. Disconnect spark plug wires and vacuum hoses noting direction for installation, then remove distributor assembly.
4. Remove fuel pump attaching bolts, then fuel pump and rod.
5. Remove crankshaft pulley attaching bolts, then crankshaft pulley, **Fig. 1. It is not necessary to remove crankshaft pulley center bolt.**
6. Remove timing belt cover attaching bolts, then timing belt cover.
7. Loosen tensioner bolt and stud, then remove timing belt from crankshaft timing belt pulley by pushing upward on tensioner with finger, **Fig. 7.**

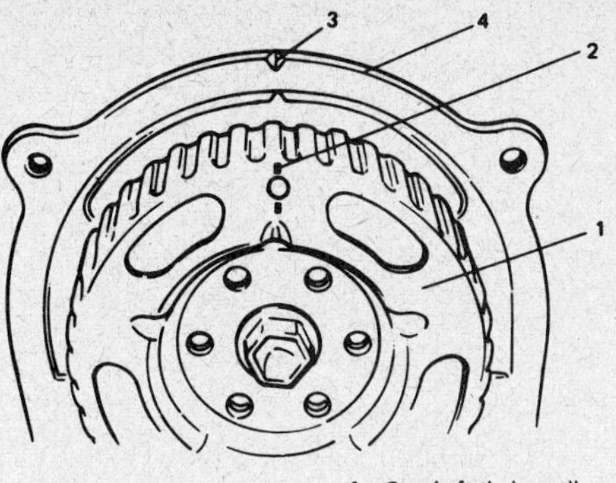

1. Camshaft timing pulley
2. Timing mark
3. "V" mark
4. Belt inside cover

Fig. 3 Camshaft pulley alignment

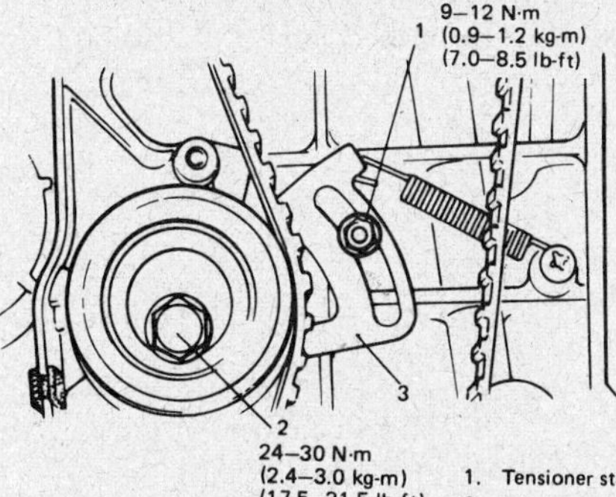

1. Tensioner stud
2. Tensioner bolt
3. Tensioner plate

Fig. 5 Adjusting timing belt tension

8. Remove timing belt tensioner, tensioner plate and spring.
9. Using Camshaft Holder Tool 09917-68210, or equivalent, remove camshaft timing belt pulley, **Fig. 8.**
10. Using Flywheel Holder 09924-17810, or equivalent, so that crankshaft will not rotate, remove crankshaft timing belt pulley bolt, pulley and belt guide, **Fig. 9.**
11. Remove crankshaft timing belt pulley key from crankshaft.
12. Remove water pump attaching bolts, then water pump.
13. Remove exhaust manifold shield attaching bolts, then shield.
14. Remove exhaust manifold attaching bolts, then exhaust manifold.
15. Remove oil filter.
16. Remove hoses from water pump inlet pipe.
17. Disconnect positive PCV hose from valve cover.
18. Remove intake manifold attaching bolts, then intake and carburetor as an assembly.
19. Remove water pump inlet pipe attaching bolts, then inlet pipe.
20. Remove valve cover attaching bolts, then valve cover.
21. Loosen all valve adjusting screws and rocker arm shaft bolts, then pull out rocker arm shaft while separating rocker arms and springs.
22. Remove camshaft from rear of engine.

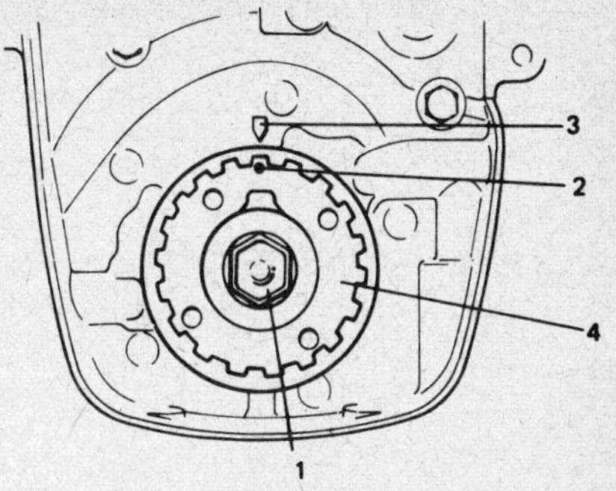

1. Crankshaft timing belt pulley bolt
2. Punch mark
3. Arrow mark
4. Crankshaft timing belt pulley

Fig. 4 Aligning timing belt pulley punch mark with oil pump arrow

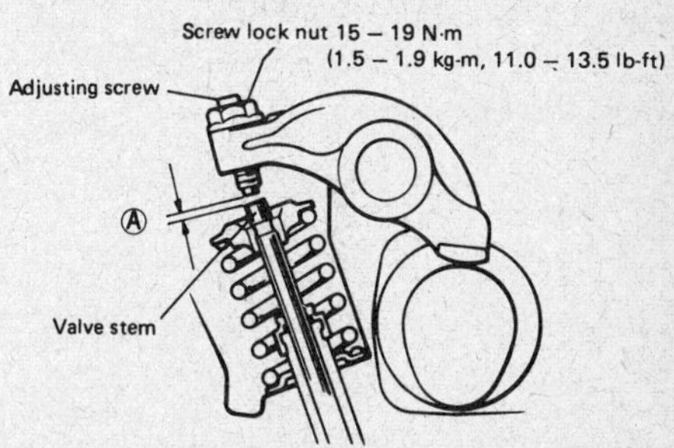

Fig. 6 Adjusting valve lash

23. Remove cylinder head attaching bolts, then cylinder head.
24. Using a suitable spring compressor, compress valve springs and remove valve locks, then spring and valve.
25. Using a suitable screwdriver, remove valve stem oil seals from valve guides, then valve spring seats. **Do not reuse oil seals after removal.**
26. Using Flywheel Holder Tool 09924-17810, or equivalent, remove flywheel attaching bolts, then flywheel.
27. Remove oil dipstick attaching bolt, then oil dipstick.
28. Remove oil pan attaching bolts, then oil pan.
29. Remove oil pump strainer attaching bolts, then oil pump strainer.
30. Remove connecting rod bearing cap bolts, then bearing caps noting direction for installation.
31. Decarbon top of each cylinder bore, before removing pistons from cylinder.
32. Remove piston and connecting rod assemblies out through top of cylinder bore. **Before removing pistons, scribe cylinder number on top of pistons and ensure each bearing cap matches rod and piston assemblies for installation.**
33. Remove oil pump attaching bolts, then oil pump and pump rotor plate.
34. Remove oil seal housing attaching bolts, then oil seal housing.
35. Remove crankshaft bearing cap bolts, then bearing caps noting direction for installation.

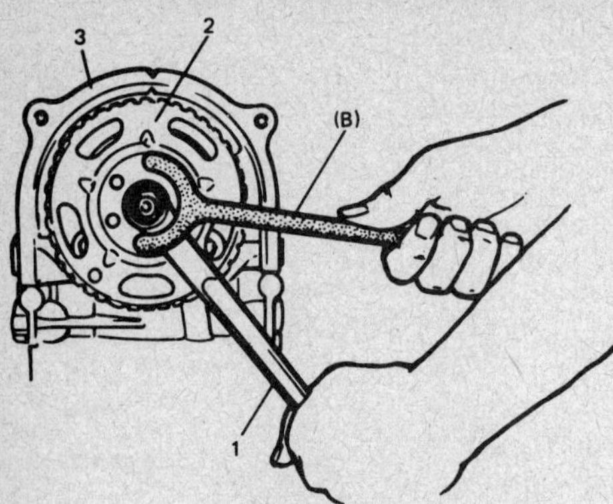

(B) Camshaft lock holder (Special tool 09917-68210)
1. Wrench
2. Camshaft timing belt pulley
3. Timing belt inside cover

Fig. 8 Timing belt sprocket removal

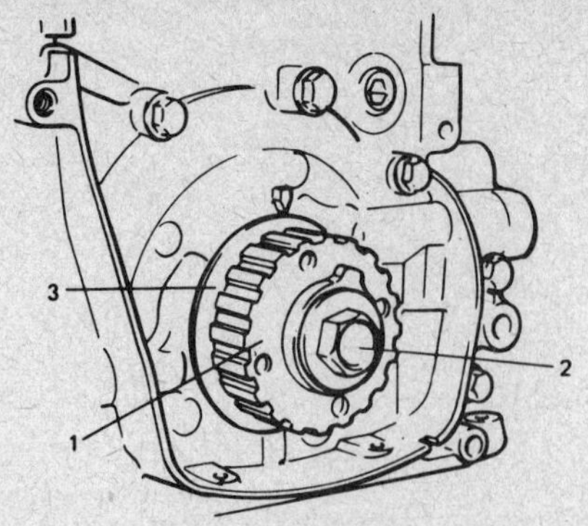

1. Crankshaft timing belt pulley
2. Pulley bolt
3. Timing belt guide

Fig. 9 Removing crankshaft timing belt pulley

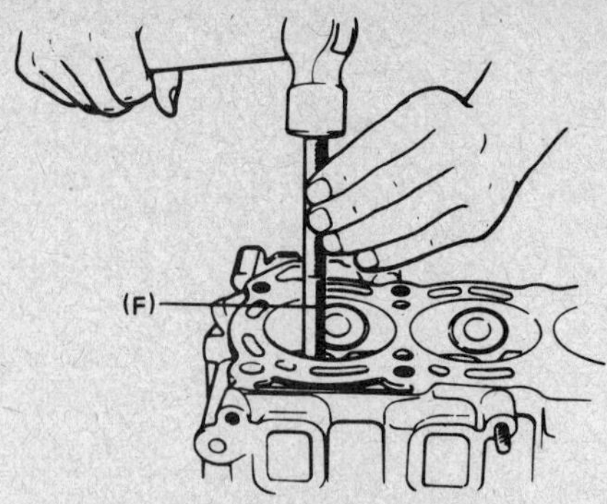

(F) Valve guide remover (Special tool 09916-44511)

Fig. 10 Removing valve guides

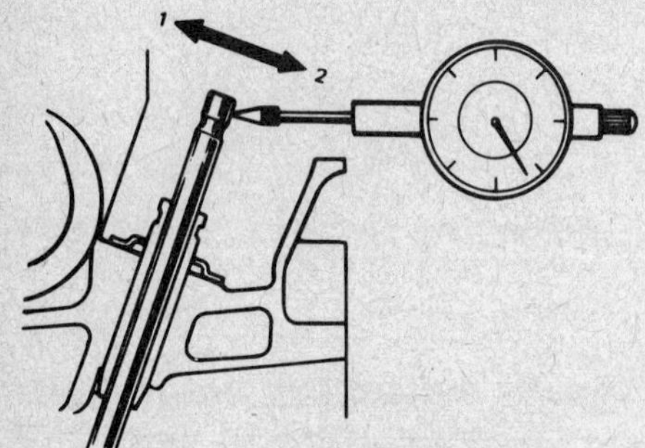

Fig. 11 Checking valve stem end deflection

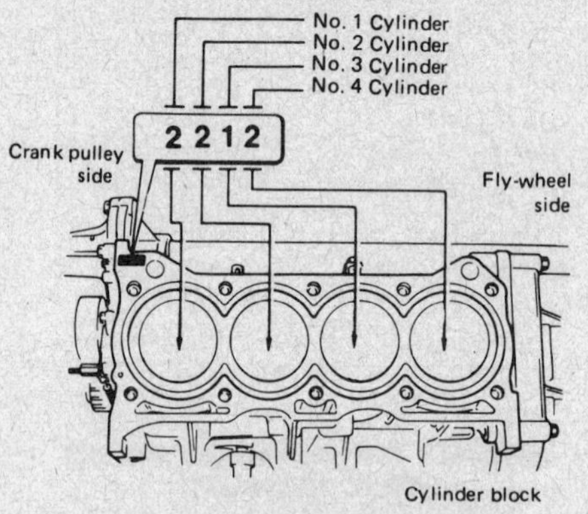

Fig. 12 Engine block stamping

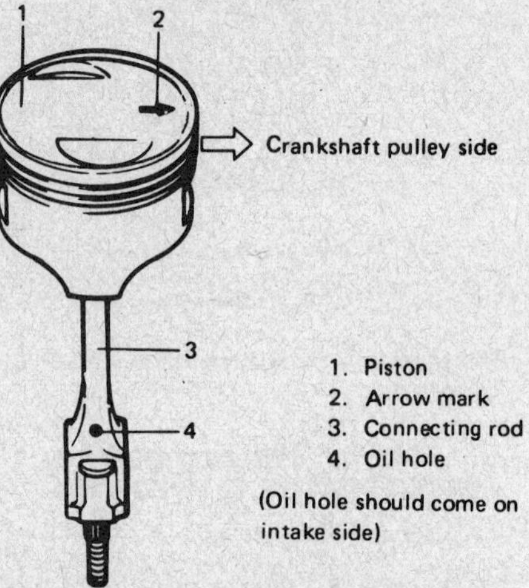

1. Piston
2. Arrow mark
3. Connecting rod
4. Oil hole

(Oil hole should come on intake side)

Fig. 13 Piston installation

36. Remove crankshaft from cylinder block.

SUBASSEMBLY SERVICE

ROCKER ARM & SHAFTS

1. Using a suitable micrometer and a bore gauge, measure rocker shaft diameter and rocker arm inside diameter. Note readings.
2. Rocker shaft diameter should be 0.628-0.629 inch (15.973-15.998 mm). If diameter is not as specified, replace shaft.
3. Rocker arm inside diameter should be 0.629-0.630 inch (16.000-16.018 mm). If diameter is not as specified, replace arm.
4. Take readings obtained in steps 2 and 3, and the difference between the two readings is arm to shaft clearance. Arm to shaft clearance should be 0.0005-0.0017 inch (0.012-0.045 mm). If clearance is not as specified, replace shaft or arm as necessary.
5. Using "V" blocks and a suitable dial indicator, check runout of rocker arm shaft. Runout should not exceed 0.004 inch (0.12 mm).

VALVE GUIDES

1. Using valve guide removal tool 09916-44511, or equivalent, remove valve guides as shown in **Fig. 10. Do not reuse valve guides after removal.**
2. Using a suitable micrometer and bore gauge, measure diameter of valve stem and valve guide inside diameter, to determine stem clearance in guide.
3. Clearances should be as follows:
   a. Intake valve stem diameter should be 0.2742-0.2748 inch (6.965-6.980 mm) and exhaust valve stem diameter 0.2737-0.2742 inch (6.950-6.965 mm).
   b. Valve guide inside diameter should be 0.2756-0.2761 inch (7.000-7.015 mm).
   c. Stem to guide clearance should be, intake; 0.0008-0.0019 inch (0.020-0.050 mm): exhaust; 0.0014-0.0025 inch (0.035-0.065 mm).
4. If bore gauge is not available, check valve stem end deflection using a suitable dial indicator as shown in **Fig. 11.** Move stem end back and forth, **Fig. 11,** and measure valve stem end deflection.
4. Valve stem end deflection should be as follows:
   a. Intake, 0.005 inch (0.14 mm).
   b. Exhaust, 0.007 inch (0.18 mm).
5. If specifications are not as specified, replace valve and guide as necessary.

PISTONS & CONNECTING RODS

Using a suitable piston ring expander, remove rings from pistons then position piston in an arbor press, and using a suitable drift, remove piston pins from pistons.

Each piston top is stamped with a No. 1 or 2, depending on its outer diameter. A No. 1 stamped piston, outer diameter should be 2.9126-2.9130 inch (73.98-73.88 mm) and a No. 2 stamped piston, outer diameter should be 2.9122-2.9126 inch (73.97-73.98 mm).

When installing piston and connecting rod assemblies, ensure number on piston top matches cylinder number stamped in block, **Fig. 12,** and arrows on top of pistons are facing front of engine, crankshaft pulley side, **Fig. 13.**

Pistons are available in standard sizes and oversizes of 0.0098 inch (0.25 mm) and 0.0196 inch (0.50 mm).

CONNECTING ROD BEARINGS

Two types of rod bearings are available, standard and 0.0098 inch (0.25 mm) undersize bearings. To distinguish then apart, the 0.0098 inch (0.25 mm) bearing has a stamped number (US025) on its back and the standard size bearing has no markings.

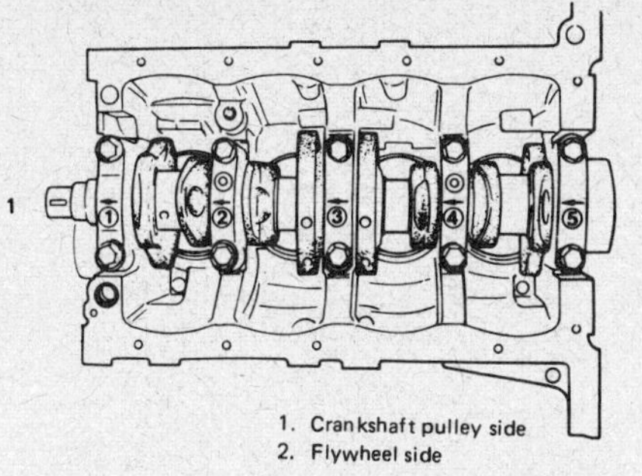

Fig. 14 Installing main bearing caps

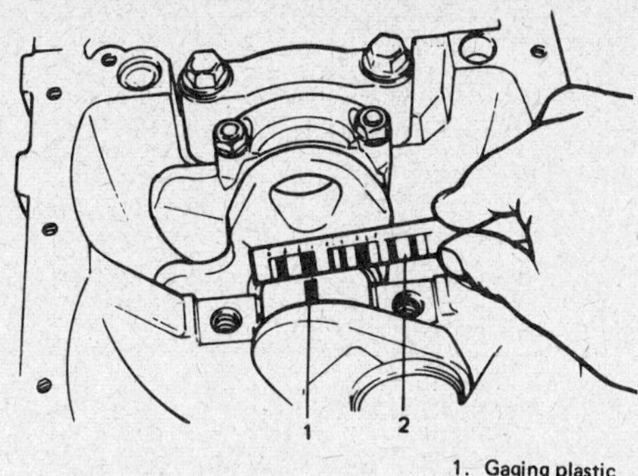

Fig. 15 Measuring Plastigage

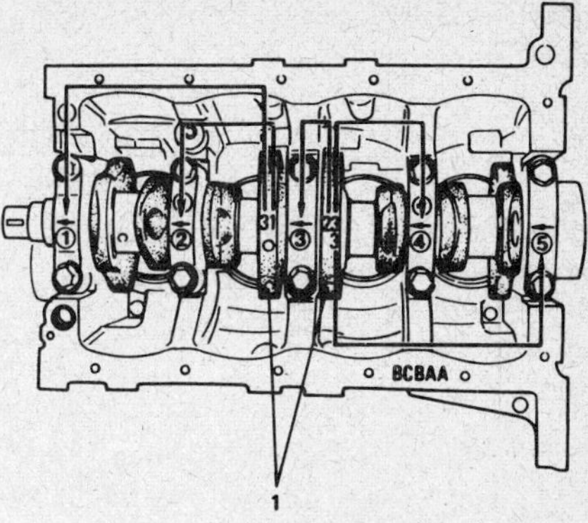

Fig. 16 Distinguishing crankshaft journal diameters

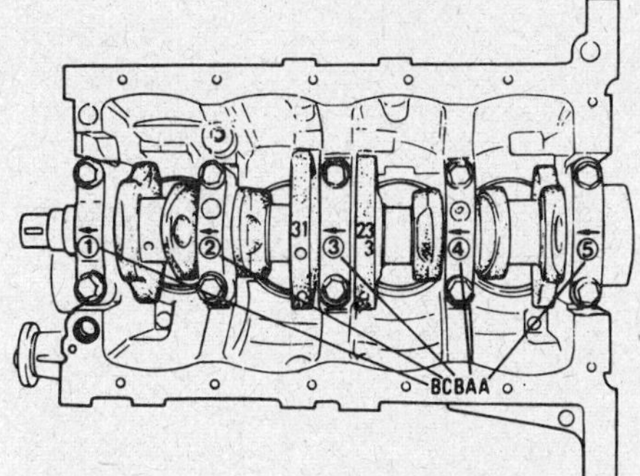

Fig. 17 Distinguishing cap bore diameters

		Numerals stamped on crank webs (Journals diameter)		
		1	2	3
Alphabets stamped on mating surface	A	Green	Black	Colorless
	B	Black	Colorless	Yellow
	C	Colorless	Yellow	Blue
		New standard bearing to be installed.		

Fig. 18 Standard bearing chart

MAIN BEARINGS

Two types of main bearings are available, standard and 0.0098 inch (0.25 mm) undersize, and each of them has five kinds of bearings differing in tolerance. Each main bearing cap is stamped with a number and an arrow. When installing bearing cap, arrow must point towards crankshaft pulley side, **Fig. 14.** Check main bearing clearance as follows:

1. Clean bearings and crankshaft main journals using a suitable solvent.
2. Place a piece of Plastigage the full width of the bearing (parallel to crankshaft) on journal, avoiding oil passage hole.
3. Install bearing cap and torque cap bolts to 36.5-41.0 ft. lbs. **Do not rotate crankshaft while Plastigage is installed.**
4. Remove bearing cap, and using Plastigage scale, measure width at its widest point, **Fig. 15.**
5. Bearing clearance should be 0.0008-0.0016 inch (0.020-0.040 mm) and must not exceed 0.0023 inch (0.060 mm). **A new standard bearing may produce proper clearance, if not, it will be necessary to regrind crankshaft journal for use of 0.0098 inch (0.25 mm) undersize bearing. After selecting appropriate bearing, recheck clearance.**

Standard Bearing Selection

1. Using a suitable micrometer, measure journal diameter. Crank webs of No. 2 and No. 3 cylinders have five stamped numbers, **Fig. 16.** These numbers represent the following journal diameters:
   a. No. 1, 1.7714-1.7716 inch (44.994-45.000 mm).
   b. No. 2, 1.7712-1.7714 inch (44.988-44.994 mm).
   c. No. 3, 1.7710-1.7712 inch (44.982-44.988 mm).
2. The first, second, third, fourth and fifth (left to right) stamped numbers on crank webs of No. 2 and No. 3 cylinders, **Fig. 16,** indicate journal diameters at bearing caps 1, 2, 3, 4 and 5. For example, the first No. 3 indicates that journal diameter at bearing No. 1 is within 1.7710-1.7712 (44.982-44.988 mm), and second No. 1 indicates that journal diameter at bearing cap No. 2 is within 1.7714-1.7716 inch (44.994-45.000 mm).
3. Using a suitable micrometer, check bearing cap bore without bearing. There are five letters stamped on mating surface of cylinder block, **Fig. 17.** These letters represents cap bore diameters as follows:
   a. Letter "A," 1.9292-1.9294 inch (49.000-49.006 mm).
   b. Letter "B," 1.9294-1.9296 inch (49.006-49.012 mm).
   c. Letter "C," 1.9296-1.9298 inch (49.012-49.018 mm).
4. The first, second, third, fourth and fifth (left to right) stamped letters indicate cap bore diameter of bearing caps 1, 2, 3, 4 and 5, **Fig. 17.** For example, the first letter "B" indicates that cap bore diameter of bearing cap No. 1 is within 1.9294-1.9296 inch (49.006-49.012 mm), and the fifth letter "A" indicates that cap bore diameter of cap No. 5 is within 1.9292-1.9294 inch (49.000-49.006 mm).
5. There are five types of standard bearings differing in thickness. Each bearing has a painted identification color on it. Each color indicates thickness at center of bearing as follows:
   a. Green, 0.0786-0.0787 inch (1.996-2.000 mm).
   b. Black, 0.0787-0.0788 inch (1.999-2.003 mm).
   c. Colorless (no paint), 0.0788-0.0789 inch (2.002-2.006 mm).
   d. Yellow, 0.0789-0.0790 inch (2.005-2.009 mm).
   e. Blue, 0.0790-0.0791 inch (2.008-2.012 mm).
6. From the number stamped on crank webs of No. 2 and No. 3 cylinders, **Fig. 16,** and the letters stamped on surface of cylinder block, **Fig. 17,** determine new standard bearing to be installed to journal, by referring to table, **Fig. 18.** For example, if number stamped on crank web is "1" and letter stamped on cylinder block is "B", install new standard bearing with a "Black" painted identification mark.
7. Using Plastigage, check bearing clearance with new standard bearing selected. If clearance exceeds limits, use next thicker bearing and recheck clearance.
8. If replacing crankshaft or cylinder block, select new standard bearings by numbers stamped on new crankshaft or letters stamped on cylinder surface.

Undersize Bearing Selection

1. 0.0098 inch (0.25 mm) undersize bearing is available in five different thicknesses. To distinguish them, each bearing has a painted identification color on it. Each color indicates thickness at center of bearing as follows:
   a. Green and red, 0.0835-0.0836 inch (2.121-2.125 mm).
   b. Black and red, 0.0836-0.0837 inch (2.124-2.128 mm).
   c. Red, 0.0837-0.0838 inch (2.127-2.131 mm).
   d. Yellow and red, 0.0838-0.0839 inch (2.130-2.134 mm).
   e. Blue and red, 0.0839-0.0840 inch (2.133-2.137 mm).

		Measured journal diameter		
		44.744 – 44.750 mm (1.7616 – 1.7618 in.)	44.738 – 44.744 mm (1.7614 – 1.7616 in.)	44.732 – 44.738 mm (1.7612 – 1.7614 in.)
Alphabets stamped on mating surface of cylinder block	A	Green & Red	Black & Red	Red only
	B	Black & Red	Red only	Yellow & Red
	C	Red only	Yellow & Red	Blue & Red
		Undersize bearing to be installed.		

Fig. 19 Undersize bearing chart

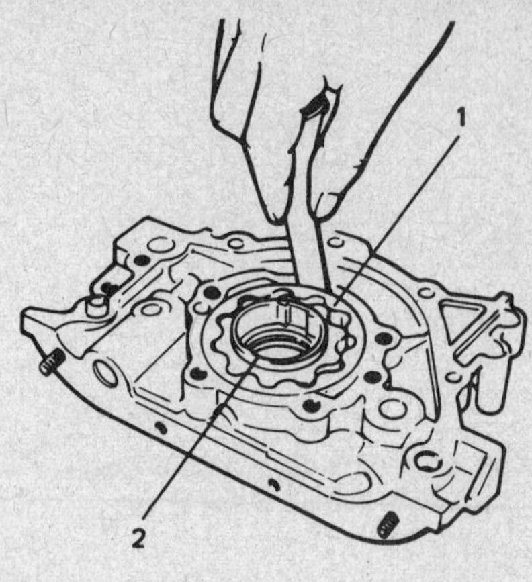

Fig. 20 Checking oil pump gear radial clearance

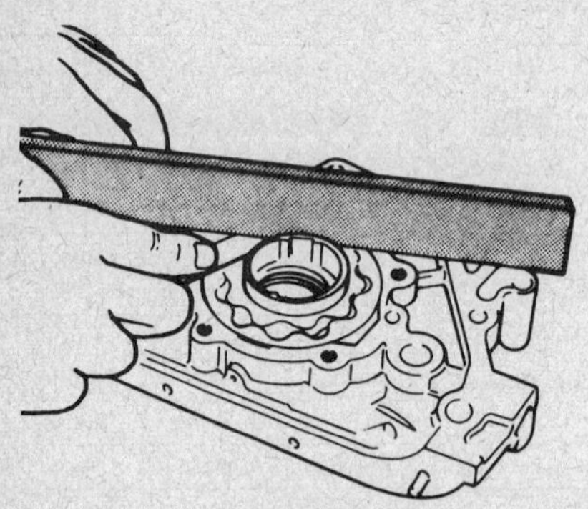

Fig. 21 Checking oil pump gear side clearance

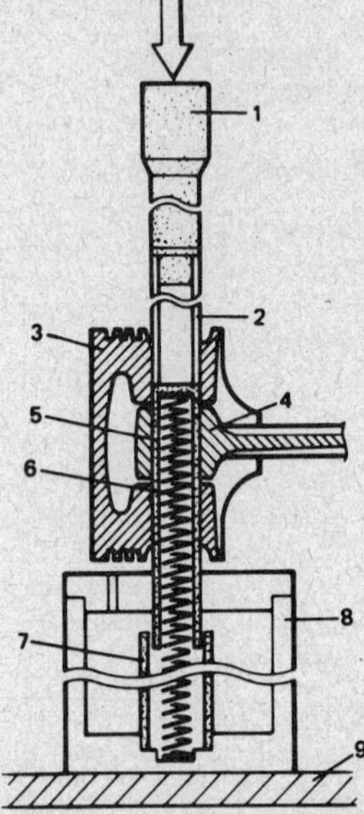

Fig. 22 Piston pin installation

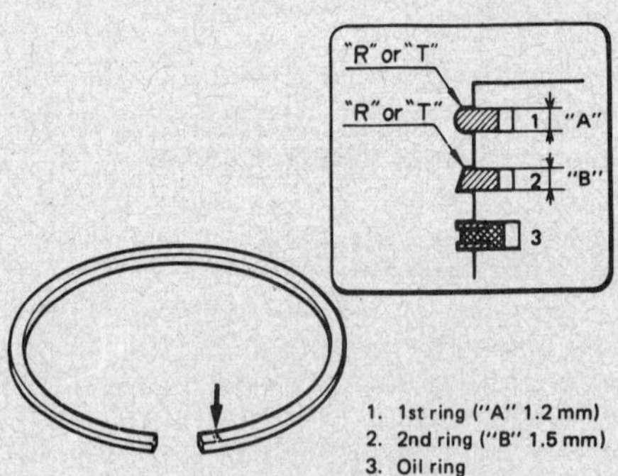

Fig. 23 Piston ring installation

2. If crankshaft has to be reground to undersize, regrind journal and select undersize bearing to be used as follows:
   a. Regrind journal to obtain a finished diameter a 1.7612-1.7618 inch (44.732-44.750 mm).
   b. Using a suitable micrometer, measure reground journal diameter. Measurement should be made in two directions perpendicular to each other in order to check for out of round condition.
   c. From journal diameter measured above and letters stamped on cylinder block, select appropriate undersize bearing to be installed referring to **Fig. 19.**
   d. Check bearing clearance with undersize bearing selected.

OIL PUMP

1. Inspect oil seal lip for damage, and replace as necessary.
2. Inspect outer and inner rotors for excessive wear or damage.
3. Using a suitable feeler gauge, measure radial clearance between outer rotor and case, **Fig. 20.** Clearance should be 0.0122 inch (0.310 mm). If clearance is not as specified, replace outer rotor or case.
4. Using a straightedge and a suitable feeler gauge, measure oil pump side clearance, **Fig. 21.** Clearance should be 0.0059 inch (0.15 mm). If clearance is not as specified, replace outer or inner rotors as necessary.

ENGINE ASSEMBLY

1. Install selected main bearings into cylinder block, then lubricate bearings with oil. **Ensure bearing half with oil hole passage is installed into cylinder block and other half without oil groove to bearing cap. Also ensure that both halves are painted with same color.**
2. Install thrust washer to cylinder block between No. 2 and No. 3 cylinders. **Ensure to face oil groove sides to crank webs.**
3. Install crankshaft into cylinder block, then lubricate journals with oil.
4. Install bearing caps onto journals. Ensure that arrow on each cap is pointing towards crankshaft pulley. Torque cap bolts to 36.5-41.0 ft. lbs., starting from crankshaft pulley side, No. 1. **After tightening cap bolts, ensure that crankshaft rotates smoothly when turned by hand.**
5. Install oil seal housing and a new gasket. Apply oil to oil seal lip before installing. Torque bolts to 7.5-9.0 ft. lbs.
6. If oil pump was disassembled, assemble as follows:
   a. Clean all components using a suitable solvent.
   b. Lubricate inner and outer rotors, oil seal lip and inside surfaces of oil pump case and plate with engine oil.
   c. Install outer and inner rotors into pump case.
   d. Install gear plate. **After installing gear plate, ensure that gears rotate smoothly by hand.**
7. Install two oil pump pins and a new gasket onto cylinder block.
8. Install Oil Guide Tool 09926-18210, or equivalent, onto crankshaft to prevent oil seal lip damage when installing oil pump assembly.
9. Install oil pump attaching pumps. Torque bolts to 7-8.5 ft. lbs.
10. install piston rings onto piston as follows:
    a. Apply engine oil to piston pin bores in piston and rod and fit connect rod to piston as shown in **Fig. 13.**
    b. Place piston on tool 09910-38210 so arrow mark on piston head faces up. Press piston pin into piston and connecting rod, **Fig. 22.**
    c. Install piston rings so mark side of each ring faces top of piston, **Fig. 23.** Note shape of of rings 1 and 2.
    d. Install oil ring spacer first, then 2 rails.

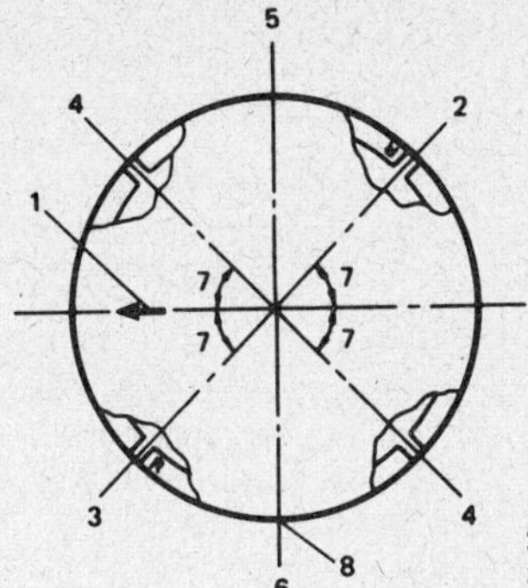

1. Arrow mark
2. 1st ring end gap
3. 2nd ring end gap
4. Oil ring rail gaps
5. Intake side
6. Exhaust side
7. 45°
8. Oil ring spacer gap

Fig. 24 Ring end gap alignment

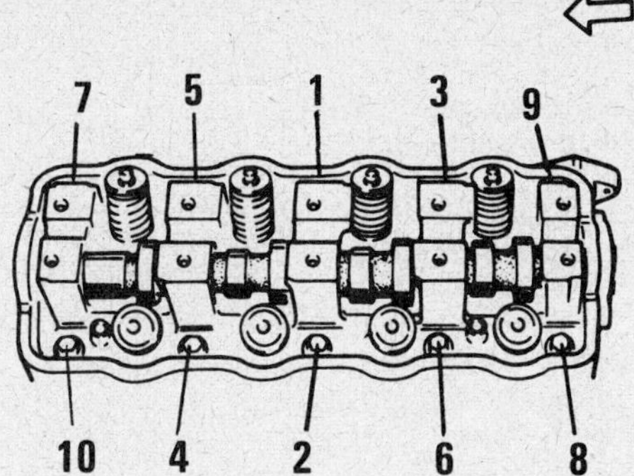

Fig. 26 Cylinder head tightening sequence

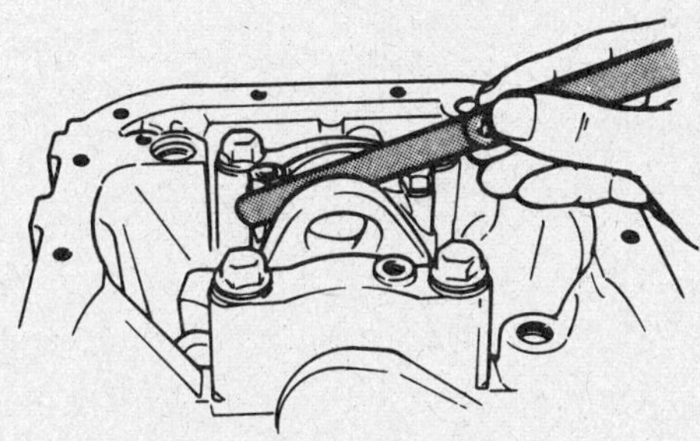

Fig. 25 Measuring rod bearing side clearance

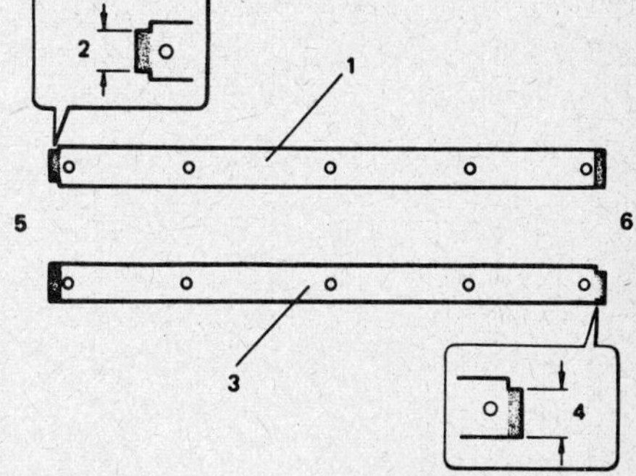

1. Intake rocker arm shaft
2. 14 mm (0.55 in)
3. Exhaust rocker arm shaft
4. 15 mm (0.59 in)
5. Camshaft pulley side
6. Distributor side

Fig. 27 Intake & exhaust rocker arm shaft identification

e. Align ring end gaps as shown in **Fig. 24.** Pistons and connecting rod assemblies must be installed in block so arrows on pistons face front (pulley end) of engine, **Fig. 13.**

11. Install connecting rod bearing caps. Torque cap nuts to 24-26.5 ft lbs. **Ensure that arrow (marked on each bearing cap) points towards crankshaft pulley side.**
12. Using a suitable feeler gauge, measure side clearance of connecting rod big end, **Fig. 25.** Big end side clearance should be 0.0039-0.0078 inch (0.10-0.20 mm), and must not exceed 0.0137 inch (0.35 mm). If clearance exceeds limit, replace connecting rod.
13. Install oil pump strainer. Torque bolts to 6.5-8.5 ft lbs.
14. Apply suitable sealant to oil pan, then install oil pan. Torque bolts, starting at center, to 7-8.5 ft. lbs.
15. Install gasket on drain plug, then drain plug into oil pan. Torque drain plug to 22-28.5 ft. lbs.
16. Install guide seal into oil pump case, then oil dipstick.
17. Install flywheel to crankshaft, then Flywheel Holder 09924-17810. Torque flywheel attaching bolts to 41.5-47 ft lbs.
18. Install valve guides into cylinder head as follows:
    a. Ream guide hole using a 12 mm reamer, to remove any burrs. Ensure guide hole diameter is 0.4736-0.4743 inch (12.030-12.048 mm) after reaming.
    b. Heat cylinder head to approximately 176-212° F (80-100° C), then using tools 09917-88210 and 09916-57321, drive in new valve guide until valve guide protrudes 0.55 inch (14 mm) from cylinder head.
    c. Using a 7 mm reamer, ream valve guide bore. After reaming, clean bore.
19. Install valve spring seat to cylinder head, then valve stem seal to valve guide.
20. Lubricate stem seal, valve guide bore and valve stem, then install valve into valve guide.
21. Install valve springs, then retainers using a suitable valve spring compressor. **Ensure to install springs with bottom end (small pitch end) down to valve spring seat.**
22. Install new head gasket, then cylinder head onto cylinder block. Torque bolts to 46-50.5 ft. lbs. as shown in **Fig. 26.**
23. Apply engine oil onto camshaft, then install camshaft from transmission case side.
24. Lubricate rocker arms and rocker arm shafts, then install rocker arms, springs and rocker shafts. **Rocker arm shafts are not identical. Dimensions of their stepped ends differ as shown in Fig. 27. Install intake rocker arm shaft, facing stepped end to camshaft pulley side and exhaust rocker arm shaft, facing its stepped end to distributor side (rear side).**
25. Torque rocker arms shaft screws to 7-8.5 ft. lbs.
26. Install water inlet pipe to cylinder block. Ensure to install new O-ring to inlet pipe before installing.
27. Install intake manifold with carburetor using a new gasket. Torque bolts to 13.5-20 ft. lbs.
28. Connect water hoses to water inlet pipe, and secure hoses with clamps.
29. Install oil filter.
30. Install exhaust manifold using a new gasket, and torque bolts to 13.5-20 ft. lbs.
31. Install water pump and new gasket. Torque bolts to 7-8.5 ft. lbs.
32. Install two rubber seats, one between oil pump and water pump and the other between water pump and cylinder head.
33. Install timing belt inside cover, then crankshaft timing belt guide, key and pulley. Torque timing belt pulley bolt to 47.5-54 ft lbs.
34. Install camshaft timing belt pulley key, then pulley. Torque pulley bolt to 41-46 ft. lbs.
35. Install timing belt tensioner, tensioner plate and spring.
36. Refer to "Timing Belt, Replace," and install timing belt as outlined.
37. Install crankshaft pulley key, then crankshaft pulley. Torque pulley bolts to 7.5-9 ft lbs.
38. Install alternator.

39. Install distributor case 0-ring to cylinder block, then distributor case. Torque bolts to 6-8.5 ft. lbs. **After tightening distributor case, fill distributor case with approximately 1 ounce of engine oil.**
40. Install fuel pump rod, gasket and fuel pump onto cylinder head. Lubricate rod with engine oil before installing.
41. Install clutch disc and cover using Alignment Tool 09923-38220, or equivalent, and torque bolts to 13.5-20 ft. lbs.
42. Install transmission assembly onto engine. Torque bolts to 16-25 ft. lbs.
43. Install distributor assembly into distributor case., then connect spark plug wires.
44. Refer to "Valves, Adjust," and adjust valve clearance as outlined.
45. Install valve cover. Torque bolts to 3-3.5 ft. lbs. and check ignition timing.

FUEL PUMP

REPLACE

1. Disconnect battery ground cable.
2. Remove fuel filler cap to release fuel pressure in tank, then reinstall cap.
3. Disconnect fuel inlet, outlet and return hoses from fuel pump.
4. Remove fuel pump attaching bolts, then fuel pump from cylinder head.
5. Remove fuel pump rod from cylinder head.
6. Reverse procedure to install. Torque fuel pump bolts to 7-11.5 ft. lbs.

WATER PUMP

REPLACE

1. Drain cooling system.
2. Remove radiator shroud attaching bolts and cooling fan assembly attaching bolts, then radiator shroud and cooling fan as an assembly.
3. Loosen water pump drive belt tensioner, then remove water pump pulley and drive belt.
4. Remove four crankshaft pulley attaching bolts, **Fig. 1,** then the crankshaft pulley. **It is not necessary to loosen crankshaft pulley center bolt, Fig. 1.**
5. Loosen tensioner bolt and stud, **Fig. 7,** then push up on tensioner plate and remove belt from crankshaft timing belt pulley and camshaft pulley.
6. Remove timing belt tensioner, plate and spring.
7. Remove water pump attaching bolts, then water pump.
8. Reverse procedure to install noting the following:
   a. Torque water pump bolts to 7-8.5 ft. lbs.
   b. Refer to "Timing Belt, Replace" to ensure timing belt is correctly installed.

MANUAL TRANSMISSION SECTION

INDEX

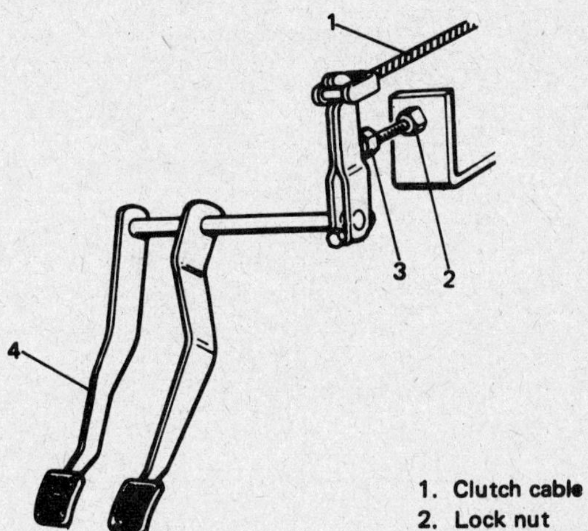

Fig. 1 Clutch pedal height adjustment

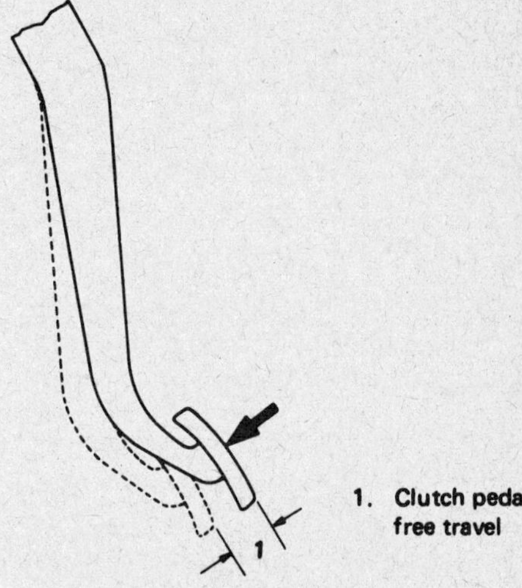

Fig. 2 Clutch pedal free travel measurement

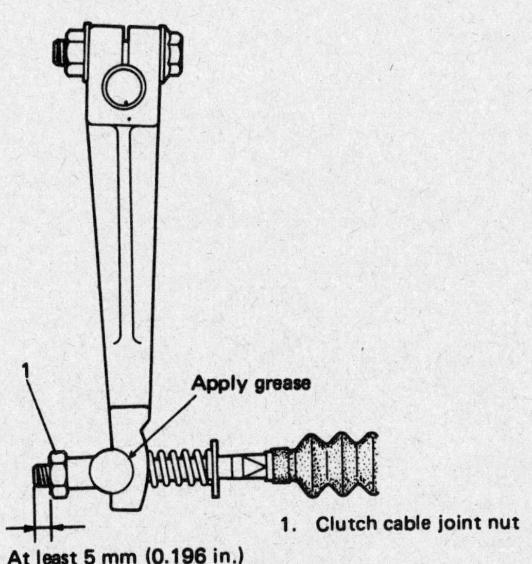

Fig. 3 Clutch pedal free travel adjustment

CLUTCH PEDAL
ADJUST

1. Loosen clutch cable locknut and turn adjusting nut as necessary until clutch pedal is even with brake pedal, **Fig. 1,** then tighten locknut.
2. Depress clutch pedal until the moment when resistance is felt and measure distance traveled, **Fig. 2.** Free travel should measure 0.8-1.1 inch.
3. Adjust free travel by turning clutch cable outer nuts as necessary, **Fig. 3.**

TRANSMISSION
REPLACE

1. Remove four bolts fastening outer gear shift lever boot and slide boot toward shift knob.
2. Unfasten inner gear shift lever boot and slide boot toward shift knob.
3. Remove three gear shift lever case bolts, then the gear shift lever from case.
4. Disconnect negative and positive cables from battery terminals.
5. Disconnect back-up light and fifth gear switch electrical connectors from transmission.

6. Disconnect wiring from starter, then remove the starter.
7. Remove fuel hose clamp from transmission case.
8. Raise and support vehicle.
9. Remove transmission drain plug and drain oil.
10. Disconnect clutch wire from clutch release lever.
11. Remove propeller shaft No. 1 from transmission to transfer case.
12. Remove propeller shaft No. 2 from transfer case to front differential.
13. Remove clutch housing lower plate from transmission case.
14. Support transmission with a suitable jack, then remove bolts securing transmission to engine.
15. Remove support pipe and exhaust center pipe.
16. Remove transmission rear mounting bracket from chassis and transmission.
17. Ensure all connectors are unfastened from transmission, then carefully lower transmission from vehicle.
18. Reverse procedure to install. Torque transmission case and extension housing bolts to 13.5-20.0 ft. lbs. and oil drain plug to 14.5-21.5 ft. lbs.

TRANSFER CASE REPLACE

1. Raise and support vehicle.
2. Remove three securing bolts from each of three universal joints from transfer case.
3. Remove clamp and boot from transfer case.
4. Remove control lever from transfer case by depressing lever guide and turning counterclockwise.
5. Drain oil from transfer case by removing drain plug.
6. Disconnect speedometer cable from transfer case.
7. Disconnect 4WD switch electrical connector from transfer case.
8. Remove transfer case-to-chassis attaching nuts and carefully lower transfer case assembly from vehicle.
9. Reverse procedure to install. Torque transfer case attaching nuts to 18.5-25.0 ft. lbs.

DISC BRAKES SECTION

INDEX

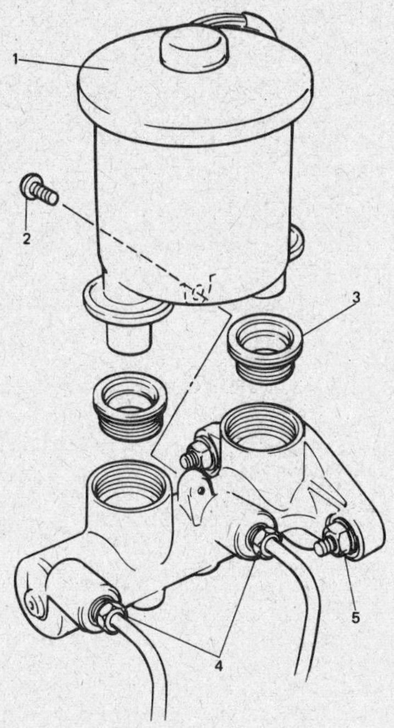

Fig. 1 Reservoir connector screw location

MASTER CYLINDER REPLACE

1. Clean any dirt from around reservoir cap. Remove cap, then brake fluid.
2. Remove reservoir connector screw, **Fig. 1,** then reservoir.
3. Disconnect brake lines from master cylinder. **Do not allow brake fluid to get on painted surfaces.**
4. Remove master cylinder attaching bolts, then master cylinder.
5. Adjust clearance of booster piston rod to master cylinder piston as follows:
   a. Push piston rod several times to ensure reaction disc is in place.
   b. Measure with gasket in place on master cylinder and booster at atmospheric pressure.
   c. Set measuring tool 09950-98210 on master cylinder and push pin until it contacts piston, **Fig. 2.**
   d. Turn tool upside down and place on booster, **Fig. 3.** Adjust booster piston rod length until rod end contacts piston head.
   e. Clearance should be 0.004-0.020 inch (0.1-0.5 mm).

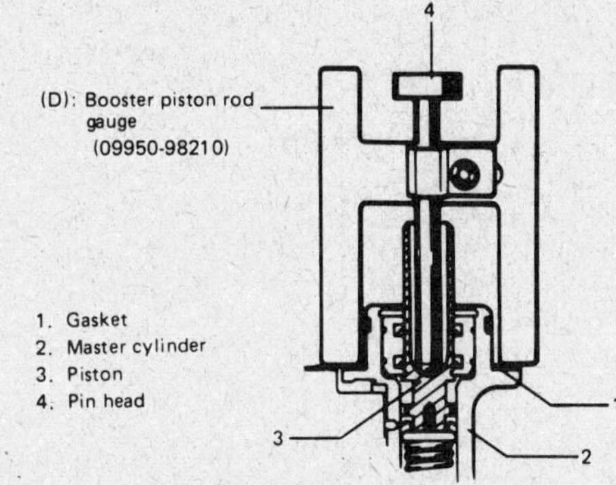

Fig. 2 Pushing pin until it contacts piston

6. Install reservoir on master cylinder, then reservoir connector screw.
7. Install master cylinder on studs, then mounting nuts.
8. Connect hydraulic lines.
9. Fill reservoir with brake fluid.

FRONT PADS REPLACE

1. Raise and support vehicle, then remove wheel assembly.
2. Remove caliper antirattle clip, **Fig. 4.**
3. Remove caliper guide pin caps.
4. Using a 6 mm Allen wrench, remove caliper guide pins.
5. Remove pad protectors, then caliper cylinder.
6. Remove pads.
7. Reverse procedure to install noting the following:
   a. Torque caliper bolts to 18.5-21.5 ft. lbs.
   b. Install wheel assemblies.
   c. Lower vehicle and perform brake test.

CALIPER SERVICE

1. Raise and support vehicle.
2. Disconnect brake hose from caliper.
3. Remove caliper guide pin caps.
4. Using a 6 mm Allen wrench, remove caliper guide pins, then caliper.
5. Clean caliper with brake fluid.
6. Using compressed air, remove piston from caliper. Keep fingers away from piston.
7. Using a suitable screwdriver, remove piston seal from caliper. **Take care not to damage bore of cylinder.**
8. Install new piston seal in cylinder.
9. Install new boot on piston as shown in **Fig. 5.**

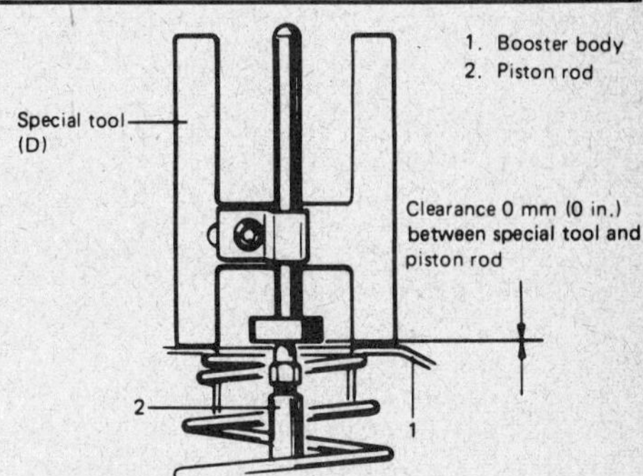

Fig. 3 Adjusting piston rod length

10. Install piston into cylinder by hand. Ensure boot fits in groove in piston.
11. Install caliper, then pads.
12. Torque caliper bolts to 18.5-21.5 ft. lbs.
13. Connect brake hose, and torque bolt to 14.5-18 ft. lbs.
14. Install wheel assembly, then lower vehicle and test brakes.

BRAKE PEDAL HEIGHT ADJUST

The brake pedal should normally be at same height as clutch pedal. Check that distance between brake booster mounting surface (with gasket) and pushrod clevis pin hole is 4.94-4.98 inch (125.5-126.5 mm).

BRAKE PEDAL TRAVEL CHECK

1. Start engine, then depress brake pedal a few times.
2. Apply approximately 66 lbs. load to brake pedal, and measure pedal arm to wall clearance, "B", **Fig. 6.**
3. Clearance should not exceed 2.95 inch (75 mm).
4. Possible causes for a low pedal are:
   a. Worn rear brake shoes.
   b. Brake lines need bleeding.
   c. Booster pushrod out of alignment.
   d. Rear brake shoes malfunctioning.

BRAKE BOOSTER REPLACE

1. Remove master cylinder from booster as described in "Master Cylinder, Replace."
2. Disconnect pushrod clevis from brake pedal arm, **Fig. 7.**
3. Disconnect vacuum hose from booster.

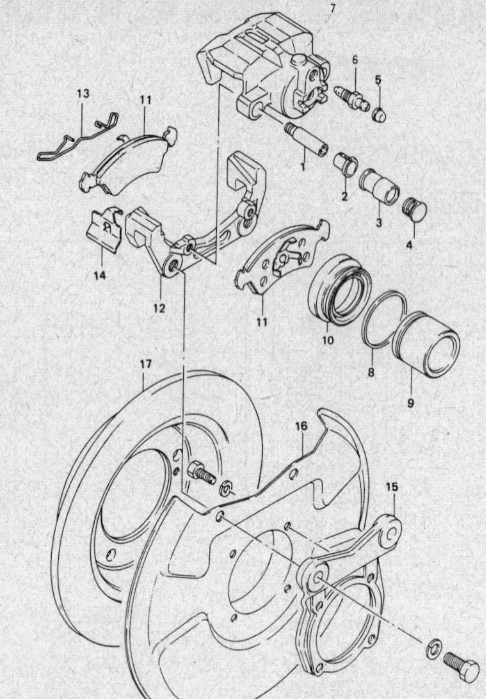

1. Caliper guide pin
2. Caliper guide pin sleeve
3. Guide pin boot
4. Guide pin cap
5. Bleeder plug cap
6. Bleeder plug
7. Disc brake caliper (Disc brake cylinder)
8. Piston seal
9. Disc brake piston
10. Cylinder boot
11. Disc brake pad
12. Disc brake carrier
13. Caliper antirattle clip
14. Pad protector
15. Caliper holder
16. Dust cover
17. Brake disc

Fig. 4 Exploded view of brake assembly

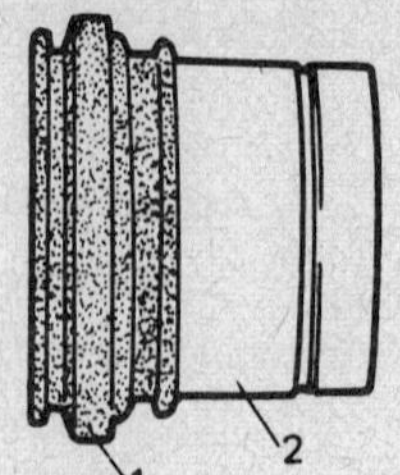

1. Boot
2. Piston

Fig. 5 Installing boot on piston

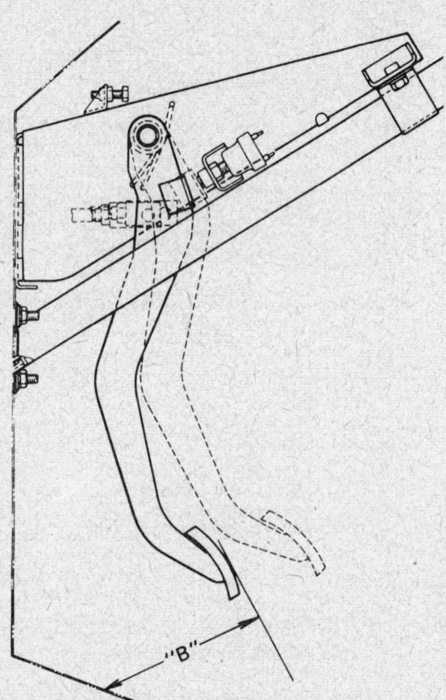

Fig. 6 Measuring pedal arm to wall clearance

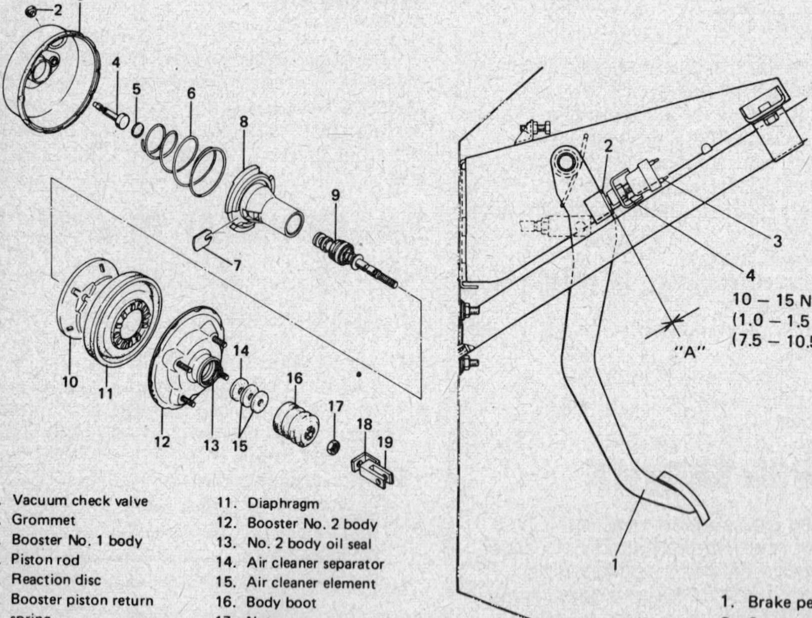

1. Vacuum check valve
2. Grommet
3. Booster No. 1 body
4. Piston rod
5. Reaction disc
6. Booster piston return spring
7. Valve stopper key
8. Booster piston
9. Booster air valve assembly
10. Pressure plate
11. Diaphragm
12. Booster No. 2 body
13. No. 2 body oil seal
14. Air cleaner separator
15. Air cleaner element
16. Body boot
17. Nut
18. Bracket
19. Push rod clevis

Fig. 7 Exploded view of booster assembly

1. Brake pedal
2. Contact plate
3. Stop light switch
4. Lock nut

Fig. 8 Brake pedal contact plate clearance check

4. Remove booster attaching nuts, then booster assembly.
5. Refer to "Master Cylinder, Replace" for adjustment procedure of the booster piston rod to master cylinder piston.
6. Reverse procedure to install. Torque booster nuts to 7.5-11.5 ft. lbs.

STOP LIGHT SWITCH

ADJUST

Pull up brake pedal and adjust switch position so that clearance between end of thread and brake pedal contact plate (A) is .02-.04 inch (0.5-1.0 mm), **Fig. 8.** Tighten locknut.

DRUM BRAKES SECTION

INDEX

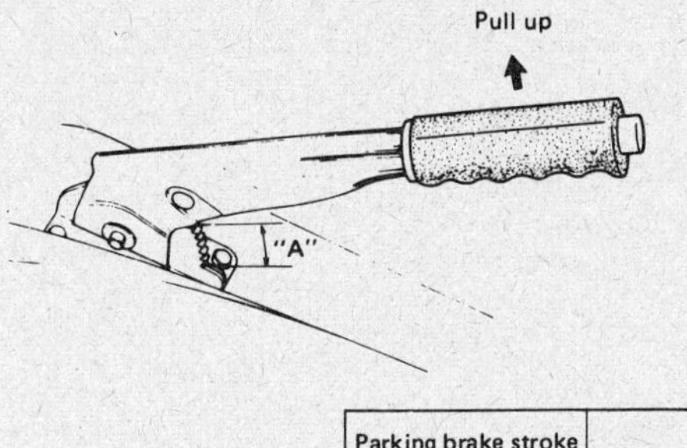

Parking brake stroke "A": When lever is pulled up at 20 kg (44 lb).	Within 3 – 8 notches

Fig. 1 Adjusting parking brake lever

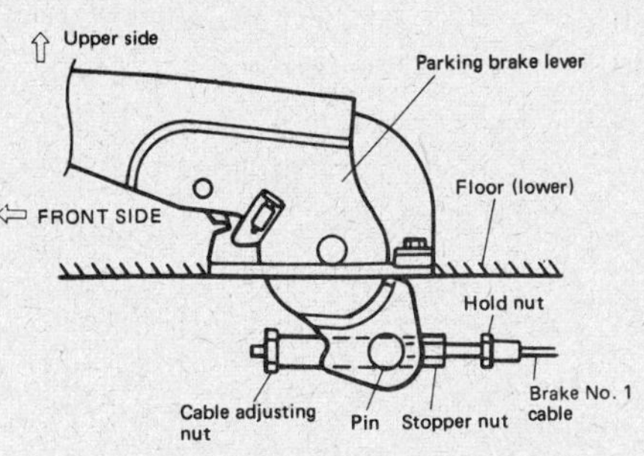

Fig. 2 Adjusting parking brake lever travel

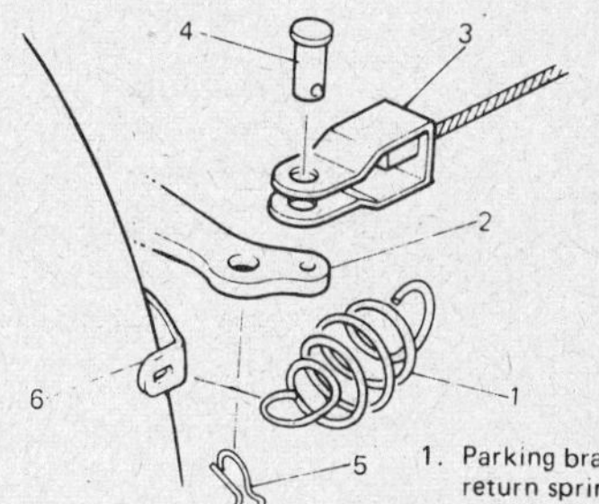

1. Parking brake shoe lever return spring
2. Parking brake shoe lever
3. Parking brake cable joint
4. Pin
5. Clip
6. Brake back plate

Fig. 3 Disconnecting parking brake cable joint

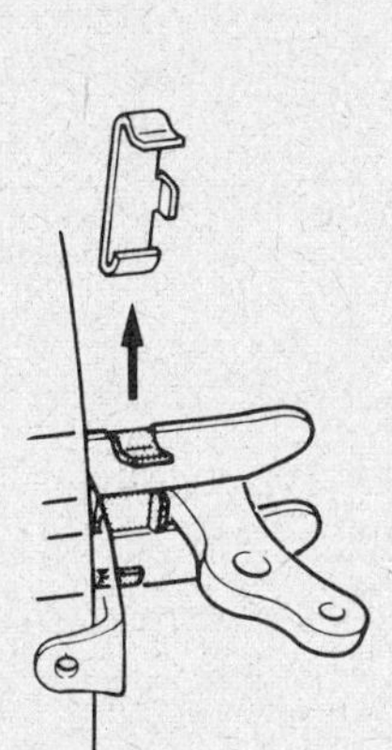
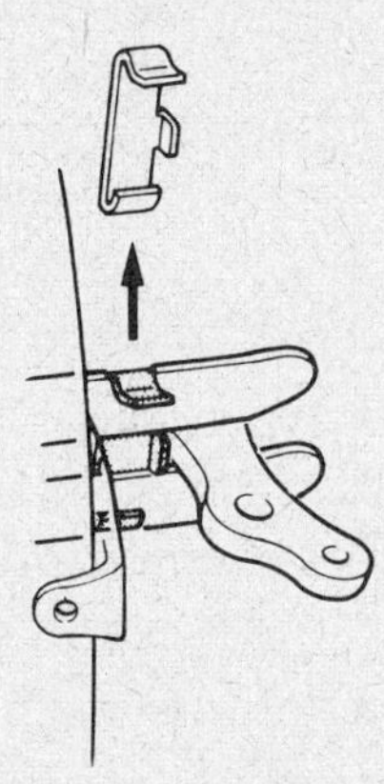

Fig. 4 Removing stopper plate

Fig. 5 Removing brake shoe hold down springs

DRUM BRAKES
ADJUST

Adjustment is accomplished automatically by depressing brake pedal 3-5 times with approximately 66 lbs. of pressure.

PARKING BRAKE
ADJUST

Parking brake lever should be adjusted so lever comes up 3-8 notches with 44 lbs. of pull applied, **Fig. 1**.

Adjust travel by loosening adjustment nuts, **Fig. 2**.

MASTER CYLINDER
REPLACE

Refer to Disc Brakes Section for master cylinder replace procedure.

BRAKE BOOSTER
REPLACE

Refer to Disc Brakes Section for brake booster replace procedure.

BRAKE PEDAL HEIGHT
ADJUST

Refer to Disc Brakes Section for brake pedal height adjustment procedure.

BRAKE PEDAL TRAVEL CHECK

Refer to Disc Brakes Section for brake pedal travel check procedure.

STOP LIGHT SWITCH
ADJUST

Refer to Disc Brakes Section for stop light switch adjust procedure.

DRUM BRAKE SERVICE

1. Raise and support vehicle
2. Remove wheel center cap.
3. Remove rear wheel assembly. En-

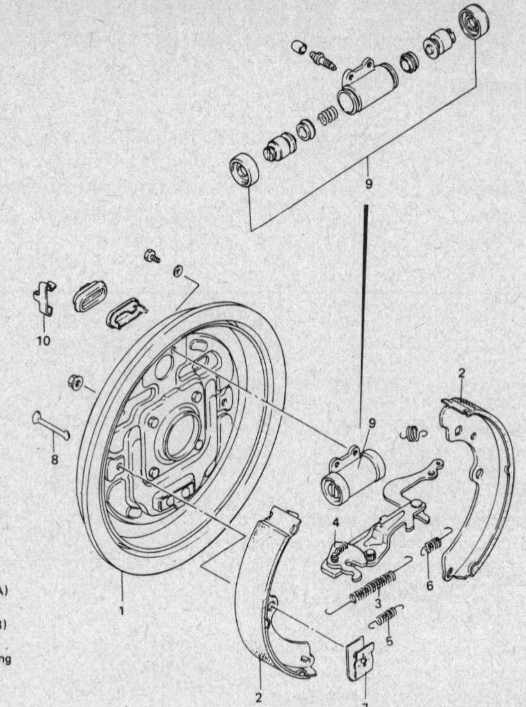

Fig. 6 Exploded view of brake assembly

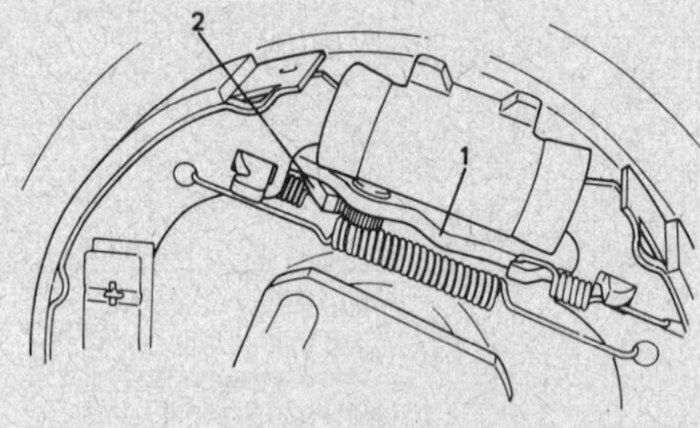

Fig. 7 Retracting brake shoes

sure that parking brake lever is not pulled up.

4. Increase the clearance between brake shoe and drum by removing parking brake shoe lever return spring (1) and disconnecting parking brake cable joint (3) from parking brake shoe lever (2), **Fig. 3.**
5. Remove parking brake shoe lever stopper plate, **Fig. 4.**
6. Remove drum to axle hub attaching bolts, then using slide hammer 09942-15510 and brake drum remover 09943-35511, pull off brake drum.
7. Remove brake shoe hold down springs by turning shoe hold down pins, then remove brake shoes, then brake shoe strut, **Fig. 5.**
8. Disconnect brake line, remove wheel cylinder attaching bolts, then wheel cylinder. Check wheel cylinder for leaks. If leakage is found, replace wheel cylinder inner components.
9. Install wheel cylinder to backing plate and torque bolts to 6-8.5 ft. lbs.
10. Install brake line and torque flare nut to 10.5-13 ft. lbs.
11. Assemble brake shoes, levers and springs as shown in **Fig. 6.**
12. Push shoe hold down springs into place, then turn hold down pins to engage springs.
13. Install parking brake shoe lever stopper plate, **Fig. 4.**
14. Connect brake cable joint to parking brake shoe lever, **Fig. 3,** then parking brake shoe lever return spring.
15. Before installing drum, maximize brake shoe to drum clearance by pushing down on ratchet using a screwdriver as shown in **Fig. 7.**
16. Install brake drum, drum to axle hub nuts and wheel assembly.
17. Install center cap.
18. Depress brake pedal several times to obtain proper drum to shoe clearance and adjust parking brake. Ensure that brake drum does not drag.
19. Lower vehicle and test brake operation.

REAR AXLE & SUSPENSION SECTION

INDEX

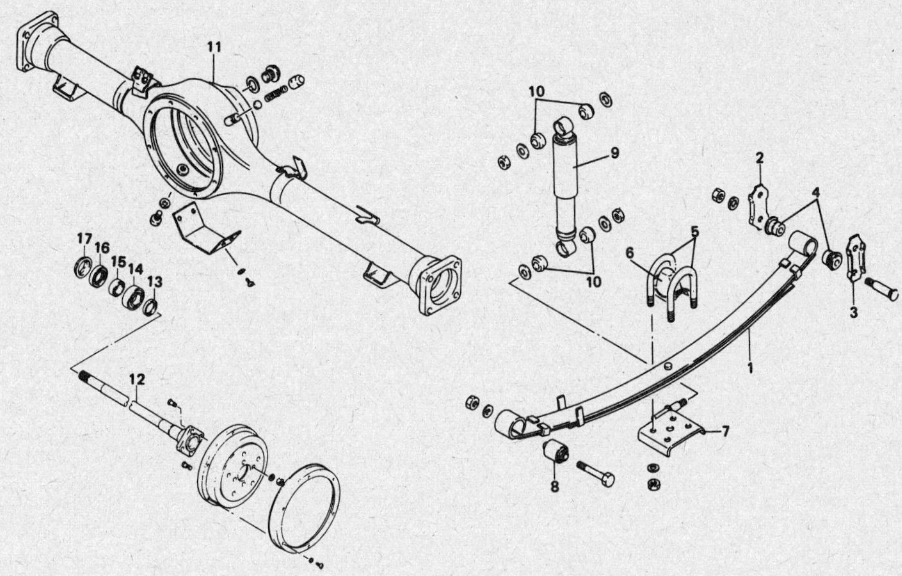

1. Leaf spring
2. Shackle plate inner
3. Shackle plate outer
4. Shackle bush
5. U bolt
6. Spring bumper
7. Spring seat
8. Spring bush
9. Shock absorber
10. Bush
11. Axle housing
12. Axle shaft
13. Spacer
14. Bearing
15. Bearing retainer ring
16. Oil seal
17. Oil seal protector

Fig. 1 Exploded view of rear suspension & axle assembly

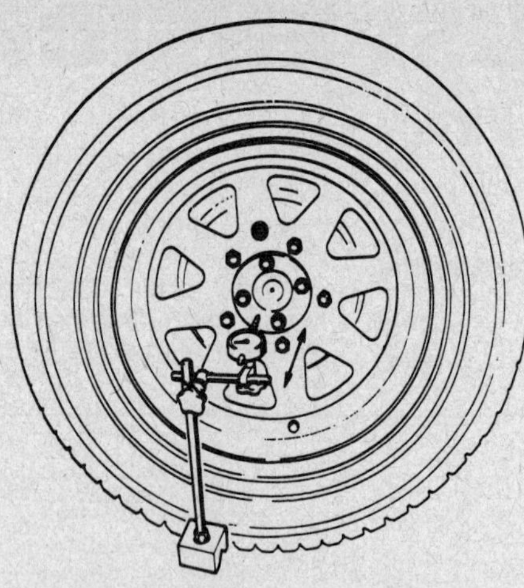

Fig. 2 Checking wheel bearing thrust play

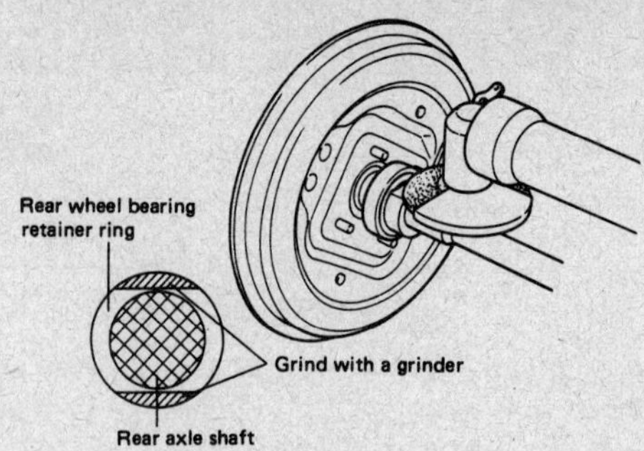

Fig. 3 Removing retaining ring

SHOCK ABSORBER

REPLACE

1. Raise and support vehicle.
2. Remove upper and lower nuts, **Fig. 1**, and remove shock.
3. Reverse procedure to install torquing upper and lower mounting bolts to 22.5-39.5 ft. lbs.

LEAF SPRING

REPLACE

1. Raise and support vehicle. Position suitable jack stands under rear axle assembly.
2. Remove rear wheel assembly.
3. Remove U-bolts nuts.
4. Remove shackle nuts, then leaf spring nuts, **Fig. 1.**
5. Pull out leaf spring bolt, then remove leaf spring from shackle pin.
6. Reverse procedure to install torquing U-bolt nuts to 43.5-57.5 ft. lbs, leaf spring nut to 33-50.5 ft. lbs and shackle pin bolt to 22-39.5 ft. lbs.

REAR AXLE SHAFT SERVICE

REAR WHEEL BEARING CHECK

1. Check wheel bearing thrust play by attaching a suitable dial indicator to drum center, **Fig. 2.**
2. Wheel bearing thrust play must not exceed 0.03 inch (0.8 mm). If measurement exceeds limit, replace bearing as outlined under "Axle Shaft, Replace."

AXLE SHAFT REMOVAL

1. Raise and support vehicle.
2. Remove wheel center cap.
3. Remove wheel assembly.
4. Using slide hammer 09942-15510 and brake drum remover 09943-35511, remove drum.
5. Remove axle housing drain plug, then drain oil from axle housing.
6. Disconnect brake line from wheel cylinder. Plug openings.
7. Remove four brake backing plate attaching bolts.
8. Using rear axle remover 09922-66010 and slide hammer 09942-15510, remove axle shaft with brake backing plate.
9. Pry seal from axle housing taking care not to damage housing.
10. Remove retaining ring from shaft by grinding two parts of bearing retainer ring until it becomes thin, **Fig. 3.**
11. Using a hammer and chisel, break retainer ring.
12. Using pulleys 09927-18410 and 09921-57810, remove bearing from shaft, then backing plate.

AXLE SHAFT INSTALLATION

1. Install oil seal so side with spring faces differential side. Grease seal lip before installing.
2. Install new bearing and spacer on shaft, ensuring wheel bearing spacer is installed with tapered side of its inner diameter facing towards brake drum side.
3. Reverse steps 1 through 10 of removal procedure to complete installation. Torque backing plate bolts to 13.5-20 ft. lbs.
4. When mounting hub bolts into rear axle shaft, ensure to fit head securely in stepped part of axle shaft.
5. Torque hub bolt nuts to 36.5-57.5 ft. lbs.

FRONT DRIVE AXLE, SUSPENSION & STEERING SECTION

INDEX

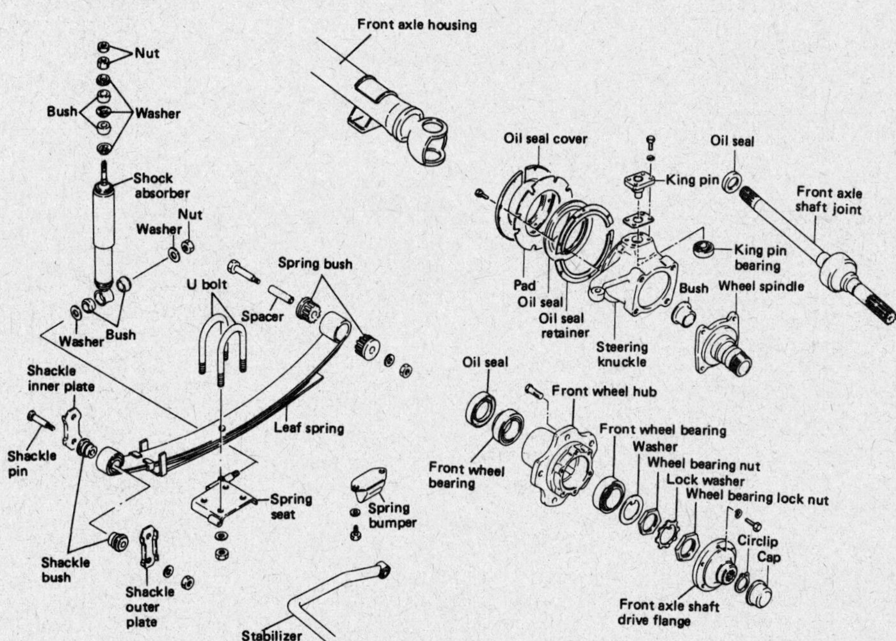

Fig. 1 Exploded view of front suspension & axle assembly

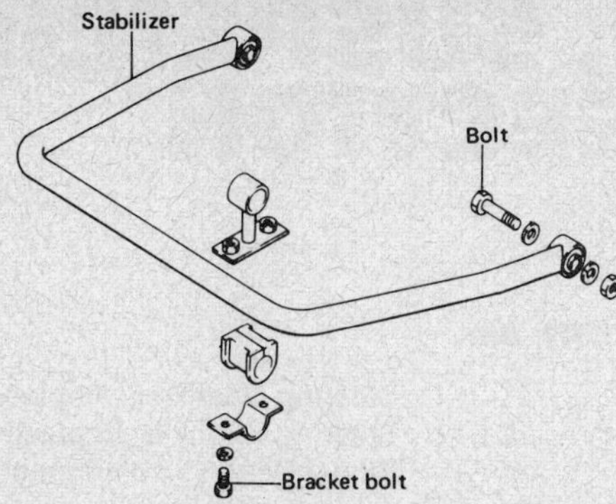

Fig. 2 Removing stabilizer bar

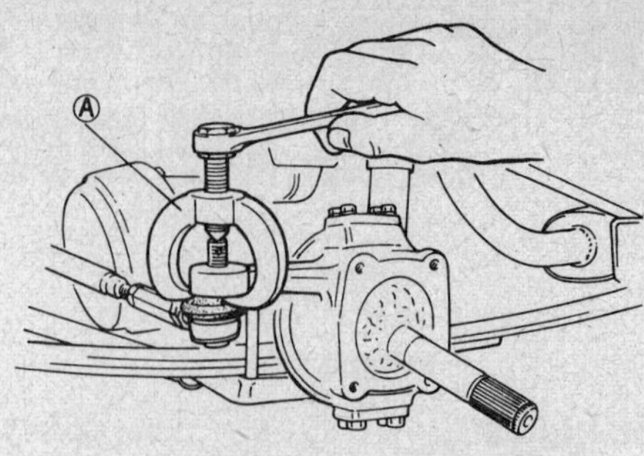

Fig. 3 Removing tie rod from steering knuckle

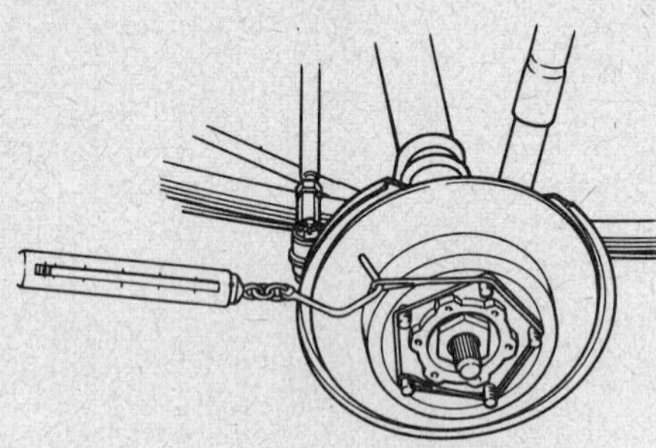

Fig. 4 Measuring wheel bearing preload

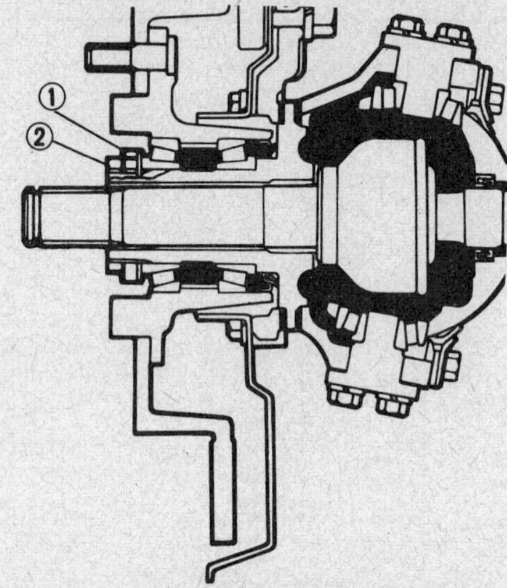

Fig. 5 Wheel bearing nut & locknut location

SHOCK ABSORBER

REPLACE

1. Raise and support vehicle, then position jack stands under frame side rails.
2. Remove upper and lower shock mounting bolts, then shock, **Fig. 1.**
3. Reverse procedure to install. Torque upper mounting bolt to 16-25 ft. lbs. and lower mounting bolt to 22.5-39.5 ft. lbs.

LEAF SPRING

REPLACE

1. Raise and support vehicle, then position suitable jack stands under axle housing.
2. Remove wheel assembly.
3. Remove stabilizer nut and bolt.
4. Remove U-bolt attaching bolts, then U-bolt.
5. Remove shackle nuts, then leaf spring nuts, **Fig. 1.**
6. Pull out leaf spring bolt, then shackle pin and remove leaf spring.
7. Reverse procedure to install. Torque U-bolt nuts to 43.5-57.5 ft. lbs., shackle pin nut to 22-39.5 ft. lbs, stabilizer bolt to 51-65 ft lbs. and leaf spring nut to 33-50.5 ft. lbs.

STABILIZER BAR

REPLACE

1. Raise and support vehicle.
2. Remove stabilizer bar attaching bolts, then stabilizer bar, **Fig. 2.**
3. Reverse procedure to install. Torque stabilizer bracket bolt to 51-65 ft. lbs. and stabilizer nuts to 16-25 ft. lbs.

HUB, ROTOR & WHEEL BEARING

REPLACE

1. Loosen wheel lug nuts, then raise and support vehicle. Position jack stands under axle housing.
2. Remove lug nuts, then wheel assembly.
3. Remove caliper carrier bolts, then support caliper with wire.
4. Remove brake disc. **If brake disc cannot be removed by hand, install two 8 mm bolts in holes provided, then tighten to remove disc.**
5. On vehicles equipped with free wheeling hubs, proceed as follows:
   a. Remove free wheeling hub cover attaching screws, then cover.
   b. Using needle nose pliers, remove free wheeling hub circlip, then free wheeling hub body.
6. On vehicles not equipped with free wheeling hub, proceed as follows:
   a. Remove front axle shaft cap.
   b. Using needle nose pliers, remove circlip retaining the front axle shaft drive flange from the front drive shaft.
   c. Remove front axle shaft drive flange attaching bolts, then drive flange.
7. On all vehicles, bend up lock washer tab and remove wheel bearing locknut using tool 09941-58010, or equivalent.
8. Using tool 09941-58010, or equivalent, remove nut from front wheel spindle, then washer.
9. Remove hub.
10. Remove oil seal and bearings from hub. If necessary, using a suitable hammer and drift, remove inner and outer bearing races from hub.
11. Reverse procedure to install, noting the following:
    a. Refer to "Wheel Bearing, Adjustment," and adjust wheel bearing preload as outlined.
    b. Torque front axle shaft drive flange bolts to 14.5-21.5 ft. lbs.

STEERING KNUCKLE

REPLACE

1. Repeat steps 1 through 9 as outlined under "Hub, Rotor & Wheel Bearings, Replace."
2. Loosen bolts securing upper and lower kingpins, **Fig. 1. Do not remove kingpins.**
3. Remove disc dust cover attaching bolts, then disc dust cover, caliper holder and wheel spindle.
4. Remove tie rod end castle nut, then using tie rod remover 09913-65210,

or equivalent, disconnect tie rod from steering knuckle, **Fig. 3.**

5. Remove joint seal attaching bolts, then oil seal cover, pad, oil seal and retainer from knuckle.
6. Remove upper and lower kingpins. **When removing kingpins, mark with identification marks for installation. Also, check number of shims used for each side.**
7. Pull off steering knuckle. **When removing steering knuckle, kingpin lower bearing may fall out. Mark upper and lower kingpin bearings for installation.**
8. Reverse procedure to install noting the following:
   a. Torque joint seal bolts to 6-8.5 ft. lbs.
   b. Torque upper and lower kingpin bolts to 14.5-21.5 ft. lbs.

AXLE SHAFT JOINT
REPLACE

1. Repeat steps 1 through 7 as outlined under "Steering Knuckle, Replace."
2. Drain oil from differential housing.
3. Remove axle shaft joint from axle housing.
4. Reverse procedure to install.

STEERING GEAR BOX
REPLACE

1. Remove steering column shaft to steering gear box coupling bolt.
2. Remove radiator under cover.
3. Using tie rod remover 09913-65210, or equivalent, disconnect ball stud of drag rod and steering damper from pitman arm.
4. Remove steering gear box attaching bolts, then steering gear box.
5. Reverse procedure to install noting the following:
   a. Torque drag rod nut to 22-50.5 ft. lbs.
   b. Torque tie rod castle nut to 22-39.5 ft. lbs.
   c. Steering gear box attaching bolts to 51-65 ft. lbs.
   d. Torque steering damper nut to 25.5-39.5 ft. lbs.

WHEEL BEARING
ADJUSTMENT

1. Remove wheel, drive flange or free wheeling hub (if equipped), caliper and holder as mentioned previously.
2. Using a suitable spring scale, measure wheel bearing preload as shown in **Fig. 4.**
3. Preload should be 2.2-6.6 ft. lbs.
4. If preload is not as specified, adjust as follows:
   a. Remove wheel bearing locknut and lock washer, then tighten bearing nut (1), **Fig. 5,** to 57.5 ft. lbs. while spinning hub by hand.
   b. Loosen bearing nut until torque becomes 0, then tighten nut to 7.5-10.5 ft. lbs. obtain a preload of 2.2-6.6 ft. lbs.
   c. After adjustment, ensure to install lock washer and tighten locknut (2), **Fig. 5,** to 43.5-65 ft. lbs.
   d. Recheck bearing preload.
5. Install axle shaft drive flange or free wheeling hub (if equipped), circlip, disc brake, caliper and holder and wheel assembly as mentioned previously.

WHEEL ALIGNMENT SECTION

INDEX

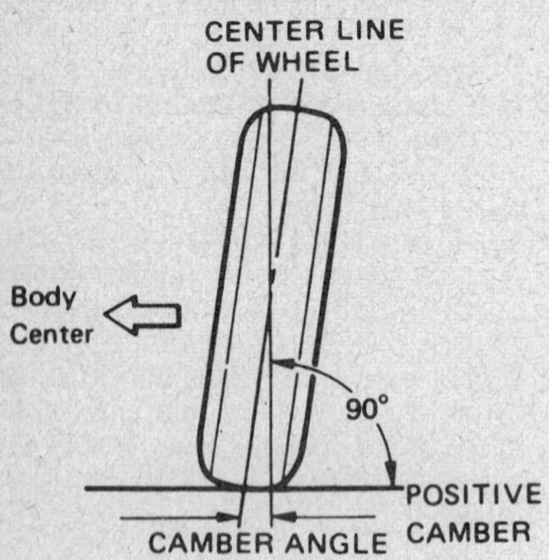

Fig. 1 Camber angle

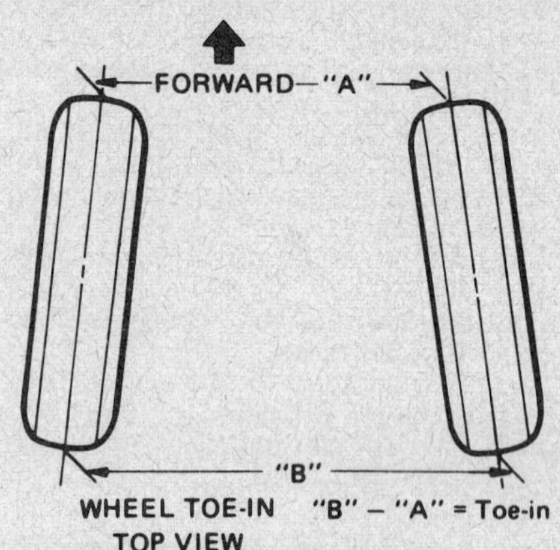

Fig. 2 Toe-in

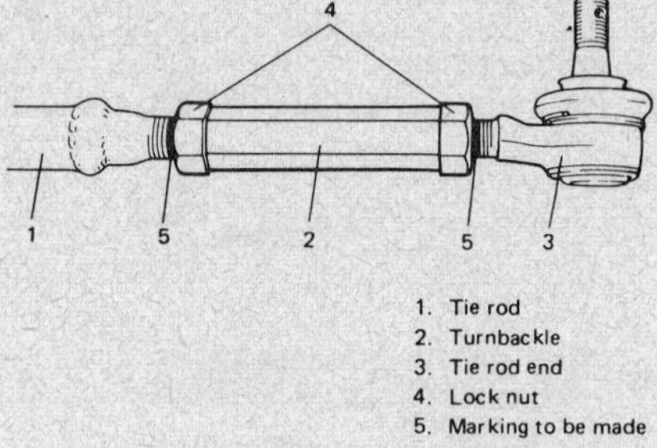

Fig. 3 Adjusting toe-in

DESCRIPTION

Wheel alignment is the angular relationship between the front wheels, front suspension attaching parts and the ground. The only adjustment required is toe. Camber and caster cannot be adjusted. Should camber or caster be out of specification due to hazardous road conditions, collision, whether the damage is in the chassis frame (body) or in suspension should be determined and body damage repaired and suspension parts replaced.

Camber is the tilting of front wheels from the vertical, when viewed from front of vehicle, **Fig. 1.** When the wheels tilt outward at the top, camber is positive. When wheels tilt inward at the top, camber is negative. Amount of tilt is measured in degrees.

Toe is the turning in or out of the front wheels, **Fig. 2.** The purpose of toe is to ensure parallel rolling of the front wheels. Excessive toe-in or toe-out may increase tire wear. Amount of toe can be obtained by subtracting "A" from "B" as shown in **Fig. 2,** and is given in inches or mm.

ADJUSTMENTS

CAMBER & CASTER

Should camber or caster be out of specification when inspecting, locate its cause. If cause is damaged, loose, bent, dented or worn suspension parts, they should be replaced. If it is chassis frame (body), repair it. To prevent incorrect reading of camber or caster, vehicle front end must be moved up and down several times before inspection.

TOE

Before making any adjustments, the following checks and inspections should be made to ensure correct alignment readings and alignment adjustments:

1. Check tires for proper inflation pressures and thread wear.
2. Check steering and suspension system for looseness. If excessive looseness is noted, it must be corrected before adjusting.
3. Check for run out of wheels and tires.
4. Consideration must be given to excess loads, such as tool boxes. If this excess load is normally carried in vehicle, it should remain in vehicle during alignment checks.
5. Vehicle must be on a level surface both fore and aft and transversely.
6. Ensure front wheels are set in straight forward driving position, and adjust toe as follows:
   a. Loosen tie rod end locknuts (4), **Fig. 3.**
   b. Rotate turnbuckle (2), **Fig. 3,** and adjust toe-in to specification.
   c. Thread lengths (5), **Fig. 3,** should be equal lengths. Tighten locknuts to 51-72 ft. lbs.

TOYOTA (Japan)

INDEX OF SERVICE OPERATIONS

Vehicle & Engine Identification

Model	Year	Engine Code	Displacement (cc)
Camry	1983–86	2S-E	1995
	1984–85	1C-TL⑤	1839
	1986	2C-T⑤	1974
	1987	3S-FE③④	1998
Celica	1983	22R	2367
	1983–85	22R-E③	2367
	1986	2S-E	1995
	1986–87	3S-GE③④	1998
	1987	3S-FE③④	1998
Corolla	1983–87	4A-C	1587
	1984–85	1C②	1839
	1986⑧	4A-GE③④	1587
	1987⑧	4A-GEC③④	1587
	1986–87⑦	4A-LC	1587
	1987⑥⑦	4A-GELC③④	1587
Cressida	1983–87	5M-GE③④	2759
MR2	1985	4A-GEL③④	1587
	1986–87	4A-GELC③④	1587

Model	Year	Engine Code	Displacement (cc)
Pickup & 4Runner	1983–87	22R	2367
	1983	L②	2188
	1984–87	22R-E③	2367
	1984–85	2L②	2446
	1985–87	22R-TE①③	2366
	1985	2L-T⑤	2466
Starlet	1983–84	4K-E③	1290
Supra	1983–Early 1986	5M-GE③④	2759
	Late 1986–87	7M-GE③④	2954
	1987	7M-GTE①③④	2954
Tercel	1983–87⑨	3A-C	1452
Tercel	1987⑩	3E	1456
Van	1984–85	3Y-EC	1998
	1986–87	4Y-EC	2237

①—Turbocharged gasoline engine.
②—Diesel engine.
③—Fuel injected engine.
④—Dual overhead cam engine.
⑤—Turbocharged diesel engine.
⑥—FX16 models.
⑦—Front wheel drive models.
⑧—Rear wheel drive models.
⑨—Exc. 1987 sedan.
⑩—1987 sedan.

General Engine Specifications

Year	Engine Displacement cu. in./cc	Fuel System	Bore & Stroke	Compression Ratio	Maximum Brake H.P. @ RPM	Maximum Torque Ft. Lbs. @ RPM
1983	4-78.7/1290	Fuel Inj.	2.95 x 2.87	9.5	58 @ 4200	74 @ 3400
	4-88.6/1452	2 Barrel	3.05 x 3.03	9.0	62 @ 4800	75 @ 2800
	4-96.8/1587	2 Barrel	3.19 x 3.03	9.0	70 @ 4800	85 @ 2800
	4-121.7/1995	Fuel Inj.	—	8.7	92 @ 4200	113 @ 2400
	4-144/2367	2 Barrel	3.62 x 3.50	9.0	96 @ 4800	129 @ 2800
	4-144/2367	Fuel Inj.	3.62 x 3.50	9.0	105 @ 4800	137 @ 2800
	6-168/2759	Fuel Inj.	3.27 x 3.35	8.8	⑤	⑥
	4-134/2188①	Fuel Inj.	3.54 x 3.39	21.5	—	—
1984	4-78.7/1290	Fuel Inj.	2.95 x 2.87	9.5	58 @ 4200	74 @ 3400
	4-88.6/1452	2 Barrel	3.05 x 3.03	9.0	62 @ 4800	76 @ 2800
	4-96.8/1587	2 Barrel	3.19 x 3.03	9.0	70 @ 4800	85 @ 2800
	4-112/1839①	Fuel Inj.	—	—	56 @ 4500	76 @ 3000
	4-112/1839⑩⑪	Fuel Inj.	—	—	72 @ 4500	104 @ 3000
	4-121.7/1995	Fuel Inj.	—	8.7	92 @ 4200	113 @ 2400
	4-122/1998	Fuel Inj.	3.38 x 3.38	8.8	90 @ 4400	120 @ 3000
	4-144/2367	2 Barrel	3.62 x 3.50	9.0	⑫	⑬
	4-144/2367	Fuel Inj.	3.62 x 3.50	9.0	106 @ 4800	137 @ 2800
	4-150/2466①	Fuel Inj.	3.62 x 3.65	—	⑭	⑮
	6-168/2759	Fuel Inj.	3.27 x 3.35	8.8	⑯	⑰

Continued

General Engine Specifications—Continued

Year	Engine Displacement cu. in./cc	Fuel System	Bore & Stroke	Compression Ratio	Maximum Brake H.P. @ RPM	Maximum Torque Ft. Lbs. @ RPM
1985	4-88.6/1452	2 Barrel	3.05 x 3.03	9.0	62 @ 4800	76 @ 2800
	4-96.8/1587 ⑱	2 Barrel	3.19 x 3.03	9.0	70 @ 4800	85 @ 2800
	4-96.8/1587 ⑲	Fuel Inj.	3.19 x 3.03	9.4	112 @ 6600	97 @ 4800
	4-112/1839 ①	Fuel Inj.	—	27.5	56 @ 4500	76 @ 3000
	4-112/1839 ⑩ ⑪	Fuel Inj.	—	—	73 @ 4500	104 @ 3000
	4-121.7/1995	Fuel Inj.	—	8.7	92 @ 4200	113 @ 2400
	4-122/1998	Fuel Inj.	3.38 x 3.38	8.8	90 @ 4400	120 @ 3000
	4-144/2366	2 Barrel	3.62 x 3.50	9.0	103 @ 4800	133 @ 2800
	4-144/2366	Fuel Inj.	3.62 x 3.50	9.3	116 @ 4800	140 @ 2800
	4-144/2366 ⑳	Fuel Inj.	3.62 x 3.50	9.3	135 @ 4800	173 @ 2800
	4-150/2466 ①	Fuel Inj.	3.62 x 3.65	22.3	75 @ 4000	114 @ 2400
	4-150/2466 ⑪	Fuel Inj.	3.62 x 3.65	22.1	84 @ 4000	137 @ 2400
	6-168/2759	Fuel Inj.	3.27 x 3.35	⑨	⑦	⑧
1986	4-88.6/1452	2 Barrel	3.05 x 3.03	9.0	62 @ 4800	76 @ 2800
	4-96.8/1587 ㉕	2 Barrel	3.2 x 3.0	9.0	②	86 @ 2800
	4-96.8/1587 ㉖	Fuel Inj.	3.2 x 3.0	9.4	112 @ 6600	97 @ 4800
	4-120.4/1974 ①	Fuel Inj.	3.39 x 3.39	23.0	74 @ 4500	117 @ 3000
	4-121.7/1995 ⑩	Fuel Inj.	3.31 x 3.54	8.7	95 @ 4400	116 @ 4000
	4-121.7/1995	Fuel Inj.	3.31 x 3.54	8.7	97 @ 4400	118 @ 4000
	4-122/1998	Fuel Inj.	3.39 x 3.39	9.2	135 @ 6000	125 @ 4800
	4-136/2237	Fuel Inj.	3.58 x 3.40	8.8	101 @ 4400	132 @ 3000
	4-144/2366	2 Barrel	3.62 x 3.50	9.3	103 @ 4800	133 @ 2800
	4-144/2366	Fuel Inj.	3.62 x 3.50	9.3	116 @ 4800	140 @ 2800
	4-144/2366 ⑳	Fuel Inj.	3.62 x 3.50	7.5	135 @ 4800	173 @ 2800
	6-168/2759 ④	Fuel Inj.	3.27 x 3.25	9.2	156 @ 5200	165 @ 4500
	6-168/2759 ③	Fuel Inj.	3.27 x 3.25	9.2	161 @ 5200	169 @ 4500
	6-180.3/2954	Fuel Inj.	3.27 x 3.58	9.2	200 @ 6000	185 @ 4800
1987	4-88.6/1452 ㉑	2 Barrel	3.05 x 3.03	9.0	㉓	㉔
	4-88.85/1456 ㉒	1 Barrel	2.87 x 3.43	9.3	78 @ 6000	87 @ 4000
	4-96.8/1587 ㉕	2 Barrel	3.2 x 3.0	9.0	②	86 @ 2800
	4-96.8/1587 ㉖	Fuel Inj.	3.2 x 3.0	9.4	㉗	97 @ 4800
	4-121.9/1998 ㉘	Fuel Inj.	3.38 x 3.38	9.3	115 @ 5200	124 @ 4400
	4-121.9/1998 ㉙	Fuel Inj.	3.38 x 3.38	9.2	135 @ 6000	125 @ 4800
	4-136/2237	Fuel Inj.	3.58 x 3.40	8.8	101 @ 4400	132 @ 3000
	4-144/2366	2 Barrel	3.62 x 3.50	9.3	103 @ 4800	133 @ 2800
	4-144/2366	Fuel Inj.	3.62 x 3.50	9.3	116 @ 4800	140 @ 2800
	4-144/2366 ⑳	Fuel Inj.	3.62 x 3.50	7.5	135 @ 4800	173 @ 2800
	6-168/2759	Fuel Inj.	3.27 x 3.25	9.2	156 @ 5200	165 @ 4500
	6-180.3/2954	Fuel Inj.	3.27 x3.58	9.2	200 @ 6000	185 @ 4800
	6-180.3/2954 ⑳	Fuel Inj.	3.27 x 3.58	8.4	230 @ 5600	246 @ 4800

① —Diesel engine.
② —Corolla FWD models, 74 @ 5200; Corolla RWD models, 74 @ 4800.
③ —Exc. Supra.
④ —Supra.
⑤ —Cressida, 143 @ 5200; Supra, 150 @ 5200.
⑥ —Cressida, 154 @ 4400; Supra, 159 @ 4400.
⑦ —Cressida, 156 @ 5200; Supra, 161 @ 5600.
⑧ —Cressida, 165 @ 4400; Supra, 169 @ 4400.
⑨ —Exc. Supra, 9.0; Supra, 8.8.
⑩ —Camry.
⑪ —Turbocharged diesel engine.
⑫ —Exc. Calif., 100 @ 4800; Calif., 96 @ 4800.
⑬ —Exc. Calif., 130 @ 2800; Calif., 129 @ 2800.
⑭ —Exc. Calif., 75 @ 4000; Calif., 70 @ 4000.
⑮ —Exc. Calif., 114 @ 2400; Calif., 108 @ 2400.
⑯ —Supra models, 150 @ 5200; Cressida models, 143 @ 5200.
⑰ —Supra models, 159 @ 4400; Cressida models, 154 @ 4400.
⑱ —Exc. MR2.
⑲ —MR2.
⑳ —Turbocharged engine.
㉑ —Exc. Tercel sedan.
㉒ —Tercel sedan.
㉓ —W/4 speed man. trans., 60 @ 4500; exc. 4 speed man. trans., 62 @ 4200.
㉔ —W/4 speed man. trans., 75 @ 2400; exc. 4 speed man. trans., 76 @ 2800.
㉕ —Exc. dual overhead cam engine.
㉖ —Dual overhead cam engine.
㉗ —Exc. FX16, 112 @ 6600; FX16, 108 @ 6600.
㉘ —3S-FE engine, Camry & Celica.
㉙ —3S-GE engine, Celica.

Alternator & Regulator Specifications

Year	Model	Alternator Maximum Output Amps	Alternator Rotor Coil Resistance Ohms	Voltage Regulator Voltage
1983	2S-E	70	3	13.5–14.3
	3A-C②	50	4.1	13.8–14.8
	3A-C①	55	2.9	13.8–14.4
	4A-C②	50	4.0	13.8–14.8
	4A-C①	55	2.9	13.8–14.4
	4K-E	55	2.9	13.8–14.4
	5M-GE	65	2.9	13.8–14.4
	22R①	40	2.9	13.8–14.4
	22R②	40	4.0	13.8–14.4
	22R①	55	2.9	13.8–14.4
	22R①	60	2.9	13.8–14.4
	22R-E	55	2.9	13.8–14.4
	22R-E	60	2.9	13.8–14.4
	L	55	4.0	13.8–14.8
1984	1C	50	4.0	13.8–14.8
	1C-T	55	2.9	13.8–14.4
	2L	55	2.9	13.8–14.4
	2S-E	70	3	13.5–15.1
	3A-C②	50	4.1	13.8–14.8
	3A-C①	55	2.9	13.8–14.4
	3Y-EC	60	3	13.5–15.1
	4A-C	55	2.9	13.8–14.4
	4K-E	55	2.9	13.8–14.4
	22R②	40	4	13.8–14.8
1984	22R①	40	2.9	14.0–14.7
	22R-E①	60	2.9	13.8–14.4
	22R-E①	55	2.9	13.8–14.4
	5M-GE	60	2.9	13.8–14.8
1985	1C	55	2.9	13.8–14.4
	1C	60	2.9	13.8–14.4
	1C-TL	55	2.9	13.8–14.4
	1C-TL	60	2.9	13.8–14.4
	2L	55	2.9	13.8–14.4
	2LT	55	2.9	13.8–14.4
	2S-E	70	2.9	13.5–15.1
	3A-C②	50	4.1	13.8–14.8
	3A-C①	55	2.9	13.5–15.1
	3Y-EC	60	2.9	13.5–15.1
	4A-C③	60	2.9	13.9–15.1
	4A-C④	55	2.9	13.5–14.3
	4A-C④	60	2.9	13.5–14.3
	4A-GE	55	2.9	13.5–14.3

Year	Model	Alternator Maximum Output Amps	Alternator Rotor Coil Resistance Ohms	Voltage Regulator Voltage
	4A-GE	60	2.9	13.5–14.3
	4A-GEL	60	2.9	13.5–16.1
	5M-GE	60	2.9	13.9–15.1
	22R	60	2.9	13.5–15.1
	22R-E	60	2.9	13.5–15.1
1986	2C-T	55	2.9	13.8–14.4
	2C-T	60	2.9	13.8–14.4
	2S-E	70	2.9	13.5–15.1
	3A-C②	50	4.1	13.8–14.8
	3A-C①	55	2.9	13.5–15.1
	3S-GE	60	2.9	13.5–15.1
	4A-C	55	2.9	13.5–14.3
	4A-C	60	2.9	13.5–14.3
	4A-GE	55	2.9	13.5–14.3
	4A-GE	60	2.9	13.5–14.3
	4A-GELC	60	2.9	13.5–15.1
	4A-LC	60	2.9	13.9–15.1
	4Y-EC	70	2.9	13.5–15.1
	5M-GE	60	2.9	13.5–15.1
	7M-GE	70	2.9	13.5–15.1
	22R	60	2.9	13.5–15.1
	22R-E	60	2.9	13.5–15.1
	22R-TE	60	2.9	13.5–15.1
1987	3A-C②	50	4.1	13.8–14.8
	3A-C①	60	2.9	13.5–15.1
	3E	45	2.9	13.5–15.1
	3E	55	2.9	13.5–15.1
	3S-FE	70	2.9	13.5–15.1
	3S-GE	60	2.9	13.5–15.1
	4A-C	55	2.9	13.5–14.3
	4A-GEC	60	2.9	13.5–14.3
	4A-GELC⑤	60	2.9	13.5–15.1
	4A-GELC⑥	70	2.9	13.5–15.1
	4A-LC	60	2.9	13.5–15.1
	4Y-EC	70	2.9	13.5–15.1
	5M-GE	60	2.9	13.5–15.1
	7M-GE	70	2.9	13.5–15.1
	7M-GTE	70	2.9	13.5–15.1
	22R	60	2.9	13.5–15.1
	22R-E	60	2.9	13.5–15.1
	22R-TE	60	2.9	13.5–15.1

①—With integral regulator.
②—Exc. integral regulator.
③—Front wheel drive models.
④—Rear wheel drive models.
⑤—FX16 models.
⑥—MR2 models.

Starting Motor Specifications

Year	Engine	Brush Spring Tension, Ounces	No Load Test		
			Amperes	Volts	RPM
1983	2S-E ①	48–64	90	11.5	3000
	2S-E ②	64–80	90	11.5	3000
	3A-C ③	35–48	50	11	5000
	3A-C ④	52–69	90	11.5	3000
	4A-C ①	64–85	90	11.5	3000
	4A-C ②	64–85	90	11.5	3500
	4K-E ③	35–48	50	11	5000
	4K-E ④	64–85	90	11.5	3000
	5M-GE ②	64–85	90	11.5	3500
	22R, R-E ①	64–85	90	11.5	3000
	22R, R-E ②	64–85	90	11.5	3500
	L ⑤	112–140	180	11	3500
1984	1C ⑥	48–128	120	—	4000
	1C ⑤	128–164	180	—	3500
	2L ⑤	112–140	180	11	3500
	2S-E ①	51–69	90	11.5	3000
	2S-E ②	62–85	90	11.5	3000
	3A-C ③	35–48	50	11	5000
	3A-C ④	62–85	90	11.5	3000
	3Y-EC ①	64–80	90	11.5	3000
	3Y-EC ②	64–80	90	11.5	3000
	4A-C ①	62–85	90	11.5	3000
	4A-C ②	62–85	90	11.5	3500
	4K-E ③	35–48	50	11	5000
	4K-E ④	62–85	90	11.5	3000
	22R, R-E ④	51–69	90	11.5	3000
	22R, R-E ⑦	62–85	90	11.5	3500
	5M-GE ②	62–85	90	11.5	3500
1985	1C ⑥	64–95	120	—	4000
	1C ⑤	85–106	180	—	3500
	1C-T ⑤	85–106	180	11	3500
	2L, LT ⑤	85–106	180	11	3500
	2S-E ④	38–51	90	11.5	3000
	2S-E ⑦	47–64	90	11.5	3000
	3A-C ③	26–36	50	11	5000
	3A-C ④	47–64	90	11.5	3000
	3Y-EC ① ②	47–64	90	11.5	3000
	4A-C, GE ④	47–64	90	11.5	3000
	4A-C, GE ⑦	47–64	90	11.5	3500
1985	4A-GEL ⑦	47–64	90	11.5	3500
	5M-GE ⑦	47–64	90	11.5	3500
	22R, R-E ④	47–64	90	11.5	3000
	22R, R-E ⑦	47–64	90	11.5	3500

Continued

Starting Motor Specifications—Continued

Year	Engine	Brush Spring Tension, Ounces	No Load Test		
			Amperes	Volts	RPM
1986	2C-T⑤	112–140	180	11	3500
	2S-E④	62–86	90	11.5	3000
	2S-E⑦	62–86	90	11.5	3000
	3A-C③	36–50	50	11	5000
	3A-C④	62–85	90	11	3000
	3S-GE④	62–85	90	11.5	3000
	3S-GE⑦	62–85	90	11.5	3000
	4A-C, GE④	62–85	90	11.5	3000
	4A-C, GE⑦	62–85	90	11.5	3500
	4A-GELC⑦	62–85	90	11.5	3500
	4A-LC④	62–85	90	11.5	3000
	4A-LC⑦	62–85	90	11.5	3500
	4Y-EC⑦	62–85	90	11.5	3000
	5M-GE	62–85	90	11.5	3500
	7M-GE	62–85	90	11.5	3500
	22R, R-E, R-TE④	62–85	90	11.5	3000
	22R, R-E, R-TE⑦	62–85	90	11.5	3500
1987	3A-C③	56	50	11	5000
	3A-C④	62–85	90	11	3000
	3E③	50–56	50	11	5000
	3E④	62–85	90	11	3000
	3S-FE, 3S-GE④	62–85	90	11	3000
	3S-FE, 3S-GE⑦	62–85	90	11	3000
	4A-C, GEC④	62–85	90	11.5	3000
	4A-C, GEC⑦	62–85	90	11.5	3500
	4A-LC, GELC④	62–85	90	11.5	3000
	4A-LC, GELC⑦	62–85	90	11.5	3500
	4Y-EC⑦	62–85	90	11.5	3000
	5M-GE	62–85	90	11.5	3500
	7M-GE, 7M-GTE	62–85	90	11.5	3500
	22R, R-E, R-TE④	62–85	90	11.5	3000
	22R, R-E, R-TE⑦	62–85	90	11.5	3500

①—Exc. heavy duty starter, 1.0 KW rating.
②—Heavy duty starter, 1.4 KW rating.
③—Conventional starter, .8 KW rating.
④—Reduction type starter, 1.0 KW rating.
⑤—Reduction type starter, 2.5 KW rating.
⑥—Reduction type starter, 2.0 KW rating.
⑦—Reduction type starter, 1.4 KW rating.

Pistons, Pins, Ring, Crankshaft & Bearings

Year	Model	Piston Clearance Bottom of Skirt	Ring End Gap		Wristpin Dia.	Rod Bearings		Main Bearings			Shaft Endplay
			Comp. (1)	Oil (1)		Shaft Dia.	Bearing Clearance	Shaft Dia.	Bearing Clearance	Thrust on Bear. No.	
1983	2S-E	.0006-.0014	(12)	.008	1.0635	1.8892-1.8898	.0009-.0022	2.1648-2.1654	.0012-.0027	3	.0008-.0087
	3A-C	.004-.0047	(4)	(5)	—	1.5742-1.5748	.0008-.002	1.8892-1.8898	.0005-.0019	3	.0008-.0073
	4A-C	.004-.0047	(10)	(11)	—	1.5742-1.5748	.0008-.002	1.8892-1.8898	.0005-.0019	3	.0008-.0073
	4K-E	.0012-.002	.006	.008	—	1.6526-1.6535	.0006-.0016	1.9676-1.9685	.0006-.0016	3	.0016-.0976
	5M-GE	.002-.0028	(4)	.008	.8663	2.0463-2.0472	.0008-.0021	2.3617-2.3627	.0013-.0023	4	.002-.0098
	22R, R-E	.002-.0028	.008	—	—	2.0865-2.0866	.001-.0022	2.3616-2.3622	.001-.0022	3	.0008-.009
	L	.0014-.0022 (8)	(9)	.0118	1.0632	2.0463-2.0472	.0012-.0028	2.4402-2.4409	.0012-.0028	3	.0016-.0098
1984	1C	.0016-.0024	(13)	.008	1.0635	1.9877-1.9882	.0014-.0025	2.2435-2.2441	.0013-.0026	3	.0016-.0094
	2L	.0020-.0028	(14)	.008	—	2.0861-2.0866	.0014-.0025	2.4403-2.4409	.0013-.0026	3	.0016-.0098
	2S-E	.0006-.0014	(12)	.008	1.0635	1.8892-1.8898	.0009-.0022	2.1648-2.1654	.0012-.0022	3	.0008-.0087
	3A-C	.004-.0047	(4)	(5)	—	1.5742-1.5748	—	1.8892-1.8898	.0012-.0026	3	.0008-.0073
	3Y-EC	.0030-.0037	(15)	.008	—	1.8892-1.8898	.0008-.002	2.2829-2.2835	.0008-.002	3	.0008-.0087
	4A-C	.004-.0047	(10)	(11)	—	1.5742-1.5748	.0008-.002	1.8892-1.8898	.0005-.0019	3	.0008-.0073
	4K-E	.0012-.002	(4)	(16)	—	1.6526-1.6535	.0006-.0016	1.9676-1.9685	.0006-.0016	3	.0016-.0976
	22R, R-E	.002-.0028	(17)	.008	—	2.0865-2.0866	.001-.0022	2.3616-2.3622	.001-.0022	3	.0008-.009
	5M-GE	.002-.0028	(4)	.008	.8863	2.0463-2.0472	.0008-.0021	2.3617-2.3627	.0013-.0023	4	.002-.0098
1985	1C	.0016-.0024	(20)	.008	1.0634	1.9877-1.9882	.0014-.0025	2.2435-2.2441	.0013-.0026	3	.0008-.0047
	1C-TL	.0016-.0024	(20)	.008	1.0633	1.9877-1.9882	.0014-.0025	2.2435-2.2441	.0013-.0026	3	.0016-.0094
	2L	.0020-.0028	(14)	.008	—	2.0861-2.0866	.0014-.0025	2.4403-2.4409	.0013-.0026	3	.0016-.0098
	2LT	.0020-.0028	(14)	.008	—	2.0861-2.0866	.0014-.0025	2.4403-2.4409	.0013-.0026	3	.0016-.0098
	2S-E	.0006-.0014	(12)	.008	—	1.8892-1.8898	.0009-.0022	2.1648-2.1654	.0012-.0022	3	.0008-.0087
	3A-C	.0039-.0047	.008	.012	—	1.5742-1.5748	.0008-.002	1.8892-1.8898	.0012-.0026	3	.0008-.0073
	3Y-EC	.0030-.0037	(18)	.008	—	1.8892-1.8898	.0008-.002	2.2829-2.2835	.0008-.002	3	.0008-.0087
	4A-C	.0039-.0047	(19)	.012	—	1.5742-1.5748	.0008-.002	1.8892-1.8898	.0005-.0019	3	.0008-.0073
	4A-GE	.0039-.0047	(19)	.012	—	1.5742-1.5748	.0008-.002	1.8892-1.8898	.0005-.0019	3	.0008-.0087
	4A-GEL	.0039-.0047	(19)	.012	—	1.5742-1.5748	—	1.8892-1.8898	.0005-.0015	3	.0008-.0087
	5M-GE	.0020-.0028	(6)	.007	—	2.0463-2.0472	.0008-.0021	2.3617-2.3627	.0013-.0023	4	.0020-.0098
	22R	.0012-.0020	(17)	.008	—	2.0861-2.0866	.001-.0022	2.3616-2.3622	.0010-.0022	3	.0008-.0087
	22R-E	.0012-.0020	(17)	.008	—	2.0861-2.0866	.001-.0022	2.3616-2.3622	.0010-.0022	3	.0008-.0087
1986	2C-T	.0018-.0026	(20)	.008	1.0633	1.9877-1.9882	.0017-.0028	2.2435-2.2441	.0013-.0026	3	.0016-.0094
	2S-E	.0006-.0014	(12)	.008	—	1.8892-1.8898	.0009-.0022	2.1648-2.1654	.0012-.0022	3	.0008-.0087
	3A-C	.0039-.0047	.008	.012	—	1.5742-1.5748	.0008-.002	1.8892-1.8898	.0005-.0015	3	.0008-.0073
	3S-GE	.0006-.0014	(12)	.008	—	1.8892-1.8898	.0009-.0022	2.1648-2.1654	.0012-.0022	3	.0008-.0087
	4A-C	.0039-.0047	(19)	.012	—	1.5742-1.5748	.0008-.002	1.8892-1.8898	.0012-.0026	3	.0008-.0073
	4A-GE	.0039-.0047	(19)	.012	—	1.5742-1.5748	.0088-.002	1.8892-1.8898	.0005-.0019	3	.0008-.0087
	4A-GELC	.0039-.0047	(19)	.012	—	1.5742-1.5748	.0008-.002	1.8892-1.8898	.0005-.0015	3	.0008-.0087
	4A-LC	.0035-.0043	(19)	.012	—	1.5742-1.5748	.0008-.002	1.8892-1.8898	.0005-.0015	3	.0008-.0073
	4Y-EC	.0026-.0033	(2)	.005	—	1.8892-1.8898	.0008-.002	2.2829-2.2835	.0008-.0020	3	.0008-.0087
	5M-GE	.0024-.0031	(3)	.007	.8663	2.0463-2.0472	.0008-.0021	2.3617-2.3627	.0013-.0023	4	.0020-.0098
	7M-GE	.0024-.0031	(6)	.004	.8663	2.0470-2.0472	.0012-.0019	2.3625-2.3627	.0012-.0022	4	.0020-.0098
	22R	.0012-.0020	(7)	.008	—	2.0861-2.0866	.0010-.0022	2.3616-2.3622	.0010-.0022	3	.0008-.0087
	22R-E	.0012-.0020	(7)	.008	—	2.0861-2.0866	.0010-.0022	2.3616-2.3622	.0010-.0022	3	.0008-.0087
	22R-TE	.0022-.0030	(7)	.008	—	2.0861-2.0866	.0010-.0022	2.3616-2.3622	.0010-.0022	3	.0008-.0087

Continued

PISTONS, PINS, RING, CRANKSHAFT & BEARINGS—Continued

Year	Model	Piston Clearance Bottom of Skirt	Ring End Gap Comp. ①	Ring End Gap Oil①	Wristpin Dia.	Rod Bearings Shaft Dia.	Rod Bearings Bearing Clearance	Main Bearings Shaft Dia.	Main Bearings Bearing Clearance	Thrust on Bear. No.	Shaft Endplay
1987	3A-C	.0039-.0047	.008	.012	—	1.5742-1.5748	.0008-.002	1.8891-1.8898	.0006-.0013	3	.0008-.0087
	3E	.0039-.0047	.008	.012	—	1.5742-1.5748	.0008-.002	1.8892-1.8898	.0005-.0015	3	.0008-.0073
	3S-FE	.0018-.0026	.0106	.008	—	1.8892-1.8898	.0009-.0022	2.1648-2.1653	.0011-.0019	—	.0008-.0087
	3S-GE	.0012-.002	㉑	.008	—	1.8892-1.8898	.0009-.0022	2.1648-2.1653	.0011-.0019	—	.0008-.0087
	4A-C	.0039-.0047	⑲	.008	—	1.5742-1.5748	.0008-.002	1.8891-1.8898	.0012-.0026	3	.0008-.0087
	4A-GEC	.0039-.0047	㉒	.012	—	1.5742-1.5748	.0008-.002	1.8891-1.8898	.0005-.0015	—	.0008-.0087
	4A-GELC	.0039-.0047	㉒	.008	—	1.5742-1.5748	.0008-.002	1.8891-1.8898	.0005-.0015	—	.0008-.0087
	4A-LC	.0035-.0043	⑲	.008	—	1.5742-1.5748	.0008-.002	1.8891-1.8898	.0006-.0013	—	.0008-.0087
	5M-GE	.0024-.0031	⑥	.004	.8663	2.0470-2.0472	.0008-.0021	2.3625-2.3627	.0012-.0048	4	.0020-.0098
	7M-GE	.0024-.0031	⑥	.004	.8663	2.0470-2.0472	.0012-.0019	2.3625-2.3627	.0012-.0022	4	.0020-.0098
	7M-GTE	.0028-.0035	③	.004	.8663	2.0470-2.0472	.0012-.0019	2.3625-2.3627	.0012-.0022	4	.0020-.0098
	22R	.0008-.0016	㉓	.008	—	2.0861-2.0866	.0010-.0022	2.3616-2.3622	.0010-.0022	3	.0008-.0087
	22R-E	.0008-.0016	㉓	.008	—	2.0861-2.0866	.0010-.0022	2.3616-2.3622	.0010-.0022	3	.0008-.0087
	22R-TE	.0022-.0030	㉓	.008	—	2.0861-2.0866	.0010-.0022	2.3616-2.3622	.0010-.0022	3	.0008-.0087

①—Tightest fit.
②—No. 1, .0091 inch; No. 2, .0063 inch.
③—No. 1, .0014 inch; No. 2, .0098 inch.
④—No. 1, .008 inch; No. 2, .006 inch.
⑤—TP type, .004 inch; Riken type, .012 inch.
⑥—No. 1, .0091 inch; No. 2, .0098 inch.
⑦—No. 1, .0138 inch; No. 2, .0098 inch.
⑧—Measurement taken approx. 1.34 inch (34 mm) up from skirt bottom edge in the thrust direction.
⑨—No. 1, .0078 inch; No. 2, .0118 inch.
⑩—TP type, No. 1, .0098 inch, No. 2, .006 inch; Riken type, No. 1, .0079 inch, No. 2, .006 inch.
⑪—TP type, .008 inch; Riken type, .012 inch.
⑫—No. 1, .011 inch; No. 2, .008 inch.
⑬—No. 1, .010 inch; No. 2, .008 inch.
⑭—No. 1, .014 inch; No. 2, .008 inch.
⑮—TPR type, No. 1, .0106 inch; No. 2, .008 inch. NPR type, No. 1, .009 inch, No. 2, .006 inch.
⑯—TP type, .008 inch; Riken type, .012 inch.
⑰—No. 1, .0094 inch; No. 2, .0071 inch.
⑱—No. 1, .0087 inch; No. 2, .0059 inch.
⑲—No. 1, .0098 inch; No. 2, .0059 inch.
⑳—No. 1, .0106 inch; No. 2, .0098 inch.
㉑—No. 1, .013 inch; No. 2, .008 inch.
㉒—No. 1, .0098 inch; No. 2, .0078 inch.
㉓—No. 2, .0098 inch; No. 2, .0236 inch.

Valve Specifications

Year	Model	Valve Lash Int.	Valve Lash Exh.	Valve Angles Seat	Valve Angles Face	Valve Spring Installed Height	Valve Spring Pressure Lbs. @ In.	Stem Clearance Intake	Stem Clearance Exhaust	Stem Diameter Intake	Stem Diameter Exhaust
1983	2S-E	①	①	45	45.5	1.555	68 @ 1.555	.0010-.0024	.0012-.0026	.3138-.3144	.3136-.3142
	3A-C	.008H	.012H	45	44.5	1.520	52 @ 1.520	.0010-.0024	.0012-.0026	.2744-.2750	.2742-.2748
	4A-C	.008H	.012H	45	45.5	1.520	52 @ 1.520	.0010-.0024	.0012-.0026	.2744-.2750	.2742-.2748
	4K-E	②	②	45	44.5	1.512	77.2 @ 1.512	.0012-.0026	.0014-.0028	.3136-.3142	.3134-.3148
	5M-GE	①	①	45	45.5	③	④	.0010-.0024	.0012-.0026	.3138-.3144	.3136-.3142
	22R, R-E	.008H	.012H	45	44.5	1.594	55 @ 1.594	.0008-.0024	.0012-.0028	.3138-.3144	.3136-.3142
	L	.010H	.014H	45	44.5	1.547	53.4 @ 1.547	.0008-.0022	.0016-.0030	.3336-.3342	.3328-.3335
1984	1C	.010C	.012C	45	44.5	1.587	53 @ 1.587	.0008-.0022	.0014-.0028	.3140-.3146	.3134-.3140
	2L	.010H	.014H	45	45.5	1.547	64 @ 1.547	.0008-.0022	.0016-.0030	.3336-.3342	.3328-.3335
	2S-E	①	①	45	45.5	1.555	68 @ 1.555	.0010-.0024	.0012-.0026	.3138-.3144	.3136-.3142
	3A-C	.008H	.012H	45	44.5	1.520	52 @ 1.520	.0010-.0024	.0012-.0026	.2744-.2750	.2742-.2748
	3Y-EC	①	①	45	45.5	1.598	63 @ 1.598	.0010-.0024	.0012-.0026	.3138-.3144	.3136-.3142
	4A-C	.008H	.012H	45	45.5	1.520	52 @ 1.520	.0010-.0024	.0012-.0026	.2744-.2750	.2742-.2748
	4K-E	①	①	45	44.5	1.512	77.2 @ 1.512	.0012-.0026	.0014-.0028	.3136-.3142	.3134-.3140
	22R, R-E	.008H	.012H	45	44.5	1.594	55 @ 1.594	.0008-.0024	.0012-.0028	.3138-.3144	.3136-.3142
	5M-GE	①	①	45	44.5	③	④	.0010-.0024	.0012-.0026	.3138-.3144	.3136-.3142

Continued

Valve Specifications—Continued

Year	Model	Valve Lash		Valve Angles		Valve Spring Installed Height	Valve Spring Pressure Lbs. @ In.	Stem Clearance		Stem Diameter	
		Int.	Exh.	Seat	Face			Intake	Exhaust	Intake	Exhaust
1985	1C	.012H	.014H	45	44.5	1.587	53 @ 1.587	.0008-.0022	.0014-.0028	.3140-.3146	.3134-.3140
	1C-TL	.012H	.014H	45	44.5	1.587	53 @ 1.587	.0008-.0022	.0014-.0028	.3140-.3146	.3134-.3140
	2L	.010H	.014H	45	44.5	1.547	64.4 @ 1.547	.0008-.0022	.-TE		
	2LT	.010H	.014H	45	44.5	1.547	64.4 @ 1.547	.0008-.0022	.0016-.0030	.3328-.3335	.3328-.3335
	2S-E	①	①	45	44.5	1.555	71.4 @ 1.555	.0010-.0024	.0012-.0026	.3138-.3144	.3136-.3142
	3A-C	.008H	.012H	45	44.5	1.520	52 @ 1.520	.0010-.0024	.0012-.0026	.2744-.2750	.2742-.2748
	3Y-EC	①	①	45	44.5	1.598	70.5 @ 1.598	.0010-.0024	.0012-.0026	.3138-.3144	.3136-.3142
	4A-C	.008H	.012H	45	45.5	1.520	52 @ 1.520	.0010-.0024	.0012-.0026	.2744-.2750	.2742-.2748
	4A-GE	.006-.010C	.008-.012C	45	44.5	1.366	34.8 @ 1.366	.0010-.0024	.0012-.0026	.2350-.2356	.2348-.2354
	4A-GEL	.006-.010C	.008-.012C	45	44.5	1.366	35.9 @ 1.366	.0010-.0024	.0012-.0026	.2350-.2356	.2348-.2354
	5M-GE	①	①	45	44.5	③	④	.0010-.0024	.0015-.0027	.3138-.3144	.3136-.3142
	22R	.008H	.012H	45	44.5	1.594	55 @ 1.594	.0008-.0024	.0012-.0028	.3138-.3144	.3136-.3142
	22R-E	.008H	.012H	45	44.5	1.594	55 @ 1.594	.0008-.0024	.0012-.0028	.3138-.3144	.3136-.3142
1986	2C-T	.008-.012C	.010-.014C	45	44.5	1.587	55.8 @ 1.587	.0008-.0022	.0014-.0028	.3140-.3146	.3134-.3140
	2S-E	①	①	45	44.5	1.555	67.9 @ 1.555	.0010-.0024	.0012-.0026	.3138-.3144	.3136-.3142
	3A-C	.008H	.012H	45	44.5	1.520	52 @ 1.520	.0010-.0024	.0012-.0026	.2744-.2750	.2742-.2748
	3S-GE	.006-.010C	.008-.012C	45	44.5	1.366	38.6 @ 1.366	.0010-.0023	.0012-.0025	.2346-.2352	.2344-.2350
	4A-C	.008H	.012H	45	45.5	1.520	52.0 @ 1.520	.0010-.0024	.0012-.0026	.2744-.2750	.2742-.2748
	4A-GE	.006-.010C	.008-.012C	45	44.5	1.366	35.9 @ 1.366	.0010-.0024	.0012-.0026	.2350-.2356	.2348-.2354
	4A-GELC	.006-.010C	.008-.012C	45	44.5	1.366	35.9 @ 1.366	.0010-.0024	.0012-.0026	.2350-.2356	.2348-.2354
	4A-LC	.008H	.012H	45	44.5	1.520	520 @ 1.520	.0010-.0024	.0012-.0026	.2744-.2750	.2742-.2748
	4Y-EC	①	①	45	44.5	1.598	70.5 @ 1.598	.0010-.0024	.0012-.0026	.3138-.3144	.3136-.3142
	5M-GE	①	①	45	44.5	③	④	.0010-.0024	.0012-.0026	.3138-.3144	.3136-.3142
	7M-GE	.006-.010	.008-.012	45	44.5	1.378	35 @ 1.378	.0010-.0024	.0012-.0026	.2350-.2356	.2348-.2354
	22R	.008H	.012H	45	44.5	1.594	66.1 @ 1.594	.0010-.0024	.0012-.0026	.3138-.3144	.3136-.3142
	22R-E	.008H	.012H	45	44.5	1.594	66.1 @ 1.594	.0010-.0024	.0012-.0026	.3138-.3144	.3136-.3142
	22R-TE	.008H	.012H	45	44.5	1.594	66.1 @ 1.594	.0010-.0024	.0012-.0027	.3138-.3144	.3136-.3142
1987	3A-C	.008H	.012H	45	44.5	1.520	52 @ 1.520	.0010-.0024	.0012-.0026	.2744-.2750	.2742-.2748
	3E	.008H	.008H	⑤	44.5	1.382	35.1 @ 1.382	.0010-.0024	.0012-.0026	.2350-.2356	.2348-.2354
	3S-FE	.007-.011C	.011-.015C	45	44.5	1.366	39.6 @ 1.366	.0010-.0024	.0012-.0026	.2350-.2356	.2348-.2354
	3S-GE	.006-.010C	.008-.012C	45	44.5	1.366	38.6 @ 1.366	.0010-.0023	.0012-.0025	.2346-.2352	.2344-.2350
	4A-C	.008H	.012H	45	45.5	1.520	52.0 @ 1.520	.0010-.0024	.0012-.0026	.2744-.2750	.2742-.2748
	4A-GEC	.006-.010C	.008-.012C	45	44.5	1.366	34.8 @ 1.366	.0010-.0024	.0012-.0026	.2350-.2356	.2348-.2354
	4A-GELC	.006-.010C	.008-.012C	45	44.5	1.366	35.9 @ 1.366	.0010-.0024	.0012-.0026	.2350-.2356	.2348-.2354
	4A-LC	.008H	.012H	45	44.5	1.520	520 @ 1.520	.0010-.0024	.0012-.0026	.2744-.2750	.2742-.2748
	4Y-EC	①	①	45	44.5	1.598	70.5 @ 1.598	.0010-.0024	.0012-.0026	.3138-.3144	.3136-.3142
	5M-GE	①	①	45	44.5	③	④	.0010-.0024	.0012-.0026	.3138-.3144	.3136-.3142
	7M-GE	.006-.010	.008-.012	45	44.5	1.378	35 @ 1.378	.0010-.0024	.0012-.0026	.2350-.2356	.2348-.2354
	7M-GTE	.006-.010	.008-.012	45	44.5	1.378	35 @ 1.378	.0010-.0024	.0012-.0026	.2350-.2356	.2348-.2354
	22R	.008H	.012H	45	44.5	1.594	66.1 @ 1.594	.0010-.0024	.0012-.0026	.3138-.3144	.3136-.3142
	22R-E	.008H	.012H	45	44.5	1.594	66.1 @ 1.594	.0010-.0024	.0012-.0026	.3138-.3144	.3136-.3142
	22R-TE	.008H	.012H	45	44.5	1.594	66.1 @ 1.594	.0010-.0024	.0012-.0027	.3138-.3144	.3136-.3142

①—Hydraulic-not adjustable.
②—One turn after zero lash.
③—Intake, 1.575; exhaust, 1.693.
④—Intake, 76.5-84.4 @ 1.575; exhaust, 73.4-80.9 @ 1.693.
⑤—Intake, 45°; exhaust, 60°.

Engine Tightening Specifications

***Torque specifications are for clean and lightly lubricated threads only. Dry or dirty threads produce increased friction which prevents accurate measurement of tightness.**

Year	Engine	Spark Plugs Ft. Lbs.	Cylinder Head Bolts Ft. Lbs.	Intake Manifold Ft. Lbs.	Rocker Arm Shaft Bracket Ft. Lbs.	Rocker Arm Cover Ft. Lbs.	Connecting Rod Cap Bolts Ft. Lbs.	Main Bearing Cap Bolts Ft. Lbs.	Flywheel To Crankshaft Ft. Lbs.	Vibration Damper Or Pulley Ft. Lbs.
1983	2S-E	—	44–50	31	⑤	—	33–39	40–47	65–72	73–86
	3A-C	11–15	40–47	15–21	17–19	—	26–32	40–47	55–61	80–94
	4A-C	11–15	40–47	15–21	17–19	—	26–32	40–47	55–61	80–94
	4K-E	11–15	40–47	15–21	14–17	—	29–37	40–47	40–47	55–75
	22R, R-E	—	58	14	—	—	46	76	80	116
	5M-GE	15–21	55–61	15–17	④	—	31–34	72–78	51–57	98–119
	L	③	84–90	8–11	11–15	—	37–43	71–81	84–90	69–75
1984	1C	⑥	62	13	⑦	—	47	76	65	72
	2L	⑥	87	17	⑦	—	43	76	90	101
	2S-E	—	47	31	⑤	—	36	43	72	80
	3A-C	11–15	40–47	15–21	17–19	—	34–39	40–47	55–61	80–94
	3Y-EC	13	①	36	17	—	36	58	61	80
	4A-C	11–15	40–47	15–21	17–19	—	34–39	40–47	54	80–94
	4K-E	11–15	40–47	15–21	14–17	—	29–37	40–47	40–47	55–75
	22R, R-E	—	58	14	—	—	46	76	80	116
	5M-GE	15–21	58	15–17	④	—	33	75	54	160
1985	1C	⑥	62	13	—	—	47	76	47	72
	1C-TL	⑥	62	13	—	—	47	76	—	72
	2L	⑥	87	17	14	—	43	76	—	101
	2LT	⑥	87	17	14	—	43	76	—	101
	2S-E	—	47	31	—	—	36	43	72	80
	3A-C	13	43	18	18	—	36	43	⑧	87
	3Y-EC	13	①	36	17	—	36	58	61	80
	4A-C	13	43	18	18	—	29	43	58	87
	4A-GE	13	43	16	—	—	36	44	54	87
1985	4A-GEL	13	44	16	—	—	36	44	54	87
	5M-GE	15–21	54–62	15–17	④	—	31–35	71–79	50–58	146–174
	22R	—	58	14	—	—	46	76	80	116
	22R-E	—	58	14	—	—	46	76	80	116
1986	2C-T	⑥	33	13	—	—	47	76	—	72
	2S-E	13	47	31	—	—	36	43	72	72
	3A-C	13	43	18	18	—	36	43	⑧	87
	3S-GE	13	40	14	—	—	43	43	65	80
	4A-C	13	43	18	18	—	36	43	58	87
	4A-GE	13	43	16	—	—	36	44	54	87
	4A-GELC	13	44	16	—	—	36	44	54	87
	4A-LC	13	43	18	18	—	36	43	58	87
	4Y-EC	13	①	36	17	—	36	58	⑩	116
	5M-GE	12	58	13	④	—	33	75	54	159
	7M-GE	13	58	13	—	13	47	75	54	195
	22R	13	58	14	②	—	46	76	80	116
	22R-E	13	58	14	②	—	46	76	80	116
	22R-TE	13	58	14	②	—	46	76	80	116

Continued

Engine Tightening Specifications—Continued

*Torque specifications are for clean and lightly lubricated threads only. Dry or dirty threads produce increased friction which prevents accurate measurement of tightness.

Year	Engine	Spark Plugs Ft. Lbs.	Cylinder Head Bolts Ft. Lbs.	Intake Manifold Ft. Lbs.	Rocker Arm Shaft Bracket Ft. Lbs.	Rocker Arm Cover Ft. Lbs.	Connecting Rod Cap Bolts Ft. Lbs.	Main Bearing Cap Bolts Ft. Lbs.	Flywheel To Crankshaft Ft. Lbs.	Vibration Damper Or Pulley Ft. Lbs.
1987	3A-C	13	43	18	18	—	36	43	⑧	87
	3E	13	⑨	14	—	—	29	42	65	112
	4A-C	13	43	18	18	—	36	43	58	87
	4A-GEC	13	43	16	—	—	36	44	54	105
	4A-GELC	13	44	16	—	—	36	44	54	105
	4A-LC	13	43	18	18	—	36	43	58	87
	4Y-EC	13	①	36	17	—	36	58	⑩	116
	5M-GE	12	58	13	④	—	33	75	54	195
	7M-GE	13	58	13	—	13	47	75	54	195
	7M-GTE	13	58	13	—	13	47	75	54	195
	22R	13	58	14	②	—	51	76	80	116
	22R-E	13	58	14	②	—	51	76	80	116
	22R-TE	13	58	14	②	—	51	76	80	116

①—14 mm bolt head, 65 ft. lbs.; 12 mm bolt head, 14 ft. lbs.
②—Rocker arm shaft bracket retained by cylinder head bolts.
③—Glow plug. Torque to 8–11 ft. lbs.
④—Camshaft housing to cylinder head, 15–17 ft. lbs.
⑤—Camshaft housing to cylinder head 9–13 ft. lbs.
⑥—Glow plug. Torque to 9 ft. lbs.
⑦—Camshaft bearing cap to cylinder head 13 ft. lbs.
⑧—Engines w/auto. trans., 47 ft. lbs.; engines w/man. trans., 58 ft. lbs.
⑨—Torque bolts in sequence to 22 ft. lbs., then repeat, tightening to 36 ft. lbs. Tighten all bolts in sequence an additional 90°.
⑩—Engines w/auto. trans., 54 ft. lbs.; engines w/man. trans., 61 ft. lbs.

Brake Specifications

Year	Model	Brake Drum Inside Diameter	Wheel Cylinder Bore Diameter		Master Cylinder Bore Diameter	Disc Brake Rotor Specifications		
			Disc Brake	Drum Brake		Nominal Thickness	Minimum Thickness	Lateral Runout (T.I.R.)
1983	Camry	7.874	—	—	⑥	.866	.827	.006
1984–86	Camry	7.874	—	—	⑦	.866	.827	.006
1987	Camry	9.000	—	—	—	.866	.827	.006
1983–84	Celica	9.000	—	—	⑥	.79	.75	.006
1985	Celica	9.000⑬	—	—	⑥	①	②	.006
1986	Celica	7.874㉕	—	—	⑤	.866㉑	.827㉒	.006
1987	Celica	7.874㉕	—	—	—	.866㉑	.827㉒	.006
1983	Corolla	9.000	—	—	⑥	—	.453	.006
1984	Corolla⑱	7.874	—	—	⑤	—	.531	.006
1985–86	Corolla⑱	7.874	—	—	⑤	.531	.492	.006
1987	Corolla⑱㉓	7.874	—	—	—	.531㉑	.492㉒	.006
1987	Corolla⑱㉔	7.874	—	—	—	.709㉑	.669㉒	.006
1984–86	Corolla⑲	9.000	—	—	⑤	.709㉑	.669㉒	.006
1987	Corolla⑲	9.000	—	—	—	.709㉑	.669㉒	.006
1983–84	Cressida	9.000⑬	—	—	⑥	.87⑭	.83⑮	.006
1985–86	Cressida	9.000⑬	—	—	⑤	.87⑭	.83⑮	.006
1987	Cressida	9.000⑬	—	—	—	.87⑭	.83⑮	.006
1985–86	MR2	—	—	—	⑤	③	④	.006
1987	MR2	—	—	—	—	㉖	㉗	.006
1983	Pickup	10.000	—	—	⑥	⑰	⑫	.006
1984	Pickup⑳	10.000	—	—	⑥	.866	.827	.006

Continued

Brake Specifications—Continued

Year	Model	Brake Drum Inside Diameter	Wheel Cylinder Bore Diameter: Disc Brake	Wheel Cylinder Bore Diameter: Drum Brake	Master Cylinder Bore Diameter	Disc Brake Rotor Specifications: Nominal Thickness	Disc Brake Rotor Specifications: Minimum Thickness	Disc Brake Rotor Specifications: Lateral Runout (T.I.R.)
1984–85	Pickup & 4Runner ⑧	10.000	—	—	⑥	.492	.453	.006
1985	Pickup ⑳	10.000	—	—	⑥	⑨	⑩	.006
1986	Pickup & 4Runner ⑧	10.000	—	—	⑤	.492	.453	.006
1986	Pickup ⑳	10.000	—	—	⑤	⑨	⑩	.006
1987	Pickup & 4Runner ⑧	10.000	—	—	—	.492	.453	.006
1987	Pickup ⑳	10.000	—	—	—	⑨	⑩	.006
1983–86	Tercel	⑯	—	—	⑥	.433	.394	.006
1987	Tercel	7.874	—	—	—	.433	.394	.006
1983–Early 1986	Supra	⑪	—	—	⑥	①	②	.006
Late 1986–87	Supra	㉘	—	—	—	㉙	㉚	.006
1983–84	Starlet	7.870	—	—	⑥	.394	.354	.006
1984–86	Van	10.000	—	—	⑥	.787	.748	.006
1987	Van ⑳	10.000	—	—	—	.787	.748	.006
1987	Van ⑧	10.000	—	—	—	.984	.945	.006

①—Front, .79 inch; rear, .71 inch.
②—Front, .75 inch; rear, .67 inch.
③—Front, .709; rear, .394.
④—Front, .669; rear, .354.
⑤—Clearance between booster pushrod & piston, .004–.020 inch.
⑥—Clearance between booster pushrod & piston at idle vacuum, .004–.020 inch; clearance between booster pushrod & piston with no vacuum, .024–.026 inch.
⑦—Clearance between booster pushrod & piston at idle vacuum, .010–.020 inch; clearance between booster pushrod & piston with no vacuum, .024–.026 inch.
⑧—4 wheel drive models.
⑨—PD60 disc, .984; FS-17 disc, .866.
⑩—PD60 disc, .945; FS-17 disc, .827.
⑪—Parking brake drum inside diameter, 6.57 inch.
⑫—Cab & chassis models, .748 inch; exc. cab. & chassis models, .453 inch.
⑬—If equipped with rear disc brakes, parking brake drum inside diameter, 6.57 inch.
⑭—If equipped with rear disc brake rotor, .71 inch.
⑮—If equipped with rear disc brake, rear disc brake rotor, .67 inch.
⑯—Exc. 4 wheel drive models, 7.087 inch; 4 wheel drive models, 7.874 inch.
⑰—Cab & chassis models, .787 inch; exc. cab & chassis models, .492 inch.
⑱—Front wheel drive.
⑲—Rear wheel drive.
⑳—Exc. 4 wheel drive models.
㉑—If equipped w/rear disc brake, rear disc brake rotor, .394 inch.
㉒—If equipped w/rear disc brake, rear disc brake rotor, .354 inch.
㉓—Exc. FX16 models.
㉔—FX16 models.
㉕—If equipped w/rear disc brakes, parking brake drum inner diameter, 6.69 inch.
㉖—Front, .866 inch; rear, .394 inch.
㉗—Front, .827 inch; rear, .354 inch.
㉘—Parking brake drum inside diameter, 7.48 inch.
㉙—Front, .866 inch; rear, .709 inch.
㉚—Front, .827 inch; rear, .669 inch.

Front Wheel Alignment Specifications

***The specifications listed below are for unloaded vehicles**

Year	Model	Caster Angle, Degrees: Limits	Caster Angle, Degrees: Desired	Camber Angle, Degrees: Limits	Camber Angle, Degrees: Desired	Toe-In Inch	Toe-Out on Turns, Deg.: Outer Wheel	Toe-Out on Turns, Deg.: Inner Wheel
1983–84	Camry ⑳	+2 to +3	+2 1/2	+1/12 to +1 1/12	+7/12	.08	28–32	36–40
	Camry ㉑	+1/2 to +1 1/2	+1	+1/12 to +1 1/12	+7/12	0	28–32	36–40
1985–86	Camry ⑳	+1/4 to +1 3/4	+1	−1/6 to +1 1/6	+7/12	.08	28–32	36–40
	Camry ㉑	+1/4 to +1 3/4	+1	−1/6 to +1 1/6	+7/12	.08	28–32	36–40
1987	Camry ④	-1/12 to +1 1/4	+7/12	+11/12 to +2 5/12	+1 2/3	.06	30 3/4	37 1/2
	Camry ⑥	−1 3/4 to +1 3/4	+1/2	+1/4 to +1 3/4	+1	.06	30 3/4	37 1/2
1983–84	Celica	+2 5/6 to +3 5/6	+3 1/3	+5/12 to +1 5/12	+11/12	①	32	33–37
1985	Celica	+2 5/6 to +3 5/6	+3 1/3	+5/12 to +1 5/12	+11/12	①	27–31	36–38
1986–87	Celica	−11/12 to +7/12	−1/6	+5/12 to +1 11/12	+1 1/6	0	30	34
1983	Corolla ④	+1 1/4 to +2 1/4	+1 3/4	+7/12 to +1 7/12	+1 1/12	.04	33 1/2	37 1/12 to 39 1/12
	Corolla ⑤	+1 1/12 to +2 1/12	+1 7/12	+7/12 to +1 7/12	+1 1/12	.04	33 1/2	37 1/12 to +39 1/12

Continued

Front Wheel Alignment Specifications—Continued

*The specifications listed below are for unloaded vehicles

Year	Model	Caster Angle, Degrees		Camber Angle, Degrees		Toe-In Inch	Toe-Out on Turns, Deg.	
		Limits	Desired	Limits	Desired		Outer Wheel	Inner Wheel
1984	Corolla (22)	+5/12 to +1 5/12	+11/12	−1 to 0	−1/2	0	(24)	(25)
	Corolla (23) (21)	+2 1/4 to +3 1/4	+2 3/4	−1/4 to +3/4	+1/4	.04	33 1/2	36 1/2 to 40 1/2
	Corolla (23) (20)	+3 1/6 to +4 1/6	+3 2/3	−1/4 to +3/4	+1/4	.04	33	36 1/2–40 1/2
1985–86	Corolla (22) (20) (5)	+5/12 to +1 5/12	+11/12	−1–0	−1/2	0	32	38–40
	Corolla (22) (21) (5)	+5/12 to +1 5/12	+11/12	−1–0	−1/2	0	31 1/2	38 1/2 to 40 1/2
	Corolla (22) (20) (9)	+1/6 to +1 3/4	+11/12	−1 1/4 to +1/4	−1/2	0	32 1/2	38–40
	Corolla (22) (21) (9)	+1/6 to +1 3/4	+11/12	−1 1/4 to +1/4	−1/2	0	33	39–41
	Corolla (22) (20)	+3 1/6 to +4 1/6	+3 2/3	−1/4 to +1 1/4	+1/4	.04	33	36 1/2–40 1/2
	Corolla (23) (21)	+2 1/4 to +3 1/4	+2 3/4	−1/4 to +1 1/4	+1/4	.04	33 1/2	36 1/2–40 1/2
1987	Corolla (20) (22)	+1/6 to +1 2/3	+11/12	39 3/4 to +1/4	−1/4	.04		32 1/2
	Corolla (21) (22)	+1/6 to +1 2/3	+11/12	40 3/4 to +1/4	−1/4	.04		33
	Corolla (21) (23)	+2 1/4 to +3 1/4	+2 3/4	−1/2 to +1	+1/4	.04	33 1/2	38 1/2
	Corolla (20) (23)	+2 1/4 to +3 1/4	+2 3/4	−1/2 to +1	+1/4	.04	33	38 1/2
1983–84	Cressida (4)	+2 to +3	+2 1/2	+1/4 to +1 1/4	+3/4	.12	28–32	36–38
	Cressida (6)	+1 2/3 to +2 2/3	+2 1/6	+1/3 to +1 1/3	+5/6	.12	28–32	36–38
1985–87	Cressida (4)	+4 1/3 to +5 1/3	+4 5/6	−1/12 to +1 1/12	+5/12	.08	33	38
	Cressida (6)	+3 3/4 to +4 3/4	+4 1/4	−1/12 to +1 1/12	+5/12	.08	33	38
1985–86	MR2	+4 3/4 to +5 3/4	+5 1/4	−1/4 to +3/4	+1/4	.04	32	35 1/2 to 37 1/2
1987	MR2	+4 7/12 to +5 7/12	+5 1/12	−1/4 to +3/4	+1/4	.04	32	35 1/2 to 37 1/2
1983	Pickup 2WD	(2)	(8)	+7/12 to +1 7/12	+1 1/12	(11)	29	36
1983	Pickup 4WD	+2 3/4 to +4 1/4	+3 1/2	+1/4 to +1 3/4	+1	(12)	29	30 1/2
1984	Pickup 2WD (26)	+1/6 to +1 1/6	+2/3	0–+1	+1/2	(28)	30	32-35
1984	Pickup 2WD (27)	+2/3 to +1 2/3	+1/6	0–+1	+1/2	(29)	30	32-35
	Pickup 4WD	+1 1/4–+3 1/4	+2 1/4	+3/4 to +1 3/4	+1	(10)	29	28 1/2–31 1/2
1985–87	Pickup 2WD (30)	−1/12 to +1 5/12	+2/3	0 to +1	+1/2	(10)	30	32–35
	Pickup 2WD (31)	+2/3 to +1 2/3	+1 1/6	0 to +1	+1/2	(34)	30	32–35
	Pickup 2WD (7)	+1/4 to +1 3/4	+1	0 to +1	+1/2	.16	30	32–35
	Pickup 2WD (32)	1/12 to +1 1/12	+7/12	0 to +1	+1/2	.16	30	32–35
	Pickup 2WD (33)	−7/12 to +7/12	+1/12	0 to +1	+1/2	.16	30	3—2-35
1985	Pickup 4WD (35)	+1 1/4 to 3 1/4	+2 1/4	+1/4 to 1 3/4	+1	(10)	29	28 1/2 to 31 1/2
	Pickup 4WD (36)	+1 to +3	+2	+1/4 to 1 3/4	+1	(10)	29	28 1/2 to 31 1/2
1986–87	Pickup 4WD (30)	+3/4 to +1 3/4	+1 1/4	+1/6 to +1 1/6	+2/3	.12	31	30 to 33
	Pickup 4WD (31)	+1 to +2	+1 1/2	+1/6 to +1 1/6	+2/3	.12	31	30 to 33
1986–87	4Runner	+1 1/3 to +2 5/6	+2 1/12	+1/6 to +1 1/6	+2/3	.12	31	30 to 33
1983–84	Starlet	+1 1/6 to +2 2/3	+1 11/12	−1/12 to +1 5/12	+2/3	.08	33 5/6	36 1/3–38 1/3
1983–Early 1986	Supra	+3 2/3 to +4 2/3	+4 1/6	+1/3 to +1 1/3	+5/6	.12	30 3/4	35 7/12–39 7/12
Late 1986–87	Supra	+6 3/4 to +8 1/4	+7 1/2	−7/12 to +8/12	+1/12	0	31 3/4	32 1/2 to 36
1983–84	Tercel 2WD	(14)	(15)	−5/6 to +5/6	+1/3	0	(16)	(17)
	Tercel 4WD	+1 3/4 to +2 3/4	+2 1/4	+1/3 to +1 1/3	+5/6	0	(18)	(19)
1985–86	Tercel 2WD (4)	(14)	(15)	+1/3 to +2/3	+1/6	−.04	(16)	(17)
	Tercel 2WD (6)	(37)	(38)	−5/12 to +7/12	+1/12	−.04	(39)	(40)
	Tercel 4WD	+1 11/12 to +2 11/12	+2 5/12	+1/6 to +1 1/6	+2/3	−.04	(13)	(3)
1987	Tercel (4) (20)	−3/4 to +3/4	0	+1 3/4 to +3 1/4	+2 1/2	0	32 2/3	37 2/3
	Tercel (4) (21)	−3/4 to +3/4	0	+1/4 to +1 3/4	+1	−.04	32 5/6	37 1/2
	Tercel (6) (20) (22)	+1 3/4 to +2 3/4	+2 1/4	−1/2 to +1/2	0	−.04	32 5/6	35 46/60
	Tercel (6) (21) (22)	+1-4 to +1 1/4	+3/4	−1/2 to +1/2	0	−.04	32 58/60	36 13/60
	Tercel (6) (20) (41)	+1 11/12 to +2 5/12	+2 5/12	+1/12 to +1 1/12	+7/12	−.04	33 2/3	36 2/3
	Tercel (6) (21) (41)	+1 3/4 to +2 3/4	+2 1/4	+1/12 to +1 1/12	+7/12	−.04	33 1/4	36 1/2

Continued

Front Wheel Alignment Specifications—Continued

*The specifications listed below are for unloaded vehicles

Year	Model	Caster Angle, Degrees Limits	Caster Angle, Degrees Desired	Camber Angle, Degrees Limits	Camber Angle, Degrees Desired	Toe-In Inch	Toe-Out on Turns, Deg. Outer Wheel	Toe-Out on Turns, Deg. Inner Wheel
1984	Van	+1 5/12 to +2 7/12	+2 1/12	0 to +1	+1/2	.04	34	34 2/3
1985-86	Van	+2 1/6 to +3 1/6	+2 2/3	0 to +1	+1/2	0	34	34 2/3
1987	Van ㉓	+2 to +3	+2 1/2	−7/12 to +5/12	−1/12	0	33	35 to 38
	Van ㊶ ㊷	+2 1/6 to +3 1/3	+2 5/6	−7/12 to +11/12	+1/6	0	33	35 to 38
	Van ㊶ ㊸	+1 2/3 to +2 2/3	+2 1/6	−7/12 to +11/12	+1/6	0	33	35 to 38

① —With power steering, .20; less power steering, .16.
② —1/2 ton models, +1/2° to +1 1/2°, 3/4 ton & cab & chassis models, 0 to +1°.
③ —With power steering, 35 1/3 to 37 1/3; less power steering, 35 1/2 to 37 1/2.
④ —Except station wagon.
⑤ —Diesel engine.
⑥ —Station wagon.
⑦ —1/2 ton extra long bed.
⑧ —1/2 ton models, +1°, 3/4 ton & cab & chassis models, +1/2°.
⑨ —Gasoline engine.
⑩ —Bias tires, .16; radial tires, .04.
⑪ —Radial tire, .08; bias tire, .20.
⑫ —Radial tire, .04; bias tire, .16.
⑬ —With power steering, 32 1/3 to 34 1/3; less power steering, 32 1/4 to 34 1/4.
⑭ —With power steering, +2 1/6° to +3 1/6°; less power steering, +2/3° to 1 2/3°.
⑮ —With power steering, +2 2/3°; less power steering, +1 1/6°.
⑯ —With power steering, 31 11/12° to 33 11/12°; less power steering, 31 2/3° to 33 2/3°.
⑰ —With power steering, 34 5/6° to 36 5/6°; less power steering, 35 1/3° to 37 1/3°.
⑱ —With power steering, 32 1/3° to 34 1/3°; less power steering, 32 1/4° to 34 1/4°.
⑲ —With power steering, 35 1/3° to 37 1/3°; less power steering, 35 1/2° to 37 1/2°.
⑳ —With power steering.
㉑ —Less power steering.
㉒ —Front wheel drive models.
㉓ —Rear wheel drive models.
㉔ —Gasoline models less power steering 33, with power steering 32 1/2; Diesel models less power steering 31 1/2, with power steering 32.
㉕ —Gasoline models less power steering 39-41, with power steering 38-40; Diesel models less power steering 39 1/2, with power steering 39.
㉖ —1/2 ton short bed & 3/4 ton models.
㉗ —1/2 ton long bed, Cab & Chassis models.
㉘ —1/2 ton short bed models with bias tires, .16; with radial tires, .04; 3/4 ton models with radial tires, .12.
㉙ —1/2 ton long bed models with bias tires, .24; Cab & Chassis models with radial tires, .12.
㉚ —1/2 ton short bed.
㉛ —1/2 ton long bed.
㉜ —1 ton.
㉝ —Cab & Chassis.
㉞ —With bias tires, .24 inch; with radial tires, .12 inch.
㉟ —Truck.
㊱ —4Runner.
㊲ —With power steering, +1 3/4 to +2 3/4; less power steering, +1/4 to +1 1/4.
㊳ —With power steering, +2 1/4; less power steering, +3/4.
㊴ —With power steering, +31 5/6 to 33 5/6; less power steering, 31 29/30 to 33 29/30.
㊵ —With power steering, 34 47/64 to 36 47/64; less power steering, 35 13/64 to37 16/64.
㊶ —Four wheel drive models.
㊷ —YR31LG models.
㊸ —YR32LV models.

Rear Wheel Alignment Specifications

*The specifications listed below are for unloaded vehicles

Year	Model	Camber Angle, Degrees Limits	Camber Angle, Degrees Desired	Toe-In Inch
1983-84	Camry	0 to +1	+1/2	0±.08
1985	Camry	0 to +1	+1/2	.16±.08
1986	Camry	−3/4 to +1 1/4	+1/2	.16±.04
1987	Camry	−1/6 to +1 1/3	+7/12	.16±.04
1983	Celica ①	+5 1/4 to +6 3/4	+6	0±.08
1984-85	Celica ①	−9 1/2 to −10 1/2	−10	0±.08
1986-87	Celica	0 to −1 1/2	−3/4	.20±.04
1984-85	Corolla ②	−1/60 to −1 1/60	−31-60	.150±.08
1986-87	Corolla ②	−1/60 to −1 1/60	−31-60	.150±.04
1983	Cressida ①	0 to +1	+1/2	.063±.08
1984	Cressida ①	−1/6 to +5/6	+1/3	−.08±.08
1985	Cressida	−11/12 to +1/12	−5/12	.12±.08
1986-87	Cressida ①	−11/12 to +1/12	−5/12	.12±.04
1985-86	MR2	−1/4 to −1 1/4	−3/4	.20±.04

Continued

Rear Wheel Alignment Specifications—Continued

*The specifications listed below are for unloaded vehicles

Year	Model	Camber Angle, Degrees		Toe-In Inch
		Limits	Desired	
1987	MR2	−5/12 to −1 5/12	−11/12	.20±.04
1983	Supra	0 to +1	+1/2	0±.08
1984—85	Supra	−2/3 to +1/3	−1/3	0±.08
Early 1986	Supra	−2/3 to +1/3	−1/3	0±.04
Late 1986—87	Supra	−1 to +1/2	−1/4	.12±.04
1983	Tercel②	−7/12 to +5/12	−1/12	0±.08
1984	Tercel②③	−7/12 to +5/12	−1/12	0±.08
	Tercel②④	−2/3 to +1/3	−1/6	0±.08
1985-86	Tercel②③	−7/12 to +5/12	−1/12	0±.04
	Tercel②④	−2/3 to +1/3	−1/6	0±.04
1987	Tercel②③	–	–	–
	Tercel②④	−3/4 to +1/4	−1/4	0±.04

①—With independent rear suspension only.
②—Front wheel drive models only.
③—Sedan models.
④—Wagon models.

Drive Axle Specifications

Year	Model	Ring Gear & Pinion		Pinion Bearing Preload			Differential Bearing Preload		
		Backlash Method	Adjustment	Method	New Bearing In. /Lbs.	Used Bearing In./Lbs.	Method	New Bearing In./Lbs.	Used Bearing In./Lbs.
1983-87	Camry	Shim	.002-.008①	Spacer & Shims	8.7-13.9	4.3-6.9	Shim	2.5-3.5②	1.3-1.7②
1983-85	Celica③	Threaded adj.	.005-.007	Spacer & Shims	8.7-13.9	4.3-6.9	Threaded adj.	2.6-4.3②	2.6-4.3②
	Celica⑤	Shim	.005-.007	Spacer & Shims	8.7-13.9	4.3-6.9	Shims	⑥	⑥
1986-87	Celica	Shim	.002-.008①	Spacer & Shims	8.7-13.9	4.3-6.9	Shim	2.5-3.5②	1.3-1.7②
1984-87	Corolla⑦⑧	Shim	.002-.008①	–	–	–	Shims	6.9-13.9	4.3-8.7
1984-85	Corolla⑦⑨	Shim	.002-.008①	–	–	–	Shims	8.9-13.9	–
1985-87	Corolla⑦⑫	Shim	.002-.008①	–	–	–	Shims	6.9-12.2	3.5-6.1
1984-87	Corolla⑦⑬	Shim	.002-.008①	Spacer & Shims	8.7-13.9	4.4-6.9	Shims	2.5-4.1②	1.3-2.0②
1983-84	Corolla⑩	Threaded adj.	.005-.007	Spacer & Shim	8.7-13.9	4.3-7.0	Threaded adj.	1.7-3.5⑪	1.7-3.5⑪
1985-87	Corolla⑩	Threaded adj.	.005-.007	Spacer & Shims	8.7-13.9	4.3-6.9	Threaded adj.	⑭	⑭
1983-87	Cressida③	Threaded adj.	.005-.007	Spacer & Shims	13.8-19	6.9-9.5	Threaded adj.	3.5-5.2②	3.5-5.2②
1983-87	Cressida⑤	Shim	.005-.007	Spacer & Shims	10.4-16.5	5.2-8.7	Shims	⑥	⑥
1985-87	MR2	Shim	.002-.008①	–	–	–	Shim	6.9-12.2	3.5-6.1
1983-85	Pickup & 4Runner⑮⑱	Threaded adj.	.005-.007	Spacer & Shims	10.4-16.5	5.2-8.7	Threaded adj.	3.5-5.2②	3.5-5.2②
	Pickup & 4Runner⑯⑱	Threaded adj.	.005-.007	Spacer & Shims	16.5-22.6	7.8-11.3	Threaded adj.	3.5-5.2②	3.5-5.2②
1986-87	Pickup & 4Runner⑮⑲	Threaded adj.	.005-.007	Spacer & Shims	10.4-16.5	5.2-8.7	Threaded adj.	3.5-5.2②	3.5-5.2②
	Pickup & 4Runner⑯⑲	Threaded adj.	.005-.007	Spacer & Shims	16.5-22.6	7.8-11.3	Threaded adj.	3.5-5.2②	3.5-5.2②
	Pickup & 4Runner⑯⑳	Shim	.005-.007	Spacer & Shims	10.4-16.5	5.2-8.7	Shim	3.5-5.2②	3.5-5.2②
1983-84	Starlet	Threaded adj.	.004-.006	Spacer	5.6-10.9	3.5-6.1	Threaded adj.	3.5-5.2②	3.5-5.2②

Continued

Drive Axle Specifications—Continued

Year	Model	Ring Gear & Pinion		Pinion Bearing Preload			Differential Bearing Preload		
		Backlash Method	Adjustment	Method	New Bearing In./Lbs.	Used Bearing In./Lbs.	Method	New Bearing In./Lbs.	Used Bearing In./Lbs.
1983–Early 1986	Supra	Shim	.005–.007	Spacer & Shims	10.4–16.5 ⑤	5.2–8.7	Shims	⑥	⑥
Late 1986–87	Supra	Shim	.005–.007	Spacer & Shims	8.7–13.9	4.3–6.9	Shims	3.5–5.2 ⑪	3.5–5.2 ⑪
1983–86	Tercel ⑰	Shim	.004–.006	Spacer & Shims	4.3–8.7	2.6–4.3	Shims	2.6–4.3 ②	2.6–4.3 ②
1983–87	Tercel ④	Threaded adj.	.004–.006	Spacer & Shims	5.6–10.9	3.5–6.1	Threaded adj.	1.7–3.5 ②	1.7–3.5 ②
1987	Tercel ⑳ ㉑	Shim	.004–.006	Spacer & Shims	4.3–8.7	2.6–4.3	Shims	2.6–4.3 ②	2.6–4.3 ②
	Tercel ㉒ ㉓	Shim	.002–.008 ①	Spacer & Shims	8.7–13.9	4.3–6.9	Shim	2.5–3.5 ⑪	1.3–1.7 ⑪
	Tercel ㉒ ㉔	Shim	.002–.008 ①	–	–	–	Shim	6.9–13.9	4.3–8.7
1984–86	Van	Threaded adj.	.005–.007	Spacer & Shims	13.9–19.1	6.9–9.5	Threaded adj.	3.5–5.2 ②	3.5–5.2 ②
1987	Van ⑲	Threaded adj.	.005–.007	Spacer & Shims	10.4–16.5	5.2–8.7	Threaded adj.	3.4–5.2 ⑪	3.4–5.2 ⑪
	Van ⑳	Shim	.005–.007	Spacer & Shims	8.7–13.9	4.3–6.9	Shims	2.6–4.3 ⑪	2.6–4.3 ⑪

①—Side gear backlash.
②—Total preload, add this to drive pinion preload.
③—Exc. models with independent rear suspension.
④—Rear axle, 1983–87 4 wheel drive models.
⑤—Models with independent rear suspension.
⑥—Differential bearing preload; for new and reused bearings should be 3.5–5.2 inches in addition to pinion bearing preload.
⑦—Front wheel drive models.
⑧—C51 & C52 manual transaxles.
⑨—S41 & 50 manual transaxles.
⑩—Rear wheel drive models.
⑪—In addition to drive pinion preload.
⑫—A240E & A240L automatic transaxles.
⑬—A130L & A131L automatic transaxles.
⑭—6.7 inch ring gear, 2.6–4.3 inches; 6.38 inch ring gear, 1.7–3.5 inches in addition to pinion bearing preload.
⑮—7.5 inch ring gear.
⑯—8 inch ring gear.
⑰—Except rear axle, 1983–86 4 wheel drive models.
⑱—Front & rear axle.
⑲—Rear axle.
⑳—Front axle.
㉑—Wagon models.
㉒—Sedan models.
㉓—Auto. trans. models.
㉔—Man. trans. models.

Cooling System & Capacity Data

Year	Model	Cooling Capacity Qts.		Radiator Cap Relief Pressure, Lbs.	Thermo. Opening Temp.	Fuel Tank Gals.	Engine Oil Refill Qts.	Transmission/Transaxle Oil			Axle Oil Pints
		Less A/C	With A/C					4 Speed Pints	5 Speed Pints	Auto. Trans. Qts.	
1983–85	Camry (23)	7.4	7.4	12.8	180	–	4.2 (19)	–	5.4	6.3	4.1 (17)
1984–85	Camry (24)	7.9	7.9	12.8	180	–	4.5 (19)	–	5.4	–	–
1986	Camry (23)	7.4	7.4	12.8	180	14.5	4.2 (19)	–	5.4	6.3	3.4 (17)
	Camry (24)	8.9	8.9	12.8	180	14.5	4.2 (19)	–	5.4	–	–
1987	Camry	6.8	6.8	12.8	180	15.9	4.3 (19)	–	5.4	5.9	3.4 (17)
1983	Celica	8.5	8.5	12.8	190	16.1	5.1 (8)	–	5.0	6.7	(4)
1984–85	Celica	8.9	8.9	12.8	190	16.1	4.9	–	5	6.7	(4)
1986	Celica (40)	7.4	7.4	12.8	180	15.9	4.2 (19)	–	5.4	6.3	3.4 (17)
	Celica (41)	7.4	7.4	12.8	180	15.9	4.1 (19)	–	5.4	6.3	3.4 (17)
1987	Celica (7)	6.8	6.84	12.8	180	15.9	4.3 (19)	–	5.4	6.3	3.4 (17)
	Celica (9)	7.4	7.4	12.8	180	15.9	4.1 (19)	–	5.4	6.3	3.4 (17)
1983	Corolla	(18)	(18)	12.8	180	(6)	3.5 (19)	3.6	3.6	(20)	2.2
1984–85	Corolla (23) (28)	(30)	(30)	12.8	180	–	3.5 (19)	–	3.6	6.0	2.2
1986–87	Corolla (1) (28)	(30)	(30)	12.8	180	13.2	3.5 (19)	–	3.6	6.0	(15)
	Corolla (2) (28)	(30)	(30)	12.8	180	13.2	3.9 (19)	–	3.6	6.0	(15)
1984–85	Corolla (23) (29)	(31)	(31)	12.8	180	–	3.5 (19)	–	(32)	5	(33)
	Corolla (24) (29)	7.7	7.7	12.8	180	–	(34)	–	(32)	5	(33)
1986	Corolla (23) (29)	6.3	6.3	12.8	180	13.2	3.5 (19)	–	5.4	(52)	(5)
1987	Corolla (1) (29)	6.4	6.4	12.8	180	13.2	3.5 (19)	–	5.4	(52)	(5)
	Corolla (2) (29)	6.3	6.3	12.8	180	13.2	3.9 (19)	–	5.4	(52)	(5)
1983–84	Cressida	8.8	8.8	12.8	190	17.2	5.4 (19)	–	5.0	6.9	3.0 (4)
1985	Cressida (38)	9.5	9.5	12.8	190	17.2	5.4 (19)	–	5	6.9	2.6
	Cressida (39)	9.5	9.5	12.8	190	17.2	5.4 (19)	–	–	6.9	3
1986	Cressida (38)	9.2	9.2	12.8	190	18.5	5.4 (19)	–	5.0	6.9	2.6
	Cressida (39)	9.2	9.2	12.8	190	18.2	5.4 (19)	–	5.0	6.9	3.0
1987	Cressida (38)	(53)	(53)	12.8	190	18.5	5.4 (19)	–	5.0	7.3	2.6
	Cressida (39)	(53)	(53)	12.8	190	18.2	5.4 (19)	–	5.0	7.3	3.0
1985	MR2	–	–	12.8	180	15.2	3.5 (19)	–	4.8	–	–
1986	MR2	(16)	(16)	12.8	180	10.8	3.6 (19)	–	5.4	5.9	(5)
1987	MR2	(54)	(54)	12.8	180	10.8	3.6 (19)	–	5.4	5.9	(5)
1983–84	Pickup (21) (23)	8.9	8.9	12.8	190	(10)	5.1 (8)	4.2	5.4	(12)	(11)
1983–84	Pickup (21) (24)	11.1	11.1	12.8	190	(10)	6.1 (19)	4.2	4.6	(12)	(11)
1983–84	Pickup (22)	8.9	8.9	12.8	190	(10)	5.1 (8)	4.2 (14)	3.8 (14)	–	4.6
1985	Pickup (23) (21)	8.9	8.9	12.8	190	(3)	5.1 (19)	5	5	6.9	(11)
1985	Pickup (23) (22)	8.9	8.9	12.8	190	17.2	5.1 (19)	5	(36)	6.9	(13)
1985	Pickup (24)	10.4	10.4	12.8	190	(3)	6.1 (19)	5	(37)	6.9	(11)
1986	Pickup & 4Runner (49)	8.9	8.9	12.8	180	(43)	4.9 (19)	5	(44)	(46)	(47)
	Pickup & 4Runner (50)	8.9	8.9	12.8	180	(43)	4.9 (19)	5	(45)	7.3	(48)
1987	Pickup & 4Runner (49)	9.6	9.6	12.8	180	(43)	4.5 (19)	5	(44)	(46)	(47)
	Pickup & 4Runner (50)	(55)	(55)	12.8	180	(43)	4.5 (19)	5	(45)	7.3	(48)
1983–84	Starlet	5.5	5.5	12.8	190	10.6	3.7 (19)	–	5.2	–	2.2
1983–85	Supra	8.5	8.5	12.8	190	16.1	5.4 (19)	–	5.2	6.9	2.6
Early 1986	Supra	(42)	(42)	13	190	16.1	6. (19)	–	5.	6.9	2.6
Late 1986–87	Supra (56)	8.5	8.5	12.8	190	18.5	4.7	–	(58)	7.6	2.8
Late 1986–87	Supra (57)	(59)	(59)	12.8	190	18.5	4.2	–	(58)	7.6	2.8
1983–84	Tercel	5.6	5.6	12.8	180	(25)	3.5 (19)	–	(26)	4.8	(27)

Continued

Cooling System & Capacity Data—Continued

Year	Model	Cooling Capacity Qts.		Radiator Cap Relief Pressure, Lbs.	Thermo. Opening Temp.	Fuel Tank Gals.	Engine Oil Refill Qts.	Transmission/Transaxle Oil			Axle Oil Pints
		Less A/C	With A/C					4 Speed Pints	5 Speed Pints	Auto. Trans. Qts.	
1985	Tercel (21)	5.6	5.6	12.8	–	11.9	3.9 (19)	–	7	4.8	2
	Tercel (22)	5.6	5.6	12.8	–	13.2	3.9 (19)	–	8.2	6.9	2.2
1986	Tercel (21)	5.6	5.6	12.8	180	(60).9	3.9 (19)	(51)	(51)	4.8	2
	Tercel (22)	5.6	5.6	12.8	180	(60)	3.9 (19)	(51)	(51)	6.9	(61)
1987	Tercel (21) (39)	5.6	5.6	12.8	180	13.2.9	3.9 (19)	(51)	(51)	4.8	2
	Tercel (22) (39)	5.6	5.6	12.8	180	13.2	3.9 (19)	(51)	(51)	6.9	(61)
	Tercel (38)	(62)	(22)	12.8	180	11.9	3.4 (19)	5.0	5.0	5.9	3.0
1984–85	Van	(35)	(35)	12.8	180	15.9	3.7	–	4.6	6.9	2.6
1986	Van	(63)	(63)	12.8	180	15.9	3.7 (19)	–	4.6	6.9	2.6
1987	Van (21)	(63)	(63)	12.8	180	15.9	3.7	–	4.6	6.9	3.0
	Van (22)	(64)	(64)	12.8	180	15.9	3.7	–	5.4	6.9	(65)

(1)—With 4A-C engine.
(2)—With 4A-GE engine.
(3)—Short wheel base, 13.7 gal.; long wheel base, 17.2 gal.; 4Runner, 14.8 gal.
(4)—Except independent rear suspension, 2.8 pts.; independent rear suspension, 2.2 pts.
(5)—Front differential, auto trans. model A131L, 3 pts.
(6)—Exc. wagon, 13.2 gals.; wagon, 12.4 gals.
(7)—With 3S-FE engine.
(8)—Total capacity.
(9)—With 3S-GE engine.
(10)—Long bed models, 16 gals.; short bed models, 13.5 gals.
(11)—7.5 inch ring gear, 3.6 pints; 8 inch ring gear, 3.8 pints.
(12)—With overdrive, 6.9 qts.; less overdrive, 6.7 qts.
(13)—Front axle, 2.4 pints; rear axle, 2.3 pints; transfer case, 3.4 pints.
(14)—Transfer case, 3.4 pints.
(15)—With 6.38 inch ring gear, 2.2 pints; with 6.7 inch ring gear, 2.8 pints.
(16)—Man. trans., 11.3 qts.; auto. trans., 12 qts.
(17)—Front differential, auto. trans. only.
(18)—Manual trans., 5.7 qts.; automatic trans., 6.6 qts.
(19)—With filter change.
(20)—With electronic overdrive, 6.2 qts.; with conventional trans., 5.8 qts.
(21)—2 wheel drive models.
(22)—4 wheel drive models.
(23)—Gasoline engine models.
(24)—Diesel engine models.
(25)—4 wheel drive models, 13.2 gals.; 2 wheel drive models, 11.9 gals.
(26)—4 wheel drive models with 6 speed overdrive, 4.1 qts. including differential. 2 wheel drive models, 3.5 qts. including differential.
(27)—Front differential oil, 2 wheel drive auto. trans., 2.0 pts. 4 wheel drive auto. trans., 2.2 pts. Rear axle oil pts., 4 wheel drive models only, 2.2 pts.
(28)—Rear wheel drive models.
(29)—Front wheel drive models.
(30)—Auto. trans. models, 5.8 qts.; man. trans. models, 5.9 qts.
(31)—Auto. trans. models, 6.6 qts.; man. trans. models, 5.7 qts.
(32)—Differential & man. trans. models S41, 50, 5.4 pts.; differential & man. trans. models C51, 4.8 pts.
(33)—Front differential, auto. trans. model A130L, 4.2 pts.; A131L, 3 pts.
(34)—Exc. California models, 4.5 qts.; California models, 4.9 qts.
(35)—Less rear heater, 7.6 qts.; with rear heater, 8.1 qts.
(36)—22R engine, 8 pts.; 22R-E engine, 6.5 pts.
(37)—2L engine, 4.6 pts.; 2L-T engine w/4WD, 6.5 pts.; 2L-T engine w/2WD, 5 pts.
(38)—Except station wagon.
(39)—Station wagon.
(40)—With 2S-E engine.
(41)—With 3S-GE engine.
(42)—With man. trans., 7.8 qts.; with auto trans. 7.7 qts.
(43)—Short wheel base, 13.7 gals.; long wheel base models and short bed 4Runner models, 17.2 gals.; longbed models, 19.3 gals.
(44)—2WD models w/W52 W55 & W56 trans. & 22R, 22R-E engines, 5 pts.; 4WD models w/W56 trans. & 22R-E, 6.4 pts.; 4WD models w/G52 trans. & 22R engines, 8.2 pts.
(45)—2WD models, 5.4 pts.; 4WD models, 8.2 pts.
(46)—2WD models, 6.9 qts.; 4WD models, 10.9 qts.
(47)—2WD models, 3.6 pts.; 4WD models, 4.6 pts.
(48)—2WD models, 3.8 pts.; 4WD models, 5 pts.
(49)—With turbocharged engine.
(50)—Less turbocharged engine.
(51)—4 speed, 7 pts.; 5 speed, 7 pts.; 6 speed, 8.2 pts.
(52)—With A240E & A240L transaxle (including differential oil), 7.6 qts.; with A131L transaxle (less differential oil), 5.8 qts.
(53)—With auto. trans., 8.7 qts.; with man. trans., 8.6 qts.
(54)—Man. trans. less A/C, 12.9 qts.; man. trans. with A/C, 13.1 qts.; auto. trans., 13.6 qts.
(55)—Exc. 4 wheel drive auto. trans. models with 22R-E engine, 8.9 qts.; 4 wheel drive auto. trans. models with 22R-E engine, 9.6 qts.
(56)—With 7M-GE engine.
(57)—With 7M-GTE engine.
(58)—With W58 transmission, 5 pints; with R154 transmission, 6.4 pints.
(59)—With auto. trans., 8.5 qts.; with man. trans., 8.7 qts.
(60)—Sedan, 11.9 gals.; wagon, 13.2 gals.
(61)—Front differential (auto. trans. only), 2.0 pints; rear differential, 2.2 pints.
(62)—With auto. trans., 5.2 qts.; with man. trans., 5.3 qts.
(63)—Less rear heater, 8.3 qts.; with rear heater, 8.9 qts.
(64)—Less rear heater, 7.4 qts.; with rear heater, 7.9 qts.
(65)—Front differential, 2.6 pints, rear differential, 4.0 pints; transfer case, 2.6 pints.

ELECTRICAL SECTION

INDEX

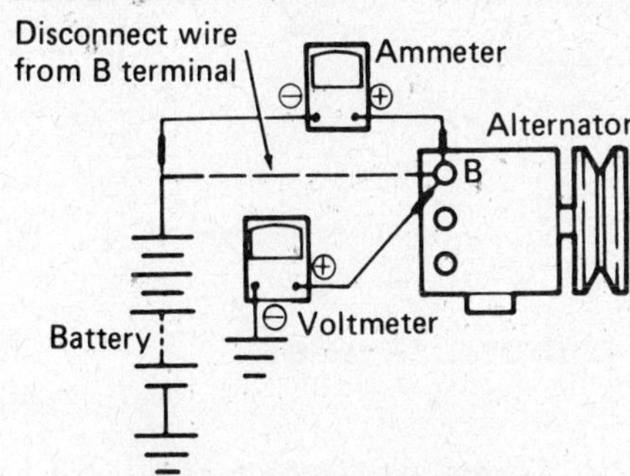

Fig. 1 Connecting voltmeter and ammeter to charging circuit

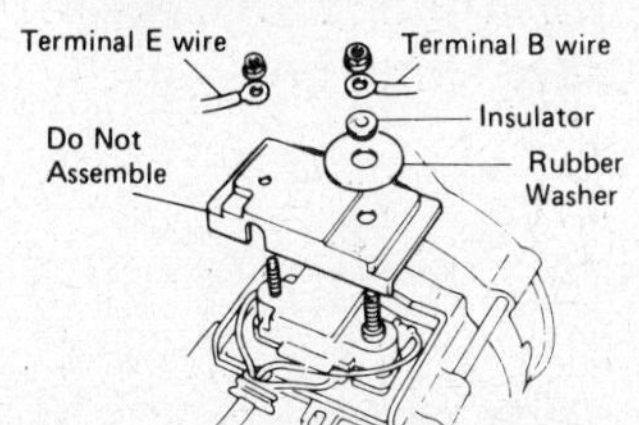

Fig. 4 Removing brush holder assembly

ALTERNATOR TESTING

The following tests should be conducted with an alternator volt-amp tester, connected in accordance with manufacturer's instructions. **If an alternator volt-amp tester is not available, connect a voltmeter and ammeter to the charging circuit as shown in Fig. 1.**

VOLTAGE & AMPERE OUTPUT

With battery in a proper state of charge, terminal voltage reading should be as indi-

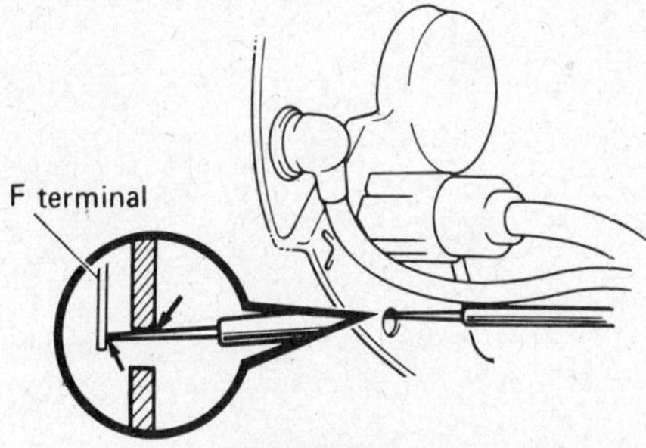

Fig. 2 Grounding terminal F (Typical). Gasoline engines

cated in Alternator & Regulator Specification chart. Ampere reading should be no more than 10 amps.

Gasoline Engines

1. If voltage reading is greater than specified in Alternator & Regulator Specification chart under Voltage Regulator Voltage, replace regulator.
2. On all except 1983 Pickup; if voltage is less than specified, ground terminal F, **Fig. 2.** If voltage remains below specification, alternator is defective. If voltage reading is greater than specified, replace regulator.
3. On 1983 Pickup, measure voltage at terminal L. If voltage reading is between one and two volts or zero, alternator is defective. If reading at terminal L indicates battery voltage, turn ignition "OFF" and connect an ohmmeter to check for continuity between terminals L and F, **Fig. 3.** If ohmmeter indicates no continuity, alternator is defective. If ohmmeter indicates continuity, replace regulator.
4. On all models, start engine and run at 2000 RPM. Turn headlights On and switch fan motor to HI, then observe ammeter. Ampere reading should be 30 amps or more. If ampere reading is

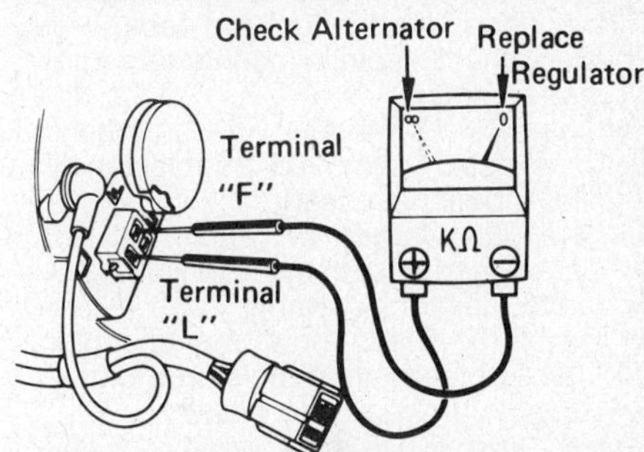

Fig. 3 Checking continuity between terminals L and F

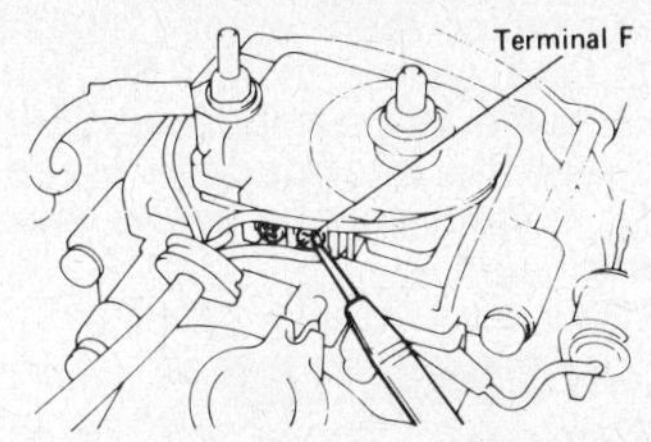

Fig. 5 Grounding terminal F. Diesel engine

less than 30 amps, alternator is defective. **If the battery is fully charged, the ampere reading may be slightly less than specified above.**

Diesel Engines

1. If voltage reading is greater than specified in "Alternator & Regulator Specification" chart under Voltage Regulator Voltage, replace regulator.
2. If voltage is less than specified, proceed as follows:
   a. Remove brush holder and connect terminal B and E wires to their original position, **Fig. 4. Before connecting terminal B, ensure that battery ground cable is disconnected.**
   b. With engine running at 2000 RPM,

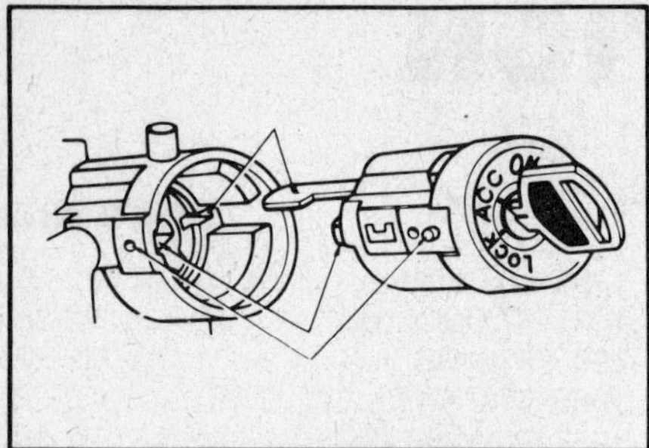

Fig. 6 Ignition lock removal

ground terminal F, **Fig. 5.** Check reading on voltmeter.

c. If voltage reading is less than specified, alternator is defective. If voltage reading is greater than specified, replace regulator.

STARTER

REPLACE

EXC. 1983–87 TERCEL & 1983–84 STARLET

1. Disconnect battery ground cable.
2. Disconnect electrical connectors from starter motor.
3. On 1985-87 models with automatic transmission, remove transmission oil filler tube if necessary.
4. On 1985 Corolla FF and 1985-86 Camry models with diesel engines, remove radiator assembly.
5. On all models, remove starter motor attaching bolts, then the starter motor.
6. Reverse procedure to install.

1983–87 TERCEL

1. Disconnect battery ground cable.
2. Disconnect electrical connectors from starter motor, then remove attaching bolts and starter motor. **On some models it may be necessary to disconnect the intermediate steering shaft to gain access to the starter motor.**
3. Reverse procedure to install.

1983–84 STARLET

1. Disconnect battery ground cable.
2. Disconnect front exhaust pipe and bracket assembly from exhaust manifold to gain access to starter motor.
3. Remove 2 mounting bolts, then raise intermediate steering shaft slightly. Disconnect intermediate shaft from steering gear, then pull shaft from mainshaft and remove from vehicle.
4. Remove two starter to clutch housing attaching bolts, then carefully lower starter and disconnect electrical connectors.
5. Reverse procedure to install.

IGNITION LOCK

REPLACE

1. Disconnect battery ground cable.
2. Turn ignition switch to "ACC" position.
3. Insert a small diameter rod into hole located on side of lock cylinder, then while holding down pin, remove lock cylinder, **Fig. 6.**
4. Reverse procedure to install. Ensure lock cylinder is in "ACC" position.

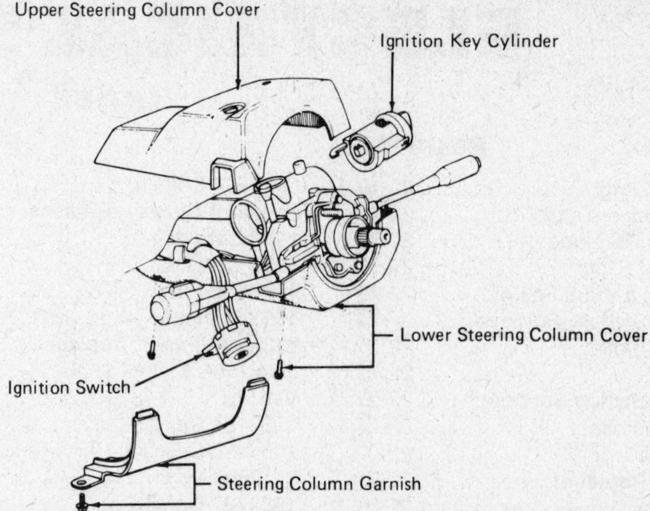

Fig. 7 Steering column & ignition switch assembly. Exc. 1983–84 Corolla & Starlet (Typical)

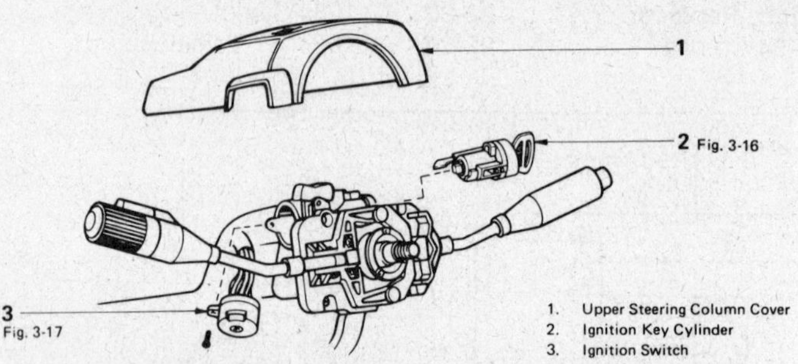

Fig. 8 Ignition switch replace. Starlet

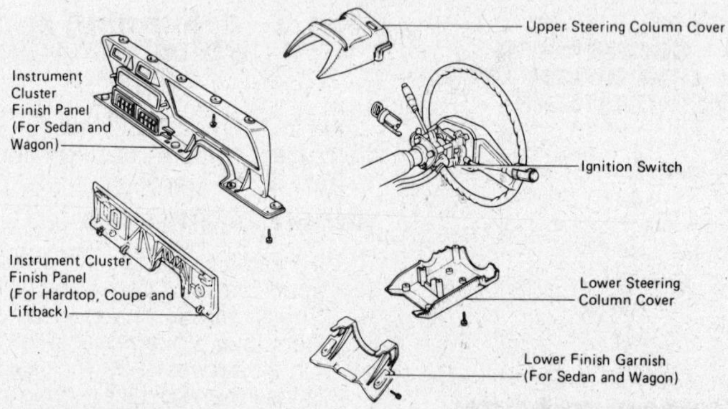

Fig. 9 Ignition switch replace. 1983–84 Corolla (Typical)

IGNITION SWITCH

REPLACE

EXC. 1983–84 COROLLA

1. Disconnect battery ground cable.
2. Remove steering wheel, if necessary, steering column garnish, if equipped, upper and lower covers, **Fig. 7.** On Starlet models, remove upper cover, **Fig. 8.**
3. Disconnect electrical connectors from ignition switch.
4. Turn ignition key to ACC position and remove ignition key cylinder.
5. Remove screw and ignition switch.
6. Reverse procedure to install.

1983–84 COROLLA

1. Disconnect battery ground cable.
2. On sedan and station wagon models, remove instrument cluster finish panel, **Fig. 9,** lower finish garnish, upper and lower steering column covers. **During removal of instrument cluster finish panel, do not bend the lower pawls.**
3. On hardtop, coupe and liftback models, remove light control rheostat knob

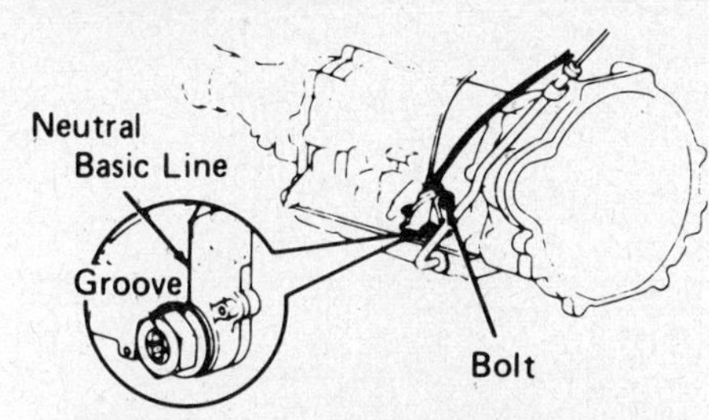

Fig. 10 Adjusting neutral safety switch. Exc. 1984 A-40 & A-41 & all 1985–86 models.

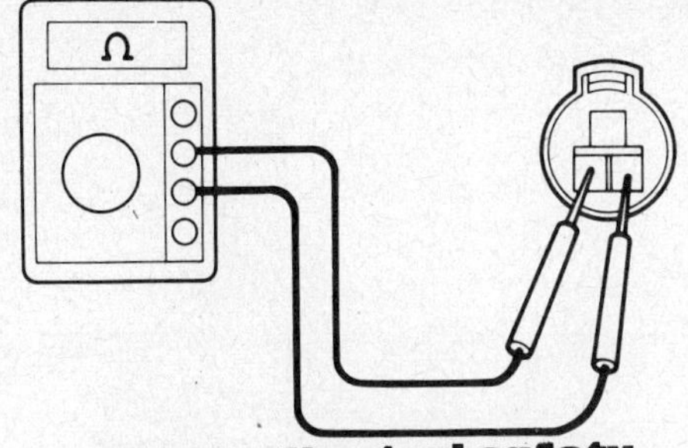

Fig. 11 Neutral safety switch ohmmeter connections. 1984 A-40 & A-41 & all 1985–86

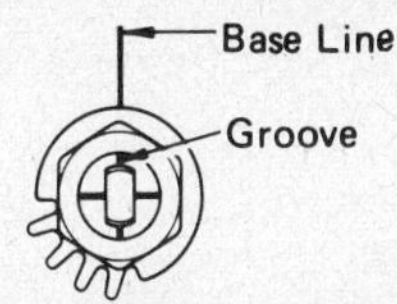

Fig. 12 Adjusting neutral safety switch. 1984 A-40 & A-41 & all 1985–86

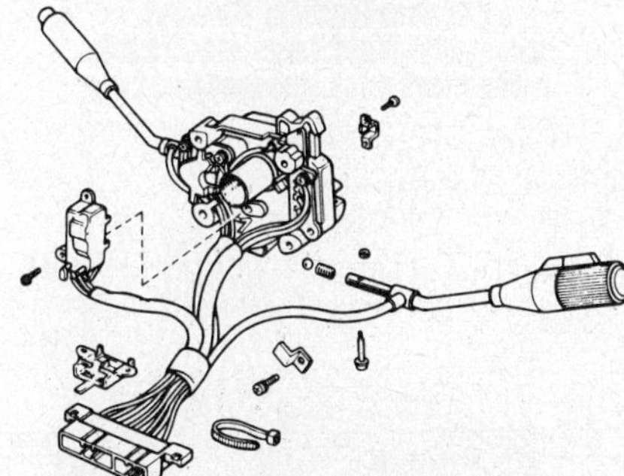

Fig. 13 Disconnecting headlight and dimmer switch from combination switch

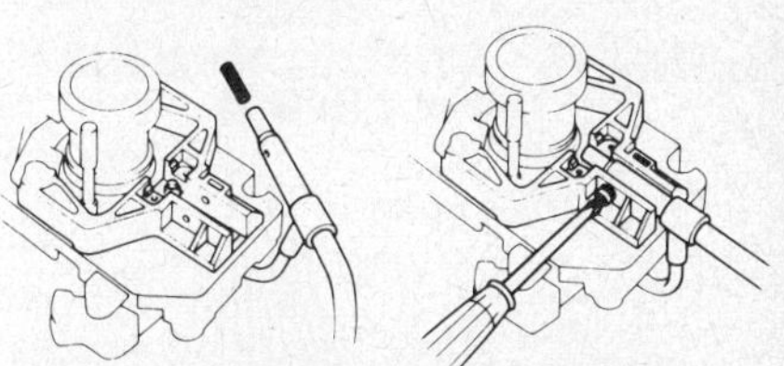

Fig. 14 Installing spring, lever and screw onto combination switch

and instrument cluster finish panel.

4. Disconnect electrical connector from ignition switch.
5. Turn ignition key to ACC position, then remove screw and ignition switch.
6. Reverse procedure to install.

STOP LIGHT SWITCH

REPLACE

1. Remove brake pedal tension spring.
2. Disconnect switch wire connector.
3. Remove switch mounting nut, then slide switch from mounting bracket.
4. Reverse procedure to install.

NEUTRAL SAFETY SWITCH

ADJUST

1. Raise and support vehicle.
2. Loosen neutral safety switch bracket bolt.
3. Position transmission shift lever into Neutral.
4. On all except 1984 A-40 and A-41 and all 1985-86 transmission models, align switch shaft groove with neutral base line, **Fig. 10.**
5. On 1984 A-40 and A-41 models and all 1985-86 automatic transmission equipped models, proceed as follows:
   a. Disconnect neutral start switch electrical connector.
   b. Connect a suitable ohmmeter between switch terminals, **Fig. 11.**
   c. Align switch shaft groove with neutral base line, **Fig. 12** and note ohmmeter reading. Ohmmeter should indicate continuity between neutral start switch connector terminals. If continuity cannot be obtained, replace switch.
   d. Connect electrical connector onto switch.

COMBINATION SWITCH REPLACE

EXC. 1983 COROLLA

1. Disconnect battery ground cable.
2. Remove horn button screws and horn button.
3. Scribe alignment marks on steering wheel and steering shaft.
4. Remove steering wheel nut.
5. Using a steering wheel puller, remove steering wheel.
6. Remove steering column upper and lower covers.
7. Remove combination switch.
8. Reverse procedure to install.

1983 COROLLA

1. Disconnect battery ground cable.
2. On sedan and station wagon models, remove the following:
   a. Instrument cluster finish panel and radio knobs.
   b. Lower finish garnish, upper and lower steering column covers.
3. On coupe and liftback models, remove the following:
   a. Instrument cluster finish panel.
   b. Indicator light electrical connector.
   c. Upper and lower steering column covers.
4. On SR-5 models, remove steering wheel pad mark. On models except SR-5, remove steering wheel pad screws from the back of the steering wheel, and pad.
5. Scribe alignment marks on steering wheel and steering wheel shaft.
6. Remove steering wheel nut and steering wheel. **Use a steering wheel puller, if necessary.**
7. Disconnect electrical connector from combination switch.
8. Remove four screws and combination switch.
9. Reverse procedure to install.

COMBINATION SWITCH SERVICE

EXC. 1983 COROLLA

Headlight & Dimmer Switch

1. Disconnect battery ground cable, then remove steering wheel and upper and lower steering column covers.
2. Disconnect combination switch connector, then using a small screwdriver, disengage headlight and dimmer switch wiring from combination switch connector. **Note position of wires.**
3. Remove screws, headlight and dimmer switch, then ball and spring assembly, **Fig. 13.**
4. Install headlight and dimmer switch onto combination switch.
5. Insert spring into headlight and dimmer lever, than install lever and screw onto combination switch, **Fig. 14.**
6. Position ball on the spring, **Fig. 15** and place headlight and dimmer switch lever into HI position. Install screws and clamp, **Fig. 15.**
7. Ensure switch operates smoothly in each position.
8. Install electrical terminals into combination switch connector in the same position as they were removed.
9. Install combination switch connector, then the steering column upper and lower covers and steering wheel.
10. Connect battery ground cable.

Hazard & Turn Signal Switch

1. Disconnect battery ground cable, then remove steering wheel and upper and lower steering column covers.
2. Disconnect hazard and turn signal switch connector, then using a small screwdriver, disengage hazard and turn signal switch wiring from combination switch connector. **Note position of wires.**
3. Remove screws, clamp, hazard and turn signal switch assembly from combination switch.
4. Reverse procedure to install.

Windshield Wiper/Washer Switch

1. Disconnect battery ground cable, then remove steering wheel and upper and lower steering column covers.

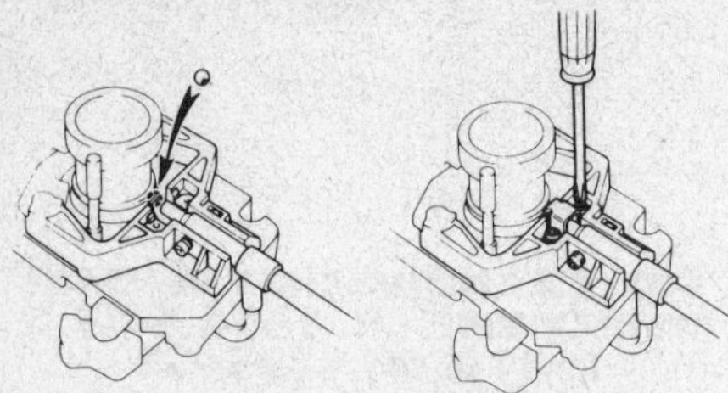

Fig. 15 Positioning ball onto spring

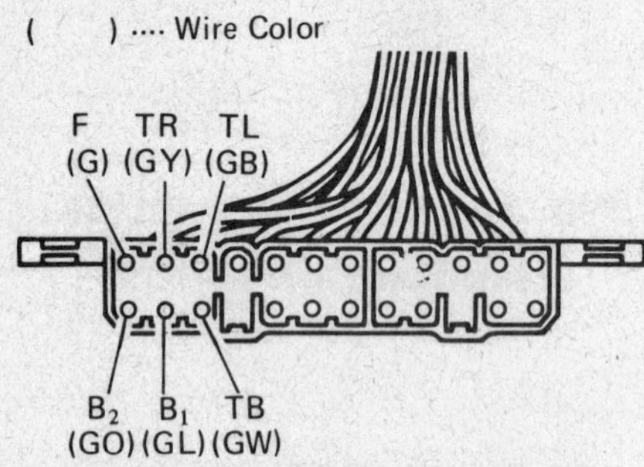

Fig. 18 Removing hazard and turn signal switch terminals from combination switch electrical connector

2. Disconnect wire terminal from horn contact (if equipped).
3. Disconnect windshield wiper/washer switch connector, then using a small screwdriver, disengage windshield wiper/washer switch wiring from combination switch connector. **Note position of wires.**
4. Remove screw, clamp and windshield wiper/washer switch assembly.
5. Reverse procedure to install.

1983 COROLLA

Headlight Switch, Replace

1. Disconnect battery ground cable.
2. Remove light control switch arm from switch body. **A steel ball will fall out when switch arm is removed. Do not lose ball.**
3. Remove terminals, **Fig. 16** from electrical connector and headlight switch from combination switch.

Headlight Dimmer Switch, Replace

1. Disconnect battery ground cable.
2. Remove screws and dimmer switch from switch body.
3. Remove terminals, **Fig. 17,** from electrical connector and headlight dimmer switch from combination switch.
4. Reverse procedure to install.

Hazard & Turn Signal Switch, Replace

1. Disconnect battery ground cable.
2. Remove screws, hazard and turn signal switch.

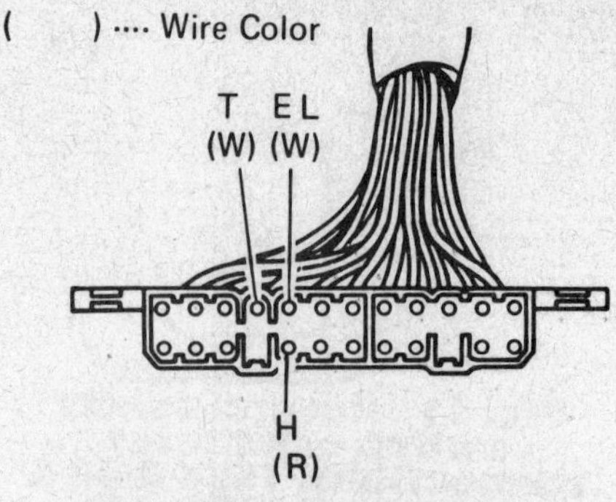

Fig. 16 Removing headlight switch terminal from combination switch electrical connector

3. Remove terminals, **Fig. 18,** from electrical connector.
4. Reverse procedure to install.

Windshield Wiper Switch, Replace

1. Disconnect battery ground cable.
2. Remove screws and wiper switch from switch body.
3. Remove terminals, **Fig. 19,** from electrical connector.
4. Reverse procedure to install.

STEERING WHEEL REPLACE

1. Remove steering wheel pad. On models with 4 spoke wheel, remove trim cover from center of steering wheel.
2. Remove nut attaching steering wheel to steering shaft.
3. Using a suitable puller, remove steering wheel.

INSTRUMENT PANEL REPLACE

1983–84 CAMRY

1. Disconnect battery ground cable.
2. Remove steering wheel.
3. Remove right and left front pillar garnish moldings, **Fig. 20.**
4. Remove nuts, then right and left cowl side trim board.
5. Remove right speaker panel.
6. Remove right speaker attaching screws, then disconnect electrical connector from right speaker. Remove right speaker.
7. Remove left speaker panel, then the speaker
8. Remove five attaching screws from lower left instrument finish panel. Disconnect electrical connectors and remove panel.
9. Disconnect hood release lever assembly from instrument panel.
10. Remove glove compartment door and door hinge.

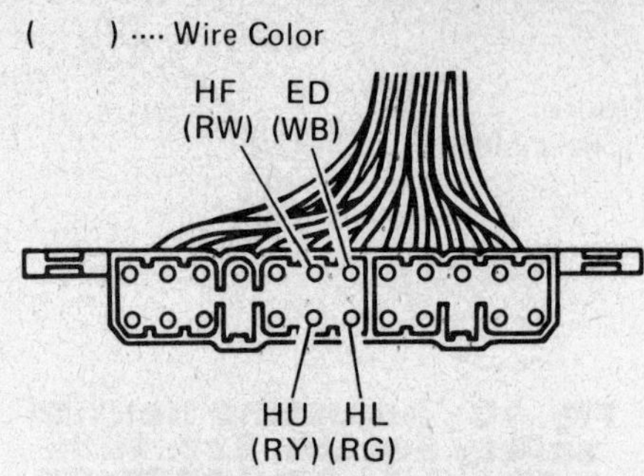

Fig. 17 Removing headlight dimmer switch terminals from combination switch electrical connector

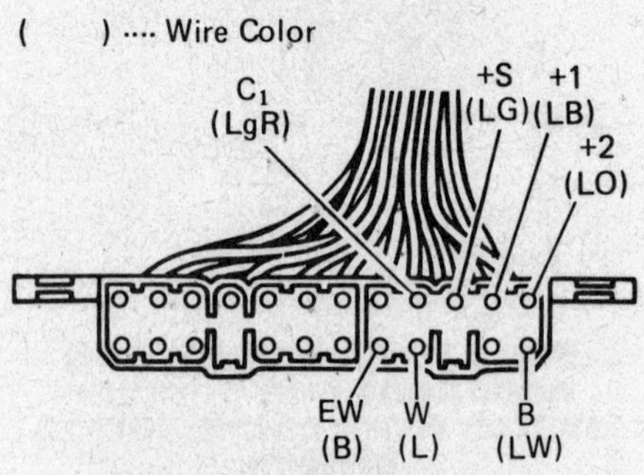

Fig. 19 Removing windshield wiper switch terminals from combination switch electrical connector

11. Remove four heater control knobs and three center cluster finish panel screws.
12. Remove center cluster finish panel.
13. Remove radio from instrument panel.
14. Remove heater control indicator lens, ashtray and ashtray retainer.
15. Remove 4 lower center finish panel attaching screws, then the panel. Disconnect electrical connector from cigar lighter.
16. Remove instrument cluster finish panel, instrument cluster and No. 2 heater duct.
17. Remove No. 1 and No. 2 defroster ducts.
18. Remove instrument panel attaching bolts, then the instrument panel.
19. Reverse procedure to install.

1984–85 CELICA & 1984–EARLY 1986 SUPRA

1. Disconnect battery ground cable.
2. Remove steering wheel and steering column cover, **Figs. 21 and 22.**
3. Remove console assembly as follows:
   a. Remove shift lever knob, if equipped.
   b. Remove ashtray.
   c. Remove heater control retainer assembly.
   d. Remove upper console panel attaching screws, then the upper console panel.
   e. Remove console assembly attach-

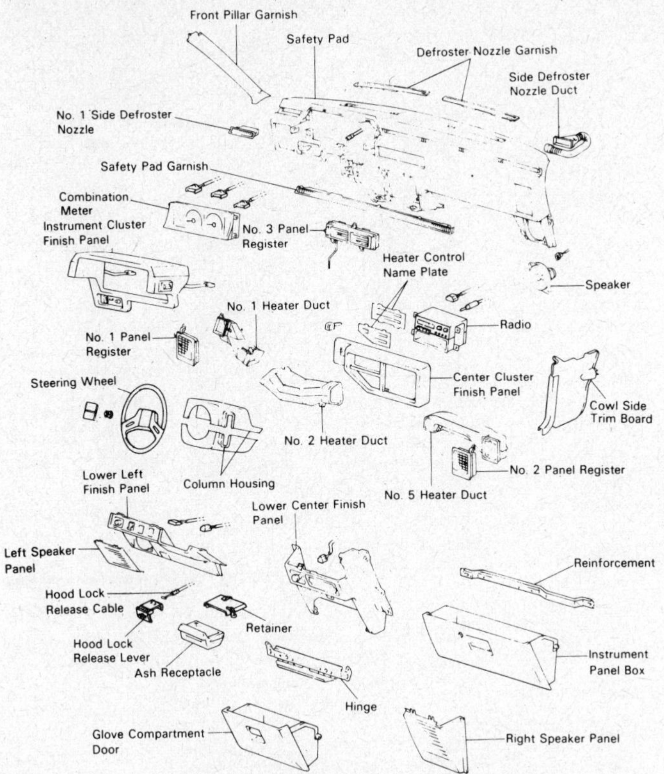

Fig. 20 Instrument panel & components. 1983–84 Camry

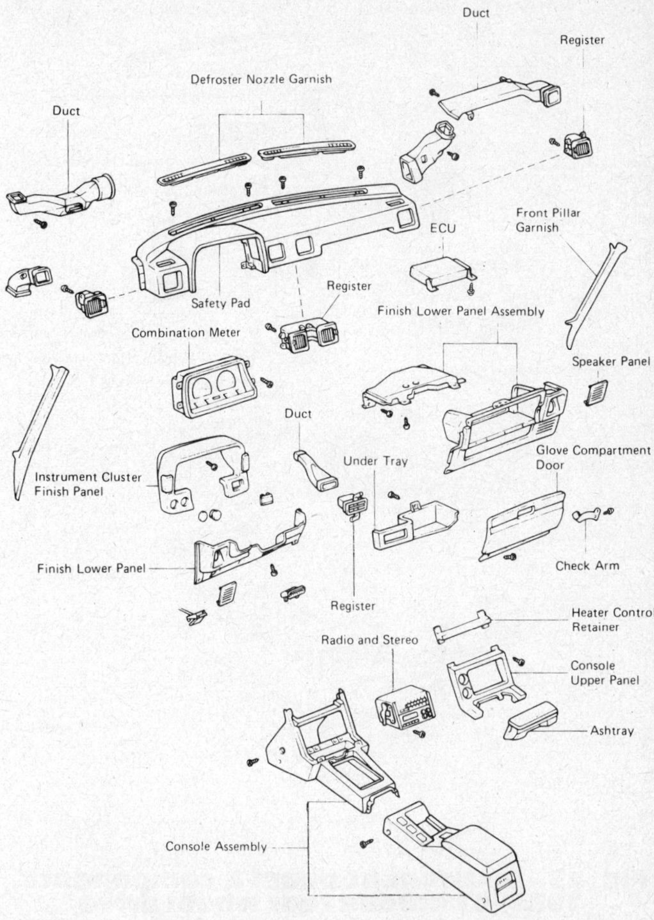

Fig. 21 Instrument panel & components. 1984 Celica. (1985 similar)

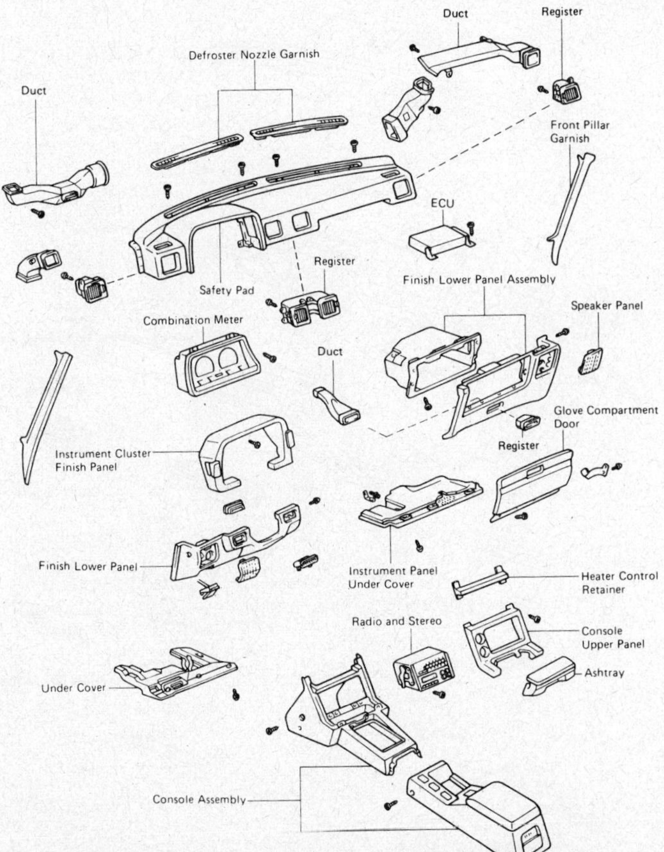

Fig. 22 Instrument panel & components. 1984 Supra. (1985–Early 1986 similar)

ing screws, then the console assembly.

4. Remove hood release lever bracket.
5. Remove left side speaker panel and lower finish panel.
6. On Supra models, remove left side under cover attaching screws, then the under cover.
7. On all models, remove instrument cluster finish panel attaching screws, then the cluster finish panel.
8. Disconnect speedometer cable and electrical connectors from instrument cluster.
9. Remove instrument cluster attaching screws, then the instrument cluster.
10. Remove right side cowl trim board.
11. On Supra models, remove right side instrument panel under cover attaching screws, then the instrument panel under cover.
12. On all models, remove right side lower finish panel as follows:
    a. Remove glove compartment door assembly.
    b. Remove right side lower finish panel attaching screws, then the panel.
    c. Disconnect electrical connectors from glove compartment.
    d. Remove right side speaker, if necessary.
13. Disconnect electrical connectors from ECU.

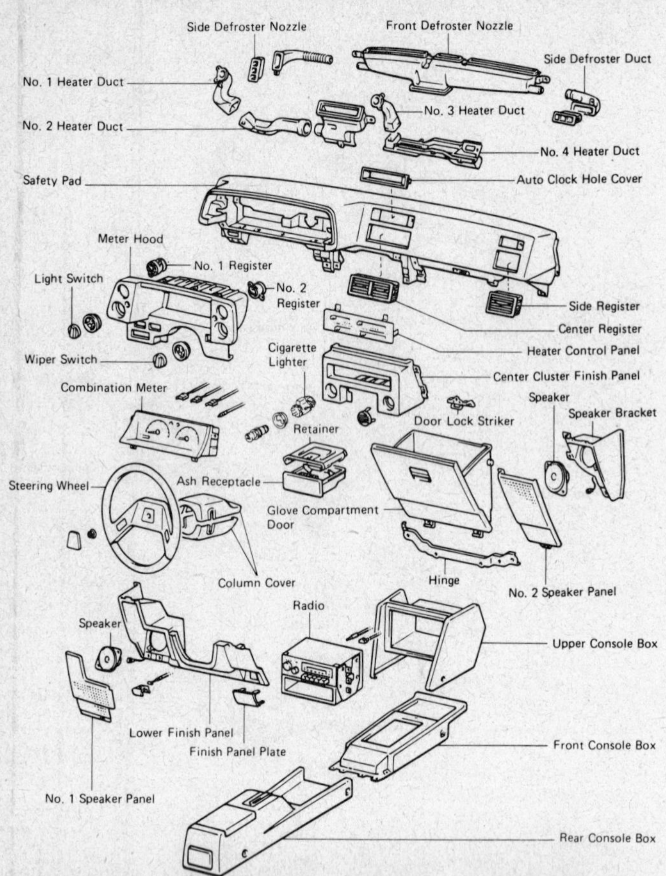

Fig. 23 Instrument panel & components. 1984–87 Corolla rear wheel drive

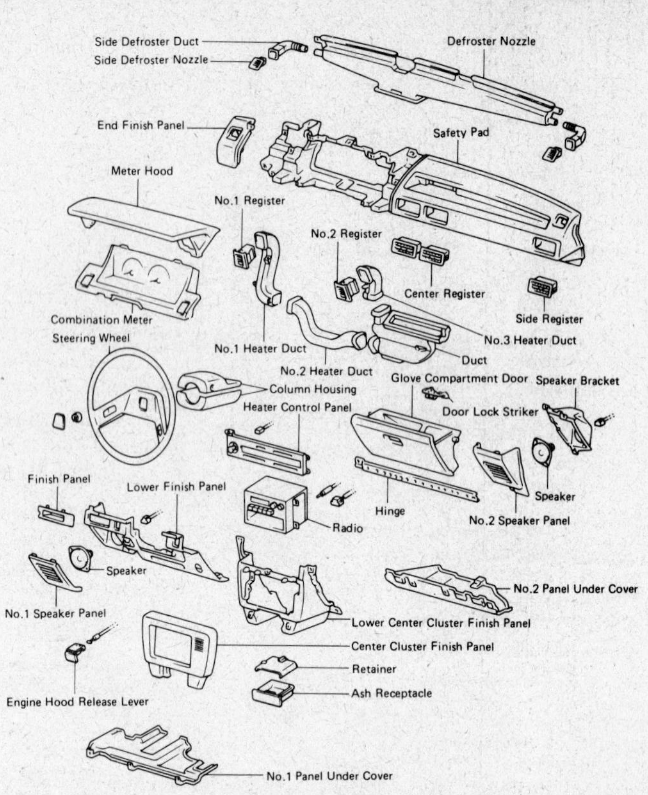

Fig. 24 Instrument panel & components. 1984–87 Corolla front wheel drive

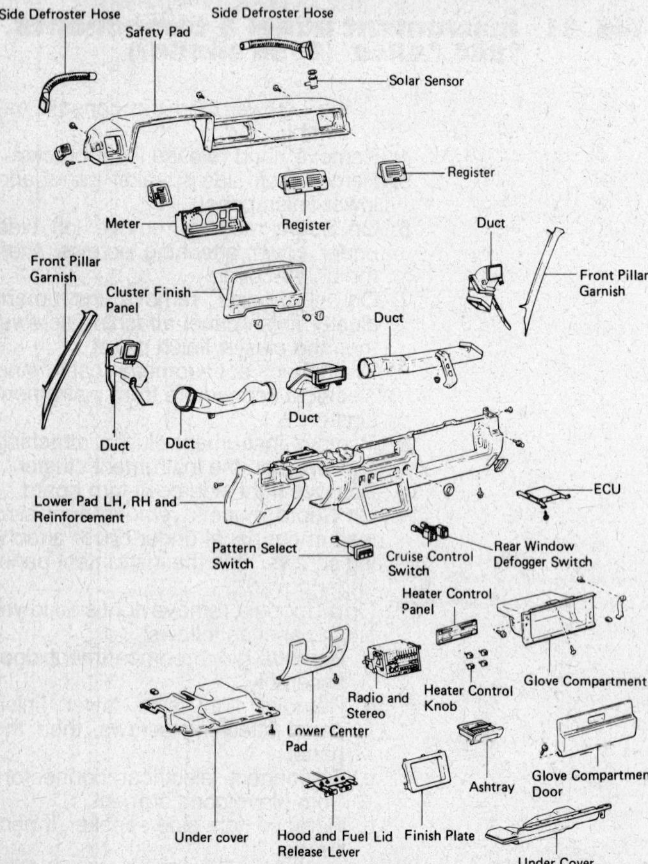

Fig. 25 Instrument panel & components. 1984 Cressida

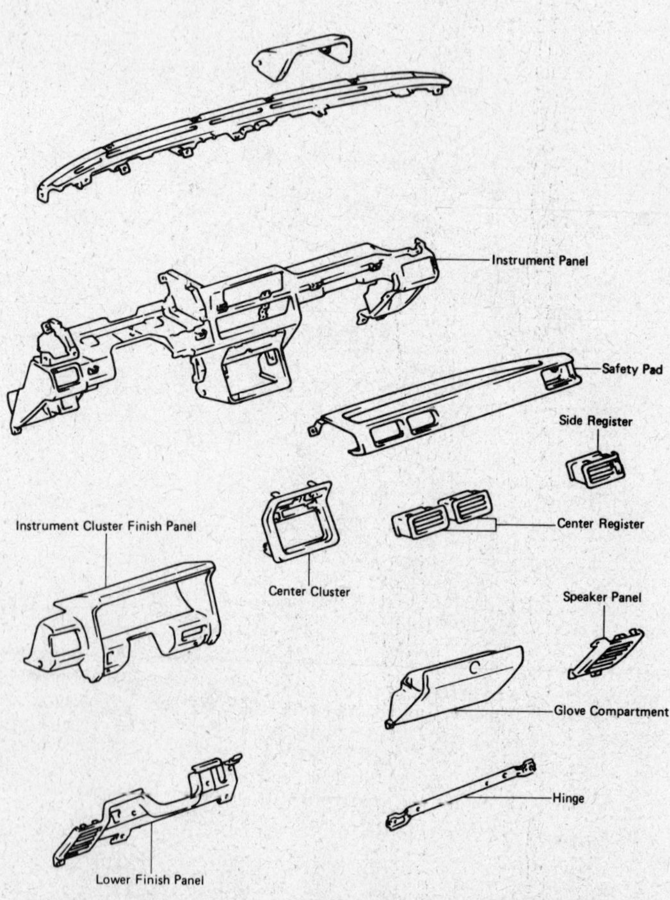

Fig. 26 Instrument panel & components. 1984–87 Pickup & 1985–87 4Runner

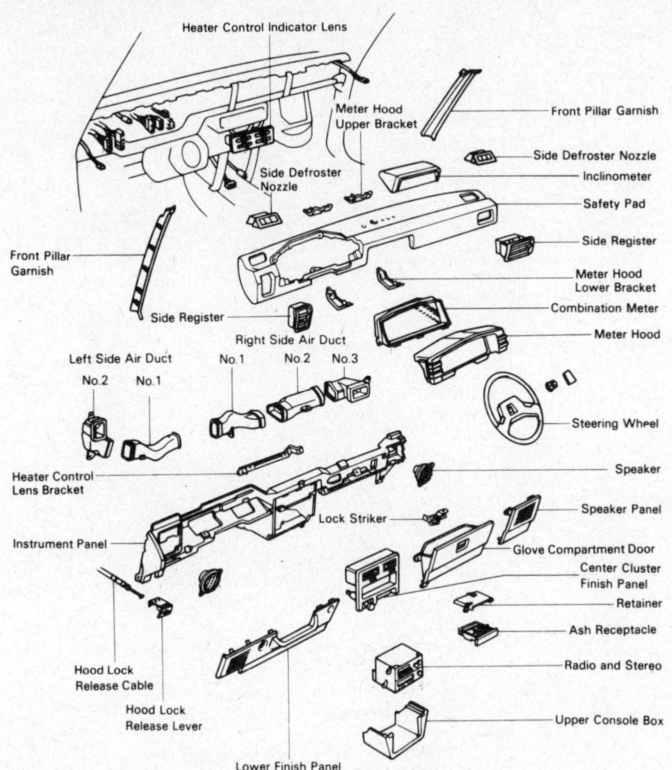

Fig. 27 Instrument panel & components. 1984–87 Tercel

Fig. 28 Instrument panel & components. 1984 Starlet

14. Remove ECU attaching screws, then the ECU.
15. Remove heater control assembly. Do not disconnect heater control cable.
16. Remove front pillar garnish assembly.
17. Remove defroster duct(s).
18. Remove instrument panel assembly as follows:
    a. Remove eight instrument panel attaching screws.
    b. Disconnect four electrical connectors from instrument panel.
    c. Remove instrument panel.
19. Reverse procedure to install.

1984–87 COROLLA

1. Disconnect battery ground cable.
2. Remove steering wheel.
3. Remove No. 1 speaker panel and clip, **Fig. 23 and 24.**
4. Remove hood release lever bracket.
5. Remove lower finish panel attaching screws, then the lower finish duct.
6. Remove No. 2 heater duct, then meter hood.
7. Remove instrument cluster attaching screws. On front wheel drive models, tip cluster outwards and disconnect speedometer cable. On all models, disconnect electrical connectors and remove instrument cluster.
8. On rear wheel drive models, remove speedometer cable from instrument panel and upper console assembly attaching screws, then the upper console assembly.
9. On front wheel drive models, remove No. 1 heater duct, end finish panel and No. 2 panel under cover.
10. On all models, remove No. 2 speaker panel attaching screws, then the speaker panel.
11. Remove speaker bracket.
12. Remove glove compartment door assembly.
13. Remove center cluster finish panel.
14. Remove heater control panel and side defroster duct.
15. On rear wheel drive models, remove auto clock cover attaching screws, then the auto clock cover.
16. Remove instrument panel attaching screws, then the instrument panel.
17. Reverse procedure to install.

1984 CRESSIDA

1. Disconnect battery ground cable.
2. Remove steering wheel and steering column cover.
3. Remove left and right front pillar garnish, **Fig. 25.**
4. Remove hood and fuel lid release lever bracket.
5. Remove left side instrument panel under cover and lower center pad.
6. Remove two left side air duct clips.
7. Remove right side instrument panel under cover and tray assembly.
8. Remove radio from instrument panel.
9. Remove glove compartment from instrument panel.
10. Disconnect electrical connectors from ECU, then remove ECU from instrument panel.
11. Remove ashtray and cigar lighter.
12. Remove instrument cluster from instrument panel.
13. Remove heater control panel attaching screws, then the panel.
14. Remove cruise control switch and rear window defogger switch, if equipped.
15. Remove pattern select switch, if equipped.
16. Remove instrument panel attaching screws, then the instrument panel.
17. Reverse procedure to install.

1984–87 PICKUP & 1985–87 4RUNNER

1. Disconnect battery ground cable.
2. Remove five instrument cluster finish panel attaching screws, then the panel, **Fig. 26. If necessary, disconnect wiring connector from finish panel.**
3. Remove instrument cluster attaching screws, then disconnect cluster wiring connectors and remove cluster.
4. If equipped, remove inclinometer hood attaching screws, then the hood. Remove inclinometer attaching screws, wiring connector and meter.
5. Remove glove compartment.
6. Remove side air duct by prying between duct and instrument panel with suitable screwdriver and releasing retaining clips.
7. If necessary, remove side air duct.
8. Remove two nuts, one bolt and five screws attaching instrument panel to cowl, then remove instrument panel.

1984–87 TERCEL

1. Disconnect battery ground cable.
2. Remove steering wheel.
3. Remove left and right front pillar garnish, **Fig. 27.**
4. Remove speaker panel attaching screws, then the speaker panel.

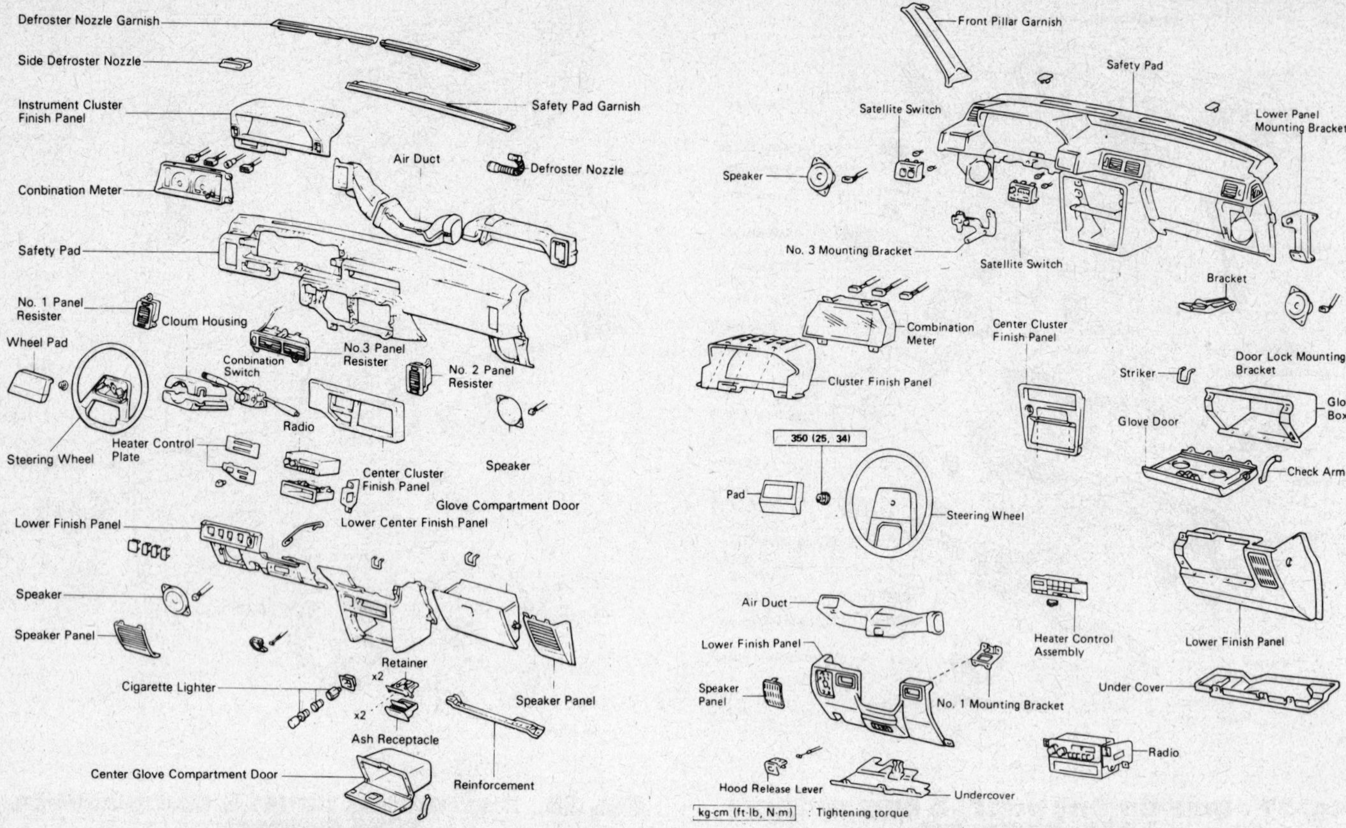

Fig. 29 Instrument panel & components. 1985–86 Camry

Fig. 30 Instrument panel & components. 1985–87 Cressida

5. Remove glove compartment door, then disconnect electrical connector from right speaker.
6. Remove No. 1 and No. 2 right side air ducts.
7. Remove instrument panel mounting nut and bolt.
8. Remove upper console assembly and radio.
9. Remove ashtray and retainer bracket.
10. Remove instrument cluster center finish panel and heater control indicator lens.
11. Remove No. 3 air duct mounting screw and lower finish panel assembly.
12. Disconnect electrical connector from left speaker.
13. Remove hood lock release lever bracket.
14. Remove No. 1 left side air duct.
15. Remove two left side instrument panel retaining bolts.
16. Remove instrument cluster front panel, then the instrument cluster.
17. Remove instrument cluster upper front panel brackets from instrument panel.
18. Remove left and right side defroster ducts and two instrument panel mounting screws.
19. Disconnect electrical connector from inclinometer, if equipped.
20. Remove instrument panel retaining clips, then the instrument panel.
21. Reverse procedure to install.

1984 STARLET

1. Disconnect battery ground cable.
2. Remove steering wheel and steering column cover.
3. Remove speaker panel attaching screws, then the speaker panel, **Fig. 28.**
4. Remove glove compartment door.
5. Disconnect electrical connector from right speaker.
6. Remove right air control door.
7. Remove right side air duct.
8. Remove computer cover attaching screws, then the computer cover assembly.
9. Remove ashtray.
10. Remove center cluster finish panel and instrument cluster cover.
11. Remove instrument cluster assembly from instrument panel.
12. Remove instrument panel attaching screws, then the instrument panel.
13. Reverse procedure to install.

1985–86 CAMRY

1. Disconnect battery ground cable.
2. Remove steering wheel and combination switch.
3. Remove left speaker panel attaching screws, then the panel, **Fig. 29.**
4. Remove left speaker attaching screws, then the speaker.
5. Remove engine hood lock release lever attaching screws, then the lever.
6. Remove five lower finish panel attaching screws, then disconnect connectors and remove panel.
7. Remove air duct, then the cluster finish panel attaching screws and panel.
8. Remove four combination meter attaching screws and pull out meter assembly.
9. Remove speedometer cable and electrical connectors from meter assembly, then the meter assembly.
10. Remove glove compartment door attaching screws, then the glove compartment door.
11. Remove right speaker panel, then the right speaker.
12. Remove right scuff plate, then the right cowl side trim.
13. Remove glove compartment door reinforcement, then the center cluster finish panel.
14. Remove ashtray assembly.
15. Remove lower center cluster finish panel attaching screws, then the cigarette lighter electrical connector and finish panel.
16. Remove heater control knobs, then the control plates.
17. Remove radio attaching screws, then the radio.
18. Remove nozzle garnishes.
19. Remove instrument panel attaching screws, then the instrument panel assembly.
20. Reverse procedure to install.

1985–87 CRESSIDA

1. Disconnect battery ground cable.

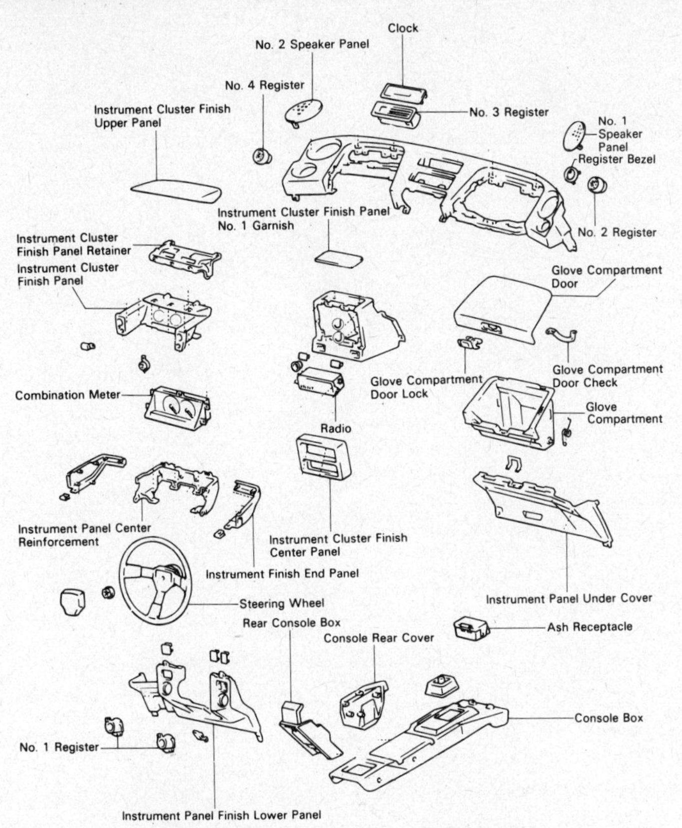

Fig. 31 Instrument panel and components. 1985–87 MR2

Fig. 32 Instrument panel and components. 1986–87 Celica

2. Remove steering wheel.
3. Remove glove box assembly attaching screws, then the glove box assembly and striker, **Fig. 30.**
4. Remove four bracket attaching screws, then the bracket.
5. Remove right side lower finish panel attaching nuts, bolts and screws, then the lower finish panel.
6. Remove engine hood release lever attaching screws, then disconnect cable from lever.
7. Remove three under cover No. 1 attaching screws, then the under cover.
8. Pry out cruise control switch using a suitable screwdriver, then disconnect switch electrical connector and remove switch.
9. Remove left speaker panel and two attaching bolts.
10. Remove left side lower finish panel attaching nuts, then the lower finish panel.
11. Remove left side air duct, then the left and right front speakers.
12. Pry off heater control panel defroster button using a suitable screwdriver, then remove heater control panel.
13. Remove center cluster finish panel attaching screws, then the cluster finish panel.
14. Remove radio attaching screws, then the radio.
15. Remove satellite switch attaching screws, then the satellite switch.
16. Remove cluster finish panel attaching screws, then the finish panel.
17. Remove four combination meter attaching screws, then disconnect meter electrical connectors and remove meter.
18. Remove heater controller attaching screws, then the heater controller.
19. Disconnect heater vacuum tube connector, then the following electrical connectors: light sensor; solar sensor for A/C; in-car sensor for A/C; glove box courtesy switch.
20. On models equipped with A/C, disconnect hose from aspirator.
21. On all models, remove instrument panel stay and No. 1 bracket.
22. Remove instrument panel attaching bolts, then pull instrument panel upward at an angle and out of vehicle.
23. Reverse procedure to install.

1985–87 MR2

1. Disconnect battery ground cable.
2. Remove steering wheel, then the rear console box, **Fig. 31.**
3. Set parking brake, then remove ashtray from console. Remove 9 console attaching screws, then with rear of console raised, remove console.
4. Remove two glove compartment door arm attaching setscrews, then the two door check setscrews with door.
5. Remove glove compartment.
6. Remove one attaching screw from front side of scuff plate, then the cowl side trim board. Remove door lock striker, then the 4 instrument panel under cover attaching screws and cover.
7. Remove one attaching screw from front side of scuff plate, then the cowl side trim board. Remove foot lock lever. Remove 4 lower panel attaching screws, then disconnect electrical connectors and remove panel.
8. Remove two upper instrument cluster finish center panel attaching screws, then the panel from lower side. Disconnect electrical connector.
9. Remove four radio tuner finish panel attaching screws, then disconnect antenna cable and remove radio. Remove instrument cluster finish panel, then the 6 attaching screws and radio tuner finish panel.
10. Remove 11 instrument cluster upper finish panel attaching screws, then pull upward and to the left to remove panel. If equipped, disconnect auto a/c electrical connector.
11. Remove instrument cluster finish panel retainer, then pull panel outward, disconnect electrical connector and remove.
12. Remove 4 combination meter attaching screws, then disconnect speedometer cable and electrical connectors. Remove meter.
13. Remove 6 instrument panel center reinforcement attachment screws, then the reinforcement.
14. Remove No. 1 speaker panel, then speaker panel No. 2.
15. Remove side speaker attaching screws, then pull speakers upward, disconnect electrical connectors and remove speakers.

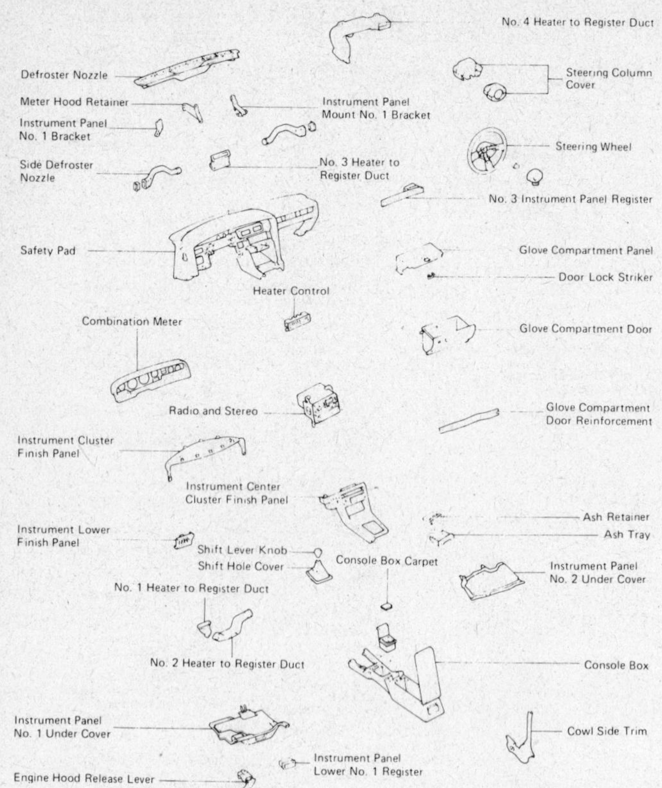

Fig. 33 Instrument panel and components. Late 1986 & 1987 Supra

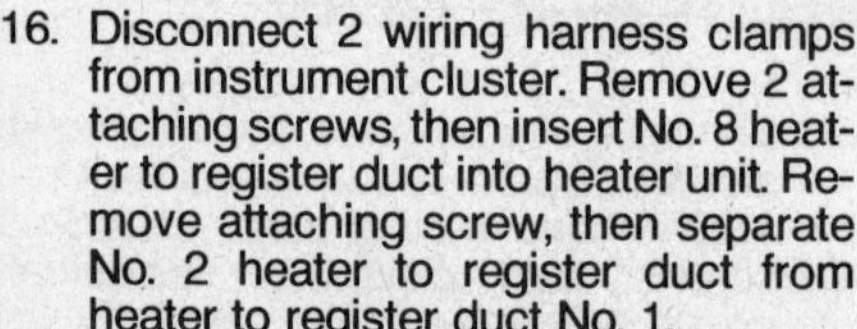

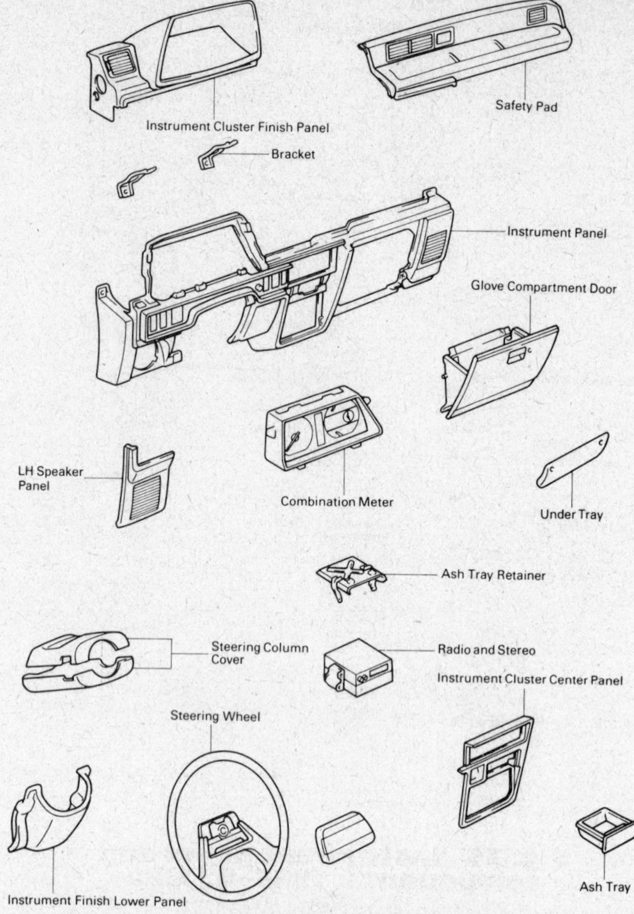

Fig. 34 Instrument panel and components. Van

16. Disconnect 2 wiring harness clamps from instrument cluster. Remove 2 attaching screws, then insert No. 8 heater to register duct into heater unit. Remove attaching screw, then separate No. 2 heater to register duct from heater to register duct No. 1.
17. Remove 6 retaining bolts and four retaining screws from instrument panel, then instrument panel outward, disconnect clock connector and remove instrument panel pad.
18. Reverse procedure to install.

1986–87 CELICA

1. Disconnect battery ground cable.
2. Remove steering wheel.
3. On models less tilt steering, remove upper and lower steering column covers.
4. On models equipped with man. trans., remove shift lever knob.
5. On all models, remove console attaching screws, then lift out console box hole cover and disconnect electrical connectors. Remove console, **Fig. 32.**
6. Remove glove compartment door.
7. Remove instrument panel speaker No. 2 attaching screws, then pull loose the clips and remove the panel.
8. Remove speaker No. 1 mounting bracket.
9. Remove remaining glove compartment door reinforcement attaching bolt, then the glove compartment door reinforcement.
10. Remove instrument panel speaker No. 1 attaching screws, then pull loose the clips and remove the panel.
11. Remove engine hood release lever attaching screws, then the lever.
12. Remove five instrument panel finish lower panel attaching screws and one bolt, then disconnect electrical connectors and remove panel.
13. Remove No. 2 heater-to-register duct.
14. Remove ashtray and instrument panel lower center panel attaching screws, then disconnect electrical connectors and remove panel.
15. Remove four radio attaching screws, then disconnect electrical connectors and antenna lead. Remove radio.
16. Pry out rear window defogger and hazard warning switches with suitable screwdriver, then disconnect electrical connectors and remove switches.
17. Remove instrument cluster finish panel attaching screws, then the panel.
18. Remove four combination meter attaching screws, then disconnect electrical connectors and remove meter.
19. Squeeze speedometer cable mounting bracket pawls together, then pull speedometer cable from instrument panel.
20. Remove four heater control panel mounting screws.
21. Remove two No. 1 instrument panel finish panel retainer mounting screws.
22. Remove cowl side trim, then disconnect instrument panel wiring from connectors mounted in cowl.
23. Remove four bolts, two screws and two nuts attaching instrument panel to cowl.
24. Remove instrument panel. **When removing instrument panel, lift off at an approximate 45° angle to disengage clips from body side.**
25. Reverse procedure to install.

LATE 1986 & 1987 SUPRA

1. Disconnect battery ground cable.
2. Remove steering wheel and steering column cover.
3. Remove hood release lever attaching screws, then the hood release lever.
4. Remove lower register.
5. Remove No. 1 under cover attaching screws, then the under cover, **Fig. 33.**
6. Remove No. 2 heater to register duct.
7. Pull instrument lower finish panel slightly away from safety pad, then disconnect switch wiring and remove lower finish panel.
8. Remove ashtray and ashtray retainer.
9. On models equipped with manual transmission, remove shift lever knob.
10. Remove three instrument center cluster finish panel attaching screws, then disconnect the panel electrical connectors and remove the panel.
11. Remove seven instrument cluster finish panel attaching screws, then the finish panel.
12. Remove four combination meter attaching screws, then disconnect elec-

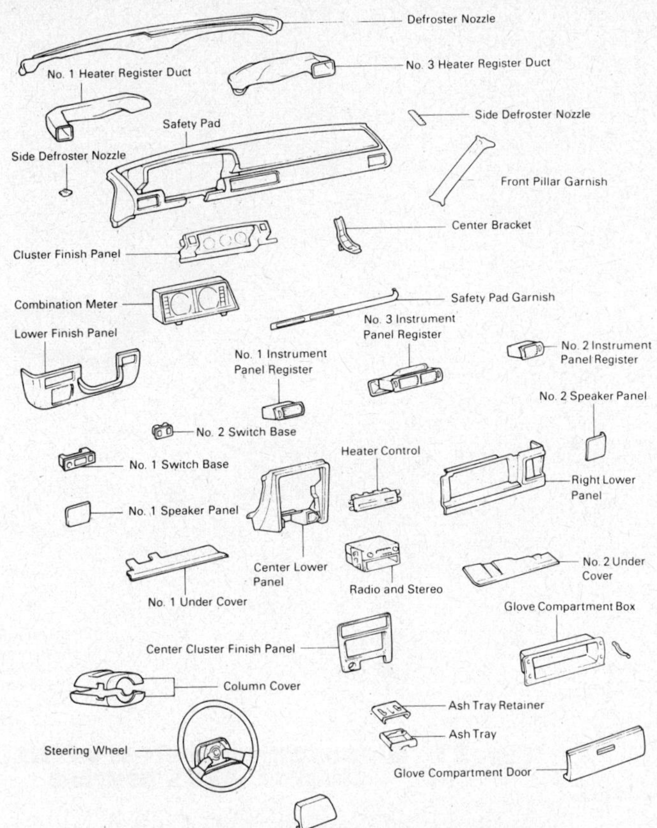

Fig. 35 Instrument panel and components. 1987 Camry

trical connectors and remove combination meter.

13. Remove console box carpet, then the six attaching screws. Disconnect electrical connectors, then remove console box.
14. Remove three heater control attaching screws, then disconnect electrical connectors and remove heater control.
15. Remove four radio attaching screws, then disconnect electrical connectors and antenna lead and remove radio.
16. Remove three instrument panel No. 2 under cover attaching screws, then the under cover.
17. Remove two glove compartment door attaching screws, then the door.
18. Remove glove compartment door lock striker attaching screws, then the striker.
19. Remove glove compartment panel attaching screws, then remove the light from the panel and the panel.
20. Remove cowl side trim attaching nut, then the trim.
21. Remove glove compartment reinforcement attaching screws and bolts, then the reinforcement.
22. Remove glove compartment door courtesy switch.
23. Remove EFI computer attaching screws, then disconnect electrical connectors and remove computer.
24. Squeeze speedometer cable mounting bracket pawls together, then withdraw cable from instrument panel.
25. Disconnect driver's side electrical harness connectors, then the passenger side.
26. Disconnect console box side wire harness from body.
27. Remove assist grip attaching screws from front pillar garnish, then the assist grip and front pillar garnish.
28. Remove five nuts, two screws and bolt attaching instrument panel to cowl.
29. Remove instrument panel. **When removing instrument panel, lift off at an approximate 45° angle to disengage clips from body side.**
30. Reverse procedure to install.

VAN

1. Disconnect battery ground cable.
2. Remove steering wheel.
3. Remove four instrument finish lower panel attaching screws, then the panel.
4. Remove upper and lower steering column covers.
5. Remove two LH speaker panel attaching screws, then remove panel, **Fig. 34.**
6. Remove five instrument cluster finish panel attaching screws, then the panel.
7. Remove four combination meter attaching screws, then disconnect electrical connectors and speedometer cable. Remove meter.
8. Remove ashtray, then the four instrument cluster center panel attaching screws. Remove panel.
9. Disconnect cigar lighter electrical connectors, then remove ashtray retainer attaching screws. Remove ashtray retainer.
10. Remove four radio attaching screws, then disconnect radio electrical connectors and antenna lead. Remove radio.
11. Remove three heater control attaching screws, then disconnect the heater control.
12. Remove glove compartment under tray attaching screws, then the under tray.
13. Remove glove compartment door attaching screws, then the door.
14. Remove six screws and two bolts attaching instrument panel to cowl, then the instrument panel.
15. Reverse procedure to install.

1987 CAMRY

1. Disconnect battery ground cable.
2. Remove steering wheel.
3. Pry out front pillar garnish retaining clips, then remove garnish by pulling upwards by hand.
4. Remove No. 1 under cover, **Fig. 35.**
5. Remove engine hood release lever attaching screws, then the lever.
6. Using suitable screwdriver, pry out switch base and No. 1 speaker panel from lower finish panel. Disconnect electrical connectors.
7. Remove seven lower finish panel attaching bolts, then the panel.
8. Remove steering column upper and lower covers.
9. Remove five instrument cluster finish panel attaching screws, then disconnect electrical connectors and remove panel.
10. Remove four combination meter attaching screws, then disconnect electrical connectors and speedometer cable. Remove meter.
11. Remove No. 2 under cover.
12. Remove glove compartment box and door.
13. Using suitable screwdriver, pry out No. 2 speaker panel from right lower panel.
14. Remove five bolts, three screws and two nuts attaching right lower panel to instrument panel, then remove right lower panel.
15. Remove two screws from top of center cluster finish panel, then the ashtray. Disconnect electrical connectors and remove center cluster finish panel.
16. Remove four radio attaching screws, then disconnect electrical connectors and antenna cable. Remove radio.
17. Remove heater control attaching screws, then the heater control.
18. Remove two two center lower panel attaching screws, then the panel.
19. Pry out side defroster nozzles with suitable screwdriver.
20. Remove center bracket-to-instrument panel attaching nut.
21. Remove two electrical junction box attaching screws located under left side of instrument panel.
22. Squeeze speedometer cable mounting bracket pawls together, then pull speedometer cable from instrument

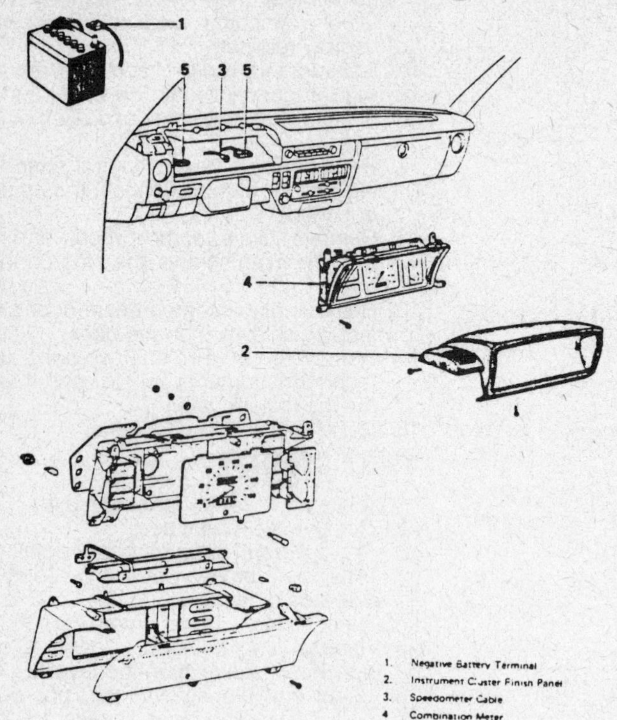

Fig. 36 Disassembled view of instrument cluster. 1983 Tercel

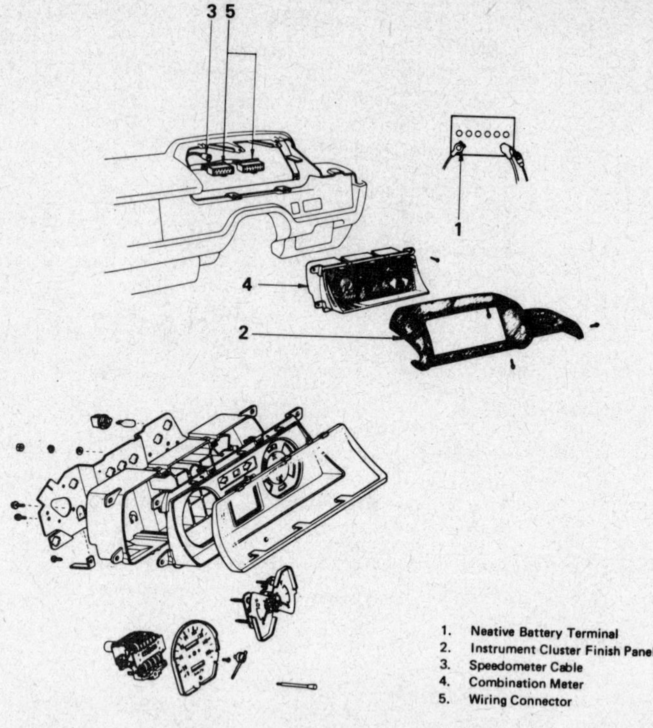

Fig. 37 Disassembled view of instrument cluster. 1983 Starlet

panel.

23. Remove four bolts, two screws and two nuts attaching instrument panel to cowl.
24. Remove instrument panel. **When removing instrument panel, lift off at an approximate 45° angle to disengage clips from body side.**
25. Reverse procedure to install.

INSTRUMENT CLUSTER

REPLACE

1983 STARLET & 1983 TERCEL

Refer to **Figs. 36 and 37** for removal and disassembly of instrument cluster.

1983 CRESSIDA

Refer to **Fig. 38** for removal and disassembly of instrument cluster.

1983 COROLLA

1. Disconnect battery ground cable.
2. On sedan and wagon models, remove radio knobs and instrument cluster finish panel. Disconnect speedometer cable from rear of speedometer, then remove instrument cluster retaining screws. Disconnect instrument cluster electrical connectors and remove cluster.
3. On coupe and liftback models, remove instrument cluster finish panel, then disconnect indicator lamp electrical connector. Disconnect cluster electrical connector and speedometer cable from cluster, then remove cluster, **Fig. 39.**
4. Reverse procedure to install.

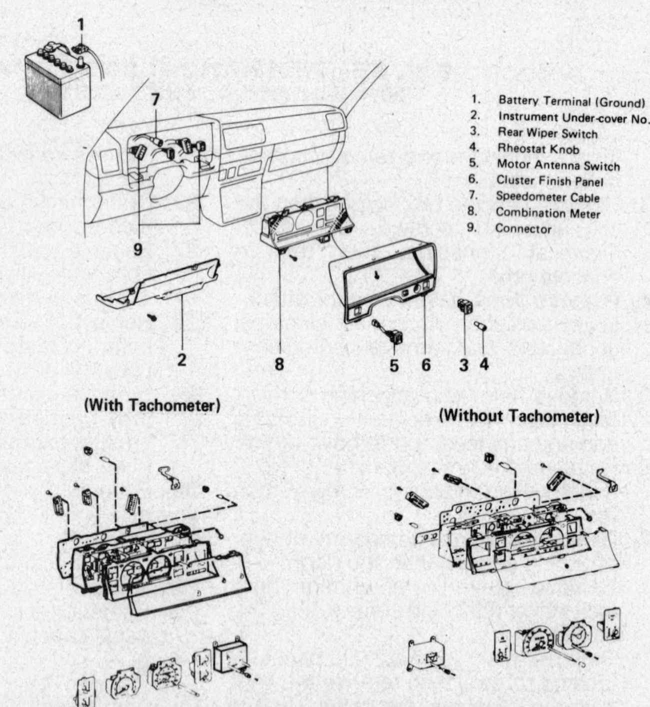

Fig. 38 Disassembled view of instrument cluster. 1983 Cressida

1983 PICKUP

1. Disconnect battery ground cable.
2. Remove steering column covers, **Fig. 40**, then remove cluster finish panel.
3. Disconnect speedometer cable from back of speedometer.
4. Remove screws securing instrument cluster, then pull instrument cluster forward and disconnect electrical connectors.
5. Remove screws securing oil pressure gauge and ammeter, then disconnect gauge electrical connectors and remove cluster, from vehicle. **1981-83 models are equipped with a voltmeter.**
6. Reverse procedure to install.

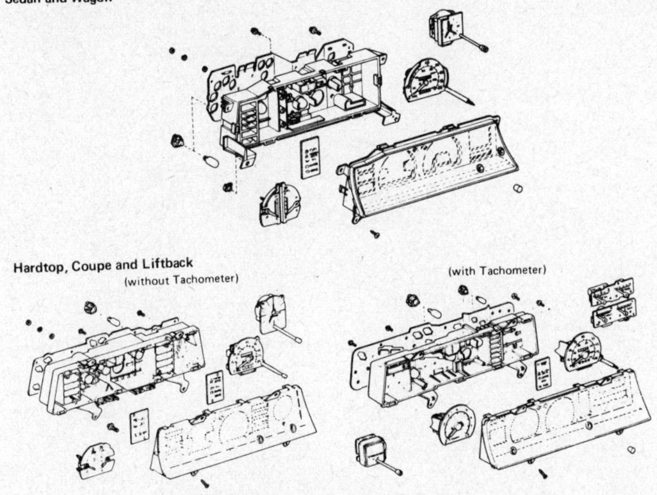

Fig. 39 Disassembled view of instrument cluster. 1983 Corolla

Fig. 40 Disassembled view of instrument cluster. 1983 Pickup

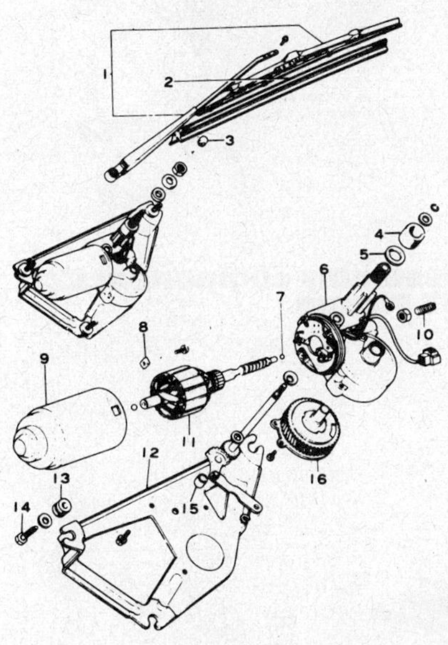

1. Windshield Wiper Arm And Blade
2. Windshield Wiper Blade
3. Cap Nut
4. Wiper Link Packing
5. Wiper Link Washer
6. Gear Housing
7. Boll
8. Nut
9. Wiper Motor Stator
10. Stop Screw
11. Wiper Motor Armature
12. Wiper Bracket
13. Bush
14. Bolt
15. Stopper
16. Wiper Motor Gear

Fig. 41 Rear wiper motor assembly

WINDSHIELD WIPER MOTOR

REPLACE

EXC. MR2

1. Disconnect battery ground cable.
2. Disconnect wiper motor wire connector, then remove wiper motor service cover, if equipped.
3. Remove wiper motor attaching bolts.
4. Using a screwdriver disconnect wiper link from wiper motor and remove wiper motor.
5. Reverse procedure to install.

MR2

1. With wiper arms in "Up" position and wiper switch on "Low," turn ignition switch "Off."
2. Disconnect battery ground cable.
3. Disconnect wiper motor electrical connector, then remove light retractor relay from wiper bracket.
4. Remove wiper motor attaching bolts. Manually lower wiper arms, then hook wiper link hook to dash panel service hole.
5. Disconnect wiper motor from wiper link.
6. Remove wiper motor.
7. Reverse procedure to install.

REAR WIPER MOTOR

REPLACE

1. Disconnect battery ground cable.
2. Remove wiper arm and rear door trim cover.
3. Disconnect wiper motor wire connector.
4. Remove wiper motor bracket attaching bolts and wiper motor and bracket, **Fig. 41.**

WINDSHIELD WIPER SWITCH

REPLACE

Refer to "Combination Switch Service & Combination Switch, Replace" procedure.

RADIO

REPLACE

Refer to "Instrument Panel, Replace" for replacement procedures.

HEATER CORE

REPLACE

1983 COROLLA

1. Disconnect battery ground cable and drain engine coolant.
2. Remove center console.
3. Remove scarf plate and front seats, **Fig. 42.**
4. Position floor carpeting aside, then remove rear heater duct, if equipped.
5. Remove under tray, **Fig. 42.**
6. Remove glove box and blower duct.
7. On sedan and station wagon models, remove the following:
   a. Heater control knobs and lens.
   b. Cluster lower center panel finish, ashtray and heater control assembly.
   c. Instrument cluster finish panel, radio and air ducts.
8. On coupe and liftback models, remove the following:
   a. Instrument cluster finish panel, instrument cluster, radio trim and radio.
   b. Ashtray, heater control knobs, heater control panel, heater control assembly and air duct.
9. On all models, disconnect heater hoses from heater core assembly, then remove heater hose grommet.
10. Remove heater core assembly retaining screws, then remove heater core assembly from vehicle.
11. Remove heater core from heater core assembly.
12. Reverse procedure to install.

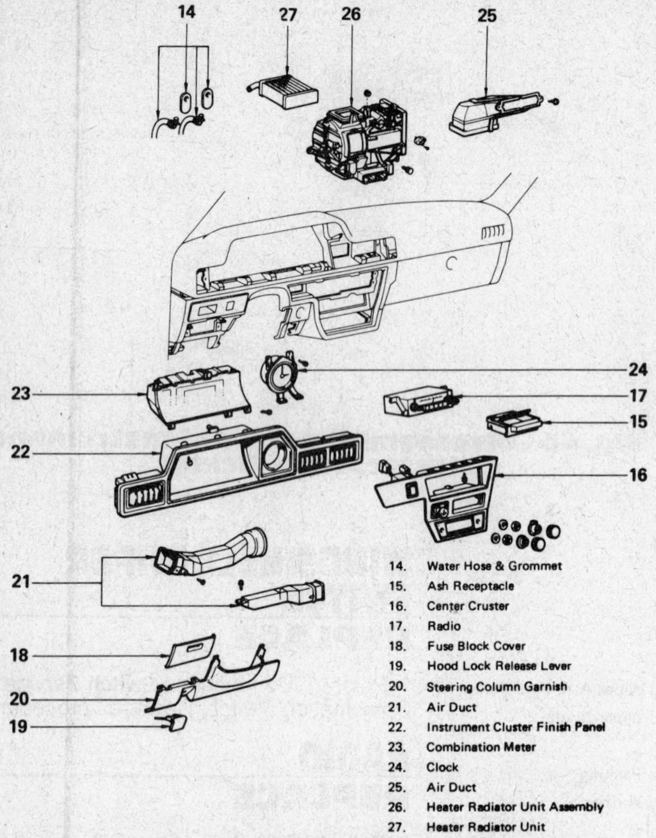

14. Water Hose & Grommet
15. Ash Receptacle
16. Center Cruster
17. Radio
18. Fuse Block Cover
19. Hood Lock Release Lever
20. Steering Column Garnish
21. Air Duct
22. Instrument Cluster Finish Panel
23. Combination Meter
24. Clock
25. Air Duct
26. Heater Radiator Unit Assembly
27. Heater Radiator Unit

Fig. 42 Heater assembly components. 1983 Corolla

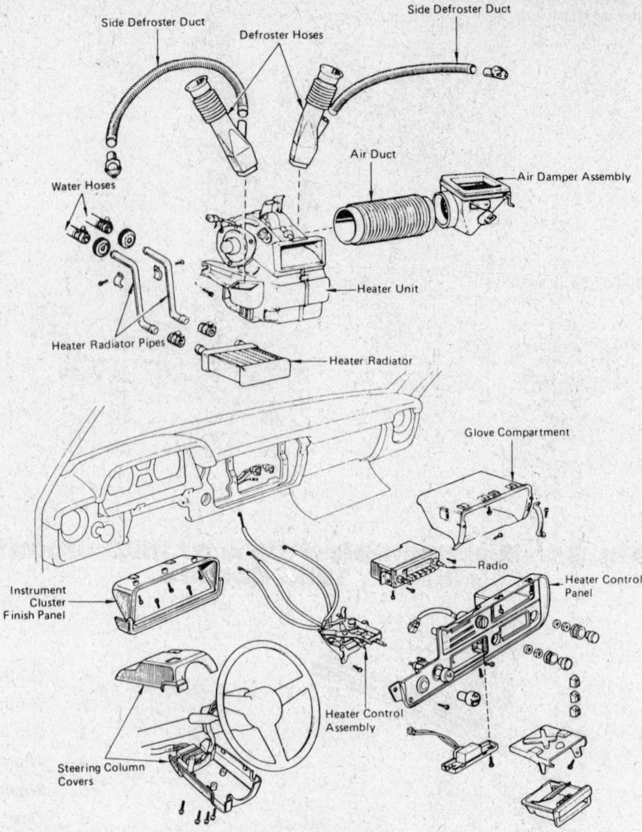

Side Defroster Duct
Defroster Hoses
Side Defroster Duct
Air Duct
Air Damper Assembly
Water Hoses
Heater Unit
Heater Radiator Pipes
Heater Radiator
Glove Compartment
Radio
Heater Control Panel
Instrument Cluster Finish Panel
Heater Control Assembly
Steering Column Covers

Fig. 43 Heater assembly components. 1983 Pickup

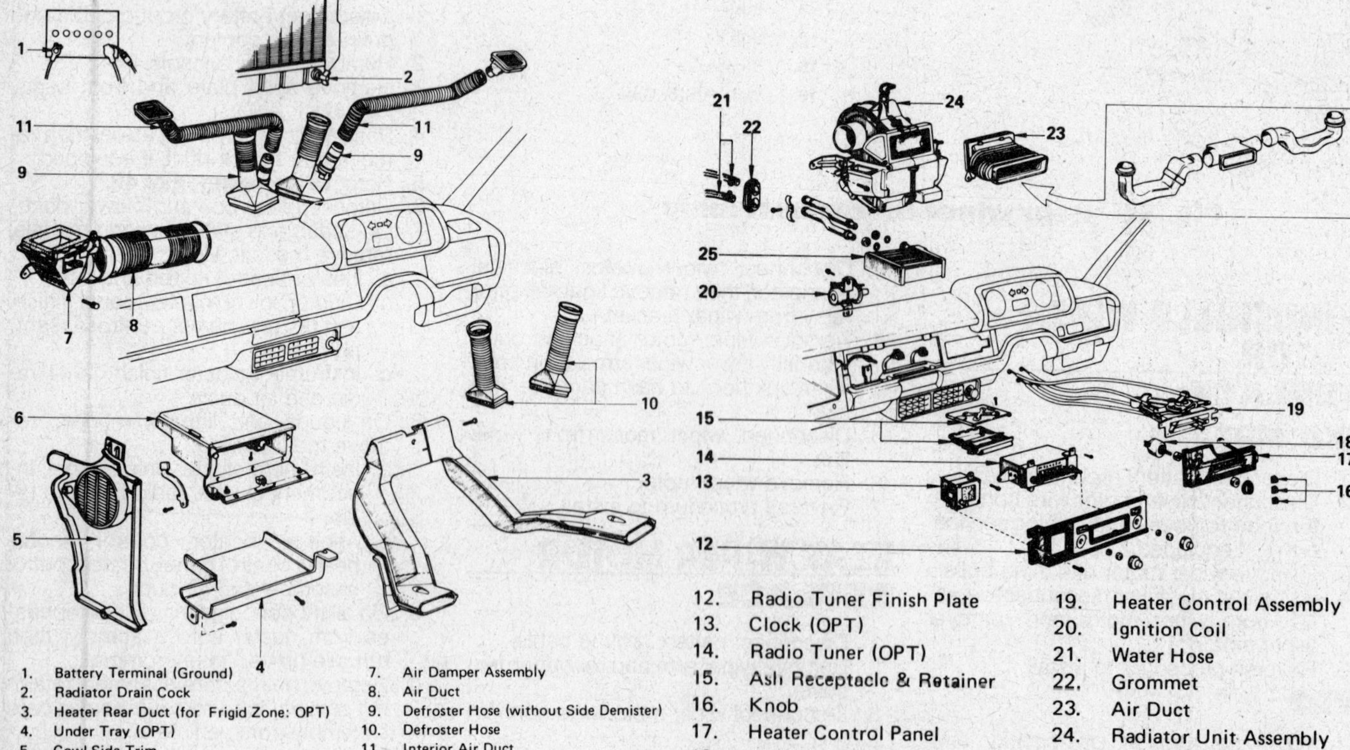

Fig. 44 Heater assembly components. 1983 Starlet

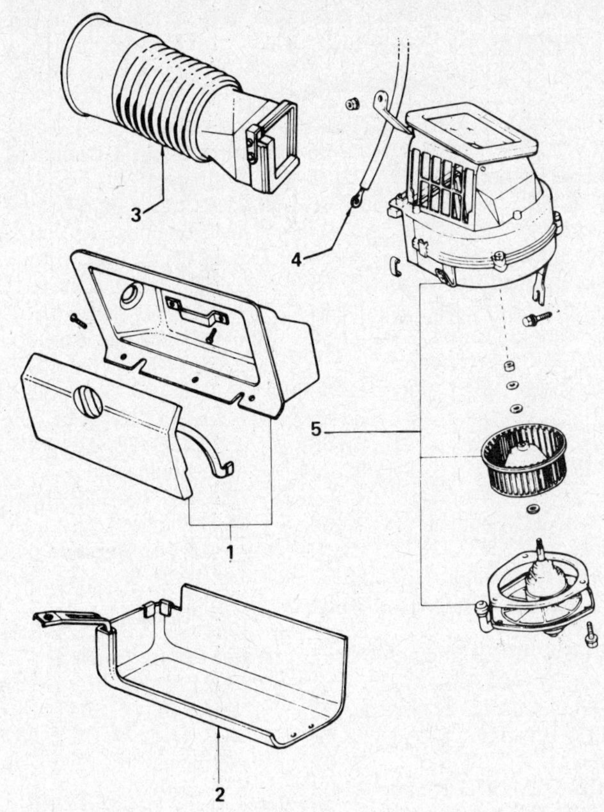

1 Glove Compartment & Door
2 Under Tray
3 Heater Air Supply Duct
4 Heater Air Inlet Butterfly Control Cable
5 Heater Blower Assembly

Fig. 45 Blower motor removal. 1983 Corolla

1983 PICKUP

1. Disconnect battery ground cable and drain coolant system.
2. Remove glove box and defroster hoses, **Fig. 43.**
3. Remove air damper assembly and air duct.
4. Remove side defroster ducts.
5. Remove steering column covers, instrument cluster finish panel and heater control panel.
6. Remove radio, then disconnect control cables from heater control assembly.
7. Disconnect heater hoses from heater core pipes, then remove heater core assembly from vehicle.
8. Remove heater water pipes from heater core assembly, then separate heater core assembly halves and remove heater core.
9. Reverse procedure to install.

1983 STARLET

1. Disconnect battery ground cable and drain coolant system.
2. Remove heater rear duct, if equipped.
3. Remove under tray, if equipped, **Fig. 44.**
4. Remove cowl side trim, glove box and air damper assembly.
5. Remove air duct, defroster hoses and inside air duct.
6. Remove radio finish plate, clock and radio.
7. Remove ashtray, heater control knobs and heater control front panel.
8. Remove heater blower switch and heater control assembly.
9. Remove ignition coil, then disconnect heater hoses from heater core assembly.
10. Remove heater hose grommet.
11. Remove screws securing heater core assembly, then remove heater core assembly from vehicle.
12. Remove heater core from heater core assembly.
13. Reverse procedure to install.

BLOWER MOTOR REPLACE

1983 COROLLA

1. Disconnect battery ground cable.
2. Remove heater air supply duct from heater unit.
3. Remove heater air inlet control cable.
4. Remove blower motor attaching bolts.
5. Disconnect wire connector and remove blower motor, **Fig. 45.**
6. Reverse procedure to install.

1983 PICKUP & 1983 STARLET

1. Disconnect blower motor electrical connector.
2. Remove blower motor from blower motor assembly.
3. Reverse procedure to install.

GASOLINE ENGINE SECTION

INDEX

ENGINE REPLACE

1983–84 TERCEL

MODELS EQUIPPED WITH MANUAL TRANSAXLE

1. Disconnect battery ground cable and drain cooling system.
2. Remove air cleaner assembly and engine compartment hood.
3. Cover driveshaft boots with shop towels to prevent damage as engine is removed.
4. Disconnect solenoid valve, water temperature switch and electric fan electrical connectors.
5. Remove stiffener plate bolt from differential, then disconnect exhaust pipe from exhaust manifold.
6. Remove radiator and windshield washer fluid tank.
7. Disconnect heater hose, fuel line, accelerator cable, choke cable and engine ground straps from engine.
8. Disconnect power brake vacuum booster hose from engine.
9. Disconnect high tension lead from ignition coil and alternator electrical connectors.
10. Disconnect clutch release cable from engine and starter motor electrical connectors from starter.
11. Remove bolts attaching engine mount and engine shock absorber to engine.
12. Remove engine to transaxle retaining bolts, then support transaxle with suitable jack.
13. Attach suitable hoist to engine, then position engine forward to clear transaxle input shaft and remove engine from vehicle.
14. Reverse procedure to install. **Torque transaxle mounting bolts to 54 ft. lbs.**

MODELS EQUIPPED WITH AUTOMATIC TRANSAXLE

1. Drain cooling system and disconnect battery ground cable.
2. Remove air cleaner assembly, grille and engine compartment hood.
3. Cover drive shaft boots with shop towels to prevent damage when engine is removed.
4. Remove radiator, then disconnect carburetor electrical connector.
5. Disconnect hose from emission canister and fuel hose from pump.
6. Disconnect power brake vacuum booster hose from engine.
7. Disconnect engine ground straps, accelerator cable and heater hose from engine.
8. Disconnect high tension lead from coil and neutral start switch and alternator electrical connectors.
9. Remove starter motor.
10. Disconnect throttle linkage, exhaust pipe and oil cooler line from engine.
11. Remove stiffener plate bolts and exhaust pipe bracket bolts from engine.
12. Disconnect oil cooler line from transaxle.
13. Raise and support vehicle, then remove bolts securing engine mounting and engine shock absorber to engine. Remove bolts securing stiffener plate, then remove torque converter cover.
14. Support transmission with suitable jack, then remove lower transaxle mounting bolts.

15. Remove remaining transaxle bolts, then remove four torque converter bolts.
16. Attach suitable hoist to engine and position engine forward two inches.
17. Using suitable pry bar, pry engine from torque converter, then remove engine from vehicle.
18. Support converter housing after engine is removed to prevent damage to transaxle.
19. Check that torque converter is properly positioned in housing by placing straightedge across housing flange. Converter should be recessed 1.02 inch (26 mm) from housing flange.
20. Install 1.18 inch (30 mm) guide bolt onto any torque converter mounting hole.
21. Remove left side engine mount insulator and right side engine mount bracket from engine prior to installation.
22. Align drive plate hole with torque converter drive bolt, then align crankshaft hole with converter hub and install engine to transaxle.
23. Temporarily install two upper transaxle mounting bolts, then remove guide bolts. Remove guide bolts and temporarily install torque converter using four .59 inch (15 mm) long bolts, tightening each bolt alternately.
24. Remove temporarily installed bolts and install regular bolts.
25. Install engine mountings, then install transaxle to engine mounting bolts. Reverse steps 1 thru 13 to complete installation. **Torque transaxle mounting bolts to 37-57 ft. lbs.**

1985–86 TERCEL & 1987 TERCEL WAGON

1. Disconnect battery ground cable, then remove engine hood.
2. Drain engine oil and engine coolant.
3. Remove battery and battery carrier, then the air cleaner assembly.
4. Remove radiator assembly.
5. On models equipped with A/C, remove A/C condenser fan, then the A/C compressor. Do not disconnect refrigerant lines.
6. On models equipped with power steering, remove power steering pump. Do not disconnect power steering pump hoses.
7. On all models, disconnect and mark all electrical connectors from engine.
8. Disconnect accelerator cable.
9. On models equipped with automatic transaxle, disconnect throttle linkage.
10. On all models, disconnect the following hoses:
    a. Heater inlet and outlet hoses.
    b. Fuel pump inlet and return hoses.
    c. Brake booster hose from intake manifold.
    d. VSV vacuum hose.
    e. Emission control hoses. **Before removing emission control hoses, note location to ensure correct installation.**
11. Disconnect air suction filter from cylinder block, if equipped.
12. Remove transaxle upper mount attaching bolts.
13. Raise and support vehicle, then remove front exhaust pipe.
14. On models equipped with automatic transaxle, remove oil cooler pipes.
15. On models equipped with manual transaxle, disconnect clutch release cable.
16. On all models, remove stiffener plates.
17. Disconnect engine mounting absorber from crossmember, then remove two engine mount attaching bolts.
18. On models equipped with automatic transaxle, remove torque converter cover, then the torque converter attaching bolts.
19. On all models, cover driveshaft boots with shop towel to prevent damage and dirt entry when engine is removed.
20. Support transaxle with a suitable jack, then remove transaxle lower mount attaching bolts.
21. Attach suitable engine hoist to engine lift brackets, then remove engine from vehicle.
22. Reverse procedure to install, noting the following:
    a. Torque transaxle mount attaching bolts to 29 ft. lbs. for 14 mm bolts and 43 ft. lbs. for 17 mm bolts.
    b. Torque stiffener plate attaching bolts to 29 ft. lbs.
    c. Torque automatic transaxle cooler pipes to 25 ft. lbs.
    d. Torque engine mount nuts to 33 ft. lbs.

1987 TERCEL EXC. WAGON

1. Disconnect battery ground cable, then remove battery and coolant reserve tank.
2. Scribe reference marks in engine hood hinge area, then remove hood.
3. Remove engine under covers.
4. Drain coolant, then drain radiator into suitable container.
5. Remove windshield washer reservoir tank.
6. On models equipped with cruise control, disconnect control cable and connector, then remove actuator attaching bolts and the actuator.
7. On all models, disconnect accelerator cable.
8. On models equipped with auto. trans., disconnect transmission throttle cable.
9. On all models, disconnect fuel hoses from fuel pump and plug open ends.
10. Remove charcoal canister.
11. Disconnect brake booster hose.
12. Disconnect heater hoses.
13. Disconnect speedometer cable from transaxle.
14. Disconnect transmission control cables from transaxle.
15. Remove clutch slave cylinder from transaxle and position aside. **Do not disconnect hydraulic lines.**
16. On models equipped with man. trans., remove gear selector bell crank.
17. On all models, disconnect the following wires:
    a. Ground strap from left front fender apron.
    b. Oxygen sensor wire.
    c. Water temperature sensor gauge wire.
    d. Cold Mixture Heater (CMH) water temperature switch wire.
    e. On models equipped with man. trans., back-up light switch wire.
    f. On models equipped with auto. trans., neutral safety switch wire.
    g. On all models, Integrated Ignition Assembly (IIA) wire.
    h. Cooling fan water temperature switch wire.
18. Disconnect wiring harness from intake manifold.
19. Remove intake manifold-to-engine block brace attaching bolt and nut, then the ground strap and bracket.
20. Disconnect the wire connectors from the following components:
    a. Solenoid and Cold Mixture Heater (CMH).
    b. Alternator.
    c. Starter.
21. Remove Vacuum Switching Valve (VSV).
22. On models equipped with power steering, remove pump from engine with hoses attached and position aside.
23. On models equipped with A/C, remove compressor with hoses attached and position aside.
24. On all models, disconnect exhaust pipe from exhaust manifold.
25. Disconnect driveshafts from transaxle.
26. Attach suitable engine lifting equipment, then remove rear mount through bolt and insulator.
27. Remove front mount through bolt, then the front mount from the cylinder block.
28. Remove right side mount through bolt and insulator.
29. Remove left side mount attaching bolts, then the mount.
30. Carefully lift engine and transaxle assembly from vehicle and place on suitable stand.
31. Remove starter from engine.
32. On models equipped with auto. trans., remove flywheel inspection cover, then rotate crankshaft as necessary to loosen six torque converter attaching bolts.
33. On all models, remove transaxle from engine.
34. Reverse procedure to install.

1983–86 CAMRY

1. Remove hood, then drain cooling system.
2. Remove battery.
3. On automatic transaxle models, disconnect throttle cable and bracket from throttle body.
4. On all models, disconnect accelerator cable from throttle body.
5. Remove cruise control actuator and bracket as follows:
    a. Disconnect vacuum hose, then remove actuator cover.
    b. Disconnect electrical connector, then remove actuator and bracket assembly.
6. Remove radiator, air cleaner, air flow

meter and air cleaner hose assembly.
7. Mark, then disconnect all electrical connections and vacuum hoses from engine.
8. Mark, then carefully disconnect the following EFI electrical connectors:
   a. All electrical connectors from left side fender apron.
   b. Solenoid resistor electrical connector.
   c. Water temperature sensor electrical connector.
   d. Start injector time switch and cold start injector electrical connectors.
   e. Air valve and throttle position sensor electrical connectors.
   f. The remaining injector electrical connectors.
   g. Oxygen sensor electrical connector.
   h. Engine ground strap.
9. Pull EFI wire harness from right side fender apron.
10. Disconnect and plug heater hoses.
11. Disconnect and plug inlet hose from fuel filter.
12. Disconnect and plug return hose from fuel return line.
13. Disconnect speedometer cable from transaxle.
14. On manual transaxle models, remove clutch release cylinder and hose bracket assembly. Do not disconnect clutch release cylinder lines.
15. On manual transaxle models, disconnect transaxle control cable as follows:
   a. Remove clips and plate washers, then disconnect each control cable from shift and selector levers.
   b. Remove clips, then disconnect each cable from control bracket.
16. On automatic transaxle models, disconnect transaxle control cable as follows.
   a. Remove retaining clip, then disconnect control cable from swivel.
   b. Remove retaining clip, then disconnect cable from bracket.
17. On all models, remove A/C compressor from engine and position aside, if equipped. Do not disconnect refrigerant lines.
18. Raise and support vehicle.
19. Wrap both front driveshaft boots with clean towels. Remove six attaching nuts from driveshaft while depressing brake pedal, then disconnect driveshafts.
20. On automatic transaxle models, disconnect left hand steering knuckle.
21. On all models, remove power steering pump from engine and position aside, if equipped. Do not disconnect power steering lines.
22. Disconnect from exhaust pipe from exhaust manifold.
23. Remove front and rear mounts from crossmember.
24. Lower vehicle.
25. Install suitable engine lifting equipment onto engine.
26. Remove engine and transaxle assembly from vehicle.
27. Reverse procedure to install. Torque front and rear mounts to 29 ft. lbs. Torque driveshaft nuts to 27 ft. lbs.

1987 CAMRY

1. Disconnect battery ground cable.
2. Drain cooling system into suitable container, then remove hood.
3. Remove engine compartment hood, then the radiator.
4. On models equipped with auto. trans., disconnect throttle valve cable and bracket from throttle body.
5. Disconnect accelerator cable from throttle body.
6. Remove cruise control actuator and bracket.
7. Disconnect ground wire from alternator upper bracket.
8. Remove air cleaner assembly, air flow meter and air cleaner hose.
9. Remove igniter, then disconnect heater hoses.
10. Disconnect and plug fuel inlet hose from fuel filter and fuel return hose from fuel return tube.
11. Disconnect speedometer cable.
12. On models equipped with man. trans., remove clutch slave cylinder and tube bracket from transaxle and position aside. **Do not disconnect any hydraulic hoses.**
13. Disconnect shift cable(s) from transaxle.
14. Remove compressor without disconnecting hoses and position aside.
15. Disconnect check connector.
16. Disconnect ground straps from left front fender apron.
17. Disconnect wire connectors from relay box and solenoid resistor.
18. Disconnect brake booster vacuum hose, then the idle-up vacuum hose.
19. Disconnect charcoal canister vacuum hose.
20. Raise and support vehicle, then drain engine oil.
21. Remove engine under covers and lower suspension crossmember.
22. Remove driveshafts.
23. Remove power steering pump without disconnecting hoses and position aside.
24. Disconnect exhaust pipe from catalytic converter.
25. Disconnect engine mount center member.
26. Lower vehicle, then disconnect three wire connectors from ECU and pull out connectors from cowl panel.
27. Attach suitable lifting equipment to engine, then remove right side mount insulator through bolt.
28. Remove left side mount through bolt, then the insulator from the bracket. Remove bracket.
29. Carefully remove engine from vehicle and place on suitable stand.
30. Remove stiffener plate. On models equipped with auto. trans., remove flywheel inspection cover, then rotate crankshaft as necessary to loosen six torque converter attaching bolts.
31. On all models, remove transaxle from engine.
32. Reverse procedure to install.

1984–86 VAN

1. Disconnect battery ground cable.
2. Remove right seat from vehicle.
3. Remove engine service cover attaching screws, then the cover.
4. Drain cooling system.
5. Disconnect and plug, radiator, heater, brake booster, reservoir tank, fuel and charcoal canister hoses.
6. Remove air cleaner assembly.
7. Remove power steering pump, if equipped.
8. Remove accelerator cable and bracket from throttle body.
9. Disconnect and mark all electrical connectors from engine.
10. Remove fan shroud, fan, fan clutch and water pump pulley.
11. Disconnect ECU electrical connectors.
12. Remove A/C compressor from engine, if equipped. **Do not disconnect refrigerant lines.**
13. Raise vehicle approximately 40 inches, then support vehicle.
14. Drain oil from engine.
15. Disconnect driveshaft from transmission.
16. Remove front exhaust pipe.
17. Disconnect transmission select and shift control cables.
18. Remove clutch release cylinder.
19. Remove starter motor from engine.
20. Disconnect speedometer cable and ground strap.
21. Disconnect back-up light switch electrical connector.
22. Disconnect rear heater control cable, if equipped.
23. Disconnect and plug heater hoses.
24. Disconnect engine ground strap from engine mount.
25. Remove engine under cover attaching screws, then the under cover.
26. On automatic transmission models, disconnect and plug transmission fluid cooler lines.
27. Remove strut bars.
28. Position suitable engine removal equipment below engine.
29. Remove engine and transmission assembly from underneath vehicle.
30. Reverse procedure to install.

1987 VAN

1. Disconnect battery ground cable.
2. Remove right front seat from vehicle.
3. Remove engine service hole cover, then drain coolant into suitable container.
4. Disconnect the following:
   a. Upper and lower radiator hoses.
   b. Radiator breather hose and radiator reservoir tank hose.
   c. Brake booster hose.
   d. Fuel inlet and outlet. Plug openings to prevent leakage and dirt entry.
   e. Charcoal canister hose.
   f. Water temperature gauge sender connector.
   g. Oil pressure switch and distributor connectors.
   h. On models equipped with A/C; compressor clutch electrical connector, A/C idle-up Vacuum Switching Valve (VSV) and Electronic Fuel Injection (EFI) VSV.
   i. On models equipped with auto. trans., disconnect three wire connectors.

j. Water temperature switch connector.
k. Alternator wiring and air flow meter wire connector.
l. Solenoid resistor connector.
m. Two connectors.
5. Remove air cleaner hose, then the power steering pump.
6. Disconnect accelerator cable from throttle linkage.
7. On models equipped with auto. trans., disconnect throttle valve cable from throttle linkage.
8. Remove radiator as follows:
   a. On models equipped with auto. trans., disconnect oil cooler hoses.
   b. Remove fan shroud, then radiator upper attaching bolt.
   c. Raise and support vehicle.
   d. Remove engine under cover from underneath vehicle.
   e. Working below vehicle, remove radiator attaching nuts and withdraw radiator from the frame.
   f. Lower vehicle.
8. Remove the left side center pillar garnish moulding, seat belt retractor and cover, then disconnect Electronic Control Unit (ECU) wire connectors.
9. On models equipped with A/C, remove compressor with hoses attached and position aside.
10. Raise vehicle approximately 40 inches, then support vehicle.
11. Drain oil from engine.
12. Disconnect driveshaft(s).
13. Remove front exhaust pipe.
14. Disconnect transmission select and shift control cables.
15. Remove clutch slave cylinder.
16. Remove starter motor from engine.
17. Disconnect speedometer cable and ground strap.
18. Disconnect back-up light switch electrical connector.
19. On four wheel drive models, disconnect transfer case indicator lamp connector.
20. On models equipped with rear heater, disconnect rear heater control cables.
21. Disconnect and plug heater hoses.
22. Disconnect engine ground strap from engine mount.
23. Disconnect oil level sensor connector.
24. On two wheel drive models, remove strut bars. On four wheel drive models, remove stabilizer bar.
25. Position suitable engine removal equipment below engine.
26. Disconnect rear engine mount, then remove the engine front member-to-frame attaching bolts.
27. On four wheel drive models, remove front suspension rear crossmember.
28. On all models, lower engine and transmission assembly to floor, then remove front member from engine.
29. Separate engine from transmission assembly.
30. Reverse procedure to install.

COROLLA

W/4A-C ENGINE

1983–87 Rear Wheel Drive Models

1. Disconnect battery ground and positive cables, then remove battery, battery carrier and engine compartment hood.
2. Remove air cleaner assembly, then drain coolant from radiator and engine block.
3. On vehicle equipped with air conditioning, remove fan shroud.
4. Disconnect radiator hoses from engine and remove radiator from vehicle.
5. On vehicles equipped with power steering, remove power steering pump drive belt, mounting bolts and power steering pump. Position pump aside.
6. On vehicles, equipped with air conditioning, remove compressor drive belt, mounting bolts, then position compressor aside. **Do not disconnect air conditioner compressor hoses.**
7. Remove cooling fan, fan pulley and drive belt.
8. Disconnect heater inlet hose, brake booster hose, fuel lines from fuel pump, canister hose, vacuum switching valve hose and emission control vacuum hoses. **Prior to removing vacuum hoses, identify them so they can be returned to their original locations.**
9. Disconnect wire from carburetor, ground strap, water temperature sending unit wire, thermo sensor wire and Cold Mixture Heater (CMH) wire.
10. Disconnect heater outlet hose, oil pressure switch electrical connector, starter wire for terminals 30 and 50, engine ground strap, alternator electrical connectors and distributor wire.
11. Disconnect engine electrical harness from engine block and position aside.
12. Disconnect electrical connectors from emission control valve assembly and position aside.
13. Disconnect electrical connector from oxygen sensor.
14. Disconnect hose, if equipped from air suction valve.
15. Disconnect transmission throttle valve cable.
16. On vehicles equipped with manual transmission, remove shift lever.
17. Raise and support vehicle.
18. Drain oil from engine.
19. Remove exhaust front pipe clamp. Disconnect and remove exhaust front pipe from exhaust manifold and catalytic converter.
20. If equipped, remove power steering gear housing.
21. Remove driveshaft from transmission. **Insert tool number 09325-12010 or equivalent into transmission output shaft to prevent oil leakage.**
22. Disconnect speedometer cable from transmission.
23. On vehicles equipped with manual transmission, disconnect electrical connector from back-up light switch.
24. On vehicles equipped with manual transmission, remove clutch slave cylinder.
25. On vehicles equipped with automatic transmission, disconnect two oil cooler lines.
26. Position a suitable jack under transmission. **Position a wooden block between jack and transmission pan to prevent damage of transmission.**
27. Remove rear engine mounts and ground strap.
28. Remove engine mount bolts.
29. Using a suitable hoist, remove engine and transmission assembly from vehicle. **If vehicle is equipped with air conditioning, use care not to damage condenser when lifting engine and transmission assembly from vehicle.**
30. Separate engine from transmission assembly.
31. Reverse procedure to install. Torque rear engine mounts to 14-22 ft. lbs. on 1983-84 models or 38 ft. lbs. on 1985 models. Torque transmission mounting bolts to 37-57 ft. lbs. Be sure to remove tool previously installed onto transmission output shaft.

1984–85 Front Wheel Drive Models

1. Disconnect battery ground cable, then remove engine hood.
2. Drain engine oil and engine coolant.
3. Remove air cleaner assembly, then the coolant reservoir tank.
4. Disconnect radiator fan electrical connector, then remove radiator hoses.
5. Remove radiator attaching bolts, then the radiator and shroud as an assembly.
6. Disconnect actuator cable, accelerator cable and throttle cable from carburetor.
7. Disconnect and mark all electrical connectors and vacuum hoses from engine.
8. Disconnect fuel hoses and fuel pump, then the coolant hoses.
9. On models equipped with power steering remove power steering pump and position aside. Do not disconnect power steering pump hoses.
10. On models equipped with A/C, remove compressor attaching bolts, then the compressor and position aside. Do not disconnect refrigerant lines.
11. On all models, disconnect speedometer cable from transaxle.
12. On models equipped with manual transaxle, remove clutch release cylinder attaching bracket, then the clutch release cylinder. Do not disconnect clutch release cylinder pipe and hose.
13. On all models, remove control cable clip and washers, then disconnect control cable from the shift outer lever and select outer lever.
14. Raise and support vehicle, then disconnect exhaust pipe from exhaust manifold.
15. Remove front and rear engine mount attaching bolts, then engine crossmember from body.
16. Remove six driveshaft to side gear shaft attaching nuts while depressing brake pedal, then disconnect driveshafts.
17. Lower vehicle, then attach engine hoist to engine lift brackets. **Ensure**

engine harness is on front side of chain.

18. Remove right and left side engine mount through bolts, then the left side engine mount from transaxle.
19. Remove left side engine mount bracket from transaxle.
20. Lift engine and transaxle from vehicle.
21. Reverse procedure to install, noting the following:
    a. Torque driveshaft to side gear shaft attaching nuts to 27 ft. lbs.
    b. Torque crossmember to body attaching nuts to 29 ft. lbs.
    c. Torque front and rear engine mount attaching nuts to 46 ft. lbs.

W/4A-GE & 4A-GEC ENGINES

1985–87 Rear Wheel Drive Models

1. Disconnect battery ground cable, then remove engine hood and under cover (if equipped).
2. Remove air cleaner hose, then disconnect actuator and accelerator cable from bracket.
3. Remove console and shift lever.
4. Drain engine and transmission oil, then disconnect two oil cooler hoses.
5. Drain coolant from radiator, then remove two heater hoses.
6. Disconnect coolant reservoir hose, then the two radiator hoses from engine.
7. Remove radiator attaching bolts, then the radiator and fan shroud as an assembly.
8. Remove air cleaner assembly.
9. On models equipped with power steering, remove power steering pump and bracket and position aside. **Do not disconnect power steering pump hoses.**
10. On all models, remove water pump drive belt, fluid coupling with fan and water pump pulley.
11. On models equipped with A/C, remove A/C compressor and bracket and position aside. **Do not disconnect refrigerant lines.**
12. Disconnect coil wire and spark plug wires cylinder head, then remove distributor attaching bolts and distributor.
13. Remove exhaust pipe bracket attaching bolts, then the exhaust pipe bracket.
14. Disconnect exhaust pipe from exhaust manifold.
15. Disconnect starter motor electrical connectors.
16. Remove fuel hoses from pulsation damper and pressure regulator.
17. Remove cold start injector pipe, then the PCV hose from intake manifold.
18. Mark and disconnect all necessary engine vacuum hoses, then remove wire harness and vacuum pipe from timing cover.
19. Mark and disconnect all engine electrical connectors.
20. Raise and support vehicle.
21. Remove engine mount attaching bolt from each side of engine.
22. Remove clutch release cylinder, then the propeller shaft.
23. Disconnect speedometer cable, then the back-up light switch electrical connector.
24. Disconnect grounding cables from clutch housing and extension housing.
25. Lower vehicle, then attach suitable hoist to engine lift brackets.
26. Support rear of engine using a suitable jack, then remove four rear engine mount attaching bolts.
27. Remove engine and transmission from vehicle as an assembly.
28. Separate engine from transmission.
29. Reverse procedure to install, noting the following:
    a. Torque rear engine mount attaching bolts to 38 ft. lbs.
    b. Torque clutch release cylinder attaching bolts to 13 ft. lbs.
    c. Torque A/C compressor and power steering pump brackets to 29 ft. lbs.
    d. Torque exhaust manifold attaching nuts and bolts to 18 ft. lbs.
    e. Torque pulsation damper to 22 ft. lbs.
    f. Torque cold start injector pipe to 13 ft. lbs.

W/4A-LC ENGINE

1986–87 Front Wheel Drive Models

1. Remove hood, then the battery.
2. Drain engine coolant, engine oil and transaxle fluid.
3. Remove air cleaner hose, then the air cleaner.
4. Remove coolant reservoir, then the radiator with shroud.
5. Disconnect actuator cables, accelerator cable and on models with automatic transaxle, the throttle cable.
6. Disconnect the following connectors:
    a. VCV and oxygen sensor.
    b. On models with manual transaxle, disconnect back-up light switch.
    c. On models with automatic transaxle, disconnect neutral start switch.
    d. On all models, disconnect water temperature switch, sender gauge and distributor.
    e. Starter connector and wire, then the engine and transaxle bond cables.
    f. Oil pressure switch and A/C compressor.
    g. EBCV, CMH and fuel cut solenoid.
7. Disconnect all necessary vacuum hoses, then the fuel hoses from pump. **Plug fuel lines to prevent gasoline leakage and/or dirt entry.**
8. Remove coolant hoses, then on models with power steering, disconnect pump.
9. On models with A/C, remove compressor and position aside. Do not disconnect pressure or return lines.
10. On all models, disconnect speedometer cable from transaxle.
11. On models with manual transaxle, remove clutch slave cylinder and position aside. Do not disconnect hydraulic lines.
12. On all models, remove clip and washers, then disconnect shift linkage.
13. Raise and support vehicle.
14. Disconnect exhaust pipe from exhaust manifold, then the engine front and rear mounting from center member.
15. Remove engine mount center member, then disconnect driveshafts from transaxle.
16. Lower vehicle.
17. Attach suitable engine lifting equipment to engine.
18. Remove RH and LH mount through bolts, then remove LH mount bracket from transaxle.
19. Remove engine and transaxle from vehicle.
20. Remove starter and flywheel/flexplate inspection cover.
21. On models equipped with auto. trans., rotate crankshaft as necessary to gain access to and remove six torque converter attaching bolts.
22. Separate engine from transaxle assembly.
23. Reverse procedure to install.

W/4A-GELC ENGINE

Corolla FX-16

1. Disconnect battery ground and positive cables, then remove battery and engine compartment hood.
2. Remove right and left side engine under covers.
3. Drain engine oil into suitable container.
4. Drain coolant from radiator and engine block into suitable container.
5. On models equipped with man. trans., drain transaxle fluid into suitable container.
6. Remove air cleaner assembly and coolant reservoir tank.
7. Remove radiator and coolant fan as an assembly.
8. Disconnect heater hoses from coolant inlet housing.
9. Disconnect fuel pressure hose from fuel filter, then the heater and air hoses from air valve.
10. Disconnect fuel return hose from fuel pressure regulator.
11. On models equipped with man. trans., remove clutch slave cylinder without disconnecting hydraulic line and position aside.
12. On all models, disconnect vacuum hose from charcoal canister.
13. Disconnect transaxle shift control cables from transaxle.
14. Disconnect speedometer cable, then the cruise control cable (if equipped), accelerator cable and accelerator link.
15. On models equipped with cruise control, remove cruise control actuator.
16. On all models, disconnect ignition coil wiring, then remove coil.
17. Remove right hand side interior cowl panel, then disconnect No. 4 junction block connectors.
18. Remove Electronic Control Unit (ECU) cover, then disconnect ECU connectors.
19. Pull engine main wire harness into engine compartment, then disconnect the following:
    a. No. 2 junction block connectors (located in engine compartment).

b. Starter cable from battery positive.
c. Ground strap terminals.
d. Washer change valve connector.
e. Cruise control vacuum pump and vacuum switch connectors (if equipped).
f. Solenoid resistor connector.

20. Disconnect brake booster hose from intake manifold.
21. Remove A/C compressor and power steering pump (if equipped) with lines attached and position aside.
22. Disconnect oxygen sensor electrical connector, then remove oxygen sensor.
23. Disconnect oil cooler hoses from oil cooler.
24. Raise and support vehicle, then disconnect catalytic converter clamp, engine pipe clamp and engine pipe from exhaust manifold.
25. Disconnect front and rear engine mounts-to-center member attaching bolts, then remove front mount through bolt and mount.
26. Remove center member-to-frame attaching bolts, then the center member.
27. Remove axle-to-side gear shaft attaching bolts, then disconnect right side lower arm from steering knuckle and separate. Remove axle shafts from side gear shafts and position aside with suitable wire.
28. Lower vehicle to ground level.
29. Attach suitable lifting equipment to engine/transaxle assembly, then remove right and left side mounts.
30. Carefully lift engine/transaxle assembly from vehicle and place on suitable stand.
31. Remove radiator fan temperature switch connector and cold start injector time switch connector.
32. Disconnect vacuum hoses from Bi-Metal Vacuum Switching Valves (BVSV), then remove coolant inlet housing attaching bolts and nut.
33. Disconnect hoses from coolant bypass tubes, then remove coolant inlet housing.
34. Disconnect back-up lamp switch connector, water temperature sensor connector and water temperature switch connector.
35. On models equipped with auto. trans., neutral start switch connectors and transaxle solenoid connector.
36. On models equipped with auto. trans., rotate crankshaft as necessary to gain access to and remove six torque converter attaching bolts.
37. Remove starter assembly, then separate transaxle from engine.
38. Reverse procedure to install.

1985 MR2

1. Disconnect battery ground cable.
2. Remove fuel tank protector and engine under cover.
3. Drain engine oil and engine coolant.
4. Remove air cleaner assembly, then the accelerator link and speedometer cable clamp.
5. Mark and disconnect all necessary engine vacuum hoses.
6. Disconnect heater hoses from cylinder head rear cover and water inlet housing, then the radiator hose from water inlet.
7. Disconnect engine air drain hose from engine air drain.
8. Disconnect radiator hose from water filler, then remove PCV hose.
9. Remove EGR vacuum modulator and bracket, then the accelerator cable clamp from engine hanger.
10. Disconnect cold start injector electrical connector, then remove two injector pipe attaching bolts and injector pipe.
11. Remove pulsation damper and two gaskets.
12. Remove fuel pipe from intake manifold and cylinder head rear cover.
13. Remove pressure regulator attaching bolts, then the pressure regulator and fuel pipe as an assembly.
14. Disconnect coil wire from distributor.
15. Mark and disconnect all necessary engine electrical connectors.
16. Raise and support vehicle.
17. Disconnect speedometer cable, then remove transaxle protector.
18. On models equipped with A/C, remove A/C compressor attaching bolts, then the compressor. Do not disconnect refrigerant lines.
19. On all models, disconnect control cables from shift outer lever and select lever.
20. Remove clutch release cylinder and control bracket.
21. Disconnect oil cooler hoses, if equipped.
22. Remove front exhaust pipe.
23. Remove six driveshaft to side gear shaft attaching nuts while depressing brake pedal, then disconnect driveshafts.
24. Remove flywheel housing under cover, then the front and rear engine mount attaching bolts.
25. Place suitable engine support under engine.
26. Lower vehicle frame, while supporting engine, then remove right and left engine mount attaching bolts.
27. Slowly raise vehicle until engine is clear from body. **Use caution not to damage throttle position sensor and oxygen sensor.**
28. Reverse procedure to install, noting the following:
    a. Torque engine mount attaching bolts to 38 ft. lbs. for 10 mm bolts or 58 ft. lbs. for 12 mm bolts.
    b. Torque driveshaft to side gear shaft attaching nuts to 27 ft. lbs.

1986–87 MR2

1. Disconnect battery ground cable.
2. Remove fuel tank protectors and engine under cover.
3. Drain engine oil into suitable container.
4. Drain engine coolant into suitable container.
5. Disconnect accelerator cable, cruise control cable (if equipped) and on models equipped with auto. trans., throttle valve cable.
6. On models equipped with cruise control, disconnect cruise control vacuum hose.
7. On all models, remove battery.
8. On 1986 models, proceed as follows:
    a. Remove air cleaner hose.
    b. Remove air cleaner assembly.
    c. Remove accelerator link and speedometer cable clamp.
9. On 1987 models, proceed as follows:
    a. Disconnect air flow meter wire connector.
    b. Disconnect air cleaner hoses from air flow meter.
    c. Remove air flow meter attaching bolts, then the air flow meter.
10. On all models, disconnect heater hoses, then the radiator hose from coolant inlet.
11. Disconnect air bleeder hose from coolant inlet housing.
12. Disconnect fuel hose from filter, then the fuel return hose.
13. Disconnect vacuum hose from charcoal canister.
14. Disconnect engine wire and engine main wire connector, then on models equipped with man. trans, the back-up light switch connector.
15. Disconnect speedometer cable, then remove transaxle protector (if equipped).
16. Remove ground strap from coolant inlet housing.
17. Remove coolant reservoir tank.
18. On models equipped with A/C, remove A/C compressor drive belt.
19. Remove alternator belt, then disconnect radiator hose from coolant outlet.
20. Disconnect brake booster hose from intake manifold.
21. Disconnect the following wire connections:
    a. Two igniter connectors.
    b. Noise filter connector.
    c. Engine compartment cooling fan wire connector.
    d. Engine-to-body ground strap connector.
    e. On models equipped with A/C, compressor clutch connector.
    f. On 1987 models, solenoid resistor connector.
22. Disconnect secondary cable from ignition coil.
23. Remove rear luggage compartment trim, then disconnect circuit opening relay connector, Electronic Control Unit (ECU) connectors, cooling fan computer connector and engine wire and engine main wire connectors. Pull wire harness into engine compartment.
24. On models equipped with A/C, remove A/C compressor without disconnecting pressure and return hoses and position aside.
25. On all models, disconnect transaxle shift linkage.
26. On models equipped with man. trans., remove clutch slave cylinder and control bracket and position aside. **Do not disconnect hydraulic hoses.**
27. Disconnect oil cooler hoses from oil cooler.
28. On models equipped with auto. trans., disconnect transmission oil cooler lines from oil cooler.
29. Remove exhaust pipe-to-exhaust

manifold attaching nuts, then lower exhaust pipe.
30. Disconnect oxygen sensor electrical connector, then remove oxygen sensor.
31. Remove flywheel/flexplate inspection cover attaching bolts and stiffener (if equipped), then remove cover.
32. Remove right side driveshaft, then disconnect left side driveshaft from side gear shaft and wire aside. **Wire shaft in such a way that inboard end is above outboard end.**
33. Remove front mount through bolt, then the mount.
34. Remove rear mount through bolt, then the mount.
35. Position suitable engine lifting and support equipment under engine/transaxle assembly, then lower vehicle.
36. Remove right side mount through bolt, then the mount.
37. Remove left side mount through bolt, then slowly raise vehicle, ensuring all wires, hoses and cables are clear. **Use caution not to damage throttle position sensor while raising vehicle.**
38. Remove engine/transaxle assembly from under vehicle.
39. Remove cold start injector time switch connector.
40. Disconnect vacuum hoses from Bi-Metal Vacuum Switching Valves (BVSV), then remove coolant inlet housing attaching bolts and nut.
41. Disconnect hoses from coolant bypass tubes, then remove coolant inlet housing.
42. On models equipped with auto. trans., disconnect back-up and neutral start switch connectors and solenoid connector.
43. On models equipped with auto. trans., rotate crankshaft as necessary to gain access to and remove six torque converter attaching bolts.
44. Remove starter assembly, then separate transaxle from engine.
45. Reverse procedure to install.

1983–84 STARLET

1. Disconnect battery ground cable and remove hood.
2. Disconnect air cleaner hose from air cleaner, then drain coolant from radiator and engine block.
3. Disconnect throttle cable.
4. Disconnect the following electrical connectors, if equipped, from the engine:
   a. Air flow meter and oxygen sensor electrical connectors.
   b. Solenoid resistor and start injector timer switch electrical connectors.
   c. Water temperature sensor and throttle positioner sensor electrical connectors.
   d. Cold start injector, air valve and injector electrical connectors.
   e. Disconnect engine ground strap and engine electrical harness clamps from engine.
   f. Disconnect clamp and electrical connector from alternator.
   g. Two grounding straps from engine.
   h. Distributor coil wire and radio noise suppressor.
5. Disconnect charcoal canister hose, fuel inlet and outlet lines, heater inlet and outlet hose and brake booster hose. **Do not disconnect brake booster portion marked with an arrow.**
6. Remove radiator and radiator grille.
7. Remove bolts, air cleaner and air flow meter assembly from engine.
8. Disconnect electrical connector from fan motor, then remove bolts, radiator upper baffle, fan shroud, fan and motor.
9. On vehicles equipped with manual transmission, remove transmission shift lever.
10. Remove engine mount bolts. Using a suitable hoist, raise and support vehicle.
11. Drain engine oil.
12. Remove driveshaft from transmission. **Insert tool number 09325-12010 or equivalent, onto transmission output shaft to prevent oil leakage.**
13. Disconnect electrical connectors, then remove bolts and starter from engine.
14. Disconnect speedometer and clutch release cables from transmission.
15. Position a suitable piece of wood between engine oil pan and front crossmember.
16. Remove rear engine mounts.
17. Lower vehicle, then using a suitable hoist, remove engine and transmission assembly.
18. Reverse procedure to install.

1983–EARLY 1986 SUPRA & 1983–87 CRESSIDA

1. Disconnect battery cables, then remove battery from vehicle.
2. Drain coolant from radiator and engine block.
3. Remove hood and windshield wiper/washer tank.
4. Disconnect air hose, remove air cleaner assembly and air flow meter from engine.
5. On vehicles equipped with automatic transmission, remove throttle cable bracket from cylinder head cover.
6. Remove accelerator and actuator cable bracket from cylinder head cover.
7. Disconnect ground strap from cylinder head, electrical connectors from oxygen sensor, oil pressure sending unit and alternator.
8. Disconnect high tension wire from ignition coil, electrical connectors from distributor, water temperature sending unit and thermo switch, if equipped.
9. Disconnect starter cables, then Electronically Controlled Transmission (ECT) connectors (if equipped).
10. Disconnect electrical connectors from solenoid resistor and knock sensor if equipped.
11. Disconnect brake booster and crulse control actuator (if equipped) hoses from intake manifold, then the EGR vacuum hose.
12. Disconnect heater hoses, then the EFI wire harness from ECU.
13. Remove screws, fan shroud and fluid coupling from vehicle.
14. Remove bolts and engine under cover from engine.
15. Remove transmission oil cooler lines, if equipped, bolts and radiator from vehicle.
16. Disconnect hoses from coolant reservoir tank, then remove attaching screws and reservoir tank from vehicle.
17. On vehicle equipped with air conditioning, remove drive belt, mounting bolts and position compressor aside. Do not disconnect compressor lines.
18. Disconnect power steering pump inlet and outlet lines. Remove bolts, pulley, drive belt and pump from bracket.
19. Remove engine mount bolts and ground strap.
20. On vehicles equipped with manual transmission, remove transmission shift lever.
21. Raise and support vehicle.
22. Drain oil from engine.
23. Disconnect exhaust pipe from exhaust manifold and remove exhaust pipe clamp from transmission housing.
24. On vehicles equipped with manual transmission, remove clutch release cylinder without disconnecting hydraulic hose and position aside.
25. Remove speedometer cable and on vehicles equipped with automatic transmission, disconnect shift linkage from shift lever.
26. On vehicles equipped with manual transmission, disconnect electrical connector from back-up light switch.
27. Remove stiffener plate and ground strap.
28. Disconnect and plug fuel lines and hose.
29. On Supra and 1985-87 Cressida models, remove power steering gear housing and suspend from under vehicle with string or wire in such a way as to protect pressure and return hoses.
30. Remove intermediate shaft from drive shaft. Position a suitable jack under transmission. **Position a wooden block between jack and transmission pan to prevent damage to transmission.**
31. Install a wooden block between firewall and rear of cylinder head to prevent damage to heater hose.
32. Remove engine rear crossmember and ground strap.
33. Using a suitable hoist, remove engine and transmission assembly from vehicle and place in suitable stand.
34. Remove starter and exhaust pipe bracket from engine, then separate transmission from engine.
35. Reverse procedure to install.

LATE 1986 & 1987 SUPRA

1. Disconnect battery ground cable, then remove engine compartment hood.
2. Remove engine under cover, then drain coolant from radiator and engine block into suitable container.
3. Drain engine oil into suitable container.
4. On models less turbo, disconnect air

flow meter wire connector and power steering air hose, then remove air cleaner case attaching bolts. Remove air cleaner case with hoses.
5. On models with turbo, remove air cleaner pipe and hose, then disconnect three air hoses and PCV hose. Disconnect air flow meter wire connector and power steering air hose, then remove air cleaner hose, air flow meter and air cleaner cap.
6. On all models, remove radiator as follows:
   a. Disconnect condenser fan motor connector.
   b. Disconnect radiator hoses and coolant reservoir tank hose.
   c. On models equipped with auto. trans., disconnect cooler hoses from radiator.
   d. Remove radiator supports, then the radiator.
7. Remove A/C belt, alternator drive belt, water pump pulley and fan clutch.
8. Remove power steering belt, then disconnect brake booster hose, heater valve hose, cruise control hose and charcoal canister hose.
9. Disconnect the following:
   a. Ground strap from left front fender apron.
   b. Battery ground cable.
   c. Noise filter connector.
   d. Theft deterrent horn connector.
   e. Check connector.
   f. Solenoid resistor connector.
   g. On models less turbo, ignition coil connector. On turbo models, igniter connectors.
   h. Main relay connector and alternator connector.
   i. On models less turbo, oxygen sensor connector.
   j. On all models, heater valve connector.
   k. Engine rear side ground connection.
   l. Electronic Control Unit (ECU) and Electronically Controlled Transmission (ECT) connectors.
10. Disconnect cruise control cable, accelerator cable, and on models equipped with auto. trans, transmission throttle valve cable.
11. Disconnect heater hoses, then remove A/C compressor.
12. On turbo models, remove air cleaner hose and radiator outlet hose.
13. Disconnect power steering hoses, then remove power steering pump.
14. On models equipped with man. trans., remove shift lever.
15. Disconnect ground strap from fuel hose clamp.
16. On turbo models, remove engine mounting shock absorber.
17. On all models, disconnect fuel hoses, then remove exhaust pipe.
18. Remove driveshaft, then disconnect speedometer cable from transmission.
19. On models equipped with auto. trans., remove manual shift linkage.
20. On all models, remove No. 1 front crossmember.
21. On models equipped with man. trans., remove clutch slave cylinder without disconnecting hydraulic hose and position aside.
22. Position suitable jack under transmission oil pan. **Place a piece of wood between jack and pan to prevent damage to transmission.**
23. On all models, place suitable piece of wood between firewall and cylinder head to prevent damaging heater hose.
24. Remove rear engine mount support member and ground strap from body.
25. Attach suitable lifting device to engine/transmission assembly, then remove engine mounting nuts and washers.
26. Carefully lift engine/transmission assembly from vehicle, then place on suitable stand.
27. On models equipped with auto. trans., remove transmission oil cooler tubes.
28. Remove transmission assembly.
29. Reverse procedure to install.

1983 CELICA

W/22R ENGINE

1. Remove hood and disconnect battery ground cable.
2. Remove air cleaner and drain cooling system.
3. Remove radiator shroud and disconnect hoses from radiator.
4. Remove radiator, upper bracket and, on vehicles equipped with air conditioning, remove condenser.
5. On vehicles equipped with automatic transmission, disconnect transmission throttle cable.
6. Disconnect heater hoses from engine, water bypass hose, fuel line from carburetor and power brake booster hose from intake manifold. Disconnect oxygen sensor electrical connector.
7. Disconnect carburetor accelerator linkage, then raise and support vehicle.
8. Drain engine oil and remove starter motor.
9. Remove two engine shock absorber bolts, then remove engine shock absorber cover.
10. Disconnect exhaust pipe, then disconnect oil pressure sender electrical connectors.
11. Remove two transmission stiffener plates and engine under cover.
12. Support transmission using suitable jack with block of wood placed between jack lifting pad and transmission pan.
13. On vehicles equipped with automatic transmission, disconnect transmission cooler lines from transmission, then remove two rubber plugs from service holes at rear of engine.
14. Remove six torque converter mounting bolts, then remove engine to transmission bolts.
15. Remove engine shock absorber from left side motor mount, then remove motor mount bolt from both sides of engine.
16. Disconnect electrical connector between coil and distributor, then disconnect distributor high tension lead.
17. Disconnect alternator electrical connectors.
18. On vehicles equipped with power steering, remove pump drive belts, then remove pump and position aside with hoses attached.
19. Disconnect electrical connector from water temperature sender and fuel cut solenoid valve.
20. On vehicles equipped with air conditioning, remove drive belts and compressor mounting bolts. Position compressor aside with all lines attached.
21. Attach suitable lifting device to engine lift brackets. Remove engine from vehicle using caution when separating engine from transmission. Check to ensure that torque converter remains with transmission.
22. Reverse procedure to install.

1983–85 CELICA

W/22R-E ENGINE

1. Disconnect battery ground cable, remove hood, drain coolant from radiator and engine block.
2. On vehicles equipped with automatic transmission, drain fluid from transmission.
3. Disconnect air cleaner hose and remove air cleaner assembly from vehicle.
4. Remove fan and disconnect heater hoses.
5. Disconnect oil cooler lines, if equipped, radiator shroud and radiator from vehicle.
6. Disconnect actuator, accelerator and throttle cables, if equipped from engine.
7. Disconnect PCV, brake booster, actuator and air control value hoses from engine.
8. Remove EGR valve and bracket.
9. Disconnect all fuel injection lines and hoses from engine.
10. Remove chamber and throttle body assembly from engine.
11. Disconnect water temperature sender gauge, overdrive thermo switch, start injection time switch, temperature sensor and injection electrical connectors from engine.
12. Disconnect electrical connector and remove alternator from engine.
13. Disconnect high tension wire from coil and remove distributor.
14. On vehicle equipped with power steering, remove drive belt, pulley, bolts and pump for vehicle.
15. Disconnect upper engine shock absorber from left engine mount.
16. On vehicles equipped with air conditioning, remove drive belt adjusting bolt, drive belt, compressor bolts and position compressor aside. Do not disconnect compressor lines.
17. On vehicles equipped with manual transmission, remove transmission shift lever.
18. Raise and support vehicle.
19. Remove bolts and engine under cover.
20. Remove lower engine shock absorber.
21. Remove exhaust front pipe clamp. Disconnect then remove exhaust

front pipe from exhaust manifold and catalytic converter.
22. On vehicles equipped with manual transmission, remove clutch release cylinder.
23. Remove steering gear housing assembly and engine mount bolts from vehicle.
24. Disconnect oil pressure sender gauge, neutral start switch, back-up light switch and starter electrical connectors.
25. Disconnect ground straps from clutch housing and engine.
26. Remove intermediate shaft from transmission. **Insert tool number 09325-22010 or equivalent, onto transmission output shaft to prevent oil leakage.**
27. On vehicles equipped with automatic transmission, disconnect shift linkage from shift lever.
28. Disconnect speedometer cable.
29. Position a suitable jack under transmission. Be sure to position a wooden block between jack and transmission pan to prevent damage to transmission.
30. Install a wooden block between firewall and rear of cylinder head to prevent damage to the heater hose.
31. Remove engine rear crossmember and grounding strap.
32. Using a suitable hoist, remove engine and transmission assembly from vehicle.
33. Reverse procedure to install.

1986–87 CELICA

W/2S-E ENGINE

1. Remove hood, then drain cooling system.
2. Remove battery.
3. On automatic transmission models, disconnect throttle cable and bracket from throttle body.
4. On all models, disconnect accelerator cable from throttle body, then remove cruise control actuator and bracket.
5. Remove radiator, air cleaner assembly, air flow meter, air cleaner hose, then the air cleaner bracket.
6. Mark, then disconnect all electrical connections and vacuum hoses from engine.
7. Mark, then carefully disconnect the following EFI components:
   a. Connectors for oxygen sensor, cold start injector, igniter, throttle position sensor, solenoid resistor and check connector.
   b. Back-up light switch, check connector and air valve connector.
   c. Transaxle connections, water temperature sensor, cold start time switch and idle-up VSV connector.
   d. Disconnect all engine ground straps, then the IIA connectors.
8. Pull EFI wire harness from right side of fender apron, then remove igniter.
9. Disconnect and plug heater hoses.
10. Disconnect and plug fuel inlet hose from filter and return hose from fuel return pipe.
11. Disconnect speedometer cable from transaxle.
12. On models with manual transaxle, remove clutch release cylinder and hose bracket. Do not disconnect clutch release cylinder lines.
13. On models with manual transaxle, disconnect transaxle control cable as follows:
   a. Remove clips and plate washers, then disconnect each control cable from shift and selector levers.
   b. Remove clips, then disconnect each cable from control bracket
14. On models with automatic transaxle, disconnect transaxle control cable as follows:
   a. Remove retaining clip, then disconnect control cable from swivel.
   b. Remove retaining clip, then disconnect control cable from bracket.
15. On all models, remove A/C compressor from engine and position aside. Do not disconnect hoses.
16. Raise and support vehicle, then drain engine oil.
17. Remove RH engine under cover, then the lower suspension crossmember.
18. Wrap both driveshaft boots with shop towels, then depress brake pedal and remove 6 attaching nuts from each shaft.
19. Remove power steering pump from bracket. Do not disconnect power steering lines.
20. Disconnect exhaust pipe from exhaust manifold, then remove engine rear mounting bolt.
21. Lower vehicle.
22. Remove engine front mounting bolts, then the power steering pump reservoir tank mounting bolts.
23. Attach suitable engine lifting equipment onto engine.
24. Remove RH and LH mount through bolts, then remove LH mount bracket from transaxle.
25. Remove engine and transaxle assembly from vehicle.
26. Reverse procedure to install.

W/3S-GE & 3S-FE ENGINE

1. Remove hood, then drain cooling system.
2. Remove battery.
3. Disconnect ignition coil connector and ignition coil wire from coil, then remove upper suspension brace attaching bolts and nuts and brace.
4. On automatic transmission models, disconnect throttle cable and bracket from throttle body.
5. Disconnect throttle cable and bracket from throttle body, then remove radiator reservoir tank.
6. Remove cruise control actuator with bracket as follows:
   a. Disconnect ground strap connector.
   b. Remove actuator cover, then disconnect vacuum hose.
   c. Disconnect actuator connector, then remove actuator with bracket.
7. Remove oxygen sensor, then the radiator.
8. Remove air cleaner assembly, air flow meter, air cleaner hose, then the air cleaner bracket.
9. Remove igniter, then disconnect heater hoses.
10. Disconnect and plug fuel inlet hose from filter and return hose from fuel return pipe.
11. Disconnect speedometer cable from transaxle.
12. On models with manual transaxle, remove clutch release cylinder and hose bracket. Do not disconnect clutch relase cylinder lines.
13. On models with manual transaxle, disconnect transaxle control cable as follows:
   a. Remove clips and plate washers, then disconnect each control cable from shift and selector levers.
   b. Remove clips, then disconnect each cable from control bracket.
14. On models with automatic transaxle, disconnect transaxle control cable as follows:
   a. Remove retaining clip, then disconnect control cable from swivel.
   b. Remove retaining clip, then disconnect control cable from bracket.
15. On all models, remove A/C compressor from engine and position aside. Do not disconnect hoses.
16. Disconnect check connector, then the ground straps from LH fender apron. Disconnect No. 2 junction block.
17. Disconnect vacuum hoses from brake booster, A/C idle-up and charcoal canister.
18. Raise and support vehicle, then drain engine oil.
19. Remove RH engine under cover, then the lower suspension crossmember.
20. Remove both driveshafts, then the power steering pump and position aside. Do not disconnect power steering pump hoses.
21. On 3S-GE engine, disconnect exhaust pipe from exhaust manifold. On 3S-FE engine, disconnect exhaust pipe from catalytic converter. On both engines, remove engine rear mount bolt.
22. Lower vehicle.
23. Pull TCCS ESU connectors into engine compartment, then disconnect the connectors.
24. Remove engine front mount bolts, then the power steering pump reservoir mount bolts.
25. Attach suitable engine lifting equipment to engine.
26. Remove RH and LH mount through bolts, then remove LH mount bracket from transaxle.
27. Remove engine and transaxle from vehicle.
28. Reverse procedure to install.

1983–84 PICKUP

W/22R ENGINE

1. Remove hood, battery and air cleaner.
2. Drain cooling system, then remove radiator, shroud and radiator hoses.
3. On vehicles equipped with air conditioning, remove drive belt and compressor mounting bolts, then position compressor aside with lines attached.
4. Remove fan, pulley and drive belt.

5. Disconnect heater inlet hose from water valve, brake booster hose from intake manifold, fuel lines from fuel pump and emission canister hoses.
6. Disconnect alternator electrical connectors and all engine ground straps.
7. Disconnect ignition coil wiring and remove high tension lead from distributor.
8. Disconnect electrical connectors from fuel cut solenoid valve and water temperature sender.
9. Disconnect accelerator linkage from carburetor and electrical connectors from thermo switch and vacuum switch. Remove bolts from vacuum switch bracket and position assembly aside. Disconnect oxygen sensor electrical connector, if equipped.
10. Remove transmission shift lever from inside vehicle, then raise and support vehicle.
11. Drain engine oil and remove driveshaft.
12. Disconnect electrical connectors from oil pressure switch, sending unit and back-up light switch.
13. Disconnect speedometer cable from transmission.
14. Disconnect exhaust pipe clamp from transmission housing.
15. Disconnect exhaust pipe from manifold, then disconnect starter electrical connectors.
16. Remove starter mount bolt and clutch release cylinder.
17. Support transmission using suitable jack with block of wood placed between jack lifting pad and transmission oil pan.
18. Remove motor mount bolts from both sides of engine, then remove rear mount bolts.
19. Attach suitable lifting device to engine lift brackets and remove engine and transmission as an assembly from vehicle. **Ensure all remaining electrical connectors are disconnected.**
20. To separate engine from transmission, remove starter and engine to transmission attaching bolts.
21. Reverse procedure to install.

1984 PICKUP

W/22R-TE ENGINE

1. Remove hood, then disconnect battery ground cable.
2. Remove engine under cover attaching screws, then the cover.
3. Drain coolant from radiator and engine block, then remove radiator.
4. On automatic transmission models, drain fluid from transmission.
5. Remove air cleaner assembly from engine.
6. Remove fan assembly from engine.
7. Disconnect and plug heater hoses.
8. Disconnect accelerator and throttle cables.
9. Disconnect and mark all electrical connectors and vacuum hoses from engine.
10. Remove throttle body.
11. Remove power steering pump, if equipped and position aside. Do not disconnect power steering pump lines.
12. Remove A/C compressor from bracket, if equipped. Do not disconnect refrigerant lines.
13. Disconnect ground straps from rear engine mounts.
14. On manual transmission models, remove transmission shift lever.
15. Raise and support vehicle.
16. Disconnect front exhaust pipe from exhaust manifold.
17. On manual transmission models, remove clutch release cylinder and bracket assembly from transmission.
18. Remove engine mount bolts.
19. Remove intermediate shaft from transmission. Insert tool No. 09325-20010 into transmission output shaft to prevent fluid leakage.
20. On automatic transmission models, disconnect shift linkage from shift lever.
21. Disconnect speedometer cable from transmission.
22. Support transmission using a suitable jack with block of wood placed between jack lifting pad and transmission fluid pan.
23. Remove rear engine mounting bracket.
24. Install suitable engine lifting equipment onto engine.
25. Remove engine and transmission assembly from vehicle.
26. Reverse procedure to install. Torque rear engine mount bolts to 19 ft. lbs. Torque mounting bracket bolts to 9 ft. lbs.

1985–87 PICKUP & 4RUNNER

1. Disconnect battery ground cable, then remove engine under cover.
2. Scribe reference marks in engine hood hinge area, then remove hood.
3. Drain engine oil into suitable container.
4. Drain coolant from radiator and engine block into suitable container.
5. On models equipped with auto. trans., drain transmission fluid into suitable container.
6. On all models, remove air cleaner hose and air cleaner.
7. On models equipped with auto. trans., disconnect transmission cooler lines from radiator.
8. On all models, disconnect upper and lower radiator hoses from engine.
9. On turbo models, disconnect turbo coolant hose.
10. On all models, disconnect coolant reservoir hose.
11. On models equipped with A/C, remove No. 2 fan shroud.
12. On all models, remove radiator and fan shroud as an assembly, then the fan and fan clutch.
13. Disconnect heater hoses, then the accelerator cable and throttle valve cable (if equipped).
14. Identify, then disconnect any cables, hoses or electrical connections that would interfere with engine removal.
15. On models equipped with EFI, remove intake plenum and throttle body as an assembly.
16. On all models, remove power steering pump (if equipped) from engine block without disconnecting pressure and return lines and position aside.
17. Disconnect ground strap from power steering bracket.
18. On models equipped with A/C, remove A/C compressor without disconnecting high and low side hoses and position aside.
19. On two wheel drive models, remove transmission. On four wheel drive models, remove transmission and transfer case.
20. Attach suitable lifting equipment to engine.
21. Remove left and right side engine mounts.
22. Slowly and carefully lift engine from vehicle. Ensure all cables, hoses and electrical connectors are disconnected during removal.
23. Reverse procedure to install.

CYLINDER HEAD REPLACE

3A-C, 4A-C & 4A-LC ENGINES

Removal

1. Disconnect battery ground cable, then remove air cleaner assembly.
2. Drain radiator coolant into suitable container.
3. Drain engine oil into suitable container.
4. Identify, then disconnect any hoses and wires that may interfere with cylinder head removal.
5. Disconnect accelerator cable from carburetor.
6. On models equipped with auto. trans., disconnect throttle valve cable from carburetor.
7. On all models, disconnect exhaust pipe from exhaust manifold.
8. Disconnect exhaust gas oxygen sensor wire connector.
9. Remove drive belts and water pump pulley.
10. Disconnect radiator outlet hose.
11. On models equipped with A/C, remove A/C idler pulley and bracket as an assembly.
12. Remove alternator upper bracket attaching nut and bolts, then the bracket.
13. Remove water outlet attaching bolts, then the outlet.
14. Remove distributor hold down bolt, then disconnect secondary wiring from spark plugs and remove distributor with distributor cap attached.
15. Remove spark plugs, then valve cover and half circle plug located in cylinder head-to-valve cover mating flange.
16. On models equipped with Air Suction (AS) system, remove AS system component parts.
17. Remove upper timing belt cover attaching bolts, then the timing cover and gasket.
18. While rotating crankshaft in a clockwise direction, bring cylinder No. 1 to TDC compression. **No. 1 cylinder is**

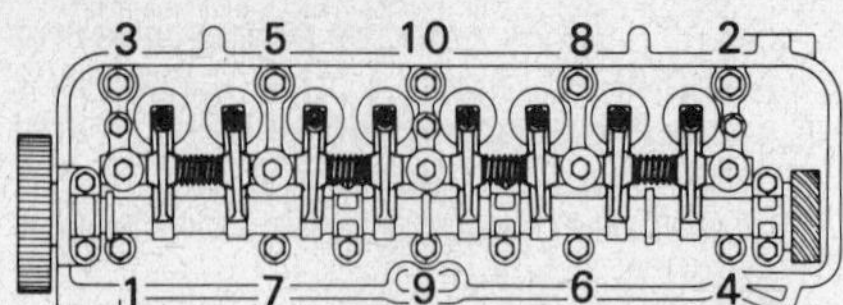

Fig. 1 Cylinder head bolt removal sequence. 3A-C, 4A-C & 4A-LC engines

Fig. 3 Measuring camshaft thrust clearance on overhead cam engine. Typical

at TDC compression when No. 1 cylinder rocker arms have freeplay. If rocker arms do not have free play, rotate crankshaft an additional turn and check again.

19. Place reference marks on camshaft pulley and belt to be used during reassembly, then loosen idler pulley set bolt and push idler pulley it as far to the left as possible to loosen camshaft belt. Temporarily tighten idler set bolt.
20. While supporting lower part of belt to maintain groove-to-teeth meshing of belt and crankshaft gear, remove belt from camshaft gear. **Do not allow any objects to drop inside lower timing belt cover. Also do not allow oil, water or dust to come into contact with timing belt.**
21. Remove bolt from exhaust manifold-to-engine bracket.
22. Loosen cylinder head bolts in increments following sequence, **Fig. 1**, then remove bolts. **If loosening sequence is not followed, cylinder head cracking or warpage could result.**
23. Remove cylinder head from engine block and place on suitable wooden blocks. **If cylinder head is difficult to remove, use suitable pry bar between cylinder head and block projection to aid in removal. Use caution not to damage cylinder head or engine block deck surfaces.**
24. Remove carburetor and fuel pump, then the intake and exhaust manifolds.
25. Loosen rocker arm attaching bolts in increments using sequence shown, **Fig. 2**, then remove rocker arm assembly.
26. While holding camshaft steady with wrench positioned at flats, remove camshaft pulley attaching bolt and pulley.
27. Position suitable dial indicator as shown in **Fig. 3**, then measure camshaft thrust clearance by prying camshaft back and forth. Standard clearance is .0031-.0071 inch. If clearance exceeds .0098 inch, cylinder head should be replaced.
28. While holding camshaft steady with wrench positioned at flats, remove distributor drive gear attaching bolt and gear.
29. Loosen camshaft bearing cap bolts in increments using sequence shown, **Fig. 4**, then remove bearing cap bolts, camshaft, oil seal and bearing caps. **Keep bearing caps in order they were removed.**

Installation

1. Install distributor drive gear, washer and attaching bolt on camshaft. Do not tighten bolt at this time.
2. Lubricate camshaft bearing journals with engine oil, then position camshaft in cylinder head.
3. Place camshaft bearing caps Nos. 2, 3 and 4 in position with stamped arrows facing camshaft gear end of head.
4. Apply multipurpose grease to camshaft oil seal inner diameter, then apply suitable liquid sealer to seal outer diameter and install seal.
5. Apply small amount of suitable sealer to corners where oil seal outer diameter intersects valve cover mounting flange.
6. Place camshaft bearing cap No. 1 in position with stamped arrows facing camshaft gear end of cylinder head.
7. Install bearing cap bolts, then tighten bolts in increments to a final torque of 9 ft. lbs. following sequence shown in **Fig. 5.**
8. Position suitable dial indicator as shown in **Fig. 3**, then measure camshaft thrust clearance by prying camshaft back and forth. Standard clearance is .0031-.0071 inch. If clearance exceeds .0098 inch, cylinder head should be replaced.
9. While holding camshaft steady with wrench positioned at flats, torque distributor drive gear attaching bolt to 22 ft. lbs.
10. Install camshaft drive gear on camshaft, then while holding camshaft steady with wrench positioned at flats, torque drive gear attaching bolts to 34 ft. lbs. **Keep camshaft drive gear free of any oil or water.**
11. Loosen rocker arm adjusting screw locknuts, then install rocker arms and attaching bolts. Tighten bolts in increments to a final torque of 18 ft. lbs. following sequence shown in **Fig. 6.**
12. Install intake and exhaust manifolds, then the fuel pump and carburetor.
13. Install new cylinder head gasket with sealer side facing up, then the cylinder head and cylinder head attaching bolts.
14. Tighten bolts in increments to a final torque of 43 ft. lbs. following sequence shown in **Fig. 7.**

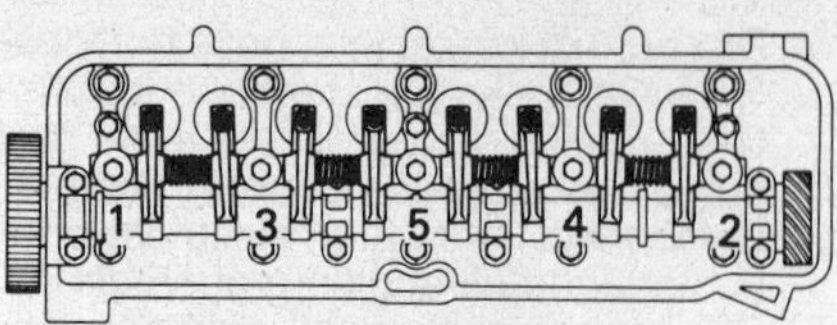

Fig. 2 Rocker arm assembly attaching bolt removal sequence. 3A-C, 4A-C & 4A-LC engines.

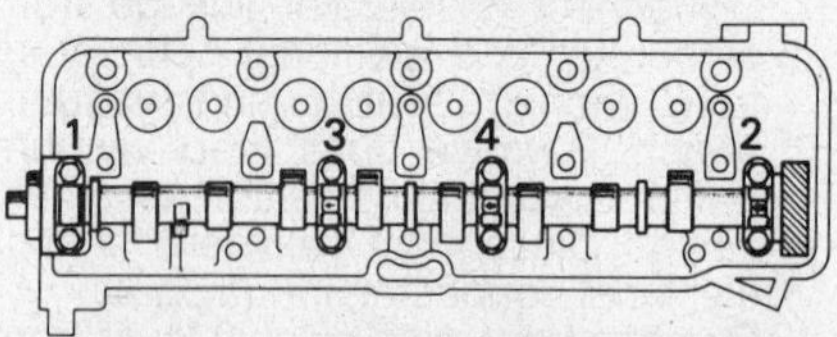

Fig. 4 Camshaft bearing cap bolt removal sequence. 3A-C, 4A-C & 4A-LC engines

15. Install bolt from exhaust manifold-to-engine bracket.
16. If equipped, install AS system components.
17. Install timing belt. Refer to "Timing Belt, Replace" for procedure.
18. Adjust valves. Refer to "Valves, Adjust" for procedure.
19. While rotating crankshaft in a clockwise direction, bring cylinder No. 1 to TDC compression. **No. 1 cylinder is at TDC compression when No. 1 cylinder rocker arms have freeplay. If rocker arms do not have freeplay, rotate crankshaft an additional turn and check again.**
20. Align distributor lower housing mark with distributor drive gear roll pin, then install distributor and hold down bolt(s).
21. Install spark plugs, then connect distributor secondary cables.
22. Install timing belt upper cover with gasket.
23. Install water pump pulley and drive belts.
24. Refill crankcase by pouring proper quantity of engine oil over rocker arms and distributor drive gear.
25. Install valve cover half-circle plug, then apply small amount of suitable sealer to corners where No. 1 camshaft bearing cap and half-circle plug intersects valve cover mounting flange.
26. Install valve cover gasket and valve cover, then connect PCV system.
27. Connect exhaust pipe-to-exhaust manifold.
28. Connect oxygen sensor, radiator upper hose, accelerator cable and throttle valve cable (if equipped).
29. Connect hoses, wires and cables that were disconnected during removal procedure.
30. Refill cooling system, then install air cleaner.
31. Connect battery ground cable, then start engine and allow to reach operating temperature while checking for leaks.
32. Retorque cylinder head bolts and readjust valve clearances.

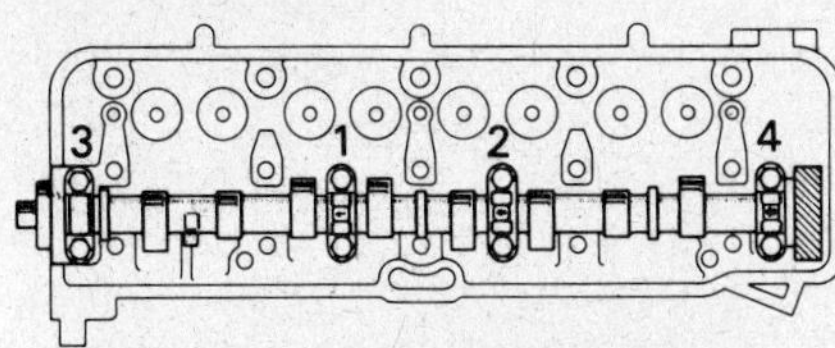

Fig. 5 Camshaft bearing cap bolt tightening sequence. 3A-C, 4A-C & 4A-LC engines

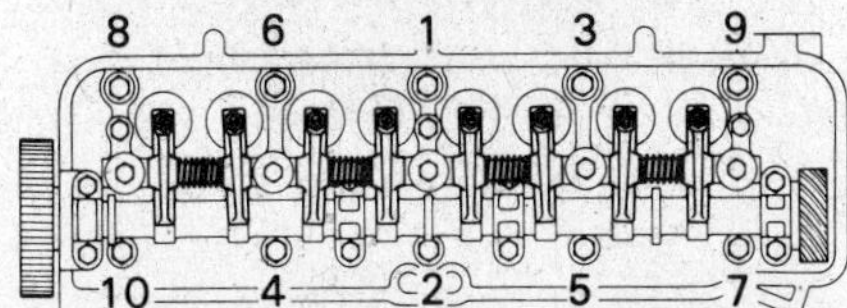

Fig. 7 Cylinder head bolt tightening sequence. 3A-C, 4A-C & 4A-LC engines

33. Adjust ignition timing and idle speed as necessary.

3E ENGINE

Removal

1. Disconnect battery ground cable.
2. Remove right side engine under cover.
3. Drain coolant from engine block and radiator into suitable container. **Engine block drain cock is located near the oil filter.**
4. On models equipped with power steering, remove power steering pump and bracket.
5. On models equipped with A/C less power steering, remove idler pulley bracket.
6. On all models, disconnect radiator hoses.
7. Disconnect accelerator cable and throttle valve cable (if equipped).
8. Remove alternator drive belt, air cleaner and spark plugs.
9. Raise engine slightly with suitable jack, then remove right side engine mount. **Place suitable block of wood between jack and engine to prevent damage.**
10. Remove valve cover, then while rotating crankshaft in a clockwise direction, bring cylinder No. 1 to TDC compression. **No. 1 cylinder is at TDC compression when No. 1 cylinder rocker arms have freeplay. If rocker arms do not have freeplay, rotate crankshaft an additional turn and check again.**
11. While holding crankshaft position with suitable tool, remove crankshaft pulley attaching nut, then remove crankshaft pulley with puller.
12. Remove upper and lower timing belt covers attaching bolts, then the covers.
13. Pull off timing belt guide from crankshaft timing gear.
14. If timing belt is to be reused, make crankshaft gear-to-timing belt reference marks and camshaft gear-to-timing belt reference marks. Also draw arrow to indicate engine rotation direction to be used during reassembly.
15. Remove timing belt idler pulley tension spring, then loosen idler pulley bolt and push idler pulley to the left as far as possible. Temporarily tighten idler pulley bolt.
16. Remove timing belt, then while holding camshaft flats with suitable wrench, remove camshaft gear attaching bolt and gear. **Do not allow timing belt to come into contact with water or oil.**
17. Disconnect heater core inlet hose, then fuel hoses.
18. On all exc. Calif. models, remove Air Suction (AS) valve and hose. On Calif. models, remove AS hose.
19. Disconnect brake booster hose from intake manifold, then coolant inlet hose.
20. Disconnect coolant hose from intake manifold.
21. Identify, then disconnect any cables, hoses or wires that may interfere with cylinder head removal.
22. Remove exhaust pipe-to-manifold attaching nuts, then disconnect exhaust pipe.
23. Remove intake manifold-to-cylinder block bracket attaching bolt and nut, then the bracket and ground strap.
24. Remove wire harness clamp bolt from intake manifold.
25. Position suitable dial indicator as shown in **Fig. 3,** then measure camshaft thrust clearance by prying camshaft back and forth. Standard clearance is .0031-.0071 inch. If clearance exceeds .0098 inch, cylinder head and/or camshaft should be replaced.
26. Loosen cylinder head bolts in increments following sequence, **Fig. 8,** then remove bolts. **If loosening sequence is not followed, cylinder head cracking or warpage could result.**
27. Remove cylinder head from engine block and place on suitable wooden blocks. **If cylinder head is difficult to remove, use suitable pry bar between cylinder head and block projection to aid in removal. Use caution not to damage cylinder head or engine block deck surfaces.**
28. Disconnect distributor secondary wiring from spark plugs, then remove two distributor hold down bolts and the distributor with cap attached.
29. Remove coolant outlet housing, then the engine hangers.
30. On Calif. models, remove AS pipe, then on all models, remove exhaust manifold attaching bolts and manifold.
31. Remove spark plugs, carburetor, accelerator cable bracket, air cleaner bracket and air pipes.
32. Remove fuel pump and intake manifold.
33. Loosen camshaft bearing cap bolts in increments using sequence shown, **Fig. 4,** then remove bearing cap bolts, camshaft, oil seal and bearing caps. **Keep bearing caps in order they were removed.**
34. Loosen rocker arm adjusting screw locknuts, then while lifting top of retaining spring, pry out lower part of spring and remove rocker arms and springs. **Keep rocker arms in order they were removed.**

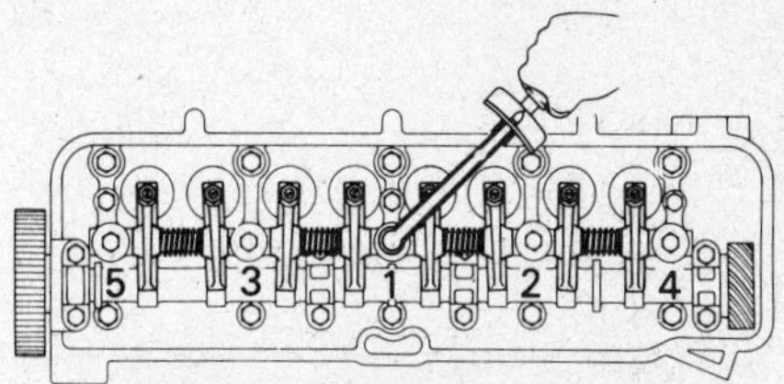

Fig. 6 Rocker arm assembly attaching bolt tightening sequence. 3A-C, 4A-C & 4A-LC engines.

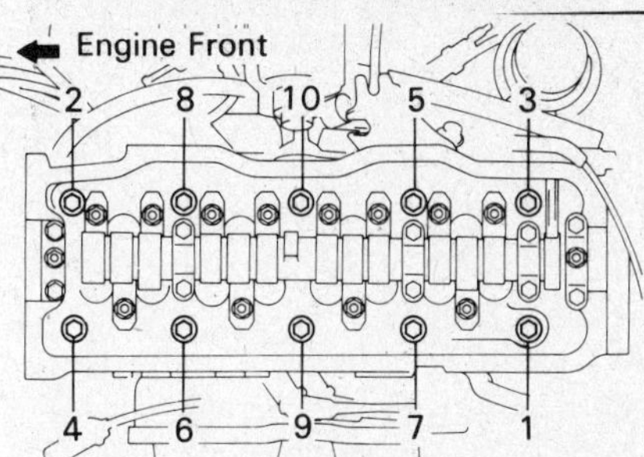

Fig. 8 Cylinder head bolt removal sequence. 3E engine

Installation

1. Ensure rocker arm adjusting screw is fully backed out, then install new rocker arm spring on rocker arm. Press bottom lip of spring until it fits into the rocker arm pivot groove.
2. Position rocker arm/spring assembly in cylinder head with rocker arm adjusting screw located in rocker arm pivot. Using suitable screwdriver, pry rocker arm spring onto rocker arm pivot. Move rocker arm up and down at pivot end to ensure there is spring tension on rocker arm and that the rocker arm does not rattle.
3. Ensure engine crankshaft is set at TDC compression stoke, then lubricate camshaft journals with engine oil and install camshaft with camshaft gear lock pin at 12 o'clock position. **Set camshaft and crankshaft as noted above to prevent damage to the sub-intake valve and/or piston head.**
4. Place camshaft bearing caps Nos. 2,3 and 4 in position with stamped arrows facing camshaft gear end of head.
5. Apply oil to camshaft oil seal inner diameter, then apply suitable liquid sealer to seal outer diameter and install seal.
6. Apply small amount of suitable sealer to corners where oil seal outer diameter intersects valve cover mounting flange.
7. Place camshaft bearing cap No. 1 in position with stamped arrows facing camshaft gear end of cylinder head.
8. Install bearing cap bolts, then tighten bolts in increments to a final torque of

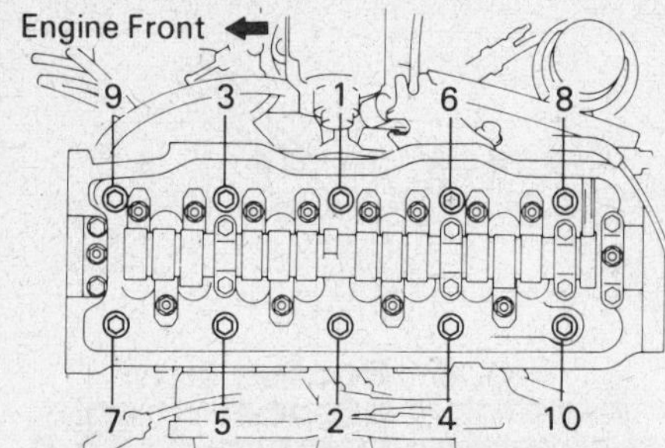

Fig. 9 Cylinder head bolt tightening sequence. 3E engine

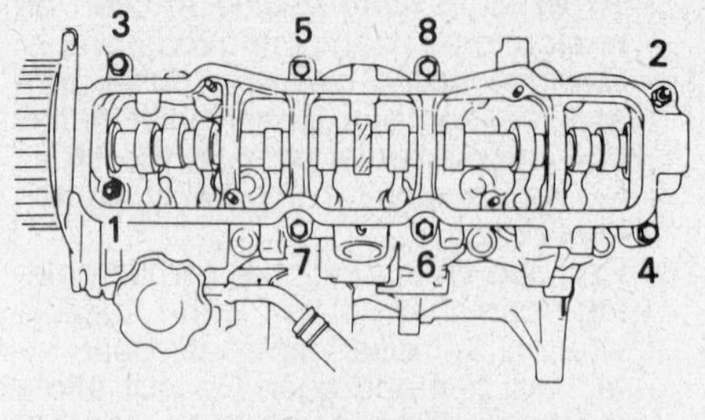

Fig. 10 Camshaft housing bolt loosening sequence. 2S-E engine

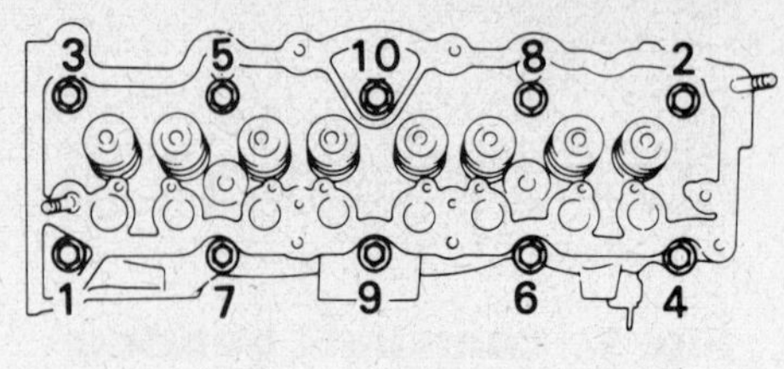

Fig. 11 Cylinder head bolt loosening sequence. 2S-E engine

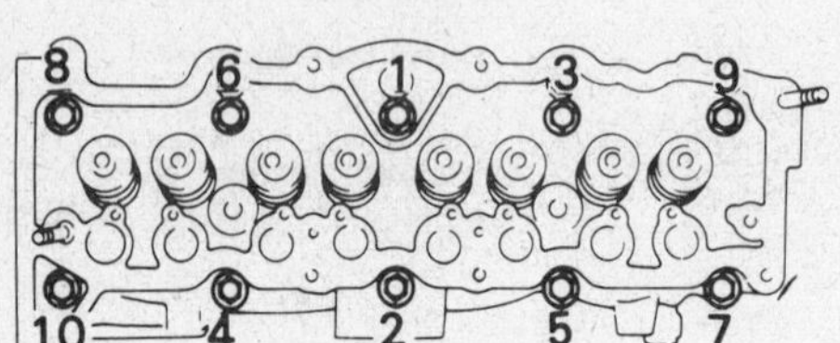

Fig. 12 Cylinder head bolt tightening sequence. 2S-E engine

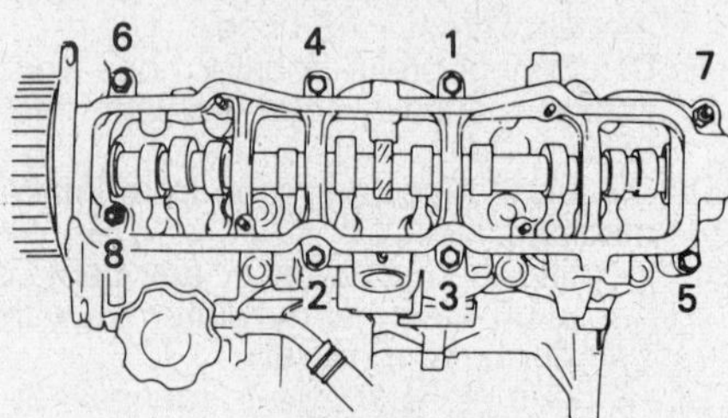

Fig. 13 Camshaft housing bolt tightening sequence. 2S-E engine

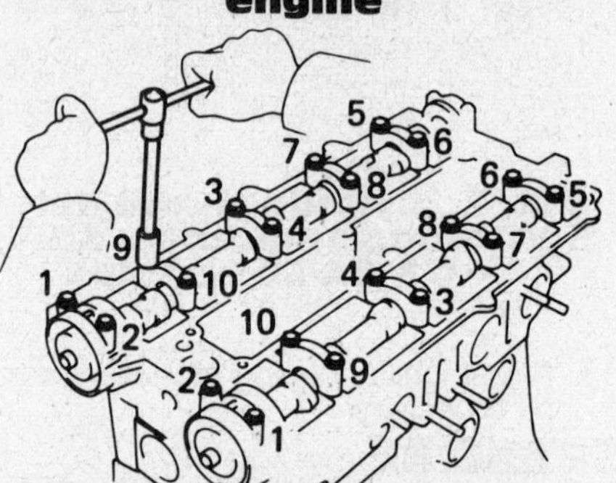
Fig. 14 Bearing cap bolt removal sequence. 3S-GE engine

10 ft. lbs. following sequence shown in **Fig. 5.**

9. Position suitable dial indicator as shown in **Fig. 3,** then measure camshaft thrust clearance by prying camshaft back and forth. Standard clearance is .0031-.0071 inch. If clearance exceeds .0098 inch, cylinder head and/or camshaft should be replaced.
10. Install intake manifold, fuel pump, carburetor, accelerator cable bracket, air cleaner bracket, carburetor and exhaust manifold.
11. Position engine hanger bracket at left front of engine, then apply suitable sealer to bracket attaching bolt threads and install. Torque attaching bolt to 15 ft. lbs.
12. Position engine hanger bracket at right rear of engine, and install attaching bolt. Torque attaching bolt to 43 ft. lbs.
13. Apply suitable sealing compound to coolant outlet housing flange, then install outlet housing.
14. Align distributor coupling groove with lower housing groove. Install distributor into cylinder head while aligning mounting flange groove with valve cover attaching stud. Install hold down bolt(s) finger tight.
15. Install new cylinder head gasket on cylinder block, then the cylinder head and cylinder head bolts. **Ensure head gasket is installed with proper side up.**
16. Tighten cylinder head bolts in sequence shown, **Fig. 9,** to 22 ft. lbs., then tighten again in soquence to 36 ft. lbs. Tighten bolts an additional 90° in sequence to achieve final tightening torque.
17. Install timing belt. Refer to "Timing Belt, Replace" for procedure.
18. Adjust valves. Refer to "Valves, Adjust" for procedure.
19. Install wire harness clamp bolt to intake manifold, then intake manifold-to-engine block bracket and ground strap.
20. Connect exhaust pipe-to-exhaust manifold, then the coolant bypass hose to carburetor. Connect belts, hoses, wires and cables that were disconnected during removal procedure.
21. Refill cooling system and crankshaft.
22. Connect battery ground cable, then start engine and allow to reach operating temperature while checking for leaks.
23. Readjust valve clearances.
24. Adjust ignition timing and idle speed as necessary.

2S-E ENGINE

1. Disconnect battery ground cable.
2. Drain cooling system, then disconnect accelerator cable from throttle body.
3. On automatic transmission models, remove throttle cable and bracket assembly from throttle body.
4. Remove air cleaner assembly from engine.
5. Mark then disconnect all EFI electrical connectors, electrical wiring and vacuum hoses for cylinder head.
6. Pull out EFI wire harness from right fender apron.
7. Remove alternator and distributor from engine.
8. Disconnect radiator upper hose and bypass hose, then remove water outlet housing.
9. Remove rear end housing and heater pipe.
10. Disconnect and plug fuel lines.
11. Raise and support vehicle, then drain oil from engine and disconnect exhaust pipe from exhaust manifold.
12. Disconnect two power steering pump vacuum lines, then remove intake manifold bracket.
13. Lower vehicle.
14. Remove timing belt. Refer to "Timing Belt, Replace" for procedure.
15. Disconnect vacuum hose from PCV valve, them remove cylinder head cover.
16. Loosen then remove camshaft housing bolts and nuts gradually in three steps in sequence shown in **Fig. 10.**
17. Remove rocker arms and valve lash adjusters.
18. Loosen then remove cylinder head bolts gradually in three steps in sequence shown in **Fig. 11.**
19. Reverse procedure to install. Torque cylinder head bolts gradually in three steps in sequence shown in **Fig. 12** to 47 ft. lbs. Torque camshaft housing bolts and nuts in three steps in sequence shown in **Fig. 13** to 11 ft. lbs.

3S-GE ENGINE

1. Disconnect battery ground cable, then drain engine coolant.
2. Remove upper suspension brace.
3. On models with automatic transaxle, disconnect throttle cable with bracket from throttle body.
4. Disconnect accelerator cable from throttle body, then remove radiator reservoir tank.
5. Remove cruise control actuator with bracket, if equipped, then the air cleaner assembly with air flow meter and air cleaner hose.
6. Remove exhaust manifold upper heat insulator, then the alternator.
7. Remove No. 1 alternator bracket.
8. Raise and support vehicle, then remove RH front wheel.
9. Remove RH engine under cover, then the suspension lower crossmember.
10. Disconnect exhaust pipe from exhaust manifold. Remove exhaust

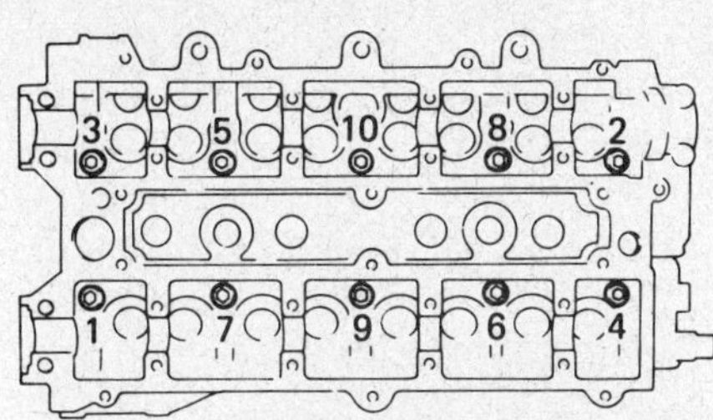

Fig. 15 Cylinder head bolt removal sequence. 3S-GE engine

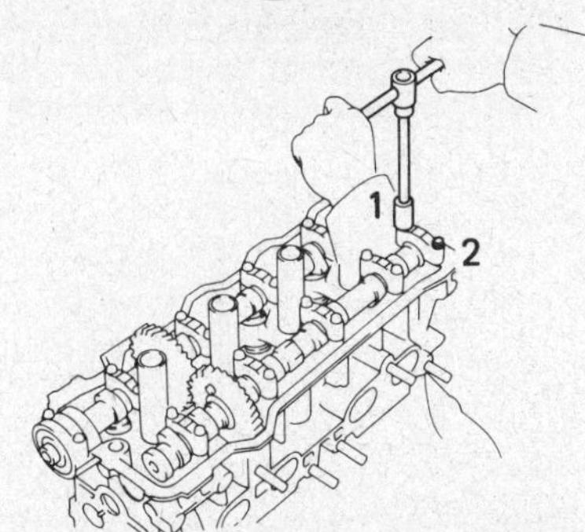

Fig. 18 Exhaust camshaft bearing cap bolts 1 and 2 removal. 3S-FE engine

manifold with lower heat insulator.

11. Remove distributor, then disconnect oil pressure switch connector.
12. Disconnect water temperature switch connector, water temperature sender gauge connector, cold start injector time switch connector, radiator and emission hoses.
13. Remove water outlet, then the water bypass pipe.
14. Remove throttle body as follows:
    a. Disconnect throttle position sensor connector, then the ventilation hose.
    b. Disconnect emission hoses, then the air valve hose.
    c. Remove four attaching bolts, then the throttle body.
15. Remove No. 2 engine hanger and No. 2 manifold stay.
16. Disconnect cold start injector connector, then remove cold start connector pipe.
17. Remove EGR vacuum modulator, then disconnect all vacuum hoses.
18. Disconnect injector connectors, then the fuel inlet and return hoses.
19. Disconnect ground strap, then the 2 VSV connectors.
20. If equipped, disconnect and plug power steering vacuum hoses.
21. Remove intake manifold and air control valve as follows:
    a. Remove intake manifold attaching bolts and nuts.
    b. Disconnect three wire harness clamps from manifold with gasket.
    c. Remove air control valve.
22. Remove delivery pipe with injectors, then the four insulators from cylinder head.
23. Remove cylinder head covers with gaskets, then the spark plugs.
24. Remove No. 1 engine hanger, then

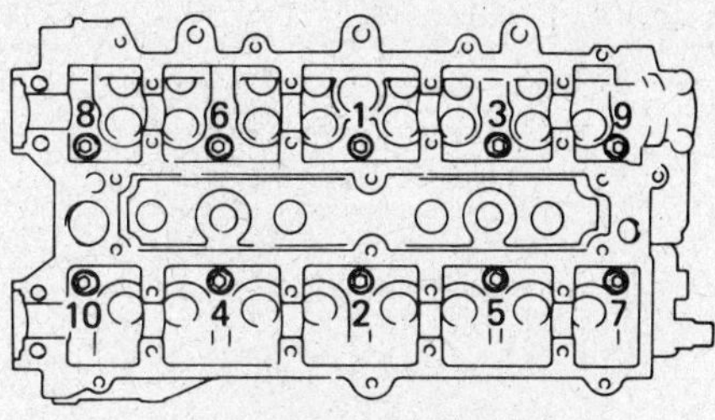

Fig. 16 Cylinder head bolt installation sequence. 3S-GE engine

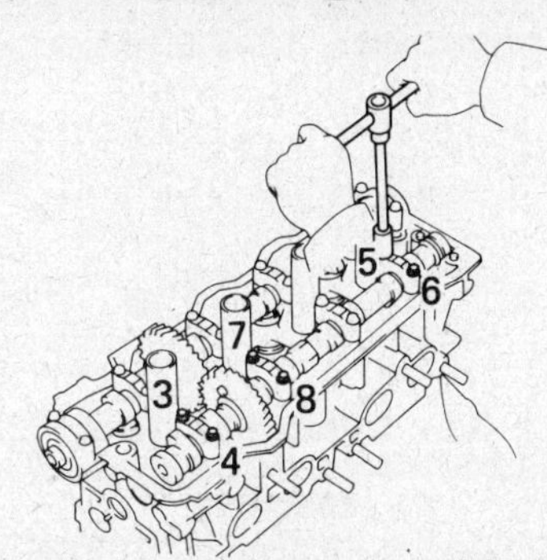

Fig. 19 Exhaust camshaft bearing cap bolt 3 through 8 removal. 3S-FE engine

the power steering reservoir. Do not disconnect hoses.

25. Remove timing belt and camshaft sprockets, refer to "Timing Belt, Replace" for procedure.
26. Loosen and remove bearing cap bolts in sequence shown, **Fig. 14.** Remove camshaft bearing caps, oil seal and camshafts.
27. Loosen and remove cylinder head bolts in sequence shown, **Fig. 15.** Lift head from dowels on cylinder block, then place head on suitable workbench.
28. Reverse procedure to install, using new gaskets and components where applicable. Torque cylinder head bolts to specifications, making several passes, in sequence shown, **Fig. 16.** Torque bearing cap bolts to 14 ft. lbs., making several passes, in sequence shown, **Fig. 17.**

3S-FE ENGINE

Removal

1. Disconnect battery ground cable.
2. Drain coolant from engine block and radiator.
3. Remove suspension upper brace.
4. On models equipped with auto. trans., disconnect transmission throttle valve cable and bracket from throttle body.
5. On all models, disconnect accelerator cable and bracket from throttle body.
6. Remove coolant reservoir tank, then cruise control actuator and bracket (if equipped).
7. Remove air cleaner assembly, air flow meter, air cleaner hose, alternator and alternator upper bracket.
8. Remove oil pressure gauge and engine hanger brackets.
9. Raise and support vehicle, then re-

Fig. 17 Bearing cap bolt installation sequence. 3S-GE engine

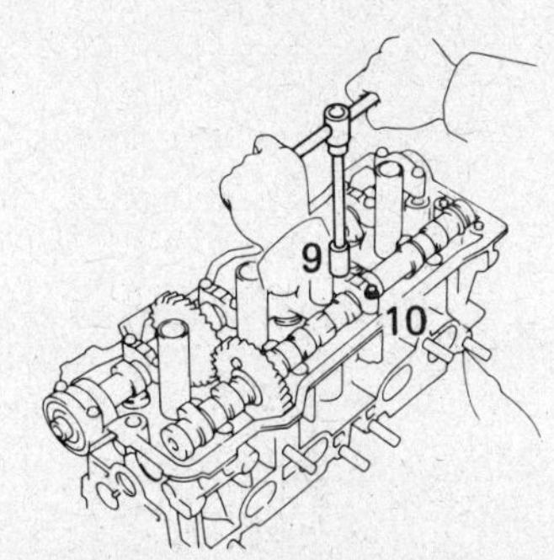

Fig. 20 Exhaust camshaft bearing cap bolt 9 & 10 removal. 3S-FE engine

move right front wheel and engine right side under cover.

10. Remove front suspension lower cross member, then disconnect exhaust pipe from catalytic converter.
11. Disconnect oxygen sensor, then remove exhaust manifold heat insulator and manifold-to-cylinder head attaching bolts. Remove exhaust manifold/catalytic converter assembly.
12. Disconnect distributor connectors and high tension leads from spark plugs, then remove distributor assembly.
13. Remove coolant outlet and coolant bypass pipe from cylinder head.
14. Remove EGR valve and modulator, then the throttle body and cold start injector delivery pipe.
15. Remove air tube from intake manifold, then the intake manifold.
16. Remove fuel delivery pipe and injectors, then the spark plugs.
17. Remove timing belt and camshaft sprocket. Refer to "Timing Belt, Replace" for procedure.
18. Remove timing belt rear cover from cylinder head.
19. Remove valve cover attaching nuts, grommets, valve cover and gasket. **If grommets are to be reused, arrange them in order so they can be installed in the same position as removed.**
20. Remove camshafts as follows: **During removal, the camshafts must remain level with top of cylinder head. If camshafts are not kept level, cylinder head damage may result.**

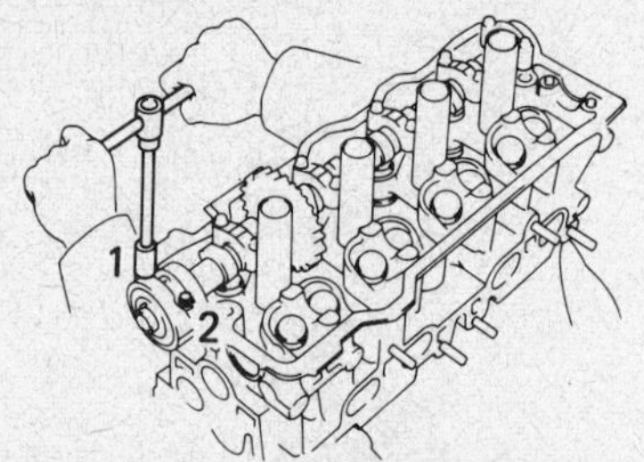

Fig. 21 Intake camshaft bearing cap bolt 9 & 10 removal. 3S-FE engine

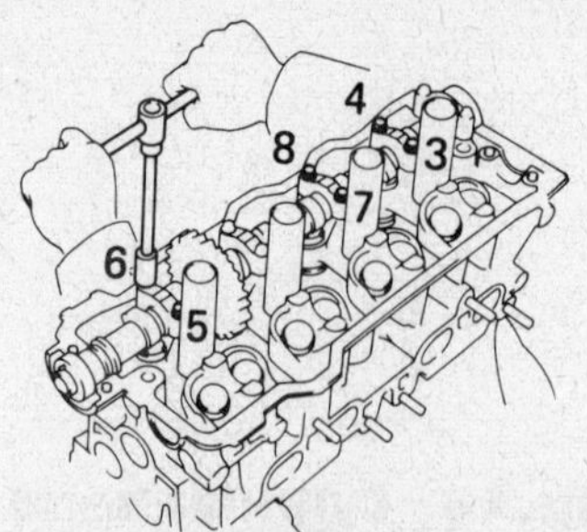

Fig. 22 Intake camshaft bearing cap bolt 3 through 8 removal. 3S-FE removal

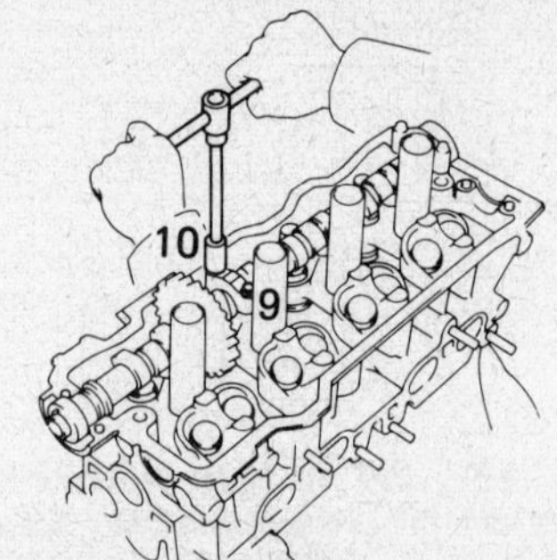

Fig. 23 Intake camshaft bearing cap bolt 9 & 10 removal. 3S-FE engine

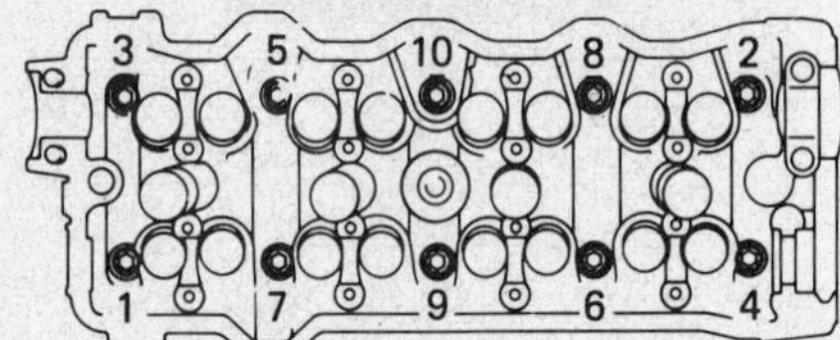

Fig. 24 Cylinder head bolt loosening sequence. 3S-FE engine

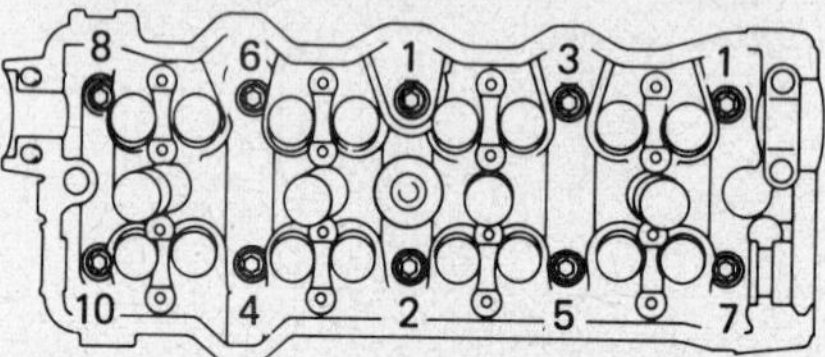

Fig. 25 Cylinder head bolt tightening sequence. 3S-FE engine

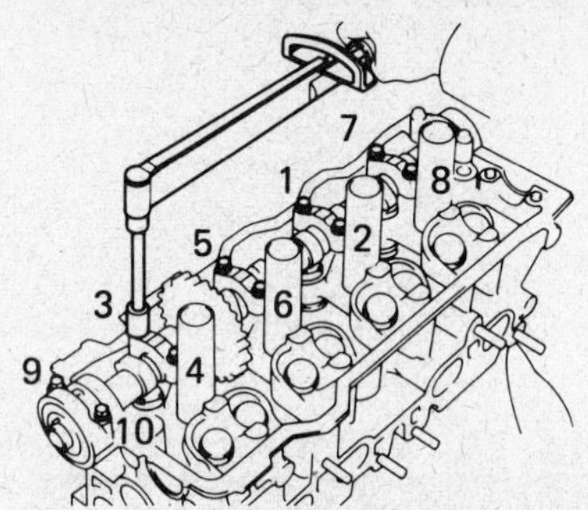

Fig. 26 Intake camshaft bearing cap bolt tightening sequence. 3S-FE engine

a. Set intake camshaft sprocket lock pin at 10-45 ° BTDC of camshaft angle. **With the intake cam set as above, the exhaust cam lobes will be applying pressure to cylinders Nos. 2 and 4 exhaust valve springs, which will aid in lifting and keeping camshaft level during removal.**

b. Secure exhaust camshaft subgear to exhaust camshaft main gear with a service bolt. The bolt must have a thread pitch of 1.0 mm, a thread diameter of 6 mm and a length of 16-20 mm. **When removing camshaft, ensure torsional spring force of sub-gear has been eliminated by above operation.**

c. Remove exhaust camshaft rear bearing cap bolts 1 and 2, **Fig. 18,** then the bearing cap.

d. Loosen bearing cap bolts 3 through 8 in small increments, following sequence, **Fig. 19.** Remove cap bolts and caps.

e. Alternately loosen and remove bearing cap bolts 9 and 10, **Fig. 20. As bearing cap bolts 9 and 10 are being loosened, ensure camshaft is being lifted level and straight from the cylinder head. If camshaft is not being lifted level and straight from the cylinder head, tighten cap bolts 9 and 10, then reverse steps c and d above to install camshaft. Repeat step a, c, d and e.**

f. Remove bearing cap, then the exhaust camshaft.

g. Set intake camshaft sprocket lock pin at 80-115 ° BTDC of camshaft angle. **With the intake cam set as above, the intake cam lobes will be applying pressure to cylinders Nos. 1 and 3 intake valve springs, which will aid in lifting and keeping camshaft level during removal.**

h. Remove intake camshaft front bearing cap bolts 1 and 2, **Fig. 21,** then the bearing cap and oil seal. **If the front bearing cap cannot be removed by hand, leave in position at this time.**

i. Loosen bearing cap bolts 3 through 8 in small increments, following sequence, **Fig. 22.** Remove cap bolts and caps.

j. Alternately loosen and remove bearing cap bolts 9 and 10, **Fig. 23. As bearing cap bolts 9 and 10 are being loosened, ensure camshaft is being lifted level and straight from the cylinder head. If camshaft is not being lifted level and straight from the cylinder head, tighten cap bolts 9 and 10, then reverse steps h and i above to install camshaft. Repeat step g, h and i.**

k. Remove bearing cap, then the intake camshaft.

21. Loosen cylinder head bolts in small increments, following sequence, **Fig. 24. If cylinder head bolt loosening sequence is not followed, head warpage or cracking could result.**
22. Lift cylinder head from block and place on wooden blocks.

Installation

1. Note installation directions, then place new gasket on engine block. Install cylinder head.
2. Lightly lubricate head bolts with clean engine oil and install.
3. Tighten cylinder head bolts in small increments, following tightening sequence, **Fig. 25.**
4. Install camshafts as follows: **During installation, the camshafts must remain level with top of cylinder head. If camshafts are not kept level, cylinder head damage may result.**

a. Apply multipurpose grease to intake camshaft thrust surface, then install camshaft with sprocket lock pin positioned at 80° BTDC.

b. Apply suitable seal packing to outer .08-.12 inch of No. 1 bearing cap mounting flange, then install bearing caps in positions removed from with arrows facing forward.

c. Lightly lubricate bearing cap bolts, then install and tighten in small increments to a final torque of 14 ft. lbs., following sequence, **Fig. 26.**

d. Apply multipurpose grease to intake camshaft oil seal lip, then install with suitable seal installer.

e. Rotate intake camshaft as necessary to position sprocket lock pin at 10° BTDC, then apply multipurpose grease to exhaust camshaft thrust surface.

f. Engage exhaust camshaft gear to intake camshaft gear by aligning timing marks, **Fig. 27,** then rolling exhaust camshaft into bearing journals while maintaining gear engagement. **Camshaft gears have two sets of timing marks. Do not use the assembly reference marks, Fig. 27.**

g. Rotate intake camshaft as necessary until exhaust camshaft is seated evenly in bearing journals.

h. Install bearing caps in positions removed from with arrows facing forward.

i. Lightly lubricate bearing cap bolts, then install and tighten in small increments to a final torque of 14 ft. lbs., following sequence, **Fig. 28.**

5. Remove service bolt from exhaust camshaft main and sub-gear assembly.

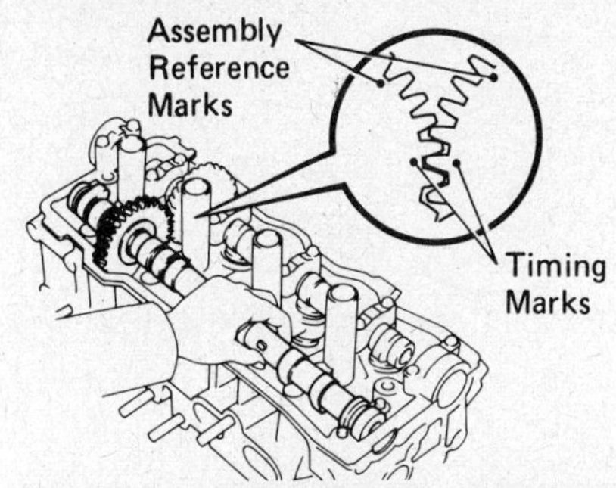

Fig. 27 Intake & exhaust camshaft alignment. 3S-FE engine

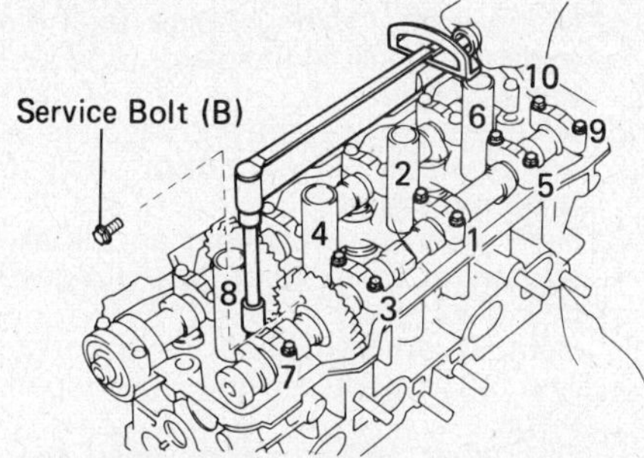

Fig. 28 Exhaust camshaft bearing cap bolt tightening sequence. 3S-FE engine

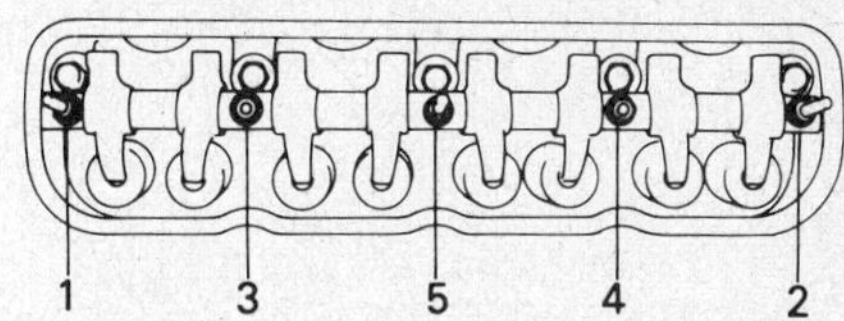

Fig. 29 Rocker arm shaft bolt removal sequence. 3Y-EC & 4Y-EC engines

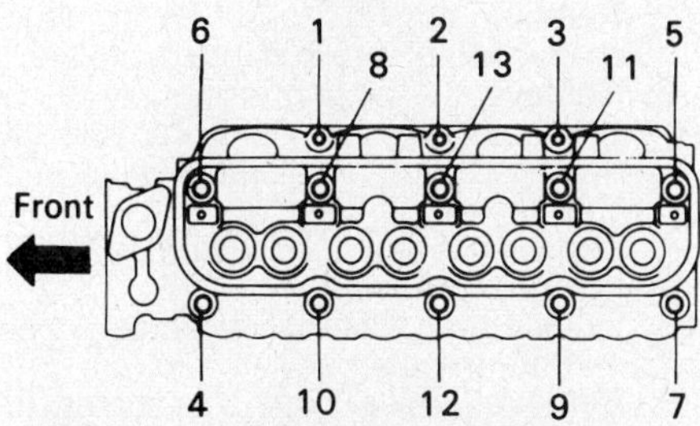

Fig. 30 Cylinder head bolt removal sequence. 3Y-EC & 4Y-EC engines

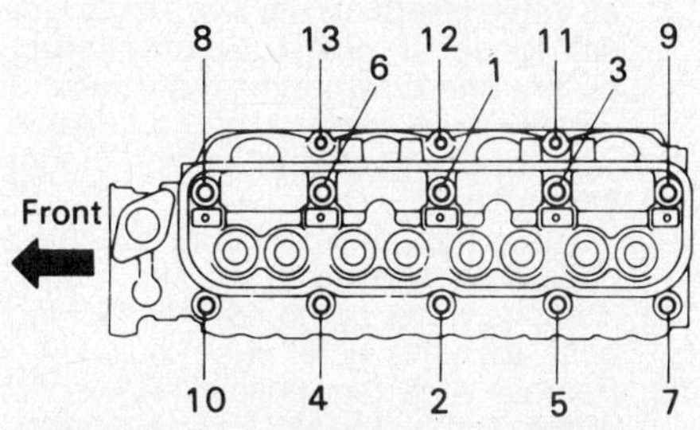

Fig. 31 Cylinder head bolt tightening sequence. 3Y-EC & 4ng sequence. 3S-FE engine

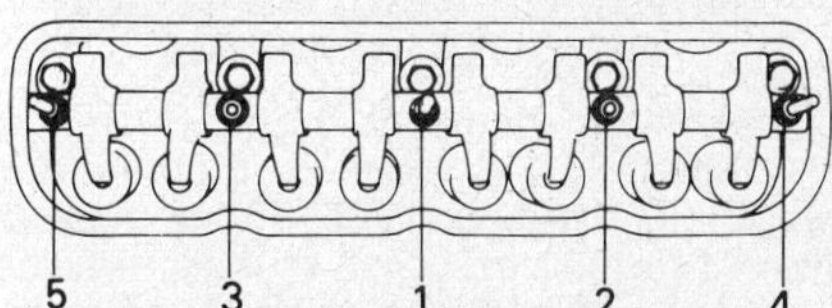

Fig. 32 Rocker arm shaft bolt tightening sequence. 3Y-EC & 4Y-EC engines

6. Reverse steps 1 through 19 to complete installation. After installation is complete, adjust valves. Refer to "Valves, Adjust" for procedure.
7. Check and adjust ignition timing and toe-in as necessary.

3Y-EC & 4Y-EC ENGINES

1. Disconnect battery ground cable.
2. Remove right seat and engine service cover.
3. Drain cooling system and engine oil.
4. Remove power steering pump.
5. Remove front exhaust pipe and bracket assembly.
6. Disconnect accelerator cable from throttle body.
7. Remove air cleaner assembly from engine.
8. Mark then disconnect all EFI electrical connectors, electrical wiring and vacuum hoses from cylinder head.
9. Disconnect radiator and heater hoses.
10. Remove throttle body from air intake chamber.
11. Remove EGR valve, then disconnect cold start in injector line, water bypass hose and pressure regulator hose.
12. Remove air intake chamber and air valve assembly from engine.
13. Remove exhaust manifold bracket, heater pipe bracket, fuel inlet line union bolt and fuel outlet hose.
14. Remove spark plugs.
15. Remove cylinder head cover attaching bolts, then the cover.
16. Remove rocker arm shaft assembly by gradually loosening shaft bolts in three steps in sequence shown in **Fig. 29.**
17. Remove pushrods from engine.
18. Loosen cylinder head bolts gradually in three steps in sequence shown in **Fig. 30.**
19. Remove cylinder head from engine.
20. Reverse procedure to install. Torque cylinder head bolts in three steps in sequence shown in **Fig. 31** to 65 ft. lbs. for 14 mm bolts and 14 ft. lbs. for 12 mm bolts. Torque rocker arm shaft assembly bolts in three steps in sequence shown in **Fig. 32** to 17 ft. lbs.

4A-GE & 4A-GEC ENGINES

1985–87 Corolla W/Rear Wheel Drive

1. Disconnect battery ground cable.
2. Remove under cover, then drain engine coolant and engine oil.
3. Disconnect air cleaner to throttle body hose.
4. Disconnect actuator cable and accelerator cable from bracket.
5. On models equipped with power steering, remove drive belt, pulley and Woodruff key, then the power steering pump attaching bolts and pump assembly. Remove power steering pump bracket.
6. On all models, remove cooling fan drive belt, fan coupling and water pump pulley.
7. Disconnect radiator upper hose from water outlet then the two heater hoses from water bypass pipe and cylinder head rear plate.
8. Disconnect coil wire and spark plug wires from cylinder head, then remove distributor attaching bolts and distributor.
9. Disconnect cold start injector electrical connector, then remove two injector pipe attaching bolts and injector pipe.
10. Remove PCV hose from cylinder head.
11. Remove fuel hoses from pulsation damper and pressure regulator.
12. Mark and disconnect all necessary vacuum hoses, then remove wire harness and vacuum pipe from timing cover.
13. Mark and disconnect all necessary engine electrical connectors.
14. Disconnect exhaust bracket and exhaust manifold from exhaust pipe.
15. Remove vacuum tank and vacuum control valve.
16. Remove exhaust manifold insulator, then the exhaust manifold.
17. Disconnect bypass pipe from water outlet housing, then remove water outlet housing attaching bolts and water outlet housing.
18. Remove delivery pipe and injectors as an assembly. Do not remove injection cover. **Use caution not to drop injectors.**
19. Remove intake manifold and intake air control valve.
20. Remove cylinder head valve covers and gaskets, then the four spark plugs.
21. Remove No. 2 and No. 3 timing belt covers and gaskets.
22. If timing belt is to be replaced, refer to "Timing Belt, Replace" for procedure. If timing belt is to be reused, proceed as follows:
    a. Turn crankshaft pulley and align groove with "0" mark on the No. 1 timing belt cover. **Ensure all valve lifters on the No. 1 cylinder are loose. If not, turn crankshaft pulley one complete revolution.**
    b. Place alignment marks on the camshaft timing pulleys and belt.
    c. Loosen idler pulley bolt, then push idler pulley as far left as possible and temporarily tighten it.
    d. Remove timing belt from camshaft timing pulleys. **Support timing belt so meshing of crankshaft timing pulley and timing belt does not shift.**
    e. Remove camshaft timing pulleys, then the No. 4 timing belt cover.

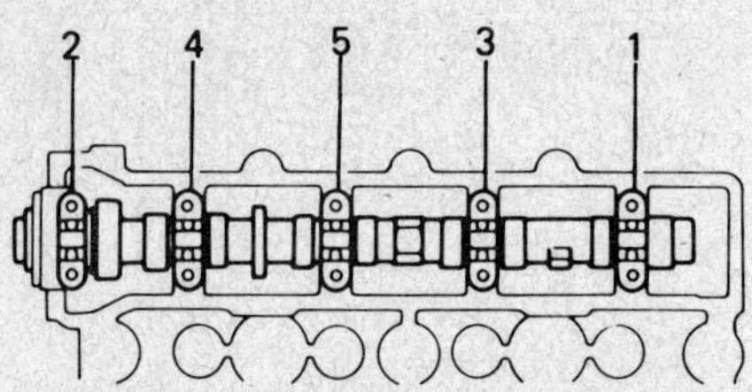

Fig. 33 Camshaft bearing cap bolt removal sequence. 4A-GE, 4A-GEC, 4A-GEL & 4A-GELC engines

23. Measure camshaft thrust clearance, **Fig. 3.** If clearance is greater than .0098 inch on 1985-86 models, or .0118 inch on 1987 models, replace camshaft and/or cylinder head.
24. Loosen and remove camshaft bearing cap attaching bolts gradually in sequence shown in **Fig. 33.**
25. Remove camshaft bearing caps, oil seal and camshaft.
26. Loosen and remove cylinder head attaching bolts gradually in sequence shown in **Fig. 34. Head warpage or cracking could result from removing cylinder head in incorrect order.**
27. Reverse procedure to install. Torque cylinder head attaching bolts gradually in three steps in reverse sequence as sequence as disassembly, **Fig 33,** to 43 ft. lbs.
28. Torque bearing cap attaching bolts gradually in three steps in reverse sequence as disassembly, **Fig. 34,** to 9 ft. lbs.

4A-GEL & 4A-GELC ENGINE

1985–87 MR2

1. Disconnect battery ground cable.
2. Remove under cover, then drain engine coolant and engine oil.
3. Disconnect air cleaner to throttle body hose, then remove air cleaner assembly.
4. Disconnect cruise control cable, if equipped, then the accelerator cable and connecting rod.
5. Remove accelerator link and speedometer cable clamp.
6. Mark and disconnect all necessary vacuum hoses.
7. Disconnect heater hose from cylinder head rear cover, then the radiator hose from water filler.
8. Remove PCV hose from cylinder head, then the EGR valve with pipes.
9. Disconnect cold start injector electrical connector, then remove two injector pipe attaching bolts and injector pipe.
10. Remove pulsation damper and pressure regulator assembly.
11. Disconnect coil wire and spark plug wires from cylinder head, then remove distributor attaching bolts and distributor.
12. Mark and disconnect all necessary electrical connectors.
13. Disconnect water bypass hoses from auxiliary air valve, then remove vacuum pipe and cylinder head rear cover.
14. Remove front exhaust pipe, then the exhaust manifold insulator and exhaust manifold.
15. Remove delivery pipe and injectors as an assembly. **Use caution not to drop injectors.**
16. Remove intake manifold and intake air control valve, then the A/C drive belt, if equipped.
17. Remove cylinder head valve covers and gaskets, then the four spark plugs.
18. Disconnect water bypass hose, then remove three bolts, water outlet with the No. 1 bypass pipe, drive belt adjusting bar and gasket.
19. Turn crankshaft pulley and align groove with idler pulley bolt. **Ensure all valve lifters on the No. 1 cylinder are loose. If not, turn crankshaft pulley one complete revolution.**
20. Slightly raise engine using a suitable jack, then remove right engine mount through bolt.
21. Remove right engine mount attaching bolts, then the engine mount.
22. Remove water pump pulley attaching bolts, then the water pump pulley.
23. Remove A/C idler pulley, if equipped with A/C, then the No. 2 and No. 3 timing belt covers.
24. If timing belt is to be replaced, refer to "Timing Belt, Replace" for procedure. If timing belt is to be reused, proceed as follows:
    a. Place alignment marks on the camshaft timing pulleys and belt.
    b. Loosen idler pulley bolt, then push idler pulley as far left as possible and temporarily tighten it.
    c. Remove timing belt from camshaft timing pulleys. **Support timing belt so meshing of crankshaft timing pulley and timing belt does not shift.**
    d. Remove camshaft timing pulleys, then the No. 4 timing belt cover.
25. Remove right mounting bracket attaching bolts, then the mounting bracket.
26. Measure camshaft thrust clearance, **Fig. 3.** If clearance is greater than .0098 inch on 1985-86 models, or .0118 inch on 1987 models, replace camshaft and/or cylinder head.
27. Loosen and remove camshaft bearing cap attaching bolts gradually in sequence shown in **Fig. 33.**
28. Remove camshaft bearing caps, oil seal and camshaft.
29. Loosen and remove cylinder head attaching bolts gradually in sequence shown in **Fig. 34. Head warpage or cracking could result from removing cylinder head in incorrect order.**
30. Reverse procedure to install. Torque cylinder head attaching bolts gradually in three steps in reverse sequence as disassembly, **Fig. 33,** to 44 ft. lbs. Torque bearing cap attaching bolts gradually in three steps in reverse sequence as disassembly, **Fig. 34,** to 9 ft. lbs.

1987 Corolla FX-16

1. Disconnect battery ground cable.

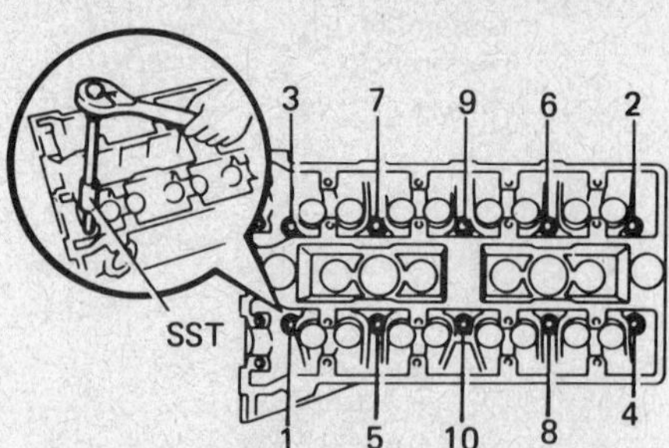

Fig. 34 Cylinder head bolt removal sequence. 4A-GE, 4A-GEC, 4A-GEL & 4A-GELC engines

2. Remove engine under cover, then drain coolant into suitable container.
3. Remove air cleaner assembly, then disconnect cruise control cable (if equipped) and accelerator cable and link.
4. Disconnect heater hose from rear cylinder head cover.
5. Identify, then disconnect vacuum hoses from throttle body.
6. Remove cruise control actuator (if equipped), ignition coil and coolant outlet hose.
7. Remove brake booster vacuum hose, then the PCV hose.
8. Remove EGR valve and tubes, then the cold start injector pressure hose.
9. Remove fuel system pulsation damper and pressure regulator.
10. Disconnect heater bypass hoses from auxiliary air valve.
11. Disconnect water temperature sensor connector and water temperature switch connector (if equipped), then identify and remove vacuum hoses from vacuum tubes. Remove vacuum tubes attaching bolts, then the vacuum tubes, cylinder head rear cover and wire clamp.
12. Disconnect all wires necessary for cylinder head removal, then lay wire harness aside.
13. Remove distributor, then the front exhaust pipe.
14. Remove exhaust manifold insulator, oxygen sensor and the manifold support bracket.
15. Remove exhaust manifold, then the oxygen sensor gasket.
16. Remove fuel delivery pipe and fuel injectors.
17. Remove intake manifold and intake air control valve.
18. Remove power steering drive belt and alternator drive belt.
19. Remove cylinder head center cover, then the valve covers.
20. Remove coolant outlet, coolant bypass pipe and drive belt adjusting bar and gasket.
21. Remove spark plugs, then set crankshaft pulley at TDC compression stroke. **Ensure valve lifters for No. 1 cylinder are loose. If not, rotate crankshaft pulley an additional 360° to set engine at TDC compression.**
22. Position suitable jack and wooden block under engine and raise slightly, then remove right side engine mount

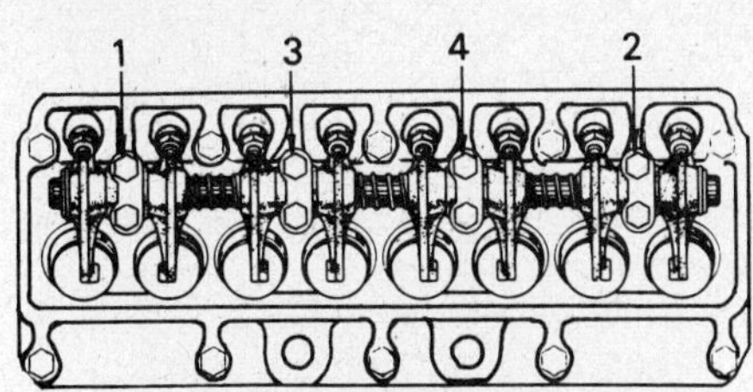

Fig. 35 Rocker arm assembly attaching bolt removal sequence. 4K-E engine

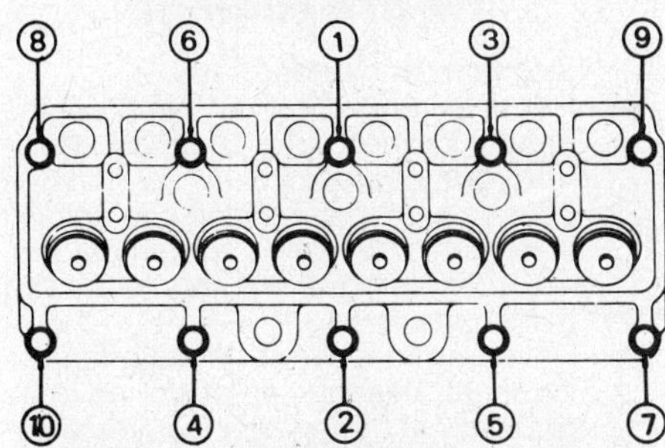

Fig. 38 Cylinder head bolt tightening sequence. 4K-E engine

through bolt and mount.

23. Remove water pump pulley, then on models equipped with A/C, the A/C compressor idler pulley. On all models, remove No. 2 and 3 timing belt covers.
24. If timing belt is to be replaced, refer to "Timing Belt, Replace" for procedure. If timing belt is to be reused, proceed as follows:
    a. Place alignment marks on the camshaft timing pulleys and belt.
    b. Loosen idler pulley bolt, then push idler pulley as far left as possible and temporarily tighten it.
    c. Remove timing belt from camshaft timing pulleys. **Support timing belt so meshing of crankshaft timing pulley and timing belt does not shift.**
    d. Remove camshaft timing pulleys, right mounting bracket attaching bolts and mount and No. 4 timing belt cover.
25. Measure camshaft thrust clearance, **Fig. 3.** If clearance is greater than .0118 inch, replace camshaft and/or cylinder head.
26. Loosen and remove camshaft bearing cap attaching bolts gradually in sequence shown in **Fig. 33.**
27. Remove camshaft bearing caps, oil seal and camshaft.
28. Loosen and remove cylinder head attaching bolts gradually in sequence shown in **Fig. 34. Head warpage or cracking could result from removing cylinder head in incorrect order.**
29. Reverse procedure to install. Torque cylinder head attaching bolts gradually in three steps in reverse sequence as disassembly, **Fig. 33,** to 44 ft. lbs. Torque bearing cap attaching bolts gradually in three steps in reverse sequence as disassembly, **Fig. 34,** to 9 ft. lbs.

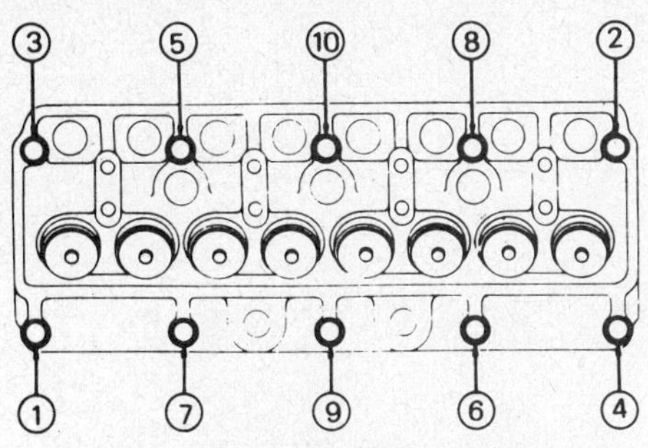

Fig. 36 Cylinder head bolt removal sequence. 4K-E engine

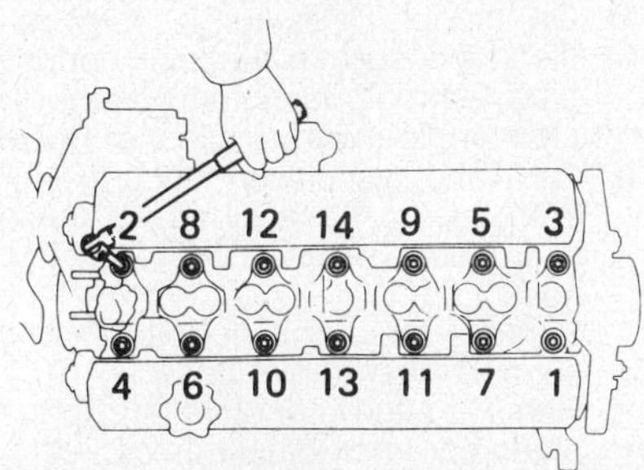

Fig. 39 Cylinder head bolt removal sequence. 5M-GE engine

4K-E ENGINE

1. Disconnect battery ground cable, drain coolant from radiator and engine block.
2. Disconnect hose from air cleaner.
3. Disconnect throttle cable from throttle body and air intake chamber.
4. Disconnect gas filter to fuel pressure regulator, gas filter to distributor and throttle body to distributor vacuum hoses. Disconnect throttle body to charcoal canister vacuum hose.
5. Disconnect spark plug wires from spark plugs.
6. Disconnect all electrical connectors, fuel lines and heater hoses from cylinder head.
7. Remove spark plugs and two air intake chamber brackets.
8. Remove air intake line, air intake chamber and air valve.
9. Disconnect EFI solenoid wire harness from fuel line.
10. Raise and support vehicle.
11. Drain engine oil, then remove front exhaust pipe and bracket.
12. Lower vehicle, then remove intake and exhaust manifolds.
13. Remove nuts, washers and cylinder head cover.
14. Remove rocker shaft assembly bolts in sequence shown in **Fig. 35,** then remove rocker shaft assembly and pushrod. **Identify pushrod so that they can be installed in their original locations.**
15. Loosen and remove cylinder head bolts in sequence shown in **Fig. 36,** then remove cylinder head.
16. Reverse procedure to install. Torque rocker shaft assembly bolts in sequence shown in **Fig. 37** to 14-17 ft. lbs. (1.8-2.4 kg-m). Torque cylinder head bolts to 40-47 ft. lbs. (5.4-6.6 kg-m) in sequence shown in **Fig. 38.**

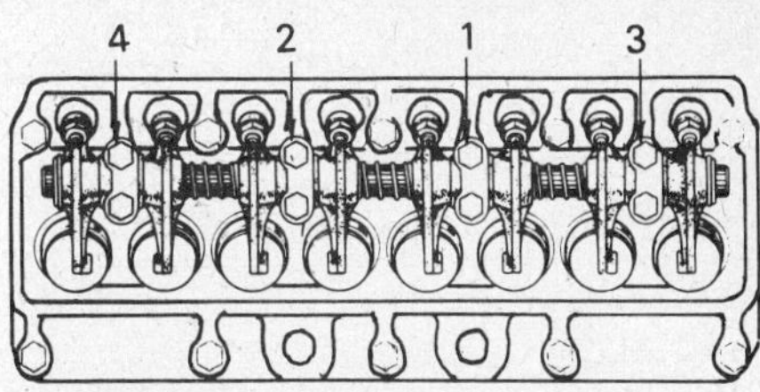

Fig. 37 Rocker arm assembly attaching bolt tightening sequence. 4K-E engine

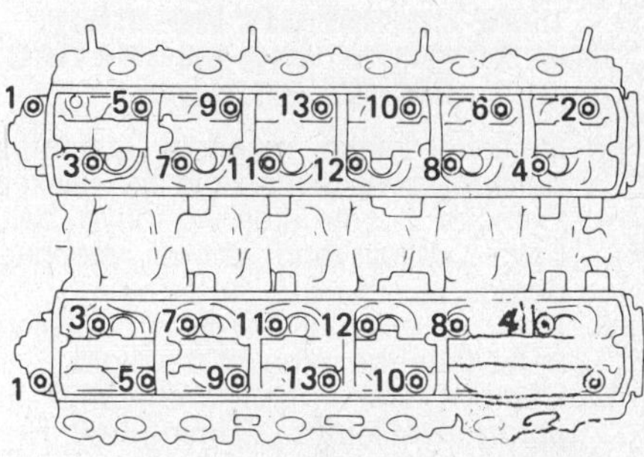

Fig. 40 Exhaust & intake side camshaft housing bolts removal sequence. 5M-GE engine

5M-GE ENGINE

1. Disconnect battery ground cable, then drain coolant from radiator and engine block.
2. Disconnect exhaust pipe from exhaust manifold.
3. On vehicles equipped with automatic transmission, remove throttle cable bracket from cylinder head cover.
4. On all models, remove accelerator and actuator cable bracket from cylinder head cover.
5. Disconnect all electrical connectors, emission control valve hoses, brake, cruise control actuator (if equipped), upper radiator hose and heater hoses from cylinder head. Disconnect fuel lines from cylinder head.
6. Remove air intake chamber bracket, bolts, vacuum line and ground strap.
7. Disconnect coil wire, then remove distributor from cylinder head.
8. Remove spark plugs, then disconnect cold start injector fuel hose from fuel line.
9. Remove air intake chamber attaching nuts and bolts, then the air intake chamber and gasket.
10. Disconnect EFI wire harness from ECU.
11. Remove pulsation damper and number 1 fuel line.
12. Remove water outlet housing attaching bolts, then the water outlet housing.

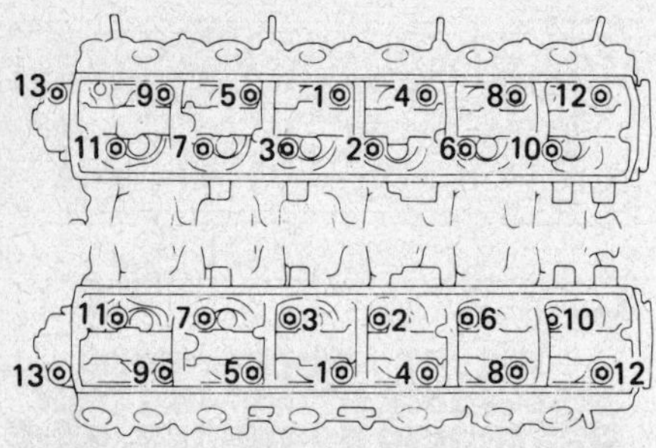

Fig. 41 Exhaust & intake side camshaft housing bolts tightening sequence. 5M-GE engine

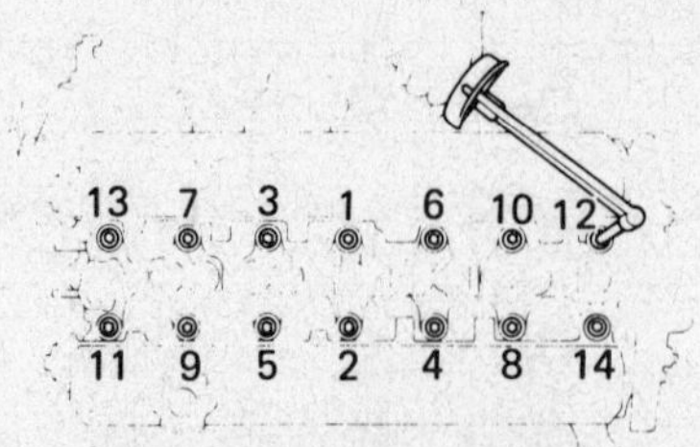

Fig. 42 Cylinder head bolt tightening sequence. 5M-GE engine

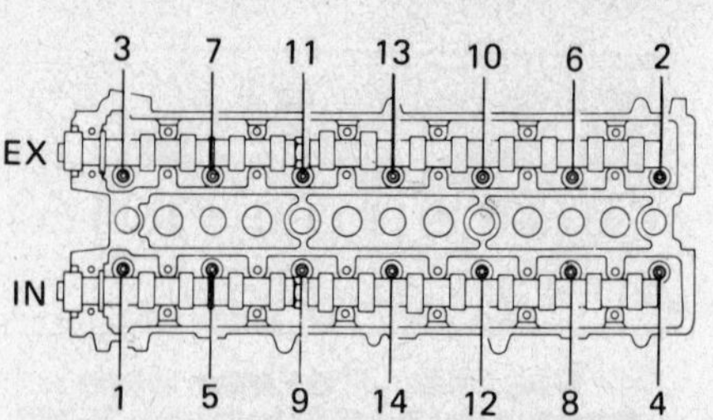

Fig. 43 Cylinder head bolt removal sequence. 7M-GE & 7M-GTE engines

13. Remove intake manifold attaching bolts, then intake manifold and gasket.
14. Remove power steering drive belt, bolts, pulley and power steering pump.
15. Remove exhaust manifold attaching bolts, then the exhaust manifold.
16. Remove timing belt and camshaft sprockets. Refer to "Timing Belt, Replace" for procedure.
17. Remove two bolts and timing belt cover bracket. Remove three bolts, oil pressure regulator and gasket.
18. Remove bolts, nuts, number 2 timing belt cover and gasket.
19. Loosen and remove cylinder head bolts a little at a time in sequence shown in **Fig. 39.**
20. Remove cylinder head from engine block.
21. Loosen and remove No. 1 and 2 camshaft housing bolts in sequence shown in **Fig. 40.** Remove camshaft housings from cylinder head.
22. Using a dial indicator as shown in **Fig. 3,** measure camshaft thrust clearance. Camshaft standard thrust clearance should be .0020-.0098 inch with a maximum clearance of .0118 inch. If camshaft thrust clearance is not within specification, replace camshaft and or camshaft housings.
23. Remove camshafts from camshaft housings.
24. Reverse procedure to install. Gradually tighten camshaft housing bolts in three steps and in sequence shown in **Fig. 41.** Torque camshaft housing bolts to 16 ft. lbs. Torque cylinder head bolts gradually in three steps in sequence shown in **Fig. 42** to 58 ft. lbs. Torque number 2 timing belt cover bolts to 9 ft. lbs. Torque exhaust manifold bolts to 29 ft. lbs. Torque intake manifold bolts to 13 ft. lbs. Torque spark plugs to 12 ft. lbs.

7M-GE & 7M-GTE ENGINES

1. Disconnect battery ground cable, then drain coolant from radiator and engine block into suitable container.
2. Disconnect exhaust pipe from exhaust manifold.
3. Disconnect cruise control cable, accelerator cable and on models equipped with auto. trans., throttle valve cable.
4. Disconnect ground strap from rear of engine.
5. On models less turbo, remove air cleaner hose with intake air connector pipe. On models w/turbo, remove air cleaner pipe with air cleaner hoses.
6. On all models, disconnect cruise control vacuum hose, charcoal canister hose and brake booster vacuum hose.
7. Remove radiator inlet hose, then disconnect heater inlet hose.
8. Remove alternator drive belt, then the alternator and adjusting bracket.
9. On turbo models, remove power steering reservoir tank, then cam position sensor.
10. On all models, remove air intake chamber with connector.
11. On turbo models, remove ignition coil cover, connectors, ground wire and attaching nut, then the ignition coil with bracket.
12. Identify, then disconnect any wiring that may interfere with cylinder head removal.
13. Remove fuel pulsation damper, vacuum switching valve and No. 1 fuel pipe.
14. Remove No. 3 fuel pipe, then on turbo models, remove auxiliary air pipe.
15. On all except turbo models, remove oil dipstick and secondary cables from spark plugs, then remove distributor.
16. On turbo models, remove turbocharger.
17. On all except turbo models, remove exhaust manifold attaching bolts, then the exhaust manifold. On turbo models, remove heat insulator, bracket and exhaust manifold attaching bolts, then the manifold.
18. On all models, remove coolant outlet housing, then the cylinder head covers and spark plugs.
19. Remove timing belt and camshaft sprockets. Refer to "Timing Belt, Replace" for procedure.
20. Loosen cylinder head bolts in increments, following sequence, **Fig. 43. If loosening sequence is not followed, cylinder head warpage or cracking could occur.**
21. Lift cylinder head from block, then disconnect No. 5 coolant bypass hose from union. Continue to remove cylinder head and place on suitable wooden blocks.
22. Remove rear timing belt cover, alternator bracket, heater inlet hose, heater union and fuel delivery pipe with injectors from cylinder head.
23. Remove intake manifold, No. 2 engine hanger, ground strap and EGR cooler from cylinder head.
24. Loosen camshaft bearing cap bolts in increments, following sequence, **Fig. 44,** then remove bearing caps and camshafts.
25. Reverse procedure to install. Torque camshaft bearing cap attaching bolts gradually in three steps in reverse sequence as disassembly, **Fig. 44,** to 14 ft. lbs. Torque cylinder head attaching bolts gradually in three steps in reverse sequence as disassembly, **Fig. 43,** to 58 ft. lbs.

22R, 22R-E & 22R-TE ENGINES

Removal

1. Disconnect battery ground cable, then drain coolant from radiator and engine block.
2. On turbo models, remove turbocharger assembly. On carbureted models, remove air cleaner. On fuel injected models less turbo, disconnect air cleaner hose from air cleaner.
3. Disconnect exhaust pipe from exhaust manifold.
4. Disconnect all electrical connectors, fuel lines, vacuum, emission and heater hoses from intake manifold, carburetor (if equipped) and cylinder head. On carbureted models, remove fuel pump.
5. Remove oil dipstick, distributor, spark plugs and radiator inlet hose, then disconnect heater water inlet hose from heater water inlet pipe.
6. Disconnect cruise control actuator (if equipped), accelerator cable and engine ground strap from cylinder head. Disconnect throttle cable, if equipped, from cylinder head.
7. Remove EGR vacuum modulator and bracket from cylinder head (if equipped).
8. On fuel injected models, remove bolts, air intake chamber and throttle body.
9. On fuel injected models, remove pulsation damper and disconnect fuel hose from fuel line.
10. On fuel injected models, disconnect air bypass hose from air valve and remove air valve from intake manifold.
11. On fuel injected models, remove auxiliary air valve.
12. On fuel injected turbo models, discon-

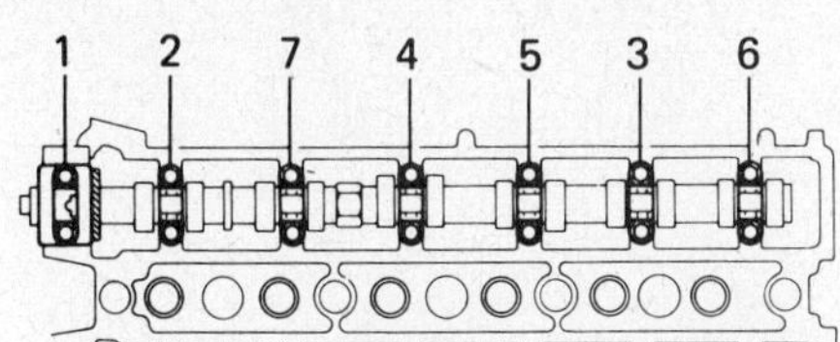

Fig. 44 Camshaft bearing cap bolt removal sequence. 7M-GE & 7M-GTE engines

nect oil cooler hose from intake manifold.

13. On vehicles equipped with power steering, remove drive belt, bolts and pulley. Remove power steering pump mounting bolts and position pump aside. Do not disconnect power steering pump hoses.
14. Remove ground strap and cylinder head cover.
15. Rotate crankshaft until No. 1 cylinder is set at TDC compression stroke. Place reference marks on timing chain and camshaft sprocket.
16. Remove semi-circular plug, camshaft sprocket bolt and distributor drive gear and fuel pump drive cam on carbureted models, or distributor drive gear and thrust plate on fuel injected models.
17. Remove camshaft sprocket and timing chain from camshaft, leaving lower part of chain engaged on lower sprocket. Remove timing chain cover bolt from front inside of cylinder head. **The timing chain cover bolt must be removed prior to removing head bolts.**
18. Gradually loosen and remove cylinder head bolts in two or three steps as shown in **Fig. 45.**
19. Remove rocker arm assembly from cylinder head, then remove cylinder head. **If rocker arm assembly is difficult to remove, a pry bar can be inserted at the front or rear of rocker arm assembly to aid in separation.**
20. Remove intake manifold.
21. Remove EGR valve and exhaust manifold, if not previously removed.
22. Remove engine hangers, ground straps and cylinder head rear cover.
23. Using suitable dial indicator positioned at front of cylinder head, measure camshaft thrust clearance, **Fig. 3.** Standard camshaft thrust clearance is .0031-.0071 inch, with a maximum clearance of .0098 inch. If measurement exceeds maximum clearance, replace cylinder head.
24. Remove camshaft bearing cap bolts, then the bearing caps and camshaft.

Installation

1. Install camshaft in cylinder head, then install bearing caps in numbered order from the front of the cylinder head with arrows facing forward. Install bearing cap bolts and torque to 14 ft. lbs.
2. Rotate camshaft to position alignment pin away from cylinder head.
3. Install cylinder head rear cover, engine hangers and ground straps.
4. Install intake manifold, EGR valve and exhaust manifold.
5. Apply a suitable sealer to where timing cover and front of engine block intersect, then install a new cylinder head gasket.
6. If camshaft sprocket was removed from timing chain, position sprocket in chain while aligning reference marks made during removal. Install cylinder head onto engine block.
7. Install rocker arm assembly, then gradually torque cylinder head bolts in three steps in sequence shown in **Fig. 46** to 58 ft. lbs.
8. Install timing chain cover bolt. Torque bolt to 9 ft. lbs.
9. Ensure camshaft alignment pin faces upward. If not, rotate camshaft as necessary to position alignment pin upwards.
10. While holding tension on camshaft sprocket and timing chain, rotate crankshaft to ensure cylinders Nos. 1 and 4 are set at TDC.
11. Position camshaft sprocket and chain onto camshaft. **If timing chain appears too short, rotate crankshaft back and forth while pulling up on chain and sprocket.**
12. Install distributor drive gear and bolt. Torque bolt to 58 ft. lbs.
13. Adjust valve clearances, refer to "Valves, Adjust" for procedure.
14. Install half circular plug, gasket and cylinder head cover.
15. Install power steering pump bolts, pulley and drive belt. Torque bolts 33 ft. lbs.
16. Reverse steps 1 through 12 of removal procedures to complete installation.

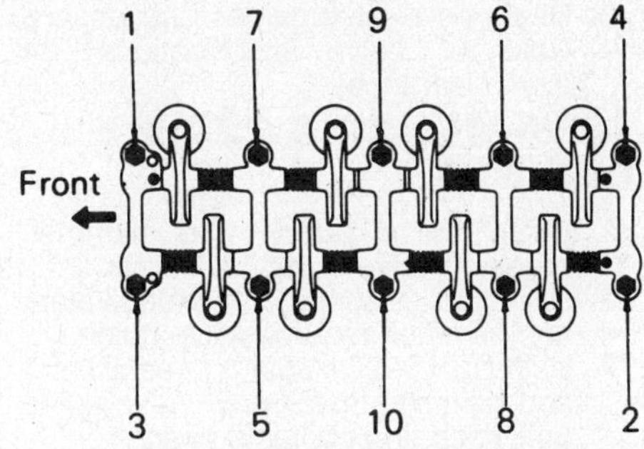

Fig. 45 Cylinder head bolt removal sequence. 20R, 22R, 22R-E & 22R-TE engines

VALVE CLEARANCE ADJUST

2S-E, 4Y-EC, 5M-GE ENGINES

These models use hydraulic valve lifters. No adjustments are required.

3A-C, 3E, 4A-C, 4A-GE, 4A-GEL, 4A-GELC & 4A-LC ENGINES

1. With No. 1 piston at TDC on compression stroke, adjust the following cylinders valves to specification:
   No. 1 Intake & Exhaust
   No. 2 Intake
   No. 3 Exhaust
2. Turn crankshaft in normal direction of rotation one full revolution (360°) and adjust the following cylinders valves to specification:
   No. 2 Exhaust
   No. 3 Intake
   No. 4 Intake and Exhaust

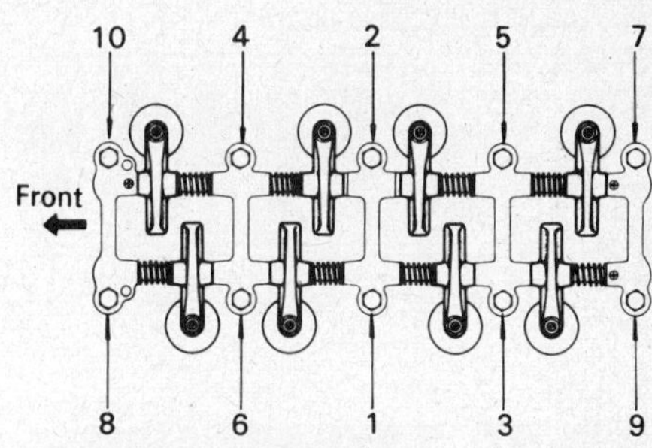

Fig. 46 Cylinder head bolt tightening sequence. 22R, 22R-E & 22R-TE engines

4K-E ENGINES

1. With No. 1 piston at TDC on compression stroke, adjust the following valves indicated in **Fig. 47** to specification:
   No. 1 Exhaust
   No. 2 Intake
   No. 3 Intake
   No. 5 Exhaust
2. Turn crankshaft in normal direction of rotation one full revolution (360°) and adjust the following valves indicated in **Fig. 47** to specification:
   No. 4 Exhaust
   No. 6 Intake
   No. 7 Intake
   No. 8 Exhaust

3S-FE, 3S-GE, 22R, 22R-E & 22R-TE ENGINES

1. Crank engine until No. 1 cylinder is at TDC compression stroke and adjust the following cylinders valves to specifications:
   Intake Nos. 1, 2
   Exhaust Nos. 1, 3
2. Rotate engine one complete revolution clockwise and adjust the following cylinders valves to specifications:
   Intake Nos. 3, 4
   Exhaust Nos. 2, 4

7M-GE & 7M-GTE ENGINES

1. With No. 1 piston at TDC on compression stroke (ensure No. 1 lifters cylinders are loose and No. 6 cylinders lifters are tight), adjust the following cylinders valves to specification:
   No. 1 Intake & Exhaust
   No. 4 Intake
   No. 5 Exhaust
2. Turn crankshaft in normal direction of rotation 2/3 turn, (240°), (ensure No. 3 cylinders lifters are loose) and adjust the following cylinders valves to spec-

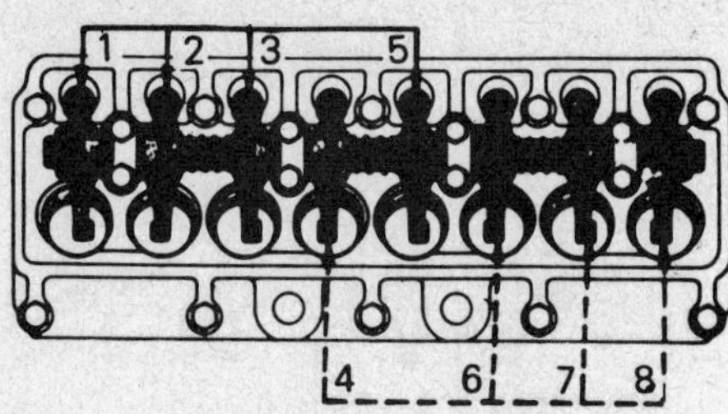

Fig. 47 Valve adjustment. 4K-E engines

Fig. 49 Aligning bearing cap mark with center of small hole on camshaft sprocket. 3A-C, 4A-C & 4A-LC engine

ifications:
No. 3 Intake and Exhaust
No. 5 Intake
No. 6 Exhaust

3. Turn crankshaft in normal direction of rotation an additional 2/3 turn, (240°), (ensure No. 2 cylinders lifters are loose) and adjust the following cylinders valves to specifications:
   No. 2 Intake and Exhaust
   No. 4 Exhaust
   No. 6 Intake

VALVE GUIDE
REPLACE
EXC. 1983–85 22R & 22R-E ENGINES

1. Using a suitable tool and hammer, strike valve guide bushing to break it off at cylinder head casting.
2. On all engine models except 4K-E engine, heat cylinder head to 176-212°F (80-100°C). On 4K-E engines, heat cylinder head to 212-266°F (100-130°C).
3. Using suitable valve guide removal tool, drive out bushing from the outside towards the combustion chamber side on all except 4A-GE, 4A-GEL, 4A-GELC, 7M-GE and 7M-GTE engines. On 4A-GE, 4A-GEL, 4A GELC, 7M-GE and 7M-GTE engines drive bushing out from combustion chamber side.
4. Install snap ring on new valve guide, then install new valve guide using tool as above and driving in from the reverse side of removal.
5. Ream new valve guide, if necessary. Refer to "Valve Specifications" for stem clearances.

1983–85 22R & 22R-E ENGINES

1. Using brass punch and hammer, break off valve guide at snap ring.
2. Using tool 09201-60011 or equivalent and hammer, remove valve guide.
3. Using tool 09201-60011 or equivalent and hammer, install new valve guide until snap ring contacts head.
4. Ream valve guide if necessary to obtain specified valve stem clearance.

HYDRAULIC VALVE LIFTERS

Check lifters for excessive wear and/or damage. Replace worn or damaged valve lifters as required. Lubricate hydraulic valve lifter before installation. **The 3Y-EC and 4Y-EC engines uses two different types of lifters, Fig. 48, a GM type and a Toyota type. The GM type lifter can be identified by a squared edged retaining clip with the lifter foot measuring .20 inch. The Toyota type lifter can be identified by a rounded edge retaining clip with the lifter foot measuring .31 inch.**

CAMSHAFT
REPLACE
EXC. 3Y-EC, 4Y-EC & 4K-E ENGINES

Refer to "Cylinder Head, Replace" for camshaft removal procedures.

3Y-EC, 4Y-EC & 4K-E ENGINES

Refer to "Timing Chain & Camshaft, Replace" for camshaft removal procedures.

CAMSHAFT HOUSING OIL SEAL
REPLACE
5M-GE ENGINE
With Camshaft Removed From Camshaft Housing

1. Using a suitable screwdriver, pry out oil seals from camshaft housings.
2. Lubricate new oil seals, then using tool number 09214-60010 or equivalent, install oil seals into camshaft housing.

With Camshaft Housing Installed On Cylinder Head

1. Using a suitable tool, split oil seals.
2. Using a suitable screwdriver, pry out oil seals from camshaft housing.
3. Check contact surface of camshaft oil seal lip for damage.
4. Lubricate new oil seals, then using tool number 09214-60010 or equivalent, install oil seals into camshaft housings.

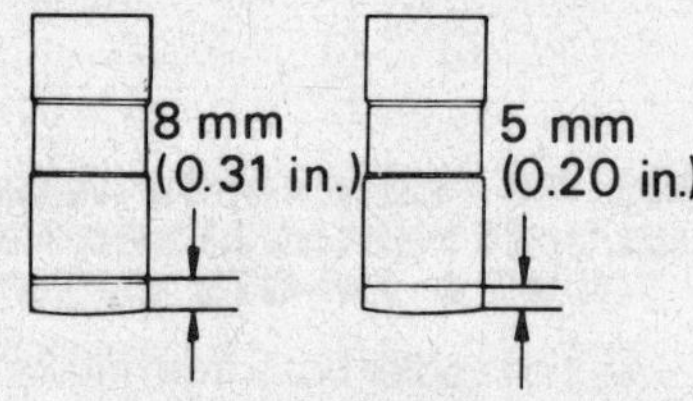

Fig. 48 Hydraulic valve lifter identification. 3Y-EC & 4Y-EC engines

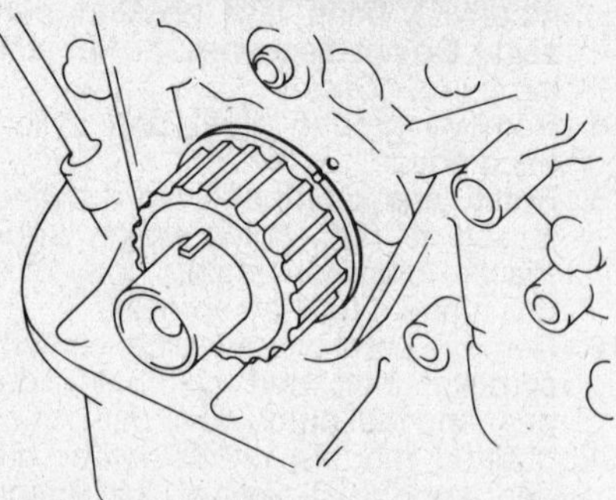

Fig. 50 Aligning TDC marks on crankshaft sprocket & oil pump body. 3A-C, 3E, 4A-C, 4A-LC engine

TIMING BELT
REPLACE
3A-C & 4A-C ENGINES
REMOVAL

1. Disconnect battery ground cable. Drain coolant from radiator and engine block. On models w/3A-C engine, remove radiator.
2. On vehicles equipped with power steering, remove fan shroud, if equipped, power steering pump mounting bolts and drive belt.
3. On vehicles equipped with air conditioning, loosen idler pulley nut, adjusting bolt and remove drive belt.
4. Remove air cleaner assembly.
5. Remove water pump pulley and drive belt.
6. Disconnect PCV hose from PCV valve.
7. Remove bolts, cylinder head cover, gasket and plug.
8. On vehicles equipped with power steering, remove No. 2 crankshaft pulley.
9. Set No. 1 piston at TDC of compression stroke. **Ensure rocker arms of No. 1 cylinder are loose. If not, turn crankshaft one full turn.**
10. Remove crankshaft pulley bolt and pulley.
11. Remove timing belt cover bolts, timing belt covers and gasket. **If timing belt is to be reused, draw arrow on belt to indicate direction of rotation and**

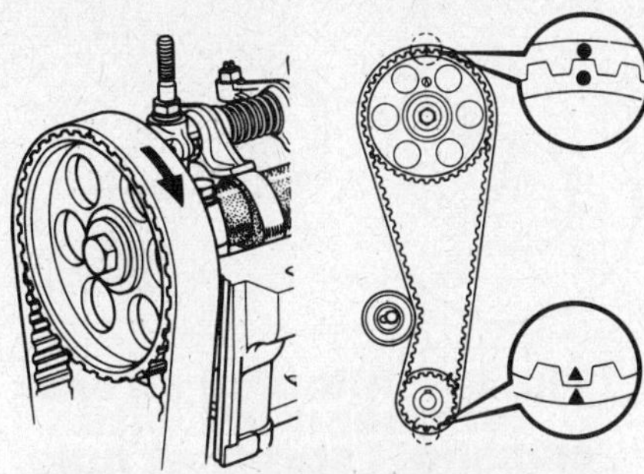

Fig. 51 Installing timing belt. 3A-C, 4A-C & 4A-LC engines

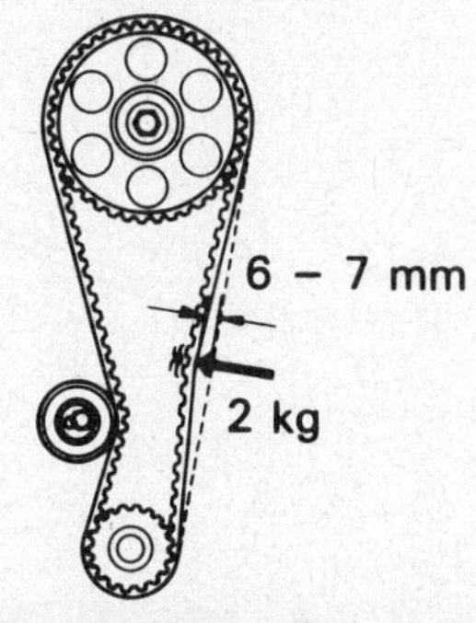

Fig. 53 Checking timing belt deflection. 3A-C, 4A-C & 4A-LC

make alignment marks between timing belt and camshaft sprocket and timing belt and camshaft sprocket.

12. Remove timing belt guide, timing belt and idler pulley. **Do not allow oil or water to contact timing belt, sprockets or idler pulley.**
13. Remove crankshaft and camshaft sprockets.

INSTALLATION

1. Check timing belt for damage, replace if necessary.
2. Align camshaft dowel pin with notch on camshaft timing sprocket.
3. Install and torque camshaft timing sprocket bolt to 29-39 ft. lbs.
4. Align bearing cap mark with small hole on camshaft sprocket, **Fig. 49.**
5. Install crankshaft timing sprocket, then align TDC marks on oil pump body and crankshaft timing sprocket, **Fig. 50.**
6. Install timing idler pulley and tension spring. Pry timing belt idler pulley toward the left and temporarily tighten the bolt.
7. Install timing belt. Loosen timing belt idler pulley bolt. **If timing belt is being reused, install in direction marked with reference marks aligned, Fig. 51.**
8. Temporarily install crankshaft sprocket bolt and turn crankshaft, in normal direction of rotation, two revolutions TDC to TDC.
9. Check valve timing. Ensure each sprocket aligns with the marks as shown in **Fig. 52.**
10. Torque idler pulley bolt to 22-32 ft. lbs.
11. Measure timing belt deflection at the middle of the long side of the belt, **Fig. 53.**
12. Timing belt deflection should be .24-.28 inch at 4.4 lb. (6-7 mm at 2 kg).
13. If measurement obtained is not within specification, loosen idler pulley bolt, then move idler pulley to obtain correct timing belt deflection. Torque idler pulley bolt to 22-32 ft. lbs.
14. Apply sealer to No. 1 camshaft bearing cap and plug.
15. Install plug, gasket and cylinder head cover. Connect hose to PCV valve.
16. Install timing belt guide and lower cover. Install timing belt cover gasket and upper cover.
17. Install crankshaft pulley and bolt. Torque bolt to 88-94 ft. lbs.
18. Install crankshaft No. 2 pulley (if equipped), water pump pulley and drive belt.
19. Install power steering pump mounting bolts and drive belt. Install fan shroud.
20. Install air cleaner assembly.

3E ENGINE

REMOVAL

1. Disconnect battery ground cable, then remove right front wheel.
2. Remove right side engine under cover.
3. Remove accessory drive belts.
4. Remove air cleaner, then the spark plugs.
5. Raise engine slightly with suitable jack. **Position block of wood between jack and engine to prevent damage to engine.**
6. Remove right side engine mount through bolt, then the engine mount.
7. Remove PCV valve from valve cover, then the valve cover.
8. Rotate crankshaft pulley in direction of rotation and align pulley groove with "0" timing mark to set engine at TDC compression stroke. **Ensure rocker arms for No. 1 cylinder are loose, otherwise engine is not set at TDC compression and crankshaft pulley must be rotated an additional 360°.**
9. On models equipped with A/C, remove compressor drive pulley. On all models, loosen crankshaft pulley bolt, then using suitable puller, remove crankshaft pulley.
10. Remove timing belt covers, then the timing belt guide from crankshaft sprocket.
11. If timing belt is to be reused, draw arrow on belt to indicate direction of rotation and make alignment marks between timing belt and camshaft sprocket and timing belt and camshaft sprocket.
12. Disconnect spring loaded idler pulley tension spring, then loosen idler pulley attaching bolt and push idler pulley as far as possible to the left and temporarily tighten bolt.
13. Remove timing belt, then the idler pulley attaching bolt, pulley and tension spring. **Do not allow oil, grease or water to contact any part of timing belt train.**
14. Remove fixed idler pulley, then using two screwdrivers pry off crankshaft sprocket.
15. While holding camshaft with suitable wrench positioned at camshaft flats, remove camshaft sprocket attaching bolt, then the sprocket.
16. While holding oil pump sprocket with suitable wrench, remove oil pump sprocket attaching nut, then the sprocket.

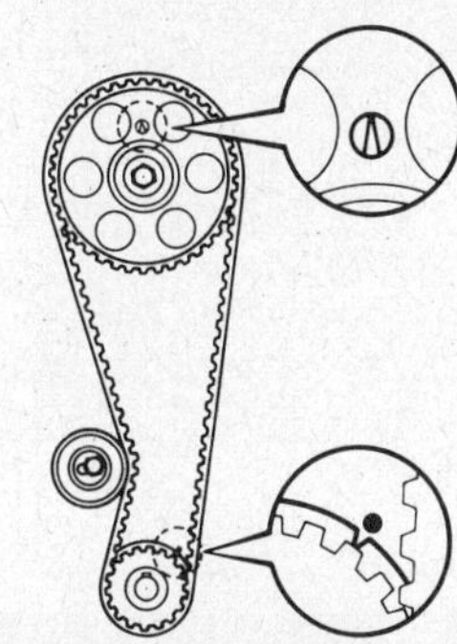

Fig. 52 Ensuring proper sprocket alignment. 3A-C, 4A-C & 4A-LC engines

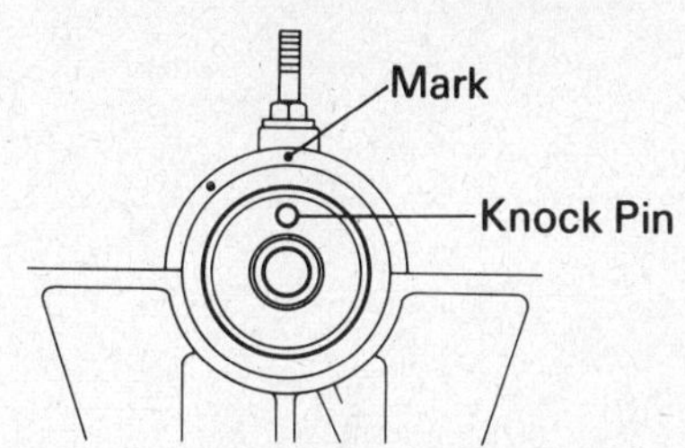

Fig. 54 Camshaft bearing cap & camshaft alignment. 3E engine

INSTALLATION

1. Install oil pump sprocket, then while holding sprocket with suitable tool, torque attaching nut to 20 ft. lbs.
2. Align camshaft sprocket drive pin with front camshaft bearing cap mark, **Fig. 54.**
3. Align camshaft sprocket "3E" marking alignment holes with camshaft drive pin and bearing cap mark, then install camshaft sprocket and attaching bolt on camshaft, **Fig. 54.**
4. While holding camshaft with suitable wrench, torque camshaft sprocket attaching bolt to 37 ft. lbs.
5. Install crankshaft sprocket, then align TDC mark on crankshaft sprocket and oil pump body, **Fig. 50.**
6. Install spring loaded idler pulley less tension spring, pry idler pulley as far as possible to the left and temporarily tighten bolt.
7. Install fixed idler pulley. Torque attaching bolt to 20 ft. lbs.
8. Install timing belt. **If timing belt is being reused, ensure arrow drawn during removal is pointing in direction of engine rotation and all reference marks are aligned.**

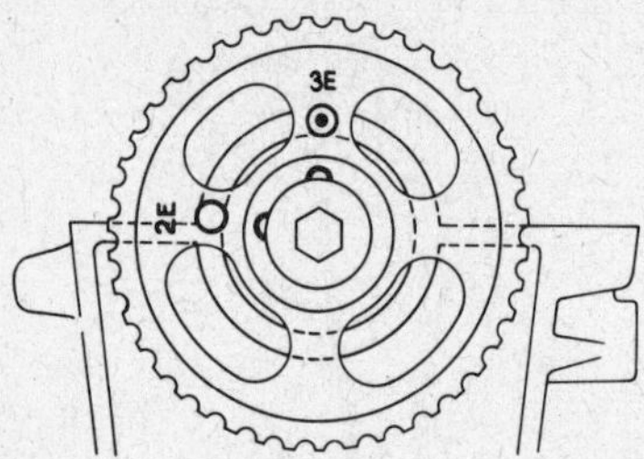

Fig. 55 Camshaft sprocket installation. 3E engine

Fig. 58 Installing crankshaft sprocket. 2S-E engine

9. Loosen spring loaded idler pulley bolt, then install tension spring.
10. Temporarily install crankshaft pulley bolt, then rotate crankshaft in clockwise direction for two revolutions, TDC to TDC.
11. Ensure timing belt alignment marks are in proper position, Fig. 56.
12. Torque spring loaded idler attaching bolt to 13 ft. lbs. **Ensure timing belt has tension between oil pump sprocket and fixed idler pulley.**
13. Remove crankshaft pulley bolt, then install timing belt guide on crankshaft sprocket.
14. Install timing belt covers, crankshaft pulley(s) and attaching bolt. Torque attaching bolt to 112 ft. lbs.
15. Install valve cover, right side engine mount, spark plugs, air cleaner, drive belts, under cover and wheel.
16. Connect battery ground cable.

2S-E ENGINE

REMOVAL

1. Disconnect battery ground cable.
2. Remove right side front wheel.
3. Remove fender apron seal.
4. Remove alternator drive belt.
5. Remove cruise control actuator and bracket.
6. Remove power steering oil reservoir tank and drive belt.
7. Raise engine slightly, then remove right side engine mount insulator and bracket.
8. Remove No. 2 timing belt cover and gasket assembly.
9. Remove spark plugs.
10. Align oil seal retainer mark with center of small hole on camshaft timing sprocket by turning crankshaft pulley clockwise, **Fig. 57.** This will position No. 1 cylinder at 90° BTDC of compression stroke. Loosen No. 1 idler pulley retaining bolt and move pulley toward the left as far as possible, then temporarily tighten retaining bolt.
11. Remove timing belt from camshaft timing sprocket.
12. Using tool No. 09278-54011 or equivalent, hold timing sprocket in place, then remove sprocket retaining bolt and sprocket.
13. Remove No. 1 idler pulley and tension spring.
14. Using tool Nos. 09213-54010 and 09330-00020 or equivalents, remove crankshaft pulley retaining bolt, then the pulley.
15. Remove No. 1 timing belt cover and gasket assembly.
16. Remove timing belt and belt guide.
17. Remove No. 2 idler pulley and crankshaft timing sprocket.

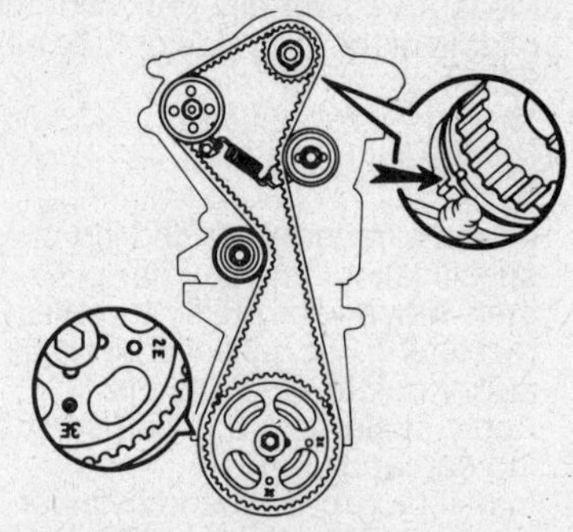

Fig. 56 Ensuring proper timing mark alignment. 3E engine

INSTALLATION

1. Slide crankshaft timing sprocket over crankshaft key, **Fig. 58.**
2. Install No. 2 idler pulley. Torque idler pulley retaining bolt, **Fig. 59**, to 31 ft. lbs.
3. Temporarily install timing belt onto sprockets.
4. Install timing belt guide.
5. Install No. 1 timing belt cover and gasket assembly.
6. Install crankshaft pulley. Torque crankshaft pulley retaining bolt to 80 ft. lbs.
7. Pull timing belt upward and align preset mark on No. 1 timing belt cover with crankshaft pulley groove, **Fig. 60.**
8. Install idler pulley and tension spring. Move idler pulley toward the left as far as possible and temporarily tighten retaining bolt, **Fig. 61.**
9. Install camshaft timing sprocket. Torque sprocket retaining bolt to 40 ft. lbs.
10. Install timing belt as follows:
    a. Align camshaft oil seal retainer preset mark with center of small hole on camshaft timing pulley.
    b. Install timing belt.
    c. Loosen No. 1 idler pulley retaining bolt 1/2 turn and release spring tension on timing belt.
    d. Turn crankshaft clockwise approximately 90° and set No. 1 cylinder to TDC of compression stroke.
    e. Torque No. 1 idler pulley retaining bolt to 31 ft. lbs.
11. Check valve timing as follows:
    a. Align camshaft oil seal retainer TDC mark with center of small hole on the camshaft timing sprocket by turning crankshaft pulley clockwise.
    b. Check crankshaft pulley angle on the No. 1 timing belt cover. Crankshaft pulley angle should be at TDC plus or minus 5°, **Fig. 62.** If not adjust valve timing.
12. To adjust valve timing proceed as follows:
    a. Turn crankshaft clockwise 1 3/4 turns (No. 1 cylinder at 90° BTDC of compression stroke) and align preset mark on No. 1 timing belt cover with crankshaft pulley groove, **Fig. 60.**
    b. Loosen No. 1 idler pulley retaining bolt and move idler pulley outward as far as possible then temporarily tighten retaining bolt.
    c. Using tool No. 09278-54011 or equivalent, secure camshaft timing sprocket and remove sprocket retaining bolt, sprocket and belt.
    d. If the timing mark is located at the BTDC side, shift camshaft sprocket to the left, **Fig. 63.**
    e. If the timing mark is located at the ATDC side, shift camshaft sprocket to the right, **Fig. 63. Changing the timing belt location by one tooth will alter the crankshaft pulley angle by 18°.**
    f. Pull camshaft timing sprocket and timing belt assembly upward, then

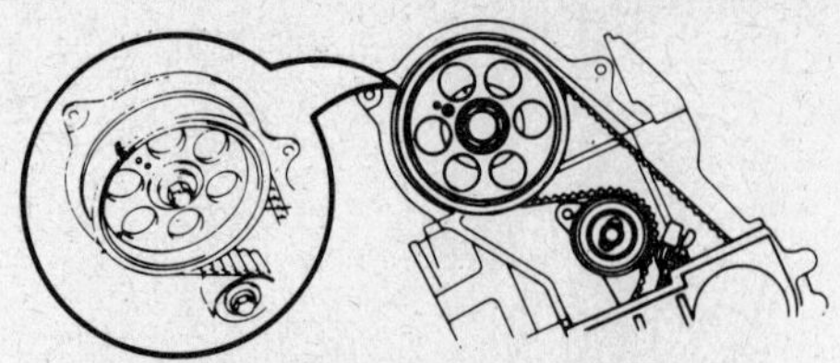

Fig. 57 Aligning oil seal retainer mark with camshaft sprocket hole. 2S-E engine

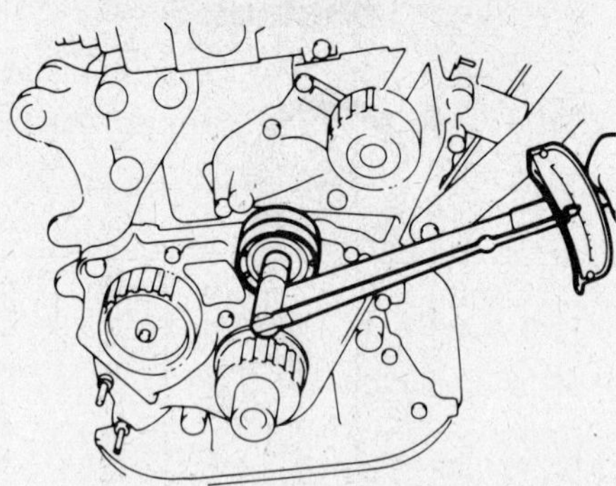

Fig. 59 Installing No. 2 idler pulley. 2S-E engine

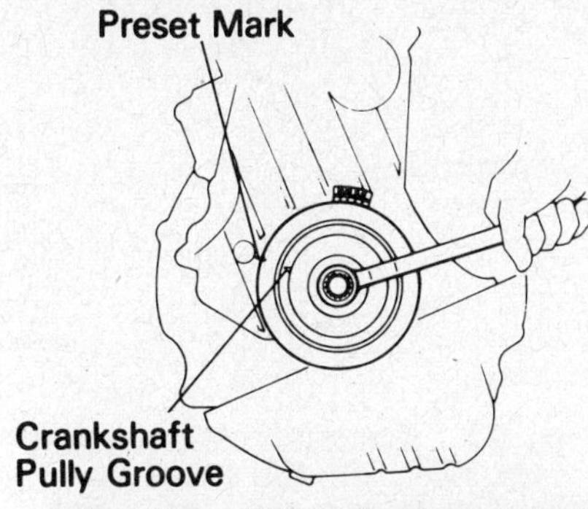

Fig. 60 Aligning preset mark on No. 1 timing belt cover with crankshaft pulley groove. 2S-E engine

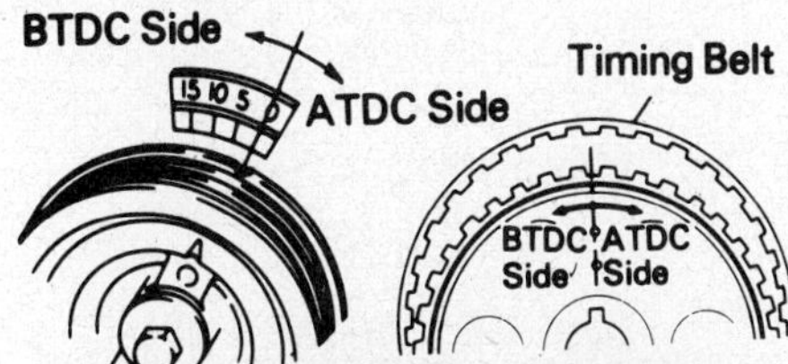

Fig. 63 Shifting camshaft sprocket position. 2S-E engine

turn crankshaft pulley slightly and install timing sprocket and belt assembly.

g. Using tool No. 09278-54011 or equivalent, secure camshaft timing sprocket and torque sprocket retaining bolt to 40 ft. lbs.
h. Loosen No. 1 idler pulley retaining bolt 1/2 turn and release spring tension on timing belt.
i. Turn crankshaft pulley until timing mark is aligned with TDC mark on tab.
j. Torque No. 1 idler pulley retaining bolt to 31 ft. lbs.

13. Install spark plugs.
14. Install No. 2 timing belt cover and gasket assembly.
15. Install right side engine mount insulator and bracket.
16. Lower engine and install power steering oil reservoir tank.
17. Install cruise control actuator and bracket.
18. Install fender apron seal and front wheel.

4A-GE, 4A-GEC, 4A-GEL & 4A-GELC

REMOVAL

1. On rear wheel drive Corolla models, proceed as follows:
   a. Disconnect battery ground cable, then remove No. 2 hose from air cleaner.
   b. Remove power steering pump and bracket assembly, if equipped.
   c. Remove drive belt, fluid coupling and water pump pulley, then the spark plugs.
2. On front wheel drive Corolla models,

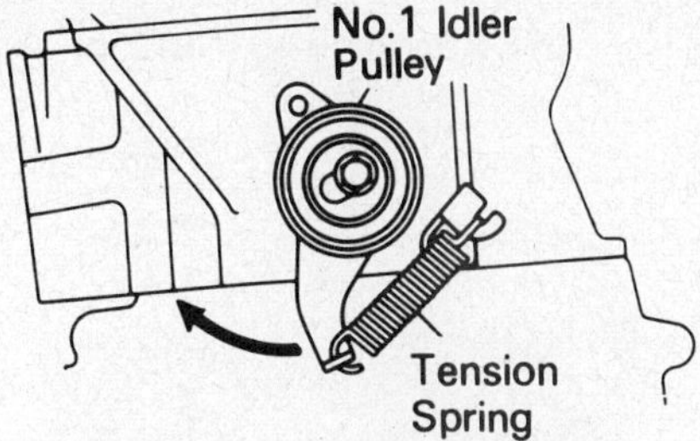

Fig. 61 Installing idler pulley & tension spring. 2S-E engine

proceed as follows:
   a. Disconnect battery ground cable, then remove right front wheel and engine under cover.
   b. Drain radiator coolant, then disconnect cruise control cable (if equipped), accelerator cable and link.
   c. Remove cruise control actuator (if equipped), then the ignition coil and coolant outlet hose.
   d. Remove accessory drive belts, then the spark plugs.
3. On MR2 models, proceed as follows:
   a. Disconnect battery ground cable, then remove right rear wheel and engine under cover.
   b. Remove accessory drive belts and spark plugs.
   c. Disconnect ignition coil high tension leads, brake booster vacuum hose and cruise control vacuum hose (if equipped).
4. Turn crankshaft pulley and align groove with "0" mark on the No. 1 timing belt cover, then remove oil filler cap and ensure cavity in camshaft is visible indicating TDC compression. If camshaft cavity is not visible, rotate crankshaft an additional 360° to set engine at TDC compression.
5. On front wheel drive Corolla models and MR2, raise engine with suitable jack, then remove right side engine mount through bolt and the mount. **Insert suitable piece of wood between jack and engine to prevent damage.** Remove crankshaft pulley using suitable tools.
6. Remove timing belt covers and gaskets, then the timing belt guide from crankshaft sprocket.
7. Loosen idler pulley bolt, then push idler pulley as far left as possible and temporarily tighten idler pulley bolt.
8. Remove timing belt, idler pulley bolt, pulley and tension spring. **If timing belt is to reused, mark direction and belt-to-sprocket reference marks to ensure correct position during installation.**
9. Remove cylinder head covers, then using suitable wrench positioned on camshaft flats, remove camshaft sprocket attaching bolts and sprockets.

INSTALLATION

1. Install camshaft sprockets, aligning marks as shown in **Fig. 64.** Install sprocket attaching bolts and torque to 34 ft. lbs.

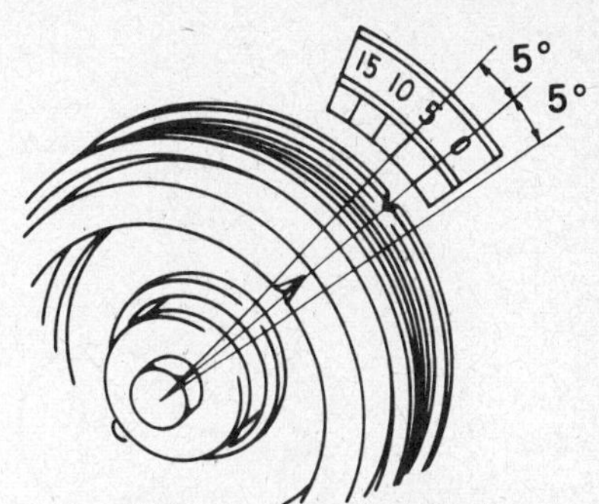

Fig. 62 Checking crankshaft pulley angle. 2S-E engine

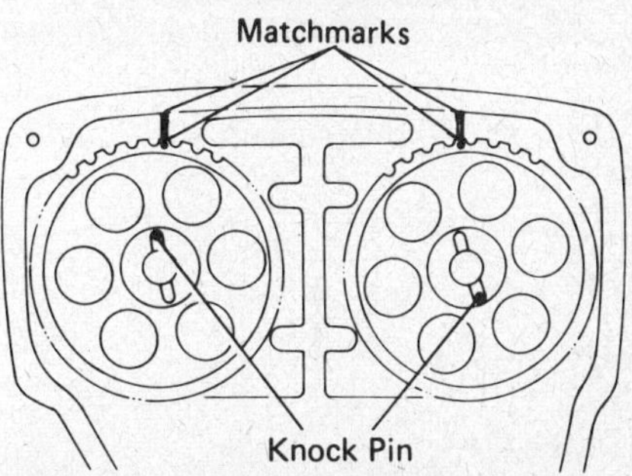

Fig. 64 Camshaft sprocket alignment. 4A-GE, 4A-GEC, 4A-GEL & 4A-GELC engines

2. Install cylinder head covers, then the crankshaft sprocket, idler pulley and tension spring. Pry idler pulley towards the left as far as possible and temporarily tighten attaching bolt.
3. Install timing belt. **If belt is being reused, ensure it is installed in the same position as removed.**
4. Slowly loosen timing belt idler bolt, then temporarily install crankshaft pulley bolt.
5. Turn crankshaft two complete revolutions clockwise from TDC of compression stroke to TDC of compression stroke.
6. Check valve timing. Ensure each sprocket is aligned as shown in **Fig. 65.**
7. Tighten timing belt idler pulley bolt to 27 ft. lbs.
8. Measure timing belt deflection as shown in **Fig. 66.** If deflection is not .16 inch with 4.4 lbs. of pressure, readjust as necessary with idler pulley.
9. Remove crankshaft pulley bolt, then install timing belt guide. Ensure guide cup side is facing outward.
10. Install timing belt covers and gaskets.
11. Reverse steps 1 through 5 of removal procedure to complete installation. When installing crankshaft pulley torque pulley bolt to 87 ft. lbs. on 1985-86 models, or 105 ft. lbs. on 1987 models.

3S-GE ENGINE

REPLACEMENT

Removal

Camshaft will have either 2 or 5 holes

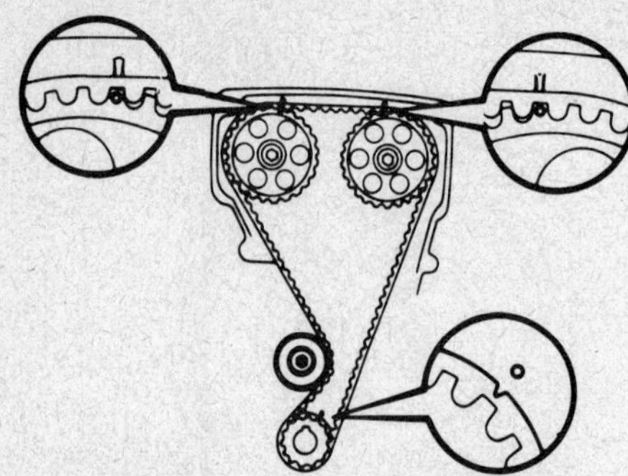

Fig. 65 Aligning timing belt marks with camshaft & crankshaft sprocket marks. 4A-GE, 4A-GEC, 4A-GEL & 4A-GELC engines

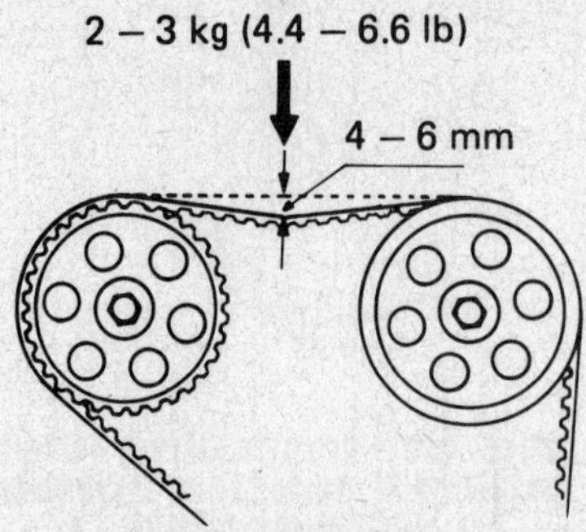

Fig. 66 Checking timing belt deflection. Engines w/dual overhead camshafts (typical)

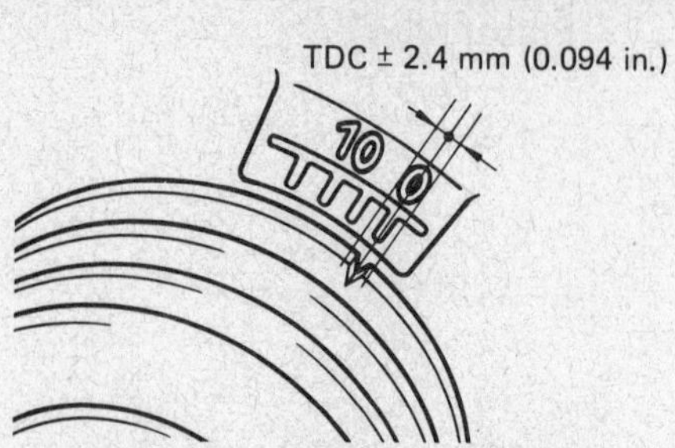

Fig. 67 Crankshaft pulley at TDC. 3S-GE engine

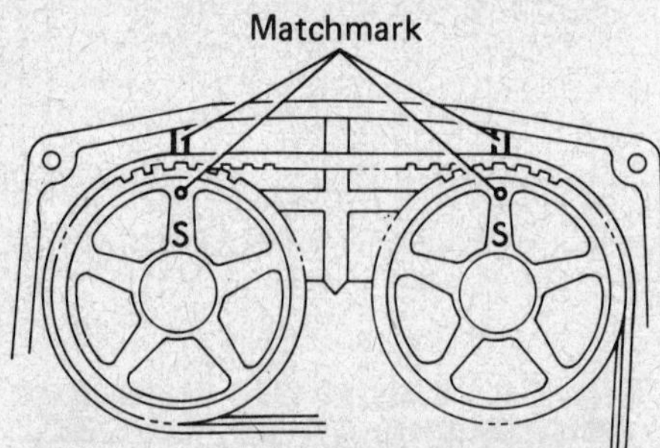

Fig. 68 Camshaft sprocket marks and No. 3 timing belt cover alignments. 3S-GE engine

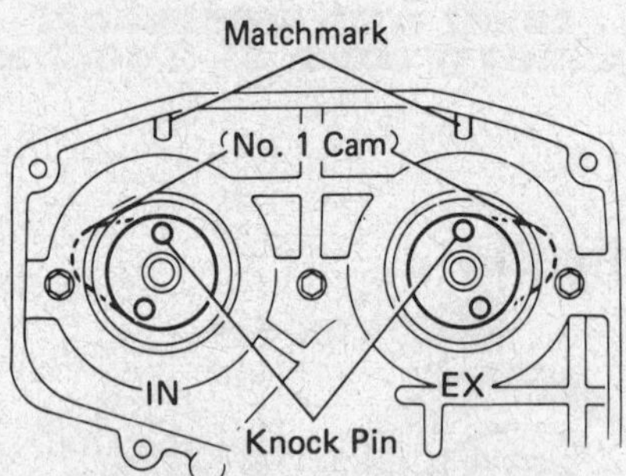

Fig. 69 Camshaft alignment. 3S-GE engine w/2 hole camshaft flange

and the camshaft sprocket will have either 1 or 5 holes. Fine adjustment of valve timing is possible only when a 5 hole camshaft and camshaft sprocket are used. If applicable, refer to "Fine Adjustment" procedure.

1. Disconnect battery ground cable, then remove right front wheel and engine under cover.
2. Remove radiator reservoir tank, then cruise control actuator and bracket.
3. Remove power steering oil reservoir attaching bolts, then position reservoir aside.
4. Remove accessory drive belts, then the alternator and alternator bracket.
5. Raise engine slightly with suitable jack. **Position suitable block of wood between jack and engine to prevent damage.**
6. Remove right side engine mount through bolt, then the mount.
7. Remove valve covers, spark plugs, then the No. 2 timing belt cover with gasket.
8. Set cylinder No. 1 to TDC by rotating crankshaft pulley until groove is aligned with "0" timing mark, **Fig. 67.** Ensure alignment marks of camshaft pulleys and No. 3 timing belt cover are aligned, **Fig. 68.** If marks are not aligned, rotate crankshaft as additional 360° to place cylinder No. 1 at TDC of compression stroke.
9. If timing belt is to be reused, draw arrow indicating direction of rotation and alignment marks between camshaft sprockets and belt and crankshaft sprocket and belt.
10. Loosen spring loaded idler pulley attaching bolt, then pry pulley as far left as possible and tighten attaching bolt temporarily.
11. Remove timing belt from camshaft timing pulleys, then hold camshaft flats with suitable wrench and remove camshaft sprocket attaching bolts, sprockets and pins. **Identify intake and exhaust camshaft sprockets for proper installation.**
12. Remove crankshaft pulley attaching bolt, then using suitable puller, remove crankshaft pulley. Remove No. 1 timing cover, then the timing belt guide from crankshaft sprocket.
13. Remove timing belt, spring loaded idler pulley, tension spring and fixed idler pulley from engine. **Do not allow belt to come into contact with water, oil or grease or damage may result.**
14. Pry off crankshaft sprocket with two screwdrivers, then while holding oil pump sprocket with suitable tool, remove oil pump sprocket nut. Remove sprocket.

Installation

1. Install oil pump pulley. Torque attaching nut to 21 ft. lbs.
2. Install crankshaft sprocket, then fixed idler pulley. Torque idler pulley attaching bolt to 32 ft. lbs.
3. Install spring loaded idler pulley and spring. Do not tighten attaching bolt. Pry idler pulley as far to the left as possible, then temporarily tighten attaching bolt.
4. Temporarily install timing belt on crankshaft sprocket, oil pump sprocket, fixed idler pulley and water pump pulleys. If belt is being reused, install in proper direction and align reference mark on crankshaft sprocket made during removal procedures. **The engine should be cold during belt installation.**
5. Install timing belt guide on crankshaft sprocket and timing cover No. 1. Torque timing cover attaching bolts to 78 inch lbs.
6. Install crankshaft pulley. Torque attaching bolt to 80 ft. lbs. Ensure crankshaft pulley groove is still aligned with "0" timing mark, **Fig. 67,** indicating No. 1 is at TDC of compression stroke.
7. On models equipped with two hole camshaft flanges, use suitable wrench to align camshaft knock pins and cam lobes as shown in **Fig. 69.** On models equipped with five hole camshaft flanges, use suitable wrench to align camshaft alignment marks as shown in **Fig. 70.**
8. Hang timing belt on camshaft sprocket pulleys with sprocket "S" markings facing outwards. If timing belt is being reused, align reference marks made during removal procedures.
9. Align camshaft sprocket alignment marks with No. 3 timing cover matchmark and install sprockets, **Fig. 68.** On models equipped with two hole camshaft flange, ensure camshaft knock pin is aligned with sprocket hole. On models equipped with five hole camshaft flange, insert knock pin into whatever holes are aligned. **On five hole flange type cams, if knock pin alignment is not exact, camshafts can be rotated slightly to compensate.**
10. While holding camshafts with suitable wrench, install camshaft sprocket attaching bolts, then torque to 43 ft. lbs.
11. Loosen spring loaded idler pulley attaching bolt just enough to allow pulley to move by itself under spring tension. Allow pulley to take up belt tension.
12. Rotate crankshaft clockwise two complete revolutions, from TDC compression stroke to TDC compression stroke, then torque spring loaded idler pulley to 32 ft. lbs. **Ensure timing belt has tension between crankshaft**

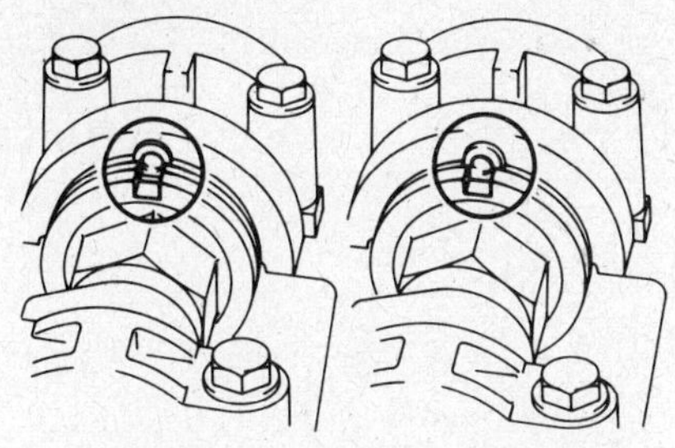

Fig. 70 Aligning marks on camshaft flange with marks on camshaft bearing caps. 3S-GE engine w/5 hole camshaft flange

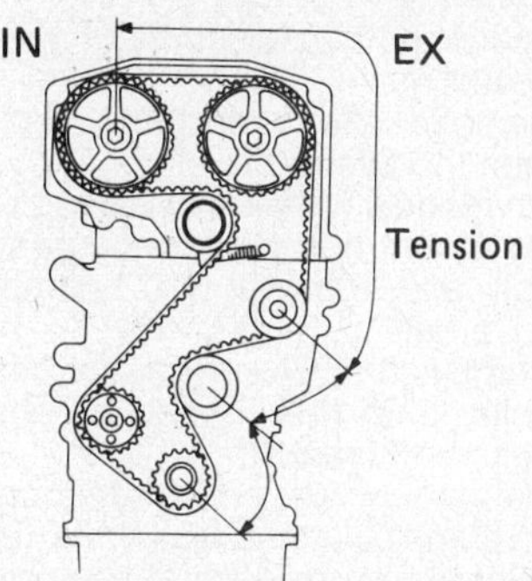

Fig. 71 Timing belt installation. 3S-GE engine

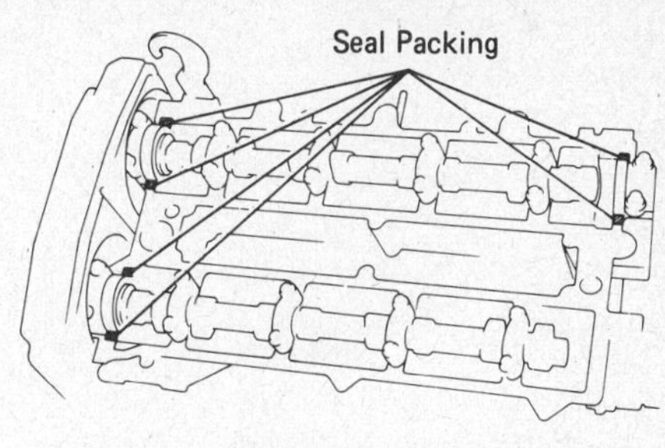

Fig. 72 Installing cylinder head packing. 3S-GE engine

sprocket and intake camshaft sprocket, Fig. 71.

13. Install timing cover No. 2 and spark plugs.
14. Apply seal packing to cylinder heads as shown, **Fig. 72**, then install cylinder head covers with new gaskets. Install center cover with new gasket.
15. Install right side engine mount and under cover, then the RH front wheel.
14. Lower vehicle, then connect battery ground cable.

FINE ADJUSTMENT

1. Disconnect battery ground cable, then raise and support vehicle.
2. Remove RH front wheel and engine under cover.
3. Remove spark plugs, then the No. 2 timing belt cover with gasket.
4. Rotate crankshaft and align its groove with "0" mark on No. 1 timing belt cover, **Fig. 67.**
5. Ensure matchmarks on camshaft sprockets are aligned with marks on No. 3 timing belt cover, **Fig. 68.**
6. If more than 1 timing sprocket tooth is between matchmarks, realign matchmarks as follows:
   a. Remove cylinder head covers with gaskets.
   b. Loosen spring loaded idler pulley attaching bolt, then shift pulley as far left as possible and tighten in position.
   c. Remove timing belt from camshaft timing sprockets, then rotate camshaft, using a suitable tool, and align matchmarks, **Fig. 68.**
   d. With engine cold, install timing belt to EX and IN side and check for tension as shown, **Fig. 71.**
   e. Loosen idler pulley attaching bolt until idler turns, then allow idler pulley to put tension against timing belt.
   f. Rotate crankshaft two complete revolutions clockwise, then torque idler pulley attaching bolt to 32 ft. lbs. Recheck camshaft timing marks.
7. Rotate crankshaft clockwise until groove on camshaft flange aligns with matchmark on camshaft bearing cap, **Fig. 70.**
8. Check crankshaft pulley angle on No. 1 timing belt cover separately for the intake and exhaust sides. Pulley movement should be within .094 inch, **Fig. 67.** If pulley movement is not within tolerance, repeat step 6.
9. Retain camshaft, using a suitable tool, then remove sprocket attaching bolts.
10. Ensure camshaft grooves are aligned with bearing cap matchmarks, **Fig. 70,** then remove knock pin from pin hole in front of camshaft sprocket using a suitable magnet.
11. Set piston of No. 1 cylinder at TDC on compression stroke. Check each of the five pin holes in camshaft sprocket and select pin hole with proper alignment. Insert knock pin into selected hole. **If there is no overlapped hole, slightly rotate crankshaft, then insert pin into hold closest to proper alignment. By moving knock pin one hole, crankshaft pulley angle can be adjusted approximately 2 degrees. Moving knock pin 2 holes can adjust crankshaft pulley angle by approximately 5 degrees.**
12. Retain camshaft, using a suitable tool, then install sprocket attaching bolt and torque to 43 ft. lbs. Rotate crankshaft two complete revolutions from TDC to TDC, then recheck valve timing.
13. Install No. 2 timing belt cover with new gasket, then the spark plugs.
14. Apply seal packing to cylinder heads as shown, **Fig. 72,** then install cylinder head covers with new gaskets. Install center cover with new gasket.
15. Install RH engine under cover, then the RH front wheel.
16. Lower vehicle, then connect battery ground cable.

3S-FE ENGINE

REMOVAL

1. Disconnect battery ground cable, then remove right front wheel and under cover.
2. Remove cruise control actuator and bracket (if equipped).
3. Remove accessory drive belts, then alternator and alternator bracket.
4. Using suitable jack, raise engine slightly. **Position block of wood between jack and engine to prevent damage.**
5. Remove right side engine mount through bolt, then the mount.
6. Remove spark plugs, then upper timing belt cover and gasket.
7. Rotate crankshaft pulley until pulley groove is aligned with "0" indication on timing marks, then ensure that camshaft sprocket hole is aligned bearing cap No. 1 alignment mark, **Fig. 73. If camshaft sprocket is not aligned properly, engine is not set at TDC compression. Rotate crankshaft an additional 360° and recheck.**
8. If timing belt is to be reused, draw arrow on belt to indicate direction of rotation and make reference marks between timing belt and camshaft sprocket.
9. Loosen spring loaded idler pulley attaching bolt, then pry pulley as far to the left as possible. Temporarily tighten attaching bolt.
10. Remove timing belt from camshaft sprocket, then remove camshaft sprocket attaching bolt, washer and sprocket.
11. Remove crankshaft pulley attaching bolt, then using suitable puller, remove crankshaft pulley.
12. Remove lower timing belt cover and gasket.
13. If timing belt is to be reused, make reference marks between timing belt and crankshaft sprocket, then remove belt and belt guide.
14. Remove spring loaded idler pulley attaching bolt, then the pulley and tension spring.
15. Remove fixed idler pulley attaching bolt, then the idler pulley.
16. Pry off crankshaft sprocket with two screwdrivers.
17. While holding oil pump sprocket with suitable tool, remove oil pump nut and sprocket.

INSTALLATION

1. Install oil pump sprocket. Torque attaching nut to 21 ft. lbs.
2. Install crankshaft sprocket, then the fixed idler pulley. Torque idler pulley attaching bolt to 31 ft. lbs.
3. Install spring loaded idler pulley and loosely install attaching bolt. Install spring, then pry pulley as far to the left as possible and tighten attaching bolt.
4. Temporarily install timing belt on crankshaft sprocket, oil pump sprocket, fixed idler pulley and water pump sprocket. If belt is being reused, install in proper direction and align reference

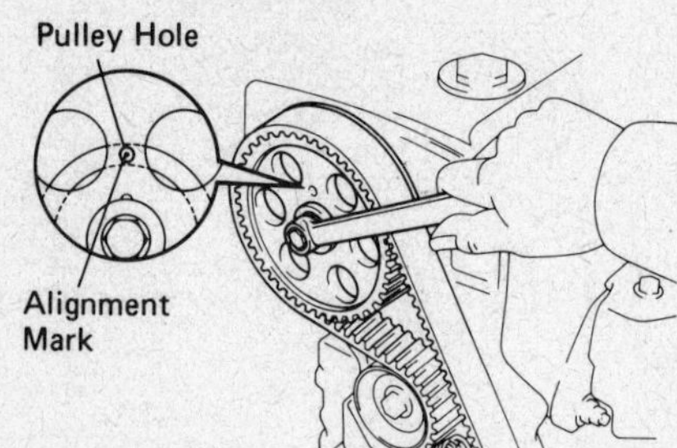

Fig. 73 Camshaft sprocket alignment. 3S-FE engine

mark on crankshaft sprocket made during removal procedures. **The engine should be cold during belt installation.**

5. Install timing belt guide, cup side up on crankshaft sprocket, then the lower timing cover.
6. Install crankshaft pulley. Torque attaching bolt to 80 ft. lbs. Ensure crankshaft pulley groove is still aligned with "0" timing mark, indicating No. 1 cylinder is at TDC of compression stroke.
7. Install camshaft sprocket, washer and attaching bolt. Torque attaching bolt to 40 ft. lbs. Rotate camshaft by turning sprocket attaching bolt to align bearing cap mark and camshaft sprocket, **Fig. 73.**
8. Install timing belt on camshaft sprocket. If timing belt is being reused, align reference marks made during removal procedures.
9. Ensure belt has tension between crankshaft sprocket, water pump sprocket and camshaft sprocket.
10. Loosen spring loaded idler pulley attaching bolt just enough to allow pulley to move by itself under spring tension. Allow pulley to take up belt tension.
11. Rotate crankshaft clockwise two complete revolutions, from TDC compression stroke to TDC compression stroke, then torque spring loaded idler pulley to 31 ft. lbs. **Ensure timing belt has tension between water pump sprocket and camshaft sprocket.**
12. Install upper timing belt cover and spark plugs.
13. Install right side engine mount, then lower engine.
14. Install alternator bracket, alternator and accessory drive belts.
15. Install cruise control actuator and bracket.
16. Install engine under cover and right front wheel, then battery ground cable.

4A-LC ENGINE

REMOVAL

1. Disconnect battery ground cable, then raise and support vehicle.
2. Remove RH wheel, then the RH under cover.
3. Drain engine coolant, then disconnect radiator inlet hose.
4. Loosen water pump pulley bolts, then remove alternator drive belts.
5. Remove alternator terminal cap, nut and wire, then disconnect wire connector.
6. Remove alternator pivot, lock bolt, then the alternator.
7. On models with A/C, loosen idler pulley mount nut, then loosen adjusting bolt and remove A/C compressor drive belt.
8. Remove 4 A/C compressor attaching bolts, then the 5 bracket attaching bolts and bracket.
9. On models with power steering, loosen pump pivot and lock bolts, then position pump aside and remove drive belt.
10. On all models, remove 4 water pump pulley attaching bolts, then disconnect water pump pulley from pump.
11. Remove upper timing belt cover with gasket, then the intermediate timing belt cover with gasket.
12. Set No. 1 piston at top dead center (TDC) of compression stroke. **Rotate crankshaft sprocket and align its groove with "0" mark on lower timing belt cover. Make sure timing marks on camshaft sprocket hole and camshaft bearing cap are aligned, Fig. 49.** If not, turn crankshaft sprocket 1 complete revolution.
13. Retain crankshaft using a suitable tool, the loosen crankshaft pulley bolt. Remove pulley bolt, then the crankshaft pulley using suitable puller.
14. Remove lower timing belt cover retaining bolts, then the cover and gasket.
15. Remove timing belt guide, timing belt, and idler pulley. **If timing belt is to be reused, draw arrow on belt to indicate direction of rotation and make reference marks between camshaft sprocket and timing belt and crankshaft sprocket and timing belt.**
16. Remove crankshaft sprocket, then the cylinder head cover with gasket.
17. Secure camshaft, then remove camshaft sprocket bolt and pulley.
18. Place a suitable jack and wooden block under engine, then remove crossmember-to-engine attaching bolts. Remove right side engine mount through bolt, then slightly raise engine and pull out timing belt.

INSTALLATION

1. Insert new timing belt, then slowly lower engine. Install RH engine mount bolts and 2 insulator nuts. Torque to 58 ft. lbs.
2. Install crossmember-to-engine attaching bolts. Torque to 29 ft. lbs.
3. Lower jack and remove.
4. Align camshaft knock pin and camshaft sprocket, the secure camshaft and torque bolt to 34 ft. lbs. Align bearing cap mark and center of small hole on camshaft timing sprocket, **Fig. 49. Remove any oil or water on camshaft sprocket and keep it clean.**
5. Apply a suitable sealant to cam bearing cap No. 1 and half circle plug on both sides. Install half circle plug, then install cylinder head cover, 2 insulators and bolts. Install PCV hose.

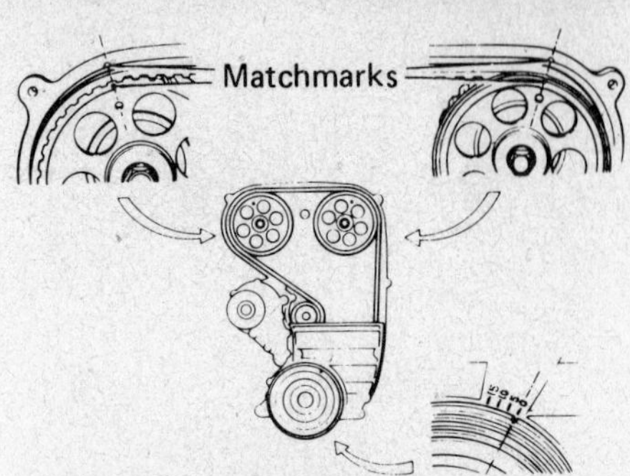

Fig. 74 Aligning marks on No. 2 timing belt cover with marks on camshaft sprockets. 5M-GE engine

6. Install crankshaft sprocket, aligning TDC marks on oil pump body with mark on sprocket, **Fig. 50. Remove any oil or water on crankshaft sprocket and keep it clean.**
7. Install timing belt idler pulley with attaching bolt, then the tension spring. Pry idler toward left as far as possible, then tighten. **Remove any oil or water on idler pulley and keep it clean.**
8. Install timing belt. If timing belt is being reused, install belt with arrow facing in correct direction of rotation and reference marks aligned, **Fig. 51.**
9. Loosen timing belt idler pulley mount bolt, then temporarily install crankshaft pulley bolt. Rotate crankshaft clockwise 2 revolutions from TDC to TDC.
10. Check valve timing, ensuring each pulley aligns with marks as shown, **Fig. 52.** Torque timing belt idler pulley mount bolt to 27 ft. lbs.
11. Measure timing belt deflection, **Fig. 53.** Deflection should be .24-.28 inch with 4.4 lbs. of force. If deflection is not as specified, readjust idler pulley. Remove temporarily installed crankshaft pulley bolt.
12. Install timing belt guide, then the lower timing belt covers with gaskets.
13. Apply engine oil to threads of crankshaft pulley set bolt, then align pulley set key with key groove of pulley and install. Torque attaching bolt to specification using suitable torque wrench.
14. Install remaining timing belt covers with new gaskets.
15. Connect water pump pulley, then if equipped, install power steering pump drive belt.
16. If equipped, install A/C compressor bracket, compressor and drive belt.
17. Install alternator and drive belt, then tighten 4 water pump pulley bolts.
18. Connect radiator inlet hose, then adjust drive belt tensions.
19. Add engine coolant and connect battery ground cable, then start engine and check for leaks.
20. Install RH under cover, then the RH wheel. Lower vehicle.

5M-GE ENGINE

VALVE TIMING CHECK & FINE ADJUSTMENT

1. Turn crankshaft in normal direction of

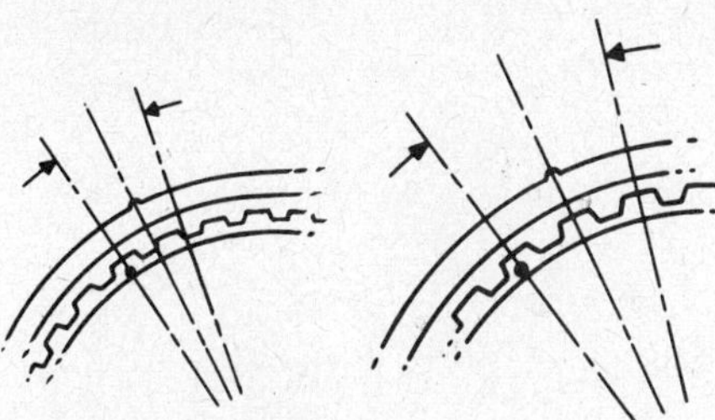

Fig. 75 Checking camshaft tooth alignment. 5M-GE engine

Fig. 76 Checking timing belt tension at points A and B. 5M-GE, 7M-GE & 7M-GTE engines

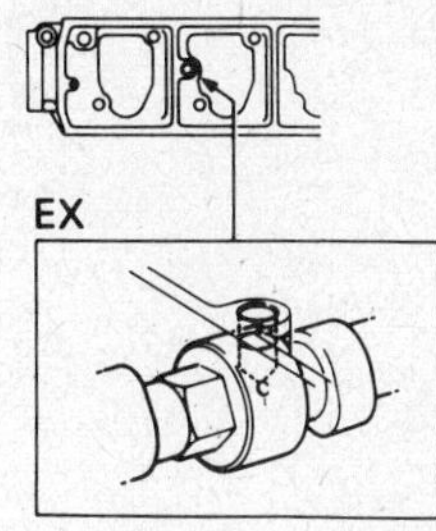

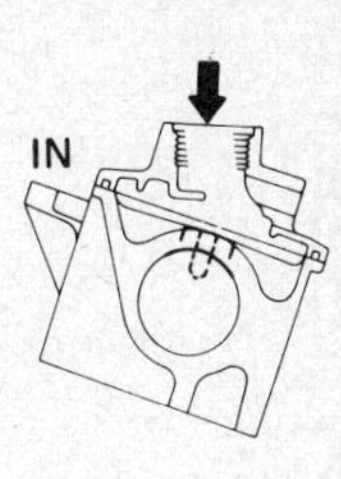

Fig. 77 Aligning hole on No. 2 camshaft journal housing w/No. 2 camshaft journal. 5M-GE engines

rotation and set No. 1 piston to TDC of compression stroke.

2. Ensure marks on camshaft sprockets are aligned with marks on No. 2 timing belt cover, **Fig. 74.**
3. If there is more than one tooth of the camshaft sprocket between marks on No. 2 timing belt cover, **Fig. 75,** note the following:
   a. Gradually loosen idler pulley bolt and move idler puller toward the alternator.
   b. Finger tighten idler pulley bolt and remove timing belt from camshaft sprockets.
   c. Using tool number 09278-54011 or equivalent, turn camshaft sprocket and align marks, **Fig. 74.**
   d. Install timing belt. Loosen idler pulley bolt and allow idler pulley to tension timing belt, then torque idler pulley bolt to 36 ft. lbs. **Ensure timing belt tension at points A and B, Fig. 76** are approximately equal. If not, loosen, then retighten idler pulley bolt.
   e. Turn crankshaft in normal direction of rotation two times and set No. 1 cylinder to TDC of compression stroke. Check camshaft sprocket marks and timing belt tension. Repeat steps 1 thru 3e, if necessary.
4. If marks are aligned properly or the differences is less than one tooth, **Fig. 75,** note the following:
   a. Using compressed air, clean out No. 2 camshaft journal housing and No. 2 camshaft journal alignment holes, **Fig. 77.**
   b. Turn crankshaft in normal direction of rotation and align No. 2 camshaft journal housing and No. 2 camshaft journal holes. **Hole alignment should be done separately for the intake and exhaust side camshafts.**
   c. After alignment of holes, place a mark on the crankshaft pulley and note degree angle on the No. 1 timing belt cover.
5. If crankshaft pulley degree angle is within 5° of TDC, crankshaft pulley degree angle is correct. If crankshaft pulley degree angle exceeds 5° of TDC, note the following:
   a. Using tool number 09278-54011 or equivalent to prevent camshaft sprockets from turning, remove camshaft sprocket bolt.
   b. Ensure No. 2 camshaft journal housing and No. 2 camshaft journal holes align, **Fig. 77.**
   c. Using a suitable magnet, remove alignment pin from camshaft sprocket pin hole.
   d. Set No. 1 piston to TDC of compression stroke, then insert alignment pin through camshaft sprocket and into camshaft. **There are five alignment pin holes on the sprockets and camshafts. Select one overlapped alignment hole and insert pin into it, Fig. 78.** If there are no overlapping alignment holes, select a hole which is nearly overlapped. Turn crankshaft slightly to overlap the alignment holes, and insert pin. Turning the crankshaft to overlap the next available alignment holes will change crankshaft sprocket angle approximately 3°.
   e. Using tool number 09278-54011 or equivalent to prevent camshaft sprockets from turning, install and torque camshaft sprocket bolts to 51 ft. lbs. (7 kg-m).
   f. Turn crankshaft in normal direction of rotation two times and set No. 1 piston to TDC of compression stroke. Recheck crankshaft pulley degree angle.
6. Using two torque wrenches positioned upright on camshaft sprocket attaching bolts, turn both intake and exhaust cams inwards with 14 ft. lbs. of torque at the same time to slacken timing belt at midposition between cams. While applying a load of 4.4-6.6 pounds, measure belt deflection, **Fig. 66.** Deflection should be .20-.28 inch on used belt or .16-.24 inch on new belt. If measurement is not within specifications, adjust with idler pulley.

REMOVAL

1. Disconnect battery ground cable.
2. Drain coolant from radiator and engine block.
3. Remove air cleaner assembly and radiator upper hose.
4. Loosen drive belts, then remove fan fluid coupling and fan shroud.
5. Remove drive belts and air intake hose.
6. Set No. 1 piston to TDC of compression stroke.
7. Remove bolts and No. 3 timing belt cover. If timing belt is to be reused, draw an arrow to indicate direction of rotation and reference marks between crankshaft sprocket and timing belt and camshaft sprockets and timing belt.
8. Loosen idler pulley bolt, the using a suitable tool, shift idler pulley toward alternator. Finger tighten idler pulley bolt.
9. Remove timing belt from camshaft sprockets.
10. Using tool number 09278-54011 or equivalent, secure camshaft in place, then remove camshaft sprocket attaching bolts and sprockets from camshafts. **The exhaust side camshaft and intake side camshaft each use a different type of sprocket and are not interchangeable. During installation of the sprockets, ensure to install the correct sprocket onto its camshaft.**
11. Remove crankshaft pulley bolt and pulley.
12. Remove air conditioner compressor bracket.
13. Remove No. 1 timing belt cover and timing belt. Remove idler pulley bolt, pulley and tension spring.
14. Remove crankshaft sprocket bolt and sprocket. Remove oil pump drive shaft sprocket bolt and sprocket.

INSTALLATION

1. Check timing belt for damage, replace if necessary.
2. Install oil pump drive shaft sprocket. Torque bolt to 16 ft. lbs.
3. Using tool number 09214-60010 or equivalent and hammer, drive crankshaft sprocket onto crankshaft.
4. Temporarily install idler pulley and tension spring. **Push idler pulley toward the alternator and finger tighten idler pulley bolt.**
5. Install timing belt onto crankshaft sprocket. **If belt is being reused, ensure direction of rotation is correct and reference marks made during removal are aligned.**
6. Install No. 1 timing cover, then the air conditioner compressor bracket.
7. Install crankshaft pulley. Torque pulley bolt to specifications.
8. Remove oil filler cap, then exhaust

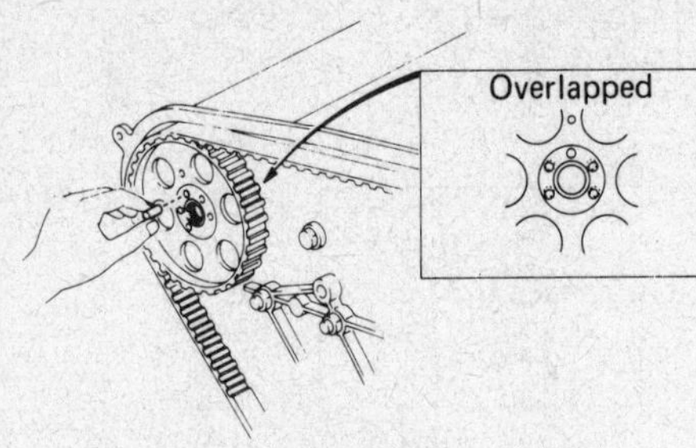

Fig. 78 Installing pin through camshaft sprocket and into camshaft. 5M-GE engine

side cylinder head cover and gasket.

9. Install camshaft sprockets and timing belt, noting the following:
   a. Ensure alignment hole on No. 2 camshaft journal housing is aligned with No. 2 camshaft journal, **Fig. 77.** If not, temporarily install camshaft sprockets as shown in **Fig. 79** and insert alignment pin into pin hole. Turn camshaft sprocket until No. 2 camshaft journal housing and No. 2 camshaft journal holes are aligned.
   b. Install camshaft sprockets with timing belt guides facing in the directions shown in **Fig. 79.**
   c. Ensure No. 1 cylinder is at TDC of compression stroke. Align marks on No. 2 timing belt cover with marks on camshaft sprockets, **Fig. 74,** and mark on crankshaft pulley with 0° mark on timing tab of No. 1 timing belt cover.
   d. Install timing belt onto camshaft sprockets. **If belt is being reused, ensure direction of rotation is correct and reference marks made during removal are aligned.**
   e. Loosen idler pulley bolt and stretch timing belt. **This will occur when the idler pulley bolt is loosened.** Torque idler pulley bolt to 36 ft. lbs.. Ensure timing belt tension at points A and B are approximately equal, **Fig. 76.**
   f. Insert alignment pin through camshaft sprockets and into the camshafts. **There are five alignment pin holes on the camshafts and sprockets. Select one overlapped camshaft and sprocket alignment hole and insert pin into it, Fig. 78.** If there are no overlapping alignment holes, select a hole which is nearly overlapped. Turn crankshaft slightly, to overlap the alignment holes and insert pin. Turning the crankshaft to overlap the alignment holes will change crankshaft sprocket angle approximately 3°.
   g. Using tool number 09278-54011 or equivalent to prevent camshaft sprockets from turning, install and torque camshaft sprocket bolts to 51 ft. lbs.
10. Loosen idler pulley bolt, then turn crankshaft in normal direction of rotation two times and tighten idler pulley bolt.
11. Check valve timing and belt tension. Refer to "Valve Timing Check & Fine Adjustment" for procedure.
12. Install exhaust side cylinder head cover gasket and cover. Install oil filler cap.
13. Install No. 3 timing belt cover gasket and cover.
14. Reverse steps 1 through 5 to complete installation procedure.

7M-GE & 7M-GTE ENGINES

REMOVAL

1. Disconnect battery ground cable, then remove radiator and spark plugs.
2. Remove coolant outlet and thermostat.
3. Remove accessory drive belts.
4. Remove upper timing belt cover and gasket.
5. Set cylinder No. 1 to TDC of compression stroke by rotating crankshaft pulley as necessary to align pulley groove with "0" timing mark. Inspect camshaft sprocket and timing cover alignment marks, **Fig. 80.** If marks are aligned, cylinder No. 1 is set at TDC of compression stroke. If marks are not aligned, rotate crankshaft pulley an additional 360° to set cylinder No. 1 to TDC.
6. If timing belt is to be reused, draw arrow on belt to indicate direction of rotation and make reference marks between timing belt and camshaft sprocket.
7. Loosen spring loaded idler pulley attaching bolt, then pry pulley as far to the left as possible. Temporarily tighten attaching bolt.
8. Remove timing belt from camshaft sprockets, then remove camshaft sprocket attaching bolts, sprockets and timing pins. **Support belt so meshing of crankshaft sprocket and belt is not lost.**
9. Remove crankshaft pulley attaching bolt, then using suitable puller, remove crankshaft pulley.
10. Remove power steering air pipe.
11. On models equipped with A/C, remove A/C compressor with low and high side hoses attached and position aside. On all models, remove lower timing belt cover attaching bolts, A/C idler pulley bracket (if equipped), compressor bracket (if equipped), lower timing cover and gasket.
12. If timing belt is to be reused, make reference marks between timing belt and crankshaft sprocket, then remove belt.
13. Remove spring loaded idler pulley attaching bolt, then the pulley and tension spring.
14. Remove crankshaft sprocket with suitable puller.
15. While holding oil pump sprocket with suitable tool, remove oil pump nut and sprocket.

INSTALLATION

1. Install oil pump sprocket and attaching nut. Torque nut to 16 ft. lbs.
2. Install crankshaft sprockets with tool No. 09214-60010 and hammer.
3. Install spring loaded idler pulley and loosely install attaching bolt. Install spring, then pry pulley as far to the left as possible and tighten attaching bolt.
4. Temporarily install timing belt on crankshaft sprocket, oil pump sprocket and idler pulley. If belt is being reused, install in proper direction and align reference mark on crankshaft sprocket made during removal procedures. **The engine should be cold during belt installation.**
5. Install lower timing cover, A/C compressor bracket (if equipped), idler pulley bracket (if equipped) and A/C compressor (if equipped).
6. Install power steering air pipe.
7. Install crankshaft sprocket. Torque attaching bolt to 195 ft. lbs. Ensure crankshaft pulley groove is still aligned with "0" timing mark, indicating No. 1 cylinder is at TDC of compression stroke.
8. Install camshaft sprockets as follows:
   a. Install camshaft sprockets while aligning reference marks, **Fig. 80.**
   b. If camshafts or sprockets are being replaced, align center holes of camshaft flange and camshaft sprocket, then install timing pins, washers and attaching bolts.
   c. If camshafts or sprockets are being replaced, install timing pins into positions removed from and install attaching bolts and washers.
   d. While restraining camshaft sprockets from turning, torque attaching bolts to 36 ft. lbs. Recheck camshaft sprocket reference mark alignment, **Fig. 80.**
9. Install timing belt on camshaft sprockets. If timing belt is being reused, align reference marks made during removal procedures.
10. Ensure timing belt has equal tension between points A and B, **Fig. 76.** If not, adjust tension with idler pulley.
11. Using two wrenches positioned upright on camshaft sprocket attaching bolts, turn both intake and exhaust cams inwards at the same time to slacken timing belt at mid-position between cams. While applying a load of 4.4-6.6 pounds, measure belt deflection, **Fig. 66.** Deflection should be .20-.28 inch on used belt or .16-.24

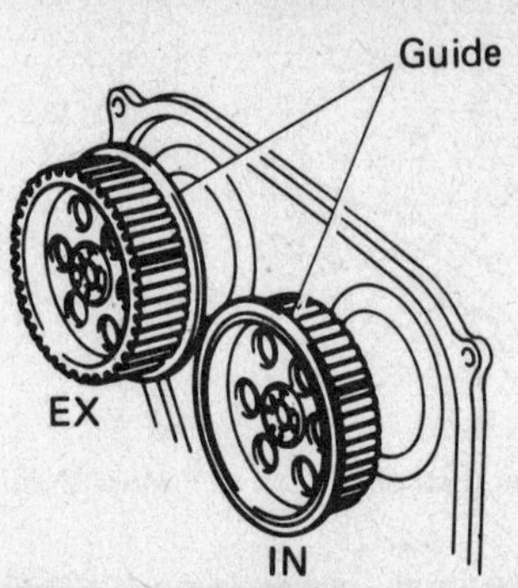

Fig. 79 Camshaft sprocket installation. 5M-GE engine

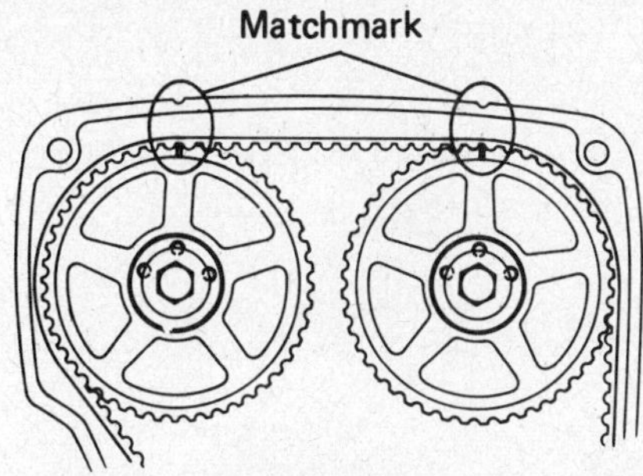

Fig. 80 Camshaft sprocket alignment. 7M-GE & 7M-GTE engines

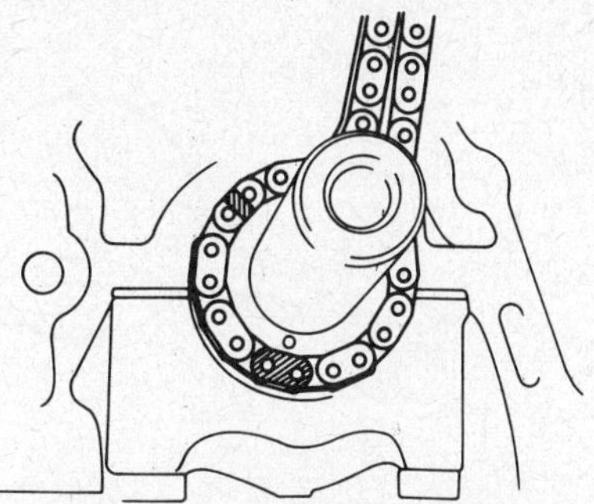

Fig. 81 Aligning timing chain on crankshaft sprocket. 22R, 22R-E & 22R-TE engines

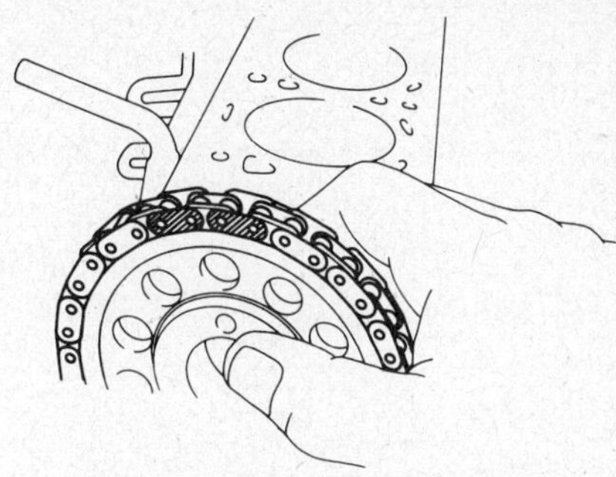

Fig. 82 Aligning timing chain on camshaft sprocket. 22R, 22R-E & 22R-TE engines

inch on new belt. If measurement is not within specifications, adjust with idler pulley.

12. Install upper timing belt cover, then the accessory drive belts.
13. Install coolant outlet, thermostat, spark plugs and radiator.
14. Install air cleaner, then connect battery ground cable.

TIMING CHAIN REPLACE

3Y-EC, 4Y-EC & 4K-E

For timing chain replacement, refer to "Timing Chain & Camshaft, Replace" for procedures.

22R, 22R-E & 22R-TE ENGINES

Removal

1. Remove cylinder head as described under "Cylinder Head, Replace."
2. Remove radiator, oil pan and all drive belts.
3. Remove air pump (if equipped), A/C compressor and bracket, alternator adjuster bracket, cooling fan, water pump pulley and crankshaft pulley.
4. Remove water bypass tube, then on all except turbo models, heater water outlet tube. On turbo models, remove turbo coolant pipe of engine.
5. Remove timing cover bolts, then using plastic mallet, loosen timing cover and remove.
6. Remove chain from damper, then remove camshaft sprocket and chain.
7. Remove oil pump drive spline, then the camshaft sprocket. **If spline and sprocket cannot be removed by hand, use a suitable puller.**

Installation

1. Rotate crankshaft until keyway is at TDC. Install sprocket onto crankshaft, then install chain onto sprocket with light colored link aligned with sprocket timing mark, **Fig. 81.**
2. Install chain onto camshaft sprocket with sprocket timing mark between two light colored links, **Fig. 82.**
3. Slide oil pump drive spline over crankshaft and key. **If installation is difficult, drive spline on with hammer and suitable socket.**
4. Install timing cover gasket, then the timing cover. Torque 8 mm bolts to 10 ft. lbs. and 10 mm bolts to 31 ft. lbs.
5. Install crankshaft pulley and torque bolt 116 ft. lbs. **Do not rotate crankshaft while tightening bolt.**
6. Install water bypass tube, then on all except turbo models, heater water outlet tube. On turbo models, install turbo coolant pipe of engine.
7. Install air pump (if equipped), A/C compressor and bracket, alternator adjuster bracket, cooling fan, water pump pulley and crankshaft pulley.
8. Install cylinder head as described under "Cylinder Head, Replace."
9. Install radiator, oil pan and all drive belts.

TIMING CHAIN & CAMSHAFT REPLACE

4K-E ENGINES

1. Disconnect battery ground cable.
2. Remove engine under cover and oil pan.
3. Remove cylinder head. Refer to "Cylinder Head, Replace" for procedure.
4. Scribe reference marks, then remove distributor.
5. Remove radiator assembly.
6. Remove accessory drive belts and water pump pulley.
7. Remove crankshaft pulley attaching bolt, then using suitable puller, remove crankshaft pulley.
8. Remove timing chain cover attaching bolts, then using suitable soft faced hammer, loosen cover and remove.
9. Remove timing chain tensioner and vibration damper.
10. Remove camshaft sprocket attaching bolt, then remove sprocket and timing chain as an assembly.
11. Remove crankshaft sprocket using suitable pry bar. **If sprocket cannot be removed with pry bar, use suitable puller.**
12. Remove valve lifters. **Label lifters so they can be reinstalled in original position.**
13. Remove thrust plate attaching screws, then the thrust plate and camshaft. **When removing camshaft, great care must be taken to avoid nicking camshaft bearings with camshaft. Installing a bolt in camshaft flange makes camshaft easier to handle.**
14. Reverse procedure to install. **During installation of timing chain and camshaft sprocket. Ensure No. 1 piston is set at TDC. Align camshaft dowel pin with mark on the thrust plate. Align timing chain and camshaft sprocket marks, then timing chain and crankshaft sprocket marks, Fig. 83.**

3Y-EC & 4Y-EC ENGINES

1. Disconnect battery ground cable, then remove radiator.
2. Remove accessory drive belts and water pump pulley.
3. Remove distributor and cold start injector.
4. Remove rocker arm shaft assembly and pushrods, **Fig. 29.**
5. Remove valve lifters. Label them so they can be reinstalled in original position.
6. Remove crankshaft pulley retaining bolt, then using suitable puller, the crankshaft pulley.
7. Remove timing chain cover bolts, then the timing chain cover.
8. Using a suitable gauge, measure timing chain tension. Timing chain tension should be .531 inch at 22 lb. applied tension. If gauge reading exceeds specified amount, replace timing chain and sprockets.
9. Remove timing chain tensioner attaching bolts, then the tensioner.
10. Remove camshaft sprocket retaining bolt.
11. Pull both camshaft and crankshaft sprockets and timing chain from engine as an assembly.
12. Using a suitable tool, remove timing chain vibration damper.
13. Remove thrust plate, then camshaft from engine. **When removing camshaft, great care must be taken to avoid nicking camshaft bearings with camshaft. Installing a bolt in camshaft flange makes camshaft easier to handle.**

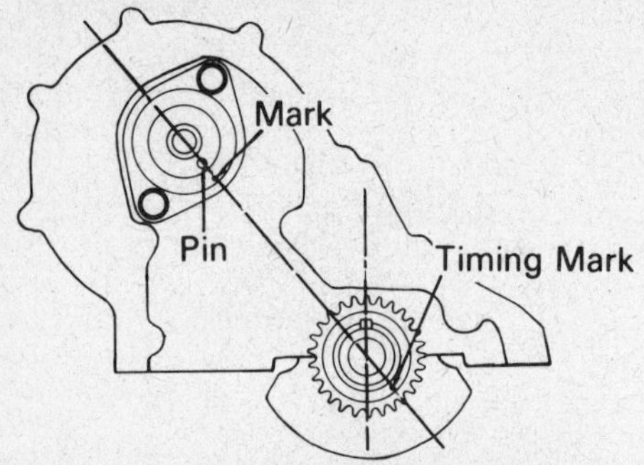

Fig. 83 Aligning camshaft & crankshaft sprockets. 4K-E engine

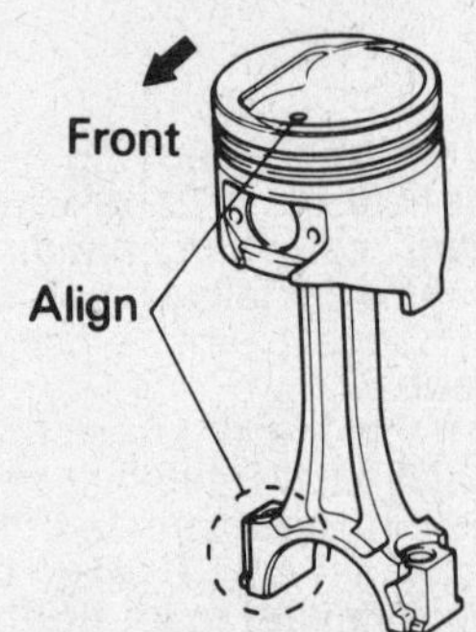

Fig. 86 Piston & connecting rod assembly. 2S-E, 3S-FE, 3S-GE & 3Y-EC engines

14. Install camshaft and thrust plate. Torque thrust plate attaching screw to 13 ft. lbs.
15. Install timing chain vibration damper. Torque attaching bolts to 13 ft. lbs.
16. Align camshaft and crankshaft as shown in **Fig. 84.**
17. Assemble sprockets and timing chain with marked links aligned at sprocket marks, **Fig. 85.**
18. Install timing chain and sprockets. Torque camshaft sprocket attaching bolt to 67 ft. lbs.
19. Install timing chain tensioner. Torque attaching bolts to 13 ft. lbs.
20. Reverse steps 1 through 7 to complete installation. Torque crankshaft pulley retaining bolt to 80 ft. lbs. on 1984-85 models, or 116 ft. lbs. on 1986-87 models.

PISTONS & CONNECTING RODS

Pistons are available in standard and oversizes of .020 inch (.50 mm), .030 inch (.75 mm) and .040 inch (1.00 mm) for all engines except 3E, 3S-FE, 3S-GE, 4A-C, 4A-LC, 4A-GE, 4A-GEC, 4A-GEL, 4A-GELC, 4Y-EC, 7M-GE, 7M-GTE, 22R, 22R-E and 22R-TE engines. On 22R, 22R-E and 22R-TE engines, pistons are available in standard and oversizes of .020 inch (.50 mm) and .040 inch (1.00 mm). On 3E, 4A-C, 4A-LC, 4Y-EC, 7M-GE and 7M-GTE engines, pistons are available in standard and oversize of .020 inch (.50 mm). On 3S-FE, 3S-GE, 4A-GE, 4A-GEC, 4A-GEL and

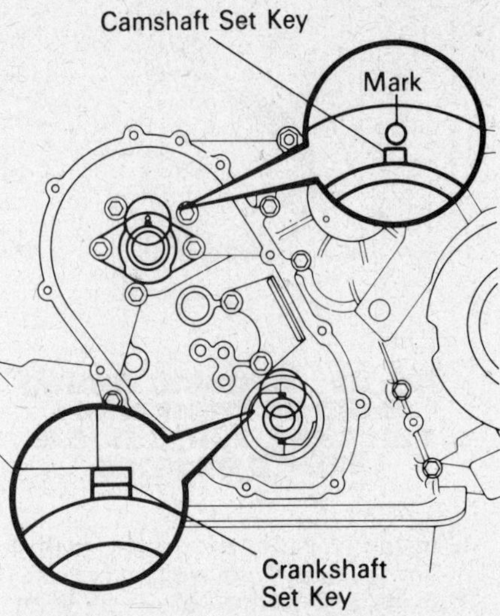

Fig. 84 Aligning camshaft & crankshaft sprockets. 3Y-EC & 4Y-EC engines

4A-GELC engines, if piston bore is not within specifications, replace piston and/or cylinder block. When assembling piston onto connecting rod, ensure mark on top of piston and mark on connecting rod are on same side, **Figs. 86 through 89.** When installing piston and connecting rod assembly, ensure mark on top of piston is facing toward front of engine.

MAIN & CONNECTING ROD BEARINGS

On 3A-C, 3E, 4A-C, 4A-GE, 4A-GEC, 4A-GEL, 4A-GELC, 4A-LC, 7M-GE, 7M-GTE, 22R, 22R-E and 22R-TE engines, main and connecting rod bearings are available in standard and undersizes of .010 inch (.25 mm).

On 4K-E and 5M-GE engines, main and connecting rod bearings are available in standard and undersizes of .010 inch (.25 mm) and .020 inch (.50 mm). On 2S-E, 3S-FE, 3S-GE, 3Y-EC and 4Y-EC engines, undersize bearings are not available. If crankshaft journals or crankpins are worn or scored, the crankshaft must be replaced.

CAMSHAFT BEARINGS

On 4K-E engines, bearings are available in standard sizes and undersizes of .005 inch (.125 mm) and .010 inch (.25 mm).

OIL PAN & OIL PUMP REPLACE

22R, 22R-E & 22R-TE ENGINES

1. Remove oil pan and oil strainer.
2. Remove crankshaft bolt and pulley.
3. Remove oil pump assembly.
4. Reverse procedure to install. On 20R, 22R & 22R-E engines, apply sealer to bolt shown in **Fig. 90.**

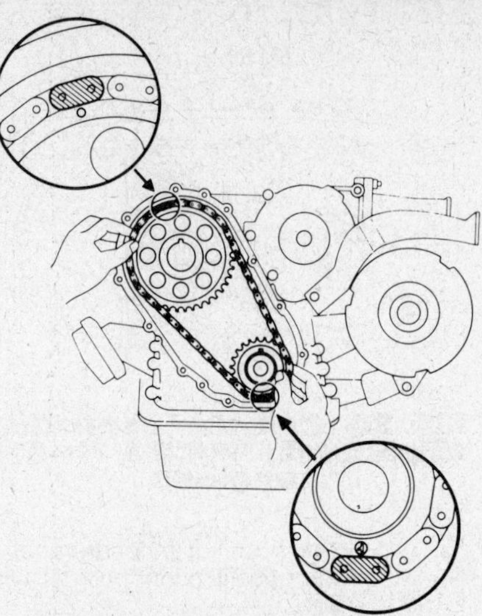

Fig. 85 Timing chain & sprocket alignment. 3Y-EC & 4Y-EC engines

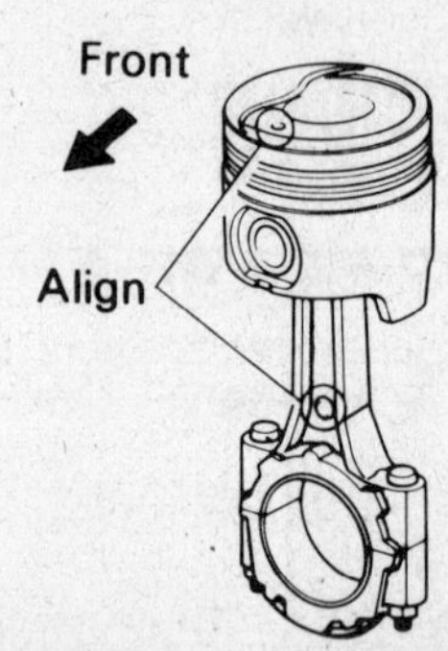

Fig. 87 Piston & connecting rod assembly. 3A-C, 3E, 4A-C, 4A-GE, 4A-GEC, 4A-GEL, 4A-GELC, 4A-LC & 4Y-EC engines

2S-E ENGINE, 1983–86 CAMRY

1. Disconnect battery ground cable.
2. Raise and support vehicle.
3. Drain oil from engine.
4. Remove right side engine under cover.
5. Remove oil level gauge.
6. Remove oil pan attaching bolts, then the oil pan.
7. Remove oil strainer attaching bolts, then the oil strainer.
8. Remove timing belt. Refer to "Timing Belt, Replace" for procedure.
9. Remove oil pump attaching bolts, then the oil pump.
10. Reverse procedure to install.

2S-E, 3S-FE & 3S-GE ENGINES, 1986–87 CELICA & 1987 CAMRY

1. Disconnect battery ground cable, then remove engine hood.
2. Raise and support vehicle.
3. Remove engine under covers, then drain engine oil.
4. On 3S-GE engines, disconnect exhaust pipe from exhaust manifold. On

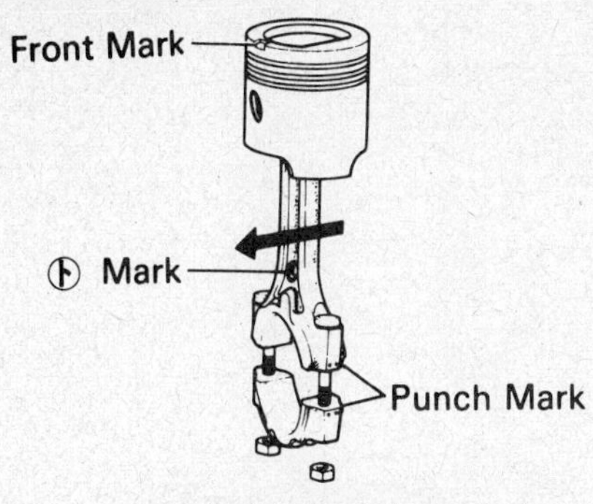

Fig. 88 Piston & connecting rod assembly. 4K-E engine

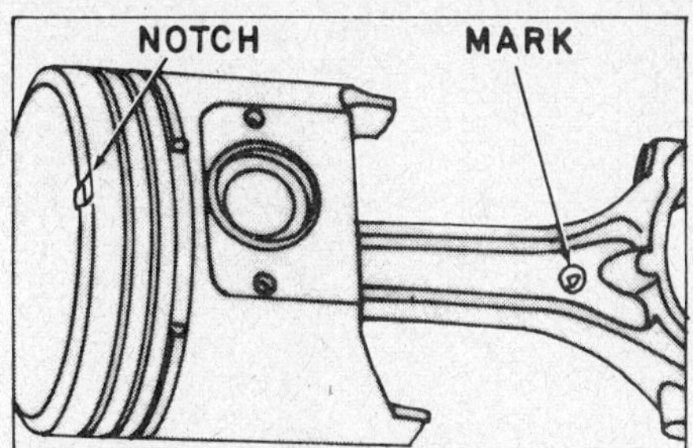

Fig. 89 Piston & connecting rod assembly. 5M-GE, 7M-GE, 7M-GTE, 22R, 22R-E & 22R-TE engines

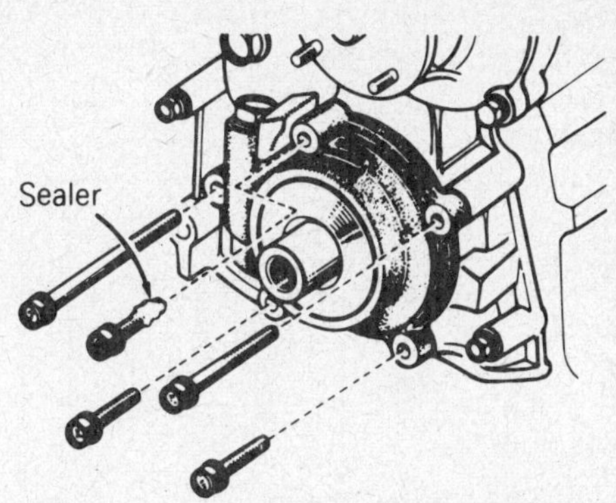

Fig. 90 Location of sealed bolt. 22R, 22R-E & 22R-TE engines

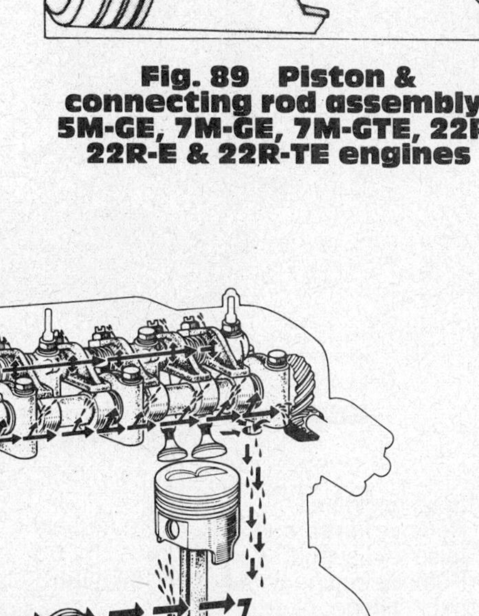

Engine lubrication system. 3A-C, 4A-C & 4A-LC engines

3S-FE engines, disconnect exhaust pipe from catalytic converter.

5. On all models, remove suspension lower crossmember, then the engine mount center member.
6. Remove stiffener plate, then the oil dipstick.
7. Remove oil pan attaching bolts, then the oil pan. **Use caution not to damage oil pan flange.**
8. On 2S-E models, remove 4 oil strainer attaching bolts, then the O-ring seal.
9. On 3S-GE and 3S-GE models, remove 2 attaching bolts, nuts, oil pan baffle plate, then the oil strainer with gasket.
10. On all models, attach a suitable hoist to engine, then lift and suspend engine with hoist.
11. Remove timing belt and pulleys. Refer to "Timing Belt, Replace" for procedure.
12. Remove oil pump attaching bolts, then the oil pump.
13. Reverse procedure to install, using new gaskets and O-ring seals as applicable.

3E ENGINE

1. Disconnect battery ground cable, then raise and support vehicle.
2. Remove right side engine under cover.
3. Disconnect exhaust pipe from exhaust manifold.
4. Remove timing belt. Refer to "Timing Belt, Replace" for procedure.
5. Remove oil filler cap and oil dipstick, then drain crankcase into suitable container.
6. Remove oil pan attaching nuts and bolts, then the oil pan.
7. Remove oil strainer attaching bolts, then the strainer and 0-ring.
8. Remove pressure regulator valve assembly.
9. Remove nine oil pump attaching bolts and the tension spring bracket, then the oil pump and 0-ring.
10. Reverse procedure to install.

3A-C ENGINE

1. Raise and support vehicle, then drain engine oil and coolant.
2. Remove radiator assembly.
3. Remove engine under cover, then the four bracket attaching bolts and lower stabilizer.
4. Remove right and left stiffener plates.
5. Remove oil pan attaching bolts, then the oil pan using a suitable tool. Use caution not to damage oil pan flange.
6. Remove oil strainer attaching bolts, then the oil strainer and gasket.
7. Remove timing belt and crankshaft timing pulley. Refer to "Timing Belt, Replace" for procedure.
8. Remove oil dipstick and tube.
9. Remove oil pump attaching bolts, then the oil pump.
10. Reverse procedure to install.

3Y-EC & 4Y-EC ENGINES

1. Disconnect battery ground cable.
2. Raise and support vehicle.
3. Drain engine oil.
4. Remove left and right stiffener plates.
5. Disconnect oil level sensor, then, if necessary, remove oil level sensor, if equipped.
6. Remove oil pan attaching bolts, then the oil pan.
7. Remove oil pump attaching bolt, then the oil pump.

4A-C, 4A-GE, 4A-GEC, 4A-GEL, 4A-GELC & 4A-LC ENGINES

1984–86 Corolla Front Wheel Drive Models

1. Disconnect battery ground cable, then drain engine oil.
2. Remove engine under cover, then the hood.
3. Remove engine mount center member from body.
4. Remove oil pan attaching bolts, then the oil pan using a suitable tool. Use caution not to damage oil pan flange.
5. Remove oil strainer attaching bolts, then the oil strainer and gaskets.
6. Attach suitable engine hoist to engine lift bracket, then lift engine.
7. Loosen water pump pulley bolts, then the alternator and power steering pump drive belts.
8. Remove water pump pulley, then the A/C compressor drive belt and idler pulley, if equipped.

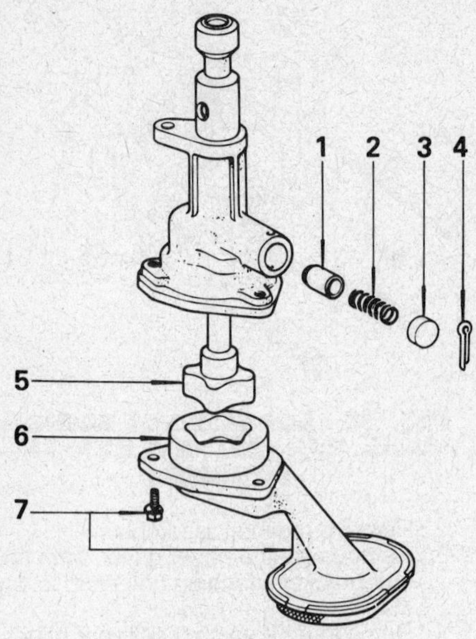

1. Oil Pump Relief Valve
2. Oil Pump Relief Valve Spring
3. Oil Pump Relief Valve Retainer
4. Cotter Pin
5. Oil Pump Drive Rotor
6. Oil Pump Driven Rotor
7. Oil Pump Cover

Fig. 91 Oil pump exploded view. 4K-E engine

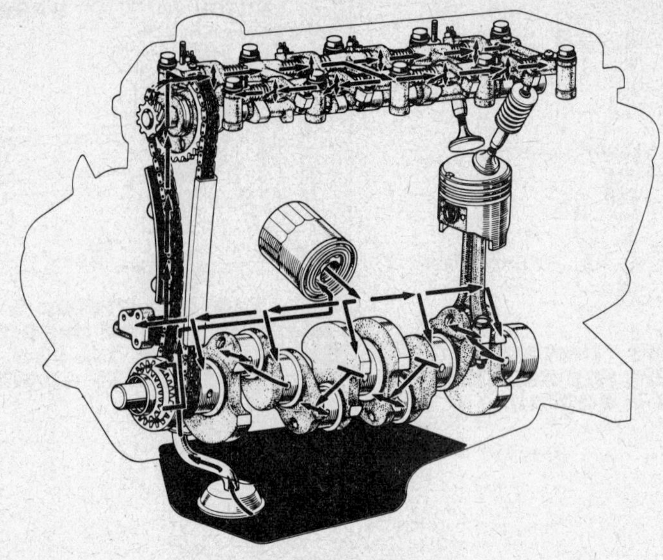

Engine lubrication system. 22R, 22R-E & 22R-TE engines

9. Remove crankshaft pulley attaching bolts, then the crankshaft pulley using a suitable tool.
10. Remove timing belt covers and gaskets, then the timing belt. Refer to "Timing Belt, Replace" for procedure.
11. Remove crankshaft timing pulley.
12. Remove oil level gauge guide and gauge.
13. Remove oil pump attaching bolts, then the oil pump assembly.
14. Reverse procedure to install.

1987 Corolla Front Wheel Drive Models

1. Disconnect battery ground cable, then make reference marks in hood hinge area and remove hood.
2. Raise and support vehicle, then drain engine oil into suitable container and remove engine under cover.
3. Remove oil pan attaching nuts and bolts, then the oil pan.
4. Remove oil strainer attaching bolts and nuts, then remove strainer and gasket.
5. Remove timing belt and crankshaft sprocket. Refer to "Timing Belt, Replace" for procedure.
6. On 4A-GE, 4A-GEC, 4A-GEL and 4A-GELC models, remove baffle plate from cylinder block.
7. On all models, remove dipstick and tube.
8. Remove seven oil pump attaching bolts, then the oil pump.
9. Reverse procedure to install.

Corolla Rear Wheel Drive Models

1. Disconnect battery ground cable, then drain engine oil.
2. Remove fan shroud, if necessary, then raise and support vehicle.
3. Remove engine under cover, then the right stiffener plate.
4. Remove oil pan attaching bolts, then the oil pan using suitable tool. Use caution not to damage oil pan flange.
5. Remove oil strainer attaching bolts, then the oil strainer.
6. Remove timing belt and crankshaft sprocket. Refer to "Timing Belt, Replace" for procedure.
7. On 4A-GE and 4A-GEC engines, remove oil baffle plate from cylinder block.
8. Remove oil level dipstick and tube.
9. Remove oil pump attaching bolts, then the oil pump assembly.
10. Reverse procedure to install.

MR2 Models

1. Disconnect battery ground cable.
2. Raise and support vehicle, then drain engine oil into suitable container.
3. Remove engine pipe-to-exhaust manifold attaching bolts, then separate exhaust pipe from manifold.
4. Remove timing belt and crankshaft sprocket. Refer to "Timing Belt, Replace" for procedure.
5. Install right side engine mount.
6. Remove oil pan attaching bolts, then the oil pan using a suitable tool. Use caution not to damage oil pan flange.
7. Remove oil strainer attaching bolts, then the oil strainer and gasket.
8. Remove baffle plate using a suitable tool. Use caution not to damage flange.
9. Remove oil level dipstick and tube.
10. Remove oil pump attaching bolts, then the oil pump assembly.
11. Reverse procedure to install.

5M-GE ENGINE

1. Disconnect battery ground cable, then drain engine oil and coolant.
2. Remove air cleaner case, then the air connector pipe and hoses.
3. Remove oil level dipstick, then disconnect upper radiator hose.
4. Loosen fan belts, then remove four fan shroud attaching bolts.
5. Remove fluid coupling flange attaching bolts, then the fluid coupling and fan shroud as an assembly.
6. Raise and support vehicle, then remove engine under cover.
7. Remove exhaust pipe clamp bolt, then the two stiffener plates.
8. Remove flywheel housing under cover, then the four motor mount attaching bolts from both sides of engine.
9. Remove oil pan attaching bolts, then the oil pan using a suitable tool. Use caution not to damage oil pan flange.
10. Remove oil pump outlet pipe union bolt and nut, then the oil pump outlet pipe.
11. Remove oil pump attaching bolts, then the oil pump assembly.
12. Reverse procedure to install.

7M-GE & 7M-GTE ENGINES

1. Disconnect battery ground cable, then make reference marks in hood hinge area and remove hood.
2. Raise and support vehicle, then remove engine under cover and drain engine oil into suitable container.
3. On models equipped with auto. trans., remove oil cooler hose clamp.
4. On all models, remove front suspension crossmember.
5. Remove front exhaust pipe bracket and brackets.
6. On turbo models, disconnect oil cooler return hose from oil pan.
7. On all models, remove brake hose brackets and clips from front suspension.
8. Disconnect steering intermediate shaft, then stabilizer links from lower control arms.
9. Attach suitable engine lifting equip-

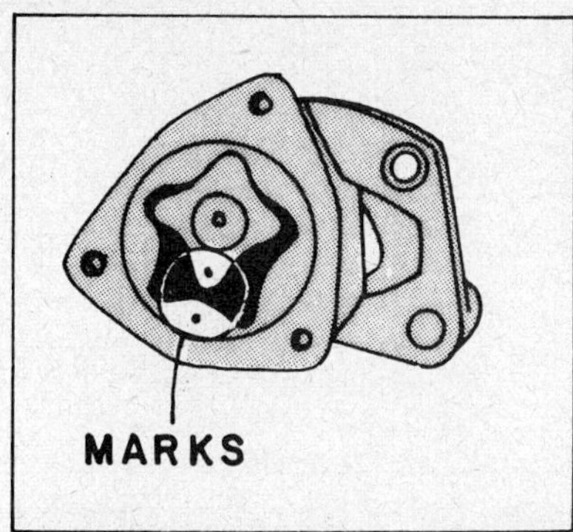

Fig. 92 Oil pump gear installation. 4K-E engine

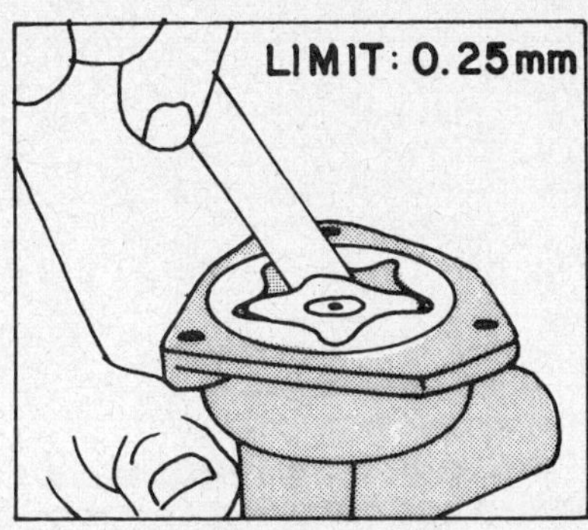

Fig. 93 Checking clearance between rotor tip & rotors. 4K-E engine

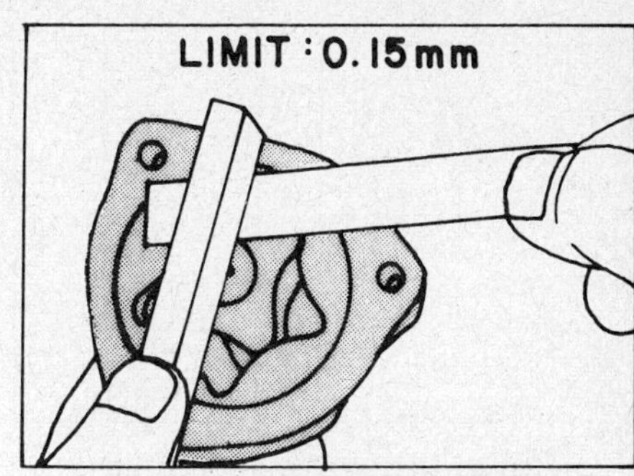

Fig. 94 Checking side clearance. 4K-E engine

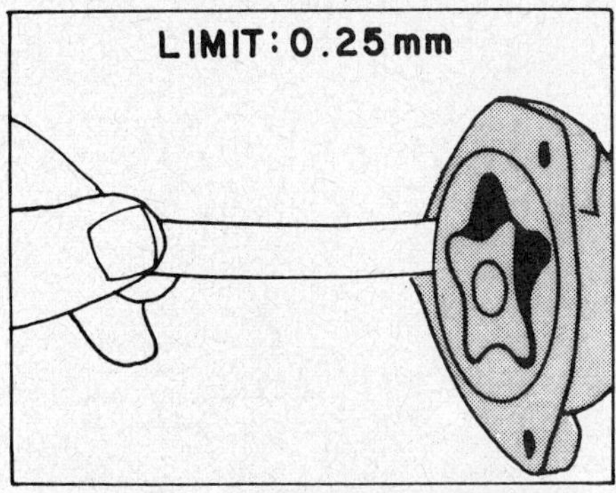

Fig. 95 Checking driven rotor to housing clearance. 4K-E engine

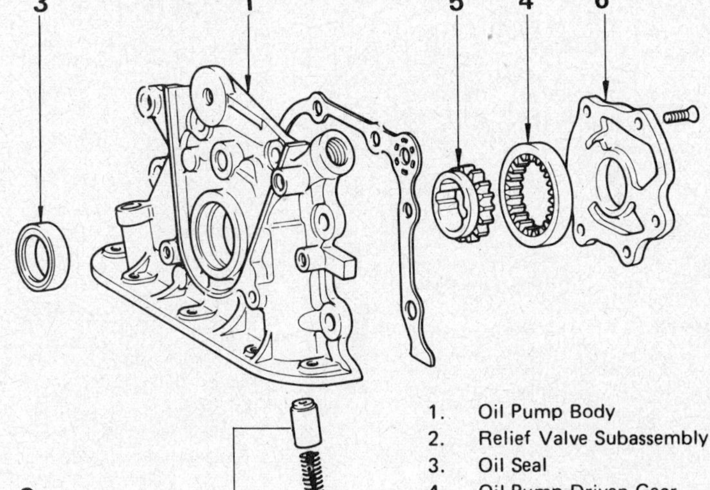

Fig. 96 Oil pump exploded view. 3A-C, 4A-C, 4A-GE, 4A-GEC, 4A-GEL, 4A-GELC & 4A-LC engines

ment, then remove engine mounting nuts and washers.

10. Remove Toyota Electronically Modulated Suspension (TEMS) actuator.
11. Remove front shock absorbers from body, then while supporting front suspension crossmember with suitable jack, remove crossmember attaching bolts. Lower and support front suspension crossmember.
12. Remove oil pan attaching nuts and bolts, then the oil pan.
13. Loosen oil pump outlet-to-engine block union nut, then remove oil pump attaching bolts and the oil pump.
14. Reverse procedure to install.

OIL PUMP SERVICE

4K-E ENGINES

Disassembly

1. Remove oil strainer subassembly and oil pump cover, **Fig. 91.**
2. Remove rotors, relief valve plug, spring and valve.
3. Reverse procedure to assemble. Make sure to install rotors with punch marks facing in the same direction, **Fig. 92.**

Inspection

1. Inspect oil pump shaft side and top end, and replace if worn or damaged.
2. Measure clearance between drive rotor and driven rotor tooth tips, **Fig. 93.** If clearance is greater than .008 inch (.2 mm), replace both rotors.
3. Place a straightedge across rotors and housing, then using a feeler gauge, measure side clearance between rotors and straightedge, **Fig. 94.** If clearance is greater than .006 inch (.15 mm), replace both rotors.
4. Measure clearance between driven rotor and housing, **Fig. 95.** If clearance is greater than .008 inch (.2 mm), replace.
5. Insert relief valve for correct fit. Check oil passages and sliding surface for damage, and replace if defective.
6. Inspect valve spring and replace if damaged or weak.
7. Inspect oil strainer and replace if damaged.

3A-C, 4A-C, 4A-GE, 4A-GEC, 4A-GEL, 4A-GELC, & 4A-LC ENGINES

1. Remove oil pump cover, drive gear and driven gear, **Fig. 96.**
2. Remove oil seal and relief valve subassembly.
3. Check contact surfaces of oil seal and drive gear for damage and wear.
4. Measure clearance between drive gear and driven gear crescents, **Fig. 97.** If clearance is greater than .0138 inch (.35 mm), replace rotor set.
5. Measure side clearance between rotor and cover, **Fig. 98.** If clearance exceeds .0039 inch (.10 mm), replace rotor or pump body as necessary.
6. Measure body clearance between driven rotor and pump body, **Fig. 99.** If clearance is greater than .0079 inch (.20 mm), replace rotor or pump body as necesary.

2S-E, 3E, 3S-FE & 3S-GE ENGINES

1. Using a suitable feeler gauge, measure clearance between driven rotor and pump case, **Figs. 100 and 101.**
2. Clearance should be .0039-.0067 inch except on 1986-87 models. On 1986-87 models, clearance should be .0039-.0063 inch. If feeler gauge clearance obtained exceeds specified

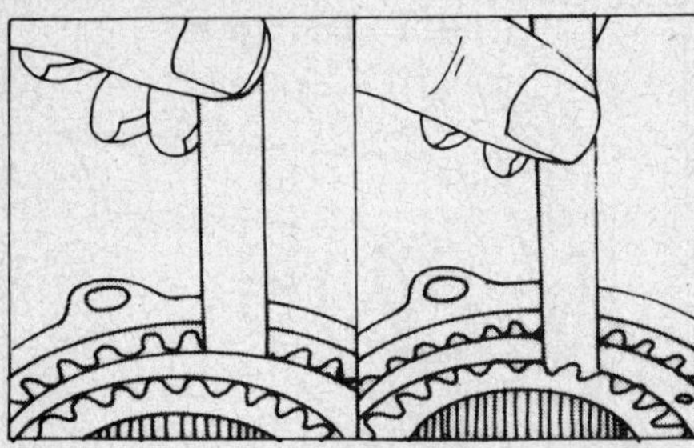

Fig. 97 Checking oil pump drive gear clearance. 3A-C, 4A-C, 4A-GE, 4A-GEC, 4A-GEL, 4A-GELC, 4A-LC, 22R, 22R-E & 22R-TE engines

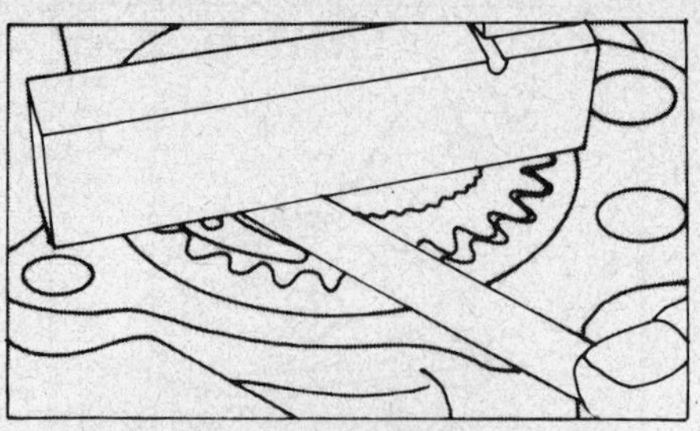

Fig. 98 Checking side clearance between rotor & cover. 3A-C, 4A-C, 4A-GE, 4A-GEC, 4A-GEL, 4A-GELC, 4A-LC, 22R, 22R-E & 22R-TE engines

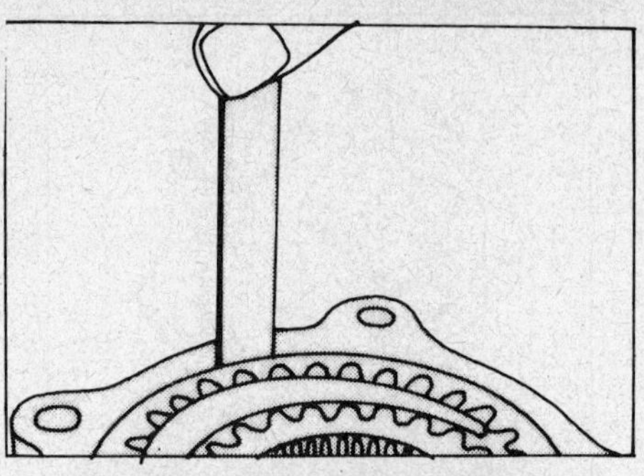

Fig. 99 Checking driven rotor & pump body clearance. 3A-C, 4A-C, 4A-GE, 4A-GEC, 4A-GEL, 4A-GELC, 4A-LC, 22R, 22R-E & 22R-TE engines

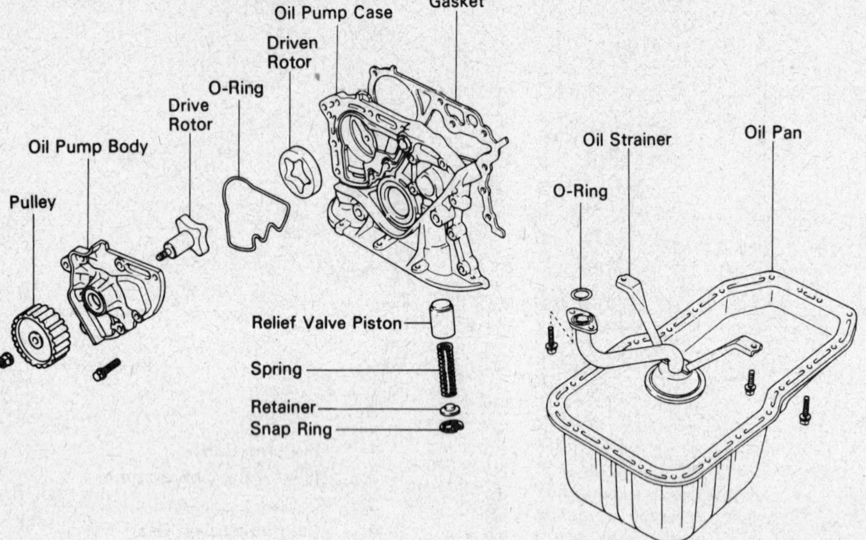

Fig. 100 Oil pump & components. 2S-E, 3E, 3S-FE & 3S-GE engines

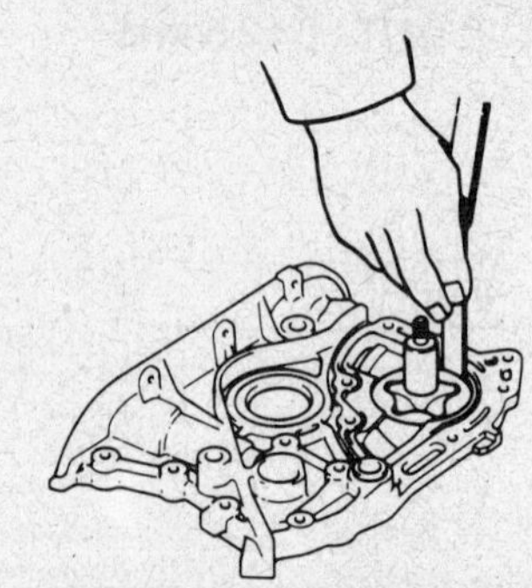

Fig. 101 Measuring clearance between driven rotor & pump case. 2S-E, 3E 3S-FE & 3S-GE engines

limits, replace oil pump rotor set and/or pump case.

3. Using a feeler gauge, measure clearance between both rotor tips. Clearance should be .0016-.0063 inch on all except 3E engine. On 3E engine clearance should be .0024-.0063 inch. If feeler gauge clearance obtained exceeds specified limit, replace oil pump rotor set.
4. On 3E engines, place suitable straightedge across pump opening and measure side clearance. Side clearance should be .0012-.0035 inch. If clearance is greater than specifications, replace oil pump rotor set and/or pump body.

3Y-EC & 4Y-EC ENGINE

1. Check relief valve for wear and/or damage, **Fig. 102.**
2. Using a suitable feeler gauge, measure clearance between driven rotor and body, **Fig. 103.** Clearance should be .0039-.0059 inch. If feeler gauge clearance obtained exceeds specified limit, replace rotor and/or body.
3. Using a feeler gauge, measure clearance between drive rotor and driven rotor, **Fig. 104.** Clearance should be .0028-.0047 inch. If feeler gauge clearance obtained exceeds specified limit, replace rotor set and/or body.
4. Using a feeler gauge, measure side clearance as shown in **Fig. 105.** Clearance should be .0012-.0028 inch. If feeler gauge clearance obtained exceeds specified limit, replace rotor set and/or body.

5M-GE, 7M-GE & 7M-GTE ENGINES

Disassembly

1. Remove oil strainer subassembly and oil pump cover, **Fig. 106.**
2. Remove rotors, relief valve plug, spring and valve.
3. Remove snap ring, spacer, driveshaft gear, key and shaft subassembly.
4. Reverse procedure to assemble.

Inspection

1. Check relief valve for scoring or wear. If damaged, replace valve or pump assembly.
2. Measure clearance between driven gear and body, **Fig. 107.** If clearance is greater than .008 inch, replace gear and/or body.
3. Measure backlash between driven and drive gears, **Fig. 108.** If backlash is greater than .035 inch, replace shaft assembly and drive gear, if necessary.
4. Place a straightedge between rotors and housing, then measure side clearance between rotors and straightedge, **Fig. 109.** If clearance is greater than .0006 inch, replace gears and/or body.

22R, 22R-E & 22R-TE ENGINES

1. To disassemble pump, remove oil pump drive spline and O-ring, then remove relief valve plug, spring, relief valve piston and gears, **Fig. 110.**
2. Inspect drive spline, drive and driven gears, pump body and timing chain cover for excessive wear or damage.
3. Measure driven gear to body clearance, **Fig. 99.** Maximum clearance is .008 inch (.2 mm).
4. Measure clearances between drive gear and crescent and driven gear and crescent, **Fig. 97.** Maximum clearance is .012 inch.
5. Measure side clearance using a straightedge placed across the housing and gears and using a feeler gauge, **Fig. 98.** Measure clearance is .006 inch (.15 mm).
6. Check relief valve piston, oil passages and sliding surfaces for burrs or scoring.
7. Inspect crankshaft front oil seal and replace if worn, damaged or cracked.

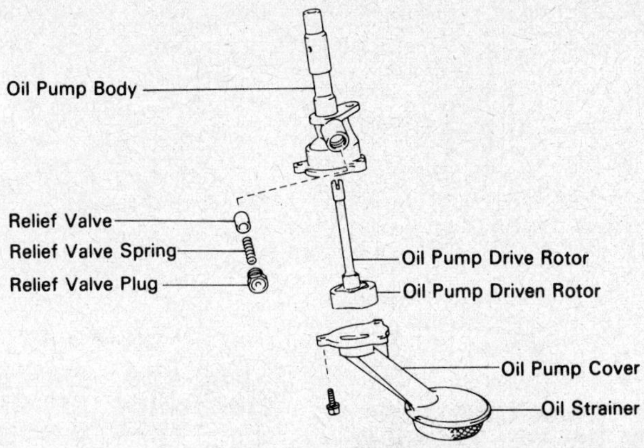

Fig. 102 Oil pump & components. 3Y-EC & 4Y-EC engines

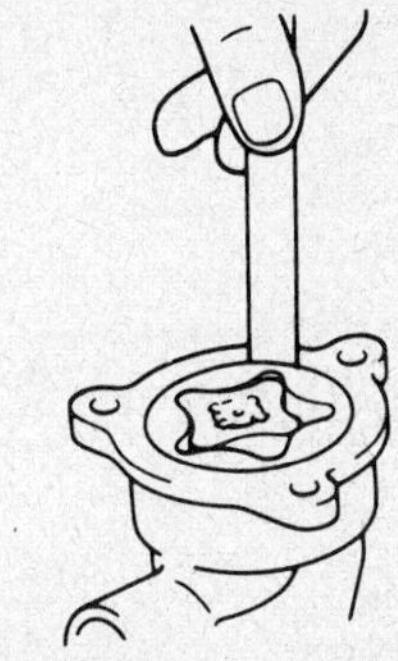

Fig. 103 measuring clearance between driven rotor & pump body. 3Y &-EC & 4Y-EC engines

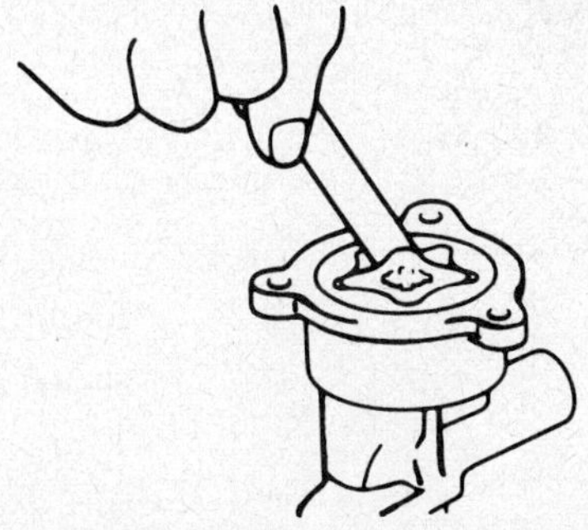

Fig. 104 Measuring rotor tip clearance. 3Y-EC & 4Y-EC engines

WATER PUMP

REPLACE

22R, 22R-E & 22R-TE ENGINES

1. Drain cooling system and remove fan belt.
2. Remove fan clutch attaching nuts, then the fan pulley and fan clutch as an assembly.
3. If necessary, remove fan from fan clutch.
4. Remove bolts and water pump.
5. Reverse procedure to install.

3A-C, 4A-C, 4A-GE & 4A-GEC ENGINES

1. Drain cooling system.
2. Remove radiator from vehicle, if necessary.
3. Loosen drive belts, then remove fan shroud, fluid coupling, if equipped, fan, and water pump pulley from water pump.
4. Remove bolts, water pump outlet housing and bypass line.
5. Remove bolts, water inlet housing and thermostat.
6. Remove timing belt upper cover.
7. Disconnect heater outlet hose from outlet line, then remove heater outlet line mounting bolt.
8. Remove oil level dipstick and guide.
9. Remove water pump attaching nuts and bolts, then the water pump.
10. Reverse procedure to install.

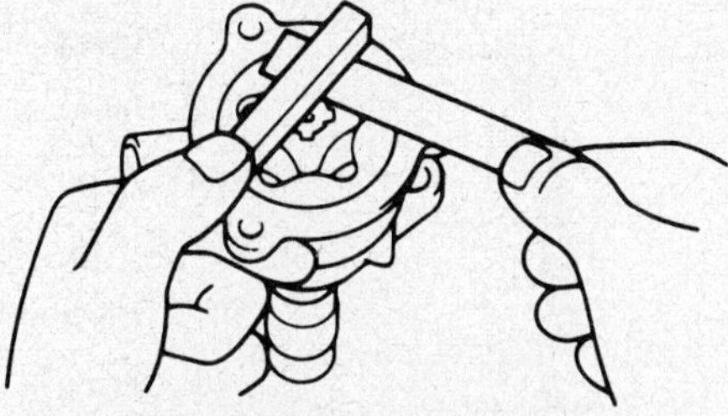

Fig. 105 Measuring side clearance. 3Y-EC & 4Y-EC engines

3E ENGINE

1. Remove right side under cover, then drain engine coolant.
2. On all exc. Calif. models, remove High Altitude Compensation (HAC) valve from bracket.
3. Remove oil dipstick and accessory drive belts.
4. Remove intake manifold support bracket.
5. Disconnect coolant bypass hose from carburetor.
6. Remove dipstick tube, alternator and alternator adjusting bracket.
7. Disconnect coolant hose from intake manifold.
8. Remove water pump pulley, then coolant inlet tube mounting bolt from engine block.
9. Remove water pump attaching nuts and bolts, then the water pump.
10. Reverse procedure to install.

4A-GEL & 4A-GELC, 1985–87 MR2 ENGINES

1. Drain cooling system.
2. Remove compressor drive belt and idle pulley, if equipped with A/C.
3. Remove alternator drive belt, then the water pump pulley attaching bolts and pump pulley.
4. Remove water inlet pipe attaching bolts, then the water inlet pipe.
5. Remove oil level gauge guide and gauge.
6. Remove No. 2 and No. 3 timing belt covers and gaskets.
7. Remove water pump attaching bolts, then the water pump.
8. Reverse procedure to install.

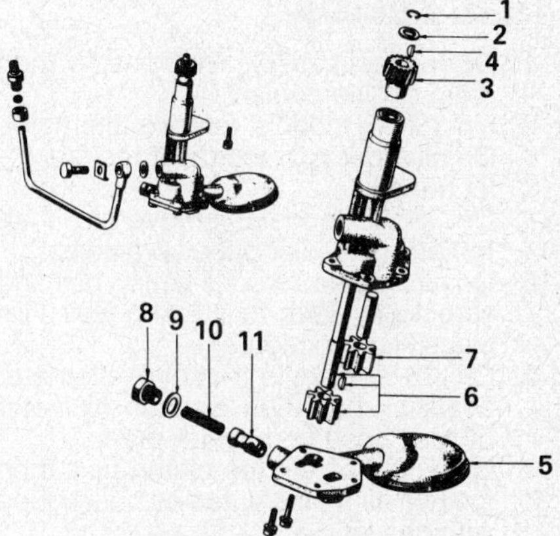

1 Shaft Snap Ring
2 Spacer
3 Oil Pump Drive Shaft Gear
4 Woodruff Key
5 Oil Pump Cover
6 Oil Pump Shaft Sub-assembly
7 Driven Gear
8 Oil Pump Relief Valve Plug
9 Gasket
10 Oil Pump Relief Valve Spring
11 Oil Pump Relief Valve

Fig. 106 Oil pump exploded view. 5M-GE, 7M-GE & 7M-GTE engines

2S-E ENGINE, 1983–86 CAMRY

1. Disconnect battery ground cable.
2. Drain cooling system.
3. Remove timing belt. Refer to "Timing Belt, Replace" for procedure.
4. Remove alternator bracket.
5. Disconnect radiator inlet hose.
6. Disconnect water temperature switch electrical connector from water inlet housing.
7. Disconnect water bypass hose from water pump.
8. Remove heater pipe.
9. Remove water pump attaching bolts, then the water pump.
10. Reverse procedure to install.

Fig. 107 Checking clearance between driven gear & body. 5M-GE, 7M-GE & 7M-GTE engines

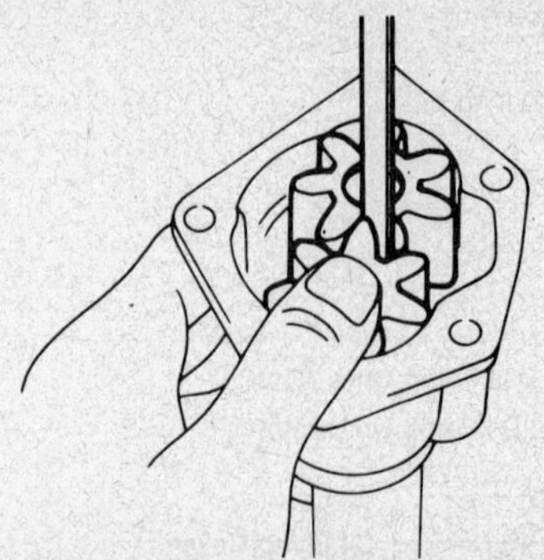

Fig. 108 Checking gear backlash. 5M-GE, 7M-GE & 7M-GTE engines

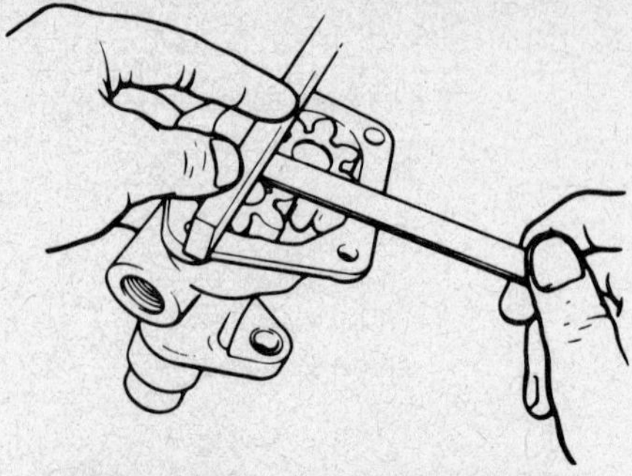

Fig. 109 Checking side clearance. 5M-GE, 7M-GE & 7M-GTE engines

2S-E & 3S-GE ENGINES, 1986 CELICA

1. Disconnect battery ground cable, then drain engine coolant.
2. On 3S-GE models, remove alternator.
3. On all models, disconnect radiator inlet hose.
4. On 3S-GE models, remove No. 1 alternator and idler pulley brackets.
5. On all models, remove timing belt and sprockets. Refer to "Timing Belt, Replace" for procedure.
6. On 2S-E models, remove alternator adjusting bar, then disconnect water bypass hose from water pump.
7. Remove heater pipe clamp bolt, then the two attaching nuts and heater pipe with gasket.
8. On 3S-GE models, remove 2 water bypass pipe to water pump attaching nuts.
9. On all models, remove center, lower, then upper water pump attaching bolts.
10. Remove water pump, O-ring and gasket, if equipped.
11. Reverse procedure to install.

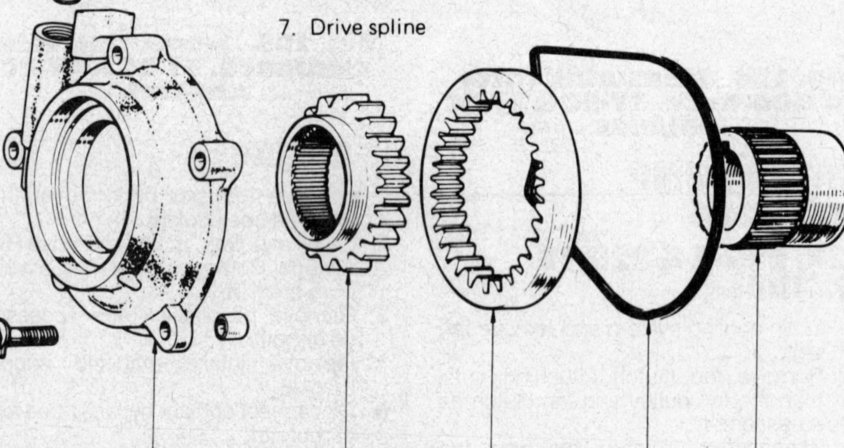

Fig. 110 Oil pump exploded view. 22R, 22R-E & 22R-TE engines

3S-FE & 3S-GE ENGINES, 1987 CAMRY & CELICA

1. Disconnect battery ground cable, then the coolant temperature switch connector.
2. Disconnect lower radiator hose from coolant inlet housing.
3. Remove timing belt and sprockets. Refer to "Timing Belt, Replace" for procedure.
4. Remove water bypass tubes-to-water pump cover attaching bolts, then the three water pump attaching bolts.
5. Remove water pump and pump cover as an assembly, then remove two 0-rings and gasket.
6. Remove water pump-to-water pump cover attaching bolts, then remove water pump.
7. Reverse procedure to install.

3Y-EC & 4Y-EC ENGINE

1. Disconnect battery ground cable.
2. Drain cooling system, then disconnect hoses from water pump.
3. Remove drive belt, fan fluid coupling and water pump pulley.
4. Remove water pump attaching bolts, then the water pump.
5. Reverse procedure to install.

4A-LC, 4A-GEL & 4A-GELC ENGINES, 1987 COROLLA FWD

1. Drain engine coolant.
2. On models equipped with 4A-GEL and 4A-GELC engines, remove power steering drive belt.
3. On all models, remove alternator drive belt.
4. Remove water pump pulley, then the coolant inlet pipe.
5. Remove oil dipstick and tube.
6. Remove timing belt cover, then the water pump.
7. Reverse procedure to install.

4K-E ENGINE

1. Drain cooling system.
2. Disconnect hose from coolant reservoir.
3. Remove air cleaner hose.
4. Disconnect upper and lower radiator hoses, then remove radiator.
5. Loosen water pump pulley bolts, then remove drive belt and pulley.
6. Remove bolts and water pump pulley.
7. Reverse procedure to install.

5M-GE ENGINE

1. Drain cooling system.
2. Loosen water pump pulley bolts and drive belt.
3. Remove air cleaner assembly.
4. Disconnect upper radiator hose, then remove fan shroud bolts.

5. Remove fluid coupling, fan, fan belt guide and water pump pulley.
6. Remove bolts and water pump.
7. Reverse procedure to install.

7M-GE & 7M-GTE ENGINES

1. Drain cooling system.
2. If equipped, remove A/C compressor belt.
3. Remove alternator drive belt, fan and fan clutch assembly and water pump pulley.
4. Remove power steering air pipe.
5. Remove water pump attaching bolts, then the water pump.

FUEL PUMP REPLACE

1. Disconnect fuel lines from pump.
2. Remove fuel pump retaining bolts or nuts and fuel pump.
3. Reverse procedure to install.

L, 2L & 2L-T DIESEL ENGINE SECTION

INDEX

TROUBLESHOOTING

STARTER DOES NOT OPERATE

1. Loose or corroded battery cables.
2. Discharge battery.
3. Defective starter.

ENGINE CRANKS SLOWLY BUT WILL NOT START

1. Loose or corroded battery cables.
2. Discharge battery.
3. Use of improper engine oil.

ENGINE CRANKS NORMALLY BUT WILL NOT START

1. No fuel delivery to an injection nozzle.
2. Fuel cut solenoid inoperative.
3. No fuel delivery to injection pump.
4. Preheat system inoperative.
5. Glow plugs inoperative.
6. Injection pipe leaking.
7. Incorrect injection timing.
8. Faulty nozzle or nozzle holder.

ROUGH IDLE WITH ENGINE WARM

1. Incorrect accelerator cable adjustment.
2. Idle speed too low.
3. Fuel leaking.
4. Incorrect injection timing.
5. Defective or inoperative nozzle or delivery valve.
6. No fuel delivery to injection pump.

ENGINE STALLS

1. Engine will not restart – refer to "Engine Cranks Normally But Will Not Start."
2. Engine starts and idles roughly – refer to "Rough Idle With Engine Warm."
3. Defective fuel cut solenoid.
4. No fuel delivery to injection pump.

ENGINE LACKS POWER

1. Restricted air cleaner.
2. Engine overheating.
3. Incorrect accelerator cable adjustment.
4. Incorrect no load maximum RPM.
5. Incorrect installation of overflow and inlet screws.
6. Fuel leaking.
7. Clogged fuel filter.
8. Improper injection timing.
9. Faulty nozzle or nozzle holder.

EXCESSIVE EXHAUST SMOKE

1. Restricted air cleaner.
2. Incorrect injection timing.
3. Clogged fuel filter.
4. Faulty nozzle or nozzle holder.

EXCESSIVE FUEL CONSUMPTION

1. Fuel leaking.
2. Idle speed too high.
3. Maximum RPM speed adjusted too high.
4. Incorrect injection timing.
5. Faulty nozzle or nozzle holder.

ENGINE NOISY WHEN WARM, EXCESSIVE VIBRATION

1. Coolant temperature too low.
2. Incorrect injection timing.
3. Faulty nozzle or nozzle holder.

ENGINE WILL NOT RETURN TO IDLE SPEED

1. Accelerator linkage binding.

ENGINE DOES NOT STOP WITH IGNITION OFF

1. Defective or inoperative fuel cut solenoid operation.

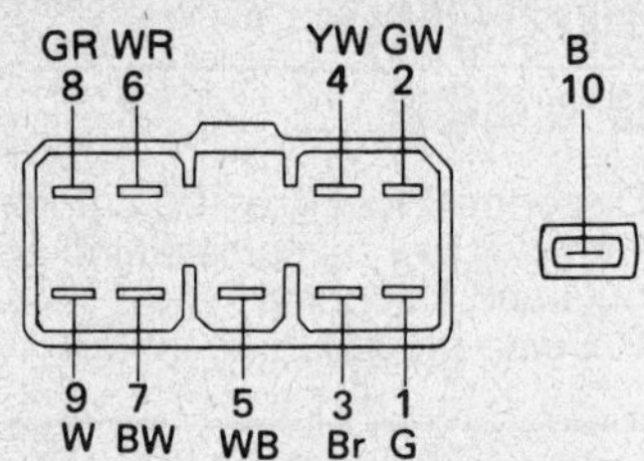

Fig. 1 Preheat timer electrical connector. L diesel engine

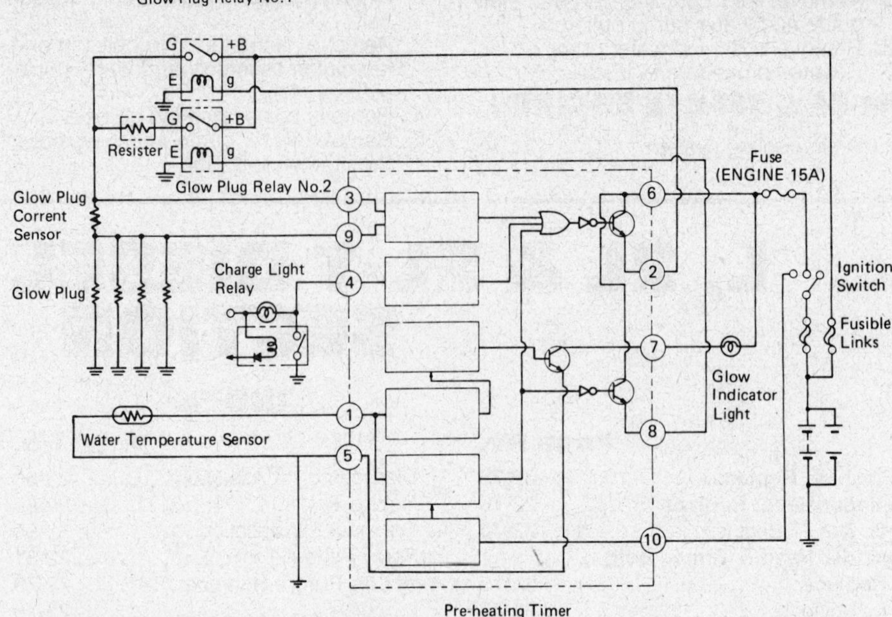

Fig. 2 Preheat circuit electrical schematic. L diesel engine

DIESEL ENGINE ELECTRICAL SYSTEM DIAGNOSIS

L ENGINE

Engine Does Not Start

1. Check preheat system by turning ignition switch On and checking operation of preheat indicator lamp. With coolant temperature below 104°F (40°C), lamp should light after 4.5 seconds. With coolant temperature above 104°F (40°C), lamp should light after .5 seconds.
2. If lamp does not operate as described, check 15 amp engine fuse. If fuse is blown, check wiring for short circuit and repair as necessary. If fuse is not blown, check indicator lamp bulb and replace if necessary.
3. If bulb is satisfactory, check for battery voltage at No. 7 terminal of preheating timer electrical connector, **Fig. 1.** If voltage is present, repair or replace preheater timer as necessary.
4. If preheater system operates as described in step 1, but engine will not start, turn ignition off, then disconnect preheater electrical connector.
5. Turn ignition On and check for battery voltage at terminal No. 2. If voltage is not present, check for reading of one volt at terminal No. 3 and No. 9. If not, repair or replace glow plug current sensor as necessary. If voltage at terminals No. 3 and No. 9 is satisfactory, replace preheater timer.
6. If battery voltage is present at preheater electrical connector terminal No. 2, **Fig. 1**, turn ignition key to Start position after time out cycle described in step 1 is completed. If no voltage is present at terminal No. 2 with ignition key in Start position and time out cycle completed, disconnect charge lamp relay electrical connector, **Fig. 2,** and perform test over. If engine starts, repair or replace relay as necessary. If engine does not start, replace preheat timer.
7. If voltage is present at preheat connector terminal No. 2 with ignition key in start position and time out cycle completed, turn ignition off.
8. Turn ignition On and check for power at terminal No. 8 of preheat timer connector. Amount of time voltage is present at terminal No. 8 will vary depending on coolant temperature. Refer to graph in **Fig. 3** for time and temperature values.
9. If no voltage is present at terminal No. 8, replace preheat timer.
10. If preheat duration is not specified for a given temperature as indicated in graph in **Fig. 3**, disconnect water temperature sensor electrical connector and check for voltage at terminal No. 8 of preheat connector.
11. Voltage should be present at terminal No. 8 of preheat connector for approximately 150 seconds with electrical connector ungrounded or for 7 seconds with electrical connector grounded. If readings are satisfactory, replace water temperature sensor. If not, replace preheat timer.
12. If voltage at terminal No. 8 of preheat connector are correct as indicated in graph in **Fig. 3**, check for voltage and terminal No. 8 with ignition key in Start position.
13. If no voltage is present, replace preheat timer. If voltage is present, turn ignition switch Off.

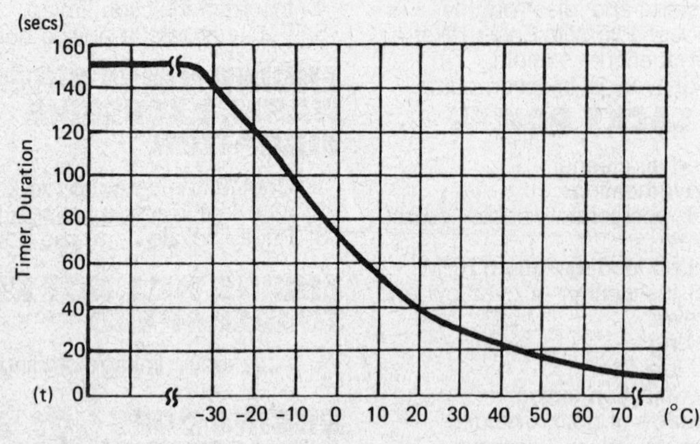

Fig. 3 Relationship between coolant temperature & preheat timer duration. L diesel engine

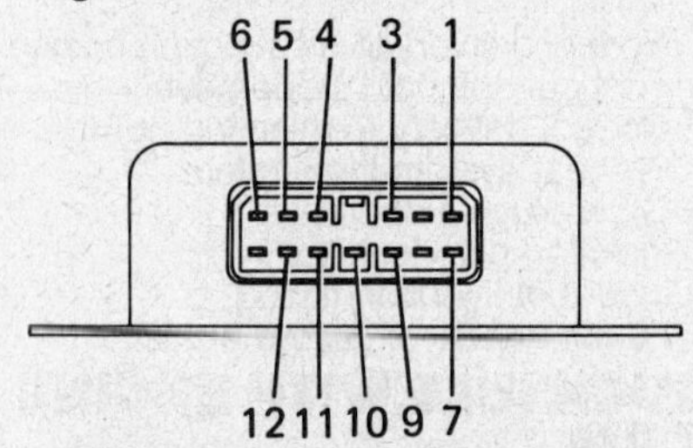

Fig. 4 Preheat timer electrical connector. 2L & 2L-T diesel engines

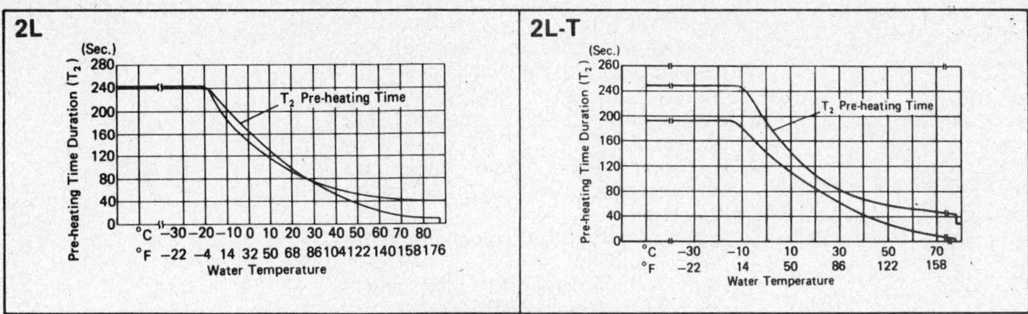

Fig. 5 Relationship between coolant temperature & preheat timer duration. 2L & 2L-T diesel engines

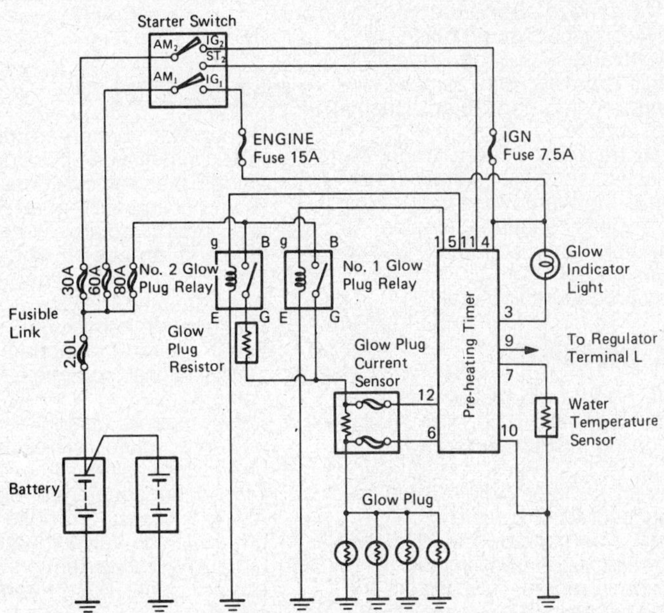

Fig. 6 Preheat circuit electrical schematic. 2L & 2L-T diesel engines

14. Turn ignition On, then wait several seconds and check voltage at glow plugs. After a short time, glow plug voltage reading should decrease to 1/2 of original reading.
15. If no voltage is present at glow plugs, check for battery voltage at positive side of glow plug current sensor. If voltage is present, replace sensor. If not, No. 1 glow plug relay is faulty and should be replaced.
16. If readings are obtained as specified in step 14, check glow plug resistance using suitable ohmmeter. If reading of zero ohms is obtained, glow plug is satisfactory. If infinite reading is obtained, replace glow plug.
17. If voltage reading does not decrease by 1/2 original reading as described in step 14, check for voltage at positive terminal of glow plug resistor. If battery voltage is present, replace resistor. If no, replace No. 2 glow plug relay.

Fuel Cut Solenoid Inoperative

1. Turn ignition switch On and Off several times while listening for click of fuel cut solenoid.
2. If clicking cannot be heard, check 15 amp engine fuse. If fuse is blown, check for short circuit and repair as necessary.
3. If fuse is not blown, apply battery voltage to fuel cut solenoid and listen for click. If clicking cannot be heard, replace fuel cut solenoid.
4. If clicking can be heard when battery voltage is applied to fuel cut solenoid, check for defective wiring between engine and fuel cut solenoid and repair as necessary.

2L & 2L-T ENGINES

Engine Does Not Start

1. Check if indicator lamp lights with ignition switch ON and coolant temperature at 68°F (20°C). If indicator lamp does not light, check engine fuse. If engine fuse is blown, check for a short circuit and repair as required. If engine fuse is not blown, check indicator light bulb and replace if necessary. If indicator light bulb is not blown, check for battery voltage to terminal 3 of preheating system timer electrical connector, **Fig. 4**. If battery voltage is present, replace preheat timer as necessary.
2. If indicator lamp lights with ignition switch ON, check for battery voltage to terminal 1 of preheating timer with ignition switch ON. If no voltage is obtained, ensure that there is 1 volt at terminals 12 and 9. If not, replace glow plug current sensor. If voltage is present, check if voltage to terminal 1 of preheating timer is switched OFF after engine is started. If no voltage is obtained, start engine and check if there is voltage at terminal 9 of preheating timer. If not, repair charging system as required. If voltage is present at terminal 9, replace preheat timer.
3. If voltage is present at terminal 1, turn ignition switch ON and check current flow to terminal 5. Voltage to terminal 5 will vary depending on coolant (water) temperature. Refer to graph in **Fig. 5** for time duration and water temperature values. If there is no voltage, replace preheat timer as necessary. If preheat duration obtained exceeds values indicated in graph, proceed as follows:
   a. Disconnect water temperature sensor, **Fig. 6** and check if preheating duration is approximately 150 seconds, or if electrical connector is grounded, preheating duration is approximately 3 seconds.
   b. If preheating duration is within time stated in step 3a, water temperature sensor is defective and should be replaced. If not, replace preheating timer.
4. After completion of preheating duration, recheck voltage at terminal 5 with ignition switch in Start position. If no voltage, replace preheating timer. If voltage is obtained, proceed as follows:
   a. Position ignition switch ON and check for voltage to glow plugs approximately 3 seconds after ignition switch is turned ON. Voltage should drop approximately one half. If voltage drops, check glow plug for continuity. If there is no continuity, replace glow plug.
   b. If no voltage is present, check for battery voltage at positive side of glow plug current sensor. If voltage is present, replace current sensor. If no voltage is present, No. 1 glow plug relay is defective and should be replaced.
   c. If voltage does not decrease by one half, check for battery voltage

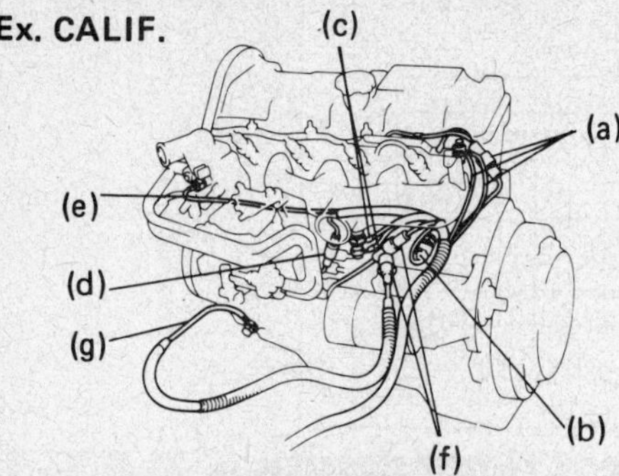

Fig. 7 Engine harness removal. 1985 2L & 2L-T exc. Calif.

at positive side of resistor. If voltage is present, replace resistor. If voltage is not present, replace No. 2 glow plug relay.

Fuel Cut Solenoid

1. With ignition switch turned ON, check for fuel cut solenoid operation (indicated by a clicking sound) while connecting and disconnecting the fuel cut solenoid.
2. If fuel cut solenoid is not operating, check engine fuse. If fuse is blown, check for a short circuit and repair as required. If fuse is not blown, apply battery voltage to solenoid and check for operation. If fuel cut solenoid operates, check and/or repair wire harness from fuse to fuel cut solenoid. If fuel cut solenoid does not operate, replace fuel cut solenoid.

ENGINE

REPLACE

L ENGINE

1. Scribe hood hinge outline on engine hood, then remove hood.
2. Remove batteries, air cleaner and drain coolant system.
3. Disconnect radiator hoses from radiator, then remove radiator and shroud.
4. On vehicles equipped with air conditioning, remove compressor drive belt and mounting bolts. Position compressor aside with hoses attached.
5. Remove alternator drive belt, fan and fan pulley.
6. Disconnect engine heater hoses, vacuum hose from rear of alternator, fuel pump return hose and sedimenter inlet hose.
7. On vehicles equipped with air conditioning, disconnect idle up vacuum hose.
8. Disconnect electrical connectors from alternator, thermo switch, oil pressure switch, B+ terminal of No. 1 glow plug relay and starter motor.
9. Disconnect accelerator wire from injection pump.
10. Remove transmission shift lever from inside vehicle using tool 09305-20012 or equivalent.
11. Raise and support vehicle and drain engine oil.
12. Remove engine under cover and disconnect back-up light switch electrical connector.
13. Remove engine shock absorber and driveshaft.
14. Disconnect speedometer cable and exhaust pipe clamp at transmission housing.
15. Disconnect exhaust pipe from exhaust manifold.
16. Remove clutch release cylinder and position aside with hydraulic lines attached.
17. Remove engine mount bolts from both sides of engine.
18. Position suitable jack under transmission, then remove engine rear mounting bracket from crossmember.
19. Attach suitable lifting equipment to engine lift brackets, then remove engine and transmission as an assembly from vehicle.
20. To separate engine from transmission, place assembly in suitable holding fixture, then remove starter motor. Remove bolts securing engine to transmission and separate engine and transmission.
21. Reverse procedure to install.

1984 2L ENGINE

1. Remove hood, then disconnect battery ground cable.
2. Drain cooling system and oil from engine.
3. Disconnect radiator hoses, then remove radiator from vehicle.
4. On manual transmission models, remove transmission from vehicle.
5. On California models, disconnect the following hoses:
   a. Vacuum pump hose from HAC valve.
   b. BVSV hose from air cleaner and VRV valve.
   c. VRV hose from vacuum damper.
   d. VRV hose from VSV valve.
   e. EGR valve hose from VSV valve.
6. On California models, remove air cleaner assembly from engine.
7. Disconnect and plug heater hoses.
8. Disconnect accelerator cable from bracket.
9. On exc. California models, disconnect A/C vacuum hose from VSV valve.
10. Disconnect oil inlet hose from vacuum pump.
11. Remove A/C compressor from bracket and position aside. Do not disconnect refrigerant lines.
12. Disconnect and plug fuel lines.
13. Disconnect all electrical connectors from engine.
14. Remove engine under cover attaching bolts, then the under cover.
15. Remove power steering pump from bracket. Do not disconnect power steering pump fluid lines.
16. Remove engine mount shock absorber from crossmember.
17. Remove engine mount nuts and bolts.
18. Install suitable engine lifting equipment onto engine.
19. Remove engine from vehicle.
20. Reverse procedure to install.

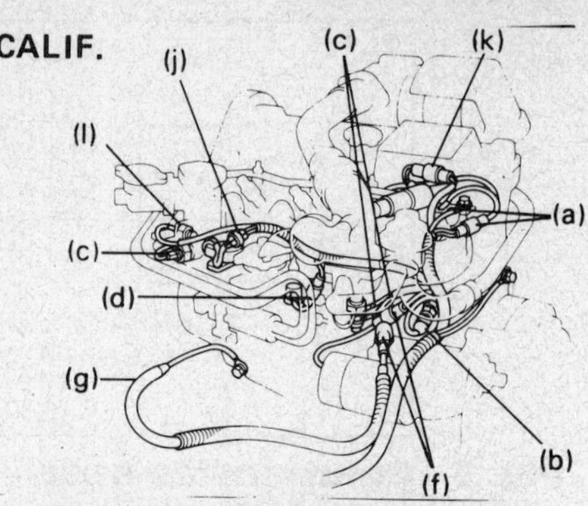

Fig. 8 Engine harness removal. 1985 2L & 2L-T Calif.

1985 2L & 2L-T

1. Disconnect battery ground cable, mark installation position of hood hinges, then remove hood.
2. Drain cooling system and engine oil.
3. Disconnect radiator hoses from engine and remove fan shroud.
4. Disconnect expansion tank hose, then remove radiator.
5. Remove transmission along with transfer case, if equipped.
6. On 2L engines, remove air cleaner assembly.
7. On all models, disconnect expansion tank and heater hoses from engine and secure aside.
8. Disconnect accelerator cable and remove A/C vacuum hose from vacuum switching valve, if equipped.
9. On 2L-T engines, remove turbocharger pressure hose from pressure switch.
10. On all models, disconnect and plug oil inlet hose to vacuum pump.
11. On models with A/C, remove 4 compressor mounting bolts and drive belt, then secure compressor aside, leaving refrigerant hoses connected.
12. Disconnect and plug fuel lines to engine.
13. Release engine harness and secure aside after disconnecting the following electrical connectors, **Figs. 7 and 8:**
   a. Glow plug current sensor.
   b. Water temperature sensor.
   c. Glow plug resistor.
   d. Injection pump.
   e. Water temperature gauge sender.
   f. Starter motor.
   g. Engine grounds.
   h. Oil pressure switch.
   i. Alternator.
   j. Throttle position sensor.
   k. EVR valve.
   l. Water temperature switch.
14. Remove engine splash guard.
15. Remove power steering pump retaining bolts and drive belt, and secure pump aside leaving hoses connected.
16. On 2 wheel drive models, remove engine vibration damper from crossmember.
17. On all models, attach suitable lifting equipment to engine, remove bolts securing engine mount insulators to

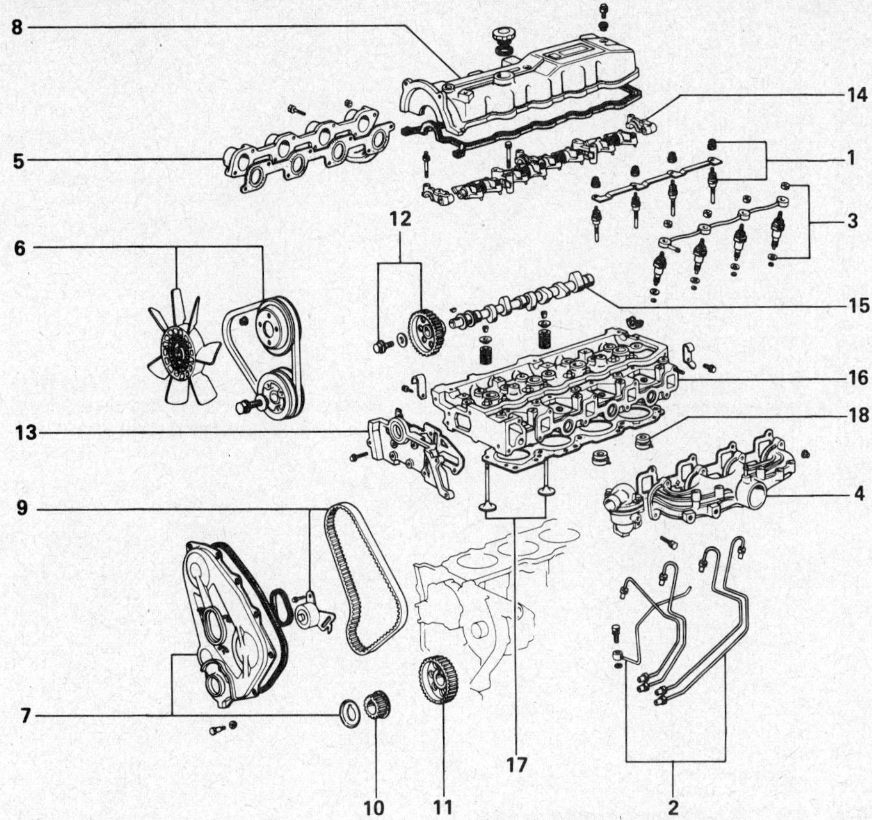

Fig. 9 Cylinder head & timing belt exploded view

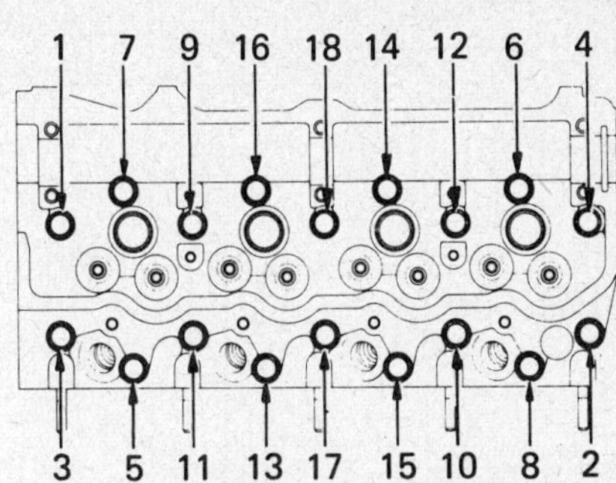

Fig. 10 Cylinder head bolt removal sequence

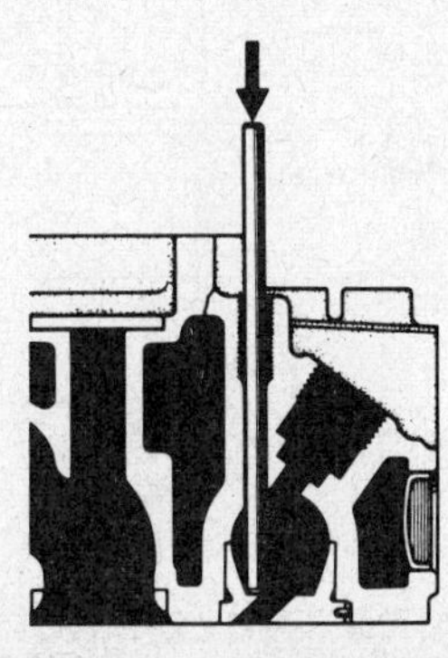

Fig. 11 Removing combustion chamber subassemblies from cylinder head. L diesel engine

crossmember and lift engine from vehicle.

18. Reverse procedure to install.

CYLINDER HEAD & TIMING BELT

REPLACE

L ENGINE

Removal

1. Rotate engine until No. 1 piston is at TDC on compression stroke.
2. Remove glow plugs, injection pipe and fuel pipe, **Fig. 9.**
3. Disconnect all hoses, wiring and cables as necessary and remove intake manifold.
4. Remove exhaust manifold, fan, fan pulley and crankshaft pulley.
5. Remove timing gear cover and belt guide.
6. Remove valve cover, idler pulley and timing belt. If timing belt is to be reused, mark relationship of belt to pulleys prior to removing.
7. Remove crankshaft timing gear and injection drive pulley.
8. Remove camshaft timing pulley and No. 2 oil seal retainer.
9. Remove rocker arm support bolts gradually and in sequence beginning with outer bolts and moving inner bolts.
10. Remove camshaft, then remove cylinder head retaining bolts in sequence shown in **Fig. 10**. Remove cylinder head.
11. Remove valves from cylinder head using suitable valve spring compressor, then remove combustion chamber subassemblies from cylinder using suitable tool, **Fig. 11.**

Installation

1. Install combustion chamber subassemblies into cylinder by aligning chamber pin with notch in cylinder head. Check for proper combustion chamber protrusion using suitable dial indicator. Chamber protrusion should be 0-.0024 inch (0-.06 mm). If protrusion is not as specified, adjust with shim, **Fig. 12.** Shims are available in the following sizes: .002 in. (.05 mm), .0039 in. (.10 mm), .0059 in. (.15 mm) and .0079 in. (.20 mm).
2. Install valves into cylinder head, then install cylinder head onto engine. Apply light coating of engine oil to cylinder head bolts, then torque to specification and in sequence shown in **Fig. 13.**
3. Install camshaft onto cylinder head. Place piece of Plastigage or equivalent onto clean camshaft bearing journal, then install bearing cap and torque to 11-15 ft. lbs. (1.5-2.2 kg-m). Remove bearing caps and check bearing oil clearance. Oil clearance should be .0009-.0030 inch (.022-.074 mm). If clearance is greater than specified, replace bearing with suitable undersize.
4. Remove all Plastigage from bearing journals, then install bearings and bearing caps and torque to 11-15 ft. lbs. (1.5-2.2 kg-m).
5. Torque rocker shaft bolts to 11-15 ft. lbs. (1.5-2.2 kg-m) gradually and in sequence beginning with inner bolts and proceeding to outer bolts.
6. Install No. 2 oil seal retainer and torque retaining bolts to 8-12 ft. lbs. (1-1.7 kg-m).
7. Install camshaft timing pulley and torque retaining bolt to 69-75 ft. lbs. (9.5-10.5 ft. lbs.)
8. Install injection pump drive pulley and torque retaining bolt to 44-50 ft. lbs. (6-7 kg-m).
9. Install crankshaft timing pulley, timing

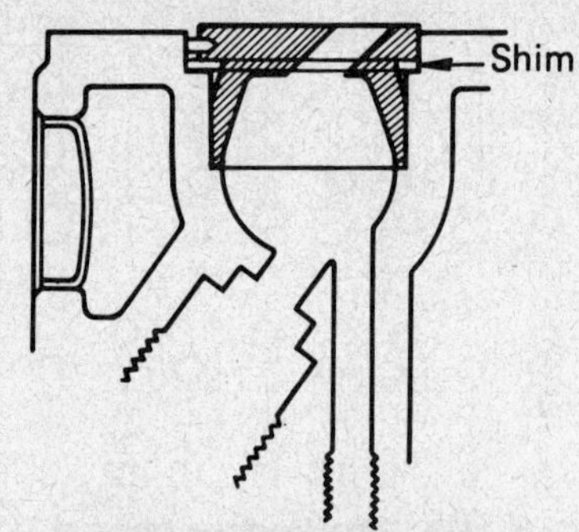

Fig. 12 Adjusting combustion chamber subassembly protrusion. L diesel engine

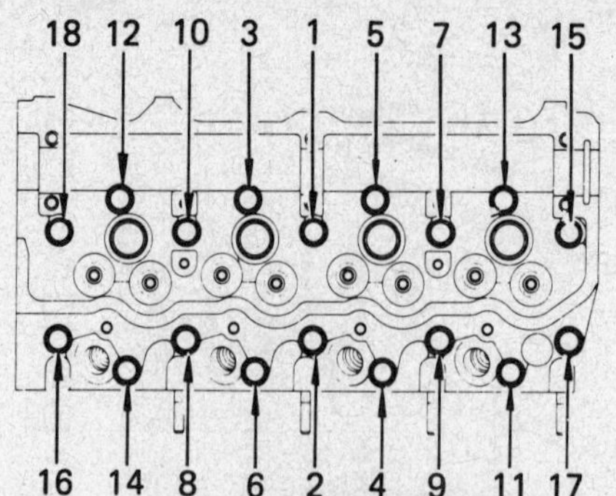

Fig. 13 Cylinder head bolt tightening sequence

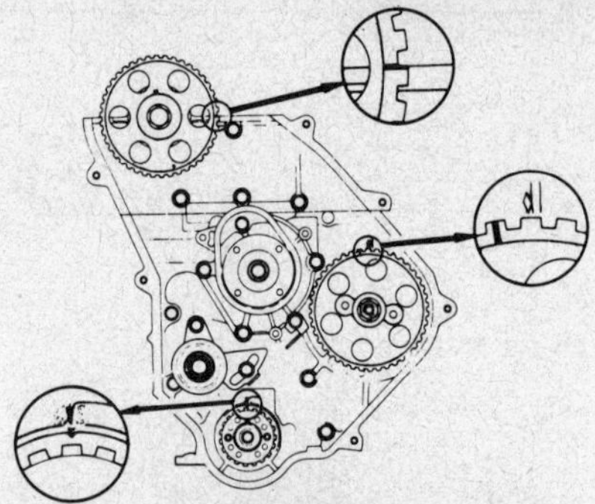

Fig. 14 Aligning timing belt with timing pulleys. L diesel engine

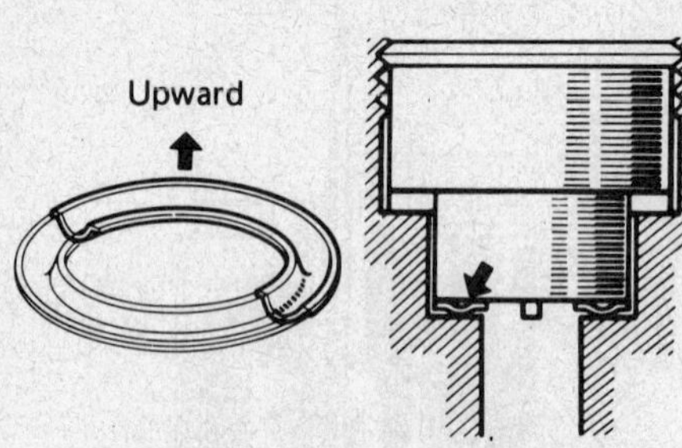

Fig. 15 Nozzle holder gasket installation position. L diesel engine

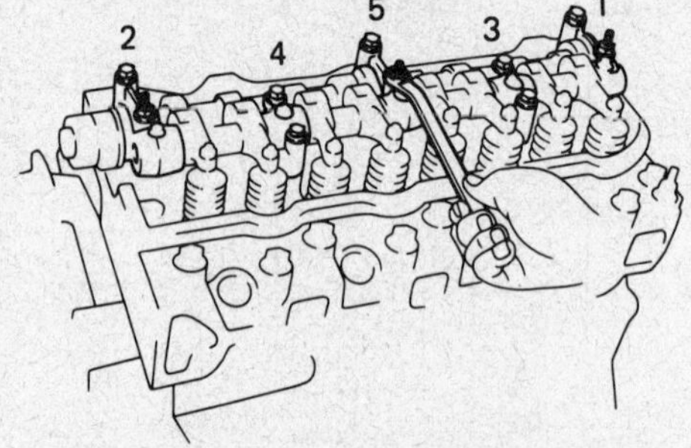

Fig. 16 Rocker shaft bolt removal sequence. 2L & 2L-T diesel engines

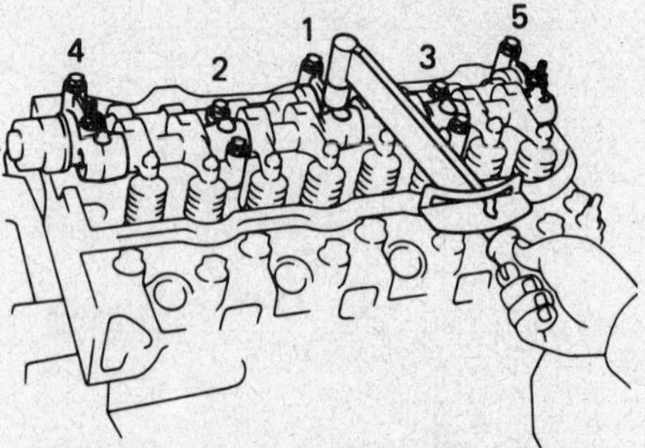

Fig. 17 Rocker shaft bolt tightening sequence. 2L & 2L-T diesel engines

belt and idler pulley. Align each pulley with proper timing mark, **Fig. 14**, then install timing belt. If old belt is to be re-used, align marks made during removal procedure.

10. Install idler pulley spring and temporarily install pulley bolt. Rotate crankshaft two complete revolutions clockwise while checking that idler pulley bracket moves when crankshaft is rotated.
11. Torque idler pulley bolts to 11-15 ft. lbs. (1.5-2.2 kg-m).
12. Install timing gear cover, belt guide and crankshaft pulley.
13. Install valve cover, intake and exhaust manifolds. Adjust valves as described under "Valves, Adjust."
14. Connect all hoses, wiring and cables disconnected during removal procedure.
15. Install glow plugs and torque to 8-11 ft. lbs. (1-1.6 kg-m).
16. Install injection nozzle holder, **Fig. 15**, and torque to 44-57 ft. lbs. (6-8 kg-m).
17. Install injection pipe and fuel pipe, then torque pipe nuts to 15-21 ft. lbs. (2-3 kg-m).
18. Install fan and pulley.

CYLINDER HEAD

REPLACE

2L & 2L-T ENGINES

1. Disconnect battery ground cable.
2. Drain cooling system, then remove radiator from vehicle.
3. Mark then disconnect all emission control hoses from cylinder head and remove air cleaner assembly as needed.
4. On 2L exc. California models, remove hose from air cleaner assembly.
5. On 2L-T engines, disconnect expansion tank hose from water outlet, then remove turbocharger.
6. Disconnect and plug heater hoses.
7. Disconnect accelerator cable from bracket.
8. Disconnect A/C vacuum hose from VSV, if equipped.
9. Remove A/C compressor from mounting bracket and position aside. Do not disconnect refrigerant lines from compressor.
10. Disconnect and plug fuel lines.
11. Disconnect glow plug current sender, water temperature sensor, glow plug resistor and water temperature sender gauge electrical connectors.
12. Mark then remove fuel injection lines, nozzles and fuel inlet line, **Fig. 9**.
13. Disconnect PCV valve hose from PCV valve, if equipped.
14. Remove cylinder head cover attaching bolts, then the cylinder head cover.
15. Remove timing belt. Refer to "Timing Belt, Replace" for procedure.
16. Remove camshaft timing sprocket.
17. Disconnect accelerator connecting rod from accelerator link.
18. On California models, remove EVR valve EGR valve and EGR valve adapter.
19. Remove intake manifold attaching bolts, then the intake manifold and left side engine bracket.
20. Remove water outlet attaching bolts, then the water outlet assembly.
21. Remove right side engine bracket, if equipped.
22. Remove A/C bracket, if equipped.
23. On turbocharged models, remove turbocharger oil pipe retaining clip and union bolt, then disconnect pipe from hose and plug hose.
24. On turbocharged models, remove heat insulator, then on all models, remove exhaust manifold retaining bolts and the manifold.
25. Remove camshaft oil seal retainer attaching bolts, then the retainer.
26. Gradually loosen then remove rocker shaft assembly retaining bolts in three steps in sequence shown in **Fig. 16**. Remove rocker shaft assembly, camshaft and bearings.
27. Gradually loosen then remove cylinder head bolts in three steps in sequence shown in **Fig. 10.**
28. Reverse procedure to install. Torque rocker shaft assembly retaining bolts in three steps in sequence shown in **Fig. 17**, to 14 ft. lbs. Torque cylinder head bolts in three steps in sequence shown in **Fig. 13**, to 87 ft. lbs.

TIMING BELT

REPLACE

2L & 2L-T ENGINES

Removal

1. Disconnect battery ground cable.
2. Drain cooling system and remove radiator from vehicle.

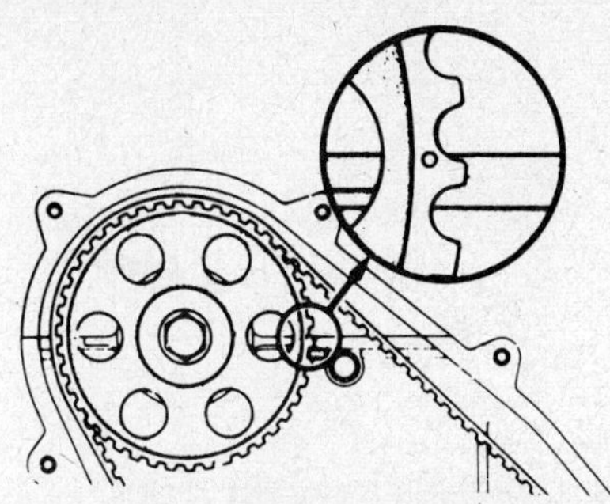

Fig. 18 Aligning TDC mark on camshaft timing sprocket with top end of cylinder head. 2L & 2L-T diesel engines

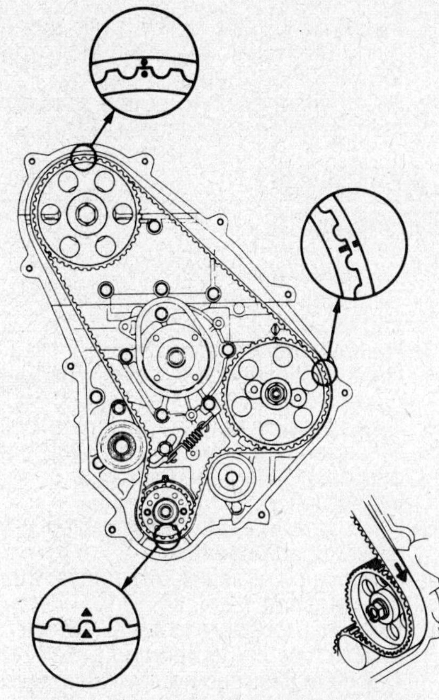

Fig. 19 Placing alignment marks on all timing sprockets & timing belt. 2L & 2L-T diesel engines

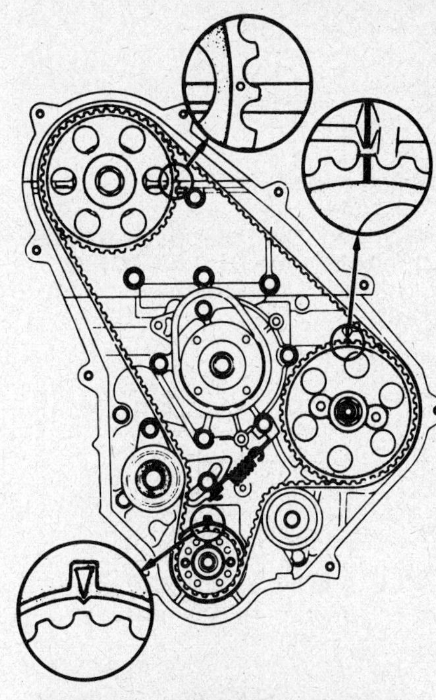

Fig. 20 Aligning timing marks on injection pump drive pulley, camshaft & crankshaft timing sprockets. 2L & 2L-T diesel engines

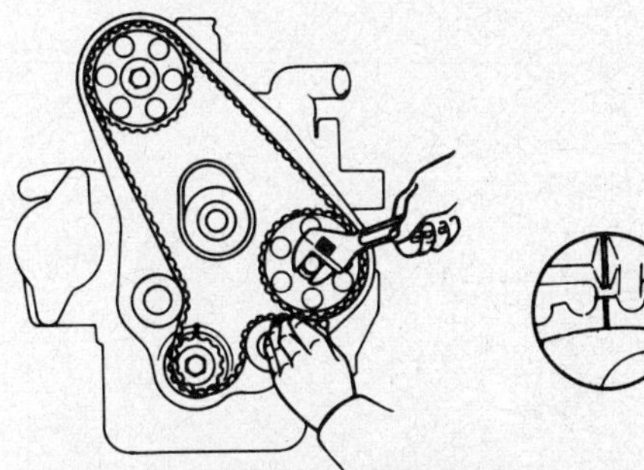

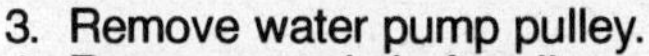

Fig. 21 Aligning marks on injection drive pulley. 2L & 2L-T diesel engines

3. Remove water pump pulley.
4. Remove crankshaft pulley.
5. Remove A/C idle pulley, if equipped.
6. Remove timing belt cover attaching bolts, then the timing belt cover.
7. Remove timing belt guide and glow plugs.
8. Position No. 1 cylinder at TDC of compression stroke and align TDC mark on camshaft timing sprocket with top end of cylinder head, **Fig. 18.**
9. Remove timing belt and injection pump drive pulley. **If original timing belt is to be reused, draw a directional mark (arrow) on the timing belt (in direction of engine rotation) and place alignment marks on all timing sprockets and timing belt as shown in Fig. 19.**
10. Remove No. 2 idler pulley and crankshaft timing sprocket.

Installation

1. Install crankshaft timing sprocket and No. 2 idler pulley. Torque idler pulley to 29 ft. lbs.
2. Install injection pump drive pulley. Torque mount nut to 47 ft. lbs.
3. Install camshaft timing sprocket. Torque sprocket retaining bolt to 73 ft. lbs.
4. Install No. 1 idler pulley.
5. Position No. 1 cylinder at TDC of compression stroke and align timing sprocket and drive pulley at each position. If original timing belt is reused, align marks on the injection pump drive pulley, **Fig. 20**. Mark on injection pump drive pulley should be at a slightly retarded position.
6. Install timing belt onto engine.
7. If installing a new timing belt, proceed as follows:
   a. Install timing belt onto camshaft timing sprocket.
   b. Align marks on the injection pump drive pulley, **Fig. 21.**
   c. Install timing belt onto No. 2 idler pulley and crankshaft timing sprocket.
8. If installing original timing belt, proceed as follows:
   a. Align points marked during removal, **Fig. 19** and install timing belt with arrow pointing in direction of engine rotation.
   b. Ensure timing belt is completely meshed with camshaft sprocket, crankshaft sprocket and injection pump drive pulley.
9. Install tension spring.
10. Check position of timing belt and sprockets by turning crankshaft 2 complete revolutions from TDC to TDC. Ensure each sprocket aligns with timing marks, **Fig. 22.**
11. Torque idler pulley mounting bolts to 14 ft. lbs. **While torquing mounting bolts, do not turn idler pulley bracket.**
12. Install glow plugs and current sensor.
13. Install timing belt guide and timing belt cover.
14. Install A/C idler pulley, if equipped.
15. Install crankshaft pulley. Torque pulley retaining bolt to 102 ft. lbs.
16. Install water pump pulley and radiator.

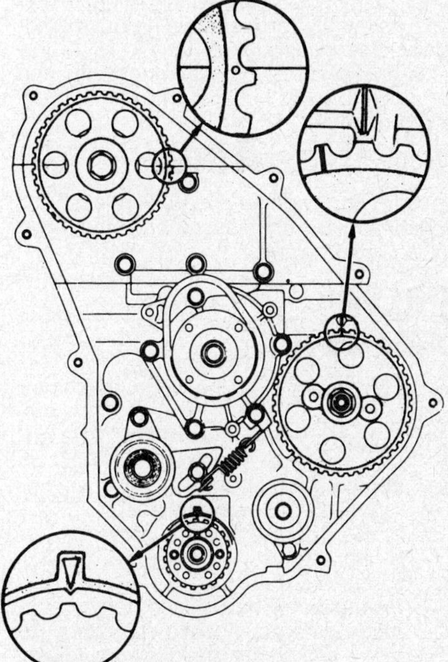

Fig. 22 Ensuring timing marks are aligned. 2L & 2L-T diesel engines

ROCKER ARMS & SHAFTS

L ENGINE

When removing rocker arms and shaft,

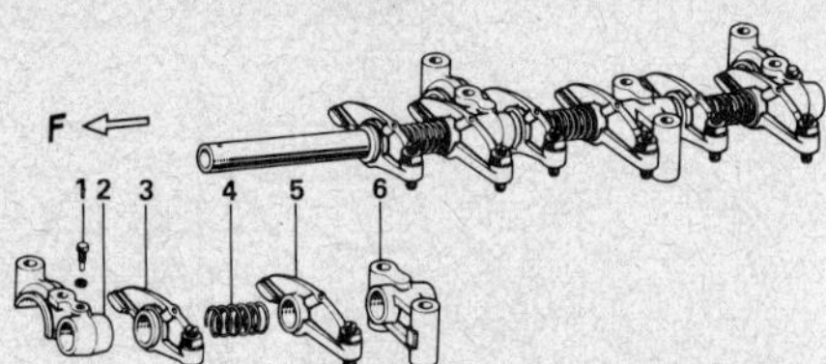

Fig. 23 Rocker arm shaft disassembly. L diesel engine

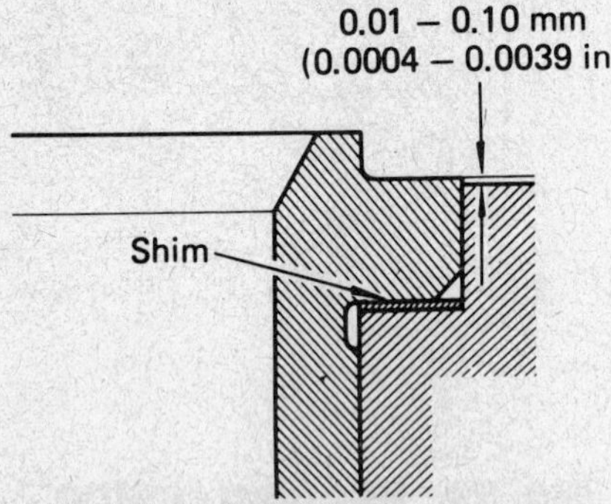

Fig. 25 Adjusting cylinder liner protrusion. L diesel engine

remove retaining bolts gradually and in sequence beginning with outer bolts and proceeding to inner bolts. Refer to **Fig. 23** for disassembly and assembly of rocker shaft assemblies. When installing rocker arm assembly, torque retaining bolts gradually and in sequence to 11-15 ft. lbs. (1.5-2.2 kg-m). Begin with inner bolts and proceed to outer bolts during bolt tightening procedure.

2L & 2L-T ENGINES

Refer to "Cylinder Head, Replace" for rocker arm and shaft assembly removal on 2L & 2L-T engines.

VALVES

ADJUST

Do not operate engine with valve cover removed.

1. Remove valve cover, then rotate engine until No. 1 piston is at TDC on compression stroke.
2. Adjust the following valves:
   a. No. 1 Intake & Exhaust.
   b. No. 2 Intake.
   c. No. 3 Exhaust.
3. Rotate crankshaft one complete revolution in normal direction of engine rotation and adjust the following valves:
   a. No. 2 Exhaust.
   b. No. 3 Intake.
   c. No. 4 Intake & Exhaust.

VALVE GUIDES

REPLACE

1. Remove valve guide from cylinder head using tool 09201-60011 or equivalent and hammer.
2. Check to ensure that valve guide bore is clean and lightly lubricated.
3. Install new valve guide until top of guide protrudes .642-.657 inch from top of cylinder head.
4. Ream valve guide to obtain specified stem to guide clearance.

CAMSHAFT

REPLACE

1. Remove valve cover.
2. Remove accessory drive belts, fan and fan pulley.
3. Remove crankshaft pulley.
4. Remove timing gear cover and belt guide.
5. Remove idler pulley and timing belt. Place reference marks on timing belt and each pulley for reference during installation.
6. Remove camshaft timing pulley and rocker shaft assembly.
7. Remove camshaft bearing caps, then the camshaft.
8. Reverse procedure to install. Check to ensure that timing belt and pulley reference marks made during disassembly align. Adjust valves as described under "Valves, Adjust."

TIMING BELT COVER

REPLACE

To replace the timing belt cover, perform steps 1 thru 4 as described under "Camshaft, Replace."

PISTON & ROD ASSEMBLIES

Assemble piston to rod with notch on piston and mark on connecting rod facing front of engine, **Fig. 24**.

MAIN & CONNECTING ROD BEARINGS

These bearings are available in standard sizes and undersizes of .010 inch (.25 mm) on all engines, .020 inch (.50 mm) on all engines, .030 inch (.75 mm) on L engines and .040 inch (1.00 mm) on L engines.

CYLINDER LINER

REPLACE

L ENGINE

The cylinder head, crankshaft and piston assemblies must be removed prior to replacing cylinder liners.

1. Remove cylinder liner using tool 09218-54011 or equivalent. Use 4400-6600 lbs. (2000-3000) of force to press liner out of block.
2. Lubricate outer surface of replacement liner with engine oil.
3. Install liner using tool 09218-54011 and 4400-6600 lbs. (2000-3000 kg) of force.
4. Measure cylinder liner protrusion with suitable dial indicator.
5. Liner protrusion should be .0016 inch (.04 mm). If protrusion is not as specified, adjust liner protrusion with shims, **Fig. 25.** Shims are available in thicknesses of .002 in. (.05 mm) and .0039 in. (.10 mm).

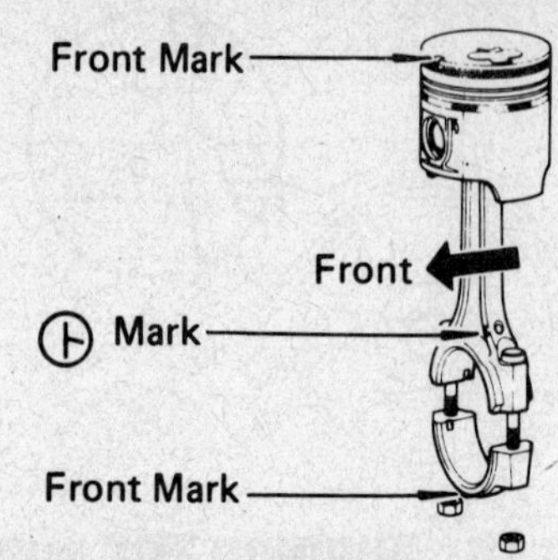

Fig. 24 Piston & rod assembly. L, 2L & 2L-T diesel engines

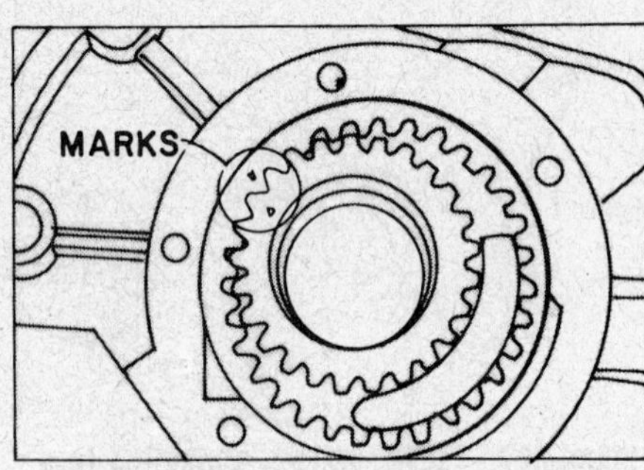

Fig. 26 Positioning oil pump drive & driven gears

OIL PAN & OIL PUMP

REPLACE

1. Remove timing belt cover as described in steps 1 thru 4 under "Camshaft, Replace".
2. Remove water pump and timing belt case.
3. Remove oil pump plate, oil pump driven gear and drive gear from timing belt case.
4. Reverse procedure to install. Refer to **Fig. 26** for proper gear alignment.

OIL PUMP SERVICE

1. Measure clearance between oil pump driven gear and body. Clearance should be .0024-.0059 inch (.06-.15 mm).
2. Measure gear tip clearances. Driven gear crescent clearance should be .0059-.0083 inch (.15-.21 mm) and drive gear crescent clearance should be .0087-.0098 inch (.22-.25 mm).
3. Measure side clearance by placing straightedge across gears and inserting feeler gauge between gears and straightedge. Side clearance should be .0012-.0035 inch.
4. If any clearances are not within specification, replace drive, gear, driven gear or oil pump body as necessary.

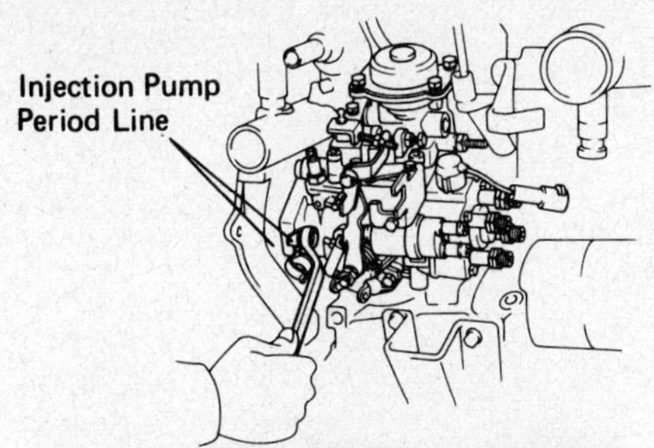

Fig. 27 Checking position of injection pump period line. 2L & 2L-T diesel engines

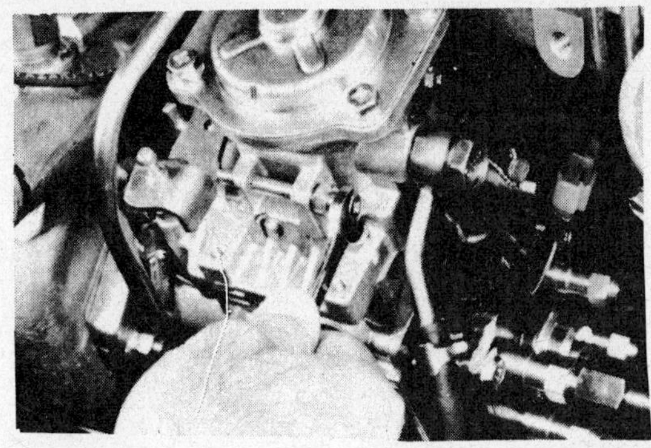

Fig. 28 Adjusting engine idle speed. L diesel engine

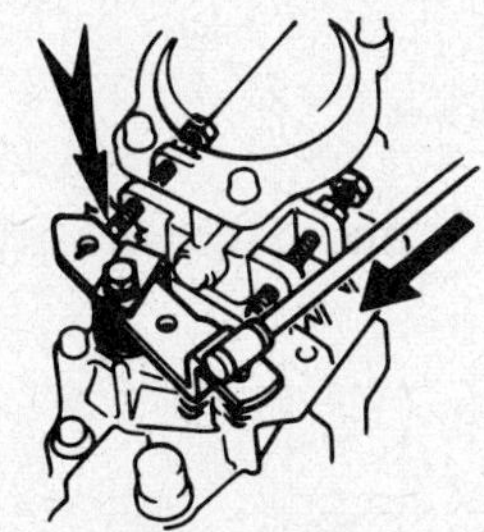

Fig. 29 Idle speed adjusting screw location. 2L & 2L-T diesel engines

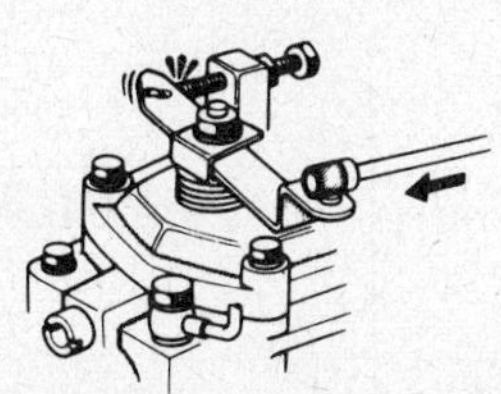

Fig. 30 Adjusting maximum speed adjusting screw. L diesel engine

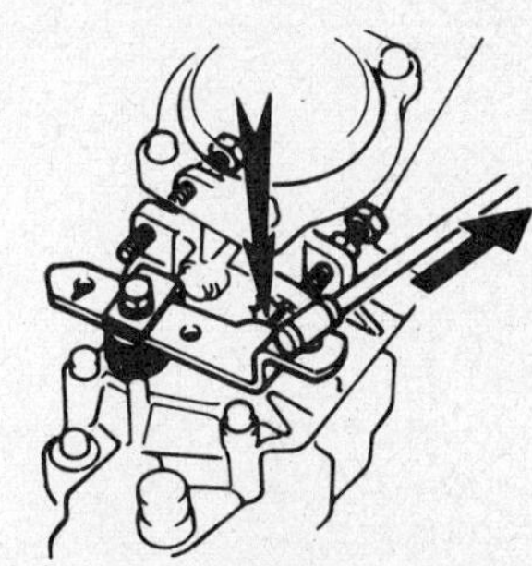

Fig. 31 Maximum speed adjusting screw location. 2L & 2L-T diesel engines

WATER PUMP

REPLACE

1. Disconnect battery ground cable.
2. Drain cooling system, then remove radiator and drive belts.
3. Remove fan fluid coupling, water pump pulley and fan assembly.
4. Remove timing belt cover. Refer to "Timing Belt Cover, Replace" for procedure.
5. Remove timing belt tension spring.
6. Remove water pump attaching bolts, then the water pump.
7. Reverse procedure to install. Torque water pump attaching bolts to 14 ft. lbs.

INJECTION PUMP

REPLACE

L ENGINE

1. Disconnect injection pipes and fuel pipe from injection pump.
2. Remove fan and fan pulley.
3. Remove crankshaft pulley, then the timing belt cover. Refer to "Timing Belt Cover, Replace" for procedure.
4. Remove idler pulley and timing belt. If timing belt is to be reused, mark relationship of timing belt to all pulleys for reference during installation.
5. Remove injection pump drive pulley.
6. Remove injection pump retaining bolts, then the injection pump.
7. Reverse procedure to install and note the following:
   a. Check to ensure that overflow screw marked "Out" is installed into injection pump.
   b. If old timing belt is to be installed, check to ensure that reference marks made during removal align.
   c. Check to ensure that injector pump housing timing mark aligns with timing gear case mark.
   d. If necessary, adjust injection pump timing as described under "Injection Pump Timing."

2L & 2L-T ENGINES

1. Disconnect battery ground cable.
2. Disconnect electrical connector from injection pump.
3. Disconnect and plug fuel hoses from fuel lines.
4. Remove accelerator connecting rod.
5. Remove fuel inlet and outlet lines.
6. Remove timing belt. Refer to "Timing Belt, Replace" for procedure.
7. Remove injection pump drive pulley.
8. Remove injection pump and note the following:
   a. Ensure position of the injection period line before removing injection pump, **Fig. 27.**
   b. Remove injection pump retaining bracket.
9. Reverse procedure to install. During installation of injection pump, align injection pump period lines on the injection pump and oil pump body, **Fig. 27.** Torque injection pump attaching bolts to 15 ft. lbs.

INJECTION PUMP TIMING

1. Remove injection pump head bolt.
2. Install tool 09275-54010 or equivalent and suitable dial indicator into injection pump head plug.
3. Manually rotate crankshaft clockwise until either No. 1 or No. 4 piston is 45° BTDC on compression stroke.
4. Zero dial indicator, then rotate crankshaft until No. 1 or No. 4 piston is at TDC on compression stroke.
5. Plunger lift should be .039 inch (1 mm) on 1983 L models, .0382-.0406 inch (.97-1.03 mm) on 1984 Calif. 2L models, .0433-.0465 inch (1.10-1.18 mm) on 1984 exc. Calif. 2L models, .035 inch (.89 mm) on 1985 Calif. 2L models, .045 inch (1.14 mm) on 1985 exc. Calif. 2L models and .039 inch (1 mm) on 1985 2L-T models.
6. If stroke is not correct, loosen injection pump retaining bolts and all union nuts connecting lines to injection pump.
7. Adjust piston plunger stroke by tilting injection pump body as necessary until specified stroke is obtained. If stroke is less than specified, tilt injection pump toward engine. If stroke is greater than specified, tilt injection pump away from engine.
8. Tighten all retaining bolts and union nuts, then recheck pump stroke to ensure it has not changed.
9. Bleed air from injection pipes by loosening fuel pipes and operating starter.

IDLE SPEED

ADJUST

L ENGINE

1. Run engine until operating temperature is reached, then rotate dash mounted idle adjuster knob counterclockwise to ensure it is in unlocked position.

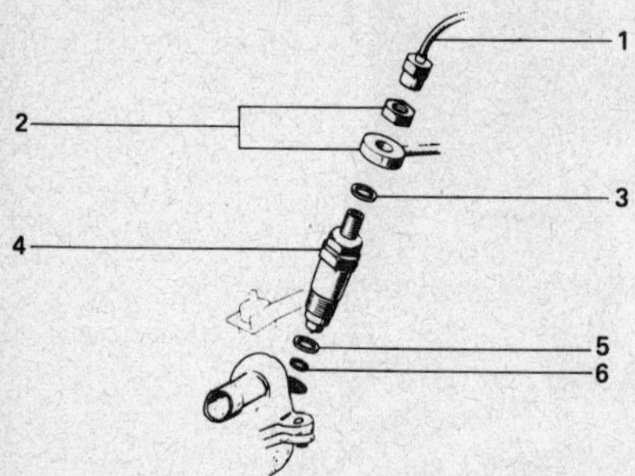

1. Injection Pipe
2. Leakage Pipe
3. Washer
4. Injection Nozzle Holder
5. Injection Nozzle Seat
6. Injection Nozzle Seat Gasket

Fig. 32 Injection nozzle replacement

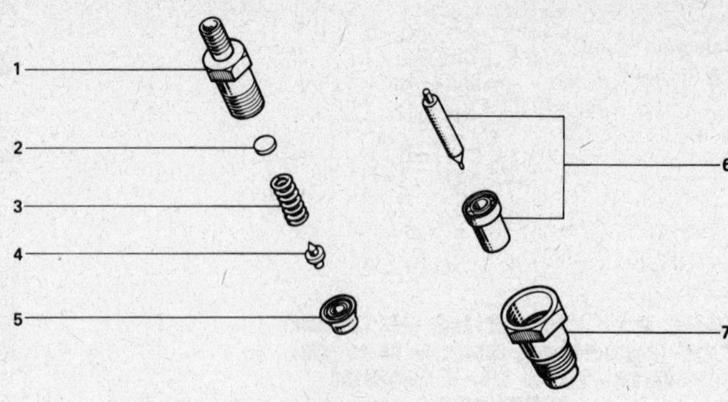

1. Nozzle Holder Retaining Nut
2. Adjusting Shim
3. Pressure Spring
4. Pressure Pin
5. Distance Piece
6. Nozzle Assembly
7. Nozzle Holder Body

Fig. 33 Injection nozzle, disassembled

Adjusting shim thickness	mm (in.)
1.00 (0.0394)	1.50 (0.0591)
1.05 (0.0413)	1.55 (0.0610)
1.10 (0.0433)	1.60 (0.0630)
1.15 (0.0453)	1.65 (0.0650)
1.20 (0.0472)	1.70 (0.0669)
1.25 (0.0492)	1.75 (0.0689)
1.30 (0.0512)	1.80 (0.0709)
1.35 (0.0531)	1.85 (0.0728)
1.40 (0.0551)	1.90 (0.0748)
1.45 (0.0571)	1.95 (0.0768)

Fig. 34 Adjusting shim thickness chart. 2L & 2L-T diesel engines

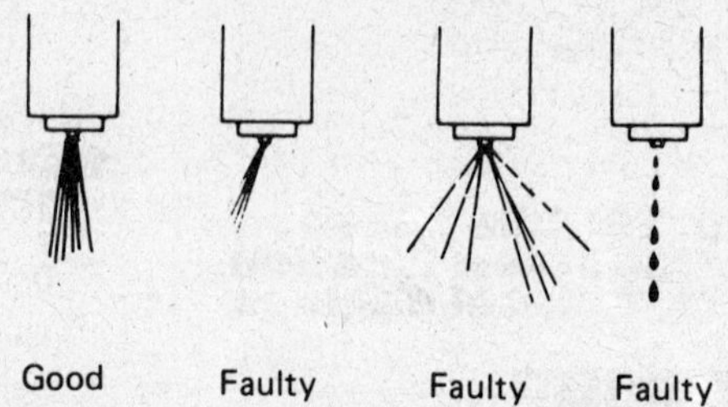

Fig. 35 Checking nozzle spray pattern

2. Disconnect accelerator rod and check for specified engine idle speed.
3. If specified idle speed cannot be obtained, adjust by rotating idle adjusting screw on injection pump, **Fig. 28.**

2L & 2L-T ENGINES

1. Operate engine until normal operating temperature is obtained.
2. Ensure adjusting lever touches idle speed adjusting screw when the accelerator pedal is released.
3. If not, disconnect accelerator linkage and loosen locknut on idle speed adjusting screw. Adjust idle speed by turning adjusting screw until correct idle speed is obtained, **Fig. 29.**

MAXIMUM SPEED ADJUST

L ENGINE

1. Run engine until operating temperature is reached, then rotate dash mounted idle adjuster counterclockwise to check that it is in unlocked position.
2. Disconnect accelerator rod and check for specified engine maximum speed. With maximum speed lever fully depressed, reading of 4900 RPM should be obtained.
3. If reading is not as specified, loosen locknut on maximum speed adjusting screw and adjust maximum speed until reading of 4900 RPM is obtained, **Fig. 30.**
4. Connect accelerator rod and adjust until there is no slack in accelerator cable.
5. Check to ensure that adjusting lever contacts maximum speed adjusting screw when accelerator is fully depressed.

2L & 2L-T ENGINES

1. Operate engine until normal operating temperature is obtained.
2. Ensure adjusting lever touches the maximum speed adjusting screw when the accelerator pedal is depressed.
3. If not, disconnect accelerator linkage, then using tool No. 09275-54020 or equivalent, loosen locknut on maximum speed adjusting screw.
4. Turn adjusting screw until 5100 RPM is obtained on 1983-84 models, or 4900 RPM is obtained on 1985 models, **Fig. 31.**

INJECTION NOZZLE SERVICE

REMOVAL & INSTALLATION

1. Remove injection fuel line from injection nozzle.
2. Remove leakage pipe from injection nozzle, **Fig. 32.**
3. Remove washer, nozzle holder and nozzle seat.
4. Remove injection nozzle seat gasket.
5. Reverse procedure to install. Check to ensure that nozzle seat gasket is installed properly.

DISASSEMBLY & ASSEMBLY

1. Remove nozzle holder retaining nut, adjusting shim and pressure spring, **Fig. 33.**
2. Remove pressure spring pin, and distance piece.
3. Remove nozzle assembly from nozzle holder body.
4. Reverse procedure to assemble. Torque retaining nut to 44-57 ft. lbs. (6-8 kg-m).

NOZZLE TESTING

L Engine

1. Install nozzle into suitable tester and bleed air from union nut.
2. Pump tester handle slowly and observe tester pressure gauge reading.
3. Nozzle opening pressure should be 1493-1778 psi (105-125 kg-cm^2).
4. If pressure reading is not as specified disassemble nozzle as described above and replace shim on top of pressure spring until opening pressure of 1636-1778 psi (115-125 kg-cm^2) is obtained. Shims are available in thicknesses ranging between .04 inch (1 mm) and .078 inch (1.95 mm) in. increments of .002 inch (.05 mm). Changing shim thickness by .002 inch (.05 mm) will change injection pressure approximately 71 psi (5 kg-cm^2).

5. Apply pressure approximately 142-284 psi (10-20 kg-cm²) less than opening pressure to nozzle. Maintain this pressure for 10 seconds, then check to ensure that nozzle does not leak. If nozzle leaks during the 10 second period, repair or replace nozzle as necessary.

2L & 2L-T Engines

1. Install nozzle into a suitable nozzle tester and bleed air from union nut. **Do not place fingers over nozzle injection orifice.**
2. Gradually pump tester handle several times to discharge any carbon build-up from injection orifice.
3. Pump tester handle slowly and note pressure gauge reading. Read pressure gauge when injection pressure begins to drop. Nozzle opening pressure for a used nozzle should be 1707-2389 psi on 1984 models or 2276-2389 psi on 1985 models.
4. If nozzle opening pressure is not within specifications, disassemble nozzle as described previously and change adjusting shim on top of nozzle pressure spring. Shims are available in different sizes as shown in **Fig. 34. Varying adjusting shim thickness by .0020 inch (.05 mm) will change injection pressure by approximately 91 psi.**
5. While maintaining pressure at approximately 142-284 psi, ensure that there is no fuel drip for 10 seconds from injection orifice or retaining nut.

SPRAY PATTERN TEST

1. The fuel injection nozzle should shudder at a pumping speed between 15-60 times per minute for a used nozzle or 30-60 times per minute for a new nozzle.
2. Check spray pattern during shuddering, **Fig. 35.** If spray pattern is not correct, replace spray nozzle(s).

1C, 1C-TL & 2C-T DIESEL ENGINE SECTION

INDEX

TROUBLESHOOTING

Refer to "L, 2L & 2L-T Diesel Engine Section" for troubleshooting procedure.

DIESEL ENGINE ELECTRICAL SYSTEM DIAGNOSIS

ENGINE DOES NOT START

1. Check if indicator lamp lights with ignition switch ON and coolant temperature at 68°F (20°C). If indicator lamp does not light, check engine fuse. If engine fuse is blown, check for a short circuit and repair as necessary. If engine fuse is not blown, check indicator light bulb and replace as necessary. If indicator light bulb is not blown, check for battery voltage to terminal 3 or A3 of preheating system timer electrical connector, **Figs. 1, 2 and 3.** If battery voltage is present, replace preheat timer as necessary.
2. If indicator lamp lights with ignition switch ON, check for battery voltage to terminal 1 or A1 of preheating timer with ignition switch ON. If no voltage is obtained, ensure that there is 1 volt at terminals 12 and 6 or A6 and A12. If not, replace glow plug current sensor. If voltage is present, check if voltage to terminal 1 or A1 of preheating timer is switched OFF after engine is started. If no voltage is obtained, start engine and check if there is voltage at terminal 9 or A9 or preheating timer. If not, repair charging system as required. If voltage is present at terminal 9 or A9, replace preheat timer.
3. If voltage is present at terminal 1, turn ignition switch ON and check current flow to terminal 5 or A5. Voltage to terminal will vary depending on coolant (water) temperature. Refer to graph in **Fig. 4,** for time duration and water temperature values. If there is no voltage, replace preheat timer as necessary. If preheat duration obtained exceeds values indicated in graph, proceed as follows:
   a. Disconnect water temperature sensor, **Fig. 5** and check if preheating duration approximately 120 seconds, or if electrical connector is ground there is no continuity.
   b. If preheating duration is within time stated in step 3a, water temperature sensor is defective and should be replaced. If not, replace preheating timer.
4. After completion of preheating duration, recheck voltage at terminal 5 or A5 with ignition switch in Start position. If no voltage, replace preheating timer. If voltage is obtained, proceed as follows:
   a. Position ignition switch ON and check for voltage to glow plugs approximately 3 seconds after ignition switch is turned ON. Voltage should drop approximately one half. If voltage drops, check glow plug for continuity. If there is no continuity, replace glow plug.
   b. If no voltage is present, check for battery voltage at positive side of glow plug current sensor. If voltage is present, replace current sensor. If no voltage is present, replace No. 1 glow plug relay.
   c. If voltage does not decrease by one half, check for battery voltage at positive side of resistor. If voltage is present, replace resistor. If voltage is not present, replace No. 2 glow plug relay.

FUEL CUT SOLENOID

1. With ignition switch turned ON, check for fuel cut solenoid operation

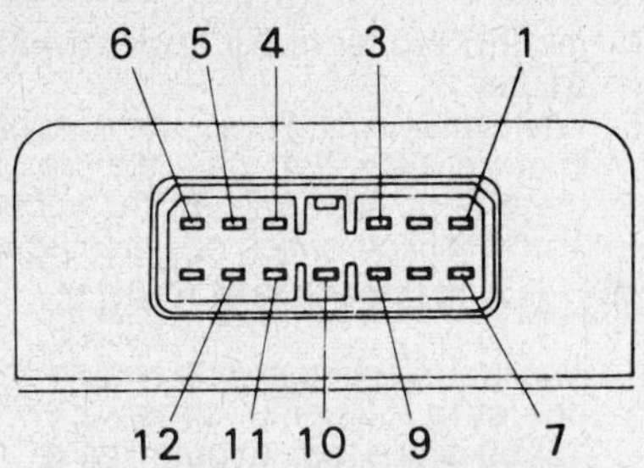

Fig. 1 Preheat timer electrical connector. 1983–84 Camry models

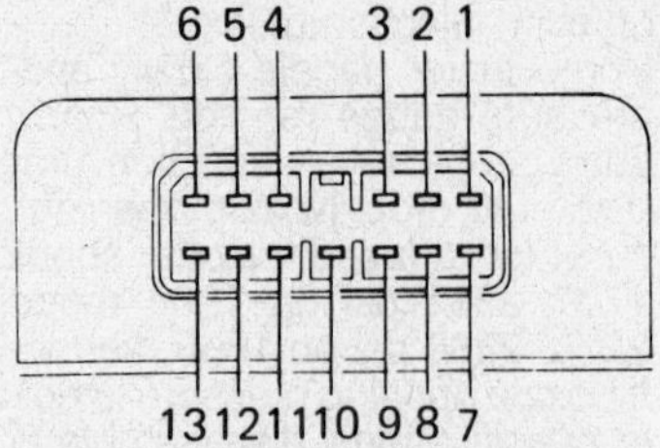

Fig. 2 Preheat timer electrical connector. Corolla models

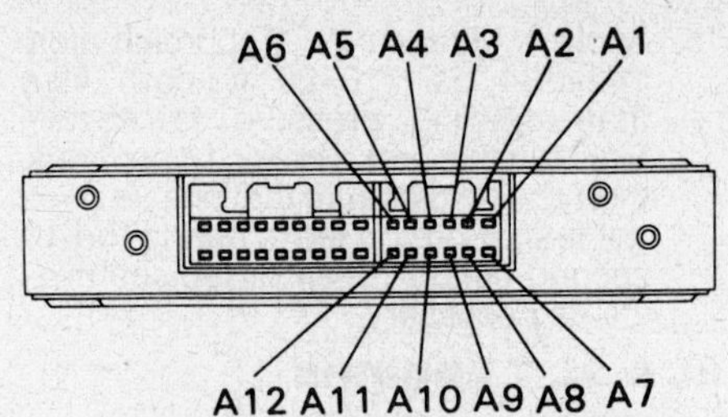

Fig. 3 Preheat timer electrical connector. 1985–86 Camry models

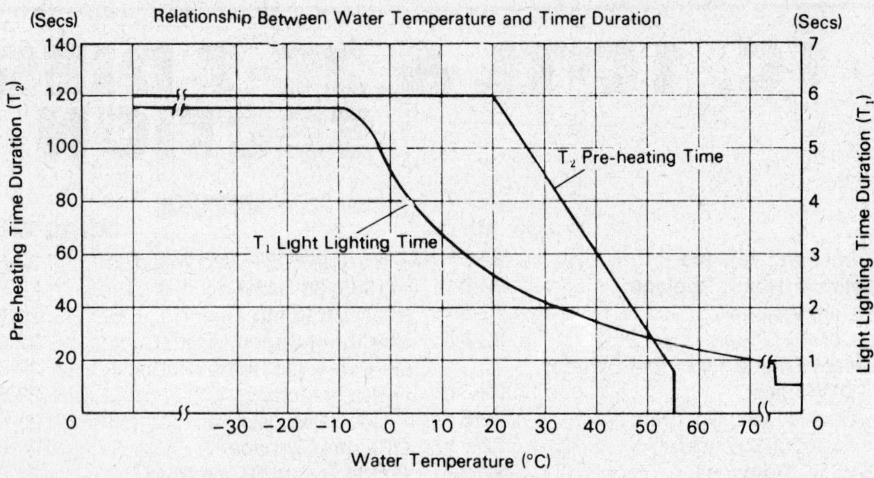

Fig. 4 Relationship between coolant temperature & preheat timer duration

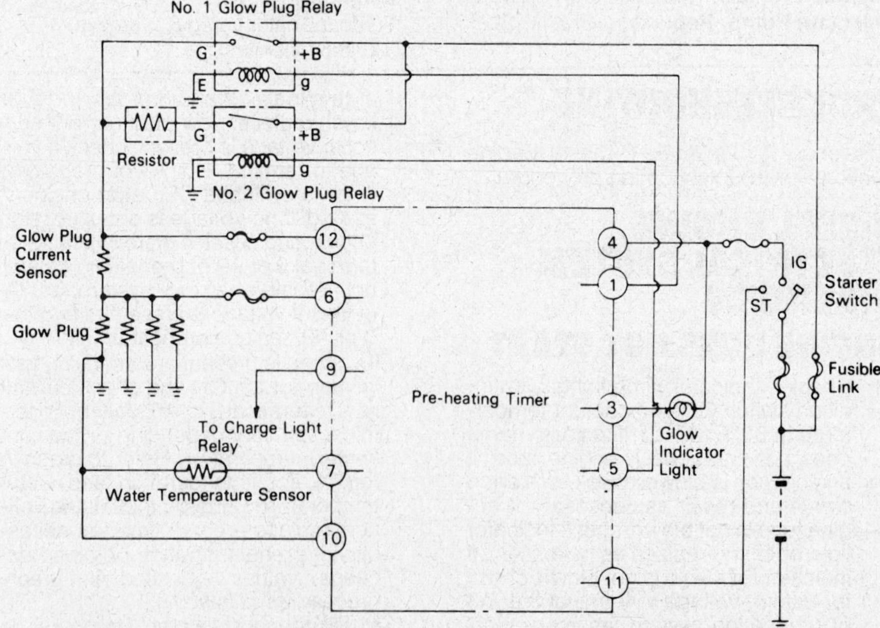

Fig. 5 Preheat circuit electrical schematic

(indicated by a clicking sound) while connecting and disconnecting the fuel cut solenoid.

2. If fuel cut solenoid is not operating, check engine fuse. If fuse is blown, check for a short circuit and repair as required. If fuse is not blown, apply battery voltage to solenoid and check for operation. If fuel cut solenoid operates, check and/or repair wire harness from fuse to fuel cut solenoid. If fuel cut solenoid does not operate, replace fuel cut solenoid.

ENGINE
REPLACE
CAMRY MODELS

1. Remove hood, battery and drain cooling system.
2. Remove relay block bracket attaching screws, then the relay block bracket and relay block assembly.
3. Remove cruise control actuator, if equipped.
4. Disconnect accelerator cable from injection pump, if equipped.
5. Remove air cleaner assembly from engine.
6. Disconnect radiator hoses, then remove radiator from vehicle.
7. Mark then disconnect all electrical connectors and vacuum hoses from engine.
8. Disconnect engine wire harness from cylinder head, heater pipe and transaxle retaining clamps.
9. Disconnect speedometer cable from transaxle.
10. Remove clutch release cylinder and bracket assembly and position aside. Do not disconnect clutch release cylinder fluid lines.
12. Remove windshield washer and radiator reservoir tanks.
13. Remove power steering pump and position aside. Do not disconnect power steering pump fluid lines.
14. Remove A/C idler pulley and bracket assembly, if equipped.
15. Remove A/C compressor and position aside. Do not disconnect refrigerant lines from compressor.
16. Raise and support vehicle.
17. Disconnect both front driveshafts as follows:
    a. Wrap both driveshaft boots with clean shop towels.
    b. Remove six attaching nuts from each driveshaft while depressing the brake pedal and disconnect drive shafts.
18. Disconnect exhaust pipe from turbocharger turbine elbow.
19. Remove rear engine mount bolts.
20. Lower vehicle, then remove front engine mount bolts.
21. Install suitable engine lifting equipment onto engine.
22. Remove engine and transaxle assembly from vehicle.

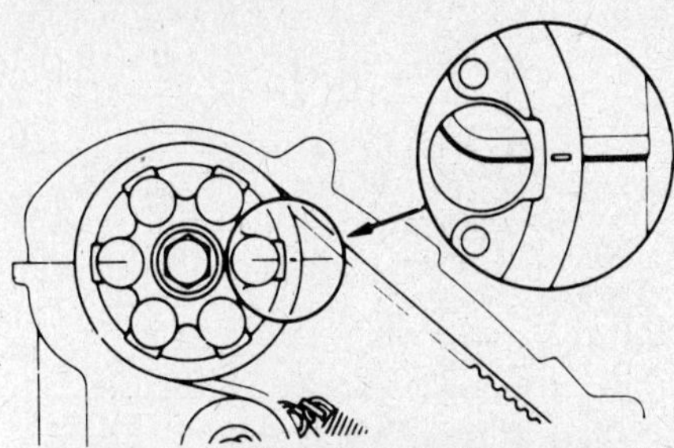
Fig. 6 Aligning line mark on camshaft timing sprocket with top end of cylinder head. Camry models

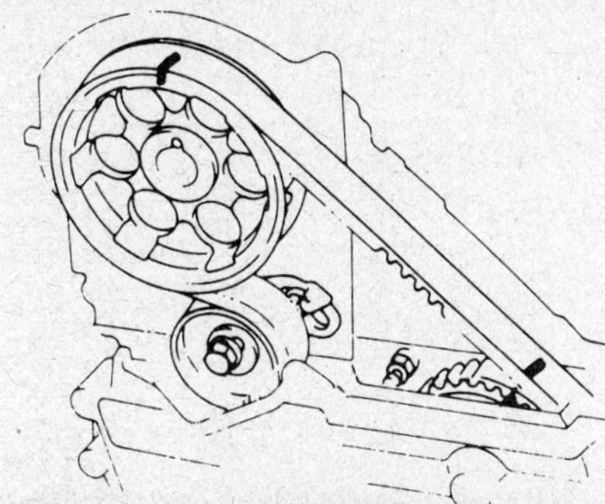
Fig. 7 Placing alignment marks on camshaft timing sprocket, injection pump pulley & timing belt. Camry models

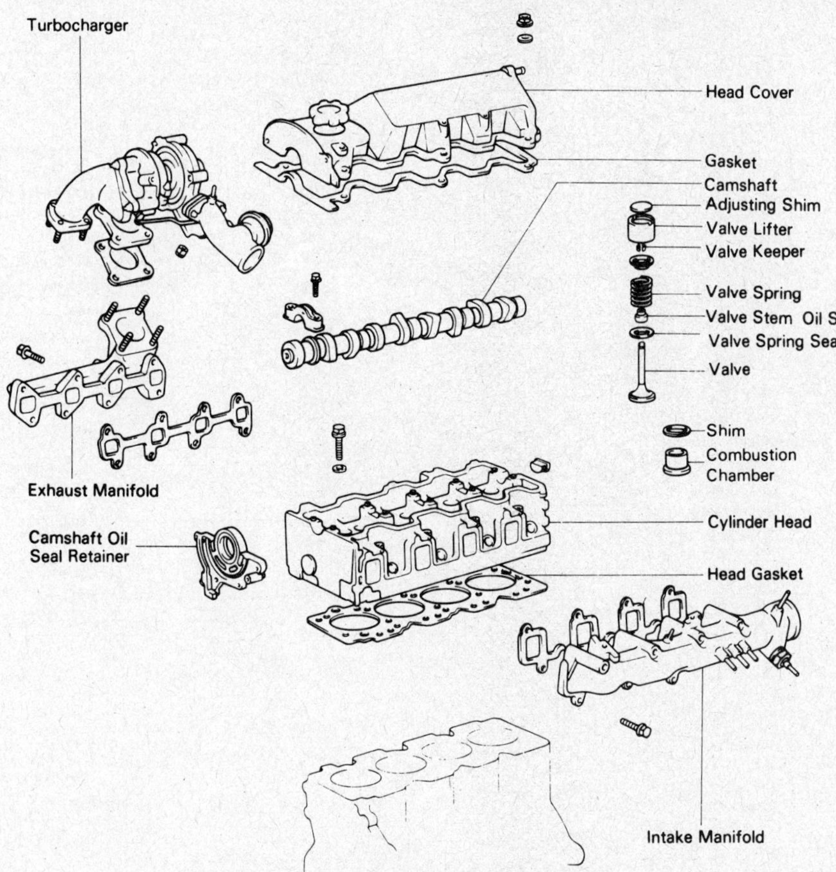

Cylinder head & components. Camry models

23. Reverse procedure to install.

COROLLA MODELS

1. Remove hood, engine under cover and battery from vehicle.
2. Disconnect accelerator and/or throttle cables from injection pump.
3. Disconnect radiator hoses, then remove radiator from vehicle.
4. Remove air cleaner assembly from engine.
5. Mark then disconnect all electrical connectors and vacuum hoses from engine.
6. Disconnect heater hose from heater pipe.
7. Disconnect and plug fuel hose from fuel line.
8. Remove power steering pump, if equipped and position aside. Do not disconnect power steering pump fluid lines.
9. Remove A/C compressor, if equipped and position aside.
10. Disconnect speedometer cable from transaxle.
11. Remove clutch release cylinder, if equipped and position aside. Do not disconnect clutch release cylinder fluid lines.
12. Disconnect transaxle control cable.
13. Raise and support vehicle.
14. Disconnect front exhaust pipe from exhaust manifold.
15. Disconnect front and rear engine mounts from crossmember.
16. Remove center engine crossmember.
17. Disconnect both driveshafts as follows:
    a. Wrap both driveshaft boots with clean shop towels.
    b. Remove attaching nuts from each driveshaft while depressing brake pedal and disconnect driveshafts.
18. Lower vehicle.
19. Install suitable engine lifting equipment onto engine.
20. Remove engine and transaxle assembly from vehicle.
21. Reverse procedure to install.

CYLINDER HEAD REPLACE

CAMRY MODELS

1. Disconnect battery ground cable.
2. Drain cooling system and oil from engine.
3. Remove cruise control actuator assembly.
4. Disconnect accelerator cable or cruise control cable from injection pump.
5. Remove air cleaner assembly from engine.
6. Mark then disconnect all electrical connectors and vacuum hoses from cylinder head.
7. Remove current sensor.
8. Raise and support vehicle.
9. Disconnect exhaust pipe from turbocharger turbine elbow.
10. Remove exhaust manifold mounting bracket bolt from exhaust manifold.
11. Lower vehicle.
12. Remove turbocharger. Refer to removal procedure under "Turbocharger Service."
13. Remove water outlet assembly.
14. Remove heater pipe.
15. Remove No. 1 water bypass hose and glow plugs.
16. Remove injection nozzle holders and level gauge guide support mounting bracket.
17. Remove No. 2 timing belt cover attaching bolts, then the cover.
18. Position No. 1 cylinder at TDC of compression stroke by aligning the line mark on camshaft timing sprocket with top end of cylinder head, **Fig. 6.**
19. Remove camshaft timing sprocket as follows:
    a. Place alignment marks on camshaft timing sprocket, injection pump pulley and timing belt, **Fig. 7.**
    b. Using a suitable screwdriver, remove tension spring.
    c. Loosen No. 1 idler pulley mount bolt.
    d. Using tool No. 09278-54011 or equivalent, to hold timing sprocket, remove camshaft timing sprocket retaining bolt and washer.

e. Remove camshaft timing sprocket and timing belt.
f. Support timing belt so that belt meshing of injection pump timing pulley and timing belt does not shift. **Do not allow oil, water or dust to come in contact with timing belt.**

20. Remove No. 3 timing belt cover attaching bolts, then the cover.
21. Remove cylinder head cover attaching bolts, then the cover.
22. Remove No. 1 engine bracket.
23. Loosen and remove cylinder head bolts in three steps and in sequence shown in **Fig. 8.**
24. Reverse procedure to install. Torque cylinder head bolts in three steps in sequence shown, **Fig. 9,** to 62 ft. lbs.

COROLLA MODELS

1. Disconnect battery ground cable.
2. Drain coolant and oil from engine.
3. Remove engine under cover.
4. Disconnect exhaust pipe from exhaust manifold.
5. Disconnect air inlet hose.
6. Disconnect accelerator and throttle cables from injection pump.
7. Remove water inlet assembly.
8. Disconnect heater hoses from heater.
9. Remove EGR valve.
10. Mark then disconnect all electrical connectors and vacuum hoses from cylinder head.
11. Disconnect water bypass hose from cylinder head union.
12. Disconnect and plug fuel hose from fuel line.
13. Remove fuel injection line.
14. Remove fuel return line and current sensor.
15. Remove glow plugs and injection nozzles.
16. Remove No. 2 timing belt cover attaching bolts, then the cover.
17. Remove timing belt from camshaft timing sprocket as follows:
    a. Turn crankshaft clockwise and position No. 1 cylinder at TDC of compression stroke.
    b. Place alignment marks on the camshaft timing sprocket, injection pump and timing belt, **Fig. 7.**
    c. Using a screwdriver, remove tension spring.
    d. Loosen No. 1 idler pulley mount bolt.
    e. Remove timing belt from camshaft timing sprocket.
18. Using tool No. 09278-54011 or equivalent, to hold sprocket, remove sprocket retaining bolt then the sprocket.
19. Support timing belt so that the meshing of the injection pump timing pulley and timing belt does not shift. **Do not allow water, oil or dust to come in contact with the timing belt.**
20. Remove cylinder head cover attaching bolts, then the cylinder head cover.
21. Remove oil level gauge guide clamp.
22. Loosen and remove cylinder head bolts in three steps and in sequence shown in **Fig. 8.**
23. Reverse procedure to install. Torque cylinder head bolts in three steps in sequence shown in **Fig. 9** to 62 ft. lbs.

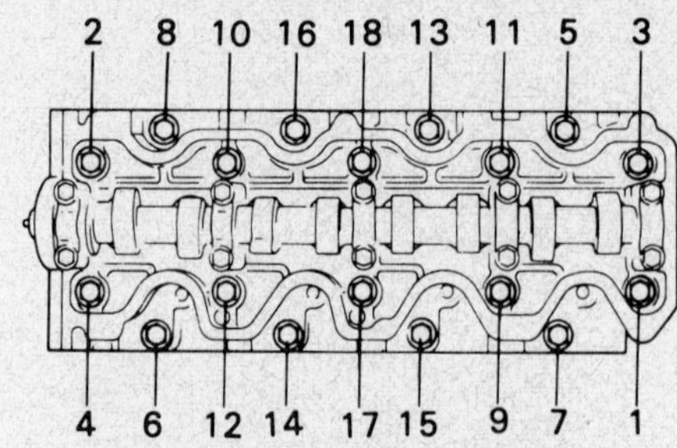

Fig. 8 Cylinder head bolt removal sequence

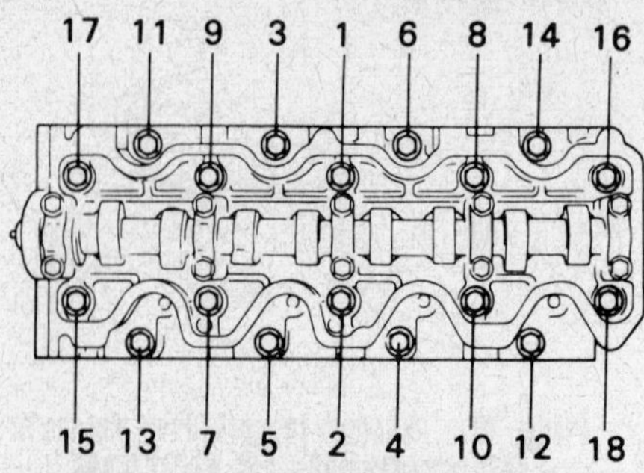

Fig. 9 Cylinder head bolt tightening sequence

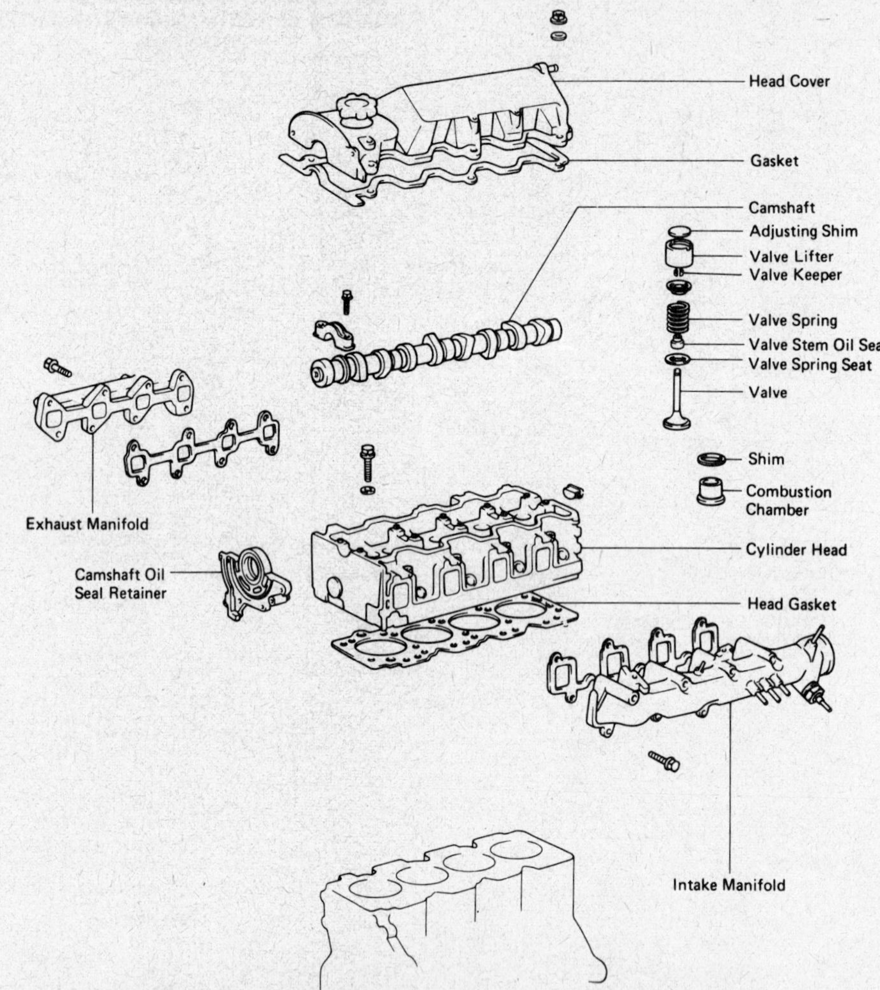

Cylinder head & components. Corolla models

TIMING BELT REPLACE

1. Disconnect battery ground cable.
2. On Camry models, proceed as follows:
    a. Remove right side front wheel.
    b. Remove fender apron seal.
    c. Remove washer and radiator reservoir tanks.
    d. Remove cruise control actuator.
    e. Remove power steering pump and position aside.
    f. Remove A/C idler pulley and bracket assembly.
    g. Remove alternator and alternator bracket.
3. On Corolla models, proceed as follows:
    a. Remove engine under cover attaching bolts, then the engine under cover.
    b. Remove power steering pump drive belts and pulley.
    c. Remove power steering pump and position aside. Do not disconnect

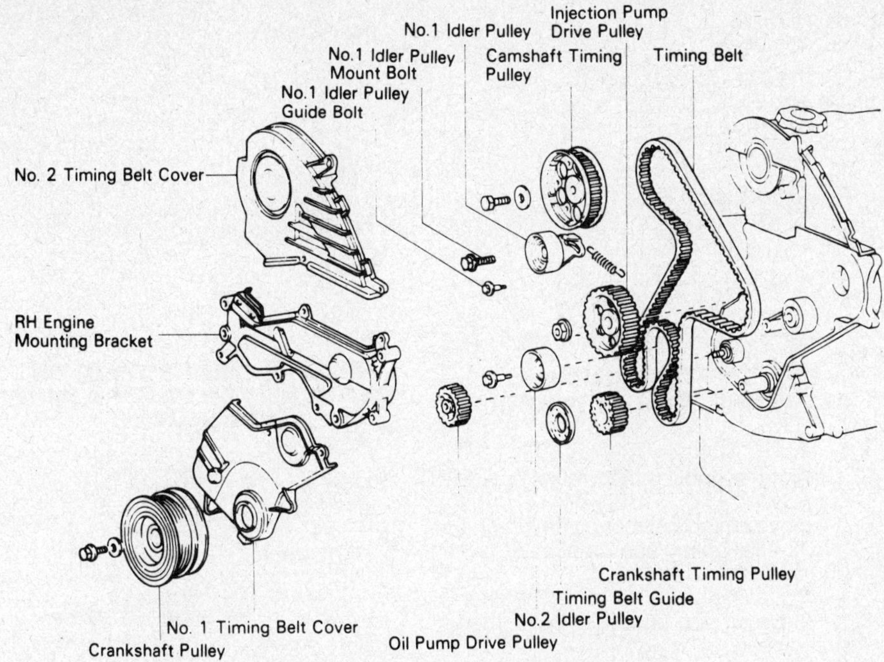

Fig. 10 Timing belt assembly

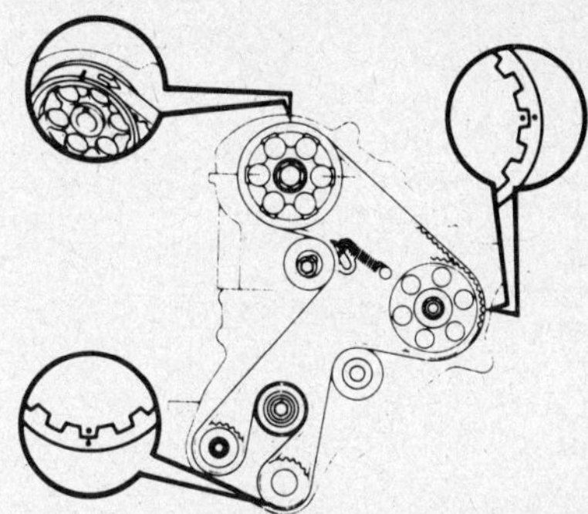

Fig. 11 Placing alignment marks on sprockets & timing belt

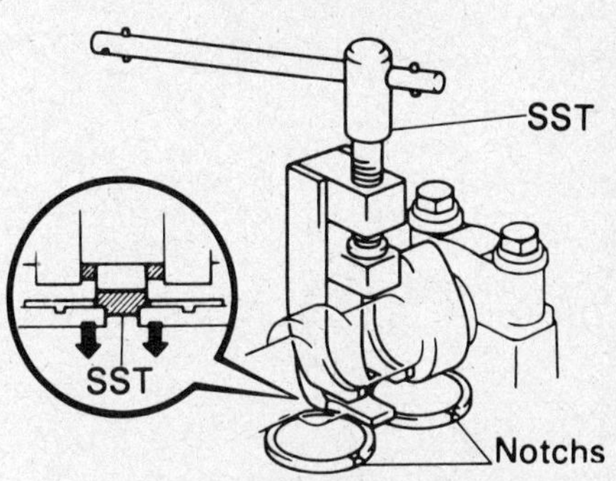

Fig. 12 Installing valve compressor tool

power steering pump fluid lines.
4. Remove No. 2 timing belt cover attaching bolts, then the cover, **Fig. 10.**
5. Position No. 1 cylinder at TDC of compression stroke.
6. Remove crankshaft pulley.
7. Remove No. 1 timing belt cover and belt guide.
8. Raise engine slightly.
9. On Camry models, remove right side engine mount insulator and bracket.
10. On Corolla models, remove engine mount center crossmember, right side engine mount and bracket.
11. Remove timing belt as follows. **If original timing belt is to be used, draw a direction arrow on timing belt (in direction of engine rotation) and place alignment marks on the sprockets and timing belt, Fig. 11.**
    a. Using a suitable screwdriver, remove tension spring.
    b. Loosen No. 1 idler pulley mount bolt.
    c. Remove timing belt from engine.
12. Remove camshaft timing sprocket, injection pump drive pulley, No. 2 idler pulley and crankshaft timing sprocket from engine.
13. Reverse procedure to install. During installation of timing belt, note the following:
    a. If original timing belt is used, align marks placed during removal and install timing belt with arrow pointing in direction of engine rotation.
    b. If a new timing belt is to be used, install timing belt with numbers and letters that can be read from the rear of the engine.
    c. After installation of timing belt, turn crankshaft 2 revolutions from TDC to TDC.
    d. Ensure timing sprocket and timing belt marks align.

VALVES
ADJUST

1. Position No. 1 cylinder to TDC of compression stroke and check clearance of the following valves. **Ensure valve lifters on the No. 1 cylinder are loose and valve lifters on No. 4 cylinder are tight.**
    a. No. 1 intake and exhaust.
    b. No. 2 intake.
    c. No. 3 exhaust.
2. Turn crankshaft one complete revolution and adjust the following valves:
    a. No. 2 exhaust.
    b. No. 3 intake.
    c. No. 4 intake and exhaust.
3. If valve clearances are not to specifications, rotate crankshaft to position intake camshaft lobe of cylinder to be adjusted upward. **Both intake and exhaust valve clearances can be adjusted in this position.**
4. Install tool No. SST 09248-64010, **Fig. 12,** between the two cam lobes, then rotate handle to compress valve lifters.
5. Remove shims, then select a suitable shim to bring valve clearances to within specifications.
6. Remove tool, then recheck valve clearances.

VALVE GUIDE BUSHING
REPLACE

1. Remove valve guide bushing snap ring.
2. Heat cylinder head to approximately 194°F.
3. Using a suitable drift and hammer, remove valve guide bushing.
4. Heat cylinder head to approximately 194°F.
5. Using a suitable drift and hammer, drive new valve guide bushing into cylinder head until snap ring contacts cylinder head.

CAMSHAFT
REPLACE

1. Disconnect battery ground cable.
2. Mark then disconnect all electrical connectors and vacuum hoses that may interfere with removal of cylinder head cover.
3. Remove cylinder head cover attaching bolts, then the cover.
4. Remove No. 2 timing belt cover attaching bolts, the the cover.
5. Position No. 1 cylinder at TDC of compression stroke by aligning the line mark on camshaft timing sprocket with top edge of cylinder head, **Fig. 6.**
6. Remove camshaft timing sprocket and camshaft as follows:
    a. Place alignment marks on camshaft timing sprocket, injection pump pulley and timing belt, **Fig. 7.**
    b. Using a suitable screwdriver, remove tension spring.
    c. Loosen No. 1 idler pulley mount bolt.
    d. Using a suitable tool to secure camshaft timing sprocket in place, remove camshaft timing sprocket retaining bolt and washer.
    e. Remove camshaft timing sprocket and camshaft.
    f. Support timing belt so that belt meshing of injection pump timing pulley and timing belt does not

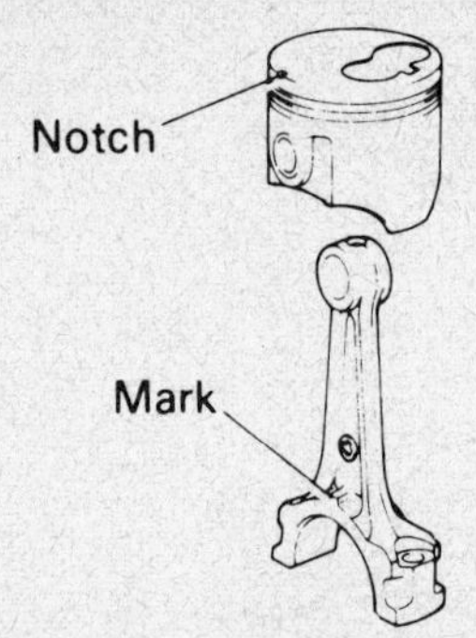

Fig. 13 Piston & rod assembly. Corolla models

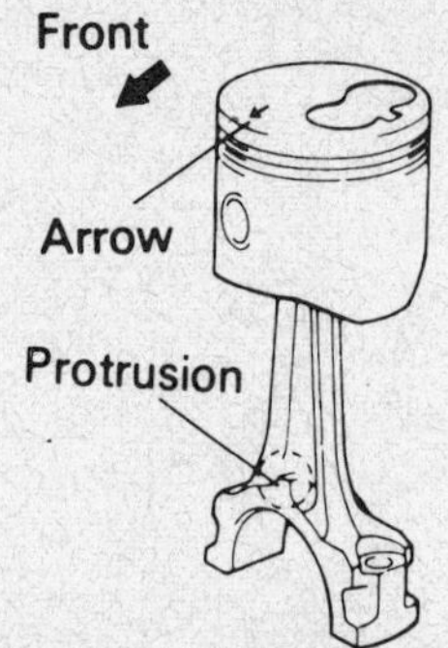

Fig. 14 Piston & rod assembly. Camry models

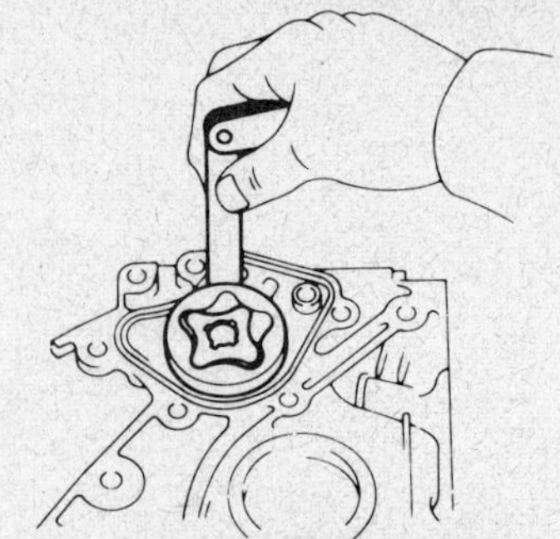

Fig. 15 Measuring oil pump driven rotor & body clearance

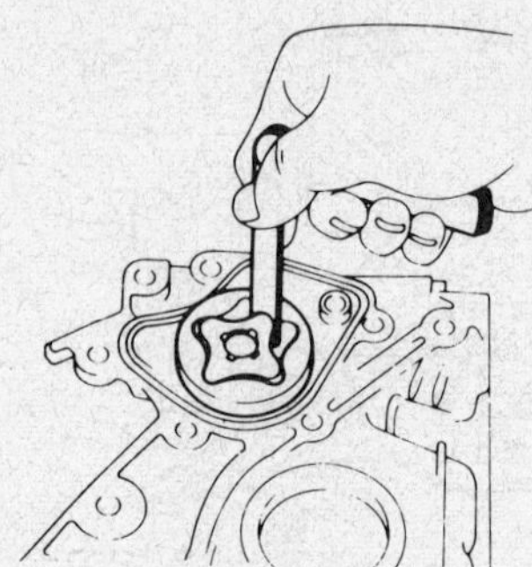

Fig. 16 Measuring rotor tip clearance

shift. **Do not allow oil, water or dust to come in contact with the timing belt.**

7. Reverse procedure to install. During installation of camshaft, ensure alignment marks placed on camshaft timing sprocket, injection pump pulley and timing belt during disassembly are correctly aligned, **Fig. 7.** Torque camshaft timing sprocket retaining bolt to 72 ft. lbs. Use a suitable tool to secure camshaft timing sprocket while torquing retaining bolt.

TIMING BELT COVER

REPLACE

To replace the timing belt cover, perform steps 1 through 4 as described under "Timing Belt, Replace."

PISTON & ROD ASSEMBLIES

Assemble piston to rod with notch or arrow on piston and mark or protrusion on connecting rod facing front of engine, **Figs. 13 and 14.**

OIL PAN & PUMP

REPLACE

CAMRY MODELS

1. Disconnect battery ground cable.
2. Raise and support vehicle.
3. Drain oil from engine.
4. Remove engine under cover(s).
5. Using a suitable hoist, raise engine slightly.
6. Remove timing belt cover, timing belt, No. 2 idler pulley and crankshaft timing sprocket.
7. Remove engine center crossmember.
8. Remove oil pan attaching bolts, then the oil pan.
9. Remove oil pump assembly.
10. Reverse procedure to install.

COROLLA MODELS

1. Disconnect battery ground cable.
2. Raise and support vehicle.
3. Remove engine under cover.
4. Drain oil from engine.
5. Using a suitable hoist, raise engine slightly.
6. Remove drive belt and pulley.
7. Remove power steering pump, if equipped and position aside.
8. Remove No. 2 timing belt cover.
9. Position No. 1 cylinder to TDC of compression stroke.
10. Remove crankshaft pulley.
11. Remove No. 1 timing belt cover and belt guide.
12. Remove right engine mount and bracket assembly.
13. Remove timing belt.
14. Remove No. 2 idler pulley and crankshaft timing sprocket.
15. Remove oil pan attaching bolts, then the pan.
16. Remove oil pump assembly.
17. Reverse procedure to install.

OIL PUMP SERVICE

1. Using a suitable feeler gauge, measure clearance between driven rotor and pump body, **Fig. 15.** Clearance should be .0039-.0067 inch. If clearance exceeds specified amount, replace oil pump rotor set and/or pump body.
2. Using a feeler gauge, measure clearance between both rotor tips, **Fig. 16.** Clearance should be .0020-.0059 inch. If clearance exceeds specified amount, replace rotor and/or pump body.
3. Using a feeler gauge and a straightedge as shown in **Fig. 17,** measure side clearance. Clearance should be .0059 inch. If clearance exceeds specified amount, replace rotor and/or pump body.

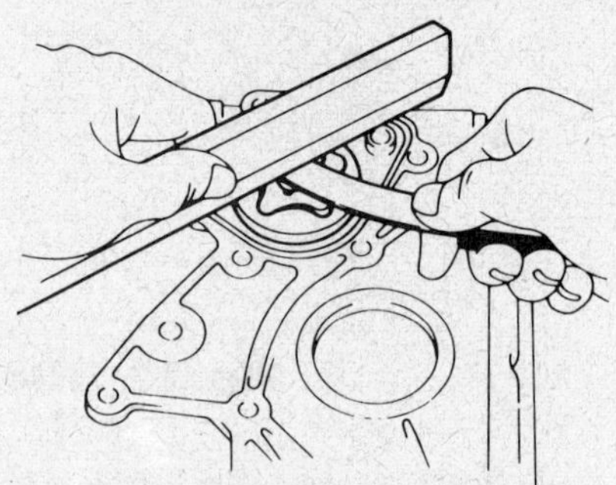

Fig. 17 Measuring side clearance

WATER PUMP

REPLACE

1. Disconnect battery ground cable.
2. Remove timing covers, timing belt and injection pump pulley.
3. Remove water pump attaching bolts, then the water pump.
4. Reverse procedure to install.

INJECTION PUMP

REPLACE

EXC. 1985–86 CAMRY MODELS

1. Disconnect battery ground cable.
2. Disconnect fuel cut solenoid electrical connector from injection pump.
3. Remove fuel injection lines, **Fig. 18.**
4. Disconnect and cap fuel return line from injection pump.
5. Disconnect water bypass hoses from injection pump.
6. Remove injection pump drive pulley.
7. Before removing injection pump, check position of injection pump period mark. Ensure mark aligns with mark on water pump.
8. Remove injection pump from engine.
9. Reverse procedure to install. Ensure injection pump period mark aligns with water pump assembly mark.

1985–86 CAMRY MODELS

1. Disconnect battery ground cable, then drain engine coolant.
2. Disconnect accelerator cable or cruise control cable and rod from injection pump.

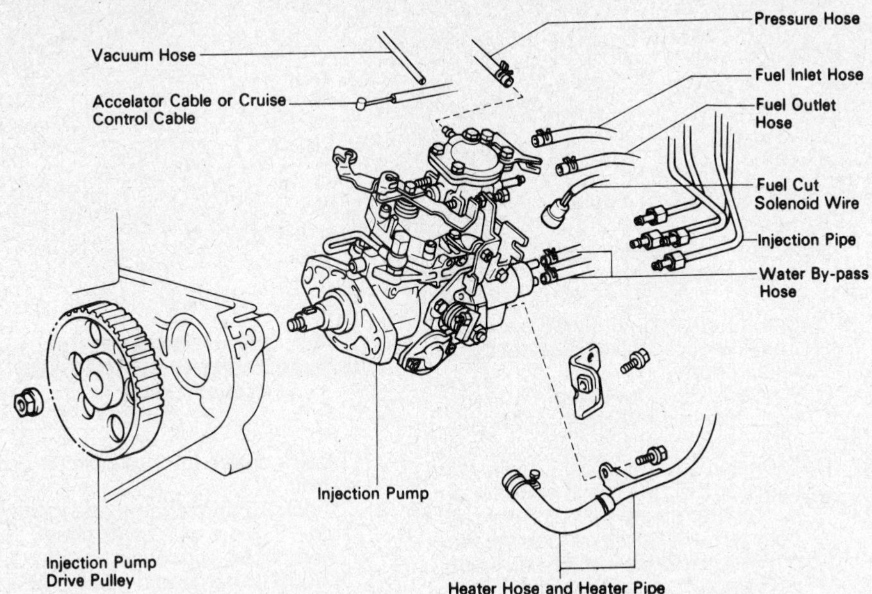

Fig. 18 Fuel injection pump assembly. Exc. 1985–86 Camry

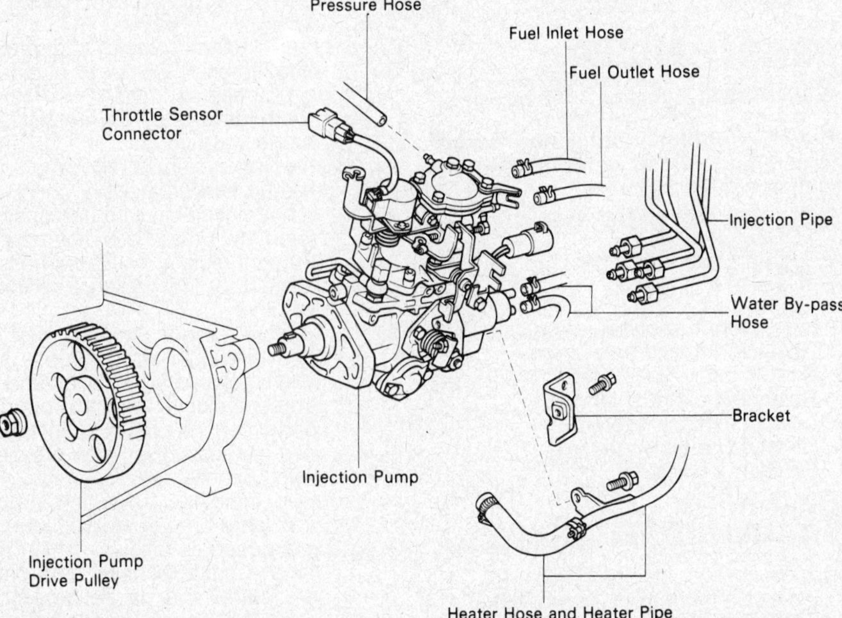

Fig. 19 Fuel injection pump assembly. 1985–86 Camry

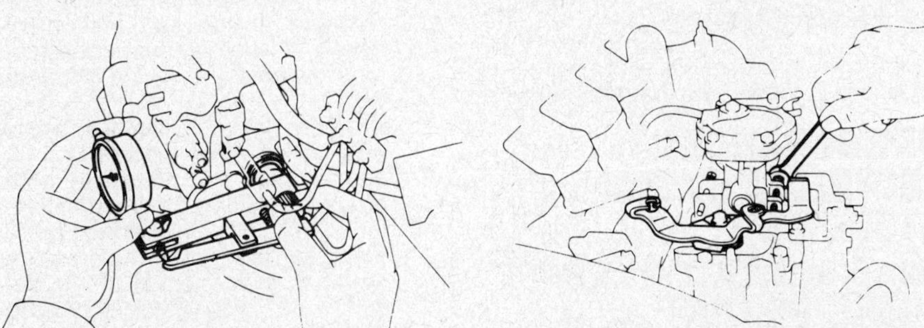

Fig. 20 Installing dial indicator onto distributive head plug

Fig. 21 Loosening idle speed adjusting bolt locknut

3. Disconnect throttle cable from injection pump, then the throttle position sensor connector, **Fig. 19.**
4. Disconnect No. 1 and No. 2 water by-pass hose, A/C or heater idle-up vacuum hose, then the heater hose with heater pipe.
5. Remove fuel injection lines, then the injection pump drive sprocket as previously described under "Timing Belt, Replace".
6. Before removing injection pump, check position of injection pump period mark. Ensure mark aligns with mark on water pump.
7. Reverse procedure to install. Ensure injection pump period mark aligns with mark on water pump.

INJECTION PUMP TIMING

1. Install a dial indicator onto the distributive head plug, **Fig. 20.**
2. Set dial indicator to zero.
3. Ensure dial indicator remains at zero, while rotating crankshaft pulley slightly to the left and right.
4. Slowly rotate crankshaft until the No. 1 or No. 4 cylinder is at TDC of compression stroke.
5. Measure plunger stroke. Plunger stroke should be .032 inch on 1984 models or .028 inch on 1985-86 models at TDC of compression stroke.
6. To adjust injection timing, proceed as follows:
   a. Loosen four injection line union nuts on the pump side.
   b. Loosen injection pump mounting bolts and nuts.
   c. Adjust plunger stroke by tilting injection pump body. If plunger stroke is less than specified amount, tilt pump toward engine. If plunger stroke exceeds specified amount, tilt pump away from engine.

IDLE SPEED

ADJUST

Before adjusting idle speed, ensure air cleaner is installed, engine at normal operating temperature, accessories Off and transmission in Neutral.

1. Connect a suitable tachometer onto engine.
2. Disconnect accelerator cable from injection pump.
3. Loosen idle speed adjusting bolt locknut, **Fig. 21.**
4. Turn idle speed adjusting screw until specified curb idle speed is obtained.

MAXIMUM SPEED

ADJUST

Before adjusting maximum speed, ensure air cleaner is installed, engine is at normal operating temperature, accessories Off and transmission in Neutral.

1. Connect a suitable tachometer onto engine.

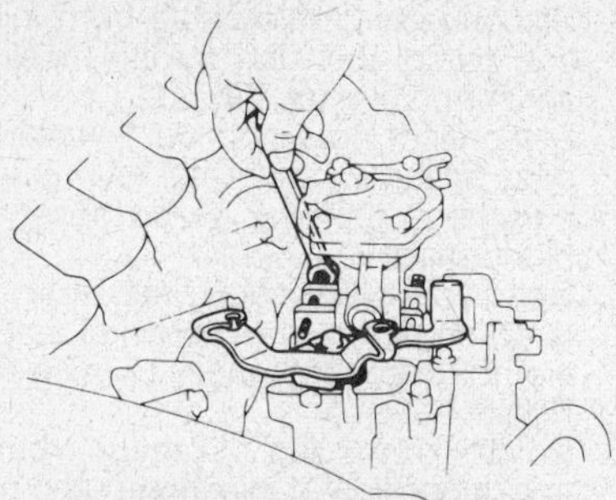

Fig. 22 Adjusting maximum speed screw

2. Remove maximum speed adjusting screw lock wire.
3. Loosen maximum speed adjusting bolt locknut.
4. Turn maximum speed adjusting screw until 5100 RPM is obtained, **Fig. 22.**

INJECTION NOZZLE REPLACE

1. Disconnect battery ground cable.
2. Loosen retaining clips, then remove fuel hoses between injection pump and fuel line.
3. Remove fuel injection lines and disconnect electrical connectors from fuel cut solenoid.
4. Disconnect fuel hose from fuel nozzle leakage line, then remove nozzle leakage line.
5. Remove injection nozzle holders and nozzles.

INJECTION NOZZLE PRESSURE TEST

1. Install a suitable nozzle hand tester onto injection nozzle, then bleed air from nozzle by loosening nozzle union nut. **Do not place fingers over nozzle injection orifice.**
2. Pump tester handle a few times to discharge any carbon build-up from injection nozzle orifice.
3. Gradually pump tester handle and note tester gauge reading. Read pressure gauge reading when injection pressure begins to drop.
4. Opening pressure for a used nozzle should be 1920-2205 psi. Opening pressure for a new nozzle should be 2062-2205 psi. **Proper nozzle operation can be determined by a swishing sound.**
5. If nozzle opening pressure is incorrect an adjustment shim must be installed at the top of the pressure spring. Shims are available in different sizes in .0010 inch (.025 mm) increments. **Varying adjusting shim thickness by .0010 inch (.025 mm) will change injection pressure by approximately 50 psi.**
6. Perform leakage test as follows:
   a. While maintaining pressure at 142-283 psi below opening pressure, ensure that there is no fuel drip for approximately 10 seconds from injection orifice or around retaining nut.
   b. If nozzle drips fuel within 10 seconds, clean or replace nozzle as required.

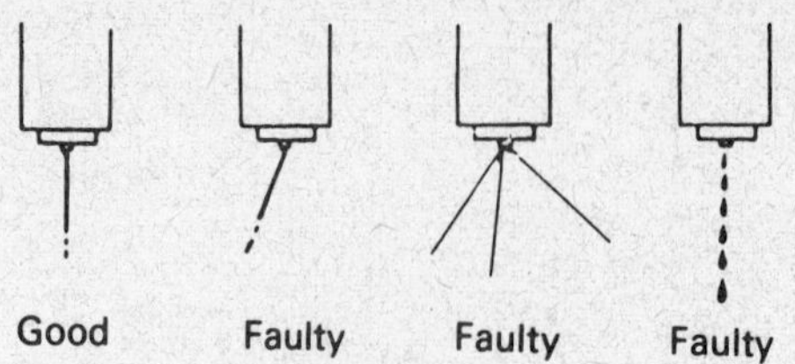

Fig. 23 Nozzle spray pattern

7. Perform spray pattern test as follows:
   a. Injection nozzle should shudder at a predetermined pumping speed between 15-60 times per minute on used nozzles or 30-60 times per minute for new nozzles.
   b. Check fuel spray pattern during shuddering period, **Fig. 23.**
   c. If fuel spray pattern is incorrect during shuddering period, replace nozzle as required.

TURBOCHARGER TROUBLESHOOTING

Before troubleshooting the turbocharger, first check valve clearances and injection timing.

LACK OF POWER OR EXCESSIVE FUEL CONSUMPTION

1. Insufficient turbocharger pressure.
2. Restricted intake air system.
3. Leak in intake air system.
4. Restricted exhaust system.
5. Leak in exhaust system.
6. Relief valve leaking.
7. Faulty turbocharger.

ABNORMAL TURBOCHARGER NOISE

1. Turbocharger insulator vibrating.
2. Exhaust pipe leaking or vibrating.
3. Faulty turbocharger.

EXCESSIVE OIL CONSUMPTION OR WHITE EXHAUST SMOKE

1. Defective turbocharger seal.
2. Oil leak in intake or exhaust systems.

TURBOCHARGER ELECTRICAL SYSTEM DIAGNOSIS

TURBO INDICATOR LAMP & WARNING LAMP OPERATION

1. Do both green indicator lamp and amber warning lamp light when ignition switch is turned ON?
2. If not, check the following:
   a. Check 7.5 gauge fuse. If fuse is blown, check for short circuit and repair.

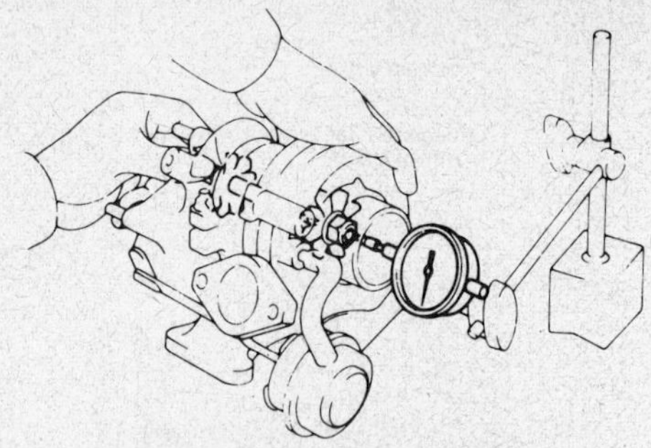

Fig. 24 Measuring turbocharger axial play clearance

   b. Check 7.5 amp charge and ignition fuse. If fuse is blown, check for short circuit and repair as required.
   c. If gauge, charge and ignition fuses are not blown, check if discharge warning light is Off. If discharge warning light is On, charging system is faulty. If discharge warning light is Off, instrument cluster is faulty.
3. If green indicator lamp and amber warning lamp are ON when engine is idling, proceed as follows:
   a. If both lamps stay On, ensure discharge warning lamp is Off. If not, charging system is defective.
   b. If green lamp stays On, check for an open circuit in wire harness between low pressure switch and instrument cluster. If wire harness is satisfactory, low pressure switch is defective.
   c. If amber lamp is On, check for an open circuit in wire harness between high pressure switch and instrument cluster and a grounded connection of switch. If wire harness is satisfactory, high pressure switch is defective.
4. If green indicator lamp and amber warning lamp are Off when engine is idling, proceed as follows:
   a. Using a suitable hand held pressure pump and gauge assembly, apply 2.0 psi to both pressure switches. If green indicator lamp does not light, check for short circuit in wire harness between low pressure switch and instrument cluster. If wire harness is satisfactory, low pressure switch is defective.
   b. If amber lamp illuminates, apply 10.4 psi on 1984 models or 11.9 psi on 1985-86 models to both pressure switches. If green indicator lamp lights with specified pressure applied to both pressure switches, instrument cluster is defective. If green indicator lamp does not light, high pressure switch is defective.
5. Apply 10.4 psi on 1984 models or 11.9 psi on 1985-86 models, to both pressure switches. If amber indicator lamp lights, turbocharger indicator warning operation lamp is satisfactory. If am-

ber indicator lamp does not light, check for short circuit in wire harness between high pressure switch and instrument cluster. If wire harness is satisfactory, high pressure switch is defective.

TURBOCHARGER SERVICE

REMOVAL

1. Disconnect battery ground cable.
2. Remove air cleaner hose with air cleaner case cover as follows:
   a. Disconnect PCV hose from cylinder head cover.
   b. Loosen retaining clamp, then disconnect air cleaner hose from turbocharger.
   c. Remove clips, air cleaner hose and air cleaner case cover assembly.
3. Mark then carefully disconnect turbocharger pressure hose from indicator and warning lights.
4. Remove compressor elbow, relief valve and air intake hose assembly as follows:
   a. Loosen clamp, then disconnect air intake hose from intake manifold.
   b. Remove elbow bracket to engine No. 2 bracket attaching bolt.
   c. Remove turbocharger compressor elbow attaching bolts, relief valve and air intake hose.
   d. Remove turbocharger elbow gasket.
5. Remove turbocharger heat insulators.
6. Disconnect exhaust pipe from turbocharger turbine elbow.
7. Remove turbocharger oil line flange retaining nuts.
8. Remove turbocharger attaching bolts from exhaust manifold.
9. Remove turbocharger turbine elbow and gasket.
10. Remove relief valve from turbocharger compressor elbow.

INSPECTION

1. Check for leakage or restrictions in the air cleaner and turbocharger inlet and between turbocharger outlet and cylinder head. Replace a restricted air cleaner as necessary. If any hoses or lines are collapsed or deformed, replace as required.
2. Check for leakage or restrictions between cylinder head and turbocharger inlet and between turbocharger outlet and exhaust pipe.
3. Check turbocharger impeller wheel rotation by turning the turbine wheel. Ensure impeller wheel rotates smoothly. If impeller wheel binds or drags, replace turbocharger assembly.
4. Check axial shaft bearing play as follows:
   a. Insert a suitable dial indicator onto turbocharger intake side as shown in **Fig. 24.**
   b. Gradually pull then push on turbine wheel edge and check axial play.
   c. Axial play clearance should be .0051 inch maximum. If not, replace turbocharger assembly.
5. Check relief valve as follows:
   a. Check outside of relief valve for excessive oil leakage.
   b. If excessive oil accumulation is found on outside of relief valve, replace valve and check valve operation.

INSTALLATION

During installation of a new turbocharger assembly, thoroughly lubricate turbocharger oil inlet and impeller wheel with clean engine oil. Turn turbocharger impeller wheel by hand several revolutions to thoroughly lubricate impeller wheel bearings.

1. Install relief valve onto turbocharger compressor elbow. Torque valve to 18 ft. lbs.
2. Install gasket and turbine elbow onto turbocharger. Torque elbow retaining nuts to 18 ft. lbs.
3. Install turbocharger assembly onto engine. Torque turbocharger to exhaust manifold attaching nuts to 38 ft. lbs.
4. Install turbocharger oil line flange nuts. Torque nuts to 13 ft. lbs.
5. Connect exhaust pipe onto turbine elbow. Torque attaching nuts to 9 ft. lbs.
6. Install turbocharger heat insulators.
7. Install turbocharger elbow, relief valve and air intake hose.
8. Connect turbocharger pressure hose onto indicator and warning lights.
9. Install air cleaner hose and air cleaner case cover.

CLUTCH & MANUAL TRANSMISSION SECTION

INDEX

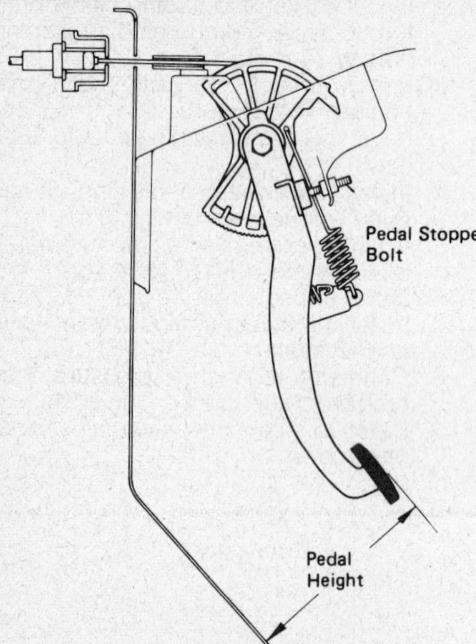

Fig. 1 Clutch pedal height adjustment. Starlet, 1983–86 Tercel & 1987 Tercel Wagon models

CLUTCH PEDAL ADJUST

STARLET, 1983–86 TERCEL & 1987 TERCEL WAGON

Clutch Pedal Height

1. Adjust distance from pedal pad to floor panel to 7.36-7.76 inch on 1983 Tercel, 7.24-7.64 inch on 1984 Tercel, 6.97-7.36 inch on 1985 Tercel, 7.13-7.44 inch on 1986 Tercel, 6.93-7.24 inch on 1987 Tercel Wagon and 6.87-7.26 inch on Starlet models, by rotating the pedal pad stopper bolt, **Fig. 1.**

Clutch Pedal Freeplay

1. Operate clutch pedal several times, then depress clutch pedal until resistance is felt. Freeplay should be .08-1.10 inch on 1983-85 and 1987 models or .08-.98 inch on 1986 models.

Clutch Release Sector & Pawl Position

1. After clutch adjustments are complete, check to ensure that six notches are remaining on sector, **Fig. 2.** If there are less than six notches remaining, the clutch disc should be replaced.

CAMRY, CELICA, COROLLA, CRESSIDA, SUPRA & 1987 TERCEL SEDAN

1. Check clutch pedal height, refer to **Fig. 3.**
2. Clutch pedal height on Camry models should be as follows:
   a. 1983-85, 7.5-7.9 inches.
   b. 1986, 7.99-8.39 inches.
   c. 1987, 7.52-7.91 inches.
3. Clutch pedal height on Celica and Supra models should be as follows:
   a. 1983-Early 1986 Supra and 1983-85 Celica, 6.06-6.46 inches.
   b. 1986-87 Celica, 6.02-6.42 inches.
   c. Late 1986-87 Supra, 6.18-6.57 inches.
4. Clutch pedal height on Corolla should be as follows:
   a. 1983, 6.46-6.85 inches.
   b. 1984 & 1986-87 FWD, 5.83-6.22 inches.
   c. 1984 RWD & 1985 FWD, 5.65-6.04 inches.
   d. 1985 RWD, 6.34-6.73 inches.
   e. 1986-87 RWD, 6.44-6.83 inches.
5. Clutch pedal height on Cressida models should be as follows:
   a. 1981-87, 6.1-6.5 inches.
6. Clutch pedal height on 1987 Tercel sedan models should be as follows:
   a. On models equipped with clutch pedal assemblies EL31L-ZGKRSA and EL31L-ZGKBSK, clutch pedal height should be 6.38-6.77 inches as measured from dash panel.
   b. On models less clutch pedal assemblies EL31L-ZGKRSA and EL31L-ZGKBSK, clutch pedal height should be 6.14-6.54 inches as measured from floor, **Fig. 3.**
7. If clutch pedal height is not as specified, loosen locknut and turn adjusting bolt until specified clutch pedal height is obtained, then tighten adjusting bolt locknut.
8. Check clutch freeplay. Clutch pedal freeplay on Camry models should be as follows:
   a. 1983-87, .20-.59 inches. **Pushrod play at top of pedal should be .039-.197 inches.**
9. Clutch freeplay on Celica and Supra models should be as follows:
   a. 1983-84 less turnover clutch, .51-.91 inch.
   b. 1983-87 Supra and 1983-86 Celica with turnover clutch, .20-.59 inch. **Pushrod play at top of pedal should be, .039-.197 inch.**
10. Clutch free play on Corolla models should be as follows:
    a. 1983 less turnover clutch, 1984-85 RWD, 1984-85 FWD gasoline engine models and 1986-87 RWD w/4A-C engine, .51-.91 inch.
    b. 1984 FWD models w/diesel engine and 1986-87 RWD w/4A-GE engine, .20-.59 inch. **Pushrod play at top of pedal should be .039-.197 inch.**
    c. 1986 FWD models, .28-.67 inch.
    d. 1987 FWD models. .20-.59 inch. **Pushrod play at top of pedal**

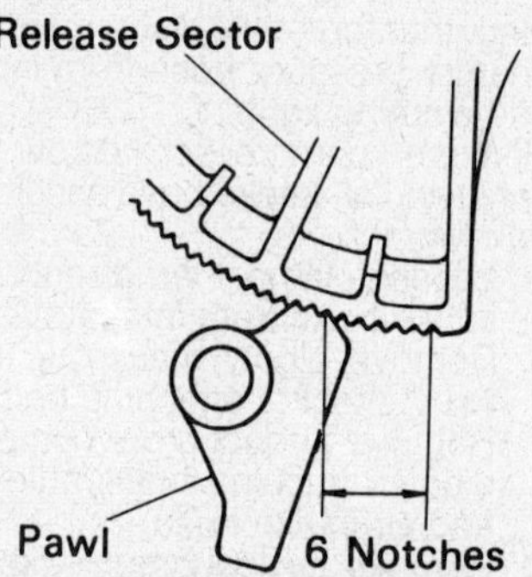

Fig. 2 Release sector & pawl position adjustment. Starlet, 1983–86 Tercel & 1987 Tercel Wagon models

Fig. 3 Clutch pedal adjustments (typical). Exc. Starlet, 1983–86 Tercel, 1987 Tercel Wagon & Van models

should be .039-.197 inch.

11. Clutch freeplay on Cressida models should be as follows:
    a. 1981-87, .20-.59 inch. **Pushrod play at top of pedal should be .039-.197 inch.**
12. Clutch freeplay on Tercel Wagon models should be as follows:
    a. 1987, .20-.59 inch. **Pushrod play at top of pedal should be .039-.197 inches.**
13. If clutch pedal freeplay is not as specified, loosen locknut and turn pushrod adjusting screw until specified pedal freeplay is obtained, **Fig. 3.**
14. Tighten locknut, then recheck clutch pedal height.

PICKUP & 4RUNNER

1. On 1983 models, check clutch pedal height, **Fig. 3.** Clutch pedal height should be 5.9-6.3 inch on gasoline engine models and 6.38-6.79 inch on diesel engine models.
2. On 1984-86 models, check clutch pedal height, **Fig. 3.** Clutch pedal height should be 5.94 inch on 1984 models and 5.67 inch on 1985-86 models.
3. On 1987 models, check clutch pedal height, **Fig. 3.** Clutch pedal height should be 6.122 inch.
4. If specified height is not as specified, loosen locknut, then rotate adjusting bolt until specified height is obtained. Tighten locknut.
5. Check clutch pedal freeplay, **Fig. 3.** Depress clutch pedal until resistance is felt, then measure freeplay distance. Freeplay should be .20-.59 inch.
6. Check clutch cylinder pushrod play at top of pedal. Play should be .039-.197 inch.
7. If clutch pedal freeplay is not as specified, loosen locknut, then rotate pushrod adjusting screw until specified freeplay is obtained.
8. Tighten locknut, then recheck pedal height.

1984–87 VAN

1. Refer to **Fig. 4** and check clutch pedal height. Clutch pedal height should be 6.57-6.97 inch on 1984-85 models and 6.73-7.13 inch on 1986-87 models. If specified clutch pedal height cannot be obtained, loosen locknut and turn adjusting bolt until specified clutch pedal height is obtained.
2. After correct clutch pedal height is obtained, tighten locknut.
3. Refer to **Fig. 4** and check clutch pedal freeplay. Depress clutch pedal until clutch resistance is obtained, then measure clutch pedal freeplay. Clutch pedal freeplay should be .20-.59 inch.
4. Check clutch cylinder pushrod play at top of pedal. Play should be .039-.197 inch.

1985–87 MR2

1. Refer to **Fig. 3** and check clutch pedal height, which should measure 6.03-6.41 inches. If specified clutch pedal height cannot be obtained, remove instrument panel lower trim panel and air duct, loosen locknut and turn adjusting bolt until specified clutch pedal height is obtained.
2. After correct clutch pedal height is obtained, tighten locknut.
3. Refer to **Fig. 3** and check pedal freeplay. Depress clutch pedal until clutch resistance is obtained, then check freeplay, which should measure .20-.59 inch.
4. Check clutch cylinder pushrod play at top of pedal. Play should be .039-.197 inch.

CLUTCH REPLACE

1. Remove transmission or transaxle from vehicle. Refer to "Transmission, Replace" for procedure.
2. Loosen pressure plate attaching bolts one turn at a time, then remove bolts, pressure plate and clutch disc.
3. Install new clutch disc and pressure plate assembly, checking to ensure that disc and plate are properly aligned. Tighten attaching bolts one turn at a time while ensuring clutch disc and pressure plate remain aligned.
4. Install transmission or transaxle and adjust clutch as described under "Clutch, Adjust."

TRANSMISSION REPLACE

1983–86 CAMRY

1. Remove hood, then drain cooling system.
2. Remove battery.
3. Disconnect accelerator cable from throttle body.
4. Remove cruise control actuator and bracket as follows:
    a. Disconnect vacuum hose, then remove actuator cover.

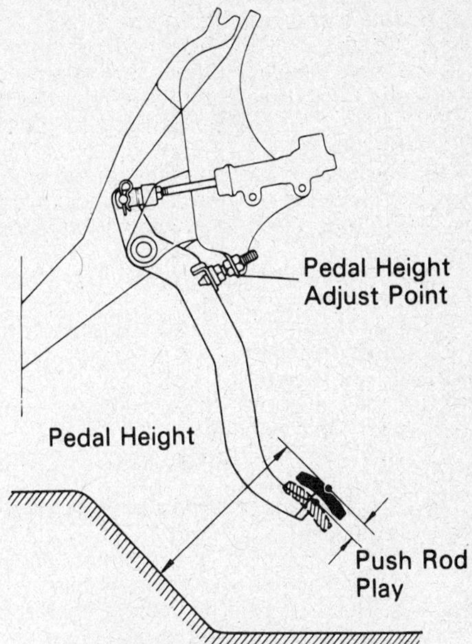

Fig. 4 Clutch pedal adjustments. Van models

    b. Disconnect electrical connector, then remove actuator and bracket assembly.
5. Remove radiator, air cleaner, air flow meter and air cleaner hose assembly.
6. Mark, then disconnect all electrical connections and vacuum hoses from engine.
7. Mark, then carefully disconnect the following EFI electrical connectors:
    a. All electrical connectors from left side fender apron.
    b. Solenoid resistor electrical connector.
    c. Water temperature sensor electrical connector.
    d. Start injector time switch and cold start injector electrical connectors.
    e. Air valve and throttle position sensor electrical connectors.
    f. The remaining injector electrical connectors.
    g. Oxygen sensor electrical connector.
    h. Engine ground strap.
8. Pull EFI wire harness from right side fender apron.
9. Disconnect and plug heater hoses.
10. Disconnect and plug inlet hose from fuel filter.
11. Disconnect and plug return hose from fuel return line.
12. Disconnect speedometer cable from transaxle.
13. Remove clutch release cylinder and hose bracket assembly. Do not disconnect clutch release cylinder lines.
14. Disconnect transaxle control cable as follows:
    a. Remove clips and plate washers, then disconnect each control cable from shift and selector levers.
    b. Remove clips, then disconnect each cable from control bracket.
15. Remove A/C compressor from engine and position aside, if equipped. Do not disconnect refrigerant lines.

16. Raise and support vehicle.
17. Wrap both front driveshaft boots with clean towels. Remove six attaching nuts from driveshaft while depressing brake pedal, then disconnect drive shafts.
18. Remove power steering pump from engine and position aside, if equipped. Do not disconnect power steering lines.
19. Disconnect from exhaust pipe from exhaust manifold.
20. Remove front and rear mounts from crossmember.
21. Lower vehicle.
22. Install suitable engine lifting equipment onto engine.
23. Remove engine and transaxle assembly from vehicle.
24. Separate engine from transaxle as follows:
    a. Remove front and rear mountings.
    b. Remove LH mounting bracket.
    c. Remove side gear shaft, then the front drive center shaft.
    d. Remove starter motor attaching bolts, then the starter motor.
    e. Remove transaxle to engine attaching bolts.
    f. Separate transaxle from engine.
25. Reverse procedure to install. Torque front and rear mounts to 29 ft. lbs. Torque drive shaft nuts to 27 ft. lbs.

1987 CAMRY

1. Disconnect battery ground cable.
2. Remove clutch release cylinder and tube clamp.
3. Remove clutch tube bracket retainer, then the bracket attaching bolt and bracket.
4. Remove control cable clips, washers and retainers.
5. Remove starter attaching bolts, then the starter.
6. Disconnect back-up light switch electrical connector and ground strap.
7. Remove transaxle upper attaching bolts.
8. Raise and support vehicle, then remove under covers.
9. Drain transaxle fluid, then disconnect speedometer cable.
10. Remove suspension lower crossmember.
11. Remove front and rear engine attaching bolts.
12. Remove engine center crossmember.
13. Depress brake pedal, then remove both driveshaft attaching nuts.
14. Remove driveshaft bearing bracket snap ring using suitable pliers.
15. Remove bearing bracket attaching bolt, then pull out center driveshaft.
16. Disconnect steering knuckle from lower arm.
17. Pull steering knuckle outward, then remove driveshaft.
18. Remove stabilizer bar.
19. Raise transaxle and engine assembly slightly using a suitable jack, then disconnect left engine mounting.
20. Remove transaxle to engine attaching bolts.
21. Lower left side of engine, then remove transaxle from engine.
22. Reverse procedure to install.

1983–85 CELICA, 1983–85 SUPRA & EARLY 1986 SUPRA

1. Remove shift boot and shift lever retainer attaching bolts, then lift out shift lever.
2. Disconnect battery ground cable.
3. Drain cooling system, then disconnect upper radiator hose.
4. Remove air cleaner and starter.
5. Disconnect back-up light switch electrical connector.
6. Disconnect exhaust pipe from exhaust manifold, then remove exhaust pipe clamp.
7. Remove steering gear housing assembly without disconnecting pressure and return lines, if necessary, then suspend unit from chassis with suitable hanger.
8. Disconnect speedometer cable from transmission.
9. Remove clutch release cylinder.
10. Mark driveshaft and pinion flanges for reassembly, then remove driveshaft. **After removing driveshaft install seal replacer tool in extension housing to prevent leakage.**
11. Support transmission using a suitable jack, then remove rear crossmember.
12. Lower jack slightly and remove clutch housing attaching bolts.
13. Pull transmission rearward and lower from vehicle.
14. Reverse procedure to install.

1986 CELICA

1. Disconnect battery ground cable.
2. Remove air cleaner with air hose, then disconnect back-up light switch electrical connector.
3. Remove speedometer cable, then disconnect ground strap.
4. Remove control cable clips, washers and retainers.
5. Remove clutch pipe bracket clip, then disconnect bracket from transaxle.
6. Remove clutch release cylinder attaching bolts, then the clutch release cylinder.
7. Remove under cover, then the exhaust pipe from manifold.
8. Remove suspension lower crossmember.
9. Remove crossmember cover, then disconnect front and rear mounting.
10. Remove engine mounting center crossmember, then disconnect both driveshafts from transaxle.
11. Disconnect steering knuckle from lower arm.
12. Pull steering knuckle outward, then remove left driveshaft.
13. Remove starter motor attaching bolts, then the starter motor.
14. Remove No. 2 engine rear plate.
15. Raise transaxle and engine assembly slightly using a suitable jack, then disconnect left engine mounting.
16. Remove engine to transaxle attaching bolts.
17. Lower left side of engine, then remove transaxle from engine.
18. Reverse procedure to install.

1987 CELICA

1. Disconnect battery ground cable.
2. Remove air cleaner with air hose.
3. Remove retainer from clutch tube bracket.
4. Remove clutch tube bracket attaching bolts, then the bracket.
5. Remove clutch release cylinder and tube clamp.
6. Remove control cable clips, washers and retainers.
7. On models equipped with 3S-FE engine, remove battery.
8. On all models, disconnect starter electrical connectors.
9. Remove starter attaching bolts, then the starter.
10. Disconnect back-up light switch electrical connector and ground strap.
11. Remove upper transaxle mounting bolts.
12. Raise and support vehicle, then remove under covers.
13. Drain transaxle fluid, then disconnect speedometer cable.
14. Disconnect exhaust pipe from manifold, then remove suspension lower crossmember.
15. Remove crossmember covers, then the front and rear member attaching bolts.
16. Remove engine center crossmember.
17. Disconnect both driveshafts from transaxle.
18. Disconnect steering knuckle from lower arm.
19. Pull steering knuckle outward, then remove driveshaft.
20. Raise transaxle and engine assembly slightly using a suitable jack, then disconnect left engine mounting.
21. Remove engine to transaxle attaching bolts.
22. Lower left side of engine, then remove transaxle from engine.
23. Reverse procedure to install.

1983 COROLLA

1. Position shift lever in Neutral, then remove shift lever boot.
2. Remove shift lever cover attaching screws.
3. Remove snap ring and lift shift lever from housing.
4. Disconnect battery negative cable and back-up light switch wire connector.
5. Drain cooling system, then disconnect upper radiator hose.
6. Disconnect bond cable at rear of engine, if equipped.
7. Remove starter.
8. Disconnect exhaust pipe at exhaust manifold, then remove exhaust pipe clamp bolt from clutch housing.
9. Remove clutch release cylinder body.
10. Disconnect speedometer cable from extension housing.
11. Mark driveshaft and pinion flanges, then remove driveshaft. **Insert seal replacer tool into extension housing after removing driveshaft.**
12. Support transmission using suitable jack, then remove engine rear support.
13. Remove clutch housing to engine mounting bolts, then slide transmission rearward and lower from vehicle.

14. Reverse procedure to install.

1984–87 COROLLA RWD

1. Disconnect battery ground cable.
2. Loosen distributor mounting bolt and turn distributor away from firewall.
3. Remove console.
4. Working from inside of vehicle, remove shift lever from bracket.
5. Raise and support vehicle, then drain fluid from transmission.
6. Remove power steering gear assembly and position aside, if equipped.
7. Disconnect front exhaust pipe from exhaust manifold.
8. Place alignment marks on propeller shaft and differential flanges, then disconnect propeller shaft from differential.
9. Remove center support bearing and heat insulator.
10. Remove propeller shaft from vehicle, then insert tool No. 09325-12010 onto transmission output shaft to prevent fluid leakage.
11. Disconnect speedometer cable and back-up light switch electrical connector from transaxle.
12. Remove clutch release cylinder.
13. Remove starter motor attaching bolts, then the starter motor.
14. Using a suitable jack, raise transmission slightly, then remove rear engine mount.
15. Remove stiffener plate attaching bolts, then the stiffener plate.
16. Remove transmission to engine mounting bolts, then lower transmission from vehicle.
17. Reverse procedure to install.

1984–86 COROLLA FWD

1. Disconnect battery ground cable, then remove air cleaner and hose.
2. Disconnect back-up lamp switch connector, then remove speedometer cable.
3. Remove retaining clips, washers, retainers, then the transaxle control cable.
4. If necessary, remove water inlet attaching bolt and nut from transaxle case, then the water inlet.
5. Remove clutch release cylinder, then the under cover.
6. Remove front and rear mounting cover, then disconnect front and rear mounting.
7. Remove engine mounting center member, then remove transaxle protector. Remove driveshaft attaching nuts, then the driveshafts.
8. Disconnect steering knuckle from lower arm, then pull steering knuckle outward and remove left driveshaft.
9. Disconnect starter cable connector, then the starter attaching bolts and starter.
10. Disconnect transaxle ground strap, then the No. 2 engine rear plate.
11. Slightly raise transaxle and engine with suitable jacks, then disconnect left engine mount.
12. Disconnect transaxle to engine mounting bolts, then lower left side of engine and separate transaxle from engine.
13. Reverse procedure to install.

1987 COROLLA FWD

1. Disconnect battery ground cable.
2. Loosen air hose clamp, then remove three air cleaner case attaching bolts. Remove air cleaner case with hose and vacuum hose.
3. Disconnect cooling fan electrical connector, then the cooling fan attaching bolts and fan.
4. Disconnect oxygen sensor connector, then the back-up lamp switch electrical connector.
5. Remove clutch release cylinder, then the two bolts and release cylinder. **Do not remove tube.**
6. Remove water inlet attaching bolt and nut, then the water inlet.
7. Remove control cable retaining clips and washers, then the retainers and control cables.
8. Disconnect speedometer cable, then the bond cable from body.
9. Remove starter attaching bolts, then disconnect electrical connector. Remove nut and disconnect cable, then remove starter.
10. Remove LH and RH engine under covers, then the front exhaust pipe.
11. Disconnect front and rear mountings, then remove engine mount center member.
12. Disconnect driveshaft as follows:
    a. Remove LH front wheel, then remove transmission protector retaining bolts and protector.
    b. Loosen 6 nuts while depressing brake pedal, then disconnect driveshaft from side gear shaft.
    c. Disconnect lower ball joint from lower arm, then pull shock absorber outward and remove driveshaft.
13. Slightly raise transaxle and engine, then remove LH engine mount attaching bolts and mount.
14. Remove 4 transaxle mounting bolts, then the two rear end plate bolts.
15. Lower LH side of engine, then separate transaxle from engine.
16. Reverse procedure to install.

1983–87 CRESSIDA

1. Disconnect battery ground cable, then drain cooling system.
2. Disconnect upper radiator hose.
3. Remove air cleaner, then disconnect torque rod from carburetor, if necessary.
4. Remove console box, if necessary, then the shift lever from inside vehicle.
5. Raise and support vehicle.
6. Drain fluid from transmission.
7. On 1983-84 models, remove propeller shaft.
8. On 1985-87 models, unfasten steering gear housing and position aside, leaving hydraulic lines attached, then remove intermediate propeller shaft.
9. On all models, disconnect exhaust pipe from tail pipe.
10. Disconnect speedometer cable and back-up lamp switch electrical connector from transmission.
11. Remove clutch release cylinder, then the starter motor.
12. Raise transmission slightly, then remove rear engine mount.
13. Remove exhaust pipe bracket and two stiffener plates, then the housing bolts.
14. Lower transmission from vehicle.
15. Reverse procedure to install.

1985–87 MR2

1. Disconnect battery ground cable, then drain gear transaxle fluid.
2. Disconnect back-up lamp switch connector, then remove speedometer cable.
3. Remove water inlet attaching bolt and nut from transaxle case, then the water inlet.
4. Remove engine under cover, then the fuel tank protector.
5. Remove retaining clips, washers, retainers, then the transaxle control cable.
6. Remove water hose clamp from control cable bracket, then the No. 2 control cable bracket. Remove control cable bracket and clutch release cylinder.
7. Disconnect exhaust pipe from manifold, then separate bracket from body. Remove exhaust pipe from rear bracket.
8. Remove transaxle protector, then disconnect driveshaft from side gear shaft.
9. Disconnect starter cable connector, then the starter attaching bolts and starter.
10. Remove No. 2 engine rear plate, then the front engine mount.
11. Remove rear engine mount, then slightly raise transaxle and engine with suitable jacks and disconnect left engine mount.
12. Disconnect transaxle to engine mounting bolts, then lower left side of engine and separate transaxle from engine.
13. Remove side gear shaft from transaxle.
14. Reverse procedure to install.

PICKUP & 4RUNNER

W/L45 & L52 TRANSMISSIONS

1. Disconnect battery ground cable. On 4WD models, remove transfer case.
2. Remove shift lever from inside vehicle, then the starter upper mount bolt.
3. Raise and support vehicle, then drain transmission fluid.
4. Disconnect propeller shaft, then remove clutch release cylinder and starter.
5. Disconnect speedometer cable, then the back-up lamp switch.
6. Remove exhaust pipe clamp from transmission housing.
7. Remove four rear engine mount attaching bolts, then slightly raise transmission, using a suitable jack. Remove four attaching bolts from support member, then remove rear mount bracket. Remove engine rear mount from transmission.
8. Remove remaining transmission attaching bolts.
9. Pull transmission assembly toward

rear of vehicle, then lower transmission forward and away from vehicle, using care not to damage extension housing dust deflector.
10. Reverse procedure to install.

W/R150 & R151F TRANSMISSIONS

1. Disconnect battery ground cable, then remove starter upper mount bolt.
2. Remove shift lever from inside vehicle, then, if equipped, the shift lever retainer.
3. Raise and support vehicle, then drain transmission fluid.
4. Disconnect propeller shaft, then the speedometer cable, back-up lamp switch and light switch connector.
5. Remove exhaust pipe clamp and exhaust pipe.
6. Remove clutch release cylinder, tube bracket and lower starter attaching bolt. Position starter aside.
7. Remove four rear engine mount attaching bolts, then slightly raise transmission, using a suitable jack. Remove four attaching bolts from support member, then remove rear mount bracket. Remove engine rear mount from transmission.
8. Place a piece of wood, approximately .8 inch (20 mm) thick, between engine oil pan and front crossmember, then lower transmission.
9. Remove exhaust pipe bracket and stiffener plate bolts.
10. Remove remaining transmission attaching bolts.
11. On all except R150 models, pull transmission assembly toward rear of vehicle, then lower transmission forward and away from vehicle, using care not to damage extension housing dust deflector.
12. On R150 models, rotate transmission clockwise approximately 45°, then slide transmission rearward. Lower transmission forward and away from vehicle.
13. Reverse procedure to install.

W/G40 & G52 TRANSMISSIONS

1. Disconnect battery ground cable.
2. Remove shift lever from inside vehicle.
3. Raise and support vehicle, then drain transmission fluid.
4. Disconnect propeller shaft, then the speedometer cable, back-up lamp switch and light switch connector.
5. Remove exhaust pipe clamp from bracket, then the exhaust pipe from manifold. Remove exhaust pipe clamp from No. 2 crossmember frame.
6. Remove clutch release cylinder and tube bracket. **Do not remove clutch line.**
7. Remove four rear engine mount attaching bolts, then slightly raise transmission, using a suitable jack. Remove four attaching bolts from support member, then remove rear mount bracket. Remove engine rear mount from transmission.
8. Place a piece of wood, approximately .8 inch (20 mm) thick, between engine oil pan and front crossmember, then lower transmission.
9. Remove starter, then the exhaust pipe bracket and stiffener plate bolts.
10. Remove remaining transmission attaching bolts.
11. Pull transmission assembly toward rear of vehicle, then lower transmission forward and away from vehicle, using care not to damage extension housing dust deflector.
12. Reverse procedure to install.

W/W42, W45, W46, W52, W55 & W56 TRANSMISSIONS

Exc. 4WD

1. Remove shift lever boot retainer and boot.
2. Remove shift lever using tool SST09305-20012 or equivalent.
3. Disconnect battery ground cable.
4. Drain cooling system, then disconnect upper radiator hose.
5. Remove clutch release cylinder hose bracket.
6. Remove accelerator torque rod.
7. Remove starter, then the clutch slave cylinder.
8. Disconnect speedometer cable and back-up switch electrical connector.
9. Disconnect exhaust pipe from exhaust manifold, then remove exhaust pipe bracket and heat insulator, if equipped.
10. Release parking brake, then disconnect parking brake cable from intermediate lever.
11. Mark driveshaft and pinion flanges for reassembly, then remove driveshaft.
12. Support transmission using suitable jack, then remove rear crossmember.
13. Lower jack and remove clutch housing to engine block attaching bolts. **To prevent oil pan from striking suspension member or EGR valve from striking dash panel, position wooden block and suitable jack under oil pan for support.**
14. Pull transmission rearward and lower from vehicle.
15. Reverse procedure to install.

4WD Models

1. Disconnect battery ground cable.
2. Using tool SST093050012 or equivalent, remove gear shift lever.
3. Using suitable long nosed pliers, remove transfer case lever retaining clip, then remove shift lever.
4. Raise and support vehicle.
5. If transmission or transfer case is to be disassembled, drain lubricant into suitable container.
6. Scribe alignment marks, then remove front and rear driveshafts.
7. Remove clutch release cylinder, then remove starter and position both aside.
8. Disconnect back-up light switch wiring and four wheel drive indicator switch wiring.
9. Disconnect speedometer cable.
10. Disconnect exhaust pipe clamp from transmission housing.
11. Remove bolts securing rear engine mount to crossmember.
12. Support transmission using suitable jack, then remove crossmember from frame rails.
13. Lower transmission slightly.
14. Position a suitable support and wooden block under engine, then remove bolts securing transmission to engine block.
15. Remove jack supporting transmission, then pull transmission and transfer case down and rearward to remove.
16. If necessary, remove transfer case from transmission by removing mounting bolts, then pulling transfer case away from transmission.
17. Reverse procedure to install.

LATE 1986 SUPRA & 1987 SUPRA

1. Disconnect battery ground cable.
2. Remove center cluster finish panel, then the shift lever from inside of vehicle.
3. Raise and support vehicle, then drain transmission oil.
4. Remove propeller shaft, then install tool 09325-20010 or equivalent into extension housing.
5. Disconnect exhaust pipe from tail pipe.
6. Disconnect speedometer cable.
7. Disconnect back-up light switch electrical connector, then the rear speed sensor electrical connector, if equipped with anti-lock braking system.
8. Remove clutch release cylinder.
9. Remove starter attaching bolts, then the starter.
10. Raise transmission enough to remove weight from rear support using a suitable jack.
11. Remove engine rear mount, then the transmission attaching bolts and flywheel housing under cover.
12. Lower transmission from vehicle.
13. Reverse procedure to install.

1983–86 TERCEL & 1987 TERCEL WAGON EXC. 4 X 4 MODELS

Steps 1 through 9 allow separation of transmission case from differential. If differential requires replacement, refer to step 10 for procedure.

1. Disconnect battery ground cable and drain coolant system.
2. Disconnect upper radiator hose from engine, then remove air cleaner inlet duct.
3. Disconnect steering column intermediate shaft, then drain transaxle oil.
4. Disconnect exhaust pipe from manifold. Disconnect gear shift control rod and shift lever housing rod.
5. Disconnect speedometer cable and back-up lamp electrical connector.
6. Support transmission with suitable jack, then remove rear support.
7. Remove transmission case to differential attaching bolts.
8. Install four 8 mm x 1.25 mm bolts into four equidistant bolt holes on differential side, then install four of the bolts removed in step 7 into same holes on

transmission case side. Tighten bolts equally until snug.

9. Separate transmission case from differential by carefully tightening bolts on the transmission case side, then remove transmission case.
10. If necessary, remove differential from vehicle as follows:
    a. Support engine, then disconnect clutch cable and remove starter.
    b. Remove upper differential housing to engine attaching bolts, then remove both driveshafts.
    c. Remove stiffener plate, if applicable, then the lower differential housing to engine attaching bolts.
    d. Lower differential and remove from vehicle.
11. Reverse procedure to install. Lubricate input shaft with suitable grease before installing transmission case. Torque transmission case to differential attaching bolts to 8-11 ft. lbs., and differential housing to engine attaching bolts to 37-57 ft. lbs.

1983–86 TERCEL & 1987 TERCEL WAGON 4 X 4 MODELS

Steps 1 through 10 allow separation of transmission case from differential. If differential requires replacement, refer to step 11 for procedure.

1. Remove battery ground cable.
2. Drain radiator upper tank, then remove upper radiator hose.
3. Remove air cleaner inlet duct.
4. Remove console, then using a suitable pair of long nose pliers, remove snap ring retaining shift lever, then remove shift lever.
5. Raise and support vehicle, then drain transmission lubricant.
6. Disconnect 4 wheel drive control linkage.
7. Scribe alignment marks, then remove rear driveshaft.
8. Remove exhaust pipe to manifold bolts, then remove exhaust clamp from transaxle.
9. Disconnect speedometer cable and back-up light switch wiring.
10. Separate transmission case from differential by using the following steps:
    a. Remove transmission case to differential attaching bolts.
    b. Install four 8 mm x 1.25 mm bolts into four equidistant bolt holes on differential side, then install four of the bolts removed in step 7 into same holes on transmission case side. Tighten bolts equally until snug.
    c. Separate transmission case from differential by carefully tightening bolts on the transmission case side, then remove transmission case.
11. If necessary, remove differential from vehicle as follows:
    a. Support engine, then disconnect clutch cable and remove starter.
    b. Remove upper differential housing to engine attaching bolts, then remove both driveshafts.
    c. Remove stiffener plate, if applicable, and 4 x 4 link, then the lower differential housing to engine attaching bolts.
    d. Lower differential and remove from vehicle.
12. Reverse procedure to install. Lubricate input shaft with suitable grease before installing transmission case. Torque transmission case to differential attaching bolts to 18 ft. lbs., and differential housing to engine attaching bolts to 37-57 ft. lbs.

1987 TERCEL SEDAN

1. On models less cruise control, disconnect battery ground cable.
2. On models with cruise control, remove battery, then the cruise control actuator with bracket.
3. Remove clutch release cylinder and tube clamp, then disconnect back-up lamp switch connector.
4. Remove clips and washers, then the control cable retainers.
5. Remove selecting bellcrank with bracket from transmission case, then the upper transaxle mounting bolts.
6. Raise and support vehicle, then remove under covers.
7. Disconnect speedometer cable, then the driveshafts.
8. Remove front and rear engine mounting brackets, then the starter attaching bolts and starter.
9. Slightly raise engine and transaxle assembly, using suitable jacks, then disconnect left engine mount.
10. Remove transaxle to engine attaching bolts, then lower left side of engine and separate transaxle from engine.

1984–87 VAN

1. Disconnect battery ground cable.
2. Raise and support vehicle, then drain transmission fluid.
3. On 2WD models, remove propeller shaft as follows:
    a. Place matchmarks on differential and propeller shaft flanges.
    b. Remove 4 attaching bolts and nuts, then disconnect propeller shaft from differential.
    c. Pull propeller shaft yoke from transmission, then insert tool No. 09325-20010 into extension housing.
4. On 4WD models, remove front and rear propeller shafts.
5. On all models, disconnect back-up lamp switch connector.
6. On 4WD models, disconnect transfer indicator switch connector.
7. On all models, disconnect speedometer cable and ground strap, then remove attaching nuts and retainers from transmission control cables.
8. Remove clutch release cylinder, then disconnect front exhaust pipe.
9. Remove starter and control cable bracket.
10. Slightly raise transmission assembly, using a suitable jack, then remove or disconnect engine rear mount.
11. Remove transmission rear mount bolts, then pull transmission assembly downward and rearward.
12. On 4WD models, separate transfer case from transmission case as follows:
    a. Remove engine rear mounting.
    b. Remove transfer case to transmission case attaching bolts, then separate transfer case from transmission case.
13. Reverse procedure to install.

DISC BRAKES SECTION

INDEX

FRONT DISC BRAKE SERVICE

1983 PICKUP W/S-16 TYPE DISC EXC. 4 WHEEL DRIVE

BRAKE PADS, REPLACE

1. Raise and support front of vehicle, then remove wheel and tire assembly.
2. Remove clips, pins, and springs, then remove brake pads and anti-squeal shims, **Fig. 1.**
3. Install pads and anti-squeal shims. Install shims so that folded portion will be facing pad and arrow mark will be facing upward. Lightly coat both sides of anti-squeal shim with anti-squeal lubricant.
4. Install springs, pins and clips.
5. Install wheel and tire assembly, then lower vehicle.

CALIPER, REPLACE

1. Remove brake pads as described under Brake Pads, Replace.
2. Disconnect brake line from caliper, then remove caliper mounting bolts and caliper, **Fig. 1.**
3. Reverse procedure to install. Bleed brake system.

DISC, REPLACE

1. Remove caliper assembly as described under "Caliper, Replace."
2. Remove hub grease cap, then remove cotter pin and castellated nut.
3. Slide disc and hub assembly off spindle.
4. Reverse procedure to install. Adjust wheel bearing and bleed brake system.

CALIPER OVERHAUL

1. Remove set ring and cylinder boot from caliper assembly, **Fig. 1.**
2. Place a suitable wooden block between pistons, then apply compressed air to brake line fitting caliper to remove pistons.
3. Remove seal rings from inside cylinder. Do not loosen bridge bolts.
4. Coat cylinder wall and seal with brake fluid, then insert seal rings into cylinder grooves.
5. Carefully push pistons into cylinders, then install cylinder boots and engage set rings.

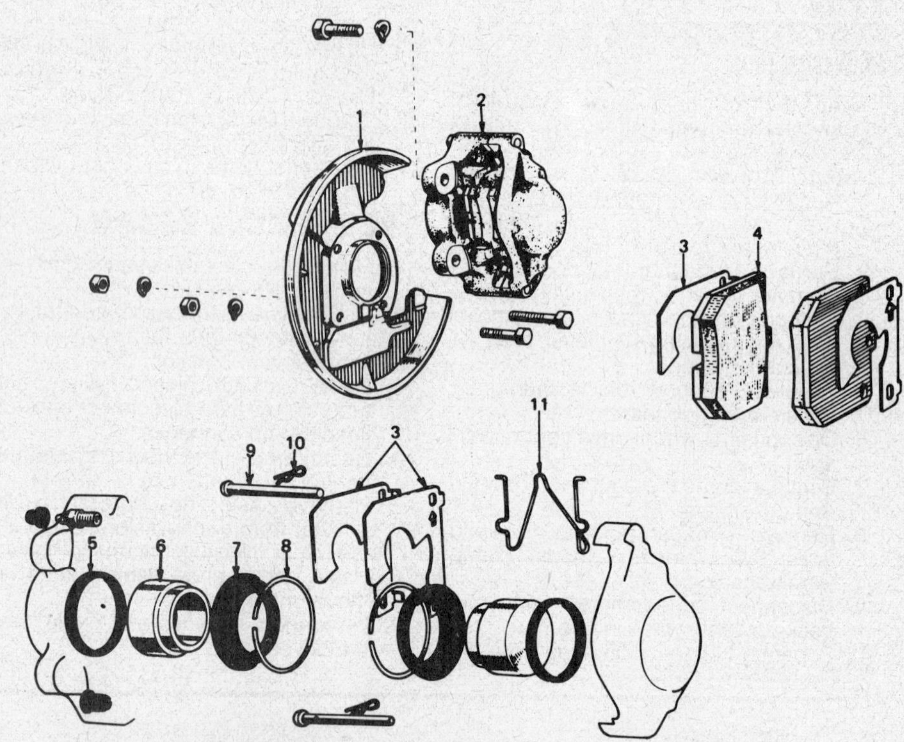

Fig. 1 S-16 type disc brake assembly. 1983 Pickup exc. 4 wheel drive

1983–84 CRESSIDA

PADS, REPLACE

1. Raise and support front of vehicle and remove wheel and tire assembly.
2. Remove lower caliper to mounting bracket retaining pin, then pivot cali-

1. Wheel
2. Brake Tube & Hose
3. Cylinder Assembly
4. Pad, Anti-squeal Shim & Pad Support Plate
5. Cylinder Mounting
6. Cylinder Boot
7. Piston
8. Piston Seal
9. Axle Hub with Disc

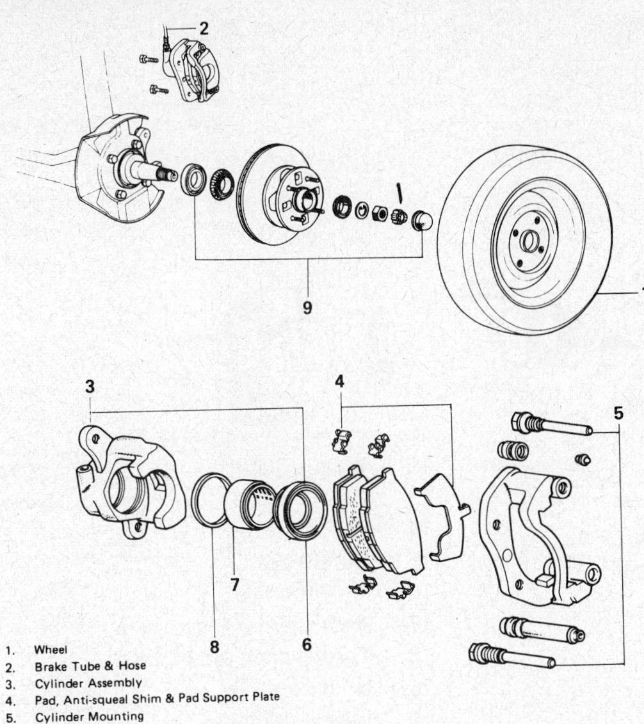

Fig. 2 Disc brake assembly. 1983–84 Cressida

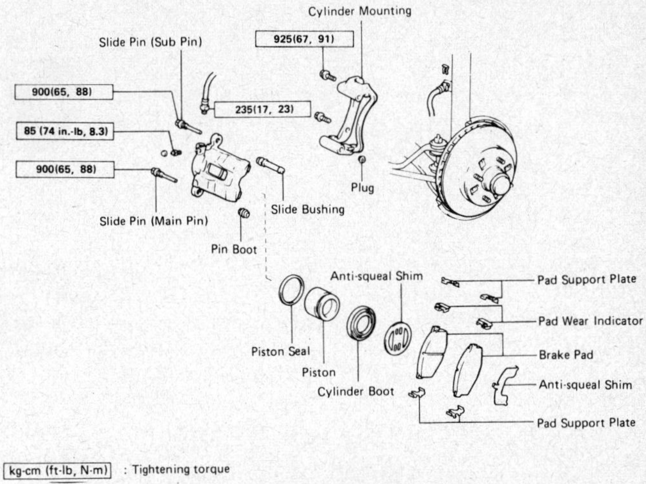

Fig. 3 Disc brake assembly. 1985–87 Cressida

per upwards.
3. Remove pads, anti-squeal shim and pad support plate.
4. Reverse procedure to install.

CALIPER, REPLACE

1. Raise and support front of vehicle and remove tire and wheel assembly.
2. Disconnect brake line from frame bracket.
3. Remove caliper from mounting bracket, **Fig. 2**, then remove pads, anti-squeal shim and pad support plate.
4. Remove caliper mounting bracket.
5. Reverse procedure to install. Bleed brake system.

DISC, REPLACE

1. Remove caliper as described under "Caliper, Replace."
2. Remove grease cap, cotter pin and locknut.
3. Remove outer wheel bearing and flat washer, then remove disc.
4. Reverse procedure to install.

CALIPER OVERHAUL

1. Remove caliper assembly as described under "Caliper, Replace."
2. Remove cylinder boot from caliper, then remove piston using compressed air.
3. Remove piston seal from caliper.
4. Reverse procedure to assemble. Bleed air from brake system.

1985–87 CRESSIDA

PADS, REPLACE

1. Raise and support vehicle and remove tire and wheel assembly.
2. Remove caliper slide pin on main pin side, **Fig. 3. Do not remove caliper slide pin on the subpin side unless necessary.**
3. Lift up caliper and suspend out of way so that brake hose is not stretched.
4. Remove pads, anti-squeal shims and the pad support plate.
5. Reverse procedure to install, torquing caliper slide pin to 65 ft. lbs.

CALIPER, REPLACE

1. Raise and support vehicle and remove wheel and tire assembly.
2. Disconnect brake hose from brake tube and caliper.
3. Remove two caliper slide pins and the caliper.
4. Remove pads, anti-squeal shim, pad support plate and pad wear indicator.
5. Reverse procedure to install. Torque caliper slide pins to 65 ft. lbs., the brake hose to 17 ft. lbs., and the brake tube to 11 ft. lbs., then bleed brakes.

DISC, REPLACE

1. Remove caliper as previously described.
2. Remove caliper mounting from knuckle.
3. Remove axle hub.
4. Remove disc from axle hub.
5. Reverse procedure to install, torquing disc attaching bolts to 47 ft. lbs.

CALIPER OVERHAUL

1. Remove caliper as previously described.
2. Using compressed air, remove piston from caliper, keeping fingers clear of piston.
3. Remove piston seal from caliper.
4. Apply lithium soap base glycol grease to piston and caliper, caliper boot and piston seal, slide pin, inner surface of mounting main pin and boot groove, outer surface of pin boot, sliding bushing and pin boot.
5. Install piston seal in caliper.
6. Install piston and caliper boot as follows:
   a. Install caliper boot in piston.
   b. Install caliper boot ridge into caliper groove.
   c. Push in piston.
   d. Install caliper boot ridge into piston groove.
7. Install pin boot on main pin side.
8. Using plastic bar, install caliper slide bushing on subpin side.

1983 COROLLA

The anti-squeal shims on 1983 Corolla models have been modified to reduce brake pad wear and noise. Refer to Fig. 4 for modification.

PADS, REPLACE

1. Raise and support front of vehicle, then remove wheel and tire assembly.
2. Remove pad protectors and anti rattle springs, **Fig. 5.**
3. Remove pins, then lift out brake pads.
4. Reverse procedure to install.

CALIPER, REPLACE

1. Remove brake pads as described under "Brake Pads, Replace."
2. Disconnect brake line from caliper, cap line and caliper fitting.
3. Remove caliper mounting bolts and caliper assembly, **Fig. 5.**
4. Reverse procedure to install. Bleed brake system.

DISC, REPLACE

1. Remove caliper assembly as described under "Caliper, Replace."
2. Remove hub grease cap, cotter pin and castellated nut.

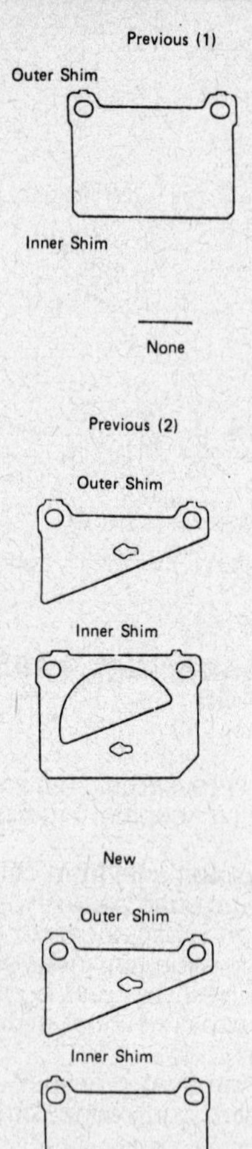

Fig. 4 Modified anti-squeal shims. 1983 Corolla

1	Caliper assy	12	Torque plate
2	Disc brake cover assy	13	Pad
3	Hole plug	14	Pad protector
4	Torque plate pin cap	15	Outer body
5	Cylinder body	16	Pin with hole
6	Dust seal	17	Anti-rattle spring
7	Dust seal retainer	18	Torque plate pin bushing
8	Piston seal	19	Bridge bolt
9	Piston	20	Bleeder plug
10	Cylinder boot	21	Bleeder plug cap
11	Ring		

Fig. 5 Disc brake assembly. 1983 Corolla

3. Reverse procedure to install. Bleed brake system and adjust wheel bearings.

CALIPER OVERHAUL

1. Loosen two bridge bolts, then separate cylinder body from outer body, then pull torque plate, **Fig. 5.**
2. Remove ring and dust boot. Apply compressed air to caliper brake line fitting to remove piston.
3. Remove piston seal, bushings, hole plugs, retainers and dust seals from cylinder.
4. Install dust seals, retainer and bushings into cylinder body.
5. Coat cylinder bore and piston seal with clean brake fluid, then install piston seal in cylinder and carefully push piston in by hand.
6. Install dust boot and ring.
7. Insert torque plate pins into cylinder body. Torque plate can be inserted smoothly if pin cap hole plug is removed before hand. After inserting, check to ensure that torque plate slides smoothly.
8. Apply castor oil or alcohol to bridge bolts and bolt on outer body. Install and torque bolts to 57.9-68.7 ft. lbs. (8-9.5 kg-cm).

1983–87 TERCEL & 1983–84 STARLET

PADS, REPLACE

1. Raise and support front of vehicle, then remove wheel and tire assembly.
2. Remove two caliper mounting bolts, then remove caliper. **Do not allow caliper to hang by brake hose.**
3. Remove inner pad, then remove outer pad and anti-squeal shim, **Figs. 6 and 7.**
4. Remove anti-rattle spring and pad guide plate.
5. Remove pad support plate and anti-squeal shim.
6. Reverse procedure to install.

CALIPER, REPLACE

1. Raise and support front of vehicle, then remove wheel and tire assembly.
2. Disconnect brake hydraulic line from frame bracket and from caliper using suitable wrench.
3. Remove caliper mounting bolts, then the caliper.
4. Reverse procedure to install and bleed brake system.

DISC, REPLACE

Tercel Models

1. Raise and support vehicle, then remove tire and wheel assembly.
2. Remove caliper assembly and torque plate.
3. Lift brake disc from hub assembly.
4. Reverse procedure to install. Torque wheel lug nuts to 65 ft. lbs.

Starlet Models

1. Remove caliper assembly as described under "Caliper, Replace."
2. Remove hub grease cap, then remove cotter pin, locknut and adjusting nut.
3. Slide disc and hub assembly off spindle.
4. Reverse procedure to install. Adjust wheel bearings and bleed brake system.

CALIPER OVERHAUL

1. Remove caliper as described under "Caliper, Replace."
2. Remove anti-squeal shim and cylinder boot set ring, **Figs. 6 and 7.**
3. Remove cylinder boot, then remove piston using compressed air.
4. Remove piston seal, caliper sliding bolt, dust boot, collar and union.
5. Install union onto caliper and torque to 19-26 ft. lbs. (2.7-3.5 kg-m).
6. Apply rubber grease to piston seal, then install piston seal onto piston.
7. Apply rubber grease to piston, then install piston into caliper.
8. Install cylinder boot and set ring, then lubricate collar and dust boot and assemble onto caliper.
9. Install caliper sliding bolt and anti-squeal shim.

1983 PICKUP W/K TYPE DISC EXC. 4 WHEEL DRIVE

PADS, REPLACE

1. Raise and support front of vehicle,

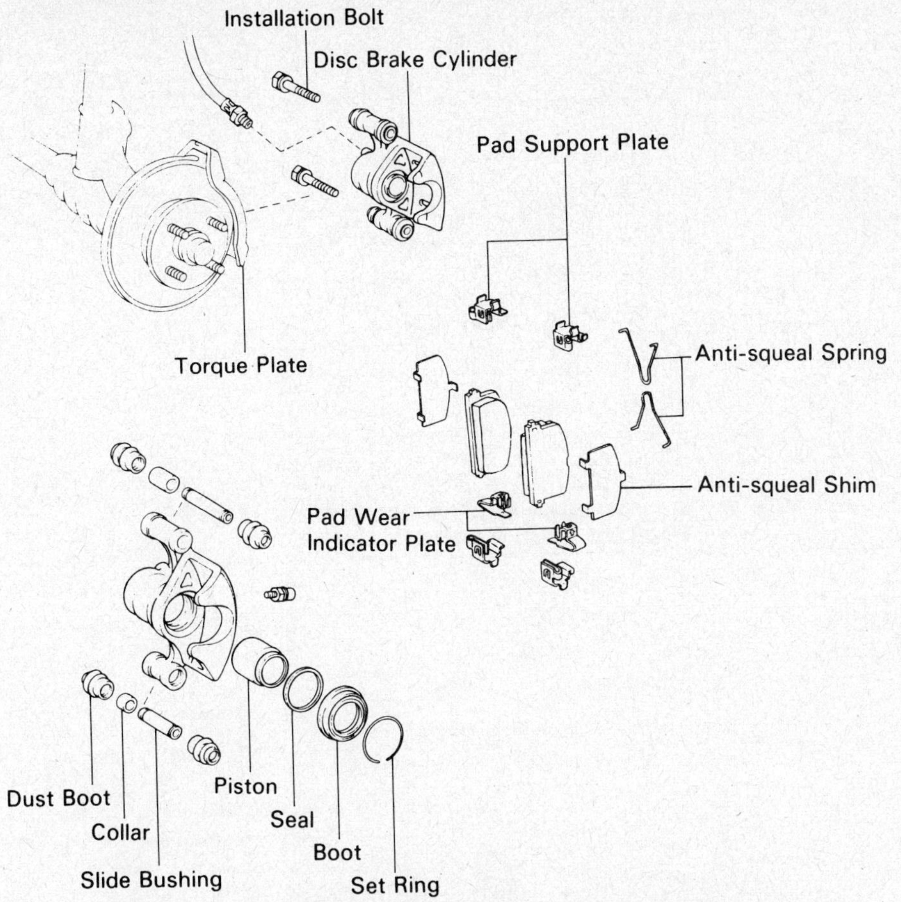

Fig. 6 Disc Brake assembly. 1983–87 Tercel

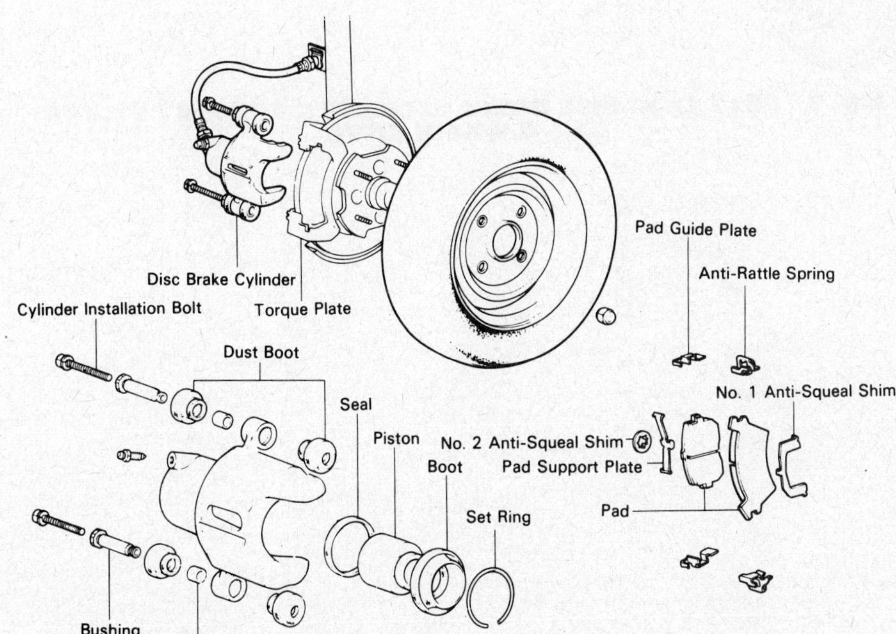

Fig. 7 Disc brake assembly. 1983–84 Starlet

then remove tire and wheel assembly.

2. Remove caliper guide plate, support spring and pad support plate, **Fig. 8.**
3. Remove caliper retaining bolt, then the caliper. **Do not allow caliper to hang by brake hose.**
4. Remove anti-rattle spring.
5. Remove outer pad, anti-squeal shim, inner pad and anti-squeal shim.
6. Reverse procedure to install.

CALIPER, REPLACE

1. Raise and support front of vehicle, then remove tire and wheel assembly.
2. Disconnect brake hydraulic line at frame bracket, then at caliper.
3. Remove cylinder guide plate, support spring and pad support plate.
4. Remove caliper retaining bolts, then the caliper.
5. Reverse procedure to install.

DISC, REPLACE

1. Remove caliper as described under "Caliper, Replace."
2. Remove grease cap, cotter pin, lock-nut and washer, then remove disc from vehicle.
3. Reverse procedure to install.

CALIPER, OVERHAUL

1. Remove caliper as described under "Caliper, Replace."
2. Remove anti-rattle spring, anti-squeal shim, outer pad, and inner pad, **Fig. 8.**
3. Remove dust boot, then remove piston using compressed air.
4. Remove piston seal.
5. Lubricate piston, seal and dust boot with rubber grease, then reverse procedure to assemble.

1984–87 PICKUP W/FS17 TYPE DISC EXC. 4 WHEEL DRIVE

PADS, REPLACE

1. Check that pad thickness is no less than .039 inch. Replace pads if thinner.
2. Raise and support vehicle and remove front wheel.
3. Remove caliper pin on subpin side, **Fig. 9.**
4. Pivot caliper up and support, leaving brake hose connected.
5. Remove brake pads, anti-squeal shim and 4 support plates.
6. Reverse procedure to install.

CALIPER, REPLACE

1. Raise and support vehicle and remove front wheel.
2. Disconnect brake hose and use suitable container to catch brake fluid.
3. Remove bracket from caliper.
4. Remove 2 slide pins and caliper.
5. Remove brake pads, anti-squeal shim, and 4 support plates.
6. If necessary, remove slide bushing and pin boots.

DISC, REPLACE

1. Remove caliper as described under "Caliper, Replace," leaving brake hose connected.
2. Remove torque plate.

3. Remove cap, cotter pin, nut lock, and nut.
4. Remove hub and disc together with outer bearing and thrust washer.
5. Remove disc from hub.
6. Reverse procedure to install. Torque disc to hub bolts 40-54 ft. lbs.

CALIPER OVERHAUL

1. Remove caliper as described under "Caliper, Replace."
2. Using screwdriver, remove cylinder boot set ring and boot.
3. Place suitable rag or block between caliper and piston. Using compressed air, remove piston.
4. Using screwdriver, remove piston seal.
5. Apply lithium soap base glycol grease to caliper boot, piston, piston seal, and both slide pins.
6. Install piston seal and piston in caliper.
7. Install caliper boot and set ring in cylinder.
8. Install pin boots to torque plate of main pin side.
9. Using a suitable driver, install slide bushing into torque plate of sub-pin side.

1985–87 PICKUP W/PD60 TYPE DISC EXC. 4 WHEEL DRIVE

PADS, REPLACE

1. Raise and support vehicle and remove tire and wheel assembly.
2. Remove caliper attaching bolts, **Fig. 10**, and the caliper, supporting caliper out of way so that brake hose is not stretched.
3. Remove two anti-rattle springs, brake pads, anti-squeal shims and the four support plates.
4. Reverse procedure to install, torquing caliper mounting bolts to 29 ft. lbs.

CALIPER, REPLACE

1. Raise and support vehicle and remove tire and wheel assembly.
2. Disconnect brake line at caliper.
3. Remove bracket from caliper.
4. Remove two caliper attaching bolts and the caliper.
5. Remove anti-rattle springs, brake pads, anti-squeal shims and support plates.
6. Reverse procedure to install. Torque bracket attaching bolts to 13 ft. lbs. and the brake line to 11 ft. lbs.

DISC, REPLACE

1. Remove caliper as previously described.
2. Remove torque plate from knuckle.
3. Remove axle hub.
4. Remove disc attaching bolts and the disc.
5. Reverse procedure to install, torquing disc attaching bolts to 47 ft. lbs.

CALIPER OVERHAUL

1. Remove caliper as previously described.
2. Remove two cylinder slide bushings,

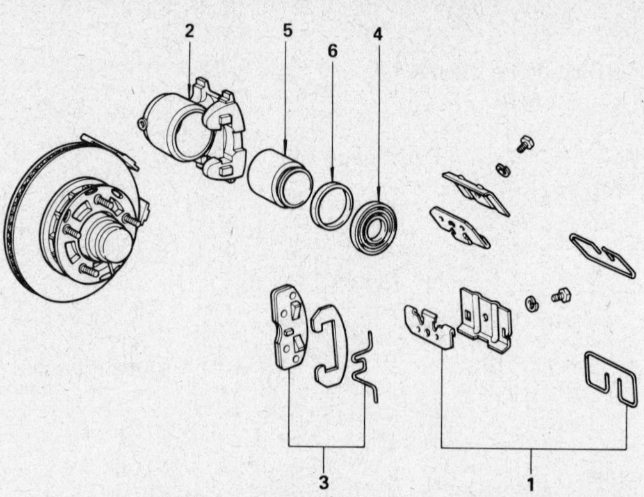

1. Cylinder Guide Plate, Support Spring & Pad Support Plate
2. Disc Brake Cylinder
3. Anti-Rattle Spring, Anti-Squeal Shim & Outer Pad
4. Dust Boot
5. Piston
6. Piston Seal

Fig. 8 K type disc brake assembly. 1983 Pickup exc. 4 wheel drive

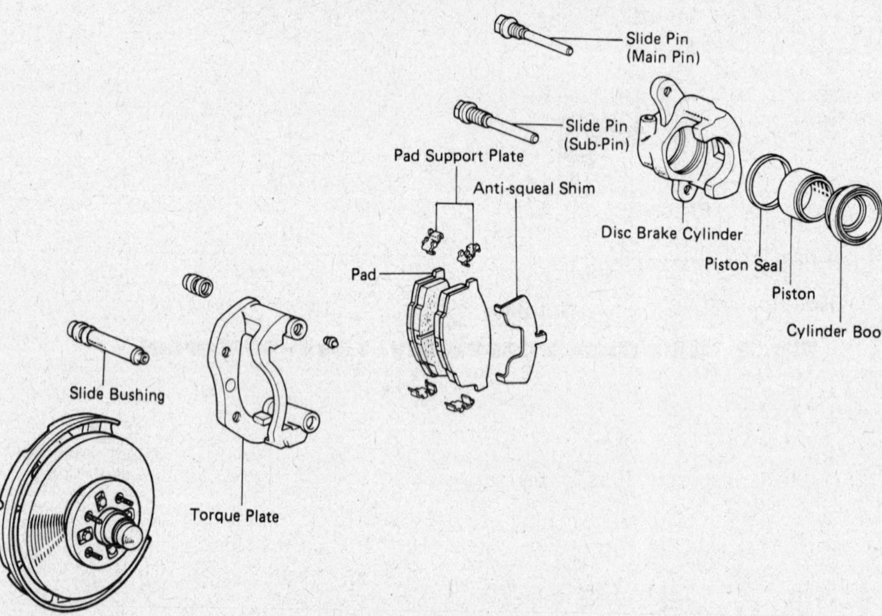

Fig. 9 FS17 type disc brake assembly. 1984–87 Pickup exc. 4 wheel drive

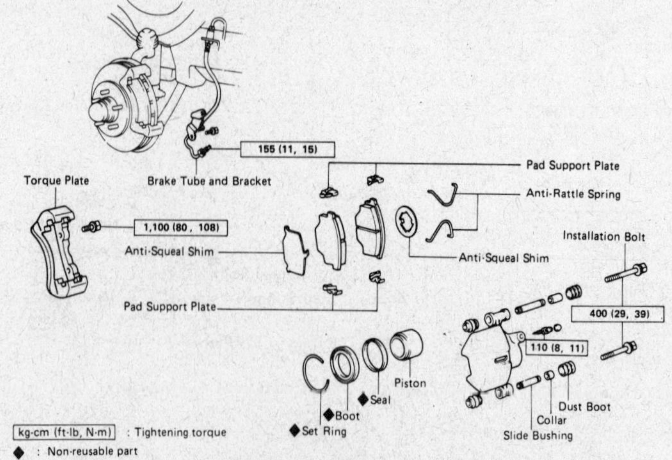

Fig. 10 PD60 type disc brake assembly. 1985–87 Pickup exc. 4 wheel drive

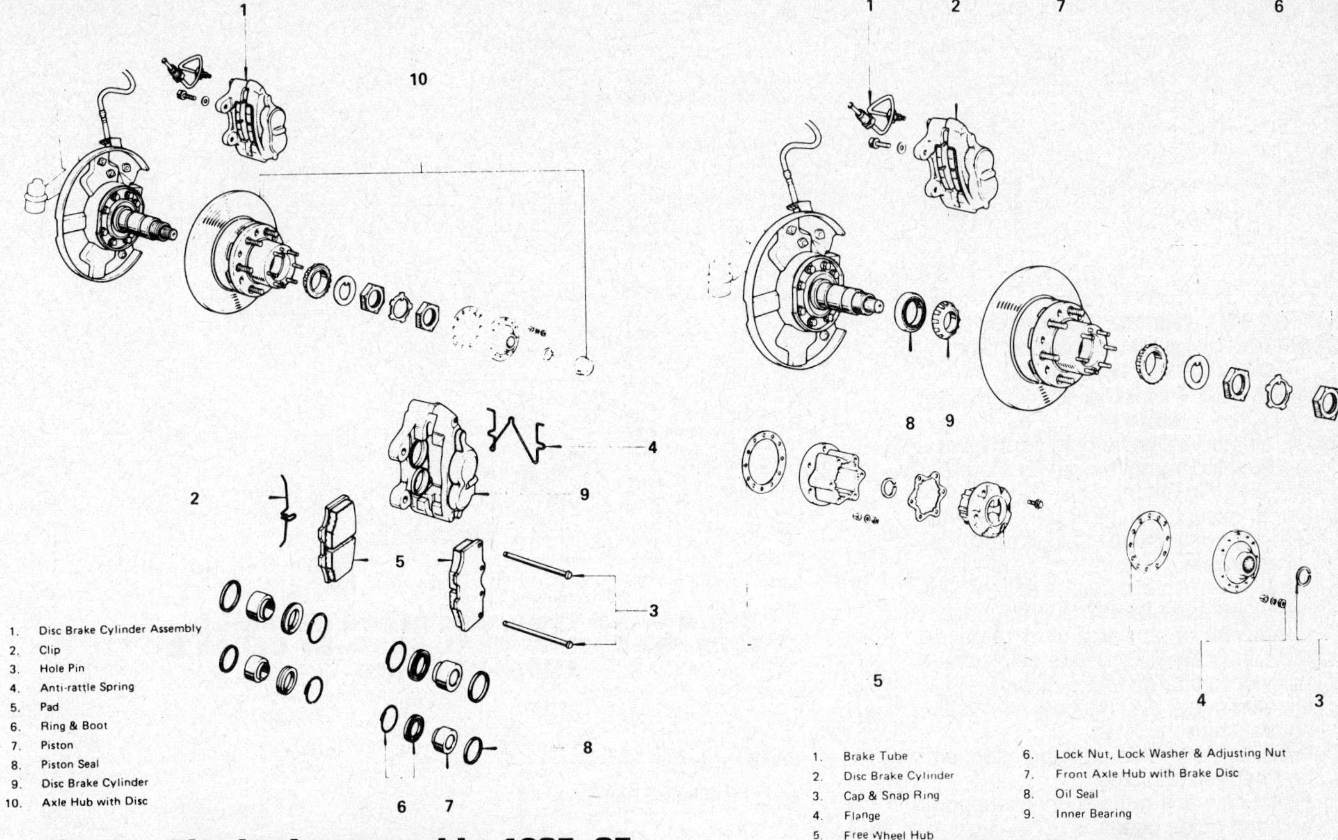

Fig. 11 Disc brake assembly. 1983–87 Pickup 4 wheel drive

Fig. 12 Removing front axle hub. 1983–87 Pickup 4 wheel drive

four dust boots and two collars.
3. Using screwdriver, remove cylinder boot set ring and boot.
4. Place a piece of cloth between piston and cylinder and, using compressed air, remove piston from cylinder.
5. Using screwdriver, remove piston seal from brake cylinder.
6. Apply lithium soap base glycol grease to all movable components.
7. Install piston seal and piston in cylinder.
8. Install cylinder boot and set ring in cylinder.
9. Install collar and dust boot in caliper, ensuring that boots are secured firmly to each brake cylinder groove.
10. Install bushing into boots, ensuring boots are secured firmly to each bushing groove.

1983–87 PICKUP 4 WHEEL DRIVE

PADS, REPLACE

1. Raise and support front of vehicle, then remove tire and wheel assembly.
2. Remove clip and hole pins, **Fig. 11.**
3. Remove anti-rattle spring, then remove brake pads.
4. Lubricate caliper housing with suitable brake grease at pad contact points.
5. Reverse procedure to install.

CALIPER, REPLACE

1. Remove pads as described under "Pads, Replace."
2. Disconnect brake hydraulic line from caliper.
3. Remove caliper retaining bolts, then the caliper.
4. Reverse procedure to install, then bleed brake system.

DISC, REPLACE

1. Remove caliper as described under "Caliper, Replace."
2. Remove cap and snap ring, **Fig. 12,** then remove cone washers with tapered punch.
3. Insert suitable length bolts into flange bolt holes, then tighten bolts evenly and remove flanges.
4. Remove free wheel hub cover and snap ring, then remove nut, spring washer and cone washer with suitable tapered punch.
5. Remove free wheel hub body and gasket.
6. Remove locknut, lock washer and adjusting nut.
7. Remove axle hub and brake disc as an assembly.
8. Remove oil seal and inner bearing from hub.
9. Reverse procedure to install. Torque adjusting nut to 43 ft. lbs. (6 kg-m), then back off nut. Retorque nut to 2.9-5.0 ft. lbs. (.4-.7 kg-m) on 1983-85 models and 18 ft. lbs. on 1986-87 models. Using spring scale attached to hub bolt, check that preload is 6.2-12.6 lbs. (2.8-5.7 kg.) on 1983 models, 2.2-8.6 lbs. (1-3.9 kg.) on 1984-85 models and 1.4-12.6 on 1986-87 models. Install lockwasher and locknut, if equipped. Torque locknut to 58-72 ft. lbs. (.4-.7 kg-m) on 1983 models, 35 ft. lbs. (450 kg-m) on 1984-87 models and recheck preload. Secure lockwasher by bending one tab inward and one tab outward.

CALIPER, OVERHAUL

1. Remove caliper as described under "Caliper, Replace."
2. Fabricate block of wood to dimensions shown in **Fig. 13.**
3. Remove snap ring and boot, **Fig. 11.**
4. Position block of wood between pistons, then remove pistons using compressed air.
5. Remove piston seals.
6. Lubricate piston and seal with suitable grease, then reverse procedure to assemble.

1984–87 COROLLA RWD, 1983–85 CELICA & 1983–1987 SUPRA

PADS, REPLACE

1. Raise and support front of vehicle, then remove tire and wheel assembly. **On late 1986 and all 1987 Supra models, temporarily install lug nuts to hold rotor in place.**
2. On late 1986 and all 1987 Supra models, remove brake hose bracket attaching bolts from steering knuckle.

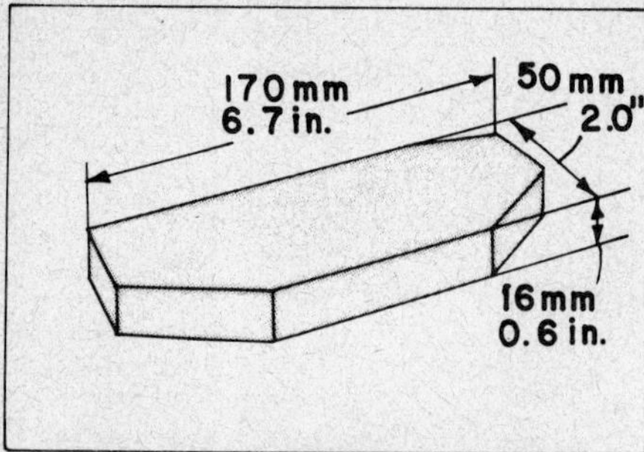

Fig. 13 Dimensions for fabricating block of wood for piston removal. 1983–87 Pickup 4 wheel drive

3. On all models, while holding the sliding bushing, remove cylinder installation bolt, **Fig. 14.**
4. On all except late 1986 and all 1987 Supra models. Rotate caliper upwards on main pin, then install a bolt into torque plate hole to secure caliper. On late 1986 and all 1987 Supra models, rotate caliper upwards and remove. Suspend caliper with wire using caution not to stretch brake hose.
5. On all models, remove pads and anti-squeal shim.
6. Remove anti-rattle springs, support and pad guide plates.
7. Install new anti-rattle springs, support and pad guide plates.
8. Siphon a small amount of fluid from master cylinder reservoir.
9. Slowly force piston into caliper bore.
10. Install new pads and anti-squeal shim. **If pads are equipped with wear indicators, install outside pad so indicator is at top side of caliper.**
11. Rotate caliper into place, then install cylinder installation bolt and torque to 12-17 ft. lbs. on all except late 1986 and all 1987 Supra models. On late 1986 and all 1987 Supra models torque bolt to 27 ft. lbs.
12. On late 1986 and all 1987 Supra models, install brake hose bracket attaching bolts. Torque attaching bolts to 14 ft. lbs.
13. On all models, fill master cylinder, then pump brake pedal until a firm pedal is obtained.

CALIPER, REPLACE

1. Disconnect brake hydraulic hose at frame bracket, then at caliper.
2. Remove caliper by following steps 1 and 2 of above procedure, then lift caliper up and pull away from torque plate main pin, **Fig. 14.**
3. Reverse procedure to install.

DISC, REPLACE

Exc. Late 1986 & All 1987 Supra Models

1. Remove caliper and torque plate as an assembly. Suspend assembly with wire.
2. Remove grease cap, cotter pin, lock cap, locknut and washer, then remove disc f rom vehicle.
3. To install, assemble disc and bearings on axle. Torque locknut to 22 ft. lbs., then seat bearings by rotating hub several times and back off nut until finger tight. Using a spring scale attached to hub stud, measure and record rotation frictional force of oil seal.
4. Tighten hub locknut until hub preload is .8-1.9 lbs. more than measurement obtained in step 3. with spring scale, then install lock cap, cotter pin and grease cap.
5. Install caliper and torque plate. Torque mount bolts to 44-57 ft. lbs.

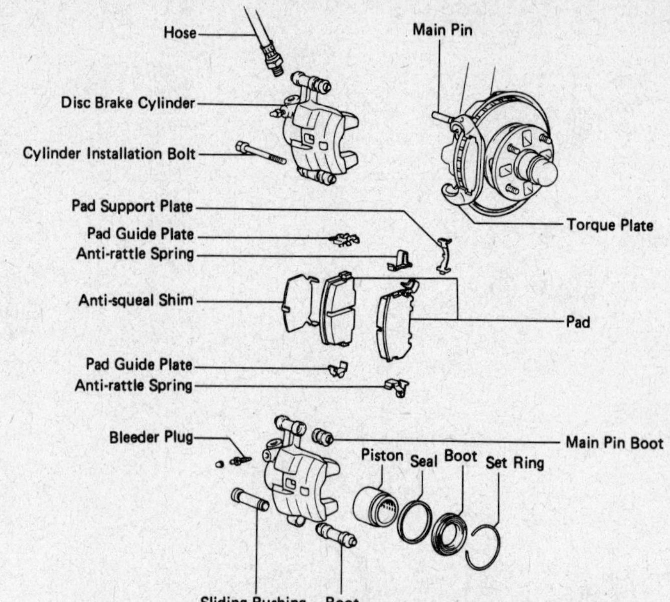

Fig. 14 AD type disc brake assembly. 1984–87 Corolla RWD, 1983–87 Celica & 1983–87 Supra

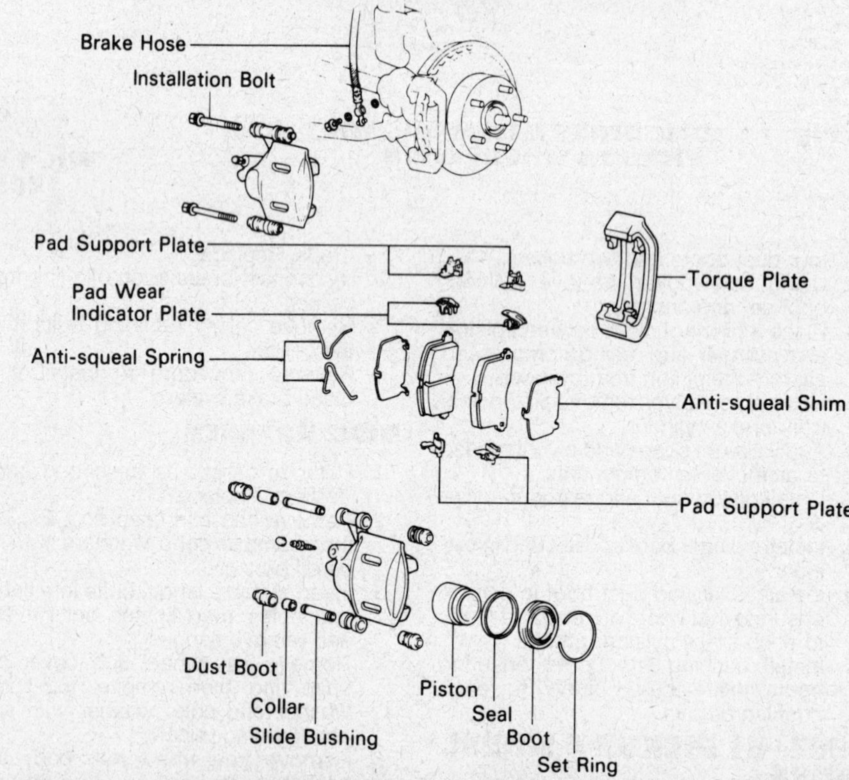

Fig. 15 Disc brake assembly. 1983–87 Camry, 1986–87 Celica & 1984–87 Corolla FWD

Late 1986 & All 1987 Supra Models

1. Raise and support front of vehicle, then remove tire and wheel assembly.
2. Remove speed sensor from steering knuckle (if equipped).
3. Remove brake hose bracket from steering knuckle.
4. Remove brake caliper and suspend with wire.
5. Scribe alignment marks between disc

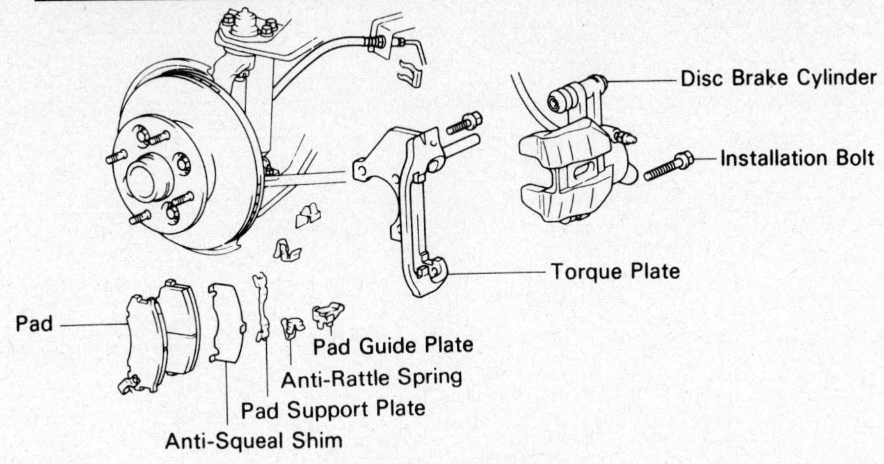

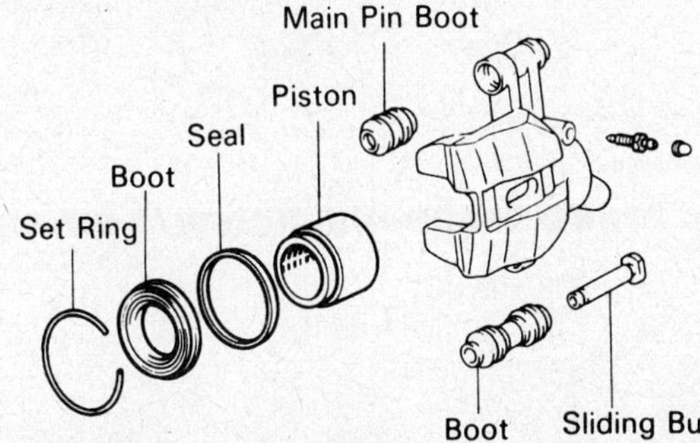

Fig. 16 Disc brake assembly. Van exc. 4 wheel drive models

and hub, then remove rotor.
6. Reverse procedure to install.

CALIPER, OVERHAUL

1. Remove caliper as described under "Caliper, Replace."
2. Remove pads, anti-squeal shims, anti-rattle springs, support and pad guide plates.
3. Remove sliding bushing and boot, **Fig. 14.**
4. Using a suitable chisel and hammer, remove main pin boot.
5. Remove piston using compressed air. **When using compressed air to remove piston, keep fingers clear of piston to avoid injury.**
6. Remove caliper boot, set ring and piston seal from caliper.
7. Lubricate main pin boot, sliding pin and boot, piston seal and boot and dust boot with suitable brake lubricant.
8. Install piston seal and piston in caliper.
9. Install cylinder boot and seat in caliper.
10. Using a 21 mm socket, press in main pin boot, then install dust and sliding bushing.
11. Install caliper.

1983–87 CAMRY, 1986–87 CELICA & 1984–87 COROLLA FWD

PADS, REPLACE

1. Remove front wheel and reinstall lug nuts to locate disc temporarily.
2. Check that brake pad thickness is at least .039 inch (1 mm). Replace pads if too thin.
3. Remove caliper from torque plate and suspend so brake hose is not under tension. Do not disconnect brake hose.
4. Refer to **Fig. 15,** and remove the following components:
   a. Brake pads.
   b. Anti-squeal shims.
   c. Pad wear indicator plates.
   d. Support plates.
   e. Anti-squeal springs.
5. Install new pad support plates.
6. Install new pad wear indicator plates on each pad with arrow pointing in direction of disc rotation.
7. Install new anti-squeal shims on each pad.
8. Install each brake pad on to each support plate.
9. Install anti-squeal springs.
10. Siphon out a small amount of brake fluid from reservoir and press caliper piston in with hammer handle. Change one brake pad at a time to prevent chance of opposite piston from flying out.
11. Install caliper taking care not to wedge dust boot. Torque attaching bolts to 18 ft. lbs. on all except 1987 Camry. On 1987 Camry, torque attaching bolts to 29 ft. lbs.
12. Install wheel and check that brake fluid level is at MAX line.

CALIPER, REPLACE

1. Raise and support vehicle and remove front wheel.
2. Remove union bolt and disconnect brake hose. Use suitable container to catch brake fluid.
3. Remove bolts and remove caliper, **Fig. 15.**
4. Remove anti-squeal shims and brake pad wear indicator plates.
5. Remove support plates.
6. Reverse procedure to install.

DISC, REPLACE

1. Remove caliper as described under "Caliper, Replace."
2. Scribe alignment marks between brake disc and hub, then remove disc.
3. Reverse procedure to install.

CALIPER OVERHAUL

1. Remove caliper as described under "Caliper, Replace."
2. Remove the following parts:
   a. Caliper slide bushings.
   b. Dust boots.
   c. Collars.
3. Using screwdriver, remove caliper boot set ring and boot.
4. Place suitable rag between caliper and piston and using compressed air, remove piston.
5. Using screwdriver, remove piston seal.
6. Apply suitable lubricant to following parts: boot, piston seal, piston, slide bushing, collar, and dust boot.
7. Install piston seal and piston in caliper.
8. Install caliper boot and set ring in caliper.
9. Install collar and dust boots in caliper.
10. Check that boots are firmly seated in caliper grooves.
11. Install bushing into boots.
12. Check that boots are firmly secured to each bushing groove.

1984–87 VAN

PADS, REPLACE

Exc. 4 Wheel Drive Models

1. Hold sliding bushing and remove installation bolt, **Fig. 16.**
2. Tilt caliper up and insert bolt into torque plate hole to secure caliper.
3. Remove anti-rattle springs, pads, and anti-squeal shims.
4. Remove anti-rattle springs, pad guide plates, and support plate.
5. Install new pad support plate, new pad guide plates, and new anti-rattle springs.
6. Install new pads on to each spring or shim. Install outside pad so wear indicator is at lower side.
7. Install anti-squeal shim toward back side of inside pad.
8. Lower caliper over pads taking care that boot is not wedged.
9. Torque installation bolt to 14 ft. lbs.

4 Wheel Drive Models

1. Raise and support front of vehicle.
2. Look through pad inspection holes in caliper. Ensure lining thickness is at least .118 inch (3.0 mm) thick. If not, pads must be replaced.
3. While holding sliding bushing, remove caliper attaching bolt, **Fig. 17.** Rotate

caliper upwards and install suitable bolt into torque plate to secure caliper.
4. Remove pads and anti-squeal shims, then the anti-rattle springs and pad guide plates.
5. Install replacement pad support plates, pad guide plates and anti-rattle springs.
6. Install pads, then anti-squeal shims.
7. Remove bolt supporting caliper, then lower caliper onto rotor. **Use caution not to pinch or wedge dust boot.**
8. Install caliper attaching bolt. Torque bolt to 27 ft. lbs.

CALIPER, REPLACE

1. Raise and support vehicle. Remove wheel.
2. Disconnect brake line. Use suitable container to catch brake fluid.
3. Remove caliper installation bolt.
4. Remove caliper from main pin of torque plate.
5. Remove following parts: anti-squeal shim, brake pad, anti-rattle spring, pad guide plate and pad support plate.
6. Reverse procedure to install.

DISC, REPLACE

Exc. 4 Wheel Drive Models

1. Remove caliper and torque plate as an assembly.
2. Remove grease cap, cotter pin and locknut.
3. Remove outer wheel bearing and flat washer, then remove disc.
4. To install, assemble disc and bearings on axle. Torque locknut 21 ft. lbs., then seat bearings by rotating hub several times and back off nut until finger tight. Using a spring scale attached to hub stud, measure and record rotation frictional force of oil seal.
5. Tighten hub locknut until starting hub preload is .8-1.9 lbs. more than measurement obtained in step 4 with spring scale, then install lock cap, cotter pin and grease cap.
6. Install caliper and torque plate assembly. Torque mount bolts to 77 ft. lbs.

4 Wheel Drive Models

1. Remove caliper and torque plate as an assembly. Suspend caliper assembly aside with suitable wire. **Leave brake hose attached.**
2. Remove hub cap from hub flange, then the bolt from end of axle shaft. Remove hub attaching nuts, then using brass drift and hammer, remove cone washers from hub.
3. Install suitable bolts into hub flange, then tighten evenly to remove flange.
4. Remove locknut (if equipped), then lock washer. Using suitable socket, remove hub attaching nut, then the disc, hub and bearings.
5. Install hub, bearings and disc assembly, then the outer bearing and nut. Torque nut to 43 ft. lbs., and rotate hub several turns in either direction to seat bearings.
6. Back off hub nut until finger tight, then torque to 11 ft. lbs. Using suitable spring scale attached to wheel stud, measure preload. Preload should be

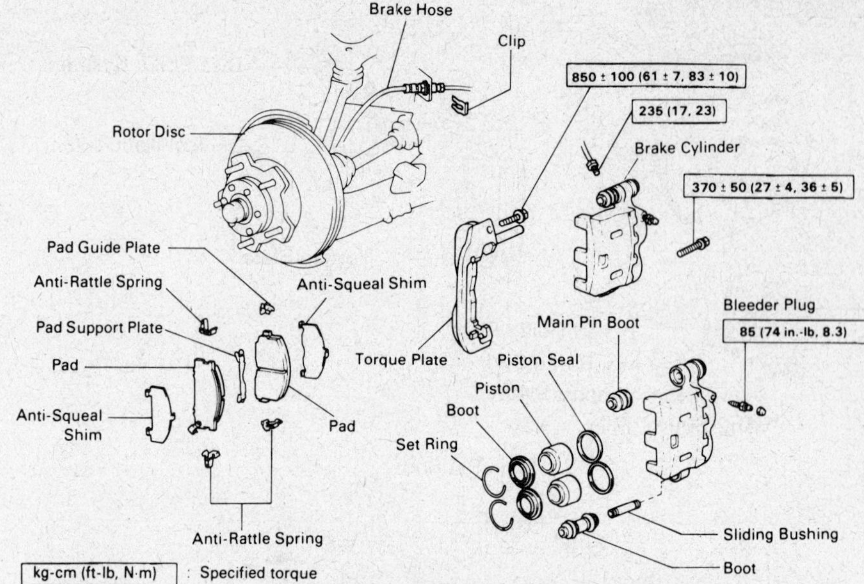

Fig. 17 Disc brake assembly. Van w/4 wheel drive

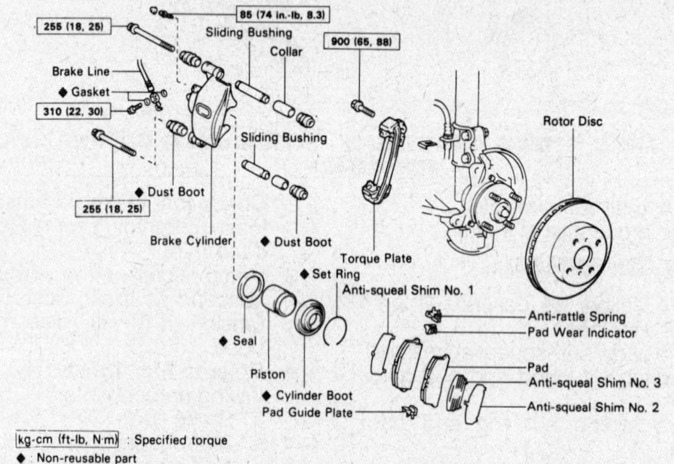

Fig. 18 Disc brake assembly. MR2

4.6-7.9 lbs.
7. Install lock washer and locknut (if equipped). Torque locknut to 35 ft. lbs. and measure preload as described in step 6. If preload is satisfactory, bend over lock washer. If preload is not satisfactory, adjust as necessary and bend over lock washer.
8. Install bolt into end of axle shaft. Torque to 13 ft. lbs.
9. Install hub, then caliper and torque plate assembly. Tighten torque plate attaching bolts to 83 ft. lbs.

CALIPER OVERHAUL

Exc. 4 Wheel Drive Models

1. Remove caliper as described under "Caliper, Replace."
2. Remove sliding bushing and boot.
3. Remove main pin boot.
4. Using compressed air, remove piston from caliper.
5. Remove caliper boot and set ring from caliper.
6. Reverse procedure to assemble. Bleed air from brake system.

4 Wheel Drive Models

1. Remove caliper as described under "Caliper, Replace."
2. Using hammer and chisel, remove main pin boot.
3. Remove caliper set rings, then using compressed air, remove pistons from caliper bores. **When removing pistons, ensure fingers are clear of pistons.**
4. Remove boots from pistons, then using soft edged tool, seals from caliper bores.
5. Reverse procedure to install. Apply suitable lithium soap based glycol grease to main pin boot, sliding bushing, sliding bushing boot, piston seals, pistons and cylinder boots prior to assembly.

1985–87 MR2

PADS, REPLACE

1. Raise and support vehicle and re-

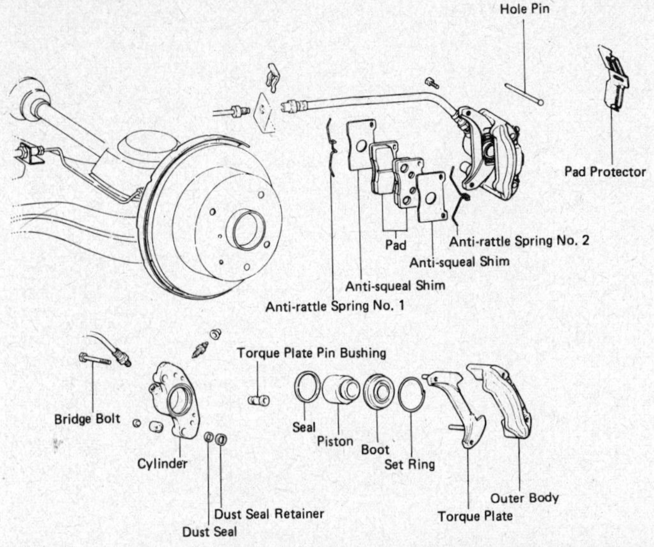

Fig. 19 Rear disc brake caliper assembly. 1983–84 Cressida (if equipped)

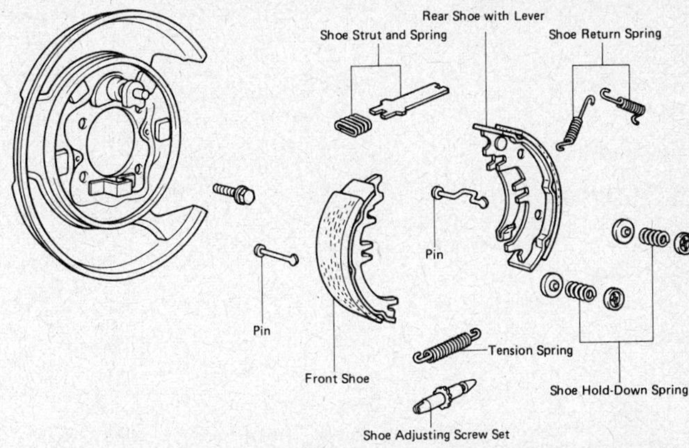

Fig. 20 Rear disc brake parking brake assembly. 1983–87 Supra, 1983–84 Cressida & 1984–87 Celica (if equipped)

move wheel and tire assembly.
2. Reinstall two wheel lug nuts to retain disc.
3. Remove two attaching bolts and the caliper from the torque plate, **Fig. 18.**
4. Remove brake pads, anti-squeal shims, pad wear indicator plates and support plates.
5. Reverse procedure to install, torquing caliper attaching bolts to 18 ft. lbs.

CALIPER, REPLACE

1. Raise and support vehicle and remove wheel and tire assembly.
2. Remove union bolt and disconnect brake line.
3. Remove two attaching bolts and the caliper from torque plate.
4. Remove brake pads, anti-squeal shims, pad wear indicator plates and support plates.
5. Reverse procedure to install, torquing union bolt to 22 ft. lbs.

DISC, REPLACE

1. Remove caliper as previously described.
2. Remove torque plate from knuckle.
3. Remove disc from knuckle.
4. Reverse procedure to install, torquing torque plate attaching bolts to 65 ft. lbs.

CALIPER OVERHAUL

1. Remove caliper as previously described.
2. Remove two caliper sliding bushings, four dust boots and two collars.
3. Using screwdriver, remove cylinder boot set ring and the cylinder boot.
4. Place a piece of cloth between piston and cylinder and, using compressed air, remove piston from cylinder.
5. Using a screwdriver, remove piston seal.
6. Apply lithium soap base glycol grease to all moveable parts.
7. Install piston seal and piston in cylinder.
8. Install cylinder boot and set ring in cylinder.
9. Install collar and dust boot, ensuring that boot is secured firmly to brake cylinder groove.
10. Install bushing into boot, ensuring that boot is secured firmly to bushing groove.

REAR DISC BRAKE SERVICE

1983–84 CRESSIDA

Pads, Replace

1. Raise and support rear of vehicle, then remove tire and wheel assembly.
2. Remove pad protector, **Fig. 19.**
3. Remove anti-rattle spring No. 2, **Fig. 19,** then hold anti-rattle spring No. 1 and remove lower hole pin.
4. Remove anti-rattle spring No. 1, then remove upper hole pin.
5. Remove pads and anti-squeal shims.
6. Siphon a small amount of brake fluid from master cylinder reservoir, then force caliper piston into bore.
7. Reverse procedure to install.

Caliper, Replace

1. Raise and support rear of vehicle, then remove tire and wheel assembly.
2. Disconnect brake hose from brake tube, then remove brake hose clip and disconnect brake hose from caliper.
3. Remove pad protector, anti-rattle springs, hole pins, brake pads and anti-squeal shims, **Fig. 19.**
4. Remove two caliper mounting bolts, then the caliper.

Rotor Disc, Replace

1. Remove caliper as described under "Caliper, Replace."
2. Remove rotor disc.

Caliper, Overhaul

1. Remove two bridge bolts from outer body, **Fig. 19,** then separate outer body from caliper.
2. Remove torque plate.
3. Remove cylinder boot and set ring.
4. Remove piston using compressed air. **When using air pressure to remove caliper piston, place a shop towel over the piston to prevent it from flying out.**
5. Remove piston seal from caliper bore.
6. Reverse procedure to install. Lubricate piston seal, caliper boot, piston and caliper bore with suitable rubber lube. Torque bridge bolts to 37-43 ft. lbs. **After assembly is complete, ensure torque plate slides smoothly.**
7. Torque caliper mounting bolts to 29-39 ft. lbs.

Parking Brake Shoes, Replace

1. Raise and support rear of vehicle, then remove tire and wheel assembly.
2. Remove rear caliper, refer to "Caliper, Replace."
3. Remove rotor disc.
4. Remove shoe return springs, **Fig. 20.**
5. Remove shoe strut and spring.
6. Slide front shoe from under shoe hold down spring, then remove shoe adjusting setscrew, tension spring and remove shoe.
7. Slide rear from shoe hold down spring, then disconnect parking brake cable from shoe lever.
8. Measure brake drum inside diameter. Maximum diameter is 6.61 inches.
9. Measure brake shoe lining thickness. Minimum thickness is .039 inch. If lining is less than minimum, replace brake shoes.
10. Measure clearance between rear parking brake shoe and parking brake lever. Clearance should be .0138 inch. If clearance is incorrect, replacement shims are available to provide proper clearance.
11. Apply non-melting grease on brake backing plate shoe flats, then on shoe sliding surface.
12. Lubricate adjusting setscrew with non-melting lubricant.
13. Connect parking brake lever to cable.
14. Slide rear shoe into position under shoe hold down spring, then install

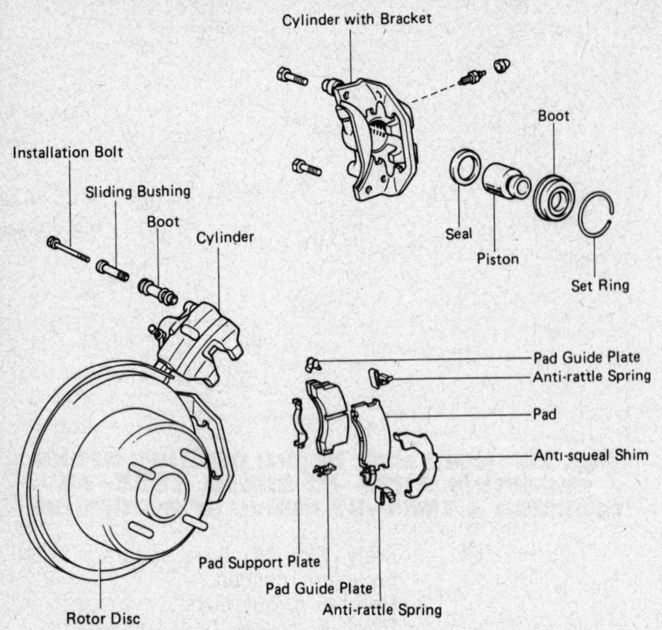

Fig. 21 Rear disc brake caliper assembly. 1983–87 Supra & 1984–87 Celica (if equipped)

Fig. 22 Rear disc brake caliper assembly. 1985–87 Corolla RWD

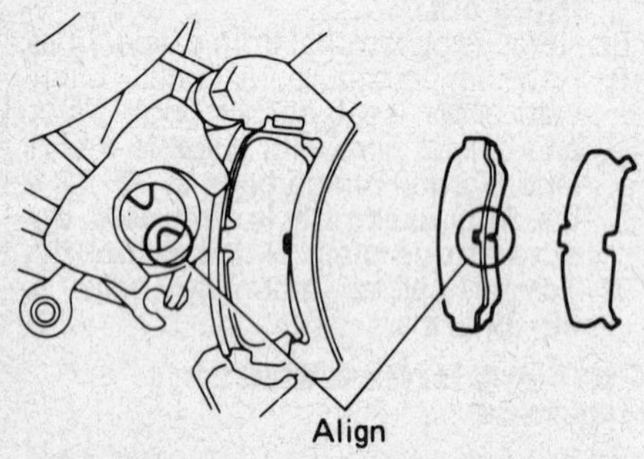

Fig. 23 Installing inboard pad. 1985–87 Corolla RWD

tension spring.
15. Install adjusting setscrew on rear shoe and partially install on front shoe.
16. Slide front shoe into position under shoe hold down spring. Ensure adjusting setscrew and tension spring are positioned properly.
17. Install front shoe return spring, then rear return spring.
18. Lightly sand brake drum inner surface, then align the service hole on disc with groove on axle shaft and install disc.
19. Install caliper, then adjust parking brake. Refer to "Parking Brake, Adjust".

1983–87 SUPRA & 1984–87 CELICA

Pads, Replace

1. Raise and support rear of vehicle, then remove tire and wheel assembly.
2. Remove caliper attaching bolts, then the caliper, **Fig. 21. Do not allow caliper to hang unsupported or damage to the brake hose may occur.**
3. Remove pads and anti-squeal shim.
4. Remove anti-rattle springs, pad guide plates and support plate.
5. Reverse procedure to install. Torque caliper attaching bolts to 14 ft. lbs.

Caliper, Replace

1. Raise and support rear of vehicle, then remove tire and wheel assembly.
2. Disconnect brake hose from brake tube and caliper using a suitable tool.
3. Remove caliper attaching bolts, then the caliper, **Fig. 21.**
4. Remove anti-squeal shim, brake pad, anti-rattle spring, pad guide plate and pad support plate.
5. Reverse procedure to install, then bleed brake system.

Rotor Disc, Replace

1. Remove caliper as described under "Caliper, Replace" procedure.
2. Remove torque plate from rear axle housing, then the rotor disc and hub attaching nuts.

Caliper Overhaul

1. Remove sliding bushing and boot, **Fig. 21.**
2. Remove main pin boot using a suitable chisel.
3. Remove piston using compressed air. **When using air pressure to remove caliper piston, place a shop towel over piston to prevent it from flying out.**
4. Remove caliper boot, set ring and piston seal from caliper.
5. Reverse procedure to install, noting the following:
   a. Apply suitable grease to the main pin boot, sliding pin and boot, piston seal and piston and dust boot.
   b. Install main pin boot using a press and suitable socket.
   c. Ensure dust boot does not fold under during installation.

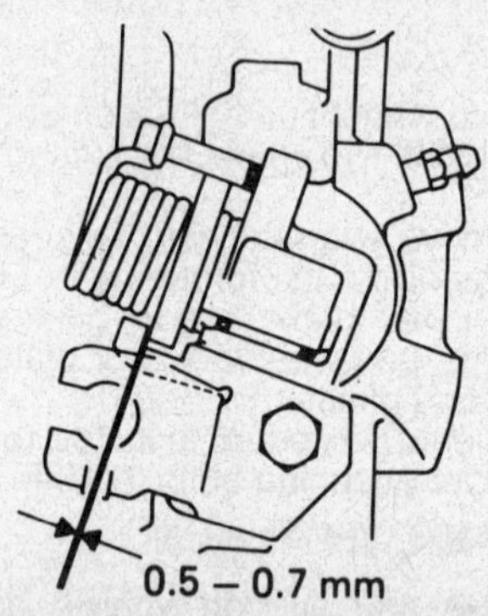

Fig. 24 Adjusting cable support bracket clearance. 1985–87 Corolla RWD

Parking Brake Shoes, Replace

Refer to "1983-84 Cressida" procedure under "Parking Brake Shoes, Replace".

1985–87 COROLLA RWD

Pads, Replace

1. Raise and support rear of vehicle, then remove tire and wheel assembly.
2. Temporarily install rotor disc with wheel attaching nuts.
3. Remove clip, cotter pin and hole pin, then pull out cable from parking brake cable bracket.
4. Remove bottom caliper attaching bolt, then lift caliper assembly, **Fig. 22. Do not remove caliper from main pin.**
5. Remove brake pads, anti-squeal shims, anti-rattle springs, pad support plate and pad guide plate.
6. Reverse procedure to install, noting the following:
   a. Using a suitable tool, slowly turn and push piston clockwise until it locks in the bore.
   b. Install inboard pad as shown in **Fig. 23.**
   c. Torque caliper attaching bolt to 14 ft. lbs.

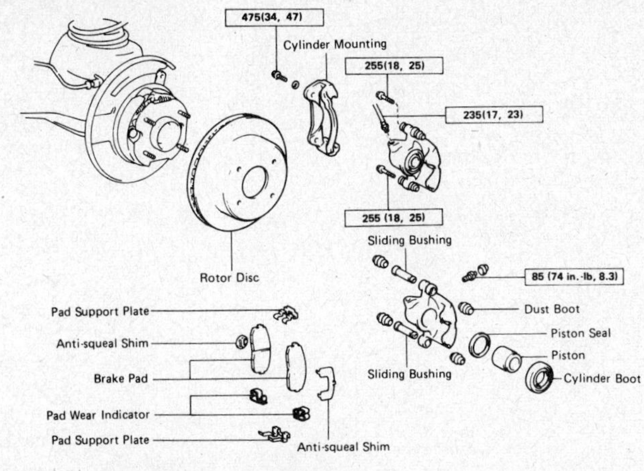

Fig. 25 Rear disc brake caliper assembly. 1985–87 Cressida

Fig. 26 Rear disc brake parking brake assembly. 1985–87 Cressida

d. Adjust parking brake automatic adjuster by fully pulling and releasing parking brake lever.

Caliper, Replace

1. Raise and support rear of vehicle, then remove tire and wheel assembly.
2. Disconnect brake hose from brake tube and caliper using a suitable tool.
3. Remove brake pads, refer to "Pads, Replace" procedure.
4. Remove main pin boot, then lift and push out caliper from main pin.
5. Reverse procedure to install, then bleed brake system.

Rotor Disc, Replace

1. Remove caliper as described under "Caliper, Replace" procedure.
2. Remove caliper mounting bracket.
3. Lift off rotor disc.

Caliper Overhaul

1. Remove sliding bushing and boot, **Fig. 22.**
2. Remove caliper boot set ring and caliper boot using a suitable screwdriver.
3. Turn piston counterclockwise using a suitable tool, then remove piston from bore.
4. Remove piston seal from cylinder using a suitable screwdriver.
5. Install tool No. 09756-00010 over adjusting nut, then tighten nut using a 14 mm socket. Use caution not to over tighten tool. **Ensure tool No. 09756-00010 is used to prevent possibility of the spring flying out, causing injury or damage to the interior surface of the cylinder.**
6. Remove snap ring from cylinder bore, then tool No. 09756-00010.
7. Remove spring retainer, spring, spring plate and stopper together with adjusting bolt. Use caution not to damage O-ring.
8. Remove strut, then the torsion spring from parking brake crank.
9. Remove parking brake crank from caliper. **Do not disassemble crank subassembly. Lever is pressure fitted to pin and should not be removed.**
10. Remove parking brake crank boot using a suitable screwdriver, if necessary.
11. Apply suitable grease to all moving parts.
12. Install parking brake crank boot in caliper, if removed.
13. Install parking brake crank in caliper. Match crank boot with groove in crank seal.
14. Install torsion spring, then ensure parking brake crank subassembly does not touch stopper pin.
15. Measure clearance of cable support bracket as shown in **Fig. 24.** If clearance is not .0197-.0275 inch (.5-.7 mm), adjust clearance with the cable support bracket attaching bolt.
16. Adjust rollers of the needle roller bearing so they do not catch on the cylinder hole, then install strut.
17. Install O-ring to adjusting bolt.
18. Assemble stopper, washer, spring and spring case to the adjusting bolt, then using tool No. 09756-00010, hand tighten adjusting bolt subassembly. **Ensure inscribed surface of stopper faces up. Also ensure notches of spring case align with notches of the stopper.**
19. Install adjusting bolt subassembly in the caliper, then the snap ring with opening toward bleeder.
20. Remove tool No. 09756-00010, then ensure adjusting bolt is in proper position.
21. Move parking brake crank by hand and ensure adjusting bolt moves smoothly.
22. Install piston seal in caliper.
23. Using a suitable tool, slowly turn and push piston clockwise until it locks in the bore.
24. Align center of piston stopper grove with the positioning protrusion of the caliper.
25. Install caliper boot and set ring in caliper.
26. Install dust boot and sliding bushing. **Ensure dust boot does not fold under during installation.**

1985–87 CRESSIDA

Pads, Replace

1. Raise and support rear of vehicle, then remove tire and wheel assembly.
2. Temporarily install rotor disc with wheel attaching nuts.
3. Remove two caliper attaching bolts, then the caliper assembly, **Fig. 25. Do not allow caliper to hang unsupported or damage to the brake hose may occur.**
4. Remove pads, anti-squeal shims and pad support plates.
5. Reverse procedure to install. Torque caliper attaching bolt to 18 ft. lbs.

Caliper, Replace

1. Raise and support rear of vehicle, then remove tire and wheel assembly.
2. Disconnect brake hose from brake tube and caliper using a suitable tool.
3. Remove caliper attaching bolts, then the caliper, **Fig. 25.**
4. Remove anti-squeal shims, brake pads with pad wear indicator, and pad support plates.
5. Reverse procedure to install, then bleed brake system.

Caliper Overhaul

1. Remove sliding bushing and boot, **Fig. 25.**
2. Remove piston using compressed air. **When using air pressure to remove caliper piston, place a shop towel over piston to prevent it from flying out.**
3. Remove caliper boot and piston seal from caliper.
4. Reverse procedure to install, noting the following:
   a. Apply suitable grease to the sliding bushing and dust boot, piston seal and piston and caliper dust boot.
   b. Ensure dust boot does not fold under during installation.

Parking Brake Shoes, Replace

1. Raise and support rear of vehicle, then remove tire and wheel assembly.
2. Remove rear caliper, refer to "Caliper, Replace" procedure.
3. Remove rotor disc, **Fig. 26.**
4. Remove shoe return springs using a suitable tool, then the shoe strut and spring.

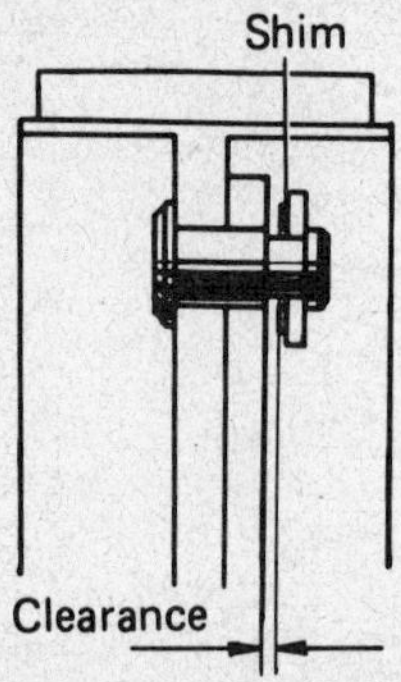

Fig. 27 Measuring clearance between parking brake shoe & lever. 1985–87 Cressida

5. Slide out front shoe, then remove shoe adjusting setscrew.
6. Remove tension spring and front shoe.
7. Slide out rear shoe, then disconnect parking brake cable from parking brake shoe lever.
8. Measure brake drum inside diameter. Maximum inside diameter should be 6.61 inch.
9. Measure brake shoe lining thickness. Minimum thickness should be .039 inch. If lining is less than minimum, replace brake shoes.
10. Measure clearance between parking brake shoe and lever, **Fig. 27.** If clearance is greater than .0138 inch, replace shim to obtain correct clearance.
11. Apply suitable grease to the backing plate, adjusting screw and sliding surfaces of the shoe.
12. Install parking brake lever to the cable.
13. Install rear shoe, tension spring, front shoe and shoe adjusting screw.
14. Install front shoe and return spring using a suitable tool.
15. Install strut and spring, then the rear shoe return spring using a suitable tool.
16. Install rotor disc, aligning groove on rear axle shaft flange and service hole on the disc, then temporarily install hub nuts.
17. Turn adjuster and expand shoes until rotor disc locks, then return adjuster eight notches.
18. Install caliper assembly and rear wheel.

1985–87 MR2 & 1986–87 COROLLA FWD

Pads, Replace

1. Raise and support vehicle and remove tire and wheel assembly.
2. Temporarily install lug nuts to restrain brake disc.
3. Remove caliper attaching bolts from torque plate, **Fig. 28.**
4. Lift caliper up out of way and suspend it. Do not remove cylinder from main pin or disconnect brake hose.
5. Remove brake pads, anti-squeal shims, anti-rattle springs, pad support plate and pad guide plate.

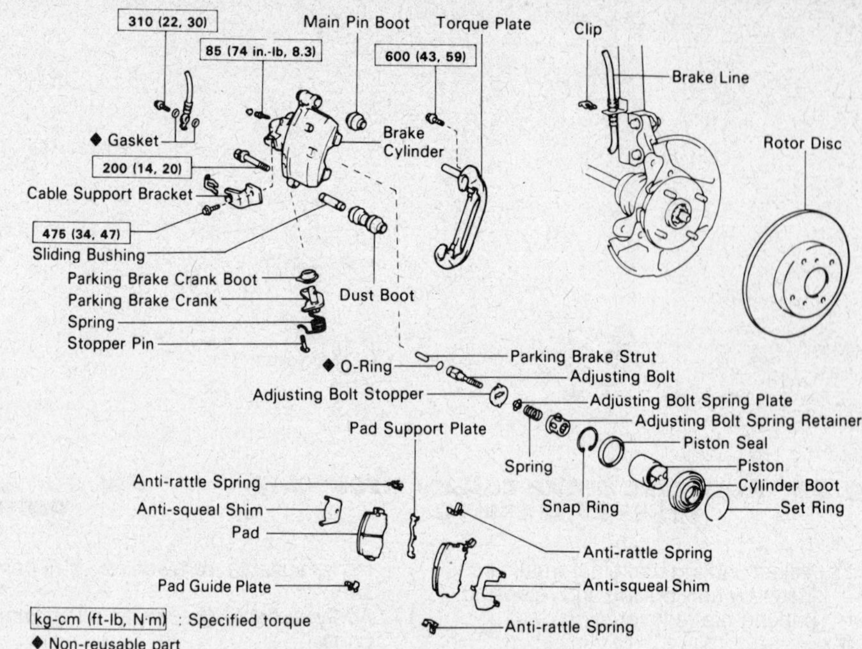

Fig. 28 Rear disc brake assembly. MR2 models (similar to 1986–87 Corolla FWD)

6. Reverse procedure to install, torquing caliper attaching bolt to 14 ft. lbs.

Caliper, Replace

1. Raise and support vehicle and remove wheel and tire assembly.
2. Remove union bolt and two gaskets and disconnect brake hose from caliper.
3. Disconnect parking brake cable as follows:
   a. Remove clip.
   b. Pull out hole pin while pushing parking brake cable.
   c. Remove retainer.
   d. Remove parking brake cable from cable support bracket.
4. Remove caliper attaching bolt and the caliper.
5. Remove brake pads, anti-squeal shims, anti-rattle springs, pad support plate and pad guide plate.
6. Reverse procedure to install, torquing brake hose union bolt to 22 ft. lbs.

Disc, Replace

1. Remove caliper as outlined under "Caliper, Replace."
2. Remove torque plate from knuckle.
3. Remove brake disc.
4. Reverse procedure to install, torquing torque plate attaching bolt to 43 ft. lbs.

Caliper Overhaul

1. Remove caliper as previously described.
2. Remove sliding bushing and boot, then the main pin boot.
3. Using screwdriver, remove cylinder boot set ring and cylinder boot.
4. Using tool 09719-14020 or equivalent, turn piston counterclockwise to remove.
5. Using screwdriver, remove piston seal.
6. Place tool 09756-00010 or equivalent onto adjusting bolt and lightly tighten bolt using 14 mm socket. **Always use tool or equivalent or spring may fly out and cause personal injury or damage interior surface of caliper. Do not tighten tool too tightly as this may damage spring retainer.**
7. Using suitable tool, remove snap ring from cylinder.
8. Pull spring retainer, spring, spring plate and stopper out of cylinder together with adjusting bolt, being careful not to damage O-ring.
9. Disassemble adjusting bolt as follows:
   a. Remove tool 09756-00010.
   b. Remove spring retainer, spring, spring plate and stopper from adjusting bolt.
   c. Remove O-ring from adjusting bolt.
10. Remove parking brake strut, then on Corolla models, the parking brake cable support bracket.
11. On all models, remove torsion spring from parking brake crank.
12. Remove parking brake crank from caliper.
13. If parking brake crank boot is to be replaced, use screwdriver to lightly tap on metal portion of boot to remove it. **If crank boot is not to be replaced, do not remove it.**
14. On MR2 models, remove cable support bracket.
15. On all models, using pin punch, tap out the stopper pin.
16. Apply lithium soap base glycol grease to all moving parts.
17. Tap stopper pin into caliper until pin extends .98 inch.
18. On MR2 models, press surface of cable support bracket flush against cylinder wall and torque bolt to 34 ft. lbs.
19. On all models, if removed, install park-

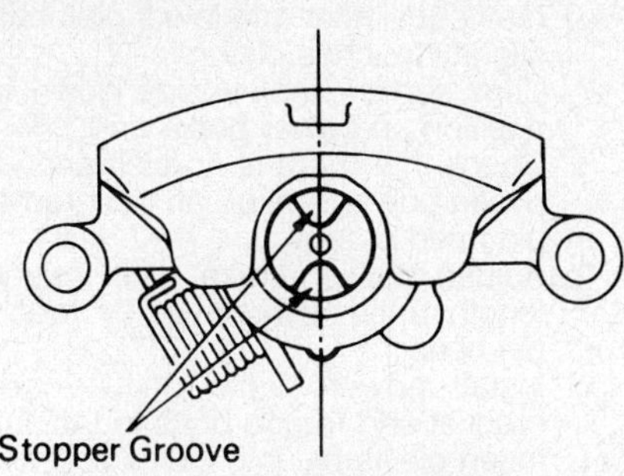

Fig. 29 Aligning piston stopper screw. MR2 & 1986–87 Corolla

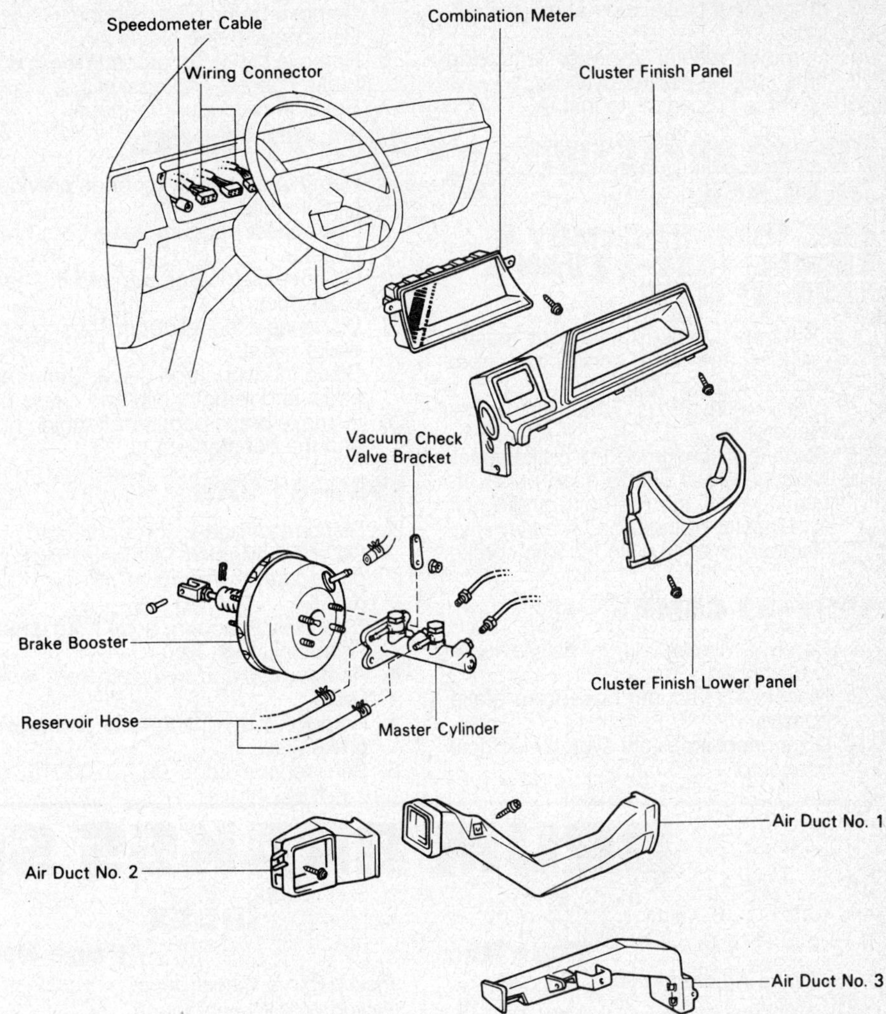

Fig. 30 Master cylinder & power brake unit. Van

ing brake crank boot in caliper.

20. Install parking brake crank in caliper, securely matching crank boot with groove of crank seal.
21. On Corolla models, press surface of cable support bracket flush against cylinder wall and torque bolt to 34 ft. lbs. **Ensure clearance between parking brake crank and cable support bracket is .236 inch.**
22. Install torsion spring, ensuring that parking brake crank subassembly is in touch with stopper pin.
23. Install parking brake strut after adjusting rollers of needle roller bearing so they do not catch on caliper hole.
24. Install new O-ring on adjusting bolt.
25. Assemble adjusting bolt as follows:
    a. Assemble stopper, plate, spring and spring retainer to adjusting bolt and, using tool 09756-00010 or equivalent, fully tighten components down manually. **Position inscribed surface of stopper upward and align notches of spring case with notches of stopper.**
    b. Install adjusting bolt subassembly into cylinder.
26. Using suitable tool, install snap ring, facing snap ring opening toward bleeder side, then remove tool from adjusting bolt and firmly pull up adjusting bolt manually to ensure that it does not move.
27. Manually move parking brake crank to ensure that adjusting bolt moves smoothly.
28. Install piston seal in cylinder.
29. Assemble piston in cylinder as follows:
    a. Using tool 09719-14020 or equivalent, slowly screw in piston clockwise until it will not descend any further.
    b. Align center of piston stopper groove with positioning protrusion of cylinder, **Fig. 29.**
30. Install cylinder boot and set ring in cylinder.
31. Install main pin boot.
32. Install dust boot, ensuring that seal does not fold under, then install bushing into boot with flange facing inside.

MASTER CYLINDER REPLACE

EXC. 1983–87 CAMRY & TERCEL, 1984–87 VAN & 1985–87 MR2

1. Disconnect brake lines from master cylinder.
2. Disconnect wire connector from brake pressure switch and then disconnect level warning switch connector, if equipped.
3. Remove master cylinder to brake unit attaching nuts, then remove master cylinder.
4. Reverse procedure to install. Bleed brake system.

1983–87 CAMRY & TERCEL

1. Disconnect level warning switch electrical connector, if equipped.
2. Disconnect brake lines at master cylinder and 3-way union.
3. Remove master cylinder attaching nuts.
4. Remove master cylinder, wire clamp if equipped, 3-way union and gasket.
5. Reverse procedure to install.

1984–87 VAN

1. Disconnect battery ground cable.
2. Refer to **Fig. 30,** and remove the following components:
    a. Instrument cluster finish panel.
    b. Instrument cluster.
    c. Instrument cluster lower finish panel.
    d. Air duct no. 3.
    e. Air duct no. 1 and no. 2.
3. Remove brake fluid with syringe.
4. Disconnect two brake lines from master cylinder.
5. Disconnect reservoir hoses from master cylinder.
6. Remove master cylinder.
7. Reverse procedure to install.

1985–87 MR2

1. Remove luggage compartment trim cover by removing two clips after disengaging inner part of clip.
2. Disconnect level warning switch electrical connector.

3. Disconnect brake lines at master cylinder.
4. Remove master cylinder attaching nuts and the master cylinder.
5. Reverse procedure to install.

POWER BRAKE UNIT REPLACE

EXC. 1983–87 CAMRY & TERCEL, 1984–87 VAN & 1985–87 MR2

1. Disconnect brake lines from master cylinder and wire connectors from brake warning switches.
2. Disconnect vacuum hose from power brake unit.
3. Disconnect pushrod from brake pedal.
4. Remove brake unit to dash panel attaching nuts, then remove brake unit and master cylinder as an assembly.
5. Remove master cylinder from brake unit.

1983–87 CAMRY

1. Remove master cylinder as previously described.
2. Disconnect vacuum hose from brake booster.
3. Disconnect stop light switch electrical connector.
4. Remove pedal return spring.
5. Remove clip and clevis pin.
6. Remove brake booster attaching nuts, brake booster and gasket.
7. Reverse procedure to install.

1983–87 TERCEL

1. Remove master cylinder as previously described.
2. Disconnect vacuum hose from brake booster.
3. Remove distributor cap and the heater air duct.
4. Disconnect pedal return spring from brake pedal.
5. Disconnect pushrod clevis from brake pedal and remove clip and clevis pin.
6. Remove brake booster attaching nuts and the booster.

1984–87 VAN

1. Disconnect battery ground cable.
2. Refer to "Master Cylinder, Replace" procedure and remove master cylinder.
3. Disconnect vacuum hose from power brake unit, **Fig. 30.**
4. Remove clip and clevis pin from brake pedal.
5. Remove 4 mounting nuts and power brake unit.
6. Set service tool 09737-00010 on master cylinder and lower pin until tip slightly touches piston.
7. Turn service tool upside down and position on power brake unit.
8. Check that there is no clearance between power brake unit pushrod and pin head of tool.
9. Adjust power brake unit pushrod length until pushrod lightly touches pin head.
10. Install power brake unit to pedal bracket and torque bolts to 9 ft. lbs.
11. Insert clevis pin into clevis and brake pedal, then insert clip in clevis pin.
12. Install brake pedal return spring.
13. Connect vacuum hose to booster.
14. Install master cylinder.
15. Fill reservoir with brake fluid and bleed system.

1985–87 MR2

1. Remove master cylinder as previously described.
2. Remove wheel guard.
3. Disconnect vacuum hose from brake booster.
4. Remove instrument lower finish panel and air duct.
5. Remove pedal return spring.
6. Remove clip and clevis pin.
7. Remove brake booster attaching bolts and the booster.
8. Reverse procedure to install.

DRUM BRAKES SECTION

INDEX

MASTER CYLINDER REPLACE

Refer to "Disc Brakes Section" for master cylinder replacement procedures.

POWER BRAKE UNIT REPLACE

Refer to "Disc Brakes Section" for power brake unit replacement procedures.

DRUM BRAKE ADJUSTMENTS

EXC. PICKUP

1. Check brake pedal reserve travel.
2. Operate parking brake lever while pressing down on lever knob.
3. Recheck brake pedal travel.
4. Check to ensure rear wheels rotate freely.

PICKUP

Measure brake drum inside diameter and maximum diameter of brake shoes using brake shoe clearance gauge, **Fig. 1.** Turn adjuster so that brake shoe diameter will be .012-.024 inch (.3-.6 mm) smaller than brake drum inner diameter.

Raise and support rear of vehicle, ensure rear wheels move freely. Remove brake shoe adjusting hole plug from backing plate, then using a suitable brake tool, expand adjuster until wheel is locked. Working through backing plate, insert a narrow tool to move self-adjuster lever away from adjuster, then loosen adjuster wheel approximately 10-12 notches. Install brake shoe adjusting hole plug.

PARKING BRAKE ADJUST

CELICA, CRESSIDA & SUPRA W/REAR DISC BRAKES

1. Apply parking brake while counting number of notches on parking brake sector. Number of notches should be 5-8 for all models.
2. If number of notches is incorrect, raise and support rear of vehicle and ensure rear wheels move freely. Working through rear disc/drum backing plate, turn adjuster until disc rotor is locked, then back off adjuster 8 notches.
3. Apply parking brake while counting number of notches on parking brake sector. If number of notches is not 5-8, remove rear console box, then

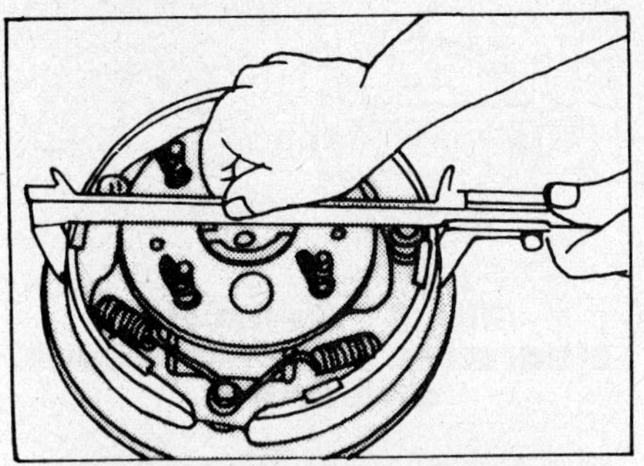

Fig. 1 Measuring brake shoe to brake drum clearance. Pickup

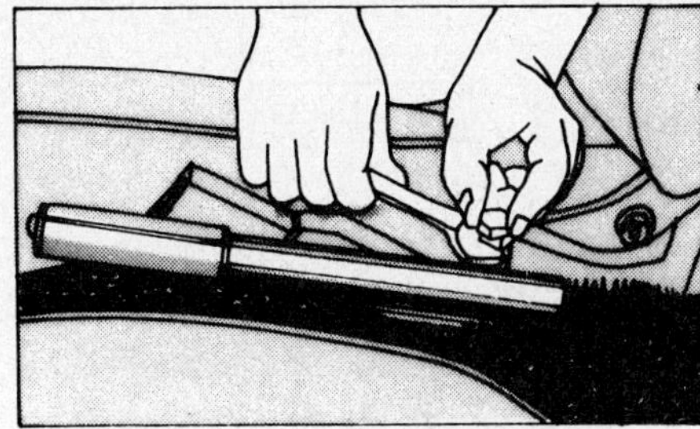

Fig. 2 Parking brake adjustment. Starlet

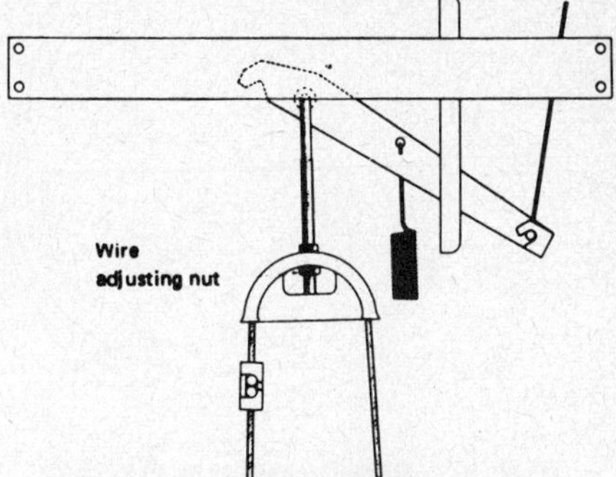

Fig. 3 Parking brake adjustment. Pickup exc. 4 wheel drive

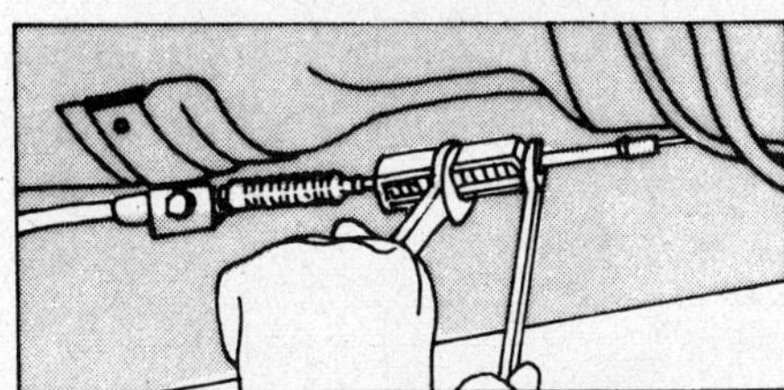

Fig. 4 Parking brake adjustment. 1983–84 Cressida less disc brakes

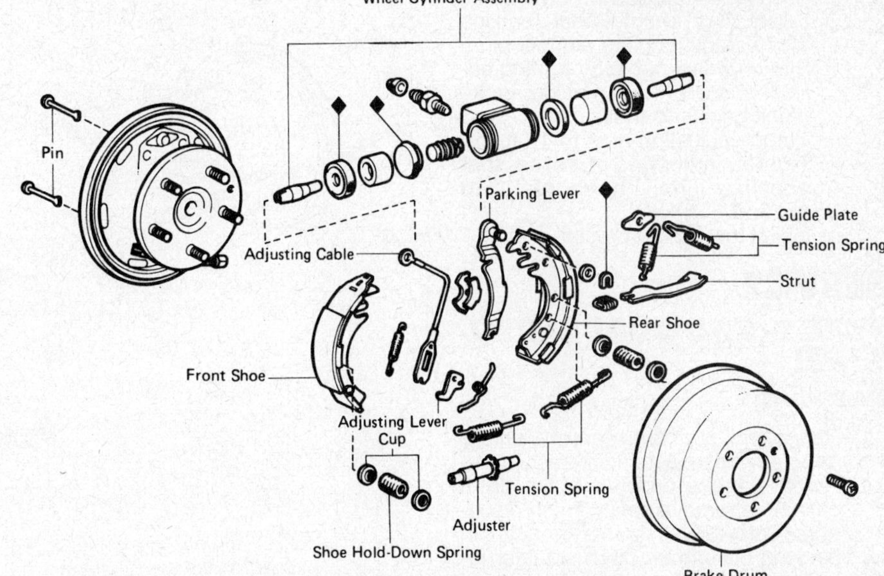

Fig. 5 Exploded view of type 1 (dual servo) brake assembly. Pickup 2WD

loosen locknut and turn adjustment screw until lever travel is correct. Tighten locknut.

CAMRY, CELICA W/DRUM BRAKES, COROLLA, STARLET, TERCEL & VAN

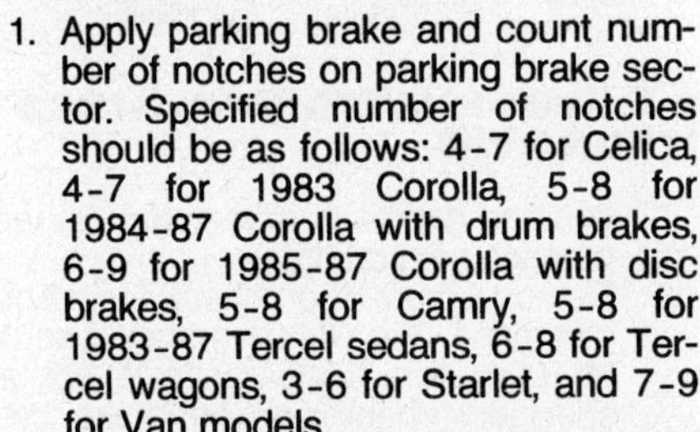

1. Apply parking brake and count number of notches on parking brake sector. Specified number of notches should be as follows: 4-7 for Celica, 4-7 for 1983 Corolla, 5-8 for 1984-87 Corolla with drum brakes, 6-9 for 1985-87 Corolla with disc brakes, 5-8 for Camry, 5-8 for 1983-87 Tercel sedans, 6-8 for Tercel wagons, 3-6 for Starlet, and 7-9 for Van models.
2. On Starlet models, adjust parking brake by loosening adjusting cap and turning nut until required number of notches is obtained, **Fig. 2.** Check to ensure that both rear wheels rotate freely, then tighten cap.
3. On Camry, Celica, Corolla, Tercel and 1984-86 Van models, adjust parking brake as follows:
   a. Remove console box, and if necessary, the shift knob.
   b. Loosen locknut and turn adjustment screw until lever travel is correct.
   c. Tighten lock nut and reinstall console, and on Van models, shift knob.
4. On 1987 Van models proceed as follows:
   a. Raise and support vehicle.
   b. Tighten or loosen adjusting nut at parking brake equalizer as necessary to bring parking brake adjustment within specifications.
   c. Lower vehicle.

PICKUP EXC. 4 WHEEL DRIVE

1. Release parking brake and check to ensure warning light switch is off. If adjustment is required, loosen parking brake warning light switch bracket and reposition switch.
2. Adjust nut at parking brake cable equalizer so that there is no looseness at No. 2 and No. 3 parking brake cables, **Fig. 3.** Check to ensure that both rear wheels rotate freely.
3. After adjusting, apply parking brake lever and count number of notches on brake lever. Specified number of notches should be 7-15 on 1983 Pickup and 10-16 on 1984-87 Pickup.

1983–84 CRESSIDA LESS DISC BRAKES

Adjust parking brake lever travel by rotating turnbuckle at parking brake equalizer, **Fig. 4.** Parking brake lever travel should be 5-8 notches.

PICKUP W/4 WHEEL DRIVE & 4RUNNER

1. Tighten bell crank stopper screw until there is no play in rear brake link. Back off screw one turn, then tighten screw locknut.
2. Tighten one intermediate lever adjusting nut while loosening the other until lever travel of 9-17 clicks is obtained. Tighten both adjusting nuts.
3. Check to ensure that bell crank stopper screw contacts backing plate.

1985–87 MR2

1. Pull parking brake lever all the way up and down two or three times, then return parking brake lever to down position.
2. Depress brake pedal several times, then pull parking brake lever all the way up, counting the number of notches of lever travel.
3. If lever does not click 5-8 times, adjust parking brake as follows:
   a. Pull parking brake lever all the way up and down tow or three times, then return parking brake lever.
   b. Depress brake pedal several times.

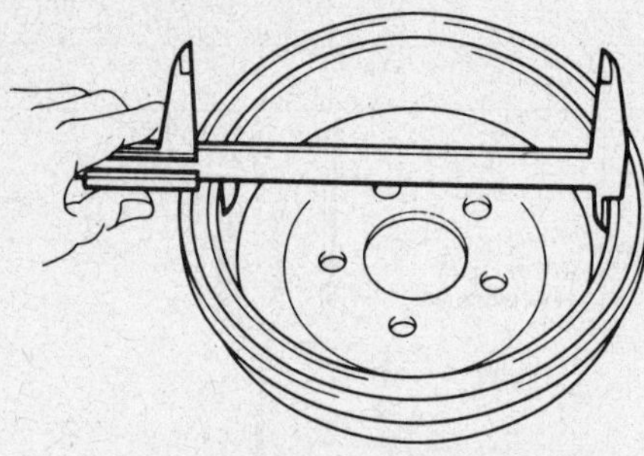

Fig. 6 Measuring brake drum inside diameter

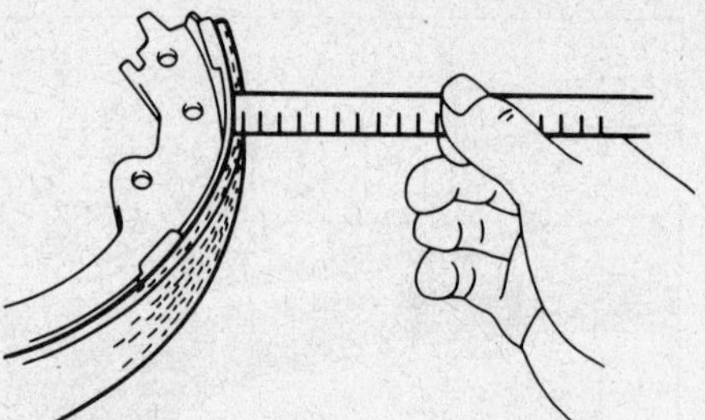

Fig. 7 Measuring brake shoe lining thickness

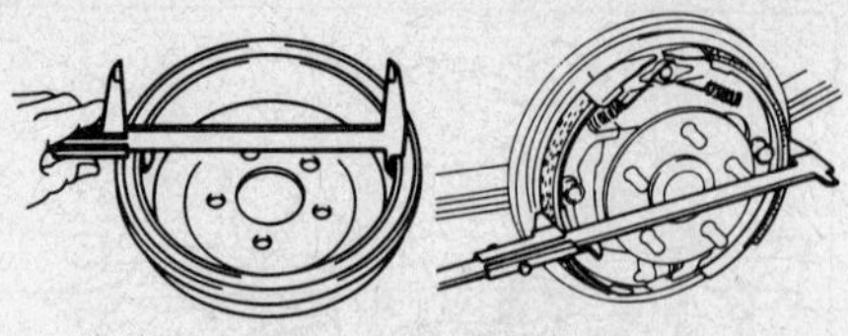

Fig. 8 Measuring clearance between shoes and drum

c. Remove fuel tank protector.
d. Loosen adjusting nut and brake cable and ensure that parking brake crank touches stopper pin.
e. Stretch brake cable by turning adjusting nut before parking brake crank begins to move.
f. Torque adjusting nuts to 12 ft. lbs. **Tighten adjusting nuts so that equalizer is horizontal to ground.**
g. Install fuel tank protector.

SERVICE

TYPE 1 (2WD DUAL SERVO TYPE)

Removal

1. Raise and support rear of vehicle, then remove wheel and tire assembly.
2. Remove brake drum. If brake drum cannot be remove easily, insert a suitable screwdriver through hole in backing plate, then push adjuster lever away from adjuster and back of adjustment tension.
3. Remove two shoe return springs, using suitable tool, **Fig. 5.**
4. Push lever upward, then remove cable, shoe guide, plate and cable guide.
5. Remove spring from lever, then the lever and spring.
6. Remove two tension springs, using a suitable tool, then the shoe hold down springs and pins.
7. Remove shoes, adjuster and strut, then disconnect parking brake cable from parking brake lever.

Inspection

1. Measure brake drum inside diameter. Inside diameter should be 10.08 inches, **Fig. 6.**
2. Measure brake shoe lining thickness, **Fig. 7.** Minimum thickness should be .04 inch.
3. Inspect brake lining and drum for proper contact and replace drum or shoes as necessary.
4. Inspect wheel cylinder for corrosion or damage.
5. Inspect backing plate for wear or damage.
6. Apply a suitable lubricant to backing plate contact areas.

Installation

1. Assemble parking brake cable to parking brake lever, **Fig. 5.**
2. Position rear brake in place with end of shoe inserted in piston rod, then install shoe hold down spring and pin, using a suitable brake tool.
3. Install strut with spring rearward, then position front brake in place with end of shoe inserted in piston rod and strut in place. Install shoe hold down spring and pin, using suitable tool.
4. Install tension springs.
5. Apply a suitable lubricant to adjuster, then install adjuster by opening shoes with screwdriver and inserting adjuster between pads.
6. Install shoe guide plate, cable guide and adjusting cable, then the front return spring and rear return spring, using a suitable tool.
7. Install tension spring to rear shoe, then hook adjusting lever with cable and insert lever. Retain adjusting lever with tension spring.
8. Pull adjusting lever cable rearward, then release and ensure adjusting bolt rotates. If bolt does not rotate, check for improper installation of rear brakes.
9. Adjust strut to shortest possible length, then install drum.
10. Rotate brake drum in reverse direction and depress brake pedal. Repeat process several times.
11. Remove drum, then check for proper clearance, **Fig. 8.** Clearance should be .024 inch. If clearance is not as specified, check parking brake system.
12. Install brake drum, then bleed and refill brake system.
13. Install wheel and tire assembly, then lower vehicle.

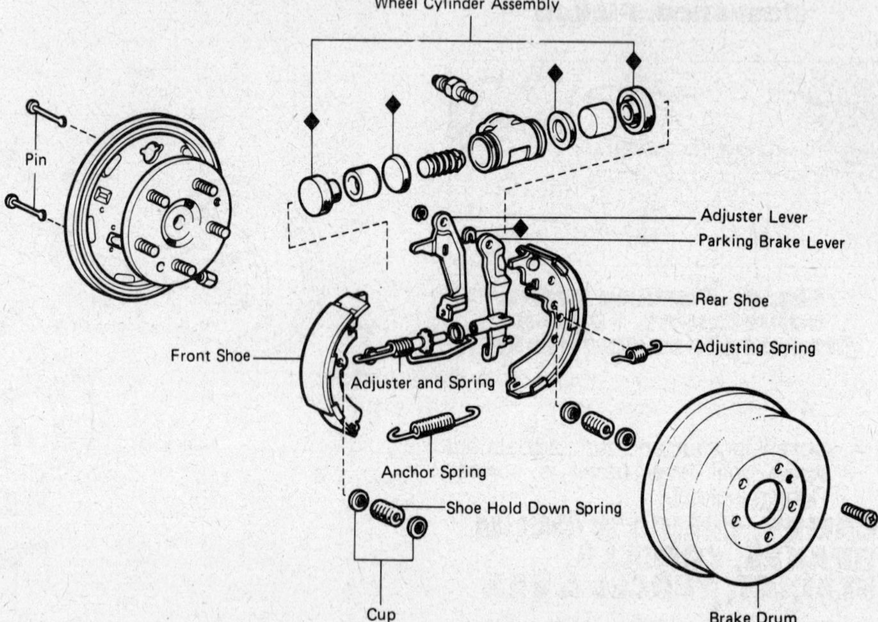

Fig. 9 Exploded view of type 2 (leading/trailing) brake assembly. Pickup 2WD

TYPE 2 (LEADING-TRAILING TYPE)

Removal

1. Raise and support rear of vehicle, then remove wheel and tire assembly.
2. Remove brake drum. If brake drum cannot be remove easily, insert a suitable screwdriver through hole in backing plate, then push adjuster lever away from adjuster and back of adjustment tension.
3. Remove return spring adjuster, using a suitable tool, then the front shoe hold down spring and pin, **Fig. 9.**
4. Remove front brake shoe, then the anchor spring.
5. Remove hold down spring and pin, then the rear shoe, using a suitable

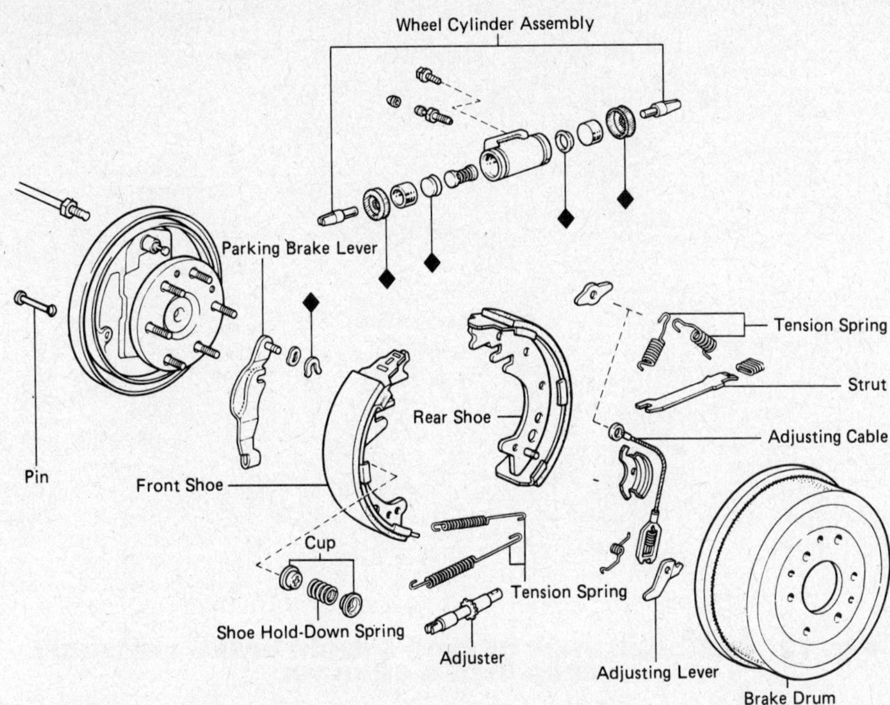

Fig. 10 Exploded view of type 3 (dual servo) brake assembly. Pickup 4WD

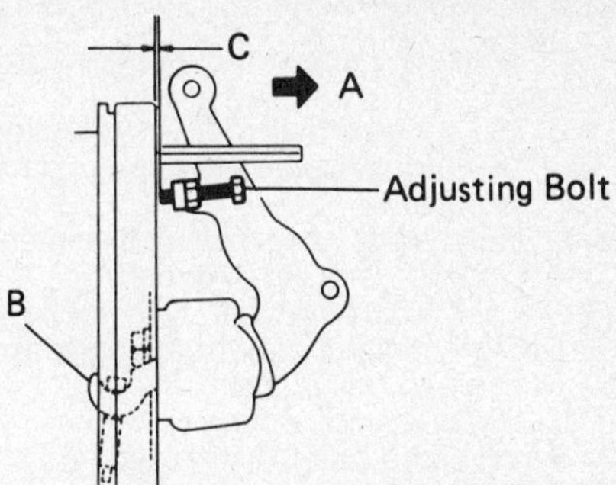

Fig. 11 Bellcrank adjustment. Pickup 4WD & 4Runner

tool.

6. Remove strut and spring from parking brake lever, then the adjusting lever spring.
7. Remove parking brake cable from parking brake lever.

Inspection

1. Measure brake drum inside diameter. Inside diameter should be 10.00 inches, **Fig. 6.**
2. Measure brake shoe lining thickness, **Fig. 7.** Minimum thickness should be .04 inch.
3. Inspect brake lining and drum for proper contact and replace drum or shoes as necessary.
4. Inspect wheel cylinder for corrosion or damage.
5. Inspect backing plate for wear or damage.
6. Apply a suitable lubricant to backing plate contact areas.

Installation

1. Apply a suitable lubricant to adjuster bolt threads and end.
2. Connect parking brake cable, then assemble strut and return spring to lever. Install adjusting lever spring using a suitable tool.
3. Position rear shoe in place with one end of shoe inserted in wheel cylinder and the other end in anchor plate. Using a suitable tool, install pin and shoe hold down spring.
4. Insert anchor spring between front and rear shoes, then position front shoe in place with end of shoe in wheel cylinder and strut in place. Using a suitable tool, install pin and shoe hold down spring.
5. Install return spring.
6. Pull adjusting lever cable upward, then release and ensure adjusting bolt rotates. If bolt does not rotate, check for improper installation of rear brakes.
7. Adjust strut to shortest possible length, then install drum.
8. Pull parking brake lever fully upward. Repeat process several times.
9. Remove drum, then check for proper clearance, **Fig. 8.** Clearance should be .024 inch. If clearance is not as specified, check parking brake system.
10. Install brake drum, then bleed and refill brake system.
11. Install wheel and tire assembly, then lower vehicle.

TYPE 3 (4WD DUAL SERVO TYPE)

Removal

1. Raise and support rear of vehicle, then remove wheel and tire assembly.
2. Remove brake drum. If brake drum cannot be remove easily, insert a suitable screwdriver through hole in backing plate, then push adjuster lever away from adjuster and back of adjustment tension.
3. Remove two shoe return springs, using suitable tool, **Fig. 10.**
4. Push lever upward, then remove cable, shoe guide, plate and cable guide.
5. Remove spring from lever, then the lever and spring.
6. Remove two tension springs, using a suitable tool, then the shoe hold down springs and pins.
7. Remove shoes, adjuster and strut, then disconnect parking brake cable from parking brake lever.

Inspection

1. Measure brake drum inside diameter. Inside diameter should be 10.00 inches, **Fig. 6.**
2. Measure brake shoe lining thickness, **Fig. 7.** Minimum thickness should be .04 inch.
3. Inspect brake lining and drum for proper contact and replace drum or shoes as necessary.
4. Inspect wheel cylinder for corrosion or damage.
5. Inspect backing plate for wear or damage.
6. Inspect bell crank components for bending, wear or damage.
7. Apply a suitable lubricant to backing plate contact areas.

Installation

1. Assemble parking brake cable to parking brake lever, **Fig. 10.**
2. Position rear brake in place with end of shoe inserted in piston rod, then install shoe hold down spring and pin, using a suitable brake tool.
3. Install strut with spring rearward, then position front brake in place with end of shoe inserted in piston rod and strut in place. Install shoe hold down spring and pin, using suitable tool.
4. Install tension springs.
5. Apply a suitable lubricant to adjuster, then install adjuster by opening shoes with screwdriver and inserting adjuster between pads.
6. Install shoe guide plate, cable guide and adjusting cable, then the front return spring and rear return spring, using a suitable tool.
7. Install tension spring to rear shoe, then hook adjusting lever with cable and insert lever. Retain adjusting lever with tension spring.
8. Pull adjusting lever cable rearward, then release and ensure adjusting bolt rotates. If bolt does not rotate, check for improper installation of rear brakes.
9. Adjust strut to shortest possible length, then install drum.
10. Rotate brake drum in reverse direction and depress brake pedal. Repeat process several times.
11. Remove drum, then check for proper clearance, **Fig. 9.** Clearance should be .024 inch. If clearance is not as specified, check parking brake sys-

tem.

12. If necessary, adjust bell crank as follows:
    a. Lightly pull bellcrank in direction "A," **Fig. 11,** until there is no slack in part "B."
    b. Rotate adjusting bolt until dimension "C" is .039-.078 inch.
    c. Lock adjusting bolt with locknut, then connect No. 2 parking brake cable to bell crank.
    d. Install tension spring.
13. Install brake drum, then bleed and refill brake system.
14. Install wheel and tire assembly, then lower vehicle.

TYPE 4

Removal

1. Raise and support rear of vehicle, then remove wheel and tire assembly.
2. Remove brake drum. If brake drum cannot be removed easily, insert a suitable screwdriver through hole in backing plate, then push adjuster lever away from adjuster and back of adjustment tension.
3. Remove tension spring, using a suitable tool, then remove rear shoe hold down spring and pin. Remove rear brake shoe and anchor spring, **Fig. 12.**
4. Remove front shoe hold down spring and pin, using suitable tool, then disconnect No. 1 parking brake cable from No. 3 parking brake bell crank.
5. Remove front brake with strut, then disconnect parking brake cable from front shoe. Remove parking brake cable No. 2.
6. Remove adjusting lever spring, then the adjuster from front shoe.

Inspection

1. Measure brake drum inside diameter. Inside diameter should be 11.61 inches, **Fig. 6.**
2. Measure brake shoe lining thickness, **Fig. 7.** Minimum thickness should be .04 inch.
3. Inspect brake lining and drum for proper contact and replace drum or shoes as necessary.
4. Inspect wheel cylinder for corrosion or damage.
5. Inspect backing plate for wear or damage.
6. Inspect bell crank components for bending, wear or damage.
7. Apply a suitable lubricant to backing plate contact areas.

Installation

1. Apply a suitable lubricant to adjuster bolt threads and end.
2. Assemble adjuster to lever, then install adjuster lever spring, **Fig. 12.**
3. Install No. 1 parking brake cable to parking brake lever shoe, then attach the other side of cable to No. 3 bell crank.
4. Position front shoe in place with end of shoe inserted into piston, then install shoe hold down spring and pin using a suitable tool.
5. Assemble anchor spring to front and rear shoe, then install rear shoe with end inserted in piston.

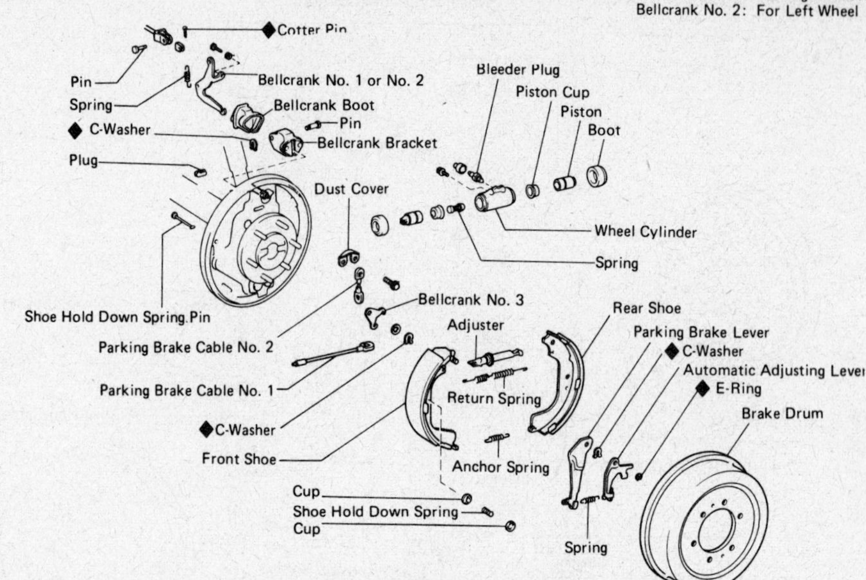

Fig. 12 Exploded view of type 4 drum brake assembly. Pickup 4WD & 4Runner

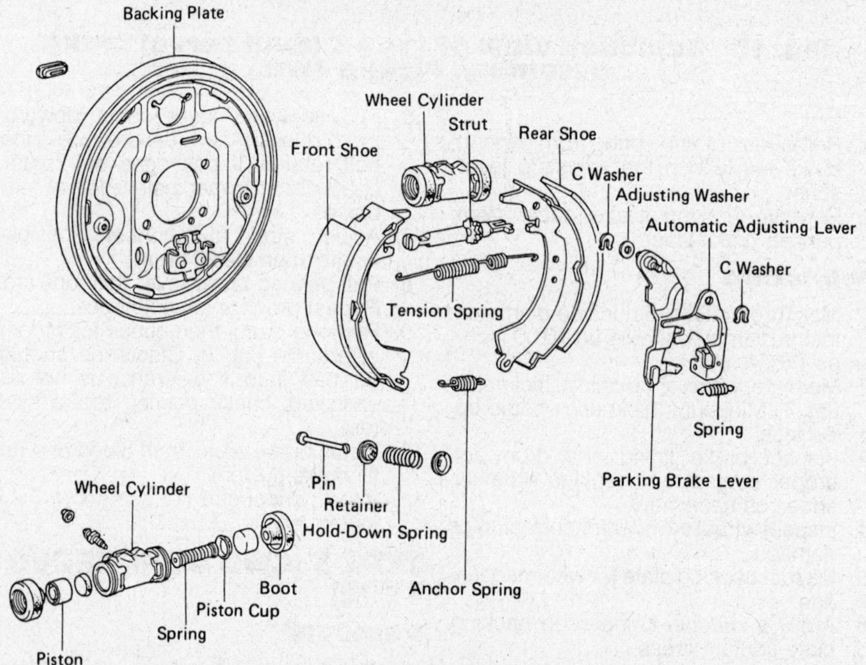

Fig. 13 Exploded view of type 5 drum brake assembly. Exc. Pickup & 4Runner

6. Install rear shoe hold down spring and pin, then the tension spring.
7. If necessary, adjust bell crank as follows:
    a. Lightly pull bell crank in direction "A," **Fig. 11,** until there is no slack in part "B."
    b. Rotate adjusting bolt until dimension "C" is .016-.031 inch.
    c. Lock adjusting bolt with locknut, when connect No. 2 parking brake cable to bell crank.
    d. Install tension spring.
8. Ensure proper parking brake travel.
9. Pull adjusting lever cable upward, then release and ensure adjusting bolt rotates. If bolt does not rotate, check for improper installation of rear brakes.
10. Adjust strut to shortest possible length, then install drum.
11. Pull parking brake lever fully upward. Repeat process several times.
12. Remove drum, then check for proper clearance, **Fig. 8.** Clearance should be .024 inch. If clearance is not as specified, check parking brake system.
13. Install brake drum, then bleed and refill brake system.

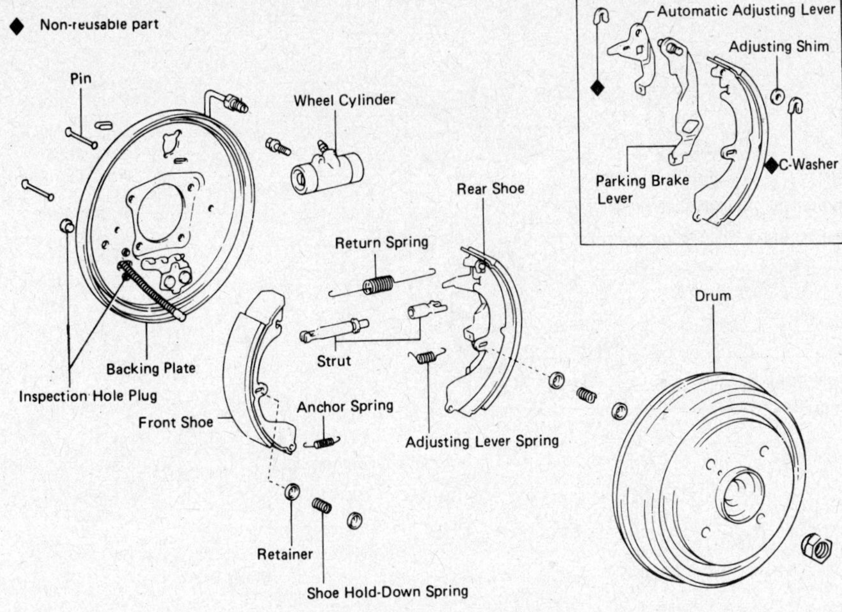

Fig. 14 Exploded view of type 6 drum brake assembly. Exc. Pickup & 4Runner

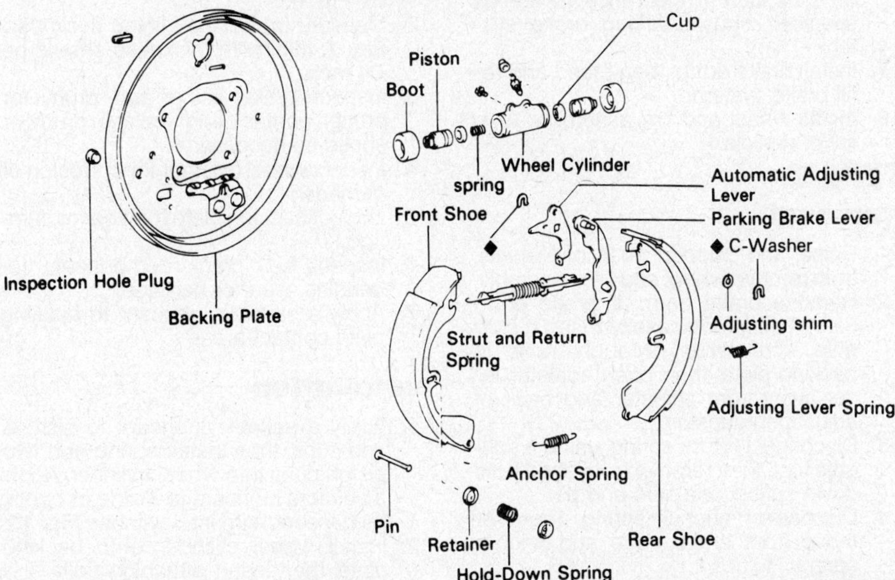

Fig. 15 Exploded view of type 7 drum brake assembly. Exc. Pickup & 4Runner

14. Install wheel and tire assembly, then lower vehicle.

TYPE 5

Removal

1. Raise and support rear of vehicle, then remove wheel and tire assembly.
2. Remove brake drum. If brake drum cannot be remove easily, insert a suitable screwdriver through hole in backing plate, then push adjuster lever away from adjuster and back of adjustment tension.
3. Remove tension spring, using a suitable tool, then remove rear shoe hold down spring and pin. Remove rear brake shoe and anchor spring, **Fig. 13.**
4. Remove rear shoe hold down spring and pin, using suitable tool, then disconnect parking brake cable from lever.
5. Remove adjusting lever spring and strut from rear shoe.
6. Position a suitable container to catch fluid, then remove two boots, two pistons, two piston cups and spring from wheel cylinder.

Inspection

1. Measure brake drum inside diameter. Inside diameter should be 9.00 inches, **Fig. 6.**
2. Measure brake shoe lining thickness, **Fig. 7.** Minimum thickness should be .04 inch.
3. Inspect brake lining and drum for proper contact and replace drum or shoes as necessary.
4. Inspect wheel cylinder for corrosion or damage.
5. Inspect backing plate for wear or damage.
6. Apply a suitable lubricant to backing plate contact areas.

Installation

1. Apply a suitable lubricant to piston cups, then insert spring and two piston cups into wheel cylinder. Apply a suitable lubricant to inside of boots, then insert them into cylinder, **Fig. 13.**
2. Apply a suitable lubricant to adjuster bolt threads and end, then install strut and adjusting lever spring.
3. Connect parking brake cable to lever, then position one end of rear shoe in wheel cylinder and the other end in anchor plate.
4. Install rear shoe pin and hold down spring.
5. Insert anchor spring between front and rear shoes, then position end of front shoe in wheel cylinder with strut in place.
6. Install front shoe hold down spring and pin.
7. Install tension spring.
8. Ensure adjusting bolt rotates while pulling parking brake upward. If bolt does not turn, check installation of rear brakes.
9. Adjust strut to shortest possible length, then install drum.
10. Pull parking brake lever fully upward then repeat step several times.
11. Remove drum, then check for proper clearance, **Fig. 8.** Clearance should be .024 inch. If clearance is not as specified, check parking brake system.
12. Install brake drum, then bleed and refill brake system.
13. Install wheel and tire assembly, then lower vehicle.

TYPE 6

Removal

1. Raise and support rear of vehicle, then remove wheel and tire assembly.
2. Remove brake drum. If brake drum cannot be remove easily, insert a suitable screwdriver through hole in backing plate, then push automatic adjuster lever away from adjuster and back of adjustment tension.
3. Disconnect return spring, using a suitable tool, then remove front shoe hold down spring, retainers and pin.
4. Disconnect anchor spring, then remove front brake shoe and anchor spring, **Fig. 14.**
5. Remove rear shoe hold down spring, retainers and pin, using suitable tool, then disconnect parking brake cable from anchor plate.
6. Disconnect parking brake cable from lever, then remove rear shoe with strut.
7. Remove adjusting lever spring, strut

and return spring from rear shoe.
8. Remove C-washer, then the shims, parking brake lever and automatic adjusting lever from rear shoe.
9. Position a suitable container to catch fluid, then disconnect brake line.
10. Remove two attaching bolts, then the wheel cylinder.
11. Remove two boots, two pistons, two piston cups and spring from wheel cylinder.

Inspection

1. Measure brake drum inside diameter. Inside diameter should be 7.87 inches, **Fig. 6.**
2. Measure brake shoe lining thickness, **Fig. 7.** Minimum thickness should be .04 inch.
3. Inspect brake lining and drum for proper contact and replace drum or shoes as necessary.
4. Inspect wheel cylinder for corrosion or damage.
5. Inspect backing plate for wear or damage.
6. Inspect bell crank components for bending, wear or damage.
7. Apply a suitable lubricant to backing plate contact areas.

Installation

1. Apply a suitable lubricant to pistons and cups, then install spring and two piston cups into wheel cylinder. Apply a suitable lubricant to inside of boots, then insert them into cylinder, **Fig. 14.**
2. Install wheel cylinder onto backing plate, then insert attaching bolts and torque to 7 ft. lbs.
3. Connect brake tube to wheel cylinder, then torque nut to 11 ft. lbs.
4. Apply a suitable lubricant to adjuster bolt contact points, then install levers, shim and new C-washer.
5. Measure clearance between shoe and lever. Clearance should be .014 inch. If clearance is not as specified, select a suitable shim to bring clearance to specified value.
6. Place strut and return spring on rear shoe, then install adjusting lever spring.
7. Connect parking brake cable to lever, then insert cable through notch in anchor plate.
8. Position one end of rear shoe in wheel cylinder and the other end in anchor plate.
9. Install rear shoe pin and hold down spring and retainers.
10. Insert anchor spring between front and rear shoes, then position end of front shoe in wheel cylinder with strut in place.
11. Install front shoe hold down spring, retainers and pin.
12. Install return spring.
13. Ensure adjusting bolt rotates while pulling parking brake upward. If bolt does not turn, check installation of rear brakes.
14. Adjust strut to its shortest possible length, then install drum.
15. Pull parking brake lever fully upward, then repeat step several times.
16. Remove drum, then check for proper clearance, **Fig. 8.** Clearance should be .024 inch. If clearance is not as specified, check parking brake system.
17. Install brake drum, then bleed and refill brake system.
18. Install wheel and tire assembly, then lower vehicle.

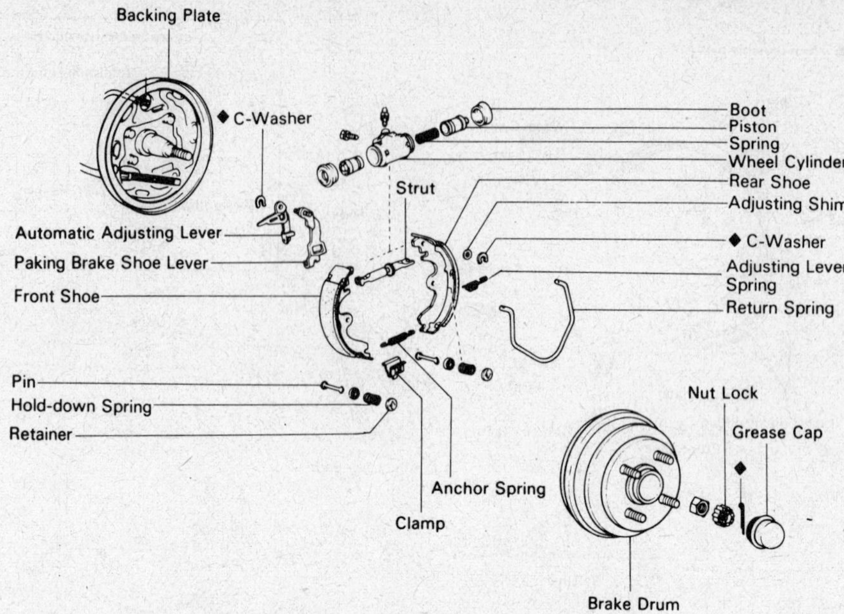

Fig. 16 Exploded view of type 8 drum brake assembly. Exc. Pickup & 4Runner

TYPE 7

Removal

1. Raise and support rear of vehicle, then remove wheel and tire assembly.
2. Remove brake drum. If brake drum cannot be remove easily, insert a suitable screwdriver through hole in backing plate, then push adjuster lever away from adjuster and back of adjustment tension.
3. Disconnect return spring, using a suitable tool, then remove front shoe hold down spring, retainers and pin.
4. Disconnect anchor spring, then remove front brake shoe and anchor spring, **Fig. 15.**
5. Remove rear shoe hold down spring, retainers and pin, using suitable tool, then disconnect parking brake cable from anchor plate.
6. Disconnect parking brake cable from lever, then remove rear shoe with strut.
7. Remove adjusting lever spring, strut and return spring from rear shoe.
8. Remove C-washer, then the shims, parking brake lever and automatic adjusting lever from rear shoe.
9. Position a suitable container to catch fluid, then disconnect brake line.
10. Remove two attaching bolts, then the wheel cylinder.
11. Remove two boots, two pistons, two piston cups and spring from wheel cylinder.

Inspection

1. Measure brake drum inside diameter. Inside diameter should be 7.87 inches, **Fig. 6.**
2. Measure brake shoe lining thickness, **Fig. 7.** Minimum thickness should be .04 inch.
3. Inspect brake lining and drum for proper contact and replace drum or shoes as necessary.
4. Inspect wheel cylinder for corrosion or damage.
5. Inspect backing plate for wear or damage.
6. Inspect bell crank components for bending, wear or damage.
7. Apply a suitable lubricant to backing plate contact areas.

Installation

1. Apply a suitable lubricant to pistons and cups, then install spring and two piston cups into wheel cylinder. Apply a suitable lubricant to inside of boots, then insert them into cylinder, **Fig. 15.**
2. Install wheel cylinder onto backing plate, then insert attaching bolts and torque to 7 ft. lbs.
3. Connect brake tube to wheel cylinder, then torque nut to 11 ft. lbs.
4. Apply a suitable lubricant to adjuster bolt contact points, then install levers, shim and new C-washer.
5. Measure clearance between shoe and lever. Clearance should be .014 inch. If clearance is not as specified, select a suitable shim to bring clearance to specified value.
6. Place strut and return spring on rear shoe, then install adjusting lever spring.
7. Connect parking brake cable to lever, then insert cable through notch in anchor plate.
8. Position one end of rear shoe in wheel cylinder and the other end in anchor plate.
9. Install rear shoe pin and hold down spring and retainers.

10. Insert anchor spring between front and rear shoes, then position end of front shoe in wheel cylinder with strut in place.
11. Install front shoe hold down spring, retainers and pin.
12. Install return spring.
13. Ensure adjusting bolt rotates while pulling parking brake upward. If bolt does not turn, check installation of rear brakes.
14. Adjust strut to its shortest possible length, then install drum.
15. Pull parking brake lever fully upward then repeat step several times.
16. Remove drum, then check for proper clearance, **Fig. 8.** Clearance should be .024 inch. If clearance is not as specified, check parking brake system.
17. Install brake drum, then bleed and refill brake system.
18. Install wheel and tire assembly, then lower vehicle.

TYPE 8

Removal

1. Raise and support rear of vehicle, then remove wheel and tire assembly.
2. Remove brake drum. If brake drum cannot be removed easily, insert a suitable screwdriver through hole in backing plate, then push adjuster lever away from adjuster and back of adjustment tension.
3. Remove shoe return spring, using a suitable tool, then remove return spring clamp.
4. Remove front shoe hold down spring, retainers and pin.
5. Disconnect anchor spring, then remove front brake shoe and anchor spring, **Fig. 16.**
6. Remove rear shoe hold down spring, retainers and pin, using suitable tool.
7. Disconnect parking brake cable from lever, then remove rear shoe with strut.
8. Remove adjusting lever spring and strut from rear shoe.
9. Remove C-washer, then the shims, parking brake lever and automatic adjusting lever from rear shoe.
10. Position a suitable container to catch fluid, then disconnect brake line.
11. Remove two attaching bolts, then the wheel cylinder.
12. Remove two boots, two pistons, two piston cups and spring from wheel cylinder.

Inspection

1. Measure brake drum inside diameter. Inside diameter should be 7.09 inches, **Fig. 6.**
2. Measure brake shoe lining thickness, **Fig. 7.** Minimum thickness should be .04 inch.
3. Inspect brake lining and drum for proper contact and replace drum or shoes as necessary.
4. Inspect wheel cylinder for corrosion or damage.
5. Inspect backing plate for wear or damage.
6. Inspect bell crank components for bending, wear or damage.
7. Apply a suitable lubricant to backing plate contact areas.

Installation

1. Apply a suitable lubricant to pistons and cups, then install spring and two piston cups into wheel cylinder. Apply a suitable lubricant to inside of boots, then insert them into cylinder, **Fig. 16.**
2. Install wheel cylinder onto backing plate, then insert attaching bolts and torque to 7 ft. lbs.
3. Connect brake tube to wheel cylinder, then torque nut to 11 ft. lbs.
4. Apply a suitable lubricant to adjuster bolt contact points, then install levers, shim and new C-washer.
5. Measure clearance between shoe and lever. Clearance should be .014 inch. If clearance is not as specified, select a suitable shim to bring clearance to specified value.
6. Place strut and return spring on rear shoe, then install adjusting lever spring.
7. Connect parking brake cable to lever, then position one end of rear shoe in wheel cylinder and the other end in anchor plate.
8. Install rear shoe pin and hold down spring.
9. Insert anchor spring between front and rear shoes, then position end of front shoe in wheel cylinder with strut in place.
10. Install front shoe hold down spring, retainers and pin.
11. Install shoe return spring clamp, then the shoe return spring.
12. Ensure adjusting bolt rotates while pulling parking brake upward. If bolt does not turn, check installation of rear brakes.
13. Adjust strut to shortest possible length, then install drum.
14. Pull parking brake lever fully upward then repeat step several times.
15. Remove drum, then check for proper clearance, **Fig. 8.** Clearance should be .024 inch. If clearance is not as specified, check parking brake system.
16. Install brake drum, then bleed and refill brake system.
17. Install wheel and tire assembly, then lower vehicle.

REAR SUSPENSION & DRIVE AXLE SECTION, EXC. CRESSIDA, MR2, SUPRA & 1983-85 CELICA WITH INDEPENDENT REAR SUSPENSION

INDEX

AXLE SHAFT, BEARING & OIL SEAL REPLACE

The following procedures apply to rear wheel drive and four wheel drive models only. For axle bearing replacement procedures on front wheel drive models, refer to "Rear Hub & Wheel Bearing, Replace."

EXC. PICKUP & 4RUNNER

Removal

1. Raise and support rear of vehicle, then remove wheel and tire assembly and brake drum or rotor, **Fig. 1.**
2. Through holes in axle shaft flange remove axle shaft outer bearing retainer attaching bolts, **Fig. 2.**
3. Using a suitable puller, remove axle shaft from axle housing. Use care not to damage oil seal.
4. To replace axle shaft bearing, grind a groove on one side of inner bearing retainer, then using a chisel, split retainer and remove from axle shaft, **Fig. 3.** Using suitable tool, press bearing from axle shaft and remove spacer (if equipped) and outer bearing retainer.
5. Remove oil seal from axle housing.

Installation

1. Coat contact surfaces of oil seal with grease, then install oil seal in axle housing using a suitable mandrel.

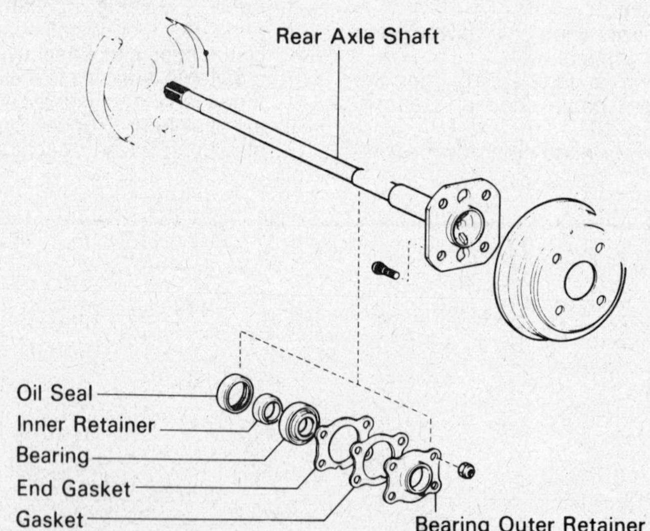

Fig. 1 Axle shaft bearing & oil seal replace. Exc. Pickup

2. Position outer bearing retainer and spacer (if equipped) on axle shaft, then press bearing onto axle shaft.
3. Heat inner bearing retainer to approximately 284° to 320°F (140° to 160°C), then press inner bearing retainer onto axle shaft with chamfered side facing toward bearing using suitable tool, **Fig. 4. When retainer is heated to 302°F (150°C), its surface will show a faint yellow color, do not heat retainer above this point.**
4. Install axle shaft in axle housing.

PICKUP & 4RUNNER

1. Raise and support vehicle, then drain rear axle fluid.
2. On two wheel drive models, remove parking brake retaining clip and clamp bolt from frame.
3. On two wheel drive models, disconnect parking brake rear cable from equalizer.
4. On four wheel drive models remove

Fig. 2 Removing axle shaft bearing retainer attaching bolts. Exc. Pickup

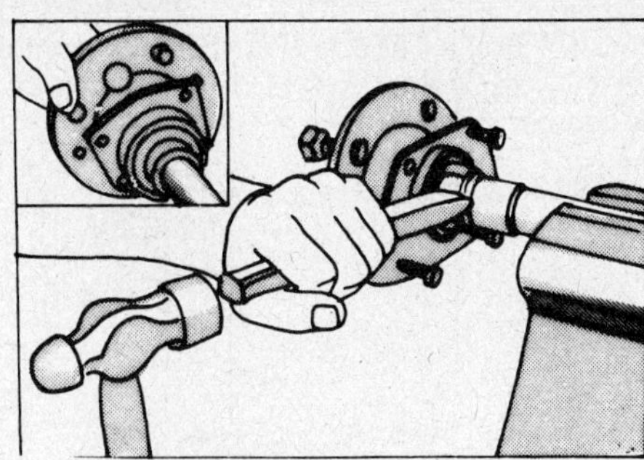

Fig. 3 Removing inner bearing retainer. Exc. Pickup

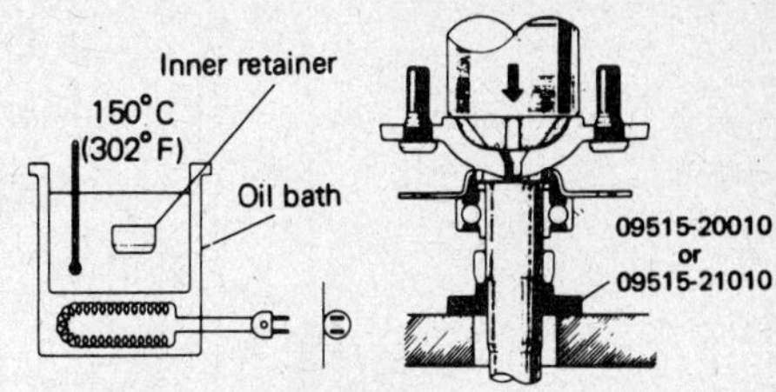

Fig. 4 Installing inner bearing retainer. Exc. Pickup

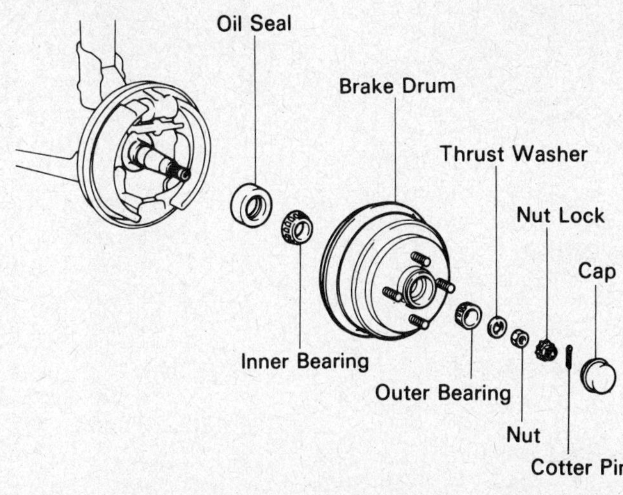

Fig. 5 Rear wheel bearing. Tercel sedan models w/front wheel drive

pin, then disconnect parking brake cable from bell crank.

5. Remove brake drum, then disconnect brake hydraulic line from wheel cylinder.
6. Remove four bolts securing backing plate to axle housing, then remove axle shaft. Use caution not to damage oil seal when removing shaft.
7. Remove snap ring, then press rear axle shaft from backing plate using tool SST 09521-25011 or equivalent.
8. To replace bearing, remove oil seal, then press bearing from flange case using tools 09608-30011 and 09228-44010 or equivalents.
9. Install new bearing using tools 09608-35012 and 09515-30010 or equivalents, then install new oil seal.
10. Coat oil seal with suitable grease, then press axle shaft onto backing plate using tool 09515-30010 or equivalent. Install snap ring.
11. Reverse steps 1 thru 6 to complete installation.

REAR HUB & WHEEL BEARING

REPLACE

The following procedures apply to front wheel drive models only.

TERCEL SEDAN MODELS W/FRONT WHEEL DRIVE

1. Raise and support rear of vehicle, then remove wheel and tire assembly.
2. Remove grease cap, cotter pin, nut lock and adjusting nut, **Fig. 5.**
3. Remove brake drum/hub assembly with outer bearing and thrust washer from axle shaft.
4. Using a suitable screwdriver, pry oil seal from hub, then remove inner bearing.
5. Inspect inner and outer bearings and races for wear and damage. If necessary, replace race(s) with suitable removal and installation tools.
6. Clean and repack bearings and fill inside of axle hub and grease cap with multipurpose grease.
7. Install inner bearing in axle hub, then install new oil seal using suitable seal installer. Grease oil seal lips with multipurpose grease.
8. Install brake drum/hub assembly on axle shaft, then install outer bearing in hub. Apply multi-purpose grease between outer bearing and thrust washer surface, then install thrust washer.
9. Install adjusting nut and torque to 22 ft. lbs., then rotate brake drum/hub assembly to seat bearings. Loosen adjusting nut until hand tight. **Ensure brakes are not dragging.**
10. Attach suitable spring scale to wheel stud and measure oil seal rotation frictional force. Oil seal frictional force should be approximately .9 lb.
11. With spring scale still attached, tighten adjusting nut until bearing preload is .9-2.2 lbs. above the oil seal frictional force determined in step 10.
12. Install locknut, cotter pin and grease cap. **If cotter pin will not line up with axle shaft hole, tighten adjusting nut as small an amount as possible to align.**
13. Adjust rear brakes as necessary.

1983–87 CAMRY, 1984–87 COROLLA W/FRONT WHEEL DRIVE, 1984–87 TERCEL WAGON LESS 4 WHEEL DRIVE & 1986–87 CELICA

1. Remove brake drum or rotor and check bearing axial play. Play should not exceed .002 inch.
2. On models w/drum brakes, disconnect brake line from wheel cylinder, **Fig. 6.**
3. Remove 4 bolts holding axle hub to axle carrier and remove axle hub and rear brake assembly.
4. Remove O-ring.
5. Place hub in suitable vise. Using hammer and chisel, loosen stake part of nut and remove nut.
6. Using special tool 09550-20014, push axle shaft off axle hub.
7. Remove inside portion of bearing inner race.
8. Using special service tool 09950-20014, pull outside portion of bearing inner race from axle shaft.
9. Remove oil seal.
10. To replace wheel bearing, place old inner race (outside) on bearing, then using special service tools 09228-22020 and 09636-20010, press out bearing.
11. Apply MP grease around bearing outer race and using special service tool 09316-60010 press new bearing into axle hub.
12. Using special service tool 09310-35010, or equivalent, drive new oil seal into axle hub.
13. Apply MP grease to oil seal lip.
14. Place inside portion of bearing inner race on bearing.
15. Using special service tool 09636-20010 and 09228-22020, press inner

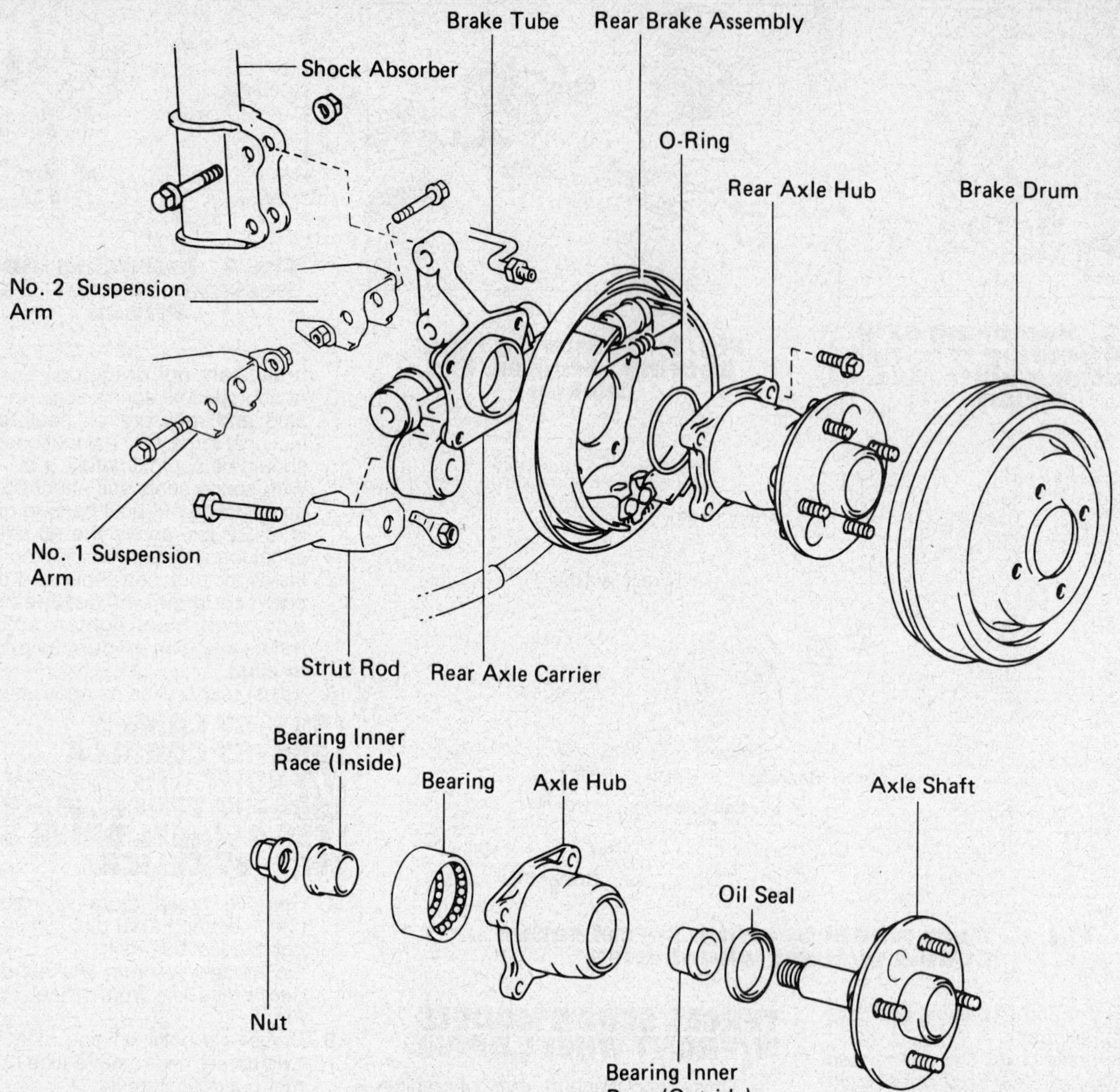

Fig. 6 Rear wheel bearing (typical). 1983–87 Camry, 1984–87 Corolla w/front wheel drive, 1984–87 Tercel Wagon less 4 wheel drive & 1986–87 Celica

race with axle hub onto axle shaft.

16. Torque nut to 90 ft. lbs. (1250 kg-cm) and stake.
17. Place new O-ring on axle carrier.
18. Install axle hub and rear brake assembly with 4 bolts. Torque bolts to 59 ft. lbs. (820 kg-cm).
19. On models w/drum brakes, connect brake line to wheel cylinder, then install brake drum and bleed brakes.
20. On models w/disc brakes, install rotor and caliper assembly.

COIL SPRING

REPLACE

REAR WHEEL DRIVE & 4 WHEEL DRIVE MODELS

1. Raise rear of vehicle and support rear axle housing on stands.
2. Disconnect shock absorber from lower mounting, **Figs. 7 and 8,** then the control rod from axle housing.
3. If equipped with rear stabilizer, remove bolts securing stabilizer bar to rear housing.
4. Lower jack until spring tension is relieved, then remove coil spring with insulator.
5. Reverse procedure to install.

1983–87 CAMRY, 1983–87 TERCEL W/FRONT WHEEL DRIVE, 1984–87 COROLLA W/FRONT WHEEL DRIVE & 1986–87 CELICA

1. Working inside vehicle, remove shock absorber cover and package tray bracket (if equipped).
2. Disconnect brake hose from wheel cylinder or caliper, then disconnect brake hose from shock absorber.
3. Working inside vehicle, loosen nut securing suspension support to shock absorber, **Figs. 9 and 10. Do not remove nut at this time.**
4. Remove bolts securing shock absorber to axle carrier, then disconnect sock absorber from carrier.
5. Working inside vehicle, remove nuts securing suspension support to vehicle body, then remove shock absorber, **Figs. 9 and 10.**
6. Install a bolt and 2 nuts in shock absorber lower mounting bracket and clamp unit in a suitable vise using lower mounting bracket as clamping surface.
7. Using a suitable spring compressor, compress coil spring.
8. Remove nut securing suspension support to shock absorber, then remove suspension support, coil spring, insulator and spring bumper, **Figs. 9 and 10. Shock absorber is filled with colorless, odorless and nonpoisonous high pressure gas.**

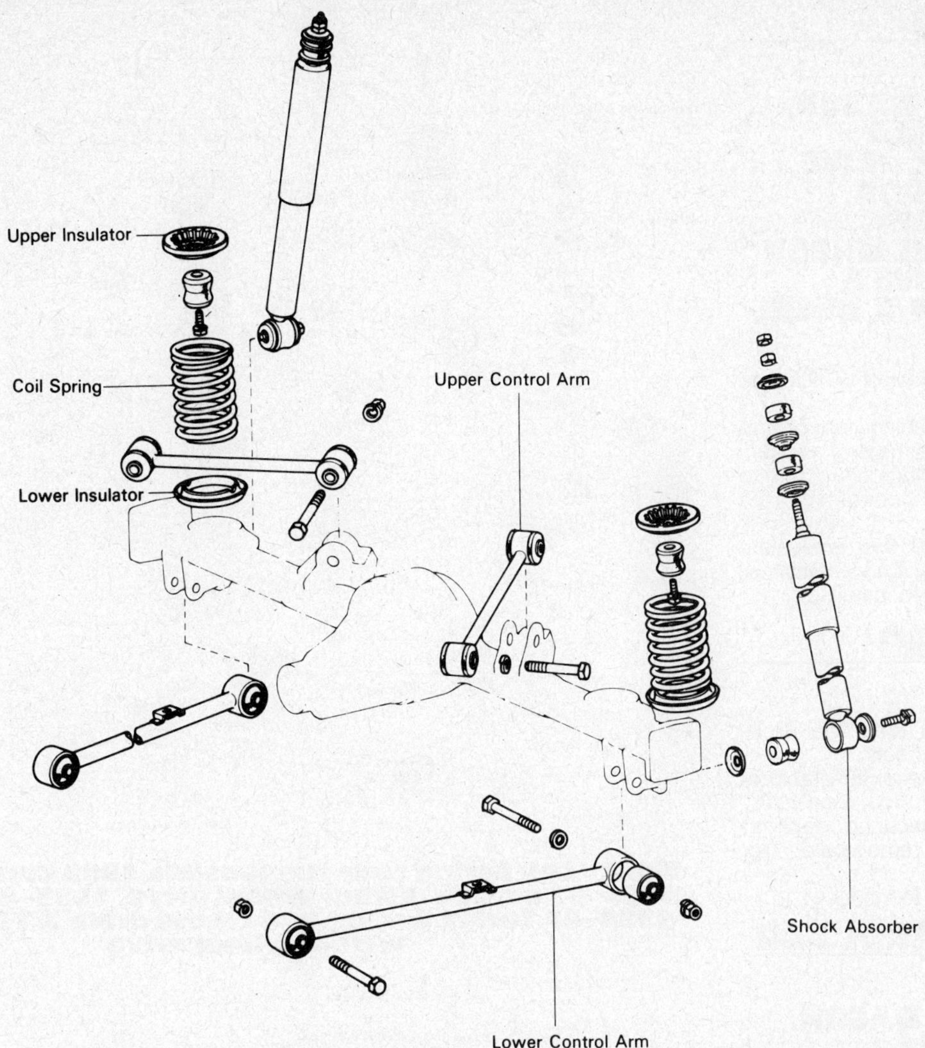

Fig. 7 Coil spring rear suspension. 1983–84 Starlet

Upon removal, handle shock absorber with care. Do not score or scratch exposed part of piston rod or allow paint or oil to come in contact with it. Do not rotate piston rod and cylinder assembly with shock absorber fully extended. When discarding shock absorber, drill a small hole in bottom of cylinder to relieve pressure.

9. Reverse procedure to install.

LEAF SPRING REPLACE

EXC. PICKUP & 4RUNNER

1. Raise rear of vehicle and support body on stands.
2. Disconnect shock absorbers from lower mounting, **Fig. 11.**
3. Remove two U-bolts at spring center.
4. Disconnect parking brake cable from rear spring guide, if necessary.
5. Support rear axle housing using a suitable jack.
6. Remove spring shackle and bushing.
7. Remove two bolts attaching bracket pin, then remove bracket pin and two bushings from rear of spring.
8. Reverse procedure to install.

PICKUP & 4RUNNER

1. Raise rear of vehicle and place stands under frame and rear axle housing.
2. Disconnect shock absorber from upper and lower mountings and remove shock absorber from vehicle, **Fig. 12.**
3. Disconnect parking brake equalizer from parking brake intermediate lever.
4. Remove three-way securing bolt.
5. Remove U-bolts and spring seats. On 4 wheel drive models, remove spring bumper.
6. Position a suitable jack under rear axle housing and raise housing to relieve weight from rear springs.
7. Remove spring shackle nuts and inner plate, then using a suitable pry bar, remove spring shackle.
8. Remove two bolts retaining spring bracket and hanger pin nut, then drive out spring hanger pin.
9. Remove spring assembly from vehicle.
10. Reverse procedure to install.

SHOCK ABSORBER REPLACE

REAR WHEEL & 4 WHEEL DRIVE MODELS

1. Raise rear of vehicle and support rear axle housing on stands.
2. Disconnect shock absorber from lower mounting.
3. Disconnect shock absorber from upper mounting and remove from vehicle.

1983–87 CAMRY, 1983–87 TERCEL W/FRONT WHEEL DRIVE, 1984–87 COROLLA W/FRONT WHEEL DRIVE & 1986–87 CELICA

Refer to "Coil Spring, Replace" for shock absorber replacement procedures.

CONTROL ARM
REPLACE

1983 COROLLA WAGON, 1984–87 COROLLA W/REAR WHEEL DRIVE, 1983–87 CRESSIDA, 1983–84 STARLET, 1984–87 TERCEL WAGON W/4 WHEEL DRIVE & 1984–87 VAN W/2 WHEEL DRIVE

1. Raise and support rear of vehicle and remove wheels.
2. Remove bolts attaching control arm to rear axle housing, **Figs. 7 and 8.**
3. Remove bolt attaching control arm to frame, then remove control arm from vehicle.
4. Use tool 09710-14010 or equivalent to replace bushings, if necessary.
5. Reverse procedure to install.

STABILIZER BAR
REPLACE

1. Raise and support rear of vehicle, then remove rear wheels.
2. Disconnect bolts securing stabilizer bar to axle housing, **Figs. 8 and 10.**
3. Disconnect bolts securing stabilizer bar to frame, then remove stabilizer bar.
4. Reverse procedure to install.

LATERAL CONTROL BAR
REPLACE

1983 COROLLA WAGON, 1984–87 COROLLA W/REAR WHEEL DRIVE, 1983–87 CRESSIDA, 1984–87 TERCEL WAGON W/4 WHEEL DRIVE & 1984–87 VAN W/2 WHEEL DRIVE

1. Raise and support rear of vehicle, then remove rear wheels.
2. Remove cotter pin, nut, washer and outer bushing as necessary from lateral control arm rear axle housing mounting.
3. Remove nut and washer from lateral control arm frame mounting, then remove bolt and lateral control arm from vehicle, **Fig. 8.**
4. Use tool 09710-14010 or equivalent to replace bushings, if necessary.
5. Reverse procedure to install.

SUSPENSION ARM
REPLACE

1983–87 CAMRY, 1983–87 TERCEL W/FRONT WHEEL DRIVE & 1984–87 COROLLA W/FRONT WHEEL DRIVE

1. Raise and support rear of vehicle.

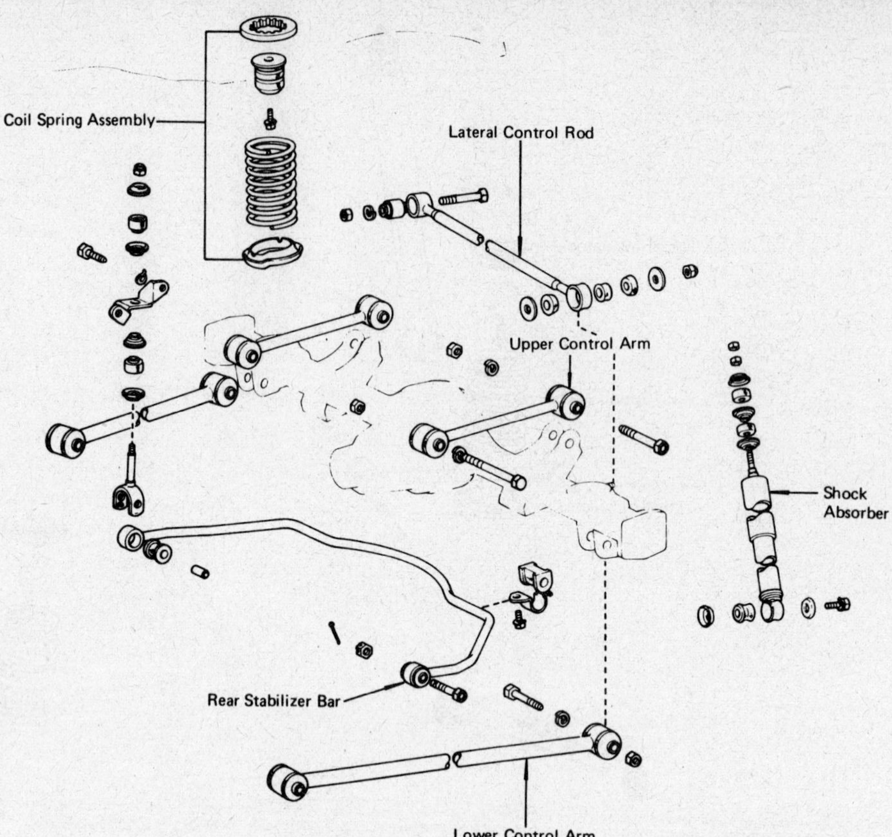

Fig. 8 Coil spring rear suspension. 1983 Corolla Wagon, 1984–87 Corolla w/rear wheel drive, 1983–87 Cressida, 1984–87 Tercel Wagon w/4 wheel drive & 1984–87 Van w/rear wheel drive

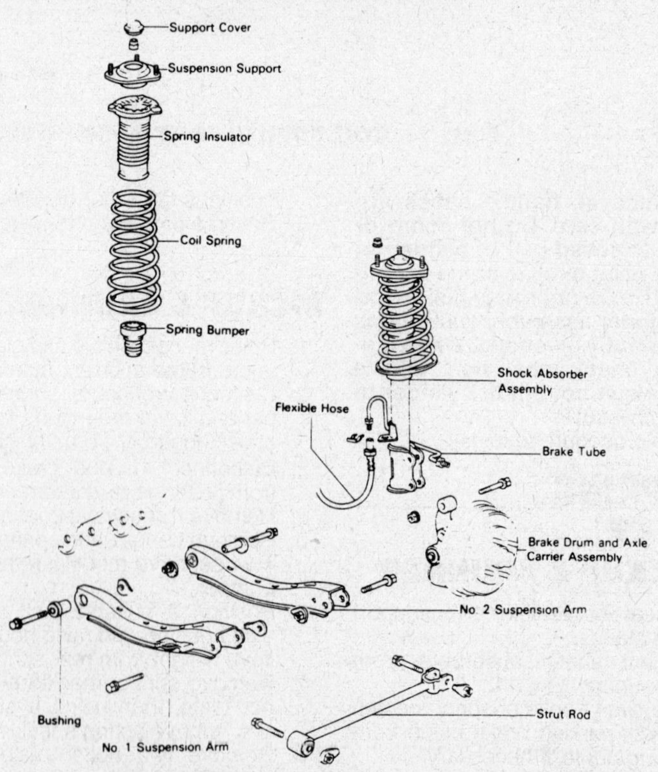

Fig. 9 Rear suspension. 1983–87 Camry, 1983–87 Tercel w/front wheel drive & 1984–87 Corolla w/front wheel drive

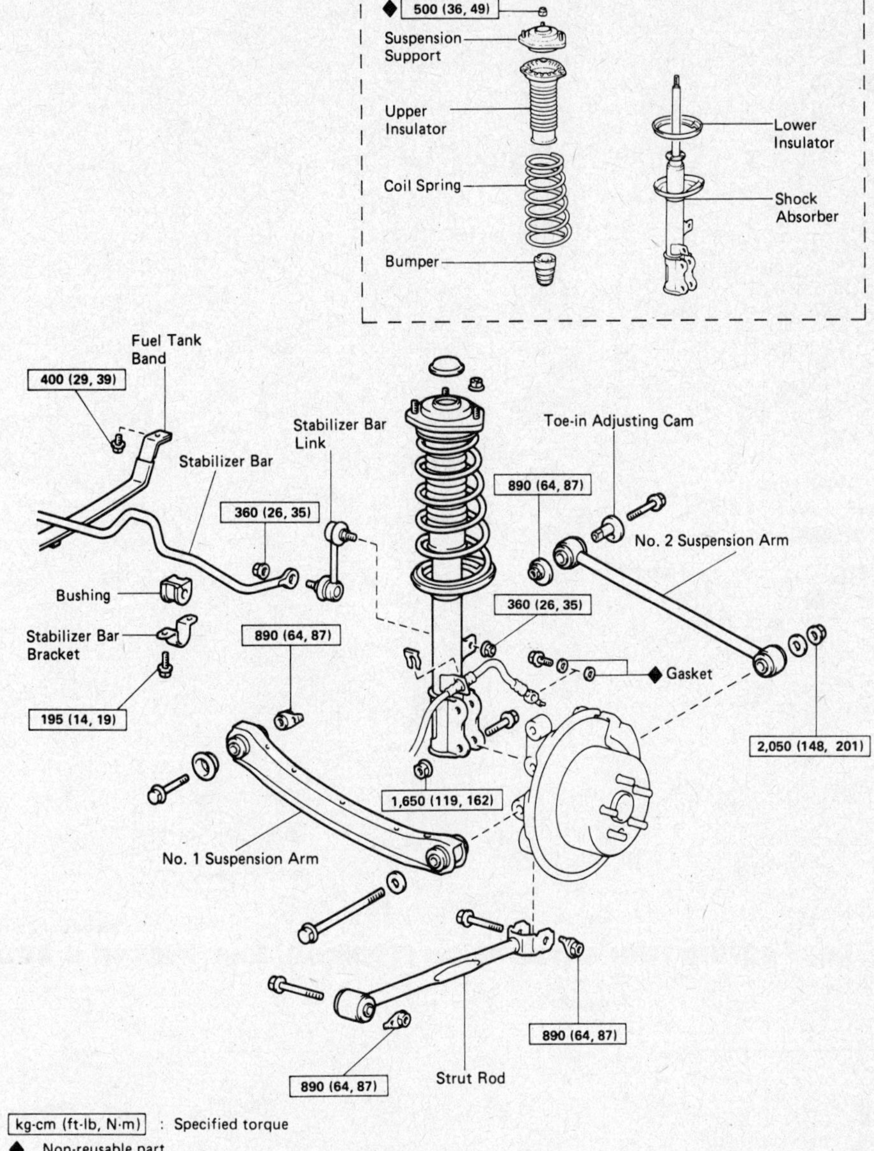

Fig. 10 Rear suspension. 1986–87 Celica

2. Remove bolt and nut securing suspension arm No. 2 to axle carrier, **Fig. 9.**
3. Scribe alignment marks on suspension arm No. 2 alignment cam plate to aid during installation, then remove bolt securing suspension arm No. 2 to body and remove arm. **When removing bolt securing suspension arm to body, turn the bolt only. Do not turn the cam.**
4. Remove bolt and nut securing suspension arm No. 1 to axle carrier, **Fig. 9.**
5. Remove bolt and nut securing suspension arm No. 1 to body, then remove arm.
6. Replace bushings with tool 09726-32010.
7. Reverse procedure to install. Torque all bolts to 64 ft. lbs. with vehicle weight on suspension.

1986–87 CELICA

Removal

1. Raise and support vehicle.
2. Remove Nos. 1 and 2 suspension arm-to-steering knuckle attaching nut and bolt, **Fig. 10.**
3. Scribe reference marks on adjusting cam, then remove No. 2 suspension arm-to-crossmember attaching nut and bolt. Remove suspension arm.
4. Remove No. 1 suspension arm attaching nut, plate and bolt, then remove suspension arm.

Installation

1. Install serrated bushing side of No. 1 suspension arm in crossmember, then install bolt, plate and nut. Do not tighten at this time. **Suspension arms are marked with "L" of "R" for installation identification.**
2. Install serrated bushing side of No. 2 suspension arm in crossmember, then install cam, bolt and nut, but do not tighten. Align cam reference marks made during removal. **Ensure side of suspension arm with spot of white paint is facing outwards.**
3. Connect Nos. 1 and 2 suspension arms on steering knuckle, then install attaching bolt and nut. Do not tighten at this time.
4. Lower vehicle to ground, then bounce vehicle up and down several times to stabilize suspension.
5. With vehicle weight on suspension, torque attaching nuts and bolts to specifications, **Fig. 10.**

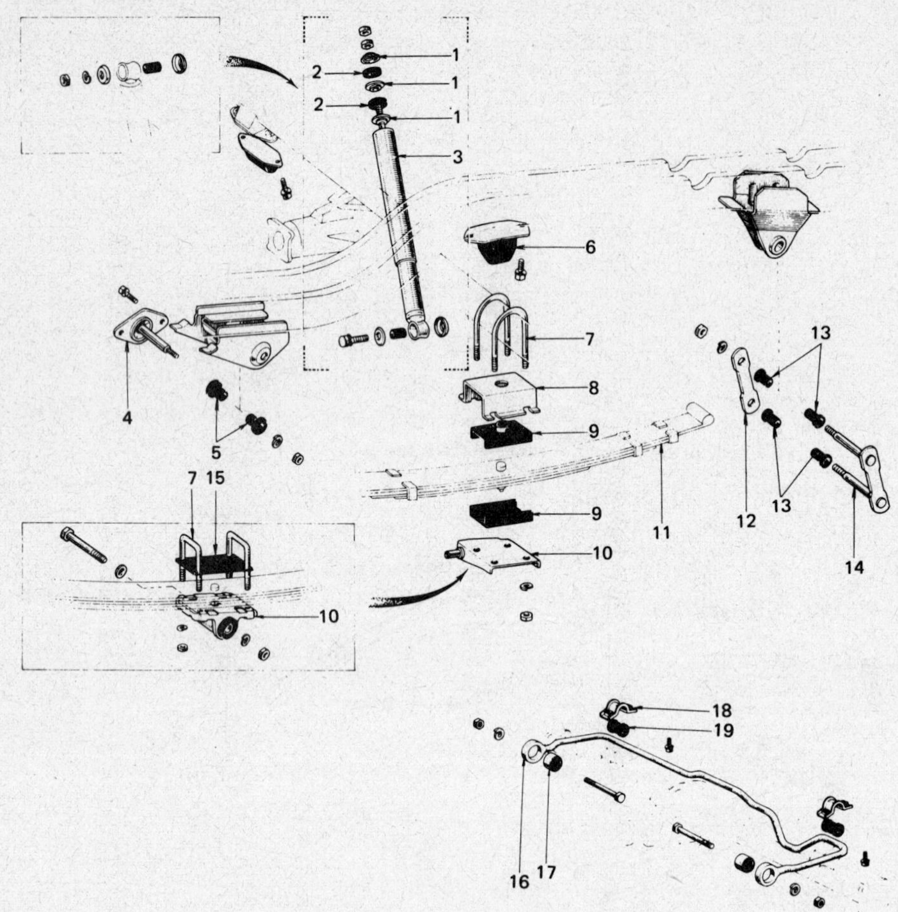

1	Cushion retainer
2	Cushion
3	Shock absorber
4	Bracket pin
5	Bushing
6	Spring bumper
7	U bolt
8	Pad retainer
9	Pad
10	Spring U bolt seat
11	Leaf spring assembly
12	Shackle plate
13	Bushing
14	Shackle pin
15	U bolt retainer
16	Stabilizer bar
17	Bushing
18	Bracket cover
19	Bushing

Fig. 11 Leaf spring rear suspension (Typical). Exc. Pickup & 4Runner

STRUT ROD REPLACE

1983–87 CAMRY, 1983–87 TERCEL W/FRONT WHEEL DRIVE, 1984–87 COROLLA W/FRONT WHEEL DRIVE & 1986–87 CELICA

1. Raise and support rear of vehicle.
2. Remove nut and bolt securing strut rod to axle carrier, **Figs. 9 and 10.**
3. Remove nut and bolt securing strut rod to body, then remove strut rod.
4. Reverse procedure to install. Prior to tightening attaching nuts and bolts, lower vehicle to ground and bounce vehicle up and down several times to stabilize suspension, then torque attaching nuts and bolts to 64 ft. lbs. with vehicle weight on suspension.

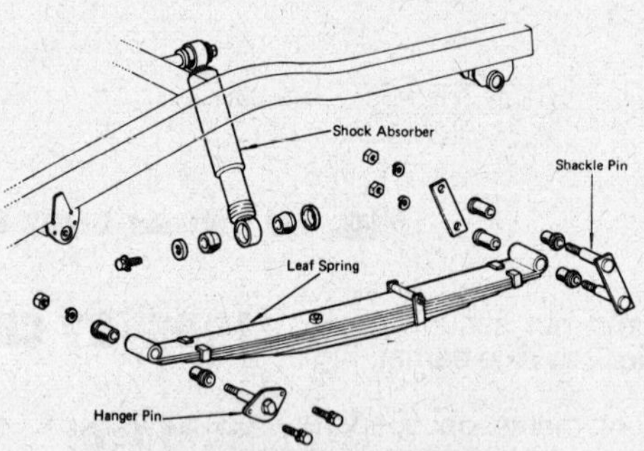

Fig. 12 Leaf spring rear suspension (Typical). Pickup & 4Runner

REAR SUSPENSION & DRIVE AXLE, CRESSIDA, MR 2, SUPRA & 1983-85 CÉLICA WITH INDEPENDENT REAR SUSPENSION SECTION

INDEX

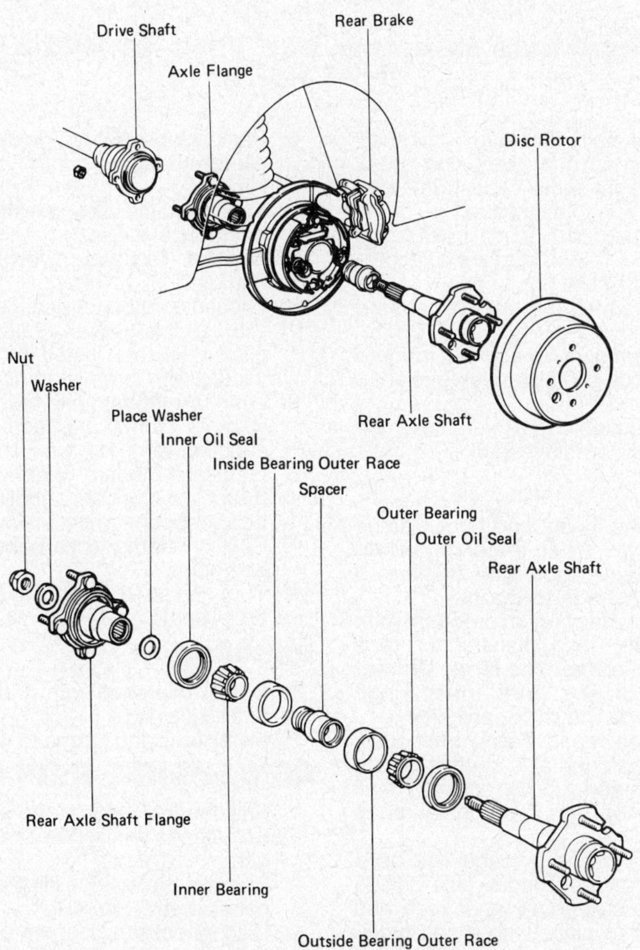

Fig. 1 Axle shaft, bearing & oil seal. Exc. 1985–87 MR2 & Early 1986–87 Supra

EXC. 1985–87 MR2 & LATE 1986–87 SUPRA

AXLE SHAFT, BEARING & OIL SEAL, REPLACE

1. Raise and support rear of vehicle.
2. Disconnect driveshaft from axle shaft and position out of the way.
3. Remove brake caliper and rotor. **If equipped with drum brakes, remove brake drum and backing plate.**
4. Using a hammer and suitable chisel, remove staked portion of axle flange nut, then remove nut and washer, **Fig. 1.**
5. Using a suitable puller, remove axle shaft flange from rear axle shaft.
6. Using an axle puller, remove axle shaft, outer oil seal, outer bearing and spacer.
7. Using a suitable seal remover, remove inner oil seal and bearing.
8. Inspect inner and outer bearings and races for wear and damage. If necessary, replace race(s) with suitable removal and installation tools.
9. Using a suitable puller, remove outer bearing from rear axle shaft.
10. Clean and repack bearings with multipurpose grease No. 2.
11. Using suitable race installer, install inner and outer races, then install inner oil seal.
12. Pack inside of rear axle housing with multipurpose grease No. 2, then lubricate new spacer with grease and install into hub.
13. Install outer bearing and new oil seal.
14. Install rear axle shaft into axle housing.
15. Apply a light coat of grease to axle flange, then assemble axle flange and place washer to axle shaft, **Fig. 1.**

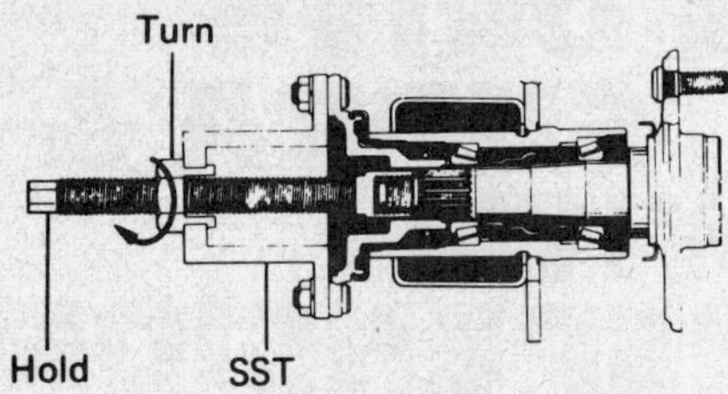

Fig. 2 Installing axle flange to axle shaft. Exc. 1985–87 MR2 & Early 1986—87 Supra

16. Using SST 09557-22022, **Fig. 2,** tighten axle shaft and flange to the point where the flange and shaft deflector are aligned. **Do not allow grease to come in contact with shaft threads.**
17. Install new axle flange washer and nut. While restraining axle shaft from turning, torque axle flange nut to 22-36 ft. lbs. **Ensure rear axle shaft has axial play.**
18. Rotate axle shaft several times in both directions to seat bearings.
19. Using a suitable inch lb. wrench on flange nut, measure and record bearing rotation resistance.
20. Torque axle flange nut to 58 ft. lbs. then remeasure bearing rotation resistance (preload). Preload should be the amount measured in step 19, plus 93.5 inch lbs. **Measure preload while turning flange one turn per six seconds.**
21. If preload is less than specifications, tighten the flange nut 5-10° at a time until specified preload is obtained. **Do not torque flange nut over 145 ft. lbs.**
22. If preload is greater than specifications, replace bearing spacer and repeat procedure.
23. Stake flange nut, install rear brake and connect driveshaft.

AXLE SHAFT SERVICE

Removal

1. Remove nuts securing axle shaft flange to differential.
2. Remove nuts securing axle shaft flange to axle shaft.
3. Remove axle shaft from vehicle.

Disassembly

1. Prior to disassembly, ensure outboard joint slides smoothly in the thrust direction, also check inboard and outboard joints for any excessive radial play.
2. Remove 4 boot clamps, **Fig. 3.**
3. Remove outboard joint large snap ring.
4. Scribe alignment marks on outer race and axle shaft, then remove outer race. Inspect outer race end cover. If worn or damaged, replace.
5. Using a soft faced hammer, remove outboard joint inner race by tapping the outer circumference of the race cage in the shaft axial direction, then lower the cage to the inboard side and remove the balls. Remove outer snap ring with snap ring pliers and press outboard joint inner race from axle shaft with suitable press.
6. Remove outboard joint inner snap ring, then remove inboard and outboard joint boots.
7. Using a screwdriver, remove inboard joint end cover.
8. Scribe alignment marks on inboard joint and axle shaft, then remove snap ring.
9. Using a suitable press, remove inboard joint from driveshaft.

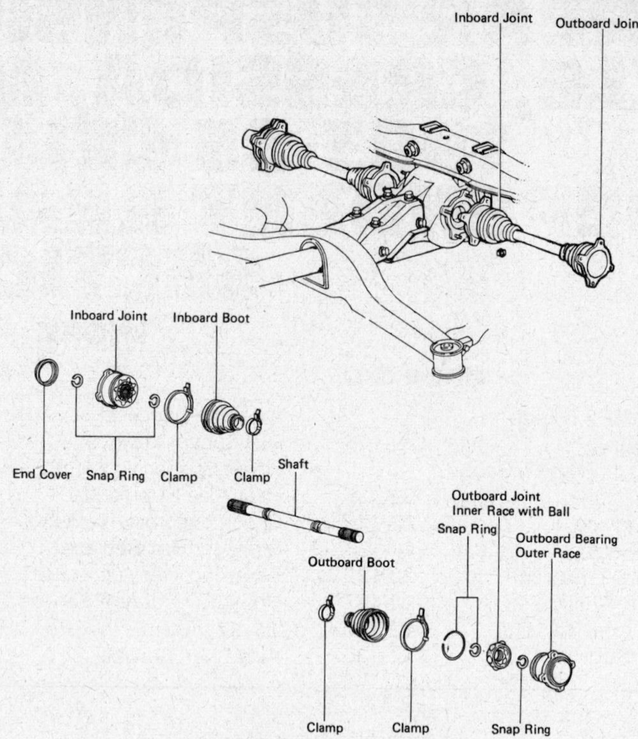

Fig. 3 Rear axle assembly. Exc. 1985–87 MR2 & Early 1986–87 Supra

Assembly

1. Position new boots and boot clamps on axle shaft. **When installing boots on axle shaft, tape axle splines to prevent damage to boots.**
2. Install new snap ring on outboard joint inner spline, then place inner race cage on axle shaft. **The larger diameter end of the joint inner cage should face the outboard side.**
3. Align scribe marks made previously on inner race and axle shaft, then using a press and suitable socket, install inner race on axle shaft. Install snap ring.
4. Lubricate inner race, cage and balls with lubricant supplied in kit. Position inner race cage over inner race and tap balls into place with a soft faced hammer.
5. Install inboard joint inner snap ring, then align scribe marks made previously on inboard joint and axle shaft. Using a suitable socket and press, install inboard joint on axle. Install inboard joint outer snap ring.
6. Pack .13 lbs. (60 gr.) of lubricant supplied with repair kit into flange side of joint.
7. Apply suitable seal packing around inboard side of end cover, then place in position. Tap end cover in joint with hammer.
8. Lubricate outboard bearing outer race with .13 lbs. (60 gr.) of lubricant supplied in kit, then install outer race and secure with large snap ring.
9. Lubricate inboard and outboard boots with .13 lbs. (60 gr.) each of lubricant supplied with kit.
10. Lubricate inboard joint with .13 lbs. (60 gr.) of lubricant supplied with kit.
11. Install boots and secure with clamps. Position clamp locks between flange bolt holes.
12. Turn and stretch boots to ensure they do not deform.

Installation

1. Install axle shaft with narrow joint at differential side.
2. Install nuts and torque to 44-57 ft. lbs.

COIL SPRING, REPLACE

1. Raise rear of vehicle and support with jack stands positioned at frame members.
2. Remove brake hose clips on rear suspension arm, **Fig. 4.**
3. Disconnect stabilizer bar end, then remove nuts securing driveshaft and remove driveshaft.
4. Position a suitable jack under suspension arm and raise suspension arm slightly.
5. Remove rear shock absorber lower mounting bolt and disconnect shock

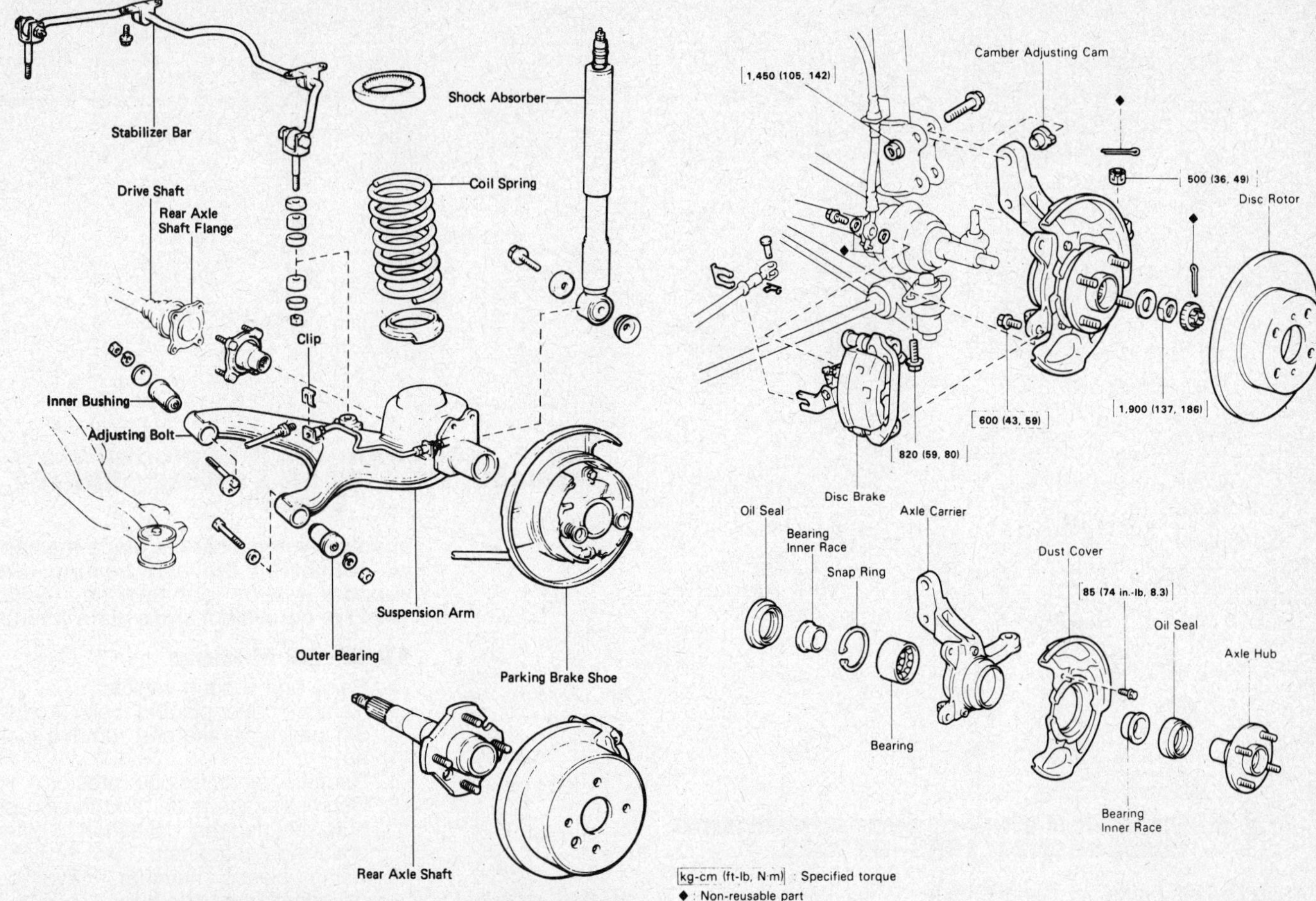

Fig. 4 Exploded view of rear suspension components (typical). Exc. 1985–87 MR2 & Early 1986–87 Supra

Fig. 5 Rear axle hub. 1985–87 MR2

absorber.

6. Slowly lower jack under suspension arm ensuring brake hose and parking brake cable are not stretched or twisted.
7. Remove coil spring and insulators from vehicle.
8. Reverse procedure to install. Torque shock absorber lower mount to 22-32 ft. lbs., torque stabilizer bar end to 11-15 ft. lbs. and torque driveshaft mounting nuts to 44-57 ft. lbs.

SHOCK ABSORBER, REPLACE

1. Raise rear of vehicle and support with jack stands positioned at suspension arms.
2. Remove shock absorber lower mounting bolt and disconnect shock absorber.
3. Using a screwdriver to restrain shock absorber from turning, remove upper mounting nut, then remove shock absorber.
4. Reverse procedure to install. Torque lower mounting bolt to 22-32 ft. lbs. and torque upper mounting nut to 14-22 ft. lbs.

STABILIZER BAR, REPLACE

1. Raise and support rear of vehicle.
2. Remove stabilizer bar brackets from frame.
3. Remove stabilizer bar nuts, cushions and links from suspension arms, then remove stabilizer bar from vehicle.
4. Install stabilizer links to arms as shown in **Fig. 4.**
5. Install stabilizer bar in vehicle, then install bar to links.
6. Install stabilizer bar brackets to frame.

SUSPENSION ARM, REPLACE

1. Raise rear of vehicle and support with jack stands positioned at frame members.
2. Disconnect stabilizer bar end from suspension arm, **Fig. 4.**
3. Disconnect driveshaft from axle shaft and position out of the way.
4. Remove rear axle shaft flange, brake drum or rotor and rear axle shaft. Refer to "Axle Shaft, Bearing & Oil Seal, Replace" procedure under Exc. 1985-87 MR2 & Late 1986-87 Supra.
5. Disconnect brake hose, then remove dust cover (disc brakes) or backing plate (drum brakes).
6. Remove brake lines on suspension arm.
7. Position a suitable jack under suspension arm and raise suspension arm slightly.
8. Remove rear shock absorber lower mounting bolt and disconnect shock absorber.
9. Slowly lower suspension arm with jack, then remove coil spring and insulators.
10. Scribe alignment marks or note setting on camber adjusting cam, then remove suspension arm mounting bolts, camber adjusting cam and suspension arm.
11. Inspect suspension arm for damage, cracks and bending. Inspect arm bushing for wear, cracks or deformation. If bushings require replacement, use tool No. 09710-22040 No. 4 and No. 5 to remove bushings and No. 5 and No. 6 to install bushings.
12. Reverse procedure to install. Torque suspension arm inside bolt to 84-108 ft. lbs. and outside bolt to 73-97 ft. lbs. Check and adjust rear wheel alignment as necessary.

1985–87 MR2

REAR AXLE HUB, REPLACE

1. Raise and support vehicle and remove tire and wheel assembly.
2. Remove cotter pin and bearing locknut cap, **Fig. 5.**

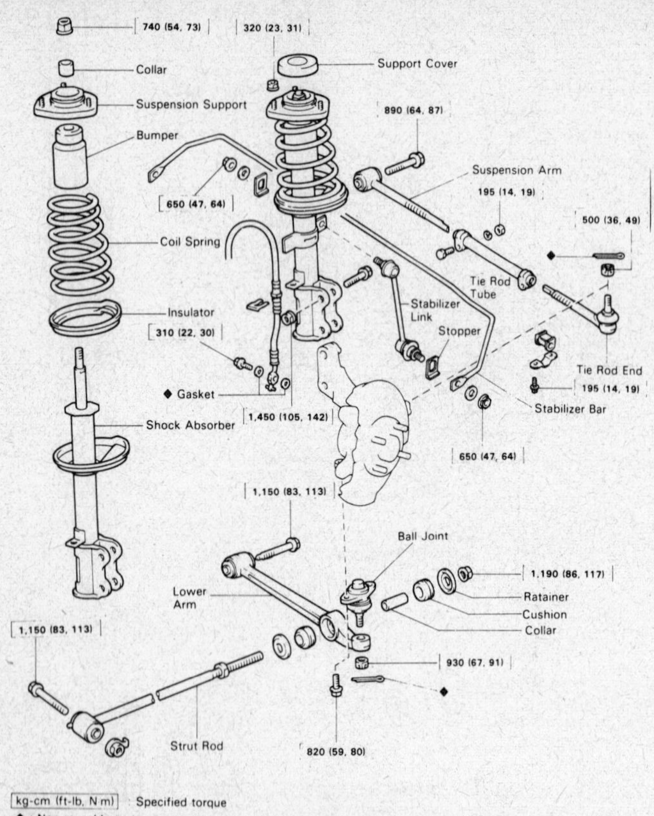

Fig. 6 Exploded view of rear suspension components. 1985–87 MR2

3. With parking brake set, remove bearing locknut.
4. Remove brake caliper from rear axle carrier and suspend out of way.
5. Remove disc rotor, then ensure that bearing play in axial direction does not exceed .002 inch.
6. Remove cotter pin and nut, then, using tool 09610-20012 or equivalent, disconnect tie rod end from rear axle carrier.
7. Disconnect rear axle carrier from lower arm.
8. Scribe alignment marks on shock absorber lower bracket and camber adjusting cam.
9. Remove two axle carrier set nuts and two bolts with camber adjusting cam.
10. Remove rear axle carrier and axle hub. **Cover driveshaft boot with cloth to prevent damage.**
11. Reverse procedure to install. Torque two axle carrier nuts to 105 ft. lbs. on 1985-86 models or 166 ft. lbs. on 1987 models, rear axle carrier to lower arm attaching nut to 59 ft. lbs., the suspension arm attaching nut to 36 ft. lbs., the brake caliper attaching bolts to 43 ft. lbs., and the bearing locknut to 137 ft. lbs.

REAR AXLE HUB SERVICE

1. Using suitable tool, remove dust deflector and inner oil seal from rear axle carrier.
2. Using suitable pliers, remove hole snap ring.
3. Remove three bolts securing disc brake dust cover to steering knuckle.
4. Using suitable puller, remove axle hub from rear axle carrier.
5. Remove inside bearing inner race from bearing.
6. Using suitable puller, remove outside inner race from rear axle carrier.
7. Using suitable puller, remove oil seal from rear axle carrier.
8. Place an outside oil inner race on bearing and, using suitable tool, press out bearing. **Always replace the bearing as an assembly.**
9. Using suitable tool, press new bearing into rear axle carrier.
10. Rotate and insert the side lip of a new oil seal into tool 09608-32010 or equivalent, then, using tool 09710-14012 or equivalent, drive oil seal into rear axle carrier.
11. Apply suitable grease to oil seal lip.
12. Install disc brake dust cover, torquing attaching bolts to 74 inch lbs.
13. Apply suitable grease to oil seal and bearing, then, using suitable tool, press hub into rear axle carrier.
14. Install hole snap ring into rear axle knuckle.
15. Using suitable tool, drive in a new oil seal and dust deflector to the rear axle knuckle surface, then apply suitable grease to oil seal.

AXLE SHAFT SERVICE

REMOVAL

The hub bearing may be damaged if it is subjected to vehicle weight, such as when moving the vehicle with the driveshaft removed. Therefore, if it is

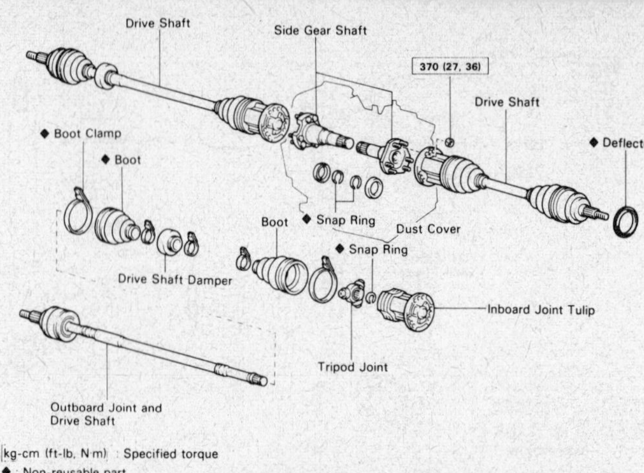

Fig. 7 Rear axle shaft exploded view (typical). 1985–87 MR2 & Late 1986–87 Supra

absolutely necessary to place the vehicle weight on the hub bearing, first support it with tool bearing, 09608-16041 or equivalent and a plate washer.

1985–86 Models

1. Raise and support vehicle.
2. Remove cotter pin and locknut cap.
3. Set parking brake and remove locknut.
4. Remove transmission protector.
5. Depress brake pedal and loosen six nuts securing rear driveshaft to differential side gear shaft.
6. Using plastic hammer, drive out driveshaft from axle hub.

1987 Models

1. Remove cotter pin from axle shaft, then the locknut cap.
2. With emergency brake applied, remove axle shaft nut.
3. With foot brake applied, remove six rear drive shaft to transaxle side gear shaft attaching nuts, then raise and support rear of vehicle.
4. Remove lower ball joint-to-rear axle carrier attaching bolts, then disconnect lower arm, **Fig. 6.**
5. Remove suspension arm-to-rear axle carrier attaching nut, then using suitable puller, remove suspension arm.
6. Using plastic hammer, tap axle shaft from axle carrier and remove.

OVERHAUL

1. Inspect axle shaft as follows:
   a. Ensure that there is no play in the inboard and outboard joint.
   b. Ensure that inboard joint slides smoothly in thrust direction.
   c. Ensure that there is not excessive play in the radial direction of the inboard joint.
   d. Check boots for damage.
2. Remove deflector (if equipped), **Fig. 7.**
3. Remove boot clamps.
4. Place alignment marks on inboard joint tulip and tripod. **Do not punch alignment marks.**
5. Remove inboard joint tulip from axle shaft.
6. Disassemble tripod joint as follows:

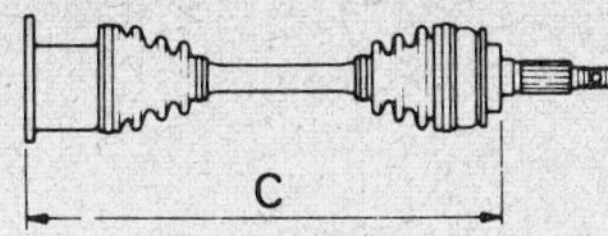

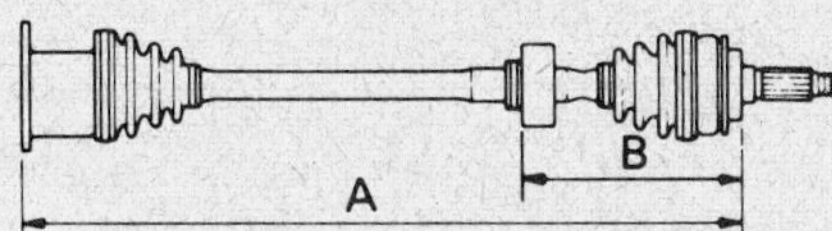

Fig. 8 Measuring driveshaft length. 1985–87 MR2 & Late 1986–87 Supra

a. Using suitable pliers, remove snap ring.
b. Using punch, place alignment marks on shaft and tripod.
c. Using hammer and brass bar, drive out tripod joint from axle shaft.

7. Remove inboard joint boot, right side axle shaft damper (if equipped) and the outboard joint boot.
8. Provisionally install boot and new boot clamp to outboard joint as follows. **Before installing boot, wrap vinyl tape around spline of shaft to prevent damaging boot.**
   a. Provisionally install new boot and clamp to outboard joint.
   b. Install right side axle shaft damper (if equipped) and new clamp.
   c. Provisionally install new boot and clamp to the outboard joint.
9. Assemble tripod joint as follows:
   a. Face beveled side of tripod axial spline toward outboard joint.
   b. Align marks made during disassembly.
   c. Using brass bar and hammer, tap tripod onto axle shaft.
10. Install new snap ring.
11. Using grease supplied in boot kit, pack .26 lb. into tulip and boot, then assemble boot to outboard joint.
12. Assemble inboard joint tulip to axle shaft as follows:
    a. Using grease supplied in boot kit, pack .47 lb. on 1985-86 and 1987 models with man. trans. or .36 lb. on 1987 models with auto. trans. into tulip and boot.
    b. Align marks made during disassembly.
    c. Install inboard joint tulip to axle shaft.
    d. Install boot to inboard joint tulip.
13. Assemble boot clamps to both boots as follows:
    a. Ensure boot is on shaft groove.
    b. Bend and lock band.
    c. On 1985-86 models, ensure that boot is not stretched or contracted when axle shaft is at standard length, **Fig. 8.** Standard length is when "A" equals 26.97 inches (685 mm), "B" equals 7.95 inches (202 mm) and "C "equals 17.28 inches (439 mm).
    d. On 1987 models, ensure boot is not stretched or contracted when driveshaft is at standard length "C", **Fig. 8.** Standard length is as follows: left side, man. trans., 17.09-17.49 inches; left side, auto. trans., 16.98-17.37 inches; right side, man. trans., 26.77-27.16 inches; right side, auto. trans., 26.84-27.24 inches.
14. Install deflector, if equipped.

INSTALLATION

1985–86 Models

1. Install outboard joint side of driveshaft to axle hub, being careful not damage boots, then finger tighten six nuts to driveshaft.
2. Install transmission case protector on left hand side.
3. Install disc rotor.
4. Install brake caliper to rear axle carrier, torquing two bolts to 43 ft. lbs.
5. Install bearing locknut, torquing to 137 ft. lbs. while depressing brake pedal.
6. Install new locknut cap and cotter pin.
7. Depress brake pedal and torque six nuts attaching rear driveshaft to intermediate shaft or differential side shaft to 27 ft. lbs.

1987 Models

1. Install outside axle shaft in axle hub, then align pins and install inboard end of axle shaft on transaxle side gear. Install attaching nuts. Do not tighten at this time.
2. While depressing brake pedal, torque axle shaft-to-side gear attaching nuts to 27 ft. lbs.
3. Install suspension arm to rear axle carrier, then the attaching nut. Torque attaching nut to 36 ft. lbs. and install cotter pin.
4. Install lower arm to rear axle carrier, then the attaching bolts. Torque attaching bolts to 83 ft. lbs.
5. While depressing brake pedal, torque bearing locknut to 137 ft. lbs., then install locknut cap and cotter pin.

COIL SPRING, REPLACE

Refer to "Shock Absorber, Replace" for coil spring replacement procedures.

SHOCK ABSORBER, REPLACE

1. Raise and support vehicle, then remove brake hose attaching clip, **Fig. 6.**
2. Remove union bolt and two gaskets and disconnect brake hose, draining brake fluid into suitable container.
3. Remove clip and brake hose from shock absorber.
4. Disconnect stabilizer link from shock absorber (if equipped).
5. Disconnect rear axle carrier as follows:
   a. Scribe alignment marks on shock absorber lower bracket and the camber adjustment cam.
   b. Remove two axle carrier set nuts and bolts with the camber adjustment cam.
6. Remove engine hood side panel.
7. Remove three upper shock absorber attaching nuts and the shock absorber. **Cover driveshaft boot with cloth to prevent damage.**

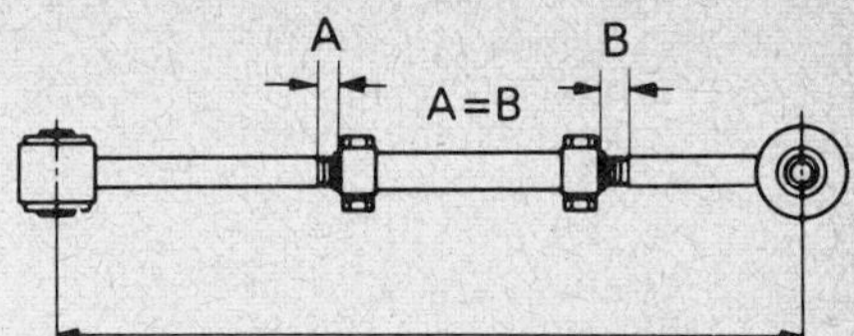

Fig. 9 Adjusting suspension arm length. 1985–87 MR2

8. Install bolt and two nuts on bracket at lower portion of shock absorber shell and secure assembly in suitable vise.
9. Remove coil spring as follows:
   a. Using tool 09727-22032 or equivalent, compress coil spring.
   b. Hold octagon head of suspension support in vise.
   c. Remove suspension support cover and the suspension support nut.
   d. Remove suspension support, coil spring, insulator and bumper.
10. Reverse procedure to install, noting the following:
    a. Use new shock absorber.
    b. Align coil spring end with lower seat hollow.
    c. Torque suspension support nut to 54 ft. lbs.
    d. Torque three upper shock absorber attaching nuts to 23 ft. lbs., being careful not to damage driveshaft boot.
    e. Torque axle carrier attaching bolts to 105 ft. lbs. on 1985-86 models, or 166 ft. lbs. on 1987 models.
    f. Torque brake hose union bolt to 22 ft. lbs.

STABILIZER BAR, REPLACE

1. Raise and support vehicle.
2. Remove nut and disconnect stabilizer link from stabilizer bar, **Fig. 6.**
3. Remove two stabilizer bar bracket bolts, then the stabilizer bar with bracket.
4. Remove bracket and cushion from stabilizer bar.
5. Remove stabilizer link from shock absorber.
6. Reverse procedure to install. Torque stabilizer link to shock absorber attaching nut to 47 ft. lbs., the stabilizer bar to body attaching nut to 14 ft. lbs., and the stabilizer link to stabilizer bar attaching nut to 47 ft. lbs.

SUSPENSION ARM, REPLACE

1. Raise and support vehicle.
2. Remove cotter pin and nut, then, using tool 09610-20012 or equivalent, disconnect suspension arm from rear axle carrier.
3. Remove suspension arm attaching nut and the suspension arm.
4. Reverse procedure to install. Torque suspension arm to rear axle carrier attaching nut to 36 ft. lbs. and the suspension arm attaching nut to 64 ft. lbs.

SUSPENSION ARM SERVICE

1. Remove tie rod tube clamp bolt.

2. Inspect ball joint as follows:
   a. Flip ball joint stud back and forth five times before installing nut.
   b. Using toque gauge, turn nut continuously one turn each 2-4 seconds, taking torque reading on fifth turn.
   c. If turning torque is not 7.4-30 inch lbs., replace ball joint.
3. Install tie rod end and suspension arm to tie rod tube.
4. Adjust tie rod end and suspension arm to 15.12 inches (384 mm) on 1985-86 models, or 13.23 inches (336 mm) on 1987 models, **Fig. 9.**

BALL JOINT SERVICE

1. Raise and support rear of vehicle, placing wooden blocks with height of 7.09-7.87 inches under one rear wheel.
2. Lower jack until there is approximately half a load on front coil spring.
3. Place safety stands under vehicle.
4. Move lower suspension arm up and down and check that ball joint has no vertical play.
5. If vertical play is evident, replace ball joint.
6. Remove cotter pin and nut from lower arm and, using tool 09610-55012 or suitable puller, disconnect ball joint from lower arm.
7. Remove two bolts and the ball joint from the rear axle carrier.
8. Flip ball joint stud back and forth five times before installing nut.
9. Using torque wrench, turn nut continuously one turn each 2-4 seconds and take torque reading on fifth turn.
10. If turning torque is not 9-26 inch lbs., replace ball joint.
11. Reverse procedure to install. Torque ball joint to rear axle carrier attaching nuts to 59 ft. lbs. and the lower arm to ball joint attaching nut to 67 ft. lbs.

LOWER ARM, REPLACE

1. Raise and support vehicle.
2. Remove cotter pin and nut and, using tool 09610-55012 or equivalent, disconnect lower arm from ball joint.
3. Remove stud rod nut and retainer from lower arm.
4. Remove lower arm to body attaching bolt and the lower arm.
5. Remove strut rod cushion, collar and retainer from lower arm.
6. Reverse procedure to install. Torque lower arm to ball joint attaching nut to 67 ft. lbs., the strut rod nut to 86 ft. lbs. and the lower arm to body attaching nut to 94 ft. lbs.

STRUT ROD, REPLACE

1. Raise and support vehicle.
2. Remove strut rod nut and retainer.
3. Remove strut rod attaching nut and bolt with cushion from body side.
4. Remove cushion collar and retainer from lower arm side of strut rod.
5. Reverse procedure to install. Prior to tightening nuts, lower vehicle to ground and bounce vehicle several times to stabilize suspension. Torque lower arm side strut rod attaching nut to 86 ft. lbs. and the body side strut rod attaching nut to 83 ft. lbs. with suspension loaded

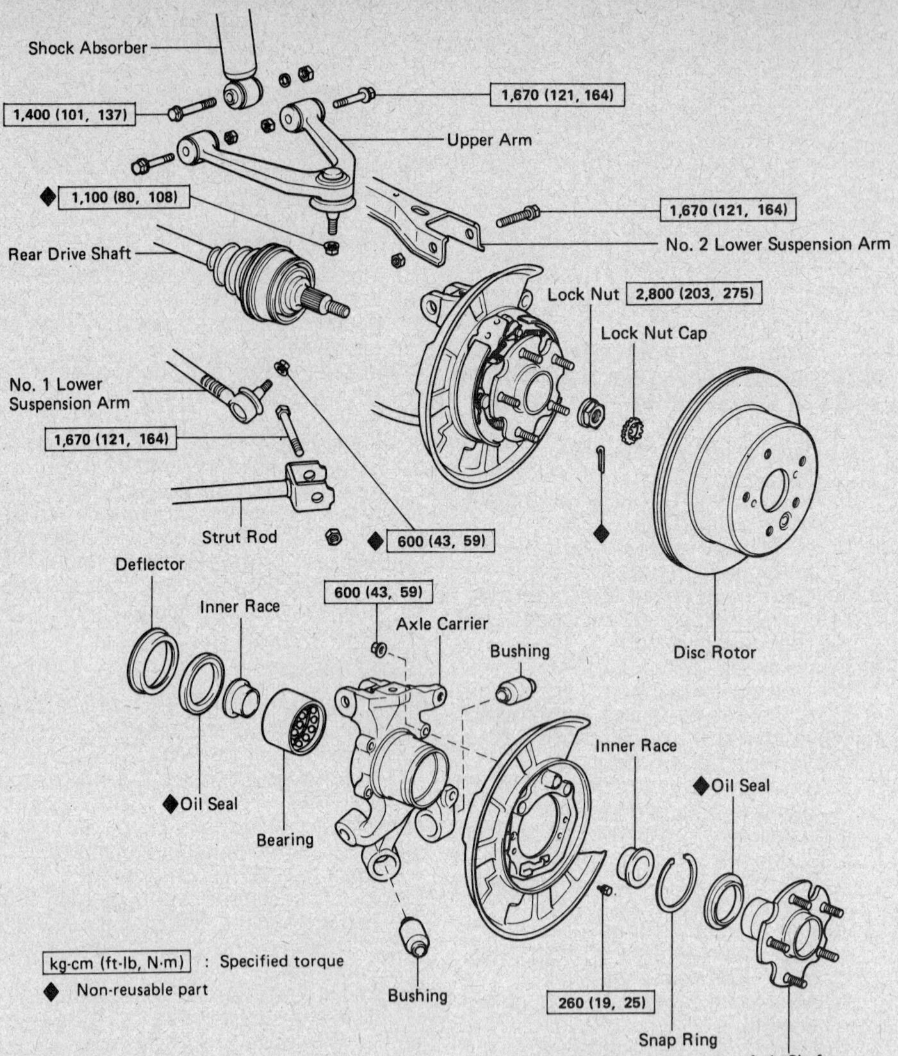

Fig. 10 Exploded view of rear axle hub. Late 1986–87 Supra

LATE 1986 & 1987 SUPRA

REAR AXLE HUB, REPLACE

Removal

1. Raise and support rear of vehicle, then remove wheel and tire assembly.
2. Remove brake caliper from axle carrier and suspend with wire.
3. Remove brake disc, then install suitable dial indicator and measure axial hub bearing play. If play is within .002 inch play is satisfactory. If play exceeds .002 inch, disassemble and inspect axle hub.
4. Check axle flange runout. If runout exceeds .002 inch, replace axle shaft.
5. Remove axle shaft. Refer to "Axle Shaft Service" for procedure.
6. Remove parking brake assembly.
7. Remove No. 1 lower suspension arm attaching nut from axle carrier, then using suitable puller, disconnect suspension arm, **Fig. 10,**
8. Disconnect No. 2 lower suspension arm and strut rod from axle carrier.
9. Disconnect shock absorber from axle carrier.
10. Disconnect upper control arm from body, then remove axle carrier and upper control arm as an assembly.
11. Remove upper arm-to-axle carrier attaching nut, then separate components.
12. Remove brake backing plate from axle carrier.

Installation

1. Install upper control arm to body. Do not tighten attaching nuts at this time.
2. Install axle carrier on upper control arm and install new nut. Do not tighten at this time.
3. Install No. 1 suspension arm on axle carrier. Torque attaching nut to 43 ft. lbs.
4. Install No. 2 suspension arm on axle carrier. Do not tighten attaching nut at this time.

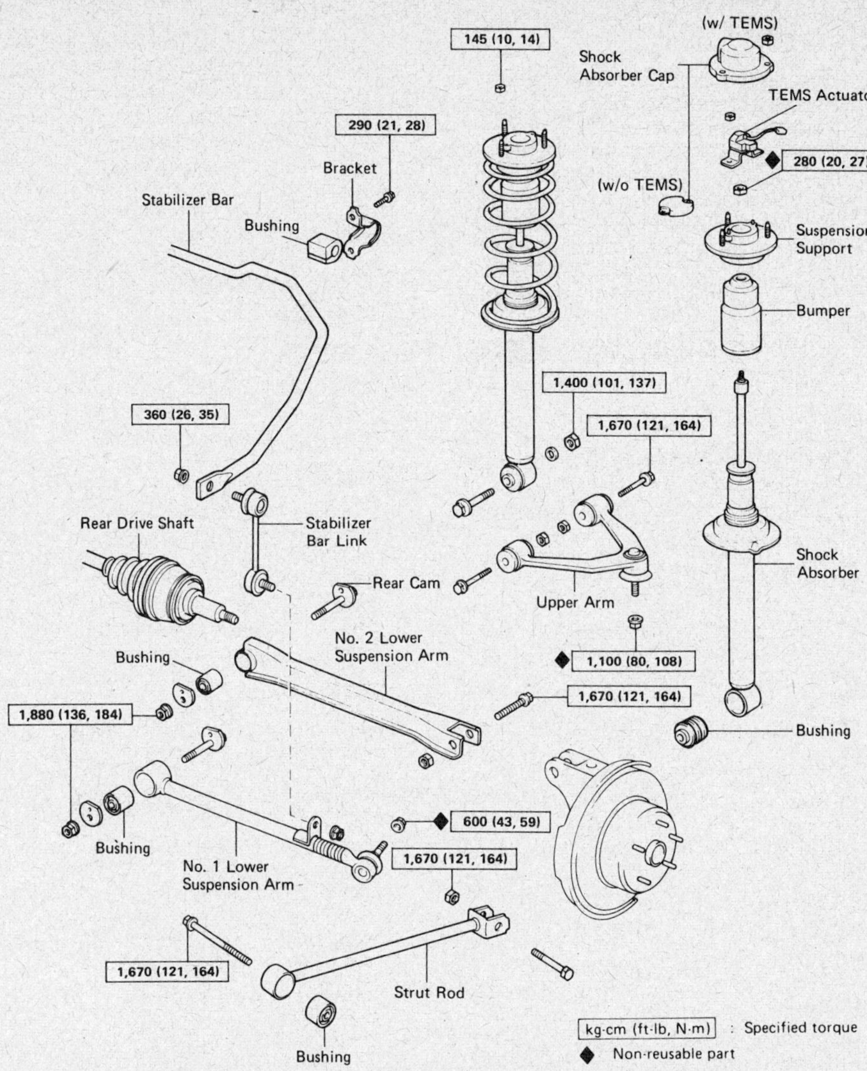

Fig. 11 Exploded view of rear suspension components. Late 1986–87 Supra

5. Install strut rod on axle carrier. Do not tighten attaching nut at this time.
6. Torque upper control arm-to-axle carrier attaching nut to 80 ft. lbs.
7. Install shock absorber on axle carrier. Torque attaching nut to 100 ft. lbs.
8. Install parking brake assembly and brake disc.
9. Install axle shaft. Refer to "Axle Shaft Service" for procedure.
10. Install brake caliper. Torque attaching bolts to 34 ft. lbs.
11. Lower vehicle to ground, then bounce vehicle up and down several times to stabilize suspension.
12. With vehicle weight on suspension, torque upper control arm-to-body attaching nuts, No. 2 lower suspension arm-to-axle carrier attaching nut and strut rod-to-axle carrier attaching nut to 120 ft. lbs.

AXLE SHAFT SERVICE

Removal

1. Raise and support rear of vehicle, then remove wheel and tire assembly.
2. Using suitable jack, raise No. 2 suspension arm, **Fig. 10,** until horizontal. Scribe reference marks between axle shaft and side gear shaft flanges.
3. With assistant applying brakes, loosen, then remove six axle shaft-to-side gear flange attaching bolts.
4. Remove cotter pin and locknut cap from outer end of drive shaft. With assistant applying brakes, loosen, then remove locknut.
5. Using suitable plastic mallet, drive axle shaft from rear wheel hub and remove from vehicle.

Overhaul

1. Inspect drive shaft as follows:
   a. Ensure that there is no play in the inboard and outboard joint.
   b. Ensure that inboard joint slides smoothly in thrust direction.
   c. Ensure that there is not excessive play in the radial direction of the inboard joint.
   d. Check boots for damage.
2. Remove inboard boot clamps.
3. Place alignment marks on inboard joint tulip and tripod. **Do not punch alignment marks.**
4. Remove inboard joint tulip from axle shaft.
5. Disassemble tripod joint as follows:
   a. Using suitable pliers, remove snap ring.
   b. Using punch, place alignment marks on shaft and tripod.
   c. Using hammer and brass bar, drive out tripod joint from axle shaft.
6. Remove inboard joint boot, then the outboard joint clamps and boot. **Do not attempt to disassemble outboard joint.**
7. Remove dust deflector with hammer and screwdriver.
8. Install dust deflector, then temporarily install boot and new boot clamp to outboard joint. **Before installing boot, wrap vinyl tape around spline of shaft to prevent damaging boot.**
9. Temporarily install boot and new boot clamps for inboard joint. **Before installing boot, wrap vinyl tape around spline of shaft to prevent damaging boot.**
10. Assemble tripod joint as follows:
    a. Face beveled side of tripod axial spline toward outboard joint.
    b. Align marks made during disassembly.
    c. Using brass bar and hammer, tap tripod onto axle shaft.
    d. Install new snap ring.
11. Using grease supplied in boot kit, apply an adequate amount to outboard joint, then assemble boot to outboard joint.
12. Assemble inboard joint tulip to driveshaft as follows:
    a. Using grease supplied in boot kit, pack grease into tulip and boot.
    b. Align marks made during disassembly.
    c. Install inboard joint tulip to axle shaft.
    d. Install boot to inboard joint tulip.
13. Assemble boot clamps to both boots as follows:
    a. Ensure boot is on shaft groove.
    b. Bend and lock band.
    c. Ensure boot is not stretched or contracted when axle shaft is at standard length "C", **Fig. 8.** Standard length is 21.724-21.842 inches (551.8-554.8 mm).

Installation

1. Apply multipurpose grease to axle shaft splines.
2. Using suitable jack, raise No. 2 suspension arm, **Fig. 10,** until horizontal.
3. Insert outboard end of axle shaft in axle hub, then install inboard end on side gear shaft flange and temporarily install axle shaft-to-side gear flange attaching washers and nuts.
4. Install axle shaft locknut, then while an assistant depresses brake pedal, torque locknut to 200 ft. lbs. Install locknut cap and cotter pin.
5. While an assistant depresses brake pedal, torque six axle shaft-to-side gear flange attaching nuts to 50 ft. lbs.
6. Install wheel and tire assembly, then

lower vehicle.

COIL SPRING, REPLACE

Refer to "Shock Absorber, Replace" procedure for coil spring replacement procedures.

SHOCK ABSORBER, REPLACE

1. Raise and support rear of vehicle, then remove wheel and tire assembly.
2. Remove speaker grille above shock absorber being replaced.
3. On models equipped with Toyota Electronically Modulated Suspension (TEMS), remove quarter panel trim.
4. Remove shock absorber-to-axle carrier attaching nut and bolt, **Fig. 11.**
5. Working inside vehicle, remove shock absorber cap, then on models equipped with TEMS, the TEMS actuator.
6. Remove three upper shock absorber attaching nuts, then the shock absorber and spring assembly. Install shock absorber and spring assembly in suitable vise, positioning vise jaws at lower shock mount.
7. Remove coil spring as follows:
   a. Using tool 09727-22032 or equivalent, compress coil spring.
   b. Remove suspension support nut, then the suspension support.
   c. Remove coil spring and bumper.
8. Reverse procedure to install, noting the following:
   a. Install bumper and coil spring on shock absorber.
   b. Align coil spring end with lower seat hollow.
   c. Torque suspension support nut to 20 ft. lbs.
   d. Torque three upper shock absorber attaching nuts to 10 ft. lbs.
   e. Torque shock absorber-to-axle carrier attaching bolts to 100 ft. lbs.

STABILIZER BAR, REPLACE

1. Raise and support rear of vehicle.
2. Disconnect stabilizer bar link from No. 1 lower suspension arm, **Fig. 11.**
3. Remove stabilizer bar bracket attaching bolts, then the stabilizer bar.
4. Remove stabilizer bar links from bar.
5. Reverse procedure to install. Torque stabilizer bar bracket attaching bolts to 21 ft. lbs. and stabilizer link-to-No. 1 lower suspension arm attaching bolts to 26 ft. lbs.

LOWER SUSPENSION ARM SERVICE

Removal

1. Raise and support rear of vehicle.
2. Remove axle shaft, then the No. 1 suspension arm-to-axle carrier attaching nut, **Fig. 11.**
3. Using suitable puller, remove suspension arm No. 1 tie rod end from axle carrier.
4. Scribe reference marks between suspension arm No. 1 adjusting cam and crossmember, then remove arm pivot nut, bolt, cams and arm.
5. Remove suspension arm No. 2-to-axle carrier attaching nut and bolt, then disconnect arm from carrier.
6. Scribe reference marks between suspension arm No. 2 adjusting cam and crossmember, then remove arm pivot nut, bolt, cams and arm.

Inspection

1. Flip tie rod end stud back and forth five times, then install nut.
2. Using torque wrench, turn nut continuously one turn each 2-4 seconds and take torque reading on fifth turn.
3. If turning torque is not 7-30 inch lbs., replace No. 1 suspension arm.

Installation

Reverse procedure to install. Prior to tightening attaching parts, lower vehicle to ground and bounce vehicle several times to stabilize suspension. Torque No. 1 suspension arm-to-axle carrier attaching nut to 43 ft. lbs., suspension arms-to-crossmember attaching nuts to 136 ft. lbs. and suspension arm-to-axle carrier attaching nuts to 121 ft. lbs.

UPPER CONTROL ARM SERVICE

Removal

Refer to "Rear Axle Hub, Replace" for upper control arm replacement procedures.

Inspection

1. Flip ball joint stud back and forth five times, then install nut.
2. Using torque wrench, turn nut continuously one turn each 2-4 seconds and take torque reading on fifth turn.
3. If turning torque is not 9-30 inch lbs., replace upper control arm.

Installation

Refer to "Rear Axle Hub, Replace" for upper control arm installation procedures.

STRUT ROD, REPLACE

1. Raise and support rear of vehicle.
2. Remove strut rod-to-axle carrier attaching nut, then the bolt and strut rod.
3. Remove strut rod-to-body attaching bolt, then the strut rod.
4. Reverse procedure to install. Prior to tightening attaching parts, lower vehicle to ground and bounce vehicle several times to stabilize suspension. Torque strut rod attaching nuts and bolts to 120 ft. lbs.

FRONT DRIVE AXLE SECTION

INDEX

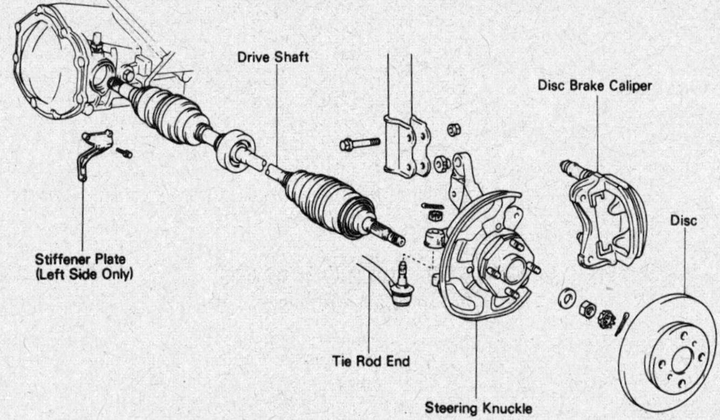

Fig. 1 Driveshaft, replace. 1983 model shown, 1984–87 models similar

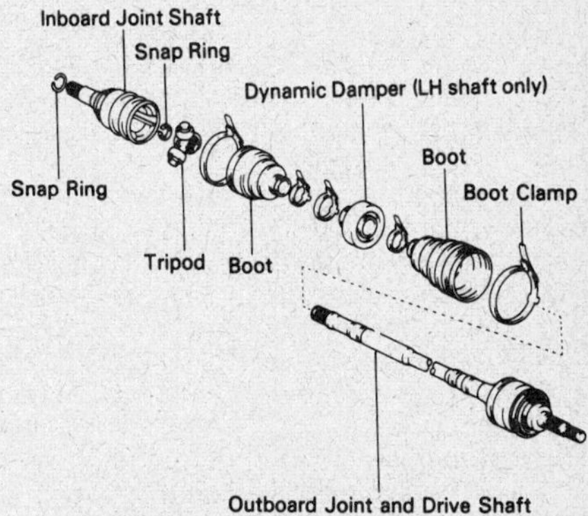

Fig. 2 Driveshaft disassembly. 1983–87 Tercel

TERCEL

DRIVESHAFT, REPLACE

1. Raise and support front of vehicle, then remove tire and wheel assembly.
2. If equipped, remove engine under cover.
3. Remove cotter pin and locknut cap.
4. Depress brake pedal to hold hub stationary, then remove bearing locknut from hub.
5. Remove brake caliper and rotor.
6. Remove tie rod end from steering knuckle, then place alignment marks on shock absorber lower bracket and camber adjust cam. Remove bolt(s) and nut(s) securing steering knuckle to shock absorber, then disconnect steering knuckle from shock absorber, **Fig. 1.**
7. Pull axle hub from driveshaft.
8. If equipped, remove stiffener plate (left side only) from transaxle.
9. Remove driveshaft from transaxle case using tool 09648-16010.
10. Install tool 09563-16010 into transaxle housing after driveshaft is removed to prevent oil leakage.
11. Reverse procedure to install.

DRIVESHAFT SERVICE

1. Inspect driveshaft for damage or wear. Check boot for leaking grease or loose clamps.
2. Remove snap ring, **Fig. 2**, then remove boot clamp.
3. Place mark across driveshaft and inboard shaft joint for reference during assembly, then remove clamp and joint.
4. Remove snap ring, then place mark across tripod and shaft for reference during assembly. Remove tripod from shaft.
5. Remove outboard joint boot clamp and boot. **Do not disassemble outboard shaft.**
6. Reverse procedure to assemble. Align matchmarks made during disassembly. Lubricate inboard joint shaft cavity with suitable grease. On 1983-84 models, right hand side driveshaft assembled length should be 28.50 inches (724 mm) and left hand side driveshaft assembled length should be 24.61 inches (625 mm). On 1985-86 and 1987 wagon models, right hand driveshaft assembled length should be approximately 24.41 inches (620 mm) and left side driveshaft assembled length should be approximately 28.43 inches (722 mm). On 1987 sedan models, right hand driveshaft assembled length should be approximately 30.882 inches (784.4 mm) and left side driveshaft assembled length should be approximately 21.815 inches (554.1 mm).

FRONT AXLE HUB, REPLACE

1. Raise and support front of vehicle, then remove tire and wheel assembly.
2. Remove wheel bearing cotter pin and locknut cap, then while depressing brake pedal, loosen bearing locknut and remove.
3. Remove caliper, then lift off brake disc.
4. Remove tie rod end cotter pin and nut, then using a suitable puller, remove tie rod end.
5. Scribe alignment marks on camber adjust cam and shock absorber lower bracket for reference during assembly, then remove nuts and bolts securing shock absorber to steering knuckle.
6. Disconnect steering knuckle from shock absorber, then remove two bolts securing ball joint to steering knuckle and pull apart.
7. Pull axle hub from driveshaft.
8. Reverse procedure to install. Torque bearing locknut to 137 ft. lbs.

FRONT AXLE HUB SERVICE

1983–86 & 1987 Wagon Models

1. Remove dust deflector from hub, then remove inner oil seal with a suitable puller.
2. Using suitable snap ring pliers, remove snap ring, **Fig. 3.**

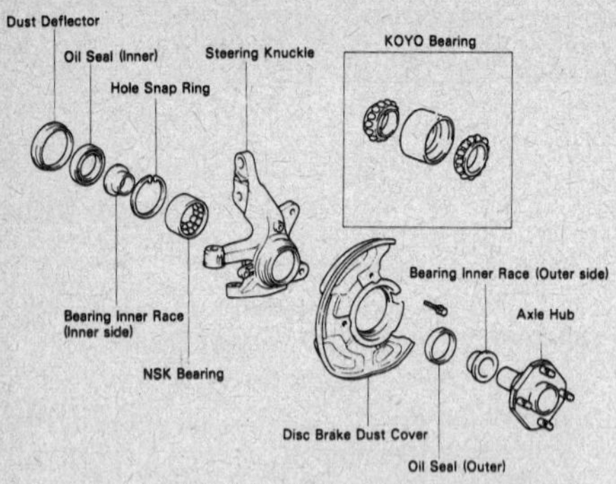

Fig. 3 Front axle hub assembly. 1983–87 Tercel

3. Remove disc brake dust cover bolts, then using a suitable puller, remove hub from steering knuckle and remove bearing race from inner bearing.
4. Using a suitable puller, remove outer bearing race from hub, then remove brake dust cover.
5. Remove outer oil seal from steering knuckle with seal remover.
6. Using a suitable press, remove bearing from steering knuckle using inner race to prevent damage to bearing.
7. Using a press and tool No. 09309-35010, install new bearing into steering knuckle.
8. Install outer bearing race, then install new outer bearing oil seal.
9. Install disc brake dust cover. **Apply suitable sealer to steering knuckle and dust cover mating surface to ensure a leak proof seal.**
10. Install inner bearing race, then using a suitable press, install axle hub into steering knuckle until inner race is tightly against hub shoulder.
11. Install snap ring.
12. Install inner oil seal. Position seal .130 ± .004 in. (3.3 ± .1 mm) from knuckle end surface.
13. Install dust deflector.

1987 Sedan Models

1. Remove ball joint from steering knuckle using suitable puller.
2. Remove inner oil seal with screwdriver.
3. Using suitable snap ring pliers, remove snap ring, **Fig. 3.**
4. Remove brake dust cover attaching bolts, then the dust cover.
5. Using suitable puller, remove axle hub from steering knuckle.
6. Remove bearing inner races and outer oil seal.
7. Place inner race in bearing, then drive bearing from knuckle with hammer and brass drift.
8. Using press and tool No. 09316-60010, press bearing into steering knuckle.
9. Install bearing inner race (outside) and outer oil seal.
10. Install brake dust cover and attaching bolts.
11. Apply suitable grease to outer oil seal lips, then install bearing inner race (inside).
12. Using suitable press, install axle hub in steering knuckle.
13. Install snap ring, inner oil seal and dust deflector (if equipped).

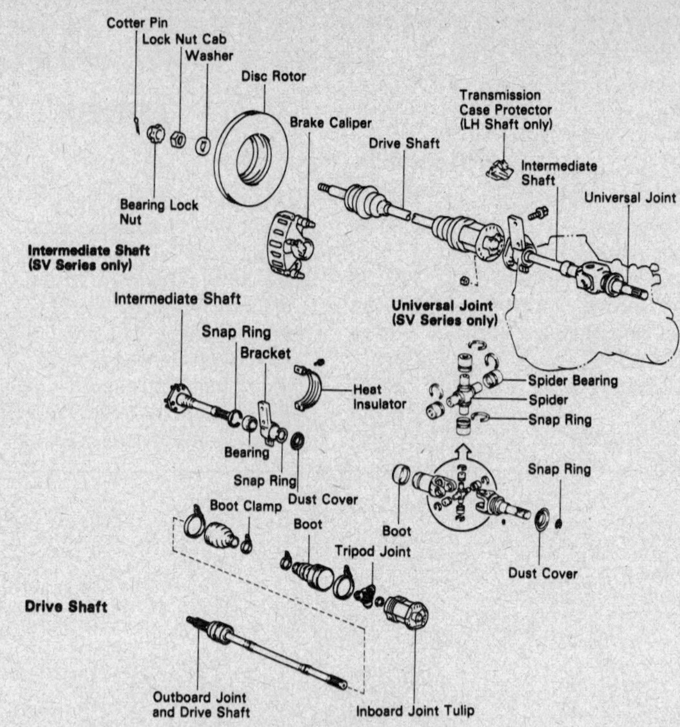

Fig. 4 Driveshaft, intermediate shaft & universal joint. 1983–84 Camry

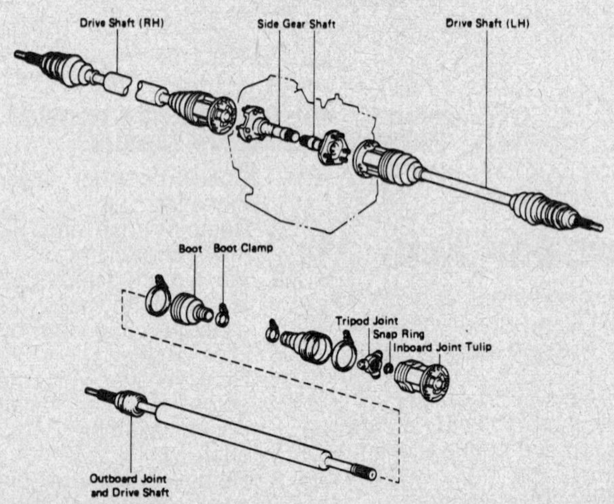

Fig. 5 Driveshaft. 1984–87 Corolla FWD

CAMRY & COROLLA FWD

DRIVESHAFT, INTERMEDIATE SHAFT & UNIVERSAL JOINT, REPLACE

1. Raise and support vehicle, then remove engine under cover (if equipped).
2. Remove cotter pin and bearing locknut cap.
3. While depressing the brake pedal, loosen bearing locknut.
4. While depressing the brake pedal, loosen six nuts attaching front driveshaft to intermediate shaft or differential side gear shaft assembly, **Figs. 4 through 7.**
5. Remove brake caliper from steering knuckle and suspend unit with piece of wire.
6. Remove disc rotor and left hand side transaxle case protector, if equipped.
7. On Corolla, 1987 Camry, 1985-86 Camry equipped with diesel engine and on left side of 1985-86 Camry equipped with gasoline engine and automatic transmission, disconnect steering knuckle from lower arm as follows:
   a. Remove two bolts attaching ball joint to steering knuckle.

[SV Series]

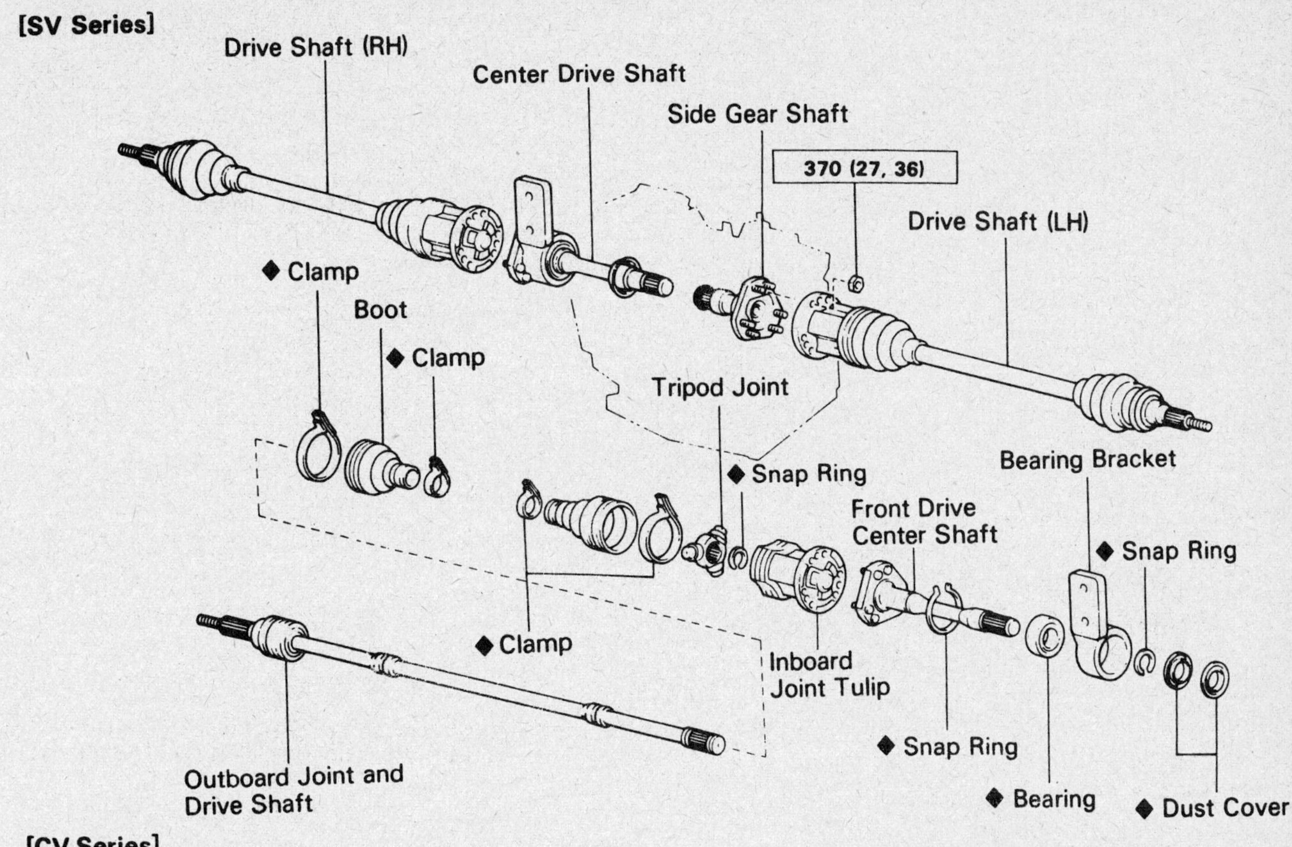

[CV Series]

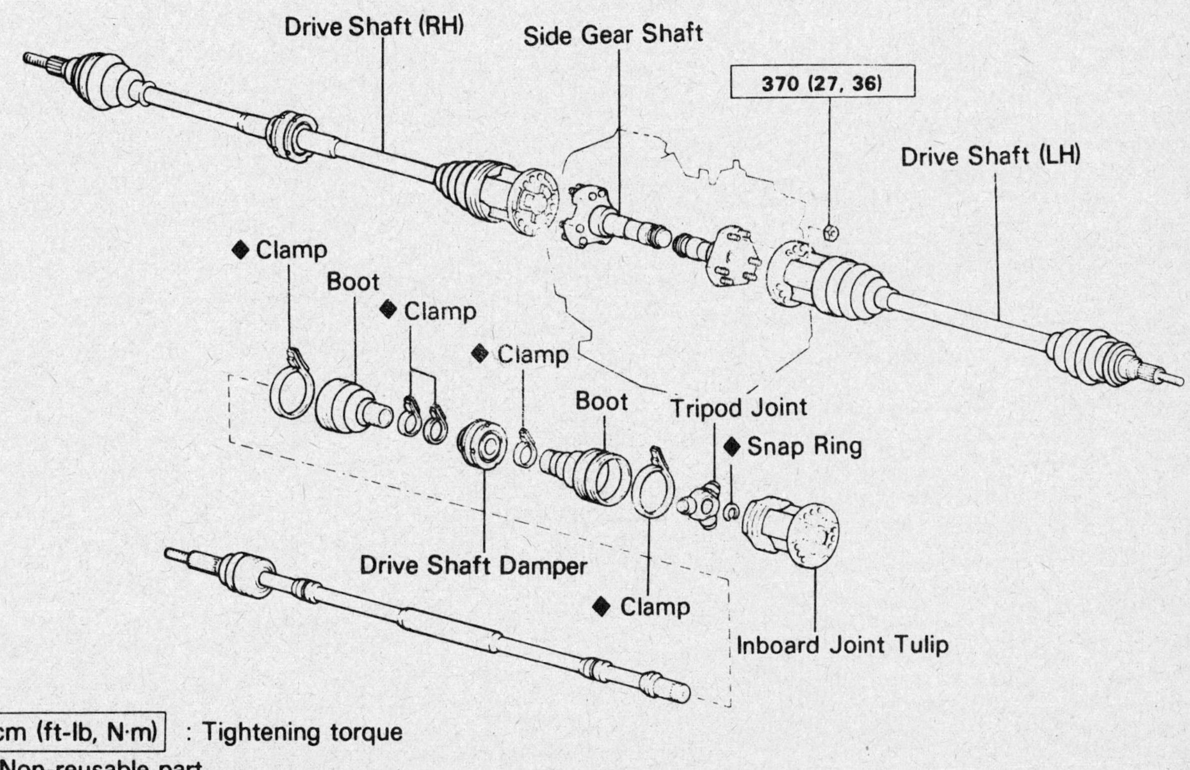

kg-cm (ft-lb, N·m) : Tightening torque
◆ : Non-reusable part

Fig. 6 Driveshaft. 1985–87 Camry

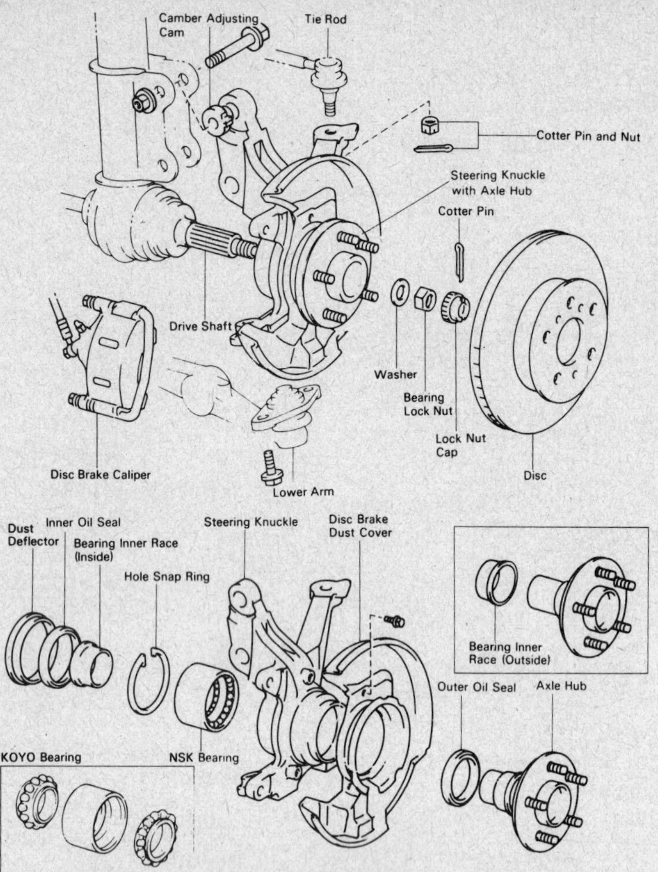

Fig. 7 Front axle hub & steering knuckle components. 1983–87 Camry & 1984–87 FWD Corolla

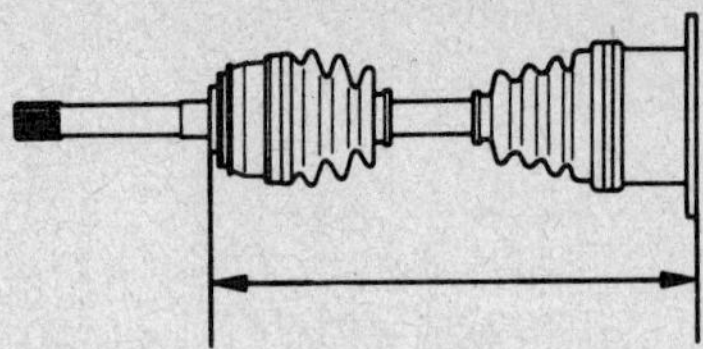

Fig. 8 Measuring front axle shaft assembled length

   b. Disconnect lower arm from steering knuckle.
8. Using tool No. 09950-20014 or equivalent, pull axle hub from front driveshaft.
9. Remove driveshaft.
10. On 1983-84 Camry gasoline models, remove bolts and bearing bracket from cylinder block, then disconnect right hand side intermediate shaft from universal joint.
11. On 1983-84 Camry gasoline models, proceed as follows:
   a. Using tool Nos. 09520-32010 and 09520-32030 or equivalents, install tools onto universal joint.
   b. Drive universal joint from transaxle case assembly.
12. If center driveshaft is to be removed on 1985-87 Camry with gasoline engine, proceed as follows:
   a. Drain transaxle fluid or differential oil into suitable container.
   b. Remove center driveshaft locknut.
   c. Remove snap ring from bearing bracket, then pull out center driveshaft.
13. Reverse procedure to install. Torque brake caliper attaching bolts to 65 ft. lbs. Torque bearing locknut while depressing brake pedal to 137 ft. lbs. Torque front driveshaft attaching nuts to 27 ft. lbs. On 1985-86 Camry with diesel engine and 1985-86 Camry with gasoline engine and automatic transmission, torque knuckle to ball joint attaching bolts to 83 ft. lbs. On 1987 Camry, torque knuckle to ball joint attaching bolts to 94 ft. lbs. On Corolla, torque knuckle to ball joint attaching bolts to 47 ft. lbs.

DRIVESHAFT SERVICE

Disassembly

Before disassembling driveshaft, ensure that there is no play in the inboard or outboard joints and that the inboard joint slides smoothly in the thrust direction.

1. Remove boot clamps, **Figs. 4 through 6.**
2. Place matchmarks on inboard joint. **Do not use a sharp tool to place matchmarks on inboard joint.**
3. Remove inboard joint from driveshaft.
4. Using snap ring pliers, remove snap ring.
5. Using a suitable punch and hammer, place matchmarks on driveshaft and tripod joint.
6. Using tool No. 09726-10010 and a suitable socket wrench, press tripod joint from driveshaft.
7. Remove boots from inboard and outboard joints.

Assembly

Before installing boot, wrap vinyl tape around driveshaft splines.

1. Temporarily install boot and new boot clamp onto outboard joint.
2. Temporarily install boot and new inboard joint clamp onto driveshaft. **The boot and clamp for the inboard joint are larger than those of the outboard joint.**
3. Assemble tripod joint as follows:
   a. Face the beveled side of tripod axial spline toward the outboard joint.
   b. Align matchmarks placed during disassembly.
   c. Using a suitable brass bar and hammer, tap tripod joint onto driveshaft.
4. Install a new snap ring onto driveshaft.
5. On Camry models, pack 6-6.4 ounces or on Corolla models pack 5.8 ounces of grease (supplied with new boot) into boot, then install boot onto outboard joint.
6. On Camry and Corolla models, pack 7.4-7.8 ounces of grease (supplied with new boot) into boot, then align matchmarks placed during disassembly and install inboard joint onto driveshaft. Install boot onto inboard joint.
7. Install both boot clamps onto boots. Ensure boot is on the driveshaft groove. Bend clamp band and lock.
8. Ensure boot is not stretched or damaged in any way when the driveshaft is at assembled length, **Fig. 8.** On 1983-86 Camry gasoline models, right and lefthand side driveshaft assembled length should be 17.87 inches (454 mm). On Camry diesel models, righthand side driveshaft assembled length should be 28.19 inches (716 mm) and lefthand side driveshaft assembled length should be 17.87 inches (454 mm). On 1983-86 Corolla gasoline models, righthand side driveshaft assembled length should be 27.48 inches (698 mm) and lefthand side driveshaft assembled length should be 16.54 inches (420 mm). On Corolla diesel models, righthand side driveshaft assembled length should be 27.76 inches (705 mm) and lefthand side driveshaft assembled length should be 16.46 inches (418 mm). On 1987 Camry models, right and left side driveshaft assembled length should be 17.744 inches (450.7 mm). On 1987 Corolla, lefthand driveshaft assembled length should be 16.54 inches (420 mm) and righthand driveshaft assembled length should be 27.48 inches (698 mm) on all exc. FX series w/man. trans. On 1987 Corolla FX series w/man. trans., righthand

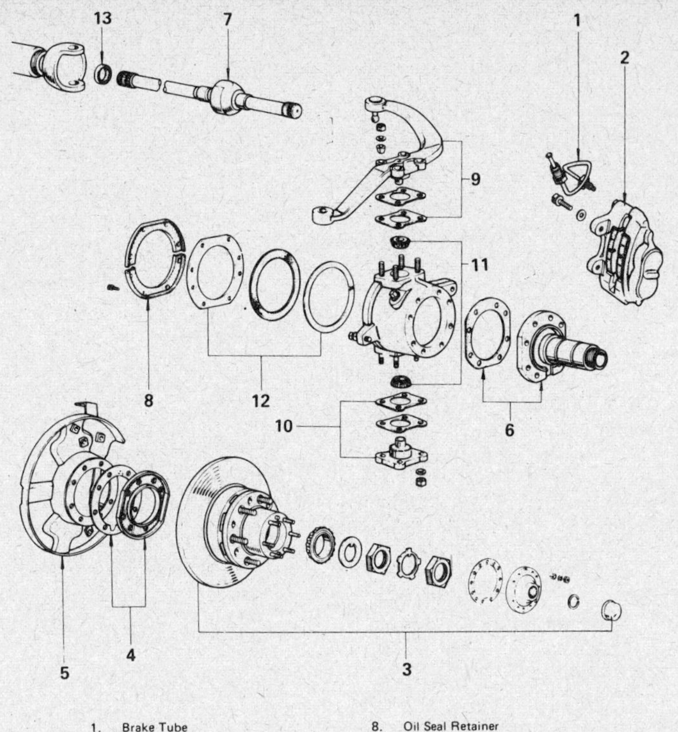

1. Brake Tube
2. Disc Brake Cylinder
3. Front Axle Hub with Brake Disc
4. Dust Seal & Gasket
5. Dust Cover
6. Knuckle Spindle & Gasket
7. Drive Shaft
8. Oil Seal Retainer
9. Knuckle Arm & Shim
10. Bearing Cap & Shim
11. Steering Knuckle & Bearing
12. Oil Seal Set
13. Oil Seal

Fig. 9 Front axle shaft and steering knuckle, replace. 1983–85 Pickup w/4WD & 1985 4Runner

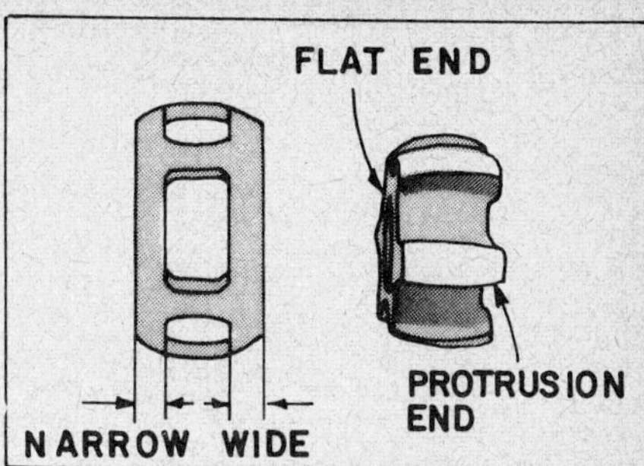

Fig. 10 Assembling inner race into cage. 1983–85 Pickup w/4WD & 4Runner

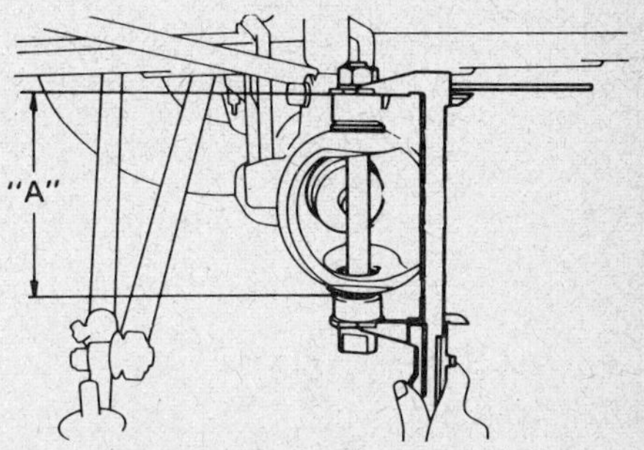

Fig. 11 Measuring axle housing dimension A with tool 09634-60013 installed

driveshaft assembled length should be 27.56 inches (700 mm).

INTERMEDIATE SHAFT

Disassembly

The following procedure applies only to righthand driveshaft on 1983-84 Camry gasoline engine models.

1. Remove heat insulator and dust cover.
2. Remove snap ring from intermediate shaft assembly.
3. Using tool No. 09950-20014 or equivalent, remove intermediate shaft.
4. Remove snap ring from intermediate shaft bearing bracket.
5. Using a suitable press and tool No. 09618-60010 or equivalent, press bearing bracket from intermediate shaft bearing bracket assembly.

Assembly

1. Using a suitable press and tool No. 09608-32030 or equivalent, press new bearing into intermediate shaft bearing bracket.
2. Install snap ring onto bearing bracket.
3. Using tool No. 09608-32030 or equivalent, install intermediate shaft.
4. Install intermediate shaft retaining snap ring.
5. Position dust cover onto tool Nos. 09506-3311 and 09608-32030 or equivalents, then place assembly into a suitable press. Press intermediate shaft into dust cover until a clearance of .04-.08 inches (1-2 mm) is obtained between dust cover and intermediate shaft bearing bracket. **Do not allow dust cover and bearing bracket to touch.**

UNIVERSAL JOINT

Disassembly

The following procedure applies only to righthand driveshaft on 1983-84 Camry gasoline engine models.

1. Remove snap ring, boot and dust cover from righthand side driveshaft.
2. Place matchmarks on driveshaft yoke and joint yoke.
3. Using two suitable screwdrivers, remove the four snap rings from universal joint.
4. To disassemble the universal joint spider bearings, proceed as follows:
   a. Using tool No. 09332-25010 or equivalent, remove bearing from universal joint.
   b. Position bearing outer race into a suitable vise, then gently tap yoke from joint. **Remove the remaining bearing in the same manner.**
   c. Using tool No. 09332-25010 or equivalent, remove bearing from yoke.
   d. Position bearing outer race into a suitable vise, then gently tap yoke from joint. **Remove the remaining bearing in the same manner.**

Assembly

1. Lubricate spider and bearings with a suitable grease.
2. Align matchmarks on the shaft yoke and joint yoke placed during disassembly.
3. Install spider into yoke.
4. Using tool No. 09332-25010 or equivalent, install new bearings onto spider. **Install bearing on the opposite side in the same manner.**
5. Install both snap rings with the same thickness which will allow a 0-.0020 inch axial clearance. Snap ring thickness and color codes are as follows:
   a. .0581-.0600 inch (1.475-1.525 mm), no color code.
   b. .0600-.0620 inch (1.525-1.575 mm), color coded brown.
   c. .0620-.0640 inch (1.575-1.625 mm), color coded blue.
6. Using a suitable hammer, tap on yoke until there is no clearance between bearing outer race and snap ring.
7. Install dust cover and snap ring.

CENTER DRIVESHAFT

The following procedure applies only to right hand driveshaft on 1985-87 Camry with gasoline engine.

1. Using suitable tools, press out dust covers.
2. Remove snap ring.
3. Using tool 09950-00020 or equivalent, remove bearing.
4. Remove the snap ring.
5. Install snap ring over shaft, then, using tool 09527-20011 or equivalent, press on a new bearing.

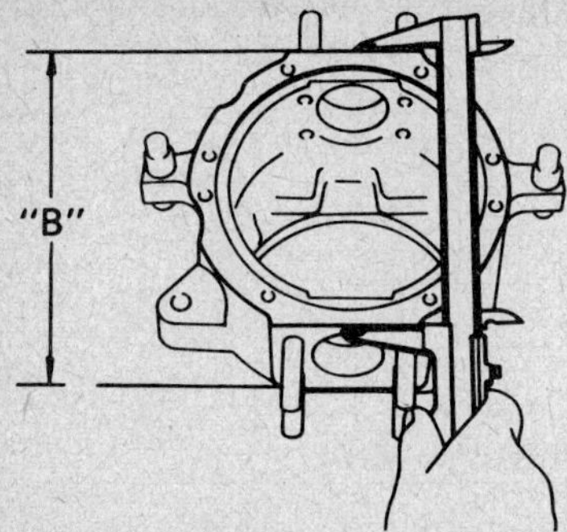

Fig. 12 Measuring steering knuckle dimension B

6. Install new snap ring.
7. Using suitable press, press in a new dust cover on driveshaft side to a clearance of .04-.08 inch, ensuring that there is clearance between dust cover and bearing.
8. Using suitable press, press in a new dust cover on transaxle side to a distance of 3.39-3.43 inches from end of shaft.

FRONT AXLE HUB, REPLACE

1. Remove cotter pin, bearing locknut cap and bearing locknut, **Fig. 7.**
2. Remove brake caliper and disc rotor.
3. Remove cotter pin and nut from tie rod end.
4. Using tool No. 09950-20014 or equivalent, disconnect tie rod from steering knuckle.
5. Disconnect steering knuckle from shock absorber as follows:
   a. Place alignment marks on shock absorber lower bracket and camber adjust cam.
   b. Remove bolt and nut assembly, then separate steering knuckle from shock absorber.
6. Disconnect steering knuckle from lower arm.
7. Using tool No. 09950-20014 or equivalent, pull axle hub assembly from driveshaft.
8. Reverse procedure to install. Torque steering knuckle to shock absorber attaching nuts to 105 ft. lbs. on 1985-87 Corolla models with gasoline engine, or 152 ft. lbs. on all other 1983-86 models. On 1987 Camry, torque steering knuckle attaching nuts to 105 ft. lbs. On all models, torque bearing locknut to 137 ft. lbs.

1983–85 PICKUP W/4 WHEEL DRIVE & 1985 4RUNNER

AXLE SHAFT, REPLACE

1. Raise and support vehicle, then remove tire and wheel assembly.
2. Remove axle hub.
3. Remove dust seal and gasket, then remove dust cover, **Fig. 9.**
4. Remove knuckle spindle and gasket, then position flattened part of outer axle shaft upwards and remove axle shaft.
5. Remove oil seal retainer, then disconnect drag link from knuckle arm. Disconnect tie rod from knuckle arm, then remove knuckle arm and shim using tool 090606-60010 or equivalent.
6. Remove bearing cap and shim using tool 09606-60010 or equivalent. Identify upper and lower bearings and shims for reference during assembly. **If original axle shaft is being replaced, original shims may be used. If new axle shaft is to be installed, new shims must be used. Refer to "Adjustments" to determine shim thickness.**

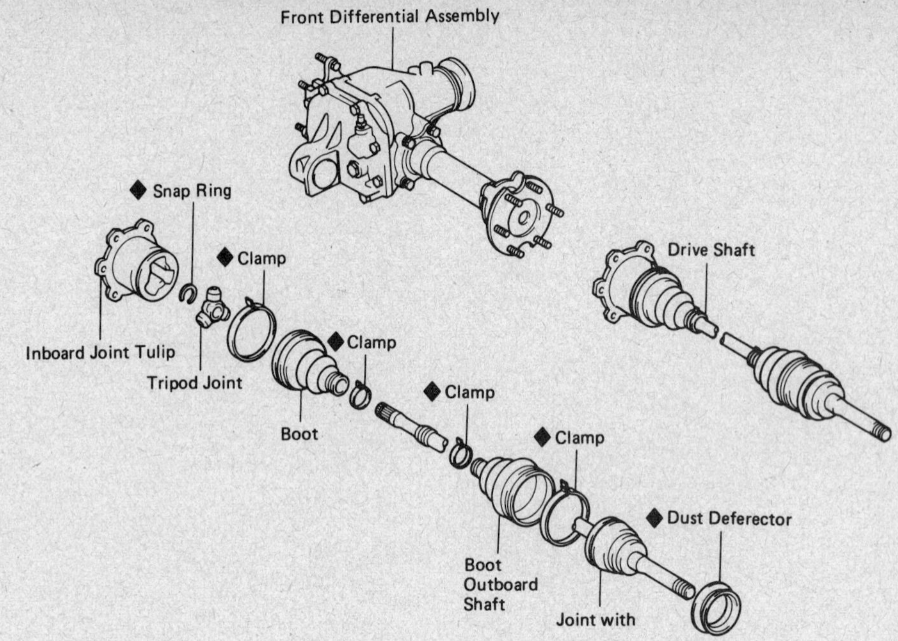

Fig. 13 Exploded view of front driveshaft assembly. 1986–87 Pickup w/4WD & 4Runner & 1987 Van w/4WD

AXLE SHAFT SERVICE

1. Place axle shaft in vise, then separate outer shaft from axle shaft using drift.
2. Remove six ball bearings by rotating inner cage until bearings can be removed.
3. Remove cage and inner race from outer shaft. Remove inner race from cage.
4. Inspect all parts for damage or wear, then assemble inner race into cage as shown in **Fig. 10.**
5. Assemble cage and inner race onto outer shaft by positioning two large openings of cage against protruded parts of outer shaft.
6. Assemble inner race and cage, then install ball bearings. Lubricate outer shaft cavity with suitable grease.
7. Install new snap ring onto inner shaft then assemble inner and outer shafts.

ADJUSTMENTS

Bearing Preload

Whenever axle housing or steering knuckle is replaced, the steering knuckle alignment and knuckle bearing preload should be adjusted with tool No. 09634-60013.

1. Using tool No. 09308-00010 or equivalent, remove oil seal.
2. Lubricate bearing with suitable grease, then install bearing and tool No. 09634-60013 into axle housing.
3. Install a suitable spring scale and measure bearing preload.
4. Bearing preload should be 4-8.4 lbs. on 1983 models, or 6.6-13.2 lbs. on 1984-85 models. Tighten nut F at top of tool No. 09634-60013 until specified bearing preload is obtained.
5. Measure distance A as shown in **Fig. 11,** then measure distance B as shown in **Fig. 12.**
6. Subtract measurement A from measurement B to obtain total adjusting shim thickness required to maintain correct bearing preload.

Axle Shaft Alignment

1. Apply light coating of red lead to center part of rod, then press tool against housing while rotating rod and scribe mark on rod.
2. Assemble knuckle spindle to knuckle, then remove tool 09634-60013 from axle housing and install onto knuckle. Rotate rod and scribe second mark onto it. Measure distance between two scribed marks.
3. Thickness of steering knuckle lower bearing shim will be distance between two scribe marks less .12 inch (3 mm).
4. Thickness of steering knuckle upper bearing shim will be difference between shim selected in step 4 and shim selected in step 6 under "Bearing Preload." Adjusting shims are available in .004 inch (.1 mm), .008 inch (.2 mm), .02 inch (.5 mm) and .04 inch (1 mm) thicknesses.

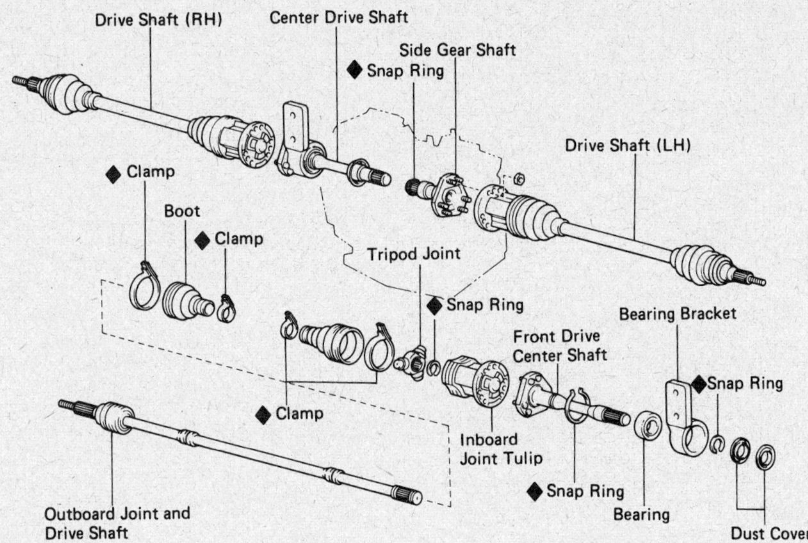

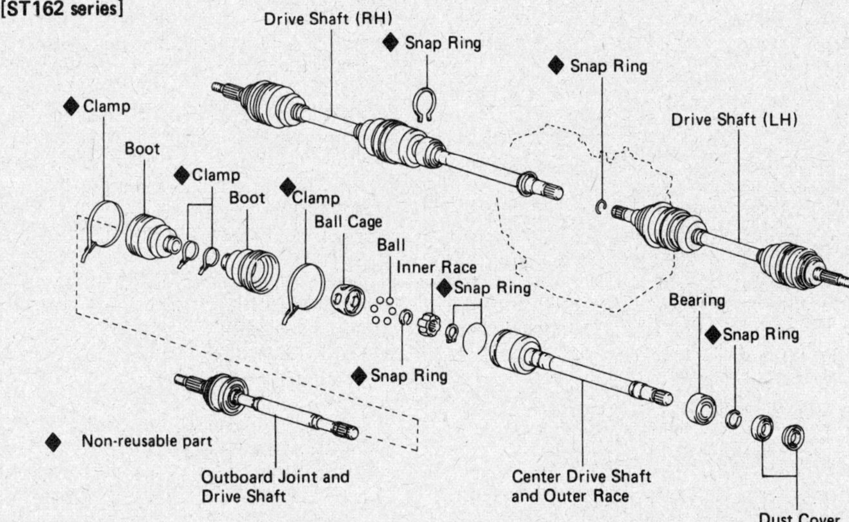

Fig. 14 Driveshaft assembly. 1986-87 Celica

1986-87 PICKUP W/4 WHEEL DRIVE & 4RUNNER & 1987 VAN W/4 WHEEL DRIVE

AXLE SHAFT REMOVAL

1. Raise and support vehicle, then remove tire and wheel assembly.
2. Depress brake pedal, then loosen six front driveshaft attaching nuts, **Fig. 13.**
3. Remove manual locking hub as follows:
   a. Place control handle to "Free" position.
   b. Remove cover attaching bolts, then the cover.
   c. Remove axle bolt with washer, then the hub body attaching nuts and washers.
   d. Remove cone washer by tapping on heads of bolts using a hammer and suitable drift.
   e. Remove manual locking hub body.
4. Remove automatic locking hub as follows:
   a. Remove hub cover.
   b. Remove axle bolt, then the washer.
   c. Remove hub body attaching nuts.
   d. Remove cone washer by tapping on heads of bolts, using a hammer and suitable drift.
   e. Remove automatic locking hub body.
5. On models less locking hubs, remove hub as follows:
   a. Remove grease cap from hub flange.
   b. Remove hub bolt and washer, then hub flange attaching nuts.
   c. Tap hub flange attaching studs with brass drift and hammer to remove cone washers.
   d. Install two bolts into hub flange opposite from each other, then tighten evenly to remove hub flange.
6. Remove driveshaft snap ring, then the spacer.
7. Pull front shaft from side gear shaft, then pull from steering knuckle.

AXLE SHAFT SERVICE

1. Place axle shaft in a suitable vise, then make sure there is no play in inboard and outboard joints.
2. Ensure inboard boot slides smoothly in thrust direction and that there in no radial play in U-joints.
3. Check boots for damage, then remove inboard joint clamps.
4. Place matchmarks on inboard joint tulip and tripod, then separate inboard joint tulip from driveshaft.
5. Remove snap ring from tripod joint, then place matchmarks on shaft and tripod, using a suitable brass punch.
6. Remove tripod joint from shaft, using a hammer and suitable drift.
7. Remove inboard joint boot, then the outboard joint boot clamps and boot. **Do not attempt to disassemble outboard joint.**
8. Remove dust deflector.
9. Temporarily install new dust deflector, then wrap vinyl tape around spline of shaft and install boot with new clamps to outboard joint.
10. Temporarily install boot with new clamps to inboard joint and driveshaft.
11. Place beveled side of tripod axial spline toward outboard joint, then align matchmarks previously marked. Tap tripod joint into driveshaft using a suitable drift, then install snap ring.
12. Apply .43-.44 lbs. of grease included with boot kit into boot, then assemble boot to outboard joint.
13. On Pickup & 4Runner models, apply .60-.62 lbs., or on Van models, apply .47-.50 lbs. of grease included in boot kit to inboard tulip and boot, then assemble inboard joint to inboard joint tulip. Align matchmarks, then insert inboard tulip to driveshaft. Install boot to inboard tulip.
14. Install both boot clamps, then bend bands rearwards and close clamps.
15. Measure assembled length of boot without boots stretched or contracted, **Fig. 8.** Length should be 15.35 inches on 1986 models, 15.705 inches on 1987 Pickup & 4Runner models, or 14.482 inches on 1987 Van models w/4 wheel drive.

AXLE SHAFT INSTALLATION

1. Apply molybdenum disulphide lithium base grease to outboard joint shaft, then insert it into steering knuckle and side gear shaft. Install 6 retaining nuts, **Fig. 13.**
2. Install spacer and snap ring to outboard joint shaft.
3. Install free wheeling hub as follows:
   a. Place new gasket on front axle hub.
   b. Install hub body with 6 cone washers and nuts, then torque attaching nuts to 23 ft. lbs.

ST161 series

Fig. 15 Measuring front axle shaft assembled length. 1986–87 Celica 161 series

c. Install hub bolt with washer, then torque to 13 ft. lbs.
d. Apply a suitable grease to inner hub splines, then place control handle in "Free" position.
e. Install new gasket on cover, then install cover on body with follower pawl tabs aligned with non-toothed portions of body.
f. Install cover attaching bolts and torque to 7 ft. lbs.

4. Install automatic locking hub as follows:
   a. Position new gasket on axle hub, then apply suitable multipurpose grease to automatic locking hub splines.
   b. Align spring ends of brake assembly in hub with hub flange alignment pins.
   c. Ensure locking hub outer cam stopper is securely in inner cam groove, then position inner cam protrusion so it is centered between outer cam protrusions and aligned with hub alignment pin holes.
   d. Install locking hub to axle hub ensuring inner cam protrusion is set between ends of hub brake spring.
   e. Install 6 cone washers and nuts and torque nuts to 23 ft. lbs. **If hub does not fit perfectly on axle hub, remove and reinstall.**
   f. Install axle bolt with washer, then torque to 13 ft. lbs.
   g. Install cover, then insert attaching bolts and torque to 7 ft. lbs.
5. On models less locking hubs, install hubs as follows:
   a. Position new gasket on axle hub, then install hub flange on axle.
   b. Install cone washers and attaching nuts. Torque attaching nuts to 23 ft. lbs.
   c. Install washer and bolt in driveshaft. Torque to 13 ft. lbs.
   d. Install grease cap on hub flange.
6. While an assistant depresses brake pedal, torque side gear shaft to drive shaft attaching nuts to 61 ft. lbs. on Pickup & 4Runner models, or 50 ft. lbs. on Van w/4 wheel drive models.

1986–87 CELICA

DRIVESHAFT, CENTER SHAFT & UNIVERSAL JOINT, REPLACE

1. Raise and support vehicle.
2. Remove cotter pin, locknut cap, then the locknut.
3. Remove engine under cover, then on 162 series, drain transaxle fluid and remove transaxle protector.
4. While depressing brake pedal, loosen 6 front driveshaft to center shaft attaching nuts or differential side bearing shaft on 161 series, **Fig. 14.**
5. Remove cotter pin and nut from tie rod end, then disconnect tie rod end from steering knuckle, using tool No. SST 09628-62011.
6. Remove bolts and attaching nuts, then separate steering knuckle from lower arm.
7. On 161 series, disconnect driveshaft from steering knuckle, then using tool No. 09950-20016 or equivalent, pull axle hub from driveshaft. Remove driveshaft.
8. On 162 series, place a mark in a convenient spot on driveshaft, then measure and note distance between transaxle case and spot marked. Using tool No. 09520-32060, remove LH driveshaft.
9. On 162 series, using tool No. 09950-20016, pull axle hub from driveshaft. Disconnect RH driveshaft from steering knuckle, then remove snap ring and pull out RH and center driveshafts.
10. On 161 series, drain transmission fluid or differential oil, then remove snap ring and center driveshaft.
11. Reverse procedures to install. Torque lower arm to steering knuckle to 94 ft. lbs. Torque tie rod end to steering knuckle nut to 36 ft. lbs. Torque bearing locknut while depressing brake pedal to 137 ft. lbs. Torque 6 front driveshaft to differential side shaft or center shaft to 27 ft. lbs.

AXLE SHAFT SERVICE

Disassembly

Before disassembling driveshaft, make sure there is no play in the inboard or outboard joints and that the inboard joint slides smoothly in the thrust direction.

1. Remove boot clamps, **Fig. 14.**
2. Place matchmarks on inboard joint. **Do not use sharp tool to place matchmarks on inboard joint.**
3. Remove inboard joint from driveshaft.
4. On 161 series, remove snap ring, then place matchmarks on shaft and tripod. Remove joint from driveshaft using a hammer and suitable drift.
5. On 162 series, place matchmarks on inboard joint outer race and driveshaft, then remove snap ring. Remove inboard joint outer race from driveshaft.
6. On 162 series, place matchmarks on driveshaft, cage and inner race, then remove six balls and cage from inner race. Remove snap ring, then, using a hammer and suitable drift, remove inner race from driveshaft.
7. Remove snap ring from shaft at end of splines, then the inboard joint.
8. Remove outboard joint boot clamps and boot.

ST162 series

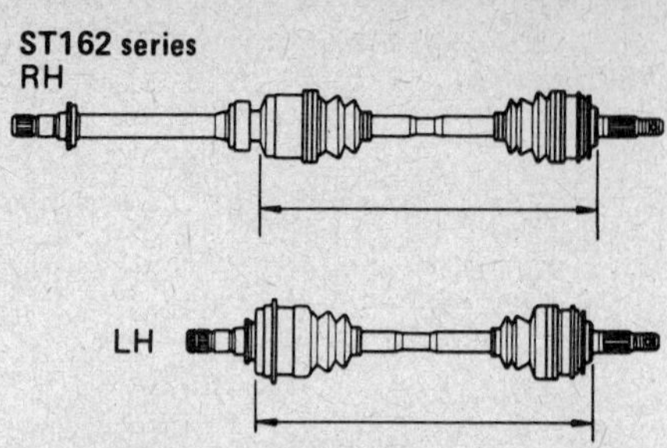

Fig. 16 Measuring front axle shaft standard length. 1986–87 Celica 162 series

9. Remove transaxle side dust cover, using a suitable press.
10. Remove driveshaft side dust cover, using tool No. 09950-00020, then release snap ring.
11. Press bearing from shaft using tool No. 09950-00020 and a suitable press, then remove snap ring.

Assembly

1. Install center driveshaft snap ring, then install bearing, using tool No. 09527-20011. Install new snap ring.
2. Install new dust covers, using a suitable press. Clearance between transaxle dust cover and bearing should be .04-.08 inch. Distance between driveshaft dust cover face and bottom of shaft splines should be 3.39-3.43 inch.
3. Wrap vinyl tape around splines, then install boot and new boot clamp to outboard joint.
4. Wrap vinyl tape around splines, then install boot and new boot clamp to driveshaft.
5. On 161 series, place beveled side of tripod axial spline toward outboard joint, then align matchmarks previously scribed. Tap tripod joint into driveshaft, using a suitable tool. Install new snap ring.
6. On 162 series, install new snap ring, then place ball cage on driveshaft with large end to inboard joint side. Align matchmarks previously made, then tap race onto driveshaft using a suitable tool. Mesh cage to inner race, then align match marks. Install 6 balls and retain with a suitable grease.
7. Pack boot with grease, then the inboard tulip and boot.
8. Align matchmarks, then assemble inboard tulip to driveshaft and install.
9. On 162 series, pack inboard outer race and boot with a suitable grease, then align matchmarks and assemble inboard outer race to driveshaft. Install new snap ring to inboard outer race, then the boot.
10. On all models, make sure boot is on shaft groove, then install band and lock into place.
11. Check shaft assembled length, **Figs. 15 and 16.** Shaft length on 161 series should be 17.53 inches. Shaft length on 162 series should be 18.29 inches on LH side and 18.37 inch on RH side.

FRONT SUSPENSION & STEERING SECTION

INDEX

WHEEL BEARINGS ADJUST

CRESSIDA, STARLET, PICKUP W/2 WHEEL DRIVE, VAN W/2 WHEEL DRIVE, 1983 COROLLA, 1984–87 COROLLA RWD, 1983–85 CELICA & 1983–EARLY 1986 SUPRA

1. Raise and support front of vehicle, then remove wheel and tire assembly and brake caliper. Wire brake caliper aside without stretching brake hose.
2. Remove hub grease cap, cotter pin and locknut, then loosen hub nut.
3. Tighten hub nut to 22 ft. lbs. (300 kg-cm), then rotate hub and disc assembly several times to ensure bearings are seated.
4. Loosen hub nut until it can be turned with fingers, then retighten nut finger tight.
5. Using a suitable spring scale, measure frictional force of axle seal and make note of it, **Fig. 1.**
6. Tighten hub nut slightly, then measure wheel bearing preload with spring scale. Preload should be as follows:
   a. On Cressida, Starlet, Van w/2WD, 1983 Celica & 1983 Supra models, preload should be 12.8-30.4 ounces, in addition to axle seal frictional force measured in step 5.
   b. On 1983 Corolla models, preload should be 11.2-24 ounces, in addition to axle seal frictional force measured in step 5.
   c. On 1984–85 Celica, 1984-87 Corolla FWD & 1984-Early 1986 Supra models, preload should be 0-37 ounces, in addition to axle seal frictional force measured in step 5.
   d. On Pickup w/2WD, preload should be 21-64 ounces, in addition to axle seal frictional force measured in step 5.
7. If preload is not as specified, tighten or loosen hub nut as necessary until proper preload is obtained.
8. Install locknut, cotter pin, grease cap, caliper and wheel and tire assembly. **If cotter pin holes do not line up, tighten nut by the least amount possible until holes are aligned.**

PICKUP W/4 WHEEL DRIVE & VAN W/4 WHEEL DRIVE

1. Raise and support vehicle, then remove tire and wheel assembly and brake caliper.
2. Remove manual locking hub as follows:

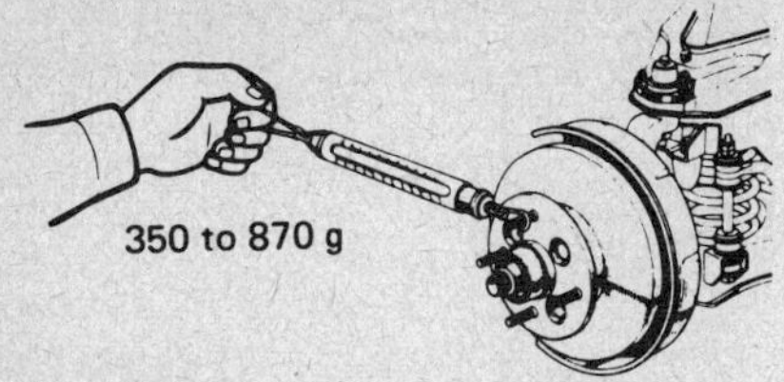

Fig. 1 Measuring wheel bearing preload

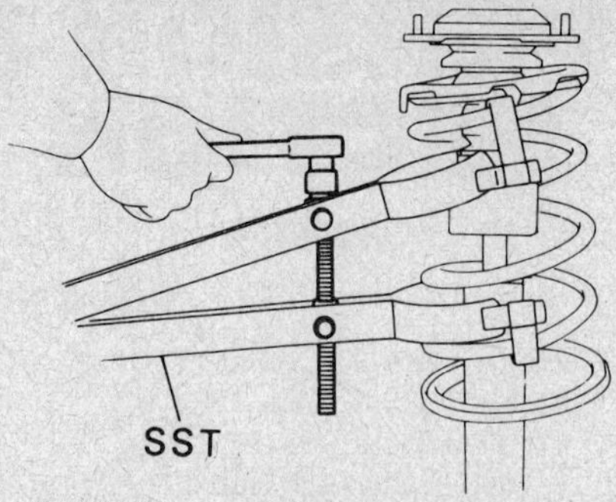

Fig. 2 Compressing coil spring on typical MacPherson strut

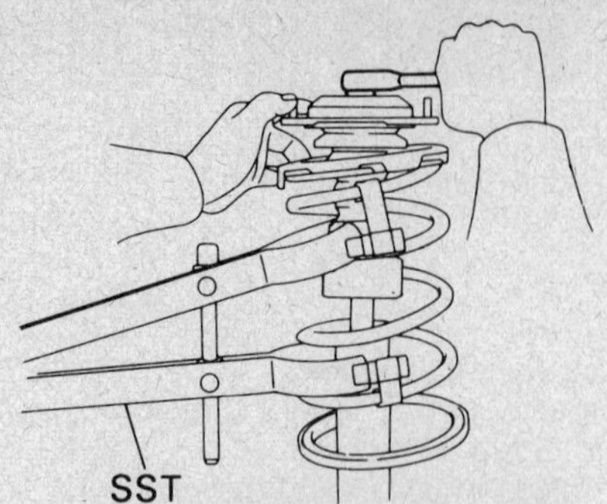

Fig. 3 Removing upper seat retaining nut on typical MacPherson strut

a. Place control handle to "Free" position.
b. Remove cover attaching bolts, then the cover.
c. Remove axle bolt with washer, then the hub body attaching nuts and washers.
d. Remove cone washer by tapping on heads of bolts using a hammer and suitable drift.
e. Remove manual locking hub body.

3. Remove automatic locking hub as follows:
   a. Remove hub cover.
   b. Remove axle bolt, then the washer.
   c. Remove hub body attaching nuts.
   d. Remove cone washer by tapping on heads of bolts, using a hammer and suitable drift.
   e. Remove automatic locking hub body.
4. On models less locking hubs, remove hub as follows:
   a. Remove grease cap from hub flange.
   b. Remove hub bolt and washer, then hub flange attaching nuts.
   c. Tap hub flange attaching studs with brass drift and hammer to remove cone washers.
   d. Install two bolts into hub flange opposite from each other, then tighten evenly to remove hub flange.
5. On models less automatic locking hubs, release lock washer, then remove locknut and lock washer. On all models, loosen hub nut.
6. Tighten hub nut to 43 ft. lbs., then rotate hub and disc assembly several times to ensure bearings are seated.
7. Loosen hub nut until it can be turned with fingers, then torque hub nut to 11 ft. lbs. on Van models, or 18 ft. lbs. on Pickup models.
8. Using a suitable spring scale, measure wheel bearing starting preload with spring scale, **Fig. 1.** Preload should be 74-125 ounces on Van models, or 102-200 on Pickup models. If preload is not as specified, tighten or loosen adjusting nut as necessary.
9. On models less automatic locking hubs, install lock washer and locknut. Torque locknut to 35 ft. lbs. and check preload as outlined in step 8. If preload is nut as specified, tighten or loosen adjusting nut as necessary.
10. If preload is within specifications, bend over lock washer.
11. Install free wheeling hub as follows:
    a. Place new gasket on front axle hub.
    b. Install hub body with 6 cone washers and nuts, then torque attaching nuts to 23 ft. lbs.
    c. Install hub bolt with washer, then torque to 13 ft. lbs.
    d. Apply a suitable grease to inner hub splines, then place control handle in "Free" position.
    e. Install new gasket on cover, then install cover on body with follower pawl tabs aligned with non-toothed portions of body.
    f. Install cover attaching bolts and torque to 7 ft. lbs.
12. Install automatic locking hub as follows:
    a. Position new gasket on axle hub, then apply suitable multipurpose grease to automatic locking hub splines.
    b. Align spring ends of brake assembly in hub with hub flange alignment pins.
    c. Ensure locking hub outer cam stopper is securely in inner cam groove, then position inner cam protrusion so it is centered between outer cam protrusions and aligned with hub alignment pin holes.
    d. Install locking hub to axle hub ensuring inner cam protrusion is set between ends of hub brake spring.
    e. Install 6 cone washers and nuts and torque nuts to 23 ft. lbs. **If hub does not fit perfectly on axle hub, remove and reinstall.**
    f. Install cover, then insert attaching bolts and torque to 7 ft. lbs.
13. On models less locking hubs, install hubs as follows:
    a. Position new gasket on axle hub, then install hub flange on axle.
    b. Install cone washers and attaching nuts. Torque attaching nuts to 23 ft. lbs.
    c. Install grease cap on hub flange.
14. Install brake caliper, wheel and tire assembly.

CAMRY, MR2, TERCEL, 1984–87 COROLLA FWD, 1986–87 CELICA & LATE 1986–87 SUPRA

These models use lubed for life, sealed front wheel bearings with no provision for adjustment.

MACPHERSON STRUT & COIL SPRING REPLACE

CRESSIDA, 1983 COROLLA, 1984–87 COROLLA RWD, 1983–85 CELICA & 1983–EARLY 1986 SUPRA MODELS

Removal

1. Raise and support front of vehicle, then remove wheel and tire assembly.
2. Disconnect brake line and hose from clamp.
3. On models equipped with Toyota Electronically Modulated Suspension (TEMS), disconnect TEMS actuator connector from top of shock absorber, then remove actuator cover and mounting bolts and pull actuator out straight and slowly to prevent binding actuator rod.
4. On all models, remove three suspension unit attaching nuts from top of fender apron.
5. Remove bolts attaching strut to steering knuckle, then remove strut. **Bolt holes in steering knuckle are provided with positioning collars that extend about 3/16 in. from arm surface and fit into bolt holes in strut lower end, therefore the lower suspension arm must be pressed downward to remove shock absorber.**
6. Attach strut stand to lower end of strut, then position holder in a vise.
7. Using suitable spring compressor, compress coil spring, **Fig. 2.**
8. Remove bearing dust cover.
9. Using a suitable tool to hold upper seat, remove nut at upper end of strut, **Fig. 3.**
10. Remove front suspension support and coil spring from strut.
11. Remove caliper and disc from spindle.
12. Reverse procedure to install. Torque piston rod to suspension support nut to 29-39 ft. lbs. (400-500 kg-cm). Torque suspension support unit to body structure attaching nuts as follows: Cressida, 1983-85 Celica and 1983-Early 1986 Supra, 22-32 ft. lbs.

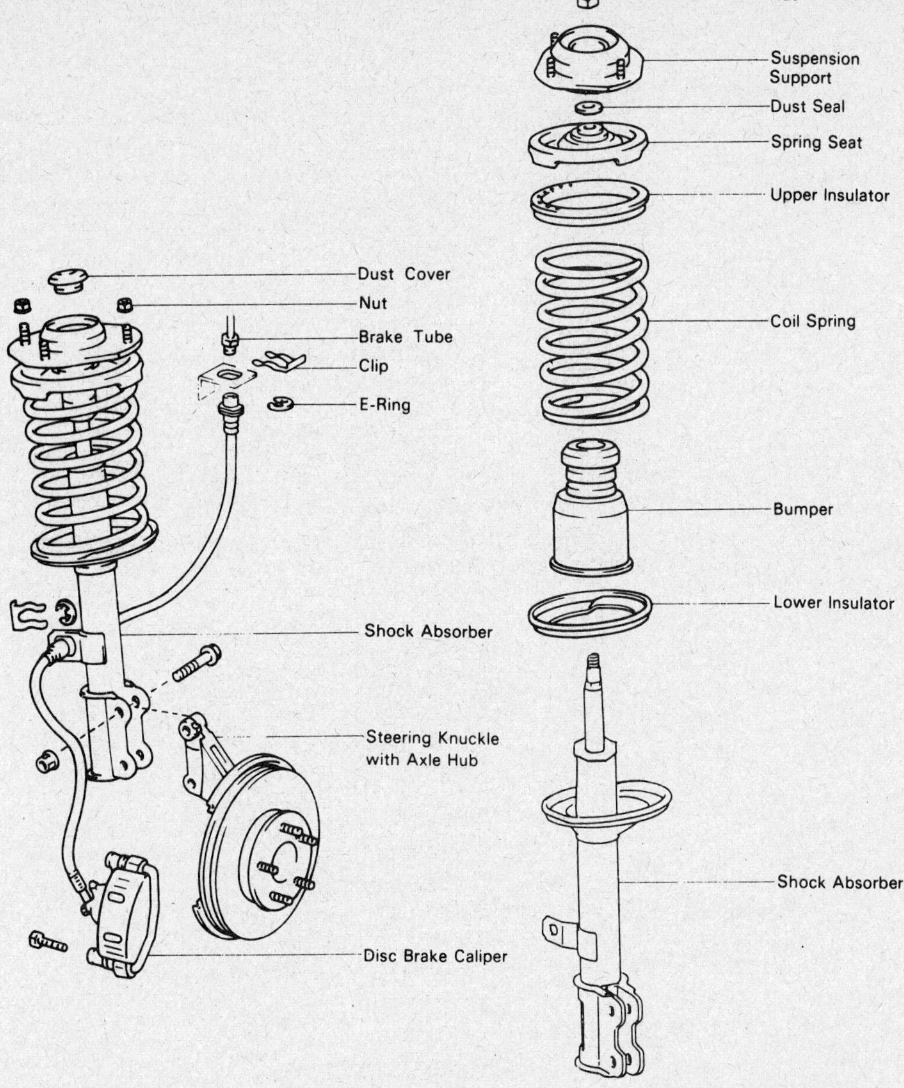

Fig. 4 Front MacPherson strut. Camry & 1984–87 Corolla FWD

(3-4.5 kg-m); 1983 Corolla and 1984-87 Corolla RWD, 11-15 ft. lbs. (1.5-2.2 kg-m); 1983-84 Starlet, 15-21 ft. lbs. (20-29 Nm). Torque strut to knuckle bolts as follows: Cressida, 1983-85 Celica and 1983-Early 1986 Supra, 58-86 ft. lbs. (8-12 kg-m); 1983 Corolla and 1984-87 Corolla RWD, 51-65 ft. lbs. (7-9 kg-m); and 1983-84 Starlet, 56 ft. lbs. (57-76 Nm). Adjust front wheel bearings and bleed brake system.

CAMRY & 1984–87 COROLLA FWD

1. Disconnect brake line from hose. Use suitable container to catch brake fluid.
2. Remove clips and E-rings, **Fig. 4.**
3. Remove 2 bolts from brake caliper and remove caliper, leaving hose attached.
4. Scribe alignment marks on lower bracket of strut and on camber adjustment cam, then remove bolts and disconnect steering knuckle and strut.
5. Remove 3 bolts holding top of strut to body structure. Remove unit from vehicle and cover driveshaft boot with rag to prevent damage.
6. Install bolt through strut bracket with nuts inside to brace bracket when clamping in vise.
7. Using suitable spring compressor, compress coil spring.
8. Using suitable tool hold spring seat to prevent it from turning, and remove nut.
9. Remove suspension support, spring seat, spring, insulators and bumper.
10. Reverse procedure to install noting the following: On 1983-84 Camry models, plugged strut mount hole, **Fig. 5,** is at front on vehicles with power steering and at rear on vehicles with manual steering; torque strut support nut to 36 ft. lbs. (47 Nm); 3 mounting nuts to 27 ft. lbs. (37 Nm); shock to steering knuckle nuts to 152 ft. lbs. (206 Nm) on 1983-85 models, or 105 ft. lbs. (142 Nm) on 1986-87 models; and brake caliper bolts to 65 ft. lbs. (88 Nm).

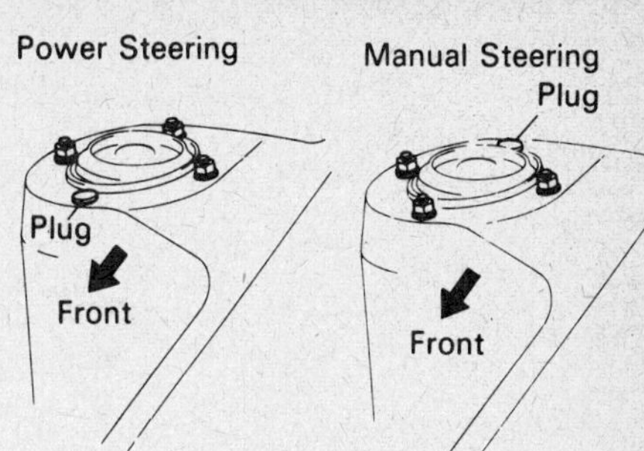

Fig. 5 MacPherson strut mounting position. 1983–84 Camry

1985–87 MR2

1. Raise and support vehicle.
2. Remove union bolt and disconnect brake hose from disc brake caliper, draining brake fluid into suitable container.
3. Remove clip from strut assembly and pull brake hose free of shock absorber.
4. Disconnect stabilizer link strut assembly.
5. Scribe alignment marks on strut lower bracket and camber adjusting cam.
6. Remove attaching nuts and bolts and disconnect steering knuckle and strut.
7. Remove three bolts securing top of suspension support and remove strut from body.
8. Install bolt and two nuts to bracket at lower portion of the strut and secure assembly in suitable vise.
9. Using suitable tool compress coil spring.
10. Using suitable tool to prevent spring seat from turning, remove top attaching nut.
11. Remove suspension support, spring seat, spring, insulator and bumper.
12. Reverse procedure to install, ensuring that "OUT" mark on spring seat faces toward outside of vehicle. Torque the three strut to body attaching nuts to 26 ft. lbs., the suspension support nut to 36 ft. lbs., the lower attaching nuts to 105 ft. lbs. and the brake line union bolt to 22 ft. lbs.

TERCEL

1. Raise and support vehicle.
2. On 1987 sedan models, remove brake hose clip from strut and disconnect brake hose from caliper, then pull brake hose from strut and allow to drain into suitable container.
3. On all except 1987 Tercel wagon, scribe alignment marks on strut lower bracket and the camber adjusting cam.
4. On all models, remove two bolts and nuts and disconnect steering knuckle.
5. Remove dust cover from suspension support, then loosen but do not remove nut.
6. Remove three nuts attaching strut to body, then remove strut from body. **Cover driveshaft boot with cloth to avoid damage.**

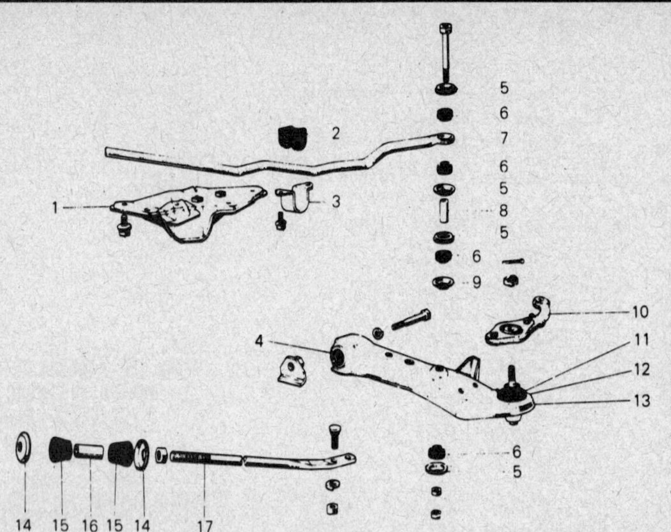

1 Strut bar bracket
2 Stabilizer bushing
3 Stabilizer bracket
4 Suspension lower arm bushing
5 Cushion retainer
6 Stabilizer cushion
7 Stabilizer bar
8 Collar
9 Cushion retainer
10 Steering knuckle arm
11 Lower ball joint dust cover
12 Set ring
13 Suspension lower arm subassy
14 Strut bar cushion retainer
15 Strut bar cushion
16 Collar
17 Strut bar

Fig. 6 Front suspension components. Cressida, 1983–85 Celica, 1983 Corolla, 1984–87 Corolla RWD & 1983–Early 1986 Supra

7. Install bolt and nuts on bracket at lower portion of strut shell and secure assembly in suitable vise.
8. Using suitable tool, compress coil spring.
9. Prevent suspension from turning with screwdriver and remove support nut.
10. Remove suspension support, spring seat, spring and dust cover.
10. Reverse procedure to install. Torque three strut upper attaching nuts to 17 ft. lbs. on 1983-86 models, or 23 ft. lbs. on 1987 models; the lower strut attaching bolts to 105 ft. lbs. on 1983-86 and 1987 wagon models, or 166 ft. lbs. on 1987 sedan models and the suspension support nut to 36 ft. lbs.

1986–87 CELICA

1. Remove union bolt and two washers, then disconnect brake hose from disc caliper.
2. Drain brake fluid into a suitable container, then remove clip from brake hose and separate brake hose from bracket.
3. Place matchmarks on strut lower bracket and camber adjust cam.
4. Remove attaching nuts, then disconnect steering knuckle from strut.
5. Remove three top suspension support attaching bolts, then remove shock from body.
6. Compress coil spring, using tool No. 09727-22032 or equivalent, **Fig. 2**, then retain seat with tool No. 09729-22031 and remove suspension support nut.
7. Remove suspension support, spring seat, spring, insulators and bumper.
8. Reverse procedure to install. Torque new suspension support nut to 34 ft. lbs., three top suspension support attaching bolts to 47 ft. lbs., steering knuckle to shock absorber nuts to 152 ft. lbs. on 1986 models, or 188 ft. lbs. on 1987 models and disc brake caliper union bolt to 22 ft. lbs.

LATE 1986–87 SUPRA

1. Remove brake caliper from steering

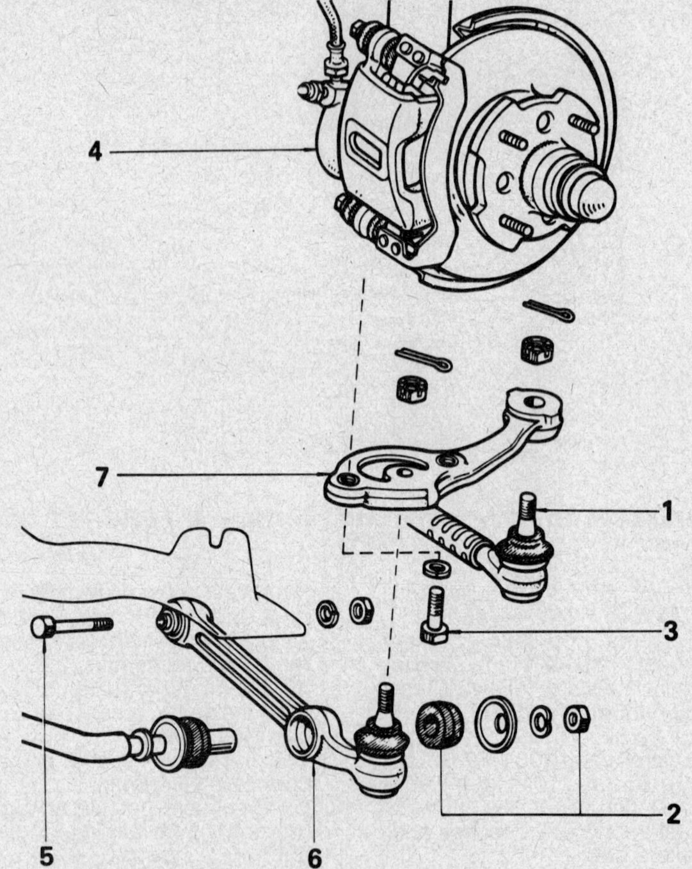

1. Tie Rod End
2. Stabilizer Bar Nut & Cushion Rubber
3. Shock Absorber Shell Lower Bolt
4. Shell Lower
5. Lower Arm Bolt
6. Lower Arm
7. Knuckle Arm

Fig. 7 Front suspension components. 1983–84 Starlet

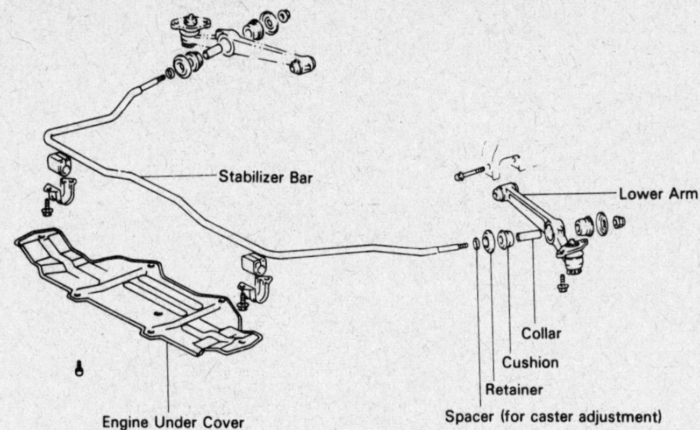

Fig. 8 Front suspension components. 1983–86 Camry

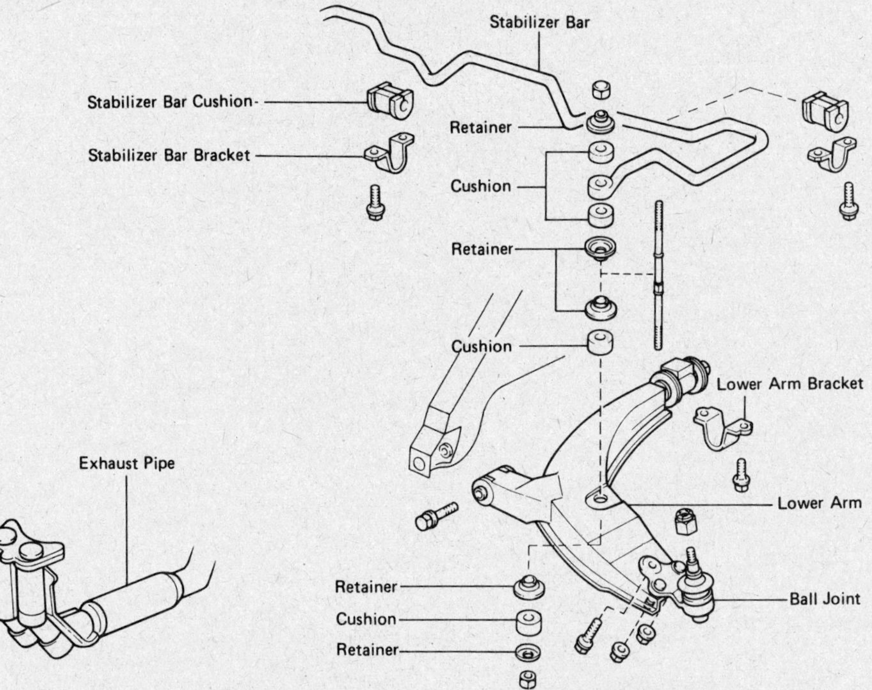

Fig. 9 Front suspension components. 1984–87 Corolla FWD & 1987 Tercel Sedan

knuckle. Suspend caliper aside with suitable wire. **Leave brake hose attached.**

2. On models equipped with Toyota Electronically Modulated Suspension (TEMS), remove TEMS actuator cover and actuator from top of strut.
3. Loosen piston rod locknut enough that it can be turned by hand.
4. Remove upper suspension arm-to-vehicle body attaching nuts and bolts, then disconnect suspension arm from body.
5. Remove three strut assembly-to-vehicle body attaching nuts.
6. Remove strut-to-lower suspension arm attaching nut and bolt, then the strut.
7. Reverse procedure to install. Torque strut-to-vehicle attaching nuts to 26 ft. lbs., strut-to-lower suspension arm attaching nut to 106 ft. lbs. Temporarily install upper suspension arm, then lower vehicle and bounce several times to stabilize suspension. With vehicle weight on suspension, torque upper suspension arm-to-vehicle body attaching nuts to 121 ft. lbs. and piston rod locknut to 22 ft. lbs.

LOWER SUSPENSION ARM

REPLACE

CRESSIDA, 1983–85 CELICA, 1983 COROLLA, 1984–87 COROLLA RWD, 1983–84 STARLET & 1983–EARLY 1986 SUPRA

1. Raise front and vehicle and support by frame members, then remove tire and wheel assembly.
2. Disconnect bolts securing steering knuckle arm to shock absorber, then push lower suspension arm down to disconnect lower arm.
3. Disconnect tie rod end from steering knuckle.
4. Disconnect strut bar (if equipped) and stabilizer bar from lower suspension arm, **Figs. 6 and 7.**
5. Remove bolt and nut securing lower suspension arm to crossmember, then remove arm.
6. Remove cotter pin and nut securing knuckle arm to ball joint, then using a suitable press, remove knuckle arm.
7. Reverse procedure to install.

1983–86 CAMRY

1. Raise front of vehicle and support with jack stands positioned at subframe.
2. Remove bolts securing lower ball joint to steering knuckle, then separate lower arm from steering knuckle **Fig. 8.**
3. Remove stabilizer bar end nut, retainer and cushion.
4. Remove lower suspension arm retaining bolt and nut, then disconnect lower arm from stabilizer bar. **When removing suspension arm from stabilizer bar, use care not to lose caster adjusting spacer.**
5. Reverse procedure to install. Torque lower arm to ball joint nut to 67 ft. lbs., the lower arm to steering knuckle attaching nuts to 83 ft. lbs., then lower vehicle to ground. Bounce vehicle several times to stabilize suspension, then while vehicle weight is on suspension, torque the stabilizer bar to lower arm attaching nut to 86 ft. lbs. and the lower arm to body attaching bolt to 83 ft. lbs.

1984–87 COROLLA FWD

1. Raise and support vehicle.
2. Remove bolt and 2 nuts to disconnect lower control arm from steering knuckle, **Fig. 9.**
3. Remove nut at stabilizer link and disconnect stabilizer bar from lower control arm.
4. Remove front and rear bracket bolts and remove lower control arm.
5. Reverse procedure to install, noting the following torque specifications: ball joint nuts and bolts, 47 ft. lbs. (64 Nm); stabilizer bar to lower control arm, 13 ft. lbs. (18 Nm); front bracket bolt, 83 ft. lbs. (113 Nm) on 1984-85 models or 105 ft. lbs. (142 Nm) on 1986-87 models; and rear bracket bolts, 64 ft. lbs. (87 Nm).

1984–87 VAN

Less 4 Wheel Drive

1. Remove shock absorber, then using suitable puller remove tie rod end from steering knuckle.
2. Disconnect stabilizer bar and bracket from lower arm.
3. Disconnect strut bar from lower arm.
4. On 1984-86 models, remove cotter pin and nut from lower ball joint, then

using suitable tool, disconnect ball joint from steering knuckle, taking care not to damage ball joint boot.
5. On 1987 models, remove lower ball joint-to-lower suspension arm attaching nuts and bolts.
6. On all models, make suitable alignment mark on control arm adjusting cam, then remove adjusting cam, then remove adjusting cam and nut. Remove lower control arm.
7. Install lower control arm. Position adjusting cam according to alignment marks made in step 6, and finger tighten nut.
8. Install lower ball joint in control arm and torque 49 ft. lbs. (67 Nm).
9. If removed, connect lower ball joint to steering knuckle and torque nut to 76 ft. lbs. (103 Nm). Install new cotter pin.
10. Install shock absorber and torque upper nut to 19 ft. lbs. (25 Nm); lower bolts to 13 ft. lbs. (18 Nm).
11. Connect strut bar to lower control arm and torque to 49 ft. lbs. (67 Nm).
12. Connect stabilizer bar and bracket to lower control arm.
13. Lower vehicle and allow the weight to rest on suspension. Bounce vehicle to settle suspension and torque adjusting cam nut to 112 ft. lbs. (152 Nm) on 1984-86 models or 152 ft. lbs. (206 Nm) on 1987 models.

W/4 Wheel Drive

1. Disconnect shock absorber from lower suspension arm.
2. Disconnect stabilizer bar from lower suspension arm.
3. Remove cotter pin from lower control arm, then the nut. Using suitable puller, disconnect lower suspension arm from lower ball joint.
4. Place reference marks between lower suspension arm front and rear alignment cams and mounting flanges.
5. Remove adjusting cam nuts, adjusting cams and lower suspension arm.
6. Reverse procedure to install, noting the following:
   a. Install lower suspension arm. Do not tighten alignment cams at this time.
   b. Torque lower suspension arm-to-ball joint attaching nut to 83 ft. lbs. (127 Nm), then install cotter pin.
   c. Torque stabilizer bar attaching bolts to 14 ft. lbs. (19 Nm).
   d. Torque shock absorber lower mounting nut and bolt to 70 ft. lbs. (95 Nm).
   e. Lower vehicle and allow the weight to rest on suspension. Bounce vehicle several times to settle suspension, then align marks made on cams. Torque adjusting cam nuts to 152 ft. lbs. (206 Nm) with vehicle weight on suspension.

1985–87 MR2

1. Raise and support vehicle.
2. Remove cotter pin and castle nut, **Fig. 10.**
3. Using tool 09610-20012 or equivalent, disconnect lower arm from ball joint.

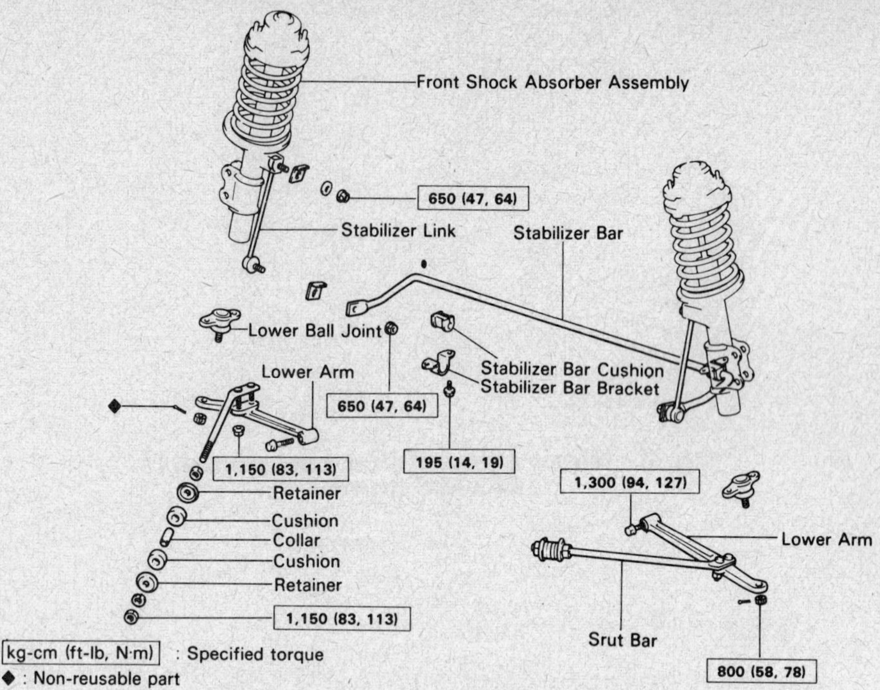

Fig. 10 Front suspension components. MR2

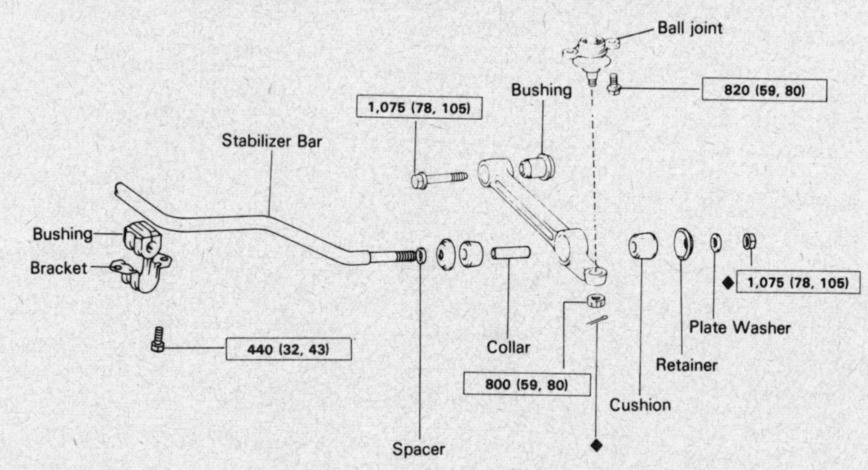

Fig. 11 Front suspension components. 1983–86 Tercel & 1987 Tercel wagon

4. Remove two nuts and disconnect strut bar from lower arm.
5. Remove the bolt and lower arm from the body.
6. Reverse procedure to install. Torque ball joint castle nut to 58 ft. lbs., the strut bar to lower arm attaching bolts to 83 ft. lbs. Lower vehicle and allow the weight to rest on suspension. Bounce vehicle several times to settle suspension, then torque lower arm to body attaching bolt to 94 ft. lbs. with suspension loaded.

1983–86 TERCEL & 1987 TERCEL WAGON

1. Raise and support vehicle.
2. Remove two bolts attaching ball joint to steering knuckle, **Fig. 11.**
3. Remove stabilizer bar nut, retainer and cushion.
4. Remove lower arm as follows:
   a. Jack up opposite wheel until vehicle body lifts off support.
   b. Loosen lower arm bolt, pry lower arm and pull out bolt.
   c. Disconnect lower arm from stabilizer bar. **Do not lose caster adjusting spacer.**
5. Reverse procedure to install. Torque lower arm to ball joint nut to 58 ft. lbs., the lower arm to steering knuckle attaching nuts to 59 ft. lbs. the stabilizer bar to lower arm attaching nut to 78 ft.

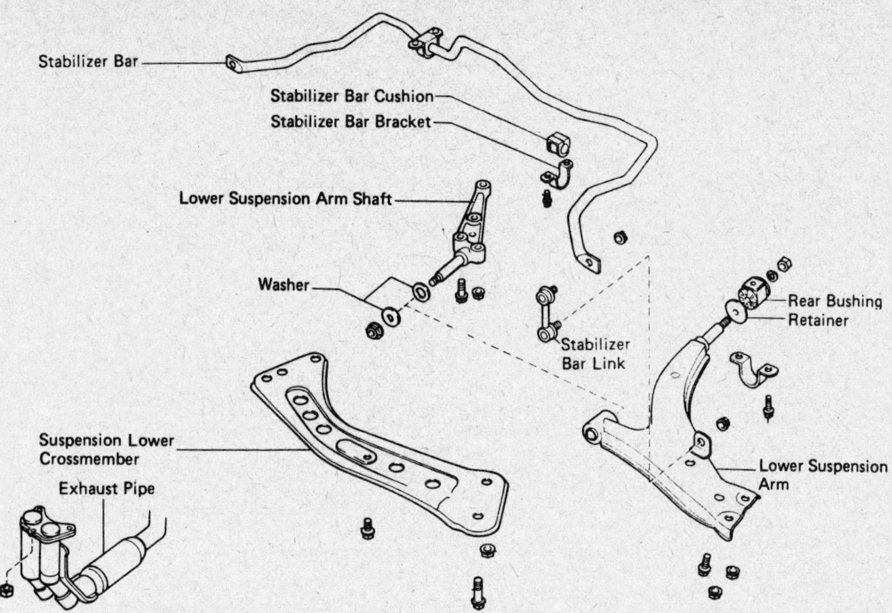

Fig. 12 Front suspension components. 1986–87 Celica

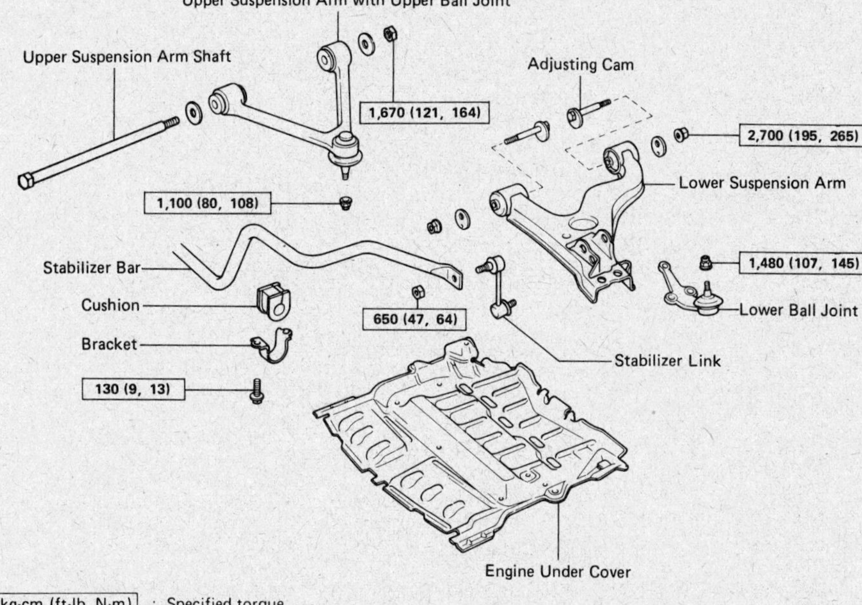

Fig. 13 Front suspension components. Late 1986–87 Supra

lbs. and the lower arm to body attaching bolt to 83 ft. lbs. on 1983-86 models, or 105 ft. lbs. on 1987 models.

1987 TERCEL SEDAN

1. Raise and support vehicle.
2. Remove bolt and 2 nuts to disconnect lower control arm from steering knuckle, **Fig. 9.**
3. Remove nut at stabilizer link and disconnect stabilizer bar from lower control arm.
4. Remove front and rear bracket bolts and remove lower control arm.
5. Reverse procedure to install, noting the following torque specifications: ball joint nuts and bolts, 59 ft. lbs. (80 Nm); stabilizer bar to lower control arm, 13 ft. lbs. (18 Nm). Lower vehicle and allow the weight to rest on suspension. Bounce vehicle several times to settle suspension, then torque front bracket bolt, 108 ft. lbs. (147 Nm) and rear bracket bolts, 64 ft. lbs. (87 Nm).

1986–87 CELICA

1. Raise and support vehicle, then remove wheel and tire assembly.
2. Remove steering knuckle to lower suspension arm attaching bolt and two nuts, **Fig. 12.**
3. Remove attaching nut, then disconnect stabilizer link from lower suspension arm.
4. Remove lower suspension arm, except LH arm on models with automatic transaxle, as follows:
   a. Remove lower suspension arm front setting nut and washer.
   b. Remove lower suspension arm rear bracket bolts, then the lower suspension arm.
   c. Remove 4 attaching bolts and two nuts, then the suspension lower crossmember.
   d. Remove attaching bolt and nut, then the lower suspension arm shaft.
5. Remove LH lower suspension arm on models with automatic transaxle as follows:
   a. Remove lower suspension arm front setting nut and washer.
   b. Remove four attaching bolts and two nuts, then the lower crossmember.
   c. Remove attaching bolt and nut, then the lower suspension arm and lower arm shaft.
6. Reverse procedure to install.
7. For lower suspension arms except LH arms on models with automatic transaxle, apply torques as follows:
   a. Torque lower suspension arm shaft nut and bolt LH, or bolt RH to 154 ft. lbs.
   b. Torque lower suspension crossmember outer attaching bolts to 154 ft. lbs. Torque center bolt to 29 ft. lbs.
   c. Torque lower suspension arm to steering knuckle attaching bolt and nuts to 94 ft. lbs.
   d. Torque front setting nut to 156 ft. lbs.
   e. Torque rear bracket bolts to 72 ft. lbs.
8. For LH arm on models with automatic transaxle, apply torques as follows:
   a. Torque lower suspension arm shaft attaching nut and bolt to 154 ft. lbs.
   b. Torque lower suspension crossmember outer attaching bolts to 154 ft. lbs. Torque center bolt to 29 ft. lbs.
   c. Torque lower suspension arm to steering knuckle attaching bolt and nuts to 94 ft. lbs.
   d. Torque front setting nut to 156 ft. lbs.
   e. Torque rear bracket bolts to 72 ft. lbs.

LATE 1986–87 SUPRA

1. Raise and support vehicle.
2. Disconnect stabilizer bar link from lower suspension arm, **Fig. 13.**
3. Remove lower ball joint locknut, then using suitable puller, disconnect ball joint from steering knuckle.
4. Remove shock absorber-to-lower suspension arm attaching nut and bolt, then disconnect shock absorber from arm.
5. Make reference marks between lower suspension arm alignment cams and their mounting surfaces, then remove nuts, alignment cams, bolts and suspension arm.

6. Reverse procedure to install, noting the following:
   a. Torque lower suspension arm-to-ball joint attaching nuts and bolts to 94 ft. lbs. (127 Nm).
   b. Install lower suspension arm. Do not tighten alignment cams at this time.
   c. When installing ball joint to steering knuckle, install conventional nut first and torque to 14 ft. lbs. (20 Nm), then install locking nut and torque to 107 ft. lbs. (145 Nm).
   d. Torque shock absorber lower mounting nut and bolt to 106 ft. lbs. (64 Nm).
   e. Torque stabilizer link attaching nut to 47 ft. lbs. (64 Nm).
   f. Lower vehicle and allow the weight to rest on suspension. Bounce vehicle several times to settle suspension, then align marks made on cams. Torque adjusting cam nuts to 177 ft. lbs. (240 Nm) with vehicle weight on suspension.

1987 CAMRY

1. Raise front of vehicle and support with jack stands positioned at subframe.
2. Remove bolts securing lower ball joint to steering knuckle, then separate lower arm from steering knuckle **Fig. 14.**
3. Remove stabilizer bar end nut, retainer and cushion.
4. Remove lower suspension arm-to-suspension arm shaft nut and retainer.
5. Remove lower suspension crossmember attaching bolts and nuts, then the crossmember.
6. Remove lower suspension arm shaft attaching nut and bolt, then remove lower suspension arm and shaft as an assembly.
7. Separate lower suspension arm from suspension arm shaft.
8. Reverse procedure to install. Torque lower arm to ball joint nut to 67 ft. lbs., lower arm to steering knuckle attaching nuts to 94 ft. lbs., lower suspension crossmember-to-engine center mounting member attaching nuts to 32 ft. lbs., lower suspension crossmember-to-chassis attaching nuts and bolts to 153 ft. lbs., then lower vehicle to ground. Bounce vehicle several times to stabilize suspension, then while vehicle weight is on suspension, torque the stabilizer bar to lower arm attaching nut to 156 ft. lbs. and the lower suspension arm-to-shaft attaching bolt to 156 ft. lbs.

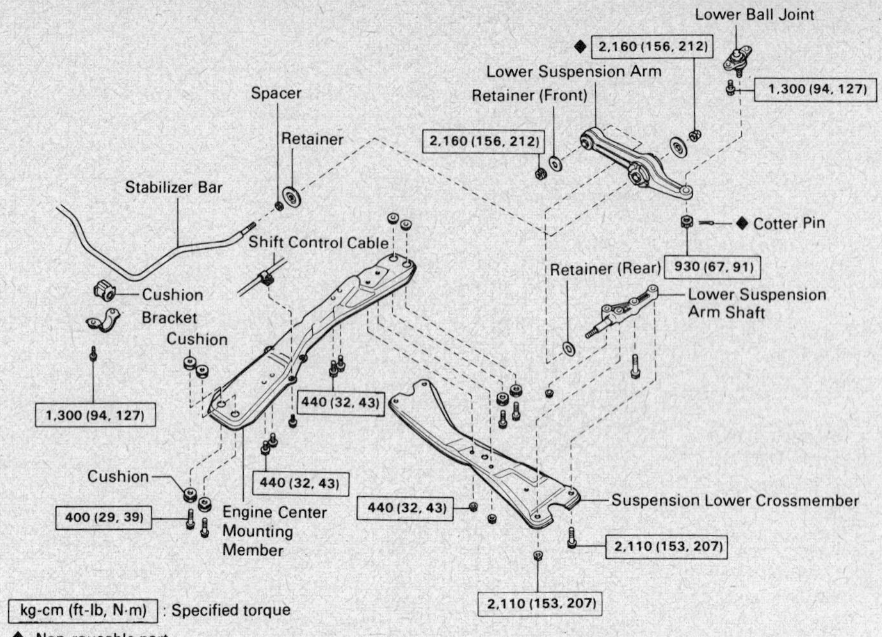

Fig. 14 Front suspension components. 1987 Camry

STABILIZER BAR REPLACE

CRESSIDA, 1983–85 CELICA, 1983 COROLLA, 1984–87 COROLLA RWD & 1983–EARLY 1986 SUPRA

1. Raise and support front of vehicle.
2. Remove engine under cover, if equipped.
3. Remove stabilizer bar to lower suspension arm attaching bolts, **Fig. 6.**
4. Remove stabilizer brackets and bushings, then the strut bar, strut bar bracket and stabilizer bar as an assembly, by pulling bar through strut bar bracket hole.
5. Reverse procedure to install.

1983–84 STARLET, 1983–86 TERCEL & 1987 TERCEL WAGON

1. Raise and support front of vehicle.
2. Remove engine under cover (if equipped).
3. Remove stabilizer bar bracket bolts, then remove brackets from crossmember.
4. Remove stabilizer to lower suspension arm attaching nuts and retainers, then remove stabilizer bar, **Figs. 7 and 11. When removing stabilizer bar from suspension arm, ensure caster adjusting spacer remains with stabilizer bar.**

1983–86 CAMRY

1. Remove engine under cover.
2. On CV series vehicles, remove center engine mounting member as follows:
   a. Remove 2 plugs.
   b. Remove 4 bolts from front and rear mounts.
   c. Remove 4 bolts and center engine mounting member.
3. On all models, remove stabilizer bar brackets from body structure, **Fig. 8.**
4. Disconnect stabilizer bar end from lower arm on one side.
5. Remove lower control arm on other side.
6. Remove stabilizer bar, spacer, cushion and collar.
7. Install stabilizer bar end on lower control arm on one side and finger tighten nut.
8. Pry stabilizer bar forward and install bracket. Torque bolts to 83 ft. lbs. (113 Nm).
9. Install lower control arm on one side.
10. Torque stabilizer bar nut to 86 ft. lbs. (117 Nm).
11. On CV series vehicles, install center engine mounting member as follows:
    a. Install center engine mount bolts and torque to 29 ft. lbs. (39 Nm).
    b. Install front and rear mounts with bolts. Torque bolts to 29 ft. lbs. (39 Nm).
    c. Install 2 plugs.
12. On all models, install engine under cover.
13. Check front wheel alignment.

1984–87 COROLLA FWD & 1987 TERCEL SEDAN

1. Disconnect stabilizer bar from front lower suspension arms, **Fig. 9.**
2. Remove stabilizer bar brackets from body structure.
3. On Corolla models, disconnect exhaust pipe from manifold.
4. Remove stabilizer bar.
5. Reverse procedure to install noting the following torques: exhaust pipe to manifold, 33 ft. lbs. (44 Nm); stabilizer bar brackets to body, 14 ft. lbs. (19 Nm); and stabilizer bar to lower arms, 13 ft. lbs. (18 Nm).

1983–85 PICKUP W/4 WHEEL DRIVE

1. Remove stabilizer bar to front suspension link bolts.
2. Remove stabilizer bar retaining brackets and rubber bushings.
3. Remove stabilizer bar from vehicle.
4. Reverse procedure to install.

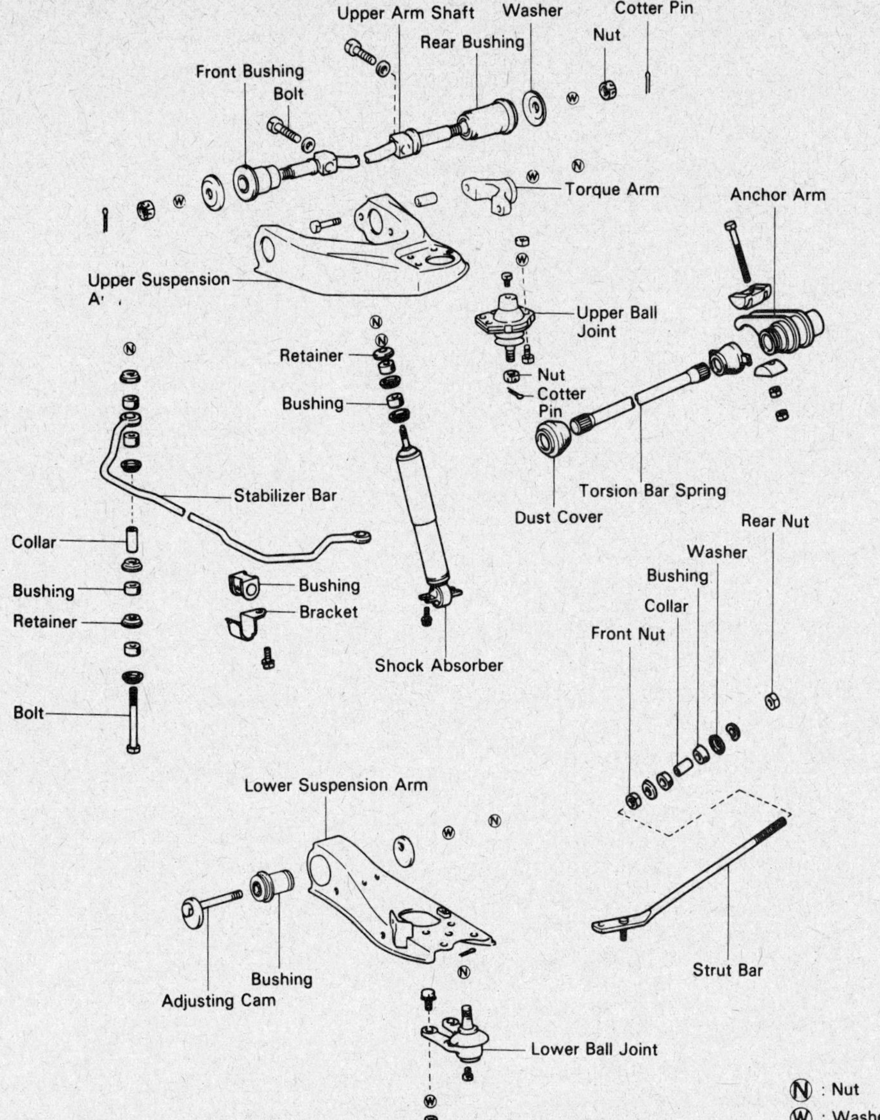

Fig. 15 Front suspension components. 1984–87 Van less 4 wheel drive

1986–87 PICKUP W/4 WHEEL DRIVE & 1987 VAN W/4 WHEEL DRIVE

1. Remove stabilizer bar to lower suspension arms retaining nuts, cushions and retainers.
2. Disconnect stabilizer bar.
3. Remove stabilizer bar brackets and cushions, then the stabilizer bar.
4. Place stabilizer bar in position, then install new cushion and brackets to frame and insert attaching bolts.
5. Connect stabilizer bar on both sides to lower arms with attaching bolts, retainers and nuts, then torque nuts to 19 ft. lbs. on Pickup models, or 14 ft. lbs. on Van models.
6. Torque bracket set bolts to 9 ft. lbs. on Pickup models, or 14 ft. lbs. on Van models.

1983–87 PICKUP LESS 4 WHEEL DRIVE

1. Remove one torsion bar as described under "Lower Control Arm & Torsion Bar, Replace."
2. Remove stabilizer bar from lower control arms.
3. Remove stabilizer brackets and bushings from frame, then remove stabilizer bar.
4. Reverse procedure to install.

1984–87 VAN LESS 4 WHEEL DRIVE

1. Remove nuts and rubber cushions from ends of bolt between lower control arms and stabilizer bar ends. Disconnect stabilizer bar, **Fig. 15.**
2. Remove stabilizer bar brackets, bushings, and stabilizer bar.
3. Reverse procedure to install. Torque bracket bolts to 14 ft. lbs. (19 Nm). Tighten nuts on stabilizer end bolts so .51-.63 inch (13-16 mm) of bolt end is exposed.

MR2

1. Raise and support vehicle.
2. Remove nut and disconnect stabilizer link from stabilizer bar.
3. Remove stabilizer bar to body attaching bolts, then the stabilizer bar and brackets.
4. Remove stabilizer link from front shock absorber assembly.
5. Remove stabilizer bracket and stabilizer bar cushion.
6. Reverse procedure to install.

LATE 1986–87 SUPRA

1. Disconnect stabilizer link from stabilizer bar, **Fig. 13.**
2. Remove stabilizer link from lower suspension arm.
3. Remove stabilizer bar bracket attaching bolts, then the stabilizer bar, cushions and brackets.
4. Reverse procedure to install. Torque all attaching nuts and bolts to 47 ft. lbs.

1987 CAMRY

1. Remove front suspension lower crossmember attaching nuts and bolts, then the lower crossmember.
2. Remove nuts and retainers attaching stabilizer bar to lower suspension arms.
3. Remove stabilizer bar bracket attaching bolts.
4. Remove shift control cable clamp bolt from engine center mounting member, then remove engine center mounting member attaching bolts and the member, **Fig. 14.**
5. Remove stabilizer bar, retainers and spacers.
6. Reverse procedure to install. Torque stabilizer bar bracket attaching bolts to 94 ft. lbs., outer engine center mounting member attaching bolts to 29 ft. lbs., inner engine center mounting member attaching bolts to 32 ft. lbs., outer suspension lower crossmember attaching bolts to 153 ft. lbs., inner suspension lower crossmember attaching bolts to 32 ft. lbs.

STRUT BAR REPLACE

CRESSIDA, 1983–85 CELICA, 1983 COROLLA, 1984–87 COROLLA RWD & 1983–EARLY 1986 SUPRA

1. Raise and support front of vehicle.
2. Remove nut and washers from strut bar, **Fig. 6.**
3. Remove strut bar to lower suspension arm attaching bolts, then remove strut bar. **If equipped, do not move strut bar staked nut unless necessary. If staked nut must be moved, check to ensure it is returned to its original position prior to installing strut bar.**
4. Reverse procedure to install. Adjust strut bar as follows: 15.6 inches (397.2 mm) on 1983-84 Cressida, no adjustment on 1985-87 Cressida, 14.7 inches (372 mm) on 1983 Corolla, 14.642 (371.9 mm) on 1984-87

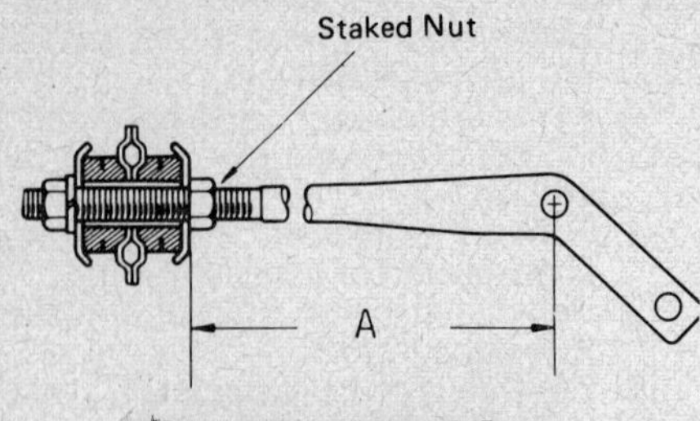

Fig. 16 Strut bar adjustment

Corolla RWD, 15.2 inches (385 mm) on 1983-85 Celica and 14.5 inches (369 mm) on 1983-Early 1986 Supra, **Fig. 16,** dimension A.

1983–87 PICKUP LESS 4 WHEEL DRIVE

On these models, mark position of staked nut to strut rod prior to removing strut rod bracket retaining bolt and washers, then disconnect strut bar from frame bracket and lower arm and remove from vehicle. When installing strut rod, check to ensure staked nut is in proper position to strut rod.

1984–87 VAN LESS 4 WHEEL DRIVE

1. Refer to "Stabilizer Bar, Replace" procedure, and remove stabilizer bar.
2. Remove stabilizer bar bracket from lower control arm, **Fig. 15.**
3. Place suitable alignment marks on strut bar.
4. Remove rear nut from strut bar.
5. Remove nuts holding strut bar to lower control arm and remove strut bar.
6. Install strut bar front nut and position according to alignment marks made in step 3. If using new bar position nut 13.07 inches (332 mm) from inner hole at opposite end of strut bar.
7. Place washer and bushing on strut bar and position bar in bracket.
8. Place collar, bushing and washer on strut bar and finger tighten rear nut.
9. Connect strut bar to lower control arm and torque bolts to 49 ft. lbs. (67 Nm).
10. Lower vehicle allowing vehicle weight to rest on tires. Bounce vehicle to settle suspension, then torque rear nut to 89 ft. lbs. (121 Nm).
11. Install stabilizer bar and check front wheel alignment.

1985–87 MR2

1. Remove strut rod nut and retainer.
2. Remove strut rod holding nut and bolt with cushion from body side.
3. Remove cushion collar and retainer from strut rod on lower control arm side.
4. Reverse procedure to install.

LOWER CONTROL ARM & TORSION BAR REPLACE

1983–87 PICKUP LESS 4 WHEEL DRIVE

1. Raise and support vehicle.

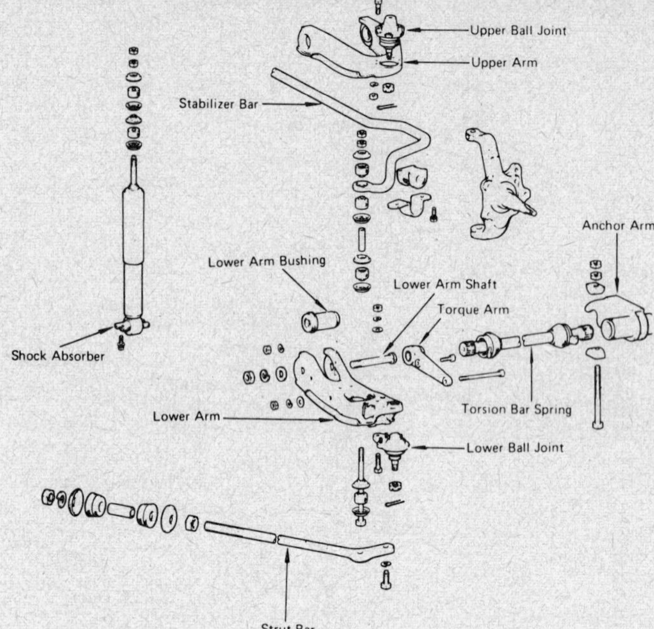

Fig. 17 Front suspension. 1983–87 Pickup less 4 wheel drive

2. Remove torsion bar boots, then place alignment mark across torsion bar, anchor arm and torque arm, **Fig. 17.**
3. Remove lock nut from torsion bar adjusting bolt and measure height of exposed bolt end. Record this value for reference when adjusting vehicle height.
4. Loosen adjusting nut, then remove anchor arm and torsion bar from vehicle.
5. Disconnect stabilizer bar end from lower suspension arm.
6. Disconnect strut bar end from lower suspension arm.
7. Remove shock absorber, refer "Shock Absorber, Replace."
8. Remove bolts securing lower ball joint to lower suspension arm, then separate ball joint from suspension arm.
9. Remove lower arm shaft nut, torque arm and lower arm shaft from lower arm, then remove lower suspension arm.
10. To install lower suspension arm, reverse steps 1 through 9 above. To install torsion bar, follow remaining steps below.
11. If original torsion bar is to be installed, apply suitable grease to splines, then align marks made during removal and install torsion bar. Check to ensure that adjusting bolt protrusion is equal to value obtained prior to removal of torsion bar.
12. If new torsion bar is to be installed, position block of wood 7.09-7.87 inches (180-200 mm) under front tire on side of vehicle from which torsion bar was removed.
13. Lower vehicle unit clearance between spring bumper on lower arm and frame is .051 inch (13 mm), **Fig. 18.** Install anchor arm onto torsion bar until adjusting bolt protrusion dimension A is .31-1.10 inch (8-28 mm), **Fig. 19,** on 1/2 ton models or .43-1.22 inch (11-31 mm) on 3/4 ton and Cab and Chassis models. Remove wooden block, then tighten adjusting nut until bolt protrusion dimension B, **Fig. 20,** is 2.72-3.50 inches (69-89 mm).
14. Install torsion bar boots and locknut, then torque locknut to 51-65 ft. lbs. (7-9 kg-m). Torque lower suspension arm shaft nuts to 145-216 ft. lbs. with vehicle suspension loaded.

LEAF SPRING REPLACE

1983–85 PICKUP W/4 WHEEL DRIVE

1. Raise and support vehicle.
2. Disconnect shock absorber and stabilizer bar from axle housing, **Fig. 21.**
3. Disconnect drag link from steering knuckle arm.
4. Disconnect brake hydraulic hose from brake dust cover.
5. Support axle housing with suitable jack, remove U-bolts, spring seats and spring bumper from leaf spring.
6. Lower axle housing, then remove shackle pin and hanger pin from leaf spring.
7. Remove leaf spring from vehicle.
8. Reverse procedure to install.

SHOCK ABSORBER REPLACE

PICKUP & VAN

1. Raise and support front of vehicle.
2. Disconnect shock absorber from upper and lower mountings.
3. Remove shock absorber from vehicle.
4. Reverse procedure to install.

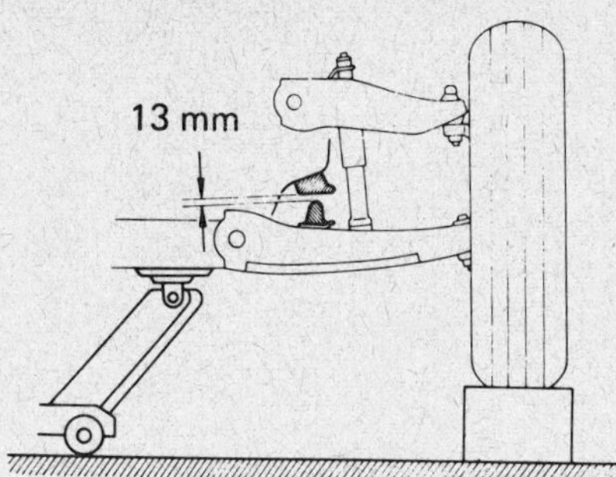

Fig. 18 Positioning front suspension for torsion bar replacement. 1983–87 Pickup less 4 wheel drive

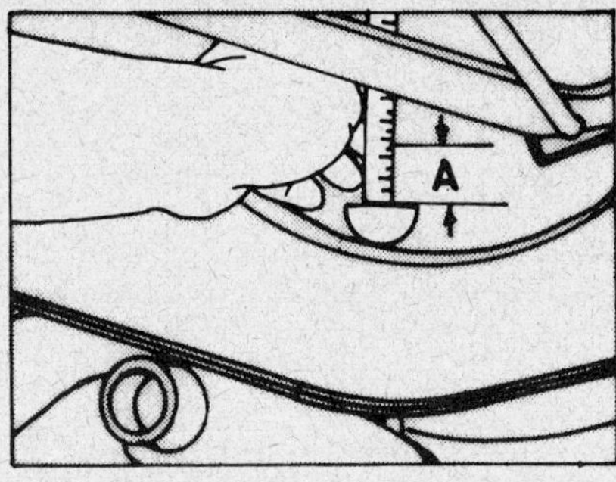

Fig. 19 Measuring torsion bar adjusting bolt height dimension A. 1983–87 Pickup less 4 wheel drive

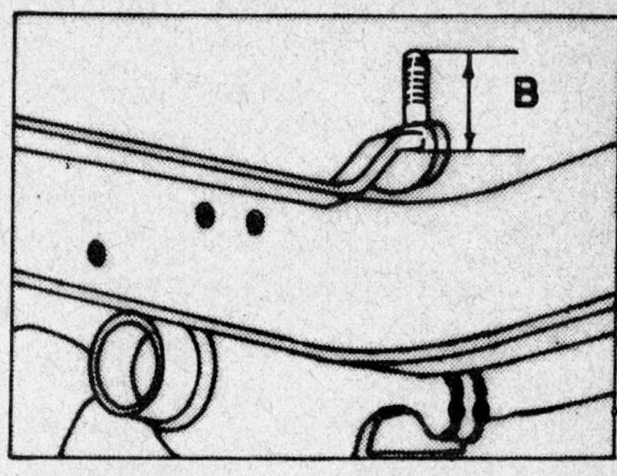

Fig. 20 Measuring torsion bar adjusting bolt height dimension B. 1983–87 Pickup less 4 wheel drive

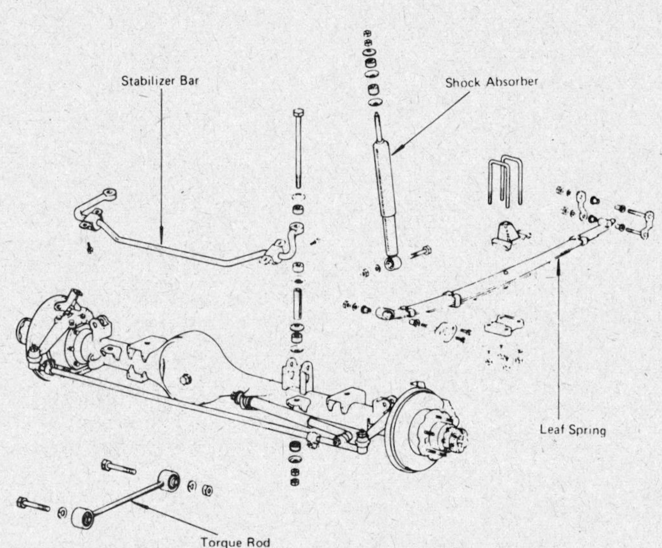

Fig. 21 Front suspension. 1983–85 Pickup w/4 wheel drive

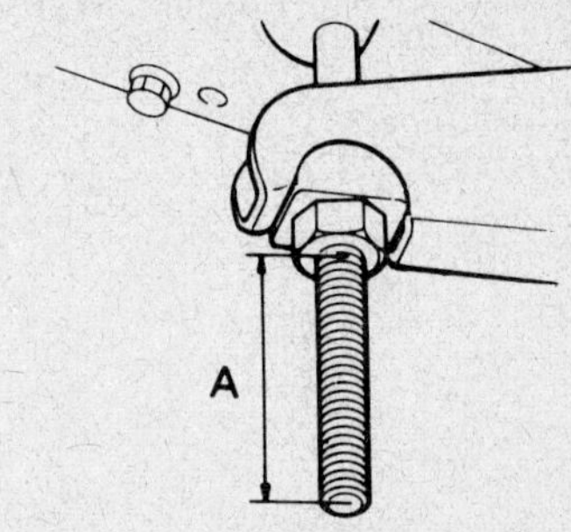

Fig. 22 Vehicle ride height reference dimension. 1984–87 Van

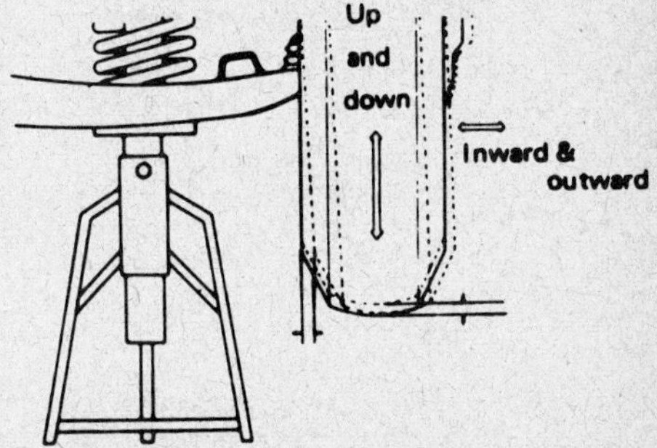

Fig. 23 Lower ball joint inspection. 1983 Pickup less 4 wheel drive & 1983–85 Pickup w/4 wheel drive

UPPER CONTROL ARM & TORSION BAR

REPLACE

1984–87 VAN LESS 4 WHEEL DRIVE

1. Raise and support vehicle.
2. Remove rubber boots, and place alignment marks on torsion bar, anchor arm, and torque arm, **Fig. 15.**
3. Remove locknut and measure protruding bolt end "A," **Fig. 22,** for reference when adjusting vehicle height.
4. Loosen adjusting nut and remove torsion bar and arm.
5. Remove air intake duct.
6. Remove cotter pin and nut from upper ball joint stud. Using suitable tool, disconnect ball joint from steering knuckle taking care not to damage ball joint boot, and remove ball joint from arm.
7. Remove bolts and upper control arm from frame.
8. Bushings can be replaced using suitable tools.
9. Reverse procedure to install, noting the following torque specifications: upper control arm front bolt, 65 ft. lbs. (88 Nm); upper control arm rear bolt, 112 ft. lbs. (152 Nm); ball joint to control arm bolts, 22 ft. lbs. (29 Nm); ball joint to steering knuckle. 58 ft. 1bs. (78 Nm).

UPPER CONTROL ARM

REPLACE

1983 PICKUP LESS 4 WHEEL DRIVE

Removal

1. Raise front of vehicle and support front suspension crossmember, then remove wheel and tire assembly.
2. Raise lower control arm using a suitable jack.
3. Remove cotter pin and nut retaining upper ball joint to steering knuckle.
4. Using tool No. SST-09628-62010, separate upper ball joint from steering knuckle.
5. Remove two bolts attaching upper control arm shaft to crossmember, then remove upper control arm and inner shaft, **Fig. 17. Record number and thickness of shims for installation.**
6. Mount control arm shaft in a vise and remove arm pivot bushings, if necessary. Remove dust seals from control arm.

Installation

1. If removed, install control arm dust seal on each end of control arm inner shaft. Position inner shaft into upper control arm. Apply grease to pivot bushing threads. Assemble pivot bushings to each side of inner shaft, tighten pivot bushings alternately an equal amount. Torque bushings to 160-181 ft. lbs. (22-25 kg-m). **When installing inner shaft on control arm, position side with offset bolt hole toward front.**

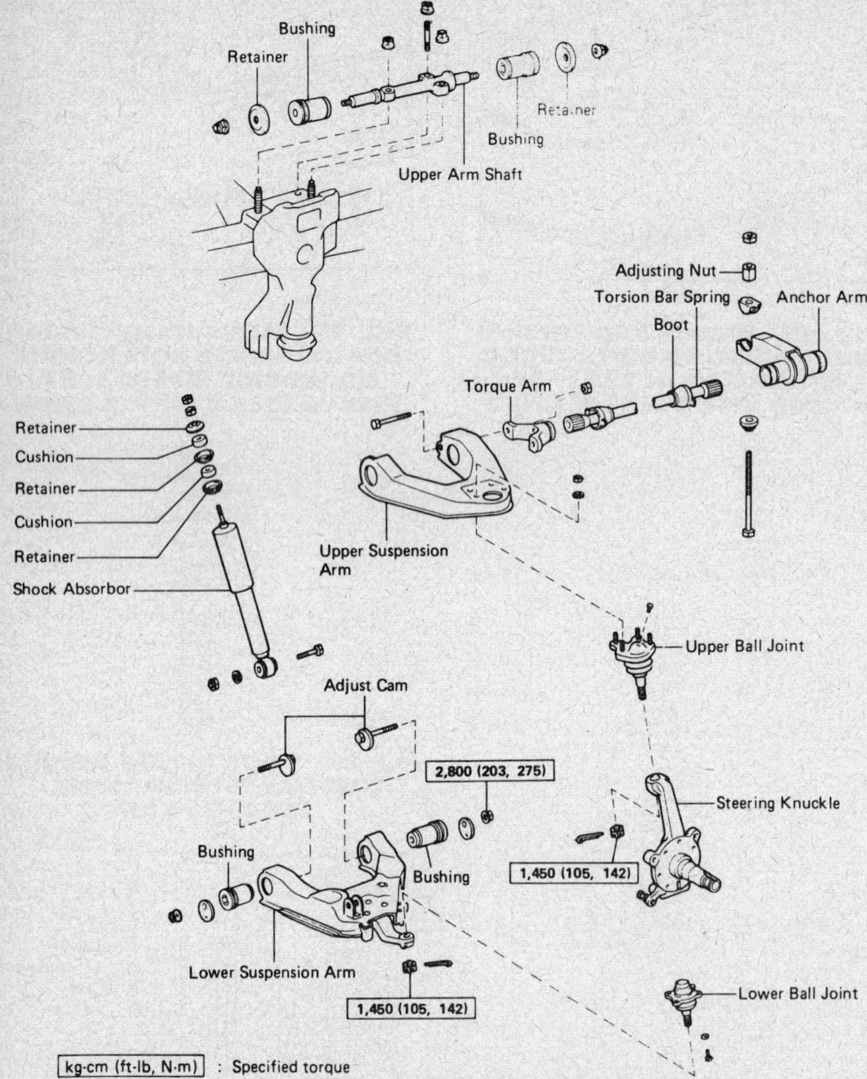

Fig. 24 Front suspension components. 1986–87 Pickup w/4 wheel drive & 4Runner

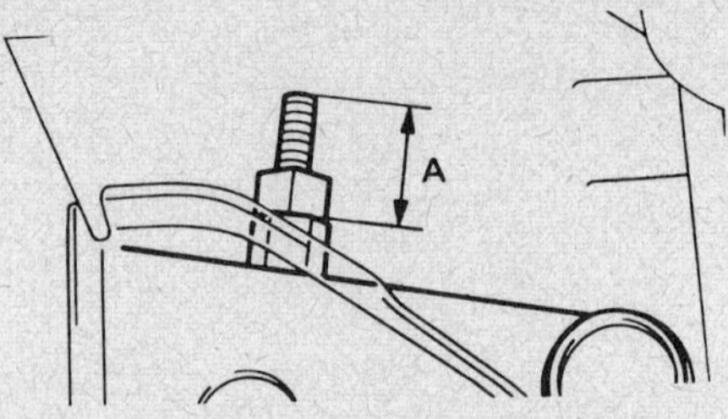

Fig. 25 Removal & installation of torsion bar spring

2. Install ball joint on upper control arm.
3. Install control arm on crossmember. Install same amount and thickness of shim as removed. Torque control arm mounting nuts to 95-153 ft. lbs. (13-21 kg-m).
4. Connect upper ball joint to steering knuckle. Torque attaching nut to 65.1-94 ft. lbs. (9-13 kg-m), then install cotter pin.
5. Install wheel and tie assembly then lower vehicle and check and adjust front wheel alignment as necessary.

BALL JOINT INSPECTION

1983 PICKUP LESS 4 WHEEL DRIVE & 1983–85 PICKUP W/4 WHEEL DRIVE

Upper Ball Joint

1. Disconnect upper control arm from steering knuckle.
2. Rotate ball stud with fingers and check for looseness in vertical and lateral directions. If looseness is noticeable, replace ball joint.
3. Attach upper ball joint to steering knuckle and install attaching nut and cotter pin.

Lower Ball Joint

1. Raise vehicle and support lower control arm.
2. With brakes applied, move wheel vertically and horizontally to check for looseness, **Fig. 23.** If tire bottom end movement exceeds .2 in. when wheel is moved inward and outward, replace ball joint. Ball joint movement should not exceed .09 in. when wheel is moved upward and downward.

CAMRY, CELICA, COROLLA, CRESSIDA, SUPRA & TERCEL

1. Raise front of vehicle and place a 7-8 inch block under one tire.
2. Lower vehicle until the front springs are about half loaded. Place stands under vehicle.
3. Chock front wheels after ensuring they are in straight forward position.
4. Using suitable lever, move lower control arm up and down to check that ball joint does not have excessive play. Maximum play should be as follows: Cressida, 1983-85 Celica, 1983-Early 1986 Supra, 1983 Corolla with spring loaded ball joint and 1984-87 Corolla RWD, .098 inch (2.5 mm); 1983 Corolla with solid ball joint, 1984-87 Corolla FWD, 1983-87 Camry, 1983-84 Starlet, 1983-87 Tercel, 1986-87 Celica & Late 1986-87 Supra, 0 inch.
5. Repeat procedure for opposite ball joint.

1984–87 PICKUP LESS 4 WHEEL DRIVE & 1984–87 VAN

Upper Ball Joint

1. Raise and support vehicle.
2. Check that front wheels are in straight ahead position and depress and hold brake pedal.
3. Move wheel up and down and check that upper ball joint play does not exceed .091 inch (2.3 mm).

Lower Ball Joint

1. Raise and support vehicle.
2. Check that front wheels are in straight ahead position and depress and hold brake pedal to eliminate wheel bearing play.
3. Move lower control arm up and down and check that lower ball joint play does not exceed .091 inch (2.3 mm) on Pickup models, or 0 inch (0 mm) on Van models.

1986–87 PICKUP W/4 WHEEL DRIVE PICKUP & 4RUNNER

Upper Ball Joint

1. Raise and support front of vehicle.
2. Position front wheels in a straight ahead position, then depress and hold brake pedal.
3. Move wheel up and down, then check ball joint play.
4. Maximum vertical play should not exceed .09 inch.

Lower Ball Joint

1. Raise and support front of vehicle.
2. Position front wheels in a straight ahead position, then depress and hold brake pedal.

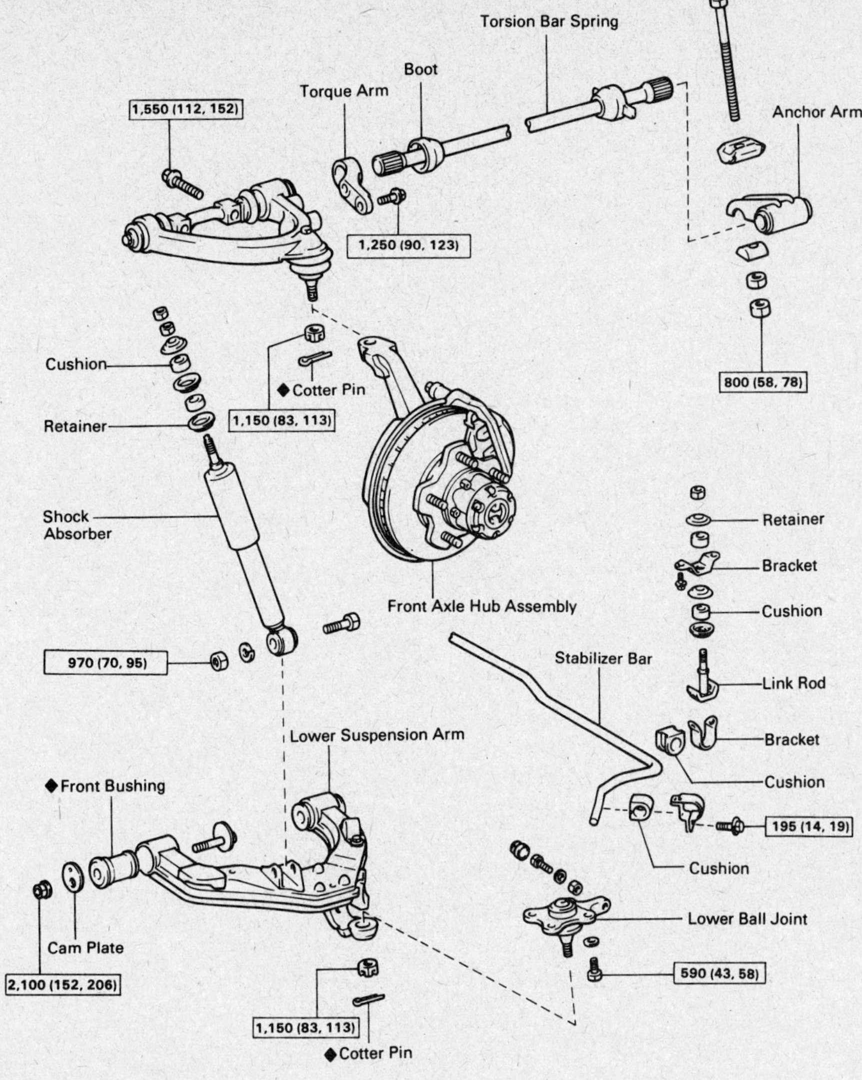

Fig. 26 Front suspension components. 1987 Van w/4 wheel drive

3. Move suspension arm up and down, then check ball joint play.
4. Maximum vertical play should be 0 inch.

TORSION BAR

REPLACE

1986–87 PICKUP W/4 WHEEL DRIVE & 4RUNNER

1. Remove boots, then mark relative position between torsion bar, anchor arm and torque arm, **Fig. 24.**
2. Measure protruding bolt end dimension "A," **Fig. 25.**
3. Loosen adjusting nut, then remove anchor arm and torsion bar. **At rear end of torsion bar there are right and left indication marks that are not to be interchanged.**
4. Apply a suitable lubricant to torsion bar spline.
5. Align matchmarks made during removal.
6. Install and tighten adjusting nut to length noted during removal, dimension "A," **Fig. 25.**

1987 VAN W/4 WHEEL DRIVE

1. Remove boots, then mark relative position between torsion bar, anchor arm and torque arm, **Fig. 26.**
2. Remove anchor arm adjusting bolt locknut.
3. Measure, and record for assembly reference, protruding bolt end dimension "A," **Fig. 22.**
4. Remove anchor arm adjusting bolt nut, then the torsion bar and anchor arm. **At rear end of torsion bar there are right and left indication marks that are not to be interchanged.**
5. Apply a suitable molybdenum disulphide lithium base lubricant to torsion bar spline.
6. Align matchmarks made during removal.
7. Install and tighten adjusting nut to length noted during removal, dimension "A," **Fig. 22.**

LOWER SUSPENSION ARM & SHOCK ABSORBER

REPLACE

1986–87 PICKUP W/4 WHEEL DRIVE & 4RUNNER

1. Remove shock absorber, **Fig. 24.**
2. Disconnect stabilizer bar from lower suspension arm.
3. Remove 4 attaching bolts, then disconnect lower suspension arm from lower ball joint.
4. Mark relative position between front and rear adjusting cams, then remove attaching nut, adjusting cams and lower suspension arm.
5. Reverse procedure to install. Torque lower suspension arm to ball joint nut to 105 ft. lbs. Torque shock absorber to lower suspension arm bracket to 101 ft. lbs. Torque adjusting cam nuts to 203 ft. lbs.

1987 VAN W/4 WHEEL DRIVE

1. Disconnect shock absorber and stabilizer bar from lower suspension arm, **Fig. 26.**
2. Remove lower ball joint cotter pin and nut, then using suitable puller, separate lower suspension arm from ball joint.
3. Mark relative position between front and rear adjusting cams, then remove attaching nut, adjusting cams and lower suspension arm.
4. Reverse procedure to install. Torque lower suspension arm to ball joint nut to 83 ft. lbs., stabilizer bar attaching bolts to 14 ft. lbs., shock absorber to lower suspension arm bracket to 70 ft. lbs. Lower vehicle to ground, then bounce vehicle several times to stabilize vehicle and torque adjusting cam nuts to 152 ft. lbs. with suspension loaded.

UPPER SUSPENSION ARM

REPLACE

1986–87 PICKUP W/4 WHEEL DRIVE & 4RUNNER

1. Remove torsion bar as previously described.
2. Remove cotter pin and nut, then disconnect upper ball joint from steering knuckle, **Fig. 24,** using tool No. 09628-62011 or equivalent.
3. Remove nut, cushion and retainer at upper end of shock absorber.
4. Disconnect intermediate shaft from steering gear housing.
5. Remove two attaching nuts and bolts, then the upper suspension arm from frame.
6. Reverse procedure to install. Torque upper suspension arm to frame at-

taching bolts to 111 ft. lbs. Upper shock absorber nut to 18 ft. lbs. Upper suspension arm to ball joint to 105 ft. lbs.

1987 VAN W/4 WHEEL DRIVE

1. Remove torsion bar as previously described.
2. Remove right front seat and console box.
3. Disconnect transmission and transfer case cables from levers, then remove the transmission and transfer case levers with retainers.
4. Disconnect parking brake cable from lever, then remove the parking brake lever assembly.
5. Disconnect parking brake cable from intermediate shaft and transmission shift cable from transmission. Remove both cables.
6. Remove seat floor panel, then the fan shroud.
7. Remove radiator mounting bolts and nuts. **Do not drain coolant from radiator.**
8. Loosen upper shock absorber mounting nut, then remove nut, cushions and retainers. Disconnect shock absorber from frame.
9. Remove upper ball joint cotter pin and nut, then using suitable puller, separate steering knuckle from upper ball joint.
10. Remove upper suspension arm shaft attaching bolts, then the shaft and arm assembly.
11. If necessary, remove torque arm attaching bolts, then the torque arm.
12. Reverse procedure to install. Torque torque arm attaching bolts to 90 ft. lbs. (123 Nm), upper suspension arm and shaft assembly attaching bolts to 112 ft. lbs. (152 Nm) and upper ball joint attaching nut to 83 ft. lbs. (113 Nm).

HUB & ROTOR

REPLACE

FRONT WHEEL DRIVE MODELS

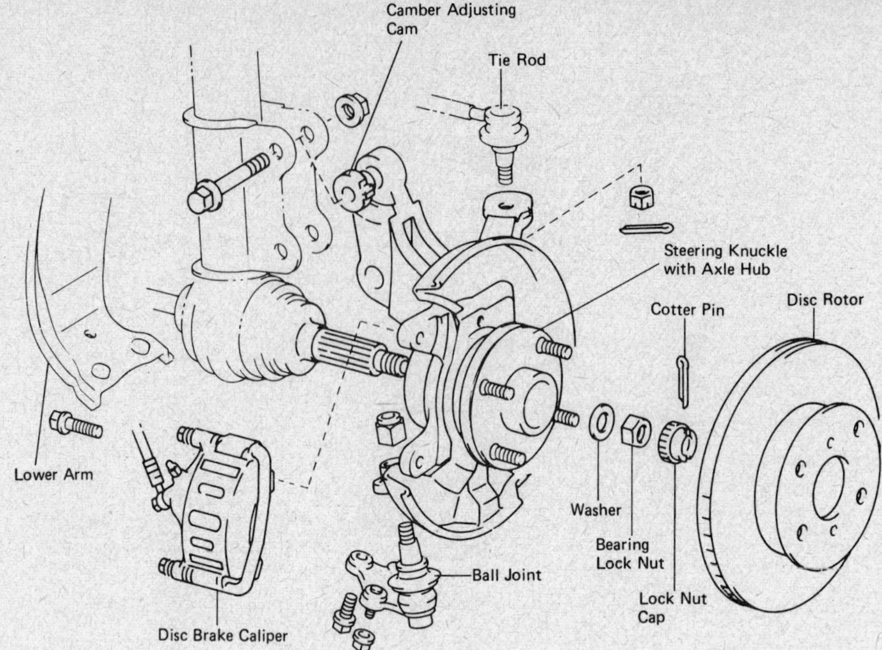

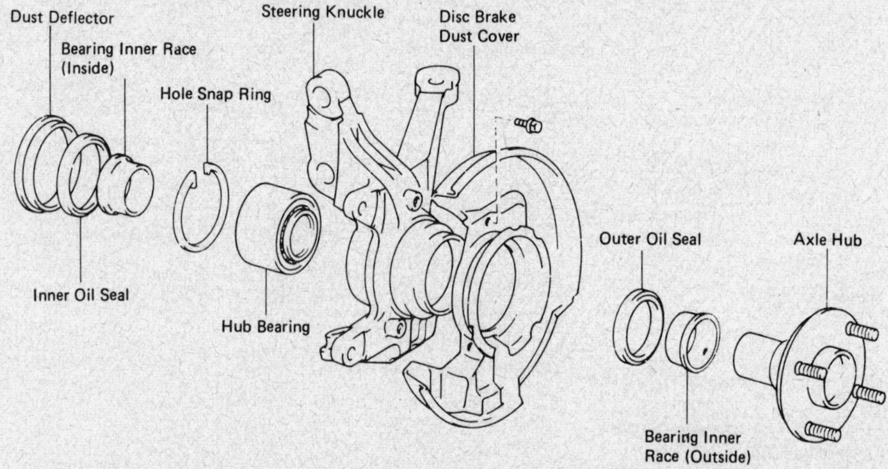

Fig. 27 Exploded view of axle hub & steering knuckle (typical). Front wheel drive models

1. Raise and support front of vehicle, then remove tire and wheel assembly.
2. Remove cotter pin and bearing locknut cap.
3. With brake pedal depressed, remove bearing locknut, **Fig. 27.**
4. Remove brake caliper from steering knuckle and suspend out of way.
5. Remove disc rotor, then ensure that bearing play in axial direction does not exceed .002 inch.
6. Remove cotter pin and nut, then, using suitable puller, disconnect tie rod end from steering knuckle.
7. Scribe alignment marks on strut lower bracket and camber adjusting cam (if equipped).
8. Remove steering knuckle-to-strut lower bracket attaching nuts and bolts.
9. Disconnect steering knuckle from lower suspension arm.
10. Using plastic hammer, tap axle shaft to loosen it while removing steering knuckle and axle hub. On some applications, it may be necessary to use puller to remove hub from axle shaft. **Cover driveshaft boot with cloth to prevent damage.**
11. If necessary, remove ball joint from steering knuckle.
12. Using suitable tool, remove dust deflector (if equipped) and inner oil seal from steering knuckle.
13. Using suitable pliers, remove axle hub snap ring.
14. Remove three bolts securing disc brake dust cover to steering knuckle.
15. Using suitable puller, remove hub from steering knuckle.
16. Remove inside bearing inner race from bearing.
17. Using suitable puller, remove outside inner race from axle hub.
18. Using suitable screwdriver, remove oil seal from steering knuckle.
19. Place an outside bearing inner race on bearing and, using suitable tool and hammer, drive out bearing. **Always replace the bearing as an assembly.**
20. Using suitable tool, press new bearing into steering knuckle.
21. Rotate and insert the side lip of a new outer oil seal into tool 09608-32010 or equivalent, then, using tool 09710-14012 or equivalent, drive oil seal into steering knuckle.
22. Apply suitable grease to oil seal lip.
23. Install disc brake dust cover.
24. Apply suitable grease to oil seal and bearing, then, using suitable tool, press hub into steering knuckle.
25. Install hub snap ring in steering knuckle.
26. Using suitable tool, drive a new oil seal and dust deflector (if equipped) into steering knuckle surface, then apply suitable grease to oil seal lip and axle shaft.
27. If removed, install ball joint.

28. Reverse procedure to install, noting the following:
    a. On 1983-87 Camry models, torque two strut-to-steering knuckle attaching nuts and bolts to 152 ft. lbs. on 1983-86 models or 166 ft. lbs. on 1987 models, steering knuckle-to-lower suspension arm attaching bolts to 83 ft. lbs. on 1983-86 models or 94 ft. lbs. on 1987 models, tie rod end attaching nut to 36 ft. lbs. and the bearing locknut to 137 ft. lbs.
    b. On 1983-87 Tercel models, torque two strut-to-steering knuckle attaching nuts and bolts to 105 ft. lbs. on 1983-86 models and 1987 Wagon models or 166 ft. lbs. on 1987 Sedan models, steering knuckle-to-lower suspension arm attaching bolts to 59 ft. lbs., tie rod end attaching nut to 36 ft. lbs. and the bearing locknut to 137 ft. lbs.
    c. On 1984-87 Corolla models, torque two strut-to-steering knuckle attaching nuts and bolts to 105 ft. lbs. on gasoline engine models or 152 ft. lbs. on diesel engine models, steering knuckle-to-lower suspension arm attaching bolts to 47 ft. lbs., tie rod end attaching nut to 36 ft. lbs. and the bearing locknut to 137 ft. lbs.
    d. On 1986-87 Celica models, torque two strut-to-steering knuckle attaching nuts and bolts to 188 ft. lbs., steering knuckle-to-lower suspension arm attaching bolts to 94 ft. lbs., tie rod end attaching nut to 36 ft. lbs. and the bearing locknut to 137 ft. lbs.

STEERING GEAR REPLACE

1983–85 PICKUP W/4 WHEEL DRIVE

1. Disconnect power steering hoses from steering gear.
2. Mark relationship of yoke and worm shaft for reference during assembly.
3. Disconnect intermediate shaft from worm shaft by loosening joint yoke bolt and compressing intermediate shaft.
4. Remove cotter pin and plug from drag link and disconnect drag link from pitman arm.
5. Disconnect pitman arm from steering gear.
6. Remove bolts securing steering gear to chassis, then remove steering gear.
7. Reverse procedure to install. Check to ensure that joint yoke and worm shaft marks align.

1983–87 PICKUP LESS 4 WHEEL DRIVE

1. Mark relative position between coupling and worm shaft, then remove coupling attaching bolt.
2. Loosen pitman arm mount nut, then disconnect relay rod from pitman arm, using tool No. 09611-22012 or equivalent.
3. Remove gear housing attaching bolts, then the gear housing.
4. Reverse procedure to install.

1986–87 PICKUP W/4 WHEEL DRIVE

1. Remove joint protector set bolt, then mark relative position between universal joint and worm shaft.
2. Remove two universal joint attaching bolts, then disconnect universal joint from worm shaft.
3. Remove pitman arm set nut, then disconnect pitman arm from steering gear housing, using tool No. 09628-62011 or equivalent.
4. Remove gear housing attaching bolts, then the gear housing.

1983–84 CRESSIDA

1. Remove coupling bolt.
2. Disconnect pressure and return lines, using tool No. 09631-22020, or equivalent.
3. Remove relay rod set nut, then disconnect relay rod from pitman arm, using tool No. 09611-20015.
4. Remove gear housing attaching bolts, then the gear housing.
5. Reverse procedure to install.

1985–87 CRESSIDA

1. Disconnect solenoid connector, then remove universal joint.
2. Position a suitable container to catch fluid, then disconnect pressure and return lines.
3. Disconnect tie rod ends from steering knuckles, then remove steering damper.
4. Remove gear housing assembly bracket set bolts.
5. Remove gear housing, then separate grommets from gear housing.
6. Reverse procedure to install.

1983–84 TERCEL & 1983–84 STARLET

1. Disconnect intermediate steering shaft, then remove cotter pin and nut from tie rod ends.
2. Disconnect tie rod ends using suitable puller, then remove suspension under cover (if equipped).
3. Remove rack housing bracket retaining bolts and rack housing brackets using caution not to damage rubber boots.
4. Remove steering assembly from vehicle.
5. Reverse procedure to install.

1983–87 CAMRY, 1983–85 CELICA, 1983–87 COROLLA & 1983–EARLY 1986 SUPRA

1. Remove two set bolts securing sliding collar between steering shaft and gear pinion, then remove collar.
2. Remove cotter pins and nuts from tie rod ends, then using suitable puller, remove tie rod ends from steering knuckle.
3. If equipped with power steering, remove pressure and return lines from control valve housing and allow fluid to drain into a suitable container.
4. Remove gear housing bracket bolts, then remove steering gear.

1984–85 VAN

1. Remove coupling bolt.
2. Loosen pitman arm set nut and loosen drag link set nut.
3. Using special service tool 09610-20012, or equivalent, disconnect pitman arm from sector shaft.
4. Using special service tool 09611-22012, or equivalent, disconnect pitman arm from drag link.
5. Remove steering gear.
6. Reverse procedure to install, noting the following torque specifications: steering gear bolts, 70 ft. lbs. (95 Nm); coupling bolt, 18 ft. lbs. (25 Nm); pitman arm to sector shaft, 90 ft. lbs. (123 Nm); and drag link to pitman arm, 67 ft. lbs. (91 Nm).

1985–87 MR2

1. Raise and support vehicle.
2. Scribe alignment marks on mainshaft, joint yoke and pinion shaft.
3. Remove two universal joint attaching bolts, then pull universal joint first from gear housing, then from mainshaft.
4. Remove front wheel and tire assemblies.
5. Remove cotter pins and nuts securing knuckle arm to tie rod.
6. Using tool 09528-62011 or equivalent, disconnect knuckle arm from tie rod end.
7. Remove center floor crossmember.
8. Remove gear housing bracket set bolts and the gear housing assembly.
9. Reverse procedure to install. Torque gear housing assembly attaching bolts to 32 ft. lbs., the crossmember attaching bolts to 19 ft. lbs., the tie rod to knuckle arm attaching nuts to 36 ft. lbs., the universal joint attaching bolts to 26 ft. lbs. and the tie rod end locknuts to 35 ft. lbs.

1985–86 TERCEL & 1987 TERCEL WAGON

1. Raise and support vehicle. If equipped with power steering, disconnect pressure and return lines from gear housing and remove union seats.
2. Remove two sliding yoke mounting bolts.
3. Pull sliding yoke first from gear housing, then from mainshaft.
4. Remove cotter pins and nuts, then using tool 09610-20012 or equivalent, disconnect tie rod end.
5. Remove four attaching bolts and two gear housing brackets, then the gear housing assembly and two bushings, being careful not to damage rack boots.
6. Reverse procedure to install. Torque gear housing attaching bolts and the tie rod to steering knuckle castle nuts to 43 ft. lbs.

1986–87 CELICA

1. Raise and support vehicle, then re-

move front tire and wheel assemblies.
2. Remove No. 1 and No. 2 under covers.
3. Remove steering shaft universal joint attaching bolts, then the joint.
4. Remove cotter pins and nuts from tie rod ends, then using suitable puller, separate tie rod ends from steering knuckles.
5. Remove suspension lower crossmember, then the engine center mounting member.
6. Remove exhaust pipe to manifold attaching nuts, then disconnect exhaust pipe from manifold.
7. Loosen exhaust pipe clamp bolt, then slide clamp towards the front.
8. Disconnect pressure and return lines from gear housing.
9. Remove two rear mount bracket attaching nuts, then the rear bracket.
10. Remove steering gear attaching bolts and brackets, then the steering gear.
11. Reverse procedure to install. Torque steering gear housing attaching bolts to 43 ft. lbs. (59 Nm), rear mount bracket attaching bolts to 43 ft. lbs. (59 Nm), power steering pressure and return lines to 29 ft. lbs. (39 Nm), exhaust pipe clamp bolt to 14 ft. lbs. (19 Nm), exhaust manifold nuts to 46 ft. lbs. (62 Nm), engine center mounting member to 29 ft. lbs. (39 Nm), center lower crossmember attaching bolt to 29 ft. lbs. (39 Nm), all other center lower crossmember attaching nuts and bolts to 154 ft. lbs. (208 Nm) and tie rod end attaching nuts to 36 ft. lbs. (49 Nm)

1986–87 VAN

Less 4 Wheel Drive

1. Raise and support front of vehicle, then remove front wheel and tire assemblies.
2. Remove cotter pins and nuts from tie rod ends, then using suitable puller, separate tie rod ends from steering knuckles.
3. Make reference marks on torque shaft and pinion shaft, then remove coupling set bolt.
4. Remove three bevel gear attaching bolts, then the bevel gear. Disconnect torque shaft from pinion shaft.
5. If equipped with power steering, disconnect power steering pressure and return lines from gear housing.
6. On all models, remove steering gear attaching bolts, then the steering gear from vehicle.
7. Reverse procedure to install. Torque steering gear housing attaching bolts to 56 ft. lbs. (76 Nm), power steering (if equipped) pressure and return lines to 33 ft. lbs. (44 Nm), bevel gear attaching bolts to 29 ft. lbs. (39 Nm), coupling set bolt to 26 ft. lbs. (35 Nm) and tie rod end attaching nuts to 43 ft. lbs. (59 Nm)

W/4 Wheel Drive

1. Remove front differential assembly.
2. Remove cotter pins and nuts from tie rod ends, then using suitable puller, separate tie rod ends from steering knuckles.
3. Remove under cover, then make reference marks on torque shaft and pinion shaft and remove coupling set bolt.
4. Remove three bevel gear attaching bolts, then the bevel gear. Disconnect torque shaft from pinion shaft.
5. Disconnect power steering pressure and return lines from gear housing.
6. Remove steering gear attaching bolts, then the steering gear from vehicle.
7. Reverse procedure to install. Torque steering gear housing attaching bolts to 56 ft. lbs. (76 Nm), power steering pressure and return lines to 33 ft. lbs. (44 Nm), bevel gear attaching bolts to 29 ft. lbs. (39 Nm), coupling set bolt to 26 ft. lbs. (35 Nm) and tie rod end attaching nuts to 43 ft. lbs. (59 Nm)

LATE 1986–87 SUPRA

1. Raise and support front of vehicle, then remove front tire and wheel assemblies.
2. Remove steering shaft universal joint bolt on pinion shaft side, then loosen universal joint bolt on main shaft side. Make alignment marks between pinion shaft and universal joint, then pull out universal joint from pinion shaft.
3. Remove power steering pressure and return lines from gear housing.
4. Remove engine under cover.
5. Remove cotter pins and nuts from tie rod ends, then using suitable puller, separate tie rod ends from steering knuckles.
6. On turbo models, remove air intake connector and air hose.
7. Remove steering damper attaching bolts, then the damper.
8. Remove power steering hose clamp bolts, then the gear housing bracket attaching bolts.
9. Remove steering gear housing from vehicle.
10. Reverse procedure to install. Torque steering gear housing attaching bolts to 56 ft. lbs. (76 Nm), tie rod end attaching nuts to 36 ft. lbs. (49 Nm), steering damper attaching bolts to 20 ft. lbs. (26 Nm), power steering pressure line to 36 ft. lbs. (49 Nm), power steering return line to 33 ft. lbs. (44 Nm) and universal joint attaching bolts to 24 ft. lbs. (32 Nm).

1987 TERCEL SEDAN

1. Raise and support front of vehicle, then remove front wheel and tire assemblies.
2. Remove cotter pins and nuts from tie rod ends, then using suitable puller, separate tie rod ends from steering knuckles.
3. Remove charcoal canister from mounting bracket, then remove mounting bracket.
4. Remove four steering column hole cover attaching bolts and the cover, then remove steering shaft universal joint attaching bolts and the joint.
5. Remove steering gear.
6. Reverse procedure to install. Torque gear housing attaching bolts to 32 ft. lbs. (43 Nm), steering shaft universal joint attaching bolts to 26 ft. lbs. and tie rod end attaching bolts to 36 ft. lbs. (49 Nm).

WHEEL ALIGNMENT SECTION

INDEX

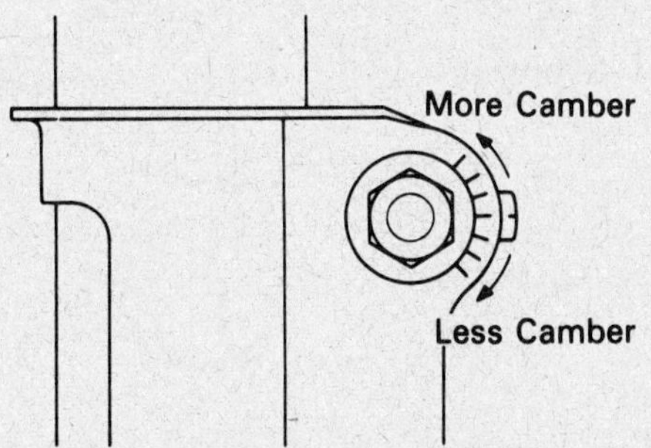

Fig. 1 Adjusting toe-in. 1983–87 Camry, 1983–86 Tercel, 1984–87 Corolla FWD, 1985–87 MR2, 1986–87 Celica & 1987 Tercel wagon

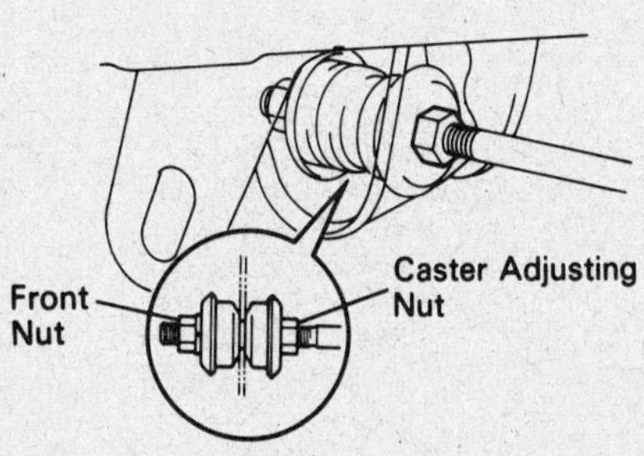

Fig. 2 Adjusting caster. 1985–87 MR2

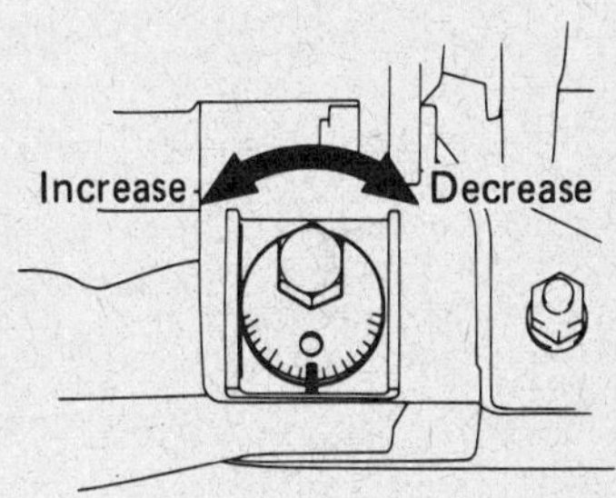

Fig. 3 Adjusting front camber angle. 1986–87 Pickup & 4Runner w/4 wheel drive

FRONT WHEEL ALIGNMENT

Prior to checking and resetting front wheel alignment, check tire pressure to ensure it is correct, check wheel bearings for looseness and correct as necessary and check wheel runout with a dial indicator. Wheel runout should not exceed .047 inch (1.2 mm).

CASTER & CAMBER

1983–85 Pickup 4 Wheel Drive & 1987 Tercel Sedan

Caster and camber are not adjustable on these models. If caster and camber are not within limits, check for worn or damaged suspension parts and replace as necessary.

1983–85 Celica, 1983 Corolla, 1984–87 Corolla RWD, 1983–Early 1986 Supra & 1983–84 Cressida

Camber is not adjustable on these models. If camber angle is not within limits, check for worn or damaged suspension parts and replace as necessary. To adjust caster rotate strut bar adjusting nuts until specified angle is obtained.

1983–87 Camry, 1983–86 Tercel, 1984–87 Corolla FWD, 1986–87 Celica & 1987 Tercel Wagon

Camber is adjusted by turning the camber nut located on the front strut, **Fig. 1.** Measure camber with suitable alignment equipment, then adjust camber by loosening shock absorber set nut and turning cam as necessary to bring camber within specification. Retorque set nut to 166 ft. lbs. on 1987 Camry. 152 ft. lbs. on 1985 Corolla FWD with diesel engine, 1985-86 Camry and 1986-87 Celica or 105 ft. lbs. on all other models.

To adjust caster, add or remove spacers as necessary to front stabilizer bar.

1983–87 Pickup Exc. 4 Wheel Drive

Caster and camber are adjusted by increasing or decreasing the number of shims between upper arm shaft and frame mounting surface. The thickness between front and rear shim packs should not exceed .16 in. (4 mm).

1983–84 Starlet

Camber is not adjustable on these models. If camber angle is not within limits,

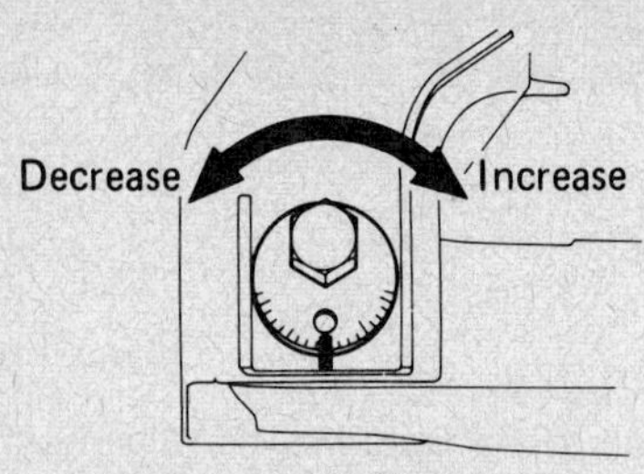

Fig. 4 Adjusting rear camber angle. 1986–87 Pickup & 4Runner w/4 wheel drive

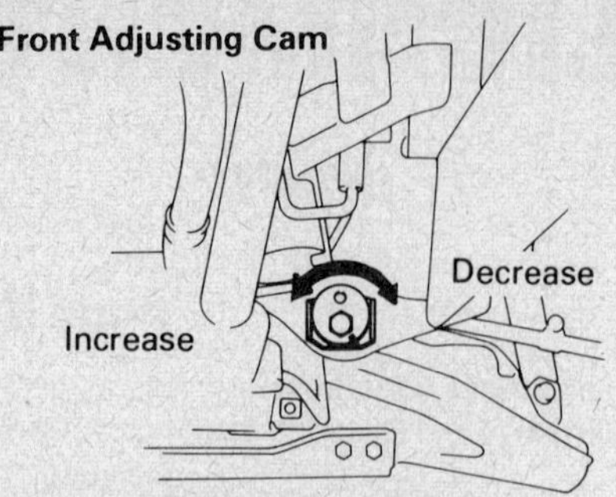

Fig. 5 Front camber/caster adjusting cam. 1987 Van w/4 wheel drive & Supra

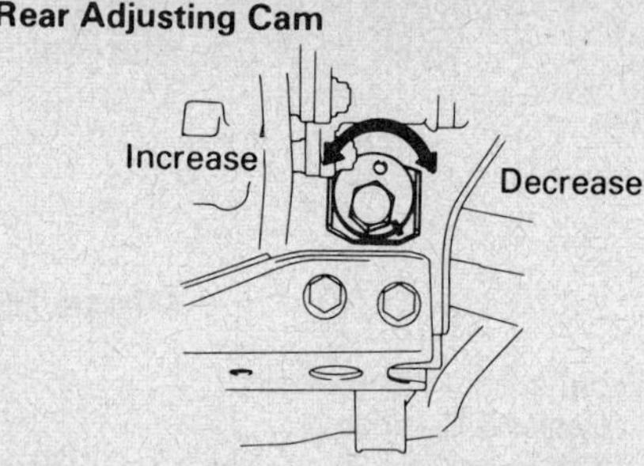

Fig. 6 Rear camber/caster adjusting cam. 1987 Van w/4 wheel drive & Supra

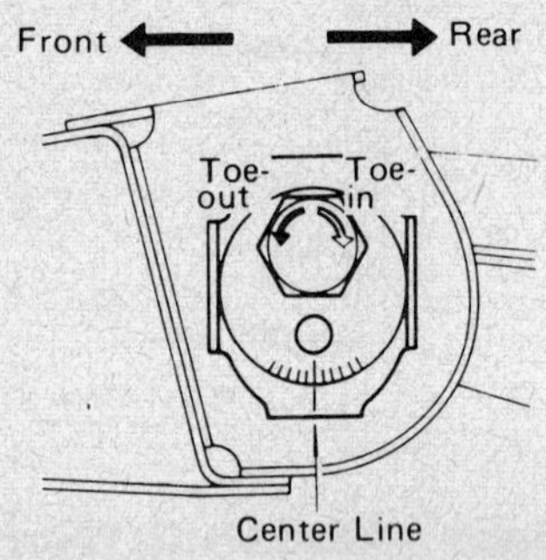

Fig. 7 Adjusting toe-in. Front wheel drive models

check for worn or damaged suspension parts and replace as necessary. To adjust caster, increase or decrease as necessary the number of stabilizer bar spacers. Each spacer will change caster angle $2/5°$. Do not install more than two spacers when performing adjustment.

1984–87 Van Exc. 4 Wheel Drive

Caster and camber are adjusted by turning the strut bar nut or the adjusting cam. Adjusting cam should not be turned more than 4.5 graduations from center position. Do not turn strut bar nut more than 3 threads from original position. Torque adjusting cam bolt to 112 ft. lbs. (152 Nm), and strut bar nut to 89 ft. lbs. (121 Nm).

1985–87 Cressida

Camber is not adjustable on these models. If camber is not within specifications, inspect front suspension components and replace as necessary. Caster is adjusted by adding or subtracting a shim between strut bar and strut bar bracket. One shim will adjust alignment $1/2$ degree. Do not add or subtract more than one shim. If caster cannot be adjusted to within specifications, inspect front suspension components and replace as necessary.

1985–87 MR2

Camber is adjusted by turning the camber adjusting nut, **Fig. 1.** Loosen shock absorber set nut and turn cam to adjust. Camber angle increases approximately $3/10$ degree with each graduation of cam. Torque shock absorber set nut to 105 ft. lbs.

Caster is adjusted by turning caster adjusting nut, **Fig. 2.** Loosen strut bar front nut and turn camber adjusting nut to adjust. Each revolution of nut alters caster angle $3/10$ degree. Torque strut bar front nut to 83 ft. lbs.

1986–87 Pickup & 4Runner W/4 Wheel Drive, 1987 Van W/4 Wheel Drive & Late 1986–87 Supra

Caster and camber are adjusted by rotating front and/or rear adjusting cams as shown, **Figs. 3 through 6.**

TOE IN, ADJUST

Measure length of tie rod on each side and adjust to be equal. Adjust toe-in by

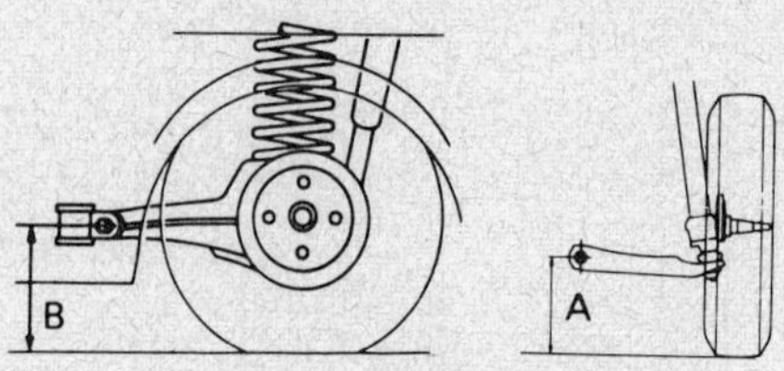

Fig. 8 Vehicle height measuring points

turning adjusting tubes equal amounts. Clamp adjusting tubes after aligning clamps with tube slots. Lock tie rod ends so that inner and outer ends are at right angles to each other.

REAR WHEEL ALIGNMENT

FRONT WHEEL DRIVE MODELS

Prior to checking and resetting rear wheel alignment, check tire pressure to ensure it is correct, check wheel bearings for looseness and correct as necessary and check wheel runout with a dial indicator. Wheel runout should not exceed .047 inch (1.2 mm).

Camber

Measure camber angle with suitable wheel alignment gauge. Camber should

Model	Tire Size	Front Height A	Front Height B
1983 Celica	185/70SR-14	8.189 inch (208 mm)	7.992 inch (203 mm)
	226/60HR-14	8.228 inch (209 mm)	8.031 inch (204 mm)
1984–85 Celica Coupe	185/70SR-14	9.055 inch (230 mm)	10.315 inch (262 mm)
	225/60HR-14	9.094 inch (231 mm)	10.354 inch (263 mm)
1984–85 Celica Liftback	185/70SR-14	9.055 inch (230 mm)	10.492 inch (266.5 mm)
	225/60HR-14	9.094 inch (231 mm)	10.531 inch (267.5 mm)
1983 Cressida	195/70SR-14	8.949 inch (227.3 mm)	10.622 inch (270 mm)
1984 Cressida	195/70SR-14	9.450 inch (240 mm)	10.24 inch (260 mm)
1985–86 Cressida	195/70SR-14	8.82 inch (224 mm)	9.69 inch (246 mm)
1987 Cressida	205/60R-15	8.62 inch (219 mm)	10.43 inch (265 mm)
1983–Early 1986 Supra	195/70SR-14	8.937 inch (227 mm)	10.512 inch (267 mm)
	225/60HR-14	8.780 inch (223 mm)	10.354 inch (263 mm)

Fig. 9 Vehicle riding height chart

be as follows: 1983-86 Tercel exc. 1984-86 front wheel drive wagon, $-1/12°$ ± $1/2°$; 1984-86 front wheel drive Tercel wagon, $-1/6°$ ± $1/2°$; 1987 front wheel drive Tercel wagon, $1/4°$ ± $1/2°$; 1983-87 Corolla with front wheel drive, $-31/60°$ ± $1/2°$; 1983-85 Camry, $1/2°$ ± $1/2°$; 1986 Camry, $1/2°$ ± $3/4°$; 1987 Camry, $-7/12°$ ± $3/4°$; 1986-87 Celica, $-3/4°$ ± $3/4°$. If reading is not within specification, check for worn or damaged bushings or bent damaged rear suspension components and replace as necessary.

Toe-In

1. Measure distance between inner wheel rim and center of lower suspension arm cam bolt. Distance should be identical for both wheels.
2. Place mark on rear center of each rear tire tread and measure distance between mark and center of cam bolt.
3. Move vehicle forward until mark on rear center of tire tread is rotated to front center of wheel. Measure distance between mark and center of cam bolt.
4. Difference between marks at rear center and front center of tire treads should be as follows: 1985-86 Tercel and 1987 Tercel wagon, 0 ± .04 inch (0 ± 1 mm); 1983-84 Camry and Tercel, 0 ± .08 inch (0 ± 2 mm); 1984-85 front wheel drive Corolla, .150 ± .08 inch (3.8 ± 2 mm); 1986-87 front wheel drive Corolla, .150 ± .04 inch (3.8 ± 1 mm); 1985 Camry, .16 ± .08 (4 ± 2 mm); 1986-87 Camry, .16 ± .04 (4 ± 1 mm); 1986-87 Celica, .20 ± .04 (5 ± 1 mm).
5. If toe-in is not within specification, rotate cam bolt(s) until specification is obtained, **Fig. 7.** Toe-in will change approximately .08 inch (2 mm) with each graduation marked on cam.

REAR WHEEL DRIVE MODELS WITH INDEPENDENT REAR SUSPENSION

EXC. 1985–87 MR2 & LATE 1986–87 SUPRA

Prior to checking and resetting rear wheel alignment, check tire pressure to ensure it is correct, check wheel bearings for looseness and correct as necessary and check wheel runout with a dial indicator. Wheel runout should not exceed .047 inch (1.2 mm). Measure vehicle ride height at point A, **Fig. 8,** for front ride height and point B, **Fig. 8,** for rear ride height. Record measurements and compare to measurements shown in **Fig. 9.** If height measurements are not correct, check for bad springs and/or loose suspension parts and repair as necessary.

Camber

Measure camber using suitable wheel alignment gauge. If reading is not within specifications, **Fig. 10,** check for worn or damaged bushings or bent or damaged rear suspension components and repair/replace as necessary.

Toe-In, Adjust

1. Using a suitable measuring device, measure distance between inner wheel rim and differential carrier cover bolt, **Fig. 11.** Both measurements

Model	Inspection Standard	Adjustment Standard	Left-Right Error
1983 Celica	1/10° ± 3/4°	1/10° ± 3/4°	1/2°
1984-85 Celica	−1/6° ± 3/4°	−1/6° ± 1/2°	1/2°
1983 Cressida	1/2° ± 3/4°	1/2° ± 1/2°	1/3°
1984 Cressida	1/3° ± 3/4°	1/3° ± 1/2°	1/2°
1985-87 Cressida	−5/12° ± 3/4°	−5/12° ± 1/2°	1/3°
1983 Supra	1/2° ± 3/4°	1/2° ± 1/2°	1/3°
1984-86 Supra	−1/6° ± 3/4°	−1/6° ± 1/2°	1/3°

Fig. 10 Camber specifications

should be the same. If the measurements are not the same, but within 0.20 in. of each other, adjust toe-in adjusting bolt to bring toe-in within limits, **Fig. 12.**

2. Place marks on rear center of each rear tire and measure distance between marks.
3. Move vehicle forward until mark on rear center of tire is rotated to front center of tire is rotated to front center of tire. Measure distance between marks.
4. Difference between marks at rear center of tires and front center of tires should be as indicated in **Fig. 13. Toe-in should be checked at the same point on the tire and at the same level.**
5. If toe-in is not within specifications, rotate left and right side adjusting bolts, **Fig. 12,** and equal amount to adjust. Toe-in will change approximately .04 inch (1 mm) with each graduation marked on cam.

1985-87 MR2

Prior to checking and resetting rear wheel alignment, check tire pressure to ensure it is correct, check wheel bearings for looseness and correct as necessary and check wheel runout with a dial indicator. Wheel runout should not exceed .039 inch. Measure front vehicle ride height, **Fig. 16,** and rear vehicle ride height, **Fig. 17.** If front ride height is not 8.7 inches (221 mm) and/or rear ride height is not 8.03 inches (204 mm), try to level vehicle by shaking it down. If vehicle height is still not correct, check for bad springs and worn or loose suspension parts.

Camber, Adjust

If camber is not −1 1/2 to 0 degrees on 1985-86 models or −1 1/6 to −1/6 degrees on 1987 models, adjust to −1 1/4 to −1/4 degrees on 1985-86 models or −1 5/12 to −5/12 degrees on 1987 models as follows:

1. Loosen shock absorber set nut.
2. Turn cam bolt, **Fig. 1,** to adjust camber. Camber changes approximately 3/10 degree with each graduation of cam nut.
3. Torque shock absorber set nut to 105 ft. lbs. on 1985-86 models or 166 ft. lbs. on 1987 models.

Toe-In, Adjust

1. Rock vehicle up and down to stabilize suspension.
2. Move vehicle forward approximately 16.4 ft. (5 mm) with front wheel in straight ahead position on a level surface. **If vehicle was backed up, move it forward the same distance.**
3. Mark center of each rear tread and measure the distance between marks.
4. Move vehicle forward until marks on rear sides of tires come to the measuring heights of the gauge on the front side. **If tire rolls too far, repeat step 2.**
5. Measure distance between marks on front of tires.
6. If toe-in is not .16-.24 inch (.4-.6 mm), adjust as follows:
   a. Loosen clamp bolts.
   b. Turn left and right adjusting tubes an equal amount.
   c. Ensure that lengths of left and right adjusting tubes are equal.

LATE 1986-87 SUPRA

Prior to checking and resetting rear wheel alignment, check tire pressure to ensure it is correct check wheel runout with a dial indicator. Wheel runout should not exceed .047 inch (1.2 mm). Measure front vehicle ride height, **Fig. 16,** and rear vehicle ride height, **Fig. 17.** If front ride height is not 8.327 inches (211.5 mm) and/or rear ride height is not 9.016 inches (229 mm), try to level vehicle by shaking it down. If vehicle height is still not correct, check for bad springs and worn or loose suspension parts.

Camber Inspection

Measure camber angle with suitable wheel alignment gauge. Camber should be within −1 to +1/2 degrees with a right to left error of no more than 1/2 degree. If not within specification, inspect rear suspension for worn and damaged parts and replace as necessary.

Toe-In Inspection

1. Rock vehicle up and down to stabilize suspension.
2. Move vehicle forward approximately 16.4 ft. (5 mm) with front wheel in straight ahead position on a level surface. **If vehicle was backed up, move it forward the same distance.**
3. Mark center of each rear tread and measure the distance between marks.
4. Roll vehicle forward until marks on rear sides of tires come to the front side. **If tire rolls too far, repeat step 2.**
5. Measure distance between marks on front of tires. Toe-in should be within .12 ± .08 inch (3 ± 2 mm).
6. If not within specification, inspect rear suspension for worn and damaged parts and replace as necessary.

Camber & Toe-In, Adjust

1. Measure distance between drive shaft to side gear shaft flange and Nos. 1 and 2 lower suspension arms on one side and compare to measurements of other side, **Fig. 18.** The measurements should be equal. 2. If measurements are not equal, turn adjusting cams as necessary until arm lengths on either side are equal. 3. Measure camber and toe-in as outlined above. If measurements are not within specifications, adjust toe-in and camber with adjusting cams.

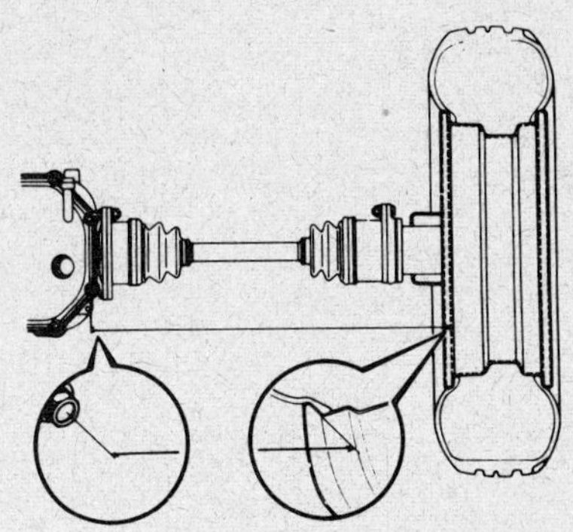

Fig. 11 Measuring wheel position

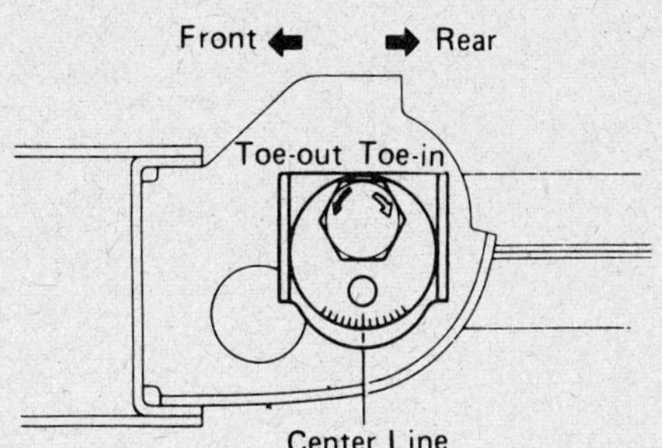

Fig. 12 Adjusting toe-in

Model	Inspection Standard	Adjustment Standard
1983–86 Celica & Supra	0 ± .16 inch (0 ± 4 mm)	0 ± .08 inch (0 ± 2 mm)
1983 Cressida	−.063 ± .16 inch (−1.6 ± 4 mm)	−.063 ± .08 inch (−1.6 ± 2 mm)
1984 Cressida	−.08 ± .16 inch (−2.0 ± 4 mm)	−.08 ± .08 inch (−2.0 ± 2 mm)
1985 Cressida	.12 ± .16 inch (3 ± 4 mm)	.12 ± .08 inch (3 ± 2 mm)
1986–87 Cressida	.12 ± .08 inch (3 ± 2 mm)	.12 ± .04 inch (3 ± 1 mm)

Fig. 13 Toe-in specifications

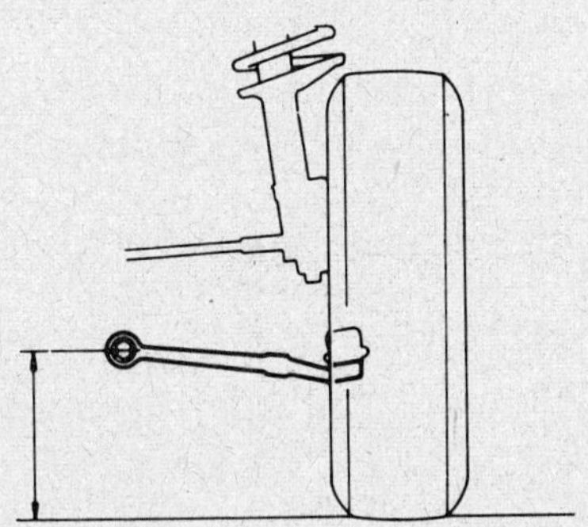

Fig. 14 Measuring front vehicle riding height. 1985–87 MR2

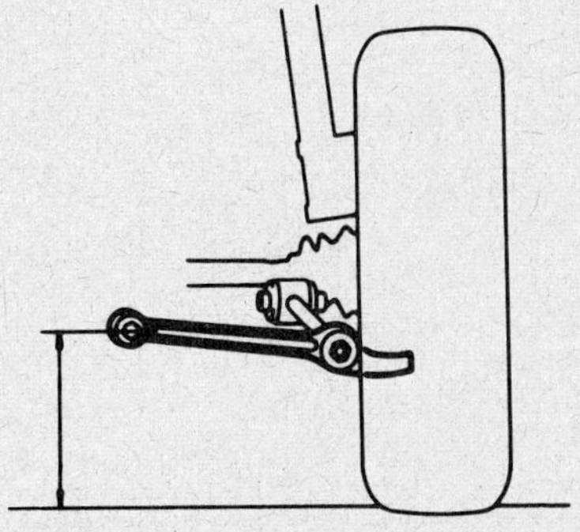

Fig. 15 Measuring rear vehicle riding height. 1985–87 MR2

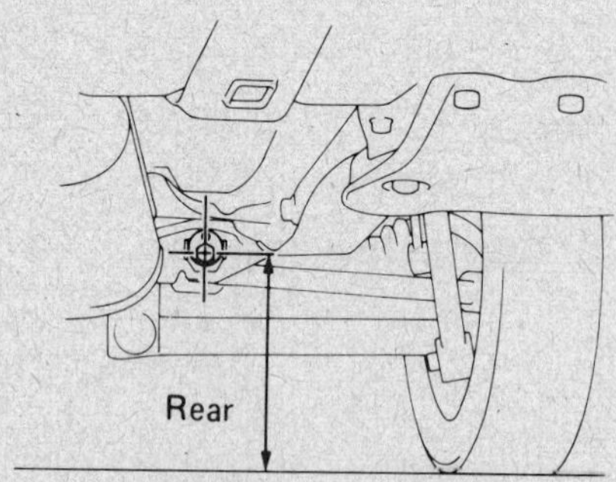

Fig. 16 Measuring front vehicle riding height. Late 1986–87 Supra

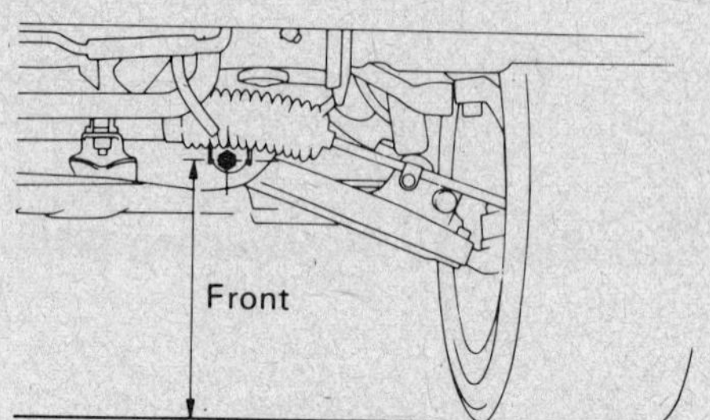

Fig. 17 Measuring rear vehicle riding height. Late 1986–87 Supra

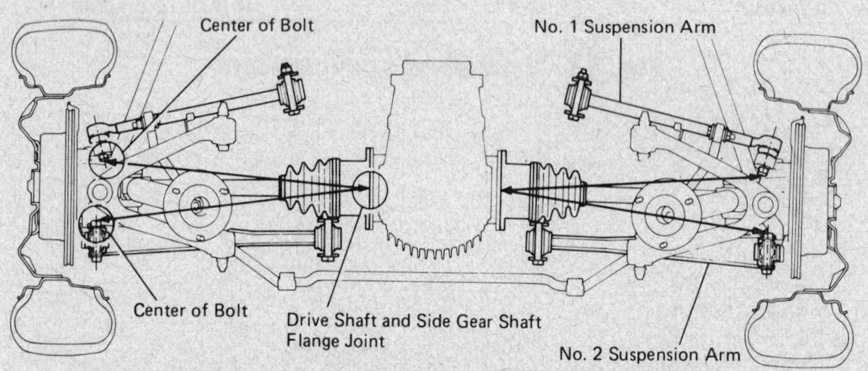

Fig. 18 Measuring points of rear suspension. Late 1986–87 Supra

VOLKSWAGEN EXC. VANAGON (Germany)

INDEX OF SERVICE OPERATIONS

General Engine Specifications

Year	Engine CID①/cc	Fuel System	Bore & Stroke Inches (mm)	Comp. Ratio	Horsepower @ RPM	Torque Lbs. Ft. @ RPM	Normal Oil Pressure Lbs.
1983②	4-105/1700cc	Fuel Inj.	3.13 x 3.40 (79.5 x 86.4mm)	8.2	⑨	⑬	28③
1983–84②⑤⑥⑧	4-96.9/1600cc	Fuel Inj.	3.01 x 3.40 (76.5 x 86.4mm)	23.5	52 @ 4800	71 @ 2000	28③
1983④⑤⑧⑩	4-105/1700cc	Fuel Inj.	3.13 x 3.40 (79.5 x 86.4mm)	8.5	74 @ 5000	90 @ 3000	28③
1983⑤⑥⑧⑩⑪	4-96.9/1600cc	Fuel Inj.	3.01 x 3.40 (76.5 x 86.4mm)	23.0	68 @ 4500	98 @ 2800	28③
1983–84⑤⑦	4-105/1700cc	1 Barrel	3.13 x 3.40 (79.5 x 86.4mm)	8.0	65 @ 5000	83 @ 2800	28③
1983–84⑫	4-109/1800cc	Fuel Inj.	3.19 x 3.40 (81 x 86.4mm)	8.5	90 @ 5500	100 @ 3000	28③
1983⑩	5-131/2100cc	Fuel Inj.	—	8.2	100 @ 5100	112 @ 3000	28③
1984⑥⑧⑩⑪	4-96.9/1600cc	Fuel Inj.	3.01 x 3.40 (76.5 x 86.4mm)	23.0	68 @ 4500	98 @ 2800	28③
1984②④⑤⑬	4-109/1800cc	Fuel Inj.	3.19 x 3.40 (79.5 x 86.4mm)	8.5	90 @ 500	100 @ 3000	28③
1984⑧⑩	4-105/1700cc	Fuel Inj.	3.13 x 3.40 (79.5 x 86.4mm)	8.2	74 @ 5000	90 @ 3000	28③
1985⑥⑩⑪	4-96.9/1600cc	Fuel Inj.	3.01 x 3.40 (76.5 x 86.4mm)	23.0	68 @ 4500	98 @ 2800	23③
1985⑩	4-109/1800cc	Fuel Inj.	—	9.0	88 @ 5500	96 @ 3250	2③
1985–86⑩	5-131/2100cc	Fuel Inj.	—	8.5	110 @ 5500	122 @ 2400	2③
1985–86④⑭	4-109/1800cc	Fuel Inj.	3.19 x 3.40 (79.5 x 86.4mm)	8.5	90 @ 5500	100 @ 3000	28③
1985–86⑧⑮	4-109/1800cc	Fuel Inj.	3.20 x 3.40 (81.0 x 86.4mm)	9.0	85 @ 5250	96 @ 3000	28③
1985–86⑧⑫⑮	4-109/1800cc	Fuel Inj.	3.20 x 3.40 (81.0 x 86.4mm)	10.0	100 @ 5500	105 @ 3000	28③
1985–86⑥⑧⑮	4-96.9/1600cc	Fuel Inj.	3.01 x 3.40 (76.5 x 86.4mm)	23.0	52 @ 4800	71 @ 2500	28③
1985–86⑥⑧⑪⑮	4-96.9/1600cc	Fuel Inj.	3.01 x 3.40 (76.5 x 86.4mm)	23.0	68 @ 4500	98 @ 2500	28③
1987	4-109/1800cc⑯	Fuel Inj.	3.20 x 3.40 (81.0 x 86.4mm)	9.0	81 @ 5500	93 @ 3250	—
	4-109/1800cc⑭	Fuel Inj.	3.20 x 3.40 (81.0 x 86.4mm)	8.5	90 @ 5500	100 @ 3000	—
	4-109/1800cc⑧	Fuel Inj.	3.20 x 3.40 (81.0 x 86.4mm)	9.0	85 @ 5250	96 @ 3000	—
	4-109/1800cc⑬	Fuel Inj.	3.20 x 3.40 (81.0 x 86.4mm)	10.0	102 @ 5250	110 @ 3250	—
	4-109/1800cc④	Fuel Inj.	3.20 x 3.40 (81.0 x 86.4mm)	8.5	90 @ 5500	100 @ 3000	—
	4-109/1800cc⑱	Fuel Inj.	3.20 x 3.40 (81.0 x 86.4mm)	10.0	123 @ 5800	120 @ 4250	—
	5-131/2100cc⑩	Fuel Inj.	—	8.5	110 @ 5500	122 @ 2400	—
	5-131/2100cc⑰	Fuel Inj.	—	8.5	115 @ 5500	126 @ 3000	—

①—Cubic inch displacement.
②—Rabbit Pickup.
③—Minimum @ 2000 RPM & normal operating temperature.
④—Scirocco.
⑤—Rabbit.
⑥—Diesel engine.
⑦—Exc. California.
⑧—Jetta.
⑨—Exc. Calif., 89 @ 3200 RPM; Calif., 90 @ 3000 RPM.
⑩—Quantum.
⑪—With turbocharger.
⑫—GTI.
⑬—Jetta GLI.
⑭—Cabriolet.
⑮—Golf.
⑯—Fox.
⑰—Quantum Synchro Wagon.
⑱—Scirocco 16-Valve.

Valve Specifications

Year	Model	Valve Lash①		Valve Angles		Valve Spring Installed Height	Valve Spring Pressure Lbs. @ In.	Stem Clearance		Stem Diameter	
		Int.	Exh.	Seat	Face			Intake②	Exhaust②	Intake	Exhaust
1983	Rabbit	.010	.018	45°	45°	—	—	.039	.051	.314	.313
1983–87	Scirocco	.010	.018	45°	45°	—	—	.039	.051	.314	.313
1983–84	Jetta	.010	.018	45°	45°	—	—	.039	.051	.314	.313
1983	Quantum	.010	.018	45°	45°	—	—	.039③	.051	.314	.313
1985–87	Cabriolet, Jetta & Golf ④	Hydraulic	Hydraulic	45°	45°	—	—	.04	.052	.319	.318
	Jetta & Golf⑤	.010	.018	45°	45°	—	—	.052	.052	.319	.318
1984–87	Quantum⑥⑦	.010	.018	45°	45°	—	—	.039	.051	.314	.313
	Quantum⑤	.010	.018	45°	45°	—	—	.051	.051	.314	.313
	Quantum⑥⑧	Hydraulic	Hydraulic	45°	45°	—	—	.039	.051	.314	.313

①—Engine warm (95°F).
②—Valve guide wear limit. Measured at valve head with dial indicator.
③—Gasoline engine, .039 in.; diesel engine, .051 in.
④—1800cc gasoline engine.
⑤—Diesel engine.
⑥—Exc. diesel.
⑦—Exc. 5-131 engine.
⑧—5-131 engine.

Pistons, Pins, Rings, Crankshaft & Bearings

Year	Engine	Piston Clearance Top of Skirt	Ring End Gap ①		Wristpin Diameter	Rod Bearings		Main Bearings			
			Comp.	Oil		Shaft Diameter	Bearing Clearance	Shaft Diameter	Bearing Clearance	Thrust on Bear. No.	Shaft Endplay
1983-84	1600cc	.0011-.0027	.012	.010	—	②	.0011-.0034	2.125	.001-.003	3	.003-.007
1983-84	1700cc	.0011-.0027	.012	.010	—	1.811	.0011-.0034	2.125	.001-.003	3	.003-.007
1983-84	1800cc	—	.012	.010	.866	1.881	—	2.125	—	3	.003-.007
1983-84	2100cc	.0010-.0031	.010	.010	—	1.810	—	2.282	.001-.003	3	.003-.007
1983-84	2000cc	.012-.0024	.012	.010	—	2.165	—	③	—	1④	.005-.005
1985-87	1600cc	.0012	.012	.010	—	1.910	—	2.158	—	3	.003-.007
	1800cc	.0012	.012	.010	—	1.910	—	2.158	—	3	.003-.007
	2100cc	.001	.010	.010	—	1.838	.0006-.002	2.318	.0006-.003	4	.003-.007

①—Minimum.
②—Exc. 1981-82 diesel, 1.811 in,; 1981-82 diesel, 1.881.
③—No. 1: with blue dot, 2.362; with red dot, 2.361. No. 3: with blue dot, 2.165; with red dot, 2.164. No. 4, 1.574.
④—Endplay adjusted by shims installed between flywheel and bearing.

Engine Tightening Specifications

*Torque specifications are for clean and lightly lubricated threads only. Dry or dirty threads produce increased friction which prevents accurate measurement of tightness.

Year	Engine	Spark Plugs Ft. Lbs.	Cylinder Head Bolts Ft. Lbs.	Intake Manifold Ft. Lbs.	Exhaust Manifold Ft. Lbs.	Camshaft Bearing Caps Ft. Lbs.	Camshaft Sprocket Bolts Ft. Lbs.	Rocker Arm Nuts Ft. Lbs.	Rocker Arm Cover Ft. Lbs.	Connecting Rod Cap Bolts Ft. Lbs.	Main Bearing Cap Bolts Ft. Lbs.	Flywheel to Crankshaft Ft. Lbs.	Vibration Damper or Pulley Ft. Lbs.
1983-84	1700cc	22	54①	17	17	14	58	—	7	35	47	④	58②
1983-84	1600cc②	③	54①	16	16	14	33	—	7	⑥⑨	47	④	108②
1983-84	1600cc⑥	③	54①	18	18	14	33	—	7	⑥	47	④	145⑦
1983-84	1800cc	22	54①	17	17	14	58	—	7	⑥	47	④	58②
1983-84	2100cc	14	54①	—	—	14	—	—	7	36	47	54	253
1985-87	1600cc② ⑤	③	⑩	—	—	14	33	—	7	⑥	47	72	130②
1985-87	1800cc	22	⑩	—	—	14	58	—	7	⑪	47	72	58②
1985-87	2100	—	⑩	—	—	14	58	—	7	⑫	47	⑬	145⑦

①—Polygon head bolts, torque to specifications plus an additional one-quarter turn.
②—Diesel engine.
③—Injectors, 51 ft. lbs.
④—Pressure plate to crankshaft, 54 ft. lbs., flywheel to pressure plate, 14 ft. lbs. (Quantum and Vanagon, 18 ft. lbs.).
⑤—Turbo diesel.
⑥—Stretch type bolt, must be replaced during assembly. Torque to 22 ft. lbs., then an additional one-half turn.
⑦—Small bolts, 18 ft. lbs.
⑧—Man. trans., 80 ft. lbs.; auto. trans., 65 ft. lbs.
⑨—Rigid type bolt, 33 ft. lbs.
⑩—Torque bolts to 30 ft. lbs. first, then to 43 ft. lbs., and an additional ½ turn.
⑪—Torque to 22 ft. lbs., then an additional ¼ turn.
⑫—Stretch bolts 22 ft. lbs. and rigid bolts 36 ft. lbs.
⑬—Bolts without shoulder, 54 ft. lbs., bolts with shoulder, 72 ft. lbs.

Starting Motor Specifications

Year	Model No.	Rotation ①	Brush Spring Tension Ounces	No Load Test			Torque Test		
				Amperes (Max.)	Volts	RPM (Min.)	Amperes (Max.)	Volts	Torque Ft. Lbs. (Min.)
1983–87	001211209 ②	—	40-48	55	11.5	6000	430	8.5	8.5
	001211223 ②	—	40-48	55	11.5	6000	430	8.5	8.5
	001212006 ②	—	40-48	55	11.5	6000	410	8.5	9.0
	001212204 ②	—	40-48	55	11.5	6000	410	8.5	9.0
	001212206 ②	—	40-48	55	11.5	6000	410	8.5	9.0
	001312105 ②	—	28-32	85	11.5	8500	730	6.0	13.75
	001314012 ②	—	40-46	80	11.5	7300	780	6.0	16.5
	001314014 ②	—	40-46	80	11.5	7300	780	6.0	16.5
	001211206 ②	—	40-48	55	11.5	6000	430	8.5	8.5
	001211218 ②	—	40-48	55	11.5	6000	430	8.5	8.5
	—	—	—	55	11.5	6000	③	8.5	—

①—Viewed from drive end.
②—Bosch part No.
③—Auto. trans., 410 amps; man. trans., 430 amps.

Brake Specifications

Year	Model	Drum Brake I.D.	Wheel Cylinder Bore			Master Cylinder Bore		Disc Brake Rotor				
			Front Disc	Rear Disc	Rear Drum	Manual	Power	Nominal Thickness Front	Nominal Thickness Rear	Min. Thickness Front	Min. Thickness Rear	Runout (T.I.R.)
1983	Rabbit	7.087	—	—	—	—	—	.472	—	.413	—	.002
1983–87	Scirocco	7.087	—	—	—	—	—	.472	—	.413	—	.002
1983–84	Jetta	7.087	—	—	—	—	—	.472	—	.413	—	.002
1983–84	Pickup	7.087 ④	—	—	—	—	—	.472	—	.413	—	.002
1983–87	Quantum ②	7.874	—	—	.687	—	—	.472	—	.394 ①	—	.002
1983–87	Quantum ③	7.874	—	—	.687	—	—	.787	—	.709 ①	—	.002
1985–86	Cabriolet, Golf & Jetta	7.087	—	—	—	—	—	.472 ⑤ ⑥	.394	.393 ⑤ ⑦	.315	.002

①—Maximum wear limit.
②—Exc. 5-131 engine.
③—5-131 engine.
④—Self-adjusting brakes, 7.874.
⑤—Solid disc.
⑥—Ventilated disc, .787 inch.
⑦—Ventilated disc, .708 inch.

Wheel Alignment Specifications

Year	Model	Caster Angle, Degrees		Camber Angle, Degrees				Toe Degrees	Toe-Out On Turns Degrees	
				Limits		Desired				
		Limits	Desired	Left	Right	Left	Right		Outer Wheel	Inner Wheel
1983–84	Rabbit, Scirocco	+1 1/3 to +2 1/3	+1 5/6	−1/6 to +5/6	−1/6 to +5/6	+1/3	+1/3	−1/12 to −1/2	—	—
1985–87	Scirocco	+1 1/3 to +2 1/3	+1 5/6	−1/6 to +5/6	−1/6 to +5/6	+1/3	+1/3	−1/12 to −1/2	—	—
1983–84	Jetta	+1 1/3 to +2 1/3	+1 5/6	−1/6 to +5/6	−1/6 to +5/6	+1/3	+1/3	−1/12 to −1/2	—	—
1983–84	Pickup	+5/6 to +1 5/6	+1 1/3	−1/6 to +5/6	−1/6 to +5/6	+1/3	+1/3	−1/12 to −1/2	—	—
1983–87	Quantum	0 to +1	+1/2	−1/6 to −1 1/6	−1/6 to −1 1/6	−2/3	−2/3	0 to +1/3	—	—
1985–87	Cabriolet	+1 1/3 to +2 1/3	+1 5/6	−1/6 to +5/6	−1/6 to +5/6	+1/3	+1/3	−1/12 to −1/2	—	—
	Golf①	+1 to +2	+1 1/2	−1/15 to −2/3	−1/15 to −2/3	−6/15	−6/15	−1/6 to +1/6	—	—
	Golf②	+1 1/20 to +2 1/20	+1 11/20	−1/4 to −1/12	−1/4 to −1/12	−7/12	−7/12	−1/6 to +1/6	—	—
	Jetta③	+1 to +2	+1 1/2	−1/6 to −5/6	−1/6 to −5/6	−1/2	−1/2	−1/6 to +1/6	—	—
	Jetta④	+1 1/20 to 2 1/20	+1 11/20	−1/4 to −1/12	−1/4 to −1/12	−7/12	−7/12	−1/6 to +1/6	—	—

①—Exc. GTI models.
②—GTI models.
③—Exc. GLI models.
④—GLI models.

Cooling System & Capacity Data

Year	Model	Cooling System Capacity Qts.	Rad. Cap Relief Pressure Lbs.	Thermostat Opening Temp. Deg. F.	Fuel Tank Capacity Gals.	Engine Oil Refill Qts. ①	Transaxle Capacity Pints			
							Manual		Automatic	
							4 Speed	5 Speed	Trans.	Final Drive
1983–84	Rabbit	⑤	17–23	185	⑥	⑨	3.2	4.2	12.8	1.6
1983–87	Scirocco	⑤	17–23	185	⑥	—	3.2	4.2	12.8	1.6
1983–84	Rabbit③	7.3	17–23	185	10	4.7	3.2	4.2	12.8	1.6
1983–84	Jetta	⑤	17–23	185	10	⑨	—	4.2	12.8	1.6
1983–84	Quantum⑦	7.3	17–21	185	16	3.7	—	4.2	12.8	1.6
1983–84	Quantum⑧	8.5	17–19	189	16	3.7	—	4.2	12.8	—
1983–84	Rabbit④	⑤	17–23	185	15.0	4.7	3.2	4.2	12.8	1.6
1985–87	Cabriolet	7.3	17–22	185	10.6	4.7	—	4.2	12.8	1.6
	Golf②	6.8	17–22	185	14.5	4.3	—	4.2	12.8	1.6
	Golf③	6.8	17–22	189	14.5	4.7	—	4.2	12.8	1.6
	Jetta②	6.8	17–22	185	14.5	4.3	—	4.2	12.8	1.6
	Jetta③	6.8	17–22	189	14.5	4.7	—	4.2	12.8	1.6
	Quantum②⑦	6.3	17–21	185	15.9	3.2	—	4.2	12.8	1.6
	Quantum③	6.3	17–21	185	15.9	3.7	—	4.2	12.8	1.6
	Quantum②⑧	8.5	17–19	189	15.9	3.7	—	5.0	12.8	2.0

①—Includes filter.
②—Exc. diesel.
③—Diesel.
④—Pickup.
⑤—Exc. diesel, 4.9 qts.; diesel, 7.3 qts.
⑥—1983 exc. diesel, 10 gals.; 1983 diesel, 11 gals.
⑦—Exc. 5-131 engine.
⑧—5-131 engine.
⑨—1983–84 exc. turbo diesel, 4.7 qts.; 1983–84 turbo diesel, 5 qts.

ELECTRICAL SECTION

INDEX

ALTERNATOR OUTPUT TEST

Two different alternators are used, one manufactured by Bosch and the other by Motorola. However, the test procedures for both alternators are identical.

1. Connect a suitable volt/amp tester, load pile, and battery cut-out switch to charging system following manufacturer's instructions.
2. Start and operate engine until normal operating temperature is obtained, then maintain engine speed at 3000 RPM. **Ensure all electrical accessories are switched off before testing system.**
3. Adjust load pile to obtain maximum ammeter reading. **Do not allow voltage to drop below 12 volts.**
4. Maximum reading should be within 16 amps of maximum hot output specification.
5. If reading is not within specification, replace voltage regulator and repeat test.
6. If reading is still not within specification, repair or replace alternator. **Before replacing alternator, ensure charging system wiring harness is properly routed, free from breaks or frayed insulation, and that connectors are free of corrosion.**

STARTER REPLACE

EXC. QUANTUM

Automatic Transaxle Models

1. Disconnect battery ground cable.
2. Remove starter splash cover clamp then the splash cover.
3. Disconnect electrical leads from starter solenoid.
4. Remove starter to housing attaching nuts and the starter.
5. Reverse procedure to install.

Manual Transaxle Models

1. Disconnect battery ground cable.
2. Disconnect electrical leads from starter solenoid.
3. Remove starter support bracket to transaxle attaching bolt.
4. Remove starter to housing mounting bolts and the starter.
5. Install starter and torque mounting bolts to 11 ft. lbs.
6. Attach support bracket to starter, place two .080 inch washers and lock washers onto starter studs, then install nuts loosely.
7. Attach support bracket to transaxle and torque attaching bolt to 11 ft. lbs.
8. Torque support bracket to starter stud nuts to 4 ft. lbs. **Both studs should have sufficient clearance in elongated holes of bracket to enable easy mounting. If not, enlarge bracket holes as necessary.**
9. Connect solenoid electrical leads and battery cable.

QUANTUM

1. Disconnect battery ground cable.
2. Disconnect electrical leads from starter solenoid.
3. Remove starter attaching bolts and the starter.
4. Reverse procedure to install.

IGNITION SWITCH REPLACE

1. Disconnect battery ground cable.
2. Remove turn signal, windshield wiper and dimmer switches as outlined under "Turn Signal, Windshield Wiper & Dimmer Switch, Replace" procedure.
3. Disconnect wire connector from ignition switch.
4. Remove steering lock housing assembly as outlined under "Steering Lock Housing, Replace" procedure.
5. Remove setscrew attaching ignition switch to lock housing assembly.
6. Remove ignition switch.
7. Reverse procedure to install.

STEERING LOCK HOUSING REPLACE

1. Disconnect battery ground cable.
2. Remove column switches as outlined under "Turn Signal, Windshield Wiper & Dimmer Switch, Replace" procedure.
3. Disconnect wire connector from ignition switch.
4. Remove retainers, if equipped, and the steering lock housing assembly.
5. Reverse procedure to install.

TURN SIGNAL, WINDSHIELD WIPER & DIMMER SWITCH REPLACE

1. Disconnect battery ground cable.
2. Pulling gently, remove steering wheel center pad.
3. Remove steering wheel retaining nut and washer, then the steering wheel.
4. Remove screws retaining switches to steering column.
5. Pull switches out gently, then disconnect multi-pin electrical plugs.
6. Remove switches from steering column.
7. Reverse procedure to install.

BRAKE LIGHT SWITCH REPLACE

The brake light switches are located at the master cylinder and are easily accessible from the engine compartment.

1. Disconnect wire connector from switch.
2. Using a suitable wrench, remove switch from master cylinder.
3. Install new switch and connect electrical connector.
4. Top up master cylinder reservoir and bleed brake system.

NEUTRAL SAFETY SWITCH REPLACE

1. Disconnect battery ground cable.
2. Loosen setscrew securing shifter selector knob to selector lever, then remove knob.
3. Remove shift indicator to selector

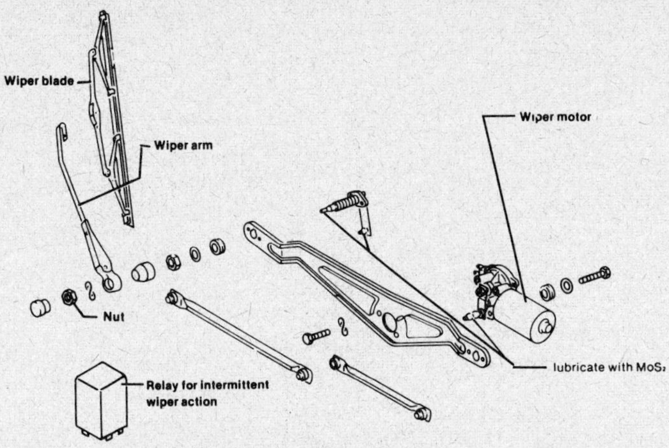

Fig. 1 Exploded view of wiper motor & transmission assembly, 1983–84 Rabbit & Jetta

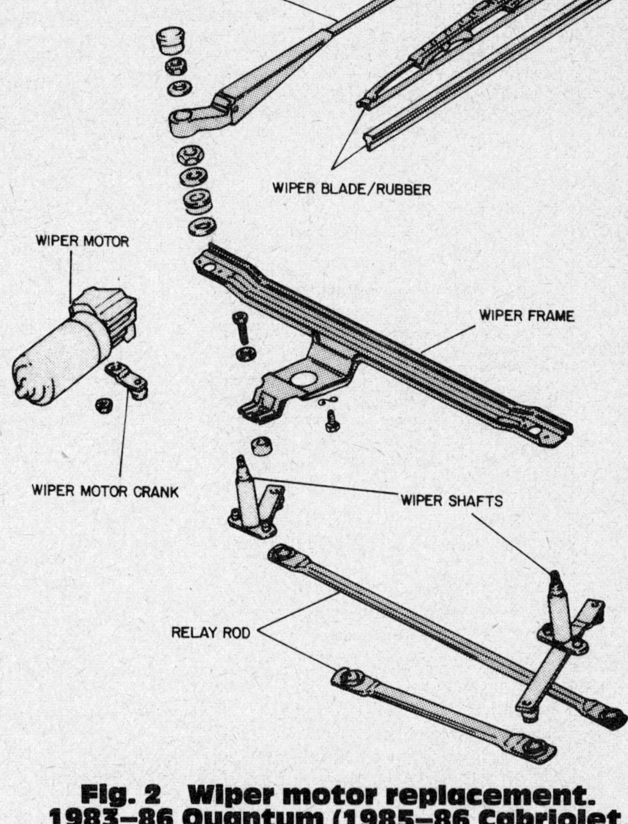

Fig. 2 Wiper motor replacement. 1983–86 Quantum (1985–86 Cabriolet, Jetta & Golf similar)

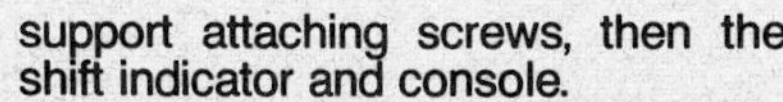

support attaching screws, then the shift indicator and console.

4. Disconnect electrical lead from switch, then remove switch attaching screws and switch.
5. Position new switch onto selector support, then install attaching screws finger tight and connect electrical connector to switch.
6. Adjust switch until starter will only operate in "Park" or "Neutral" positions, then tighten switch attaching screws.
7. Reverse procedure to complete installation.

INSTRUMENT CLUSTER REPLACE

1983–84 RABBIT EXC. CONVERTIBLE

1. Disconnect battery ground cable.
2. Remove LH speaker grille, headlamp switch knob and shaft, and radio knobs.
3. Remove 6 screws securing cluster bezel and remove bezel.
4. Remove 4 screws securing cluster and pull cluster away from dash.
5. Disconnect wiring harness connectors and speedometer cable, and remove cluster.
6. Reverse procedure to install.

1983–86 JETTA, 1983–84 RABBIT CONVERTIBLE & 1985–86 GOLF & CABRIOLET

1. Disconnect battery ground cable.
2. Remove steering wheel trim and retaining nut, then remove steering wheel using a suitable puller.
3. Remove radio or storage tray, heater control knobs, and control trim plate.
4. On Rabbit models, remove trim rings from around each switch panel.
5. On all models remove screws securing instrument cluster bezel and pull bezel away from dash.
6. If equipped, press switches out of bezel and remove bezel.
7. Remove screws securing instrument cluster, disconnect wiring harness connectors and speedometer cable, then remove cluster.
8. Reverse procedure to install, ensuring that steering wheel is properly centered.

1983–86 QUANTUM

1. Disconnect battery ground cable.
2. Remove steering wheel trim and retaining nut, then the wheel using a suitable puller.
3. Pry off cluster bezel cover, then remove bezel attaching screws and the bezel.
4. Remove attaching screw from top of instrument cluster and tilt cluster away from dash.
5. Disconnect speedometer cable and electrical connectors from cluster and remove cluster from vehicle.
6. Reverse procedure to install.

1983–86 SCIROCCO

1. Disconnect battery ground cable.
2. Remove 2 screws securing cluster bezel and remove bezel.
3. Remove screw at top of instrument cluster and tilt cluster away from dash.
4. Disconnect wiring harness connectors and speedometer cable and remove cluster.
5. Reverse procedure to install.

WIPER MOTOR REPLACE

RABBIT, JETTA & 1985–86 CABRIOLET & GOLF

1. Disconnect battery ground cable.
2. Disconnect wiper assembly connecting rods from wiper motor crank arm, **Figs. 1 and 2.**
3. Disconnect multi-pin electrical connector from wiper motor.
4. Remove wiper motor to mounting frame attaching bolts and the wiper motor.
5. Reverse procedure to complete installation.

1983–86 SCIROCCO

1. Disconnect battery ground cable.
2. Hold wiper arm near base and remove retaining nut, then remove arm.
3. Remove nut securing wiper transmission to cowl and remove spacer.
4. Disconnect wiring harness electrical connector to wiper motor and remove wiper frame bolts.
5. Remove motor, frame and transmission as an assembly.
6. Remove crank retaining nut and crank, then remove wiper motor.
7. Place wiper motor to park position, then install onto wiper frame.
8. Install crank facing away from motor so motor attaching bolt is not visible.

9. Reverse procedure to complete installation, installing wiper arm with joint 1.968 inches above windshield molding.

1983–86 QUANTUM

Refer to **Fig. 3** for wiper motor replacement procedure on this model.

HEATER CORE REPLACE

1983–84 RABBIT, JETTA, PICKUP & 1983–86 SCIROCCO

1. Disconnect battery ground cable and drain cooling system.
2. Remove windshield washer reservoir from mounting bracket.
3. Remove ignition coil.
4. From inside engine compartment, disconnect heater hoses from heater core.
5. Pull knobs off heater control assembly to dash panel attaching screws and the control assembly, **Fig. 4.**
6. Remove console and dash trim panels as needed to gain access to fresh air housing.
7. Disconnect wiring harness electrical connectors from housing, then pry housing from retainers and remove lower housing.
8. Remove heater core cover from LH side of housing and pull out core.
9. Reverse procedure to install.

1983–86 QUANTUM

Refer to **Figs. 3 and 4** for heater core replacement procedure on these models.

1985–86 JETTA, GOLF & CABRIOLET

Refer to **Fig. 5** for heater core replacement procedure on these models.

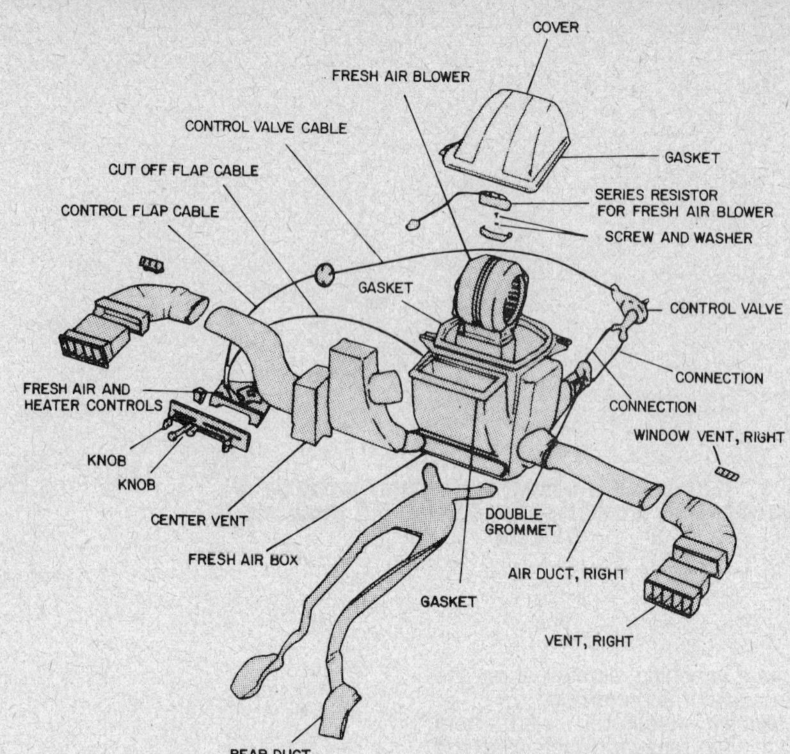

Fig. 3 Heater assembly removal. Quantum

BLOWER MOTOR REPLACE

1983–84 RABBIT, JETTA, PICKUP & 1983–86 SCIROCCO

1. Disconnect battery ground cable.
2. If equipped with A/C, remove screws securing air distribution flap housing to cowl and partially remove cover.
3. Remove screws securing heater cover to cowl and remove cover.
4. Remove resistor retaining bolts and lay resistor aside.
5. Remove clamp and screws securing motor, then remove fan and motor assembly.
6. Reverse procedure to install.

1983–86 QUANTUM

Refer to **Fig. 5** for blower motor replacement procedure on these models.

1985–86 JETTA, GOLF & CABRIOLET

Refer to **Fig. 5** for blower motor replacement procedure on these models.

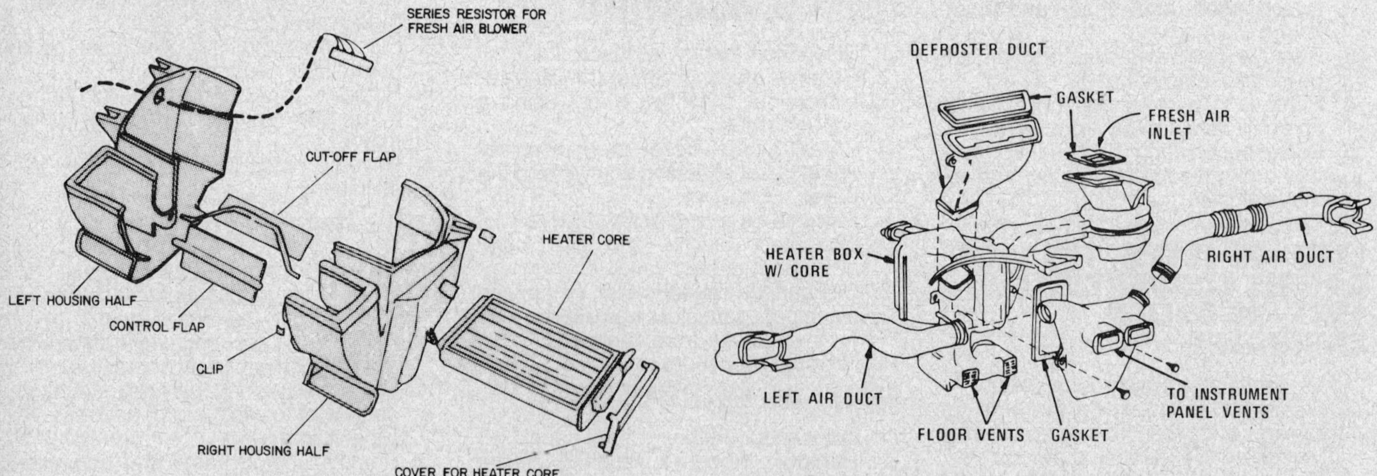

Fig. 4 Exploded view of heater assembly. Quantum

Fig. 5 Exploded view of heater assembly. 1985–86 Jetta, Golf & Cabriolet

GASOLINE ENGINE SECTION

INDEX

ENGINE REPLACE

1983–84 JETTA, PICKUP, RABBIT & 1983–86 SCIROCCO

The engine and transaxle are removed as an assembly on these vehicles.

1. Disconnect battery ground cable.
2. On models equipped with automatic transaxle, place shift selector in Park position.
3. Open fuel filler cap to relieve tank pressure.
4. Remove air intake pipe between fuel distributor and throttle valve assembly.
5. Remove radiator cap.
6. Remove thermostat housing to engine attaching bolts, open heater control valve and drain cooling system.
7. Remove thermostat housing, then disconnect upper radiator hose.
8. Mark, then disconnect all electrical connectors from engine.
9. Remove radiator side retaining nuts.
10. Remove upper radiator clip, then the radiator upper clamp.
11. Remove radiator assembly with electric cooling fan from vehicle.
12. Remove pre-heater pipe, then disconnect vacuum hoses from distributor and EGR temperature valve.
13. Remove coil wire, then disconnect heater hoses from engine.
14. Disconnect fuel line from cold start valve and warm-up regulator.
15. On automatic transaxle models, disconnect speedometer cable.
16. Disconnect vacuum hoses from brake booster, front and rear vacuum amplifiers and vacuum booster (if equipped).
17. Disconnect PCV hose.
18. On manual transaxle models, disconnect accelerator cable from linkage ball stud and cylinder head cover attaching bracket.
19. Remove fuel injectors, fuel lines and vacuum hoses and position aside.
20. Disconnect ground cable strap from transaxle.
21. On manual transaxle models, disconnect clutch cable from clutch lever and speedometer cable from transaxle, then remove upper starter bolt.
22. On automatic transaxle models, disconnect selector cable and accelerator pedal cable from transaxle bracket, then disconnect accelerator pedal cable from operating rod.
23. Remove nuts and bolts securing exhaust flex pipe to exhaust manifold.
24. On manual transaxle models, remove relay shaft retaining nut and relay shaft.
25. Disconnect driveshafts from transaxle drive flanges.
26. On manual transaxle models, remove starter.
27. Remove horn assembly and position aside.
28. Remove front mount cup to body attaching bolts, then the front mount and cup.
29. Remove both driveshaft to bearing housing attaching bolts, then the ball joint lock bolts.
30. Separate both ball joints from bearing housings, then remove both drive shafts from vehicle. After removing driveshafts, connect ball joints and lock bolts to enable vehicle to be lowered.
31. Remove rear transaxle mount and right front wheel/tire assembly.
32. Attach engine replacement tool US-1105 or equivalent and lift engine slightly with hoist. **Always attach lifting eye tool 055103390A to cylinder head when removing engine to ensure equal weight distribution.**
33. On manual transaxle models, disconnect all shift linkages that will interfere with engine/transaxle removal.
34. Remove left and right side engine mount to body attaching bolts, then the mounts.
35. Lower engine/transaxle assembly onto suitable floor dolly, raise vehicle and remove engine/transaxle assembly out from underneath vehicle.
36. Reverse procedure to install.

1985–86 CABRIOLET, JETTA & GOLF

The engine and transaxle are removed as an assembly on these vehicles.

1. On models equipped with air conditioning, proceed as follows:
   a. Remove engine trim panel and lower apron.
   b. Remove consider from crossmember and radiator, then all ducts.
   c. Disconnect electrical connectors from radiator fan shroud and A/C compressor.
   d. Remove alternator and A/C compressor V-belts.
   e. Disconnect idle boost valve vacuum hoses.
   f. Disconnect air filter assembly along with air flow assembly and position aside.
   g. Remove compressor and condenser.
2. On all models, disconnect driveshafts from transmission, then suspend driveshafts from body with wire.
3. Remove exhaust manifold spring clamp.
4. On models equipped with power steering, proceed as follows:
   a. Remove bolts attaching adjusting bracket, then bolts attaching pivot bracket.
   b. Remove V-belt, then suspend pump from body crossmember with wire.
   c. Remove fluid reservoir with mount and suspend with wire from body crossmember.
5. On all models, remove front apron attaching bolt and trim, then apron and trim.
6. Disconnect and remove battery.
7. Remove coolant reservoir cap, then drain coolant from coolant hose and/or thermostat flange.
8. Remove radiator grille.
9. Disconnect headlight and radiator support electrical connectors, then remove radiator mounts.
10. Disconnect hood release cable from hood latch and disconnect cable from support.
11. Disconnect cooling fan electrical connector.
12. Remove radiator support, coolant hoses, radiator and fan shroud assembly.
13. Disconnect necessary fuel injection and ignition system wiring.

14. Disconnect ground connections.
15. On manual transaxle models, disconnect upshift indicator vacuum switch, transaxle switch, then starter.
16. On automatic transaxle models, disconnect battery cable to starter, then starter cable CIS-E wire harness.
17. On GTI and GLI models, disconnect idle stabilizer control valve, throttle plate switch and knock sensor.
18. On manual transaxle models, disconnect clutch cable from transaxle.
19. On all models, disconnect speedometer cable from transaxle. Plug all openings.
20. On automatic transaxle models, position selector lever in Park position, then disconnect accelerator cable and selector lever cable from actuator levers and mounts.
21. On all models, remove gear shift rods and bracket.
22. On manual transaxle models, disconnect accelerator cable at throttle linkage and at mounting bracket. **Do not remove throttle linkage.**
23. On all models, remove cold start valve, but leave fuel line connected.
24. Disconnect vacuum hose from intake manifold, then connecting hose.
25. If equipped, remove warm up regulator.
26. Disconnect fuel injectors, then plug all openings.
27. Remove intake manifold pre-heat hose, then purple hose from "T" connection on throttle body.
28. If equipped, remove hose from throttle body to idle boost valve.
29. Disconnect crankcase ventilation hose from air cleaner housing.
30. Remove rear engine mount attaching bolts, then rear mount.
31. Disconnect transaxle mount.
32. Remove front mount attaching bolt, then carefully remove transaxle from mount by turning slightly.
33. Attach suitable engine lifting equipment onto engine, and remove engine from vehicle.
34. Reverse procedure to install.

QUANTUM

4 Cylinder Engine

1. Disconnect battery ground cable.
2. Place temperature control lever in Warm position, then open radiator cap.
3. Remove 5 power steering pump attaching bolts and the pump drive belt, then position pump aside, leaving fluid lines attached.
4. Disconnect lower hose from water pump and drain cooling system.
5. Disconnect coolant hose from cylinder head.
6. Disconnect electrical connectors from thermo-time switch, alternator, oil pressure switch and control pressure regulator.
7. Disconnect vacuum hoses from distributor.
8. Remove control pressure regulator attaching bolts and position aside, leaving fuel lines attached.
9. Disconnect electrical connectors from radiator fan switch and fan.
10. Remove radiator, air duct and fan as an assembly.
11. On manual transaxle models, disconnect clutch cable from transaxle.
12. On all models, remove attaching nut from left engine mount.
13. Disconnect hall sender electrical connector and coil wire from distributor.
14. Disconnect electrical connectors from coolant temperature sender and oxygen sensor thermo-switch.
15. Disconnect remaining coolant hoses.
16. Disconnect electrical connectors from cold start valve, frequency valve and oxygen sensor.
17. Remove charcoal filter valve from air duct and remove the duct.
18. Remove pre-heater hose, then the cold start valve with fuel line attached.
19. Disconnect vacuum hoses from intake manifold, then remove accelerator cable.
20. Disconnect crankcase breather and brake booster hoses.
21. Disconnect electrical connector from auxiliary air regulator.
22. Remove injectors, leaving fuel lines attached.
23. Loosen fuel distributor and air filter housing and position aside.
24. On models without air conditioning, remove front engine mount.
25. On all models, disconnect front exhaust pipe from exhaust manifold.
26. Disconnect electrical connectors from starter motor.
27. Remove right engine mount attaching nuts.
28. Remove starter motor attaching bolts, then lower transaxle-to-engine attaching bolts.
29. Remove flywheel cover plate.
30. On automatic transaxle models, remove starter motor, then torque converter attaching bolts.
31. On all models, support transaxle with tool VW-785/1B or equivalent.
32. On models equipped with air conditioning, proceed as follows:
    a. Remove front engine mount attaching bolts and the mount.
    b. Loosen crankshaft pulley outer nuts and remove drive belt.
    c. Remove both upper bolts from compressor mounting bracket.
    d. Remove 3 lower bolts from compressor mounting bracket, then position compressor and bracket aside, leaving refrigerant lines attached.
33. On all models, attach engine lifting tool US-1105 or equivalent to engine and raise engine slightly.
34. Remove right engine mount, then tension transaxle supporting tool and remove upper transaxle-to-engine attaching bolts.
35. Separate engine from transaxle, then carefully lift engine from vehicle.
36. Reverse procedure to install.

5 Cylinder Engine

1. Disconnect battery ground cable.
2. Place temperature control lever in warm position, then remove cap from coolant expansion tank.
3. Remove power steering pump drive belt cover, then loosen pump and position aside, leaving lines attached.
4. Remove front grille, then the radiator cover.
5. Disconnect radiator lower hose and drain cooling system.
6. Remove front bumper with energy absorber.
7. Disconnect vacuum hoses from intake manifold, then remove upper radiator hose.
8. Disconnect coolant hose from thermostat housing.
9. Disconnect hose from heater pipe and drain residual coolant.
10. Disconnect electrical connectors from oil pressure switch, control pressure regulator and thermo-time switches.
11. Disconnect ground wire from valve cover, then remove control pressure regulator, leaving fuel lines attached.
12. Remove circlip and disconnect ball joint from pushrod.
13. Remove alternator drive belt, then unfasten alternator and bracket and position aside.
14. Loosen clamps and remove intake air duct.
15. Disconnect electrical connectors from cold start valve, throttle switch, frequency valve, idle stabilizer valve, oxygen sensor and hall sender at distributor.
16. Remove snap ring and disconnect accelerator rod.
17. Remove distributor cap, then disconnect injection cooling hose.
18. Remove injectors, leaving fuel lines attached, then disconnect vacuum hose from thermo-pneumatic valve.
19. Remove fuel distributor with air filter housing and position aside with injectors, control pressure regulator and cold start valve.
20. Remove air filter housing.
21. Disconnect coolant hoses from transmission oil cooler and the heater hose.
22. Remove pipe bracket with transaxle-to-engine attaching bolt.
23. Remove air conditioner compressor drive belt and disconnect compressor clutch wire.
24. Attach engine support No. 2084 or equivalent, then remove crankshaft bolt.
25. Remove two crankshaft pulley bolts and loosen bolts. Tap lightly against remaining two bolts, then remove bolts and the pulley.
26. Remove front engine mount, then disconnect exhaust pipe from exhaust manifold.
27. Loosen air conditioner compressor and bracket, then position aside leaving refrigerant lines connected.
28. Remove exhaust pipe support attaching bolt.
29. Remove both front subframe attaching bolts.
30. Remove starter motor, then the torque converter attaching bolts.
31. Remove lower transaxle-to-engine attaching bolts, then disconnect shift rod clip.
32. Remove rubber plugs from side mem-

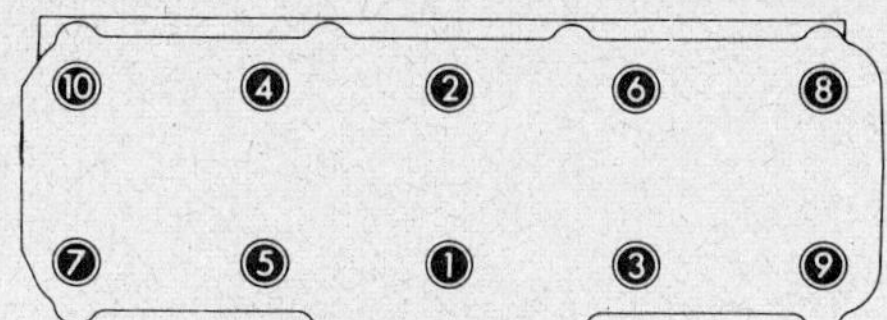

Fig. 1 Cylinder head bolt tightening sequence

ber, then attach tool VW-785/1 or equivalent to support transaxle.
33. Remove engine mount attaching nuts.
34. Remove upper transaxle-to-engine attaching bolts, leaving the most easily accessible bolt installed.
35. Attach suitable lifting equipment to engine and lift engine slightly.
36. Remove remaining transaxle-to-engine attaching bolt and separate engine from transaxle.
37. Carefully lift engine out of vehicle.
38. Reverse procedure to install.

CYLINDER HEAD

REPLACE

EXC. 5-131 ENGINE

1. Drain cooling system.
2. Remove valve cover to cylinder head attaching bolts, then the valve cover and camshaft cover.
3. Loosen alternator adjusting bolt, then remove alternator drive belt.
4. Disconnect all hoses and wires that will interfere with cylinder head removal.
5. Disconnect intake and exhaust manifolds from cylinder head.
6. Remove timing belt as outlined under "Timing Belt, Replace" procedure.
7. Loosen cylinder head bolts in reverse order shown in **Fig. 1.**
8. Remove bolts and the cylinder head.
9. Reverse procedure to install. Torque head bolts using sequence shown in **Fig. 1**, as follows:
   a. Insert bolts 8 and 10 first to align cylinder head and gasket, then tighten all bolts hand tight.
   b. Tighten bolt (12 pt. M11 bolts), in 2 steps: 29 ft. lbs., then 43 ft. lbs., and turn each bolt an additional 1/2 turn. No retorquing is necessary.

5-131 ENGINE

Removal

Refer to **Fig. 2** for cylinder head removal procedure.

Installation

Before installing cylinder head, turn crankshaft so pistons are at approximately equal distances below TDC. Otherwise, engine damage may result.

1. Clean cylinder head and engine block mating surfaces, then install cylinder head and gasket. **Use no sealing compound.**
2. Install bolt Nos. 8 and 10 first, **Fig. 3,** to center head.
3. Torque bolts to 29 ft. lbs. first, then to 43 ft. lbs. and a final 1/2 turn (180°), in sequence shown in **Fig. 3.**

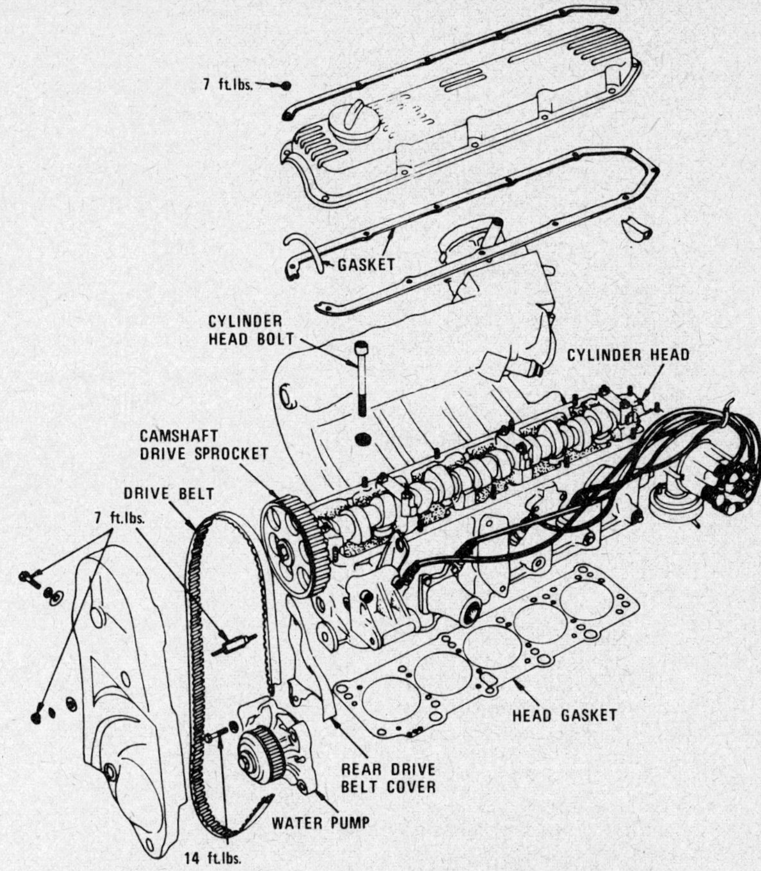

Fig. 2 Exploded view of 5-131 engine

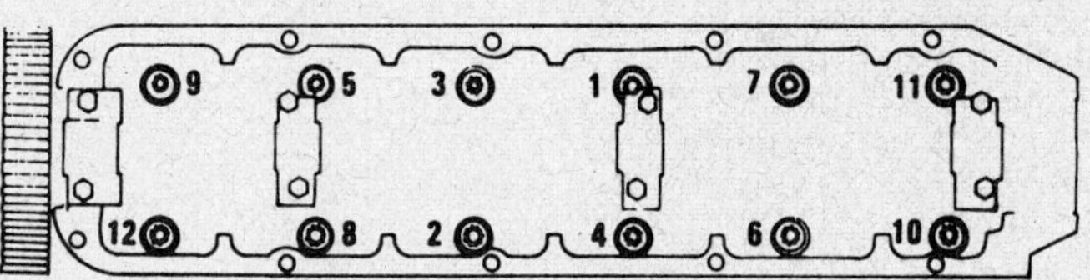

Fig. 3 Cylinder head bolt tightening sequence. 5-131 engine

4. Turn camshaft until marking on sprocket is aligned with upper edge of gasket or rear drive belt cover.
5. Coat threads of bolt with Loctite 573 or equivalent, then install drive belt with drive belt sprocket onto crankshaft.
6. Using tool Nos. 2084 and 2079 or equivalent, torque pulley bolt to 253 ft. lbs.
7. If engine is installed in vehicle, align TDC symbol O (arrow) on flywheel with lug cast on clutch housing.
8. If engine is removed from vehicle, align notch (arrow) on V-belt pulley with upper arrow on oil pump housing. Install drive belt onto camshaft and water pump sprocket.
9. If engine is removed from vehicle, adjust belt tension by loosening water pump bolts and turning pump counterclockwise to tighten belt. Belt is correctly tensioned when it can be twisted 90 degrees (between camshaft and water pump/drive belt sprocket) with thumb and index finger.
10. If engine is installed in vehicle, adjust belt tension as follows:
    a. Remove upper radiator cover.
    b. Loosen water pump bolts, then install a suitable screwdriver through hole in radiator side cover and turn pump counterclockwise to tighten belt.
    c. Belt tension is correct when it can be twisted 90 degrees (between camshaft and water pump/drive belt sprocket) with thumb and index finger.
    d. Install upper radiator cover and lower and upper drive belt cover.
    e. Install power steering pump if equipped, then V-belts and adjust.

VALVES

ADJUST

1. Start engine and allow it to idle for several minutes. (95°F).
2. Turn engine off, then remove spark plug wires and valve cover.

Fig. 4 Aligning valve timing marks

Fig. 5 Aligning camshaft sprocket timing mark

3. Bump starter until camshaft lobes of valves being adjusted are positioned upward.
4. Using a suitable feeler gauge, check valve clearance.
5. If measured clearance is larger or smaller than specifications, replace adjusting disc with tools US4476 and VW546 or equivalents. **The dimension between valve guides has been increased on some late model engines. This revision necessitates the use of tools US-4476 and 2078 to replace adjusting disc. Engines including this modification are identified by a sticker on the valve cover. Adjusting disc thicknesses range from .118 through .167 in .002 inch increments. Adjusting disc part Nos. range from 056 109 55 through 056 109 580. Adjusting disc 056 109 55 being the .118 inch thick adjusting disc and 056 109 580 being the .167 inch thick adjusting disc.**

TIMING COVER

REPLACE

EXC. 5-131 ENGINE

1. Loosen alternator adjusting bolts, then remove alternator drive belt.
2. Remove water pump pulley retaining bolts and the water pump pulley.
3. Remove timing cover to engine attaching bolts and the timing cover.
4. Reverse procedure to install.

5-131 ENGINE

Refer to **Fig. 2** for removal and installation of timing belt cover.

TIMING BELT

REPLACE

EXC. 5-131 ENGINE

1. Remove timing cover as outlined under "Timing Cover, Replace" procedure.
2. Remove timing belt guide, if equipped.
3. Loosen timing belt tensioner adjusting nut, then remove timing belt.
4. Align crankshaft pulley notch with intermediate sprocket mark at TDC pointer, **Fig. 4.**
5. Align camshaft sprocket mark with valve cover flange, **Fig. 5.**
6. Install timing belt onto sprockets, then tighten belt tensioner adjusting nut until belt can be twisted 90 degrees.
7. Install timing belt guide, if equipped, then the timing cover.

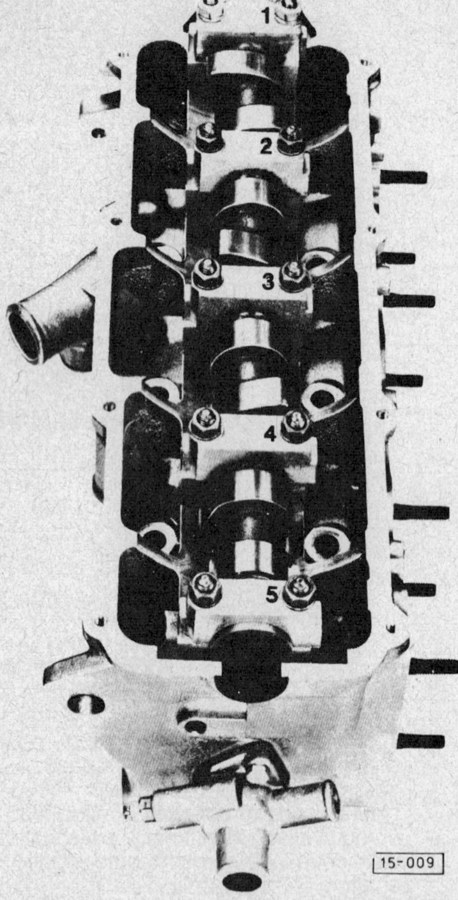

Fig. 6 Camshaft & bearing caps

5-131 ENGINE

Refer to **Fig. 2** and "Cylinder Head, Replace," for timing belt replace procedure.

VALVE GUIDES

Worn valve guides can be removed using tool 10-206. Press worn guides out from combustion chamber side of cylinder head. Coat new guides with engine oil and press into cold cylinder head from camshaft side. Press guides in as far as they will go. Ream guides by hand using proper cutting lubricant. **Once valve guide shoulder is seated, do not use more than one ton pressure or guide shoulder may break.**

CAMSHAFT

REPLACE

1. Remove valve cover to cylinder head attaching bolts, then the valve cover.
2. Remove timing cover and timing belt as outlined previously.
3. Remove camshaft sprocket attaching bolt and the camshaft sprocket.
4. Exc. 5-131 engine, working from front of engine, remove No. 5, No. 1 and No. 3 bearing caps.
5. Exc. 5-131 engine, diagonally loosen, then remove, No. 2 and No. 4 bearing caps, **Fig. 6.**
6. On 5-131 engine, diagonally loosen bearing caps No. 2 and No. 4, then remove **Fig. 7.**
7. On 5-131 engine, diagonally loosen bearing caps No. 1 and No. 3, then remove, **Fig. 7.**
8. Remove camshaft from cylinder head.
9. Lubricate bearing shells, journals and contact surface of bearing caps with engine oil.
10. Position camshaft onto bearing saddles and install new camshaft oil seal.
11. Install bearing caps, ensure caps align correctly, **Fig. 8.**
12. Lightly tighten No. 2 and No. 4 bearing caps diagonally, then torque all caps to 14 ft. lbs., **Fig. 6.**
13. Install camshaft sprocket onto camshaft and torque attaching bolt to 58 ft. lbs.
14. Align timing marks, then install timing belt, timing cover and valve cover.

PISTON & ROD ASSEMBLY

Assemble the piston to the rod with the

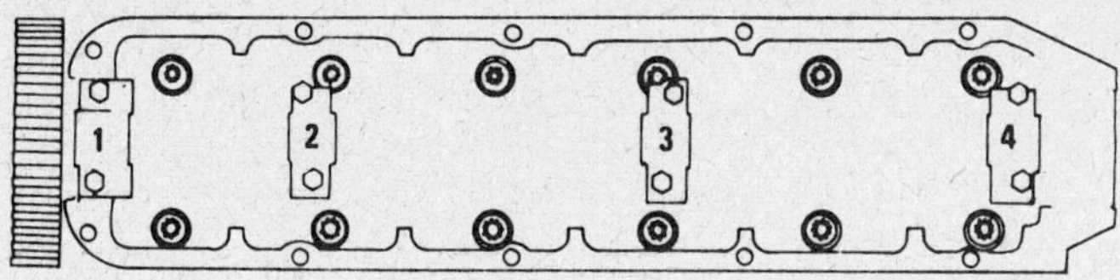

Fig. 7 Camshaft & bearing caps. 5-131 engine

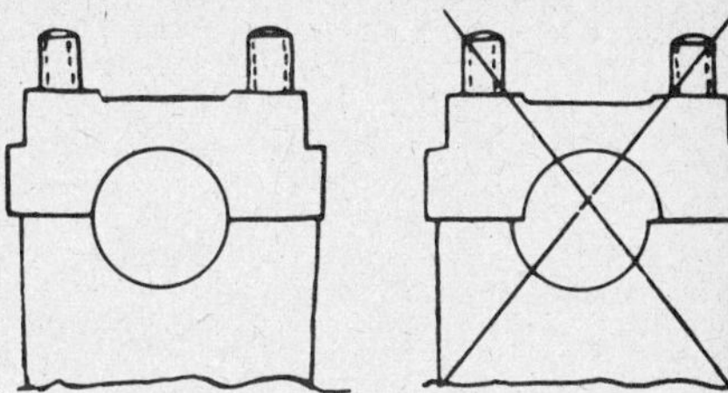
Fig. 8 Camshaft bearing alignment

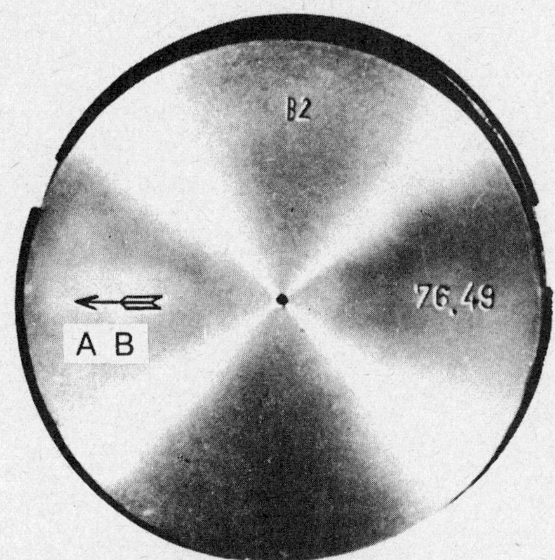

Fig. 9 Piston crown markings

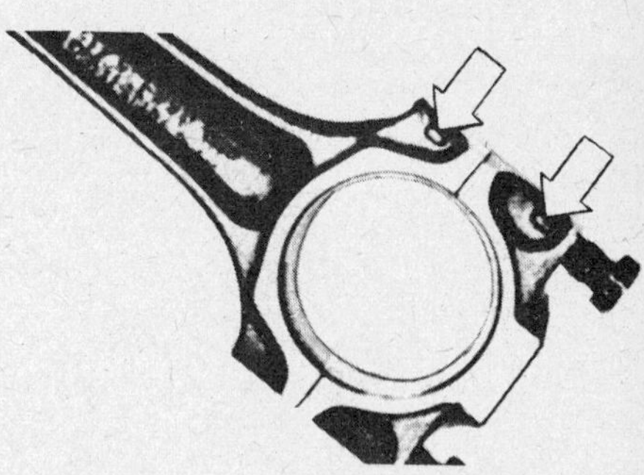
Fig. 10 Connecting rod casting marks

arrow on piston crown pointing toward front of engine and casting marks on rod facing intermediate shaft, **Figs. 9 and 10.**

PISTONS, PINS & RINGS

Pistons and rings are available in .010 inch, .020 inch and .040 inch oversize. Oversize piston pins are not available.

MAIN & ROD BEARINGS

Main and connecting rod bearings are available in .010 inch, .020 inch and .030 inch undersizes.

CRANKSHAFT REAR OIL SEAL REPLACE

1. On manual transaxle models, remove transaxle, flywheel, pressure plate, clutch disc and intermediate plate.
2. On automatic transaxle models, remove transaxle, torque converter and torque converter drive plate.
3. On except 5-131 engine, pry oil seal out of oil seal flange using a screwdriver or equivalent.
4. On 5-131 engine, pry out oil seal using tool No. 2086 or equivalent.
5. On all engines, lubricate new seal, center seal in seal flange and press until fully seated.
6. Reverse procedure to complete installation.

OIL PAN REPLACE

EXC. QUANTUM

1. Remove oil pan drain plug and drain engine oil.
2. Remove oil pan to engine attaching bolts and the oil pan.
3. Reverse procedure to install.

QUANTUM

1. Loosen alternator V-belt, then remove air conditioner compressor and power steering pump if equipped.
2. Loosen crankshaft pulley bolt, then loosen water pump attaching bolts.
3. Remove upper radiator cover, then loosen water pump attaching bolts.
4. Using a suitable screwdriver, working through hole in side duct panel, turn water pump clockwise to loosen drive belt.
5. Remove front bolts on subframe, oil pan attaching bolts, then oil pan.
6. Reverse procedure to install. Refer to "Cylinder Head, Replace" for adjustment of drive belt.

WATER PUMP REPLACE

EXC. 5-131 ENGINE

1. Drain cooling system.
2. Loosen alternator adjusting bolt, then remove alternator drive belt.
3. Remove water pump pulley attaching bolts and the water pump pulley.
4. Remove water pump to housing attaching bolts and the water pump, **Fig. 11.**
5. Reverse procedure to install.

5-131 ENGINE

Refer to **Fig. 2** for removal and installation of water pump.

FUEL PUMP REPLACE

MECHANICAL

1. Disconnect inlet and outlet lines at pump.
2. Remove two fuel pump to engine block attaching bolts and the fuel pump.
3. Reverse procedure to install. **Replacement fuel pumps have a longer actuator lever. On early model vehicles, use insulating flange and M8x30 bolts when installing new pump.**

ELECTRIC

1. Remove fuel tank cap to relieve tank pressure.
2. Clean fuel pump and fuel line unions thoroughly to prevent entry of dirt into fuel system.
3. Disconnect fuel lines and electrical connections from pump.
4. Remove retaining bracket and clamp, then the fuel pump.
5. Reverse procedure to install.

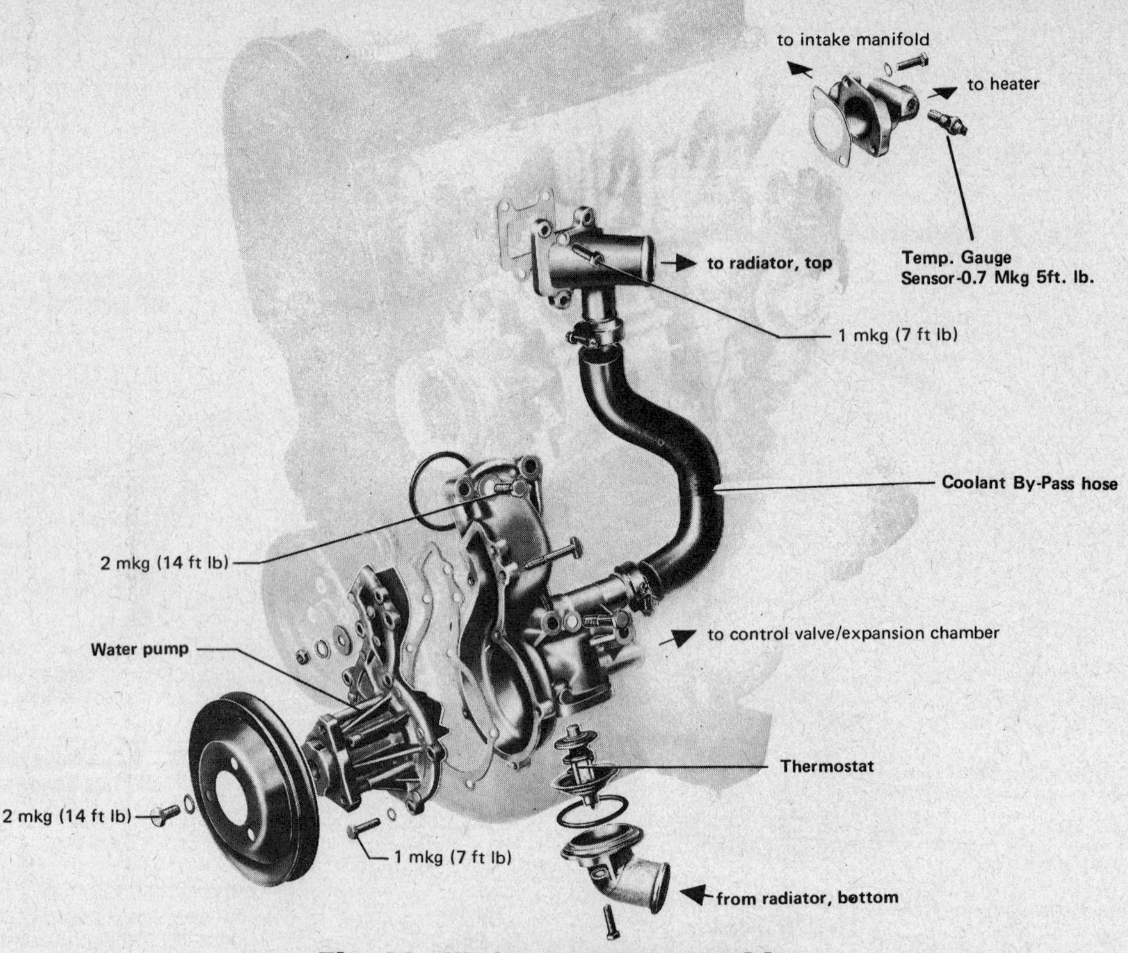

Fig. 11 Water pump assembly

DIESEL ENGINE SECTION

INDEX

ENGINE REPLACE

1983–84 RABBIT, PICKUP & JETTA

Engine and transaxle is removed as an assembly and is lowered out of vehicle.

1. Disconnect battery ground cable and drain cooling system.
2. Disconnect fuel filter from body and position aside.
3. Disconnect electrical connectors from radiator fan motor and thermoswitch.
4. Remove expansion hose from expansion tank.
5. Remove radiator side retainer nuts, disconnect upper and lower radiator hoses, then remove radiator assembly from vehicle.
6. Disconnect vacuum hose from brake booster pump, if equipped.
7. Disconnect electrical connector, then remove alternator attaching bolts and the alternator.
8. Disconnect wires at fuel shut-off solenoid, glow plugs, oil pressure switch and coolant temperature switch.
9. Disconnect heater hoses from engine and fuel inlet and return lines from injection pump.
10. Disconnect accelerator cable from injection pump lever, then remove accelerator cable and bracket from injection pump body.
11. Disconnect cold start cable from injection pump, remove attaching clip from cable bracket and slide cable out of bracket.
12. If equipped with A/C, remove compressor as follows:
    a. Remove timing belt cover, loosen belt tensioner and remove timing belt.
    b. Loosen injection pump sprocket retaining nut slightly, and carefully apply pressure to sprocket using a suitable puller.
    c. Tap center bolt of puller to loosen sprocket from pump shaft, then remove puller and sprocket.
    d. Disconnect fuel lines from injection

pump, plug lines and open fittings, and remove pump from bracket.
e. Remove A/C drive belt tensioner, water pump pulley and drive belts.
f. Remove washer pump reservoir and set aside.
g. Disconnect wiring harness from compressor, remove compressor mounting bolts, remove compressor leaving refrigerant lines connected, and secure aside.
h. Remove compressor mounting brackets from engine.

13. Disconnect wires from starter solenoid and back-up light switch, then remove ground strap on transaxle.
14. Loosen clutch cable locknut, then remove retaining clip and clutch cable from clutch lever.
15. Remove speedometer cable attaching clamp, then disconnect speedometer cable.
16. Remove upper starter bolt and exhaust flex pipe attaching bolts.
17. Remove nut from transaxle relay shaft, then disconnect lever.
18. Disconnect both driveshafts from transaxle drive flanges.
19. Remove lower starter bolt, then the starter.
20. Remove horn assembly and position aside.
21. Remove front mount cup bolts, then the front mount and cup.
22. Remove oil filter.
23. Remove left and right axle shaft retaining nuts from bearing housing assemblies.
24. Remove right side ball joint lock bolt, then separate ball joint from bearing housing. Repeat procedure for left side.
25. Pull right wheel and strut assembly away from vehicle and remove driveshaft. Repeat procedure for left side.
26. Connect ball joints to bearing housings, then remove rear transaxle mount.
27. Remove right front wheel and tire assembly, then attach tool US1105 or equivalent, to engine and lift slightly.
28. Disconnect gearshift lever rod from selector shaft lever, then remove relay shaft complete with gearshift lever rod.
29. Disconnect selector rod from relay lever.
30. Remove bolts holding right and left side mounts to body.
31. Lower engine/transaxle assembly onto dolly, raise vehicle and remove assembly out from underneath vehicle.
32. Reverse procedure to install. Ensure rear mount is straight and left and right mounts are centered in brackets.

1985–86 CABRIOLET, JETTA & GOLF

The engine and transaxle are removed as an assembly on these vehicles.

1. On air conditioned models, proceed as follows:
   a. Remove engine trim panel and lower apron.
   b. Remove condenser from crossmember and radiator, then all ducts.
   c. Disconnect electrical connectors from radiator fan shroud and A/C compressor.
   d. Remove alternator and A/C compressor V-belts.
   e. Disconnect idle boost valve vacuum hoses.
   f. Disconnect air filter assembly along with air flow assembly and position aside.
   g. Remove compressor and condenser.
2. On all models, disconnect driveshafts from transaxle, then suspend driveshafts from body with wire.
3. Remove exhaust manifold spring clamp.
4. On models equipped with power steering, proceed as follows:
   a. Remove bolts attaching adjusting pivot bracket.
   b. Remove V-belt, then suspend pump from body crossmember with wire.
   c. Remove fluid reservoir with mount and suspend with wire from body crossmember.
5. On all models, remove front apron attaching bolt and trim, then apron and trim.
6. Disconnect and remove battery.
7. Remove coolant reservoir cap, then drain coolant from coolant hose and/or thermostat flange.
8. Remove radiator grille.
9. Disconnect headlight and radiator support electrical connectors, then remove radiator mounts.
10. Disconnect hood release cable from hood latch and disconnect cable from support.
11. Disconnect cooling fan electrical connector.
12. Remove radiator support, coolant hoses, radiator and fan shroud assembly.
13. Disconnect necessary fuel injection and ignition system wiring.
14. Disconnect ground connections.
15. On manual transaxle models, disconnect upshift indicator vacuum switch, transaxle switch and the starter connectors.
16. On automatic transaxle models, disconnect battery cable to starter and starter cable CIS-E wire harness.
17. On GTI and GLI models, disconnect idle stabilizer control valve, throttle plate switch and knock sensor.
18. On manual transaxle models, disconnect clutch cable from transaxle.
19. On all models, disconnect speedometer cable from transaxle. Close all openings.
20. On automatic transaxle models, position selector lever in Park position, then disconnect accelerator cable and selector lever cable from actuator levers and mounts.
21. On all models, remove gear shift rods and bracket.
22. On manual transaxle models, disconnect accelerator cable at throttle linkage and at mounting bracket. **Do not remove throttle linkage.**
23. On all models, remove cold start valve, but leave fuel line connected.
24. Disconnect vacuum hose from intake manifold, then connecting hose.
25. If equipped, remove warm up regulator.
26. Disconnect fuel injectors and close all openings.
27. Remove intake manifold pre-heat hose, then purple hose from "T" connection on throttle body.
28. If equipped, remove hose from throttle body to idle boost valve.
29. Disconnect crankcase ventilation hose from air cleaner housing
30. Remove rear engine mount attaching bolts, then rear mount.
31. Disconnect transaxle mount.
32. Remove front mount attaching bolt, then carefully remove transaxle from mount by turning slightly.
33. Attach suitable engine lifting equipment onto engine, and remove engine from vehicle.
34. Reverse procedure to install.

QUANTUM

1. Disconnect battery ground cable.
2. Remove horn assembly, then the engine and transaxle cover plates.
3. Open heater control valve and coolant expansion tank cap, then drain cooling system.
4. Disconnect electrical connectors from fan and thermoswitch, then the coolant hoses from engine or expansion tank.
5. Remove radiator, then disconnect fuel lines and accelerator cable from injection pump. Disconnect accelerator cable from support.
6. On automatic transaxle models, remove accelerator cable with bracket.
7. On all models, disconnect cold start cable from pin and remove lockwasher from support.
8. Disconnect fuel shut-off solenoid electrical connector.
9. Disconnect gearshift indicator switch from bracket.
10. Disconnect vacuum hose between air filter and turbocharger at air filter.
11. Disconnect electrical connectors from oil pressure switch, coolant temperature sensors and glow plugs.
12. Disconnect coolant hose from engine.
13. Loosen power steering pump and bracket and position aside, leaving lines attached.
14. Disconnect hose from vacuum pump, then remove lock plate and disconnect clutch cable.
15. Remove attaching nuts from left and right engine mounts.
16. Remove alternator, then the engine stop bracket bolts.
17. On air conditioned models, loosen A/C compressor bracket bolts and position aside, leaving refrigerant lines connected.
18. On all models, remove turbocharger exhaust pipe and bracket from transaxle.
19. Remove starter motor, then the flywheel cover plate attaching bolts.
20. On automatic transaxle models, remove transaxle cover plate, then the

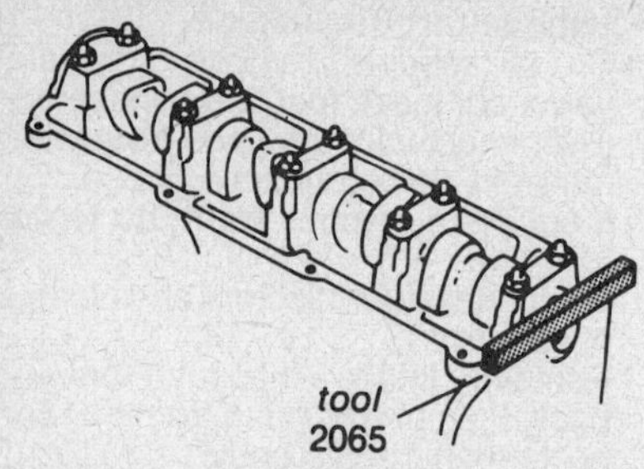

Fig. 1 Camshaft locking tool installation

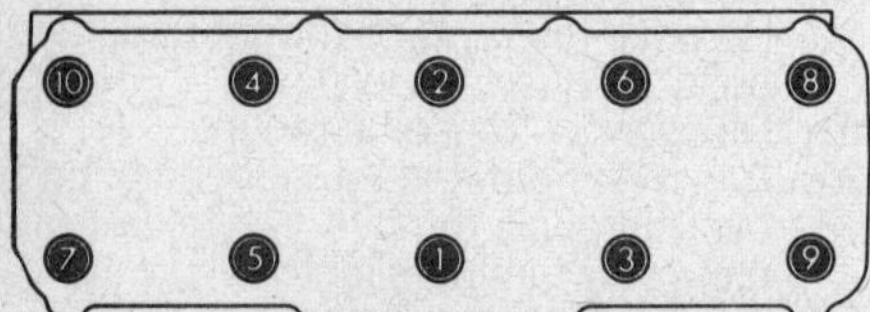

Fig. 3 Cylinder head bolt tightening sequence

torque converter mounting bolts.
21. On all models, install transaxle support bar VW785/1B or equivalent.
22. Attach tool No. US1105 or equivalent to engine, then raise engine and transaxle slightly using a suitable hoist.
23. Adjust transaxle support bar to contact transaxle, then remove transaxle-to-engine attaching bolts.
24. Separate transaxle from engine, then carefully lift engine assembly from vehicle.
25. Reverse procedure to install.

TIMING BELT REPLACE

1. Remove air cleaner assembly, duct and upper engine cover on Vanagon.
2. Loosen alternator mounting bolts, then A/C drive belt tensioner and remove drive belts.
3. Remove crankshaft pulley, if necessary, timing belt and camshaft covers.
4. Disconnect wiring harness connectors to fuel shut-off solenoid.
5. Rotate engine until TDC mark on flywheel is aligned with pointer and slot on camshaft is parallel to cylinder head gasket surface, then disconnect battery ground cable. **Do not rotate engine opposite normal direction of rotation (counterclockwise) using crankshaft center bolt, as torque setting may be disturbed allowing sprocket to loosen.**
6. Install camshaft locking tool No. 2065 or 2065A on rear of camshaft, **Fig. 1.** Center tool by inserting equal thickness shims between each side of tool and cylinder head surface.
7. Insert locking pin 2064 into injector pump sprocket, ensuring that marks on sprocket, pump and bracket are properly aligned. (Refer to "Injection Pump Timing").
8. Loosen timing belt tensioner and remove belt. **Do not rotate camshaft or crankshaft with belt removed, as engine damage will result.**
9. Prior to installation, check that all timing marks are properly aligned, loosen camshaft sprocket retaining bolt 1/2 turn and loosen sprocket on shaft by tapping with suitable hammer.
10. Install timing belt, then remove locking pin from injection pump sprocket.
11. Adjust belt tension by turning tensioner to right, and check tension as follows:
    a. Install tension gauge VW 210 or equivalent, on belt between camshaft and injection pump, **Fig. 2.**
    b. Adjust tension until gauge reads 12-13, then torque tensioner locknut and camshaft retaining nuts to specifications.
    c. Remove camshaft tool and rotate engine two complete turns clockwise, stopping with TDC mark on flywheel aligned with pointer.
    d. Strike belt once with rubber mallet between camshaft and injection pump, then check tension with gauge.
12. Check that injection pump timing is within specifications, then reverse procedure to complete installation.

CYLINDER HEAD SERVICE

Cylinder head service procedures on diesel engines are similar to procedures found in "Gasoline Engine Section."

CYLINDER HEAD REPLACE

1. Disconnect battery ground cable, remove air cleaner and duct assembly, and remove engine covers on Vanagon models.
2. Remove expansion tank cap and drain cooling system by removing thermostat, or by disconnecting hose from water pump at radiator pipe on Vanagon models.
3. Disconnect all coolant hoses from cylinder head.
4. Disconnect wiring harness connectors to temperature sensors and glow plugs, and remove wiring harness from cylinder head.
5. Disconnect and remove injector fuel pipe assemblies, then plug open fittings.
6. Remove fuel injectors and glow plugs, then plug openings in cylinder head.
7. Remove timing belt as outlined in "Timing Belt, Replace." **Do not rotate crankshaft or camshaft with timing belt removed, as engine damage will result.**
8. Raise and support vehicle. Disconnect exhaust pipe from manifold, remove exhaust manifold retaining bolts, then lower vehicle.
9. Remove cylinder head retaining bolts in reverse order of tightening sequence, **Fig. 3.**
10. Ensure hoses, cables, and wiring harness components are disconnected from cylinder head and that camshaft is properly secured, then remove head.

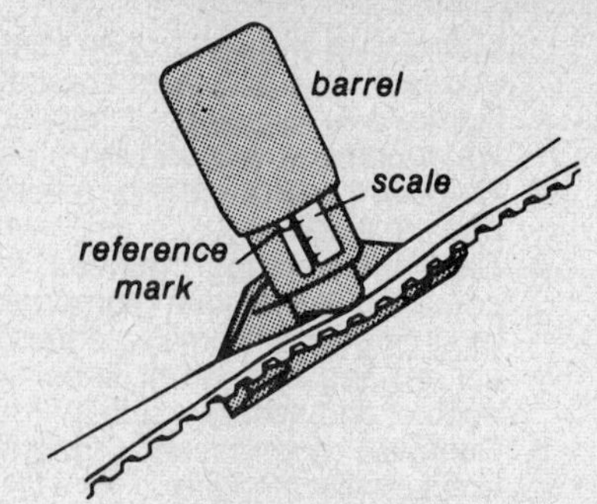

Fig. 2 Timing belt tension tool installation

Fig. 4 Piston installation. Piston marked ".9" in direction of installation

11. Remove camshaft as outlined in steps 4-10 of "Camshaft, Replace — Gasoline Engine Section."
12. Thoroughly clean cylinder head, checking for cracks, and check gasket surface for flatness. Check valve guides as outlined in "Gasoline Engine Section." **Diesel engine cylinder heads cannot be resurfaced. If more than .003 inch warpage is measured, cylinder head must be replaced.**
13. Check piston deck height to determine head gasket thickness as follows:
    a. Ensure that TDC mark on flywheel is aligned with pointer, and measure piston projection using a suitable dial indicator.
    b. Select head gasket thickness according to chart below. **Cylinder head gaskets can be identified by part number and notches in edge of gasket. Install gasket with "OBEN" marking toward cylinder head.**

Piston Projection	Gasket Thickness	Notches	
		1500cc	1600cc
.025-.032	.055	3	1
.033-.036	.059	4	2
.037-.040	.063	5	3

14. Install cylinder head gasket without sealer, check that camshaft is locked and that TDC mark on flywheel is

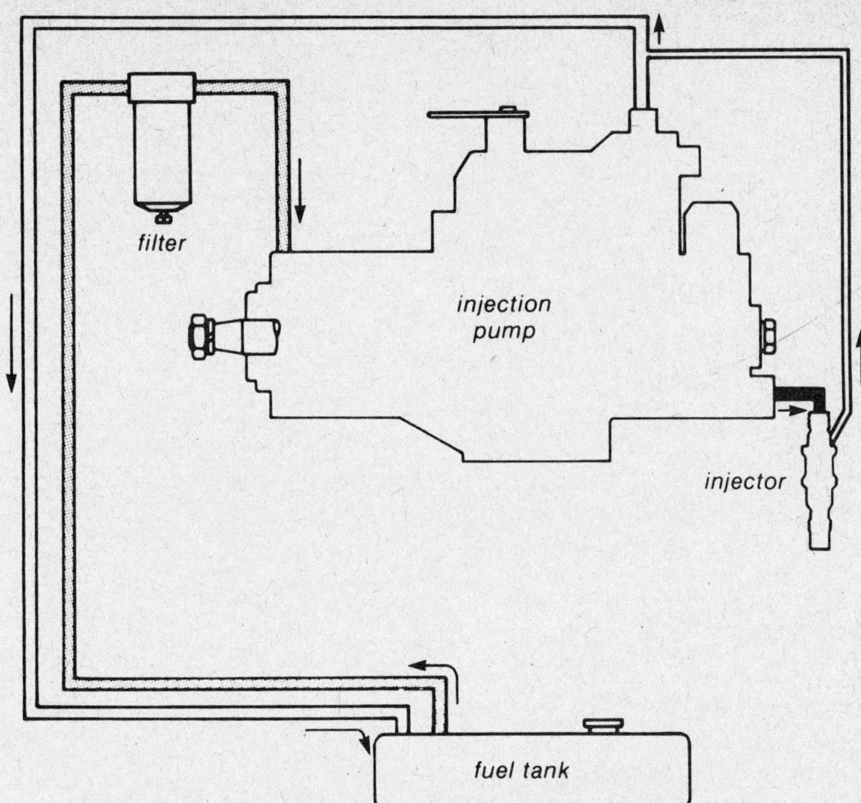

Fig. 5 Diesel fuel system

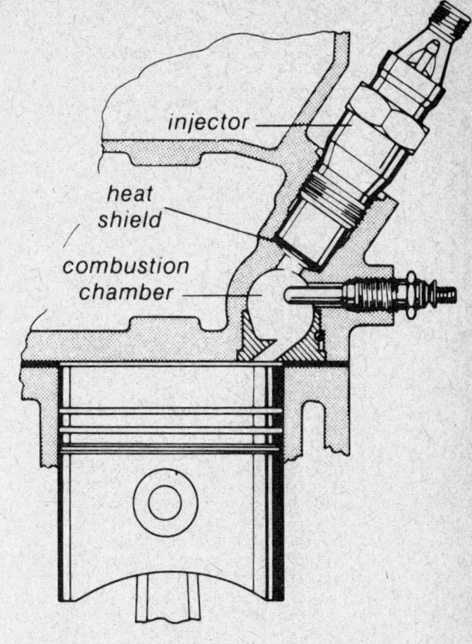

Fig. 6 Injector installation

properly aligned with pointer. Install head using guide pins in bolt holes 8 and 10 to align head and gasket.

15. Install cylinder head bolts and torque in sequence, **Fig. 3,** as follows:
    a. Tighten all bolts hand tight.
    b. Torque 12 pt. 12mm Polygon bolts to 29 ft. lbs. and 43 ft. lbs., then turn each bolt an additional 1/2 turn. **Bolts must be torqued after initial warm up.**
16. Reverse procedure to complete installation, ensure injection pump timing is within specifications. Check valve adjustment as outlined in "Gasoline Engine Section."
17. Run engine until cooling fan cycles and torque head bolts in sequence, **Fig. 3.** Torque 12 pt. 12mm Polygon bolts an additional 1/4 turn, without backing bolts off.
18. After 1000 miles of operation, turn each 12 pt. Polygon cylinder head bolts an additional 1/4 turn in sequence shown in **Fig. 3,** without backing off.

PISTONS, RINGS & CONNECTING RODS

1. Prior to removal, mark pistons and rods to match cylinder number.
2. Remove circlips from piston, press pin out by hand and separate assembly. **If pin is too tight in bore, heat piston to approximately 140°F.**
3. Check piston to cylinder wall clearance at right angles to piston pin, 3/8 in. from top and bottom and in center of travel.
4. Check that ring end gaps are within specifications by installing ring approximately 9/16 inch from top of cylinder and centering with an inverted piston.
5. Assemble piston and rod combinations with casting marks and bearing attaching lugs on rod face intermediate shaft, and markings on piston crown, **Fig. 4,** face drive belt. **If piston pin is tight in pin bore, heat piston to approximately 140°F to aid installation. Ensure pin attaching locks are properly seated.**
6. Install piston rings with "TOP" markings facing piston crown. Side clearance for compression rings should measure .002-.004 inch on upper rings and .002-.003 inch on lower rings and must not exceed .008 inch. Side clearance for oil rings should measure .001-.002 inch and must not exceed .006 inch.
7. Install assemblies with piston marking facing drive belt, using a suitable ring compressor. Ensure connecting rod side clearance is less than .004 inch. **Ensure "stretch" type connecting rod bolts are used. Bolts are not reusable, and must be replaced during assembly. During installation, torque nuts to specified value, then turn each nut an additional 1/2 turn to obtain proper stretch.**

DIESEL FUEL SYSTEM

FUEL SUPPLY

Fuel is drawn through the filter from the tank by the injection pump, **Fig. 5.** The injection pump meters and distributes fuel under pressure to the injectors in the correct firing order.

Excess fuel from the pump and injectors returns to the tank through a separate line.

The fuel circulation cools and lubricates the injection pump and injectors and also warms the fuel in the tank slightly to help prevent wax formation during cold weather.

INJECTORS

Diesel injectors spray fuel directly into the combustion chamber near the end of each compression stroke, **Fig. 6.** The injectors are threaded into the cylinder head and are subject to the direct heat of combustion like a gasoline engine spark plug. Each injector is protected by a heat shield between the cylinder head and injector body. The heat shield acts as an insulating and sealing washer.

Fuel pressure from the injection pump forces the needle up against spring pressure so that the injector sprays a cone-shaped mist of diesel fuel at the proper time. A small quantity of fuel leaks around the injector needle to lubricate and cool the injector. This fuel returns to the tank through a separate fuel line, **Fig. 7.**

REMOVAL & TESTING

Always keep hands/arms away from nozzle end of injector when it is installed in the "pop" tester. The high pressure spray can penetrate skin and cause serious injury.

1. Using compressed air, clean fuel connections and area around injectors.
2. Remove injector lines as an assembly.
3. Remove injectors.
4. Install injector on a suitable "pop" tester (tools US1322, US1111 or equivalent). Ensure knob is closed, **Fig. 8.**
5. Operate gauge lever with rapid strokes to prime tester and injector.

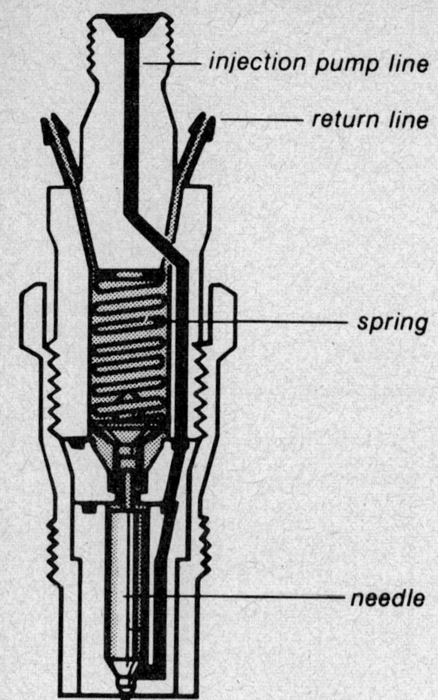

Fig. 7 Injector

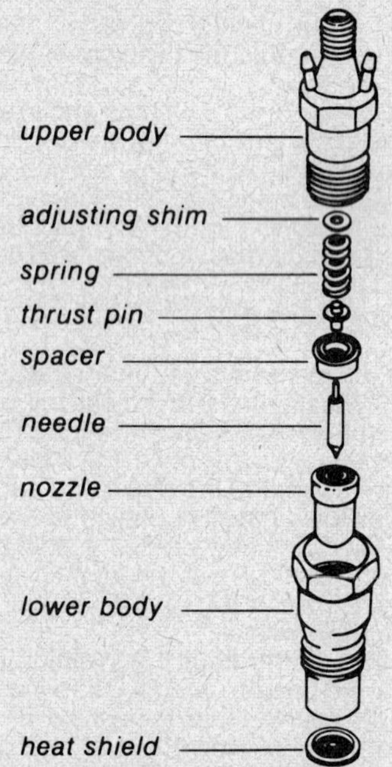

Fig. 10 Exploded view of injector assembly

Ensure injector sprays with compact, even cone pattern.

6. Operate lever with slow strokes. Injector should make creaking sound if nozzle is in good condition.
7. Turn knob out to open gauge and operate lever slowly. Note gauge reading when injector begins to spray.
8. Operate lever carefully to hold pressure specified for leak test. The injector should not drip within approximately 10 seconds.

INSTALLATION

1. Install new injector heat shields with larger diameter sealing surface facing injector, **Fig. 9.**

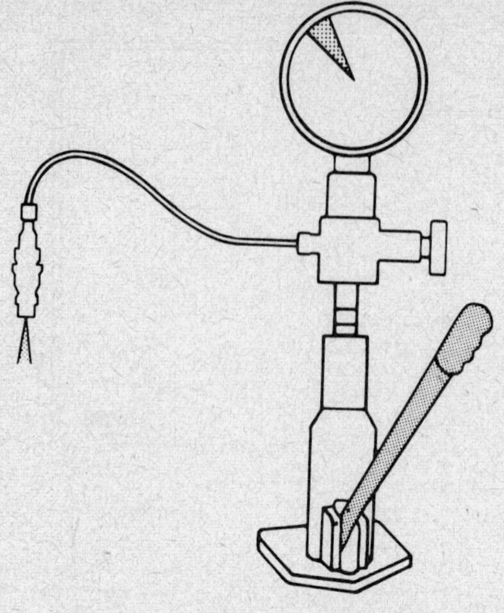

Fig. 8 Injector testing

2. Install injectors in cylinder head and torque to 51 ft. lbs.

REPAIRS

1. Invert injector and place into a suitable vise. Grip upper body along flats.
2. Carefully remove lower body.
3. Visually inspect needle and nozzle assembly, ensure needle and nozzle are in satisfactory condition. Clean assembly in suitable solvent or replace needle/nozzle unit. **Brass scrapers and brushes (used gently) can be used to remove hardened carbon deposits. Do not apply excessive pressure when removing carbon deposits or needle and/or nozzle damaging will result.**
4. Adjust opening pressure, if necessary. Using a suitable micrometer, check shim thickness and substitute shims, if necessary. Each .0019 inch (.05 mm) shim thickness adjusts nozzle opening pressure by approximately 71 psi.
5. Install all six internal parts in upper body as shown in **Fig. 10.**
6. Install and torque lower body to 51 ft. lbs. Recheck injector on tester. **Always use new heat shields when reinstalling injectors, compression leaks can occur if heat shields are reused, or if injectors are excessively or insufficiently torqued.**

ENGINE COMPRESSION CHECK

1. Disconnect fuel shut-off solenoid electrical connector from injection pump and insulate end. **This prevents mechanical fuel pump from spraying fuel during cranking. Ensure electrical connector does not contact any conductor (metallic component) in engine compartment.**
2. Remove injectors as outlined in "Injectors – Removal & Testing," and remove all heat shields.

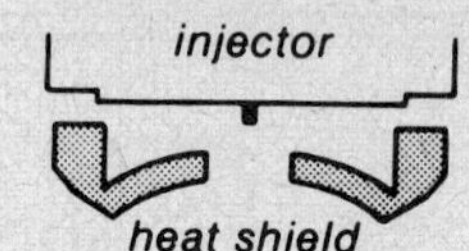

Fig. 9 Heat shield installation

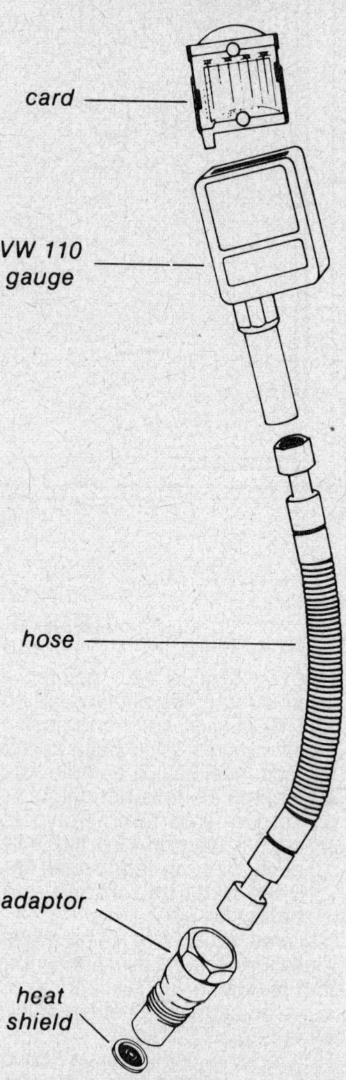

Fig. 11 Compression tester

3. Install threaded adapter into injector opening, using an old heat shield for sealing, and connect gauge VW 1110 or equivalent to adapter, **Fig. 11.**
4. Crank engine to obtain highest gauge reading, note reading, and release pressure.
5. Repeat procedure on remaining cylinders.
6. If readings are not within specifications, or if there is more than 7-73 psi difference between readings, check the following:
   a. Low readings on adjacent cylinders can mean head gasket leakage between cylinders.
   b. Low readings on one cylinder usually means valve leakage.
   c. Low readings on all cylinders could mean worn piston rings.

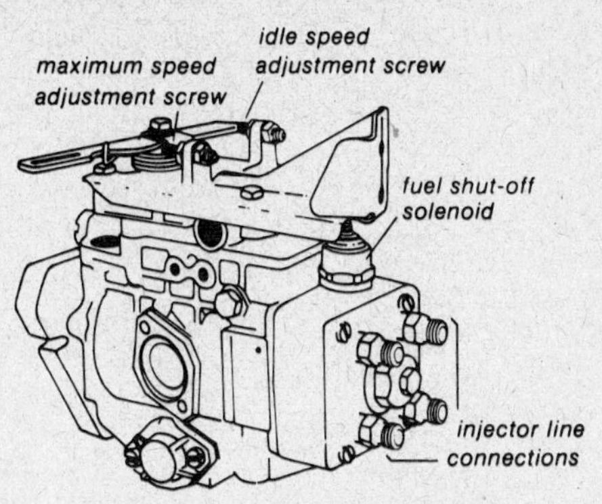

Fig. 12 Front view of injection pump

Fig. 13 Rear view of injection pump

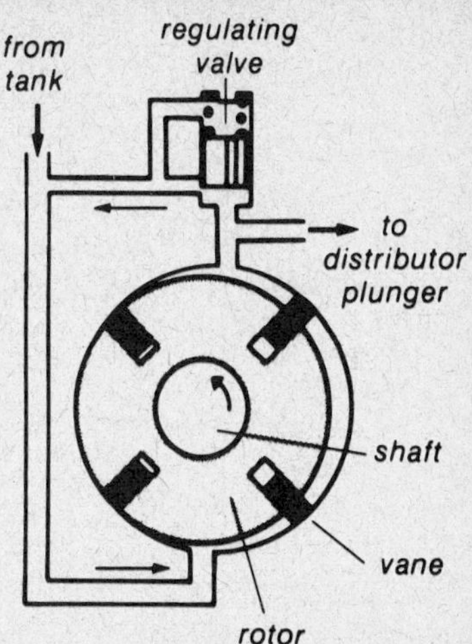

Fig. 14 Vane type fuel supply pump

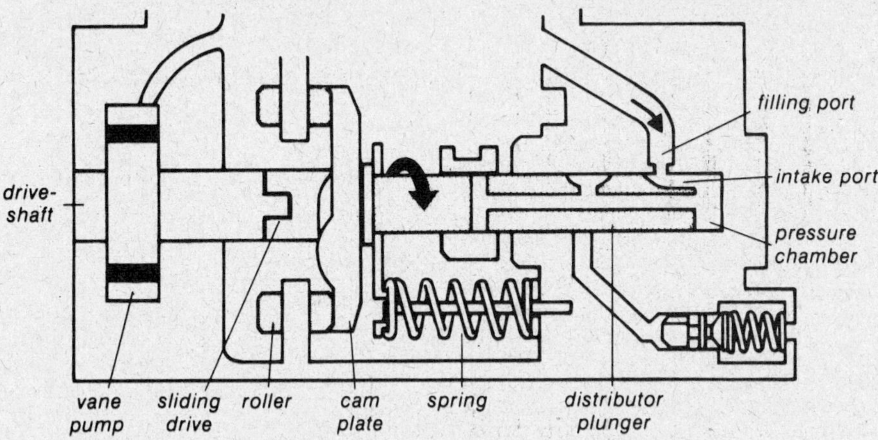

Fig. 15 Plunger & roller

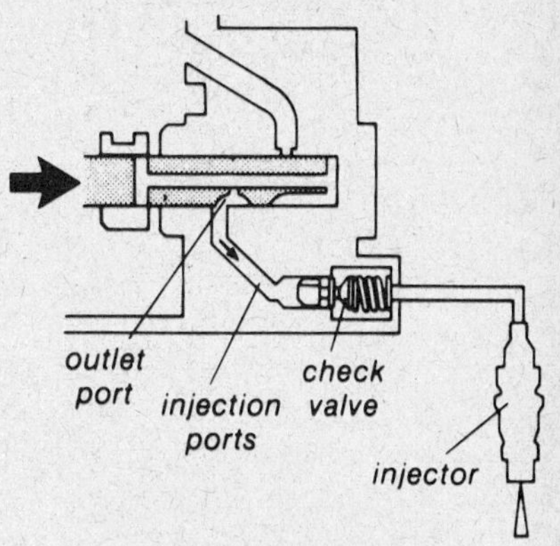

Fig. 16 Plunger installation

7. A low cylinder can be checked again after squirting about a tablespoon of engine oil onto the piston through the injector opening, prceed as follows:
   a. If compression reading remains low during the second check, inspect for burnt or improperly seated valves.
   b. If the second reading increases, piston rings are probably worn.

INJECTION PUMP

The injection pump is a single-plunger mechanical pump, **Figs. 12 and 13,** which meters and distributes fuel to the injectors in the correct firing order. The pump is driven by the camshaft spur belt at one-half engine speed. All internal pump components are lubricated by diesel fuel so the pump is maintenance free. Diesel pumps operate reliably for a long time if clean fuel is used. Idle speed, maximum speed, and injection timing can be adjusted with workshop equipment. The fuel shut-off solenoid can be replaced separately, but any internal problem means pump replacement. Since diesel pumps should not be disassembled, normal service consists only of troubleshooting to determine whether a pump may necessitate replacement.

Fuel Supply Pump

The rotary-vane fuel supply pump inside the injection pump draws fuel through the filter from the tank and supplies it to the distributor plunger, **Fig. 14.** The vane pump is driven by the engine camshaft spur belt. As the rotor spins, centrifugal force holds the vanes against the walls of the pressure chamber. The off center configuration of the rotor and pressure chamber "squeezes" fuel trapped between the vanes and forces it out the delivery port.

Vane pump delivery pressure varies from 44-102 psi depending on engine speed and is controlled by the regulating valve. The relief port is actually a series of small holes which open progressively to allow vane pump pressure to vary with engine speed. Vane pump pressure lubricates the internal components in the pump, supplies fuel to the distributor plunger for the injector and controls injection timing advance mechanism.

Injection pump manufacturers use a special test bench to set and check internal pump pressures. The vane pump and distributor plunger injection pressures cannot be checked easily with normal workshop equipment. If clean fuel is used, diesel injection pumps operate reliably for a long time. Diesel pumps should not be disassembled or adjusted. Normal service consists only of troubleshooting to determine whether a pump might need replacement.

Injection & Distribution

The injection pump driveshaft turns the vane pump, distributor plunger, and cam plate as a unit. Springs hold the cam plate against stationary rollers. In this position, the plunger also moves back and forth as it turns.

Whenever an intake port in the plunger is in line with the filling port in the pump body, fuel from the vane pump fills the pressure chamber, **Fig. 15.** As the plunger turns, the intake port is covered up so that fuel is trapped in the pressure chamber. The cam plate and rollers push the plunger and pressurize the fuel to approximately 1800 psi.

As the plunger continues to turn, the outlet port in the plunger lines up with the injection passage in the pump body, opening the check valve and supplying high-pressure fuel to the injector, **Fig. 16.**

The pump and plunger are designed with ports to supply each injector with fuel in the proper firing order, **Fig. 17.**

Fuel Metering

The amount of fuel is controlled by changing the injection cut-off point according to engine speed and load conditions.

The injection cut-off point is controlled by the position of a metering sleeve on the distributor plunger. The metering sleeve usually covers a relief port in the plunger, uncovering the relief port stops injection. The position of the metering sleeve is controlled by linkage connected to a centrifugal governor and also to the accelerator pedal.

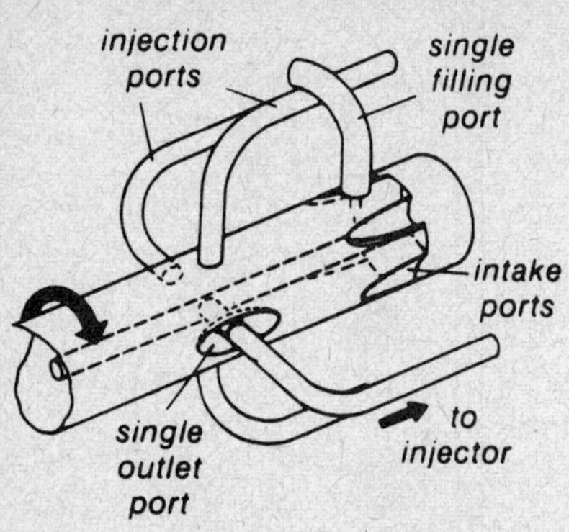

Fig. 17 Plunger & ports

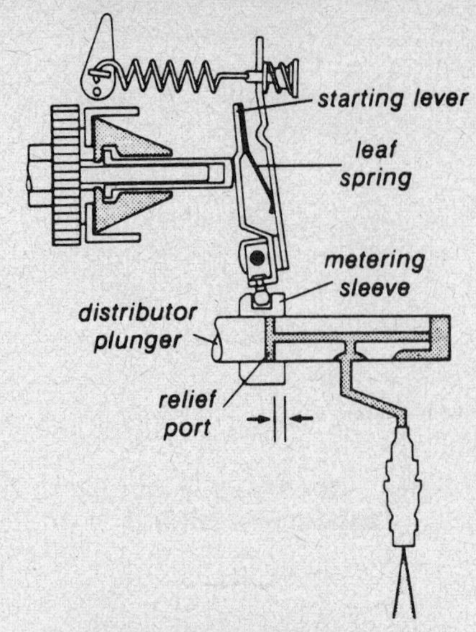

Fig. 18 Starting fuel metering

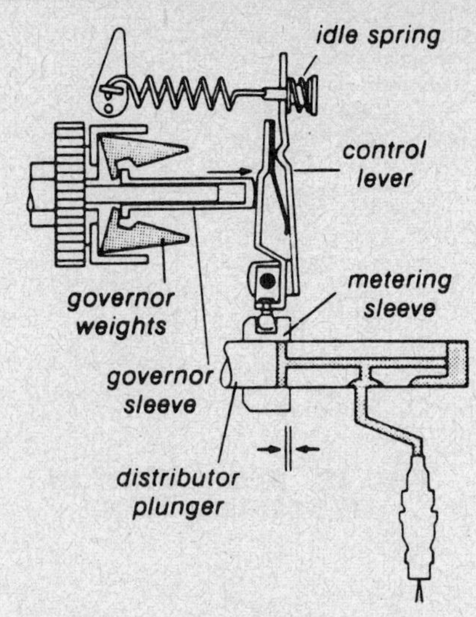

Fig. 19 Idle fuel metering

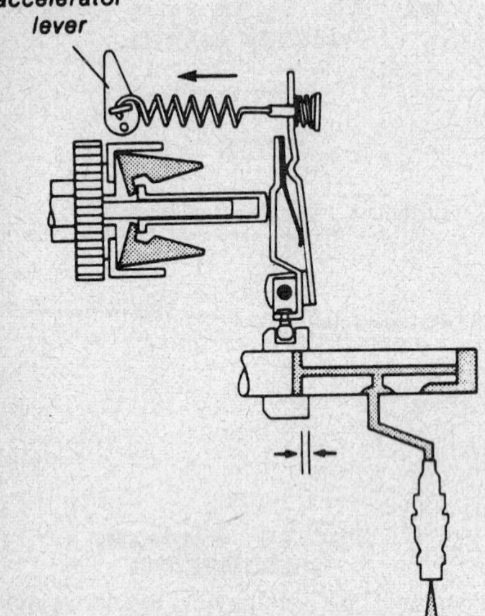

Fig. 20 Acceleration fuel metering

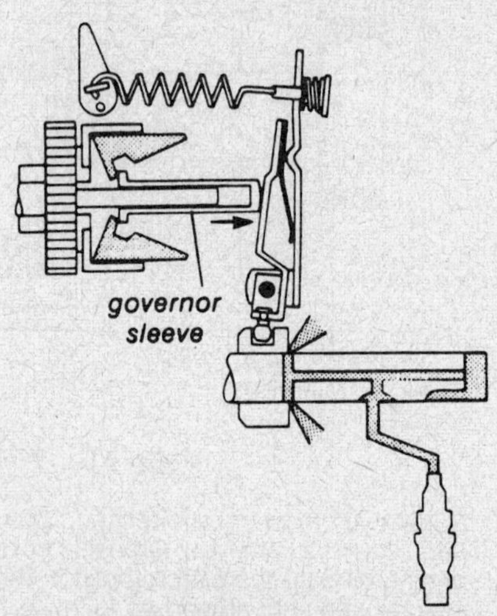

Fig. 21 Maximum speed fuel metering

During the starting procedure, (when the engine is not running) the leaf spring presses the starting lever to the left, so the metering sleeve moves to the right. The distributor plunger must move farther before the relief port is exposed. Injection lasts longer so that more fuel is supplied during starting, **Fig. 18.**

At idle speed, the weights in the centrifugal governor are partly expanded so the governor sleeve moves to the right. The starting lever is pushed against the control lever so the metering sleeve moves to the left. The distributor plunger now moves a short distance before the relief port is uncovered. Injection lasts a short time so that a small amount of fuel is supplied at idle applications, **Fig. 19.**

The injection pump automatically compensates for effects of temperature and load changes at idle. When idle speed begins to drop, the governor weights and the governor sleeve retract. The idle spring then pushes the metering sleeve to the right, increasing the amount of fuel to correct the idle speed.

During acceleration, the control lever is pulled to the left by linkage from the accelerator pedal. The metering sleeve is moved to the right so more fuel is injected before the relief port is uncovered. Engine speed increases until the movement of the governor neutralizes the effect of the pedal linkage, **Fig. 20.**

With pedal linkage at "full load," engine speed increases to about 5400 RPM. At this point, the governor is spinning with enough force for the governor sleeve to stretch the pedal linkage spring and force the control lever to the right, **Fig. 21.**

The metering sleeve moves far enough to the left to uncover the relief port at the beginning of the distributor plunger stroke. There is no pressure for injection until engine speed drops and the metering sleeve moves to the right again. This provision acts as a speed limiter and is designed to react slowly enough so that engine performance simply "flattens out" at the top limit.

Injection Timing Advance

Near the end of each compression stroke, diesel fuel is injected directly into the combustion chamber. Injection must continue well beyond piston TDC in order to burn the necessary amount of fuel to provide engine power. As engine speed increases, stroke duration time becomes shorter and injection time becomes longer. Burning must begin sooner to ensure peak combustion pressures still occur at the most efficient point after TDC.

Diesel injection timing is advanced by a hydraulic piston in the injection pump. As engine speed increases, fuel pressure from the vane pump also increases. Vane pump pressure pushes the injection advance piston to the left against the spring so that the roller housing turns slightly. Since the cam plate is turning in the opposite direction, the ramps on the cam plate engage the rollers sooner whenever the injection advance piston moves to the left. This means that the distributor plunger begins injection sooner, **Fig. 22.** The injection timing advance piston is located in the bottom of the injection pump body, **Fig. 23.**

The only cold start and warm-up device necessary for the diesel fuel system is a manual control which advances injection timing at idle and during low speed running. A cable-operated lever turns a cam which pushes the piston to the left. This advances injection timing about 5°.

This injection advance provides more time for fuel to burn, which improves performance and prevents smoking during cold starts and warm-up, **Fig. 24.** The cold start cam does not advance the complete range of injection timing. Above approximately 2200 RPM the piston operates normally and does not contact the cam, **Fig. 25.**

CHECKING INJECTION TIMING

Injection timing is checked by determining injection pump plunger movement at piston TDC with a dial gauge, **Fig. 26.**

1. Check that cold start lever is in the off position. Reading will be incorrect if cold start cam is on. Adjust cable, if necessary.
2. Remove hex plug from injection pump cover and install adapter 2066 and suitable dial indicator **Fig. 26.** Preload indicator to read approximately .097 inch.

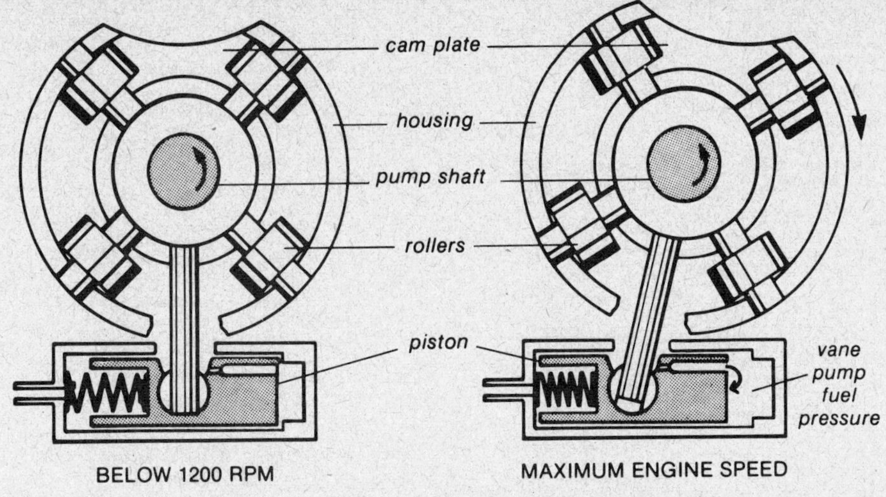

Fig. 22 Injection timing advance

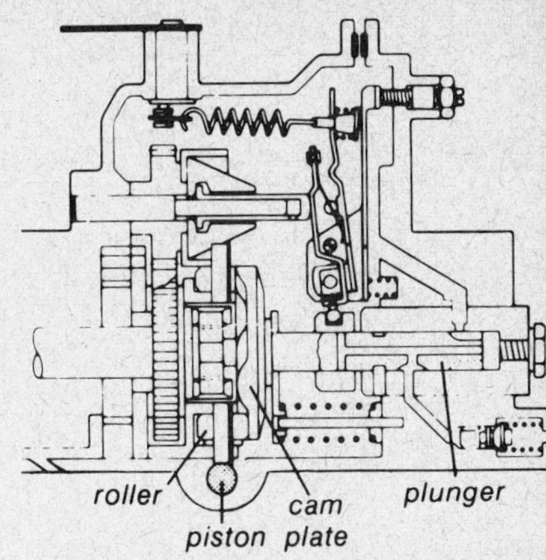

Fig. 23 Advance piston location

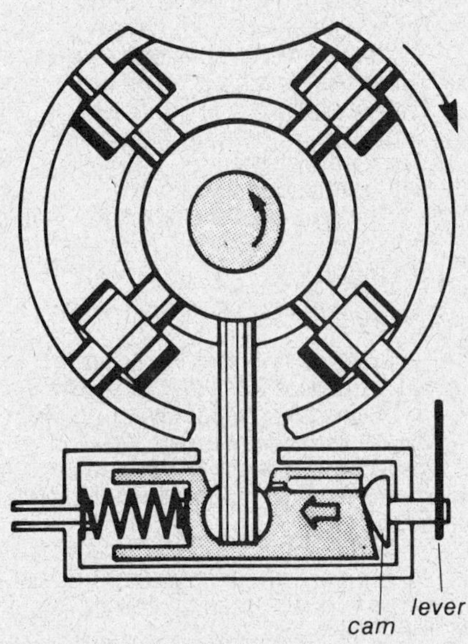

Fig. 24 Cold start advance

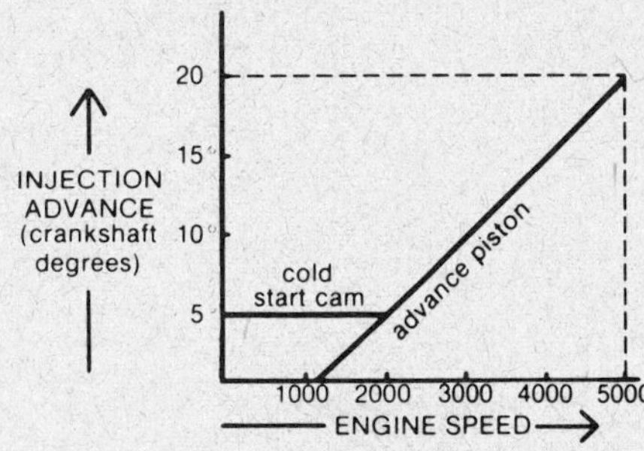

Fig. 25 Injection advance curve

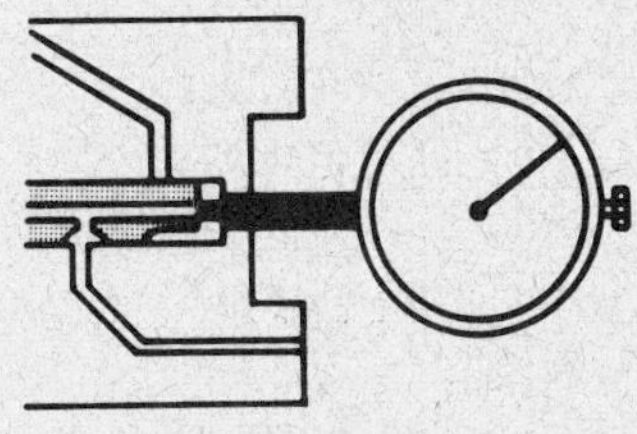

Fig. 26 Dial gauge installation

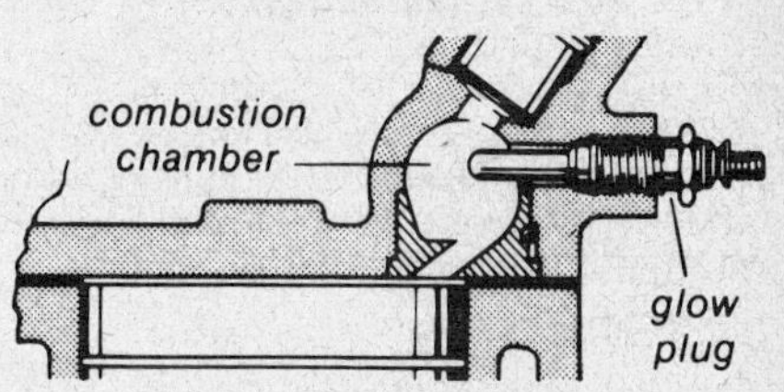

Fig. 27 Glow plug installation

3. Rotate engine counterclockwise slowly until gauge needle stops moving, then zero indicator. **Do not rotate engine in opposite direction of normal rotation by turning crankshaft center bolt. Torque setting of bolt may be disturbed, allowing sprocket to loosen.**
4. Rotate engine clockwise (normal rotation) slowly until TDC mark on flywheel is aligned with pointer. Dial indicator should read within .001 ± inch of specification.
5. If reading is not within specifications, loosen four pump mounting bolts and rotate pump until indicator reading is correct.
6. Tighten pump mounting bolts and repeat steps 3 and 4 to check adjustment. **Tighten all bolts securely, including bolt on left hand lower side of pump body. Pump looseness will cause engine surge and poor performance.**
7. With injection pump properly installed and timing within specifications, marks on sprocket, pump and bracket should be aligned with No. 1 cylinder at TDC on compression stroke. If pump position must be altered to reset injection timing, scribe a new mark on pump. **Some models have two timing marks on the injection pump sprocket. The mark crossed out with yellow paint should be disregarded.**

INJECTION PUMP, REPLACE

1. Remove timing belt as outlined in "Timing Belt, Replace."
2. Loosen injection pump sprocket retaining bolt slightly.
3. Install puller VW203b or equivalent so that jaws are at 90° angle to crossbar and facing direction of spindle rotation.
4. Carefully apply pressure to sprocket and tap puller spindle with a light hammer until sprocket is released from shaft taper. **Do not apply excessive force with puller, as sprocket will be damaged.**
5. Remove puller, retaining bolt and sprocket.
6. Disconnect fuel lines from pump and plug lines and open fittings.
7. Disconnect accelerator and cold start cable from pump, and wiring harness connector to fuel shut-off solenoid.
8. Remove lower bolt securing pump mounting plate, bolts securing pump to mounting plate and braces (if equipped) and remove pump. **Do not loosen bolts on fuel distributor head, as distributor will be damaged.**
9. Install pump on mounting bracket with marks on pump and bracket aligned. Torque bolts to 18 ft. lbs.
10. Install pump sprocket and torque retaining bolt to 33 ft. lbs. Align mark on pump sprocket with marks on pump and bracket and lock position with pin 2064.
11. Reverse procedure to complete installation. Install timing belt as outlined in "Timing Belt, Replace," adjust cold start and accelerator cables, and check injection timing.

GLOW PLUGS

During cold starts, diesel compression heat is dissipated rapidly through the cold engine so that a pre-heating provision is necessary to ensure compression ignition. The glow plugs are threaded into the cylinder head so they project into each combustion chamber, **Fig. 27.** A heating element in each plug gets red hot whenever current is applied to the plug terminals.

Current is supplied to the glow plugs directly from the battery by a relay which is

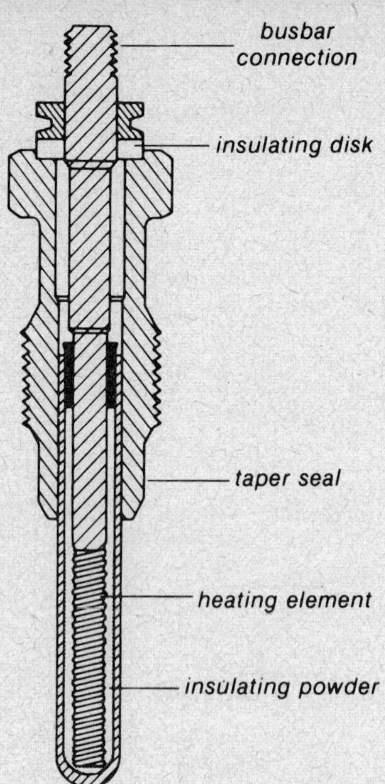

Fig. 28 Glow plug

controlled by the ignition switch. A temperature sensor connected to a time circuit in the relay controls pre-heating time. The colder the temperature, the longer the pre-heating time. The glow plug light is on when the plugs are being heated and goes off when the engine is ready to start.

Testing

Defective glow plugs cause hard starting and rough running during warm-up. Most problems in the pre-heat system can be found with a test light.

1. Connect test light clip to ground and touch test light probe to any glow plug connection with key in glow position. Test light should light up if key switch and relay are working properly.
2. Remove busbar from glow plug connections, **Fig. 28.**
3. Connect test light clip to battery positive post and probe to each glow plug connection. Test light should light up each time if heating elements are satisfactory, **Fig. 29.**

Glow plugs can also be checked with an ohmmeter. The resistance value is about .25 ohms. Carbon deposits can insulate the heating element. If the system seems satisfactory, but the engine is hard to start, the glow plugs should be removed for cleaning.

FUEL SHUT-OFF SOLENOID

Since diesels do not use spark ignition systems, the engine is switched off by a fuel shut-off solenoid on the injection pump.

Current is supplied to the fuel shut-off solenoid whenever the ignition key is on. The magnetic coil pulls the solenoid plunger up against the spring, opening the injection port for injection, **Fig. 30.**

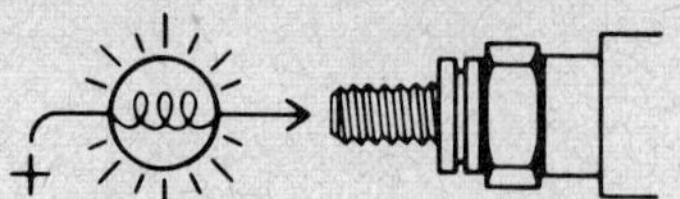

Fig. 29 Glow plug continuity check

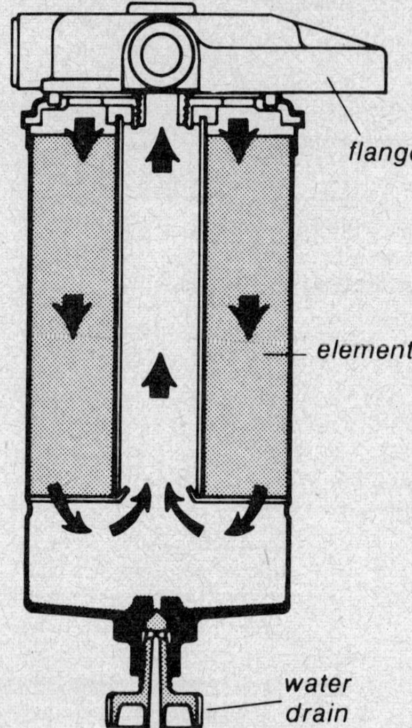

Fig. 31 Fuel filter

Whenever the ignition key is turned off, the solenoid closes the intake port, cutting off the supply of fuel for injection from the vane pump.

The engine will not run if the fuel shut-off solenoid sticks closed. If it sticks open, the engine will continue to run after the ignition key is turned off.

FUEL FILTER

Diesel fuel systems operate reliably as long as the fuel is free from dirt and water. Internal components inside the injection pump and injectors can be damaged by a small amount of dirt or corrosion.

The diesel fuel filter is designed to allow unrestricted flow or fuel from the tank but stops any dirt or water before it reaches the pump.

The replaceable element is similar to an oil filter. It threads onto a removable flange in the engine compartment, **Fig. 31.**

Some filter elements have a water drain in the bottom. If poor quality fuel is used, water separated by the filter can be drained to prevent freezing and blocking of the filter in cold weather.

Replacement

The filter element should be replaced at normal maintenance intervals to ensure reliable operation of the pump and injectors.

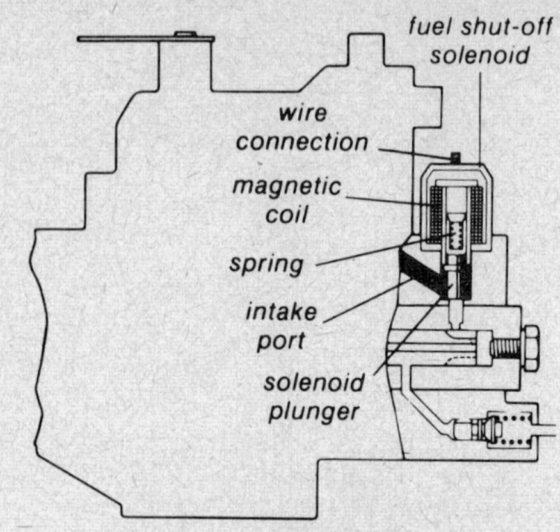

Fig. 30 Fuel shut-off solenoid

1. Remove filter flange with element from body panel and invert the assembly on the mounting studs.
2. Remove element from flange.
3. Fill new element with clean diesel fuel (no further priming should be necessary when filter is full of fuel).
4. Coat rubber seal with diesel fuel and install new element on flange.
5. Remount flange to body.
6. Start engine and check for fuel leaks at flange.

CHECKING IDLE & MAXIMUM SPEED

1. Run engine until radiator is warm.
2. Mount sensor VW 1324, or equivalent, on valve cover (magnetic end). **Since diesel engines do not need spark ignition systems, RPM signals are generated through this vibration sensor.**
3. Connect tachometer positive cable to sensor post and tachometer negative cable to ground sensor cables to battery posts.
4. Idle speed indicated on tachometer should be within specifications.
5. Adjust, if necessary. Loosen locknut, first turn IN to raise idle speed or turn OUT to lower idle speed, then tighten locknut.
6. Now accelerate engine briefly to "full load" position. Engine speed should be within specifications.
7. Adjust, if necessary. Loosen locknut, first turn OUT to raise maximum speed or turn IN to lower maximum speed, then tighten locknut. If maximum speed is set too low, the engine will not produce full power. If maximum speed is set too high, the engine and injection pump can be damaged by over revving of the engine.

TURBOCHARGER

The turbocharger is an exhaust driven device which compresses the air/fuel mixture to increase engine power on a demand basis.

A turbine in the exhaust gas flow is connected through a shaft to the impeller (compressor). During normal, steady operation, the turbine does not rotate with suffi-

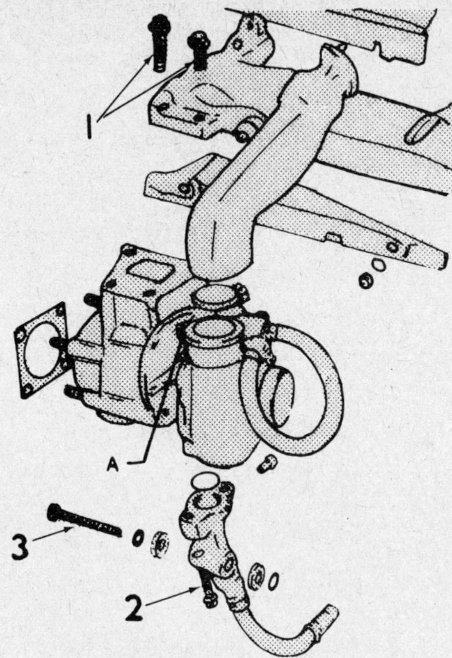

Fig. 32 Turbocharger replacement

cient speed to boost pressure to compress the air/fuel mixture. As engine speed increases, the mixture is compressed, allowing the denser mixture to enter the combustion chambers and develop more engine power during the combustion cycle.

The intake manifold boost pressure is controlled by a wastegate valve which is used to bypass a portion of the exhaust gases around the turbine at a predetermined point in the engine cycle, limiting the boost pressure.

TURBOCHARGER, REPLACE

1. Disconnect battery ground cable.
2. Remove lower engine and transmission cover plate.
3. Disconnect oil return line from turbocharger.
4. Loosen engine carrier inner bolt, then disconnect heat shield and oil return line from turbocharger.
5. Remove air hose between turbocharger and intake manifold.
6. Disconnect oil supply line and exhaust pipe from turbocharger.
7. Remove turbocharger-to-exhaust manifold attaching bolts and the turbocharger, **Fig. 32.**
8. Reverse procedure to install, noting the following:
   a. Apply suitable grease to turbocharger-to-exhaust manifold attaching bolts.
   b. Tighten bolts hand tight in sequence shown in **Fig. 32**, then torque bolts in sequence to the following specifications. Torque turbocharger-to-manifold bolts to 29 ft. lbs., and oil return line attaching bolts to 18 ft. lbs.
   c. Prior to connecting oil supply line, fill turbocharger connection branch with engine oil.
   d. Following completion of installation, run engine at idle speed for one minute to properly distribute oil supply.

TURBOCHARGER TESTING

1. Connect a suitable pressure gauge between injection pump and intake pipe, **Fig. 33.** Position gauge so it is visible from driver's seat.
2. Open gauge stop valve by pushing in direction of gauge dial.
3. Measure turbocharger boost pressure with engine at full throttle using one of the following methods:
   a. Using a dynamometer, measure boost pressure at 4000 RPM in third gear on models equipped with automatic transaxle, or second gear on models equipped with manual transaxle.

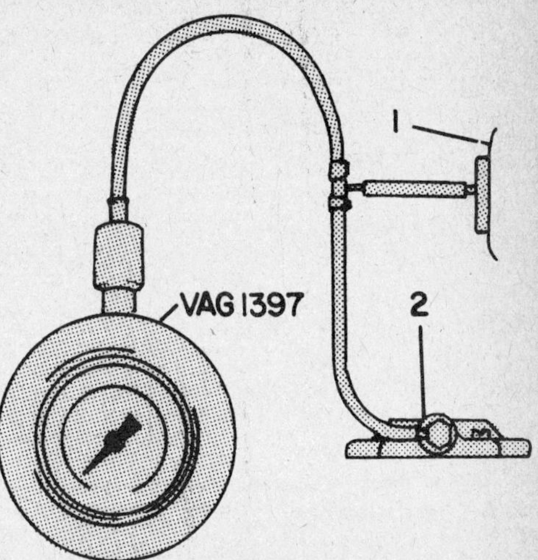

Fig. 33 Turbocharger boost pressure test connections

   b. On a road test, measure boost pressure while applying brake to hold vehicle speed to 35 miles per hour in second gear on models equipped with manual transaxle, or first gear on models equipped with automatic transaxle. **To make boost pressure reading easier while road testing, pull gauge stop valve away from gauge dial to lock reading on indicator.**
4. Boost pressure should measure 9-10 psi. If pressure is high, the wastegate is defective and the turbocharger must be replaced. If pressure is low, proceed to step 5.
5. Disconnect blow-off valve hose from intake air hose, then block air hose with a 1 inch plug and tighten with a clamp. Repeat boost pressure test and note reading. If pressure is now within specifications, replace blow-off valve. If pressure is still low, replace turbocharger.

CLUTCH & MANUAL TRANSAXLE SECTION

INDEX

CLUTCH PEDAL ADJUST

1983–84 JETTA, PICKUP, RABBIT, 1983–86 SCIROCCO & QUANTUM

1. Loosen clutch cable adjusting sleeve at transaxle case.
2. Adjust sleeve until clutch pedal freeplay is approximately 9/16 inch on 1983-86 Quantum models. On all other models, freeplay should measure between 27/32 and 1 inch.

1985–86 CABRIOLET, JETTA & GOLF

1. Fully depress clutch pedal approximately 5 times.
2. Loosen locknut A, **Fig. 1.**
3. Install adjusting gage US 5043 or equivalent as shown in **Fig. 1.**
4. Raise clutch release lever at transmission until resistance is felt.
5. Adjust adjusting sleeve B, **Fig. 1** until zero freeplay is obtained.
6. Torque cable locknut A to 3-4 ft. lbs., then remove adjusting tool.
7. Clutch freeplay at clutch release lever

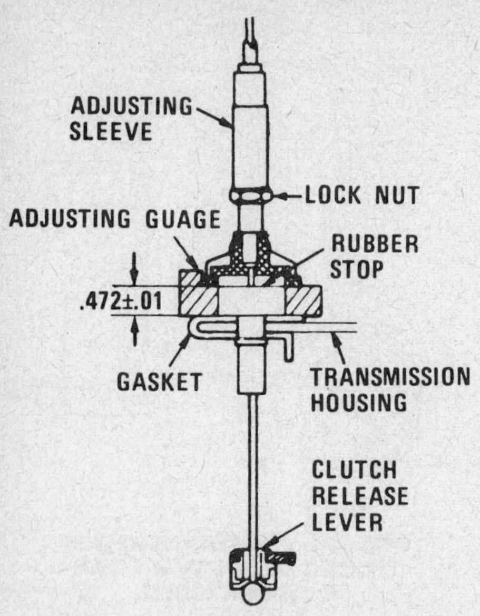

Fig. 1 Adjusting freeplay

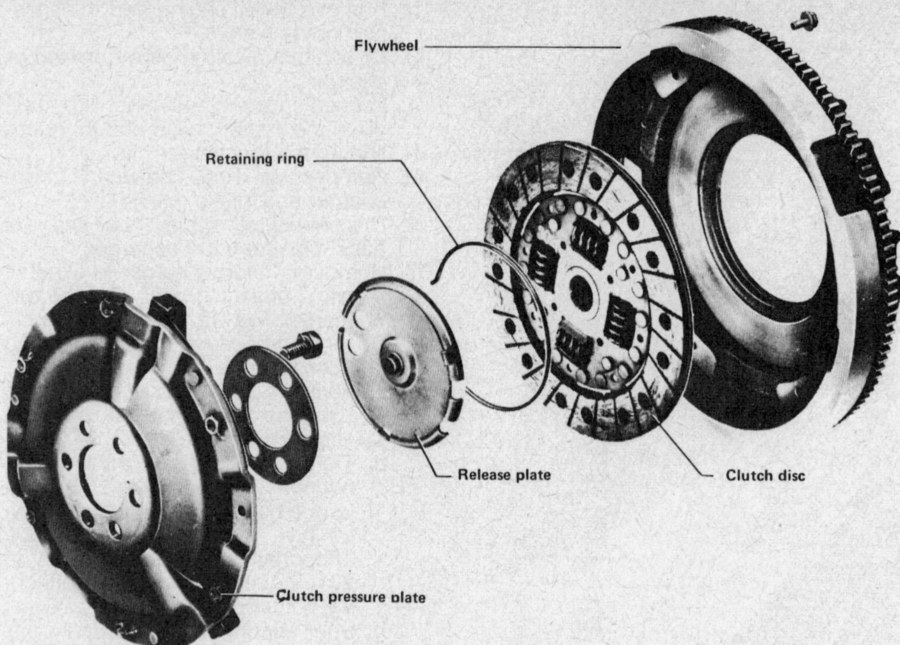

Fig. 2 Disassembled view of clutch assembly

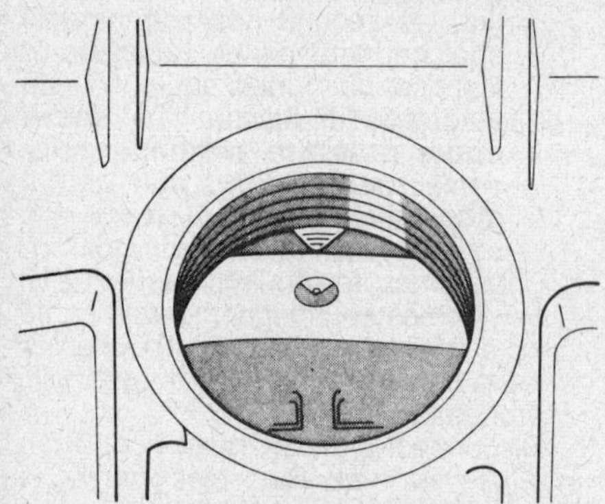

Fig. 3 Aligning flywheel lug w/bellhousing boss

should be .236 inch plus or minus .012 inch.

CLUTCH

REPLACE

1. Remove transaxle as outlined under "Transaxle, Replace" procedure.
2. Lock flywheel with suitable tool, then remove flywheel to pressure plate attaching bolts.
3. Remove flywheel, clutch disc, release plate retaining ring and the release plate, **Fig. 2.**
4. Lock pressure plate using tool VW 558 or equivalent, then remove pressure plate to crankshaft retaining bolts and the pressure plate.
5. To install, position pressure plate to crankshaft, coat retaining bolts with thread locking compound and install bolts finger tight.
6. Install pressure plate locking tool and torque retaining bolts to 54 ft. lbs.
7. Lubricate release plate contact surface and pushrod socket with lithium grease, then install release plate and retaining ring to pressure plate.
8. Install clutch disc, flywheel and flywheel attaching bolts.
9. Using tool VW 547, center clutch disc in flywheel and torque attaching bolts to 14 ft. lbs.
10. Install transaxle assembly.

MANUAL TRANSAXLE

REPLACE

1983–84 JETTA, PICKUP, RABBIT & 1983–86 SCIROCCO

1. Disconnect battery ground cable.
2. Install engine support bar 10-222 or equivalent and support transaxle with suitable jack.
3. Remove left mount.
4. Disconnect wires from back-up light switch connector, clutch cable, and speedometer drive cable and plug hole.
5. Remove upper transaxle-to-engine bolts.
6. Remove starter motor.
7. Turn engine until lug on flywheel aligns with boss in sender unit hole, **Fig. 3.** The engine and transaxle can only be separated in this position.
8. Disconnect shift linkage by opening clips with screwdriver.
9. Remove front selector rod.
10. Remove exhaust pipe bracket.
11. Remove transaxle rear mount from body and transaxle.
12. Disconnect right and left side driveshafts from transaxle and wire up.
13. Remove bolts from large cover plate and bolt from small cover plate.
14. Remove remaining transaxle bolt or nut near the differential.
15. Pull transaxle away from engine.

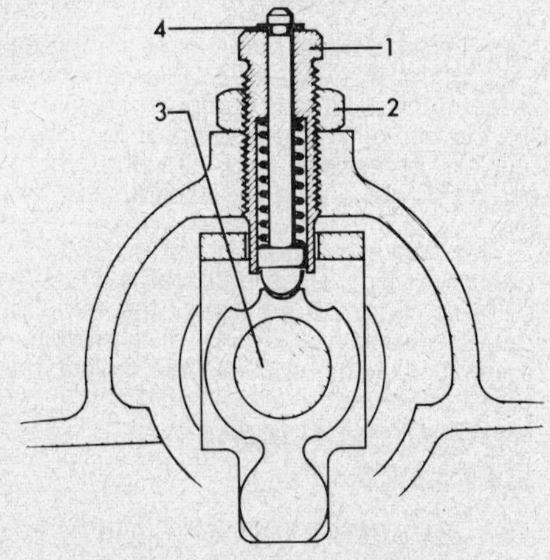

Fig. 4 Selector shaft detent plunger adjustment

16. Lower and remove transaxle from vehicle.
17. Reverse procedure to install transaxle. Note the following:
    a. Ensure large cover plate is properly seated.
    b. Torque bolts on large and small cover plates to 78 inch lbs.
    c. Torque upper transaxle to engine bolt and lower engine to transaxle bolt near differential to 58 ft. lbs.
    d. Torque starter, rear mount, and driveshaft flange bolts to 33 ft. lbs.
    e. Align engine transaxle in mounts.

1985–86 CABRIOLET, JETTA & GOLF

Engine remains installed in vehicle, while transmission is lowered out of vehicle.

1. Disconnect battery ground cable, then connector at reverse/upshift light switch.

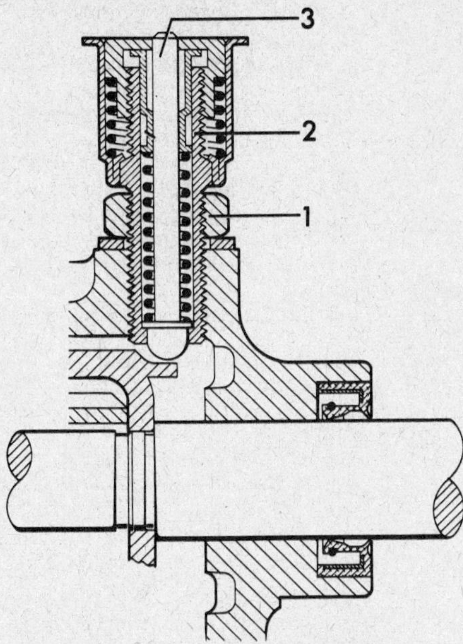

Fig. 5 5th gear detent plunger adjustment

2. Disconnect speedometer at transmission, then plug all openings to prevent contamination.
3. Remove upper bolts attaching engine to transmission, then disconnect clutch cable at clutch release lever and transmission housing.
4. Remove right side engine support attaching bolts.
5. Disconnect short selector rod, then connecting rod from gear shift lever shaft.
6. Remove long selector rod from relay lever, than bolt from left transmission mount.
7. Remove the two upper left side engine support attaching bolts.
8. Install engine support bar 10-222A or equivalent onto engine.
9. Remove left side wheel house liner, then detach axle shafts and support with wire.
10. Remove two clutch cover plates, then starter motor and suspend with wire.
11. Remove front mount assembly, then the remaining left side engine support attaching bolt.
12. Lower transmission housing slightly, then remove left transmission mounting bolts.
13. Position engine/transmission assembly as far to right as possible, then position a suitable transmission jack under transmission and remove lower transmission attaching bolts.
14. Separate transmission off engine centering pins, then remove transmission.
15. Reverse procedure to install noting the following:
    a. Clean input shaft splines and lubricate with a suitable lubricant.
    b. Ensure clutch cover plate is positioned correctly.
    c. Check clutch freeplay, and adjust, if necessary.
    d. Torque engine to transmission bolts to 55 ft. lbs., starter bolts to 44 ft. lbs., axle shaft to flange attaching bolts to 33 ft. lbs. and left transmission housing to mount bolts to 44 ft. lbs.

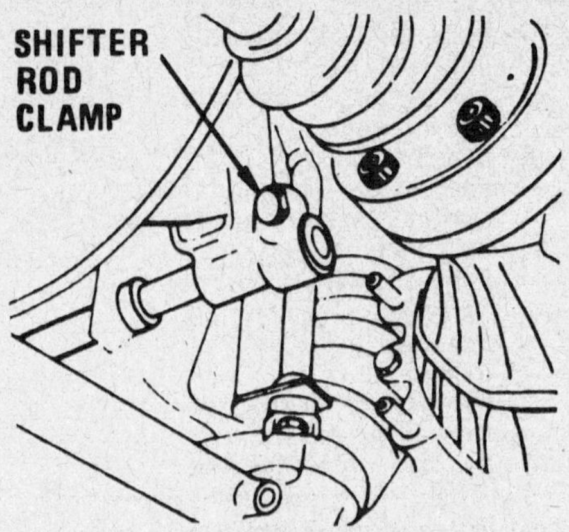

Fig. 6 Shifter rod clamp bolt location

QUANTUM

1. Disconnect battery ground cable.
2. Remove upper transaxle-to-engine attaching bolts.
3. Disconnect speedometer cable and clutch cable from transaxle.
4. Disconnect exhaust pipe from exhaust manifold.
5. Remove front engine support bolts, then the front muffler and exhaust pipe.
6. Disconnect right and left side driveshafts from transaxle.
7. Disconnect back-up light electrical connector, then remove cover plate attaching bolts and the starter attaching bolt.
8. Remove shift rod coupling bolt from transaxle, then pry off shift rod coupling ball and pull shift rod coupling off shift rod.
9. Raise transaxle slightly using a suitable jack.
10. Remove transaxle support bolts, then pivot support rearward and remove rubber mount.
11. Remove front transaxle support attaching bolts, then the lower transaxle-to-engine attaching bolts.
12. Separate transaxle from engine, then carefully lower transaxle from vehicle.
13. Reverse procedure to install.

SHIFT LINKAGE

ADJUST

1983–84 JETTA, PICKUP, RABBIT & 1983–86 SCIROCCO

Lever Bearing Assembly

1. Align holes in lever baring plate with corresponding holes in lever housing. **When installing lever bearing plate, threaded holes in lever housing should be centered in plate slots. If not, turn plate 180° and torque plate bolts to 74 inch lbs.**

Shift Rod

1. Loosen bolts holding lever housing.

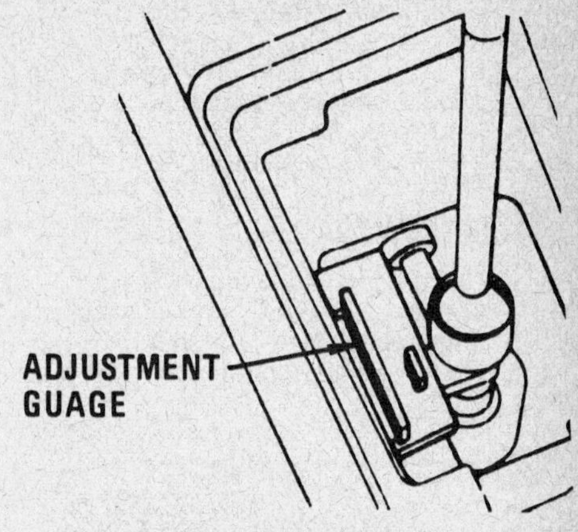

Fig. 7 Installing adjustment gauge

2. Pull boot from lever housing and move aside.
3. Loosen shift rod clamp so selector lever moves easily on shift rod.
4. Adjust shift finger in center of lock out plate so front and rear spacing are equal.
5. Adjust shift rod end so that distance between shift finger and lock out bracket is 3/4 inch on 4 speed models or 9/16 inch on 5 speed models.
6. Torque shift rod clamps to 14 ft. lbs.
7. Ensure gears engage easily without jamming. Ensure reverse lock out works properly.
8. If shift linkage is spongy or jams after adjustments, adjust selector shaft detent plunger according to following procedure:
    a. Ensure transaxle is in neutral.
    b. Loosen locknut 2 and turn adjusting sleeve 1 in until lock ring 4 lifts off sleeve, **Fig. 4.**
    c. Turn adjusting sleeve back until lock ring just contacts sleeve. Tighten locknut 2.
    d. Turn shaft 3 slightly. Ensure lock ring lifts as soon as shaft is turned.
9. On 5 speed transaxles only, adjust 5th gear detent plunger, if necessary, as follows:
    a. Ensure transaxle is in neutral.
    b. Remove adjusting sleeve protection cap.
    c. Loosen locknut 1, **Fig. 5.**
    d. Tighten adjusting sleeve 2 until detent plunger 3 just begins to rise.
    e. From this position loosen adjusting sleeve 1/3 turn.
    f. Tighten locknut.

1985–86 CABRIOLET, JETTA & GOLF

1. Position gearshift lever in neutral.
2. Loosen shifter rod clamp bolt, **Fig. 6,** and ensure selector lever moves freely on shifter rod.
3. Remove gearshift lever knob and boot.
4. Position adjustment gauge 3104 or equivalent as shown in **Fig. 7.**
5. With transmission in neutral, align shift rod with selector lever. **Shift linkage should not be under pressure**

during adjustment.

6. Move gearshift lever through all gears, including reverse. Gears should engage smoothly and without jamming.
7. Install shift boot and gearshift lever knob.

QUANTUM

1. Place gearshift lever in neutral.
2. Loosen clamp nut and ensure shift finger slides freely on shift rod.
3. Remove shift boot and gearshift lever knob.
4. Loosen lever bearing plate attaching bolts, then align gearshift lever housing centering holes with gearshift lever bearing housing and tighten attaching bolts.
5. Install adjusting tool 3057 over gearshift lever. Position locating pin in front centering hole, then place gearshift lever in right cutout (5/R) and tighten lower knurled nut on tool.
6. Move gearshift lever and slide to right stop and tighten upper knurled nut on tool.
7. Place gearshift lever in left cutout (3/4), then align shift rod to shift finger with transaxle in neutral position.
8. Tighten clamp nut, then remove tool.
9. Check that, when gearshift lever is placed in first or fifth gear and lever is pressed against left or right stop and then released, the lever springs back approximately the same distance. If lever does not spring back equally from both stops, adjust gearshift lever housing in elongated slots.
10. Check that gears engage easily without jamming. Ensure reverse lockout works properly.
11. Install shift boot and gearshift lever knob.

DISC BRAKES SECTION

INDEX

GIRLING SINGLE PISTON TYPE

Volkswagen uses four different disc brake calipers. These calipers are manufactured by Girling, Teves and Kelsey-Hayes. Before removing pads, determine which caliper is used, Figs. 1, 2, 3 and 4.

EXC. QUANTUM

Disc Pads, Replace

1. Raise and support front of vehicle, then remove wheels.
2. Remove lower caliper to pad carrier attaching bolt, then swing caliper upward and lift out pads.
3. Install anti-rattle springs onto new pads, then position pads into brake pad carrier, **Fig. 5.**
4. Push piston fully into caliper bore, then swing caliper over pads.
5. Install new mounting bolt and torque to 25 ft. lbs.

Caliper, Replace

1. Remove two caliper to brake pad carrier mounting bolts.
2. Disconnect brake line from caliper, then remove caliper from vehicle.
3. Reverse procedure to install and bleed brake system.

Caliper Overhaul

1. Remove caliper as outlined previously.
2. Remove piston dust cup from piston assembly.
3. Position a suitable piece of wood between piston and outer caliper flange, then apply low pressure compressed air to fluid port and carefully blow piston out of cylinder.

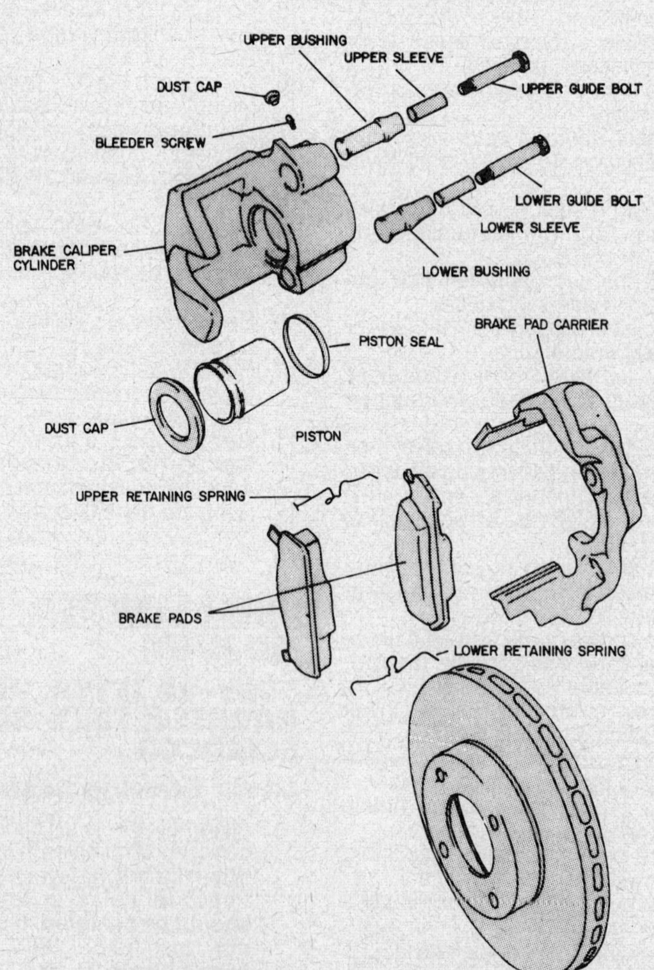

Fig. 1 Girling single piston caliper assembly. Quantum

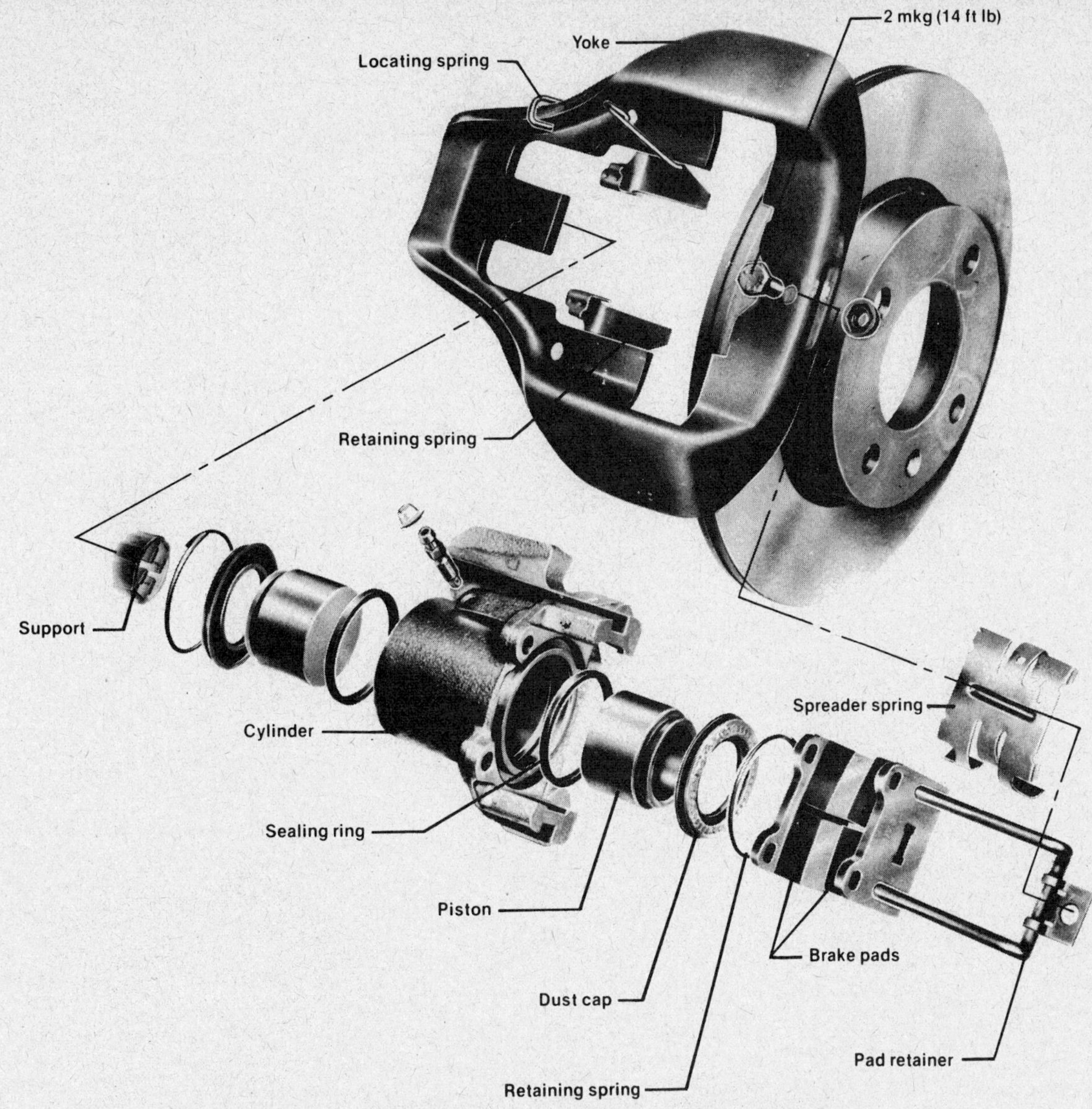

Fig. 2 Girling dual piston caliper assembly

4. Using a plastic rod, pry piston seal out of cylinder bore.
5. Slide dust cap onto piston, then coat new piston seal and piston with brake cylinder paste and install into cylinder bore.
6. Assemble caliper to brake pad carrier, then bleed brake system.

QUANTUM

Disc Pads, Replace

1. Raise and support front of vehicle, then remove wheels.
2. Loosen attaching springs at top and bottom of brake pads, then remove upper and lower guide pins, **Fig. 1.**
3. Loosen caliper and wire it to the frame.
4. Remove brake pads from carrier.
5. Reverse procedure to install. Torque guide pins to 29 ft. lbs.

Caliper, Replace

1. Remove retaining springs and guide pins.
2. Loosen caliper, then disconnect brake line and remove caliper from vehicle.
3. Reverse procedure to install and bleed brake system.

Caliper Overhaul

1. Remove caliper as outlined previously.
2. Pry piston dust cap from piston assembly, **Fig. 1.**
3. Apply low pressure compressed air to fluid port and blow piston out of cylinder bore.
4. Using a plastic rod, pry piston seal out of caliper bore.
5. Coat new piston seal and piston with brake cylinder paste, then install into caliper bore.
6. Install dust boot onto piston assembly.
7. Install caliper assembly, then bleed brake system.

GIRLING DUAL PISTON TYPE

BRAKE PADS, REPLACE

1. Raise and support front of vehicle, then remove wheels.
2. Pry off spreader spring, then remove pad retainer bolt and pull retainer out of caliper, **Fig. 6.**
3. Using pliers, or equivalent, pull pads out of caliper yoke.
4. Using tool US 1023-4, push caliper piston fully into bore.
5. Install new pads and pad retainer, then torque pad retainer nut to 14 ft. lbs.
6. Snap spreader spring over pad. Ensure arrow on spring points upward.

CALIPER, REPLACE

1. Remove disc brake pads as outlined previously.
2. Remove yoke retainers, then the yoke and caliper as an assembly.

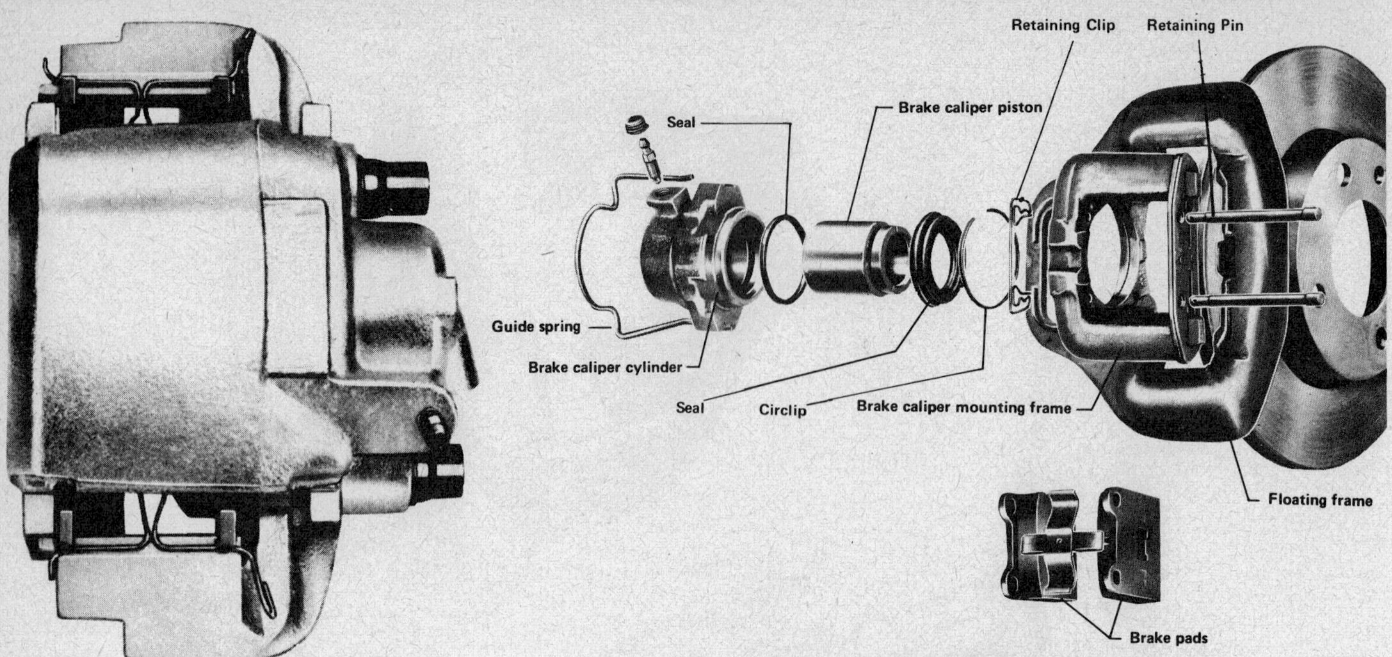

Fig. 3 Kelsey-Hayes caliper assembly

Fig. 4 Teves caliper assembly

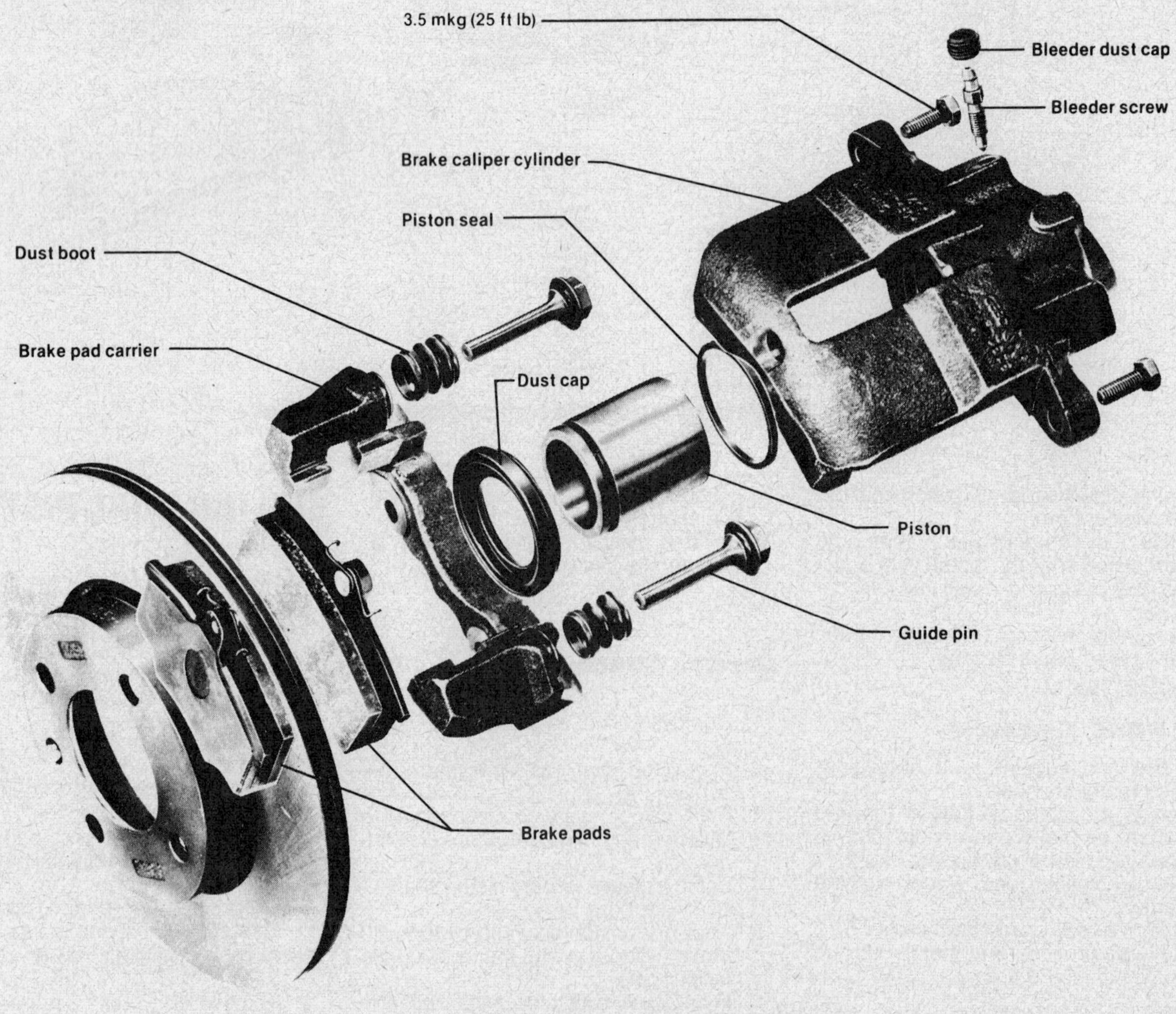

Fig. 5 Girling single piston caliper assembly. Exc. Quantum

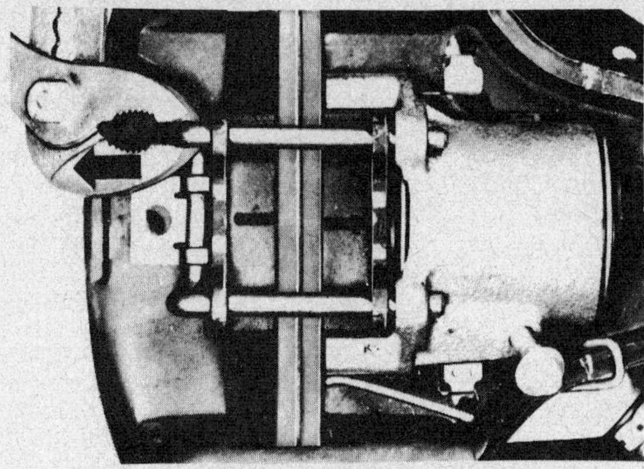

Fig. 6 Pad retainer removal. Girling dual piston caliper

Fig. 7 Driving caliper from yoke. Girling dual piston caliper

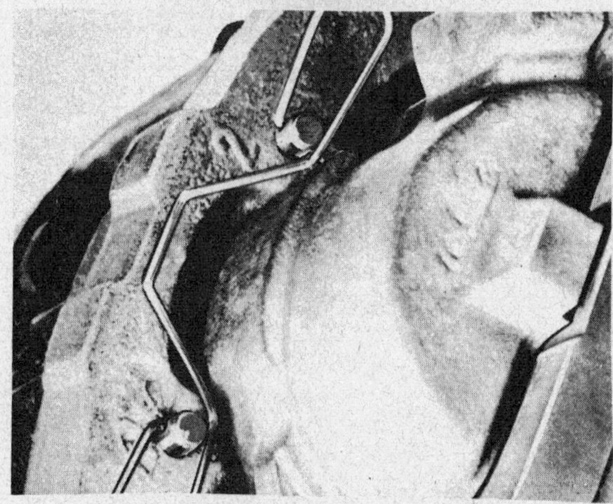

Fig. 8 Pad retainer pin spring clip. Teves caliper

3. Disconnect brake line from caliper.
4. Place yoke and caliper on workbench, then using a wooden drift, drive caliper out of yoke, **Fig. 7.**
5. Reverse procedure to install and bleed brake system.

CALIPER OVERHAUL

1. Remove caliper as outlined previously.
2. Remove two piston dust boot retaining rings, then the dust boots, **Fig. 2.**
3. Position caliper in a suitable vise and support with wooden blocks.
4. Apply low pressure compressed air to fluid port and blow pistons out of cylinders.
5. Using a plastic rod, pry piston seals out of cylinder bores.
6. Coat new piston seals and pistons with brake cylinder paste, then install into cylinder bores.
7. Install dust boots and attaching rings onto pistons.
8. Install cylinder assembly into yoke.
9. Install cylinder and yoke assembly, then bleed brake system.

KELSEY-HAYES TYPE

BRAKE PADS, REPLACE

1. Raise and support vehicle, then remove wheels.
2. Remove anti-rattle springs and two caliper guide pins, **Fig. 3.**
3. Swing caliper outward and remove from support. Wire caliper to frame.
4. Remove brake pads from caliper support.
5. Install new brake pads into caliper support. Inner pad has chamfered edges.
6. Using tool 1023-4 or equivalent, push caliper piston completely into bore.
7. Position caliper over pads, install guide pins and torque to 30 ft. lbs.

CALIPER, REPLACE

1. Remove anti-rattle springs and two caliper guide pins.
2. Swing caliper outward and remove from support.
3. Disconnect brake line from caliper, then caliper from vehicle.
4. Reverse procedure to install and bleed brake system.

CALIPER OVERHAUL

1. Remove caliper as outlined previously.
2. Pry piston dust boot from piston assembly.
3. Place folded rag into caliper assembly, then apply low pressure compressed air to fluid port and blow piston out of caliper.
4. Using a plastic rod, pry piston seal out of caliper bore.
5. Coat new piston seal and piston with brake cylinder paste, then install into caliper bore.
6. Install dust boot onto piston assembly.
7. Install caliper assembly, then bleed brake system.

TEVES TYPE

BRAKE PADS, REPLACE

1. Raise and support front of vehicle, then remove wheels.
2. Remove pad retainer pin spring clip, then drive retaining pins out of caliper, **Fig. 8.**
3. Pull inner pad out of caliper, press caliper outward, then remove outer pad.
4. Using tool 1023-4 or equivalent, push caliper piston fully into bore.
5. Position piston as necessary, then install new brake pads.
6. Insert new spreader spring over pads, then drive new retaining pins into caliper and install retaining pin spring clip.

CALIPER, REPLACE

1. Remove brake pads as outlined previously.
2. Remove caliper, caliper mounting frame and caliper floating frame, **Fig. 4,** then disconnect brake line.
3. Pressing outward, separate mounting frame from caliper.
4. Position caliper and floating frame on workbench. Using a brass drift, or equivalent, drive caliper from floating frame.
5. Reverse procedure to install and bleed brake system.

CALIPER OVERHAUL

1. Remove caliper as outlined previously.
2. Remove dust seal circlip and dust seal, then support piston on a wooden block.
3. Apply low pressure compressed air to fluid port and blow piston out of cylinder bore.
4. Using a plastic rod, pry piston seal out of cylinder bore.

5. Coat new piston seal and piston with brake cylinder paste, then install into cylinder bore.
6. Install dust seal and circlip onto piston.
7. Install caliper assembly, then bleed brake system.

MASTER CYLINDER
REPLACE

1. Siphon brake fluid from reservoir, then disconnect brake lines from master cylinder and electrical connectors from brake light switches.
2. Remove master cylinder to firewall or brake booster, if equipped, attaching nuts, then the master cylinder and seal.
3. Position new master cylinder and seal to firewall or brake booster, then install attaching nuts.
4. Transfer brake light switches to new master cylinder, then connect brake lines and electrical connectors.
5. Fill fluid reservoir with clean brake fluid and bleed brake system.

POWER BRAKE UNIT
REPLACE

1. Remove master cylinder as previously described.
2. Disconnect vacuum line from brake booster.
3. Disconnect brake booster pushrod clevis pin from brake pedal.
4. Remove brake booster to mounting bracket attaching bolts and the brake booster.
5. Position new brake booster to mounting bracket and torque attaching nuts to 11 ft. lbs. on Quantum models, or 15 ft. lbs. on Jetta, Pickup, Rabbit and Scirocco models.
6. Connect booster push rod clevis pin to brake pedal.
7. Connect vacuum line to brake booster, install master cylinder and bleed brake system. **When bleeding brake system, push lever on brake pressure regulator located at rear axle, toward rear of vehicle.**

DRUM BRAKES SECTION

INDEX

BRAKE SHOES
REPLACE

1983–84 JETTA, PICKUP & RABBIT & 1983–86 SCIROCCO

Models Less Self Adjusters

Refer to **Fig. 1** for brake shoe removal and installation. Adjust wheel bearings as outlined under "Wheel Bearings, Adjust."

Models With Self Adjusters

1. Raise and support vehicle, then remove rear wheel assembly.
2. Using tool VW 637/2 or equivalent, remove grease cap, then cotter pin and axle nut.
3. Remove brake drum, then spring retainers by pressing in and turning, **Fig. 2.**
4. Remove brake shoes from anchor pins, then lower return spring.
5. Disconnect parking brake cable from lever.
6. Disconnect spring for adjusting wedge, then upper return spring using suitable pliers.
7. Remove brake shoes.
8. Reverse procedure to install, then adjust wheel bearings as outlined under "Wheel Bearing, Adjust."

1983–86 QUANTUM & 1985–86 CABRIOLET, GOLF & JETTA

Refer to "1983-84 Jetta, Pickup & Rabbit & 1983-86 Scirocco, Models With Self Adjusters," for brake shoe removal and installation.

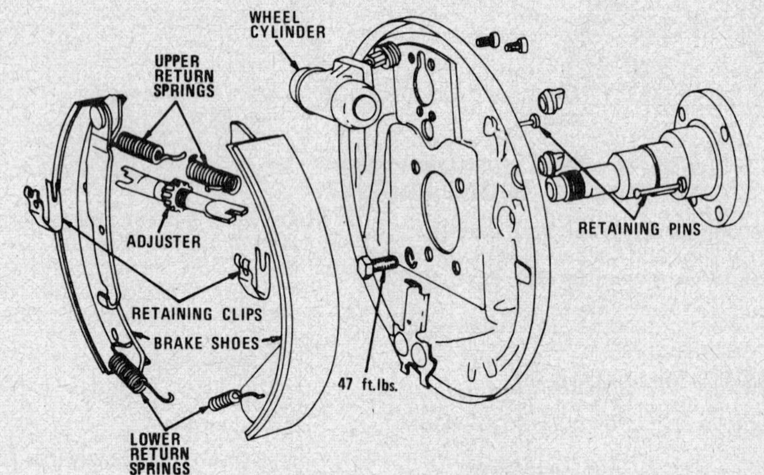

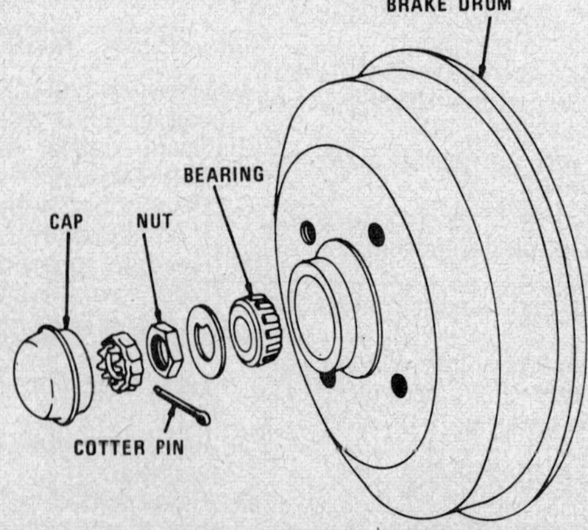

Fig. 1 Exploded view of brake assembly. Models less belt adjusters

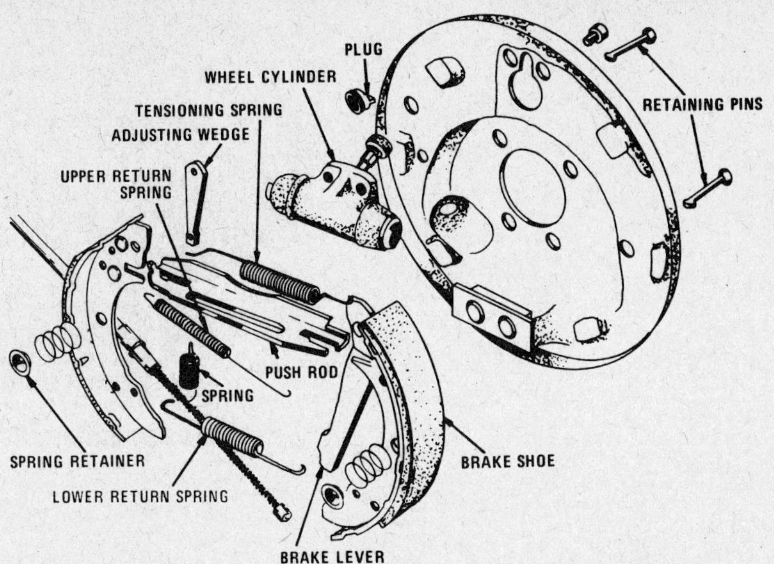

Fig. 2 Exploded view of brake assembly. Models w/belt adjusters

PARKING BRAKE

ADJUST

EXC. 1983–84 JETTA, PICKUP, RABBIT & 1983–86 SCIROCCO

1. Raise and support vehicle.
2. Pull parking brake lever up to second click.
3. Working from underneath vehicle, tighten adjusting nut until both rear wheels can just be turned by hand.
4. Release parking brake and check that rear wheels rotate freely.

1983–84 JETTA, PICKUP, RABBIT & 1983–86 SCIROCCO

With Adjustable Brakes

1. Raise and support vehicle.
2. Loosen parking brake cable adjusting nuts.
3. Adjust rear brakes.
4. Pull parking brake lever to second notch.
5. Tighten adjusting nuts until neither rear wheel can be turned by hand.
6. Release parking brake and ensure that both rear wheels turn freely.
7. Tighten lock nuts.

With Self-Adjusting Brakes

1. Raise and support vehicle.
2. Firmly apply brake pedal one time.
3. Pull parking brake lever to second notch.
4. Tighten adjusting nuts until neither rear wheel can be turned by hand.
5. Release parking brake and ensure that both rear wheels turn freely.
6. Tighten lock nuts.

SERVICE BRAKE

ADJUST

On models equipped with adjustable rear brakes the rear brakes should be re-adjusted whenever replacing shoes or whenever brake pedal travel becomes excessive. To adjust, raise and support rear of vehicle and turn star adjuster with screwdriver until linings touch brake drum. Then back-off adjuster until wheel can be turned freely by hand. **If vehicle is equipped with brake pressure regulator, the lever on the regulator must be pushed toward rear axle before adjusting brakes.**

MASTER CYLINDER

REPLACE

Refer to "Disc Brakes Section" for service procedure.

POWER BRAKE UNIT

REPLACE

Refer to "Disc Brakes Section" for service procedure.

DRIVE AXLE SECTION

INDEX

Page No.

DRIVE AXLE

REPLACE

1. With vehicle on ground, remove drive axle retaining nut from wheel assembly.
2. Remove drive axle to transaxle drive flange attaching bolts.
3. On all models except Quantum, separate ball joint from wheel bearing housing.
4. On Quantum models equipped with manual transaxle, mark position of ball joint to right side control arm and separate ball joint from control arm.
5. On Quantum models equipped with automatic transaxle, mark position of ball joints to both right and left side control arms and separate ball joints from control arms.
6. On all models, pull wheel and tire assembly outward and remove drive axle from vehicle.
7. Reverse procedure to install.

CONSTANT VELOCITY JOINT

REPLACE

OUTER JOINT

1. Remove drive axle as outlined previously.
2. Secure drive axle in a suitable vise.
3. Remove outer joint boot retaining clamp, then pull boot toward inner joint, **Fig. 1.**
4. Spread ears of circlip inside hub and tap on front of shaft to drive joint off shaft, **Fig. 2.**
5. Mark ball hub in relation to cage and housing, then turn cage until large openings are level with outer housing. Remove cage together with hub.
6. Position hub until one segment can be pushed into larger opening of cage, then remove hub from cage, **Fig. 3. Always replace hub, outer ring, ball cage and balls together, since**

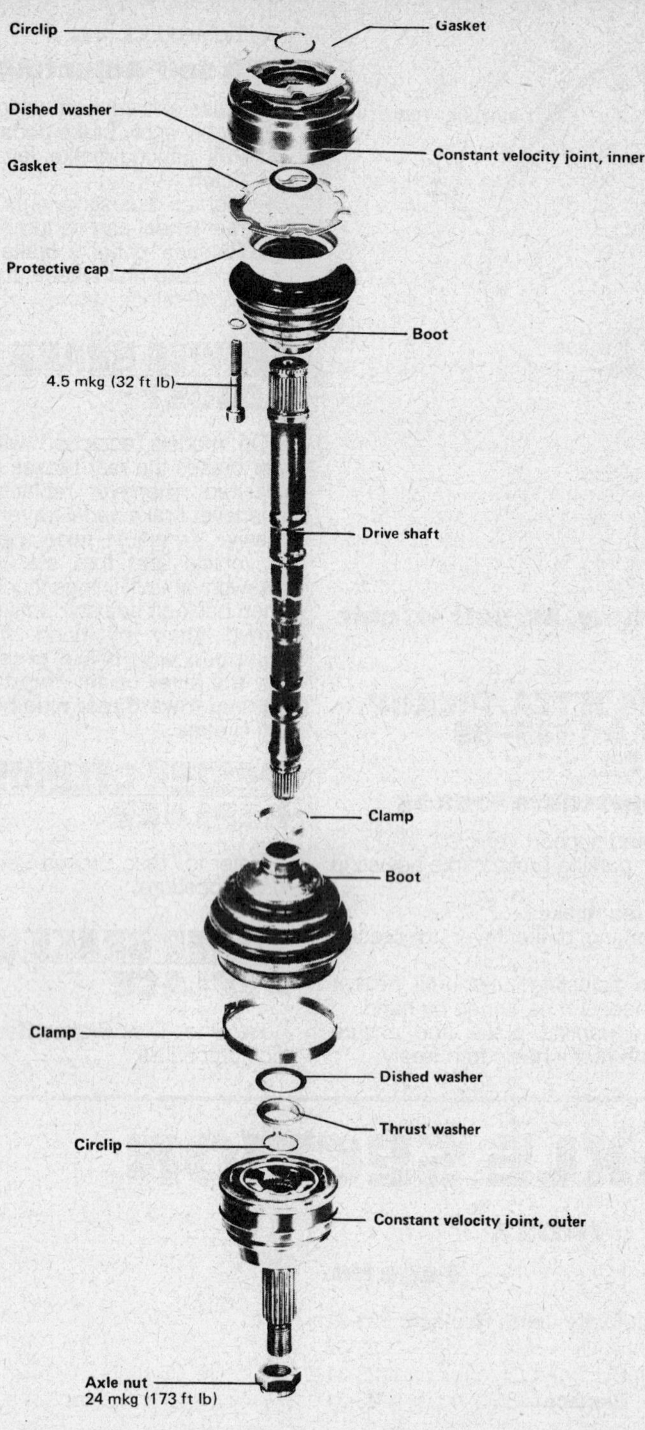

Fig. 1 Disassembled view of drive axle

Fig. 2 Outer joint circlip

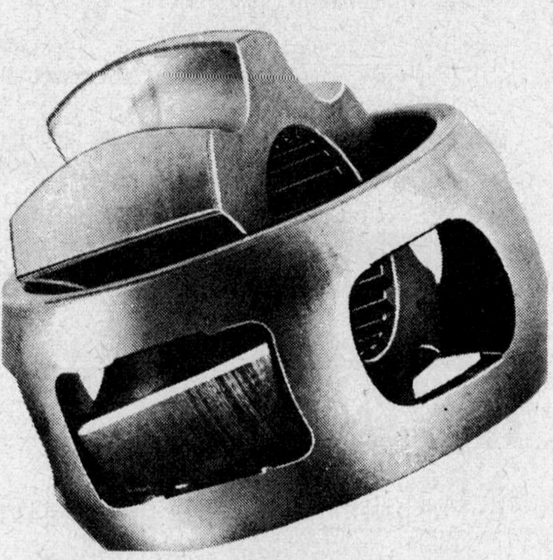

Fig. 3 Removing hub from ball cage

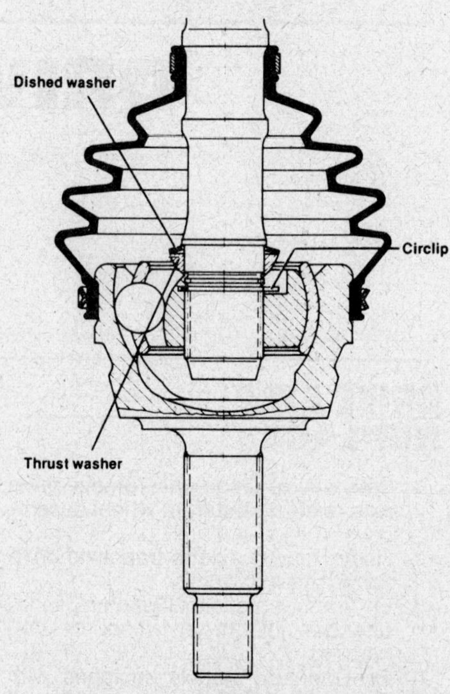

Fig. 4 Positioning dished and thrust washers. Outer joint

each belong to one specific tolerance group.

7. Reverse procedure to install. Ensure dished side of dished washer and convex side of thrust washer face toward joint, **Fig. 4**.

INNER JOINT

1. Compress circlip with pliers and remove from joint.
2. Using drift and hammer, carefully drive protective cap off joint.
3. Using tools VW 408a & VW 402 or equivalent, remove joint from drive axle **Fig. 5.**
4. Pivot ball hub and cage and remove from outer ring, then press balls out of cage.

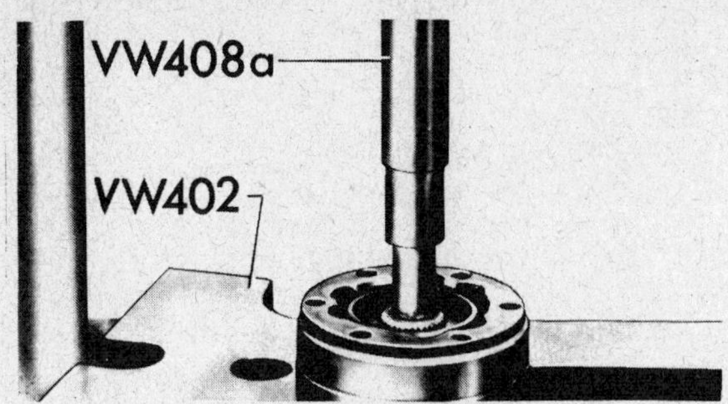

Fig. 5 Removing inner joint

5. Align grooves, then remove ball hub from cage.
6. Reverse procedure to install, ensuring:
   a. Chamfer on inside diameter of ball hub faces shoulder on drive axle.
   b. Wide ball groove in outer ring and narrow groove in hub are together on one side.
   c. Dished side of dished washer faces splined area of drive axle, **Fig. 6.**

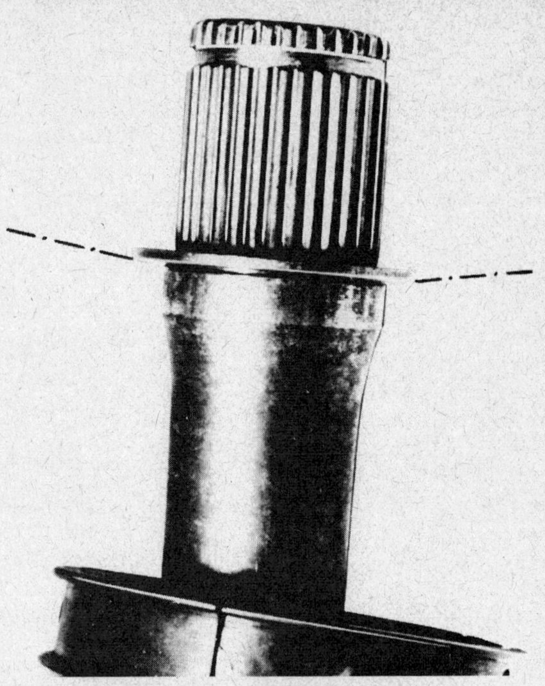

Fig. 6 Positioning inner joint dished washer

REAR AXLE & SUSPENSION SECTION

INDEX

REAR AXLE REPLACE

1983–84 JETTA, RABBIT & 1983–86 SCIROCCO

1. Raise and support rear of vehicle.
2. Working from inside vehicle, disconnect parking brake cable from parking brake lever.
3. Disconnect and plug brake hoses.
4. Raise rear axle beam with a suitable floor jack, then remove upper strut to body attaching nut, **Fig. 1. Always disconnect struts one at a time, since personal injury and/or damage to vehicle may result.**
5. Remove rear axle mount to rear axle attaching bolts, then the rear axle.
6. Reverse procedure to install. **When installing rear axle assembly, ensure that upper edge of rear mount (A), Fig. 2, parallel to line (B). If not, loosen nut (C), adjust mount as required, then torque nut to 43 ft. lbs.**

1985–86 CABRIOLET, JETTA & GOLF

Refer to **Fig. 3**, for removal and installation of rear axle.

PICKUP

1. Disconnect parking brake cables at parking brake handle.
2. Raise and support vehicle.
3. Remove parking brake cables from side member and spring bracket.
4. Remove cable ties and pull cables out of tubes.
5. Unhook brake equalizer springs, noting direction.
6. Attach tools US 4489 or equivalents to body and axle.
7. Disconnect brake lines from axle hose attachments, then plug lines and hoses.
8. Remove brake equalizer pivot bolt on axle.
9. Remove brake hose attachment plate from axle.
10. Remove lower shock absorber mounting bolts, **Fig. 4.**
11. Remove U-bolts and spring plates.
12. Lower vehicle to ground, then remove tools US 4489.
13. Raise vehicle, leaving axle on ground.
14. Reverse procedure to install, then bleed brakes and adjust parking brake.

QUANTUM

1. Raise and support rear of vehicle.
2. Disconnect parking brake cable from pull rod, **Fig. 5.**
3. Disconnect and plug brake hoses. **If mounting brackets are to remain on body, remove axle retaining bolts. When installing bolts, ensure axle is horizontal and level prior to tightening bolts.**
4. Disconnect brake equalizer, then remove mounting bracket nuts, leaving one nut installed on each side.
5. Loosen exhaust pipe attaching rings, then lower vehicle while supporting axle with a suitable jack.
6. Disconnect strut upper mounts, then remove remaining nut from both mount brackets.
7. Raise rear of vehicle slowly. Lift parking brake cable over exhaust pipe and

CAUTION

If rear axle beam is removed, always bleed brake system and readjust brakes.

CAUTION

Do not attempt to straighten or weld rear axle beam or stub axles.

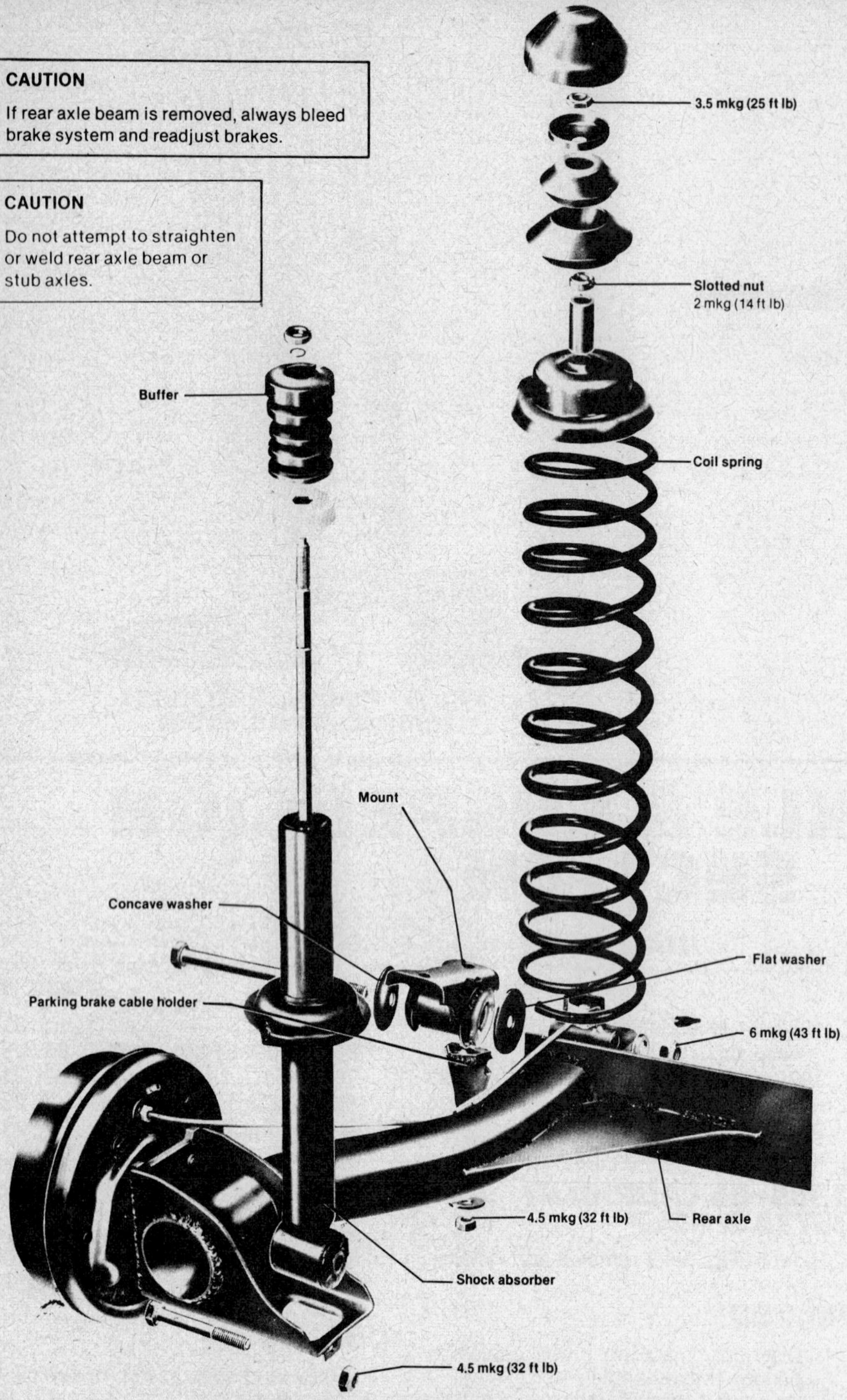

3.5 mkg (25 ft lb)
Slotted nut 2 mkg (14 ft lb)
Buffer
Coil spring
Mount
Concave washer
Flat washer
Parking brake cable holder
6 mkg (43 ft lb)
4.5 mkg (32 ft lb)
Rear axle
Shock absorber
4.5 mkg (32 ft lb)

Fig. 1 Rear axle & suspension. 1983–84 Jetta, Rabbit & 1983–86 Scirocco

slide axle assembly from under vehicle.

8. Reverse procedure to install. **Install mount brackets onto axle at an approximate angle of 15-19°.**

SHOCK ABSORBER

REPLACE

Whenever replacing shock absorbers, always remove and install one shock absorber at a time, since personal injury and/or damage to vehicle may result.

1983–84 JETTA, RABBIT & 1983–86 SCIROCCO

1. Raise and support rear of vehicle.
2. Position a suitable floor jack under axle beam, then remove upper strut to body attaching nut.
3. Carefully lower floor jack, then remove shock to axle beam mounting bolt.
4. Remove shock and coil spring from vehicle.
5. Secure shock/coil spring assembly in a suitable vise, then carefully remove

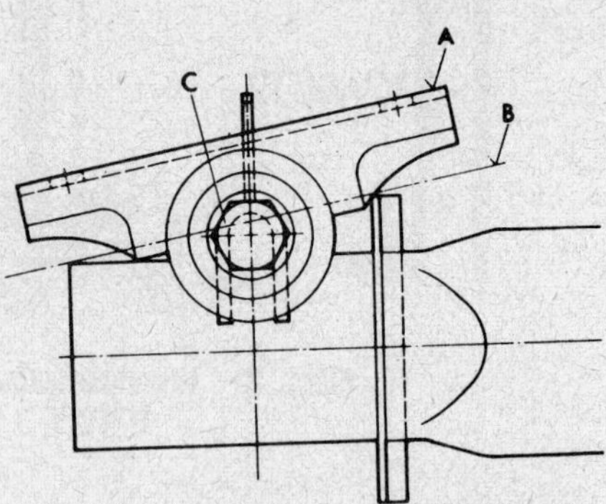

Fig. 2 Rear axle mount alignment. 1983–84 Jetta, Rabbit & 1983–86 Scirocco

slotted nut using tool 50-200.

6. Assemble spring and spring components to new shock as shown in **Fig. 1.**
7. Reverse procedure to complete installation.

1985–86 CABRIOLET, JETTA & GOLF

Refer to **Fig. 3** for removal and installation of shock absorber.

PICKUP

1. Raise and support vehicle.
2. Install tool US 4489 or equivalent, to body and axle.
3. Remove upper and lower shock absorber mounting bolts, noting direction of bolts for installation.
4. Remove shock absorber, **Fig. 4.**
5. Reverse procedure to install.

QUANTUM

1. Remove shock absorber upper cover, then disconnect strut from body, **Fig. 5.**
2. Raise rear of vehicle slowly and remove strut-to-axle attaching bolt.
3. Disconnect strut from lower mounting while pressing down on wheel slightly.
4. Guide strut assembly out between wheel and wheel housing.
5. Reverse procedure to install.

WHEEL BEARING

ADJUST

1. Raise and support rear of vehicle, then remove the wheel/tire assembly.
2. Remove grease cap, then the cotter pin and locknut.
3. Tighten adjusting nut while turning wheel to settle bearings.
4. Loosen, then retighten adjusting nut, until thrust washer can be moved slightly with screwdriver.
5. Install locknut and new cotter pin, then the grease cap.
6. Install wheel/tire assembly and lower vehicle to ground.

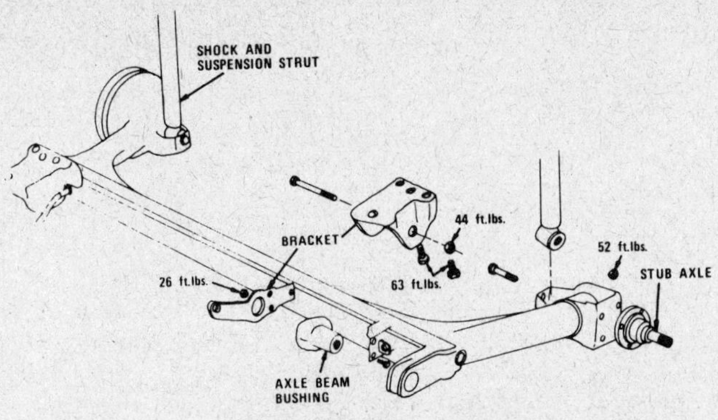

Fig. 3 Exploded view of rear axle assembly. 1985–86 Cabriolet, Jetta & Golf

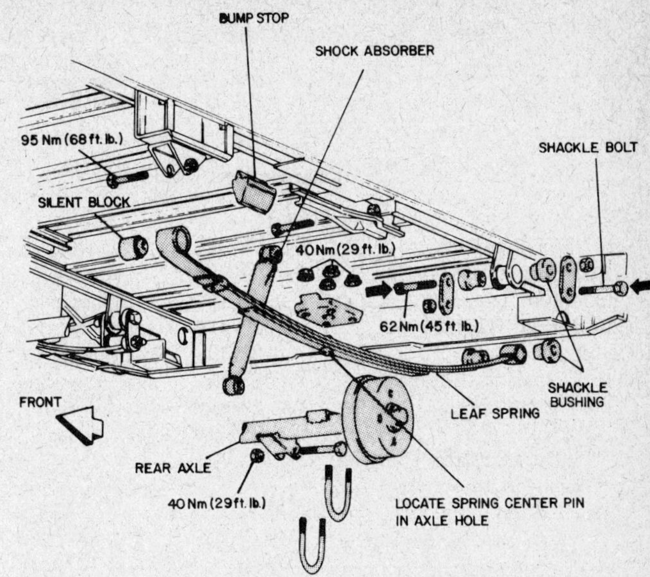

Fig. 4 Rear axle & suspension. Pickup

LEAF SPRING

REPLACE

PICKUP

Removal

1. Raise and support vehicle.
2. Remove parking brake cable from spring bracket and cut tie wrap.
3. Install tool US 4489 or equivalent, to body and axle.
4. Remove lower shock absorber mounting nuts.
5. Remove U-bolts and spring plates.
6. Loosen upper and lower shackle bolts.
7. If removing left spring, proceed as follows:
   a. Remove three bolts from exhaust system flange on flex pipe.
   b. Remove exhaust system hangers.
   c. Remove exhaust system.
8. Remove lower shackle bolt.
9. Remove front spring bolt.
10. Remove spring, **Fig. 3.**
11. Reverse procedure to install.

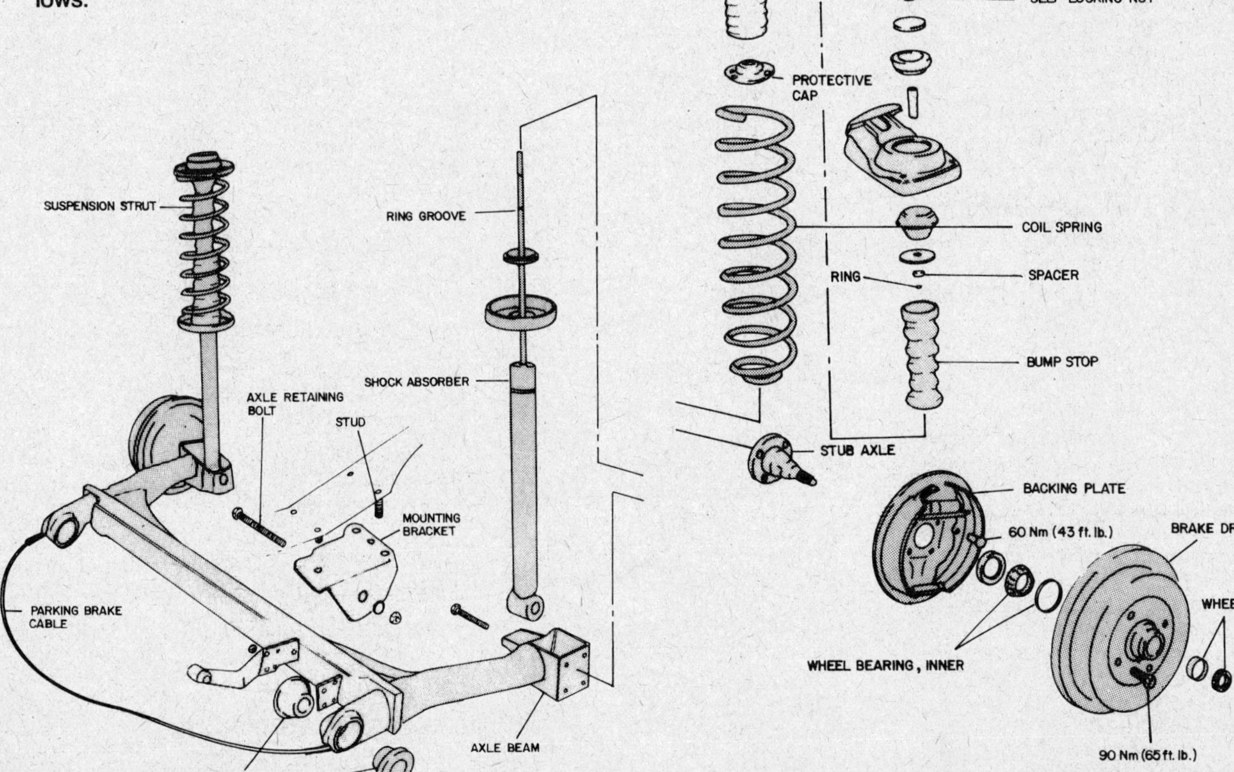

Fig. 5 Rear axle & suspension (Part 1 of 2). Quantum

Fig. 5 Rear axle & suspension (Part 2 of 2). Quantum

FRONT SUSPENSION & STEERING SECTION

INDEX

DESCRIPTION

These vehicles use a MacPherson strut type front suspension. The upper part of strut is attached to the upper fender reinforcement. On Quantum models, the wheel bearing housing is integral with the strut assembly and is attached to the lower control arm through a ball joint, **Fig. 1.** On all models except Quantum, the strut and wheel bearing housing are separate and distinct parts, with the strut attached to the housing with through bolts. The assembly is attached to the lower control arm through a ball joint, **Figs. 2 and 3.** During steering maneuvers, the strut and housing rotate as an assembly.

The driveshafts are attached inboard to the transaxle output drive flanges and outboard to the driven wheel hub.

SUSPENSION STRUT REPLACE

1983–84 JETTA, PICKUP, RABBIT & 1983–86 SCIROCCO

Mark position of strut cam bolt to aid installation.

1. Raise and support vehicle, then remove front wheels.
2. Disconnect caliper brake hose from brake line.
3. Remove lower control arm to frame attaching bolts and disconnect control arm from frame.
4. Raise wheel bearing housing assembly with a suitable jack, then remove the strut bracket to housing cam and through bolts.
5. Lower wheel bearing housing assembly and disconnect from strut.
6. Remove the two strut to fender reinforcement attaching nuts, then the strut assembly.
7. Reverse procedure to install.

1985–86 CABRIOLET, GOLF & JETTA

Refer to **Fig. 3** for removal and installation of suspension strut.

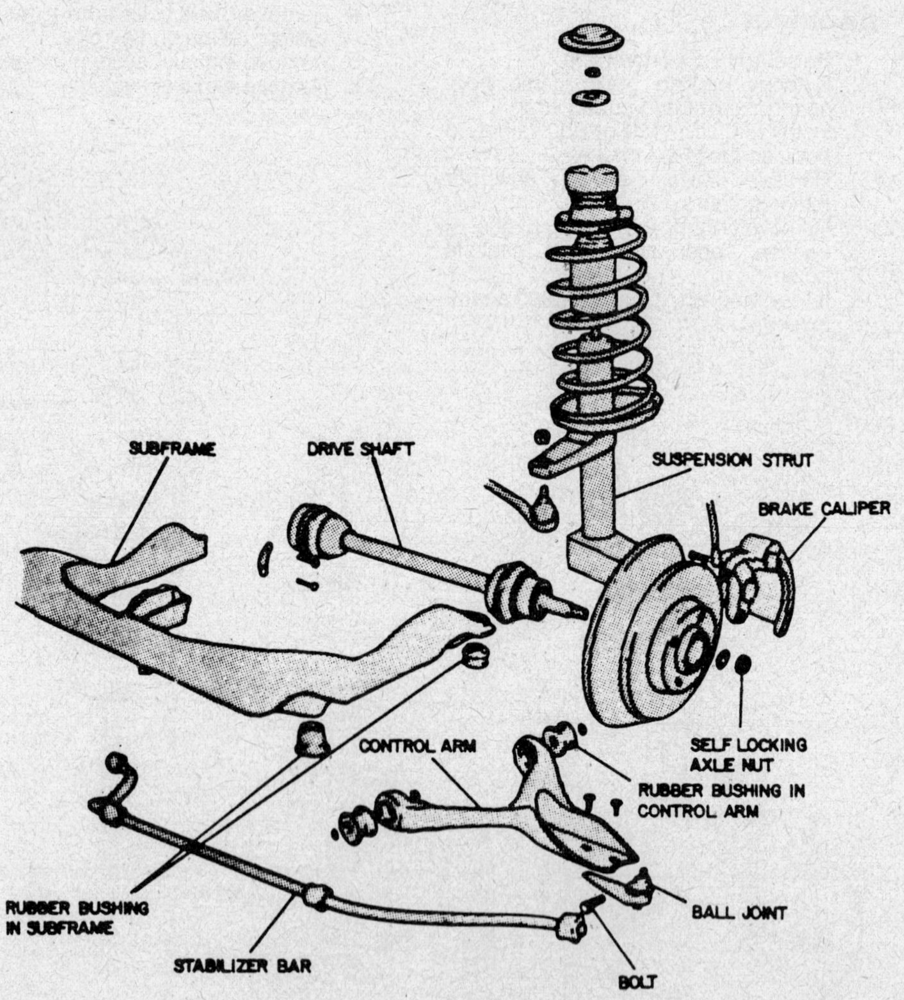

Fig. 1 Front suspension. Quantum

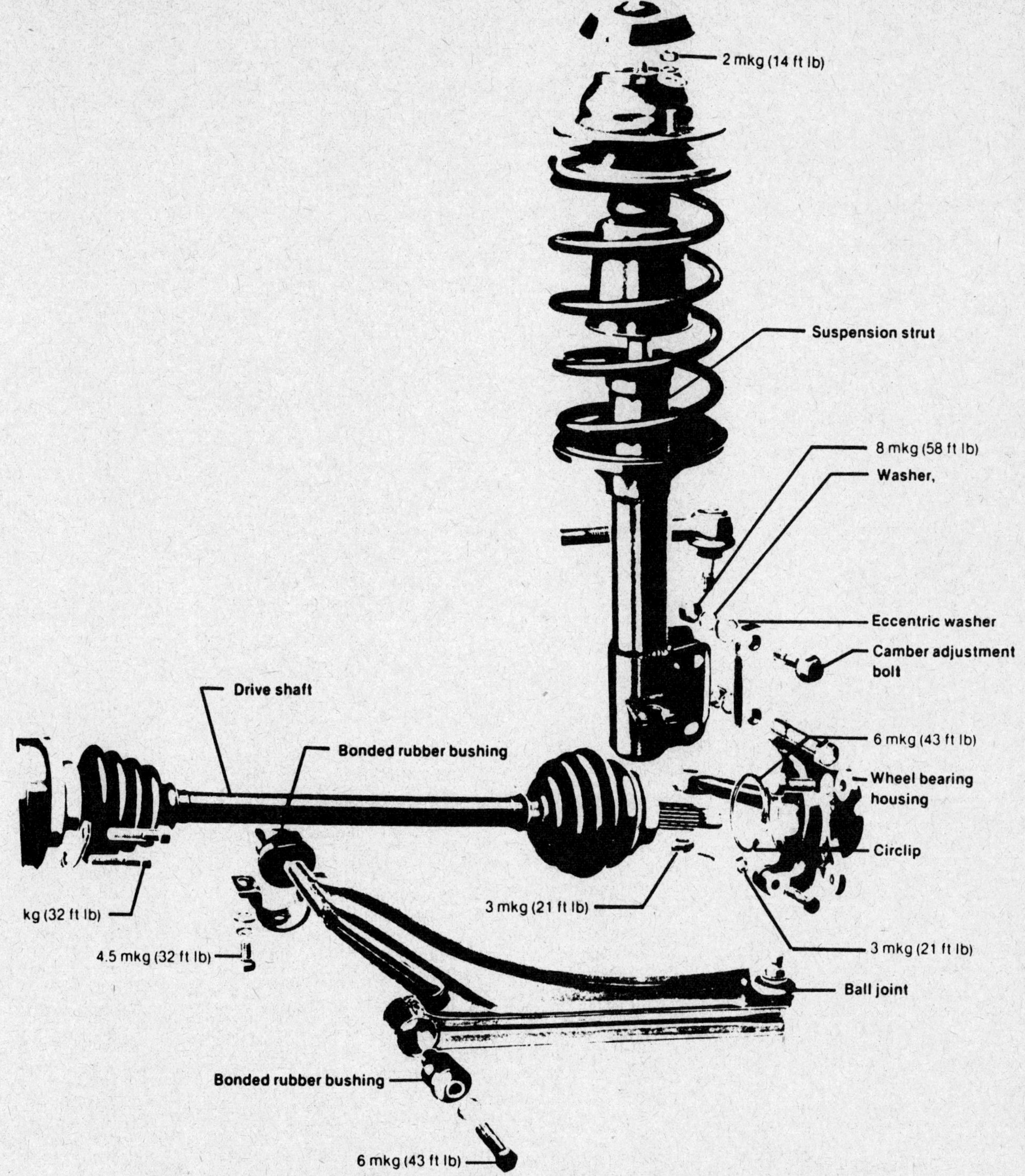

Fig. 2 Front suspension. Jetta, Pickup, Rabbit & Scirocco

QUANTUM

1. Raise and support front of vehicle and remove front wheel.
2. Remove brake caliper attaching bolts, then the brake line bracket.
3. Remove wheel bearing housing-to-ball joint clamp bolt, then disconnect tie rod from strut steering arm.
4. Disconnect stabilizer bar from lower control arm.
5. Remove axle nut, then push control arm down and disconnect driveshaft from wheel bearing housing.
6. Remove upper mounting nut, then carefully lower strut from vehicle.
7. Reverse procedure to install.

COIL SPRING REPLACE

1. Remove strut assembly as outlined previously. **Mark position of upper mount in relation to strut. Scribe mark on upper mount to aid installation.**
2. Using tool US 4475, or equivalent, compress coil spring.
3. Hold shock absorber shaft with hex key, then remove attaching nut.
4. Carefully release tension on spring compressor, then remove retainer, end collar and mount, rubber damper, bearing, upper spring seat and the coil spring.
5. Inspect rubber components for deterioration, retainers and seats for cracks or distortion and bearing for binding. Replace, if necessary.
6. Position coil spring onto strut and compress, using tool US 4475.
7. Install upper spring seat, bearing rubber damper, end collar and mount,

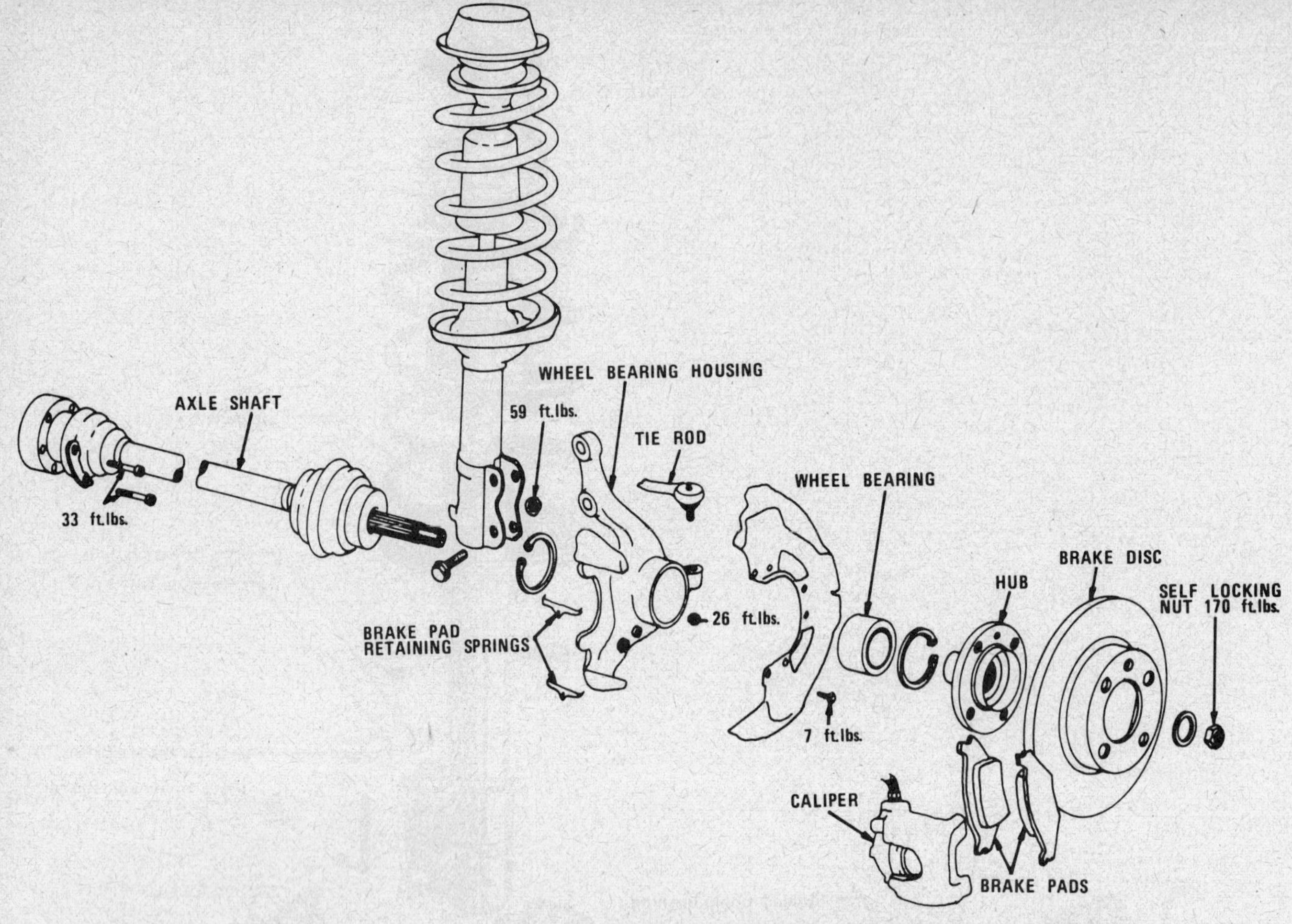

Fig. 3 Front suspension. 1985–86 Cabriolet, Golf & Jetta

then the retainer and nut. Torque nut to 36 ft. lbs. on Quantum models, 51 ft. lbs. on 1983-84 Jetta, Pickup and Rabbit and 1983-86 Scirocco, and 30 ft. lbs. on 1985-86 Cabriolet, Golf and Jetta.

8. Remove spring compressor.

STRUT CARTRIDGE REPLACE

These vehicles incorporate an integral, non-serviceable shock absorber built into the strut assembly.

1. Remove coil spring as previously outlined.
2. Secure strut assembly in a suitable vise, then remove the strut tube threaded cap.
3. Remove strut cartridge from strut assembly.
4. Reverse procedure to install. Torque strut tube threaded cap to 108 ft. lbs.

BALL JOINT REPLACE

EXC. QUANTUM

1. Raise and support vehicle, then remove front wheel.
2. Remove ball joint to wheel bearing housing clamp bolt, then separate ball joint from housing.
3. Using a 1/4 inch drill bit, drill out rivets, then chisel off rivet heads and remove ball joint from control arm.
4. Position new ball joint to control arm, install retaining bolts, spring washers and nuts and torque to 18 ft. lbs.
5. Reverse procedure to complete installation.

QUANTUM

1. Raise and support vehicle, then remove front wheel.
2. Scribe mark where ball joint flange meets lower control arm to aid installation.
3. Remove ball joint to wheel bearing housing clamp bolt, then separate ball joint from wheel bearing housing.
4. Disconnect stabilizer bar from lower control arm.
5. Remove ball joint to lower control arm retaining bolts and the ball joint.
6. Install new ball joint to control arm, align scribe mark and torque retaining bolts to 47 ft. lbs.
7. Reverse procedure to complete installation.

LOWER CONTROL ARM REPLACE

1983–84 JETTA, PICKUP, RABBIT & 1983–86 SCIROCCO W/MANUAL TRANSAXLE

1. Raise and support vehicle, then remove front wheel.
2. Remove lower control arm to frame attaching bolts, then disconnect control arm from frame.
3. Remove ball joint to wheel bearing housing clamp bolt, then separate ball joint from housing.
4. Disconnect stabilizer bar from control arm, if equipped, then remove control arm from vehicle.
5. Reverse procedure to install.

1983–84 JETTA, PICKUP, RABBIT & 1983–86 SCIROCCO W/AUTOMATIC TRANSAXLE

1. Raise and support vehicle, then remove front wheel.
2. Remove left front engine mount, then the rear mount attaching nut.

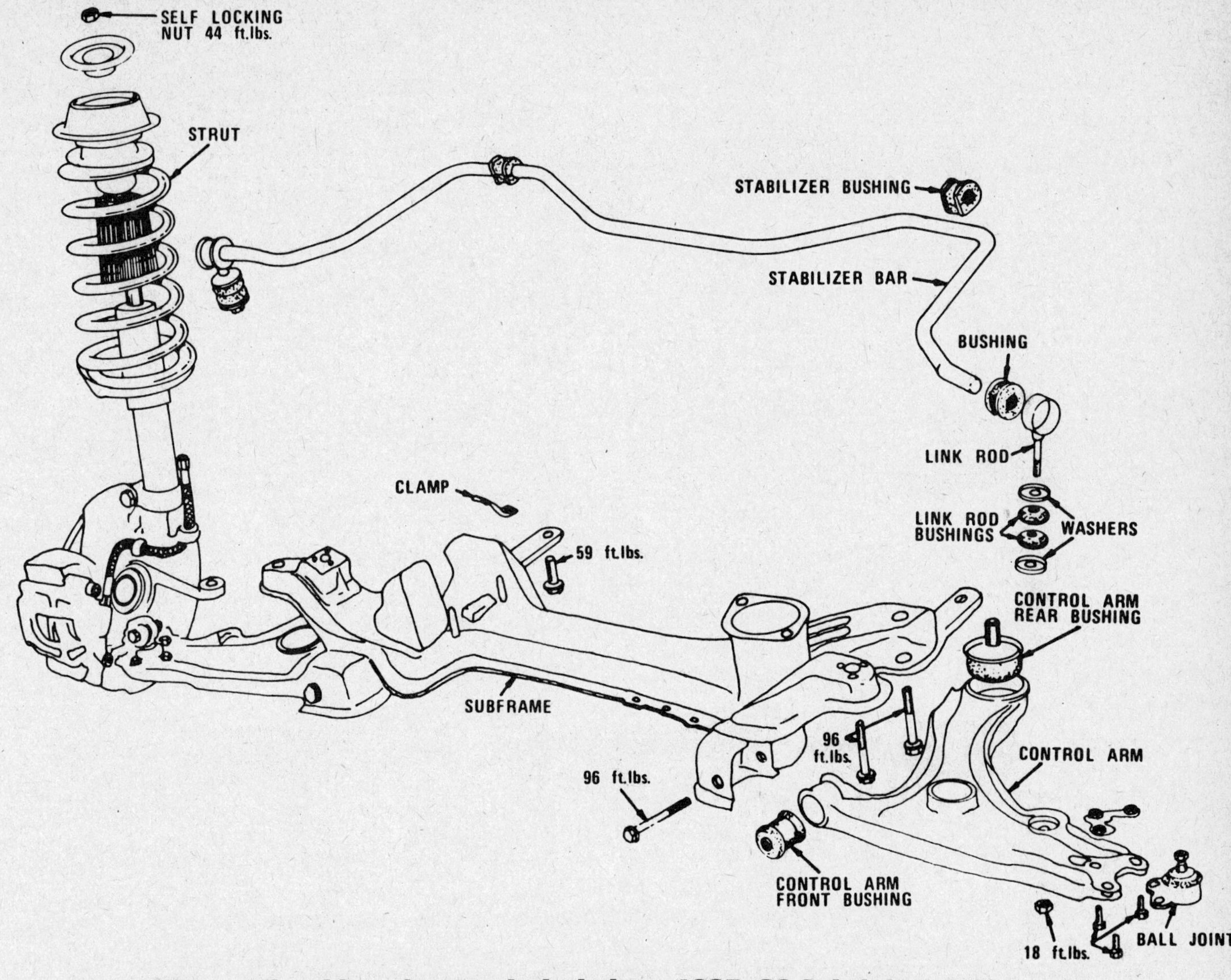

Fig. 4 Wheel bearing exploded view. 1985–86 Cabriolet, Golf & Jetta

3. Remove engine mount support, then install engine support bar 10-222 or equivalent, across engine compartment.
4. Lift engine with support bar until lower control arm attaching bolts can be removed.
5. Remove control arm to frame attaching bolts.
6. Remove ball joint to wheel bearing housing clamp bolt, then separate ball joint from housing.
7. Disconnect stabilizer bar from control arm, if equipped, then remove control arm.
8. Reverse procedure to install.

1985–86 CABRIOLET, GOLF & JETTA

Refer to **Fig. 3** for removal and installation of lower control arm.

WHEEL BEARING HOUSING

REPLACE

QUANTUM

Since the wheel bearing housing is integral with the strut assembly, it is necessary to remove the strut assembly to service the housing, **Figs. 1 and 2.**

1983–84 JETTA, PICKUP, RABBIT & 1983–86 SCIROCCO

Removal

1. Remove drive shaft to hub retaining nut.
2. Raise and support vehicle. Remove wheel assembly.
3. Remove brake caliper and support using a length of wire.
4. Remove brake rotor.
5. Remove tie rod to wheel bearing housing retaining nut, then separate tie rod from wheel bearing housing.
6. Remove ball joint to wheel bearing housing clamp bolt, then separate ball joint from wheel bearing housing.
7. Mark location of camber adjusting bolt, then remove the camber and through bolts, **Fig. 2.**
8. Support driveshaft, pull housing from strut and remove housing from vehicle.

Installation

1. Insert driveshaft into hub, then install wheel bearing housing onto strut bracket. Install cam and through bolts. Align reference marks on cam bolt and torque bolt to 58 ft. lbs. Torque through bolt to 50 ft. lbs. on models with self-locking bolts, or 36 ft. lbs. on models less self-locking bolts.
2. Install ball joint and clamp bolt. Torque clamp bolt to 36 ft. lbs.
3. Connect tie rod to wheel bearing housing and torque retaining nut to 21 ft. lbs. Install new cotter pin.
4. Install brake rotor and caliper.
5. Install driveshaft to hub retaining nut, lower vehicle and torque nut to 173 ft. lbs.

1985–86 CABRIOLET, GOLF & JETTA

Refer to **Fig. 4** for removal and installation of wheel bearing housing.

Fig. 5 Positioning rack assembly. Exc. Quantum

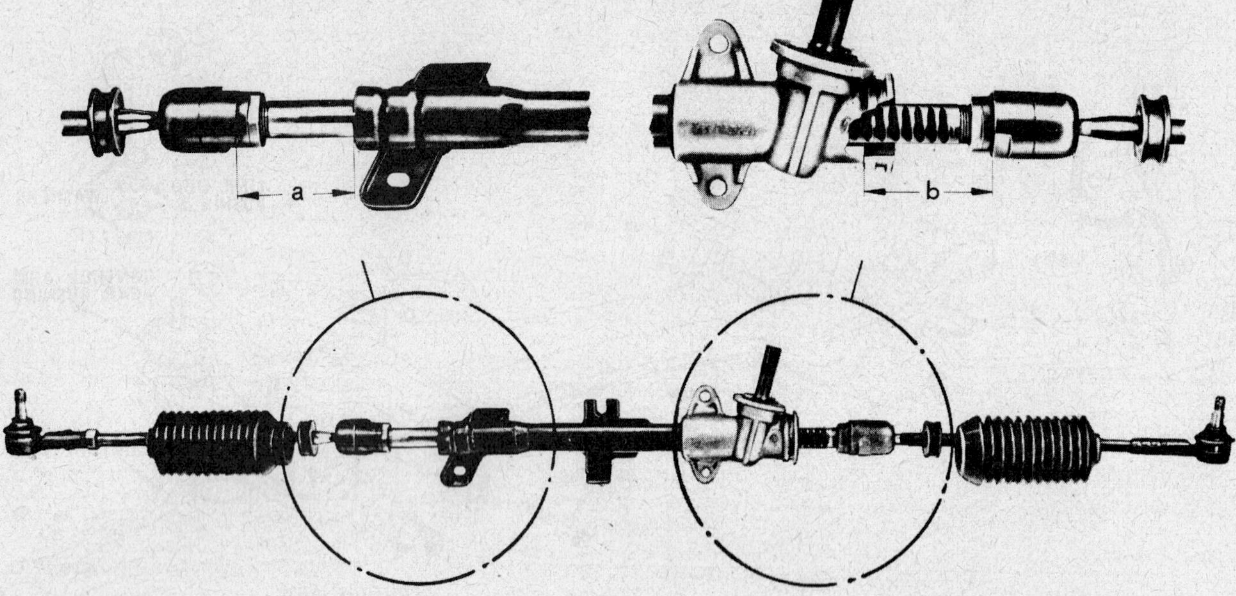

Fig. 6 Adjusting steering rack. Exc. Quantum

HUB & BEARING

REPLACE

REMOVAL

1. On Quantum models, remove strut assembly as outlined previously. On all other models, remove wheel bearing housing as outlined previously.
2. On all models, press hub from wheel bearing housing.
3. Remove brake dust shield from wheel bearing housing.
4. With a suitable puller, remove wheel bearing inner race from hub.
5. Remove retaining clips, then press bearing and outer race from wheel bearing housing. **Damage will occur to the wheel bearing as it is pressed from the housing. Therefore, it will be necessary to install a new bearing.**

INSTALLATION

1. Install outer retaining clip, then press new bearing and outer race into housing. Install inner retaining clip.
2. Press wheel bearing inner race onto hub assembly.

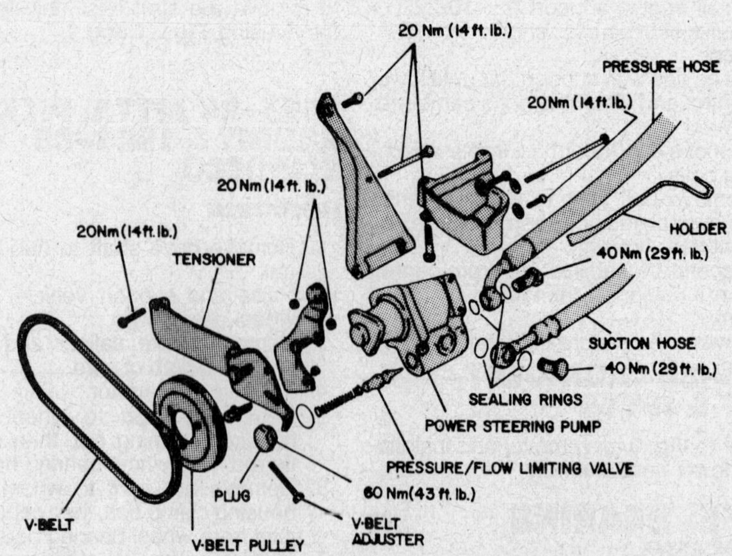

Fig. 7 Power steering pump replacement. Quantum W/4 cylinder engine

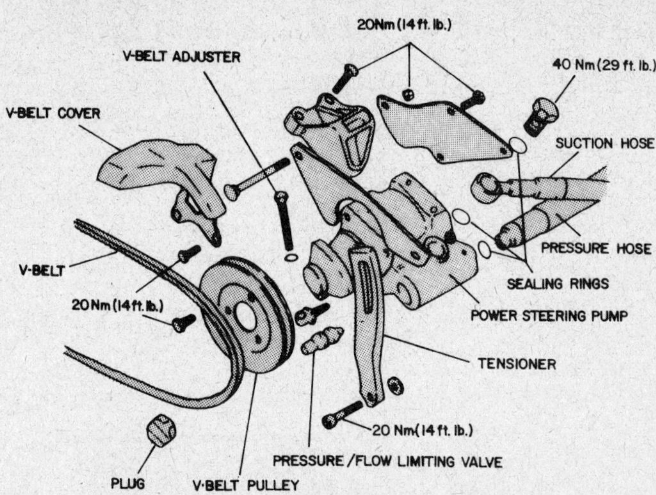

Fig. 8 Power steering pump replacement. Quantum W/5 cylinder engine

3. Install brake dust shield on wheel bearing housing.
4. Press hub assembly into wheel bearing housing.
5. Install strut or wheel bearing housing as outlined previously.

STEERING GEAR REPLACE

EXC. QUANTUM

Manual Steering

1. Raise and support front vehicle. Remove front wheels.
2. Remove universal joint to steering gear pinch bolt, then disconnect shaft from steering gear.
3. Position rubber boots over tie rods, then disconnect inner tie rods from steering gear.
4. Remove steering gear assembly retaining bolts and the steering gear from vehicle.
5. Reverse procedure to install and note the following:
   a. When installing the gear, position the rack so that dimension "a" is equal on both sides, **Fig. 5.**
   b. After the tie rods are connected, an adjustment is required. On automatic transaxle equipped vehicles, set dimension "a", **Fig. 6** to 2.638 inches and dimension "b", **Fig. 6,** to 2.716 inches. On manual transaxle equipped vehicles, set dimensions "a" and "b" to 2.716 inches, **Fig. 6.**
   c. Adjust toe setting as required.

Power Steering

1. Raise and support front of vehicle.
2. Remove front wheels.
3. Drain and discard power steering fluid.
4. Disconnect pressure hose at steering gear.
5. Disconnect return hose at steering gear.
6. Disconnect tie rod ends at steering arm.
7. Remove left tie rod end from tie rod.
8. Remove rear motor/transaxle mount.
9. Remove exhaust pipe.
10. Remove clamp bolt at steering shaft.
11. Remove nuts from steering gear mounting clamps and remove steering gear assembly.
12. Reverse procedure to install, torquing steering gear assembly mounting clamp nuts to 22 ft. lbs., then fill power steering reservoir and bleed system.

POWER STEERING PUMP REPLACE

EXC. QUANTUM

1. Raise and support vehicle.
2. Remove right front wheel.
3. Disconnect pressure, return, and feed hoses at pump.
4. Drain and discard power steering fluid.
5. Remove power steering belt by removing three power steering pulley attaching bolts, noting location of shims.
6. Remove power steering pump.
7. Using tools VW402 and VW411 or equivalents, press pulley hub from old pump.
8. Secure hub in vise with protective jaw covers.
9. Insert shaft of replacement pump into hub.
10. Using 3/8-16 bolt and heavy washer, pull hub onto shaft by tightening bolt until face of hub is level with face of shaft.
11. Reverse procedure to install, noting the following:
   a. With pump installed in vehicle, assemble pulley halves, shims, and fan belt onto hub and hand tighten nuts. Shims should be installed in position noted in removal.
   b. Using center hex in pump shaft, rotate pulley at least one complete turn.
   c. Torque nut closest to crankshaft pulley to 13 ft. lbs., rotate pulley 1/3 turn and torque nut closest to crankshaft pulley to 13 ft. lbs., and again rotate pulley 1/3 turn and torque final nut to 13 ft. lbs.
   d. Rotate pulley at least three turns to ensure that fan belt turns freely.
   e. Torque nuts to 13 ft. lbs.

QUANTUM

Refer to **Figs. 7 and 8** for power G-306 steering pump replacement procedure.

WHEEL ALIGNMENT SECTION

INDEX

CASTER ADJUSTMENT

The caster angle on these vehicles cannot be adjusted.

CAMBER ADJUSTMENT

FRONT

Exc. Quantum

To adjust camber, loosen the cam and through bolts at strut bracket. Rotate the upper cam bolt until specified camber angle is achieved. Torque cam bolt to 58 ft. lbs. Torque through bolt to 50 ft. lbs. on models with self-locking bolts, or 36 ft. lbs. on models less self-locking bolts.

Quantum

To adjust camber, loosen both ball joint mounting nuts on lower control arm and install tools US 4490 and VW 552 or equivalent. Tighten tensioner nut to break joint loose from control arm, then loosen tensioner. Adjust tensioner nut until wheel has desired camber angle, then torque mounting bolts to 47 ft. lbs. and remove tools.

REAR

Camber on rear axle assembly is not adjustable.

TOE SETTING ADJUSTMENT

FRONT

The toe setting is adjusted by the right tie rod only on all models except Quantum. On Quantum models, the toe setting is adjusted by both tie rods, however, centering tool 3075 or equivalent must be used. Install tool with bracket over mounting nut on left tie rod.

Loosen clamp and locknut on tie rod. Rotate tie rod until specified toe setting is obtained, then tighten locknut securely.

REAR

Toe setting or rear axle assembly is not adjustable.

VOLKSWAGEN VANAGON (Germany)

INDEX OF SERVICE OPERATIONS

General Engine Specifications

Year	Engine CID/cc	Fuel System	Bore & Stroke Inches (mm)	Comp. Ratio	Horsepower @ RPM	Torque Lbs. Ft. @ RPM	Normal Oil Pressure Lbs.
1983	4-120.2/2000 ① ②	Fuel Inj.	3.70 x 2.80 (94 x 71 mm)	7.3	67 @ 4200	101 @ 3000	28 ③
1983-85	4-117/1900 ② ④	Fuel Inj.	3.70 x 2.72 (94 x 69 mm)	8.6	82 @ 4800	106 @ 2600	28 ③
1986-87	4-129/2100 ④	Fuel Inj.	—	—	—	—	—

①—Air cooled.
②—For Vanagon models with diesel engine, refer to "Volkswagen - Exc. Vanagon" chapter.
③—With oil temperature at 176°F @ 2000 RPM.
④—Water cooled.

Alternator & Regulator Specifications

Year	Alternator					Regulator
	Model	Rated Hot Output		Output Test ①		
		Amps.	Volts	Amps @ RPM ②	Amps @ RPM ②	
1983-85	All	—	13.5-14.5	③	—	Integral
1986-87	—	—	—	—	—	—

—Not available.
①—Using load pile & battery cut-out to obtain values below, voltage must be within specifications.
②—Engine RPM.
③—16 amps. below rated output stamped on case @ 3000 RPM.

Starting Motor Specifications

Year	Engine	Model No.	Rotation ①	Brush Spring Tension Ounces	No Load Test			Torque Test		
					Amperes (Max.)	Volts	RPM (Min.)	Amperes (Max.)	Volts	Torque Ft. Lbs. (Min.)
1983	2000 ③ ⑤	0/001/211/005 ④	—	44.0	35-55	11.5	6000-9000	340-430	8.5	8.7
								290-380	7.5	7.2
	2000 ② ⑤	0/001/212/208 ④	—	41.0	35-55	11.5	6000-8000	320-410	8.5	9.0
								280-370	7.5	8.0
1983-85	1900 ⑥	—	—	—	—	—	—	—	—	—
1986-87	2100 ⑥	—	—	—	—	—	—	—	—	—

—Not available.
①—Viewed from drive end.
②—All w/manual transmission.
③—All w/auto. transmission.
④—Bosch part No.
⑤—Air cooled.
⑥—Water cooled.

Engine Tightening Specifications

*Torque specifications are for clean and lightly lubricated threads only. Dry or dirty threads produce increased friction which prevents accurate measurement of tightness.

Year	Engine cc	Spark Plugs Ft. Lbs.	Cylinder Head Bolts Ft. Lbs.	Crankcase Halves Ft. Lbs.	Rocker Arm Shaft Ft. Lbs.	Connecting Rod Ft. Lbs.	Drive Plate To Crankshaft Ft. Lbs.	Flywheel To Crankshaft Ft. Lbs.	Vibration Damper Or Pulley Ft. Lbs.
1983	2000①	22	22	②	11	25	65	80	22③
1983–85	1900④	14	25	⑤	18	33	65	80	25⑧
1986–87	2100④	—	—	—	—	—	—	—	—

①—Air cooled.
②—Inner crankcase nut, 14 ft. lbs.; outer nut, 22 ft. lbs. Apply sealing compound to thread contact area.
③—Fan hub to crankshaft.
④—Water cooled.
⑤—Inner crankcase nut 14 ft lbs.; outer nut, 25 ft. lbs. Apply sealing compound to thread contact area.

Pistons, Pins, Rings, Crankshaft & Bearings

Year	Engine	Piston Clearance Top of Skirt	Ring End Gap		Wristpin Diameter	Rod Bearings		Main Bearings			
			Comp.	Oil		Shaft Diameter	Bearing Clearance	Shaft Diameter	Bearing Clearance	Thrust on Bearing No.	Shaft Endplay
1983	2000①	.001–.002②	.016–.026	.010–.016	③	—	—	—	—	1	.003–.005
1983–85	1900④	.001–.002②	⑤	.010–.016	③	2.1646–2.1651	—	⑥	—	1	.003–.005
1986–87	2100④	—	—	—	—	—	—	—	—	—	—

①—Air cooled.
②—Measured at bottom of skirt at right angles to piston pin.
③—Slip fit. If too tight in piston, heat piston to approximately 140°F.
④—Water cooled.
⑤—Upper ring, .012–.018 inch; lower ring, .012–.020 inch.
⑥—No. 1: with blue dot, 2.3614–2.3618 inch; with red dot, 2.3610–2.3613 inch. No. 2, 2.1642–2.1649 inch; No. 3, with blue dot, 2.1645–2.1649 inch; with red dot, 2.1642–2.1645 inch. No. 4, 1.5741–1.5748 inch.

Valve Specifications

Year	Engine	Valve Lash		Valve Angles		Valve Spring Installed Height	Valve Spring Pressure Lbs. @ In.	Stem Clearance		Stem Diameter	
		Int.	Exh.	Seat	Face			Intake⑦	Exhaust⑦	Intake	Exhaust
1983	2000①	③	③	④	⑤⑥	1.142	177 @ 1.15	.018–.035	.014–.047	.311–.313	.349–.351
1983–85	1900②	③	③	45	45	—	—	.047⑧	.047⑧	.313–.314	.350–.351
1986–87	2100②	—	—	—	—	—	—	—	—	—	—

①—Air cooled.
②—Water cooled.
③—Hydraulic lifters, at TDC 2 turns after zero lash.
④—Intake 30°; exhaust 45°.
⑤—Intake 29° 30'; exhaust 45 °.
⑥—It is not recommended to machine work exhaust valves, hand lap only.
⑦—Valve guide wear measured at valve head with dial indicator.
⑧—With valve stem flush against valve guide end, rock valve back and forth against valve face installed dial indicator.

Front Wheel Alignment Specifications

Year	Model	Caster Angle, Degrees		Camber Angle, Degrees				Toe-In Inch	Toe-Out On Turn Degrees	
				Limits		Desired				
		Limits	Desired	Left	Right	Left	Right		Outer Wheel	Inner Wheel
1983–85	All	+7° to +7½°	+7¼°	−½° to +½°	−½ to +½°	0°	0°	.08	—	—

—Not available.

Rear Wheel Alignment Specifications

Year	Model	Camber Angle, Degrees		Toe, Degrees
		Limits	Desired	
1983--85	All	−⅓ to +¼	−⅚	−¾ to +⅙

Brake Specifications

Year	Model	Brake Drum Inside Dia.				Brake Disc Thickness		Wheel Cylinder Bore Dia. (Inches)			Master Cylinder Bore Diameter (Inches)
		Nominal Diameter (Inches)		Maximum Diameter (Inches) ①		Nominal Thickness (Inches)	Minimum Thickness (Inches) ①	Disc Brake	Front Drum Brake	Rear Drum Brake	
		Front	Rear	Front	Rear						
1983–85	All	—	9.921	—	9.960	.512	.453②	—	—	—	—

—Not available.
①—After machining.
②—Equal amounts must be removed from each side of disc during machining.

Differential Specifications

Year	Model	Pinion Bearing Preload			Differential Bearing Preload			Ring Gear	
		New Bearings Inch Lbs.	Used Bearings Inch Lbs.	Method	New Bearings Inch Lbs.	Used Bearings Inch Lbs.	Method	Backlash Inches	Method
1983–85	Vanagon	—	—	—	27-31	2.7–6.2	①	.006–.010	①
	Vanagon④	12.4	③	Shim	②	②	①	.006–.010	①

①—Threaded adjusting rings.
②—At least 1.8 in. lbs. greater than pinion bearing preload.
③—Measure pinion turning torque in lbs. before disassembly and tighten to the same torque upon installation.
④—Automatic transmission.

Capacity Data

Year	Engine or Model	Fuel Tank Gals.	Engine Oil Refill Qts.	Transaxle	
				Man. Transaxle Qts.	Auto. Transaxle Qts.
1983	2000 ① ⑦	18.4	②	③	④
1983–85	1900 ⑤ ⑦	18.4	⑥	③	④

①—Air cooled.
②—With filter, 3.7 quarts; without filter, 3.2 quarts.
③—With transaxle model No. 091, 3.7 quarts; 091/1, 3.2 quarts; 094, 4.2 quarts.
④—Dry fill, 6.4 qts.; refill, 3.2 qts.; final drive, 1.25 qts.
⑤—Water cooled.
⑥—With filter, 4.7 quarts; without filter, 4.2 quarts.
⑦—For capacity data on diesel engine models, refer to Volkswagen - "Exc. Vanagon" chapter.

ELECTRICAL SECTION

INDEX

STARTER
REPLACE

1. Disconnect battery ground cable.
2. Disconnect wires from starter solenoid.
3. While an assistant holds nut inside engine compartment, remove upper starter mounting bolt, then remove the lower nut and remove starter. **On vehicles with Bosch starters, inspect bushing in transmission case. If bushing is worn or damaged, it should be replaced.**
4. Reverse procedure to install.

IGNITION/STEERING LOCK, IGNITION SWITCH & LOCK CYLINDER
REPLACE

1. Remove turn signal and windshield wiper switch as outlined in this chapter.
2. Loosen ignition/steering lock housing clamp bolt. Turn ignition "On."
3. Using tool No. VW 267a clamp steering column coupling together.
4. Using a suitable puller, remove ignition/steering lock housing together with spacing sleeve.
5. To remove ignition switch, remove screw securing switch to bottom of ignition/steering lock and pull switch out.
6. To remove steering lock cylinder, refer to **Fig. 1.** Dimension a= 12 mm (1/2 inch); b= 10 mm (3/8 inch). Using a 1/8 inch drill, make a hole where specified then, using a piece of wire or a punch, press in lock pin and remove lock cylinder.
7. To reinstall, place ignition/steering lock housing over column tube.
8. Using tool No. VW420 drive spacing sleeve on column until clearance between top of spacing sleeve and top of steering shaft is 51 mm (2 inches) and tighten lock housing clamp bolt.
9. Reverse remaining procedure to install. Torque steering wheel nut to 36 ft. lbs.

HEADLIGHT SWITCH
REPLACE

1. Disconnect battery ground cable.
2. Reach behind instrument cluster cover and lift up cover by recesses in lower edge of cover.
3. Remove cover and instrument cluster retaining screws.
4. Disconnect wiring harness connector to headlamp switch and remove by depressing lock tabs on sides of switch.
5. Reverse procedure to install.

STOP LIGHT SWITCH
REPLACE

Switches are located on master cylinder. Switch is accessible after removing instrument cluster.

1. Determine which switch is defective (this is accomplished by disconnecting wiring on one switch at a time and depressing the brake pedal. If brake lights are operative, reconnect wiring and disconnect other switch, recheck operation).
2. Disconnect battery ground cable.
3. Disconnect wiring from defective switch noting position of each wire, then remove switch.
4. Remove sealing washer from old switch and reinstall on new switch (if equipped) and install new switch. Torque to 14 ft. lbs.
5. Reconnect wiring and battery ground cable. Check operation of brake lights and brake warning light.
6. Bleed brakes if necessary.

NEUTRAL SAFETY SWITCH
REPLACE

The neutral safety switch is located under the housing at the base of the shift lever.

1. Disconnect battery ground cable and remove shifter knob after loosening setscrew.
2. Remove shifter cover retaining screws and the cover.
3. Remove 2 retaining screws, disconnect wiring harness connector, and remove switch.
4. Reverse procedure to install, then check that engine only starts with selector in park or neutral position.
5. Adjust switch as needed by loosening retaining screws and moving switch body.

TURN SIGNAL & WINDSHIELD WIPER/WASHER SWITCH
REPLACE

The windshield wiper/washer switch is incorporated into the steering column with an operating lever like the turn signal switch. The three switches are removed as a unit but can be replaced individually.

1. Disconnect battery ground cable.
2. Remove steering column upper and lower shrouds.
3. Pull off steering wheel cover and remove horn wires.
4. Remove nut and washer securing steering wheel, center wheel and remove.
5. Remove three screws securing turn signal and windshield/washer switches to ignition/steering lock housing flange.
6. Disconnect wiring and remove switch.
7. Reverse procedure to install, noting the following; lubricate turn signal cancelling ring with multi-purpose grease. Torque steering wheel nut to 36 ft. lbs.

SPEEDOMETER & INSTRUMENT CLUSTER
REPLACE

1. Disconnect battery ground cable.
2. Reach behind cluster cover and insert fingertips into recesses. Pull cluster cover up and away from dashboard.
3. Remove hazard warning switch and brake warning light housing.
4. Remove four instrument cluster retaining screws and pull cluster rearward.
5. Remove speedometer cable and wiring connector. Remove cluster.
6. Reverse procedure to install.

WINDSHIELD WIPER MOTOR
REPLACE

Refer to **Fig. 2** for wiper motor removal and installation.

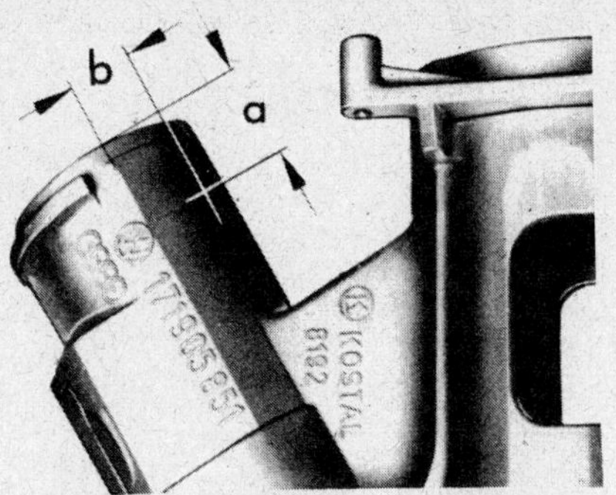

Fig. 1 Drilling hole in steering lock housing.

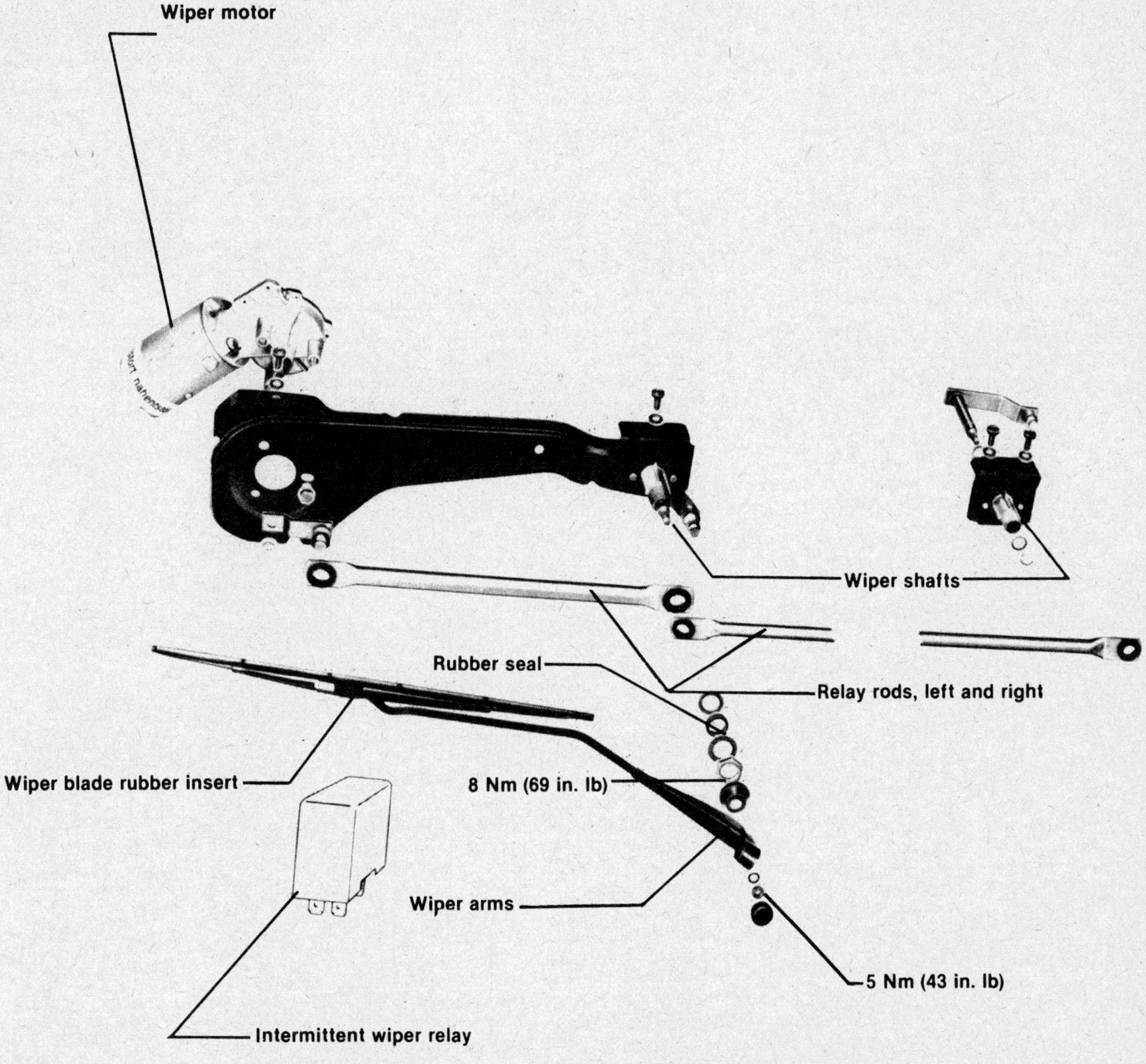

Wiper motor

Wiper shafts

Rubber seal

Relay rods, left and right

Wiper blade rubber insert

8 Nm (69 in. lb)

Wiper arms

5 Nm (43 in. lb)

Intermittent wiper relay

Fig. 2 Wiper motor & transmission assembly

AIR COOLED ENGINE SECTION

INDEX

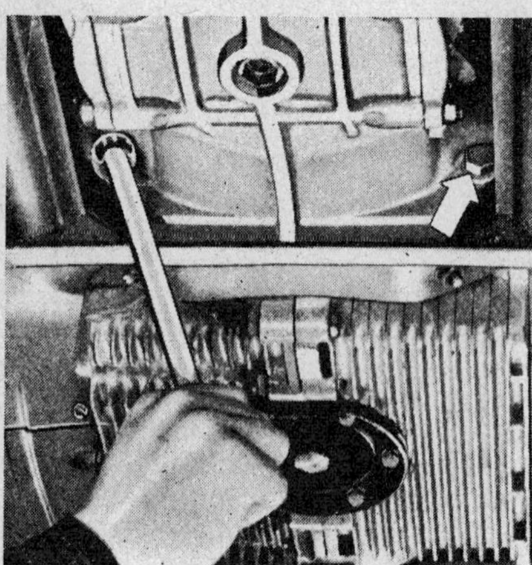

Fig. 1 Removing lower transmission to engine attaching bolts

ENGINE

REPLACE

1. Disconnect battery ground cable, then remove rear body plate.
2. Remove air cleaner, throttle linkage, air flow sensor and intake duct.
3. Disconnect wiring from engine, alternator, fuel injection and starter.
4. Disconnect heater fan hoses. Then remove oil filler pipe and fuel injection control unit connector.
5. Disconnect vacuum hoses and fuel lines.
6. On models equipped with automatic transmission, remove plug from transmission housing and remove three bolts securing torque converter to driven plate. Turn crankshaft to position each bolt in the opening.
7. On models equipped with automatic transmission, remove ATF dipstick and filler tube.
8. On all models, pull accelerator cable free of engine.
9. Remove engine rear and side cover plates, then remove heater control cables and heat exchanger to connectors.
10. Remove two upper engine mounting bolts.
11. Using a suitable support, place it under transmission to support it after and during engine removal.
12. Remove two lower engine mounting bolts, **Fig. 1.**
13. Using a floor jack, raise engine enough so engine weight is off engine carrier bolts and remove bolts.
14. Lower jack slightly until transmission weight is now resting on transmission support.
15. Separate engine from transmission. Pull engine assembly back far enough to ensure the engine is separated completely from transmission. On Automatic Transmission models, install a suitable restraining device to prevent the torque converter from falling out of bellhousing.
16. Remove engine.
17. Reverse procedure to install.

ENGINE SERVICE

DISASSEMBLE

1. Remove all remaining external parts from engine.
2. On models equipped with manual transmission, remove clutch and flywheel assembly. On models equipped with automatic transmission, remove driven plate and flywheel.
3. Unbolt muffler and heat exchange boxes.
4. Unclip valve covers then, remove rocker arm assemblies and pushrods as follows:
   a. Remove pushrod tube retaining wire, **Fig. 2.**
   b. Store rocker arm assemblies with homemade retaining pins in stud holes.
   c. Twist pushrod tubes and slide out.
   d. Remove air deflectors under cylinder barrels.
   e. Remove cam followers.
5. Remove all eight cylinder head nuts—start from outside corners and work to middle to prevent distortion.
6. Lift off cylinder heads, **Fig. 3.**
7. Mark cylinder number on each barrel, then slide off cylinder barrels, **Fig. 4.**
8. Remove all eight piston pin circlips. If ridge has formed on outside of circlip groove, scrape clean before removing pins.
9. Tap out piston pins carefully and remove pistons—warm piston slightly if pin is tight.
10. Unbolt oil cooler and oil strainer plate with screen.
11. Remove all hex nuts and bolts holding crankcase halves together. (Bus only: don't forget one behind flywheel and on side of case).
12. Remove six large sealing nuts around cylinder openings.

Fig. 2 Removing pushrod tube retaining clips. Vanagon

13. Remove oil pump retaining nuts and slide out housing, **Fig. 5,** then the insert from housing, **Fig. 6.**
14. Separate crankcase halves, then lift out camshaft and crankshaft, **Fig. 7.**
15. Unscrew oil control valve plugs: slide out pistons and springs.
16. Remove connecting rod nuts and separate caps.
17. Remove crankshaft circlip and press off gears with bearing "splitter" or suitable pieces of "flatstock," **Fig. 7. All parts should be rinsed clean in fresh solvent and blown dry with compressed air before reassembly. Check all parts according to dimensions given in specification section.**

ASSEMBLE

1. Dip connecting rod bearing shells in clean oil and seat in connecting rod "halves"—oil under bearing shell will help "squeeze out" small particles of dirt and doesn't affect bearing clearance.
2. Install connecting rods onto crankshaft, noting the following:
   a. Install connecting rod so stamping on big end faces up with rod in installed position.
   b. Install cap, ensuring that stamping on cap is aligned with stamping on big end of rod. **Tap assembly lightly to avoid pinching bearing when torquing retaining nuts.**
   c. Install retaining nuts and torque to 25 ft. lbs.

1. Cam follower (8)
2. Exhaust valve (4)
3. Intake valve (4)
4. Pushrod tube (8)
5. Exhaust valve guide (4)
6. Intake valve guide (4)
7. Cylinder head (2)
8. Washer (16)
9. M 10 nut (16)
10. Oil deflector ring (8)
11. Valve spring (8)
12. Spring retainer (8)
13. Valve keeper (16)
14. Spring washer (8)
15. M 7 nut (8)
16. Black sealing ring (8)
17. Pushrod (8)
18. White sealing ring (8)
19. Deflector plate (2)
20. Washer (4)
21. M 6 fillister head screw
22. Washer (2)
23. M 5 fillister head screw
24. Support (8)
25. Exhaust rocker arm (4)
26. Thrust washer (discontinued in early 1974) (8)
27. Spacer spring (4)
28. Rocker shaft (4)
29. Intake rocker arm (4)
30. Adjusting screw (8)
31. M 8 nut (8)
32. Pushrod tube retaining wire (2)
33. Cylinder head cover gasket (2)
34. Cylinder head cover (2)

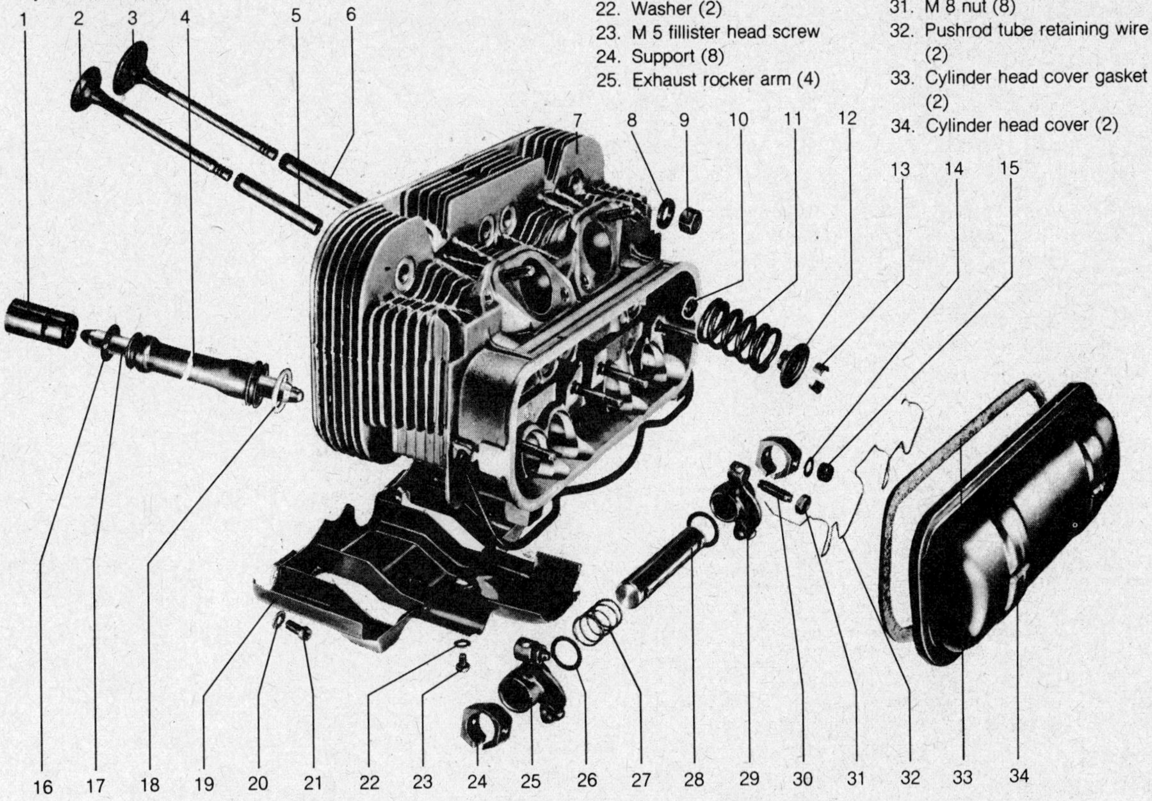

Fig. 3 Cylinder head assembly, exploded view

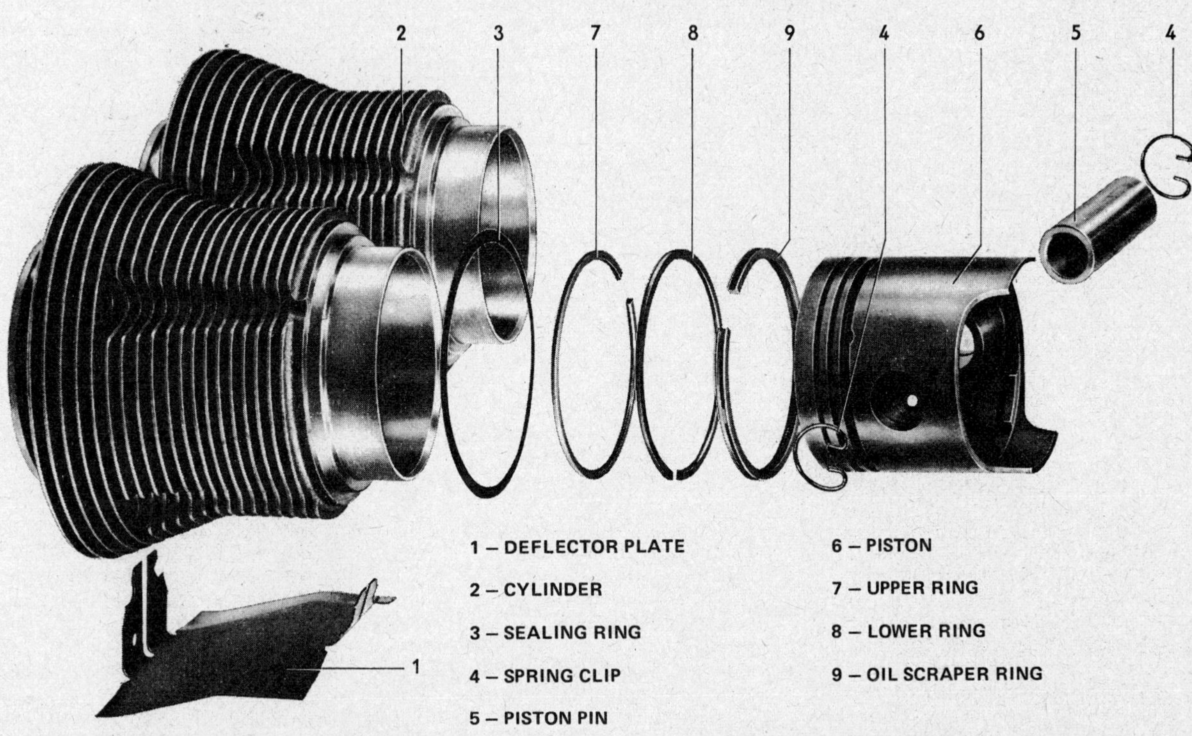

Fig. 4 Piston & cylinder assembly, exploded view

1. Oil filter mounting flange
2. M 8 nut (2)
3. Spring washer (2)
4. Oil cooler seal (2)
5. Oil pressure switch
6. Breather seal
7. Oil breather
8. Oil pressure control valve plunger*
9. Oil pressure control valve spring*
10. Sealing ring*
11. Control valve plug*
12. Rubber bellows
13. Oil pump bearing plate
14. Oil pump driven gear
15. Oil pump drive gearshaft
16. Oil filler pipe
17. Oil dipstick
18. Oil filler clamp
19. Oil filler with cover
20. Oil cooler
21. Washer (3)
22. Spring washer (3)
23. M 6 nut (3)
24. Sealing ring
25. Plug
26. Oil filter
27. Oil strainer gasket (2)
28. Oil strainer
29. Oil strainer cover
30. Drain plug seal
31. Oil drain plug
32. Relief valve plug
33. Sealing ring
34. Oil pressure relief valve spring
35. Oil pressure relief valve plunger
36. Filter flange gasket
37. Oil filler pipe gasket
38. Oil pump gasket
39. Spring washer (2)
40. M 8 nut (2)
41. Oil pump O-ring
42. M 6 self-locking nut
43. Spring washer (4)
44. Oil pump housing
45. Spring washer (4)
46. M 8 nut (4)

* Discontinued after November 1975.

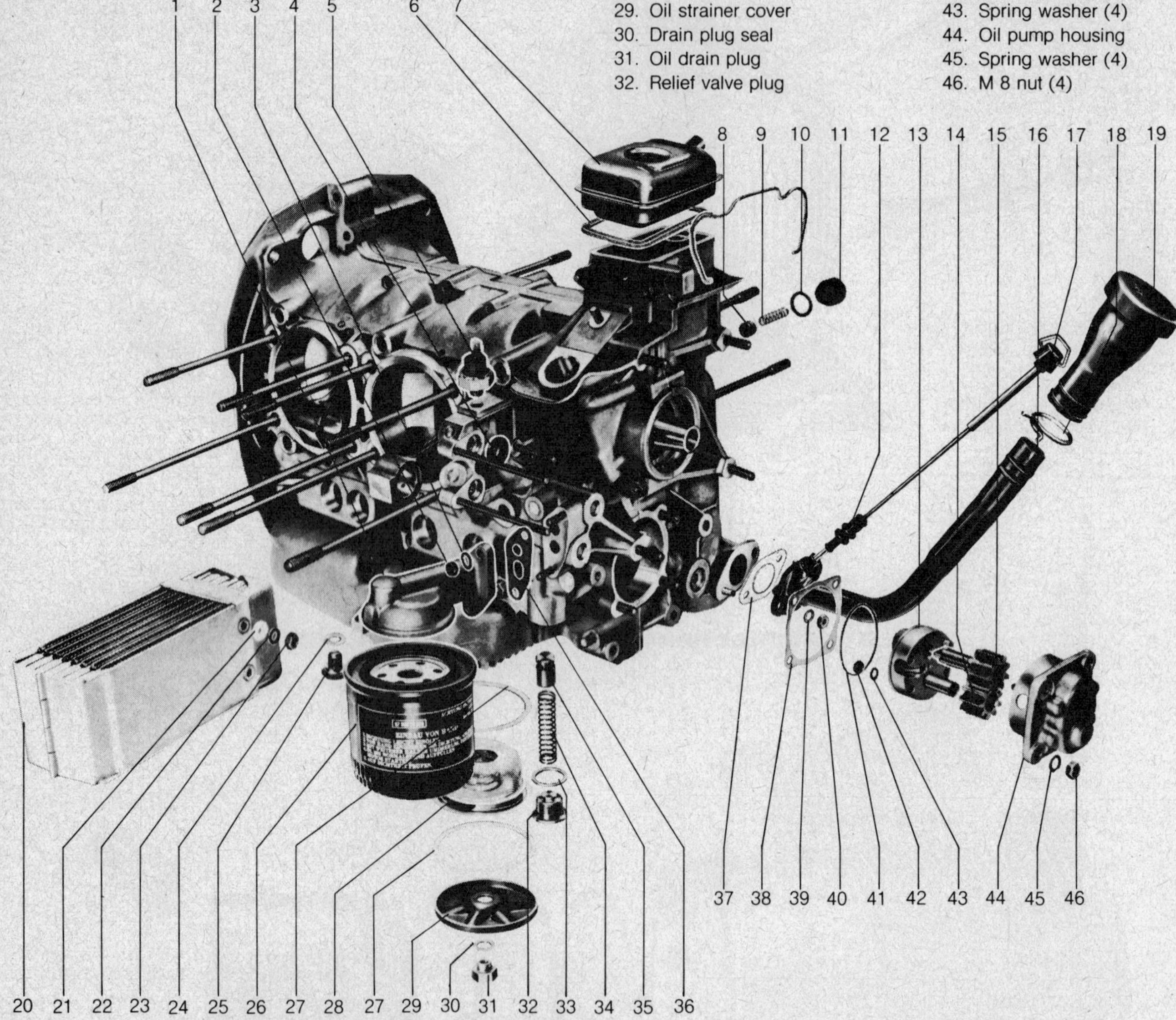

Fig. 5 Engine crankcase assembly

3. Dip new main bearings in clean engine oil. Install large bearing without thrust shoulder on crankshaft journal beside cam gear location.
4. Heat gears and slide on crankshaft in the following order: cam gear, spacer, distributor drive gear, and circlip.
5. Slide small main bearing onto crankshaft (also install oil "slinger" and Woodruff key or O-ring on crankshaft).
6. Slide on shouldered thrust bearing behind flywheel mating surface.
7. Install small dowel pins in main bearing saddles in left-hand crankcase half.
8. Install two-piece main bearing in "middle" saddle of both case halves.
9. Hold #1 and #2 connecting rods and lay crankshaft assembly into left-hand crankcase half. Number 3 and 4 rods should hang through cylinder openings. **Rotate bearings to seat dowel pins before continuing.**
10. Install all six camshaft bearing shells into case (dip in oil first).
11. Lay camshaft in case with mark on cam gear tooth between marks on crankshaft gear teeth (marks ensure correct valve timing), **Fig. 8.** If camshafts with different pitch circle radius numbers (on side of gear) are available, use shaft with largest number that will fit without binding when crankshaft is turned.
12. Position existing endplay shims and crankshaft seals in left case half.

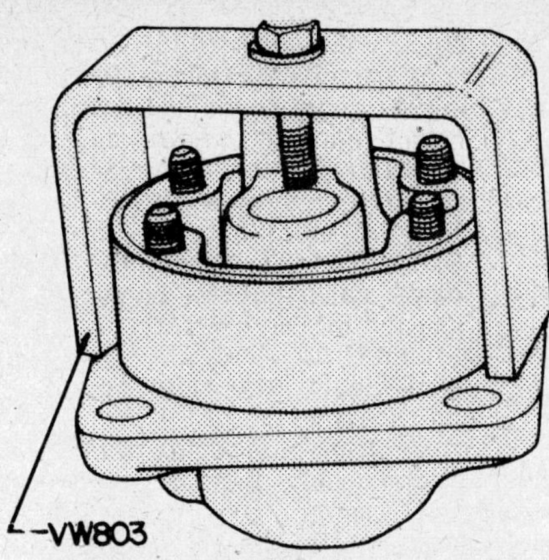

Fig. 6 Oil pump insert removal

Fig. 8 Cam & crankshaft timing mark alignment

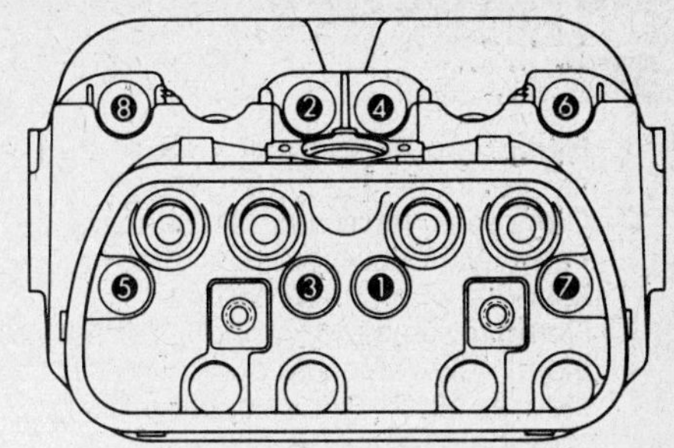

Fig. 9 Cylinder head tightening sequence

13. Torque 6 large sealing nuts to specifications, then torque remaining case retaining nuts to specifications. Check that crankshaft rotates freely.
14. Install flywheel. Torque bolts to 80 ft. lbs.
15. To check endplay:
    a. Check crankshaft endplay with dial gauge and holder or with feeler gauges through cylinder #3 opening.
    b. If endplay measurement is incorrect, remove flywheel and seal. Install different size shims to bring endplay within specifications.
    c. Be sure to install seal and retorque flywheel after adjustment is correct.
16. Use ring expander to install rings on pistons—manufacturer's markings should face toward combustion chamber.
17. Install pistons on connecting rods: arrows on piston crown should face toward flywheel (do not forget all eight piston pin circlips).
18. Use piston ring compressor to install cylinder barrels—seat barrels against crankcase without sealing gasket (gaskets are still provided in some overhaul kits, but have been discontinued to improve sealing).
19. Install cylinder heads.
20. Torque cylinder head nuts to specifications in sequence shown in **Fig. 9. Over-torquing cylinder head nuts causes cylinder head leakage; thermal expansion of aluminum head increases torque and can pull out studs or "dig in" barrel.**
21. Install air deflector shields, cam followers, and pushrod tubes.
22. Install pushrods and rocker arm assemblies. Adjust valve clearance between adjuster and valve stem end to specifications at TDC position.
23. Install distributor drive gear with shims so that distance from top of drive gear to case surface is 1.76 in. (44.6 mm).
24. With No. 1 piston at TDC on compression stroke, install distributor drive so that slot is at 12° angle to engine centerline. Small segment should be toward coil.
25. Install cooling air ducts and heat exchange boxes.
26. Fit fan housing (with alternator).
27. Install fan hub: 22 ft. lbs. (3 mkg) and fan: 14 ft. lbs. (2 mkg).
28. Install fan belt—adjust belt tension. (1/2 inch deflection).
29. Bolt on muffler.

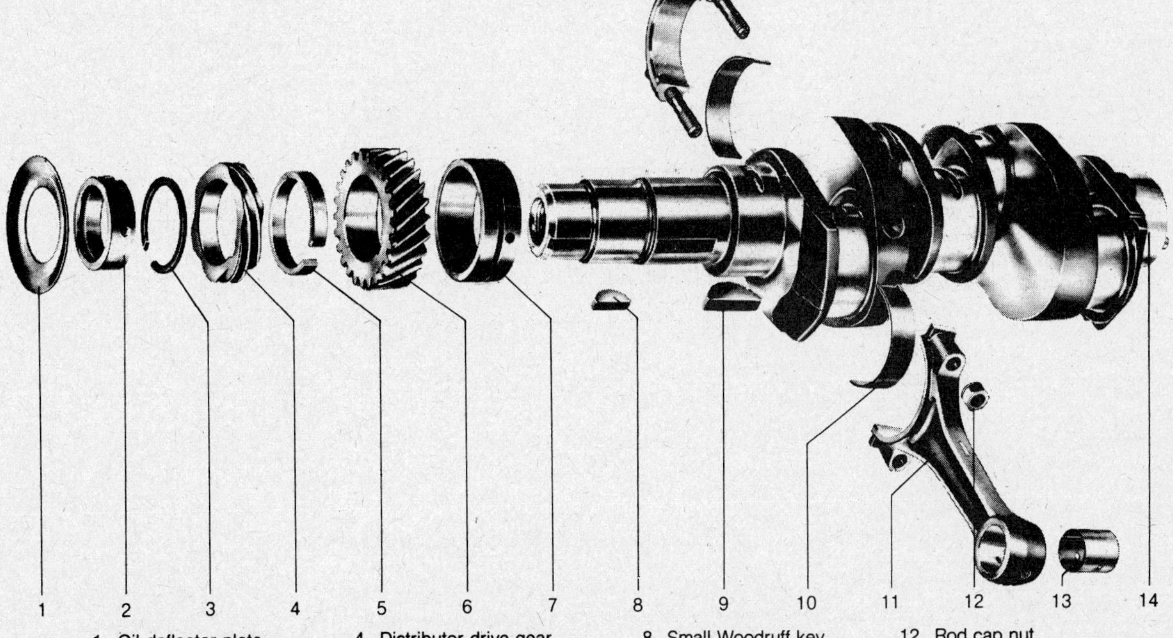

1. Oil deflector plate
2. No. 4 main bearing
3. Circlip
4. Distributor drive gear
5. Spacer
6. Crankshaft gear
7. No. 3 main bearing
8. Small Woodruff key
9. Large Woodruff key
10. Rod bearing shell
11. Connecting rod
12. Rod cap nut
13. Piston pin bushing
14. Crankshaft

Fig. 7 Crankshaft assembly, exploded view

CYLINDER HEAD SERVICE

1. Remove cylinder heads from engine as previously described, **Fig. 3.**
2. Compress valve springs with suitable valve spring compressor and remove keepers with small magnet.
3. Remove retainers, springs and valves.
4. Insert new valve into guide until end of stem is flush with top of guide, and check clearance as follows:
   a. Install a dial indicator on cylinder head, suitable to measure total deflection of valve head.
   b. Push valve head as far as it will go toward spark plug opening, then "zero" dial indicator.
   c. Push valve head as far as it will go away from spark plug opening, and measure total deflection.
   d. If deflection is greater than 0.047 inch, valve guide must be replaced. **Specifications given in 4d are wear limit specifications. For proper service, valve guides should be replaced if worn more than 0.010 inch above minimum specification.**
5. To remove worn guides, cut thread in rocker arm end of guide about 1/2 inch deep using 3/8 inch or 10 mm tap: now install soft threaded rod in guide and place old piston pin around rod; place flat washer on wrist pin and screw on nut until valve guide has been extracted into pin. **Do not hammer out guides from combustion chamber side as guide end can "mushroom" and enlarge hole in cylinder head so that new guide does not fit tightly.**
6. Press in new guides from rocker shaft side, supporting cylinder plate in supporting cylinder plate in suitable angle plate. Use at least 1 ton to seat guide, but do not exceed 2 tons of force. **Oversize guides are available but require special machine work for proper fit.**
7. Check inside diameter of installed guide with reamer (standard size guides usually do not require reaming).
8. Now install seat re-facing pilot in valve guide.
9. Reface valve seat to 45° angle and check with seat runout gauge if possible (30° angle on intake seats).
10. Correct seat width if necessary, using a 15° cutter, to the following specifications: Intake valve seat, 1.8-2.2 mm (.070-.088 inch); exhaust valve seat, 2.5-3.5 mm (.060-.098 inch).
11. Reface valve contact angle to 45° (30° for intake valves) and reface stem end.
12. Valve "margin" should be at least .020 inch (.5 mm).
13. Check spark plug threads and install heli-coil inserts if threads are damaged (use bushing inserts only for emergency repairs with engine in car).
14. Make sure heads and parts are rinsed clean in fresh solvent. Oil valve stems and place in guides (although valve seals are included in some repair kits, do not use them on horizontally-opposed air-cooled engines).
15. Install valve springs (if spring is progressively wound, place closely wound coils next to head).
16. Install retainers, compress springs and install valve keepers.

WATER COOLED GASOLINE ENGINE SECTION

INDEX

Page No.

VALVES ADJUST

1. Remove valve cover, then back out adjusting screws on rocker arms until ball shaped end is flush with surface of arm.
2. Rotate crankshaft until No. 1 cylinder is at TDC, indicated by mark on rotor in alignment with mark on distributor housing.
3. Turn adjusting screws in until they just contact valve stems, then continue to turn screws in an additional 2 turns and tighten locknuts.
4. Rotate crankshaft 180° and adjust valves of next cylinder.
5. Repeat procedure until all cylinders are adjusted.

PUSHROD TUBES REPLACE

1. Remove valve cover and rocker arm shaft and pull pushrod out.
2. Remove lower cover plate, then pull pushrod tube out using suitable pliers or a screwdriver.
3. Reverse procedure to install, using new O-rings. Install tube with seam facing upward and the small end toward cylinder head.

ENGINE DISASSEMBLE

Refer to **Fig. 1** to disassemble engine, noting the following:

1. Use puller VW-228b or equivalent to remove distributor driveshaft.
2. Lock flywheel with tool No. VW-215c or equivalent when removing flywheel.
3. Remove torque converter drive plate by locking plate with tool No. VW-802 or equivalent and pressing plate off with an M18 1.5 60 bolt at least 1.77 inches long.
4. Remove triple V-belt pulley after locking pulley with tool No. 3102 or equivalent. Insert large pin of tool into small hole in pulley and small pin of tool into right engine mount bolt hole.
5. Prior to removing pistons or cylinder sleeves, scribe matching numbers on pistons and sleeves for assembly reference.
6. Remove cylinder sleeves using tool No. 3092 or equivalent, with piston at TDC position.
7. Remove piston pins using tool No. 3091 or equivalent.
8. Remove circlip from crankshaft using tool No. VW-161a or equivalent.
9. Remove distributor drive gear and crankshaft timing gear from crankshaft using tool No. VW-402 or equivalent.
10. Remove crankshaft pilot bearing using tool US-8028, US-1039 and US-1039/3 or equivalents.
11. Remove valve springs using tools US-1020 and US-1020/1 or equivalents.

ENGINE ASSEMBLE

Refer to **Fig. 1** to assemble engine, noting the following:

1. Position No. 1 cylinder at TDC when installing distributor driveshaft. Install driveshaft with offset slot facing bolt and small segment facing water pump.
2. When assembling crankcase halves, first tighten M8 nut indicated in **Fig. 2,** then tighten all M10 nuts, and finally the remaining M8 nuts.
3. On models equipped with single V-belt pulley, install crankshaft front oil

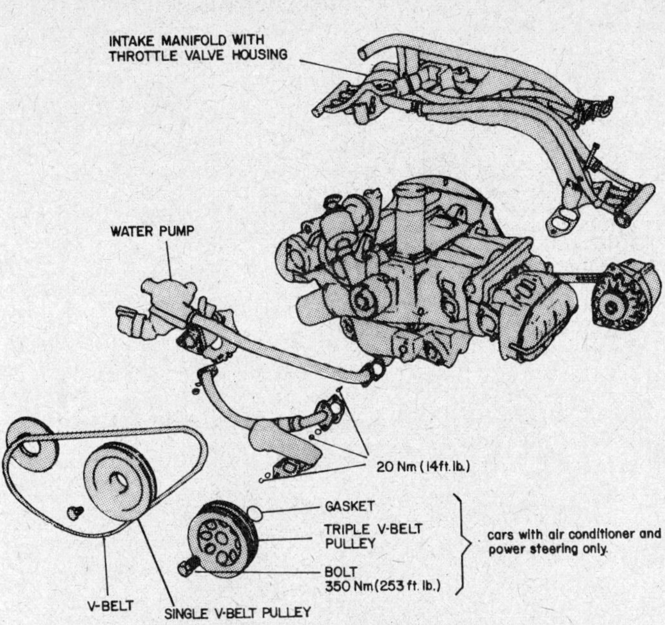

Fig. 1 Engine disassembly & assembly. Vanagon (1 of 7)

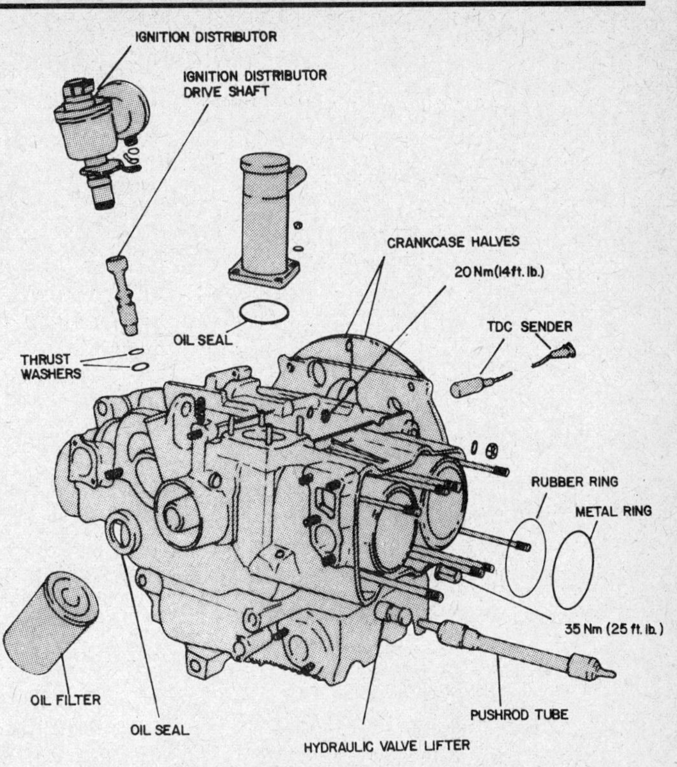

Fig. 1 Engine disassembly & assembly. Vanagon (2 of 7)

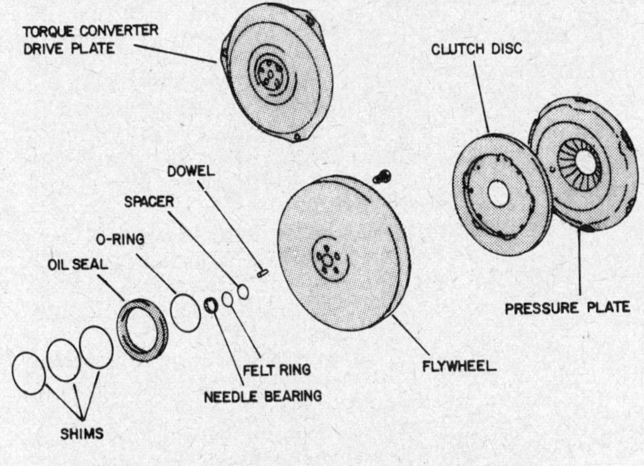

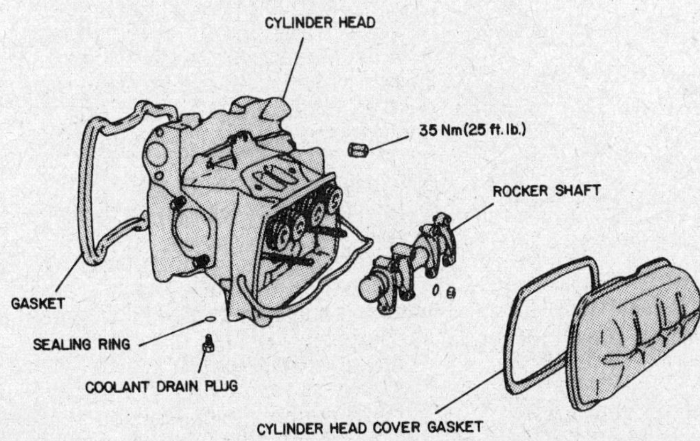

Fig. 1 Engine disassembly & assembly. Vanagon (3 of 7)

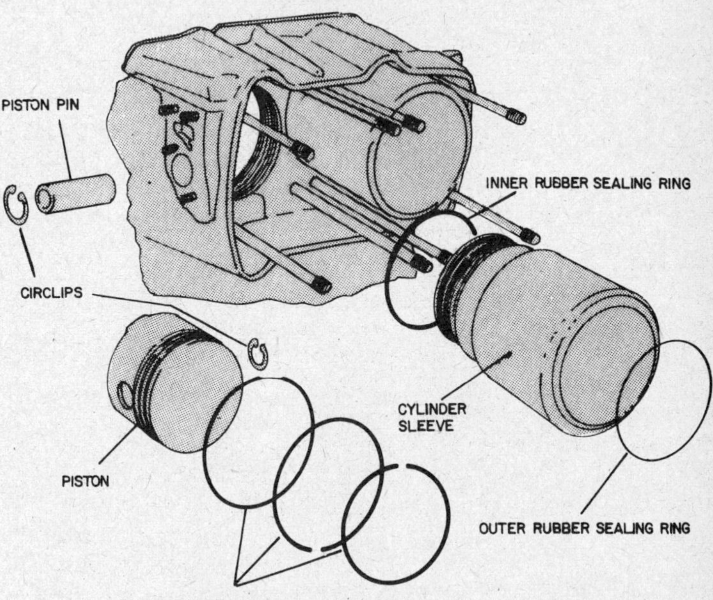

Fig. 1 Engine disassembly & assembly. Vanagon (4 of 7)

seal using tool No. 3088 and pulley bolt without washer, then tighten bolt with washer until stop.

4. On models equipped with triple V-belt pulley, install crankshaft front oil seal using tool No. 3088 and pulley bolt without washer and tighten bolt until stop.
5. Install crankshaft rear oil seal using tool No. VW-191 or equivalent.
6. Drive TDC sender into place using a piston pin and a plastic hammer, being careful to avoid damaging inner ring.

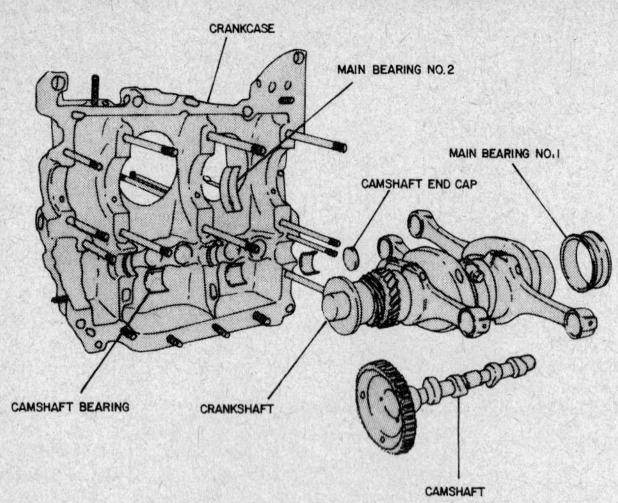

Fig. 1 Engine disassembly & assembly. Vanagon (5 of 7)

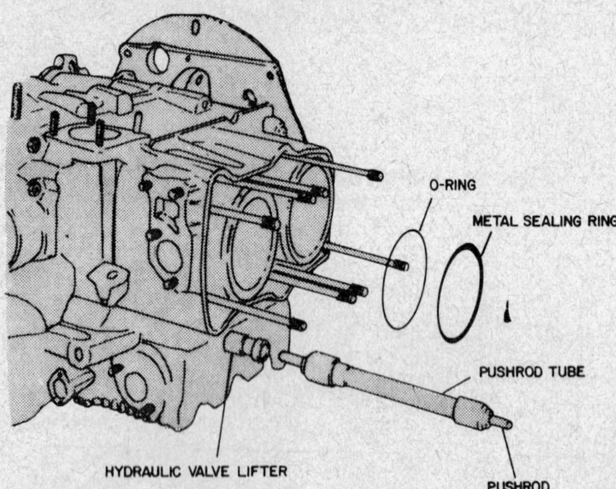

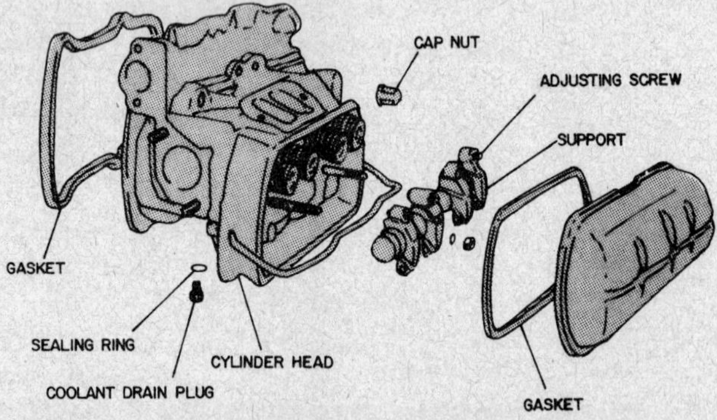

Fig. 1 Engine disassembly & assembly. Vanagon (7 of 7)

Fig. 1 Engine disassembly & assembly. Vanagon (6 of 7)

CONNECTING ROD BEARING
MAIN BEARING NO.3
CRANKSHAFT
MAIN BEARING NO.4
CRANKSHAFT PILOT BEARING
SPACER
OIL THRUST RING
CIRCLIP
CRANKSHAFT TIMING GEAR
CONNECTING ROD NUTS
DISTRIBUTOR DRIVE GEAR
CONNECTING ROD

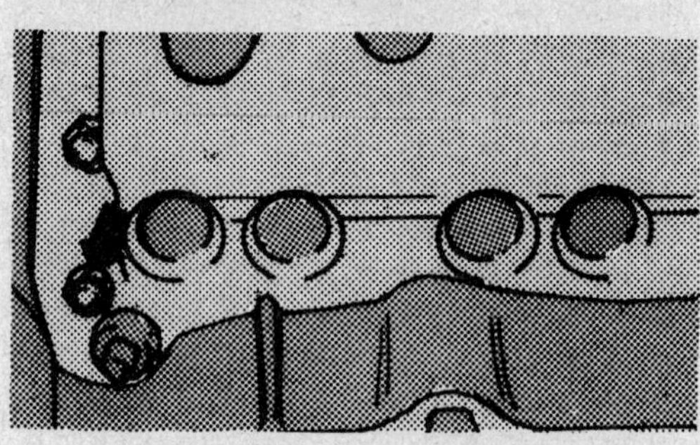

Fig. 2 Assembling crankcase halves. Vanagon

7. Install pistons with stamped arrow on piston head facing flywheel.
8. Install piston rings as shown in **Fig. 3,** ensuring "Top" mark on rings faces top of piston. Stagger ring gaps 180°.
9. Install piston pins using tool No. 3091 or equivalent.
10. Install camshaft with mark on camshaft gear tooth between marks on crankshaft gear teeth.
11. Install circlip onto crankshaft using tools VW-428a, VW-471 and VW-415a or equivalents.
12. Install distributor drive gear and crankshaft timing gear using tools VW-428a and VW-415a or equivalents. Heat gears to approximately 175°F prior to installation.
13. Ensure numbers on connecting rod and cap match when installing connecting rods. Forged marks on rods must face up during installation.
14. Install valve springs using tools US-1020 and US-1020/1 or equivalents.
15. Install pushrod tubes with seam facing upward and small end toward cylinder head.
16. Install cylinder head as follows:
    a. Install new water jacket gasket on crankcase and apply a narrow bead of suitable sealant to center of gasket.
    b. Tighten cylinder head attaching nut No. 1, **Fig. 4,** just enough to allow installation of remaining nuts.
    c. Apply suitable sealant to nuts and torque in sequence, **Fig. 4,** to 10 ft. lbs.
    d. Ensure pushrod tubes are properly seated, then torque cylinder head nuts in sequence to 25 ft. lbs.
17. Ensure valve lifters are properly bled prior to installation. If lifters can be compressed using hand force, they must be bled as follows:
    a. Disassemble lifter, **Fig. 5.**
    b. Fill valve body with oil up to bleed hole.
    c. Install plunger spring, then the plunger with ball check valve, spring and spring retainer. Depress assembly while simultaneously opening ball check valve with scribe.
    d. Insert pushrod in socket and slowly press together with valve guide or section of a pushrod in a suitable vise or press until lock ring can be installed, then install the lock ring. Ensure bore faces upward when compressing lifter.

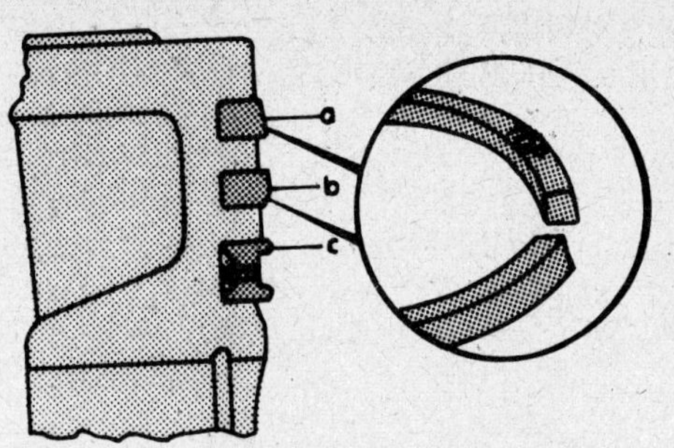

Fig. 3 Positioning piston rings. Vanagon

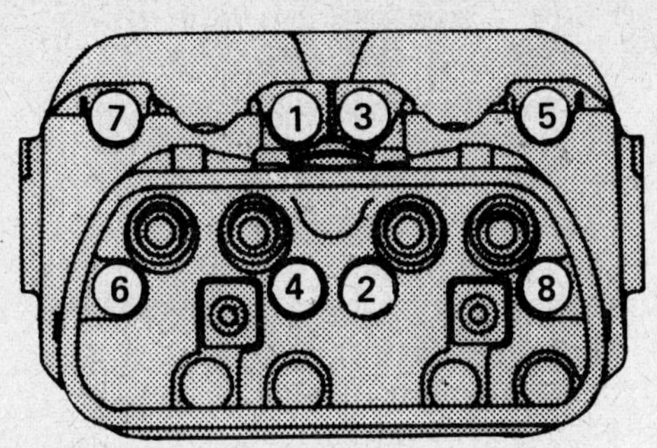

Fig. 4 Cylinder head cap nut torque sequence. Vanagon

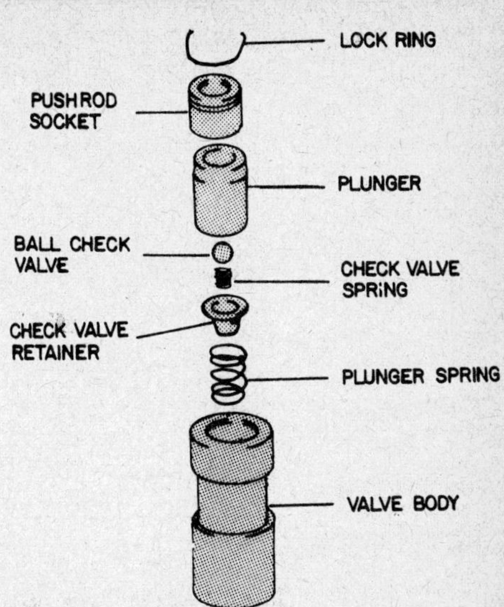

Fig. 5 Hydraulic valve lifter exploded view. Vanagon

DIESEL ENGINE SECTION

ENGINE REPLACE

1. Disconnect battery ground cable and remove air cleaner and lower engine cover.
2. Remove coolant expansion tank cap and drain cooling system.
3. Disconnect coolant hoses from engine, hoses between engine and oil cooler, and hoses to vacuum pump.
4. Disconnect wiring harness connectors to engine accessories, oil pressure and temperature sending units, glow plugs and fuel shut-off solenoid, then disconnect harness from clamps and remove from engine.
5. Disconnect fuel supply and return lines from injection pump, and plug lines and open fittings.
6. Remove coolant expansion tank, oil filler cap and dipstick.
7. Disconnect accelerator cable from pump lever and remove cable and bracket. Disconnect cold start cable from pump and remove from bracket.
8. Remove nuts from left and right rear engine mount bolts, leaving bolts in place.
9. Remove seven engine to transaxle mounting bolts, engine support member retaining bolts and support member.
10. Support engine and transaxle assembly using a suitable hoist and adapter No. 3058 or equivalent.
11. Remove nuts from left and right front engine mount bolts, remove front and rear mount bolts, and lower engine until it can be separated from transaxle.
12. Support transaxle with cradle 785/1B or equivalent, then remove engine.
13. Reverse procedure to install, adjusting angle of engine to transaxle prior to installation.

ENGINE SERVICE

Refer to the Diesel Engine Section in the "Volkswagen, Exc. Vanagon" chapter for complete service procedures on this engine.

CLUTCH & TRANSMISSION SECTION

INDEX

CLUTCH

REPLACE

1. Remove engine as previously described.
2. Carefully unbolt clutch pressure plate from flywheel, keep plate parallel to flywheel until spring tension is released.
3. Remove clutch disk and replace if worn or oil-soaked.
4. Check friction surface on flywheel and replace if scored or blue.
5. Check pilot needle bearing in crankshaft (in "gland nut" on convertible engines) and replace if needles are missing or feel rough.
6. Place a dab of wheel bearing grease in pilot needle bearing.
7. Seat clutch disc against flywheel friction surface, using an old mainshaft to center the clutch disc. If disc is not centered properly, engine will not bolt up to transmission housing.
8. Place pressure plate on flywheel and install bolts finger tight. Keep plate parallel to flywheel while tightening bolts and torque to 18 ft. lbs. (2 1/2 mkg).
9. Remove clutch "pilot" and reinstall engine. If replacement pressure plate has tensioning clips, be sure to remove the clips with a screwdriver before reinstalling the engine.
10. Check clutch freeplay after reinstalling engine; should be at least 1/2 inch freeplay at pedal and reverse gear should engage without grinding. Adjust at cable wing nut on release lever.

CLUTCH

ADJUST

The hydraulic clutch linkage is not adjustable. The only service required is change of brake/clutch fluid every two years. The hydraulic system can only be bled with a pressure bleeder.

TRANSMISSION

REPLACE

1. Disconnect battery ground cable.
2. Remove clutch hydraulic line from transmission bracket, then remove two bolts securing hydraulic slave cylinder and wire out of the way.
3. Remove two engine to transmission upper mounting bolts, then shift linkage.
4. Disconnect starter wiring, back-up light switch wiring and transmission ground strap.
5. Remove left and right side driveshafts and wire out of the way.
6. Position a suitable jack stand under the engine.
7. Remove two engine to transmission lower mounting bolts.
8. Remove transmission front mount.
9. Lower engine and transmission slightly until front of transmission is clear of frame and remove transmission.
10. Reverse procedure to install.

SHIFT LEVER

ADJUST

1. Remove spare tire.
2. Pull up shift boot, place shift lever in neutral and loosen two upper bearing bracket bolts.
3. Align sight holes in upper bearing plate with those of lower plate and tighten bolts.
4. Working under vehicle, loosen center shift rod to rear shift rod clamp until both rods move freely. At shift mechanism housing, move front shift rod until shift rod stop contacts rubber cushion.
5. Move shift rod away from rubber cushion until clearance between shift rod and opposite end of shift mechanism housing measures 3/4 inch (19 mm) on models with chassis number up to 25BH137155, or 7/8 inch (22 mm) on models with chassis number after 25BH137155.
6. Tighten clamp between center shift rod and rear shift rod.
7. Test shift "H" pattern and reverse lock-out for correct operation.

DISC BRAKES SECTION

INDEX

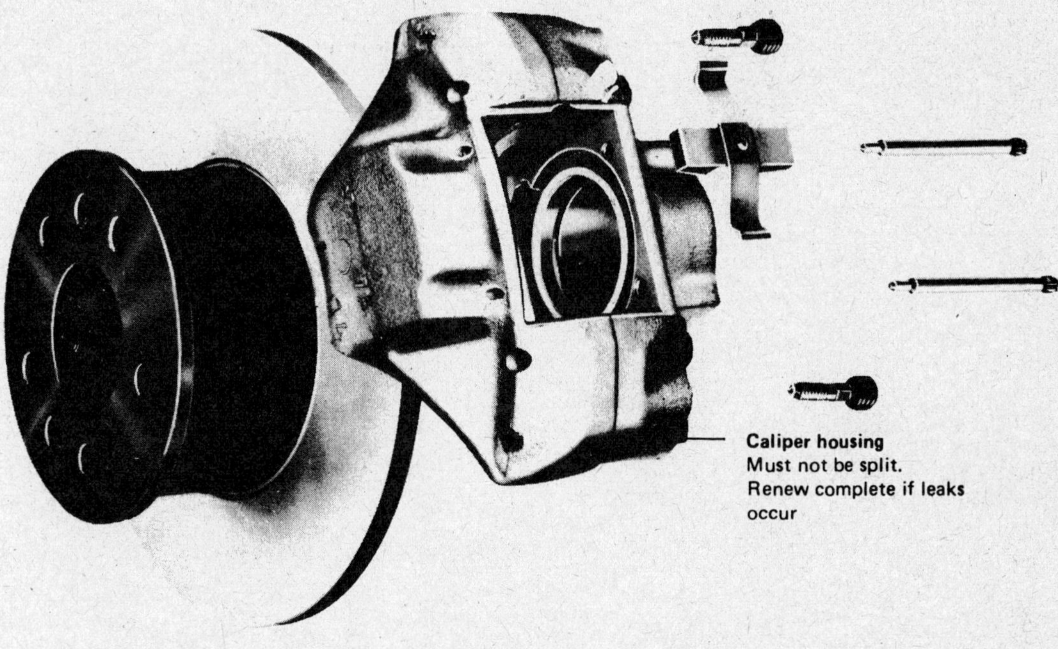

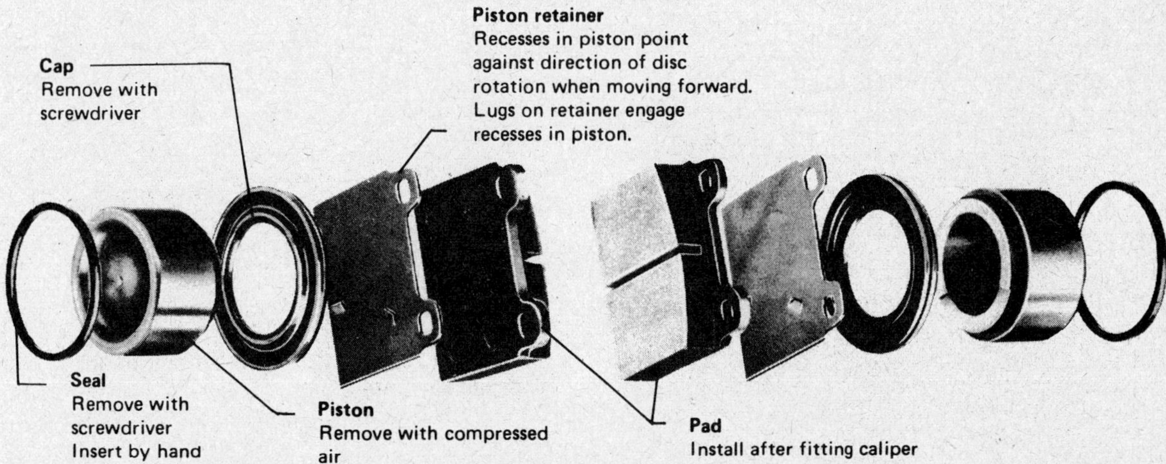

Fig. 1 Teves disc brake caliper, exploded view

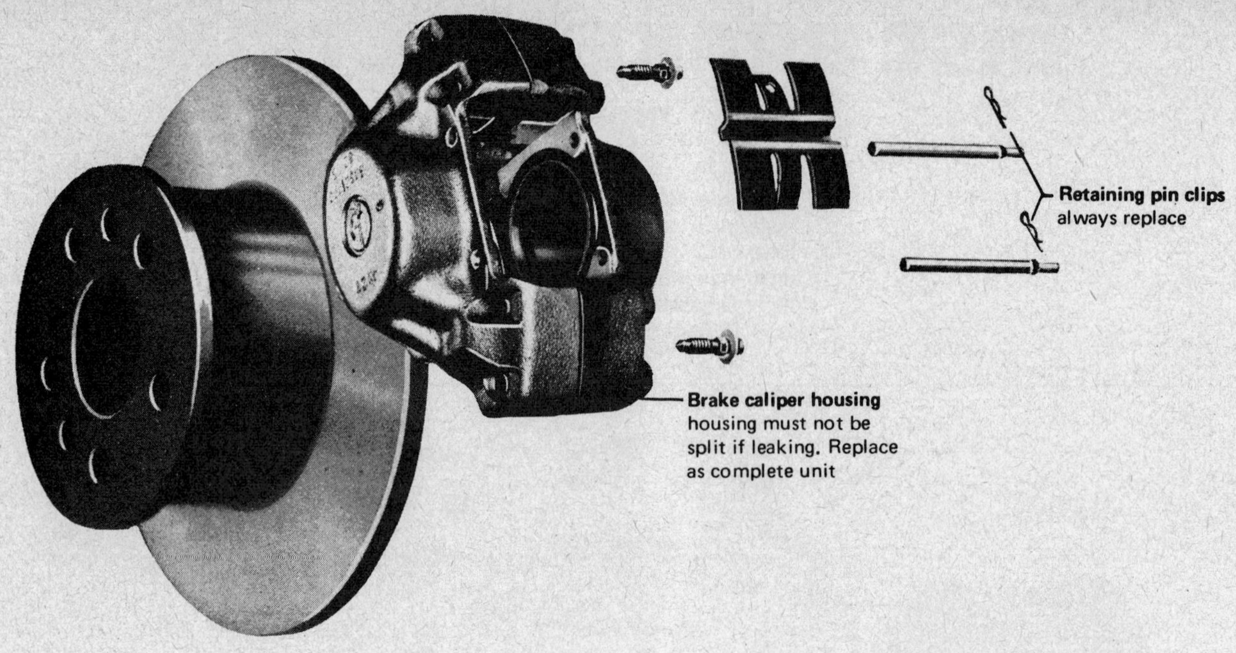

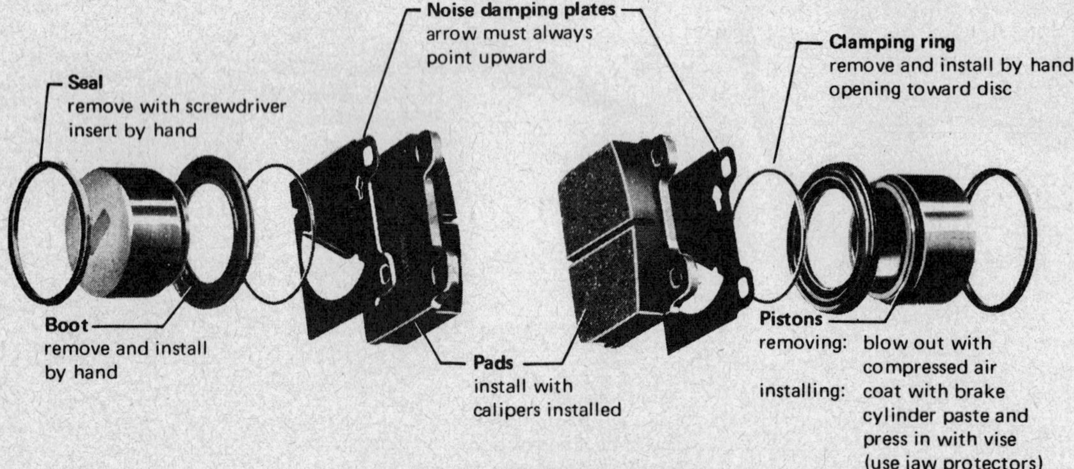

Fig. 2 Girling disc brake caliper, exploded view

BRAKE PADS REPLACE

These models use two types of opposed piston fixed brake calipers, one is Girling, the other Teves. Refer to **Figs. 1 and 2**, for service procedures on these calipers. The friction pads must be checked for wear every 6000 miles. Pads that have worn down to the thickness of 5/64" must be replaced with new ones. **All four friction pads must always be renewed together. It is not permissible to renew single friction pads or both pads of only one wheel. In addition, the spreader springs of both calipers must also be renewed with the friction pads. All necessary parts are furnished in a repair kit.**

REMOVAL

1. Remove front wheel.
2. Using a punch, drive out pad upper retaining pin.
3. Remove pad spreader spring.
4. Using a punch, drive out pad lower retaining pin.
5. Pull pads out of caliper, using a suitable hook. **If the friction pads are to be reused, they must be marked as it is not permissible to change the pads from the outside to the inside and vice versa or from the right to the left wheel.**

INSTALLATION

1. Oily friction pads and those with deep cracks or which have become detached from the metal plate must be renewed. In this case, all four friction pads must be renewed.
2. If pads are to be reused, remove excess dirt from grooves.
3. Push both pistons into their end positions with retaining pliers. **When doing this, the brake fluid behind the piston in the cylinder is forced back into the fluid reservoir. To prevent the reservoir overflowing, some of the fluid must be removed from the reservoir with a container**

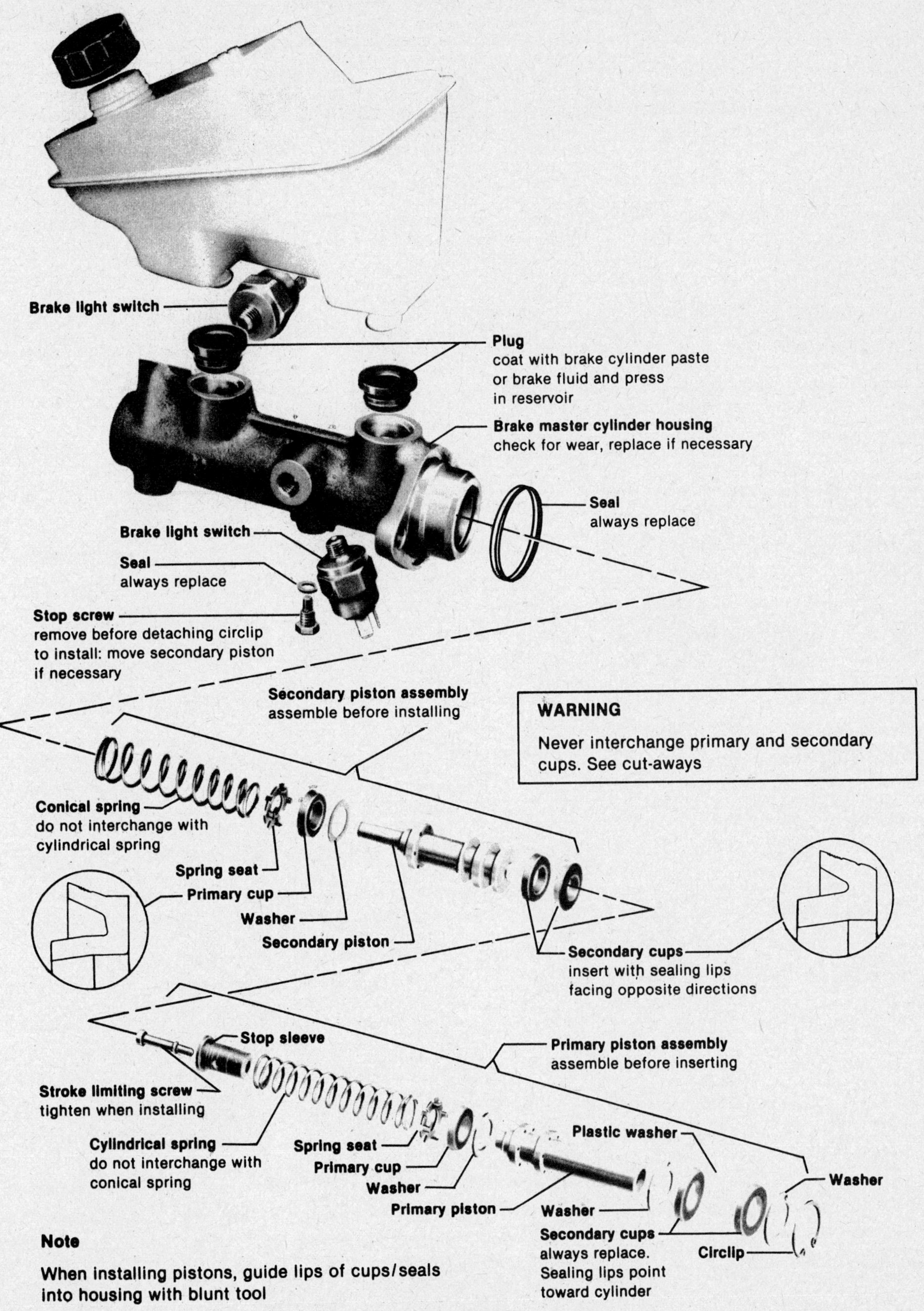
Brake light switch
Plug
coat with brake cylinder paste
or brake fluid and press
in reservoir
Brake master cylinder housing
check for wear, replace if necessary
Seal
always replace
Brake light switch
Seal
always replace
Stop screw
remove before detaching circlip
to install: move secondary piston
if necessary
Secondary piston assembly
assemble before installing
WARNING
Never interchange primary and secondary
cups. See cut-aways
Conical spring
do not interchange with
cylindrical spring
Spring seat
Primary cup
Washer
Secondary piston
Secondary cups
insert with sealing lips
facing opposite directions
Stop sleeve
Primary piston assembly
assemble before inserting
Stroke limiting screw
tighten when installing
Cylindrical spring
do not interchange with
conical spring
Spring seat
Primary cup
Washer
Primary piston
Plastic washer
Washer
Washer
Secondary cups
always replace.
Sealing lips point
toward cylinder
Circlip
Note
When installing pistons, guide lips of cups/seals
into housing with blunt tool

Fig. 3 Master cylinder assembly, exploded view

that is used only for brake fluid. Brake fluid is poisonous and must not be siphoned off with a hose.

4. Clean seating and sliding surfaces of friction pads in brake caliper. To do this, remove piston retaining plates. Never use petroleum products for cleaning. After cleaning, blow out with compressed air.
5. Check rubber boot for damage. Hardened, brittle or cracked boots must be replaced. To replace a rubber boot the brake caliper must be removed.
6. Check brake disc for wear.
7. Insert pads into brake caliper. The pads must be free enough to move to freely in caliper.
8. Insert pad lower retaining pin into caliper. **The retaining pin must not be driven in with a punch smaller in diameter than the pin as the front shoulder can easily be sheared off by the split clamping bushing. It is advisable to drive in the retaining pins with a hammer only and no additional tools.**
9. Install new pad spreader spring.
10. Push in pad upper retaining pin after first pressing spreader spring down with thumb. **Depress brake pedal several times while vehicle is stationary to enable pistons and pads to assume their correct positions to the brake disc.**

CALIPER DISASSEMBLE

The caliper consists of two paired halves which are bolted together. Under no circumstances should the two halves be separated.

1. Raise and support front of vehicle. Remove wheels then calipers.
2. Position caliper ear in a suitable vise.
3. Carefully pry out dust boot with a screwdriver.
4. Restrain one piston with a C-clamp, then position a block of wood between the two pistons. Apply compressed air to hydraulic fluid inlet to force unrestrained piston outward in the block of wood, remove piston.
5. Remove piston seal carefully with a screwdriver.
6. Assemble caliper as explained in "Caliper Assemble" and repeat procedure for other caliper piston.

CALIPER ASSEMBLE

1. Lubricate new piston seal with brake cylinder paste and install in bore.
2. Using a C-clamp or other suitable tool press piston into bore. Before piston is fully seated install dust seal engaging sealing lip into piston and caliper bore.
3. Using hand pressure fully seat piston. Ensure dust boot is fully seated. **On Teves caliper, place noise dampening plates in position in caliper. Notches in piston must align with lugs on dampening plates, if not rotate piston, notches must face down against forward rotor rotation, Fig. 1.**
4. Install caliper, torque caliper retaining bolts to 116 ft. lbs. then bleed brakes.

MASTER CYLINDER REPLACE

Refer to **Fig. 3**, for service procedures on this master cylinder.

DRUM BRAKES SECTION

INDEX

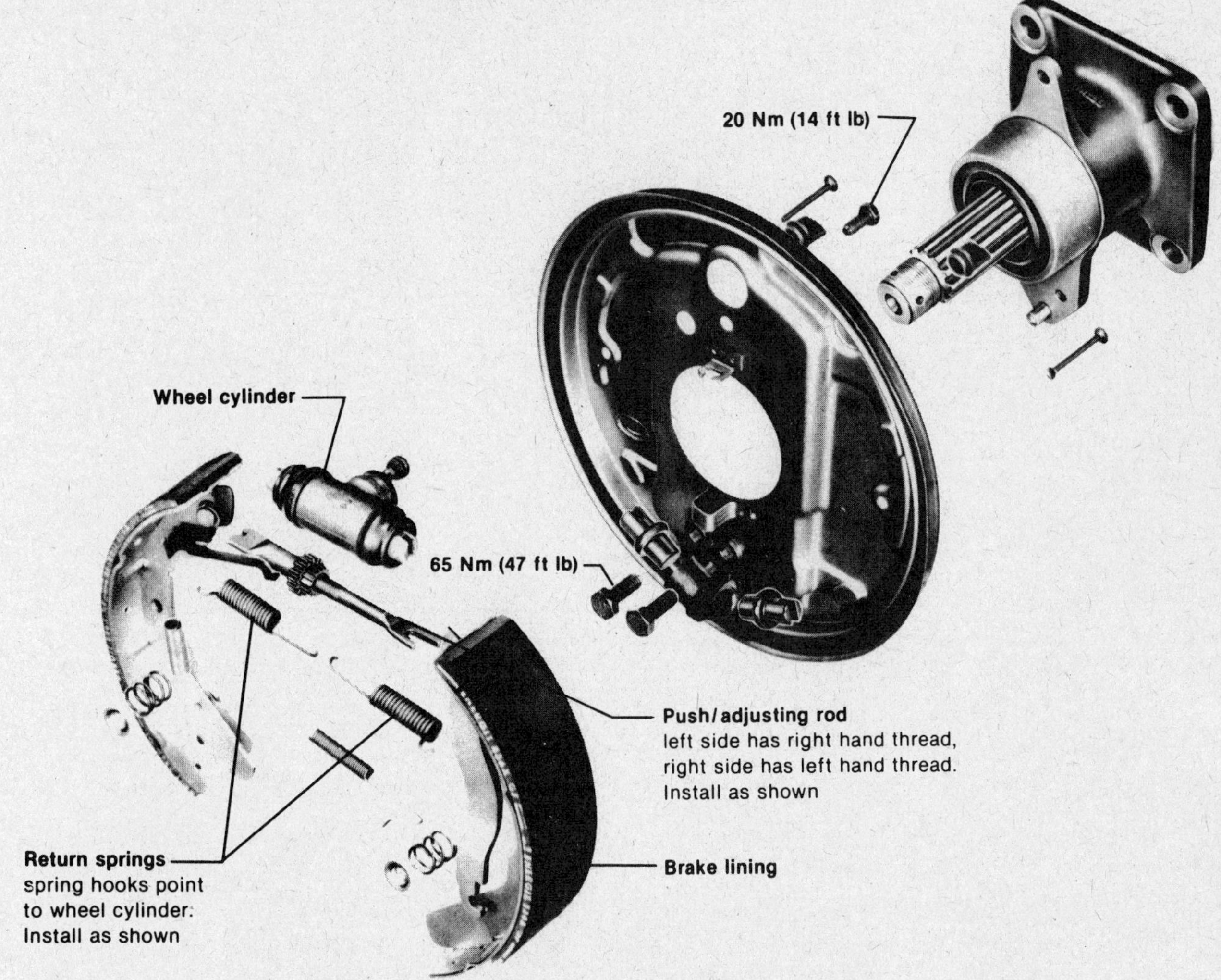

Fig. 1 Rear brake assembly, exploded view. (Part 1 of 2)

DRUM BRAKES
ADJUST

Rear drum brakes, **Fig. 1,** are self-adjusting whenever the brakes are applied. After relining rear brakes make an initial adjustment by measuring the brake drum inside diameter and transferring that measurement to the brake linings by turning the adjuster, **Fig. 1,** before installing the brake drum.

MASTER CYLINDER
REPLACE

For master cylinder replacement procedures, refer to "Disc Brakes Section."

PARKING BRAKE
ADJUST

1. Release parking brake.
2. Tighten parking brake equalizer adjusting nut until all slack is removed from brake cables.
3. Apply emergency brake 2-4 notches, ensure parking brake holds vehicle.
4. Release parking brake, ensure rear wheels rotate freely.

BRAKE SHOES
REPLACE

1. Raise and support vehicle, then remove wheel assembly.

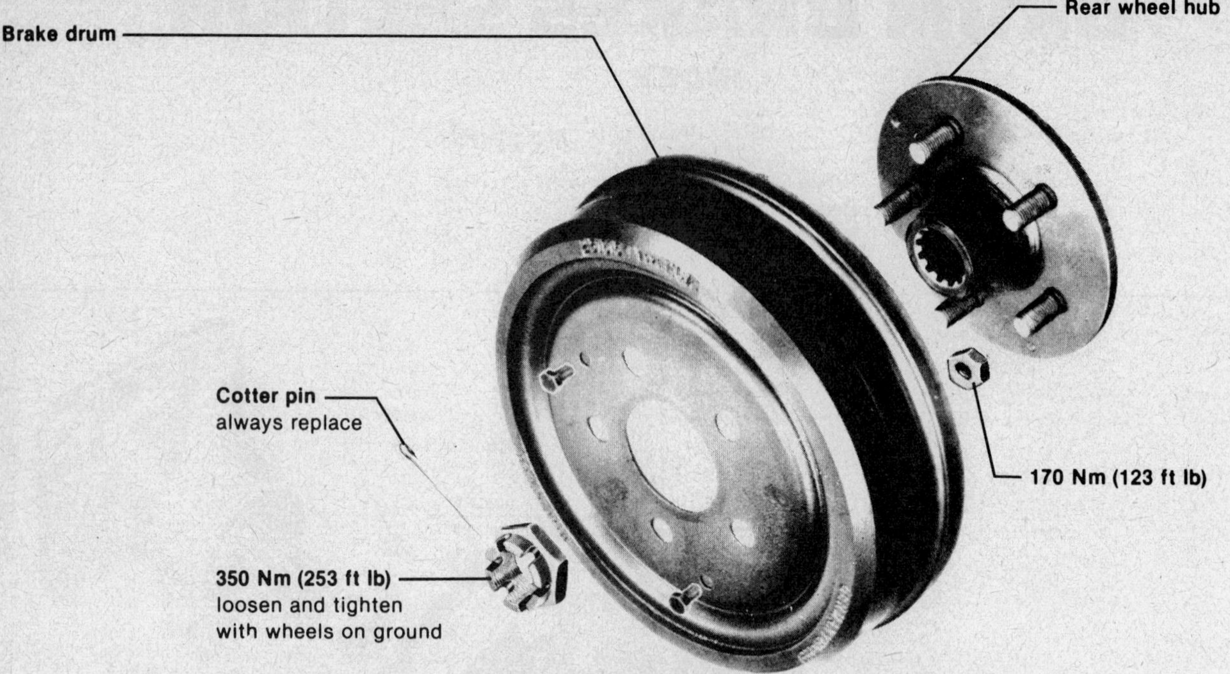

Fig. 1 Rear brake assembly, exploded view. (Part 2 of 2)

2. Loosen nuts at parking brake equalizer and release parking brake cables, then loosen adjuster through hole in backing plate.
3. Using puller OTC 827-B or equivalent, remove brake drum.
4. Remove spring retainers and hold down springs, then disconnect parking brake cable from lever on brake shoe.
5. Remove lower return spring and adjuster spring, then move shoe out of lower support.
6. Disconnect return springs and remove brake shoes along with push/adjusting rod.
7. Reverse procedure to install.

REAR AXLE & SUSPENSION SECTION

INDEX

Fig. 1 Removing velocity joint to transmission drive flange bolts

Fig. 2 Pressing driveshaft from ball hub

Fig. 3 Removing hub & ball cage

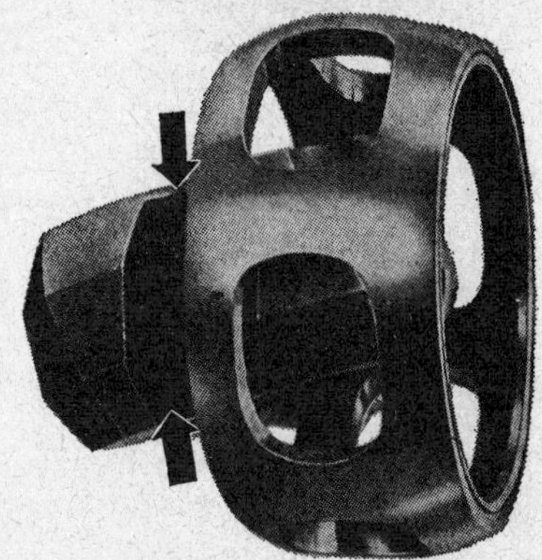

Fig. 4 Removing ball hub from cage

Fig. 5 Assembling hub, cage, balls & outer rings

Fig. 6 Aligning chamfer, ball hub splines & large diameter end with outer ring face

CONSTANT VELOCITY JOINTS

REPLACE

1. Remove 12-point socket head bolts holding joints to transmission drive flange and stub axle, **Fig. 1.**
2. Remove driveshaft assemblies from vehicle.
3. Loosen clamps on boots. Late models have no clamps, large end is crimped into sheet metal caps.
4. Use drift to tap off caps.
5. Remove circlip on shaft and press shaft out of ball hub, **Fig. 2.**
6. Remove concave washer from driveshaft.
7. Repack or replace joints. When repacking joints, use G-6 grease. **Don't mix up outer rings and hubs since they are matched.**
8. Turn ball hub and cage then push out of outer ring, **Fig. 3.**
9. Push balls out of cage.
10. Align ball grooves in hub with edge of cage and slide hub out, **Fig. 4.**
11. Check all parts for wear.
12. Reassemble hub, cage, balls and outer ring, **Fig. 5.** Make sure chamfer on inside splines of ball hub, **Fig. 6,** and the larger diameter end on the outer ring face in the same direction.
13. Ball hub can be moved back and forth if joint is assembled properly, but there should be little or no radial play.
14. Place concave washer against step on driveshaft and press inner hub onto shaft—make sure chamfer on inner splines of hub faces toward concave washer.
15. Install new circlip on shaft and

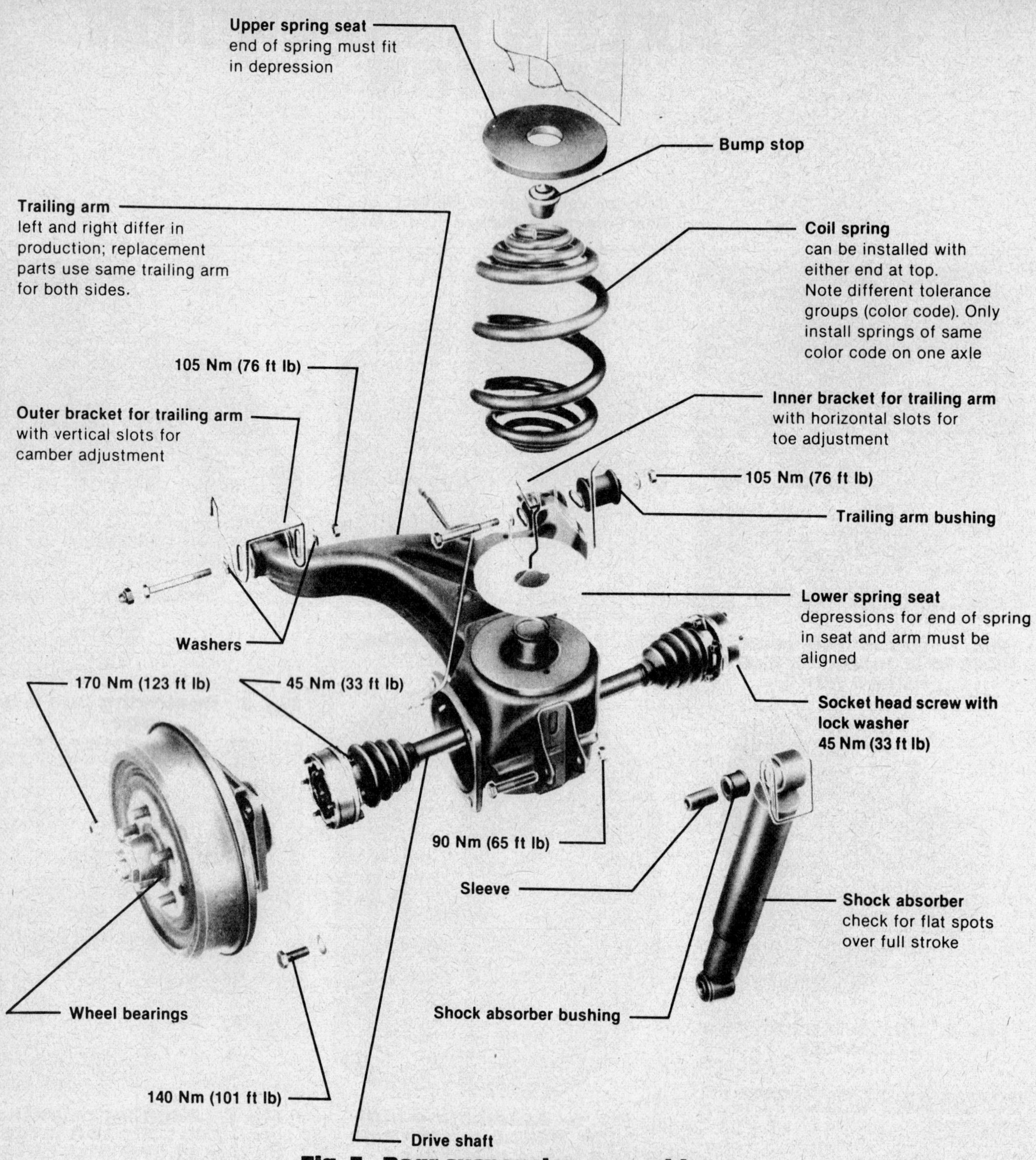

Fig. 7 Rear suspension assembly, exploded view

squeeze with pliers until fully seated.

16. Install shafts into vehicle. Torque 12-point socket head bolts to 33 ft. lbs. (45 Nm).

REAR SUSPENSION
REPLACE

Refer to **Fig. 7** for service procedures on this vehicle

FRONT SUSPENSION & STEERING SECTION

INDEX

Page No.

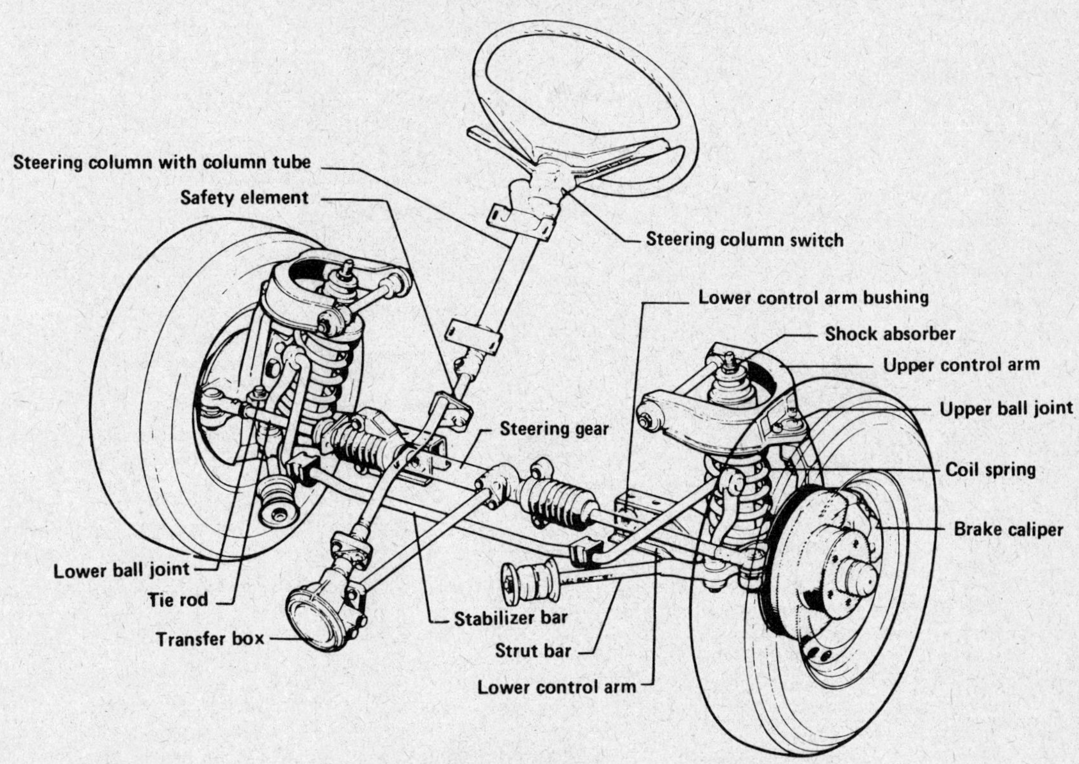

Fig. 1 Front suspension & steering

FRONT SUSPENSION SERVICE

WHEEL BEARINGS, ADJUST

1. Raise and support front of vehicle.
2. Using a suitable tool, pry off the grease cap, **Fig. 1.**
3. Remove and discard wheel bearing adjustment nut.
4. Install new nut and snug with fingers.
5. While spinning wheel, firmly tighten the adjustment nut.
6. Back nut off slowly while trying to move thrust washer with a screwdriver and finger pressure (do not pry or twist screwdriver). When thrust washer moves freely bearing is correctly adjusted.
7. Using a blunt chisel or other suitable tool, peen nut onto shoulder of steering knuckle.
8. Reinstall grease cap and lower vehicle to ground.

SHOCK ABSORBER, REPLACE

1. Raise and support front of vehicle.
2. Remove shock absorber lower retaining nut and bolt (it may be necessary to lower vehicle to floor to release tension on bolt), **Fig. 2.**
3. Remove nut securing top shock mount to body and remove shock.
4. Reverse procedure to install.

BALL JOINT, REPLACE

1. Raise and support front of vehicle.
2. Remove front wheels, then remove front stabilizer bar, **Fig. 2.**
3. Remove three nuts securing lower ball joint adapter to lower control arm and discard.
4. Remove bolts, then brake caliper and disconnect brake hose bracket. Wire out of the way.
5. Using a suitable tie rod end press remove tie rod ends. Then lift out steering knuckle.
6. Place steering knuckle in a suitable vise, then, using tool No. VW267a, press out lower ball joint adapter, then the upper joint.
7. Remove lower ball joint circlip and use a press to remove lower ball joint.
8. Press in upper and lower ball joints, install circlip on lower ball joint and loosely install ball joint adapter.
9. Reverse procedure to install. Refer to **Fig. 2** for torque specifications.

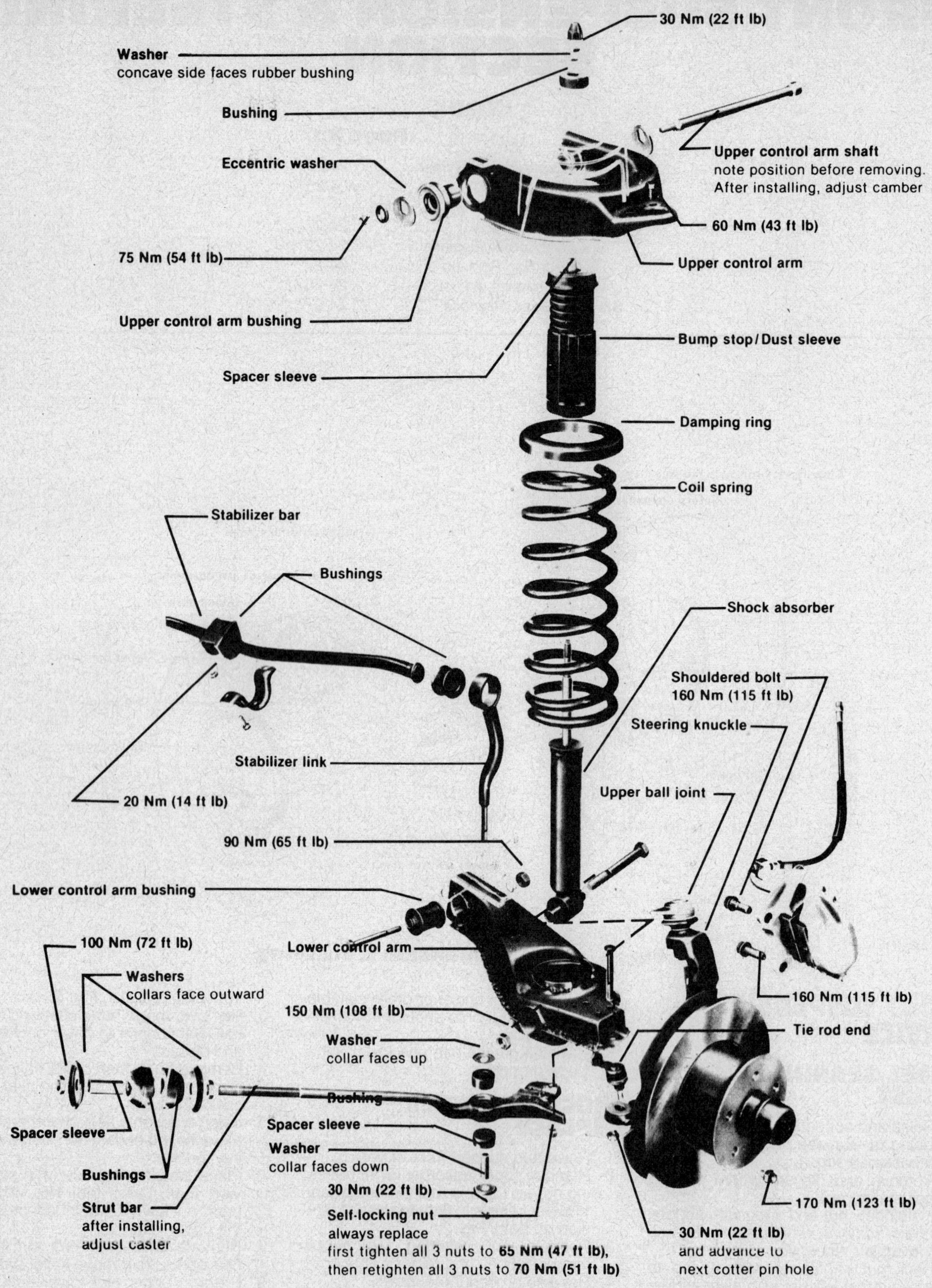
30 Nm (22 ft lb)
Washer
concave side faces rubber bushing
Bushing
Upper control arm shaft
note position before removing.
After installing, adjust camber
Eccentric washer
60 Nm (43 ft lb)
75 Nm (54 ft lb)
Upper control arm
Upper control arm bushing
Bump stop/Dust sleeve
Spacer sleeve
Damping ring
Coil spring
Stabilizer bar
Bushings
Shock absorber
Shouldered bolt
160 Nm (115 ft lb)
Steering knuckle
Stabilizer link
Upper ball joint
20 Nm (14 ft lb)
90 Nm (65 ft lb)
Lower control arm bushing
100 Nm (72 ft lb)
Lower control arm
Washers
collars face outward
160 Nm (115 ft lb)
150 Nm (108 ft lb)
Tie rod end
Washer
collar faces up
Bushing
Spacer sleeve
Spacer sleeve
Washer
collar faces down
Bushings
30 Nm (22 ft lb)
170 Nm (123 ft lb)
Strut bar
after installing,
adjust caster
Self-locking nut
always replace
first tighten all 3 nuts to 65 Nm (47 ft lb),
then retighten all 3 nuts to 70 Nm (51 ft lb)
30 Nm (22 ft lb)
and advance to
next cotter pin hole

Fig. 2 Front suspension, exploded view

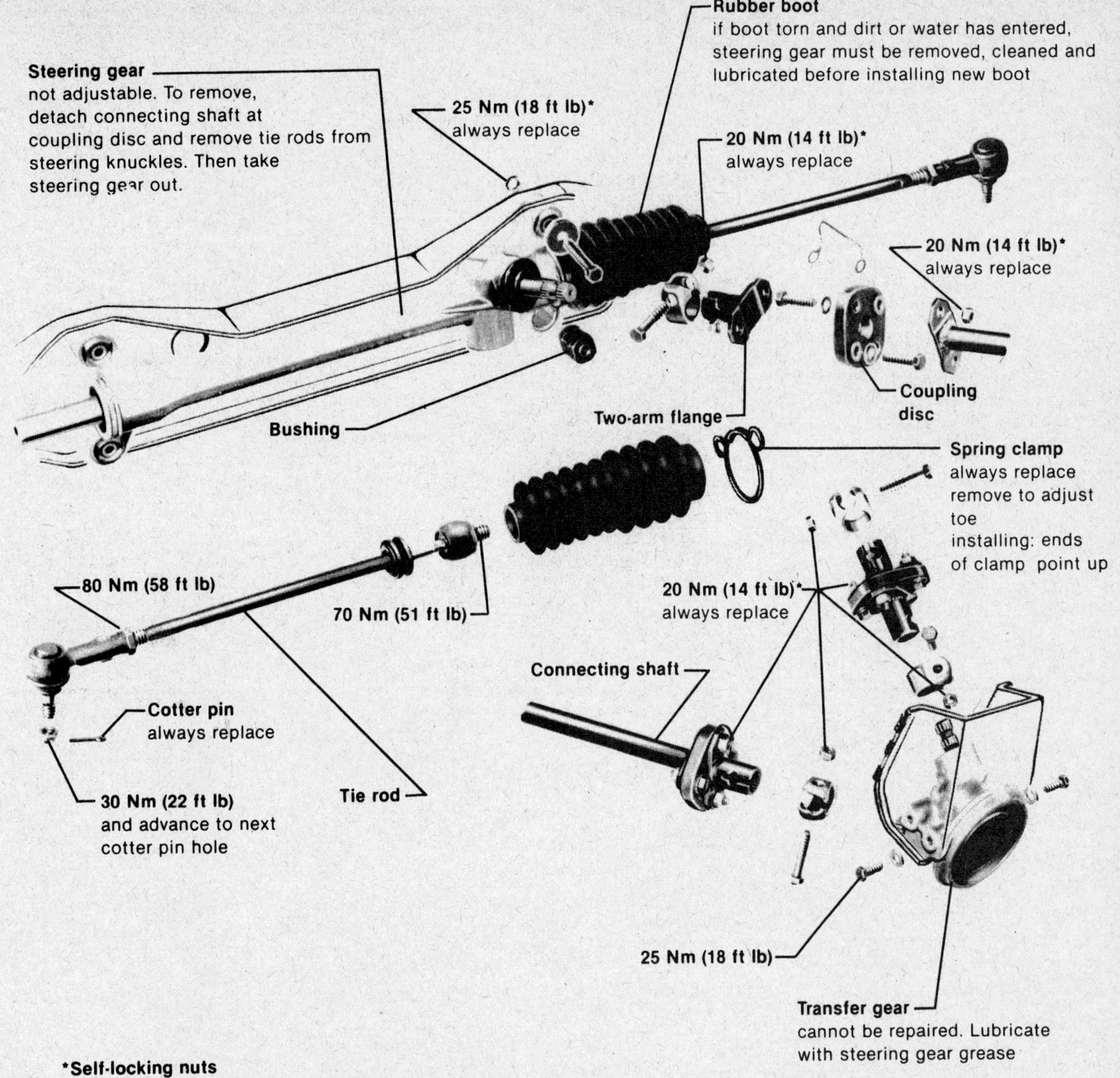

Fig. 3 Steering gear, exploded view

LOWER CONTROL ARM & COIL SPRING, REPLACE

Follow steps 1 through 5 of "Ball Joints, Replace" then continue with the following steps:

1. Raise and support vehicle.
2. Remove shock absorber lower retaining nut, do not remove bolt as it is restraining the coil spring, **Fig. 2.**
3. Position a floor jack under lower control arm and carefully raise control arm to ease tension on the lower shock bolt, remove bolt. Slowly lower jack and remove coil spring. Remove lower control arm bushing bolt and remove control arm, **Fig. 2.**
4. Reverse procedure to install. Ensure the lower end of spring is seated in the lower control spring depression. Refer to **Fig. 2** for torque specifications.

STABILIZER BAR, REPLACE

Refer to **Fig. 2** for service procedures on this component.

STEERING GEAR REPLACE

Refer to **Fig. 3** for service procedures on this steering gear.

WHEEL ALIGNMENT SECTION

INDEX

2 WHEEL DRIVE MODELS

Check rear wheel alignment first and correct as needed, then service front wheels. When adjusting front wheel alignment angles, set caster first, followed by camber, then toe.

FRONT WHEELS

Caster

1. Loosen strut bar nut.
2. Adjust caster to specifications by adjusting length of strut bar.
3. Tighten strut bar nut to 72 ft. lbs.

Camber

1. Loosen upper control arm shaft nut.
2. Adjust camber to specifications by turning the upper control arm shaft.
3. Tighten upper control arm shaft nut to 54 ft. lbs.

Toe

1. Center steering wheel by turning steering wheel from lock to lock and counting number of turns.
2. Turn steering wheel back 1/2 number of turns until lug on rubber washer of pinion shaft aligns with notch in steering housing.
3. Loosen tie rod locknuts, then adjust toe to specifications by turning both tie rods equal amounts. **Ensure that tie rod boots are not twisted.**
4. Tighten locknuts to 58 ft. lbs.

REAR WHEELS

Camber

1. Loosen trailing arm outer bolt.
2. Using a suitable screwdriver, adjust camber to specifications by moving trailing arm up and down.
3. Tighten trailing arm outer bolt to 76 ft. lbs.

Toe

1. Loosen trailing arm inner bolt.
2. Using a suitable screwdriver, adjust toe to specifications by moving trailing arm to the front or rear.
3. Tighten trailing arm inner bolt to 76 ft. lbs.

VOLVO (Sweden)

INDEX OF SERVICE OPERATIONS

General Engine Specifications

Year	Model	Engine	Fuel System	Bore & Stroke	Compression Ratio	Maximum Brake HP @ RPM	Maximum Torque Lbs. Ft. @ RPM	Normal Oil Pressure Pounds
1983	DL	4-130/2127 ①	Fuel Inj.	3.620 x 3.150 (92 x 80 mm)	7.5	127 @ 5400	150 @ 3750	35–85
	DL, GL	4-142/2320 ②	Fuel Inj.	3.780 x 3.150 (96 x 80 mm)	10.3	107 @ 5400	127 @ 3500	35–85
	DL, GL	6-145/2383 ③	Fuel Inj.	3.0118 x 3.4016 (76.6x 86.4 mm)	23.0	76 @ 4800	98 @ 2800	28
	GLT	4-130/2127 ①	Fuel Inj.	3.620 x 3.150 (92 x 80 mm)	7.5	127 @ 5400	150 @ 3750	35–85
	760GLE	V6-174/2849 ④	Fuel Inj.	3.580 x 2.870 (91 x 73 mm)	8.8	130 @ 5500	153 @ 2750	14–57
	760GLE	6-145/2383 ⑤	Fuel Inj.	3.0118 x 3.4016 (76.5 x 86.4 mm)	23.0	103 @ 4800	139 @ 2400	28
1984	DL	4-142/2320 ②	Fuel Inj.	3.780 x 3.150 (96 x 80 mm)	9.5	111 @ 5400	136 @ 2750	35–85
	GL	6-145/2383 ③	Fuel Inj.	3.0118 x 3.4016 (76.5 x 86.4 mm)	23	80 @ 4800	103 @ 2800	28
	GLT	4-130/2127 ① ⑥	Fuel Inj.	3.620 x 3.150 (92 x 80 mm)	7.5	162 @ 5100	181 @ 3900	35–85
	760 GLE Turbo	4-142/2320 ⑦	Fuel Inj.	3.780 x 3.150 (96 x 80 mm)	157 @ 5300	184 @ 2900	35–85	
	760 GLE	V6-174/2849 ④	Fuel Inj.	3.580 x 2.870 (91 x 73 mm)	8.8	134 @ 5500	159 @ 2750	14–57
	760 GLE	6-145/2383 ⑤	Fuel Inj.	3.0118 x 3.4016 (76.5 x 86.4 mm)	23	106 @ 4800	140 @ 2400	28
1985	DL Sedan	4-142/2320 ⑧	Fuel Inj.	3.780 x 3.150 (96 x 80 mm)	9.5	111 @ 5400	136 @ 2750	35–85
	DL Wagon	4-142/2320 ⑧	Fuel Inj.	3.780 x 3.150 (96 x 80 mm)	9.5	114 @ 5400	136 @ 2750	35–85
	DL Turbo	4-130/2127 ① ⑥	Fuel Inj.	3.620 x 3.150 (92 x 80 mm)	7.5	162 @ 5100	181 @ 3900	35–85
	740 GLE	4-142/2320 ⑧	Fuel Inj.	3.780 x 3.150 (96 x 80 mm)	9.5	114 @ 5400	136 @ 2750	35–85
	740 GT Turbo	4-142/2320 ⑥ ⑨	Fuel Inj.	3.780 x 3.150 (96 x 80 mm)	8.7	160 @ 5300	187 @ 2900	35–85
	740 Wagon	6-145/2383 ⑤	Fuel Inj.	3.0118 x 3.4016 (76.5 x 86.4 mm)	23.0	106 @ 4800	140 @ 2400	28
	760 GLE Turbo	4-142/2320 ⑥ ⑨	Fuel Inj.	3.780 x 3.150 (96 x 80 mm)	8.3	157 @ 5300	184 @ 2900	35–85
	760 GLE Sedan	V6-174/2849 ④	Fuel Inj.	3.580 x 2.870 (91 x 73 mm)	8.8	134 @ 5500	159 @ 2750	14–57
	760 GLE Turbo	6-145/2383 ⑤	Fuel Inj.	3.0118 x 3.4016 (76.5 x 86.4 mm)	23.0	106 @ 4800	140 @ 2400	28
	760 GLE Turbo Wagon	4-142/2320 ⑨	Fuel Inj.	3.780 x 3.150 (96 x 80 mm)	8.7	160 @ 5300	187 @ 2900	35–85
1986	240 DL/GL	4-142/2320 ⑧	Fuel Inj.	3.780 x 3.150 (96 x 80 mm)	9.8	114 @ 5400	136 @ 2750	35–85
	740 GLE	4-142/2320 ⑧	Fuel Inj.	3.780 x 3.150 (96 x 80 mm)	9.8	114 @ 5400	136 @ 2750	35–85
	740/760 Turbo	4-142/2320 ⑥ ⑨	Fuel Inj.	3.780 x 3.150 (96 x 80 mm)	8.7	160 @ 5300	187 @ 2900	35–85
	760 GLE	V6-174/2849 ④	Fuel Inj.	3.580 x 2.870 (91 x 73 mm)	8.8	136 @ 5500	159 @ 2700	14–57
	740 Turbo Diesel	6-145/2383 ⑤	Fuel Inj.	3.0118 x 3.4016 (76.5 x 86.4 mm)	23.0	106 @ 4800	140 @ 2400	28
1987	240 DL/GL	4-142/2320 ⑧	Fuel Inj.	3.780 x 3.150 (96 x 80 mm)	9.8	114 @ 5400	136 @ 2750	35–85
	740 GLE	4-142/2320 ⑧	Fuel Inj.	3.780 x 3.150 (96 x 80 mm)	9.8	114 @ 5400	136 @ 2750	35–85
	740 GT	4-142/2320 ⑨	Fuel Inj.	3.780 x 3.150 (96 x 80 mm)	8.7	160 @ 5300	187 @ 2900	35–85
	760 GLE Sedan	V6-174/2849 ⑩	Fuel Inj.	3.580 x 2.870 (91 x 73 mm)	9.5	145 @ 5100	173 @ 3750	14–57
	760 GLE Wagon	4-142/2320 ⑨	Fuel Inj.	3.780 x 3.150 (96 x 80 mm)	8.3	160 @ 5300	189 @ 2900	35–85
	780 Coupe	V6-174/2849 ⑩	Fuel Inj.	3.580 x 2.870 (91 x 73 mm)	9.5	145 @ 5100	173 @ 3750	14–57

①—B21F Turbo.
②—B23F LH-Jetronic.
③—D24 Diesel.
④—B28F.
⑤—D24T Diesel.
⑥—Intercooled engine.
⑦—B23F Turbo.
⑧—B230F.
⑨—B230F Turbo.
⑩—B280F.

Alternator & Regulator Specifications

	Alternator				Regulator	
Year	Model	Rated Hot Output Amps	Field Winding Resistance Ohms	Output @ 14 Volts 3000 RPM Amps	Type	Voltage @ 125°F
1983–87	Bosch K1	55	4.2	47	Integral	①
	Bosch N1	70	3.6	58	Integral	②
	Bosch N1	90	3.0	60③	Integral	②
1987	Bosch N1	80	2.6	80④	Integral	13.8–14.6
	Bosch N1	100	2.6	100④	Integral	13.8–14.6

①—1983-84, 13.8-14.3; 1985-87, 13.8-14.6.
②—1983-84, 13.8-14.3; 1985-87, 13.8-14.6.
③—At 2000 RPM.
④—At 6000 RPM.

Starting Motor Specifications

			No Load Test			Torque Test	
Year	Part No.	Brush Spring Tension, Ounces	Amperes	Volts	RPM	Amperes	Volts
1983–87	Bosch GE	3.1–3.5	30-50	11.5	5800-7800	185-220	9
	Bosch JF	5.1–5.5	65–95	11.5	6500-8500	—	—
	Bosch 0001362	—	95	11.5	6500	700–800①	4.5①
	Bosch 00013111	—	70	11.5	7500	410–490①	6.5①
	Bosch 0001108030	—	80	11.5	6500	700–880①	4.5①

①—Locked starter motor current consumption.

Pistons, Pins, Rings, Crankshaft & Bearings

			Ring End Gap			Rod Bearings		Main Bearings			
Year	Engine	Piston Clearance Top of Skirt	Comp.	Oil	Wrist-Pin Dia.	Shaft Diameter	Bearing Clearance	Shaft Diameter	Bearing Clearance	Thrust on Bear. No.	Shaft End Play
1983–84	B23F	.0004–.0016	.014	.010	.946	2.1271–2.1276	.0009–.0028	2.5000–2.5005	.0011–.0033	5	.0098①
	B23F Turbo	.0020–.0028	.016	.012	.946	2.1271–2.1276	.0009–.0028	2.5000–2.5005	.0011–.0033	5	.0098①
1983–85	B21F Turbo	.0008–.0016	.014	.010	.946	2.1271–2.1276	.0009–.0028	2.500–2.5005	.0011–.0033	5	.0098①
1983–86	B28F	.0007–.0015	.016	.016	②	2.0577–2.0585	.0011–.0031	2.7575–2.7583	.0014–.0034	4	.0027–.0106
	D24, D24T Diesel	.0012–.0019	.012	.010	—	1.8802–1.8810	.0005–.0024	2.2816–2.2824	.0006–.0029	4	.0027–.0071
1985–87	B230F, Turbo	.0004–.0012	.012	.012	.906	1.9285–1.9293	.0009–.0026	2.1648–2.1654	.0009–.0028	—	.0032–.0106
1987	B280F	.0028–.0035	.016	.016	.985	2.3629–2.3636	—	2.7575–2.7583	—	4	.0027–.0106

—Not available.
①—Maximum.
②—Piston marking, blue, .9255-9257 inch; white, .9254-.9255 inch; red, .9253-.9254 inch.

Valve Specifications

Year	Model	Valve Lash		Valve Angles		Valve Spring Pressure Lbs. @ In.	Stem Clearance		Stem Diameter	
		Int.	Exh.	Seat	Face		Intake	Exhaust	Intake	Exhaust
1983–84	B23F	.017H	.017H	45	44.5	165 @ 1.08	.0012–.0024	.0024–.0035	.3132–.3138	.3128–.3134
	B23F Turbo	.016H	.016H	45	44.5	158 @ 1.08	.0012–.0024	.0012–.0024	.3134–.3140	.3130–.3136
1983–85	B21F Turbo	.017H	.017H	45	45.5	165 @ 1.06	.0012–.0024	.0024–.0035	.3132–.3138	.3128–.3134
1983–86	B28F	.007H	.013H	①	②	145 @ 1.18	③	④	⑤	⑥
	D24, D24T Diesel	.010H	.018H	45	⑦	⑧	.012–.051⑨	.012–.051⑨	.314	.313
1985–87	B230F	.017H	.017H	45	44.5	165 @ 1.08	.0012–.0024	.0024–.0035	.3132–.3138	.3128–.3134
	B230F Turbo	.017H	.017H	45	44.5	165 @ 1.08	.0012–.0024	.0024–.0035	.3132–.3138	.3136–.3142
1987	B280F	.007H	.013H	45	44.5	145 @ 1.18	③	④	⑤	⑥

—Not available.
①—Intake, 30°; exhaust, 45° (venturi seats: 15° and 60° angles can be used to reduce seat width).
②—Intake, 29.5°; exhaust, 44.5°.
③—Tapered valve stem; diameter taken approximately 1.04 inch from end of valve should be .3135–.3141 inch, diameter taken just below valve collet groove should be .3139–.3145 inch.
④—Tapered valve stem; diameter take approximately 1.25 inch from end of valve should be .3127–.3133 inch, diameter taken just below valve collet groove should be .3135–.3141 inch.
⑤—Tapered valve stem; diameter, .3135–.3141 to .3139–.3145 inch.
⑥—Tapered valve stem, diameter, .3127–.3133 to .3135–.3141 inch.
⑦—Intake, 44.5°; exhaust, 45°.
⑧—D24 engine, inner 48.5 @ .720; outer 100 @ .878; D24T engine, inner 49.5 @ .720, outer 103 @ .878.
⑨—Measured with new valve installed and stem positioned equal with top of guide.

Engine Tightening Specifications

*Torque specifications are for clean and lightly lubricated threads only. Dry or dirty threads produce increased friction which prevents accurate measurement of tightness.

Year	Engine	Spark Plugs Ft. Lbs.	Cylinder Head Bolts Ft. Lbs.	Intake Manifold Ft. Lbs.	Camshaft Sprocket Bolt Ft. Lbs.	Camshaft Carrier Bolts Ft. Lbs.	Connecting Rod Cap Bolts Ft. Lbs.	Main Bearing Cap Bolts Ft. Lbs.	Flywheel to Crankshaft Ft. Lbs.	Vibration Damper or Pulley Ft. Lbs.
1983–84	B23F, Turbo	15–22	①	15	37	15	45	80	50	120
1983–85	B21F Turbo	15–22	①	15	37	15	45	80	50	120
1983–86	B28F	7.5–10.5	①	7–11	52–66	—	33–37	①	33–37	177–206
	D24, D24T Diesel	—	①	18	②	15	33	48	55	330③
1985–87	B230F, Turbo	14–22	④	—	35	14	⑤	80	50	⑥
1987	B280F	7.5–10.5	—	—	52–66	—	33–37	①	33–37	177–206

—Not available.
①—See text.
②—Front gear, 33 ft. lbs.; rear gear, 73 ft. lbs.
③—Hex head screws, 15 ft. lbs.
④—Torque bolts in three steps: Step 1, 15 ft. lbs.; Step 2, 45 ft. lbs.; Step 3, tighten each bolt an additional 90° from that in Step 2.
⑤—Torque bolts in two steps: Step 1, 14 ft. lbs.; Step 2, tighten each bolt an additional 90° from that in Step 1.
⑥—Torque bolt in two steps: Step 1, 4 ft. lbs.; Step 2, tighten bolt an additional 60° from that in Step 1.

Brake Specifications

Year	Model	Wheel Cyl. Bore		Disc Brake Rotor								
				Nominal Thickness		Minimum Thickness		Thickness Variation (Parallelism)		Run Out (TIR)		Master Cyl. I.D.
		Front	Rear	Front	Rear	Front	Rear	Front	Rear	Front	Rear	
1983–87	①	—	—	②	.380	③	.331	.0008	.0008	.004	.004	④
	740, 760	—	—	⑤	.378	⑥	.330	—	—	.003	.004	⑦
1987	780	—	—	⑤	.378	⑥	.330	—	—	.003	.004	⑧

—Not available.
①—240 DL, GL & GLT.
②—Ventilated, .866 inch; non-ventilated, .563 inch.
③—Ventilated, .803 inch; non-ventilated, .500 inch.
④—Primary bore, .877 inch; secondary bore, .620 inch.
⑤—Ventilated, .867 inch; non-ventilated, .551 inch.
⑥—Ventilated, .788 inch; non-ventilated, .433 inch.
⑦—Early production models: primary bore, .880 inch; secondary bore, .620 inch. Late production models: primary bore, .940 inch; secondary bore, .660 inch.
⑧—Primary bore, .940 inch; secondary bore, .660 inch.

Rear Axle Specifications

Year	Model	Carrier Type	Ring Gear & Pinion Backlash		Pinion Bearing Preload			Differential Bearing Preload		
			Method	Adjustment	Method	New Bearings Inch Lbs.	Used Bearings Inch Lbs.	Method	New Bearings Inch Lbs.	Used Bearings Inch Lbs.
1983–87	All	Integral	Shims	.005–.007	Shims	22–31	13–22	Shims	—	—

—Not available.

Cooling System & Capacity Data

Year	Engine	Cooling Capacity Qts.		Radiator Cap Relief Pressure Lbs.		Thermo Opening Temp.	Fuel Tank Gals.	Engine Oil Refill Qts.①	Transmission Oil		
		With Heater	With A/C	With A/C	Less A/C				5 Speed Pints	Auto. Trans. Qts.②	Axle Oil Pints
1983–84	B23F, Turbo	10	10	9–12	9–12	190	15.8	3.6	4.8	7.8	③
1983–85	B21F Turbo	10	10	9–12	9–12	190	15.8	3.5	4.8	7.8	③
1983–86	B28F	10.6	10.6	9–12	9–12	198	15.8	6.3	4.8	7.9	3.4
	D24, D24T Diesel	④	④	9–12	9–12	⑤	⑥	7.4⑦	4.8	⑧	③
1985–87	B230F, Turbo	9.8	9.8	9–12	9–12	—	15.8	3.5	4.8	7.8	③
1987	B280F	10.6	10.6	21	21	190	15.8	5.6	4.8	7.8	③

—Not available.
①—Add 1/2 qt. with filter change.
②—Approximate, make final check with dipstick.
③—type 1030, 2.8; type 1031, 3.4.
④—Exc. turbo models, 10; turbo models, 10.6.
⑤—Exc. turbo models, 190; turbo models, 198.
⑥—Exc. turbo models, 15.8; turbo models, 21.6.
⑦—Includes filter.
⑧—Exc. turbo models, 7.1; turbo models, 7.9.

Wheel Alignment Specifications

Year	Model	Caster Angle, Degrees ①		Camber Angle, Degrees ①				Toe-In, Inch
				Limits		Desired		
		Limits	Desired	Left	Right	Left	Right	
1983–84	GLT	①	②	+1/4 to +3/4	+1/4 to +3/4	+1/2	+1/2	③
1983–86	240 DL, GL	①	②	+1 to +1 1/2	+1 to +1 1/2	+1 1/4	+1 1/4	③
	760	+5	+5	+2/5	+2/5	+2/5	+2/5	1/6
1984–86	740	+5	+5	+2/5	+2/5	+2/5	+2/5	1/6
1987	240 DL, GL	+3 to +4	+3 1/2	+1/4 to +3/4	+1/4 to +3/4	+1/2	+1/2	1/6
	740, 760, 780	+5	+5	+2/5	+2/5	+2/5	+2/5	1/6

①—Except power steering, +2 to +3; power steering, +3 to +4.
②—Except power steering, +2 1/2; power steering, +3 1/2.
③—Exc. power steering, 3/16; power steering, 1/8.

ELECTRICAL SECTION

INDEX

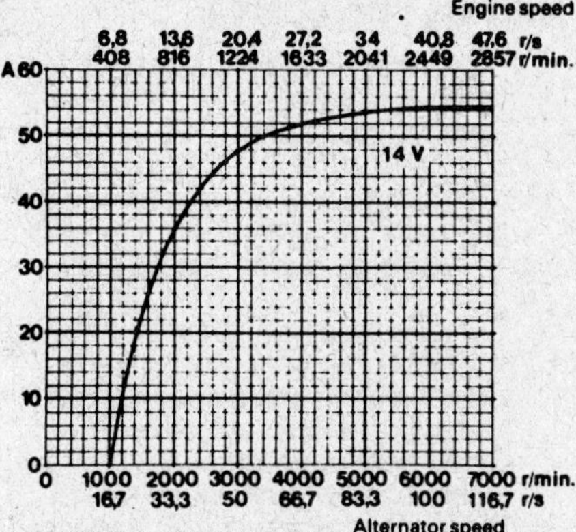

Fig. 1 Alternator output test. Bosch 55 amp alternator with integral regulator

Fig. 2 Alternator output test. Bosch 70 amp alternator with integral regulator

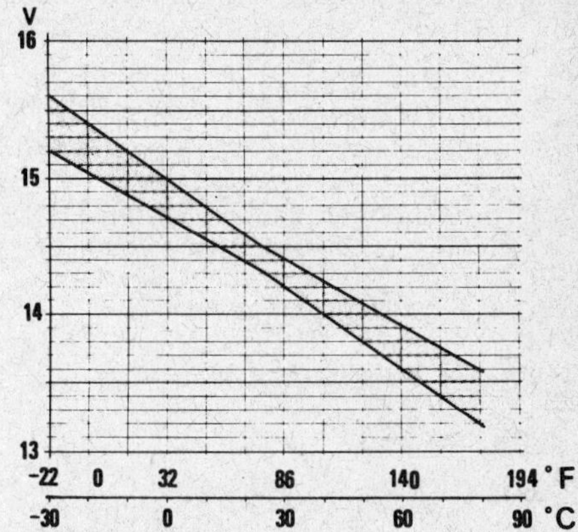

Fig. 3 Charging voltage graph (w/external temperature sensor connected)

ALTERNATOR IN CAR TESTS

When testing an alternator, it is important that a fully charged battery be used.

BOSCH ALTERNATOR W/INTEGRAL REGULATOR

Alternator Output Test

1. With alternator at normal operating temperature, run engine at 3000 RPM for 3 minutes.
2. Using a suitable shunt or loading alternator with accessories to require 40 amps, check output and compare to **Fig. 1** for 55 amp alternator or **Fig. 2** for 70 amp alternator.
3. If alternator does not produce current within specifications, check brushes. If brushes are satisfactory, repeat test using a known good regulator. Indicator on dash must not glow during any part of the testing procedure, if so one or more diodes are defective. Also maximum voltage difference between B+ and D+/61 is 1/2 volt.

Voltage Regulator Test

1. Run alternator until normal operating temperature is reached.
2. With the engine running at 3000 RPM, measure the voltage between B+ and D− terminals on back of alternator.
3. Correct reading should be 13.4-14.2 volts. If voltage is incorrect, make sure alternator brush length is correct. Minimum brush length is .2 in. (5 mm). If brush length is satisfactory, replace regulator.

Temperature Sensor Test

Some 1985-87 model vehicles use an external temperature sensor located underneath the battery. This sensor, directly connected to the voltage regulator, senses battery temperature and relays this information to the regulator. During cold weather operation, the alternator delivers higher voltage to the battery, thereby charging it at a faster rate. As the battery warms, the charging rate is reduced to prevent excessive gassing. To check sensor operation, proceed as follows:

1. Note and record battery temperature.
2. Connect voltmeter across battery terminals, then with all accessories off, start engine and allow to run at 2000 RPM. Observe charging voltage.
3. With battery temperature as noted in step 1, charging voltage should be within shaded areas of graph, **Fig. 3.** If voltage is as specified, temperature sensor is functioning properly. If not, proceed to next step.
4. Disconnect external temperature sensor from regulator, then repeat steps 1 and 2. With battery temperature as noted, charging voltage should be within shaded areas of graph, **Fig. 4.** If voltage is as specified, replace temperature sensor. If voltage is not as specified, replace voltage regulator.

STARTER REPLACE

1. Disconnect battery cable.
2. Disconnect starter leads.
3. Remove two starter mounting bolts, then the starter.
4. Reverse procedure to install.

IGNITION SWITCH REPLACE

1987 vehicles with "SRS" designation on steering wheel are equipped with air bag restraint system. Use extreme caution when working around steering column to avoid personal injury.

240 DL, GL & GLT

1. Disconnect battery ground cable.
2. Remove noise insulation panel and center side panel.
3. Disconnect terminal block from ignition switch.
4. Remove ignition switch.

740, 760 & 780

1. Disconnect battery ground cable.
2. Remove noise insulation panel below instrument panel, then disconnect electrical connector from switch.
3. Remove upper steering column cover and casing around switch.
4. Loosen switch mounting screw, then install key and position switch in Start position.
5. Working through hole beneath holder, depress catch and remove switch from vehicle.
6. Insert key into new switch, depress locking tab, the remove key.
7. Position switch in holder and reinsert key to release locking tab.
8. Tighten switch mounting screw, then install column casing and cover.
9. Connect electrical connector, then install noise insulation panel.

LIGHT SWITCH
REPLACE

240 DL, GL & GLT

1. Disconnect defroster hose from defroster outlet.
2. Remove screws retaining outlet.
3. Pull out switch knob.
4. Lift out defroster outlet.
5. Remove nut and lift out switch.

740, 760 & 780 SERIES

1. Disconnect battery ground cable.
2. Remove trim panel under dashboard, then disconnect switch wires.
3. Remove switch retaining nut and switch.

TURN SIGNAL SWITCH
REPLACE

1987 vehicles with "SRS" designation on steering wheel are equipped with air bag restraint system. Use extreme caution when working around steering column to avoid personal injury.

1. Remove screws holding upper and lower switch covers and remove covers.
2. Where necessary, remove overdrive switch bracket.
3. Remove turn signal switch mounting screws and remove switch.

INSTRUMENT CLUSTER
REPLACE

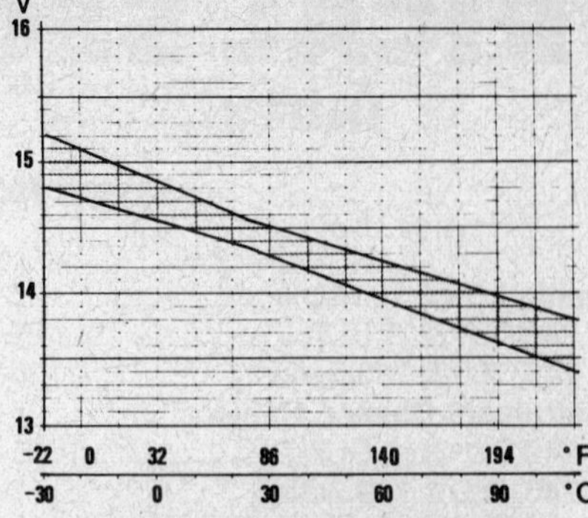

Fig. 4 Charging voltage graph (w/external temperature sensor disconnected)

1987 vehicles with "SRS" designation on steering wheel are equipped with air bag restraint system. Use extreme caution when working around steering column to avoid personal injury.

240 DL, GL & GLT

1. Remove covers over the steering column.
2. Remove attaching screws for the bracket and allow it to drop down towards the steering column. Remove the cluster attaching screws.
3. Disconnect speedometer cable.
4. Take hold of back side of the speedometer unit and press upwards and out until the snap lock in the upper edge releases.
5. Lift out the cluster and disconnect the electrical leads.

740, 760 & 780 SERIES

1. Remove insulation and sound proofing from under dash panel.
2. Remove two attaching screws and catches, located at both ends of instrument cluster.
3. Press cluster forward to remove from catches, then lift up and partially pull out cluster.
4. Disconnect speedometer and electrical connections from cluster, then remove cluster.

STOP LIGHT SWITCH
REPLACE

1. Disconnect battery ground cable.
2. Disconnect switch wires.
3. Remove switch retaining nut. Remove switch.
4. When installing switch, be sure that distance between brake pedal when fully released, and thread bronze hub on switch is 4 mm (.008). If necessary, adjust by loosening bracket attaching screw and moving bracket.

NEUTRAL SAFETY SWITCH
REPLACE

The switch is located inside the passenger compartment and is mounted directly beneath the gear shift selector. Remove the selector cover and loosen the two retaining bolts to adjust or replace the switch.

WINDSHIELD WIPER SWITCH
REPLACE

1987 vehicles with "SRS" designation on steering wheel are equipped with air bag restraint system. Use extreme caution when working around steering column to avoid personal injury.

1. Remove covers over steering column.
2. Remove switch retaining screws.
3. Transfer wires to new switch and install retaining screws and covers.

W/S WIPER MOTOR
REPLACE

240 DL, GL & GLT

1. Disconnect battery ground cable. Remove side panel.
2. Remove glove box.
3. Disconnect the linkage to motor retaining nut and remove retaining bolts. Lift motor off of firewall.

740, 760 & 780 SERIES

1. Remove wiper arm, then lift hood and disconnect battery ground cable.
2. Remove cover plate attaching screws and clips, then lift out cover plate.
3. Close hood and remove motor cover located below the windshield.
4. Disconnect all electrical connections, then remove attaching screws and wiper assembly.
5. Remove motor from wiper assembly.

BLOWER MOTOR
REPLACE

240 DL, GL & GLT

1. Disconnect battery ground cable.
2. Remove trim panels from both sides of center console.
3. Snap off retaining clips for both side covers of heater unit.
4. Slip retaining clips off turbine wheels on each side of the heater.
5. Move the heater control valve capillary tube to one side.
6. Remove the left inner end of the central unit.
7. Remove the motor retainer, disconnect the wires and lift out the motor.

740, 760 & 780 SERIES

1. Disconnect battery ground cable.
2. Remove trim panel under glove compartment.
3. Remove blower motor attaching screws, then lower motor and disconnect all hoses and electrical connections.
4. Remove fan and blower motor.

HEATER CORE
REPLACE

240 DL, GL & GLT

1. Drain coolant, then disconnect battery ground cable.

2. Remove heater hoses from connections at firewall and plug connections.
3. On air conditioned models, remove holding clamps from evaporator hoses. **Do not discharge the air conditioning system, simply loosen the retaining clamps to allow removal of the firewall door.**
4. Remove instrument cluster.
5. Disconnect air ducts and vacuum hoses.
6. Remove unit mounting bolts.
7. Carry out Steps 2-6 under "Blower Motor, Replace" procedure.
8. Remove evaporator from central unit without disconnecting evaporator hoses.
9. Disconnect heater valve hoses and remove the heater core.

740, 760 & 780 SERIES

1. Drain coolant, then disconnect battery ground cable.
2. Remove heater hose from connections at fire wall and plug connections.
3. Remove ashtray and holder, lighter and storage compartment, then remove center console.
4. Remove left side trim panel from under dash, then remove air duct under steering column.
5. Remove glove compartment and electrical connections, then upper console side panels.
6. Remove radio compartment attaching bolts, then radio compartment.
7. Remove panel around heater control, radio console and control panel attaching screws.
8. Remove control panel cables and electrical connections, then remove control panel.
9. Remove center panel vents, distribution unit attaching screws and remaining air ducts.
10. Remove vacuum motor hoses, then aspirator hoses, if equipped with Automatic Climate Control (ACC).
11. Remove distribution unit, then four heater core attaching bolts and heater core.

GASOLINE ENGINE SECTION

INDEX

ENGINE REPLACE

240 DL, GL & GLT

B-21, B-23 & B-230 Engines

The engine and transmission are removed as an assembly.

1. Open hood, then scribe hood hinge locations and remove hood.
2. Disconnect battery ground cable.
3. Remove air filter.
4. Drain coolant from radiator and oil from engine.
5. Disconnect radiator hoses, then remove radiator and fan cover.
6. On turbocharged models, loosen attaching bolts, then disconnect exhaust pipe from turbocharger assembly.
7. If equipped, remove attaching bolts, then move servo pump and A/C compressor aside. **Do not disconnect lines and/or hoses.**
8. Label, then disconnect all necessary vacuum lines, fuel lines, electrical connectors and water hoses from engine.
9. Raise and support front of vehicle.
10. Remove engine splash guard attaching bolts, then the splash guard.
11. On naturally aspirated models, disconnect exhaust pipe from manifolds.
12. Remove engine to front axle crossmember mount bolts.
13. Remove front exhaust pipe support from transmission.
14. On manual transmission models, disconnect clutch cable, then remove gearshift lever.
15. On automatic transmission models, disconnect selector linkage from transmission.
16. Disconnect speedometer cable from transmission.
17. Disconnect driveshaft from transmission.
18. Position a suitable jack under transmission assembly, then remove transmission crossmember.
19. Disconnect electrical connectors from transmission.
20. Install suitable engine lifting equipment onto engine lifting eyes.
21. Carefully lift engine and transmission assembly from vehicle.
22. Reverse procedure to install.

740 SERIES

B-230 Engine

Refer to B-23/B-230 Engines under "760 Series" for procedures.

760 SERIES

B-28/B-280 Engines

The engine, transmission and front exhaust pipe are removed as an assembly.

1. Disconnect battery ground cable.
2. Scribe hood hinge locations, then remove hood.
3. Remove air cleaner, then the engine splash shield.
4. Disconnect gearshift and accelerator linkages.
5. Drain engine coolant.
6. On automatic transmission models,

disconnect transmission oil cooler lines at radiator.
7. Remove front grille, then the radiator and cover and fan shroud.
8. Remove air conditioning compressor attaching bolts and drive belt and position compressor aside. **Do not disconnect lines from compressor.**
9. Remove air conditioning condenser attaching bolts and position condenser aside. **Do not disconnect lines from condenser.**
10. Disconnect all electrical connectors, water hoses and vacuum lines necessary for engine removal.
11. Raise and support vehicle and drain engine oil.
12. Disconnect driveshaft from transmission.
13. Attaching suitable lifting equipment to engine, then remove front and rear engine mount bolts and the crossmember.
14. Lower vehicle and support transmission with a suitable jack.
15. Remove engine lifting equipment, then attach suitable hoist and remove engine and transmission assembly from vehicle.

B-23/B-230 Engines

The engine and transmission are removed as an assembly.

1. Disconnect battery ground cable, then drain cooling system and crankcase.
2. Remove distributor cap, if necessary.
3. Remove preheating hose and fan shroud, then the front grille, if necessary.
4. If applicable, disconnect exhaust pipe at turbocharger assembly.
5. If equipped, remove attaching bolts and position power steering pump and A/C compressor aside. **Do not disconnect lines and/or hoses.**
6. Disconnect all electrical wires, hoses, lines and cables that will interfere will engine removal. Label all vacuum hoses to aid in installation.
7. Raise and support vehicle, then remove engine splash guard attaching screws and guard.
8. On naturally aspirated models, disconnect exhaust pipe from manifold.
9. On all models, remove engine mount to front crossmember attaching bolts.
10. Remove front exhaust pipe support from transmission.
11. On manual transmission equipped vehicles, disconnect clutch cable and remove gearshift lever.
12. On automatic transmission equipped vehicles, disconnect selector linkage from transmission.
13. On all models, disconnect speedometer cable, then remove driveshaft from transmission. **On some models, the front U-joint is insulated for vibration with a rubber mount. Use care when separating joint from output flange to prevent damage to rubber mounting.**
14. Support transmission with suitable jack, remove rear crossmember, then disconnect all electrical connectors from transmission.
15. Attach suitable engine lifting equipment to engine, then carefully lift engine/transmission assembly from vehicle.
16. Reverse procedure to install.

Fig. 1 Cylinder head tightening sequence. B-21, B-23 & B-230 engines

780 SERIES

B-280 Engine

Refer to B-28/B-280 Engines under "760 Series" for procedures.

CYLINDER HEAD REPLACE

B-21, B-23 & B-230 ENGINES

1. Drain coolant by opening nipple on right hand side of engine.
2. Disconnect battery ground cable.
3. Disconnect upper radiator hose from engine.
4. Disconnect vacuum hoses from intake manifold.
5. Disconnect hoses from diverter valve.
6. If applicable, remove air injection reactor pump retaining bolts and position pump aside.
7. On B-21 and B-23 engines, remove fan shroud and drive belts. On B-230 engines, remove fan, preheater hose clamp, fan shroud, drive belts and water pump pulley.
8. If applicable, remove bolts from intake manifold brace.
9. On some air conditioned models, it may be necessary to discharge system and disconnect suction hose from compressor in order to gain sufficient clearance.
10. Remove exhaust pipe flange nuts from manifold or turbocharger.
11. Disconnect spark plug leads from plugs.
12. Disconnect vacuum hoses from wax thermostat and wires from temperature sensor and thermal time switch, if applicable.
13. Disconnect heater hose from rear of cylinder head.
14. Remove timing belt cover retaining bolts and remove cover (upper cover on B-230 engines).
15. On B-230 engines, rotate crankshaft clockwise until mark on camshaft gear is aligned with mark on inner cover and mark on crankshaft pulley is aligned with "0" mark on timing indicator. On B-21 and B-23 engines, rotate crankshaft clockwise until marks on camshaft and intermediate shaft pulleys are aligned with marks on inner casing.
16. On B-230 engines, loosen nut for belt tensioner and press idler roller back. Lock roller by inserting a 3 mm drill through the pusher rod and remove timing belt. On B-21 and B-23 engines, loosen belt tensioner nut, pull belt outward to compress tensioner spring, then tighten tensioner nut and lift timing belt off camshaft pulley.
17. On B-230 engines, remove camshaft pulley, spacer and timing belt tensioner stud bolt.
18. Remove vacuum pump, if applicable.
19. Remove cylinder head retaining bolts and cylinder head together with intake manifold.
20. Reverse procedure to install. When installing head, follow tightening sequence in **Fig. 1** and note the following:
    a. On B-21 and B-23 engines equipped with Allen-head type bolts, torque bolts in two steps. Step 1: 44 ft. lbs.; step 2: 81 ft. lbs.
    b. On B-21 and B-23 engines equipped with hex-head type bolts, and all B-230 engines, torque bolts in three steps. Step 1: 15 ft. lbs.; step 2: 45 ft. lbs.; step 3: tighten bolts an additional 90° from that in step 2.
    c. Follow instructions given under "Timing Belt, Replace" procedure to install and correctly adjust timing belt.

B-28 ENGINE

1. Disconnect battery ground cable, then drain engine coolant.
2. Remove fuel filler cap to release any pressure in fuel tank, then reinstall the cap.
3. Remove air intake duct, then the oil filler cap and hoses.
4. Disconnect fuel lines from filter and the fuel return pipe.
5. Remove air control valve from intake manifold.
6. Disconnect leads from spark plugs, ignition coil and wire holders.
7. Remove fuel injectors from cylinder head and plug openings to prevent contamination.
8. Loosen distributor cap retaining clips.
9. Disconnect vacuum hose from fuel vapor canister.
10. Disconnect all vacuum hoses at intake manifold.
11. Remove front section of manifold. Plug openings to prevent contamination.
12. Disconnect throttle cable, kickdown cable and, if equipped, cruise control cable from throttle control pulley.
13. Disconnect wiring harness and position aside.
14. Remove control pressure regulator attaching bolts and position regulator aside.
15. Remove intake manifold attaching bolts, then the intake manifold.
16. If removing right cylinder head, proceed as follows:
    a. Remove air conditioning compressor attaching bolts and position

Fig. 2 Cylinder head tightening sequence. B-28 engine

Fig. 4 Cylinder liner retainers installed. B-28 engine

compressor aside.

b. Remove oil dipstick and tube, then disconnect upper radiator hose.
c. Disconnect heater hoses from cylinder head.
d. Disconnect ground lead and ignition timing sender electrical connector from cylinder head.
e. Remove distributor cap with ignition cables, then rotate crankshaft until rotor aligns with notch in distributor body, and remove distributor.

17. If removing left cylinder head, proceed as follows:
    a. Remove vacuum pump, then the air intake heater tube.
    b. Disconnect lower radiator hose from water pump, then the hose between water pump and cylinder head.
18. Remove exhaust crossover pipe flange nuts and the exhaust pipe support bolts at transmission.
19. Pry off rubber support rings at center muffler, then slide exhaust system rearward.
20. Remove valve cover attaching bolts, then the valve cover.
21. Remove cover plate from rear of cylinder head.
22. Remove timing gear cover plug using an 8 mm Allen wrench, and on right side, remove cover plate.
23. Remove four upper timing gear cover attaching bolts.
24. Loosen timing gear sprocket bolt using a 10 mm Allen wrench.
25. Remove rocker arm shaft assembly. Bolts must be removed in the proper sequence, **Fig. 2.**
26. Loosen camshaft lock plate bolt and move plate to one side, **Fig. 3.**
27. Install tool 5213. Hook holder under timing chain and tighten nut hand tight, then fasten holder to timing gear cover. Tension the chain and sprocket by turning knob on tool. The tool holds tension on the timing chain when the camshaft is removed. If the chain loosens, the tensioner will take up any slack. If this occurs, the timing gear cover will have to be removed.
28. Remove camshaft sprocket center bolt, then move camshaft to the rear and disconnect it from sprocket.
29. Pry up cylinder head at inner edge with the wooden handle of a hammer, then remove cylinder head from block. **Do not pull head straight up during removal, as cylinder liners may be disturbed. As soon as cylinder head is removed, install cylinder liner retainers, Fig. 4.**
30. Reverse procedure to install. Note the following:
    a. Torque cylinder head bolts in three steps, in sequence, **Fig. 2.** Torque first to 10 Nm (7 ft. lbs.), then to 30 Nm (22 ft. lbs.) and finally to 60 Nm (44 ft. lbs.). Allow head to stabilize for at least 10-15 minutes.
    b. While head is stabilizing, install camshaft into timing gear sprocket and install retaining bolt and camshaft lock.
    c. Loosen cylinder head bolts in sequence, **Fig. 2,** then retorque to 15-20 Nm (11-15 ft. lbs.). Install tool 5098 onto socket, then, using protractor, tighten bolts an additional 113-117°.

VALVE GUIDES

1. On B-21, B-23 and B-230 engines,

Fig. 3 Camshaft locking fork installed. B-28 engine

Fig. 5 Valve adjustment. B-21 & B-23 engines

heat cylinder head to approximately 212°F., then press out old guides using tool 5218. On B-28 engines, press guides out with cylinder head at room temperature using tool mentioned.

2. On B-21, B-23 and B-230 engines, press in new guides with cylinder head at room temperature using tool 5027 for intake guides and tool 5028 for exhaust guides. On B-28 engines, heat cylinder head to approximately 300°F., cool new valve guide to −95°F. using carbon dioxide gas or equivalent, then press new guides into position using tool 5108 for intake guides and tool 5109 for exhaust guides. **Installation must be completed within 3-4 seconds to prevent temperatures from stabilizing.** On all engines, press guides down until the tools mentioned above are fully bottomed.
3. On all engines, lightly clean valve guides using reamer 5224 or equivalent.

VALVE ADJUSTMENT

B-21, B-23 & B-230 ENGINES

1. Remove valve cover.

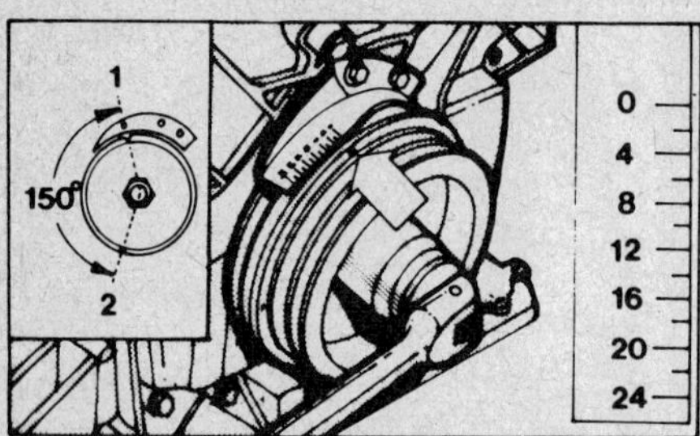

Fig. 6 Crankshaft pulley timing marks. B-28 engine

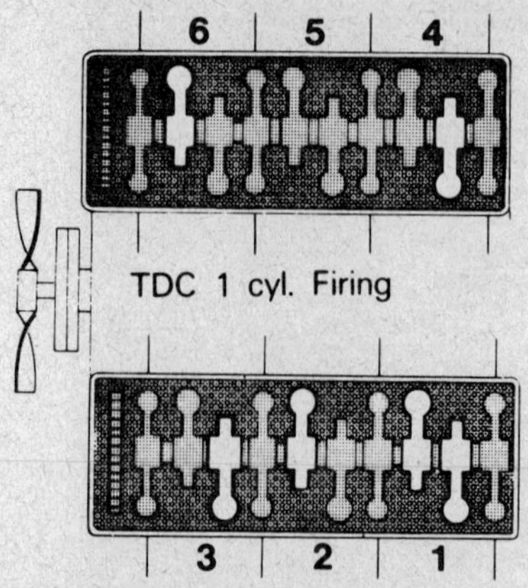

Fig. 7 Valve adjustment, No. 1 cylinder at TDC position. B-28 engine

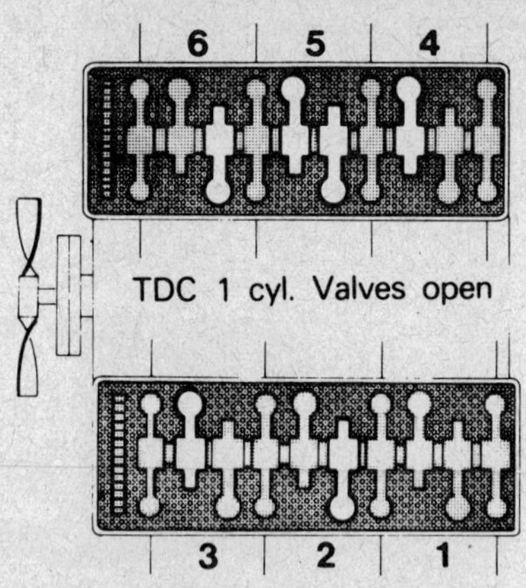

Fig. 8 Valve adjustment, No. 6 cylinder at TDC position. B-28 engine

2. Rotate engine until both valves for #1 cylinder are on the heel of cam lobes.
3. Insert feeler gauge between cam lobe and valve shim to check clearance. If clearance is incorrect, line up valve depressors so notches are at right angles to engine center line arrows in **Fig. 5.**
4. Attach tool 5022. Screw down tool spindle until depressor groove is just above edge of head and accessible with pliers, **Fig. 5.**
5. Use special pliers 5026 to remove valve shim.
6. Use a micrometer to measure shim thickness. Calculate shim thickness necessary to obtain correct clearance.
7. Coat new shim with oil and install it in valve depressor with marking facing downward.
8. Repeat adjustment procedure for cylinders 3, 4 and 2.

B-28 ENGINE

1. Remove valve covers.
2. Rotate crankshaft until No. 1 cylinder is at TDC position. The crankshaft pulley has two timing marks on it, **Fig. 6.** Mark #1 is the only one to be used on valve adjustment.
3. With No. 1 cylinder at TDC, adjust the following valves: Intake, Nos. 1, 2 and 4; Exhaust, Nos. 1, 3 and 6 as shown, **Fig. 7.**
4. Rotate engine one full revolution clockwise to bring timing mark back in line with the "0" on the timing plate. Engine is now in No. 6 cylinder firing position.
5. With engine positioned as outlined above, adjust the following valves: Intake, Nos. 3, 5 and 6; Exhaust, Nos. 2, 4 and 5 as shown, **Fig. 8.**
6. Replace valve covers.

TIMING COVER REPLACE

B-21 & B-23 ENGINES

1. Disconnect battery ground cable, if necessary.
2. Remove cooling fan shroud and drive belts.
3. Remove timing cover attaching bolts, then the cover.

B-230 ENGINE

This engine is equipped with both upper and lower timing covers. To remove covers, proceed as follows:

1. Disconnect battery ground cable, if necessary.
2. Remove cooling fan, preheater hose clamp at fan shroud, if applicable, then the shroud.
3. Remove drive belts and water pump pulley.
4. Remove upper timing cover attaching bolts and screws, then the upper cover.
5. Remove lower cover attaching bolts, then the lower cover.

B-28 ENGINE

1. Disconnect battery ground cable, then drain cooling system.
2. Disconnect oil tube from cooler.
3. Disconnect electrical leads and fan shroud from radiator, then remove radiator and shroud.
4. Remove engine splash guard.
5. Loosen drive belts, then remove power steering pump and bracket and A/C compressor, and position aside. Do not disconnect hoses from pump or compressor.
6. Remove drive belts, cooling fan and water pump pulley.
7. Remove air intake duct, vacuum pump and left hand valve cover.
8. Remove oil filler cap, control pressure regulator, electrical wiring and right hand valve cover.
9. Position No. 1 cylinder at TDC compression stroke, then lock flywheel using suitable tool and remove crankshaft pulley.
10. Position wiring harness to one side, then remove attaching bolts and timing gear cover.

TIMING BELT REPLACE

B-21 & B-23 ENGINES

1. Remove timing cover as outlined previously.
2. Rotate crankshaft until timing marks are aligned as shown in **Fig. 9.**
3. Loosen belt tensioner retaining nut, pull belt outward until tensioner spring is compressed, then tighten retaining nut and remove timing belt.
4. Ensure timing marks are still in alignment, then place belt around crankshaft and intermediate shaft pulleys so that two lines on belt are aligned with timing mark on crankshaft, **Fig. 9.**
5. Stretch belt over camshaft pulley and tensioner roller, taking care not to damage belt.
6. Loosen tensioner nut to permit spring tension to act on roller, then tighten tensioner nut.
7. Check to ensure belt has not slipped, then install timing cover.
8. Start engine and allow to reach normal operating temperature, then shut engine off. Remove rubber plug from timing cover, loosen tensioner nut to readjust belt, then retighten nut and install rubber plug. Readjust belt after vehicle has been driven 600 miles.

B-230 ENGINE

1. Remove upper timing cover, then turn crankshaft clockwise and align timing marks as shown in **Fig. 10.**
2. Remove belt tensioner retaining nut and washer, then install holding tool 5284 or equivalent onto vibration damper.
3. Remove retaining nut, vibration damper and lower timing cover.
4. Pull timing belt outward, then lock tensioner roller by inserting a 3 mm drill bit through the pusher rod. Remove timing belt. **Do not turn crankshaft with timing belt removed.**
5. Reverse procedure to install, ensuring timing marks are aligned properly. To adjust belt, remove drill bit and pull belt until tensioner spring is fully depressed, then tighten tensioner nut. Start engine and allow to reach normal operating temperature, then shut engine off. Remove rubber plug from timing cover, loosen tensioner nut to readjust belt, then retighten nut and install rubber plug. Readjust belt after vehicle has been driven 600 miles.

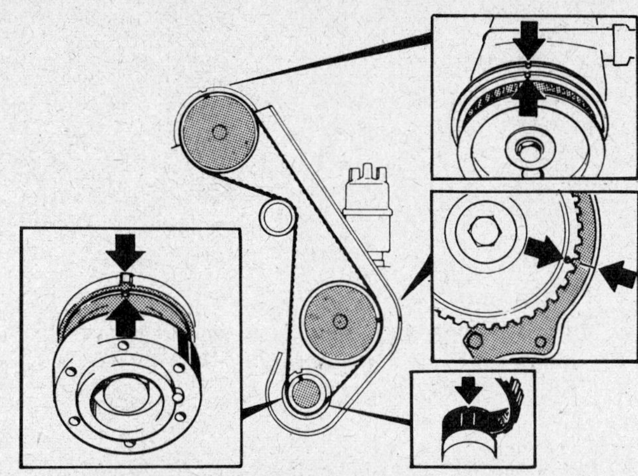

Fig. 9 Aligning timing marks. B-21 & B-23 engines

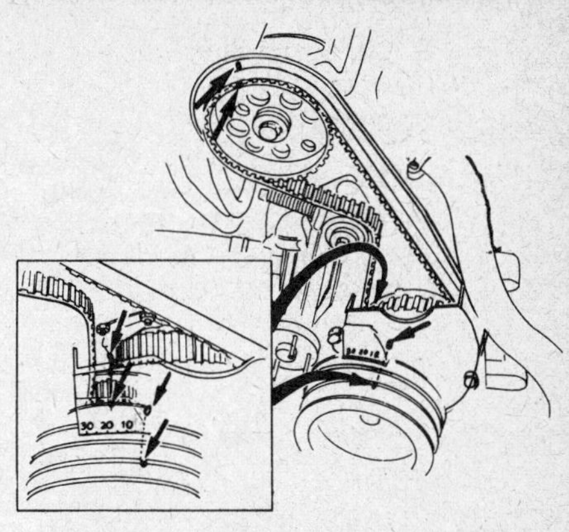

Fig. 10 Aligning timing marks. B-230 engine

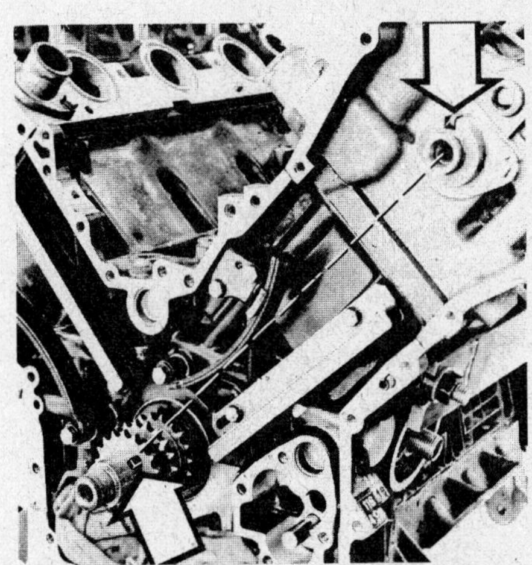

Fig. 11 Positioning left camshaft for sprocket installation. B-28 engine

TIMING CHAIN
REPLACE
B-28 ENGINE

1. Remove timing cover as outlined previously.
2. Loosen right and left camshaft sprocket center bolts, then release tension on both chains by turning each lock 1/4 turn counterclockwise and pushing piston in.
3. Remove oil pump sprocket and chain, chain tensioners, oil strainers, chain dampers and camshaft sprockets and chains.
4. Remove outer sprocket, spacer sleeve (if applicable), woodruff key, inner sprocket and woodruff key from crankshaft snout.
5. Install inner key, sprocket (with line facing outward), spacer sleeve, if applicable, outer woodruff key and sprocket onto crankshaft snout.
6. Install new oil strainers, chain tensioners and dampers.
7. To install left timing chain, position crankshaft so crankshaft woodruff key points to left camshaft (one o'clock) position. Position left camshaft so its keyway points to twelve o'clock position, **Fig. 11.**
8. Slip chain over camshaft sprocket, being sure that timing mark on camshaft sprocket is between two painted timing marks on the chain.
9. Holding chain on camshaft sprocket, slip the other end of the chain over the crankshaft inner sprocket. Be sure that timing mark on gear aligns with painted link on the chain.
10. Install sprocket onto camshaft. Pin in sprocket must go into slot in camshaft.
11. Install sprocket bolt. Insert a screwdriver through sprocket to prevent engine from turning and torque retaining bolt to 70-80 Nm (51-59 ft. lbs.).
12. Rotate engine clockwise to position crankshaft woodruff key at six o'clock. Position right camshaft so its groove is at seven o'clock.
13. Install chain on camshaft sprocket, being sure timing mark on sprocket is between two painted marks on chain.
14. Holding chain on camshaft sprocket, slip other end of chain over crankshaft intermediate sprocket. Be sure that timing mark on gear aligns with painted link on chain.
15. Install sprocket on camshaft. Pin in sprocket must go into slot in sprocket.
16. Install sprocket bolt. Insert a screwdriver through sprocket to prevent engine from turning and torque retaining bolt to 70-80 Nm (51-59 ft. lbs.).
17. Turn lock screw on each chain tensioner 1/4 turn clockwise to release tensioner shoes, then turn crankshaft clockwise two complete revolutions until woodruff key faces twelve o'clock position.
18. Install oil pump sprocket and drive chain. Be sure to center pump while installing to prevent binding of the gears against aluminum housing.
19. Install timing gear cover and torque retaining bolts to 10-15 Nm (7-11 ft. lbs.).

Fig. 12 Camshaft tensioning tool. B-21, B-23 & B-230 engines

CAMSHAFT
REPLACE
B-21, B-23 & B-230 ENGINES

1. Remove timing belt, distributor (if applicable) and camshaft pulley.
2. Remove center camshaft bearing cap. **The camshaft bearing caps are matched to bores and must not be interchanged.**
3. Attach tool 5021, **Fig. 12,** and tighten handle to hold camshaft in place while removing other bearing caps.
4. Remove four remaining caps.
5. Back off tool handle and release camshaft. Remove camshaft.
6. When installing camshaft, oil all bearing caps and position camshaft on cylinder head with dowel for sprocket upward. On B-230 engines, coat cylinder head front and rear bearing cap sealing surfaces with sealant 1161027-6 or equivalent.
7. Position rear camshaft bearing cap. Do not tighten cap.
8. Attach tool 5021 and press down camshaft.
9. Install all but the center bearing caps.
10. Remove tool 5021 and install the center bearing cap. Torque bearing cap retaining nuts to 20 Nm (15 ft. lbs.).
11. Install camshaft pulley and distributor (if applicable).

12. Install and adjust timing belt as outlined previously.

B-28 ENGINE

Left Bank

1. Remove cylinder head. Refer to "Cylinder Head, Replace" for procedure.
2. Slide camshaft out rear of cylinder head.
3. Reinstall camshaft and install cylinder head as outlined.

Right Bank

The camshaft can be removed from right bank without removing cylinder head.

1. Remove valve cover.
2. Attach tool 5213 as outlined under "Cylinder Head, Replace."
3. Remove timing sprocket retaining bolt, camshaft lock and access cover at rear of cylinder head.
4. Remove cap from coolant expansion tank.
5. Remove cylinder head retaining bolts and rocker arm assembly. **Do not disturb cylinder head.**
6. Remove access cover from firewall. Slide camshaft rearward and through firewall into passenger compartment.

PISTON & ROD ASSEMBLY

B-21, B-23 & B-230 ENGINES

Assembly connecting rods to pistons so pistons can be installed with notch on piston top facing forward. Mark on connecting rod and cap should also face forward.

To install pistons, use tool 5031 or other suitable ring compressor.

B-28 ENGINE

The B-28 engine uses a Mahle piston with a height of 62.8 mm. Pistons are available only as a piston/cylinder liner set. Piston pins are press fit in piston and connecting rod. Pins are removed by pressing them out with the aid of special tool 5092. To install a new piston pin, the piston end of the connecting rod is heated on an electric heater. To gauge the correct heat, place a small piece of solder on the connecting rod. The solder will melt when the rod reaches the proper temperature. When the rod is sufficiently heated, place it and the piston in the tool fixture. Arrow on the piston should face upward.

The tool fixture has a side for rods 1, 2 and 3 and the opposite side for rods 4, 5 & 6. It is important that the rods face in the proper direction. With the piston and rod correctly set in the tool, install the piston pin in the mandrill, dip the pin in oil and quickly push the mandrel pin assembly into the piston until it is stopped by the tool.

PISTON PINS

B-21, B-23 & B-230 ENGINES

Piston pins are available in .002" oversize. If pin hole in piston is so worn as to require an oversize pin, the hole should first be reamed until the pin can be pushed through by hand with only a light pressure.

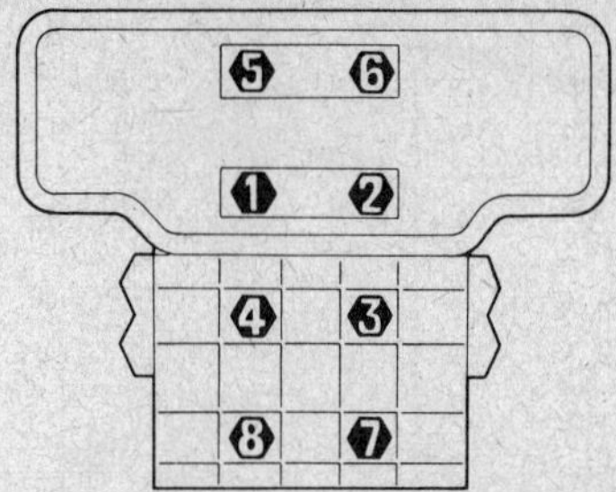

Fig. 13 Main bearing torque sequence. B-28 & B-280 engines

PISTONS & RINGS

PISTON RING END GAP

1. Using a piston turned upside-down, push each ring down into the cylinder in which it is to be installed.
2. Measure the gap between ends of the ring with a feeler gauge. End gap should be as specified in "Pistons, Pins, Rings, Crankshaft & Bearings" chart at the beginning of this chapter.
3. After installing rings on pistons, check to be sure rings are not binding in their grooves, and that gaps are 120° apart.

CRANKSHAFT REAR OIL SEAL

REPLACE

B-21, B-23 & B-230 ENGINES

1. Remove transmission, clutch (if applicable) and flywheel.
2. Using a suitable screwdriver, carefully pry out old seal from between holder and crankshaft.
3. Press in new seal using tools 1801 and 5276 or equivalents. Inspect seal surface of crankshaft. The seal can be installed to different depths to compensate for wear. If old seal was flush with holder, remove one spacer ring from tool 5276. If seal was approximately .120 inch inside holder, remove two spacer rings from service tool.
4. Reinstall flywheel, clutch (if applicable) and transmission.

B-28 ENGINE

1. Remove transmission, clutch (if applicable) and flywheel.
2. Using a suitable screwdriver, carefully pry out old seal from between holder and crankshaft.
3. Lubricate seal and holder groove, then pack grease between sealing lips of seal. Press in new seal using tools 1801 and 5953 or equivalents, until seal is bottomed in crankshaft.

CAMSHAFT, CRANKSHAFT & INTERMEDIATE SHAFT FRONT SEALS

REPLACE

B-21, B-23 & B-230 ENGINES

Before suspecting that the camshaft, crankshaft or intermediate shaft front seals are leaking, check engine flame guard, if equipped. A restricted flame guard will cause the engine oil dipstick to jump out of the pipe seat, engine knock and oil leakage at front seals. If any of these symptoms are encountered, thoroughly clean flame guard and engine assembly, then check for oil leaks.

1. Remove timing belt as outlined previously.
2. On B-230 engines, remove tensioner and inner timing belt cover.
3. If seals require replacement, proceed as follows:
   a. Remove pulley(s) using tool 5034 or equivalent.
   b. Using a suitable screwdriver, remove front seal(s). Do not damage sealing surface when removing seal.
   c. Check sealing surfaces for wear and/or damage.
   d. Coat new seal with suitable grease.
   e. Using tool 5025 or equivalent, install camshaft or intermediate sprocket seal and seal seat.
   f. Using tool 5024 for B-21 and B-23 engines or tool 5283 for B-230 engine, install crankshaft seal and seal seat.
   g. Install sprocket (s). Ensure camshaft sprocket side plates face outward from sprocket. Torque sprocket attaching bolt to 37 ft. lbs. Use tool 5034 to hold sprocket from turning when tightening. Install intermediate sprocket with marking (indentation) facing outward. Torque sprocket attaching bolt to 37 ft. lbs. Use tool 5034 to hold sprocket from turning while tightening.
   h. Install inner timing cover and belt tensioner, if applicable.
   i. Ensure timing marks are correctly aligned, then install timing belt and cover(s) as outlined previously. **Never turn crankshaft or camshaft with timing belt removed or serious engine damage will result.**

MAIN BEARING TORQUE SEQUENCE

B-28 & B-280 ENGINES

Whenever replacing main bearings on B-28 and B-280 engines, the following torque sequence should be followed:

1. Torque main bearing nuts 1 through 8, **Fig. 13,** to 22 ft. lbs.

2. Loosen nut 1, retorque to 24 ft. lbs., then tighten an additional 75° using a suitable protractor.
3. Repeat step 2 with remaining nuts, following sequence shown in **Fig. 13.**

OIL PAN

REPLACE

240 DL, GL & GLT

1. Raise and support vehicle and drain oil. Replace drain plug and torque to 44 ft. lbs. (60 Nm).
2. Remove splash guard under engine and remove engine mount nuts from underside of crossmember.
3. Disconnect steering shaft at steering gear. On vehicles with manual steering gear, pull shield up. On all models, remove lower bolt and loosen upper bolt, then slide flange assembly up steering shaft.
4. Raise engine slightly and support with tools 5033, 5006 and 5115 or equivalents.
5. Remove left side engine mount.
6. Support front crossmember, remove retaining bolts, then lower crossmember and remove support bracket at rear of oil pan.
7. Remove oil pan from vehicle by turning front of oil pan towards left and lowering oil pan.
8. Reverse procedure to install noting the following: torque oil pan bolts to 8 ft. lbs. (11 Nm), torque steering shaft coupling bolts to 18 ft. lbs. (25 Nm) and lock with cotter pins.

740 & 760 SERIES

B-23 & B-230 Engines

1. Raise and support vehicle and drain oil. Replace drain plug and torque to 44 ft. lbs. (60 Nm).
2. Remove splash guard under engine.
3. Disconnect battery ground cable, then disconnect exhaust pipe from front muffler flange and remove engine mount retaining nuts.
4. Remove steering shaft lower clamp bolt and loosen upper bolt, then slide flange assembly up steering shaft.
5. Loosen fan shroud, remove dipstick, then raise and support engine using tools 5033, 5115 and 5006 or equivalents.
6. Remove power steering hose retaining strap, then remove left side engine mount.
7. Remove front crossmember attaching bolts, disconnect hoses from power steering fluid reservoir, then remove reinforcing bracket and lower crossmember.
8. Remove retaining bolts, then turn oil pan and remove from vehicle.
9. Reverse procedure to install noting the following: torque oil pan bolts to 8 ft. lbs. (11 Nm), torque steering shaft coupling bolts to 18 ft. lbs. (25 Nm) and lock with cotter pins.

B-28 & B-280 Engines

1. Raise and support vehicle and drain oil.
2. Remove splash guard under engine.
3. Remove oil pan retaining bolts and the oil pan.
4. Reverse procedure to install.

780 SERIES

Refer to B-28 & B-280 Engines under "740 & 760 Series" for procedures.

OIL PUMP

REPLACE

B-21, B-23 & B-230 ENGINES

1. Remove oil pan as outlined previously.
2. Remove oil pump retaining bolts and remove pump together with delivery pipe.
3. When installing oil pump, always use new seals on delivery pipe. Attach oil trap drain hose clamp, if applicable, to one of the pump retaining bolts. Ensure hose is properly positioned behind oil pump shoulder.

B-28 & B280 ENGINES

1. Remove timing cover as outlined previously.
2. Remove three oil pump sprocket attaching bolts and remove sprocket and chain.
3. Remove four oil pump attaching bolts and remove pump.
4. When reinstalling pump, use extreme caution to prevent binding of pump gears against aluminum bore. Be sure to rotate pump as pump retaining bolts are torqued (7-11 ft. lbs.). Any binding will then be evident.

WATER PUMP

REPLACE

B-21, B-23 & B-230 ENGINES

1. Drain cooling system and remove radiator shroud retaining screws and move shroud to rear. Remove fan and fan clutch.
2. Loosen and remove accessory drive belts .
3. Remove fan pulley.
4. Remove timing cover.
5. Remove lower radiator hose.
6. Remove coolant pipe retaining bolt and pull pipe rearward.
7. Remove water pump.
8. Reverse procedure to install.

B-28 ENGINE

1. Disconnect battery ground cable and drain cooling system.
2. Remove intake manifold.
3. Disconnect expansion tank hoses from radiator.
4. Remove upper radiator hose.
5. With automatic transmission, disconnect transmission oil cooler pipes from radiator.
6. Remove screws from fan shroud and slide shroud to the rear.
7. Remove radiator.
8. Remove fan.
9. Remove water pump to cylinder head hoses. Remove coolant return hoses at pump.
10. Remove fan belts and water pump pulley.
11. Disconnect thermal timer and temperature sender wires.
12. Remove water pump from engine block.
13. Reverse procedure to install. Torque water pump attaching bolts to 13 ft. lbs.

TURBOCHARGER

The turbocharger is an exhaust driven device which compresses the intake air to increase engine power on a demand basis. This allows for performance equal to that of a larger displacement naturally aspirated engine without the added weight and fuel consumption. Other benefits of a turbocharged engine are lower noise and emission levels. Most 1984-87 models equipped with turbocharged engines use an intercooler. The intercooler is an air to air heat exchanger (similar to a radiator in appearance and function) and is mounted in front of the radiator.

As air travels from the turbocharger to the cylinder head it passes through the intercooler, which reduces the air charge temperature. This results in greater combustion efficiency, horsepower and torque.

FUEL PUMP

REPLACE

On some late model vehicles, an auxiliary fuel pump, located in the fuel tank, is used to supplement the main pump.

B-21, B-23, B-230, B-28 & B280 ENGINES

The main fuel pump may be located on the left side of the fuel tank, or attached to a bracket under the rear seat.

1. Clamp off the tank to pump hose with suitable pliers. Disconnect fuel lines from pump.
2. Disconnect wire connector from pump.
3. Remove pump retaining bolts and remove the pump.

DIESEL ENGINE SECTION

INDEX

ENGINE

REPLACE

EXC. TURBOCHARGED ENGINE

1. On manual transmission models, remove gear shift lever. On automatic transmission models, move selector to P position.
2. Disconnect battery ground cable, windshield washer hose at T-fitting, then remove hood.
3. Remove splash pan under engine and expansion tank cap. Disconnect lower hose at radiator and drain coolant. Disconnect lower hose from cold start device and turn end down to drain remaining coolant from engine.
4. On automatic transmission models, disconnect oil cooler lines. On all models, remove lower radiator hose, disconnect upper radiator hose at engine and disconnect expansion tank hose at radiator. Remove radiator.
5. Disconnect harness connector from firewall, heater control valve hoses, vacuum pump hose, and accelerator cable.
6. Disconnect fuel supply line at fuel filter and fuel return line at injection pump. Plug all connections to prevent dirt from entering fuel system. **Absolute cleanliness is extremely important. All connections must be cleaned thoroughly before disconnecting.**
7. Remove glow plug relay screws and hang relay and harness on engine. Remove and suspend power steering pump.
8. Remove cooling fan, pulley and drive belts. Remove air cleaner cover and disconnect alternator wire harness at voltage regulator.
9. Disconnect exhaust pipes from manifolds and drain engine oil.
10. On manual transmission models, disconnect clutch cable and return spring. On automatic transmission models, disconnect shift lever from transmission.
11. Disconnect speedometer cable, driveshaft, and gear lever. Loosen Allen head lock screw, push out pin and push shift lever up into vehicle.
12. Support transmission with suitable jack and remove transmission crossmember. Disconnect engine mounts and support engine using lifting hooks 5185 and 5186 or equivalent and lifting beam 2810 or equivalent.
13. Raise engine enough to unload mounts and remove left engine mount assembly. Remove jack from under transmission and lift out engine.
14. Reverse procedure to install.

TURBOCHARGED ENGINE

1. Disconnect battery cables.
2. Remove upper exhaust pipe to turbocharger attaching nut.
3. Disconnect air filter hose.
4. Remove rear preheat panel assembly.
5. Raise and support vehicle.
6. Disconnect red lead electrical connector from alternator assembly, then remove engine splash guard.
7. Remove lower right and left engine mount attaching nuts.
8. On manual transmission models, disconnect clutch cable from clutch fork.
9. Disconnect exhaust pipe from turbocharger assembly, transmission crossmember and coupling support brackets.
10. Loosen starter motor attaching bolts, then suspend starter motor from control arm strut. Use a piece of wire to suspend starter motor.
11. Remove flywheel housing attaching bolts. Leave at least 2 or 3 bolts in place to keep housing in position. Different size bellhousing bolts are used. Ensure to install correct bolt into its proper location. On manual transmission models, ensure to retain the two thick washers from either end of bellhousing and note positions from which they were removed for installation. On automatic transmission models, spring washers are used on all attaching bolts except the dipstick tube attaching bolts.
12. Disconnect coolant hoses from engine and allow engine coolant to drain as follows:
    a. On models without drain tap, disconnect lower hose from cold start unit.
    b. Disconnect lower hose from radiator.
    c. On models with drain tap, loosen drain tap and allow coolant to drain.
    d. Disconnect expansion tank hoses from radiator and upper radiator hose from engine.
13. Remove grille and fan shroud.
14. Remove radiator mounts and radiator.
15. Remove power steering pump and A/C compressor, then position aside.
16. Remove air filter.
17. Disconnect upper hose from heat exchanger. Disconnect vacuum hose from pump.
18. Disconnect and cap fuel lines from fuel filter and fuel connector manifold.
19. Disconnect throttle pulley cable.
20. Disconnect kickdown cable, if equipped.
21. On vehicles with cruise control, disconnect throttle cable and vacuum hose.
22. Disconnect glow plug relay from wheel housing. Separate cable harness, then disconnect spade terminal and positive lead from relay assembly.
23. Attach suitable engine lifting equipment onto engine.
24. On automatic transmission models, remove torque converter attaching bolts.
25. On manual transmission models, remove remaining bolts from flywheel housing.
26. Remove engine from vehicle.
27. Reverse procedure to install.

CYLINDER HEAD

REPLACE

EXC. TURBOCHARGED ENGINE

1. Disconnect battery ground cable and remove splash guard under engine. Disconnect exhaust pipe from transmission bracket, rear exhaust manifold, and front exhaust manifold.
2. Disconnect air cleaner cover, remove expansion tank cap, and disconnect lower radiator hose to drain coolant. Disconnect lower hose at cold start device and point down to drain remaining coolant.
3. Disconnect upper radiator hose and cold start device hose from cylinder

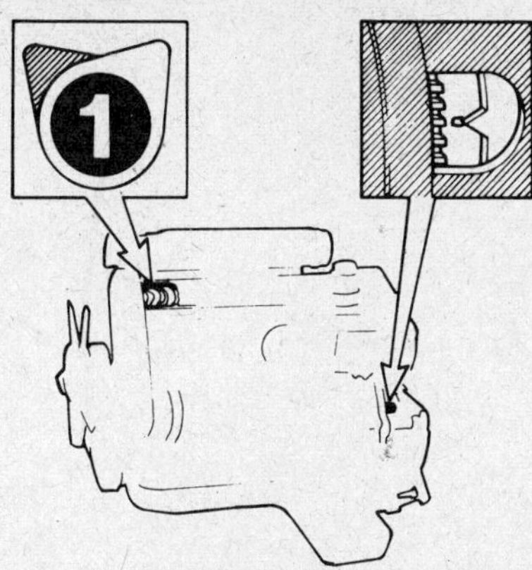

Fig. 1 Engine at TDC and injection

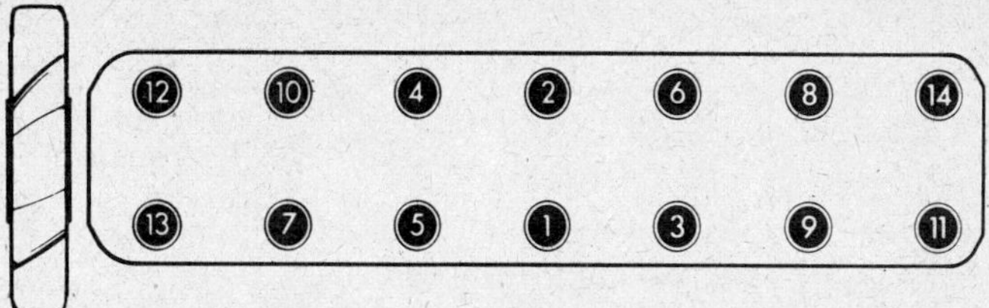

Fig. 2 Cylinder head bolt tightening sequence

head. Remove vacuum pump and plunger.

4. Remove fuel delivery pipes and plug all ends and connections to prevent entry of dirt. **Absolute cleanliness is extremely important. All connections must be cleaned thoroughly before disconnecting.**
5. Disconnect the following from cylinder head: wires for temperature gauge sender and glow plugs, wire harness for rear glow plug, return hose from rear injector, and temperature gauge sender wire holder.
6. Remove valve cover, front and rear timing belt covers. Set engine to TDC and injection position (compression stroke) for No. 1 cylinder. Both No. 1 cylinder camshaft lobes should point up at equal angles and flywheel timing mark should be at zero (0), **Fig. 1.**
7. Remove timing belt shield using care to avoid washer on inner retaining screw from falling inside timing gear lower cover.
8. Loosen retaining bolts for coolant pumps and belt idler pulley and remove belt from camshaft gear.
9. Using wrench 5199 or equivalent to hold gear, tap gear loose from camshaft. Do not allow camshaft to rotate.
10. Loosen injection pump bracket bolts to release belt tension and remove belt.
11. Using wrench 5199 or equivalent and wrench 5201 or equivalent to loosen bolt, remove camshaft rear gear. Camshaft must not be allowed to rotate.
12. Remove cylinder head bolts in reverse of tightening sequence, **Fig. 2.** Make sure that rear glow plug clears injection pump bracket and that valves do not contact cylinder walls.
13. Remove cylinder head and place on wooden blocks. Do not allow cylinder head to rest on valves. Clean gasket surfaces and check cylinder head for warpage, using steel rule and feeler gauge. Clearance should not exceed 0.008 inch lengthwise and 0.002 inch crosswise. Cracks between valve seats do not require replacement of cylinder head as long as they do not exceed 0.02 inch.
14. Reverse procedure to install, noting the following:
    a. Three sizes of head gaskets are available as indicated by 1, 2, or 3 notches on the tab adjacent to the No. 2 cylinder opening in the gasket. Number of notches must be the same as old gasket if pistons, connecting rods or crankshaft assemblies have not been disturbed. If pistons, connecting rods, or crankshaft have been replaced or serviced, piston projection above cylinder block face must be measured and a new gasket selected. For a piston projection of 0.026-0.031" use a gasket with a thickness of 0.055" (1 notch), for a piston projection of 0.032-0.035" use a gasket with a thickness of 0.059" (2 notches), and for a piston projection of 0.036-0.040" use a gasket with a thickness of 0.063" (3 notches).
    b. If cylinder head bolts are 11 mm diameter, torque cylinder head according to sequence in **Fig. 2**, in two steps: first to 30 ft. lbs. and then to 65 ft. lbs.
    c. If cylinder head bolts are 12 mm diameter, torque cylinder head bolts in steps as follows: Step 1, torque bolts in sequence, **Fig. 2**, to 30 ft. lbs., then 44 ft. lbs. and finally 55 ft. lbs. Step 2, tighten bolts 1/2 additional turn with continuous motion. Step 3, run engine until oil temperature reaches 120°F., then tighten bolts 1/4 additional turn with continuous motion.
    d. Refer to "Timing Belts, Replace" to set camshaft position.
    e. Refer to "Injection Pump Setting" to set pump.
    f. Torque fuel delivery pipes to 18 ft. lbs.

TURBOCHARGED ENGINE

Removal

1. Disconnect battery ground cable and remove engine splash guard.
2. Remove air filter, preheat and inlet hose.
3. Disconnect crankcase breather and blowoff valve hose.
4. Label, disconnect and cap all electrical connectors, vacuum and fuel lines from cylinder head.
5. Disconnect front exhaust pipe from turbocharger assembly. If necessary, apply anti-rust oil to the attaching bolts.
6. Disconnect exhaust pipe from transmission and coupling brackets. Cover exhaust pipe opening with suitable tape.
7. Remove expansion tank cap.
8. On vehicles without drain tap, disconnect lower radiator hose and drain coolant.
9. On vehicles with drain tap, carefully loosen drain tap and drain coolant. Disconnect lower hose from radiator.
10. Disconnect lower hose form cold start unit, point hose end downward and drain remaining coolant.
11. Disconnect and cap oil feed and return lines from oil cooler and turbocharger assembly.
12. Disconnect upper radiator hose and cold start unit hose from cylinder head.
13. Loosen power steering pump attaching bolts and position pump aside. Do not disconnect power steering pump lines.
14. Remove vacuum pump and pump plunger. Position vacuum pump aside.
15. Remove fuel delivery lines from cylinder head.
16. Remove valve cover.
17. Remove front and rear timing belt covers.
18. Set No. 1 cylinder to TDC and injection position (compression stroke). Both No. 1 cylinder camshaft lobes should be face upward at equal angles and the flywheel timing mark should be at zero (0), **Fig. 1.**
19. Remove cylinder head timing belt cover attaching screws.
20. Loosen water pump attaching bolts and release tension from timing belt tensioner.
21. Using tool 5199 or equivalent, to hold camshaft sprocket in place, loosen front camshaft sprocket attaching bolt. Using a suitable mallet, tap camshaft sprocket from camshaft. Remove sprocket and timing belt.
22. Loosen injection pump bracket attaching bolts to release belt tension. Leave one attaching bolts in place and lift off belt.
23. Using tool 5199 or equivalent, hold rear camshaft sprocket in place. Using tool 5201 or equivalent, loosen rear camshaft sprocket attaching bolt. **While loosening attaching bolt, do not allow camshaft to rotate.**
24. Carefully and gradually loosen cylinder head attaching bolts in reverse of tightening sequence shown in **Fig. 2.**
25. Carefully remove cylinder head from cylinder block. Ensure rear glow plug clears injection pump bracket and valves do not contact cylinder walls.

Installation

1. Place cylinder head on wooden blocks. Ensure cylinder head is not

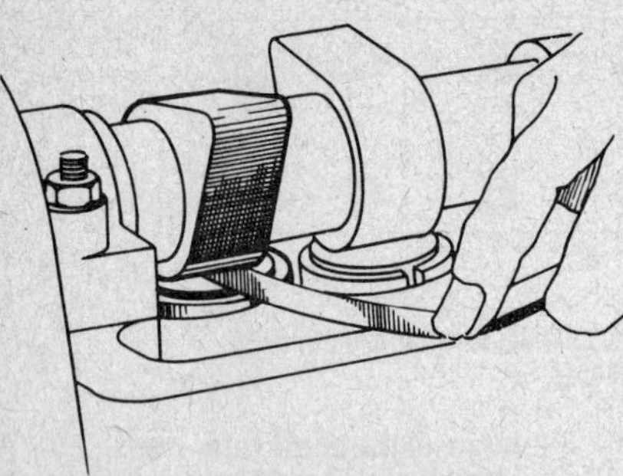

Fig. 3 Checking valve clearance

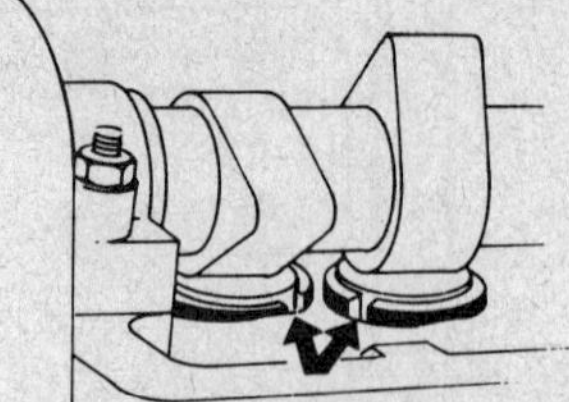

Fig. 4 Aligning valve tappets

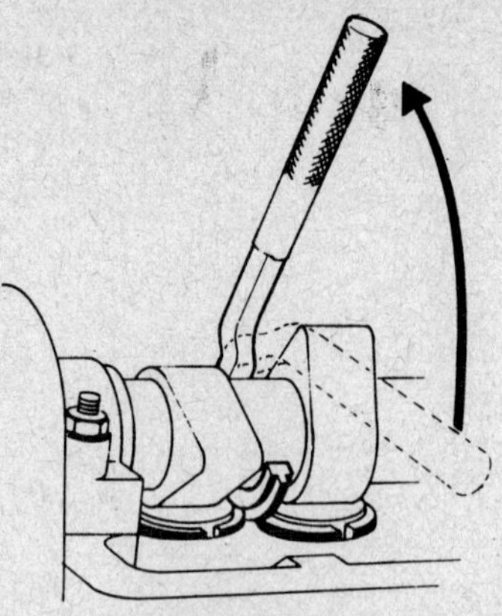

Fig. 5 Depressing valve tappets

resting on valves.

2. Clean gasket surfaces on cylinder head and cylinder head bolt holes.
3. Check cylinder head for damage and/or warpage. Measure cylinder head for warpage lengthwise and crosswise. Cylinder head warpage measured lengthwise should not exceed .020 inch. Cylinder head warpage measured crosswise should not exceed .008 inch. Replace cylinder head if warpage measurements obtained exceed specifications.
4. If cracks are found, ensure cracks are no longer than .020 inch. If cracks exceed .020 inch, replace cylinder head.
5. If pistons, connecting rods and bearings are replaced, piston height must be measured and correct cylinder head gasket installed. If measured piston height above cylinder block is .032-.035 inch, a .059 inch thick cylinder head gasket (indicated by 2 notches on gasket) must be used. If measured piston height above cylinder block is .036-.040 inch, a .063 inch gasket (indicated by 3 notches on gasket) must be used.
6. Install cylinder head gasket onto cylinder block with "UP" marking facing upward. When installing a new gasket, ensure to check date code located on gasket and packet. The gasket must be used before the indicated date. Only gaskets with code designation M2 or later may be used on turbocharged engines (D24T engines). To avoid reducing the sealing properties of the gasket do not open gasket packet until just before gasket is to be installed. When installing, ensure not to damage the Teflon strip or rubber seal.
7. Place No. 1 cylinder to TDC. In this position the flywheel timing mark should be at zero (0).
8. Set camshaft so that No. 1 cylinder is at the injection position (both camshaft lobes pointing diagonally upward.)
9. Install tool 5190 or equivalent, to prevent camshaft from rotating.
10. Lubricate, then install new cylinder head bolts.
11. Torque all cylinder head bolts one at a time in sequence shown in **Fig. 2** in four steps as follows:
    a. First step, torque bolts to 29 ft. lbs.
    b. Second step, torque bolts to 44 ft. lbs.
    c. Third step, torque bolts to 55 ft. lbs.
    d. Fourth step, angle tighten cylinder head bolts an additional 180° in one movement without stopping.
    e. After the cylinder head and all removed engine accessories are installed, vacuum lines, fuel lines and electrical connectors properly connected and engine properly filled with correct coolant, start and operate engine until normal operating temperature has been obtained. With engine properly warmed, turn cylinder head bolts an additional 90 degrees.
12. Reverse remaining removal procedure to complete installation.

VALVES
ADJUST

1. Remove valve cover and turn engine to firing position for No. 1 cylinder. Flywheel timing mark should be at 0 and No. 1 cylinder cam lobes should point up at equal angles.
2. Check valve clearance by placing feeler gauge between cam and tappet, **Fig. 3**. Refer to "Valve Specifications."
3. If clearances are not within specifications, turn engine approximately 1/4 turn to allow adequate clearance for depressing valves.
4. Turn valve tappets until notches point slightly inward, **Fig. 4**. Use tool 5196 or equivalent to depress valve tappets, **Fig. 5**. Tappet grooves must point so that disc can be gripped with pliers 5195 or equivalent.
5. Remove disc and use micrometer to measure disc thickness. Determine disc thickness necessary to obtain correct clearance. Discs are available in thicknesses of 0.1299 inch (3.30 mm) to 0.1673 inch (4.25 mm) in increments of 0.002 inch (0.05 mm). Use only new discs.
6. Oil disc and position with numbers facing down.
7. Check remaining cylinders in 1-5-3-6-2-4 sequence. Always check valve clearance with cylinder at TDC. Always turn engine 1/4 turn after TDC to set valve clearance.
8. Rotate engine several turns and check clearances. Adjust if necessary. Install valve cover using new gasket if necessary.

TIMING COVER
REPLACE

The timing belt cover is secured with clips to the rear plate which is bolted to the engine. To remove cover, snap open clips.

TIMING BELTS
REPLACE

1. Remove expansion tank cap and splash guard under engine. Disconnect lower hose at radiator.
2. Remove radiator, cooling fan with spacer and pulley, fan belt, and power steering pump drive belt.
3. Remove valve cover and front and rear timing gear covers.
4. Set engine to TDC and injection position (compression stroke) for No. 1 cylinder. Both No. 1 cylinder camshaft lobes should point up at equal angles and flywheel timing mark should be at zero (0), **Fig. 1.**
5. Using wrench 5187 or equivalent to hold vibration damper, remove bolt with wrench 5188 or equivalent. Engine may be turned slightly to allow wrench to rest on cooling fan journal. Engine must be returned to TDC position.
6. Remove four Allen head bolts and pull vibration damper, tapping damper and crankshaft sprocket apart, if necessary.
7. Remove lower belt shield, loosen water pump bolts and remove timing belt.
8. Idler pulley must be replaced when timing belt is replaced. Remove center bolt, then using puller 5202 or equivalent remove idler pulley. Tap new idler pulley into position and install center bolt.
9. Using wrench 5199 or equivalent hold rear sprocket and remove center bolt with wrench 5201 or equivalent. Do not let camshaft rotate. Remove rear sprocket.
10. Remove valve cover gasket. Place gauge 5190 or equivalent in groove on camshaft gear rear end. Place a 0.008 inch (0.2 mm) feeler gauge under the left side of the gauge, **Fig. 6**, to compensate for play in timing sprockets.
11. Use wrench 5199 or equivalent to hold gear and tap gear loose from camshaft tapered end. Camshaft must not be allowed to rotate.

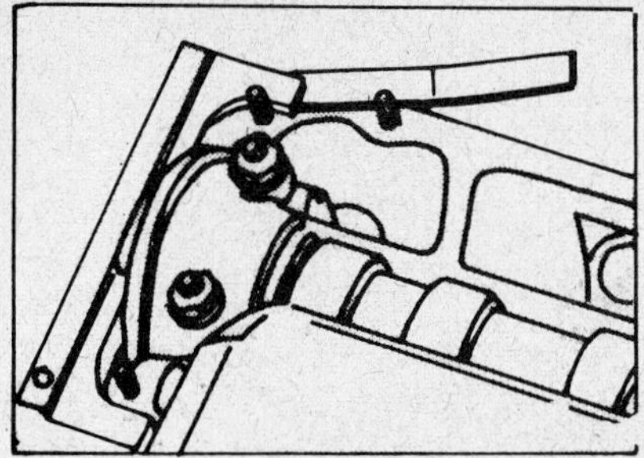

Fig. 6 Camshaft setting gauge

12. Install timing belt and sprocket. Make sure timing belt fits securely on all sprockets. Install sprocket bolt finger tight so sprocket can rotate. Camshaft must not be rotated.
13. Install lower belt shield and vibration damper. Pin on crankshaft sprocket locates damper. Torque four Allen head bolts to 15 ft. lbs. (20 Nm).
14. Apply suitable thread locking compound to bolt threads, using wrench 5187 or equivalent to hold vibration damper torque center bolt to 255 ft. lbs. (350 Nm) with wrench 5188 or equivalent. **Torque value is only applicable when using wrench 5188. Torque wrench must be in line with wrench.**
15. Make sure that cylinder No. 1 is at top dead center and flywheel mark is at zero (0), **Fig. 1.**
16. Install belt tension gauge 5197 or equivalent on timing belt, **Fig. 7.** Set gauge 5197 to 12.5. Using water pump, tighten timing belt until mark on plunger is flush with gauge sleeve. Press belt heavily and recheck tension. Adjust if necessary.
17. Tighten front camshaft sprocket using wrench 5199 to hold sprocket. Make sure camshaft or sprocket is not allowed to rotate. Torque sprocket center bolt to 33 ft. lbs. (45 Nm).
18. Remove gauge 5190 and feeler gauge and refer to "Injection Pump Setting" procedure.
19. Install the following: valve cover, front and rear timing belt covers, cooling fan with spacer and pulley (torque bolts to 6.5 ft. lbs. (9 Nm), fan belt and power steering pump drive belt, radiator, radiator hoses, and splash guard under engine.
20. Set heater control to MAX and fill cooling system through expansion tank. After running engine up to operating temperature, recheck coolant level and fill as necessary.

CAMSHAFT

REPLACE

1. Remove valve cover, then the front and rear timing belt covers.
2. Set engine to TDC and injection position (compression stroke) for No. 1 cylinder. Both No. 1 cylinder camshaft lobes should point up at equal angles and flywheel timing mark should be at zero (0), **Fig. 1.**
3. Loosen water pump retaining bolts to relieve timing belt tension. Tighten two lower bolts to avoid coolant loss and remove timing belt.
4. Using wrench 5199 or equivalent to hold sprocket, remove camshaft center bolt. Camshaft must not be allowed to rotate. Tap sprocket to loosen it from tapered end.
5. Remove two upper belt shield retaining bolts, then push shield away so it clears end of camshaft.
6. Loosen injection pump bracket bolts to relieve belt tension and remove pump timing belt.
7. Using wrench 5199 or equivalent to hold camshaft, remove sprocket bolt with wrench 5201 or equivalent. Camshaft must not be allowed to rotate.
8. Remove vacuum pump and plunger and place pump on wheel house.
9. Remove camshaft bearing caps 1 and 4.
10. Loosen cap nuts alternately to avoid unequal stresses on camshaft and remove bearing caps 2 and 3.
11. Lift out camshaft and remove seals.
12. Lubricate bearings and contact areas. Place gauge 5190 or equivalent on camshaft rear end and position camshaft on cylinder head. Both No. 1 cylinder cam lobes should point up at equal angles.
13. Install bearing caps 2 and 3 noting that centers are staggered. Tighten bearing caps alternately to avoid unequal stresses on camshaft.
14. Place new oil seals on camshaft making sure they are not cocked. Do not bottom seals.
15. Install camshaft bearing caps 1 and 4 and fit bearing cap 4 against thrust bearing. Torque cap nuts to 15 ft. lbs. (20 Nm).
16. Press ear seal into position using adapter 5200 or equivalent with bolt for rear camshaft sprocket. Tap front seal into position using adapter 5200 or equivalent.
17. Attach front timing belt shield, install front camshaft sprocket and timing belt. Install center bolt so sprocket turns freely. Camshaft must not be allowed to rotate.
18. Move water pump to adjust timing belt tension. Place tension gauge 5197 or equivalent on belt and set to 12.5, **Fig. 7.** Tighten timing belt until mark on gauge plunger is flush with sleeve. Press heavily on timing belt and recheck belt tension.
19. Place gauge 5190 or equivalent on rear end of camshaft. Place a 0.008 inch (0.2 mm) feeler gauge under left side of gauge, **Fig. 6.** Feeler gauge compensates for timing gear clearances.
20. Using wrench 5199 to hold sprocket torque center bolt to 33 ft. lbs. Camshaft and sprocket must not be allowed to rotate. Remove gauge and feeler gauge.
21. Refer to "Injection Pump Setting" in order to set injection pump.
22. Install vacuum pump and plunger. Inspect O-ring on pump and replace if necessary.

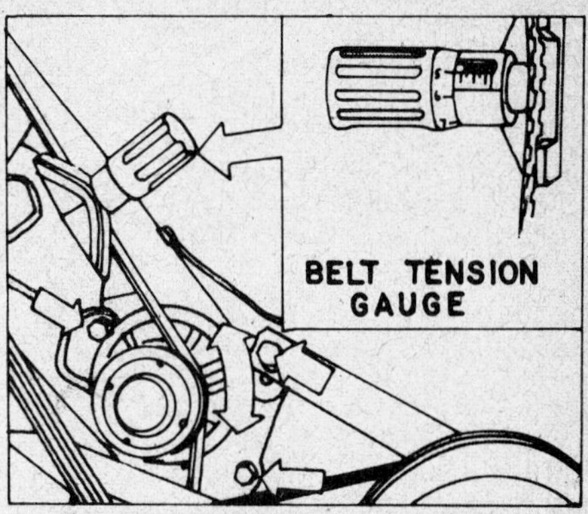

Fig. 7 Adjusting timing belt tension

23. Refer to "Valves, Adjust" procedure to adjust valve clearance. Install valve cover and front and rear timing belt covers.

PISTON & ROD ASSEMBLY

Assemble connecting rod to pistons so pistons can be installed with valve reliefs opposite oil filter side of engine. Connecting rods must be installed with casting marks on cap and rod facing oil filter side of engine.

CRANKSHAFT REAR OIL SEAL

REPLACE

1. Remove transmission.
2. Remove pressure plate and clutch disc, if applicable.
3. Lock flywheel using tool 5112 or equivalent, then remove flywheel bolts and flywheel.
4. Using screwdriver, pry out rear crankshaft oil seal. Clean and inspect surfaces on seal holder and crankshaft.
5. Apply oil to contact surfaces and new seal lips. Using tool 5208 or equivalent press seal in place until it bottoms.
6. Install flywheel using new bolts. Apply thread locking compound Volvo P/N 277961-9 or equivalent to bolt threads. Torque bolts to 55 ft. lbs. (75 Nm).
7. If applicable, install clutch disc with hub facing out, then the pressure plate. Tighten bolts in alternating sequence.
8. Install transmission.

OIL PAN & PUMP

REPLACE

Removing the oil pump requires removal of oil pan which requires removal of engine. Refer to "Engine, Replace" procedure.

The triangular mark on pump outer gear, **Fig. 8,** must face rear oil pump cover. If oil pressure is incorrect, make sure relief valve plunger slides freely in oil pump bore and inspect spring. As separate parts are

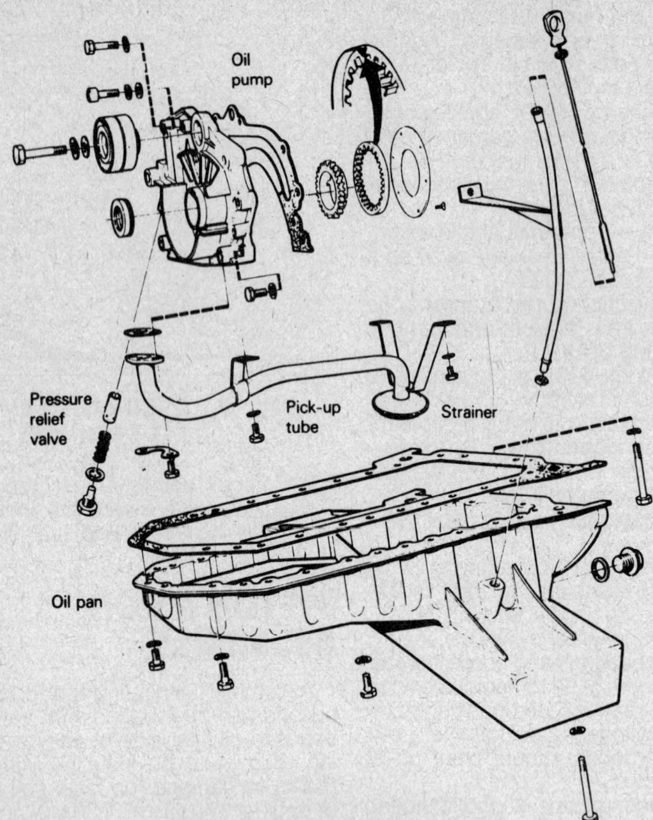

Fig. 8 Oil pan & pump

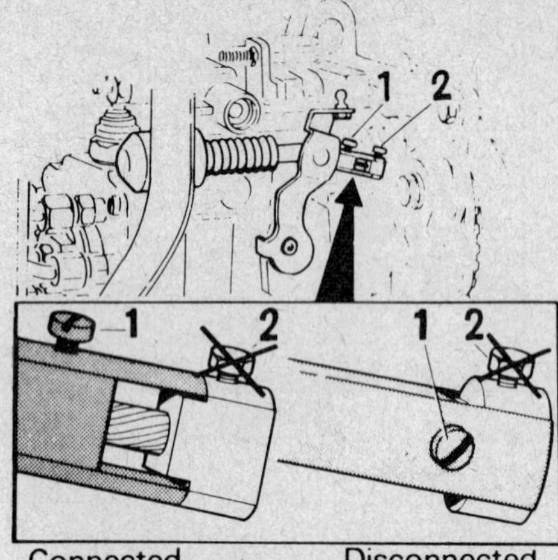

Fig. 9 Connecting and disconnecting cold start device

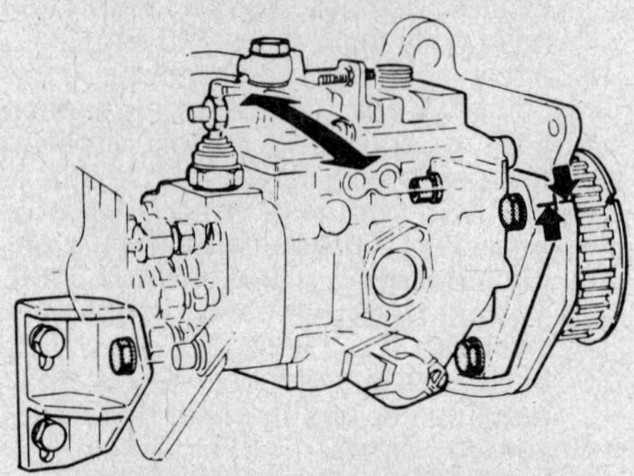

Fig. 10 Alignment of injection pump marks

not available, oil pump must be serviced as an assembly.

WATER PUMP
REPLACE

1. Remove splash guard under engine and expansion tank cap. Disconnect lower hose at radiator and drain coolant.
2. Remove radiator, cooling fan with spacer and pulley, drive belts, and front timing belt cover.
3. Disconnect cold start device, **Fig. 9.** Loosen screw 1, push lever forward and rotate sleeve 90°. Push lever backward against stop. Do not loosen screw 2 or cold start device will have to be reset on test bench.
4. Remove plug at end of injection pump distributor and install holder 5194 and dial indicator with range of 0-3 mm (0-0.118 inch). Set indicator to 2 mm (0.079 inch).
5. Turn engine to TDC (flywheel mark at zero (0), **Fig. 1**) and injection position (compression stroke). Markings on injection pump sprocket should align with marking on injection pump bracket, **Fig. 10.** Turn engine 1/4 turn past 0 mark and then back to 0 mark to place slack of timing belt on drive side.
6. Zero dial indicator. Pointer must not move during remainder of procedure or camshaft will have to be reset in relation to crankshaft. If camshaft has moved, follow steps 10 through 12 and 15 through 17 of "Timing Belts, Replace" procedure and then entire "Injection Pump Setting" procedure. If pointer has not moved, checking and adjusting injection pump setting will be adequate.
7. Follow steps 5 through 7 of "Timing Belts, Replace" procedure.
8. Loosen bracket for cooling fan and alternator and move away from engine.
9. Remove belt shield and water pump.
10. Clean pump surfaces on block. Grease new O-ring and fit into pump groove. Install water pump, noting that longest bolt goes in upper hole.

INJECTION PUMP
REPLACE
EXC. TURBOCHARGED ENGINE

1. Clamp and disconnect hoses at cold start device. Disconnect accelerator cable, kickdown cable, if equipped, and wire at stop valve.
2. Remove rear timing belt cover, clean and disconnect fuel line connections at injection pump. Plug open connections to prevent entry of dirt.
3. Remove vacuum pump and plunger. Clean and remove fuel delivery pipes and plug all connections to prevent entry of dirt.
4. Turn engine to No. 1 cylinder TDC and injection, **Fig. 1.** With flywheel mark at zero (0), pump sprocket notch must be aligned with mark on bracket and pump, **Fig. 10.**
5. Loosen injection pump bracket bolts and remove pump belt.
6. Remove camshaft rear sprocket using wrench 5199 or equivalent to hold gear, and wrench 5201 to loosen sprocket center nut. Do not allow camshaft to rotate, sprocket should rotate on camshaft.
7. Lock injection pump sprocket with stop 5193 or equivalent and using wrench 5201 or equivalent remove sprocket nut. Use puller 5204 or equivalent to remove sprocket.
8. Remove injection pump bracket bolts and remove pump with bracket. Remove Allen head bolts and separate pump from bracket.
9. Install new pump so mark on pump body aligns with mark on bracket. Install pump sprocket making sure that shaft key is correctly installed.
10. Refer to "Injection Pump Setting" procedure and set pump.
11. Fill pump with fuel if necessary and install rear timing belt cover.
12. Connect fuel supply and return lines. Do not switch connector screws. Screw for fuel return line has small hole and is marked OUT. Torque to 18 ft. lbs. (25 Nm).
13. Install fuel delivery pipes and torque cap nuts to 18 ft. lbs. (25 Nm). Install vacuum pump and plunger.
14. Connect cold start device hoses, stop valve wires, accelerator cable, and kickdown cable on automatic transmission models.

15. Set accelerator controls, **Fig. 11,** as follows:
    a. Disconnect cold start device, **Fig. 9,** and link rod at injection pump lever.
    b. Adjust accelerator cable by turning cable sheath until cable is under tension but does not alter pulley position. Pulley should be at idle stop.
    c. Depress accelerator pedal fully and check maximum accelerator position. Pulley should contact full throttle stop.
    d. On automatic transmission models, kickdown cable should move about 2 inches between end positions when accelerator is floored. Cable should be under tension in idle position, and distance between kickdown cable clip and cable sheath should be 0.01-0.04 inch (0.25-1.00 mm).
    e. Connect link rod to injection pump lever. Turn pulley to full throttle position and adjust link rod length so that pump lever contacts maximum speed adjusting screw.
    f. Turn pulley to idle stop and move link rod ball joint in slot in injection pump lever until lever contacts idle adjusting screw.
    g. Readjust link rod by repeating steps e and f until control is correctly adjusted. A maximum clearance of 0.012 inch (0.3 mm) is permissible at pulley stops.
    h. Reconnect cold start device.

TURBOCHARGED ENGINE

Removal

1. Using suitable pliers, pinch cold start unit hoses, then disconnect and cap hoses.
2. Disconnect throttle cable and kickdown cable, if equipped from injection pump.
3. Disconnect fuel valve electrical connector.
4. Disconnect hose from intake manifold.
5. Remove rear timing gear cover.
6. Remove vacuum pump and plunger.
7. thoroughly clean fuel delivery lines, then disconnect and cap lines.
8. Disconnect and cap fuel supply and return lines from injection pump.
9. Rotate crankshaft (in direction of engine rotation) until No.1 piston is at TDC and injection position (compression stroke). Mark on injection pump sprocket should be properly aligned with mark on mounting bracket. Flywheel wheel mark should be at zero (0).
10. Loosen injection pump mounting bolts to release belt tension. Leave one bolt in place to secure injection pump in position, then lift off belt.
11. Install tool 5199 or equivalent, to prevent camshaft from turning. Using tool 5201 or equivalent, loosen camshaft rear sprocket attaching bolt, then the camshaft rear sprocket.
12. Using tool 5193 or equivalent, secure injection pump sprocket from turning. Using tool 5201 or equivalent, remove sprocket attaching bolt and washer.
13. Using tools 5204 and 5193 or equivalents, pull sprocket from shaft.
14. Remove front mounting bracket from engine, then the injection pump from rear mounting bracket.

Installation

1. Position injection pump onto engine, install attaching bolts and front mounting bracket. Hand tighten bolts only.
2. Align mark on injection pump mounting flange with mark on mounting bracket.
3. With marks properly aligned, tighten injection pump to mounting bracket attaching bolts.
4. Install injection pump sprocket as follows:
    a. Install key into injection pump axle keyway.
    b. Install sprocket, washer and nut.
    c. Using tool 5193 or equivalent, secure sprocket from turning.
    d. Install tool 5201 onto sprocket attaching nut.
    e. Install a suitable torque wrench onto tool 5201, and torque attaching nut to 33 ft. lbs. **Ensure tool 5201 and torque wrench, when installed, form a right angle, otherwise torque reading obtained will be incorrect.**
5. Loosen cold start unit screw closest to injection pump lever and rotate cold start unit sleeve 90 degrees.
6. Press injection pump connecting lever back against lever stop.
7. With injection pump connecting lever properly set, proceed as follows:
    a. Loosen, then remove injection pump distributor plug.
    b. Install tool holder 5194 or equivalent and a suitable dial indicator onto injection pump. Ensure dial indicator has a measuring range of at least 0-.12 inch.
    c. Set dial indicator to approximately .08 inch.
    d. Turn injection pump sprocket in normal direction of rotation, until mark on sprocket and mounting bracket are aligned.
    e. Turn injection pump sprocket back slightly until a minus reading registers on dial indicator, then zero (0) dial indicator.
    f. Turn injection pump sprocket forward until mark on sprocket and injection pump mounting bracket are aligned.
    g. With marks properly aligned, install tool 5193 or equivalent, to lock sprocket in this position.
8. Install belt onto injection pump sprocket. Adjust belt tension by moving pump either slightly upward or downward.
9. Install measuring gauge tool 5197 or equivalent to check belt tension. Set gauge to 12.5. Stretch belt until mark on gauge plunger is flush with sleeve, then tighten attaching bolts. Depress belt firmly by hand and check belt tension. Adjust, if necessary.
10. Using tool 5199 or equivalent, secure camshaft rear sprocket. Install wrench 5201 or equivalent, onto sprocket attaching nut. Install a suitable torque wrench onto wrench tool 5201. Ensure torque wrench and wrench tool form a right angle. Using tool 5199 or equivalent, turn sprocket slowly clockwise until dial indicator indicates the following:
    a. On 1983 models, dial indicator reading obtained should be .031 inch.
    b. On 1984-86 except California models, dial indicator reading obtained should be .033 inch.
    c. On 1984-86 California models, dial indicator reading obtained should be .029 inch.
    d. On 1983-86 high altitude models, normal setting at sea level should be .033 inch. Setting should be advanced .0028 inch for every 3300 ft. increase in altitude above sea level.
11. With sprocket secured from turning, torque rear camshaft sprocket attaching bolt to 73 ft. lbs. Ensure while torquing attaching bolt that camshaft and sprocket do not turn.
12. Remove tool 5193 from injection pump gear.
13. Check pump setting as described under "Injection Pump Setting."
14. Remove dial indicator and tool 5194.
15. Install injection pump plug and new seal. Torque plug to 6.5 ft. lbs.
16. Press injection pump connecting lever forward, then turn lever sleeve 90 degrees and tighten attaching screw closest to injection pump lever.
17. If necessary, fill injection pump with clean diesel fuel. This is necessary only if the injection pump has been drained or a new pump installed.
18. Install rear timing belt cover. Clamp wiring harness onto left side retaining bolt on cover assembly.
19. Connect all electrical connectors, vacuum lines and fuel lines that were disconnected during removal procedure. Ensure not to interchange electrical connectors, vacuum and fuel lines. The fuel return line connections are smaller in width and are labeled OUT. Torque fuel delivery and return line connections to 18 ft. lbs. Do not use a screwdriver to hold the fuel line during tightening.
20. Install plunger and vacuum pump. Check seal ring. Replace, if necessary.
21. Ensure No. 1 cylinder is at TDC and injection position. Marks on pump sprocket and mounting bracket should be aligned properly. The flywheel timing mark should be at zero (0).
22. Connect cold start unit hoses.
23. Connect electrical connector onto fuel valve.
24. Connect throttle cable and kickdown cable, if equipped.

INJECTION PUMP SETTING

1. Disconnect cold start device by loos-

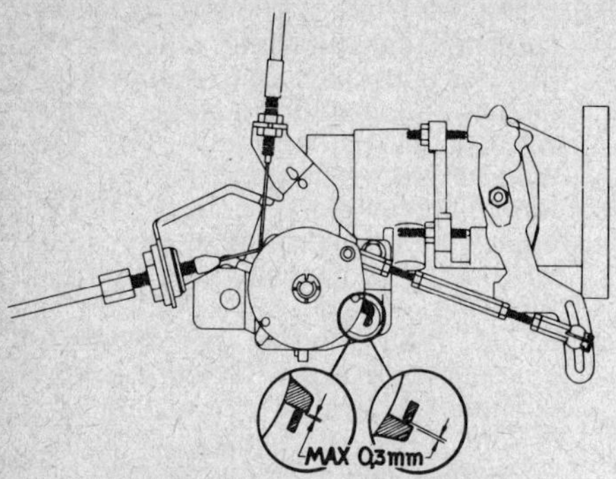

Fig. 11 Setting accelerator controls

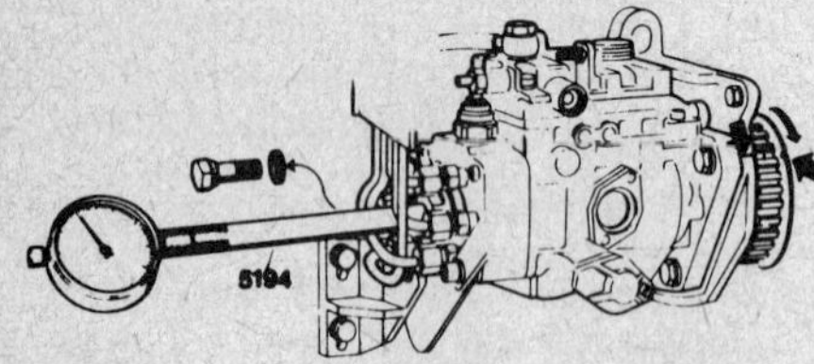

Fig. 12 Installing dial indicator on injection pump

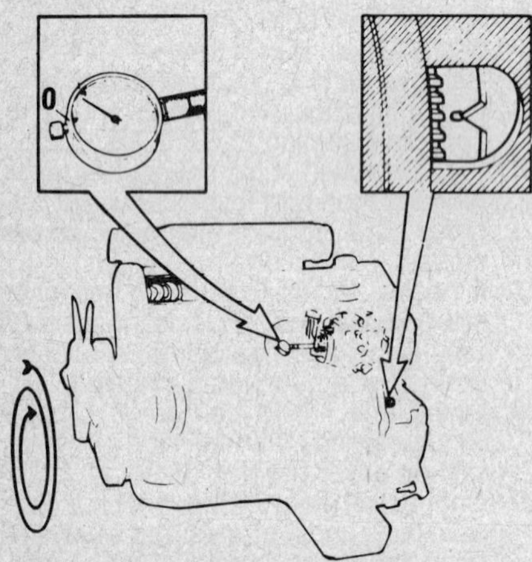

Fig. 13 Checking injection pump setting

FAULT Symtom	Cause	Check/remedy
CHARGE PRESSURE TOO LOW (pressure gauge connected)	Air filter clogged	Replace air filter
	Engine controls incorrectly adjusted	Adjust
	Engine fault (low compression, incorrect valve clearance, not enough fuel supply)	Check and remedy if necessary
	Leakage between compressor housing and cylinder head or between cylinder head and turbine housing	Replace damaged gaskets, connections, etc. Tighten screws, nuts, clamps
	Wastegate valve stuck in open position (fully or partly)	Replace wastegate valve and housing
	Exhaust system partly clogged	Replace
	Wastegate valve leaks	Replace
	Turbocharger faulty	Replace complete or overhaul as required
CHARGE PRESSURE TOO HIGH	Leakage from hose between compressor housing and pressure actuator	Replace hose and clamps
	Pressure actuator (diaphragm) damaged	Replace
	Wastegate valve stuck in closed position	Replace wastegate valve and housing
ENGINE KNOCKS	Incorrect fuel (too low cetane number) Incorrect injection timing Charge pressure too high	Change fuel Check and adjust Check charge pressure
NOISE FROM WASTEGATE VALVE	Wastegate valve housing or exhaust manifold loose	Tighten. Replace if required
NOISE OR VIBRATIONS FROM TURBOCHARGER	Preheater plates loose or cracked	Replace, tighten
	Leakage from intake or exhaust system	Tighten loose connections, replace seals, etc.
	Poor lubrication of turbocharger	Check oil pressure and oil flow to turbo. If fault remains after checking, replace turbocharger
	Imbalance in turbo shaft, turbine wheel or compressor wheel because of damage	Replace turbocharger
OIL LEAKAGE AT TURBO SHAFT SEALS *Oil smoke in exhaust gas*	Air filter clogged (oil leakage on intake side causes smoke)	Replace air filter
	Exhaust system loose or leaks	Tighten or replace
	Excessive pressure in crankcase	Clean crankcase ventilation
	Return oil line clogged	Clean return oil line
	Turbo shaft seal damaged	Replace turbocharger

Fig. 14 Troubleshooting D24T turbodiesel engine

ening screw 1, **Fig. 9.** Push lever forward and rotate sleeve 90°. Then push lever back against stop. Do not loosen screw 2 or cold start device will have to be reset on test bench.

2. Remove injection pump drive belt. Loosen injection pump mounting screws (6 mm Allen head screws) and turn injection pump so marks on pump and bracket are aligned, **Fig. 10.** Tighten retaining screws.
3. Use stop 5193 or equivalent to lock injection pump gear. No. 1 cylinder should be at position for injection.
4. Remove plug at end of injection pump distributor and install holder 5194 and a dial indicator with a range of 0-3 mm (0-0.118 inch), **Fig. 12.** Set indicator at 2 mm (0.079 inch) and turn injection pump sprocket until marks on sprocket and bracket coincide, **Fig. 10.**
5. Turn injection pump sprocket slightly counterclockwise until dial indicator shows minimum reading. Set indicator to zero. Turn sprocket slightly clockwise until marks on sprocket and bracket coincide. Lock sprocket in this position with stop 5193 or equivalent. Insert stop through hole in sprocket and bracket.
6. Install rear sprocket on camshaft. Tighten center bolt so sprocket can rotate on camshaft and install drive belt.
7. Use injection pump bracket to tighten pump drive belt. Set belt tension using gauge 5197 or equivalent. Place gauge on belt and set to 12.5 and tighten belt until mark on plunger is flush with tool sleeve. Tighten pump bolts and recheck tension.
8. Use wrench 5199 or equivalent to hold rear camshaft sprocket and place wrench 52 01 on center bolt. Place torque wrench on wrench 5201 at right angle to get accurate readings. Turn sprocket until indicator reads 0.70 mm (0.028 inch) on D24 engine, or 0.80 mm (0.031 inch) on D24T engine. Hold sprocket in this position and torque center bolt to 73 ft. lbs. (100 Nm). Make sure camshaft and sprocket do not change position.
9. Rotate crankshaft two full turns until No. 1 cylinder is at TDC and injection position (compression stroke), **Fig. 13.** If engine is turned too far, turn crankshaft back 1/4 turn and then to 0 mark. Dial indicator should now read 0.70 mm (0.028 inch) on D24 engine, or 0.80 mm (0.031 inch) on D24T engine.
10. If reading is correct, remove dial indicator and holder, install plug and torque to 6.5 ft. lbs. (9 Nm). Push cold start lever forward, turn sleeve 90° and tighten screw 1. If reading is incorrect and less than 0.70 mm (0.028 inch) on D24 engine, or 0.80 mm (0.031 inch) on D24T engine, loosen pump retaining bolts and turn pump inward (toward engine) to obtain reading of 0.70 mm (0.028 inch) on D24 engine, or 0.80 mm (0.031 inch) on D24T engine. Tighten retaining bolts and repeat step 9. If reading is more than 0.70 mm on D24 engine, or 0.80 mm (0.031 inch) on D24T engine, turn pump outward (away from engine) to obtain reading of 0.60 mm (0.024 inch). Then turn pump inward

(towards engine) to obtain reading of 0.70 mm (0.028 inch) on D24 engine, or 0.80 mm (0.031 inch) on D24T engine. Tighten retaining bolts. Repeat step 9. **Injection pump must not be disturbed as settings will be altered.**

TURBOCHARGER

DESCRIPTION

The turbocharger is an exhaust driven device which compresses the intake air to increase engine power on a demand basis. This allows for performance equal to that of a larger displacement naturally aspirated engine without the added weight and fuel consumption. Other benefits of a turbocharged engine are lower noise and emission levels.

CONTROLS

In order to obtain high torque at low engine RPM, the turbocharger is designed to generate high boost pressure even at relatively low engine RPM. A wastegate which is set to open at 10.9 psi is used to prevent excessive boost pressure at high RPM.

Should the wastegate fail to open and boost pressure continue to rise, a safety blow-off valve mounted on the intake manifold will open at 11.4 psi and return some of the air flow back to the turbocharger inlet. When the blow-off valve opens, it also triggers a warning light on the instrument panel.

TROUBLESHOOTING

Refer to chart, **Fig. 14,** to troubleshoot turbocharger equipped diesel vehicles.

LUBRICATION

Proper lubrication is essential for proper turbocharger operation. Since it is lubricated by engine oil pressure, three important practices should be observed:

1. Do not race engine immediately after starting. Let engine idle to provide initial lubrication.
2. Do not switch engine off while running at high RPM as turbocharger will continue to spin at high RPM without oil pressure. Letting engine idle before shut down will also lower turbine temperatures.

TESTS & ADJUSTMENTS

Boost Pressure, Check

1. Connect pressure gauge between fuel limiter and intake manifold hose. Place gauge so it can be read from inside vehicle.
2. With engine at normal operating temperature, drive at 1500 RPM in 3rd gear with manual transmission models; 2nd gear with automatic transmission models.
3. Depress throttle pedal to floor for full throttle acceleration. On automatic transmission models, do not depress pedal enough to cause transmission to downshift.
4. On all vehicles, when engine reaches 3000 RPM, apply brakes while keeping throttle pedal depressed and read boost pressure. Pressure should not exceed 10-11 psi. Low boost pressure is not necessarily caused by a turbocharger fault. Refer to "Troubleshooting."
5. Reconnect hose to fuel limiter.

Blow-Off Valve, Check

1. Connect pressure gauge between fuel limiter and intake manifold hose. Place gauge so it can be read from inside vehicle.
2. Disconnect electrical connector from blow-off valve. Short connector terminals and turn on ignition to check that instrument panel warning light illuminates.
3. Remove short and reconnect connector to valve.
4. Clamp hose between turbocharger housing and pressure actuator using hose pliers. **Do not race engine with pliers clamped on hose as engine could over-rev due to unlimited boost pressure.**
5. Drive in 3rd gear on manual transmission models, 2nd gear on automatic transmission models.
6. Carefully apply throttle until engine reaches 3000 RPM while applying brakes. Check that warning light illuminates and blow-off valve opens when pressure gauge reads 11.4-12.1 psi. Do not allow boost pressure to become too high.
7. Remove hose pliers, pressure gauge, and hoses.
8. Reconnect hose to fuel limiter.

TURBOCHARGER, REPLACE

1. Disconnect battery ground cable.
2. Remove inlet hose from turbocharger pipe.
3. Remove air cleaner and heated air hose.
4. Remove snap ring from turbocharger intake pipe and remove intake pipe. Disconnect hose to blow-off valve.
5. Disconnect turbocharger oil drain pipe and position aside. Plug openings.
6. Disconnect oil supply pipe from turbocharger and plug openings.
7. Push turbocharger outlet pipe up into intake manifold.
8. Disconnect exhaust pipe from turbocharger.
9. Raise and support vehicle.
10. Disconnect exhaust pipe at front support bracket located at transmission and disconnect at flange.
11. Remove nuts and lower front end of turbocharger to remove.
12. Reverse procedure to install. Torque turbocharger mounting bolts to 44 ft. lbs.

CLUTCH & MANUAL TRANSMISSION SECTION

INDEX

CLUTCH PEDAL

ADJUST

MODELS W/MECHANICAL ACTUATION

Adjustment is carried out at point at which cable attaches to fork, or by turning adjusting nuts on clutch actuating cable where cable attaches to side of clutch housing. To check adjustment, push clutch fork fully toward front (models with return spring) or rear (models without return spring) of vehicle. Clutch lever play should be .04-.12 inch.

MODELS W/HYDRAULIC ACTUATION

This system is designed so clutch fork and throw-out bearing touch lightly on pressure plate. No provision for adjustment is provided.

CLUTCH MASTER CYLINDER

REPLACE

1. Remove panel from under dash.
2. Remove locking spring and pin from clutch pedal assembly.
3. Drain fluid, then disconnect line from fluid reservoir.
4. Remove master cylinder attaching

bolts and master cylinder.

5. Reverse procedure to install. Ensure that .04 inch clearance exists between push rod and piston, then bleed hydraulic system.

SLAVE CYLINDER REPLACE

1. Disconnect hose from pipe and bracket.
2. Remove slave cylinder to bellhousing attaching bolts, then the slave cylinder.
3. Reverse procedure to install, then bleed hydraulic system.

CLUTCH REPLACE

240 DL, GL & GLT

1. Remove transmission as described under "Transmission, Replace" procedure.
2. Remove upper bolt from starter motor.
3. Remove release bearing. Disconnect cable from release fork, then remove cable sleeve from bracket, if applicable.
4. Remove flywheel housing.
5. Remove bolt holding release fork ball joint. Remove ball joint and fork.
6. Remove clutch retaining bolts and remove clutch.
7. Reverse procedure to install.

740, 760 & 780 SERIES

1. Remove transmission as described under "Transmission, Replace" procedure.
2. Install suitable centering mandrel.
3. Loosen, then remove, clutch to flywheel attaching bolts in a criss-cross pattern.
4. Remove pressure plate and disc.
5. Remove pilot bearing, using tool No. 4090, or equivalent.
6. Disconnect clutch release fork and remove release bearing.

TRANSMISSION REPLACE

240 DL, GL & GLT

1. Disconnect battery ground cable.
2. Disconnect back-up light wire harness connector at firewall.
3. From underneath vehicle, disconnect gearshift lever from gearshift rod.
4. From inside vehicle, remove rubber bellows. Remove fork for reverse gear detent. Remove lock ring and gearshift lever.
5. Disconnect clutch cable and return spring or slave cylinder linkage, whichever is applicable. It is not necessary to open any hydraulic lines.
6. Remove front exhaust pipe bracket or turbocharger assembly.
7. Place a jack under transmission to support it and remove rear transmission mounting bolts. Remove crossmember.
8. Disconnect front universal joint from transmission flange. Disconnect speedometer cable.
9. Lower transmission jack and remove bellhousing to engine retaining bolts. Remove all of these bolts except one at top right.
10. Remove starter motor front bracket bolts and pull starter out until it is free of bellhousing.
11. Remove bellhousing bolt at top right and remove transmission.

740, 760 & 780 SERIES

Exc. Models W/B-230 Engine

1. Raise and support vehicle.
2. Start and run engine with the overdrive engaged, then depress clutch pedal and stop engine to unload the overdrive.
3. Disconnect battery ground cable.
4. Remove gearshift lever as follows:
   a. Remove ashtray and holder assembly.
   b. Remove gear shift lever frame, then disconnect gearshift lever cover from floor and remove the snap ring.
   c. Disconnect gearshift lever from gearshift rod under vehicle. Remove lock screw and press out pivot pin using tool No. 5181, then push up and remove the gearshift lever.
5. Using tool No. 5244, disconnect propeller shaft from transmission.
6. Separate exhaust pipe at joint and remove bracket from exhaust pipe.
7. Remove crossmember, then the rear transmission support.
8. Disconnect overdrive, back-up light and solenoid connectors from transmission case.
9. Cut the plastic clamp at gearshift assembly wiring harness.
10. Remove starter motor attaching bolts.
11. Remove cover plate under bellhousing, then the starter motor opening cover plate, if applicable.
12. If equipped with hydraulic clutch, remove slave cylinder from bellhousing and the upper bellhousing attaching bolts.
13. If equipped with mechanical clutch, disconnect clutch cable from release fork and bellhousing.
14. Support transmission with suitable jack, then remove lower bellhousing attaching bolts and lower transmission from vehicle.

Models W/B-230 Engine

1. Install lifting beam tool 5006 or equivalent onto engine lifting eyes. Ensure beam tool is correctly positioned at each inner fender lip.
2. Attach beam tool hook and tighten to support rear of engine.
3. Disconnect battery ground cable.
4. Raise and support vehicle.
5. Using a suitable tool, remove propeller shaft from transmission mounting flange.
6. Disconnect propeller shaft support bearing from crossmember.
7. Move propeller shaft rearward approximately 8 inches.
8. Disconnect front exhaust pipe from front exhaust coupling.
9. Loosen lock screw, then remove gear shift lever pin.
10. Remove locking ring, then push gear shift lever upward.
11. Remove crossmember and bracket. Cut wire straps and disconnect electrical connectors from transmission.
12. Disconnect clutch control cable, or remove clutch slave cylinder, whichever is applicable.
13. Disconnect exhaust pipe from transmission bracket.
14. Position a suitable jack under transmission.
15. Remove transmission to flywheel cover attaching bolts.
16. Pull transmission assembly rearward and lower from vehicle.
17. Reverse procedure to install.

DISC BRAKES SECTION

INDEX

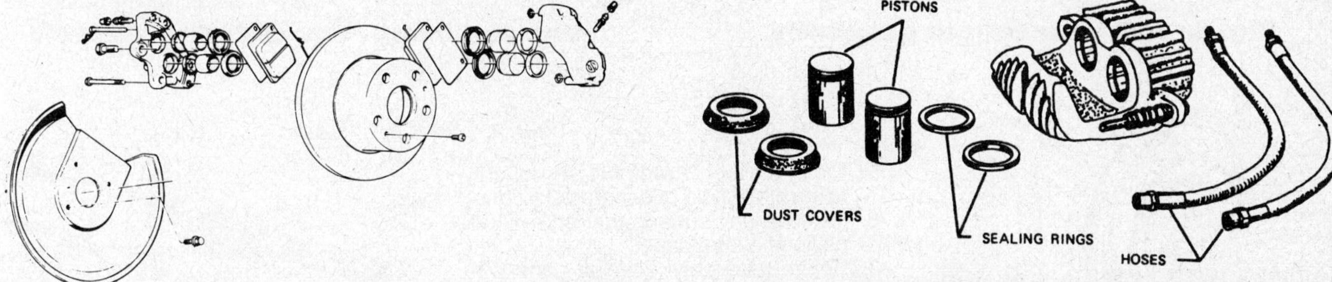

Fig. 1 Girling front caliper assembly. 240 DL, GL & GLT

Fig. 2 Disassembled view of Girling front caliper assembly. 740, 760 & 780 series

FRONT DISC BRAKE SERVICE

BRAKE PADS, REPLACE

240 DL, GL & GLT

1. Raise car and remove wheels.
2. Remove hairpin shaped locking clips for guide pins. Tap out one of guide pins while holding damper springs in place. Remove springs and other guide pin.
3. Pull out pads using tool No. 2917 or equivalent.
4. Carefully clean out cavity in which pads are located. Replace any dust covers that are damaged. If dirt has penetrated into cylinder due to a damaged cover, recondition brake caliper. Check brake disc and resurface if necessary.
5. Press caliper pistons back into their bores with tool 2809 or a suitable wide bladed screwdriver. Use caution if a screwdriver is used to avoid damage to rubber dust covers. When pistons are pressed back into their bores, brake fluid in master cylinder can overflow.
6. Reverse procedure to install, noting the following:
   a. If caliper has previously been equipped with intermediate shims, rubber coated spacers or damper washers, they should be reinstalled. In the case of round damper washers, smaller contact face should face pad. Do not install spacers or shims with round damper washers.

740, 760 & 780 Series

1. Raise vehicle and remove wheels.
2. Using a 17 mm wrench, hold caliper guide pin and remove lower caliper attaching bolt.
3. Loosen upper caliper attaching bolt, then lift caliper and remove springs and pads. **Do not depress brake pedal when caliper is removed.**
4. Press caliper pistons back into bores using suitable clamp.
5. Install new brake pads with springs and lower caliper, then install lower attaching bolt. Torque bolts to 25 ft. lbs.
6. Install wheels and lower vehicle. After replacing pads on any disc brake system, caliper pistons will be retracted in their bores and will require one full application of brakes to assume correct position. **Do not attempt to move car until a firm brake pedal has been achieved.**

CALIPER REMOVAL & OVERHAUL

240 DL, GL & GLT

1. Raise vehicle and remove wheels.
2. Disconnect brake lines. Before loosening mounting bolts, loosen all bleeder screws.
3. Remove caliper mounting bolts and remove caliper. Do not loosen bridge bolts.
4. Remove retaining ring and rubber dust cover from each caliper piston, **Fig. 1.** Place a thick piece of wood between pistons and apply air pressure to brake line connection of caliper to blow pistons out. Remove seals. The caliper must not be separated or leaks may result after reassembly.
5. Coat pistons and cylinders with brake fluid before assembling.
6. Install seals in cylinders, then install pistons, dust covers and lock rings.
7. Reinstall calipers and bleed system. Torque caliper retaining bolts to 70 ft. lbs.

740, 760 & 780 Series

1. Raise vehicle and remove wheels.
2. Mark hoses, then disconnect from brake pipes.
3. Remove caliper to spring strut attaching bolts, then the caliper.
4. Remove rubber dust cover from each piston, **Fig. 2.** Place a thick shop towel between pistons and outer portion of caliper, then apply air pressure to brake line connection of caliper to blow pistons out. Remove inner seals.
5. Clean all passages with compressed air, then coat pistons and cylinders with brake fluid before assembling.
6. Install inner seals into cylinders.
7. Position dust covers onto lower edges of pistons, then pull covers outward so that they are fully extended.
8. Insert lower edge of dust covers onto groove in cylinders, then press pistons fully inward.
9. Inspect guide pins and bushings for excessive wear or damage. Replace as necessary.
10. Reinstall calipers and bleed system. Torque caliper attaching bolts to 72 ft. lbs.

REAR DISC BRAKE SERVICE

The following procedures are applicable to all models. 1983-87 models may use either Girling or ATE type rear caliper assemblies, **Figs. 3 and 4.**

BRAKE PADS, REPLACE

1. Raise and support rear of vehicle, then remove rear wheels and tires.
2. Using a suitable punch, remove lock pins and spring clips, then remove pads.
3. Using a suitable clamp, press pistons back into bore.

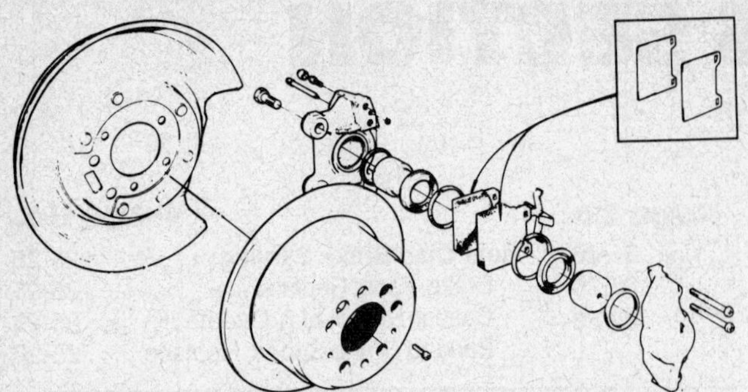
Fig. 3 ATE rear caliper assembly

Fig. 4 Girling rear caliper assembly

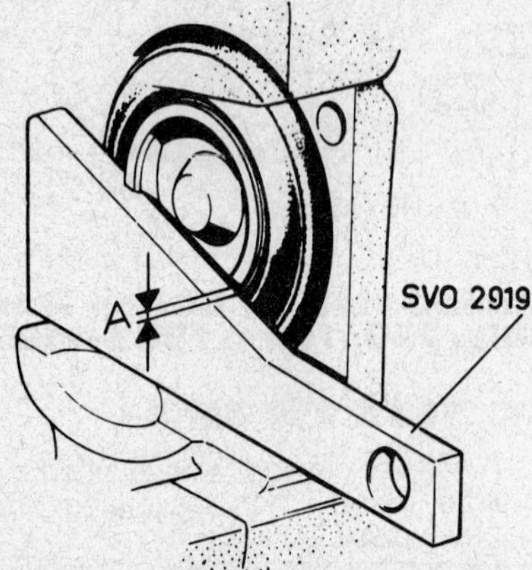

Fig. 5 Checking caliper piston position. ATE rear caliper

4. Install new pads, then replace lock pins and spring clips.
5. Install wheels and lower vehicle. After replacing pads on any disc brake system, caliper pistons will be retracted in their bores and will require at least one full application of brakes to assume correct position. **Do not attempt to move car until a firm brake pedal has been achieved.**

CALIPER REMOVAL & OVERHAUL

1. Raise and support rear of vehicle, then remove rear tires.
2. Disconnect brake lines, then remove two caliper attaching bolts and caliper.
3. Remove piston dust cover, then place a piece of wood or suitable material between both pistons. Force pistons out of bore using low pressure compressed air.
4. Using a suitable screwdriver, remove sealing rings, then bleeder screw. **Do not separate brake caliper into two separate halves.**
5. Clean caliper assembly thoroughly using brake fluid or denatured alcohol.
6. Remove any surface rust on cylinder using fine sandpaper.
7. Before assembly, coat all parts with power steering fluid, then install new seal rings and pistons.
8. On ATE calipers, check to be sure caliper pistons are in proper position to avoid squeals. Piston recess should incline 20° in relation to lower guide area of caliper. Check using tool No. 2919, **Fig. 5.** If necessary, rotate piston with tool No. 2918.
8. Install new dust cover and bleeder screw.

PARKING BRAKE SHOES, REPLACE

1. Loosen parking brake cable adjusting screw. Refer to "Parking Brake Adjustment" for procedure.
2. Raise and support vehicle, then remove rear wheels.
3. Remove caliper.
4. Remove brake disc, then remove brake shoe springs, brake shoes and adjuster, if applicable. On some models, it may be necessary to work through holes in axle shaft flange to gain access to springs.
5. Before assembly, apply a thin layer of heat resistant graphite grease or equivalent on brake shoe sliding surface.
6. Install brake shoes, springs and adjuster, if applicable.
7. Install brake disc and caliper.
8. Adjust parking brake as outlined under "Parking Brake Adjustment."

PARKING BRAKE ADJUSTMENT

1. Remove rear ashtray.

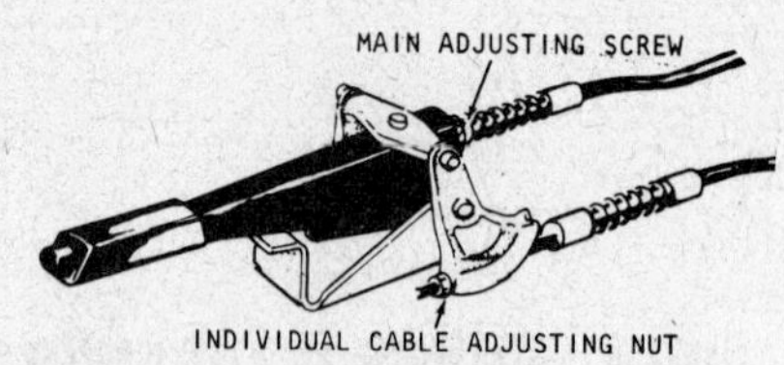

Fig. 6 Parking brake adjustment

2. Working through ashtray hole, tighten adjusting nut at rear of parking lever so that brake is fully applied after 2-5 notches, **Fig. 6**

POWER BRAKE UNIT REPLACE

1. Remove master cylinder, then disconnect vacuum hose from power brake unit.
2. Disconnect link arm from brake pedal, then remove bracket with clutch pedal stop.
3. Remove nuts attaching power brake unit to dash panel.
4. Pull power brake unit forward, then disconnect fork from link arm and remove brake unit.

MASTER CYLINDER REPLACE

1. Place a cover over the fender to protect paint from brake fluid.
2. Disconnect brake lines and install plastic plugs.
3. Remove retaining nuts and remove cylinder.
4. Before installing, be sure to bleed master cylinder.

REAR AXLE & SUSPENSION SECTION

INDEX

REAR AXLE ASSEMBLY REPLACE

240 DL, GL & GLT

1. Position fixture No. 2714 on a suitable jack, then position jack and fixture under rear axle assembly and raise rear of vehicle.
2. Place jack stands in front of rear jack supports, then slightly lower rear of vehicle and remove rear wheels.
3. Disconnect shock absorbers from upper mountings.
4. Disconnect brake lines from rear axle, then remove caliper retaining screws.
5. Use wire to hook calipers to top shock absorber supports to prevent brake lines from becoming damaged.
6. Remove brake discs, then remove parking brake shoes.
7. Press out pins attaching parking brake cables to levers.
8. Remove screws and pull out cable and hose with seals, then remove springs retaining parking brake cable to rear axle.
9. Disconnect propeller shaft at pinion flange.
10. Disconnect track rod from body bracket.
11. Disconnect springs from trailing arms, then lower rear axle and remove springs.
12. Remove screws retaining rear axle and remove rear axle assembly from vehicle.

740, 760 & 780 SERIES

1. Raise and support vehicle, then remove rear wheels.
2. Remove brake caliper attaching bolts, then hang caliper away from spring.
3. Remove brake discs and parking brake cable from equalizer and clamps, located on the rear axle assembly.
4. Remove torque rod attaching bolts then position lifting fixture 2714 on a suitable jack and raise rear axle assembly slightly.
5. Remove track rod from differential.
6. Disconnect speedometer sender from rear of differential, then remove propeller shaft at pinion flange using tool 5244.
7. Remove upper torque rod at rear axle, then shock absorber lower attaching

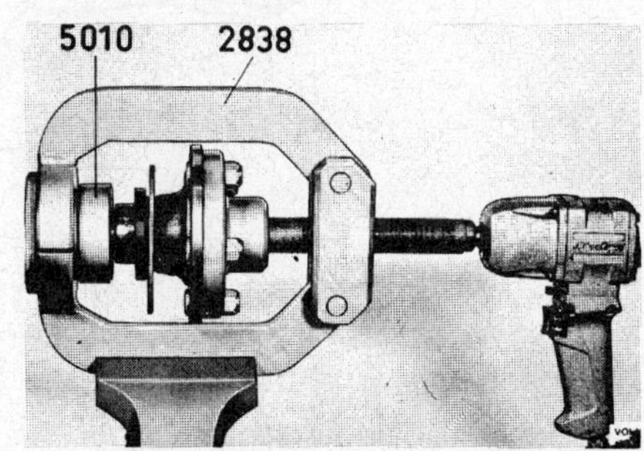

Fig. 1 Axle shaft bearing installation

bolts.

8. Remove trailing arm front bracket. Using a suitable pry bar, remove trailing arms from chassis.
9. Remove rear axle breather hose, then lower axle assembly and remove from vehicle.

AXLE SHAFT, BEARING & SEAL REPLACE

1. Raise rear of vehicle and support on jack stands.
2. Remove brake caliper and disc.
3. Remove axle shaft retaining nuts. Using tool 2709 or other suitable puller, pull out axle shaft.
4. Pull out inner seal ring with a screwdriver.
5. Remove and reinstall bearing using tool Nos. 2838 & 5010 or equivalent, **Fig. 1.**
6. Install inner seal in axle housing using tool Nos. 5009 and 1801 or equivalent.

SHOCK ABSORBER REPLACE

1. Raise car and place stands under the jacking points of body.
2. Remove the wheel. Unload axle by jacking up the axle.
3. Remove upper and lower retaining bolts and remove shock absorber.

REAR SPRINGS REPLACE

1. Raise car and place stands under jacking points of body.
2. Remove wheel, then raise rear axle so spring compresses. Loosen upper and lower spring attachments.
3. Remove upper attachment for shock absorber. Lower jack carefully and remove spring, **Figs. 2 and 3.**
4. Install upper screw, washer and rubber spacer inside spring and firmly secure spring to upper attachment.
5. Raise jack and secure spring to the lower attachment with washer and screw.
6. Install shock absorber and wheel.

ROLL BAR REPLACE

1. Raise rear of vehicle, then position jack stands in front of rear shock absorber mountings.
2. Disconnect roll bar at axle and frame mounting brackets, then remove roll bar.
3. Reverse procedure to install.

TORQUE ROD REPLACE

740, 760 & 780 SERIES

1. Raise vehicle and place stands under the jacking points of body.
2. Remove torque rod attaching bolts, then the torque rod, **Fig. 2.**
3. Install rear end of torque rod first, then install the front end with X-link.
4. Torque front end bolts to 103 ft. lbs., sub-frame mount bolts to 63 ft. lbs., then the rear end bolts to 103 ft. lbs.

TRACK ROD REPLACE

1. Raise vehicle and place stands under jacking points of body.
2. Remove track rod attaching bolts, then the track rod, **Figs. 2 and 3.** Remove body end of rod first.
3. Reverse procedure to install. Install rear axle end of rod first. Torque trailing arm to axle attaching bolt to 45 ft.

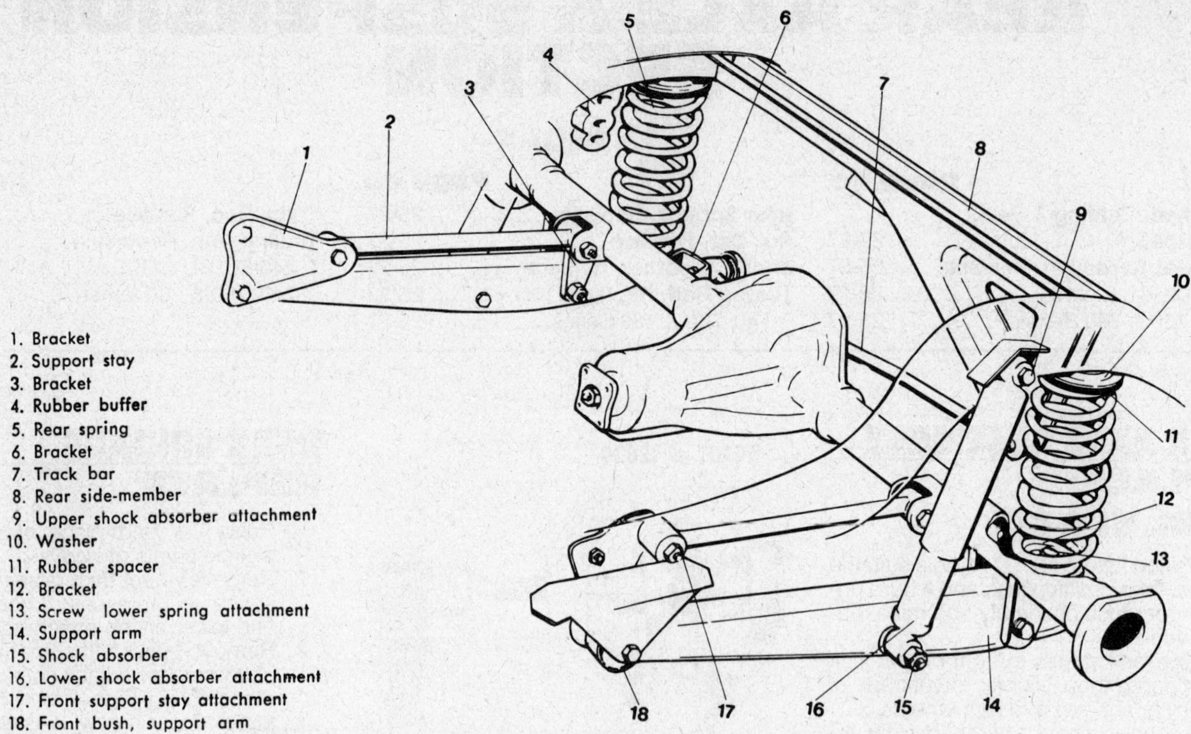

Fig. 2 Rear suspension. 240 DL, GL & GLT(Typical)

lbs. and trailing arm to body bolt to 65 ft. lbs.

TRAILING ARM REPLACE

240 DL, GL & GLT

1. Raise and support rear of vehicle.
2. Position a suitable jack under rear axle housing, then raise rear axle housing to compress springs.
3. Disconnect lower shock absorber at lower mounting, then remove lower spring attaching screw.
4. Slowly lower jack until spring releases from trailing arm, then move spring backwards so that it is free from arm.
5. Raise jack until axle housing is in a level position.
6. Disconnect trailing arm from axle and frame mounting brackets and remove arm.
7. Reverse procedure to install. Torque trailing arm to mounting bracket attaching bolts to 85 ft. lbs., shock absorber lower mounting bolt and nut to 65 ft.lbs., and spring attaching screw to 15 ft. lbs.

740, 760 & 780 SERIES

1. Raise and support vehicle. Support front end under control arm brackets so the vehicle will not be front heavy and the rear springs difficult to compress.
2. Remove rear wheel and brake caliper assembly. Hang caliper from rear spring.

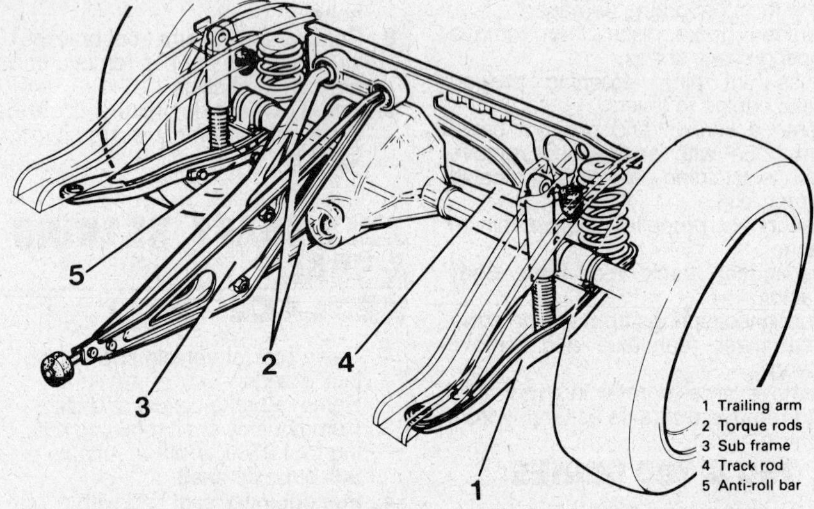

Fig. 3 Rear suspension. 740, 760 & 780 Series

3. Remove propeller shaft rear flange attaching bolts and lower the shaft slightly.
4. Support trailing arm with a suitable jack, then remove roll bar attaching bolts on both sides.
5. Remove shock absorber lower bolt on side trailing arm is being removed and loosen bolt on opposite side, then slowly lower rear axle to unload springs.
6. Remove trailing arm rear bracket and rubber supports, then the front bracket and trailing arm.
7. Reverse procedure to install. Note the following torques: trailing arm rear bracket bolts, 33 ft. lbs.; roll bar nuts, 35 ft. lbs.; shock absorber lower bolt, 63 ft. lbs.; trailing arm front bracket bolts, 35 ft. lbs. and nuts, 63 ft. lbs.; brake caliper bolts, 43 ft. lbs.

FRONT SUSPENSION & STEERING SECTION

INDEX

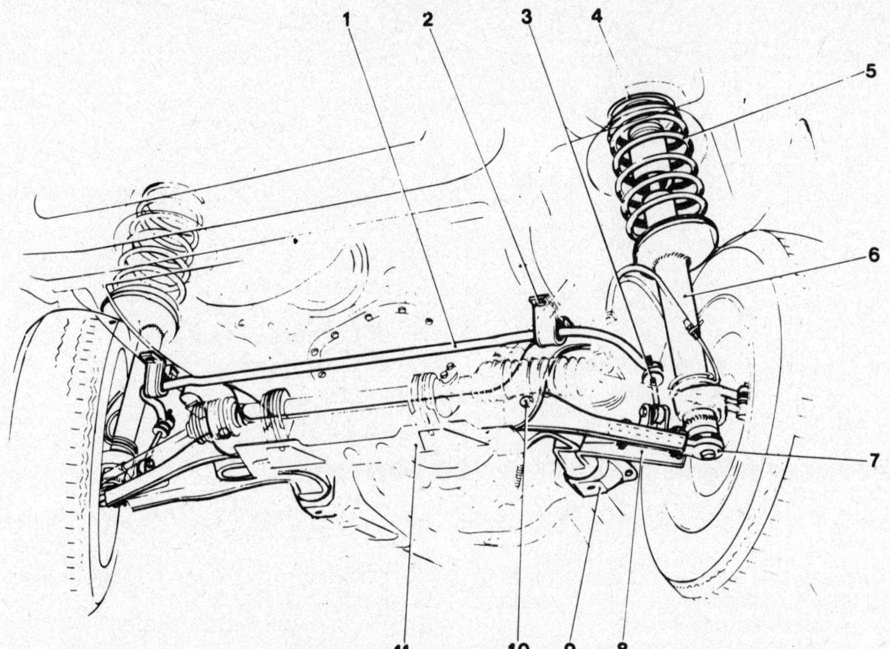

1. Stabilizer bar
2. Bracket
3. Link
4. Strut upper pivot point
5. Spring
6. Strut assembly
7. Ball joint
8. Control arm
9. Rear bracket for control arm
10. Front bracket for control arm
11. Front axle member

Fig. 1 Front suspension. 240 DL, GL & GLT

WHEEL BEARINGS
ADJUST

240 DL, GL & GLT

Adjust front wheel bearings by first tightening nut with a torque wrench to 70 Nm (50 ft. lbs.). Then loosen nut $1/3$ of a turn. If slot in nut does not coincide with cotter pin hole in spindle, loosen it further to enable cotter pin to be installed. Be sure to rotate wheel while tightening nut to be sure wheel bearings are properly seated.

740, 760 & 780 SERIES

Adjust front wheel bearings by first tightening nut to 57 Nm (42 ft. lbs.), then loosening nut $1/2$ turn. Torque nut to 1 ft. lb. and install cotter pin. If slot in nut does not align with hole in spindle, tighten nut to the next notch.

BALL JOINTS
REPLACE

240 DL, GL & GLT

1. Raise and support vehicle, then remove front wheel.
2. Remove ball joint housing to strut retaining bolts and lock washers (if applicable), then separate housing from strut.
3. Remove ball joint and housing assembly to control arm retaining nuts and bolts, then separate and remove joint assembly from control arm.
4. Position ball joint and housing on suitable bench, remove retaining nut, then press ball joint from housing.
5. Install new ball joint into housing and torque retaining nut to 44 ft. lbs. **Different ball joints are used for left and right sides of vehicle. Ensure correct one is used when replacing joints.**
6. Install ball joint housing to strut, using new bolts and lock washers (if applicable). Torque retaining bolts to 17 ft. lbs.
7. Install ball joint to control arm, then torque attaching nuts to 85 ft. lbs.

740, 760 & 780 SERIES

1. Raise and support vehicle.
2. Remove anti-roll bar link to control arm attaching bolt.
3. Remove ball joint stud cotter pin and nut.
4. Press ball joint out of control arm using tool 5259.
5. Remove ball joint to strut attaching bolts, then press control arm down and remove ball joint.
6. Reverse procedure to install. Torque attaching bolts to 30 Nm (22 ft. lbs.) then tighten an additional $1/4$ turn. Torque ball joint stud nut to 60 Nm (44 ft. lbs.).

CONTROL ARM & BUSHING
REPLACE

240 DL, GL & GLT

1. Raise and support front of vehicle and remove wheel.
2. Disconnect stabilizer link and ball joint from control arm, **Fig. 1.**
3. Remove rear bushing bracket to side member attaching bolts.
4. Remove front retaining bolt, then the control arm together with rear bushing bracket. Separate control arm from bracket.
5. Using tools 5085 and 5091 positioned in a vise, press out control arm bushing. Press in new bushing using tools 5084 and 5085.
6. Using tools 5082, 5083 and 1801, press bushing from rear bracket. Press in new bushing using tools 5081, 5082 and 1801.
7. Connect rear bushing bracket to control arm, then install washer and retaining nut. Tighten nut sufficiently, while still allowing rotation of washer.
8. Install control arm and front retaining

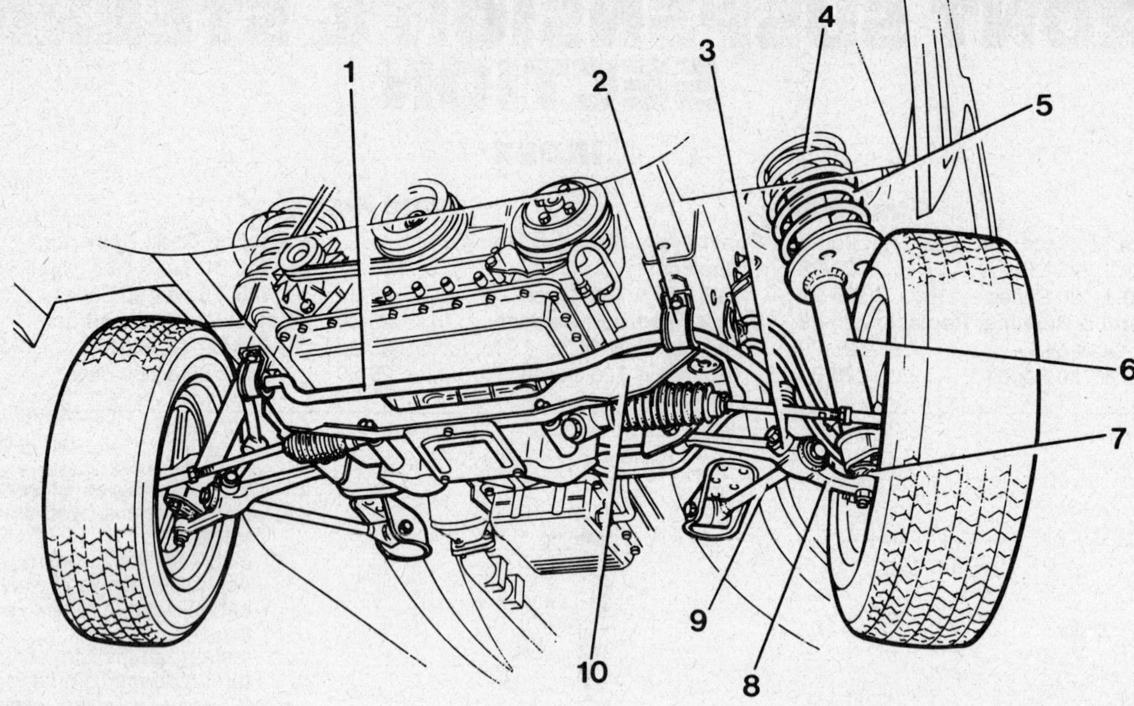

1 Anti-roll bar
2 Anti-roll bar mounting bracket
3 Anti-roll bar link
4 Spring strut upper mount
5 Coil spring
6 Spring strut
7 Ball joint
8 Control arm
9 Control arm strut
10 Cross member

Fig. 2 Front suspension. 740, 760 & 780 Series

bolt. Do not tighten nut at this time.

9. Guide stabilizer link into position, then connect ball joint to control arm and torque attaching nuts to 85 ft. lbs.
10. Attach rear bushing bracket to side member, then install attaching bolts and torque to 30 ft. lbs.
11. Tighten stabilizer link at control arm, lower vehicle, then bounce vehicle several times to allow control arm to set in position.
12. Torque control arm to rear bushing bracket attaching nut to 40 ft. lbs. and control arm front retaining bolt to 55 ft. lbs.

740, 760 & 780 SERIES

1. Raise and support front of vehicle and remove wheel.
2. Remove ball joint stud cotter pin and nut.
3. Remove anti-roll bar link and control arm strut attaching bolt, **Fig. 2,** then drive out front bushing.
4. Press ball joint out of control arm using tool 5259, then remove control arm from crossmember.
5. Secure control arm in a vise and press out bushing using tools 5091 and 5240. Press in rear bushing using tools 2904 and 5240.
6. Align control arm strut with control arm, attach control arm to crossmember, then install retaining bolt. Do not tighten bolt at this time.
7. Install ball joint to control arm, then torque attaching nut to 44 ft. lbs. and install cotter pin.
8. Install control arm strut bushing, washer and retaining bolt. Torque bolt to 70 ft. lbs.
9. Attach anti-roll bar link to control arm and torque retaining bolt to 63 ft. lbs.
10. Lower vehicle, then bounce vehicle several times to allow control arm to set in position. Torque control arm to crossmember retaining bolt to 63 ft. lbs.

SHOCK ABSORBER REPLACE

The following procedures allow servicing of the shock absorbers without removing the strut assembly from vehicle.

240 DL, GL & GLT

1. Raise vehicle and place stands under jacking points, then remove wheel.
2. Using tool 5039 (hydraulic shocks) or 5173 (gas shocks), loosen shock absorber retaining nut several turns.
3. Disconnect steering rod from steering arm using tool 5043.
4. Disconnect stabilizer bar from link attachment.
5. Disconnect brake line bracket.
6. Remove cover for spring and strut assembly upper attachment.
7. Using tool 5036 and 5037, loosen center nut, **Fig. 3.**
8. Place alignment marks on nut plate and wheel housing, then remove strut upper retaining nuts. Lower jack, support strut assembly when lowering jack so that brake lines and hoses do not become damaged. Hook tool No. 5045 to strut assembly and stabilizer bar.
9. Install two 5040 spring compressors. Be sure compressor spans five coils or spring will not be sufficiently compressed. Tighten compressors.
10. Remove center nut using tools mentioned above, then remove spring seat, rubber bumper and shock absorber protector.
11. Loosen spring compressors and remove coil spring.
12. Using tool 5039 (hydraulic shocks) or 5173 (gas shocks), remove shock absorber retaining nut. Use a pipe wrench to hold the outer housing. Be sure to place the pipe wrench on the weld of the housing.
13. Pull shock absorber out of housing.
14. Reverse procedure to install, ensuring that marks on nut plate and wheel housing are aligned. Torque strut upper retaining nuts to 15 ft. lbs.

740, 760 & 780 SERIES

1. Raise and support front of vehicle and

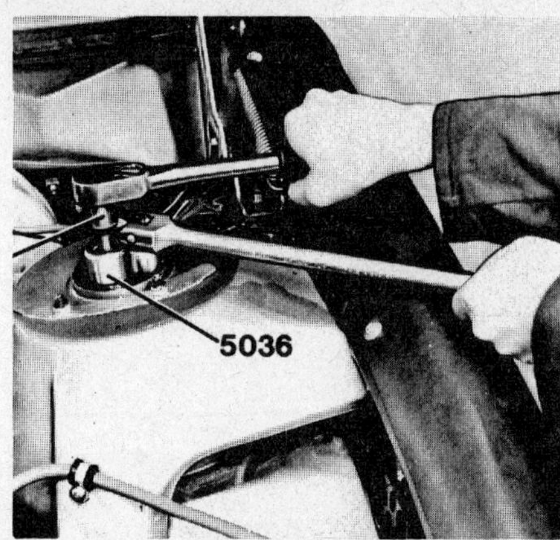

Fig. 3 Loosening/removing strut center nut

remove wheel.
2. Disconnect steering rod from steering arm using tool 5259.
3. Support control arm with a suitable jack, then disconnect anti-roll bar from link attachment.
4. Remove brake line bracket attaching bolt, then disconnect brake lines from retaining clips.
5. Remove rubber boot from upper strut nut, then disconnect high tension lead from ignition coil.
6. Loosen strut center nut using tools 5036 and 5037, **Fig. 3.**
7. Mark position of upper mount, then remove mount attaching nuts and washers.
8. Lower jack while supporting strut assembly to avoid damage to brake lines and fender. Hook tool 5045 to strut and anti-roll bar.
9. Install two 5040 spring compressors. Position compressors so that claws span three spring coils and compress each side alternately.
10. Remove strut center nut, then the upper mount, spring retainer, spring and rubber bumper, or rubber bellows and disc on gas pressure shocks.
11. Remove shock absorber retaining nut, then the shock absorber.
12. Reverse procedure to install.

STEERING GEAR REPLACE

240 DL, GL & GLT

1. Loosen steering shaft flange from pinion shaft.
2. Raise vehicle and support front end on jack stands.
3. Using tool 5043, disconnect steering rods from steering arms.
4. Remove lower splash pan.
5. On power steering units, disconnect hoses at steering gear.
6. Remove four steering gear retaining nuts and bolts. Remove steering gear.

740, 760 & 780 SERIES

1. Raise and support front of vehicle.
2. Remove splash pan, then the jack support panel on front crossmember.
3. Disconnect lower steering shaft from steering gear.
4. Remove snap rings from lower universal joint.
5. Loosen upper bolt and remove lower bolt from universal joint clamp, then slide joint up steering shaft.
6. Remove ball joint nut, then disconnect tie rods.
7. Disconnect oil lines from steering gear.
8. Remove anti-roll bar brackets from side members and position aside.
9. Remove steering gear attaching bolts, then the steering gear from vehicle.
10. Reverse procedure to install. Torque steering gear attaching bolts to 32 ft. lbs.

CONTROL ARM STRUT & BUSHING REPLACE

740, 760 & 780 SERIES

1. Raise and support front of vehicle and remove wheel.
2. Remove strut to control arm attaching bolt, then detach strut and remove bushing.
3. Remove strut rear mount attaching bolt, then remove strut from vehicle.
4. Press rear bushing out of strut using tool 2731.
5. Reverse procedure to install. Press rear bushing into strut using tool 2731 and a V-block. Torque strut to control arm attaching bolt to 70 ft. lbs. Torque rear mount attaching bolt to 63 ft. lbs. if M12 bolt is used, or 73 ft. lbs. for M14 bolt.

WHEEL ALIGNMENT SECTION

INDEX

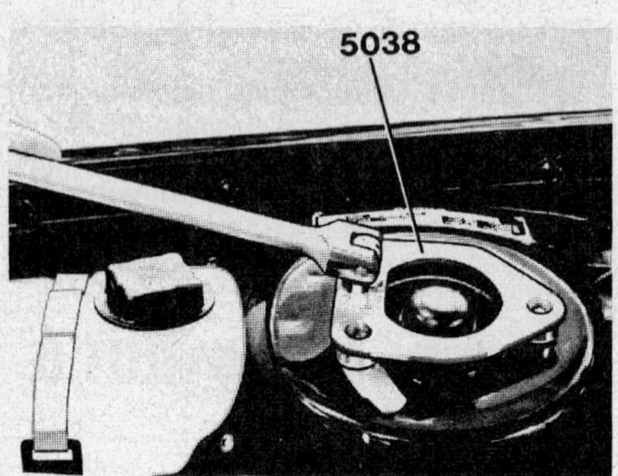

Fig. 1 Adjusting camber. 240 DL, GL & GLT

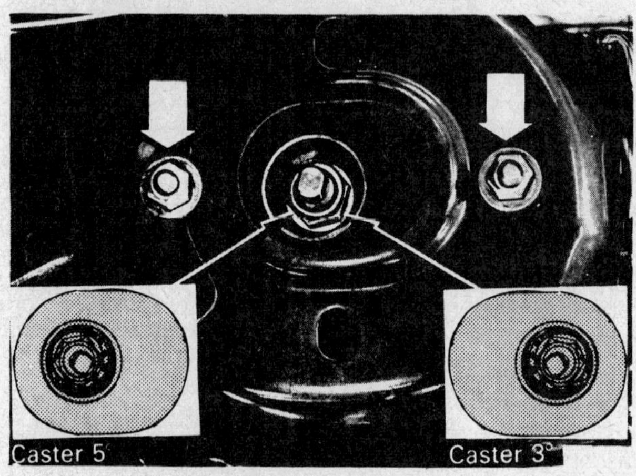

Fig. 2 Adjusting caster. 740, 760 & 780 Series

240 DL, GL & GLT

CASTER ADJUSTMENT

Caster is not adjustable. If caster angle is not within specifications, check for damaged or worn suspension components and replace as needed.

CAMBER ADJUSTMENT

1. Bounce vehicle up and down several times to set control arms in normal position.
2. Loosen upper strut attaching nuts.
3. Adjust camber using tool 5038, **Fig. 1.**
4. Tighten strut attaching nuts, then recheck caster angle.

TOE-IN ADJUSTMENT

1. Loosen locknut on each tie rod.
2. Turn each tie rod to obtain proper toe-in. Length of tie rods may not differ more than 2 mm (.080 inch).
3. If after toe-in adjustment, steering wheel is not properly centered, remove steering wheel and reinstall in correct alignment. **1987 vehicles with "SRS" designation on steering wheel are equipped with air bag restraint system. Use extreme caution when working on steering wheel to avoid personal injury.**

740, 760 & 780 SERIES

CASTER ADJUSTMENT

If caster measures $+3°$, the spring strut upper mount is set at the wrong position. Remove nuts and move mount to the correct position, **Fig. 2.**

CAMBER ADJUSTMENT

Camber is not adjustable on these models. If camber is not within specifications, check for damaged or worn components and replace as needed.

TOE-IN ADJUSTMENT

1. Loosen locknut on each tie rod, then turn each tie rod to obtain proper toe-in. Length of tie rods must not differ more than 2 mm (.080 inch).
2. If, after adjustment, steering wheel is not properly centered, remove steering wheel and reinstall in correct alignment. **1987 vehicles with "SRS" designation on steering wheel are equipped with air bag restraint system. Use extreme caution when working on steering wheel to avoid personal injury.**

YUGO (Yugoslavia)

INDEX OF SERVICE OPERATIONS

General Engine Specifications

Year	Engine	Carb. Type	Bore & Stroke Inches (mm)	Comp. Ratio	Horsepower @ RPM	Torque Lbs. Ft. @ RPM	Normal Oil Pressure Psi
1986–87	4-68/1116	2 Barrel	3.15 x 2.185 (80 x 55.5)	9.2	55 @ 6000	57 @ 3000	50–70

Alternator & Regulator Specifications

Alternator		Regulator
Model No.	Output @ 13 Volts 6000 RPM	Model
AAK1163	54 Amps	Iskra AER

Starter Motor Specifications

Model No.	Rotation	Brush Spring Tension Lbs.	No Lead Test				Torque Test		
			Amps	Volts	Speed RPM	Break Away Resistance Ohms	Amps	Volts	Torque Ft. Lbs. (Min.)
AZE 3502	Clockwise	2.49–2.8	30–40	11.2–11.5	6500–7500	.021–.023	300–330	7–7.2	5.9

Drive Axle Specifications

Year	Carrier Type	Ring Gear & Pinion Backlash		Pinion Bearing Preload		Differntial Bearing Preload	
		Method	Adjustment	Method	Adjustment	Method	Adjustment
1986–87	Integral	Shims	.004	Shims	①	Shims	—

①—Shim thickness equals P–H + .003 inch where P is distance between cover mounting surface and outer race of bearing and H is height of cover.

Pistons, Pins, Rings, Crankshaft & Bearings

Engine	Piston Clearance	Ring End Gap		Wristpin Diameter	Rod Bearings		Main Bearings			
		Comp.	Oil		Shaft Diameter	Bearing Clearance	Shaft Diameter	Bearing Clearance	Thrust on Bear. No.	Bearing Clearance
4-68/1116cc	.001–.002	.012	.008	.8652	1.7913–1.7920	.0014–.0034	1.9994–2.0002	.0016–.0033	5	.002–.010

Valve Specifications

Engine	Valve Lash		Valve Angles		Valve Spring Free Length	Valve Spring Pressure Lbs. @ In.	Stem Clearance		Stem Diameter	
	Int.	Exh.	Int.	Exh.			Intake	Exhaust	Intake	Exhaust
4-68/1116cc	.0157C	.019C	45	45	①	②	.0020–.0039	.0020–.0039	.3139–.3146	.3139–.3146

①—Inner spring, 1.646 inch; outer spring, 2.122 inch.

②—Inner spring, 64 @ .846; outer spring, 141 @ 1.043

Front Wheel Alignment Specifications

Year	Caster Angle, Degrees		Camber Angle, Degrees		Toe-In, Inches	
	Limits	Desired	Limits	Desired	Limits	Desired
1986–87	+1¾ to +2¾	+2¼	+1 to +2	+1½	−3/32 to −1/32	−1/16

Rear Wheel Alignment Specifications

Year	Camber Angle, Degrees		Toe-In Inches	
	Limits	Desired	Limits	Desired
1986–87	−1 to 0	−½	+⅛ to +¼	+3/16

Engine Tightening Specifications

Year	Engine	Spark Plug Ft. Lbs.	Cylinder Head Bolts Ft. Lbs.	Intake Manifold Ft. Lbs.	Exhaust Manifold Ft. Lbs.	Connecting Rod Cap Nuts Ft. Lbs.	Main Bearing Cap Bolts Ft. Lbs.	Flywheel Bolt Ft. Lbs.	Camshaft Housing Nuts Ft. Lbs.	Crankshaft Pulley Nut, Ft. Lbs.	Camshaft Sprocket Bolt Ft. Lbs.
1986–87	4-68/1116cc	27	69	—	—	38	59	38	—	101	20

Brake Specifications

Year	Drum Brake I.D.	Wheel Cylinder Bore		Master Cylinder Bore	Disc Brake Rotor		
		Front Disc	Rear Drum		Nominal Thickness	Minimum Thickness	Runout (T.I.R.)
1986–87	7.3	1.889	.75	.75	.425	.354	.006

Cooling System & Capacity Data

Year	Cooling Capacity Qts.	Radiator Cap Relief Pressure Lbs.	Thermo. Opening Temp. °F.	Fuel Tank Gals.	Engine Oil Refill Qts.	Trans. Oil Qts.
1986–87	6.9	12	180	10	4.5	3.35

ELECTRICAL SECTION

INDEX

ALTERNATOR TESTING

1. Check resistance of rotor winding by connecting ohmmeter leads to two slip rings. Resistance should be 3-3.75 ohms.
2. Check rotor windings for short circuits by connecting ohmmeter test leads between a slip ring and the rotor.
3. Connect leads between stator commutator and ground. There should be no current flow.
4. Inspect stator winding live wires for short circuits as follows:
   a. Connect ohmmeter leads between each winding live wire end on energizing and power diode plate and the stator winding core.
   b. Connect ohmmeter leads to stator live wire ends in three possible combinations.
   c. If resistance is near zero in one of the three measurements in 4a or 4b and much higher in the other two measurements, an open exists in a stator winding live wire.
5. Connect test leads between live wire ends and ground. There should be no current flow.

STARTER
REPLACE

1. Disconnect battery ground cable.
2. Raise and support vehicle.
3. Disconnect electrical connectors at starter.
4. Remove starter attaching bolts and washers and the starter.
5. Reverse procedure to install.

IGNITION SWITCH
REPLACE

1. Disconnect battery ground cable.
2. Remove upper and/or lower steering column covers as necessary to gain access to switch.
3. Disconnect electrical connections at switch.
4. Remove switch attaching screw and the switch.
5. Reverse procedure to install.

STOP LIGHT SWITCH
REPLACE

1. Disconnect switch electrical connectors at brake pedal.
2. Remove switch attaching nut and the switch.
3. Reverse procedure to install.

LIGHT SWITCH
REPLACE

1. Disconnect battery ground cable.
2. Disconnect light switch electrical connectors from behind switch.
3. Remove switch retaining ring, if equipped, and remove switch from dashboard.
4. Reverse procedure to install.

TURN SIGNAL SWITCH
REPLACE

1. Disconnect battery ground cable.
2. Center steering wheel and front wheels.
3. Pry horn button off steering wheel.
4. Remove horn button spring.
5. Remove steering wheel attaching nut.
6. Mark position steering wheel in relation to shaft, then remove steering wheel using suitable puller.
7. Remove upper and lower steering column covers.
8. Loosen turn signal switch retaining clamp.
9. Disconnect electrical connectors at and remove switch.
10. Reverse procedure to install.

WINDSHIELD WIPER SWITCH
REPLACE

1. Disconnect battery ground cable.
2. Center steering wheel and front wheels.
3. Pry horn button off steering wheel.
4. Remove horn button spring.
5. Remove steering wheel attaching nut.
6. Mark position of, then remove steering wheel.
7. Remove upper and lower steering column covers.
8. Loosen windshield wiper switch retaining clamp.
9. Disconnect electrical connectors at and remove switch.
10. Reverse procedure to install.

REAR WIPER SWITCH
REPLACE

1. Disconnect battery ground cable.
2. Disconnect switch electrical connectors from behind switch.
3. Remove switch retaining ring, if equipped, and remove switch from dashboard.
4. Reverse procedure to install.

INSTRUMENT CLUSTER
REPLACE

1. Disconnect battery ground cable.
2. Remove spare tire from engine compartment.
3. Remove speedometer cable retainer plate screw and the cable.
4. Remove cluster attaching screws and the cluster.
5. Reverse procedure to install.

WINDSHIELD WIPER MOTOR & LINKAGE
REPLACE

1. Disconnect battery ground cable.
2. Remove wiper blade arm.
3. Remove wiper assembly attaching nuts.
4. Open hood and remove two wiper mechanism attaching bolts.
5. Disconnect electrical connectors at wiper motor.
6. Remove windshield wiper mechanism.
7. Reverse procedure to install.

REAR WIPER MOTOR & LINKAGE
REPLACE

1. Disconnect battery ground cable.
2. Remove wiper blade arm.
3. Remove attaching nut with washer and two spacers.
4. Open hatch and remove protective plastic cap attaching bolts and the cap.
5. Disconnect electrical connectors at motor.
6. Remove wiper motor attaching bolt and the wiper motor.
7. Reverse procedure to install.

RADIO
REPLACE

1. Disconnect antenna lead and electrical connectors.
2. Remove radio attaching bolts and the

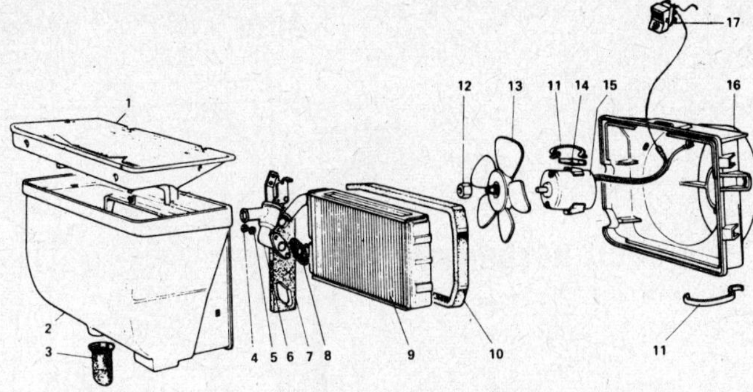

Heater assembly components

1. Water shield
2. Housing
3. Water drain plug
4. Nut
5. Spring washer
6. Valve
7. Gasket
8. Gasket
9. Radiator
10. Gasket
11. Spring clips
12. Nut, attaching impeller to motor
13. Impeller
14. Rubber pad
15. Motor
16. Fan housing
17. Switch

Fig. 1 Exploded view of heater assembly

radio.

3. Reverse procedure to install.

BLOWER MOTOR REPLACE

1. Disconnect battery ground cable.
2. Drain coolant from radiator and heater core. To drain heater core, move top heater control lever fully to right.
3. Loosen heater hose clamps at heater core.
4. Remove air admission shutter actuator rod attaching screw and nut.
5. Remove air conveyor and slide out radiator housing spring clips, **Fig. 1.**
6. Remove outside air admission shutter actuating rod.
7. Remove heater valve control cable.
8. Remove heater core.
9. Remove fan housing attaching nuts.
10. Disconnect electrical connectors at blower motor and fan switch.
11. Disconnect blower motor ground wire at radiator.
12. Remove heater assembly from vehicle.
13. Remove two spring clips attaching blower motor to housing and slide motor out of housing.
14. Reverse procedure to install, ensuring gasket between fan housing and body is correctly installed.

HEATER CORE REPLACE

1. Disconnect battery ground cable.
2. Drain coolant from radiator and heater core. To drain heater core, move top heater control lever fully to right.
3. Loosen heater hose clamps at heater core.
4. Remove air admission shutter actuator rod attaching screw and nut.
5. Remove air conveyor and slide out radiator housing spring clips, **Fig. 1.**
6. Remove outside air admission shutter actuating rod.
7. Remove heater valve control cable.
8. Remove heater core.
9. Reverse procedure to install.

ENGINE SECTION

INDEX

ENGINE REPLACE

The engine, transmission and differential are removed as an assembly from under the vehicle.

1. Disconnect battery ground cable and drain cooling system. Remove spare tire from engine compartment.
2. Disconnect air cleaner snorkel flexible hose from front of vehicle, then the hoses from beneath the air cleaner. Remove air cleaner.
3. Disconnect primary and secondary wiring from distributor.
4. Disconnect wiring from alternator, starter, oil pressure and water temperature sending units, and the back-up light switch.
5. Disconnect air hoses and vacuum valve from air injection diverter valve.
6. Disconnect accelerator cable and the choke and shutoff solenoid wiring from carburetor.
7. Disconnect vacuum and fuel evaporative hoses from carburetor and intake manifold.
8. Disconnect fuel hoses and lines from carburetor.
9. Disconnect exhaust pipe from exhaust manifold.
10. Disconnect radiator hoses from thermostat housing and the heater hoses from engine.
11. Disconnect speedometer cable from transmission and clutch cable from clutch release lever.
12. Raise and support vehicle so that the assembly may be lowered from vehicle.
13. Support engine and transmission assembly with suitable equipment.
14. Remove front wheels.
15. Disconnect tie rods from steering knuckle.
16. Remove bolts securing sway bar brackets to body and the sway bar-to-control rod nuts. Remove sway bar from vehicle.
17. Remove bolts securing struts to steering knuckle.
18. Remove axle shaft retaining nuts and work constant velocity joints from seat in steering knuckle. Support each axle shaft with wire to retain shafts in differential seats.
19. Remove exhaust pipe support bracket and the ground strap from transmission.
20. Disconnect shift linkage from transmission.
21. Remove crossmember and disconnect reaction strut from engine.
22. Remove engine front, right side mount bolt.
23. Lower assembly from vehicle.
24. Reverse procedure to install.

ENGINE DISASSEMBLY

1. Place engine in suitable work stand.
2. Remove oil dipstick and oil filter, then drain crankcase oil.
3. Disconnect starter wiring, then remove three starter attaching bolts and the starter.
4. Remove transmission to engine attaching bolts and nuts and the transmission.
5. Mark relationship of clutch pressure plate to flywheel for proper assembly.
6. Remove clutch to flywheel attaching bolts and the clutch.

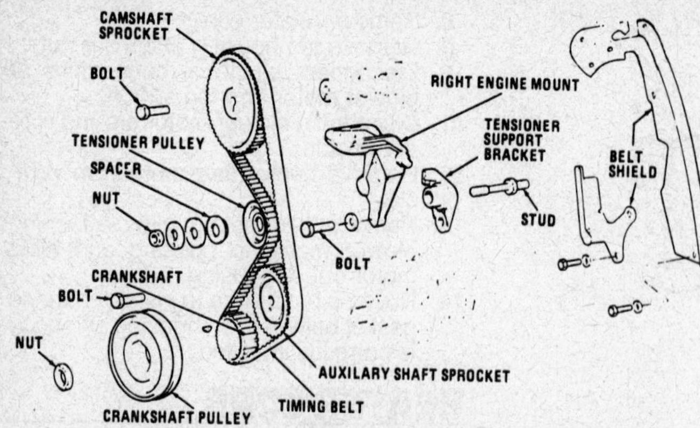

Fig. 1 Exploded view of timing belt assembly

7. Disconnect vacuum hose at distributor.
8. Disconnect spark plug wires at plugs, then remove distributor holding clamp and the distributor.
9. Remove crankcase breather attaching bolt, then the breather and gasket.
10. Remove bolts, washers and nuts securing alternator to mounting brackets, then remove alternator and drive belt.
11. Remove alternator mounting bracket to engine attaching bolts and washer, then the bracket.
12. Disconnect air hose at check valve, then remove air pump attaching bolts and washers and remove air pump with hoses attached.
13. Remove check valve.
14. Disconnect EGR tube from carburetor base and exhaust manifold and remove spacer and gasket.
15. Remove EGR tube to valve attaching bolts and washers and separate tube and valve.
16. Disconnect vacuum hose at EGR valve, then remove EGR valve attaching bolts and washers and the valve.
17. Remove EGR base attaching bolts and washers, then the base and gasket.
18. Disconnect coolant hoses at thermostat housing.
19. Remove coolant pipe to water pump attaching bolts and the pipe.
20. Remove water pump attaching bolts and washers, then the pump and gasket.
21. Remove thermostat housing attaching bolts and washers, then the housing and gasket.
22. Remove timing bolt cover attaching bolts and washers and the cover.
23. Install tool A 60360 or equivalent on flywheel to inhibit engine rotation.
24. Remove camshaft sprocket bolt, **Fig. 1,** and the auxiliary shaft sprocket bolt.
25. Using suitable tool, remove crankshaft pulley.
26. Remove nut, washers and spacer, then press bracket against tensioner in right engine mount and remove pulley and timing belt.
27. Remove tensioner support bracket from stud and remove stud.
28. Remove three right engine mount attaching bolts and the mount.
29. Remove camshaft sprocket, auxiliary shaft sprocket, crankshaft pulley and the crankshaft sprocket.
30. Remove bolts and nuts attaching belt shields, then the shields.
31. Disconnect fuel pump line at caburetor, leaving filter and fuel pump lines attached to pump.
32. Remove fuel pump, ensuring that actuating rod is removed.
33. Remove carburetor.
34. Remove cylinder head, with manifolds and camshaft housing, by removing cylinder head attaching nuts and bolts. Remove gasket.
35. Remove auxiliary shaft cover and seal and the auxiliary shaft.
36. Remove six flywheel attaching bolts and washer plate, then the flywheel.
37. Invert engine on stand and remove oil pan attaching bolts, then the pan and gasket.
38. Remove six flywheel end cover plate attaching bolts and lock washers, then the end cover plate and gasket, **Fig. 2.**
39. Remove five timing gear end cover plate attaching bolts and lock washers, then the plate and gasket.
40. Remove three oil pump assembly attaching bolts and lockwashers, then the pump with oil pickup tube and gasket.
41. Remove oil return pipe attaching bolt and the pipe.
42. Remove connecting rod caps, complete with bearing inserts, from crankshaft.
43. Remove four piston-rod assemblies from top of cylinder block, turning crankshaft as necessary to facilitate removal.

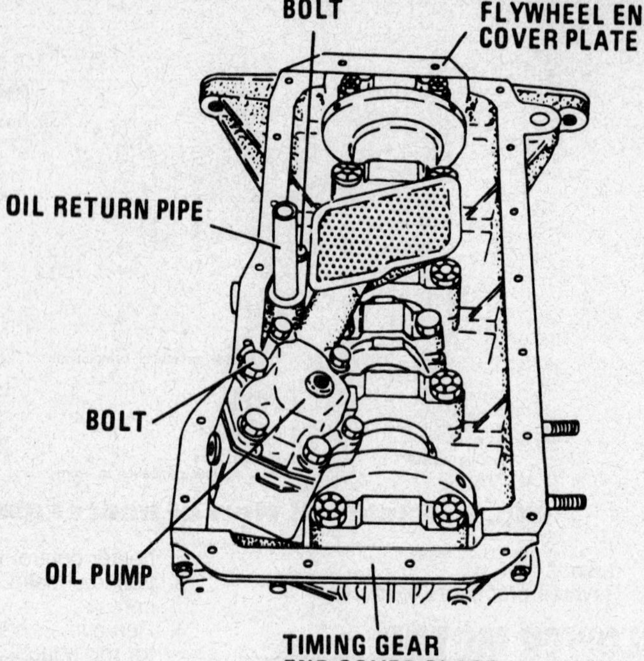

Fig. 2 Lower crankcase

44. Remove main bearing caps together with bearing inserts.
45. Remove crankshaft and take out upper bearing inserts.
46. Remove thrust ring halves from rear main bearing saddle.

ENGINE ASSEMBLY

1. Thoroughly lubricate bearing inserts with clean engine oil.
2. Place main bearing inserts in position and install crankshaft. **Thrust ring halves are positioned at rear main bearing saddle bore and may be installed before or after installing crankshaft.**
3. Install main bearing caps and bearing inserts, ensuring caps are installed in proper location. Cap without notch goes at timing gear end of crankcase, then cap with one notch and so on.
4. Install new seal and gasket on flywheel end cover plate.
5. Install cover on crankcase, ensuring distance between cover seal and crankshaft is equal along entire circumference.
6. Secure flywheel to crankshaft with washer plate and six bolts, then block crankshaft with tool A 60369 or equivalent and torque flywheel bolts to 61 ft. lbs.
7. Thoroughly lubricate pistons and cylinder bores with clean engine oil and install piston and rod assemblies in cylinder bores with suitable piston ring compressors. Refer to "Pistons & Connecting Rods."
8. Thoroughly lubricate connecting rod bearing inserts and journals with clean engine oil.
9. Position connecting rod, with bearing inserts, on journals.

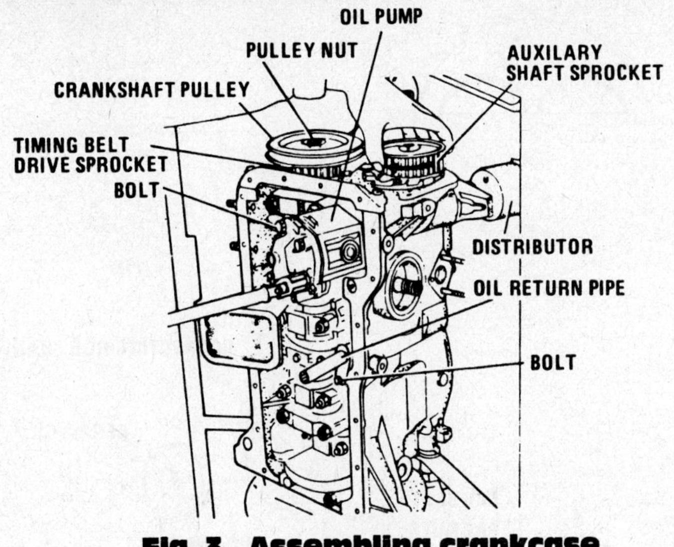

Fig. 3 Assembling crankcase

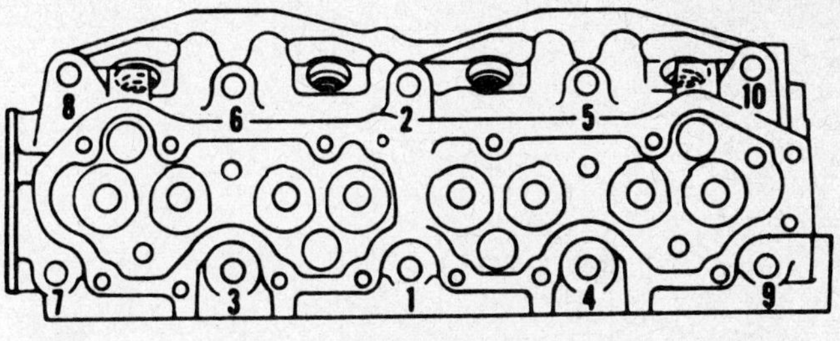

Fig. 4 Cylinder head bolt tightening sequence

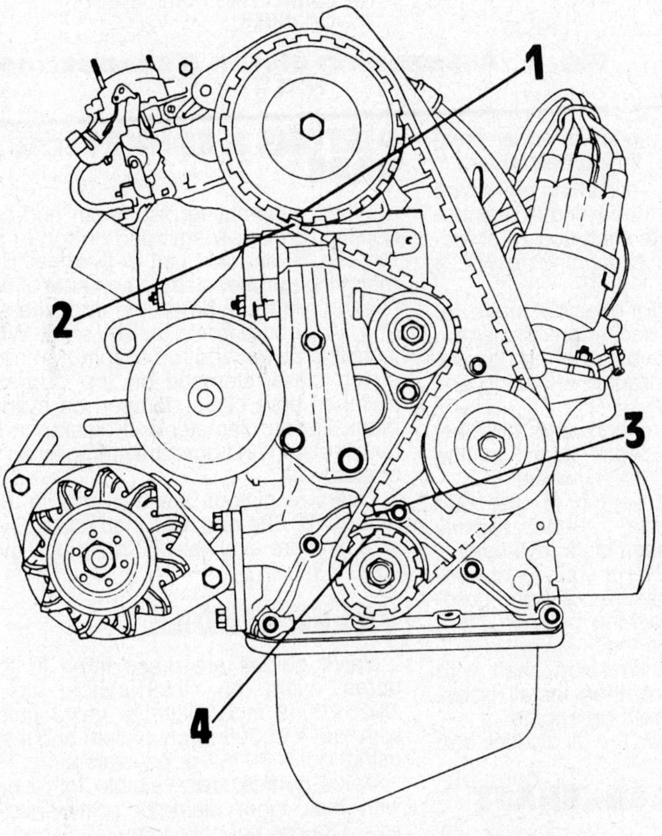

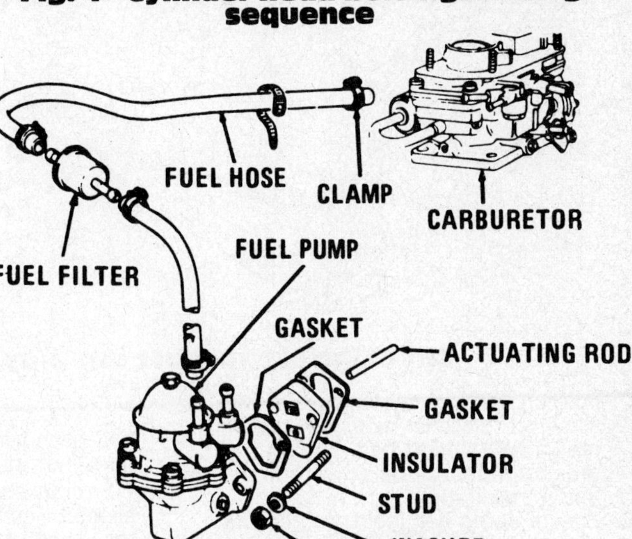

Fig. 6 Installing fuel pump

Fig. 5 Installing timing belt

10. Install caps with bearing inserts and torque nuts to 38 ft. lbs.
11. Thoroughly lubricate auxiliary shaft bushings with clean engine oil.
12. Install shaft, then place gasket on lock plate and secure shaft in place with three bolts, lock washers, lock plate and new seal.
13. Install auxiliary shaft sprocket with bolt washer but do not tighten bolt fully.
14. Install new seal and gasket on timing gear end cover plate and install plate on crankshaft, ensuring indexing marks on cover plate are properly aligned.
15. Install oil pump and gasket, **Fig. 3.** Before final tightening of oil pump bolts, install oil pump and distributor drive gear, coupling it to gear on auxiliary shaft.
16. Temporarily install distributor.
17. Rotate auxiliary shaft, using sprocket, while tightening oil pump bolts alternately. If auxiliary shaft binds or crawls during rotation, loosen pump and repeat operation.
18. Install oil return pipe with one bolt and lock washer.
19. Install crankshaft sprocket and crankshaft pulley, then install pulley nut and, with flywheel blocked, torque pulley nut to 101 ft. lbs.
20. Install oil pan and gasket.
21. Install cylinder head assembly and new gasket complete with valves, springs, camshaft housing, manifolds and carburetor.
22. Gradually torque cylinder head bolts in proper sequence, **Fig. 4,** in two stages; torque to approximately 29 ft. lbs., torque to 69 ft. lbs.
23. Install timing belt shields.
24. Install camshaft sprocket with bolt and washer but do not fully tighten bolt at this time.
25. Install right engine mount with three bolts and lock washers.
26. Install spring tensioner in its seat in engine mount.
27. Install tensioner pulley support stud and bracket on crankcase.
28. Install tension pulley on bracket and secure temporarily with nut washers and spacer, but do not fully tighten at this time.
29. Using suitable tool, turn engine until mark (4), **Fig. 5,** on crankshaft sprocket is aligned with reference index (3).
30. Position camshaft sprocket so that marks (1 and 2) are aligned. **Auxiliary shaft sprocket does not have to be aligned.**
31. Move tensioner pulley toward engine mount and tighten nut to hold pulley in

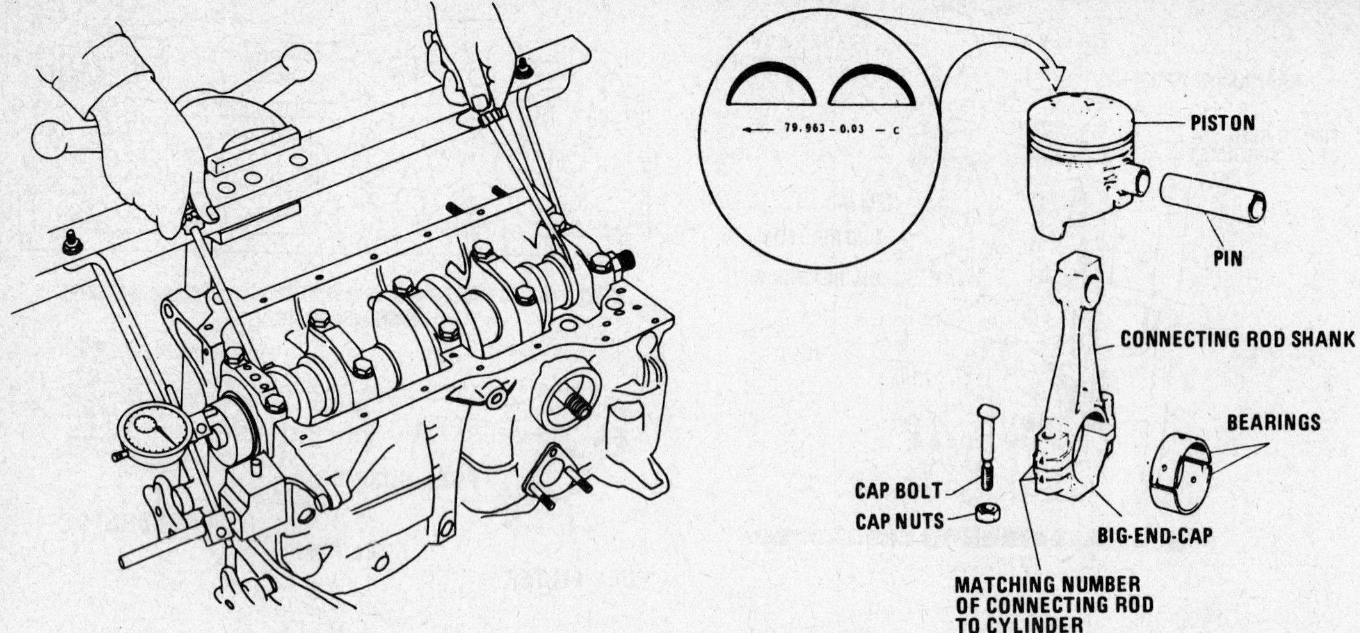

Fig. 7 Checking crankshaft endplay

Fig. 8 Assembling piston & connecting rod

position, then install timing belt with slack on tensioner side. **Always install a new timing belt. Timing belt tension must not be adjusted after initial installation.**

32. Ensure timing belt teeth are perfectly coupled with sprockets.
33. Loosen nut holding tensioner pulley to allow tensioner to tighten belt, then torque tensioner pulley nut to 33 ft. lbs. and ensure timing marks are still aligned.
34. With flywheel blocked, torque auxiliary shaft sprocket bolt and camshaft sprocket bolt to 61 ft. lbs.
35. Install fuel pump with gaskets, insulator, actuating rod, two nuts and washers in order shown, **Fig. 6. Gasket comes in three different sizes which are used to adjust pump stroke.**
36. Connect fuel line at carburetor.
37. Screw check valve into cylinder head and secure with locknut.
38. Install air pump and connect air hoses to air pump and check valve.
39. Install thermostat housing and gasket on crankcase.
40. Install water pump and gasket, torquing attaching bolts to 22 ft. lbs.
41. Install coolant pipe and gasket to water pump.
42. Connect coolant hoses to thermostat housing.
43. Install new air pump belt and check for approximately 1/2 inch deflection with moderate finger pressure.
44. Install EGR valve base, gasket, EGR valve and gasket.
45. Connect vacuum hose and EGR tube to EGR valve.
46. Connect EGR tube to carburetor base and exhaust manifold with spacer and gasket.
47. Install alternator mounting bracket, then the alternator.
48. Install new alternator drive belt, checking for approximately 1/2 inch deflection with moderate finger pressure, then install timing belt cover.
49. Turn crankshaft until timing marks are aligned, **Fig. 5,** then remove distributor cap and rotate shaft until rotor faces terminal corresponding to No. 4 cylinder.
50. Ensuring that rotor does not move, install distributor, securing with clamp.
51. Install crankcase breather and gasket on crankcase, torquing attaching bolt to 18.5 ft. lbs.
52. After ensuring clutch and flywheel surfaces are clean, align mating marks on clutch and flywheel.
53. With protruding portion of disc hub facing away from flywheel, loosely fasten clutch assembly to flywheel.
54. Using tool A 70210 or equivalent, center disc with pressure plate and gradually torque attaching bolts to 28 ft. lbs., then remove tool.
55. Lightly coat transmission shaft with suitable lubricant, then install transmission and covers on engine.
56. Install starter, then the oil dipstick and oil filter.

CHECKING CRANKSHAFT ENDPLAY

1. After installing crankshaft, check end play between thrust rings on rear main bearing saddle and crankshaft shoulders.
2. Install magnetic base dial gage and wedge two screwdrivers, **Fig. 7.**
3. Using screwdrivers, pry crankshaft back and forth and check on dial gage to see if end movement is .002-.010 inch.
4. If end play exceeds .0137 inch, replace thrust rings with .005 inch oversize rings.
5. When installing service thrust rings, ensure grooves on thrust ring face crankshaft shoulder.

PISTONS & CONNECTING RODS

When assembling piston, pin and connecting rod, arrow stamped on top of piston, **Fig. 8,** should point to flywheel. Bore matching number stamped on side of connecting rod must be on the opposite side of cylinder bore from auxiliary shaft. When installing piston and rod assembly, ensure piston class, stamped on top of piston, matches bore class stamped on cylinder block. Piston diameter and clearance between piston and bore are stamped on top of piston.

Oversize pistons are available in .004, .008, .016, .024 and .031 inch sizes. Oversize pins are available in .0079 inch oversize.

VALVE GUIDES

Valve guides are press fitted in their bores with an interference fit of .0025-.0043 inch. Remove valve guides with tool A 60395 or equivalent and install using tool A 60462 or equivalent.

Valve guides are available for service with their inner diameter prefinished to size. They do not have to be refinished unless a minor fault occurs during press fitting.

VALVES

ADJUST

1. Remove camshaft cover.
2. Turn crankshaft until lobe controlling tappet being checked is pointing upward and is at right angles to tapped plate.
3. Using feeler gage, measure clearance between shim and camshaft lobe. Clearance with cold engine should be .0157 inch for intake valves and .0190 for exhaust valves.

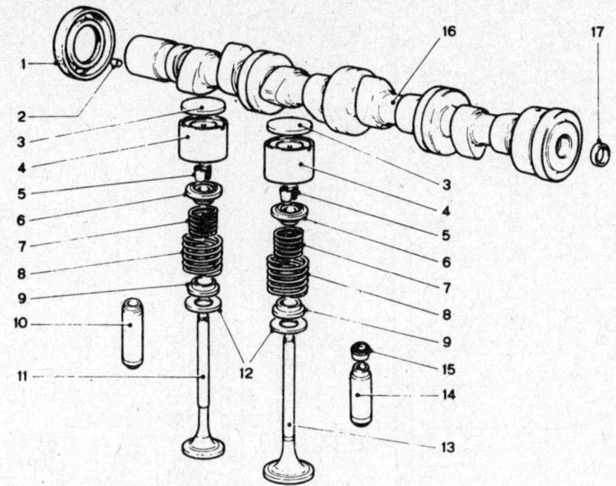

1. Seal
2. Dowel
3. Plates for adjusting valve clearance
4. Tappets
5. Locks
6. Upper cups
7. Inner springs
8. Outer springs
9. Lower cups
10. Exhaust valve guide
11. Exhaust valve
12. Flat washers
13. Intake valve
14. Intake valve guide
15. Oil seal
16. Camshaft
17. Weich plug

Fig. 9 Exploded view of valve assembly

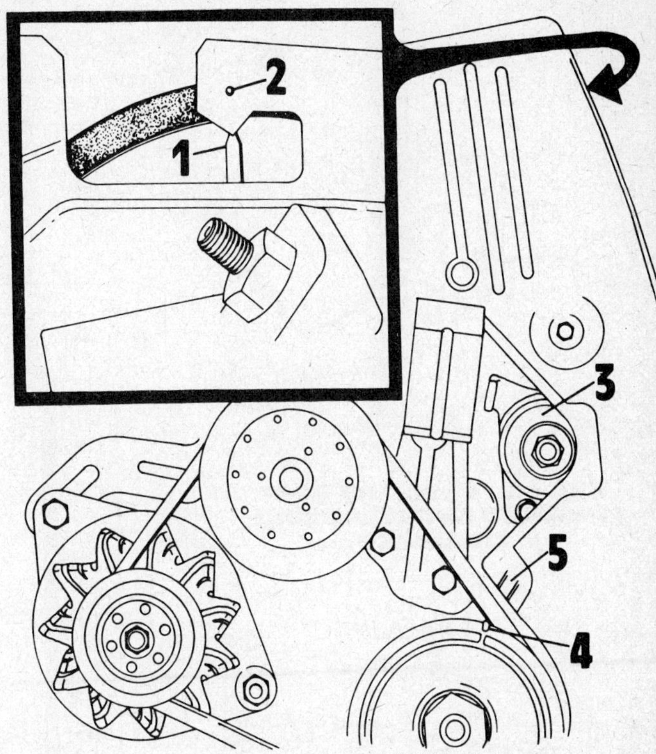

Fig. 10 Adjusting valve timing

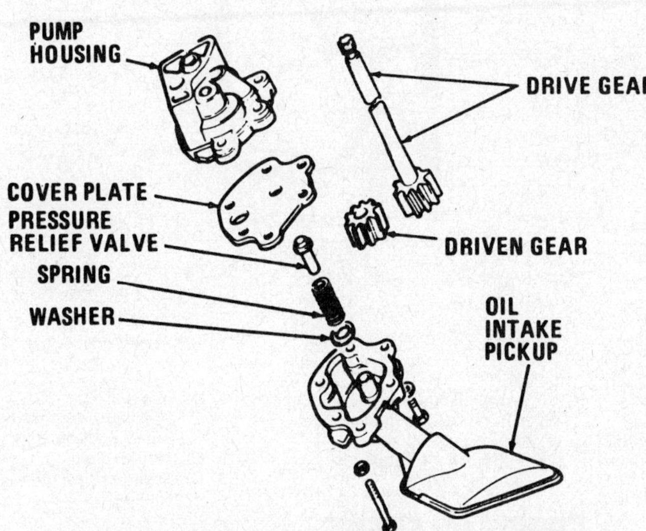

Fig. 11 Exploded view of oil pump

4. If clearance is not within specifications, insert tool A 60421 or equivalent on both intake and exhaust valve tappets, then, using suitable tool, remove plate from its seat on tappet, **Fig. 9.**
5. After determining needed thickness, install new shim. Shims are available in a range of thicknesses from .128 to .185 inch in .002 inch increments. The thickness of the shim is shown on one of the flat surfaces which should be assembled toward the tappet.

VALVE TIMING

ADJUST

1. Temporarily install timing belt cover.
2. Turn crankshaft until timing mark (4), **Fig. 10,** on crankshaft pulley is aligned with index (5) on timing belt cover.
3. Turn camshaft sprocket and align index mark (1) on back of sprocket with index mark (2) on timing belt shield.
4. Move belt tensioner (3) to compress spring and secure it in place.
5. Install timing belt with slack on tensioner side, ensuring timing belt teeth are perfectly coupled with sprockets.
6. Loosen nut holding tensioner pulley to allow tensioner to tighten belt, then torque tensioner pulley nut in this position to 33 ft. lbs.
7. Install timing belt cover and ensure timing marks are still aligned.

CYLINDER HEAD

REPLACE

1. Disconnect battery ground cable and drain cooling system. Remove spare tire from engine compartment.
2. Disconnect air cleaner snorkel flexible hose from front of vehicle, then the hoses from beneath the air cleaner. Remove air cleaner.
3. Disconnect accelerator cable and the choke and shutoff solenoid wiring from carburetor.
4. Disconnect vacuum and fuel evaporative hoses from carburetor and intake manifold.
5. Disconnect fuel hoses and lines from carburetor.
6. Remove carburetor.
7. Remove thermostat housing, leaving coolant hoses attached.
8. Remove timing belt cover.
9. Remove air pump and support bracket.
10. Remove alternator and position aside, leaving wiring connected.
11. Loosen timing belt tensioner and remove timing belt.
12. Remove upper timing belt shield.
13. Disconnect exhaust pipe from exhaust manifold.
14. Disconnect lines from EGR valve and remove valve from maifold.
15. Disconnect high tension wires from spark plugs.
16. Disconnect wiring from sending units located in cylinder head.
17. Remove cylinder head attaching bolts and stud nuts.
18. Remove cylinder head with intake and exhaust manifolds.
19. Reverse procedure to install. Torque cylinder head bolts and nuts, in sequence, **Fig. 4.** Torque bolts and nuts in two steps. First step, torque to 29 ft. lbs. Second step, torque to 61 ft. lbs.

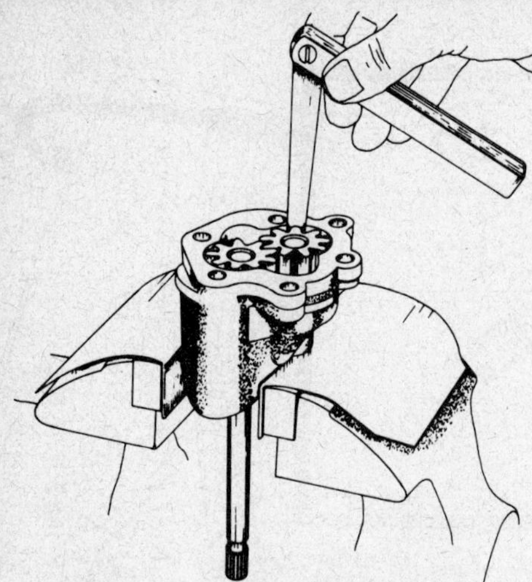

Fig. 12 Checking gear tooth to pump housing clearance

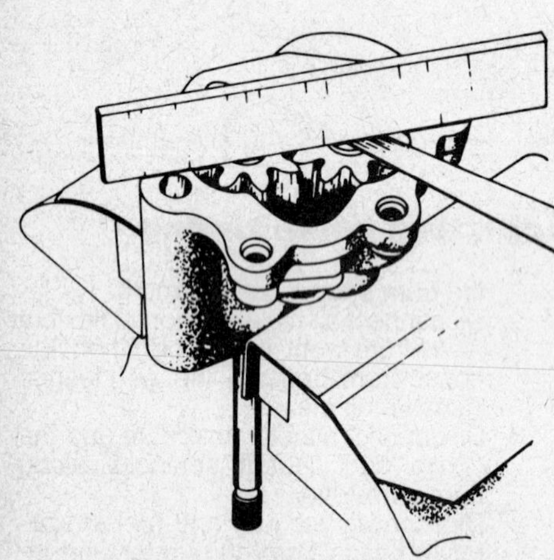

Fig. 13 Checking clearance between gears & cover mating surface

1. Oil filler
2. Oil spray outlets for camshaft lobes and tappets
3. Camshaft
4. Auxiliary shaft
5. Main oil gallery
6. Oil pump and distributor drive gear oil duct
7. Full-flow oil filter
8. By-pass valve
9. Oil pump
10. Oil pressure relief valve
11. Oil pump suction pipe
12. Oil return pipe
13. Oil spray outlet for cylinder walls

Engine oil circuit

TIMING BELT REPLACE

1. Remove timing belt cover. Lower cover retaining screw must be removed from under vehicle after removing right guard.
2. Check timing by aligning timing mark on back of camshaft sprocket with timing mark on shield. Timing mark on crankshaft pulley should coincide with timing mark on cover.
3. Apply hand brake and engage a low gear to prevent crankshaft from turning.
4. Loosen alternator adjusting nut and the alternator to bracket attaching bolt and remove drive belt.
5. Loosen tensioner retaining nut, move tensioner toward engine nut and tighten nut, then remove timing belt with slack on tensioner side.
6. Install new timing belt, ensuring timing belt teeth are perfectly coupled with sprockets.
7. Loosen nut holding tensioner to allow tensioner to tighten belt, then torque tensioner nut in this position to 33 ft. lbs. Ensure that timing marks are still correctly aligned.
8. Install drive belt, adjusting its tension to approximately 1/2 inch deflection with moderate finger pressure.
9. Install timing belt cover.
10. Check and adjust ignition timing as necessary.

OIL PUMP SERVICE

1. Disconnect battery ground cable.
2. Raise and support vehicle and drain crankcase.
3. Remove oil pan.
4. Remove three oil pump attaching bolts and washers, then the pump and gasket.
5. Carefully clamp oil pump body in vise.
6. Remove three bolts holding pickup housing to pump housing and remove pickup.
7. Remove spring, relief valve and cover, **Fig. 11,** the slide driveshaft with drive gear and driven gear out of housing.
8. Clean all disassembled parts in suitable solvent and blow dry with compressed air.
9. Check housing and cover for cracks and the intake pickup and oil duct for clogging.
10. Reverse steps 6 and 7 to assemble pump.
11. Check backlash between gears. Backlash is .006 inch for new pump and maximum allowable backlash is .010 inch.
12. Check gear tooth to pump housing clearance, **Fig. 12.** Clearance should be .004-.007 inch on new pump with maximum allowable clearance being .010 inch.
13. Replace housing and gears if maximum clearances are exceeded in

steps 11 and 12.

14. Check clearance between gears and the cover mating face. Using straightedge and feeler gage, **Fig. 13,** clearance range should be .008-.0041 inch. If a value of more than .006 inch is found, gears and/or pump housing must be replaced.
15. To determine if gears are worn, measure their length. The range for new gears is 1.101-1.102 inch. The drive gear is mounted on its shaft with an interference fit. Check for signs of play.
16. Clearance between driven gear and its shaft is .0006-.002 inch with a maximum allowable clearance of .004 inch.
17. Check clearance between pump drive shaft and pump housing. Clearance range is .0006-.002 inch with a maximum allowable clearance of .004 inch.
18. Reverse steps one through four to install oil pump, installing all new gaskets and ensuring pump is properly seated before tightening bolts.

WATER PUMP
REPLACE

1. Disconnect battery ground cable.
2. Remove timing belt cover.
3. Remove air pump and drive belt.
4. Loosen alternator and remove drive belt.
5. Drain sufficient amount of coolant to bring level below that of water pump.
6. Remove two intake pipe to water pump attaching bolts and disconnect pipe.
7. Remove four water pump to engine block attaching bolts and lock washers, then the water pump and gasket.
8. Reverse procedure to install, using new gaskets.

CLUTCH & MANUAL TRANSAXLE SECTION

INDEX

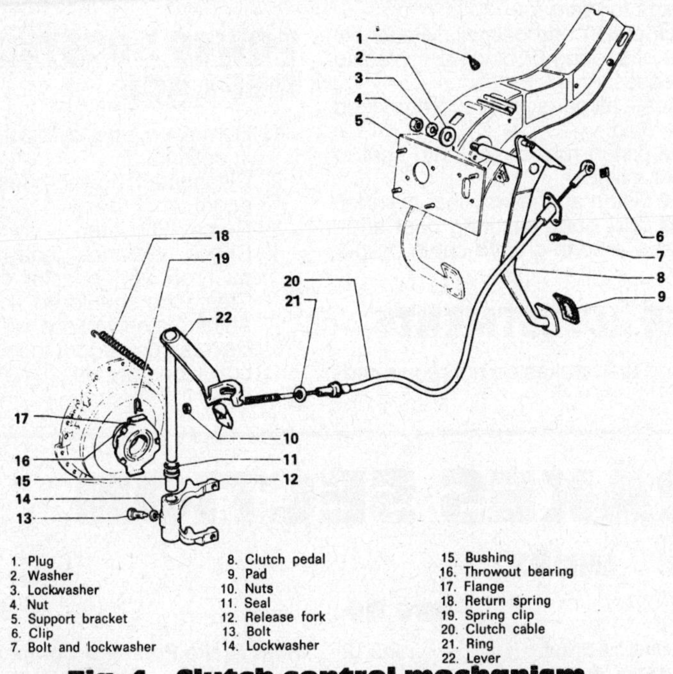

Fig. 1 Clutch control mechanism

CLUTCH PEDAL
ADJUST

1. Raise and support vehicle.
2. Loosen clutch cable locknut.
3. Turn clutch cable adjusting nut in or out as necessary to provide 1 inch free travel at clutch pedal.
4. Tighten clutch cable locknut.

CLUTCH
REPLACE

1. Remove transaxle as described under "Transaxle, Replace."
2. Mark relationship of clutch assembly and flywheel for proper installation.
3. Remove clutch assembly by gradually loosening and then removing six bolts.
4. If flywheel was removed, torque mounting bolts to 61 ft. lbs.
5. Ensure that clutch and flywheel surfaces are clean and align marks made during disassembly.
6. With protruding part of disc hub facing away from flywheel, loosely attach clutch assembly on flywheel.
7. Using tool A 70210 or equivalent, center disc in pressure plate.
8. Gradually torque mounting bolts to 28 ft. lbs., then remove tool.
9. Lightly coat transaxle shaft with suitable lubricant, then install transaxle.

TRANSAXLE
REPLACE

1. Disconnect battery ground cable and remove spare tire.
2. Disconnect speedometer cable at transaxle housing by unscrewing ring nut.
3. Disconnect clutch cable from release lever and unhook return spring.
4. Install suitable engine supporting device.
5. Remove bellhousing bolt and nut that is accessible from above.
6. Remove hubcaps from front wheels and unscrew constant velocity joint hub nuts.
7. Raise and support vehicle and remove left front wheel.
8. Using suitable tool, disconnect left tie rod from steering arm.
9. Remove sway bar.
10. Remove control arm to body attaching bolt.
11. Disconnect back-up light switch electrical connectors.
12. Disconnect exhaust pipe bracket.
13. Disconnect gearshift linkage.
14. Remove starter and the flywheel cover.
15. Remove lower support crossmember.
16. Remove bellhousing bolt not previously removed.
17. Disconnect ground cable at transaxle.
18. Tie axle shafts and CV joints to transaxle.
19. Carefully lower transaxle assembly from vehicle.
20. Reverse procedure to install.

DISC BRAKES SECTION

INDEX

BRAKE PADS
REPLACE

1. Raise and support vehicle and remove front wheels.
2. Remove cotter pins from locking blocks.
3. Using suitable tool, drive out locking blocks.
4. Remove caliper and tie out of way. **Do not let caliper hang by brake hose.**
5. Remove brake pads and springs.
6. Reverse procedure to install.

CALIPER
REPLACE

1. Raise and support vehicle and remove front wheels.
2. Plug outlet ports in brake fluid reservoir.
3. Disconnect brake hose at caliper.
4. Remove cotter pins from locking blocks.
5. Using suitable tool, drive out locking blocks.
6. Lift off caliper.
7. Reverse procedure to install.

CALIPER SERVICE

1. Remove dust cap, **Fig. 1.**
2. Remove piston from caliper by introducing compressed air into fluid inlet.
3. Remove inner seal from caliper.

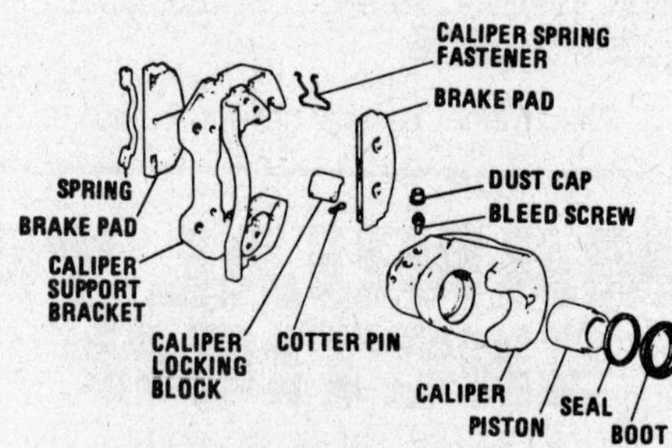

Fig. 1 Exploded view of disc brake assembly

4. Wash all parts in hot water and blow dry with compressed air, then inspect all parts for damage.
5. Check piston and caliper cylinder for signs of scoring or binding, replacing as necessary.
6. Lubricate all parts with recommended brake fluid.
7. Install piston rubber seal into seat in caliper cylinder.
8. Install piston all the way into cylinder.
9. Install dust boot, ensuring boot edge is well seated in groove cut in caliper body.

BRAKE ADJUSTMENTS

Front and rear brakes do not require adjustment.

MASTER CYLINDER
REPLACE

1. Remove spare tire from engine compartment.
2. Remove fluid reservoir cover and plug outlet.
3. Disconnect tubes from reservoir to master cylinder.
4. Disconnect brake lines at master cylinder.
5. Remove master cylinder attaching nuts and the master cylinder.
6. Reverse procedure to install, torquing master cylinder attaching nuts to 18.5 ft. lbs.

POWER BOOSTER
REPLACE

1. Remove master cylinder as previously described.
2. Disconnect power booster at brake pedal.
3. Remove booster.
4. Check distance between booster pushrod and booster body at rest. Clearance should be .032-.040 inch. Adjust as necessary.
5. Reverse procedure to install, torquing brake booster attaching nut to 11 ft. lbs.

DRUM BRAKES SECTION

INDEX

PARKING BRAKE
ADJUST

1. Fully depress brake pedal several times.
2. Starting from released position, pull up ratchet lever three or four clicks.
3. Loosen locknut and turn adjusting nut until wheels are locked securely.
4. Tighten adjusting nut and locknut.

REAR BRAKE PRESSURE COMPENSATOR
ADJUST

1. Secure compensator, with bar and boot, to its brackets by means of two bolts (7), **Fig. 1,** leaving bolts loose.
2. Attach bar (3) to body with bracket.
3. Bring end of bar (3b) to 2.165-2.559 inch from center of buffer mounting hole (2).
4. Raise dust boot (9) to check contact between regulator and bar.
5. Rotate regulator body on either bolt (7) until end of piston (8) is in contact with bar end (3a).
6. Torque bolts (7) to 18.5 ft. lbs. Torque bottom bolt first.
7. Attach link (4) to bracket (6) pin at control arm (11).
8. Install spring fastener on link pin (5).

BRAKE SHOES
REPLACE

1. Raise and support vehicle and remove rear wheels.
2. Plug outlet ports in brake fluid reservoir.
3. Remove two brake drum attaching screws and the drum.
4. Install tool A 72257 or equivalent on wheel cylinder, then, using suitable tool, unhook upper and lower brake shoe return springs, **Fig. 2.**
5. Tilt shoe guide pins and lift them out together with cups and springs, then withdraw shoe assemblies. **Groove**

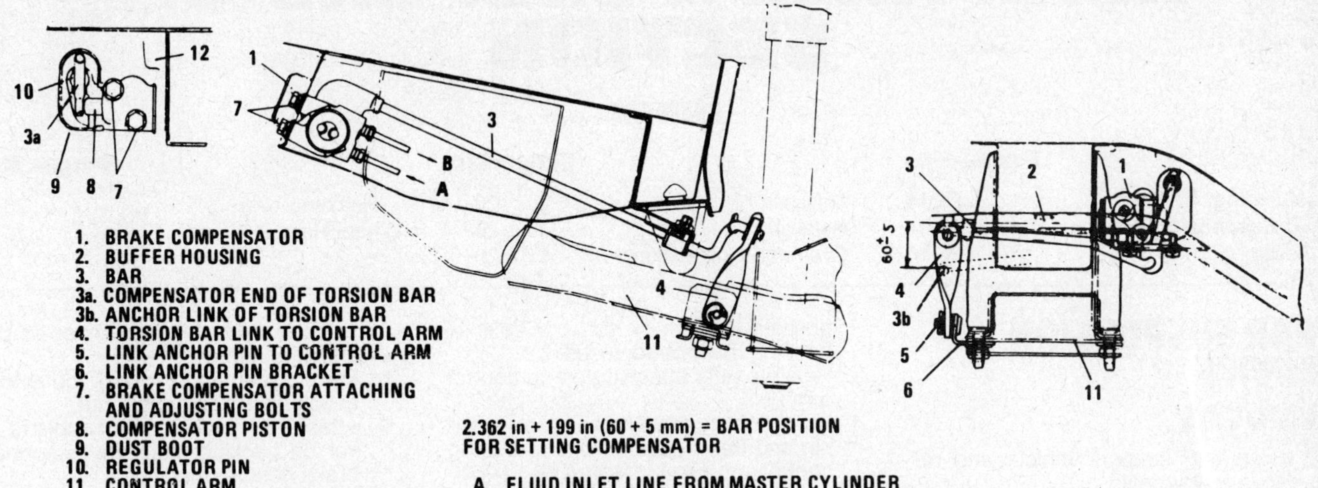

Fig. 1 Adjusting rear brake pressure compensator

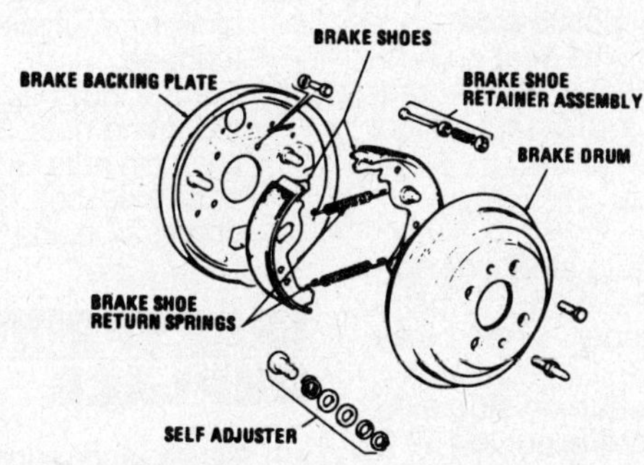

Fig. 2 Exploded view of drum brake assembly

cut on wheel hub should face toward self-adjusting mechanism to facilitate shoe removal.

6. Disconnect brake line at wheel cylinder.
7. Remove wheel cylinder attaching screws and washers and the wheel cylinder.
8. Temporarily install both brake shoes and hook up return springs, then push shoes outward onto self adjusters to see if they stay in position. If brake shoes do not stay in position, shoe return springs or self adjuster springs must be replaced.
9. Install wheel cylinder on backing plate, torquing attaching screws to 7 ft. lbs.
10. Connect brake line to wheel cylinder, torquing to 14 ft. lbs.
11. Install brake shoes, ensuring shoe ends are properly seated on wheel cylinder and backing plate.
12. Place spring and the inner and outer cups in position, then slide guide pins on shoes.
13. Connect upper and lower return springs.
14. Install brake drum and tighten two attaching screws.

MASTER CYLINDER
REPLACE

Refer to Disc Brakes Section.

POWER BOOSTER
REPLACE

Refer to Disc Brakes Section.

REAR AXLE & SUSPENSION SECTION

INDEX

REAR SUSPENSION SERVICE

REMOVAL

1. Raise and support vehicle and remove rear wheels.
2. Plug outlet hose of brake fluid reservoir.
3. Disconnect flex hose from metal pipe.
4. Release hand brake and detach cable from levers on brake backing plate.
5. Disconnect brake compensator bar from right control arm.
6. Place suitable jack under control arm, raise suspension and detach shock absorbers in luggage compartment, then remove jack.
7. Detach rubber pads attaching leaf spring to control arm.
8. Remove nuts attaching swivels of control arms to the body.
9. Slide off control arms complete with shock absorbers.

DISASSEMBLY

1. Remove nut attaching shock absorber and control arm to stub axle and slip off screw and control arm. Note number and thickness of shims.
2. Remove nut attaching shock absorber to stub axle and slide off screw and shock absorber.
3. Remove brake drum by unscrewing wheel centering stud and the drum attachment screw.
4. Remove dust cover.
5. Remove nut attaching hub to stub axle and remove washer.
6. Using tool A 47017 or equivalent, remove hub with bearing.
7. Remove safety plate and disconnect brake hose at wheel cylinder.
8. Remove brake backing plate to stub axle attaching screws and remove backing plate.

OVERHAUL & INSPECTION

1. Check control arms for distortion, replacing as necessary.
2. Check condition of rubber bushings inserted in control arms. The inside surface should not show friction marks with the pin. If rubber part of bushing is worn or not fully flexible, bushing must be replaced.
3. Remove nuts attaching pin to control arm.
4. Using tool A 47057 and press, push pin and free bushing from its seat in control arm. **First bushing should be only partly extracted from control arm so that pin is properly centered for removal of second bushing.**
5. Using tool A 47057 or equivalent, extract rubber bushing from control arm on outer end.
6. Repeat setp 5 on opposite side.
7. Insert new bushing in its seat on control arm and install tool A 47057 complete with cap, then turn screw on tool to force bushing into place.

ASSEMBLY

1. Attach backing plate to stub axle, torquing attaching bolts to 18.5 ft. lbs.
2. Install wheel cylinder and brake shoes.
3. Assemble complete hub on stub axle, insert washer and torque nut to 159 ft. lbs., then, using suitable tool, stake nut.
4. Install brake drum and dust cover.
5. Connect bottom end of shock absorber to stub axle and control arm, being sure to insert shims between bushings and shock absorber mounting bracket.
6. Loosely install self locking nut.

INSTALLATION

1. Torque upper shock absorber to spindle attaching nut to 53 ft. lbs.
2. Connect brake hose to wheel cylinder, securing with plate and srew.
3. Attach control arm to body over two studs protruding through plate and tighten nuts finger tight.
4. Attach rubber pads used to anchor leaf spring.
5. Attach bar of brake pressure regulator to right control arm.
6. Slip bottom rubber bushing on top stud of shock absorber, then place suitable jack under suspension and lift whole assembly so that top stud of shock absorber enters body.
7. Mount top rubber bushing, retaining cap and self locking nut on top stud of shock absorber.
8. Using suitable tool to lock top stud of shock absorber, tighten nut.
9. Attach handbrake control cable to lever on backing plate and reconnect brake hose to metal pipe.
10. Fill brake fluid reservoir and bleed brake system.
11. Install wheels and lower vehicle. **Nuts of rubber bushings must be tightened with vehicle loaded to prevent premature wear.**
12. Set wheel straight ahead and load vehicle to equivalent of 4 persons plus luggage.
13. Torque nuts as follows: control arm mounting nuts, 36 ft. lbs.; control arm pivot pin nuts, 30 ft. lbs.; control arm to stub axle bolt, 58 ft. lbs.; spring anchors, 27 ft. lbs.

LEAF SPRING REPLACE

1. Raise and support vehicle and remove rear wheels.
2. Using suitable jack, raise left end of spring and free anchor pad on control arm.
3. Repeat step 2 to free other end of spring.
4. Remove two guides securing spring to body and remove spring.
5. Reverse procedure to install.

WHEEL HUB REPLACE

1. Raise and support vehicle and remove rear wheels.
2. Remove dust cover.
3. Remove wheel centering stud and attaching screw, then the brake drum.
4. Remove hub to spindle attaching nut.
5. Remove washer, then, using suitable puller, the entire hub. **Rear wheel hubs are supplied for service complete with bearings and whole assembly must be replaced when overhauling unit.**
6. Reverse procedure to install.

FRONT SUSPENSION, DRIVE AXLE & STEERING SECTION

INDEX

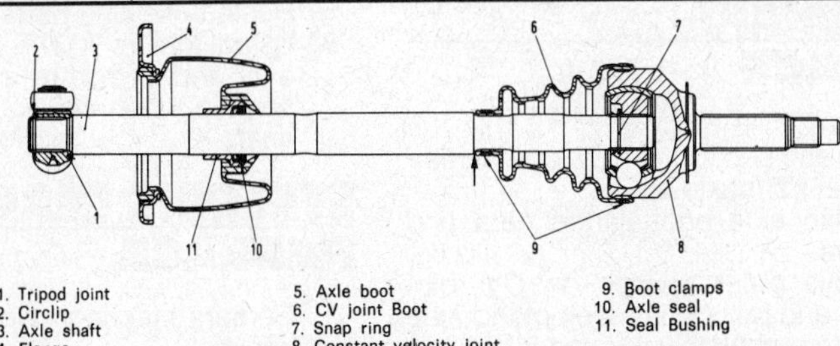

Fig. 1 Cross sectional view of axle shaft

FRONT SUSPENSION SERVICE

REMOVAL

1. Raise and support vehicle and remove front wheels.
2. Remove three brake caliper to knuckle attaching bolts, then remove caliper and support out of way.
3. Remove tie rod ball joint to steering knuckle attaching nut and, using suitable puller, remove ball joint from steering knuckle.
4. Remove nut and adjustment shims securing sway bar to control arm, noting number of adjustment shims between end of bar and control arm bushing.
5. Remove control arm to body bracket attaching bolt and nut.
6. Remove hub nut.
7. Support front suspension and remove three strut to body attaching nuts in engine compartment.
8. Slide suspension assembly off CV joint shaft and remove assembly from vehicle. Secure axle shaft to keep it from slipping out of differential.

DISASSEMBLY

1. Remove two strut assembly to knuckle attaching bolts and nuts and remove strut assembly.
2. Remove locating pin and bolt securing brake disc to hub, then remove disc and plate.
3. Remove control arm ball joint to knuckle attaching nut, then, using suitable puller, remove ball joint from knuckle.
4. Place knuckle in press and remove hub.
5. Using suitable tool, remove ring nut retaining bearing in knuckle and remove bearing.
6. Place tool A 74278 or equivalent on strut assembly and place strut assembly in tool A 74277 or equivalent.
7. Ensure one bolt at each end of strut assembly is in depression used to position spring on plate.
8. Tighten three bolts on tool A 74278 until they contact spring check plate.
9. Crank tool A 74277 until spring is compressed approximately one inch.
10. Using suitable wrench to hold shock absorber stud, remove nut holding upper mount to shock absorber.
11. Carefully uncrank tool A 74277 until spring is fully relaxed.
12. Remove strut from tool and separate parts.

INSPECTION

Control Arms

1. Check control arms for cracks or distortion, replacing as necessary.
2. Check ball joint for excessive play. Check swivels and protective boots for cracks or breaks. Replace entire control arm if damaged.
3. Check rubber bushing for wear or deterioration. If replacement is necessary, proceed as follows:
   a. Place control arm in press and, using suitable tool, press bushing out of control arm.
   b. Mount control arm on tool A 74271 or equivalent.
   c. Coat new bushing with suitable lubricant and place bushing on tool, then, using press, install bushing in control arm. Press installer down so that tabs on installer contact tool.
   d. Place a new spacer for bushing on installer with the tool spacer on installer.
   e. Screw tip onto installer and install spacer in control arm bushing, then remove tip and tool.

Knuckle

Carefully check knuckle for cracks. Ensure that areas of contact with outer ring of hub bearing are smooth and free from signs of binding. Replace knuckle if damage or wear is evident.

Coil Springs

Check coils for cracks or distortion. Check spring performance. Check support plates for condition. Replace parts as necessary.

Shock Absorber

Check shock absorber for leaks or faulty performance and replace as necessary.

Sway Bar

Check sway bar for cracks or distortion and the mounting pads and rubber bushings for wear, replacing as necessary.

ASSEMBLY

1. Press bearing into knuckle until seated, then screw octagonal lock ring into threaded sections. **Bearing must be replaced every time wheel hub is disassembled.**
2. Using suitable tools, press hub in knuckle.
3. Install control arm on knuckle and secure ball joint to knuckle, torquing nut to 40 ft. lbs.
4. Install brake disc on hub with locator pin and bolt.
5. Using suitable tools, reassemble shock absorber and coil spring, then mount strut assembly on knuckle with two bolts and nuts but do not tighten bolts.

INSTALLATION

1. Install sway bar, if removed.
2. Position studs on top of strut assembly through bolt holes in engine compartment and loosely secure strut assembly with nuts and washers.
3. Slide shaft of CV joint through hub and secure shaft in hub with flat washer and nut.
4. Attach tie rod to steering arm, torquing attaching nut to 25 ft. lbs.
5. Apply suitable lubricant to sway bar bushing in control arm.
6. Using same number of shims as were removed, loosely attach sway bar to control arm.
7. Loosely attach control arm to bracket on body.
8. Install brake caliper and support on knuckle.
9. Torque hub nut to 159 ft. lbs. and stake collar of nut.

10. Install wheels and tighten strut upper mounting bolts in engine compartment.
11. Set wheels straight ahead and load vehicle to equivalent of 4 persons plus luggage.
12. Torque nuts as follows: sway bar nut at control arm, 43 ft. lbs.; control arm bolt at body, 29 ft. lbs.; sway bar bracket bolt or nut, 36 ft. lbs.; strut lower mounting bolts, 53 ft. lbs.

WHEEL HUB
REPLACE

1. Raise and support vehicle and remove front wheels.
2. Remove hub nut, then the brake caliper and disc.
3. Remove two strut assembly to knuckle attaching bolts and nuts.
4. Remove control arm to knuckle retaining nut and, using suitable tool, remove ball joint from knuckle.
5. Remove tie rod ball joint to steering arm securing nut and, using suitable tool, remove ball joint.
6. Slide knuckle and hub off CV joint shaft.
7. Reverse procedure to install. Torque hub nut to 159 ft. lbs. and stake in position. Torque suspension nuts and bolts to specification under load as described under "Front Suspension Service."

SHOCK ABSORBER
REPLACE

1. Raise and support vehicle and remove front wheel.
2. Remove two strut assembly to knuckle attaching bolts and nuts.
3. Remove strut assembly to body attaching bolts located in engine compartment.
4. Disassemble strut as described under "Front Suspension Service."
5. Reverse procedure to install.

AXLE SHAFT
REPLACE

1. Raise and support vehicle and partially drain transaxle oil.
2. Remove axle boot flange nuts and screws.
3. Remove outer clamps on CV joint boots and pull boots back along axle shaft to completely expose joints.
4. Clean grease from joints.
5. Open snap ring on joints and remove shaft ends from their seats in joint.
6. Turn wheels as necessary to facilitate removal of shafts from their differential seats.
7. Reverse procedure to install. Ensure axle shaft snap ring is properly seated in groove by moving shaft inward and outward several times. Arrow, **Fig. 1**, indicates shoulder that boot should contact after installation.
8. Apply suitable lubricant to CV joint sockets and the protective boot. Use 3 ounces of lubricant for each joint.

DRIVE AXLE SERVICE
AXLE BOOT & SEAL REPLACEMENT

1. Remove axle shaft as previously described.
2. Remove snap ring from inner end of axle and slide tripod joint off spline.
3. Remove boot, bushing and seal as an assembly.
4. Clean polished surface of axle with suitable solvent and fine emery cloth to provide proper sealing surface.
5. Replace sealing parts as necessary.
6. Using tool A 70375 J or equivalent over end of axle to avoid damage to seal lip when sliding boot onto axle shaft.

STEERING GEAR
REPLACE

1. Center steering wheel and front wheels.
2. Mark relationship of universal joint steering gear shaft for proper assembly.
3. Remove universal joint to steering gear shaft attaching bolt and nut.
4. Raise and support vehicle.
5. Remove tie rod ball joint to steering knuckle securing nut.
6. Using suitable tool, separate ball joints from steering knuckle.
7. Remove steering gear to body attaching bolts and remove steering gear from vehicle.
8. Reverse procedure to install, then check toe-in and adjust as necessary.

WHEEL ALIGNMENT SECTION

INDEX

FRONT ALIGNMENT
CASTER & CAMBER

1. Caster and camber are adjusted by adding or removing shims as necessary at junction of control arm and sway bar.

TOE-IN

1. Toe-in can be adjusted by turning tie rod ends in or out as necessary. Either of two types of tie rods may be used, **Fig. 1.** If tie rod is supplied with sleeve, separate from tie rod end, adjust toe by loosening locknuts and turning sleeve. If rod is supplied with sleeve and tie rod end in one piece, adjust toe by loosening locknut and turning steering rack ball joint stud.

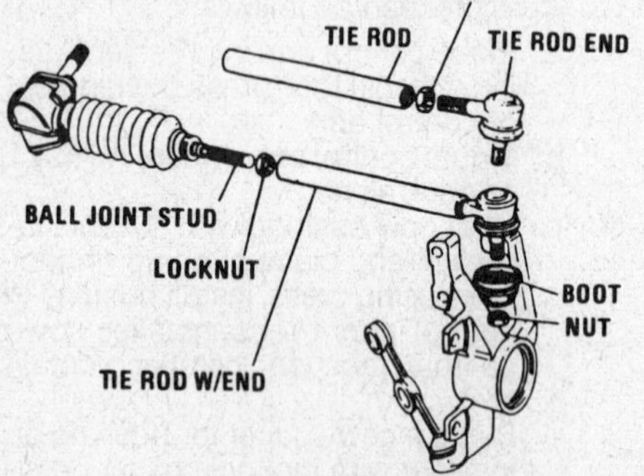

Fig. 1 Exploded view of tie rod assembly

REAR ALIGNMENT
CAMBER & TOE-IN

1. Camber and toe-in are adjusted by adding or removing shims between control arm pin and body.